Scott 7, graded 98
PF certificate 462135

Scott 11, graded 100
PF certificates 521651, 176262

Scott 17, graded 100-J
PF certificate 535539

Scott 233, graded 98-J
PF certificate 431008

Scott 261, graded 98
PF certificate 509957

Scott 354, graded 100
PF certificates 479469, 380288

Scott 313, graded 95
PF certificates 445953, 309419

Scott 404, graded 98
PF certificate 523114

Scott E8, graded 100-J
PF certificate 525203

SCOTT®

2023 Specialized Catalogue of United States Stamps & Covers

ONE-HUNDRED-FIRST EDITION

CONFEDERATE STATES • CANAL ZONE • DANISH WEST INDIES
GUAM • HAWAII

UNITED STATES ADMINISTRATION:
Cuba • Puerto Rico • Philippines • Ryukyu Islands

EDITOR-IN-CHIEF	Jay Bigalke
EDITOR EMERITUS	James E. Kloetzel
EDITOR-AT-LARGE	Donna Houseman
CONTRIBUTING EDITOR	Charles Snee
SENIOR EDITOR /NEW ISSUES AND VALUING	Martin J. Frankevicz
ADMINISTRATIVE ASSISTANT/CATALOGUE LAYOUT	Eric Wiessinger
PRINTING AND IMAGE COORDINATOR	Stacey Mahan
SENIOR GRAPHIC DESIGNER	Cinda McAlexander
SALES DIRECTOR	David Pistello
SALES DIRECTOR	Eric Roth
SALES DIRECTOR	Brenda Wyen
SALES REPRESENTATIVE	Julie Dahlstrom

Released October 2022
Includes New Stamp Listings through the September 2022 *Linn's Stamp News Monthly* Catalogue Update

AMOS MEDIA

1660 Campbell Road, Suite A, Sidney, OH 45365
Publishers of *Linn's Stamp News,*
Linn's Stamp News Monthly, Coin World and *Coin World Monthly.*

Copyright Notice

COPYRIGHT NOTE

Permission is hereby given for the use of material in this book and covered by copyright if:

(a) The material is used in advertising matter, circulars or price lists for the purpose of offering stamps for sale or purchase at the prices listed therein; and

(b) Such use is incidental to the business of buying and selling stamps and is limited in scope and length, i.e., it does not cover a substantial portion of the total number of stamps issued by any country or of any special category of stamps of any country; and

(c) Such material is not used as part of any catalogue, stamp album or computerized or other system based upon the Scott catalogue numbers, or in any updated valuations of stamps not offered for sale or purchase; and

(d) Such use is not competitive with the business of the copyright owner; and

(e) Such use is for editorial purposes in publications in the form of articles or commentary, except for computer software or the serialization of books in such publications, for which separate written permission is required.

Any use of the material in this book which does not satisfy all the foregoing conditions is forbidden in any form unless permission in each instance is given in writing by the copyright owner.

Trademark Notice

The terms SCOTT, SCOTT'S, SCOTT CATALOGUE NUMBERING SYSTEM, SCOTT CATALOGUE NUMBER, SCOTT NUMBER and abbreviations thereof, are trademarks of Amos Media Co., used to identify its publications and its copyrighted system for identifying and classifying postage stamps for dealers and collectors. These trademarks are to be used only with the prior consent of Amos Media Co.

Please Note

Effective as of 1978, designs of all United States stamps are copyrighted.

Scott Catalogue accepts all advertisements in good faith, but does not endorse or assume any responsibility for the contents of advertisements.

ISBN 0-89487-666-0

Library of Congress Card No. 2-3301

Scott Catalogue Mission Statement

The Scott Catalogue Team exists to serve the recreational, educational and commercial hobby needs of stamp collectors and dealers.

We strive to set the industry standard for philatelic information and products by developing and providing goods that help collectors identify, value, organize and present their collections.

Quality customer service is, and will continue to be, our highest priority. We aspire toward achieving total customer satisfaction.

SCOTT

What's new for 2023 Scott Specialized Catalogue of United States Stamps and Covers?

Many important value and editorial changes enhance the historic 101st edition of the Scott *Specialized Catalogue of United States Stamps and Covers*. Before we turn our attention to specific examples, we salute Scott editor emeritus James E. Kloetzel for working tirelessly on the thousands of value changes and hundreds of editorial changes. Kloetzel and the rest of the Scott editors have been busy adding and expanding listings and making significant improvements throughout the catalog.

VALUING OVERVIEW

Strong auction, retail and internet sales during the past year indicate that the U.S. market is strong, and catalog values well represent the market. Some values advance in certain areas of the catalog, as always, and some of these changes are discussed below.

Most collectors will be interested to hear that the 1847 5¢ Franklin and 10¢ Washington stamps (Scott 1 and 2) move significantly higher in used condition because of continuing high demand. The 5¢ Franklin jumps to $425 in this year's Scott U.S. Specialized catalog, up from $350 in the 2023 Vol. 1A of the Scott *Standard Postage Stamp Catalogue*. The 10¢ Washington shows a similar move, to $900 from $750. The 1875 reproductions of these stamps (3 and 4) each add $100 to the values shown in Vol. 1A, moving to $1,000 unused and $1,250 unused, respectively. The 1855 10¢ green type IV (16) shows a huge increase in value in unused, original gum condition, as it has become clearer that this stamp with gum and in nice condition is a real rarity. From $37,500 in Vol. 1A, its value now shoots to $50,000.

A few extremely scarce 20th-century stamps drop in value somewhat. The used 1901 2¢ Pan-American Exposition issue with center inverted (Scott 295a) drops from $55,000 to $50,000 following a poor auction realization for the finest known used example. The 1908 4¢ brown coil stamp with Schermack type III perforations (314A) drops from $100,000 for an unused single to $85,000, and a used single drops from $50,000 to 45,000. And the used 2¢ deep rose type Ia with Schermack type III perforations (482A) falls from $65,000 to $55,000.

On the other hand, quite a few 20th-century unused coil pairs and line pairs rise in value. See especially the Scott 385-388 coils. In 20th-century sheet stamps, the 1929 2¢ Ohio River Canalization issue in the scarce lake shade (Scott 681a) has a value added for the plate block of six, which had been valued with a dash previously. The new value is $6,000 for a never-hinged plate block. This rare item is not recorded hinged.

For unused stamps in the Postage section valued at the 25¢ minimum value, most if not all have been updated to 30¢. Used values remain at the 25¢ minimum.

Values of forever stamps were also updated to reflect the new 60¢ postage rate that took effect in July 2022.

Collectors of recent new issues will also want to pay particular attention to a number of se-tenant issues and wedding-related stamp issues of the past decade. Many saw notable increases in this edition of the catalog.

Among the back-of-the-book stamps, the stand-out section showing value increases is the newspaper and periodicals issues. Some nice auction sales of these stamps in unused, high-quality condition caught the eyes of some serious collectors, and the spirited bidding has resulted in almost across-the-board value increases for the 1875 issues (Scott PR9-PR32 and PR36-PR50).

The Vending and Affixing Machine Perforations section was another active area for value increases and editorial enhancements. Comprehensive collections seldom are offered, but this year was an exception. Occasional items have slipped in value, but the vast majority of the value changes made are upward, significant and seen throughout the section. Interested collectors and dealers will want to carefully review this section of the catalog this year.

Essays, proofs and specimen stamps see more value changes than usual, and the specimens especially show a great many changes, universally being increases and very often significant increases.

The Test Stamps section sees its normal editorial and value change enhancements, with more value changes than in recent years. Here we see a mix of increases and decreases.

And for encased postage stamps, for the second year in a row, it has been possible to review new comprehensive auctions of this material, resulting in more value changes than usual, almost all of which are increases.

EDITORIAL ENHANCEMENTS

Many editorial improvements have been made in the 2023 Scott U.S. Specialized catalog. Notes have been added in the Introduction concerning premiums for cancellations on classic stamps, rotary press sheet waste issues and unofficial bisects. Many footnotes have been added or expanded to make understanding the listings and values even clearer. Nine new earliest documented uses have been added, from No. 153 through No. 554c in the Postage section and No. 384H in the Imperforate Flat Plate Coils section.

An important, long note has been added in the Newspaper and Periodical Stamps section concerning the so-called Colman "special printing" newspaper stamps of 1894. These stamps, though not officially issued, exist both imperforate and unofficially perforated, and they are in great demand by newspaper stamp specialists. The note explains what they are and why they were produced, how they got into the marketplace, how to identify them and how to value them.

In the Vending and Affixing Machine Perforations section, an enormous number of additions have been made throughout the listings. This is because of the auction sale of the comprehensive Melvin Getlan collection of vending- and affixing-machine perforations. Collectors of this area will want to review these

Continued on page 8A

Table of contents

Letter from the Editor 5A
Acknowledgments 8A
Expertizing Services 9A
Addresses of philatelic societies 10A
Information on catalogue values, grade and condition 11A
Grading illustrations 12A
Catalogue values for stamps on covers 14A
Understanding the listings 16A
Catalogue listing policy 18A
Scott numbering practices and special notices 19A
Postmasters General of the United States 21A
Basic stamp information 22A
Territorial and statehood dates 42A
Domestic letter rates 44A
Domestic air mail letter rates 45A
Subject index of regular, commemorative and air post issues 46A
2023 U.S. Specialized additions, deletions & number changes 62A
Glossary of Philatelic Terms 1195
Index to Advertisers 1216
Dealer Directory Yellow Pages 1217

United States 1

Entries in this subsection are arranged alphabetically to facilitate use. Where applicable, the Scott number prefix or consistent suffix for a section is included in parentheses.

Air post stamped envelopes & air letter sheets (UC) 674
Air post first day covers 468
Air post postal cards (UXC) 705
Air post semi-official stamps (CL) 414
Air post special delivery (CE) 413
Air post stamps (C) 403
Booklet panes, booklets (BK) 470
Carriers' stamps (LO, LB) 610
Certified mail stamp (FA) 421
Christmas seals (WX) 1061
Commemorative panels (CP) 1002
Commemorative stamps, quantities issued 604
Computer vended postage (CVP) 577
Machine set-up and test labels (CVPT) 583
Die & plate proofs (-P) 952
Duck (Hunting permit) stamps (Federal) 793
Duck (Hunting permit) stamps (State) 804
Duck (Hunting permit) stamps (Indian Reservation) 831
Encased postage stamps (EP) 1076
Envelopes & wrappers (U, W) 645
Essays (-E) 846
1861 First Design Essays and Trial Color Proofs 950
First day covers, postage, semi-postal, air post 442
Imperforate flat plate coil stamps (-H, -V) 602
International reply coupons (IRC) 1016
Local stamps (L, LU) 614
Local handstamped covers 641
Newspaper & periodical stamps (PR) 435
Offices in China (K) 426
Official envelopes & wrappers (UO, WO) 678
Official postal cards (UZ) 707
Official seals (OXF, OXA, OX, LOX) 1018
Official stamps (O) 426
Parcel post postage due stamps (JQ) 440
Parcel post stamps (Q) 438
Non-Personalizable Postage 595
Nonpostal and revenue counterfeits 1035
Personal Computer Postage 586
Postage 4
Postage currency (PC) 1081
Postage due stamps (J) 422
Postal cards (UX, UY) 682
Computer vended (CVUX) 585
Postal counterfeits [-(CF)] 1027
Postal insurance stamps (QI) 441
Postal markings 36A
Postal note stamps (PN) 438
Postal savings mail (O) 433
Postal savings stamps (PS) 837
Postal savings envelopes (UO) 680
Postal stationery 645
Postmasters' provisionals (X, XU) 1
Confederate States 1082
Post office seals (OXF, OXA, OX, LOX) 1018
Proofs (-P) 952
Quantities issued, Commemorative stamps 604
Registry Exchange Labels (FX) 420
Registration stamp (F) 421
Revenue Stamps 709
Beer (REA) 734
Boating (RVB) 790
Camp Stamps (RVC) 790
Cigarette tubes (RH) 743
Consular service fee (RK) 748
Cordials & Wines (RE) 732
Customs fee (RL) 748
Distilled spirits excise tax (RX) 792
Documentary (R) 709
Duck (Hunting permit, Federal RW) 793
Duck (Hunting permit, State & Indian Reservation) 804
Embossed Revenue Stamped Paper (RM-RN) 749
Fermented fruit juice (REF) 739
Firearms transfer (RY) 792
Future delivery (RC) 727
General (R) 709
Hunting permit, Federal (RW) 793
States 804
Indian Reservations 831
Marihuana tax (RJM) 747
Match & Medicine (RO, RS) 758
Motor vehicle use (RV) 789
Narcotic tax (RJA) 745
National Park Service Golden Eagle Pass Stamp (RVP) 791
Playing cards (RF) 740
Potato tax (RI) 744
Private die proprietary (RO-RU) 758
Proprietary (RB) 725
Rectification (RZ) 793
Rectified spirits, Puerto Rico (RE) 1165
Revenue stamped paper (RM-RN) 753
Silver tax (RG) 742
Stock transfer (RD) 728
Tobacco sale tax (RJ) 744
Trailer Permit (RVT) 791
Virgin Islands (Danish West Indies) (R) 1130
Wines (RE) 732
R.F. Overprints (CM) 417
Sanitary Fair stamps (WV) 1074
Savings stamps (S, PS) 837
Treasury savings stamp (TS) 839
War savings stamps (WS) 838
SCADTA stamps (CLEU) 415
Semi-Postal (B) 402
Shanghai (Offices in China) (K) 426
Souvenir cards, philatelic (SC) 998
Souvenir pages (SP) 1007
Special delivery (E) 418
Special handling (QE) 440
Specimen (-S) 994
Stamped envelopes & wrappers (U, W) 645
Telegraph stamps (T) 840
Test stamps 1036
Test booklets: panes & covers 1048
Test stamp essays, trial color, and plate proofs 1060
Trial color proofs (-TC) 952
Vending & affixing machine perforations 595
Wrappers 645

Confederate States 1082

General issues 1100
U.S. stamps used in the Confederacy 1082
3¢ 1861 postmasters' provisionals (AX, AXU) 1083
Confederate postmasters' provisionals (X, XU) 1084

Canal Zone 1106
Cuba 1126
Danish West Indies 1130
Guam 1135
Hawaii 1136
Philippines 1144
Puerto Rico 1163
Ryukyu Islands 1167

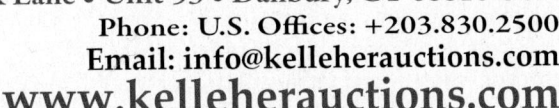

Acknowledgments

Our appreciation and gratitude go to the following individuals who have assisted us in preparing information included in this year's Scott catalogues. Some helpers prefer anonymity. These individuals have generously shared their stamp knowledge with others through the medium of the Scott catalogue.

Those who follow provided information that is in addition to the hundreds of dealer price lists and advertisements and scores of auction catalogues and realizations that were used in producing the catalogue values. It is from those noted here that we have been able to obtain information on items not normally seen in published lists and advertisements. Support from these people goes beyond data leading to catalogue values, for they also are key to editorial changes.

Roland Austin
Jim Bardo
(Bardo Stamps)
Charles R. Biro
Brian M. Bleckwenn
(The Philatelic Foundation)
John D. Bowman
"Albert "Chip" Briggs
Roger S. Brody
Randall Brooksbank
Tom Brougham
(Canal Zone Study Group)
Lewis E. Bussey
Lawrence A. Bustillo
(Suburban Stamp Inc.)
James R. Callis, Jr.
(precancels.com)
A. Bryan Camarda
(University Stamp Co.)
Harry Corrigan
Francis J. Crown, Jr.
Tony L. Crumbley
(Carolina Coin and Stamp, Inc.)
Charles Deaton
John Denune, Jr.
Bob and Rita Dumaine
(Sam Houston Duck Co.)
Mark Eastzer
Charles Epting (H.R. Harmer)
Mike Farrell
Robert S. Freeman
Richard Friedberg
Henry L. Gitner
(Henry Gitner Philatelists, Inc.)
Stan Goldfarb
Dan Harding
Bruce Hecht
(Bruce L. Hecht Co.)
Alexander Haimann
Peter Hoffman
John M. Hotchner
Doug Iams
Tom Jacks
(Mountainside Stamps, Coins and Currency)
Eric Jackson
Michael Jaffe
(Michael Jaffe Stamps, Inc.)
Allan Katz
(Ventura Stamp Co.)
Lewis Kaufman
Patricia A. Kaufmann
(Civil War Philatelic Society)
Jon Kawaguchi
(Ryukyu Philatelic Specialist Society)
Matt Kewriga
Rev. Stephen A. Knapp
Lester C. Lanphear III
Ken Lawrence
James E. Lee
Ronald E. Lesher, Sr.
Nicholas Lombardi
Peter Martin
(State Revenue Society)
William K. McDaniel
Timothy M. McRee
Brian Metz
William E. Mooz
Gary Morris
(Pacific Midwest Co.)
Peter Mosiondz, Jr.
Scott Murphy
Leonard Nadybal
George Painter
Michael O. Perry
Peter W. W. Powell
Bob Prager
(Gary Posner, Inc.)
Ed Reiser
(Century Stamp Co.)
Robert G. Rufe
Dennis W. Schmidt
Terry R. Scott
Craig Selig
J. Randall Shoemaker
(Philatelic Stamp Authentication and Grading, Inc.)
Ray Simrak
Sergio & Liane Sismondo
(The Classic Collector)
Alfred E. Staubus
Philip Stevens
Jay B. Stotts
Don Sundman
(Mystic Stamp Co.)
Robert E. Thompson
Alan Thomson
(Plate Number Coil Collectors Club)
David R. Torre
Scott R. Trepel
(Siegel Auction Galleries, Inc.)
Dan Undersander
Steven Unkrich
Philip T. Wall
Gary B. Weiss
John P. Zuckerman
(Siegel Auction Galleries, Inc.)

Editor's letter continued from page 5A

changes thoroughly, along with the revaluing of existing items.

It has been common in the last few years to see many new listings in the Essays section, and this trend seems to have even accelerated for 2023. New listings appear in some earlier issues as well as many in the modern period. A major reworking of the 1873-76 safety paper essays has been done and should be carefully examined by collectors of this interesting area. In proofs, standing out amidst the many additions are many major listings and new lettered minor listings for shades in the Officials section. And the Specimens section sees some rather major editorial improvements worth examining.

Finally, the Test Stamps section once again sees a thorough review, with new listings (both major and minor) and corrections based on new research. One major addition should be mentioned: the 1995 Antique Auto test stamp precursors to the issued stamps (Scott 3019-3023). These test stamps have been researched for several years, and now the extensive listings may be viewed in the 2023 Scott U.S. Specialized catalog.

Best wishes in your stamp collecting pursuits!

Jay Bigalke, Scott catalog editor-in-chief

Expertizing services

The following organizations will, for a fee, provide expert opinions about stamps submitted to them. Collectors should contact these organizations to find out about their fees and requirements before submitting philatelic material to them. The listing of these groups here is not intended as an endorsement by Amos Media Co.

General Expertizing Services

American Philatelic Expertizing Service (a service of the American Philatelic Society)
100 Match Factory Place
Bellefonte PA 16823-1367
Ph: (814) 933-3803
Fax: (814) 933-6128
www.stamps.org
E-mail: apsinfo@stamps.org
Areas of expertise: Worldwide

Philatelic Foundation
22 E. 35th St., 4th Floor
New York NY 10016
Ph: (212) 221-6555
Fax: (212) 221-6208
www.philatelicfoundation.org
E-mail: philatelicfoundation@verizon.net
Areas of expertise: U.S. and Worldwide

Philatelic Stamp Authentication and Grading, Inc.
PO Box 41-0880
Melbourne FL 32941-0880
Customer Service: (305) 345-9864
www.psaginc.com
E-mail: info@psaginc.com
Areas of expertise: U.S., Canal Zone, Hawaii, Philippines, Canada & Provinces

Professional Stamp Experts
PO Box 539309
Henderson NV 89053-9309
Ph: (702) 776-6522
www.gradingmatters.com
www.psestamp.com
E-mail: info@gradingmatters.com
Areas of expertise: U.S., U.S. Possessions, British Commonwealth

Expertizing Services Covering Specific Fields Or Countries

Civil War Philatelic Society Authentication Service
C/O Stefan T. Jaronski
P.O. Box 232
Sidney, MT 59270-0232
www.civilwarphilatelicsociety.org/authentication/
authentication@civilwarphilatelicsociety.org
Areas of expertise: Confederate stamps and postal history

Errors, Freaks and Oddities Collectors Club Expertizing Service
138 East Lakemont Drive
Kingsland GA 31548
Ph: (912) 729-1573
Areas of expertise: U.S. errors, freaks and oddities

Hawaiian Philatelic Society Expertizing Service
PO Box 10115
Honolulu HI 96816-0115
Areas of expertise: Hawaii

Addresses, telephone numbers, web sites, email addresses of general and specialized philatelic societies

Collectors can contact the following groups for information about the philately of the areas within the scope of these societies, or inquire about membership in these groups. Aside from the general societies, we limit this list to groups that specialize in particular fields of philately, particular areas covered by the Scott *Standard Postage Stamp Catalogue*, and topical groups. Many more specialized philatelic society exist than those listed below. These addresses are updated yearly, and they are, to the best of our knowledge, correct and current. Groups should inform the editors of address changes whenever they occur. The editors also want to hear from other such specialized groups not listed.

Unless otherwise noted all website addresses begin with http://

American Air Mail Society
Stephen Reinhard
P.O. Box 110
Mineola NY 11501
www.americanairmailsociety.org
E-mail: sreinhard1@optonline.net

American First Day Cover Society
P.O. Box 246
Colonial Beach VA 22443-0246
Ph: (520) 321-0880
www.afdcs.org
E-mail: afdcs@afdcs.org

American Philatelic Society
100 Match Factory Place
Bellefonte PA 16823-1367
Ph: (814) 933-3803
www.stamps.org
E-mail: apsinfo@stamps.org

American Revenue Association
Lyman Hensley
473 E. Elm St.
Sycamore IL 60178-1934
www.revenuer.org
E-mail: ilrno2@netzero.net

American Society for Philatelic Pages and Panels
Ron Walenciak
P.O. Box 1042
Washington Township NJ 07676
www.asppp.org
E-mail: rwalenciak@aol.com

American Stamp Dealers Association
P.O. Box 513
Centre Hall PA 16828
Ph: (800) 369-8207
www.americanstampdealer.com
E-mail: asda@americanstampdealer.com

American Topical Association
Jennifer Miller
P.O. Box 2143
Greer SC 29652-2143
www.americantopicalassn.org
E-mail: americantopical@msn.com

Auxiliary Markings Club
Jerry Johnson
6621 W. Victoria Ave.
Kennewick WA 99336
www.postal-markings.org
E-mail: membership-2016@postal-markings.org

Canal Zone Study Group
Mike Drabik
P.O. Box 281
Bolton MA 01740
www.canalzonestudygroup.com
E-mail: czsgsecretary@gmail.com

Carriers and Locals Society
John Bowman
14409 Pentridge Drive
Corpus Christi TX 78410
www.pennypost.org
E-mail: jbowman@stx.rr.com

Christmas Seal & Charity Stamp Society
John Denune
234 East Broadway
Granville OH 43023
Ph: (740) 814-6031
www.seal-society.org
E-mail: john@christmasseals.net

Civil War Philatelic Society
Patricia A. Kaufmann
10194 N. Old State Road
Lincoln DE 19960
Ph. (302) 422-2656
www.civilwarphilatelicsociety.org
E-mail: trishkauf@comcast.net

Errors, Freaks, and Oddities Collectors Club
Scott Shaulis
P.O. Box 549
Murrysville PA 15668-0549
Ph: (724) 733-4134
www.efocc.org
E-mail: scott@shaulisstamps.com

Hawaiian Philatelic Society
P O Box 10115
Honolulu HI 96816-0115
www.hawaiicollectibles.org/hawaii-philatelic-society
E-mail: hiphilsoc@gmail.com

International Philippine Philatelic Society
James R. Larot, Jr.
4990 Bayleaf Court
Martinez CA 94553
Ph: (925) 260-5425
www.theipps.info
E-mail: jlarot@ccwater.com

International Society of Reply Coupon Collectors
Peter Robin
P.O. Box 353
Bala Cynwyd PA 19004
E-mail: peterrobin@verizon.net

National Duck Stamp Collectors Society
Anthony J. Monico
P.O. Box 43
Harleysville PA 19438-0043
www.ndscs.org
E-mail: ndscs@hwcn.org

National Stamp Dealers Association
Sheldon Ruckens, President
3643 Private Road 18
Pinckneyville IL 62274-3426
Ph: (800) 875-6631
www.nsdainc.org
E-mail: nsda@nsdainc.org

Plate Number Coil Collectors Club
Gene Trinks
16415 W. Desert Wren Court
Surprise AZ 85374
Ph: (623) 322-4619
www.pnc3.org
E-mail: gctrinks@cox.net

Post Mark Collectors Club
Bob Milligan
7014 Woodland Oaks Drive
Magnolia TX 77354
Ph: (281) 259-2735
www.postmarks.org
E-mail: bob.milligan0@gmail.com

Postal History Society
Douglas Clark
P.O. Box 427
Marston Mills MA 02548-0427
www.postalhistorysociety.org
E-mail: dnc@math.uga.edu

Precancel Stamp Society
Frank J. Bird III
Promotional Secretary
1095 S. Pinellas Point Dr.
St. Petersburg, FL 33705-6377
www.precancels.com
E-mail: promo@precancels.com

Ryukyu Philatelic Specialists Society
Laura Edmonds, Secy.
P.O. Box 240177
Charlotte NC 28224-0177
Ph: (704) 519-5157
www.ryukyustamps.org
E-mail: secretary@ryukyustamps.org

Souvenir Card Collectors Society
William V. Kriebel
1923 Manning St.
Philadelphia PA 12103-5728
E-mail: krebewv@drexel.edu

State Revenue Society
Kent Gray
P. O. Box 67842
Albuquerque NM 87193
www.staterevenue.org
E-mail: srssecretary@comcast.net

United Nations Philatelists
Anthony F. Dewey
157 Warrenton Ave.
Hartford CT 06105
www.unpi.com
E-mail: afdewey@sbcglobal.net

United Postal Stationery Society
Dan Undersander
3804 Dolphin Drive
Madison WI 53719-1864
www.upss.org
E-mail: djunders@wisc.edu

U.S. Cancellation Club
Roger Curran
20 University Avenue
Lewisburg PA 17837
E-mail: rcurran@dejazzd.com

U.S. Philatelic Classics Society
Rob Lund
2913 Fulton St.
Everett WA 98201-3733
www.uspcs.org
E-mail: membershipchairman@uspcs.org

U.S. Possessions Philatelic Society
Daniel F. Ring
P.O. Box 113
Woodstock IL 60098
www.uspps.net
E-mail: danielfring@hotmail.com

United States Stamp Society
Executive Secretary
Rod Juell
P.O. Box 3508
Joliet IL 60434-3508
www.usstamps.org
E-mail: execsecretary@usstamps.org

Information on Catalogue Values, Grade and Condition

Catalogue Value

The Scott Catalogue value is a retail value; that is, an amount you could expect to pay for a stamp in the grade of Very Fine with no faults. Any exceptions to the grade valued will be noted in the text. The general introduction on the following pages and the individual section introductions further explain the type of material that is valued. The value listed for any given stamp is a reference that reflects recent actual dealer selling prices for that item.

Dealer retail price lists, public auction results, published prices in advertising and individual solicitation of retail prices from dealers, collectors and specialty organizations have been used in establishing the values found in this catalogue. Amos Media Co. values stamps, but Amos Media is not a company engaged in the business of buying and selling stamps as a dealer.

Use this catalogue as a guide for buying and selling. The actual price you pay for a stamp may be higher or lower than the catalogue value because of many different factors, including the amount of personal service a dealer offers, or increased or decreased interest in the country or topic represented by a stamp or set. An item may occasionally be offered at a lower price as a "loss leader," or as part of a special sale. You also may obtain an item inexpensively at public auction because of little interest at that time or as part of a large lot.

Stamps that are of a lesser grade than Very Fine, or those with condition problems, generally trade at lower prices than the values shown in this catalogue. Stamps of exceptional quality in both grade and condition often command higher prices than the values listed.

Values for pre-1879 unused issues are for stamps with approximately half or more of their original gum. Stamps with most or all of their original gum may be expected to sell for more, and stamps with less than half of their original gum may be expected to sell for somewhat less than the values listed. On rarer stamps, it may be expected that the original gum will be somewhat more disturbed than it will be on more common issues. Post-1879 unused issues are assumed to have full original gum. From breakpoints in most countries' listings, stamps are valued as never hinged, due to the wide availability of stamps in that condition. These notations are prominently placed in the listings and in the country information preceding the listings. Some countries also feature listings with dual values for hinged and never-hinged stamps.

Grade

A stamp's grade and condition are crucial to its value. The accompanying illustrations show examples of Very Fine stamps from different time periods, along with examples of stamps in Fine to Very Fine and Extremely Fine grades as points of reference. When a stamp seller offers a stamp in any grade from fine to superb without further qualifying statements, that stamp should not only have the centering grade as defined, but it also should be free of faults or other condition problems.

FINE stamps (illustrations not shown) have designs that are noticeably off center on two sides. Imperforate stamps may have small margins, and earlier issues may show the design touching one edge of the stamp design. For perforated stamps, perfs may barely clear the design on one side, and very early issues normally will have the perforations slightly cutting into the design. Used stamps may have heavier than usual cancellations.

FINE-VERY FINE stamps may be somewhat off center on one side, or slightly off center on two sides. Imperforate stamps will have two margins of at least normal size, and the design will not touch any edge. For perforated stamps, the perfs are well clear of the design, but are still noticeably off center. *However, early issues of a country may be printed in such a way that the design naturally is very close to the edges. In these cases, the perforations may cut into the design very slightly.* Used stamps will not have a cancellation that detracts from the design.

VERY FINE stamps may be slightly off center on one or two sides, but the design will be well clear of the edge. The stamp will present a nice, balanced appearance. Imperforate stamps will have three normal-sized margins. *However, early issues of many countries may be printed in such a way that the perforations may touch the design on one or more sides. Where this is the case, a boxed note will be found defining the centering and margins of the stamps being valued.* Used stamps will have light or otherwise neat cancellations. This is the grade used to establish Scott Catalogue values.

EXTREMELY FINE stamps are close to being perfectly centered. Imperforate stamps will have even margins that are larger than normal. Even the earliest perforated issues will have perforations clear of the design on all sides.

Amos Media Co. recognizes that there is no formally enforced grading scheme for postage stamps, and that the final price you pay or obtain for a stamp will be determined by individual agreement at the time of transaction.

Condition

Grade addresses only centering and (for used stamps) cancellation. *Condition* refers to factors other than grade that affect a stamp's desirability.

Factors that can increase the value of a stamp include exceptionally wide margins, particularly fresh color, the presence of selvage, and plate or die varieties. Unusual cancels on used stamps (particularly those of the 19th century) can greatly enhance their value as well.

Factors other than faults that decrease the value of a stamp include loss of original gum, regumming, a hinge remnant or foreign object adhering to the gum, natural inclusions, straight edges, and markings or notations applied by collectors or dealers.

Faults include missing pieces, tears, pin or other holes, surface scuffs, thin spots, creases, toning, short or pulled perforations, clipped perforations, oxidation or other forms of color changelings, soiling, stains, and such man-made changes as reperforations or the chemical removal or lightening of a cancellation.

Grading Illustrations

On the following page are illustrations of 11 different representative stamps from various time periods, 1847 to the modern era. Beginning with the 1847 10¢ Washington, examples are shown from the 1851-57 imperforates, two examples from the difficult 1857-61 perforated issues, a Black Jack representative of the 1861-67 issues, a Franklin stamp from the 1869 issue, a Bank Note stamp representative of the 1870-88 issues, an 1898 commemorative, a stamp from the 1902-03 issue, a representative 1908-22 Washington-Franklin design, and a 20th century definitive from the 1922 issue.

The editors believe these illustrations will prove useful in showing the margin size and centering that will be seen in the different time periods of U.S. stamp production.

In addition to the matters of margin size and centering, collectors are reminded that the very fine stamps valued in the Scott catalogues also will possess fresh color and intact perforations, and they will be free from defects.

Examples shown are computer-manipulated images made from single digitized master illustrations.

Stamp Illustrations Used in the Catalogue

It is important to note that the stamp images used for identification purposes in this catalogue may not be indicative of the grade of stamp being valued. Refer to the written discussion of grades on this page and to the grading illustrations on the following two pages for grading information.

	1847 ISSUE	1851-57 ISSUES	1857-61 ISSUES	1857-61 ISSUES	1861-67 ISSUES	1869 ISSUE
Fine-Very Fine →						
SCOTT CATALOGUES VALUE STAMPS IN THIS GRADE Very Fine →						
Extremely Fine →						

	1870-88 ISSUES	1898 TRANS-MISSISSIPPIS	1902-03 ISSUES	1908-20 WASHINGTON-FRANKLIN ISSUES	1922-25 ISSUES
Fine-Very Fine →					
SCOTT CATALOGUES VALUE STAMPS IN THIS GRADE Very Fine →					
Extremely Fine →					

For purposes of helping to determine the gum condition and value of an unused stamp, Scott presents the following chart which details different gum conditions and indicates how the conditions correlate with the Scott values for unused stamps.

Used together, the Illustrated Grading Chart on the previous page and this Illustrated Gum Chart should allow catalogue users to better understand the grade and gum condition of stamps valued in the *Scott U.S. Specialized Catalogue.*

Gum Categories:	MINT N.H.	ORIGINAL GUM (O.G.)				NO GUM
	 **Mint Never Hinged** *Free from any disturbance*	 **Lightly Hinged** *Faint impression of a removed hinge over a small area*	 **Hinge Mark or Remnant** *Prominent hinged spot; may have part or all of the hinge remaining*	 **Large part o.g.** *Approximately half or more of the gum intact*	**Small part o.g.** *Approximately less than half of the gum intact*	**No gum** *Only if issued with gum*
Commonly Used Symbol:	★★	★	★	★	★	(★)
PRE-1879 ISSUES	*Very fine pre-1879 stamps in these categories trade at a premium over Scott value*		Scott Value for "Unused" (Actual value will be affected by the degree of hinging and completeness of the gum.)			Scott "No Gum" Values thru No. 218
1879-1935 ISSUES	Scott "Never Hinged" Values for Nos. 182-771	Scott Value for "Unused" (Actual value will be affected by the degree of hinging of the full o.g.)				
1935 TO DATE	Scott Value for "Unused"					

Never Hinged (NH; ★★): A never-hinged stamp will have full original gum that will have no hinge mark or disturbance. The presence of an expertizer's mark does not disqualify a stamp from this designation.

Original Gum (OG; ★): Pre-1890 stamps should have approximately half or more of their original gum. On rarer stamps, it may be expected that the original gum will be somewhat more disturbed than it will be on more common issues. Stamps issued in 1890 or later should have full original gum. Original gum will show some disturbance caused by a previous hinge(s) which may be present or entirely removed. The actual value of an 1890 or later stamp will be affected by the degree of hinging of the full original gum.

Disturbed Original Gum: Gum showing noticeable effects of humidity, climate or hinging over more than half of the gum. The significance of gum disturbance in valuing a stamp in any of the Original Gum categories depends on the degree of disturbance, the rarity and normal gum condition of the issue and other variables affecting quality.

Regummed (RG; (★)): A regummed stamp is a stamp without gum that has had some type of gum privately applied at a time after it was issued. This normally is done to deceive collectors and/or dealers into thinking that the stamp has original gum and therefore has a higher value. A regummed stamp is considered the same as a stamp with none of its original gum for purposes of grading.

IMPORTANT INFORMATION REGARDING VALUES FOR NEVER-HINGED STAMPS

Collectors should be aware that the values given for never-hinged stamps from No. 182 on are for stamps in the grade of very fine. The never-hinged premium as a percentage of value will be larger for stamps in extremely fine or superb grades, and the premium will be smaller for fine-very-fine, fine or poor examples. This is particulary true of the issues of the late-19th and early 20th centuries. For example, in the grade of very fine, an unused stamp from this time period may be valued at $100 hinged and $200 never hinged. The never-hinged premium is thus 100%. But in a grade of extremely fine, this same stamp will not only sell for more hinged, but the never-hinged premium will increase, perhaps to 200%-400% or more over the higher extremely fine value. In a grade of superb, a hinged copy will sell for much more than a very fine copy, and additionally the never-hinged premium will be much larger, perhaps as large as 500%-1,000%. On the other hand, the same stamp in a grade of fine or fine-very fine not only will sell for less than a very fine stamp in hinged condition, but additionally the never-hinged premium will be smaller than the never-hinged premium on a very fine stamp, perhaps as small as 15%-30%.

Please note that the above statements and percentages are NOT a formula for arriving at the values of stamps in hinged or never-hinged condition in the grades of very good, fine, fine to very fine, extremely fine or superb. The percentages given apply only to the size of the premium for never-hinged condition that might be added to the stamp value for hinged condition. Further, the percentages given are only generalized estimates. Some stamps or grades may have percentages for never-hinged condition that are higher or lower than the ranges given. For values of the most popular U.S. stamps in the grades of very good, fine, fine to very fine, very fine to extremely fine, extremely fine, extremely fine to superb and superb, see the *Scott Stamp Values* section of this catalog.

Never-Hinged Plate Blocks

Values given for never-hinged plate blocks are for blocks in which all stamps have original gum that has never been hinged and has no disturbances, and all selvage, whether gummed or ungummed, has never been hinged.

Catalogue Values for Stamps on Covers

Definition of a Cover

Covers are philatelically defined as folded letters, folded covers or envelopes, with or without postage stamps, that have passed through the mail and bear postal or other markings of philatelic interest. Before the introduction of envelopes about 1840, people folded letters and wrote the address on the outside. Used stamped envelopes and wrappers and other items of postal stationery also are considered covers, as is a postage stamp used on a post card.

Catalogue Value

The Scott Catalogue value for a stamp on cover, as for a stamp off cover, is a retail value; that is, an amount you could expect to pay for that cover in a grade of Very Fine, as defined below. Folded letters, folded covers, envelopes, postcards, stationery entires and newspapers are valued as whole and complete, not as fronts of letter sheets or envelopes or as fragments of newspapers or circulars. Values given are for covers bearing stamps that are "tied on" by the cancellation. A stamp is said to be "tied" to a cover when the cancellation or postmark falls on both the stamp and the cover. Exceptions always will be noted. Values for bisected stamps on cover are for items on which the cancellation ties the stamp across the cut. Values for U.S. patriotic covers of the Civil War period (bearing pictorial designs of a patriotic nature) are for the most common designs.

It should be noted that conventions observed for calculating the catalogue value of a cover with several different stamps vary somewhat between types of covers. In a general way, however, the most common procedure may be summarized as follows: the stamp which has the highest "value on cover" is counted with its on-cover value, while the other stamps are added on to the total with their normal value as used stamps "off cover."

The value generally is given for the stamps as they are most commonly found on a cover. In some cases a stamp is most commonly found alone, paying a specified rate for the envelope, given its weight, destination and method of intended delivery. For instance, beginning July 1, 1863, and continuing through September 30, 1883, a one-half ounce letter sent domestically by ordinary first-class mail required three cents postage. Because such letters were very common, it follows that stamps with denominations of three cents are most often found on envelopes paying that one-half ounce domestic rate. Three-cent stamps also are found on letters together with other stamps making up different rates. A pair of three-cent stamps paid for a one-ounce domestic letter, four three-cent stamps paid for a one-ounce letter addressed to England (rate effective January 1, 1870, through June 30, 1875), and so forth. Because letters addressed abroad are less common than letters addressed domestically, the on-cover value of the three-cent stamps refers to the single usage. That is not true in all instances, because there are some stamps issued during the 19th century that are more scarce used singly than in combination with other stamps. In all these other cases, the value given is for the least scarce of the combinations. For most stamps issued during 1922-31, the value is for a specific use. For example, the value for the 1922 15-cent Statue of Liberty stamp (Scott 566) is for that stamp on a registered cover with a two-cent stamp, to pay the two-cent domestic first-class letter rate and 15-cent registry fee.

If the value of a single stamp on a cover is of particular philatelic importance, as in the case of certain stamps used to pay for reduced rates for the delivery of newspapers or other printed matter, then their different value for this use may be indicated in footnotes or as a separate listing. For example, the 3-cent George Washington stamp of 1851 (Scott 10) is specifically valued paying the 3-cent rate for a circular mailed a distance of 1,000 miles to 1,500 miles from the point of mailing. It clearly is impossible to add to a specialized catalogue of U.S. stamps the detailed information regarding the relative scarcity and value of all rates and combinations. We have limited ourselves to some of the more noteworthy and important cases.

In the majority of cases, the value of a cover assumes that the stamps on it have been used in the period contemporaneous with their issuance. Late uses are sometimes considered premium items, but in most cases late and very late uses are of no significance and detract from the value of the cover.

Condition

When evaluating a cover, care must be given to the factors that determine the overall condition of the item. It is generally more difficult to grade and evaluate a cover than a stamp. The condition of the stamps affixed to the cover must be taken into account — always in relation to the criteria for the particular issue. The Scott Catalogue does specify the grade and condition of the stamps for which a value is given, so it is important to consult this information. In addition, the condition of the cover must be taken into account. Values are for covers that are reasonably well preserved given the period of usage and the country of origin. A tiny nick or tear, or slight reduction from opening, are normal for 19th century covers. Folded letters may be expected to have tears on the reverse from opening, and often they will have file folds. Unless these factors affect the stamps or postal markings, they should not detract from the on-cover values given in the catalogue.

Just as with stamps, various factors can lower the value of a cover. Missing pieces, serious tears, holes, creases, toning, stains and alterations of postal markings are examples of factors that lower the value of a cover. The necessity of considering these factors for the cover, as well as having to consider the condition of the stamps on the cover, helps to explain why it is more difficult to determine the value of a cover than a stamp off cover.

Factors Enhancing the Value of a Cover

A further difficulty in the valuation of covers is the necessity of considering factors other than the stamps used on a cover and the condition of the stamps and the cover. As stated previously, catalogue values listed herein generally reflect the most common uses of stamps on covers that are reasonably well preserved given the period of usage. Consideration of factors that may enhance the value of covers for the most part is beyond the scope of the Scott Catalogue. However, it is critical to understand that there are many such factors. Following is a list of many of the factors that often will increase the value of a cover.

- postal markings indicating origin, transit and arrival;
- postal markings indicating rates paid, which include postage, registration, acknowledgment of receipt, express charges, insurance, postage due, forwarding and many others;
- postal markings indicating carriers such as stagecoaches, trains, ships, aircraft, etc.;
- markings applied by censors, other civilian or military authorities, and others;
- scarce or rare destinations and routings;
- interruptions in the delivery system due to accidents, wars, natural calamities, etc.;
- unusual combinations of stamps;
- printed or hand-drawn pictorial, advertising or patriotic cover designs;
- unusual quality of stamps, postal markings or cover;
- and, outside of postal history, particularly noteworthy addressee, sender or contents.

Understanding the Listings

On the opposite page is an enlarged "typical" listing from this catalogue. Following are detailed explanations of each of the highlighted parts of the listing.

1 Scott number — Stamp collectors use Scott numbers to identify specific stamps when buying, selling, or trading stamps, and for ease in organizing their collections. Each stamp issued by a country has a unique number. Therefore, U.S. Scott 219 can only refer to a single stamp. Although the Scott Catalogue usually lists stamps in chronological order by date of issue, when a country issues a set of stamps over a period of time the stamps within that set are kept together without regard to date of issue. This follows the normal collecting approach of keeping stamps in their natural sets.

When a country is known to be issuing a set of stamps over a period of time, a group of consecutive catalogue numbers is reserved for the stamps in that set, as issued. If that group of numbers proves to be too few, capital-letter suffixes are added to numbers to create enough catalogue numbers to cover all items in the set. Scott uses a suffix letter, e.g., "A," "b," etc., only once. If there is a Scott 296B in a set, there will not be a Scott 296b also.

There are times when the block of numbers is too large for the set, leaving some numbers unused. Such gaps in the sequence also occur when the editors move an item elsewhere in the catalogue or remove it from the listings entirely. Scott does not attempt to account for every possible number, but rather it does attempt to assure that each stamp is assigned its own number.

Scott numbers designating regular postage normally are only numerals. Scott numbers for other types of stamps, e.g., air post, special delivery, and so on, will have a prefix of either a capital letter or a combination of numerals and capital letters.

2 Illustration number — used to identify each illustration. Where more than one stamp in a set uses the same illustration number, that number needs to be used with the description line (noted below) to be certain of the exact variety of the stamp within the set. Illustrations normally are 75, 100, or 150 percent of the original size of the stamp. An effort has been made to note all illustrations not at those percentages. Overprints are shown at 100 percent of the original, unless otherwise noted. Letters *in parentheses* which follow an illustration number refer to illustrations of overprints or surcharges.

3 Listing styles — there are two principal types of catalogue listings: major and minor.

Majors may be distinguished by having as their catalogue number a numeral with or without a capital-letter suffix and with or without a prefix.

Minors have a small-letter suffix (or, only have the small letter itself shown if the listing is immediately beneath its major listing). These listings show a variety of the "normal," or major item. Examples include color variation or a different watermark used for that stamp only.

Examples of major numbers are 9X1, 16, 28A, 6LB1, C13, RW1, and TS1. Examples of minor numbers are 22b, 279Bc and C3a.

4 Denomination — normally value printed on the stamp (generally known as the *face value*), which is — unless otherwise stated — the cost of the stamp at the time of issue.

5 Basic information on stamp or set — introducing each stamp issue, this section normally includes the date of issue, method of printing, perforation, watermark, and sometimes additional information. New information on method of printing, watermark or perforation measurement will appear when that information changes. Dates of issue are as precise as Scott is able to confirm, either year only, month and year, or month, day and year.

In stamp sets issued over more than one date, the year or span of years will be in bold type above the first catalogue number. Individual stamps in the set will have a date-of-issue appearing in italics. Stamps without a year listed appeared during the first year of the span. Dates are not always given for minor varieties.

6 Color or other description — this line provides information to solidify identification of the stamp. Historically, when stamps normally were printed in a single color, only the color appeared here. With modern printing techniques, which include multicolor presses which mix inks on the paper, earlier methods of color identification are no longer applicable. When space permits, a description of the stamp design will replace the terms "multi" or "multicolored." The color of the paper is noted in italic type when the paper used is not white.

7 Date of issue — As precisely as Scott is able to confirm, either year only; month and year, or month, day and year. In some cases, the earliest documented use (edu) is given. All dates, especially where no official date of issue has been given, are subject to change as new information is obtained. Many cases are known of inadvertent sale and use of stamps prior to dates of issue announced by postal officials. These are not listed here.

8 Value unused and Value used — the catalogue values are in U. S. dollars and are based on stamps that are in a grade of Very Fine unless stated otherwise. Unused values refer to items that have not seen postal or other duty for which they were intended. For pre-1890 issues, unused stamps must have at least most of their original gum; for later issues, complete gum is expected. Stamps issued without gum are noted. Unused values are for never-hinged stamps beginning at the point immediately following a prominent notice in the actual listing. Scott values for used self-adhesive stamps are for examples either on piece or off piece. Premium values for used stamps with certain cancellations are listed under the heading "Cancellations" below the main listings. These values are to be added to the used values for the stamps. In those cases where a stamp has a cancel with two or more characteristics, the premium values are combined and then added to the used value.

Some sections in this book have more than two columns for values. Check section introductions and watch for value column headers. See the sections "Catalogue Values" and "Understanding Valuing Notations" for an explanation of the meaning of these values.

9 Changes in basic set information — bold or other type is used to show any change in the basic data between stamps within a set of stamps, e.g., perforation from one stamp to the next or a different paper or printing method or watermark.

10 Other varieties — these include additional shades, plate varieties, multiples, used on cover, plate number blocks. coil line pairs, coil plate number strips of three or five, ZIP blocks, etc.

On early issues, there may be a "Cancellation" section. Values in this section refer to single stamps off cover, unless otherwise noted. Values with a "+" are added to the basic used value. See "Basic Stamp Information" for more details on stamp and cancellation varieties.

11 Footnote — Where other important details about the stamps can be found.

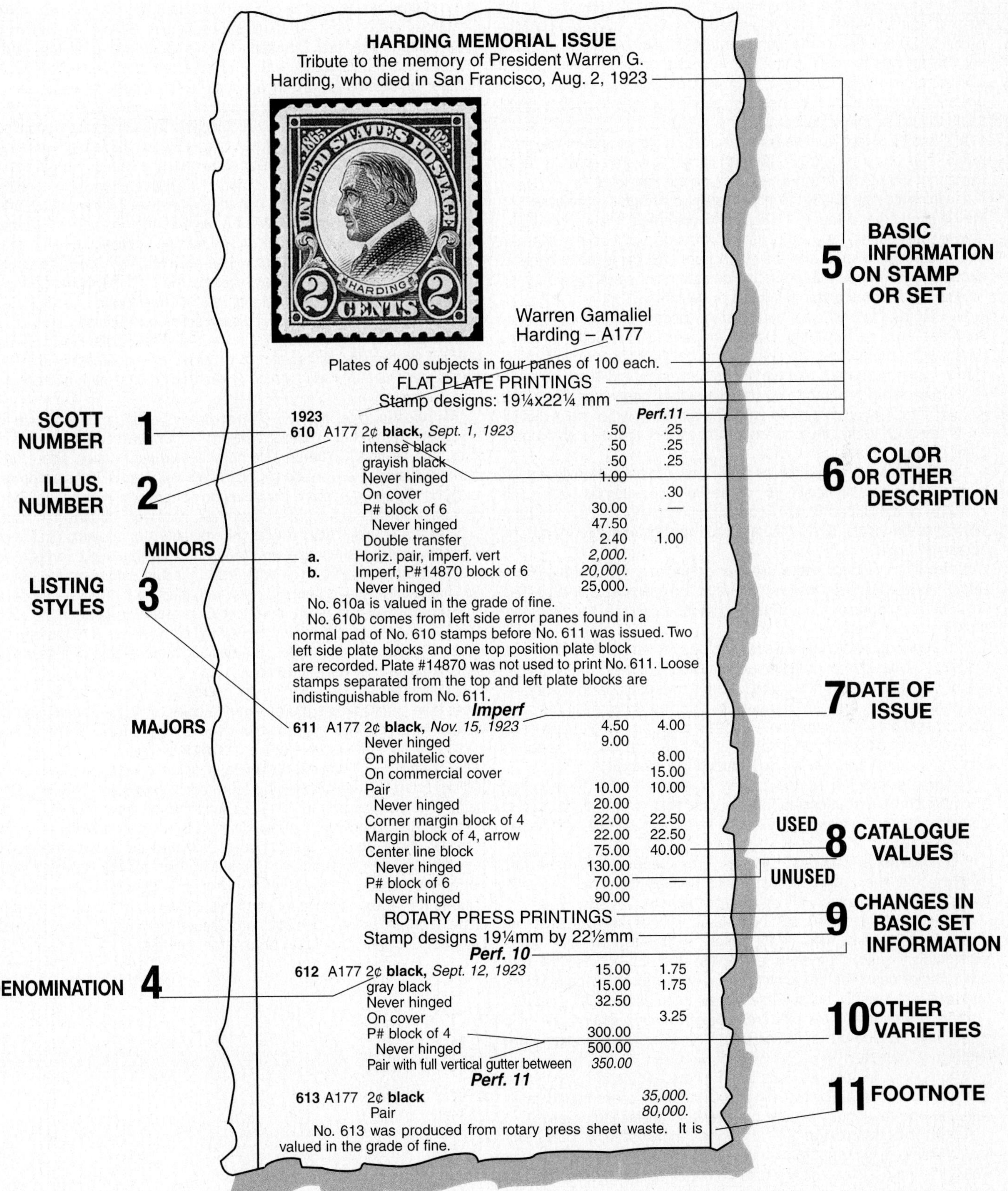

HARDING MEMORIAL ISSUE

Tribute to the memory of President Warren G. Harding, who died in San Francisco, Aug. 2, 1923

Warren Gamaliel Harding – A177

Plates of 400 subjects in four panes of 100 each.

FLAT PLATE PRINTINGS

Stamp designs: 19¼x22¼ mm

1923			*Perf.11*
610	A177 2¢ **black,** *Sept. 1, 1923*	.50	.25
	intense black	.50	.25
	grayish black	.50	.25
	Never hinged	1.00	
	On cover		.30
	P# block of 6	30.00	—
	Never hinged	47.50	
	Double transfer	2.40	1.00
a.	Horiz. pair, imperf. vert	*2,000.*	
b.	Imperf, P#14870 block of 6	*20,000.*	
	Never hinged	25,000.	

No. 610a is valued in the grade of fine.

No. 610b comes from left side error panes found in a normal pad of No. 610 stamps before No. 611 was issued. Two left side plate blocks and one top position plate block are recorded. Plate #14870 was not used to print No. 611. Loose stamps separated from the top and left plate blocks are indistinguishable from No. 611.

Imperf

611	A177 2¢ **black,** *Nov. 15, 1923*	4.50	4.00
	Never hinged	9.00	
	On philatelic cover		8.00
	On commercial cover		15.00
	Pair	10.00	10.00
	Never hinged	20.00	
	Corner margin block of 4	22.00	22.50
	Margin block of 4, arrow	22.00	22.50
	Center line block	75.00	40.00
	Never hinged	130.00	
	P# block of 6	70.00	—
	Never hinged	90.00	

ROTARY PRESS PRINTINGS

Stamp designs 19¼mm by 22½mm

Perf. 10

612	A177 2¢ **black,** *Sept. 12, 1923*	15.00	1.75
	gray black	15.00	1.75
	Never hinged	32.50	
	On cover		3.25
	P# block of 4	300.00	
	Never hinged	500.00	
	Pair with full vertical gutter between	*350.00*	

Perf. 11

613	A177 2¢ **black**		*35,000.*
	Pair		*80,000.*

No. 613 was produced from rotary press sheet waste. It is valued in the grade of fine.

Catalogue Listing Policy

It is the intent of Amos Media Co. to list all postage stamps of the world in the *Scott Standard Postage Stamp Catalogue.* The only strict criteria for listing is that stamps be decreed legal for postage by the issuing country and that the issuing country actually have an operating postal system. Whether the primary intent of issuing a given stamp or set was for sale to postal patrons or to stamp collectors is not part of our listing criteria. Scott's role is to provide basic comprehensive postage stamp information. It is up to each stamp collector to choose which items to include in a collection.

It is Scott's objective to seek reasons why a stamp should be listed, rather than why it should not. Nevertheless, there are certain types of items that will not be listed. These include the following:

1. Unissued items that are not officially distributed or released by the issuing postal authority. If such items are officially issued at a later date by the country, they will be listed. Unissued items consist of those that have been printed and then held from sale for reasons such as change in government, errors found on stamps or something deemed objectionable about a stamp subject or design.

2. Stamps "issued" by non-existent postal entities or fantasy countries, such as Nagaland, Occusi-Ambeno, Staffa, Sedang, Torres Straits and others. Also, stamps "issued" in the names of legitimate, stamp-issuing countries that are not authorized by those countries.

3. Semi-official or unofficial items not required for postage. Examples include items issued by private agencies for their own express services. When such items are required for delivery, or are valid as prepayment of postage, they are listed.

4. Local stamps issued for local use only. Postage stamps issued by governments specifically for "domestic" use, such as Haiti Scott 219-228, or the United States non-denominated stamps, are not considered to be locals, since they are valid for postage throughout the country of origin.

5. Items not valid for postal use. For example, a few countries have issued souvenir sheets that are not valid for postage. This area also includes a number of worldwide charity labels (some denominated) that do not pay postage.

6. Egregiously exploitative issues such as stamps sold for far more than face value, stamps purposefully issued in artificially small quantities or only against advance orders, stamps awarded only to a selected audience such as a philatelic bureau's standing order customers, or stamps sold only in conjunction with other products. All of these kinds of items are usually controlled issues and/or are intended for speculation. These items normally will be included in a footnote.

7. Items distributed by the issuing government only to a limited group, such as a stamp club, philatelic exhibition or a single stamp dealer, or other private company. These items normally will be included in a footnote.

8. Stamps not available to collectors. These generally are rare items, all of which are held by public institutions such as museums. The existence of such items often will be cited in footnotes.

The fact that a stamp has been used successfully as postage, even on international mail, is not in itself sufficient proof that it was legitimately issued. Numerous examples of so-called stamps from non-existent countries are known to have been used to post letters that have successfully passed through the international mail system.

There are certain items that are subject to interpretation. When a stamp falls outside our specifications, it may be listed along with a cautionary footnote.

A number of factors are considered in our approach to analyzing how a stamp is listed. The following list of factors is presented to share with you, the catalogue user, the complexity of the listing process.

Additional printings — "Additional printings" of a previously issued stamp may range from an item that is totally different to cases where it is impossible to differentiate from the original. At least a minor number (a small-letter suffix) is assigned if there is a distinct change in stamp shade, noticeably redrawn design, or a significantly different perforation measurement. A major number (numeral or numeral and capital-letter combination) is assigned if the editors feel the "additional printing" is sufficiently different from the original that it constitutes a different issue.

Commemoratives — Where practical, commemoratives with the same theme are placed in a set. For example, the U.S. Civil War Centennial set of 1961-65 and the Constitution Bicentennial series of 1989-90 appear as sets. Countries such as Japan and Korea issue such material on a regular basis, with an announced, or at least predictable, number of stamps known in advance. Occasionally, however, stamp sets that were released over a period of years have been separated. Appropriately placed footnotes will guide you to each set's continuation.

Definitive sets — Blocks of numbers generally have been reserved for definitive sets, based on previous experience with any given country. If a few more stamps were issued in a set than originally expected, they often have been inserted into the original set with a capital-letter suffix, such as U.S. Scott 1059A. If it appears that many more stamps than the originally allotted block will be released before the set is completed, a new block of numbers will be reserved, with the original one being closed off. In some cases, such as the U.S. Transportation and Great Americans series, several blocks of numbers exist. Appropriately placed footnotes will guide you to each set's continuation.

New country — Membership in the Universal Postal Union is not a consideration for listing status or order of placement within the catalogue. The index will tell you in what volume or page number the listings begin.

"No release date" items — The amount of information available for any given stamp issue varies greatly from country to country and even from time to time. Extremely comprehensive information about new stamps is available from some countries well before the stamps are released. By contrast some countries do not provide information about stamps or release dates. Most countries, however, fall between these extremes. A country may provide denominations or subjects of stamps from upcoming issues that are not issued as planned. Sometimes, philatelic agencies, those private firms hired to represent countries, add these later-issued items to sets well after the formal release date. This time period can range from weeks to years. If these items were officially released by the country, they will be added to the appropriate spot in the set. In many cases, the specific release date of a stamp or set of stamps may never be known.

Overprints — The color of an overprint is always noted if it is other than black. Where more than one color of ink has been used on overprints of a single set, the color used is noted. Early overprint and surcharge illustrations were altered to prevent their use by forgers.

Se-tenants — Connected stamps of differing features (se-tenants) will be listed in the format most commonly collected. This includes pairs, blocks or larger multiples. Se-tenant units are not always symmetrical. An example is Australia Scott 508, which is a block of seven stamps. If the stamps are primarily collected as a unit, the major number may be assigned to the multiple, with minors going to each component stamp. In cases where continuous-design or other unit se-tenants will receive significant postal use, each stamp is given a major Scott number listing. This includes issues from the United States, Canada, Germany and Great Britain, for example.

Scott Numbering Practices and Special Notices

Classification of stamps

The Scott *Specialized Catalogue of United States Stamps and Covers* lists the stamps of the United States and its possessions and territories and the stamps of the United Nations. The next level is a listing by section on the basis of the function of the stamps or postal stationery. In each case, the items are listed in specialized detail. The principal sections cover regular postage stamps; air post stamps; postage due stamps, special delivery, and so on. Except for regular postage, catalogue numbers for most sections include a prefix letter (or number-letter combination) denoting the class to which the stamp belongs.

The Table of Contents notes each section and, where pertinent, the prefix used. Some, such as souvenir cards and encased postage, do not have prefixes. Some sections, such as specimens and private perforations, have suffixes only.

New issue listings

Updates to this catalogue appear each month in the *Linn's Stamp News Monthly* magazine. Included are corrections and updates to the current edition of this catalogue.

From time to time there will be changes in the listings from the *Linn's Stamp News Monthly* to the next edition of the catalogue, as additional information becomes available.

The catalogue update section of the *Linn's Stamp News Monthly* is the most timely presentation of this material available. For current subscription rates, see advertisements in this catalogue or write Linn's Stamp News, Box 926, Sidney, OH 45365-0926.

Additions, deletions & number changes

A list of catalogue additions, deletions, and number changes from the previous edition of the catalogue appears in each volume. See Catalogue Additions, Deletions & Number Changes in the Table of Contents for the location of this list.

Understanding valuing notations

The *absence of a value* does not necessarily suggest that a stamp is scarce or rare. In the U.S. listings, a dash in the value column means that the stamp is known in a stated form or variety, but information is lacking or insufficient for purposes of establishing a usable catalogue value. These could include rarities, such as Scott 3X4 on cover, or items that have a limited market, such as used plate blocks of Scott 1097.

Stamp values in *italics* generally refer to items which are difficult to value accurately. For expensive items, e.g., value at $1,000 or more, a value in italics represents an item which trades very seldom, such as a unique item. For inexpensive items, a value in italics represents a warning.

The Scott Catalogue values for used stamps reflect canceled-to-order material when such are found to predominate in the marketplace for the issue involved. Frequently notes appear in the stamp listings to specify items which are valued as canceled-to-order (Canal Zone Scott O1-O8) or if there is a premium for postally used examples.

Scott values for used stamps are not for precanceled examples, unless so stated. Precanceled copies must not have additional postal cancellations.

An example of a warning to collectors is a stamp that used has a value considerably higher than the unused version. Here, the collector is cautioned to be certain the used version has a readable, contemporaneous cancellation.

The *minimum catalogue value* of a stamp is 25 cents, to cover a dealer's costs of purchase and preparation for resale. The minimum catalogue value of a first day cover is one dollar. As noted, the sum of these values does not properly represent the "value" of a packet of unsorted or unmounted stamps sold in bulk. Such large collections, mixtures or packets generally consist of the lower-valued stamps. There are examples where the catalogue value of a block of stamps is less than the sum of the values of the individual stamps. This situation is caused by the overhead involved in handling single stamps, and should not be considered a suggestion that all blocks be separated into individual stamps to achieve a higher market value.

Values in the "unused" column are for stamps with original gum, if issued with gum. The stamp is valued as hinged if the listing appears *before* the point at which stamps are valued as never hinged. This point is marked by prominent notes in many sections. A similar note will appear at the beginning of the section's listing, noting exactly where the dividing point between hinged and never hinged is for each section of the listings. Where a value for a used stamp is considerably higher than for the unused stamp, the value applies to a stamp showing a distinct contemporaneous cancellation.

Cancellations

A complete treatment of this subject is impossible in a catalogue of this limited size. Only postal markings of meaning — those which were necessary to the proper function of the postal service — are recorded here, while those of value owing to their fanciness only are disregarded. The latter are the results of the whim of some postal official. Many of these odd designs, however, command high prices, based on their popularity, scarcity and clearness of impression.

Although there are many types of most of the cancellations listed, only one of each is illustrated. The values quoted are for the most common type of each.

Values for cancellation varieties are for stamp specimens off cover. Some cancellation varieties (e.g., pen, precancel, cut) are valued individually. Other varieties on pre-1900 stamps (e.g., less common colors, specific dates, foreign usages) are valued using premiums (denoted by "+") which are added to the stated value for the used stamp. When listed on cover, the distinctive cancellation must be on the stamp in order to merit catalogue valuation. Postal markings that denote origin or a service (as distinguished from canceling a stamp) merit catalogue valuation when on a cover apart from the stamp, provided the stamp is otherwise tied to the cover by a cancellation.

One type of "Paid" cancellation used in Boston, and shown in this introduction under "Postal Markings," is common and values given are for types other than this.

Examination

Amos Media Co. will not pass upon the genuineness, grade or condition of stamps, because of the time and responsibility involved. Rather, there are several expertizing groups which undertake this work for both collectors and dealers. Neither will Amos Media Co. appraise or identify philatelic material. The Company cannot take responsibility for unsolicited stamps or covers sent by individuals.

All letters, E-mails, etc. are read attentively, but they are not always answered due to time considerations

How to order from your dealer

It is not necessary to write the full description of a stamp as listed in this catalogue. All that you need is the name of the country or *U.S. Specialized* section, the Scott Catalogue number and whether the item is unused or used. For example, "U.S. Scott 833" is sufficient to identify the stamp of the United States listed as the 2-dollar value of a set of stamps issued between 1938-43. This stamp was issued September 29, 1938. It is yellow green and black in color, has a perforation of 11, and is printed on paper without a watermark by a flat plate press. Sections without a prefix or suffix must be mentioned by name.

Abbreviations

Amos Media Co. uses a consistent set of abbreviations throughout this catalogue and the *Standard Postage Stamp Catalogue* to conserve space while still providing necessary information. The first block shown here refers to color names only:

COLOR ABBREVIATIONS

amb	amber	ind	indigo
anil	aniline	int	intense
ap	apple	lav	lavender
aqua	aquamarine	lem	lemon
az	azure	lil	lilac
bis	bister	lt	light
bl	blue	mag	magenta
bld	blood	man	manila
blk	black	mar	maroon
bril	brilliant	mv	mauve
brn	brown	multi	multicolored
brnsh	brownish	mlky	milky
brnz	bronze	myr	myrtle
brt	bright	ol	olive
brnt	burnt	olvn	olivine
car	carmine	org	orange
cer	cerise	pck	peacock
chlky	chalky	pnksh	pinkish
cham	chamois	Prus	Prussian
chnt	chestnut	pur	purple
choc	chocolate	redsh	reddish
chr	chrome	res	reseda
cit	citron	ros	rosine
cl	claret	ryl	royal
cob	cobalt	sal	salmon
cop	copper	saph	sapphire
crim	crimson	scar	scarlet
cr	cream	sep	sepia
dk	dark	sien	sienna
dl	dull	sil	silver
dp	deep	sl	slate
db	drab	stl	steel
emer	emerald	turq	turquoise
gldn	golden	ultra	ultramarine
grysh	grayish	ven	venetian
grn	green	ver	vermilion
grnsh	greenish	vio	violet
hel	heliotrope	yel	yellow
hn	henna	yelsh	yellowish

When no color is given for an overprint or surcharge, black is the color used. Abbreviations for colors used for overprints and surcharges are: "(B)" or "(Blk)," black; "(Bl)," blue; "(R)," red; "(G)," green; etc.

Additional abbreviations used in this catalogue are shown below:

Adm. .... Administration
AFL .... American Federation of Labor
Anniv. .... Anniversary
APU .... Arab Postal Union
APS .... American Philatelic Society
ASEAN .... Association of South East Asian Nations
ASPCA .... American Society for the Prevention of Cruelty to Animals
Assoc. .... Association

b. .... Born
BEP .... Bureau of Engraving and Printing
Bicent. .... Bicentennial
Bklt. .... Booklet
Brit. .... British
btwn. .... Between
Bur. .... Bureau

c. or ca. .... Circa
CAR .... Central African Republic
Cat. .... Catalogue
Cent. .... Centennial, century, centenary
CEPT .... Conference Europeenne des Administrations des Postes et des Telecommunications
CIO .... Congress of Industrial Organizations
Conf. .... Conference
Cong. .... Congress
Cpl. .... Corporal
CTO .... Canceled to order

d. .... Died
Dbl. .... Double
DDR .... German Democratic Republic (East Germany)

EC .... European Community
ECU .... European currency unit
EDU .... Earliest documented use
EEC .... European Economic Community
Engr. .... Engraved
Exhib. .... Exhibition
Expo. .... Exposition

FAO .... Food and Agricultural Organization of the United Nations
Fed. .... Federation
FIP .... Federation International de Philatelie

GB .... Great Britain
Gen. .... General
GPO .... General post office

Horiz. .... Horizontal

ICAO .... International Civil Aviation Organization
ICY .... International Cooperation Year
ILO .... International Labor Organization
Imperf. .... Imperforate
Impt. .... Imprint
Intl. .... International
Invtd. .... Inverted
IQSY .... International Quiet Sun Year
ITU .... International Telecommunications Union
ITY .... International Tourism Year
IWY .... International Women's Year
IYC .... International Year of the Child
IYD .... International Year of the Disabled
IYSH .... International Year of Shelter for the Homeless
IYY .... International Youth Year

L. .... Left
Lieut. .... Lieutenant
Litho. .... Lithographed

LL.............. Lower left
LR.............. Lower right

mm .... Millimeter
Ms.............. Manuscript

NASA.......... National Aeronautics and Space Administration
Natl. .... National
NATO .... North Atlantic Treaty Organization
No.............. Number
NY.............. New York
NYC .... New York City

OAU........... Organization of African Unity
OPEC......... Organization of Petroleum Exporting Countries
Ovpt........... Overprint
Ovptd......... Overprinted

P# .... Plate number
Perf. .... Perforated, perforation
Phil............. Philatelic
Photo. .... Photogravure
PO .... Post office
Pr. .... Pair
P.R. .... Puerto Rico
PRC .... People's Republic of China (Mainland China)
Prec. .... Precancel, precanceled
Pres. .... President

R................. Right
Rio .... Rio de Janeiro
ROC........... Republic of China (Taiwan)

SEATO .... South East Asia Treaty Organization
Sgt. .... Sergeant
Soc. .... Society
Souv........... Souvenir
SSR .... Soviet Socialist Republic
St. .... Saint, street
Surch. .... Surcharge

Typo. .... Typographed
UAE .... United Arab Emirates
UAMPT....... Union of African and Malagasy Posts and Telecommunications
UL.............. Upper left
UN .... United Nations
UNESCO .... United Nations Educational, Scientific and Cultural Organization
UNICEF...... United Nations Children's Fund
Univ .... University
UNPA.......... United Nations Postal Administration
Unwmkd ..... Unwatermarked
UPU............ Universal Postal Union
UR .... Upper right
US.............. United States
USPO.......... United States Post Office Department
USPS.......... United States Postal Service (also "U.S. Postage Stamp" when referring to the watermark)
USSR.......... Union of Soviet Socialist Republics

Vert .... Vertical
VP .... Vice president

WCY .... World Communications Year
WFUNA....... World Federation of United Nations Associations
WHO.......... World Health Organization
Wmk .... Watermark
Wmkd .... Watermarked
WMO .... World Meteorological Organization
WRY........... World Refugee Year
WWF.......... World Wildlife Fund
WWI........... World War I
WWII.......... World War II

YAR............ Yemen Arab Republic
Yemen PDR. Yemen People's Democratic Republic

Postmasters General of the United States

1775 Benjamin Franklin, July 26.
1776 Richard Bache, Nov. 7.
1782 Ebenezer Hazard, Jan. 28.
1789 Samuel Osgood, Sept. 26.
1791 Timothy Pickering, Aug. 12.
1795 Joseph Habersham, Feb. 25.
1801 Gideon Granger, Nov. 28.
1814 Return J. Meigs, Jr., Apr. 11.
1823 John McLean, July 1.
1829 William T. Barry, Apr. 6.
1835 Amos Kendall, May 1.
1840 John M. Niles, May 26.
1841 Francis Granger, Mar. 8.
1841 Charles A. Wickliffe, Oct. 13.
1845 Cave Johnson, Mar. 7.
1849 Jacob Collamer, Mar. 8.
1850 Nathan K. Hall, July 23.
1852 Samuel D. Hubbard, Sept. 14.
1853 James Campbell, Mar. 8.
1857 Aaron V. Brown, Mar. 7.
1859 Joseph Holt, Mar. 14.
1861 Horatio King, Feb. 12.
1861 Montgomery Blair, Mar. 9.
1864 William Dennison, Oct. 1.
1866 Alexander W. Randall, July 25.
1869 John A.J. Creswell, Mar. 6.
1874 Jas. W. Marshall, July 7.
1874 Marshall Jewell, Sept. 1.
1876 James N. Tyner, July 13.
1877 David McK. Key, Mar. 13.
1880 Horace Maynard, Aug. 25.
1881 Thomas L. James, Mar. 8.
1882 Timothy O. Howe, Jan. 5.
1883 Walter Q. Gresham, Apr. 11.
1884 Frank Hatton, Oct. 14.
1885 Wm. F. Vilas, Mar. 7.
1888 Don M. Dickinson, Jan. 17.
1889 John Wanamaker, Mar. 6.
1893 Wilson S. Bissell, Mar. 7.
1895 William L. Wilson, Apr. 4.
1897 James A. Gary, Mar. 6.
1898 Charles Emory Smith, Apr. 22.
1902 Henry C. Payne, Jan. 15.
1904 Robert J. Wynne, Oct. 10.
1905 Geo. B. Cortelyou, Mar. 7.
1907 Geo. von L. Meyer, Mar. 4.
1909 Frank H. Hitchcock, Mar. 6.
1913 Albert S. Burleson, Mar. 5.
1921 Will H. Hays, Mar. 5.
1922 Hubert Work, Mar. 4.
1923 Harry S. New, Mar. 4.
1929 Walter F. Brown, Mar. 6.
1933 James A. Farley, Mar. 4.
1940 Frank C. Walker, Sept. 11.
1945 Robert E. Hannegan, July 1.
1947 Jesse M. Donaldson, Dec. 16.
1953 Arthur E. Summerfield, Jan. 21.
1961 J. Edward Day, Jan. 21.
1963 John A. Gronouski, Sept. 30.
1965 Lawrence F. O'Brien, Nov. 3.
1968 W. Marvin Watson, Apr. 26.
1969 Winton M. Blount, Jan. 22.

U.S. POSTAL SERVICE

1971 Elmer T. Klassen, Dec. 7.
1975 Benjamin Bailar, Feb. 15.
1978 William F. Bolger, Mar. 1.
1985 Paul N. Carlin, Jan. 1.
1986 Albert V. Casey, Jan. 6.
1986 Preston R. Tisch, Aug. 17.
1988 Anthony M. Frank, Mar. 1.
1992 Marvin T. Runyon, Jr., July 6.
1998 William J. Henderson, May 16.
2001 John E. Potter, June 1
2010 Patrick R. Donahoe, Oct. 25
2015 Megan J. Brennan, Feb. 1
2020 Louis DeJoy, June 16

Basic Stamp Information

A stamp collector's knowledge of the combined elements that make a given issue of a stamp unique determines his or her ability to identify stamps. These elements include paper, watermark, method of separation, printing, design and gum. On the following pages these important areas are described in detail.

The guide below will direct you to those philatelic terms which are not major headings in the following introductory material. The major headings are:

Plate	Paper	Gum	Postal Markings
Printing	Separation	Luminescence	General Glossary

Subheadings are shown in parentheses after the major heading for a given term.

Guide to Subjects

Arrows	See Plate (Sheet Stamps)
Bisect	See General Glossary
Blind Perforations	See General Glossary
Blocks	See Plate (Sheet Stamps)
Booklet Panes	See Plate (Sheet Stamps)
Booklets	See Plate (Sheet Stamps), General Glossary
Booklets A.E.F.	See Plate (Sheet Stamps)
Bureau Precancels	See Postal Markings
Cancellations	See Postal Markings, General Glossary
Carrier Postmarks	See Postal Markings
Coarse Perforation	See Separation (Perforations)
Coils	See Plate (Coil Stamps)
Coil Waste	See Plate (Coil Stamps)
Color Changeling	See Printing (Additional Terms
Color Registration Markings	See Plate (Sheet Stamps)
Color Trials	See Printing (Additional Terms)
Commemorative Stamps	See General Glossary
Compound Perforation	See Separation (Perforations)
Covers	See General Glossary
Cracked Plate	See Printing (Common Flaws)
Die	See Plate (Line Engraving)
Die Cutting	See Separation
Double Impression	See Printing (Additional Terms)
Double Paper	See Paper
Double Perforation	See Separation (Perforations)
Double Transfer	See Plate (Line Engraving)
Dry Printings	See note after Scott 1029
Electric Eye	See Separation (Perforations)
Embossed Printing	See Printing
End Roller Grills	See Paper (Grills)
Engraved	See Printing
Error	See General Glossary
Essay	See Printing (Additional Terms)
Fine Perforation	See Separation (Perforations)
First Day Cover	See General Glossary
Flat Plate Printing	See Printing (Additional Terms)
Fluorescent Papers	See Luminescence
Foil Application	See Printing
Foreign Entry	See Plate
Giori Press	See Printing
Gridiron Cancellation	See Postal Markings
Grills	See Paper
Gripper Cracks	See Printing (Common Flaws)
Gouge	See Printing (Additional Terms)
Guide Lines	See Plate (Sheet Stamps)
Gum Breaker Ridges	See General Glossary
Gutter	See Plate (Sheet Stamps)
Hidden Plate Number	See Plate (Coil Stamps)
Holograms	See Printing
Imperforate	See General Glossary
Imprint	See Plate (Sheet Stamps)
India Paper	See Paper
Intaglio	See Plate (Line Engraving), Printing
Inverted Center	See Printing (Additional Terms)
Joint Line	See Plate (Coil Stamps)
Laid Paper	See Paper
Line Engraved	See Printing
Line Pair	See Plate (Coil Stamps)
Lithography	See Printing
Manila Paper	See Paper
Margin	See Plate (Sheet Stamps)
Military Postmarks	See Postal Markings
Multicolored Stamps	See Printing (Additional Terms)
New York City Foreign Mail	See Postal Markings
Offset Lithography	See Printing
Original Gum	See General Glossary
Overprint	See Printing (Additional Terms), General Glossary
Pair Imperf. Between	See General Glossary
Pane	See Plate (Plate Arrangement)
Part-Perforate	See General Glossary
Paste-up	See Plate (Coil Stamps)
Paste-up Pair	See Plate (Coil Stamps)
Patent Cancellations	See Postal Markings
Pelure Paper	See Paper
Perforation Gauge	See Separation (Perforations)
Phosphor Tagged	See Luminescence
Photogravure	See Printing
Plate Flaws	See Printing (Common Flaws)
Plate Markings	See Plate (Sheet Stamps)
Plate Numbers	See Plate (Sheet Stamps)
Postmarks	See Postal Markings
Precancels	See Postal Markings
Printed on Both Sides	See Printing (Additional Terms)
Proofs	See Printing (Additional Terms)
Railroad Postmarks	See Postal Markings
Receiving Mark	See Postal Markings
Re-cut	See Plate (Line Engraving)
Re-engraved	See Plate (Line Engraving)
Re-entry	See Plate (Line Engraving)
Reissue	See Printing (Additional Terms)
Relief	See Plate (Line Engraving)
Reprint	See Printing (Additional Terms)
Retouch	See Plate (Line Engraving)
Ribbed Paper	See Paper
Rosette Crack	See Printing (Common Flaws)
Rotary Press Printing	See Printing (Additional Terms)
Rough Perforation	See Separation (Perforations)
Rouletting	See Separation
Se-Tenant	See General Glossary
Service Indicators	See Postal Markings
Sheet	See Plate (Plate Arrangement)
Shifted Transfer	See Plate (Line Engraving)
Ship Postmarks	See Postal Markings
Short Transfer	See Plate (Line Engraving)
Silk Paper	See Paper
Specimens	See General Glossary
Splice	See General Glossary
Split Grill	See Paper (Grills)
Stitch Watermark	See Paper
Supplementary Mail	See Postal Markings
Surcharge	See Printing (Additional Terms), General Glossary

Tagged Stamps .... See Luminescence
Tete Beche .... See General Glossary
Tied On .... See Postal Markings
Transfer .... See Plate (Line Engraving)
Transfer Roll .... See Plate (Line Engraving)
Triple Transfer .... See Plate (Line Engraving)
Typeset .... See Printing
Typeset Stamps .... See Printing
Typography .... See Printing
Watermarks .... See Paper
Wet Printings .... See Note after Scott 1029
Wove Paper .... See Paper

PLATE

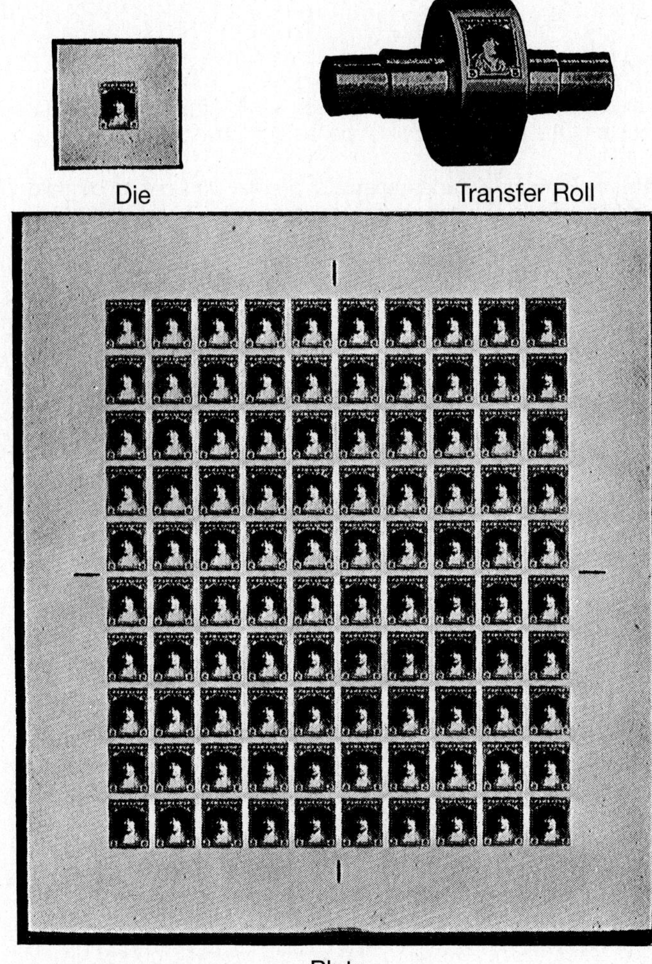

Die Transfer Roll

Plate

Line Engraving (Intaglio)

Die — Making the die is the initial operation in developing the intaglio plate. The die is a small flat piece of soft steel on which the subject (design) is recess-engraved in reverse. Dies are usually of a single-subject type, but dies exist with multiple subjects of the same design, or even different designs. After the engraving is completed, the die is hardened to withstand the stress of subsequent operations.

Transfer Roll — The next operation is making the transfer roll, which is the medium used to transfer the subject from the die to the plate. A blank roll of soft steel, mounted on a mandrel, is placed under the bearers of a transfer press. The hardened die is placed on the bed of the press and the face of the roll is brought to bear on the die. The bed is then rocked backed and forth under increasing pressure until the soft steel of the roll is forced into every line of the die. The resulting impression on the roll is known as a "relief" or "relief transfer." Several reliefs usually are rocked in on each roll. After the required reliefs are completed, the roll is hardened.

Relief — A relief is the normal reproduction of the design on the die, in reverse. A defective relief, caused by a minute piece of foreign material lodging on the die, may occur during the rocking-in process, or from other causes. Imperfections in the steel of the transfer roll may also result in a breaking away of parts of the design. If the damaged relief is continued in use, it will transfer a repeating defect to the plate. Also, reliefs sometimes are deliberately altered. "Broken relief" and "altered relief" are terms used to designate these changed conditions.

Plate — A flat piece of soft steel replaces the die on the bed of the transfer press and one of the reliefs on the transfer roll is brought to bear on this soft steel. The position of the plate is determined by guide dots, which have been lightly marked on the plate in advance. After the position of the relief is determined, pressure is brought to bear and, by following the same method used in the making of the transfer roll, a transfer is entered. This transfer reproduces, in reverse, every detail of the design of the relief. As many transfers are entered on the plate as there are to be subjects printed at one time.

After the required transfers have been entered, the guide dots, layouts and lines, scratches, etc., are burnished out. Also, any required guide lines, plate numbers, or other marginal markings are added. A proof impression is then taken and if certified (approved), the plate is machined for fitting to the press, hardened and sent to the plate vault until used.

Rotary press plates, after being certified, require additional machining. They are curved to fit the press cylinder and gripper slots are cut into the back of each plate to receive the grippers, which hold the plate securely to the press. The rotary press plate is not hardened until these additional processes are completed.

Transfer — An impression entered on the plate by the transfer roll. A relief transfer is made when entering the design of the die onto the transfer roll.

Double Transfer — The condition of a transfer on a plate that shows evidence of a duplication of all or a portion of the design. A double transfer usually is the result of the changing of the registration between the relief and the plate during the rolling of the original entry.

Occasionally it is necessary to remove the original transfer from a plate and enter the relief a second time. When the finished re-transfer shows indications of the original transfer, because of incomplete erasure, the result is known as a double transfer.

Triple Transfer — Similar to a double transfer, this situation shows evidence of a third entry or two duplications.

Foreign Entry — When original transfers are erased incompletely from a plate, they can appear with new transfers of a different design which are entered subsequently on the plate.

Re-entry — When executing a re-entry, the transfer roll is reapplied to the plate at some time after the latter has been put to press. Thus, worn-out designs may be resharpened by carefully re-entering the transfer roll. If the transfer roll is not carefully entered, the registration will not be true and a double transfer will result. With the protective qualities of chromium plating, it is no longer necessary to resharpen the plate. In fact, after a plate has been curved for the rotary press, it is impossible to make a re-entry.

Shifted Transfer (Shift) — In transferring, the metal displaced on the plate by the entry of the ridges, constituting the design on the transfer roll, is forced ahead of the roll as well as pressed out at the sides. The amount of displaced metal increases with the depth of the entry. When the depth is increased evenly, the design will be uniformly entered. Most of the displaced metal is pressed ahead of the roll. If too much pressure is exerted on any pass (rocking), the impression on the previous partial entry may be floated (pushed) ahead of the roll and cause a duplication of the final design. The duplication appears as an increased width of frame lines or a doubling of the lines.

The ridges of the displaced metal are flattened out by the hammering or rolling back of the plate along the space occupied by the subject margins.

Short Transfer — Occasionally the transfer roll is not rocked its entire length in the entering of a transfer onto a plate, with the result that the finished transfer fails to show the complete design. This is known as a short transfer.

Short transfers are known to have been made deliberately, as in the Type III of the 1-cent issue of 1851-60 (Scott 8, 21), or accidentally, as in the 10-cent 1847 (Scott 2).

Re-engraved — Either the die that has been used to make a plate or the plate itself may have its temper drawn (softened) and be re-cut. The resulting impressions for such re-engraved die or plate may differ very slightly from the original issue and are given the label "re-engraved."

Re-cut — A re-cut is the strengthening or altering of a line by use of an engraving tool on unhardened plates.

Retouch — A retouch is the strengthening or altering of a line by means of etching.

Plate Arrangement

Arrangement — The first engraved plates used to produce U.S. postage stamps in 1847 contained 200 subjects. The number of subjects to a plate varied between 100 and 300 until the issue of 1890, when the 400-subject plate was first laid down. Since that time, this size of plate has been used for a majority of the regular postal issues (those other than commemoratives). Exceptions to this practice exist, particularly among the more recent issues, and are listed under the headings of the appropriate issues in the catalogue.

Sheet — In single-color printings, the complete impression from a plate is termed a sheet. A sheet of multicolored stamps (two or more colors) may come from a single impression of a plate, i.e., many Giori-type press printings from 1957, or from as many impressions from separate plates as there are inks used for the particular stamp. Combination process printings may use both methods of multicolor production: Giori-type intaglio with offset lithography or with photogravure.

The Huck multicolor press used plates of different format (40, 72 or 80 subjects). The sheet it produced had 200 subjects for normal-sized commemoratives or 400 subjects for regular-issue stamps, similar to the regular products of other presses.

See the note on the Combination Press following the listing for Scott 1703 in this catalogue.

In casual usage, a "pane" often is referred to as a "sheet."

Pane — A pane is the part of the original sheet that is issued for sale at post offices. A pane may be the same as an entire sheet, where the plate is small, or it may be a half, quarter, or some other fraction of a sheet where the plate is large.

The illustration shown later under the subtopic "Sheet Stamps" shows the layout of a 400-subject sheet from a flat plate, which for issuance would have been divided along the intersecting guide lines into four panes of 100.

Panes are classified into normal reading position according to their location on the printed sheet: U.L., upper left; U.R., upper right; L.L., lower left; and L.R., lower right. Where only two panes appear on a sheet, they are designed "R" (right) and "L" (left) or "T" (top) and "B" (bottom), on the basis of the division of the sheet vertically or horizontally.

To fix the location of a particular stamp on any pane, except for those printed on the Combination press, the pane is held with the subjects in the normal position, and a position number is given to each stamp starting with the first stamp in the upper left corner and proceeding horizontally to the right, then staring on the second row at the left and counting across to the right, and so on to the last stamp in the lower right corner.

In describing the location of a stamp on a sheet of stamps issued prior to 1894, the practice is to give the stamp position number first, then the pane position and finally the plate number, i.e., "1R22." Beginning with the 1894 issue and on all later issues the method used is to give the plate number first, then the position of the pane, and finally the position number of the stamp, i.e., "16807LL48" to identify an example of Scott 619 or "2138L2" to refer to an example of Scott 323.

Booklet Stamps

Plates for Stamp Booklets — These are illustrated and described preceding the listing of booklet panes and covers in this catalogue.

Booklet Panes — Panes specially printed and cut to be sold in booklets which are a convenient way to purchase and store stamps. U.S. Booklet panes are straight-edged on three sides, but perforated between the stamps. Die cut, ATM and other panes will vary from this. Except for BK64 and BK65, the A.E.F. booklets, booklets were sold by the Post Office Department for a one-cent premium until 1962. Other sections of this catalogue with listings for booklet panes include Savings stamps, Telegraph stamps and Canal Zone.

A.E.F. Booklets — These were special booklets prepared principally for use by the U.S. Army Post Office in France during World War I. They were issued in 1-cent and 2-cent denominations with 30 stamps to a pane (10 x 3), bound at right or left. As soon as Gen. John J. Pershing's organization reached France, soldiers' mail was sent free by means of franked envelopes.

Stamps were required during the war for the civilian personnel, as well as for registered mail, parcel post and other types of postal service. See the individual listings for Scott 498f and 499f and booklets BK64 and BK65.

Coil Stamps

First issued in 1908-09, coil stamps originally were produced in two roll sizes, 500 and 1,000 stamps, with the individual stamps arranged endways or sideways and with or without perforations between.

Rolls of stamps for use in affixing or vending machines were first constructed by private companies and later by the Bureau of Engraving and Printing. Originally, it was customary for the Post Office Department to sell to the private vending companies and others imperforate sheets of stamps printed from the ordinary 400-subject flat plates. These sheets were then pasted together end-to-end or side-to-side by the purchaser and cut into rolls as desired, with the perforations being applied to suit the requirements of the individual machines. Such stamps with private perforations are listed in this catalogue under "Vending and Affixing Machine Perforations."

Later the Bureau produced coils by the same method, also in rolls of 500 and 1,000. These coils were arranged endways or sideways and were issued with or without perforations.

With the introduction of the Stickney rotary press, curved plates made for use on these presses were put into use at the Bureau of Engraving and Printing, and the sale of imperforate sheets was discontinued. This move marked the end of the private perforation. Rotary press coils have been printed on a number of presses over the years and have been made in roll sizes of 100, 500, 1,000, 3,000 and 10,000 stamps, etc.

Paste-up — The junction of two flat-plate printings joined by pasting the edge of one sheet onto the edge of another sheet to make coils. A two-stamp example of this joining is a "paste-up pair." See Splice.

Guide Line Pair — Attached pair of flat-plate-printed coil stamps with printed line between. This line is identical with the guide line (See listing under (Sheet Stamps) found in sheets.

Joint Line — The edges of two curved plates do not meet exactly on the press and the small space between the plates takes ink and prints a line. A pair of rotary-press-printed stamps with such a line is called a "joint line pair."

Coil stamps printed on the Multicolor Huck Press do not consistently produce such lines. Occasionally accumulated ink will print partial lines in one or more colors, and very occasionally complete lines will be printed. Stamps resulting from such situations are not listed in this catalogue. The "B" and "C" presses do not print joint lines at all.

Plate Number — for U.S. coil stamps prior to Scott 1891, Scott 1947, War Savings coils and Canal Zone:

On a rotary-press horizontal coil the top or bottom part of a plate number may show. On a vertical coil, the left or right part of a plate number may show. The number was entered on the plate to be cut off when the web was sliced into coils and is found only when the web was sliced off center. Every rotary press coil plate number was adjacent to a joint line, so both features could occur together in one strip.

For U.S. coil stamps from Scott 1891 onward (excluding Scott 1947) and Official coils:

The plate number is placed in the design area of the stamp, so it will not be trimmed off. Such items are normally collected unused with the stamp containing the plate number in the center of a strip of three or five stamps. They normally are collected used as singles. The line, if any, will be at the right of the plate-number stamp. On the Bureau's Cottrell press, the number occurs every 24th stamp, on the "B" press every 52nd stamp, on the "C," "D" and "F" presses every 48th stamp. On modern private contractor presses, the number occurs in a range from every 5th stamp to every 31st stamp, depending on the press used.

Unused plate-number strips of three and five are valued in this catalogue.

Hidden Plate Number — A plate number may be found entirely on a coil made from flat plates, but usually is hidden by a part of the next sheet which has been lapped over it.

Coil Waste — an occurrence brought about by stamps issued in perforated sheets from a printing intended for coils. These stamps came from short lengths of paper at the end of the coil run. Sometimes the salvaged sections were those which had been laid aside for mutilation because of some defect. Because the paper had been moistened during printing, it sometimes stretched slightly and provided added printing area. Sheets of 70, 100, and 170 are known. See Scott 538-541, 545-546, 578-579, and 594-595. See also "Rotary Press Sheet Waste" on the next page.

"T" — Letter which appears in the lower design area of Scott 2115b, which was printed on an experimental pre-phosphored paper. The stamp with the plate number is inscribed "T1."

Sheet Stamps

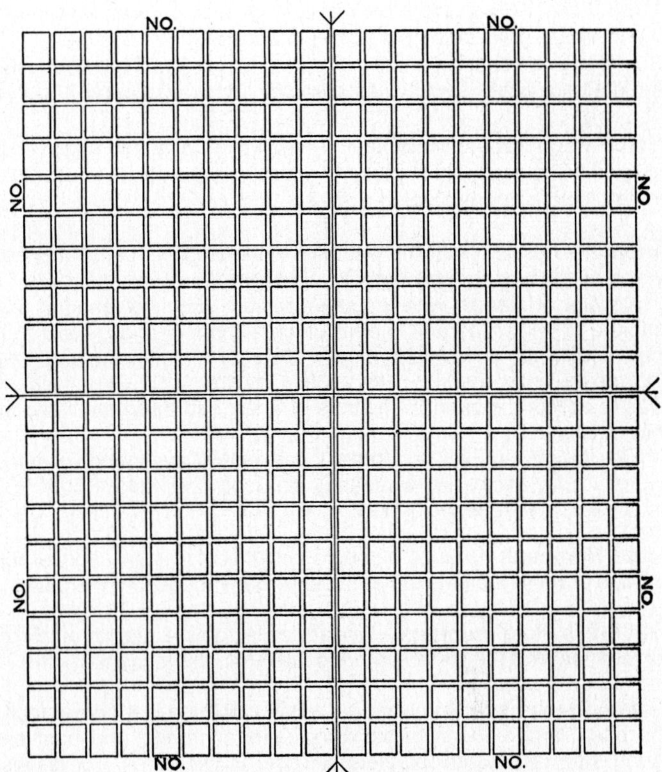

A typical 400-subject plate of 1922

Plate Markings — The illustration above shows a typical 400-subject plate of the 1922 issue, with markings as found on this type of plate. Other layouts and markings are found further in the catalogue text.

Guide Lines — Horizontal or vertical colored lines between the stamps, extending wholly or partially across the sheet. They serve as guides for the operators of perforating machines or to indicate the point of separation of the sheet into panes.

A block of stamps divided by any of the guide lines is known as a "line block" or "guide line block." The block of stamps from the exact center of the sheet, showing the crossed guide lines, is a "center line block."

Gutter — When guide lines are used to mark the division of the sheet into panes, the space between the stamps at the edge of the pane is no different than the space between any other stamps on the sheet. Some plates provide a wide space, or gutter, between the panes. These plates do not produce guide lines.

A pair of stamps with the wide space between is known as a "gutter pair," and blocks with that feature are "gutter blocks." A block of stamps from the position where four panes meet, showing the two wide spaces crossing, is a "center gutter block" or "cross gutter block."

Gutter pairs or gutter blocks must contain complete stamp images on both sides of the gutter. On pairs or blocks that had a paper foldover before proper perforating, the stamps on each side of the gutter must be complete and show perforation teeth all around, unless imperforate. Gutter pairs or blocks caused by a paper foldover may or may not contain creased stamps from the foldover; either way they qualify as the listed variety. Some gutter pairs or blocks are the result of misplaced perforations and improper cutting of the panes. These pairs or blocks may have perforations running through the stamps, either straight or at an angle. In these cases, there must be complete stamp-size images on each side of the gutter to be considered gutter pairs or blocks. These errors may have parts of two or more designs in the stamp-size images.

Arrows — Arrow-shaped markings were used in the margins of stamp sheets, in place of guide lines, on the issues of 1870 through 1894. Since 1894, guide lines with arrows at both ends have been the standard practice on flat-plate printings.

A margin block of at least four stamps, showing the arrow centered at one edge, is known as a "margin block with arrow."

Color Registration Markings — marks of different sizes and shapes, used as an aid in properly registering the colors in producing a bicolored or multicolored stamp.

Imprint — design containing the name of the producer of the stamps, which appears on the sheet margin usually near the plate number.

A block of stamps with the sheet margin attached, bearing the imprint, is known as an "imprint block." Imprints and plate numbers usually are collected in blocks of six, or of sufficient length to include the entire marking. From 1894 until about 1907, one fashion was to collect the imprints in strips of three, and these are listed in this catalogue.

The imprint and plate number combination are found in eight types I-VIII, which are illustrated at Scott 245 and Scott E3. Example: "T V" refers to Type V.

Plate Numbers — Serial numbers assigned to plates, appearing on one or more margins of the sheet or pane to identify the plate.

Flat Press Plate Numbers — usually collected in a margin block of six stamps with the plate number centered in the margin.

Rotary Press Plate Numbers — usually collected in a corner margin block large enough to show the plate number(s) and position along the margin and complete selvage on two sides. For issues with a single plate number at the corner of the pane, a block of four normally suffices.

During 1933-39, some plates had the number opposite the third stamp (up or down) from the corner of the sheet and for these the number is customarily collected in a corner block of no less than eight stamps, with most collectors preferring a block of ten stamps. Multicolored stamps may have more than one plate number in the margin and the "plate block" may then be expanded to suit the collector's desire.

The catalogue listing for plate blocks includes enough stamps to accommodate all numbers on the plate. Plate block listings for se-tenant issues include all the designs as part of the block. When a continuous design is involved, such as Scott 1629-31, the complete design will be included in the plate number block. The entire pane constitutes the plate number block for issues such as the State Birds and Flowers (Scott 1953-2002, 1953A-2002A).

Plate numbers take a further designation from the position on the sheet on which they appear, e.g. U.L. refers to upper left pane, etc.

See note following Scott 1703 for description of combination press markings.

Private Contractor Marks — On rotary plates from Scott 1789 onward: "A" denotes issues produced by private contractor American Bank Note Co., "B" by Banknote Corp of America, "D" by Dittler Brothers, "G" by Guilford Gravure, "K" by KCS Industries, "M" by 3M Corp., "P" by Ashton-Potter (USA) Ltd., "S" by Stamp Venturers, Inc. (now Sennett Security Products), "U" by U.S. Bank Note Co., "V" by Avery Dennison.

Rotary Press Sheet Waste — an occurence brought about by stamps regular printed in sheet form having lengths of printed paper being run through perforators of a different gauge. See Scott 544, 596 and 613. Also see "Coil Waste" on the previous page.

Stars — used on the flat plates to indicate a change from the previous spacing of the stamps. They also were used as a check on the assignment of the printed sheets to a perforating machine of the proper setting. Stars appear on certain rotary plates used for printing stamps for coils, appearing adjacent to the plate joint line and above stamp No. 1 on the 170-subject plates, and to the left of stamp No. 141 on the 150-subject plates.

"A" — on flat plates; used on plates having uniform vertical spacing between rows of subjects, but wider than those with the star marking.

"C.S." and "C" — plate has been chromium plated.
"E.I." — abbreviation for Electrolytic Iron. The designation is for plates made by the electrolytic process.
"F" — used to indicate the plate is ready for hardening. This appears only on flat plates and generally precedes the upper right plate number.

"O" — plate has undergone an experimental oil-hardening process during manufacture.

"Top" — marking on the top sheet margin of printings from both plates of some bicolored issues. This marking is used to check printings for "inverts." Beginning with the 6-cent bicolored airpost issue of 1938 (Scott C23), bicolored crosses also were used as an additional check.

"Coil Stamps" — appearing on the side sheet margins, designates plates used in the production of endwise coils.

"S 20," "S 30," "S 40" — marginal markings appearing on certain 150- and 170-subject rotary press plates to designate experimental variations in the depth and character of the frame line to over-come excess inking. "S 30" was adopted as the standard. Blocks showing these markings are listed as "Margin Block with S 20," etc., in this catalogue.

Initials — used in sheet margins to identify individuals in the Bureau of Engraving and Printing who participated in the production or use of the plates.

Gutter Dashes — on the first 400-subject rotary plates, 3/16-inch horizontal dashes appear in the gutter between the 10th and 11th vertical rows of stamps. This arrangement was superseded by dashes 3/16-inch at the extreme ends of the vertical and horizontal gutters, and a ¼-inch cross at the central gutter intersection. This latter arrangement continued until replaced by the scanning marks on the Electric Eye plates. See Electric Eye.

Margin — border outside the printed design or perforated area of a stamp, also known as selvage, or the similar border of a sheet of stamps. A block of stamps from the top, side or bottom of a sheet or pane to which is attached the selvage (margin) is known as a "margin block." A block of stamps from the corner of a sheet with full selvage attached to two adjoining sides is known as a "corner block."

NOTE: The descriptions and definitions above indicate that a certain number of stamps make up an arrow or plate number block. Any block of stamps, no matter how large or small, which had an arrow or plate number on its margin would be considered by that name. The usual practice is to collect flat-plate numbers in margin blocks of six and arrow blocks in margin blocks of four. Plate number blocks from rotary press printings generally are collected in blocks of 4 when the plate number appears beside the stamp at any of the four corners of the sheet. Particularly relative to bi-colored stamps, an arrow block is now separated from a plate number block. Thus, in those situations, the two individual types of blocks might form a block of eight or 10, as the situation dictates.

PRINTING

Methods Used — all four basic forms of printing have been used in producing U.S. stamps, engraved, photogravure, lithography, and typography. Holography has been used on some stamps and stamped envelopes.

Engraved (Recess or Intaglio) — process where ink is received and held in lines depressed below the surface of the plate. Initially, in printing from such plates, damp paper was forced into the depressed lines and therefore picked up ink. Consequently, ink lines on the stamp are slightly raised. This also is noted from the back of the stamp, where depressions mark where ink is placed on the front.

When the ornamental work for a stamp is engraved by a machine, the process is called "engine turned" or lathe-work engraving. An example of such lathe-work background is the 3-cent stamp of 1861 (Scott Illustration No. A25).

Engraved stamps were printed only with flat plates until 1914, when rotary press printing was introduced. "Wet" and "dry" printings are explained in the note in the text of the catalogue following Scott 1029. The various Giori presses, used to print some U.S. stamps from 1957 (see Scott 1094, 4-cent Flag issue until the early 1990s), applied two or three different colored inks simultaneously.

The Huck Multicolor press, put into service at the Bureau of Engraving and Printing in 1968, was first used to produce the 1968 Christmas stamp (Scott 1363) and the 6-cent Flag coil of 1969 (Scott 1338A). Developed by the Bureau's technical staff and the firm of graphic arts engineers whose name it bears, the Huck press printed, tagged with phosphor ink, gummed and perforated stamps in a continuous operation. Printing was accomplished in as many as nine colors. Fed by paper from a roll, the Huck Multicolor used many recess-engraved plates of smaller size than any used previously for U.S. stamp printing. Its product has certain characteristics which other U.S. stamps do not have. Post office panes of the 1969 Christmas stamp, for example, show seven or eight plate numbers in the margins. Joint lines appear after every two or four stamps. Other presses providing multiple plate numbers are the Andreotti, Champlain, Combination, Miller Offset, A Press, D Press and more.

Photogravure — the design of a stamp to be printed by photogravure usually is photographed through an extremely fine screen, lined in minute quadrille. The screen breaks up the reproduction into tiny dots, which are etched onto the plate and the depressions formed hold the ink. Somewhat similarly to engraved printing, the ink is lifted out of the recesses by the paper, which is pressed against the plate. Unlike engraved printing, however, the ink does not appear to be raised relative to the surface of the paper.

Gravure is most often used for multicolored stamps, generally using the three primary colors (red, yellow and blue) and black. By varying the dot matrix pattern and density of these colors, virtually any color can be reproduced. A typical full-color gravure stamp will be created from four printing cylinders (one for each color). The original multicolored image will have been photographically separated into its component colors.

For U.S. stamps, photogravure first appeared in 1967, with the Thomas Eakins issue (Scott 1335). The early photogravure stamps were printed by outside contractors until the Bureau obtained the multicolor Andreotti press in 1971. The earliest stamp printed on that press was the 8-cent Missouri Statehood issue of 1971 (Scott 1426).

Color control bars, dashes or dots are printed in the margin of one pane in each "Andreotti" sheet of 200, 160 or 128 stamps. These markings generally are collected in blocks of 20 or 16 (two full rows of one pane), which include the full complement of plate numbers, Mr. Zip and the Zip and Mail Early slogans.

Details on the Combination Press follow the listing for Scott 1703.

Modern gravure printing may use computer-generated dot-matrix screens, and modern plates may be of various types including metal-coated plastic. The catalogue designation of Photogravure (or "Photo") covers any of these older and more modern gravure methods of printing.

Lithography — this is the most common and least expensive process for printing stamps. In this method, the design is drawn by hand or transferred in greasy ink from an original engraving to the surface of a lithographic stone or metal plate. The stone or plate is wet with an acid fluid, which causes it to repel the printing ink except at the greasy lines of the design. A fine lithographic print closely resembles an engraving, but the lines are not raised on the face or depressed on the back. Thus there usually is a more dull appearance to the lithograph than to the engraving.

Offset Lithography (Offset Printing) — a modern development of the lithographic process. Anything that will print — type, woodcuts, photoengravings, plates engraved or etched in intaglio, halftone plates, linoleum blocks, lithographic stones or plates, photogravure plates, rubber stamps, etc. — may be used. Greasy ink is applied to the dampened plate or form and an impression made on a rubber blanket. Paper immediately is pressed against the blanket, which transfers the ink. Because of its greater flexibility, offset printing has largely displaced lithography.

Because the processes and results obtained are similar, stamps printed by either of these two methods normally are considered to be "lithographed."

The first application of lithographic printing for any U.S. items listed in this catalogue was for Post Office seals, probably using stone printing bases. See also some Confederates States general issues. Offset lithography was used for the 1914 documentary revenues (Scott R195-R216). Postage stamps followed in 1918-20 (Scott 525-536) because of war-time shortages of ink, plates and manpower relative to the regular intaglio production.

The next use of offset lithography for postage stamps was in 1964 with the Homemakers issue (Scott 1253), in combination with intaglio printing. Many similar issues followed, all of which were produced by the combination of offset lithography and intaglio. The combination process serves best for soft backgrounds and tonal effects.

Typography — an exact reverse of engraved-plate printing, this process provides for the parts of the design which are to show in color to be left at the original level of the plate and the spaces between cut away. Ink is applied to the raised lines, and the pressure of the printing forces these lines more or less into the paper. The process impresses the lines on the face of the stamp and slightly raises them on the back. Normally, a large number of electrotypes of the original are made and assembled into a plate with the requisite number of designs for printing a sheet of stamps. Stamps printed by this process show greater uniformity, and the stamps are less expensive to print than with intaglio printing.

The first U.S. postal usage of an item printed by typography, or letterpress, under national authority was the 1846 "2" surcharge on the United States City Despatch Post 3-cent carrier stamp (Scott 6LB7). The next usage was the 1865 newspaper and periodical stamp issue, which for security reasons combined the techniques of machine engraving, colorless embossing and typography. This created an unusual first.

Most U.S. stamp typography consists of overprints, such as those for the Canal Zone, the Molly Pitcher and Hawaii Sesquicentennial stamps of 1928 (Scott 646-648), the Kansas-Nebraska control markings (Scott 658-679), Bureau-printed precancels, and "specimen" markings.

Embossed (relief) Printing — method in which the design is sunk in the metal of the die and the printing is done against a platen that is forced into the depression, thus forming the design on the paper in relief. Embossing may be done without ink (blind embossing), totally with ink, or a combination thereof. The U.S. stamped envelopes are an example of this form of printing.

Typeset — made from movable type.

Typeset Stamps — printed from ordinary printer's type. Sometimes electrotype or stereotype plates are made, but because such stamps usually are printed only in small quantities for temporary use, movable type often is used for the purpose. This method of printing is apt to show broken type and lack of uniformity. See Hawaii Scott 1-4 and 12-26.

Holograms — for objects to appear as holograms on stamps, a model exactly the same size as it is to appear on the hologram must be created. Rather than using photographic film to capture the image, holography records an image on a photoresist material. In processing, chemicals eat away at certain exposed areas, leaving a pattern of constructive and destructive interference. When the photoresist is developed, the result is a pattern of uneven ridges that acts as a mold. This mold is then coated with metal, and the resulting form is used to press copies in much the same way phonograph records are produced.

A typical reflective hologram used for stamps consists of a reproduction of the uneven patterns on a plastic film that is applied to a reflective background, ususally a silver or gold foil. Light is reflected off the background through the film, making the pattern present on the film visible. Because of the uneven pattern of the film, the viewer will perceive the objects in their proper three-dimensional relationships with appropriate brightness.

The first hologram on a stamp was produced by Austria in 1988 (Scott 1441).

Foil Application — A modern technique of applying color to stamps involves the application of metallic foil to the stamp paper. A pattern of foil is applied to the stamp paper by use of a stamping die. The foil usually is flat, but it may be textured. Canada Scott 1735 has three different foil applications in pearl, bronze, and gold. The gold foil was texured using a chemical-etch copper embossing die. The printing of this stamp also involved two-colored offset lithography plus embossing.

Additional Terms

Multicolored Stamps — Until 1957 when the Giori press was introduced, bicolored stamps were printed on a flat-bed press in two runs, one for each color (example: Norse-American Issue of 1925, Scott 620-621). In the flat-press bicolors, if the sheet were fed to the press on the second run in reversed position, the part printed in the second color would be upside down, producing an "invert" such as the famed Scott C3a.

With the Giori press and subsequent presses, stamps could be printed in more than one color at the same time.

Many bicolored and multicolored stamps show varying degrees of poor color registration (alignment). Such varieties are not listed in this catalogue.

Color Changeling — a stamp which, because of exposure to the environment, has naturally undergone a change of ink colors. Orange U.S. stamps of the early 1900's are notorious for turning brown as the ink reacts with oxygen. Exposure to light can cause some inks to fade. These are not considered color-omitted errors. Exposure to other chemicals can cause ink colors to change. These stamps are merely altered stamps, and their value to collectors is greatly diminished.

Color Trials — printings in various colors, made to facilitate selection of color for the issued stamp.

Double Impression — a second impression of a stamp over the original impression.

This is not to be confused with a "double transfer," which is a plate imperfection and generally shows just bits of doubling of the design. See also "Printed on Both Sides."

Essay — a proposed design, a designer's model or an incomplete engraving. Its design differs in some way — great or small — from the issued item.

Inverted Center — bicolored or multicolored stamp with the center printed upside down relative to the remainder of the design. A stamp may be described as having an inverted center even if the center is printed first. See "Multicolored Stamps."

Flat Plate Printing — stamp printed on a flat-bed press, rather than on a rotary press. See "Plate."

Overprint — any word, inscription or image printed across the face of a stamp to alter its use or locality or otherwise to serve a special purpose. An example is U.S. Scott 646, the "Molly Pitcher" overprint, which is Scott 634 with a black overprinted inscription as a memorial to the Revolutionary War heroine. See "Surcharge."

Printed on Both Sides — Occasionally a sheet of stamps already printed will, through error, be turned over and passed through the press a second time, creating the rare "printed on both sides" variety. On one side the impression is almost always poor or incomplete. This often is confused with an "offset," which occurs when sheets of stamps are stacked while the ink is still wet.

The "printed on both sides" variety will show the design as a positive (all inscriptions reading correctly) and the offset shows a reverse impression. See "Double Impression."

Progressive Proof — a type of essay that is an incomplete engraving of the finished, accepted die.

Proofs — trial printings of a stamp made from the original die or the finished plate.

Reprints and Reissues — are impressions of stamps (usually obsolete) made from the original plates or stones. If they are valid for postage and reproduce obsolete issues (such as U.S. Scott 102-111), the stamps are *reissues*. If they are from current issues, they are designated as *second, third,* etc., *printing*. If designated for a particular purpose, they are called *special printings.*

When special printings are not valid for postage, but are made from original dies and plates by authorized persons, they are *official reprints. Private reprints* are made from the original plates and dies by private hands. An example of a private reprint is that of the 1871-1932 reprints made from the original die of the 1845 New Haven, Conn., postmaster's provisional. *Official reproductions* or imitations are made from new dies and plates by government authorization. Scott will list those reissues that are valid for postage if they differ significantly from the original printing.

The U.S. government made special printings of its first postage stamps in 1875. Produced were official imitations of the first two stamps (listed as Scott 3-4), reprints of the demonetized pre-1861 issues (Scott 40-47) and reissues of the 1861 stamps, the 1869 stamps and the then-current 1875 denominations. Even though the official imitations and the reprints were not valid for postage, Scott lists all of these U.S. special printings.

Most reprints or reissues differ slightly from the original stamp in some characteristic, such as gum, paper, perforation, color or watermark. Sometimes the details are followed so meticulously that only a student of that specific stamp is able to distinguish the reprint or reissue from the original.

Rotary Press Printing — stamps which have been printed on a rotary-type press from curved plates. Rotary press-printed stamps are longer or wider than stamps of the same design printed from flat plates. All rotary press printings through 1953, except coil waste (such as Scott 538), exist with horizontal "gum breaker ridges" varying from one to four per stamp. See: "Plate."

Surcharge — overprint which alters or restates the face value or denomination of the stamp to which it is applied. An example is Scott K1-K18, U.S. stamps that were surcharged for use by U.S. offices in China. Many surcharges are typeset. See: "Overprint" and "Typeset."

Common Flaws

Cracked Plate — A term to describe stamps that show evidence that the plate from which they were printed was cracked.

Plate cracks have various causes, each which may result in a different formation and intensity of the crack. Cracks similar to the above illustration are quite common in older issues and are largely due to the plate being too quickly immersed in the cooling bath when being tempered. These cracks are known as *crystallization cracks*. A jagged line running generally in one direction and most often in the gutter between stamps is due to the stress of the steel during the rolling in or transferring process.

In curved (rotary) plates, there are two types of cracks. Once is the bending or curving crack, which is quite marked and always runs in the direction in which the plate is curved.

The accompanying illustration shows the second type, the *gripper crack*. This type is caused by the cracking of the plate over the slots cut in the underside of the plate, which receive the "grippers" that fasten the plate to the press. These occur only on curved plates and are to be found in the row of stamps adjoining the plate joint. These appear on the printed impression as light, irregularly colored lines, usually parallel to the plate joint line.

Rosette Crack — cluster of fine cracks radiating from a central point in irregular lines. These usually are caused by the plate receiving a blow.

Scratched Plate — caused by foreign matter scratching the plate, these usually are too minor to mention. See: "Gouge."

Gouge — exceptionally heavy and usually short scratches, these may be caused by a tool falling onto the plate.

Surface Stains — irregular surface marks resembling the outline of a point on a map. Experts differ on the cause. These are too minor to list.

PAPER

Paper falls broadly into two types: wove and laid. The difference in the appearance is caused by the wire cloth upon which the pulp is first formed.

Paper also is distinguished as thick or thin, hard or soft, and by its color (such as bluish, yellowish, greenish, etc.).

Wove — where the wire cloth is of even and closely woven nature, producing a sheet of uniform texture throughout. This type shows no light or dark figures when held to the light.

Laid — where the wire cloth is formed of closely spaced parallel wires crossed at much wider intervals by cross wires. The resultant paper shows alternate light and dark lines. The distances between the widely spaced lines and the thickness of these lines may vary, but on any one piece of paper they will be the same.

Pelure — type of paper which is very thin and semi-transparent. It may be either wove or laid.

Bluish — The 1909 so-called "bluish" paper was made with 35 percent rag stock instead of all wood pulp. The bluish (actually grayish-blue) color goes through the paper, showing clearly on back and face. See the note with Scott 331.

Manila — a coarse paper formerly made of Manila hemp fiber. Since about 1890, so-called "manila" paper has been manufactured entirely from wood fiber. It is used for cheaper grades of envelopes and newspaper wrappers and normally is a natural light brown. Sometimes color is added, such as in the U.S. "amber manila" envelopes. It may be either wove or laid.

Silk — refers to two kinds of paper found by stamp collectors.

One type has one or more threads of silk embedded in the substance of the paper, extending across the stamp. In the catalogues, this type of paper usually is designated as "with silk threads."

The other type, used to print many U.S. revenue stamps, has short silk fibers strewn over it and impressed into it during manufacture. This is simply called "silk paper."

Ribbed — paper which shows fine parallel ridges on one or both sides of a stamp.

India — a soft, silky appearing wove paper, usually used for proof impressions.

Double Paper — as patented by Charles F. Steel, this style of paper consists of two layers, a thin surface paper and a thicker backing paper. Double paper was supposed to be an absolute safeguard against cleaning cancellations off stamps to permit reuse, for any attempt to remove the cancellation would result in the destruction of the upper layer. The Continental Bank Note Co. experimented with this paper in the course of printing Scott 156-165. See "Rotary Press Double Paper."

China Clay Paper — See note preceding Scott 331.

Fluorescent or Bright Paper — See "Luminescence."

Rotary Press Double Paper — Rotary press printings occasionally are found on a double sheet of paper. The web (roll) of paper used on the press must be continuous. Therefore, any break in the web during the process of manufacture must be lapped and pasted. The overlapping portion, when printed upon, is known as a "double paper" variety. In some cases, the lapped ends are joined with colored or transparent adhesive tape.

Such results of splicing normally are removed from the final printed material, although some slip through quality control efforts.

In one instance known, two splices have been made, thus leaving three thicknesses of paper. All rotary press stamps may exist on double paper.

Watermarks — Closely allied to the study of paper, watermarks normally are formed in the process of paper manufacture. Watermarks used on U.S. items consist of the letters "USPS" (found on postage stamps). "USPOD" (found on postal cards), the Seal of the United States (found on official seals), "USIR" (found on revenue items), and various monograms of letters, numbers, and so on, found on stamped envelopes.

The letters may be single- or double-lined and are formed from dies made of wire or cut from metal and soldered to the frame on which the pulp is caught or to a roll under which it is passed. The action of these dies is similar to the wires causing the prominent lines of laid paper, with the designs making thin places in the paper which show by more easily transmitting light.

The best method of detecting watermarks is to lay the stamp face down on a dark tray and immerse the stamp in a commercial brand of watermark fluid, which brings up the watermark in dark lines against a lighter background. **When collectors discuss watermarks, they refer to their appearance as viewed from the back of the stamp.**

Note: This method of detecting watermarks may damage certain stamps printed with inks that run when immersed (such as U.S. Scott 1260 and 1832). It is advisable to first test a damaged stamp of the same type, if possible.

Wmk. 191
PERIOD OF USE
Postage: 1895-1910 Revenue: none

In the 1895-1903 U.S. issues, the paper was fed through the press so that the watermark letters read horizontally on 400 subject sheets and vertically on 200 subject sheets.

The "USPS" in watermark 191 is known in two different orientations: a "backward-stepping" version in which each row of letters begins one letter to the left of the row above (shown above), and a second variety, called a "forward-stepping" variety, in which each row of letters begins one letter to the right of the row above. For more detail, see the notes and diagrams before No. 264 in the postage section of this catalogue.

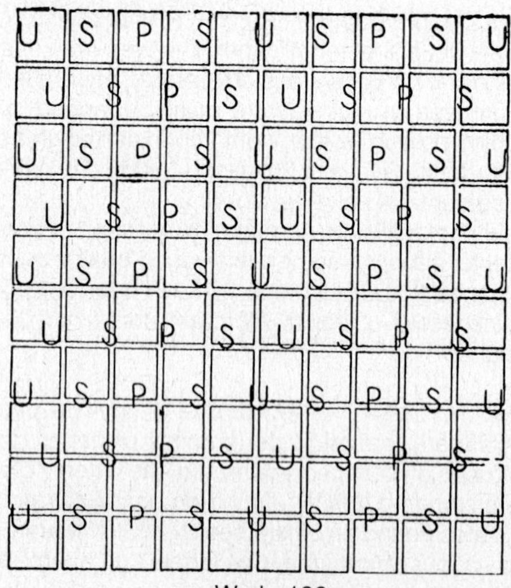

Wmk. 190
PERIOD OF USE
Postage: 1910-1916 Revenue: 1914

USIR

Wmk. 191R
PERIOD OF USE
Postage (unintentionally): 1895 (Scott 271a, 272a), 1951 (832b) Revenue: 1878-1958

Paper watermarked "USPOD" was used for postal cards from 1873 to 1875. For watermarks used on stamped envelopes, see Stamped Envelopes & Wrappers section in this catalogue.

Watermarks may be found normal, reversed, inverted, inverted reversed and sideways, as seen from the back of the stamp. See illustrated diagrams before No. 264.

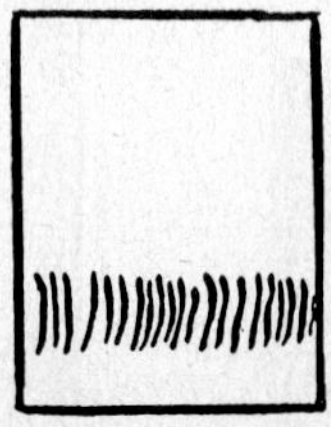

Stitch Watermark — a type of watermark consisting of a row of short parallel lines. This is caused by the stitches which join the ends of the band on which the paper pulp is first formed. Stitch watermarks have been found on a great many issues, and may exist on all.

Grills

The grill consists of small square pyramids in parallel rows, impressed or embossed on the stamp. The object of the process is to break the fibers of the paper so that the ink from the cancellation would soak into the paper and make washing for reuse impossible. Grill impressions, when viewed from the face of the stamp, may be either "points up" or "points down." This process was used on U.S. Scott 79-101, 112-122 and 134-144, as well as some examples of 156-165 and 178-179.

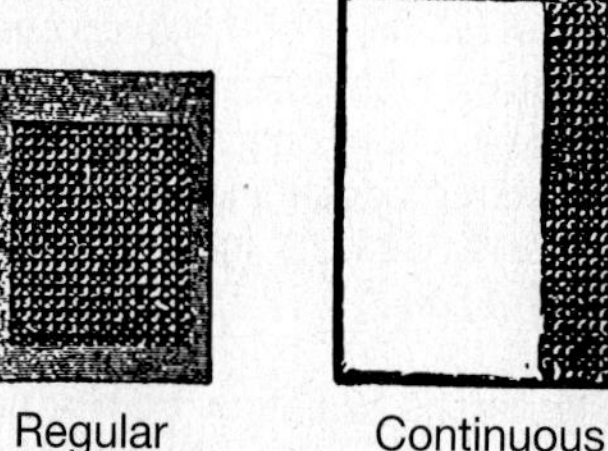

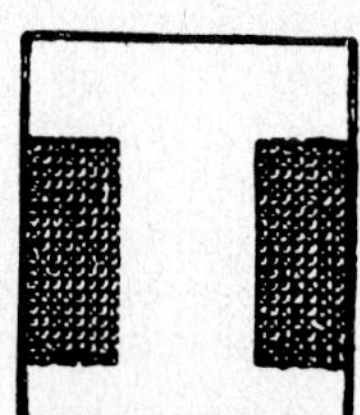

Regular Grill — Continuous Marginal Grill — Split Grill

Continuous Marginal Grill — includes continuous rows of grill points impressed by the untrimmed parts of the ends of the grill rollers, noted as "end roller grill" on the 1870 and 1873 issues, and those grills which came from a continuous band lengthwise of the roller.

Split Grill — situation on a stamp showing parts of two or more grills, caused by a sheet being fed under the grill roller off center.

Double (or Triple) Grill — stamp showing two or more separate grill impressions. This is not to be confused with a split grill, which shows two or four partial impressions from a single grill impression.

Rotary Grills — grilled appearance occasionally found on rotary press printings that was produced unintentionally by a knurled roller during the perforating process.

Similarly, grill-like impressions can be left on stamps dispensed from vending machines.

SEPARATION

"Separation" is the general term used to describe methods used to separate stamps. The standard forms currently in use in the United States are perforating and die-cutting. These methods are done during the stamp production process, after printing. Sometimes these methods are done on-press or sometimes as a separate step. The earliest issues, such as the 1847 5¢ Franklin (Scott 1), did not have any means provided for separation. It was expected the stamps would be cut apart with scissors or folded and torn. These are examples of imperforate stamps. Many stamps were first issued in imperforate formats and were later issued with perforations. Therefore, care must be observed in buying single imperforate stamps, to be certain they were issued imperforate and are not perforated examples that have been altered by having the perforations trimmed away. Stamps issued imperforate usually are valued as singles. However, imperforate varieties of normally perforated stamps should be collected in pairs or larger multiples as indisputable evidence of their imperforate character.

Perforations

The chief style of separation of U.S. stamps has been perforating. This is produced by cutting away the paper between the stamps in a line of holes (usually round) and leaving little bridges of paper between the stamps. These little bridges are the "teeth" of the perforation and, of course, project from the stamp when it is torn from the pane.

Because the gauge of the perforation often is the distinguishing difference among stamps, it is necessary to measure and describe perforations by a gauge number. The standard for this measurement is the number of such teeth within two centimeters. Thus, we say that a stamp is perforated 12 or 10½ to note that there are either 12 or 10½ teeth counted within two centimeters.

Some later U.S. stamps are "stroke" perforated rather than "line" perforated. While it is difficult to tell the difference on a single stamp, with a block of four or more stamps the difference is more easily seen where the horizontal and vertical perforations cross. On the stroke-perforated items, the crossing point is clean and no holes are out of line. On the line-perforated stamps, the crossing point only rarely is perfect and generally there is a roughness.

Perforation Gauge — tool for measuring perforation, as described above.

Fine Perforation — perforation with small holes and teeth close together.

Coarse Perforation — perforation with large holes and teeth far apart, frequently irregularly spaced.

Rough Perforation — holes not clean cut, but jagged.

Compound Perforation — normally where perforations at the top and bottom differ from the perforations at the sides of the stamp. In describing compound perforations, the gauge of the top is given first, then the sides.

Some stamps are found where one side will differ from the other three, and in this case the reading will be the top first, then the right side, then the bottom, then the left side.

Double Perforation — often found on early U.S. revenue stamps and occasionally on postage issues, double perforations are applied in error. They do not generally command a premium over catalogue values of properly perforated stamps and are not to be confused with a variety found on occasional rotary press printings, where stamps adjacent to the center gutters will show the entire width of the gutter and a line of perforations on the far end of the gutter. These are caused by the sheet having been cut off center and are called "gutter snipes." They command a small premium.

Many double perforations were privately made to increase the value of the stamp, and are to be considered damaged stamps.

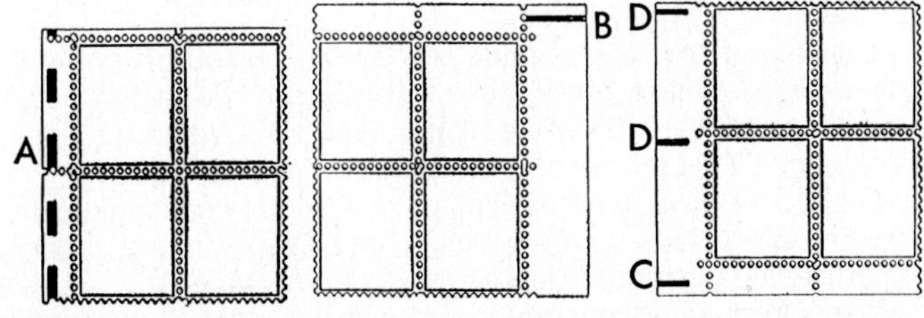

Electric Eye — an electronically controlled mechanical device acting as a guide in the operation of the perforating machine. Positive identification of stamps perforated by the electric eye process may be made by means of the distinctive marks in the gutters and margins of the full sheets on the printed web of paper. The original marks consisted of a series of heavy dashes dividing the vertical sheet gutter between the left and right panes (illustration A), together with a single line (margin line, illustration B), in the right sheet margin at the end of the horizontal sheet gutter between the upper and lower panes.

They first were used in 1933 on 400-subject plates for Scott 634, which was distributed to post offices in 1935 (used were plates 21149-50 and 21367-68). On these plates the plate numbers were placed opposite the ends of the third row of stamps from the top or bottom of the full sheet.

In later experiments, the margin line was broken into closely spaced thin vertical lines. Then it was again returned to its original form, but somewhat narrower.

In 1939, the Bureau of Engraving and Printing installed a new perforating machine which required a different layout to operate the centering mechanism. The vertical dashes remained the same, but the margin line was removed from the right sheet margin and a corresponding line ("gutter bar," illustration C) was placed in the left sheet margin at the end of the horizontal sheet gutter. Additional horizontal lines ("frame bars," illustration D) were added in the left sheet margin opposite the top frame line of the adjacent stamp design of all horizontal rows except the upper horizontal row of each left pane, where the frame bar is omitted. The plate numbers were moved back to their normal positions adjoining the corner stamps. Plates for the two types of machines could not be interchanged.

Later in 1939, a "convertible" plate was employed, consisting of a combination of the two previous layouts, the current one with the addition of a margin line (B) in its former position in the right sheet margin, thus making the perforation possible on either machine.

Originally laid out as 400-subject plates, electric-eye plates were later used for 200-subject horizontal or vertical format (commemorative, special delivery and airpost issues), 280-subject (Famous Americans and those with similar formats) and 180- and 360-subject plates (booklet panes of definitives, airpost, postal savings and war savings issues).

In laying out the plates for the 400-subject and 200-subject horizontal format issues, the marks retained the same relative position to the stamp designs. This was changed, however, in entering the design for the stamps of the 200-subject vertical format and 280-subject issues because the stamp designs were turned 90 degrees. That is, the designs were entered on the plates with the longer dimension horizontal. Although the electric eye marks were entered on the plates in the usual positions, on the printed sheet they appear as though shifted 90 degrees when the stamps are held in the customary upright position.

Thus a "horizontal" mark on a 400-subject or 200-subject horizontal format sheet would become a "vertical" mark on a 200-subject vertical format or 280-subject sheet. This situation has caused confusion among collectors and dealers in determining a definite description of the various marks. The designation of the position of the plate numbers also has not been uniform for the "turned" designs.

To solve this confusion, the United States Stamp Society (formerly the Bureau Issues Association) adopted a standard terminology for all the marks appearing on the electric eye sheets. Dashes (A), Margin Line (B), Gutter Bar (C) and Frame Bars (D), whereby each type of mark may be identified readily without referring to its plate-number position. The plate-number designation of the panes will continue to be established by holding the pane of stamps with the designs in an upright position; the corner of the pane on which the plate number appears will determine whether the pane is upper left, upper right, lower left, or lower right.

Die Cutting

The other major form of U.S. stamp separation is die-cutting. This is a method where a die in the pattern of separation is created that later cuts the stamp paper in a stroke motion. This process is used for self-adhesive postage stamps. Die-cutting can appear in straight lines, such as U.S. Scott 2522; shapes, such as U.S. Scott 1552; or imitating the appearance of perforations, such as U.S. Scott 2920. On stamps where the die cutting is unintentionally omitted, the terms "die cutting omitted" or "imperforate" may be used interchangeably.

Rouletting

A third type of separation is seen on a few revenue stamps. In rouletting, the stamp paper is cut partly or wholly through in a series of short consecutive cuts, with no paper removed. The number of cuts made in a two-centimeter space determines the gauge of the rouletting, just as the number of perforations in two centimeters determines the gauge of the perforation.

GUM

The Illustrated Gum Chart in the first part of this introduction shows and defines various types of gum condition. Because gum condition has an important impact on the value of unused stamps, we recommend studying this chart and the accompanying text carefully.

The gum on the back of a stamp may be shiny, dull, smooth, rough, dark, white, colored or tinted. Most stamp gumming adhesives use gum arabic or dextrine as a base. Certain polymers such as polyvinyl alcohol (PVA) have been used extensively since World War II.

The Scott *Standard Postage Stamp Catalogue* does not list items by types of gum. The Scott *Specialized Catalogue of United States Stamps and Covers* does differentiate among some types of gum for certain issues.

Because collectors generally prefer unused stamps with original gum, many unused stamps with no gum have been regummed to make them more desirable (and costly) to collectors who want stamps with full original gum. Some used stamps with faint cancels have had these cancels chemically removed and have been regummed. Skillful regumming can be difficult to detect, particularly on imperforate stamps. Certification of such stamps by competent authorities is suggested.

Reprints of stamps may have gum differing from the original issues. In addition, some countries have used different gum formulas for different seasons. These adhesives have different properties that may become more apparent over time.

Many stamps have been issued without gum, and this catalogue will note this fact. See United States Scott PR33-PR56.

LUMINESCENCE

Kinds of Luminescence — Fluorescence and phosphorescence, two different luminescent qualities, are found in U.S. postage stamps and postal stationery. While all luminescent stamps glow when exposed to short-wave ultraviolet (UV) light, only those with phosphorescent properties display brief afterglow when the UV light source is extinguished.

Fluorescent or "Hi-Bright" Papers — The Bureau of Engraving and Printing, at one point accepting paper for the printing of stamps without regard to fluorescent properties, unknowingly used a mix of paper with infinitely varying amounts of fluorescent optical brighteners added during the papermaking process. In March 1964, to preserve uniformity of product and as a safeguard for an emerging but still incomplete plan for nationwide use of luminescent stamps, BEP purchasing specifications were amended to limit the use of fluorescent paper brighteners. The amended specification permitted paper with some brightener content, but excluded brilliantly glowing papers known in the printing trade as "hi-bright."

Stamps printed on such papers emit a distinctive, intense whitish-violet glow when viewed with either long or short-wave UV. In following years, stamps were produced on papers with lower levels of fluorescence permitted by amended specifications.

Tagged Stamps — The Post Office Department (now the U.S. Postal Service) field-tested automated mail-handling equipment to face, cancel and sort mail at rates up to 30,000 pieces an hour, by sensing UV-light-activated afterglow from phosphorescent substances. For the first tests at Dayton, Ohio, started after August 1, 1963, the 8-cent carmine airpost stamp (Scott C64a) was overprinted (tagged) with a so-called "nearly-invisible" calcium silicate compound which phosphoresces orange-red when exposed to short-wave UV. A facer-canceler, with modifications that included a rapidly cycling on-off UV light, activated the phosphor-tagged airpost stamps and extracted envelopes bearing them from the regular flow of mail.

While the airpost extraction test was still in progress, the entire printing of the City Mail Delivery commemorative (Scott 1238) was ordered tagged with a yellow-green glowing zinc orthosilicate compound intended for use with the automated recognition circuits to be tested with surface-transported letter mail.

After the first-day ceremonies October 26, 1963, at Washington, D.C., it was learned the stamps had been tagged to publicize the innovative test by coupling tagging with stamps memorializing "100 years of postal progress" and to provide the first national distribution of tagged stamps for collectors. Between October 28 and November 2, to broaden the scope of the test in the Dayton area, the 4-cent and 5-cent denominations of the regular issue then in use were issued with the same yellow-green glowing compound applied in an experimental tagging format (Scott 1036e, 1213b, 1213c, and 1229a).

By June 1964, testing had proven sufficiently effective for the Post Office Department to order all 8-cent airpost adhesive stamps phosphor-tagged for general distribution. By January 1966, all airpost stamps, regardless of denomination, were ordered tagged. Meanwhile, from 1963 through 1965, limited quantities of the Christmas issues were tagged for use in the continuing test in the Dayton area on the use of tagging to automatically position (face) and cancel mail. (Scott 1240a, 1254a-1257a, and 1276a).

On May 19, 1966, the use of phosphor-tagged stamps was expanded to the Cincinnati Postal Region, which then included offices in Ohio, Kentucky and Indiana. During the last half of 1966, primarily to meet postal needs of that region, phosphor-tagged issues were authorized to include additional denominations of regular issues, some postal stationery, and about 12 percent of each commemorative issue, starting with the National Park Service 5-cent issue (Scott 1314a) and continuing through the Mary Cassatt 5-cent commemorative (Scott 1322a). After January 1, 1967, most regular values through the 16-cent, all commemoratives, and additional items of postal stationery were ordered tagged.

Adhesive stamps precanceled by the Bureau of Engraving and Printing (Bureau precancels), however, were not tagged, with the exception of Scott 1394, 1596, 1608, and 1610. Because there was no need to cancel mail with these stamps and since precancel permit holders post such mail already faced, postal officials by-passed facer-canceler operations and avoided the cost of tagging.

Overall phosphorescent overprints, when newly issued, are practically invisible in ordinary light. After aging three to five years, the tagging can discolor and become more easily visible. When viewed with UV light, there is little change in the hue of either orange-red or yellow-green emitted light. Even though observable discoloration exists, the presence or absence of tagging is best determined by examination with UV light.

Bar, or block, tagging, instead of the usual overall phosphorescent overprint, was used for some stamps beginning with the Andreotti-printed Mail Order Business commemorative (Scott 1468). These are much easier to identify than the overall overprint, often without need for a UV light.

Band tagging, a bar extending across two or more stamps, was first used with Scott 1489-1498.

Beginning in the 1990s, many stamps are printed on prephosphored paper. Unlike overall tagging, in which the tagging substance is applied to the entire stamp after it is printed, prephosphored paper has the tagging substance added to the surface of the paper during the paper-making process, before printing occurs.

In the late 1990s, some stamps appeared with the tagging formed in the shape of the stamp design elements.

Most of the luminescent issues exist with the luminescent coating unintentionally omitted. Such stamps are termed "tagging omitted" errors and should not be confused with stamps printed intentionally without tagging, which are termed "untagged."

In some postal stationery, such as Scott U551, UC40, UX48a and UX55, the luminescent element is in the ink with which the stamp design is printed. The luminescent varieties of Scott U550 and UC37 were made by adding a vertical phosphorescent bar or panel to the left of the stamp imprint. On Scott UC42, this "glow-bar" passes through the tri-globe design.

The Scott *Specialized Catalogue of United States Stamps and Covers* lists different tagging types when more than one type is known on a stamp. Currently, these types can be large or small block tagging, overall tagging and prephosphored paper. Prephosphored paper is further broken down into two types, each listed separately. In the first case, the tagging compound is applied to uncoated paper, seeping into its fibers and creating a highly mottled, or blotchy, appearance under short-wave UV light. This type is designated in the catalogue listings as "prephosphored uncoated paper with embedded tagging showing a mottled appearance." Some specialists shorten this to "embedded phosphor paper (EP)." In the second case, the tagging compound is mixed with the substance used to coat the surface when making coated paper. The taggant lies on top of the paper and can be removed if the coating is scraped off. This surface phosphor can have a number of different appearances, including solid (or smooth), grainy solid, uneven or randomly wavy. These variations should not be confused with the heavy and irregular mottled appearance of embedded tagging. This second type of prephosphored paper is designated in the catalogue listings as "prephosphored coated paper with surface tagging showing a solid [or grainy solid, or uneven, etc.] appearance." Some specialists shorten this to "surface phosphor paper (SP)." In instances where different prephosphored coated papers are used in the printing or printings of a single stamp, giving rise to surface phosphor paper with different appearances as noted above, such differences are mentioned in footnotes.

NOTE: Users of UV light should avoid prolonged exposure, which can burn the eyes. Sunglasses (particularly those that feature a "UV block") or prescription eyeglasses, tinted or plain, screen the rays and provide protection.

POSTAL MARKINGS

Postal markings are those marks placed by postal employees of this and other countries on the stamp or cover or both. These marks may indicate the mailing place of a letter, date, rate, route, accounting between post offices, and so on.

In addition to the basic town designations, there are many varieties of supplemental markings. Among these are rate marks, route marks, obliterators, special dating markings usually found on advertised or dead-letter covers, transportation markings (rail, steam, ship, airpost, etc.), and service markings (advertised, forwarded, missent, second delivery, mail route, too late, charged, paid box, due, returned for postage, soldier's letter, held for postage, short paid, unpaid, not paid, paid, free, dead letter office, etc.).

These markings originated, for material mailed in what is now the United States, in the Colonial period when manuscript postal markings were first introduced under the Ordinance of December 10, 1672, of New York, which established an inland postal system between the colonies. A "Post Payd" is found on the first letter ever sent under the system, on January 22, 1673. Manuscript postal markings continued in use right through the pre-stamp period and even can be found on some letters today.

The earliest handstamp associated with American service is a "NEW/YORK" blank handstamp found on letters conveyed via the Bristol Packet line in 1710-12 between New York and England. Following the demise of this operation, the first regular handstamp postal markings were introduced at New York in 1756, when a post office packet service was established between Falmouth, England, and New York. The marking merely was "NEW YORK" on two lines of type. The marking (see illustration), with each word of the city name on a separate line, is represented in presentations such as this as "NEW/YORK." Similar markings were later introduced at other towns, such as ANNA/POLIS, by 1766; CHARLES/TOWN, by 1770; PHILA/DELPHIA, by 1766; HART/FORD, by 1766; while other offices received a single-line marking: BOSTON, by 1769; ALBANY, by 1773; PENSACOLA, by 1772; SAVANNA, by 1765; BALTIMORE, by 1772; and WMSBURG, by 1770.

Some of these early letters also bear a circular datestamp containing the month in abbreviated form, i.e., "IV" for June and "IY" for July, and the date in a 14-17mm circle (see illustration). Known from at least nine towns, these are called "Franklin marks" after Benjamin Franklin, then deputy postmaster general for the English crown. The marks also are known as "American Bishopmarks," to distinguish them from the Bishopmark used in England, which has a center line.

First U.S. Handstamp

Franklin Mark

During 1774-75, an American provisional postal system was established in opposition to that of the English crown. Both manuscript and handstamp markings have been attributed to it. This system was taken over by Congress on July 26, 1775, and the same markings were continued in use. The earliest reported Congressional marks are a manuscript "Camb Au 8" and a blue-green straightline "NEW*YORK*AU*24." Postal markings are known throughout Revolution, including English occupation markings. Most are manuscript.

In the post-war Confederation period, handstamped circular markings were introduced at Charleston, South Carolina, in 1778-1780, and later at New London, Connecticut. Straightlines and manuscripts continued to dominate until the use of oval markings became widespread about 1800, with circles becoming the predominant markings shortly thereafter.

Handstamp rate markings are known as early as the 1789 pennyweight markings of Albany. Such types of markings became more common in the 1830's and almost the standard by the "5"and- "10"-cent rate period which began on July 1, 1845. This period also is when envelopes began to replace folded letter sheets. Before that date, envelopes were charged with an extra rate of postage. These "5," "10," and succeeding "3," "6," "5," and "10" rates of 1851-56 were common on domestic mail until prepayment became compulsory April 1, 1855, on all but drop or local letters domestically. The markings were common on foreign mail through about 1875.

Only 1.3 percent of all letters posted between 1847 and 1852 bore stamps. This proportion increased to 25 percent in 1852, 32 percent in 1853, 34 percent in 1854, 40 percent in 1855, and 64 percent in 1856. Stampless covers are commonplace, although there are some that are highly prized on the basis of their markings. Most are more common than stamped covers of the same period.

While the government began issuing handstamps as early as 1799 and obliterators in 1847, many postmasters were required, or at least permitted, to purchase their own canceling devices or to use pen strokes. Pen cancellations continued to be common in the smaller offices into the 1880's. Because of collector prejudice against pen-canceled stamps, many have ended up being "cleaned" (having the pen cancel removed). These are sold either as unused or with a different, faked cancellation to cover the evidence of cleaning. Ultraviolet light (long-wave) usually will reveal traces of the original pen markings.

From around 1850 until 1900, many postmasters used obliterators cut from wood or cork. Many bear fanciful designs, such as bees, bears, chickens, locks, eagles, Masonic symbols, flags, numerals and so on. Some of the designs symbolized the town of origin. These are not listed in this catalogue, for they owe their origin to the whim of some individual rather than a requirement of the postal regulations. Many command high prices and are eagerly sought by collectors. This has led to extensive forgery of such markings so that collectors are advised to check them carefully.

Rapid machine cancellations were introduced at Boston in 1880-90 and later spread across the country. Each of the various canceling machine types had identifiable characteristics, and collectors form collections based on type. One sub-specialty is that of flag cancellations. While handstamp flag designs are known earlier, the first machine flag cancellation was that of Boston in November-December 1894.

Specialists have noted that different canceling inks are used at different times, depending partly on the type of canceling device used. Rubber handstamps, prohibited in 1893 although used for parcel post and precanceling after that date, require a different type of ink from the boxwood or type-metal cancelers of the classic period, while a still different ink is used for the steel devices of the machine cancels.

Registry of letters was first authorized in this country in the Dutch colony of New Netherlands on overseas mail. Records of valuable letters were kept by postmasters throughout the stampless period while an "R" marking was introduced at Philadelphia in 1845 for registered mail. Cincinnati also had such a registry system. The first appearance of the word "registered" is on mail in November 1847, in manuscript, and in handstamp in May 1850. The official registration for U.S. mail, however, did not begin until July 1, 1855.

In recent years, the handstamped and machine types of cancellations have been standardized by the U.S. Postal Service and supplied to the various post offices.

Postmarks — markings to indicate the office of origin or manner of postal conveyance. In general terms, the postmark refers to the post office of origin, but sometimes there also are receiving postmarks of the post office of destination or of transit. Other post office markings include: advertised, forwarded, mail route, missent, paid, not paid, second delivery, too late, etc. Postmarks often serve to cancel postage stamps with or without additional obliterating cancels.

Cancellations — postal markings that make further use of stamps impossible. As used in the listings in this catalogue, cancellations include both postmarks used as cancellations and obliterations intended primarily to cancel (or "kill") the stamp.

Carrier Postmarks — usually show the words "Carrier" "City Delivery," or "U.S.P.O. Dispatch." They were applied to letters to indicate the delivery of mail by U.S. Government carriers. These markings should not be confused with those of local posts or other private mail services that used postmarks of their own. Free delivery of city mail by carriers was begun on July 1, 1863.

Free — handstamp generally used on free, franked mail. The marking occasionally is seen on early adhesives of the United States, used as a canceling device.

Railroad Postmarks — usually handstamps, the markings were used to postmark unpouched mail received by route agents of the Post Office Department traveling on trains on railway mail route. The route name in an agent's postmark often was similar to the name of the railroad or included the terminals of the route. The earliest known use of the word "Railroad" as a postmark is 1838. Route agents gradually became R.P.O. clerks, and some continued to use their handstamps after the route-agent service ceased June 30, 1882. The railroad postmarks of the 1850 period and later usually carried the name of the railroad.

A sub-group of railroad postmarks is made up of those applied in the early days by railroad station agents, using the railroad's ticket dating handstamp as a postmark. Sometimes the station agent was also the postmaster.

In 1864, the Post Office Department equipped cars for the general distribution of mails between Chicago and Clinton, Iowa.

Modern railroad marks, such as "R.P.O.," indicate transportation by railroad, and include Railway Post Office, Terminal Railway Post Office, Transfer Office, Closed Mail Service, Air Mail Field, and Highway Post Office.

Effective November 1, 1949, the Railway Mail Service was merged with others of like nature under the consolidated title Postal Transportation Service (PTS). The service was discontinued June 30, 1977.

The modern "railway marks" are quite common and are not the types referred to under cancellations as listed in this catalogue.

Way Markings — Way letters are those received by a mail carrier on his way between post offices and delivered at the first post office he reached. The postmaster ascertained where the carrier received them and charged, in his postbills, the postage from those places to destination. He wrote "Way" against those charges in his bills and also wrote or stamped "Way" on each letter. If the letter was exempt from postage, it should have been marked "Free."

The term "mail carrier" above refers to any carrier under contract to carry U.S. mail: a stage line, a horseback rider, or a steamboat or railroad that did not have a route agent on board. Only unpouched mail (not previously placed in a post office) was eligible for a Way fee of one cent. The postmaster paid this fee to the carrier, if demanded, for the carrier's extra work of bringing the letter individually to the post office. For a limited time at certain post offices, the Way fee was added to the regular postage. This explains the use of a numeral with the "Way" marking.

Packet Markings — Packet markings listed in this catalogue are those applied on a boat traveling on inland or coastal waterways. This group does not include mail to foreign countries that contains the words "British Packet," "American Packet," etc, or their abbreviations. These are U.S. foreign-mail exchange-office markings.

Listed packet markings are in two groups: 1) waterways route-agent markings that denote service exactly the same as that of the railroad route-agent markings, except that the route agent traveled on a boat instead of a train; 2) name-of-boat markings placed on the cover to advertise the boat or, as some believe, to expedite payment of Way and Steam fees at the post office where such letters entered the U.S. mails.

Occasionally waterways route-agent markings included the name of a boat, "S.B.," "STEAMBOAT," or merely a route number. Such supplemental designations do not alter the character of the markings as those of a route-agent.

19th Century U.S. Express Mail Postmarks — In pre-stamp days these represented either an extra-fast mail service or mail under the care of an express-mail messenger who also carried out-of-mail express packages. The service was permitted as a practical means of competing with package express companies that also carried mail in competition with the U.S. Mail. Several of these early postmarks were later used by U.S. Mail route agents on the New York-Boston and New York-Albany runs, or by U.S. steamboat letter carriers on the coastal run between Boston and St. John, New Brunswick.

Steamboat or Steam Markings — Except for the circular markings "Maysville Ky. Steam" and "Terre Haute Stb." and the rectangular "Troy & New York Steam Boat," these markings contain only the word "STEAMBOAT" or "STEAM," with or without a rating numeral. They represent the same service as that of Way markings, except that the carrier was an inland or coastal steamer that had no contract to carry U.S. mails. Such boats, however, were required by law to carry to the nearest post office any mail given them at landings. The boat owner was paid a two-cent fee for each letter so delivered, except on Lake Erie where the fee was one-cent. At some post offices, the Steamboat fee was added to regular postage. In 1861, the two-cent fee was again added to the postage, and in 1863 double postage was charged.

Ship Postmarks — postal markings indicating arrival on a private ship (one not under contract to carry mail). This marking was applied to letters delivered by such ships to the post office at their port of entry as required by law, for which they received a fee and the letters were taxed with a specified fee for the service in place of the ordinary open postage.

The use of U.S. postage stamps on ship letters is unusual, except for letters from Hawaii, because the U.S. inland postage on ship letters from a foreign point did not need to be prepaid. "U.S. SHIP" is a special marking applied to mail posted on naval vessels, especially during the Civil War period.

Steamship Postmarks — akin to Ship postmarks, but they appear to have been used mostly on mail from Caribbean or Pacific ports to New Orleans or Atlantic ports carried on steamships having a U.S. mail contract. An associated numeral usually designates the through rate from where the letter was received by the ship to its inland destination.

Receiving Mark — postal marking placed on the back of envelopes by the receiving post office to indicate the name of the office and date of arrival. It also is known as a "backstamp." Generally discontinued about 1913, the marking was employed for a time on airmail service until it was found the practice slowed the service. Receiving markings now are used on regisered and special-delivery mail.

Miscellaneous Route Markings — wordings associated with the previously described markings include "Bay Route," "River Mail," "Steamer," "Mail Route," etc. Classification of the marking ordinarily is evident from the use, or it can be identified from publications on postal markings.

U.S. Foreign-Mail Exchange-Office Markings — These served to meet the accounting requirements of the various mail treaties before the Universal Postal Union was established. The markings usually designate the exchange office or the carrier (British Packet, Bremen Packet, American Packet, etc.). Sometimes these markings are a restatement of the through rate, or a numeral designating the amount credited or debited to the foreign country as a means of allocating the respective parts of the total postage, according to conditions of route, method of transit, weight, etc.

Gridiron Cancellation — most common type of cancellation on early U.S. stamps. The marking consists of a circle enclosing parallel lines. There are many varieties of grid cancellations.

Paid Markings — generally consist of the word "PAID," sometimes within a frame, indicating regular postage prepaid by the sender of a letter. They are found as separate handstamps, within town or city postmarks, and as a part of obliterating cancels. In each case, the "paid" marking may be used with or without an accompanying or combined rate numeral indication.

Precancels — stamps having the cancellation applied before the article is presented for mailing. The purpose is to reduce handling and speed up the mails. A permit is required for use by the public, except for special cases, such as the experiments using Scott 1384a, 1414a-1418a, or 1552 for Christmas mail. Normally the precanceling is done with devices not used for ordinary postal service. Most precancellations consist of the city and state names between two lines or bars.

Precancels are divided into two groups: locals and Bureaus. Locals were printed, usually from 100-subject plates, or handstamped, usually by means of a 10- or 25-subject device having a rubber, metal or vinyl surface, at the town using the stamps. Most locals were made with devices furnished by the Post Office Department and the Postal Service, but a number were made with devices created in the city using them. Early locals include the printed "PAID" or "paid" on Scott 7 and 9, "CUMBERLAND, ME." on Scott 24-26 and the Glen Allen, Virginia stars. The U.S. Postal Service discontinued the practice of local precanceling as of July 5, 2007.

Many styles of precancellation are known. More than 600,000 different precancels exist from more than 20,000 post offices in the United States.

The Bureaus, or Bureau Prints, were precancels furnished to the post offices by the Post Office Department in Washington. For 75 years these were printed by the Bureau of Engraving and Printing, hence the name "Bureaus."

In late 1991, the American Bank Note Co. and J.W. Fergusson and Sons for Stamp Venturers also began producing precanceled stamps under contract with the Postal Service. Other companies have followed. Because the stamps go to the local post office from the same source, the Postal Service, and the method of production is essentially the same as used by the BEP, the term "Bureau precancel" has been retained in this catalogue. The cancellations consist of the name of the city and state where the stamps are to be used, lines or the class of mail. They originated in 1916, when postal officials were seeking ways to reduce costs as well as increase the legibility of the overprint. The BEP was low bidder in three cities, which resulted in the "experimentals." These 16 denominations, including two postage dues, were issued for Augusta, Maine (one value); Springfield, Massachusetts (14 values); and New Orleans (six values) in quanities ranging from 4,000,000 down to 10,000. Electrotype plates mounted on a flat-bed press were used to print the precancellations.

Regular production of Bureau precancels began on May 2, 1923, with Scott 581 precanceled "New York, N.Y." All regular Bureaus until 1954 were produced by the Stickney rotary press, whereby the stamps, immediately after printing, pass under the precanceling plates. Then the roll is gummed, perforated and cut into sheets or coils. Since 1954, a variety of printing methods have been used.

Precancels are listed in this catalogue only if the precanceled stamp is different from the nonprecanceled version (untagged stamps such as Scott 1582a); or, if the stamp only exists precanceled (Scott 2265). Classic locals and experimental Bureaus also are included as cancellations. See Service Indicator.

Service Indicator — inscription included in the design of the stamp to indicate the category of postal service to be rendered. The first regular postage stamp to include a service indicator was the 1976 7.9-cent Drum coil stamp of the Americana series (Scott 1615), which was for bulk rate mailings. This stamp was issued with Bureau precancels for proper usage from 107 cities. Examples without the Bureau precancellation were for philatelic purposes.

A second category of service indicator came about when the USPS began to include the service inscription between the lines of the Bureau precancellation. Examples of this group are "Bulk Rate" and "Nonprofit Organization."

Finally, with the 16.7-cent Transportation coil (Scott 2261), issued July 7, 1988, the USPS went back to including the service indicator in the design, with the indicator serving as the cancellation. With the precancellation now part of the design, the USPS stopped offering tagged versions of the stamps for collectors. The only so-called precancels currently in use are the service class/rate inscribed coils, and mailers' postmarks. This change was announced in *Postal Bulletin* 22210, dated July 5, 2007.

In all cases, the "service indicator" stamp does not normally receive an additional cancellation when used for the indicated service. For examples see Postal Markings - Bureau Precancels.

Tied On — when the cancellation (or postmark) extends from the stamp to the envelope.

Postal Markings - Cancellation Examples

Numerals
Values are for rating marks such as those illustrated. Later types of numerals in grids targets, etc., are common.

The common Boston Paid cancellation
(Values are for types other than this)

PAID ALL

PAID

Steamship

STEAMBOAT

SHIP STEAM

FREE

Steamboat
(Route agent marking)

ST. LOUIS, CAIRO AND NEW ORLEANS
RAILROAD LINE STEAMER
CHAMPION
LEAVES NEW ORLEANS FOR
CAIRO AND ST LOUIS.
MAR 25

Packet Boat
(Name-of-boat marking)

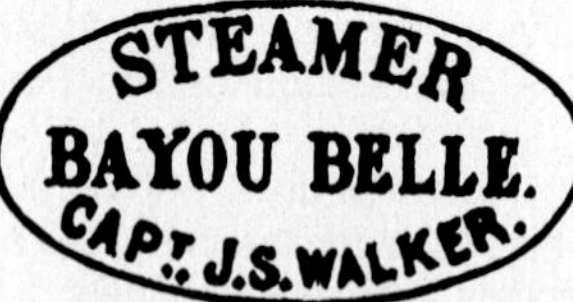

Packet Boat
(Name-of-boat marking)

Packet Boat
(Name-of-boat marking)

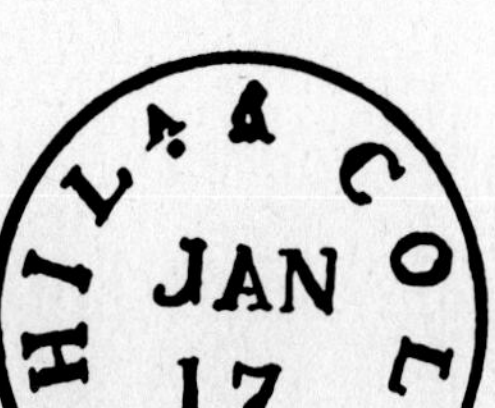

Railroad
(Route agent marking)

U.S. Express Mail
(Route agent marking)

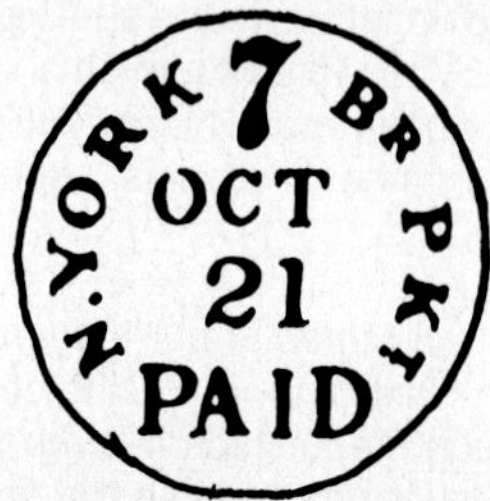

(In red on letter to Germany via Prussian Closed Mail, via British Packet. Credits 7 cents to Prussia.)

Express Company

Carrier

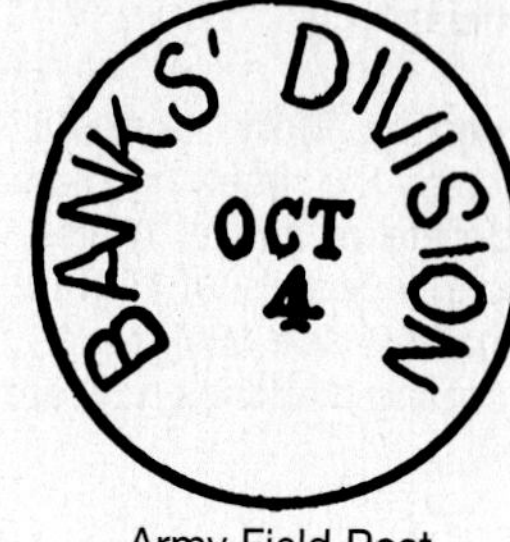

Army Field Post

Canadian

Town

Fort

Year dated

Vera Cruz, Mexico 1914

U.S. Postmark used in China

Exposition Station
Used while exposition is open. Many styles.

U.S. Postmark
used in Japan

1 WORLD'S FAIR ST LOUIS 1903

Exposition advertising
Used before exposition opens. Many styles.

New York City Foreign Mail – A group of design cancellations used between 1871 and 1877 in New York City on outgoing foreign mail only. This group of handstamps totals about 200 different fancy stars, geometric designs, wheels conventionalized flowers, etc., the majority within a circle 26-29 mm in diameter.

Patent Defacing Cancellations – When adhesive stamps came into general use, the Post Office Department made constant efforts to find a type of cancellation which would make the reuse of the stamp impossible. Many patents were granted to inventors, and some of the cancellations (killers) came into more or less general use. Some of them appear in combination with the town postmarks.

About 125 different types are known on the stamps issued up to about 1887. Their principal use and greatest variety occur on Scott 65, 147, 158, 183 and 184.

Patent cancellations generally fall into three groups:

1) Small pins or punches which pierce the paper or depress it sufficiently to break the fiber.

2) Sharp blades or other devices for cutting the paper.

3) Rotation of a portion of the canceler so that part of the paper is scraped away.

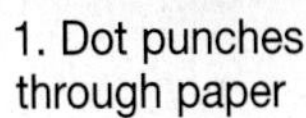

1. Dot punches through paper

2. Blades cut the paper

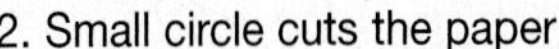

2. Small circle cuts the paper

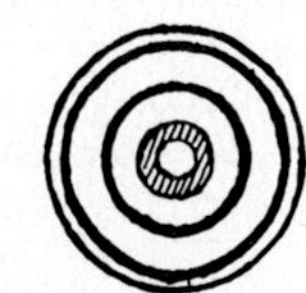

3. Scraped in the shaded circle

Supplementary Mail – markings which designate the special post office service of dispatching mail after the regular mail closed. Two kinds of supplementary mail were available:

1. Foreign mail. For New York, the postmaster general established in 1853 a fee of double the regular rate. This paid to get the mail aboard ship after the regular mail closing and before sailing time. The service continued until 1939. Postmark Types A, D, E, F, and G were used.

2. Domestic mail. For Chicago, at no extra fee, supplementary mail entitled a letter to catch the last eastbound train. Postmark Types B and C were used. No foreign destination was implied.

Similar service with "Supplementary" in the postmark apparently was available in Philadelphia and possibly elsewhere.

Type A

Type D

Type E

Type F
Combination Handstamp
(Also comes with numeral "1")
(Stamps with numeral cancel alone do not qualify for Supplementary Mail cancel premiums.)

Type G (also with other numerals)

Type B

Type C

Military Postmarks - Although mail from soldiers and sailors exists for all of the wars back to the American Revolution, such early letters were ordinarily sent through nearby civilian post offices. In fact, the first postal stations specifically for the handling of military mail were opened during the Spanish-American War in 1898. They were initially set up at training camps in the U.S. However, as the actual conflict took place in the Spanish colonies in the Caribbean and the Pacific, 77 special post offices were opened to handle military mail in Cuba, Puerto Rico, Guam and the Philippines. Most of these offices were issued cancels inscribed "Military Postal Station No. __" with the name of the town and territory in which they were located.

For many years, the warships of the U.S. Navy did not have post offices, so sailors' mail was simply deposited at the next convenient port. However, in 1908 the creation of on-board postal facilities was authorized, resulting in new postmarks showing the name of each vessel, thus creating a vast new collecting field. During both World Wars, these were replaced with generic cancels reading simply "U.S. Navy" so that they would not provide any information about ships' names or locations to enemy agents.

When the United States entered World War I on April 6, 1917, a vast expansion of U.S. military forces was required. This had to be met with an equally large expansion of postal facilities. Many post offices were opened at training camps in the U.S. In addition, an entirely new system of Army Post Offices (APOs) was created overseas, with the first being opened at St. Nazaire, France, on July 10, 1917. This system eventually involved about 200 different military stations. Most were located in France, but some were in Italy. Following the Armistice on November 11, 1918, other offices were opened in Belgium, Germany, Luxembourg and The Netherlands.

At first, members of the AEF were allowed to send mail from the APOs to the U.S., its territories and possessions at domestic postage rates, which were 1¢ for postcards and 2¢ for letters. However, from October 4, 1917, the troops were granted free postage for such items, although they were still required to pay at domestic rates for special services such as registration, special delivery and parcel post.

Civilians serving with the army, war correspondents and workers with welfare organizations, including the American Red Cross, YMCA, Knights of Columbus and Salvation Army, were permitted to use the APOs but had to pay domestic postage, including the war tax of 1¢ per piece that was in effect from November 2, 1917, until June 30, 1919.

Some American units participated in the Allied intervention in Russia in 1918-1920, including Siberia and North Russia. A U.S. postal agency was opened in Vladivostok, Siberia, to handle mail from the AEF-Siberia, but the troops in North Russia used the British postal facilities (with their so-called "Polar Bear" markings).

Elsewhere, American forces were involved in military interventions in China, the Caribbean and Latin America (Cuba, Dominican Republic, Haiti, Mexico and Nicaragua). In each case, U.S. military postal facilities were opened to serve the troops, thus creating new postal markings that are collected by specialists.

During World War II, the first new U.S. military post offices were opened in connection with the bases acquired from Great Britain in exchange for a fleet of old destroyers. The first of these offices was opened on January 15, 1941, using a postmark inscribed "American Forces in Newfoundland." When other offices opened, the inscription was changed to "American Base Forces" and an APO number added. After the U.S. entered the war on December 7, 1941, there was a vast expansion of the system, and the postmarks were changed to "U.S. Army Postal Service" with an APO number.

During the course of the war and its aftermath, more than 1,000 APOs were created, serving Army and Air Force personnel around the world. Some of these were open for very short periods, and their postmarks are scarce. As in World War I, the troops were granted free franking for surface cards and letters from April 1, 1942, to December 31, 1947, but postage was required for special services, including airmail, at normal domestic rates.

More recently, of course, there is military mail from the conflicts in Korea, Vietnam, Kuwait, Afghanistan and Iraq, not to mention smaller events in places like Grenada, Panama and Kosovo. It should be noted that the APO numbering system was switched over to five digits in 1965, to bring it in line with the civilian zip code designations.

In looking at covers, collectors will find that most military mail from World War I on bears evidence of military and/or civilian censorship, after which the letters were permitted to be forwarded.

Readers desiring more information on military postal markings, censorship and the handling of military mail, or a list of available publications on these and related subjects, are invited to visit www.MilitaryPHS.org, the website of the Military Postal History Society.

Postal Markings - Bureau Precancels

AUGUSTA MAINE

NEW ORLEANS LA.

SPRINGFIELD MASS.

Experimentals

PERU IND.

LANSING MICH.

SAINT LOUIS MO.

New Orleans La.

San Francisco Calif.

PORTLAND ME.

LAKEWOOD N. J.

KANSAS CITY MO.

POUGHKEEPSIE N. Y.

LONG ISLAND CITY, N. Y.

CORPUS CHRISTI TEXAS

ATLANTA GEORGIA

ATLANTA GA.

PEORIA IL

CINCINNATI OH

Postal Markings - Service Indicators

Blk. Rt. CAR-RT SORT

Bulk Rate

Nonprofit Org.

Nonprofit Org.

PRESORTED FIRST-CLASS

ZIP+4

Postal Markings - Local Precancels

QUINCY ILLINOIS

FITCHBURG MASS.

LOS ANGELES CALIF.

Fergus Falls Minn.

COVINGTON KY.

REDWOOD CITY CALIF.

BELMONT CALIF.

ELGIN ILLINOIS

Electroplates

Ashland Wis.

PALMYRA N. Y.

Northhampton MASS.

DES PLAINES ILL.

RICHMOND VA.

BROOKFIELD ILLINOIS

PAONIA COLO.

GOSHEN IND

TOWER CITY N. DAK.

NEW BRUNSWICK N. J.

ORLANDO, FLA.

RICHTON PARK ILL.

MULINO, OREG.

PINE HILL N.Y.

FARRELL, PA

SACRAMENTO CA

Handstamps

GENERAL GLOSSARY

Scott Publishing Co. uses the following terms in its catalogues, as appropriate. Definitions follow each term.

Imperforate — stamps without perforations, rouletting, or other form of separation. Some self-adhesive stamps are die cut with straight lines. They look imperforate, but they are not.

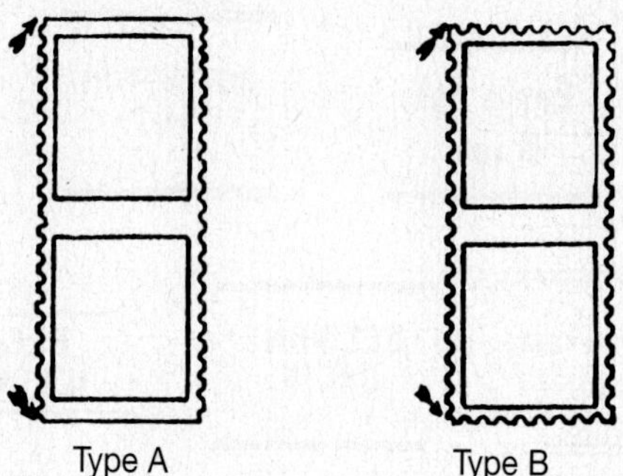

Part-Perforate — Stamps with perforations on the two opposite sides, the other two sides remaining imperforate. See Coil Stamps.

Vertical Pair, Imperforate Horizontally — (Type A illustrated) indicating that a pair of stamps is fully perforated vertically, but has no horizontal perforations.

Horizontal Pair, Imperforate Vertically — (Type A) indicating that a pair of stamps is fully perforated horizontally but has no vertical perforations.

Vertical Pair, Imperforate Between — (Type B illustrated) indicating that the vertical pair is fully perforated at the top, sides and bottom, but has no perforations between the stamps.

Horizontal Pair, Imperforate Between — (Type B) indicating that the horizontal pair is fully perforated at the top, sides and bottom, but has no perforations between the stamps.

Note: Of the above two types (A and B), Type A is the more common.

Blind Perforations — the slight impressions left by the perforating pins if they fail to puncture the paper. While multiples of stamps showing blind perforations may command a slight premium over normally perforated stamps, they are not imperforate errors. Fakers have removed gum from stamps to make blind perforations less evident.

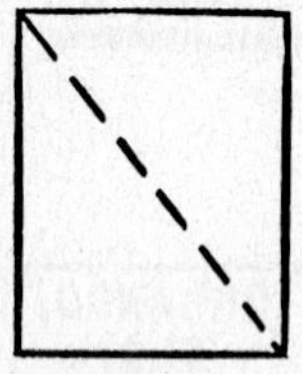

Diagonal

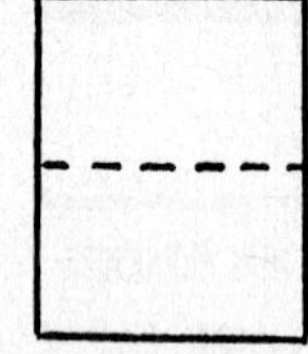

Horizontal

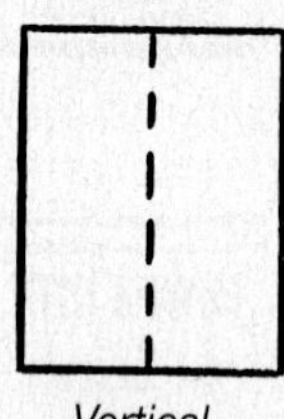

Vertical

Bisect — Stamps cut in half so that each part prepaid postage. These items were used in emergencies where no stamps of the lower denomination were available. These may be diagonal, horizontal or vertical,as shown. Listings are for bisects on full covers with the bisected stamp tied to the cover on the cut side. Those on piece or part of a cover sell for considerably less. "Half-stamps" that receive a surcharge or overprint are not considered bisects.

This catalogue does not list unofficial bisects after 1880.

Block of Four, Imperforate Within — Examples exist of blocks of four stamps that are perforated on all four outside edges, but lack both horizontal and vertical perforations within the block. Scott 2096c, the Smokey the Bear commemorative, is an accidental example of this phenomenon. Scott RS173j and RS174j are examples of a situation where internal perforations were omitted intentionally to create 4-cent "stamps" from four 1-cent stamps.

Rouletting — short consecutive cuts in the paper to facilitate separation of the stamps, made with a toothed wheel or disc.

Booklets — Many countries have issued stamps in booklets for the convenience of users. This idea is becoming increasingly popular today in many countries. Booklets have been issued in all sizes and forms, often with advertising on the covers, on the panes of stamps or on the interleaving.

The panes may be printed from special plates or made from regular sheets. All panes from booklets issued by the United States and many from those of other countries are imperforate on three sides, but perforated between the stamps. Any stamplike unit in the pane, either printed or blank, which is not a postage stamp, is considered a *label* in the catalogue listings. The part of the pane through which stitches or staples bind the booklet together, or which affixes the pane to the booklet cover, is considered to be a *binding stub* or tab.

Scott lists and values booklets in this volume. Except for panes from Canal Zone, handmade booklet panes are not listed when they are fashioned from existing sheet stamps and, therefore, are not distinguishable from the sheet-stamp foreign counterparts.

Panes usually do not have a "used" value because there is little market activity in used panes, even though many exist used.

Cancellations — the marks or obliterations put on a stamp by the authorities to show that it has done service and is no longer valid for use. If made with a pen, it is a "pen cancellation." When the location of the post office appears in the cancellation, it is a "town cancellation." When calling attention to a cause or celebration, it is a "slogan cancellation." Many other types and styles of cancellations exist, such as duplex, numerals, targets, etc.

Coil Stamps — stamps issued in rolls for use in dispensers, affixing and vending machines. Those of the United States and its territories are perforated horizontally or vertically only, (with the exception of No. 3785) with the other edges imperforate. Coil stamps of some countries, such as Great Britain, are perforated on all four sides.

Commemorative Stamps — Special issues that commemorate some anniversary or event or person. Usually such stamps are available for a limited period concurrently with the regular issue of stamps. Examples of commemorative issues are Scott 230-245, 620-621, 946, 1266, C68, and U218-U221.

Covers — envelopes, with or without adhesive postage stamps, which have passed through the mail and bear postal or other markings of philatelic interest. Before the introduction of envelopes in about 1840, people folded letters and wrote the address on the outside. Many people covered their letters with an extra sheet of paper on the outside for the address, producing the term "cover." Used air letter sheets and stamped envelopes also are considered covers. Stamps on paper used to cover parcels are said to be "on wrapper." ("Wrapper" also is the term used for postal stationery items that were open at both sides and wrapped around newspapers or pamphlets.) Often stamps with high face values are rare on cover, but more common on wrapper. Some stamps and postal stationery items are difficult to find used in the manner for which they were intended, but quite common when used to make philatelic items such as flight or first day covers. High face-value stamps also may be more common on package address tags. See Postal Cards.

Earliest Documented Use (EDU) — For stamps that do not have a designated first day of issue, the earliest documented use is the date when a stamp was first used in the U.S. mails. These dates are listed in the U.S. Specialized catalogue, and new dates must be documented with recognized certificates from leading expertizing committees.

Error — stamps having some unintentional major deviation from the normal. Errors include, but are not limited to, mistakes in color, paper, or watermark; inverted centers or frames on multicolor printing; missing color;inverted or double surcharges or overprints; imperforates and part-perforates; unintentionally omitted tagging; and double impressions. A factually wrong or misspelled inscription, if it appears on all examples of a stamp, even if corrected later, is not classified as a philatelic error.

Color-Omitted Errors — This term refers to stamps where a missing color is caused by the complete failure of the printing plate to deliver ink to the stamp paper or any other paper. Generally, this is caused by the printing plate not being engaged on the press or by the ink station running dry of ink during printing.

Color-Missing Errors — This term refers to stamps where a color or colors were printed somewhere but do not appear on the finished stamp. There are four different classes of color-missing errors, and this catalogue indicates with a two-letter code appended to each such listing what caused the color to be missing. This same terminology is used in the listings of many modern perforation/die cutting missing errors.

FO = A foldover of the stamp sheet during printing may block ink from appearing on a stamp. Instead, the color will appear on the back of the foldover (where it might fall on the back of the selvage or perhaps on the back of another stamp). FO also will be used in the case of foldunders, where the paper may fold underneath the other stamp paper and the color will print on the platen.

EP = A piece of *extraneous paper* falling across the plate or stamp paper will receive the printed ink. When the extraneous paper is removed, an unprinted area of stamp paper remains and shows partially or totally missing colors.

CM = A misregistration of the printing plates during printing will result in a *color misregistration,* and such a misregistration may result in a color not appearing on the finished stamp.

PS = A *perforation shift* after printing may remove a color from the finished stamp. Normally, this will occur on a row of stamps at the edge of the stamp pane.

First Day Cover — A philatelic term to designate the use of a certain stamp (on cover) or postal stationery item on the first day of issue at a place officially designated for such issue or so postmarked. Current U.S. stamps may have such a postal marking applied considerably after the actual issue date.

Gum Breaker Ridges — Colorless marks across the backs of some rotary press stamps, impressed during manufacture to prevent curling. Many varieties of "gum breaks" exist.

Measurements — When measurements are given in the Scott catalogues for stamp size, grill size or any other reason, the first measurement given is always for the top and bottom dimension, while the second measurement will be for the sides (just as perforation gauges are measured). Thus, a stamp size of 15mm x 21mm will indicate a vertically oriented stamp 15mm wide at top and bottom, and 21mm tall at the sides. The same principle holds for measuring or counting items such as U.S. grills. A grill count of 22x18 points (B grill) indicates that there are 22 grill points across by 18 grill points down.

Original Gum — A stamp is described as "O.G." if it has the original gum as applied when printed. Some are issued without gum, such as Scott 730, 731, 735, 752, etc; government reproductions, such as Scott 3 and 4; and official reprints.

Overprinted and Surcharged Stamps — Overprinting is a wording or design placed on stamps to alter the place of use (e.g., "Canal Zone" on U.S. stamps), to adapt them for a special purpose ("I.R." on 1-cent and 2-cent U.S. stamps of the 1897-1903 regular issue for use as revenue stamps. Scott R153-R155A), or for a special occasion (U.S. Scott 647-648).

Surcharge is an overprint that changes or restates the face value of the item.

Surcharges and overprints may be handstamped, typeset or, occasionally, lithographed or engraved. A few handwritten overprints and surcharges are known. The world's first surcharge was a handstamped "2" on the United States City Despatch Post stamps of 1846.

Postal Cards — cards that have postage printed on them. Ones without printed stamps are referred to as "postcards."

Proofs and Essays — *Proofs* are impressions taken from an approved die, plate or stone in which the design and color are the same as the stamp issued to the public. *Trial color proofs* are impressions taken from approved dies, plates or stones in varying colors. An *essay* is the impression of a design that differs in some way from the stamp as issued.

Provisionals — stamps issued on short notice and intended for temporary use pending the arrival of regular (definitive) issues. They usually are issued to meet such contingencies as changes in government or currency, shortage of necessary denominations, or military occupation.

In the 1840's, postmasters in certain American cities issued stamps that were valid only at specific post offices. Postmasters of the Confederate States also issued stamps with limited validity. These are known as "postmaster's provisionals." See U.S. Scott 9X1-9X3 and Confederate States Scott 51X1.

Se-Tenant — joined, referring to an unsevered pair, strip or block of stamps differing in design, denomination or overprint. See U.S. Scott 2158a. Unless the se-tenant item has a continuous design (see U.S. Scott 1451a, 1694a), the stamps do not have to be in the same order as shown in the catalogue (see U.S. Scott 2158a).

Tete Beche — A pair of stamps in which one is upside down in relation to the other. Some of these are the result of intentional sheet arrangements, i.e. Morocco Scott B10-B11. Others occurred when one or more electrotypes accidentally were placed upside down on the plate. See Hawaii Scott 21a and 22a. Separation of the stamps, of course, destroys the tete beche variety.

Specimens — One of the regulations of the Universal Postal Union requires member nations to send samples of all stamps they put into service to the International Bureau in Switzerland. Member nations of the UPU receive these specimens as samples of what stamps are valid for postage. Many are overprinted, handstamped or initial-perforated "Specimen," "Canceled" or "Muestra."Stamps distributed to government officials or for publicity purposes, and stamps submitted by private security printers for official approval also may receive such defacements.

These markings prevent postal use, and all such items generally are known as "specimens." There is a section in this catalogue devoted to this type of material. U.S. officials with "specimen" overprints and printings are listed in the Special Printings section.

Splice — The junction of two rotary-press printings by butting the ends of the web (roll) of paper together and pasting a strip of perforated translucent paper on the back of the junction. The two-stamp specimen to show this situation is a "spliced pair."

Splices occur when a web breaks and is repaired or when one web is finished and another begins.

Territorial and Statehood Dates

	Territorial Date	Statehood Date	
Alabama	Sept. 25, 1817	Dec. 14, 1819	Territory by enabling act of March 3, 1817, effective Sept. 25, 1817. Created out of part of existing Mississippi Territory.
Alaska	Oct. 18, 1867	Jan. 3, 1959	A district from Oct. 18, 1867, until it became an organized territory Aug. 24, 1912.
Arizona	Feb. 24, 1863	Feb. 14, 1912	This region was sometimes called Arizona before 1863 though still in the Territory of New Mexico.
Arkansas	July 5, 1819*	June 15, 1836	The territory was larger than the state. After statehood, the left-over area to the west had post offices that continued for some years to use an Arkansas abbreviation in the postmarks although really they were in the "Indian Country."
California		Sept. 9, 1850	Ceded by Mexico by the Treaty of Guadalupe-Hidalgo, concluded Feb. 2, 1848, and proclaimed July 4, 1848. From then until statehood, California had first a military government until Dec. 20, 1849, and then a local civil government. It never had a territorial form of government.
Colorado	Feb. 28, 1861	Aug. 1, 1876	
Connecticut		Jan. 9, 1788	The fifth of the original 13 colonies.
Delaware		Dec. 7, 1787	The first of the original 13 colonies.
Dakota	March 2, 1861	Nov. 2, 1889	Became two states: North and South Dakota.
Deseret	March 5, 1849		Brigham Young created the unofficial territory of Deseret. In spite of the fact that Utah Territory was created Sept. 9, 1850, Deseret continued to exist unofficially, in what is now Utah, at least as late as 1862.
Frankland or Franklin			This unofficial state was formed in Aug. 1784, in the northeast corner of what is now Tennessee, and the government existed until 1788. In reality it was part of North Carolina.
Florida	March 30, 1822	March 3, 1845	
Georgia		Jan. 2, 1788	The fourth of the original 13 colonies.
Hawaii	Aug. 12, 1898	Aug. 21, 1959	The territorial date given is that of the formal transfer to the United States, with Sanford B. Dole as first Governor.
Idaho	March 3, 1863	July 3, 1890	
Illinois	March 2, 1809*	Dec. 3, 1818	
Indiana	July 5, 1800*	Dec. 11, 1816	There was a residue of Indiana Territory which continued to exist under that name from Dec. 11, 1816 until Dec. 3, 1818, when it was attached to Michigan Territory.
Indian Territory		Nov. 16, 1907	In the region first called the "Indian Country," established June 30, 1834. It never had a territorial form of government. Finally, with Oklahoma Territory, it became the State of Oklahoma on Nov. 16, 1907.
Iowa	July 4, 1838	Dec. 28, 1846	
Jefferson	Oct. 24, 1859		An unofficial territory from Oct. 24, 1859, to Feb. 28, 1861. In reality it included parts of Kansas, Nebraska, Utah and New Mexico Territories, about 30% being in each of the first three and 10% in New Mexico. The settled portion was mostly in Kansas Territory until Jan. 29, 1861, when the State of Kansas was formed from the eastern part of Kansas Territory. From this date the heart of "Jefferson" was in unorganized territory until Feb. 28, 1861, when it became the Territory of Colorado.
Kansas	May 30, 1854	Jan. 29, 1861	
Kentucky		June 1, 1792	Never a territory, it was part of Virginia until statehood.
District of Louisiana	Oct. 1, 1804		An enormous region, it encompassed all of the Louisiana Purchase except the Territory of Orleans. Created by Act of March 26, 1804, effective Oct. 1, 1804, and attached for administrative purposes to the Territory of Indiana.
Territory of Louisiana	July 4, 1805		By Act of March 3, 1805, effective July 4, 1805, the District of Louisiana became the Territory of Louisiana.
Louisiana		April 30, 1812	With certain boundary changes, had been the Territory of Orleans.
District of Maine		March 16, 1820	Before statehood, what is now the State of Maine was called the District of Maine and belonged to Massachusetts.
Maryland		April 28, 1788	The seventh of the original 13 colonies.

	Territorial Date	Statehood Date	
Massachusetts		Feb. 6, 1788	The sixth of the original 13 colonies.
Michigan	July 1, 1805	Jan. 26, 1837	
Minnesota	March 3, 1849	May 11, 1858	
Mississippi	May 7, 1798	Dec. 10, 1817	Territory by Act of April 7, 1798, effective May 7, 1798.
Missouri	Dec. 7, 1812	Aug. 10, 1821	The state was much smaller than the territory. The area to the west and northwest of the state, which had been in the territory, was commonly known as the "Missouri Country" until May 30, 1854, and certain of the post offices in this area show a Missouri abbreviation in the postmark.
Montana	May 26, 1864	Nov. 8, 1889	
Nebraska	May 30, 1854	March 1, 1867	
Nevada	March 2, 1861	Oct. 31, 1864	
New Hampshire		June 21, 1788	The ninth of the original 13 colonies.
New Jersey		Dec. 18, 1787	The third of the original 13 colonies.
New Mexico	Dec. 13, 1850	Jan. 6, 1912	
New York		July 26, 1788	The 11th of the original 13 colonies.
North Carolina		Nov. 21, 1789	The 12th of the original 13 colonies.
North Dakota		Nov. 2, 1889	Had been part of the Territory of Dakota.
Northwest Territory	July 13, 1787		Ceased to exist March 1, 1803, when Ohio became a state. The date given is in dispute, Nov. 29, 1802 often being accepted.
Ohio		March 1, 1803	Had been part of Northwest Territory until statehood.
Oklahoma	May 2, 1890	Nov. 16, 1907	The state was formed from Oklahoma Territory and Indian Territory.
Oregon	Aug. 14, 1848	Feb. 14, 1859	
Orleans	Oct. 1, 1804		A territory by Act of March 26, 1804, effective Oct. 1, 1804. With certain boundary changes, it became the State of Louisiana, April 30, 1812.
Pennsylvania		Dec. 12, 1787	The second of the original 13 colonies.
Rhode Island		May 29, 1790	The 13th of the original 13 colonies.
South Carolina		May 23, 1788	The eighth of the original 13 colonies.
South Dakota		Nov. 2, 1889	Had been part of Dakota Territory.
Southwest Territory			Became the State of Tennessee, with minor boundary changes, June 1, 1796.
Tennessee		June 1, 1796	Had been Southwest Territory before statehood.
Texas		Dec. 29, 1845	Had been an independent Republic before statehood.
Utah	Sept. 9, 1850	Jan. 4, 1896	
Vermont		March 4, 1791	Until statehood, had been a region claimed by both New York and New Hampshire.
Virginia		June 25, 1788	The 10th of the original 13 colonies.
Washington	March 2, 1853	Nov. 11, 1889	
West Virginia		June 20, 1863	Had been part of Virginia until statehood.
Wisconsin	July 4, 1836	May 29, 1848	The state was smaller than the territory, and the left-over area continued to be called the Territory of Wisconsin until March 3, 1849.
Wyoming	July 29, 1868	July 10, 1890	

* The dates followed by an asterisk are one day later than those generally accepted. The reason is that the Act states, with Arkansas for example, "from and after July 4." While it was undoubtedly the intention of Congress to create Arkansas as a Territory on July 4, the U.S. Supreme Court decided that "from and after July 4," for instance, meant "July 5."

Territorial and statehood data compiled by Dr. Carroll Chase and Richard McP. Cabeen.

Domestic Letter Rates

Effective Date	Prepaid	Collect
1845, July 1		
Reduction from 6¢ to 25¢ range on single-sheet letters		
Under 300 miles, per ½ oz	5¢	5¢
Over 300 miles, per ½ oz	10¢	10¢
Drop letters	2¢	
1847-1848		
East, to or from Havana (Cuba) per ½ oz	12½¢	12½¢
East, to or from Chagres (Panama) per ½ oz	20¢	20¢
East, to or from Panama, across Isthmus, per ½ oz.	30¢	30¢
To or from Astoria (Ore.) or Pacific Coast, per ½ oz	40¢	40¢
Along Pacific Coast, per ½ oz	12½¢	12½¢
1847, July 1		
Unsealed circulars		
1 oz. or less	3¢	
1851, July 1		
Elimination of rates of 1847-1848 listed above		
Up to 3,000 miles, per ½ oz.	3¢	5¢
Over 3,000 miles, per ½ oz	6¢	10¢
Drop letters	1¢	
Unsealed circular		
1 oz. or less up to 500 miles	1¢	
Over 500 miles to 1,500 miles	2¢	
Over 1,500 miles to 2,500 miles	3¢	
Over 2,500 miles to 3,500 miles	4¢	
Over 3,500 miles	5¢	
1852, September 30		
Unsealed circulars		
3 oz. or less anywhere in U.S.	1¢	
Each additional ounce	1¢	
(Double charge if collect)		
1855, April 1		
Prepayment made compulsory		
Not over 3,000 miles, per ½ oz.	3¢	
Over 3,000 miles, per ½ oz.	10¢	
Drop letters	1¢	
1863, July 1		
Distance differential eliminated		
All parts of United States, per ½ oz.	**3¢**	
1883, October 1		
Letter rate reduced one-third		
All parts of United States, per ½ oz.	2¢	
1885, July 1		
Weight increased to 1 oz.		
All parts of United States, per 1 oz.	2¢	
1896, October 1		
Rural Free Delivery started		

Effective Date	Prepaid
1917, November 2	
War emergency	
All parts of United States, per 1 oz.	3¢
1919, July 1	
Restoration of pre-war rate	
All parts of United States, per 1 oz.	2¢
1932, July 6	
Rise due to depression	
All parts of United States, per 1 oz.	3¢

Effective Date	Prepaid
1958, August 1	
All parts of United States, per 1 oz.	4¢
1963, January 7	
All parts of United States, per 1 oz.	5¢
1968, January 7	
All parts of United States, per 1 oz.	6¢
1971, May 16	
All parts of United States, per 1 oz.	8¢
1974, March 2	
All parts of United States, per 1 oz.	10¢
1975, December 31	
All parts of United States, 1st oz.	13¢
1978, May 29	
All parts of United States, 1st oz.	15¢
1981, March 22	
All parts of United States, 1st oz.	18¢
1981, November 1	
All parts of United States, 1st oz.	20¢
1985, February 17	
All parts of United States, 1st oz.	22¢
1988, April 3	
All parts of United States, 1st oz.	25¢
1991, February 3	
All parts of United States, 1st oz.	29¢
1995, January 1	
All parts of United States, 1st oz.	32¢
1999, January 10	
All parts of United States, 1st oz.	33¢
2001, January 7	
All parts of United States, 1st oz.	34¢
2002, June 30	
All parts of United States, 1st oz.	37¢
2006, January 8	
All parts of United States, 1st oz.	39¢
2007, May 14	
All parts of United States, 1st oz.	41¢
2008, May 12	
All parts of United States, 1st oz.	42¢
2009, May 11	
All parts of United States, 1st oz.	44¢
2012, January 22	
All parts of United States, 1st oz.	45¢
2013, January 27	
All parts of United States, 1st oz.	46¢
2014, January 26	
All parts of United States, 1st oz.	49¢
2016, April 10	
All parts of United States, 1st oz.	47¢
2017, January 22	
All parts of United States, 1st oz.	49¢
2018, January 21	
All parts of United States, 1st oz.	50¢
2019, January 27	
All parts of United States, 1st oz.	55¢
2021, August 29	
All parts of United States, 1st oz.	58¢
2022, July 10	
All parts of United States, 1st oz.	60¢

Domestic Air Mail Rates

Effective Date	Prepaid
1911-1916 – The Pioneer Period	
Special official Post Office Flights at Fairs, aviation meets, etc., per 1 oz.	2¢
Postal cards and postcards	1¢
(Regulations prohibited an additional charge for air service on Post Office authorized flights.)	
1918, May 15 - July 13, 1918	
Service between Washington, DC, New York and Philadelphia (including 10¢ special delivery fee), per 1 oz.	24¢
1918, July 15-Dec. 14, 1918	
Service between Washington, DC, New York and Philadelphia (including 10¢ special delivery fee), per 1 oz.	16¢
Additional ounces	6¢
1918, Dec. 15-July 17, 1919	
Service between selected cities (other cities added later, special delivery no longer included), per 1 oz.	6¢
1919, July 18-June 29, 1924	
No specific airmail rate: mail carried by airplane on space available basis but airmail service not guaranteed, per 1 oz.	2¢
Postal cards and postcards, per 1 oz.	1¢
1924, June 30-Jan. 31, 1927	
Airmail service per zone (New York-Chicago; Chicago-Cheyenne, Wyo.; Cheyenne-San Francisco), per 1 oz. (each zone or portion thereof)	8¢
1925, July 1-Jan. 31, 1927	
Special overnight service New York-Chicago (with three intermediate stops), per 1 oz.	10¢
1926, Feb. 15-Jan. 31, 1927	
Contract routes not exceeding 1,000 miles (first flight Feb. 15) per 1 oz. (each route or portion thereof)	10¢
Contract routes between 1,000 and 1,500 miles (Seattle-Los Angeles, first flight Sept. 15) per 1 oz.	15¢
Mail traveling less than entire Seattle-Los Angeles route per 1 oz.	10¢
Contract routes exceeding 1,500 miles (none established during this rate period) per 1 oz.	20¢
Additional service on govt. route, per 1 oz. (each route or portion thereof)	5¢
1927, Feb. 1-July 31, 1928	
All contract routes or govt. zones, or combinations thereof, per ½ oz.	10¢
1928, Aug. 1-July 5, 1932	
All routes, 1st oz.	5¢
Each additional ounce or fraction thereof	10¢

Effective Date	Prepaid
1932, July 6-June 30, 1934	
All routes, 1st oz.	8¢
Each additional ounce or fraction thereof	13¢
1934, July 1-Mar. 25, 1944	
All routes, per oz.	6¢
1944, Mar. 26-Sept. 30, 1946	
All routes, per oz.	8¢
1946, Oct. 1-Dec. 31, 1948	
All routes, per oz.	5¢
1949, Jan. 1-July 31, 1958	
All routes, per oz.	6¢
Postal cards and postcards, per oz.	4¢
1958, Aug. 1-Jan. 6, 1963	
All routes, per oz.	7¢
Postal cards and postcards, per oz.	5¢
1963, Jan. 7-Jan. 6, 1968	
All routes, per oz.	8¢
Postal cards and postcards, per oz.	6¢
1968, Jan. 7-May 15, 1971	
All routes, per oz.	10¢
Postal cards and postcards, per oz.	8¢
1971, May 16-Mar. 1, 1974	
All routes, per oz.	11¢
Postal cards and postcards, per oz.	9¢
1974, Mar. 2-Oct. 10, 1975	
All routes, per oz.	13¢
Postal cards and postcards, per oz.	11¢

As of Oct. 11, 1975, separate domestic airmail service was abolished, although at least one more airmail rate was published; effective Dec. 28, 1975, 17¢ per 1st oz., 15¢ each additional oz., 14¢ for postal cards and postcards. It lasted until May 1, 1977.

Many thanks to the American Air Mail Society for sharing information on airmail rates. For further study, we highly recommend the society's book, *Via Airmail, An Aerophilatelic Survey of Events, Routes, and Rates;* Simine Short, editor; James R. Adams, author (available from the American Airmail Society, P.O. Box 110, Mineola, NY 11501. Price: $20, plus $2.50 postage to U.S. addresses; $3.50 to addresses outside the U.S.).

SUBJECT INDEX OF REGULAR, COMMEMORATIVE & AIR POST ISSUES

A Charlie Brown Christmas ... 5021-5030
A Streetcar Named Desire ... 3186n
Abbey, Edwin Austin ... 3502k
Abbott, Bud ... 2566
Abby Cadabby ... 5394h
Abstract Expressionists ... 4444
Acadia National Park ... 746, 762, 5080d, C138
Accounting, Certified Public ... 2361
Acheson, Dean ... 2755
Acoma Pot ... 1709, 3873g
Acuff, Roy ... 3812
Adams, Abigail ... 2146
Adams, Ansel ... 3649p
Adams, John ... 806, 841, 850, 2216b
Adams, John Q. ... 811, 846, 2216f
Addams, Jane ... 878
Admiralty Head Lighthouse, WA ... 2470
Adoption ... 3398
Adriatic, S.S. ... 117, 128
Advances in Aviation ...]3916-3925
Adventures of Huckleberry Finn ... 2787
African Daisy ... 5680
African Elephant Herd ... 1388
African Violet ... 2486
Agave ... 1943
Aging Together ... 2011
AIDS Awareness ... 2806
Ailey, Alvin ... 3841
Aircraft, Classic American ... 3142
Air Force Cross ... 5067
Air Force Medal of Honor ... 4988
Air Force One ... 4144
Air Force, U.S. ... C49, 3167
Air Mail, 50th Anniversary ... C74
Air Mail, 100th Anniversary ... 5281-5282
Air Service Emblem ... C5
Airborne Attack Units ... 2838d
Airlift $1 ... 1341
Alabama Flag ... 1654, 4274
Alabama Statehood ... 1375, 5360
Alamo, The ... 1043
Alaska Flag ... 1681, 4275
Alaska Highway ... 2635
Alaska Purchase ... C70
Alaska Statehood ... 2066, 4374, C53
Alaska Territory ... 800
Alaska-Yukon Pacific Exposition ... 370, 371
Alaskan Brown Bear ... 2310
Alaskan Malamute ... 2100
Albania, Flag ... 918
Alcoholism ... 1927
Alcott, Louisa May ... 862
Aleutian Islands, Japanese Invasion of ... 2697e
Alexandria, Virginia ... C40
Alfred Hitchcock Presents ... 4414o
Alger, Horatio ... 2010
All in the Family ... 3189b
Allen, Richard ... 5056
Alley Oop ... 3000n
Alliance for Progress ... 1234
Allied Nations ... 907
Alligator ... 1428
Allosaurus ... 3136g
Aloha Shirts ... 4592-4601, 4682-4686
Alpha Airplane ... 3142e
Alphabet Cone ... 5165, 5167
Alpine Buttercup ... 5673, 5678
Alpine Skiing ... 3180
Alpine Tundra ... 4198
Alta California ... 1725
Altocumulus Castellanus ... 3878i
Altocumulus Lenticularis ... 3878j
Altocumulus Stratiformis ... 3878f
Altocumulus Undulatus ... 3878h
Altostratus Translucidus ... 3878g
Alyssum ... 4758
Alzheimer's Disease Awareness ... 4358, B6
Amateur Radio ... 1260
Amber Alert ... 4031
Ambulance ... 2128, 2231
American Alligator ... 4033
American Arts ... 1484-1487, 1553-1555, 3236
American Automobile Association ... 1007
American Bald Eagle ... 1387, 2309
American Bankers Association ... 987
American Bar Association ... 1022
American Beaver ... 4064
American Bicentennial ... 1456-1459, 1476-1479, 1480-1483, 1543-1546, 1559-1568, 1629-1631, 1686-1694, 1704, 1716-1720, 1722, 1726, 1728, 1753, 1789, 1937-1938, 2052
American Buffalo ... 569, 700, 1392, 1883, 2320, 3467, 3468, 3475, 3484, 3484A, 4041
American Bullfrog ... 4055
American Chemical Society ... 1002, 1685
American Clock ... 3757, 3762, 3763
American Cream Draft Horse ... 5590
American Crocodile ... 3105d
American Design Issue ... 3612, 3749, 3749A, 3750-3756, 3756A, 3757-3758, 3758A. 3758B, 3759, 3761-3763
American Elk ... 2328
American Folklore ... 1317, 1330, 1357, 1370, 1470, 1548
American Foxhound ... 2101
American Gardens ... 5461-5470
American Goldfinch ... 4890
American Illustrators ... 3502
American Indian ... 565, 695, 1364
American Indian Dances ... 3072-3076
American Institute of Architects ... 1089
American Kestrel ... 2476-2477, 3031-3031A, 3044
American Legion ... 1369
American Lobster ... 2304
American Lotus ... 4046
American Mammoth Jackstock Donkey ... 5587
American Music ... 1252, 2721-2737, 2767-2778, 2849-2861, 2982-2992, 3096-3103, 3154-3165, 3212-3219, 3339-3350
American Philatelic Society ... 750
American Realism (art) ... 3184n
American Red Cross ... 1910
American Revolution Bicentennial ... 1432
American Samoa ... 3389
American Samoa Flag ... 4276
American Shoals Lighthouse, FL ... 2473
American Treasures ... 3524-3527, 3650, 3804-3807, 3872, 3926-3929, 4089-4098, 4165, 4346, 4473, 4653
American Woman ... 1152
Americana Issue ... 1581-1585, 1590, 1590A, 1591-1599, 1603-1606, 1608, 1610-1615, 1615C, 1616-1618, 1618C, 1619
AMERIPEX '86 ... 2145, 2216-2219
Amethyst ... 1540
Amish Horse and Buggy ... C150
Amphipod ... 3442
Anadarko, Oklahoma Post Office Mural ... 5375
Anderson, C. Alfred "Chief" ... 4879
Anderson, Marian ... 3896
Anemone ... 3029
Angelou, Maya ... 4979
Angus Cattle ... 1504
Animal (Muppet) ... 3944g
Animal Rescue ... 4451-4460
Annapolis Tercentenary ... 984
Antarctic Treaty ... 1431, C130
Anthony, Susan B. ... 784, 1051
Antibiotics ... 3186b
Antietam, Battle of ... 4665
Antillean Euphonia ... 3222
Antioch Dunes Evening Primrose ... 1786
Anti-aircraft Gun ... 900
Anti-Pollution ... 1410-1413
Apgar, Virginia ... 2179
Apollo 8 ... 1371
Apollo-Soyuz Space Project ... 1569-1570
Appalachians ... 4045
Appaloosa Horse ... 2158
Apple ... 3491, 3493, 4727-4734, 5037
Appleseed, Johnny ... 1317
Appomattox Surrender ... 1182, 4981
Apprenticeship ... 1201
Apte Tarpon Fly ... 2547
Aquaman ... 4084h, 4084r
Arbor Day ... 717
Arches National Park ... 5080h
Archie ... 4469
Architecture, American ... 1779-1782, 1838-1841, 1928-1931, 2019-2022, 3910
Arctic Animals ... 3288-3292
Arctic Explorations ... 1128
Arctic Fox ... 3289
Arctic Hare ... 3288
Arctic Tundra ... 3802
Arizona Flag ... 1680, 4277
Arizona Statehood ... 1192, 4627
Arkansas Flag ... 1657, 4278
Arkansas River Navigation ... 1358
Arkansas Statehood ... 782, 2167
Arlen, Harold ... 3100
Arlington Amphitheater ... 570, 701
Arlington Green Bridge ... 4738
Armadillo ... 2296
Armed Forces Reserve ... 1067
Armory Show ... 3183d
Armstrong, Edwin ... 2056
Armstrong, Louis ... 2982, 2984
Army ... 785-789, 934
Army, Continental ... 1565
Army Medal of Honor ... 4823
Arnold, H.H. "Hap" ... 2191
Arsenal of Democracy ... 2559e
Art Deco Bird ... 4495
Art Deco Style ... 3184j
Art Direction ... 3772f
Art of the American Indian ... 3873
Art of Magic, The ... 5301-5306
Arthur, Chester A. ... 826, 2218c
Articles of Confederation ... 1726
Artists ... 884-888
Asawa, Ruth, Wire Sculptures by ... 5504-5513
Ash Can School ... 3182h
Ashe, Arthur ... 3936
Assateague Island National Seashore ... 5080f
Assassin Bug ... 3351g
Assiniboin Headdress ... 2501
Aster ... 2993, 4762
Atlantic Cable Centenary ... 1112
Atlas Statue ... 3520, 3770
Atomic Energy Act ... 1200
Atoms for Peace ... 1070
Audubon, John J. ... 874, 1241, 1863, 3236e, 3650, C71
Aurora Australis ... 4123b, 4204
Aurora Borealis ... 4123a. 4203
Australia Bicentennial ... 2370
Austria, Flag ... 919
Authors ... 859-863
Automated Post Office ... 1164
Automobile, Electric ... 296
Automobiles ... 2381-2385, 2905-2906, 3019-3023, 4353-4357
Automobile Tail Fin ... 2908-2910
Autry, Gene ... 4449
Autumn Fern ... 4850, 4876, 4974

Auxiliary Steamship (Merchant Marine) 4549
Azalea Bonsai 4622
Azurite 2700

B-10 Airplane 3142f
B-24 Liberator 3922
B-29 Superfortress 3923
Baby Boom 3186l
Baby Buggy 1902
Backyard Games 5627-5634
Badger 2312
Badminton 5633
Bailey Gatzert Riverboat 3095
Bailey, Mildred 2860
Baker, Ella 4384f
Balanchine, George 3843
Balboa, Vasco Nunez de 397, 401
Bald Eagle 1387, 2309
Baldwin, Abraham 1850
Baldwin, James 3871
Ball, Lucille 3523
Ballet 1749, 3237
Balloons 2032-2035, 2530, C54
Ballot Box 1584
Balls, Sports 5203-5210
Baltimore Cathedral 1780
Baltimore Checkerspot Butterfly 4592-4601
Baltimore & Ohio Railroad 1006
Baltimore Oriole 4886
Banana Split 5095
Bandelier National Monument 5080k
Bankers Association, American 987
Banking and Commerce 1577-1578
Banneker, Benjamin 1804
Banyan Bonsai 4620
Bara, Theda 2827
Barbados Blackbelly Sheep 5592
Barber, Samuel 3162
Barbie Doll 3188i
Bardeen, John 4227
Barge Fleeting 4710l
Barney Google 3000i
Barn Swallow 2286
Barns 5546-5553, 5684-5687
Barred Owl 1762
Barrel Cactus 1942
Barry, John 790
Barrymore, John, Ethel & Lionel 2012
Bartholdi, Frederic Auguste 2147
Barton, Clara 967, 2975c
Bartram, John & William 3314
Baseball 855, 1381, 2619, 3186c, 3187c, 3187j, 3402, 3408, 5207, 5631
Baseball Stadiums 3510-3519
Basie, Count 3096
Basilone, Sgt. John 3963
Basketball 1189, 2560, 3399, 5208
Bass, Largemouth 2207
Bastogne & Battle of the Bulge 2838j
Bat Signal 4928-4931
Bates, Daisy Gaston 4384c
Batman 4084e, 4084o, 4932-4935
Bats 3661-3664, 5423
Beach Umbrella 2443
Beacon on Rocky Mountains C11
Beagle 2098
Beaker and Dr. Bunsen Honeydew 3944h
Beans 4004, 4011, 4017
Bearberry 2687
Beard, James 4925
Bearden, Romare 4566-4569
Beau Geste 2447
Beautification of America 1318, 1365-1368, 4716a, 4716b, 4716c, 4716d, 4716e
Beautyberry 5417
Beaver 2316, 4064
Beavertail Cactus 1944
Beckwourth, Jim 2869q, 2870
Beechcraft 35 Bonanza 3924
Beetle Bailey 4467
Bel Geddes, Norman 4546g
Belgian Malinois 5407
Belgium, Flag 914
Bell, Alexander Graham 893
Benedict, Ruth 2938
Benet, Stephen Vincent 3221
Benny, Jack 2564
Bergen, Edgar 2563
Bergman, Ingrid 5012
Bering Glacier 4036
Bering Land Bridge C131
Berlin Airlift 3211
Berlin, Irving 3669
Bernstein, Leonard 3521
Berra, Lawrence "Yogi" 5608
Bert 5394c
Best Friend of Charleston Locomotive 2363
Best Wishes 2271, 2396
Bethesda Fountain 5348
Bethune, Mary McLeod 2137
Betta Fish 5107
Bicentennial Celebrations 3189f
Bicycle 1901, 3119, 3228-3229, 4687-4690
Bierstadt, Albert 3236m, 4346
Big Bend National Park 5429
Big Bird 5394a
Big Brothers/Big Sisters 2162
Bighorn Sheep 1467, 1880, 1949, 2288, 4138, 4140
Biglin Brothers 1335
Bill of Rights 1312, 2421
Biloxi Lighthouse, MS 4411
Biltmore Estate Gardens 5467
Biltmore House 1929
Bingham, George Caleb 3236f
Bingham IV, Hiram 4076c
Bioluminescent Life 5264-5273
Biomedicine 5515
Biplane 2436, 2438c
Big Band Sound 3186j
Bird of Paradise Flower 3310
Birds and Flowers, State 1953-2002
Birds, Coastal 4991-4998
Birds in Winter 5126-5129, 5317-5320
Birds of Prey 4608-4612
Birds, Tropical 3222-3225
Birth of Liberty 618
Bishop, Elizabeth 4659
Bison (See American Buffalo)
Bissell, Emily 1823
Bixby Creek Bridge 4439
Black and Tan (movie) 4336
Black and Tan Coonhound 2101
Black Bear 2299
Black Heritage 1744, 1771, 1804, 1875, 2016, 2044, 2073, 2137, 2203, 2249, 2371, 2402, 2442, 2567, 2617, 2746, 2816, 2956, 3058, 3121, 3181, 3273, 3371, 3501, 3557, 3746, 3834, 3896, 3996, 4120, 4222, 4408, 4464, 4565, 4624, 4803, 4856, 4958, 5056, 5171, 5259, 5349, 5432, 5555, 5663
"Black Jack" 73
Black, Hugo L. 2172
Black Pine Bonsai 4619
Black Widow 3351a
Black-capped Chickadee 5317
Black-footed Ferret 2333, 3105a
Black-necked Crane 2867
Black-tailed Jack Rabbit 2305
Black-tailed Prairie Dog 2325
Blackberries 3297, 3301, 3304, 3406
Blacksmith 1718
Blackwell, Elizabeth 1399
Blair, Montgomery C66
Blake, Eubie 2988
Blondie 3000l
Blood Donor 1425
Blue Flag 2663
Blue Jay 1757d, 2318, 2483, 3048, 3053, 5320
Blue Paloverde 3194
Blue Whale 4069
Blueberries 3294, 3298, 3302, 3404, 5488, 5652-5653
Bluebird, Eastern 2478, 3033
Bluebird, Mountain 4883
Bluets 2656
Blue-spotted Salamander 3815
Bly, Nellie 3665
BMX Biking 3322
Bobcat 2332, 2482, 4672, 4802
Bobwhite 2301
Bocce 5628
Boeing 247 Airplane 3916
Bogart, Humphrey 3152
Bohlen, Charles E. 4076e
Bolivar, Simon 1110-1111
Bombardier Beetle 3351m
Bone Shaker 5327
Bonsai 4618-4622
Books, Bookmark, and Eyeglasses 1585
Boone, Daniel 1357
Boston Harbor Lighthouse, MA 4793
Boston State House 1781
Boston Tea Party 1480-1483
Boston Terrier 2098
Botanical Art 5042-5051
Botanical Prints by M. S. Merian 3126-3129
Botanical Congress 1376-1379
Boulder (Hoover) Dam 774, 4269
Boutonniere 5199, 5457
Bow, Clara 2820
Bowling 2963
Box Turtle 2326
Boy Scouts 995, 1145, 2161, 3183j, 4472
Boys' Clubs of America 1163
Brachiosaurus 3136d
Braddock's Field 688
Bradley, Gen. Omar N. 3394
Brain Coral 1827, 5364, 5370
Brandeis, Louis D. 4422c
Bread Wagon 2136
Breast Cancer Awareness 3081, B1, B5
Breckinridge, Mary 2942
Breeder Reactor 2008
Brenda Starr 3000t
Brennan, William J., Jr. 4422b
Brice, Fanny 2565
Bridge at Niagara Falls 297
Bridge, Mississippi River 293
Bridger, Jim 2869c, 2870
Bringing Up Father 3000d
Brinker, Maureen Connolly 5377
Bristlecone Pines 4049
Broad-billed Hummingbird 2643
Broad-tailed Hummingbird 2289
Broadbill Decoy 2138
Brodsky, Joseph 4654
Brontosaurus 2425
Brooklyn Botanic Garden 5461
Brooklyn Bridge 2041
Brooklyn, Battle of 1003
Brooks, Gwendolyn 4655
Brother Jonathan Locomotive 2365
Brown Bear 1884
Brown Pelican 1466, 3105h
Brown v. Board of Education 3937j
Brush Rabbit 5544-5545
Brussels International Exhibition 1104
Bryan, William Jennings 2195
Bryant, Bear 3143, 3148
Bryce Canyon National Park C139
Buchanan, James 820, 2217f
Buchanan's No. 999 2847
Buck, Pearl 1848
Buckboard 2124
Buffalo (See American Buffalo)
Buffalo Soldiers 2818
Bugs Bunny 3137-3138, 5494-5503

Building a Nation ... 4801
Bull Run, First Battle of ... 4523
Bunchberry ... 2675
Bunche, Ralph ... 1860
Bunker Hill Monument ... 1034, 1056
Bunker Hill, Battle of ... 1564
Burbank, Luther ... 876
Bureau of Engraving and Printing ... 2875
Burgos, Julia de ... 4476
Burgoyne, Surrender of ... 644, 1728, 2590
Burke, Admiral Arleigh A. ... 4441
Burma Road ... 2559a
Burns and Allen ... 4414p
Burroughs, Edgar Rice ... 4702
Bush, George Herbert Walker ... 5393
Butte ... 2902, 2902B, 4710d
Butterflies ... 1712-1715, 3105f, 4000-4002, 4462, 4603, 4736, 4859, 4999, 5136, 5568
Butterfly Garden Flowers ... 5664-5665
Buzz Lightyear ... 5709-5712
Byodo-In Temple ... 5257
Byrd Antarctic ...]733, 753, 768
Byrd, Richard E. ... 2388

C-3PO ... 5579
Cabbage Patch Kids ... 3190i
Cable Car ... 1442, 2263
Cable TV ... 3190f
Caboose ... 1905
Cabrillo, Juan Rodriguez ... 2704
Cacti ... 1942-1945
Cactus Flowers ... 5350-5359
Cadabby, Abby ... 5394h
Cadillac Eldorado ... 4353
Cadillac, Landing of ... 1000
Caffe Latte ... 5569
Caffe Mocha ... 5571
Cagney, James ... 3329
Calder, Alexander ... 3198-3202
Caldonia (movie) ... 4339
Calendula ... 4755
Calico Scallop Shell ... 2120
California Condor ... 1430, 3105i
California Dogface Butterfly ... 5346
California Flag ... 1663, 4279
California Gold ... 954
California Gold Rush ... 3316
California Poppy ... 2651
California Sea Lion ... 2329
California Settlement ... 1373
California Statehood ... 997, 3438
California-Pacific Exposition ... 773
Calliope Hummingbird ... 2646
Calvin and Hobbes ... 4468
Calvin, Melvin ... 4541
Camarasaurus ... 3136c
Camellia ... 1877
Camilla the Chicken and The Great Gonzo ... 3944j
Camp, Walter ... 3810
Camp Fire Girls ... 1167
Camp Fire, Inc. ... 2163
Campanella, Roy ... 4080
Camptosaurus ... 3136b
Canada Centenary ... 1324
Canada Goose ... 1757c, 2334
Canada-U.S. Friendship ... 961
Canal Boat ... 2257
Canal Locks at Sault Ste. Marie ... 298
Cancer ... 1263, 1754
Canoe ... 2453, 2454
Canoeing ... 5476
Cantaloupes ... 5006
Canvasback Decoy ... 2140
Cape Hatteras Lighthouse, NC ... 2471
Cape Hatteras National Seashore ... 1448-1451
Cape Lookout Lighthouse, NC ... 3788
CAPEX '78 ... 1757
Cappucino ... 5572
Capra, Frank ... 4669
Captain America ... 4159e, 4159o
Captain Hook from "Peter Pan" ... 5217
Caraway, Hattie ... 3431, 3432
Cardinal ... 1465, 1757a, 2480, 5128, 5318
Cardinal Honeyeater ... 3225
CARE ... 1439
Caribou, Woodland ... 3105l
Carlsbad Caverns National Park ... 5080o
Carlson, Chester ... 2180
Carmel Mission ... 4650
Carmichael, Hoagy ... 3103
Carnegie, Andrew ... 1171
Carnivorous Plants ... 3528-3531
Carolina Charter ... 1230
Carolina-Charleston ... 683
Carousel Animals ... 2390-2393, 2976-2979
Carpenter's Hall ... 1543
Carreta ... 2255
Carrots ... 5486
Carson, Kit ... 2869n, 2870
Carson, Rachel ... 1857
Carter Family ... 2773, 2777
Caruso, Enrico ... 2250
Carved Figures ... 2426, C121
Carver, George Washington ... 953, 3183c
Cash, Johnny ... 4789
Cashman, Nellie ... 2869k, 2870
Cassatt, Mary ... 1322, 2181, 3236o,3804-3807
Castillod de San Marcos ... 5554
Cat and Raven ... 5420
Catfish ... 2209
Cather, Willa ... 1487
Catlin, George ... 3236k
Cats ... 2372-2375, 3232, 4452, 4453, 4456, 4457, 4460, 5122
"Cats" Broadway Show ... 3190b
Catt, Carrie Chapman ... 959
Cattle ... 1504
Cayuga Duck ... 5591
Cedar Waxwing ... 5127
Celebrate ... 4196, 4335, 4407, 4502, 5019, 5434
Celebrate the Century ... 3182-3191
Celebrity Chefs ... 4922-4926
Cellular Phones ... 3191o
Center-pivot Irrigation ... 4710h
Century of Progress ... 728-731, 766-767
Ceratosaurus ... 3136a
Certified Public Accounting ... 2361
Ceviche ... 5197
Cha Cha Cha ... 3941
Chalice Coral ... 1829
Chamberlain, Wilt ... 4950-4951
Champions of Liberty ... 1096, 1110-1111, 1117-1118, 1125-1126, 1136-1137, 1147-1148, 1159-1160, 1165-1166, 1168-1169, 1174-1175
Champlain, East Coast Explorations of Samuel de ... 4073-4074
Chancellorsville, Battle of ... 2975p
Chaney, Lon ... 2822, 3168
Chaney, Lon, Jr. ... 3172
Chanute, Octave ... C93-C94
Chaplains, Four ... 956
Chaplin, Charlie ... 2821, 3183a
Chapman, Dave ... 4546h
Charles, Ray ... 4807
Charles W. Morgan Ship ... 1441
Chautauqua ... 1505
Chavez, Cesar E. ... 3781
Chavez, Dennis ... 2186
Checkerspot Butterfly ... 1713
Chemical Society, American ... 1002
Chemistry ... 1685
Chen, Joyce ... 4924
Chennault, Claire ... 2187
Cherokee Strip ... 1360, 2754
Cherry Blossom Centennial ... 4651-4652
Cherry Orchard ... 4710i
Chesapeake Bay ... 4038
Chesapeake Bay Retriever ... 2099
Chesnut, Mary ... 2975o
Chesnutt, Charles W. ... 4222
Chevrolet Chevelle SS ... 4746
Chevrolet Corvette ... 3933
Chevrolet truck ... 5102
Cheyenne Headdress ... 2502
Chicago Botanic Garden ... 5465
Chief Joseph ... 1364
Child Building Sandcastle ... 5475
Child Health ... 3938
Child, Julia ... 4926
Child Labor Reform ... 3183o
Children's Friendship ... 1085
Children's Stick Drawing ... 2104
Chile Relleno ... 5196
Chili Peppers ... 4003, 4012, 4013
China Clipper ... C20-C22
Chinchilla ... 5119
Chinese Hibiscus ... 3313
Chinese New Year ... 2720, 2817, 2876, 3060, 3120, 3179, 3272, 3370, 3500, 3559, 3747, 3832, 3895, 3997, 4221, 4375, 4435, 4492, 4623, 4726, 4846, 4957, 5057, 5154, 5254, 5340, 5428, 5556, 5662
Chinese Resistance ... 906
Chipmunk ... 1757f, 2297
Chippendale Chair ... 3755, 3761, 3761A
Chisholm, Shirley ... 4856
Chopper Droid ... 5582
Chopper Motorcycle ... 4087
Choreographers ... 4698-4701
Christmas ... 1205, 1240, 1254-1257, 1276, 1321, 1336, 1363, 1384, 1414-1418, 1444-1445, 1471-1472, 1507-1508, 1550-1552, 1579-1580B, 1701-1703, 1729-1730, 1768-1769, 1799-1800, 1842-1843, 1939-1940, 2025-2030, 2063-2064, 2107-2108, 2165-2166, 2244-2245, 2367-2368, 2399-2400, 2427-2429, 2514-2516, 2578-2585, 2710-2719, 2789-2803, 2871-2874, 3003-3018, 3107-3117, 3176-3177, 3244-3252, 3355-3367, 3536-3544, 3675-3691, 3820-3828, 3879, 3883-3894, 3949-3960, 4100-4116, 4206-4218, 4359-4371, 4424-4432, 4477-4485, 4570-4582, 4711-4715, 4813-4821, 4945-4949, 5021-5030, 5143-5148, 5247-5250, 5331-5336, 5424-5427, 5525-5529, 5644-5647
Chrysanthemum ... 2994, 5460
Chrysler Building ... 3910b
Chrysler 300C ... 4357
Church, Frederick ... 3236n, 4919
Churchill, Winston S. ... 1264, 2559d
CIA Invert ... 1610c
Cinematography ... 3772g
Cinco de Mayo ... 3203, 3309
CIPEX ... 948
Circus, American ... 1309, 2750-2753
Circus Posters ... 4898-4905
Circus Wagon ... 2452, 2452B, 2452D, 4905c
Cirrocumulus Undulatus ... 3878c
Cirrostratus Fibratus ... 3878b
Cirrus Radiatus ... 3878a
Citizen Kane ... 3186o
City Mail Delivery ... 1238
Civil Defense ... 2559g
Civil Rights Act of 1964 ... 3937g
Civil Rights Pioneers ... 4384
Civil Service ... 2053
Civil War ... 1178-1182, 2975, 4522-4523, 4664-4665, 4787-4788, 4910-4911, 4980-4981
Civilian Conservation Corps ... 2037
Claret Cup Cactus ... 2660
Clarion River ... 5381l
Clark, Eugenie ... 5693
Clark, George Rogers ... 651
Clark, Grenville ... 1867
Clark, William ... 3854, 3856
Classics Forever ... 5079
Clay, Henry ... 140, 151, 162, 173, 198, 227, 259, 274, 284, 309, 1846
Clemens, Samuel L. ... 863, 4545
Clemente, Roberto ... 2097, 3408j
Cleveland, Grover ... 564, 693, 827, 2218d

Cleveland Motorcycle....4086
Cliff Palace....4039
Clifford, J. R.....4384b
Cline, Patsy....2772, 2777
Clipper Ship (Merchant Marine)....4548
Cloudscapes....3878
Coal Car....2259
Coast and Geodetic Survey....1088
Coast Guard....936, 5008
Coast Guard Cross....5068
Coast Redwoods....4063
Coastal Maine Botanical Gardens....5464
Cobb, Ty....3408d
Cobra Lily....3530
Coburn, Alvin Langdon....3649f
Cochran, Jacqueline....3066
Cochrane, Mickey....3408g
Cocker Spaniel....2099
Cod, Atlantic....2206
Code Deciphering....2697f
Cody, Buffalo Bill....2177, 2869b, 2870
Cog Railroad....2463
Cohan, George M.....1756
Cole, Nat "King"....2852
Cole, Thomas....4920
Coleman, Bessie....2956
Collective Bargaining....1558
Collie....2100
Collins, Eddie....3408b
Colonial Communications....1476-1479
Colonial Craftsmen....1456-1459
Colorado Flag....1670, 4280
Colorado Hairstreak Butterfly....5568
Colorado Statehood....1001, 1711
Colorful Celebrations....5081-5090
Coltrane, John....2991
Columbia River Gorge....5041
Columbia University....1029
Columbian Exposition....230-245, 2624-2629
Columbus' Discovery....2426, 2512, 2620-2623, 2805, C121, C127, C131
Comanche Headdress....2503
Comedians....2562-2566
Comic Strips....3000, 4467-4471
Comiskey Park....3517
Commerce....1578
Commercial Aviation....1684
Common Buckeye Butterfly....4000-4002
Common Sunflower....2666
Commonwealth of the Northern Mariana Islands....2804
Communications for Peace....1173
Compact Discs....3190h
Compact, Signing of the....550
Composers....879-883, 3100-3103
Computer Art and Graphics....3191f
Computer Technology....3106
Computing....5514
Comstock, Henry....1130
Condor, California....1430, 3105i
Conestoga Wagon....2252
Confederate Veterans, United....998
Confederation, Articles of....1726
Congratulations....2267
Congressional....3334
Connecticut Flag....1637, 4281
Connecticut Statehood....2340
Connecticut Tercentenary....772
Connolly, Maureen....5377
Constellation Airplane....3142m
Constellations....3945-3948
Constitution Bicentennial....2412-2414
Constitution Drafting....2355-2359
Constitution Ratification....835, 2336-2348
Constitution Signing....798, 2360
Constitution, U.S. Frigate....951, 4703
Construction Toys....3182n
Consumer Education....2005
Container Ship (Merchant Marine)....4548
Contemplation of Justice....1592, 1617
Continental Army....1565
Continental Marines....1567
Continental Navy....1566
Contra Costa Wallflower....1785
Contributors to the Cause....1559-1562
Cook, Capt. James....1732-1733
Cookie Monster....5394d
Coolidge, Calvin....834, 2219b
Cooper, Anna Julia....4408
Cooper, Gary....2447, 4421
Cooper, James Fenimore....860
Copernicus, Nicolaus....1488
Copley, John Singleton....1273
Copper....2701
Coral Pink Rose....3052
Coral Reefs....1827-1830, 5363-5370
Coral Sea, Battle of....2697c
Cord (automobile)....2383
Cori, Gerty....4224
Corn....4007, 4008, 4014, 5005
Corn Snake....5116
Cornhole....5634
Cornish-Windsor Covered Bridge....4070
Cornwell, Dean....3502j
Coronado Expedition....898
Corregidor....925, 2697d
Corsair Airplane....3142g
Corsage....5200, 5458
Corythosaurus....3136m
"Cosby Show, The"....3190j
Cosmos....4761
Costello, Lou....2566
Costume Design....3772c
Cotton Patch Goose....5588
Cottontail....2290
Count, The....5394f
Cowboys of the Silver Screen....4446-4449
CPA....2361
Cranberry Harvest....4710j
Cranes....1097, 2867-2868
Crater Lake....745, 761, 4040
Crayola Crayons....3182d
Crazy Horse....1855
Credit Union Act....2075
Credo....1139-1144
Crested Honeycreeper....3224
Crime, Take a Bite out of....2102
Crippled, Hope for....1385
Crockett, Davy....1330
Crocodile, American....3105d
Crocus....3025
Croquet....5630
Crosby, Bing....2850
Crosley Field....3512
Cross-country Skiing....5479
Crossword Puzzle, First....3183l
Cruella De Vil from "One Hundred and One Dalmatians"....5219
Cruz, Celia....4501
Cub Airplane....3142c
Cueva del Indio, La....5040
Cummings, E. E.....4662
Cumulonimbus Incus....3878e
Cumulonimbus Mammatus....3878d
Cumulonimbus with Tornado....3878o
Cumulus Congestus....3878n
Cumulus Humilis....3878m
Cunningham, Imogen....3649q
Curious George....3992
Curtiss Jenny....C1-C3, 3142s
Curtiss, Glenn....C100
Cushing, Harvey....2188
Cycling....3119, 5478
Czechoslovakia, Flag....910

D-O....5576
Daffodil....2761, 3901
Daffy Duck....3306-3307
Dahlia....1878, 2995
Daly, Sgt. Major Daniel J.....3964
Dance, American....1749-1752
Dances, American Indian....3072-3076
Dante....1268
Dare, Virginia....796
Daredevil Comic Book....4159s
Dartmouth College Case....1380
Daspletosaurus....3136k
Davis, Dr. Allison....2816
Davis, Benjamin O.....3121
Davis, Bette....4350
Davis, Jefferson....2975f
Davis, Miles....4693
Davis, Stuart....1259, 4748c
Day of the Dead....5640-5643
Daylight....3333
DC Comics Superheroes....4084
DC-3 Airplane....3142q
DC-4 Skymaster....C32-C33, C37, C39, C41
D-Day....2838c
De Burgos, Julia....4476
De Haviland Biplane....C6
De la Renta, Oscar....5173
De Mille, Agnes....3842
Dean, Dizzy....3408s
Dean, James....3082
Death Valley....4070
Decatur House....1440
Decatur, Stephen....791
Declaration of Independence....120, 130, 627,1545, 1691-1695
Declaration of War on Japan....2559j
Deep Sea Creatures....3439-3443
Deer (Fawn)....2479
Deer Mouse....2324
Defense, National....899-901
Delaware Flag....1633, 4282
Delaware Statehood....2336
Delta Wing....C77
Deming New Mexico Post Office Mural....5376
Dempsey, Jack....3183m
Demuth, Charles....4748a
Denmark, Flag....920
Dennis the Menace....4471
Dental Health....1135
Deora II....5329
Depression....3185m
Deschutes River....5381i
Desegregating Public Schools....3187f
Desert Fire Spot....2690
Desert Plants....1942-1945
Desert Shield/Desert Storm....2551-2552
Deskey, Donald....4546d
Destroyer Reuben James....2559f
Devils Tower....1084
Dewey, George....793
Dewey, John....1291
Diabetes Awareness....3503
Diamond Head Lighthouse, HI....4146
Dickinson, Emily....1436
Dickson, William....3064
Dick Tracy....3000m
Digitalis....4756
DiMaggio, Joe....4697
Dinah Shore Show, The....4414i
Diner....3208, 3208A
Dinosaurs....2422-2425, 3136
Diplomats, Distinguished American....4076
Directing....3772b
Dirksen, Everett....1874
Disabled, Intl. Year of the....1925
Disabled Veterans....1421
Disco Music....3189d
Disney, Walt....1355
Disney Characters....3865-3868, 3912-3915, 4025-4028, 4192-4195, 4342-4345, 5213-5222
Disney-Pixar Films Characters....4553-4557, 4677-4681

Distinguished Americans Issue 3420,3422, 3426-3427, 3427A, 3428, 3430-3432, 3432A, 3432B, 3433-3436, 4510, 4666, 4879, 5191, 5699
Distinguished Service Cross 5065
District of Columbia 2561, 3813
District of Columbia Flag 4283
Diwali 5142
Dix, Dorothea 1844
Doby, Larry 4695
Dr. Seuss' "The Cat in the Hat" 3187h
Doctors 949
Dodge Charger Daytona 4743
Dogbane Beetle 3351e
Dogface Butterfly 1714
Dog Sled 2135
Dogs...... 2098-2101, 3230, 4451, 4454, 4455, 4458, 4459, 5125
Dogs at Work 4604-4607
Dogs, Military Working 5405-5408
Dolls 3151
Dolphin 2511, 4388
Dome of Capitol 1590-1591, 1616, 1809, 3472
Dorsey, Tommy & Jimmy 3097
Douglas, Aaron 4748g
Douglass, Frederick 1290, 2975h
Dove, Arthur 4748l
Dracula 3169
Dragnet 4414e
Dragonfly 4267
Dragons 5307-5310
Drew, Charles R. 1865
Dreyfuss, Henry 4546f
Drive-In Movies 3187i
Drug Abuse, Prevent 1438
Drug Free USA 5542
Drum 1615
Du Bois, W.E.B. 2617, 3182l
Du Sable, Jean Baptiste Pointe 2249
Duchamp, Marcel 4748k
Duck Decoys 2138-2141
Duck, Wood 2484-2485
Duesenberg 2385
Dulles Airport 2022
Dulles, John Foster 1172
Dumbarton Oaks 5463
Dunbar, Paul Laurence 1554
Duncan, Isadora 4698
Dung Beetle 3351n
Dunham, Katherine 4700
Dunn, Harvey 3502o
Durand, Asher B. 3236g, 4918
Dutch Shepherd 5408
Dutchman's Breeches 2682

"E. T. The Extra-Terrestrial" 3190m
Eagan, Eddie 2499
Eagle............ 1735-1736, 1743, 1818-1820, 1909, 1946-1948, 2111-2113, 2122, 2309, 2394, 2540, 2541, 2542, 2598, 3471-3471A, 3646, 4585-4590, 5013-5018, C48, C50, C67
Eagle and Shield............116, 127, 771, 1596, 2431, 2595-2597, 2602-2604, 2907, 3270-3271, 3792-3801, 3844-3853, CE1-CE2
Eagle Holding Shield, etc. 121, 131, C23
Eagle Nebula 3384
Eakins, Thomas 1335
Eames, Charles and Ray 4333
Earhart, Amelia C68
Early Football Heroes 3808-3811
Early TV Memories 4414
Earp, Wyatt 2869j, 2870
Earth 2277, 2279, 2282, 2570, 4740, 5071
Earth Day 2951-2954, 3189a, 5459
Earthscapes 4710
Eastern Bluebird 2478, 3033
Eastern Chipmunk 2297
Eastern Hercules Beetle 3351l
Eastern Tailed-Blue Butterfly 5136
Eastern Tiger Swallowtail Butterfly 4999
Eastman, George 1062
Ebbets Field 3510
Ebony Jewelwing 3351h
Echeveria 5198
Echo I 1173
Ed Sullivan Show, The 4414j
Eddy's No. 242 2845
Edison, Thomas A. 654-656, 945
Edmontonia 3136i
Education 1833
Educators 869-873
Egg Cream 5094
Egg Nebula 3387
Eggplants 5492
Eid 3532, 3674, 4117, 4202, 4351, 4416, 4552, 4800, 5092
Einiosaurus 3136j
Einstein, Albert 1285, 1774
Eisenhower, Dwight D. 1383, 1393-1395, 1401-1402, 2219g, 2513
Elderberry Longhorn 3351b
Electric Auto 296, 1906
Electric Light 654-656
Electric Toy Trains 3184d
Electronics 1500-1502, C86
Elektra 41591, 4159s
Elevator 2254
Eliot, Charles W. 871
Eliot, T.S. 2239
Elk 1886
Elkhorn Coral 1828, 5363, 5369
Elks, B.P.O. 1342
Ellington, "Duke" 2211
Ellison, Ralph 4866
Ellsworth, Lincoln 2389
Elmo 5394m
Ely's No. 10 2846
Emancipation Proclamation 1233, 4721
Emerson, Ralph Waldo 861
Emigration, Hardships of 290
Empanadas 5195
Emperor Penguins 4989-4990
Empire State Building 3185b
Empire State Express 295
Endangered Flora 1783-1786
Endangered Species 3105
Energy 1723-1724, 2006-2009
Energy Conservation 1547
Engineering Education 5278
Engineers, American Society of Civil 1012
English Sundew 3531
Enjoy the Great Outdoors 5475-5479
Envelopes 2150
Eohippus 3077
Ercoupe 415 3920
Ericsson, John, Statue of 628
Erie Canal 1325
Erie Harbor Lighthouse, PA 5623
Erikson, Leif 1359
Ernie 5394b
Escalante, Jaime 5100
Espresso 5570
Etiquette 3184
Evans, Walker 3649m
Evening Grosbeak 4887
Everglades National Park 952, 5080l
Evers, Medgar 4384e
Ewry, Ray 2497
Executive Branch of Gov't 2414
Executive Order 9981 .... 3937a
Exeter Academy Library 3910k
Experiment Steamboat 2405
Explorer II Balloon 2035
Explorers 2024, 2093, 2220-2223, 2386-2389
EXPO '74 1527

F6F Hellcat 3918
Fairbanks, Douglas 2088
Fairs, State and County 5401-5404
Fall of the Berlin Wall 3190k
Fallen Timbers, Battle of 680
Fallingwater 2019
Family Planning 1455
Family Unity 2104
Famous Americans 859-893
Fanfin Anglerfish 3439
Fangtooth 3441
Fantastic Four, The 4159n
Far West Riverboat 3093
Farley, Carl 2934
Farmers Markets 4912-4915
Farming in the West 286
Farnsworth, Philo T. 2058
Farragut, David G. 311, 792, 2975g
Fashions, 1970s 3189k
Faulkner, William 2350
Fawcett, Robert 3502d
Fawn 2479
Federal Deposit Insurance Corp. 2071
Federal Reserve System 3183b
Federated States of Micronesia 2506
Fenway Park 3516
Ferber, Edna 3433, 3434
Fermi, Enrico 3533
Ferns 4848-4852, 4874-4878, 4973-4977
Ferrer, Jose 4666
Ferret, Black-footed 2333, 3105a
Ferryboat 2466
Feynman, Richard 3909
Fiedler, Arthur 3159
Fields, Dorothy 3102
Fields, W.C. 1803
Figs 5493
Figure Skating 3190e
Fillmore, Millard 818, 2217d
Film Directors 4668-4671
Film Editing 3772h
Filmmaking 3772
Films 2445-2448
Fine Arts 1259
Finger Coral 1830
Finnish Independence 1334
FIPEX 1075
Fire Engine 2264
Fire Pumper 1908
Fireweed 2679
First Continental Congress 1543-1546
First Moon Landing 5399-5400
First Responders 5316
Fish 2205-2209, 2863-2866 3231, 3317-3320
Fishing Boat 2529, 2529C
Fishing Flies 2545-2549
Fitzgerald, Ella 4120
Fitzgerald, F. Scott 3104
Five Finger Lighthouse, AK 4147
Five Forks, Battle of 4980
Flag Act of 1818 5284
Flag, Foreign 909-921
Flag, Fort McHenry............ 1346, 1597-1598, 1618, 1618C, 4853-4855, 4868-4871
Flag, U.S. 1094, 1132, 1153, 1208, 1338-1338G, 1345-1354, 1509, 1519, 1597, 1618C, 1622-1623B, 1625, 1890-1891, 1893-1896, 2114-2116, 2276, 2278, 2280, 2285A, 2475, 2522, 2523, 2523A, 2528, 2531, 2593-2594, 2605-2609, 2879-2893, 2897, 2913-2916, 2919-2921, 3133, 3277-3282, 3283, 3403, 3448-3450, 3469-3470, 3495, 3549-3550A, 3620-3625, 3629F-3637, 3965-3970, 3972-3975, 3978-3983, 3985, 4129-4135, 4186-4191, 4228-4247, 4273, 4302, 4303, 4332, 4391-4396, 4487, 4489, 4491, 4519, 4560, 4562, 4564, 4629-4648, 4673-4676, 4706-4709, 4766-4785, 4796-4799, 4894-4897, 4961-4963, 5052-5055, 5158-5162, 5260-5263, 5342-5345, 5654-5659, 5684-5687
Flagg, James Montgomery 3502a
Flags of Our Nation 4273-4332
Flags on Barns 5684-5687
Flags, 50 States 1633-1682
Flags, Historic 1345-1354
Flamingo 2707

Flan 5193
Flanagan, Father Edward Joseph 2171
Flappers 3184h
Flash, The 4084f, 4084p
Flash Gordon 3000p
Flathead Headdress 2504
Flathead River 5381f
Flax 4506, 4517
Flight of Wright Brothers, First 3783
Floral Geometry 5700-5701
Florence, Colorado Post Office Mural 5373
Florida Flag 1659, 4284
Florida Manatee 3105o
Florida, Naming of, 500th Anniv. 4750-4753
Florida Panther 3105m, 4137, 4139, 4141, 4142
Florida Settlement 1271
Florida Statehood 927, 2950
Flower Fly 3351f
Flowers 1876-1879, 2076-2079, 2517-2520, 2524-2527, 2647-2696, 2760-2764, 2829-2833, 2993-2997, 3025-3029, 3310-3313, 3454-3465, 3478-3481, 3487-3490, 3836-3837, 4166-4185, 4722-4725, 4750-4753, 4754-4763, 4764-4765, 4862-4865, 4881, 5001, 5233-5240, 5664-5665, 5672-5679, 5680, 5681-5682
Flowers and Birds, State 1953-2002
Flushing Remonstrance 1099
Flying Disc 5629
Flying Fortress Airplane 3142k
Folk Art, American 1706-1709, 1745-1748, 1775-1778, 1834-1837, 2138-2141, 2240-2243, 2351-2354, 2390-2393
Fonda, Henry 3911
Fontanne, Lynn & Lunt, Alfred 3287
Food for Peace 1231
Football 3400, 5203
Football, Intercollegiate 1382
For Defense 899-901
Forbes Field 3515
Ford, Gerald R. 4199
Ford, John 4668
Ford, Henry 1286A
Ford F-1 truck 5103
Ford F-100 truck 5104
Ford Mustang 3188h
Ford Mustang Shelby GT 4745
Ford Roadster Hot Rods 4908-4909
Ford Thunderbird 3935
Forest Conservation 1122
Forestry Congress, 5th World 1156
Forget-me-nots 4987
Fort Bliss 976
Fort Duquesne 1123
Fort Jefferson Lighthouse, FL 4413
Fort Kearny 970
Fort McHenry, Bombardment of 4921
Fort Nisqually 1604
Fort Orange, Landing at ....]615
Fort Snelling 1409
Fort Sumter 1178, 4522
Fort Ticonderoga 1071
Fortune's Holly Fern 4848, 4874, 4977
Fosse, Bob 4701
Fossil Fuels 2009
Foster, John 3236a
Foster, Rube 4466
Foster, Stephen Collins 879
Four Freedoms 908
Four-H Clubs 1005
Four Horseman of Notre Dame 3184l
Fox, Red 1757g, 3036
Fox in Socks 3989
Foxglove 4507, 4513
Foxx, Jimmie 3408n
Fozzie Bear 3944b
Fragrant Water Lily 2648
France, Flag 915
Francis of Assisi 2023
Francisco, Peter 1562
Frankenstein 3170
Frankfurter, Felix 4422a
Franklin, Benjamin 1, 3, 5-5A, 6-8A, 9, 18-24, 38, 40, 46, 63, 71, 81, 85, 85A, 86, 92, 100, 102, 110, 112, 123, 133-134, 145, 156, 167, 182, 192, 206, 212, 219, 246-247, 264, 279, 300, 314, 316, 318, 331, 343, 348, 352, 357, 374, 383, 385, 387, 390, 392, 414-423, 431-440, 460, 470-478, 497, 508-518, 523-524, 547, 552, 575, 578, 581, 594, 596-597, 604, 632, 658, 669, 803, 1030, 1073, 1393D, 1690, 3139, 4021-4024, 5079b, 5079f
Frederick 3994
Freedom from Hunger 1231
Freedom of the Press 1119
Freedom Riders 3937f
Fremont, John C. 2869i, 2870
Fremont on the Rocky Mountains 288
French Alliance 1753
French Revolution C120
French, Daniel Chester 887
Frigatebird 4994, 4996
Frilled Dogwinkle Shell 2117
Fringed Gentian 2672
Frogs 5395-5398
From Me to You 4978
Frost, A. B. 3502g
Frost, Robert 1526
Frozen Treats 5285-5294
Fruit 5037-5039, 5177-5178, 5201, 5256
Fruit Berries 3294-3305, 3404-3407
Fruit, Tropical 4253-4262
Fruits and Vegetables 5484-5493
Fulbright Scholarships 3065
Fuller, R. Buckminster 3870
Fulton, Robert 1270
Fur Seal 1464
Future Farmers 1024
Futuristic Mail Delivery C122-C126

Gable, Clark & Leigh, Vivien 2446
Gadsden Purchase 1028
Galaxy NGC1316 3388
Gallatin, Albert 1279
Gallaudet, Thomas H. 1861
Galvez, Gen. Bernardo de 1826
Games, Backyard 5627-5634
Gandhi, Mahatma 1174-1175
Garbo, Greta 3943
Gardel, Carlos 4500
Garden Beauty 5558-5567
Garden of Love 4531-4540
Gardening-Horticulture 1100
Garfield (comic strip) ....]4470
Garfield, James A. 205, 205C, 216, 224, 256, 271, 282, 305, 558, 587, 638, 664, 675, 723, 825, 2218b
Garibaldi, Giuseppe 1168-1169
Garland, Judy 2445, 4077
Garner, Erroll 2992
Gasoline Alley 3000h
Gaston from "Beauty and the Beast" 5221
Gateway Arch 4044, 5157
Gato Class Submarine 3377
Gatsby Style 3184b
Gaye, Marvin 5371
Gecko 5121
Gee's Bend, Alabama Quilts 4089-4098
Geebee Airplane 3142i
Gehrig, Lou 2417, 3408t
Geisel, Theodor Seuss 3835
Gellhorn, Martha 4248
Genome Sequencing 5516
George, Walter F. 1170
Georgia Bicentennial 726
Georgia Flag 1636, 4285
Georgia Statehood 2339
Geothermal Spring 4710c
Gerbil 5120
German Immigration 2040
German Shepherd 5405
Geronimo 2869m, 2870
Gershwin, George 1484, 3345
Gershwin, Ira 3345
Get Well 2268
Gettysburg Address 978
Gettysburg, Battle of 1180, 2975t, 4788
Ghosts 5421
GI Bill 3186i
Giannini, Amadeo P. 1400
Giant Sequoia 1764
Gibbs, Josiah Willard 3907
Gibson, Althea 4803
Gibson Girl 3182m
Gibson, Josh 3408r
Gifts of Friendship 4982-4985
Gila Trout 3105j
Gilbert, John 2823
Gilbreth, Lillian M. 1868
Giant Panda 2706
Giraffe 2705
Girl Scouts 974, 1199, 2251, 3182k, 4691
Giving & Sharing 3243
Glacier and icebergs 4710a
Glacier Bay National Park and Preserve 5080a
Glacier National Park 748, 764, C149
Glade Creek Grist Mill 4927
Gladiola 2831
Glass, American 3325-3328
Glass House 3910h
Gloriosa Lily 3312
Go For Broke 5593
Go Green 4524
Goddard, Robert H. C69
Gold Star Banner 2765i
Gold Star Mothers 969
Golden-crowned Kinglets 5126
Golden Eagle 4610
Golden Gate 399, 403, 567, 698, 3185l
Golden Gate Exposition 852
Golden Spike 5379
Goldfish 5110
Goldie's Wood Fern 4851, 4877, 4975
Golf 2965
Golf Ball 5206
Gompers, Samuel 988
Gone With the Wind 2446, 3185i
Goniopholis 3136e
Gonk Droid 5580
Goodman, Benny 3099
Goodnight, Charles 2869l, 2870
Gorky, Arshile 4444e
Gottlieb, Adolph 4444i
Gottschalk, Louis Moreau 3165
Gowan & Marx Locomotive 2366
Graf Zeppelin C13-C15, C18
Graham, Katherine 5699
Graham, Martha 3840
Grand Army of the Republic 985
Grand Canyon 741, 757 2512, 3183h, 4054, 5080e, C135
Grand Central Terminal 4739
Grand Coulee Dam 1009
Grand Island Ice Caves 5430
Grand Teton National Park C147
Grange 1323
Grange, Red 3811
Grant, Cary 3692
Grant, U.S. 223, 255, 270, 281, 303, 314A, 560, 589, 640, 666, 677, 787, 823, 2217i, 2975d
Grapes 5038, 5177, 5489
Gray, Asa 4542
Gray Birch 1767
Gray Squirrel 2295
Gray Wolf 2322, 3292
Grays Harbor Lighthouse, WA 4148
Great Americans Issue 1844-1869, 2168-2173, 2175-2197, 2933-2936, 2938, 2940-2943
Great Basin 4051
Great Gonzo and Camilla the Chicken 3944j
Great Gray Owl 1760

Great Horned Owl ... 1763
Great Lakes Dunes ... 4352
Great Plains Prairie ... 3506
Great River Road ... 1319
Great Sand Dunes ... 4037
Great Smoky Mountains National Park ... 749, 765, 797, C140
Great Spangled Fritillary Butterfly ... 4859
Great Train Robbery, The ... 3182c
Great White Shark ... 5227
Greece, Flag ... 916
Greeley, Horace ... 1177
Greely, Adolphus W. ... 2221
Green Arrow ... 4084d, 4084n
Green Bay Packers ... 3188d
Green Lantern ... 4084b, 4084l
Green-throated Carib ... 3223
Greenberg, Hank ... 4081
Greene, Nathanael ... 785
Greetings From America ... 3561-3610, 3696-3745
Griffith, D.W. ... 1555
Grofe, Ferde ... 3163
Gropius House ... 2021
Grosbeak ... 2284
Grosbeak, Evening ... 4887
Grosbeak, Rose-breasted ... 4889
Grove, Lefty ... 3408k
Grover ... 5394o
Guadalcanal, Battle of ... 2697i
Guam Flag ... 4286
Guava ... 4257, 4259
Guggenheim Museum ... 3910a
Guinea Pig ... 5114
Guitar ... 1613
Gulf Islands National Seashore ... 5080p
Gulf War ... 3191b
Gunston Hall ... 1108
Gutenberg Bible ... 1014
Guthrie, Woody ... 3213
Guy Smiley ... 5394k

Habib, Philip C. ... 4076d
Hagatna Bay, Guam ... C143
Haida Canoe ... 1389
Halas, George ... 3146, 3150
Hale, Nathan ... 551, 653
Haleakala National Park ... 5080m
Haley, Bill ... 2725, 2732
Half Moon and Steamship ... 372-373
Hallelujah (movie) ... 4340
Hamer, Fannie Lou ... 4384e
Hamilton, Alexander ... 143, 154, 165, 176, 190, 201, 217, 1053, 1086
Hamilton, Alice ... 2940
Hammarskjold, Dag ... 1203-1204
Hammerhead Shark ... 5226
Hammerstein II, Oscar & Rodgers, Richard ... 3348
Hamster ... 3234, 5109
Hancock Center, Chicago ... 3910l
Hancock, Winfield ... 2975n
Handcar ... 1898
Handicapped ... 1155
Handy, W.C. ... 1372
Hansom Cab ... 1904
Hanson, John ... 1941
Hanukkah ... 3118, 3352, 3547, 3672, 3880, 4118, 4219, 4372, 4433, 4583, 4824, 5153, 5338, 5530
Happy Birthday ... 2272, 2395, 3558, 3695, 4079, 5635
Happy New Year ... 2720, 2817, 2876, 3060, 3120, 3179, 3272, 3369, 3370, 3500, 3559, 3747, 3832, 3895, 3997, 4221, 4375, 4435, 4492, 4623
Harbor of Refuge Lighthouse, DE ... 5624
Harbor Seal ... 1882
Harburg, Edgar Y. "Yip" ... 3905
Harding, Warren G. ... 553, 576, 582, 598, 605, 610-613, 631, 633, 659, 670, 684, 686, 833, 2219a
Hardy, Oliver ... 2562
Harebell ... 2689
Harlem Renaissance ... 5471-5474
Harlequin Lupine ... 2664
Harley-Davidson Electra-Glide Motorcycle ... 4088
Harnett, William M. ... 1386, 3236i
Harris, Joel Chandler ... 980
Harris, Patricia Roberts ... 3371
Harrison, Benjamin ... 308, 622, 694, 828, 1045, 2218e
Harrison, William H. ... 814, 996, 2216i
Harry Potter Movie Characters ... 4825-4844
Hart, Lorenz ... 3347
Hart, Moss ... 3882
Hart, William S. ... 4448
Harte, Bret ... 2196
Hartley, Marsden ... 4748d
Harvard, John ... 2190
Hawaii ... C46
Hawaii Flag ... 1682, 4287
Hawaii Sesquicentennial ... 647-648
Hawaii Statehood ... 2080, 4415, C55
Hawaii Territory ... 799
Hawaiian Missionary Stamps ... 3694
Hawaiian Monk Seal ... 3105c
Hawaiian Rain Forest ... 4474
Hawaiian Wild Broadbean ... 1784
Hawes, Josiah Johnson & Southworth, Albert Sands ... 3649a
Hawkins, Coleman ... 2983
Hawkman ... 4084j, 4084t
Hawthorne, Nathaniel ... 2047
Hayden, Robert ... 4657
Hayes, Helen ... 4525
Hayes, Rutherford B. ... 563, 692, 824, 2218a
Head of Freedom Statue, Capitol Dome ... 573, 4075c
Heade, Martin Johnson ... 3872
Healing Post-Traumatic Stress Disorder ... B7
Health Research ... 2087
Heart Health ... 4625
Height, Dorothy ... 5171
Held, John, Jr. ... 3502t
Help Find Missing Children ... 4987
Helping Children Learn ... 3125
Hemingway, Ernest M. ... 2418
HemisFair '68 ... 1340
Hendrix, Jimi ... 4880
Henry, O. ... 4705
Henry, Patrick ... 1052
Henson, Jim ... 3944k
Henson, Matthew, & Peary, Robert E. ... 2223
Hepburn, Audrey ... 3786
Hepburn, Katharine ... 4461
Herb Robert ... 2657
Herbert, Victor ... 881
Heritage Animal Breeds ... 5583-5592
Herkimer at Oriskany ... 1722
Hermit Crab ... 5118
Hermitage, The ... 786, 1037, 1059
Heroes of 2001 ... B2
Herrmann, Bernard ... 3341
Herry Monster ... 5394i
Hersey, John ... 4249
Hershey, Milton ... 2933
Hesburgh, Father Ted ... 5241-5242
Heston, Charlton ... 4892
Hiawatha ... 3336
Hickok, Wild Bill ... 2869o, 2870
Higgins, Marguerite ... 3668
High Museum of Art ... 3910j
Higher Education ... 1206
Highway Interchange ... 4710o
Hiking ... 5477
Hillsboro Inlet Lighthouse, FL ... 3791
Hine, Lewis W. ... 3649e
Hines, Gregory ... 5349
Hines, Maj. Gen. John L. ... 3393
Hip-hop Culture ... 3190o, 5480-5483
Hispanic Americans ... 2103
Historic Preservation ... 1440-1443
History of Ice Hockey ... 5252-5253
Hitchcock, Alfred ... 3226
Ho-Chunk Bag ... 3873d
Hoban, James ... 1935-1936
Hobby, Oveta Culp ... 4510
Hofmann, Hans ... 4444a
Holiday, Billie ... 2856
Holly, Buddy ... 2729, 2736
Holmes, Oliver Wendell ... 1288, 1288B, 1305E
Home on the Range ... 2869a, 2870
Homemakers ... 1253
Homer, Winslow ... 1207, 3236j, 4473
Homestead Act ... 1198
Honest John from "Pinocchio" ... 5214
Honeybee ... 2281
Honeydew, Dr. Bunsen, and Beaker ... 3944h
Honeymooners, The ... 4414t
Honoring Those Who Served ... 3331
Honoring U.S. Servicemen ... 1422
Honoring Veterans ... 3508
Hoover (Boulder) Dam ... 774, 4269
Hoover, Herbert C. ... 1269, 2219c
Hopalong Cassidy ... 4414g
Hope, Bob ... 4406
Hopi Pottery ... 1708
Hopkins, Johns ... 2194
Hopkins, Mark ... 870
Hopper, Edward ... 3236p, 4558
Horne, Lena ... 5259
Hornsby, Rogers ... 3408f
Horse Racing ... 1528
Horses ... 2155-2158, 2756-2759, 5123
Horseshoes ... 5627
Horticulture ... 1100
Hospice Care ... 3276
Hospitals ... 2210
Hostages in Iran Return ... 3190d
Hot Fudge Sundae ... 5097
Hot Rods ... 4908-4909
Hot Wheels Toy Cars ... 5321-5330
Houdini, Harry ... 3651
Household Conveniences ... 3185g
House of Representatives, U.S. ... 2412
Houston, Charles Hamilton ... 4384d
Houston, Sam ... 776, 1242
Hovercraft ... C123, C126b
Howdy Doody ... 4414d
Howe, Elias ... 892
Howe, Julia Ward ... 2176
Howlin' Wolf ... 2861
Hubble, Edwin ... 4226
Hubble Space Telescope ... 3384-3388, 3409a
Hudson-Fulton Celebration ... 372-373
Hudson River School Paintings ... 4917-4920
Hudson's General ... 2843
Hughes, Charles Evans ... 1195
Hughes, Langston ... 3557
Huguenot-Walloon Tercentenary ... 614-616
Hulk, The Incredible ... 4159b, 4159l
Hull, Cordell ... 1235
Humane Treatment of Animals ... 1307
Hummingbirds ... 2642-2646, 4857-4858
Humphrey, Hubert ... 2189
Hunger, Help End ... 2164
Huntington Botanical Gardens ... 5469
Hurley, Ruby ... 4384f
Hurston, Zora Neale ... 3748
Huston, John ... 4671
HW40 ... 5328
Hyacinth ... 2760, 3900
Hydrangea ... 2996

I Love Lucy ... 3187l, 4414b
Ice Cream Cone ... 5093
Ice Hockey, History of ... 5252-5253
Iceboat ... 2134
Idaho Flag ... 1675, 4288
Idaho Statehood ... 896, 2439
Ifill, Gwen ... 5432
IG-11 ... 5572
Iguana ... 5108

Iiwi 2311
Illinois Flag 1653, 4289
Illinois Institute of Technology 2020
Illinois Statehood 1339, 5274
Immigrants Arrive 3182i
Improving Education 3191e
Independence Hall 1044, 1546, 1622, 1622C, 1625
Independence Spirit, Rise of 1476-1479
Independence, Skilled Hands for 1717-1720
Indian Centenary 972
Indian Headdresses 2501-2505
Indian Head Penny 1734
Indian Hunting Buffalo 287
Indian Masks, Pacific Northwest 1834-1837
Indian Motorcycle 4085
Indian Paintbrush 2647
Indian Pond Lily 2680
Indiana Flag 1651, 4290
Indiana Statehood 1308, 5091
Indiana Territory 996
Indianapolis 500 4530
Industrial Design, Pioneers of American 4546
Inkwell and Quill 1581, 1811, 4496
Inland Marsh 4710e
Innovation 5514-5518
Insects & Spiders 3351
Integrated circuit 3188j
Int'l Aeronautics Conference 649-650
International Cooperation Year 1266
International Geophysical Year 1107
International Harvester D-2 truck 5101
International Peace Garden 2014
International Philatelic Exhibition 630, 778, 1075-1076, 1310-1311, 1632, 1757, 2145, 2216-2219
International Polar Year 4123
Int'l Telecommunications Union 1274
International Women's Year 1571
International Year of the Child 1772
Int'l Year of the Disabled 1925
International Youth Year 2160-2163
Interphil '76 1632
Intrepid Balloon 2032
Inventors 889-893, 2055-2058
Inverted Jenny C3a, 4806
Iowa Flag 1661, 4291
Iowa Statehood 942, 3088-3089
Iowa Territory 838
Iris 2763, 3903
Irish Immigration 3286
Iron "Betty" Lamp 1608
Iron Man 4159h, 4159r
Irving, Washington 859
Italy, Invasion of 2765f
Ives, Charles 3164
Ives, Frederic E. 3063
Iwo Jima 929

Jack-in-the-pulpit 2650
Jack-O'-Lanterns 5137-5140
Jackson, Andrew 73, 84-85, 85B, 87, 93, 103, 135, 146, 157, 168, 178, 180, 183, 193, 203, 211, 211D, 215, 221, 253, 268, 302, 786, 812, 941, 1209, 1225, 1286, 2216g, 2592
Jackson, Mahalia 3216
Jackson, "Stonewall" 788, 2975s
Jacob's Ladder 2684
James, Henry 5105
Jamestown Exposition 328-330
Jamestown Festival 1091
Jamestown, Founding of 329, 4136
Japan 1021, 1158
Japanese Diet 4984
Jay, John 1046
Jazz 4503
Jazz Flourishes 3184k
Jeffers, Robinson 1485
Jefferson Memorial 1510, 1520, 3647-3647A, 4652
Jefferson, Thomas 12, 27-30A, 42, 67, 75-76, 80, 95, 105, 139, 150, 161, 172, 187-188, 197, 209, 228, 260, 275, 310, 324, 561, 590, 641, 667, 678, 807, 842, 851, 1033, 1055, 1278, 1299, 2185, 2216c
Jenny Airplane C1-C3, 3142s
Jenny Invert C3a
Jet Airliner Silhouette C51-C52, C60-C61, C78, C82
Jitterbug 3186g
Jock Scott 2546
John Bull Locomotive 2364
John Henry 3085
Johnson, Andrew 822, 2217h
Johnson, James P. 2985
Johnson, James Weldon 2371
Johnson, John H. 4624
Johnson, Joshua 3236h
Johnson, Lady Bird 4716f
Johnson, Lyndon B. 1503, 2219i
Johnson, Robert 2857
Johnson, Walter 3408i
Johnson, William H. 4653
Johnston, Joseph E. 2975m
Jolson, Al 2849
Jones, Casey 993
Jones, John Paul 790, 1789-1789B
Jones, Robert Tyre (Bobby) 1933, 3185n
Joplin, Janis 4916
Joplin, Scott 2044
Jordan, Barbara 4565
Joseph, Chief 1364, 2869f, 2870
Joshua Tree 5347
Journalists, American 4248-4252
Juke Box 2911-2912B, 3132
Julia 5394j
Julian, Percy Lavon 2746
Jumbo Jets 3189n
Jumping Spider 3351t
Juniper Berry 5416
Jupiter 2573, 5073
Jupiter Balloon C54
Jupiter Locomotive 5378
Jurassic Park 3191k
Jury Duty 4200
Just, Ernest E. 3058

K-2SO 5575
Kahanamoku, Duke 3660
Kahlo, Frida 3509
Kaiser Darrin 3932
Kaleidoscope Flowers 4722-4725
Kane, Elisha Kent 2220
Kansas City, Missouri 994
Kansas Flag 1666, 4292
Kansas Hard Winter Wheat 1506
Kansas Statehood 1183, 4493
Kansas Territory 1061
Karloff, Boris 3170, 3171
Karman, Theodore von 2699
Kasebier, Gertrude 3649d
Katzenjammer Kids 3000b
Kearny Expedition 944
Keaton, Buster 2828
Keep in Touch 2274
Keller, Helen, & Anne Sullivan 1824
Kelly, Ellsworth 5382-5391
Kelly, Grace 2749
Kelp Forest 4423
Kenilwoth Park and Aquatic Gardens 5080j
Kennedy, John F. 1246, 1287, 2219h, 5175
Kennedy, Robert F. 1770
Kent, Rockwell 3502q
Kentucky Flag 1647, 4293
Kentucky Settlement 1542
Kentucky Statehood 904, 2636
Kermit the Frog 3944a
Kern, Jerome 2110
Kerosene Table Lamp 1611
Kertesz, Andre 3649r
Kestrel, American 2476-2477, 3031, 3044
Key, Francis Scott 962
Keystone Cops 2826
Kickball 5210
Kilauea Volcano 4067
Killer Whale 2508
King, Jr., Dr. Martin Luther 1771, 3188a
King Eider 4992, 4998
King Penguins 2708
Kinglets, Golden-crowned 5126
Kitten 3670, 5111
Kitten and Puppy 2025
Kiwi 4255, 4262
Kline, Franz 3236s
Klondike Gold Rush 3235
Knox, Henry 1851
Knoxville World's Fair 2006-2009
Kooning, Willem de 4444b
Korea, Flag 921
Korean War 3187e
Korean War Veterans Memorial 3803
Kosciuszko, Gen. Tadeusz 734
Kossuth, Lajos 1117-1118
Koyukuk River 5381c
Krazy Kat 3000e
Kukla, Fran and Ollie 4414k
Kutenai Parfleche 3873b
Kwanzaa 3175, 3368, 3548, 3673, 3881, 4119, 4220, 4373, 4434, 4584, 4845, 5141, 5337, 5531

L3-37 5577
La Florida 4750-4753
Labor Day 1082
Labrador Retriever 5406
Lacemaking 2351-2354
Lady Tremaine from "Cinderella" 5215
Ladybeetle, Ladybug 2315, 3351c
Lafayette, Marquis de 1010, 1097, 1716
Lagoon Nebula 3386
LaGuardia, Fiorello H. 1397
Lake Erie, Battle of 4805
Lake Shore Drive Buildings, Chicago 3910f
Lake Superior 4047
Lancaster County, Pennsylvania C150
Land-Grant Colleges 1065, 1206
Landing of Columbus 118-119, 129
Lange, Dorothea 3649l
Langley, Samuel P. C118
Lanier, Sidney 1446
Large-flowered Trillium 2652
Larsen, Nella 5471
Lasers 3188k
Lasker, Mary 3432B
Lassie 4414f
Latin American Dishes 5192-5197
Latin Jazz 4349
Latin Music Legends 4497-4501
Laubach, Frank C. 1864
Laurel, Stanley 2562
Lavender 4508, 4514
Law and Order 1343
Le Guin, Ursula K. 5619
Leadbelly (Huddie Ledbetter) 3212
Leatherworker 1720
Lee, Jason 964
Lee, Robert E. 788, 1049, 2975b
Lefty's Deceiver 2548
Legend of Sleepy Hollow 1548
Legends of Baseball 3408
Legends of Hollywood 2967, 3082, 3152, 3226, 3329, 3446, 3523, 3692, 3786, 3876, 3911, 4077, 4197, 4350, 4421, 4461, 4526, 4892, 5012, 5060
Legends of the West 2869-2870
Leigh, Vivien & Gable, Clark 2446
Lejeune, Lt. Gen. John A. 3961
Lemons 5256, 5487
Lend Lease 2559c
Lennon, John 5312-5315
Leo Constellation 3945
Leon, Ponce de 2024
Lerner, Alan Jay & Loewe, Frederick 3346
Letter Carriers 2420

Letters Lift Spirits ... 1807
Letters Mingle Souls ... 1530, 1532, 1534, 1536
Letters Preserve Memories ... 1805
Letters Shape Opinions ... 1809
Lettuce ... 5490
Levertov, Denise ... 4661
Lewis and Clark Expedition ... 1063, 3854-3856
Lewis, Edmonia ... 5663
Lewis, Edna ... 4922
Lewis, Meriwether ... 3854, 3855
Lewis, Sinclair ... 1856
Lexington-Concord ... 617-619, 1563
Leyendecker, J. C. ... 3502c
Leyte Gulf, Battle of ... 2838i
Liberation of Rome and Paris ... 2838f
Liberty Bell ... 627, 1518, 1595, 1618, 4125-4128, 4437, C57, C62
Liberty Issue ... 1030-1031, 1031A, 1032-1041, 1041B, 1042, 1042A, 1043-1044, 1044A, 1045-1054, 1054A, 1055-1059, 1059A
Liberty Ships ... 2559h, 4550
Libraries, America's ... 2015
Library of Congress ... 2004, 3390
Life Magazine ... 3185c
Lighthouses ... 1605, 2470-2474, 2969-2973, 3787-3791, 4146-4150, 4409-4413, 4791-4795, 5621-5625
Lightning Airplane ... 3142n
Lightning Whelk Shell ... 2121
Lightyear, Buzz ... 5709-5712
Li'l Abner ... 3000q
Lilac ... 2764
Lili'uokalani Gardens ... 5156
Lily ... 1879, 2829
Limner, The Freake ... 3236b
Limon, Jose ... 4699
Lincoln Memorial ... 571, 4075a, 4982
Lincoln, Abraham ... 77, 85F, 91, 98, 108, 122, 132, 137, 148, 159, 170, 186, 195, 208, 222, 254, 269, 280, 304, 315, 317, 367-369, 555, 584, 600, 635, 661, 672, 821, 906, 978, 1036, 1058, 1113-1116, 1282, 1303, 2217g, 2433, 2975j, 4380-4383, 4860-4861, 5079e, C59
Lincoln-Douglas Debates ... 1115
Lincoln Premiere ... 4356
Lindbergh Flight ... 1710, 3184m, C10
Linum ... 4757
Lion, New York Public Library ... 3447, 3769
Lions International ... 1326
Lippmann, Walter ... 1849
Literary Arts ... 1773, 1832, 2047, 2094, 2239, 2350, 2418, 2449, 2538, 2698, 2862, 3002, 3104, 3134, 3221, 3308, 3444, 3659, 3748, 3871, 3904, 4030, 4124, 4223, 4386, 4476, 4545, 4705, 4866, 5003, 5105, 5414, 5619
Little House on the Prairie ... 2786
Little Mo ... 5377
Little Nemo in Slumberland ... 3000c
Little Orphan Annie ... 3000j
Little Rock Nine ... 3937d
Little Women ... 2788
Livingston, Robert R. ... 323
Lloyd, Harold ... 2825
Locke, Alain ... 5474
Lockwood, Belva Ann ... 2178
Locomobile ... 2381
Locomotive ... 114, 125, 1897A, 2226, 2362-2366, 2843-2847
Loesser, Frank ... 3350
Loewe, Frederick & Lerner, Alan Jay ... 3346
Loewy, Raymond ... 4546c
Log Rafts ... 4710g
Lombardi, Vince ... 3145, 3147
London, Jack ... 2182, 2197
Lone Ranger, The ... 4414m
Long, Dr. Crawford W. ... 875
Longfellow, Henry W. ... 864, 4124
Longleaf Pine Forest ... 3611
Los Angeles Class Submarine ... 3372, 3374
Louis, Joe ... 2766
Louisiana Flag ... 1650, 4294
Louisiana Purchase ... 1020, 3782
Louisiana Purchase Exposition ... 323-327
Louisiana Purchase, Map of ... 327
Louisiana Statehood ... 1197, 4667
Louisiana World Exposition ... 2086
Love ... 1475, 1951-1951A, 2072, 2143, 2202, 2248, 2378-2379, 2398, 2440-2441, 2535-2535A, 2536-2537, 2618, 2813-2815, 2948-2949, 2957-2960, 3030, 3123-3124, 3274-3275, 3496-3499, 3551, 3657-3658, 3833, 3898, 3976, 4029, 4122, 4270, 4404-4405, 4450, 4531-4540, 4626, 4741, 4847, 4955-4956, 5036, 5155, 5255, 5339, 5431, 5542, 5660-5661
Love You, Dad ... 2270
Love You, Mother ... 2273
Low, Juliette Gordon ... 974
Lowell, James Russell ... 866
Luce, Henry R. ... 2935
Ludington, Sybil ... 1559
Lugosi, Bela ... 3169
Luiseno Basket ... 3873j
Luna Moth ... 2293
Lunch Counter Sit-ins ... 3937c
Lunch Wagon ... 2464
Lunt, Alfred & Fontanne, Lynn ... 3287
Luther, Martin ... 2065
Luxembourg, Flag ... 912
Lyndhurst ... 1841
Lyon, Mary ... 2169
Lyra Constellation ... 3947

Maass, Clara ... 1699
MacArthur, Gen. Douglas ... 1424
MacDonough, Thomas ... 791
MacDowell, Edward ... 882
Mach Speeder ... 5325
Mackinac Bridge ... 1109, 4438
Maclay Gardens State Park ... 5468
Madison, Dolley ... 1822
Madison, Helene ... 2500
Madison, James ... 262, 277, 312, 479, 808, 843, 2216d, 2875a, 3545
Magic, The Art of ... 5301-5306
Magna Carta ... 1265
Magsaysay, Ramon ... 1096
Mail Automobile ... 2437, 2438d
Mail Order Business ... 1468
Mail Transport - ZIP Code ... 1511
Mail Wagon ... 1903
Maine Flag ... 1655, 4295
Maine Statehood ... 1391, 5456
Maisy ... 3990
Makeup ... 3772e
Mako Shark ... 5223
Malaria ... 1194
Malcolm X ... 3273
Maleficent from "Sleeping Beauty" ... 5218
Mallard ... 1757b
Mallard Decoy ... 2139
Mambo ... 3942
Mammoth Cave ... 4068
Mammoth, Woolly ... 3078
Manatee, Florida ... 3105o
Mancini, Henry ... 3839
Mann, Horace ... 869
Mannerheim, Baron Gustaf Emil ... 1165-1166
Mantle, Mickey ... 4083
Map of Sea Surface Temperatures ... 4893
Map, U.S. ... C7-C9
Marathon ... 3067
Marblehead Lighthouse ... 2972
March on Washington ... 3937h, 4804
Marciano, Rocky ... 3187k
Mariachi ... 5703-5707
Mariana Islands ... 2804
Marigold ... 2832
Marin, John ... 4748b
Marin, Luis, Munoz ... 2173
Marine Corps Reserve ... 1315
Marine One ... 4145
Mariner 10 ... 1557
Marines ... 3961-3964
Marines, Continental ... 1567
Marines, World War II ... 929
Maris, Roger ... 3188n
Marquette on the Mississippi ... 285
Marquette, Jacques ... 1356
Mars ... 2572, 5072
Mars Pathfinder and Sojourner ... 3178
Marsh-Billings-Rockefeller National Historic Park ... 5080c
Marsh Marigold ... 2658
Marshall, George C. ... 1289
Marshall Islands ... 2507
Marshall, John ... 263, 278, 313, 480, 1050, 2415
Marshall Plan ... 3141
Marshall, Thurgood ... 3746
Martin, Roberta ... 3217
Marvel Comics Superheroes ... 4159
Maryland Flag ... 1639, 4296
Maryland Statehood ... 2342
Maryland Tercentenary ... 736
Masaryk, Thomas G. ... 1147-1148
Mason, George ... 1858
Massachusetts Bay Colony ... 682
Massachusetts Flag ... 1638, 4297
Massachusetts Statehood ... 2341
Masters, Edgar Lee ... 1405
Masters of American Photography ... 3649
Masterson, Bat ... 2869h, 2870
Mastodon ... 3079
Matagorda Island Lighthouse, TX ... 4409
Mathematics Education ... 5279
Mathewson, Christy ... 3408c
Mauldin, Bill ... 4445
Mayer, Maria Goeppert ... 4543
Mayflower ... 548, 5524
Matzeliger, Jan ... 2567
Mayo, Drs. William and Charles ... 1251
Mazzei, Philip ... C98-C98A
McClintock, Barbara ... 3906
McCloy, Lt. Commander John ... 4442
McCormack, John ... 2090
McCormick, Cyrus Hall ... 891
McDaniel, Hattie ... 3996
McDowell, Dr. Ephraim ... 1138
McKinley, William ... 326, 559, 588, 639, 665, 676, 829, 2218f
McLoughlin, John ... 964
McMahon, Brien ... 1200
McMein, Neysa ... 3502m
McPhatter, Clyde ... 2726, 2733
McQueen's Jupiter ... 2844
Mead, Margaret ... 3184g
Meadow Beauty ... 2649
Meany, George ... 2848
Medal of Honor ... 2045, 4822-4823, 4988
Medical Imaging ... 3189o
Medusa ... 3443
Mellon, Andrew W. ... 1072
Melville, Herman ... 2094
Mendez v. Westminster ... 4201
Mendoza, Lydia ... 4786
Mentoring a Child ... 3556
Merced River ... 5381a
Mercer, Johnny ... 3101
Merchant Marine ... 939, 4548-4551
Mercury ... 2568, 5069
Merengue ... 3939
Mergenthaler, Ottmar ... 3062
Merman, Ethel ... 2853
Mesa Verde ... 743, 759
Message Monsters ... 5636-5639
Messenger Spacecraft ... 4528
Metropolitan Opera ... 2054
Mexican Hat ... 2688
Mexican Independence ... 1157
Michael, Moina ... 977
Micheaux, Oscar ... 4464
Michener, James A. ... 3427A
Michigan Centenary ... 775

Michigan Flag 1658, 4298
Michigan State College 1065
Michigan Statehood 2246
Micronesia, Federated States of 2506
Midway, Battle of 2697g
Migratory Bird Treaty 1306
Mighty Casey 3083
Mighty Mississippi 5698
Military Dog 4606
Military Medics 2765b
Military Services Bicentenary 1565-1568
Military Uniforms 1565-1568
Military Working Dogs 5405-5408
Militia, American 1568
Milk, Harvey 4906
Milk Wagon 2253
Milking Devon Cow 5585
Millay, Edna St. Vincent 1926
Miller, Doris 4443
Miller, Glenn 3098
Millikan, Robert 1866
Mimbres Bowl 3873a
Minerals 1538-1541, 2700-2703
Mingus, Charles 2989
Mining Prospector 291
Minnesota Flag 1664, 4299
Minnesota Statehood 1106, 4266
Minnesota Territory 981
Minute Man, The 619
Miranda, Carmen 4498
Miss Piggy 3944d
Mississippi Flag 1652, 4300
Mississippi River 5698
Mississippi River Delta 4058
Mississippi Statehood 1337, 5190
Mississippi Territory 955
Mississippi-Missouri River System 4065
Mississippian Effigy 3873f
Missouri Flag 1656, 4301
Missouri River 5381g
Missouri Statehood 1426, 5626
Mister Rogers 5275
Mitchell, Joan 4444h
Mitchell, Margaret 2168
Mitchell, Gen. William "Billy" L. 3330
Mix, Tom 4447
Mobile, Battle of 1826
Mobile Bay, Battle of 4910
Mockingbird 2330
Model B Airplane 3142b
Model T Ford 3182a
Modern Art 4748
Moloka'i 4034
Monarch Butterfly 2287, 3351k, 4462
Monarch Caterpillar 3351j
Monday Night Football .... 3189 l
Monitor and Virginia, Battle of 2975a
Monk, Thelonious 2990
Monmouth, Battle of 646
Monopoly Game 3185o
Monroe, James 325, 562, 591, 603, 642, 668, 679, 810, 845, 1038, 1105, 2216e
Monroe, Marilyn 2967
Monsters, Message 5636-5639
Montana Flag 1673, 4304
Montana Statehood 858, 2401
Montauk Point Lighthouse, NY 5621
Montgomery, Ala. Bus Boycott 3937e
Monticello 1047
Monument Valley 5666
Moon 2571, 5058
Moon Landing 2419, 2841-2842, 3188c, 3413, C76
Moon Rover 1435, C124, C126c
Moore, John Bassett 1295
Moore, Marianne 2449
Moose 1757e, 1887, 2298
Moran, Thomas 3236l, 4917
More than Meets the Eye 5614
Morgan Horse 2156
Morocco-U.S. Diplomatic Relations 2349
Morrill, Justin S. 2941
Morris Island Lighthouse, SC 3789
Morris Township School, ND 1606
Morrison, George 5688-5692
Morse, Samuel F.B. 890
Morton, Jelly Roll 2986
Moses, (Grandma) Anna Mary Robertson 1370
Moses, Horace 2095
Moss Campion 2686
Mother Teresa 4475
Mothers of America 737-738, 754
Motherwell, Robert 4444g
Motion Pictures 926
Motorcycle 1899, 4085-4088
Mott, Lucretia 959
Mount McKinley 1454, C137
Mount Rainier National Park 742, 758, 770, 5080b
Mount Rushmore 1011, 2523, 2523A, 4268, C88
Mount Vernon 785, 1032
Mount Wai'ale'ale 4066
Mount Washington 4053
Mountain 2903-2904B
Mountain Bluebird 4883
Mountain Flora 5672-5679
Mountain Goat 2323
Mountain Lion 2292
Mouse 5117
Movies Go 3-D 3187o
Muddler Minnow 2549
Muir, John 1245, 3182j
Mule Deer 2294
Mulefoot Hog 5583
Muller-Munk, Peter 4546a
Mummy, The 3171
Munoz Marin, Luis 2173
Muppets 3944a-3944j
Murphy, Second Lt. Audie L. 3396
Murphy, Gerald 4748j
Murphy, Robert D. 4076a
Murrow, Edward R. 2812
Muscle Cars 4743-4747
Music (films) 3772d
Music Icons 4786, 4789, 4807, 4880, 4916, 5009, 5059, 5312-5315, 5371, 5708
Muskellunge 2205
Mustang Airplane 3142a
Muybridge, Eadweard 3061
My Fair Lady 2770
Mystery Message 5614

Nagurski, Bronko 3808
Naismith-Basketball 1189
Nancy 3000o
Narragansett Turkey 5586
Nash Healey 3934
Nash, Ogden 3659
Nassau Hall 1083
Nation of Readers 2106
National Academy of Science 1237
National Archives 2081
National Capital Sesquicentennial 989-992
National Gallery of Art 3910g
National Grange 1323
National Guard 1017
National Letter Writing Week 1805-1810
National Marine Sanctuaries 5713
National Museum of African American History and Culture 5251
National Park Service 1314, 5080
National Parks 740-749, 756-765, 769-770, 1448-1454, C84
National Postal Museum 2779-2782
National Recovery Administration 732
National Stamp Exhibition 735
National World War II Memorial 3862
Native American Culture 2869e, 2870
NATO 1008, 1127, 3354
Natural History Museum 1387-1390
Navajo Blankets 2235-2238
Navajo Necklace 3750-3753, 3758B
Navajo Weaving 3873h
Naval Aviation 1185
Naval Review 1091
Navesink Twin Lighthouses, NJ 5622
Navigation, Lake 294
Navigation, Ocean 299
Navy, Continental 1566
Navy Cross 5066
Navy Medal of Honor 4822
Navy, U.S. 790-794, 935
Nebraska Flag 1669, 4305
Nebraska Statehood 1328, 5179
Nebraska Territory 1060
Negro Leagues Baseball 4465-4466
Neptune 2576, 5076
Netherlands 2003
Netherlands, Flag 913
Neumann, John von 3908
Neuter and Spay 3670-3671
Nevada Flag 1668, 4306
Nevada Settlement 999
Nevada Statehood 1248, 4907
Nevelson, Louise 3379-3383
Nevers, Ernie 3809
Nevin, Ethelbert 883
New Baseball Records 3191a
New Deal 3185e
New England Neptune Shell 2119
New Guinea, Allied Recapture of 2838a
New Hampshire 1068
New Hampshire Flag 1641, 4307
New Hampshire Statehood 2344
New Horizons Probe 5078
New Jersey Flag 1635, 4308
New Jersey Statehood 2338
New Jersey Tercentenary 1247
New London Harbor Lighthouse, CT 4795
New Mexico Flag 1679, 4309
New Mexico Statehood 1191, 4591
New Netherland 614
New Orleans, 1815 Battle of 1261, 4952
New Orleans, 1862 Battle of 4664
New Orleans Steamboat 2407
New River Gorge Bridge 4511
New Sweden Settlement C117
New York City 1027, C38
New York Coliseum 1076
New York Flag 1643, 4310
New York Skyline & Statue of Liberty C35
New York Statehood 2346
New York Stock Exchange 2630
New York University Library 1928
New York World's Fair 853, 1244
Newburgh, New York 727
Newman, Alfred 3343
Newman, Barnett 4444j
Newman, Paul 5020
Newspaper Boys 1015
Niagara Falls 568, 699, C133
Nimitz, Chester M. 1869
Nine-Mile Prairie C136
Nineteenth Amendment 3184e
Niobrara River 5381d
Nixon, Richard 2955
No. 119 Locomotive 5380
Nobel Prize 3504
Noguchi, Isamu 3857-3861
Non-Denominated 1735-1736, 1743, 1818-1820, 1946-1948, 2111-2113, 2277, 2279, 2282, 2517-2522, 2602-2604, 2877-2893, 2902, 2902B, 2903-2904, 2904A, 2904B, 2905-2912, 2912A, 2912B, 2948-2949, 3207, 3207A, 3208, 3208A, 3228-3229, 3257-3258, 3260, 3264-3271, 3447-3465, 3496, 3520, 3522
Norfolk Botanical Garden 5470
Norris, George W. 1184

Norse-American 620, 621
North African Invasion 2697j
North Carolina Flag 1644, 4311
North Carolina Statehood 2347
North Dakota Flag 1671, 4312
North Dakota Statehood 858, 2403
Northeast Deciduous Forest 3899
Northern Goshawk 4608
Northern Harrier 4612
Northern Mariana Islands, Commonwealth of the 2804
Northern Marianas Flag 4313
Northwest Ordinance 795
Northwest Territory 837
Norway, Flag 911
Noyes, Eliot 4546j
NRA 732
Numismatics 2558
Nursing 1190
Nuthatches, Red-breasted 5129

O Beautiful 5298
Oakley, Annie 2869d, 2870
Ocelot 3105e
Ochoa, Severo 4544
Ochs, Adolph S. 1700
O'Connor, Flannery 5003
Off the Florida Keys, Reef 4042
Oglethorpe, Gen. James Edward 726
Ohi'a Lehua 2669
Ohio Class Submarine 3375
Ohio Flag 1649, 4314
Ohio River Canalization 681
Ohio Statehood 1018, 3773
Oil Wagon 2130
O'Keeffe, Georgia 3069, 4748e
Okefenokee Swamp C142
Oklahoma! (musical) 2722, 2769
Oklahoma Flag 1678, 4315
Oklahoma Statehood 1092, 4121
Old Cape Henry Lighthouse, VA 3787
Old Faithful, Yellowstone 744, 760, 1453, 4379
Old Glory 3776-3780
Old North Church, Boston 1603
Olivia 3993
Olmsted, Frederick Law 3338
Olympics 716, 718-719, 1146, 1460-1462, 1695-1698, 1790-1798, 1795A-1798A, 2048-2051, 2067-2070, 2082-2085, 2369, 2380, 2528, 2496-2500, 2539-2542, 2553-2557, 2611-2615, 2619, 2637-2641, 2807-2811, 3068, 3087, 3552-3555, 3863, 3995, 4334, 4436, C85, C97, C101-C112
Omnibus 1897, 2225
O'Neill, Eugene 1294, 1305C
O'Neill, Rose 3502i
Ontonagon River 5381k
Opisthias 3136h
Orange 3492, 3494
Orange-tip Butterfly 1715
Orchids 2076-2079
Orchids, Wild 5435-5444
Oregano 4505, 4516
Oregon Flag 1665, 4316
Oregon Statehood 1124, 4376
Oregon Territory 783, 964
Oregon Trail 2747
Organ & Tissue Donation 3227
Organized Labor 1831
Orion Constellation 3946
Oriskany, Battle of 1722
Ormandy, Eugene 3161
Ornate Box Turtle 3818
Ornate Chorus Frog 3817
Ornithomimus 3136n
Oroville Dam 4056
Oscar the Grouch 5394g
Osprey 2291, 4611
Osteopathic Medicine 1469
O'Sullivan, Timothy H. 3649b
Ott, Mel 4082
Otters in Snow 5648-5651
Ouimet, Francis 2377
Overland Mail 1120, 2869t, 2870
Overrun Countries 909-921
Ovington, Mary White 4384a
Owatonna, Minnesota Bank 1931
Owens, Jesse 2496, 3185j
Owl 1760-1763, 2285, 3290
Owney, the Postal Dog 4547
Owyhee River 5381b
Ozzie and Harriet 4414q

P-47 Thunderbolt 3919
P-51s Escortng B-17s 2838b
P-80 Shooting Star 3921
Pacific Calico Scallop 5164, 5170
Pacific Calypso Orchid 2079
Pacific Coast Rain Forest 3378
Pacific Coral Reef 3831
Pacific Crest Trail 4043
Pacific Dogwood 3197
Pacific 97 .... 3130-3131, 3139-3140
Packard 2384
Paderewski, Ignacy Jan 1159-1160
Paige, Satchel 3408p
Paine, Thomas 1292
Painted Bunting 4885
Painted Fern 4852, 4878, 4976
Palace of Fine Arts, San Francisco 1930, 5667
Palace of the Governors, Santa Fe 1031A, 1054A
Palaeosaniwa 3136l
Palau 2999
Palmer, Arnold 5455
Palmer, Nathaniel 2386
Palomar Observatory 966
Pan American Games 2247, C56
Pan American Union 895, C34
Pan-American Exposition 294-299
Pan-American Exposition, Cent. 3505
Panama Canal 856, 3183f
Panama Canal, Pedro Miguel Locks 398, 402
Panama-Pacific Exposition 397-404
Panara, Robert 5191
Pansy 3027
Panther, Florida 3105m, 4137, 4139, 4141, 4142
Papanicolaou, Dr. George 1754
Papaya 4256, 4258
Parakeets 3233, 5124
Parasaurolophus 3136o
Parent Teacher Association 1463
Parker, Al 3502f
Parker, Charlie 2987
Parker, Dorothy 2698
Parkman, Francis 1281, 1297
Parks, Rosa 4742
Parrish, Maxfield 3502b
Parrot 5115
Parrot, Thick-Billed 3105b
Partridge, Alden 1854
Pasqueflower 2676, 5675, 5676
Passionflower 2674
Patriotic Banner 4157-4158, 4385
Patriotic Spiral 5130-5131
Patriotic Star 4749
Patriotic Waves 4953-4954
Patrol Wagon 2258
Patton, Gen. George S., Jr. 1026
Paul, Alice 2943
Paul Bunyan 3084
Pauling, Linus 4225
Payne, Ethel L. 3667
PBY Catalina 3916
Peace Bridge 1721
Peace Corps 1447, 3188f
Peace of 1783 .... 727, 752
Peace Rose 5280
Peace Symbol 3188m
Peacetime Draft 2559b
Peach 2487, 2493, 2495
Peale, Rembrandt 3236d
Peanuts Comic Strip Characters 3507, 5021-5030
Pear 2488, 2494, 2495A, 5039, 5178
Pearl Harbor 2559i
Peary, Robert E., & Matthew Henson 2223
Peashooter Airplane 3142o
Peck, Gregory 4526
Pecos Bill 3086
Pegasus Constellation 3948
Pelican Island National Wildlife Refuge 3774
Pember, Phoebe 2975r
Penguins, Emperor 4989-4990
Penn, William 724
Pennsylvania Academy 1064, 1840
Pennsylvania Flag 1634, 4317
Pennsylvania State University 1065
Pennsylvania Statehood 2337
Pennsylvania Toleware 1775-1778, 3612
Pepper, Claude 3426
Peppers, Chili 4003, 4012, 4013
Peregrine Falcon 4057, 4609
Performing Arts 1755-1756, 1801, 1803, 2012, 2088, 2090, 2110, 2211, 2250, 2411, 2550
Periodical Cicada 3351r
Perkins, Frances 1821
Perry, Commodore Matthew C. 1021
Perry, Commodore O.H. 144, 155, 166, 177, 191, 202, 218, 229, 261-261A, 276-276A
Perry Mason 4414n
Pershing, Gen. John J. 1214
Persistent Trillium 1783
Personal Computers 3190n
Petersburg, Battle of 4910
Petrified Wood 1538
Petroleum Industry 1134
Pets 5106-5125
Phantom of the Opera, The 3168
Pharmacy 1473
Pheasant 2283, 3050-3051A, 3055
Phil Silvers Show, The 4414l
Philadelphia Exchange 1782
Phillips, Ammi 3236c
Phillips, Coles 3502e
Phlox 4754
Phoenix Steamboat 2406
Photography 1758, 3649
Physical Fitness 2043
Physical Fitness-Sokol 1262
Piaf, Edith 4692
Piano 1615C
Pickett, Bill 2869g, 2870
Pickup Trucks 5101-5104
Pierce, Franklin 819, 2217e
Pierce-Arrow 2382
Piggott, Arkansas Post Office Mural 5372
Pika 2319
Pilgrim Tercentenary 548-550
Pilgrims, Landing of the 549, 1420
Pillar Coral 5365, 5367
Pine Cone 1257, 2491
Pinks 4760
Pioneer 10 .... 1556, 3189i
Pioneers of American Industrial Design 4546
Piper, William C129, C132
Piping Plover 3105n
Pitcher, Molly 646
Pitts, Zasu 2824
Pittsburgh Steelers 3189e
Plains Prickly Pear 2685
Plan for Better Cities 1333
Plane and Globes C89-C90
Plastic Man 4084g, 4084q
Plath, Sylvia 4658
Pledge of Allegiance 2594, 2594B
Ploesti Refineries, Bombing of 2765d
Plover, Piping 3105n
Plums 5484

Pluto ... 2577, 5077
Plymouth Hemi Barracuda ... 4747
Pocahontas ... 330
Poe, Edgar Allan ... 986, 4377
Poets ... 864-868, 4654-4663
Point Judith Lighthouse, RI ... 4794
Poinsettia ... 5311
Poland, Flag ... 909
Polar Bear ... 1429, 1885, 3291, 4387, 4389
Polio ... 1087, 3187a
Polish Millennium ... 1313
Polk, George ... 4250
Polk, James K. ... 816, 2217b, 2587
Pollination ... 4153-4156
Pollock, Jackson ... 3186h, 4444d
Polo Grounds ... 3514
Pomegranate ... 4253, 4260
Pons, Lily ... 3154
Ponselle, Rosa ... 3157
Pontiac GTO ... 4744
Pontiac Safari ... 4355
Pony Express ... 894, 1154
Poor, Salem ... 1560
Popcorn Wagon ... 2261
Popeye ... 3000k
Poppy, Memorial ... 977
Porgy & Bess ... 2768
Porky Pig ... 3534-3535
Porter, Cole ... 2550
Porter, David D. ... 792
Porter, Katherine Anne ... 4030
Portland Head Lighthouse, ME ... 4791
Portsmouth Harbor Lighthouse, NH ... 4792
Post Horse & Rider ... 113, 124
Post, Emily ... 3182f
Post Office Murals ... 5372-5375
Post, Wiley ... C95-C96
Postal Service Bicentenary ... 1572-1575
Postal Service Emblem ... 1396
Postal Service Employees ... 1489-1498
Post-Traumatic Stress Disorder ... B7
Poultry Industry ... 968
POW/MIA ... 2966
Powell, John Wesley ... 1374
Powered Flight ... 3783, C47
PrairieCrab Apple ... 3196
Preserve Wetlands ... 2092
Presidential Issue ... 803-834, 839-851
Presidential Libraries ... 3930
Presidents of the United States ... 2216-2219
Presley, Elvis ... 2721, 2724, 2731, 5009
Priestley, Joseph ... 2038
Primrose ... 4763
Prince Valiant ... 3000s
Prinsesse Tam-Tam (movie) ... 4338
Printing ... 857
Printing Press, Early American ... 1593
Prisoners of War/Missing in Action ... 1422, 2966
Professional Management ... 1920
Prohibition Enforced ... 3184c
Project Mercury ... 1193
Prominent Americans Issue ... 1278-1283, 1283B, 1284-1286, 1286A, 1287-1288, 1288B, 1289-1295, 1297-1299, 1303, 1304, 1304C, 1305, 1305E, 1305C, 1393, 1393D, 1394-1402
Pronghorn ... 1889, 2313, 4048
Propeller and Radiator ... C4
Prostate Cancer Awareness ... 3315
Protect Pollinators ... 5228-5232
P.S. Write Soon ... 1806, 1808, 1810
PTA ... 1463
Pteranodon ... 2423
PTSD, Healing ... B7
Public Education ... 2159
Pueblo Pottery ... 1706-1709
Puente, Tito ... 4497
Puerto Rico Elections ... 983
Puerto Rico Flag ... 4318
Puerto Rico Territory ... 801
Puffins, Tufted ... 4737-4737A
Pulaski, Gen. Casimir ... 690
Pulitzer, Joseph ... 946
Puller, Lt. Gen. Lewis B. ... 3962
Puma ... 1881
Pumpkinseed Sunfish ... 2481
Puppy ... 3671, 5106
Puppy and Kitten ... 2025
Pure Food and Drug Act ... 3182f
Purple Heart ... 3784-3784A, 4032, 4164, 4263-4264, 4390, 4529, 4704, 5035, 5419
Purple Passion ... 5321
Pushcart ... 2133
Pyle, Ernie T. ... 1398
Pyle, Howard ... 3502h

Quaking Aspen ... 4072
Quarter Horse ... 2155
Queen Conch ... 5163, 5169
Queen from "Snow White and the Seven Dwarves" ... 5213
Queen of Hearts from "Alice in Wonderland" ... 5216
Quill and Inkwell ... 4496
Quilts ... 1745-1748, 3524-3527, 4089-4098, 5098-5099
Quimby, Harriet ... C128

R2-D2 ... 5574
Rabbit ... 3272, 5112, 5544-5545
Raccoon ... 1757h, 2331
Racing Car ... 2262
Radio Entertains America ... 3184i
Railroad Conductor's Lantern ... 1612
Railroad Engineers ... 993
Railroad Mail Car ... 2265
Railroad Roundhouse ... 4710m
Railroad, Transcontinental ... 922, 5378-5380
Rainbow Bridge ... 4060
Rainey, Ma ... 2859
Ramirez, Martin ... 4968-4972
Rand, Ayn ... 3308
Randolph, Asa Philip ... 2402
Range Conservation ... 1176
Raspberries ... 3295, 3300, 3303, 3407
Ration Coupons ... 2697b
Raven and Cat ... 5420
Raven Story ... 5620
Rawlings, Marjorie Kinnan ... 4223
Ray, Man ... 3649i, 4748f
Rayburn, Sam ... 1202
Readers, Nation of ... 2106
Reagan, Nancy ... 5702
Reagan, Ronald ... 3897, 4078, 4494
Rebecca Everingham Riverboat ... 3094
Rebecca of Sunnybrook Farm ... 2785
Recognizing Deafness ... 2783
Recovering Species ... 3191g
Red Ball Express ... 2838h
Red Cloud ... 2175
Red Cross ... 702, 967, 1016, 1239, 1910
Red Fox ... 1757g, 2335, 3036
Red Knot ... 4991, 4997
Red Maid ... 2692
Red Skelton Show, The ... 4414c
Red-breasted Nuthatches ... 5129
Red-bellied Woodpecker ... 5319
Red-headed Woodpecker ... 3032, 3045
Red-winged Blackbird ... 2303
Redding, Otis ... 2728, 2735
Redhead Decoy ... 2141
Redwood Forest ... 4378
Reed, Dr. Walter ... 877
Register and Vote ... 1249, 1344
Religious Freedom ... 1099
Remember The Maine ... 3192
Remington, Frederic ... 888, 1187, 1934, 3502p
Repeal of the Stamp Act ... 5064
Reptiles, Age of ... 1390
Reptiles and Amphibians ... 3814-3818
Rescue Dog ... 4607
Residential Subdivision ... 4710k
Restaurationen, sloop ... 620
Retarded Children ... 1549
Reticulate Collared Lizard ... 3816
Reticulated Helmet Shell ... 2118
Return to Space ... 3191h
Reuter, Ernst ... 1136-1137
Revel, Bernard ... 2193
Revere, Paul ... 1048, 1059A
Rhead, Frederick Hurten ... 4546b
Rhode Island Flag ... 1645, 4319
Rhode Island Statehood ... 2348
Rhode Island Tercentenary ... 777
Rhodochrosite ... 1541
Ribault, Jan, Monument to ... 616
Rickenbacker, Eddie ... 2998
Ride, Sally ... 5283
Rigor Motor ... 5323
Riley, James Whitcomb ... 868
Ring Nebula ... 3385
Ringtail ... 2302
Rio Grande ... C134
Rio Grande Blankets ... 3926-3929
Rise of Spirit of Independence ... 1476-1479
River Otter ... 2314
Riverboats ... 3091-3095
Rivers ... 5381
Road Runner & Wile E. Coyote ... 3391-3392
Roanoke Voyages ... 2093
Robeson, Paul ... 3834
Robie House ... 3182o
Robinson, Edward G. ... 3446
Robinson, Jackie ... 2016, 3186c, 3408a
Robinson, Sugar Ray ... 4020
Robotics ... 5517
Robt. E. Lee Riverboat ... 3091
Rocket-Bye-Baby ... 5322
Rockne, Knute ... 2376
Rock 'n Roll ... 3187m
Rockville, Maryland Post Office Mural ... 5374
Rockwell, Norman ... 2839-2840, 3502s
Rocky Mountains ... 4062
Rodger Dodger ... 5324
Rodgers, Jimmie ... 1755
Rodgers, Richard & Hammerstein II, Oscar ... 3348
Roethke, Theodore ... 4663
Rogers, Fred ... 5275
Rogers, Roy ... 4446
Rogers, Will ... 975, 1801
Rohde, Gilbert ... 4546l
Rojas-Lombardi, Felipe ... 4923
Roosevelt, Eleanor ... 1236, 2105, 3185d
Roosevelt, Franklin D. ... 930-933, 1284, 1298, 1305, 1950, 2219d, 2559d, 3185a
Roosevelt, Theodore ... 557, 586, 602, 637, 663, 674, 830, 1039, 2218g, 3182b
Root Beer Float ... 5096
Roseate Spoonbill ... 2308
Rosebud Orchid ... 2670
Rose-breasted Grosbeak ... 4889
Roses ... 1737, 1876, 2378-2379, 2490, 2492, 2833, 3049, 3052E, 3054, 4520, 4959, 5280
Rosita ... 5394e
Ross, Betsy ... 1004
Rotary International ... 1066
Rothko, Mark ... 3236t, 4444c
Rough Riders ... 973
Round-lobed Hepatica ... 2677
Rowlf the Dog ... 3944i
Royal Poinciana ... 3311
Royal Wulff ... 2545
Rube Goldberg ... 3000f
Ruby-throated Hummingbird ... 2642
Rudbeckia ... 2997
Rudolph, Wilma ... 3422, 3436
Rue Anemone ... 2694
Rufous Hummingbird ... 2645
Rural America ... 1504-1506

Rural Electrification Administration 2144
Rural Free Delivery 3090
Rush Lamp and Candle Holder 1610
Rushing, Jimmy 2858
Russell, Charles M. 1243
Russell, Richard 1853
Ruth, Babe 2046, 3184a, 3408h

S Class Submarine 3373
Saber-tooth Cat 3080
Sabin, Dr. Albert 3435
Sabine Pass Lighthouse, LA 4410
Sacagawea 2869s, 2870
Saddlebred Horse 2157
Sagamore Hill 1023
Sage 4509, 4515
Saguaro 1945, 4035
Saint-Gaudens, Augustus 886
St. George Reef Lighthouse, CA 4150
St. John, VI C145
St. Joseph Lighthouse 2970
St. Lawrence Seaway 1131, 2091
St. Louis World's Fair 3182e
Saipan, Battle of 2838g
Salazar, Ruben 4251
Salk, Dr. Jonas 3428
Salomon, Haym 1561
Salsa 3940
Salt Evaporation Ponds 4710f
Salvation Army 1267
Sam the Eagle 3944c
Sampson, Adm. William T. 793
San Clemente Island Goat 5589
San Francisco Bay, Discovery of 400-400A, 404
San Francisco Garter Snake 3105k
San Francisco Maritime National Historic Park 5080g
San Francisco-Oakland Bay Bridge C36
San Francisco 49ers 3190c
San Ildefonso Pottery 1707
San Juan 1437
San Martin, Jose de 1125-1126
San Xavier del Bac Mission 1443
Sanchez, Emilio, Paintings by 5594-5597
Sancocho 5194
Sand Island Lighthouse, AL 4412
Sandburg, Carl 1731
Sandy Hook Lighthouse, NJ 1605
Saratoga, Surrender at 1728, 2590
Saroyan, William 2538
Satellite Launched 3187d
Saturn 2574, 5074
Save Our Air, Cities, Soil, Water 1410-1413
Save Vanishing Species B4
Savings & Loan 1911
Savings Bonds, 50th Anniv. 2534
Savings Bonds-Servicemen 1320
Saw-whet Owl 1761
Sawyer, Tom 1470
Saxhorns 1614
Scar from "The Lion King" 5222
Scarlet Kingsnake 3814
Scarlet Tanager 2306, 4888
Scenic American Landscapes Issue C133-C148
Schaus Swallowtail Butterfly 3105f
Schley, Adm. Winfield S. 794
Schomburg, Arturo 5472
School Bus 2123
Schurz, Carl 1847
Science Education 5276
Science & Industry 2031
Science, National Academy of 1237
Scientists 874-878, 4224-4227, 4541-4544
Scooby-Doo 5299
Scorpionfly 3351s
Scott, Blanche Stuart C99
Scott, Gen. Winfield 142, 153, 164, 175, 200, 786
Scouting 4472
Screenwriting 3772a
Scuba Diving 2863-2866
Sea Coast 3693, 3775, 3785, 3864, 3874-3875, 4348
Sea Creatures 2508-2511
Sea Cucumber 3440
Sea Lions, Northern 2509
Sea Otter 2510
Sea Shells 2117-2121, 5163-5170
Seal, Hawaiin Monk 3105c
Seamstress 1717
Seaplane 2468
Search for Peace 1326
Seashells 2117-2121
SEATO 1151
Seattle World's Fair 1196
Secretariat 3189g
Seeger, Pete 5708
Seeing Eye Dogs 1787, 4604
Sego Lily 2667
Seinfeld 3191c
Selena 4499
Selma, Ala. March 3937i
Seminole Doll 3873e
Semmes, Raphael 2975i
Senate, U.S. 2413
Seneca Carving 3873i
Sequoyah 1859
Serra, Father Junipero C116
Service Women 1013
Servicemen 1422
Servicemen-Savings Bonds 1320
Sesame Street 3189c, 5394
Sesquicentennial Exposition 627
Sessile Bellwort 2662
Sevareid, Eric 4252
Sevier, John 941
Seward, William H. 370-371
Shakespeare, William 1250
Sharkruiser 5330
Sharks 5223-5227
Sheeler, Charles 3236r, 4748h
Shepard, Alan B., Jr. 4527
Sheridan, Philip H. 787
Sherman, William T. 225, 257, 272, 787, 2975a
Shibe Park 3518
Shiloh, Battle of 1179, 2975e
Shipbuilding 1095
Shooting Star 2654
Shoshone Headdress 2505
"Shot Heard 'Round the World" 3187c
Show Boat 2767
Showy Evening Primrose 2671
Sicily, Invasion of 2765c
Sickle Cell Disease Awareness 3877
Sierra Juniper Bonsai 4618
Sign Language 2783-2784
Sikorsky, Igor C119
Silhouettes, Sppoky 5420-5423
Silver Bells Wreath 4936
Silver Centennial 1130
Silver Coffeepot 3754, 3759
Silver Surfer 4159f, 4159p
Silverstein, Shel 5683
Simpsons, The 4399-4403
Sims, Admiral William S. 4440
Sinatra, Frank 4265
SIPEX 1310-1311
Sisler, George 3408e
Sister Rosetta 3219
Sitting Bull 2183
Skagit River 5381h
Skateboarding 3321
Skating, Inline 3324
Skiing 3180
Skilled Hands for Independence 1717-1720
Skylab 1529
Skyscraper Apartments 4710n
Sleeping Bear Dunes 5258
Sleepy Hollow 1548
Sleigh 1900
Slinky 3186m
Sloan, John 1433
Smiley Face 3189m
Smiley, Guy 5394k
Smith, Alfred E. 937
Smith, Bessie 2854
Smith, Capt. John 328
Smith, Jessie Willcox 3502l
Smith, Kate 4463
Smith, Margaret Chase 3427
Smith, W. Eugene 3649n
Smithsonian Institution 943, 1838, 3059
Smokey the Bear 2096
Smooth Soloman's Seal 2691
Snake River 5381e
Snake, San Francisco Garter 3105k
Snowboarding 3323
Snowdrop 3028
Snowflakes 4808-4812, 5031-5034
Snow White & the Seven Dwarfs 3185h
Snowy Day, The 5243-5246
Snowy Egret 2321, 3829-3830D
Snowy Owl 3290
Snuffleupagus 5394l
Soapberry 5418
Soccer Ball 5205
Soccer, Youth 3401
Social Security Act 2153
Society of Philatelic Americans 797
Soda Fountain Favorites 5080a
Soft Shield Fern 4849, 4875, 4973
Softball 2962
Soil Conservation 1133
Soil and Water Conservation 2074
Sokol-Physical Fitness 1262
Solar Energy 2006
Solar Technology 5518
Songbirds 4882-4891, 5126-5129
Sonoran Desert 3293
Soo Locks 1069
Sound (film) 3772j
Sound Recording 1705
Sousa, John Philip 880
South Carolina Flag 1640, 4320
South Carolina Statehood 2343
South Carolina Tercentenary 1407
South Dakota Flag 1672, 4321
South Dakota Statehood 858, 2416
Southern Florida Wetland 4099
Southern Magnolia 3193
Southwest Carved Figure 2426
Southworth, Albert Sands & Hawes, Josiah Johnson 3649a
Space Accomplishments 1331-1332, 1529, 1556-1557, 1569-1570, 1759, 1912-1919, 2568-2577, 2631-2634, 3409-3413
Space Achievement Decade 1434-1435
Space Discovery 3238-3242
Spacecraft C122, C126a
Space Fantasy 2543, 2741-2745
Space Shuttle 1913-1914, 1917-1918, 2544-2544A, 3261-3262, 3190a, 3411a, C125, C126d
Spanish-American War 3192
Spanish Settlement In Southwest 3220
Speaker, Tris 3408l
Speaker's Stand 1582
Special Effects 3772i
Special Occasions 2267-2274, 2395-2398
Special Olympics 1788, 2142, 3191i, 3771
Special Olympics World Games 4986
Spectacle Reef Lighthouse 2971
Speedboats, Mahogany 4160-4163
Spencer, Anne 5473
Sperry, Lawrence and Elmer C114
Spicebush Swallowtail Butterfly 4736
Spider and Web 5422
Spider-man 4159a, 4159k
Spider-woman 4159g, 4159q

Spingarn, Joel Elias 4384b
Spinybacked Spider 3351q
Spirit of '76 1629-1631
Spirit of St. Louis C10
Split Rock Lighthouse 2969
Spooky Silhouettes 5420-5423
Spoonbill 4993, 4995
Sport of the Gods, The (movie) 4337
Sport Utility Vehicles 3191m
Sports, Extreme 3321-3324, 3191d
Spotted Water Beetle 3351o
Spreading Pogonia Orchid 2078
Squashes 4006, 4009, 4015
Squirrel 2489
Stagecoach 1898A, 2228, 2434, 2438a
Stagecoach (film) 2448
Staggerwing Airplane 3142j
Staghorn Coral 5366, 5368
Stamp Act, Repeal of 5064
Stamp Centenary 947
Stamp Collecting 1474, 2198-2201
Stampin' the Future 3414-3417
Stan Hywet Hall and Gardens 5462
Standing Cypress 2695
Stanley Steamer 2132
Stanton, Edwin M. 138, 149, 160, 171, 196
Stanton, Elizabeth 959
Star 3613-3615, 4749
Star and Stripes 5433
Star Fruit 4254, 4261
Star Quilts 5098-5099
Star Ribbon 5361-5362
Star Route Truck 2125
Star Trek 3188e, 5132-5135
Star Wars 4143, 5573-5582
Stargell, Willie 4696
Stars C72-C73
Stars and "6" 1892
"Stars and Stripes Forever" 3153
State and County Fairs 5401-5404
State Birds and Flowers 1953-2002, 1953A-2002A
State Flags 1633-1682
Statehood: North Dakota, South Dakota, Montana, Washington 858
Statler and Waldorf 3944e
Statue of Freedom 989, 5295-5297
Statue of Liberty 566, 696, 899, 1035, 1041-1042, 1044A, 1057, 1075, 1594, 1599, 1619, 1816, 2147, 2224, 2599, 3122, 3122E, 3451-3453, 3466, 3476-3477, 3485, 3965-3970, 3972-3975, 3978-3983, 3985, C58, C63, C80, C87
Statue of Liberty & New York Skyline C35
Statue of Liberty Replica, Las Vegas, NV 4486, 4488, 4490, 4518, 4559, 4561, 4563
Steam Carriage 2451
Steamboat Geyser 4059
Steamboats 2405-2409, 2435, 2438b
Steamship Savannah 923
Stearman Airplane 3142l
Steel Industry 1090
Stefansson, Vilhjalmur 2222
Stegosaurus 2424, 3136f
Steichen, Edward 3649g
Steinbeck, John 1773
Steiner, Max 3339
Steinmetz, Charles 2055
Stella, Joseph 4748i
Steuben, Baron Friedrich von 689
Stevens, Wallace 4660
Stevenson, Adlai E. 1275
Stewart, James 4197
Stieglitz, Alfred 3649h
Still, Clyfford 4444f
Stilwell, Gen. Joseph W. 3420
Stock Car Racing 3187n
Stock Market Crash 3184o
Stokowski, Leopold 3158
Stone Mountain Memorial 1408
Stone, Harlan Fiske 965
Stone, Lucy 1293
Stop Family Violence B3
Story, Joseph 4422d
Stourbridge Lion Locomotive 2362
Stowe, Harriet Beecher 3430
Strand, Paul 3649o
Stratford Hall 788
Stratocumulus Undulatus 3878k
Stratojet Airplane 3142h
Stratus Opacus 3878l
Stravinsky, Igor 1845
Strawberries 3296, 3299, 3305, 3405, 5201, 5491
Streamline Design 3185k
Stream Violet 2655
Streetcars 2059-2062
Stuart, Gilbert Charles 884
Studebaker Golden Hawk 4354
Studebaker Starliner 3931
Stutz Bearcat 2131
Stuyvesant, Peter 971
Sub-mariner 4159c, 4159m
Submarines 3372-3377
Submarines in Pacific 2838e
Sullivan, Anne, and Helen Keller 1824
Sullivan, Maj. Gen. John 657
Summer Harvest 5004-5007
Summer Sports 3397
Sun 3410
Sun Science 5598-5607
Sun Yat-sen 906, 1188
Sunday Funnies 4467-4471
Sunflower 4347, 5682
Sunflower and Seeds 4005, 4010, 4016
Sunshine Skyway Bridge 4649
Super Bowl I 3188l
Super Chief 3337
Supergirl 4084i, 4084s
Superman 3185f, 4084a, 4084k
Supersonic Flight 3173
Supreme Court Bicentennial 2415
Supreme Court Building 991
Supreme Court Justices 4422
Surrender of Burgoyne at Saratoga 2590
Surrender of Cornwallis at Yorktown 1686
Surrey 1907
Swallowtail Buttterfly 1712
Sweden-U.S. Treaty 2036
Swedish Chef, The 3944f
Swedish Pioneers 958
Swedish-Finnish Tercentenary 836
Sweet White Violet 2659
Switzerland, 700th Anniv. 2532
Sylvan Dell Riverboat 3092
Sylvester the Cat 3204-3205
Synthetic Fuels 2007
Szell, George 3160

2-1B Droid 5581
Taft, Robert A. 1161
Taft, William H. 685, 687, 831, 2218h
Tail Fins & Chrome 3187g
Take Me Out to the Ballgame 4341
Talking Pictures 1727
Tamales 5192
Tandem Bicycle 2266
Tanner, Henry Ossawa 1486
Tap Dance 5609-5613
Tarawa, Invasion of 2765j
Tarbell, Ida M. 3666
Taylor, Robert Robinson 4958
Taylor, Zachary 179, 181, 185, 204, 817, 2217c
Teachers 1093
Teague, Walter Dorwin 4546e
Technology Education 5277
Teddy Bear Centennial 3653-3656
Teddy Bear Created 3182k
Teen Fashions 3187b
Telegraph Centenary 924
Telephone Centenary 1683
Telescopes 3409
Television 3186f
Telly 5394n
Temple, Shirley 5060
Tennessee Flag 1648, 4322
Tennessee Statehood 941, 3070-3071
Tennessee Valley Authority 2042
Tennis 2964
Tennis Ball 5209
Terrell, Mary Church 4384a
Terry and the Pirates 3000r
Terry, Sonny 3214
Tesla, Nikola 2057
Tetherball 5632
Texaco Star Theater 4414a
Texas Flag 1660, 4323
Texas Independence 776
Texas Republic 2204
Texas Statehood 938, 2968
Thank You 2269, 5519-5522
Thanksgiving 3546
Thanksgiving Day Parade 4417-4420
Tharpe, Sister Rosetta 3219
That's All Folks 3534-3535
Thayer, Sylvanus 1852
Theodore Roosevelt National Park 5080i
Therapy Dog 4605
Thick-billed Parrot 3105b
Thinking of You 2397
Thing, The 4159d, 4159n
Third International Philatelic Exhibition 778
Thirteen-Mile Woods, NH C144
Thirteenth Amendment 902
35 Bonanza Airplane 3924
Thirty Mile Point Lighthouse 2973
Thomas, Danny 4628
Thomas Point Shoal Lighthouse, MD 5625
Thoreau, Henry David 1327, 5202
Thorpe, Jim 2089, 3183g
314 Clipper Airplane 3142r
Thresher Shark 5225
Thurber, James 2862
Tibbett, Lawrence 3156
Tickseed 2653
Tiffany Lamp 3749, 3749A, 3758, 3758A
Tiffany, Louis Comfort 4165
Tiger Stadium 3511
Tiger Swallowtail 2300
Tilghman, Bill 2869r, 2870
Tiomkin, Dimitri 3340
Titanic 3191l
Title IX Civil Rights Law 5668-5671
Tlikakila River 5381j
Tlingit Sculptures 3873c
To Form a More Perfect Union 3937
Toad, Wyoming 3105g
Tokyo Clock Tower 4985
Tokyo Raid 2697a
Toleware 1775-1778, 3612, 3756, 3756A
Tom Sawyer 1470
Tomatoes 5007, 5485
Tonight Show, The 4414r
Toonerville Folks 3000g
Torch 901, 1594, 1816, 2531A
Tortoise 5113
Toscanini, Arturo 2411
Total Solar Eclipse 5211
Tourmaline 1539
Touro Synagogue 2017
Tow Truck 2129
Toys, Antique 3626-3629, 3638-3645
Tractor 2127
Tractor Trailer 2457, 2458
Traditional Mail Delivery 2434-2438
Traffic Safety 1272
Trains 3333-3337
Transcontinental Telephone Line 3183e

Transcontinental Railroad....922, 5378-5380
Trans-Mississippi Exposition....285-293
Trans-Mississippi Philatelic Exposition....751
Trans-Mississippi Stamps, Cent.....3209-3210
Transpacific Airmail....C115
Transportation Coil Issue....1897, 1897A, 1898, 1898A, 1899-1909, 2123-2136, 2225, 2226, 2228, 2231, 2252-2266, 2451-2452, 2452B, 2452D, 2453-2454, 2457-2458, 2463-2464, 2466, 2468
Transport Plane....C25-C31
Traynor, Pie....3408o
Treaty of Paris....2052
Trees, American....1764-1767, 3193-3197
Tricycle....2126
Trident Maple Bonsai....4621
Tri-Motor Airplane....3142p
Trinity Church, Boston....1839
Troops Guarding Train....289
Trout....1427, 3105j
Trucking Industry....1025
Trudeau, Edward....3432A
True Katydid....3351p
Truman, Harry S.....1499, 1862, 2219f, 3186d
Trumbull, John....1361
Trumpet Honeysuckle....2683
Trunk Bay, St. John, VI....C145
Truth, Sojourner....2203
Tubman, Harriet....1744, 2975k
Tucker, Richard....3155
Tufted Puffins....4737-4737A
Tugboat....2260
Tulip.....2517-2520, 2524-2527, 2762, 3902, 4960, 5002, 5681
Tuna, Bluefin....2208
Turk's Cap Lily....2681
Turners, American Society of....979
TWA Terminal, New York....3910d
Twain, Mark....863, 4545
20th Century Limited....3335
Tweety Bird....3204-3205
Twilight Zone, The....4414s
Twin Mill....5326
Twinflower....2665
247 Airplane....3916
Tybee Island Lighthouse, GA....3790
Tyler, John....815, 847, 2217a
Tyrannosaurus Rex....2422, 5410-5413

U-boat Battles....2765a
Umbrella....2443
Umpqua River Lighthouse, OR....4149
Uncle Sam....3259, 3263, 3353
Uncle Sam's Hat....3260, 3264-3269, 5174, 5341
United Confederate Veterans....998
United Nations....1419, 2974
United Nations Conference....928
United Nations Secretariat....3186k
U.S. Air Force Academy....3838
U.S. Capitol....572, 992, 1590-1591, 1616, 1623, 1623B, 1809, 2114-2116, 3472, 3648, 4075b, 4983, C64-C65
U.S. Military Academy....789, 3560
U.S.-Canada Friendship....961
U.S.-Canada Peace Bridge....1721
U.S.-Japan Treaty....1158
U.S.-Morocco Diplomatic Relations....2349
U.S. Naval Academy....794, 3001
U.S.-Netherlands Diplomatic Relations....2003
U.S.-Sweden Treaty....2036
United Way....2275
United We Stand....3549-3550A
Universal Postal Congress....2434-2438, C122-C126
Universal Postal Union....1530-1537, 3332, C42-C44
Uranus....2575, 5075
Urban Planning....1333
Ursula from "The Little Mermaid"....5220
{USA{ and Jet....C75, C81
{USA{ and Star....5061, 5172
USPS Emblem....1396
USPS Emblem & Olympic Rings....2539
USS Arizona Memorial....4873
USS Constellation....3869
USS Constitution....951, 4703
USS Holland....3376
USS Missouri....5392
Utah Flag....1677, 4324
Utah Settlement....950
Utah Statehood....3024

Valens, Ritchie....2727, 2734
Valentino, Rudolph....2819
Valley Forge....645, 1729
Van Buren, Martin....813, 2216h
VanDerZee, James....3649k
Vanna Venturi House....3910c
Varela, Felix....3166
Variscite....2702
Vaughan, Sarah....5059
VCRs....3189h
Vega Airplane....3142d
Velvet Ant....3351i
Venus....2569, 5070
Venus Flytrap....3528
Vermont Flag....1646, 4325
Vermont Sesquicentennial....643
Vermont Statehood....903, 2533
Verrazano-Narrows Bridge....1258, 4052, 4872
Verville, Alfred V.....C113
Very Hungry Caterpillar, The....3987
Veterans....3508
Veterans Administration....1825
Veterans of Foreign Wars....1525
Veterans, Korean War....2152
Veterans, Viet Nam War....1802
Veterans, World War I....2154
Veterans, World War II....940
Vicksburg, Battle of....4787
Victory....537
Video Games....3190 l
Viet Nam Veterans' Memorial....2109, 3190g
Viet Nam War....3188g
Viking Missions to Mars....1759
Viking Ship....621
Villard, Oswald Garrison....4384b
Vintage Black Cinema....4336-4340
Vintage Seed Packets....4754-4763
Violins....1813
Virgin Islands Flag....4326
Virgin Islands Territory....802
Virginia Bluebells....2668
Virginia Capes, Battle of....1938
Virginia Flag....1642, 4327
Virginia Rotunda....1779
Virginia Statehood....2345
Virtual Reality....3191j
V-mail....2765e
Voice of America....1329
Volcanic Crater....4710b
Volleyball....2961, 5204
Volunteer, Lend a Hand....2039
Volunteer Firemen....971
Von Karman, Theodore....2699
Von Nessen, Greta....4546i
Von Neumann, John....3908
Voting Rights Act of 1965....3937b
Voyages of Columbus....2620-2629
Voyageurs National Park....C148

Wagner, Honus....3408q
Walk in the Water Steamboat....2409
Walker, C. J.....3181
Walker, Dr. Mary E.....2013
Wallace, Lila and DeWitt....2936
Wallenberg, Raoul....3135
Walt Disney Concert Hall....3910e
War of 1812....4703, 4805, 4921, 4952
War Savings Bonds & Stamps....2765g
Ward, Clara....3218
Warhol, Andy....3652
Warner, Pop....3144, 3149
Warren, Earl....2184
Warren, Robert Penn....3904
Washington and Lee University....982
Washington at Cambridge....617
Washington Crossing the Delaware....1688
Washington Flag....1674, 4328
Washington Mounument....2149, 3473, 4651
Washington Reviewing Army at Valley Forge....1689
Washington Statehood....858, 2404
Washington Steamboat....2408
Washington Territory....1019
Washington 2006 World Philatelic Exhibition....4075
Washington, Booker T.....873, 1074
Washington, D.C.....989-992, 2561
Washington, Dinah....2730, 2737
Washington, George....2, 4, 10-11A, 13-17, 25-26A, 31-37, 39, 41, 43-45, 47, 62B, 64-66, 68-70, 72, 74, 78-79, 82-83, 85, 85C-85E, 88-90, 94, 96-97, 99, 101, 104, 106-107, 109, 111, 115, 126, 136, 147, 158, 169, 184, 194, 207, 210-211, 211B, 213-214, 219D, 220, 248-252, 265-267, 279B, 301, 319-322, 332-342, 344-347, 349-351, 353-356, 358-366, 375-382, 384, 386, 388-389, 391, 393-396, 405-413, 423A-423E, 424-430, 441-450, 452-459, 461-469, 481-496, 498-507, 519, 525-536, 538-546, 554, 577, 579, 583, 595, 599-599A, 606, 634-634A, 660, 671, 704-715, 720-722, 785, 804, 839, 848, 854, 947-948, 1003, 1031, 1054, 1213, 1229, 1283, 1283B, 1304, 1304C, 1686, 1688-1689, 1704, 1729, 1952, 2149, 2216a, 2592, 3140, 3468A, 3475A, 3482-3483, 3616-3619, 3819, 4504, 4512, 5079a, 5079c, 5079d
Washington, Martha....306, 556, 585, 601, 636, 662, 673, 805, 840, 849
Water Conservation....1150
Water Lilies....4964-4967
Waterfowl Conservation....1362
Waterfowl Preservation Act....2092
Watermelon....5004
Waters, Ethel....2851
Waters, Muddy....2855
Watie, Stand....2975l
Watkins, Carleton E.....3649c
Waves of Color....4717-4720
Waxman, Franz....3342
Waxwing, Cedar....5127
Wayne, Gen. Anthony....680
Wayne, John....2448, 3876
Weather Vane....3257-3258, 4613-4617
Webster, Daniel....141, 152, 163, 174, 189, 199, 226, 258, 273, 282C, 283, 307, 725, 1380
Webster, Noah....1121
Wedding Cake....4398, 4521, 4602, 4735, 4867, 5000
Wedding Doves....3998-3999
Wedding Flowers....4764-4765
Wedding Hearts....4151-4152, 4271-4272
Wedding Rings....4397
Wedding Roses....4520
Wells, Ida B.....2442
West, Benjamin....1553
Western Cattle in Storm....292
Western Meadowlark....4882
Western Tanager....4884
Western Wear....5615-5618
Western Wildlife....2869p, 2870
West Point....789, 3560
West Quoddy Head Lighthouse, ME....2472
West Virginia Flag....1667, 4329
West Virginia Statehood....1232, 4790
Weston, Edward....3649j
Wetlands....3207-3207A
Whale Shark....5224
Wharton, Sr., Clifton R.....4076f
Wharton, Edith....1832
Wharton, Joseph....1920
Wheat Fields....1506
Wheatland....1081
Wheel Chair....2256
Wheels of Freedom....1162

Wheelwright........1719
Whistler, James A. McNeill........885
Whitcomb, Jon........3502n
White Bengal Tiger........2709
White House........809, 844, 1338, 1338D, 1338A, 1338F, 1338G, 2219e, 2609, 3445
White Mountain Avens........2661
White Oak........1766
White Pine........1765
White Plains, Battle of........629-630
White Sturgeon........4061
White, Josh........3215
White, Minor........3649t
White, Paul Dudley........2170
White, Walter........4384d
White, William Allen........960
White-tailed Deer........1888, 2317
White-throated Sparrow........4891
Whitman, Walt........867, 5414
Whitney, Eli........889
Whittier, John Greenleaf........865
Whooping Crane........1098, 2868
Wilbur........3988
Wildcat Airplane........3142t
Wild Columbine........2678
Wild Flax........2696
Wild Animals........2705-2709
Wild Orchids........5435-5444
Wild Pink Orchid........2076
Wild Thing........3991
Wilder, Billy........4670
Wilder, Thornton........3134
Wilderness, Battle of the........1181
Wildlife........1921-1924, 2286-2335
Wildlife Conservation........1077-1079, 1098, 1392, 1427-1430, 1464-1467, 1760-1763
Wile E. Coyote & Road Runner........3391-3392
Wiley, Harvey W.........1080
Wilkes, Lt. Charles........2387
Wilkins, Roy........3501
Willard, Frances E.........872
Williams, Hank........2723-2723A, 2771, 2775
Williams, Ted........4694
Williams, Tennessee........3002
Williams, William Carlos........4656
Willie and Joe........2765h
Willis, Frances E.........4076b
Willkie, Wendell........2192
Wills, Bob........2774, 2778
Willson, Meredith........3349
Wilson, August........5555
Wilson, Woodrow........623, 697, 832, 1040, 2218i
Win the War........905
Windmills........1738-1742
Winged Airmail Envelope........C79-C83
Winged Globe........C12, C16-C17, C19, C24
Winogrand, Garry........3649r
Winter Aconite........3026
Winter Fun........4937-4944
Winter Scenes........5532-5541
Winterberry........5415
Winterthur Garden........5466
Wisconsin Flag........1662, 4330
Wisconsin Statehood........957, 3206
Wisconsin Tercentenary........739, 755
Wisdom Statue........3766
Wizard of Oz, The........2445
Wolf Trap Farm Park........1452, 2018
Wolfe, Thomas........3444
Wolfman, The........3172
Wolverine........2327
Wolverine (comic book character)........4159j
Woman Suffrage........1406, 2980, 3184e, 5523
Women........1152
Women, Armed Services........1013, 3174
Women in Journalism........3665-3668
Women in War Effort........2697h, 3186e
Women, Progress of........959
Womens' Clubs........1316
Women's Rights Movement........3189j
Women's Rowing........5694-5697
Wonder Woman........4084c, 4084m, 5149-5152
Wonders of America........4033-4072
Wonders of the Sea........2863-2866
Wood Carvings........2240-2243
Woodchuck........2307
Wood Duck........2484-2485
Wood, Grant........3236q
Wood Lily........5672, 5675
Woodland Caribou........3105l
Woodpecker, Red-bellied........5319
Woodpecker, Red-headed........3032
Woods' Rose........5674, 5679
Woodson, Carter G.........2073
Woodstock Music Festival........3188b, 5409
Woody Wagon........3522
Wool Industry........1423
Woolly Mammoth........3078
Workman's Compensation........1186
Works Progress Administration Posters........5180-5189
World Columbian Stamp Expo........2616
World Cup Soccer Championships........2834-2837
World Peace Through Law........1576
World Peace Through World Trade........1129
World Refugee Year........1149
World Series........3182n, 3187j
World Stamp Expo '89........2410, 2433
World Stamp Show 2016........5010-5011, 5062-5063
World's Fair........853, 1196, 1244, 2006-2009, 2086, 3182e
World University Games........2748
World War I, Cent.........5300
World War I, U.S. Involvement........3183i
World War II........2559, 2697, 2765, 2838, 2981, 3186a
World War II Memorial........3862
World Wide Web........3191n
WPA Posters........5180-5189
Wright Brothers........649, C45, C47, C91-C92, 3182g, 3783
Wright, Frank Lloyd........1280
Wright, Richard........4386
Wright, Russel........4546k
Wrigley Field........3519
Wu, Chien-shiung........5557
Wulfenite........2703
Wyandotte Chicken........5584
Wyeth, Andrew........5212
Wyeth, N. C.........3502r
Wyoming Flag........1676, 4331
Wyoming Statehood........897, 2444
Wyoming Toad........3105g

X-Men........4159t
X-Planes........4018-4019

Yale Art and Architecture Building........3910i
Yankee Stadium........3513
YB-49 Flying Wing........3925
Year 2000........3369
Yellow Garden Spider........3351d
Yellow Kid........3000a
Yellow Lady's Slipper........2077, 2673
Yellow Poplar........3195
Yellow Skunk Cabbage........2693
Yellow Submarine, The Beatles........3188o
Yellow Trumpet........3529
Yellowstone National Park........744, 760, 1453, 5080n
YMCA Youth Camping........2160
Yoda........4143n, 4205
York, Sgt. Alvin C.........3395
Yorktown, Battle of........1937
Yorktown, Surrender of........703
Yorktown, Sinking of the........2697g
Yosemite Falls........4050
Yosemite National Park........740, 756, 769, 2280, C141
You Bet Your Life........4414h
Young, Cy........3408m
Young, Whitney Moore........1875
Youth Month........963
Youth, Support Our........1342
Youth Team Sports........3399-3402
Yugoslavia, Flag........917

Zaharias, Mildred Didrikson........1932
Zebra Nerite........5166, 5168
Zeppelin, Graf........C13-C15, C18
Zia Pottery........1706
Zinnia........2830, 4759
Zion National Park........747, 763, C146
ZIP Code........1511
Zoe........5394p

Additions, deletions and number changes

Number in 2022 Catalogue	Number in 2023 Catalogue
Postage	
new	442a
new	474a
new	512c
new	527d
new	554e
new	1238b
new	1727a
new	2015e
new	2562a
new	5434a
Special Delivery	
E5b	deleted
Official Stamps	
O48a	deleted
new	O49b
new	O54a
new	O56a
new	O59b
new	O74b
new	O77a
new	O82a
Vending and Affixing Machine Perforations	
new	Attleboro 343a
new	Brinkerhoff 345a
Imperforate Flat Plate Coil Stamps	
new	345V
Revenue Stamps	
R1f	deleted
new	R718a
Stock Transfer	
new	RD65a
Silver Tax	
RG129a	deleted
Narcotic Tax	
RJA59a	deleted
Embossed Revenue Stamped Paper	
RM42	RM43
new	RM42
Firearms Transfer Tax Stamps	
new	RY13
Essays	
new	79-E28i
72-E7c	deleted
new	160-E1
new	161-E2
new	165-E1
new	156-E3
new	156-E4
new	156-E4a
new	158-E2
new	158-E3
new	158-E3a
new	158-E3b
158-E2	deleted
158-E3	deleted
294-E5	294-E8
new	294-E5
new	294-E6
new	294-E7
296-E3	296-E4
new	296-E3
555-E2	555-E3
new	555-E2
new	1193-E1
new	2376-E1-E10

Number in 2022 Catalogue	Number in 2023 Catalogue
Essays	
new	2403-E1
new	2538-E1-E12
new	2545-2549-E1
new	2551-E1
new	2558-E1
new	2602-E1
new	2635-E1
new	2636-E1-E2
new	2704-E1
new	2746-E1-E2
new	2747-E1-E3
new	2749-E1
Trial Color, Die and Plate Proofs	
new	62BP2b
new	62BP2c
new	209TC6
261TC1a	deleted
261TC1ae	deleted
261ATC1a	261TC1a
261AP1	261P1
261AP2	261P2
261AP2a	261P2a
251P2	deleted
new	886P1
new	C128P1
new	J3TC1al
new	O3TC1ag
new	O11TC3b
new	O27TC3e
new	O27TC3f
new	O36TC5b
new	O57TC3a
new	O61TC3a
new	O62TC3a
new	O85TC1ah
new	O85TC1ai
PR1TC1a	PR1TCb
PR82P5	deleted
PR83P5	deleted
PR84P5	deleted
PR85P5	deleted
PR86P5	deleted
PR87P5	deleted
PR88P5	deleted
PR89P5	deleted
Specimen	
new	78S
146S B	deleted
155S B	deleted
new	146S Aa
new	147S Aa
new	148S Aa
new	149S Aa
new	150S Aa
new	152S Aa
new	152S Aa
new	157S B
new	161S B
PR57S E - PR81S E	deleted
Counterfeits	
new	4387(CF1)
Test Stamps	
new	TD120Cd
new	TD121, TD121A-TD121V
Test Booklets: Panes & Covers	
TDB80b	TDB80d
new	TDB80b
new	TDB80c
Test Stamp Essays, Trial Color, and Plate Proofs	
TD28TC2	TD28TC1d

Number in 2022 Catalogue	Number in 2023 Catalogue
Confederate Postmasters' Provisionals	
new	46XU2a
Philippines	
new	269S T
new	272S T
new	274S T
new	287AS T
new	290S T
new	291S T
new	294S T
new	295S T
new	296S T
new	297S T
new	299S T
new	300S T
new	302S T
new	340S T-353ST
340aS S-353aS S	340aS T-353aS T
new	E5aS T
E6aS S	E6aS T
new	E6S T
Puerto Rico	
new	RE7A
Ryukyus Islands	
new	18a
3X17c	deleted
3X19a	deleted
3X20b	deleted
UZE22b	UZE22a

POSTMASTERS' PROVISIONALS

The Act of Congress of March 3, 1845, effective July 1, 1845, established rates of postage as follows:

"For every single letter in manuscript or paper of any kind by or upon which information shall be asked or communicated in writing or by marks designs, conveyed in the mail, for any distance under 300 miles, five cents; and for any distance over 300 miles, ten cents; and for a double letter there shall be charged double these rates; and for a treble letter, treble these rates; and for a quadruple letter, quadruple these rates; and every letter or parcel not exceeding half an ounce in weight shall be deemed a single letter, and every additional weight of half an ounce, shall be charged with an additional single postage. All drop letters, or letters placed in any post office, not for transmission through the mail but for delivery only, shall be charged with postage at the rate of two cents each."

Circulars were charged 2 cents, magazines and pamphlets 2½ cents; newspapers according to size.

Between the time of the Act of 1845, effecting uniform postage rates, and the Act of Congress of March 3, 1847, authorizing the postmaster-general to issue stamps, postmasters in various cities issued provisional stamps.

Before adhesive stamps were introduced, prepaid mail was marked "Paid" either with pen and ink or handstamps of various designs. Unpaid mail occasionally was marked "Due." Most often, however, unpaid mail did not have a "Due" marking, only the amount of postage to be collected from the recipient, e.g. "5," "10," "18¾," etc. Thus, if a letter was not marked "Paid," it was assumed to be unpaid. These "stampless covers" are found in numerous types and usually carry the town postmark.

New York Postmaster Robert H. Morris issued the first postmaster provisional in July 1845. Other postmasters soon followed. The provisionals served until superseded by the federal government's 5c and 10c stamps issued July 1, 1847.

Postmasters recognized the provisionals as indicating postage prepaid. On several provisionals, the signature of initials of the postmaster vouched for their legitimate use.

On July 12, 1845, Postmaster Morris sent examples of his new stamp to the postmasters of Boston, Philadelphia, Albany and Washington, asking that they be treated as unpaid until they reached the New York office. Starting in that year, the New York stamps were distributed to other offices. Postmaster General Cave Johnson reportedly authorized this practice with the understanding that these stamps were to be sold for letters directed to or passing through New York. This was an experiment to test the practicality of the use of adhesive postage stamps.

ALEXANDRIA, VA.

Daniel Bryan, Postmaster

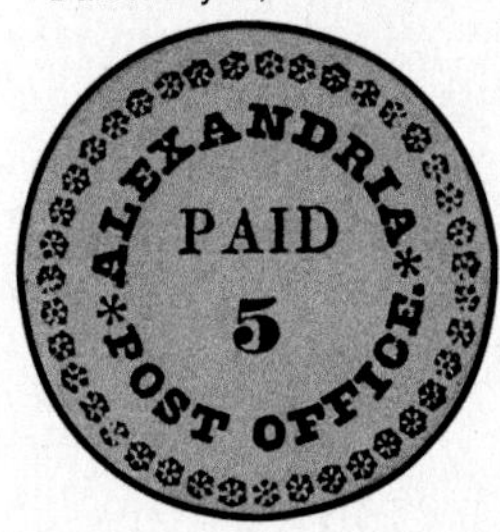

A1

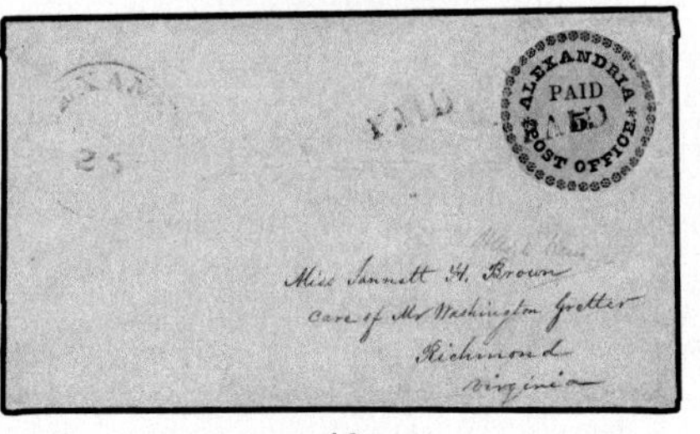

A2

All known examples are cut to shape.
Type I — 40 asterisks in circle.
Type II — 39 asterisks in circle.

1846	Typeset		Imperf.
1X1	A1 5c **black,** *buff,* type I		325,000.
a.	5c black, *buff,* type II	625,000.	
	On cover (I or II)		500,000.
1X2	A2 5c **black,** *blue,* type I, on cover		1,180,000.

Cancellations

Red circular town
Black "PAID"
Black ms. accounting number ("No. 45," "No. 70")

The approximately 6 examples of Nos. 1X1 and 1X1a known on cover or cover front are generally not tied by postmark and some are uncanceled. The value for "on cover" is for a stamp obviously belonging on a cover which bears the proper circular dated town, boxed "5" and straight line "PAID" markings.

No. 1X2 is unique. Value represents realization in a 2019 auction sale.

ANNAPOLIS, MD.

Martin F. Revell, Postmaster
ENVELOPE

E1

1846	Printed in upper right corner of envelope	
2XU1	E1 5c **carmine red,** *white*	500,000.

No. 2XU1 exists in two sizes of envelope.

Envelopes and letter sheets are known showing the circular design and figure "2" handstamped in blue or red. They were used locally. Value, blue $17,500, red $30,000.

Letter sheets are known showing the circular design and figure "5" handstamped in blue or red. Value, blue $10,000, red $12,500.

Similar circular design in blue without numeral or "PAID" is known to have been used as a postmark.

BALTIMORE, MD.

James Madison Buchanan, Postmaster

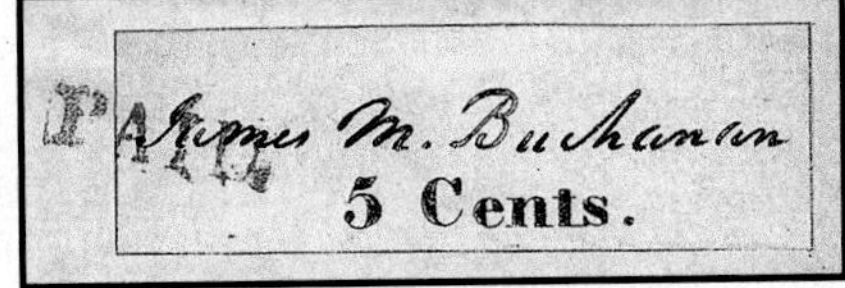

Signature of Postmaster — A1

Printed from a plate of 12 (2x6) containing nine 5c stamps (Pos. 1-6, 8, 10, 12) and three 10c (Pos. 7, 9, 11). The thin horizontal and vertical lines between stamps are not frame lines. Rather, they are dividing lines between stamps.

1845	Engr.		Imperf.
3X1	A1 5c **black**		6,000.
	On cover		12,500.
	Vertical pair on cover		75,000.
3X2	A1 10c **black,** on cover		80,000.
3X3	A1 5c **black,** *bluish*	65,000.	8,000.
	On cover		12,500.
3X4	A1 10c **black,** *bluish*		50,000.
	On cover		—

Earliest documented uses: Jan. 15, 1846 (No. 3X1); Aug. 3, 1845 (No. 3X3).

Nos. 3X3-3X4 preceded Nos. 3X1-3X2 in use.

No. 3X3 unused is unique. Value is based on 1997 auction sale.

Cancellations

Blue circular town
Blue straight line
"PAID"
Blue "5" in oval
Blue "10" in oval
Black pen

Off cover values are for stamps canceled by either pen or handstamp. Stamps on covers tied by handstamps command premiums.

Envelopes

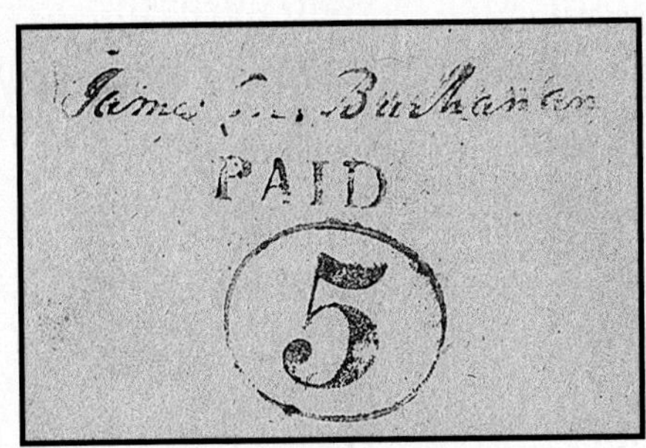

E1

Three Separate Handstamps

The "PAID" and "5" in oval were handstamped in blue or red, always both in the same color on the same entire. "James M. Buchanan" was handstamped in black, blue or red. Blue town and rate with black signature was issued first and sells for more.

The paper is manila, buff, white, salmon or grayish. Manila is by far the most frequently found 5c envelope. All 10c envelopes are rare, with manila or buff the more frequent. Of the 10c on salmon, only one example is known.

The general attractiveness of the envelope and the clarity of the handstamps primarily determine the value.

The color listed is that of the "PAID" and "5" in oval.

1845	Various Papers	Handstamped
3XU1	E1 5c **blue**	4,500.
3XU2	E1 5c **red**	10,000.
3XU3	E1 10c **blue**	20,000.
3XU4	E1 10c **red**	20,000.

Earliest documented uses: Sept. 7, 1845 (No. 3UX1); Apr. 27, 1846 (No. 3XU2); Nov. 16, 1845 (No. 3XU3); June 12, 1846 (No. 3XU4).

Cancellations

Blue circular town
Blue "5" in oval

The second "5" in oval on the unlisted "5 + 5" envelopes is believed not to be part of the basic prepaid marking, but envelopes bearing this marking merit a premium over the values for Nos. 3XU1-3XU2.

BOSCAWEN, NH.

Worcester Webster, Postmaster

A1

1846 (?) **Typeset** ***Imperf.***

4X1 A1 5c **dull blue,** *yellowish,* on cover *300,000.*

One example known, uncanceled on cover with ms. postal markings.

BRATTLEBORO, VT.

Frederick Niles Palmer, Postmaster

Initials of Postmaster (FNP) — A1

Printed from plate of 10 (5x2) separately engraved subjects with imprint "Eng'd by Thos. Chubbuck, Bratto." below the middle stamp of the lower row (Pos. 8). There are thin horizontal and vertical lines outside the thicker frame lines. These thin lines are dividing lines between stamps, not frame lines.

1846 ***Imperf.***

Thick Softwove Paper Colored Through

5X1 A1 5c **black,** *buff*	*7,500.*
On cover	*17,500.*
Two singles on cover	*230,000.*

Earliest documented use: Aug. 28, 1846.

The cover bearing two singles of No. 5X1 is unique. Value reflects 2007 auction sale.

Cancellations

Red straight line "PAID"
Red pen
Blue "5" (unique)
Red grid (unique)

The red pen-marks are small and lightly applied. They were used to invalidate a single sample sheet. One example of each plate position is known so canceled.

LOCKPORT, N.Y.

Hezekiah W. Scovell, Postmaster

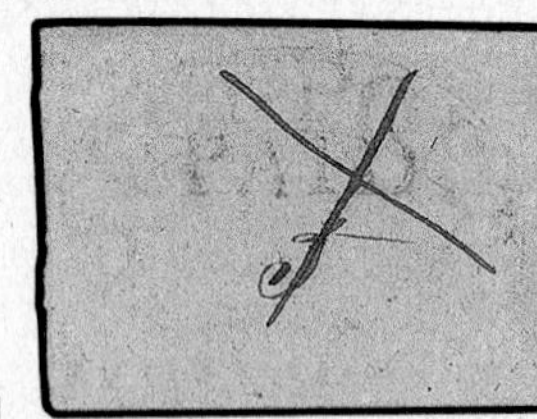

A1

"Lockport, N.Y." oval and "PAID" separately handstamped in red, "5" in black ms.

1846 ***Imperf.***

6X1 A1 5c **red,** *buff,* on cover *120,000.*

Cancellation

Black ms. "X"

No. 6X1 is unique. Value is based on a 2020 auction sale.

Small fragments of two other stamps adhering to one cover also exist.

MILLBURY, MASS.

Asa H. Waters, Postmaster

George Washington — A1

Printed from a woodcut, singly, on a hand press.

1846 ***Imperf.***

7X1 A1 5c **black,** *bluish*	—	*50,000.*
On cover		*250,000.*

Earliest documented use: Aug. 21, 1846.

Cancellations

Red straight line "PAID"
Red circular "MILBURY, MS.," date in center

NEW HAVEN, CONN.

Edward A. Mitchell, Postmaster
ENVELOPES

E1

Impressed from a brass handstamp at upper right of envelope.

Signed in blue, black or magenta ms., as indicated in parentheses.

1845

8XU1 E1 5c **red** (M)	*100,000.*
Cut square	*50,000.*
Cut to shape	*15,000.*
8XU2 E1 5c **red,** *light bluish* (Bk)	*125,000.*
8XU3 E1 5c **dull blue,** *buff* (Bl)	*75,000.*
Cut to shape (Bk)	*55,000.*
8XU4 E1 5c **dull blue** (Bl)	*60,000.*

Values of Nos. 8XU1-8XU4 are a guide to value. They are based on auction realizations and other sales, and take condition into consideration. All New Haven envelopes are of equal rarity (each is unique), with the exception of No. 8XU2, of which two exist. An entire of No. 8XU2 is the finest example known, and this is reflected in the value shown. The other envelopes are valued according to condition, and cut squares also are valued according to condition as much as rarity.

REPRINTS

Twenty reprints in dull blue on white paper, signed by E. A. Mitchell in lilac rose ink, were made in 1871 for W. P. Brown and others, value $1,750. Thirty reprints in carmine on hard white paper, signed in dark blue, red or black (rare), were made in 1874 for Cyrus B. Peets, Chief Clerk for Mitchell, value $1,200. Unsigned reprints in dull red on soft yellowish white paper were made for N. F. Seebeck and others about 1872, value $400.

Edward A. Mitchell, grandson of the Postmaster, in 1923 delivered reprints in lilac on soft white wove paper, dated "1923" in place of the signature, value $400.

In 1932, the New Haven Philatelic Society bought the original handstamp and gave it to the New Haven Colony Historical Society. To make the purchase possible (at the $1000 price) it was decided to print 260 stamps from the original handstamp. Of these, 130 were in red and 130 in dull blue, all on hard, white wove paper, value approximately $250 each.

According to Carroll Alton Means' booklet on the New Haven Provisional Envelope, after this last reprinting the brass handstamp was so treated that further reprints cannot be made. The reprints were sold originally at $5 each. A facsimile signature of the postmaster, "E. A. Mitchell," (blue on the red reprints, black on the blue) was applied with a rubber handstamp. These 260 reprints are all numbered to correspond with the number of the booklet issued then.

NEW YORK, N.Y.

Robert H. Morris, Postmaster

George Washington — A1

Printed by Rawdon, Wright & Hatch from a plate of 40 (5x8). The die for Washington's head on the contemporary bank notes was used for the vignette. It had a small flaw—a line extending from the corner of the mouth down the chin—which is quite visible on the paper money. This was corrected for the stamp.

The stamps were usually initialed "ACM" (Alonzo Castle Monson) in magenta ink as a control before being sold or passed through the mails. There are four or five styles of these initials. The most common is "ACM" without periods. The scarcest is "A.C.M.", believed written by Marcena Monson. The rare initials "RHM" (Robert H. Morris, the postmaster) and "MMJr" (Marcena Monson) are listed separately.

The stamps were printed on a variety of wove papers varying in thickness from pelure to thick, and in color from gray to bluish and blue. A thick brown gum was used first, succeeded by a thin whitish transparent gum. Some stamps appear to have a slight ribbing or mesh effect. A few also show letters of a double-line papermaker's watermark, a scarce variety. All used true blue copies carry "ACM" without periods; of the three unused copies, two lack initials.

Nos. 9X1-9X3 and varieties unused are valued without gum. Examples with original gum are extremely scarce and will command higher prices.

Earliest documented use: July 15, 1845 (No. 9X1e).

1845-46 **Engr.** **Bluish Wove Paper** ***Imperf.***

9X1 A1 5c **black,** signed ACM, connected, *1846*	1,500.	450.
On cover		550.
On cover to France or England		*2,200.*
On cover to other European countries		*5,500.*
Pair	5,750.	1,400.
Pair on cover		2,000.
Pair on cover to England		*4,500.*
Pair on cover to Canada		*5,500.*
Vertical pair, 9X1 and 9X1e	*85,000.*	
Strip of 3		*5,000.*
Strip of 3 on cover		*9,000.*
Strip of 4	*12,500.*	
Strip of 4 on cover		*85,000.*
Block of 4		*50,000.*
Double transfer at bottom (Pos. 2)	1,700.	525.
Double transfer at top (Pos. 7)	1,700.	525.
Bottom frame line double (Pos. 31)	1,700.	525.
Top frame line double (Pos. 36)	1,700.	525.

The unused pair of Nos. 9X1 and 9X1e is unique.

The only blocks currently known are a used block of 4 off cover (faulty), a repaired block of 6 on cover, and a block of 9 on cover.

Cancellations

Blue pen		450.
Black pen		+25.
Magenta pen		+100.
Red square grid (New York)		+100.
Black circular date stamp		—
Red round grid (Boston)		+350.
Blue numeral (Philadelphia)		+750.
Red "U.S" in octagon frame (carrier)		+1,200.
Red "PAID"		+90.
Red N.Y. circular date stamp		+150.
Large red N.Y. circular date stamp containing "5"		+125.
Small red "5"		—
Large red "5"		+1,000.
a. Signed ACM, AC connected	1,750.	525.
On cover		675.
On cover to France or England		*2,250.*
On cover to other European countries		*6,000.*
Pair	5,750.	1,700.
Pair, on cover		*2,200.*
Strip of 4, on cover		*100,000.*
Pair, Nos. 9X1, 9X1a	—	*5,000.*
Pair, Nos. 9X1 and 9X1a, on cover		*15,000.*
Double transfer at bottom (Pos. 2)	1,800.	650.
Double transfer at top (Pos. 7)	1,800.	650.
Bottom frame line double (Pos. 31)	1,800.	650.
Top frame line double (Pos. 36)	1,800.	650.

Cancellations

Blue pen		550.
Black pen		+25.
Magenta pen		+100.
Red N.Y. circular date stamp		+125.
Large red N.Y. circular date stamp with "5"		+150.
Red square grid		+100.
Red "PAID"		+60.
b. Signed A.C.M.	*4,500.*	*675.*
On cover		*825.*
On cover to France or England		*2,750.*

On cover to other European countries		6,000.
Pair		2,400.
Pair on cover		3,250.
Double transfer at bottom (Pos. 2)	—	925.
Double transfer at top (Pos. 7)	—	925.
Bottom frame line double (Pos. 31)		925.
Top frame line double (Pos. 36)		925.

Cancellations

Blue pen	675.
Black pen	+25.
Red square grid	+100.
Red N.Y. circular date stamp	+100.
Large red N.Y. circular date stamp containing "5"	+150.
Red "PAID"	+75.

c.	Signed MMJr		10,000.
	On cover		—
	Pair on cover front		26,500.

The No. 9X1c pair on cover front is unique. Value reflects auction sale price in 1992.

d.	Signed RHM	13,000.	3,500.
	Pair		12,000.
	On cover		5,500.
	On cover from New Hamburgh, N.Y.		12,500.

Cancellations

Blue pen	3,500.
Black pen	+150.
Red square grid	+250.
Red N.Y. circular date stamp	+400.
Red "PAID"	+300.

Earliest documented use: July 17, 1845.

e.	Without signature	3,750.	900.
	On cover		1,250.
	On cover to France or England		2,500.
	On cover to other European countries		6,000.
	On cover, July 15, 1845		27,500.
	Pair		2,600.
	Pair on cover		2,900.
	Double transfer at bottom (Pos. 2)	4,000.	1,000.
	Double transfer at top (Pos. 7)	4,000.	1,000.
	Bottom frame line double (Pos. 31)	4,000.	1,000.
	Top frame line double (Pos. 36)	4,000.	1,000.
	Ribbed paper	—	—

Cancellations

Blue pen	900.
Black pen	+25.
Magenta pen	+100.
Red square grid	+100.
Red N.Y. circular date stamp	+100.
Large red N.Y. circular date stamp containing "5"	+150.
Red "PAID"	+100.

Known used from Albany, Boston, Jersey City, N.J., New Hamburgh, N.Y., Philadelphia, Sing Sing, N.Y., Washington, D.C., and Hamilton, Canada, as well as by route agents on the Baltimore R.R. Covers originating in New Hamburgh are known only with No. 9X1d (one also bearing the U.S. City Despatch Post carrier); one also known used to Holland.

1847 Engr. Blue Wove Paper *Imperf.*

9X2	A1 5c **black,** signed ACM connected	6,500.	4,000.
	On cover		5,750.
	Pair		13,000.
	Pair on cover		—
	Double transfer at bottom (Pos. 2)		4,250.
	Double transfer at top (Pos. 7)		4,250.
	Bottom frame line double (Pos. 31)		4,250.
	Top frame line double (Pos. 36)		4,250.
a.	Signed RHM		—
b.	Signed ACM, AC connected		8,000.
d.	Without signature	25,000.	7,500.

Earliest documented use: Mar. 4, 1847.

Cancellations

Red square grid	3,750.
Red "PAID"	+100.
Red N.Y. circular date stamp	+650.

All used true blue examples carry "ACM" without periods; of the three unused examples, two lack initials.

On the only example known of No. 9X2a the "R" is illegible and does not match those of the other "RHM" signatures.

No. 9X2b is unique.

1847 Engr. Gray Wove Paper *Imperf.*

9X3	A1 5c **black,** signed ACM connected	5,250.	3,250.
	On cover		5,250.
	On cover to Europe		8,500.
	Pair		7,750.
	Pair on cover		8,750.
	Double transfer at bottom (Pos. 2)		2,600.
	Double transfer at top (Pos. 7)		2,600.
	Bottom frame line double (Pos. 31)		2,600.
	Top frame line double (Pos. 36)		2,600.
a.	Signed RHM		8,500.
b.	Without signature		13,000.

Earliest documented use: Feb. 8, 1847.

Cancellations

Red square grid	2,250.
Red N.Y. circular date stamp	2,250.
Red "PAID"	+100.

All known used examples of No. 9X3a have red square grid or red "PAID" in arc cancel.

The first plate was of nine subjects (3x3). Each subject differs slightly from the others, with Position 8 showing the white stock shaded by crossed diagonal lines. At some point prints were struck from this plate in black on deep blue and white bond paper, as well as in blue, green, scarlet and brown on white bond paper. These are listed in the Proof and Trial Color Proof sections. Stamps from this plate were not issued, and it is possible that it is an essay, as the design differs slightly from the issued stamps from the sheet of 40. No examples from the plate of nine are known used.

ENVELOPES

Postmaster Morris, according to newspaper reports of July 2 and 7, 1845, issued envelopes. The design was not stated and no example has been seen. It is possible that these items were envelopes to which stamps had been affixed.

PROVIDENCE, R.I.

Welcome B. Sayles, Postmaster

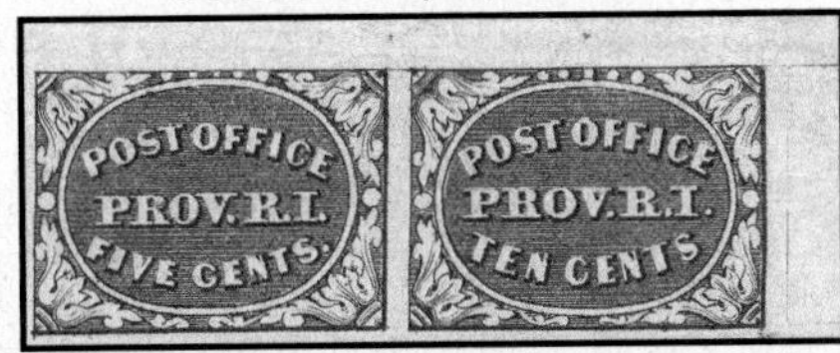

A1 & A2

Engraved on copper plate containing 12 stamps (3x4). Upper right corner stamp (Pos. 3) "TEN"; all others "FIVE." The stamps were engraved directly on the plate, each differing from the other. The "TEN" and Pos. 4, 5, 6, 9, 11 and 12 have no period after "CENTS."

Yellowish White Handmade Paper

Earliest documented use: Aug. 25, 1846 (No. 10X1).

1846, Aug. 24 *Imperf.*

10X1	A1 5c **gray black**	350.	2,250.
	No gum	200.	
	On cover, tied by postmark		21,500.
	On cover, tied by pen cancel		11,000.
	On cover, pen canceled		7,000.
	Two on cover		—
	Pair	725.	
	Block of four	1,450.	
10X2	A2 10c **gray black**	1,150.	16,500.
	No gum	700.	
	On cover, pen canceled		45,000.
a.	Se-tenant with 5c	2,000.	
	Complete sheet	5,500.	
	No gum	3,500.	

Cancellations

Black pen check mark
Red circular town
Red straight line "PAID" (2 types)
Red "5"

All canceled examples of Nos. 10X1-10X2, whether or not bearing an additional handstamped cancellation, are obliterated with a black pen check mark. There is only one known certified used example off cover of No. 10X2, and it has a minor fault. Value represents a 1997 sale. All genuine covers must bear the red straight line "PAID," the red circular town postmark, and the red numeral "5" or "10" rating mark.

The reprints with no printing on the reverse can be determined by their size, which is approximately 27.3x21.5mm, whereas the original stamps are approximately 28x20mm in size.

Beware of fakes of Nos. 10X1 and 10X2, which are fairly common. The genuine stamps are engraved, whereas most fakes are lithographed. On the fakes, the "O" in "PROV." is smaller and somewhat misshapen, especially on the inner right side, as shown below.

Reprints were made in 1898. In general, each stamp bears one of the following letters on the back: B O G E R T D U R B I N. However, some reprint sheets received no such printing on the reverse. All reprints are without gum. Value for 5c, $75; for 10c, $190; for sheet, $1,250. Reprints without the printing on the reverse sell for more.

"O" in "PROV." smaller and somewhat misshapen on the fakes.

ST. LOUIS, MO.

John M. Wimer, Postmaster

A1

A2

Missouri Coat of Arms — A3

Printed from a copper plate of 6 (2x3) subjects separately engraved by J. M. Kershaw.

The plate in its first state, referred to as Plate 1, comprised: three 5c stamps in the left vertical row and three 10c in the right vertical row. The stamps vary slightly in size, measuring from 17¾ to 18¼ by 22 to 22½mm.

Later a 20c denomination was believed necessary. So two of the 5c stamps, types I (pos. 1) and II (pos. 3) were changed to 20c by placing the plate face down on a hard surface and hammering on the back of the parts to be altered until the face was driven flush at those points. The new numerals were then engraved. Both 20c stamps show broken frame lines and the paw of the rights bear on type II is missing. The 20c type II (pos. 3) also shows retouching in the dashes under "SAINT" and "LOUIS." The characteristics of types I and II of the 5c also serve to distinguish the two types of the 20c. This altered, second state of the plate is referred to as Plate 2. It is the only state to contain the 20c.

The demand for the 20c apparently proved inadequate, and the plate was altered again. The "20" was erased and the "5" engraved in its place, resulting in noticeable differences from the 5c stamps from Plate 1. In type I (pos. 1) reengraved, the "5" is twice as far from the top frame line as in the original state, and the four dashes under "SAINT" and "LOUIS" have disappeared except for about half of the upper dash under each word. In type II (pos. 3) reengraved, the ornament in the flag of the "5" is a diamond instead of a triangle; the diamond in the bow is much longer than in the first state, and the ball of the "5," originally blank, contains a large dot. At right of the shading of the "5" is a short curved line which is evidently a remnant of the "0" of "20." Type III (pos. 5) of the 5c was slightly retouched. This second alteration of the plate is referred to as Plate 3.

Type characteristics common to Plates 1, 2 and 3:

5 Cent. Type I (pos. 1). Haunches of both bears almost touch frame lines.

Type II (pos. 3). Bear at right almost touches frame line, but left bear is about ¼mm from it.

Type III (pos. 5). Haunches of both bears about ½mm from frame lines. Small spur on "S" of "POST."

10 Cent. Type I (pos. 2). Three dashes below "POST OFFICE."

Type II (pos. 4). Three pairs of dashes.

Type III (pos. 6). Pairs of dashes (with rows of dots between) at left and right. Dash in center with row of dots above it.

20 Cent. Type I. See 5c Type I.

Type II. See 5c Type II.

Nos. 11X1-11X8 unused are valued without gum.

Values for used off-cover examples of Nos. 11X1-11X8 are for pen-canceled examples. Handstamp-canceled stamps sell for much more. Values for stamps on cover are for examples with pen cancels. Covers with the stamps tied by handstamp sell at considerable premiums depending upon the condition of the stamps and the general attractiveness of the cover. In general, covers with multiple frankings (unless separately valued) are valued at the "on cover" value of the highest-valued stamp, plus the "off cover" value of the other stamps.

Earliest documented use of St. Louis "Bears": Nov. 13, 1845 (No. 11X2).

Wove Paper Colored Through

1845, Nov.-1846 *Imperf.*

11X1	A1 5c **black,** *greenish*	47,500.	8,000.
	On cover		17,500.
	Pair	—	18,000.
	Two on cover		25,000.
	Strip of 3		35,000.
	Strip of 3 plus single on cover		45,000.
11X2	A2 10c **black,** *greenish*	47,500.	8,000.
	On cover		14,000.
	Pair		18,000.
	Pair on cover		22,500.
	Strip of 3		32,500.
	Strip of 3 on cover		70,000.
	Five on cover		225,000.
	On cover, #11X2, 11X6		125,000.
11X3	A3 20c **black,** *greenish*		160,000.
	On cover		—
	On cover, #11X5, two #11X3		325,000.

Printed from Plate 1 (3 varieties each of the 5c and 10c) and Plate 2 (1 variety of the 5c, 3 of the 10c, 2 of the 20c).

1846

No.	Description	Unused	Used
11X4	A1 5c **black,** (III), *gray lilac*	—	*50,000.*
	On cover		—
11X5	A2 10c **black,** *gray lilac*	*50,000.*	*11,500.*
	On cover		*16,000.*
	Pair		*29,000.*
	Pair, 10c (III), 5c (III)		*90,000.*
	Strip of 3		*52,500.*
	Strip of 3 on cover		*160,000.*
	Pair 10c (II), 10c (III) se-tenant with 5c (III)		*70,000.*
	Strip of 3 10c (I, II, III) se-tenant with 5c (III)		*300,000.*

Earliest documented use: Feb. 27, 1846.

No.	Description	Unused	Used
11X6	A3 20c **black,** *gray lilac*	*100,000.*	*60,000.*
	On cover		*70,000.*
	Pair		*130,000.*
	Pair on cover		*145,000.*
	On cover, #11X6 and #11X5		*75,000.*
	On cover, #11X6 and 2 #11X4, tied by handstamp cancel (unique)		*125,000.*
	Pair, #11X6 and #11X5		*155,000.*
	Pair, #11X6 and #11X5, on cover		*210,000.*
	Strip of 3, 2#11X6 and #11X4		*175,000.*

Printed from Plate 2 (1 variety of the 5c, 3 of the 10c, 2 of the 20c).

No. 11X6 unused is unique. It is in the grade of fine and is valued thus.

The used pair of No. 11X6 is unique. The left margin cuts into the frameline, and it is valued thus.

1847 **Pelure Paper**

No.	Description	Unused	Used
11X7	A1 5c **black,** *bluish*	—	*11,000.*
	On cover		*16,000.*
	Pair		*40,000.*
	Two on cover		*37,500.*
11X8	A2 10c **black,** *bluish*	*17,500.*	*15,000.*
	On cover		*20,000.*
a.	Impression of 5c on back		*77,500.*

Printed from Plate 3 (3 varieties each of the 5c, 10c).
Earliest documented use: Nov. 25, 1846 (#11X8).
No. 11X8 unused is unique. No. 11X8a is unique.

Cancellations, Nos. 11X1-11X8

Black pen
Ms. initials of postmaster (#11X2, type I)
Red circular town
Red straight line "PAID"
Red grid (#11X7)

Values of Nos. 11X7-11X8, on and off cover, reflect the usual poor condition of these stamps, which were printed on fragile pelure paper. Attractive examples with minor defects sell for considerably more.

POSTAGE

GENERAL ISSUES

Please Note:

Stamps are valued in the grade of very fine unless otherwise indicated.

Values for early and valuable stamps are for examples with certificates of authenticity from acknowledged expert committees, or examples sold with the buyer having the right of certification. This applies to examples with original gum as well as examples without gum. Beware of stamps offered "as is," as the gum on some unused stamps offered with "original gum" may be fraudulent, and stamps offered as unused without gum may in some cases be altered or faintly canceled used stamps.

Color Cancellations

Additional values for color cancellations listed in the "cancellations" section after stamps from No. 1 through No. 218 are for full or nearly full unfaded strikes on very fine stamps. Premiums for such strikes on extremely fine or superb stamps often are much larger, and premiums for strikes on stamps in grades lower than very fine are smaller.

Issues from 1847 through 1894 are unwatermarked.

Benjamin Franklin — A1

Double transfer of top frame line — (A) position 80R1

Double transfer of top and bottom frame lines — (B) position 90R1

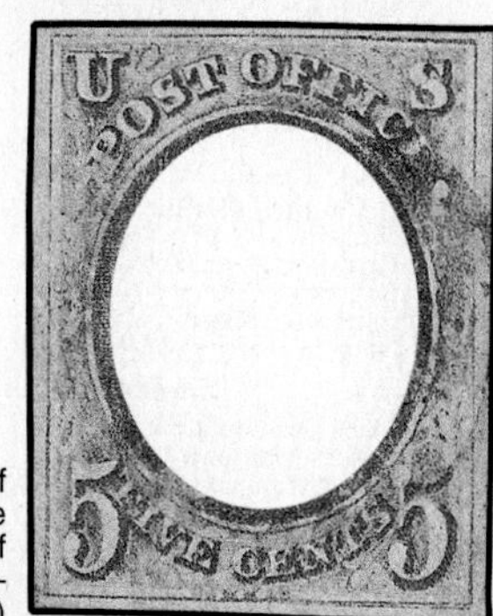

Double transfer of bottom frame line and lower part of left frame line — (C)

Double transfer of top, bottom and left frame lines, also numerals — (D)

Double transfer of "U," "POST OFFICE" and left numeral — (E)

Double transfer of top frame line, upper part of side frame lines, "U," and "POST OFFICE" — (F)

This issue was authorized by an Act of Congress, approved March 3, 1847, to take effect July 1, 1847, from which date the use of Postmasters' Stamps or any which were not authorized by the Postmaster General became illegal.

This issue was declared invalid as of July 1, 1851.

Produced by Rawdon, Wright, Hatch & Edson.
Plates of 200 subjects in two panes of 100 each.

1847, July 1 **Engr.** ***Imperf.***

Thin Bluish Wove Paper

No.	Description	Unused	Used
1	A1 5c **red brown**	6,000.	425.
	pale brown	6,000.	425.
	brown	6,500.	425.
	No gum	2,100.	
	On cover		500.
	On cover to England or France		2,500.
	On cover to other European countries		3,000.
	Pair	15,000.	950.
	Pair on cover		1,150.
	Strip of 3	*25,000.*	2,150.
	Strip of 4		5,000.
	Block of 4	*50,000.*	*27,500.*
	Block of 4 on cover		*80,000.*
	Dot in "S" in upper right corner	7,000.	500.
	Cracked plate (69R1)		*2,000.*
	Recut left frame line	—	*1,150.*
a.	5c **dark brown**	7,000.	525.
	No gum	2,400.	
	On cover		625.
	Pair	*21,000.*	1,250.
	Block of 4	*55,000.*	*60,000.*
	Block of 4 on cover		25,000.
	grayish brown	9,000.	625.
	No gum	3,500.	
	Pair		1,500.
	blackish brown	10,000.	*1,500.*
	No gum	3,750.	

		Unused	Used
	Pair	*25,000.*	*3,250.*
b.	5c **orange brown**	10,000.	675.
	No gum	3,500.	
	On cover		775.
	Pair		1,800.
	Block of 4 on cover		*240,000.*
c.	5c **red orange**	*25,000.*	*8,500.*
	No gum	*9,500.*	
	On cover		*10,000.*
	Pair		*30,000.*
d.	5c **brown orange**	—	1,000.
	No gum	*4,500.*	
	On cover		1,150.
	Pair on cover		—
	Dot in "S" in upper right corner		*1,250.*
(A)	Double transfer of top frame line (80R1)		800.
(B)	Double transfer of top and bottom frame lines (90R1)	*50,000.*	800.
	No gum	*5,000.*	
(C)	Double transfer shows best on bottom frame line and lower part of left frame line, also shows on top and right frame lines and in "5"s and "Five Cents"		*8,500.*
(D)	Double transfer on all frame lines (most noticeable at top right and lower left corners), also numerals	—	*11,000.*
(E)	Double transfer of "U," "POST OFFICE" and left numeral		*1,750.*
	On cover		*3,500.*
(F)	Double transfer of top frame line, upper part of side frame lines, "U," and "POST OFFICE"		*10,000.*

The "B double transfer" with original gum is in a pair and is valued thus. A second example with original gum is known, a single with faults.

The unused "D" double transfer is unique. It is in a block of 4 and is cut in at the top.

Some students believe that the "E double transfer" actually shows plate scratches instead.

Three blocks of 4 on cover exist for the 5c first issue, as listed. The No. 1 cover on a rebacked cover front to Canada, the No. 1a on reverse of cover to England, and the No. 1b to Albany, NY. Values are based on recent auction sales and reflect usages and condition.

Earliest documented use: July 7, 1847.

Cancellations

Red	425.
Red town	+150.
Orange red	+50.
Orange red town	+220.
Blue	+40.
Blue town	+125.
Black	+75.
Black town	+300.
Magenta	+275.
Orange	+750.
Ultramarine	+900.
Violet	+1,000.
Violet town	—
Green	+1,250.
"Paid"	+50.
"Paid" in grid (demonetized usage)	+300.
"Free"	+400.
Railroad	+200.
U. S. Express Mail (on the cover)	+100.
U. S. Express Mail (on stamp)	—
U. S. Express Mail in black (on stamp) (demonetized usage)	+12,500.
"Way"	+250.
"Way" with numeral	+500.
"Steamboat"	+350.
"Steam"	+200.
"Steamship"	+300.
Philadelphia RR	+250.
On cover	+500.
Hotel (on the cover)	*+2,000.*
Numeral	+100.
Canada	+3,000.
Wheeling, Va., grid	+25,000.
Pen Cancel	250.

George Washington — A2

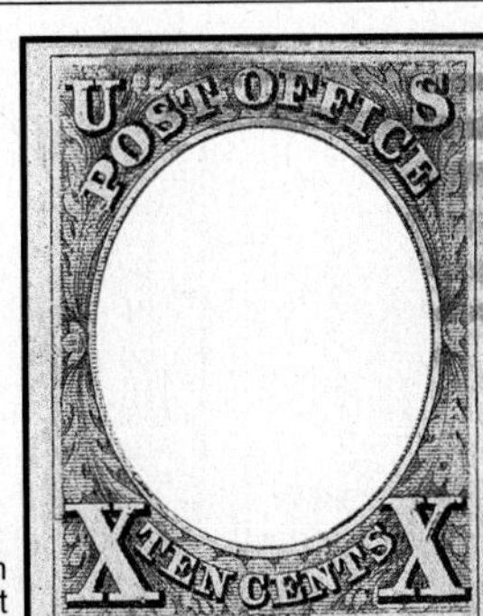
Double transfer in "X" at lower right — (A)

Double transfer in "Post Office" — (B)

Double transfer in "X" at lower left and lower right, plus bottom frame line — (C)

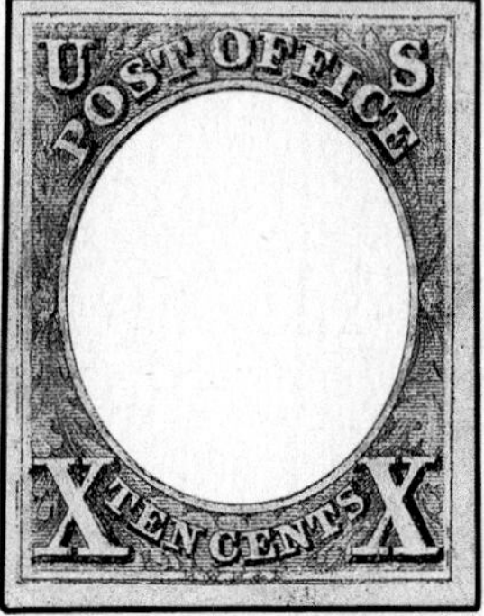

Double transfer of left and bottom frame lines plus parts of frame lines at top right and bottom right. Much of the lettering plus the left "X" also affected. — (D)

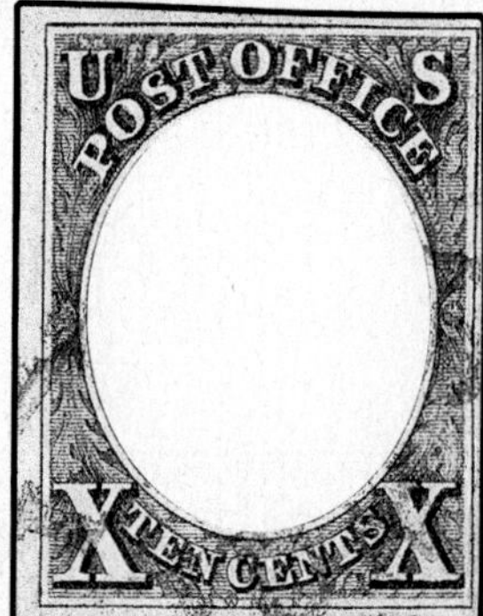

Double transfer of several letters at top, also top frame line recut — (E)

No.	Description	Unused	Used
2	A2 10c **black**	37,500.	900.
	gray black	37,500.	900.
	No gum	16,000.	
	greenish black	—	—
	On cover		1,200.
	On cover to Canada		1,750.
	On cover to Great Britain		3,250.
	On cover to France		*5,250.*
	On cover with 5c No. 1, singles of each, paying separate rates		*50,000.*
	On cover with 5c No. 1, singles of each, paying triple 5-cent rate		*7,500.*
	Pair	90,000.	2,750.
	Pair on cover		*3,250.*
	Strip of 3	125,000.	*10,000.*
	Block of 4	500,000.	*75,000.*
	Short transfer at top	40,000.	1,150.
	Vertical line through second "F" of "OFFICE" (68R1)	—	1,800.
	With "Stick Pin" in tie (52L1)	—	3,000.
	With "harelip" (57L1)	—	2,750.
a.	Diagonal half used as 5c on cover		*12,500.*
b.	Vertical half used as 5c on cover		*30,000.*
c.	Horizontal half used as 5c on cover		*30,000.*
(A)	Double transfer in "X" at lower right (1R1)	52,500.	1,650.
(B)	Double transfer in "Post Office" (31R1)	—	*4,000.*
(C)	Double transfer in "X" at lower left and lower right, plus bottom frame line (2R1)	—	*3,250.*
(D)	Double transfer of left and bottom frame line (41R1)	—	2,250.
(E)	Double Transfer of several letters at top, also top frame line recut		2,250.

Earliest documented use: July 2, 1847.

Two examples of the unused block are recorded, only one of which is available to collectors.

The value for the used block of 4 represents a block with manuscript cancel. One block is recorded with a handstamp cancellation and it is worth significantly more.

Cancellations

Red	900.
Red town	+150.
Orange red	+100.
Blue	+50.
Orange	+500.
Black	+250.
Magenta	+650.
Violet	+950.
Green	+3,250.
Ultramarine	+1,500.
"Paid"	+100.
"Paid" in grid (demonetized usage)	+400.
"Free"	+900.
Railroad	+1,000.
Philadelphia RR straightline	+500.
U.S. Express Mail (on the cover)	+500.
"Way"	+550.
Numeral	+250.
"Steam"	+350.
"Steamship"	+400.
"Steamboat"	+650.
"Steamer 10"	+1,000.
Canada	+3,000.
Panama	—
Wheeling, Va., grid	+22,500.
Pen Cancel	575.

REPRODUCTIONS of 1847 ISSUE

A3

A4

Actually, official imitations made from new plates of 50 subjects made by the Bureau of Engraving and Printing by order of the Post Office Department. These were not valid for postal use.

Reproductions. The letters R. W. H. & E. at the bottom of each stamp are less distinct on the reproductions than on the originals.

5c. On the originals the left side of the white shirt frill touches the oval on a level with the top of the "F" of "Five." On the reproductions it touches the oval about on a level with the top of the figure "5." On the originals, the bottom of the right leg of the "N" in "CENTS" is blunt. On the reproductions, the "N" comes to a point at the bottom.

10c. On the originals line of coat at left points to "T" of TEN and at right it points between "T" and "S" of "CENTS."

On the reproductions line of coat at left points to right tip of "X" and line of coat at right points to center of "S."

The bottom of the right leg of the "N" of "CENTS" shows the same difference as on the 5c originals and reproductions.

On the reproductions, the gap between the bottom legs of the left "X" is noticeably wider than the gap on the right "X." On the originals, the gaps are of equal width.

On the reproductions the eyes have a sleepy look, the line of the mouth is straighter, and in the curl of the hair near the left cheek is a strong black dot, while the originals have only a faint one.

(See Nos. 948a and 948b for 1947 reproductions — 5c blue and 10c brown orange in larger size.)

1875 Bluish paper, without gum *Imperf.*

No.	Description	Value
3	A3 5c **red brown** *(4779)*	1,000.
	brown	1,000.
	dark brown	1,000.
	Pair	2,250.
	Block of 4	*8,750.*
4	A4 10c **black** *(3883)*	1,250.
	gray black	1,250.
	Pair	2,750.
	Block of 4	*11,000.*

Numbers in parentheses are quantities sold.

Except as noted here and in footnotes for selected issues, values for 1851-57 issues are for examples that clearly show all of the illustrated type characteristics. Stamps that have weakly defined or missing type characteristics sell for less.

In Nos. 5-17, the 1¢, 3¢ and 12¢ have very small margins between the stamps. The 5¢ and 10¢ have moderate size margins. The values of these stamps take the margin size into consideration.

Values for Nos. 5A, 6b and 19b are for the less distinct positions. Best examples sell for more.

Values for No. 16 are for outer line recut at top. Other recuts sell for more.

Produced by Toppan, Carpenter, Casilear & Co.

Stamps of the 1851-57 series were printed from plates consisting of 200 subjects and the sheets were divided into two panes of 100 each. Stamps printed from different positions on the plate often have characteristics which make them more valuable than the basic listing. It is, therefore, necessary to be able to clearly identify each position on the plates used to print these stamps. In order that each stamp in the sheet and within each pane could be identified easily in regard to its relative position it was devised that the stamps in each pane be numbered from one to one hundred, starting with the top horizontal row and numbering consecutively from left to right. Thus the first stamp at the upper left corner would be 1 and the last stamp at the bottom right corner, would be 100. The left and right panes are indicated by the letters "L" or "R." The number of the plate is given last. As an example, the best-known of the scarce type III, one cent 1851 being the 99th stamp in the right pane of Plate No. 2 is listed as (99R2), *i.e.* 99th stamp, right pane, Plate No. 2.

One plate of the one cent and several plates of the three cents were reentered after they had been in use. The original state of the plate is called "Early" and the reentered state is termed "Late." If the plate was reentered twice, the inbetween state is called "Intermediate." Identification of "Early," "Intermediate" or "Late" state is explained by the addition of the letters "E," "i" or "L" after the plate numbers. The sixth stamp of the right pane of Plate No. 1 from the "Early" state would be 6R1E. The same plate position from the "Late" state would be 6R1L. Many varieties occur on the same position in each of the states of the plate. The state of the plate is mentioned only if that variety does not show on the other states.

One plate of the three cent stamp never had a plate number and is referred to by specialists as "Plate O."

The position of the stamp in the sheet is placed within parentheses, for example: (99R2).

The different values of this issue were intended primarily for the payment of specific rates, though any value might be used in making up a rate. The one cent stamp was to pay the postage on newspapers, drop letters and circulars, and the one cent carrier fee in some cities from 1856. The three cent stamp represented the rate on ordinary letters and two of them made up the rate for distances over 3000 miles prior to April 1, 1855. The five cent stamp was originally for the registration fee but the fee was usually paid in cash. Occasionally two of them were used to pay the rate over 3000 miles, after it was changed in April, 1855. Singles paid the "Shore to ship" rate to certain foreign countries and, from 1857, triples paid the fifteen-cent rate to France. Ten cents was the rate to California and points distant more than 3000 miles. The twelve cent stamp was for quadruple the ordinary rate. Twenty-four cents represented the single letter rate to Great Britain. Thirty cents was the rate to Germany. The ninety cent stamp was apparently intended to facilitate the payment of large amounts of postage.

Act of Congress, March 3, 1851. "From and after June 30, 1851, there shall be charged the following rates: Every single letter not exceeding 3000 miles, prepaid postage, 3 cents; not prepaid, 5 cents; for any greater distance, double these rates. Every single letter or paper conveyed wholly or in part by sea, and to or from a foreign country over 2500 miles, 20 cents; under 2500 miles, 10 cents. Drop or local letters, 1 cent each. Letters uncalled for and advertised, to be charged 1 cent in addition to the regular postage."

Act of Congress, March 3, 1855. "For every single letter, in manuscript or paper of any kind, in writing, marks or signs, conveyed in the mail between places in the United States not exceeding 3000 miles, 3

cents; and for any greater distance, 10 cents. Drop or local letters, 1 cent."

The Act of March 3, 1855, made the prepayment of postage on domestic letters compulsory April 1, 1855, and prepayment of postage on domestic letters compulsory by stamps effective January 1, 1856.

The Act authorized the Postmaster to establish a system for the registration of valuable letters, and to require prepayment of postage on such letters as well as registration fee of five cents. Stamps to prepay the registry fee were not required until June 1, 1867.

Franklin — A5

Type I

Type Ib

ONE CENT. Issued July 1, 1851.

Type I. Has complete curved lines outside the labels with "U. S. Postage" and "One Cent." The scrolls below the lower label are turned under, forming little balls. The ornaments at top are substantially complete.

Type Ib. As type I, but balls below bottom label are not as clear. Plume-like scrolls at bottom are incomplete.

1851-57 ***Imperf.***

No.		Unused	Used
5	A5 1c **blue,** type I (7R1E)	*115,000.*	*50,000.*
	dark blue		—
	On cover		*110,000.*
	Pair, types I, Ib		*85,000.*
	On cover, pair, one stamp type I		95,000.
	Strip of 3, one stamp type I		*110,000.*
	On cover, strip of 3, one stamp type I		*180,000.*
	Block of 8, one stamp No. 5	125,000.	

Only one example of No. 5 in the dark blue shade is recorded.

Earliest documented use: July 5, 1851.

Cancellations

Blue	+1,000.
Blue town	—
Red grid	+3,000.
Red town	—
Red "Paid"	—

Values for No. 5 are for examples with margins touching or cutting slightly into the design, or for examples with four margins and minor faults. Very few sound examples with the design untouched exist, and these sell for much more than the values shown.

Value for No. 5 unused is for a stamp with no gum. Only one example unused with original gum is recorded. It is in a multiple and is creased.

No.		Unused	Used
5A	A5 1c **blue,** type Ib, *July 1, 1851* (Less distinct examples 3-5, 9R1E)	*32,500.*	*6,500.*
	No gum	*12,000.*	
	Pair	*70,000.*	*15,000.*
	On cover		*7,000.*
	blue, type Ib (Best examples 6, 8R1E)	*45,000.*	*11,000.*
	No gum	*18,000.*	
	On cover		*15,500.*
	Pair, type Ib, II		*12,000.*
	Block of 4, pair type Ib, pair type IIIa (8-9, 18-19R1E)		—

Earliest documented use: July 1, 1851 (FDC).

Cancellations

Blue town	+300.
Red town	+550.
Red Carrier	+550.
Red "Paid"	+550.
Pen (3, 4, 5 or 9R1E)	*3,250.*
Pen (6 or 8R1E)	*5,500.*

Values for No. 5A are for sound examples with margins just clear to just touching the design on one or two sides. Examples with margins well clear of the design all around are scarce and will sell for more than the values shown.

A6

Type Ic

Type Ia. Same as type I at bottom, but top ornaments and outer line at top are partly cut away. Type Ia comes only from the bottom row of both panes of Plate 4. All type Ia stamps have the flaw below "U" of "U.S.," but this flaw also appears on some stamps of types Ic, III and IIIa of Plate 4.

Type Ic. Same as type Ia, but bottom right plume and ball ornament incomplete. Bottom left plume is complete or nearly complete. Best examples are from bottom row, "F" relief, positions 91 and 96R4. Less distinct examples are "E" reliefs from 5th and 9th rows, positions 47L, 49L, 83L, 49R, 81R, 82R, and 89R, Plate 4, and early impressions of 41R4.

No.		Unused	Used
6	A6 1c **blue,** type Ia, *1857*	*45,000.*	*9,250.*
	No gum	*20,000.*	
	On cover		*14,000.*
	Pair	—	*22,500.*
	Strip of 3 on cover		*67,500.*
	Pair, types Ia, Ic		*22,000.*
	Horizontal strip of 3, (95-97R4) types Ia, Ic, Ia		*37,500.*
	Vertical pair, types Ia, III	*75,000.*	*14,000.*
	Vertical pair, types Ia, IIIa	*55,000.*	*15,000.*
	Block of 4, types Ia, IIIa	*120,000.*	
	"Curl on shoulder" (97L4)	*47,500.*	*10,500.*
	"Curl in C" (97R4)	*47,500.*	*10,500.*

The horizontal strip of 3 represents positions 95-97R4, position 96R4 being type 1c.

Earliest documented use: Apr. 19, 1857.

Cancellations

Blue	+300.
Black Carrier	+350.
Red Carrier	+700.
Pen Cancel	*4,500.*

No.		Unused	Used
6b	A6 1c **blue,** type Ic ("E" relief, less distinct examples)	*7,000.*	*3,750.*
	No gum	*3,000.*	
	On cover		*4,750.*
	Horizontal pair (81-82R4)		—
	Pair, types Ic, III		—
	Pair, types Ic, IIIa		—
	blue, type Ic ("F" relief, best examples, 91, 96R4)	*27,500.*	*9,000.*
	No gum	*12,500.*	
	On cover		*10,000.*
	Vertical pair (81-91R4)		—

Earliest documented use: May 20, 1857 (dated cancel on off-cover stamp); June 6, 1857 (on cover).

Cancellations

Blue ("E" relief)	—
Red ("E" relief)	—
Blue town ("F" relief)	—
Red ("F" relief)	—
Black carrier ("F" relief)	—
Pen ("E" relief)	*2,000.*
Pen ("F" relief)	*4,750.*

A7

Type II — Same as Type I at top, but the little balls of the bottom scrolls and the bottoms of the lower plume ornaments are missing. The side ornaments are substantially complete.

No.		Unused	Used
7	A7 1c **blue,** type II, (Plates 1E, 2); *July 1, 1851* (Plate 1E)	1,000.	150.
	No gum	375.	
	On cover		175.
	Pair	2,300.	325.
	Strip of 3	8,500.	500.
	Block of 4 (Plate 1E)	—	—
	Block of 4 (Plate 2)	*9,500.*	1,150.
	P# block of 8, Impt. (Plate 2)	*47,500.*	
	Design complete at top (10R1E only)	—	*2,000.*
	Pair, types II, IIIa (Plate 1E)	7,500.	1,450.
	Double transfer (Plate 1E or 2)	1,100.	175.
	Double transfer (65R1E)		*500.*
	Double transfer (89R2)	1,150.	225.
	Double transfer, one inverted (71L1E)	1,500.	400.
	Triple transfer, one inverted (91L1E)	1,500.	425.
	Major cracked plate (2L, 13L, 23L, Plate 2)	1,300.	460.
	Intermediate cracked plate (12L2)	900.	350.
	Minor cracked plate (33L2)	900.	235.
	Plate 1L (4R1L only, double transfer), *June 1852*	2,000.	360.
	Pair, types II (4R1L), IV	*3,800.*	*650.*
	Plate 3, *June, 1856*	*2,000.*	360.
	On cover		550.
	Pair	—	775.
	Strip of 3		—
	Block of 4	—	—
	Double transfer		460.
	Major plate crack (22L, 24L, 31L, 33L, 34L, 8R, Plate 3)		825.
	Plate 4, *April, 1857*	*3,250.*	*900.*
	On cover		*1,250.*
	Pair	—	*2,100.*
	Pair (vert.), types II, III	—	—
	Pair (vert.), types II, IIIa	—	—
	Vertical strip of 3 (9L, 19L, 29L; Plate 4), types II, III, III, on cover		—
	Block of 4, type II and types III, IIIa	—	
	"Curl in hair" (3R, 4R4)	—	*1,100.*
	Double transfer (10R4)	—	—
	Perf. 12½, unofficial	*22,500.*	*8,000.*
	On cover		*35,000.*
	On cover with strip of 3 No. 11		*25,000.*

Please note: Regardless of the strength or weakness of the design at bottom, all stamps originating from the top row of plate 4 are classified as type II.

See note concerning unofficial perfs following listings for No. 11.

Earliest documented uses: July 1, 1851 (Plate 1E) (FDC); Dec. 5, 1855 (Plate 2); June 25, 1856 (Plate 3).

Cancellations

Blue	+7.50
Red	+20.00
Magenta	+80.00
Ultramarine	+175.00
Green	+400.00
Orange	+500.
1855 year date	+10.00
1856 year date	+5.00
1857 year date	+2.50
1858 year date	—
"Paid"	+5.00
"Way"	+35.00
Red "Too Late"	+200.00
Numeral	+25.00

Railroad	+50.00
"Steam"	+60.00
"Steamboat"	+80.00
Red Carrier	+45.00
Black Carrier	+25.00
U. S. Express Mail	+25.00
Territorial	+200.00
Printed precancel "PAID"	+2,500.
Printed precancel "paid"	+2,500.
Pen Cancel	60.00

A8

Type IIIa

Type III — The top and bottom curved lines outside the labels are broken in the middle. The side ornaments are substantially complete.

The most desirable examples of type III are those showing the widest breaks in the top and bottom framelines.

A special example is 99R2. All other stamps come from plate 4 and almost all show the breaks in the lines less clearly defined. Some of these breaks, especially of the bottom line, are very small.

Type IIIa — Similar to III with the outer line broken at top or, rarely, at bottom but not both. The side ornaments are substantially complete.

8	A8 1c **blue,** type III (Plate 4) see below for 99R2	*25,000.*	1,500.
	No gum	*7,500.*	
	On cover		1,800.
	Pair	*55,000.*	3,250.
	Pair, types III, IIIa	*35,000.*	*2,900.*
	Pair, types III, II	—	—
	Strip of 3		*8,250.*
	Block of 4, types II, III	—	
	Block of 4, types III, IIIa	—	—

Earliest documented use: July 7, 1857 (on off-cover stamp); May 1, 1857 (on cover).

Cancellations

Blue	+75.
Red	+200.
Red Carrier	+250.
Black Carrier	+250.
Pen Cancel	800.

Values for type III are for at least a 2mm break in each outer line. Examples of type III with wider breaks in outer lines command higher prices; those with smaller breaks sell for much less.

(8)	A8 1c **blue,** type III (99R2)	*35,000.*	*5,250.*
	No gum	*10,000.*	
	On cover (99R2)		*15,000.*
	Pair, types III (99R2), II	—	*10,500.*
	Pair, types III (99R2), IIIa	*42,500.*	—
	Block of 4, type III (99R2), 3 type II	*42,500.*	
	Block of 9, one type III (99R2), others type II	*47,500.*	

Cancellations

Blue	+150.00
Green	—
"Paid"	—
Red Carrier	+500.00

8A	A8 1c **blue,** type IIIa (Plate 1E) *July 1, 1851*	6,000.	800.
	No gum	2,250.	
	On cover		875.
	Pair	*12,500.*	2,300.
	Double transfer, one inverted (81L1E)	*6,500.*	1,100.
	Plate 1E (100R), break in lower line	—	—
	Plate 2 (100R), break in lower line	—	—
	Plate 4, *April, 1857*	*6,250.*	1,250.
	No gum	2,350.	
	On cover		1,400.
	Pair	*13,500.*	2,500.
	Block of 4	—	*9,500.*

Earliest documented uses: July 3, 1851 (Plate 1E); Apr. 4, 1857 (Plate 4).

Cancellations

Blue	+50.00
Red	+125.00
"Paid"	+90.00
Black Carrier	+175.00
Red Carrier	+175.00
Pen Cancel	400.00

Values are for stamps with at least a 2mm break in the top outer line. Examples with a wider break or a break in the lower line command higher prices, those with a smaller break sell for less.

"Paid" Cancellations

Values for "Paid" cancellations are for those OTHER than the common Boston type. See Postal Markings in the Introduction for illustrations.

A9

Type IV. Similar to type II, but with the curved lines outside the labels recut at top or bottom or both.

9	A9 1c **blue,** type IV, *1852*	725.00	100.00
	No gum	260.00	
	On cover		120.00
	Pair	1,650.	210.00
	Strip of 3	2,600.	340.00
	Block of 4	3,500.	*1,750.*
	P# block of 8, Impt. (Plate 1)	—	
	Double transfer	850.00	110.00
	Triple transfer, one inverted (71L, 81L and 91L Plate 1L)	900.00	160.00
	Cracked plate	900.00	160.00
	On cover		—
	Bottom frameline broken (30L, 50L, 67R, 89R, 90R, 99R Plate 1L), late printings	—	250.00
	Perf. 12½, unofficial		*10,000.*
	Strip of 3		—
a.	Printed on both sides, reverse inverted		*40,000.*
b.	Diagonal half used as ½c on cover		*60,000.*

No. 9a is unique.

The No. 9b cover, a printed-matter circular mailed in 1853, is unique. The circular likely should have been sent at the 1c rate for printed matter in effect at the time. However, both the sending (New Haven, Conn.) and receiving (Hartford, Conn.) post offices treated it as fully prepaid with ½c postage applied. Value is based on 2013 auction realization.

See note concerning unofficial perfs following listings for No. 11.

VARIETIES OF RECUTTING

Stamps of this type were printed from Plate 1 after it had been reentered and recut in 1852. All but one stamp (4R, see No. 7 for listings) were recut and all varieties of recutting are listed below:

Recut once at top and once at bottom, (113 on plate)	750.00	95.00
Recut once at top, (40 on plate)	775.00	100.00
Recut once at top and twice at bottom, (21 on plate)	800.00	105.00
Recut twice at bottom, (11 on plate)	825.00	120.00
Recut once at bottom, (8 on plate)	850.00	125.00
Recut once at bottom and twice at top, (4 on plate)	900.00	135.00
Recut twice at bottom and twice at top, (2 on plate)	950.00	240.00

Earliest documented use: June 5, 1852.

Cancellations

Blue	+5.00
Red	+40.00
Ultramarine	+150.00
Brown	+90.00
Green	+400.00
Violet	+350.00
1853 year date	+250.00
1855 year date	+10.00
1856 year date	+7.50
1857 year date	+10.00
"Paid"	+10.00
"U. S. PAID"	+50.00
"Way"	+50.00
"Free"	+75.00
Railroad	+75.00
"Steam"	+60.00
Numeral	+10.00
"Steamboat"	+90.00
"Steamship"	+60.00
Red Carrier	+15.00
Black Carrier	+25.00
U. S. Express Mail	+60.00
Express Company	—
Packet boat	+500.00
Printed precancel "PAID"	+2,500.
Printed precancel "paid"	+2,500.
Pen Cancel	47.50

These 1c stamps were often cut apart carelessly, destroying part or all of the top and bottom lines. When this was done, it is difficult to determine whether a stamp is type II, III, IIIa or IV without identifying the position. Such mutilated examples sell for much less.

PLEASE NOTE:

Stamps are valued in the grade of very fine unless otherwise indicated.

Values for early and valuable stamps are for examples with certificates of authenticity from acknowledged expert committees, or examples sold with the buyer having the right of certification. This applies to examples with original gum as well as examples without gum. Beware of stamps offered "as is," as the gum on some unused stamps offered with "original gum" may be fraudulent, and stamps offered as unused without gum may in some cases be altered or faintly canceled used stamps.

VALUES FOR NEVER-HINGED STAMPS PRIOR TO SCOTT No. 182

This catalogue does not value pre-1879 stamps in never-hinged condition. Premiums for never-hinged condition in the classic era invariably are even larger than those premiums listed for the 1879 and later issues. Generally speaking, the earlier the stamp is listed in the catalogue, the larger will be the never-hinged premium.

Washington — A10

All of the 3c stamps of the 1851 and 1857 issues were recut at least to the extent of the outer frame lines, sometimes the inner lines at the sides (type II stamps), and often other lines in triangles, diamond blocks, label blocks and/or top/bottom frame lines. Some of the most prominent varieties are listed below each major listing (others are described in "The 3c Stamp of U.S. 1851-57 Issue," by Carroll Chase).

Type I

THREE CENTS. Issued July 1, 1851 (Plate 1E).

Type I — There is an outer frame line on all four sides. The outer frame lines at the sides are always recut.

10	A10 3c **orange brown,** type I (Plates 1E, 1i)	4,000.	190.00
	No gum	1,600.	
	deep orange brown	4,250.	220.00

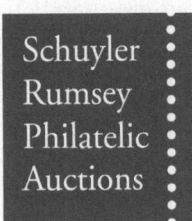

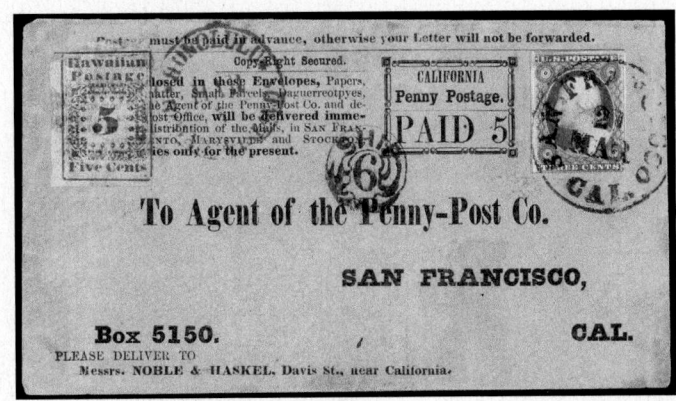

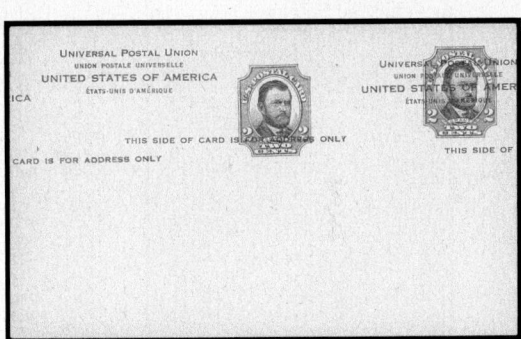

No gum	1,750.	
On cover, orange brown		260.00
On cover (3c circular rate - 1000-1500 miles)		1,000.
Pair	9,000.	550.00
Pair on cover (double rate)		650.00
Pair on cover (6c West Coast rate)		800.00
Strip of 3	*15,000.*	1,200.
Block of 4	*23,500.*	—
Pair, types I, II	*12,000.*	*825.00*
Double transfer		220.00
Gash on shoulder		220.00
On part India paper		*1,000.*

VARIETIES OF RECUTTING

1 line recut in upper left triangle	4,250.	210.00
1 line recut in upper left triangle, 2 lines recut at top of upper right diamond block (27R1E)		500.00

Earliest documented uses: July 1, 1851 (Plate 1E) (FDC); July 12, 1851 (Plate 1i).

Cancellations

Blue	+10.00
Red	+20.00
Orange red	+25.00
Brown	+40.00
Ultramarine	+100.00
Green	+235.00
Violet	+250.00
1851 year date	*+1,500.*
1852 year date	+750.00
"Paid"	+5.00
"Way"	+40.00
"Way" with numeral	+150.00
"Free"	+50.00
Numeral	+15.00
Railroad	+50.00
U. S. Express Mail	+20.00
"Steam"	+35.00
"Steamship"	+60.00
"Steamboat"	+70.00
Packet Boat	+300.00
Black Carrier (circular)	+400.00
Blue Carrier (circular)	+600.00
Blue Carrier (New Orleans "snowshovel")	+400.00
Green Carrier (New Orleans "snowshovel")	+500.00
Canadian	—
Territorial	+200.00
Pen Cancel	70.00

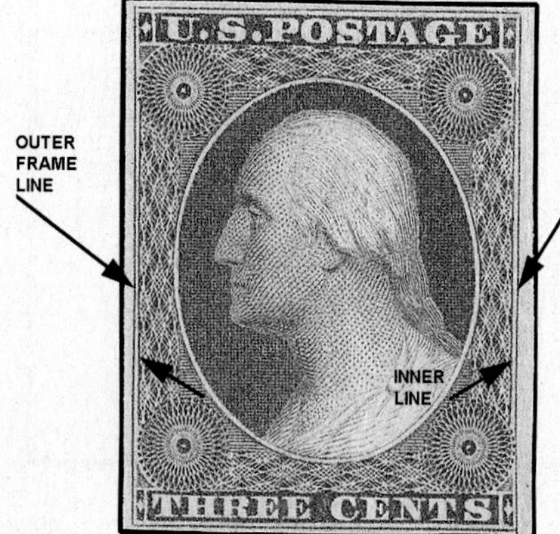

Type II

Type II — As type I, but with the inner lines at the sides added by recutting on the plate.

10A A10 3c **orange brown,** type II (Plates 1E, 1i, 2E, 5E, 0)

10A A10 3c **orange brown,** type II (Plates 1E, 1i, 2E, 5E, 0)	3,250.	150.00
No gum	1,350.	
deep orange brown	3,500.	190.00
No gum	1,300.	
copper brown (Plate 2E only)	*4,250.*	900.00
No gum	*1,600.*	
On cover, orange brown		200.00
On cover, copper brown		*1,100.*
On cover (3c circular rate - 1000-1500 miles)		1,000.
Pair	6,750.	500.00
Pair on cover (double rate)		550.00
Pair on cover (6c West Coast rate)		675.00
Strip of 3	*10,500.*	1,200.
Block of 4	*12,000.*	—
Double transfer		170.00
Triple transfer		450.00
Gash on shoulder		160.00
Dot in lower right diamond block (69L5E)		325.00
On part-India paper		*1,100.*
b. Printed on both sides		*55,000.*

Only one example of No. 10Ab is recorded.

VARIETIES OF RECUTTING

All of these stamps also were recut at least to the extent of the outer frame lines at the sides and the inner lines at the sides (the basic type II criteria).

Left inner line only recut		200.00
Right inner line only recut		160.00
1 line recut in upper left triangle		160.00
2 lines recut in upper left triangle		160.00
3 lines recut in upper left triangle		180.00
5 lines recut in upper left triangle (47L0)		*1,500.*
1 line recut in lower left triangle		160.00
1 line recut in lower right triangle		160.00
2 lines recut in lower right triangle (57L0)		*1,500.*
2 lines recut in upper left triangle and 1 line recut in lower right triangle		220.00
1 line recut in upper right triangle		170.00
1 line recut in both upper left and upper right triangles (68, 70L0)	4,000.	260.00
Upper part of top label and diamond block recut	3,750.	155.00
Top label and right diamond block joined		180.00
Top label and left diamond block joined at top (6R2E, 100R2E)		300.00
Lower label and right diamond block joined		210.00
1 line recut at bottom of lower left diamond block (34R2E)		1,500.
Vertical line ties upper left corner of upper left diamond block to top frame line (45R2E)		1,000.

Earliest documented uses: July 1, 1851 (Plate 1E) (FDC); July 12, 1851 (Plate 1i); July 19, 1851 (Plate 2E); July 19, 1851 (Plate 5E); Sept. 6, 1851 (Plate 0).

Cancellations

Blue	+5.00
Red	+15.00
Orange red	+20.00
Orange	—
Brown	+40.00
Ultramarine	+100.00
Green	+225.00
Violet	+250.00
1851 year date	*+1,000.*
1852 year date	+750.00
"Paid"	+5.00
"Way"	+40.00
"Way" with numeral	+150.00
"Free"	+100.00
Numeral	+15.00
Railroad	+50.00
U. S. Express Mail	+20.00
"Steam"	+35.00
"Steamship"	+60.00
"Steamboat"	+70.00
Packet Boat	+300.00
Black Carrier (circular)	+400.00
Blue Carrier (circular)	+600.00
Blue Carrier (New Orleans "snowshovel")	+400.00
Green Carrier (New Orleans "snowshovel")	+500.00
Canadian	—
Territorial	+200.00
Pen Cancel	70.00

11 A10 3c **dull red** (1855), type I (Plates 4, 6, 7, 8)	250.00	17.50
orange red (1855)	250.00	17.50
rose red (1855)	250.00	17.50
No gum	100.00	
brownish carmine (1856)	275.00	20.00
No gum	110.00	
claret (1857)	325.00	25.00
No gum	120.00	
deep claret (1857)	350.00	30.00
No gum	125.00	
plum (1857)	—	*2,200.*
No gum	—	
pinkish		*5,750.*
On cover, dull red		20.00
On cover, orange red		21.00
On cover, brownish carmine		26.00
On cover, claret		30.00
On cover, plum		*3,750.*
On propaganda cover, dull red		400.00
Pair	650.00	62.50
Pair on cover (double rate)		70.00
Pair on cover (6c West Coast rate)		—
Pair, types I, II	—	
Strip of 3	1,100.	140.00
Block of 4	2,100.	1,000.
P# block of 8, Impt.	*7,500.*	
Double transfer	300.00	22.50
Gash on shoulder	300.00	20.00
Worn plate	275.00	15.00
Perf. 12½, unofficial		*5,000.*
On cover		*8,000.*

The unofficial perf varieties listed under Nos. 7, 11 and 11A represent the first perforated stamps in the U. S. made using a true perforating machine. Known as the "Chicago perfs," both the perf. 11 and perf. 12½ stamps were made by Dr. Elijah W. Hadley, using a machine of his construction. None of the perf 11 stamps are believed to have been used.

VARIETIES OF RECUTTING

All of these stamps were recut at least to the extent of three outer frame lines (including both sides) and often other lines in triangles, diamond blocks, label blocks and/or top/bottom frame lines. Some of the most prominent varieties are listed below.

Lines on bust and bottom of medallion circle recut (47R6)	*1,400.*	600.00
Top label and right diamond block joined	300.00	19.00
Top label and right diamond block joined at top and bottom (68R4)	325.00	20.00
Lower label and right diamond block joined	325.00	20.00
Extra line at right	325.00	20.00

Earliest documented uses: Mar. 28, 1855 (Plate 4); Feb. 18, 1856 (Plate 6); Feb. 9, 1856 (Plate 7); Apr. 14, 1856 (Plate 8).

Cancellations

Blue	+4.00
Red	+10.00
Orange red	+5.00
Orange	+250.00
Brown	+75.00
Magenta	+50.00
Ultramarine	+40.00
Green	+125.00
Violet	+250.00
Purple	+250.00
Olive	+200.00
Yellow	+7,500.
1855 year date	+50.00
1856 year date	+12.50
1857 year date	+12.50
1858 year date	+1.00
1859 year date	+25.00
"Paid"	+1.50
"Way"	+10.00
"Free"	+25.00
Numeral, "3" or "5"	+25.00
Numeral, number greater than "5"	—
Railroad	+20.00
Supplemental Mail Type A	*+2,500.*
"Steam"	+25.00
"Ship"	+25.00
"New York Ship"	+35.00
"Steamboat"	+45.00
"Steamship"	+45.00
Packet boat	+120.00
Express Company	+120.00
Black Carrier	+60.00
Red Carrier (New York)	+100.00
Blue Carrier (New Orleans)	+300.00
Green Carrier (New Orleans)	+500.00
Canada	—
Territorial	+200.00
Pen Cancel	9.00

11A A10 3c **dull red** (1852-53-54-55), type II (Plates 1L, 2L, 3, 5L)	250.00	15.00
orange red (1855)	250.00	15.00
rose red (1854-55)	250.00	15.00
No gum	85.00	
brownish carmine (1851-52)	280.00	20.00
No gum	95.00	
claret (1851-52)	300.00	22.50
No gum	115.00	
experimental orange brown (1851-52, Plate 1L))	—	300.00
plum (1857)		*2,200.*
pinkish		*6,000.*
On cover, dull red		17.50
On cover, orange red		19.00
On cover, brownish carmine		26.00
On cover, claret		27.50
On cover, experimental orange brown (Plate 1L)		700.00
On cover, plum		*3,500.*
On propaganda cover, dull red		400.00
On cover (3c circular rate - 1000-1500 miles)		850.00
Pair	550.00	62.50
Pair on cover (double rate)		70.00
Pair on cover (6c West Coast rate)		100.00
Strip of 3	1,050.	140.00
Block of 4	2,000.	1,000.
P# block of 8, Impt.	*4,500.*	
Double transfer in "Three Cents"	275.00	20.00
Double transfer line through "Three Cents" and rosettes double (92L1L)	400.00	70.00
Double transfer, "Gents" instead of "Cents" (66R2L)	400.00	55.00
Triple transfer (92L2L)	400.00	55.00
Gash on shoulder	275.00	17.00
Dot in lower right diamond block (69L5L)	350.00	45.00
Major cracked plate (84L, 94L, 9R, Plate 5L)	*775.00*	160.00
Intermediate cracked plate (80L, 96L, 71R, Plate 5L)	*500.00*	80.00
Minor cracked plate (8L, 27L, 31L, 44L, 45L, 51L, 55L, 65L, 71L, 72L, 74L, 78L, 79L, 7R, Plate 5L)	*375.00*	60.00
Worn plate	250.00	13.00
Perf. about 11, unofficial	*6,500.*	
Block of 4	*27,500.*	
Perf. 12½, unofficial		*5,000.*
On cover		*8,000.*
Pair on cover		—
c. Vertical half used as 1c on cover		*5,000.*
Strip of 4 No. 11Ac used as 6c on cover		*15,000.*
d. Diagonal half used as 1c on cover		*5,000.*
e. Double impression		*30,000.*

The unofficial perf varieties listed represent the first perforated stamps in the U. S. made using a true perforating machine. Known as the "Chicago perfs," both were made by Dr. Elijah W. Hadley, using a machine of his construction. None of the perf 11 stamps are believed to have been used.

The strip of 4 No. 11Ac on cover is the only recorded multiple of a bisected stamp in United States philately.

The "Gents" instead of "Cents" double transfer must show three vertical lines recut in the upper left triangle.

VARIETIES OF RECUTTING

All of these stamps also were recut at least to the extent of the outer lines at the sides and the inner frame lines at the sides (the basic type II criteria).

Right inner line only recut	300.00	17.50
1 line recut in upper left triangle	300.00	16.00
2 lines recut in upper left triangle	300.00	16.00
3 lines recut in upper left triangle	325.00	16.00
5 lines recut in upper left triangle (95L1L)	650.00	200.00
1 line recut in lower left triangle	325.00	16.00
1 line recut in lower right triangle	300.00	16.00
1 line recut in upper right triangle	425.00	18.00
1 line recut in UL, LL and LR triangles (49L1L, 95R3)	475.00	32.50
2 lines recut in UL triangle, 1 line recut in LL triangle (9L1L)	475.00	32.50
Recut button on shoulder (10R2L)	600.00	175.00
Upper part of top label and diamond block recut	275.00	16.00
Top label and right diamond block joined	300.00	16.00
Top label and left diamond block joined	325.00	17.50
Lower label and right diamond block joined	325.00	17.50
1 extra vertical line outside of left frame line (29L, 39L, 49L, 59L, 69L, 79L, Plate 3)	300.00	17.50
2 extra vertical lines outside of left frame line (89L, 99L, Plate 3)	375.00	32.50
1 extra vertical line outside of right frame line (58L, 68L, 78L, 88L, 98L, Plate 3)	425.00	20.00
No inner line and frame line close to design at right (9L, 19L, Plate 3)	375.00	32.50
No inner line and frame line close to design at left (70, 80, 90, 100L, Plate 3)	325.00	19.00

Earliest documented uses: Jan. 7, 1852 (Plate 1L); Jan. 7, 1852 (Plate 2L); Jan. 15, 1852 (Plate 3); July 13, 1855 (Plate 5L).

Cancellations

Blue	+1.00
Red	+7.50
Orange red	+25.00
Orange	+260.00
Brown	+75.00
Magenta	+50.00
Ultramarine	+40.00
Green	+175.00
Violet	+250.00
Purple	+250.00
Olive	+200.00
Yellow	*+7,500.*
Yellow, on cover	*15,000.*
1852 year date	*+300.00*
1852 year date, on cover	1,000.
1853 year date	+100.00
1854 year date	—
1855 year date	+50.00
1856 year date	+12.50
"Paid"	+1.50
"Way"	+10.00
"Way" with numeral	+60.00
"Free"	+25.00
Numeral	+7.50
Railroad	+20.00
U. S. Express Mail	+5.00
Supplemental Mail Type A	*+2,500.*
"Steam"	+15.00
"Ship"	+20.00
"New York Ship"	+35.00
"Steamboat"	+45.00
"Steamship"	+45.00
Packet boat	+120.00
Express Company	+120.00
Black Carrier	+60.00
Red Carrier (New York)	+50.00
Blue Carrier (New Orleans)	+200.00
Green Carrier (New Orleans)	+350.00
Canada	—
Territorial	+100.00
Pen Cancel	7.50

Thomas Jefferson — A11

FIVE CENTS

Type I — Projections on all four sides.

12 A11 5c **red brown,** type I, *1856*	*30,000.*	775.
dark red brown	*30,000.*	775.
No gum	*11,000.*	
On domestic cover		1,200.
Single on cover to France		1,600.
Strip of 3 on cover to France		5,750.
Pair	*67,500.*	1,700.
Strip of 3	*100,000.*	3,750.
Block of 4	*300,000.*	*45,000.*
Double transfer (40R1)		*1,000.*
Defective transfer (23R1)		*1,200.*

Earliest documented use: Mar. 24, 1856.

Cancellations

Red	+175.
Magenta	+200.
Blue	+150.
Brown	+100.
Green	+1,000.
1856 year date	+25.
1857 year date	+25.
1858 year date	—
"Paid"	+200.
"Steamship"	+200.
U.S. Express Mail	+200.
Express Company	+400.
"Steamboat"	+350.
Railroad	+400.
Numeral	+1,000.
Pen Cancel	385.

Washington — A12

TEN CENTS

Type I — The "shells" at the lower corners are practically complete. The outer line below the label is very nearly complete. The outer lines are broken above the middle of the top label and the "X" in each upper corner. Beware of type V perforated (No. 35) trimmed to resemble type I imperforate (No. 13). Note that the pearls on No. 35 normally will be missing from each end of the lower label.

Types I, II, III and IV have complete ornaments at the sides of the stamps, and three pearls at each outer edge of the bottom panel.

Type I comes only from the bottom row of both panes of Plate 1.

13 A12 10c **green,** type I, *1855*	*19,000.*	750.
dark green	*19,000.*	750.
yellowish green	*19,000.*	750.
No gum	*8,500.*	
On domestic cover		850.
Pair	*42,500.*	1,700.
Strip of 3		2,750.
Vert. pair, types III, I	*26,000.*	1,400.
Vert. pair, types IV, I (86, 96L1)		*10,000.*
Vertical strip of 3, types II, III, I		4,250.
Block of 4, types III, I	*55,000.*	*10,500.*
Block of 4, types III, IV, I		*16,000.*
Double transfer (100R1)	*20,000.*	825.
"Curl" in left "X" (99R1)	*20,000.*	825.

Earliest documented use: July 11, 1855.

Cancellations

Blue	+50.
Red	+100.
Magenta	+200.
Orange	—
1855 year date	+25.
1856 year date	+25.
1857 year date	+25.
"Paid"	+50.
"Steamship"	+150.
Railroad	+175.
Territorial	+400.
Numeral	+50.
U.S. Express Mail	—
Pen Cancel	375.

A13

Type II — The design is complete at the top. The outer line at the bottom is broken in the middle. The shells are partly cut away, as shown.

14 A13 10c **green,** type II, *1855*	5,000.	145.
dark green	5,000.	145.
yellowish green	5,000.	145.
No gum	1,800.	
On domestic cover		190.
Pair	11,000.	310.
Strip of 3	17,000.	625.
Block of 4	*25,000.*	*4,000.*
Pair, types II, III	11,000.	325.
Pair, types II, IV	*42,500.*	*2,100.*
Vertical strip of 3, types II, III, IV		*2,400.*
Block of 4, types II, III	—	*3,500.*
Block of 4, types II, IV		—
Block of 4, types II, III, IV		*10,000.*
Double transfer (31L, 51L, and 20R, Plate 1)	5,500.	225.
"Curl" opposite "X" (10R1)	5,500.	250.

Earliest documented use: May 12, 1855.

Cancellations

Blue	+15.
Red	+25.
Brown	+75.
Ultramarine	+100.
Magenta	+150.
Green	+200.
Violet	+150.
1855 year date	+100.
1856 year date	+50.
1857 year date	+10.
1858 year date	+10.

"Paid"		+25.
"Way"		+75.
"Free"		+75.
Railroad		+75.
Steamship		+75.
Steamboat		+100.
Numeral		+50.
Territorial		+150.
Express Company		+200.
U. S. Express Mail		+75.
Pen Cancel		62.50

A14

Type III — The outer lines are broken above the top label and the "X" numerals. The outer line at the bottom and the shells are partly cut away, as shown, similar to type II.

15	A14 10c **green,** type III, *1855*	5,000.	145.
	dark green	5,000.	145.
	yellowish green	5,000.	145.
	No gum	1,800.	
	On domestic cover		190.
	Pair	11,000.	310.
	Strip of 3	17,000.	625.
	Pair, types III, IV	*40,000.*	*2,100.*
	Double transfer at top and at bottom		—
	"Curl" on forehead (85L1)	5,500.	240.
	"Curl" to right of left "X" (87R1)	5,500.	250.

Earliest documented use: May 19, 1855.

Cancellations

Blue	+15.
Red	+25.
Orange red	+35.
Magenta	+100.
Violet	+150.
Brown	+75.
Orange	+150.
Green	+300.
1855 year date	—
1856 year date	+50.
1857 year date	+10.
1858 year date	+10.
"Paid"	+25.
Steamship	+75.
U. S. Express Mail	+75.
"MAIL ROUTE"	+1,500.
Express Company	+200.
Packet boat	—
"too late"	+500.
Canada (on cover)	+1000.
Territorial	+150.
Railroad	+75.
Numeral	+50.
Pen Cancel	62.50

A15

Type IV — The outer lines have been recut at top or bottom or both.

16	A15 10c **green,** type IV, *1855*	*50,000.*	1,700.
	dark green	*50,000.*	1,700.
	yellowish green	*50,000.*	1,700.
	No gum	*27,500.*	
	On domestic cover		2,000.
	Pair	—	4,500.
	Block of 4 (54-55, 64-65L)		—

VARIETIES OF RECUTTING

Eight stamps on Plate 1 were recut. All are listed below.

Outer line recut at top (65L, 74L, 86L, and 3R, Plate 1)	*37,500.*	1,700.
Outer line recut at bottom (54L, 55L, 76L, Plate 1)	*39,000.*	1,800.
Outer line recut at top and bottom (64L1)	*45,000.*	2,250.

Positions 65L1 and 86L1 have both "X" ovals recut at top, as well as the outer line.

Earliest documented use: June 4, 1855.

Cancellations

Blue	+90.
Red	+185.
Brown	+250.
1857 year date	—
1859 year date	—
"Paid"	+150.
Steamship	+300.
Territorial	+500.
Express Company	+800.
Numeral	+150.
Pen Cancel	850.

Types I, II, III and IV occur on the same sheet, so it is possible to obtain pairs and blocks showing combinations of types. For listings of type combinations in pairs and blocks, see Nos. 13-15.

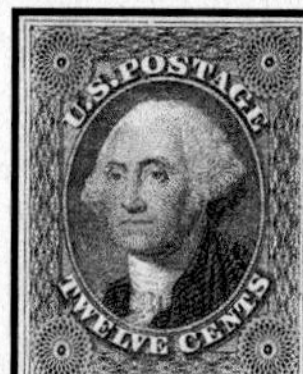

Washington — A16

17	A16 12c **gray black,** *July 1, 1851*	6,250.	260.
	No gum	2,100.	
	black	7,500.	325.
	No gum	2,500.	
	Single, on cover		1,500.
	Single on cover with No. 11 to France		1,100.
	Pair	*17,500.*	600.
	Pair, on cover to England		750.
	Block of 4	*45,000.*	*5,500.*
	Double transfer	6,500.	290.
	Triple transfer (5R1 & 49R1)	6,750.	425.
	Not recut in lower right corner	6,500.	300.
	Recut in lower left corner (43L, 53L, 63L, 73L and 100L, Plate 1)	6,500.	375.
	Cracked plate (32R1)		—
	On part-India paper	*7,000.*	*1,200.*
	On very thin paper		*1,750.*
	No gum	*4,500.*	
a.	Diagonal half used as 6c on cover		*2,500.*
	Diagonal half used as 6c on "Via Nicaragua" cover		*5,000.*
b.	Vertical half used as 6c on cover		*8,500.*
c.	Printed on both sides		*35,000.*

Earliest documented use: Aug. 4, 1851.

Cancellations

Red	+30.
Orange red	+55.
Blue	+15.
Brown	+60.
Magenta	+75.
Orange	+200.
Green	+600.
"Paid"	+25.
"Way"	+75.
Steamship	+100.
Steamboat	+125.
Supplementary Mail Type A	+125.
Railroad	+100.
"Honolulu" in red (on cover)	+400.
U. S. Express Mail	+125.
Pen Cancel	130.

Please Note:

Stamps are valued in the grade of very fine unless otherwise indicated.

Values for early and valuable stamps are for examples with certificates of authenticity from acknowledged expert committees, or examples sold with the buyer having the right of certification. This applies to examples with original gum as well as examples without gum. Beware of stamps offered "as is," as the gum on some unused stamps offered with "original gum" may be fraudulent, and stamps offered as unused without gum may in some cases be altered or faintly canceled used stamps.

Values for 1857-61 issues are for examples that clearly show all the illustrated type characteristics. Stamps that have weakly defined or missing type characteristics sell for less.

Nos. 18-39 have small or very small margins. The values take into account the margin size. See footnotes for more specific information on selected issues.

SAME DESIGNS AS 1851-57 ISSUES

Printed by Toppan, Carpenter & Co.

1857-61 ***Perf. 15½***

18	A5 1c **blue,** type I (Plate 12), *1861*	2,100.	500.
	No gum	800.	
	On cover		650.
	On patriotic cover		1,500.
	Pair	4,500.	1,100.
	Strip of 3	7,000.	2,000.
	Block of 4	*14,000.*	
	Short ornaments at either top or bottom		—
	Pair, types I, II	3,500.	850.
	Pair, types I, IIIa	4,700.	1,075.
	Block of 4, types I, II	*8,750.*	5,000.
	Block of 4, types I, II, IIIa	*10,500.*	6,250.
	Double transfer	2,600.	575.
	Cracked plate (91R12)		750.

Plate 12 consists of types I & II. A few positions are type IIIa. Late printings of position 46L12 are type III.

Earliest documented use: Jan. 25, 1861.

Cancellations

Blue	+20.
Red	+70.
Violet	+150.
Steamboat	+100.
"Paid"	+25.
"Free"	+750.
Black Carrier	+85.
Red Carrier	+95.
Numeral	—
Pen Cancel	260.

19	A6 1c **blue,** type Ia (Plate 4)	*42,500.*	*9,500.*
	No gum	*20,000.*	
	On cover		*10,500.*
	Pair	*95,000.*	*22,000.*
	Strip of 3	*140,000.*	*35,000.*
	Vertical pair, types Ia, III	*65,000.*	*13,500.*
	Vertical pair, types Ia, IIIa	*50,000.*	*11,000.*
	Pair, types Ia, Ic	—	—
	Strip of 3, types Ia, Ia, Ic (94-96R4 or 96-98R4)		—
	Block of 4, types Ia, Ic, and IIIa	*100,000.*	
	Block of 4, pair type Ia and types III or IIIa	—	—
	"Curl on shoulder" (97L4)	*45,000.*	*10,500.*

No. 19 is valued in the grade of fine.

Examples of this stamp exist with perforations not touching the design at any point. Such examples command very high prices.

Type Ia comes only from the bottom row of both panes of Plate 4. Two strips of three, types Ia, Ia, Ic ("F" relief) are recorded.

Earliest documented use: Sept. 9, 1857. No. 19 is known on a folded circular with Aug. 1 postmark, but the year of use has not been certified.

Cancellations

Red Carrier	+200.
Blue	—
Green	+1,750.
Pen Cancel	4,500.

19b	A6 1c **blue,** type Ic ("E" relief, less distinct examples)	*4,250.*	*3,750.*
	No gum	*1,750.*	
	On cover		*4,500.*
	Horizontal pair (81-82R4)		—
	Pair, types Ic, III	—	—
	Pair, types Ic, IIIa		—
	blue, type Ic ("F" relief, best examples, 91, 96R4)	*20,000.*	*7,250.*
	No gum	*9,000.*	
	On cover		*8,750.*

Type Ic — Same as Ia, but bottom right plume and ball ornament incomplete. Bottom left plume complete or nearly complete. Best examples are from bottom row, "F" relief, positions 91 and 96R4. Less distinct examples are "E" reliefs from 5th and 9th rows, positions 47L, 49L, 83L, 49R, 81R, 82R, and 89R, Plate 4, and early impressions of 41R4. Several combination type multiples can be found in the unused complete left pane of 100 from Plate 4.

Examples of the "F" relief type Ic stamps exist with perforations not touching the design at any point. Such examples command a substantial premium.

Cancellations

Pen ("E" relief)		*1,000.*
Blue ("F" relief)		—
Red ("F" relief)		—
Pen ("F" relief)		*3,000.*

20 A7 1c **blue,** type II (Plate 2)	850.	275.
No gum	375.	
On cover		340.
Pair	1,800.	675.
Strip of 3	3,000.	1,050.
Block of 4	*6,000.*	2,600.
Double transfer (Plate 2)	900.	325.
Double transfer (89R2)	*2,250.*	*1,500.*
Major cracked plate (2L, 13L, 23L, Plate 2)	3,400.	1,400.
Intermediate cracked plate (12L2)	2,400.	1,200.
Minor cracked plate (33L2)	2,400.	800.
Reconstruction of the major plate crack (5 stamps: 2L2, 12L2, 13L2, 23L2, 33L2)		*5,000.*
Plate 1L (4R1L only, double transfer), *July 1857*		1,000.
Pair, types II (4R1L), IV		*2,500.*
Plate 4	3,500.	*1,250.*
On cover		*1,500.*
Pair	7,500.	*2,750.*
Vertical pair, types II, III	—	—
Strip of 3	—	—
Double transfer (10R4)	3,750.	*1,800.*
"Curl in hair" (3R, 4R4)	—	*1,350.*
Plate 11	1,700.	750.
On cover		1,000.
On patriotic cover		—
Pair	3,600.	1,650.
Strip of 3		—
Double transfer	—	—
Plate 12	1,050.	325.
On cover		375.
On patriotic cover		700.
Pair	2,200.	675.
Strip of 3	3,500.	1,100.
Block of 4	*6,000.*	*2,500.*
Double transfer	—	—

Earliest documented uses: July 26, 1857 (Plate 2); July 26, 1857 (Plate 4); Jan. 5, 1861 (dated cancel on off-cover stamp), Jan. 12, 1861 (on cover) (Plate 11); Jan. 21, 1861 (Plate 12).

No. 20, plate 2, is also known on two folded circulars dated July 24 and July 25, respectively, but no postal year date or docketing verifies the actual day of mailing.

Cancellations

Blue	+15.
Red	+35.
Green	+200.
1857 year date	+10.
1858 year date	+5.
1861 year date	+5.
"FREE"	—
1863 year date	+200.
"Paid"	+15.
Railroad	+60.
"Way"	+75.
Steamboat	+75.
STEAM SHIP	—
Red Carrier	+40.
Black Carrier	+50.
"Old Stamps / Not Recognized"	—
Pen Cancel	135.

21 A8 1c **blue,** type III (Plate 4), see below for 99R2	*17,500.*	1,400.
No gum	*6,000.*	
On cover		1,800.
Pair	*40,000.*	3,250.
Strip of 3		5,750.
Block of 4	—	
Pair, types III, IIIa	*22,500.*	2,500.
Vert. strip of 3, types II, IIIa, III		*2,800.*
On cover		6,000.
Block of 4, types III, IIIa	—	
Plate 12 (46L12)	*9,000.*	*6,000.*
a. Horiz. pair, imperf between		*20,000.*

Earliest documented use: Sept. 18, 1857.

Cancellations

Blue	+50.
Red	+90.
Green	+1,250.
1858 year date	+35.
"Paid"	+60.
Black Carrier	+175.
Red Carrier	+200.
Pen Cancel	850.

Values for type III are for at least a 2mm break in each outer line. Examples of type III with wider breaks in outer lines command higher prices; those with smaller breaks sell for less.

No. 21a is unique and is contained in a strip of three. Value reflects auction sale in 1999.

(21) A8 1c **blue,** type III (99R2)	—	*7,250.*
On cover		*11,000.*
Pair, types III (99R2), II		—
Pair, types III (99R2), IIIa		—
Strip of 3, types III (99R2), II, IIIa		—
Block of 9, one type III (99R2), others type II	*115,000.*	

Two unused examples of No. 21, position 99R2, are recorded; one is in a block of 9. Only three covers are recorded bearing No. 21 (99R2).

Earliest documented use: Oct. 27, 1857.

22 A8 1c **blue,** type IIIa (Plate 4)	2,200.	475.
No gum	850.	
On cover		525.
Pair	4,850.	1,050.
Vertical pair, types IIIa, II	—	*1,850.*
Strip of 3	7,250.	1,700.
Block of 4	*13,000.*	*5,500.*
Block of 4, types IIIa, II	—	—
Double transfer	2,400.	525.
Plate 2 (100R)	—	—
Plate 11 and Plate 12	2,400.	500.
On cover		550.
On patriotic cover		1,000.
Pair	*5,400.*	1,100.
Vert. pair, types IIIa, II (Plate 11)	*4,750.*	1,500.
Strip of 3	*8,500.*	1,750.
Strip of 3, types IIIa, II, I (46-48L12)		—
Block of 4	*13,000.*	
Block of 4, types IIIa, II (Plate 11)	*12,500.*	*4,250.*
Double transfer	2,500.	525.
Triple transfer (Plate 11)	*3,250.*	*1,900.*
Bottom line broken (46L12)	—	*1,900.*

Beware of pairs of No. 22 with faint blind perforations between that sometimes are offered as pairs imperf. between.

Earliest documented uses: July 26, 1857 (Plate 4), Dec. 1860 (day unknown) (dated cancel on off-cover stamp) (Plate 11), Dec. 31, 1860, (on cover) (Plate 11), Jan. 25, 1861 (Plate 12).

Cancellations

Blue	+20.
Red	+75.
Green	+350.
1857 year date	—
1858 year date	—
1861 year date	—
1863 year date	—
"Paid"	+50.
"Steamboat"	—
Red Carrier	+50.
Black Carrier	+85.
Blue Carrier	+120.
Pen Cancel	250.

23 A9 1c **blue,** type IV	*10,000.*	550.
No gum	4,250.	
On cover		1,000.
Pair	*22,500.*	1,800.
Strip of 3	*35,000.*	2,600.
Block of 4		*25,000.*
Double transfer	*11,000.*	900.
Triple transfer, one inverted (71L1L, 81L1L and 91L1L)	*17,500.*	2,500.
On cover		—
Cracked plate	*10,500.*	*975.*
Bottom line broken (89R1L)	—	*1,750.*

No. 23 is valued in the grade of fine with perforations touching or cutting slightly on one or two sides.

Three or four used blocks of No. 23 are presently known. Value of used block of four is based on 1998 auction sale of the well-centered block of 5 sold at auction in 1998. Other blocks are poorly centered and will sell for much less.

VARIETIES OF RECUTTING

Recut once at top and once at bottom, (113 on plate)	10,000.	550.
Recut once at top, (40 on plate)	10,250.	600.
Recut once at top and twice at bottom, (21 on plate)	10,500.	600.
Recut twice at bottom, (11 on plate)	10,250.	625.
Recut once at bottom, (8 on plate)	10,500.	650.
Recut twice at top and once at bottom, (4 on plate)	11,000.	675.
Recut twice at top and twice at bottom, (2 on plate)	11,500.	675.

One example of the "recut twice at top and once at bottom" variety is pos. 71L1L, valued separately under the main listing.

Earliest documented use: July 25, 1857.

Cancellations

Blue	+25.
Red	+100.
1857 year date	+50.
"Paid"	+25.
Red Carrier	+125.
Black Carrier	+150.
Railroad	+150.
"Way"	+120.
"Steamboat"	+135.
"Steam"	+100.
Pen Cancel	275.

Franklin — A20

Type V — Similar to type III of 1851-57 but with side ornaments partly cut away. About one-half of all positions have side scratches. Wide breaks in top and bottom framelines.

Type Va — Stamps from Plate 5 with almost complete ornaments at right side and no side scratches. Many, but not all, stamps from Plate 5 are Type Va, the remainder being Type V.

24 A20 1c **blue,** type V (Plates 5, 7, 8, 9, 10) *1857*	140.00	40.00
No gum	60.00	
On cover		45.00
On patriotic cover		300.00
Pair	300.00	82.50
Strip of 3	475.00	140.00
Block of 4	800.00	425.00
P# strip of 4, Impt.	1,400.	
P# block of 8, Impt.	4,500.	—
Double transfer at top (8R and 10R, Plate 8)	200.00	82.50
Double transfer at bottom (52R9)	260.00	90.00
Curl on shoulder, (57R, 58R, 59R, 97R, 98R, 99R, Plate 7)	200.00	65.00
Long curl in hair and curl over "C" of "Cent" (52, 92R8)	290.00	130.00
With "Earring" below ear (10L9)	575.00	90.00
Curl over "C" of "Cent" (92R8)	210.00	65.00
Curl over "E" of "Cent" (41R and 81R8)	230.00	77.50
Curl in hair, 23L7; 39, 69L8; 34, 74R9	200.00	55.00
Horizontal dash in hair (24L7)	310.00	80.00
Horizontal dash in hair (36L8)	310.00	80.00
Plate 5, type V	*1,250.*	120.00
On cover		140.00
No gum	*400.00*	
Pair	*2,750.*	*260.00*
Strip of 3	—	*500.00*
Pair, types V, Va	*1,500.*	*675.00*
Curl on shoulder (48L5)	—	300.00
Curl in "O" of "ONE" (62L5)	—	300.00
Plate 5, type Va	1,000.	300.00
No gum	400.00	
On cover (Type Va)		400.00
Pair (Type Va)	—	—
Strip of 3 (Type Va)	—	—
Block of 4 (Type Va)	—	—
b. Laid paper		*7,500.*

Earliest documented uses: Dec. 2, 1857 (Plate 5); Dec. 31, 1857 (Plate 7); Nov. 17, 1857 (Plate 8); Aug. 2, 1859 (Plate 9); May 5, 1860 (Plate 10).

Cancellations

Blue	+2.50
Red	+15.00
Green	+250.00
Brown	+150.00
Magenta	+150.00
Ultramarine	+100.00
1857 year date	+70.00
1858 year date	+2.50
1859 year date	+2.50
1860 year date	+2.50
1861 year date	+2.50
1862 year date	—
1863 year date	+250.00
Printed Precancel "CUMBERLAND, ME." (on cover)	*25,000.*
"Paid"	+5.00
"Free"	+25.00
Railroad	+50.00
Numeral	+12.50
Express Company	+90.00
Steamboat	+55.00
"Steam"	+30.00
Steamship	+40.00
Packet boat	—
Supp. Mail Type A, B, or C	+55.00
"Way"	+30.00
Red Carrier	+20.00
Black Carrier	+12.50
Blue Carrier	+50.00
"Old Stamps-Not Recognized"	+1,500.
Territorial	+80.00
Pen Cancel	17.50

25 A10 3c **rose,** type I (Plates 4, 6, 7, 8)	3,000.	190.00
rose red	3,000.	190.00
dull red	3,000.	190.00
No gum	1,050.	
On cover		210.00
brownish carmine		225.00
On cover		375.00
claret	3,250.	200.00
No gum	1,000.	
On patriotic cover		525.00
Pair	*6,250.*	400.00
Strip of 3	*10,000.*	600.00
Block of 4	*16,000.*	7,000.
Double transfer	3,250.	220.00
Worn plate	3,000.	180.00
Major cracked plate (47R, 48R, Plate 7)	*4,750.*	700.00
Gash on shoulder	3,250.	210.00
b. Vert. pair, imperf. horizontally		*25,000.*

No. 25 is valued in the grade of fine with perforations touching or cutting slightly on one or two sides.

All type I perforated stamps were printed from 4 of the plates used to print the imperf. stamps, so many varieties exist both imperf. and perf.

VARIETIES OF RECUTTING

Lines on bust and bottom of medallion circle recut (47R6)	—	1,750.
Top label and right diamond block joined	—	600.00
Top label and right diamond block joined at top and bottom (68R4)	—	1,250.

Lower label and right diamond block joined	—	600.00
Extra line at right	—	750.00

All varieties of recutting listed under No. 11 are found on No. 25.

Earliest documented use: May 9, 1857 (Plate 4); April 30, 1857 (Plate 6); Feb. 28, 1857 (Plate 7); April 15, 1857 (Plate 8).

Cancellations

Blue	+7.50
Red	+20.00
Orange red	+40.00
Orange	+175.00
Brown	+100.00
Ultramarine	+125.00
Green	+250.00
1857 year date	+10.00
1858 year date	+10.00
1859 year date	+10.00
"Paid"	+5.00
"Way"	+20.00
Numeral	+10.00
Railroad	+25.00
"Steam"	+20.00
Steamship	+35.00
Steamboat	+45.00
Packet Boat	+50.00
Supplementary Mail Type A	+40.00
U. S. Express Mail	+7.50
Express Company	+65.00
Black Carrier	+30.00
"Old Stamps-Not Recognized"	+1,000.
Territorial	+50.00
Printed precancel "Cumberland, Me." (on cover)	—
Pen Cancel	75.00

25A A10 3c **rose,** type II, (Plates 2L, 3, 5L)	9,000.	900.
rose red	9,000.	900.
dull red	9,000.	900.
No gum	4,000.	
On cover		1,000.
claret	9,250.	1,000.
No gum	4,250.	
Pair	*19,500.*	2,000.
Strip of 3	*32,500.*	3,250.
Block of 4	—	—
Double transfer "Gents" instead of "Cents" (66R2L)	—	2,000.
Triple transfer	—	1,700.
Dot in lower right diamond block (69L5L)	—	1,000.
Major cracked plate (84L, 94L, 9R, Plate 5L)	*10,000.*	1,500.
Intermediate cracked plate (80L, 96L, 71R, Plate 5L)	*10,000.*	1,100.
Minor cracked plate (8L, 27L, 31L, 44L, 45L, 51L, 55L, 65L, 71L and 72L, 74L, 78L, 79L, 7R, Plate 5L)	*9,250.*	1,000.
Gash on shoulder	9,250.	1,000.
Worn plate	9,000.	900.

No. 25A is valued in the grade of fine with perforations touching or cutting slightly on one two sides.

The used block of four, a right margin block showing the center line, is believed to be unique.

All type II perforated stamps were printed from 3 of the plates used to print the imperf. stamps, so most varieties exist both imperf. and perf. See "Varieties of Recutting" under No. 11A — All these varieties also exist on No. 25A except the "5 lines recut in upper left triangle" variety. Nos. 25A printed from plates 2L and 5L are much scarcer than stamps printed from plate 3.

VARIETIES OF RECUTTING

Recut inner line only at right		1,100.
1 extra vertical line outside of left frame line (29L, 39L, 49L, 59L, 69L, 79L, Plate 3)	—	1,150.
2 extra vertical lines outside of left frame line (89L, 99L, Plate 3)	—	1,250.
1 extra vertical line outside of right frame line (58L, 68L, 78L, 88L, 98L, Plate 3)	—	1,250.
No inner line and frame line close to design at right (9L, 19L, Plate 3)	—	1,200.
No inner line and frame line close to design at left (70L, 80L, 90L, 100L, Plate 3)	—	1,150.
Lower label and lower right diamond block joined at top (25L5L)		*2,300.*
Recut button (10R2L)		1,900.

Earliest documented use: July 16, 1857 (Plate 2L); July 16, 1857 (Plate 3); April 15, 1857 (Plate 5L).

Cancellations

Blue	+50.00
Red	+100.00
Orange red	+150.00
Orange	+300.00
Brown	+150.00
Ultramarine	+200.00
Green	+500.00
1857 year date	+20.00
1858 year date	+20.00
1859 year date	+20.00
"Paid"	+20.00
"Way"	+50.00
Numeral	+50.00
Railroad	+70.00
"Steam"	+40.00
Steamship	+50.00
Steamboat	+90.00
Packet Boat	+80.00
Supplementary Mail Type A	+80.00
Express Company	+120.00
Black Carrier	+50.00
Green Carrier (New Orleans "snow shovel")	—
Territorial	+100.00
Pen Cancel	475.00

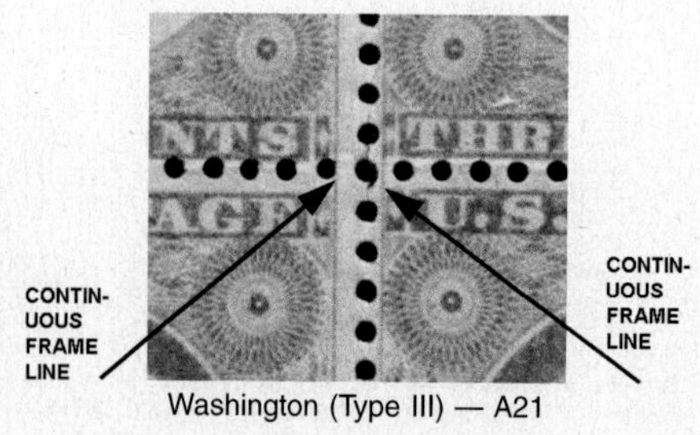

Washington (Type III) — A21

Type III — There are no outer frame lines at top and bottom. The side frame lines were recut so as to be continuous from the top to the bottom of the plate. Stamps from the top or bottom rows show the ends of the side frame lines and may be mistaken for Type IV.

Beware of type III stamps with frame lines that stop at the top of the design (from top row of plate) or bottom of the design (from bottom row of plate). These are often mistakenly offered as No. 26A.

26	A21 3c **dull red,** type III (Plates 9, 12-28)	65.00	10.00
	red	65.00	10.00
	rose	65.00	10.00
	No gum	27.50	
	brownish carmine	140.00	21.00
	No gum	47.50	
	claret	160.00	26.00
	No gum	55.00	
	orange brown	—	550.00
	plum		*5,000.*
	On cover, dull red		11.00
	On cover, brownish carmine		40.00
	On cover, orange brown		*700.00*
	On patriotic cover		150.00
	On Confederate patriotic cover		2,000.
	On Pony express cover		—
	Pair	150.00	22.50
	Strip of 3	220.00	42.50
	Block of 4	450.00	175.00
	P# block of 8, Impt.	4,250.	
	Double transfer	100.00	21.00
	Double transfer, rosettes double and line through "Postage" and "Three Cents" (87R15)	—	*2,500.*
	Left frame line double	100.00	21.00
	Right frame line double	100.00	21.00
	Cracked plate (71L18)	*1,000.*	*400.00*
	Cracked plate (62L, 72L, Plate 18)	*750.00*	*250.00*
	Damaged transfer above lower left rosette	75.00	12.00
	Same, retouched	95.00	13.00
	Same, retouched with 2 vertical lines	130.00	14.00
	Same, both damaged areas retouched	310.00	100.00
	Pair, both damaged areas retouched (8, 9R20)	500.00	175.00
	"Quadruple" plate flaw (18L28)	—	*2,000.*
	1 line recut in upper left triangle	200.00	75.00
	5 lines recut in upper left triangle (52L25)		500.00
	Inner line recut at left		*500.00*
	Inner line recut at right	—	*1,000.*
	Worn plate	65.00	10.00
b.	Horiz. pair, imperf. vertically	*14,000.*	
	On cover		—
c.	Vert. pair, imperf. horizontally		*16,000.*
d.	Horizontal pair, imperf. between		—
e.	Double impression		*15,000.*
	On cover		—

Frame line double varieties are separate and distinct for virtually the entire length of the stamp. Examples with partly split lines are worth considerably less.

Earliest documented use: Sept. 14, 1857.

Cancellations

Blue	+1.00
Red	+3.00
Orange red	+10.00
Orange	+150.00
Brown	+100.00
Ultramarine	+120.00
Violet	+100.00
Green	+150.00
1857 year date	+3.00
1858-1861 year date	+1.00
Printed Circular Precancel "Cumberland, Me." (on cover)	—
"Paid"	+1.00
"Paid All"	+15.00
"Free"	+20.00
"Collect"	+40.00
Numeral, "3" or "5"	+2.50
Numeral, number greater than "5"	—
"Steam"	+12.50
Steamer	—
Steamboat	+22.50
Steamship	+22.50
"Way"	+12.50
Railroad	+15.00
U. S. Express Mail	+20.00
Express Company	+65.00
Packet boat	+65.00
Supp. Mail Type A, B or C	+500.00
Black Carrier	+30.00
Red Carrier	+25.00
"Southn. Letter Unpaid"	+750.00
Territorial	+20.00
"Old Stamps-Not Recognized"	+500.00
On cover	*12,500.*
Pen Cancel	4.00

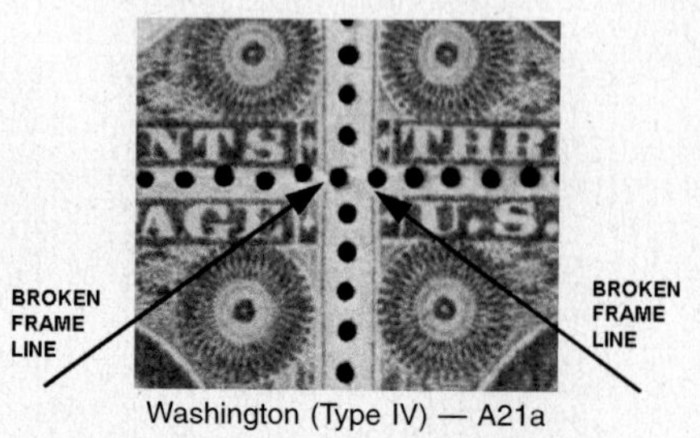

Washington (Type IV) — A21a

Type IV — As type III, but the side frame lines extend only to the top and bottom of the stamp design. All Type IV stamps are from plates 10 and 11 (each of which exists in three states), and these plates produced only Type IV. The side frame lines were recut individually for each stamp, thus being broken between the stamps vertically.

Beware of type III stamps with frame lines that stop at the top of the design (from top row of plate) or bottom of the design (from bottom row of plate). These are often mistakenly offered as No. 26A.

26A	A21a 3c **dull red,** type IV (Plates 10-11)	600.00	150.00
	brownish carmine	600.00	150.00
	rose	600.00	150.00
	No gum	260.00	
	claret	650.00	170.00
	No gum	275.00	
	orange red	—	*190.00*
	On cover		*225.00*
	orange brown	—	*1,600.*
	On patriotic cover		450.00
	Pair	1,250.	325.00
	Strip of 3	2,000.	600.00
	Block of 4	*4,750.*	*2,500.*
	P# block of 8, Impt.	*16,000.*	
	Double transfer	675.00	225.00
	Double transfer, line through rosettes (61R10i, 61R10L, 98R10i, 98R10L)	—	925.00
	Double transfer of rosettes and lower part of stamp (91R11L)	—	270.00
	Triple transfer	—	475.00
	Damaged transfer above lower left rosette	650.00	175.00
	Same, retouched	625.00	170.00
	Same, both damaged areas retouched (10R11)		325.00
	Inner line recut at right	—	325.00
	Inner line recut at left (79L10)	—	525.00
	Left frame line double (70, 80, 90, 100R11)	—	225.00
	Worn plate	600.00	140.00
f.	Horiz. strip of 3, imperf. vert., on cover		*27,000.*

No. 26Af is unique.

Earliest documented use: July 11, 1857.

Cancellations

Blue	+10.00
Red	+20.00
Orange red	+30.00
Orange	+150.00
Brown	+100.00
Ultramarine	+100.00
Violet	+150.00
Green	+175.00
1857 year date	+2.50
1858 or 1859 year date	+1.50
"Paid"	+2.50
"Paid All"	+15.00
"Free"	+20.00
"Collect"	+40.00
Numeral	+2.50
"Steam"	+15.00
Steamer	—
Steamboat	+25.00
Steamship	+25.00
"Way"	+15.00
Railroad	+17.50
U. S. Express Mail	+17.50
Express Company	+65.00
Packet boat	+65.00
Black Carrier	+30.00
Red Carrier	+20.00
Territorial	+30.00
Pen Cancel	40.00

27	A11 5c **brick red,** type I, *1858*	*80,000.*	1,450.
	No gum	*20,000.*	
	On cover		1,800.
	On patriotic cover		4,750.
	Pair	*175,000.*	3,500.
	Strip of 3		*6,000.*
	Block of 4	*475,000.*	*40,000.*
	Defective transfer (23R1)	—	—

The unused block of 4 is unique. Value reflects 2019 auction sale price.

Earliest documented use: Oct. 6, 1858.

Cancellations

Blue	+225.
Red	+250.
Ultramarine	+500.
1859 year date	+50.
1860 year date	+50.
"Paid"	+50.
Supplementary Mail Type A	+150.
"Steamship"	+150.
N.Y. Ocean Mail	+1,000.
Pen Cancel	850.

28 A11 5c **red brown,** type I	*60,000.*	1,100.
pale red brown	*60,000.*	1,100.
No gum	15,000.	
On cover		1,300.
Pair	*125,000.*	2,500.
Strip of 3		4,000.
Block of 4	*90,000.*	*8,000.*
Defective transfer (23R1)		—
b. **Bright red brown**	*70,000.*	*2,000.*
No gum	*20,000.*	
Defective transfer (23R1)		*2,500.*

The value of the block of 4 of No. 28 is based on the 2009 auction sale of the finest original-gum block, which grades Average-Fine.

Earliest documented use: Aug. 23, 1857 (No. 28).

Cancellations

Blue	+75.
Ultramarine	+200.
Red	+125.
1857 year date	+20.
1858 year date	+15.
"Paid"	+35.
Railroad	+75.
"Short Paid"	—
Pen Cancel	525.

28A A11 5c **Indian red,** type I, *1858*	*160,000.*	3,750.
No gum	*40,000.*	
On cover		5,250.
Pair		*8,000.*
Strip of 3		*13,000.*
Block of 4		—

There are only five recorded examples of No. 28A with any amount of original gum. Value is for a fine stamp, the highest recorded grade (two thus).

Earliest documented use: Mar. 31, 1858.

Cancellations

Red	+250.
Blue	+350.
1858 year date	+50.
1859 year date	+25.
Pen Cancel	1,650.

29 A11 5c **brown,** type I, *1859*	5,500.	325.
pale brown	5,500.	325.
deep brown	5,500.	325.
yellowish brown	5,500.	325.
No gum	1,750.	
On cover		475.
Pair	*12,000.*	700.
Strip of 3	*19,000.*	1,10.
Block of 4	*90,000.*	*5,000.*
Defective transfer (23R1)	—	—

Earliest documented use: Mar. 21, 1859.

Cancellations

Blue	+25.
Ultramarine	+175.
Red	+75.
Brown	+100.
Magenta	+150.
Green	+550.
1859 year date	+10.
1860 year date	+10.
"Paid"	+15.
"Steam"	+75.
Steamship	+100.
Numeral	+80.
Pen Cancel	150.

Jefferson — A22

FIVE CENTS.

Type II — The projections at top and bottom are partly cut away. Several minor types could be made according to the extent of cutting of the projections.

30 A22 5c **orange brown,** Type II, *1861*	1,200.	*1,300.*
deep orange brown	1,200.	*1,300.*
No gum	500.	
On cover		*2,250.*
On patriotic cover		—
Pair	2,700.	*3,250.*
Strip of 3	4,250.	—
Block of 4	*7,000.*	—

Earliest documented use: May 8, 1861.

Cancellations

Blue	+30.
Red	+75.
Green	+1,000.
"Paid"	+75.
Steamship	+110.
Supplementary Mail Type A	+150.
Railroad	—
Pen Cancel	650.

30A A22 5c **brown,** type II, *1860*	2,250.	300.
dark brown	2,250.	300.
yellowish brown	2,250.	300.
No gum	850.	
On cover		350.
On patriotic cover		—
Pair	5,000.	625.
Strip of 3	*7,500.*	950.
Block of 4	*25,000.*	*3,250.*
Cracked plate	—	
b. Printed on both sides		*35,000.*

Earliest documented use: May 4, 1860.

Cancellations

Blue	+50.
Red	+75.
Magenta	+100.
Brown	+100.
Green	+400.
"Paid"	+20.
Supplementary Mail Type A	+50.
"Steamship"	+50.
"Steam"	+50.
Express Company	+300.
Railroad	—
Packet boat	—
Pen Cancel	150.

31 A12 10c **green,** type I	*35,000.*	1,100.
dark green	*35,000.*	1,100.
bluish green	*35,000.*	1,100.
yellowish green	*35,000.*	1,100.
No gum	*11,500.*	
On domestic cover		1,300.
On patriotic cover		3,500.
Pair	*75,000.*	2,400.
Vertical pair, types III, I	*45,000.*	1,500.
Vertical pair, types IV, I (86, 96 L 1)		—
Strip of 3		—
Vertical strip of 3, types II, III, I		—
Block of 4, types III, I	*80,000.*	—
Block of 4, types III, IV, I		*9,500.*
Vertical block of 6, 2 each types II, III, I	*100,000.*	
Double transfer (100R1)	*37,500.*	1,250.
"Curl" in left "X" (99R1)	*37,500.*	1,250.

Type I comes only from the bottom row of both panes of Plate 1.

Earliest documented use: Aug. 25, 1857.

Cancellations

Blue	+50.
Red	+100.
Green	+850.
Supplementary Mail Type A	—
"Steamship"	+100.
Canadian	—
Pen Cancel	600.

Act of February 27, 1861. Ten cent rate of postage to be prepaid on letters conveyed in the mail from any point in the United States east of the Rocky Mountains to any State or Territory on the Pacific Coast and vice versa, for each half-ounce.

32 A13 10c **green,** type II	5,750.	190.
dark green	5,750.	190.
bluish green	5,750.	190.
yellowish green	5,750.	190.
No gum	2,000.	
On domestic cover		230.
On pony express cover		8,500.
Pair	*12,000.*	400.
Strip of 3	—	600.
Block of 4	*30,000.*	*4,500.*
Pair, types II, III	*12,000.*	450.
Pair, types II, IV	*60,000.*	2,500.
Vertical strip of 3, types II, III, IV		—
On cover		—
Block of 4, types II, III	*30,000.*	*3,500.*
Block of 4, types II, IV		—
Block of 4, types II, III, IV	*95,000.*	*18,000.*
Double transfer (31L, 51L and 20R, Plate 1)	6,250.	235.
"Curl opposite left X" (10R1)		260.

Earliest documented use: July 27, 1857 (dated cancel on off-cover stamp), Aug. 8, 1857 (on cover).

Cancellations

Blue	+15.
Red	+35.
Orange "PAID"	—
Brown	+125.
Green	+300.
"Paid"	+20.
1857 year date	+10.
Supplementary Mail Type A	—
Steamship	+50.
Packet boat	—
Railroad	—
Express Company	—
Pen Cancel	90.

33 A14 10c **green,** type III	5,750.	190.
dark green	5,750.	190.
bluish green	5,750.	190.
yellowish green	5,750.	190.
No gum	2,000.	
On domestic cover		230.
Pair	*12,000.*	400.
Strip of 3	—	600.
Pair, types III, IV		2,500.
"Curl" on forehead (85L1)	—	250.
"Curl in left X" (87R1)		250.

Earliest documented use: Aug. 8, 1857.

Cancellations

Blue	+15.
Red	+35.
Brown	+125.
Ultramarine	+150.
Green	+900.
1857 year date	+10.
"Paid"	+20.
"Steam"	+45.
Steamboat	—
Steamship	+50.
Numeral	+20.
Packet boat	—
Pen Cancel	90.

34 A15 10c **green,** type IV	*50,000.*	2,200.
dark green	*50,000.*	2,200.
bluish green	*50,000.*	2,200.
yellowish green	*50,000.*	2,200.
No gum	*20,000.*	
On domestic cover		2,600.
Pair		*5,750.*
Block of 4 (54-55, 64-65L)		—

VARIETIES OF RECUTTING

Eight stamps on Plate I were recut. All are listed below.

Outer line recut at top (65L, 74L, 86L and 3R, Plate I)	*50,000.*	2,200.
Outer line recut at bottom (54L, 55L, 76L, Plate 1)	*52,500.*	2,400.
Outer line recut at top and bottom (64L1)	*55,000.*	2,750.

Earliest documented use: Oct. 5, 1857.

Cancellations

Blue	+100.
Red	+175.
Steamship	+200.
Packet boat	—
Pen Cancel	1,200.

Types I, II, III and IV occur on the same sheet, so it is possible to obtain pairs and blocks showing combinations of types. For listings of type combinations in pairs and blocks, see Nos. 31-33.

Example I Example II

Washington (Two typical examples) — A23

Type V — The side ornaments are slightly cut away. Usually only one pearl remains at each end of the lower label, but some examples show two or three pearls at the right side. At the bottom the outer line is complete and the shells nearly so. The outer lines at top are complete except over the right "X."

35 A23 10c **green,** type V, (Plate 2), *1859*	210.00	55.00
dark green	210.00	55.00
yellowish green	210.00	55.00
No gum	95.00	
On domestic cover		67.50
On patriotic cover		625.00
On pony express cover		—
On cover to Canada		120.00
Pair	450.00	120.00
Block of 4	1,100.	600.00
P# block of 8, Impt.	*17,500.*	
Double transfer at bottom (47R2)	275.00	80.00
Small "Curl" on forehead (37, 78L2)	250.00	120.00
Curl in "e" of "cents" (93L2)	300.00	80.00
Curl in "t" of "cents" (73R2)	300.00	80.00
Cracked plate		—

Earliest documented use: Apr. 29, 1859.

Cancellations

Red	+7.50
Orange red	+12.50
Orange	+150.00
Brown	+100.00
Blue	+5.00
Magenta	+100.00

Green	+275.00
1859 year date	+5.00
"Paid"	+5.00
"Paid All"	—
"Free"	+75.00
Red carrier	—
Railroad	+40.00
Steamship	+35.00
"Steam"	+30.00
Numerals	+15.00
Supp. Mail Type A or C	+60.00
Express Company	+135.00
"Southn Letter Unpaid"	—
Territorial	—
Pen Cancel	25.00

TWELVE CENTS. Printed from two plates.

Plate 1 (No. 36) — Outer frame lines were recut on the plate and are complete. Very narrow spacing of stamps on the plate.

No. 36, Outer frame lines recut on plate

36	A16 12c **black** (Plate 1)	1,700.	300.
	gray black	1,700.	300.
	No gum	600.	
	Single on cover		700.
	Single on cover with No. 26 to France		475.
	Pair on cover to England		850.
	Pair on patriotic cover		—
	Pair	4,000.	700.
	Block of 4	*10,000.*	3,500.
	Not recut in lower right corner	2,000.	350.
	Recut in lower left corner (43, 53, 63, 73, 100L)	2,000.	350.
	Double transfer	2,000.	350.
	Triple transfer	2,200.	—
a.	Diagonal half used as 6c on cover		*17,500.*
c.	Horizontal pair, imperf. between		*12,500.*

Earliest documented use: July 30, 1857.

Cancellations

Blue	+10.
Red	+20.
Brown	+75.
Magenta	+75.
Green	+350.
1857 year date	+100.
"Paid"	+10.
Supplementary Mail Type A	+60.
Express Company	—
Railroad	+60.
Numeral	+20.
"Southn Letter Unpaid"	—
Pen Cancel	150.

Typical No. 36B, outer frame lines not recut

Plate 3 (No. 36B) — Weak outer frame lines from the die were not recut and are noticeably uneven or broken, sometimes partly missing. Somewhat wider spacing of stamps on the plate.

36B	A16 12c **black** (Plate 3)	775.	275.
	intense black	775.	275.
	No gum	375.	
	Single on cover		1,150.
	Single on cover with No. 26 to France		475.
	Pair on cover to England		800.
	Pair	1,650.	650.
	Block of 4	5,000.	3,250.
	Double frame line at right	825.	300.
	Double frame line at left	825.	300.
	Vertical line through rosette (95R3)	950.	350.

Earliest documented use: June 1, 1860. (The previously listed Dec. 3, 1859, cover requires expertization in order to be considered.)

Cancellations

Blue	+20.
Red	+40.
Brown	+85.
Magenta	+60.
Green	+275.
1860 year date	+100.
1861 year date	+50.
"Paid"	+12.
Supplementary Mail Type A	+300.
Express Company	—
Railroad	+65.
Numeral	+25.
"Southn Letter Unpaid"	—
Pen Cancel	140.

Washington — A17

Franklin — A18

37	A17 24c **gray lilac**, *1860*	1,450.	400.
a.	24c **gray**	1,450.	400.
	No gum	500.	
	On cover to England		1,000.
	On patriotic cover		*4,000.*
	Pair	3,150.	850.
	Block of 4	*10,000.*	*6,500.*
	P# block of 12, Impt.	*40,000.*	

The technical configuration of a No. 37 plate block is eight stamps. The unique plate block currently is contained in the listed block of twelve stamps.

Earliest documented use: July 7, 1860.

Cancellations

Blue	+20.
Red	+65.
Magenta	+110.
Violet	+175.
Green	+650.
1860 year date	+15.
"Paid"	+25.
"Paid All"	+50.
"Free"	+150.
Supplementary Mail Type A	+150.
Railroad	+150.
Packet Boat	+200.
Red Carrier	—
Numeral	+40.
"Southn Letter Unpaid"	—
Mexico	—
Pen Cancel	200.

See Trial Color Proofs for the 24c red lilac.

38	A18 30c **orange**, *1860*	1,900.	500.
	yellow orange	1,900.	500.
	reddish orange	1,900.	500.
	No gum	700.	
	On cover to Germany or France		*1,350.*
	On patriotic cover		*7,500.*
	Pair	*4,250.*	1,100.
	Block of 4	*14,000.*	*6,750.*
	Double transfer (89L1 and 99L1)	2,150.	575.
	Recut at bottom (52L1)	2,400.	625.
	Cracked plate	—	—
	Curl above "U" of "U.S." (64R1)	—	—

Earliest documented use: Aug. 8, 1860.

Cancellations

Blue	+30.
Red	+50.
Magenta	+90.
Violet	+250.
Green	+1,200.
1860 year date	+30.
"Paid"	+35.
"Free"	—
Black town	+30.
Supplementary Mail Type A	+125.
Steamship	—
N.Y. Ocean Mail	+100.
Express Company	—
Pen Cancel	250.

Washington — A19

39	A19 90c **blue**, *1860*	3,000.	*10,000.*
	deep blue	3,000.	*10,000.*
	No gum	1,400.	
	On cover		*225,000.*
	Pair	*6,250.*	—
	Block of 4	*75,000.*	*45,000.*
	Double transfer at bottom	3,250.	—
	Double transfer at top	3,250.	—
	Short transfer at bottom right and left (13L1 and 68R1)	3,250.	

The used block of 4 is believed to be unique and has perfs trimmed off at left and bottom clear of design. Value is based on 1993 auction sale.

Earliest documented use: Sept. 11, 1860.

Cancellations

Red	10,500.
Black	+200.
Blue	+400.
Red town	+1,200.
Black town	+1,000.
1861 year date	+1,000.
Boston "Paid"	+750.
Red Carrier	—
N.Y. Ocean Mail	+1,000.
Pen Cancel	3,250.

Genuine cancellations on the 90c are very scarce.

All used examples of No. 39 must be accompanied by certificates of authenticity issued by recognized expertizing committees.

See Die and Plate Proofs for imperfs. on stamp paper.

REPRINTS OF 1857-60 ISSUE

These were not valid for postal use, though one example each of Nos. 43 and 45 are known with contemporaneous cancels.

Produced by the Continental Bank Note Co.

White paper, without gum.

The 1, 3, 10 and 12c were printed from new plates of 100 subjects each differing from those used for the regular issue.

1875 ***Perf. 12***

40	A5 1c **bright blue** *(3846)*	*600.*	
	Pair	*1,250.*	
	Block of 4	*3,300.*	
	Cracked plate, pos. 91	*725.*	
	Double transfer, pos. 94	*725.*	
41	A10 3c **scarlet** *(479)*	*2,850.*	
42	A22 5c **orange brown** *(878)*	*1,200.*	
	Pair	*2,750.*	
	Vertical margin strip of 4, Impt. & P#	*11,500.*	
43	A12 10c **blue green** *(516)*	*2,500.*	13,000.
	Pair	*6,000.*	
44	A16 12c **greenish black** *(489)*	*2,750.*	
	Pair	*7,000.*	
45	A17 24c **blackish violet** *(479)*	*3,000.*	10,000.
46	A18 30c **yellow orange** *(480)*	*3,000.*	
47	A19 90c **deep blue** *(454)*	*3,750.*	

Nos. 41-46 are valued in the grade of fine.

Nos. 40-47 exist imperforate. Very infrequent sales preclude establishing a value at this time. One set of imperforate pairs is recorded and it sold for $110,000 in a 2009 auction. An imperforate horizontal strip of 3 of No. 44 also is recorded.

Numbers in parentheses are quantities sold.

Produced by the National Bank Note Co.

Franklin

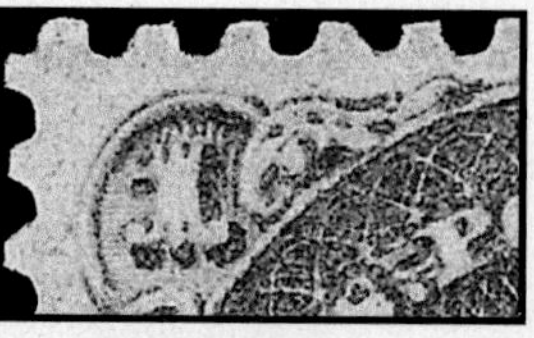

A24

Washington

A25

Jefferson

A26

Washington — A27

A27

A27a

Washington

A28

Washington — A29

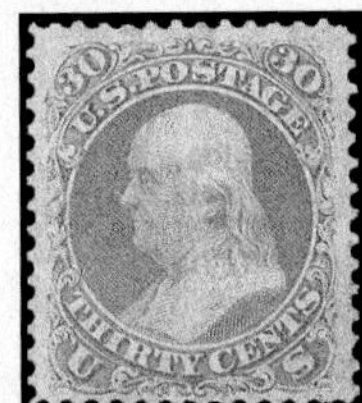

Franklin — A30

Washington

A31

1c — There is a dash under the tip of the ornament at right of the numeral in upper left corner.

3c — Ornaments at corners end in a small ball.

5c — There is a leaflet in the foliated ornaments at each corner.

10c (A27) — A heavy curved line has been cut below the stars and an outer line added to the ornaments above them.

12c — There are corner ornaments consisting of ovals and scrolls.

90c — Parallel lines form an angle above the ribbon with "U. S. Postage"; between these lines there is a row of dashes and a point of color at the apex of the lower line.

Patriotic Covers covering a wide range of historical interest were used during the Civil War period, in the North as well as the South, and are collected by manufacturer and topic as well as generally, both used and unused. There are believed to be 12,500 or more Northern varieties and 300 or more Southern varieties.

During the war, these stamps were used as small change until Postage Currency was issued.

The Act of Congress of March 3, 1863, effective July 1, 1863, created a rate of three cents for each half ounce, first class domestic mail. This Act was the first law which established uniform rate of postage regardless of the distance. This rate remained in effect until Oct. 1, 1883.

Plates of 200 subjects in two panes of 100 each.

The following items, formerly listed here as Nos. 55-62, are considered to be essays or trial color proofs. They will be found in a separate listing between the Essay section and the Proof section of this catalog. Previous No. 58 has been combined with No. 62B.

Formerly	Currently	Formerly	Currently
55	63-E11e	59	69-E6e
56	65-E15h	60	70TC6
57	67-E9e	61	71TC6
58	62B	62	72-E7h

The paper of Nos. 62B-72 is thicker and more opaque than the essays and trial color proofs, except Nos. 62B, 70c, and 70d.

1861 ***Perf. 12***

62B	A27a 10c **dark green**	*8,500.*	1,750.
	dark yellow green	*8,250.*	1,750.
	No gum	*3,600.*	
	On cover		2,250.
	On patriotic cover		3,250.
	Pair	*18,000.*	3,750.
	Block of 4	*37,500.*	*13,500.*
	Foreign entry 94R4	*9,500.*	—
	Block of 4, one stamp 94R4	*40,000.*	

The foreign entry is of the 90c 1861.

Earliest documented use: Sept. 17, 1861.

Cancellations

Red	+110.
Blue	+70.
"Paid"	+60.
Steamship	+100.
Express Company	+200.
Supplementary Mail Type A	+125.

1861-62 ***Perf. 12***

63	A24 1c **blue,** *Aug. 17, 1861*	275.00	45.00
	pale blue	275.00	45.00
	bright blue	275.00	45.00
	pale milky blue		—
	No gum	100.00	
	On cover (single)		52.50
	On prisoner's letter		—
	On patriotic cover		275.00
	Pair	600.00	95.00
	Block of 4	1,600.	500.00
	P# block of 8, Impt.	*6,500.*	
	Double transfer	—	57.50
	Dot in "U"	300.00	50.00
a.	1c **ultramarine**	*2,500.*	*1,900.*
	No gum	*1,000.*	
	dark ultramarine	*5,000.*	*2,000.*
	No gum	*2,250.*	
b.	1c **dark blue**	800.00	*875.00*
	No gum	300.00	
c.	Laid paper, horiz. or vert.	*8,500.*	*4,500.*
	Block of four		*27,500.*
d.	Vertical pair, imperf. horiz.		—
e.	Printed on both sides, reverse inverted	—	*35,000.*

The editors would like to see authenticated evidence of the existence of No. 63d.

The pale milky blue shade of No. 63 is very rare.

Earliest documented use: Aug. 17, 1861 (dated cancel on off-cover stamp); Aug. 21, 1861 (on cover).

Cancellations

Blue	+5.00
Red	+15.00
Magenta	+50.00
Green	+250.00
Violet	+70.00
1861 year date	+7.50
1865 year date	+2.00
1866 year date	+2.00
"Free"	+40.00
"Paid"	+2.50
"Paid All"	+15.00
Supp. Mail Type A or B	+30.00
Steamship	+35.00
Steam	+40.00
Express Company	+175.00
Red Carrier	+20.00
Black Carrier	+25.00
Railroad	+40.00
Numeral	+20.00
"Steamboat"	+50.00
Printed Precancel "CUMBERLAND, ME."	—

64	A25 3c **pink,** *Aug. 17, 1861*	*14,000.*	575.00
	No gum	*5,000.*	
	On cover		750.00
	On patriotic cover		1,400.
	Pair	*30,000.*	*1,600.*
	Block of 4	*65,000.*	—

Earliest documented use: Aug. 17, 1861 (FDC).

Cancellations

Blue	+50.00
Red	+150.00
Green	+500.00
1861 date	—
"Paid"	+25.00
"Free"	+175.00
"Ship"	+85.00
Supplementary Mail Type B	+150.00
Railroad	+125.00
Steamboat	+175.00

a.	3c **pigeon blood pink**	*55,000.*	*4,250.*
	No gum	*17,500.*	
	On cover		*4,750.*
	On patriotic cover		*7,000.*

Earliest documented use: Aug. 21, 1861.

b.	3c **rose pink,** *Aug. 17, 1861*	600.00	140.00
	No gum	250.00	
	On cover		170.00
	On patriotic cover		250.00
	Pair	1,350.	300.00
	Block of 4	3,250.	850.00

Earliest documented use: Aug. 17, 1861 (FDC).

Cancellations

Blue	+15.00
Red	+30.00
Orange red	+40.00
Green	+180.00
Orange	—
"Paid"	+10.00
"Free"	+75.00
Supplementary Mail Type C	—
Numeral "15" (on No. 64b)	—
"Ship"	+30.00
Railroad	+60.00
Steamboat	+90.00

65	A25 3c **rose**	125.00	3.00
	bright rose	125.00	3.00
	dull red	125.00	3.00
	rose red	125.00	3.00
	No gum	50.00	
	On cover		3.50
	On patriotic cover		110.00
	On prisoner's letter		150.00
	On pony express cover		—
	Pair	270.00	6.75
	Block of 4	700.00	42.50
	P# block of 8, Impt.	4,750.	
	Double transfer	160.00	10.00
	Cracked plate	—	—
	brown red	*275.00*	5.50
	No gum	100.00	
	pale brown red	*210.00*	5.50
	No gum	70.00	
	dull brown red	*250.00*	5.50
	No gum	90.00	
	Block of 4	*1,250.*	
	deep pinkish rose	*290.00*	30.00
	On cover		—
	Indian red		*5,000.*
b.	Laid paper, horiz. or vert.	—	*1,100.*
d.	Vertical pair, imperf. horiz.	*12,500.*	*1,500.*
	No gum	*5,000.*	
e.	Printed on both sides, reverse inverted	*40,000.*	*8,000.*
	Pair	*82,500.*	
	Printed on both sides, reverse not inverted		*8,000.*
f.	Double impression		*11,000.*

See Die and Plate Proofs for imperfs. on stamp paper.

Earliest documented use: Aug. 19, 1861.

Cancellations

Blue	+1.00
Ultramarine	+2.75
Brown	+50.00
Red	+3.00
Orange red	+3.50
Violet	+75.00
Magenta	+8.00
Green	+100.00
Olive	+100.00
Orange	+150.00
Yellow	*+3,500.*
1861 year date	+2.00
1867 or 1868 year date	+1.00
"Paid"	+.35

"Paid All"	+7.50
"Returned for Postage"	+35.00
"Mails Suspended"	—
Railroad	+12.50
"Way"	+20.00
"Free"	+20.00
"Collect"	+35.00
"Ship"	+15.00
"U. S. Ship"	+35.00
"Steam"	+12.00
Steamship	+15.00
Steamboat	+20.00
"Ship Letter"	+35.00
Red Carrier	+15.00
Blue Carrier	+25.00
Black Carrier	+20.00
Supplementary Mail Type A, B or C	+15.00
Numeral, "3" or "5"	+3.00
Numeral, number greater than "5"	—
Express Company	+90.00
Army Field Post	+60.00
Packet Boat	+40.00
"Registered"	+30.00
"Postage Due"	+25.00
"Advertised"	+15.00
"U.STATES"	+300.00
Territorial	+25.00
St. Thomas	—
China	—

The 3c lake can be found under No. 66TC6 in the Trial Color, Die and Plate Proofs section.

67	A26 5c **buff**	*30,000.*	750.
	No gum	*12,500.*	
	On cover		1,000.
	On patriotic cover		*3,750.*
	Pair	*65,000.*	1,900.
	Block of 4	*25,000.*	*13,000.*
a.	5c **brown yellow**	*32,500.*	1,100.
	No gum	*14,000.*	
b.	5c **olive yellow**	—	4,850.

The unused block of 4 is unique but very faulty. Value is based on 2019 auction sale.

Earliest documented uses: Aug. 19, 1861 (No. 67); Aug. 21, 1861 (No. 67a); Sept. 18, 1861 (on off-cover No. 67b).

Cancellations

Red	+60.00
Blue	+30.00
Magenta	+250.00
Green	+900.00
1861 year date	+10.00
"Paid"	+25.00
Supplementary Mail Type A	+100.00
Express Company	+250.00
Numeral	+50.00
"Steamship"	+100.00

Values of Nos. 67, 67a, 67b reflect the normal small margins.

68	A27 10c **green**	950.	60.00
	yellow green	900.	60.00
	No gum	375.	
	On cover		80.00
	On patriotic cover		400.00
	On cover to Canada		100.00
	Pair	2,100.	125.00
	Block of 4	*5,500.*	650.00
	P# block of 8, Impt.	*20,000.*	
	Double transfer	1,150.	65.00
	deep yellow green on thin paper	1,250.	67.50
a.	10c **dark green**	1,350.	90.00
	blue green	1,350.	90.00
	No gum	500.	
b.	Vertical pair, imperf. horiz.		*30,000.*

Earliest documented use: Aug. 20, 1861.

Cancellations

Blue	+5.00
Red	+10.00
Purple	+50.00
Magenta	+50.00
Brown	+50.00
Green	+250.00
1865 year date	+3.50
"Paid"	+2.50
"Collect"	+32.50
"Short Paid"	+50.00
"P.D." in circle	+30.00
"Free"	+100.00
Numeral	+7.50
Red Carrier	+65.00
Railroad	+20.00
Steamship	+15.00
"Steamboat"	+35.00
Supplementary Mail Type A	+30.00
Red Supp. Mail Type D	+1,000.
Express Company	+70.00
China	—
Japan	+200.00
St. Thomas	—
"U. States"	+300.00

Stamps are valued in the grade of very fine unless otherwise indicated.

Please Note:

Values for early and valuable stamps are for examples with certificates of authenticity from acknowledged expert committees, or examples sold with the buyer having the right of certification.

This applies to unused examples with original gum as well as examples without gum. It also applies to used stamps.

Beware of stamps offered "as is," as the gum on some unused stamps offered with "original gum" may be fraudulent, and stamps offered as unused without gum may in some cases be altered or faintly canceled used stamps.

69	A28 12c **black**	1,700.	95.00
	gray black	1,700.	105.00
	No gum	675.	
	intense black	1,800.	110.00
	No gum	700.	
	On domestic cover		135.00
	On patriotic cover		850.00
	On cover to France or Germany with #65		160.00
	Pair	3,750.	230.00
	Block of 4	*10,000.*	1,100.
	Double transfer of top frame line	1,800.	125.00
	Double transfer of bottom frame line	1,800.	125.00
	Double transfer of top and bottom frame lines	1,900.	130.00

Earliest documented use: Aug. 30, 1861.

Cancellations

Blue	+15.00
Ultramarine	+500.
Red	+40.00
Purple	+110.00
Magenta	+100.00
Green	+550.00
1861 year date	+5.00
"Paid"	+5.00
"Registered"	+35.00
Supp. Mail Type A, B or C	+45.00
Express Company	+175.00
Railroad	+50.00
Numeral	+15.00

70	A29 24c **red lilac**	2,900.	300.00
	No gum	1,100.	
	On cover		350.00
	On patriotic cover		*3,000.*
	Pair	6,250.	625.00
	Block of 4	*15,000.*	*3,000.*
	Scratch under "A" of "Postage"		—
a.	24c **brown lilac**	3,250.	325.00
	No gum	1,250.	
	Block of 4	*17,000.*	*3,500.*
b.	24c **steel blue** ('61)	*16,500.*	825.00
	No gum	*6,250.*	
	On cover		1,300.
	Block of 4	*75,000.*	
c.	24c **violet,** thin paper, *Aug. 20, 1861*	*35,000.*	2,250.
	reddish violet		—
	No gum	*13,500.*	
d.	24c **pale gray violet,** thin paper	*25,000.*	3,000.
	No gum	*6,000.*	

There are numerous shades of the 24c stamp in this and the following issue.

Color changelings, especially of No. 78, are frequently offered as No. 70b. Obtaining a certificate from an acknowledged expert committee is strongly advised.

Nos. 70c and 70d are on a thinner, harder and more transparent paper than Nos. 70, 70a, 70b or the latter Nos. 78, 78a, 78b and 78c. No. 70eTC (formerly No. 60, see Trial Color Proofs section) is distinguished by its distinctive dark color.

Earliest documented uses: Jan. 7, 1862 (No. 70); Feb. 5, 1862 (No. 70a); Sept. 21, 1861 (No. 70b); Aug. 20, 1861 (No. 70c); Sept. 10, 1861 (No. 70d).

Cancellations, No. 70

Blue	+25.00
Red	+40.00
Magenta	+200.00
Brown	+125.00
Green	+400.00
1865 year date	+5.00
"Paid"	+15.00
Supp. Mail Types A or B	+75.00
Express Company	+350.00

71	A30 30c **orange**	2,600.	250.
	deep orange	2,600.	275.
	No gum	900.	
	On cover to France or Germany		400.
	On patriotic cover		*3,500.*
	Pair	5,750.	550.
	Block of 4	*17,000.*	*2,600.*
	P# strip of 4, Impt.	—	
a.	Printed on both sides		—

Values for No. 71 are for examples with small margins, especially at sides. Large-margined examples sell for much more.

Earliest documented use: Aug. 20, 1861.

Cancellations

Blue	+15.00
Magenta	+100.00
Brown	+100.00
Red	+45.00
Green	—
"Paid"	+20.00
"Paid All"	+50.00
"Returned for Postage"	+65.00
"Registered"	—
Railroad	—
Packet Boat	—
"Steamship"	+75.00
Supplementary Mail Type A	+75.00
Red Supp. Mail Type D	—
Express Company	+350.00
Japan	—

72	A31 90c **blue**	3,000.	625.
	dull blue	3,000.	625.
	No gum	1,200.	
	On cover		*25,000.*
	Pair	*6,500.*	1,300.
	Block of 4	*32,500.*	*5,000.*
	P# strip of 4, Impt.	*50,000.*	
a.	90c **pale blue**	3,000.	675.
	No gum	1,200.	
b.	90c **dark blue**	3,750.	950.
	No gum	1,500.	

The unique plate number and imprint strip of 4 of No. 72 has no gum and is valued thus.

Earliest documented use: Nov. 27, 1861.

Cancellations

Blue	+60.
Red	+125.
Green	+1,000.
1865 year date	+35.
"Paid"	+25.
"Registered"	+75.
Express Company	+500.
Supplementary Mail Type A	+100.

Nos. 68a, 69, 71 and 72 exist as imperforate sheet-margin singles with pen cancel. They were not regularly issued.

The 90c was distributed to several post offices in the last two weeks of August, 1861.

Owing to the Civil War, stamps and stamped envelopes in current use or available for postage in 1860, were demonetized by various post office orders, beginning in August, 1861, and extending to early January, 1862.

P. O. Department Bulletin.

"A reasonable time after hostilities began in 1861 was given for the return to the Department of all these (1851-56) stamps in the hands of postmasters, and as early as 1863 the Department issued an order declining to longer redeem them."

The Act of Congress, approved March 3, 1863, abolished carriers' fees and established a prepaid rate of two cents for drop letters, making necessary the 2-cent Jackson (No. 73).

Free City Delivery was authorized by the Act of Congress of March 3, 1863, effective in 49 cities with 449 carriers, beginning July 1, 1863.

Produced by the National Bank Note Co.
DESIGNS AS 1861 ISSUE

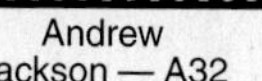

Andrew Jackson — A32

Abraham Lincoln — A33

1861-66 ***Perf. 12***

73	A32 2c **black,** *1863*	350.00	65.00
	gray black	350.00	60.00
	intense black	350.00	65.00
	No gum	150.00	
	On cover		80.00
	On prisoner's letter		—
	On patriotic cover		*1,800.*
	Pair	750.00	130.00
	Block of 4	*2,750.*	*3,250.*
	P# strip of 4, Impt.	*4,500.*	
	P# block of 8, Impt.	*15,000.*	
	Double transfer	400.00	65.00
	Major double transfer of top left corner and "Postage" ("Atherton shift")		*12,000.*
	Major double transfer of right side, pos. 81, right pane ("Preston shift")	*5,000.*	*4,000.*
	Major double transfer of frame in all corners plus hair and chin ("Metzger shift")		—
	Triple transfer		—
	Short transfer	375.00	65.00
	Cracked plate	—	—
a.	Diagonal half used as 1c as part of 3c rate on cover		1,500.
	Diagonal half used as 1c as part of 2c drop rate on cover		—
b.	Diagonal half used alone as 1c on cover		*3,000.*
c.	Horiz. half used as 1c as part of 3c rate on cover		*3,500.*
d.	Vert. half used as 1c as part of 3c rate on cover		2,000.
e.	Vert. half used alone as 1c on cover		*4,000.*
f.	Printed on both sides, reverse not inverted		*27,500.*

Printed on both sides, reverse inverted 6,500. 20,000.
g. Laid paper — 11,500.

No. 73f unused is unique. It has perfs cut off on two sides and is valued thus.

Earliest documented use: July 1, 1863 (dated cancel on off-cover stamp); July 6, 1863 (on cover).

Cancellations

Blue +15.00
Brown +75.00
Red +50.00
Orange red +70.00
Magenta +200.00
Ultramarine +150.00
Orange +200.00
Green +600.00
1863 year date +5.00
Printed Precancel "Jefferson, Ohio" —
"PAID ALL" +40.00
"Paid" +10.00
Numeral +15.00
"Way" +150.00
Railroad +300.00
"Steam" +40.00
Steamship +100.00
"Steamboat" +65.00
"Ship Letter" +150.00
Black Carrier +20.00
Blue Carrier +35.00
Supp. Mail Type A or B +100.00
Express Company +300.00
"Short Paid" +250.00
Territorial +100.00
"Forwarded by U.S. Consul . . . Japan" +2,000.
China —

The 3c scarlet, design A25, can be found under No. 74TC6 in the Trial Color, Die and Plate Proofs section.

75 A26 5c **red brown** 5,500. 425.
dark red brown 6,250. 1,000.
Bright red brown —
No gum 2,000.
On cover 700.
On patriotic cover 4,000.
Pair 12,000. 1,100.
Block of 4 62,500. 7,500.
Double transfer 5,750. 475.

Values for No. 75 reflect the normal small margins.

Earliest documented use: Jan. 2, 1862.

Cancellations

Blue +30.
Red +60.
Magenta +90.
Green +3,000.
"Paid" +25.
Supplementary Mail Type A +50.
Express Company +300.

76 A26 5c **brown**, *1863* 1,400. 125.
pale brown 1,400. 125.
dark brown 1,400. 140.
No gum 550.
On cover 180.
On patriotic cover 2,000.
Pair 3,000. 290.
Block of 4 8,250. 1,250.
P# strip of 4, Impt. 15,000.
Double transfer of top frame line 1,450. 145.
Double transfer of bottom frame line 1,450. 145.
Double transfer of top and bottom frame lines 1,550. 165.
a. 5c **black brown** 2,250. 400.
No gum 850.
Block of 4 9,000. 2,200.
b. Laid paper —

Values of Nos. 76, 76a reflect the normal small margins. The plate no. strip of 4 with imprint of No. 76 is unique.

Earliest documented use: Feb. 3, 1863.

Cancellations

Blue +15.00
Ultramarine +150.
Magenta +75.00
Red +45.00
Brown +150.00
Green +750.00
1865 year date +10.00
"Paid" +15.00
"Short Paid" +75.00
Supp. Mail Type A or F +55.00
Express Company +175.00
"Steamship" +65.00
Packet boat —
"Forwarded by U.S. Consul . . . Japan" —

77 A33 15c **black**, *April 1866* 5,000. 175.
full black 5,000. 175.
No gum 1,900.
On cover to France or Germany 225.
Pair 10,000. 375.
Block of 4 32,500. 1,500.
P# block of 8, Impt. —
Double transfer 5,000. 240.
Cracked plate — 240.

Earliest documented use: April 21, 1866.

Cancellations

Blue +15.
Indigo +25.
Purple +175.
Lavender (Philadelphia) +135.
Violet +90.
Magenta +100.
Red +50.
Brown +125.
Green +500.
Ultramarine +100.
"Paid" +20.
"Short Paid" +85.
"Insufficiently Paid" or "Insufficiently Prepaid" +130.
"Ship" +50.
Steamship +50.
Supplementary Mail Type A +90.
French anchor in lozenge +75.

78 A29 24c **lilac**, *1862* 2,750. 400.
No gum 950.
dark lilac 2,750. 425.
No gum 950.
On cover 425.
Pair 6,000. 850.
Block of 4 18,000. 2,750.
Scratch under "A" of "Postage" — —
a. 24c **grayish lilac** 2,750. 425.
No gum 950.
b. 24c **gray** 2,750. 450.
No gum 950.
c. 24c **blackish violet** 95,000. 16,000.
No gum 30,000.
On cover 24,000.

Only three examples are recorded of No. 78c unused with original gum. No. 78c unused with and without gum are valued in the grade of fine-very fine.

d. Printed on both sides, reverse inverted 22,500.
On cover 35,000.

No. 78d off cover and on cover are each unique.

Earliest documented uses: Oct. 23, 1862 (No. 78a); Oct. 29, 1862 (No. 78b); May 1, 1863 (No. 78c).

Cancellations

Blue +20.00
Ultramarine +250.
Red +40.00
Magenta +90.00
Green +600.00
"Paid" +15.00
Numeral +20.00
Supplementary Mail Type A +50.00
"Free" +100.00

Nos. 73, 76-78 exist as imperforate sheet-margin singles, all with pen cancel except No. 76 which is uncanceled. They were not regularly issued.

SAME DESIGNS AS 1861-66 ISSUES

Printed by the National Bank Note Co.

Grill

Embossed with grills of various sizes. Some authorities believe that more than one size of grill probably existed on one of the grill rolls.

A peculiarity of the United States issues from 1867 to 1870 is the grill or embossing. The object was to break the fiber of the paper so that the ink of the canceling stamp would soak in and make washing for a second using impossible. The exact date at which grilled stamps came into use is unsettled. Luff's "Postage Stamps of the United States" places the date as probably August 8, 1867.

Horizontal measurements are given first.

GRILL WITH POINTS UP

Grills A and C were made by a roller covered with ridges shaped like an inverted V. Pressing the ridges into the stamp paper forced the paper into the pyramidal pits between the ridges, causing irregular breaks in the paper. Grill B was made by a roller with raised bosses.

A. GRILL COVERING THE ENTIRE STAMP

1867-68 ***Perf. 12***

79 A25 3c **rose** 8,500. 1,300.
No gum 2,750.
On cover 2,250.
Pair 18,000. 3,250.
Block of 4 55,000.
b. Printed on both sides —

Earliest documented use: Aug. 13, 1867.

Cancellations

Blue +125.
Ultramarine +325.
Railroad —

Values for No. 79 are for fine-very fine examples with minor perf. faults. Examples with complete or virtually complete perforations sell for much more.

An essay (#79-E15) which is often mistaken for No. 79 shows the points of the grill as small squares faintly impressed in the paper but not cutting through it. On the issued stamp the grill generally breaks through the paper. Examples without defects are rare.

See Die and Plate Proofs for imperf. on stamp paper.

80 A26 5c **brown** 400,000.
a. 5c **dark brown** 400,000.
81 A30 30c **orange** 225,000.

Four examples of Nos. 80 and 80a (two of each shade), and eight examples of No. 81 (one in the New York Public Library Miller collection and not available to collectors) are known. All are more or less faulty and/or off center. Values are for off-center examples with small perforation faults.

B. GRILL ABOUT 18x15mm (22x18 POINTS)

82 A25 3c **rose** 900,000.

The four known examples of No. 82 are valued in the grade of fine.

Earliest documented use: Feb. 1?, 1869 (dated cancel on off-cover stamp).

C. GRILL ABOUT 13x16mm (16 TO 17 BY 18 TO 21 POINTS)

The grilled area on each of four C grills in the sheet may total about 18x15mm when a normal C grill adjoins a fainter grill extending to the right or left edge of the stamp. This is caused by a partial erasure on the grill roller when it was changed to produce C grills instead of the all-over A grill. Do not mistake these for the B grill. Unused exists and is very rare, value unused $7,500; value used $2,750; on cover $4,500.

83 A25 3c **rose** 5,500. 1,100.
No gum 2,000.
On cover 1,250.
Pair 12,000. 3,250.
Block of 4 30,000. —
Double grill 6,750. 2,000.
Grill with points down 6,250. 1,400.

Earliest documented use: Nov. 16, 1867.

Cancellation

Blue +100.

See Die and Plate Proofs for imperf. on stamp paper.
The 1c, 3c, 5c, 10c, 12c, 30c of 1861 are known with experimental C grills. They are listed in the Essays section. The 3c differs slightly from No. 83.

GRILL WITH POINTS DOWN

The grills were produced by rollers with the surface covered, or partly covered, by pyramidal bosses. On the D, E and F grills the tips of the pyramids are vertical ridges. On the Z grill the ridges are horizontal.

D. GRILL ABOUT 12x14mm (15 BY 18 TO 19 POINTS)

84 A32 2c **black** 16,000. 5,250.
No gum 6,500.
On cover 5,750.
Pair 35,000. 11,000.
Block of 4 100,000. —
Double transfer — —
Split grill — 5,500.

No. 84 is valued in the grade of fine.

Earliest documented use: Feb. 15, 1868.

Cancellations

Red +400.
Blue +750.
"Paid All" +100.

85 A25 3c **rose** 8,000. 1,050.
No gum 2,400.
On cover 1,200.
Pair 17,000. 2,400.
Block of 4 45,000. —
Double grill —
Split grill 1,150.

Earliest documented use: Feb. 1, 1868 (on cover front); Feb. 2, 1868 (on full cover).

Cancellations

Blue +50.
Green +450.
"Paid" +50.

Z. GRILL ABOUT 11x14mm (14 TO 15 BY 17 OR 18 POINTS)

(1c, 10c, 15c 17 rows; 2c, 3c, 12c 18 rows)

85A A24 1c **blue** 3,000,000.

Two examples of No. 85A are currently recorded. One is contained in the New York Public Library collection, which is on long-term loan to the Smithsonian National Postal Museum.

85B A32 2c **black** 17,500. 1,100.
No gum 6,750.
On cover 1,300.
Pair 32,500. 2,750.
Block of 4 75,000. 10,000.
Double transfer 19,000. 1,200.
Major double transfer ("Preston shift") 3,250.
Double grill —
Split grill —

Earliest documented use: Jan. 17, 1868 (on piece); Jan. 20, 1868 (on cover).

Cancellations

Cancellation	Value
Blue	+250.
Red	+350.
Black Carrier	+75.
"Paid All"	+75.

85C A25 3c **rose**	25,000.	3,500.
No gum	9,000.	
On cover		4,000.
Pair		—
Block of 4	120,000.	
Double grill	27,000.	

Earliest documented use: Jan. 29, 1868.

Cancellations

Cancellation	Value
Green	+600.
Blue	+100.
Red	+250.
"Paid"	+50.

85D A27 10c **green**	750,000.	

Six examples of No. 85D are known. One is contained in the New York Public Library collection. Value is for a well-centered example with small faults.

85E A28 12c **intense black**	25,000.	2,250.
black	25,000.	2,250.
No gum	8,500.	
On cover		2,750.
Strip of 3		—
Block of 4	77,500.	—
Double grill		—
Double transfer of top frame line		2,400.

Earliest documented use: Feb. 12, 1868.

The unused block of four of No. 85E is unique, and it has fine centering and a small fault. Value is based on 2019 auction sale.

Cancellations

Cancellation	Value
Blue	+200.
Red	+200.

85F A33 15c **black**	2,000,000.	

Two examples of No. 85F are documented, one in the grade of very good, the other extremely fine. Value is for the extremely fine example.

E. GRILL ABOUT 11x13mm (14 BY 16 TO 18 POINTS)

86 A24 1c **blue**	3,000.	450.
No gum	1,100.	
a. 1c **dull blue**	3,000.	425.
No gum	1,100.	
On cover		575.
Pair	6,500.	950.
Block of 4	20,000.	3,500.
Double grill	—	575.
Split grill	3,250.	575.
Very thin paper		—

Earliest documented use: Mar. 9, 1868.

Cancellations

Cancellation	Value
Blue	+25.
Red	+80.
Green	+450.
"Paid"	+25.
Steamboat	+90.
Red Carrier	+110.

87 A32 2c **black**	1,700.	200.
gray black	1,700.	200.
No gum	650.	
intense black	1,800.	225.
No gum	700.	
On cover		275.
Pair	3,750.	420.
Block of 4	8,750.	6,250.
P# strip of 4, Impt.	9,750.	
Double grill	—	—
Double grill, one split	—	
Triple grill		—
Split grill	2,000.	220.
Grill with points up	—	
Double transfer	1,850.	220.
Major double transfer ("Preston shift")		—
a. Diagonal half used as 1c on cover		2,000.
b. Vertical half used as 1c on cover		2,000.
c. Horizontal half used as 1c on cover		2,000.

Earliest documented use: Feb. 28, 1868.

Cancellations

Cancellation	Value
Blue	+10.00
Purple	+100.00
Brown	+40.00
Red	+65.00
Magenta	+200.00
Green	+1,000.
"Paid"	+10.00
Steamship	+60.00
Black Carrier	+35.00
"Paid All"	+20.00
"Short Paid"	+65.00
Japan	—

88 A25 3c **rose**	1,050.	30.00
pale rose	1,050.	30.00
rose red	1,050.	30.00
No gum	400.	
On cover		35.00
Pair	2,200.	65.00
Block of 4	6,000.	350.00
P# block of 8, Impt.	13,000.	
Double grill	—	—
Double grill, one split	—	—
Triple grill	—	—
Split grill	1,150.	35.00
Very thin paper	1,150.	35.00
a. 3c **lake red**	1,250.	80.00
No gum	475.	
b. Two diagonal halves from different stamps used as 3c stamp (fraudulent use), one half having grill with points up, on cover		—

Earliest documented use: Feb. 12, 1868.

Cancellations

Cancellation	Value
Blue	+5.00
Red	+10.00
Ultramarine	+40.00
Green	+125.00
"Paid"	+5.00
"Way"	+30.00
Numeral, "3" or "5"	+5.00
Numeral, number greater than "5"	—
Steamboat	+35.00
Railroad	+25.00
Express Company	+80.00

89 A27 10c **green**	5,000.	350.
dark green	5,000.	350.
blue green	5,000.	350.
No gum	2,000.	
On cover		450.
Pair	10,000.	750.
Block of 4	24,000.	3,500.
Double grill	6,500.	525.
Split grill	5,250.	375.
Double transfer	—	375.
Very thin paper	5,250.	375.

Earliest documented use: Feb. 21, 1868.

Cancellations

Cancellation	Value
Blue	+30.
Red	+75.
"Paid"	+15.
Steamship	+50.
French anchor in lozenge	—
Japan	+225.

90 A28 12c **black**	4,750.	400.
gray black	4,750.	400.
intense black	4,750.	400.
No gum	1,900.	
On cover		550.
Pair	10,000.	850.
Block of 4	35,000.	3,000.
Double transfer of top frame line	5,000.	425.
Double transfer of bottom frame line	5,000.	475.
Double transfer of top and bottom frame lines	5,250.	475.
Double grill	5,500.	700.
Split grill	5,000.	425.

Earliest documented use: Mar. 3, 1868.

Cancellations

Cancellation	Value
Blue	+25.
Red	+75.
Purple	+150.
Green	+400.
Railroad	+100.
"Paid"	+30.

91 A33 15c **black**	12,500.	575.
gray black	12,500.	575.
No gum	4,500.	
On cover		700.
Pair	26,000.	1,250.
Block of 4	65,000.	12,500.
Double grill	—	925.
Split grill	—	650.

Earliest documented use: May 2, 1868.

Cancellations

Cancellation	Value
Blue	+30.
Magenta	+150.
Red	+125.
"Paid"	+30.
Supplementary Mail Type A	+150.

F. GRILL ABOUT 9x13mm (12 BY 16 TO 18 POINTS)

92 A24 1c **blue**	2,800.	425.
dark blue	2,800.	425.
No gum	900.	
a. 1c **pale blue**	2,300.	400.
No gum	700.	
On cover		475.
Pair	6,000.	900.
Block of 4	16,000.	3,250.
Double transfer	3,000.	475.
Double grill	—	800.
Split grill	3,000.	500.
Double grill, one split		—
Very thin paper	3,000.	750.

Earliest documented use: Aug. 11, 1868.

Cancellations

Cancellation	Value
Blue	+20.00
Red	+50.00
Green	+450.00
"Paid"	+10.00
Red Carrier	+60.00
"Paid All"	+15.00

93 A32 2c **black**	450.	55.00
gray black	450.	55.00
No gum	155.	
On cover		70.00
Pair	950.	120.00
Block of 4	2,600.	525.00
P# strip of 4, Impt.	6,500.	
P# block of 8, Impt.	—	
Double transfer	500.	62.50
Double grill	—	170.00
Split grill	500.	60.00
Double grill, one split		—
Double grill, one quadruple split	1,100.	—
Very thin paper	550.	60.00
a. Vertical half used as 1c as part of 3c rate on cover		1,250.
b. Diagonal half used as 1c as part of 3c rate on cover		1,250.
c. Horizontal half used alone as 1c on cover		2,500.
d. Diagonal half used alone as 1c on cover		2,500.

Earliest documented use: Mar. 27, 1868.

Cancellations

Cancellation	Value
Blue	+8.00
Red	+20.00
Green	+250.00
"Paid"	+5.00
"Paid All"	+15.00
Black Carrier	+20.00
Red Carrier	+30.00
Japan	+350.00

94 A25 3c **red**	350.	12.50
rose red	350.	12.50
a. 3c **rose**	350.	12.50
No gum	150.	
On cover		14.00
Pair	750.	27.50
Block of 4	3,000.	180.00
P# block of 8, Impt.	9,500.	
Double transfer	400.	27.50
Double grill		—
Double grill, one normal, one partial with points up		—
Triple grill	—	300.00
End roller grill		450.00
Split grill	375.	17.50
Quadruple split grill	650.	175.00
Double grill, one quadruple split		—
Grill with points up		—
On cover		7,500.
Very thin paper	375.	13.00
c. Vertical pair, imperf. horiz.	15,000.	
Block of 4	40,000.	
d. Printed on both sides	9,000.	35,000.

Seven examples of No. 94d are recorded. Six are in the top row of an unused top margin imprint block of 18 (6x3).

Earliest documented use: Mar. 21, 1868.

Cancellations

Cancellation	Value
Blue	+.25
Ultramarine	+30.00
Red	+15.00
Violet	+70.00
Green	+70.00
Numeral, "3" or "5"	+3.00
Numeral, number greater than "5"	—
"Paid"	+2.25
"Paid All"	+12.50
"Free"	+20.00
Railroad	+30.00
Steamboat	+40.00
Packet boat	+80.00
Express Company	+50.00

See Die and Plate Proofs for imperf. on stamp paper.

95 A26 5c **brown**	3,250.	850.
No gum	1,100.	
dark brown	3,500.	950.
No gum	1,300.	
On cover		900.
Pair	6,750.	1,800.
Block of 4	17,000.	9,000.
Double transfer of top frame line	—	—
Double transfer of bottom frame line	—	
Double grill	—	—
Split grill	4,000.	900.
Very thin paper	3,750.	900.
a. 5c **black brown**	5,000.	2,400.
No gum	2,000.	
Double grill		—

Earliest documented use: Aug. 19, 1868.

Cancellations

Cancellation	Value
Blue	+25.
Magenta	+90.
Violet	+90.
Red	+80.
Green	+500.
"Paid"	+25.
"Free"	+250.
"Steamship"	+150.

Values of Nos. 95, 95a reflect the normal small margins.

96 A27 10c **yellow green**	2,500.	250.
green	2,750.	250.
blue green	2,500.	250.
dark green	2,500.	325.
No gum	825.	
On cover		290.
Pair	5,250.	525.
Block of 4	26,000.	3,500.
P# strip of 4, Impt.	50,000.	
Double transfer	—	—
Double grill	—	390.
Split grill	2,750.	280.
Quadruple split grill		685.
Very thin paper	2,750.	270.

Earliest documented use: May 28, 1868.

Cancellations

Cancellation	Value
Blue	+10.00
Red	+35.00
Magenta	+40.00
Green	+300.00
"Paid"	+10.00
"Free"	+50.00
Supplementary Mail Type A	—

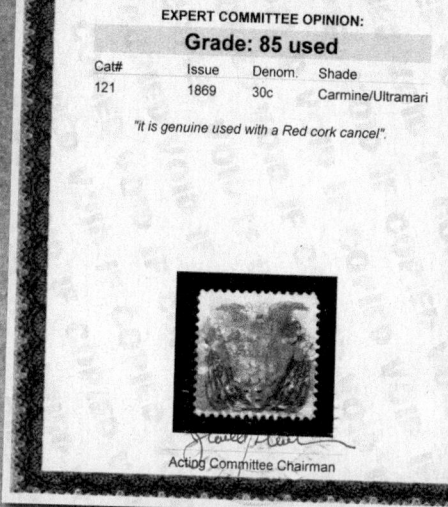

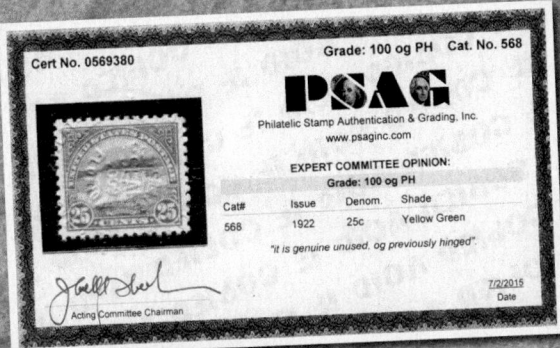

Steamship		+75.00
Japan		+200.00
China		—
97 A28 12c **black**	2,800.	250.
gray black	2,800.	250.
No gum	1,000.	
On cover		300.
Pair	6,000.	525.
Block of 4	*40,000.*	*2,500.*
P# strip of 4, Impt.	*50,000.*	
Double transfer of top frame line	3,250.	280.
Double transfer of bottom frame line	3,250.	280.
Double transfer of top and bottom frame lines	—	300.
Double grill	—	475.
Triple grill		—
Split grill	3,250.	280.
End roller grill		—
Very thin paper	3,250.	325.

Earliest documented use: May 27, 1868.

Cancellations

Blue	+10.00
Red	+50.00
Magenta	+50.00
Brown	+50.00
Green	+250.00
Purple	+150.00
"Paid"	+20.00
"Insufficiently Prepaid"	+100.00
"Paid All"	+25.00
Supplementary Mail Type A	+50.00

98 A33 15c **black**	4,250.	275.
gray black	4,250.	275.
No gum	1,600.	
On cover		300.
Pair	*9,000.*	600.
Block of 4	*35,000.*	*6,000.*
P# block of 8, Impt.	*165,000.*	
Double transfer of upper right corner	—	500.
Double grill	4,750.	425.
Split grill	4,500.	300.
Quadruple split grill	5,000.	575.
Very thin paper	4,750.	475.

Earliest documented use: May 4, 1868.

The plate block of No. 98 is unique; value reflects sale price in 2019 auction.

Cancellations

Blue	+20.00
Magenta	+75.00
Red	+100.00
Orange red	+40.00
Green	+300.00
Orange	+190.00
Purple	+100.00
Lavender (Philadelphia)	+160.00
"Paid"	+20.00
"Insufficiently Prepaid"	+135.00
"Insufficiently Paid"	+135.00
Japan	+300.00
Supplementary Mail Type A	+90.00
French anchor in lozenge	+75.00

99 A29 24c **gray lilac**	8,500.	1,600.
gray	8,500.	1,600.
No gum	3,250.	
On cover		2,500.
Pair	*18,000.*	3,500.
Block of 4	*45,000.*	*11,000.*
P# block of 8, Impt.	*155,000.*	
Double grill	9,500.	2,400.
Split grill	8,750.	1,700.
Scratch under "A" of "Postage"	—	

Earliest documented use: Jan. 5, 1869.

The plate block of No. 99 is unique; value reflects sale price in 2019 auction.

Cancellations

Blue	+100.
Red	+200.
"Paid"	+50.

100 A30 30c **orange**	12,500.	1,000.
deep orange	12,500.	1,050.
No gum	4,500.	
On cover		1,800.
Pair	*26,000.*	2,100.
Block of 4	*57,500.*	*10,000.*
Double grill	15,000.	1,150.
Split grill	13,000.	1,100.
Double grill, one split		—
Double grill, one quadruple split		—
Triple grill, two split		—

Values for No. 100 are for examples with small margins, especially at sides. Large-margined examples sell for much more.

Earliest documented use: Nov. 10, 1868.

Cancellations

Blue	+50.
Red	+120.
Magenta	+150.
Green	+700.
"Paid"	+50.
Steamship	+1,250.
Supplementary Mail Type A	+100.
French anchor in lozenge	—
Japan	+400.

101 A31 90c **blue**	14,500.	2,500.
dark blue	14,500.	2,500.
No gum	5,750.	
On cover		*100,000.*
Pair	*31,500.*	5,500.
Block of 4	*75,000.*	*25,000.*
Double grill	*19,000.*	
Split grill	15,000.	2,400.

Two usages on cover are recorded (one being a cover front). Value is for use on full cover to Peru.

Some authorities believe that more than one size of grill probably existed on one of the grill rolls.

Earliest documented use: May 8, 1869.

Cancellations

Blue	+150.
Red	+300.
Japan	+600.
"Paid"	+50.

RE-ISSUE OF 1861-66 ISSUES

Produced by the National Bank Note Co.

Without grill, hard white paper, with white crackly gum.

The 1, 2, 5, 10 and 12c were printed from new plates of 100 subjects each.

1875		*Perf. 12*
102 A24 1c **blue** *(3195)*	*750.*	*1,700.*
No gum	*350.*	
On cover		—
Block of 4	*7,000.*	—
103 A32 2c **black** *(979)*	*3,500.*	*10,500.*
No gum	*1,600.*	
Block of 4	*65,000.*	
104 A25 3c **brown red** *(465)*	*3,750.*	*13,000.*
No gum	*1,700.*	
Block of 4	*90,000.*	
105 A26 5c **brown** *(672)*	*2,500.*	*6,000.*
No gum	*1,150.*	
Block of 4	*90,000.*	
106 A27 10c **green** *(451)*	*2,900.*	*100,000.*
No gum	*1,400.*	
Block of 4	*90,000.*	
107 A28 12c **black** *(389)*	*3,750.*	*12,000.*
No gum	*1,750.*	
Block of 4	*115,000.*	
108 A33 15c **black** *(397)*	*4,500.*	*30,000.*
No gum	*2,100.*	
Block of 4	*90,000.*	
109 A29 24c **deep violet** *(346)*	*6,000.*	*17,500.*
No gum	*2,750.*	
Block of 4	*115,000.*	
110 A30 30c **brownish orange** *(346)*	*5,750.*	*17,500.*
No gum	*2,800.*	
Pair	*15,500.*	
Block of 4	*115,000.*	
111 A31 90c **blue** *(317)*	*7,000.*	*225,000.*
No gum	*3,500.*	

Earliest documented uses: No. 102, July 25, 1881; No. 104, July ?, 1883 (dated cancel on off-cover stamp); No. 111, Nov. 30, 1888 (dated cancel on off-cover stamp). Any 2c with the "star-on-cheek" variety that is not grilled is a No. 103. Some examples of the "F" grill, No. 93, also show the "star-on-cheek" variety.

These stamps can be distinguished from the 1861-66 issue by the brighter colors, the sharper proof-like impressions and the paper which is very white instead of yellowish. The gum is almost always somewhat yellowed with age, and unused stamps with original gum are valued with such gum.

Numbers in parentheses are quantities sold.

While it was legal to use Nos. 102-111 as postage, their actual use is generally rare and is mostly confined to dealers using them on registered mail. Examination by recognized expert authorities is recommended.

Five examples are recorded of No. 111 used, one of which has a non-contemporaneous cancel. Value is for centered and sound example (two are known thus).

PLEASE NOTE:

Stamps are valued in the grade of very fine unless otherwise indicated.

Values for early and valuable stamps are for examples with certificates of authenticity from acknowledged expert committees, or examples sold with the buyer having the right of certification. This applies to examples with original gum as well as examples without gum. Beware of stamps offered "as is," as the gum on some unused stamps offered with "original gum" may be fraudulent, and unused stamps offered without may in some cases be altered or faintly canceled used stamps.

VALUES FOR NEVER-HINGED STAMPS PRIOR TO SCOTT No. 182

This catalogue does not value pre-1879 stamps in never-hinged condition. Premiums for never-hinged condition in the classic era invariably are even larger than those premiums listed for the 1879 and later issues. Generally speaking, the earlier the stamp is listed in the catalogue, the larger will be the never-hinged premium.

Produced by the National Bank Note Co.

Plates for the 1c, 2c, 3c, 6c, 10c and 12c consisted of 300 subjects in two panes of 150 each. For the 15c, 24c, 30c and 90c plates of 100 subjects each.

NOTE: Stamps of the 1869 issue without grill cannot be guaranteed except when unused and with the original gum or traces of the original gum.

Franklin — A34

Post Horse and Rider — A35

G. Grill measuring 9½x9mm (12 by 11 to 11½ points)

1869	**Hard Wove Paper**	*Perf. 12*
112 A34 1c **buff**	575.	140.
brown orange	575.	140.
dark brown orange	625.	180.
No gum	210.	
On cover, single		270.
Pair	1,200.	300.
Block of 4	*5,500.*	*2,250.*
Margin block of 4, arrow	*5,750.*	
Margin block of 4, P#	*6,250.*	
Double transfer	—	—
Double grill	1,350.	300.
Split grill	725.	190.
Double grill, one split		—
Double grill, one quadruple split		—
b. Without grill, original gum	*32,500.*	

Earliest documented use: Apr. 1, 1869.

Cancellations

Blue	+25.
Ultramarine	+600.
Magenta	+150.
Purple	+175.
Red	+100.
Green	+700.
"Paid"	+50.
Numeral	+100.
Steamship	+135.
Black town	+30.
Blue town	+30.
Red town	+90.
Black Carrier	+80.
Blue Carrier	+100.
Japan	+1,000.
China (Shanghai fancy star), on cover	*+11,000.*

113 A35 2c **brown**	500.	80.
pale brown	500.	80.
dark brown	525.	90.
yellow brown	500.	80.
No gum	190.	
On cover, single		140.
Pair	1,100.	170.
Block of 4	3,750.	1,350.
Margin block of 4, arrow	3,850.	
P# block of 10, Impt.	*55,000.*	
Double grill	—	310.
Split grill	650.	125.
Quadruple split grill	—	
End roller grill	925.	
Double transfer		110.
b. Without grill, original gum	*14,000.*	
c. Half used as 1c on cover, diagonal, vertical or horizontal		*6,000.*
d. Printed on both sides		*62,500.*

Earliest documented use: Mar. 20, 1869.

Cancellations

Blue	+50.
Red	+75.
Orange red	+90.
Orange	+250.
Magenta	+80.
Purple	+100.
Ultramarine	+150.
Green	+500.
Brown	+160.
"FREE"	—
"Paid"	+15.
"Paid All"	+25.
Steamship	+75.
Black town	+10.
Blue town	+30.
Japan	+400.
Blue Carrier	+90.
Black Carrier	+80.
China	—
Printed Precancellation "Jefferson, Ohio"	+6,500.

Locomotive — A36

Washington — A37

114 A36 3c **ultramarine**	225.	18.00
pale ultramarine	225.	16.00
dark ultramarine	250.	19.00
No gum	90.	
blue	625.	100.00
No gum	225.	

	On cover		24.00
	Pair	525.	35.00
	Block of 4	1,250.	450.00
	Margin block of 4, arrow	1,450.	
	P# block of 10, Impt.	*7,500.*	
	Double transfer	300.	35.00
	Double grill	525.00	95.00
	Triple grill	—	—
	Sextuple grill	—	*7,000.*
	Split grill	275.	40.00
	Quadruple split grill	550.	130.00
	Double grill, one split		—
	Double grill, one quadruple split		—
	End roller grill	—	—
	Grill with points up		—
	Gray paper	—	100.00
	On cover		750.00
	Without grill		—
	Cracked plate	—	160.00
a.	Without grill, original gum	*13,000.*	*18,000.*
	Without grill, gray paper		3,750.
b.	Vert. one-third used as 1c on cover		—
c.	Vert. two-thirds used as 2c on cover		*10,000.*
e.	Printed on both sides, reverse inverted		*55,000.*

The grill-with-points-up variety is found on a unique margin "pair" of stamps where the paper was folded over prior to perforating and grilling. The stamps have drastic freak perfs.

Two examples used are recorded for No. 114a on normal paper and two used examples on gray paper. On normal paper, there exist a used single with original gum and black pen cancel (2015 Philatelic Foundation certificate), and a single on cover that was lifted to check for grill and replaced (2011 Philatelic Foundation certificate). No. 114a used on gray paper exists as a strip of three on piece (1978 Philatelic Foundation certificate), and as a single on advertising cover, lifted and hinged back in place (2015 Philatelic Foundation certificate).

No. 114e is unique.

Earliest documented use: Mar. 27, 1869.

Cancellations

Blue	+5.
Ultramarine	+25.
Magenta	+35.
Purple	+75.
Violet	+65.
Red	+15.
Orange red	+20.
Brown	+200.
Green	+300.
Orange	—
Yellow	—
Black town	+3.
Blue town	+7.
Red town	+30.
Numeral	+15.
"Paid"	+20.
"Paid All"	+15.
"Steamboat"	—
"Lake Champlain S.B." (steamboat), on cover	—
"Steamship"	+50.
Ship	+35.
"U. S. Ship"	+450.
Railroad	+30.
Packet Boat	+100.
Blue Carrier	+40.
Black Carrier	+30.
Express Company	+250.
"Way"	—
"Free"	+150.
Alaska	—
French anchor in lozenge	—
Japan	+600.

The authenticity of the yellow cancel has been questioned by some specialists. The editors would like to see an expertizing certificate for this stamp and cancel.

115	A37 6c **ultramarine**	2,600.	225.
	pale ultramarine	2,600.	
	No gum	1,050.	
	On cover		475.
	Pair	5,500.	500.
	Block of 4	*16,750.*	*9,000.*
	Margin block of 4, arrow	*18,000.*	
	Double grill	—	550.
	Split grill	3,150.	280.
	Quadruple split grill	—	750.
	Double transfer		250.
b.	Vertical half used as 3c on cover		*50,000.*

Earliest documented use: Apr. 26, 1869.

No. 115b is unique.

Cancellations

Blue	+25.
Brown	+125.
Magenta	+50.
Purple	+85.
Red	+75.
Green	+1,000.
"Paid"	+15.
"Paid All"	+25.
Black town	+30.
"Short Paid"	+75.
"Insufficiently Paid"	+75.
Steamship	+45.
Railroad	+50.
Japan	+1,500.

Shield and Eagle — A38

S.S. "Adriatic" — A39

116	A38 10c **yellow**	1,850.	110.
	yellowish orange	1,850.	110.
	No gum	750.	
	On cover		375.
	Pair	4,000.	270.
	Block of 4	*14,000.*	*8,000.*
	Margin block of 4, arrow	*14,500.*	
	Double grill	—	350.
	Split grill	2,100.	150.
	End roller grill	—	—

Earliest documented use: Apr. 1, 1869.

Cancellations

Blue	+35.
Magenta	+80.
Purple	+250.
Violet	—
Red	+40.
Ultramarine	+300.
Green	+5,000.
Black town	+20.
Numeral	—
Steamship	+35.
Railroad	+45.
"Paid"	+15.
"Paid All"	+30.
"Insufficiently Paid"	+50.
Supplementary Mail Type A	+150.
Express Company	—
Alaska	+5,000.
St. Thomas	—
Hawaii	—
Japan	+200.
China, Shanghai circle of wedges	—

117	A39 12c **green**	1,850.	130.
	yellowish green	1,850.	130.
	bluish green	2,100.	175.
	No gum	725.	
	On cover		450.
	Pair	4,000.	310.
	Block of 4	*14,000.*	*1,800.*
	Margin block of 4, arrow	*14,500.*	
	Double grill	—	400.
	Split grill	2,150.	170.
	Double grill, one quadruple split		—
	End roller grill	—	575.

Earliest documented use: Apr. 1, 1869.

Cancellations

Blue	+125.
Magenta	+125.
Purple	+250.
Brown	+300.
Red	+150.
Green	+3,500.
Numeral	+125.
"Paid"	+25.
"Paid All"	+40.
"Too Late"	+100.
"Insufficiently Paid"	+125.
Black town	+35.
Red town	+250.
Japan	+950.

Landing of Columbus — A40

No. 118 has horizontal shading lines at the left and right sides of the vignette.

118	A40 15c **brown & blue,** type I, Picture unframed	9,000.	850.
	dark brown & blue	9,000.	850.
	No gum	3,250.	
	On cover		1,800.
	Pair	*20,000.*	1,850.
	Block of 4	*60,000.*	*30,000.*

	Double grill	*15,000.*	1,150.
	Split grill	10,500.	1,000.
a.	Without grill, original gum	*11,500.*	

Earliest documented use: Mar. 31, 1869 (dated cancel on off-cover stamp); Apr. 2, 1869 (on cover).

Cancellations

Blue	+75.
Red	+135.
Magenta	+250.
Brown	+150.
"Paid"	+50.
"Paid All"	+100.
"Insufficiently Paid"	+150.
Black town	+50.
Blue town	+150.
Steamship	+100.

A40a

No. 119 has diagonal shading lines at the left and right sides of the vignette.

119	A40a 15c **brown & blue,** type II, Picture framed	2,600.	190.
	dark brown & blue	2,600.	190.
	No gum	925.	
	On cover		800.
	Pair	5,500.	425.
	Block of 4	*15,750.*	*9,000.*
	P# block of 8, Impt.	*45,000.*	
	Double transfer	—	—
	Double grill	4,750.	475.
	Split grill	3,000.	300.
b.	Center inverted	*1,000,000.*	*22,500.*
	No gum	*700,000.*	
c.	Center double, one inverted		*80,000.*

Earliest documented use: Apr. 5, 1869.

Cancellations

Blue	+60.
Ultramarine	—
Purple	+150.
Magenta	+135.
Red	+150.
Brown	+200.
Green	+1,500.
Numeral	+75.
"Paid"	+25.
"Paid All"	+35.
Black town	+30.
Blue town	+75.
Red town	+200.
"Steamship"	+75.
Supp. Mail Type A or F	+40.
Japan	+500.

Most examples of No. 119b are faulty. Values are for fine centered examples with only minimal faults. Three examples of No. 119b unused are recorded; only one has original gum.

Three examples of No. 119c are recorded. Value is for the finer of the two sound examples.

The Declaration of Independence — A41

120	A41 24c **green & violet**	8,000.	650.
	bluish green & violet	8,000.	650.
	No gum	3,000.	
	On cover, domestic usage		*12,500.*
	On cover, foreign usage		*35,000.*
	Pair	*22,500.*	1,400.
	Block of 4	*52,500.*	*20,000.*
	Double grill	—	2,000.
	Split grill	8,500.	800.
a.	Without grill, original gum	*14,000.*	
b.	Center inverted	*750,000.*	*37,500.*
	On cover		*130,000.*
	Pair		*110,000.*
	Block of 4		*750,000.*

Earliest documented use: Apr. 7, 1869 (No. 120); Mar. 1874 (No. 120b).

Cancellations

Blue	+300.
Red	+500.
Black town	+100.
Red town	+400.
"Paid All"	+150.
"Steamship"	+250.
Supp. Mail Type A	+200.
China	+750.

Most examples of No. 120b are faulty. Values are for fine centered examples with only minimal faults. No. 120b unused is valued without gum, as all of the three examples available to collectors are without gum.

Shield, Eagle and Flags — A42

Lincoln — A43

No.	Description	Unused	Used
121	A42 30c **ultramarine & carmine**	4,000.	450.
	ultramarine & dark carmine	4,000.	500.
	No gum	1,450.	
	On cover, domestic usage		*17,500.*
	On cover, foreign usage		*35,000.*
	Pair	*9,500.*	1,050.
	Block of 4	*40,000.*	*3,750.*
	Double grill	—	1,350.
	Split grill	5,000.	575.
	Double grill, one split		—
	Double paper (without grill), original gum	*7,000.*	
	Block of 4	—	
a.	Without grill, original gum	*10,000.*	
	Block of 4	*45,000.*	
	P# block of 8, Impt.	*100,000.*	
b.	Flags inverted	*750,000.*	*85,000.*
	No gum	*300,000.*	

Seven examples of No. 121b unused are recorded. Only one has part of its original gum.

Earliest documented use: May 22, 1869.

Cancellations

Blue	+250.
Red	+250.
Brown	+600.
Purple	+1,000.
Green	+7,500.
"Paid"	+50.
"Paid All"	+250.
Black town	+100.
Steamship	+85.
"Steam"	+70.
Supp. Mail Type A	+75.
French anchor in lozenge	+400.
Japan	+800.
China, Shanghai circle of wedges	—

No.	Description	Unused	Used
122	A43 90c **carmine & black**	11,000.	1,900.
	carmine rose & black	11,000.	1,900.
	No gum	4,000.	
	On cover		*430,000.*
	Pair	*28,000.*	*8,500.*
	Block of 4	*75,000.*	*55,000.*
	Block of 6	*140,000.*	
	Split grill	—	—
a.	Without grill, original gum	*22,500.*	

Cancellations

Blue	+1,100.
Red	+1,000.
Orange red	+750.
Brown	+2,000.
Purple	+3,000.
Ultramarine	+1,750.
Black town	+1,500.
Red town	+1,750.
Magenta town	+2,500.
"Paid"	—
"Paid All"	—
N.Y. steamship	+1,000.

Nos. 112, 114, 117, 118, 120b, 121, 122 exist as imperf. singles. They were not regularly issued.

No. 122 on cover is unique. Value reflects 2009 auction sale price. The block of six (two recorded) is the largest multiple known of No. 122.

CANCELLATIONS

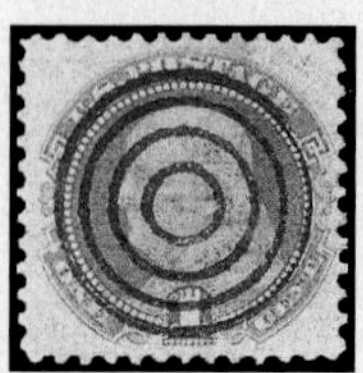

The common type of cancellation on the 1869 issue is the block or cork similar to illustrations above. Japanese cancellations seen on this issue (not illustrated) resulted from the sale of U.S. stamps in Japanese cities where post offices were maintained for mail going from Japan to the United States.

RE-ISSUE OF 1869 ISSUE

Produced by the National Bank Note Co.

Without grill, hard white paper, with white crackly gum.

The gum is almost always somewhat yellowed with age, and unused stamps with original gum are valued with such gum.

A new plate of 150 subjects was made for the 1c. The plate for the frame of the 15c was made using the same die as that used to make the type I frame for No. 118. For No. 118, the lines on each side of the vignette area were entered onto the plate itself, one position at a time. Upon close examination, each stamp position will be found to exhibit minute differences in these horizontal fringe lines.

1875 ***Perf. 12***

No.	Description	Unused	Used
123	A34 1c **buff** *(10,000)*	525.	425.
	No gum	220.	
	Block of 4	*5,500.*	
	On cover		*3,000.*
124	A35 2c **brown** *(4755)*	600.	750.
	No gum	250.	
	Block of 4	*7,000.*	
	On cover		*12,500.*
125	A36 3c **blue** *(1406)*	*5,000.*	*25,000.*
	No gum	2,500.	
	On cover		—

Cancellation

Supplementary Mail Type F	—

Very few authenticated sound used examples of No. 125 are recorded. The used value is for an attractive fine to very fine example with minimal faults. Examples of No. 114 with faint or pressed-out grill are frequently offered as No. 125. Expertization by competent authorities is required.

No.	Description	Unused	Used
126	A37 6c **blue** *(2226)*	1,900.	*3,000.*
	No gum	900.	
	Block of 4	*40,000.*	
	On cover		—
127	A38 10c **yellow** *(1947)*	1,600.	1,800.
	No gum	750.	
	Block of 4	*22,500.*	
	On cover		*22,500.*
128	A39 12c **green** *(1584)*	2,000.	*3,000.*
	No gum	1,000.	
	Block of 4	*45,000.*	
	On cover		—

A40b

No. 129 (type III) is similar to No. 118 (type I) but without the shading lines at each side of the vignette.

No.	Description	Unused	Used
129	A40b 15c **brown & blue,** type III, *(1981)*	1,300.	1,000.
	No gum	625.	
	Pair		*6,000.*
	Block of 4	*42,500.*	
	On cover		*22,500.*
a.	Imperf. horizontally, single	*14,000.*	*30,000.*
	No gum	*5,000.*	

Two used examples of No. 129a are recorded. Both have faults and are valued thus.

No.	Description	Unused	Used
130	A41 24c **green & violet** *(2091)*	2,000.	1,600.
	No gum	1,000.	
	Pair		*10,000.*
	On cover		*27,500.*
131	A42 30c **ultra & carmine** *(1535)*	2,250.	2,750.
	No gum	1,100.	
	Pair		*28,000.*
132	A43 90c **carmine & black** *(1356)*	3,750.	*6,000.*
	No gum	1,750.	
	Pair		*32,500.*
	Block of 4	*35,000.*	
	P# block of 10, Impt.	*325,000.*	

Numbers in parentheses are quantities sold.

While use of Nos. 123-133 for postage was legal, such use is scarce. Expertization is recommended.

Earliest documented uses:

No. 123, Dec. 9, 1877;
No. 124, Mar. 20, 1880;
No. 127, Nov. 11, 1880;
No. 128, Mar. 20, 1880.
No. 129, Mar. 20, 1880;
No. 130, Mar. 27, 1880.

RE-ISSUE OF 1869 ISSUE

Produced by the American Bank Note Co.

Without grill, soft porous paper.

1880-82

No.	Description	Unused	Used
133	A34 1c **buff,** issued with gum (5,000)	350.	*550.*
	No gum	150.	
	Block of 4, with gum	1,650.	*12,500.*
	Margin block of 10, Impt. & P#	*22,500.*	
	On cover		1,900.
a.	1c **brown orange,** issued without gum, *1881-82* (18,252)	400.	*650.*
	Block of 4, without gum	1,750.	
	Margin block of 10, Impt. & P#, without gum	*24,000.*	

Earliest documented use: Oct. 5, 1880 (No. 133).

Beware of No. 133 unused without gum offered as No. 133a. Certification is recommended for No. 133a.

PRODUCED BY THE NATIONAL BANK NOTE COMPANY

Plates of 200 subjects in two panes of 100 each.

Franklin

A44

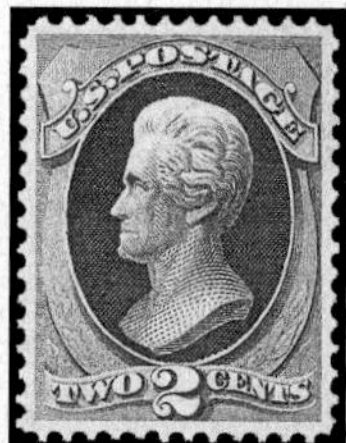

Jackson

A45

Washington

A46

Lincoln

A47

Edwin M. Stanton

A48

Jefferson

A49

Henry Clay

A50

Daniel Webster

A51

General Winfield Scott — A52

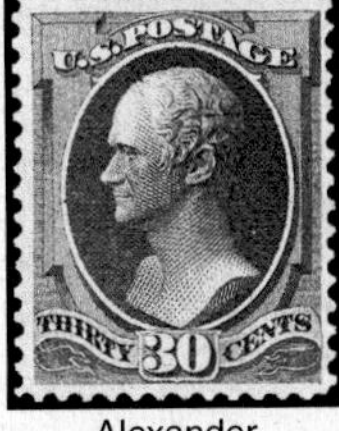

Alexander Hamilton — A53

Commodore Oliver Hazard Perry — A54

H. GRILL ABOUT 10x12mm (11 TO 13 BY 14 TO 16 POINTS)

The "H" grills can be separated into early state and late state, based on the shape of the tip of the grill. Early-state grills show a point or very small vertical line at the tip of the pyramid, while late-state grills show the pyramid tips truncated and flat.

Early-state "H" grills tend to be on vertical-mesh wove paper, while later printings and all late-state grills were printed on horizontal-mesh wove paper, resulting in stamp designs being approximately ¼mm shorter than the designs printed on vertical-mesh wove paper. The late-stage "H" grills virtually all seem to have been used only after Jan. 1873.

Poor printing quality often resulted in grills that show only a few grill points or a very few rows of points. This is especially true of the "H" grills. When there are not enough grill points to clearly identify whether the grill is an "H" or an "I," it must be assumed it is the lower-valued "H" grill variety. Authentication is advised for these stamps with high catalogue values.

Killer cancellation of the oval grid type with letters or numeral centers was first used in 1876 Bank Note issues. By order of the Postmaster-General (July 23, 1860) it was prohibited to use the town mark as a canceling instrument, and a joined town-and-killer duplex cancellation was developed.

Numeral cancellations-see "Postal Markings-Examples."

White Wove Paper, Thin to Medium Thick.

1870-71 ***Perf. 12***

134 A44	1c **ultramarine,** *Apr. 1870*	2,000.	200.00
	pale ultramarine	2,000.	200.00
	dark ultramarine	2,000.	200.00
	No gum	700.	
	On cover		240.00
	Pair	*4,250.*	450.00
	Block of 4	*12,000.*	1,250.
	Double transfer	2,250.	225.00
	Double grill	—	340.00
	Split grill	2,500.	225.00
	Quadruple split grill	—	525.00
	End roller grill		675.00
b.	Pair, one without grill	—	

Earliest documented use: Apr. 9, 1870.

Cancellations

Blue	+25.00
Red	+50.00
Green	+150.00
"Paid"	+10.00
"Paid All"	+20.00
"Steamship"	+45.00

135 A45	2c **red brown,** *Apr. 1870*	1,000.	80.00
	pale red brown	1,000.	80.00
	dark red brown	1,000.	80.00
	No gum	360.	
	On cover		100.00
	Pair	2,100.	170.00
	Block of 4	5,500.	525.00
	Double grill	1,400.	150.00
	Split grill	1,050.	95.00
	Quadruple split grill	*2,250.*	240.00
	End roller grill	*1,750.*	*400.00*
	Grill with points up		*500.00*
b.	Diagonal half used as 1c on cover		—
c.	Vertical half used as 1c on cover		—
d.	Pair, one without grill	—	
	Strip of 6, five without grill	—	

Earliest documented use: July 14, 1870.

Cancellations

Blue	+10.00
Red	+20.00
Brown	+15.00
Green	+100.00
"Paid"	+5.00
"Paid All"	+10.00
Numeral	+5.00
China	—

136 A46	3c **green,** *Mar. 1870*	575.	32.50
	pale green	575.	32.50
	yellow green	575.	32.50
	deep green	575.	32.50
	No gum	190.	
	On cover		37.50
	Pair	1,200.	67.50
	Block of 4	3,000.	240.00
	P# block of 10, Impt.	*52,500.*	
	Double transfer	—	37.50
	Double grill	950.	90.00
	Split grill	625.	37.50
	Quadruple split grill	—	150.00
	End roller grill		275.00
	Cracked plate	—	100.00
c.	Printed on both sides	—	

Earliest documented use: Mar. 24, 1870.

Cancellations

Blue	+5.00
Purple	+10.00
Magenta	+10.00
Red	+10.00
Orange red	+10.00
Orange	+25.00
Brown	+2.50
Green	+60.00
"Paid"	+2.50
Railroad	+10.00
"Steamship"	+20.00
"Paid All"	+15.00
Numeral	+4.00
"Free"	+25.00

See Die and Plate Proofs for imperf. on stamp paper.

137 A47	6c **carmine,** *Apr. 1870*	5,000.	425.
	pale carmine	5,000.	425.
	carmine rose	5,000.	425.
	No gum	1,750.	
	On cover		525.
	Pair	*10,000.*	900.
	Block of 4	*27,500.*	
	Double grill	—	775.
	Split grill	*5,250.*	500.
	Quadruple split grill	—	1,000.
	End roller grill	*6,500.*	*850.*
b.	Pair, one without grill		—
	Strip of 4 + single, one in strip without grill, on cover		—

Earliest documented use: Apr. 11, 1870.

Cancellations

Blue	+50.
Red	+75.
"Paid"	+35.

138 A48	7c **vermilion,** *1871*	4,250.	525.
	deep vermilion	4,250.	525.
	No gum	1,550.	
	On cover		700.
	Pair	9,000.	1,100.
	Block of 4	*24,000.*	
	Double grill		800.
	Split grill	4,500.	550.
	Quadruple split grill		950.
	End roller grill		*975.*
b.	Pair, one without grill	—	
	Strip of 3, two without grill	—	

Earliest documented use: Feb. 12, 1871.

Cancellations

Blue	+25.00
Purple	+35.00
Red	+50.00
Green	+300.00
"Paid"	+25.00

The 7c stamps, Nos. 138 and 149, were issued for a 7c rate of July 1, 1870, to Prussia, German States and Austria, including Hungary, via Hamburg (on the Hamburg-American Line steamers), or Bremen (on North German Lloyd ships), but issue was delayed by the Franco-Prussian War.

The rate for this service was reduced to 6c in 1871.

For several months there was no 7c rate, but late in 1871 the Prussian closed mail rate via England was reduced to 7c which revived an important use for the 7c stamps.

The rate to Denmark direct via Baltic Lloyd ships, or via Bremen and Hamburg as above, was 7c from Jan. 1, 1872.

139 A49	10c **brown,** *Apr. 1870*	7,500.	800.
	yellow brown	7,500.	800.
	dark brown	7,500.	800.
	No gum	2,700.	
	On cover		1,000.
	Pair	*15,500.*	1,650.
	Block of 4	*37,500.*	—
	Double grill	—	1,350.
	Split grill	7,750.	825.
	End roller grill		*1,650.*
b.	Pair, one without grill, one with split grill, on cover		—

Earliest documented use: May 6, 1870.

Cancellations

Blue	+50.
Red	+100.
"Steamship"	+50.
Supplementary Mail Type A	—
"Honolulu Paid All"	—

140 A50	12c **dull violet,** *Apr. 1870*	*32,500.*	3,750.
	No gum	*17,500.*	
	On cover		*7,000.*
	Pair	*65,000.*	*8,250.*
	Strip of 3		*15,000.*
	Strip of 4		*20,000.*
	Block of 4	*190,000.*	
	Double grill		—
	Split grill	—	4,250.
	End roller grill		*7,500.*

Earliest documented use: June 17, 1870.

Cancellations

Blue	+200.
Red	+375.
"Paid all"	—

141 A51	15c **orange,** *Apr. 1870*	7,500.	1,500.
	bright orange	7,500.	1,500.
	deep orange	7,500.	1,500.
	No gum	2,500.	
	On cover		2,250.
	Pair	16,000.	3,250.
	Block of 4	*45,000.*	—
	Double grill		*4,500.*
	Double grill, one split		—
	Split grill	7,750.	1,600.
	Quadruple split grill		—

Earliest documented use: June 2, 1870.

Cancellations

Blue +50.
Purple +100.
Red +150.
Green +1,000.
"PAID" —

142 A52 24c **purple** — 6,500.
On cover —
Pair, double grill —
Split grill —
End roller grill —
Grill with points up —

Earliest documented use: July 11, 1872.

Cancellations

Red +750.
Blue +4,000.
Purple +2,500.

The pair of No. 142 is the unique multiple of this stamp.

143 A53 30c **black,** *Apr. 1870* 20,000. 3,750.
full black 20,000. 3,750.
No gum 7,500.
On cover 4,750.
Pair *42,500.* 8,000.
Block of 4 *100,000.* —
Double grill —
End roller grill *5,250.*

Earliest documented use: Aug. 18, 1870.

Cancellations

Blue +100.
Red +200.

144 A54 90c **carmine,** *Apr. 12, 1870* 25,000. 2,250.
dark carmine 25,000. 2,250.
No gum 10,000.
On cover —
Pair *55,000.* 5,000.
Block of 4 *125,000.* *13,500.*
Double grill —
Split grill 2,500.

Cancellations

Blue +120.
Red +200.

I. GRILL ABOUT 8½x10mm (10 TO 11 BY 10 TO 13 POINTS)

The "I" grills can be separated into early state and late state, based on the shape of the tip of the grill. Early state grills show small tips of the pyramid, while late state grills show the pyramid tips truncated and flat.

Early state "I" grills tend to be on vertical-mesh wove paper, while later printings and all late-state grills were printed on horizontal-mesh wove paper, resulting in stamp designs being approximately ¼mm shorter than the designs printed on vertical-mesh wove paper. The late-stage "I" grills all seem to have been used only after Jan. 1873.

Values are for stamps with grills that are clearly identifiable. Poor printing quality often resulted in grills that show only a few grill points or a very few rows of points. When there are not enough grill points to clearly identify whether the grill is an "H" or an "I," it must be assumed it is the lower-valued "H" grill variety. Authentication is advised for these stamps with high catalogue values.

134A A44 1c **ultramarine,** *1870* *2,750.* *400.00*
pale ultramarine —
No gum *800.00*
Pair *9,000.*
Block of 4 *30,000.*
On cover —
Split grill — *450.00*

Cancellations

Blue +150.00
Green +150.00
"Paid" +20.00

135A A45 2c **red brown,** *1870* *2,000.* *300.00*
On cover —
Split grill — —
Quadruple split grill —

Earliest documented use: July 21, 1870.

Cancellations

Blue +100.00

136A A46 3c **green,** *1870* *850.00* *100.00*
On cover —
Pair — —
Block of 4 — —
Double grill —
Split grill *1,200.* —
Quadruple split grill — —
a. Pair, one without grill —
On cover —

Earliest documented use: June 27, 1870.

Cancellations

Blue —
Red —
Green —
"Paid All" —

137A A47 6c **carmine,** *1870* *8,500.* *950.00*
On cover *1,250.*
Strip of 3 —
Quadruple split grill —

Cancellations

Blue town —

138A A48 7c **vermilion,** *1871* *6,500.* *800.00*
No gum *2,200.*
Split grill —
Double grill, both split —
Quadruple split grill —

Cancellations

Blue +200.00
Red +150.00

139A A49 10c **brown,** *1870* *17,500.* *10,000.*
Pair, on cover 13,000.
Split grill —
b. Strip of 3, one without grill, two with split grill —

There are four unused examples of No. 139A recorded. One is fine and the other is very fine plus. The catalogue value is for the latter. The pair on cover is the only example of No. 139A on cover. One stamp in the pair is defective, and the cover is valued thus.

Earliest documented use: Mar. 8, 1871.

Cancellation

Red +100.00

140A A50 12c **dull violet,** *1870* *30,000.* —

Two examples are recorded of No. 140A unused, and it is valued in the grade of fine.

One used example is recorded, centered to the left.

141A A51 15c **orange,** *1870* *16,500.* *8,500.*
On cover —
Block of 4 —

Seven singles and a block of 4 are recorded of No. 141A unused. Value for unused single is for a fine example. The unique unused block has original gum and faults.

Earliest documented use: June 15, 1870.

Cancellations

Red +100.00
N. YORK STEAMSHIP —

143A A53 30c **black,** *1870* *75,000.*

Only one recorded example of No. 143A, which is valued in the grade of fine-very fine.

144A A54 90c **carmine,** *1870* — *15,000.*

The unused No. 144A has a vertically split grill and is unique.

PRODUCED BY THE NATIONAL BANK NOTE COMPANY.

White Wove Paper, Thin to Medium Thick.
Issued (except 3c, 6c and 7c) in April, 1870.
Without Grill.

1870-71 ***Perf. 12***

145 A44 1c **ultramarine** 650. 20.00
pale ultramarine 650. 20.00
dark ultramarine 650. 20.00
gray blue 650. 20.00
No gum 240.
On cover 22.50
Pair 1,350. 42.50
Block of 4 3,500. 100.00
P# block of 12, Impt. *9,000.*
Double transfer — 25.00
Worn plate 650. 20.00

Only one plate block of No. 145 is known in private hands. It is of average condition and is without gum. Value is based on 2019 auction sale.

Earliest documented use: May 7, 1870.

Cancellations

Blue +1.50
Ultramarine +2.50
Magenta +2.00
Purple +2.00
Brown +2.00
Red +5.00
Green +55.00
"Paid" +3.00
"Paid All" +15.00
"Steamship" +25.00
Railroad +20.00
Numeral +2.00

146 A45 2c **red brown** 350. 17.50
pale red brown 350. 17.50
dark red brown 350. 17.50
No gum 150.
orange brown 375. 20.00
No gum 160.
On cover 20.00
Pair 725. 37.50
Block of 4 1,900. 125.00
P# block of 10, Impt. *13,000.*
Double transfer — 20.00
a. Diagonal half used as 1c on cover *800.00*
b. Vertical half used as 1c on cover *900.00*
c. Horiz. half used as 1c on cover *900.00*
d. Double impression *9,000.*

The No. 146 plate block is unique. Value is based on 2019 auction sale. No. 146d is also unique. It has VG-Fine centering and faults and is valued thus.

Earliest documented use: May 7, 1870.

Cancellations

Blue +1.00
Purple +1.25
Red +3.00
Green +55.00
Brown +1.25
"Paid" +2.00
"Paid All" +10.00
Numeral +2.00
"Steamship" +22.50
Black Carrier +12.50
Japan —
China —
Curacao —

Major Plate Crack At Bottom

147 A46 3c **green** 200. 1.80
pale green 200. 1.80
dark green 200. 1.80
No gum 80.
yellow green 225. 1.90
No gum 90.
On cover 2.30
Pair 425. 3.75
Block of 4 1,200. 24.00
P# block of 10, Impt. *6,000.*
Double transfer — 11.00
Short transfer at bottom 225. 20.00
Cracked plate — 55.00
Major plate crack at bottom (91L, plate ?) *400.00*
On cover *800.00*
Worn plate 220. 1.80
a. Printed on both sides, reverse inverted *17,500.*
b. Double impression *30,000.*
On cover —

Nos. 147a and 147b are valued in the grade of fine.

See Die and Plate Proofs for imperf. on stamp paper.

Earliest documented use: Mar. 1, 1870.

Cancellations

Blue +.25
Purple +.50
Magenta +.50
Brown +1.50
Red +2.50
Ultramarine +2.00
Green +55.00
Orange +750.00
"Paid" +2.00
"Paid All" +10.00
"Free" +15.00
Numeral +2.00
Railroad +10.00
Express Company —
"Steamboat" +20.00
"Steamship" +17.50
Ship +15.00
Japan +75.00

148 A47 6c **carmine** 900. 22.50
dark carmine 900. 22.50
rose 900. 22.50
No gum 290.
On cover 27.50
Pair 1,900. 55.00
Block of 4 4,750. 325.00
Double transfer 32.50
brown carmine 1,050. 65.00
No gum 340.
violet carmine 1,200. 190.00
No gum 400.
a. Vertical half used as 3c on cover *6,500.*
b. Double impression, on cover *20,000.*
c. Double paper — *100.00*

No. 148b is unique.

Earliest documented use: Mar. 28, 1870.

Cancellations

Blue +1.50
Purple +3.00
Violet +4.00
Ultramarine +5.00
Brown +2.00
Red +5.00
Claret +10.00
Orange red +7.00
Orange +20.00
Green +150.00
"Paid" +3.00
"Steamship" +25.00
"Paid All" +15.00
Numeral —
Supp. Mail Type A or D +35.00
China +90.00
Japan +150.00

149 A48 7c **vermilion,** *Mar. 1871* 900. 100.00
deep vermilion 900. 100.00
No gum 290.
On cover 150.00
Pair 1,900. 225.00
Block of 4 5,500. *800.00*
Cracked plate 170.00

Earliest documented use: May 11, 1871.

Cancellations

Blue +2.50
Purple +7.50
Ultramarine +12.50
Red +10.00
Green +450.00
Japan +150.00

150 A49 10c **brown** 2,000. 35.00
dark brown 2,000. 35.00
yellow brown 2,000. 35.00
No gum 800.
On cover 47.50
Pair 4,250. 72.50

	Block of 4	10,000.	*275.00*
	P# block of 10, Impt.	—	
	Double transfer	—	85.00

Earliest documented use: May 14, 1870 (stamp on piece); May 19, 1870 (on cover).

Cancellations

Blue	+1.00
Purple	+2.00
Magenta	+2.00
Ultramarine	+4.00
Red	+4.00
Orange red	+5.00
Orange	+10.00
Green	+120.00
Brown	+3.00
"Paid All"	+20.00
"Steamship"	+20.00
Supp. Mail Type A or D	+25.00
Japan	+120.00
China	—
St. Thomas	—

151	A50 12c **dull violet**	2,850.	200.00
	violet	2,850.	200.00
	dark violet	2,850.	200.00
	No gum	1,050.	
	On cover		450.00
	Pair	6,000.	425.00
	Block of 4	*14,000.*	*2,250.*

Earliest documented use: July 9, 1870.

Cancellations

Blue	+25.00
Ultramarine	+1,000.
Magenta	+10.00
Red	+15.00
Orange	—
Green	+150.00
"Paid All"	+25.00
"Steamship"	+50.00
Supp. Mail Type A or D	+40.00
Japan	—

152	A51 15c **bright orange**	3,500.	225.00
	deep orange	3,500.	225.00
	No gum	1,300.	
	On cover		350.00
	Pair	7,500.	475.00
	Block of 4	*17,500.*	*1,850.*
a.	Double impression		*9,000.*

No. 152a is unique. It has fine centering and faults and is valued thus.

Earliest documented use: June 24, 1870.

Cancellations

Blue	+7.50
Magenta	+7.50
Ultramarine	+10.00
Red	+15.00
Purple	+250.00
"Paid"	+12.50
"Steamship"	+40.00
Supp. Mail Type A or F	+30.00
China	—

153	A52 24c **purple**	1,700.	225.00
	bright purple	1,700.	225.00
	No gum	650.	
	On cover		*1,500.*
	Pair	3,600.	475.00
	Block of 4	*13,000.*	*3,500.*
a.	Double paper	—	—

Earliest documented use: Sept. 8, 1870.

Cancellations

Red	+15.00
Blue	+5.00
Purple	+7.50
China	—
"Paid"	+25.00
Town	+15.00
"Steamship"	—
Supp. Mail Type A, D or F	+30.00

154	A53 30c **black**	7,000.	300.00
	full black	7,000.	325.00
	No gum	2,600.	
	On cover		875.00
	Pair	*15,000.*	625.00
	Block of 4	*37,500.*	

Earliest documented use: July 9, 1870.

Cancellations

Blue	+5.00
Brown	+50.00
Magenta	+15.00
Red	+50.00
"Steamship"	+55.00
Supplementary Mail Type A	+40.00

155	A54 90c **carmine**	5,000.	350.00
	dark carmine	5,000.	350.00
	No gum	1,800.	
	On cover		—
	Pair	*10,500.*	725.00
	Block of 4	*25,000.*	2,400.
	P# strip of 5, Impt.	*35,000.*	

Earliest documented use: Sept. 1, 1872.

Cancellations

Blue	+10.00
Purple	+15.00
Magenta	+15.00
Green	+275.00
Red	+50.00
Town	+20.00
Supp. Mail Type A or F	+40.00
Japan	—

PLEASE NOTE:

Stamps are valued in the grade of very fine unless otherwise indicated.

Values for early and valuable stamps are for examples with certificates of authenticity from acknowledged expert committees, or examples sold with the buyer having the right of certification. This applies to examples with original gum as well as examples without gum. Beware of stamps offered "as is," as the gum on some unused stamps offered with "original gum" may be fraudulent, and stamps offered as unused without gum may in some cases be altered or faintly canceled used stamps.

VALUES FOR NEVER-HINGED STAMPS PRIOR TO SCOTT No. 182

This catalogue does not value pre-1879 stamps in never-hinged condition. Premiums for never-hinged condition in the classic era invariably are even larger than those premiums listed for the 1879 and later issues. Generally speaking, the earlier the stamp is listed in the catalogue, the larger will be the never-hinged premium.

PRINTED BY THE CONTINENTAL BANK NOTE COMPANY

Plates of 200 subjects in two panes of 100 each.

Designs of the 1870-71 Issue with secret marks on the values from 1c to 15c, as described and illustrated:

The object of secret marks was to provide a simple and positive proof that these stamps were produced by the Continental Bank Note Company and not by their predecessors.

Almost all of the stamps of the Continental Bank Note Co. printing including the Department stamps and some of the Newspaper stamps may be found upon a paper that shows more or less the characteristics of a ribbed paper. The ribbing may be oriented either vertically or horizontally, with horizontal ribbing being far more common than vertical ribbing. Values are for the most common varieties.

Franklin — A44a

1c. In the pearl at the left of the numeral "1" there is a small crescent.

Jackson — A45a

2c. Under the scroll at the left of "U. S." there is a small diagonal line. This mark seldom shows clearly. The stamp, No. 157, can be distinguished by its color.

Washington — A46a

3c. The under part of the upper tail of the left ribbon is heavily shaded.

Lincoln — A47a

6c. The first four vertical lines of the shading in the lower part of the left ribbon have been strengthened.

Stanton — A48a

7c. Two small semi-circles are drawn around the ends of the lines that outline the ball in the lower right hand corner.

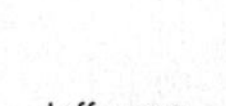

Jefferson — A49a

10c. There is a small semi-circle in the scroll at the right end of the upper label.

Clay — A50a

12c. The balls of the figure "2" are crescent shaped.

Webster — A51a

15c. In the lower part of the triangle in the upper left corner two lines have been made heavier forming a "V." This mark can be found on some of the Continental and American (1879) printings, but not all stamps show it.

Secret marks were added to the dies of the 24c, 30c and 90c but new plates were not made from them. The various printings of the 30c and 90c can be distinguished only by the shades and paper.

Experimental J. Grill about 7x9½mm exists on all values except 24c and 90c. Grill was composed of truncated pyramids and was so strongly impressed that some points often broke through the paper.

White Wove Paper, Thin to Thick Without Grill

1873, July (?) ***Perf. 12***

156	A44a 1c **ultramarine**	200.	5.75
	pale ultramarine	200.	5.75
	gray blue	200.	5.75
	blue	200.	5.75
	No gum	90.	
	dark ultramarine	225.	5.75
	No gum	95.	
	On cover		7.25
	Pair	425.	12.00

	Block of 4	1,000.	47.50
	P# block of 12, Impt.	7,000.	
	P# block of 14, Impt.	9,500.	
	Double transfer	275.	10.00
	Ribbed paper	325.	25.00
	Paper with silk fibers	—	35.00
	Cracked plate		—
	Paper cut with "cogwheel" punch	425.	
a.	Double paper	2,000.	500.00
e.	With grill	2,000.	
f.	Imperf., pair	—	1,500.

The No. 156 plate block is unique. Value is 1998 auction sale. No. 156f may not have been regularly issued.

Earliest documented use: Aug. 22, 1873.

Cancellations

Blue	+.25
Purple	+.35
Magenta	+.35
Ultramarine	+1.00
Red	+3.50
Orange red	+4.00
Orange	+5.00
Brown	+20.00
Green	+60.00
"Paid All"	+7.00
"Paid"	+1.00
Railroad	+12.00
"Free"	+12.00
Black carrier	+15.00
Numeral	+2.50
Alaska	—
Japan	—
Printed "G." Precancel (Glastonbury, Conn.)	+200.00
Printed Star Precancel (Glen Allen, Va.)	+100.00

157	A45a 2c **brown**	325.	25.00
	dark brown	325.	25.00
	dark reddish brown	325.	25.00
	yellowish brown	325.	25.00
	No gum	125.	
	With secret mark	350.	27.50
	No gum	140.	
	On cover		30.00
	Pair	675.	52.50
	Block of 4	1,650.	190.00
	P# block of 12, Impt.	12,000.	
	P# block of 14, Impt.	13,000.	
	Ribbed paper	475.	57.50
	Double transfer	—	32.50
	Cracked plate		—
a.	Double paper	1,500.	200.00
	On cover		2,500.
c.	With grill	1,850.	750.00
d.	Double impression		16,500.
e.	Vertical half used as 1c on cover		1,000.

No. 157d is unique.

Earliest documented use: July 12, 1873.

Cancellations

Blue	+.75
Magenta	+1.00
Purple	+1.00
Red	+5.00
Orange red	+5.50
Orange	+7.50
Green	+100.00
"Paid"	+2.50
"Insufficiently Paid"	—
"Paid All"	+13.50
"P. D." in circle	+15.00
Town	+2.00
Numeral	+1.50
Black Carrier	+8.50
"Steamship"	+15.00
Supplementary Mail Type F	+5.00
China	—
Japan	+100.00
Printed Star Precancellation (Glen Allen, Va.)	—

158	A46a 3c **green**	110.	1.00
	bluish green	110.	1.00
	yellow green	110.	1.00
	dark yellow green	110.	1.00
	dark green	110.	1.00
	No gum	40.	
	olive green, ribbed paper	375.	15.00
	No gum	140.	
	On cover		1.20
	Pair	230.	2.10
	Block of 4	550.	14.50
	P# strip of 5, Impt.	700.	
	P# strip of 6, Impt.	825.	
	P# block of 10, Impt.	2,600.	
	P# block of 12, Impt.	3,750.	
	P# block of 14, Impt.	5,000.	
	Paper cut with "cogwheel" punch	290.	400.
	On cover		—
	Ribbed paper	290.	10.00
	Paper with silk fibers	—	10.00
	Cracked plate	—	32.50
	Double transfer	—	6.00
	Short transfer at bottom		15.00
a.	Double paper	600.	100.00
	P# strip of 6, Impt.	4,250.	
e.	With grill	550.	
	End roller grill	1,250.	425.
h.	Horizontal pair, imperf. vert.		—
i.	Horizontal pair, imperf. between		1,300.
j.	Double impression		7,000.
k.	Printed on both sides		20,000.

Nos. 158j and 158k are valued in the grade of fine.

See Die and Plate Proofs for imperfs. on stamp paper, with and without grill.

Earliest documented use: July 17, 1873.

Cancellations

Blue	+.10
Magenta	+.20
Purple	+.20
Ultramarine	+1.25
Red	+2.50
Orange red	+2.75
Orange	+3.50
Green	+25.00
Town	+.05
"Paid"	+2.50
"Paid All"	+20.00
"Free"	+15.00
Numeral	+1.00
China	—
Railroad	+7.00
"R. P. O."	+1.50
"P. D." in circle	—
"Steamboat"	—
"Steamship"	—
Supplementary Mail Type D	+11.00
Supplementary Mail Type F	+8.50
Express Company	—
Black Carrier	+8.00
Red Carrier	+25.00
Japan	+65.00
Alaska	—

159	A47a 6c **dull pink**	375.	18.00
	brown rose	450.	18.00
	No gum	120.	
	On cover		27.50
	Pair	800.	37.50
	Block of 4	2,250.	130.00
	P# block of 12, Impt. (dull pink)	15,000.	
	P# block of 12, Impt. (brown rose)	16,500.	
	Ribbed paper	—	60.00
	Paper with colored fibers	—	700.00
a.	Diagonal half used as 3c on cover		7,250.
b.	With grill	1,800.	
	End roller grill	2,400.	
c.	Double paper	—	900.00

Earliest documented use: June 8, 1873.

No. 159a is unique.

No. 159b is valued in the grade of fine.

Cancellations

Blue	+1.00
Indigo	+2.50
Magenta	+1.50
Purple	+1.50
Violet	+3.00
Ultramarine	+2.50
Red	+7.50
Orange red	+9.00
Green	+100.00
Numeral	+1.50
"Paid"	+10.00
"Paid All"	+15.00
Supp. Mail Type D, E or F	+35.00
Japan	+100.00
China	+125.00
Railroad	+6.00
"R. P. O."	+3.00

160	A48a 7c **orange vermilion**	1,000.	85.00
	vermilion	1,000.	85.00
	No gum	350.	
	On cover		160.00
	Pair	2,300.	180.00
	Block of 4	6,000.	
	P# block of 12, Impt.	18,500.	
	Double transfer of "7 cents" (1R22)	—	200.00
	Double transfer in lower left corner	—	150.00
	Ribbed paper	—	140.00
	Paper with silk fibers	1,900.	200.00
a.	With grill	3,500.	
b.	Double paper		—

The plate block of 12 is in fine condition. It is unique.

Earliest documented use: Sept. 10, 1873.

Cancellations

Blue	+4.00
Red	+10.00
Purple	+10.00
Brown	+5.00
"Paid"	+15.00

161	A49a 10c **brown**	800.	25.00
	dark brown	800.	25.00
	yellow brown	800.	25.00
	No gum	275.	
	On cover		40.00
	Pair	1,800.	52.50
	Block of 4	4,750.	200.00
	P# block of 10, Impt.	18,500.	
	P# block of 12, Impt.	21,500.	
	Ribbed paper	—	90.00
	Paper with silk fibers	1,400.	100.00
	Double transfer	—	52.50
a.	Double paper	3,500.	900.00
c.	With grill	3,750.	
d.	Horizontal pair, imperf. between		15,000.

Earliest documented use: Aug. 2, 1873.

No. 161d is unique. It has a small fault and is valued thus.

Cancellations

Blue	+1.50
Ultramarine	—
Purple	+2.00
Red	+6.00
Orange red	+7.00
Orange	+10.00
Magenta	+2.00
Brown	+20.00
Green	+100.00
"Paid"	+4.00
"P. D." in circle	+20.00
"Steamship"	+15.00
Supplementary Mail Type E	+7.00
Supplementary Mail Type F	+2.50
Japan	+100.00
China	—
Alaska	—

162	A50a 12c **blackish violet**	2,200.	140.00
	No gum	775.	
	On cover		325.00
	Pair	4,750.	280.00
	Block of 4	12,000.	1,000.
	Ribbed paper	—	350.00
a.	With grill	5,500.	

Earliest documented use: Jan. 3, 1874.

Cancellations

Blue	+2.50
Ultramarine	+15.00
Brown	+5.00
Red	+15.00
Magenta	+200.00
Purple	+500.00
Supplementary Mail Type D	+15.00
Japan	+200.00

163	A51a 15c **yellow orange**	2,250.	160.00
	pale orange	2,250.	160.00
	reddish orange	2,250.	160.00
	No gum	775.	
	On cover		350.00
	Pair	4,000.	350.00
	Block of 4	11,000.	1,150.
	P# strip of 5, Impt.	15,000.	
	Paper with silk fibers	3,000.	250.00
	Vertical ribbed paper	3,000.	250.00
a.	With grill	5,750.	
b.	Double paper		1,250.

Earliest documented use: July 22, 1873.

Cancellations

Blue	+5.00
Purple	+50.00
Red	+20.00
Green	+350.00
Brown	—
Supplementary Mail Type E	—
Supplementary Mail Type F	+10.00
"Steamship"	—
Numeral	+7.50
Puerto Rico	—
China	—

164	A52 24c **purple**		357,500.

The Philatelic Foundation has certified as genuine a 24c on vertically ribbed paper, and that is the unique stamp listed as No. 164. Specialists believe that only Continental used ribbed paper. It is not known for sure whether or not Continental also printed the 24c value on regular paper; if it did, specialists currently are not able to distinguish these from No. 153. The catalogue value represents a 2004 auction sale price realized.

165	A53 30c **gray black**	4,000.	140.
	greenish black	4,000.	140.
	No gum	1,300.	
	On cover		700.
	Pair	8,000.	290.
	Block of 4	19,000.	1,200.
	P# strip of 5, Impt.	15,000.	
	Double transfer	—	160.
	Ribbed paper	4,500.	150.
	Paper with silk fibers		—
a.	Double paper	—	
c.	With grill	22,500.	

Earliest documented use: Oct. 14, 1874.

Cancellations

Purple	+10.00
Blue	+5.00
Red	+25.00
Brown	+30.00
Magenta	+10.00
"Steamship"	—
Supplementary Mail Type E	+10.00
Supplementary Mail Type F	+5.00
Japan	+200.00

166	A54 90c **rose carmine**	2,100.	300.00
	pale rose carmine	2,100.	300.00
	No gum	700.	
	On cover		7,500.
	Pair	4,500.	650.00
	Block of 4	12,500.	2,650.
	P# strip of 5, Impt.	13,000.	

Earliest documented use: June 25, 1875.

Cancellations

Blue	+10.
Purple	+40.
Red	+40.
Supplementary Mail Type F	+30.

SPECIAL PRINTING OF 1873 ISSUE

Produced by the Continental Bank Note Co.

1875 *Perf. 12*

Hard, white wove paper, without gum

167 A44a 1c **ultramarine**	*14,000.*	
168 A45a 2c **dark brown**	*6,000.*	
169 A46a 3c **blue green**	*21,500.*	—
On cover		—
170 A47a 6c **dull rose**	*20,000.*	
171 A48a 7c **reddish vermilion**	*4,250.*	
172 A49a 10c **pale brown**	*19,000.*	
173 A50a 12c **dark violet**	*5,500.*	
Horizontal pair	—	
174 A51a 15c **bright orange**	*19,000.*	
175 A52 24c **dull purple**	*3,500.*	*22,500.*
Horizontal pair	—	
176 A53 30c **greenish black**	*12,000.*	
177 A54 90c **violet carmine**	*18,000.*	

Although perforated, these stamps were usually cut apart with scissors. As a result, the perforations are often much mutilated and the design is frequently damaged.

These can be distinguished from the 1873 issue by the shades; also by the paper, which is very white instead of yellowish.

These and the subsequent issues listed under the heading of "Special Printings" are special printings of stamps then in current use which, together with the reprints and re-issues, were made for sale to collectors. They were available for postage except for the Officials, Newspaper and Periodical, and demonetized issues.

Only No. 169 is documented on cover (unique; postmarked Mar. 5, 1876).

Only three examples of No. 175 used have been certified. They all have small faults and are valued thus.

While use of Nos. 167-177 for postage was legal, actual use was almost non-existent. Expertization strongly recommended.

PRINTED BY THE CONTINENTAL BANK NOTE COMPANY

REGULAR ISSUE

Yellowish Wove Paper

1875 *Perf. 12*

178 A45a 2c **vermilion,** *June 1875*	325.	15.00
No gum	100.	
On cover		17.50
Pair	675.	32.50
Block of 4	1,650.	130.00
P# strip of 6, Impt.	*3,000.*	
P# block of 12, Impt.	—	
P# block of 14, Impt.	*7,250.*	
Double transfer		—
Ribbed paper	—	—
Paper with silk fibers	400.	30.00
a. Double paper	—	—
b. Half used as 1c on cover		*850.00*
c. With grill	*1,200.*	*2,750.*

See Die and Plate Proofs for imperf. on stamp paper.

The previously listed EDU has been found to be erroneous. The editors welcome new verified early dates in 1875.

Cancellations

Blue	+.50
Purple	+.75
Magenta	+.75
Red	+6.00
"Paid"	+8.00
"Steamship"	—
Supplementary Mail Type F	+5.50
Black Carrier	+15.00
Railroad	+12.50

Zachary Taylor — A55

179 A55 5c **blue,** *June 1875*	700.	27.50
dark blue	725.	27.50
bright blue	700.	27.50
light blue	700.	27.50
No gum	225.	
greenish blue	725.	32.50
No gum	240.	
On cover		42.50
Pair	1,500.	57.50
Block of 4	3,750.	380.00
Cracked plate	—	*170.00*
Double transfer	—	40.00
Ribbed paper	—	—
Paper with silk fibers	—	52.50
a. Double paper	*950.*	
c. With grill	9,500.	
End roller grill	—	

Earliest documented use: July 10, 1875.

Cancellations

Blue	+1.00
Ultramarine	+3.00
Purple	+2.00
Magenta	+2.00
Red	+10.00
Green	+70.00
Numeral	+5.00
Railroad	+17.50
"Steamship"	+12.50
Ship	+12.50
Supplementary Mail Type E	+5.00
Supplementary Mail Type F	+2.00
China	—
Japan	+125.00
Peru	—

The five cent rate to foreign countries in the Universal Postal Union began on July 1, 1875. No. 179 was issued for that purpose.

SPECIAL PRINTING OF 1875 ISSUE

Produced by the Continental Bank Note Co.

Hard, White Wove Paper, without gum

1875

180 A45a 2c **carmine vermilion**	*70,000.*
181 A55 5c **bright blue**	*450,000.*

Unlike Nos. 167-177, Nos. 180-181 were seldom cut apart with scissors.

Numbers sold: No. 180, 917; No. 181, 317. However, fewer than 25 No. 180 and fewer than 10 No. 181 have been expertized and are available to collectors.

IMPORTANT INFORMATION REGARDING VALUES FOR NEVER-HINGED STAMPS

Collectors should be aware that the values given for never-hinged stamps from No. 182 on are for stamps in the grade of very fine, just as the values for all stamps in the catalogue are for very fine stamps unless indicated otherwise. The never-hinged premium as a percentage of value will be larger for stamps in extremely fine or superb grades, and the premium will be smaller for fine-very fine, fine or poor examples. This is particularly true of the issues of the late-19th and early-20th centuries.

VALUES FOR NEVER-HINGED STAMPS PRIOR TO SCOTT 182

This catalogue does not value pre-1879 stamps in never-hinged condition. Premiums for never-hinged condition in the classic era invariably are even larger than those premiums listed for the 1879 and later issues. Generally speaking, the earlier the stamp is listed in the catalogue, the larger will be the never-hinged premium.

NEVER-HINGED PLATE BLOCKS

Values given for never-hinged plate blocks are for blocks in which all stamps have original gum that has never been hinged and has no disturbances, and all selvage, whether gummed or ungummed, has never been hinged.

For values of the most popular U.S. stamps in various conditions, including never hinged from No. 182 on, and in the grades of fine, fine to very fine, very fine, very fine to extremely fine, extremely fine, extremely fine to superb, superb, and gem, see the *Scott Stamp Values U.S. Specialized by Grade*booklet, updated and issued each year.

PRINTED BY THE AMERICAN BANK NOTE COMPANY

The Continental Bank Note Co. was consolidated with the American Bank Note Co. on February 4, 1879. The American Bank Note Company used many plates of the Continental Bank Note Company to print the ordinary postage, Departmental and Newspaper stamps. Therefore, stamps bearing the Continental Company's imprint were not always its product.

The A. B. N. Co. also used the 30c and 90c plates of the N. B. N. Co. Some of No. 190 and all of No. 217 were from A. B. N. Co. plate 405.

Early printings of No. 188 were from Continental plates 302 and 303 which contained the normal secret mark of 1873. After those plates were re-entered by the A. B. N. Co. in 1880, pairs or multiple pieces contained combinations of normal, hairline or missing marks. The pairs or other multiples usually found contain at least one hairline mark which tended to disappear as the plate wore.

A. B. N. Co. plates 377 and 378 were made in 1881 from the National transfer roll of 1870. No. 187 from these plates has no secret mark.

Identification by Paper Type:

Collectors traditionally have identified American Bank Note Co. issues by the soft, porous paper on which they were printed. However, the Continental Bank Note Co. used some intermediate papers as early as 1877 and a soft paper from August 1878 through early 1879, before the consolidation of the companies. When the consolidation occurred in the late afternoon of Feb. 4, 1879, American Bank Note Co. took over the presses, plates, paper, ink, and the employees of Continental. Undoubtedly they also acquired panes of finished stamps and sheets of printed stamps that had not yet been gummed and/or perforated. Since the soft paper that was in use at the time of the consolidation and after is approximately the same texture and thickness as the soft paper that American Bank Note Co. began using regularly in June or July of 1879, all undated soft paper stamps have traditionally been classified as American Bank Note Co. printings.

However, if a stamp bears a dated cancellation or is on a dated cover from Feb. 4, 1879 or earlier, collectors (especially specialist collectors) must consider the stamp to be a Continental Bank Note printing. Undated stamps off cover, and stamps and covers dated Feb. 5 or later, traditionally have been considered to be American Bank Note Co. printings since that company held the contract to print U.S. postage stamps beginning on that date. The most dedicated and serious specialist students sometimes attempt to determine the stamp printer of the issues on soft, porous paper in an absolute manner (by scientifically testing the paper and/or comparing printing records).

Earliest documented uses for American Bank Note Co. issues are given for stamps on the soft, porous paper that has been traditionally associated with that company. But, for reasons given above, sometimes that date will precede the Feb. 4, 1879 consolidation date.

SAME AS 1870-75 ISSUES

Soft Porous Paper

1879 *Perf. 12*

182 A44a 1c **dark ultramarine**	200.	6.00
blue	200.	6.00
gray blue	200.	6.00
Never hinged	675.	
No gum	80.	
On cover		6.50
Pair	425.	12.50
Block of 4	1,200.	67.50
P# block of 12, Impt.	*7,000.*	
P# block of 10, Impt.	*6,000.*	
Double transfer	—	12.50

Earliest documented use: Jan. 3, 1879.

Cancellations

Blue	+.20
Magenta	+.30
Purple	+.30
Red	+7.00
Printed Star Precancellation (Glen Allen, Va.)	+125.00
Green	+35.00
"Paid"	+4.00
Supplementary Mail Type F	+10.00
Railroad	+12.50
Printed "G." Precancellation (Glastonbury, Conn.)	+100.00

183 A45a 2c **vermilion**	100.	5.00
orange vermilion	100.	5.00
Never hinged	370.	
No gum	40.	
On cover		5.50
Pair	210.	11.00
Block of 4	550.	55.00
P# block of 10, Impt.	*4,000.*	
P# block of 12, Impt.	*4,500.*	
Double transfer	—	—
a. Double impression	—	*5,500.*
b. Half used as 1c on cover		*750.00*

No. 183a is valued in the grade of fine.

Earliest documented use: Aug. 19, 1878.

Cancellations

Blue	+.25
Purple	+.40
Magenta	+.40
Red	+6.00
Green	+175.00
"Paid"	+5.00
"Paid All"	—
"Ship"	—
Numeral	+4.00
Railroad	+15.00
Supplementary Mail Type F	+8.00
China	—
Printed Star Precancellation in black (Glen Allen, Va.)	+350.00
Printed Star Precancellation in red (Glen Allen, Va.)	+1,750.

184 A46a 3c **green**	90.	1.00
light green	90.	1.00
dark green	90.	1.00
Never hinged	325.	
No gum	35.	
On cover		1.10
Pair	190.	2.10
Block of 4	450.	12.50
P# block of 10, Impt.	1,300.	
Never hinged	*3,000.*	
P# block of 12, Impt.	1,525.	
P# block of 14, Impt.	1,900.	
Double transfer	—	—
Short transfer	—	7.00
b. Double impression		*5,000.*

No. 184b is valued in the grade of fine.

See Die and Plate Proofs for imperf. on stamp paper.

Earliest documented use: July 2, 1878.

Cancellations

Blue		+.10
Magenta		+.15
Purple		+.15
Violet		+.15
Brown		+1.00
Red		+7.50
Green		+25.00
"Paid"		+3.00
"Free"		+15.00
Numeral		+2.00
Railroad		+12.50
"Steamboat"		—
Supplementary Mail Type F		+8.00
Printed Star Precancel (Glen Allen, Va.)		—
China		+60.00
Alaska		—

185 A55 5c **blue**	500.	16.00
light blue	500.	16.00
bright blue	500.	16.00
dark blue	500.	16.00
Never hinged	*1,600.*	
No gum	155.	
On cover		27.50
Pair	1,050.	35.00
Block of 4	2,500.	190.00
P# block of 10, Impt.	*17,500.*	
Double transfer	—	
Short transfer at top	—	

Earliest documented use: Jan. 16, 1879.

Cancellations

Blue		+.25
Purple		+1.00
Magenta		+1.00
Ultramarine		+3.50
Red		+7.50
Railroad		+20.00
Numeral		+2.00
Supplementary Mail Type F		+1.50
"Steamship"		+35.00
China		+60.00
Peru		—
Panama		—

186 A47a 6c **pink**	900.	22.50
dull pink	900.	22.50
brown rose	900.	22.50
Never hinged	*3,100.*	
No gum	275.	
On cover		27.50
Pair	2,000.	50.00
Block of 4	4,000.	*475.00*

Earliest documented use: April 18, 1879.

Cancellations

Blue		+.50
Ultramarine		+3.50
Purple		+1.00
Magenta		+1.00
Red		+12.00
Supplementary Mail Type F		+8.00
Railroad		+20.00
Numeral		+4.00
China		+100.00

187 A49 10c **brown,** without secret mark	3,000.	45.00
yellow brown	3,000.	45.00
Never hinged	*10,000.*	
No gum	1,000.	
On cover		62.50
Pair	6,250.	95.00
Block of 4	*14,000.*	—
Double transfer	—	62.50
a. Double paper	*10,000.*	—

Earliest documented use: Sept. 5, 1879.

Cancellations

Blue		+.50
Magenta		+1.50
Red		+10.00
"Paid"		+3.50
Supplementary Mail Type F		+3.00
China		+70.00

188 A49a 10c **brown,** with secret mark	1,800.	30.00
yellow brown	1,800.	30.00
Never hinged	*6,000.*	
No gum	650.	
black brown	2,100.	60.00
Never hinged	*6,500.*	
No gum	750.	
On cover		45.00
Pair	3,750.	62.50
Block of 4	*9,500.*	325.00
Pair, one stamp No. 187	*9,000.*	725.00
Double transfer		47.50
Cracked plate	—	—

Earliest documented use: Oct. 5, 1878.

Cancellations

Blue		+.50
Ultramarine		+3.00
Purple		+2.00
Magenta		+2.00
Red		+10.00
Green		+70.00
"Paid"		+7.50
Supplementary Mail Type F		+5.00
Numeral		+3.00
Printed Star Precancel (Glen Allen, Va.)		—

189 A51a 15c **red orange**	180.	27.50
orange	180.	27.50
yellow orange	180.	27.50
Never hinged	600.	
No gum	70.	
On cover		82.50
Pair	375.	60.00
Block of 4	1,100.	250.00
P# block of 12, Impt.	*5,000.*	
Never hinged	*8,500.*	
Double transfer		—

Earliest documented use: Jan. 20, 1879.

Cancellations

Blue		+1.50
Purple		+3.00
Magenta		+3.00
Ultramarine		+5.00
Red		+12.00
"Steamship"		+22.50
Supplementary Mail Type E		—
Supplementary Mail Type F		+5.00
Japan		+120.00
China		—

190 A53 30c **full black**	850.	90.00
greenish black	850.	90.00
Never hinged	*2,800.*	
No gum	300.	
On cover		450.00
Pair	1,800.	200.00
Block of 4	4,250.	575.00
P# block of 10, Impt.	*17,000.*	

Earliest documented use: April 5, 1881.

Cancellations

Blue		+1.50
Purple		+3.00
Magenta		+3.00
Red		+20.00
Supplementary Mail Type F		+6.00
"Steamship"		+35.00
Tahiti		—
Samoa		—

191 A54 90c **carmine**	2,100.	375.00
rose	2,100.	375.00
carmine rose	2,100.	375.00
Never hinged	*7,250.*	
No gum	700.	
On cover		*5,000.*
Pair	4,750.	800.00
Block of 4	*12,500.*	2,100.
P# strip of 5, Impt.	*13,000.*	
a. Double paper	—	

See Die and Plate Proofs for imperf. on stamp paper.

Earliest documented use: May 27, 1882 (dated cancel on off-cover stamp), June 24, 1882 (on cover).

Cancellations

Blue		+15.00
Purple		+20.00
Red		+45.00
Supplementary Mail Type F		+20.00

SPECIAL PRINTING OF 1879 ISSUE

Produced by the American Bank Note Co.

1880 ***Perf. 12***

Soft porous paper, without gum

192 A44a 1c **dark ultramarine**	*57,500.*
193 A45a 2c **brown**	*16,000.*
194 A46a 3c **blue green**	*120,000.*
195 A47a 6c **dull rose**	*67,500.*
196 A48a 7c **scarlet vermilion**	*6,750.*
197 A49a 10c **deep brown**	*37,500.*
Double transfer	—
198 A50a 12c **blackish purple**	*9,500.*
199 A51a 15c **orange**	*30,000.*
200 A52 24c **dark violet**	*9,000.*
201 A53 30c **greenish black**	*22,500.*
202 A54 90c **dull carmine**	*30,000.*
203 A45a 2c **scarlet vermilion**	*100,000.*
204 A55 5c **deep blue**	*240,000.*

Nos. 192 and 194 are valued in the grade of fine.

No. 197 was printed from Continental plate 302 (or 303) after plate was re-entered. Therefore, the stamp may show normal, hairline or missing secret mark.

The Post Office Department did not keep separate records of the 1875 and 1880 Special Printings of the 1873 and 1879 issues, but the total quantity sold of both is recorded. Census research indicates that numbers sold of the two sets were approximately equal.

Unlike the 1875 hard-paper Special Printings (Nos. 167-177), the 1880 soft-paper Special Printings were never cut apart with scissors.

While use of Nos. 192-204 for postage was legal, no used examples are recorded. Expertization by competent authorities would be required to establish use.

Numbers Sold of 1875 and 1880 Special Printings.

1c ultramarine & dark ultramarine *(388)*
2c dark brown & black brown *(416)*
2c carmine vermilion & scarlet vermilion *(917)*
3c blue green *(267)*
5c bright blue & deep blue *(317)*
6c dull rose *(185)*
7c reddish vermilion & scarlet vermilion *(473)*
10c pale brown & deep brown *(180)*
12c dark violet & blackish purple *(282)*
15c bright orange & orange *(169)*
24c dull purple & dark violet *(286)*
30c greenish black *(179)*
90c violet carmine & dull carmine *(170)*

REGULAR ISSUE

Printed by the American Bank Note Co.

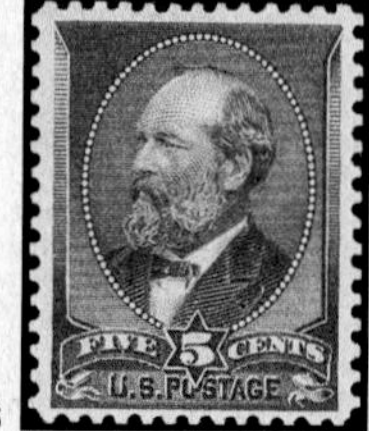

James A. Garfield — A56

1882

205 A56 5c **yellow brown**	240.	15.00
brown	240.	15.00
gray brown	240.	15.00
Never hinged	775.	
No gum	90.	
On cover		27.50
Pair	500.	32.50
Block of 4	1,150.	135.00
P# strip of 5, Impt.	1,750.	
P# block of 10, Impt., no gum	*5,750.*	
P# block of 12, Impt.	*9,750.*	

Earliest documented use: Feb. 18, 1882.

Cancellations

Blue		+.75
Purple		+1.00
Magenta		+1.00
Red		+7.00
"Ship"		—
Numeral		+2.00
Supplementary Mail Type F		+2.50
Red Express Co.		—
China		+125.00
Japan		+125.00
Samoa		+150.00
Puerto Rico		—

SPECIAL PRINTING

Printed by the American Bank Note Co.

1882 ***Perf. 12***

Soft porous paper, without gum

205C A56 5c **gray brown**	*50,000.*

Although Post Office records indicate that 2,463 examples of the 5c Garfield Special Printing were sold, almost all of these stamps appear to have been from supplies of the regular issue No. 205. The actual Special Printings, No. 205C, came from a small supply sent to the Third Assistant Post Master General before the regular issue was available. Only 22 examples have been certified as genuine Special Printings.

While use of No. 205C for postage was legal, no used examples are recorded.

DESIGNS OF 1873 RE-ENGRAVED

Franklin — A44b

1c — The vertical lines in the upper part of the stamp have been so deepened that the background often appears to be solid. Lines of shading have been added to the upper arabesques.

1881-82

206 A44b 1c **gray blue,** *Aug. 1881*	70.00	1.00
ultramarine	70.00	1.25
dull blue	70.00	1.00
slate blue	70.00	1.25
Never hinged	225.00	
No gum	25.00	
On cover		1.75
Pair	160.00	2.60
Block of 4	375.00	17.50
P# strip of 5, Impt.	500.00	
P# strip of 6, Impt.	575.00	
P# block of 10, Impt.	*1,800.*	
Never hinged	*2,750.*	
P# block of 12, Impt.	*2,000.*	
Never hinged	*3,000.*	
Double transfer	105.00	6.00
Punched with 8 small holes in a circle	*200.00*	
P# block of 10, Impt. (8-hole punch)	*2,750.*	
a. Double impression		—

No. 206a is a partial double impression, with "ONE 1 CENT," etc. at bottom doubled.

Earliest documented use: Oct. 11, 1881.

Cancellations

Purple		+.10
Magenta		+.10
Blue		+.20
Red		+3.00
Orange red		+3.50
Orange		+5.00
Green		+50.00
"Paid"		+4.75
"Paid All"		+12.00
Numeral		+3.50
Supplementary Mail Type F		+5.00
Railroad		+10.00

Printed Star Precancel (Glen Allen, Va.)	+80.00
China	—

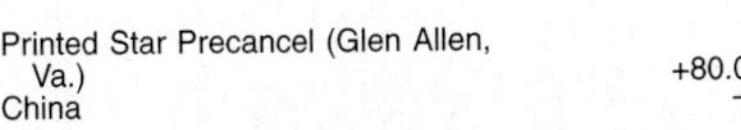

Washington — A46b

3c. The shading at the sides of the central oval appears only about one-half the previous width. A short horizontal dash has been cut about 1mm below the "TS" of "CENTS."

207 A46b 3c **blue green,** *July 16, 1881*	80.00	.80
green	80.00	.80
yellow green	80.00	.80
Never hinged	250.00	
No gum	27.50	
On cover		.95
Pair	170.00	1.70
Block of 4	375.00	30.00
P# strip of 5, Impt.	525.00	
P# block of 10, Impt.	*1,750.*	
Never hinged	*2,750.*	
Double transfer	—	12.00
Cracked plate	—	
Punched with 8 small holes in a circle	*220.00*	
P# block of 10, Impt. (8-hole punch)	*3,000.*	
c. Double impression		*10,000.*
On cover		*5,500.*

Earliest documented use: Aug. 7, 1881.

The No. 207c on cover has faults and is valued thus.

Cancellations

Purple	+.10
Magenta	+.10
Blue	+.25
Brown	+1.50
Red	+2.50
"Paid"	+3.00
"Paid All"	—
Numeral	+2.50
"Ship"	—
Railroad	+5.00
Supplementary Mail Type F	+8.00
Printed Star Precancellation (Glen Allen, Va.)	+750.00

Lincoln — A47b

6c. On the original stamps four vertical lines can be counted from the edge of the panel to the outside of the stamp. On the re-engraved stamps there are but three lines in the same place.

208 A47b 6c **rose**	825.	110.00
dull rose	825.00	110.00
Never hinged	2,600.	
No gum	250.	
On cover (rose)		140.00
Pair (rose)	1,750.	230.00
Block of 4 (rose)	4,000.	1,000.
P# block of 10, Impt.	*11,500.*	
Double transfer	875.	150.00
a. 6c **deep brown red**	600.	190.00
Never hinged	1,900.	
No gum	170.	
pale brown red	525.	140.00
Never hinged	1,550.	
No gum	150.	
On cover (deep brown red)		*450.00*
Pair (deep brown red)	1,300.	775.00
Block of 4 (deep brown red)	3,000.	1,400.
P# strip of 5, Impt.	3,750.	
P# strip of 6, Impt.	*4,600.*	
P# block of 10, Impt.	*9,500.*	
P# block of 12, Impt.	—	

Earliest documented use: June 1, 1882.

Cancellations

Magenta	+3.00
Purple	+5.00
Blue	+5.00
Red	+15.00
Supplementary Mail Type F	+10.00

Jefferson — A49b

10c. On the original stamps there are five vertical lines between the left side of the oval and the edge of the shield. There are only four lines on the re-engraved stamps. In the lower part of the latter, also, the horizontal lines of the background have been strengthened.

209 A49b 10c **brown,** *Apr. 1882*	160.	6.00
yellow brown	160.	6.00
orange brown	160.	6.00
Never hinged	500.	
No gum	65.	
dark brown	175.	10.00
purple brown	200.	20.00
olive brown	200.	20.00
Never hinged	550.	
No gum	55.	
On cover		11.00
Pair	350.	12.50
Block of 4	875.	40.00
P# strip of 5, Impt.	1,175.	
P# strip of 6, Impt.	1,375.	
P# block of 10, Impt.	*3,750.*	
P# block of 12, Impt.	*4,500.*	
Never hinged	*8,750.*	
b. 10c **black brown**	3,000.	375.00
Never hinged	6,000.	
No gum	950.	
On cover		*550.00*
Pair	—	775.00
Block of 4	—	*6,000.*
c. Double impression		—

Specimen stamps (usually overprinted "Sample") without overprint exist in a brown shade that differs from No. 209. The unoverprinted brown specimen is cheaper than No. 209. Expertization is recommended.

Earliest documented use: May 4, 1882.

Cancellations

Purple	+.50
Magenta	+.50
Blue	+1.00
Red	+4.00
Green	+35.00
Numeral	+2.00
"Paid"	+2.50
Supplementary Mail Type F	+3.00
Express Company	—
Japan	+75.00
China	—
Samoa	—

Printed by the American Bank Note Company.

Washington — A57

Jackson — A58

Nos. 210-211 were issued to meet the reduced first class rate of 2 cents for each half ounce, and the double rate, which Congress approved Mar. 3, 1883, effective Oct. 1, 1883.

1883, Oct. 1 ***Perf. 12***

210 A57 2c **red brown**	45.	.75
dark red brown	45.	.75
orange brown	45.	.75
Never hinged	135.	
No gum	17.	
On cover		.85
Pair	95.	1.60
Block of 4	230.	12.50
P# strip of 5, Impt.	275.	
P# strip of 6, Impt.	340.	
P# block of 10, Impt.	*1,050.*	
P# block of 12, Impt.	*1,300.*	
Double transfer	50.	2.25

See Die and Plate Proofs for imperf. on stamp paper.

Earliest documented use: Oct. 1, 1883 (FDC).

Cancellations

Purple	+.10
Magenta	+.10
Blue	+.20
Violet	+.30
Brown	+.30
Red	+3.50
Green	+25.00
Numeral	+2.50
"Paid"	+3.00
Railroad	+5.00
Express Company	—
Supplementary Mail Type F	+5.00
"Ship"	—
"Steamboat"	—
China	—

211 A58 4c **blue green**	225.	25.00
deep blue green	225.	25.00
Never hinged	800.	
No gum	80.	
On cover		50.00
Pair	475.	52.50
Block of 4	1,075.	130.00
P# strip of 5, Impt.	1,700.	
P# strip of 6, Impt.	2,000.	
P# block of 10, Impt.	*6,500.*	
P# block of 12, Impt.	*7,500.*	
Never hinged	*8,250.*	
Double transfer	—	—
Cracked plate	—	

See Die and Plate Proofs for imperf. on stamp paper.

Earliest documented use: Oct. 1, 1883 (FDC).

Cancellations

Purple	+1.00
Magenta	+1.00
Green	+50.00
Blue	+1.00
Numeral	+2.00
Supplementary Mail Type F	+5.00

SPECIAL PRINTING

Printed by the American Bank Note Company.

1883-85 **Soft porous paper** ***Perf. 12***

211B A57 2c **pale red brown,** with gum ('85)	400.	—
Never hinged	1,000.	
No gum	140.	
Block of 4	1,750.	
c. Horizontal pair, imperf. between	*2,250.*	
Never hinged	*3,250.*	
Top margin strip of 6, "Steamer-American Bank Note Co." imprint	*20,000.*	
Top margin block of 16 (8x2), full "Steamer-American Bank Note Co." imprint	*25,000.*	

Earliest documented use: May 23, 1885 (dated cancel on off-cover stamp).

No. 211B is from a special trial printing by a new steam-powered American Bank Note Company press. Approximately 1,000 of these stamps (in sheets of 200 with an imperf gutter between the panes of 100) were delivered as samples to the Third Assistant Postmaster General and subsequently made their way to the public market.

While use of No. 211B for postage was legal, actual usage was rare. Expertization is strongly recommended for suspected used examples.

211D A58 4c **deep blue green,** without gum *47,500.*

Postal records indicate that 26 examples of No. 211D were sold. Records also indicate an 1883 delivery and sales of 55 examples of the 2c red brown stamp, but there is no clear evidence that these can be differentiated from no gum examples of No. 210. No used examples of No. 211D are recorded.

REGULAR ISSUE

Printed by the American Bank Note Company.

Franklin — A59

1887 ***Perf. 12***

212 A59 1c **ultramarine,** *June*	90.00	2.50
bright ultramarine	90.00	2.50
Never hinged	290.00	
No gum	35.00	
On cover		3.25
Pair	190.00	5.25
Block of 4	425.00	37.50
P# strip of 5, Impt.	575.00	
P# strip of 6, Impt.	675.00	
P# block of 10, Impt.	*1,500.*	
Never hinged	*3,250.*	
P# block of 12, Impt.	*1,850.*	
Double transfer		—

See Die and Plate Proofs for imperf. on stamp paper.

Earliest documented use: June 22, 1887.

Cancellations

Purple	+.10
Magenta	+.10
Blue	+.10
Red	+5.50
Numeral	+2.00
Railroad	+10.00
Supplementary Mail Type F	+5.00
China	—

213 A57 2c **green,** *Sept. 10*	40.00	.60
bright green	40.00	.60
dark green	40.00	.60
Never hinged	120.00	
No gum	15.00	
On cover		.75
Pair	85.00	1.30
Block of 4	190.00	10.50
P# strip of 5, Impt.	275.00	
P# strip of 6, Impt.	340.00	
P# block of 10, Impt.	*1,250.*	
Never hinged	*2,250.*	
P# block of 12, Impt.	*1,500.*	
Double transfer	—	3.25
b. Printed on both sides		—

See Die and Plate Proofs for imperf. on stamp paper.

Earliest documented use: Sept. 20, 1887 (dated cancel on off-cover stamp); Sept. 21, 1887 (on cover).

Cancellations

Purple	+.10
Magenta	+.10
Blue	+.90

Red +5.00
Green +25.00
"Paid" +5.00
Railroad +12.00
Numeral +2.00
"Steam" —
"Steamboat" —
Supplementary Mail Type F +7.50
China —
Japan —

214 A46b 3c **vermilion**, *Sept.* 60.00 50.00
Never hinged 190.00
No gum 25.00
On cover (single) 90.00
Pair 130.00 110.00
Block of 4 300.00 *350.00*
P# strip of 5, Impt. 400.00
P# strip of 6, Impt. 475.00
P# block of 10, Impt. *1,300.*
Never hinged *2,750.*
P# block of 12, Impt. *1,500.*

Earliest documented use: Sept. 23, 1887.

Cancellations

Purple +5.00
Magenta +5.00
Green +150.00
Blue +10.00
Supplementary Mail Type F +15.00
Railroad +30.00

Printed by the American Bank Note Company.
SAME AS 1870-83 ISSUES

1888 ***Perf. 12***

215 A58 4c **carmine**, *Nov.* 180. 30.00
rose carmine 180. 30.00
pale rose 180. 30.00
Never hinged 525.
No gum 60.
On cover 50.00
Pair 375. 62.50
Block of 4 850. 210.00
P# strip of 5, Impt. 1,350.
Never hinged *3,500.*
P# strip of 6, Impt. 1,600.
P# block of 10, Impt. *4,500.*
Never hinged *6,500.*
P# block of 12, Impt. *5,300.*

Earliest documented use: Dec. 26, 1888.

The earliest documented use of No. 215 has been questioned by specialists, even though the cover currently has a certificate of genuineness. The owner of this cover should contact the Scott editor for resubmission information.

Cancellations

Blue +1.00
Red +5.00
Purple +2.00
Magenta +2.00
Supplementary Mail Type F +5.00

216 A56 5c **indigo**, *Feb.* 220. 20.00
deep blue 220. 20.00
Never hinged 675.
No gum 75.
On cover 37.50
Pair 475. 42.50
Block of 4 1,050. 160.00
P# strip of 5, Impt. 1,300.
P# strip of 6, Impt. 1,750.
P# block of 10, Impt. *8,000.*
P# block of 12, Impt. *8,750.*

Earliest documented use: Mar. 15, 1888.

Cancellations

Purple +1.00
Magenta +1.00
Blue +1.00
Supplementary Mail Type F +3.00
China +85.00
Japan +85.00
Puerto Rico +75.00
Samoa —

217 A53 30c **orange brown**, *Jan.* 300. 90.00
deep orange brown 300. 90.00
Never hinged 1,075.
No gum 90.
On cover *1,400.*
Pair 675. 210.00
Block of 4 1,600. 650.00
P# strip of 5, Impt. *2,400.*
P# block of 10, Impt. *8,500.*
P# block of 12, Impt. —

Earliest documented use: April 16, 1888.

Cancellations

Blue +5.00
Magenta +10.00
Supplementary Mail Type F +10.00
"Paid All" +25.00
"Paid" +15.00

218 A54 90c **purple**, *Feb.* 800. 225.00
bright purple 800. 225.00
Never hinged 2,500.
No gum 250.
On cover *10,000.*
Pair 1,800. 500.
Block of 4 *4,750.* 1,400.
P# strip of 5, Impt. *5,750.*
P# block of 10, Impt. *22,500.*
P# block of 12, Impt. —

Earliest documented use: June 26, 1888 (dated cancel on off-cover stamp); Oct. 29, 1888 (on cover).

Cancellations

Blue +80.00
Purple +100.00
Supplementary Mail Type F +25.00

See Die and Plate Proofs for imperfs. on stamp paper.

Printed by the American Bank Note Company.

Plates for the 1c were of 400 subjects in four panes of 100 each. Plates for the 2c were first of 400 subjects in four panes of 100 each, and later of 200 subjects in two panes of 100 each. All other values were from plates of 200 subjects in two panes of 100 each. Plates of 400 of the 1c and 2c show imprints in the side margins.

Franklin — A60

Washington — A61

Jackson — A62

Lincoln — A63

Ulysses S. Grant — A64

Garfield — A65

William T. Sherman — A66

Daniel Webster — A67

Henry Clay — A68

Jefferson — A69

Perry — A70

1890-93 ***Perf. 12***

219 A60 1c **dull blue**, *Feb. 22, 1890* 20.00 .75
deep blue 20.00 .75
ultramarine 20.00 .75
Never hinged 65.00
On cover .80
Block of 4 85.00 5.25
P# strip of 5, Impt. & letter 125.00
P# strip of 6, Impt. & letter 150.00
P# strip of 7, Impt. & letter 175.00
P# block of 10, Impt. & letter 775.00
P# block of 12, Impt. & letter 1,075.
P# block of 14, Impt. & letter 1,450.
Never hinged *5,000.*
Double transfer — —

Earliest documented use: Feb 27, 1890.

Cancellations

Samoa —
China —

219D A61 2c **lake**, *Feb. 22, 1890* 160.00 5.75
Never hinged 500.00
On cover 7.75
Block of 4 700.00 47.50
P# strip of 5, Impt. 975.00
P# block of 10, Impt. 3,250.
Never hinged *6,000.*
Double transfer — —

Earliest documented use: Feb. 22, 1890 (FDC).

Cancellation

Supplementary Mail Type F +3.00

Normal Right 2

Damaged Right 2

Cap only on left 2

Cap on both 2s

220 A61 2c **carmine**, *1890* 20.00 .70
dark carmine 20.00 .70
carmine rose 20.00 .70
rose 20.00 .70
Never hinged 60.00
On cover .75
Block of 4 85.00 3.00
P# strip of 5, Impt. & letter 125.00
P# strip of 6, Impt. & letter 150.00
Never hinged 290.00
P# strip of 7, Impt. & letter 175.00
P# block of 10, Impt. & letter 575.00
P# block of 12, Impt. & letter 900.00
Never hinged *1,350.*
P# block of 14, Impt. & letter 1,050.
Never hinged —
Double transfer — 3.25
Damaged "2" at lower right —

a. Cap on left "2" (Plates 235-236, 246-247-248) 150.00 12.50
Never hinged 450.00
Block of 4 675.00 *150.00*
P# block of 10, Impt. *12,000.*
Never hinged *25,000.*
Pair, Nos. 220, 220a — —
Never hinged —

c. Cap on both "2's" (Plates 245, 246) 650.00 35.00
Never hinged 1,800.
Pair, Nos. 220a, 220c — —
Never hinged —

The No. 220 with "cap on right 2" variety is due to imperfect inking, not a plate defect.

Earliest documented uses: Feb. 18, 1890 (No. 220); Sept. 9, 1892 (No. 220a); July 7, 1892 (No. 220c).

Cancellations

Blue +.05
Purple +.05
Supp. Mail Types F or G +3.00
China +20.00

221 A62 3c **purple**, *Feb. 22, 1890* 55.00 9.00
bright purple 55.00 9.00
dark purple 55.00 9.00
Never hinged 175.00
On cover 17.50

Block of 4	250.00	55.00
P# strip of 5, Impt.	375.00	
P# block of 10, Impt.	2,750.	
Never hinged	*4,000.*	

Earliest documented use: Feb. 28, 1890.

Cancellation

Samoa		—
222 A63 4c **dark brown,** *June 2, 1890*	80.00	4.75
blackish brown	80.00	4.75
Never hinged	240.00	
On cover		10.00
Block of 4	400.00	35.00
P# strip of 5, Impt.	500.00	
P# block of 10, Impt.	3,500.	
Never hinged	*9,000.*	
Double transfer	95.00	25.00

Earliest documented use: July 16, 1890.

Cancellation

China		+50.00
223 A64 5c **chocolate,** *June 2, 1890*	60.00	4.75
yellow brown	60.00	4.75
Never hinged	185.00	
On cover		12.50
Block of 4	260.00	27.50
P# strip of 5, Impt.	350.00	
P# block of 10, Impt.	2,800.	
Never hinged	6,250.	
Double transfer	85.00	5.25

Earliest documented use: June 14, 1890.

Cancellations

China		+35.00
Samoa		—
Supp. Mail Types F or G		+7.50
224 A65 6c **brown red,** *Feb. 22, 1890*	50.00	25.00
dark brown red	50.00	25.00
Never hinged	160.00	
On cover		40.00
Block of 4	250.00	130.00
P# strip of 5, Impt.	350.00	
P# block of 10, Impt.	2,750.	
Never hinged	*4,500.*	

Earliest documented use: May 8, 1890.

Cancellation

Supplementary Mail Type F		+3.00
225 A66 8c **lilac,** *Mar. 21, 1893*	45.00	17.00
grayish lilac	45.00	17.00
magenta	45.00	17.00
Never hinged	135.00	
On cover		32.50
Block of 4	200.00	100.00
P# strip of 5, Impt.	275.00	
P# block of 10, Impt.	1,900.	
Never hinged	3,250.	

The 8c was issued because the registry fee was reduced from 10 to 8 cents effective Jan. 1, 1893.

Earliest documented use: May 4, 1893.

226 A67 10c **green,** *Feb. 22, 1890*	160.00	5.00
bluish green	160.00	5.00
dark green	160.00	5.00
Never hinged	475.00	
On cover		10.00
Block of 4	700.00	42.50
P# strip of 5, Impt.	925.00	
P# block of 10, Impt.	3,750.	
Never hinged	*7,500.*	
Double transfer	—	—

Earliest documented use: Mar. 5, 1890.

Cancellations

Samoa		—
Supp. Mail Type F or G		+2.50
227 A68 15c **indigo,** *Feb. 22, 1890*	180.00	25.00
deep indigo	180.00	25.00
Never hinged	550.00	
On cover		60.00
Block of 4	800.00	135.00
P# strip of 5, Impt.	1,250.	
P# block of 10, Impt.	*8,500.*	
Never hinged	*15,000.*	
Double transfer	—	—
Triple transfer		—

Earliest documented use: May 16, 1890.

Cancellation

Supplementary Mail Type F		+3.00
228 A69 30c **black,** *Feb. 22, 1890*	300.00	30.00
gray black	300.00	30.00
full black	300.00	30.00
Never hinged	900.00	
On cover		*600.00*
Block of 4	1,400.	200.00
P# strip of 5, Impt.	1,900.	
P# block of 10, Impt.	*22,500.*	
Never hinged	—	
Double transfer	—	—

Earliest documented use: April 14, 1890.

Cancellation

Supplementary Mail Type F		+5.00
229 A70 90c **orange,** *Feb. 22, 1890*	475.00	140.00
yellow orange	475.00	135.00
red orange	475.00	135.00
Never hinged	1,600.	
On cover		—
Block of 4	2,100.	775.00
P# strip of 5, Impt.	2,900.	
P# block of 10, Impt.	*27,500.*	
Never hinged	*42,500.*	
Short transfer at bottom	—	—
Nos. 219-229 (12)	1,605.	267.70

Earliest documented use: May 16, 1890 (dated cancel on off-cover stamp); Feb. 7, 1892 (on cover).

Cancellation

Supp. Mail Type F or G		+10.00

VALUES FOR VERY FINE STAMPS
Please note: Stamps are valued in the grade of Very Fine unless otherwise indicated.

See Die and Plate Proofs for imperfs. on stamp paper.

COLUMBIAN EXPOSITION ISSUE

World's Columbian Exposition, Chicago, Ill., May 1 - Oct. 30, 1893, celebrating the 400th anniv. of the discovery of America by Christopher Columbus.

See Nos. 2624-2629 for souvenir sheets containing stamps of designs A71-A86 but with "1992" at upper right.

Columbus in Sight of Land — A71

Landing of Columbus — A72

"Santa Maria," Flagship of Columbus — A73

Fleet of Columbus — A74

Columbus Soliciting Aid from Queen Isabella — A75

Columbus Welcomed at Barcelona — A76

Columbus Restored to Favor — A77

Columbus Presenting Natives — A78

Columbus Announcing His Discovery — A79

Columbus at La Rábida — A80

Recall of Columbus — A81

Queen Isabella Pledging Her Jewels — A82

Columbus in Chains — A83

Columbus Describing His Third Voyage — A84

Queen Isabella and Columbus — A85

Columbus — A86

P AMERICAN BANK NOTE COMPANY. No.67

Type of imprint and plate number

Exposition Station Handstamp Postmark

Printed by the American Bank Note Company.
Plates of 200 subjects in two panes of 100 each (1c, 2c).
Plates of 100 subjects in two panes of 50 each (2c-$5).
Issued (except 8c) Jan. 1 (a Sunday) and Jan. 2 (Monday), 1893. Jan. 1 and Jan. 2 first day covers are documented for the 1c, 2c, 3c, 4c, 5c and 10c. Jan. 2-only first day covers exist for the 6c and $2. See the First Day Cover section for values.

1893 *Perf. 12*

230	A71 1c **deep blue**	14.00	.40
	blue	14.00	.40
	pale blue	14.00	.40
	Never hinged	32.50	
	On cover		.90
	Pair on cover, Expo. station machine canc.		100.00
	Pair on cover, Expo. station duplex handstamp canc.		175.00
	Block of 4	60.00	7.00
	P# strip of 3, Impt.	60.00	
	P# strip of 4, Impt. & letter	95.00	
	P# block of 6, Impt.	450.00	
	Never hinged	625.00	
	P# block of 8, Impt. & letter	700.00	
	Never hinged	1,000.	
	Double transfer	19.00	.75
	Cracked plate	80.00	

Earliest documented use: Jan. 1, 1893 (FDC).

Cancellations

China	—
Philippines	—

"Broken hat" variety

Broken Frame Line

231	A72 2c **brown violet**	12.50	.30
	deep brown violet	12.50	.30
	gray violet	12.50	.30
	Never hinged	31.00	
	On cover		.35
	On cover or card, Expo. station machine cancel		55.00
	On cover or card, Expo. station duplex handstamp cancel		110.00
	Block of 4	55.00	4.50
	P# strip of 3, Impt.	55.00	
	P# strip of 4, Impt. & letter	90.00	
	Never hinged	225.00	
	P# block of 6, Impt.	550.00	
	Never hinged	750.00	
	P# block of 8, Impt. & letter	800.00	
	Never hinged	1,100.	
	Double transfer	17.50	.35
	Triple transfer	50.00	—
	Quadruple transfer	80.00	
	Broken hat on third figure to left of Columbus	55.00	3.50
	Never hinged	160.00	
	P# block of 6, Impt., all stamps the "broken hat" variety	1,250.	
	P# block of 6, Impt., mixed normal stamps and "broken hat" varieties	1,250.	
	Broken frame line	16.00	.45
	Recut frame lines	16.00	—
	Cracked plate	65.00	—

There are a number of different versions of the broken hat variety, some of which may be progressive.
Earliest documented use: Jan. 1, 1893 (FDC).

Cancellations

China	—
Supplementary Mail Type G	+3.50

See Die and Plate Proofs for the 2c, imperf. on stamp paper.

232	A73 3c **green**	35.00	15.00
	dull green	35.00	15.00
	dark green	35.00	15.00
	Never hinged	97.50	
	On cover		30.00
	On cover, Expo. station machine canc.		225.00
	On cover, Expo. station duplex handstamp cancel		325.00
	Block of 4	150.00	130.00
	P# strip of 3, Impt.	150.00	
	Never hinged	290.00	
	P# strip of 4, Impt. & letter	230.00	
	Never hinged	475.00	
	P# block of 6, Impt.	700.00	
	Never hinged	1,250.	
	P# block of 8, Impt. & letter	1,175.	
	Never hinged	2,000.	
	Double transfer	52.50	—

Earliest documented use: Jan. 1, 1893 (FDC).

Cancellations

China	—
Supp. Mail Type F or G	+7.50

233	A74 4c **ultramarine**	55.00	8.00
	dull ultramarine	55.00	8.00
	deep ultramarine	55.00	8.00
	Never hinged	150.00	
	On cover		22.50
	On cover, Expo. station machine canc.		275.00
	On cover, Expo. station duplex handstamp cancel		400.00
	Block of 4	250.00	67.50
	P# strip of 3, Impt.	250.00	
	Never hinged	440.00	
	P# strip of 4, Impt. & letter	400.00	—
	Never hinged	700.00	
	P# block of 6, Impt.	1,000.	
	Never hinged	1,700.	
	P# block of 8, Impt. & letter	1,800.	
	Never hinged	3,150.	
	Double transfer	90.00	—
a.	4c **blue** (error)	*20,000.*	*15,000.*
	Never hinged	*35,000.*	
	Block of 4	*100,000.*	—
	Never hinged	*150,000.*	
	P# strip of 4, Impt., letter	*150,000.*	

No. 233a exists in two shades. No. 233a used is valued with small faults, as almost all examples come thus.

Earliest documented use: Jan. 1, 1893 (FDC).

Cancellation

Supplementary Mail Type G	+3.00

234	A75 5c **chocolate**	55.00	8.50
	pale brown	55.00	8.50
	yellow brown	55.00	8.50
	dark chocolate	55.00	8.50
	Never hinged	150.00	
	On cover		22.50
	On cover, Expo. station machine canc.		275.00
	On cover, Expo. station duplex handstamp cancel		400.00
	Block of 4	250.00	75.00
	P# strip of 3, Impt.	250.00	
	Never hinged	440.00	
	P# strip of 4, Impt. & letter	400.00	
	Never hinged	700.00	
	P# block of 6, Impt.	1,300.	
	Never hinged	2,275.	
	P# block of 8, Impt. & letter	2,750.	
	Never hinged	4,700.	
	Double transfer	110.00	—

Earliest documented use: Jan. 1, 1893 (FDC).

Cancellations

China	—
Philippines	—
Supplementary Mail Type F	+3.00

235	A76 6c **purple**	55.00	22.50
	dull purple	55.00	22.50
	Never hinged	150.00	
a.	6c **red violet**	65.00	22.50
	Never hinged	175.00	
	On cover		45.00
	On cover, Expo. station machine canc.		300.00
	On cover, Expo. station duplex handstamp cancel		450.00
	Block of 4	250.00	150.00
	P# strip of 3, Impt.	250.00	
	Never hinged	440.00	
	P# strip of 4, Impt. & letter	400.00	
	Never hinged	700.00	
	P# block of 6, Impt.	1,250.	
	Never hinged	2,150.	
	P# block of 8, Impt. & letter	1,950.	
	Never hinged	3,400.	
	Double transfer	75.00	30.00

Earliest documented use: Jan. 2, 1893 (FDC).

Cancellations

China	—
Supplementary Mail Type F	+5.00

236	A77 8c **brn pur,** *Mar. 1893*	50.00	10.00
	light magenta	50.00	10.00
	dark magenta	50.00	10.00
	Never hinged	140.00	
	On cover		20.00
	On cover, Expo. station machine canc.		300.00
	On cover, Expo. station duplex handstamp cancel		475.00
	Block of 4	250.00	85.00
	P# strip of 3, Impt.	220.00	
	Never hinged	385.00	
	P# strip of 4, Impt. & letter	360.00	
	Never hinged	625.00	
	P# block of 6, Impt.	1,075.	
	Never hinged	1,750.	
	P# block of 8, Impt. & letter	1,625.	
	Never hinged	2,700.	
	Double transfer	60.00	—

Earliest documented use: Mar. 18, 1893.

Cancellations

China	—
Supplementary Mail Type F	+4.50

237	A78 10c **black brown**	95.00	8.00
	dark brown	95.00	8.00
	gray black	95.00	8.00
	Never hinged	265.00	
	On cover		27.50
	On cover, Expo. station machine canc.		400.00
	On cover, Expo. station duplex handstamp cancel		550.00
	Block of 4	425.00	80.00
	P# strip of 3, Impt.	425.00	
	Never hinged	750.00	
	P# strip of 4, Impt. & letter	625.00	
	Never hinged	1,400.	
	P# block of 6, Impt.	3,000.	
	Never hinged	*4,500.*	
	P# block of 8, Impt. & letter	4,500.	
	Never hinged	*8,000.*	
	Double transfer	120.00	12.50
	Triple transfer	—	

Earliest documented use: Jan. 1, 1893 (FDC).

Cancellations

Philippines	—
Supp. Mail Types F or G	+4.00

238	A79 15c **dark green**	200.00	80.00
	green	200.00	80.00
	dull green	200.00	80.00
	Never hinged	600.00	
	On cover		220.00
	On cover, Expo. station machine canc.		700.00
	On cover, Expo. station duplex handstamp cancel		*1,000.*
	Block of 4	850.	650.00
	P# strip of 3, Impt.	825.	
	P# strip of 4, Impt. & letter	1,350.	
	P# block of 6, Impt.	*4,000.*	
	Never hinged	*6,500.*	
	P# block of 8, Impt. & letter	*6,000.*	
	Never hinged	*12,000.*	
	Double transfer	—	—

Earliest documented use: Jan. 26, 1893.

Cancellations

China	+75.00
Supp. Mail Type F or G	+10.00

239	A80 30c **orange brown**	225.00	90.00
	bright orange brown	225.00	90.00
	Never hinged	675.00	
	On cover		375.00
	On cover, Expo. station machine canc.		*1,250.*
	On cover, Expo. station duplex handstamp cancel		*1,750.*
	Block of 4	1,075.	850.00
	P# strip of 3, Impt.	1,000.	
	P# strip of 4, Impt. & letter	1,450.	—
	P# block of 6, Impt.	*7,500.*	
	Never hinged	*12,500.*	
	P# block of 8, Impt. & letter	*9,500.*	
	Never hinged	*15,000.*	

Earliest documented use: Jan. 4, 1893 (dated cancel on off-cover stamp); Feb. 8, 1893 (cover).

Cancellation

Supp. Mail Types F or G	+25.00

240	A81 50c **slate blue**	450.	200.
	dull state blue	450.	200.
	Never hinged	1,400.	
	No gum	200.	
	On cover		600.
	On cover, Expo. station machine canc.		*1,750.*
	On cover, Expo. station duplex handstamp cancel		2,250.
	Block of 4	1,850.	2,000.
	P# strip of 3, Impt.	1,850.	
	P# strip of 4, Impt. & letter	*3,250.*	—
	Never hinged	6,750.	
	P# block of 6, Impt.	*10,500.*	
	Never hinged	*18,000.*	
	P# block of 8, Impt. & letter	*17,000.*	

Never hinged	*27,000.*	
Double transfer	—	—
Triple transfer	—	—

Earliest documented use: Feb. 8, 1893.

Cancellation

Supp. Mail Types F or G		+30.00
241 A82 $1 **salmon**	1,000.	525.
dark salmon	1,000.	525.
Never hinged	3,400.	
No gum	500.	
On cover		*1,800.*
On cover, Expo. station machine canc.		*3,500.*
On cover, Expo. station duplex handstamp cancel		4,500.
Block of 4	4,500.	*5,000.*
P# strip of 3, Impt.	4,750.	
P# strip of 4, Impt. & letter	8,250.	
P# block of 6, Impt.	*45,000.*	
P# block of 8, Impt. & letter	*75,000.*	
Never hinged	*130,000.*	
Double transfer	—	—

Earliest documented use: Jan. 11, 1893 (dated cancel on off-cover stamp); Jan. 21, 1893 (on cover).

Cancellation

Supp. Mail Types F or G		+50.
242 A83 $2 **brown red**	1,100.	525.
deep brown red	1,100.	525.
Never hinged	3,600.	
No gum	550.	
On cover		*1,900.*
On cover, Expo. station machine canc.		*3,500.*
On cover, Expo. station duplex handstamp cancel		*4,500.*
Block of 4	4,800.	*5,500.*
P# strip of 3, Impt.	5,500.	
P# strip of 4, Impt. & letter	8,750.	
P# block of 6, Impt.	*150,000.*	
P# block of 8, Impt. & letter	*225,000.*	

Earliest documented use: Jan. 2, 1893 (FDC).

Cancellations

Supplementary Mail Type G		+50.

The No. 242 plate block of 8 is believed to be unique.

243 A84 $3 **yellow green**	1,500.	775.
pale yellow green	1,500.	775.
Never hinged	4,750.	
No gum	750.	
a. $3 **olive green**	1,400.	775.
Never hinged	4,350.	
No gum	700.	
On cover		*2,500.*
On cover, Expo. station machine canc.		*5,000.*
On cover, Expo. station duplex handstamp cancel		*7,000.*
Block of 4	*8,750.*	*10,000.*
P# strip of 3, Impt.	*8,000.*	
P# strip of 4, Impt. & letter	*14,000.*	
P# block of 6, Impt.	*200,000.*	

Earliest documented use: Mar. 24, 1893.

244 A85 $4 **crimson lake**	2,100.	975.
Never hinged	7,250.	
No gum	1,000.	
a. $4 **rose carmine**	2,000.	975.
pale aniline rose	2,000.	1,025.
Never hinged	7,000.	
No gum	950.	
On cover		*4,000.*
On cover, Expo. station machine canc.		*6,500.*
On cover, Expo. station duplex handstamp cancel		*9,000.*
Block of 4	*10,500.*	*15,000.*
P# strip of 3, Impt.	*12,000.*	
P# strip of 4, Impt. & letter	*40,000.*	
P# block of 6, Impt.	*500,000.*	
P# block of 8, Impt. & letter	—	

The No. 244 plate block of 8 is unique; it has full original gum with light hinge marks.

Earliest documented use: Mar. 24, 1893.

Cracked Plate

245 A86 $5 **black**	2,400.	1,200.
grayish black	2,400.	1,200.
Never hinged	9,750.	
No gum	1,250.	
On cover		*4,750.*
On cover, Expo. station machine canc.		*15,000.*
On cover, Expo. station duplex handstamp cancel		*17,500.*
Block of 4	*12,000.*	*15,000.*
P# strip of 3, Impt.	*14,000.*	
P# strip of 4, Impt. & letter	*55,000.*	
Never hinged	*150,000.*	
P# block of 6, Impt.	*290,000.*	
Never hinged	—	
P# block of 8, Impt. & letter	*325,000.*	
Cracked plate		—

Earliest documented use: Jan. 6, 1893.

The No. 245 plate block of 8 is unique; it has traces of original gum.

See Nos. 2624-2629 for souvenir sheets containing stamps of designs A71-A86 but with "1992" at upper right.

Nos. 230-245 exist imperforate; not issued. See Die and Plate proofs for the 2c.

Never-Hinged Stamps

See note before No. 182 regarding premiums for never-hinged stamps.

BUREAU ISSUES

In the following listings of postal issues mostly printed by the Bureau of Engraving and Printing at Washington, D.C., the editors acknowledge with thanks the use of material prepared by the Catalogue Listing Committee of the Bureau Issues Association.

The Bureau-printed stamps until 1965 were engraved except the Offset Issues of 1918-19 (Nos. 525-536). Engraving and lithography were combined for the first time for the Homemakers 5c (No. 1253). The Bureau used photogravure first in 1971 on the Missouri 8c (No. 1426).

Stamps in this section that were not printed by the Bureau begin with Nos. 909-921 and are so noted.

"*On cover*" listings carry through No. 701. Beyond this point a few covers of special significance are listed. Many Bureau Issue stamps are undoubtedly scarce properly used on cover. Most higher denominations exist almost exclusively on pieces of package wrapping and usually in combination with other values. Collector interest in covers is generally limited to fancy cancellations, attractive corner cards, uses abroad and other special usages.

Plate number blocks are valued unused. Although many exist used, and are scarcer in that condition, they tend to sell for less than the value of the unused examples because they are less sought after.

IMPRINTS AND PLATE NUMBERS

In listing the Bureau of Engraving & Printing Imprints, the editors have followed the classification of types adopted by the Bureau Issues Association.

Types I, II, IV, V and VIII occur on postage issues and are illustrated below. Types III, VI and VII occur only on Special Delivery plates, so are illustrated with the listings of those stamps; other types are illustrated with the listings of the issues on which they occur.

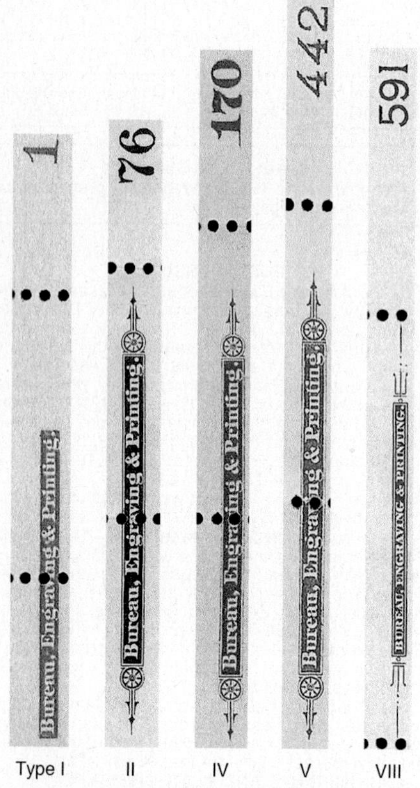

Type I II IV V VIII

In listing Imprint blocks and strips, the editors have designated for each stamp the various types known to exist. If, however, the Catalogue listing sufficiently describes the Imprint, no type number is given. Thus a listing reading: "P# block of 6, Impt. (Imprint) & A" in the 1912-14 series would not be followed by a type number as the description is self-explanatory. Values are for the most common types.

PLATE POSITIONS

At the suggestion of the Catalogue Listing Committee of the Bureau Issues Association (now the United States Stamp Society), all plate positions of these issues are indicated by giving the plate number first, next the pane position, and finally the stamp position. For example: 20234 L.L. 58.

Franklin — A87

Washington — A88

Jackson — A89

Lincoln — A90

Grant — A91

Garfield — A92

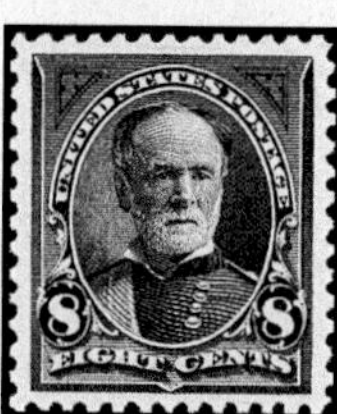

Sherman — A93

Webster — A94

Clay — A95

Jefferson — A96

Perry A97

James Madison A98

John Marshall — A99

Designed by Thomas F. Morris.

REGULAR ISSUE

Plates for the issue of 1894 were of two sizes: 400 subjects for all 1c, 2c and 10c denominations; 200 subjects for all 6c, 8c, 15c, 50c, $1.00, $2.00 and $5.00, and both 400 and 200 subjects for the 3c, 4c and 5c denominations; all issued in panes of 100 each.

1894 **Unwmk.** ***Perf. 12***

246 A87 1c **ultramarine,** *Oct. 1894*	30.00	7.00
bright ultramarine	30.00	7.00
dark ultramarine	30.00	7.00
Never hinged	90.00	
On cover		22.50
Block of 4	130.00	45.00
P# strip of 3, Impt., T I	135.00	
Never hinged	300.00	
P# block of 6, Impt., T I	500.00	
Never hinged	1,000.	
Double transfer	37.50	8.00

Earliest documented use: Oct. 17, 1894.

Cancellation

China		—
247 A87 1c **blue**	62.50	4.00
bright blue	62.50	4.00
dark blue	62.50	4.00
Never hinged	180.00	
On cover		18.50
Block of 4	270.00	27.50
P# strip of 3, Impt., T I or II	285.00	
Never hinged	600.00	
P# block of 6, Impt., T I or II	850.00	
Never hinged	1,750.	
Double transfer	—	5.00

Earliest documented use: Nov. 5, 1894.

Triangle A (Type I)

TWO CENTS

Type I (Triangle A). The horizontal lines of the ground work run across the triangle and are of the same thickness within it as without.

Triangle B (Type II)

Type II (Triangle B). The horizontal lines cross the triangle but are thinner within it than without. Other minor design differences exist, but the change to Triangle B is a sufficient determinant.

Triangle C (Types III and IV)

Type III (Triangle C). The horizontal lines do not cross the double lines of the triangle. The lines within the triangle are thin, as in Type II. The rest of the design is the same as Type II, except that most of the designs had the dot in the "S" of "CENTS" removed. Stamps with this dot present are listed; some specialists refer to them as "Type IIIa" varieties.

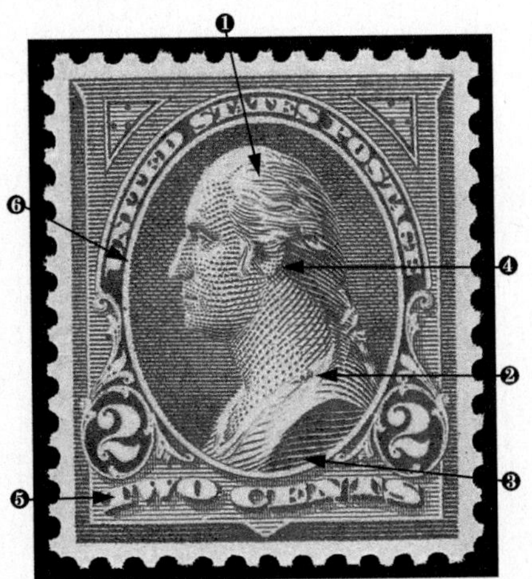

Type IV (Triangle C). See No. 279B and its varieties. Type IV is from a new die with many major and minor design variations including, (1) re-cutting and lengthening of hairline, (2) shaded toga button, (3) strengthening of lines on sleeve, (4) additional dots on ear, (5) "T" of "TWO" straight at right, (6) background lines extend into white oval opposite "U" of "UNITED." Many other differences exist.

For further information concerning type IV, see also George Brett's article in the Sept. 1993 issue of the "The United States Specialist" and the 23-part article by Kenneth Diehl in the Dec. 1994 through Aug. 1997 issues of the "The United States Specialist."

248 A88 2c **pink,** type I, *Oct. 1894* 32.50 10.00
pale pink 32.50 10.00
Never hinged 97.50
On cover 17.50
Block of 4 135.00 52.50
P# strip of 3, Impt., T I or II 130.00
Never hinged 310.00
P# block of 6, Impt., T I or II 300.00
Never hinged 750.00
Double transfer — —
a. Vert. pair, imperf horiz. *5,500.*

Earliest documented use: Oct. 16, 1894.

249 A88 2c **carmine lake,** type I, *Oct. 1894* 175.00 7.00
dark carmine lake 175.00 7.00
Never hinged 500.00
On cover 12.50
Block of 4 750.00 45.00
P# strip of 3, Impt., T I or II 750.00
Never hinged 1,500.
P# block of 6, Impt., T I or II 2,750.
Never hinged 5,750.
Double transfer — 8.00
a. Double impression —

250 A88 2c **carmine,** type I, *Oct. 1894* 29.00 3.00
dark carmine 30.00 5.00
Never hinged 85.00
On cover 4.00
Block of 4 125.00 20.00
P# strip of 3, Impt., T I or II 120.00
Never hinged 290.00
P# block of 6, Impt., T I or II 375.00
Never hinged 800.00
a. 2c **rose,** type I, *Oct. 1894* 40.00 8.50
Never hinged 115.00
On cover 10.00
Block of 4 170.00 40.00
P# strip of 3, Impt., T I or II 170.00
Never hinged 400.00
P# block of 6, Impt., T I or II 475.00
Never hinged 1,000.
b. 2c **scarlet,** type I, *Jan. 1895* 26.00 2.75
Never hinged 80.00
On cover 5.75
Block of 4 110.00 30.00
P# strip of 3, Impt., T I or II 105.00
Never hinged 250.00
P# block of 6, Impt., T I or II 350.00
Never hinged 750.00
Double transfer — 5.00
d. Horizontal pair, imperf. between *2,000.*

Earliest documented uses: Oct. 11, 1894 (No. 250), Oct. 13, 1894 (No. 250a), Jan. 17, 1895 (No. 250b).

Counterfeits exist of No. 250. See the Postal Counterfeits section of this catalog.

251 A88 2c **carmine,** type II, *Feb. 1895* 400.00 17.50
dark carmine 400.00 17.50
Never hinged 1,200.
On cover 25.00
Block of 4 1,700. 110.00
P# strip of 3, Impt., T II 1,600.
Never hinged 4,500.
P# block of 6, Impt., T II 4,000.
Never hinged 8,000.
a. 2c **scarlet,** type II, *Feb. 1895* 375.00 15.00
Never hinged 1,125.
On cover 22.50
Block of 4 1,600. 100.00
P# strip of 3, Impt., T II 1,500.
Never hinged 4,250.
P# block of 6, Impt., T II 3,500.
Never hinged 7,500.

Earliest documented uses: Feb. 12, 1895 (No. 251, dated cancel on off-cover stamp); Feb. 16, 1895 (No. 251, on cover); Feb. 19, 1895 (No. 251a).

252 A88 2c **carmine,** type III, *Mar. 1895* 135.00 13.00
pale carmine 135.00 13.00
Never hinged 400.00
On cover 22.50
Block of 4 600.00 120.00
P# strip of 3, Impt., T II or IV 600.00
Never hinged 1,400.
P# block of 6, Impt., T II or IV 2,100.
Never hinged 4,500.
a. 2c **scarlet,** type III, *Mar. 1895* 120.00 15.00
Never hinged 360.00
On cover 20.00
Block of 4 500.00 115.00
P# strip of 3, Impt., T II or IV 500.00
Never hinged 1,200.
P# block of 6, Impt., T II or IV 1,850.
Never hinged 4,000.
Dot in "S" of "CENTS" (carmine) 140.00 16.50
Never hinged 400.00
b. Horiz. pair, imperf. vert. *5,000.*
c. Horiz. pair, imperf. between *5,500.*

Earliest documented uses: Apr. 2, 1895 (dated cancel tying No. 252 dot in "S" variety on piece); Apr. 5, 1895 (No. 252); Apr. 17, 1895 (No. 252a).

No. 252b is unique and exists only as a horizontal top plate-number strip of 3. A right vertical plate-number strip of 3 from the same plate exists containing three stamps imperforate at left and right.

Counterfeits exist of No. 252. See the Postal Counterfeits section of this catalog.

253 A89 3c **purple,** *Sept. 1894* 120.00 12.00
dark purple 120.00 12.00
Never hinged 360.00
On cover 27.50
Block of 4 500.00 85.00
Margin block of 4, arrow, R or L 525.00
P# strip of 3, Impt., T I or II 475.00
Never hinged 1,200.
P# block of 6, Impt., T I or II 1,500.
Never hinged 3,250.

Earliest documented use: Oct. 20, 1894 (dated cancel on off-cover stamp); Nov. 15, 1894 (on cover).

See Die and Plate Proofs for imperf. on stamp paper.

254 A90 4c **dark brown,** *Sept. 1894* 200.00 11.00
brown 200.00 11.00
Never hinged 600.00
On cover 22.50
Block of 4 850.00 60.00
Margin block of 4, arrow, R or L 875.00
P# strip of 3, Impt., T I or II 800.00
Never hinged 1,950.
P# block of 6, Impt., T I or II 2,300.
Never hinged 5,000.

Earliest documented use: Oct. 16, 1894 (dated cancel on off-cover stamp); Nov. 2, 1894 (on cover).

See Die and Plate Proofs for imperf. on stamp paper.

Cancellation

Supplementary Mail Type F +2.00

255 A91 5c **chocolate,** *Sept. 1894* 120.00 9.00
deep chocolate 120.00 9.00
yellow brown 120.00 9.00
Never hinged 360.00
On cover 22.50
Block of 4 500.00 52.50
Margin block of 4, arrow, R or L 525.00
P# strip of 3, Impt., T I, II or IV 500.00
Never hinged 1,200.
P# block of 6, Impt., T I, II or IV 1,500.
Never hinged 3,000.
Double transfer 150.00 10.00
Worn plate, diagonal lines missing in oval background 140.00 10.00
c. Vert. pair, imperf. horiz. *4,000.*
P# block of 6, Impt., T IV *17,500.*

The plate block of No. 255c is in a unique block of 9 stamps. Beware of a No. 255P5 plate block that is known to have been reperforated to resemble No. 255c.

Earliest documented use: Oct. 23, 1894.

See Die and Plate Proofs for imperf. on stamp paper.

Cancellations

Supplementary Mail Type G +2.00
China —

256 A92 6c **dull brown,** *July 1894* 160.00 27.50
Never hinged 475.00
On cover 50.00
Block of 4 700.00 185.00
Margin block of 4, arrow, R or L 725.00
P# strip of 3, Impt., T I 675.00
Never hinged 1,650.
P# block of 6, Impt., T I 3,250. —
Never hinged *6,500.*
a. Vert. pair, imperf. horiz. *3,000.*
P# block of 6, Impt., T I *30,000.*

Earliest documented use: Aug. 11, 1894.

257 A93 8c **violet brown,** *Mar. 1895* 160.00 20.00
bright violet brown 160.00 20.00
Never hinged 475.00
On cover 50.00
Block of 4 700.00 130.00
Margin block of 4, arrow, R or L 725.00
P# strip of 3, Impt., T I 675.00
Never hinged 1,600.
P# block of 6, Impt., T I 2,500.
Never hinged *5,500.*

Earliest documented use: May 8, 1895.

258 A94 10c **dark green,** *Sept. 1894* 275.00 20.00
green 275.00 20.00
dull green 275.00 20.00
Never hinged 850.00
On cover 37.50
Block of 4 1,150. 100.00
P# strip of 3, Impt., T I 1,250.
Never hinged 2,700.
P# block of 6, Impt., T I 3,250.
Never hinged *6,750.*
Double transfer 325.00 22.50

Earliest documented use: Oct. 2, 1894.

See Die and Plate Proofs for imperf. on stamp paper.

Cancellations

China —
Supp. Mail Types F, G +2.00

259 A95 15c **dark blue,** *Oct. 1894* 275.00 65.00
indigo 275.00 65.00
Never hinged 850.00
On cover 125.00
Block of 4 1,150. 425.00
Margin block of 4, arrow, R or L 1,200.
P# strip of 3, Impt., T I 1,250.
Never hinged 2,750.
P# block of 6, Impt., T I 4,750.
Never hinged *9,500.*

Earliest documented use: Dec. 6, 1894.

Cancellation

China —

260 A96 50c **orange,** *Nov. 1894* 475. 140.
deep orange 475. 140.
Never hinged 1,425.
On cover 950.
Block of 4 2,250. 1,100.
Margin block of 4, arrow, R or L 2,350.
P# strip of 3, Impt., T I 2,300.
Never hinged *4,750.*
P# block of 6, Impt., T I 20,000.
Never hinged *32,500.*

Earliest documented use: Dec. 12, 1894 (dated cancel on off-cover stamp); Jan. 15, 1895 (on cover).

Cancellations

Supp. Mail Type F or G —
China —

Type I

Type II

ONE DOLLAR

Type I. The circles enclosing "$1" are broken where they meet the curved line below "One Dollar."

Type II. The circles are complete.

The fifteen left columns of impressions from the plate of 200 subjects are Type I, the other five columns being Type II.

261	A97 $1 **black,** type I, *Nov. 1894*	1,000.	350.
	grayish black	1,000.	350.
	Never hinged	3,200.	
	No gum	400.	
	On cover		*2,750.*
	Block of 4	4,500.	*2,100.*
	Margin block of 4, arrow, L	4,750.	
	P# strip of 3, Impt., T V	4,250.	
	P# block of 6, Impt., T V	*20,000.*	

Earliest documented use: Jan. 18, 1895.

261A	A97 $1 **black,** type II, *Nov. 1894*	2,100.	800.
	Never hinged	6,500.	
	No gum	850.	
	On cover		*4,500.*
	Block of 4	*9,000.*	*5,000.*
	Margin block of 4, arrow, R	*9,500.*	
	Horizontal pair, types I and II	*4,000.*	*1,400.*
	Block of 4, two each of types I and II	*9,500.*	—
	P# strip of 3, Impt., T V, one stamp No. 261	10,000.	
	P# block of 6, Impt., T V, two stamps No. 261	*75,000.*	

Earliest documented use: Mar. 22, 1895. A Mar. 11, 1895, cover has been reported. The editors would like to see evidence of certification of this date.

262	A98 $2 **bright blue,** *Dec. 1894*	2,750.	1,200.
	Never hinged	9,000.	
	No gum	1,100.	
	dark blue	2,900.	1,250.
	Never hinged	9,250.	
	On cover		*5,000.*
	Block of 4	*12,500.*	*9,500.*
	Margin block of 4, arrow, R or L	*13,000.*	
	P# strip of 3, Impt., T V	*13,500.*	
	P# block of 6, Impt., T V	*45,000.*	

The only recorded plate block of 6 of No. 262 has average centering and is valued as such.

Earliest documented use: July 6, 1895 (dated cancel on off-cover stamp); July 15, 1895 (on cover).

263	A99 $5 **dark green,** *Dec. 1894*	4,000.	2,600.
	Never hinged	15,000.	
	No gum	2,100.	
	On cover		—
	Block of 4	*20,000.*	*16,000.*
	Margin block of 4, arrow, R or L	*21,000.*	
	P# strip of 3, Impt., T V	*25,000.*	

Earliest documented use: July 6, 1896 (dated cancel on off-cover stamp).

Top plate block positions on the unwatermarked dollar-denomination stamps, Nos. 261, 261A, 262 and 263, do not exist. The Bureau of Engraving and Printing trimmed the top selvage before issuing the panes. Therefore, only bottom position plate blocks exist for these stamps.

REGULAR ISSUE

Designed by Thomas F. Morris.

(Actual size of letter)

repeated in rows, thus

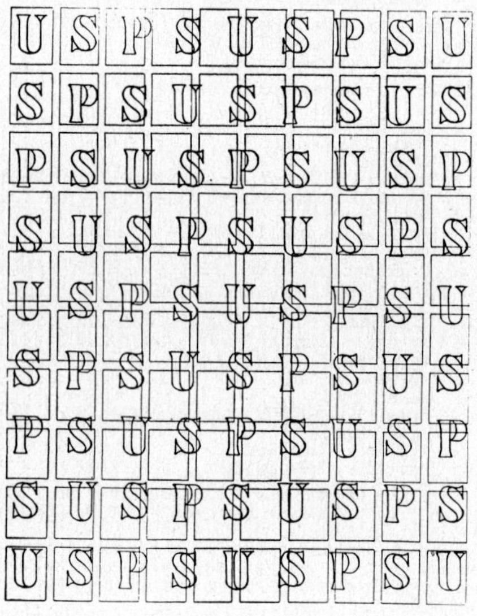

Watermarks are viewed from the back of the stamp.

Note that the letters "USPS" in watermark 191 occur in a pattern called "backward stepping." That is, each row of letters begins one letter to the left of the row above. A second variety of this watermark was discovered in 2009. In this "forward-stepping" watermark, each row of letters begins one letter to the right of the row above.

All watermarked Bureau issues printed before Jan. 1903 were on paper with the backward-stepping watermark. After 1902, stamps printed in fiscal years 1902-03, 1903-04, 1906-07 and 1909-10 have backward-stepping watermarks, while stamps printed in fiscal years 1904-05, 1905-06, 1907-08 and 1908-09 have forward-stepping watermarks.

Some issues are found only on paper with the forward-stepping watermark. These include Nos. 357-366, 367-369 and TD10.

Twelve stamps have been confirmed on which both types of watermark appear. They are Nos. 300, 301, 319, 331a, 332a, 343, 344, E6 and J39-J42. Many more are expected to exist thus and should be reported to the editors.

It is expected that exceptions to the general rules will be found occasionally, and the editors welcome new reports by collectors and dealers.

HORIZONTAL WATERMARK ORIENTATIONS

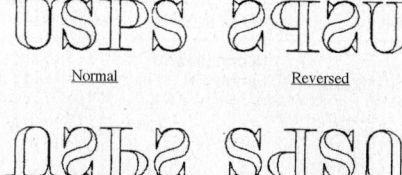

USPS — Normal

Reversed

Inverted

Inverted Reversed

VERTICAL WATERMARK ORIENTATIONS

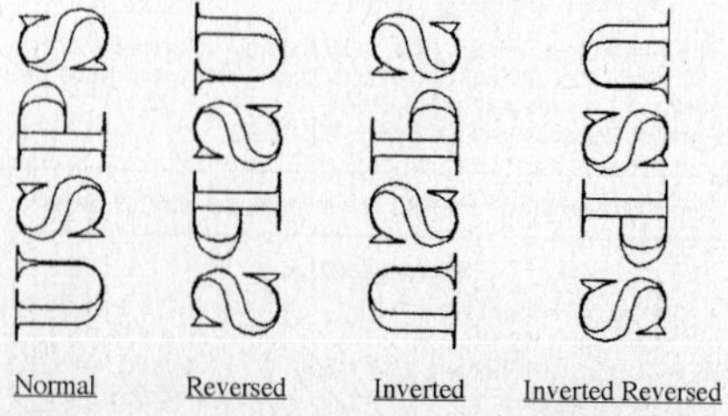

Normal   Reversed   Inverted   Inverted Reversed

This catalog does not list the different watermark orientations shown above for individual stamps. What research has been done indicates many stamp issues show most or all of the orientations, and most orientations do not appear to be very much scarcer than the others.

Watermark 191

The letters stand for "United States Postage Stamp."

Plates for the 1895 issue were of two sizes:

400 subjects for all 1c, 2c and 10c denominations; 200 subjects for all 3c, 4c, 5c, 6c, 8c, 15c, 50c, $1, $2 and $5; all issued in panes of 100 each.

Printings from the 400 subject plates show the watermark reading horizontally, on the 200 subject printings the watermark reads vertically.

Same as 1894 Issue

Wmk. 191 Horizontally or Vertically

1895 ***Perf. 12***

264	A87 1c **blue,** *Apr. 1895*	6.00	.60
	dark blue	6.00	.60
	pale blue	6.00	.60
	Never hinged	17.50	
	On cover		1.25
	Block of 4	26.00	5.00
	P# strip of 3, Impt., T I, II, IV or V	26.00	
	Never hinged	65.00	
	P# block of 6, Impt., T I, II, IV or V	240.00	
	Never hinged	450.00	
	Double transfer	—	1.10

Earliest documented use: May 16, 1895.

The bottom margin plate-number strip of 3, imperforate vertically, formerly No. 264a, is now listed in the Proofs section as No. 264P5a.

Cancellations

China	—
Philippines	—
Samoa	—

265	A88 2c **carmine,** type I, *May 1895*	35.00	3.50
	deep carmine	35.00	3.50
	Never hinged	105.00	
	On cover		5.50
	Block of 4	150.00	18.00
	P# strip of 3, Impt., T II	130.00	
	Never hinged	325.00	
	P# block of 6, Impt., T II	450.00	
	Never hinged	900.00	
	Double transfer	50.00	7.25

Earliest documented use: May 2, 1895.

266	A88 2c **carmine,** type II, *May 1895*	40.00	15.00
	Never hinged	120.00	
	On cover		20.00
	Block of 4	240.00	100.00
	Horizontal pair, types II and III	220.00	27.50
	Never hinged	600.00	
	P# strip of 3, Impt., T II or IV	150.00	
	Never hinged	375.00	
	P# block of 6, Impt., T II or IV	525.00	
	Never hinged	1,100.	

Earliest documented use: May 27, 1895.

267	A88 2c **carmine,** type III, *May 1895*	5.50	.60
	deep carmine	5.50	.60
	reddish carmine	5.50	.60
	Never hinged	16.00	
	On cover		.75
	Block of 4	24.00	4.00
	P# strip of 3, Impt., T II, IV or V	22.50	
	Never hinged	57.50	
	P# block of 6, Impt., T II, IV or V	190.00	
	Never hinged	325.00	
	Dot in "S" of "CENTS"	7.50	.70
	Never hinged	22.50	
	Double transfer	16.50	1.50
a.	2c **pink,** type III, *Nov. 1897*	20.00	5.00
	Never hinged	60.00	
	bright pink	25.00	7.50
	Never hinged	75.00	
	On cover		6.00
	Block of 4	90.00	32.50
	P# strip of 3, Impt., T II, IV or V	75.00	
	Never hinged	200.00	
	P# block of 6, Impt., T II, IV or V	425.00	
	Never hinged	825.00	
	Dot in "S" of "CENTS"	35.00	5.50
	Never hinged	110.00	
b.	2c **vermilion,** type III, *early 1899*	*50.00*	15.00
c.	2c **rose carmine,** type III, *Mar. 1899*	—	—

No. 267-267c type III plate numbers run through plate #503.

No. 279B type IV plate numbers start at #505.

Earliest documented uses:

No. 267, May 23, 1895;

No. 267 with dot in "S", July 15, 1895;

No. 267a, Dec. 8, 1897;

No. 267a with dot in "S", Mar. 18, 1898.

Cancellations

Green	—
China	—
Hawaii	—
Philippines	—
Samoa	—

The three left vertical rows of impressions from plate 170 are Type II, the balance being Type III.

268	A89 3c **purple,** *Oct. 1895*	37.50	2.25
	dark purple	37.50	2.25
	Never hinged	115.00	
	On cover		8.00
	Block of 4	160.00	21.00
	Margin block of 4, arrow, R or L	175.00	
	P# strip of 3, Impt., T II or V	150.00	
	Never hinged	400.00	
	P# block of 6, Impt., T II or IV	725.00	
	Never hinged	1,300.	
	Double transfer	45.00	4.75

Earliest documented use: Dec. 1, 1895.

Cancellations

Guam	—
China	—
Philippines	—

269 A90 4c **dark brown,** *June, 1895* 42.50 3.50
dark yellow brown 42.50 3.50
Never hinged 125.00
On cover 8.00
Block of 4 180.00 35.00
Margin block of 4, arrow, R or L 200.00
P# strip of 3, Impt., T I, II, IV or V 180.00
Never hinged 450.00
P# block of 6, Impt., T I, II, IV or V 775.00
Never hinged 1,600.
Double transfer 50.00 5.50

Earliest documented use: June 24, 1895.

Cancellations

Philippines —
China —
Samoa —

270 A91 5c **chocolate,** *June, 1895* 35.00 3.50
deep brown 35.00 3.50
chestnut 35.00 3.50
Never hinged 105.00
On cover 8.00
Block of 4 150.00 30.00
Margin block of 4, arrow, R or L 160.00
P# strip of 3, Impt., T I, II, IV or V 145.00
Never hinged 375.00
P# block of 6, Impt., T I, II, IV or V 675.00
Never hinged 1,300.
Double transfer 42.50 5.00
Worn plate, diagonal lines missing in oval background 37.50 3.75

Earliest documented use: Sept. 12, 1895.

Cancellations

China —
Supplementary Mail G +2.50

271 A92 6c **dull brown,** *Aug. 1895* 110.00 8.50
claret brown 110.00 8.50
Never hinged 325.00
On cover 27.50
Block of 4 525.00 70.00
Margin block of 4, arrow, R or L 550.00
P# strip of 3, Impt., T I, IV or V 475.00
Never hinged 1,200.
P# block of 6, Impt., T I, IV or V 2,900.
Never hinged 5,500.
Very thin paper 130.00 9.50
a. Wmkd. USIR *15,000.* *8,000.*
Pair — —

Earliest documented use: Sept. 14, 1895.

Cancellation

Philippines —

No. 271a unused is valued in the grade of fine.

Nos. 271a, 272a must have an identifiable portion of the letters "I" or "R." Single stamps from the same sheets, but showing the "U" or "S" are considered to be Nos. 271 and 272.

272 A93 8c **violet brown,** *July 1895* 70.00 2.75
dark violet brown 70.00 2.75
Never hinged 210.00
On cover 14.00
Block of 4 300.00 17.50
Margin block of 4, arrow, R or L 310.00
P# strip of 3, Impt., T I, IV or V 300.00
Never hinged 750.00
P# block of 6, Impt., T I, IV or V 975.00
Never hinged 2,100.
Double transfer 85.00 4.25
a. Wmkd. USIR *7,000.* 950.00
Block of 4 *5,500.*
P# strip of 3 Impt., T I *22,500.*

Earliest documented use: Sept. 11, 1895.

Cancellations

China —
Guam —
Philippines —
Puerto Rico, 1898 —
Samoa —
Supplementary Mail Type G +2.50

273 A94 10c **dark green,** *June 1895* 95.00 2.25
green 95.00 2.25
Never hinged 280.00
On cover 15.00
Block of 4 400.00 21.00
P# strip of 3, Impt., T I or IV 410.00
Never hinged 1,000.
P# block of 6, Impt., T I or IV 1,750.
Never hinged 3,500.
Double transfer 120.00 4.75

Earliest documented use: July 25, 1895.

Cancellations

Green —
China —
Cuba —
Philippines —
Supp. Mail Types F, G +2.00

274 A95 15c **dark blue,** *Sept. 1895* 200.00 17.50
indigo 200.00 17.50
Never hinged 600.00
On cover 55.00
Block of 4 875.00 105.00
Margin block of 4, arrow, R or L 900.00
P# strip of 3, Impt., T I or IV 825.00
Never hinged 2,200.
P# block of 6, Impt., T I or IV 4,500.
Never hinged *10,000.*

Earliest documented use: May 5, 1896.

Cancellations

China —
Philippines —
Supplementary Mail Type G +3.00

275 A96 50c **orange,** *Nov. 1895* 240. 40.00
Never hinged 725.
On cover 400.00
Block of 4 1,075. 225.00
Margin block of 4, arrow, R or L 1,125.
P# strip of 3, Impt., T I 1,000.
P# block of 6, Impt., T I *7,500.*
Never hinged *17,500.*
a. 50c **red orange** 325. 47.50
Never hinged 975.
On cover 425.00
Block of 4 1,500. 275.00
Margin block of 4, arrow, R or L 1,550.
P# strip of 3, Impt., T I 1,500.
P# block of 6, Impt., T I *7,000.*

Earliest documented use: May 5, 1896.

Cancellations

China —
Philippines —
Supp. Mail Types F, G +5.

276 A97 $1 **black,** type I, *Aug. 1895* 600. 95.
greenish black 600. 95.
Never hinged 1,800.
No gum 250.
On cover *2,250.*
Block of 4 2,600. 750.
Margin block of 4, arrow, L 2,700.
P# strip of 3, Impt., T V *3,000.*
Never hinged *6,000.*
P# block of 6, Impt., T V *40,000.*

Earliest documented use: April 9, 1897.

Cancellation

Philippines —

276A A97 $1 **black,** type II, *Aug. 1895* 1,250. 200.
greenish black 1,250. 200.
Never hinged 3,750.
No gum 500.
On cover *3,750.*
Block of 4 5,500. 1,500.
Margin block of 4, arrow, R 5,750.
Horizontal pair, types I and II *2,250.* *2,600.*
Block of 4, two each of types I and II *6,000.* *6,500.*
P# strip of 3, Impt., T V, one stamp No. 276 *5,000.*
P# block of 6, Impt., T V, two stamps No. 276 *125,000.*

Earliest documented use: Apr. 6, 1896.

Cancellations

China —
Philippines —

The fifteen left columns of impressions from the plate of 200 subjects are Type I, the other five columns being Type II.

277 A98 $2 **bright blue** 900. 400.
Never hinged 2,900.
No gum 375.
a. $2 **dark blue** 900. 400.
Never hinged 2,900.
No gum 375.
On cover *3,500.*
Block of 4 *4,000.* *3,000.*
Margin block of 4, arrow, R or L *4,250.*
P# strip of 3, Impt., T V *4,500.* *2,000.*
P# block of 6, Impt., T V *90,000.*

Earliest documented use: July 18, 1895.

Cancellation

Supplementary Mail Type G —

278 A99 $5 **dark green,** *Aug. 1895* 2,000. 600.
Never hinged 6,250.
No gum 800.
On cover *10,000.*
Block of 4 *9,000.* *4,000.*
Margin block of 4, arrow, R or L *9,500.*
P# strip of 3, Impt., T V *9,750.*
P# block of 6, Impt., T V *200,000.*

The plate block of 6 of No. 278 is unique.

Earliest documented use: Nov. 3, 1896.

See Die and Plate Proofs for imperf. or horiz. pair, imperf. vert. (1c) on stamp paper.

REGULAR ISSUE

Designed by Thomas F. Morris.

Plates for the sheet stamps for the 1897-1903 issue were of two sizes:

400 subjects for the 1c and 2c denominations; 200 subjects for all 4c, 5c, 6c and 15c denominations; and both 400 and 200 for the 10c denomination; all issued in panes of 100 each.

Printings from the 400 subject plates show the watermark reading horizontally. On the 200 subject plate printings the watermark reads vertically.

Plates for booklet panes for the 1897-1903 issue were of two sizes: 360 subjects and 180 subjects. Printings from the 360-subject plates show the watermark reading horizontally, while printings from the 180-subject plates show the watermark reading vertically.

In January, 1898, the color of the 1-cent stamp was changed to green and in March, 1898, that of the 5-cents to dark blue in order to conform to the colors assigned these values by the Universal Postal Union. These changes necessitated changing the colors of the 10c and 15c denominations in order to avoid confusion.

Wmk. 191 Horizontally or Vertically

1897-1903 ***Perf. 12***

279 A87 1c **deep green,** horizontal watermark, *Jan. 1898* 9.00 .50
green 9.00 .50
yellow green 9.00 .50
dark yellow green 9.00 .50
Never hinged 25.00
On cover .60
Block of 4 37.50 5.00
P# strip of 3, Impt., T V 37.50 —
Never hinged 85.00
P# block of 6, Impt., T V 185.00
Never hinged 350.00
Double transfer 12.00 1.10
a. 1c **deep green, vertical** watermark (error), *May 1902* *80.00* *7.50*
Never hinged *240.00*
On cover *22.50*
Block of 4 *325.00*
P# strip of 3, Impt., T V *350.00*
Never hinged *700.00*

Earliest documented use: Jan. 31, 1898

Cancellations

China —
Guam —
Puerto Rico, 1898 —
Philippines —

279B A88 2c **red,** type IV *May 1899* 9.00 .40
light red, *May 1899* 9.00 .40
Never hinged 25.00
deep red, *Sept. 1901* 13.50 1.25
Never hinged 32.50
On cover .50
Block of 4 37.50 3.00
P# strip of 3, Impt., T V 37.50
Never hinged 85.00
P# block of 6, Impt., T V 200.00
Never hinged 360.00
P# strip of 4, Impt., T V (plate 802, UR position) *250.00*
P# block of 8, Impt., T V (plate 802, UR position) *750.00*
Double transfer 18.00 .75
Triple transfer —
Triangle at upper right without shading 22.50 6.00
c. 2c **rose carmine,** type IV, *Mar. 1899* 275.00 230.00
bright carmine rose, *Mar. 1899* 275.00 230.00
Never hinged 850.00
pinkish rose carmine —
Never hinged —
Block of 4 1,200. —
P# strip of 3, Impt., T V 1,150.
Never hinged 2,750.
P# block of 6, Impt., T V 4,000.

No. 279Bc in the pinkish rose carmine shade is essentially the same shade as the rose carmine stamp, but the ink contains a pink pigment from an aniline ink that causes fluorescence under ultraviolet light.

d. 2c **orange red,** type IV, horizontal watermark, *June 1900* 11.50 2.00
pale orange red 11.50 2.00
dark orange red, *Sept. 1902* 11.50 2.00
deep orange red, *Jan. 1903* 11.50 2.00
Never hinged 32.50
On cover 2.50
Block of 4 50.00 12.50
P# strip of 3, Impt., T V 42.50
Never hinged 115.00
P# block of 6, Impt., T V 220.00
Never hinged 400.00
e. 2c **orange red,** type IV, **vertical** watermark (error), *May 1902* *80.00* *12.50*
Never hinged *240.00*
On cover *22.50*
Block of 4 *250.00*
P# strip of 3, Impt., T V *325.00*
Never hinged *800.00*
P# block of 6, Impt., T V, never hinged *2,850.*
f. 2c **carmine,** type IV, *Nov. 1897* 10.00 2.00
reddish carmine, *Dec. 1898* 10.00 2.00
Never hinged 27.50
On cover 2.25
Block of 4 42.50 12.50
P# strip of 3, Impt., T V 40.00
Never hinged 95.00
P# block of 6, Impt., T V 220.00
Never hinged 385.00
g. 2c **pink,** type IV, *Nov. 1897* 55.00 7.50
Never hinged 165.00
bright pink 65.00 15.00
Never hinged 200.00
On cover 8.00
Block of 4 250.00 40.00
P# strip of 3, Impt., T V 190.00
Never hinged 550.00
P# block of 6, Impt., T V 625.00
Never hinged 1,250.
h. 2c **vermilion,** type IV, *Jan. 1899* 12.50 3.00
pale vermilion 12.50 3.00
Never hinged 35.00
On cover 5.00
Block of 4 47.50 20.00
P# strip of 3, Impt., T V 45.00
Never hinged 120.00
P# block of 6, Impt., T V 235.00
Never hinged 425.00
i. 2c **brown orange,** type IV, *Jan. 1899* *400.00* *100.00*
Never hinged *950.00*
P# strip of 3, Impt., T V *1,500.*

j.	Booklet pane of 6, **red,** type IV, horizontal watermark, *Apr. 18, 1900*	500.00	*3,000.*
	light red	500.00	*3,000.*
	orange red, *1901*	500.00	*3,000.*
	Never hinged	1,000.	
k.	Booklet pane of 6, **red,** type IV, vertical watermark ('02)	500.00	—
	Never hinged	1,000.	
	orange red	750.00	—
	Never hinged	1,500.	
l.	As No. 279B, all color missing (FO)	*500.00*	

No. 279Bl must be collected se-tenant with a partially printed stamp.

Earliest documented uses:
No. 279B, July 6, 1899;
No. 279Bc, Mar 30, 1899;
No. 279Bc in bright rose carmine, July 16, 1899;
No. 279Bd, June 8, 1900;
No. 279Be, June 23, 1902;
No. 279Bf, Nov. 18, 1897;
No. 279Bg, Dec. 1, 1897;
No. 279Bh, Feb. 27, 1899;
No. 279Bj booklet single (red), May 4, 1900;
No. 279Bj booklet single (orange red), May 7, 1902.

Cancellations

Puerto Rico, 1898	—
Philippines, 1898	—
Guam, 1899 or 1900	—
Supplementary Mail Type G	+4.00
Cuba, 1898	—
China	+35.00
Samoa	+20.00

280	A90 4c **rose brown,** *Oct. 1898*	30.00	3.25
	Never hinged	80.00	
a.	4c **lilac brown**	30.00	3.25
	brownish claret	30.00	4.00
	Never hinged	80.00	
b.	4c **orange brown**	30.00	3.00
	Never hinged	80.00	
	On cover		7.50
	Block of 4	130.00	25.00
	Margin block of 4, arrow, R or L	140.00	
	P# strip of 3, Impt., T V	110.00	
	Never hinged	300.00	
	P# block of 6, Impt., T V	700.00	
	Never hinged	1,250.	
	Double transfer	35.00	5.00
	Extra frame line at top (Plate 793 R 62)	55.00	9.50

Earliest documented use: Nov. 13, 1898.

Cancellations

Supplementary Mail Type G	+3.00
China	+35.00
Philippines	+20.00
Samoa	—

281	A91 5c **dark blue,** *Mar. 1898*	32.50	2.25
	blue	32.50	2.25
	bright blue	32.50	2.25
	Never hinged	100.00	
	On cover		10.00
	Block of 4	140.00	14.00
	Margin block of 4, arrow, R or L	150.00	
	P# strip of 3, Impt., T V	135.00	
	Never hinged	340.00	
	P# block of 6, Impt., T V	650.00	
	Never hinged	1,250.	
	Double transfer	42.50	4.50
	Worn plate (diagonal lines missing in oval background)	37.50	2.75

Earliest documented use: Mar. 19, 1898.

Cancellations

Puerto Rico, 1898	—
Supplementary Mail Type G	+4.00
China	—
Cuba	—
Guam	—
Philippines	—
Samoa	—

282	A92 6c **lake,** *Dec. 1898*	45.00	6.50
	claret	45.00	6.50
	Never hinged	140.00	
	On cover		17.50
	Block of 4	190.00	50.00
	Margin block of 4, arrow, R or L	200.00	
	P# strip of 3, Impt., T V	190.00	
	Never hinged	475.00	
	P# block of 6, Impt., T V	900.00	
	Never hinged	1,650.	
	Double transfer	55.00	9.00
a.	6c **purple lake**	80.00	20.00
	Never hinged	240.00	
	Block of 4	375.00	110.00
	Margin block of 4, arrow	400.00	
	P# strip of 3, Impt., T V	340.00	
	Never hinged	840.00	
	P# block of 6, Impt., T V	1,300.	
	Never hinged	2,300.	

Earliest documented use: Mar. 13, 1899.

Cancellations

Supplementary Mail Type G	+4.00
China	—
Philippines	—

Type I. The tips of the foliate ornaments do not impinge on the white curved line below "ten cents."

282C	A94 10c **brown,** type I, *Nov. 1898*	175.00	6.50
	dark brown	175.00	6.50
	Never hinged	525.00	
	On cover		18.00
	Block of 4	750.00	57.50
	P# strip of 3, Impt., T IV or V	725.00	
	Never hinged	1,750.	
	P# block of 6, Impt., T IV or V	2,600.	
	Never hinged	*4,500.*	
	Double transfer	220.00	11.00

Earliest documented use: Dec. 10, 1898.

Cancellation

Supplementary Mail Type G	+2.50

Type II. The tips of the ornaments break the curved line below the "e" of "ten" and the "t" of "cents."

283	A94 10c **orange brown,** type II, horizontal watermark	150.00	6.00
	brown	150.00	6.00
	yellow brown	150.00	6.00
	Never hinged	450.00	
	On cover		17.50
	Block of 4	650.00	50.00
	P# strip of 3, Impt., T V	550.00	
	Never hinged	1,500.	
	P# block of 6, Impt., T V	1,900.	
	Never hinged	3,750.	
	Double transfer		—
	Pair, type I and type II	*15,000.*	*6,000.*
a.	10c **orange brown,** type II, vertical watermark, *early 1900*	*250.00*	*15.00*
	Never hinged	*775.00*	
	On cover		*35.00*
	Block of 4	*1,050.*	
	Margin block of 4, arrow, R or L	1,100.	—
	P# strip of 3, Impt., T V	*1,100.*	
	Never hinged	*2,750.*	
	P# block of 6, Impt., T V	*3,000.*	
	Never hinged	*5,500.*	

Earliest documented use: Mar. 13, 1899.

Cancellations

Supplementary Mail Type G	+2.50
China	—
Puerto Rico	—

On the 400 subject plate 932, all are Type I except the following: UL 20; UR 11, 12, 13; LL 61, 71, 86, these 7 being Type II.

284	A95 15c **olive green,** *Nov. 1898*	150.00	13.00
	dark olive green	150.00	13.00
	Never hinged	475.00	
	On cover		32.50
	Block of 4	650.00	90.00
	Margin block of 4, arrow, R or L	700.00	
	P# strip of 3, Impt., T IV	600.00	
	Never hinged	1,575.	
	P# block of 6, Impt., T IV	2,250.	
	Never hinged	4,250.	

Earliest documented use: Mar. 3, 1899.

Cancellations

Supp. Mail Type F or G	+2.50
China	—
Samoa	—

Nos. 279-284 (8)	600.50	38.40

For "I.R." overprints, see Nos. R153-R155A.

VALUES FOR VERY FINE STAMPS

Please note: Stamps are valued in the grade of Very Fine unless otherwise indicated.

TRANS-MISSISSIPPI EXPOSITION ISSUE

Omaha, Nebr., June 1 - Nov. 1, 1898.

Jacques Marquette on the Mississippi A100

Farming in the West — A101

Indian Hunting Buffalo — A102

John Charles Frémont on the Rocky Mountains A103

Troops Guarding Wagon Train — A104

Hardships of Emigration A105

Western Mining Prospector A106

Western Cattle in Storm — A107

Mississippi River Bridge, St. Louis — A108

Exposition Station Handstamp Postmark

Designed by Raymond Ostrander Smith.

Plates of 100 (10x10) subjects, divided vertically into 2 panes of 50.

See Nos. 3209-3210 for bi-colored reproductions of Nos. 285-293.

1898, June 17 Wmk. 191 *Perf. 12*

285 A100 1c **dark yellow green**	27.50	7.00
yellow green	27.50	7.00
green	27.50	7.00
Never hinged	75.00	
On cover		10.00
On card, Expo. station canc.		200.00
Pair, on cover, Expo. station canc.		300.00
Block of 4	120.00	47.50
Margin block of 4, arrow, R or L	130.00	—
P# pair, Impt., T VIII	65.00	
Never hinged	175.00	
P# strip of 3, Impt., T VIII	115.00	
Never hinged	275.00	
P# block of 4, Impt., T VIII	275.00	
Never hinged	440.00	
P# block of 6, Impt., T VIII	500.00	
Never hinged	800.00	
Double transfer	37.50	8.00

Earliest documented use: June 17, 1898 (FDC).

Cancellations

Supp. Mail Type F or G		+1.50
China		—
Philippines		—
Puerto Rico, 1898		—
286 A101 2c **copper red**	25.00	2.75
brown red	25.00	2.75
light brown red	25.00	2.75
Never hinged	72.50	
On cover		3.75
On cover, Expo. station canc.		175.00
Block of 4	110.00	16.00
Margin block of 4, arrow, R or L	120.00	—
P# pair, Impt., T VIII	60.00	
Never hinged	160.00	
P# strip of 3, Impt., T VIII	105.00	
Never hinged	250.00	
P# block of 4, Impt., T VIII	260.00	
Never hinged	430.00	
P# block of 6, Impt., T VIII	500.00	
Never hinged	800.00	
Double transfer	35.00	4.00
Worn plate	27.50	3.25

Earliest documented use: June 17, 1898 (FDC).

Cancellations

China		—
Hawaii		—
Puerto Rico, 1898		—
Philippines		—
287 A102 4c **orange**	110.00	25.00
deep orange	110.00	25.00
Never hinged	330.00	
On cover		60.00
On cover, Expo. station canc.		750.00
Block of 4	475.00	190.00
Margin block of 4, arrow, R or L	460.00	—
P# pair, Impt., T VIII	275.00	
Never hinged	725.00	
P# strip of 3, Impt., T VIII	425.00	
Never hinged	1,050.	
P# block of 4, Impt., T VIII	850.00	
Never hinged	1,550.	
P# block of 6, Impt., T VIII	1,750.	
Never hinged	3,250.	

Earliest documented use: June 17, 1898 (FDC).

Cancellations

Supp. Mail Type F or G		+5.00
China		—
Philippines		—
288 A103 5c **dull blue**	100.00	25.00
bright blue	100.00	25.00
Never hinged	300.00	
On cover		50.00
On cover, Expo. station canc.		500.00
Block of 4	430.00	160.00
Margin block of 4, arrow, R or L	450.00	—
P# pair, Impt., T VIII	260.00	—
Never hinged	675.00	
P# strip of 3, Impt., T VIII	400.00	
Never hinged	950.00	
P# block of 4, Impt., T VIII	800.00	
Never hinged	1,600.	
P# block of 6, Impt., T VIII	1,600.	
Never hinged	3,250.	

Earliest documented use: June 17, 1898 (FDC).

Cancellations

Supp. Mail Type F or G		+5.00
China		—
Philippines		—
Puerto Rico, 1898		—
289 A104 8c **violet brown**	140.00	47.50
dark violet brown	140.00	47.50
Never hinged	425.00	
On cover		120.00
On cover, Expo. station canc.		1,000.
Block of 4	600.00	300.00
Margin block of 4, arrow, R or L	625.00	—
P# pair, Impt., T VIII	350.00	
Never hinged	875.00	
P# strip of 3, Impt., T VIII	625.00	
P# block of 4, Impt., T VIII	1,950.	
Never hinged	3,400.	
P# block of 6, Impt., T VIII	3,250.	
Never hinged	5,500.	
a. Vert. pair, imperf. horiz.	*27,500.*	
P# block of 4, Impt., T VIII	*160,000.*	

Earliest documented use: June 17, 1898 (FDC).

Cancellations

Philippines		—
Samoa		—
290 A105 10c **gray violet**	140.00	35.00
blackish violet	140.00	35.00
Never hinged	425.00	
On cover		90.00
On cover, Expo. station canc.		750.00
Block of 4	600.00	210.00
Margin block of 4, arrow, R or L	625.00	—
P# pair, Impt., T VIII	375.00	
Never hinged	1,025.	
P# strip of 3, Impt., T VIII	550.00	
Never hinged	1,500.	
P# block of 4, Impt., T VIII	2,100.	
Never hinged	3,600.	
P# block of 6, Impt., T VIII	3,500.	
Never hinged	6,000.	

Earliest documented use: June 17, 1898 (FDC).

Cancellations

Supplementary Mail Type G		+5.00
China		—
Philippines		—
291 A106 50c **sage green**	600.00	175.00
dark sage green	600.00	175.00
Never hinged	1,750.	
On cover		1,750.
Block of 4	2,750.	1,250.
Margin block of 4, arrow, R or L	3,000.	—
P# pair, Impt., T VIII	1,800.	
Never hinged	4,250.	
P# strip of 3, Impt., T VIII	*2,750.*	
Never hinged	*6,750.*	
P# block of 4, Impt., T VIII	*15,000.*	
Never hinged	*25,000.*	
P# block of 6, Impt., T VIII	*30,000.*	
Never hinged	*70,000.*	

Earliest documented use: June 17, 1898 (FDC).

Cancellations

Supp. Mail Type F or G		+25.
Cuba		—
Philippines		—
292 A107 $1 **black**	1,500.	700.
Never hinged	3,750.	
No gum	850.	
On cover		*4,500.*
Block of 4	*7,000.*	*4,000.*
Margin block of 4, arrow, R or L	*7,250.*	
P# pair, Impt., T VIII	*4,000.*	
Never hinged	*8,750.*	
P# strip of 3, Impt., T VIII	*6,500.*	
Never hinged	*15,000.*	
P# block of 4, Impt., T VIII	*31,000.*	
Never hinged	*45,000.*	
P# block of 6, Impt., T VIII	*65,000.*	
Never hinged	*100,000.*	

Earliest documented use: June 17, 1898 (FDC).

Cancellation

Philippines		—
293 A108 $2 **orange brown**	1,900.	1,000.
dark orange brown	1,900.	1,050.
Never hinged	5,750.	
No gum	950.	
On cover		*12,500.*
Block of 4	*8,000.*	*6,000.*
Margin block of 4, arrow, R or L	*8,250.*	
P# pair, Impt., T VIII	*9,000.*	
Never hinged	*16,500.*	
P# strip of 3, Impt., T VIII	*15,000.*	
P# block of 4, Impt., T VIII	*90,000.*	
Never hinged	—	
P# block of 6, Impt., T VIII	*175,000.*	
Nos. 285-293 (9)	4,543.	2,017.

Earliest documented use: June 24, 1898.

Never-Hinged Stamps

See note before No. 182 regarding premiums for never-hinged stamps.

PAN-AMERICAN EXPOSITION ISSUE

Buffalo, N.Y., May 1 - Nov. 1, 1901.
On sale May 1-Oct. 31, 1901.

Fast Lake Navigation (Steamship "City of Alpena") — A109

Empire State Express — A110

Electric Automobile in Washington — A111

Bridge at Niagara Falls — A112

Canal Locks at Sault Ste. Marie — A113

Fast Ocean Navigation (Steamship "St. Paul") — A114

Exposition Station Duplex Handstamp Cancellation

Exposition Station Machine Cancellation

Designed by Raymond Ostrander Smith.

Plates of 200 subjects in two panes of 100 each.

1901, May 1 Wmk. 191 *Perf. 12*

294 A109 1c **green & black**	16.00	3.00
dark blue green & black	16.00	3.00
Never hinged	40.00	
On cover		4.50

	Unused	Used
On Expo. cover or card, Expo. station machine canc.		50.00
On Expo. cover or card, Expo. station duplex handstamp canc.		170.00
Block of 4	67.50	25.00
Margin block of 4, top arrow & markers	70.00	
Margin block of 4, bottom arrow & markers & black P#	72.50	
P# strip of 3, Impt., T V	75.00	
Never hinged	150.00	
P# block of 6, Impt., T V	325.00	
Never hinged	500.00	
P# strip of 5, bottom Impt. T V, two P#, arrow & markers	110.00	
Never hinged	250.00	
Margin block of 10, bottom Impt., T V, two P#, arrow & markers	700.00	
Never hinged	1,100.	
Double transfer	25.00	5.25
a. Center inverted	*12,500.*	*22,500.*
Never hinged	*22,500.*	
On cover		—
Block of 4	*75,000.*	
P# strip of 4, Impt.	*167,500.*	

Earliest documented uses: May 1, 1901 (No. 294 FDC); Aug. 2, 1901 (No. 294a). The No. 294a cover sold at auction in 1999 for $121,000. Two other uses on cover are recorded.

	Unused	Used
295 A110 2c **carmine & black**	15.00	1.00
carmine & gray black	15.00	1.00
dark carmine & black	15.00	1.00
rose carmine & black	15.00	1.00
scarlet & black	15.00	1.00
Never hinged	37.50	
On cover		1.50
On Expo. cover or card, Expo. sta. machine cancel		60.00
On Expo. cover or card, Expo. sta. duplex handstamp canc.		200.00
Block of 4	62.50	8.00
Margin block of 4, top arrow & markers	65.00	
P# block of 4, bottom arrow & markers and black P#	67.50	
P# strip of 3, Impt., T V	62.50	
Never hinged	135.00	
P# block of 6, Impt., T V	325.00	
Never hinged	500.00	
P# strip of 5, bottom Impt., T V, two P#, arrow & markers	125.00	
Never hinged	240.00	
P# block of 10, bottom Impt., T V, two P#, arrow & markers	600.00	
Never hinged	1,000.	
Double transfer	24.00	2.25
a. Center inverted	*50,000.*	*50,000.*
Block of 4	*900,000.*	

Almost all unused examples of No. 295a have partial or disturbed gum. Values are for examples with full original gum that is slightly disturbed. Value for No. 295a used is for a well-centered example with faults, as there are no known fault-free examples.

Earliest documented use: May 1, 1901 (No. 295 FDC); Feb. 26, (1902?) (No. 295a, dated cancel on off-cover stamp). The dated No. 295a stamp is the only used example showing a date of any kind. Sold at auction in 2007 for $83,375.

The block of 4 of No. 295a is unique. Value reflects sale price at 2009 auction.

	Unused	Used
296 A111 4c **deep red brown & black**	70.00	18.00
chocolate & black	70.00	18.00
Never hinged	170.00	
On cover		42.50
On cover, Expo. station machine cancel		350.00
On cover, Expo. station duplex handstamp canc.		*750.00*
Block of 4	300.00	140.00
Margin block of 4, top arrow & markers	320.00	
P# block of 4, bottom arrow & markers & black P#	340.00	
P# strip of 3, Impt., T V	300.00	
Never hinged	650.00	
P# block of 6, Impt., T V	2,000.	
Never hinged	*3,250.*	
P# strip of 5, bottom Impt., T V, two P#, arrow & markers	550.00	
Never hinged	1,125.	
P# block of 10, bottom Impt., T V, two P#, arrow & markers	*4,000.*	
Never hinged	*5,750.*	
a. Center inverted	*80,000.*	—
Block of 4	*400,000.*	
P# strip of 4, Impt.	*450,000.*	

No. 296a was a Special Printing and not regularly issued.

Almost all unused examples of No. 296a have partial or disturbed gum. Values are for examples with full orginal gum that is slightly disturbed.

See No. 296a-S, "Specimen" Stamps.

Earliest documented use: May 1, 1901 (FDC).

	Unused	Used
297 A112 5c **ultramarine & black**	75.00	17.00
dark ultramarine & black	75.00	17.00
Never hinged	180.00	
On cover		45.00
On cover, Expo. station machine cancel		350.00
On cover, Expo. station duplex handstamp canc.		*750.00*
Block of 4	325.00	130.00
Margin block of 4, top arrow & markers	350.00	
P# block of 4, bottom arrow & markers & black P#	375.00	
P# strip of 3, Impt., T V	310.00	
Never hinged	625.00	
P# block of 6, Impt., T V	2,100.	
Never hinged	*3,600.*	
P# strip of 5, bottom Impt., T V, two P#, arrow & markers	625.00	
Never hinged	1,250.	
P# block of 10, bottom Impt., T V, two P#, arrow & markers	*4,250.*	
Never hinged	*6,000.*	

Earliest documented use: May 1, 1901 (FDC).

	Unused	Used
298 A113 8c **brown violet & black**	90.00	50.00
purplish brown & black	90.00	50.00
Never hinged	230.00	
On cover		110.00
On cover, Expo. station machine cancel		*750.00*
On cover, Expo. station duplex handstamp canc.		*1,250.*
Block of 4	400.00	425.00
Margin block of 4, top arrow & markers	425.00	
P# block of 4, bottom arrow & markers & black P#	475.00	
P# strip of 3, Impt., T V	400.00	
Never hinged	850.00	
P# block of 6, Impt., T V	*3,800.*	
Never hinged	*6,000.*	
P# strip of 5, bottom Impt., T V, two P#, arrow & markers	800.00	
Never hinged	1,600.	
P# block of 10, bottom Impt., T V, two P#, arrow & markers	*6,500.*	
Never hinged	*9,000.*	

Earliest documented use: May 1, 1901 (FDC).

	Unused	Used
299 A114 10c **yellow brown & black**	115.00	30.00
dark yellow brown & black	115.00	32.50
Never hinged	325.00	
On cover		125.00
On cover, Expo. station machine cancel		*1,000.*
On cover, Expo. station duplex handstamp canc.		*1,500.*
Block of 4	525.00	250.00
Margin block of 4, top arrow & markers	550.00	
P# block of 4, bottom arrow & markers & black P#	625.00	
P# strip of 3, Impt., T V	525.00	
Never hinged	1,100.	
P# block of 6, Impt., T V	6,000.	
Never hinged	*8,500.*	
P# strip of 5, bottom Impt., T V, two P#, arrow & markers	1,075.	
Never hinged	2,150.	
P# block of 10, bottom Impt., T V, two P#, arrow & markers	*9,000.*	
Never hinged	*13,000.*	
Nos. 294-299 (6)	381.00	119.00
Nos. 294-299, never hinged	957.50	

Earliest documented use: May 1, 1901 (FDC).

VALUES FOR VERY FINE STAMPS

Please note: Stamps are valued in the grade of Very Fine unless otherwise indicated.

Franklin — A115

Washington — A116

Jackson — A117

Grant — A118

Lincoln — A119

Garfield — A120

Martha Washington — A121

Daniel Webster — A122

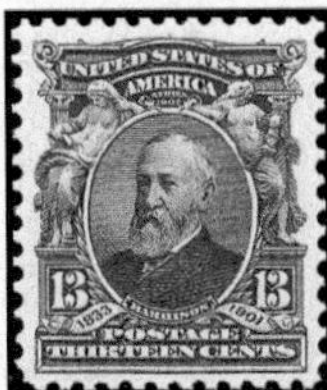

Benjamin Harrison — A123

Henry Clay — A124

Jefferson — A125

David G. Farragut — A126

Madison — A127

Marshall — A128

REGULAR ISSUE

Designed by Raymond Ostrander Smith and/or Clair Aubrey Huston.

Plates of 400 subjects in four panes of 100 each for all values from 1c to 15c inclusive. Certain plates of 1c, 2c type A129, 3c and 5c show a round marker in margin opposite the horizontal guide line at right or left.

Plates of 200 subjects in two panes of 100 each for 15c, 50c, $1, $2 and $5.

Many stamps of this issue are known with blurred printing due to having been printed on dry paper.

1902-03 **Wmk. 191** ***Perf. 12***

300 A115 1c **blue green,** *Feb. 1903*	12.00	.25
green	12.00	.25
deep green	12.00	.25
gray green	12.00	.25
yellow green	12.00	.25
Never hinged	30.00	
On cover		.75
Block of 4	52.50	3.50
P# strip of 3, Impt., T V	50.00	
Never hinged	100.00	
Bottom P# strip of 3, Impt. T V, plate number on left side of imprint (plate 3394)	—	
P# block of 6, Impt., T V	225.00	
Never hinged	350.00	
Double transfer	17.50	1.00
Worn plate	13.00	.35
Cracked plate	14.00	.30
b. Booklet pane of 6, *Mar. 6, 1907*	600.00	*11,500.*
Never hinged	1,150.	
Wmk. horiz.	*2,000.*	

Earliest documented uses: Feb. 3, 1903 (No. 300); Mar. 22, 1907 (No. 300b single).

301 A116 2c **carmine,** *Jan. 22, 1903*	15.00	.50
bright carmine	15.00	.50
deep carmine	15.00	.50
carmine rose	15.00	.50
Never hinged	37.50	
On cover		1.00
Block of 4	62.50	5.50
P# strip of 3, Impt., T V	60.00	
Never hinged	120.00	
Bottom P# strip of 3, Impt. T V, plate number on left side of imprint (plate 1568)	—	
P# block of 6, Impt., T V	275.00	
Never hinged	425.00	
Double transfer	27.00	1.40
Cracked plate	—	1.40
c. Booklet pane of 6, *Jan. 24, 1903*	500.00	*6,000.*
Never hinged	950.00	

Earliest documented use: Jan. 26, 1903 (No. 301); Mar. 28, 1903 (No. 301c single); Apr. 4, 1903 (No. 301c pane).

Four unused single imperforate sheet margin examples of No. 301 are recorded. These are considered printer's waste, but they are sought by specialists. Value, $5,000.

302 A117 3c **bright violet,** *Feb. 1903*	55.00	3.75
violet	55.00	3.75
deep violet	55.00	3.75
Never hinged	140.00	
On cover		11.00
Block of 4	230.00	32.50
P# strip of 3, Impt., T V	215.00	
Never hinged	425.00	
P# block of 6, Impt., T V	750.00	
Never hinged	1,300.	
Double transfer	77.50	4.50
Cracked plate	—	—

Earliest documented use: Mar. 14, 1903.

303 A118 4c **brown,** *Feb. 1903*	55.00	2.25
dark brown	60.00	2.25
yellow brown	55.00	2.25
orange brown	55.00	2.25
red brown	55.00	2.25
Never hinged	140.00	
On cover		12.00
Block of 4	230.00	25.00
P# strip of 3, Impt., T V	220.00	
Never hinged	450.00	
P# block of 6, Impt., T V	825.00	
Never hinged	1,500.	
Double transfer	72.50	2.50

Earliest documented use: Mar. 10, 1903.

304 A119 5c **blue,** *Jan. 1903*	60.00	2.00
pale blue	60.00	2.00
bright blue	60.00	2.00
dark blue	65.00	2.00
Never hinged	150.00	
On cover		6.00
Block of 4	250.00	12.50
P# strip of 3, Impt., T V	240.00	
Never hinged	500.00	
P# block of 6, Impt., T V	775.00	—
Never hinged	1,350.	
Double transfer	82.50	3.50
Cracked plate	75.00	5.00

Earliest documented use: Feb. 9, 1903.

305 A120 6c **claret,** *Feb. 1903*	60.00	5.50
deep claret	60.00	5.50
brownish lake	65.00	5.50
dull brownish lake	65.00	5.50
Never hinged	150.00	
On cover		16.00
Block of 4	260.00	50.00
P# strip of 3, Impt., T V	260.00	
Never hinged	575.00	
P# block of 6, Impt., T V	850.00	
Never hinged	1,500.	
Double transfer	65.00	6.25

Earliest documented use: April 14, 1903.

306 A121 8c **violet black,** *Dec. 1902*	45.00	3.25
black	45.00	3.25
slate black	45.00	3.25
gray lilac	45.00	3.25
Never hinged	110.00	
lavender	65.00	4.00
Never hinged	160.00	
On cover		8.00
Block of 4	190.00	30.00
P# strip of 3, Impt., T V	175.00	
Never hinged	360.00	
P# block of 6, Impt., T V	700.00	
Never hinged	1,150.	
Double transfer	50.00	4.50

Earliest documented use: Dec. 27, 1902.

307 A122 10c **pale red brown,** *Feb. 1903*	60.00	3.00
red brown	60.00	3.00
dark red brown	75.00	3.00
Never hinged	150.00	
On cover		9.50
Block of 4	260.00	19.00
P# strip of 3, Impt., T V	250.00	
Never hinged	525.00	
P# block of 6, Impt., T V	1,000.	
Never hinged	1,800.	
Double transfer	70.00	11.00

Earliest documented use: Mar. 7, 1903.

308 A123 13c **purple black,** *Nov. 1902*	40.00	10.00
brown violet	40.00	10.00
Never hinged	100.00	
On cover		37.50
Block of 4	175.00	100.00
P# strip of 3, Impt., T V	165.00	
Never hinged	350.00	
P# block of 6, Impt., T V	675.00	
Never hinged	1,150.	

Earliest documented use: Nov. 18, 1902.

309 A124 15c **olive green,** *May 27, 1903*	185.00	12.50
dark olive green	185.00	12.50
Never hinged	475.00	
On cover		75.00
Block of 4	775.00	100.00
Margin block of 4, arrow	800.00	
P# strip of 3, Impt., T V	750.00	
Never hinged	1,650.	
P# block of 6, Impt., T V	3,250.	
Never hinged	5,500.	
Double transfer	210.00	16.00

Earliest documented use: July 1903 (on registry tag); Sept. 11, 1903 (on cover).

310 A125 50c **orange,** *Mar. 23, 1903*	425.	35.00
deep orange	425.	35.00
Never hinged	1,225.	
On cover		700.00
Block of 4	1,900.	250.00
Margin block of 4, arrow	2,000.	
P# strip of 3, Impt., T V	1,800.	
Never hinged	4,500.	
P# block of 6, Impt., T V	*7,250.*	

Earliest documented use: Oct. 6, 1903 (on cover front).

311 A126 $1 **black,** *June 5, 1903*	600.00	90.00
grayish black	600.00	90.00
Never hinged	1,800.	
No gum	240.00	
On cover		1,500.
Block of 4	2,750.	600.00
Margin block of 4, arrow	3,000.	
P# strip of 3, Impt., T V	3,000.	
P# block of 6, Impt., T V	*27,500.*	

Earliest documented use: Sept. 30, 1903.

312 A127 $2 **dark blue,** *June 5, 1903*	825.00	200.00
blue	825.00	200.00
Never hinged	2,500.	
No gum	325.00	
On cover		2,500.
Block of 4	3,600.	2,000.
Margin block of 4, arrow	3,750.	
P# strip of 3, Impt., T V	4,250.	
P# block of 6, Impt., T V	*35,000.*	

Earliest documented use: Feb. 17, 1904.

313 A128 $5 **dark green,** *June 5, 1903*	2,100.	700.00
Never hinged	*6,500.*	
No gum	800.00	
On cover		*5,000.*
Block of 4	*11,000.*	*6,000.*
Margin block of 4, arrow	*11,500.*	
P# strip of 3, Impt., T V	*9,750.*	
P# block of 6, Impt., T V	*170,000.*	

Earliest documented use: Feb. 17, 1904.

Nos. 300-313 (14)	4,537.	1,068.

For listings of designs A127 and A128 with Perf. 10 see Nos. 479 and 480.

Earliest documented use dates for imperforates are for the imperforate sheet stamps, not for imperforate stamps with vending and affixing machine perforations or for flat plate imperforate coil stamps. EDU dates for VAMP and flat plate imperf coil stamps are shown in their respective sections later in the catalogue.

1906-08 ***Imperf.***

314 A115 1c **blue green,** *Oct. 2, 1906*	14.00	17.50
green	14.00	17.50
deep green	14.00	17.50
Never hinged	30.00	
On cover		32.50
Pair	30.00	40.00
Never hinged	60.00	
Block of 4	62.50	*95.00*
Never hinged	130.00	
Corner margin block of 4	70.00	*100.00*
Margin block of 4, arrow	72.50	*105.00*
Margin block of 4, arrow & round marker	170.00	150.00
Center line block	130.00	130.00
Never hinged	250.00	
P# block of 6, Impt.	200.00	—
Never hinged	325.00	
Double transfer	28.00	22.50

Earliest documented use: Dec. 20, 1906.

For imperforate coil varieties of No. 314, see the Imperforate Flat Plate Coil Stamps section in this catalogue.

314A A118 4c **brown,** *May 12, 1908*	*85,000.*	*45,000.*
Never hinged	*200,000.*	
On cover		*140,000.*
Pair	*200,000.*	
Strip of 3		*230,000.*
Guide line pair	*250,000.*	

This stamp was issued imperforate but all examples were privately perforated with large oblong perforations at the sides (Schermack type III).

Two guide line pairs of No. 314A are recorded, one fine-very fine and the other extremely fine. The extremely fine example sold for $460,000 in a 2009 auction.

Beware of examples of No. 303 with trimmed perforations and fake private perfs. added.

Used and on-cover values are for contemporaneous usage.

Earliest documented use: May 27, 1908.

315 A119 5c **blue,** *Mar. 30, 1908*	350.	*1,250.*
Never hinged	600.	
On cover, pair		*70,000.*
Pair	725.	*11,000.*
Never hinged	1,250.	
Block of 4	1,450.	*27,500.*
Never hinged	2,500.	
Corner margin block of 4	1,500.	
Margin block of 4, arrow	1,800.	
Margin block of 4, arrow & round marker	2,500.	
Never hinged	*3,750.*	
Center line block	*8,500.*	
Never hinged	*12,500.*	
P# block of 6, Impt.	3,000.	—
Never hinged	4,750.	

Earliest documented use: Sept. 15, 1908 (pair on piece).

Beware of examples of No. 304 with perforations removed.

Used examples of No. 315 must have contemporaneous cancels and certificate of authenticity issued by a recognized expertizing committee. Single examples of No. 315 on cover must be accompanied by a certificate of authenticity.

COIL STAMPS

Warning! Imperforate stamps are known fraudulently perforated to resemble coil stamps and part-perforate varieties. Fully perforated stamps and booklet stamps also are known with perforations fraudulently trimmed off to resemble coil stamps.

1908 ***Perf. 12 Horizontally***

316 A115 1c **blue green,** *Feb. 18*	*150,000.*	
Pair	*375,000.*	
Guide line pair	*500,000.*	

See No. 314V in the Imperforate Flat Plate Coil Stamps section of this catalogue for the imperforate counterpart to this perforated coil stamp.

317 A119 5c **blue,** *Feb. 24*	*6,000.*	—
Never hinged	*12,000.*	
Pair	*15,000.*	
Never hinged	*45,000.*	
Guide line pair	*70,000.*	
Never hinged	*160,000.*	

Earliest documented use: Sept. 18, 1908.

Perf. 12 Vertically

318 A115 1c **blue green,** *July 31*	*4,500.*	
Never hinged	*9,500.*	
Pair	*11,000.*	
Guide line pair	*35,000.*	
Double transfer	—	

See No. 314H in the Imperforate Flat Plate Coil Stamps section of this catalogue for the imperforate counterpart to this perforated coil stamp.

No. 316 is valued in the grade of fine to very fine. There are no very fine examples recorded.

The No. 317 mint, never hinged guide line pair is valued in the grade of fine-very fine.

The No. 318 mint never hinged single is valued in the grade of fine.

Coil stamps for use in vending and affixing machines are perforated on two sides only, either horizontally or vertically. They were first issued in 1908, using perf. 12. This was changed to 8½ in 1910, and to 10 in 1914.

Imperforate sheets of certain denominations were sold to the vending machine companies which applied a variety of private perforations and separations (see Vending and Affixing Machine Perforations section of this catalogue).

Several values of the 1902 and later issues are found on an apparently coarse-ribbed paper. This is caused by worn blankets on the printing presses and is not a true paper variety.

All examples of Nos. 316-318 must be accompanied by certificates of authenticity issued by recognized expertizing committees.

Washington — A129

Plate of 400 subjects in four panes of 100 each.

Type I

Type II

Designed by Clair Aubrey Huston.

The two large arrows in the illustrations highlight the two major differences of the type II stamps: closing of the thin left border line next to the laurel leaf, and strengthening of the inner frame line at the lower left corner. The small arrows point out three minor differences that are not always easily discernible: strengthening of shading lines under the ribbon just above the "T" of "TWO," a shorter shading line to the left of the "P" in "POSTAGE," and shortening of a shading line in the left side ribbon.

Type I

1903 Wmk. 191 *Perf. 12*

319	A129 2c **carmine,** *Nov. 12*	6.00	.25
	bright carmine	6.00	.25
	red	6.00	.25
	Never hinged	15.00	
	On cover		.30
	Block of 4	25.00	2.50
	P# strip of 3, Impt., T V	24.00	
	Never hinged	55.00	
	P# block of 6, Impt., T V	180.00	
	Never hinged	310.00	
	Double transfer	12.50	2.00
a.	2c **lake**	—	
b.	2c **carmine rose**	15.00	.40
	Never hinged	45.00	
	On cover		.60
	Block of 4	65.00	9.00
	P# strip of 3, Impt., T V	60.00	
	Never hinged	175.00	
	P# block of 6, Impt., T V	375.00	
	Never hinged	650.00	
c.	2c **scarlet**	10.00	.30
	Never hinged	25.00	
	On cover		.40
	Block of 4	42.50	6.00
	P# strip of 3, Impt., T V	40.00	
	Never hinged	85.00	
	P# block of 6, Impt., T V	250.00	
	Never hinged	375.00	
d.	Vert. pair, imperf. horiz., No. 319	*7,500.*	
	Never hinged	*17,500.*	
e.	Vert. pair, imperf. between	—	
r.	Vert. pair, rouletted between	*4,000.*	

During the use of No. 319, the postmaster of San Francisco discovered in his stock panes that had the perforations missing between the top two rows of stamps. To facilitate their separation, the imperf rows were rouletted, and the stamps were sold over the counter. These vertical pairs with regular perfs all around and rouletted between are No. 319r. No 319e is from a different source. One example has been authenticated, and collectors are warned that other pairs exist with faint blind perfs or indentations from the perforating machine.

g.	Booklet pane of 6, **carmine**	125.00	*450.00*
	Never hinged	240.00	
	Wmk. horizontal	*3,000.*	
	Never hinged	*5,000.*	
n.	Booklet pane of 6, **carmine rose**	275.00	*700.00*
	Never hinged	500.00	
p.	Booklet pane of 6, **scarlet**	185.00	*625.00*
	Never hinged	350.00	

Earliest documented uses:
No. 319, Nov. 18, 1903;
No. 319b, Nov. 3, 1903;
No. 319c, Dec. 16, 1903;
No. 319g single, Dec. 7, 1903;
No. 319p single, Apr. 12, 1904.

"Gash on Face" Variety, Type II

The gash may appear as double lines due to different plate wiping techniques.

Type II

1908 Wmk. 191 *Perf. 12*

319F	A129 2c **lake**	10.00	.30
	carmine lake	10.00	.30
	Never hinged	25.00	
	On cover		.75
	Block of 4	42.50	5.50
	P# strip of 3, Impt., T V	45.00	
	Never hinged	95.00	
	P# block of 6, Impt., T V	325.00	
	Never hinged	475.00	
	"Gash on face" plate flaw (carmine lake, 4671 LL 16)	—	
i.	2c **carmine**	65.00	*50.00*
	red	65.00	*50.00*
	Never hinged	150.00	
	Block of 4	275.00	
	P# strip of 3, Impt., T V	*250.00*	
	Never hinged	*500.00*	
	P# block of 6, Impt., T V	*1,750.*	
	Never hinged	*2,500.*	
	On cover		*150.00*
j.	2c **carmine rose**	100.00	1.75
	Never hinged	225.00	
	Block of 4	450.00	20.00
	P# strip of 3, Impt., T V	525.00	
	P# block of 6, Impt., T V	*1,400.*	
k.	2c **scarlet**	70.00	2.00
	Never hinged	160.00	
	Block of 4	300.00	15.00
	P# strip of 3, Impt., T V	350.00	
	P# block of 6, Impt., T V	*1,100.*	
h.	Booklet pane of 6, **carmine**	900.00	—
	Never hinged	1,500.	
l.	Booklet pane of 6, **scarlet**	—	
q.	Booklet pane of 6, **lake**	300.00	*800.00*
	Never hinged	575.00	

Earliest documented uses:
No. 319F, Sept. 25, 1908;
No. 319Fi, June 5, 1908;
No. 319Fj, June 30, 1908;
No. 319Fk, June 11, 1908;
No. 319Fh single, June 8, 1908.

Type I

1906 Wmk. 191 *Imperf.*

320	A129 2c **carmine,** *Oct. 2*	15.00	*19.00*
	Never hinged	32.50	
	On cover		25.00
	Pair	32.50	*42.50*
	Never hinged	70.00	
	Block of 4	65.00	*87.50*
	Corner margin block of 4	67.50	*110.00*
	Margin block of 4, arrow	70.00	*120.00*
	Margin block of 4, arrow & round marker	—	
	Center line block	145.00	*225.00*
	Never hinged	240.00	
	P# block of 6, Impt., T V, carmine	200.00	—
	Never hinged	325.00	
	Double transfer	24.00	21.50

Earliest documented use: Oct. 16, 1906.

b.	2c **scarlet**	17.50	15.00
	Never hinged	37.50	
	On cover		22.50
	Pair	37.50	
	Never hinged	80.00	
	Block of 4	72.50	
	Corner margin block of 4	75.00	
	Margin block of 4, arrow	77.50	—
	Center line block	200.00	—
	Never hinged	320.00	
	P# block of 6, Impt., T V	225.00	
	Never hinged	350.00	
c.	2c **carmine rose**	75.00	42.50
	Never hinged	150.00	

For imperforate coil varieties of No. 320, see the Imperforate Flat Plate Coil Stamps section in this catalogue.

Type II

1908 Wmk. 191 *Imperf.*

320A	A129 2c **lake**	45.00	50.00
	carmine lake	45.00	50.00
	Never hinged	100.00	
	On cover		*100.00*
	Pair	100.00	*120.00*
	Never hinged	225.00	
	Block of 4	200.00	*275.00*
	Corner margin block of 4	205.00	
	Margin block of 4, arrow	210.00	
	Center line block	425.00	—
	Never hinged	700.00	
	P# block of 6, Impt., T V	725.00	—
	Never hinged	1,150.	
	"Gash on face" plate flaw (see No. 319F)	—	
d.	2c **carmine**	*135.00*	—
	Never hinged	*200.00*	
	On cover		*2,000.*
	Pair	*290.00*	
	Never hinged	*525.00*	
	Guide line pair	*500.00*	*6,000.*

No. 320Ad was issued imperforate, but all examples were privately perforated with large oblong perforations at the sides (Schermack type III).

COIL STAMPS

1908 *Perf. 12 Horizontally*

321 A129 2c **carmine,** type I, pair, *Feb. 18*	*1,000,000.*	
On cover, single		*310,000.*

See No. 320V in the Imperforate Flat Plate Coil Stamps section of this catalogue for the imperforate counterpart to this perforated coil stamp.

Four authenticated unused pairs of No. 321 are known and available to collectors. A fifth, unauthenticated pair is in the New York Public Library Miller collection, which is on long-term loan to the Smithsonian National Postal Museum. The value for an unused pair is for a fine-very fine example. Four fine pairs are recorded and one fine-very fine pair.

There are no authenticated unused or off-cover used single stamps recorded. Two on-cover singles are known, both used from Indianapolis in 1908.

The Oct. 2, 1908, cover with No. 321 alone sold in 2018 and is the cover valued. The second cover bears a single No. 321 and also a pair of No. 315, which was separated from the cover for more than 48 years until it was discovered off cover in the marketplace and finally reunited with the cover bearing the No. 321. This second cover sold for $130,000 in a 2020 auction.

Numerous counterfeits exist.

Earliest documented use: Oct. 2, 1908.

Perf. 12 Vertically

322 A129 2c **carmine,** type II, *July 31*	*7,000.*	—
Never hinged	*15,000.*	
Pair	*17,500.*	
Guide line pair	*35,000.*	
Double transfer	—	

See No. 320H in the Imperforate Flat Plate Coil Stamps section of this catalogue for the imperforate counterpart to this perforated coil stamp.

This Government Coil Stamp should not be confused with those of the International Vending Machine Co., which are perforated 12½.

All examples of Nos. 321-322 must be accompanied by certificates of authenticity issued by recognized expertizing committees.

VALUES FOR VERY FINE STAMPS
Please note: Stamps are valued in the grade of Very Fine unless otherwise indicated.

LOUISIANA PURCHASE EXPOSITION ISSUE
St. Louis, Mo., Apr. 30 - Dec. 1, 1904

Robert R. Livingston — A130

Thomas Jefferson — A131

James Monroe — A132

William McKinley — A133

Map of Louisiana Purchase — A134

Designed by Clair Aubrey Huston.

Plates of 100 (10x10) subjects, divided vertically into 2 panes of 50.

Exposition Station Machine Cancellation

1904, Apr. 30 — Wmk. 191 — *Perf. 12*

No.	Description	Unused	Used
323	A130 1c **green**	22.50	4.75
	dark green	22.50	4.75
	Never hinged	60.00	
	On cover		7.00
	On Expo. card, Expo. station machine canc.		40.00
	On Expo. card, Expo. station duplex handstamp canc.		100.00
	Block of 4	100.00	35.00
	Margin block of 4, arrow, R or L	110.00	—
	P# pair, Impt., T V	70.00	
	Never hinged	160.00	
	P# strip of 3, Impt., T V	95.00	
	Never hinged	210.00	
	P# block of 4, Impt., T V	190.00	
	Never hinged	325.00	
	P# block of 6, Impt., T V	400.00	
	Never hinged	600.00	
	Diagonal line through left "1" (2138 L 2)	45.00	12.50
	Double transfer	—	

Earliest documented use: Apr. 30, 1904 (FDC).

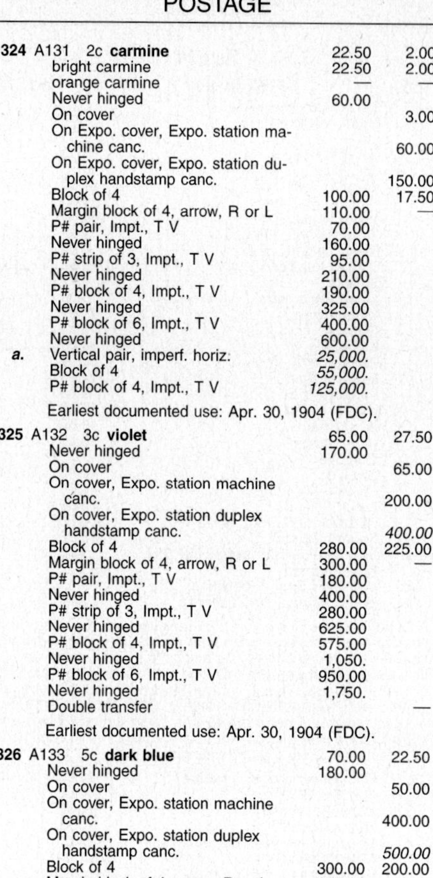

No.	Description	Unused	Used
324	A131 2c **carmine**	22.50	2.00
	bright carmine	22.50	2.00
	orange carmine	—	—
	Never hinged	60.00	
	On cover		3.00
	On Expo. cover, Expo. station machine canc.		60.00
	On Expo. cover, Expo. station duplex handstamp canc.		150.00
	Block of 4	100.00	17.50
	Margin block of 4, arrow, R or L	110.00	—
	P# pair, Impt., T V	70.00	
	Never hinged	160.00	
	P# strip of 3, Impt., T V	95.00	
	Never hinged	210.00	
	P# block of 4, Impt., T V	190.00	
	Never hinged	325.00	
	P# block of 6, Impt., T V	400.00	
	Never hinged	600.00	
a.	Vertical pair, imperf. horiz.	*25,000.*	
	Block of 4	*55,000.*	
	P# block of 4, Impt., T V	*125,000.*	

Earliest documented use: Apr. 30, 1904 (FDC).

No.	Description	Unused	Used
325	A132 3c **violet**	65.00	27.50
	Never hinged	170.00	
	On cover		65.00
	On cover, Expo. station machine canc.		200.00
	On cover, Expo. station duplex handstamp canc.		*400.00*
	Block of 4	280.00	225.00
	Margin block of 4, arrow, R or L	300.00	—
	P# pair, Impt., T V	180.00	
	Never hinged	400.00	
	P# strip of 3, Impt., T V	280.00	
	Never hinged	625.00	
	P# block of 4, Impt., T V	575.00	
	Never hinged	1,050.	
	P# block of 6, Impt., T V	950.00	
	Never hinged	1,750.	
	Double transfer		—

Earliest documented use: Apr. 30, 1904 (FDC).

No.	Description	Unused	Used
326	A133 5c **dark blue**	70.00	22.50
	Never hinged	180.00	
	On cover		50.00
	On cover, Expo. station machine canc.		400.00
	On cover, Expo. station duplex handstamp canc.		*500.00*
	Block of 4	300.00	200.00
	Margin block of 4, arrow, R or L	325.00	—
	P# pair, Impt., T V	190.00	
	Never hinged	425.00	
	P# strip of 3, Impt., T V	300.00	
	Never hinged	675.00	
	P# block of 4, Impt., T V	625.00	
	Never hinged	1,150.	
	P# block of 6, Impt., T V	1,000.	
	Never hinged	1,850.	

Earliest documented use: Apr. 30, 1904 (FDC).

No.	Description	Unused	Used
327	A134 10c **red brown**	125.00	27.50
	dark red brown	125.00	27.50
	Never hinged	300.00	
	On cover		125.00
	On cover, Expo. station machine canc.		450.00
	On cover, Expo. station duplex handstamp canc.		*750.00*
	Block of 4	525.00	225.00
	Margin block of 4, arrow, R or L	575.00	—
	P# pair, Impt., T V	325.00	
	Never hinged	800.00	
	P# strip of 3, Impt., T V	600.00	
	Never hinged	1,400.	
	P# block of 4, Impt., T V	1,250.	
	Never hinged	2,150.	
	P# block of 6, Impt., T V	2,250.	
	Never hinged	4,000.	

Earliest documented use: Apr. 30, 1904 (FDC).

	Nos. 323-327 (5)	305.00	84.25
	Nos. 323-327, never hinged	770.00	

JAMESTOWN EXPOSITION ISSUE
Hampton Roads, Va., Apr. 26 - Dec. 1, 1907

Captain John Smith — A135

Founding of Jamestown — A136

Pocahontas — A137

Plates of 200 subjects in two panes of 100 each.

Exposition Station Machine Cancellation

Designed by Clair Aubrey Huston.

1907 — Wmk. 191 — *Perf. 12*

No.	Description	Unused	Used
328	A135 1c **green,** *Apr. 26*	30.00	4.50
	dark green	30.00	4.50
	Never hinged	75.00	
	On cover		8.00
	On Expo. card, Expo. station machine canc.		25.00
	On Expo. card, Expo. station duplex handstamp canc.		125.00
	Block of 4	125.00	50.00
	Margin block of 4, arrow	130.00	—
	P# strip of 3, Impt., T V	120.00	
	Never hinged	275.00	
	P# block of 6, Impt., T V	600.00	
	Never hinged	900.00	
	Double transfer	32.50	5.50

Earliest documented use: Apr. 26, 1907 (FDC).

No.	Description	Unused	Used
329	A136 2c **carmine,** *Apr. 26*	32.50	4.00
	bright carmine	32.50	4.00
	Never hinged	85.00	
	On cover		6.00
	On Expo. cover, Expo. station machine canc.		100.00
	On Expo. cover, Expo. station duplex handstamp canc.		150.00
	Block of 4	140.00	35.00
	Margin block of 4, arrow	150.00	—
	P# strip of 3, Impt., T V	132.50	
	Never hinged	310.00	
	P# block of 6, Impt., T V	650.00	
	Never hinged	950.00	
	Double transfer	42.50	5.50
a.	2c **carmine lake**	—	

Earliest documented use: Apr. 26, 1907 (FDC).

No.	Description	Unused	Used
330	A137 5c **blue**	150.00	30.00
	deep blue	150.00	30.00
	Never hinged	375.00	
	On cover		80.00
	On cover, Expo. station machine canc.		350.00
	On cover, Expo. station duplex handstamp canc.		*500.00*
	Block of 4	625.00	225.00
	Margin block of 4, arrow	650.00	—
	P# strip of 3, Impt., T V	575.00	
	Never hinged	1,350.	
	P# block of 6, Impt., T V	3,200.	
	Never hinged	6,000.	
	Double transfer	175.00	35.00

Earliest documented use: May 8, 1907.

	Nos. 328-330 (3)	212.50	38.50
	Nos. 328-330, never hinged	535.00	

REGULAR ISSUE

Plates of 400 subjects in four panes of 100 each for all values 1c to 15c inclusive.

Plates of 200 subjects in two panes of 100 each for 50c and $1 denominations.

In 1909 the Bureau prepared certain plates with horizontal spacings of 3mm between the outer seven vertical stamp rows and 2mm between the others. This was done to try to counteract the effect of unequal shrinkage of the paper. *However, some unequal shrinkage still did occur and intermediate spacings are frequently found.* The listings of 2mm and 3mm spacings are for exact measurements. Intermediate spacings sell for approximately the same as the cheaper of the two listed spacings.

All such plates were marked with an open star added to the imprint and exist on the 1c, 2c, 3c, 4c, and 5c denominations only. A small solid star was added to the imprint and plate number for 1c plate No. 4980, 2c plate No. 4988 and for the 2c Lincoln. All other plates for this issue are spaced 2mm throughout.

There are several types of some of the 2c and 3c stamps of this and succeeding issues. These types are described under the dates at which they first appeared. Illustrations of Types I-VII of the 2c (A140) and Types I-IV of the 3c (A140) are reproduced by permission of H. L. Lindquist.

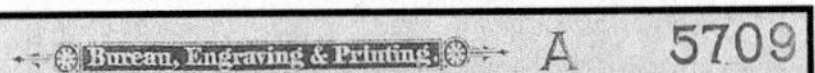

Imprint, plate number and open star

Imprint, plate number and small solid star

Imprint, plate number and "A"

(Illustrations reduced in size)

"A" and number only

Number only

The above illustrations are several of the styles used on plates of issues from 1908 to date.

The previously listed "China Clay Paper" stamps, formerly Scott 331b-332b and 333a-340a, have been removed from the catalogue. Research has shown that the "experimental paper" explanation for the existence of these stamps was incorrect. The only paper experiment during this time period was the 35 percent rag stock paper (Blue Paper, Scott 357-366, 369) of 1909. The stamps previously known as "China Clay Paper" stamps were, in fact, normal stamps printed on paper that was defective to varying degrees. These interesting varieties, which have nothing to do with China clay, can appear to be thin, thick, translucent, opaque, somewhat dark or very dark, but they are not the kind of items that the Scott catalogue or other catalogues normally list. This is not to say that these various paper varieties are of no value or are not of great interest to specialists of the stamps from this period. It is only to say that these various types and degrees of paper varieties are subjects which are beyond the scope of stamp catalogues. Specialist collectors will no doubt continue to study and treasure these varieties.

Franklin — A138

Washington — A139

1908-09 **Wmk. 191** ***Perf. 12***

331	A138 1c **green**, *Dec. 1908*	6.50	.40
	bright green	6.50	.40
	dark green	6.50	.40
	yellow green	6.50	.40
	Never hinged	16.50	
	On cover		.55
	Block of 4 (2mm spacing)	30.00	2.50
	Block of 4 (3mm spacing)	32.50	3.00
	P# block of 6, Impt., T V	100.00	
	Never hinged	175.00	
	P# block of 6, Impt. & star	95.00	
	Never hinged	160.00	
	P# block of 6, Impt. & small solid star (plate 4980)	*1,500.*	
	Never hinged	*2,250.*	
	Double transfer	100.00	100.00
	Cracked plate	—	—
a.	Booklet pane of 6, *Dec. 1908*	150.00	*700.00*
	Never hinged	300.00	

No. 331 exists in horizontal pair, imperforate between, a variety resulting from booklet experiments. Not regularly issued. Value in the grade of fine, $3,750.

No. 331a used is valued with a contemporaneous cancel. A certificate of authenticity is advised.

Earliest documented uses: Dec. 1, 1908 (No. 331); Dec. 2, 1908 (No. 331a single) (FDC).

332	A139 2c **carmine**, *Nov. 1908*	6.00	.35
	light carmine	6.00	.35
	dark carmine	6.00	.35
	Never hinged	14.50	
	On cover		.40
	Block of 4 (2mm spacing)	26.00	2.00
	Block of 4 (3mm spacing)	29.00	2.50
	P# block of 6, Impt., T V	90.00	
	Never hinged	150.00	
	P# block of 6, Impt. & star	85.00	
	Never hinged	140.00	
	P# block of 6, Impt. & small solid star (plate 4988)	*1,750.*	
	Never hinged	*2,750.*	
	Double transfer	12.00	—
	Foreign entry, design of 1c (plate 5299)	*2,250.*	*2,750.*
	On cover		*8,000.*
	Rosette crack	—	
	Cracked plate	—	—
a.	Booklet pane of 6	135.00	*500.00*
	Never hinged	240.00	
b.	2c **lake**	*4,250.*	
	On cover		—

No. 332a used is valued with a contemporaneous cancel. A certificate of authenticity is advised.

No. 332 with foreign entry, used, is valued in the grade of fine and with a contemporaneous cancel.

No. 332b is valued in the grade of fine.

Earliest documented uses: Dec. 2, 1908 (No. 332), Nov. 16, 1908 (No. 332a single) (FDC).

Washington — A140

TYPE I

THREE CENTS

Type I. The top line of the toga rope is weak and the rope shading lines are thin. The 5th line from the left is missing. The line between the lips is thin. (For descriptions of 3c types II, III and IV, see notes and illustrations preceding Nos. 484, 529-530.)

Used on both flat plate and rotary press printings.

333	A140 3c **deep violet,** type I, *Dec. 1908*	30.00	3.00
	violet	30.00	3.00
	light violet	30.00	3.00
	Never hinged	75.00	
	On cover		8.50
	Block of 4 (2mm spacing)	130.00	26.50
	Block of 4 (3mm spacing)	135.00	29.00
	P# block of 6, Impt., T V	390.00	
	Never hinged	625.00	
	P# block of 6, Impt. & star	410.00	
	Never hinged	675.00	
	Double transfer	37.50	5.75

Earliest documented use: Jan. 8, 1909.

334	A140 4c **orange brown,** *Dec. 1908*	35.00	1.50
	brown	35.00	1.50
	light brown	35.00	1.50
	dark brown	35.00	1.50
	Never hinged	87.50	
	On cover		7.00
	Block of 4 (2mm spacing)	150.00	12.50
	Block of 4 (3mm spacing)	160.00	14.00
	P# block of 6, Impt., T V	450.00	
	Never hinged	725.00	
	P# block of 6, Impt. & star	450.00	
	Never hinged	725.00	
	Double transfer	52.50	—

Earliest documented use: Jan. 12, 1909.

335	A140 5c **blue,** *Dec. 1908*	45.00	2.25
	bright blue	45.00	2.25
	dark blue	45.00	2.25
	Never hinged	110.00	
	On cover		8.50
	Block of 4 (2mm spacing)	190.00	20.00
	Block of 4 (3mm spacing)	200.00	17.50
	P# block of 6, Impt., T V	525.00	
	Never hinged	1,000.	
	P# block of 6, Impt. & star	550.00	
	Never hinged	1,050.	
	Double transfer	55.00	—

Earliest documented use: Jan. 10, 1909.

336	A140 6c **red orange,** *Jan. 1909*	62.50	6.00
	pale red orange	62.50	6.00
	orange	62.50	6.00
	Never hinged	145.00	
	On cover		22.50
	Block of 4	270.00	50.00
	P# block of 6, Impt., T V	750.00	
	Never hinged	1,500.	

Earliest documented use: Jan. 6, 1909.

337	A140 8c **olive green,** *Dec. 1908*	45.00	2.75
	deep olive green	45.00	2.75
	Never hinged	105.00	
	On cover		18.00
	Block of 4	190.00	22.50
	P# block of 6, Impt., T V	525.00	
	Never hinged	875.00	
	Double transfer	57.50	—

Earliest documented use: Jan. 8, 1909.

338	A140 10c **yellow,** *Jan. 1909*	70.00	1.80
	Never hinged	165.00	
	On cover		10.00
	Block of 4	290.00	15.00
	P# block of 6, Impt., T V	800.00	
	Never hinged	1,500.	
	Double transfer	—	—
	Very thin paper	—	
a.	10c **brown yellow,** on cover		—

Earliest documented use: Jan. 18, 1909.

339	A140 13c **blue green,** *Jan. 1909*	37.50	17.50
	deep blue green	37.50	17.50
	Never hinged	90.00	
	On cover		110.00
	Block of 4	160.00	175.00
	P# block of 6, Impt., T V	500.00	
	Never hinged	875.00	
	Line through "TAG" of "POSTAGE" (4948 LR 96)	70.00	—

Earliest documented use: Mar. 5, 1909.

340	A140 15c **pale ultramarine,** *Jan. 1909*	67.50	6.00
	ultramarine	67.50	6.00
	Never hinged	160.00	
	On cover		125.00
	Block of 4	280.00	65.00
	P# block of 6, Impt., T V	650.00	
	Never hinged	1,250.	

Earliest documented use: Mar. 12, 1909.

341	A140 50c **violet,** *Jan. 13, 1909*	275.00	20.00
	dull violet	275.00	20.00
	Never hinged	650.00	
	On cover		*5,000.*
	Block of 4	1,200.	150.00
	Margin block of 4, arrow, right or left	1,250.	
	P# block of 6, Impt., T V	*6,000.*	—
	Never hinged	*13,500.*	

Earliest documented use: Oct. 21, 1909 (on registered cover front); June 2, 1916 (on complete cover).

342	A140 $1 **violet brown,** *Jan. 29, 1909*	450.00	95.00
	light violet brown	450.00	95.00
	Never hinged	1,050.	
	On cover		*6,000.*
	Block of 4	2,000.	700.00
	Margin block of 4, arrow, right or left	2,150.	740.00
	P# block of 6, Impt., T V	*20,000.*	
	Never hinged	*32,500.*	
	Double transfer	—	—

Earliest documented use: July 3, 1909 (on parcel tag with two No. 334); July 26, 1909 (on cover).

Nos. 331-342 (12)	1,130.	156.55

For listings of other perforated sheet stamps of A138, A139 and A140 see:

Nos. 357-366 Bluish paper
Nos. 374-382, 405-407 Single line wmk. Perf. 12
Nos. 423A-423C Single line wmk. Perf 12x10
Nos. 423D-423E Single line wmk. Perf 10x12
Nos. 424-430 Single line wmk. Perf. 10
Nos. 461 Single line wmk. Perf. 11
Nos. 462-469 unwmk. Perf. 10

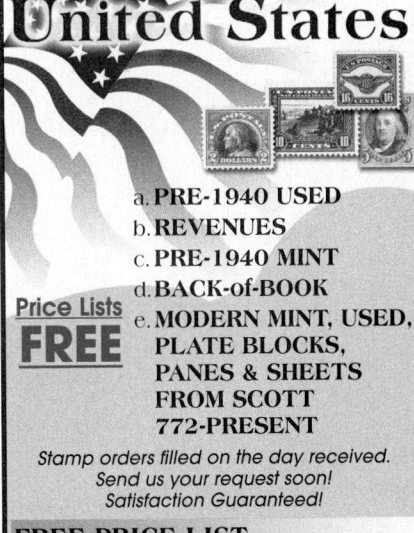

Nos. 498-507 unwmk. Perf. 11
Nos. 519 Double line wmk. Perf. 11
Nos. 525-530 and 536 Offset printing
Nos. 538-546 Rotary press printing

Plate Blocks

Scott values for plate blocks printed from flat plates are for very fine side and bottom positions. Top position plate blocks with full wide selvage sell for more.

Earliest documented use dates for imperforates are for the imperforate sheet stamps, not for imperforate stamps with vending and affixing machine perforations or for flat plate imperforate coil stamps. EDU dates for VAMP and flat plate imperf coil stamps are shown in their respective sections later in the catalogue.

Imperf

343 A138 1c **green,** *Dec. 1908* 5.50 5.00
dark green 5.50 5.00
yellowish green 5.50 5.00
Never hinged 9.00
On cover 12.00
Pair 11.50 11.00
Never hinged 20.00
Block of 4 (2mm or 3mm spacing) 25.00 25.00
Corner margin block of 4, 2mm or 3mm 26.50 27.50
Margin block of 4, arrow, 2mm or 3mm 28.00 27.50
Center line block 35.00 40.00
Never hinged 65.00
P# block of 6, Impt., T V 50.00 —
Never hinged 80.00
P# block of 6, Impt. & star 62.50 —
Never hinged 97.50
P# block of 6, Impt. & small solid star (plate 4980) 675.00
Never hinged 1,050.
Double transfer 12.50 8.00

Earliest documented use: Jan. 4, 1909.

344 A139 2c **carmine,** *Dec. 1908* 5.50 2.75
light carmine 5.50 2.75
dark carmine 5.50 2.75
Never hinged 9.00
On cover 8.00
Pair 11.50 7.00
Never hinged 20.00
Block of 4 (2mm or 3mm spacing) 25.00 16.00
Corner margin block of 4, 2mm or 3mm 26.00 22.50
Margin block of 4, arrow, 2mm or 3mm 28.00 22.50
Center line block 37.50 40.00
Never hinged 67.50
P# block of 6, Impt., T V 77.50 —
Never hinged 120.00
P# block of 6, Impt. & star 70.00 —
Never hinged 110.00
Double transfer 12.50 3.50
Foreign entry, design of 1c (plate 5299) — —

Earliest documented use: Dec. 7, 1908.

The existence of the foreign entry on the imperforate sheet stamp No. 344 has been questioned by specialists. The editors would like to see evidence of the existence of the item, either unused or used.

345 A140 3c **deep violet,** type I, *1909* 11.00 20.00
violet 11.00 20.00
Never hinged 19.00
On cover 65.00
Pair 23.00 50.00
Never hinged 47.50
Block of 4 47.50 110.00
Corner margin block of 4 50.00 115.00
Margin block of 4, arrow 50.00 115.00
Center line block 90.00 140.00
Never hinged 150.00
P# block of 6, Impt., T V 155.00 —
Never hinged 240.00
Double transfer 25.00 —

Earliest documented use: Feb. 13, 1909.

346 A140 4c **orange brown,** *Feb. 25, 1909* 15.00 20.00
brown 15.00 20.00
Never hinged 25.00
On cover 100.00
Pair 32.50 60.00
Never hinged 55.00
Block of 4 (2 or 3mm spacing) 67.50 130.00
Corner margin block of 4 (2 or 3mm spacing) 72.50 135.00
Margin block of 4, arrow, (2 or 3mm spacing) 77.50 135.00
Center line block 135.00 220.00
Never hinged 225.00
P# block of 6, Impt., T V 175.00 —
Never hinged 275.00
P# block of 6, Impt. & star 210.00 —
Never hinged 325.00
Double transfer 35.00 —

Earliest documented use: Mar. 13, 1909.

347 A140 5c **blue,** *Feb. 25, 1909* 30.00 32.50
dark blue 30.00 32.50
Never hinged 50.00
On cover 140.00
Pair 65.00 100.00
Never hinged 110.00
Block of 4 125.00 220.00
Corner margin block of 4 130.00 235.00
Margin block of 4, arrow 140.00 245.00
Center line block 230.00 325.00
Never hinged 400.00
P# block of 6, Impt., T V 275.00 —
Never hinged 500.00
Cracked plate —

Earliest documented use: Mar. 4, 1909.

Nos. 343-347 (5) 67.00 80.25
Nos. 343-347, never hinged 129.00

For listings of other imperforate stamps of designs A138, A139 and A140 see Nos. 383, 384, 408, 409 and 459 Single line wmk.
Nos. 481-485 unwmk.
Nos. 531-535 Offset printing

The values for used coil singles, pairs and line pairs are for examples with contemporaneous cancels that can be authenticated by expertizing committees. Used coils with cancels most commonly from the 1950s exist, and these and stamps with other non-contemporaneous cancels sell for less than the values shown.

COIL STAMPS

1908-10 ***Perf. 12 Horizontally***

348 A138 1c **green,** *Dec. 29, 1908* 45.00 60.00
dark green 45.00 60.00
Never hinged 80.00
On cover 95.00
Pair 110.00 170.00
Never hinged 225.00
Guide line pair 325.00 800.00
Never hinged 650.00

Earliest documented use: Jan. 25, 1909.

349 A139 2c **carmine,** *Jan. 1909* 110.00 160.00
dark carmine 110.00 160.00
Never hinged 235.00
On cover 190.00
Pair 260.00 425.00
Never hinged 600.00
Guide line pair 550.00 1,350.
Never hinged 1,350.
Foreign entry, design of 1c (plate 5299) — 3,000.

Earliest documented use: May 14, 1909.

350 A140 4c **orange brown,** *Aug. 15, 1910* 155.00 250.00
Never hinged 325.00
On cover 390.00
Pair 375.00 800.00
Never hinged 900.00
Guide line pair 1,175. 4,000.
Never hinged 2,600.

Earliest documented use: Mar. 22, 1912.

351 A140 5c **blue,** *Jan. 1909* 155.00 300.00
dark blue 155.00 300.00
Never hinged 325.00
On cover 625.00
Pair 400.00 825.00
Never hinged 850.00
Guide line pair 1,075. 3,500.
Never hinged 2,350.
Nos. 348-351 (4) 465.00 770.00

Earliest documented use: Sept. 21, 1909.

See Nos. 343V-347V in the Imperforate Flat Plate Coil Stamps section of this catalogue for the imperforate counterparts to these perforated coil stamps.

1909 ***Perf. 12 Vertically***

352 A138 1c **green,** *Jan. 1909* 110.00 225.00
dark green 110.00 225.00
Never hinged 235.00
On cover 350.00
Pair (2mm spacing) 260.00 650.00
Never hinged 570.00
Pair (3mm spacing) 250.00 625.00
Never hinged 550.00
Guide line pair 825.00 1,650.
Never hinged 1,800.
Double transfer — —

353 A139 2c **carmine,** *Jan. 12, 1909* 100.00 220.00
dark carmine 100.00 220.00
Never hinged 210.00
On cover 375.00
Pair (2mm spacing) 240.00 600.00
Never hinged 525.00
Pair (3mm spacing) 230.00 575.00
Never hinged 500.00
Guide line pair 750.00 4,000.
Never hinged 1,750.

Earliest documented use: June 14, 1909.

354 A140 4c **orange brown,** *Feb. 23, 1909* 220.00 275.00
Never hinged 425.00
On cover 450.00
Pair (2mm spacing) 525.00 825.00
Never hinged 1,100.
Pair (3mm spacing) 500.00 825.00
Never hinged 1,050.
Guide line pair 1,400. 2,000.
Never hinged 3,000.

Earliest documented use: June 9, 1909.

355 A140 5c **blue,** *Feb. 23, 1909* 230.00 300.00
Never hinged 450.00
On cover 475.00
Pair 525.00 875.00
Never hinged 1,100.
Guide line pair 1,500. 4,000.
Never hinged 3,250.

Earliest documented use: Oct. 25, 1909.

See Nos. 343H-347H in the Imperforate Flat Plate Coil Stamps section of this catalogue for the imperforate counterparts to these perforated coil stamps.

These Government Coil Stamps, Nos. 352-355, should not be confused with those of the International Vending Machine Co., which are perf. 12½-13.

356 A140 10c **yellow,** *Jan. 7, 1909* 3,500. 6,250.
Never hinged 8,000.
On cover 10,000.
Pair 8,250. 15,000.
Never hinged 17,500.
Guide line pair 16,000. 29,000.
Never hinged 45,000.

Earliest documented uses: Mar. 9, 1909 (dated cancel on off-cover stamp); July 6, 1909 (on cover).

The used guide line pair of No. 356 is unique. Value reflects price realized at auction in 2002.
For listings of other coil stamps of designs A138 A139 and A140 see:
Nos. 385-396, 410-413, 441-459, single line watermark.
Nos. 486-496, unwatermarked.

Beware of stamps offered as No. 356 which may be examples of No. 338 with perfs. trimmed at top and/or bottom. Beware also of plentiful fakes in the marketplace of Nos. 348-355, made by fraudulently perforating imperforate stamps or by fraudulently trimming perforations off fully perforated stamps. Authentication of all these coils is advised.

BLUISH PAPER

This was made with 35 percent rag stock instead of all wood pulp. The "bluish" color (actually grayish blue) goes through the paper showing clearly on the back as well as on the face.

1909 ***Perf. 12***

357 A138 1c **green,** *Feb. 16, 1909* 90.00 160.00
Never hinged 190.00
On postcard 185.00
On cover 260.00
Block of 4 (2mm spacing) 380.00 1,000.
Block of 4 (3mm spacing) 750.00
P# block of 6, Impt., T V 1,100.
Never hinged 1,850.
P# block of 6, Impt. & star 3,100.
Never hinged 5,200.

Earliest documented use: Feb. 21, 1909.

358 A139 2c **carmine,** *Feb. 16, 1909* 80.00 150.00
Never hinged 170.00
On cover 200.00
Block of 4 (2mm spacing) 350.00 1,000.
Block of 4 (3mm spacing) 450.00
P# block of 6, Impt., T V 1,000.
Never hinged 1,800.
P# block of 6, Impt. & star 1,650.
Never hinged 2,750.
Double transfer 750.00

Earliest documented use: Feb. 23, 1909.

359 A140 3c **deep violet,** type I 1,800. 12,500.
Never hinged 4,000.
On cover —
Block of 4 7,750.
P# block of 6, Impt., T V 25,000.
Never hinged 35,000.

Earliest documented use: Dec. 27, 1910.

360 A140 4c **orange brown** 27,500.
Never hinged 80,000.
Block of 4 125,000.
P# strip of 3, Impt., T V 165,000.

The No. 360 plate number strip of three is unique.

361 A140 5c **blue** 6,500. 20,000.
Never hinged 15,000.
On cover 27,500.
Block of 4 27,500. —
P# block of 6, Impt., T V 140,000.

Only two examples of No. 361 used off cover (three additional on cover) are recorded. Value used is for the better of the two examples, which is well-centered but has two reattached perforations.
The No. 361 plate block is unique.

Earliest documented use: May 18, 1910.

362 A140 6c **red orange** 1,250. 12,500.
Never hinged 3,000.
On cover 22,500.
Block of 4 5,250.
P# block of 6, Impt., T V 17,500.
Never hinged 30,000.

Earliest documented use: Sept. 14, 1911.

363 A140 8c **olive green** 30,000.
Never hinged 90,000.
Block of 4 135,000.
P# strip of 3, Impt., T V 125,000.

The No. 363 plate number strip of three is unique.

364 A140 10c **yellow**	1,600.	*10,000.*
Never hinged	4,000.	
On cover		—
Block of 4	7,000.	
P# block of 6, Impt., T V	*40,000.*	

Earliest documented use: Feb. 3, 1910.

365 A140 13c **blue green**	2,600.	*3,750.*
Never hinged	6,000.	
On cover		—
Block of 4	*11,500.*	*17,500.*
P# strip of 3, Impt. T V	*10,000.*	
P# block of 6, Impt., T V	*52,500.*	—
Never hinged	*90,000.*	
366 A140 15c **pale ultramarine**	1,300.	*16,000.*
Never hinged	3,000.	
On cover		—
Block of 4	*6,250.*	
P# block of 6, Impt., T V	*16,000.*	
Never hinged	*30,000.*	

Earliest documented use: Jan. 15, 1911.

Nos. 360 and 363 were not regularly issued.

Used examples of Nos. 357-366 must bear contemporaneous cancels, and Nos. 359-366 used must be accompanied by certificates of authenticity issued by recognized expertizing committees.

IMPORTANT INFORMATION
REGARDING VALUES FOR
NEVER-HINGED STAMPS

Collectors should be aware that the values given for never-hinged stamps from No. 182 on are for stamps in the grade of very fine, just as the values for all stamps in the catalogue are for very fine stamps unless indicated otherwise. The never-hinged premium as a percentage of value will be larger for stamps in extremely fine or superb grades, and the premium will be smaller for fine-very fine, fine or poor examples. This is particularly true of the issues of the late-19th and early-20th centuries.

VALUES FOR NEVER-HINGED STAMPS
PRIOR TO SCOTT 182

This catalogue does not value pre-1879 stamps in never-hinged condition. Premiums for never-hinged condition in the classic era invariably are even larger than those premiums listed for the 1879 and later issues. Generally speaking, the earlier the stamp is listed in the catalogue, the larger will be the never-hinged premium.

NEVER-HINGED PLATE BLOCKS

Values given for never-hinged plate blocks are for blocks in which all stamps have original gum that has never been hinged and has no disturbances, and all selvage, whether gummed or ungummed, has never been hinged.

For values of the most popular U.S. stamps in various conditions, including never hinged from No. 182 on, and in the grades of very good, fine, fine to very fine, very fine, very fine to extremely fine, extremely fine, extremely fine to superb, and superb, see the *Scott Stamp Values U.S. Specialized by Grade*, updated and issued each year as part of this U.S. specialized catalogue. This section is located after Postage and before Semi-Postal Stamps.

LINCOLN CENTENARY OF BIRTH ISSUE

Lincoln — A141

Designed by Clair Aubrey Huston.

Plates of 400 subjects in four panes of 100 each

1909 **Wmk. 191** ***Perf. 12***

367 A141 2c **carmine,** *Feb. 12*	4.50	1.75
bright carmine	4.50	1.75
Never hinged	9.50	
On cover		4.00
Block of 4 (2mm spacing)	19.00	15.00
Block of 4 (3mm spacing)	19.00	15.00
P# block of 6, Impt. & small solid star	200.00	
Never hinged	275.00	
Double transfer	7.50	2.75

Earliest documented use: Feb. 12, 1909 (FDC).

Imperf

368 A141 2c **carmine,** *Feb. 12*	12.50	19.00
Never hinged	24.00	
On cover		37.50
Pair	27.50	45.00
Never hinged	57.50	
Block of 4 (2mm or 3mm spacing)	55.00	90.00
Corner margin block of 4	60.00	90.00
Margin block of 4, arrow	62.50	95.00
Center line block	140.00	125.00
Never hinged	250.00	
P# block of 6, Impt. & small solid star	200.00	—
Never hinged	390.00	
Double transfer	35.00	27.50

Earliest documented use: Feb. 12, 1909 (FDC).

See Nos. 368V and 368H in the Imperforate Flat Plate Coil Stamps section of this catalogue for imperforate coil stamps of this design.

BLUISH PAPER

Perf. 12

369 A141 2c **carmine,** *Feb.*	150.00	*225.00*
Never hinged	300.00	
On cover		375.00
Block of 4 (2mm or 3mm spacing)	650.00	*1,250.*
P# block of 6, Impt. & small solid star	*2,750.*	
Never hinged	*4,000.*	
Double transfer	*225.00*	—

Earliest documented use: Feb. 27, 1909 (dated cancel on off-cover stamp); Mar. 27, 1909 (on cover).

Used examples of No. 369 must bear contemporaneous cancels. Expertizing is recommended.

ALASKA-YUKON-PACIFIC EXPOSITION ISSUE

Seattle, Wash., June 1 - Oct. 16, 1909

William H. Seward — A142

Designed by Clair Aubrey Huston.

Plates of 280 subjects in four panes of 70 each

1909 **Wmk. 191** ***Perf. 12***

370	A142 2c **carmine,** *June 1*	6.75	2.00
	bright carmine	6.75	2.00
	Never hinged	15.00	
	On cover		5.00
	On Expo. card or cover, Expo. station machine canc.		65.00
	On Expo. card or cover, Expo. station duplex handstamp canc.		250.00
	Block of 4	29.00	18.00
	P# block of 6, Impt., T V	200.00	
	Never hinged	320.00	
	Double transfer (5249 UL 8)	10.00	4.75
a.	Imperf. (error), P#5209 block of 6	*3,500.*	

Earliest documented use: June 1, 1909 (FDC).

No. 370a comes from error panes found in perforated stock. Plate 5209 was used only to print the perforated Alaska-Yukon-Pacific Exposition issue. No 370a can only be collected as a plate-number stamp or multiple. Without an attached plate number 5209, the stamps from this pane cannot be differentiated from No. 371.

Imperf

371 A142 2c **carmine,** *June*	14.00	21.00
Never hinged	30.00	
On cover		40.00
On cover, Expo. station machine canc.		*450.00*
Pair	30.00	47.50
Never hinged	65.00	
Block of 4	67.50	120.00
Corner margin block of 4	72.50	—
Margin block of 4, arrow	75.00	130.00
Center line block	160.00	175.00
Never hinged	275.00	
P# block of 6, Impt., T V	225.00	—
Never hinged	350.00	
Double transfer	27.50	27.50

Earliest documented use: June 7, 1909.

HUDSON-FULTON CELEBRATION ISSUE

Tercentenary of the discovery of the Hudson River and the centenary of Robert Fulton's steamship, the "Clermont."

Henry Hudson's "Half Moon" and Fulton's Steamship "Clermont" A143

Designed by Clair Aubrey Huston.

Plates of 240 subjects in four panes of 60 each

1909, Sept. 25 **Wmk. 191** ***Perf. 12***

372 A143 2c **carmine**	10.00	4.75
Never hinged	21.00	
On cover		8.50
Block of 4	42.50	30.00
P# block of 6, Impt., T V	280.00	
Never hinged	425.00	
Double transfer (5393 and 5394)	20.00	5.00

Earliest documented use: Sept. 25, 1909 (FDC).

Imperf

373 A143 2c **carmine**	20.00	27.50
Never hinged	40.00	
On cover		40.00
Pair	42.50	60.00
Never hinged	87.50	
Block of 4	90.00	130.00
Corner margin block of 4	95.00	—
Margin block of 4, arrow	100.00	135.00
Center line block	210.00	160.00
Never hinged	360.00	
P# block of 6, Impt., T V	240.00	—
Never hinged	375.00	
Double transfer (5393 and 5394)	55.00	32.50

Earliest documented use: Sept. 25, 1909 (FDC).

Earliest documented use dates for imperforates are for the imperforate sheet stamps, not for imperforate stamps with vending and affixing machine perforations or for flat plate imperforate coil stamps. EDU dates for VAMP and flat plate imperf coil stamps are shown in their respective sections later in the catalogue.

REGULAR ISSUE
DESIGNS OF 1908-09 ISSUES

In this issue the Bureau used three groups of plates:

(1) The old standard plates with uniform 2mm spacing throughout (6c, 8c, 10c and 15c values);

(2) Those having an open star in the margin and showing spacings of 2mm and 3mm between stamps (for all values 1c to 10c); and

(3) A third set of plates with uniform spacing of approximately 2¾mm between all stamps. These plates have imprints showing

a. "Bureau of Engraving & Printing," "A" and number.
b. "A" and number only.
c. Number only.
(See above No. 331)

These were used for the 1c, 2c, 3c, 4c and 5c values.

On or about Oct. 1, 1910 the Bureau began using paper watermarked with single-lined letters:

(Actual size of letter)

repeated in rows, this way:

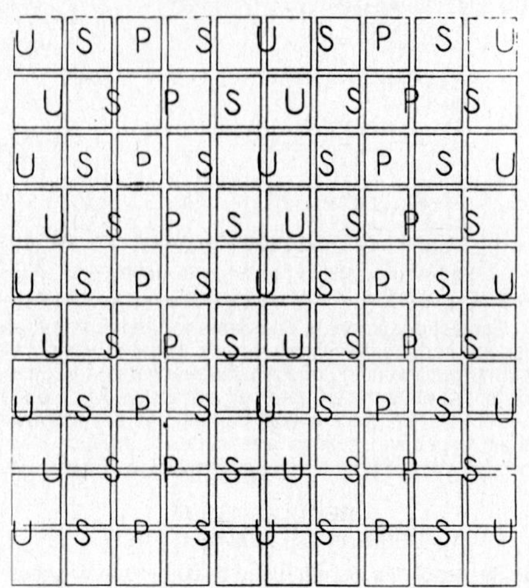

Watermark 190

Plates of 400 subjects in four panes of 100 each

1910-11 Wmk. 190 *Perf. 12*

No.		Unused	Used
374	A138 1c **green,** *Nov. 23, 1910*	6.00	.25
	light green	6.00	.25
	dark green	6.00	.25
	Never hinged	14.00	
	On cover		.30
	Block of 4 (2mm spacing)	26.00	3.25
	Block of 4 (3mm spacing)	28.00	3.00
	P# block of 6, Impt., & star	100.00	
	Never hinged	160.00	
	P# block of 6, Impt. & "A"	125.00	—
	Never hinged	175.00	
	Double transfer	13.00	—
	Cracked plate	—	—
	Pane of 60	*2,250.*	—
a.	Booklet pane of 6, *Oct. 7, 1910*	225.00	*400.00*
	Never hinged	375.00	
b.	Double impression		*300.00*

Earliest documented uses: Dec. 31, 1910 (No. 374); Feb. 28, 1911 (No. 374a single).

Panes of 60 of No. 374 were regularly issued in Washington, D.C. during Sept. and Oct., 1912. They were made from the six outer vertical rows of imperforate "Star Plate" sheets that had been rejected for use in vending machines on account of the 3mm spacing. Therefore, these sheets of 60 are correctly termed the first coil waste issues in U.S. philately.

These panes have sheet margins on two adjoining sides and are imperforate along the other two sides. Upper and lower right panes show plate number, star and imprint on both margins; upper and lower left panes show plate number, star and imprint on side margins, but only the imprint on top or bottom margins. Certification by expertizing committees is strongly recommended, because these panes of 60 could be faked by cutting down full panes of No. 374.

No.		Unused	Used
375	A139 2c **carmine,** *Nov. 23, 1910*	6.00	.25
	bright carmine	6.00	.25
	dark carmine	6.00	.25
	Never hinged	14.00	
	On cover		.30
	Block of 4 (2mm spacing)	26.00	2.00
	Block of 4 (3mm spacing)	25.00	1.75
	P# block of 6, Impt. & star	125.00	
	Never hinged	185.00	
	P# block of 6, Impt. & "A"	135.00	
	Never hinged	200.00	
	Cracked plate	—	—
	Double transfer	12.00	—
	Foreign entry, design of 1c (plate 5299)	—	*1,450.*
a.	Booklet pane of 6, *Nov. 30, 1910*	125.00	*300.00*
	Never hinged	200.00	
b.	2c **lake**	*825.00*	—
	Never hinged	*1,800.*	
c.	As "b," booklet pane of 6	*10,000.*	
d.	Double impression	*750.00*	—
	Never hinged	*1,500.*	

Earliest documented uses: Dec. 3, 1910 (No. 375); April 27, 1911 (No. 375a single).

No.		Unused	Used
376	A140 3c **deep violet,** type I, *Jan. 16, 1911*	18.00	2.00
	violet	18.00	2.00
	Never hinged	40.00	
	lilac	22.50	2.25
	Never hinged	50.00	
	On cover		8.00
	Block of 4 (2mm spacing)	77.50	15.00
	Block of 4 (3mm spacing)	80.00	14.00
	P# block of 6, Impt. & star	300.00	
	Never hinged	450.00	
	P# block of 6	325.00	
	Never hinged	475.00	

Earliest documented use: June 9, 1911.

No.		Unused	Used
377	A140 4c **brown,** *Dec. 1910*	27.50	1.00
	dark brown	27.50	1.00
	orange brown	27.50	1.00
	Never hinged	65.00	
	On cover		7.50
	Block of 4 (2mm spacing)	125.00	6.50
	Block of 4 (3mm spacing)	120.00	6.00
	P# block of 6, Impt. & star	325.00	
	Never hinged	450.00	
	P# block of 6	350.00	
	Never hinged	550.00	
	Double transfer	—	—

Earliest documented use: Dec. 23, 1910.

No.		Unused	Used
378	A140 5c **blue,** *Jan. 25, 1911*	27.50	.75
	light blue	27.50	.75
	dark blue	27.50	.75
	bright blue	27.50	.75
	Never hinged	65.00	
	On cover		5.25
	Block of 4 (2mm spacing)	125.00	6.00
	Block of 4 (3mm spacing)	120.00	5.00
	P# block of 6, Impt., T V	350.00	
	Never hinged	550.00	
	P# block of 6, Impt. & star	350.00	
	Never hinged	550.00	
	P# block of 6, "A"	400.00	
	Never hinged	625.00	
	P# block of 6	400.00	
	Never hinged	625.00	
	Double transfer	—	—

Earliest documented use: Feb. 14, 1911.

No.		Unused	Used
379	A140 6c **red orange,** *Jan. 1911*	37.50	1.25
	light red orange	37.50	1.25
	Never hinged	85.00	
	On cover		13.00
	Block of 4 (2mm spacing)	160.00	13.50
	Block of 4 (3mm spacing)	155.00	12.00
	P# block of 6, Impt., T V	500.00	
	Never hinged	800.00	
	P# block of 6, Impt. & star	440.00	
	Never hinged	700.00	

Earliest documented use: Jan. 12, 1911.

No.		Unused	Used
380	A140 8c **olive green,** *Feb. 8, 1911*	90.00	15.00
	dark olive green	90.00	15.00
	Never hinged	200.00	
	On cover		45.00
	Block of 4 (2mm spacing)	400.00	100.00
	Block of 4 (3mm spacing)	400.00	95.00
	P# block of 6, Impt., T V	1,100.	
	Never hinged	1,900.	
	P# block of 6, Impt., & star	*1,300.*	
	Never hinged	*2,200.*	

Earliest documented use: May 27, 1911.

No.		Unused	Used
381	A140 10c **yellow,** *Jan. 1911*	85.00	6.00
	Never hinged	200.00	
	On cover		22.50
	Block of 4 (2mm spacing)	360.00	50.00
	Block of 4 (3mm spacing)	360.00	47.50
	P# block of 6, Impt., T V	1,150.	
	Never hinged	2,000.	
	P# block of 6, Impt. & star	1,250.	
	Never hinged	2,250.	

Earliest documented use: Jan. 21, 1911.

No.		Unused	Used
382	A140 15c **pale ultramarine,** *Mar. 1, 1911*	225.00	20.00
	Never hinged	500.00	
	On cover		100.00
	Block of 4	950.00	125.00
	P# block of 6, Impt., T V	2,500.	
	Never hinged	4,500.	

Earliest documented use: April 25, 1911.

	Nos. 374-382 (9)	522.50	46.50

Earliest documented use dates for imperforates are for the imperforate sheet stamps, not for imperforate stamps with vending and affixing machine perforations or for flat plate imperforate coil stamps. EDU dates for VAMP and flat plate imperf coil stamps are shown in their respective sections later in the catalogue.

1910, Dec. *Imperf.*

No.		Unused	Used
383	A138 1c **green**	2.50	*2.75*
	dark green	2.50	*2.75*
	yellowish green	2.50	*2.75*
	bright green	2.50	*2.75*
	Never hinged	5.00	
	On cover		6.00
	Pair	5.25	*6.00*
	Never hinged	11.00	
	Block of 4 (2mm or 3mm spacing)	12.50	*20.00*
	Corner margin block of 4	13.50	
	Margin block of 4, arrow	14.00	*22.50*
	Center line block	27.50	*55.00*
	Never hinged	47.50	
	P# block of 6, Impt., & star	50.00	—
	Never hinged	80.00	
	P# block of 6, Impt. & "A"	85.00	—
	Never hinged	130.00	
	Double transfer	6.75	—

Earliest documented use: Jan. 28, 1911.

The top and bottom arrow blocks of 16 with star and plate number are from panes of 160 stamps requisitioned for sale to vending companies. No full panes of 160 are known to the Scott editors. These imperforate sheets tie directly to the panes of 60 of No. 374. See footnote for No. 374. The No. 383 arrow blocks of 16 are from the inner eight columns of panes that have 2mm spacing and were therefore acceptable for vending company manufacturing.

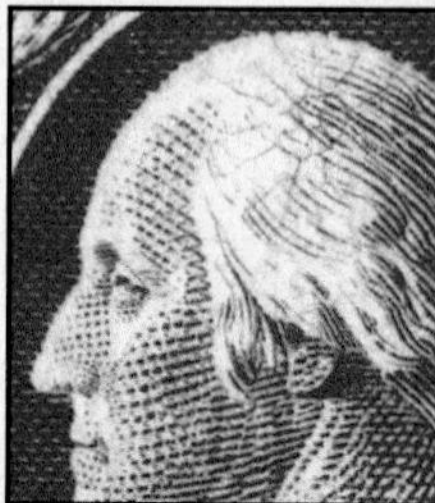

Rosette plate crack on head

No.		Unused	Used
384	A139 2c **carmine**	4.00	2.75
	light carmine	4.00	2.75
	Never hinged	8.00	
	dark carmine	55.00	14.00
	On cover		4.00
	Horizontal pair	11.00	8.25
	Never hinged	22.00	
	Vertical pair	9.00	6.75
	Never hinged	18.00	
	Block of 4 (2mm or 3mm spacing)	25.00	17.50
	Corner margin block of 4	27.50	21.50
	Margin block of 4, arrow	29.00	22.50
	Center line block	52.50	*100.00*
	Never hinged	85.00	
	P# block of 6, Impt. & star	130.00	—
	Never hinged	200.00	
	P# block of 6, Impt. & "A"	170.00	—
	Never hinged	260.00	
	Double transfer	8.00	—
	Rosette plate crack on head	*150.00*	—

Earliest documented use: Dec. 8, 1910.

The values for used coil singles, pairs and line pairs are for examples with contemporaneous cancels that can be authenticated by expertizing committees. Used coils with cancels most commonly from the 1950s exist, and these and stamps with other non-contemporaneous cancels sell for less than the values shown.

COIL STAMPS

1910, Nov. 1 *Perf. 12 Horizontally*

No.		Unused	Used
385	A138 1c **green**	50.00	*50.00*
	dark green	50.00	*50.00*
	Never hinged	100.00	
	On cover		90.00
	Pair	120.00	*250.00*
	Never hinged	260.00	
	Guide line pair	450.00	*850.00*
	Never hinged	1,000.	
386	A139 2c **carmine**	130.00	90.00
	light carmine	130.00	90.00
	Never hinged	260.00	
	On cover		175.00
	Pair	325.00	*2,500.*
	Never hinged	700.00	
	Guide line pair	1,600.	*4,000.*
	Never hinged	3,500.	

Earliest documented use: Dec. 9, 1910.

See Nos. 383V-384V in the Imperforate Flat Plate Coil Stamps section of this catalogue for the imperforate counterparts to these perforated coil stamps.

1910-11 *Perf. 12 Vertically*

No.		Unused	Used
387	A138 1c **green,** *Nov. 1, 1910*	200.00	140.00
	Never hinged	400.00	
	On cover		250.00
	Pair (2mm spacing)	500.00	*500.00*
	Never hinged	1,100.	
	Pair (3mm spacing)	525.00	*500.00*
	Never hinged	1,150.	
	Guide line pair	1,250.	*2,500.*
	Never hinged	2,500.	

Earliest documented use: Nov. 5, 1910.

No.		Unused	Used
388	A139 2c **carmine,** *Nov. 1, 1910*	1,600.	*2,250.*
	Never hinged	4,000.	
	On cover		*3,000.*
	Pair (2mm spacing)	3,750.	*7,500.*
	Never hinged	8,250.	
	Pair (3mm spacing)	4,000.	*8,000.*
	Never hinged	8,500.	
	Guide line pair	*9,000.*	*30,000.*
	Never hinged	*24,000.*	

Stamps offered as No. 388 frequently are privately perforated examples of No. 384, or examples of No. 375 with top and/or bottom perfs trimmed.

Earliest documented use: Jan. 4, 1911.

See Nos. 383H-384H in the Imperforate Flat Plate Coil Stamps section of this catalogue for the imperforate counterparts to these perforated coil stamps.

No.		Unused	Used
389	A140 3c **deep vio.,** type I, *Jan. 24, 1911*	*110,000.*	*10,000.*
	Never hinged	*325,000.*	
	On cover		*25,000.*
	Pair	*240,000.*	*42,500.*

No. 389 is valued in the grade of fine.

Only a small supply of this coil was used at Orangeburg, N.Y. The used pair listed is part of a strip of 3 (three such strips exist). Each strip is in average grade or condition, and the pairs are valued thus. No other used multiples are recorded. There is only one mint, never-hinged example recorded.

Stamps offered as No. 389 sometimes are examples of No. 376 with top and/or bottom perfs trimmed. Expertization by competent authorities is recommended.

Earliest documented use: Mar. 8, 1911.

Beware of plentiful fakes in the marketplace of Nos. 385-389, made by fraudulently perforating the 1c and 2c imperforate stamps or by fraudulently trimming perforations off fully perforated stamps. It is advised that these coils should be accompanied by certificates of authenticity issued by recognized expertizing committees.

1910 ***Perf. 8½ Horizontally***

390 A138 1c **green,** *Dec. 12, 1910* 4.50 *14.00*
dark green 4.50 *14.00*
Never hinged 10.00
On cover 17.50
Pair 10.50 *45.00*
Never hinged 22.00
Guide line pair 35.00 *125.00*
Never hinged 72.50
Double transfer — —

Earliest documented use: Oct. 5, 1911.

391 A139 2c **carmine,** *Dec. 23, 1910* 42.50 *50.00*
light carmine 42.50 *50.00*
Never hinged 90.00
On cover 70.00
Pair 110.00 170.00
Never hinged 240.00
Guide line pair 260.00 *1,500.*
Never hinged 575.00

Earliest documented use: April 30, 1911 (on cover front); May 3, 1911 (on full cover).

See Nos. 383V-384V in the Imperforate Flat Plate Coil Stamps section of this catalogue for the imperforate counterparts to these perforated coil stamps.

1910-13 ***Perf. 8½ Vertically***

392 A138 1c **green,** *Dec. 12, 1910* 32.50 *50.00*
dark green 32.50 *50.00*
Never hinged 65.00
On cover 75.00
Pair 75.00 *145.00*
Never hinged 145.00
Guide line pair 190.00 *500.00*
Never hinged 400.00
Double transfer — —

Earliest documented use: Dec. 16, 1910.

393 A139 2c **carmine,** *Dec. 16, 1910* 52.50 *55.00*
dark carmine 52.50 55.00
Never hinged 105.00
On cover 90.00
Pair 135.00 140.00
Never hinged 260.00
Guide line pair 300.00 *450.00*
Never hinged 650.00

Earliest documented use: Dec. 27, 1910.

See Nos. 383H-384H in the Imperforate Flat Plate Coil Stamps section of this catalogue for the imperforate counterparts to these perforated coil stamps.

394 A140 3c **deep violet,** type I, *Sept. 1911* 67.50 65.00
violet 67.50 65.00
red violet 67.50 65.00
Never hinged 135.00
On cover 125.00
Pair (2mm spacing) 155.00 *220.00*
Never hinged 350.00
Pair (3mm spacing) 150.00 *200.00*
Never hinged 330.00
Guide line pair 425.00 *650.00*
Never hinged 925.00

Earliest documented use: Sept. 18, 1911.

395 A140 4c **brown,** *Apr. 15, 1912* 67.50 *65.00*
dark brown 67.50 *65.00*
Never hinged 135.00
On cover 125.00
Pair (2mm spacing) 155.00 190.00
Never hinged 350.00
Pair (3mm spacing) 150.00 190.00
Never hinged 330.00
Guide line pair 475.00 *650.00*
Never hinged 1,100.

Earliest documented use: June 21, 1912.

396 A140 5c **blue,** *Mar. 1913* 67.50 *65.00*
dark blue 67.50 *65.00*
Never hinged 135.00
On cover 120.00
Pair 160.00 190.00
Never hinged 375.00
Guide line pair 425.00 *825.00*
Never hinged 975.00

Earliest documented use: April 5, 1913.

Beware of plentiful fakes in the marketplace of Nos. 390-393, made by fraudulently perforating imperforate stamps.

PANAMA-PACIFIC EXPOSITION ISSUE

San Francisco, Cal., Feb. 20 - Dec. 4, 1915

Vasco Nunez de Balboa — A144

Pedro Miguel Locks, Panama Canal — A145

Golden Gate — A146

Discovery of San Francisco Bay — A147

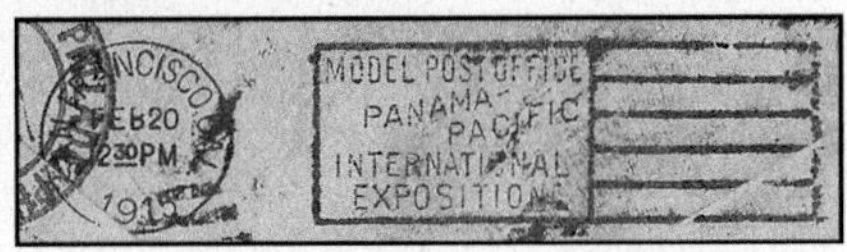

Exposition Station Cancellation.

Designed by Clair Aubrey Huston.

Plates of 280 subjects in four panes of 70 each.

1913 **Wmk. 190** ***Perf. 12***

397 A144 1c **green,** *Jan. 1, 1913* 15.00 2.00
deep green 15.00 2.00
yellowish green 15.00 2.00
Never hinged 35.00
On cover 3.50
On Expo. card, Expo. station 1915 machine cancel *30.00*
Pair on cover, Expo. station 1915 duplex handstamp cancel *150.00*
Block of 4 65.00 14.00
P# block of 6 300.00
Never hinged 450.00
Double transfer 20.00 3.25

Earliest documented use: Jan. 1, 1913 (FDC).

398 A145 2c **carmine,** *Jan. 1913* 16.00 1.00
deep carmine 16.00 1.00
Never hinged 35.00
On cover 1.75
On cover, Expo. station 1915 machine cancel 75.00
On cover, Expo. station 1915 duplex handstamp cancel *250.00*
Block of 4 67.50 10.00
P# block of 6 400.00
Never hinged 625.00
Double transfer 35.00 3.50
a. 2c **carmine lake** *1,600.*
Never hinged *2,500.*
b. 2c **lake** *5,250.* 3,000.
Never hinged *8,500.*

Earliest documented use: Jan. 17, 1913.

399 A146 5c **blue,** *Jan. 1, 1913* 70.00 10.00
dark blue 70.00 10.00
Never hinged 160.00
On cover 27.50
On cover, Expo. station 1915 machine cancel 300.00
Block of 4 280.00 70.00
P# block of 6 1,900.
Never hinged 3,200.

Earliest documented use: Jan. 1, 1913 (FDC).

400 A147 10c **orange yellow,** *Jan. 1, 1913* 115.00 20.00
Never hinged 260.00
On cover 57.50
On cover, Expo. station 1915 machine cancel 500.00
Block of 4 500.00 150.00
P# block of 6 2,250.
Never hinged 3,750.

Earliest documented use: Jan. 1, 1913 (FDC).

400A A147 10c **orange,** *Aug. 1913* 175.00 22.50
Never hinged 390.00
On cover 75.00
On cover, Expo. station 1915 machine cancel 550.00
Block of 4 725.00 120.00
P# block of 6 *9,500.*
Never hinged *16,000.*

Earliest documented use: Nov. 12, 1913.

Nos. 397-400A (5) 391.00 55.50
Nos. 397-400A, never hinged 850.00

1914-15 ***Perf. 10***

401 A144 1c **green,** *Dec. 1914* 25.00 7.00
dark green 25.00 7.00
Never hinged 60.00
On cover 16.00
On Expo. card, Expo. station 1915 machine cancel 75.00
Block of 4 110.00 47.50
P# block of 6 400.00
Never hinged 650.00

Earliest documented use: Dec. 21, 1914.

402 A145 2c **carmine,** *Jan. 1915* 70.00 3.00
deep carmine 70.00 3.00
red 70.00 3.00
Never hinged 170.00
On cover 6.50
On cover, Expo. station 1915 machine cancel 150.00
On cover, Expo. station 1915 duplex handstamp cancel 450.00
Block of 4 300.00 20.00
P# block of 6 1,200.
Never hinged 3,000.

Earliest documented use: Jan. 13, 1915.

403 A146 5c **blue,** *Feb. 1915* 160.00 17.50
dark blue 160.00 17.50
Never hinged 400.00
On cover 55.00
On cover, Expo. station 1915 machine cancel 450.00
Block of 4 700.00 125.00
P# block of 6 3,800.
Never hinged 6,500.

Earliest documented use: Feb. 6, 1915.

404 A147 10c **orange,** *July 1915* 675.00 70.00
Never hinged 1,650.
On cover 175.00

	On cover, Expo. station 1915 machine cancel		600.00
	Block of 4	*3,100.*	500.00
	P# block of 6	*9,500.*	
	Never hinged	*16,500.*	
	Nos. 401-404 (4)	930.00	97.50
	Nos. 401-404, never hinged	2,280.	

Earliest documented use: Aug. 27, 1915.

VALUES FOR VERY FINE STAMPS

Please note: Stamps are valued in the grade of Very Fine unless otherwise indicated.

REGULAR ISSUE

Washington — A140

The plates for this and later issues were the so-called "A" plates with uniform spacing of 2¾mm between stamps.

Plates of 400 subjects in four panes of 100 each for all values 1c to 50c inclusive.

Plates of 200 subjects in two panes of 100 each for $1 and some of the 50c (No. 422) denomination.

1912-14 Wmk. 190 ***Perf. 12***

405	A140 1c **green,** *Feb. 1912*	6.50	.25
	light green	6.50	.25
	dark green	6.50	.25
	yellowish green	6.50	.25
	Never hinged	15.00	
	On cover		.30
	Block of 4	28.00	2.50
	P# block of 6, Impt. & "A"	125.00	
	Never hinged	200.00	
	P# block of 6, "A"	115.00	
	Never hinged	185.00	
	P# block of 6	110.00	
	Never hinged	170.00	
	Cracked plate	14.50	—
	Double transfer	8.50	—
a.	Vert. pair, imperf. horiz.	*2,000.*	—
b.	Booklet pane of 6, *1912*	65.00	*90.00*
	Never hinged	110.00	
c.	Double impression		*5,500.*

Earliest documented uses: Jan. 28, 1912 (No. 405); Jan. 16, 1912 (No. 405b single).

TYPE I

TWO CENTS

Type I. There is one shading line in the first curve of the ribbon above the left "2" and one in the second curve of the ribbon above the right "2."

The button of the toga has only a faint outline.

The top line of the toga rope, from the button to the front of the throat, is also very faint.

The shading lines of the face terminate in front of the ear with little or no joining, to form a lock of hair.

Used on both flat plate and rotary press printings.

406	A140 2c **carmine,** type I, *Feb. 1912*	6.50	.25
	bright carmine	6.50	.25
	Never hinged	15.00	
	dark carmine	7.00	.25
	Never hinged	16.00	
	On cover		.30
	Block of 4	28.00	2.50
	P# block of 6, Impt. & "A"	150.00	
	Never hinged	240.00	
	P# block of 6, "A"	140.00	
	Never hinged	230.00	
	P# block of 6	125.00	
	Never hinged	200.00	
	P# single, Electrolytic, (Pl. 6023)	*2,500.*	
	Never hinged	*4,000.*	
	Double transfer	9.00	—
a.	Booklet pane of 6, *Feb. 8, 1912*	65.00	*90.00*
	Never hinged	110.00	
b.	Double impression	*1,250.*	—
c.	2c **lake,** type I	*2,000.*	*6,000.*
	Never hinged	*4,500.*	

Earliest documented uses: Feb. 15, 1912 (No. 406); May 2, 1912 (No. 406a single).

407	A140 7c **black,** *Apr. 1914*	70.00	14.00
	grayish black	70.00	14.00
	intense black	70.00	14.00
	Never hinged	150.00	
	On cover		75.00
	Block of 4	310.00	100.00
	P# block of 6	1,200.	
	Never hinged	2,000.	

Earliest documented use: May 1, 1914.

Earliest documented use dates for imperforates are for the imperforate sheet stamps, not for imperforate stamps with vending and affixing machine perforations or for flat plate imperforate coil stamps. EDU dates for VAMP and flat plate imperf coil stamps are shown in their respective sections later in the catalogue.

Plate Blocks

Scott values for plate blocks printed from flat plates are for very fine side and bottom positions. Top position plate blocks with full wide selvage sell for more.

1912 ***Imperf.***

408	A140 1c **green,** *Mar. 1912*	1.00	1.00
	yellowish green	1.00	1.00
	dark green	1.00	1.00
	Never hinged	2.00	
	On cover		1.75
	Pair	2.10	2.10
	Never hinged	4.20	
	Block of 4	4.20	4.20
	Corner margin block of 4	4.30	4.30
	Margin block of 4, arrow	4.40	4.40
	Center line block	10.00	*35.00*
	Never hinged	17.50	
	P# block of 6, Impt. & "A," T, B or L	45.00	—
	Never hinged	75.00	
	P# block of 6, Impt. & "A," at right	*550.00*	—
	Never hinged	*850.00*	
	P# block of 6, "A"	26.00	—
	Never hinged	45.00	
	P# block of 6	18.00	—
	Never hinged	29.00	
	Double transfer	2.40	2.40
	Cracked plate	—	—

Earliest documented use: April 26, 1912.

409	A140 2c **carmine,** type I, *Feb. 1912*	1.20	1.20
	deep carmine	1.20	1.20
	scarlet	1.20	1.20
	Never hinged	2.40	
	On cover		2.00
	Pair	2.50	2.50
	Never hinged	5.00	
	Block of 4	5.00	5.00
	Corner margin block of 4	5.25	
	Margin block of 4, arrow	5.50	5.50
	Center line block	11.00	*70.00*
	Never hinged	19.00	
	P# block of 6, Impt. & "A"	47.50	—
	Never hinged	80.00	
	P# block of 6, "A"	45.00	—
	Never hinged	75.00	
	P# block of 6	35.00	—
	Never hinged	57.50	
	Cracked plate (Plates 7580, 7582)	14.00	—

Earliest documented use: Apr. 15, 1912.

In late 1914, the Post Office at Kansas City, Mo., had on hand a stock of imperforate sheets of 400 of stamps Nos. 408 and 409, formerly sold for use in vending machines, but not then in demand. In order to make them salable, they were rouletted with ordinary tracing wheels and were sold over the counter with official approval of the Post Office Department given Jan. 5, 1915.

These stamps were sold until the supply was exhausted. Except for one full sheet of 400 of each value, all were cut into panes of 100 before being rouletted and sold. They are known as "Kansas City Roulettes". Value, authenticated blocks of 4, 1c *$100*, 2c *$200*. No. 408 is known as a block of four imperforate between vertically. Approximately 20 uses on cover are recorded. Most unused examples have authentication initials on reverse (CAS, MOC, ERW, WW, WDW, WCM).

Other private roulettes and perforations on imperforate stamps exist for various imperforates before and after the "Kansas City Roulettes" were issued, and these are also very collectable, but the "Kansas City Roulettes" were the only officially issued roulettes.

Earliest documented uses of "Kansas City Roulettes": Oct. 22, 1914 (No. 408); Nov. 25, 1914 (No. 409).

COIL STAMPS

1912 ***Perf. 8½ Horizontally***

410	A140 1c **green,** *Mar. 1912*	6.00	*12.50*
	dark green	6.00	*12.50*
	Never hinged	13.00	
	On cover		17.50
	Pair	15.00	*42.50*
	Never hinged	32.50	
	Guide line pair	30.00	*100.00*
	Never hinged	65.00	
	Double transfer	—	—

Earliest documented use: Apr. 17, 1912.

411	A140 2c **carmine,** type I, *Mar. 1912*	10.00	*17.50*
	deep carmine	10.00	*17.50*
	Never hinged	22.50	
	On cover		22.50
	Pair	25.00	*55.00*
	Never hinged	55.00	
	Guide line pair	55.00	*175.00*
	Never hinged	125.00	
	Double transfer	12.50	—

Earliest documented use: June 5, 1912.

See Nos. 408V-409V in the Imperforate Flat Plate Coil Stamps section of this catalogue for the imperforate counterparts to these perforated coil stamps.

Perf. 8½ Vertically

412	A140 1c **green,** *Mar. 18, 1912*	25.00	*40.00*
	deep green	25.00	40.00
	Never hinged	55.00	
	On cover		50.00
	Pair	60.00	120.00
	Never hinged	130.00	
	Guide line pair	120.00	*250.00*
	Never hinged	260.00	

Earliest documented use: May 21, 1912.

413	A140 2c **carmine,** type I, *Mar. 1912*	60.00	50.00
	dark carmine	60.00	50.00
	Never hinged	130.00	
	On cover		60.00
	Pair	125.00	100.00
	Never hinged	260.00	
	Guide line pair	275.00	*325.00*
	Never hinged	575.00	
	Double transfer	70.00	—
	Nos. 410-413 (4)	101.00	120.00

Earliest documented use: April 16, 1912.

See Nos. 408H-409H in the Imperforate Flat Plate Coil Stamps section of this catalogue for the imperforate counterparts to these perforated coil stamps.

Beware of plentiful fakes in the marketplace of Nos. 410-413, made by fraudulently perforating imperforate stamps.

Franklin — A148

1912-14 Wmk. 190 ***Perf. 12***

414	A148 8c **pale olive green,** *Feb. 1912*	40.00	2.00
	olive green	40.00	2.00
	Never hinged	100.00	
	On cover		15.00
	Block of 4	170.00	15.00
	P# block of 6, Impt. & "A"	475.00	
	Never hinged	800.00	

Earliest documented use: May 23, 1912.

415	A148 9c **salmon red,** *Apr. 1914*	50.00	14.00
	rose red	50.00	14.00
	Never hinged	120.00	
	On cover		50.00
	Block of 4	210.00	125.00
	P# block of 6	650.00	
	Never hinged	1,100.	

Earliest documented use: May 1, 1914.

416	A148 10c **orange yellow,** *Jan. 1912*	40.00	.80
	yellow	40.00	.80
	Never hinged	100.00	
	On cover		2.75
	Block of 4	170.00	5.25
	P# block of 6, Impt. & "A"	500.00	
	Never hinged	825.00	
	P# block of 6, "A"	550.00	
	Never hinged	900.00	
	Double transfer	—	—
a.	10c **brown yellow**	*1,250.*	—
	Never hinged	*2,750.*	
	On cover		—

Earliest documented use: Feb. 12, 1912 (No. 416); Mar. 30, 1914 (No. 416a).

417	A148 12c **claret brown,** *Apr. 1914*	40.00	5.00
	deep claret brown	40.00	5.00
	Never hinged	100.00	
	On cover		25.00
	Block of 4	170.00	37.50
	P# block of 6	625.00	
	Never hinged	1,050.	
	Double transfer	52.50	—
	Triple transfer	75.00	—

Earliest documented use: May 5, 1914.

418	A148 15c **gray,** *Feb. 1912*	80.00	4.00
	dark gray	80.00	4.00
	Never hinged	190.00	
	On cover		17.50
	Block of 4	340.00	35.00
	P# block of 6, Impt. & "A"	675.00	
	Never hinged	1,400.	
	P# block of 6, "A"	850.00	
	Never hinged	1,550.	
	P# block of 6	1,000.	
	Never hinged	1,700.	
	Double transfer	—	—

Earliest documented use: Apr. 26, 1912.

419 A148 20c **ultramarine,** *Apr. 1914* 190.00 17.50
dark ultramarine 190.00 17.50
Never hinged 400.00
On cover *150.00*
Block of 4 800.00 130.00
P# block of 6 2,000.
Never hinged 3,500.

Earliest documented use: May 1, 1914.

420 A148 30c **orange red,** *Apr. 1914* 115.00 17.50
dark orange red 115.00 17.50
Never hinged 250.00
On cover *250.00*
Block of 4 475.00 130.00
P# block of 6 1,450.
Never hinged 2,400.

Earliest documented use: May 1, 1914.

421 A148 50c **violet,** *1914* 350.00 27.50
bright violet 350.00 27.50
Never hinged 775.00
On cover *2,000.*
Block of 4 1,500. 200.00
P# block of 6 *10,000.*
Never hinged *16,000.*

Earliest documented use: May 1, 1914.

No. 421 almost always has an offset of the frame lines on the back under the gum. No. 422 does not have this offset.

1912, Feb. 12 **Wmk. 191**

422 A148 50c **violet** 225.00 25.00
Never hinged 500.00
On cover *3,250.*
Block of 4 950.00 160.00
Margin block of 4, arrow, R or L 1,000.
P# block of 6, Impt. & "A" *4,750.*
Never hinged *7,500.*

Earliest documented use: Oct. 31, 1914.

423 A148 $1 **violet brown** 475.00 85.00
Never hinged 1,000.
On cover *7,000.*
Block of 4 2,000. 1,000.
Margin block of 4, arrow, R or L 2,100.
P# block of 6, Impt. & "A" *13,500.*
Never hinged *70,000.*
Double transfer (5782 L 66) 600.00 —

Earliest documented use: July 15, 1915.

During the United States occupation of Vera Cruz, Mexico, from April to November, 1914, letters sent from there show Provisional Postmarks.

For other listings of perforated sheet stamps of design A148, see:

Nos. 431-440 — Single line wmk. Perf. 10
Nos. 460 — Double line wmk. Perf. 10
Nos. 470-478 — Unwmkd. Perf. 10
Nos. 508-518 — Unwmkd. Perf. 11

1914 Compound Perforations

As the Bureau of Engraving and Printing made the changeover to perf 10 from perf 12, in the normal course of their stamp production they perforated limited quantities of 1c, 2c and 5c stamps with the old 12-gauge perforations in one direction and the new 10-gauge perforations in the other direction. These were not production errors. These compound-perforation stamps previously were listed as Nos. 424a, 424b, 425c, 425d and 428a.

All examples of Nos. 423A-423E must be accompanied by certificates of authenticity issued by a recognized expertizing committee. Fakes made from perf 12, perf 10 and imperfs exist.

1914 **Wmk. 190** ***Perf. 12x10***

423A A140 1c **green** *12,500.* *5,000.*
Never hinged —
Pair — *13,000.*
Block of 4 — *27,500.*
On postcard *11,000.*
On cover, pair *17,500.*

Formerly No. 424a. Twenty-one unused, 53 used and 4 on-cover examples are recorded. Value for unused is for a sound stamp with perfs touching or just cutting the design. Value for used is for a sound stamp in the grade of fine-very fine. Of the used examples, 23 are precanceled Quincy IL (very scarce) or Chicago (usually inverted). The unused block of four, used block of four and pair on cover are each unique (top stamp of pair on cover with small piece missing and valued thus). Both the unused and used blocks have perforations slightly cutting into the design of each stamp at top. Values are for blocks with such centering.

423B A140 2c **rose red,** type I *175,000.* *10,000.*

Formerly No. 425d. One unused (a plate #7082 single) and 32 used examples are recorded. Value for used is for a sound stamp in the grade of fine-very fine. There are no precancels known on this issue.

423C A140 5c **blue** *15,000.*
Pair —

Formerly No. 428a. 25 used examples are recorded. No unused examples are recorded. Three examples are precanceled: Tampa FL (2) and Rahway NJ (1). Value is for a sound stamp in the grade of fine-very fine. The pair is unique (one stamp creased, the other with a small tear).

Earliest documented use: April 14, 1915 (dated cancel on off-cover stamp).

1914 **Wmk. 190** ***Perf. 10x12***

423D A140 1c **green** *8,500.*
On postcard *22,500.*

Formerly No. 424b. Fifty-one used and 5 covers are recorded. No unused examples are recorded.The majority of stamps are precanceled Dayton OH (most common), Buffalo NY, and Elkhart IN (last two extremely scarce). Value is for a sound stamp in the grade of fine-very fine.
Earliest documented use: Dec. 19, 1914.

423E A140 2c **rose red,** type I —

Formerly No. 425c. Only one used example has been certified (by the Philatelic Foundation). It is well centered, has a machine cancel, and has small thinning and a crease.

Plates of 400 subjects in four panes of 100 each.

Type of plate number and imprint used for the 12 special 1c and 2c plates designed for the production of coil stamps.

1913-15 **Wmk. 190** ***Perf. 10***

424 A140 1c **green,** *Sept. 5, 1914* 2.25 .25
bright green 2.25 .25
deep green 2.25 .25
yellowish green 2.25 .25
Never hinged 4.75
On cover .25
Block of 4 9.50 1.50
P# block of 6 60.00
Never hinged 90.00
Block of 10 with imprint "COIL STAMPS" and number (6581-82, 85, 89) 175.00
Never hinged 350.00
L or R P# block of 6 without imprint "COIL STAMPS" (#6581-82, 85, 89) *850.00*
Cracked plate — —
Double transfer 4.75 —
c. Vert. pair, imperf. horiz. *3,000.* *2,750.*
Never hinged *4,500.*
d. Booklet pane of 6 ('13) 5.25 *7.50*
Never hinged 8.75
f. Vert. pair, imperf. between and with straight edge at top *13,000.*

For former Nos. 424a and 424b, see Nos. 423A and 423D.
The unique example of No. 424f is never hinged, and it is valued thus.

Earliest documented uses: Oct. 11, 1914 (No. 424); Dec. 18, 1913 (No. 424d single); Sept. 24, 1915 (block with "COIL STAMPS" and plate number in selvage).

Research has proven beyond doubt that all examples of the previously listed No. 424e, booklet pane of 6, imperforate and without gum, are unissued fabrications made from an ungummed press sheet on stamp paper once undoubtedly housed in the Smithsonian philatelic collection.

425 A140 2c **rose red,** type I, *Sept. 5, 1914* 2.25 .25
dark rose red 2.25 .25
carmine rose 2.25 .25
carmine 2.25 .25
dark carmine 2.25 .25
scarlet 2.25 .25
red 2.25 .25
Never hinged 5.00
On cover .25
Block of 4 9.50 1.50
P# block of 6 40.00
Never hinged 75.00
Block of 10 with imprint "COIL STAMPS" and number (6568, 70-72) 175.00
Never hinged 350.00
Cracked plate 9.75 —
Double transfer — —
e. Booklet pane of 6, *1913* 17.50 *25.00*
Never hinged 30.00

For former Nos. 425c and 425d, see Nos. 423E and 423B.
The aniline inks used on some printings of Nos. 425, 426 and 435a caused a pink tinge to permeate the paper and appear on the back. These are called "pink backs."

Earliest documented uses: Oct. 27, 1914 (No. 425); Dec. 23, 1913 (No. 425e pair).

426 A140 3c **deep violet,** type I, *Sept. 18, 1914* 15.00 1.25
violet 16.00 1.25
bright violet 16.00 1.25
reddish violet 16.00 1.25
Never hinged 35.00
On cover 3.50
Block of 4 62.50 11.00
P# block of 6 250.00
Never hinged 400.00

See "pink backs" note after No. 425.

Earliest documented use: Oct. 14, 1914.

427 A140 4c **brown,** *Sept. 7, 1914* 32.50 .90
dark brown 32.50 .90
orange brown 32.50 .90
yellowish brown 32.50 .90
Never hinged 75.00
On cover 5.00
Block of 4 135.00 8.50
P# block of 6 475.00
Never hinged 775.00
Double transfer 42.50 —

Earliest documented use: Jan. 2, 1915.

428 A140 5c **blue,** *Sept. 14, 1914* 32.50 .90
bright blue 32.50 .90
dark blue 32.50 .90
indigo blue 32.50 .90
Never hinged 75.00
On cover 3.00
Block of 4 135.00 8.00
P# block of 6 425.00
Never hinged 650.00

For former No. 428a, see No. 423C.

Earliest documented use: Nov. 27, 1914.

429 A140 6c **red orange,** *Sept. 28, 1914* 45.00 2.00
deep red orange 45.00 2.00
pale red orange 45.00 2.00
Never hinged 105.00
On cover 9.00
Block of 4 (2mm spacing) 200.00 15.00
Block of 4 (3mm spacing) 190.00 14.00
P# block of 6, Impt. & star 425.00
Never hinged 725.00
P# block of 6 525.00
Never hinged 875.00

430 A140 7c **black,** *Sept. 10, 1914* 85.00 4.75
gray black 85.00 4.75
intense black 85.00 4.75
Never hinged 190.00
On cover 37.50
Block of 4 360.00 40.00
P# block of 6 1,000.
Never hinged 1,650.

Earliest documented use: April 14, 1915.

431 A148 8c **pale olive green,** *Sept. 26, 1914* 40.00 3.00
olive green 40.00 3.00
Never hinged 80.00
On cover 8.00
Block of 4 175.00 22.50
P# block of 6, Impt. & "A" 525.00
Never hinged 850.00
P# block of 6, "A" 625.00
Never hinged 1,000.
Double transfer — —
a. Double impression —

Earliest documented use: Jan. 20, 1915.

432 A148 9c **salmon red,** *Oct. 6, 1914* 40.00 8.00
dark salmon red 40.00 8.00
Never hinged 80.00
On cover 27.50
Block of 4 175.00 70.00
P# block of 6 725.00
Never hinged 1,150.

Earliest documented use: Oct. 7, 1915 (dated cancel on off-cover block of 4); Feb. 25, 1916 (on cover).

433 A148 10c **orange yellow,** *Sept. 9, 1914* 40.00 1.00
golden yellow 40.00 1.00
Never hinged 80.00
On cover 7.50
Block of 4 170.00 6.00
P# block of 6, Impt. & "A" 650.00
Never hinged 1,100.
P# block of 6, "A" 950.00
Never hinged 1,600.
P# block of 6 825.00
Never hinged 1,400.
a. 10c **brown yellow** —
On cover —

Earliest documented use: Nov. 13, 1914.

434 A148 11c **dark green,** *Aug. 12, 1915* 30.00 8.00
bluish green 30.00 8.00
Never hinged 75.00
On cover 25.00
Block of 4 130.00 65.00
P# block of 6 350.00
Never hinged 550.00

Earliest documented use: Sept. 23, 1915.

435 A148 12c **claret brown,** *Sept. 10, 1914* 30.00 5.50
deep claret brown 30.00 5.50
Never hinged 75.00
On cover 17.50
Block of 4 130.00 45.00
P# block of 6 400.00
Never hinged 600.00
Double transfer 40.00 —
Triple transfer 45.00 —
a. 12c **copper red** 30.00 6.50
Never hinged 75.00
On cover 20.00
Block of 4 130.00 50.00
P# block of 6 350.00
Never hinged 550.00

All so-called vertical pairs, imperf. between, have at least one perf. hole or "blind perfs" between the stamps.
See "pink backs" note after No. 425.

Earliest documented use: Feb. 22, 1915.

437 A148 15c **gray,** *Sept. 16, 1914* 120.00 8.00
dark gray 120.00 8.00
Never hinged 275.00
On cover 52.50
Block of 4 550.00 70.00
P# block of 6, Impt. & "A" 1,100.

Never hinged	2,100.	
P# block of 6, "A"	1,225.	
Never hinged	2,250.	
P# block of 6	1,125.	
Never hinged	2,150.	

Earliest documented use: May 6, 1915.

438 A148 20c **ultramarine**, *Sept. 19, 1914*	200.00	7.00
dark ultramarine	200.00	7.00
Never hinged	450.00	
On cover		*150.00*
Block of 4	850.00	45.00
P# block of 6	3,250.	
Never hinged	*5,500.*	

Earliest documented use: Nov. 28, 1914.

439 A148 30c **orange red**, *Sept. 19, 1914*	225.00	20.00
dark orange red	225.00	20.00
Never hinged	500.00	
On cover		*250.00*
Block of 4	950.00	135.00
P# block of 6	*4,000.*	
Never hinged	*6,750.*	

Earliest documented use: Feb. 13, 1915.

440 A148 50c **violet**, *Dec. 10, 1915*	450.00	20.00
Never hinged	1,100.	
On cover		*1,750.*
Block of 4	2,000.	135.00
P# block of 6	*13,000.*	
Never hinged	—	
Nos. 424-440 (16)	1,390.	90.80

The values for used coil singles, pairs and line pairs are for examples with contemporaneous cancels that can be authenticated by expertizing committees. Used coils with cancels most commonly from the 1950s exist, and these and stamps with other non-contemporaneous cancels sell for less than the values shown.

COIL STAMPS

1914 ***Perf. 10 Horizontally***

441 A140 1c **green**, *Nov. 14, 1914*	1.00	*1.50*
deep green	1.00	*1.50*
Never hinged	2.00	
On cover		2.75
Pair	2.75	*7.00*
Never hinged	5.75	
Guide line pair	8.00	*40.00*
Never hinged	17.50	
442 A140 2c **carmine**, type I, *July 22, 1914*	10.00	*45.00*
deep carmine	10.00	*45.00*
Never hinged	22.50	
On cover		60.00
Pair	25.00	*130.00*
Never hinged	55.00	
Guide line pair	60.00	*300.00*
Never hinged	130.00	
a. 2c lake, type I, on cover		—

See Nos. 408V-409V in the Imperforate Flat Plate Coil Stamps section of this catalogue for the imperforate counterparts to these perforated coil stamps.

At the current time, No. 442a is known only as an example on cover. The editors would like to see authenticated evidence of the existence of unused or used off-cover examples, if such exist.

1914 ***Perf. 10 Vertically***

443 A140 1c **green**, *May 29, 1914*	30.00	*45.00*
deep green	30.00	*45.00*
Never hinged	65.00	
On cover		60.00
Pair	75.00	*135.00*
Never hinged	160.00	
Guide line pair	155.00	*250.00*
Never hinged	325.00	

Earliest documented use: June. 19, 1914.

444 A140 2c **carmine**, type I, *Apr. 25, 1914*	50.00	40.00
deep carmine	50.00	40.00
red	50.00	40.00
Never hinged	120.00	
On cover		57.50
Pair	120.00	125.00
Never hinged	250.00	
Guide line pair	300.00	210.00
Never hinged	650.00	
a. 2c **lake**		*2,000.*

Earliest documented use: May 19, 1914.

See Nos. 408H-409H in the Imperforate Flat Plate Coil Stamps section of this catalogue for the imperforate counterparts to these perforated coil stamps.

445 A140 3c **violet**, type I, *Dec. 18, 1914*	210.00	*250.00*
deep violet	210.00	250.00
Never hinged	500.00	
On cover		*500.00*
Pair	500.00	*750.00*
Never hinged	1,100.	
Guide line pair	1,200.	*2,750.*
Never hinged	2,600.	

Earliest documented use: August 13, 1915.

446 A140 4c **brown**, *Oct. 2, 1914*	130.00	*150.00*
Never hinged	280.00	
On cover		200.00
Pair	300.00	*425.00*
Never hinged	650.00	
Guide line pair	700.00	*1,250.*
Never hinged	1,550.	

Earliest documented use: June 4, 1915.

447 A140 5c **blue**, *July 30, 1914*	45.00	*110.00*
Never hinged	100.00	
On cover		140.00
Pair	105.00	*375.00*
Never hinged	220.00	
Guide line pair	240.00	*950.00*
Never hinged	525.00	

Earliest documented use: May 9, 1916.

Beware of plentiful fakes in the marketplace of Nos. 441-447, made by fraudulently perforating imperforate stamps or by fraudulently trimming perforations off fully perforated stamps.

ROTARY PRESS STAMPS

The Rotary Press Stamps are printed from plates that are curved to fit around a cylinder. This curvature produces stamps that are slightly larger, either horizontally or vertically, than those printed from flat plates. Designs of stamps from flat plates measure about 18½-19mm wide by 22mm high.

When the impressions are placed sidewise on the curved plates the designs are 19½-20mm wide; when they are placed vertically the designs are 22½ to 23mm high. A line of color (not a guide line) shows where the curved plates meet or join on the press.

Rotary Press Coil Stamps were printed from plates of 170 subjects for stamps coiled sidewise, and from plates of 150 subjects for stamps coiled endwise.

Double paper varieties of Rotary Press stamps are not listed in this catalogue. Collectors are referred to the note on "Rotary Press Double Paper" in the "Information for Collectors" in the front of the catalogue.

ROTARY PRESS COIL STAMPS

Stamp designs: 18½-19x22½mm

1915 ***Perf. 10 Horizontally***

448 A140 1c **green**, *Dec., 1915*	12.50	*17.50*
light green	12.50	*17.50*
Never hinged	25.00	
On cover		30.00
Pair	30.00	*50.00*
Never hinged	65.00	
Joint line pair	80.00	*250.00*
Never hinged	170.00	

Earliest documented use: Dec. 11, 1915.

TYPE II

TWO CENTS

Type II. Shading lines in ribbons as on type I.

The toga button, rope and rope shading lines are heavy.

The shading lines of the face at the lock of hair end in a strong vertical curved line.

Used on rotary press printings only.

TYPE III

Type III. Two lines of shading in the curves of the ribbons.

Other characteristics similar to type II.

Used on rotary press printings only.

449 A140 2c **red**, type I, *1915*	2,500.	650.00
Never hinged	5,500.	
carmine rose, type I	2,750.	
On cover, type I		1,500.
Pair, type I	6,000.	*8,000.*
Never hinged	*12,500.*	
Joint line pair, type I	*13,500.*	*25,000.*
Never hinged	*28,000.*	

Earliest documented uses: Oct. 29, 1915 (on cover front or dated cancel on off-cover stamp); Nov. 4, 1915 (on cover).

450 A140 2c **carmine**, type III, *1915*	15.00	*25.00*
carmine rose, type III	15.00	*25.00*
red, type III	15.00	*25.00*
Never hinged	30.00	
On cover, type III		45.00
Pair, type III	30.00	*70.00*
Never hinged	65.00	
Joint line pair, type III	240.00	*300.00*
Never hinged	550.00	

Earliest documented use: Dec. 10, 1915 (dated cancel tying stamp to piece); Dec. 21, 1915 (on cover).

1914-16 ***Perf. 10 Vertically***

Stamp designs: 19½-20x22mm

452 A140 1c **green**, *Nov. 11, 1914*	15.00	*17.50*
Never hinged	30.00	
On cover		30.00
Pair	35.00	*55.00*
Never hinged	75.00	
Joint line pair	90.00	*200.00*
Never hinged	190.00	

Earliest documented use: Nov. 25, 1914.

453 A140 2c **carmine rose**, type I, *July 3, 1914*	140.00	45.00
Never hinged	300.00	
On cover, type I		55.00
Pair, type I	300.00	140.00
Never hinged	625.00	
Joint line pair, type I	675.00	*600.00*
Never hinged	1,450.	
Cracked plate, type I	—	—

Earliest documented use: Sept. 26, 1914.

454 A140 2c **red**, type II, *June, 1915*	70.00	22.50
carmine, type II	70.00	22.50
Never hinged	160.00	
On cover, type II		50.00
Pair, type II	165.00	70.00
Never hinged	360.00	
Joint line pair, type II	400.00	*600.00*
Never hinged	850.00	

Earliest documented use: July 7, 1915.

455 A140 2c **carmine**, type III, *Dec. 1915*	8.00	3.50
carmine rose, type III	8.00	3.50
Never hinged	18.00	
On cover, type III		8.00
Pair, type III	20.00	*27.50*
Never hinged	42.50	
Joint line pair, type III	47.50	*200.00*
Never hinged	105.00	

Earliest documented use: Dec. 15, 1915.

Fraudulently altered examples of Type III (Nos. 455, 488, 492 and 540) have had one line of shading scraped off to make them resemble Type II (Nos. 454, 487, 491 and 539).

456 A140 3c **violet**, type I, *Feb. 2, 1916*	250.00	170.00
deep violet	250.00	170.00
red violet	250.00	170.00
Never hinged	550.00	
On cover		250.00
Pair	575.00	650.00
Never hinged	1,200.	
Joint line pair	1,300.	*3,000.*
Never hinged	2,700.	

Earliest documented use: Apr. 13, 1916.

457 A140 4c **brown**, *1915*	30.00	30.00
light brown	30.00	30.00
Never hinged	60.00	
On cover		50.00
Pair	70.00	95.00
Never hinged	150.00	
Joint line pair	190.00	*275.00*
Never hinged	390.00	
Cracked plate	40.00	—

Earliest documented use: Nov. 5, 1915.

458 A140 5c **blue**, *Mar. 9, 1916*	32.50	30.00
Never hinged	65.00	
On cover		50.00
Pair	75.00	95.00
Never hinged	160.00	
Joint line pair	180.00	*250.00*
Never hinged	375.00	
Double transfer	—	—

Earliest documented use: Apr. 6, 1916.

Horizontal Coil

1914, June 30 ***Imperf.***

459 A140 2c **carmine**, type I	275.	*1,300.*
Never hinged	400.	
Pair	600.	*3,500.*
Never hinged	875.	
Joint line pair, with crease	700.	—
Never hinged	1,200.	
Joint line pair, without crease	1,200.	*50,000.*
Never hinged	2,000.	

Most line pairs of No. 459 are creased. The value for joint line pair with crease is for a pair creased vertically between the stamps, but not touching the design.

When the value for a used stamp is higher than the unused value, the stamp must have a contemporaneous cancel. Valuable stamps of this type should be accompanied by certificates of authenticity issued by recognized expertizing committees. The used value for No. 459 is for an example with such a certificate.

Beware of examples of No. 453 with perforations fraudulently trimmed to resemble single examples of No. 459.

Earliest documented use: Dec. 1914 (dated cancel on a used joint line pair, off cover).

FLAT PLATE PRINTINGS

1915 Wmk. 191 *Perf. 10*

460 A148 $1 **violet black,** *Feb. 8* 650. 140.
Never hinged 1,450.
On cover *12,000.*
Block of 4 2,400. 750.
Margin block of 4, arrow, R or L 3,000.
P# block of 6, Impt. & "A" *11,000.*
Never hinged *17,000.*
Double transfer (5782 L. 66) 800. 175.

Earliest documented uses: May 25, 1916 (dated cancel on stamp on mailing tag); June 2, 1916 (unique usage on cover is from Shanghai, China).

Wmk. 190 *Perf. 11*

461 A140 2c **pale car. red,** type I, *June 17* 160. *375.*
Never hinged 330.
On cover *1,200.*
Block of 4 675. *3,000.*
P# block of 6 *1,500.*
Never hinged *2,600.*

Beware of fraudulently perforated examples of No. 409 being offered as No. 461.
See note on used stamps following No. 459.

Earliest documented use: June 24, 1915.

VALUES FOR VERY FINE STAMPS
Please note: Stamps are valued in the grade of Very Fine unless otherwise indicated.

FLAT PLATE PRINTINGS

Plates of 400 subjects in four panes of 100 each for all values 1c to 50c inclusive.

Plates of 200 subjects in two panes of 100 each for $1, $2 and $5 denominations.

The Act of Oct. 3, 1917, effective Nov. 2, 1917, created a 3 cent rate. Local rate, 2 cents.

1916-17 Unwmk. *Perf. 10*

462 A140 1c **green,** *Sept. 27, 1916* 7.00 .35
light green 7.00 .35
dark green 7.00 .35
bluish green 7.00 .35
blackish green — —
Never hinged 16.00
On cover .50
Block of 4 30.00 3.25
P# block of 6 160.00
Never hinged 275.00
Experimental bureau precancel, New Orleans 8.00
Experimental bureau precancel, Springfield, Mass. 8.00
Experimental bureau precancel, Augusta, Me. 17.50
a. Booklet pane of 6, *Oct. 15, 1916* 9.50 *12.50*
Never hinged 16.00
Cracked plate at right (Plate 7449, pane 9) 250.00 —
Never hinged 350.00
Cracked plate at left (Plate 7449, pane 10) 310.00
Never hinged 425.00

Earliest documented uses: Oct. 3, 1916 (No. 462); Apr. 5, 1917 (No. 462a single).

463 A140 2c **carmine,** type I, *Sept. 1916* 4.50 .40
dark carmine 4.50 .40
rose red 4.50 .40
Never hinged 10.00
On cover .45
Block of 4 20.00 3.50
P# block of 6 150.00
Never hinged 250.00
Double transfer 6.50 —
Experimental bureau precancel, New Orleans *1,000.*
Experimental bureau precancel, Springfield, Mass. 22.50
a. Booklet pane of 6, *Oct. 8, 1916* 110.00 *110.00*
Never hinged 180.00

See No. 467 for P# block of 6 from plate 7942.

Earliest documented uses: Sept. 12, 1916 (No. 463).

464 A140 3c **violet,** type I, *Nov. 11, 1916* 65.00 17.50
deep violet 65.00 17.50
Never hinged 165.00
On cover 40.00
Block of 4 300.00 150.00
P# block of 6 1,500.
Never hinged 2,500.
Double transfer in "CENTS" *90.00* —
Experimental bureau precancel, New Orleans *1,500.*
Experimental bureau precancel, Springfield, Mass. 400.00

Beware of fraudulently perforated examples of No. 483 being offered as No. 464.

Earliest documented use: Mar. 9, 1917.

465 A140 4c **orange brown,** *Oct. 7, 1916* 60.00 2.25
deep brown 60.00 2.25
brown 60.00 2.25
Never hinged 125.00
On cover 10.00
Block of 4 250.00 22.50
P# block of 6 950.00
Never hinged 1,550.
Double transfer — —
Experimental bureau precancel, Springfield, Mass. 300.00

Earliest documented use: Jan. 20, 1917.

466 A140 5c **blue,** *Oct. 17, 1916* 65.00 2.25
dark blue 65.00 2.25
Never hinged 150.00
On cover 12.00
Block of 4 270.00 22.50
P# block of 6 950.00
Never hinged 1,600.
Experimental bureau precancel, Springfield, Mass. 250.00

Earliest documented use: Dec. 7, 1916.

467 A140 5c **carmine** (error in plate of 2c) 425.00 *3,250.*
Never hinged 800.00
On cover *7,500.*
Block of 9, #467 in middle 900.00 *3,750.*
Never hinged 1,550.
Block of 12, two middle stamps #467 1,750. *5,250.*
Never hinged 2,900.
P# block of 6 2c stamps (#463), P#7942 140.00
Never hinged 250.00

No. 467 is an error caused by using a 5c transfer roll in re-entering three subjects: 7942 UL 74, 7942 UL 84, 7942 LR 18; the balance of the subjects on the plate being normal 2c entries. No. 467 imperf. is listed as No. 485. The error perf 11 on unwatermarked paper is No. 505.

The first value given for the error in blocks of 9 and 12 is for blocks with the error stamp(s) never hinged. The second value given is for blocks in which all stamps are never hinged. See note on used stamps following No. 459.

Earliest documented use: May 22, 1917.

468 A140 6c **red orange,** *Oct. 10, 1916* 100.00 8.00
Never hinged 225.00
On cover 35.00
Block of 4 425.00 70.00
P# block of 6 1,500.
Never hinged 2,750.
Double transfer — —
Experimental bureau precancel, New Orleans *3,000.*
Experimental bureau precancel, Springfield, Mass. 350.00

Earliest documented use: Feb. 27, 1917 (dated cancel on off-cover block of 4); April 19, 1917 (on cover).

469 A140 7c **black,** *Oct. 10, 1916* 120.00 13.00
gray black 120.00 13.00
Never hinged 270.00
On cover 45.00
Block of 4 500.00 125.00
P# block of 6 1,350.
Never hinged 2,500.
Experimental bureau precancel, Springfield, Mass. 250.00

Earliest documented use: Feb. 19, 1917.

470 A148 8c **olive green,** *Nov. 13, 1916* 80.00 7.00
dark olive green 80.00 7.00
Never hinged 165.00
On cover 25.00
Block of 4 350.00 60.00
P# block of 6, Impt. & "A" 650.00
Never hinged 1,050.
P# block of 6, "A" 700.00
Never hinged 1,225.
Experimental bureau precancel, Springfield, Mass. 200.00

Earliest documented use: Dec. 29, 1916 (dated cancel on off-cover block of 4); Feb. 13, 1917 (on cover).

471 A148 9c **salmon red,** *Nov. 16, 1916* 90.00 17.50
Never hinged 190.00
On cover 40.00
Block of 4 375.00 140.00
P# block of 6 825.00
Never hinged 1,375.
Experimental bureau precancel, Springfield, Mass. 200.00

Earliest documented use: Aug. 6, 1917.

472 A148 10c **orange yellow,** *Oct. 17, 1916* 120.00 3.00
Never hinged 250.00
On cover 8.50
Block of 4 490.00 17.50
P# block of 6 1,400.
Never hinged 2,350.
Experimental bureau precancel, Springfield, Mass. 175.00

Earliest documented use: Oct. 24, 1916.

473 A148 11c **dark green,** *Nov. 16, 1916* 50.00 19.00
Never hinged 110.00
On cover 47.50
Block of 4 210.00 140.00
P# block of 6 425.00
Never hinged 750.00
Experimental bureau precancel, Springfield, Mass. *1,000.*

Earliest documented use: Apr. 13, 1917.

474 A148 12c **claret brown,** *Oct. 1916* 55.00 8.00
Never hinged 120.00
On cover 22.50
Block of 4 230.00 55.00
P# block of 6 675.00
Never hinged 1,125.
Double transfer 80.00 9.00
Triple transfer 92.50 12.00
Experimental bureau precancel, Springfield, Mass. 300.00
a. 12c **copper red** 75.00 12.50
Never hinged 170.00

Earliest documented uses: Oct. 6, 1916 (dated cancel on off-cover pair); Oct. 13, 1916 (on cover).

475 A148 15c **gray,** *Nov. 16, 1916* 170.00 15.00
dark gray 170.00 15.00
Never hinged 375.00
On cover 85.00
Block of 4 725.00 120.00
P# block of 6 3,000.
Never hinged 5,250.
P# block of 6, Impt. & "A" *8,000.*
Experimental bureau precancel, Springfield, Mass. 200.00

Earliest documented use: Mar. 2, 1917.

476 A148 20c **light ultramarine,** *Dec. 5, 1916* 240.00 17.50
ultramarine 240.00 17.50
Never hinged 500.00
On cover *725.00*
Block of 4 1,000. 130.00
P# block of 6 3,750.
Never hinged *6,400.*
Experimental bureau precancel, Springfield, Mass. 125.00

476A A148 30c **orange red** *2,000.*
Never hinged *4,250.*
Block of 4 *10,000.*
Never hinged *20,000.*
P# block of 6 *30,000.*
Never hinged *50,000.*

No. 476A is valued in the grade of fine.

477 A148 50c **light violet,** *Mar. 2, 1917* 850. 80.00
Never hinged 2,000.
On cover *2,250.*
Block of 4 3,750. 575.00
P# block of 6 *60,000.*
Never hinged —

Earliest documented use: Aug. 31, 1917.

478 A148 $1 **violet black,** *Dec. 22, 1916* 600. 27.50
Never hinged 1,400.
On cover *3,000.*
Block of 4 2,600. 200.00
Margin block of 4, arrow, R or L 2,800.
P# block of 6, Impt. & "A" *10,000.*
Never hinged *17,500.*
Double transfer (5782 L 66) 675. 30.00

Earliest documented use: May 24, 1917 (on large part of parcel label).

TYPES OF 1902-03 ISSUE

1917, Mar. 22 Unwmk. *Perf. 10*

479 A127 $2 **dark blue** 210.00 40.00
Never hinged 475.00
On cover (other than first flight or Zeppelin) *1,250.*
On first flight cover *350.00*
On Zeppelin flight cover *750.00*
Block of 4 925.00 325.00
Margin block of 4, arrow, R or L 1,050.
P# block of 6 4,000.
Never hinged *6,500.*
Double transfer —

Earliest documented use (on large piece of reg'd parcel wrapper): Apr. 6, 1917.

480 A128 $5 **light green** 170.00 35.00
Never hinged 375.00
On cover *1,250.*
Block of 4 750.00 280.00
Margin block of 4, arrow, R or L 850.00
P# block of 6 3,000. —
Never hinged *5,000.*

Earliest documented use: Apr. 6, 1917 (on large piece of reg'd parcel wrapper).

Earliest documented use dates for imperforates are for the imperforate sheet stamps, not for imperforate stamps with vending and affixing machine perforations or for flat plate imperforate coil stamps. EDU dates for VAMP and flat plate imperf coil stamps are shown in their respective sections later in the catalogue.

1916-17 *Imperf.*

481 A140 1c **green,** *Nov. 1916* 1.25 .95
bluish green 1.25 .95
deep green 1.25 .95
Never hinged 1.90
On cover 1.50
Pair 2.60 2.00
Never hinged 4.00
Block of 4 5.25 4.00
Corner margin block of 4 5.50 4.25
Margin block of 4, arrow 5.75 4.40
Center line block 10.00 *22.50*
Never hinged 16.50
P# block of 6 30.00 —
Never hinged 45.00
Margin block of 6, Electrolytic (Pl. 13376) 450.00
Never hinged 800.00

Margin block of 6, Electrolytic (Pl. 13377) 1,000.
Never hinged 1,500.
Single, Electrolytic 5.00
Never hinged 10.00
Double transfer 2.75 2.75

Earliest documented use: Nov. 17, 1916.

During September 1921, the Bureau of Engraving and Printing issued a 1c stamp printed from experimental electrolytic plates made in accordance with a patent granted to George U. Rose. Tests at that time did not prove satisfactory, and the method was discontinued. Four plates were made: 13376, 13377, 13389 and 13390, from which stamps were issued. They are difficult to distinguish from the normal varieties, but can be authenticated by experts. Singles and blocks must be certified. (See No. 498).

TYPE Ia

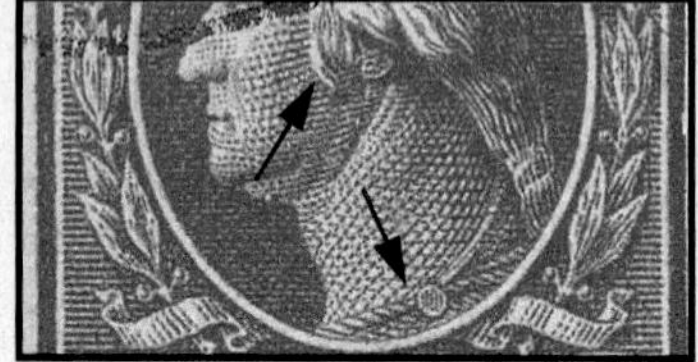

TWO CENTS

Type Ia. The design characteristics are similar to type I except that all of the lines of the design are stronger.

The toga button, toga rope and rope shading lines are heavy.

The latter characteristics are those of type II, which, however, occur only on impressions from rotary plates.

Used only on flat plates 10208 and 10209.

482 A140 2c **carmine,** type I, *Dec. 8, 1916* 1.50 1.30
deep carmine 1.50 1.30
carmine rose 1.50 1.30
deep rose 1.50 1.30
Never hinged 2.60
On cover 2.50
Pair 3.20 2.75
Never hinged 5.50
Block of 4 6.50 6.50
Corner margin block of 4 6.75 *6.75*
Margin block of 4, arrow 7.00 *7.00*
Center line block 9.50 *20.00*
Never hinged 15.00
P# block of 6 30.00 —
Never hinged 45.00
Cracked plate — —

Earliest documented use: Dec. 16, 1916.

See No. 485 for P# block of 6 from plate 7942.

482A A140 2c **deep rose,** type Ia — *55,000.*
On cover *70,000.*
Pair *147,500.*

Earliest documented use: Feb. 17, 1920.

The imperforate, type Ia, was issued but all known examples were privately perforated with large oblong perforations at the sides (Schermack type III). See the vending and affixing machine perforations section of this catalogue.

The No. 482A pair is unique.

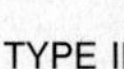
TYPE II

THREE CENTS

Type II. The top line of the toga rope is strong and the rope shading lines are heavy and complete.

The line between the lips is heavy.

Used on both flat plate and rotary press printings.

483 A140 3c **violet,** type I, *Oct. 13, 1917* 12.00 10.00
light violet 12.00 10.00
Never hinged 24.00
On cover 25.00
Pair 25.00 22.50
Never hinged 50.00
Block of 4 50.00 45.00
Corner margin block of 4 52.50 47.50
Margin block of 4, arrow 55.00 50.00
Center line block 80.00 *100.00*
Never hinged 140.00
P# block of 6 125.00 —
Never hinged 200.00
Double transfer 20.00 —
Triple transfer —

Earliest documented use: Nov. 8, 1917.

484 A140 3c **violet,** type II 10.00 8.00
deep violet 10.00 8.00
Never hinged 20.00
On cover 14.00
Pair 21.00 17.00
Never hinged 42.50
Block of 4 42.50 35.00
Corner margin block of 4 45.00 37.50
Margin block of 4, arrow 47.50 40.00
Center line block 75.00 *100.00*
Never hinged 140.00
P# block of 6 95.00 —
Never hinged 160.00
Double transfer 14.00 —

Earliest documented use: Apr. 30, 1918.

485 A140 5c **carmine** (error), *Mar. 1917* *10,000.*
Never hinged *14,000.*
Block of 9, #485 in middle *17,500.*
Never hinged *23,500.*
Block of 12, two middle stamps #485 *26,000.*
Never hinged *33,500.*
P# block of six 2c stamps (#482), P#7942 130.00
Never hinged 220.00

No. 485 is usually seen either as the center stamp in a block of 9 with 8 No. 482 (the first value given being with No. 485 never hinged) or as two center stamps in a block of 12 (the first value given being with both examples of No. 485 never hinged). A second value is given for each block with all stamps in the block never hinged.

See note under No. 467.

ROTARY PRESS COIL STAMPS
(See note over No. 448)

1916-18 ***Perf. 10 Horizontally***

Stamp designs: 18½-19x22½mm

486 A140 1c **green,** *Jan. 1918* .85 .85
yellowish green .85 .85
Never hinged 1.75
On cover 1.15
Pair 2.00 *2.50*
Never hinged 4.25
Joint line pair 4.50 *15.00*
Never hinged 9.50
Cracked plate — —
Double transfer 2.25 —

Earliest documented use: June 30, 1918.

487 A140 2c **carmine,** type II, *Nov. 15, 1916* 12.50 14.00
Never hinged 27.50
On cover 19.00
Pair 30.00 37.50
Never hinged 65.00
Joint line pair 120.00 *140.00*
Never hinged 275.00
Cracked plate *600.00*

Earliest documented use: Sept. 21, 1917.

(See note after No. 455)

488 A140 2c **carmine,** type III, *1916* 3.00 *5.00*
carmine rose 3.00 *5.00*
Never hinged 6.50
On cover 7.00
Pair 8.00 *17.50*
Never hinged 17.50
Joint line pair 40.00 *110.00*
Never hinged 90.00
Cracked plate 12.50 10.00

Earliest documented use: Feb. 12, 1917.

489 A140 3c **violet,** type I, *Oct. 10, 1917* 4.50 2.25
dull violet 4.50 2.25
bluish violet 4.50 2.25
Never hinged 10.00
On cover 3.50
Pair 10.50 9.00
Never hinged 22.50
Joint line pair 32.50 *40.00*
Never hinged 70.00

Earliest documented use: Nov. 23, 1917.

Rosette plate crack on head

1916-22 ***Perf. 10 Vertically***

Stamp designs: 19½-20x22mm

490 A140 1c **green,** *Nov. 17, 1916* .50 *.60*
yellowish green .50 *.60*
Never hinged 1.05
On cover .80
Pair 1.25 *2.25*
Never hinged 2.60
Joint line pair 3.25 *12.50*
Never hinged 7.00
Double transfer — —
Cracked plate (horizontal) 7.50 —
Cracked plate (vertical) retouched 9.00 —
Rosette plate crack on head *60.00* —
a. Small holes, pair —
Joint line pair —
Never hinged —

Earliest documented use: No. 490: Jan. 3, 1917 (dated cancel on off-cover pair); Feb. 14, 1917 (on cover).

491 A140 2c **carmine,** type II, *Nov. 17, 1916* 2,500. 800.00
Never hinged 5,250.
On cover, type II 1,100.
Pair, type II 5,750. 3,750.
Never hinged *12,500.*
Joint line pair, type II *13,000.* *17,500.*
Never hinged *26,000.*

Earliest documented use: Dec. 5, 1916 (dated cancel on off-cover rejoined pair); Dec. 5, 1916 (on cover).

See note after No. 455.

492 A140 2c **carmine,** type III 9.00 1.00
carmine rose, type III 9.00 1.00
Never hinged 19.00
On cover, type III 1.40
Pair, type III 21.50 5.00
Never hinged 45.00
Joint line pair, type III 55.00 *35.00*
Never hinged 115.00
Double transfer, type III — —
Cracked plate — —
a. Small holes, joint line pair — —

Earliest documented use: Jan. 13, 1917 (No. 492).

493 A140 3c **violet,** type I, *July 23, 1917* 14.00 4.50
reddish violet, type I 14.00 4.50
Never hinged 30.00
On cover, type I 8.00
Pair, type I 35.00 12.50
Never hinged 75.00
Joint line pair, type I 110.00 *90.00*
Never hinged 230.00

Earliest documented use: Nov. 2, 1917.

494 A140 3c **violet,** type II, *Feb. 4, 1918* 10.00 2.50
dull violet, type II 10.00 2.50
gray violet, type II 10.00 2.50
Never hinged 21.50
On cover, type II 4.00
Pair, type II 24.00 9.00
Never hinged 50.00
Joint line pair, type II 75.00 50.00
Never hinged 160.00

Earliest documented use: Apr. 16, 1918.

495 A140 4c **orange brown,** *Apr. 15, 1917* 10.00 7.00
Never hinged 21.50
On cover 10.00
Pair 24.00 20.00
Never hinged 50.00
Joint line pair 75.00 45.00
Never hinged 160.00
Cracked plate 25.00 —
a. Small holes, pair —
Joint line pair —
Never hinged —

Earliest documented use: June 20, 1917 (No. 495).

496 A140 5c **blue,** large holes, *Jan. 15, 1919* 3.25 2.50
Never hinged 7.00
On cover 3.00
Pair 8.00 10.00
Never hinged 17.50
Joint line pair 30.00 22.50
Never hinged 65.00
a. Small holes *100.00* —
Pair *225.00* —
Never hinged *450.00*
Joint line pair *375.00*
Never hinged *750.00*

See note concerning large and small perforation holes following No. 1053.

Earliest documented use: April 15, 1919.

497 A148 10c **orange yellow,** *Jan. 31, 1922* 17.50 17.50
Never hinged 35.00
On cover 22.50
Pair 40.00 *57.50*
Never hinged 85.00
Joint line pair 120.00 *200.00*
Never hinged 260.00

Earliest documented use: Jan. 31, 1922 (FDC).

Blind Perfs

Listings of imperforate-between varieties are for examples which show no trace of "blind perfs," traces of impressions from the perforating pins which do not cut into the paper.

Some unused stamps have had the gum removed to eliminate the impressions from the perforating pins. These stamps do not qualify as the listed varieties.

TYPES OF 1913-15 ISSUE

FLAT PLATE PRINTINGS

Plates of 400 subjects in four panes of 100.

1917-19 **Unwmk.** ***Perf. 11***

498 A140 1c **green,** *Mar. 1917* .50 .25
light green .50 .25
dark green .50 .25
yellowish green .50 .25
Never hinged 1.00
On cover .30
Block of 4 2.00 1.50
P# block of 6 22.50
Never hinged 35.00
Margin block of 6, Electrolytic (Pl, 13376-7, 13389-90) *See note after No. 481* *1,250.*
Never hinged *2,000.*
Single, Electrolytic (See note after No. 481) *25.00*
Never hinged *50.00*

	Single, Electrolytic, pl. #13390, on postcard		—
	Cracked plate (10656 UL and 10645 LR)	35.00	—
	Double transfer	5.50	2.00
a.	Vertical pair, imperf. horiz.	800.00	
	Never hinged	*1,600.*	
b.	Horizontal pair, imperf. between	700.00	
	Never hinged	*1,500.*	
c.	Vertical pair, imperf. between	*700.00*	—
d.	Double impression	250.00	*3,750.*
e.	Booklet pane of 6, *March 1917*	2.50	*2.00*
	Never hinged	4.25	
f.	Booklet pane of 30, *Aug. 1917*	*1,050.*	*12,500.*
	Never hinged	*1,700.*	
	On post card, single, pre-war rate		750.00
	On cover, single, pre-war letter rate		1,000.
	On post card, single, war rate		500.00
	On cover, single plus single No. 499f, war letter rate		1,500.
g.	Perf. 10 at top or bottom	*15,000.*	*20,000.*
	Never hinged	*27,500.*	

Earliest documented use: March 30, 1917 (No. 498e booklet pair); Aug. 8, 1917 (No. 498f single).

No. 498g used is valued in the grade of fine. No. 498g also known as a transitional stamp gauging 10 at left bottom and 11 at right bottom (bottom center stamp in a plate block of 6).

No. 499g, Stamp 15mm Wide

Recut In Hair, Type I

499	A140 2c **rose,** type I, *Mar. 1917*	.50	.25
	dark rose, type I	.50	.25
	carmine rose, type I	.50	.25
	deep rose, type I	.50	.25
	Never hinged	1.00	
	On cover, type I		.30
	Block of 4, type I	2.00	1.50
	P# block of 6, type I	22.50	
	Never hinged	35.00	
	Cracked plate, type I	—	—
	Recut in hair, type I	*1,750.*	*2,300.*
	Never hinged	*3,500.*	
	Double transfer, type I	6.00	—
a.	Vertical pair, imperf. horiz., type I	*3,000.*	*2,500.*
	Never hinged	*4,250.*	
b.	Horiz. pair, imperf. vert., type I	*550.00*	*600.00*
	Never hinged	*1,100.*	
c.	Vert. pair, imperf. btwn., type I	*900.00*	*300.00*
e.	Booklet pane of 6, type I, *Mar. 31, 1917*	4.00	*2.50*
	Never hinged	6.75	
f.	Booklet pane of 30, type I, *Aug. 1917*	*20,000.*	—
	Never hinged	*28,000.*	
	On cover, single, pre-war letter rate		1,000.
	On post card, single, war rate		500.00
g.	Double impression, type I	200.00	*2,000.*
	Never hinged	*400.00*	
	On cover		—
	As "g," stamp design 15mm wide	*1,000.*	
	Never hinged	*1,500.*	
h.	2c **lake,** type I	600.00	800.00
	Never hinged	*1,250.*	
	On cover		—
i.	As "e," single stamp, **lake**		*3,250.*

For Nos. 498f and 499f, the war-rate period was Nov. 2, 1917 to June 30, 1919.

No. 499b is valued in the grade of fine. No 499g used is valued in the grade of fine.

See No. 505 for P# block of 6 from plate 7942.

No. 499h occurs in two different lake shades. The true lake is similar to the lake on other lake shades noted elsewhere in this catalogue. A somewhat more common lake shade is known as "Boston lake," and it is a very distinctive and duller lake shade. Certificates of authenticity recommended for these and all listed lake shades.

Earliest documented uses: Mar. 27, 1917 (No. 499); July 19, 1917 (No. 499e single); Aug. 7, 1917 (No. 499f single).

500	A140 2c **deep rose,** type Ia	260.00	240.00
	Never hinged	570.00	
	On cover, type Ia		*650.00*
	Block of 4, type Ia	1,150.	*1,500.*
	P# block of 6, type Ia	2,100.	
	Never hinged	3,750.	—
	P# block of 6, two stamps type I (P# 10208 LL)	*15,000.*	
	Never hinged	*22,500.*	
	Pair, types I and Ia (10208 LL 95 or 96)	*1,500.*	

Earliest documented use: Dec. 15, 1919.

No. 500 exists with imperforate top sheet margin. Examples have been altered by trimming perforations. Some also have faked Schermack perfs.

501	A140 3c **light violet,** type I, *Mar. 1917*	9.00	.40
	violet, type I	9.00	.40
	dark violet, type I	9.00	.40
	reddish violet, type I	9.00	.40
	Never hinged	20.00	
	On cover, type I		.50
	Block of 4, type I	37.50	4.00
	P# block of 6, type I	140.00	
	Never hinged	240.00	
	Double transfer, type I	11.00	
b.	Bklt. pane of 6, type I, *Oct. 17, 1917*	75.00	*80.00*
	Never hinged	125.00	
c.	Vert. pair, imper. horiz., type I	*2,100.*	
	Never hinged	*3,250.*	
d.	Double impression	*3,500.*	*3,500.*
	Never hinged	*5,000.*	

Earliest documented uses: Mar. 29, 1917 (No. 501); Feb. 8, 1918 (No. 501b single).

No. 501d is valued in the grade of fine.

No. 502d

502	A140 3c **dark violet,** type II	12.00	.75
	violet, type II	12.00	.75
	Never hinged	27.50	
	On cover, type II		1.00
	Block of 4, type II	50.00	5.50
	P# block of 6, type II	160.00	
	Never hinged	275.00	
b.	Bklt. pane of 6, type II, *Feb. 25, 1918*	60.00	*75.00*
	Never hinged	100.00	
c.	Vert. pair, imperf. horiz., type II	*1,400.*	*850.00*
	Never hinged	*2,750.*	
	On cover		*1,400.*
d.	Double impression	800.00	*1,000.*
	Never hinged	1,600.	
e.	Perf. 10 at top or bottom	—	*30,000.*
	Never hinged	*21,500.*	

Earliest documented uses: Jan. 30, 1918 (No. 502); June 12, 1918 (No. 502b single).

503	A140 4c **brown,** *Mar. 1917*	8.50	.40
	dark brown	8.50	.40
	orange brown	8.50	.40
	yellow brown	8.50	.40
	Never hinged	19.00	
	On cover		2.10
	Block of 4	35.00	3.50
	P# block of 6	150.00	
	Never hinged	250.00	
	Double transfer	14.00	—
b.	Double impression	—	
504	A140 5c **blue,** *Mar. 1917*	7.50	.35
	light blue	7.50	.35
	dark blue	7.50	.35
	Never hinged	17.00	
	On cover		.45
	Block of 4	32.50	3.00
	P# block of 6	140.00	
	Never hinged	225.00	
	Double transfer	10.00	—
a.	Horizontal pair, imperf. between	*20,000.*	—
b.	Double impression	*1,750.*	*1,600.*

Earliest documented use: June 5, 1917.

505	A140 5c **rose** (error)	325.00	*600.00*
	Never hinged	625.00	
	On cover		2,250.
	Block of 9, middle stamp #505	650.00	*1,100.*
	Never hinged	1,000.	
	Block of 12, two middle stamps #505	1,200.	*3,000.*
	Never hinged	1,850.	
	P# block of six 2c stamps (#499), P# 7942	40.00	
	Never hinged	70.00	

Earliest documented use: Mar. 27, 1917.

Value notes under No. 467 also apply to No. 505.

No. 506b

506	A140 6c **red orange,** *Mar. 1917*	11.00	.40
	orange	11.00	.40
	Never hinged	25.00	
	On cover		2.50
	Block of 4	47.50	4.00
	P# block of 6	180.00	
	Never hinged	300.00	
	Double transfer	—	—
a.	Perf. 10 at top or bottom	*30,000.*	*8,000.*
b.	Double impression, never hinged	*2,000.*	

No. 506a also exists as a transitional stamp gauging partly perf 10 and partly perf 11 at top. Value thus the same as normal 506a.

No. 506b is a partial double impression. Two authenticated examples are documented.

507	A140 7c **black,** *Mar. 1917*	24.00	1.25
	gray black	24.00	1.25
	intense black	24.00	1.25
	Never hinged	55.00	
	On cover		7.75
	Block of 4	100.00	12.50
	P# block of 6	250.00	
	Never hinged	450.00	
	Double transfer	—	—
508	A148 8c **olive bister,** *Mar. 1917*	11.00	.65
	dark olive green	11.00	.65
	olive green	11.00	.65
	Never hinged	25.00	
	On cover		2.75
	Block of 4	47.50	6.50
	P# block of 6, Impt. & "A"	170.00	
	Never hinged	285.00	
	P# block of 6, "A"	220.00	
	Never hinged	370.00	
	P# block of 6	140.00	
	Never hinged	240.00	
b.	Vertical pair, imperf. between	—	—
c.	Perf. 10 at top or bottom		*9,000.*
509	A148 9c **salmon red,** *Mar. 1917*	11.00	1.60
	salmon	11.00	1.60
	Never hinged	25.00	
	On cover		13.00
	Block of 4	47.50	18.00
	P# block of 6	150.00	
	Never hinged	250.00	
	Double transfer	18.00	4.50
a.	Perf. 10 at top or bottom		*7,500.*
	Never hinged	*37,500.*	

No. 509a also exists as a transitional stamp gauging partly perf 10 and partly perf 11 at top or bottom. Value thus the same as normal 509a.

Earliest documented use: Nov. 23, 1917.

510	A148 10c **orange yellow,** *Mar. 1917*	15.00	.25
	golden yellow	15.00	.25
	Never hinged	34.00	
	On cover		2.00
	Block of 4	62.50	2.00
	P# block of 6, "A"	290.00	
	Never hinged	475.00	
	P# block of 6	200.00	
	Never hinged	325.00	
a.	10c **brown yellow**	*1,400.*	
	Never hinged	*3,250.*	
	On cover		—

Earliest documented use: Mar. 27, 1917 (No. 510); Dec. 23, 1918 (No. 510a used on dated label on piece).

511	A148 11c **light green,** *May 1917*	7.50	2.25
	green	7.50	2.25
	Never hinged	17.00	
	dark green	8.50	2.25
	Never hinged	18.00	
	On cover		8.50
	Block of 4	32.50	20.00
	P# block of 6	150.00	
	Never hinged	260.00	
	Double transfer	11.00	3.00
a.	Perf. 10 at top or bottom	*3,000.*	*3,250.*
	Never hinged	*6,000.*	
	Block of 4, two stamps No. 511a	7,000.	*9,000.*
	P# block of 6, top, bottom 3 stamps No. 511a	*22,500.*	

No. 511a also exists as a transitional stamp gauging partly perf 10 and partly perf 11 at top or bottom. Value thus the same as normal 511a.

512	A148 12c **claret brown,** *May 1917*	8.50	.50
	Never hinged	19.00	
	On cover		4.00
	Block of 4	32.50	4.00
	P# block of 6	150.00	
	Never hinged	260.00	
	Double transfer	11.00	—
	Triple transfer	20.00	—
a.	12c **brown carmine**	8.50	.50
	Never hinged	19.00	
	On cover		4.50
	Block of 4	36.00	4.50
	P# block of 6	150.00	
	Never hinged	260.00	
b.	Perf. 10 at top or bottom	*25,000.*	*15,000.*

	On cover		—
c.	12c **claret red**	8.50	.50
	Never hinged	19.00	

Earliest documented use: Aug. 15, 1917 (No. 512a); Aug. 26, 1924 (No. 512b).

513	A148 13c **apple green,** *Jan. 10, 1919*	9.50	5.50
	pale apple green	9.50	5.50
	Never hinged	21.00	
	deep apple green	11.50	6.00
	Never hinged	26.00	
	On cover		19.00
	Block of 4	40.00	45.00
	P# block of 6	140.00	
	Never hinged	240.00	

Earliest documented use: Jan. 25, 1919.

514	A148 15c **gray,** *May 1917*	32.50	1.40
	dark gray	32.50	1.40
	Never hinged	75.00	
	On cover		25.00
	Block of 4	140.00	12.50
	P# block of 6	550.00	—
	Never hinged	900.00	
	Double transfer	—	—
a.	Perf. 10 at bottom		*10,000.*

Earliest documented use: Nov. 15, 1917.

No. 515c

515	A148 20c **light ultramarine,** *May 1917*	40.00	.45
	gray blue	40.00	.45
	Never hinged	85.00	
	deep ultramarine	45.00	.55
	Never hinged	95.00	
	On cover		75.00
	Block of 4	175.00	3.50
	P# block of 6	600.00	
	Never hinged	1,000.	
	Double transfer	—	—
b.	Vertical pair, imperf. between	*1,750.*	*3,250.*
c.	Double impression	*1,250.*	
	Never hinged	*2,750.*	
d.	Perf. 10 at top or bottom	—	*11,000.*

No. 515b is valued in the grade of fine.

Beware of pairs with blind perforations inside the design of the top stamp that are offered as No. 515b.

No. 515c is a partial double impression.

Earliest documented use: May 4, 1918.

516	A148 30c **orange red,** *May 1917*	30.00	1.50
	dark orange red	30.00	1.50
	Never hinged	70.00	
	On cover		150.00
	Block of 4	130.00	12.50
	P# block of 6	600.00	
	Never hinged	925.00	
	Double transfer	—	
	Dropped transfer (6921 LL 49)	*1,150.*	
a.	Perf. 10 at top or bottom	*20,000.*	*15,000.*
	Never hinged	*37,500.*	
b.	Double impression		—

No. 516a used is valued in the grade of fine.

Earliest documented use: Jan. 12, 1918.

517	A148 50c **red violet,** *May 1917*	50.00	.75
	Never hinged	120.00	
	violet	60.00	.75
	Never hinged	145.00	
	light violet	62.50	.75
	Never hinged	150.00	
	On cover		*400.00*
	Block of 4	225.00	5.00
	P# block of 6	1,600.	
	Never hinged	2,550.	
	Double transfer	95.00	1.75
b.	Vertical pair, imperf. between & with natural straight edge at bottom		*6,000.*
c.	Perf. 10 at top or bottom		*17,000.*

No. 517b is valued in average condition and may be a unique used pair (precanceled). The editors would like to see authenticated example of an unused pair.

Earliest documented use: Dec. 28, 1917 (on registry tag).

518	A148 $1 **violet brown,** *May 1917*	37.50	1.50
	violet black	37.50	1.50
	Never hinged	95.00	
	On cover		*550.00*
	Block of 4	165.00	12.50
	Margin block of 4, arrow right or left	220.00	
	P# block of 6, Impt. & "A"	1,300.	—
	Never hinged	2,100.	
	Double transfer (5782 L. 66)	57.50	2.00
b.	$1 **deep brown**	*2,000.*	*1,100.*
	Never hinged	*4,000.*	
	Block of 4	*9,000.*	*5,500.*
	P# block of 6, Impt. & "A," never hinged	*32,500.*	
	Nos. 498-504,506-518 (20)	585.50	260.40

Earliest documented use: May 19, 1917.

No. 518b is valued in the grade of fine to very fine.

TYPE OF 1908-09 ISSUE

This is the result of an old stock of No. 344 which was returned to the Bureau in 1917 and perforated with the then current gauge 11. Only lower left panes of No. 344 were perforated 11, and therefore only left and bottom plate blocks exist.

1917, Oct. 10 Wmk. 191 *Perf. 11*

519	A139 2c **carmine**	425.00	*1,800.*
	Never hinged	900.00	
	On cover		*3,500.*
	Block of 4	1,900.	*9,250.*
	P# block of 6, T V, Impt.	3,500.	—
	Never hinged	*6,500.*	

Beware of examples of No. 344 fraudulently perforated and offered as No. 519. Obtaining a certificate from a recognized expertizing committee is strongly recommended.

Warning: See note following No. 459 regarding used stamps.

Earliest documented use: Oct. 10, 1917.

Franklin — A149

Plates of 100 subjects.

1918, Aug. Unwmk. *Perf. 11*

523	A149 $2 **orange red & black**	525.	240.
	red orange & black	525.	240.
	Never hinged	1,175.	
	On cover		*2,000.*
	Block of 4	2,200.	1,300.
	Margin block of 4, arrow	2,300.	
	Center line block	2,500.	1,400.
	P# block of 8, 2# & arrow	*12,000.*	—
	Never hinged	*18,000.*	

Earliest documented use: Dec. 17, 1918.

524	A149 $5 **deep green & black**	160.	40.
	Never hinged	340.	
	yellow green & black	—	—
	Never hinged	—	
	On cover		*2,500.*
	Block of 4	675.	250.
	Margin block of 4, arrow	700.	260.
	Center line block	950.	300.
	P# block of 8, 2# & arrow	3,500.	
	Never hinged	*5,000.*	

Earliest documented use: Mar. 10, 1919 (strip of nine with Nos. 516, 517 and 537 on piece); Mar. 20, 1920 (on cover).

For other listing of design A149 see No. 547.

TYPES OF 1917-19 ISSUE

Plates of 400, 800 or 1600 subjects in panes of 100 each, as follows:

No. 525 — 400 and 1600 subjects
No. 526 — 400 subjects
No. 527 — 400 and 1600 subjects
No. 528 — 400 and 1600 subjects
No. 528A — 400, 800 and 1600 subjects
No. 528B — 400, 800 and 1600 subjects
No. 529 — 400 subjects
No. 531 — 400 subjects
No. 532 — 400, 800 and 1600 subjects
No. 533 — 400 and 1600 subjects
No. 534 — 400 subjects
No. 534A — 400, 800 and 1600 subjects
No. 534B — 400 subjects
No. 535 — 400 subjects
No. 536 — 400 and 1600 subjects

1918-20 Unwmk. OFFSET PRINTING *Perf. 11*

525	A140 1c **gray green,** *Dec. 1918*	2.50	.90
	Never hinged	6.00	
	emerald	7.50	1.25
	Never hinged	17.50	
	On cover		1.75
	Block of 4	10.50	6.00
	P# block of 6	30.00	
	Never hinged	50.00	
	"Flat nose"	—	
a.	1c **dark green**	10.00	1.75
	Never hinged	25.00	
c.	Horizontal pair, imperf. between	*750.00*	*650.00*
d.	Double impression	40.00	*750.00*
	Never hinged	90.00	

No. 525c is valued in the grade of fine and with natural straight edge at right, as virtually all recorded examples come thus. No. 525d used is valued in the grade of very good.

Earliest documented use: Dec. 24, 1918.

TYPE IV

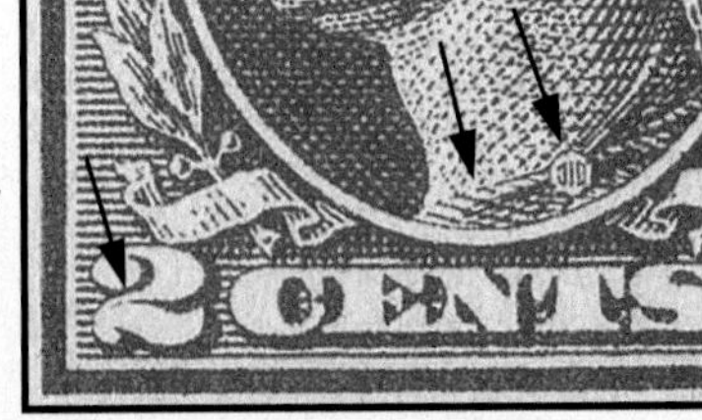

TWO CENTS

Type IV — Top line of the toga rope is broken.

The shading lines in the toga button are so arranged that the curving of the first and last form "D (reversed) ID."

The line of color in the left "2" is very thin and usually broken.

Used on offset printings only.

TYPE V

Type V — Top line of the toga is complete.

There are five vertical shading lines in the toga button.

The line of color in the left "2" is very thin and usually broken.

The shading dots on the nose are as shown on the diagram.

Used on offset printings only.

TYPE Va

Type Va — Characteristics are the same as type V except in the shading dots of the nose. The third row of dots from the bottom has four dots instead of six. The overall height is ⅓mm shorter than the other types.

Used on offset printings only.

TYPE VI

Type VI — General characteristics the same as type V except that the line of color in the left "2" is very heavy.

Used on offset printings only.

TYPE VII

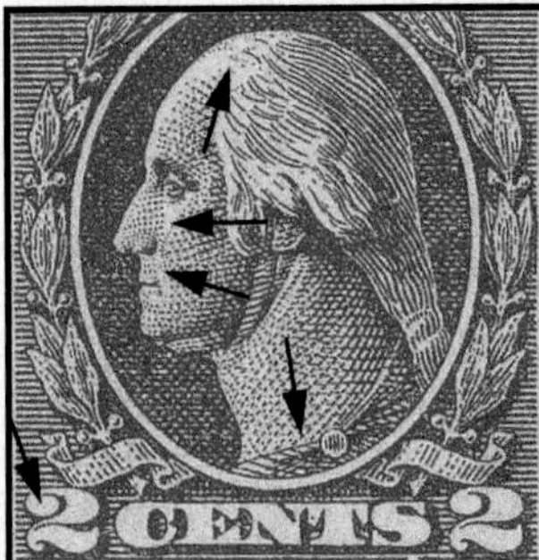

Type VII — The line of color in the left "2" is invariably continuous, clearly defined and heavier than in type V or Va but not as heavy as type VI.

An additional vertical row of dots has been added to the upper lip.

Numerous additional dots have been added to the hair on top of the head.

Used on offset printings only.

Dates of issue of types after type IV are not known but official records show the first plate of each type to have been certified as follows:

Type IV, Mar. 6, 1920
Type V, Mar. 20, 1920
Type Va, May 4, 1920
Type VI, June 24, 1920
Type VII, Nov. 3, 1920

Gash on Forehead

No.	Description	Unused	Used
526	A140 2c **carmine,** type IV, *1920*	25.00	4.00
	rose carmine, type IV	25.00	4.00
	Never hinged	57.50	
	On cover, type IV		11.00
	Block of 4, type IV	110.00	30.00
	P# block of 6, type IV	240.00	
	Never hinged	450.00	
	Gash on forehead, type IV	60.00	—
	Never hinged	125.00	
	Malformed "2" at left, type IV (10823 LR 93)	40.00	6.00

Earliest documented use: Mar. 15, 1920 (FDC).

No.	Description	Unused	Used
527	A140 2c **carmine,** type V, *1920*	18.00	1.25
	bright carmine, type V	18.00	1.25
	rose carmine, type V	18.00	1.25
	Never hinged	40.00	
	On cover, Type V		2.75
	Block of 4, type V	77.50	10.00
	P# block of 6, type V	185.00	
	Never hinged	350.00	
	Line through "2" & "EN," type V	35.00	—
	Never hinged	75.00	
a.	Double impression, type V	100.00	—
	Never hinged	225.00	
b.	Vert. pair, imperf. horiz., type V	*850.00*	
c.	Horiz. pair, imperf. vert., type V	*1,000.*	—
d.	All color missing (FO)	—	—

Earliest documented use: Apr. 16, 1920.

No.	Description	Unused	Used
528	A140 2c **carmine,** type Va, *1920*	10.00	.40
	Never hinged	22.50	
	On cover, type Va		.75
	Block of 4, type Va	42.50	3.50
	P# block of 6, type Va	110.00	
	Never hinged	190.00	
	P# block of 6, monogram over P#	200.00	
	Never hinged	300.00	
	Retouches in "P" of Postage type Va	*55.00*	—
	Retouched on toga, type Va	—	—
	Variety C"R"NTS, type Va	*40.00*	
	Never hinged	87.50	
	Top margin P# block of 6 containing the C"R"NTS variety, type Va	*450.00*	
c.	Double impression, type Va	62.50	
	Never hinged	150.00	
g.	Vert. pair, imperf. between	*3,250.*	

Earliest documented use: June 18, 1920.

No.	Description	Unused	Used
528A	A140 2c **carmine,** type VI, *1920*	47.50	2.00
	bright carmine, type VI	47.50	2.00
	Never hinged	115.00	
	On cover, type VI		3.75
	Block of 4, type VI	200.00	15.00
	P# block of 6, type VI	425.00	
	Never hinged	800.00	
	P# block of 6, monogram over P#	525.00	
	Never hinged	900.00	
d.	Double impression, type VI	200.00	*900.00*
	Never hinged	450.00	
f.	Vert. pair, imperf. horiz., type VI	—	
h.	Vert. pair, imperf. between	*5,000.*	

Earliest documented use: July 30, 1920.

Counterfeits exist of No. 528A. See the Postal Counterfeits section of this catalog.

No.	Description	Unused	Used
528B	A140 2c **carmine,** type VII, *1920*	20.00	.75
	Never hinged	50.00	
	On cover, type VII		1.00
	Block of 4, type VII	85.00	6.00
	P# block of 6, type VII	200.00	
	Never hinged	375.00	
	Gash on cheek, type VII	*325.00*	—
	Retouched on cheek, type VII	*750.00*	—
	Vertical plate scratch through face, type VII	*200.00*	
e.	Double impression, type VII	77.50	*400.00*

No. 528Be used is valued in the grade of very good to fine.

Earliest documented use: Nov. 10, 1920.

TYPE III

THREE CENTS

Type III — The top line of the toga rope is strong but the 5th shading line is missing as in type I.

Center shading line of the toga button consists of two dashes with a central dot.

The "P" and "O" of "POSTAGE" are separated by a line of color.

The frame line at the bottom of the vignette is complete.

Used on offset printings only.

TYPE IV

Type IV — The shading lines of the toga rope are complete.

The second and fourth shading lines in the toga button are broken in the middle and the third line is continuous with a dot in the center.

The "P" and "O" of "POSTAGE" are joined.

The frame line at the bottom of the vignette is broken.

Used on offset printings only.

No.	Description	Unused	Used
529	A140 3c **violet,** type III, *Mar. 1918*	3.50	.50
	light violet, type III	3.50	.50
	dark violet, type III	3.50	.50
	Never hinged	7.75	
	On cover, type III		.60
	Block of 4, type III	14.50	4.00
	P# block of 6, type III	75.00	
	Never hinged	125.00	
a.	Double impression, type III	50.00	*1,250.*
	Never hinged	115.00	
b.	Printed on both sides, type III	*2,500.*	

No. 529a used is valued in the grade of fine.

Earliest documented use: Apr. 4, 1918 (No. 529); June 24, 1918 (No. 529a).

No.	Description	Unused	Used
530	A140 3c **purple,** *June 1918* type IV	2.00	.30
	light purple, type IV	2.00	.30
	deep purple, type IV	2.00	.30
	violet, type IV	2.00	.30
	Never hinged	4.50	
	On cover, type IV		.35
	Block of 4, type IV	8.50	2.00
	P# block of 6, type IV	32.50	
	Never hinged	55.00	
	"Blister" under "U.S.," type IV	5.00	—
	Recut under "U.S.," type IV	5.00	—
a.	Double impression, type IV	40.00	*800.00*
	Never hinged	90.00	
	On cover		*1,600.*
	P# block of 6, type IV, never hinged	1,250.	
b.	Printed on both sides, type IV	*750.00*	
	Never hinged	*1,100.*	
c.	Triple impression, type IV	*1,750.*	—
	Nos. 525-530 (8)	128.50	10.10

No. 530a used is valued in the grade of fine.

Earliest documented use: June 30, 1918.

Earliest documented use dates for imperforates are for the imperforate sheet stamps, not for imperforate stamps with vending and affixing machine perforations or for flat plate imperforate coil stamps. EDU dates for VAMP and flat plate imperf coil stamps are shown in their respective sections later in the catalogue.

1918-20 *Imperf.*

Dates of issue of 2c types are not known, but official records show that the first plate of each type known to have been issued imperforate was certified as follows:

Type IV, Mar. 1920
Type V, May 4, 1920
Type Va, May 25, 1920
Type VI, July 26, 1920
Type VII, Dec. 2, 1920

No.	Description	Unused	Used
531	A140 1c **green,** *Jan. 1919*	14.00	12.00
	gray green	14.00	12.00
	emerald	14.00	12.00
	Never hinged	21.00	
	On cover		17.50
	Pair	30.00	*52.50*
	Never hinged	47.50	
	Block of 4	60.00	*75.00*
	Corner margin block of 4	62.50	—
	Margin block of 4, arrow	65.00	*80.00*
	Center line block	100.00	*90.00*
	Never hinged	150.00	
	P# block of 6	125.00	—
	Never hinged	190.00	

Earliest documented use: Mar. 17, 1919 (dated cancel on off-cover plate block); April 2, 1919 (pair on cover).

No.	Description	Unused	Used
532	A140 2c **carmine rose,** type IV, *1920*	50.00	42.50
	Never hinged	80.00	
	On cover		75.00
	Pair	100.00	*120.00*
	Never hinged	175.00	
	Block of 4	210.00	*250.00*
	Corner margin block of 4	220.00	
	Margin block of 4, arrow	230.00	
	Center line block	300.00	*250.00*
	Never hinged	525.00	
	P# block of 6	400.00	—
	Never hinged	675.00	

Earliest documented use: July 22, 1920 (dated cancel on used pair); April 12, 1923 (on cover).

No.	Description	Unused	Used
533	A140 2c **carmine,** type V, *1920*	120.00	*150.00*
	Never hinged	200.00	
	On cover		225.00
	Pair	250.00	*350.00*
	Never hinged	425.00	
	Block of 4	450.00	*650.00*
	Corner margin block of 4	460.00	*700.00*
	Margin block of 4, arrow	475.00	*700.00*
	Center line block	800.00	*1,200.*
	Never hinged	1,350.	
	P# block of 6	1,100.	—
	Never hinged	1,800.	
	Line through "2" and "EN," type V	225.00	
	Never hinged	245.00	

Earliest documented use: Sept. 29, 1920 (dated cancel on off-cover center line block of 4).

No.	Description	Unused	Used
534	A140 2c **carmine,** type Va, *1920*	16.50	15.00
	carmine rose	16.50	15.00
	Never hinged	26.50	
	On cover		17.50
	Pair	34.00	*35.00*
	Never hinged	55.00	
	Block of 4	67.50	*70.00*
	Corner margin block of 4	70.00	
	Margin block of 4, arrow	72.50	*72.50*
	Center line block	95.00	*150.00*
	Never hinged	155.00	
	P# block of 6	140.00	—
	Never hinged	200.00	
	Block of 6, monogram over P#	225.00	
	Never hinged	360.00	

Earliest documented use: June 24, 1920.

No.	Description	Unused	Used
534A	A140 2c **carmine,** type VI, *1920*	52.50	40.00
	Never hinged	90.00	
	On cover		45.00
	Pair	110.00	85.00
	Never hinged	190.00	
	Block of 4	220.00	230.00
	Corner block of 4	225.00	250.00
	Block of 4, arrow	230.00	—
	Center line block	300.00	*300.00*
	Never hinged	550.00	
	P# block of 6	450.00	—
	Never hinged	725.00	

Earliest documented use: Aug. 31, 1920.

No.	Description	Unused	Used
534B	A140 2c **carmine,** type VII, *1920*	2,500.	1,500.
	Never hinged	3,750.	
	On cover		*5,000.*
	Pair	5,250.	*4,500.*
	Never hinged	9,000.	
	Block of 4	10,500.	*7,250.*
	Corner margin block of 4	10,750.	
	Margin block of 4, arrow	11,000.	
	Center line block	*12,500.*	*20,000.*
	Never hinged	*13,000.*	
	P# block of 6	*17,500.*	
	Never hinged	*25,000.*	

Earliest documented use: Oct. 1, 1921 (dated cancel on on-piece pair); Mar. 22, 1923 (on cover). A cover purported to be an Oct. 20, 1920, usage is believed to exist. The editors would like to see authenticated evidence of its genuineness.

Beware of perforated 2c offset stamps that may have been fraudulently trimmed to resemble Nos. 532-534B.

Examples of the 2c type VII with Schermack type III vending machine perforations have been cut down at sides to simulate the rarer No. 534B imperforate. The No. 534B with Schermack type III perforations is much less expensive than the fully imperforate No. 534B listed here.

No.	Description	Unused	Used
535	A140 3c **violet,** type IV, *1918*	11.00	6.00
	Never hinged	18.00	
	On cover		12.50
	Pair	22.50	15.00
	Never hinged	37.50	
	Block of 4	45.00	32.50
	Corner margin block of 4	47.50	35.00
	Margin block of 4, arrow	50.00	35.00
	Center line block	75.00	*50.00*
	Never hinged	125.00	
	P# block of 6	90.00	—
	Never hinged	130.00	
a.	Double impression	100.00	—
	Never hinged	200.00	
	Nos. 531-534A,535 (6)	264.00	265.50

Earliest documented use: Sept. 30, 1918.

Cancellation

Haiti	—

1919, Aug. 12 ***Perf. 12½***

No.	Description	Unused	Used
536	A140 1c **gray green**	20.00	*35.00*
	Never hinged	45.00	
	On postcard, single		225.00
	On cover, pair		300.00
	Block of 4	85.00	*175.00*
	P# block of 6	250.00	
	Never hinged	400.00	
a.	Horiz. pair, imperf. vert.	*900.00*	
	Never hinged	*1,400.*	

Earliest documented use: Aug. 18, 1919.

VICTORY ISSUE

Victory of the Allies in World War I

"Victory" and Flags of Allies — A150

Designed by Clair Aubrey Huston

FLAT PLATE PRINTING

Plates of 400 subjects in four panes of 100 each

1919, Mar. 3 Unwmk. Engr. ***Perf. 11***

No.	Description	Unused	Used
537	A150 3c **violet**	10.00	3.25
	Never hinged	20.00	
	On cover		11.00
	Block of 4	42.50	17.50
	P# block of 6	260.00	
	Never hinged	350.00	
	Double transfer	—	—
a.	3c **deep red violet**	*1,300.*	*1,800.*
	Never hinged	*2,400.*	
	On cover		—
	Block of 4	*5,250.*	*11,000.*
	P# block of 6	*10,000.*	
	Never hinged	*16,000.*	
b.	3c **light reddish violet**	150.00	50.00
	Never hinged	300.00	
	On cover		250.00
	Block of 4	650.00	250.00
	P# block of 6	1,500.	
	Never hinged	2,500.	
c.	3c **red violet**	200.00	60.00
	Never hinged	400.00	
	On cover		275.00
	Block of 4	875.00	
	P# block of 6	1,750.	
	Never hinged	2,750.	

No. 537a is valued in the grade of fine.

Earliest documented date: Mar. 3, 1919 (FDC).

REGULAR ISSUE

ROTARY PRESS PRINTINGS

(See note over No. 448)

Issued in panes of 170 stamps (coil waste), later in panes of 70 and 100 (#538, 540)

1919 Unwmk. ***Perf. 11x10***

Stamp designs: 19½-20x22-22¼mm

No.	Description	Unused	Used
538	A140 1c **green,** *June*	10.00	9.00
	yellowish green	10.00	9.00
	bluish green	10.00	9.00
	Never hinged	23.00	
	On cover		22.50
	Block of 4	42.50	*55.00*
	P# block of 4 & "S 30"	95.00	
	Never hinged	160.00	
	P# block of 4	110.00	
	Never hinged	180.00	
	P# block of 4, star	140.00	
	Never hinged	225.00	
	Double transfer	16.00	—
a.	Vert. pair, imperf. horiz.	60.00	*125.00*
	Never hinged	125.00	
	Block of 4	130.00	*300.00*
	Never hinged	275.00	
	P# block of 4	900.00	
	Never hinged	1,375.	

No. 538a used is valued with a contemporaneous cancel. A certificate of authenticity is advised.

Earliest documented use: June 28, 1919 (No. 538); Sept. 5, 1927 (No. 538a).

No.	Description	Unused	Used
539	A140 2c **carmine rose,** type II	2,700.	*16,000.*
	Never hinged	4,250.	
	On cover, type II		*50,000.*
	Block of 4, type II	*12,000.*	*75,000.*
	P# block of 4, type II, & "S 20"	*17,500.*	
	Never hinged	*25,000.*	

No. 539 is valued in the grade of fine.

(See note after No. 455.)

Earliest documented use: June 30, 1919. This is the unique usage on cover. The used block of four also is unique.

No.	Description	Unused	Used
540	A140 2c **carmine rose,** type III, *June 14*	12.00	9.50
	carmine	12.00	9.50
	Never hinged	27.50	
	On cover, type III		25.00
	Block of 4, type III	50.00	*60.00*
	Never hinged	115.00	
	P# block of 4, type III, & "S 30"	105.00	
	Never hinged	175.00	
	P# block of 4, type III, & "S 30" inverted	450.00	
	Never hinged	725.00	
	P# block of 4, type III	105.00	
	Never hinged	175.00	
	P# block of 4, type III, star	160.00	
	Never hinged	275.00	
	Double transfer, type III	21.00	—

Earliest documented use: June 17, 1919.

No.	Description	Unused	Used
a.	Vert. pair, imperf. horiz., type III	60.00	*140.00*
	Never hinged	125.00	
	Block of 4	130.00	*350.00*
	Never hinged	275.00	
	P# block of 4, type III	1,000.	
	Never hinged	1,500.	
	P# block of 4, type III, Star	1,050.	
	Never hinged	1,600.	
b.	Horiz. pair, imperf. vert., type III	*2,750.*	

No. 540a used is valued with a contemporaneous cancel. A certificate of authenticity is advised.

Earliest documented use: June 17, 1919 (No. 540); Nov. 4, 1922 (No. 540a).

No.	Description	Unused	Used
541	A140 3c **violet,** type II, *June 14*	40.00	37.50
	gray violet, type II	40.00	37.50
	Never hinged	100.00	
	On cover		100.00
	Block of 4	170.00	*260.00*
	P# block of 4	360.00	
	Never hinged	625.00	

Earliest documented use: June 14, 1919 (FDC).

Plates of 400 subjects in four panes of 100.

1920, May 26 ***Perf. 10x11***

Stamp design: 19x22½-22¾mm

No.	Description	Unused	Used
542	A140 1c **green**	12.50	1.50
	bluish green	12.50	1.50
	Never hinged	30.00	
	On cover		5.50
	Block of 4	55.00	12.50
	Vertical margin block of 6, P# opposite center horizontal row	165.00	
	Never hinged	300.00	

Earliest documented use: May 26, 1920 (FDC).

Plates of 400 subjects in four panes of 100 each.

1921, May ***Perf. 10***

Stamp design: 19x22½mm

No.	Description	Unused	Used
543	A140 1c **green**	.70	.40
	deep green	.70	.40
	Never hinged	1.75	
	On cover		.45
	Block of 4	2.80	2.00
	Vertical margin block of 6, P# opposite center horizontal row	32.50	
	Never hinged	57.50	
	Corner margin block of 4, P# only	20.00	
	Never hinged	35.00	
	Double transfer		—
	Triple transfer	—	—
a.	Horizontal pair, imperf. between	*4,500.*	

Earliest documented use: May 21, 1921.

Rotary Press Sheet Waste

1922 ***Perf. 11***

Stamp design: 19x22½mm

No.	Description	Unused	Used
544	A140 1c **green**	*22,500.*	3,500.
	Never hinged	*35,000.*	
	On cover		*5,250.*

No. 544 is valued in the grade of fine.

Earliest documented use: Dec. 17, 1922.

Issued in panes of 170 stamps (coil waste), later in panes of 70 and 100.

1921, May

Stamp designs: 19½-20x22mm

No.	Description	Unused	Used
545	A140 1c **green**	225.00	200.00
	yellowish green	225.00	210.00
	Never hinged	550.00	
	On cover		*1,800.*
	Block of 4	9,250.	*1,050.*
	P# block of 4, "S 30"	1,350.	
	Never hinged	2,750.	
	P# block of 4	1,400.	
	Never hinged	2,750.	
	P# block of 4, star	1,450.	
	Never hinged	2,850.	

Earliest documented use: June 25, 1921.

No.	Description	Unused	Used
546	A140 2c **carmine rose,** type III	105.00	*190.00*
	deep carmine rose	105.00	*190.00*
	Never hinged	230.00	
	On cover		*800.00*
	Block of 4	450.00	*1,000.*
	P# block of 4, "S 30"	700.00	
	Never hinged	1,300.	
	P# block of 4	775.00	
	Never hinged	1,450.	
	P# block of 4, star	800.00	
	Never hinged	1,500.	
	Recut in hair	140.00	*210.00*
a.	Perf. 10 on left side	*7,500.*	*17,500.*

No. 546a used is valued in the grade of very good. It is unique used.

Earliest documented use: May 5, 1921.

FLAT PLATE PRINTING

Plates of 100 subjects

1920, Nov. 1 ***Perf. 11***

No.	Description	Unused	Used
547	A149 $2 **carmine & black**	125.	40.
	Never hinged	275.	
	On cover (commercial)		1,000.
	On flown cover (philatelic)		250.
	Block of 4	525.	200.
	Margin block of 4, arrow	540.	
	Center line block	750.	—
	Margin block of 8, two P#, & arrow	3,500.	
	Never hinged	5,000.	
a.	$2 **lake & black**	200.	40.
	Never hinged	425.	
	Margin block of 8, two P#, & arrow	4,250.	

Earliest documented use: Dec. 6, 1920 (on piece).

From No. 548 forward, almost all U.S. stamps have had officially designated first days of sale and use. Therefore, from this point, earliest documented uses are given only for those stamps for which there were not designated first days of sale. For first day covers, see the First Day Cover section later in the catalogue.

PILGRIM TERCENTENARY ISSUE

Landing of the Pilgrims at Plymouth, Mass.

The "Mayflower" — A151

Landing of the Pilgrims — A152

Signing of the Compact — A153

Designed by Clair Aubrey Huston

Plates of 280 subjects in four panes of 70 each

1920, Dec. 21 **Unwmk.** ***Perf. 11***

548 A151 1c **green**	4.00	2.00
dark green	4.00	2.00
Never hinged	10.00	
On cover		3.50
Block of 4	17.00	13.00
P# block of 6	70.00	
Never hinged	115.00	
Double transfer	—	—
549 A152 2c **carmine rose**	5.50	1.60
carmine	5.50	1.60
rose	5.50	1.60
Never hinged	14.00	
On cover		2.50
Block of 4	23.00	9.00
P# block of 6	85.00	
Never hinged	135.00	
Cancellation		
China		—
550 A153 5c **deep blue**	32.50	12.50
dark blue	32.50	12.50
Never hinged	70.00	
On cover		22.50
Block of 4	150.00	75.00
P# block of 6	435.00	
Never hinged	700.00	
Nos. 548-550 (3)	42.00	16.10
Nos. 548-550, never hinged	94.00	

IMPORTANT INFORMATION REGARDING VALUES FOR NEVER-HINGED STAMPS

Collectors should be aware that the values given for never-hinged stamps from No. 182 on are for stamps in the grade of very fine, just as the values for all stamps in the catalogue are for very fine stamps unless indicated otherwise. The never-hinged premium as a percentage of value will be larger for stamps in extremely fine or superb grades, and the premium will be smaller for fine-very fine, fine or poor examples. This is particularly true of the issues of the late-19th and early-20th centuries.

VALUES FOR NEVER-HINGED STAMPS PRIOR TO SCOTT 182

This catalogue does not value pre-1879 stamps in never-hinged condition. Premiums for never-hinged condition in the classic era invariably are even larger than those premiums listed for the 1879 and later issues. Generally speaking, the earlier the stamp is listed in the catalogue, the larger will be the never-hinged premium.

NEVER-HINGED PLATE BLOCKS

Values given for never-hinged plate blocks are for blocks in which all stamps have original gum that has never been hinged and has no disturbances, and all selvage, whether gummed or ungummed, has never been hinged.

For values of the most popular U.S. stamps in various conditions, including never hinged from No. 182 on, and in the grades of very good, fine, fine to very fine, very fine, very fine to extremely fine, extremely fine, extremely fine to superb, and superb, see the *Scott Stamp Values U.S. Specialized by Grade*, updated and issued each year as part of this U.S. specialized catalogue. This section is located after Postage and before Semi-Postal Stamps.

REGULAR ISSUE

Nathan Hale — A154

Franklin — A155

Warren G. Harding — A156

Washington — A157

Lincoln — A158

Martha Washington — A159

Theodore Roosevelt — A160

Garfield — A161

McKinley — A162

Grant — A163

Jefferson — A164

Monroe — A165

Rutherford B. Hayes — A166

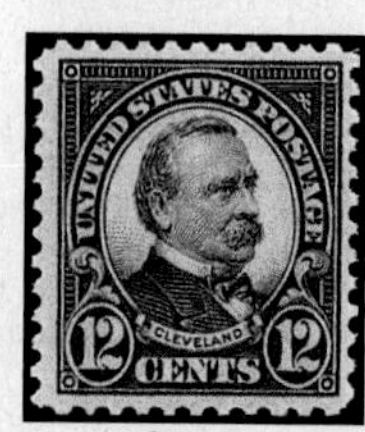
Grover Cleveland — A167

American Indian — A168

Statue of Liberty — A169

Golden Gate — A170

Niagara Falls — A171

American Buffalo — A172

Arlington Amphitheater — A173

Lincoln Memorial — A174

United States Capitol — A175

Head of Freedom Statue, Capitol Dome — A176

Plates of 400 subjects in four panes of 100 each for all values ½c to 50c inclusive.

Plates of 200 subjects for $1 and $2. The sheets were cut along the horizontal guide line into two panes, upper and lower, of 100 subjects each.

Plates of 100 subjects for the $5 denomination, and sheets of 100 subjects were issued intact.

The Bureau of Engraving and Printing in 1925 in experimenting to overcome the loss due to uneven perforations, produced what is known as the "Star Plate." The vertical rows of designs on these plates are spaced 3mm apart in place of 2¾mm as on the regular plates. Most of these plates were identified with a star added to the plate number.

Designed by Clair Aubrey Huston.

"Special" Booklet Paper

For a limited period of time in 1928 the Bureau of Engraving and Printing produced eleven stamps on "special" booklet paper, being sheets of paper specifically ordered and purchased for booklet pane production. A significant inventory of this paper remained when the BEP stopped printing booklets on the flat plate press and began printing all booklets on rotary presses. The "special" booklet paper had the grain running horizontally rather than the vertical grain paper normally used for sheet stamps. After being produced on moistened

paper, stamps shrank four times more across the grain than with the grain. Thus, the stamps printed on "special" booklet paper shrank differently when dried than stamps printed on normal stamp paper, and the differences in design dimensions are readily identifiable.

The eleven stamps involved, with their minor-lettered numbers, are Nos. 563b, 564b, 566a, 567b, 568a, 569a, C11b, E13a, QE1, QE2 and QE3. All of the first printings of Nos. QE1, QE2 and QE3 were printed on "special" booklet paper.

Nos. 563b, 564b and 566a are slightly wider and shorter than the varieties printed on normal paper; Nos. 567b, 568a and 569a are slightly narrower and taller than their counterparts; and Nos. C11b, E13a, QE1, QE2 and QE3 are slightly shorter and noticeably wider than their counterparts.

FLAT PLATE PRINTINGS

1922-25 Unwmk. *Perf. 11*

551 A154 ½c **olive brown,** *Apr. 4, 1925* .25 .25
pale olive brown .25 .25
deep olive brown .25 .25
Never hinged .50
On 1c stamped envelope (3rd class) 2.50
Block of 4 1.00 .50
P# block of 6 15.00
Never hinged 25.00
"Cap" on fraction bar (Pl. 17041) 12.50 2.00

552 A155 1c **deep green,** *Jan. 17, 1923* 1.25 .25
green 1.25 .25
pale green 1.25 .25
Never hinged 2.75
On postcard .25
Block of 4 5.50 .40
P# block of 6 37.50
Never hinged 55.00
Double transfer 3.25 —
a. Booklet pane of 6, *after Oct. 27, 1923* 7.50 *4.00*
Never hinged 12.50

Earliest documented use: Dec. 21, 1923 (No. 552a pair).

553 A156 1½c **yellow brown,** *Mar. 19, 1925* 2.00 .25
pale yellow brown 2.00 .25
brown 2.00 .25
Never hinged 4.10
On 3rd class cover 2.25
Block of 4 8.25 1.10
P# block of 6 67.50 —
Never hinged 87.50
Double transfer — —

554 A157 2c **carmine,** *Jan. 15, 1923* 1.10 .25
light carmine 1.10 .25
deep claret —
Never hinged 2.50
On cover .25
Block of 4 4.75 .40
P# block of 6 42.50
Never hinged 55.00
P# block of 6 & small 5-point star, top only 550.00
Never hinged 850.00
P# block of 6 & large 5-point star, side only 65.00
Never hinged 97.50
Same, large 5-point star, top 600.00
Never hinged 1,250.
Same, large 6-point star, top 950.00
Never hinged 1,850.
Same, large 6-point star, side only (Pl. 17196) 1,000.
Never hinged 1,750.
Double transfer 2.40 .80
a. Horiz. pair, imperf. vert. 250.00
Never hinged 400.00
b. Vert. pair, imperf. horiz. *6,000.*
Never hinged *10,000.*
c. Booklet pane of 6, *Mar. 27, 1923 (No. 554c single)* 7.00 *3.00*
Never hinged 12.00
d. Perf. 10 at top or bottom *9,000.* *5,000.*
Never hinged *12,000.*
On cover *10,000.*
e. Imperf., pair —

Virtually all top plate blocks of No. 554 with the 5-point star have narrow top selvage. Plate blocks with wide top selvage are rare and are worth much more.

Thirteen examples of No. 554e are contained in a partly perforated pane of 100. The other stamps in the pane are No. 554a with horizontal performations running at an angle. The plate number on the pane is 16269, which was only used to print perforated stamps.

Earliest documented uses: Feb. 10, 1923 (No. 554c single); Nov. 23, 1923 (No. 554d).

555 A158 3c **violet,** *Feb. 12, 1923* 13.00 1.20
deep violet 15.00 1.20
dark violet 15.00 1.20
red violet 13.00 1.20
bright violet 13.00 1.20
Never hinged 27.50
On cover with 2c (single UPU rate) 7.50
Block of 4 55.00 9.00
P# block of 6 240.00
Never hinged 400.00

556 A159 4c **yellow brown,** *Jan. 15, 1923* 16.00 .50
brown 16.00 .50
Never hinged 35.00
On cover 9.00
Block of 4 70.00 3.00
P# block of 6 250.00
Never hinged 375.00
Double transfer — —
a. Vert. pair, imperf. horiz. *12,500.*
b. Perf. 10 at top or bottom *7,000.* *7,000.*

No. 556a is unique. It resulted from a sheet that was damaged and patched during production.

No. 556b used also exists as a transitional stamp gauging 10 at left top and 11 at right top. Value the same.

557 A160 5c **dark blue,** *Oct. 27, 1922* 16.00 .30
deep blue 16.00 .30
Never hinged 35.00
On UPU-rate cover 6.00
Block of 4 70.00 2.00
P# block of 6 250.00
Never hinged 375.00
Double transfer (15571 UL 86) — *350.00*
a. Imperf., pair *2,000.*
Never hinged *3,500.*
P# block of 6 *29,000.*
b. Horiz. pair, imperf. vert. —
c. Perf. 10 at top or bottom — *9,500.*
On cover *12,500.*

Earliest documented use: Nov. 12, 1923 (No. 557c).

558 A161 6c **red orange,** *Nov. 20, 1922* 30.00 1.00
pale red orange 30.00 1.00
Never hinged 65.00
Pair on special delivery cover 17.50
Block of 4 125.00 7.50
P# block of 6 400.00
Never hinged 600.00
Double transfer (Plate 14169 LR 60 and 70) 55.00 2.00
Same, recut 55.00 2.00

559 A162 7c **black,** *May 1, 1923* 7.25 .75
gray black 7.25 .75
Never hinged 15.50
On registered cover with other values 27.50
Block of 4 32.50 6.00
P# block of 6 120.00
Never hinged 170.00
Double transfer — —

560 A163 8c **olive green,** *May 1, 1923* 37.50 1.00
pale olive green 37.50 1.00
Never hinged 80.00
Pair on airmail cover 12.50
Block of 4 160.00 7.50
P# block of 6 575.00
Never hinged 850.00
Double transfer — —

561 A164 9c **rose,** *Jan. 15, 1923* 11.00 1.25
pale rose 11.00 1.25
Never hinged 25.00
On registered cover with other values 22.50
Block of 4 47.50 9.00
P# block of 6 250.00
Never hinged 375.00
Double transfer — —

562 A165 10c **orange,** *Jan. 15, 1923* 13.50 .35
pale orange 13.50 .35
Never hinged 30.00
On special delivery cover with 2c 6.00
Block of 4 60.00 2.00
P# block of 6 275.00
Never hinged 400.00
a. Vert. pair, imperf. horiz. *2,000.*
Never hinged *3,250.*
b. Imperf., pair *1,850.*
Block of 4 *6,000.*
P# block of 6 *24,000.*
c. Perf. 10 at top or bottom *25,000.* *7,500.*
Pair *15,000.*

No. 562a is valued in the grade of fine, with gum and without blue defacing lines. No. 562b is valued without gum and without blue pencil defacing lines. No. 562c is valued in the grade of fine.

563 A166 11c **greenish blue,** *Oct. 4, 1922* 1.25 .60
Never hinged 2.75
light blue 1.60 .60
Never hinged 3.25
On registered cover with other values 12.50
Block of 4 5.50 3.50
P# block of 6 55.00
Never hinged 70.00
a. 11c **light bluish green** 1.25 .60
light yellow green 1.25 .60
Never hinged 2.75
On registered cover with other values 14.00
Block of 4 5.50 4.00
P# block of 6 40.00
Never hinged 60.00
b. 11c **light bluish green,** printed on "special" booklet paper, *1928* (see note before #551) 1.75 .90
Never hinged 4.00
On registered cover with other values 25.00
Block of 4 45.00
P# block of 6 90.00
Never hinged 120.00
d. Imperf., horiz. pair *15,000.*
Imperf., vert. strip of 3 *20,000.*

Many other intermediate shades exist for Nos. 563 and 563a, all falling within the blue or green color families.

No. 563d is known only as the two listings shown.

564 A167 12c **brown violet,** *Mar. 20, 1923* 4.75 .35
deep brown violet 4.75 .35
Never hinged 10.50
On special delivery cover 12.50
Block of 4 21.00 3.00
P# block of 6 115.00
Never hinged 160.00
P# block of 6 & large 5 point star, side only 150.00
Never hinged 225.00
P# block of 6 & large 6 point star, side only 250.00
Never hinged 400.00
Double transfer, (14404 UL 73 & 74) 11.00 1.10
a. Horiz. pair, imperf. vert. *3,750.*
b. Printed on "special" booklet paper, *1928* (see note before #551) 10.00 1.00
Never hinged 25.00
On special delivery cover 25.00
Block of 4 45.00
P# block of 6 325.00
Never hinged 650.00

565 A168 14c **blue,** *May 1, 1923* 4.25 .90
deep blue 4.25 .90
Never hinged 9.50
On registered cover with other values 15.00
Block of 4 18.00 7.50
P# block of 6 80.00
Never hinged 120.00
Double transfer — —

Horizontal pairs of No. 565 are known with spacings up to 3mm instead of 2mm between. These are from the 5th and 6th vertical rows of the right panes of Plate 14515 and also between stamps Nos. 3 and 4 of the same pane. A plate block of Pl. 14512 is known with 3mm spacing.

566 A169 15c **gray,** *Nov. 11, 1922* 16.00 .30
light gray 16.00 .30
Never hinged 35.00
On registered cover with 2c 3.50
Block of 4 70.00 2.00
P# block of 6 275.00
Never hinged 400.00
P# block of 6 & large 5 point star, side only 550.00
Never hinged 825.00
a. Printed on "special" booklet paper, *1928* (see note before #551) 30.00 2.00
Never hinged 65.00
On cover 12.00
Block of 4 130.00
P# block of 6 450.00
Never hinged 800.00

567 A170 20c **carmine rose,** *May 1, 1923* 16.00 .30
deep carmine rose 16.00 .30
Never hinged 35.00
On registered UPU-rate cover 12.50
Block of 4 70.00 2.00
P# block of 6 275.00
Never hinged 400.00
P# block of 6 & large 5 point star, side only 575.00
Never hinged 850.00
a. Horiz. pair, imperf. vert. *2,500.*
Never hinged *5,000.*
b. Printed on "special" booklet paper, *1928* (see note before #551) 35.00 3.00
Never hinged 70.00
On registered UPU-rate cover 20.00
Block of 4 150.00
P# block of 6 500.00
Never hinged 900.00

No. 567a is valued in the grade of fine.

"Bridge over Falls" plate scratches

568 A171 25c **yellow green,** *Nov. 11, 1922*	13.50	.75
green	13.50	.75
deep green	13.50	.75
Never hinged	30.00	
On contract airmail cover		27.50
Block of 4	60.00	6.00
P# block of 6	300.00	
Never hinged	425.00	
Double transfer	—	—
Plate scratches ("Bridge over Falls") (17445 LL 26)	*475.00*	—
Never hinged	*675.00*	
a. Printed on "special" booklet paper, *1928* (see note before #551)	35.00	2.25
Never hinged	75.00	
On contract airmail cover		35.00
Block of 4	150.00	
P# block of 6	600.00	
Never hinged	900.00	
b. Vert. pair, imperf. horiz.	*3,250.*	
c. Perf. 10 at one side	*12,000.*	*9,000.*
Never hinged	*16,000.*	

No. 568b is valued in the grade of fine. No. 568c used is valued in the grade of fine.

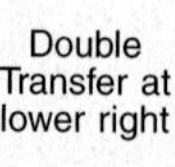
Double Transfer at lower right

569 A172 30c **olive brown,** *Mar. 20, 1923*	22.50	.60
Never hinged	50.00	
On registered cover with other values		20.00
Block of 4	100.00	5.00
P# block of 6	325.00	
Never hinged	475.00	
Double transfer at lower right (16065 UR 52)	450.00	—
Double transfer at left (14438 LR 79)	—	—
a. Printed on "special" booklet paper, *1928* (see note before #551)	45.00	3.50
Never hinged	100.00	
On registered cover with other values		35.00
Block of 4	200.00	
P# block of 6	500.00	
Never hinged	900.00	
Double transfer at lower right (16065 UR 52)	*800.00*	
570 A173 50c **lilac,** *Nov. 11, 1922*	32.50	.40
dull lilac	32.50	.40
Never hinged	70.00	
On Federal airmail cover		27.50
Block of 4	140.00	2.00
P# block of 6	550.00	
Never hinged	750.00	
571 A174 $1 **violet brown,** *Feb. 12, 1923*	35.00	.80
Never hinged	75.00	
violet black	42.50	1.00
Never hinged	85.00	
On post-1932 registered cover with other values		27.50
Block of 4	150.00	4.50
Margin block of 4, arrow, top or bottom	160.00	
P# block of 6	300.00	
Never hinged	525.00	
Double transfers, Pl. 18642 L 30 and Pl. 18682	90.00	2.00
572 A175 $2 **deep blue,** *Mar. 20, 1923*	55.00	9.00
Never hinged	120.00	
On post-1932 registered cover with other values		55.00
Block of 4	240.00	65.00
Margin block of 4, arrow, top or bottom	300.00	
P# block of 6	700.00	
Never hinged	1,000.	
573 A176 $5 **carmine & blue,** *Mar. 20, 1923*	90.00	15.00
Never hinged	180.00	
On post-1932 registered cover with other values		175.00
Block of 4	380.00	95.00
Margin block of 4, arrow	400.00	
Center line block	460.00	*105.00*
Never hinged	825.00	
P# block of 8, two P# & arrow	1,650.	—
Never hinged	2,600.	
a. $5 **carmine lake & dark blue**	180.00	30.00
Never hinged	375.00	
On post-1932 registered cover with other values		190.00
Block of 4	825.00	175.00
Margin block of 4, arrow	850.00	
Center line block	925.00	*225.00*
Never hinged	1,650.	
P# block of 8, two P# & arrow	2,500.	
Never hinged	3,750.	
Nos. 551-573 (23)	439.60	36.35
Nos. 551-573, never hinged	940.60	

For other listings of perforated stamps of designs A154 to A173 see:
Nos. 578 & 579, Perf. 11x10
Nos. 581-591, Perf. 10
Nos. 594-596, Perf. 11
Nos. 632-642, 653, 692-696, Perf. 11x10½
Nos. 697-701, Perf. 10½x11
This series also includes #622-623 (perf. 11), 684-687 & 720-723.

Plate Blocks

Scott values for plate blocks printed from flat plates are for very fine side and bottom positions. Top position plate blocks with full wide selvage sell for more.

Earliest documented use dates for imperforates are for the imperforate sheet stamps, not for imperforate stamps with vending and affixing machine perforations or for flat plate imperforate coil stamps. EDU dates for VAMP and flat plate imperf coil stamps are shown in their respective sections later in the catalogue.

1923-25 ***Imperf.***

Stamp design 19¼x22¼mm

575 A155 1c **green,** *Mar. 1923*	6.00	5.00
deep green	6.00	5.00
Never hinged	11.00	
On commercial cover		*100.00*
On philatelic cover		8.50
Pair	12.50	*12.50*
Never hinged	24.00	
Block of 4	25.00	27.50
Corner margin block of 4	27.50	*27.50*
Corner margin block of 4 (UR), "O" in selvage		—
Margin block of 4, arrow	30.00	*30.00*
Center line block	45.00	40.00
Never hinged	70.00	
P# block of 6	80.00	—
Never hinged	115.00	

Earliest documented use: Mar. 16, 1923.

576 A156 1½c **yellow brown,** *Apr. 4, 1925*	1.50	*1.50*
pale yellow brown	1.50	*1.50*
brown	1.50	*1.50*
Never hinged	2.70	
On commercial cover		*25.00*
On philatelic cover		6.00
Pair	3.25	*3.75*
Never hinged	6.00	
Block of 4	6.25	*8.50*
Corner margin block of 4	6.50	*9.00*
Margin block of 4, arrow	6.75	*10.00*
Center line block	13.00	*20.00*
Never hinged	22.50	
P# block of 6	30.00	—
Never hinged	45.00	
Double transfer	—	—

The 1½c A156 Rotary press imperforate is listed as No. 631.

577 A157 2c **carmine**	1.50	1.25
light carmine	1.50	1.25
Never hinged	2.70	
On commercial cover		*20.00*
On philatelic cover		6.00
Pair	3.25	3.00
Never hinged	6.00	
Block of 4	6.25	7.00
Corner margin block of 4	6.50	*8.00*
Margin block of 4, arrow	6.75	*10.00*
Center line block	13.00	*15.00*
Never hinged	22.50	
P# block of 6	30.00	—
Never hinged	45.00	
P# block of 6, large 5 point star	175.00	—
Never hinged	250.00	
a. 2c **carmine lake**		—
Nos. 575-577 (3)	9.00	7.75
Nos. 575-577, never hinged	16.40	

ROTARY PRESS PRINTINGS
(See note over No. 448)

Issued in sheets of 70, 100 or 170 stamps, coil waste of Nos. 597, 599.

1923 ***Perf. 11x10***

Stamp designs: 19¾x22¼mm

578 A155 1c **green**	75.00	*160.00*
Never hinged	150.00	
On cover		*700.00*
Block of 4	325.00	*1,000.*
P# block of 4, star	1,000.	
Never hinged	1,500.	

Earliest documented use: Nov. 7, 1923.

579 A157 2c **carmine**	70.00	*140.00*
deep carmine	70.00	*140.00*
Never hinged	140.00	
Block of 4	300.00	*1,750.*
On cover		*400.00*
P# block of 4, star	550.00	
Never hinged	900.00	
V-shaped gouge from eye down into cheek and back to hair in front of ear, plate 14731, pos. 3	—	—
Recut in eye, plate 14731, pos. 3	*110.00*	*150.00*

Earliest documented use: Feb. 20, 1923.

Warning: See note following No. 459 regarding used stamps.

Plates of 400 subjects in four panes of 100 each.

1923-26 ***Perf. 10***

Stamp designs: 19¼x22½mm

581 A155 1c **green,** *Apr. 21, 1923*	10.00	.75
yellow green	10.00	.75
pale green	10.00	.75
Never hinged	21.00	
On postcard		.85
On 3rd class cover		1.75
Block of 4	42.50	4.50
P# block of 4	175.00	
Never hinged	250.00	

Earliest documented use: May 18, 1923.

582 A156 1½c **brown,** *Mar. 19, 1925*	6.00	.65
dark brown	6.00	.65
Never hinged	13.00	
On 3rd class cover		6.00
Block of 4	26.00	4.00
P# block of 4	85.00	
Never hinged	125.00	
Pair with full horiz. gutter btwn.	*350.00*	
Pair with full vert. gutter btwn.	*350.00*	

No. 582 was available in full sheets of 400 subjects but was not regularly issued in that form.

583 A157 2c **carmine,** *Apr. 14, 1924*	3.00	.30
deep carmine	3.00	.30
Never hinged	6.25	
On cover		2.50
Block of 4	14.00	2.00
P# block of 4	70.00	
Never hinged	110.00	
a. Booklet pane of 6, *Aug. 27, 1926*	110.00	*150.00*
Never hinged	200.00	

Earliest documented use (unprecanceled): May 15, 1924.

584 A158 3c **violet,** *Aug. 1, 1925*	27.50	3.00
Never hinged	60.00	
On cover with 2c (single UPU rate)		6.50
Block of 4	130.00	17.50
P# block of 4	275.00	
Never hinged	425.00	
585 A159 4c **yellow brown,** *Mar. 1925*	17.50	.65
deep yellow brown	17.50	.65
Never hinged	37.50	
On cover		15.00
Block of 4	77.50	4.00
P# block of 4	275.00	
Never hinged	425.00	
586 A160 5c **blue,** *Dec. 1924*	17.50	.40
deep blue	17.50	.40
Never hinged	37.50	
On UPU-rate cover		6.00
Block of 4	77.50	3.00
P# block of 4	275.00	
Never hinged	425.00	
Double transfer	—	—
a. Horizontal pair, imperf. vertically		*7,500.*

No. 586a is unique, precanceled, with average centering and small faults, and it is valued as such.

587 A161 6c **red orange,** *Mar. 1925*	9.25	.60
pale red orange	9.25	.60
Never hinged	20.00	
On registered cover with other values		15.00
Block of 4	40.00	4.00
P# block of 4	225.00	
Never hinged	325.00	
588 A162 7c **black,** *May 29, 1926*	12.50	6.25
Never hinged	26.00	
On registered cover with other values		30.00
Block of 4	57.50	45.00
P# block of 4	275.00	
Never hinged	425.00	
589 A163 8c **olive green,** *May 29, 1926*	27.50	4.50
pale olive green	27.50	4.50
Never hinged	57.50	
On airmail cover		22.50
Block of 4	125.00	25.00
P# block of 4	300.00	
Never hinged	450.00	
590 A164 9c **rose,** *May 29, 1926*	6.00	2.50
Never hinged	12.50	
On registered cover with other values		22.50
Block of 4	26.00	17.50
P# block of 4	150.00	
Never hinged	225.00	
591 A165 10c **orange,** *June 8, 1925*	40.00	.50
Never hinged	85.00	
On airmail cover		17.50
Block of 4	200.00	3.00
P# block of 4	475.00	
Never hinged	750.00	
Nos. 581-591 (11)	176.75	20.10
Nos. 581-591, never hinged	371.25	

Bureau Precancels: 1c, 64 diff., 1½c, 76 diff., 2c, 58 diff., 3c, 41 diff., 4c, 36 diff., 5c, 38 diff., 6c, 36 diff., 7c, 18 diff., 8c, 18 diff., 9c, 13 diff., 10c, 39 diff.

Issued in sheets of 70 or 100 stamps, coil waste of Nos. 597, 599.

1923 *Perf. 11*

Stamp designs approximately 19¾x22¼mm

594 A155 1c **green** *35,000. 10,500.*
With gum *65,000.*
On cover *17,500.*
Pair *25,000.*

The main listing for No. 594 unused is for an example without gum; both unused and used are valued with perforations just touching frameline on one side.

Earliest documented use: Mar. 25, 1924.

595 A157 2c **carmine** 240.00 *375.00*
deep carmine 240.00 *375.00*
Never hinged 450.00
On cover 550.00
Block of 4 1,050. *1,750.*
P# block of 4, star 2,100. —
Never hinged 3,000.
V-shaped gouge from eye down into cheek and back to hair in front of ear, plate 14731, pos.3 — —
Recut in eye, plate 14731, pos. 3 —

Earliest documented uses: Mar. 31, 1923 (dated cancel on off-cover pair of stamps); June 29, 1923 (on cover).

Rotary press sheet waste

Stamp design approximately 19¼x22½mm

596 A155 1c **green,** machine cancel *250,000.*
With Bureau precancel *200,000.*

Fifteen examples of No. 596 are recorded, all used. Ten of the fifteen carry the Bureau precancel "KANSAS CITY/MO" between lines, only two or three of the non-precenceled example are completely sound, and only three or four of the precanceled examples are completely sound. Values are for sound stamps in the grade of fine.

COIL STAMPS

ROTARY PRESS

1923-29 ***Perf. 10 Vertically***

Stamp designs approximately 19¾x22¼mm

597 A155 1c **green,** *July 18, 1923* .30 .25
yellow green .30 .25
grayish green — —
Never hinged .60
Three on cover 2.25
Pair .65 .25
Never hinged 1.40
Joint line pair 2.00 .75
Never hinged 4.00
Gripper cracks 2.60 1.00
Double transfer 2.60 1.00

598 A156 1½c **brown,** *Mar. 19, 1925* .90 .25
deep brown .90 .25
Never hinged 1.80
On 3rd class cover 6.00
Pair 1.90 .25
Never hinged 3.80
Joint line pair 4.50 .75
Never hinged 9.00

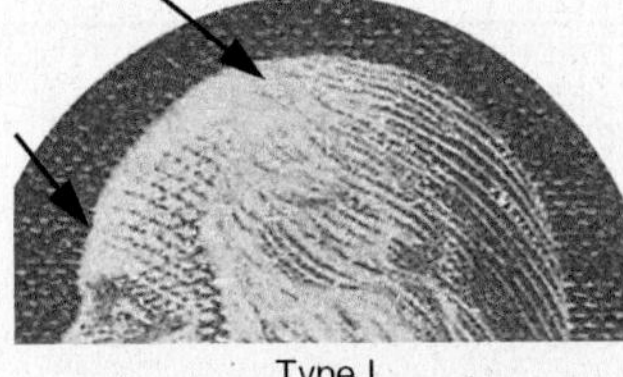

Type I

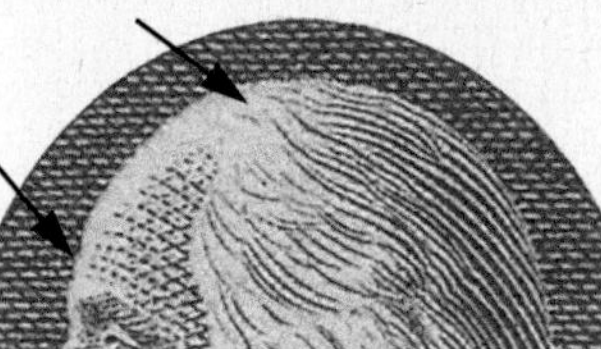

Type II

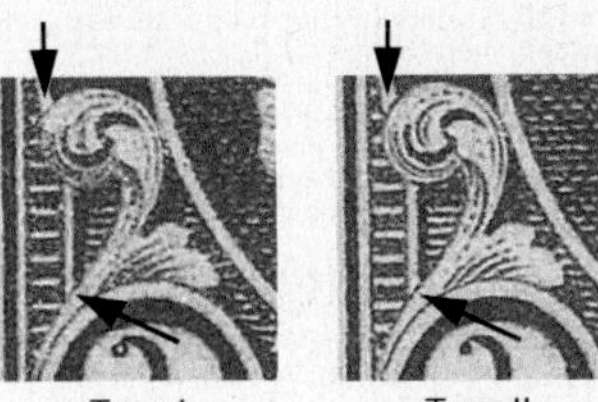

Type I Type II

TYPE I. No line outlining forehead. No heavy hair lines at top center of head. Outline of left acanthus scroll generally faint at top and toward base at left side.

TYPE II. Thin line outlining forehead. Three heavy hair lines at top center of head; two being outstanding in the white area. Outline of left acanthus scroll very strong and clearly defined at top (under left edge of lettered panel) and at lower curve (above and to left of numeral oval). This type appears only on Nos. 599A and 634A.

599 A157 2c **carmine,** type I, *Jan. 1923* .35 .25
deep carmine, type I .35 .25
Never hinged .70
On cover 1.10
Pair, type I .75 .25
Never hinged 1.50
Joint line pair, type I 2.25 1.00
Never hinged 4.50
Double transfer, type I 1.90 1.00
Gripper cracks, type I 2.30 2.00
V-shaped gouge from eye down into cheek and back to hair in front of ear, plate 14731, pos. 3 — —
Recut in eye, plate 14731, pos. 3 — —
b. 2c **carmine lake,** type I, never hinged *300.00* —
Pair, never hinged *650.00*
Joint line pair *700.00*
Never hinged *950.00*

Earliest documented use: Jan. 10, 1923 (precanceled version).

599A A157 2c **carmine,** type II, *Mar. 1929* 120.00 16.00
Never hinged 240.00
On cover 32.50
Pair, type II 250.00 60.00
Never hinged 500.00
Joint line pair, type II 575.00 400.00
Never hinged 1,150.
Joint line pair, types I & II 700.00 *1,100.*
Never hinged 1,350.

Earliest documented use: Mar. 29, 1929.

600 A158 3c **violet,** *May 10, 1924* 5.25 .25
deep violet 5.25 .25
Never hinged 10.50
On cover 6.00
Pair 11.00 .45
Never hinged 22.00
Joint line pair 30.00 4.00
Never hinged 60.00
Cracked plate — 1.00

601 A159 4c **yellow brown,** *Aug. 5, 1923* 3.75 .35
brown 3.75 .35
Never hinged 7.50
On cover 14.00
Pair 8.25 .95
Never hinged 16.50
Joint line pair 27.50 10.00
Never hinged 55.00

Earliest documented use: Sept. 14, 1923.

602 A160 5c **dark blue,** *Mar. 5, 1924* 1.75 .25
Never hinged 3.50
On UPU-rate cover 6.00
Pair 3.75 .35
Never hinged 7.50
Joint line pair 11.00 3.00
Never hinged 22.50

603 A165 10c **orange,** *Dec. 1, 1924* 3.50 .25
Never hinged 7.00
On special delivery cover with 2c 22.50
Pair 8.00 .25
Never hinged 16.00
Joint line pair 25.00 4.50
Never hinged 50.00

The 6c design A161 coil stamp is listed as No. 723.

Bureau Precancels: 1c, 296 diff., 1½c, 188 diff., 2c, type I, 113 diff., 2c, type II, Boston, Detroit, 3c, 62 diff., 4c, 34 diff., 5c, 36 diff., 10c, 32 diff.

1923-25 ***Perf. 10 Horizontally***

Stamp designs: 19¼x22½mm

604 A155 1c **green,** *July 19, 1924* .40 .25
yellow green .40 .25
Never hinged .80
Three on cover 6.00
Pair .85 .25
Never hinged 1.70
Joint line pair 3.50 1.25
Never hinged 7.00

605 A156 1½c **yellow brown,** *May 9, 1925* .40 .25
brown .40 .25
Never hinged .80
On 3rd class cover 17.50
Pair .85 .35
Never hinged 1.70
Joint line pair 3.50 *4.00*
Never hinged 7.00

606 A157 2c **carmine,** *Dec. 31, 1923* .40 .25
Never hinged .80
On cover 12.50
Pair .85 .45
Never hinged 1.70
Joint line pair 2.50 *3.50*
Never hinged 5.00
Cracked plate 5.25 2.00
a. 2c **carmine lake** *75.00* —
Never hinged *150.00*
Pair *170.00*
Never hinged *350.00*
Joint line pair, never hinged *775.00*

Nos. 597-599,600-606 (10) 17.00 2.60
Nos. 597-599, 600-606, never hinged 36.00

HARDING MEMORIAL ISSUE

Tribute to the memory of President Warren G. Harding, who died in San Francisco, Aug. 2, 1923.

Warren Gamaliel Harding — A177

Plates of 400 subjects in four panes of 100 each

FLAT PLATE PRINTING

Stamp designs: 19¼x22¼mm

1923 ***Perf. 11***

610 A177 2c **black,** *Sept. 1, 1923* .50 .25
intense black .50 .25
grayish black .50 .25
Never hinged 1.00
On cover .30
P# block of 6 30.00 —
Never hinged 47.50
Double transfer 2.40 1.00
a. Horiz. pair, imperf. vert. *2,000.*
b. Imperf. (error), P#14870 block of 6 *20,000.*
Never hinged 25,000.

No. 610a is valued in the grade of fine.

No. 610b comes from left side error panes found in a normal pad of No. 610 stamps before No. 611 was issued. Two left side plate blocks and one top position plate block are recorded. Plate #14870 was not used to print No. 611. Loose stamps separated from the top and left plate blocks are indistinguishable from No. 611.

Imperf

611 A177 2c **black,** *Nov. 15, 1923* 4.50 4.00
Never hinged 9.00
On philatelic cover 8.00
On commercial cover 15.00
Pair 10.00 10.00
Never hinged 20.00
Corner margin block of 4 22.00 22.50
Margin block of 4, arrow 22.00 22.50
Center line block 75.00 40.00
Never hinged 130.00
P# block of 6 70.00 —
Never hinged 90.00

ROTARY PRESS PRINTING

Stamp designs: 19¼x22½mm

Perf. 10

612 A177 2c **black,** *Sept. 12, 1923* 15.00 1.75
gray black 15.00 1.75
Never hinged 32.50
On cover 3.25
P# block of 4 300.00
Never hinged 500.00
Pair with full vertical gutter between *350.00*

Perf. 11

613 A177 2c **black** *35,000.*
Pair *80,000.*

No. 613 was produced from rotary press sheet waste. It is valued in the grade of fine.

HUGUENOT-WALLOON TERCENTENARY ISSUE

300th anniversary of the settling of the Walloons, and in honor of the Huguenots.

Ship "Nieu Nederland" A178

Walloons Landing at Fort Orange (Albany) — A179

Jan Ribault Monument at Duval County, Fla. — A180

"Broken Circle" flaw

Designed by Clair Aubrey Huston

FLAT PLATE PRINTINGS

Plates of 200 subjects in four panes of 50 each

1924, May 1 ***Perf. 11***

614 A178 1c **dark green** 2.30 *3.00*
green 2.30 *3.00*
Never hinged 4.25
On cover 4.50
P# block of 6 40.00 —
Never hinged 60.00
Double transfer 6.00 6.00

615 A179 2c **carmine rose** 3.75 2.25
dark carmine rose 3.75 2.25
Never hinged 7.00
On cover 3.50
P# block of 6 60.00 —
Never hinged 85.00
Double transfer 12.00 3.50

616 A180 5c **dark blue** 15.00 13.00
deep blue 15.00 13.00
Never hinged 27.50
On UPU-rate cover 20.00
P# block of 6 250.00 —
Never hinged 375.00
Added line at bottom of white circle around right numeral, "broken circle" plate flaw (15754 UR 2, 3, 4, 5) 60.00 20.00
Never hinged 120.00
Nos. 614-616 (3) 21.05 18.25
Nos. 614-616, never hinged 38.75

LEXINGTON-CONCORD ISSUE

150th anniv. of the Battle of Lexington-Concord.

Washington at Cambridge A181

"Birth of Liberty," by Henry Sandham A182

The Minute Man, by Daniel Chester French — A183

Plates of 200 subjects in four panes of 50 each

1925, Apr. 4 ***Perf. 11***

617 A181 1c **deep green** 2.00 2.50
green 2.00 2.50
Never hinged 3.75
On cover 3.75
P# block of 6 40.00 —
Never hinged 67.50

618 A182 2c **carmine rose** 3.50 4.00
pale carmine rose 3.50 4.00
Never hinged 6.50
On cover 5.50
P# block of 6 60.00 —
Never hinged 85.00

619 A183 5c **dark blue** 14.00 13.00
blue 14.00 13.00
Never hinged 26.00
On UPU-rate cover 20.00
P# block of 6 200.00 —
Never hinged 275.00
Line over head (16807 LL 48) 42.50 19.00
Nos. 617-619 (3) 19.50 19.50
Nos. 617-619, never hinged 36.25

NORSE-AMERICAN ISSUE

Arrival in New York, on Oct. 9, 1825, of the sloop "Restaurationen" with the first group of immigrants from Norway.

Sloop "Restaurationen" A184

Viking Ship A185

Designed by Clair Aubrey Huston.

Plates of 100 subjects.

1925, May 18 ***Perf. 11***

620 A184 2c **carmine & black** 3.00 2.75
deep carmine & black 3.00 2.75
Never hinged 6.00
On cover 4.50
Margin block of 4, arrow 15.00
Center line block 20.00
Never hinged 37.50
P# block of 8, two P# & arrow 160.00 —
Never hinged 275.00
P# block of 8, carmine & arrow; black P# omitted *6,000.* —
Never hinged 6,500.

621 A185 5c **dark blue & black** 9.00 9.00
Never hinged *19.00*
On UPU-rate cover 17.50
Margin block of 4, arrow 52.50
Center line block 65.00
Never hinged 115.00
P# block of 8, two P# & arrow 450.00 —
Never hinged 700.00

REGULAR ISSUE

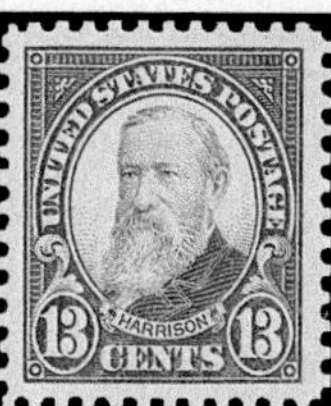
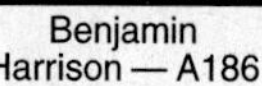

Benjamin Harrison — A186

Woodrow Wilson — A187

Plates of 400 subjects in four panes of 100.

1925-26 ***Perf. 11***

622 A186 13c **green,** *Jan. 11, 1926* 9.00 .75
light green 9.00 .75
Never hinged 19.00
On registered cover with other values 17.50
P# block of 6 210.00 —
Never hinged 300.00
P# block of 6, large 5 point star, right side only *2,100.* —
Never hinged *3,250.*

623 A187 17c **black,** *Dec. 28, 1925* 9.00 .30
gray black 9.00 .30
Never hinged 19.00
On registered cover 6.00
P# block of 6 250.00 —
Never hinged 325.00

Plate Blocks

Scott values for plate blocks printed from flat plates are for very fine side and bottom positions. Top position plate blocks with full wide selvage sell for more.

SESQUICENTENNIAL EXPOSITION ISSUE

Sesquicentennial Exposition, Philadelphia, Pa., June 1 - Dec. 1, 1926, and 150th anniv. of the Declaration of Independence.

Liberty Bell — A188

Designed by Clair Aubrey Huston.

Plates of 200 subjects in four panes of 50.

1926, May 10 ***Perf. 11***

627 A188 2c **carmine rose** 2.25 .50
Never hinged 4.00
On cover 1.00
On cover, Expo. station machine canc. 7.50
On cover, Expo. station duplex hand-stamp canc. 35.00
P# block of 6 35.00 —
Never hinged 50.00
Double transfer — —

ERICSSON MEMORIAL ISSUE

Unveiling of the statue of John Ericsson, builder of the "Monitor," by the Crown Prince of Sweden, Washington, D.C., May 29, 1926.

Statue of John Ericsson — A189

Designed by Clair Aubrey Huston.

Plates of 200 subjects in four panes of 50.

1926, May 29 ***Perf. 11***

628 A189 5c **gray lilac** 5.00 3.25
Never hinged 8.50
On UPU-rate cover 8.00
P# block of 6 57.50 —
Never hinged 82.50

BATTLE OF WHITE PLAINS ISSUE

150th anniv. of the Battle of White Plains, N. Y.

Alexander Hamilton's Battery — A190

Designed by Clair Aubrey Huston.

Plates of 400 subjects in four panes of 100.

1926, Oct. 18 ***Perf. 11***

629 A190 2c **carmine rose** 1.60 1.70
Never hinged 2.75
On cover 2.25
P# block of 6 35.00 —
Never hinged 50.00

INTERNATIONAL PHILATELIC EXHIBITION ISSUE
Souvenir Sheet

A190a

Illustration reduced.

Plates of 100 subjects in four panes of 25 each, separated by one inch wide gutters with central guide lines.

Condition valued:

Centering: Overall centering will average very fine, but individual stamps may be better or worse.

Perforations: No folds along rows of perforations.

Gum: There may be some light gum bends but no gum creases.

Hinging: There may be hinge marks in the selvage and on up to two or three stamps, but no heavy hinging or hinge remnants (except in the ungummed portion of the wide selvage.

Margins: Top panes should have about ½ inch bottom margin and 1 inch top margin.

Bottom panes should have about ½ inch top margin and just under ¾ inch bottom margin. Both will have one wide side (usually 1 inch plus) and one narrow (½ inch) side margin. The wide margin corner will have a small diagonal notch on top panes.

1926, Oct. 18 ***Perf. 11***

630 A190a 2c **carmine rose,** pane of 25 275.00 *450.00*
Never hinged 500.00
On cover —

Dot over first "S" of "States" 18774 LL 9 or 18773 LL 11, sheet 350.00 *500.00*
Never hinged 575.00
a. Single stamp (see footnote) *10.00* —
Never hinged 14.00
P# block of 6 (#18770, 18771, 18773 or 18774) 70.00 —
Never hinged 100.00
Dot over first "S" of "States," 18773 LL 11, single stamp 15.00 —
Never hinged 20.00
P# block of 6, L or R side, containing dot over first "S" of "States," 18774 LL 9 or 18773 LL 11 90.00 —
Never hinged 125.00

Issued in panes measuring 158-160¼x136-146½mm containing 25 stamps with inscription "International Philatelic Exhibition, Oct. 16th to 23rd, 1926" in top margin.

No. 630a can be identified only when attached to the distinctive selvage as shown in illustration A190a. The four plate numbers used to print the White Plains souvenir sheets were distinct from the plate numbers used to print No. 629, and therefore all stamps in a plate block, for instance, are identifiable as No. 630a.

VALUES FOR VERY FINE STAMPS
Please note: Stamps are valued in the grade of Very Fine unless otherwise indicated.

TYPES OF 1922-26 ISSUE
REGULAR ISSUE
ROTARY PRESS PRINTINGS
(See note above No. 448.)
Plates of 400 subjects in four panes of 100 each
Stamp designs 19¼x22½mm

1926, Aug. 27 ***Imperf.***

631 A156 1½c **yellow brown** 2.00 1.70
light brown 2.00 1.70
Never hinged 3.00
On philatelic cover 12.50
Pair 4.25 4.00
Never hinged 6.25
Pair, vert. gutter between 4.75 *5.00*
Pair, horiz. gutter between 4.75 *5.00*
Margin block with dash (left, right, top or bottom) 11.00 *14.00*
Center block with crossed gutters and dashes 35.00 *40.00*
Never hinged 55.00
P# block of 4 55.00 —
Never hinged 75.00
Without gum breaker ridges 50.00
Never hinged 75.00
Pair, vert. gutter between *110.00*
Pair, horiz. gutter btwn. *110.00*
Margin block with dash (left right, top or bottom) *275.00*
Center block with crossed gutters and dashes *600.00*
Never hinged *900.00*
P# block of 4 375.00
Never hinged 575.00

1926-34 ***Perf. 11x10½***

632 A155 1c **green,** *June 10, 1927* .25 .25
yellow green .25 .25
Never hinged .35
Three on cover 1.25
P# block of 4 2.00 —
Never hinged 3.25
Pair with full vertical gutter btwn. 150.00 —
Pair with full horizontal gutter btwn. —
Cracked plate — —
a. Booklet pane of 6, *Nov. 2, 1927* 5.00 *4.00*
Never hinged 8.00
b. Vertical pair, imperf. between *3,000.* *3,250.*
Never hinged *5,500.*
c. Horiz. pair, imperf. between *5,000.*

No. 632b is valued in the grade of fine. No. 632c is valued in the grade of fine and never hinged. It is possibly unique.

633 A156 1½c **yellow brown,** *May 17, 1927* 1.70 .25
deep brown 1.70 .25
Never hinged 2.60
On 3rd class cover 2.50
P# block of 4 70.00 —
Never hinged 115.00

Normal

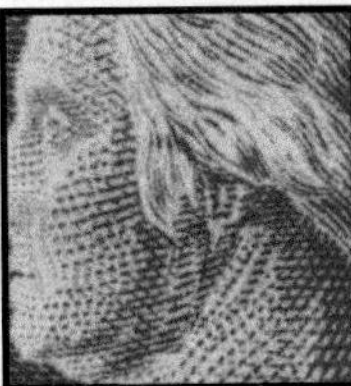

"Long ear"
Recut

"Smiling George"
Recut

634 A157 2c **carmine,** type I, *Dec. 10, 1926* .25 .25
carmine red .25 .25
carmine rose .25 .25
Never hinged .30
On cover .35
P# block of 4, type I, # opposite corner stamp 3.75 —
Never hinged 6.50
Vertical P# block of 10, # opposite 3rd horizontal row from top or bottom (Experimental Electric Eye plates) 7.50 —
Never hinged 12.50
Margin block of 4, Electric Eye marking .45 .25
Pair with full vertical gutter between 200.00
Recut ("long ear"), type I, 20342 UR 34 *90.00* —
Never hinged *175.00*
Gash and recut ("smiling George"), type I, 21423 UL 23 *120.00* —
Never hinged 250.00
Recut face, type I, 20234 LL 58 —
b. 2c **carmine lake,** type I *180.00* *500.00*
Never hinged *425.00*
P# block of 4 *2,250.*
Never hinged *4,250.*
c. Horizontal pair, type I, imperf. between *6,000.*
d. Booklet pane of 6, **carmine,** type I, *mid-April, 1927* 1.50 1.50
Never hinged 2.50
e. As "d," **carmine lake** *400.00* *1,000.*
Never hinged *750.00*
f. 2c **lake,** type I, on cover —
g. 2c **carmine,** type I, on thin, tough experimental paper — —

No. 634c is valued in the grade of fine.

Earliest documented use: FDC (No. 634); Dec. 20, 1929 (No. 634b); May 9, 1927 (5 No. 6634d singles on cover).

Counterfeits exist of No. 634. See the Postal Counterfeits section of this catalog.

634A A157 2c **carmine,** type II, *Dec. 1928* 300.00 13.50
Never hinged 600.00
On cover 21.00
P# block of 4, type II 2,000. —
Never hinged 3,000.
Pair with full horiz. gutter btwn. 750.00 —
Never hinged *1,250.*
Pair with full vert. gutter btwn. 750.00 —
Never hinged *1,250.*
Center block with crossed gutters 2,750.
Never hinged *4,250.*

Earliest documented use: Dec. 15, 1928.

An unused, never-hinged block of four in a distinctive dark carmine shade was authenticated as genuine in 2013. To date, unused (hinged) examples and used examples have not been reported. This shade is likely extremely scarce, and the editors would like to receive reports of additional examples.

No. 634A, Type II, was available in full sheet of 400 subjects but was not regularly issued in that form.

635 A158 3c **violet,** *Feb. 3, 1927* .75 .25
Never hinged 1.20
On cover 2.00
P# block of 4 17.50 —
Never hinged 35.00
a. 3c **bright violet,** *Feb. 7, 1934* re-issue, Plates 21185 & 21186 .35 .25
Never hinged .45
On cover .25
P# block of 4 10.00 —
Never hinged 18.00
Gripper cracks 3.25 2.00

636 A159 4c **yellow brown,** *May 17, 1927* 1.90 .25
Never hinged 3.00
On cover 8.00
P# block of 4 65.00 —
Never hinged 92.50
Pair with full vert. gutter btwn. *200.00*

637 A160 5c **dark blue,** *Mar. 24, 1927* 1.90 .25
Never hinged 3.00
On UPU-rate cover 4.50
P# block of 4 12.50 —
Never hinged 17.50
Pair with full vert. gutter btwn. *275.00*
Double transfer — —

638 A161 6c **red orange,** *July 27, 1927* 2.00 .25
Never hinged 3.20
On airmail cover 6.00
P# block of 4 15.00 —
Never hinged 20.00
Pair with full horiz. gutter btwn. —
Pair with full vert. gutter btwn. *300.00*

639 A162 7c **black,** *Mar. 24, 1927* 2.00 .25
Never hinged 3.20
On registered cover with other values 15.00
P# block of 4 15.00 —
Never hinged 20.00
a. Vertical pair, imperf. between 550.00 400.00
Never hinged 1,000.

640 A163 8c **yellow brown,** *June 10, 1927* 2.00 .25
olive bister 2.00 .25
Never hinged 3.20
On airmail cover 8.00
P# block of 4 15.00 —
Never hinged 20.00

641 A164 9c **rose,** *May 17, 1927* 1.90 .25
salmon rose 1.90 .25
orange red, *1931* 1.90 .25
Never hinged 3.00
On registered cover with other values 8.00
P# block of 4 12.50 —
Never hinged 17.50
Pair with full vert. gutter btwn. —

642 A165 10c **orange,** *Feb. 3, 1927* 3.25 .25
Never hinged 5.50
On special delivery cover with 2c 6.00
P# block of 4 17.00 —
Never hinged 22.50
Double transfer — —
Pair with full vert. gutter btwn. *300.00*
Nos. 632-634,635-642 (11) 17.90 2.75
Nos. 632-634, 635-642 never hinged 28.00

The 1½c, 2c, 4c, 5c, 6c, 8c imperf. (dry print) are printer's waste.

See No. 653.

Bureau Precancels: 1c, 292 diff., 1½c, 147 diff., 2c, type I, 99 diff., 2c, type II, 4 diff., 3c, 101 diff., 4c, 60 diff., 5c, 91 diff., 6c, 78 diff., 7c, 66 diff., 8c, 78 diff., 9c, 60 diff., 10c, 97 diff.

VERMONT SESQUICENTENNIAL ISSUE

Battle of Bennington, 150th anniv. and State independence.

Green Mountain Boy — A191

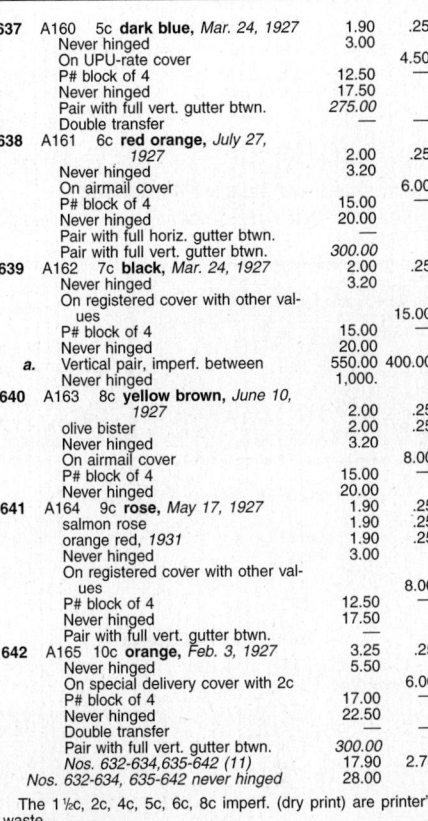

FLAT PLATE PRINTING

Plates of 400 subjects in four panes of 100.

1927, Aug. 3 ***Perf. 11***

643	A191 2c **carmine rose**	1.20	.80
	Never hinged	2.00	
	On cover		1.50
	P# block of 6	32.50	—
	Never hinged	45.00	

BURGOYNE CAMPAIGN ISSUE

Battles of Bennington, Oriskany, Fort Stanwix and Saratoga.

"The Surrender of General Burgoyne at Saratoga," by John Trumbull A192

Plates of 200 subjects in four panes of 50.

1927, Aug. 3 ***Perf. 11***

644	A192 2c **carmine rose**	3.00	2.10
	Never hinged	5.25	
	On cover		3.00
	P# block of 6	32.50	—
	Never hinged	42.50	

VALLEY FORGE ISSUE

150th anniversary of Washington's encampment at Valley Forge, Pa.

Washington at Prayer — A193

Plates of 400 subjects in four panes of 100.

1928, May 26 ***Perf. 11***

645	A193 2c **carmine rose**	1.15	.50
	Never hinged	1.80	
	On cover		.75
	P# block of 6	25.00	—
	Never hinged	37.50	
a.	2c **lake**	—	
	Never hinged	—	

BATTLE OF MONMOUTH ISSUE

150th anniv. of the Battle of Monmouth, N.J., and "Molly Pitcher" (Mary Ludwig Hayes), the heroine of the battle.

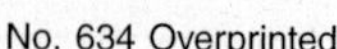
No. 634 Overprinted

ROTARY PRESS PRINTING

1928, Oct. 20 ***Perf. 11x10½***

646	A157 2c **carmine**	1.00	1.00
	Never hinged	1.60	
	On cover		1.60
	P# block of 4	37.50	—
	Never hinged	52.50	
	Wide spacing, vert. pair	50.00	—
a.	"Pitcher" only	*675.00*	
b.	2c **carmine lake**		*2,500.*

No. 646a is valued in the grade of fine.

Normally the overprints were placed 18mm apart vertically, but pairs exist with a space of 28mm between the overprints.

HAWAII SESQUICENTENNIAL ISSUE

Sesquicentennial Celebration of the discovery of the Hawaiian Islands.

Nos. 634 and 637 Overprinted

ROTARY PRESS PRINTING

1928, Aug. 13 ***Perf. 11x10½***

647	A157 2c **carmine**	4.00	4.00
	Never hinged	7.25	
	On cover		5.75
	P# block of 4	110.00	—
	Never hinged	180.00	
	Wide spacing, vert. pair	125.00	
648	A160 5c **dark blue**	11.00	12.50
	Never hinged	21.50	
	On cover		20.00
	P# block of 4	200.00	—
	Never hinged	375.00	

Nos. 647-648 were sold at post offices in Hawaii and at the Postal Agency in Washington, D.C. They were valid throughout the nation.

Normally the overprints were placed 18mm apart vertically, but pairs exist with a space of 28mm between the overprints.

AERONAUTICS CONFERENCE ISSUE

Intl. Civil Aeronautics Conf., Washington, D.C., Dec. 12 - 14, 1928, and 25th anniv. of the 1st airplane flight by the Wright Brothers, Dec. 17, 1903.

Wright Airplane A194

Globe and Airplane A195

"Prairie Dog" plate flaw

FLAT PLATE PRINTING

Plates of 200 subjects in four panes of 50.

1928, Dec. 12 ***Perf. 11***

649	A194 2c **carmine rose**	1.10	.80
	Never hinged	1.75	
	On cover		1.50
	P# block of 6	11.50	—
	Never hinged	17.50	
650	A195 5c **blue**	4.50	3.25
	Never hinged	7.00	
	On UPU-rate cover		5.00
	P# block of 6	42.50	—
	Never hinged	60.00	
	Plate flaw "prairie dog" (19658 LL 50)	35.00	20.00

GEORGE ROGERS CLARK ISSUE

150th anniv. of the surrender of Fort Sackville, the present site of Vincennes, Ind., to Clark.

Surrender of Fort Sackville A196

Plates of 100 subjects in two panes of 50.

1929, Feb. 25 ***Perf. 11***

651	A196 2c **carmine & black**	.70	.50
	deep carmine & black	.70	.50
	Never hinged	1.15	
	On cover		1.00
	Margin block of 4, arrow (line only) right or left	3.25	
	P# block of 6, two P# & "Top"	11.00	—
	Never hinged	20.00	
	P# block of 10, red P# only	—	—
	Double transfer (19721 R 14, 29 & 44)	4.25	2.25

TYPE OF 1922-26 ISSUE

REGULAR ISSUE

ROTARY PRESS PRINTING

Plates of 400 subjects in four panes of 100.

1929, May 25 ***Perf. 11x10½***

653	A154 ½c **olive brown**	.25	.25
	Never hinged	.35	
	On 1c stamped envelope (3rd class)		1.00
	P# block of 4	2.00	—
	Never hinged	3.00	
	Damaged plate, (19652 LL 72)	2.00	1.00
	Retouched plate, (19652 LL 72)	2.00	1.00
	Pair with full vert. gutter btwn.	*200.00*	
	Pair with full horiz. gutter btwn.	*150.00*	

Bureau Precancels: 99 diff.

ELECTRIC LIGHT'S GOLDEN JUBILEE ISSUE

Invention of the 1st incandescent electric lamp by Thomas Alva Edison, Oct. 21, 1879, 50th anniv.

Edison's First Lamp — A197

Designed by Alvin R. Meissner.

FLAT PLATE PRINTING

Plates of 400 subjects in four panes of 100.

1929 ***Perf. 11***

654	A197 2c **carmine rose,** *June 5*	.65	.65
	Never hinged	1.10	
	On cover		1.10
	P# block of 6	25.00	—
	Never hinged	40.00	
a.	2c **lake**	—	

ROTARY PRESS PRINTING

Perf. 11x10½

655	A197 2c **carmine rose,** *June 11*	.65	.25
	Never hinged	1.10	
	On cover		.25
	P# block of 4	32.50	—
	Never hinged	45.00	
	Pair with full horiz. gutter btwn.	—	

ROTARY PRESS COIL STAMP

Perf. 10 Vertically

656	A197 2c **carmine rose,** *June 11*	10.00	1.75
	Never hinged	20.00	
	On cover		2.75
	Pair	22.50	4.00
	Never hinged	45.00	
	Joint line pair	55.00	27.50
	Never hinged	110.00	

SULLIVAN EXPEDITION ISSUE

150th anniversary of the Sullivan Expedition in New York State during the Revolutionary War.

Major General John Sullivan — A198

FLAT PLATE PRINTING

Plates of 400 subjects in four panes of 100.

1929, June 17 *Perf. 11*

657 A198 2c **carmine rose** .55 .55
Never hinged .95
On cover 1.00
P# block of 6 17.50 —
Never hinged 27.50
a. 2c **lake** 375.00 250.00
Never hinged 625.00
P# block of 6 *2,500.*
Never hinged *3,500.*
b. Vert. pair, imperf. btwn. *4,000.*

The unique No. 657b resulted from a paper foldover before perfing, and it has angled errant perfs from another row of horiz. perfs through the left side of the stamps.

REGULAR ISSUE

Nos. 632 to 642 Overprinted

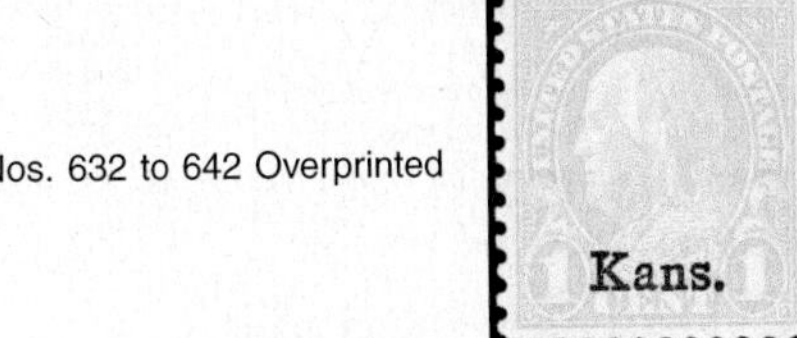

Officially issued May 1, 1929.

Some values known canceled as early as Apr. 15.

This special issue was authorized as a measure of preventing losses from post office burglaries. Approximately a year's supply was printed and issued to postmasters. The P.O. Dept. found it desirable to discontinue the State overprinted stamps after the initial supply was used.

On-cover values are for commercial contemporaneous (1929-31) uses from Kansas or Nebraska. Later (post 1932) uses and philatelic uses such as first-flight commemorations sell for less.

ROTARY PRESS PRINTING

1929, May 1 *Perf. 11x10½*

658 A155 1c **green** 2.50 2.00
Never hinged 5.00
On cover 6.50
Single franking on drop letter 15.00
Pair on first-class letter 15.00
P# block of 4 60.00 —
Never hinged 85.00
Wide spacing, pair 32.50
a. Vertical pair, one without ovpt. *300.00*
Never hinged *500.00*
659 A156 1½c **brown** 3.25 2.90
Never hinged 6.50
Pair on first-class (after July 6, 1932) letter 20.00
Single franking on third-class unsealed advertising cover 25.00
Single franking on third-class greeting card with contents 30.00
P# block of 4 60.00 —
Never hinged 85.00
Wide spacing, pair 70.00
a. Vertical pair, one without ovpt. *475.00*
660 A157 2c **carmine** 4.00 1.00
Never hinged 7.50
On cover 6.00
Single franking on UPU treaty rate cover *90.00*
P# block of 4 60.00 —
Never hinged 80.00
Wide spacing, pair 55.00
661 A158 3c **violet** 17.50 15.00
Never hinged 35.00
On domestic airmail cover *90.00*
On registered cover with return receipt *150.00*
Single franking on UPU postcard *200.00*
Single franking on first-class (after July 6, 1932) cover *45.00*
P# block of 4 250.00 —
Never hinged 325.00
a. Vertical pair, one without ovpt. *600.00*
Never hinged *800.00*
662 A159 4c **yellow brown** 17.50 9.00
Never hinged 35.00
Single franking on double-weight first-class letter *95.00*
Single franking on double-weight UPU treaty rate cover *130.00*
P# block of 4 225.00 —
Never hinged 300.00
a. Vertical pair, one without ovpt. *500.00*
663 A160 5c **deep blue** 12.50 9.75
Never hinged 25.00
Single franking on domestic airmail cover *95.00*
Single franking on UPU cover to Germany *80.00*
Single franking on UPU cover to other destinations *160.00*
On registered or special delivery cover *135.00*
P# block of 4 200.00 —
Never hinged 650.00
664 A161 6c **red orange** 25.00 18.00
Never hinged 50.00
On registered or special delivery cover *145.00*
Single franking on triple-weight first-class cover *175.00*
P# block of 4 450.00 —
Never hinged 600.00
665 A162 7c **black** 25.00 27.50
Never hinged 50.00
On registered or special delivery cover *175.00*
P# block of 4 500.00 —
Never hinged 700.00
666 A163 8c **olive green** 72.50 65.00
Never hinged 145.00
On registered or special delivery cover *300.00*
Single franking on quadruple-weight first-class letter *275.00*
Single franking on double-weight UPU foreign letter rate cover *375.00*
P# block of 4 700.00 —
Never hinged 1,000.
667 A164 9c **light rose** 14.00 11.50
Never hinged 27.50
On registered or special delivery cover *235.00*
P# block of 4 275.00 —
Never hinged 375.00
668 A165 10c **orange yellow** 22.50 12.50
Never hinged 45.00
On registered special delivery cover *185.00*
Pair on registered first-class cover with return receipt *225.00*
P# block of 4 375.00 —
Never hinged 525.00
Pair with full horizontal gutter between *4,750.*
Nos. 658-668 (11) 216.25 174.15
Nos. 658-668, never hinged 431.50

See notes following No. 679.

Overprinted

Nebr.

1929, May 1

669 A155 1c **green** 3.25 2.25
Never hinged 6.50
On cover 6.50
Single franking on drop letter 15.00
Pair on first-class letter 15.00
P# block of 4 60.00 —
Never hinged 80.00
Wide spacing, pair 60.00 —
b. No period after "Nebr." (19338, 19339 UR 26, 36 and 19339 LR 26, 36) 50.00
670 A156 1½c **brown** 3.00 2.50
Never hinged 6.00
Pair on first-class (after July 6, 1932) letter 20.00
Single franking on third-class unsealed advertising cover 25.00
Single franking on third-class greeting card with contents 30.00
P# block of 4 65.00 —
Never hinged 95.00
Wide spacing, pair 60.00
671 A157 2c **carmine** 3.00 1.30
Never hinged 6.00
On cover 6.00
Single franking on UPU treaty rate cover *90.00*
P# block of 4 60.00 —
Never hinged 85.00
Wide spacing, pair 75.00
672 A158 3c **violet** 11.00 12.00
Never hinged 22.00
On domestic airmail cover *90.00*
On registered cover with return receipt *150.00*
Single franking on UPU postcard *200.00*
Single franking on first-class (after July 6, 1932) cover *45.00*
P# block of 4 260.00 —
Never hinged 350.00
Wide spacing, pair 175.00
a. Vertical pair, one without ovpt. *500.00*
673 A159 4c **yellow brown** 17.50 15.00
Never hinged 35.00
Single franking on double-weight first-class letter *95.00*
Single franking on double-weight UPU treaty rate cover *130.00*
P# block of 4 275.00 —
Never hinged 375.00
Wide spacing, pair 175.00
674 A160 5c **deep blue** 15.00 15.00
Never hinged 30.00
Single franking on domestic airmail cover *95.00*
Single franking on UPU cover to Germany *80.00*
Single franking on UPU cover to other destinations *160.00*
On registered or special delivery cover *135.00*
P# block of 4 300.00 —
Never hinged 400.00
675 A161 6c **red orange** 35.00 24.00
Never hinged 70.00
On registered or special delivery cover *145.00*
Single franking on triple-weight first-class cover *175.00*
P# block of 4 525.00 —
Never hinged 750.00
676 A162 7c **black** 22.50 18.00
Never hinged 45.00
On registered or special delivery cover *175.00*
P# block of 4 325.00 —
Never hinged 500.00
677 A163 8c **olive green** 30.00 25.00
Never hinged 60.00
On registered or special delivery cover *300.00*
Single franking on quadruple-weight first-class letter *275.00*
Single franking on double-weight UPU foreign letter rate cover *375.00*
P# block of 4 400.00 —
Never hinged 550.00
Wide spacing, pair 150.00
Never hinged 225.00
678 A164 9c **light rose** 35.00 27.50
Never hinged 70.00
On registered or special delivery cover *235.00*
P# block of 4 500.00 —
Never hinged 700.00
Wide spacing, pair 160.00
a. Vertical pair, one without ovpt. *800.00*
679 A165 10c **orange yellow** 90.00 22.50
Never hinged 180.00
On registered special delivery cover *185.00*
Pair on registered first-class cover with return receipt *225.00*
P# block of 4 925.00 —
Never hinged 1,275.
Nos. 669-679 (11) 265.25 165.05
Nos. 669-679, never hinged 530.50

Nos. 658-661, 669-673, 677-678 are known with the overprints on vertical pairs spaced 32mm apart instead of the normal 22mm.

Important: Nos. 658-679 with original gum have either one horizontal gum breaker ridge per stamp or portions of two at the extreme top and bottom of the stamps, 21mm apart. Multiple complete gum breaker ridges indicate a fake overprint. Absence of the gum breaker ridge indicates either regumming or regumming and a fake overprint.

BATTLE OF FALLEN TIMBERS ISSUE

Memorial to Gen. Anthony Wayne and for 135th anniv. of the Battle of Fallen Timbers, Ohio.

General Wayne Memorial — A199

FLAT PLATE PRINTING

Plates of 400 subjects in four panes of 100.

1929, Sept. 14 *Perf. 11*

680 A199 2c **carmine rose** .65 .65
deep carmine rose .65 .70
Never hinged 1.00
On cover 1.10
P# block of 6 20.00 —
Never hinged 30.00

OHIO RIVER CANALIZATION ISSUE

Completion of the Ohio River Canalization Project, between Cairo, Ill. and Pittsburgh, Pa.

Lock No. 5, Monongahela River — A200

Plates of 400 subjects in four panes of 100.

1929, Oct. 19 *Perf. 11*

681 A200 2c **carmine rose** .55 .55
Never hinged .90
On cover 1.10
P# block of 6 12.50 —
Never hinged 20.00
a. 2c **lake** *425.00* —
Never hinged *650.00*
P# block of 6, never hinged *6,000.*
b. 2c **carmine lake**, never hinged —

MASSACHUSETTS BAY COLONY ISSUE

300th anniversary of the founding of the Massachusetts Bay Colony.

Massachusetts Bay Colony Seal — A201

Plates of 400 subjects in four panes of 100.

1930, Apr. 8		***Perf. 11***	
682	A201 2c **carmine rose**	.65	.50
	Never hinged	.95	
	On cover		1.00
	P# block of 6	20.00	—
	Never hinged	26.00	

CAROLINA-CHARLESTON ISSUE

260th anniv. of the founding of the Province of Carolina and the 250th anniv. of the city of Charleston, S.C.

Gov. Joseph West and Chief Shadoo, a Kiowa — A202

Plates of 400 subjects in four panes of 100.

1930, Apr. 10		***Perf. 11***	
683	A202 2c **carmine rose**	1.00	1.00
	Never hinged	1.50	
	On cover		1.40
	P# block of 6	37.50	—
	Never hinged	50.00	

TYPES OF 1922-26 ISSUE
REGULAR ISSUE

Harding — A203

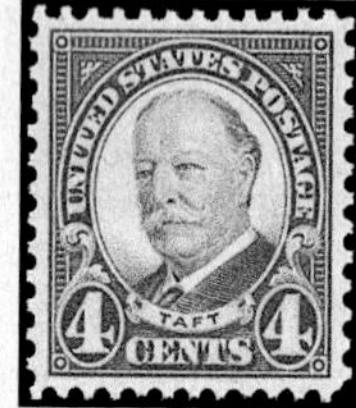

Taft — A204

REGULAR ISSUE
ROTARY PRESS PRINTING

1930		***Perf. 11x10½***	
684	A203 1½c **brown,** *Dec.1*	.50	.25
	yellow brown	.50	.25
	Never hinged	.70	
	On 3rd class cover		2.00
	P# block of 4	2.25	—
	Never hinged	2.75	
	Pair with full horiz. gutter btwn.	*175.00*	
	Pair with full vert. gutter btwn.	—	
685	A204 4c **brown,** *June 4*	.80	.25
	deep brown	.80	.25
	Never hinged	1.25	
	On cover		5.00
	P# block of 4	15.00	—
	Never hinged	20.00	
	Gouge on right "4" (20141 UL 24)	2.50	.65
	Recut right "4" (20141 UL 24)	2.50	.65
	Pair with full horiz. gutter btwn.	—	

Bureau Precancels: 1½c, 96 diff., 4c, 46 diff.

ROTARY PRESS COIL STAMPS
Perf. 10 Vertically

686	A203 1½c **brown,** *Dec. 1*	1.75	.25
	Never hinged	2.60	
	On 3rd class cover		5.00
	Pair	3.75	.30
	Never hinged	5.75	
	Joint line pair	7.50	.75
	Never hinged	11.50	
687	A204 4c **brown,** *Sept. 18*	3.00	.45
	Never hinged	4.50	
	On cover		10.00
	Pair	6.25	1.00
	Never hinged	9.50	
	Joint line pair	11.00	2.50
	Never hinged	22.00	

Bureau Precancels: 1½c, 107 diff., 4c, 23 diff.

BRADDOCK'S FIELD ISSUE

175th anniversary of the Battle of Braddock's Field, otherwise the Battle of Monongahela.

Statue of George Washington — A205

Designed by Alvin R. Meissner.

FLAT PLATE PRINTING

Plates of 400 subjects in four panes of 100.

1930, July 9		***Perf. 11***	
688	A205 2c **carmine rose**	.85	.85
	Never hinged	1.30	
	On cover		1.00
	P# block of 6	30.00	—
	Never hinged	40.00	

VON STEUBEN ISSUE

Baron Friedrich Wilhelm von Steuben (1730-1794), participant in the American Revolution.

General von Steuben — A206

FLAT PLATE PRINTING

Plates of 400 subjects in four panes of 100.

1930, Sept. 17		***Perf. 11***	
689	A206 2c **carmine rose**	.50	.50
	Never hinged	.75	
	On cover		1.05
	P# block of 6	16.00	—
	Never hinged	25.00	
a.	Imperf., pair	*2,000.*	
	Never hinged	*3,000.*	
	P# block of 6	*12,500.*	
b.	2c **carmine lake,** never hinged	*950.00*	

The No. 689a plate block is unique but damaged. The value is for the item in its damaged condition.

PULASKI ISSUE

150th anniversary (in 1929) of the death of Gen. Casimir Pulaski, Polish patriot and hero of the American Revolutionary War.

General Casimir Pulaski — A207

Plates of 400 subjects in four panes of 100.

1931, Jan. 16		***Perf. 11***	
690	A207 2c **carmine rose**	.30	.25
	deep carmine rose	.30	.25
	Never hinged	.40	
	On cover		.50
	P# block of 6	10.00	—
	Never hinged	15.00	

TYPE OF 1922-26 ISSUES

REGULAR ISSUE
ROTARY PRESS PRINTING

1931		***Perf. 11x10½***	
692	A166 11c **light blue,** *Sept. 4*	2.50	.25
	Never hinged	3.75	
	On registered cover with other values		10.00
	P# block of 4	15.00	—
	Never hinged	25.00	
	Retouched forehead (20617 LL 2, 3)	30.00	2.50
693	A167 12c **brown violet,** *Aug. 25*	5.00	.25
	violet brown	5.00	.25
	Never hinged	8.00	
	Pair on registered cover		8.00
	P# block of 4	22.50	—
	Never hinged	35.00	
694	A186 13c **yellow green,** *Sept. 4*	2.25	.25
	light yellow green	2.25	.25
	blue green	2.25	.25
	Never hinged	3.50	
	On special delivery cover		27.50
	P# block of 4	15.00	
	Never hinged	27.50	
	Pair with full vert. gutter btwn.	150.00	
695	A168 14c **dark blue,** *Sept. 8*	4.00	.60
	Never hinged	6.25	
	On registered cover with other values		20.00
	P# block of 4	24.00	—
	Never hinged	37.50	
696	A169 15c **gray,** *Aug. 27*	7.75	.25
	dark gray	8.00	.25
	Never hinged	12.00	
	On registered cover with 3c		5.00
	P# block of 4	40.00	—
	Never hinged	55.00	

Perf. 10½x11

697	A187 17c **black,** *July 25*	4.75	.25
	Never hinged	7.25	
	On registered cover		5.00
	P# block of 4	37.50	—
	Never hinged	50.00	
698	A170 20c **carmine rose,** *Sept. 8*	7.75	.25
	Never hinged	12.50	
	On registered UPU-rate cover		12.50
	P# block of 4	40.00	—
	Never hinged	60.00	
	Double transfer (20538 LR 26)	20.00	—
699	A171 25c **blue green,** *July 25*	8.00	.25
	Never hinged	13.00	
	On Federal airmail cover		20.00
	P# block of 4	40.00	—
	Never hinged	60.00	
700	A172 30c **brown,** *Sept. 8*	12.50	.25
	Never hinged	21.00	
	On Federal airmail cover		17.50
	P# block of 4	70.00	
	Never hinged	95.00	
	Retouched in head (20552 UL 83)	50.00	1.00
	Cracked plate (20552 UR 30)	45.00	1.00
701	A173 50c **lilac,** *Sept. 4*	30.00	.25
	red lilac	30.00	.25
	Never hinged	50.00	
	On Federal airmail cover		25.00
	P# block of 4	160.00	—
	Never hinged	230.00	
	Nos. 692-701 (10)	84.50	2.85
	Nos. 692-701, never hinged	137.25	

Bureau Precancels: 11c, 33 diff., 12c, 33 diff., 13c, 28 diff., 14c, 27 diff., 15c, 33 diff., 17c, 29 diff., 20c, 37 diff., 25c, 29 diff., 30c, 31 diff., 50c, 28 diff.

RED CROSS ISSUE

50th anniversary of the founding of the American Red Cross Society.

"The Greatest Mother" — A208

FLAT PLATE PRINTING

Plates of 200 subjects in two panes of 100.

1931, May 21		***Perf. 11***	
702	A208 2c **black & red**	.25	.25
	Never hinged	.35	
	Margin block of 4, arrow right or left	1.10	
	P# block of 4, two P#	2.25	—
	Never hinged	3.25	
	Double transfer	1.50	.50
a.	Red cross missing (FO)	*40,000.*	

The cross tends to shift, appearing in many slightly varied positions.

One example of No. 702a is documented; believed to be unique. Value reflects most recent sale price at auction in 1994.

YORKTOWN ISSUE

Surrender of Cornwallis at Yorktown, 1781.

Rochambeau, Washington, de Grasse A209

First Plate Layout — Border and vignette plates of 100 subjects in two panes of 50 subjects each. Plate numbers between 20461 and 20602.

Second Plate Layout — Border plates of 100 subjects in two panes of 50 each, separated by a 1 inch wide vertical gutter with central guide line and vignette plates of 50 subjects. Plate numbers between 20646 and 20671.

Issued in panes of 50 subjects.

1931, Oct. 19		***Perf. 11***	
703	A209 2c **carmine rose & black**	.35	.25
	Never hinged	.50	
	Margin block of 4, arrow marker, right or left	1.70	
	Center line block	1.80	
	P# block of 4, 2#	3.00	—
	Never hinged	4.00	
	P# block of 4, 2# & arrow & marker block	3.00	—
	Never hinged	4.00	
	P# block of 6, 2# & "TOP," arrow & marker	3.50	—
	Never hinged	4.50	
	P# block of 8, 2# & "TOP"	3.75	—
	Never hinged	5.00	
	Double transfer	1.75	.75
a.	2c **lake & black**	4.50	.75
	Never hinged	6.25	
b.	2c **dark lake & black**	*500.00*	
	Never hinged	*950.00*	
	P# block of 4, 2#	*2,750.*	

	Never hinged	*4,250.*
c.	Horiz. pair, imperf. vertically	*7,000.*
	Never hinged	*8,500.*
	Center line block of 10	*35,000.*
	P# block of 10, top, 2#, arrow, marker and "TOP," block	*37,500.*
	P# block of 10, bottom, 2#, arrow and marker	*35,000.*

No. 703c is valued in the grade of fine.

WASHINGTON BICENTENNIAL ISSUE

200th anniversary of the birth of George Washington. Various Portraits of George Washington.

By Charles Willson Peale, 1777 — A210

From Houdon Bust, 1785 — A211

By Charles Willson Peale, 1772 — A212

By Gilbert Stuart, 1796 — A213

By Charles Willson Peale, 1777 — A214

By Charles Peale Polk — A215

By Charles Willson Peale, 1795 — A216

By John Trumbull, 1792 — A217

By John Trumbull, 1780 — A218

By Charles B. J. F. Saint Memin, 1798 — A219

By W. Williams, 1794 — A220

By Gilbert Stuart, 1795 — A221

Broken Circle

ROTARY PRESS PRINTINGS

Plates of 400 subjects in four panes of 100 each

1932, Jan. 1 ***Perf. 11x10½***

704 A210	½c **olive brown**	.25	.25
	Never hinged	.35	
	P# block of 4	5.00	—
	Never hinged	10.00	
	Broken circle (20560 UR 8)	2.00	.50
705 A211	1c **green**	.25	.25
	Never hinged	.35	
	P# block of 4	4.00	—
	Never hinged	5.50	
	Gripper cracks (20742 UL and UR)	2.75	1.75
706 A212	1½c **brown**	.45	.25
	Never hinged	.60	
	P# block of 4	14.00	—
	Never hinged	27.50	

Cracked Plate

Broken "E" Plate Flaw

707 A213	2c **carmine rose**	.30	.25
	Never hinged	.45	
	P# block of 4	1.40	—
	Never hinged	2.20	
	Pair with full vert. gutter between	—	
	Cracked plate (20768 UL 1)	—	—
	Broken "E" plate flaw (20772 UR 8)	—	—
	Gripper cracks (20752 LR, 20755 LL & LR, 20756 LL, 20774 LR, 20792 LL & LR, 20796 LL & LR)	1.75	.65

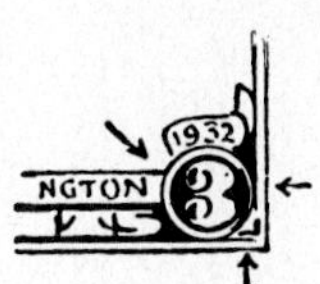

Double Transfer

Broken Frame Line

708 A214	3c **purple**	.55	.25
	Never hinged	.80	
	P# block of 4	15.00	—
	Never hinged	20.00	
	Double transfer	1.75	.65
	Broken top frame line (20847 LL 8)	5.00	1.00

Spot Between Eyes

Original

Retouched Eyes

Broken Frame Line

709 A215	4c **light brown**	.60	.25
	Never hinged	.85	
	P# block of 4	5.00	—
	Never hinged	7.00	
	Double transfer (20568 LR 60)	2.00	.25
	Spot between eyes plate defect (20568 LR 89)	5.00	1.00
	Retouch in eyes (20568 LR 89)	3.00	.50
	P# block of 4 with variety	—	
	Broken bottom frame line (20568 LR 100)	2.50	.75
	P# block of 4 with broken bottom frame line (20568 LR 100)	12.50	
	P# block of 4 with spot between eyes (20568 LR 89) and broken bottom frame line (20568 LR 100)	20.00	

Gash On Forehead — 5c

Cracked Plate — 5c

710 A216	5c **blue**	1.40	.25
	Never hinged	2.25	
	P# block of 4	15.00	—
	Never hinged	22.50	

Plate defect over right eye (Gash on Forehead - 20636 LR 8) 25.00 —
Cracked plate (20637 UR 80) 10.00 1.10

No. 710 Gash on Forehead variety is progressive in several degrees of severity.

711 A217 6c **red orange** 2.75 .25
Never hinged 4.50
P# block of 4 50.00 —
Never hinged 70.00

Double Transfer

712 A218 7c **black** .60 .25
Never hinged .85
P# block of 4 8.50 —
Never hinged 12.00
Double transfer (20563 UL 1 or 20564 LL 91) 7.50 .50
P# block of 4 with variety 17.50
713 A219 8c **olive bister** 2.50 .50
Never hinged 4.00
P# block of 4 47.50 —
Never hinged 60.00
Pair with full vert. gutter between —
714 A220 9c **pale red** 2.00 .25
orange red 2.00 .25
Never hinged 3.25
P# block of 4 32.50 —
Never hinged 45.00
715 A221 10c **orange yellow** 9.00 .25
Never hinged 15.00
P# block of 4 85.00 —
Never hinged 110.00
Nos. 704-715 (12) 20.65 3.25
Nos. 704-715, never hinged 33.25

OLYMPIC WINTER GAMES ISSUE

3rd Olympic Winter Games, held at Lake Placid, N.Y., Feb. 4-13, 1932.

Skier — A222

Colored Snowball

FLAT PLATE PRINTING
Plates of 400 subjects in four panes of 100.

1932, Jan. 25 *Perf. 11*
716 A222 2c **carmine rose** .35 .25
carmine .35 .25
Never hinged .55
P# block of 6 8.00 —
Never hinged 11.00
Cracked plate (20823 UR 41, 42; UL 48, 49, 50) 5.00 1.65
Recut (20823 UR 61) 3.50 1.50
Colored "snowball" (20815 UR 64) 25.00 5.00
a. 2c **lake** *700.00*
Never hinged *1,050.*
carmine lake —
Never hinged —

No. 716a should be accompanied by a certificate of authenticity issued by a recognized exertizing committee.

ARBOR DAY ISSUE

1st observance of Arbor Day in the state of Nebraska, Apr. 1872, 60th anniv., and cent. of the birth of Julius Sterling Morton, who conceived the plan and the name "Arbor Day," while he was a member of the Nebraska State Board of Agriculture.

Boy and Girl Planting Tree — A223

ROTARY PRESS PRINTING
Plates of 400 subjects in four panes of 100.

1932, Apr. 22 *Perf. 11x10½*
717 A223 2c **carmine rose** .25 .25
Never hinged .35
P# block of 4 5.50 —
Never hinged 7.00

OLYMPIC GAMES ISSUE

Issued in honor of the 10th Olympic Games, held at Los Angeles, Calif., July 30 to Aug. 14, 1932.

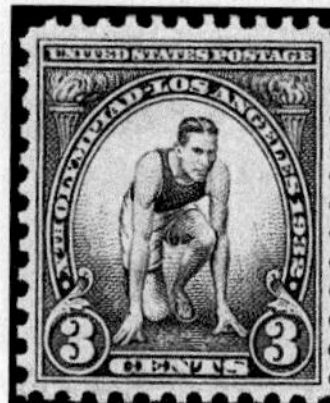

Runner at Starting Mark — A224

Myron's Discobolus — A225

Designed by Victor S. McCloskey, Jr.

ROTARY PRESS PRINTING
Plates of 400 subjects in four panes of 100.

1932, June 15 *Perf. 11x10½*
718 A224 3c **purple** 1.50 .25
deep purple 1.50 .25
Never hinged 2.00
P# block of 4 12.00 —
Never hinged 17.00
Gripper cracks (20906 UL 1) 4.25 .75
P# block of 4 with variety —
719 A225 5c **blue** 2.25 .25
deep blue 2.25 .25
Never hinged 2.90
P# block of 4 17.50 —
Never hinged 25.00
Gripper cracks (20868 UL & UR) 4.25 1.00

Washington, by Gilbert Stuart — A226

REGULAR ISSUE

ROTARY PRESS PRINTING
Plates of 400 subjects in four panes of 100.

1932 *Perf. 11x10½*
720 A226 3c **purple,** *June 16* .35 .25
light purple .35 .25
Never hinged .45
P# block of 4 1.75 —
Never hinged 2.25
Double transfer 1.00 .30
Recut face (20986 UR 15) 4.00 1.00
Gripper cracks 1.25 .30
Pair with full vert. gutter btwn. *200.00*
Pair with full horiz. gutter btwn. *200.00*
b. Booklet pane of 6, *July 25* 35.00 *12.50*
Never hinged 60.00
c. Vertical pair, imperf. between *725.00* *1,750.*
Never hinged *1,450.*

Bureau Precancels: 64 diff.

ROTARY PRESS COIL STAMPS

1932 *Perf. 10 Vertically*
721 A226 3c **purple,** *June 24* 2.75 .25
light purple 2.75 .25
Never hinged 3.50
Pair 5.75 .25
Never hinged 7.50
Joint line pair 10.00 1.50
Never hinged 13.00
Gripper cracks — —
Recut face (20995, pos. 29) — —

Recut lines around eyes — —

Perf. 10 Horizontally

722 A226 3c **purple,** *Oct. 12* 1.50 .35
light purple 1.50 .35
Never hinged 2.00
Pair 3.25 .80
Never hinged 4.25
Joint line pair 6.25 2.75
Never hinged 8.00

Bureau Precancels: No. 721, 46 diff.

TYPE OF 1922-26 ISSUES

1932, Aug. 18 *Perf. 10 Vertically*
723 A161 6c **deep orange** 11.00 .30
Never hinged 15.00
Pair 24.00 .70
Never hinged 32.50
Joint line pair 60.00 5.00
Never hinged 82.50

Bureau Precancels: 5 diff.

WILLIAM PENN ISSUE

250th anniv. of the arrival in America of Penn (1644-1718), English Quaker and founder of Pennsylvania.

William Penn — A227

FLAT PLATE PRINTING
Plates of 400 subjects in four panes of 100 each

1932, Oct. 24 *Perf. 11*
724 A227 3c **purple** .45 .25
Never hinged .60
P# block of 6 7.50 —
Never hinged 12.50
a. Vert. pair, imperf. horiz. —

DANIEL WEBSTER ISSUE

Daniel Webster (1782-1852), Statesman — A228

FLAT PLATE PRINTING
Plates of 400 subjects in four panes of 100.

1932, Oct. 24 *Perf. 11*
725 A228 3c **purple** .45 .25
light purple .45 .25
Never hinged .60
P# block of 6 15.00 —
Never hinged 20.00

GEORGIA BICENTENNIAL ISSUE

200th anniv. of the founding of the Colony of Georgia, and honoring Oglethorpe, who landed from England, Feb. 12, 1733, and personally supervised the establishing of the colony.

Gen. James Edward Oglethorpe — A229

FLAT PLATE PRINTING
Plates of 400 subjects in four panes of 100.

1933, Feb. 12 *Perf. 11*
726 A229 3c **purple** .50 .25
Never hinged .65
P# block of 6 9.00 —
Never hinged 15.00
P# block of 10, "C.S." in selvage 12.00
Never hinged 18.00
Bottom margin block of 20, no P# —

PEACE OF 1783 ISSUE

150th anniv. of the issuance by George Washington of the official order containing the Proclamation of Peace marking officially the ending of hostilities in the War for Independence.

Washington's Headquarters at Newburgh, N.Y. — A230

ROTARY PRESS PRINTING

Plates of 400 subjects in four panes of 100 each

1933, Apr. 19 *Perf. 10½x11*

727	A230 3c **violet**	.25	.25
	Never hinged	.30	
	P# block of 4	3.00	—
	Never hinged	5.50	

No. 727 was not regularly issued in full sheets of 400 with gum. Gutter pairs and blocks with crossed gutters come from a very few non-issued full sheets. Those varieties should not be confused with similar pairs and blocks without gum, which are from the No. 752 Special Printing.

See No. 752 in the Special Printings following No. 751.

CENTURY OF PROGRESS ISSUES

"Century of Progress" Intl. Exhibition, Chicago, which opened June 1, 1933, and centenary of the incorporation of Chicago as a city.

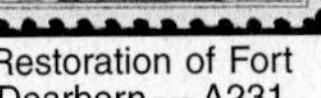

Restoration of Fort Dearborn — A231

Federal Building — A232

ROTARY PRESS PRINTING

Plates of 400 subjects in four panes of 100.

1933, May 25 *Perf. 10½x11*

728	A231 1c **yellow green**	.25	.25
	Never hinged	.30	
	On card, Expo. station machine canc.		1.00
	On card, Expo. station duplex handstamp canc.		3.00
	P# block of 4	1.75	—
	Never hinged	3.00	
	Gripper cracks (21133 UR & LR)	2.00	—
729	A232 3c **purple**	.25	.25
	Never hinged	.35	
	On cover, Expo. station machine canc.		2.00
	On cover, Expo. station duplex handstamp canc.		5.00
	P# block of 4	2.40	—
	Never hinged	4.00	

Nos. 728 and 729 were not regularly issued in full sheets of 400 with gum. Gutter pairs and blocks with cross gutters and dashes, with gum, exist from a very few non-issued sheets that were retained by Postmaster General James A. Farley.

AMERICAN PHILATELIC SOCIETY ISSUE

SOUVENIR SHEETS

A231a

A232a

Illustrations reduced.

FLAT PLATE PRINTING

Plates of 225 subjects in nine panes of 25 each.

1933, Aug. 25 ***Imperf.***

Without Gum

730	A231a 1c **deep yellow green,** pane of 25	20.00	*25.00*
a.	Single stamp	.70	.50
	Single on card, Expo. station machine canc.		1.50
	Single on card, Expo. station duplex handstamp canc.		5.00
731	A232a 3c **purple,** pane of 25	20.00	*22.50*
a.	Single stamp	.65	.50
	Single on cover, Expo. station machine canc.		3.00
	Single on cover, Expo. station duplex handstamp canc.		7.50

Issued in panes measuring 134x120mm containing twenty-five stamps, inscribed in the margins:

PRINTED BY THE TREASURY DEPARTMENT, BUREAU OF ENGRAVING AND PRINTING, — UNDER AUTHORITY OF JAMES A. FARLEY, POSTMASTER-GENERAL, AT CENTURY OF PROGRESS, — IN COMPLIMENT TO THE AMERICAN PHILATELIC SOCIETY FOR ITS CONVENTION AND EXHIBITION — CHICAGO, ILLINOIS, AUGUST, 1933. PLATE NO. 21145.

Also used were plates 21159 (1c), 21146 and 21160 (3c). Each different plate number used is inscribed in the bottom selvage of the respective souvenir sheets.

See Nos. 766-767 in the Special Printings following No. 751.

NATIONAL RECOVERY ACT ISSUE

Issued to direct attention to and arouse the support of the nation for the National Recovery Act.

Group of Workers — A233

Gripper Crack

ROTARY PRESS PRINTING

Plates of 400 subjects in four panes of 100.

1933, Aug. 15 *Perf. 10½x11*

732	A233 3c **purple**	.25	.25
	Never hinged	.30	
	P# block of 4	1.50	—
	Never hinged	2.00	
	Gripper cracks (21151 UL & UR, 21153 UR & LR)	1.50	—
	Recut at right (21151 UR 47)	4.00	

BYRD ANTARCTIC ISSUE

Issued in connection with the Byrd Antarctic Expedition of 1933 and for use on letters mailed through the Little America Post Office established at the Base Camp of the Expedition in the territory of the South Pole.

A Map of the World (on van der Grinten's Projection) — A234

Designed by Victor S. McCloskey, Jr.

FLAT PLATE PRINTING

Plates of 200 subjects in four panes of 50 each

1933, Oct. 9 *Perf. 11*

733	A234 3c **dark blue**	.50	.50
	Never hinged	.60	
	P# block of 6	12.00	—
	Never hinged	15.00	
	Double transfer (21167 LR 2)	2.75	1.00

In addition to the postage charge of 3 cents, letters sent by the ships of the expedition to be canceled in Little America were subject to a service charge of 50 cents each.

See No. 753 in the Special Printings following No. 751.

KOSCIUSZKO ISSUE

Kosciuszko (1746-1817), Polish soldier and statesman served in the American Revolution, on the 150th anniv. of the granting to him of American citizenship.

Statue of General Tadeusz Kosciuszko — A235

Designed by Victor S. McCloskey, Jr.

FLAT PLATE PRINTING

Plates of 400 subjects in four panes of 100 each

1933, Oct. 13 *Perf. 11*

734	A235 5c **blue**	.55	.25
	Never hinged	.65	
	P# block of 6	22.00	—
	Never hinged	28.00	
	Cracked plate	—	
a.	Horizontal pair, imperf. vertically	*1,750.*	
	Never hinged	*2,750.*	
	P# block of 8	*35,000.*	

The No. 734a plate block is unique but damaged.

NATIONAL STAMP EXHIBITION ISSUE

SOUVENIR SHEET

A235a

Illustration reduced.

TYPE OF BYRD ISSUE

Plates of 150 subjects in 25 panes of six each.

1934, Feb. 10 *Imperf.*

Without Gum

735	A235a 3c **dark blue,** pane of 6	10.00	9.00
a.	Single stamp	1.60	1.25

Issued in panes measuring 87x93mm containing six stamps, inscribed in the margins: "Printed by the Treasury Department, Bureau of Engraving and Printing, under authority of James A. Farley, Postmaster General, in the National Stamp Exhibition of 1934. New York, N. Y., February 10-18, 1934. Plate No. 21184." Plate No. 21187 was used for sheets printed at the Exhibition, but all these were destroyed.

See No. 768 in the Special Printings following No. 751.

MARYLAND TERCENTENARY ISSUE

300th anniversary of the founding of Maryland.

"The Ark" and "The Dove" — A236

Designed by Alvin R. Meissner.

FLAT PLATE PRINTING

Plates of 400 subjects in four panes of 100.

1934, Mar. 23 *Perf. 11*

736	A236 3c **carmine rose**	.30	.25
	Never hinged	.40	
	P# block of 6	6.25	—
	Never hinged	9.50	
	Double transfer (21190 UL 1)	—	—
a.	Horizontal pair, imperf between	*4,000.*	
b.	3c **lake**	*1,000.*	—
c.	3c **carmine lake,** never hinged	—	

The unique No. 736a resulted from a paper foldover before perfing, and it has angled errant perfs from another column of vert. perfs through the upper-left corner of the left stamp.

MOTHERS OF AMERICA ISSUE

Issued to commemorate Mother's Day.

Adaptation of Whistler's Portrait of his Mother A237

Designed by Victor S. McCloskey, Jr.

Plates of 200 subjects in four panes of 50.

ROTARY PRESS PRINTING

1934, May 2 *Perf. 11x10½*

737	A237 3c **purple**	.25	.25
	Never hinged	.30	
	P# block of 4	1.00	—
	Never hinged	1.30	

FLAT PLATE PRINTING

Perf. 11

738	A237 3c **purple**	.25	.25
	Never hinged	.30	
	P# block of 6	4.50	—
	Never hinged	6.50	

See No. 754 in the Special Printings following No. 751.

WISCONSIN TERCENTENARY ISSUE

Arrival of Jean Nicolet, French explorer, on the shores of Green Bay, 300th anniv. According to historical records, Nicolet was the 1st white man to reach the territory now comprising the State of Wisconsin.

Nicolet's Landing A238

Designed by Victor S. McCloskey, Jr.

FLAT PLATE PRINTING

Plates of 200 subjects in four panes of 50.

1934. July 7 *Perf. 11*

739	A238 3c **purple**	.25	.25
	violet	.25	.25
	Never hinged	.40	
	P# block of 6	3.50	—
	Never hinged	5.00	
a.	Vert. pair, imperf. horiz.	*575.00*	
	Never hinged	*1,050.*	
b.	Horiz. pair, imperf. vert.	*1,000.*	
	Never hinged	*1,750.*	
	P# block of 10	*6,500.*	

See No. 755 in the Special Printings following No. 751.

NATIONAL PARKS YEAR ISSUE

El Capitan, Yosemite (California) — A239

Old Faithful, Yellowstone (Wyoming) — A243

View of Grand Canyon (Arizona) A240

Mt. Rainier and Mirror Lake (Washington) A241

Cliff Palace, Mesa Verde Park (Colorado) A242

Crater Lake (Oregon) A244

Great Head, Acadia Park (Maine) A245

Great White Throne, Zion Park (Utah) — A246

Great Smoky Mountains (North Carolina) — A248

Mt. Rockwell (Mt. Sinopah) and Two Medicine Lake, Glacier National Park (Montana) A247

FLAT PLATE PRINTING

Plates of 200 subjects in four panes of 50.

1934 **Unwmk.** *Perf. 11*

740	A239 1c **green,** *July 16*	.25	.25
	light green	.25	.25
	Never hinged	.40	
	P# block of 6	1.80	—
	Never hinged	2.50	
	Recut	1.50	.50
a.	Vert. pair, imperf. horiz., with gum	*1,750.*	
	Never hinged	*3,000.*	
741	A240 2c **red,** *July 24*	.30	.25
	orange red	.30	.25
	Never hinged	.40	
	P# block of 6	1.55	—
	Never hinged	2.00	
	Double transfer	1.25	—
a.	Vert. pair, imperf. horiz., with gum	*800.00*	
	Never hinged	*1,450.*	
	P# block of 6	—	
b.	Horiz. pair, imperf. vert., with gum	*1,000.*	
	Never hinged	*1,750.*	
	P# block of 6	*3,500.*	
	Never hinged	*4,750.*	
c.	Imperf. P# 21261 block of 20	*7,500.*	

No. 741c is a unique bottom margin plate #21261 block of 20. This plate was not used to print the imperforate Farley special printing, No. 757. Loose stamps separated from this block or from other possible imperforate No. 741 Plate #21261 blocks are indistinguishable from gummed examples of No. 757.

742	A241 3c **purple,** *Aug. 3*	.40	.25
	Never hinged	.50	
	P# block of 6	2.25	—
	Never hinged	3.00	
	Recut	1.50	—
a.	Vert. pair, imperf. horiz., with gum	*1,150.*	
	Never hinged	*2,000.*	
	P# block of 6	—	
743	A242 4c **brown,** *Sept. 25*	.50	.40
	light brown	.50	.40
	Never hinged	.70	
	P# block of 6	6.50	—
	Never hinged	8.00	
a.	Vert. pair, imperf. horiz., with gum	*3,750.*	
	Never hinged	*8,500.*	
744	A243 5c **blue,** *July 30*	.80	.65
	light blue	.80	.65
	Never hinged	1.10	
	P# block of 6	9.00	—
	Never hinged	11.00	
a.	Horiz. pair, imperf. vert., with gum	*1,400.*	
	Never hinged	*3,500.*	
	P# block of 6	—	
745	A244 6c **dark blue,** *Sept. 5*	1.20	.85
	Never hinged	1.65	
	P# block of 6	15.00	—
	Never hinged	20.00	
746	A245 7c **black,** *Oct. 2*	.80	.75
	Never hinged	1.10	
	P# block of 6	9.00	—
	Never hinged	12.00	
	Double transfer	3.25	1.40
a.	Horiz. pair, imperf. vert., with gum	*1,250.*	
	Never hinged	*2,000.*	
	P# block of 6, never hinged	*6,000.*	
747	A246 8c **sage green,** *Sept. 18*	1.75	1.50
	Never hinged	2.70	
	P# block of 6	15.00	—
	Never hinged	25.00	
748	A247 9c **red orange,** *Aug. 27*	1.60	.65
	orange	1.60	.65
	Never hinged	2.40	
	P# block of 6	15.00	—
	Never hinged	20.00	
749	A248 10c **gray black,** *Oct. 8*	3.25	1.25
	gray	3.25	1.25
	Never hinged	5.00	

P# block of 6	21.00	—
Never hinged	30.00	
Nos. 740-749 (10)	10.85	6.80
Nos. 740-749, never hinged	15.95	
Nos. 740-749, P# blks of 6	100.00	

In 1934, Postmaster General James A. Farley had full sheets of Nos. 727, 729, 730, 735, 738, 739, 740-749, 750-751 and CE1 delivered to himself and "gifted" most of these to friends and family, including President Franklin Roosevelt, Secretary of the Interior Harold Ickes, Third Assistant Postmaster General Clinton Eilenberger, and others. Nos. 738, 739 and 740-749 were delivered imperforate, and the souvenir sheets Nos. 730-731, 735 and 750-751 were delivered uncut. Nos. 740-749 and 750-751 were delivered with gum, the others without gum.

The sheets of these stamps were signed in the selvage by Farley and/or the recipients. As a result, stamps from these sheets can be and have been certified by expertizing committees as varieties of the original issues rather the 1935 Special Printings (Nos. 752-771) known as "Farley's Follies."

Sheets of these 1934 varieties have reached the marketplace from the sheets given to Roosevelt, Ickes and Eilenberger. As unissued varieties that were improperly distributed through private gifts from Postmaster General Farley rather than sold across the counter by the Post Office Department, these varieties are not listed in the Scott catalogs.

Imperforate varieties of the 2c and 5c exist as errors of the perforated Parks set, but are virtually impossible to distinguish from gummed examples from the imperforate sheets of 200.

Also, beware of fakes of the part-perforate errors of Nos. 740-749, including those with gum (see "without gum" note before No. 752.)

AMERICAN PHILATELIC SOCIETY ISSUE

SOUVENIR SHEET

A248a

Illustration reduced.

Plates of 120 subjects in 20 panes of 6 stamps each.

1934, Aug. 28 *Imperf.*

750	A248a 3c **purple**, pane of 6	20.00	*27.50*
	Never hinged	30.00	
a.	Single stamp	3.25	3.25
	Never hinged	4.00	

Issued in panes measuring approximately 98x93mm containing six stamps, inscribed in the margins: PRINTED BY THE TREASURY DEPARTMENT, BUREAU OF ENGRAVING AND PRINTING, — UNDER AUTHORITY OF JAMES A. FARLEY, POSTMASTER GENERAL, — IN COMPLIMENT TO THE AMERICAN PHILATELIC SOCIETY FOR ITS CONVENTION AND EXHIBITION, — ATLANTIC CITY, NEW JERSEY, AUGUST, 1934. PLATE NO. 21303.

See No. 770 in the Special Printings following No. 751.

TRANS-MISSISSIPPI PHILATELIC EXPOSITION ISSUE

SOUVENIR SHEET

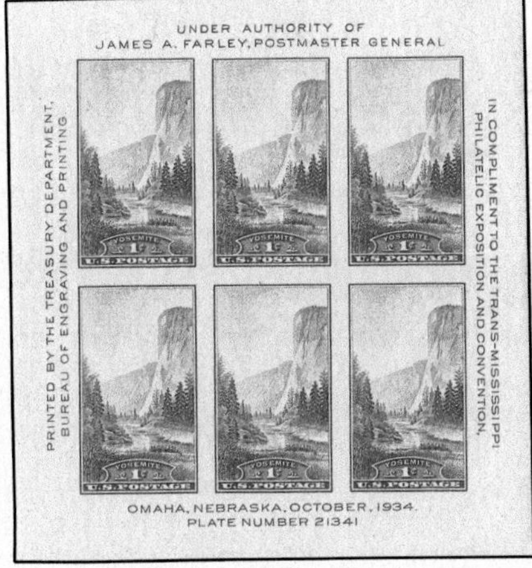

A248b

Illustration reduced.

Plates of 120 subjects in 20 panes of 6 stamps each.

1934, Oct. 10 *Imperf.*

751	A248b 1c **green**, pane of 6	10.00	12.50
	Never hinged	15.00	
a.	Single stamp	1.65	1.60
	Never hinged	2.25	

Issued in panes measuring approximately 92x99mm containing six stamps, inscribed in the margins: PRINTED BY THE TREASURY DEPARTMENT, BUREAU OF ENGRAVING AND PRINTING, — UNDER AUTHORITY OF JAMES A. FARLEY, POSTMASTER GENERAL, — IN COMPLIMENT TO THE TRANS-MISSISSIPPI PHILATELIC EXPOSITION AND CONVENTION, OMAHA, NEBRASKA, — OCTOBER, 1934. PLATE NO. 21341.

See No. 769 in the Special Printings that follow.

SPECIAL PRINTING

(Nos. 752-771 inclusive)

"Issued for a limited time in full sheets as printed, and in blocks thereof, to meet the requirements of collectors and others who may be interested." — From Postal Bulletin No. 16614.

Issuance of the following 20 stamps in complete sheets resulted from the protest of collectors and others at the practice of presenting, to certain government officials, complete sheets of unsevered panes, imperforate (except Nos. 752 and 753) and generally ungummed.

Designs of Commemorative Issues

Without Gum

NOTE: In 1940 the P.O. Department offered to and did gum full sheets of Nos. 756-765 and 769-770 sent in by owners. No other Special Printings were accepted for gumming.

TYPE OF PEACE ISSUE

Issued in sheets of 400, consisting of four panes of 100 each, with vertical and horizontal gutters between and plate numbers at outside corners at sides.

ROTARY PRESS PRINTING

1935, Mar. 15 **Unwmk.** *Perf. 10½x11*

752	A230 3c **purple**	.25	.25
	Pair with horiz. gutter between	5.75	—
	Pair with vert. gutter between	9.50	—
	Gutter block of 4 with dash (left or right)	15.00	—
	Gutter block of 4 with dash (top or bottom)	20.00	—
	Center block with crossed gutters and dashes	60.00	—
	P# block of 4	27.50	—

TYPE OF BYRD ISSUE

Issued in sheets of 200, consisting of four panes of 50 each, with vertical and horizontal guide lines in gutters between panes, and plate numbers centered at top and bottom of each pane. This applies to Nos. 753-765 and 771.

FLAT PLATE PRINTING

Perf. 11

753	A234 3c **dark blue**	.50	.45
	Pair with horiz. line between	2.00	—
	Pair with vert. line between	32.50	—
	Margin block of 4, arrow & guide line (left or right)	8.00	—
	Margin block of 4, arrow & guideline (top or bottom)	70.00	—
	Center line block	75.00	100.00
	P# block of 6, number at top or bottom	15.00	—

No. 753 is similar to No. 733. Positive identification is by blocks or pairs showing guide line between stamps. These lines between stamps are found only on No. 753.

TYPE OF MOTHERS OF AMERICA ISSUE

Issued in sheets of 200

FLAT PLATE PRINTING

Imperf

754	A237 3c **deep purple**	.60	.60
	Pair with horiz. line between	1.75	—
	Pair with vert. line between	1.50	—
	Margin block of 4, arrow & guideline (left or right)	3.75	—
	Margin block of 4, arrow & guideline (top or bottom)	3.25	—
	Center line block	7.25	9.00
	P# block of 6, number at top or bottom	11.00	—

TYPE OF WISCONSIN ISSUE

Issued in sheets of 200

FLAT PLATE PRINTING

Imperf

755	A238 3c **deep purple**	.60	.60
	Pair with horiz. line between	1.75	—
	Pair with vert. line between	1.50	—
	Margin block of 4, arrow & guideline (left or right)	3.75	—
	Margin block of 4, arrow & guideline (top or bottom)	3.25	—
	Center line block	8.00	13.00
	P# block of 6, number at top or bottom	11.00	—

TYPES OF NATIONAL PARKS ISSUE

Issued in sheets of 200

FLAT PLATE PRINTING

Imperf

756	A239 1c **green**	.25	.25
	With original gum, never hinged	1.60	
	Pair with horiz. line between	.55	—
	With original gum, never hinged	4.25	
	Pair with vert. line between	.65	—
	With original gum, never hinged	5.75	
	Margin block of 4, arrow & guideline (left or right)	1.25	—
	With original gum, never hinged	9.00	
	Margin block of 4, arrow & guideline (top or bottom)	1.50	—
	With original gum, never hinged	13.00	
	Center line block	3.25	3.50
	With original gum, never hinged	27.50	
	P# block of 6, number at top or bottom	4.25	—
	With original gum, never hinged	37.50	

See note above No. 766.

757	A240 2c **red**	.25	.25
	With original gum, never hinged	1.75	
	Pair with horiz. line between	.70	—
	With original gum, never hinged	7.00	
	Pair with vert. line between	.55	—
	With original gum, never hinged	5.00	
	Margin block of 4, arrow & guideline (left or right)	1.60	—
	With original gum, never hinged	17.50	
	Margin block of 4, arrow & guideline (top or bottom)	1.25	—
	With original gum, never hinged	11.50	
	Center line block	4.25	5.00
	With original gum, never hinged	35.00	
	P# block of 6, number at top or bottom	5.50	—
	With original gum, never hinged	47.50	
	Double transfer	—	
758	A241 3c **deep purple**	.50	.45
	With original gum, never hinged	4.00	
	Pair with horiz. line between	1.40	—
	With original gum, never hinged	15.00	
	Pair with vert. line between	1.25	—
	With original gum, never hinged	12.00	
	Margin block of 4, arrow & guideline (left or right)	3.10	—
	With original gum, never hinged	35.00	
	Margin block of 4, arrow & guideline (top or bottom)	2.75	—
	With original gum, never hinged	26.00	
	Center line block	5.25	6.00
	With original gum, never hinged	47.50	
	P# block of 6, number at top or bottom	12.50	—
	With original gum, never hinged	130.00	
759	A242 4c **brown**	1.00	.95
	With original gum, never hinged	8.00	
	Pair with horiz. line between	2.75	—
	With original gum, never hinged	30.00	
	Pair with vert. line between	2.25	—
	With original gum, never hinged	22.50	
	Margin block of 4, arrow & guideline (left or right)	5.75	—
	With original gum, never hinged	65.00	
	Margin block of 4, arrow & guideline (top or bottom)	4.75	—
	With original gum, never hinged	47.50	
	Center line block	8.75	10.00
	With original gum, never hinged	100.00	
	P# block of 6, number at top or bottom	20.00	—
	With original gum, never hinged	150.00	
760	A243 5c **blue**	1.60	1.40
	With original gum, never hinged	12.00	
	Pair with horiz. line between	3.75	—
	With original gum, never hinged	35.00	
	Pair with vert. line between	4.50	—
	With original gum, never hinged	45.00	

Margin block of 4, arrow & guideline (left or right) 8.00 —
With original gum, never hinged 70.00
Margin block of 4, arrow & guideline (top or bottom) 10.00 —
With original gum, never hinged 92.50
Center line block 16.00 16.00
With original gum, never hinged 140.00
P# block of 6, number at top or bottom 27.50 —
With original gum, never hinged 230.00
Double transfer —

761 A244 6c **dark blue** 2.40 2.25
With original gum, never hinged 19.00
Pair with horiz. line between 6.00 —
With original gum, never hinged 70.00
Pair with vert. line between 5.00 —
With original gum, never hinged 50.00
Margin block of 4, arrow & guideline (left or right) 12.00 —
With original gum, never hinged 140.00
Margin block of 4, arrow & guideline (top or bottom) 11.00 —
With original gum, never hinged 120.00
Center line block 18.00 22.50
With original gum, never hinged 180.00
P# block of 6, number at top or bottom) 35.00 —
With original gum, never hinged 340.00

762 A245 7c **black** 1.60 1.40
With original gum, never hinged 12.00
Pair with horiz. line between 4.25 —
With original gum, never hinged 45.00
Pair with vert. line between 3.75 —
With original gum, never hinged 37.50
Margin block of 4, arrow & guideline (left or right) 9.25 —
With original gum, never hinged 95.00
Margin block of 4, arrow & guideline (top or bottom) 8.25 —
With original gum, never hinged 85.00
Center line block 14.00 16.00
With original gum, never hinged 135.00
P# block of 6, number at top or bottom 30.00 —
With original gum, never hinged 280.00
Double transfer —

763 A246 8c **sage green** 1.90 1.50
With original gum, never hinged 12.50
Pair with horiz. line between 5.25 —
With original gum, never hinged 37.50
Pair with vert. line between 4.25 —
With original gum, never hinged 50.00
Margin block of 4, arrow & guideline (left or right) *12.50* —
With original gum, never hinged 85.00
Margin block of 4, arrow & guideline (top or bottom) *15.00* —
With original gum, never hinged 80.00
Center line block 20.00 22.50
With original gum, never hinged 175.00
P# block of 6, number at top or bottom 35.00 —
With original gum, never hinged 350.00

764 A247 9c **red orange** 2.00 1.75
With original gum, never hinged 14.00
Pair with horiz. line between 5.00 —
With original gum, never hinged 50.00
Pair with vert. line between 4.50 —
With original gum, never hinged 42.50
Margin block of 4, arrow & guideline (left or right) 11.50 —
With original gum, never hinged 125.00
Margin block of 4, arrow & guideline (top or bottom) 10.50 —
With original gum, never hinged 97.50
Center line block 22.50 25.00
With original gum, never hinged 210.00
P# block of 6, number at top or bottom 40.00 —
With original gum, never hinged 400.00

765 A248 10c **gray black** 4.00 3.50
With original gum, never hinged 27.50
Pair with horiz. line between 9.00 —
With original gum, never hinged 82.50
Pair with vert. line between 10.50 —
With original gum, never hinged 115.00
Margin block of 4, arrow & guideline (left or right) 20.00 —
With original gum, never hinged 175.00
Margin block of 4, arrow & guideline (top or bottom) 24.00 —
With original gum, never hinged 240.00
Center line block 30.00 35.00
With original gum, never hinged 275.00
P# block of 6, number at top or bottom 45.00 —
With original gum, never hinged 475.00
Nos. 756-765 (10) 15.50 13.70
Nos. 756-765, with original gum, never hinged 114.35
Nos. 756-765, P# blocks of 6 254.75

Hinged examples of Nos. 756-765 and 769-770 with original gum sell for approximately half the values shown for never-hinged stamps.

Gum skips and light gum bends are normal on the Bureau of Engraving & Printing gummed Farley issues that were originally issued without gum.

SOUVENIR SHEETS

Note: Single items from these sheets are identical with other varieties, 766 and 730, 766a and 730a, 767 and 731, 767a and 731a, 768 and 735, 768a and 735a, 769a and 756, 770a and 758.

Positive identification is by blocks or pairs showing wide gutters between stamps. These wide gutters occur only on Nos. 766-770 and measure, horizontally, 13mm on Nos. 766-767; 16mm on No. 768, and 23mm on Nos. 769-770.

TYPE OF CENTURY OF PROGRESS ISSUE

Issued in sheets of 9 panes of 25 stamps each, with vertical and horizontal gutters between panes.

FLAT PLATE PRINTING
Imperf

766 A231a 1c **yellow green,** pane of 25 30.00 30.00
a. Single stamp .85 .50
Pair with horiz. gutter between 5.00 —
Pair with vert. gutter between 7.00 —
Block with crossed gutters 22.50 22.50
Block of 50 stamps (two panes) 70.00

767 A232a 3c **deep purple,** pane of 25 30.00 30.00
a. Single stamp .85 .50
Pair with horiz. gutter between 5.00 —
Pair with vert. gutter between 6.50 —
Block with crossed gutters 22.50 22.50
Block of 50 stamps (two panes) 70.00

NATIONAL EXHIBITION ISSUE TYPE OF BYRD ISSUE

Issued in sheets of 25 panes of 6 stamps each, with vertical and horizontal gutters between panes.

FLAT PLATE PRINTING
Imperf

768 A235a 3c **dark blue,** pane of 6 20.00 15.00
a. Single stamp 2.80 2.40
Pair with horiz. gutter between 7.00 —
Pair with vert. gutter between 8.00 —
Block of 4 with crossed gutters 20.00 17.50
Block of 12 stamps (two panes) 45.00
Top margin single with "F" and "C.S." in selvage —

TYPES OF NATIONAL PARKS ISSUE

Issued in sheets of 20 panes of 6 stamps each, with vertical and horizontal gutters between panes.

FLAT PLATE PRINTING
Imperf

769 A248b 1c **green,** pane of 6 11.00 11.00
With original gum, never hinged 80.00
a. Single stamp 1.85 1.80
Pair with horiz. gutter between 5.50 —
With original gum, never hinged 40.00
Pair with vert. gutter between 7.50 —
With original gum, never hinged 65.00
Block of 4 with crossed gutters 15.00 12.50
With original gum, never hinged 120.00
Block of 12 stamps (two panes) 25.00

770 A248a 3c **deep purple,** pane of 6 30.00 24.00
With original gum, never hinged 275.00
a. Single stamp 3.25 3.10
Pair with horiz. gutter between 12.00 —
With original gum, never hinged 130.00
Pair with vert. gutter between 10.50 —
With original gum, never hinged 100.00
Block of 4 with crossed gutters 27.50 27.50
With original gum, never hinged 300.00
Block of 12 stamps (two panes) 65.00

Hinged examples of Nos. 769-770 with original gum sell for approximately half the values shown for never-hinged stamps.

TYPE OF AIR POST SPECIAL DELIVERY

Issued in sheets of 200, with vertical and horizontal guide lines between panes.

FLAT PLATE PRINTING
Imperf

771 APSD1 16c **dark blue** 2.50 2.60
Pair with horiz. line between 7.75 —
Pair with vert. line between 6.50 —
Margin block of 4, arrow & guideline (left or right) 17.50 —
Margin block of 4, arrow & guideline (top or bottom) 15.00 —
Center line block 65.00 72.50
P# block of 6, number at top or bottom 55.00 —

Catalogue values for unused stamps in this section, from this point to the end, are for Never Hinged items.

VALUES FOR HINGED STAMPS AFTER NO. 771

This catalogue does not value unused stamps after No. 771 in hinged condition. Hinged unused stamps from No. 772 to the present are worth considerably less than the values given for unused stamps, which are for never-hinged examples.

CONNECTICUT TERCENTENARY ISSUE

300th anniv. of the settlement of Connecticut.

The Charter Oak — A249

Defect in Cent Sign

ROTARY PRESS PRINTING
Plates of 200 subjects in four panes of 50.

1935, Apr. 26 **Unwmk.** ***Perf. 11x10½***
772 A249 3c **rose purple** .35 .25
deep rose purple .35 .25
P# block of 4 2.25 —
Defect in cent sign (21395 UR 4) 5.00 4.00

CALIFORNIA PACIFIC EXPOSITION ISSUE

California Pacific Exposition at San Diego.

View of San Diego Exposition A250

ROTARY PRESS PRINTING
Plates of 200 subjects in four panes of 50.

1935, May 29 **Unwmk.** ***Perf. 11x10½***
773 A250 3c **purple** .35 .25
On cover, Expo. station machine canc. (non-first day) *2.50*
On cover, Expo. station duplex handstamp canc. (non-first day) *20.00*
P# block of 4 1.50 —
Pair with full vertical gutter between —

BOULDER DAM ISSUE

Dedication of Boulder Dam.

Boulder Dam (Hoover Dam) — A251

FLAT PLATE PRINTING
Plates of 200 subjects in four panes of 50.

1935, Sept. 30 **Unwmk.** ***Perf. 11***
774 A251 3c **purple** .35 .25
deep purple .35 .25
P# block of 6 2.50 —

MICHIGAN CENTENARY ISSUE

Advance celebration of Michigan Statehood centenary.

Michigan State Seal — A252

Designed by Alvin R. Meissner.

ROTARY PRESS PRINTING
Plates of 200 subjects in 4 panes of 50.

1935, Nov. 1 **Unwmk.** ***Perf. 11x10½***
775 A252 3c **purple** .35 .25
P# block of 4 2.25 —

TEXAS CENTENNIAL ISSUE

Centennial of Texas independence.

Sam Houston, Stephen F. Austin and the Alamo — A253

Designed by Alvin R. Meissner.

ROTARY PRESS PRINTING

Plates of 200 subjects in four panes of 50.

1936, Mar. 2 **Unwmk.** ***Perf. 11x10½***

776 A253 3c **purple** .35 .25
On cover, Expo. station machine canc. 2.00
On cover, Expo. station duplex hand-stamp canc. *40.00*
P# block of 4 2.00 —
Pair with full horizontal gutter between *225.00*

RHODE ISLAND TERCENTENARY ISSUE

300th anniv. of the settlement of Rhode Island.

Statue of Roger Williams — A254

ROTARY PRESS PRINTING

Plates of 200 subjects in four panes of 50.

1936, May 4 **Unwmk.** ***Perf. 10½x11***

777 A254 3c **purple** .35 .25
bright purple .35 .25
P# block of 4 2.00 —
Pair with full gutter between *200.00*

THIRD INTERNATIONAL PHILATELIC EXHIBITION ISSUE

SOUVENIR SHEET

A254a

Illustration reduced.

Plates of 120 subjects in thirty panes of 4 each.

FLAT PLATE PRINTING

1936, May 9 **Unwmk.** ***Imperf.***

778 A254a **purple,** pane of 4 1.75 1.25
a. 3c Type A249 .40 .30
b. 3c Type A250 .40 .30
c. 3c Type A252 .40 .30
d. 3c Type A253 .40 .30

Issued in panes measuring 98x66mm containing four stamps, inscribed in the margins: "Printed by the Treasury Department, Bureau of Engraving and Printing, under authority of James A. Farley, Postmaster General, in compliment to the third International Philatelic Exhibition of 1936. New York, N. Y., May 9-17, 1936. Plate No. 21557."

Also used was plate 21558. Each different plate number used is inscribed in the bottom selvage of the respective souvenir sheets.

ARKANSAS CENTENNIAL ISSUE

100th anniv. of the State of Arkansas.

Arkansas Post, Old and New State Houses A255

ROTARY PRESS PRINTING

Plates of 200 subjects in four panes of 50.

1936, June 15 **Unwmk.** ***Perf. 11x10½***

782 A255 3c **purple** .35 .25
P# block of 4 2.00 —

OREGON TERRITORY ISSUE

Opening of the Oregon Territory, 1836, 100th anniv.

Map of Oregon Territory A256

ROTARY PRESS PRINTING

Plates of 200 subjects in four panes of 50.

1936, July 14 **Unwmk.** ***Perf. 11x10½***

783 A256 3c **purple** .35 .25
P# block of 4 1.25 —
Double transfer (21579 UL 3) 4.00 2.50

SUSAN B. ANTHONY ISSUE

Susan Brownell Anthony (1820-1906), woman-suffrage advocate, and 16th anniv. of the ratification of the 19th Amendment which grants American women the right to vote.

Susan B. Anthony — A257

Original

No Period After "B"

ROTARY PRESS PRINTING

Plates of 400 subjects in four panes of 100.

1936, Aug. 26 **Unwmk.** ***Perf. 11x10½***

784 A257 3c **purple** .30 .25
rose purple .30 .25
P# block of 4 1.10 —
Period missing after "B" (21590 LR 100) 4.00 2.00
P# block of 4 (21590 LR) 6.50

ARMY ISSUE

Issued in honor of the United States Army.

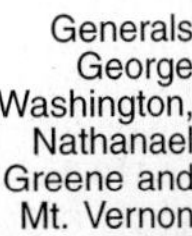

Generals George Washington, Nathanael Greene and Mt. Vernon A258

Maj. Gen. Andrew Jackson, Gen. Winfield Scott and the Hermitage A259

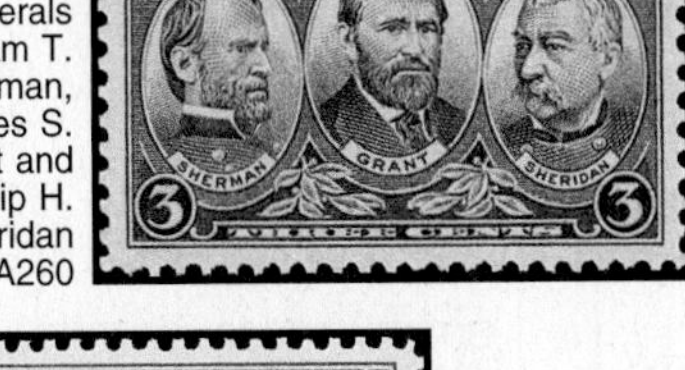

Generals William T. Sherman, Ulysses S. Grant and Philip H. Sheridan A260

Generals Robert E. Lee, "Stonewall" Jackson and Stratford Hall — A261

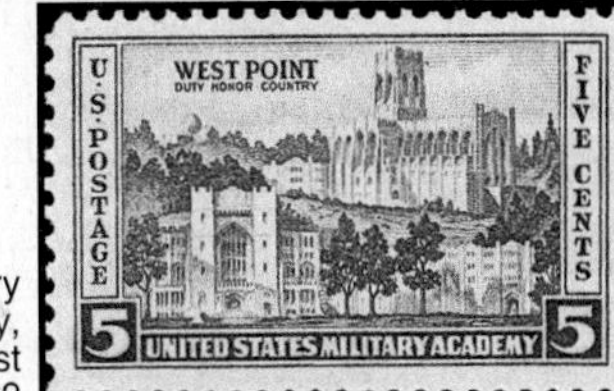

U. S. Military Academy, West Point — A262

ROTARY PRESS PRINTING

Plates of 200 subjects in four panes of 50.

1936-37 **Unwmk.** ***Perf. 11x10½***

785 A258 1c **green,** *Dec. 15, 1936* .30 .25
yellow green .30 .25
P# block of 4 1.20 —
Pair with full vertical gutter between *500.00*
786 A259 2c **carmine,** *Jan. 15, 1937* .30 .25
P# block of 4 1.20 —
787 A260 3c **purple,** *Feb. 18, 1937* .40 .25
P# block of 4 2.50 —
788 A261 4c **bl gray,** *Mar. 23, 1937* .60 .25
P# block of 4 7.50 —
789 A262 5c **ultramarine,** *May 26, 1937* .75 .25
P# block of 4 6.50 —
Nos. 785-789 (5) 2.35 1.25

NAVY ISSUE

Issued in honor of the United States Navy.

John Paul Jones and John Barry — A263

Stephen Decatur and Thomas MacDonough A264

Admirals David G. Farragut and David D. Porter — A265

Admirals William T. Sampson, George Dewey and Winfield S. Schley A266

Seal of US Naval Academy and Naval Midshipmen A267

ROTARY PRESS PRINTING

Plates of 200 subjects in four panes of 50.

1936-37 **Unwmk.** ***Perf. 11x10½***

790 A263 1c **green,** *Dec. 15, 1936* .30 .25
yellow green .30 .25
P# block of 4 1.20 —
791 A264 2c **carmine,** *Jan. 15, 1937* .30 .25
P# block of 4 1.20 —
792 A265 3c **purple,** *Feb. 18, 1937* .40 .25
P# block of 4 1.60 —
793 A266 4c **gray,** *Mar. 23, 1937* .60 .25
P# block of 4 8.50 —
794 A267 5c **ultramarine,** *May 26, 1937* .75 .25
P# block of 4 8.00 —
Pair with full vert. gutter btwn. —
Nos. 790-794 (5) 2.35 1.25

ORDINANCE OF 1787 SESQUICENTENNIAL ISSUE

150th anniv. of the adoption of the Ordinance of 1787 and the creation of the Northwest Territory.

Manasseh Cutler, Rufus Putnam and Map of Northwest Territory A268

ROTARY PRESS PRINTING

Plates of 200 subjects in four panes of 50.

1937, July 13 **Unwmk.** ***Perf. 11x10½***

795 A268 3c **rose purple** .30 .25
P# block of 4 1.75 —

VIRGINIA DARE ISSUE

350th anniv. of the birth of Virginia Dare, 1st child born in America of English parents (Aug. 18, 1587), and the settlement at Roanoke Island.

Virginia Dare and Parents — A269

FLAT PLATE PRINTING

Plates of 192 subjects in four panes of 48 each, separated by 1¼ inch wide gutters with central guide lines.

1937, Aug. 18 **Unwmk.** ***Perf. 11***

796 A269 5c **gray blue** .35 .25
P# block of 6 6.50 —

SOCIETY OF PHILATELIC AMERICANS ISSUE

SOUVENIR SHEET

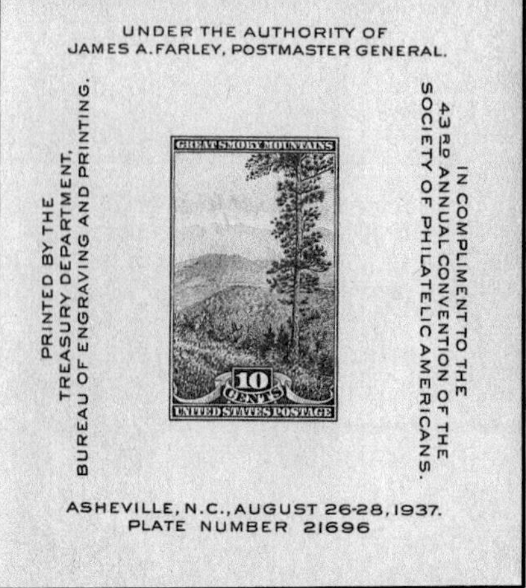

A269a

Illustration reduced.

TYPE OF NATIONAL PARKS ISSUE

Plates of 36 subjects

FLAT PLATE PRINTING

1937, Aug. 26 **Unwmk.** ***Imperf.***

797 A269a 10c **blue green** .60 .40

Issued in panes measuring 67x78mm, inscribed in margins: "Printed by the Treasury Department, Bureau of Engraving and Printing — Under the Authority of James A. Farley, Postmaster General — In Compliment to the 43rd Annual Convention of the Society of Philatelic Americans - Asheville, N.C., August 26-28, 1937. Plate Number 21695."

Also used was plate 21696. Each different plate number used is inscribed in the bottom selvage of the respective souvenir sheets.

CONSTITUTION SESQUICENTENNIAL ISSUE

150th anniversary of the signing of the Constitution on September 17, 1787.

"Adoption of the Constitution" A270

ROTARY PRESS PRINTING

Plates of 200 subjects in four panes of 50.

1937, Sept. 17 **Unwmk.** ***Perf. 11x10½***

798 A270 3c **bright reddish purple** .40 .25
P# block of 4 2.00 —

TERRITORIAL ISSUES

Hawaii

Statue of Kamehameha I, Honolulu — A271

Alaska

Mt. McKinley A272

Puerto Rico

La Fortaleza, San Juan — A273

Virgin Islands

Charlotte Amalie Harbor, St. Thomas A274

ROTARY PRESS PRINTING

Plates of 200 subjects in panes of 50.

1937 **Unwmk.** ***Perf. 10½x11***

799 A271 3c **violet,** *Oct. 18* .35 .25
P# block of 4 2.00 —

Perf. 11x10½

800 A272 3c **violet,** *Nov. 12* .40 .25
P# block of 4 2.25 —
Pair with full gutter between —
801 A273 3c **bright purple,** *Nov. 25* .40 .25
P# block of 4 2.25 —
802 A274 3c **rose violet,** *Dec. 15* .40 .25
P# block of 4 2.25 —
Pair with full vertical gutter between *275.00*
Nos. 799-802 (4) 1.55 1.00

PRESIDENTIAL ISSUE

Benjamin Franklin — A275

George Washington — A276

Martha Washington — A277

John Adams — A278

Thomas Jefferson — A279

James Madison — A280

The White House — A281

James Monroe — A282

Ulysses S. Grant — A295

Rutherford B. Hayes — A296

John Quincy Adams — A283

Andrew Jackson — A284

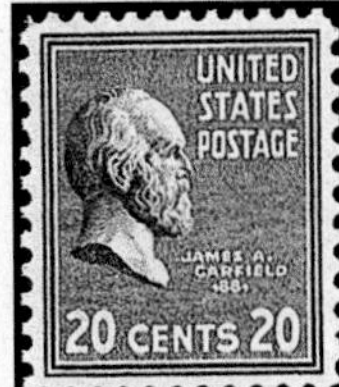

James A. Garfield — A297

Chester A. Arthur — A298

Martin Van Buren — A285

William H. Harrison — A286

Grover Cleveland — A299

Benjamin Harrison — A300

John Tyler — A287

James K. Polk — A288

William McKinley — A301

Theodore Roosevelt — A302

Zachary Taylor — A289

Millard Fillmore — A290

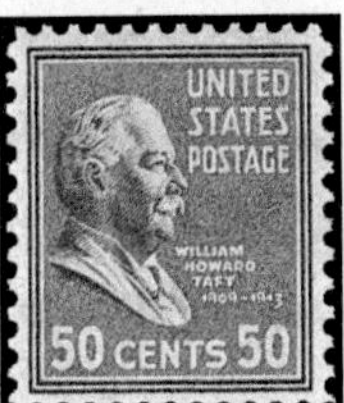

William Howard Taft — A303

Woodrow Wilson — A304

Franklin Pierce — A291

James Buchanan — A292

Warren G. Harding — A305

Calvin Coolidge — A306

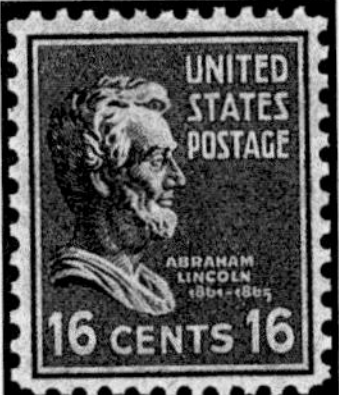

Abraham Lincoln — A293

Andrew Johnson — A294

ROTARY PRESS PRINTING

Ordinary and Electric Eye (EE) Plates of 400 subjects in four panes of 100. (For details of EE Markings, see Information for Collectors in first part of this Catalogue.)

1938 **Unwmk.** ***Perf. 11x10½***

803 A275 ½c **deep orange,** *May 19* .30 .25
On cover 2.50
P# block of 4 .50 —

804 A276 1c **green,** *Apr. 25* .30 .25
light green .30 .25
On cover .50
Single franking on local cover at non-carrier post office 60.00
Single franking on certificate of mailing, btwn. 1938 and Feb. 1, 1954 10.00
P# block of 4 1.10 —
Pair with full vert. gutter btwn. *160.00* —
b. Booklet pane of 6 2.00 *.50*
On domestic airmail cover 75.00
c. Horiz. pair, imperf between (from booklet pane) —

805 A277 1½c **bister brown,** *May 5* .30 .25
buff ('43) .30 .25
On cover .50
Single franking on int'l printed matter cover 25.00
Single franking on pre-1949 domestic third-class (up to 2 ozs) cover 10.00
P# block of 4 .50 —
Pair with full horiz. gutter btwn. *175.00*
Pair with full vert. gutter btwn. —
b. Horiz. pair, imperf. between 100.00 20.00

No. 805b unused is not precanceled. Precanceled examples are considered used and are valued in the used column. They are valued with gum; pairs without gum are worth less.

806 A278 2c **rose carmine,** *June 3* .30 .25
rose pink ('43) .30 .25
On cover .50
Single franking on post-1949 third-class (up to 2 ozs.) cover 10.00
Single franking on local cover at carrier post office 10.00
Single franking on local cover at non-carrier post office *350.00*
P# block of 4, # opposite corner stamp 1.10 —
Vertical margin block of 10, P# opposite 3rd horizontal row (Experimental EE plates) 12.00
Recut at top of head, Pl. 22156 U.L. 3 3.00 1.50
Pair with full horiz. gutter btwn. *125.00*
Pair with full vert. gutter btwn. —
b. Booklet pane of 6 5.50 *1.00*
On double-weight domestic airmail cover *300.00*

807 A279 3c **light violet,** *June 16* .30 .25
violet .30 .25
On cover .50
Single franking on private carrier cover *150.00*
Single franking on int'l surface mail postcard until 1953 15.00
Single franking on first-class cover to UPU countries of the Americas and Spain 20.00
Single franking on post-1949 double-weight third-class cover *50.00*
Single franking on penalty-permit cover with return receipt *150.00*
Single franking on certificate of mailing, btwn. Feb. 1, 1954, and July 1, 1957 *50.00*
P# block of 4, # opposite corner stamp 1.10 .25
Vertical margin block of 10, P# opposite 3rd horizontal row (Experimental EE plates) 125.00
Pair with full vert. gutter btwn. *150.00*
Pair with full horiz. gutter btwn. *200.00*
a. Booklet pane of 6 8.50 *2.00*
Horiz. booklet pair with full vert. gutter between —
b. Horiz. pair, imperf. between *2,000.* —
c. Imperf., pair *3,500.*
d. As "a," imperf between vert. *5,000.*

No. 807d is a booklet pane of nine, the error resulting from a foldover and miscutting.

Counterfeits exist of No. 807. See the Postal Counterfeits section of this catalog.

808 A280 4c **bright rose purple,** *July 1* .75 .25
rose purple ('43) .75 .25
On cover 3.00
Single franking on domestic third-class cover 25.00
Single franking on domestic airmail postcard 25.00
Single franking on penalty-permit cover with return receipt *250.00*
Single franking on post-1949 third-class cover *125.00*
Single franking on international surface postcard 30.00
Single franking on double weight local letter 150.00
Single franking on post Aug. 1, 1958 first-class letter 75.00
P# block of 4 3.25 —
Single frank on airmail return receipt (pays domestic air mail postcard rate on a return receipt form) *250.00*

809 A281 4½c **dark gray,** *July 11* .40 .25
gray ('43) .40 .25
On cover 20.00
Single franking on triple-weight third-class cover 75.00
Single franking on third-class cover with minimum insurance *125.00*
P# block of 4 2.00 —

810 A282 5c **bright blue,** *July 21* .35 .25
light blue .35 .25
On cover 1.00
Single franking on UPU surface cover 10.00
Single franking on domestic airmail cover 30.00
Single franking paying dead letter office return fee *75.00*
Single franking on certificate of mailing, after July 1, 1957 *250.00*
P# block of 4 1.75 —
Pair with full vert. gutter btwn. *1,350.*

811 A283 6c **red orange,** *July 28* .40 .25
On cover 1.00
Single franking on double-weight first-class cover 15.00

Single franking on 1944-45 airmail cover to POW 100.00
P# block of 4 2.00 —
Pair with full vert. gutter btwn. *1,200.*

812 A284 7c **sepia**, *Aug. 4* .40 .25
violet brown .40 .25
On cover 10.00
Single franking on 1958 domestic airmail cover 100.00
Single franking on domestic third-class cover 75.00
Single franking on penalty permit cover with return receipt *350.00*
P# block of 4 2.00 —

813 A285 8c **olive green**, *Aug. 11* .40 .25
light olive green ('43) .40 .25
bright olive green .40 .25
olive ('42) .40 .25
On cover 3.00
Single franking on domestic airmail cover 10.00
Single franking on pre-1953 double-weight UPU surface cover 75.00
Single franking on post-1953 UPU surface cover 25.00
Single franking on post-1958 third-class 150.00
Single franking paying 3c airmail to exchange office, 5c UPU surface to another country 500.00
P# block of 4 2.25 —

814 A286 9c **rose pink**, *Aug. 18* .45 .25
pink ('43) .45 .25
On cover 3.00
Single franking on triple-weight first-class cover 30.00
P# block of 4 2.25 —
Pair with full vert. gutter btwn. —

815 A287 10c **brown red**, *Sept. 2* .40 .25
pale brown red ('43) .40 .25
On cover 2.00
Single franking on airmail cover to the Caribbean 10.00
Single franking on international airmail postcard 25.00
Single franking on aerogramme or private air letter *500.00*
Single franking on airmail cover from Midway Island to Hawaii *350.00*
Single franking paying airmail from Midway to Hawaii and surface transport to continental U.S. *250.00*
P# block of 4 2.25 —

816 A288 11c **ultramarine**, *Sept. 8* .75 .25
bright ultramarine .75 .25
dull ultramarine .75 .25
On cover 5.00
Single franking on international airmail postcard *150.00*
Single franking on surface mail cover with airmail surcharge in US and Europe *1,150.*
Single franking on pre-1953 three-ounce UPU surface cover *600.00*
P# block of 4 3.50 —

817 A289 12c **bright mauve**, *Sept. 14* 1.00 .25
On cover 3.00
Single franking on double weight domestic airmail, 1939-44 30.00
Single franking on double weight domestic airmail, 1949-58 60.00
Single franking on quadruple-weight first-class cover 50.00
Single franking on local special delivery cover *250.00*
Single franking on international printed-matter cover *200.00*
Single franking on post-1953 double-weight UPU surface cover *250.00*
Single franking paying 2c local letter rate plus 10c special delivery *500.00*
P# block of 4 4.50 —

818 A290 13c **blue green**, *Sept. 22* 1.30 .25
deep blue green 1.30 .25
On cover 5.00
Single franking on special delivery cover *75.00*
P# block of 4 7.00 —

819 A291 14c **blue**, *Oct. 6* 1.00 .25
On cover 15.00
Single franking on 1958 double-weight domestic airmail cover *750.00*
Single franking on parcel post cover *200.00*
Single franking on pre-1953 four-ounce UPU surface cover *750.00*
P# block of 4 5.00 —

820 A292 15c **blue gray**, *Oct. 13* .80 .25
On cover 5.00
Single franking on 1945-46 airmail cover to or from Hawaii 25.00
Single franking on international airmail cover 15.00
Single franking paying quintuple first-class rate 100.00
Single frank on airmail cover between Wake Island and Hawaii 1,000.
P# block of 4 4.00 —

821 A293 16c **black**, *Oct. 20* 1.50 .25
On cover 15.00
Single franking on first-class special delivery cover *130.00*
Single franking on airmail special delivery cover *100.00*
Single franking on pre-1944 double-weight first-class special delivery cover *150.00*
Single franking on double-weight airmail cover *125.00*
P# block of 4 7.00 —

822 A294 17c **rose red**, *Oct. 27* 1.00 .25
deep rose red 1.10 .25
On cover 10.00
Single franking on local registered cover 100.00
Single franking on registered local territorial cover *2,750.*
P# block of 4 5.00 —

823 A295 18c **brown carmine**, *Nov. 3* 2.25 .25
rose brown ('43) 2.25 .25
On cover 5.00
Single franking on registered first-class cover 10.00
Single franking on 1938-44 or 1949-58 triple-weight airmail cover *100.00*
Single franking on airmail special delivery cover *150.00*
P# block of 4 12.00 —

824 A296 19c **bright mauve**, *Nov. 10* 1.30 .35
On cover 20.00
Single franking on parcel post cover *250.00*
Single franking on registered cover with unindemnified excess value *2,500.*
Single franking on double-weight local registered cover *3,000.*
Single franking on double-weight first-class special delivery cover *2,750.*
Single frank on insured third class cover *750.00*
P# block of 4 7.00 —

825 A297 20c **bright blue green**, *Nov. 10* 1.20 .25
deep blue green ('43) 1.20 .25
On cover 3.00
Single franking on airmail cover to or from Hawaii 10.00
Single franking on registered local letter with return receipt *100.00*
Single franking paying 2c local letter, 3c return receipt, 15c minimum registry *100.00*
P# block of 4 5.50 —
Pair with full horiz. gutter btwn. —
Pair with full vert. gutter btwn. —

826 A298 21c **dull blue**, *Nov. 22* 1.30 .25
On cover 10.00
Single franking on registered airmail cover 25.00
Single franking on double-weight first-class registered cover 35.00
On 1944-46 airmail special delivery cover *150.00*
On 1949-51 airmail special delivery cover *200.00*
P# block of 4 7.00 —

827 A299 22c **vermilion**, *Nov. 22* 1.20 .40
On cover 20.00
Single franking on insured third-class cover *850.00*
Single franking on registered cover with return receipt and unindemnified excess value *2,000.*
Single franking on registered local cover with return receipt *2,000.*
P# block of 4 8.00 —

828 A300 24c **gray black**, *Dec. 2* 3.25 .25
On cover 5.00
Single franking on registered penalty cover with return receipt 50.00
Single franking on 1944-46 or 1949-58 triple-weight airmail cover *175.00*
Single franking on 1938-44 quadruple-weight airmail cover *150.00*
P# block of 4 14.50 —

829 A301 25c **deep red lilac**, *Dec. 2* 1.20 .25
rose lilac ('43) 1.20 .25
On cover 5.00
Single franking on airmail cover to Asia, Africa and Australia 25.00
Single frank on registered airmail cover October 1946-January 1949 100.00
P# block of 4 5.50 —
Pair with full vert. gutter btwn. *900.00*

830 A302 30c **deep ultra**, *Dec. 8* 3.50 .25
On cover 5.00
Single franking on airmail cover to Europe 25.00
Single franking on cover to or from Midway Island *250.00*
P# block of 4 16.00 —
a. 30c **blue** 20.00 —
P# block of 4 150.00
b. 30c **deep blue** *375.00* —
P# block of 4 *1,850.* —

831 A303 50c **mauve**, *Dec. 8* 5.50 .25
On cover 10.00
Single franking on airmail cover to the Philippines 50.00
Single franking on double-weight airmail cover to Asia, Africa and Australia 60.00
Single franking on airmail cover from Hawaii to Europe *350.00*
P# block of 4 25.00 —

Bureau Precancels: ½c, 199 diff., 1c, 701 diff., 1½c, 404 diff., 2c, 161 diff., 3c, 87 diff., 4c, 30 diff., 4½c, 27 diff., 5c, 44 diff., 6c, 45 diff., 7c, 44 diff., 8c, 44 diff., 9c, 38 diff., 10c, 43 diff.

Also, 11c, 41 diff., 12c, 33 diff., 13c, 28 diff., 14c, 23 diff., 15c, 38 diff., 16c, 6 diff., 17c, 27 diff., 18c, 5 diff., 19c, 8 diff., 20c, 39 diff., 21c, 5 diff., 22c, 4 diff., 24c, 8 diff., 25c, 23 diff., 30c, 27 diff., 50c, 24 diff.

FLAT PLATE PRINTING
Plates of 100 subjects

1938 ***Perf. 11***

832 A304 $1 **purple & black**, *Aug. 29* 7.00 .25
On cover 10.00
On registered bank tag 5.00
Single franking on double-weight airmail cover to the Philippines *350.00*
Single franking on quadruple-weight airmail cover to Asia, Africa and Australia *400.00*
Single franking on quintuple-weight airmail cover to or from Hawaii *275.00*
Margin block of 4, bottom or side arrow 30.00 —
Center line block 32.50 *4.00*
Top P# block of 4, 2# 32.50 —
Top P# block of 20, 2#, arrow, 2 TOP, 2 registration markers and denomination 160.00 —
a. Vert. pair, imperf. horiz. *1,100.*
Top P# blk of 8, imperf horiz. *7,500.*
b. Watermarked USIR ('51) 200.00 65.00
Hinged 120.00
Center line block *1,700.*
P# block of 4, 2# *2,000.*
Top P# block of 20, 2#, arrow, 2 TOP, 2 registration markers and denomination 5,000.
c. $1 **red violet & black**, *Aug. 31, 1954* 6.00 .25
On cover 60.00
On registered bank tag 20.00
Single franking on quadruple-weight airmail cover to Asia, Africa and Australia *500.00*
Top or bottom P# block of 4, 2# 30.00 —
d. As "c," vert. pair, imperf. horiz. *900.00*
e. Vertical pair, imperf. between *7,500.*
f. As "c," vert. pair, imperf. btwn. *10,000.*
g. As "c," **bright magenta & black** *70.00* 50.00
Top or bottom P# block of 4, 2# *400.00*
h. As No. 832, **red violet & black** — —
Top or bottom P# block of 4, 2# —

No. 832c is dry printed from 400-subject flat plates on thick white paper with smooth, colorless gum.

No. 832g is the far end of the color spectrum for the No. 832c stamp, trending toward a more pinkish shade, but the shade is not pink. No. 832g is known in bright magenta and in deep bright magenta; both shades qualify as No. 832g.

No. 832h is a shade variety of the wet printing (No. 832), but the shade essentially matches the red violet normally seen on the dry printing (No. 832c).

833 A305 $2 **yellow green & black**, *Sept. 29* 16.00 3.75
green & black ('43) 16.00 3.75
On cover 500.00
On registered bank tag 35.00
Single franking on airmail cover to the Philippines *2,000.*
Single franking on registered airmail cover to Europe *3,000.*
Margin block of 4, bottom or side arrow 70.00 —
Center line block 80.00 35.00
Top P# block of 4, 2# 85.00 —
Top P# block of 20, 2#, arrow, 2 TOP, 2 registration markers and denominations 400.00 —
Top P# block of 20, 2#, black # and marginal markings only (yellow green # and markings omitted) *15,000.*

834 A306 $5 **carmine & black**, *Nov. 17* 75.00 3.00
Hinged 40.00
On registered bank tag 40.00
On cover, one example with other stamps on registered domestic cover *3,500.*
Multiple examples with other stamps on domestic registered cover *6,000.*
On international airmail cover with other stamps *7,500.*
dark red & black *700.00* *450.00*
Margin block of 4, bottom or side arrow 325.00 —
Center line block 350.00 *25.00*
Top P# block of 4, 2# 325.00 —
Top P# block of 20, 2#, arrow, 2 TOP, 2 registration markers and denominations 2,000.
a. $5 **red brown & black** *3,000.* *7,000.*
Hinged *1,850.*
Top P# block of 4, 2# *15,000.*
Hinged *15,000.*
Nos. 803-834 (32) 131.10 14.50
Nos. 803-834, P# blocks of 4 670.95

Top plate number blocks of Nos. 832, 833 and 834 are found both with and without top arrow or registration markers.

No. 834 can be chemically altered to resemble Scott 834a. No. 834a should be purchased only with competent expert certification.

Watermarks
All stamps from No. 835 on are unwatermarked.

CONSTITUTION RATIFICATION ISSUE
150th anniversary of the ratification of the United States Constitution.

Old Courthouse, Williamsburg, Va. — A307

ROTARY PRESS PRINTING

Plates of 200 subjects in four panes of 50.

1938, June 21 *Perf. 11x10½*

835 A307 3c **deep violet** .45 .25
P# block of 4 3.50 —

SWEDISH-FINNISH TERCENTENARY ISSUE

Tercentenary of the founding of the Swedish and Finnish Settlement at Wilmington, Delaware.

"Landing of the First Swedish and Finnish Settlers in America," by Stanley M. Arthurs — A308

FLAT PLATE PRINTING

Plates of 192 subjects in four panes of 48 each, separated by 1¼ inch wide gutters with central guide lines.

1938, June 27 *Perf. 11*

836 A308 3c **bright reddish purple** .35 .25
P# block of 6 2.25 —

NORTHWEST TERRITORY SESQUICENTENNIAL

"Colonization of the West," by Gutzon Borglum — A309

ROTARY PRESS PRINTING

Plates of 400 subjects in four panes of 100.

1938, July 15 *Perf. 11x10½*

837 A309 3c **bright rose purple** .30 .25
P# block of 4 5.00 —

IOWA TERRITORY CENTENNIAL ISSUE

Old Capitol, Iowa City — A310

ROTARY PRESS PRINTING

Plates of 200 subjects in four panes of 50.

1938, Aug. 24 *Perf. 11x10½*

838 A310 3c **violet** .40 .25
P# block of 4 6.00 —
Pair with full vertical gutter between —

TYPES OF 1938
REGULAR ISSUE
ROTARY PRESS COIL STAMPS

1939, Jan. 20 *Perf. 10 Vertically*

839 A276 1c **green** .30 .25
light green .30 .25
On cover .50
Pair .60 .50
Joint line pair 1.40 .70
Small holes —
Pair —
Joint line pair —

840 A277 1½c **bister brown** .30 .25
buff .30 .25
On cover 2.00
Single franking on third-class cover 15.00
Pair .60 .50
Joint line pair 1.50 .75
Small holes — —
Pair — —
Joint line pair —

841 A278 2c **rose carmine** .40 .25
On cover 2.00
Single franking on local cover 25.00
Pair .80 .50
Joint line pair 1.75 .85
Small holes —
Pair —
Joint line pair —

842 A279 3c **light violet**, large holes .50 .25
violet .50 .25
On cover .50
Pair 1.00 .50
Joint line pair 2.00 1.00
Gripper cracks —
Thin translucent paper — —
Small holes —
Pair —
Joint line pair —

See note concerning large and small perforation holes following No. 1053.

843 A280 4c **red violet** 7.50 .40
On cover 5.00
Single franking on domestic first-class cover 100.00
Single franking on domestic third-class cover 75.00
Single franking on domestic airmail postcard *100.00*
Single franking on international postcard *150.00*
Pair 16.50 .90
Joint line pair 27.50 12.50
Small holes —
Pair —
Joint line pair —

844 A281 4½c **dark gray** .70 .40
On cover 40.00
Single franking on triple-weight third-class cover *275.00*
Single franking on third-class cover with minimum insurance *375.00*
Pair 1.50 .90
Joint line pair 5.00 2.25
Small holes —
Pair —
Joint line pair —

845 A282 5c **bright blue** 5.00 2.50
On cover 15.00
Single franking on domestic airmail cover 75.00
Single franking on UPU surface cover *150.00*
Pair 10.50 .75
Joint line pair 27.50 5.00
Small holes —
Pair —
Joint line pair —

846 A283 6c **red orange** 1.10 .55
On cover 5.00
Single franking on domestic airmail cover 15.00
Pair 2.25 .50
Joint line pair 7.50 1.50
Small holes —
Pair —
Joint line pair —

847 A287 10c **brown red** 11.00 1.00
On cover *300.00*
Single franking on international airmail postcard *2,500.*
Single franking on airmail cover the Carribean and Central and South America *3,000.*
Pair 24.00 2.50
Joint line pair 42.50 10.00
Small holes —
Pair —
Joint line pair —

Bureau Precancels: 1c, 269 diff., 1½c, 179 diff., 2c, 101 diff., 3c, 46 diff., 4c, 13 diff., 4½c, 3 diff., 5c, 6 diff., 6c, 8 diff., 10c, 4 diff.

1939, Jan. 27 *Perf. 10 Horizontally*

848 A276 1c **green** .85 .25
On cover 5.00
Single franking on domestic postcard 25.00
Pair 1.75 .50
Joint line pair 2.75 1.25
Small holes —
Pair —
Joint line pair —

849 A277 1½c **bister brown** 1.25 .30
On cover 20.00
Single franking on third-class cover 100.00
Pair 2.50 .65
Joint line pair 4.50 2.00
Small holes —
Pair —
Joint line pair —

850 A278 2c **rose carmine** 2.50 .40
On cover 10.00
Single franking on third-class cover 75.00
Pair 5.00 .90
Joint line pair 7.50 3.50
Small holes —
Pair —
Joint line pair —

851 A279 3c **light violet** 2.50 .40
violet 2.50 .40
On cover 15.00
Single franking on domestic first-class cover 30.00
Pair 5.00 .90
Joint line pair 8.50 3.75
Thin translucent paper —
Same, joint line pair *750.00*
Small holes —
Pair —
Joint line pair —
Nos. 839-851 (13) 33.90 7.20
Nos. 839-851, joint line pairs (13) 139.90 29.65

GOLDEN GATE INTL. EXPOSITION, SAN FRANCISCO

"Tower of the Sun" — A311

ROTARY PRESS PRINTING

Plates of 200 subjects in four panes of 50.

1939, Feb. 18 *Perf. 10½x11*

852 A311 3c **bright purple** .30 .25
On cover, Expo. station machine canc. (non-first day) 3.00
On cover, Expo. station duplex handstamp canc. (non-first day) 15.00
P# block of 4 1.50 —

NEW YORK WORLD'S FAIR ISSUE

Trylon and Perisphere — A312

ROTARY PRESS PRINTING

Plates of 200 subjects in four panes of 50.

1939, Apr. 1 *Perf. 10½x11*

853 A312 3c **violet** .30 .25
On cover, Expo. station machine canc. (non-first day) 3.00
On cover, Expo. station duplex handstamp canc. 10.00
P# block of 4 2.00 —

WASHINGTON INAUGURATION ISSUE

Sesquicentennial of the inauguration of George Washington as First President.

Washington Taking Oath of Office, Federal Building, New York City — A313

FLAT PLATE PRINTING

Plates of 200 subjects in four panes of 50.

1939, Apr. 30 *Perf. 11*

854 A313 3c **bright purple** .60 .25
P# block of 6 3.50 —

BASEBALL CENTENNIAL ISSUE

Sandlot Baseball Game — A314

Designed by William A. Roach.

ROTARY PRESS PRINTING

Plates of 200 subjects in four panes of 50.

1939, June 12		*Perf. 11x10½*	
855 A314 3c **violet**		1.75	.25
P# block of 4		7.50	—

PANAMA CANAL ISSUE

25th anniv. of the opening of the Panama Canal.

Theodore Roosevelt, Gen. George W. Goethals and Ship in Gaillard Cut — A315

Designed by William A. Roach.

FLAT PLATE PRINTING

Plates of 200 subjects in four panes of 50.

1939, Aug. 15		*Perf. 11*	
856 A315 3c **reddish purple**		.40	.25
P# block of 6		3.50	—

PRINTING TERCENTENARY ISSUE

Issued in commemoration of the 300th anniversary of printing in Colonial America. The Stephen Daye press is in the Harvard University Museum.

Stephen Daye Press — A316

Designed by William K. Schrage.

ROTARY PRESS PRINTING

E.E. Plates of 200 subjects in four panes of 50.

1939, Sept. 25		*Perf. 10½x11*	
857 A316 3c **violet**		.30	.25
P# block of 4		1.00	—

50th ANNIVERSARY OF STATEHOOD ISSUE

Map of North and South Dakota, Montana and Washington A317

ROTARY PRESS PRINTING

E.E. Plates of 200 subjects in four panes of 50.

1939, Nov. 2		*Perf. 11x10½*	
858 A317 3c **rose purple**		.35	.25
P# block of 4		2.25	—

FAMOUS AMERICANS ISSUES

ROTARY PRESS PRINTING

E.E. Plates of 280 subjects in four panes of 70.

AMERICAN AUTHORS

Washington Irving — A318

James Fenimore Cooper — A319

Ralph Waldo Emerson — A320

Louisa May Alcott — A321

Samuel L. Clemens (Mark Twain) — A322

1940		*Perf. 10½x11*	
859 A318 1c **bright blue green,** *Jan. 29*		.30	.25
P# block of 4		1.00	—
860 A319 2c **rose carmine,** *Jan. 29*		.30	.25
P# block of 4		1.25	—
861 A320 3c **bright purple,** *Feb. 5*		.30	.25
P# block of 4		1.25	—
862 A321 5c **ultramarine,** *Feb. 5*		.35	.25
P# block of 4		8.00	—
863 A322 10c **dark brown,** *Feb. 13*		1.75	1.20
P# block of 4		22.50	—
Nos. 859-863 (5)		3.00	2.20

AMERICAN POETS

Henry Wadsworth Longfellow — A323

John Greenleaf Whittier — A324

James Russell Lowell — A325

Walt Whitman — A326

James Whitcomb Riley — A327

864 A323 1c **bright blue green,** *Feb. 16*		.30	.25
P# block of 4		2.00	—
865 A324 2c **rose carmine,** *Feb. 16*		.30	.25
P# block of 4		1.75	—
866 A325 3c **bright purple,** *Feb. 20*		.30	.25
P# block of 4		2.25	—
867 A326 5c **ultramarine,** *Feb. 20*		.50	.25
P# block of 4		8.50	—
868 A327 10c **dark brown,** *Feb. 24*		1.75	1.25
P# block of 4		22.50	—
Nos. 864-868 (5)		3.15	2.25

AMERICAN EDUCATORS

Horace Mann — A328

Mark Hopkins — A329

Charles W. Eliot — A330

Frances E. Willard — A331

Booker T. Washington — A332

869 A328 1c **bright blue green,** *Mar. 14*		.30	.25
P# block of 4		2.25	—
870 A329 2c **rose carmine,** *Mar. 14*		.30	.25
P# block of 4		1.75	—
871 A330 3c **bright purple,** *Mar. 28*		.30	.25
P# block of 4		2.00	—
872 A331 5c **ultramarine,** *Mar. 28*		.50	.25
P# block of 4		8.00	—
873 A332 10c **dark brown,** *Apr. 7*		2.25	1.10
P# block of 4		22.50	—
Nos. 869-873 (5)		3.65	2.10

AMERICAN SCIENTISTS

John James Audubon — A333

Dr. Crawford W. Long — A334

Luther Burbank — A335

Dr. Walter Reed — A336

Jane Addams — A337

874 A333 1c **bright blue green,** *Apr. 8* .30 .25
P# block of 4 1.00 —
875 A334 2c **rose carmine,** *Apr. 8* .30 .25
P# block of 4 1.00 —
876 A335 3c **bright purple,** *Apr. 17* .30 .25
P# block of 4 1.10 —
877 A336 5c **ultramarine,** *Apr. 17* .50 .25
P# block of 4 5.50 —
878 A337 10c **dark brown,** *Apr. 26* 1.50 .85
P# block of 4 15.00 —
Nos. 874-878 (5) 2.90 1.85

AMERICAN COMPOSERS

Stephen Collins Foster — A338

John Philip Sousa — A339

Victor Herbert — A340

Edward A. MacDowell — A341

Ethelbert Nevin — A342

879 A338 1c **bright blue green,** *May 3* .30 .25
P# block of 4 1.00 —
880 A339 2c **rose carmine,** *May 3* .30 .25
P# block of 4 1.00 —
881 A340 3c **bright purple,** *May 13* .30 .25
P# block of 4 1.10 —
882 A341 5c **ultramarine,** *May 13* .50 .25
P# block of 4 9.00 —
883 A342 10c **dark brown,** *June 10* 3.75 1.35
P# block of 4 20.00 —
Nos. 879-883 (5) 5.15 2.35

AMERICAN ARTISTS

Gilbert Charles Stuart — A343

James A. McNeill Whistler — A344

Augustus Saint-Gaudens — A345

Daniel Chester French — A346

Frederic Remington — A347

884 A343 1c **bright blue green,** *Sept. 5* .30 .25
P# block of 4 1.00 —
885 A344 2c **rose carmine,** *Sept. 5* .30 .25
P# block of 4 1.00 —
886 A345 3c **bright purple,** *Sept. 16* .30 .25
P# block of 4 1.50 —
887 A346 5c **ultramarine,** *Sept. 16* .50 .25
P# block of 4 8.00 —
888 A347 10c **dark brown,** *Sept. 30* 1.75 1.25
P# block of 4 15.00 —
Nos. 884-888 (5) 3.15 2.25

AMERICAN INVENTORS

Eli Whitney — A348

Samuel F. B. Morse — A349

Cyrus Hall McCormick — A350

Elias Howe — A351

Alexander Graham Bell — A352

889 A348 1c **bright blue green,** *Oct. 7* .30 .25
P# block of 4 2.25 —
890 A349 2c **rose carmine,** *Oct. 7* .30 .25
P# block of 4 2.00 —
891 A350 3c **bright purple,** *Oct. 14* .30 .25
P# block of 4 1.50 —
892 A351 5c **ultramarine,** *Oct. 14* 1.10 .30
P# block of 4 11.00 —
893 A352 10c **dark brown,** *Oct. 28* 11.00 2.00
P# block of 4 40.00 —
Nos. 889-893 (5) 13.00 3.05
Nos. 859-893 (35) 34.00 16.05
Nos. 859-893, P# blocks of 4 245.70

PONY EXPRESS, 80th ANNIV. ISSUE

Pony Express Rider — A353

ROTARY PRESS PRINTING
E.E. Plates of 200 subjects in four panes of 50.

1940, Apr. 3 ***Perf. 11x10½***
894 A353 3c **henna brown** .50 .25
P# block of 4 3.50 —

PAN AMERICAN UNION ISSUE

Founding of the Pan American Union, 50th anniv.

The Three Graces (Botticelli) — A354

ROTARY PRESS PRINTING
E.E. Plates of 200 subjects in four panes of 50.

1940, Apr. 14 ***Perf. 10½x11***
895 A354 3c **bright rose purple** .30 .25
P# block of 4 2.75 —

IDAHO STATEHOOD, 50th ANNIV.

Idaho State Capitol A355

ROTARY PRESS PRINTING
E.E. Plates of 200 subjects in four panes of 50.

1940, July 3 ***Perf. 11x10½***
896 A355 3c **bright mauve** .35 .25
P# block of 4 2.25 —

WYOMING STATEHOOD, 50th ANNIV.

Wyoming State Seal — A356

ROTARY PRESS PRINTING
E.E. Plates of 200 subjects in four panes of 50.

1940, July 10 ***Perf. 10½x11***
897 A356 3c **brown violet** .35 .25
P# block of 4 2.25 —

CORONADO EXPEDITION, 400th ANNIV.

"Coronado and His Captains" Painted by Gerald Cassidy A357

ROTARY PRESS PRINTING

E.E. Plates of 200 subjects in four panes of 50.

1940, Sept. 7 *Perf. 11x10½*

898 A357 3c **bright violet** .35 .25
P# block of 4 2.25 —

NATIONAL DEFENSE ISSUE

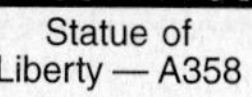

Statue of Liberty — A358

90-millimeter Anti-aircraft Gun — A359

Torch of Enlightenment — A360

ROTARY PRESS PRINTING

E.E. Plates of 400 subjects in four panes of 100

1940, Oct. 16 *Perf. 11x10½*

899 A358 1c **bright blue green**	.30	.25
P# block of 4	1.00	—
Cracked plate (22684 UR 10)	3.00	
Gripper cracks	3.00	
Pair with full vert. gutter between	*200.00*	
a. Vertical pair, imperf. between	*600.00*	—
b. Horizontal pair, imperf. between	32.50	—
900 A359 2c **rose carmine**	.30	.25
P# block of 4	1.00	—
Pair with full vert. gutter between	*275.00*	
a. Horizontal pair, imperf. between	37.50	—
901 A360 3c **bright mauve**	.30	.25
P# block of 4	1.00	—
Pair with full vert. gutter between	—	
a. Horizontal pair, imperf. between	22.50	—
Nos. 899-901 (3)	.90	.75

Bureau Precancels: 1c, 316 diff., 2c, 25 diff., 3c, 22 diff.

THIRTEENTH AMENDMENT ISSUE

75th anniv. of the 13th Amendment to the Constitution abolishing slavery.

Emancipation Monument; Lincoln and Kneeling Slave, by Thomas Ball — A361

Designed by William A. Roach.

ROTARY PRESS PRINTING

E.E. Plates of 200 subjects in four panes of 50.

1940, Oct. 20 *Perf. 10½x11*

902 A361 3c **violet** .50 .25
dark violet .50 .25
P# block of 4 3.50 —

VERMONT STATEHOOD, 150th ANNIV.

State Capitol, Montpelier A362

Designed by Alvin R. Meissner.

ROTARY PRESS PRINTING

E.E. Plates of 200 subjects in four panes of 50.

1941, Mar. 4 *Perf. 11x10½*

903 A362 3c **light violet** .45 .25
P# block of 4 3.00 —

KENTUCKY STATEHOOD, 150th ANNIV.

Daniel Boone and Three Frontiersmen, from Mural by Gilbert White — A363

Designed by William A. Roach.

ROTARY PRESS PRINTING

E.E. Plates of 200 subjects in four panes of 50.

1942, June 1 *Perf. 11x10½*

904 A363 3c **purple** .30 .25
P# block of 4 1.75 —

WIN THE WAR ISSUE

American Eagle — A364

ROTARY PRESS PRINTING

E.E. Plates of 400 subjects in four panes of 100.

1942, July 4 *Perf. 11x10½*

905 A364 3c **bright lilac**	.30	.25
light violet	.30	.25
P# block of 4	2.25	—
Pair with full vert. gutter between	*200.00*	
Pair with full horiz. gutter between	*600.00*	
b. 3c **reddish purple**	*750.00*	*500.00*

Bureau Precancels: 26 diff.

All examples of No. 905b are precanceled either Los Angeles, Calif., Fremont, Ohio, or St. Paul, Minn. Value is for Los Angeles, which is the more common. Value of Fremont, unused, $1,500. Value of St. Paul, used (without gum), $2,500. The stamps with St. Paul precancel are slightly less reddish than Los Angeles or Fremont, but they are in the same reddish purple/purple color family.

CHINESE RESISTANCE ISSUE

Issued to commemorate the Chinese people's five years of resistance to Japanese aggression.

Map of China, Abraham Lincoln and Sun Yat-sen, Founder of the Chinese Republic A365

ROTARY PRESS PRINTING

E.E. Plates of 200 subjects in four panes of 50.

1942, July 7 *Perf. 11x10½*

906 A365 5c **bright blue** *4.00* .50
P# block of 4 *22.00* —

ALLIED NATIONS ISSUE

Allegory of Victory — A366

Designed by Leon Helguera.

ROTARY PRESS PRINTING

E.E. Plates of 400 subjects in four panes of 100.

1943, Jan. 14 *Perf. 11x10½*

907 A366 2c **rose carmine** .30 .25
P# block of 4 1.00 —
Pair with full vert. or horiz. gutter between *225.00*

Bureau Precancels: Denver, Baltimore.

FOUR FREEDOMS ISSUE

Liberty Holding the Torch of Freedom and Enlightenment — A367

Designed by Paul Manship.

ROTARY PRESS PRINTING

E.E. Plates of 400 subjects in four panes of 100.

1943, Feb. 12 *Perf. 11x10½*

908 A367 1c **bright blue green** .30 .25
P# block of 4 1.00 —

Bureau Precancels: 20 diff.

OVERRUN COUNTRIES ISSUE

Due to the failure of the printers to divulge detailed information as to printing processes used, the editors omit listings of irregularities, flaws and blemishes which are numerous in this issue. Exceptions are made for certified double impressions, the widely recognized "KORPA" variety, and "reverse" vs. "normal" printings of the flag colors.

Flag of Poland A368

Printed by the American Bank Note Co.

FRAMES ENGRAVED, CENTERS OFFSET LETTERPRESS

ROTARY PRESS PRINTING

Plates of 200 subjects in four panes of 50.

1943-44 *Perf. 12*

909 A368 5c **blue violet, bright red & black,** *June 22, 1943*	.30	.25
Margin block of 4, Inscribed "Poland"	3.50	—
Top margin block of 6, with red & blue violet guide markings and "Poland"	4.75	—
Bottom margin block of 6, with red & black guide markings	1.65	—
a. Double impression of "Poland"	*200.00*	
b. Double impression of black flag color and red "Poland"		—
c. Reverse printing of flag colors (bright red over black)	*25.00*	*150.00*

Flag of Czechoslovakia — A368a

910 A368a 5c **blue violet, blue, bright red & black,** *July 12, 1943*	.30	.25
Margin block of 4, inscribed "Czechoslovakia"	2.75	—

Top margin block of 6, with red & blue violet guide markings and "Czechoslovakia" 3.25 —
a. Double impression of "Czechoslovakia" *600.00*
b. Reverse printing of flag colors (blue and bright red over black) — *150.00*
c. Partial reverse printing of flag colors (bright red over black and black over blue) —

Flag of Norway — A368b

911 A368b 5c **blue violet, dark rose, deep blue & black,** *July 27, 1943* .30 .25
Margin block of 4, inscribed "Norway" 1.30 —
Bottom margin block of 6 with dark rose & blue violet guide markings 1.65 —
a. Double impression of "Norway" *225.00*
b. Reverse printing of flag colors (dark rose and deep blue over black) —

Flag of Luxembourg — A368c

912 A368c 5c **blue violet, dark rose, light blue & black,** *Aug. 10, 1943* .30 .25
Margin block of 4, inscribed "Luxembourg" 1.30 —
Top margin block of 6 with light blue & blue violet guide markings & "Luxembourg" 1.65 —
a. Double impression of "Luxembourg" —
b. Reverse printing of flag colors (dark rose and light blue over black) — —
c. Partial reverse printing of flag colors (dark rose over black and black over light blue) —

Flag of Netherlands — A368d

913 A368d 5c **blue violet, dark rose, blue & black,** *Aug. 24, 1943* .30 .25
Margin block of 4, inscribed "Netherlands" 1.25 —
Bottom margin block of 6 with blue & blue violet guide markings 1.65 —
a. Reverse printing of flag colors (dark rose and blue over black) — *150.00*
b. Partial reverse printing of flag colors (blue over black and black over dark rose) .30 .25
c. Double impression of black 90.00

Flag of Belgium — A368e

914 A368e 5c **blue violet, dark rose, yellow & black,** *Sept. 14, 1943* .30 .25
Margin block of 4, inscribed "Belgium" 1.10 —
Top margin block of 6, with yellow & blue violet guide markings and "Belgium" 1.50 —
a. Double impression of "Belgium" *200.00*
b. Reverse printing of flag colors (red and yellow over black) .30 .25

c. Partial reverse printing of flag colors (yellow over black and black over red) —

Flag of France — A368f

915 A368f 5c **blue violet, deep blue, dark rose & black,** *Sept. 28, 1943* .30 .25
Margin block of 4, inscribed "France" 1.25 —
Bottom margin block of 6 with dark rose & blue violet guide markings 1.65 —
a. Reverse printing of flag colors (deep blue and dark rose over black) *20.00 150.00*
b. Partial reverse printing of flag colors (dark rose over black and black over deep blue) —

Flag of Greece — A368g

916 A368g 5c **blue vio, pale blue, grnsh blue & blk,** reverse printing of flag colors (pale blue flag stripes over pale blue shading), *Oct. 12, 1943* .50 .25
Margin block of 4, inscribed "Greece" 6.50 —
Top margin block of 6 with pale blue & blue violet guide markings & "Greece" 11.50 —
a. "Normal" printing of flag colors (dark blue shading over pale blue flag stripes) — —

Flag of Yugoslavia — A368h

Normal

Reverse Printing of Flag Colors

917 A368h 5c **blue violet, blue, dark rose & black,** *Oct. 26, 1943* .40 .25
Margin block of 4, inscribed "Yugoslavia" 4.25 —
Bottom margin block of 6 with dark rose & blue violet guide markings 2.60 —
a. Reverse printing of flag colors (blue and dark rose over black) *20.00* —
b. Double impression of black *250.00 200.00*

c. Partial reverse printing of flag colors (dark rose over black and black over blue) —

Flag of Albania — A368i

918 A368i 5c **blue violet, dark red & black,** *Nov. 9, 1943* .30 .25
Margin block of 4, inscribed "Albania" 4.25 —
Top margin block of 6, with dark red & blue violet guide markings & "Albania" 6.50 —
a. Double impression of "Albania" — *600.00*
b. Reverse printing of flag colors (red over black) — —

Flag of Austria — A368j

919 A368j 5c **blue violet, red & black,** *Nov. 23, 1943* .30 .25
Margin block of 4, inscribed "Austria" 3.50 —
Bottom margin block of 6, with red & blue violet guide markings 2.00 —
a. Double impression of "Austria" *300.00*
b. Reverse printing of flag colors (red over black) —
c. Double impression of black —

Flag of Denmark — A368k

920 A368k 5c **blue violet, red & black,** *Dec. 7, 1943* .30 .25
Margin block of 4, inscribed "Denmark" 5.25 —
Top margin block of 6, with red & blue violet guide markings & "Denmark" 6.00 —
a. Reverse printing of flag colors (red over black) — *150.00*
b. 5c **blue violet, red & gray** .30 .25
c. As "b," reverse printing of flag colors (red over gray) — —

Flag of Korea — A368m

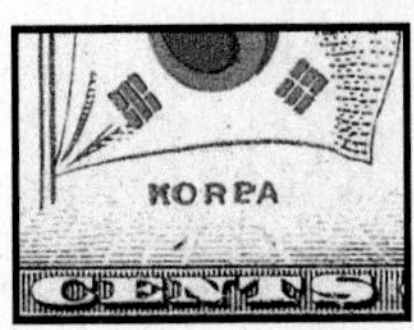

"KORPA" plate flaw

921 A368m 5c **blue violet, red, light blue & gray,** reverse printing of flag colors (light blue over gray), *Nov. 2, 1944* .30 .25
Margin block of 4, inscribed "Korea" 4.50 —
Top margin block of 6 with blue & black guide markings and "Korea" 5.25 —
"KORPA" plate flaw 22.50 12.50
a. Double impression of light blue (including "Korea") —

b.	"Normal" printing of flag colors (gray over light blue)	.30	.25
c.	Double impression of red	—	—

The "P" of "KORPA" is actually a mangled "E." Occurs only on some panes, position 26.

Nos. 909-921 (13)	4.20	3.25
Nos. 909-921, Name blocks of 4	43.60	

TRANSCONTINENTAL RAILROAD ISSUE

Completion of the 1st transcontinental railroad, 75th anniv.

"Golden Spike Ceremony" Painted by John McQuarrie
A369

ENGRAVED
ROTARY PRESS PRINTING
E.E. Plates of 200 subjects in four panes of 50.

1944, May 10 — ***Perf. 11x10½***

922 A369 3c **violet**	.30	.25
P# block of 4	2.50	—

STEAMSHIP ISSUE

1st steamship to cross the Atlantic, 125th anniv.

"Savannah"
A370

ROTARY PRESS PRINTING
E.E. Plates of 200 subjects in four panes of 50.

1944, May 22 — ***Perf. 11x10½***

923 A370 3c **violet**	.30	.25
P# block of 4	1.25	—

TELEGRAPH ISSUE

1st message transmitted by telegraph, cent.

Telegraph Wires and Morse's First Transmitted Words "What Hath God Wrought"
A371

ROTARY PRESS PRINTING
E.E. Plates of 200 subjects in four panes of 50.

1944, May 24 — ***Perf. 11x10½***

924 A371 3c **bright purple**	.30	.25
P# block of 4	1.00	—

PHILIPPINE ISSUE

Final resistance of the US and Philippine defenders on Corregidor to the Japanese invaders in 1942.

Aerial View of Corregidor, Manila Bay — A372

ROTARY PRESS PRINTING
E.E. Plates of 200 subjects in four panes of 50.

1944, Sept. 27 — ***Perf. 11x10½***

925 A372 3c **deep violet**	.30	.25
P# block of 4	1.50	—

MOTION PICTURE, 50th ANNIV.

Motion Picture Showing for Armed Forces in South Pacific — A373

ROTARY PRESS PRINTING
E.E. Plates of 200 subjects in four panes of 50.

1944, Oct. 31 — ***Perf. 11x10½***

926 A373 3c **deep violet**	.30	.25
P# block of 4	1.00	—

FLORIDA STATEHOOD, CENTENARY

State Seal, Gates of St. Augustine and Capitol at Tallahassee
A374

ROTARY PRESS PRINTING
E.E. Plates of 200 subjects in four panes of 50.

1945, Mar. 3 — ***Perf. 11x10½***

927 A374 3c **bright red violet**	.30	.25
P# block of 4	1.40	—

UNITED NATIONS CONFERENCE ISSUE

United Nations Conference, San Francisco, Calif.

"Toward United Nations, April 25, 1945" — A375

ROTARY PRESS PRINTING
E.E. Plates of 200 subjects in four panes of 50.

1945, Apr. 25 — ***Perf. 11x10½***

928 A375 5c **ultramarine**	.30	.25
P# block of 4	1.00	—

IWO JIMA (MARINES) ISSUE

Battle of Iwo Jima and honoring the achievements of the US Marines.

Marines Raising American Flag on Mount Suribachi, Iwo Jima, from a photograph by Joe Rosenthal — A376

ROTARY PRESS PRINTING
E.E. Plates of 200 subjects in four panes of 50.

1945, July 11 — ***Perf. 10½x11***

929 A376 3c **yellow green**	.30	.25
P# block of 4	2.00	—

FRANKLIN D. ROOSEVELT ISSUE

Franklin Delano Roosevelt (1882-1945).

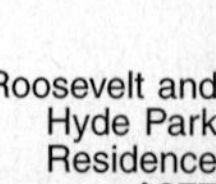

Roosevelt and Hyde Park Residence
A377

Roosevelt and the "Little White House" at Warm Springs, Ga. — A378

Roosevelt and White House — A379

Roosevelt, Map of Western Hemisphere and Four Freedoms
A380

ROTARY PRESS PRINTING
E.E. Plates of 200 subjects in four panes of 50.

1945-46 — ***Perf. 11x10½***

930 A377 1c **blue green,** *July 26, 1945*	.30	.25
P# block of 4	1.00	—
931 A378 2c **carmine rose,** *Aug. 24, 1945*	.30	.25
P# block of 4	1.00	—
932 A379 3c **purple,** *June 27, 1945*	.30	.25
P# block of 4	1.00	—
933 A380 5c **bright blue,** *Jan. 30, 1946*	.30	.25
P# block of 4	1.00	—
Nos. 930-933 (4)	1.20	1.00

ARMY ISSUE

Achievements of the US Army in World War II.

United States Troops Passing Arch of Triumph, Paris — A381

ROTARY PRESS PRINTING
E.E. Plates of 200 subjects in four panes of 50.

1945, Sept. 28 — ***Perf. 11x10½***

934 A381 3c **olive**	.30	.25
P# block of 4	1.00	—

NAVY ISSUE

Achievements of the U.S. Navy in World War II.

United States Sailors — A382

ROTARY PRESS PRINTING
E.E. Plates of 200 subjects in four panes of 50.

1945, Oct. 27 — ***Perf. 11x10½***

935 A382 3c **blue**	.30	.25
P# block of 4	1.00	—

COAST GUARD ISSUE

Achievements of the US Coast Guard in World War II.

Coast Guard Landing Craft and Supply Ship — A383

ROTARY PRESS PRINTING

E.E. Plates of 200 subjects in four panes of 50.

1945, Nov. 10 ***Perf. 11x10½***

936 A383 3c **bright blue green** .30 .25
P# block of 4 1.00 —

ALFRED E. SMITH ISSUE

Alfred E. Smith, Governor of New York — A384

ROTARY PRESS PRINTING

E.E. Plates of 400 subjects in four panes of 100.

1945, Nov. 26 ***Perf. 11x10½***

937 A384 3c **purple** .30 .25
P# block of 4 1.00
Pair with full vert. gutter btwn. —
Pair with full horiz. gutter btwn. 300.00

TEXAS STATEHOOD, 100th ANNIV.

Flags of the United States and the State of Texas — A385

ROTARY PRESS PRINTING

E.E. Plates of 200 subjects in four panes of 50.

1945, Dec. 29 ***Perf. 11x10½***

938 A385 3c **dark blue** .30 .25
P# block of 4 1.00 —

MERCHANT MARINE ISSUE

Achievements of the US Merchant Marine in World War II.

Liberty Ship Unloading Cargo — A386

ROTARY PRESS PRINTING

E.E. Plates of 200 subjects in four panes of 50.

1946, Feb. 26 ***Perf. 11x10½***

939 A386 3c **blue green** .30 .25
P# block of 4 1.00 —

VETERANS OF WORLD WAR II ISSUE

Issued to honor all veterans of World War II.

Honorable Discharge Emblem — A387

ROTARY PRESS PRINTING

E.E. Plates of 400 subjects in four panes of 100.

1946, May 9 ***Perf. 11x10½***

940 A387 3c **dark violet** .30 .25
P# block of 4 1.00 —
Pair with full vert. gutter btwn. 225.00

TENNESSEE STATEHOOD, 150th ANNIV.

Andrew Jackson, John Sevier and State Capitol, Nashville A388

ROTARY PRESS PRINTING

E.E. Plates of 200 subjects in four panes of 50.

1946, June 1 ***Perf. 11x10½***

941 A388 3c **dark violet** .30 .25
P# block of 4 1.00 —

IOWA STATEHOOD, 100th ANNIV.

Iowa State Flag and Map — A389

ROTARY PRESS PRINTING

E.E. Plates of 200 subjects in four panes of 50.

1946, Aug. 3 ***Perf. 11x10½***

942 A389 3c **deep blue** .30 .25
P# block of 4 1.00 —

SMITHSONIAN INSTITUTION ISSUE

100th anniversary of the establishment of the Smithsonian Institution, Washington, D.C.

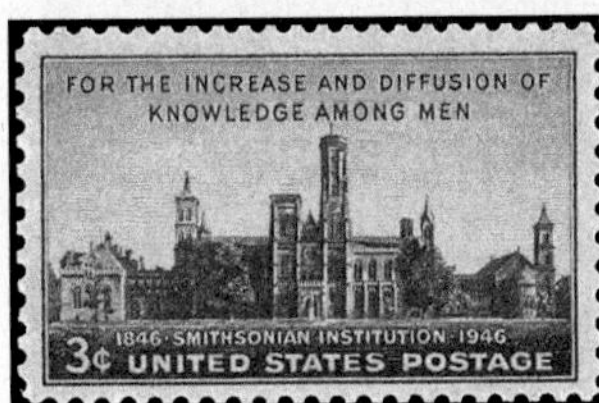

Smithsonian Institution A390

ROTARY PRESS PRINTING

E.E. Plates of 200 subjects in four panes of 50.

1946, Aug. 10 ***Perf. 11x10½***

943 A390 3c **violet brown** .30 .25
P# block of 4 1.00 —

KEARNY EXPEDITION ISSUE

100th anniversary of the entry of General Stephen Watts Kearny into Santa Fe.

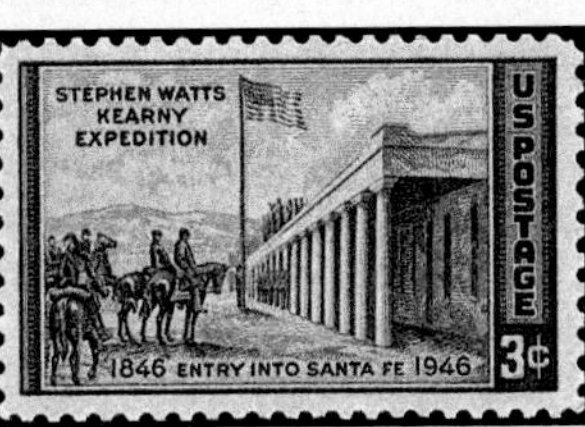

"Capture of Santa Fe" by Kenneth M. Chapman A391

ROTARY PRESS PRINTING

E.E. Plates of 200 subjects in four panes of 50.

1946, Oct. 16 ***Perf. 11x10½***

944 A391 3c **brown violet** .30 .25
P# block of 4 1.00 —

THOMAS A. EDISON ISSUE

Thomas A. Edison (1847-1931), Inventor — A392

ROTARY PRESS PRINTING

E.E. Plates of 280 subjects in four panes of 70.

1947, Feb. 11 ***Perf. 10½x11***

945 A392 3c **bright red violet** .30 .25
P# block of 4 1.00 —

JOSEPH PULITZER ISSUE

Joseph Pulitzer (1847-1911), Journalist, and Statue of Liberty A393

Designed by Victor S. McCloskey, Jr.

ROTARY PRESS PRINTING

E.E. Plates of 200 subjects in four panes of 50.

1947, Apr. 10 ***Perf. 11x10½***

946 A393 3c **purple** .30 .25
P# block of 4 1.00 —

POSTAGE STAMP CENTENARY ISSUE

Centenary of the first postage stamps issued by the United States Government

Washington and Franklin, Early and Modern Mail-carrying Vehicles A394

Designed by Leon Helguera.

ROTARY PRESS PRINTING

E.E. Plates of 200 subjects in four panes of 50.

1947, May 17 ***Perf. 11x10½***

947 A394 3c **deep blue** .30 .25
P# block of 4 1.00 —

CENTENARY INTERNATIONAL PHILATELIC EXHIBITION ISSUE

SOUVENIR SHEET

A395

Illustration reduced.

FLAT PLATE PRINTING

Plates of 30 subjects

1947, May 19 ***Imperf.***

948 A395 Pane of 2 .60 .45
a. 5c **blue**, type A1 .30 .25
b. 10c **brown orange**, type A2 .30 .25

Pane inscribed below stamps: "100th Anniversary United States Postage Stamps" and in the margins:

"PRINTED BY THE TREASURY DEPARTMENT, BUREAU OF ENGRAVING AND PRINTING. — UNDER AUTHORITY OF ROBERT E. HANNEGAN, POSTMASTER GENERAL. — IN COMPLIMENT TO THE CENTENARY INTERNATIONAL PHILATELIC EXHIBITION. — NEW YORK, N.Y., MAY 17-25, 1947."

Pane size varies: 96-98x66-68mm.

DOCTORS ISSUE

Issued to honor the physicians of America.

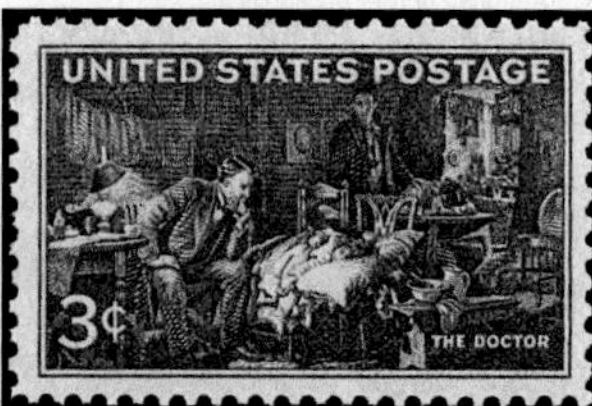

"The Doctor" by Sir Luke Fildes — A396

Designed by Charles R. Chickering.

ROTARY PRESS PRINTING

E.E. Plates of 200 subjects in four panes of 50.

1947, June 9 ***Perf. 11x10½***

949 A396 3c **brown violet** .30 .25
P# block of 4 1.00 —

UTAH ISSUE

Centenary of the settlement of Utah.

Pioneers Entering the Valley of Great Salt Lake — A397

Designed by Charles R. Chickering.

ROTARY PRESS PRINTING

E.E. Plates of 200 subjects in four panes of 50.

1947, July 24 ***Perf. 11x10½***

950 A397 3c **dark violet** .30 .25
P# block of 4 1.00 —

U.S. FRIGATE CONSTITUTION ISSUE

150th anniversary of the launching of the U.S. frigate Constitution ("Old Ironsides").

Naval Architect's Drawing of Frigate Constitution A398

Designed by Andrew H. Hepburn.

ROTARY PRESS PRINTING

E.E. Plates of 200 subjects in four panes of 50.

1947, Oct. 21 ***Perf. 11x10½***

951 A398 3c **blue green** .30 .25
P# block of 4 1.00 —

EVERGLADES NATIONAL PARK ISSUE

Dedication of the Everglades National Park, Florida, Dec. 6, 1947.

Great White Heron and Map of Florida — A399

Designed by Robert I. Miller, Jr.

ROTARY PRESS PRINTING

E.E. Plates of 200 subjects in four panes of 50.

1947, Dec. 5 ***Perf. 10½x11***

952 A399 3c **bright green** .30 .25
P# block of 4 1.00 —

GEORGE WASHINGTON CARVER ISSUE

5th anniversary of the death of Dr. George Washington Carver, (1864-1943), botanist.

Dr. George Washington Carver — A400

ROTARY PRESS PRINTING

E.E. Plates of 280 subjects in four panes of 70.

1948, Jan. 5 ***Perf. 10½x11***

953 A400 3c **bright red violet** .30 .25
P# block of 4 1.00 —

CALIFORNIA GOLD CENTENNIAL ISSUE

Sutter's Mill, Coloma, California A401

Designed by Charles R. Chickering.

ROTARY PRESS PRINTING

E.E. Plates of 200 subjects in four panes of 50.

1948, Jan. 24 ***Perf. 11x10½***

954 A401 3c **dark violet** .30 .25
P# block of 4 1.00 —

MISSISSIPPI TERRITORY ISSUE

Mississippi Territory establishment, 150th anniv.

Map, Seal of Mississippi Territory and Gov. Winthrop Sargent A402

Designed by William K. Schrage.

ROTARY PRESS PRINTING

E.E. Plates of 200 subjects in four panes of 50.

1948, Apr. 7 ***Perf. 11x10½***

955 A402 3c **brown violet** .30 .25
P# block of 4 1.00 —

FOUR CHAPLAINS ISSUE

George L. Fox, Clark V. Poling, John P. Washington and Alexander D. Goode, the 4 chaplains who sacrificed their lives in the sinking of the S.S. Dorchester, Feb. 3, 1943.

Four Chaplains and Sinking S.S. Dorchester A403

Designed by Charles R. Chickering.

ROTARY PRESS PRINTING

E.E. Plates of 200 subjects in four panes of 50.

1948, May 28 ***Perf. 11x10½***

956 A403 3c **gray black** .30 .25
P# block of 4 1.00 —

WISCONSIN STATEHOOD, 100th ANNIV.

Map on Scroll and State Capitol — A404

Designed by Victor S. McCloskey, Jr.

ROTARY PRESS PRINTING

E.E. Plates of 200 subjects in four panes of 50.

1948, May 29 ***Perf. 11x10½***

957 A404 3c **dark violet** .30 .25
P# block of 4 1.00 —

SWEDISH PIONEER ISSUE

Centenary of the coming of the Swedish pioneers to the Middle West.

Swedish Pioneer with Covered Wagon Moving Westward A405

Designed by Charles R. Chickering.

ROTARY PRESS PRINTING

E.E. Plates of 200 subjects in four panes of 50.

1948, June 4 ***Perf. 11x10½***

958 A405 5c **deep blue** .30 .25
P# block of 4 1.00 —

PROGRESS OF WOMEN ISSUE

Century of progress of American Women.

Elizabeth Stanton, Carrie Chapman Catt and Lucretia Mott — A406

Designed by Victor S. McCloskey, Jr.

ROTARY PRESS PRINTING

E.E. Plates of 200 subjects in four panes of 50.

1948, July 19 ***Perf. 11x10½***

959 A406 3c **dark violet** .30 .25
P# block of 4 1.00 —
Pair with full vert. gutter btwn. 950.00

WILLIAM ALLEN WHITE ISSUE

William Allen White (1868-1944), Writer and Journalist — A407

ROTARY PRESS PRINTING

E.E. Plates of 280 subjects in four panes of 70.

1948, July 31 ***Perf. 10½x11***

960 A407 3c **bright red violet** .30 .25
P# block of 4 1.00 —

UNITED STATES-CANADA FRIENDSHIP ISSUE

Century of friendship between the US and Canada.

Niagara Railway Suspension Bridge — A408

Designed by Leon Helguera, modeled by V. S. McCloskey, Jr.

ROTARY PRESS PRINTING

E.E. Plates of 200 subjects in four panes of 50.

1948, Aug. 2 ***Perf. 11x10½***

961 A408 3c **blue** .30 .25
P# block of 4 1.00 —

FRANCIS SCOTT KEY ISSUE

Francis Scott Key (1779-1843), Maryland lawyer and author of "The Star-Spangled Banner" (1813).

Francis Scott Key and American Flags of 1814 and 1948 — A409

Designed by Victor S. McCloskey, Jr.

ROTARY PRESS PRINTING

E.E. Plates of 200 subjects in four panes of 50.

1948, Aug. 9 ***Perf. 11x10½***

962 A409 3c **rose pink** .30 .25
P# block of 4 1.00 —

SALUTE TO YOUTH ISSUE

Issued to honor the Youth of America and to publicize "Youth Month," September, 1948.

Girl and Boy Carrying Books — A410

ROTARY PRESS PRINTING

E.E. Plates of 200 subjects in four panes of 50.

1948, Aug. 11 ***Perf. 11x10½***

963 A410 3c **deep blue** .30 .25
P# block of 4 1.00 —

OREGON TERRITORY ISSUE

Centenary of the establishment of Oregon Territory.

John McLoughlin, Jason Lee and Wagon on Oregon Trail — A411

ROTARY PRESS PRINTING

E.E. Plates of 200 subjects in four panes of 50.

1948, Aug. 14 ***Perf. 11x10½***

964 A411 3c **brown red** .30 .25
P# block of 4 1.00 —

HARLAN F. STONE ISSUE

Harlan Fiske Stone (1872-1946) of New York, Associate Justice of the Supreme Court, 1925-1941, and Chief Justice, 1941-1946 — A412

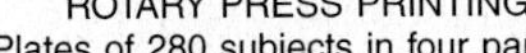

ROTARY PRESS PRINTING

E.E. Plates of 280 subjects in four panes of 70.

1948, Aug. 25 ***Perf. 10½x11***

965 A412 3c **bright red violet** .30 .25
P# block of 4 1.00 —

PALOMAR MOUNTAIN OBSERVATORY ISSUE

Dedication, August 30, 1948.

Observatory, Palomar Mountain, California — A413

Designed by Victor S. McCloskey, Jr.

ROTARY PRESS PRINTING

E.E. Plates of 280 subjects in four panes of 70.

1948, Aug. 30 ***Perf. 10½x11***

966 A413 3c **blue** .30 .25
P# block of 4 1.00 —
a. Vert. pair, imperf. between *300.00*

CLARA BARTON ISSUE

Clara Barton (1821-1912), Founder of the American Red Cross in 1882 — A414

Designed by Charles R. Chickering.

ROTARY PRESS PRINTING

E.E. Plates of 200 subjects in four panes of 50.

1948, Sept. 7 ***Perf. 11x10½***

967 A414 3c **rose pink** .30 .25
P# block of 4 1.00 —

POULTRY INDUSTRY CENTENNIAL ISSUE

Light Brahma Rooster A415

Designed by Charles R. Chickering.

ROTARY PRESS PRINTING

E.E. Plates of 200 subjects in four panes of 50.

1948, Sept. 9 ***Perf. 11x10½***

968 A415 3c **sepia** .30 .25
P# block of 4 1.10 —

GOLD STAR MOTHERS ISSUE

Issued to honor the mothers of deceased members of the United States armed forces.

Star and Palm Frond — A416

Designed by Charles R. Chickering.

ROTARY PRESS PRINTING

E.E. Plates of 200 subjects in four panes of 50.

1948, Sept. 21 ***Perf. 10½x11***

969 A416 3c **orange yellow** .30 .25
P# block of 4 1.00 —

FORT KEARNY ISSUE

Establishment of Fort Kearny, Neb., centenary.

Fort Kearny and Pioneer Group — A417

ROTARY PRESS PRINTING

E.E. Plates of 200 subjects in four panes of 50.

1948, Sept. 22 ***Perf. 11x10½***

970 A417 3c **violet** .30 .25
P# block of 4 1.00 —

VOLUNTEER FIREMEN ISSUE

300th anniv. of the organization of the 1st volunteer firemen in America by Peter Stuyvesant.

Peter Stuyvesant, Early and Modern Fire Engines A418

ROTARY PRESS PRINTING

E.E. Plates of 200 subjects in four panes of 50.

1948, Oct. 4 ***Perf. 11x10½***

971 A418 3c **bright rose carmine** .30 .25
P# block of 4 1.00 —

INDIAN CENTENNIAL ISSUE

Centenary of the arrival in Indian Territory, later Oklahoma, of the Five Civilized Indian Tribes: Cherokee, Chickasaw, Choctaw, Muscogee and Seminole.

Map of Indian Territory and Seals of Five Tribes — A419

ROTARY PRESS PRINTING

E.E. Plates of 200 subjects in four panes of 50.

1948, Oct. 15 ***Perf. 11x10½***

972 A419 3c **dark brown** .30 .25
P# block of 4 1.00 —

ROUGH RIDERS ISSUE

50th anniversary of the organization of the Rough Riders of the Spanish-American War.

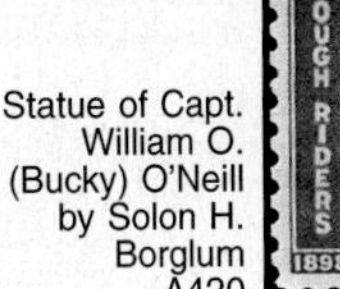

Statue of Capt. William O. (Bucky) O'Neill by Solon H. Borglum A420

Designed by Victor S. McCloskey, Jr.

ROTARY PRESS PRINTING

E.E. Plates of 200 subjects in four panes of 50.

1948, Oct. 27 ***Perf. 11x10½***

973 A420 3c **violet brown** .30 .25
P# block of 4 1.20 —

JULIETTE LOW ISSUE

Low (1860-1927), founder of the Girl Scouts of America. Mrs. Low organized the 1st Girl Guides troop in 1912 at Savannah. The name was changed to

Girl Scouts in 1913 and headquarters moved to New York.

Juliette Gordon Low and Girl Scout Emblem A421

Designed by William K. Schrage.

ROTARY PRESS PRINTING

E.E. Plates of 200 subjects in four panes of 50.

1948, Oct. 29 *Perf. 11x10½*

974 A421 3c **blue green** .30 .25
P# block of 4 1.00 —

WILL ROGERS ISSUE

Will Rogers, (1879-1935), Humorist and Political Commentator. — A422

ROTARY PRESS PRINTING

E.E. Plates of 280 subjects in four panes of 70.

1948, Nov. 4 *Perf. 10½x11*

975 A422 3c **bright red violet** .30 .25
P# block of 4 1.00 —

FORT BLISS CENTENNIAL ISSUE

Fort Bliss, El Paso, Texas, and Rocket Firing — A423

Designed by Charles R. Chickering.

ROTARY PRESS PRINTING

E.E. Plates of 280 subjects in four panes of 70.

1948, Nov. 5 *Perf. 10½x11*

976 A423 3c **henna brown** .30 .25
P# block of 4 1.00 —

MOINA MICHAEL ISSUE

Moina Michael (1870-1944), educator who originated (1918) the Flanders Field Poppy Day idea as a memorial to the war dead.

Moina Michael and Poppy Plant — A424

ROTARY PRESS PRINTING

E.E. Plates of 200 subjects in four panes of 50.

1948, Nov. 9 *Perf. 11x10½*

977 A424 3c **rose pink** .30 .25
P# block of 4 1.00 —

GETTYSBURG ADDRESS ISSUE

85th anniversary of Abraham Lincoln's address at Gettysburg, Pennsylvania.

Abraham Lincoln and Quotation from Gettysburg Address A425

Designed by Charles R. Chickering.

ROTARY PRESS PRINTING

E.E. Plates of 200 subjects in four panes of 50.

1948, Nov. 19 *Perf. 11x10½*

978 A425 3c **bright blue** .30 .25
P# block of 4 1.25 —

AMERICAN TURNERS ISSUE

Formation of the American Turners Soc., cent.

Torch and Emblem of American Turners — A426

Designed by Alvin R. Meissner.

ROTARY PRESS PRINTING

E.E. Plates of 200 subjects in four panes of 50.

1948, Nov. 20 *Perf. 10½x11*

979 A426 3c **carmine** .30 .25
P# block of 4 1.00 —

JOEL CHANDLER HARRIS ISSUE

Joel Chandler Harris (1848-1908), Georgia Writer, Creator of "Uncle Remus" and newspaperman. — A427

ROTARY PRESS PRINTING

E.E. Plates of 280 subjects in four panes of 70.

1948, Dec. 9 *Perf. 10½x11*

980 A427 3c **bright red violet** .30 .25
P# block of 4 1.00 —

MINNESOTA TERRITORY ISSUE

Establishment of Minnesota Territory, cent.

Pioneer and Red River Oxcart — A428

ROTARY PRESS PRINTING

E.E. Plates of 200 subjects in four panes of 50.

1949, Mar. 3 *Perf. 11x10½*

981 A428 3c **blue green** .30 .25
P# block of 4 1.00 —

WASHINGTON AND LEE UNIVERSITY ISSUE

Bicentenary of Washington and Lee University.

George Washington, Robert E. Lee and University Building, Lexington, Va. — A429

ROTARY PRESS PRINTING

E.E. Plates of 200 subjects in four panes of 50.

1949, Apr. 12 *Perf. 11x10½*

982 A429 3c **ultramarine** .30 .25
P# block of 4 1.00 —

PUERTO RICO ELECTION ISSUE

First gubernatorial election in the Territory of Puerto Rico, Nov. 2, 1948.

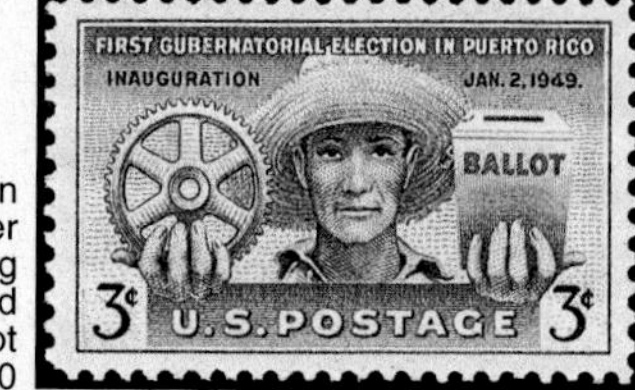

Puerto Rican Farmer Holding Cogwheel and Ballot Box — A430

ROTARY PRESS PRINTING

E.E. Plates of 200 subjects in four panes of 50.

1949, Apr. 27 *Perf. 11x10½*

983 A430 3c **green** .30 .25
P# block of 4 1.00 —

ANNAPOLIS TERCENTENARY ISSUE

Founding of Annapolis, Maryland, 300th anniv.

James Stoddert's 1718 Map of Regions about Annapolis, Redrawn A431

ROTARY PRESS PRINTING

E.E. Plates of 200 subjects in four panes of 50.

1949, May 23 *Perf. 11x10½*

984 A431 3c **aquamarine** .30 .25
P# block of 4 1.00 —

G.A.R. ISSUE

Final encampment of the Grand Army of the Republic, Indianapolis, Aug. 28 - Sept. 1, 1949.

Union Soldier and G.A.R. Veteran of 1949 — A432

Designed by Charles R. Chickering.

ROTARY PRESS PRINTING

E.E. Plates of 200 subjects in four panes of 50.

1949, Aug. 29 *Perf. 11x10½*

985 A432 3c **bright rose carmine** .30 .25
P# block of 4 1.00 —

EDGAR ALLAN POE ISSUE

Edgar Allan Poe (1809-1849), Boston-born Poet, Story Writer and Editor — A433

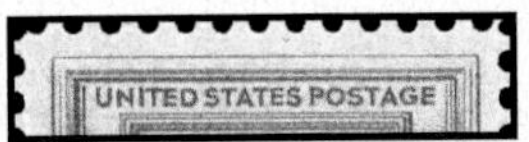

Inner Frame Line Missing

ROTARY PRESS PRINTING

E.E. Plates of 280 subjects in four panes of 70.

1949, Oct. 7 ***Perf. 10½x11***

986 A433 3c **bright red violet** .30 .25
P# block of 4 1.00 —
Thin outer frame line at top, inner line missing (24143 LL 42) 6.00

AMERICAN BANKERS ASSOCIATION ISSUE

75th anniv. of the formation of the Association.

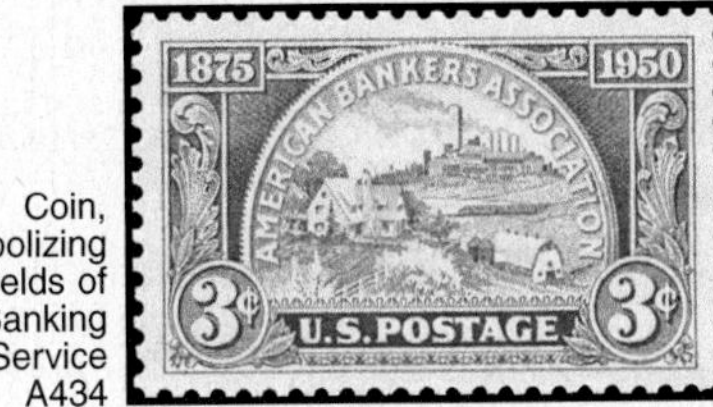

Coin, Symbolizing Fields of Banking Service A434

Designed by Charles R. Chickering.

ROTARY PRESS PRINTING

E.E. Plates of 200 subjects in four panes of 50.

1950, Jan. 3 ***Perf. 11x10½***

987 A434 3c **yellow green** .30 .25
P# block of 4 1.00 —

SAMUEL GOMPERS ISSUE

Samuel Gompers (1850-1924), British-born American Labor Leader — A435

ROTARY PRESS PRINTING

E.E. Plates of 280 subjects in four panes of 70.

1950, Jan. 27 ***Perf. 10½x11***

988 A435 3c **bright red violet** .30 .25
P# block of 4 1.00 —

NATIONAL CAPITAL SESQUICENTENNIAL ISSUE

150th anniversary of the establishment of the National Capital, Washington, D.C.

Statue of Freedom on Capitol Dome — A436

Executive Mansion A437

Supreme Court Building A438

United States Capitol — A439

ROTARY PRESS PRINTING

E.E. Plates of 200 subjects in four panes of 50.

1950 ***Perf. 10½x11, 11x10½***

989 A436 3c **bright blue,** *Apr. 20* .30 .25
P# block of 4 1.00 —
990 A437 3c **deep green,** *June 12* .30 .25
P# block of 4 1.00 —
991 A438 3c **light violet,** *Aug. 2* .30 .25
P# block of 4 1.00 —
992 A439 3c **bright red violet,** *Nov. 22* .30 .25
P# block of 4 1.20 —
Gripper cracks (24285 UL 11) 4.50 3.00
Nos. 989-992 (4) 1.20 1.00

RAILROAD ENGINEERS ISSUE

Issued to honor the Railroad Engineers of America. Stamp portrays John Luther (Casey) Jones (1864-1900), locomotive engineer killed in train wreck near Vaughn, Miss.

"Casey" Jones and Locomotives of 1900 and 1950 — A440

ROTARY PRESS PRINTING

E.E. Plates of 200 subjects in four panes of 50.

1950, Apr. 29 ***Perf. 11x10½***

993 A440 3c **violet brown** .30 .25
P# block of 4 1.00 —

KANSAS CITY, MISSOURI, CENTENARY ISSUE

Kansas City, Missouri, incorporation.

Kansas City Skyline, 1950 and Westport Landing, 1850 — A441

ROTARY PRESS PRINTING

E.E. Plates of 200 subjects in four panes of 50.

1950, June 3 ***Perf. 11x10½***

994 A441 3c **violet** .30 .25
P# block of 4 1.00 —

BOY SCOUTS ISSUE

Honoring the Boy Scouts of America on the occasion of the 2nd National Jamboree, Valley Forge, Pa.

Three Boys, Statue of Liberty and Scout Badge A442

ROTARY PRESS PRINTING

E.E. Plates of 200 subjects in four panes of 50.

1950, June 30 ***Perf. 11x10½***

995 A442 3c **sepia** .30 .25
P# block of 4 1.00 —

INDIANA TERRITORY ISSUE

Establishment of Indiana Territory, 150th anniv.

Gov. William Henry Harrison and First Indiana Capitol, Vincennes A443

ROTARY PRESS PRINTING

E.E. Plates of 200 subjects in four panes of 50.

1950, July 4 ***Perf. 11x10½***

996 A443 3c **bright blue** .30 .25
P# block of 4 1.00 —

CALIFORNIA STATEHOOD ISSUE

Gold Miner, Pioneers and S.S. Oregon A444

ROTARY PRESS PRINTING

E.E. Plates of 200 subjects in four panes of 50.

1950, Sept. 9 ***Perf. 11x10½***

997 A444 3c **yellow orange** .30 .25
P# block of 4 1.00 —

UNITED CONFEDERATE VETERANS FINAL REUNION ISSUE

Final reunion of the United Confederate Veterans, Norfolk, Virginia, May 30, 1951.

Confederate Soldier and United Confederate Veteran A445

ROTARY PRESS PRINTING

E.E. Plates of 200 subjects in four panes of 50.

1951, May 30 ***Perf. 11x10½***

998 A445 3c **gray** .30 .25
P# block of 4 1.00 —

NEVADA CENTENNIAL ISSUE

Centenary of the settlement of Nevada.

Carson Valley, c. 1851 — A446

Designed by Charles R. Chickering.

ROTARY PRESS PRINTING

E.E. Plates of 200 subjects in four panes of 50.

1951, July 14 ***Perf. 11x10½***

999 A446 3c **light olive green** .30 .25
P# block of 4 1.00 —

LANDING OF CADILLAC ISSUE

250th anniversary of the landing of Antoine de la Mothe Cadillac at Detroit.

Detroit Skyline and Cadillac Landing A447

ROTARY PRESS PRINTING
E.E. Plates of 200 subjects in four panes of 50.

1951, July 24 ***Perf. 11x10½***
1000 A447 3c **blue** .30 .25
P# block of 4 1.00 —

COLORADO STATEHOOD, 75th ANNIV.

Colorado Capitol, Mount of the Holy Cross, Columbine and Bronco Buster by Proctor A448

ROTARY PRESS PRINTING
E.E. Plates of 200 subjects in four panes of 50.

1951, Aug. 1 ***Perf. 11x10½***
1001 A448 3c **blue violet** .30 .25
P# block of 4 1.00 —

AMERICAN CHEMICAL SOCIETY ISSUE

75th anniv. of the formation of the Society.

A.C.S. Emblem and Symbols of Chemistry A449

ROTARY PRESS PRINTING
E.E. Plates of 200 subjects in four panes of 50.

1951, Sept. 4 ***Perf. 11x10½***
1002 A449 3c **violet brown** .30 .25
P# block of 4 1.00 —

BATTLE OF BROOKLYN, 175th ANNIV.

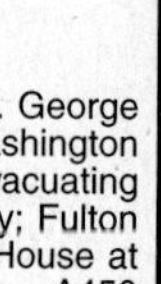

Gen. George Washington Evacuating Army; Fulton Ferry House at Right — A450

ROTARY PRESS PRINTING
E.E. Plates of 200 subjects in four panes of 50.

1951, Dec. 10 ***Perf. 11x10½***
1003 A450 3c **violet** .30 .25
P# block of 4 1.00 —

BETSY ROSS ISSUE

200th anniv. of the birth of Betsy Ross, maker of the first American flag.

"Birth of Our Nation's Flag," by Charles H. Weisgerber — Betsy Ross Showing Flag to Gen. George Washington, Robert Morris and George Ross — A451

ROTARY PRESS PRINTING
E.E. Plates of 200 subjects in four panes of 50.

1952, Jan. 2 ***Perf. 11x10½***
1004 A451 3c **carmine rose** .30 .25
P# block of 4 1.00 —

4-H CLUB ISSUE

Farm, Club Emblem, Boy and Girl — A452

ROTARY PRESS PRINTING
E.E. Plates of 200 subjects in four panes of 50.

1952, Jan. 15 ***Perf. 11x10½***
1005 A452 3c **blue green** .30 .25
P# block of 4 1.00 —

B. & O. RAILROAD ISSUE

125th anniv. of the granting of a charter to the Baltimore and Ohio Railroad Company by the Maryland Legislature.

Charter and Three Stages of Rail Transportation A453

ROTARY PRESS PRINTING
E.E. Plates of 200 subjects in four panes of 50.

1952, Feb. 28 ***Perf. 11x10½***
1006 A453 3c **bright blue** .30 .25
P# block of 4 1.00 —

A. A. A. ISSUE

50th anniversary of the formation of the American Automobile Association.

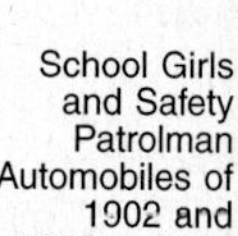

School Girls and Safety Patrolman Automobiles of 1902 and 1952 — A454

ROTARY PRESS PRINTING
E.E. Plates of 200 subjects in four panes of 50.

1952, Mar. 4 ***Perf. 11x10½***
1007 A454 3c **deep blue** .30 .25
P# block of 4 1.00 —

NATO ISSUE

Signing of the North Atlantic Treaty, 3rd anniv.

Torch of Liberty and Globe — A455

ROTARY PRESS PRINTING
E.E. Plates of 400 subjects in four panes of 100.

1952, Apr. 4 ***Perf. 11x10½***
1008 A455 3c **deep violet** .30 .25
P# block of 4 1.00 —

GRAND COULEE DAM ISSUE

50 years of Federal cooperation in developing the resources of rivers and streams in the West.

Spillway, Grand Coulee Dam — A456

ROTARY PRESS PRINTING
E.E. Plates of 200 subjects in four panes of 50.

1952, May 15 ***Perf. 11x10½***
1009 A456 3c **blue green** .30 .25
P# block of 4 1.00 —

LAFAYETTE ISSUE

175th anniversary of the arrival of Marquis de Lafayette in America.

Marquis de Lafayette, Flags, Cannon and Landing Party — A457

Designed by Victor S. McCloskey, Jr.

ROTARY PRESS PRINTING
E.E. Plates of 200 subjects in four panes of 50.

1952, June 13 ***Perf. 11x10½***
1010 A457 3c **bright blue** .30 .25
P# block of 4 1.00 —

MT. RUSHMORE MEMORIAL ISSUE

Dedication of the Mt. Rushmore National Memorial in the Black Hills of South Dakota, 25th anniv.

Sculptured Heads on Mt. Rushmore — A458

Designed by William K. Schrage.

ROTARY PRESS PRINTING
E.E. Plates of 200 subjects in four panes of 50.

1952, Aug. 11 ***Perf. 10½x11***
1011 A458 3c **blue green** .30 .25
P# block of 4 1.00 —

ENGINEERING CENTENNIAL ISSUE

American Society of Civil Engineers founding.

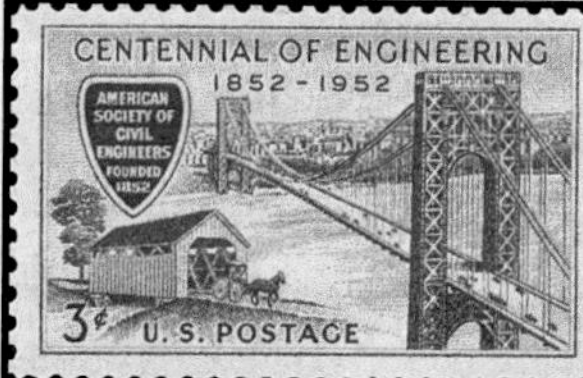

George Washington Bridge and Covered Bridge of 1850's — A459

ROTARY PRESS PRINTING
E.E. Plates of 200 subjects in four panes of 50.

1952, Sept. 6 ***Perf. 11x10½***
1012 A459 3c **violet blue** .30 .25
P# block of 4 1.00 —

SERVICE WOMEN ISSUE

Women in the United States Armed Services.

Women of the Marine Corps, Army, Navy and Air Force — A460

ROTARY PRESS PRINTING

E.E. Plates of 200 subjects in four panes of 50.

1952, Sept. 11 *Perf. 11x10½*

1013 A460 3c **deep blue** .30 .25
P# block of 4 1.00 —

GUTENBERG BIBLE ISSUE

Printing of the 1st book, the Holy Bible, from movable type, by Johann Gutenberg, 500th anniv.

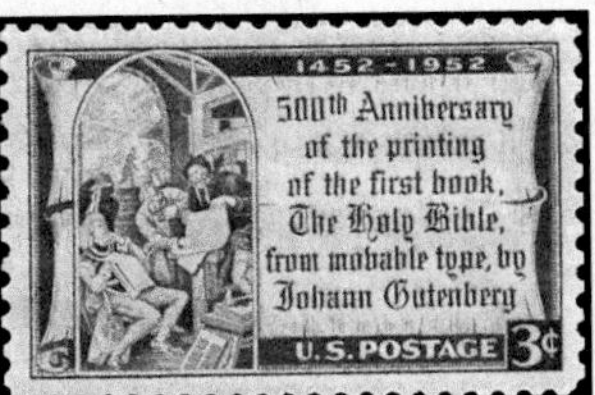

Gutenberg Showing Proof to the Elector of Mainz — A461

ROTARY PRESS PRINTING

E.E. Plates of 200 subjects in four panes of 50.

1952, Sept. 30 *Perf. 11x10½*

1014 A461 3c **violet** .30 .25
P# block of 4 1.00 —

NEWSPAPER BOYS ISSUE

Newspaper Boy, Torch and Group of Homes A462

ROTARY PRESS PRINTING

E.E. Plates of 200 subjects in four panes of 50.

1952, Oct. 4 *Perf. 11x10½*

1015 A462 3c **violet** .30 .25
P# block of 4 1.00 —

RED CROSS ISSUE

Globe, Sun and Cross — A463

ROTARY PRESS PRINTING

Cross Typographed

E.E. Plates of 200 subjects in four panes of 50.

1952, Nov. 21 *Perf. 11x10½*

1016 A463 3c **deep blue & carmine** .30 .25
P# block of 4 1.00 —

NATIONAL GUARD ISSUE

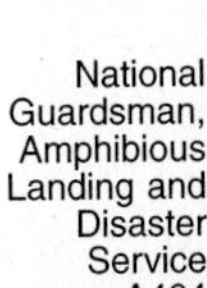

National Guardsman, Amphibious Landing and Disaster Service A464

ROTARY PRESS PRINTING

E.E. Plates of 200 subjects in four panes of 50.

1953, Feb. 23 *Perf. 11x10½*

1017 A464 3c **bright blue** .30 .25
P# block of 4 1.00 —

OHIO STATEHOOD, 150th ANNIV.

Ohio Map, State Seal, Buckeye Leaf — A465

ROTARY PRESS PRINTING

E.E. Plates of 280 subjects in four panes of 70.

1953, Mar. 2 *Perf. 11x10½*

1018 A465 3c **chocolate** .30 .25
P# block of 4 1.00 —

WASHINGTON TERRITORY ISSUE

Organization of Washington Territory, cent.

Medallion, Pioneers and Washington Scene — A466

ROTARY PRESS PRINTING

E.E. Plates of 200 subjects in four panes of 50.

1953, Mar. 2 *Perf. 11x10½*

1019 A466 3c **green** .30 .25
P# block of 4 1.00 —

LOUISIANA PURCHASE, 150th ANNIV.

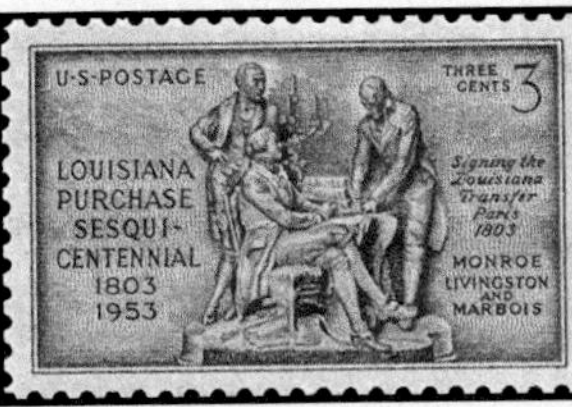

James Monroe, Robert R. Livingston and Marquis Francois de Barbé-Marbois A467

ROTARY PRESS PRINTING

E.E. Plates of 200 subjects in four panes of 50.

1953, Apr. 30 *Perf. 11x10½*

1020 A467 3c **violet brown** .30 .25
P# block of 4 1.00 —

OPENING OF JAPAN CENTENNIAL ISSUE

Centenary of Commodore Matthew Calbraith Perry's negotiations with Japan, which opened her doors to foreign trade.

Commodore Matthew C. Perry and First Anchorage off Tokyo Bay — A468

ROTARY PRESS PRINTING

E.E. Plates of 200 subjects in four panes of 50.

1953, July 14 *Perf. 11x10½*

1021 A468 5c **green** .30 .25
P# block of 4 1.00 —

AMERICAN BAR ASSOCIATION, 75th ANNIV.

Section of Frieze, Supreme Court Room — A469

ROTARY PRESS PRINTING

E.E. Plates of 200 subjects in four panes of 50.

1953, Aug. 24 *Perf. 11x10½*

1022 A469 3c **rose violet** .30 .25
P# block of 4 1.00 —

SAGAMORE HILL ISSUE

Opening of Sagamore Hill, Theodore Roosevelt's home, as a national shrine.

Home of Theodore Roosevelt A470

ROTARY PRESS PRINTING

E.E. Plates of 200 subjects in four panes of 50.

1953, Sept. 14 *Perf. 11x10½*

1023 A470 3c **yellow green** .30 .25
P# block of 4 1.00 —

FUTURE FARMERS ISSUE

25th anniversary of the organization of Future Farmers of America.

Agricultural Scene and Future Farmer A471

ROTARY PRESS PRINTING

E.E. Plates of 200 subjects in four panes of 50.

1953, Oct. 13 *Perf. 11x10½*

1024 A471 3c **deep blue** .30 .25
P# block of 4 1.00 —

TRUCKING INDUSTRY ISSUE

50th anniv. of the Trucking Industry in the US.

Truck, Farm and Distant City — A472

ROTARY PRESS PRINTING

E.E. Plates of 200 subjects in four panes of 50.

1953, Oct. 27 *Perf. 11x10½*

1025 A472 3c **violet** .30 .25
P# block of 4 1.00 —

GENERAL PATTON ISSUE

Honoring Gen. George S. Patton, Jr. (1885-1945), and the armored forces of the US Army.

Gen. George S. Patton, Jr., and Tanks in Action — A473

ROTARY PRESS PRINTING

E.E. Plates of 200 subjects in four panes of 50.

1953, Nov. 11 *Perf. 11x10½*

1026 A473 3c **blue violet** .30 .25
P# block of 4 1.00 —

NEW YORK CITY, 300th ANNIV.

Dutch Ship in New Amsterdam Harbor A474

ROTARY PRESS PRINTING

E.E. Plates of 200 subjects in four panes of 50.

1953, Nov. 20 ***Perf. 11x10½***

1027 A474 3c **bright red violet**	.30	.25
P# block of 4	1.00	—

GADSDEN PURCHASE ISSUE

Centenary of James Gadsden's purchase of territory from Mexico to adjust the US-Mexico boundary.

Map and Pioneer Group — A475

ROTARY PRESS PRINTING

E.E. Plates of 200 subjects in four panes of 50.

1953, Dec. 30 ***Perf. 11x10½***

1028 A475 3c **copper brown**	.30	.25
P# block of 4	1.00	—

COLUMBIA UNIVERSITY, 200th ANNIV.

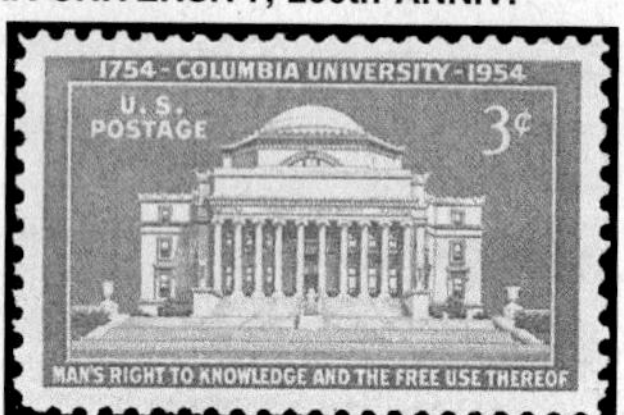

Low Memorial Library A476

ROTARY PRESS PRINTING

E.E. Plates of 200 subjects in four panes of 50.

1954, Jan. 4 ***Perf. 11x10½***

1029 A476 3c **blue**	.30	.25
P# block of 4	1.00	—

Wet and Dry Printings

In 1953 the Bureau of Engraving and Printing began experiments in printing on "dry" paper (moisture content 5-10 per cent). In previous "wet" printings the paper had a moisture content of 15-35 per cent.

The new process required a thicker, stiffer paper, special types of inks and greater pressure to force the paper into the recessed plates. The "dry" printings show whiter paper, a higher sheen on the surface, feel thicker and stiffer, and the designs stand out more clearly than on the "wet" printings.

Nos. 832c and 1041 (flat plate) were the first "dry" printings to be issued of flat-plate, regular-issue stamps. No. 1063 was the first rotary press stamp to be produced entirely by "dry" printing. Nos. QE1a, QE2a and QE3a, RF26A and RW21 (all flat plate) were the first "dry" printings of back-of-the-book issue stamps.

Stamps printed by both the "wet" and "dry" process are Nos. 1030, 1031, 1035, 1035a, 1036, 1039, 1049, 1050-1052, 1054, 1055, 1057, 1058, C34-C36, C39, C39a, J78, J80-J84, QE1-QE3, RF26-RF28, S1, S1a, S2, S2a, S3. The "wet" printed 4c coil, No. 1058b, exists only Bureau precanceled.

In the Liberty Issue listings that follow, wet printings are listed first, followed by dry printings, except for Nos. 1058 and 1058b. Where only one type of printing of a stamp is indicated, it is "dry."

All postage stamps have been printed by the "dry" process since the late 1950s.

LIBERTY ISSUE

Benjamin Franklin — A477

George Washington — A478

Palace of the Governors, Santa Fe — A478a

Thomas Jefferson — A480

Statue of Liberty — A482

The Hermitage, Home of Andrew Jackson, near Nashville — A484

Theodore Roosevelt — A486

Statue of Liberty — A488

The Alamo, San Antonio — A490

Mount Vernon — A479

Bunker Hill Monument and Massachusetts Flag, 1776 — A481

Abraham Lincoln — A483

James Monroe — A485

Woodrow Wilson — A487

Statue of Liberty — A489

Independence Hall — A491

Statue of Liberty — A491a

Benjamin Harrison — A492

John Jay — A493

Monticello, Home of Thomas Jefferson, near Charlottesville, Va. — A494

Paul Revere — A495

Robert E. Lee — A496

John Marshall — A497

Susan B. Anthony — A498

Patrick Henry — A499

Alexander Hamilton — A500

ROTARY PRESS PRINTING

E.E. Plates of 400 subjects in four panes of 100

1954-68 ***Perf. 11x10½***

1030	A477	½c **red orange,** wet printing, *Oct. 20, 1955*	.30	.25
		On cover		1.50
		P# block of 4	1.00	—
a.		½c **red orange**, dry printing, *May 1958*	.30	.25
		On cover		1.50
		P# block of 4 (#25980 and up)	1.00	—

Counterfeits exist of No. 1030. See the Postal Counterfeits section of this catalog.

1031	A478	1c **dark green,** wet printing, *Aug. 28, 1954*	.30	.25
		On cover		1.50
		P# block of 4	1.00	—
b.		1c **dark green**, dry printing, *Mar. 1956*	.30	.25
		On cover		1.50
		P# block of 4 (#25326 and up)	1.00	—
		Pair with full vert. gutter between	*150.00*	

Pair with full horiz. gutter between 150.00

Perf. 10½x11

1031A A478a 1¼c **turquoise,** *June 17, 1960* .30 .25
On cover 1.00
P# block of 4 1.00 —

1032 A479 1½c **brown carmine,** *Feb. 22, 1956* .30 .25
On cover 1.00
Precanceled single on bulk rate cover 3.00
P# block of 4 1.00 —

Perf. 11x10½

1033 A480 2c **carmine rose,** *Sept. 15, 1954* .30 .25
On cover .50
Single franking on noncarrier drop-rate cover 125.00
P# block of 4 1.00 —
Pair with full vert. gutter btwn. —
Pair with full horiz. gutter btwn. —
a. Silkote paper 275.
P# block of 4 2,000.
Single franking on third-class cover 15,000.

Silkote paper was used in 1954 for an experimental printing of 50,000 stamps. The stamps were put on sale at the Westbrook, Maine post office in Dec. 17, 1954. Only plates 25061 and 25062 were used to print No. 1033a (these plates also used to print No. 1033 on normal paper). Competent expertization is required for No. 1033a.

1034 A481 2½c **gray blue,** *June 17, 1959* .30 .25
On cover 1.00
P# block of 4 1.00 —

1035 A482 3c **deep violet,** wet printing, *June 30, 1954* .30 .25
On cover .50
Single franking on noncarrier drop-rate cover 350.00
P# block of 4 1.00 —
a. Booklet pane of 6, *June 30, 1954* 3.50 1.25
b. Horiz. pairs, imperf. btwn in #1035a with foldover (two pairs recorded in two full panes) or miscut (three pairs from pane) 5,000.
c. 3c **deep violet,** dry printing .30 .25
On cover .50
Single franking on certificate of mailing 10.00
P# block of 4 (#25235 and up) 1.00 —
Pair with full vert. gutter between 150.00
Pair with full horiz. gutter between 150.00
d. Booklet pane of 6, dry printing 4.50 1.50
e. Tagged, *July 6, 1966* .35 .25
On cover 25.00
P# block of 4 5.75 —
f. Imperf., pair 3,000.
g. Horiz. pair, imperf. between 1,000.

No. 1057b measures about 19½x22mm; No. 1035f, about 18¾x22½mm.

1036 A483 4c **red violet,** wet printing, *Nov. 19, 1954* .30 .25
On cover .50
Single franking on noncarrier drop-rate cover 400.00
P# block of 4 1.00 —
a. 4c **red violet,** dry printing .30 .25
On cover .50
P# block of 4 (#25445 and up) 1.00 —
Pair with full vert. gutter between 600.00
Pair with full horiz. gutter between 850.00
b. Booklet pane of 6, *July 31, 1958* 2.75 1.25
c. As "b," imperf. horiz. 10,000.
d. Horiz. pair, imperf between 4,150.
e. Tagged, *Nov. 2, 1963* .65 .40
On cover 30.00
P# block of 4 9.00 —

No. 1036d resulted from a booklet pane foldover after perforating and before cutting into panes.
Counterfeits exist of No. 1036. See the Postal Counterfeits section of this catalog.

Perf. 10½x11

1037 A484 4½c **blue green,** *Mar. 16, 1959* .30 .25
On cover 5.00
Single franking on third-class cover 15.00
P# block of 4 1.00 —

Perf. 11x10½

1038 A485 5c **deep blue,** *Dec. 2, 1954* .30 .25
On cover 3.00
Single franking on certificate of mailing 5.00
Precanceled single franking on international printed matter cover 20.00
P# block of 4 1.00 —
Pair with full vert. gutter btwn. 200.00

1039 A486 6c **carmine,** wet printing, *Nov. 18, 1955* .40 .25
On cover 1.00
P# block of 4 2.00 —
Pair with full vert. gutter btwn. 2,750.
a. 6c **carmine,** dry printing .30 .25
On cover 1.00
P# block of 4 (#25427 and up) 1.20 —
b. Imperf, block of 4 (unique) 23,000.

1040 A487 7c **rose carmine,** *Jan. 10, 1956* .30 .25
On cover 1.00
P# block of 4 1.00 —
a. 7c **dark rose carmine** .30 .25
P# block of 4 1.20 —

FLAT PLATE PRINTING
Plates of 400 subjects in four panes of 100 each
Size: 22.7mm high
Perf. 11

1041 A488 8c **dark violet blue & carmine,** *Apr. 9, 1954* .30 .25
On cover 2.00
P# block of 4, 2# 1.80 —
Corner P# block of 4, blue # only 2,000.
Corner P# block of 4, red # only —
a. Double impression of carmine 575.00 —

FLAT PRINTING PLATES
Frame: 24912-13-14-15, 24926, 24929-30, 24932-33.
Vignette: 24916-17-18-19-20, 24935-36-37, 24939.
See note following No. 1041B.

ROTARY PRESS PRINTING
Plates of 400 subjects in four panes of 100 each
Size: 22.9mm high
Perf. 11

1041B A488 8c **dark violet blue & carmine,** *Apr. 9, 1954* .40 .25
On cover 2.00
P# block of 4, 2# 4.25 —

ROTARY PRINTING PLATES
Frame: 24923-24, 24928, 24940, 24942.
Vignette: 24927, 24938.
No. 1041B is slightly taller than No. 1041, about the thickness of one line of engraving.

GIORI PRESS PRINTING
Plates of 400 subjects in four panes of 100 each
Redrawn design
Perf. 11

1042 A489 8c **dark violet blue & carmine rose,** *Mar. 22, 1958* .30 .25
On cover 2.00
P# block of 4 1.00 —

The 8c John J. Pershing stamp, formerly No. 1042A, is now included with the regular issue of 1961-66. See No. 1214.

ROTARY PRESS PRINTING
E.E. Plates of 400 subjects in four panes of 100 each
Perf. 10½x11

1043 A490 9c **rose lilac,** *June 14, 1956* .30 .25
On cover 3.00
P# block of 4 1.50 —
a. 9c **dark rose lilac** .30 .25
P# block of 4 1.50 —

1044 A491 10c **rose lake,** *July 4, 1956* .30 .25
On cover 2.00
Single franking on private aerogramme 300.00
P# block of 4 1.25 —
b. 10c **dark rose lake** .30 .25
P# block of 4 1.00 —
d. Tagged, *July 6, 1966* 2.00 1.00
On cover 30.00
P# block of 4 35.00 —

No. 1044b is from later printings and is on a harder, whiter paper than No. 1044.
Counterfeits exist of No. 1044. See the Postal Counterfeits section of this catalog.

GIORI PRESS PRINTING
Plates of 400 subjects in four panes of 100.
Perf. 11

1044A A491a 11c **carmine & dark violet blue,** *June 15, 1961* .30 .25
On cover 2.00
Single franking on international airmail postcard 5.00
Single franking on private aerogram 50.00
P# block of 4 1.40 —
c. Tagged, *Jan. 11, 1967* 3.00 1.60
On cover 200.00
P# block of 4 60.00 —

ROTARY PRESS PRINTING
E.E. Plates of 400 subjects in four panes of 100 each
Perf. 11x10½

1045 A492 12c **red,** *June 6, 1959* .35 .25
On cover 3.00
P# block of 4 1.60 —
a. Tagged, *1968* .35 .25
On cover 30.00
Single franking on third-class cover 75.00
P# block of 4 4.00 —

1046 A493 15c **rose lake,** *Dec. 12, 1958* .60 .25
On cover 3.00
Single franking on international airmail cover 10.00
P# block of 4 2.75 —
a. Tagged, *July 6, 1966* 1.10 .80
On cover 25.00
P# block of 4 13.00

Perf. 10½x11

1047 A494 20c **ultramarine,** *Apr. 13, 1956* .50 .25
On cover 3.00
Single franking on double-weight airmail cover to Central America 50.00
P# block of 4 2.25 —
a. 20c **deep bright ultramarine** .50 .25
P# block of 4 2.25 —

No. 1047a is from later printings and is on a harder, whiter paper than No. 1047.

Perf. 11x10½

1048 A495 25c **green,** *Apr. 18, 1958* 1.00 .75
On cover 2.00
Single franking on airmail cover to Asia 10.00
P# block of 4 4.25 —

1049 A496 30c **black,** wet printing, *Sept. 21, 1955* 1.20 .75
On cover 2.00
P# block of 4 5.25 —
a. 30c **black,** dry printing, *June 1957* .90 .25
On cover 2.00
Single franking on international airmail cover 10.00
P# block of 4 (#25487 and up) 4.00 —
b. 30c **intense black** .80 .25
P# block of 4 3.75 —

No. 1049b is from later printings and is on a harder, whiter paper than Nos. 1049 or 1049a.
Counterfeits exist of No. 1049. See the Postal Counterfeits section of this catalog.

1050 A497 40c **brown red,** wet printing, *Sept. 24, 1955* 1.75 .25
On cover 5.00
P# block of 4 9.00 —
a. 40c **brown red,** dry printing, *Apr. 1958* 1.50 .25
On cover 5.00
Single franking on international airmail cover 50.00
P# block of 4 (#25571 and up) 7.00 —

Cracked Plate

1051 A498 50c **bright purple,** wet printing, *Aug. 25, 1955* 1.75 .25
On cover 10.00
P# block of 4 11.00 —
Cracked plate (25231 UL 1) 50.00 —
P# block of 4, UL stamp cracked plate 100.00 —
a. 50c **bright purple,** dry printing, *Apr. 1958* 1.50 .25
On cover 10.00
Single franking on international airmail cover 40.00
P# block of 4 (#25897 and up) 7.00 —

1052 A499 $1 **purple,** wet printing, *Oct. 7, 1955* 5.00 1.00
On cover 25.00
P# block of 4 21.00 —
a. $1 **purple,** dry printing, *Oct. 1958* 4.50 .25
On cover 25.00
Single franking on international airmail cover 150.00
P# block of 4 (#25541 and up) 18.00 —

Counterfeits exist of No. 1052. See the Postal Counterfeits section of this catalog.

FLAT PLATE PRINTING
Plates of 400 subjects in four panes of 100.
Perf. 11

1053 A500 $5 **black,** *Mar. 19, 1956* 47.50 6.75
On registered bank tag 25.00
On air parcel-post tag 75.00
On commercial cover 1,800.
Single franking on registered cover 7,000.
P# block of 4 210.00 —
Nos. 1030-1053 (27) 65.25 15.00

Bureau Precancels: ½c, 37 diff., 1c, 113 diff., 1¼c, 142 diff., 1½c, 45 diff.

2c, 86 diff., 2½c, 123 diff., 3c, 106 diff., 4c, 95 diff., 4½c, 23 diff., 5c, 20 diff., 6c, 23 diff., 7c, 16 diff.
Also, No. 1041, 12 diff., No. 1042, 12 diff., 9c, 15 diff., 10c, 16 diff., 11c, New York, 12c, 6 diff.
15c, 12 diff., 20c, 20 diff., 25c, 11 diff., 30c, 17 diff., 40c, 10 diff., 50c, 19 diff., $1, 5 diff.

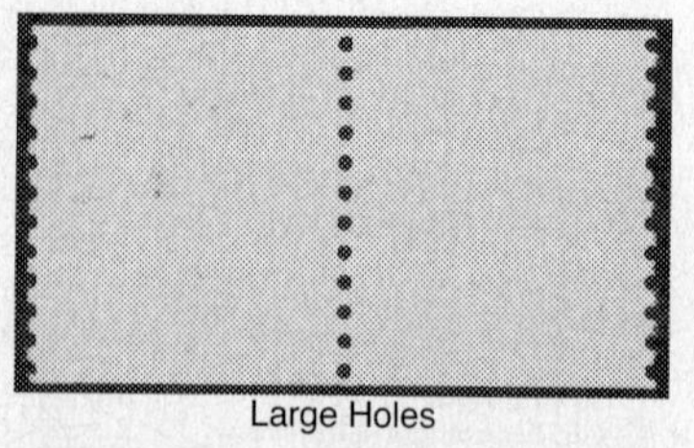
Large Holes

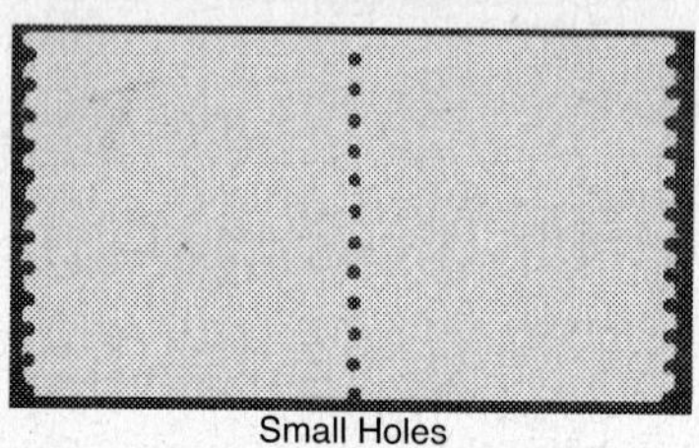
Small Holes

With the change from 384-subject plates to 432-subject plates the size of the perforation holes was reduced. While both are perf. 10 the later holes are smaller than the paper between them. The difference is most noticeable on pairs.

Gripper Crack

ROTARY PRESS COIL STAMPS

1954-80 *Perf. 10 Vertically*

1054 A478 1c **dark green,** large holes, wet printing, *Oct. 8, 1954* .60 .25
On cover 3.00
Pair 1.20 .40
Joint line pair 2.75 .90
Gripper crack — —
b. 1c **dark green,** large holes, dry printing, *Aug. 1957* 1.00 .25
On cover 3.00
Pair 2.00 .50
Joint line pair 4.00 .65
Small holes, dry printing, *Feb. 1960* .30 .25
On cover 3.00
Pair .50 .50
Joint line pair 1.00 .65
c. Imperf., pair — —

Perf. 10 Horizontally

1054A A478a 1¼c **turquoise,** *June 17, 1960,* small holes .30 .25
On cover 2.00
Pair .50 .50
Joint line pair 2.25 1.00
Large holes *3.50* .25
Pair *7.00* .50
Joint line pair *90.00* 1.25
d. Imperf., pair — —
Joint line pair —

All examples of No. 1054Ad are precanceled "SEATTLE/WASH." No. 1054A with large holes exists non-precanceled as well as precanceled. The values shown are for the non-precanceled variety; precanceled stamps with large holes are quite common.

Perf. 10 Vertically

1055 A480 2c **carmine rose,** large holes, wet printing, *Oct. 22, 1954* .60 .25
On cover .50
Pair 1.20 .50
Joint line pair 3.50 .60
Small holes —
Pair —
Joint line pair —
a. 2c **carmine rose,** large holes, dry printing, *May 1957* .35 .25
On cover .50
Pair .80 .50
Joint line pair 1.50 .60
Small holes, *Aug. 1961* 7.00 .25
Pair 17.50 .50
Joint line pair 50.00 .60
b. Tagged, small holes, shiny gum, *May 6, 1968* .30 .25
On cover 2.00
Pair .50 .50
Joint line pair .75 .60
Dull gum, tagged, small holes .75
Pair 1.50
Joint line pair 6.00
Large holes, *May 6, 1968* —
c. Imperf., pair, untagged, shiny gum (Bureau precanceled, Riverdale, MD) *325.00*
Joint line pair *700.00*
d. Imperf. pair, tagged, shiny gum *425.00*
Joint line pair *1,100.*

1056 A481 2½c **gray blue,** large holes *Sept. 9, 1959* .30 .25
On cover 2.00
Pair .60 .50
Joint line pair 3.50 1.75
Small holes, *Jan. 1961* *400.00* *100.00*
Pair *850.00* *200.00*
Joint line pair *3,000.* *400.00*

No. 1056 with small holes only known with Bureau precancels. It was against postal regulations to make mint precanceled stamps available other than to permit holders for their use. Resale was prohibited. Since some mint examples do exist in the marketplace, values are furnished here.

1057 A482 3c **deep violet,** large holes, wet printing, *July 20, 1954* .35 .25
On cover .50
Pair .80 .50
Joint line pair 2.75 .60
Small holes, *Jan. 1961* —
Pair —
Joint line pair —
a. 3c **deep violet,** large holes, dry printing, *Oct. 1956* .35 .25
On cover .50
Pair .80 .50
Joint line pair 2.75 .60
Gripper cracks —
Small holes, *Mar. 1958* .25 .25
Pair .25 .50
Joint line pair .55 .60
b. Imperf., pair *1,250.* *800.00*
Joint line pair *2,750.* —
c. Tagged, small holes, Look magazine printing, *Oct. 1966* 8.00 4.00
On "Look" cover *10,000.*
Pair 17.50 8.00
Joint line pair *350.00*
d. Tagged, small holes, philatelic printing, *June 26, 1967* 1.00 .50
On cover *250.00*
Pair 3.00 1.00
Joint line pair 25.00 —

Earliest documented use: Dec. 29, 1966 (No. 1057c).

No. 1057b measures about 19½x22mm; No. 1035f, about 18¾x22½mm.

The second tagged printing (No. 1057d) was a "philatelic reprint" made when the original stock of tagged stamps was exhausted. The original tagged printing (No. 1057c, specially printed for "Look" magazine) has a less intense color, the impression is less sharp and the tagging is brighter.

The reprint was printed on a slightly fluorescent paper, while the original paper is dead under longwave UV light.

1058 A483 4c **red violet,** large holes, dry printing, *July 31, 1958* .75 .25
On cover .50
Pair 1.60 .50
Joint line pair 2.50 .60
Small holes .25 .25
Pair .55 .50
Joint line pair .75 .60
a. Imperf., pair 75.00 70.00
Joint line pair *225.00*
b. 4c **red violet,** large holes, wet printing, (Bureau precanceled) *22.50* *2.25*
On cover 250.00
Pair *47.50* —
Joint line pair *300.00*

It was against postal regulations to make mint precanceled examples of No. 1058b available other than to permit holders for their use. Resale was prohibited. Since some mint examples do exist in the marketplace, values are furnished here.

Perf. 10 Horizontally

1059 A484 4½c **blue green,** large holes, *May 1, 1959* 1.50 1.00
On cover 15.00
Single franking on third-class cover *200.00*
Pair 3.25 2.25
Joint line pair 14.00 3.00
Small holes 12.00 —
Pair 35.00 —
Joint line pair *450.00* —

Perf. 10 Vertically

1059A A495 25c **green,** *Feb. 25, 1965* .50 .30
On cover 2.00
Pair 1.00 .60
Joint line pair 2.00 1.20
b. Tagged, shiny gum, *Apr. 3, 1973* .80 .25
On cover 2.00
Pair 1.60 .50
Joint line pair 3.25 1.25
Thin translucent paper — —
Tagged, dull gum, *1980* 4.00
Pair 8.00
Joint line pair 12.00
c. Imperf., pair, untagged —
Joint line pair —
d. Imperf., pair, tagged 30.00
Joint line pair 60.00

Value for No. 1059Ad is for fine centering.

Bureau Precancels: 1c, 118 diff., 1¼c, 105 diff., 2c, 191 diff., 2½c, 94 diff., 3c, 142 diff., 4c, 83 diff., 4½c, 23 diff.

The editors question the existence of No. 1059Ac. Evidence of its existence is necessary to maintain this listing.

NEBRASKA TERRITORY ISSUE

Establishment of the Nebraska Territory, centenary.

"The Sower," Mitchell Pass and Scotts Bluff — A507

ROTARY PRESS PRINTING
E.E. Plates of 200 subjects in four panes of 50.

1954, May 7 *Perf. 11x10½*
1060 A507 3c **violet** .30 .25
P# block of 4 1.00 —

KANSAS TERRITORY ISSUE

Establishment of the Kansas Territory, centenary.

Wheat Field and Pioneer Wagon Train — A508

ROTARY PRESS PRINTING
E.E. Plates of 200 subjects in four panes of 50.

1954, May 31 *Perf. 11x10½*
1061 A508 3c **brown orange** .30 .25
P# block of 4 1.00 —

GEORGE EASTMAN ISSUE

Eastman (1854-1932), inventor of photographic dry plates, flexible film and the Kodak camera; Rochester, N.Y., industrialist. — A509

ROTARY PRESS PRINTING
E.E. Plates of 280 subjects in four panes of 70.

1954, July 12 *Perf. 10½x11*
1062 A509 3c **violet brown** .30 .25
P# block of 4 1.00 —

LEWIS AND CLARK EXPEDITION

150th anniv. of the Lewis and Clark expedition.

Meriwether Lewis, William Clark and Sacagawea Landing on Missouri Riverbank A510

ROTARY PRESS PRINTING
E.E. Plates of 200 subjects in four panes of 50.

1954, July 28 *Perf. 11x10½*
1063 A510 3c **violet brown** .30 .25
P# block of 4 1.00 —

PENNSYLVANIA ACADEMY OF THE FINE ARTS ISSUE

150th anniversary of the founding of the Pennsylvania Academy of the Fine Arts, Philadelphia.

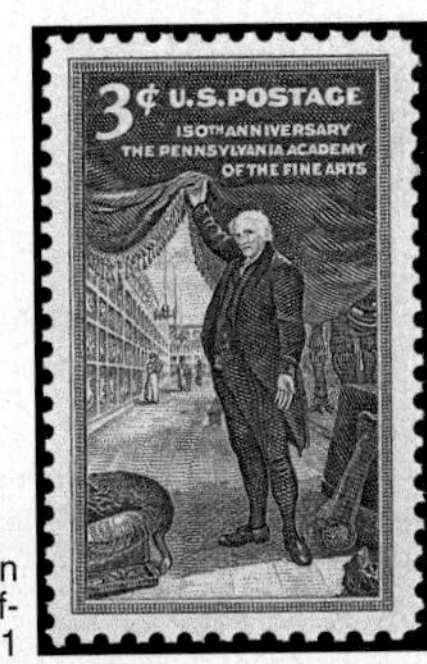

Charles Willson Peale in his Museum, Self-portrait — A511

ROTARY PRESS PRINTING

E.E. Plates of 200 subjects in four panes of 50.

1955, Jan. 15 ***Perf. 10½x11***

1064 A511 3c **rose brown** .30 .25
P# block of 4 1.00 —

LAND GRANT COLLEGES ISSUE

Centenary of the founding of Michigan State College and Pennsylvania State University, first of the land grant institutions.

Open Book and Symbols of Subjects Taught — A512

ROTARY PRESS PRINTING

E.E. Plates of 200 subjects in four panes of 50.

1955, Feb. 12 ***Perf. 11x10½***

1065 A512 3c **green** .30 .25
P# block of 4 1.00 —

ROTARY INTERNATIONAL, 50th ANNIV.

Torch, Globe and Rotary Emblem A513

ROTARY PRESS PRINTING

E.E. Plates of 200 subjects in four panes of 50.

1955, Feb. 23 ***Perf. 11x10½***

1066 A513 8c **deep blue** .30 .25
P# block of 4 1.25 —

ARMED FORCES RESERVE ISSUE

Marine, Coast Guard, Army, Navy and Air Force Personnel A514

ROTARY PRESS PRINTING

E.E. Plates of 200 subjects in four panes of 50.

1955, May 21 ***Perf. 11x10½***

1067 A514 3c **bright red violet** .30 .25
P# block of 4 1.00 —

NEW HAMPSHIRE ISSUE

Sesquicentennial of the discovery of the "Old Man of the Mountains."

Great Stone Face — A515

ROTARY PRESS PRINTING

E.E. Plates of 200 subjects in four panes of 50.

1955, June 21 ***Perf. 10½x11***

1068 A515 3c **green** .30 .25
P# block of 4 1.00 —

SOO LOCKS ISSUE

Centenary of the opening of the Soo Locks.

Map of Great Lakes and Two Steamers A516

ROTARY PRESS PRINTING

E.E. Plates of 200 subjects in four panes of 50.

1955, June 28 ***Perf. 11x10½***

1069 A516 3c **blue** .30 .25
P# block of 4 1.00 —

ATOMS FOR PEACE ISSUE

Issued to promote an Atoms for Peace policy.

Atomic Energy Encircling the Hemispheres A517

Designed by George R. Cox.

ROTARY PRESS PRINTING

E.E. Plates of 200 subjects in four panes of 50.

1955, July 28 ***Perf. 11x10½***

1070 A517 3c **deep blue** .30 .25
P# block of 4 1.10 —

FORT TICONDEROGA ISSUE

Bicentenary of Fort Ticonderoga, New York.

Map of the Fort, Ethan Allen and Artillery A518

Designed by Enrico Arno.

ROTARY PRESS PRINTING

E.E. Plates of 200 subjects in four panes of 50.

1955, Sept. 18 ***Perf. 11x10½***

1071 A518 3c **light brown** .30 .25
P# block of 4 1.10 —

ANDREW W. MELLON ISSUE

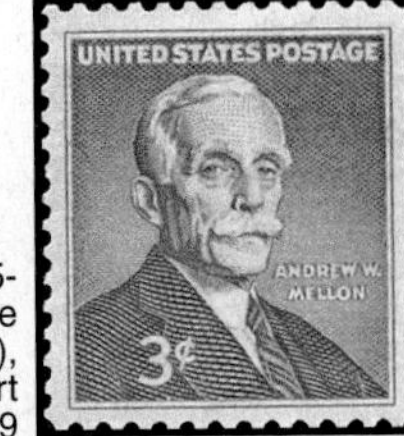

Andrew W. Mellon (1855-1937), US Secretary of the Treasury (1921-32), Financier and Art Collector — A519

Designed by Victor S. McCloskey, Jr.

ROTARY PRESS PRINTING

E.E. Plates of 280 subjects in four panes of 70.

1955, Dec. 20 ***Perf. 10½x11***

1072 A519 3c **rose carmine** .30 .25
P# block of 4 1.10 —

BENJAMIN FRANKLIN ISSUE

250th anniv. of the birth of Benjamin Franklin.

"Franklin Taking Electricity from the Sky," by Benjamin West — A520

Designed by Charles R. Chickering.

ROTARY PRESS PRINTING

E.E. Plates of 200 subjects in four panes of 50.

1956, Jan. 17 ***Perf. 10½x11***

1073 A520 3c **bright carmine** .30 .25
P# block of 4 1.10 —

BOOKER T. WASHINGTON ISSUE

Washington (1856-1915), black educator, founder and head of Tuskegee Institute in Alabama.

Log Cabin — A521

Designed by Charles R. Chickering.

ROTARY PRESS PRINTING

E.E. Plates of 200 subjects in four panes of 50.

1956, Apr. 5 ***Perf. 11x10½***

1074 A521 3c **deep blue** .30 .25
P# block of 4 1.00 —

FIFTH INTERNATIONAL PHILATELIC EXHIBITION ISSUES

FIPEX, New York City, Apr. 28 - May 6, 1956.

SOUVENIR SHEET

A522

Illustration reduced.

FLAT PLATE PRINTING
Plates of 24 subjects

1956, Apr. 28 ***Imperf.***

1075	A522	Pane of 2	1.20	1.50
a.	A482	3c deep violet	.75	.60
b.	A488	8c dark violet blue & carmine	.85	.75

No. 1075 measures 108x73mm. Nos. 1075a and 1075b measure 24x28mm.

Inscriptions printed in dark violet blue; scrolls and stars in carmine.

New York Coliseum and Columbus Monument A523

Designed by William K. Schrage.

ROTARY PRESS PRINTING
E.E. Plates of 200 subjects in four panes of 50.

1956, Apr. 30 ***Perf. 11x10½***

1076	A523	3c **deep violet**	.30	.25
		P# block of 4	1.10	—

WILDLIFE CONSERVATION ISSUE

Issued to emphasize the importance of Wildlife Conservation in America.

Wild Turkey A524

Pronghorn Antelope A525

King Salmon — A526

Designed by Robert W. (Bob) Hines.

ROTARY PRESS PRINTING
E.E. Plates of 200 subjects in four panes of 50.

1956 ***Perf. 11x10½***

1077	A524	3c **rose lake,** *May 5*	.30	.25
		P# block of 4	1.00	—
1078	A525	3c **brown,** *June 22*	.30	.25
		P# block of 4	1.00	—
1079	A526	3c **blue green,** *Nov. 9*	.30	.25
		P# block of 4	1.00	—
		Nos. 1077-1079 (3)	.90	.75

PURE FOOD AND DRUG LAWS, 50th ANNIV.

Harvey Washington Wiley — A527

Designed by Robert L. Miller

ROTARY PRESS PRINTING
E.E. Plates of 200 subjects in four panes of 50.

1956, June 27 ***Perf. 10½x11***

1080	A527	3c **dark blue green**	.30	.25
		P# block of 4	1.00	—

WHEATLAND ISSUE

Pres. Buchanan's Home, Lancaster, Pa. — A528

ROTARY PRESS PRINTING
E.E. Plates of 200 subjects in four panes of 50.

1956, Aug. 5 ***Perf. 11x10½***

1081	A528	3c **black brown**	.30	.25
		P# block of 4	1.00	—

LABOR DAY ISSUE

Mosaic, AFL-CIO Headquarters — A529

Designed by Victor S. McCloskey, Jr.

ROTARY PRESS PRINTING
E.E. Plates of 200 subjects in four panes of 50.

1956, Sept. 3 ***Perf. 10½x11***

1082	A529	3c **deep blue**	.30	.25
		P# block of 4	1.00	—

NASSAU HALL ISSUE

200th anniv. of Nassau Hall, Princeton University.

Nassau Hall, Princeton, N.J. — A530

ROTARY PRESS PRINTING
E.E. Plates of 200 subjects in four panes of 50.

1956, Sept. 22 ***Perf. 11x10½***

1083	A530	3c **black,** *orange*	.30	.25
		P# block of 4	1.00	—

DEVILS TOWER ISSUE

Issued to commemorate the 50th anniversary of the Federal law providing for protection of American natural antiquities. Devils Tower National Monument, Wyoming, is an outstanding example.

Devils Tower — A531

Designed by Charles R. Chickering.

ROTARY PRESS PRINTING
E.E. Plates of 200 subjects in four panes of 50.

1956, Sept. 24 ***Perf. 10½x11***

1084	A531	3c **violet**	.30	.25
		P# block of 4	1.00	—
		Pair with full horiz. gutter btwn.	*400.00*	

CHILDREN'S ISSUE

Issued to promote friendship among the children of the world.

Children of the World — A532

Designed by Ronald Dias.

ROTARY PRESS PRINTING
E.E. Plates of 200 subjects in four panes of 50.

1956, Dec. 15 ***Perf. 11x10½***

1085	A532	3c **dark blue**	.30	.25
		P# block of 4	1.00	—

ALEXANDER HAMILTON (1755-1804)

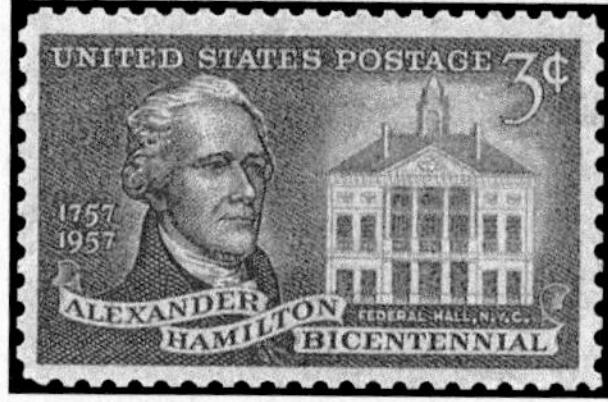

Alexander Hamilton and Federal Hall — A533

Designed by William K. Schrage.

ROTARY PRESS PRINTING
E.E. Plates of 200 subjects in four panes of 50.

1957, Jan. 11 ***Perf. 11x10½***

1086	A533	3c **rose red**	.30	.25
		P# block of 4	1.00	—

POLIO ISSUE

Honoring "those who helped fight polio," and on for 20th anniv. of the Natl. Foundation for Infantile Paralysis and the March of Dimes.

Allegory — A534

Major Plate Crack

Designed by Charles R. Chickering.

ROTARY PRESS PRINTING
E.E. Plates of 200 subjects in four panes of 50.

1957, Jan. 15 ***Perf. 10½x11***

1087	A534	3c **red lilac**	.30	.25
		P# block of 4	1.00	—
		Major plate crack (25605 UL 1)	—	

COAST AND GEODETIC SURVEY ISSUE

150th anniversary of the establishment of the Coast and Geodetic Survey.

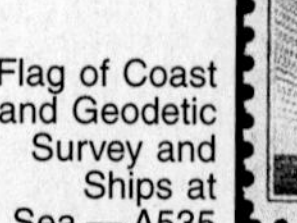

Flag of Coast and Geodetic Survey and Ships at Sea — A535

Designed by Harold E. MacEwen.

ROTARY PRESS PRINTING

E.E. Plates of 200 subjects in four panes of 50.

1957, Feb. 11 ***Perf. 11x10½***

1088 A535 3c **dark blue** .30 .25
P# block of 4 1.00 —

ARCHITECTS ISSUE

American Institute of Architects, centenary.

Corinthian Capital and Mushroom Type Head and Shaft — A536

Designed by Robert J. Schultz.

ROTARY PRESS PRINTING

E.E. Plates of 200 subjects in four panes of 50.

1957, Feb. 23 ***Perf. 11x10½***

1089 A536 3c **red lilac** .30 .25
P# block of 4 1.00 —

STEEL INDUSTRY ISSUE

Centenary of the steel industry in America.

American Eagle and Pouring Ladle — A537

Designed by Anthonio Petruccelli.

ROTARY PRESS PRINTING

E.E. Plates of 200 subjects in four panes of 50.

1957, May 22 ***Perf. 10½x11***

1090 A537 3c **bright ultramarine** .30 .25
P# block of 4 1.00 —

INTERNATIONAL NAVAL REVIEW ISSUE

Issued to commemorate the International Naval Review and the Jamestown Festival.

Aircraft Carrier and Jamestown Festival Emblem A538

Designed by Richard A. Genders.

ROTARY PRESS PRINTING

E.E. Plates of 200 subjects in four panes of 50.

1957, June 10 ***Perf. 11x10½***

1091 A538 3c **blue green** .30 .25
P# block of 4 1.00 —

OKLAHOMA STATEHOOD, 50th ANNIV.

Map of Oklahoma, Arrow and Atom Diagram A539

Designed by William K. Schrage.

ROTARY PRESS PRINTING

E.E. Plates of 200 subjects in four panes of 50.

1957, June 14 ***Perf. 11x10½***

1092 A539 3c **dark blue** .30 .25
P# block of 4 1.00 —

SCHOOL TEACHERS ISSUE

Teacher and Pupils — A540

ROTARY PRESS PRINTING

E.E. Plates of 200 subjects in four panes of 50.

1957, July 1 ***Perf. 11x10½***

1093 A540 3c **rose lake** .30 .25
P# block of 4 1.00 —

FLAG ISSUE

"Old Glory" (48 Stars) — A541

Designed by Victor S. McCloskey, Jr.

GIORI PRESS PRINTING

Plates of 200 subjects in four panes of 50.

1957, July 4 ***Perf. 11***

1094 A541 4c **dark blue & deep carmine** .30 .25
P# block of 4 1.00 —

SHIP BUILDING ISSUE

350th anniversary of shipbuilding in America.

"Virginia of Sagadahock" and Seal of Maine — A542

Designed by Ervine Metzel, Mrs. William Zorach, A. M. Main, Jr., and George F. Cary II.

ROTARY PRESS PRINTING

E.E. Plates of 280 subjects in four panes of 70.

1957, Aug. 15 ***Perf. 10½x11***

1095 A542 3c **deep violet** .30 .25
P# block of 4 1.00 —

CHAMPION OF LIBERTY ISSUE

Magsaysay (1907-57), Pres. of the Philippines.

Ramon Magsaysay — A543

Designed by Arnold Copeland, Ervine Metzl and William H. Buckley.

GIORI PRESS PRINTING

Plates of 192 subjects in four panes of 48 each.

1957, Aug. 31 ***Perf. 11***

1096 A543 8c **carmine, ultramarine & ocher** .30 .25
P# block of 4, 2# 1.00 —
P# block of 4, ultra. # omitted —

LAFAYETTE BICENTENARY ISSUE

Marquis de Lafayette (1757-1834) — A544

Designed by Ervine Metzl.

ROTARY PRESS PRINTING

E.E. Plates of 200 subjects in four panes of 50.

1957. Sept. 6 ***Perf. 10½x11***

1097 A544 3c **rose lake** .30 .25
P# block of 4 1.00 —

WILDLIFE CONSERVATION ISSUE

Issued to emphasize the importance of Wildlife Conservation in America.

Whooping Cranes — A545

Designed by Bob Hines and C.R. Chickering.

GIORI PRESS PRINTING

Plates of 200 subjects in four panes of 50.

1957, Nov. 22 ***Perf. 11***

1098 A545 3c **blue, ocher & green** .30 .25
P# block of 4 1.00 —

RELIGIOUS FREEDOM ISSUE

300th anniv. of the Flushing Remonstrance.

Bible, Hat and Quill Pen — A546

Designed by Robert Geissmann.

ROTARY PRESS PRINTING

E.E. Plates of 200 subjects in four panes of 50.

1957, Dec. 27 ***Perf. 10½x11***

1099 A546 3c **black** .30 .25
P# block of 4 1.00 —

GARDENING HORTICULTURE ISSUE

Issued to honor the garden clubs of America and in connection with the centenary of the birth of Liberty Hyde Bailey, horticulturist.

"Bountiful Earth" — A547

Designed by Denver Gillen.

ROTARY PRESS PRINTING

E.E. Plates of 200 subjects in four panes of 50.

1958, Mar. 15 ***Perf. 10½x11***

1100 A547 3c **green** .30 .25
P# block of 4 1.00 —

BRUSSELS EXHIBITION ISSUE

Issued in honor of the opening of the Universal and International Exhibition at Brussels, April 17.

US Pavilion at Brussels A551

Designed by Bradbury Thompson.

ROTARY PRESS PRINTING

E.E. Plates of 200 subjects in four panes of 50.

1958, Apr. 17 ***Perf. 11x10½***

1104 A551 3c **deep claret** .30 .25
On cover, Expo. station ("U.S. Pavilion") canc. 3.00
P# block of 4 1.00 —

JAMES MONROE ISSUE

James Monroe (1758-1831), 5th President of the US — A552

Designed by Frank P. Conley.

ROTARY PRESS PRINTING

E.E. Plates of 280 subjects in four panes of 70.

1958, Apr. 28 ***Perf. 11x10½***

1105 A552 3c **purple** .30 .25
P# block of 4 1.00 —

MINNESOTA STATEHOOD, 100th ANNIV.

Minnesota Lakes and Pines — A553

Designed by Homer Hill.

ROTARY PRESS PRINTING

E.E. Plates of 200 subjects in four panes of 50.

1958, May 11 ***Perf. 11x10½***

1106 A553 3c **green** .30 .25
P# block of 4 1.00 —

GEOPHYSICAL YEAR ISSUE

International Geophysical Year, 1957-58.

Solar Disc and Hands from Michelangelo's "Creation of Adam" — A554

Designed by Ervine Metzl.

GIORI PRESS PRINTING

Plates of 200 subjects in four panes of 50.

1958, May 31 ***Perf. 11***

1107 A554 3c **black & red orange** .30 .25
P# block of 4 1.00 —

GUNSTON HALL ISSUE

Issued for the bicentenary of Gunston Hall and to honor George Mason, author of the Constitution of Virginia and the Virginia Bill of Rights.

Gunston Hall, Virginia A555

Designed by Rene Clarke.

ROTARY PRESS PRINTING

E.E. Plates of 200 subjects in four panes of 50.

1958, June 12 ***Perf. 11x10½***

1108 A555 3c **light green** .30 .25
P# block of 4 1.00 —

MACKINAC BRIDGE ISSUE

Dedication of Mackinac Bridge, Michigan.

Mackinac Bridge — A556

Designed by Arnold J. Copeland.

ROTARY PRESS PRINTING

E.E. Plates of 200 subjects in four panes of 50.

1958, June 25 ***Perf. 10½x11***

1109 A556 3c **bright greenish blue** .30 .25
P# block of 4 1.00 —

CHAMPION OF LIBERTY ISSUE

Simon Bolívar, South American freedom fighter.

Simon Bolívar — A557

ROTARY PRESS PRINTING

E.E. Plates of 280 subjects in four panes of 70.

1958, July 24 ***Perf. 10½x11***

1110 A557 4c **olive bister** .30 .25
P# block of 4 1.00 —

GIORI PRESS PRINTING

Plates of 288 subjects in four panes of 72 each.

Perf. 11

1111 A557 8c **carmine, ultramarine & ocher** .30 .25
P# block of 4, 2# 1.25 —
P# block of 4, ocher # only —

ATLANTIC CABLE CENTENNIAL ISSUE

Centenary of the Atlantic Cable, linking the Eastern and Western hemispheres.

Neptune, Globe and Mermaid A558

Designed by George Giusti.

ROTARY PRESS PRINTING

E.E. Plates of 200 subjects in four panes of 50.

1958, Aug. 15 ***Perf. 11x10½***

1112 A558 4c **reddish purple** .30 .25
P# block of 4 1.00 —

LINCOLN SESQUICENTENNIAL ISSUE

Sesquicentennial of the birth of Abraham Lincoln. No. 1114 also for the centenary of the founding of Cooper Union, New York City. No. 1115 marks the centenary of the Lincoln-Douglas Debates.

Lincoln by George Healy — A559

Lincoln by Gutzon Borglum — A560

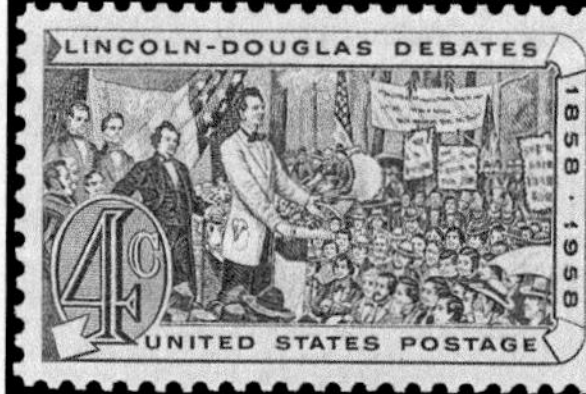

Lincoln and Stephen A. Douglas Debating, from Painting by Joseph Boggs Beale — A561

Daniel Chester French Statue of Lincoln as Drawn by Fritz Busse — A562

Designed by Ervine Metzl.

ROTARY PRESS PRINTING

E.E. Plates of 200 subjects in four panes of 50.

1958-59 ***Perf. 10½x11***

1113 A559 1c **green**, *Feb. 12, 1959* .30 .25
P# block of 4 .50 —
1114 A560 3c **dark rose**, *Feb. 27, 1959* .30 .25
P# block of 4 1.00 —

Perf. 11x10½

1115 A561 4c **sepia**, *Aug. 27, 1958* .30 .25
P# block of 4 1.00 —
1116 A562 4c **dark blue**, *May 30, 1959* .30 .25
P# block of 4 1.00 —
Nos. 1113-1116 (4) 1.20 1.00

CHAMPION OF LIBERTY ISSUE

Lajos Kossuth, Hungarian freedom fighter.

Lajos Kossuth — A563

ROTARY PRESS PRINTING
E.E. Plates of 280 subjects in four panes of 70.

1958, Sept. 19 *Perf. 10½x11*
1117 A563 4c **green** .30 .25
P# block of 4 1.00 —

GIORI PRESS PRINTING
Plates of 288 subjects in four panes of 72 each.
Perf. 11

1118 A563 8c **carmine, ultramarine & ocher** .30 .25
P# block of 4, 2# 1.00 —

FREEDOM OF PRESS ISSUE

Honoring Journalism and freedom of the press in connection with the 50th anniv. of the 1st School of Journalism at the University of Missouri.

Early Press and Hand Holding Quill — A564

Designed by Lester Beall and Charles Goslin.

ROTARY PRESS PRINTING
E.E. Plates of 200 subjects in four panes of 50.

1958, Sept. 22 *Perf. 10½x11*
1119 A564 4c **black** .30 .25
P# block of 4 1.00 —

OVERLAND MAIL ISSUE

Centenary of Overland Mail Service.

Mail Coach and Map of Southwest US — A565

Designed by William H. Buckley.

ROTARY PRESS PRINTING
E.E. Plates of 200 subjects in four panes of 50.

1958, Oct. 10 *Perf. 11x10½*
1120 A565 4c **crimson rose** .30 .25
P# block of 4 1.00 —

NOAH WEBSTER ISSUE

Webster (1758-1843), lexicographer and author.

Noah Webster — A566

Designed by Charles R. Chickering.

ROTARY PRESS PRINTING
E.E. Plates of 280 subjects in four panes of 70.

1958, Oct. 16 *Perf. 10½x11*
1121 A566 4c **dark carmine rose** .30 .25
P# block of 4 1.00 —

FOREST CONSERVATION ISSUE

Issued to publicize forest conservation and the protection of natural resources and to honor Theodore Roosevelt, a leading forest conservationist, on the centenary of his birth.

Forest Scene — A567

Designed by Rudolph Wendelin.

GIORI PRESS PRINTING
Plates of 200 subjects in four panes of 50.

1958, Oct. 27 *Perf. 11*
1122 A567 4c **green, yellow & brown** .30 .25
P# block of 4 1.00 —

FORT DUQUESNE ISSUE

Bicentennial of Fort Duquesne (Fort Pitt) at future site of Pittsburgh.

British Capture of Fort Duquesne, 1758; Brig. Gen. John Forbes on Litter, Colonel Washington Mounted A568

Designed by William H. Buckley and Douglas Gorsline.

ROTARY PRESS PRINTING
E.E. Plates of 200 subjects in four panes of 50.

1958, Nov. 25 *Perf. 11x10½*
1123 A568 4c **blue** .30 .25
P# block of 4 1.00 —

OREGON STATEHOOD, 100th ANNIV.

Covered Wagon and Mt. Hood — A569

Designed by Robert Hallock.

ROTARY PRESS PRINTING
E.E. Plates of 200 subjects in four panes of 50.

1959, Feb. 14 *Perf. 11x10½*
1124 A569 4c **blue green** .30 .25
P# block of 4 1.00 —

CHAMPION OF LIBERTY ISSUE

San Martin, So. American soldier and statesman.

José de San Martin — A570

ROTARY PRESS PRINTING
E.E. Plates of 280 subjects in four panes of 70.

1959, Feb. 25 *Perf. 10½x11*
1125 A570 4c **blue** .30 .25
P# block of 4 1.00 —
a. Horiz. pair, imperf. between *900.00*

GIORI PRESS PRINTING
Plates of 288 subjects in four panes of 72 each.
Perf. 11

1126 A570 8c **carmine, ultramarine & ocher** .30 .25
P# block of 4 1.10 —

NATO ISSUE

North Atlantic Treaty Organization, 10th anniv.

NATO Emblem — A571

Designed by Stevan Dohanos.

ROTARY PRESS PRINTING
E.E. Plates of 280 subjects in four panes of 70.

1959, Apr. 1 *Perf. 10½x11*
1127 A571 4c **blue** .30 .25
P# block of 4 1.00 —

ARCTIC EXPLORATIONS ISSUE

Conquest of the Arctic by land by Rear Admiral Robert Edwin Peary in 1909 and by sea by the submarine "Nautilus" in 1958.

North Pole, Dog Sled and "Nautilus" A572

Designed by George Samerjan.

ROTARY PRESS PRINTING
E.E. Plates of 200 subjects in four panes of 50.

1959, Apr. 6 *Perf. 11x10½*
1128 A572 4c **bright greenish blue** .30 .25
P# block of 4 1.00 —

WORLD PEACE THROUGH WORLD TRADE ISSUE

Issued in conjunction with the 17th Congress of the International Chamber of Commerce, Washington, D.C., April 19-25.

Globe and Laurel — A573

Designed by Robert Baker.

ROTARY PRESS PRINTING
E.E. Plates of 200 subjects in four panes of 50.

1959, Apr. 20 *Perf. 11x10½*
1129 A573 8c **rose lake** .30 .25
P# block of 4 1.00 —

SILVER CENTENNIAL ISSUE

Discovery of silver at the Comstock Lode, Nevada.

Henry Comstock at Mount Davidson Site — A574

Designed by Robert L. Miller and W.K. Schrage.

ROTARY PRESS PRINTING
E.E. Plates of 200 subjects in four panes of 50.

1959, June 8 *Perf. 11x10½*

1130 A574 4c **black**	.30	.25
P# block of 4	1.00	—

ST. LAWRENCE SEAWAY ISSUE

Opening of the St. Lawrence Seaway.

Great Lakes, Maple Leaf and Eagle Emblems A575

Designed by Arnold Copeland, Ervine Metzl, William H. Buckley and Gerald Trottier.

GIORI PRESS PRINTING
Plates of 200 subjects in four panes of 50.

1959, June 26 *Perf. 11*

1131 A575 4c **red & dark blue**	.30	.25
P# block of 4	1.00	—
Pair with full horiz. gutter btwn.	—	

See Canada No. 387.

49-STAR FLAG ISSUE

U.S. Flag, 1959 — A576

Designed by Stevan Dohanos.

GIORI PRESS PRINTING
Plates of 200 subjects in four panes of 50.

1959, July 4 *Perf. 11*

1132 A576 4c **ocher, dark blue & deep carmine**	.30	.25
P# block of 4	1.00	—

SOIL CONSERVATION ISSUE

Issued as a tribute to farmers and ranchers who use soil and water conservation measures.

Modern Farm — A577

Designed by Walter Hortens.

GIORI PRESS PRINTING
Plates of 200 subjects in four panes of 50.

1959, Aug. 26 *Perf. 11*

1133 A577 4c **blue, green & ocher**	.30	.25
P# block of 4	1.00	—

PETROLEUM INDUSTRY ISSUE

Centenary of the completion of the nation's first oil well at Titusville, Pa.

Oil Derrick — A578

Designed by Robert Foster.

ROTARY PRESS PRINTING
E.E. Plates of 200 subjects in four panes of 50.

1959, Aug. 27 *Perf. 10½x11*

1134 A578 4c **brown**	.30	.25
P# block of 4	1.00	—

DENTAL HEALTH ISSUE

Issued to publicize Dental Health and for the centenary of the American Dental Association.

Children A579

Designed by Charles Henry Carter.

ROTARY PRESS PRINTING
E.E. Plates of 200 subjects in four panes of 50.

1959, Sept. 14 *Perf. 11x10½*

1135 A579 4c **green**	.30	.25
P# block of 4	1.00	—

No. 1135 exists tagged as a Pitney-Bowes tagging essay.

CHAMPION OF LIBERTY ISSUE

Ernst Reuter, Mayor of Berlin, 1948-53.

Ernst Reuter — A580

ROTARY PRESS PRINTING
E.E. Plates of 280 subjects in four panes of 70.

1959, Sept. 29 *Perf. 10½x11*

1136 A580 4c **gray**	.30	.25
P# block of 4	1.00	—

GIORI PRESS PRINTING
Plates of 288 subjects in four panes of 72 each.
Perf. 11

1137 A580 8c **carmine, ultramarine & ocher**	.30	.25
P# block of 4	1.10	—
a. Ocher missing (EP)	*3,000.*	
b. Ultramarine missing (EP)	*3,750.*	
c. Ocher & ultramarine missing (EP)	*4,000.*	
d. All colors missing (EP)	*2,000.*	

DR. EPHRAIM McDOWELL ISSUE

Honoring McDowell (1771-1830) on the 150th anniv. of the 1st successful ovarian operation in the US, performed at Danville, Ky., 1809.

Dr. Ephraim McDowell — A581

Designed by Charles R. Chickering.

ROTARY PRESS PRINTING
E.E. Plates of 280 subjects in four panes of 70.

1959, Dec. 3 *Perf. 10½x11*

1138 A581 4c **rose lake**	.30	.25
P# block of 4	1.00	—
a. Vert. pair, imperf. btwn.	*375.00*	
b. Vert. pair, imperf. horiz.	*200.00*	

VALUES FOR HINGED STAMPS AFTER NO. 771

This catalogue does not value unused stamps after No. 771 in hinged condition. Hinged unused stamps from No. 772 to the present are worth considerably less than the values given for unused stamps, which are for never-hinged examples.

AMERICAN CREDO ISSUE

Issued to re-emphasize the ideals upon which America was founded and to honor those great Americans who wrote or uttered the credos.

Quotation from Washington's Farewell Address, 1796 — A582

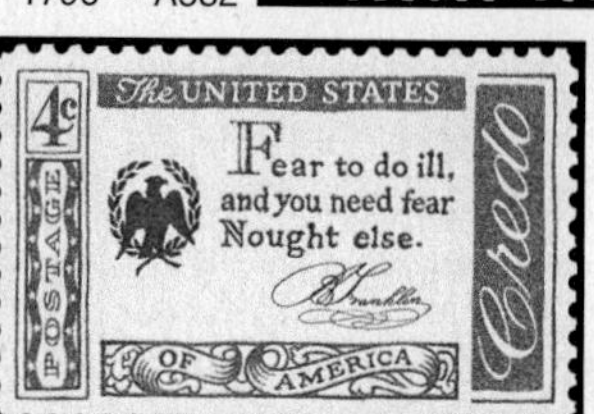

Benjamin Franklin Quotation A583

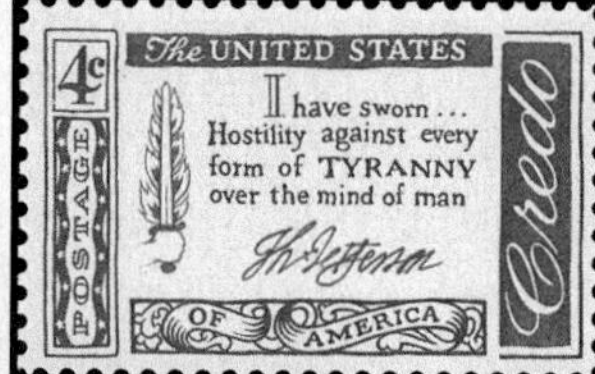

Thomas Jefferson Quotation A584

Francis Scott Key Quotation A585

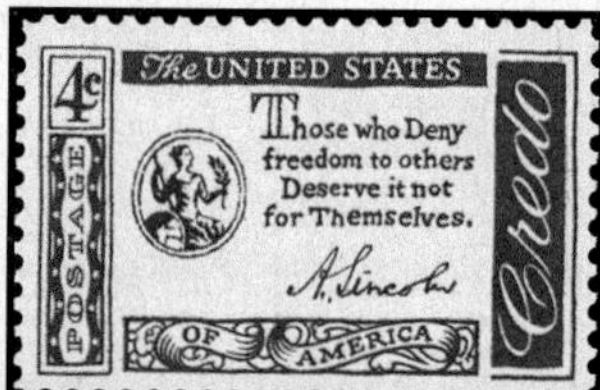

Abraham Lincoln Quotation A586

Patrick Henry Quotation A587

Designed by Frank Conley.

GIORI PRESS PRINTING
Plates of 200 subjects in four panes of 50.

1960-61 *Perf. 11*

1139 A582 4c **dark violet blue, & carmine,** *Jan. 20, 1960*	.30	.25
P# block of 4	1.00	—
1140 A583 4c **olive bister & green,** *Mar. 31, 1960*	.30	.25
P# block of 4	1.00	—
1141 A584 4c **gray & vermilion,** *May 18, 1960*	.30	.25
P# block of 4	1.00	—
1142 A585 4c **carmine & dark blue,** *Sept. 14, 1960*	.30	.25
P# block of 4	1.00	—
1143 A586 4c **magenta & green,** *Nov. 19, 1960*	.30	.25
P# block of 4	1.00	—
Pair with full horiz. gutter between	525.00	
1144 A587 4c **green & brown,** *Jan. 11, 1961*	.30	.25
P# block of 4	1.00	—
Nos. 1139-1144 (6)	1.80	1.50

BOY SCOUT JUBILEE ISSUE

50th anniv. of the Boy Scouts of America.

Boy Scout Giving Scout Sign — A588

Designed by Norman Rockwell.

GIORI PRESS PRINTING

Plates of 200 subjects in four panes of 50.

1960, Feb. 8 *Perf. 11*

1145 A588 4c **red, dark blue & dark bister** .30 .25
P# block of 4 1.00 —

No. 1145 exists tagged as a Pitney-Bowes tagging essay.

OLYMPIC WINTER GAMES ISSUE

Opening of the 8th Olympic Winter Games, Squaw Valley, Feb. 18-29, 1960.

Olympic Rings and Snowflake — A589

Designed by Ervine Metzl.

ROTARY PRESS PRINTING

E.E. Plates of 200 subjects in four panes of 50.

1960, Feb. 18 *Perf. 10½x11*

1146 A589 4c **dull blue** .30 .25
P# block of 4 1.00 —

CHAMPION OF LIBERTY ISSUE

Issued to honor Thomas G. Masaryk, founder and president of Czechoslovakia (1918-35), on the 110th anniversary of his birth.

Thomas G. Masaryk — A590

ROTARY PRESS PRINTING

E.E. Plates of 280 subjects in four panes of 70.

1960, Mar. 7 *Perf. 10½x11*

1147 A590 4c **blue** .30 .25
P# block of 4 1.00 —
a. Vert. pair, imperf. between *1,900.*

GIORI PRESS PRINTING

Plates of 288 subjects in four panes of 72 each.

Perf. 11

1148 A590 8c **carmine, ultramarine & ocher** .30 .25
P# block of 4 1.00 —
a. Horiz. pair, imperf. between —

WORLD REFUGEE YEAR ISSUE

World Refugee Year, July 1, 1959-June 30, 1960.

Family Walking Toward New Life — A591

Designed by Ervine Metzl.

ROTARY PRESS PRINTING

E.E. Plates of 200 subjects in four panes of 50.

1960, Apr. 7 *Perf. 11x10½*

1149 A591 4c **gray black** .30 .25
P# block of 4 1.00 —

WATER CONSERVATION ISSUE

Issued to stress the importance of water conservation and to commemorate the 7th Watershed Congress, Washington, D.C.

Water: From Watershed to Consumer A592

Designed by Elmo White.

GIORI PRESS PRINTING

Plates of 200 subjects in four panes of 50.

1960, Apr. 18 *Perf. 11*

1150 A592 4c **dark blue, brown orange & green** .30 .25
P# block of 4 1.00 —
a. Brown orange missing (EP) *2,750.*

SEATO ISSUE

South-East Asia Treaty Organization and for the SEATO Conf., Washington, D.C., May 31-June 3.

SEATO Emblem — A593

Designed by John Maass.

ROTARY PRESS PRINTING

E.E. plates of 280 subjects in four panes of 70.

1960, May 31 *Perf. 10½x11*

1151 A593 4c **blue** .30 .25
P# block of 4 1.00 —
a. Vertical pair, imperf. between *125.00*

AMERICAN WOMAN ISSUE

Issued to pay tribute to American women and their accomplishments in civic affairs, education, arts and industry.

Mother and Daughter A594

Designed by Robert Sivard.

ROTARY PRESS PRINTING

E.E. Plates of 200 subjects in four panes of 50.

1960, June 2 *Perf. 11x10½*

1152 A594 4c **deep violet** .30 .25
P# block of 4 1.00 —

50-STAR FLAG ISSUE

US Flag, 1960 — A595

Designed by Stevan Dohanos.

GIORI PRESS PRINTING

Plates of 200 subjects in four panes of 50.

1960, July 4 *Perf. 11*

1153 A595 4c **dark blue & red** .30 .25
P# block of 4 1.00 —

PONY EXPRESS CENTENNIAL ISSUE

Pony Express Rider — A596

Designed by Harold von Schmidt.

ROTARY PRESS PRINTING

E.E. Plates of 200 subjects in four panes of 50.

1960, July 19 *Perf. 11x10½*

1154 A596 4c **sepia** .30 .25
P# block of 4 1.00 —

EMPLOY THE HANDICAPPED ISSUE

Promoting the employment of the physically handicapped and publicizing the 8th World Congress of the Intl. Soc. for the Welfare of Cripples, New York City.

Man in Wheelchair Operating Drill Press — A597

Designed by Carl Bobertz.

ROTARY PRESS PRINTING

E.E. Plates of 200 subjects in four panes of 50.

1960, Aug. 28 *Perf. 10½x11*

1155 A597 4c **dark blue** .30 .25
P# block of 4 1.00 —

WORLD FORESTRY CONGRESS ISSUE

5th World Forestry Cong., Seattle, Wash., Aug. 29-Sept. 10.

World Forestry Congress Seal — A598

ROTARY PRESS PRINTING
E.E. Plates of 200 subjects in four panes of 50.

1960, Aug. 29 *Perf. 10½x11*
1156 A598 4c **green** .30 .25
P# block of 4 1.00 —

MEXICAN INDEPENDENCE, 150th ANNIV.

Independence Bell — A599

Designed by Leon Helguera and Charles R. Chickering.

GIORI PRESS PRINTING
Plates of 200 subjects in four panes of 50.

1960, Sept. 16 *Perf. 11*
1157 A599 4c **green & rose red** .30 .25
P# block of 4 1.00 —

See Mexico No. 910.

US-JAPAN TREATY ISSUE

Centenary of the United States-Japan Treaty of Amity and Commerce.

Washington Monument and Cherry Blossoms — A600

Designed by Gyo Fujikawa.

GIORI PRESS PRINTING
Plates of 200 subjects in four panes of 50.

1960, Sept. 28 *Perf. 11*
1158 A600 4c **blue & pink** .30 .25
P# block of 4 1.00 —

CHAMPION OF LIBERTY ISSUE

Jan Paderewski, Polish statesman and musician.

Ignacy Jan Paderewski — A601

ROTARY PRESS PRINTING
E.E. Plates of 280 subjects in four panes of 70.

1960, Oct. 8 *Perf. 10½x11*
1159 A601 4c **blue** .30 .25
P# block of 4 1.00 —

GIORI PRESS PRINTING
Plates of 288 subjects in four panes of 72 each.
Perf. 11

1160 A601 8c **carmine, ultramarine & ocher** .30 .25
P# block of 4 1.00 —

SENATOR TAFT MEMORIAL ISSUE

Senator Robert A. Taft (1889-1953) of Ohio.

Robert A. Taft — A602

Designed by William K. Schrage.

ROTARY PRESS PRINTING
E.E. Plates of 280 subjects in four panes of 70.

1960, Oct. 10 *Perf. 10½x11*
1161 A602 4c **dull violet** .30 .25
P# block of 4 1.00 —

WHEELS OF FREEDOM ISSUE

Issued to honor the automotive industry and in connection with the National Automobile Show, Detroit, Oct. 15-23.

Globe and Steering Wheel with Tractor, Car and Truck — A603

Designed by Arnold J. Copeland.

ROTARY PRESS PRINTING
E.E. Plates of 200 subjects in four panes of 50.

1960, Oct. 15 *Perf. 11x10½*
1162 A603 4c **dark blue** .30 .25
P# block of 4 1.00 —

BOYS' CLUBS OF AMERICA ISSUE

Boys' Clubs of America movement, centenary.

Profile of Boy — A604

Designed by Charles T. Coiner.

GIORI PRESS PRINTING
Plates of 200 subjects in four panes of 50.

1960, Oct. 18 *Perf. 11*
1163 A604 4c **indigo, slate & rose red** .30 .25
P# block of 4 1.00 —

FIRST AUTOMATED POST OFFICE IN THE US ISSUE

Publicizing the opening of the 1st automated post office in the US at Providence, R.I.

Architect's Sketch of New Post Office, Providence, R.I. — A605

Designed by Arnold J. Copeland and Victor S. McCloskey, Jr.

GIORI PRESS PRINTING
Plates of 200 subjects in four panes of 50.

1960, Oct. 20 *Perf. 11*
1164 A605 4c **dark blue & carmine** .30 .25
P# block of 4 1.00 —
a. Red missing (PS) *250.00*

CHAMPION OF LIBERTY ISSUE

Baron Karl Gustaf Emil Mannerheim (1867-1951), Marshal and President of Finland.

Baron Gustaf Mannerheim — A606

ROTARY PRESS PRINTING
E.E. Plates of 280 subjects in four panes of 70.

1960, Oct. 26 *Perf. 10½x11*
1165 A606 4c **blue** .30 .25
P# block of 4 1.00 —

GIORI PRESS PRINTING
Plates of 288 subjects in four panes of 72 each.
Perf. 11

1166 A606 8c **carmine, ultramarine & ocher** .30 .25
P# block of 4 1.00 —

CAMP FIRE GIRLS ISSUE

50th anniv. of the Camp Fire Girls' movement and in connection with the Golden Jubilee Convention celebration of the Camp Fire Girls.

Camp Fire Girls Emblem — A607

Designed by H. Edward Oliver.

GIORI PRESS PRINTING
Plates of 200 subjects in four panes of 50.

1960, Nov. 1 *Perf. 11*
1167 A607 4c **dark blue & bright red** .30 .25
P# block of 4 1.00 —

CHAMPION OF LIBERTY ISSUE

Giuseppe Garibaldi (1807-1882), Italian patriot and freedom fighter.

Giuseppe Garibaldi — A608

ROTARY PRESS PRINTING
E.E. Plates of 280 subjects in four panes of 70.

1960, Nov. 2 *Perf. 10½x11*
1168 A608 4c **green** .30 .25
P# block of 4 1.00 —

GIORI PRESS PRINTING
Plates of 288 subjects in four panes of 72 each.
Perf. 11

1169 A608 8c **carmine, ultramarine & ocher** .30 .25
P# block of 4 1.00 —

SENATOR GEORGE MEMORIAL ISSUE

Walter F. George (1878-1957) of Georgia.

Walter F. George — A609

Designed by William K. Schrage.

ROTARY PRESS PRINTING
E.E. Plates of 280 subjects in four panes of 70.

1960, Nov. 5 *Perf. 10½x11*
1170 A609 4c **dull violet** .30 .25
P# block of 4 1.00 —

ANDREW CARNEGIE ISSUE

Carnegie (1835-1919), industrialist & philanthropist.

Andrew Carnegie — A610

Designed by Charles R. Chickering.

ROTARY PRESS PRINTING
E.E. Plates of 280 subjects in four panes of 70.

1960, Nov. 25 *Perf. 10½x11*
1171 A610 4c **deep claret** .30 .25
P# block of 4 1.00 —

JOHN FOSTER DULLES MEMORIAL ISSUE

Dulles (1888-1959), Secretary of State (1953-59).

John Foster Dulles — A611

Designed by William K. Schrage.

ROTARY PRESS PRINTING
E.E. Plates of 280 subjects in four panes of 70.

1960, Dec. 6 *Perf. 10½x11*
1172 A611 4c **dull violet** .30 .25
P# block of 4 1.00 —

ECHO I — COMMUNICATIONS FOR PEACE ISSUE

World's 1st communications satellite, Echo I, placed in orbit by the Natl. Aeronautics and Space Admin., Aug. 12, 1960.

Radio Waves Connecting Echo I and Earth — A612

Designed by Ervine Metzl.

ROTARY PRESS PRINTING
E.E. Plates of 200 subjects in four panes of 50.

1960, Dec. 15 *Perf. 11x10½*
1173 A612 4c **deep violet** .30 .25
P# block of 4 1.00 —

CHAMPION OF LIBERTY ISSUE

Mohandas K. Gandhi, leader in India's struggle for independence.

Mahatma Gandhi — A613

ROTARY PRESS PRINTING
E.E. Plates of 280 subjects in four panes of 70.

1961, Jan. 26 *Perf. 10½x11*
1174 A613 4c **red orange** .30 .25
P# block of 4 1.00 —

GIORI PRESS PRINTING
Plates of 288 subjects in four panes of 72 each.
Perf. 11

1175 A613 8c **carmine, ultramarine & ocher** .30 .25
P# block of 4 1.00 —

RANGE CONSERVATION ISSUE

Issued to stress the importance of range conservation and to commemorate the meeting of the American Society of Range Management. "The Trail Boss" from a drawing by Charles M. Russell is the Society's emblem.

The Trail Boss and Modern Range — A614

Designed by Rudolph Wendelin.

GIORI PRESS PRINTING
Plates of 200 subjects in four panes of 50.

1961, Feb. 2 *Perf. 11*
1176 A614 4c **blue, slate & brown orange** .30 .25
P# block of 4 1.00 —

HORACE GREELEY ISSUE

Horace Greeley (1811-1872), Publisher and Editor — A615

Designed by Charles R. Chickering.

ROTARY PRESS PRINTING
E.E. Plates of 280 subjects in four panes of 70.

1961, Feb. 3 *Perf. 10½x11*
1177 A615 4c **dull violet** .30 .25
P# block of 4 1.00 —

CIVIL WAR CENTENNIAL ISSUE

Centenaries of the firing on Fort Sumter (No. 1178), the Battle of Shiloh (No. 1179), the Battle of Gettysburg (No. 1180), the Battle of the Wilderness (No. 1181) and the surrender at Appomattox (No. 1182).

Sea Coast Gun of 1861 — A616

Rifleman at Battle of Shiloh, 1862 — A617

Blue and Gray at Gettysburg, 1863 — A618

Battle of the Wilderness, 1864 — A619

Appomattox, 1865 — A620

Designed by Charles R. Chickering (Sumter), Noel Sickles (Shiloh), Roy Gjertson (Gettysburg), B. Harold Christenson (Wilderness), Leonard Fellman (Appomattox).

ROTARY PRESS PRINTING
E.E. Plates of 200 subjects in four panes of 50.

1961-65 *Perf. 11x10½*
1178 A616 4c **light green,** *Apr. 12, 1961* .30 .25
P# block of 4 1.00 —
1179 A617 4c **black,** *peach blossom, Apr. 7, 1962* .30 .25
P# block of 4 1.00 —

GIORI PRESS PRINTING
Plates of 200 subjects in four panes of 50.
Perf. 11

1180 A618 5c **gray & blue,** *July 1, 1963* .30 .25
P# block of 4 1.00 —
1181 A619 5c **dark red & black,** *May 5, 1964* .30 .25
P# block of 4 1.00 —
Margin block of 4, Mr. Zip and "Use Zip Code" 1.00 —
1182 A620 5c **Prus. blue & black,** *Apr. 9, 1965* .30 .25
P# block of 4 1.25 —
Margin block of 4, Mr. Zip and "Use Zip Code" 1.25 —
a. Horiz. pair, imperf. vert. *3,500.*
Nos. 1178-1182 (5) 1.50 1.25

KANSAS STATEHOOD, 100th ANNIV.

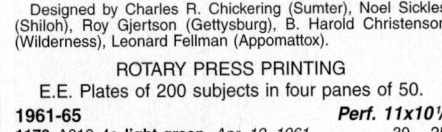

Sunflower, Pioneer Couple and Stockade A621

GIORI PRESS PRINTING
Plates of 200 subjects in four panes of 50.

1961, May 10 *Perf. 11*
1183 A621 4c **brown, dark red & green,** *yellow* .30 .25
P# block of 4 1.00 —

SENATOR NORRIS ISSUE

Senator George W. Norris of Nebraska, and Norris Dam — A622

Designed by Charles R. Chickering.

ROTARY PRESS PRINTING

E.E. Plates of 200 subjects in four panes of 50.

1961, July 11 *Perf. 11x10½*

1184 A622 4c **blue green** .30 .25
P# block of 4 1.00 —

NAVAL AVIATION, 50th ANNIV.

Navy's First Plane (Curtiss A-1 of 1911) and Naval Air Wings — A623

Designed by John Maass.

ROTARY PRESS PRINTING

E.E. Plates of 200 subjects in four panes of 50.

1961, Aug. 20 *Perf. 11x10½*

1185 A623 4c **blue** .30 .25
P# block of 4 1.00 —
Pair with full vert. gutter btwn. *150.00*

WORKMEN'S COMPENSATION ISSUE

50th anniv. of the 1st successful Workmen's Compensation Law, enacted by the Wisconsin legislature.

Scales of Justice, Factory, Worker and Family — A624

Designed by Norman Todhunter.

ROTARY PRESS PRINTING

E.E. Plates of 200 subjects in four panes of 50.

1961, Sept. 4 *Perf. 10½x11*

1186 A624 4c **ultramarine,** *grayish* .30 .25
P# block of 4 1.00 —
P# block of 4 inverted 1.10 —

FREDERIC REMINGTON ISSUE

Remington (1861-1909), artist of the West. The design is from an oil painting, Amon Carter Museum of Western Art, Fort Worth, Texas.

"The Smoke Signal" — A625

Designed by Charles R. Chickering.

GIORI PRESS PRINTING

Panes of 200 subjects in four panes of 50.

1961, Oct. 4 *Perf. 11*

1187 A625 4c **multicolored** .30 .25
P# block of 4 1.00 —

REPUBLIC OF CHINA ISSUE

50th anniversary of the Republic of China.

Sun Yat-sen — A626

ROTARY PRESS PRINTING

E.E. Plates of 200 subjects in four panes of 50.

1961, Oct. 10 *Perf. 10½x11*

1188 A626 4c **blue** .35 .25
P# block of 4 1.50 —

NAISMITH — BASKETBALL ISSUE

Honoring basketball and James Naismith (1861-1939), Canada-born director of physical education, who invented the game in 1891 at Y.M.C.A. College, Springfield, Mass.

Basketball — A627

Designed by Charles R. Chickering.

ROTARY PRESS PRINTING

E.E. Plates of 200 subjects in four panes of 50.

1961, Nov. 6 *Perf. 10½x11*

1189 A627 4c **brown** .30 .25
P# block of 4 1.00 —

NURSING ISSUE

Issued to honor the nursing profession.

Student Nurse Lighting Candle — A628

Designed by Alfred Charles Parker.

GIORI PRESS PRINTING

Plates of 200 subjects in four panes of 50.

1961, Dec. 28 *Perf. 11*

1190 A628 4c **blue, green, orange & black** .30 .25
P# block of 4, 2# 1.00 —

NEW MEXICO STATEHOOD, 50th ANNIV.

Shiprock A629

Designed by Robert J. Jones.

GIORI PRESS PRINTING

Plates of 200 subjects in four panes of 50.

1962, Jan. 6 *Perf. 11*

1191 A629 4c **lt. blue, maroon & bister** .30 .25
P# block of 4 1.00 —

ARIZONA STATEHOOD, 50th ANNIV.

Giant Saguaro Cactus — A630

Designed by Jimmie E. Ihms and James M. Chemi.

GIORI PRESS PRINTING

Plates of 200 subjects in four panes of 50.

1962, Feb. 14 *Perf. 11*

1192 A630 4c **carmine, violet blue & green** .30 .25
P# block of 4 1.00 —

PROJECT MERCURY ISSUE

1st orbital flight of a US astronaut, Lt. Col. John H. Glenn, Jr., Feb. 20, 1962.

"Friendship 7" Capsule and Globe — A631

GIORI PRESS PRINTING

Plates of 200 subjects in four panes of 50.

1962, Feb. 20 *Perf. 11*

1193 A631 4c **dark blue & yellow** .30 .25
P# block of 4 1.00 —

Imperfs. are printers waste.

MALARIA ERADICATION ISSUE

World Health Organization's drive to eradicate malaria.

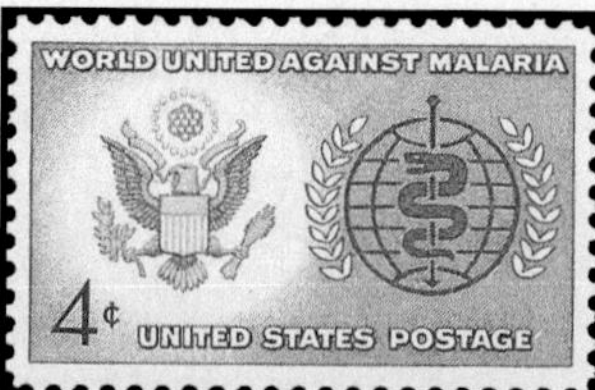

Great Seal of US and WHO Symbol A632

Designed by Charles R. Chickering.

GIORI PRESS PRINTING

Plates of 200 subjects in four panes of 50.

1962, Mar. 30 *Perf. 11*

1194 A632 4c **blue & bister** .30 .25
P# block of 4 1.00 —

CHARLES EVANS HUGHES ISSUE

Hughes (1862-1948), Governor of New York, Chief Justice of the US.

Charles Evans Hughes — A633

Designed by Charles R. Chickering.

ROTARY PRESS PRINTING

E.E. Plates of 200 subjects in four panes of 50.

1962, Apr. 11 *Perf. 10½x11*

1195 A633 4c **black,** *buff* .30 .25
P# block of 4 1.00 —

SEATTLE WORLD'S FAIR ISSUE

"Century 21" International Exposition, Seattle, Wash., Apr. 21-Oct. 21.

"Space Needle" and Monorail — A634

Designed by John Maass.

GIORI PRESS PRINTING

Plates of 200 subjects in four panes of 50.

1962, Apr. 25 *Perf. 11*

1196 A634 4c **red & dark blue** .30 .25
On cover, "Century 21" Expo. cancel 5.00
On cover, "Space Needle" Expo. cancel 2.00
P# block of 4 1.00 —

LOUISIANA STATEHOOD, 150th ANNIV.

Riverboat on the Mississippi A635

Designed by Norman Todhunter.

GIORI PRESS PRINTING

Plates of 200 subjects in four panes of 50.

1962, Apr. 30 *Perf. 11*

1197 A635 4c **blue, dark slate green & red** .30 .25
P# block of 4 1.00 —

HOMESTEAD ACT, CENTENARY

Sod Hut and Settlers A636

Designed by Charles R. Chickering.

ROTARY PRESS PRINTING

E.E. Plates of 200 subjects in four panes of 50.

1962, May 20 *Perf. 11x10½*

1198 A636 4c **slate** .30 .25
P# block of 4 1.00 —

GIRL SCOUTS ISSUE

50th anniversary of the Girl Scouts of America.

Senior Girl Scout and Flag — A637

Designed by Ward Brackett.

ROTARY PRESS PRINTING

E.E. Plates of 200 subjects in four panes of 50.

1962, July 24 *Perf. 11x10½*

1199 A637 4c **rose red** .30 .25
P# block of 4 1.00 —
Pair with full vertical gutter between *250.00*

SENATOR BRIEN McMAHON ISSUE

McMahon (1903-52) of Connecticut had a role in opening the way to peaceful uses of atomic energy through the Atomic Energy Act establishing the Atomic Energy Commission.

Brien McMahon and Atomic Symbol A638

Designed by V. S. McCloskey, Jr.

ROTARY PRESS PRINTING

E.E. Plates of 200 subjects in four panes of 50.

1962, July 28 *Perf. 11x10½*

1200 A638 4c **purple** .30 .25
P# block of 4 1.00 —

APPRENTICESHIP ISSUE

National Apprenticeship Program and 25th anniv. of the National Apprenticeship Act.

Machinist Handing Micrometer to Apprentice A639

Designed by Robert Geissmann.

ROTARY PRESS PRINTING

E.E. Plates of 200 subjects in four panes of 50.

1962, Aug. 31 *Perf. 11x10½*

1201 A639 4c **black,** *yellow bister* .30 .25
P# block of 4 1.00 —

SAM RAYBURN ISSUE

Sam Rayburn (1882-1961), Speaker of the House of Representatives — A640

Designed by Robert L. Miller.

GIORI PRESS PRINTING

Plates of 200 subjects in four panes of 50.

1962, Sept. 16 *Perf. 11*

1202 A640 4c **dark blue & red brown** .30 .25
P# block of 4 1.00 —

DAG HAMMARSKJOLD ISSUE

UN Headquarters and Dag Hammarskjold, UN Sec. Gen., 1953-61 A641

Designed by Herbert M. Sanborn.

GIORI PRESS PRINTING

Plates of 200 subjects in four panes of 50.

1962, Oct. 23 *Perf. 11*

1203 A641 4c **black, brown & yellow** .30 .25
P# block of 4, 2# 1.00 —
a. Yellow inverted, on cover, see note —
Vert. pair, on piece *4,250.*

No. 1203a can only be collected on a cover postmarked before Nov. 16, 1962 (the date the Hammarskjold Special Printing, No. 1204, was issued), or tied on dated piece (unique used pair). Covers are known machine postmarked Cuyahoga Falls, Ohio, Nov. 14, 1962, and notarized in the lower left corner by George W. Schwartz, Notary Public. Other covers are reported postmarked Oct. 26, 1962, Brooklyn, NY, Vanderveer Station. Unaddressed, uncacheted first day covers also exist, but are believed by experts to have been backdated using examples of No. 1204.

An unused pane of 50 was signed in the selvage by ten well-known philatelists attesting to its genuineness. This pane was donated to the American Philatelic Society in 1987.

An unknown number of "first day covers" exist bearing Artmaster cachets. These were contrived using examples of No. 1204.

Hammarskjold Special Printing

No. 1204 was issued following discovery of No. 1203 with yellow background inverted.

GIORI PRESS PRINTING

Plates of 200 subjects in four panes of 50.

1962, Nov. 16 *Perf. 11*

1204 A641 4c **black, brown & yel** (yellow inverted) .30 .25
P# block of 4, 2#, yellow # inverted 1.00 —

The inverted yellow impression is shifted to the right in relation to the black and brown impression. Stamps of first vertical row of UL and LL panes show no yellow at left side for a space of 11-11½mm in from the perforations.

Stamps of first vertical row of UR and LR panes show vertical no-yellow strip 9¾mm wide, covering UN Building. On all others, the vertical no-yellow strip is 3½mm wide, and touches UN Building.

CHRISTMAS ISSUE

Wreath and Candles — A642

Designed by Jim Crawford.

GIORI PRESS PRINTING

Plates of 400 subjects in four panes of 100.
Panes of 90 and 100 exist
without plate numbers due to provisional use of smaller paper.
Value per pane thus $50.

1962, Nov. 1 *Perf. 11*

1205 A642 4c **green & red** .30 .25
P# block of 4 1.00 —

HIGHER EDUCATION ISSUE

Higher education's role in American cultural and industrial development and the centenary celebrations of the signing of the law creating land-grant colleges and universities.

Map of U.S. and Lamp — A643

Designed by Henry K. Bencsath.

GIORI PRESS PRINTING
Plates of 200 subjects in panes of 50.

1962, Nov. 14 *Perf. 11*
1206 A643 4c **blue green & black** .30 .25
P# block of 4, 2# 1.00 —

WINSLOW HOMER ISSUE

Homer (1836-1910), painter, showing his oil, "Breezing Up," which hangs in the National Gallery, Washington, D.C.

"Breezing Up" — A644

Designed by Victor S. McCloskey, Jr.

GIORI PRESS PRINTING
Plates of 200 subjects in four panes of 50.

1962, Dec. 15 *Perf. 11*
1207 A644 4c **multicolored** .30 .25
P# block of 4 1.00 —
a. Horiz. pair, imperf. btwn. and at right *7,000.*

FLAG ISSUE

Flag over White House — A645

Designed by Robert J. Jones.

GIORI PRESS PRINTING
Plates of 400 subjects in four panes of 100.

1963-66 *Perf. 11*
1208 A645 5c **blue & red,** *Jan. 9, 1963* .30 .25
P# block of 4 1.00 —
Pair with full horiz. gutter between —
a. Tagged, *Aug. 25, 1966* .30 .25
P# block of 4 2.25 —
b. Horiz. pair, imperf. between, tagged *2,250.*

Beware of pairs with faint blind perfs between offered as No. 1208b.

REGULAR ISSUE

Andrew Jackson — A646

George Washington — A650

John J. Pershing — A651

Designed by William K. Schrage.

ROTARY PRESS PRINTING
E.E. Plates of 400 subjects in four panes of 100.

1961-66 *Perf. 11x10½*
1209 A646 1c **green,** *Mar. 22, 1963* .30 .25
P# block of 4 1.00 —
Pair with full vert. gutter btwn. —
a. Tagged, *July 6, 1966* .30 .25
P# block of 4 .50 —
1213 A650 5c **dark blue gray,** *Nov. 23, 1962* .30 .25
P# block of 4 1.00 —
Pair with full vert. gutter btwn. *250.00*
Pair with full horiz. gutter btwn. *425.00*
a. Booklet pane of 5 + label 2.00 *2.00*
b. Tagged, *Oct. 28, 1963* .50 .25
P# block of 4 4.50 —
c. As "a," tagged, *Oct. 28, 1963* 2.00 *1.50*
d. Horiz. pair, imperf. between, in #1213a with foldover or miscut *1,750.*

Counterfeits exist of No. 1213. See the Postal Counterfeits section of this catalog.

1214 A651 8c **brown,** *Nov. 17, 1961* .30 .25
P# block of 4 1.00

Bureau Precancels: 1c, 10 diff., 5c, 18 diff., 8c, 16 diff.

No. 1213d resulted from a paper foldover after perforating and before cutting into panes. At least six individually unique panes exist, including at least one that contains two error pairs. Recent auction prices for panes have ranged between $1,400 and $4,000.

COIL STAMPS
(Rotary Press)

1962-66 *Perf. 10 Vertically*
1225 A646 1c **green,** *May 31, 1963* .40 .25
Pair .80 .25
Joint line pair 2.25 .25
a. Tagged, *July 6, 1966* .40 .25
Joint line pair .90 .25
1229 A650 5c **dark blue gray,** *Nov. 23, 1962* 1.50 .25
Pair 3.00 .25
Joint line pair 4.00 .35
a. Tagged, *Oct. 28, 1963* 2.50 .25
Joint line pair 12.00 .25
b. Imperf., pair *300.00*
Joint line pair *900.00*

Bureau Precancels: 1c, 5 diff., 5c, 14 diff.

See Luminescence note in "Basic Stamp Information" in the introduction.

CAROLINA CHARTER ISSUE

Tercentenary of the Carolina Charter granting to 8 Englishmen lands extending coast-to-coast roughly along the present border of Virginia to the north and Florida to the south. Original charter on display at Raleigh.

First Page of Carolina Charter A662

Designed by Robert L. Miller.

GIORI PRESS PRINTING
Plates of 200 subjects in four panes of 50.

1963, Apr. 6 *Perf. 11*
1230 A662 5c **dark carmine & brown** .30 .25
P# block of 4 1.00 —

FOOD FOR PEACE-FREEDOM FROM HUNGER ISSUE

American "Food for Peace" program and the "Freedom from Hunger" campaign of the FAO.

Wheat — A663

Designed by Stevan Dohanos.

GIORI PRESS PRINTING
Plates of 200 subjects in four panes of 50.

1963, June 4 *Perf. 11*
1231 A663 5c **green, buff & red** .30 .25
P# block of 4 1.00 —

WEST VIRGINIA STATEHOOD, 100th ANNIV.

Map of West Virginia and State Capitol A664

Designed by Dr. Dwight Mutchler.

GIORI PRESS PRINTING
Plates of 200 subjects in four panes of 50.

1963, June 20 *Perf. 11*
1232 A664 5c **green, red & black** .30 .25
P# block of 4 1.00 —

EMANCIPATION PROCLAMATION ISSUE

Centenary of Lincoln's Emancipation Proclamation freeing about 3,000,000 slaves in 10 southern states.

Severed Chain — A665

Designed by Georg Olden.

GIORI PRESS PRINTING
Plates of 200 subjects in four panes of 50.

1963, Aug. 16 *Perf. 11*
1233 A665 5c **dark blue, black & red** .30 .25
P# block of 4 1.00 —

ALLIANCE FOR PROGRESS ISSUE

2nd anniv. of the Alliance for Progress, which aims to stimulate economic growth and raise living standards in Latin America.

Alliance Emblem A666

Designed by William K. Schrage.

GIORI PRESS PRINTING
Plates of 200 subjects in four panes of 50.

1963, Aug. 17 *Perf. 11*
1234 A666 5c **ultramarine & green** .30 .25
P# block of 4 1.00 —
Pair with full vert. gutter between *750.00*

CORDELL HULL ISSUE

Hull (1871-1955), Secretary of State (1933-44).

Cordell Hull — A667

Designed by Robert J. Jones.

ROTARY PRESS PRINTING
E.E. Plates of 200 subjects in four panes of 50.

1963, Oct. 5 *Perf. 10½x11*
1235 A667 5c **blue green** .30 .25
P# block of 4 1.00 —

ELEANOR ROOSEVELT ISSUE

Mrs. Franklin D. Roosevelt (1884-1962).

Eleanor Roosevelt A668

Designed by Robert L. Miller.

ROTARY PRESS PRINTING
E.E. Plates of 200 subjects in four panes of 50.

1963, Oct. 11 *Perf. 11x10½*
1236 A668 5c **bright purple** .30 .25
P# block of 4 1.00 —

SCIENCE ISSUE

Honoring the sciences and in connection with the centenary of the Natl. Academy of Science.

"The Universe" A669

Designed by Antonio Frasconi.

GIORI PRESS PRINTING
Plates of 200 subjects in four panes of 50.

1963, Oct. 14 *Perf. 11*
1237 A669 5c **Prussian blue & black** .30 .25
P# block of 4 1.00 —

CITY MAIL DELIVERY ISSUE

Centenary of free city mail delivery.

Letter Carrier, 1863 — A670

Designed by Norman Rockwell.

GIORI PRESS PRINTING
Plates of 200 subjects in four panes of 50.

1963, Oct. 26 **Tagged** *Perf. 11*
1238 A670 5c **gray, dark blue & red** .30 .25
P# block of 4 1.00 —
a. Tagging omitted 10.00
b. Dark blue missing (PS) —

RED CROSS CENTENARY ISSUE

Cuban Refugees on S.S. Morning Light and Red Cross Flag — A671

Designed by Victor S. McCloskey, Jr.

GIORI PRESS PRINTING
Plates of 200 subjects in four panes of 50.

1963, Oct. 29 *Perf. 11*
1239 A671 5c **bluish black & red** .30 .25
P# block of 4 1.00 —

CHRISTMAS ISSUE

National Christmas Tree and White House — A672

Designed by Lily Spandorf; modified by Norman Todhunter.

GIORI PRESS PRINTING
Plates of 400 subjects in four panes of 100.

1963, Nov. 1 *Perf. 11*
1240 A672 5c **dark blue, bluish black & red** .30 .25
P# block of 4 1.00 —
a. Tagged, *Nov. 2, 1963* .65 .50
P# block of 4 5.00 —
Pair with full horiz. gutter between —
b. Horiz. pair, imperf between *7,500.*
c. Red missing (PS) *500.00*

JOHN JAMES AUDUBON ISSUE

Audubon (1785-1851), ornithologist and artist. The birds pictured are actually Collie's magpie jays. See No. C71.

"Columbia Jays" by Audubon — A673

Designed by Robert L. Miller.

GIORI PRESS PRINTING
Plates of 200 subjects in four panes of 50.

1963, Dec. 7 *Perf. 11*
1241 A673 5c **dark blue & multicolored** .30 .25
P# block of 4 1.00 —

SAM HOUSTON ISSUE

Houston (1793-1863), soldier, president of Texas, US senator.

Sam Houston — A674

Designed by Tom Lea.

ROTARY PRESS PRINTING
E.E. Plates of 200 subjects in four panes of 50.

1964, Jan. 10 *Perf. 10½x11*
1242 A674 5c **black** .30 .25
P# block of 4 1.00 —
Margin block of 4, Mr. Zip and "Use Zip Code" 1.00 —

CHARLES M. RUSSELL ISSUE

Russell (1864-1926), painter. The design is from a painting, Thomas Gilcrease Institute of American History and Art, Tulsa, Okla.

"Jerked Down" — A675

Designed by William K. Schrage.

GIORI PRESS PRINTING
Plates of 200 subjects in four panes of 50.

1964, Mar. 19 *Perf. 11*
1243 A675 5c **multicolored** .30 .25
P# block of 4 1.00 —
Margin block of 4, Mr. Zip and "Use Zip Code" 1.00 —

NEW YORK WORLD'S FAIR ISSUE

New York World's Fair, 1964-65.

Mall with Unisphere and "Rocket Thrower" by Donald De Lue — A676

Designed by Robert J. Jones.

ROTARY PRESS PRINTING
E.E. Plates of 200 subjects in four panes of 50.

1964, Apr. 22 *Perf. 11x10½*
1244 A676 5c **blue green** .30 .25
On cover, Expo. station machine cancel (non-first day) 2.00
On cover, Expo. station handstamp cancel (non-first day) 10.00
P# block of 4 1.00 —
Margin block of 4, Mr. Zip and "Use Zip Code" 1.00 —
a. All color omitted —

On No. 1244a, a clear albino impression of the design is present.

JOHN MUIR ISSUE

Muir (1838-1914), naturalist and conservationist.

John Muir and Redwood Forest — A677

Designed by Rudolph Wendelin.

GIORI PRESS PRINTING
Plates of 200 subjects in four panes of 50.

1964, Apr. 29 *Perf. 11*
1245 A677 5c **brown, green, yellow green & olive** .30 .25
P# block of 4 1.00 —

KENNEDY MEMORIAL ISSUE

President John Fitzgerald Kennedy, (1917-1963).

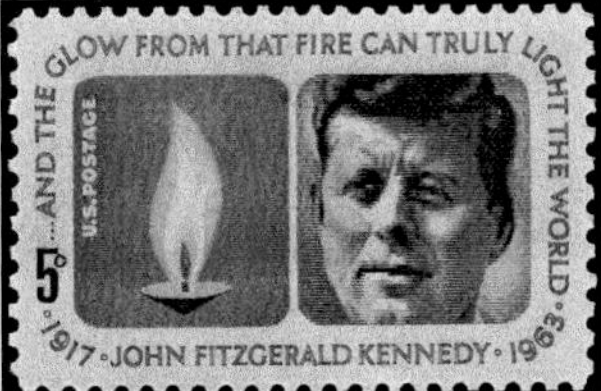

John F. Kennedy and Eternal Flame — A678

Designed by Raymond Loewy/William Snaith, Inc.

Photograph by William S. Murphy.

ROTARY PRESS PRINTING

E.E. Plates of 200 subjects in four panes of 50.

1964, May 29 *Perf. 11x10½*

1246 A678 5c **blue gray** .30 .25
P# block of 4 1.00 —

NEW JERSEY TERCENTENARY ISSUE

300th anniv. of English colonization of New Jersey. The design is from a mural by Howard Pyle in the Essex County Courthouse, Newark, N.J.

Philip Carteret Landing at Elizabethtown, and Map of New Jersey — A679

Designed by Douglas Allen.

ROTARY PRESS PRINTING

E.E. Plates of 200 subjects in four panes of 50.

1964, June 15 *Perf. 10½x11*

1247 A679 5c **brt ultramarine** .30 .25
P# block of 4 1.00 —
Margin block of 4, Mr. Zip and "Use Zip Code" 1.00 —

NEVADA STATEHOOD, 100th ANNIV.

Virginia City and Map of Nevada A680

Designed by William K. Schrage.

GIORI PRESS PRINTING

Plates of 200 subjects in four panes of 50.

1964, July 22 *Perf. 11*

1248 A680 5c **red, yellow & blue** .30 .25
P# block of 4 1.00 —
Margin block of 4, Mr. Zip and "Use Zip Code" 1.00 —

REGISTER AND VOTE ISSUE

Campaign to draw more voters to the polls.

Flag — A681

Designed by Victor S. McCloskey, Jr.

GIORI PRESS PRINTING

Plates of 200 subjects in four panes of 50.

1964, Aug. 1 *Perf. 11*

1249 A681 5c **dark blue & red** .30 .25
P# block of 4 1.00 —
Margin block of 4, Mr. Zip and "Use Zip Code" 1.00 —

SHAKESPEARE ISSUE

William Shakespeare (1564-1616).

William Shakespeare — A682

Designed by Douglas Gorsline.

ROTARY PRESS PRINTING

E.E. Plates of 200 subjects in four panes of 50.

1964, Aug. 14 *Perf. 10½x11*

1250 A682 5c **black brown,** *tan* .30 .25
P# block of 4 1.00 —
Margin block of 4, Mr. Zip and "Use Zip Code" 1.00 —

DOCTORS MAYO ISSUE

Dr. William James Mayo (1861-1939) and his brother, Dr. Charles Horace Mayo (1865-1939), surgeons who founded the Mayo Foundation for Medical Education and Research in affiliation with the Univ. of Minnesota at Rochester. Heads on stamp are from a sculpture by James Earle Fraser.

Drs. William and Charles Mayo — A683

ROTARY PRESS PRINTING

E.E. Plates of 200 subjects in four panes of 50.

1964, Sept. 11 *Perf. 10½x11*

1251 A683 5c **green** .30 .25
P# block of 4 1.00 —
Margin block of 4, Mr. Zip and "Use Zip Code" 1.00 —

AMERICAN MUSIC ISSUE

50th anniv. of the founding of the American Society of Composers, Authors and Publishers (ASCAP).

Lute, Horn, Laurel, Oak and Music Score — A684

Designed by Bradbury Thompson.

GIORI PRESS PRINTING

Plates of 200 subjects in four panes of 50.

1964, Oct. 15 *Perf. 11*

Gray Paper with Blue Threads

1252 A684 5c **red, black & blue** .30 .25
P# block of 4 1.00 —
Margin block of 4, Mr. Zip and "Use Zip Code" 1.00 —
a. Blue omitted *450.00*
b. Blue missing (PS) *500.00*

Beware of examples offered as No. 1252a which have traces of blue.

HOMEMAKERS ISSUE

Honoring American women as homemakers and for the 50th anniv. of the passage of the Smith-Lever Act. By providing economic experts under an extension service of the U.S. Dept. of Agriculture, this legislation helped to improve homelife.

Farm Scene Sampler A685

Designed by Norman Todhunter.

Plates of 200 subjects in four panes of 50.

Engraved (Giori Press); Background Lithographed

1964, Oct. 26 *Perf. 11*

1253 A685 5c **multicolored** .30 .25
P# block of 4 1.00 —
Margin block of 4, Mr. Zip and "Use Zip Code" 1.00 —

CHRISTMAS ISSUE

Holly — A686

Mistletoe — A687

Poinsettia — A688

Sprig of Conifer — A689

Designed by Thomas F. Naegele.

GIORI PRESS PRINTING

Plates of 400 subjects in four panes of 100.

Panes contain 25 subjects each of Nos. 1254-1257

1964, Nov. 9 *Perf. 11*

1254 A686 5c **green, carmine & black** .30 .25
a. Tagged, *Nov. 10* .75 .50
b. Printed on gummed side *1,850.*
c. All color missing (FO) 2,000.
1255 A687 5c **carmine, green & black** .30 .25
a. Tagged, *Nov. 10* .75 .50
1256 A688 5c **carmine, green & black** .30 .25
a. Tagged, *Nov. 10* .75 .50
1257 A689 5c **black, green & carmine** .30 .25
a. Tagged, *Nov. 10* .75 .50
b. Block of 4, #1254-1257 1.00 1.00
P# block of 4 1.00 —
Margin block of 4, Zip and "Use Zip Code" 1.00 —
c. Block of 4, tagged 3.00 2.25
P# block of 4 6.00 —
Zip block of 4 3.25 —

No. 1254b resulted from a paper foldover before printing and perforating.

No. 1254c is unique and is in a block of four with the other three stamps missing parts of the designs.

VERRAZANO-NARROWS BRIDGE ISSUE

Opening of the Verrazano-Narrows Bridge connecting Staten Island and Brooklyn.

Verrazano-Narrows Bridge and Map of New York Bay — A690

ROTARY PRESS PRINTING
E.E. Plates of 200 subjects in four panes of 50.

1964, Nov. 21 *Perf. 10½x11*

1258 A690 5c **blue green**	.30	.25
P# block of 4	1.00	—
Margin block of 4, Mr. Zip and "Use Zip Code"	1.00	—

FINE ARTS ISSUE

Abstract Design by Stuart Davis — A691

GIORI PRESS PRINTING
Plates of 200 subjects in four panes of 50.

1964, Dec. 2 *Perf. 11*

1259 A691 5c **ultra., black & dull red**	.30	.25
P# block of 4, 2#	1.00	—
Margin block of 4, Mr. Zip and "Use Zip Code"	1.00	—

AMATEUR RADIO ISSUE

Issued to honor the radio amateurs on the 50th anniversary of the American Radio Relay League.

Radio Waves and Dial — A692

Designed by Emil J. Willett.

ROTARY PRESS PRINTING
E.E. Plates of 200 subjects in four panes of 50.

1964, Dec. 15 *Perf. 10½x11*

1260 A692 5c **red lilac**	.30	.25
P# block of 4	1.00	—
Margin block of 4, Mr. Zip and "Use Zip Code"	1.00	—

BATTLE OF NEW ORLEANS ISSUE

Battle of New Orleans, Chalmette Plantation, Jan. 8-18, 1815, established 150 years of peace and friendship between the US and Great Britain.

General Andrew Jackson and Sesquicentennial Medal — A693

Designed by Robert J. Jones.

GIORI PRESS PRINTING
Plates of 200 subjects in four panes of 50.

1965, Jan. 8 *Perf. 11*

1261 A693 5c **deep carmine, violet blue & gray**	.30	.25
P# block of 4	1.00	—
Margin block of 4, Mr. Zip and "Use Zip Code"	1.00	—

PHYSICAL FITNESS-SOKOL ISSUE

Publicizing the importance of physical fitness and for the centenary of the founding of the Sokol (athletic) organization in America.

Discus Thrower — A694

Designed by Norman Todhunter.

GIORI PRESS PRINTING
Plates of 200 subjects in four panes of 50.

1965, Feb. 15 *Perf. 11*

1262 A694 5c **maroon & black**	.30	.25
P# block of 4	1.00	—
Margin block of 4, Mr. Zip and "Use Zip Code"	1.00	—

CRUSADE AGAINST CANCER ISSUE

Issued to publicize the "Crusade Against Cancer" and to stress the importance of early diagnosis.

Microscope and Stethoscope — A695

Designed by Stevan Dohanos.

GIORI PRESS PRINTING
Plates of 200 subjects in four panes of 50.

1965, Apr. 1 *Perf. 11*

1263 A695 5c **black, purple & red orange**	.30	.25
P# block of 4, 2#	1.00	—
Margin block of 4, Mr. Zip and "Use Zip Code"	1.00	—

CHURCHILL MEMORIAL ISSUE

Sir Winston Spencer Churchill (1874-1965), British statesman and World War II leader.

Winston Churchill — A696

Designed by Richard Hurd.

ROTARY PRESS PRINTING
E.E. Plates of 200 subjects in four panes of 50.

1965, May 13 *Perf. 10½x11*

1264 A696 5c **black**	.30	.25
P# block of 4	1.00	—
Margin block of 4, Mr. Zip and "Use Zip Code"	1.00	—

MAGNA CARTA ISSUE

750th anniversary of the Magna Carta, the basis of English and American common law.

Procession of Barons and King John's Crown — A697

Designed by Brook Temple.

GIORI PRESS PRINTING
Plates of 200 subjects in four panes of 50.

1965, June 15 *Perf. 11*

1265 A697 5c **black, yellow ocher & red lilac**	.30	.25
P# block of 4, 2#	1.00	—
Margin block of 4, Mr. Zip and "Use Zip Code"	1.00	—
Corner block of 4, black # omitted	—	

INTERNATIONAL COOPERATION YEAR

ICY, 1965, and 20th anniv. of the UN.

International Cooperation Year Emblem A698

Designed by Herbert M. Sanborn and Olav S. Mathiesen.

GIORI PRESS PRINTING
Plates of 200 subjects in four panes of 50.

1965, June 26 *Perf. 11*

1266 A698 5c **dull blue & black**	.30	.25
P# block of 4	1.00	—
Margin block of 4, Mr. Zip and "Use Zip Code"	1.00	—

SALVATION ARMY ISSUE

Centenary of the founding of the Salvation Army by William Booth in London.

A699

Designed by Sam Marsh.

GIORI PRESS PRINTING
Plates of 200 subjects in four panes of 50.

1965, July 2 *Perf. 11*

1267 A699 5c **red, black & dark blue**	.30	.25
P# block of 4	1.00	—
Margin block of 4, Mr. Zip and "Use Zip Code"	1.00	—

DANTE ISSUE

Dante Alighieri (1265-1321), Italian poet.

Dante after a 16th Century Painting — A700

Designed by Douglas Gorsline.

ROTARY PRESS PRINTING

E.E. Plates of 200 subjects in four panes of 50.

1965, July 17 ***Perf. 10½x11***

1268 A700 5c **maroon,** *tan* .30 .25
P# block of 4 1.00 —
Margin block of 4, Mr. Zip and "Use Zip Code" 1.00 —

HERBERT HOOVER ISSUE

President Herbert Clark Hoover, (1874-1964).

Herbert Hoover — A701

Designed by Norman Todhunter; photograph by Fabian Bachrach, Sr.

ROTARY PRESS PRINTING

E.E. Plates of 200 subjects in four panes of 50.

1965, Aug. 10 ***Perf. 10½x11***

1269 A701 5c **rose red** .30 .25
P# block of 4 1.00 —
Margin block of 4, Mr. Zip and "Use Zip Code" 1.00 —

ROBERT FULTON ISSUE

Fulton (1765-1815), inventor of the 1st commercial steamship.

Robert Fulton and the Clermont A702

Designed by John Maass; bust by Jean Antoine Houdon.

GIORI PRESS PRINTING

Plates of 200 subjects in four panes of 50.

1965, Aug. 19 ***Perf. 11***

1270 A702 5c **black & blue** .30 .25
P# block of 4 1.00 —
Margin block of 4, Mr. Zip and "Use Zip Code" 1.00 —

FLORIDA SETTLEMENT ISSUE

400th anniv. of the settlement of Florida, and the 1st permanent European settlement in the continental US, St. Augustine, Fla.

Spanish Explorer, Royal Flag of Spain and Ships — A703

Designed by Brook Temple.

GIORI PRESS PRINTING

Plates of 200 subjects with four panes of 50.

1965, Aug. 28 ***Perf. 11***

1271 A703 5c **red, yellow & black** .30 .25
P# block of 4, 3# 1.00 —
Margin block of 4, Mr. Zip and "Use Zip Code" 1.00 —
a. Yellow omitted *200.00*

See Spain No. 1312.

TRAFFIC SAFETY ISSUE

Issued to publicize traffic safety and the prevention of traffic accidents.

Traffic Signal — A704

Designed by Richard F. Hurd.

GIORI PRESS PRINTING

Plates of 200 subjects in four panes of 50.

1965, Sept. 3 ***Perf. 11***

1272 A704 5c **emerald, black & red** .30 .25
P# block of 4, 2# 1.00 —
Margin block of 4, Mr. Zip and "Use Zip Code" 1.00 —

JOHN SINGLETON COPLEY ISSUE

Copley (1738-1815), painter. The portrait of the artist's daughter is from the oil painting "The Copley Family," which hangs in the National Gallery of Art, Washington, D.C.

Elizabeth Clarke Copley — A705

Designed by John Carter Brown.

GIORI PRESS PRINTING

Plates of 200 subjects in four panes of 50.

1965, Sept. 17 ***Perf. 11***

1273 A705 5c **black, brown & olive** .30 .25
P# block of 4 1.00 —
Margin block of 4, Mr. Zip and "Use Zip Code" 1.00 —

INTERNATIONAL TELECOMMUNICATION UNION, 100th ANNIV.

Galt Projection World Map and Radio Sine Wave — A706

Designed by Thomas F. Naegele.

GIORI PRESS PRINTING

Plates of 200 subjects with four panes of 50.

1965, Oct. 6 ***Perf. 11***

1274 A706 11c **black, carmine & bister** .35 .25
P# block of 4, 2# 1.60 —
Margin block of 4, Mr. Zip and "Use Zip Code" 1.50 —

ADLAI STEVENSON ISSUE

Adlai Ewing Stevenson (1900-65), governor of Illinois, US ambassador to the UN.

Adlai E. Stevenson — A707

Designed by George Samerjan; photograph by Philippe Halsman.

LITHOGRAPHED, ENGRAVED (Giori)

Plates of 200 subjects in four panes of 50.

1965, Oct. 23 ***Perf. 11***

1275 A707 5c **pale blue, black, carmine & violet blue** .30 .25
P# block of 4 1.10 —

CHRISTMAS ISSUE

Angel with Trumpet, 1840 Weather Vane — A708

Designed by Robert Jones.

After a watercolor by Lucille Gloria Chabot of the 1840 weather vane from the People's Methodist Church, Newburyport, Mass.

GIORI PRESS PRINTING

Plates of 400 subjects in four panes of 100.

1965, Nov. 2 ***Perf. 11***

1276 A708 5c **carmine, dark olive green & bister** .30 .25
P# block of 4 1.00 —
Margin block of 4, Mr. Zip and "Use Zip Code" 1.00 —
Pair with full vert. gutter btwn. *400.00*
a. Tagged, *Nov. 15* .75 .25
P# block of 4 5.50 —
Zip block of 4 3.50 —

PROMINENT AMERICANS ISSUE

Thomas Jefferson — A710

Albert Gallatin — A711

Frank Lloyd Wright and Guggenheim Museum, New York — A712

Francis Parkman — A713

Abraham Lincoln — A714

George Washington — A715

George Washington (redrawn) — A715a

Franklin D. Roosevelt — A716

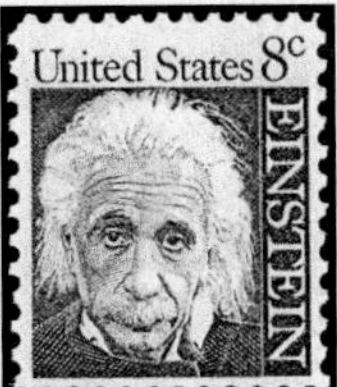

Albert Einstein — A717

Andrew Jackson — A718

Henry Ford and 1909 Model T — A718a

John F. Kennedy — A719

Oliver Wendell Holmes — A720

Type III — A720a

George Catlett Marshall — A721

Frederick Douglass — A722

John Dewey — A723

Thomas Paine — A724

Lucy Stone — A725

Eugene O'Neill — A726

John Bassett Moore — A727

Designers: 1c, Robert Geissmann, after portrait by Rembrandt Peale. 1¼c, Robert Gallatin. 2c, Patricia Amarantides; photograph by Blackstone-Shelburne. 3c, Bill Hyde. 4c, Bill Hyde; photograph by Mathew Brady. 5c, Bill Hyde, after portrait by Rembrandt Peale. 5c, No. 1283B, Redrawn by Stevan Dohanos. 6c, 30c, Richard L. Clark. 8c, Frank Sebastiano; photograph by Philippe Halsman. 10c, Lester Beall. 12c, Norman Todhunter. 13c, Stevan Dohanos; photograph by Jacques Lowe. 15c, Richard F. Hurd. 20c, Robert Geissmann. 25c, Walter DuBois Richards. 40c, Robert Geissmann, after portrait by John Wesley Jarvis. 50c, Mark English. $1, Norman Todhunter. $5, Tom Laufer.

ROTARY PRESS PRINTING

E.E. Plates of 400 subjects in four panes of 100

1965-78 ***Perf. 11x10½, 10½x11***

1278 A710 1c **green,** tagged, shiny gum, *Jan. 12, 1968* .30 .25
On cover 4.00
P# block of 4 .50 —
Margin block of 4, "Use Zip Codes" .50 —
Dull gum (from bklt. pane) .30
a. Booklet pane of 8, shiny gum, *Jan. 12, 1968* 1.00 .75
Dull gum 1.75
b. Bklt. pane of 4+2 labels, *May 10, 1971* .75 .60
c. Untagged (Bureau precanceled) 6.25 1.25
P# block of 4 175.00
Margin block of 4, "Use Zip Codes" 30.00
d. Tagging omitted (not Bureau precanceled), shiny gum 4.00 —
dull gum —
e. As "a," dull gum, tagging omitted *85.00*

1279 A711 1¼c **light green,** *Jan. 30, 1967* .30 .25
On cover 6.00
Single franking on third-class nonprofit cover *125.00*
P# block of 4 3.50 —

1280 A712 2c **dark blue gray,** tagged, shiny gum, *June 8, 1966* .30 .25
On cover 4.00
Single franking on third-class nonprofit cover 10.00
Single franking on certificate of mailing *100.00*
P# block of 4 .50 —
Margin block of 4, "Use Zip Codes" .50 —
Pair with full vert. gutter between —
Pair with full horiz. gutter between —
Dull gum (from bklt. pane) .30
a. Bklt. pane of 5 + label, *Jan. 8, 1968* 1.25 .80
b. Untagged (Bureau precanceled) 2.00 .40
P# block of 4 27.50
Margin block of 4, "Use Zip Codes" 7.50
c. Bklt. pane of 6, shiny gum, *May 7, 1971* 1.00 .75
Dull gum 1.10
d. Tagging omitted (not Bureau precanceled) 4.00 —

1281 A713 3c **violet,** tagged, *Sept. 16, 1967* .30 .25
On cover 4.00
Single franking on third-class nonprofit cover 15.00
P# block of 4 .50 —
Margin block of 4, "Use Zip Codes" .50 —
Pair with full horiz. gutter between —
a. Untagged (Bureau precanceled) 3.00 .75
P# block of 4 —
Margin block of 4, "Use Zip Codes" 30.00
b. Tagging omitted (not Bureau precanceled) 6.00 —

1282 A714 4c **black,** *Nov. 19, 1965* .30 .25
On cover 4.00
Single franking on third-class cover 5.00
Single franking on third-class bulk-rate cover 30.00
P# block of 4 1.00 —
a. Tagged, *Dec. 1, 1965* .30 .25
P# block of 4 1.00 —
Pair with full horiz. gutter between *800.00*

1283 A715 5c **blue,** *Feb. 22, 1966* .30 .25
On cover 2.00
Single franking on int'l surface printed-matter cover 15.00
Single franking on certificate of mailing 20.00
P# block of 4 1.00 —
a. Tagged, *Feb. 23, 1966* .30 .25
P# block of 4 1.00 —
Pair with full vert. gutter between *350.00*

1283B A715a 5c **blue,** tagged, shiny gum, *Nov. 17, 1967* .30 .25
On cover 2.00
Single franking on third-class bulk-rate cover 10.00
P# block of 4 1.00 —
Pair with full horiz. gutter between *175.00*
Dull gum .30
P# block of 4 1.40
d. Untagged (Bureau precanceled) 12.50 1.00
P# block of 4 —
e. Tagging omitted (not Bureau precanceled), shiny gum 6.00
Dull gum 5.50

No. 1283B is redrawn; highlights, shadows softened.

1284 A716 6c **gray brown,** *Jan. 29, 1966* .30 .25
On cover 2.00
Single franking on third-class cover 10.00
P# block of 4 1.00 —
Margin block of 4, "Use Zip Codes" (Bureau precanceled) 3.00
Pair with full horiz. gutter between *150.00*
Pair with full vert. gutter between *150.00*
a. Tagged, *Dec. 29, 1966* .30 .25
P# block of 4 1.00 —
Margin block of 4, "Use Zip Codes" 1.00 —
b. Booklet pane of 8, *Dec. 28, 1967* 1.50 1.00
c. Bklt. pane of 5+ label, *Jan. 9, 1968* 1.40 1.00
d. Horiz. pair, imperf. between *2,250.*
e. As "b," tagging omitted *90.00* —

For untagged sheet stamps, "Use Zip Codes" and "Mail Early in the Day" marginal markings are found only on panes with Bureau precancels.

Counterfeits exist of No. 1284. See the Postal Counterfeits section of this catalog.

1285 A717 8c **violet,** *Mar. 14, 1966* .30 .25
On cover 4.00
Single franking on first-class cover 4.00
Single franking on third-class cover 15.00
Single franking on international surface-rate postcard —
P# block of 4 1.00 —
a. Tagged, *July 6, 1966* .30 .25
P# block of 4 1.10 —
Margin block of 4, "Use Zip Codes" 1.00 —

1286 A718 10c **lilac,** tagged, *Mar. 15, 1967* .30 .25
On cover 4.00
Single franking on int'l surface postcard 10.00
P# block of 4 1.10 —
Margin block of 4, "Use Zip Codes" 1.00 —
b. Untagged (Bureau precanceled) 50.00 1.75
P# block of 4 —
Margin block of 4, "Use Zip Codes" 275.00
e. Tagging omitted (not Bureau precanceled) 10.00

1286A 718a 12c **black,** tagged, *July 30, 1968* .30 .25
On cover 8.00
Single franking on domestic surface postcard 8.00
Single franking on int'l surface postcard 15.00
P# block of 4 1.30
Margin block of 4, "Use Zip Codes" 1.00 —
c. Untagged (Bureau precanceled) 4.75 1.00
P# block of 4 145.00

Margin block of 4, "Use Zip Codes" 27.50
d. Tagging omitted (not Bureau precanceled) 35.00

1287 A719 13c **brown,** tagged, *May 29, 1967* .30 .25
On cover 8.00
Single franking on int'l airmail postcard 10.00
Single franking on first-class airmail cover 15.00
Single franking on int'l surface cover 15.00
P# block of 4 1.50 —
Pair with full horiz. gutter between *500.00*
a. Untagged (Bureau precanceled) 6.00 1.00
P# block of 4 100.00
b. Tagging omitted (not Bureau precanceled) *15.00* —

Counterfeits exist of No. 1287. See the Postal Counterfeits section of this catalog.

Type I

Type II

Type III

Types of 15c:
I. Necktie barely touches coat at bottom; crosshatching of tie strong and complete. Flag of "5" is true horizontal. Crosshatching of "15" is colorless when visible.
II. Necktie does not touch coat at bottom; LL to UR crosshatching lines strong, UL to LR lines very faint. Flag of "5" slants down slightly at right. Crosshatching of "15" is colored and visible when magnified.
III. Used only for No. 1288B; smaller in overall size and "15¢" is ¾mm closer to head.

1288 A720 15c **magenta,** type I, tagged, *Mar. 8, 1968* .30 .25
On cover 4.00
Single franking on first-class cover 4.00
Single franking on certificate of mailing 15.00
P# block of 4 1.25 —
Margin block of 4, "Use Zip Codes" 1.25 —
Pair with full horiz. gutter between *200.00*
Pair with full vert. gutter between *325.00*
a. Untagged (Bureau precanceled) .75 .75
P# block of 4 29.50
Margin block of 4, "Use Zip Codes" 7.50
d. Type II .55 .25
On cover 4.00
P# block of 4 8.00 —
Zip block of 4 3.50 —
Pair with full vert. gutter between —
f. As "d," tagging omitted (not Bureau precanceled) 7.50 —
h. As No. 1288, tagging omitted (not Bureau precanceled) 40.00
Imperforates exist from printer's waste.

Counterfeits exist of No. 1288. See the Postal Counterfeits section of this catalog.
Earliest documented use: July 16, 1979 (No. 1288d).
Values for No. 1288a are for the bars-only precancel. Also exists with city precancels, and worth more thus.
The existence of the No. 1288d pair with vert. gutter between has been questioned by specialists. The editors would like to see evidence of its existence.

1288B A720a 15c **magenta,** type III, tagged, perf. 10 (from blkt. pane) .35 .25
On cover 6.00
c. Booklet pane of 8, *June 14, 1978* 2.80 1.75
e. As "c," vert. imperf. between *1,500.*
g. Tagging omitted *10.00* —
i. As "c," tagging omitted *80.00* *50.00*

No. 1288B issued in booklets only. All stamps have one or two straight edges. Plates made from redrawn die.

1289 A721 20c **deep olive,** shiny gum, *Oct. 24, 1967* .40 .25
On cover 2.00
Single franking on int'l airmail cover to Europe 15.00
Single franking on domestic airmail cover 10.00
Single franking on int'l surface cover 20.00
P# block of 4 1.75 —
Margin block of 4, "Use Zip Codes" 1.65 —
a. Tagged, shiny gum, *Apr. 3, 1973* .40 .25
P# block of 4 1.75 —
Zip block of 4 1.65 —
Dull gum .45
P# block of 4 2.10
Zip block of 4 1.90
b. 20c **black olive,** tagged, dull gum .50 .25
P# block of 4 3.50 —
Zip block of 4 2.25 —
c. As "a," double impression *500.00*
d. As "b," tagging omitted —

1290 A722 25c **rose lake,** *Feb. 14, 1967* .55 .25
On cover 2.00
Single franking on int'l airmail cover to Asia 15.00
P# block of 4 2.25 —
Margin block of 4, "Use Zip Codes" 2.20 —
a. Tagged, shiny gum, *Apr. 3, 1973* .45 .25
P# block of 4 2.00 —
Zip block of 4 1.90 —
Dull gum .45
P# block of 4 2.00
Zip block of 4 1.90
b. 25c **magenta** *25.00* —
On cover —
P# block of 4 *175.00*

Shades of No. 1290 rose lake exist that tend toward magenta, but are not. Competent identification is important for No. 1290b.

1291 A723 30c **red lilac,** *Oct. 21, 1968* .65 .25
On cover 10.00
Single franking on double-weight airmail cover to Central/South America 15.00
P# block of 4 2.90 —
Margin block of 4, "Use Zip Codes" 2.70 —
a. Tagged, *Apr. 3, 1973* .50 .25
P# block of 4 2.25 —
Zip block of 4 2.10 —

1292 A724 40c **blue black,** shiny gum, *Jan. 29, 1968* .80 .25
On cover 6.00
Single franking on double-weight airmail cover to Europe 10.00
P# block of 4 3.25 —
Margin block of 4, "Use Zip Codes" 3.25 —
Pair with full vert. gutter btwn. —
a. Tagged, shiny gum, *Apr. 3, 1973* .75 .25
P# block of 4 3.75 —
Zip block of 4 3.00 —
Dull gum .75
P# block of 4 3.00
Zip block of 4 3.00
b. As "a" with dull gum, tagging omitted —

1293 A725 50c **rose magenta,** *Aug. 13, 1968* 1.00 .25
On cover 4.00
Single franking on double-weight airmail cover to Asia 20.00
P# block of 4 4.25 —
Margin block of 4, "Use Zip Codes" 4.00 —
Pair with full vert. gutter btwn. —
a. Tagged, *Apr. 3, 1973* .80 .25
P# block of 4 3.50 —
Zip block of 4 3.25 —
Pair with full horiz. gutter btwn. —

Counterfeits exist of No. 1293. See the Postal Counterfeits section of this catalog.

1294 A726 $1 **dull purple,** *Oct. 16, 1967* 2.25 .25
On cover 5.00
Single franking on registered airmail cover 10.00
Single franking on quadruple-weight int'l airmail cover to Asia 20.00
P# block of 4 10.00 —
Margin block of 4, "Use Zip Codes" 9.25 —
a. Tagged, *Apr. 3, 1973* 1.75 .25
P# block of 4 7.25 —
Zip block of 4 7.00 —
b. **black violet** 200.00 *350.00*
P# block of 4 *1,250.*
Zip block of 4 *500.00*

1295 A727 $5 **gray black,** *Dec. 3, 1966* 10.00 2.25
On cover 20.00
Single franking on registered first-class cover *500.00*
Single franking on fourth-class cover *750.00*
P# block of 4 42.50 —
a. Tagged, *Apr. 3, 1973* 8.50 2.00
P# block of 4 35.00 —
Nos. 1278-1295 (21) 19.90 7.25
Nos. 1278-1288, 1289-1295, P# blocks of 4 (20) 78.65

Counterfeits exist of No. 1295. See the Postal Counterfeits section of this catalog.

Bureau Precancels: 1c, 19 diff., 1¼c, 14 diff., 2c, 41 diff., 3c, 11 diff., 4c, 49 diff., No. 1283, 7 diff., No. 1283B, 29 diff., 6c, 35 diff., 8c, 18 diff., 10c, 12 diff., 12c, 3 diff., 13c, 3 diff., No. 1288a, 9 diff., 20c, 14 diff., 25c, 9 diff., 30c, 14 diff., 40c, 7 diff., 50c, 14 diff., $1, 8 diff.
See Luminescence note in the catalogue introduction.

COIL STAMPS

1967-75 **Tagged** ***Perf. 10 Horizontally***

1297 A713 3c **violet,** shiny gum, *Nov. 4, 1975* .30 .25
On cover 3.00
Pair .50 .50
Joint line pair .60 .60
Dull gum .75
Joint line pair 3.00
a. Imperf., pair, shiny gum 22.50
Imperf., joint line pair 45.00
Imperf, pair, dull gum 22.50
Imperf, joint line pair 45.00
b. Untagged (Bureau precanceled), shiny gum .40 .25
Single franking on third-class nonprofit cover 5.00
Pair .80 .50
Joint line pair 62.50 3.75
Dull gum .30
Pair .50
Joint line pair 3.75
c. As "b," imperf. pair 8.00 —
Joint line pair 20.00

No. 1297c is precanceled "Nonprofit Org. / CAR RT SORT."

1298 A716 6c **gray brown,** *Dec. 28, 1967* .30 .25
On cover 4.00
Single franking on third-class cover 10.00
Pair .50 .50
Joint line pair 1.10 .60
a. Imperf., pair *1,500.*
Imperf., joint line pair *4,500.*
b. Tagging omitted 3.50

Bureau Precancels: 3c, 9 diff.

Franklin D. Roosevelt — A727a

Revised design by Robert J. Jones and Howard C. Mildner.

COIL STAMPS

1966-81 **Tagged** ***Perf. 10 Vertically***

1299 A710 1c **green,** *Jan. 12, 1968* .30 .25
On cover 4.00
Pair .50 .50
Joint line pair .60 .60

a.	Untagged (Bureau precanceled)	8.00	1.75
	Pair	17.50	4.00
	Joint line pair	*290.00*	—
b.	Imperf., pair	*22.50*	—
	Imperf., joint line pair	*50.00*	
c.	Tagging omitted (not Bureau precanceled)	—	
1303	A714 4c **black,** *May 28, 1966*	.30	.25
	On cover		8.00
	Pair	.50	.50
	Joint line pair	.75	.60
a.	Untagged (Bureau precanceled)	8.75	.75
	Pair	19.00	1.75
	Joint line pair	*250.00*	—
b.	Imperf., pair	*400.00*	
	Imperf., joint line pair	*1,300.*	
c.	Tagging omitted (not Bureau precanceled)	*15.00*	—
1304	A715 5c **blue,** shiny gum, *Sept. 8, 1966*	.30	.25
	On cover		3.00
	Pair	.50	.50
	Joint line pair	.75	.60
	Dull gum	.75	
	Joint line pair	5.00	
a.	Untagged (Bureau precanceled)	6.50	.65
	Single franking on third-class bulk rate cover		6.00
	Pair	14.00	1.40
	Joint line pair	*175.00*	—
b.	Imperf., pair	*110.00*	
	Joint line pair	*250.00*	
e.	As "a," imperf., pair	*250.00*	
	Joint line pair	*800.00*	
f.	Tagging omitted (not Bureau precanceled)	—	—

No. 1304b is valued in the grade of fine.

No. 1304e is precanceled Mount Pleasant, Iowa. Also exists from Chicago, Illinois; value $1,500 for pair.

1304C	A715a 5c **blue,** *Jan., 1981*	.30	.25
	On cover		3.00
	Pair	.50	.50
	Joint line pair	1.25	—
d.	Imperf., pair	*375.00*	
	Joint line pair	*675.00*	
1305	A727a 6c **gray brown,** *Feb. 28, 1968*	.30	.25
	On cover		2.00
	Single franking on third-class cover		10.00
	Pair	.50	.50
	Joint line pair	.75	.60
a.	Imperf., pair	55.00	
	Joint line pair	*115.00*	
b.	Untagged (Bureau precanceled)	20.00	1.00
	Pair	42.50	2.25
	Joint line pair	*675.00*	—
k.	Tagging omitted (not Bureau precanceled)	4.00	—
m.	Pair, imperf. between	*250.00*	
	Joint line pair	*500.00*	
1305E	A720 15c **magenta,** type I, shiny gum, *June 14, 1978*	.30	.25
	On cover		2.00
	Pair	.50	.50
	Joint line pair	1.10	.60
	Dull gum	.75	
	Joint line pair	4.50	
f.	Untagged (Bureau precanceled, Chicago, IL)	32.50	—
	Pair	75.00	—
	Joint line pair	*1,100.*	—
g.	Imperf., pair, type I, shiny gum	20.00	
	Joint line pair	50.00	
	Imperf., pair, dull gum	22.50	
	Joint line pair	60.00	
h.	Pair, imperf. between	125.00	
	Joint line pair	*400.00*	
i.	Type II, dull gum	1.50	.25
	On cover		2.00
	Single franking on first-class cover		5.00
	Joint line pair	5.00	—
j.	Type II, dull gum, Imperf., pair	*55.00*	
	Joint line pair	*150.00*	
l.	Tagging omitted		—

Earliest documented use: July 16, 1979 (No. 1305Ei).

1305C	A726 $1 **dull purple,** shiny gum, *Jan. 12, 1973*	3.25	.40
	blackish purple	4.00	.60
	On cover		8.00
	Single franking on first-class insured cover		35.00
	Pair	6.50	.80
	Joint line pair	9.50	1.50
	Dull gum	4.75	
	Pair	9.50	
	Joint line pair	15.00	
d.	Imperf., pair	*1,250.*	
	Joint line pair	*3,000.*	
	Nos. 1297-1305C (9)	5.65	2.40

Bureau Precancels: 1c, 5 diff., 4c, 35 diff., No. 1304a, 45 diff., 6c, 30 diff.

MIGRATORY BIRD TREATY ISSUE

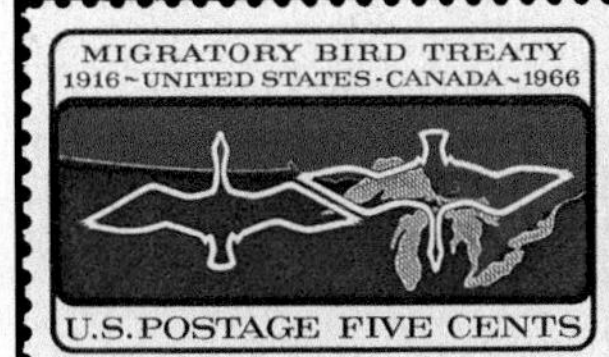

Migratory Birds over Canada-US Border
A728

Designed by Burt E. Pringle.

GIORI PRESS PRINTING

Plates of 200 subjects in four panes of 50.

1966, Mar. 16 ***Perf. 11***

1306	A728 5c **black, crimson & dark blue**	.30	.25
	P# block of 4, 2#	1.00	—
	Margin block of 4, Mr. Zip and "Use Zip Code"	1.00	—

HUMANE TREATMENT OF ANIMALS ISSUE

Issued to promote humane treatment of all animals and for the centenary of the American Society for the Prevention of Cruelty to Animals.

Mongrel
A729

Designed by Norman Todhunter.

LITHOGRAPHED, ENGRAVED (Giori)

Plates of 200 subjects in four panes of 50.

1966, Apr. 9 ***Perf. 11***

1307	A729 5c **orange brown & black**	.30	.25
	P# block of 4	1.00	—
	Margin block of 4, Mr. Zip and "Use Zip Code"	1.00	—

INDIANA STATEHOOD, 150th ANNIV.

Sesquicentennial Seal; Map of Indiana with 19 Stars and old Capitol at Corydon — A730

Designed by Paul A. Wehr.

GIORI PRESS PRINTING

Plates of 200 subjects in four panes of 50.

1966, Apr. 16 ***Perf. 11***

1308	A730 5c **ocher, brown & violet blue**	.30	.25
	P# block of 4, 2#	1.00	—
	Margin block of 4, Mr. Zip and "Use Zip Code"	1.00	—
	Pair with full vert. gutter btwn.	325.00	

AMERICAN CIRCUS ISSUE

Issued to honor the American Circus on the centenary of the birth of John Ringling.

Clown — A731

Designed by Edward Klauck.

GIORI PRESS PRINTING

Plates of 200 subjects in four panes of 50.

1966, May 2 ***Perf. 11***

1309	A731 5c **multicolored**	.30	.25
	P# block of 4, 2#	1.00	—
	Margin block of 4, Mr. Zip and "Use Zip Code"	1.00	—

SIXTH INTERNATIONAL PHILATELIC EXHIBITION ISSUES

Sixth International Philatelic Exhibition (SIPEX), Washington, D.C., May 21-30.

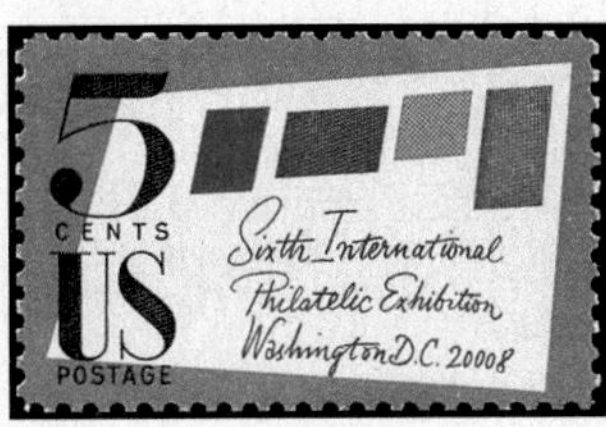

Stamped Cover — A732

Designed by Thomas F. Naegele.

LITHOGRAPHED, ENGRAVED (Giori)

Plates of 200 subjects in four panes of 50.

1966 ***Perf. 11***

1310	A732 5c **multicolored,** *May 21*	.30	.25
	P# block of 4	1.00	—
	Margin block of 4, Mr. Zip and "Use Zip Code"	1.00	—

Souvenir Sheet

A733

Designed by Brook Temple.

Plates of 24 subjects

Imperf

1311	A733 5c **multicolored,** *May 23*	.30	.25

No. 1311 measures 108x74mm. Below the stamp appears a line drawing of the Capitol and Washington Monument. Marginal inscriptions and drawing are green.

BILL OF RIGHTS, 175th ANNIV.

"Freedom" Checking "Tyranny" — A734

Designed by Herbert L. Block (Herblock).

GIORI PRESS PRINTING

Plates of 200 subjects in four panes of 50.

1966, July 1 ***Perf. 11***

1312	A734 5c **carmine, dark & light blue**	.30	.25
	P# block of 4, 2#	1.00	—
	Margin block of 4, Mr. Zip and "Use Zip Code"	1.00	—

POLISH MILLENNIUM ISSUE

Adoption of Christianity in Poland, 1000th anniv.

Polish Eagle and Cross — A735

Designed by Edmund D. Lewandowski.

ROTARY PRESS PRINTING
E.E. Plates of 200 subjects in four panes of 50.

1966, July 30 *Perf. 10½x11*

1313 A735 5c **red** .30 .25
P# block of 4 1.00 —
Margin block of 4, Mr. Zip and "Use Zip Code" 1.00 —

Tagging Extended

During 1966, experimental use of tagged stamps was extended to the Cincinnati Postal Region covering offices in Indiana, Kentucky and Ohio. To supply these offices about 12 percent of the following nine issues (Nos. 1314-1322) were tagged.

NATIONAL PARK SERVICE ISSUE

50th anniv. of the Natl. Park Service of the Interior Dept. The design "Parkscape U.S.A." identifies Natl. Park Service facilities.

National Park Service Emblem A736

Designed by Thomas H. Geismar.

LITHOGRAPHED, ENGRAVED (Giori)
Plates of 200 subjects in four panes of 50.

1966, Aug. 25 *Perf. 11*

1314 A736 5c **yellow, black & green** .30 .25
P# block of 4 1.00 —
Margin block of 4, Mr. Zip and "Use Zip Code" 1.00 —
a. Tagged, *Aug. 26* .35 .35
P# block of 4 2.25 —
Zip block of 4 1.50 —

MARINE CORPS RESERVE ISSUE

US Marine Corps Reserve founding, 50th anniv.

Combat Marine, 1966; Frogman; World War II Flier; World War I "Devil Dog" and Marine, 1775 — A737

Designed by Stella Grafakos.

LITHOGRAPHED, ENGRAVED (Giori)
Plates of 200 subjects in four panes of 50.

1966, Aug. 29 *Perf. 11*

1315 A737 5c **black, bister, red & ultra** .30 .25
P# block of 4 1.00 —
Margin block of 4, Mr. Zip and "Use Zip Code" 1.00 —
a. Tagged .40 .25
P# block of 4 2.25 —
Zip block of 4 1.70 —
b. Black & bister (engraved) missing (EP) *16,000.*

GENERAL FEDERATION OF WOMEN'S CLUBS ISSUE

75 years of service by the General Federation of Women's Clubs.

Women of 1890 and 1966 — A738

Designed by Charles Henry Carter.

GIORI PRESS PRINTING
Plates of 200 subjects in four panes of 50.

1966, Sept. 12 *Perf. 11*

1316 A738 5c **black, pink & blue** .30 .25
P# block of 4, 2# 1.00 —
Margin block of 4, Mr. Zip and "Use Zip Code" 1.00 —
a. Tagged, *Sept. 13* .40 .25
P# block of 4, 2# 2.25 —
Zip block of 4 1.70 —

AMERICAN FOLKLORE ISSUE
Johnny Appleseed

Issued to honor Johnny Appleseed (John Chapman 1774-1845), who wandered over 100,000 square miles planting apple trees, and who gave away and sold seedlings to Midwest pioneers.

Johnny Appleseed — A739

Designed by Robert Bode.

GIORI PRESS PRINTING
Plates of 200 subjects in four panes of 50.

1966, Sept. 24 *Perf. 11*

1317 A739 5c **green, red & black** .30 .25
P# block of 4, 2# 1.00 —
Margin block of 4, Mr. Zip and "Use Zip Code" 1.00 —
Pair with full horiz. gutter between —
a. Tagged, *Sept. 26* .40 .25
P# block of 4, 2# 2.25 —
Zip block of 4 1.70 —

BEAUTIFICATION OF AMERICA ISSUE

Issued to publicize President Johnson's "Plant for a more beautiful America" campaign.

Jefferson Memorial, Tidal Basin and Cherry Blossoms A740

Designed by Miss Gyo Fujikawa.

GIORI PRESS PRINTING
Plates of 200 subjects in four panes of 50.

1966, Oct. 5 *Perf. 11*

1318 A740 5c **emerald, pink & black** v .25
P# block of 4, 2# 1.00 —
Margin block of 4, Mr. Zip and "Use Zip Code" 1.00 —
a. Tagged .40 .25
P# block of 4, 2# 2.25 —
Zip block of 4 1.70 —

Compare with No. 4716c.

GREAT RIVER ROAD ISSUE

Issued to publicize the 5,600-mile Great River Road connecting New Orleans with Kenora, Ontario, and following the Mississippi most of the way.

Map of Central United States with Great River Road — A741

Designed by Herbert Bayer.

LITHOGRAPHED, ENGRAVED (Giori)
Plates of 200 subjects in four panes of 50.

1966, Oct. 21

1319 A741 5c **vermilion, yellow, blue & green** .30 .25
P# block of 4 1.00 —
Margin block of 4, Mr. Zip and "Use Zip Code" 1.00 —
a. Tagged, *Oct. 22* .45 .25
P# block of 4 2.50 —
Zip block of 4 1.90 —

SAVINGS BOND-SERVICEMEN ISSUE

25th anniv. of US Savings Bonds, and honoring American servicemen.

Statue of Liberty and "Old Glory" — A742

Designed by Stevan Dohanos, photo by Bob Noble.

LITHOGRAPHED, ENGRAVED (Giori)
Plates of 200 subjects in four panes of 50.

1966, Oct. 26 *Perf. 11*

1320 A742 5c **red, dark blue, light blue & black** .30 .25
P# block of 4 1.00 —
Margin block of 4, Mr. Zip and "Use Zip Code" 1.00 —
a. Tagged, *Oct. 27* .40 .25
P# block of 4 2.00 —
Zip block of 4 1.70 —
b. Red, dark blue & black missing (EP) *3,750.*
c. Dark blue (engr.) missing (EP) *5,000.*

CHRISTMAS ISSUE

Madonna and Child, by Hans Memling — A743

Designed by Howard C. Mildner.

Modeled after "Madonna and Child with Angels," by the Flemish artist Hans Memling (c.1430-1494), Mellon Collection, National Gallery of Art, Washington, D.C.

LITHOGRAPHED, ENGRAVED (Giori)
Plates of 400 subjects in four panes of 100.

1966, Nov. 1 *Perf. 11*

1321 A743 5c **multicolored** .30 .25
P# block of 4 1.00 —
Margin block of 4, Mr. Zip and "Use Zip Code" 1.00 —
a. Tagged, *Nov. 2* .40 .25
P# block of 4 2.00 —
Zip block of 4 1.70 —

MARY CASSATT ISSUE

Cassatt (1844-1926), painter. The painting "The Boating Party" is in the Natl. Gallery of Art, Washington, D.C.

"The Boating Party" — A744

Designed by Robert J. Jones.

GIORI PRESS PRINTING

Plates of 200 subjects in four panes of 50.

1966, Nov. 17 ***Perf. 11***

1322 A744 5c **multicolored** .30 .25
P# block of 4, 2# 1.00 —
Margin block of 4, Mr. Zip and "Use Zip Code" 1.00 —
a. Tagged .40 .25
P# block of 4, 2# 2.00 —
Zip block of 4 1.70 —

NATIONAL GRANGE ISSUE

Centenary of the founding of the National Grange, American farmers' organization.

Grange Poster, 1870 — A745

Designed by Lee Pavao.

GIORI PRESS PRINTING

Plates of 200 subjects in four panes of 50.

1967, Apr. 17 **Tagged** ***Perf. 11***

1323 A745 5c **orange, yellow, brown, green & black** .30 .25
P# block of 4, 2# 1.00 —
Margin block of 4, Mr. Zip and "Use Zip Code" 1.00 —
a. Tagging omitted *6.00* —

Phosphor Tagging

From No. 1323 onward, all postage issues are tagged, unless otherwise noted.

Inadvertent omissions of tagging occurred on Nos. 1238, 1278, 1281, 1298 and 1305. In addition many tagged issues from 1967 on exist with tagging unintentionally omitted, and these errors are listed herein.

CANADA CENTENARY ISSUE

Centenary of Canada's emergence as a nation.

Canadian Landscape A746

Designed by Ivan Chermayeff.

GIORI PRESS PRINTING

Plates of 200 subjects in four panes of 50.

1967, May 25 **Tagged** ***Perf. 11***

1324 A746 5c **lt. blue, dp. green, ultra, olive & black** .30 .25
On cover, Expo. station ("U.S. Pavilion") machine canc. 1.00
On cover, Expo. station handstamp canc. 2.50
P# block of 4, 2# 1.00 —
Margin block of 4, Mr. Zip and "Use Zip Code" 1.00 —
a. Tagging omitted *7.50* —

ERIE CANAL ISSUE

150th anniversary of the Erie Canal ground-breaking ceremony at Rome, N.Y. The canal links Lake Erie and New York City.

Stern of Early Canal Boat — A747

Designed by George Samerjan.

LITHOGRAPHED, ENGRAVED (Giori)

Plates of 200 subjects in four panes of 50.

1967, July 4 **Tagged** ***Perf. 11***

1325 A747 5c **ultra, grnsh blue, blk & crim** .30 .25
P# block of 4 1.00 —
Margin block of 4, Mr. Zip and "Use Zip Code" 1.00 —
a. Tagging omitted *20.00* —

"SEARCH FOR PEACE" — LIONS ISSUE

Issued to publicize the search for peace. "Search for Peace" was the theme of an essay contest for young men and women sponsored by Lions International on its 50th anniversary.

Peace Dove — A748

Designed by Bradbury Thompson.

GIORI PRESS PRINTING

Plates of 200 subjects in four panes of 50.

1967, July 5 **Tagged** ***Perf. 11***

Gray Paper with Blue Threads

1326 A748 5c **blue, red & black** .30 .25
P# block of 4 1.00 —
Margin block of 4, Mr. Zip and "Use Zip Code" 1.00 —
a. Tagging omitted *10.00* —

HENRY DAVID THOREAU ISSUE

Henry David Thoreau (1817-62), Writer — A749

Designed by Leonard Baskin.

GIORI PRESS PRINTING

Plates of 200 subjects in four panes of 50.

1967, July 12 **Tagged** ***Perf. 11***

1327 A749 5c **carmine, black & blue green** .30 .25
P# block of 4 1.00 —
Margin block of 4, Mr. Zip and "Use Zip Code" 1.00 —
a. Tagging omitted *200.00*
b. Carmine missing (PS) *700.00*

NEBRASKA STATEHOOD, 100th ANNIV.

Hereford Steer and Ear of Corn — A750

Designed by Julian K. Billings.

LITHOGRAPHED, ENGRAVED (Giori)

Plates of 200 subjects in four panes of 50.

1967, July 29 **Tagged** ***Perf. 11***

1328 A750 5c **dark red brown, lemon & yellow** .30 .25
P# block of 4 1.00 —
Margin block of 4, Mr. Zip and "Use Zip Code" 1.00 —
a. Tagging omitted *7.50* —

VOICE OF AMERICA ISSUE

25th anniv. of the radio branch of the United States Information Agency (USIA).

Radio Transmission Tower and Waves — A751

Designed by Georg Olden.

LITHOGRAPHED, ENGRAVED (Giori)

Plates of 200 subjects in four panes of 50.

1967, Aug. 1 **Tagged** ***Perf. 11***

1329 A751 5c **red, blue, black & carmine** .30 .25
P# block of 4 1.00 —
Margin block of 4, Mr. Zip and "Use Zip Code" 1.00 —
a. Tagging omitted *20.00* —

AMERICAN FOLKLORE ISSUE

Davy Crockett (1786-1836), frontiersman, hunter, and congressman from Tennessee who died at the Alamo.

Davy Crockett and Scrub Pine — A752

Designed by Robert Bode.

LITHOGRAPHED, ENGRAVED (Giori)

Plates of 200 subjects in four panes of 50.

1967, Aug. 17 **Tagged** ***Perf. 11***

1330 A752 5c **green, black, & yellow** .30 .25
P# block of 4 1.00 —
Margin block of 4, Mr. Zip and "Use Zip Code" 1.00 —
a. Vertical pair, imperf. between *7,500.*
b. Green (engr.) missing (FO) —
c. Black & green (engr.) missing (FO) —
e. Tagging omitted *10.00* —

A foldover on a pane of No. 1330 resulted in one example each of Nos. 1330b-1330c. Part of the colors appear on the back of the selvage and one freak stamp. An engraved black-and-green-only impression appears on the gummed side of one almost-complete "stamp."

ACCOMPLISHMENTS IN SPACE ISSUE

US accomplishments in space. Printed with continuous design in horizontal rows of 5. In the left panes the astronaut stamp is 1st, 3rd and 5th, the spaceship 2nd and 4th. This arrangement is reversed in the right panes.

Space-Walking Astronaut — A753

Gemini 4 Capsule — A754

Designed by Paul Calle.

LITHOGRAPHED, ENGRAVED (Giori)
Plates of 200 subjects in four panes of 50.

1967, Sept. 29 **Tagged** ***Perf. 11***

1331 A753 5c **multicolored**	.55	.25
a. Tagging omitted	*25.00*	—
1332 A754 5c **multicolored**	.55	.25
P# block of 4	2.50	—
Margin block of 4, Mr. Zip and "Use Zip Code"	2.40	—
Plate flaw (red stripes of flag on capsule omitted; 29322, 29325 UL 19)	200.00	
a. Tagging omitted	*25.00*	—
b. Pair, #1331-1332	1.25	1.25
c. As "b," tagging omitted	*60.00*	—

URBAN PLANNING ISSUE

Publicizing the importance of Urban Planning in connection with the Intl. Conf. of the American Institute of Planners, Washington, D.C., Oct. 1-6.

View of Model City — A755

Designed by Francis Ferguson.

LITHOGRAPHED, ENGRAVED (Giori)
Plates of 200 subjects in four panes of 50.

1967, Oct. 2 **Tagged** ***Perf. 11***

1333 A755 5c **dark blue, light blue & black**	.30	.25
P# block of 4	1.00	—
Margin block of 4, Mr. Zip and "Use Zip Code"	1.00	—
a. Tagging omitted	*50.00*	

FINNISH INDEPENDENCE, 50th ANNIV.

Finnish Coat of Arms — A756

Designed by Bradbury Thompson.

ENGRAVED (Giori)
Plates of 200 subjects in four panes of 50.

1967, Oct. 6 **Tagged** ***Perf. 11***

1334 A756 5c **blue**	.30	.25
P# block of 4	1.00	—
Margin block of 4, Mr. Zip and "Use Zip Code"	1.00	—
a. Tagging omitted	*100.00*	

THOMAS EAKINS ISSUE

Eakins (1844-1916), painter and sculptor. The painting is in the Natl. Gallery of Art, Washington, D.C.

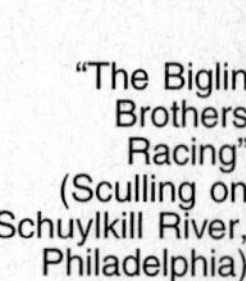

"The Biglin Brothers Racing" (Sculling on Schuylkill River, Philadelphia) A757

Printed by Photogravure & Color Co., Moonachie, N.J.

PHOTOGRAVURE
Plates of 200 subjects in four panes of 50.

1967, Nov. 2 **Tagged** ***Perf. 12***

1335 A757 5c **gold & multicolored**	.30	.25
P# block of 4, 6#	1.00	—
a. Tagging omitted	*40.00*	—

Plate number blocks from upper left or lower left panes show clipped corner of margin.

CHRISTMAS ISSUE

Madonna and Child, by Hans Memling — A758

LITHOGRAPHED, ENGRAVED (Giori)
Plates of 200 subjects in four panes of 50.

1967, Nov. 6 **Tagged** ***Perf. 11***

1336 A758 5c **multicolored**	.30	.25
P# block of 4	1.00	—
Margin block of 4, Mr. Zip and "Use Zip Code"	1.00	—
a. Tagging omitted	*5.50*	—

See note on painting above No. 1321.

MISSISSIPPI STATEHOOD, 150th ANNIV.

Magnolia A759

Designed by Andrew Bucci.

GIORI PRESS PRINTING
Plates of 200 subjects in four panes of 50.

1967, Dec. 11 **Tagged** ***Perf. 11***

1337 A759 5c **brt. greenish blue, green & red brown**	.30	.25
P# block of 4, 2#	1.00	—
Margin block of 4, Mr. Zip and "Use Zip Code"	1.00	—
a. Tagging omitted	*10.00*	—

FLAG ISSUE

Flag and White House — A760

Designed by Stevan Dohanos.

GIORI PRESS PRINTING
Plates of 400 subjects in four panes of 100.

1968, Jan. 24 **Tagged** ***Perf. 11***
Size: 19x22mm

1338 A760 6c **dark blue, red & green**	.30	.25
P# block of 4	1.00	—
Margin block of 4, "Use Zip Code"	1.00	—
Pair with full vert. gutter btwn.	550.00	
k. Vert. pair, imperf. btwn.	*250.00*	*150.00*
m. Tagging omitted	*4.50*	—
s. Red missing (FO)		—
u. Vert. pair, imperf horiz.	*275.00*	
v. All color omitted		—
w. Green missing (FO)		—

No. 1338s is unique.

Beware of regumming on No. 1338u. Most examples have had the gum washed off to make it difficult or impossible to detect blind perfs. Check carefully for blind perfs. Value is for pair with original gum.

On No. 1338v, an albino impression of the engraved plate is present.

COIL STAMP
MULTICOLOR HUCK PRESS

1969, May 30 **Tagged** ***Perf. 10 Vertically***
Size: 18¼x21mm

1338A A760 6c **dark blue, red & green**	.30	.25
Pair	.50	.50
b. Imperf., pair	*350.00*	
q. Tagging omitted	*10.00*	—

MULTICOLOR HUCK PRESS
Panes of 100 (10x10) each

1970-71 **Tagged** ***Perf. 11x10½***
Size: 18¼x21mm

1338D A760 6c **dark blue, red & green,** *Aug. 7, 1970*	.30	.25
Margin block of 20+	4.00	—
e. Horiz. pair, imperf. between	*115.00*	
n. Tagging omitted	*5.00*	—
1338F A760 8c **dark blue, red & slate green,** *May 10, 1971*	.30	.25
Margin block of 20+	3.50	—
i. Imperf., vert. pair	35.00	
j. Horiz. pair, imperf. between	45.00	
o. Tagging omitted	*5.00*	—
p. Slate green omitted	*350.00*	
t. Horiz. pair, imperf. vertically	—	

+ Margin blocks of 20 come in four versions: (1) 2 P#, 3 ME, 3 zip; (2) 3 P#, 2 ME, 2 zip; (3) 2 P#, 3 ME, 2 zip; (4) 3 P#, 2 ME, 3 zip.

COIL STAMP
MULTICOLOR HUCK PRESS

1971, May 10 **Tagged** ***Perf. 10 Vertically***
Size: 18¼x21mm

1338G A760 8c **dk blue, red & slate green**	.30	.25
Pair	.60	.50
h. Imperf., pair	*45.00*	
r. Tagging omitted	*5.00*	—

ILLINOIS STATEHOOD, 150th ANNIV.

Farm Buildings and Fields of Ripening Grain — A761

Designed by George Barford.

LITHOGRAPHED, ENGRAVED (Giori)
Plates of 200 subjects in four panes of 50.

1968, Feb. 12 **Tagged** ***Perf. 11***

1339 A761 6c **dk blue, blue, red & ocher**	.30	.25
P# block of 4	1.00	—
Margin block of 4, Mr. Zip and "Use Zip Code"	1.00	—
a. Tagging omitted	*170.00*	

HEMISFAIR '68 ISSUE

HemisFair '68 exhibition, San Antonio, Texas, Apr. 6-Oct. 6, for the 250th anniv. of San Antonio.

Map of North and South America and Lines Converging on San Antonio — A762

Designed by Louis Macouillard.

LITHOGRAPHED, ENGRAVED (Giori)

Plates of 200 subjects in four panes of 50.

1968, Mar. 30	**Tagged**	***Perf. 11***	
1340 A762 6c **blue, rose red & white**		.30	.25
On cover, Expo. station machine canc.			10.00
On cover, Expo. roller canc.			25.00
P# block of 4		1.00	—
Margin block of 4, Mr. Zip and "Use Zip Code"		1.00	—
a. White omitted		*650.00*	

AIRLIFT ISSUE

Issued to pay for airlift of parcels from and to US ports to servicemen overseas and in Alaska, Hawaii and Puerto Rico. Valid for all regular postage. On Apr. 26, 1969, the Post Office Department ruled that henceforth No. 1341 "may be used toward paying the postage or fees for special services on *airmail* articles."

Eagle Holding Pennant A763

Designed by Stevan Dohanos.

After a late 19th century wood carving, part of the Index of American Design, National Gallery of Art.

LITHOGRAPHED, ENGRAVED (Giori)

Plates of 200 subjects in four panes of 50.

1968, Apr. 4	**Untagged**	***Perf. 11***	
1341 A763 $1 **sepia, dk. blue, ocher & brown red**		2.00	1.25
P# block of 4		8.25	—
Margin block of 4, Mr. Zip and "Use Zip Code"		8.00	—
Pair with full horiz. gutter btwn.			—

"SUPPORT OUR YOUTH" — ELKS ISSUE

Support Our Youth program, and honoring the Benevolent and Protective Order of Elks, which extended its youth service program in observance of its centennial year.

Girls and Boys — A764

Designed by Edward Vebell.

LITHOGRAPHED, ENGRAVED (Giori)

Plates of 200 subjects in four panes of 50.

1968, May 1	**Tagged**	***Perf. 11***	
1342 A764 6c **ultramarine & orange red**		.30	.25
P# block of 4		1.00	—
Margin block of 4, Mr. Zip and "Use Zip Code"		1.00	—
a. Tagging omitted		10.00	—

LAW AND ORDER ISSUE

Publicizing the policeman as protector and friend and to encourage respect for law and order.

Policeman and Boy — A765

Designed by Ward Brackett.

GIORI PRESS PRINTING

Plates of 200 subjects in four panes of 50 each

1968, May 17	**Tagged**	***Perf. 11***	
1343 A765 6c **chalky blue, black & red**		.30	.25
P# block of 4		1.00	—
Margin block of 4, Mr. Zip and "Use Zip Code"		1.00	—
a. Tagging omitted		*175.00*	*90.00*

REGISTER AND VOTE ISSUE

Campaign to draw more voters to the polls. The weather vane is from an old house in the Russian Hill section of San Francisco, Cal.

Eagle Weather Vane — A766

Designed by Norman Todhunter and Bill Hyde; photograph by M. Halberstadt.

LITHOGRAPHED, ENGRAVED (Giori)

Plates of 200 subjects in four panes of 50.

1968, June 27	**Tagged**	***Perf. 11***	
1344 A766 6c **black, yellow & orange**		.30	.25
P# block of 4		1.00	—
Margin block of 4, Mr. Zip and "Use Zip Code"		1.00	—
a. Tagging omitted		—	

HISTORIC FLAG SERIES

Flags carried by American colonists and by citizens of the new United States. Printed se-tenant in vertical columns of 10. The flag sequence on the 2 upper panes is as listed. On the 2 lower panes the sequence is reversed with the Navy Jack in the 1st row and the Fort Moultrie flag in the 10th.

Ft. Moultrie, 1776 — A767

Ft. McHenry, 1795-1818 A768

Washington's Cruisers, 1775 — A769

Bennington, 1777 — A770

Rhode Island, 1775 — A771

First Stars and Stripes, 1777 — A772

Bunker Hill, 1775 — A773

Grand Union, 1776 — A774

Philadelphia Light Horse, 1775 — A775

First Navy Jack, 1775 — A776

ENGR. (Giori) (#1345-1348, 1350);
ENGR. & LITHO. (#1349, 1351-1354)

Plates of 200 subjects in four panes of 50.

1968, July 4	**Tagged**	***Perf. 11***	
1345 A767 6c **dark blue**		.40	.25
1346 A768 6c **dark blue & red**		.40	.25
1347 A769 6c **dark blue & olive green**		.30	.25
1348 A770 6c **dark blue & red**		.30	.25
1349 A771 6c **dark blue, yellow & red**		.30	.25
1350 A772 6c **dark blue & red**		.30	.25
1351 A773 6c **dark blue, olive green & red**		.30	.25
1352 A774 6c **dark blue & red**		.30	.25
1353 A775 6c **dark blue, yellow & red**		.30	.25
1354 A776 6c **dark blue, red & yellow**		.30	.25
a. Strip of ten, #1345-1354		3.25	*3.25*
P# block of 20, inscriptions, #1345-1354		6.75	—
b. #1345b-1354b, any single, tagging omitted		*65.00*	
c. As "a," imperf		*4,500.*	
d. As "a," tagging omitted		*650.00*	

WALT DISNEY ISSUE

Walt Disney (1901-1966), cartoonist, film producer and creator of Mickey Mouse.

Walt Disney and Children of the World — A777

Designed by C. Robert Moore.

Designed after portrait by Paul E. Wenzel.
Printed by Achrovure Division of Union-Camp Corp., Englewood, N.J.

PHOTOGRAVURE
Plates of 400 subjects in eight panes of 50.

1968, Sept. 11 **Tagged** ***Perf. 12***

1355	A777 6c **multicolored**	.40	.25
	P# block of 4, 5#	1.75	—
	P# block of 4, 5#, 5 dashes	1.75	—
	Margin block of 4, Mr. Zip and "Use Zip Code"	1.60	—
a.	Ocher omitted ("Walt Disney," "6c," etc.)	*300.00*	—
b.	Vert. pair, imperf. horiz.	*575.00*	
c.	Imperf., pair	*425.00*	
d.	Black omitted	*1,750.*	
e.	Horiz. pair, imperf. between	*5,000.*	
f.	Blue omitted	*1,500.*	
g.	Tagging omitted	*17.50*	—

FATHER MARQUETTE ISSUE

Father Jacques Marquette (1637-1675), French Jesuit missionary, who together with Louis Jolliet explored the Mississippi River and its tributaries.

Father Marquette and Louis Jolliet Exploring the Mississippi A778

Designed by Stanley W. Galli.

LITHOGRAPHED, ENGRAVED (Giori)
Plates of 200 subjects in four panes of 50.

1968, Sept. 20 **Tagged** ***Perf. 11***

1356	A778 6c **black, apple green & orange brown**	.30	.25
	P# block of 4	1.00	—
	Margin block of 4, Mr. Zip and "Use Zip Code"	1.00	—
a.	Tagging omitted	*7.50*	—

AMERICAN FOLKLORE ISSUE

Daniel Boone (1734-1820), frontiersman and trapper.

Pennsylvania Rifle, Powder Horn, Tomahawk Pipe and Knife — A779

Designed by Louis Macouillard.

LITHOGRAPHED, ENGRAVED (Giori)
Plates of 200 subjects in four panes of 50.

1968, Sept. 26 **Tagged** ***Perf. 11***

1357	A779 6c **yellow, deep yellow, maroon & black**	.30	.25
	P# block of 4	1.00	—
	Margin block of 4, Mr. Zip and "Use Zip Code"	1.00	—
a.	Tagging omitted	*275.00*	

ARKANSAS RIVER NAVIGATION ISSUE

Opening of the Arkansas River to commercial navigation.

Ship's Wheel, Power Transmission Tower and Barge — A780

Designed by Dean Ellis.

LITHOGRAPHED, ENGRAVED (Giori)
Plates of 200 subjects in four panes of 50.

1968, Oct. 1 **Tagged** ***Perf. 11***

1358	A780 6c **bright blue, dark blue & black**	.30	.25
	P# block of 4	1.00	—
	Margin block of 4, Mr. Zip and "Use Zip Code"	1.00	—
a.	Tagging omitted	*200.00*	

LEIF ERIKSON ISSUE

Leif Erikson, 11th century Norse explorer, called the 1st European to set foot on the American continent, at a place he called Vinland. The statue by the American sculptor A. Stirling Calder is in Reykjavik, Iceland.

Leif Erikson by A. Stirling Calder — A781

Designed by Kurt Weiner.

LITHOGRAPHED & ENGRAVED
Plates of 200 subjects in four panes of 50.

1968, Oct. 9 **Tagged** ***Perf. 11***

1359	A781 6c **light gray brown & black brown**	.30	.25
	P# block of 4	1.25	—
	Margin block of 4, Mr. Zip and "Use Zip Code"	1.00	—

The luminescent element is in the light gray brown ink of the background. The engraved parts were printed on a rotary currency press.

CHEROKEE STRIP ISSUE

75th anniversary of the opening of the Cherokee Strip to settlers, Sept. 16, 1893.

Racing for Homesteads in Cherokee Strip, 1893 — A782

Designed by Norman Todhunter.

ROTARY PRESS PRINTING
E.E. Plates of 200 subjects in four panes of 50.

1968, Oct. 15 **Tagged** ***Perf. 11x10½***

1360	A782 6c **brown**	.30	.25
	P# block of 4	1.10	—
	Margin block of 4, Mr. Zip and "Use Zip Code"	1.00	—
a.	Tagging omitted	*10.00*	—

JOHN TRUMBULL ISSUE

Trumbull (1756-1843), painter. The stamp shows Lt. Thomas Grosvenor and his attendant Peter Salem. The painting hangs at Yale University.

Detail from "The Battle of Bunker's Hill" — A783

Modeled by Robert J. Jones.

LITHOGRAPHED, ENGRAVED (Giori)
Plates of 200 subjects in four panes of 50.

1968, Oct. 18 **Tagged** ***Perf. 11***

1361	A783 6c **multicolored**	.30	.25
	P# block of 4	1.00	—
	Margin block of 4, Mr. Zip and "Use Zip Code"	1.00	—
a.	Tagging omitted	*125.00*	—
b.	Black (engr.) missing (FO)	*11,000.*	—

WATERFOWL CONSERVATION ISSUE

Wood Ducks — A784

Designed by Stanley W. Galli.

LITHOGRAPHED, ENGRAVED (Giori)
Plates of 200 subjects in four panes of 50.

1968, Oct. 24 **Tagged** ***Perf. 11***

1362	A784 6c **black & multicolored**	.30	.25
	P# block of 4	1.00	—
	Margin block of 4, Mr. Zip and "Use Zip Code"	1.00	—
a.	Vertical pair, imperf. between	*250.00*	—
b.	Red & dark blue omitted	*350.00*	
c.	Red omitted		*1,750.*

Dangerous fakes exist of Nos. 1362b and 1362c. Authentication by experts is required.

CHRISTMAS ISSUE

"The Annunciation" by the 15th century Flemish painter Jan van Eyck is in the National Gallery of Art, Washington, D.C.

Angel Gabriel, from "The Annunciation" by Jan van Eyck — A785

Designed by Robert J. Jones.

ENGRAVED (Multicolor Huck press)
Panes of 50 (10x5)

1968, Nov. 1 **Tagged** ***Perf. 11***

1363	A785 6c **multicolored**	.30	.25
	P# block of 10 (see note)	2.50	—
a.	Untagged, *Nov. 2*	.30	.25
	P# block of 10 (see note)	2.50	—
b.	Imperf., pair, tagged	*140.00*	
c.	Light yellow omitted	*60.00*	—
d.	Imperf., pair, untagged	*200.00*	

P# blocks come in two versions: (1) 7 P#, 3 ME; (2) 8 P#, 2 ME.

AMERICAN INDIAN ISSUE

Honoring the American Indian and to celebrate the opening of the Natl. Portrait Gallery, Washington, D.C. Chief Joseph (Indian name, Thunder Traveling over the Mountains), a leader of the Nez Percé, was born in eastern Oregon about 1840 and died at the Colville Reservation in Washington State in 1904.

Chief Joseph, by Cyrenius Hall — A786

Designed by Robert J. Jones; lettering by Crimilda Pontes.

LITHOGRAPHED, ENGRAVED (Giori)
Plates of 200 subjects in four panes of 50.

1968, Nov. 4 **Tagged** ***Perf. 11***

1364 A786 6c **black & multi** .30 .25
P# block of 4 1.00 —
Margin block of 4, Mr. Zip and "Use Zip Code" 1.00 —
a. Tagging omitted — —

BEAUTIFICATION OF AMERICA ISSUE

Publicizing the Natural Beauty Campaign for more beautiful cities, parks, highways and streets. In the left panes Nos. 1365 and 1367 appear in 1st, 3rd and 5th place, Nos. 1366 and 1368 in 2nd and 4th place. This arrangement is reversed in the right panes.

Capitol, Azaleas and Tulips — A787

Washington Monument, Potomac River and Daffodils A788

Poppies and Lupines along Highway A789

Blooming Crab Apples Lining Avenue A790

Designed by Walter DuBois Richards.

LITHOGRAPHED, ENGRAVED (Giori)
Plates of 200 subjects in four panes of 50.

1969, Jan. 16 **Tagged** ***Perf. 11***

1365 A787 6c **multicolored** .30 .25
1366 A788 6c **multicolored** .30 .25
1367 A789 6c **multicolored** .30 .25
1368 A790 6c **multicolored** .30 .25
a. Block of 4, #1365-1368 1.00 *1.25*
P# block of 4 1.10 —
Margin block of 4, Mr. Zip and "Use Zip Code" 1.00 —
b. #1365b-1368b, tagging omitted, any single *75.00*
c. As "a," tagging omitted 325.00

Compare with Nos. 4716a, 4716b, 4716d, 4716e.

AMERICAN LEGION, 50th ANNIV.

Eagle from Great Seal — A791

Designed by Robert Hallock.

LITHOGRAPHED, ENGRAVED (Giori)
Plates of 200 subjects in four panes of 50.

1969, Mar. 15 **Tagged** ***Perf. 11***

1369 A791 6c **red, blue & black** .30 .25
P# block of 4 1.00 —
Margin block of 4, Mr. Zip and "Use Zip Code" 1.00 —
a. Tagging omitted *225.00*

AMERICAN FOLKLORE ISSUE

Grandma Moses (Anna Mary Robertson Moses, 1860-1961), primitive painter of American life.

July Fourth, by Grandma Moses — A792

Designed by Robert J. Jones.

LITHOGRAPHED, ENGRAVED (Giori)
Plates of 200 subjects in four panes of 50.

1969, May 1 **Tagged** ***Perf. 11***

1370 A792 6c **multicolored** .30 .25
P# block of 4 1.00 —
Margin block of 4, Mr. Zip and "Use Zip Code" 1.00 —
a. Horizontal pair, imperf. between *140.00* —
b. Engraved black ("6c U.S. Postage") & Prus. blue ("Grandma Moses") omitted *400.00*
c. Tagging omitted 10.00 —

Beware of pairs with blind perfs. being offered as No. 1370a.
No. 1370b often comes with mottled or disturbed gum. Such stamps sell for about two-thirds as much as examples with perfect gum.

APOLLO 8 ISSUE

Apollo 8 mission, which 1st put men into orbit around the moon, Dec. 21-27, 1968. The astronauts were: Col. Frank Borman, Capt. James Lovell and Maj. William Anders.

Moon Surface and Earth — A793

Designed by Leonard E. Buckley after a photograph by the Apollo 8 astronauts.

LITHOGRAPHED, ENGRAVED (Giori)
Plates of 200 subjects in four panes of 50.

1969, May 5 **Tagged** ***Perf. 11***

1371 A793 6c **black, blue & ocher** .30 .25
P# block of 4 1.00 —
Margin block of 4, Mr. Zip and "Use Zip Code" 1.00 —
a. Tagging omitted —

Imperfs. exist from printer's waste.

W.C. HANDY ISSUE

Handy (1873-1958), jazz musician and composer.

William Christopher Handy — A794

Designed by Bernice Kochan.

LITHOGRAPHED, ENGRAVED (Giori)
Plates of 200 subjects in four panes of 50.

1969, May 17 **Tagged** ***Perf. 11***

1372 A794 6c **violet, deep lilac & blue** .30 .25
P# block of 4 1.00 —
Margin block of 4, Mr. Zip and "Use Zip Code" 1.00 —
a. Tagging omitted 10.00 —

CALIFORNIA SETTLEMENT, 200th ANNIV.

Carmel Mission Belfry — A795

Designed by Leonard Buckley and Howard C. Mildner.

LITHOGRAPHED, ENGRAVED (Giori)
Plates of 200 subjects in four panes of 50.

1969, July 16 **Tagged** ***Perf. 11***

1373 A795 6c **orange, red, black & light blue** .30 .25
P# block of 4 1.00 —
Margin block of 4, Mr. Zip and "Use Zip Code" 1.00 —
a. Tagging omitted 10.00 —
b. Red (engr.) missing (CM) *400.00*

JOHN WESLEY POWELL ISSUE

Powell (1834-1902), geologist who explored the Green and Colorado Rivers 1869-75, and ethnologist.

Major Powell Exploring Colorado River, 1869 — A796

Designed by Rudolph Wendelin.

LITHOGRAPHED, ENGRAVED (Giori)
Plates of 200 subjects in four panes of 50.

1969, Aug. 1 **Tagged** ***Perf. 11***

1374 A796 6c **black, ocher & light blue** .30 .25
P# block of 4 1.00 —
Margin block of 4, Mr. Zip and "Use Zip Code" 1.00 —
a. Tagging omitted 10.00 —

ALABAMA STATEHOOD, 150th ANNIV.

Camellia and Yellow-shafted Flicker — A797

Designed by Bernice Kochan

LITHOGRAPHED, ENGRAVED (Giori)
Plates of 200 subjects in four panes of 50.

1969, Aug. 2 **Tagged** ***Perf. 11***

1375	A797 6c **magenta, rose red, yellow, dark green & brown**	.30	.25
	P# block of 4	1.00	—
	Margin block of 4, Mr. Zip and "Use Zip Code"	1.00	—
a.	Tagging omitted	*160.00*	—

BOTANICAL CONGRESS ISSUE

11th Intl. Botanical Cong., Seattle, Wash., Aug. 24-Sept. 2. In left panes Nos. 1376 and 1378 appear in 1st, 3rd and 5th place; Nos. 1377 and 1379 in 2nd and 4th place. This arrangement is reversed in right panes.

Douglas Fir (Northwest) A798

Lady's-slipper (Northeast) A799

Ocotillo (Southwest) A800

Franklinia (Southeast) A801

Designed by Stanley Galli.

LITHOGRAPHED, ENGRAVED (Giori)
Plates of 200 subjects in four panes of 50.

1969, Aug. 23 **Tagged** ***Perf. 11***

1376	A798 6c **multicolored**	.35	.25
1377	A799 6c **multicolored**	.35	.25
1378	A800 6c **multicolored**	.35	.25
1379	A801 6c **multicolored**	.35	.25
a.	Block of 4, #1376-1379	1.40	*1.75*
	P# block of 4	1.50	—
	Margin block of 4, Mr. Zip and "Use Zip Code"	1.45	—

DARTMOUTH COLLEGE CASE ISSUE

150th anniv. of the Dartmouth College Case, which Daniel Webster argued before the Supreme Court, reasserting the sanctity of contracts.

Daniel Webster and Dartmouth Hall — A802

Designed by John R. Scotford, Jr.

ROTARY PRESS PRINTING
E.E. Plates of 200 subjects in four panes of 50.

1969, Sept. 22 **Tagged** ***Perf. 10½x11***

1380	A802 6c **green**	.30	.25
	P# block of 4	1.00	—
	Margin block of 4, Mr. Zip and "Use Zip Code"	1.00	—

PROFESSIONAL BASEBALL, 100th ANNIV.

Batter — A803

Designed by Alex Ross.

LITHOGRAPHED, ENGRAVED (Giori)
Plates of 200 subjects in four panes of 50.

1969, Sept. 24 **Tagged** ***Perf. 11***

1381	A803 6c **yellow, red, black & green**	.45	.25
	P# block of 4	2.00	—
	Margin block of 4, Mr. Zip and "Use Zip Code"	1.90	—
a.	Black omitted ("1869-1969, United States, 6c, Professional Baseball")	*500.00*	
b.	Tagging omitted	—	
c.	Double impression of black (engr.)	*5,750.*	

INTERCOLLEGIATE FOOTBALL, 100th ANNIV.

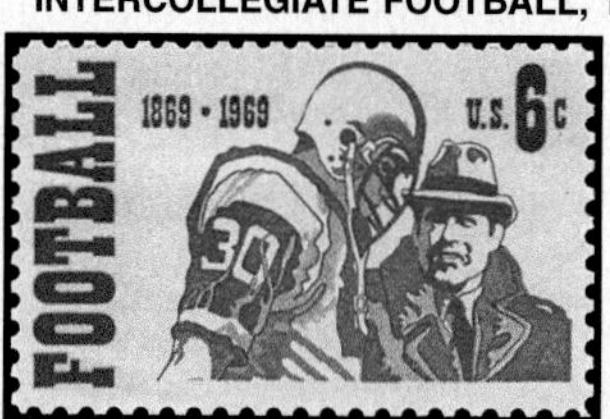

Football Player and Coach — A804

Designed by Robert Peak.

LITHOGRAPHED, ENGRAVED (Giori)
Plates of 200 subjects in four panes of 50.

1969, Sept. 26 **Tagged** ***Perf. 11***

1382	A804 6c **red & green**	.30	.25
	P# block of 4	1.10	—
	Margin block of 4, Mr. Zip and "Use Zip Code"	1.00	—
a.	Tagging omitted	—	—
b.	Vert. pair, imperf horiz.	*5,750.*	
c.	Double impression	*2,500.*	

The engraved parts were printed on a rotary currency press.
No. 1382b is unique.

Two examples of No. 1382c are recorded, with the double impression on the left part of the left stamps within a lower left plate block of 4. Value given is for the plate block.

DWIGHT D. EISENHOWER ISSUE

Dwight D. Eisenhower, 34th President (1890-1969) — A805

Designed by Robert J. Jones; photograph by Bernie Noble.

GIORI PRESS PRINTING
Plates of 128 subjects in 4 panes of 32 each.

1969, Oct. 14 **Tagged** ***Perf. 11***

1383	A805 6c **blue, black & red**	.30	.25
	P# block of 4	1.00	—
	Margin block of 4, Mr. Zip and "Use Zip Code"	1.00	—
a.	Tagging omitted		—
b.	Blue ("U.S. 6c Postage") missing (PS)	*600.00*	

CHRISTMAS ISSUE

The painting, painted about 1870 by an unknown primitive artist, is the property of the N.Y. State Historical Association, Cooperstown, N.Y.

Winter Sunday in Norway, Maine A806

Designed by Stevan Dohanos.

ENGRAVED (Multicolor Huck)
Panes of 50 (5x10)

1969, Nov. 3 **Tagged** ***Perf. 11x10½***

1384	A806 6c **dark green & multicolored**	.30	.25
	P# block of 10, 5#, 2-3 zip, 2-3 Mail Early	2.00	—
	Precancel	.60	.25
b.	Imperf., pair	*700.00*	
c.	Light green omitted	30.00	
d.	Light green, red & yellow omitted	*600.00*	—
e.	Yellow omitted	*1,250.*	
f.	Tagging omitted	5.00	—
g.	Red & yellow omitted	*2,250.*	
h.	Light green and yellow omitted	*500.00*	
i.	Light green and red omitted	—	
j.	Vert. pair, top stamp Baltimore precancel, bottom stamp precancel missing (FO)	—	
k.	Baltimore precancel printed on gum side	*175.00*	
l.	Baltimore precancel, vert. pair, one stamp missing precancel, other stamp with precancel printed inverted on reverse (FO)	*500.00*	
m.	Inverted Baltimore precancel	*225.00*	
n.	Baltimore precancel printed inverted on reverse (FO)	*150.00*	
o.	Baltimore precancel, tagging omitted	*50.00*	
p.	Double impression of New Haven precancel	—	
q.	Inverted Memphis precancel	*100.00*	
r.	Memphis precancel, tagging omitted	—	
s.	New Haven precancel, tagging omitted	—	
t.	Inverted Atlanta precancel	*500.00*	

The precancel value applies to the least expensive of experimental precancels printed locally in four cities, on tagged stamps, with the names between lines 4½mm apart: in black or green, "ATLANTA, GA" and in green only "BALTIMORE, MD," "MEMPHIS, TN" and "NEW HAVEN, CT." They were sold freely to the public and could be used on any class of mail at all post offices during the experimental program and thereafter.

Most examples of No. 1384c show orange where the offset green was. Value is for this variety. Examples without orange sell for more.

On No. 1384i, almost all of the yellow is also omitted. Do not confuse with No. 1384d.

HOPE FOR CRIPPLED ISSUE

Issued to encourage the rehabilitation of crippled children and adults and to honor the National Society for Crippled Children and Adults (Easter Seal Society) on its 50th anniversary.

Cured Child — A807

Designed by Mark English.

LITHOGRAPHED, ENGRAVED (Giori)
Plates of 200 subjects in four panes of 50.

1969, Nov. 20	**Tagged**	***Perf. 11***	
1385 A807 6c **multicolored**		.30	.25
P# block of 4		1.00	—
Margin block of 4, Mr. Zip and "Use Zip Code"		1.00	—
a. Tagging omitted		—	

WILLIAM M. HARNETT ISSUE

Harnett (1848-1892), painter. The painting hangs in the Museum of Fine Arts, Boston.

"Old Models" — A808

Designed by Robert J. Jones.

LITHOGRAPHED, ENGRAVED (Giori)
Plates of 128 subjects in 4 panes of 32 each.

1969, Dec. 3	**Tagged**	***Perf. 11***	
1386 A808 6c **multicolored**		.30	.25
P# block of 4		1.00	—
Margin block of 4, Mr. Zip and "Use Zip Code"		1.00	—
a. Red (engr.) missing (CM)		—	

NATURAL HISTORY ISSUE

Centenary of the American Museum of Natural History, New York City. Nos. 1387-1388 alternate in 1st row, Nos. 1389-1390 in 2nd row. This arrangement is repeated throughout the pane.

American Bald Eagle — A809

African Elephant Herd — A810

Tlingit Chief in Haida Ceremonial Canoe — A811

Brontosaurus, Stegosaurus and Allosaurus from Jurassic Period — A812

Designers: No. 1387, Walter Richards; No. 1388, Dean Ellis; No. 1389, Paul Rabut; No. 1390, detail from mural by Rudolph Zallinger in Yal Peabody Museum, adapted by Robert J. Jones.

LITHOGRAPHED, ENGRAVED (Giori)
Plates of 128 subjects in 4 panes of 32 each (4x8).

1970, May 6	**Tagged**	***Perf. 11***	
1387 A809 6c **multicolored**		.30	.25
1388 A810 6c **multicolored**		.30	.25
1389 A811 6c **multicolored**		.30	.25
1390 A812 6c **multicolored**		.30	.25
a. Block of 4, #1387-1390		1.00	*1.00*
P# block of 4		1.10	—
Margin block of 4, Mr. Zip and "Use Zip Code"		1.00	—
b. As "a," tagging omitted		—	—

MAINE STATEHOOD, 150th ANNIV.

The painting hangs in the Metropolitan Museum of Art, New York City.

The Lighthouse at Two Lights, Maine, by Edward Hopper A813

Designed by Stevan Dohanos.

LITHOGRAPHED, ENGRAVED (Giori)
Plates of 200 subjects in four panes of 50.

1970, July 9	**Tagged**	***Perf. 11***	
1391 A813 6c **black & multi**		.30	.25
P# block of 4		1.00	—
Margin block of 4, Mr. Zip and "Use Zip Code"		1.00	—
a. Tagging omitted		*175.00*	—

WILDLIFE CONSERVATION ISSUE

American Buffalo — A814

Designed by Robert Lougheed.

ROTARY PRESS PRINTING
E.E. Plates of 200 subjects in four panes of 50.

1970, July 20	**Tagged**	***Perf. 11x10½***	
1392 A814 6c **black,** *light brown*		.30	.25
P# block of 4		1.00	—
Margin block of 4, Mr. Zip and "Use Zip Code"		1.00	—

REGULAR ISSUE
Dwight David Eisenhower

Dot between "R" and "U" — A815

No Dot between "R" and "U" — A815a

Benjamin Franklin — A816

U.S. Postal Service Emblem — A817

Fiorello H. LaGuardia A817a

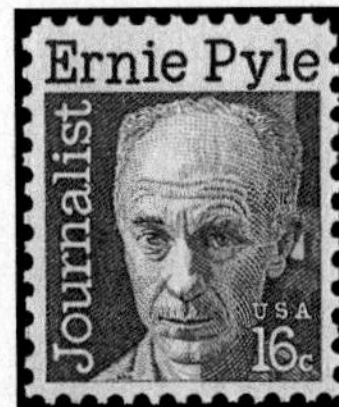

Ernest Taylor Pyle — A818

Dr. Elizabeth Blackwell — A818a

Amadeo P. Giannini A818b

Designers: Nos. 1393-1395, 1401-1402, Robert Geissman; photograph by George Tames. 7c, Bill Hyde. No. 1396, Raymond Loewy/William Smith, Inc. 14c, Robert Geissman; photograph by George Fayer. 16c, Robert Geissman; photograph by Alfred Eisenstadt. 18c, Robert Geissman; painting by Joseph Kozlowski. 21c, Robert Geissman.

ROTARY PRESS PRINTING
E.E. Plates of 400 subjects in four panes of 100.

1970-74	**Tagged**	***Perf. 11x10½***	
1393 A815 6c **dark blue gray,** shiny gum, *Aug. 6, 1970*		.30	.25
On cover			2.00
Single franking on certificate of mailing			*100.00*
P# block of 4		1.00	—
Margin block of 4, "Use Zip Codes"		1.00	—
Dull gum		.30	
P# block of 4		1.40	
Zip block of 4		1.00	
a. Booklet pane of 8, shiny gum		2.00	2.00
Dull gum		2.25	
b. Booklet pane of 5 + label		1.40	1.40
c. Untagged (Bureau precanceled)		12.75	3.00
P# block of 4		*175.00*	
Margin block of 4, "Use Zip Codes"		75.00	
g. Tagging omitted (not Bureau precanceled)		*150.00*	—
h. As "a," tagging omitted, shiny gum		*250.00*	—
Dull gum		*325.00*	

Counterfeits exist of No. 1393. See the Postal Counterfeits section of this catalog.

Perf. 10½x11

1393D A816 7c **bright blue,** shiny gum, *Oct. 20, 1972*		.30	.25
On cover			4.00
Single franking on first-class postcard			8.00
P# block of 4		1.00	—
Margin block of 4, "Use Zip Codes"		1.00	—
Dull gum		.30	
P# block of 4		1.25	
Zip block of 4		1.00	
e. Untagged (Bureau precanceled)		4.25	1.00
P# block of 4		52.50	
Margin block of 4, "Use Zip Codes"		22.50	
f. Tagging omitted (not Bureau precanceled)		5.00	—

GIORI PRESS PRINTING
Plates of 400 subjects in four panes of 100.
Perf. 11

1394 A815a 8c **black, red & blue gray,** *May 10, 1971* .30 .25
On cover 2.00
P# block of 4 1.00 —
Margin block of 4, "Use Zip Codes" 1.00 —
Pair with full vert. gutter btwn. —
a. Tagging omitted 5.00 —
b. Red missing (PS) *150.00*
c. Red missing (FO) *1,250.*
d. Red and blue gray missing (PS) —
e. Red and blue gray missing (FO or preprinting paper crease) *1,000.*
f. All colors and tagging missing (FO) *1,000.*
g. Printed on gum side, tagged *1,000.*

No. 1394f must be collected se-tenant with No. 1394c, 1394e, or with a partially printed No. 1394.
Counterfeits exist of No. 1394. See the Postal Counterfeits section of this catalog.

ROTARY PRESS PRINTING
Perf. 11x10½ on 2 or 3 Sides

1395 A815 8c **deep claret,** shiny gum (from blkt. pane) .30 .25
Dull gum .30
On cover 2.00
a. Booklet pane of 8, shiny gum, *May 10, 1971* 2.00 2.00
b. Booklet pane of 6, shiny gum, *May 10, 1971* 1.50 1.50
c. Booklet pane of 4 + 2 labels, dull gum, *Jan. 28, 1972* 1.65 1.10
d. Booklet pane of 7 + label, dull gum, *Jan. 28, 1972* 1.90 1.90
e. Vert. pair, imperf. between, in #1395a or 1395d with foldover *750.00*
f. As "a," tagging omitted — —
g. As "b," tagging omitted *80.00* —
h. As "c," tagging omitted *55.00* —
i. As "d," tagging omitted —
j. As No. 1395, tagging omitted 7.50 —
dull gum 7.50 —

No. 1395 was issued only in booklets.
At least 4 pairs of No. 1395e are recorded from 3 panes (one No. 1395a and two 1395d) with different foldover patterns. A pane of No. 1395d also is known with a foldover resulting in a vertical pair of stamp and label, imperf between.

PHOTOGRAVURE (Andreotti)
Plates of 400 subjects in four panes of 100.
Perf. 11x10½

1396 A817 8c **multicolored,** *July 1, 1971* .30 .25
P# block of 12, 6# 2.50
P# block of 20, 6#, "Mail Early in the Day," "Use Zip Codes" and rectangular color contents (UL pane) 4.00
Margin block of 4, "Use Zip Codes" 1.00 —

ROTARY PRESS PRINTING
E.E. Plates of 400 subjects in four panes of 100.

1397 A817a 14c **gray brown,** *Apr. 24, 1972* .30 .25
On cover 10.00
Single franking on airmail postcard 30.00
Single franking on int'l printed-matter surface cover 25.00
P# block of 4 1.10 —
Margin block of 4, "Use Zip Codes" —
Pair with full vert. gutter btwn. 900.00
a. Untagged (Bureau precanceled) *100.00* 17.50
P# block of 4 —
Margin block of 4, "Use Zip Codes" —
1398 A818 16c **brown,** *May 7, 1971* .35 .25
On cover 6.00
Single franking on double-weight air-mail cover 40.00
Single franking on third-class cover *70.00*
P# block of 4 2.50 —
Margin block of 4, "Use Zip Codes" 1.50 —
a. Untagged (Bureau precanceled) 22.50 5.00
P# block of 4 —
Margin block of 4, "Use Zip Codes" 175.00
b. Tagging omitted (not Bureau precanceled) *125.00* —
1399 A818a 18c **violet,** *Jan. 23, 1974* .35 .25
On cover 10.00
Single franking on int'l surface cover 30.00
Single franking on int'l airmail post-card 30.00
Single franking on double-weight third-class cover *60.00*
P# block of 4 1.50 —
Margin block of 4, "Use Zip Codes" 1.40 —
1400 A818b 21c **green,** *June 27, 1973* .40 .25
On cover 10.00
Single franking on int'l airmail cover 15.00
P# block of 4 1.65 —
Margin block of 4, "Use Zip Codes" 1.60 —
Nos. 1393-1400 (9) 2.90 2.25

Bureau Precancels: 6c, 6 diff., 7c, 13 diff., No. 1394, 24 diff., 14c, 3 diff., 16c, NYC, 3 diff. Greensboro, NC.

COIL STAMPS
ROTARY PRESS PRINTING

1970-71 **Tagged** ***Perf. 10 Vert.***

1401 A815 6c **dark blue gray,** shiny gum, *Aug. 6, 1970* .30 .25
On cover 2.00
Pair .50 .50
Joint line pair .60 .60
Dull gum .85
Joint line pair 7.00
a. Untagged (Bureau precanceled) 19.50 3.00
Pair 42.50 6.50
Joint line pair *525.00* —
b. Imperf., pair *2,500.*
Joint line pair —
1402 A815 8c **deep claret,** *May 10, 1971* .30 .25
On cover 2.00
Single franking on third-class bulk qty discount cover 10.00
Pair .50 .50
Joint line pair .60 .60
a. Imperf., pair 37.50
Joint line pair 70.00
b. Untagged (Bureau precanceled) 6.75 .75
Pair 15.00 1.60
Joint line pair *185.00* —
c. Pair, imperf. between *6,250.*

No. 1401b often found with small faults and/or without gum. Such examples sell for considerably less.

Bureau Precancels: 6c, 4 diff., 8c, 34 diff.

EDGAR LEE MASTERS ISSUE

Edgar Lee Masters (1869-1950), Poet — A819

Designed by Fred Otnes.

LITHOGRAPHED, ENGRAVED (Giori)
Plates of 200 subjects in four panes of 50.

1970, Aug. 22 **Tagged** ***Perf. 11***

1405 A819 6c **black & olive bister** .30 .25
P# block of 4 1.00 —
Margin block of 4, Mr. Zip and "Use Zip Code" 1.00 —
a. Tagging omitted 140.00 —

WOMAN SUFFRAGE ISSUE

50th anniversary of the 19th Amendment, which gave the vote to women.

Suffragettes, 1920, and Woman Voter, 1970 — A820

Designed by Ward Brackett.

GIORI PRESS PRINTING
Plates of 200 subjects in four panes of 50.

1970, Aug. 26 **Tagged** ***Perf. 11***

1406 A820 6c **blue** .30 .25
P# block of 4 1.00 —
Margin block of 4, Mr. Zip and "Use Zip Code" 1.00 —

SOUTH CAROLINA ISSUE

300th anniv. of the founding of Charles Town (Charleston), the 1st permanent settlement of South Carolina. Against a background of pine wood the line drawings of the design represent the economic and historic development of South Carolina: the spire of St. Phillip's Church, Capitol, state flag, a ship, 17th century man and woman, a Fort Sumter cannon, barrels, cotton, tobacco and yellow jasmine.

Symbols of South Carolina A821

Designed by George Samerjan.

LITHOGRAPHED, ENGRAVED (Giori)
Plates of 200 subjects in four panes of 50.

1970, Sept. 12 **Tagged** ***Perf. 11***

1407 A821 6c **bister, black & red** .30 .25
P# block of 4 1.00 —
Margin block of 4, Mr. Zip and "Use Zip Code" 1.00 —

STONE MOUNTAIN MEMORIAL ISSUE

Dedication of the Stone Mountain Confederate Memorial, Georgia, May 9, 1970.

Robert E. Lee, Jefferson Davis and "Stonewall" Jackson A822

Designed by Robert Hallock.

GIORI PRESS PRINTING
Plates of 200 subjects in four panes of 50.

1970, Sept. 19 **Tagged** ***Perf. 11***

1408 A822 6c **gray** .30 .25
P# block of 4 1.00 —
Margin block of 4, Mr. Zip and "Use Zip Code" 1.00 —

FORT SNELLING ISSUE

150th anniv. of Fort Snelling, Minnesota, an important outpost for the opening of the Northwest.

Fort Snelling, Keelboat and Tepees A823

Designed by David K. Stone.

LITHOGRAPHED, ENGRAVED (Giori)
Plates of 200 in four panes of 50.

1970, Oct. 17 **Tagged** ***Perf. 11***

1409 A823 6c **yellow & multicolored** .30 .25
P# block of 4 1.00 —
Margin block of 4, Mr. Zip and "Use Zip Code" 1.00 —
a. Tagging omitted — —

ANTI-POLLUTION ISSUE

Issued to focus attention on the problems of pollution.
In left panes Nos. 1410 and 1412 appear in 1st, 3rd and 5th place; Nos. 1411 and 1413 in 2nd and 4th place. This arrangement is reversed in right panes.

Globe and Wheat — A824

Globe and City — A825

Globe and Bluegill A826

Globe and Seagull
A827

Designed by Arnold Copeland and Walter DuBois Richards.
Printed by Bureau of Engraving and Printing at Guilford Gravure, Inc., Guilford, Conn.

PHOTOGRAVURE

Plates of 200 subjects in four panes of 50.

1970, Oct. 28 Tagged *Perf. 11x10½*

1410	A824 6c **multicolored**	.30	.25
1411	A825 6c **multicolored**	.30	.25
1412	A826 6c **multicolored**	.30	.25
1413	A827 6c **multicolored**	.30	.25
a.	Block of 4, #1410-1413	1.00	*1.25*
	P# block of 10, 5#	2.50	—
	Margin block of 4, Mr. Zip and "Use Zip Code"	1.10	—

CHRISTMAS ISSUE

In left panes Nos. 1415 and 1417 appear in 1st, 3rd and 5th place; Nos. 1416 and 1418 in 2nd and 4th place. This arrangement is reversed in right panes.

Nativity, by Lorenzo Lotto — A828

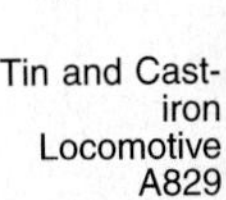

Tin and Cast-iron Locomotive
A829

Toy Horse on Wheels
A830

Mechanical Tricycle
A831

Doll Carriage
A832

Designers: No. 1414, Howard C. Mildner, from a painting by Lorenzo Lotto (1480-1556) in the National Gallery of Art, Washington, D.C. Nos. 1415-1418, Stevan Dohanos, from a drawing (locomotive) by Charles Hemming and from "Golden Age of Toys" by Fondin and Remise.
Printed by Guilford Gravure, Inc., Guilford, Conn.

PHOTOGRAVURE

Plates of 200 subjects in four panes of 50.

1970, Nov. 5 Tagged *Perf. 10½x11*

1414	A828 6c **multicolored**	.30	.25
	P# block of 8, 4#	1.10	—
	Margin block of 4, Mr. Zip and "Use Zip Code"	.50	—
a.	Precanceled	.30	.25
	P# block of 8, 4#	2.00	—
	Margin block of 4, Mr. Zip and "Use Zip Code"	1.00	—
b.	Black omitted	*400.00*	
c.	As "a," blue omitted	*1,100.*	
d.	Type II	.30	.25
	P# block of 8, 4#	3.25	—
	Zip block of 4	1.00	—
	Pair with full horiz. gutter btwn.	—	
e.	Type II, precanceled	.30	.25
	P# block of 8, 4#	4.25	—
	Zip block of 4	1.25	—

No. 1414 has a slightly blurry impression, snowflaking in the sky and no gum breaker ridges. No. 1414d has shiny surfaced paper, sharper impression, no snowflaking and vertical and horizontal gum breaker ridges.

No. 1414a has a slightly blurry impression, snowflaking in the sky, no gum breaker ridges and the precancel is grayish black. No. 1414e has sharper impression, no snowflaking, gum breaker ridges and the precancel is intense black.

Perf. 11x10½

1415	A829 6c **multicolored**	.30	.25
a.	Precanceled	.65	.25
b.	Black omitted	*1,750.*	
c.	Tagging omitted	—	—
1416	A830 6c **multicolored**	.30	.25
a.	Precanceled	.65	.25
b.	Black omitted	1,750.	
c.	Imperf., pair (#1416, 1418)	—	*2,500.*
d.	Tagging omitted	—	
1417	A831 6c **multicolored**	.30	.25
a.	Precanceled	.65	.25
b.	Black omitted	*1,750.*	
c.	Tagging omitted	—	—
1418	A832 6c **multicolored**	.30	.25
a.	Precanceled	.65	.25
b.	Block of 4, #1415-1418	1.25	*1.40*
	P# block of 8, 4#	3.00	—
	Margin block of 4, Mr. Zip and "Use Zip Code"	1.25	—
c.	As "b," precanceled	3.75	*3.50*
	P# block of 8, 4P#	5.50	—
	Margin block of 4, Mr. Zip and "Use Zip Code"	3.00	—
d.	Black omitted	*1,750.*	
e.	As "b," black omitted	*8,000.*	
f.	As "b," black omitted on #1417 & 1418	*4,000.*	
g.	P# block of 8, black omitted on #1415 & 1416	*4,000.*	
h.	As "b," tagging omitted on #1415 and 1417	—	
i.	Tagging omitted	—	
	Nos. 1415-1418 (4)	1.20	1.00

Nos. 1415-1418 and 1415a-1418a are known both without gum breaker ridges (common) and with gum breaker ridges (scarce).

The precanceled stamps, Nos. 1414a-1418a, were furnished to 68 cities. The plates include two straight (No. 1414a) or two wavy (Nos. 1415a-1418a) black lines that make up the precancellation. Unused values are for stamps with gum and used values are for stamps with an additional cancellation or without gum.

UNITED NATIONS, 25th ANNIV.

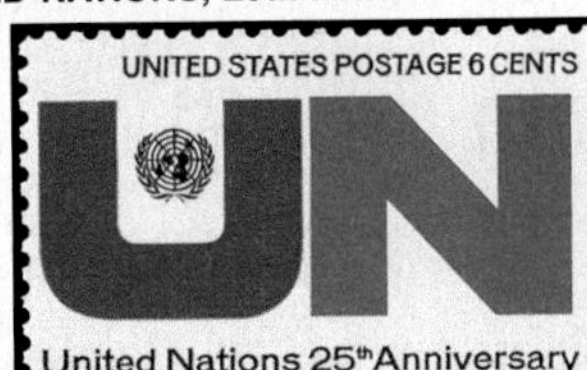

"UN" and UN Emblem
A833

Designed by Arnold Copeland.

LITHOGRAPHED, ENGRAVED (Giori)

Plates of 200 subjects in four panes of 50.

1970, Nov. 20 Tagged *Perf. 11*

1419	A833 6c **black, verm & ultra**	.30	.25
	P# block of 4	1.00	—
	Margin block of 4, Mr. Zip and "Use Zip Code"	1.00	—
	Pair with full horiz. gutter btwn.	—	
a.	Tagging omitted	*75.00*	—

LANDING OF THE PILGRIMS ISSUE

350th anniv. of the landing of the Mayflower.

Mayflower and Pilgrims — A834

Designed by Mark English.

LITHOGRAPHED, ENGRAVED (Giori)

Plates of 200 subjects in four panes of 50.

1970, Nov. 21 Tagged *Perf. 11*

1420	A834 6c **blk, org, yel, magenta, bl & brn**	.30	.25
	P# block of 4	1.00	—
	Margin block of 4, Mr. Zip and "Use Zip Code"	1.00	—
a.	Orange & yellow omitted	*425.00*	
b.	Tagging omitted	—	—

DISABLED AMERICAN VETERANS AND SERVICEMEN ISSUE

No. 1421 for the 50th anniv. of the Disabled Veterans of America Organization; No. 1422 honors the contribution of servicemen, particularly those who were prisoners of war, missing or killed in action. Nos. 1421-1422 are printed se-tenant in horizontal rows of 10.

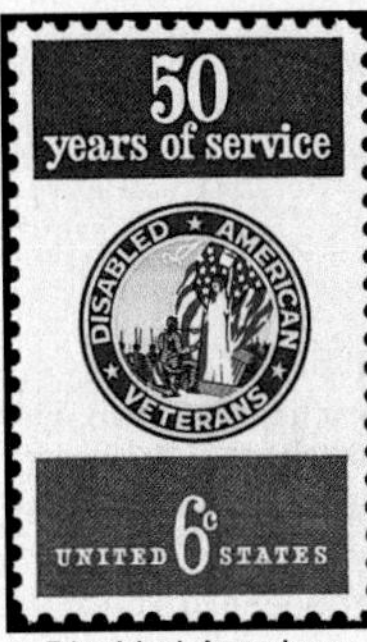

Disabled American Veterans Emblem — A835

A836

Designed by Stevan Dohanos.

LITHOGRAPHED, ENGRAVED (Giori)

Plates of 200 subjects in four panes of 50.

1970, Nov. 24 Tagged *Perf. 11*

1421	A835 6c **dark blue, red & multicolored**	.30	.25

ENGRAVED

1422	A836 6c **dark blue, black & red**	.30	.25
a.	Pair, #1421-1422	.50	.50
	P# block of 4	1.00	—
	Margin block of 4, Mr. Zip and "Use Zip Code"	1.00	—
b.	As "a," tagging omitted	90.00	—

AMERICAN WOOL INDUSTRY ISSUE

450th anniv. of the introduction of sheep to the North American continent and the beginning of the American wool industry.

Ewe and Lamb — A837

Designed by Dean Ellis.

LITHOGRAPHED, ENGRAVED (Giori)
Plates of 200 subjects in four panes of 50.

1971, Jan. 19 Tagged *Perf. 11*
1423 A837 6c **multicolored** .30 .25
P# block of 4 1.00 —
Margin block of 4, Mr. Zip and "Use Zip Code" 1.00 —
a. Tagging omitted 11.00 —
b. Teal blue ("United States") missing (CM) *325.00*

GEN. DOUGLAS MacARTHUR ISSUE

MacArthur (1880-1964), Chief of Staff, Supreme Commander for the Allied Powers in the Pacific Area during World War II and Supreme Commander in Japan after the war.

Gen. Douglas MacArthur — A838

Designed by Paul Calle; Wide World photograph.

GIORI PRESS PRINTING
Plates of 200 subjects in four panes of 50.

1971, Jan. 26 Tagged *Perf. 11*
1424 A838 6c **black, red & dark blue** .30 .25
P# block of 4 1.00 —
Margin block of 4, Mr. Zip and "Use Zip Code" 1.00 —
a. Red missing (PS) —
b. Tagging omitted *300.00* —
c. Blue missing (PS) —

BLOOD DONOR ISSUE

Salute to blood donors and spur to increased participation in the blood donor program.

"Giving Blood Saves Lives" — A839

Designed by Howard Munce.

LITHOGRAPHED, ENGRAVED (Giori)
Plates of 200 subjects in four panes of 50.

1971, Mar. 12 Tagged *Perf. 11*
1425 A839 6c **blue, scarlet & indigo** .30 .25
P# block of 4 1.00 —
Margin block of 4, Mr. Zip and "Use Zip Code" 1.00 —
a. Tagging omitted 10.00 —

MISSOURI STATEHOOD, 150th ANNIV.

The stamp design shows a Pawnee facing a hunter-trapper and a group of settlers. It is from a mural by Thomas Hart Benton in the Harry S Truman Library, Independence, Mo.

"Independence and the Opening of the West," Detail, by Thomas Hart Benton — A840

Designed by Bradbury Thompson.

PHOTOGRAVURE (Andreotti)
Plates of 200 subjects in four panes of 50.

1971, May 8 Tagged *Perf. 11x10½*
1426 A840 8c **multicolored** .30 .25
P# block of 12, 6# 3.00 —
Margin block of 4, Mr. Zip and "Use Zip Code" 1.00 —
a. Tagging omitted — —

See note on Andreotti printings and their color control markings in Information for Collectors under Printing, Photogravure.

WILDLIFE CONSERVATION ISSUE

Nos. 1427-1428 alternate in first row, Nos. 1429-1430 in second row. This arrangement repeated throughout pane.

Trout A841

Alligator — A842

Polar Bear and Cubs A843

California Condor — A844

Designed by Stanley W. Galli.

LITHOGRAPHED, ENGRAVED (Giori)
Plates of 128 subjects in 4 panes of 32 each (4x8).

1971, June 12 Tagged *Perf. 11*
1427 A841 8c **multicolored** .30 .25
a. Red omitted *1,250.*
b. Green (engr.) omitted —
1428 A842 8c **multicolored** .30 .25
1429 A843 8c **multicolored** .30 .25
1430 A844 8c **multicolored** .30 .25
a. Block of 4, #1427-1430 1.00 1.00
P# block of 4 1.25 —
Margin block of 4, Mr. Zip and "Use Zip Code" 1.00 —
b. As "a," light green & dark green omitted from #1427-1428 *3,250.*
c. As "a," red omitted from #1427, 1429-1430 *3,000.*
d. As "a," tagging omitted —

ANTARCTIC TREATY ISSUE

Map of Antarctica A845

Designed by Howard Koslow.

Adapted from emblem on official documents of Consultative Meetings.

GIORI PRESS PRINTING
Plates of 200 subjects in four panes of 50.

1971, June 23 Tagged *Perf. 11*
1431 A845 8c **red & dark blue** .30 .25
P# block of 4 1.00 —
Margin block of 4, Mr. Zip and "Use Zip Code" 1.00 —
a. Tagging omitted *10.00*
b. Both colors missing (EP) *500.00*

No. 1431b should be collected se-tenant with a normal stamp and/or a partially printed stamp.

AMERICAN REVOLUTION BICENTENNIAL

Bicentennial Commission Emblem — A846

Designed by Chermayeff & Geismar.

LITHOGRAPHED, ENGRAVED (Giori)
Plates of 200 subjects in four panes of 50.

1971, July 4 Tagged *Perf. 11*
1432 A846 8c **gray, red, blue & black** .30 .25
P# block of 4 1.25 —
Margin block of 4, Mr. Zip and "Use Zip Code" 1.00 —
a. Gray & black missing (EP) *325.00*
b. Gray ("U.S. Postage 8c") missing (EP) *650.00*
c. Tagging omitted 125.00

JOHN SLOAN ISSUE

John Sloan (1871-1951), painter. The painting hangs in the Phillips Gallery, Washington, D.C.

The Wake of the Ferry — A847

Designed by Bradbury Thompson.

LITHOGRAPHED, ENGRAVED (Giori)
Plates of 200 subjects in four panes of 50.

1971, Aug. 2 Tagged *Perf. 11*
1433 A847 8c **multicolored** .30 .25
P# block of 4 1.00 —
Margin block of 4, Mr. Zip and "Use Zip Code" 1.00 —
a. Tagging omitted —
b. Red engr. ("John Sloan" and "8") missing (CM) *1,000.*

SPACE ACHIEVEMENT DECADE ISSUE

Decade of space achievements and the Apollo 15 moon exploration mission, July 26-Aug. 7. In the left panes the earth and sun stamp is 1st, 3rd and 5th, the rover 2nd and 4th. This arrangement is reversed in the right panes.

Earth, Sun and Landing Craft on Moon — A848

Lunar Rover and Astronauts A849

Designed by Robert McCall.

LITHOGRAPHED, ENGRAVED (Giori)
Plates of 200 subjects in four panes of 50.

1971, Aug. 2 Tagged *Perf. 11*

1434	A848 8c **black, blue, gray, yellow & red**	.30	.25
a.	Tagging omitted	*45.00*	
1435	A849 8c **black, blue, gray, yellow & red**	.30	.25
a.	Tagging omitted	*45.00*	
b.	Pair, #1434-1435	.50	.50
	P# block of 4	1.00	—
	Margin block of 4, Mr. Zip and "Use Zip Code"	1.00	—
c.	As "b," tagging omitted	*125.00*	
d.	As "b," blue & red (litho.) omitted	*950.00*	

EMILY DICKINSON ISSUE

Emily Elizabeth Dickinson (1830-1886), Poet — A850

Designed by Bernard Fuchs after a photograph.

LITHOGRAPHED, ENGRAVED (Giori)
Plates of 200 subjects in four panes of 50.

1971, Aug. 28 Tagged *Perf. 11*

1436	A850 8c **multicolored**, *greenish*	.30	.25
	P# block of 4	1.00	—
	Margin block of 4, Mr. Zip and "Use Zip Code"	1.00	—
a.	Black & olive (engr.) omitted	*500.00*	
b.	Pale rose missing (EP)	*5,000.*	
c.	Red omitted	—	
d.	Tagging omitted	130.00	—

SAN JUAN ISSUE

450th anniversary of San Juan, Puerto Rico.

Sentry Box, Morro Castle, San Juan — A851

Designed as a woodcut by Walter Brooks.

LITHOGRAPHED, ENGRAVED (Giori)
Plates of 200 subjects in four panes of 50.

1971, Sept. 12 Tagged *Perf. 11*

1437	A851 8c **pale brown, black, yellow, red brown & dark brown**	.30	.25
	P# block of 4	1.50	—
	Margin block of 4, Mr. Zip and "Use Zip Code"	1.10	—
a.	Tagging omitted	*10.00*	—
b.	Dark brown (engr.) omitted	*1,500.*	—

No. 1437b used is a 1971 on-cover single expertized in 2014.

VALUES FOR HINGED STAMPS AFTER NO. 771
This catalogue does not value unused stamps after No. 771 in hinged condition. Hinged unused stamps from No. 772 to the present are worth considerably less than the values given for unused stamps, which are for never-hinged examples.

PREVENT DRUG ABUSE ISSUE

Drug Abuse Prevention Week, Oct. 3-9.

Young Woman Drug Addict — A852

Designed by Miggs Burroughs.

PHOTOGRAVURE (Andreotti)
Plates of 200 subjects in four panes of 50.

1971, Oct. 4 Tagged *Perf. 10½x11*

1438	A852 8c **blue, deep blue & black**	.30	.25
	P# block of 6, 3#	1.00	—
	Margin block of 4, "Use Zip Code"	1.00	—
a.	Tagging omitted	—	

CARE ISSUE

25th anniversary of CARE, a US-Canadian Cooperative for American Relief Everywhere.

Hands Reaching for CARE — A853

Designed by Soren Noring

PHOTOGRAVURE (Andreotti)
Plates of 200 subjects in four panes of 50.

1971, Oct. 27 Tagged *Perf. 10½x11*

1439	A853 8c **blue, blk, vio & red lilac**	.30	.25
	P# block of 8, 4#	1.75	—
	Margin block of 4, Mr. Zip and "Use Zip Code"	1.00	—
a.	Black omitted	*1,100.*	
b.	Tagging omitted	5.00	—

HISTORIC PRESERVATION ISSUE

Nos. 1440-1441 alternate in 1st row, Nos. 1442-1443 in 2nd row. This arrangement is repeated throughout the pane.

Decatur House, Washington, D.C. — A854

Whaling Ship Charles W. Morgan, Mystic, Conn. — A855

Cable Car, San Francisco — A856

San Xavier del Bac Mission, Tucson, Ariz. — A857

Designed by Melbourne Brindle.

LITHOGRAPHED, ENGRAVED (Giori)

1971, Oct. 29 Tagged *Perf. 11*

1440	A854 8c **black brown & ocher**, *buff*	.30	.25
1441	A855 8c **black brown & ocher**, *buff*	.30	.25
1442	A856 8c **black brown & ocher**, *buff*	.30	.25
1443	A857 8c **black brown & ocher**, *buff*	.30	.25
a.	Block of 4, #1440-1443	1.00	*1.00*
	P# block of 4	1.00	—
	Margin block of 4, Mr. Zip and "Use Zip Code"	1.00	—
b.	As "a," black brown omitted	*600.00*	
c.	As "a," ocher omitted	*2,500.*	
d.	As "a," tagging omitted	*75.00*	

CHRISTMAS ISSUE

Adoration of the Shepherds, by Giorgione — A858

"Partridge in a Pear Tree" — A859

Designers: No. 1444, Bradbury Thompson, using a painting by Giorgione in the National Gallery of Art, Washington, D.C. No. 1445, Jamie Wyeth.

PHOTOGRAVURE (Andreotti)
Plates of 200 subjects in four panes of 50.

1971, Nov. 10 **Tagged** ***Perf. 10½x11***

1444 A858 8c **gold & multi** .30 .25
P# block of 12, 6# 1.80 —
Margin block of 4, Mr. Zip and "Use Zip Code" 1.00 —
a. Gold omitted *350.00*
b. Tagging omitted —
1445 A859 8c **dark green, red & multicolored** .30 .25
P# block of 12, 6# 1.80
Margin block of 4, Mr. Zip and "Use Zip Code" 1.00 —

SIDNEY LANIER ISSUE

Lanier (1842-81), poet, musician, lawyer, educator.

Sidney Lanier — A860

Designed by William A. Smith.

GIORI PRESS PRINTING
Plates of 200 subjects in four panes of 50.

1972, Feb. 3 **Tagged** ***Perf. 11***

1446 A860 8c **black, brown & light blue** .30 .25
P# block of 4 1.00 —
Margin block of 4, Mr. Zip and "Use Zip Code" 1.00 —
a. Tagging omitted 60.00

PEACE CORPS ISSUE

Peace Corps Poster, by David Battle — A861

Designed by Bradbury Thompson.

PHOTOGRAVURE (Andreotti)
Plates of 200 subjects in four panes of 50.

1972, Feb. 11 **Tagged** ***Perf. 10½x11***

1447 A861 8c **dark blue, light blue & red** .30 .25
P# block of 6, 3# 1.50 —
Margin block of 4, Mr. Zip and "Use Zip Code" 1.00 —
a. Tagging omitted 5.00

NATIONAL PARKS CENTENNIAL ISSUE

Centenary of Yellowstone National Park, the 1st National Park, and of the entire National Park System. See No. C84.

A862 A863

A864 A865

Cape Hatteras National Seashore

Wolf Trap Farm, Va. — A866

Old Faithful, Yellowstone — A867

Mt. McKinley, Alaska — A868

Designers: 2c, Walter D. Richards; 6c, Howard Koslow; 8c, Robert Handville; 15c, James Barkley.

LITHOGRAPHED, ENGRAVED (Giori)

1972 **Tagged** ***Perf. 11***

Plates of 400 subjects in 4 panes of 100 each

1448 A862 2c **black & multi.**, *Apr. 5* .30 .25
1449 A863 2c **black & multi.**, *Apr. 5* .30 .25
1450 A864 2c **black & multi.**, *Apr. 5* .30 .25
1451 A865 2c **black & multi.**, *Apr. 5* .30 .25
a. Block of 4, #1448-1451 .50 .50
P# block of 4 .60 —
Margin block of 4, "Use Zip Codes" .50 —
b. As "a," black (litho.) omitted *800.00*
c. As "a," tagging omitted *150.00*

Plates of 200 subjects in four panes of 50 each

1452 A866 6c **black & multicolored**, *June 26* .30 .25
P# block of 4 1.00 —
Margin block of 4, Mr. Zip and "Use Zip Code" 1.00 —
a. Tagging omitted *10.00*

Plates of 128 subjects in four panes of 32 (8x4)

1453 A867 8c **blk, blue, brn & multi**, *Mar. 1* .30 .25
P# block of 4 1.00 —
Margin block of 4, Mr. Zip and "Use Zip Code" 1.00 —
a. Tagging omitted 140.00

Plates of 200 subjects in four panes of 50 each

1454 A868 15c **black & multi.**, *July 28* .30 .25
P# block of 4 1.30 —
Margin block of 4, Mr. Zip 1.25 —
a. Tagging omitted 150.00
b. Yellow omitted *3,000.*

FAMILY PLANNING ISSUE

Family — A869

LITHOGRAPHED, ENGRAVED (Giori)
Plates of 200 subjects in four panes of 50.

1972, Mar. 18 **Tagged** ***Perf. 11***

1455 A869 8c **black & multicolored** .30 .25
P# block of 4 1.00 —
Margin block of 4, Mr. Zip and "Use Zip Code" 1.00 —
a. Yellow omitted *300.00*
c. Dark brown missing (FO) *9,500.*
d. Tagging omitted *275.00*

AMERICAN BICENTENNIAL ISSUE
Colonial American Craftsmen

In left panes Nos. 1456 and 1458 appear in 1st, 3rd and 5th place; Nos. 1457 and 1459 in 2nd and 4th place. This arrangement is reversed in right panes.

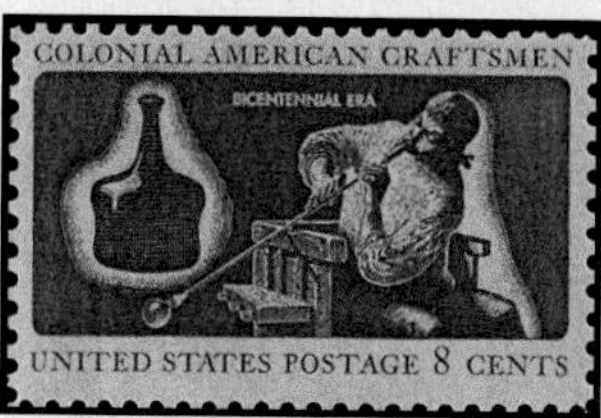

Glass Blower — A870

Silversmith A871

Wigmaker A872

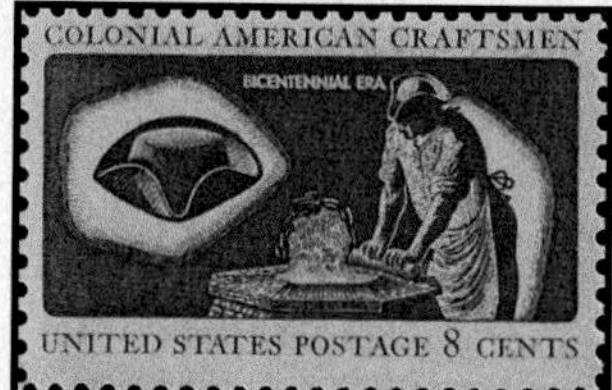

Hatter — A873

Designed by Leonard Everett Fisher.

ENGRAVED
E.E. Plates of 200 subjects in four panes of 50.

1972, July 4 **Tagged** ***Perf. 11x10½***

1456 A870 8c **deep brown**, *dull yellow* .30 .25
1457 A871 8c **deep brown**, *dull yellow* .30 .25
1458 A872 8c **deep brown**, *dull yellow* .30 .25
1459 A873 8c **deep brown**, *dull yellow* .30 .25
a. Block of 4, #1456-1459 1.00 1.00
P# block of 4 1.00 —
Margin block of 4, Mr. Zip and "Use Zip Code" 1.00 —
b. As "a," tagging omitted *150.00*

Margin includes Bicentennial Commission emblem and inscription: USA BICENTENNIAL / HONORS COLONIAL / AMERICAN CRAFTSMEN.

OLYMPIC GAMES ISSUE

11th Winter Olympic Games, Sapporo, Japan, Feb. 3-13 and 20th Summer Olympic Games, Munich, Germany, Aug. 26-Sept. 11. See No. C85.

Bicycling and Olympic Rings — A874

Bobsledding and Olympic Rings — A875

Running and Olympic Rings — A876

"Broken red ring" Cylinder Flaw

Designed by Lance Wyman.

PHOTOGRAVURE (Andreotti)

Plates of 200 subjects in four panes of 50.

1972, Aug. 17 Tagged *Perf. 11x10½*

1460 A874 6c **black, blue, red, emerald & yellow** .30 .25
- P# block of 10, 5# 1.50 —
- Margin block of 4, Mr. Zip and "Use Zip Code" 1.00 —
- Cylinder flaw (broken red ring) (33313 UL 43) 10.00

1461 A875 8c **black, blue, red, emerald & yellow** .30 .25
- P# block of 10, 5# 1.75 —
- Margin block of 4, Mr. Zip and "Use Zip Code" 1.00 —
- *a.* Tagging omitted 7.50

1462 A876 15c **black, blue, red, emerald & yel** .30 .25
- P# block of 10, 5# 3.00 —
- Margin block of 4, Mr. Zip and "Use Zip Code" 1.20 —
- *a.* Tagging omitted —
- *Nos. 1460-1462 (3)* .90 .75

PARENT TEACHER ASSN., 75th ANNIV.

Blackboard A877

Designed by Arthur S. Congdon III.

PHOTOGRAVURE (Andreotti)

Plates of 200 subjects in four panes of 50.

1972, Sept. 15 Tagged *Perf. 11x10½*

1463 A877 8c **yellow & black** .30 .25
- P# block of 4, 2# 1.00 —
- P# block of 4, yellow # reversed 1.00 —
- Margin block of 4, Mr. Zip and "Use Zip Code" 1.00 —
- *a.* Tagging omitted *175.00*

WILDLIFE CONSERVATION ISSUE

Nos. 1464-1465 alternate in 1st row, Nos. 1468-1469 in 2nd row. This arrangement repeated throughout pane.

Fur Seals A878

Cardinal — A879

Brown Pelican — A880

Bighorn Sheep — A881

Designed by Stanley W. Galli.

LITHOGRAPHED, ENGRAVED (Giori)

Plates of 128 subjects in 4 panes of 32 (4x8).

1972, Sept. 20 Tagged *Perf. 11*

1464 A878 8c **multicolored** .30 .25

1465 A879 8c **multicolored** .30 .25

1466 A880 8c **multicolored** .30 .25

1467 A881 8c **multicolored** .30 .25
- *a.* Block of 4, #1464-1467 1.00 *1.00*
- P# block of 4 1.10 —
- Margin block of 4, Mr. Zip and "Use Zip Code" 1.00 —
- *b.* As "a," brown omitted *2,750.*
- *c.* As "a," green & blue omitted *2,750.*
- *d.* As "a," red & brown omitted *3,250.*
- *e.* As "a," tagging omitted *300.00*

MAIL ORDER BUSINESS ISSUE

Centenary of mail order business, originated by Aaron Montgomery Ward, Chicago. Design based on Headsville, W.Va., post office in Smithsonian Institution, Washington, D.C.

Rural Post Office Store — A882

Designed by Robert Lambdin.

PHOTOGRAVURE (Andreotti)

Plates of 200 subjects in four panes of 50.

1972, Sept, 27 Tagged *Perf. 11x10½*

1468 A882 8c **multicolored** .30 .25
- P# block of 12, 6# 1.75 —
- Margin block of 4, Mr. Zip and "Use Zip Code" 1.00 —

The tagging on No. 1468 consists of a vertical bar of phosphor 10mm wide.

OSTEOPATHIC MEDICINE ISSUE

75th anniv. of the American Osteopathic Assoc., founded by Dr. Andrew T. Still (1828-1917), who developed the principles of osteopathy in 1874.

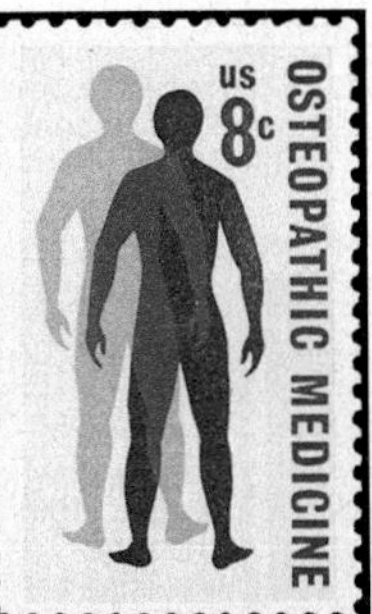

Man's Quest for Health — A883

Designed by V. Jack Ruther.

PHOTOGRAVURE (Andreotti)

Plates of 200 subjects in four panes of 50.

1972, Oct. 9 Tagged *Perf. 10½x11*

1469 A883 8c **multicolored** .30 .25
- P# block of 6, 3# 1.10 —
- Margin block of 4, Mr. Zip and "Use Zip Code" 1.00 —

AMERICAN FOLKLORE ISSUE

Tom Sawyer, by Norman Rockwell — A884

Designed by Bradbury Thompson.

LITHOGRAPHED, ENGRAVED (Giori)

Plates of 200 subjects in four panes of 50.

1972, Oct. 13 Tagged *Perf. 11*

1470 A884 8c **black, red, yellow, tan, blue & rose red** .30 .25
- P# block of 4 1.00 —
- Margin block of 4, Mr. Zip and "Use Zip Code" 1.00 —
- *a.* Horiz. pair, imperf. between *6,750.*
- *b.* Red & black (engr.) omitted *800.00*
- *c.* Yellow & tan (litho.) omitted *1,300.*
- *d.* Tagging omitted *110.*
- *e.* Red (engr. 8c) missing (CM) *750.*

CHRISTMAS ISSUE

Angels from "Mary, Queen of Heaven" — A885

Santa Claus — A886

Designers: No. 1471, Bradbury Thompson, using detail from a painting by the Master of the St. Lucy legend, in the National Gallery of Art, Washington, D.C. No. 1472, Stevan Dohanos.

PHOTOGRAVURE (Andreotti)

Plates of 200 subjects in four panes of 50.

1972, Nov. 9 Tagged *Perf. 10½x11*

1471 A885 8c **multicolored** .30 .25
- P# block of 12, 6# 1.75 —
- Margin block of 4, Mr. Zip and "Use Zip Code" 1.00 —
- *a.* Pink omitted *100.00*
- *b.* Black omitted *2,500.*

1472 A886 8c **multicolored** .30 .25
- P# block of 12, 6# 1.75 —
- Margin block of 4, Mr. Zip and "Use Zip Code" 1.00 —
- *a.* Tagging omitted —

PHARMACY ISSUE

Honoring American druggists in connection with the 120th anniversary of the American Pharmaceutical Association.

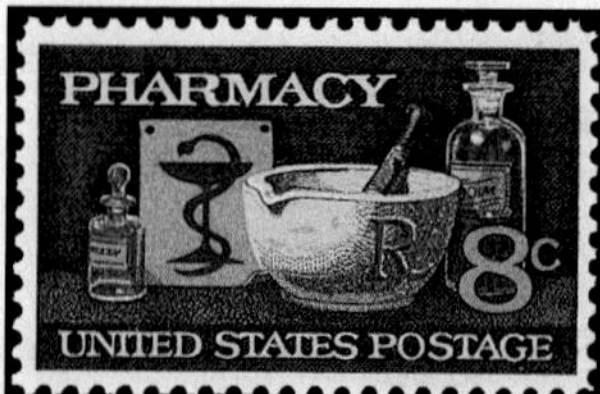

Mortar and Pestle, Bowl of Hygeia, 19th Century Medicine Bottles — A887

Designed by Ken Davies.

LITHOGRAPHED, ENGRAVED (Giori)
Plates of 200 subjects in four panes of 50.

1972, Nov. 10 **Tagged** ***Perf. 11***
1473 A887 8c **black & multi** .30 .25
P# block of 4 1.00 —
Margin block of 4, Mr. Zip and "Use Zip Code" 1.00 —
a. Blue & orange omitted *600.00*
b. Blue omitted *1,250.*
c. Orange omitted *1,250.*
d. Tagging omitted 225.00 —
e. Vertical pair, imperf horiz. *2,000.*

STAMP COLLECTING ISSUE

Issued to publicize stamp collecting.

U.S. No. 1 under Magnifying Glass — A888

Designed by Frank E. Livia.

LITHOGRAPHED, ENGRAVED (Giori)
Plates of 160 subjects in four panes of 40.

1972, Nov. 17 **Tagged** ***Perf. 11***
1474 A888 8c **multicolored** .30 .25
P# block of 4 1.00 —
Margin block of 4, Mr. Zip and "Use Zip Code" 1.00 —
a. Black (litho.) omitted *325.00*
b. Tagging omitted 4.50

Counterfeits exist of No. 1474. See the Postal Counterfeits section of this catalog.

LOVE ISSUE

"Love," by Robert Indiana A889

Designed by Robert Indiana.

PHOTOGRAVURE (Andreotti)
Plates of 200 subjects in four panes of 50.

1973, Jan. 26 **Tagged** ***Perf. 11x10½***
1475 A889 8c **red, emerald & violet blue** .30 .25
P# block of 6, 3# 1.00 —
Margin block of 4, Mr. Zip and "Use Zip Code" 1.00 —

AMERICAN BICENTENNIAL ISSUE
Communications in Colonial Times

Printer and Patriots Examining Pamphlet A890

Posting a Broadside A891

Postrider A892

Drummer A893

Designed by William A. Smith.

GIORI PRESS PRINTING
Plates of 200 subjects in four panes of 50.

1973 **Tagged** ***Perf. 11***
1476 A890 8c **ultra, greenish blk & red,** *Feb. 16* .30 .25
P# block of 4 1.00 —
Margin block of 4, Mr. Zip and "Use Zip Code" 1.00 —
a. Tagging omitted 45.00
b. Red missing (PS) *300.00*
1477 A891 8c **black, vermilion & ultra,** *Apr. 13* .30 .25
P# block of 4 1.00 —
Margin block of 4, Mr. Zip and "Use Zip Code" 1.00 —
Pair with full horiz. gutter btwn *500.00*
a. Tagging omitted —

LITHOGRAPHED, ENGRAVED (Giori)

1478 A892 8c **blue, black, red & green,** *June 22* .30 .25
P# block of 4 1.00 —
Margin block of 4, Mr. Zip and "Use Zip Code" 1.00 —
Pair with full vert. gutter btwn. —
a. Red missing (CM) *1,300.*
1479 A893 8c **blue, black, yellow & red,** *Sept. 28* .30 .25
P# block of 4 1.00 —
Margin block of 4, Mr. Zip and "Use Zip Code" 1.00 —
a. Blue missing (CM) —
b. Red missing (CM) —
Nos. 1476-1479 (4) 1.20 1.00

Margin of Nos. 1477-1479 includes Bicentennial Commission emblem and inscription.

AMERICAN BICENTENNIAL ISSUE
Boston Tea Party

In left panes Nos. 1480 and 1482 appear in 1st, 3rd and 5th place, Nos. 1481 and 1483 appear in 2nd and 4th place. This arrangement is reversed in right panes.

British Merchantman A894

British Three-master A895

Boats and Ship's Hull — A896

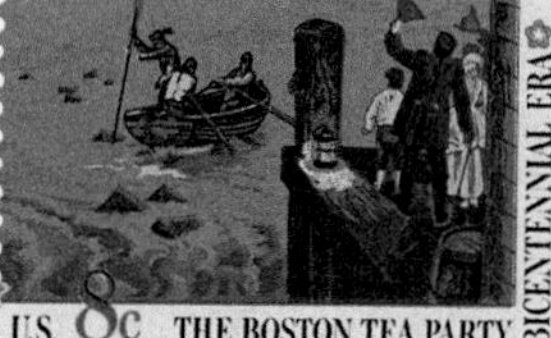

Boat and Dock — A897

Designed by William A. Smith.

LITHOGRAPHED, ENGRAVED (Giori)
Plates of 200 subjects in four panes of 50.

1973, July 4 **Tagged** ***Perf. 11***
1480 A894 8c **black & multicolored** .30 .25
1481 A895 8c **black & multicolored** .30 .25
1482 A896 8c **black & multicolored** .30 .25
1483 A897 8c **black & multicolored** .30 .25
a. Block of 4, #1480-1483 1.00 1.00
P# block of 4 1.00 —
Margin block of 4, Mr. Zip and "Use Zip Code" 1.00 —
b. As "a," black (engraved) omitted *750.00*
c. As "a," black (litho.) omitted *900.00*
d. As "a," tagging omitted *200.00* —
e. As "a," dk blue omitted *1,500.* *750.00*
On cover —

Margin includes Bicentennial Commission emblem and inscription.

AMERICAN ARTS ISSUE

George Gershwin (1898-1937), composer (No. 1484); Robinson Jeffers (1887-1962), poet (No. 1485); Henry Ossawa Tanner (1859-1937), black painter (No. 1486); Willa Cather (1873-1947), novelist (No. 1487).

Gershwin, Sportin' Life, Porgy and Bess — A898

Robinson Jeffers, Man and Children of Carmel with Burro — A899

Henry Ossawa Tanner, Palette and Rainbow A900

Willa Cather, Pioneer Family and Covered Wagon A901

Designed by Mark English.

PHOTOGRAVURE (Andreotti)
Plates of 160 subjects in four panes of 40.

1973	Tagged	Perf. 11	
1484	A898 8c **dp. green & multi.**, *Feb. 28*	.30	.25
	P# block of 12, 6#	2.00	—
	Margin block of 4, Mr. Zip, "Use Zip Code" and "Mail Early in the Day"	1.00	—
	P# block of 16, 6#, Mr. Zip and slogans	3.00	—
a.	Vertical pair, imperf. horiz.	*160.00*	
1485	A899 8c **Prussian blue & multi.**, *Aug. 13*	.30	.25
	P# block of 12, 6#	2.00	—
	Margin block of 4, Mr. Zip, "Use Zip Code" "Mail Early in the Day"	.60	—
	P# block of 16, 6#, Mr. Zip and slogans	3.00	—
a.	Vertical pair, imperf. horiz.	*160.00*	
1486	A900 8c **yellow brown & multi.**, *Sept. 10*	.30	.25
	P# block of 12, 6#	2.00	—
	Margin block of 4, Mr. Zip, "Use Zip Code" "Mail Early in the Day"	1.00	—
	P# block of 16, 6#, Mr. Zip and slogans	3.00	—
1487	A901 8c **deep brown & multi.**, *Sept. 20*	.30	.25
	P# block of 12, 6#	2.50	—
	Margin block of 4, Mr. Zip, "Use Zip Code" "Mail Early in the Day"	1.00	—
	P# block of 16, 6#, Mr. Zip and slogans	3.00	—
a.	Vertical pair, imperf. horiz.	*175.00*	
	Nos. 1484-1487 (4)	1.20	1.00

COPERNICUS ISSUE

Nicolaus Copernicus (1473-1543), Polish Astronomer — A902

Designed by Alvin Eisenman after 18th century engraving.

LITHOGRAPHED, ENGRAVED (Giori)
Plates of 200 subjects in four panes of 50.

1973, Apr. 23	Tagged	Perf. 11	
1488	A902 8c **black & orange**	.30	.25
	P# block of 4	1.00	—
	Margin block of 4, Mr. Zip and "Use Zip Code"	1.00	—
a.	Orange omitted	*400.00*	
b.	Black (engraved) omitted	*600.00*	
c.	Tagging omitted	*125.00*	

The orange can be chemically removed. Expertization of No. 1488a is required.

POSTAL SERVICE EMPLOYEES ISSUE

A tribute to US Postal Service employees. Nos. 1489-1498 are printed se-tenant in horizontal rows of 10. Emerald inscription on back, printed beneath gum in water-soluble ink, includes Postal Service emblem, "People Serving You" and a statement, differing for each of the 10 stamps, about some aspect of postal service.

Each stamp in top or bottom row has a tab with blue inscription enumerating various jobs in postal service.

Stamp Counter — A903

Mail Collection — A904

Letter Facing on Conveyor Belt — A905

Parcel Post Sorting — A906

Mail Canceling — A907

Manual Letter Routing — A908

Electronic Letter Routing — A909

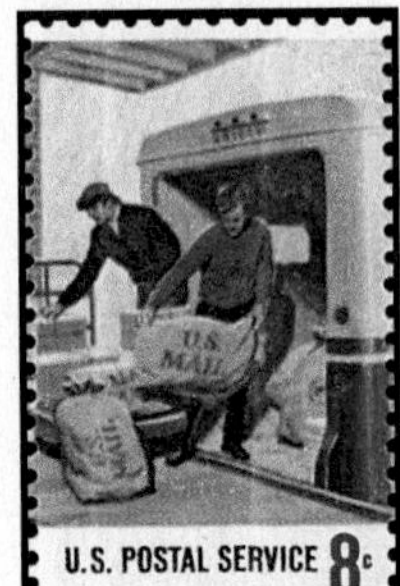

Loading Mail on Truck — A910

Mailman — A911

Rural Mail Delivery — A912

Designed by Edward Vebell.

PHOTOGRAVURE (Andreotti)
Plates of 200 subjects in four panes of 50.

1973, Apr. 30	Tagged	Perf. 10½x11	
1489	A903 8c **multicolored**	.30	.25
1490	A904 8c **multicolored**	.30	.25
1491	A905 8c **multicolored**	.30	.25
1492	A906 8c **multicolored**	.30	.25
1493	A907 8c **multicolored**	.30	.25
1494	A908 8c **multicolored**	.30	.25
1495	A909 8c **multicolored**	.30	.25
1496	A910 8c **multicolored**	.30	.25
1497	A911 8c **multicolored**	.30	.25
1498	A912 8c **multicolored**	.30	.25
a.	Strip of 10, #1489-1498	2.50	2.50
	P# block of 20, 5# and 10 tabs	4.00	—
b.	As "a," tagging omitted	*250.00*	—

The tagging on Nos. 1489-1498 consists of a ½-inch horizontal band of phosphor.

HARRY S. TRUMAN ISSUE

Harry S Truman, 33rd President, (1884-1972) — A913

Designed by Bradbury Thompson; photograph by Leo Stern.

GIORI PRESS PRINTING
Plates of 128 subjects in four panes of 32 each.

1973, May 8	Tagged	Perf. 11	
1499	A913 8c **carmine rose, black & blue**	.30	.25
	P# block of 4	1.00	—
a.	Tagging omitted	7.50	

ELECTRONICS PROGRESS ISSUE

Marconi's Spark Coil and Spark Gap — A914

Transistors and Printed Circuit Board — A915

Microphone, Speaker, Vacuum Tube and TV Camera Tube — A916

Designed by Walter and Naiad Einsel.

LITHOGRAPHED, ENGRAVED (Giori)
Plates of 200 subjects in four panes of 50.

1973, July 10	Tagged	Perf. 11	
1500	A914 6c **lilac & multicolored**	.30	.25
	P# block of 4	1.00	—
	Margin block of 4, Mr. Zip and "Use Zip Code"	1.00	—
a.	Tagging omitted	90.00	
1501	A915 8c **tan & multicolored**	.30	.25
	P# block of 4	1.00	—
	Margin block of 4, Mr. Zip and "Use Zip Code"	1.00	—

a.	Black (inscriptions & "U.S. 8c") omitted	*300.00*	
b.	Tan (background) & lilac omitted	*600.00*	
c.	Tagging omitted	*175.00*	

Many examples of No. 1501b are hinged. Value about one-half never hinged value.

1502	A916 15c **gray green & multicolored**	.30	.25
	P# block of 4	1.30	—
	Margin block of 4, Mr. Zip and "Use Zip Code"	1.20	—
a.	Black (inscriptions & "U.S. 15c") omitted	*850.00*	
	Nos. 1500-1502 (3)	.90	.75

See No. C86.

LYNDON B. JOHNSON ISSUE

Lyndon B. Johnson, 36th President (1908-1973) — A917

Designed by Bradbury Thompson, portrait by Elizabeth Shoumatoff.

PHOTOGRAVURE (Andreotti)

Plates of 128 subjects in four panes of 32 each.

1973, Aug. 27 Tagged *Perf. 11*

1503	A917 8c **black & multicolored,** *Aug. 27*	.30	.25
	P# block of 12, 6#	2.50	—
a.	Horiz. pair, imperf. vert.	*200.00*	

RURAL AMERICA ISSUE

Centenary of the introduction of Aberdeen Angus cattle into the US (#1504); of the Chautauqua Institution (#1505); and of the introduction of hard winter wheat into Kansas by Mennonite immigrants (#1506).

Angus and Longhorn Cattle — A918

Chautauqua Tent and Buggies A919

Wheat Fields and Train — A920

No. 1504 modeled by Frank Waslick after painting by F. C. "Frank" Murphy. Nos. 1505-1506 designed by John Falter.

LITHOGRAPHED, ENGRAVED (Giori)

Plates of 200 subjects in four panes of 50.

1973-74 Tagged *Perf. 11*

1504	A918 8c **multicolored,** *Oct. 5, 1973*	.30	.25
	P# block of 4	1.00	—
	Margin block of 4, Mr. Zip and "Use Zip Code"	1.00	—
a.	Green & red brown omitted	*600.00*	
b.	Vert. pair, imperf. between		*5,000.*
c.	Tagging omitted	100.00	
d.	Blue (engr.) missing (PS)	—	
1505	A919 10c **multicolored,** *Aug. 6, 1974*	.30	.25
	P# block of 4	1.00	—
	Margin block of 4, Mr. Zip and "Use Zip Code"	1.00	—
a.	Black (litho.) omitted		*1,750.*
b.	Tagging omitted	—	
1506	A920 10c **multicolored,** *Aug. 16, 1974*	.30	.25
	P# block of 4	1.00	—
	Margin block of 4, Mr. Zip and "Use Zip Code"	1.00	—
	Pair with full vert. gutter btwn.	—	
a.	Black and blue (engr.) omitted	*500.00*	
b.	Tagging omitted	100.00	
	Nos. 1504-1506 (3)	.90	.75

CHRISTMAS ISSUE

Small Cowper Madonna, by Raphael — A921

Christmas Tree in Needlepoint — A922

Designers: No. 1507, Bradbury Thompson, using a painting in the National Gallery of Art, Washington, D.C. No. 1508, Dolli Tingle.

PHOTOGRAVURE (Andreotti)

Plates of 200 subjects in four panes of 50.

1973, Nov. 7 Tagged *Perf. 10½x11*

1507	A921 8c **multicolored**	.30	.25
	P# block of 12, 6#	2.00	—
	Margin block of 4, Mr. Zip and "Use Zip Code"	1.00	—
	Pair with full vert. gutter btwn.	—	
1508	A922 8c **multicolored**	.30	.25
	P# block of 12, 6#	2.00	—
	Margin block of 4, Mr. Zip and "Use Zip Code"	1.00	—
	Pair with full horiz. gutter btwn.	750.00	
a.	Vertical pair, imperf. between	*225.00*	

The tagging on Nos. 1507-1508 consists of a 20x12mm horizontal bar of phosphor.

50-Star and 13-Star Flags — A923

Jefferson Memorial and Signature — A924

Mail Transport — A925

Liberty Bell — A926

Designers: No. 1509, Ren Wicks. No. 1510, Dean Ellis. No. 1511, Randall McDougall. 6.3c, Frank Lionetti.

MULTICOLOR HUCK PRESS

Panes of 100 (10x10)

1973-74 Tagged *Perf. 11x10½*

1509	A923 10c **red & blue,** *Dec. 8, 1973*	.30	.25
	P# block of 20, 4-6#, 2-3 "Mail Early" and 2-3 "Use Zip Code"	4.25	—
a.	Horizontal pair, imperf. between	*40.00*	—
b.	Blue omitted	*150.00*	—
c.	Imperf., vert. pair	*450.00*	
d.	Horiz. pair, imperf. vert.	*900.00*	
e.	Tagging omitted	*10.00*	
f.	Vert. pair, imperf between	—	

No. 1509 exists imperf and with red omitted from printer's waste.

Counterfeits exist of No. 1509. See the Postal Counterfeits section of this catalog.

ROTARY PRESS PRINTING

E.E. Plates of 400 subjects in four panes of 100.

1510	A924 10c **blue,** *Dec. 14, 1973*	.30	.25
	P# block of 4	1.00	—
	Margin block of 4, "Use Zip Codes"	1.00	—
	Pair with full horiz. gutter btwn.	—	
a.	Untagged (Bureau precanceled)	4.00	1.00
	P# block of 4	50.00	
	Margin block of 4, "Use Zip Codes"	25.00	
b.	Booklet pane of 5 + label	1.65	1.25
c.	Booklet pane of 8	2.00	2.00
	Pair of bklt panes with full vert. gutter btwn.	*1,750.*	
	Pair of bklt. singles with full vert. gutter btwn.	500.00	
d.	Booklet pane of 6, *Aug. 5, 1974*	5.00	1.75
e.	Vert. pair, imperf. horiz.	*300.00*	
f.	Vert. pair, imperf. btwn., in #1510c with miscut or with foldover	*600.00*	
g.	As No. 1510, tagging omitted (not Bureau precanceled)	10.00	
h.	As "c," tagging omitted	—	—
i.	As "b," double booklet pane of 10 plus stamps with 2 horiz. pairs imperf. btwn. plus stamp and label imperf. btwn. (FO)	*1,750.*	
j.	As "d," tagging omitted	—	

Counterfeits exist of No. 1510. See the Postal Counterfeits section of this catalog.

Bureau Precancels: 10 different.

No. 1510 varieties and 1510f resulted from paper foldovers after perforating and before cutting into booklet panes.

PHOTOGRAVURE (Andreotti)

Plates of 400 subjects in four panes of 100.

1511	A925 10c **multicolored,** *Jan. 4, 1974*	.30	.25
	P# block of 8, 4#	2.00	—
	Margin block of 4, "Use Zip Codes"	1.00	—
	Pair with full horiz. gutter btwn.	—	
a.	Yellow omitted	*40.00*	

Beware of stamps with yellow chemically removed offered as No. 1511a.

COIL STAMPS

ROTARY PRESS PRINTING

1973-74 Tagged *Perf. 10 Vert.*

1518	A926 6.3c **brick red,** *Oct. 1, 1974*	.30	.25
	Pair	.50	.50
	Joint line pair	.80	—
a.	Untagged (Bureau precanceled)	.35	.25
	Pair	.70	.50
	Joint line pair	1.65	1.65
b.	Imperf., pair	*130.00*	
	Joint line pair	*375.00*	
c.	As "a," imperf., pair	*75.00*	
	Joint line pair	*175.00*	

A total of 129 different Bureau precancels were used by 117 cities.

No. 1518c is precanceled Washington, DC., Columbus, Ohio and Garden City, N.Y. Values for Columbus pair $400, for Garden City pair $850.

MULTICOLOR HUCK PRESS

1519	A923 10c **red & blue,** *Dec. 8, 1973*	.30	.25
	Pair	.50	.50
a.	Imperf., pair	35.00	
b.	Tagging omitted	*9.00*	

Huck press printings often show parts of a joint line, but this feature is not consistent.

ROTARY PRESS PRINTING

1520	A924 10c **blue,** *Dec. 14, 1973*	.30	.25
	Pair	.50	.50
	Joint line pair	.75	—
a.	Untagged (Bureau precanceled)	5.50	1.25
	Pair	12.00	2.75
	Joint line pair	*185.00*	—
b.	Imperf., pair	30.00	
	Joint line pair	50.00	
c.	Tagging omitted		—

Bureau Precancels: No. 1520a, 14 diff.

VETERANS OF FOREIGN WARS ISSUE

75th anniversary of Veterans of Spanish-American and Other Foreign Wars.

Emblem and Initials of Veterans of Foreign Wars — A928

Designed by Robert Hallock.

GIORI PRESS PRINTING

Plates of 200 subjects in 4 plates of 50.

1974, Mar. 11 **Tagged** ***Perf. 11***

1525 A928 10c **red & dark blue** .30 .25
P# block of 4 1.00 —
Margin block of 4, Mr. Zip and "Use Zip Code" 1.00 —
a. Tagging omitted *90.00*
b. Blue missing (PS) 350.00

ROBERT FROST ISSUE

Robert Frost (1873-1963), Poet — A929

Designed by Paul Calle; photograph by David Rhinelander.

ROTARY PRESS PRINTING

E.E. Plates of 200 subjects in four panes of 50.

1974, Mar. 26 **Tagged** ***Perf. 10½x11***

1526 A929 10c **black** .30 .25
P# block of 4 1.00 —
Margin block of 4, Mr. Zip and "Use Zip Code" 1.00 —

EXPO '74 WORLD'S FAIR ISSUE

EXPO '74 World's Fair "Preserve the Environment," Spokane, Wash., May 4-Nov. 4.

"Cosmic Jumper" and "Smiling Sage" — A930

Designed by Peter Max.

PHOTOGRAVURE (Andreotti)

Plates of 160 subjects in four panes of 40.

1974, Apr. 18 **Tagged** ***Perf. 11***

1527 A930 10c **multicolored** .30 .25
On cover, Expo. station handstamp canc. 12.50
P# block of 12, 6# 3.00 —
Margin block of 4, Mr. Zip, "Use Zip Code" and "Mail Early in the Day" 1.00 —
P# block of 16, 6#, Mr. Zip and slogans 4.00 —

HORSE RACING ISSUE

Kentucky Derby, Churchill Downs, centenary.

Horses Rounding Turn — A931

Designed by Henry Koehler.

PHOTOGRAVURE (Andreotti)

Plates of 200 subjects in four panes of 50.

1974, May 4 **Tagged** ***Perf. 11x10½***

1528 A931 10c **yellow & multicolored** .30 .25
P# block of 12, 6# 3.25 —
Margin block of 4, Mr. Zip and "Use Zip Code" 1.10 —
a. Blue ("Horse Racing") omitted *500.00*
b. Red ("U.S. postage 10 cents") omitted *1,750.*
c. Tagging omitted 90.00

Beware of stamps offered as No. 1528b that have traces of red.

SKYLAB ISSUE

First anniversary of the launching of Skylab I, honoring all who participated in the Skylab project.

Skylab — A932

Designed by Robert T. McCall.

LITHOGRAPHED, ENGRAVED (Giori)

Plates of 200 subjects in four panes of 50.

1974, May 14 **Tagged** ***Perf. 11***

1529 A932 10c **multicolored** .30 .25
P# block of 4 1.00 —
Margin block of 4, Mr. Zip and "Use Zip Code" 1.00 —
a. Vert. pair, imperf. between —
b. Tagging omitted *10.00*
c. Vert. pair, imperf. horiz. —
d. Double impression of magenta —

UNIVERSAL POSTAL UNION ISSUE

UPU cent. In the 1st row Nos. 1530-1537 are in sequence as listed. In the 2nd row Nos. 1534-1537 are followed by Nos. 1530-1533. Every row of 8 and every horizontal block of 8 contains all 8 designs. The letter writing designs are from famous works of art; some are details. The quotation on every second stamp, "Letters mingle souls," is from a letter by poet John Donne.

Michelangelo, from "School of Athens," by Raphael, 1509 — A933

"Five Feminine Virtues," by Hokusai, c. 1811 — A934

"Old Scraps," by John Fredrick Peto, 1894 — A935

"The Lovely Reader," by Jean Etienne Liotard, 1746 — A936

"Lady Writing Letter," by Gerard Terborch, 1654 — A937

Inkwell and Quill, from "Boy with a Top," by Jean-Baptiste Simeon Chardin, 1738 — A938

Mrs. John Douglas, by Thomas Gainsborough, 1784 — A939

Don Antonio Noriega, by Francisco de Goya, 1801 — A940

Designed by Bradbury Thompson.

PHOTOGRAVURE (Andreotti)

Plates of 128 subjects in four panes of 32 each.

1974, June 6	**Tagged**	***Perf. 11***	
1530 A933 10c **multicolored**		.30	.25
1531 A934 10c **multicolored**		.30	.25
1532 A935 10c **multicolored**		.30	.25
1533 A936 10c **multicolored**		.30	.25
1534 A937 10c **multicolored**		.30	.25
1535 A938 10c **multicolored**		.30	.25
1536 A939 10c **multicolored**		.30	.25
1537 A940 10c **multicolored**		.30	.25
a. Block or strip of 8 (#1530-1537)		2.40	2.00
P# block of 16, 5#, "Mail Early in the Day," Mr. Zip and "Use Zip Code"		4.00	—
P# block of 10, 5#; no slogans		3.00	—
b. As "a," (block), imperf. vert.		*2,500.*	

MINERAL HERITAGE ISSUE

The sequence of stamps in 1st horizontal row is Nos. 1538-1541, 1538-1539. In 2nd row Nos. 1540-1541 are followed by Nos. 1538-1541.

Petrified Wood A941

Tourmaline — A942

Amethyst A943

Rhodochrosite — A944

Designed by Leonard F. Buckley.

LITHOGRAPHED, ENGRAVED (Giori)

Plates of 192 subjects in four panes of 48 (6x8).

1974, June 13	**Tagged**	***Perf. 11***	
1538 A941 10c **blue & multicolored**		.30	.25
a. Light blue & yellow (litho.) omitted		—	
1539 A942 10c **blue & multicolored**		.30	.25
a. Light blue (litho.) omitted		—	
b. Black & purple (engr.) omitted		—	
1540 A943 10c **blue & multicolored**		.30	.25
a. Light blue & yellow (litho.) omitted		—	
1541 A944 10c **blue & multicolored**		.30	.25
a. Block or strip of 4, #1538-1541		1.20	1.00
P# block of 4		1.20	—
Margin block of 4, Mr. Zip and "Use Zip Code"		1.20	—
b. As "a," light blue & yellow (litho.) omitted		*900.00*	—
c. Light blue (litho.) omitted		—	
d. Black & red (engr.) omitted		—	
e. Block of 4, two right stamps being Nos. 1539b and 1541d		*7,000.*	
f. As "a," tagging omitted		*225.00*	

No. 1541e is usually collected as a transition block of six or larger.

KENTUCKY SETTLEMENT, 200th ANNIV.
Fort Harrod, first settlement in Kentucky.

Covered Wagons at Fort Harrod — A945

Designed by David K. Stone.

LITHOGRAPHED, ENGRAVED (Giori)

Plates of 200 subjects in four panes of 50.

1974, June 15	**Tagged**	***Perf. 11***	
1542 A945 10c **green & multicolored**		.30	.25
P# block of 4		1.00	—
Margin block of 4, Mr. Zip and "Use Zip Code"		1.00	—
a. Dull black (litho.) omitted		*400.00*	
b. Green (engr. & litho.), black (engr. & litho.) & blue missing (EP)		*1,750.*	
c. Green (engr.) missing (EP)		*3,000.*	
d. Green (engr.) & black (litho.) missing (EP)			—
e. Tagging omitted			150.00
f. Blue (litho.) omitted			—

No. 1542f was caused by an occurrence that seems to be unique for U.S. total color omitted/missing errors. According to the BEP, oil on the printing blanket made a small area unreceptive to the blue ink. No blue at all was printed on one unique error stamp.

AMERICAN REVOLUTION BICENTENNIAL ISSUE
First Continental Congress

Nos. 1543-1544 alternate in 1st row, Nos. 1545-1546 in 2nd row. This arrangement is repeated throughout the pane.

Carpenters' Hall, Philadelphia A946

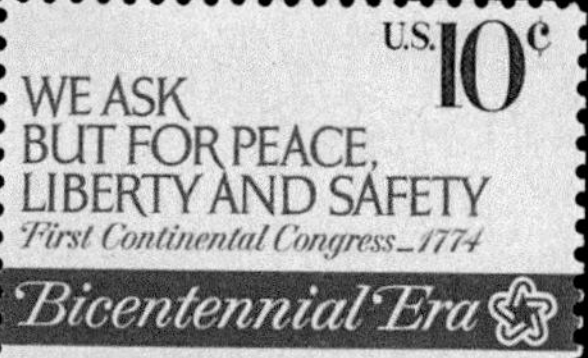

"We ask but for peace . . ." A947

"Deriving their just powers . . ." A948

Independence Hall — A949

Designed by Frank P. Conley

GIORI PRESS PRINTING

Plates of 200 subjects in four panes of 50.

1974, July 4	**Tagged**	***Perf. 11***	
1543 A946 10c **dark blue & red**		.30	.25
1544 A947 10c **gray, dark blue & red**		.30	.25
1545 A948 10c **gray, dark blue & red**		.30	.25
1546 A949 10c **red & dark blue**		.30	.25
a. Block of 4, #1543-1546		1.20	1.00
P# block of 4		1.20	—
Margin block of 4, Mr. Zip and "Use Zip Code"		1.20	—
b. As "a," tagging omitted		*65.00*	

Margin includes Bicentennial Commission emblem and inscription.

ENERGY CONSERVATION ISSUE

Publicizing the importance of conserving all forms of energy.

Molecules and Drops of Gasoline and Oil — A950

Designed by Robert W. Bode.

LITHOGRAPHED, ENGRAVED (Giori)
Plates of 200 subjects in four panes of 50.

1974, Sept. 23 **Tagged** ***Perf. 11***

1547 A950 10c **multicolored** .30 .25
P# block of 4 1.00 —
Margin block of 4, Mr. Zip and "Use Zip Code" 1.00 —
a. Blue & orange omitted *400.00*
b. Orange & green omitted *275.00*
c. Green omitted *400.00*
d. Tagging omitted 10.00

AMERICAN FOLKLORE ISSUE
Legend of Sleepy Hollow

The Headless Horseman in pursuit of Ichabod Crane from "Legend of Sleepy Hollow," by Washington Irving.

Headless Horseman and Ichabod A951

Designed by Leonard Everett Fisher.

LITHOGRAPHED, ENGRAVED (Giori)
Plates of 200 subjects in four panes of 50.

1974, Oct. 10 **Tagged** ***Perf. 11***

1548 A951 10c **dk bl, blk, org & yel** .30 .25
P# block of 4 1.00 —
Margin block of 4, Mr. Zip and "Use Zip Code" 1.00 —
a. Tagging omitted *225.00* —

RETARDED CHILDREN ISSUE

Retarded Children Can Be Helped, theme of annual convention of the National Association of Retarded Citizens.

Retarded Child — A952

Designed by Paul Calle.

GIORI PRESS PRINTING
Plates of 200 subjects in four panes of 50.

1974, Oct. 12 **Tagged** ***Perf. 11***

1549 A952 10c **brown red & dark brown** .30 .25
P# block of 4 1.00 —
Margin block of 4, Mr. Zip and "Use Zip Code" 1.00 —
a. Tagging omitted 11.00

WARNING: DO NOT SOAK ⓢ

Beginning with No. 1552, the first U.S. self-adhesive stamp, the symbol shown above, a black "S" inside a red circle, accompanies listings or appears in footnotes for self-adhesive stamps that will not separate from paper or otherwise do not respond well to a standard warm-water soak. In general, the symbol appears with the issue title, or on the listing line, next to the color description. The editors strongly recommend that such stamps be collected on piece.

CHRISTMAS ISSUE

Angel From Pérussis Altarpiece, 1480 — A953

"The Road-Winter," by Currier and Ives — A954

Designers: No. 1550, Bradbury Thompson, using detail from the Pérussis altarpiece painted by anonymous French artist, 1480, in Metropolitan Museum of Art, New York City. No. 1551, Stevan Dohanos, using Currier and Ives print from drawing by Otto Knirsch.

PHOTOGRAVURE (Andreotti)
Plates of 200 subjects in four panes of 50.

1974, Oct. 23 **Tagged** ***Perf. 10½x11***

1550 A953 10c **multicolored** .30 .25
P# block of 10, 5# 2.50 —
Margin block of 4, Mr. Zip and "Use Zip Code" 1.00 —

Perf. 11x10½

1551 A954 10c **multicolored** .30 .25
P# block of 12, 6# 3.00 —
Margin block of 4, Mr. Zip and "Use Zip Code" 1.00 —
a. Buff omitted 12.50
b. Tagging omitted *175.00*

No. 1551a is difficult to identify. Competent expertization is necessary.

Dove Weather Vane atop Mount Vernon — A955

Designers: Don Hedin and Robert Geissman.

Die Cut, Paper Backing Rouletted

1974, Nov. 15 **Untagged**

Self-adhesive; Inscribed "Precanceled"

1552 A955 10c **multicolored** ⓢ .30 .25
P# block of 20, 6#, 5 slogans 4.50
P# block of 12, 6#, 5 different slogans 3.00
Nos. 1550-1552 (3) .90 .75

Unused value of No. 1552 is for stamp on rouletted paper backing as issued. Used value is for stamp on piece, with or without postmark. **Most examples are becoming discolored from the adhesive. The Catalogue value is for discolored examples.**

Die cutting includes crossed slashes through dove, applied to prevent removal and re-use of the stamp. The stamp will separate into layers if soaked.

Two different machines were used to roulette the sheet.

See note after No. 1549.

AMERICAN ARTS ISSUE

Benjamin West (1738-1820), painter (No. 1553); Paul Laurence Dunbar (1872-1906), poet (No. 1554); David (Lewelyn) Wark Griffith (1875-1948), motion picture producer (No. 1555).

Self-portrait — A956

A957

A958

Designers: No. 1553, Bradbury Thompson; No. 1554, Walter D. Richards; No. 1555, Fred Otnes.

PHOTOGRAVURE (Andreotti)
Plates of 200 subjects in four panes of 50.

1975 **Tagged** ***Perf. 10½x11***

1553 A956 10c **multicolored**, *Feb. 10* .30 .25
P# block of 10, 5# 2.50 —
Margin block of 4, Mr. Zip and "Use Zip Code" 1.00 —

Perf. 11

1554 A957 10c **multicolored**, *May 1* .30 .25
P# block of 10, 5# 2.50 —
Margin block of 4, Mr. Zip and "Use Zip Code" 1.00 —
a. Imperf., pair *600.00*
b. Tagging omitted *350.00*

LITHOGRAPHED, ENGRAVED (Giori)

Perf. 11

1555 A958 10c **brown & multicolored**, *May 27* .30 .25
P# block of 4 1.00 —
Margin block of 4, Mr. Zip and "Use Zip Code" 1.00 —
a. Brown (engr.) omitted *450.00*
b. Tagging omitted *175.00*
Nos. 1553-1555 (3) .90 .75

SPACE ISSUES

US space accomplishments with unmanned craft. Pioneer 10 passed within 81,000 miles of Jupiter, Dec. 10, 1973. Mariner 10 explored Venus and Mercury in 1974 and Mercury again in 1975.

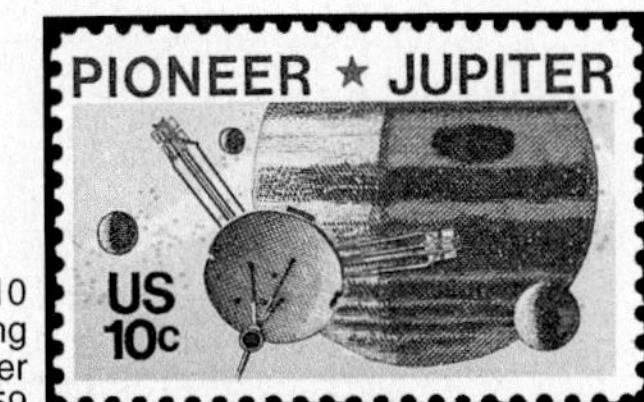

Pioneer 10 Passing Jupiter A959

Mariner 10, Venus and Mercury A960

Designed by Robert McCall (No. 1556); Roy Gjertson (No. 1557).

LITHOGRAPHED, ENGRAVED (Giori)
Plates of 200 subjects in four panes of 50.

1975 **Tagged** ***Perf. 11***

1556 A959 10c **light yellow, dark yellow, red, blue & 2 dark blues** *Feb. 28* .30 .25
P# block of 4 1.00 —
Margin block of 4, Mr. Zip and "Use Zip Code" 1.00 —
a. Red & dark yellow omitted *750.00*

b. Dark blues (engr.) omitted *400.00*
c. Tagging omitted *12.50*
d. Dark yellow omitted —

Imperfs. exist from printer's waste.

1557 A960 10c **black, red, ultra & bister,** *Apr. 4* .30 .25
P# block of 4 1.00 —
Margin block of 4, Mr. Zip and "Use Zip Code" 1.00 —
a. Red omitted *275.00* —
b. Ultramarine & bister omitted *750.00*
c. Tagging omitted *12.50*
d. Red missing (PS) *525.00*

COLLECTIVE BARGAINING ISSUE

Collective Bargaining law, enacted 1935, in Wagner Act.

"Labor and Management" A961

Designed by Robert Hallock.

PHOTOGRAVURE (Andreotti)
Plates of 200 subjects in four panes of 50.

1975, Mar. 13 **Tagged** ***Perf. 11***
1558 A961 10c **multicolored** .30 .25
P# block of 8, 4# 2.00 —
Margin block of 4, Mr. Zip and "Use Zip Code" 1.00 —

Imperforates exist from printer's waste.

AMERICAN BICENTENNIAL ISSUE

Contributors to the Cause

Sybil Ludington, age 16, rallied militia, Apr. 26, 1777; Salem Poor, black freeman, fought in Battle of Bunker Hill; Haym Salomon, Jewish immigrant, raised money to finance Revolutionary War; Peter Francisco, Portuguese-French immigrant, joined Continental Army at 15. Emerald inscription on back, printed beneath gum in water-soluble ink, gives thumbnail sketch of portrayed contributor.

Sybil Ludington A962

Salem Poor — A963

Haym Salomon A964

Peter Francisco A965

Designed by Neil Boyle.

PHOTOGRAVURE (Andreotti)
Plates of 200 subjects in four panes of 50.

1975, Mar. 25 **Tagged** ***Perf. 11x10½***
1559 A962 8c **multicolored** .30 .25
P# block of 10, 5# 2.50 —
Margin block of 4, Mr. Zip and "Use Zip Code" 1.00 —
a. Back inscriptions omitted *110.00*
1560 A963 10c **multicolored** .30 .25
P# block of 10, 5# 2.50 —
Margin block of 4, Mr. Zip and "Use Zip Code" 1.00 —
a. Back inscription omitted *110.00*
b. Black missing (PS) —
1561 A964 10c **multicolored** .30 .25
P# block of 10, 5# 2.50 —
Margin block of 4, Mr. Zip and "Use Zip Code" 1.00 —
a. Back inscription omitted *110.00*
1562 A965 18c **multicolored** .35 .25
P# block of 10, 5# 3.60 —
Margin block of 4, Mr. Zip and "Use Zip Code" 1.45 —
Nos. 1559-1562 (4) 1.25 1.00

On No. 1560, two black plates were used. No. 1560b is missing the impression from one of those plates ("Salem Poor - U.S. Bicentennial symbol - Gallant Soldier") due to an upward shift of the horizontal perforations.

Dangerous fakes exist of No. 1561 with red apparently omitted. Professional authentication is mandatory in order to establish such a stamp as a genuine error.

Lexington-Concord Battle, 200th Anniv.

"Birth of Liberty," by Henry Sandham A966

Designed by Bradbury Thompson.

PHOTOGRAVURE (Andreotti)
Plates of 160 subjects in four panes of 40.

1975, Apr. 19 **Tagged** ***Perf. 11***
1563 A966 10c **multicolored** .30 .25
P# block of 12, 6# 2.50 —
Margin block of 4, Mr. Zip, "Use Zip Code" and "Mail Early in the Day" 1.00 —
P# block of 16, 6 P#, Mr. Zip and slogans 3.40 —
a. Vert. pair, imperf. horiz. *300.00*

Bunker Hill Battle, 200th Anniv.

Battle of Bunker Hill, by John Trumbull — A967

Designed by Bradbury Thompson.

PHOTOGRAVURE (Andreotti)
Plates of 160 subjects in four panes of 40.

1975, June 17 **Tagged** ***Perf. 11***
1564 A967 10c **multicolored** .30 .25
P# block of 12, 6# 2.50 —
Margin block of 4, Mr. Zip, "Use Zip Code" and "Mail Early in the Day" 1.00 —
P# block of 16, 6#, Mr. Zip and slogans 3.40 —

Military Uniforms

Bicentenary of US Military Services. Nos. 1565-1566 alternate in one row, Nos. 1567-1568 in next row.

Soldier with Flintlock Musket, Uniform Button — A968

Sailor with Grappling Hook, First Navy Jack, 1775 — A969

Marine with Musket, Fullrigged Ship — A970

Militiaman with Musket and Powder Horn — A971

Designed by Edward Vebell.

PHOTOGRAVURE (Andreotti)
Plates of 200 subjects in four panes of 50.

1975, July 4 **Tagged** ***Perf. 11***
1565 A968 10c **multicolored** .30 .25
a. Tagging omitted —
1566 A969 10c **multicolored** .30 .25
1567 A970 10c **multicolored** .30 .25
1568 A971 10c **multicolored** .30 .25
a. Block of 4, #1565-1568 1.20 1.00
P# block of 12, 6# 2.50 —
P# block of 20, 6#, Mr. Zip and slogans 4.50 —
Margin block of 4, Mr. Zip and "Use Zip Code" 1.20 —
b. As "a," tagging omitted on #1565 and 1566 —

APOLLO SOYUZ SPACE ISSUE

Apollo Soyuz space test project, Russo-American cooperation, launched July 15; link-up, July 17. Nos. In the 1st row, No. 1569 is in 1st and 3rd space, No. 1570 is 2nd space; in the 2nd row No. 1570 is in 1st and 3rd space, No. 1569 in 2nd space, etc.

Participating US and USSR crews: Thomas P. Stafford, Donald K. Slayton, Vance D. Brand, Aleksei A. Leonov, Valery N. Kubasov.

Apollo and Soyuz after Link-up, and Earth — A972

Spacecraft before Link-up, Earth and Project Emblem — A973

Illustrations reduced.

Designed by Robert McCall (No. 1569) and Anatoly M. Aksamit of USSR (No. 1570).

PHOTOGRAVURE (Andreotti)

Plates of 96 subjects in four panes of 24 each.

1975, July 15 **Tagged** ***Perf. 11***

1569 A972 10c **multicolored** .30 .25
Pair with full horiz. gutter btwn. —
1570 A973 10c **multicolored** .30 .25
a. Pair, #1569-1570 .60 .50
P# block of 12, 6# 2.50 —
Margin block of 4, Mr. Zip, "Use Zip Code" 1.00 —
P# block of 16, 6#, Mr. Zip, "Use Zip Code" 3.40 —
Pair with full horiz. gutter btwn. —
b. As "a," tagging omitted *30.00* —
c. As "a," vert. pair, imperf. horiz. *800.00*
d. As "a," yellow omitted *900.00*

Nos. 1569-1570 totally imperforate are printer's waste.
See Russia Nos. 4339-4340.

INTERNATIONAL WOMEN'S YEAR ISSUE

International Women's Year 1975.

Worldwide Equality for Women A974

Designed by Miriam Schottland.

PHOTOGRAVURE (Andreotti)

Plates of 200 subjects in four panes of 50.

1975, Aug. 26 **Tagged** ***Perf. 11x10½***

1571 A974 10c **blue, orange & dark blue** .30 .25
P# block of 6, 3# 1.30 —
Margin block of 4, Mr. Zip and "Use Zip Code" 1.00 —
a. Tagging omitted 10.00

US POSTAL SERVICE BICENTENNIAL ISSUE

Nos. 1572-1573 alternate in 1st row, Nos. 1574-1575 in 2nd row. This arrangement is repeated throughout the pane.

Stagecoach and Trailer Truck — A975

Old and New Locomotives A976

Early Mail Plane and Jet — A977

Satellite for Transmission of Mailgrams A978

Designed by James L. Womer.

PHOTOGRAVURE (Andreotti)

Plates of 200 subjects in four panes of 50.

1975, Sept. 3 **Tagged** ***Perf. 11x10½***

1572 A975 10c **multicolored** .30 .25
1573 A976 10c **multicolored** .30 .25
1574 A977 10c **multicolored** .30 .25
1575 A978 10c **multicolored** .30 .25
a. Block of 4, #1572-1575 1.20 1.00
P# block of 12, 6# 2.50 —
P# block of 20, 6#, Mr. Zip and slogans 4.50 —
Margin block of 4, Mr. Zip and "Use Zip Code" 1.20 —
b. As "a," red "10c" omitted, tagging omitted —

WORLD PEACE THROUGH LAW ISSUE

A prelude to 7th World Law Conference of the World Peace Through Law Center at Washington, D.C., Oct. 12-17.

Law Book, Gavel, Olive Branch and Globe — A979

Designed by Melbourne Brindle.

GIORI PRESS PRINTING

Plates of 200 subjects in four panes of 50.

1975, Sept. 29 **Tagged** ***Perf. 11***

1576 A979 10c **green, Prussian blue & rose brown** .30 .25
P# block of 4 1.00 —
Margin block of 4, Mr. Zip and "Use Zip Code" 1.00 —
a. Tagging omitted 10.00
b. Horiz. pair, imperf vert. *7,500.*
c. All colors omitted 725.00

No. 1576c is collected in a horiz. strip as two errors se-tenant with a partially printed stamp.

BANKING AND COMMERCE ISSUE

Banking and commerce in the U.S., and for the Centennial Convention of the American Bankers Association.

Engine Turning, Indian Head Penny, Morgan-type Silver Dollar — A980

Seated Liberty Quarter, $20 Gold Double Eagle and Engine Turning A981

Designed by V. Jack Ruther.

LITHOGRAPHED, ENGRAVED (Giori)

Plates of 160 subjects in four panes of 40.

1975, Oct. 6 **Tagged** ***Perf. 11***

1577 A980 10c **multicolored** .30 .25
1578 A981 10c **multicolored** .30 .25
a. Pair, #1577-1578 .60 .50
P# block of 4 1.00 —
Margin block of 4, Mr. Zip and "Use Zip Code" 1.00 —
b. As "a," brown & blue (litho) omitted *1,100.*
c. As "a," brown, blue & yellow (litho) omitted *1,750.*
d. As No. 1578a, tagging omitted —

CHRISTMAS ISSUE

Madonna and Child, by Domenico Ghirlandaio — A982

Christmas Card, by Louis Prang, 1878 — A983

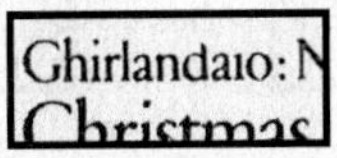

Ghirlandaio: N
Christmas

Plate flaw ("d" damaged and no dot on the second "i" in "Ghirlandaio")

Designed by Stevan Dohanos.

PHOTOGRAVURE (Andreotti)

Plates of 200 subjects in four panes of 50.

1975, Oct. 14 **Tagged** ***Perf. 11***

1579 A982 (10c) **multicolored** .30 .25
P# block of 12, 6# 2.50 —
Margin block of 4, Mr. Zip and "Use Zip Code" 1.00 —
Plate flaw ("d" damaged and no dot on the second "i" in "Ghirlandaio") (36741-36746 LL 47) 5.00 —
a. Imperf., pair *75.00*

Perf. 11.2

1580 A983 (10c) **multicolored** .30 .25
P# block of 12, 6# 2.50 —
Margin block of 4, Mr. Zip and "Use Zip Code" 1.00 —
a. Imperf., pair *85.00*
c. Perf. 10.9 .30 .25
P# block of 12, 6# 3.50 —
Margin block of 4, Mr. Zip and "Use Zip Code" 1.00 —

Perf. 10.5x11.3

1580B A983 (10c) **multicolored,** .65 .25
P# block of 12, 6# 14.00 —
Margin block of 4, Mr. Zip and "Use Zip Code" 2.75 —

AMERICANA ISSUE

Inkwell and Quill — A984

Speaker's Stand — A985

Early Ballot Box — A987

Books, Bookmark, Eyeglasses — A988

Dome of Capitol — A994

Contemplation of Justice, by J. E. Fraser — A995

Early American Printing Press — A996

Torch, Statue of Liberty — A997

Liberty Bell — A998

Eagle and Shield — A999

Fort McHenry Flag (15 Stars) — A1001

Head, Statue of Liberty — A1002

Old North Church, Boston — A1003

Fort Nisqually, Wash. — A1004

Sandy Hook Lighthouse, NJ — A1005

Morris Township School No. 2, Devils Lake, ND — A1006

Iron "Betty" Lamp, Plymouth Colony, 17th-18th Centuries — A1007

Rush Lamp and Candle Holder — A1008

Kerosene Table Lamp — A1009

Railroad Conductor's Lantern, c. 1850 — A1010

Designed by: 2c, 4c, 15c, V. Jack Ruther and Robert Hallock. 3c, Clarence Holbert. 9c, 10c, 11c, Walter Brooks. 12c, George Mercer. No. 1595, Bernard Glassman. No. 1596, James L. Womer.

ROTARY PRESS PRINTING

E.E. Plates of 400 subjects in four panes of 100.

1975-81 Tagged ***Perf. 11¼x10½***

Size: 18½x22½mm

1581 A984 1c **dark blue,** *greenish,* shiny gum, *Dec. 8, 1977* .30 .25
P# block of 4 .60 —
Margin block of 4, "Use Zip Code" .30 —
Dull gum .30
P# block of 4 .60
Zip block of 4 .30
Pair with full vert. gutter btwn. —
a. Untagged (Bureau precanceled) 4.50 1.50
P# block of 4 30.00
Margin block of 4, "Use Zip Codes" 18.50
c. White paper, dull gum — —
d. Tagging omitted (not Bureau precanceled), shiny gum 7.50
Dull gum 7.50

1582 A985 2c **red brown,** *greenish,* shiny gum, *Dec. 8, 1977* .30 .25
P# block of 4 .60 —
Margin block of 4, "Use Zip Code" .30 —
Dull gum .30
P# block of 4 2.50
Zip block of 4 1.00
a. Untagged (Bureau precanceled) 4.50 1.50
P# block of 4 30.00
Zip block of 4 18.50
b. Cream paper, dull gum, *1981* .30 .25
P# block of 4 .60
Zip block of 4 .30
c. Tagging omitted (not Bureau precanceled) 7.50

1584 A987 3c **olive,** *greenish,* shiny gum, *Dec. 8, 1977* .30 .25
P# block of 4 .60 —
Margin block of 4, "Use Zip Code" .60 —
Dull gum .30
P# block of 4 .60
Zip block of 4 .60
Pair with full horiz. gutter btwn. *275.00*
a. Untagged (Bureau precanceled), dull gum .75 .50
P# block of 4 9.50
Zip block of 4 5.00
b. Tagging omitted (not Bureau precanceled), shiny gum 10.00
dull gum 10.00

Values for No. 1584a are for the lines-only precancel. Also known with city precancels, and valued at $50 thus.

1585 A988 4c **rose magenta,** *cream,* shiny gum, *Dec. 8, 1977* .30 .25
P# block of 4 .75 —
Margin block of 4, "Use Zip Code" .60 —
Dull gum .30
P# block of 4 1.10
Zip block of 4 1.00
Pair with full horiz. gutter btwn. *150.00*
a. Untagged (Bureau precanceled) 1.00 .75
P# block of 4 13.50
Zip block of 4 6.00
b. Tagging omitted (not Bureau precanceled), dull gum *65.00*
Shiny gum *40.00*

The pair with horiz. gutter between also is misperfed through the stamps horizontally.

Also known with city precancels, and valued at $100 thus.

Size: 17½x20½mm

Perf. 11x10½ on 3 Sides

1590 A994 9c **slate green** (from bklt. pane #1623a), *Mar. 11, 1977* .45 *1.00*
Pair with full horiz. gutter between —
b. Tagging omitted —

Perf. 10x9¾ on 3 Sides

1590A A994 9c **slate green** (from bklt. pane #1623Bc), *Mar. 11, 1977* 12.50 12.50

Size: 18½x22½mm

Perf. 11¼x10½

1591 A994 9c **slate green,** *gray,* shiny gum, *Nov. 24, 1975* .30 .25
P# block of 4 1.00 —
Margin block of 4, "Use Zip Code" 1.00 —
Dull gum 1.00
P# block of 4 5.00
Zip block of 4 4.25
a. Untagged (Bureau precanceled) 1.75 1.00
P# block of 4 45.00
Zip block of 4 8.00
b. Tagging omitted (not Bureau precanceled) 6.00

Values for No. 1591a are for the lines-only precancel. Also known with city precancels, and valued at $32.50 thus.

1592 A995 10c **violet,** *gray,* shiny gum, *Nov. 17, 1977* .30 .25
P# block of 4 1.00 —
Margin block of 4, "Use Zip Code" 1.00 —
Dull gum .30
P# block of 4 1.00
Zip block of 4 1.00
a. Untagged (Bureau precanceled, Chicago) 9.50 5.00
P# block of 4 95.00
Zip block of 4 42.50
b. Tagging omitted (not Bureau precanceled), dull gum 7.50

1593 A996 11c **orange,** *gray, Nov. 13, 1975* .30 .25
P# block of 4 1.00 —
Margin block of 4, "Use Zip Code" 1.00 —
Pair with full horiz. gutter between —
a. Tagging omitted 5.00

1594 A997 12c **red brown,** *beige,* dull gum, *Apr. 8, 1981* .30 .25
brownish red .30 .25
P# block of 4 1.60 —
Zip block of 4 1.10 —
a. Tagging omitted 10.00

Perf. 11¼x10½ on 2 or 3 Sides

1595 A998 13c **brown** (from bklt. pane), *Oct. 31, 1975* .30 .25
a. Booklet pane of 6 2.25 1.50
b. Booklet pane of 7 + label 2.25 1.50
c. Booklet pane of 8 2.25 1.50
d. Booklet pane of 5 + label, *Apr. 2, 1976* 1.75 1.25
e. Vert. pair, imperf. btwn., in #1595c with foldover *1,500.*
f. Tagging omitted — —
g. Horiz. pair, imperf. btwn., in #1595d with foldover —
h. As "a," miscut and inserted upside down into booklet cover, imperf below bottom stamps and with "tab" at bottom —
i. As "b," tagging omitted —
j. As "d," tagging omitted —

Nos. 1595e and 1595g resulted from paper foldovers after perforating and before cutting into panes. Beware of printer's waste consisting of complete panes with perfs around all outside edges.

Counterfeits exist of No. 1595. See the Postal Counterfeits section of this catalog.

PHOTOGRAVURE (Andreotti)

Plates of 400 subjects in four panes of 100.

Perf. 11¼ Bullseye

1596 A999 13c **multicolored,** *Dec. 1, 1975* .30 .25
On cover 50.00
P# block of 12, 6# 3.25 —
P# block of 20, 6# and slogans 5.50 —
Margin block of 4, "Use Zip Code" 1.00 —
Pair with full horiz. gutter btwn. *150.00*
a. Imperf., pair *40.00* —
b. Yellow omitted *75.00*
d. Line perforated 11 *27.50* —
P# block of 12, 6# *350.00* —

On No. 1596 the entire sheet is perforated at one time so the perforations meet perfectly at the corners of the stamp. On No. 1596d the perforations do not line up perfectly.

ENGRAVED (Combination Press)

Plates of 460 subjects (20x23) in panes of 100 (10x10)

Perf. 11x11¼

1597 A1001 15c **gray, dark blue & red,** large block tagging, *June 30, 1978* .30 .25
P# block of 6 1.90 —
P# block of 20, 1-2# 6.50 —
a. Small block tagging .30 .25
P# block of 6 1.90 —
P# block of 20, 1-2# 6.50 —
b. Gray omitted *300.00*
c. Vert. pair, imperf btwn and with natural straight edge at bottom *350.00*
d. Tagging omitted 5.00
e. Imperf., vert. pair *15.00*
f. As "e," tagging omitted —

Plate number appears 3 times on each plate of 23 rows. With no separating gutters, each pane has only left or right sheet margin. Plate numbers appear on both margins; there are no slogans.

ENGRAVED

Perf. 11x10½ on 2 or 3 Sides

1598 A1001 15c **gray, dark blue & red** (from bklt. pane), *June 30, 1978* .40 .25
a. Booklet pane of 8 3.75 1.50

Perf. 11¼x10½

1599 A1002 16c **blue,** *Mar. 31, 1978* .35 .25
P# block of 4 1.90 —
Margin block of 4, "Use Correct Zip Code" 1.40 —

1603 A1003 24c **red,** *blue, Nov. 14, 1975* .50 .25
P# block of 4 2.25 —
Margin block of 4, "Use Zip Code" 2.00 —
a. Tagging omitted 7.50
b. **red,** *greenish blue* .50 .25
P# block of 4 2.25 —
Margin block of 4, "Use Zip Code" 2.00

1604 A1004 28c **brown,** *blue,* shiny gum, *Aug. 11, 1978* .55 .25
P# block of 4 3.00 —
Margin block of 4, "Use Correct Zip Code" 2.25 —
Dull gum 1.10
P# block of 4 10.00
Zip block of 4 5.00

1605 A1005 29c **blue,** *light blue,* shiny gum, *Apr. 14, 1978* .60 .25
P# block of 4 3.00 —
Margin block of 4, "Use Correct Zip Code" 2.40 —
Dull gum 2.00

P# block of 4 15.00
Zip block of 4 9.00
1606 A1006 30c **green,** *blue, Aug. 27, 1979* .55 .25
P# block of 4 2.40 —
Margin block of 4, "Use Correct Zip Code" 2.25 —
a. Tagging omitted 55.00

LITHOGRAPHED AND ENGRAVED

Perf. 11

1608 A1007 50c **tan, black & orange,** *Sept. 11, 1979* .85 .25
P# block of 4 3.75 —
Margin block of 4, "Use Correct Zip Code" 3.50 —
a. Black omitted *375.00*
b. Vert. pair, imperf. horiz. *1,200.*
c. Tagging omitted 20.00

Beware of examples offered as No. 1608b that have blind perfs.

1610 A1008 $1 **tan, brown, orange & yellow,** *July 2, 1979* 2.00 .25
P# block of 4 8.50 —
Margin block of 4, "Use Correct Zip Code" 8.00 —
Pair with full vert. gutter btwn. —
a. Brown (engraved) omitted *175.00*
b. Tan, orange & yellow omitted *175.00*
c. Brown (engraved) inverted *17,000.*
d. Tagging omitted *20.00*
1611 A1009 $2 **tan, dark green, orange & yellow,** *Nov. 16, 1978* 3.75 .75
dark tan, dark green, orange & yellow 3.75 .75
P# block of 4 16.00 —
Margin block of 4, "Use Correct Zip Code" 15.00 —
a. Tagging omitted — —
1612 A1010 $5 **tan, red brown, yellow & orange,** *Aug. 23, 1979* 8.50 1.75
P# block of 4 36.00 —
Margin block of 4, "Use Correct Zip Code" 34.00 —
Nos. 1581-1612 (23) 34.30 20.75

Nos. 1590, 1590A, 1595, 1598, 1623 and 1623b were issued only in booklets. All stamps have one or two straight edges.

Bureau Precancels: 1c, 3 diff., 2c, Chicago, Greensboro, NC, 3c, 6 diff., 4c, Chicago, lines only, No. 1591a, 4 diff., No. 1596, 5 diff., 30c, lines only, 50c, 3 spacings, lines only, $1, 2 spacings, lines only. The 30c, 50c, $1 and No. 1596 are precanceled on tagged stamps.

Six-string Guitar — A1011

Saxhorns — A1012

Drum — A1013

Steinway Grand Piano, 1857 — A1014

Designers: 3.1c, George Mercer. 7.7c, Susan Robb. 7.9c, Bernard Glassman. 10c, Walter Brooks. 15c, V. Jack Ruther.

COIL STAMPS
ENGRAVED

1975-79 ***Perf. 10 Vertically***

1613 A1011 3.1c **brown,** *yellow, Oct. 25, 1979* .30 .25
Pair .50 .50
Joint line pair 1.25 —
a. Untagged (Bureau precanceled, lines only) .35 .35
Pair .70 .70
Joint line pair 7.00 —
b. Imperf., pair *850.00*
Joint line pair —
1614 A1012 7.7c **brown,** *bright yellow, Nov. 20, 1976* .30 .25
Pair .50 .50
Joint line pair .90 —
a. Untagged (Bureau precanceled) .40 .30
Pair .80 .60
Joint line pair 3.25 —
b. As "a," imperf., pair *1,250.*
Joint line pair *3,000.*

A total of 160 different Bureau precancels were used by 153 cities.

No. 1614b is precanceled Washington, DC. Also exists with Marion, OH precancel; value $1,950 for pair.

1615 A1013 7.9c **carmine,** *yellow,* shiny gum, *Apr. 23, 1976* .30 .25
Pair .50 .50
Joint line pair .75 —
Dull gum 1.00
Pair 2.00
Joint line pair 6.00
a. Untagged (Bureau precanceled), shiny gum .40 .40
Pair .80 .80
Joint line pair 2.75 —
Dull gum .45
Pair .90
Joint line pair 4.50
b. Imperf., pair *300.00*

A total of 109 different Bureau precancels were used by 107 cities plus two types of CAR. RT./SORT.

1615C A1014 8.4c **dark blue,** *yellow,* shiny gum, *July 13, 1978* .30 .25
Pair .50 .50
Joint line pair 3.25 .60
d. Untagged (Bureau precanceled), shiny gum .50 .40
Pair 1.00 .80
Joint line pair 4.25 —
Dull gum .40
Pair .80
Joint line pair 3.25
e. As "d," pair, imperf. between 45.00
Joint line pair *110.00*
f. As "d," imperf. pair, shiny gum 15.00
Joint line pair *35.00*
Dull gum *15.00*
Joint line pair *35.00*

A total of 145 different Bureau precancels were used by 144 cities.

No. 1615Ce is precanceled with lines only. No. 1615Cf is precanceled with lines only (value shown) and also exists in pairs precanceled Newark, N.J. ($25)., Brownstown, Ind. ($900), Oklahoma City, Okla. ($1,500.) and Washington, DC ($500).

1616 A994 9c **slate green,** *gray, Mar. 5, 1976* .30 .25
Pair .50 .50
Joint line pair .90 —
a. Imperf., pair *125.00*
Joint line pair *260.00*
b. Untagged (Bureau precanceled), shiny gum 1.15 .75
Pair 2.30 1.50
Joint line pair 42.50 —
Dull gum .75
Pair 1.50
Joint line pair 19.50
c. As "b," imperf., pair *600.00*
Joint line pair —

Values for No. 1616b with shiny gum are for the lines-only precancel. Also known with city precancels, and worth more thus.

No. 1616c is precanceled Pleasantville, NY.

1617 A995 10c **violet,** *gray,* shiny gum, *Nov. 4, 1977* .30 .25
Pair .50 .50
Joint line pair 1.00 —
Dull gum .30
Pair .60
Joint line pair 2.50
a. Untagged (Bureau precanceled, shiny gum) 42.50 1.35
Pair 90.00 2.75
Joint line pair *1,150.* —
Dull gum 1.35
Pair 2.75
Joint line pair 47.50
b. Imperf., pair, shiny gum 80.00
Joint line pair, shiny gum *150.00*
Imperf., pair, dull gum 55.00
Joint line pair, dull gum *115.00*
c. As "a," imperf pair, dull gum *3,750.*
Joint line pair, dull gum *4,750.*
1618 A998 13c **brown,** shiny gum, *Nov. 25, 1975* .30 .25
Pair .50 .50
Joint line pair .75 —
Dull gum 1.50
Pair 3.00
Joint line pair 9.00
a. Untagged (Bureau precanceled), shiny gum 5.75 .75
Pair 12.00 1.50
Joint line pair 100.00 —
Dull gum .75
Pair 1.50
Joint line pair 32.50
b. Imperf., pair 22.50
Joint line pair 45.00
g. Pair, imperf. between *600.00*
h. As "a," imperf., pair —
j. As No. 1618, shiny gum, tagging omitted —

Values for No. 1618a with shiny gum are for the lines-only precancel. Also known with city precancels, and worth more thus. No. 1618a with dull gum and lines-only precancel is extremely scarce and is worth much more than the values shown.

1618C A1001 15c **gray, dark blue & red,** small block tagging, *June 30, 1978* .75 .25
Pair 1.50 .50
d. Imperf., pair, small block tagging 20.00
e. Pair, imperf. between *100.00*
f. Gray omitted 30.00
i. Tagging omitted 65.00
k. As "d," tagging omitted —

l. Large block tagging .90 .35
Pair 1.80 .70
1619 A1002 16c **ultramarine,** overall tagging, *Mar. 31, 1978* .35 .25
Pair .70 .50
Joint line pair 1.75 —
a. Block tagging .50 .25
Pair 1.00 .50
Nos. 1613-1619 (9) 3.20 2.25

No. 1619a (the B press printing) has a white background without bluish tinge, is a fraction of a millimeter smaller than No. 1619 (the Cottrell press printing) and has no joint lines.

Bureau Precancels: 9c, 7 diff., 10c, 3 diff., 13c, 12 diff.

See Nos. 1811, 1813, 1816.

13-Star Flag over Independence Hall — A1015

Designer: No. 1622, Melbourne Brindle.

Panes of 100 (10x10) each.

1975-81 ***Perf. 11x10¾***

1622 A1015 13c **dk blue, red & brown red,** *Nov. 15, 1975* .30 .25
P# block of 20, 2-3#, 2-3 Zip, 2-3 Mail Early 6.00 —
a. Horiz. pair, imperf. between 40.00
b. Vertical pair, imperf. *225.00*
e. Horiz. pair, imperf. vert. —
f. Tagging omitted 9.00
g. As "a," tagging omitted —

No. 1622 was printed on the Multicolored Huck Press. Plate markings are at top or bottom of pane. It has large block tagging and nearly vertical multiple gum ridges.

See note after No. 1338F for marginal markings.

Perf. 11¼

1622C A1015 13c **dk blue, red & brown red,** *1981* 1.00 .25
P# block of 20, 1-2#, 1-2 Zip 35.00 —
P# block of 6 25.00 —
d. Vertical pair, imperf 100.00
h. As "d," tagging omitted —

No. 1622C was printed on the Combination Press. Plate markings are at sides of pane. It has small block tagging and shiny flat gum.

See note after No. 1703.

Flag over Capitol — A1016

Designer: No. 1623, Esther Porter.

BOOKLET STAMPS

Perf. 11x10½ on 2 or 3 Sides

1977, Mar. 11 **Engr.**

1623 A1016 13c **blue & red** .30 .25
a. Booklet pane, 1 #1590 + 7 #1623 2.25 2.00
d. Pair, #1590 & #1623 .70 *1.25*
f. Tagging omitted —
g. As "a," tagging omitted —

Perf. 10x9¾ on 2 or 3 Sides

1623B A1016 13c **blue & red** .65 .75
c. Booklet pane, 1 #1590A + 7 #1623B 15.00 15.00
e. Pair, #1590A & #1623B 14.00 14.00

COIL STAMP

1975, Nov. 15 ***Perf. 10 Vertically***

1625 A1015 13c **dk blue, red & brown red** .35 .25
Pair .70 .50
a. Imperf., pair 20.00
b. Tagging omitted —

No. 1625 was printed on both the Huck and "B" presses. Huck press printings have pebbled gum (gummed on press), while "B" press printings have smooth gum (pregummed paper). Huck press printings often show portions of a joint line, but this feature is not consistent. Values for coils and imperf coils the same for both varieties.

AMERICAN BICENTENNIAL ISSUE
The Spirit of '76

Designed after painting by Archibald M. Willard in Abbot Hall, Marblehead, Massachusetts. Nos. 1629-1631 printed in continuous design.

Left panes contain 3 No. 1631a and one No. 1629; right panes contain one No. 1631 and 3 No. 1631a.

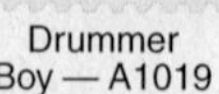
Drummer Boy — A1019

Old Drummer — A1020

Fifer — A1021

Designed by Vincent E. Hoffman.

PHOTOGRAVURE (Andreotti)

Plates of 200 subjects in four panes of 50.

1976, Jan. 1	**Tagged**	***Perf. 11***	
1629	A1019 13c **blue violet & multi**	.30	.25
a.	Imperf., vert. pair	—	
1630	A1020 13c **blue violet & multi**	.30	.25
1631	A1021 13c **blue violet & multi**	.30	.25
a.	Strip of 3, #1629-1631	.75	.75
	P# block of 12, 5#	3.50	—
	P# block of 20, 5#, slogans	5.75	—
b.	As "a," imperf.	*700.00*	
c.	Imperf., vert. pair, #1631	*500.00*	

INTERPHIL ISSUE

Interphil 76 International Philatelic Exhibition, Philadelphia, Pa., May 29-June 6.

"Interphil 76" A1022

Designed by Terrence W. McCaffrey.

LITHOGRAPHED, ENGRAVED (Giori)

Plates of 200 subjects of four panes of 50.

1976, Jan. 17	**Tagged**	***Perf. 11***	
1632	A1022 13c **dark blue & red (engr.), ultra. & red (litho.)**	.30	.25
	P# block of 4	1.00	—
	Margin block of 4, Mr. Zip and "Use Zip Code"	1.00	—
a.	Dark blue & red (engr.) missing (CM)	—	
b.	Tagging omitted	75.00	—
c.	Red (engr,) missing (CM)	—	

AMERICAN BICENTENNIAL ISSUE

Illustration reduced.

Designed by Walt Reed.

PHOTOGRAVURE (Andreotti)

Plates of 200 subjects in four panes of 50.

1976, Feb. 23	**Tagged**	***Perf. 11***	
1633	A1023 13c Delaware	.30	.25
1634	A1024 13c Pennsylvania	.30	.25
1635	A1025 13c New Jersey	.30	.25
1636	A1026 13c Georgia	.30	.25
1637	A1027 13c Connecticut	.30	.25
1638	A1028 13c Massachusetts	.30	.25
1639	A1029 13c Maryland	.30	.25
1640	A1030 13c South Carolina	.30	.25
1641	A1031 13c New Hampshire	.30	.25
1642	A1032 13c Virginia	.30	.25
1643	A1033 13c New York	.30	.25
1644	A1034 13c North Carolina	.30	.25
1645	A1035 13c Rhode Island	.30	.25
1646	A1036 13c Vermont	.30	.25
1647	A1037 13c Kentucky	.30	.25
1648	A1038 13c Tennessee	.30	.25
1649	A1039 13c Ohio	.30	.25
1650	A1040 13c Louisiana	.30	.25
1651	A1041 13c Indiana	.30	.25
1652	A1042 13c Mississippi	.30	.25
1653	A1043 13c Illinois	.30	.25
1654	A1044 13c Alabama	.30	.25
1655	A1045 13c Maine	.30	.25
1656	A1046 13c Missouri	.30	.25
1657	A1047 13c Arkansas	.30	.25
1658	A1048 13c Michigan	.30	.25
1659	A1049 13c Florida	.30	.25
1660	A1050 13c Texas	.30	.25
1661	A1051 13c Iowa	.30	.25
1662	A1052 13c Wisconsin	.30	.25
1663	A1053 13c California	.30	.25
1664	A1054 13c Minnesota	.30	.25
1665	A1055 13c Oregon	.30	.25
1666	A1056 13c Kansas	.30	.25
1667	A1057 13c West Virginia	.30	.25
a.	Tagging omitted		—
1668	A1058 13c Nevada	.30	.25
1669	A1059 13c Nebraska	.30	.25
1670	A1060 13c Colorado	.30	.25
1671	A1061 13c North Dakota	.30	.25
1672	A1062 13c South Dakota	.30	.25
1673	A1063 13c Montana	.30	.25
1674	A1064 13c Washington	.30	.25
1675	A1065 13c Idaho	.30	.25
1676	A1066 13c Wyoming	.30	.25
1677	A1067 13c Utah	.30	.25
1678	A1068 13c Oklahoma	.30	.25
1679	A1069 13c New Mexico	.30	.25
1680	A1070 13c Arizona	.30	.25
1681	A1071 13c Alaska	.30	.25
1682	A1072 13c Hawaii	.30	.25
a.	Pane of 50	17.50	15.00

TELEPHONE CENTENNIAL ISSUE

Centenary of first telephone call by Alexander Graham Bell, March 10, 1876.

Bell's Telephone Patent Application, 1876 — A1073

Designed by George Tscherny.

ENGRAVED (Giori)

Plates of 200 subjects in four panes of 50.

1976, Mar. 10	**Tagged**	***Perf. 11***	
1683	A1073 13c **black, purple & red,** *tan*	.30	.25
	P# block of 4	1.10	—
	Margin block of 4, Mr. Zip and "Use Zip Code"	1.00	—
a.	Black & purple missing (EP)	*450.00*	
b.	Red missing (EP)	—	
c.	All colors missing (EP)	725.00	
d.	Tagging omitted	—	

On No. 1683a, the errors have only tiny traces of red present, so are best collected as a horiz. strip of 5 with 2 or 3 error stamps. No. 1683c also must be collected as a transitional strip.

COMMERCIAL AVIATION ISSUE

50th anniversary of first contract airmail flights: Dearborn, Mich. to Cleveland, Ohio, Feb. 15, 1926; and Pasco, Wash. to Elko, Nev., Apr. 6, 1926.

Ford-Pullman Monoplane and Laird Swallow Biplane A1074

Designed by Robert E. Cunningham.

PHOTOGRAVURE (Andreotti)

Plates of 200 subjects in four panes of 50 each

1976, Mar. 19	**Tagged**	***Perf. 11***	
1684	A1074 13c **blue & multicolored**	.30	.25
	P# block of 10, 5#	2.75	—
	Margin block of 4, Mr. Zip and "Use Zip Code"	1.00	—
a.	Tagging omitted		—

CHEMISTRY ISSUE

Honoring American chemists, in conjunction with the centenary of the American Chemical Society.

Various Flasks, Separatory Funnel, Computer Tape — A1075

Designed by Ken Davies.

PHOTOGRAVURE (Andreotti)

Plates of 200 subjects in four panes of 50.

1976, Apr. 6	**Tagged**	***Perf. 11***	
1685	A1075 13c **multicolored**	.30	.25
	P# block of 12, 6#	3.25	—
	Margin block of 4, Mr. Zip and "Use Zip Code"	1.00	—
	Pair with full vert. gutter btwn.	—	

AMERICAN BICENTENNIAL ISSUES

SOUVENIR SHEETS

Designs, from Left to Right, No. 1686: a, Two British officers. b, Gen. Benjamin Lincoln. c, George Washington. d, John Trumbull, Col. Cobb, von Steuben, Lafayette, Thomas Nelson. e, Alexander Hamilton, John Laurens, Walter Stewart (all vert.).

No. 1687: a, John Adams, Roger Sherman, Robert R. Livingston. b, Jefferson, Franklin. c, Thomas Nelson, Jr., Francis Lewis, John Witherspoon, Samuel Huntington. d, John Hancock, Charles Thomson. e, George Read, John Dickinson, Edward Rutledge (a, d, vert., b, c, e, horiz.).

No. 1688: a, Boatsman. b, Washington. c, Flag bearer. d, Men in boat. e, Men on shore (a, d, horiz., b, c, e, vert.).

No. 1689: a, Two officers. b, Washington. c, Officer, black horse. d, Officer, white horse. e, Three soldiers (a, c, e, horiz., b, d, vert.).

Surrender of Cornwallis at Yorktown, by John Trumbull — A1076

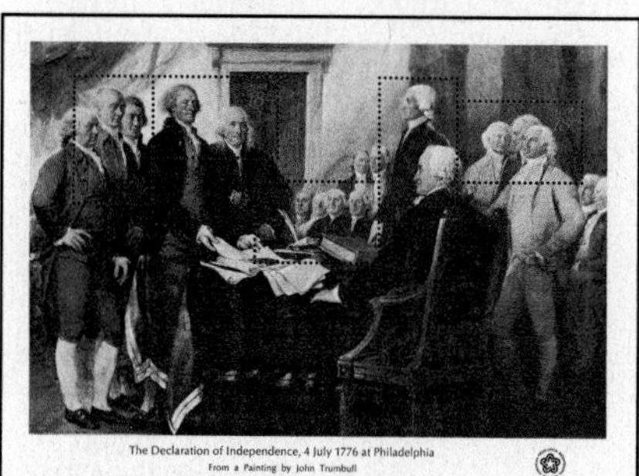

Declaration of Independence, by John Trumbull — A1077

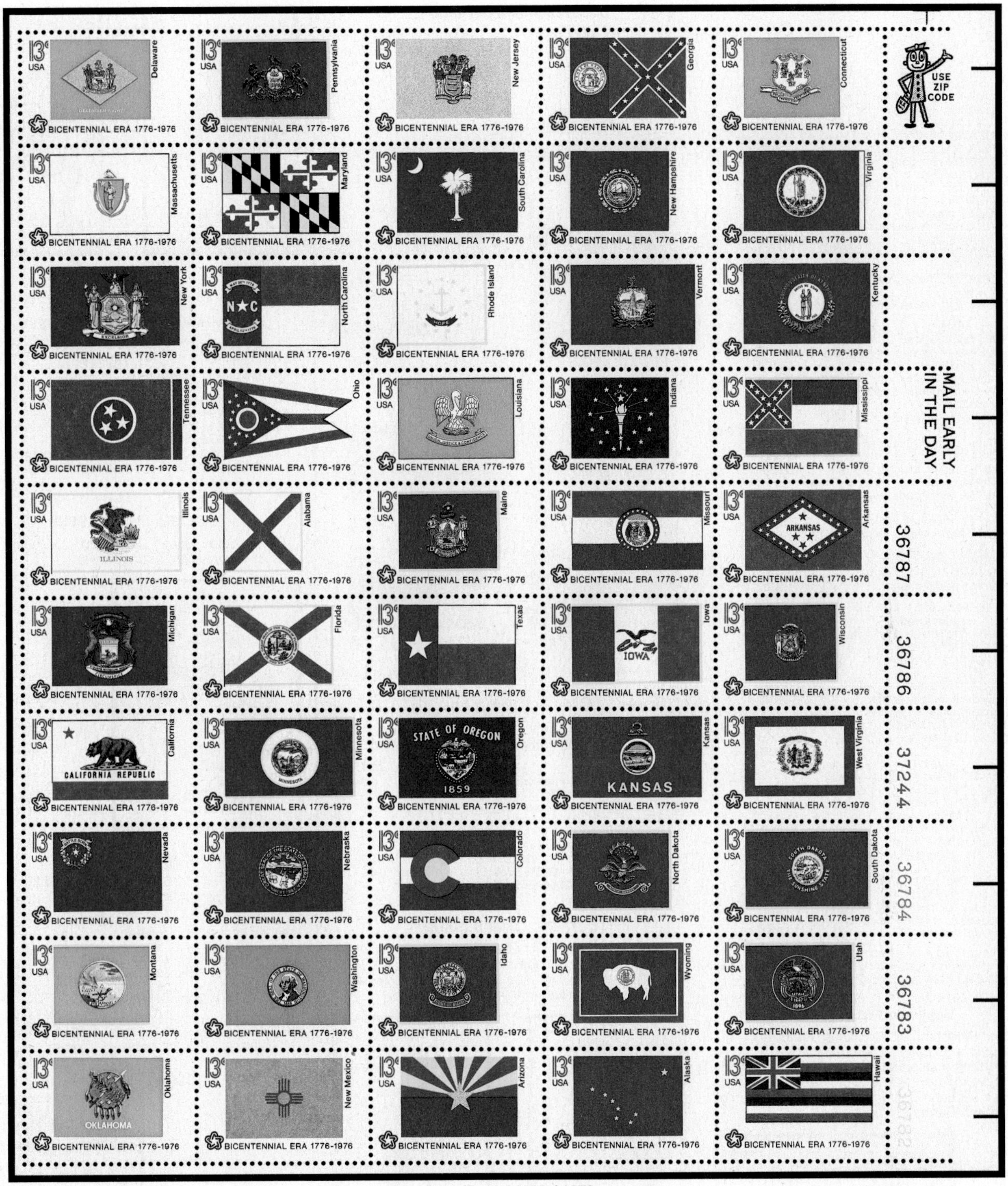

State Flags A1023-A1072

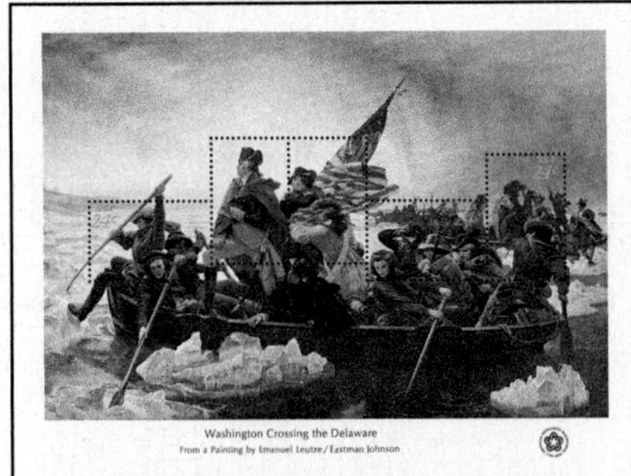

Washington Crossing the Delaware, by Emmanuel Leutze / Eastman Johnson — A1078

Washington Reviewing Army at Valley Forge, by William T. Trego — A1079

Illustrations reduced.

Designed by Vincent E. Hoffman.

LITHOGRAPHED

Plates of 30 subjects in six panes of 5 each.

1976, May 29 **Tagged** ***Perf. 11***

1686	A1076 Pane of 5		2.75	2.25
a.-e.	13c **multicolored**		.40	.40
f.	"USA/13c" omitted on "b," "c" & "d," imperf, tagging omitted		—	*1,750.*
g.	"USA/13c" omitted on "a" & "e"		*500.00*	*300.00*
h.	Imperf., tagging omitted			*2,000.*
i.	"USA/13c" omitted on "b," "c" & "d"		*500.00*	
j.	"USA/13c" double on "b"		—	
k.	"USA/13c" omitted on "c" & "d"		*750.00*	
l.	"USA/13c" omitted on "e"		*475.00*	
m.	"USA/13c" omitted, imperf., tagging omitted			—
n.	As "g," imperf., tagging omitted			*1,400.*
o.	"USA/13c" missing on "a" (PS)		*450.00*	
p.	As No. 1686, tagging omitted			—
q.	"USA/13c" omitted on "a"		*750.00*	
r.	Imperf., tagged			—

s.	"USA/13c" missing on "b" and "d" (PS)	—	
1687	A1077 Pane of 5	3.75	3.25
a.-e.	18c **multicolored**	.50	.50
f.	Design & marginal inscriptions omitted	*2,500.*	
g.	"USA/18c" omitted on "a" & "c"	*550.00*	*1,800.*
h.	"USA/18c" omitted on "b," "d" & "e"	*350.00*	
i.	"USA/18c" omitted on "d"	*425.00*	*475.00*
j.	Black omitted in design	*1,500.*	
k.	"USA/18c" omitted, imperf., tagging omitted	*1,250.*	
m.	"USA/18c" omitted on "b" & "e"	*500.00*	
n.	"USA/18c" omitted on "b" & "d"	*1,000.*	
p.	Imperf. (tagged)	*1,000.*	
q.	"USA/18c" missing on "c" (CM)	—	
r.	Yellow omitted	*5,000.*	
s.	"USA/18c" missing on "a," "c" and "d" (PS)	—	
t.	"USA/18c" missing on "a" and "d" (PS)	*300.00*	
u.	"USA/18c" omitted on "a"	*5,000.*	
1688	A1078 Pane of 5	4.75	4.25
a.-e.	24c **multicolored**	.65	.65
f.	"USA/24c" omitted, imperf., tagging omitted	*950.00*	
g.	"USA/24c" omitted on "d" & "e"	*400.00*	*400.00*
h.	Design & marginal inscriptions omitted	*2,500.*	
i.	"USA/24c" omitted on "a," "b" & "c"	*400.00*	*400.00*
j.	Imperf., tagging omitted	*1,250.*	
k.	"USA/24c" of "d" & "e" inverted	*12,500.*	
l.	As "i," imperf, tagging omitted	*3,250.*	—
m.	Tagging omitted on "e" and "f"	—	
n.	As No. 1688, perfs inverted and reversed	*7,500.*	
o.	As No. 1688, tagging omitted	*850.00*	
p.	"USA/24c" missing on "d" and "e" (CM)	—	
q.	"USA/24c" omitted on "b" and "c"	—	
r.	"USA/24c" omitted on "a"	*400.00*	
s.	As No. 1688, imperf.	*1,250.*	
1689	A1079 Pane of 5	5.75	5.25
a.-e.	31c **multicolored**	.80	.80
f.	"USA/31c" omitted, imperf.	*1,600.*	
g.	"USA/31c" omitted on "a" & "c"	*375.00*	
h.	"USA/31c" omitted on "b," "d" & "e"	*450.00*	—
i.	"USA/31c" omitted on "e"	*375.00*	
j.	Black omitted in design	*1,700.*	
k.	Imperf., tagging omitted		*2,000.*
l.	"USA/31c" omitted on "b" & "d"	*300.00*	
m.	"USA/31c" omitted on "a," "c" & "e"	*750.00*	
n.	As "m," imperf., tagging omitted	—	
p.	As "h," imperf., tagging omitted		*1,250.*
q.	As "g," imperf., tagging omitted	*2,500.*	
r.	"USA/31c" omitted on "d" & "e"	*600.00*	
s.	As "f," tagging omitted	*2,000.*	
t.	"USA/31c" omitted on "d"	*500.00*	
u.	As No. 1689, tagging omitted	—	
v.	As No. 1689, perfs and tagging inverted	*10,000.*	
w.	"USA/31c" missing on "a," "b," "c" and "d" (PS)	*500.00*	
x.	"USA/31c" missing on "e" (CM)	—	
y.	"USA/31c" omitted on "a"	—	
	Nos. 1686-1689 (4)	17.00	

Issued in connection with Interphil 76 International Philatelic Exhibition, Philadelphia, Pa., May 29-June 6. Size of panes: 203x152mm; size of stamps: 25x39½mm, 39½x25mm.

Benjamin Franklin

American Bicentennial: Benjamin Franklin (1706-1790), deputy postmaster general for the colonies (1753-1774) and statesman. Design based on marble bust by anonymous Italian sculptor after terra cotta bust by Jean Jacques Caffieri, 1777. Map published by R. Sayer and J. Bennett in London.

Franklin and Map of North America, 1776 — A1080

Designed by Bernard Reilander (Canada).

LITHOGRAPHED, ENGRAVED (Giori)

Plates of 200 subjects in four panes of 50.

1976, June 1	**Tagged**	***Perf. 11***	
1690	A1080 13c **multicolored**	.30	.25
	P# block of 4	1.10	—
	Margin block of 4, Mr. Zip and "Use Zip Code"	1.00	—
a.	Light blue omitted	*150.00*	
b.	Tagging omitted	10.00	

See Canada No. 691.

Declaration of Independence

Designed after painting of Declaration of Independence, by John Trumbull, in the Rotunda of the Capitol, Washington, D.C. Nos. 1691-1694 printed in continuous design. Left panes contain 10 No. 1694a and 5 each of Nos. 1691-1692; right panes contain 5 each of Nos. 1693-1694 and 10 No. 1694a.

A1081

A1082

A1083

A1084

Designed by Vincent E. Hoffman.

PHOTOGRAVURE (Andreotti)

Plates of 200 subjects in four panes of 50.

1976, July 4	**Tagged**	***Perf. 11***	
1691	A1081 13c **multicolored**	.30	.25
1692	A1082 13c **multicolored**	.30	.25
1693	A1083 13c **multicolored**	.30	.25
1694	A1084 13c **multicolored**	.30	.25
a.	Strip of 4, #1691-1694	1.20	1.10
	P# block of 20, 5#, "Mail Early in the Day," Mr. Zip and "Use Zip Code"	7.00	—
	P# block of 16, 5#, "Mail Early in the Day"	6.50	—
	Margin block of 4, Mr. Zip and "Use Zip Code"	1.25	—

OLYMPIC GAMES ISSUE

12th Winter Olympic Games, Innsbruck, Austria, Feb. 4-15, and 21st Summer Olympic Games, Montreal, Canada, July 17-Aug. 1. Nos. 1695-1696 alternate in one row, Nos. 1697-1698 in other row.

Diving — A1085

Skiing — A1086

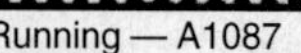

Running — A1087

Skating — A1088

Designed by Donald Moss.

PHOTOGRAVURE (Andreotti)

Plates of 200 subjects in four panes of 50.

1976, July 16	**Tagged**	***Perf. 11***	
1695	A1085 13c **multicolored**	.30	.25
1696	A1086 13c **multicolored**	.30	.25
1697	A1087 13c **multicolored**	.30	.25
1698	A1088 13c **multicolored**	.30	.25
a.	Block of 4, #1695-1698	1.20	1.20
	P# block of 12, 6#	4.00	—
	P# block of 20, 6#, Mr. Zip and slogans	8.75	—
	Margin block of 4, Mr. Zip and "Use Zip Code"	1.40	—
b.	As "a," imperf.	*375.00*	

CLARA MAASS ISSUE

Clara Louise Maass (1876-1901), volunteer in fight against yellow fever, birth centenary.

Clara Maass and Newark German Hospital Pin — A1089

Designed by Paul Calle.

PHOTOGRAVURE (Andreotti)

Plates of 160 subjects in four panes of 40.

1976, Aug. 18	**Tagged**	***Perf. 11***	
1699	A1089 13c **multicolored**	.30	.25
	P# block of 12, 6#	4.00	—
	Margin block of 4, Mr. Zip, "Use Zip Code" and "Mail Early in the Day"	1.00	—
a.	Horiz. pair, imperf. vert.	*350.00*	
b.	Dark blue missing (PS)	*700.00*	

On No. 1699, two blue plates were used. No 1699b is missing the dark blue ("She gave her life") at bottom due to an upward shift of the horizontal perforations.

ADOLPH S. OCHS ISSUE

Adolph S. Ochs (1858-1935), Publisher of the New York Times, 1896-1935 — A1090

Designed by Bradbury Thompson; photograph by S. J. Woolf.

GIORI PRESS PRINTING

Plates of 128 subjects in four panes of 32 (8x4).

1976, Sept. 18 **Tagged** ***Perf. 11***

1700 A1090 13c **black & gray** .30 .25
P# block of 4 1.10 —
Margin block of 4, Mr. Zip and "Use Zip Code" 1.00 —
a. Tagging omitted *45.00* —

CHRISTMAS ISSUE

Nativity, by John Singleton Copley A1091

"Winter Pastime," by Nathaniel Currier A1092

Designers: No. 1701, Bradbury Thompson after 1776 painting in Museum of Fine Arts, Boston. No. 1702, Stevan Dohanos after 1855 lithograph in Museum of the City of New York.

PHOTOGRAVURE (Andreotti)

Plates of 200 subjects in four panes of 50.

1976, Oct. 27 **Tagged** ***Perf. 11***

1701 A1091 13c **multicolored** .30 .25
P# block of 12, 6# 3.25 —
Margin block of 4, Mr. Zip and "Use Zip Code" 1.00 —
a. Imperf., pair *85.00*
1702 A1092 13c **multi,** overall tagging .30 .25
P# block of 10, 5# 2.75 —
Margin block of 4, Mr. Zip and "Use Zip Code" 1.00 —
a. Imperf., pair *75.00*

COMBINATION PRESS

Plates of 230 (10x23) subjects in panes of 50 (5x10)

Tagged, Block

1703 A1092 13c **multicolored** .30 .25
P# block of 20, 5-8# 6.00 —
a. Imperf., pair *75.00*
b. Vert. pair, imperf. between *275.00*
c. Tagging omitted 17.50
d. Red omitted *500.00*
e. Yellow omitted *675.00*

No. 1702 has overall tagging. Lettering at base is black and usually ½mm below design. As a rule, no "snowflaking" in sky or pond. Pane of 50 has margins on 4 sides with slogans. Plate Nos. 37465-37478.

No. 1703 has block tagging the size of printed area. Lettering at base is gray black and usually ¾mm below design. "Snowflaking" generally in sky and pond. Plate Nos. 37617-37621 or 37634-37638.

Examples of No. 1703 are known with various amounts of red or yellow missing. Nos. 1703d-1703e are stamps with the colors totally omitted. Expertization is recommended.

COMBINATION PRESS

Cylindrical plates consist of 23 rows of subjects, 10 across for commemoratives (230 subjects), 20 across for definitives (460 subjects), with selvage on the two outer edges only. Guillotining through the perforations creates individual panes of 50 or 100 with selvage on one side only.

Failure of the guillotine to separate through the perforations resulted in straight edges on some stamps. Perforating teeth along the center column and the tenth rows were removed for issues released on or after May 31, 1984 (the 10c Richard Russell, for definitives; the 20c Horace Moses, for commemoratives), creating panes with straight edged stamps on three sides.

Three sets of plate numbers, copyright notices (starting with No. 1787), and zip insignia (starting with No. 1927) are arranged identically on the left and right sides of the plate so that each pane has at least one of each marking. The markings adjacent to any particular row are repeated either seven or eight rows away on the cylinder.

Fifteen combinations of the three marginal markings and blank rows are possible on panes.

AMERICAN BICENTENNIAL ISSUE
Washington at Princeton

Washington's Victory over Lord Cornwallis at Princeton, N.J., bicentenary.

Washington, Nassau Hall, Hessian Prisoners and 13-star Flag, by Charles Willson Peale — A1093

Designed by Bradbury Thompson.

PHOTOGRAVURE (Andreotti)

Plates of 160 subjects in four panes of 40.

1977, Jan. 3 **Tagged** ***Perf. 11***

1704 A1093 13c **multicolored** .30 .25
P# block of 10, 5# 2.75 —
Margin block of 4, Mr. Zip and "Use Zip Code", "Mail Early in the Day" 1.00 —
a. Horiz. pair, imperf. vert. *425.00*
b. Black (inscriptions) missing (PS) —

SOUND RECORDING ISSUE

Centenary of the invention of the phonograph by Thomas Alva Edison and development of sophisticated recording industry.

Tin Foil Phonograph A1094

Designed by Walter and Naiad Einsel.

LITHOGRAPHED, ENGRAVED (Giori)

Plates of 200 subjects in four panes of 50.

1977, Mar. 23 **Tagged** ***Perf. 11***

1705 A1094 13c **black & multicolored** .30 .25
P# block of 4 1.10 —
Margin block of 4, Mr. Zip and "Use Zip Code" 1.00 —
a. Tagging omitted —

AMERICAN FOLK ART SERIES
Pueblo Pottery

Pueblo art, 1880-1920, from Museums in New Mexico, Arizona and Colorado.

Nos. 1706-1709 are printed in blocks and strips of 4 in panes of 40. In the 1st row Nos. 1706-1709 are in sequence as listed. In the 2nd row Nos. 1708-1709 are followed by Nos. 1706-1709, 1708-1709.

Zia Pot — A1095

San Ildefonso Pot — A1096

Hopi Pot — A1097

Acoma Pot — A1098

Designed by Ford Ruthling.

PHOTOGRAVURE (Andreotti)

Plates of 160 subjects in four panes of 40.

1977, Apr. 13 **Tagged** ***Perf. 11***

1706 A1095 13c **multicolored** .30 .25
1707 A1096 13c **multicolored** .30 .25
1708 A1097 13c **multicolored** .30 .25
1709 A1098 13c **multicolored** .30 .25
a. Block or strip of 4, #1706-1709 1.20 1.00
P# block of 10, 5# 2.75 —
P# block of 16, 5#; Mr. Zip and slogans 4.25 —
Margin block of 6, Mr. Zip and "Use Zip Code" "Mail Early in the Day" 1.50 —
b. As "a," imperf. vert. *1,100.*

LINDBERGH FLIGHT ISSUE

Charles A. Lindbergh's solo transatlantic flight from New York to Paris, 50th anniversary.

Spirit of St. Louis — A1099

Designed by Robert E. Cunningham.

PHOTOGRAVURE (Andreotti)

Plates of 200 subjects in four panes of 50.

1977, May 20 **Tagged** ***Perf. 11***

1710 A1099 13c **multicolored** .30 .25
P# block of 12, 6# 3.25 —
Margin block of 4, Mr. Zip and "Use Zip Code" 1.00 —
a. Imperf., pair *700.00*
b. Tagging omitted —

Beware of private overprints on No. 1710.

COLORADO STATEHOOD ISSUE

Issued to honor Colorado as the "Centennial State." It achieved statehood in 1876.

Columbine and Rocky Mountains — A1100

Designed by V. Jack Ruther.

PHOTOGRAVURE (Andreotti)

Plates of 200 subjects in four panes of 50.

1977, May 21 **Tagged** ***Perf. 11***

1711 A1100 13c **multicolored** .30 .25
P# block of 12, 6# 3.25 —
Margin block of 4, Mr. Zip and "Use Zip Code" 1.00 —
a. Horiz. pair, imperf. between and with natural straight edge at right *650.00*
b. Horiz. pair, imperf. vertically *500.00*
c. Perf. 11.2 .75 .25
P# block of 12, 6# 20.00

Perforations do not run through the sheet margin on about 10 percent of the sheets of No. 1711.

BUTTERFLY ISSUE

Nos. 1712-1713 alternate in 1st row, Nos. 1714-1715 in 2nd row. This arrangement is repeated throughout the pane. Butterflies represent different geographic US areas.

Swallowtail A1101

Checkerspot A1102

Dogface A1103

Orange-Tip A1104

Designed by Stanley Galli.

PHOTOGRAVURE (Andreotti)

Plates of 200 subjects in four panes of 50.

1977, June 6 **Tagged** ***Perf. 11***

1712 A1101 13c **tan & multicolored** .30 .25
1713 A1102 13c **tan & multicolored** .30 .25
1714 A1103 13c **tan & multicolored** .30 .25
1715 A1104 13c **tan & multicolored** .30 .25
a. Block of 4, #1712-1715 1.20 1.00
P# block of 12, 6# 3.25 —
P# block of 20, 6#, Mr. Zip and slogans 5.50 —
Margin block of 4, Mr. Zip and "Use Zip Code" 1.05 —
b. As "a," imperf. horiz. *9,500.*

AMERICAN BICENTENNIAL ISSUES
Marquis de Lafayette

200th anniversary of Lafayette's Landing on the coast of South Carolina, north of Charleston.

Marquis de Lafayette — A1105

Designed by Bradbury Thompson.

GIORI PRESS PRINTING

Plates of 160 subjects in four panes of 40.

1977, June 13 **Tagged** ***Perf. 11***

1716 A1105 13c **blue, black & red** .30 .25
P# block of 4 1.10 —
Margin block of 4, Mr. Zip and "Use Zip Code" 1.00 —
a. Red missing (PS) *300.00*

Skilled Hands for Independence

Nos. 1717-1718 alternate in 1st row, Nos. 1719-1720 in 2nd row. This arrangement is repeated throughout the pane.

Seamstress A1106

Blacksmith A1107

Wheelwright A1108

Leatherworker A1109

Designed by Leonard Everett Fisher.

PHOTOGRAVURE (Andreotti)

Plates of 200 subjects in four panes of 50.

1977, July 4 **Tagged** ***Perf. 11***

1717 A1106 13c **multicolored** .30 .25
1718 A1107 13c **multicolored** .30 .25
1719 A1108 13c **multicolored** .30 .25
1720 A1109 13c **multicolored** .30 .25
a. Block of 4, #1717-1720 1.20 1.00
P# block of 12, 6# 3.25
P# block of 20, 6#, Mr. Zip and slogans 5.50 —
Margin block of 4, Mr. Zip and "Use Zip Code" 1.05 —

PEACE BRIDGE ISSUE

50th anniversary of the Peace Bridge, connecting Buffalo (Fort Porter), N.Y. and Fort Erie, Ontario.

Peace Bridge and Dove — A1110

Designed by Bernard Brussel-Smith (wood-cut).

ENGRAVED

Plates of 200 subjects in four panes of 50.

1977, Aug. 4 **Tagged** ***Perf. 11x10½***

1721 A1110 13c **blue** .30 .25
P# block of 4 1.10 —
Margin block of 4, Mr. Zip and "Use Zip Code" 1.00 —

AMERICAN BICENTENNIAL ISSUE
Battle of Oriskany

200th anniv. of the Battle of Oriskany, American Militia led by Brig. Gen. Nicholas Herkimer (1728-77).

Herkimer at Oriskany, by Frederick Yohn — A1111

Designed by Bradbury Thompson after painting in Utica, N.Y. Public Library.

PHOTOGRAVURE (Andreotti)

Plates of 160 subjects in four panes of 40.

1977, Aug. 6 **Tagged** ***Perf. 11***

1722 A1111 13c **multicolored** .30 .25
P# block of 10, 5# 2.75 —
Margin block of 6, Mr. Zip and "Use Zip Code" and "Mail Early in the Day" 1.50 —

ENERGY ISSUE

Conservation and development of nation's energy resources. Nos. 1723-1724 se-tenant vertically.

"Conservation" A1112

"Development" A1113

Designed by Terrance W. McCaffrey.

PHOTOGRAVURE (Andreotti)

Plates of 160 subjects in four panes of 40.

1977, Oct. 20 **Tagged** ***Perf. 11***

1723 A1112 13c **multicolored** .30 .25
1724 A1113 13c **multicolored** .30 .25
a. Pair, #1723-1724 .60 .50
P# block of 12, 6# 3.25 —
Margin block of 4, Mr. Zip, "Use Zip Code" and "Mail Early in the Day" 1.00 —

ALTA CALIFORNIA ISSUE

Founding of El Pueblo de San José de Guadalupe, first civil settlement in Alta California, 200th anniversary.

Farm Houses
A1114

Designed by Earl Thollander.

LITHOGRAPHED, ENGRAVED (Giori)
Plates of 200 subjects in four panes of 50.

1977, Sept. 9 **Tagged** ***Perf. 11***

1725 A1114 13c **black & multicolored** .30 .25
P# block of 4 1.10 —
Margin block of 4, Mr. Zip and "Use Zip Code" 1.00 —
a. Tagging omitted *250.00* —

AMERICAN BICENTENNIAL ISSUE
Articles of Confederation

200th anniversary of drafting the Articles of Confederation, York Town, Pa.

Members of Continental Congress in Conference
A1115

Designed by David Blossom.

ENGRAVED (Giori)
Plates of 200 subjects in four panes of 50.

1977, Sept. 30 **Tagged** ***Perf. 11***

1726 A1115 13c **red & brown,** *cream* .30 .25
P# block of 4 1.10 —
Margin block of 4, Mr. Zip and "Use Zip Code" 1.00 —
Pane of 50 12.50
a. Tagging omitted 100.00
b. Red omitted *500.00*
c. Red & brown omitted *300.00*

No. 1726b also has most of the brown omitted. No. 1726c must be collected as a transition multiple, certainly with No. 1726b and preferably also with No. 1726.

TALKING PICTURES, 50th ANNIV.

Movie Projector and Phonograph
A1116

Designed by Walter Einsel.

LITHOGRAPHED, ENGRAVED (Giori)
Plates of 200 subjects in four panes of 50.

1977, Oct. 6 **Tagged** ***Perf. 11***

1727 A1116 13c **multicolored** .30 .25
P# block of 4 1.10 —
Margin block of 4, Mr. Zip and "Use Zip Code" 1.00 —
Pane of 50 12.50
a. Brown & black omitted —

AMERICAN BICENTENNIAL ISSUE
Surrender at Saratoga

200th anniversary of Gen. John Burgoyne's surrender at Saratoga.

Surrender of Burgoyne, by John Trumbull
A1117

Designed by Bradbury Thompson.

PHOTOGRAVURE (Andreotti)
Plates of 160 subjects in four panes of 40.

1977, Oct. 7 **Tagged** ***Perf. 11***

1728 A1117 13c **multicolored** .30 .25
P# block of 10, 5# 2.75 —
Margin block of 6, Mr. Zip, "Use Zip Code" and "Mail Early in the Day" 1.50 —
Pane of 40 10.00
a. Tagging omitted —

CHRISTMAS ISSUE

Washington at Valley Forge — A1118

Rural Mailbox — A1119

Designers: No. 1729, Stevan Dohanos, after painting by J. C. Leyendecker. No. 1730, Dolli Tingle.

PHOTOGRAVURE (Combination Press)
Plates of 460 subjects (20x23) in panes of 100 (10x10).

1977, Oct. 21 **Tagged** ***Perf. 11***

1729 A1118 13c **multicolored** .30 .25
P# block of 20, 5-8# 5.75 —
Pane of 100 25.00
a. Imperf., pair *50.00*

See Combination Press note after No. 1703.

PHOTOGRAVURE (Andreotti)
Plates of 400 subjects in 4 panes of 100.

1730 A1119 13c **multicolored** .30 .25
P# block of 10, 5# 2.75 —
Margin block of 4, Mr. Zip and "Use Zip Code" 1.00 —
Pair with full vert. gutter btwn. —
Pair with full horiz. gutter btwn. —
Pane of 100 25.00
a. Imperf., pair *175.00*

CARL SANDBURG ISSUE

Carl Sandburg (1878-1967), poet, biographer and collector of American folk songs, birth centenary.

Carl Sandburg, by William A. Smith, 1952 — A1120

Designed by William A. Smith.

GIORI PRESS PRINTING
Plates of 200 subjects in four panes of 50.

1978, Jan. 6 **Tagged** ***Perf. 11***

1731 A1120 13c **black & brown** .30 .25
P# block of 4 1.25 —
Margin block of 4, Mr. Zip 1.05 —
Pane of 50 12.50
a. Brown omitted *1,750.*
b. Tagging omitted *225.00*
c. All colors omitted —

No. 1731c is tagged and has a faint black tagging ghost. Authentication is advised.

CAPTAIN COOK ISSUE

Capt. James Cook, 200th anniversary of his arrival in Hawaii, at Waimea, Kauai, Jan. 20, 1778, and of his anchorage in Cook Inlet, near Anchorage, Alaska, June 1, 1778. Nos. 1732-1733 printed in panes of 50, containing 25 each of Nos. 1732-1733 including 5 No. 1733b.

Capt. Cook, by Nathaniel Dance — A1121

"Resolution" and "Discovery," by John Webber
A1122

Designers: No. 1732, Robert F. Szabo. No. 1733, Jak Katalan.

GIORI PRESS PRINTING
Plates of 200 subjects in four panes of 50.

1978, Jan. 20 **Tagged** ***Perf. 11***

1732 A1121 13c **dark blue** .30 .25
1733 A1122 13c **green** .30 .25
a. Vert. pair, imperf. horiz. *1,000.*
b. Pair, #1732-1733 .60 .50
P# block of 4, #1732 or 1733 1.10 —
Margin block of 4, Mr. Zip, #1732 or 1733 1.05 —
P# block of 20, 10 each #1732-1733, P# and slogans 5.25 —
Pane of 50 12.50
c. As "b," imperf. between *4,000.*
d. As "b," tagging omitted *250.00*

Indian Head Penny, 1877 — A1123

Eagle — A1124

Red Masterpiece and Medallion Roses — A1126

ENGRAVED (Giori)
Plates of 600 subjects in four panes of 150.

1978 **Tagged** ***Perf. 11***

1734 A1123 13c **brown & blue green,** *bister, Jan. 11, 1978* .30 .25
P# block of 4 1.10 —
Margin block of 4, "Use Correct Zip Code" 1.00 —
Pane of 150 37.50
Vert. pair with full horiz. gutter between 200.00
a. Horiz. pair, imperf. vert. *175.00*
b. Tagging omitted *175.00*

PHOTOGRAVURE (Andreotti)
Plates of 400 subjects in four panes of 100.

1735 A1124 (15c) **orange,** *May 22, 1978* .30 .25
P# block of 4 1.40 —
Margin block of 4, "Use Zip Code" 1.25 —
Pane of 100 30.00
Vert. pair with full horiz. gutter between 500.00
a. Imperf., pair *70.00*
b. Vert. pair, imperf. horiz. *500.00*
c. Perf. 11.2 .35 .25
P# block of 4 1.80 —
Zip block of 4 1.50 —

BOOKLET STAMPS
ENGRAVED
Perf. 11x10½ on 2 or 3 Sides

1736 A1124 (15c) **orange** .30 .25
a. Booklet pane of 8, *May 22, 1978* 2.50 1.50
b. As "a," tagging omitted —
c. Vert. pair, imperf. btwn., in #1736a with foldover *1,000.*
d. As No. 1736, tagging omitted —

Perf. 10 on 2 or 3 Sides

1737 A1126 15c **multicolored** .30 .25
a. Booklet pane of 8, *July 11, 1978* 2.50 2.00
b. Imperf, pair *450.00*
c. As "a," imperf *2,250.*
d. As "a," tagging omitted *60.00*
e. As No. 1737, tagging omitted 6.50
f. Orange omitted —
g. As "a," orange omitted —

A1127 A1128  A1129

A1130 A1131

Designed by Ronald Sharpe.

BOOKLET STAMPS
ENGRAVED

1980, Feb. 7 Tagged *Perf. 11 on 2 or 3 Sides*

1738 A1127 15c **sepia,** *yellow* .30 .25
1739 A1128 15c **sepia,** *yellow* .30 .25
1740 A1129 15c **sepia,** *yellow* .30 .25
1741 A1130 15c **sepia,** *yellow* .30 .25
1742 A1131 15c **sepia,** *yellow* .30 .25
a. Booklet pane of 10, 2 each #1738-1742 3.50 3.00
b. Strip of 5, #1738-1742 1.50 1.40

COIL STAMP

1978, May 22 *Perf. 10 Vert.*

1743 A1124 (15c) **orange** .30 .25
Pair .60 .25
Joint line pair .75 —
a. Imperf., pair 65.00
Joint line pair 140.00

No. 1743a is valued in the grade of fine.

BLACK HERITAGE SERIES

Harriet Tubman (1820-1913), born a slave, helped more than 300 slaves escape to freedom.

Harriet Tubman and Cart Carrying Slaves — A1133

Designed by Jerry Pinkney after photograph.

PHOTOGRAVURE (Andreotti)
Plates of 200 subjects in four panes of 50.

1978, Feb. 1 Tagged *Perf. 10½x11*

1744 A1133 13c **multicolored** .30 .25
P# block of 12, 6# 3.25 —
Margin block of 4, Mr. Zip 1.00 —
Pane of 50 12.50

AMERICAN FOLK ART SERIES
Quilts

Nos. 1745-1746 alternate in 1st row, Nos. 1747-1748 in 2nd.

Basket Design

A1134

A1135

A1136

A1137

Designed by Christopher Pullman after 1875 quilt made in New York City. Illustration reduced.

PHOTOGRAVURE (Andreotti)
Plates of 192 subjects in four panes of 48 (6x8).

1978, Mar. 8 Tagged *Perf. 11*

1745 A1134 13c **multicolored** .30 .25
1746 A1135 13c **multicolored** .30 .25
1747 A1136 13c **multicolored** .30 .25
1748 A1137 13c **multicolored** .30 .25
a. Block of 4, #1745-1748 1.20 1.00
P# block of 12, 6# 3.25 —
P# block of 16, 6#, Mr. Zip and copyright 4.50 —
Margin block of 4, Mr. Zip, copyright 1.05 —
Pane of 48 12.00

AMERICAN DANCE ISSUE

Nos. 1749-1750 alternate in 1st row, Nos. 1751-1752 in 2nd.

Ballet
A1138

Theater
A1139

Folk Dance
A1140

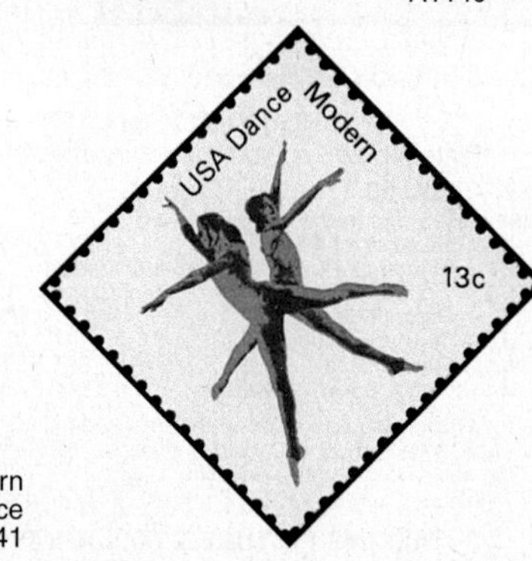

Modern
Dance
A1141

Designed by John Hill.

PHOTOGRAVURE (Andreotti)
Plates of 192 subjects in four panes of 48 (6x8).

1978, Apr. 26 Tagged *Perf. 11*

1749 A1138 13c **multicolored** .30 .25
1750 A1139 13c **multicolored** .30 .25
1751 A1140 13c **multicolored** .30 .25
1752 A1141 13c **multicolored** .30 .25
a. Block of 4, #1749-1752 1.20 1.00
P# block of 12, 6# 3.25 —
P# block of 16, 6#, Mr. Zip and copyright 4.50 —
Margin block of 4, Mr. Zip, copyright 1.05 —
Pane of 48 12.00

AMERICAN BICENTENNIAL ISSUE

French Alliance, signed in Paris, Feb. 6, 1778 and ratified by Continental Congress, May 4, 1778.

King Louis XVI and Benjamin Franklin, by Charles Gabriel Sauvage — A1142

Designed by Bradbury Thompson after 1785 porcelain sculpture in Du Pont Winterthur Museum, Delaware.

GIORI PRESS PRINTING

Plates of 160 subjects in four panes of 40.

1978, May 4	**Tagged**	***Perf. 11***	
1753 A1142 13c **blue, black & red**		.30	.25
P# block of 4		1.10	—
Margin block of 4, Mr. Zip		1.00	—
Pane of 40		10.00	
a. Red missing (PS)		—	

EARLY CANCER DETECTION ISSUE

George Papanicolaou, M.D. (1883-1962), cytologist and developer of Pap Test, early cancer detection in women.

Dr. Papanicolaou and Microscope — A1143

Designed by Paul Calle.

ENGRAVED

Plates of 200 subjects in four panes of 50.

1978, May 18	**Tagged**	***Perf. 10½x11***	
1754 A1143 13c **brown**		.30	.25
P# block of 4		1.10	—
Margin block of 4, Mr. Zip		1.00	—
Pane of 50		12.50	

PERFORMING ARTS SERIES

Jimmie Rodgers (1897-1933), the "Singing Brakeman, Father of Country Music" (No. 1755); George M. Cohan (1878-1942), actor and playwright (No. 1756).

Jimmie Rodgers with Guitar and Brakeman's Cap, Locomotive — A1144

George M. Cohan, "Yankee Doodle Dandy" and Stars — A1145

Designed by Jim Sharpe.

PHOTOGRAVURE (Andreotti)

Plates of 200 subjects in four panes of 50.

1978	**Tagged**	***Perf. 11***	
1755 A1144 13c **multicolored,** *May 24*		.30	.25
P# block of 12, 6#		4.00	—
Margin block of 4, Mr. Zip		1.25	—
Pane of 50		12.50	
1756 A1145 15c **multicolored,** *July 3*		.30	.25
P# block of 12, 6#		4.00	—
Margin block of 4, Mr. Zip		1.25	—
Pane of 50		15.00	

CAPEX ISSUE

CAPEX '78, Canadian International Philatelic Exhibition, Toronto, Ont., June 9-18.

Wildlife from Canadian-United States Border — A1146

Illustration reduced.

Designed by Stanley Galli.

LITHOGRAPHED, ENGRAVED (Giori)

Plates of 24 subjects in four panes of 6 each.

1978, June 10	**Tagged**	***Perf. 11***	
1757 A1146 Block of 8, **multicolored**		2.40	2.00
a. 13c Cardinal		.30	.25
b. 13c Mallard		.30	.25
c. 13c Canada goose		.30	.25
d. 13c Blue jay		.30	.25
e. 13c Moose		.30	.25
f. 13c Chipmunk		.30	.25
g. 13c Red fox		.30	.25
h. 13c Raccoon		.30	.25
P# block of 8		2.40	—
Margin block of 8, Mr. Zip and copyright		2.25	—
Pane of 48		13.00	—
i. As No. 1757, yellow, green, red, brown, blue, black (litho) omitted		*6,000.*	
j. Strip of 4 (a-d), imperf. vert.		*5,000.*	
k. Strip of 4 (e-h), imperf. vert.		*2,000.*	
l. As No. 1757, "d" and "h" with black (engr.) omitted		—	
m. As No. 1757, "b" with blue missing (PS)		—	
n. As No. 1757, tagging omitted		—	
o. Strip of 4 (e-h), all colors except black missing on "e," "f" and "g," all colors except black and brown missing on "h" (PS)		*1,250.*	
p. As No. 1757, yellow, red, brown omitted, pane of 48		—	

No. 1757k is worth more when contained in the block of 8. Value is for strip only.

PHOTOGRAPHY ISSUE

Photography's contribution to communications and understanding.

Camera, Lens, Color Filters, Adapter Ring, Studio Light Bulb and Album — A1147

Designed by Ben Somoroff.

PHOTOGRAVURE (Andreotti)

Plates of 160 subjects in four panes of 40.

1978, June 26	**Tagged**	***Perf. 11***	
1758 A1147 15c **multicolored**		.30	.25
P# block of 12, 6#		4.00	—
Margin block of 4, Mr. Zip and copyright		1.25	—
P# block of 16, 6#, Mr. Zip and copyright		5.00	—
Pane of 50		12.00	

VIKING MISSIONS TO MARS ISSUE

Second anniv. of landing of Viking 1 on Mars.

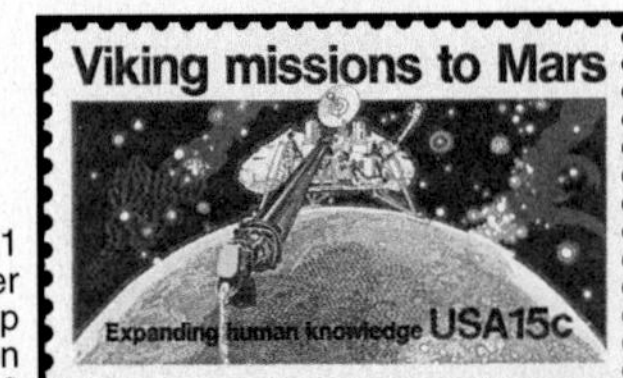

Viking 1 Lander Scooping up Soil on Mars — A1148

Designed by Robert McCall.

LITHOGRAPHED, ENGRAVED (Giori)

Plates of 200 subjects in four panes of 50.

1978, July 20	**Tagged**	***Perf. 11***	
1759 A1148 15c **multicolored**		.30	.25
P# block of 4		1.35	—
Margin block of 4, Mr. Zip		1.25	—
Pane of 50		15.00	
a. Tagging omitted		*75.00*	

WILDLIFE CONSERVATION

Nos. 1760-1761 alternate in one horizontal row. Nos. 1762-1763 in the next.

Great Gray Owl — A1149

Saw-whet Owl — A1150

Barred Owl — A1151

Great Horned Owl — A1152

Designed by Frank J. Waslick.

LITHOGRAPHED, ENGRAVED (Giori)

Plates of 200 subjects in four panes of 50.

1978, Aug. 26	**Tagged**	***Perf. 11***	
1760 A1149 15c **multicolored**		.30	.25
1761 A1150 15c **multicolored**		.30	.25
1762 A1151 15c **multicolored**		.30	.25
1763 A1152 15c **multicolored**		.30	.25
a. Block of 4, #1760-1763		1.25	1.25
P# block of 4		1.40	—
Margin block of 4, Mr. Zip		1.25	—
Pane of 50		15.00	
b. As "a," tagging omitted			—
c. As "a," yellow and orange (litho.) omitted		—	

Two panes of No. 1763c have been reported. On one pane, the black (engr.) is shifted to the left.

AMERICAN TREES ISSUE

Nos. 1764-1765 alternate in 1st row, Nos. 1766-1767 in 2nd.

Giant Sequoia A1153

White Pine — A1154

White Oak — A1155

Gray Birch — A1156

Designed by Walter D. Richards.

PHOTOGRAVURE (Andreotti)

Plates of 160 subjects in four panes of 40.

1978, Oct. 9 **Tagged** ***Perf. 11***

1764 A1153 15c **multicolored** .30 .25
1765 A1154 15c **multicolored** .30 .25
1766 A1155 15c **multicolored** .30 .25
1767 A1156 15c **multicolored** .30 .25
a. Block of 4, #1764-1767 1.25 1.25
P# block of 12, 6# 4.00 —
P# block of 16, 6#, Mr. Zip and copyright 5.25 —
Margin block of 4, Mr. Zip, copyright 1.30 —
Pane of 40 12.00
b. As "a," imperf. horiz. *17,500.*

No. 1767b is unique.

CHRISTMAS ISSUE

Madonna and Child with Cherubim, by Andrea della Robbia — A1157

Child on Hobby Horse and Christmas Trees — A1158

Designed by Bradbury Thompson (No. 1768) after terra cotta sculpture in National Gallery, Washington, D.C. by Dolli Tingle (No. 1769).

PHOTOGRAVURE (Andreotti)

Plates of 400 subjects in four panes of 100.

1978, Oct. 18 ***Perf. 11***

1768 A1157 15c **blue & multicolored** .30 .25
P# block of 12, 6# 4.00 —
Margin block of 4, "Use Correct Zip Code" 1.25 —
Pane of 100 30.00
Pair with full horiz. gutter between 150.00
a. Imperf., pair *70.00*

Value for No. 1768a is for an uncreased pair.

1769 A1158 15c **red & multicolored** .30 .25
P# block of 12, 6# 4.00 —
Margin block of 4, "Use Correct Zip Code" 1.25 —
Pair with full horiz. gutter btwn. —
Pane of 100 30.00
a. Imperf., pair *75.00*
b. Vert. pair, imperf. horiz. *900.00*

ROBERT F. KENNEDY ISSUE

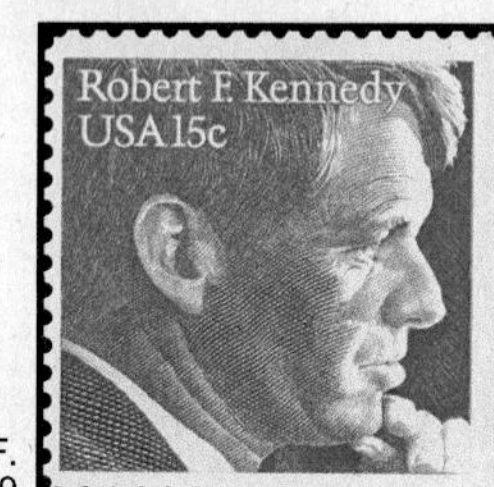

Robert F. Kennedy — A1159

Designed by Bradbury Thompson after photograph by Stanley Tretick.

ENGRAVED

Plates of 192 subjects in four panes of 48 (8x6).

1979, Jan. 12 **Tagged** ***Perf. 11***

1770 A1159 15c **blue** .35 .25
P# block of 4 1.50 —
Margin block of 4, Mr. Zip 1.40 —
Pane of 48 16.75
a. Tagging omitted *50.00*

BLACK HERITAGE SERIES

Dr. Martin Luther King, Jr. (1929-1968), Civil Rights leader.

Martin Luther King, Jr. and Civil Rights Marchers — A1160

Designed by Jerry Pinkney.

PHOTOGRAVURE (Andreotti)

Plates of 200 subjects in four panes of 50.

1979, Jan. 13 **Tagged** ***Perf. 11***

1771 A1160 15c **multicolored** .40 .25
P# block of 12, 6# 5.75 —
Margin block of 4, Mr. Zip 1.75 —
Pane of 50 20.00
a. Imperf., pair *800.00*
b. Tagging omitted —

INTERNATIONAL YEAR OF THE CHILD ISSUE

Children of Different Races A1161

Designed by Paul Calle.

ENGRAVED

Plates of 200 subjects in four panes of 50.

1979, Feb. 15 **Tagged** ***Perf. 11***

1772 A1161 15c **orange red** .30 .25
P# block of 4 1.40 —
Margin block of 4, Mr. Zip 1.25 —

LITERARY ARTS SERIES

John Steinbeck (1902-1968), Novelist — A1162

Designed by Bradbury Thompson after photograph by Philippe Halsman.

ENGRAVED

Plates of 200 subjects in four panes of 50.

1979, Feb. 27 **Tagged** ***Perf. 10½x11***

1773 A1162 15c **dark blue** .30 .25
P# block of 4 1.40 —
Margin block of 4, Mr. Zip 1.25 —
Pane of 50 15.00

ALBERT EINSTEIN ISSUE

Albert Einstein (1879-1955), Theoretical Physicist — A1163

Designed by Bradbury Thompson after photograph by Hermann Landshoff.

ENGRAVED

Plates of 200 subjects in four panes of 50.

1979, Mar. 4 **Tagged** ***Perf. 10½x11***

1774 A1163 15c **chocolate** .30 .25
P# block of 4 1.60 —
Margin block of 4, Mr. Zip 1.45 —
Pane of 50 15.00
Pair, horiz. gutter btwn. —

AMERICAN FOLK ART SERIES

Pennsylvania Toleware, c. 1800.

Coffeepot — A1164

Tea Caddy — A1165

Sugar Bowl — A1166

Coffeepot — A1167

Designed by Bradbury Thompson.

PHOTOGRAVURE (Andreotti)
Plates of 160 subjects in four panes of 40.

1979, Apr. 19 Tagged *Perf. 11*

1775 A1164 15c **multicolored**	.30	.25
1776 A1165 15c **multicolored**	.30	.25
1777 A1166 15c **multicolored**	.30	.25
1778 A1167 15c **multicolored**	.30	.25
a. Block of 4, #1775-1778	1.25	1.25
P# block of 10, 5#	3.25	—
P# block of 16, 5#; Mr. Zip and copyright	5.25	—
Margin block of 6, Mr. Zip and copyright	2.00	—
Pane of 40	12.00	
b. As "a," imperf. horiz.	*2,000.*	

AMERICAN ARCHITECTURE SERIES

Nos. 1779-1780 alternate in 1st row, Nos. 1781-1782 in 2nd.

Virginia Rotunda, by Thomas Jefferson — A1168

Baltimore Cathedral, by Benjamin Latrobe — A1169

Boston State House, by Charles Bulfinch — A1170

Philadelphia Exchange, by William Strickland — A1171

Designed by Walter D. Richards.

ENGRAVED (Giori)
Plates of 192 subjects in four panes of 48 (6x8).

1979, June 4 Tagged *Perf. 11*

1779 A1168 15c **black & brick red**	.30	.25
1780 A1169 15c **black & brick red**	.30	.25
1781 A1170 15c **black & brick red**	.30	.25

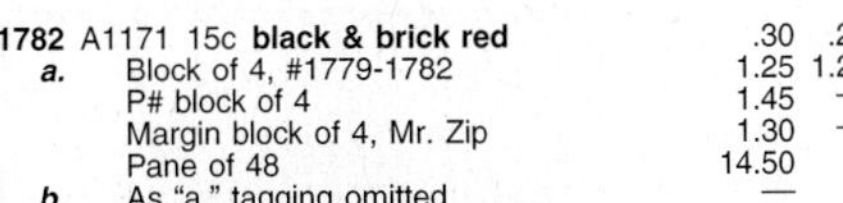

1782 A1171 15c **black & brick red**	.30	.25
a. Block of 4, #1779-1782	1.25	1.25
P# block of 4	1.45	—
Margin block of 4, Mr. Zip	1.30	—
Pane of 48	14.50	
b. As "a," tagging omitted	—	

ENDANGERED FLORA ISSUE

Nos. 1783-1784 alternate in one horizontal row. Nos. 1785-1786 in the next.

Persistent Trillium — A1172

Hawaiian Wild Broadbean — A1173

Contra Costa Wallflower — A1174

Antioch Dunes Evening Primrose — A1175

Designed by Frank J. Waslick.

PHOTOGRAVURE (Andreotti)
Plates of 200 subjects in four panes of 50.

1979, June 7 Tagged *Perf. 11*

1783 A1172 15c **multicolored**	.30	.25
1784 A1173 15c **multicolored**	.30	.25
1785 A1174 15c **multicolored**	.30	.25
1786 A1175 15c **multicolored**	.30	.25
a. Block of 4, #1783-1786	1.25	1.25
P# block of 12, 6#	4.00	—
P# block of 20, 6#, Mr. Zip and copyright	6.50	—
Margin block of 4, Mr. Zip	1.30	—
Pane of 50	15.00	
As "a," full vert. gutter btwn.	*800.00*	
b. As "a," imperf.	*200.00*	

SEEING EYE DOGS ISSUE

1st guide dog program in the US, 50th anniv.

German Shepherd Leading Man — A1176

Designed by Joseph Csatari.

PHOTOGRAVURE (Combination Press)
Plates of 230 (10x23) subjects in panes of 50 (10x5).

1979, June 15 Tagged *Perf. 11*

1787 A1176 15c **multicolored**	.30	.25
P# block of 20, 5-8#, 1-2 copyright	6.50	—
Pane of 50	15.00	
a. Imperf., pair	*325.00*	
b. Tagging omitted	15.00	

See Combination Press note after No. 1703.

SPECIAL OLYMPICS ISSUE

Special Olympics for special children, Brockport, N.Y., Aug. 8-13.

Child Holding Winner's Medal — A1177

Designed by Jeff Cornell.

PHOTOGRAVURE (Andreotti)
Plates of 200 subjects in four panes of 50.

1979, Aug. 9 Tagged *Perf. 11*

1788 A1177 15c **multicolored**	.30	.25
P# block of 10, 5#	3.25	—
Zip block of 4	1.25	—
Pane of 50	15.00	

JOHN PAUL JONES ISSUE

John Paul Jones (1747-1792), Naval Commander, American Revolution.

John Paul Jones, by Charles Willson Peale — A1178

Designed after painting in Independence National Historical Park, Philadelphia.
Printed by American Bank Note Co. and J. W. Fergusson and Sons.

Designed by Bradbury Thompson.

PHOTOGRAVURE (Champlain)
Plates of 200 subjects in four panes of 50.

1979, Sept. 23 Tagged *Perf. 11x12*

1789 A1178 15c **multicolored**	.30	.25
P# block of 10, 5#+A	3.25	—
Zip block of 4	1.25	—
Pane of 50	15.00	
c. Vert. pair, imperf. horiz.	*125.00*	

Imperforates on gummed stamp paper, including gutter pairs and blocks, are proofs from the ABNCo. archives. See No. 1789P in Proofs section.

Perf. 11

1789A A1178 15c **multicolored**	.55	.25
P# block of 10, 5#+A	5.75	—
Zip block of 4	3.25	—
Pane of 50	27.50	
d. Vertical pair, imperf. horiz.	*115.00*	

Perf. 12

1789B A1178 15c **multicolored**	*3,000.*	*3,500.*
On cover		*14,000.*
P# block of 10, 5#+A	*37,500.*	
Zip block of 4	*15,000.*	—

OLYMPIC GAMES ISSUE

22nd Summer Olympic Games, Moscow, July 19-Aug. 3, 1980. Nos. 1791-1792 alternate in one horizontal row, Nos. 1793-1794 in next.

Javelin — A1179

Running
A1180

Swimming
A1181

Rowing
A1182

Equestrian
A1183

Designed by Robert M. Cunningham.

PHOTOGRAVURE

Plates of 200 subjects in four panes of 50.

1979, Sept. 5	**Tagged**	***Perf. 11***	
1790 A1179 10c **multicolored**		.30	.25
P# block of 12, 6#		3.25	—
Zip block of 4		1.00	—
Pane of 50		12.50	

1979, Sept. 28		
1791 A1180 15c **multicolored**	.30	.25
1792 A1181 15c **multicolored**	.30	.25
1793 A1182 15c **multicolored**	.30	.25
1794 A1183 15c **multicolored**	.30	.25
a. Block of 4, #1791-1794	1.25	1.25
P# block of 12, 6#	4.00	—
Zip block of 4	1.30	—
P# block of 20, 6#, zip, copyright	6.50	—
Pane of 50	15.00	
b. As "a," imperf.	*900.00*	

OLYMPIC GAMES ISSUE

13th Winter Olympic Games, Lake Placid, N.Y., Feb. 12-24. Nos. 1795-1796 alternate in one horizontal row, Nos. 1797-1798 in next.

Speed Skating
A1184

Downhill Skiing
A1185

Ski
Jump — A1186

Ice Hockey
A1187

Designed by Robert M. Cunningham

PHOTOGRAVURE

Plates of 200 subject in four panes of 50.

1980, Feb. 1	**Tagged**	***Perf. 11¼x10½***	
1795 A1184 15c **multicolored**		.35	.25
1796 A1185 15c **multicolored**		.35	.25
1797 A1186 15c **multicolored**		.35	.25
1798 A1187 15c **multicolored**		.35	.25
b. Block of 4, #1795-1798		1.50	1.40
P# block of 12, 6#		4.50	—
Zip block of 4		1.55	—
P# block of 20, 6#, zip and copyright		7.50	—
Pane of 50		17.50	

Perf. 11

1795A A1184 15c **multicolored**	1.00	.60
1796A A1185 15c **multicolored**	1.00	.60
1797A A1186 15c **multicolored**	1.00	.60
1798A A1187 15c **multicolored**	1.00	.60
c. Block of 4, #1795A-1798A	4.00	3.50
P# block of 12, 6#	14.00	—
Zip block of 4	4.25	—
P# block of 20, 6#, zip and copyright	26.00	—
Pane of 50	50.00	

CHRISTMAS ISSUE

Virgin and Child by Gerard David — A1188

Santa Claus, Christmas Tree Ornament — A1189

Designed by Bradbury Thompson (No. 1799) and by Eskil Ohlsson (No. 1800).

No. 1799 is designed after a painting in National Gallery of Art, Washington, D.C.

PHOTOGRAVURE (Andreotti)

Plates of 400 subjects in four panes of 100.

1979, Oct. 18	**Tagged**	***Perf. 11***	
1799 A1188 15c **multicolored**		.30	.25
P# block of 12, 6#		4.00	—
Zip block of 4		1.25	—
P# block of 20, 6#, zip, copyright		6.50	—
Pane of 100		30.00	
a. Imperf., pair		70.00	
b. Vert. pair, imperf. horiz.		*450.00*	
c. Vert. pair, imperf. between		*950.00*	
d. Tagging omitted			—

Perf. 11x10½

1800 A1189 15c **multicolored**	.30	.25
P# block of 12, 6#	4.00	—
Zip block of 4	1.25	—
P# block of 20, 6#, zip, copyright	6.50	—
Pane of 100	30.00	
a. Green & yellow omitted	*400.00*	
b. Green, yellow & tan omitted	*400.00*	
c. Vert. se-tenant pair, #1800a & 1800b	*850.00*	

Nos. 1800a and 1800b always have the remaining colors misaligned.

Nos. 1800a, 1800b and 1800c are valued in the grade of fine.

VALUES FOR HINGED STAMPS AFTER NO. 771

This catalogue does not value unused stamps after No. 771 in hinged condition. Hinged unused stamps from No. 772 to the present are worth considerably less than the values given for unused stamps, which are for never-hinged examples.

PERFORMING ARTS SERIES

Will Rogers (1879-1935), Actor and Humorist — A1190

Designed by Jim Sharpe.

PHOTOGRAVURE (Andreotti)

Plates of 200 subjects in four panes of 50.

1979, Nov. 4	**Tagged**	***Perf. 11***	
1801 A1190 15c **multicolored**		.30	.25
P# block of 12, 6#		4.00	—
Zip block of 4		1.25	—
P# block of 20, 6#, zip, copyright		6.50	—
Pane of 50		15.00	
a. Imperf., pair		*135.00*	

VIETNAM VETERANS ISSUE

A tribute to veterans of the Vietnam War.

Ribbon for Vietnam Service Medal A1191

Designed by Stevan Dohanos.

PHOTOGRAVURE (Andreotti)

Plates of 200 subjects in four panes of 50.

1979, Nov. 11	**Tagged**	***Perf. 11***	
1802 A1191 15c **multicolored**		.30	.25
P# block of 10, 5#		3.25	—
Zip block of 4		1.25	—
Pane of 50		15.00	

PERFORMING ARTS SERIES

W.C. Fields (1880-1946), actor and comedian.

W.C. Fields — A1192

Designed by Jim Sharpe.

PHOTOGRAVURE

Plates of 200 subjects in four panes of 50.

1980, Jan. 29	**Tagged**	***Perf. 11***	
1803 A1192 15c **multicolored**		.30	.25
P# block of 12, 6#		4.00	—
Zip block of 4		1.25	—
P# block of 20, 6#, zip, copyright		6.50	—
Pane of 50		15.00	
a. Imperf., pair		—	

BLACK HERITAGE SERIES

Benjamin Banneker (1731-1806), astronomer and mathematician.

Benjamin Banneker — A1193

Designed by Jerry Pinkney.

Printed by American Bank Note Co. and J. W. Fergusson and Sons.

PHOTOGRAVURE

Plates of 200 subjects in four panes of 50.

1980, Feb. 15 **Tagged** ***Perf. 11***

1804	A1193	15c **multicolored**	.30	.25
		P# block of 12, 6#+A	4.00	—
		Zip block of 4	1.25	—
		Plate block of 20, 6#+A, zip, copyright	6.50	—
		Pane of 50	15.00	
a.		Horiz. pair, imperf. vert.	*275.00*	

Imperfs, including gutter pairs and blocks, exist from printer's waste. These have been fraudulently perforated to simulate No. 1804a. Genuine examples of No. 1804a do not have colors misregistered.

NATIONAL LETTER WRITING WEEK ISSUE

National Letter Writing Week, Feb. 24-Mar. 1. Nos. 1805-1810 are printed vertically se-tenant.

Letters Preserve Memories — A1194

P.S. Write Soon — A1195

Letters Lift Spirits — A1196

Letters Shape Opinions — A1197

Designed by Randall McDougall.

Plates of 240 subjects in four panes of 60 (10x6) each.

PHOTOGRAVURE

1980, Feb. 25 **Tagged** ***Perf. 11***

1805	A1194	15c **multicolored**	.30	.25
1806	A1195	15c **purple & multi**	.30	.25
1807	A1196	15c **multicolored**	.30	.25
1808	A1195	15c **green & multi**	.30	.25
1809	A1197	15c **multicolored**	.30	.25
1810	A1195	15c **red & multi**	.30	.25
a.		Vertical strip of 6, #1805-1810	1.85	*2.00*
		P# block of 36, 6#	13.00	—
		Zip block of 12	3.75	—
		Pane of 60	18.00	
		Nos. 1805-1810 (6)	1.80	1.50

AMERICANA TYPE

Weaver Violins — A1199

Designer: 3.5c, George Mercer.

COIL STAMPS

1980-81 **Engr.** ***Perf. 10 Vertically***

1811	A984	1c **dark blue,** *greenish,* shiny gum, *Mar. 6, 1980*	.30	.25
		Pair	.50	.50
		Joint line pair	.60	—
		Dull gum	.35	
		Joint line pair	1.75	
a.		Imperf., pair	*60.00*	
		Joint line pair	*150.00*	
b.		Tagging omitted	—	
1813	A1199	3.5c **purple,** *yellow, June 23, 1980*	.30	.25
		Pair	.50	.50
		Joint line pair	1.00	—
a.		Untagged (Bureau precanceled, lines only)	.25	.25
		Pair	.50	.50
		Joint line pair	1.95	—
b.		Imperf., pair	*125.00*	
		Joint line pair	*375.00*	
1816	A997	12c **red brown,** *beige, Apr. 8, 1981*	.30	.25
		Pair	.50	.50
		Joint line pair	2.00	—
a.		Untagged (Bureau precanceled), **red brown,** *beige*	1.25	1.25
		Pair	2.60	2.60
		Joint line pair	40.00	—
b.		Imperf., pair	135.00	
		Joint line pair	275.00	
c.		As "a," **brownish red,** *reddish beige*	1.25	1.25
		Pair	2.60	2.60
		Joint line pair	*37.50*	—
		Nos. 1811-1816 (3)	.90	.75

Bureau Precancels: No. 1816a, lines only (valued), lines and PRESORTED/FIRST CLASS (values: unused $75, pair $150, joint line pair $2,250); No. 1816c, lines and PRESORTED/FIRST CLASS.

Eagle — A1207

PHOTOGRAVURE

Plates of 400 subjects in four panes of 100.

1981, Mar. 15 **Tagged** ***Perf. 11x10½***

1818	A1207	(18c) **violet**	.35	.25
		P# block of 4	1.60	—
		Zip block of 4	1.50	—
		Pane of 100	35.00	
		Pair with full vert. gutter between	—	
		Cross gutter block of 10	*3,000.*	

The cross gutter block, caused by a foldover and misperforated horizontally, is unique.

BOOKLET STAMP

ENGRAVED

Perf. 10 on 2 or 3 Sides

1819	A1207	(18c) **violet**	.40	.25
a.		Booklet pane of 8	3.50	2.25

COIL STAMP

Perf. 10 Vert.

1820	A1207	(18c) **violet**	.40	.25
		Pair	.80	.50
		Joint line pair	1.60	—
a.		Imperf., pair	*75.00*	
		Joint line pair	*120.00*	

FRANCES PERKINS ISSUE

Frances Perkins (1882-1965), Secretary of Labor, 1933-1945 (first woman cabinet member).

Frances Perkins — A1208

Designed by F.R. Petrie.

ENGRAVED

Plates of 200 subjects in four panes of 50.

1980, Apr. 10 **Tagged** ***Perf. 10½x11***

1821	A1208	15c **Prussian blue**	.30	.25
		P# block of 4	1.30	—
		Zip block of 4	1.25	—
		Pane of 50	30.00	

DOLLEY MADISON ISSUE

Dolley Madison (1768-1849), First Lady, 1809-1817.

Dolley Madison — A1209

Designed by Esther Porter.

ENGRAVED

Plates of 600 subjects in four panes of 150.

1980, May 20 **Tagged** ***Perf. 11***

1822	A1209	15c **red brown & sepia**	.30	.25
		P# block of 4	1.40	—
		Zip block of 4	1.25	—
		Pane of 150	45.00	
a.		Red brown missing (PS)	*575.00*	

EMILY BISSELL ISSUE

Emily Bissell (1861-1948), social worker; introduced Christmas seals in United States.

Emily Bissell — A1210

Designed by Stevan Dohanos.

ENGRAVED

Plates of 200 subjects in four panes of 50.

1980, May 31 **Tagged** ***Perf. 11***

1823	A1210	15c **black & red**	.30	.25
		P# block of 4	1.60	—
		Zip block of 4	1.45	—
		Pane of 50	15.00	
a.		Vert. pair, imperf. horiz.	*250.00*	
b.		All colors missing (EP)	—	
c.		Red missing (FO)	—	
d.		Red omitted	—	

On No. 1823d, traces of black are present.

HELEN KELLER ISSUE

Helen Keller (1880-1968), blind and deaf writer and lecturer taught by Anne Sullivan (1867-1936).

Helen Keller and Anne Sullivan — A1211

Designed by Paul Calle.

LITHOGRAPHED AND ENGRAVED

Plates of 200 subjects in four panes of 50.

1980, June 27	**Tagged**	***Perf. 11***	
1824 A1211 15c **multicolored**		.30	.25
P# block of 4		1.30	—
Zip block of 4		1.25	—
Pane of 50		15.00	

VETERANS ADMINISTRATION, 50th ANNIV.

Veterans Administration Emblem — A1212

Designed by Malcolm Grear.

Printed by American Bank Note Co. and J. W. Fergusson and Sons.

PHOTOGRAVURE

Plates of 200 subjects in four panes of 50.

1980, July 21	**Tagged**	***Perf. 11***	
1825 A1212 15c **carmine & violet blue**		.30	.25
P# block of 4, 2#+A		1.30	—
Zip block of 4		1.25	—
Pane of 50		15.00	
a. Horiz. pair, imperf. vert.		*375.00*	

BERNARDO DE GALVEZ ISSUE

Gen. Bernardo de Galvez (1746-1786), helped defeat British in Battle of Mobile, 1780.

Gen. Bernardo de Galvez — A1213

Designed by Roy H. Andersen.

LITHOGRAPHED & ENGRAVED

Plates of 200 subjects in four panes of 50.

1980, July 23	**Tagged**	***Perf. 11***	
1826 A1213 15c **multicolored**		.30	.25
P# block of 4		1.30	—
Zip block of 4		1.25	—
Pane of 50		15.00	
a. Red, brown & blue (engr.) omitted		*550.00*	
b. Light yellow, red, blue & brown (litho.) omitted		*550.00*	

CORAL REEFS ISSUE

Nos. 1827-1828 alternate in one horizontal row, Nos. 1829-1830 in the next.

Brain Coral, Beaugregory Fish — A1214

Elkhorn Coral, Porkfish — A1215

Chalice Coral, Moorish Idol — A1216

Finger Coral, Sabertooth Blenny — A1217

Normal

Cylinder Flaw

Designed by Chuck Ripper.

PHOTOGRAVURE

Plates of 200 subjects in four panes of 50.

1980, Aug. 26	**Tagged**	***Perf. 11***	
1827 A1214 15c **multi**		.30	.25
1828 A1215 15c **multi**		.30	.25
1829 A1216 15c **multi**		.30	.25
1830 A1217 15c **multi**		.30	.25
Cylinder flaw (period between "Finger coral" and "Hawaii" instead of colon) (39390 LR 48)		—	—
a. Block of 4, #1827-1830		1.25	1.10
P# block of 12, 6#		5.00	—
Zip block of 4		1.30	—
Pane of 50		15.00	
b. As "a," imperf.		*250.00*	
c. As "a," vert. imperf. between		*1,750.*	
d. As "a," imperf. vert.		*2,750.*	

ORGANIZED LABOR ISSUE

American Bald Eagle — A1218

Designed by Peter Cocci.

PHOTOGRAVURE

Plates of 200 subjects in four panes of 50.

1980, Sept. 1	**Tagged**	***Perf. 11***	
1831 A1218 15c **multi**		.30	.25
P# block of 12, 6#		3.50	—
Zip block of 4		1.25	—
Pane of 50		15.00	
a. Imperf., pair		*275.00*	

LITERARY ARTS SERIES

Edith Wharton (1862-1937), novelist.

Edith Wharton — A1219

Designed by Bradbury Thompson after 1905 photograph.

ENGRAVED

Plates of 200 subjects in four panes of 50.

1980, Sept. 5	**Tagged**	***Perf. 10½x11***	
1832 A1219 15c **purple**		.30	.25
P# block of 4		1.30	—
Zip block of 4		1.25	—
Pane of 50		15.00	

EDUCATION ISSUE

"Homage to the Square: Glow" by Josef Albers — A1220

Designed by Bradbury Thompson

Printed by American Bank Note Co. and J. W. Fergusson and Sons.

PHOTOGRAVURE

Plates of 200 subjects in four panes of 50.

1980, Sept. 12	**Tagged**	***Perf. 11***	
1833 A1220 15c **multi**		.30	.25
P# block of 6, 3#+A		1.90	—
Zip block of 4		1.25	—
Pane of 50		15.00	
a. Horiz. pair, imperf. vert.		*150.00*	

AMERICAN FOLK ART SERIES

Pacific Northwest Indian Masks

Heiltsuk, Bella Bella Tribe — A1221

Chilkat Tlingit Tribe — A1222

Tlingit Tribe — A1223

Bella Coola Tribe — A1224

Designed by Bradury Thompson after photographs.

PHOTOGRAVURE

Plates of 160 subjects in four panes of 40.

1980, Sept. 25 **Tagged** ***Perf. 11***

1834	A1221 15c **multi**	.35	.25
1835	A1222 15c **multi**	.35	.25
1836	A1223 15c **multi**	.35	.25
1837	A1224 15c **multi**	.35	.25
a.	Block of 4, #1834-1837	1.50	1.25
	P# block of 10, 5#	5.00	—
	Zip, copyright block of 6	2.25	—
	Pane of 40	14.00	

AMERICAN ARCHITECTURE SERIES

Smithsonian A1225

Trinity Church A1226

Penn Academy A1227

AJ Davis 1803-1892 Lyndhurst Tarrytown NY
Architecture USA 15c

Lyndhurst A1228

Designed by Walter D. Richards.

ENGRAVED (Giori)

Plates of 160 subjects in four panes of 40.

1980, Oct. 9 **Tagged** ***Perf. 11***

1838	A1225 15c **black & red**	.30	.25
a.	Red missing (PS)		—
1839	A1226 15c **black & red**	.30	.25
1840	A1227 15c **black & red**	.30	.25
1841	A1228 15c **black & red**	.30	.25
a.	Block of 4, #1838-1841	1.25	1.25
	P# block of 4	1.50	—
	Zip block of 4	1.30	—
	Pane of 40	12.00	
b.	As "a," red missing on Nos. 1838, 1839 (PS)	*400.00*	
c.	As "a," tagging omitted	—	

CHRISTMAS ISSUE

Madonna and Child — A1229

Wreath and Toys — A1230

Designed by Esther Porter (No. 1842) after Epiphany Window, Washington Cathedral, and by Bob Timberlake (No. 1843).

PHOTOGRAVURE

Plate of 200 subjects in four panes of 50.

1980, Oct. 31 **Tagged** ***Perf. 11***

1842	A1229 15c **multi**	.30	.25
	P# block of 12, 6#	4.00	—
	Zip block of 4	1.25	—
	Pane of 50	15.00	
	Pair with full vert. gutter btwn.	—	
a.	Imperf., pair	40.00	

PHOTOGRAVURE (Combination Press)

Plates of 230 subjects (10x23) in panes of 50 (10x5).

1843	A1230 15c **multi**	.30	.25
	P# block of 20, 5-8 #, 1-2 copyright	6.50	—
	Pane of 50	15.00	
a.	Imperf., pair	45.00	
b.	Buff omitted	22.50	
c.	Vert. pair, imperf. horiz.	—	
d.	Horiz. pair, imperf. between	*3,250.*	
e.	Tagging omitted	125.00	—

No. 1843b is difficult to identify and should have a competent certificate.

See Combination Press note after No. 1703.

GREAT AMERICANS ISSUE

Dorothea Dix — A1231

Igor Stravinsky — A1232

Henry Clay — A1233

Carl Schurz — A1234

Pearl Buck — A1235

Walter Lippmann — A1236

Abraham Baldwin — A1237

Henry Knox — A1238

Sylvanus Thayer — A1239

Richard Russell — A1240

Alden Partridge — A1241

Crazy Horse — A1242

Sinclair Lewis — A1243

Rachel Carson — A1244

George Mason — A1245

Sequoyah — A1246

Ralph Bunche — A1247

Thomas H. Gallaudet — A1248

Harry S. Truman — A1249

John J. Audubon — A1250

Frank C. Laubach — A1251

Charles R. Drews MD — A1252

Robert Millikan — A1253

Grenville Clark — A1254

Lillian M. Gilbreth — A1255

Chester W. Nimitz — A1256

Designers: 1c, Bernie Fuchs. 2c, Burt Silverman, 3c, 17c, 40c, Ward Brackett. 4c, 7c, 10c, 18c, 30c, Richard Sparks. 5c, Paul Calle. 6c, No. 1861, Dennis Lyall. 8c, Arthur Lidov. 9c, 11c, Robert Alexander Anderson. 13c, Brad Holland. 14c, Bradbury Thompson. 19c, 39c, Roy H. Andersen. No. 1860, Jim Sharpe. No. 1862, 22c, 50c, 37c, Christopher Calle. 35c, Nathan Jones.

ENGRAVED

Perf. 11x10½, 11 (1c, 6c-11c, 14c, No. 1862, 22c, 30c, 39c, 40c, 50c)

1980-85 **Tagged**

1844 A1231 1c **black,** perf. 11.2, small block tagging, *Sept. 23, 1983* .30 .25
On cover 2.00
P# block of 6 .75 —
P# block of 20, 1-2 #, 1-2 copyright 3.50 —
Pane of 100 6.00
a. Imperf., pair *250.00*
b. Vert. pair, imperf. btwn. and with natural straight edge at bottom *1,000.*
c. Perf. 10.9, small block tagging .30 .25
P# block of 6 1.50 —
P# block of 20, 1-2 #, 1-2 copyright 3.50 —
Pane of 100 6.00
d. Perf. 10.9, large block tagging, *1985* .30 .25
P# block of 6 1.50 —
P# block of 20, 1-2 #, 1-2 copyright 3.50 —
Pane of 100 6.00
e. Vert. pair, imperf. horiz. *1,000.*

1845 A1232 2c **brn blk,** overall tagging, *Nov. 18, 1982* .30 .25
On cover 2.00
P# block of 4 .60 —
Zip block of 4 .50 —
Pair with full horiz. gutter between —
Pane of 100 6.00
a. Tagging omitted 125.00

The pair with gutter between of No. 1845 is also misperfed, with horiz. perfs running through the stamps.

1846 A1233 3c **olive green,** overall tagging, *July 13, 1983* .30 .25
On cover 2.00
deep olive green .30 .25
P# block of 4 1.00 —
Zip block of 4 .80 —
Pane of 100 6.00
a. Tagging omitted 9.00

1847 A1234 4c **violet,** overall tagging, *June 3, 1983* .30 .25
On cover 4.00
P# block of 4 1.00 —
Zip block of 4 1.00 —
Pane of 100 8.00
a. Tagging omitted 9.00

1848 A1235 5c **henna brown,** overall tagging, *June 25, 1983* .30 .25
On cover 2.00
P# block of 4 1.50 —
Zip block of 4 1.25 —
Pane of 100 12.00

1849 A1236 6c **orange vermilion,** large block tagging, *Sept. 19, 1985* .30 .25
On cover 4.00
P# block of 6 1.50 —
P# block of 20, 1-2 #, 1-2 zip, 1-2 copyright 5.00 —
Pane of 100 12.00
a. Vert. pair, imperf. between and with natural straight edge at bottom *1,000.*

1850 A1237 7c **bright carmine,** small block tagging, *Jan. 25, 1985* .30 .25
On cover 4.00
P# block of 6 1.50 —
P# block of 20, 1-2 #, 1-2 zip, 1-2 copyright 4.00 —
Pane of 100 14.00

1851 A1238 8c **olive black,** overall tagging, *July 25, 1985* .30 .25
On cover 4.00
P# block of 4 1.00 —
Zip block of 4 1.00 —
Pane of 100 16.00
a. Tagging omitted *150.00*

1852 A1239 9c **dark green,** small block tagging, *June 7, 1985* .30 .25
On cover 4.00
P# block of 6 1.50 —
P# block of 20, 1-2 #. 1-2 zip, 1-2 copyright 5.00 —
Pane of 100 18.00

1853 A1240 10c **Prussian blue,** small block tagging, *May 31, 1984* .30 .25
On cover 4.00
P# block of 6 2.00 —
P# block of 20, 1-2 #, 1-2 copyright, 1-2 zip 9.00 —
Pane of 100 25.00
a. Large block tagging .30 .25
P# block of 6 2.25 —
P# block of 20, 1-2 #, 1-2 copyright, 1-2 zip 9.00 —
Pane of 100 30.00
b. Vert. pair, imperf. between *550.00*
c. Horiz. pair, imperf. between *1,250.*
d. Vert. pair, imperf horiz. —

Almost all examples of No. 1853b also have a natural straight edge at bottom. At least one pair has perfs at bottom and partial perfs at top.

Completely imperforate tagged or untagged stamps are from printer's waste. Known unused and used.

1854 A1241 11c **dark blue,** overall tagging, *Feb. 12, 1985* .40 .25
On cover 4.00
P# block of 4 2.00 —
Zip block of 4 1.60 —
Pane of 100 40.00
a. Tagging omitted 30.00

1855 A1242 13c **light maroon,** overall tagging, *Jan. 15, 1982* .40 .25
On cover 2.00
P# block of 4 2.25 —
Zip block of 4 1.60 —
Pane of 100 40.00
Pair with full vert. gutter btwn. —
a. Tagging omitted 22.50

1856 A1243 14c **slate green,** small block tagging, *Mar. 21, 1985* .30 .25
On cover 2.00
P# block of 6 2.25 —
P# block of 20, 1-2 #, 1-2 zip, 1-2 copyright 10.00 —
Pane of 100 30.00
a. Large block tagging .30 .25
P# block of 6 2.25 —
P# block of 20, 1-2 #, 1-2 zip, 1-2 copyright 9.00 —
Pane of 100 30.00
b. Vert. pair, imperf. horiz. *90.00*
c. Horiz. pair, imperf. between 8.00 —
d. Vert. pair, imperf. between *1,250.*
e. All color omitted —

No. 1856e comes from a partially printed pane and should be collected as a vertical strip of 10, one stamp normal, one stamp transitional and 8 stamps with color omitted.

1857 A1244 17c **green,** overall tagging, *May 28, 1981* .35 .25
On cover 2.00
P# block of 4 2.00 —
Zip block of 4 1.40 —
Pane of 100 35.00
Pair with full vert. gutter btwn. —
a. Tagging omitted 17.50

1858 A1245 18c **dark blue,** overall tagging, *May 7, 1981* .35 .25
On cover 2.00
P# block of 4 3.00 —
Zip block of 4 1.40 —
Pane of 100 35.00
Pair with full horiz. gutter between —
a. Tagging omitted 15.00

1859 A1246 19c **brown,** overall tagging, *Dec. 27, 1980* .45 .25
On cover 4.00
Single franking on international surface postcard 8.00
P# block of 4 2.75 —
Zip block of 4 1.90 —
Pane of 100 45.00

1860 A1247 20c **claret,** overall tagging, *Jan. 12, 1982* .40 .25
On cover 2.00
Single franking on first-class Canada/Mexico letter 8.00
Single franking on domestic surface postcard 6.00
P# block of 4 3.25 —
Zip block of 4 1.65 —
Pane of 100 40.00
a. Tagging omitted 12.50

1861 A1248 20c **green,** overall tagging, *June 10, 1983* .50 .25
On cover 2.00
Single franking on first-class Canada/Mexico letter 8.00
Single franking on domestic surface postcard 6.00
P# block of 4 4.00 —
Zip block of 4 2.00 —
Pane of 100 50.00
a. Tagging omitted *225.00*

1862 A1249 20c **black,** perf 10.9, small block tagging, dull gum, *Jan. 26, 1984* .40 .25
On cover 2.00
Single franking on first-class Canada/Mexico letter 8.00
P# block of 6 4.50 —
P# block of 20, 1-2 #, 1-2 copyright, 1-2 zip 11.00 —
Pane of 100 40.00
a. Perf. 11.2, large block tagging, dull gum .75 .25
Corner P# block of 4 4.50 —
Zip block of 4 3.00 —
Pane of 100 75.00
b. Perf. 11.2, overall tagging, dull gum, *1990* .40 —
Corner P# block of 4 3.75 —
Zip block of 4 1.60 —
Pane of 100 40.00
c. Tagging omitted, perf. 11.2 10.00
d. Prephosphored uncoated paper with embedded tagging showing a mottled appearance, shiny gum, perf. 11.2, *1993* .40 .25
Corner P# block of 4 2.50
Zip block of 4 1.60
Pane of 100 40.00

1863 A1250 22c **dark chalky blue,** small block tagging, *Apr. 23, 1985* .75 .25
On cover 2.00
Single franking on first-class Canada/Mexico letter 8.00
P# block of 6 9.00 —
P# block of 20, 1-2 #, 1-2 zip, 1-2 copyright 16.00 —
Pane of 100 75.00
a. Large block tagging 1.00 .25
P# block of 6 12.50 —
P# block of 20, 1-2 #, 1-2 zip, 1-2 copyright 22.50 —
Pane of 100 100.00
b. Perf. 11.2, large block tagging, *1987* .75 .25
Corner P# block of 4 8.00 —
Zip block of 4 3.25 —
Pane of 100 75.00
c. Tagging omitted 17.50
d. Vert. pair, imperf. horiz. *1,300.*
f. Horiz. pair, imperf. between *1,300.*
g. Vert. pair, imperf. between —

1864 A1251 30c **olive gray,** small block tagging, *Sept. 2, 1984* .60 .25
On cover 4.00
Single franking on first-class Canada letter 8.00
P# block of 6 3.75 —
P# block of 20, 1-2 #, 1-2 copyright, 1-2 zip 17.50 —
Pane of 100 60.00
a. Perf. 11.2, large block tagging .70 .25
Corner P# block of 4 4.50 —
Zip block of 4 3.00 —
Pane of 100 70.00

b.	Perf. 11.2, overall tagging	3.75	.25
	Corner P# block of 4	30.00	—
	Zip block of 4	16.00	—
	Pane of 100	375.00	
c.	Tagging omitted	*225.00*	
1865	A1252 35c **gray,** overall tagging, *June 3, 1981*	.75	.25
	On cover		4.00
	Double-weight first-class letter		10.00
	International airmail letter to Canada, South America		15.00
	International surface postcard		10.00
	Double-weight Mexico letter		20.00
	First-class Mexico postcard		10.00
	P# block of 4	4.25	—
	Zip block of 4	3.25	—
	Pane of 100	75.00	
a.	Tagging omitted	85.00	
1866	A1253 37c **blue,** overall tagging, *Jan. 26, 1982*	.80	.25
	On cover		4.00
	Double-weight first-class letter		5.00
	International surface letter		15.00
	P# block of 4	3.75	—
	Zip block of 4	3.25	—
	Pane of 100	80.00	
a.	Tagging omitted	30.00	
1867	A1254 39c **rose lilac,** perf 10.9, small block tagging, *Mar. 20, 1985*	1.00	.25
	On cover		4.00
	Double-weight first-class letter		5.00
	UPU international air letter		15.00
	International air letter Canada, South America		20.00
	Single franking on aerogramme		20.00
	P# block of 6	6.50	—
	P# block of 20, 1-2 #, 1-2 zip, 1-2 copyright	21.00	—
	Pane of 100	100.00	
a.	Vert. pair, imperf. horiz.	*350.00*	
b.	Vert. pair, imperf. between	*1,500.*	
c.	Large block tagging, perf 10.9	.90	.25
	P# block of 6	5.75	—
	P# block of 20, 1-2 #, 1-2 zip, 1-2 copyright	20.00	—
	Pane of 100	90.00	
d.	Perf. 11.2, large block tagging	.90	.25
	Corner P# block of 4	8.00	—
	Zip block of 4	3.75	—
	Pane of 100	90.00	
1868	A1255 40c **dark green,** perf 10.9, small block tagging, *Feb. 24, 1984*	1.00	.25
	On cover		4.00
	International surface letter		15.00
	International printed matter/packets		20.00
	Certificate of mailing		30.00
	First-class Canada letter		8.00
	International airmail postcard		15.00
	First-class Canada postcard		8.00
	P# block of 6	6.50	—
	P# block of 20, 1-2 #, 1-2 copyright, 1-2 zip	21.00	—
	Pane of 100	100.00	
a.	Perf. 11.2, large block tagging	.90	.25
	Corner P# block of 4	5.50	—
	Zip block of 4	3.75	—
	Pane of 100	90.00	
1869	A1256 50c **brown,** perf 10.9, overall tagging, shiny gum, *Feb. 22, 1985*	1.00	.25
	On cover		4.00
	P# block of 4	7.50	—
	Zip block of 4	4.25	—
	Pane of 100	100.00	
a.	Perf. 11.2, medium block tagging, dull gum	1.00	.25
	P# block of 4	6.25	—
	Zip block of 4	4.25	—
	Pane of 100	100.00	
b.	Tagging omitted, perf. 10.9, shiny gum	22.50	
c.	Tagging omitted, perf. 11.2, dull gum	12.50	
d.	Perf. 11.2, overall tagging, dull gum	3.50	.25
	P# block of 4	35.00	—
	Zip block of 4	15.00	—
	Pane of 100	350.00	
e.	Perf. 11.2, prephosphored uncoated paper with embedded tagging showing a mottled appearance, shiny gum, *1992*	1.00	.25
	P# block of 4	5.00	—
	Zip block of 4	4.25	—
	Pane of 100	100.00	
f.	Perf. 11.2, large block tagging, dull gum	—	
	P# block of 4	—	
	Pane of 100	—	
	Nos. 1844-1869 (26)	12.45	6.50

The medium block tagging, No. 1869a, measures 19x21.5mm. The large block tagging, No. 1869f, measures 20x24mm.

EVERETT DIRKSEN (1896-1969)

Senate minority leader, 1960-1969.

A1261

Designed by Ron Adair.

ENGRAVED

Plates of 200 subjects in four panes of 50.

1981, Jan. 4	**Tagged**	***Perf. 11***	
1874 A1261 15c **gray**		.30	.25
P# block of 4		1.40	—
Zip block of 4		1.25	—
Pane of 50		15.00	
a. All color omitted		*500.00*	

No. 1874a comes from a partially printed pane and may be collected as a vertical strip of 3 or 5 (1 or 3 stamps normal, one stamp transitional and one stamp with color omitted) or as a pair with one partially printed stamp.

BLACK HERITAGE SERIES

Whitney Moore Young, Jr. (1921-1971), civil rights leader.

A1262

Designed by Jerry Pinkney.

PHOTOGRAVURE

Plates of 200 subjects in four panes of 50.

1981, Jan. 30	**Tagged**	***Perf. 11***	
1875 A1262 15c **multi**		.35	.25
P# block of 4, 6#		1.60	—
Zip block of 4		1.50	—
Pane of 50		17.50	

FLOWER ISSUE

A1263

A1264

A1265

A1266

Illustration reduced.

Designed by Lowell Nesbitt.

PHOTOGRAVURE

Plates of 192 subjects in four panes of 48 (8x6).

1981, Apr. 23	**Tagged**	***Perf. 11***	
1876 A1263 18c **multicolored**		.35	.25
1877 A1264 18c **multicolored**		.35	.25
1878 A1265 18c **multicolored**		.35	.25
1879 A1266 18c **multicolored**		.35	.25
a. Block of 4, #1876-1879		1.40	1.25
P# block of 4, 6#		1.75	—
Zip block of 4		1.45	—
Pane of 48		16.75	

AMERICAN WILDLIFE

A1267

A1268

A1269

A1270

A1271

A1272

A1273

A1274

A1275

A1276

Designs from photographs by Jim Brandenburg.

No. 1880, Bighorn. No. 1881, Puma. No. 1882, Harbor seal. No. 1883, American Buffalo. No. 1884, Brown bear. No. 1885, Polar bear. No. 1886, Elk (wapiti). No. 1887, Moose. No. 1888, White-tailed deer. No. 1889, Pronghorn.

ENGRAVED

Perf. 11 on 2 or 3 Sides

1981, May 14	**Tagged**	**Dark brown**	
1880 A1267 18c multicolored		.50	.25
a. Tagging omitted			—
1881 A1268 18c multicolored		.50	.25
1882 A1269 18c multicolored		.50	.25
1883 A1270 18c multicolored		.50	.25
1884 A1271 18c multicolored		.50	.25
1885 A1272 18c multicolored		.50	.25
1886 A1273 18c multicolored		.50	.25
a. Tagging omitted			—
1887 A1274 18c multicolored		.50	.25
a. Tagging omitted			—
1888 A1275 18c multicolored		.50	.25
1889 A1276 18c multicolored		.50	.25
a. Booklet pane of 10, #1880-1889		5.00	5.00
b. Tagging omitted			—
Nos. 1880-1889 (10)		5.00	2.50

Nos. 1880-1889 issued in booklet only. All stamps have one or two straight edges.

Imperfs are from printer's waste.

FLAG AND ANTHEM ISSUE

A1277

A1278

A1279

A1280

Designed by Peter Cocci.

ENGRAVED

Plates of 460 subjects (20x23) in panes of 100 (10x10).

1981, Apr. 24	**Tagged** *Perf. 11*		
1890 A1277 18c **multicolored**		.35	.25
P# block of 6		2.25	—
P# block of 20, 1-2 #		10.00	—
Pane of 100		35.00	
a. Imperf., pair		75.00	
b. Vert. pair, imperf. horiz.		*550.00*	
c. Vert. pair, imperf. between		*550.00*	
d. Tagging omitted		125.00	—
e. As "a," tagging omitted		—	

See Combination Press note after No. 1703.

Coil Stamp

Perf. 10 Vert.

No.	Description	Unused	Used
1891	A1278 18c **multicolored**	.35	.25
	Pair	.70	.25
	P# strip of 3, #1	45.00	
	P# strip of 3, #2	11.50	
	P# strip of 3, #3	80.00	
	P# strip of 3, #4	3.00	
	P# strip of 3, #5	3.00	
	P# strip of 3, #6	*525.00*	
	P# strip of 3, #7	7.50	
	P# strip of 5, #1	100.00	
	P# strip of 5, #2	27.50	
	P# strip of 5, #3	550.00	
	P# strip of 5, #4	3.50	
	P# strip of 5, #5	3.50	
	P# strip of 5, #6	*1,900.*	
	P# strip of 5, #7	8.00	
	P# single, #1	—	2.50
	P# single, #2	—	.80
	P# single, #3	—	9.00
	P# single, #4	—	.80
	P# single, #5	—	1.00
	P# single, #6	—	*500.00*
	P# single, #7	—	9.00
a.	Imperf., pair	17.50	—
b.	Pair, imperf. between	*1,750.*	
c.	Tagging omitted		—

Beware of pairs offered as No. 1891b that have faint blind perfs.

Vertical pairs and blocks exist from printer's waste.

Booklet Stamps

Perf. 11x10½ on 3 Sides

No.	Description	Unused	Used
1892	A1279 6c **dark blue & red**	.50	.25
a.	Tagging omitted	35.00	

Perf. 11x10½ on 2 or 3 Sides

No.	Description	Unused	Used
1893	A1280 18c **multicolored**	.30	.25
a.	Booklet pane of 8 (2 #1892, 6 #1893)	3.00	2.50
b.	As "a," vert. imperf. between	60.00	
c.	Se-tenant pair, #1892 & #1893	.90	1.00
d.	As "a," tagging omitted	*675.00*	
e.	As No. 1893, tagging omitted	100.00	

Bureau Precanceled Coils

Starting with No. 1895b, Bureau precanceled coil stamps are valued unused as well as used. The coils issued with dull gum may be difficult to distinguish.

When used normally these stamps do not receive any postal markings so that used stamps with an additional postal cancellation of any kind are worth considerably less than the values shown here.

FLAG OVER SUPREME COURT ISSUE

A1281

Designed by Dean Ellis

ENGRAVED

Plates of 460 subjects (20x23) in panes of 100 (10x10)

1981, Dec. 17	**Tagged** *Perf. 11*		
1894	A1281 20c **black, dark blue & red,** dull gum	.40	.25
	P# block of 6	2.75	—
	P# block of 20, 1-2 #	9.00	—
	Pane of 100	40.00	
a.	As "e," vert. pair, imperf.	30.00	
b.	Vert. pair, imperf. horiz.	*250.00*	
c.	Dark blue omitted	*60.00*	
d.	Black omitted	*225.00*	
e.	Perf. 11.2, shiny gum	.35	.25
	P# block of 6	2.50	—
	P# block of 20, 1-2 #	8.50	—
	Pane of 100	35.00	
f.	Tagging omitted	—	

Counterfeits exist of No. 1894. See the Postal Counterfeits section of this catalog.

Coil Stamp

Perf. 10 Vert.

No.	Description	Unused	Used
1895	A1281 20c **black, dark blue & red,** wide block tagging	.40	.25
	Pair	.80	.50
	P# strip of 3, #1	1.75	
	P# strip of 3, #2	3.00	
	P# strip of 3, #3	3.00	
	P# strip of 3, #5	3.00	
	P# strip of 3, #11	3.00	
	P# strip of 3, #13, 14	3.00	
	P# strip of 5, #1	25.00	
	P# strip of 5, #2	3.75	
	P# strip of 5, #3	3.25	
	P# strip of 5, #5	3.25	
	P# strip of 5, #11	3.75	
	P# strip of 5, #13, 14	3.25	
	P# single, #1	—	.75
	P# single, #2-3	—	.50
	P# single, #5	—	.50
	P# single, #11	—	3.00
	P# single, #13, 14	—	.50
a.	Narrow block tagging	.40	.25
	Pair	.80	.50
	P# strip of 3, #4	110.00	
	P# strip of 3, #6	35.00	
	P# strip of 3, #8	2.75	
	P# strip of 3, #9-10	2.75	
	P# strip of 3, #12	3.00	
	P# strip of 5, #4	*250.00*	
	P# strip of 5, #6	85.00	
	P# strip of 5, #8	8.00	
	P# strip of 5, #9	3.50	
	P# strip of 5, #10	4.25	
	P# strip of 5, #12	4.00	
	P# single, #4	—	.80
	P# single, #6	—	2.25
	P# single, #8	—	.40
	P# single, #9	—	.40
	P# single, #10	—	.60
	P# single, #12	—	.40
b.	Untagged (Bureau precanceled, lines only)	.50	.50
	P# strip of 3, #14	27.50	
	P# strip of 5, #14	32.50	
	P# single, #14		30.00
c.	Tagging omitted (not Bureau precanceled)	*25.00*	
	P# strip of 3, #4		—
	P# strip of 3, #3, 5, 8, 10, 11, 14	—	
	P# strip of 5, #5, 10, 11, 14	—	
	P# single, #5, 8-11, 14	—	—
d.	Imperf., pair, narrow block tagging	8.00	—
e.	Pair, imperf. between	*600.00*	
f.	Black omitted	*45.00*	
g.	Dark blue omitted	*1,000.*	
h.	Black field of stars instead of blue		—
i.	As "d," tagging omitted	—	
j.	Imperf., pair, wide block tagging	20.00	—

The wide block tagging on No. 1895 and narrow block tagging on No. 1895a differentiate stamps printed on two different presses. The wide blocks are approximately 20-21mm high by 18mm wide with a 4mm untagged gutter between tagging blocks.

The narrow blocks are approximately 21-22mm high and approximately 16-16½mm wide with a 5½-6½ untagged gutter between tagging blocks.

BOOKLET STAMP

Perf. 11x10½ on 2 or 3 Sides

No.	Description	Unused	Used
1896	A1281 20c **black, dark blue & red,** small block tagging	.40	.25
a.	Booklet pane of 6	3.00	2.25
	Scored perforations	3.00	2.25
b.	Booklet pane of 10, *June 1, 1982*	5.25	3.25
	Scored perforations	7.50	5.00
c.	As "b," tagging omitted	—	—
d.	Large block tagging ('83)	.40	.25
e.	As "d," booklet pane of 10	5.25	3.25
	Scored perforations	5.25	3.25
f.	As "a," tagging omitted	—	—
g.	As No. 1896, tagging omitted	—	

Booklets containing two panes of ten of No. 1896e were issued Nov. 17, 1983.

The small block tagging is 16x18mm (Nos. 1896-1896b). The large block tagging is 18x21mm (Nos. 1896d-1896e).

TRANSPORTATION ISSUE

Omnibus 1880s — A1283

Locomotive 1870s — A1284

Designer: 1c, 2c, David Stone.

COIL STAMPS

ENGRAVED

1981-84	**Tagged** *Perf. 10 Vert.*		
1897	A1283 1c **violet,** *Aug. 19, 1983*	.30	.25
	Pair	.30	.25
	P# strip of 3, line, #1, 2	.40	
	P# strip of 3, line, #3, 4	.50	
	P# strip of 3, line, #5, 6	.40	
	P# strip of 5, line, #1, 2	.50	
	P# strip of 5, line, #3, 4	.50	
	P# strip of 5, line, #5, 6	.50	
	P# single, #1, 2	—	.25
	P# single, #3, 4	—	.55
	P# single, #5, 6	—	.30
b.	Imperf., pair	*325.00*	
	Joint line pair, P#	—	
e.	Tagging omitted	*150.00*	

See No. 2225.

No.	Description	Unused	Used
1897A	A1284 2c **black,** *May 20, 1982*	.30	.25
	Pair	.30	.25
	P# strip of 3, line, #2-4, 6, 8, 10	.45	
	P# strip of 5, line, #2-4, 6, 8, 10	.50	
	P# single, #2-4, 6, 8, 10	—	.40
c.	Imperf., pair	45.00	
	Joint line pair, P#	—	
d.	Tagging omitted	40.00	

See No. 2226.

Handcar 1880s — A1284a

Stagecoach 1890s — A1285

Designers: 3c, Walter Brooks. 4c, Jim Schleyer.

No.	Description	Unused	Used
1898	A1284a 3c **dark green,** *Mar. 25, 1983*	.30	.25
	Pair	.30	.25
	P# strip of 3, line, #1-4	.55	
	P# strip of 5, line, #1-4	.75	
	P# single, #1-4	—	.50
1898A	A1285 4c **reddish brown,** *Aug. 19, 1982*	.30	.25
	Pair	.30	.25
	P# strip of 3, line, #1-4	.75	
	P# strip of 3, line, #5-6	1.25	
	P# strip of 5, line, #1-4	.90	
	P# strip of 5, line, #5-6	1.75	
	P# single, #1-4	—	.75
	P# single, #5-6	—	1.50
b.	Untagged (Bureau precanceled, Nonprofit Org.)	.30	.25

P# strip of 3, line, #3-6 — 2.50
P# strip of 5, line, #3-6 — 3.00
P# single, #3, 4 — — 2.90
P# single, #5, 6 — — 2.90
c. As "b," imperf., pair — *300.00*
d. As No. 1898A, imperf. pair — *400.00* —
e. Tagging omitted (not Bureau precanceled) — *50.00* *35.00*

See No. 2228.

Motorcycle 1913 — A1286

Sleigh 1880s — A1287

Designers: 5c, 5.2c, Walter Brooks.

1899 A1286 5c **gray green,** *Oct. 10, 1983* — .30 .25
Pair — .30 .25
P# strip of 3, line, #1-4 — .80
P# strip of 5, line, #1-4 — .90
P# single, #1-4 — — .65
a. Imperf., pair — *1,500.*
b. Tagging omitted — 25.00 —

1900 A1287 5.2c **carmine,** *Mar. 21, 1983* — .30 .25
Pair — .35 .35
P# strip of 3, line, #1-2 — 2.00
P# strip of 3, line, #3 — 150.00
P# strip of 3, line, #5 — 90.00
P# strip of 5, line, #1-2 — 3.00
P# strip of 5, line, #3 — 190.00
P# strip of 5, line, #5 — 125.00
P# single, #1-2 — — 2.50
P# single, #3 — — *110.00*
P# single, #5 — — *100.00*
a. Untagged (Bureau precanceled, lines only) — .30 .25
P# strip of 3, line, #1-3 — 3.75
P# strip of 3, line, #4 — 4.75
P# strip of 3, line, #5 — 4.00
P# strip of 3, line, #6 — 4.50
P# strip of 5, line, #1-3 — 4.50
P# strip of 5, line, #4, 6 — 7.50
P# strip of 5, line, #5 — 4.50
P# single, #1, 2 — — 2.25
P# single, #3 — — 1.50
P# single, #4 — — 7.00
P# single, #5 — — 1.75
P# single, #6 — — 7.50
b. Tagging omitted — *150.00*

Bicycle 1870s — A1288

Baby Buggy 1880s — A1289

Designers: 5.9c, David Stone. 7.4c, Jim Schleyer.

1901 A1288 5.9c **blue,** *Feb. 17, 1982* — .30 .25
Pair — .50 .50
P# strip of 3, line, #3-4 — 2.75
P# strip of 5, line, #3-4 — 3.75
P# single, #3-4 — — 3.50
a. Untagged (Bureau precanceled, lines only) — .30 .25
P# strip of 3, line, #3-4 — 10.00
P# strip of 3, line, #5-6 — 50.00
P# strip of 5, line, #3-4 — 17.50
P# strip of 5, line, #5-6 — 75.00
P# single, #3-4 — — 5.00
P# single, #5-6 — — 50.00
b. As "a," imperf., pair — *140.00*

1902 A1289 7.4c **brown,** *Apr. 7, 1984* — .30 .25
Pair — .50 .50
P# strip of 3, #2 — 3.25
P# strip of 5, #2 — 3.50
P# single, #2 — — 4.00
a. Untagged (Bureau precanceled, Blk. Rt. CAR-RT SORT) — .30 .25
P# strip of 3, #2 — 3.00
P# strip of 5, #2 — 3.25
P# single, #2 — — 3.50

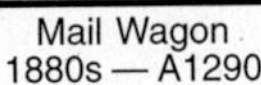
Mail Wagon 1880s — A1290

Hansom Cab 1890s — A1291

Designers: 9.3c, Jim Schleyer. 10.9c, David Stone.

1903 A1290 9.3c **carmine rose,** *Dec. 15* — .30 .25
Pair — .60 .50
P# strip of 3, line, #1-2 — 3.00
P# strip of 3, line, #3-4 — 5.00
P# strip of 3, line, #5-6 — 125.00
P# strip of 5, line, #1-2 — 3.75
P# strip of 5, line, #3-4 — 11.00
P# strip of 5, line, #5-6 — 260.00
P# single, #1-2 — — 2.00
P# single, #3-4 — — 7.50
P# single, #5-6 — — 150.00
a. Untagged (Bureau precanceled, lines only) — .30 .25
P# strip of 3, line, #1 — 3.25
P# strip of 3, line, #2 — 3.25
P# strip of 3, line, #3 — 5.25
P# strip of 3, line, #4 — 3.50
P# strip of 3, line, #5-6 — 1.25
P# strip of 3, line, #8 — 150.00
P# strip of 5, line, #1 — 5.00
P# strip of 5, line, #2 — 5.00
P# strip of 5, line, #3 — 10.00
P# strip of 5, line, #4 — 5.50
P# strip of 5, line, #5-6 — 1.75
P# strip of 5, line, #8 — 200.00
P# single, #1-2 — — 3.25
P# single, #3 — — 5.25
P# single, #4 — — 3.50
P# single, #5-6 — — 1.25
P# single, #8 — — 150.00
b. As "a," imperf., pair — 90.00

1904 A1291 10.9c **purple,** *Mar. 26, 1982* — .30 .25
Pair — .60 .50
P# strip of 3, line, #1-2 — 4.00
P# strip of 5, line, #1-2 — 9.00
P# single, #1-2 — — 6.00
a. Untagged (Bureau precanceled, lines only) — .30 .25
P# strip of 3, line, #1-2 — 10.00
P# strip of 3, line, #3-4 — 50.00
P# strip of 5, line, #1-2 — 15.00
P# strip of 5, line, #3-4 — 200.00
P# single, #1-2 — — 7.00
P# single, #3-4 — — 50.00
b. As "a," imperf., pair — 125.00
Joint line pair, P# — —

RR Caboose 1890s — A1292

Electric Auto 1917 — A1293

Designers: 11c, Jim Schleyer. 17c Chuck Jaquays.

1905 A1292 11c **red,** *Feb. 3, 1984* — .30 .25
Pair — .60 .50
P# strip of 3, #1 — 1.90
P# strip of 5, #1 — 2.25
P# single, #1 — — 2.25
a. Untagged *Sept. 1991* — .25 .25
Pair — .50 .50
P# strip of 3, #1 — 1.50
P# strip of 3, #2 — 1.70
P# strip of 5, #1 — 2.25
P# strip of 5, #2 — 2.25
P# single, #1 — — 2.25
P# single, #2 — — 2.00

Untagged stamps from plate 1 come only Bureau precanceled with lines. Untagged stamps from plate 2 come only without precancel lines.

1906 A1293 17c **ultramarine,** *June 25* — .35 .25
Pair — .70 .50
P# strip of 3, line, #1-5 — 1.50
P# strip of 3, line, #6 — 6.00
P# strip of 3, line, #7 — 2.25
P# strip of 5, line, #1-5 — 2.00
P# strip of 5, line, #6 — 7.00
P# strip of 5, line, #7 — 2.75
P# single, #1-5 — — 1.50
P# single, #6 — — 7.50
P# single, #7 — — 3.00
a. Untagged (Bureau precanceled, Presorted First Class) — .35 .35
P# strip of 3, line, #1, 2 — 4.00
P# strip of 3, line, #3-5 — 2.50
P# strip of 3, line, #6, 7 — 6.00
P# strip of 5, line, #1, 2 — 6.00
P# strip of 5, line, #3-5 — 5.00
P# strip of 5, line, #6-7 — 7.00
P# single, #1, 2 — — 6.00
P# single, #3-5 — — 3.00
P# single, #6, 7 — — 7.50
b. Imperf., pair — 130.00
c. As "a," imperf., pair — *400.00*
d. As No. 1906, tagging omitted — —

Three different precancel styles exist with differences in the font used: Type A has thin lines and the "T" in "PRESORTED" is tall with a short cross bar (most common); Type B has thicker lines and the "T" is shorter with a longer cross bar (least common); Type C has thicker lines still and the "T" has a shorter stem with a cross bar longer than on Types A or B. Lengths of the precancel increase with the types and the wider spacing of the letters, though the imprecise manufacture of the precancel mats led to significant variations in length. Combination pairs exist of Types A and B.

Surrey 1890s — A1294

Fire Pumper 1860s — A1295

Designers: 18c, David Stone. 20c, Jim Schleyer.

1907 A1294 18c **dark brown,** *May 18* — .35 .25
Pair — .70 .50
P# strip of 3, line, #1 — 15.00
P# strip of 3, line, #2 — 2.00
P# strip of 3, line, #3, 4 — 17.50
P# strip of 3, line, #5, 6 — 2.50
P# strip of 3, line, #7 — 6.00
P# strip of 3, line, #8 — 2.50
P# strip of 3, line, #9-12 — 4.75
P# strip of 3, line, #13, 14 — 2.50
P# strip of 3, line, #15, 16 — 6.00
P# strip of 3, line, #17, 18 — 2.50
P# strip of 5, line, #1 — 45.00
P# strip of 5, line, #2 — 3.00
P# strip of 5, line, #3-4 — 45.00
P# strip of 5, line, #5, 6 — 3.00
P# strip of 5, line, #7 — 7.00
P# strip of 5, line, #8 — 3.00
P# strip of 5, line, #9-12 — 6.00
P# strip of 5, line, #13, 14 — 3.00
P# strip of 5, line, #15, 16 — 7.50
P# strip of 5, line, #17, 18 — 3.00
P# single, #1 — — 8.00

	P# single, #2	—	.75
	P# single, #3, 4	—	8.00
	P# single, #5, 6	—	.75
	P# single, #7	—	7.00
	P# single, #8	—	.75
	P# single, #9-14	—	3.25
	P# single, #15, 16	—	10.00
	P# single, #17, 18	—	2.75
a.	Imperf., pair	95.00	
b.	Tagging omitted	—	
1908	A1295 20c **vermilion,** *Dec. 10*	.35	.25
	Pair	.70	.50
	P# strip of 3, line, #1	12.50	
	P# strip of 3, line, #2	90.00	
	P# strip of 3, line, #3, 4	2.50	
	P# strip of 3, line, #5	2.25	
	P# strip of 3, line, #6	9.00	
	P# strip of 3, line, #7, 8	20.00	
	P# strip of 3, line, #9, 10	2.25	
	P# strip of 3, line, #11	9.00	
	P# strip of 3, line, #12	4.00	
	P# strip of 3, line, #13	2.50	
	P# strip of 3, line, #14	4.00	
	P# strip of 3, line, #15, 16	2.75	
	P# strip of 5, line, #1	55.00	
	P# strip of 5, line, #2	400.00	
	P# strip of 5, line, #3, 4	3.00	
	P# strip of 5, line, #5	2.75	
	P# strip of 5, line, #6	20.00	
	P# strip of 5, line, #7-8	140.00	
	P# strip of 5, line, #9-10	2.75	
	P# strip of 5, line, #11	50.00	
	P# strip of 5, line, #12	5.00	
	P# strip of 5, line, #13	3.25	
	P# strip of 5, line, #14	5.00	
	P# strip of 5, line, #15-16	3.25	
	P# single, #1	—	.65
	P# single, #2	—	7.50
	P# single, #3, 4	—	.65
	P# single, #5	—	.75
	P# single, #6	—	1.25
	P# single, #7, 8	—	1.10
	P# single, #9, 10	—	.75
	P# single, #11	—	1.00
	P# single, #12	—	5.00
	P# single, #13	—	.65
	P# single, #14	—	5.00
	P# single, #15, 16	—	2.00
a.	Imperf., pair	75.00	
b.	Tagging omitted	*100.00*	—
	Nos. 1897-1908 (14)	4.35	3.50

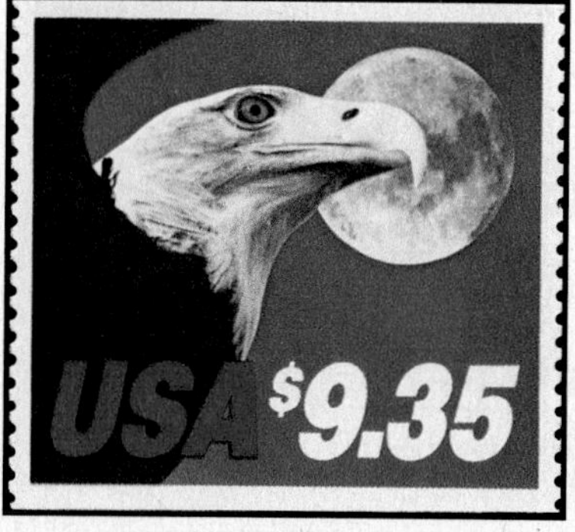

Eagle and Moon A1296

Booklet Stamp

PHOTOGRAVURE

Perf. 10 Vert. on 1 or 2 Sides

1983, Aug. 12 **Untagged**

1909	A1296 $9.35 **multicolored**	19.00	15.00
a.	Booklet pane of 3	57.50	—

AMERICAN RED CROSS CENTENNIAL

A1297

Designed by Joseph Csatari.

PHOTOGRAVURE

Plates of 200 subjects in four panes of 50.

1981, May 1 **Tagged** ***Perf. 10½x11***

1910	A1297 18c **multicolored**	.35	.25
	P# block of 4, 6#	1.75	—
	Zip block of 4	1.40	—
	Pane of 50	17.50	

SAVINGS & LOAN SESQUICENTENNIAL

A1298

Designed by Don Hedin.

PHOTOGRAVURE

Plates of 200 subjects in four panes of 50.

1981, May 8 **Tagged** ***Perf. 11***

1911	A1298 18c **multicolored**	.35	.25
	P# block of 4, 6#	1.75	—
	Zip block of 4	1.40	—
	Pane of 50	17.50	

SPACE ACHIEVEMENT ISSUE

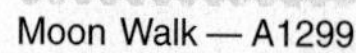

Moon Walk — A1299

Skylab — A1302

Space Shuttle Columbia A1300

Space Shuttle Columbia A1301

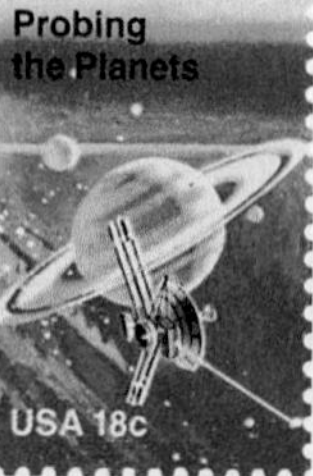

Pioneer 11 — A1303

Telescope — A1306

Space Shuttle Columbia A1304

Space Shuttle Columbia A1305

Designed by Robert McCall.

PHOTOGRAVURE

Plates of 192 subjects in four panes of 48 each.

1981, May 21 **Tagged** ***Perf. 11***

1912	A1299 18c **multicolored**	.35	.25
1913	A1300 18c **multicolored**	.35	.25
1914	A1301 18c **multicolored**	.35	.25
1915	A1302 18c **multicolored**	.35	.25
1916	A1303 18c **multicolored**	.35	.25
1917	A1304 18c **multicolored**	.35	.25
1918	A1305 18c **multicolored**	.35	.25
1919	A1306 18c **multicolored**	.35	.25
a.	Block of 8, #1912-1919	2.80	3.00
	P# block of 8, 6#	3.00	—
	Zip, copyright block of 8	2.90	—
	Pane of 48	16.75	
	Nos. 1916, 1912 with full horiz. gutter btwn.	—	
b.	As "a," imperf.	*5,500.*	
c.	As "a," imperf. vert.	*2,000.*	
d.	As "a," tagging omitted	*1,000.*	
e.	As "a," top 4 stamps part perf, bottom 4 stamps imperf	2,700.	

No. 1919c is unique and has blind horiz. perfs.

PROFESSIONAL MANAGEMENT EDUCATION CENTENARY

Joseph Wharton (Founder of Wharton School of Business) A1307

Designed by Rudolph de Harak.

PHOTOGRAVURE

Plates of 200 subject in four panes of 50.

1981, June 18 **Tagged** ***Perf. 11***

1920	A1307 18c **blue & black**	.35	.25
	P# block of 4, 2#	1.50	—
	Zip block of 4	1.40	—
	Pane of 50	17.50	

PRESERVATION OF WILDLIFE HABITATS

Great Blue Heron — A1308

Badger — A1309

Grizzly Bear — A1310

Ruffed Grouse — A1311

Designed by Chuck Ripper

PHOTOGRAVURE

Plates of 200 subjects in four panes of 50.

1981, June 26 **Tagged** ***Perf. 11***

1921	A1308 18c **multicolored**	.35	.25
1922	A1309 18c **multicolored**	.35	.25
1923	A1310 18c **multicolored**	.35	.25
1924	A1311 18c **multicolored**	.35	.25
a.	Block of 4, #1921-1924	1.50	1.25
	P# block of 4, 5#	2.50	—
	Zip block of 4	1.50	—
	Pane of 50	17.50	

INTERNATIONAL YEAR OF THE DISABLED

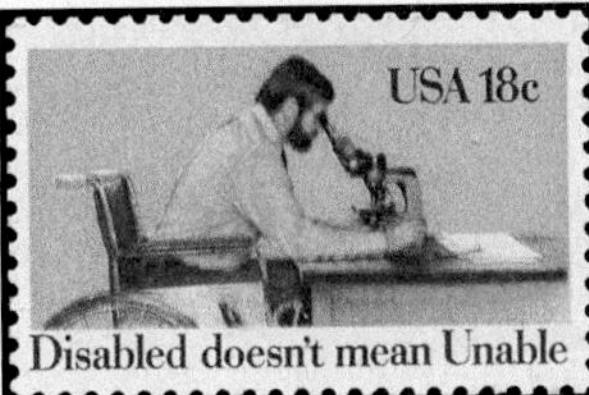

Man Using Microscope A1312

Designed by Martha Perske

PHOTOGRAVURE

Plates of 200 subjects in four panes of 50.

1981, June 29 **Tagged** ***Perf. 11***

1925	A1312 18c **multicolored**	.35	.25
	P# block of 4, 6#	1.50	—
	Zip block of 4	1.40	—
	Pane of 50	17.50	
a.	Vert. pair, imperf. horiz.	*1,500.*	

EDNA ST. VINCENT MILLAY ISSUE

A1313

Designed by Glenora Case Richards

LITHOGRAPHED AND ENGRAVED

Plates of 200 subjects in four panes of 50.

1981, July 10 **Tagged** ***Perf. 11***

1926	A1313 18c **multicolored**	.35	.25
	P# block of 4, 7#	1.50	—
	Zip block of 4	1.40	—
	Pane of 50	17.50	
a.	Black (engr., inscriptions) omitted	*200.00*	—

ALCOHOLISM

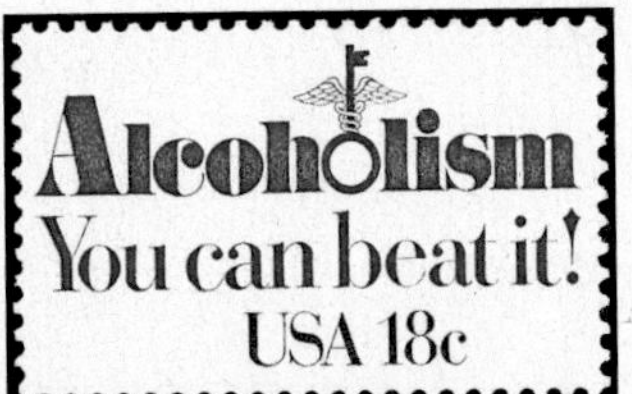

A1314

Designed by John Boyd

ENGRAVED

Plates of 230 (10x23) subjects in panes of 50 (5x10)

1981, Aug. 19 **Tagged** ***Perf. 11***

1927	A1314 18c **blue & black**, large block tagging	.45	.25
	P# block of 6	9.00	—
	P# block of 20, 1-2 #, 1-2 copyright, 1-2 Zip	15.00	—
	Pane of 50	22.50	
a.	Imperf., pair	*325.00*	
b.	Vert. pair, imperf. horiz.	*2,000.*	
c.	Small block tagging	*2.50*	

See Combination Press note after No. 1703.

AMERICAN ARCHITECTURE SERIES

New York University Library by Stanford White A1315

Biltmore House By Richard Morris Hunt — A1316

Palace of the Arts by Bernard Maybeck A1317

National Farmer's Bank by Louis Sullivan A1318

Designed by Walter D. Richards.

ENGRAVED

Plates of 160 subjects in four panes of 40.

1981, Aug. 28 **Tagged** ***Perf. 11***

1928	A1315 18c **black & red**	.40	.25
a.	Tagging omitted	—	
1929	A1316 18c **black & red**	.40	.25
a.	Red missing (PS)	—	
1930	A1317 18c **black & red**	.40	.25
a.	Tagging omitted	—	
b.	Red missing (PS)	—	
1931	A1318 18c **black & red**	.40	.25
a.	Block of 4, #1928-1931	1.65	1.65
	P# block of 4	2.10	—
	Zip block of 4	1.80	—
	Pane of 40	16.00	
b.	As "a," tagging omitted	—	

SPORTS PERSONALITIES

Mildred Didrikson Zaharias — A1319

Robert Tyre Jones — A1320

Designed by Richard Gangel

ENGRAVED

Plates of 200 subjects in four panes of 50.

1981, Sept. 22 **Tagged** ***Perf. 10½x11***

1932	A1319 18c **purple**	.40	.25
	P# block of 4	3.00	—
	Zip block of 4	1.75	—
	Pane of 50	20.00	
1933	A1320 18c **green**	.60	.25
	P# block of 4	3.25	—
	Zip block of 4	2.50	—
	Pane of 50	30.00	

FREDERIC REMINGTON

Coming Through the Rye — A1321

Designed by Paul Calle

LITHOGRAPHED AND ENGRAVED

Plates of 200 in four panes of 50.

1981, Oct. 9 **Tagged** ***Perf. 11***

1934	A1321 18c **gray, olive green & brown**	.35	.25
	P# block of 4, 3#	1.75	—
	Zip block of 4	1.50	—
	Pane of 50	17.50	
a.	Vert. pair, imperf. between	*160.00*	
b.	Brown omitted	*190.00*	

JAMES HOBAN

Irish-American Architect of the White House A1322

Designed by Ron Mercer and Walter D. Richards.

PHOTOGRAVURE

Plates of 200 in four panes of 50.

1981, Oct. 13 **Tagged** ***Perf. 11***

1935	A1322 18c **multicolored**	.35	.25
	P# block of 4, 6#	1.60	—
	Zip block of 4	1.50	—
	Pane of 50	17.50	
1936	A1322 20c **multicolored**	.35	.25
	P# block of 4, 6#	2.00	—
	Zip block of 4	1.50	—
	Pane of 50	17.50	

See Ireland No. 504.

AMERICAN BICENTENNIAL

Battle of Yorktown A1323

Battle of the Virginia Capes A1324

Designed by Cal Sacks.

LITHOGRAPHED AND ENGRAVED
Plates of 200 in four panes of 50.

1981, Oct. 16	**Tagged**	***Perf. 11***	
1937 A1323 18c **multicolored**		.35	.25
1938 A1324 18c **multicolored**		.35	.25
a. Pair, #1937-1938		.90	.75
P# block of 4, 7#		2.00	—
Zip block of 4		1.65	—
Pane of 50		17.50	
b. As "a," black (engr., inscriptions) omitted		*275.00*	
c. As "a," tagging omitted		*120.00*	
d. As "a," black (litho.) omitted		—	

CHRISTMAS

Madonna and Child, Botticelli — A1325

Felt Bear on Sleigh A1326

Designed by Bradbury Thompson (No. 1939) and by Naiad Einsel (No. 1940).

PHOTOGRAVURE
Plates of 400 in four panes of 100 (No. 1939)
Plates of 200 in four panes of 50 (No. 1940)

1981, Oct. 28	**Tagged**	***Perf. 11***	
1939 A1325 (20c) **multicolored**		.40	.25
P# block of 4, 6#		1.75	—
Zip block of 4		1.65	—
Pane of 100		40.00	
a. Imperf., pair		*90.00*	
b. Vert. pair, imperf. horiz.		*750.00*	
c. Tagging omitted		*17.50*	
1940 A1326 (20c) **multicolored**		.40	.25
P# block of 4, 5#		1.75	—
Zip block of 4		1.65	—
Pane of 50		20.00	
Pair with full horiz. gutter btwn.		—	
a. Imperf., pair		*175.00*	
b. Vert. pair, imperf. horiz.		*1,750.*	

JOHN HANSON

First President of the Continental Congress — A1327

Designed by Ron Adair.

PHOTOGRAVURE
Plates of 200 in panes of 50

1981, Nov. 5	**Tagged**	***Perf. 11***	
1941 A1327 20c **multicolored**		.40	.25
P# block of 4, 5#		1.75	—
Zip block of 4		1.65	—
Pane of 50		20.00	

DESERT PLANTS

Barrel Cactus — A1328

Agave — A1329

Beavertail Cactus — A1330

Saguaro — A1331

Designed by Frank J. Waslick.

LITHOGRAPHED AND ENGRAVED
Plates of 160 in four panes of 40

1981 Dec. 11	**Tagged**	***Perf. 11***	
1942 A1328 20c **multicolored**		.35	.25
1943 A1329 20c **multicolored**		.35	.25
1944 A1330 20c **multicolored**		.35	.25
1945 A1331 20c **multicolored**		.35	.25
a. Block of 4, #1942-1945		1.50	1.25
P# block of 4, 7#		1.90	—
Zip block of 4		1.55	—
Pane of 40		14.00	
b. As "a," deep brown (litho.) omitted		*3,000.*	
c. No. 1945 imperf., vert. pair		*3,000.*	
d. As "a," dark green & dark blue (engr.) missing (EP)		*1,800.*	
e. As "a," dark green (engr.) missing on left stamp (EP)		*2,500.*	
f. As "a," tagging omitted		—	

A1332

A1333

Designed by Bradbury Thompson.

PHOTOGRAVURE
Plates of 400 in panes of 100.

1981, Oct. 11	**Tagged**	***Perf. 11x10½***	
1946 A1332 (20c) **brown**		.40	.25
P# block of 4		2.00	—
Zip block of 4		1.65	—
Pane of 100		60.00	
a. Tagging omitted		10.00	
b. All color omitted		*425.00*	

No. 1946b comes from a partially printed pane with most stamps normal. It must be collected as a vertical pair or strip with normal or partially printed stamps attached.

Counterfeits exist of No. 1946. See the Postal Counterfeits section of this catalog.

ENGRAVED
COIL STAMP
Perf. 10 Vert.

1947 A1332 (20c) **brown**		.60	.25
Pair		1.20	.25
Joint line pair		1.50	—
a. Imperf. pair		*700.00*	
Joint line pair		—	

BOOKLET STAMPS
Perf. 11 on 2 or 3 Sides

1948 A1333 (20c) **brown**		.40	.25
a. Booklet pane of 10		4.50	3.25
b. Tagging omitted		—	

Rocky Mountain Bighorn — A1334

BOOKLET STAMP
ENGRAVED

1982, Jan. 8	**Tagged**	***Perf. 11 on 2 or 3 Sides***	
1949 A1334 20c **dark blue**		.50	.25
a. Booklet pane of 10		4.75	2.50
b. As "a," imperf. vert.		*90.00*	
c. Type II		1.25	.25
d. Type II, booklet pane of 10		12.50	—
e. As #1949, tagging omitted		5.00	—
f. As "e," booklet pane of 10		*55.00*	—

No. 1949 is 18¾mm wide and has overall tagging. No. 1949c is 18½mm wide and has block tagging.

See No. 1880.

FRANKLIN DELANO ROOSEVELT

A1335

Designed by Clarence Holbert.

ENGRAVED
Plates of 192 in four panes of 48

1982, Jan. 30	**Tagged**	***Perf. 11***	
1950 A1335 20c **blue**		.40	.25
P# block of 4		1.75	—
Zip block of 4		1.65	—
Pane of 48		19.00	

LOVE ISSUE

A1336

Designed by Mary Faulconer.

PHOTOGRAVURE

Plates of 200 in four panes of 50.

1982, Feb. 1 **Tagged** ***Perf. 11¼***

1951	A1336 20c **multicolored**	1.00	.25
	P# block of 4, 5#	4.00	—
	Zip block of 4	4.00	—
	Pane of 50	50.00	
b.	Imperf., pair	*200.00*	
c.	Blue omitted	*200.00*	
d.	Yellow omitted	*600.00*	
e.	Purple omitted	—	
f.	Tagging omitted	75.00	—

No. 1951c is valued in the grade of fine.

Perf. 11¼x10½

1951A	A1336 20c **multicolored**	1.00	.25
	P# block of 4, 5#	4.00	—
	Zip block of 4	4.00	—
	Pane of 50	50.00	

GEORGE WASHINGTON

A1337

Designed by Mark English.

PHOTOGRAVURE

Plates of 200 in four panes of 50.

1982, Feb. 22 **Tagged** ***Perf. 11***

1952	A1337 20c **multicolored**	.40	.25
	P# block of 4, 6#	1.75	—
	Zip block of 4	1.65	—
	Pane of 50	20.00	

STATE BIRDS AND FLOWERS ISSUE

Illustration reduced.

Designed by Arthur and Alan Singer.

PHOTOGRAVURE (Andreotti)

Plates of 200 subjects in four panes of 50.

1982, Apr. 14 **Tagged** ***Perf. 10½x11¼***

1953	A1338 20c Alabama	.55	.30
1954	A1339 20c Alaska	.55	.30
1955	A1340 20c Arizona	.55	.30
1956	A1341 20c Arkansas	.55	.30
1957	A1342 20c California	.55	.30
1958	A1343 20c Colorado	.55	.30
1959	A1344 20c Connecticut	.55	.30
1960	A1345 20c Delaware	.55	.30
1961	A1346 20c Florida	.55	.30
1962	A1347 20c Georgia	.55	.30
1963	A1348 20c Hawaii	.55	.30
1964	A1349 20c Idaho	.55	.30
1965	A1350 20c Illinois	.55	.30
1966	A1351 20c Indiana	.55	.30
1967	A1352 20c Iowa	.55	.30
1968	A1353 20c Kansas	.55	.30
1969	A1354 20c Kentucky	.55	.30
1970	A1355 20c Louisiana	.55	.30
1971	A1356 20c Maine	.55	.30
1972	A1357 20c Maryland	.55	.30
1973	A1358 20c Massachusetts	.55	.30
1974	A1359 20c Michigan	.55	.30
1975	A1360 20c Minnesota	.55	.30
1976	A1361 20c Mississippi	.55	.30
1977	A1362 20c Missouri	.55	.30
1978	A1363 20c Montana	.55	.30
1979	A1364 20c Nebraska	.55	.30
1980	A1365 20c Nevada	.55	.30
1981	A1366 20c New Hampshire	.55	.30
b.	Black missing (EP)	*4,000.*	

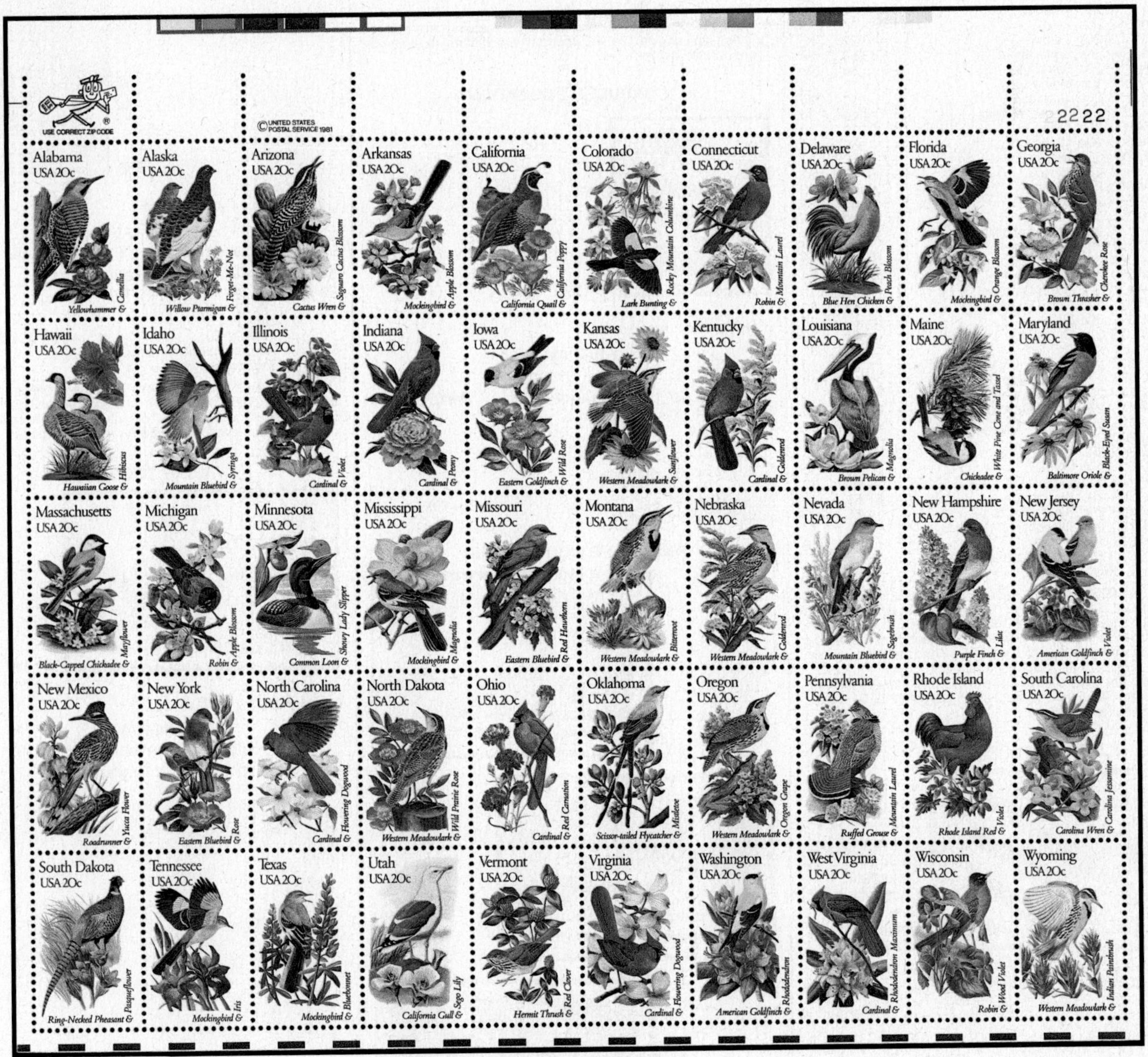

State Birds and Flowers
A1338-A1387

1982	A1367	20c	New Jersey	.55	.30
1983	A1368	20c	New Mexico	.55	.30
1984	A1369	20c	New York	.55	.30
1985	A1370	20c	North Carolina	.55	.30
1986	A1371	20c	North Dakota	.55	.30
1987	A1372	20c	Ohio	.55	.30
1988	A1373	20c	Oklahoma	.55	.30
1989	A1374	20c	Oregon	.55	.30
1990	A1375	20c	Pennsylvania	.55	.30
1991	A1376	20c	Rhode Island	.55	.30
b.			Black missing (EP)	*4,000.*	
1992	A1377	20c	South Carolina	.55	.30
1993	A1378	20c	South Dakota	.55	.30
1994	A1379	20c	Tennessee	.55	.30
1995	A1380	20c	Texas	.55	.30
1996	A1381	20c	Utah	.55	.30
1997	A1382	20c	Vermont	.55	.30
1998	A1383	20c	Virginia	.55	.30
1999	A1384	20c	Washington	.55	.30
2000	A1385	20c	West Virginia	.55	.30
2001	A1386	20c	Wisconsin	.55	.30
b.			Black missing (EP)	*4,000.*	
2002	A1387	20c	Wyoming	.55	.30
b.			A1338-A1387 Pane of 50, Nos. 1953-2002	27.50	20.00
d.			Pane of 50, imperf.	*21,000.*	

Perf. 11¼x11

1953A	A1338	20c	Alabama	.60	.30
1954A	A1339	20c	Alaska	.60	.30
1955A	A1340	20c	Arizona	.60	.30
1956A	A1341	20c	Arkansas	.60	.30
1957A	A1342	20c	California	.60	.30
1958A	A1343	20c	Colorado	.60	.30
1959A	A1344	20c	Connecticut	.60	.30
1960A	A1345	20c	Delaware	.60	.30
1961A	A1346	20c	Florida	.60	.30
1962A	A1347	20c	Georgia	.60	.30
1963A	A1348	20c	Hawaii	.60	.30
1964A	A1349	20c	Idaho	.60	.30
1965A	A1350	20c	Illinois	.60	.30
1966A	A1351	20c	Indiana	.60	.30
1967A	A1352	20c	Iowa	.60	.30
1968A	A1353	20c	Kansas	.60	.30
1969A	A1354	20c	Kentucky	.60	.30
1970A	A1355	20c	Louisiana	.60	.30
1971A	A1356	20c	Maine	.60	.30
1972A	A1357	20c	Maryland	.60	.30
1973A	A1358	20c	Massachusetts	.60	.30
1974A	A1359	20c	Michigan	.60	.30
1975A	A1360	20c	Minnesota	.60	.30
1976A	A1361	20c	Mississippi	.60	.30
1977A	A1362	20c	Missouri	.60	.30
1978A	A1363	20c	Montana	.60	.30
1979A	A1364	20c	Nebraska	.60	.30
1980A	A1365	20c	Nevada	.60	.30
1981A	A1366	20c	New Hampshire	.60	.30
1982A	A1367	20c	New Jersey	.60	.30
1983A	A1368	20c	New Mexico	.60	.30
1984A	A1369	20c	New York	.60	.30
1985A	A1370	20c	North Carolina	.60	.30
1986A	A1371	20c	North Dakota	.60	.30
1987A	A1372	20c	Ohio	.60	.30
1988A	A1373	20c	Oklahoma	.60	.30
1989A	A1374	20c	Oregon	.60	.30
1990A	A1375	20c	Pennsylvania	.60	.30
1991A	A1376	20c	Rhode Island	.60	.30
1992A	A1377	20c	South Carolina	.60	.30
1993A	A1378	20c	South Dakota	.60	.30
1994A	A1379	20c	Tennessee	.60	.30
1995A	A1380	20c	Texas	.60	.30
1996A	A1381	20c	Utah	.60	.30
1997A	A1382	20c	Vermont	.60	.30
1998A	A1383	20c	Virginia	.60	.30
1999A	A1384	20c	Washington	.60	.30
2000A	A1385	20c	West Virginia	.60	.30
2001A	A1386	20c	Wisconsin	.60	.30
2002A	A1387	20c	Wyoming	.60	.30
c.			A1338-A1387 Pane of 50, Nos. 1953A-2002A	30.00	22.50

Nos. 1953-2002 are line perforated. The perforations do not meet perfectly at the corners of each stamp and extend into the narrow selvage margins of an intact pane. Nos. 1953A-2002A are comb perforated. The perforations meet perfectly at the corners of each stamp and do not extend into the narrow selvage margins of an intact pane (shown).

The dull, dry gum on this State Birds and Flowers issue is essentially invisible, making the stamps appear to have no gum. This is normal for the issue.

US-NETHERLANDS

200th Anniv. of Diplomatic Recognition by The Netherlands
A1388

Designed by Heleen Tigler Wybrandi-Raue.

PHOTOGRAVURE

Plates of 230 (10x23) subjects in panes of 50 (5x10).

1982, Apr. 20 **Tagged** ***Perf. 11***

2003	A1388	20c	**multicolored**	.40	.25
			P# block of 6	3.50	—
			P# block of 20, 1-2 #, 1-2 copyright, 1-2 zip	10.00	—
			Pane of 50	20.00	
a.			Imperf., pair	*250.00*	

See Combination Press note after No. 1703.
See Netherlands Nos. 640-641.

LIBRARY OF CONGRESS

A1389

Designed by Bradbury Thompson.

ENGRAVED

Plates of 200 subjects in four panes of 50.

1982, Apr. 21 **Tagged** ***Perf. 11***

2004	A1389	20c	**red & black**	.40	.25
			P# block of 4	1.75	—
			Zip block of 4	1.65	—
			Pane of 50	20.00	
a.			All color missing	—	

No. 2004a must be collected as a right margin horiz. strip of 3, 4 or 5 with one No. 2004a, one transitional stamp and one or more normal stamps.

CONSUMER EDUCATION

A1390

Designed by John Boyd.

ENGRAVED

Coil Stamp

1982, Apr. 27 **Tagged** ***Perf. 10 Vert.***

2005	A1390	20c	**sky blue**	.55	.25
			Pair	1.10	.50
			P# strip of 3, line, #1-4	9.00	
			P# strip of 5, line, #1-2	40.00	
			P# strip of 5, line, #3-4	40.00	
			P# single, #1-4	—	1.50
a.			Imperf., pair	70.00	
b.			Tagging omitted	*15.00*	

KNOXVILLE WORLD'S FAIR

A1391

A1392

A1393

A1394

Designed by Charles Harper.

PHOTOGRAVURE

Plates of 200 in four panes of 50.

1982, Apr. 29 **Tagged** ***Perf. 11***

2006	A1391	20c	**multicolored**	.45	.25
2007	A1392	20c	**multicolored**	.45	.25
2008	A1393	20c	**multicolored**	.45	.25
2009	A1394	20c	**multicolored**	.45	.25
			Any single on cover, Expo. station handstamp cancel		10.00
a.			Block of 4, #2006-2009	1.80	1.50
			P# block of 4, 6#	2.40	—
			Zip block of 4	1.90	—
			Pane of 50	22.50	

HORATIO ALGER

A1395

Designed by Robert Hallock.

ENGRAVED

Plates of 200 in four panes of 50.

1982, Apr. 30 **Tagged** ***Perf. 11***

2010	A1395	20c	**red & black,** *tan*	.40	.25
			P# block of 4	1.75	—
			Zip block of 4	1.65	—
			Pane of 50	20.00	
a.			Red and black omitted	—	
b.			Tagging omitted		—

The Philatelic Foundation has issued a certificate for a pane of 50 with red and black colors omitted. Recognition of this error is by the paper and by a tiny residue of red ink from the tagging roller. The engraved plates did not strike the paper.

AGING TOGETHER

A1396

Designed by Paul Calle.

ENGRAVED

Plates of 200 in four panes of 50.

1982, May 21 **Tagged** ***Perf. 11***

2011	A1396	20c	**brown**	.40	.25
			P# block of 4	1.75	—
			Zip block of 4	1.65	—
			Pane of 50	20.00	

PERFORMING ARTS SERIES

John, Ethel and Lionel Barrymore — A1397

Designed by Jim Sharpe.

PHOTOGRAVURE
Plates of 200 in four panes of 50.

1982, June 8 **Tagged** ***Perf. 11***

2012	A1397 20c **multicolored**	.40	.25
	P# block of 4, 6#	1.75	—
	Zip block of 4	1.65	—
	Pane of 50	20.00	
a.	Black missing (EP)	—	

John (1882-1942), Ethel (1879-1959), and Lionel (1878-1954) Barrymore, actors.

DR. MARY WALKER

Dr. Mary Walker — A1398

Designed by Glenora Richards.

PHOTOGRAVURE
Plate of 200 in four panes of 50.

1982, June 10 **Tagged** ***Perf. 11***

2013	A1398 20c **multicolored**	.40	.25
	P# block of 4, 6#	1.75	—
	Zip block of 4	1.65	—
	Pane of 50	20.00	

Dr. Mary Walker (1832-1919), 1865 recipient of Medal of Honor.

INTERNATIONAL PEACE GARDEN

Dunseith, ND-Boissevain, Manitoba A1399

Designed by Gyo Fujikawa.

LITHOGRAPHED AND ENGRAVED
Plate of 200 in four panes of 50.

1982, June 30 **Tagged** ***Perf. 11***

2014	A1399 20c **multicolored**	.45	.25
	P# block of 4, 5#	2.00	—
	Zip block of 4	1.90	—
	Pane of 50	20.00	
a.	Black (engr.) omitted	*200.00*	

AMERICA'S LIBRARIES

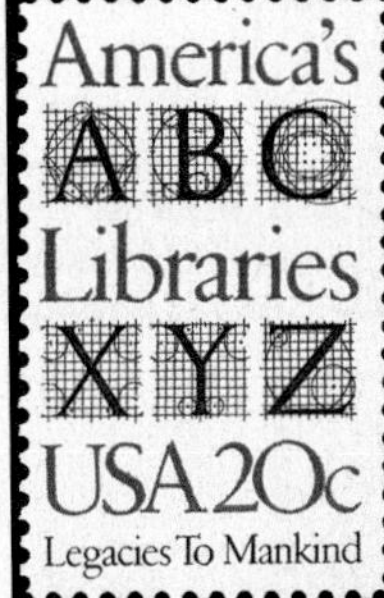

A1400

Designed by Bradbury Thompson.

ENGRAVED
Plate of 200 subjects in four panes of 50.

1982, July 13 **Tagged** ***Perf. 11***

2015	A1400 20c **red & black**	.40	.25
	P# block of 4	1.75	—
	Zip block of 4	1.65	—
	Pane of 50	20.00	
a.	Vert. pair, imperf. horiz.	*200.00*	
b.	Tagging omitted	*12.50*	
c.	All colors missing (EP)	*175.00*	
d.	Imperf. pair	*500.00*	
e.	Horz. pair, imperf. vert.	—	

On No. 2015c, an albino impression of the design is present.

BLACK HERITAGE SERIES

Jackie Robinson (1919-72), baseball player.

A1401

Designed by Jerry Pinkney.

PHOTOGRAVURE
Plate of 200 subjects in four panes of 50.

1982, Aug. 2 **Tagged** ***Perf. 10½x11***

2016	A1401 20c **multicolored**	1.00	.25
	P# block of 4, 5#	5.00	—
	Zip block of 4	4.25	—
	Pane of 50	50.00	

TOURO SYNAGOGUE

Oldest Existing Synagogue Building in the U.S. — A1402

Designed by Donald Moss and Bradbury Thompson.

PHOTOGRAVURE AND ENGRAVED
Plates of 230 (10x23) subjects in panes of 50 (5x10).

1982, Aug. 22 **Tagged** ***Perf. 11***

2017	A1402 20c **multicolored**	.40	.25
	P# block of 20, 6-12 #, 1-2 copyright, 1-2 zip	11.50	—
	Pane of 50	20.00	
a.	Imperf., pair	*1,400.*	

See Combination Press note after No. 1703.

WOLF TRAP FARM PARK

A1403

Designed by Richard Schlecht.

PHOTOGRAVURE
Plates of 200 in four panes of 50.

1982, Sept. 1 **Tagged** ***Perf. 11***

2018	A1403 20c **multicolored**	.40	.25
	P# block of 4, 5#	1.75	—
	Zip block of 4	1.65	—
	Pane of 50	20.00	

AMERICAN ARCHITECTURE SERIES

A1404

A1405

A1406

A1407

Designed by Walter D. Richards.

ENGRAVED
Plates of 160 subjects in four panes of 40.

1982, Sept. 30 **Tagged** ***Perf. 11***

2019	A1404 20c **black & brown**	.45	.25
a.	Tagging omitted		—
b.	Red missing (PS)	—	
2020	A1405 20c **black & brown**	.45	.25
a.	Red missing (PS)	—	
2021	A1406 20c **black & brown**	.45	.25
2022	A1407 20c **black & brown**	.45	.25
a.	Block of 4, #2019-2022	2.00	1.75
	P# block of 4	2.50	—
	Zip block of 4	2.10	—
	Pane of 40	18.00	

FRANCIS OF ASSISI

A1408

Designed by Ned Seidler.

Printed by American Bank Note Co. and J.W. Fergusson and Sons.

PHOTOGRAVURE
Plates of 200 subjects in four panes of 50.

1982, Oct. 7	**Tagged**	***Perf. 11***	
2023 A1408 20c **multicolored**		.40	.25
	P# block of 4, 6#+A	1.75	—
	Zip block of 4	1.65	—
	Pane of 50	20.00	

PONCE DE LEON

A1409

Designed by Richard Schlecht.

PHOTOGRAVURE (Combination press)
Plates of 230 subjects (10x23) in panes of 50 (5x10).

1982, Oct. 12	**Tagged**	***Perf. 11***	
2024 A1409 20c **multicolored**		.40	.25
	P# block of 6, 5#	3.00	—
	P# block of 20, 5 or 10 #, 1-2 zip, 1-2 copyright	10.50	—
	Pane of 50	20.00	
a.	Imperf., pair	*250.00*	
b.	Vert. pair, imperf. between and at top	*500.00*	
c.	Tagging omitted	—	

See Combination Press note after No. 1703.

CHRISTMAS ISSUES

A1410

A1411

A1412

A1413

A1414

A1415

PHOTOGRAVURE
Plates of 200 subjects in four panes of 50

Designed by Chuck Ripper.

1982, Nov. 3		**Tagged**	
2025 A1410 13c **multicolored**		.30	.25
	P# block of 4	1.40	—
	Zip block of 4	1.10	—
	Pane of 50	12.50	
a.	Imperf., pair	*300.00*	

PHOTOGRAVURE (Combination Press)
Plates of 230 subjects (10x23) in panes of 50 (5x10).

Designed by Bradbury Thompson.

1982, Oct. 28		**Tagged**	
2026 A1411 20c **multicolored**		.40	.25
	P# block of 6	3.00	—
	P# block of 20, 5 or 10 #, 1-2 copyright, 1-2 zip	11.00	—
	Pane of 50	20.00	
a.	Imperf. pair	90.00	
b.	Horiz. pair, imperf. vert.	*900.00*	
c.	Vert. pair, imperf. horiz.	—	

See Combination Press note after No. 1703.

PHOTOGRAVURE
Plates of 200 in four panes of 50.

Designed by Dolli Tingle.

2027 A1412 20c **multicolored**		.60	.25
2028 A1413 20c **multicolored**		.60	.25
2029 A1414 20c **multicolored**		.60	.25
2030 A1415 20c **multicolored**		.60	.25
a.	Block of 4, #2027-2030	2.40	1.50
	P# block of 4, 4#	2.50	—
	Zip block of 4	2.40	—
	Pane of 50	30.00	
b.	As "a," imperf.	*1,250.*	
c.	As "a," imperf. horiz.	*700.00*	
	Nos. 2025-2030 (6)	3.10	1.50

SCIENCE & INDUSTRY

A1416

Designed by Saul Bass.

LITHOGRAPHED AND ENGRAVED
Plates of 200 in four panes of 50.

1983, Jan. 19	**Tagged**	***Perf. 11***	
2031 A1416 20c **multicolored**		.40	.25
	P# block of 4, 4#	1.75	—
	Zip block of 4	1.65	—
	Pane of 50	20.00	
a.	Black (engr.) omitted	*750.00*	
b.	Tagging omitted		—

BALLOONS

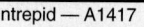

Intrepid — A1417

Explorer II — A1420

A1418

A1419

Designed by Davis Meltzer.

PHOTOGRAVURE
Plates of 160 in four panes of 40.

1983, Mar. 31	**Tagged**	***Perf. 11***	
2032 A1417 20c **multicolored**		.50	.25
2033 A1418 20c **multicolored**		.50	.25
2034 A1419 20c **multicolored**		.50	.25
2035 A1420 20c **multicolored**		.50	.25
a.	Block of 4, #2032-2035	2.00	1.50
	P# block of 4, 5#	2.25	—
	Zip block of 4	2.10	—
	Pane of 50	20.00	
b.	As "a," imperf.	*2,750.*	
c.	As "a," right stamp perf., otherwise imperf.	*2,750.*	

US-SWEDEN

Benjamin Franklin A1421

Designed by Czeslaw Slania, court engraver of Sweden.

ENGRAVED
Plates of 200 in four panes of 50.

1983, Mar. 24	**Tagged**	***Perf. 11***	
2036 A1421 20c **blue, blk & red brn**		.40	.25
	P# block of 4	1.75	—
	Zip block of 4	1.65	—
	Pane of 50	20.00	

See Sweden No. 1453.

CCC, 50th ANNIV.

A1422

Designed by David K. Stone.

PHOTOGRAVURE
Plates of 200 in four panes of 50.

1983, Apr. 5	**Tagged**	***Perf. 11***	
2037 A1422 20c **multicolored**		.40	.25
	P# block of 4, 6#	1.75	—
	Zip block of 4	1.65	—
	Pane of 50	20.00	
a.	Imperf., pair	*2,250.*	
b.	Vert. pair, imperf. horiz.	—	

JOSEPH PRIESTLEY

Joseph Priestley (1733-1804), Discoverer of Oxygen — A1423

Designed by Dennis Lyall.

Printed by American Bank Note Company and J.W. Ferguson and Sons.

PHOTOGRAVURE
Plates of 200 in four panes of 50.

1983, Apr. 13	**Tagged**	***Perf. 11***	
2038 A1423 20c **multicolored**		.40	.25
	P# block of 4, 6#+A	1.75	—
	Zip block of 4	1.65	—
	Pane of 50	20.00	

VOLUNTEERISM

A1424

Designed by Paul Calle.

ENGRAVED (Combination Press)
Plates of 230 subjects (10x23) in panes of 50 (5x10).

1983, Apr. 20	**Tagged**	***Perf. 11***	
2039 A1424 20c **red & black**		.40	.25
	P# block of 6	3.00	—
	P# block of 20, 1-2 #, 1-2 copyright, 1-2 zip	10.00	—
	Pane of 50	20.00	
a.	Imperf., pair	*225.00*	

See Combination Press note after No. 1703.

US-GERMANY

A1425

Designed by Richard Schlecht.

ENGRAVED
Plates of 200 in four panes of 50.

1983, Apr. 29	**Tagged**	***Perf. 11***	
2040 A1425 20c **brown**		.40	.25
	P# block of 4	1.75	—
	Zip block of 4	1.65	—
	Pane of 50	20.00	
a.	Tagging omitted	—	—

See Germany No. 1397.

BROOKLYN BRIDGE

A1426

Normal

"Unfinished Bridge"
Short Transfer

Designed by Howard Koslow.

ENGRAVED
Plates of 200 in four panes of 50.

1983, May 17	**Tagged**	***Perf. 11***	
2041 A1426 20c **blue**		.40	.25
	P# block of 4	1.75	—
	Zip block of 4	1.65	—
	Short transfer (unfinished bridge) (UL 2)	9.00	.75
	P# block of 4	15.00	—
	Pane of 50	20.00	
a.	Tagging omitted	*125.00*	
b.	All color missing (EP)	*90.00*	

On No. 2041b, an albino impression of part of the design is evident.

TVA

Norris Hydroelectric Dam — A1427

Designed by Howard Koslow.

PHOTOGRAVURE AND ENGRAVED (Combination Press)
Plates of 230 in panes of 50

1983, May 18	**Tagged**	***Perf. 11***	
2042 A1427 20c **multicolored**		.40	.25
	P# block of 20, 5-10 #, 1-2 copyright, 1-2 zip	10.00	—
	Pane of 50	20.00	

Runners, Electrocardiograph Tracing — A1428

Designed by Donald Moss.

PHOTOGRAVURE (Combination Press)
Plates of 230 in panes of 50.

1983, May 14	**Tagged**	***Perf. 11***	
2043 A1428 20c **multicolored**		.40	.25
	P# block of 6, 4#	3.00	—
	P# block of 20, 4-8 #, 1-2 copyright, 1-2 zip	10.00	—
	Pane of 50	20.00	

BLACK HERITAGE SERIES

Scott Joplin (1868-1917), Ragtime composer.

A1429

Designed by Jerry Pinkney.

PHOTOGRAVURE
Plates of 200 in four panes of 50.

1983, June 9	**Tagged**	***Perf. 11***	
2044 A1429 20c **multicolored**		.50	.25
	P# block of 4, 6#	2.40	—
	Zip block of 4	2.10	—
	Pane of 50	25.00	
a.	Imperf., pair	*300.00*	
b.	Tagging omitted	*300.00*	—

MEDAL OF HONOR

A1430

Designed by Dennis J. Hom.

LITHOGRAPHED AND ENGRAVED
Plates of 160 in four panes of 40.

1983, June 7	**Tagged**	***Perf. 11***	
2045 A1430 20c **multicolored**		.55	.25
	P# block of 4, 5#	2.50	—
	Zip block of 4	2.25	—
	Pane of 40	22.00	
a.	Red omitted	*150.00*	

GEORGE HERMAN RUTH (1895-1948)

A1431

Designed by Richard Gangel.

ENGRAVED
Plates of 200 in four panes of 50.

1983, July 6	**Tagged**	***Perf. 10½x11***	
2046 A1431 20c **blue**		1.00	.25
	P# block of 4	5.00	—
	Zip block of 4	4.25	—
	Pane of 50	50.00	

LITERARY ARTS SERIES

Nathaniel Hawthorne (1804-1864), novelist.

A1432

Designed by Bradbury Thompson after 1851 painting by Cephus Giovanni Thompson.

PHOTOGRAVURE

Plates of 200 in four panes of 50.

1983, July 8 **Tagged** ***Perf. 11***

2047 A1432 20c **multicolored**		.40	.25
	P# block of 4, 4#	1.90	—
	Zip block of 4	1.70	—
	Pane of 50	20.00	

1984 SUMMER OLYMPICS

Los Angeles, July 28-August 12

Discus
A1433

High Jump — A1434

Archery
A1435

Boxing
A1436

Designed by Bob Peak.

PHOTOGRAVURE

Plates of 200 in four panes of 50.

1983, July 28 **Tagged** ***Perf. 11***

2048 A1433 13c **multicolored**		.35	.25
2049 A1434 13c **multicolored**		.35	.25
2050 A1435 13c **multicolored**		.35	.25
2051 A1436 13c **multicolored**		.35	.25
a.	Block of 4, #2048-2051	1.50	1.25
	P# block of 4, 4#	1.75	—
	Zip block of 4	1.65	—
	Pane of 50	17.50	

SIGNING OF TREATY OF PARIS

John Adams, B. Franklin, John Jay, David Hartley
A1437

Designed by David Blossom after an unfinished painting by Benjamin West in Winterthur Museum.

PHOTOGRAVURE

Plates of 160 in four panes of 40.

1983, Sept. 2 **Tagged** ***Perf. 11***

2052 A1437 20c **multicolored**		.40	.25
	P# block of 4, 4#	1.75	—
	Zip block of 4	1.65	—
	Pane of 40	16.00	
a.	Tagging omitted		—

CIVIL SERVICE

A1438

Designed by MDB Communications, Inc.

PHOTOGRAVURE AND ENGRAVED

Plates of 230 in four panes of 50.

1983, Sept. 9 **Tagged** ***Perf. 11***

2053 A1438 20c **buff, blue & red**		.40	.25
	P# block of 20, 1-2P#, 1-2 Zip, 1-2 Copyright	10.00	—
	Pane of 50	20.00	
a.	Tagging omitted	—	—

METROPOLITAN OPERA

Original State Arch and Current 5-arch Entrance
A1439

Designed by Ken Davies.

LITHOGRAPHED AND ENGRAVED

Plates of 200 in four panes of 50.

1983, Sept. 14 **Tagged** ***Perf. 11***

2054 A1439 20c **yellow & maroon**		.40	.25
	P# block of 4, 2#	1.75	—
	Zip block of 4	1.65	—
	Pane of 50	20.00	
a.	Tagging omitted	*12.50*	

AMERICAN INVENTORS

Charles Steinmetz and Curve on Graph
A1440

Edwin Armstrong and Frequency Modulator
A1441

Nikola Tesla and Induction Motor
A1442

Philo T. Farnsworth and First Television Camera
A1443

Designed by Dennis Lyall.

LITHOGRAPHED AND ENGRAVED

Plates of 200 in four panes of 50.

1983, Sept. 21 **Tagged** ***Perf. 11***

2055 A1440 20c **multicolored**		.50	.25
2056 A1441 20c **multicolored**		.50	.25
2057 A1442 20c **multicolored**		.50	.25
2058 A1443 20c **multicolored**		.50	.25
a.	Block of 4, #2055-2058	2.00	1.50
	P# block of 4, 2#	2.75	—
	Zip block of 4	2.10	—
	Pane of 50	25.00	
b.	As "a," black omitted	*275.00*	

STREETCARS

A1444

A1445

A1446

St. Charles streetcar, New Orleans, La., 1923 — USA20c

A1447

Designed by Richard Leech.

PHOTOGRAVURE AND ENGRAVED

Plates of 200 in four panes of 50.

1983, Oct. 8 Tagged *Perf. 11*

2059 A1444 20c **multicolored** .50 .25
2060 A1445 20c **multicolored** .50 .25
a. Horiz. pair, black (engr.) missing on Nos. 2059, 2060 (EP) —
2061 A1446 20c **multicolored** .50 .25
a. Vert. pair, black (engr.) missing on Nos. 2059, 2061 (EP) —
2062 A1447 20c **multicolored** .50 .25
a. Block of 4, #2059-2062 2.00 1.50
P# block of 4, 5# 2.75 —
Zip block of 4 2.10 —
Pane of 50 25.00
b. As "a," black (engr.) omitted *250.00*
c. As "a," black (engr.) omitted on #2059, 2061 —

CHRISTMAS

Niccolini-Cowper Madonna, by Raphael — A1448

Santa Claus — A1449

Designed by Bradbury Thompson (No. 2063), and John Berkey (No. 2064).

PHOTOGRAVURE

Plates of 200 in four panes of 50 (No. 2063),
Plates of 230 in panes of 50 (Combination Press, No. 2064)

1983, Oct. 28 Tagged *Perf. 11*

2063 A1448 20c **multicolored** .40 .25
P# block of 4, 5# 1.75 —
Zip block of 4 1.65 —
Pane of 50 20.00
2064 A1449 20c **multicolored** .40 .25
P# block of 6, 5# 3.00 —
P# block of 20, 5-10 P#, 1-2 copyright, 1-2 zip 11.50 —
Pane of 50 20.00
a. Imperf., pair *100.00*
b. Tagging omitted —

See Combination Press note after No. 1703.

MARTIN LUTHER

Martin Luther (1483-1546), German Religious Leader, Founder of Lutheran Church — A1450

Designed by Bradbury Thompson.

Printed by American Bank Note Company.

PHOTOGRAVURE

Plates of 200 in four panes of 50.

1983, Nov. 11 Tagged *Perf. 11*

2065 A1450 20c **multicolored** .40 .25
P# block of 4, 5#+A 1.75 —
Zip block of 4 1.65 —
Pane of 50 20.00

ALASKA STATEHOOD, 25th ANNIV.

Caribou and Alaska Pipeline — A1451

Designed by Bill Bond.

Printed by American Bank Note Company and J.W. Ferguson and Sons.

PHOTOGRAVURE

Plates of 200 in four panes of 50.

1984, Jan. 3 Tagged *Perf. 11*

2066 A1451 20c **multicolored** .40 .25
P# block of 4, 5#+A 1.75 —
Zip block of 4 1.65 —
Pane of 50 20.00
a. Vert. pair, imperf. horiz. —

14th WINTER OLYMPIC GAMES

Sarajevo, Yugoslavia, Feb. 8-19

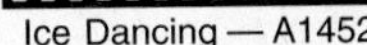

Ice Dancing — A1452

Downhill Skiing — A1453

Cross-country Skiing — A1454

Hockey — A1455

Designed by Bob Peak.

PHOTOGRAVURE

Plates of 200 in four panes of 50.

1984, Jan. 6 Tagged *Perf. 10½x11*

2067 A1452 20c **multicolored** .55 .25
2068 A1453 20c **multicolored** .55 .25
2069 A1454 20c **multicolored** .55 .25
2070 A1455 20c **multicolored** .55 .25
a. Block of 4, #2067-2070 2.20 1.75
P# block of 4, 4# 3.00 —
Zip block of 4 2.25 —
Pane of 50 27.50

FEDERAL DEPOSIT INSURANCE CORPORATION, 50TH ANNIV.

Pillar, Dollar Sign — A1456

Designed by Michael David Brown.

PHOTOGRAVURE

Plates of 200 in four panes of 50

(1 pane each #2071, 2074, 2075 and 2081)

1984, Jan. 12 Tagged *Perf. 11*

2071 A1456 20c **multicolored** .40 .25
P# block of 4, 6#, UL only 2.00 —
Zip block of 4 1.65 —
Pane of 50 20.00

LOVE

A1457

Designed by Bradbury Thompson.

PHOTOGRAVURE AND ENGRAVED (Combination Press)

Plates of 230 in four panes of 50.

1984, Jan. 31 Tagged *Perf. 11x10½*

2072 A1457 20c **multicolored** .40 .25
P# block of 20, 6-12#, 1-2 copyright, 1-2 zip 10.00 —
Pane of 50 20.00
a. Horiz. pair, imperf. vert. *125.00*
b. Tagging omitted *10.00*

See Combination Press note after No. 1703.

BLACK HERITAGE SERIES

Carter G. Woodson (1875-1950), Historian.

A1458

Designed by Jerry Pinkney.

Printed by American Bank Note Company.

PHOTOGRAVURE

Plates of 200 in four panes of 50.

1984, Feb. 1 Tagged *Perf. 11*

2073 A1458 20c **multicolored** .40 .25
P# block of 4, 6#+A 2.00 —
Zip block of 4 1.65 —
Pane of 50 20.00
a. Horiz. pair, imperf. vert. *800.00*

SOIL & WATER CONSERVATION

A1459

Designed by Michael David Brown.

See No. 2071 for printing information.

1984, Feb. 6 **Tagged** ***Perf. 11***

2074 A1459 20c **multicolored** .40 .25
P# block of 4, 6#, UR only 1.75 —
Zip block of 4 1.65 —
Pane of 50 20.00

50TH ANNIV. OF CREDIT UNION ACT

Dollar Sign, Coin — A1460

Designed by Michael David Brown.

See No. 2071 for printing information.

1984, Feb. 10 **Tagged** ***Perf. 11***

2075 A1460 20c **multicolored** .40 .25
P# block of 4, 6#, LR only 1.75 —
Zip block of 4 1.65 —
Pane of 50 20.00

ORCHIDS

Wild Pink — A1461

Yellow Lady's-slipper A1462

Spreading Pogonia — A1463

Pacific Calypso — A1464

Designed by Manabu Saito.

PHOTOGRAVURE

Plates of 192 in four panes of 48.

1984, Mar. 5 **Tagged** ***Perf. 11***

2076 A1461 20c **multicolored** .50 .25
2077 A1462 20c **multicolored** .50 .25
2078 A1463 20c **multicolored** .50 .25
2079 A1464 20c **multicolored** .50 .25
a. Block of 4, #2076-2079 2.00 1.50
P# block of 4, 5# 2.50 —
Zip block of 4 2.10 —
Pane of 48 24.00

HAWAII STATEHOOD, 25th ANNIV.

Eastern Polynesian Canoe, Golden Plover, Mauna Loa Volcano A1465

Designed by Herb Kane.

Printed by American Bank Note Company.

PHOTOGRAVURE

Plates of 200 in four panes of 50.

1984, Mar. 12 **Tagged** ***Perf. 11***

2080 A1465 20c **multicolored** .40 .25
P# block of 4, 5#+A 2.00 —
Zip block of 4 1.65 —
Pane of 50 20.00

50TH ANNIV., NATIONAL ARCHIVES

Abraham Lincoln, George Washington — A1466

Designed by Michael David Brown.

See No. 2071 for printing information.

1984, Apr. 16 **Tagged** ***Perf. 11***

2081 A1466 20c **multicolored** .40 .25
P# block of 4, 6#, LL only 2.00 —
Zip block of 4 1.65 —
Pane of 50 20.00

LOS ANGELES SUMMER OLYMPICS

July 28-August 12

Diving — A1467

Long Jump — A1468

Wrestling — A1469

Kayak — A1470

Designed by Bob Peak.

PHOTOGRAVURE

Plates of 200 in four panes of 50.

1984, May 4 **Tagged** ***Perf. 11***

2082 A1467 20c **multicolored** .55 .25
2083 A1468 20c **multicolored** .55 .25
2084 A1469 20c **multicolored** .55 .25
2085 A1470 20c **multicolored** .55 .25
a. Block of 4, #2082-2085 2.40 1.90
P# block of 4, 4# 3.00 —
Zip block of 4 2.50 —
Pane of 50 27.50
b. As "a," imperf between vertically *9,500.*

LOUISIANA WORLD EXPOSITION

New Orleans, May 12-Nov. 11

Bayou Wildlife A1471

Designed by Chuck Ripper.

PHOTOGRAVURE

Plates of 160 in four panes of 40.

1984, May 11 **Tagged** ***Perf. 11***

2086 A1471 20c **multicolored** .50 .25
On cover, Expo. station pictorial hand-stamp cancel 2.50
P# block of 4, 5# 2.60 —
Zip block of 4 2.10 —
Pane of 50 20.00

HEALTH RESEARCH

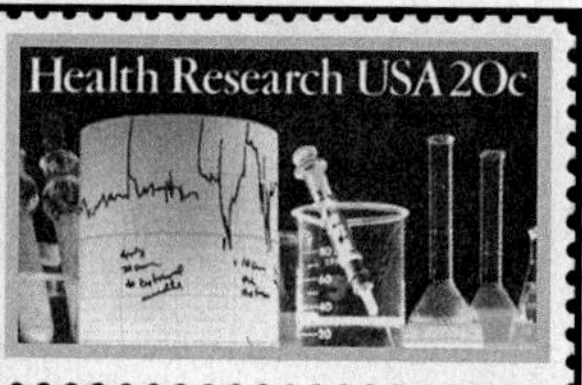

Lab Equipment A1472

Designed by Tyler Smith.

Printed by American Bank Note Company.

PHOTOGRAVURE

Plates of 200 in four panes of 50.

1984, May 17 **Tagged** ***Perf. 11***

2087 A1472 20c **multicolored** .40 .25
P# block of 4, 5#+A 2.00 —
Zip block of 4 1.65 —
Pane of 50 20.00

PERFORMING ARTS

Douglas Fairbanks (1883-1939), Actor — A1473

Designed by Jim Sharpe.

PHOTOGRAVURE AND ENGRAVED (Combination Press)
Plates of 230 in panes of 50.

1984, May 23 **Tagged** ***Perf. 11***

2088 A1473 20c **multicolored** .40 .25
P# block of 20, 5-10#, 1-2 copyright, 1-2 zip 12.50 —
Pane of 50 20.00
a. Tagging omitted *20.00*
b. Horiz. pair, imperf between —

See Combination Press note after No. 1703.

JIM THORPE

Jim Thorpe (1888-1953), Athlete — A1474

Designed by Richard Gangel.

ENGRAVED
Plates of 200 in four panes of 50.

1984, May 24 **Tagged** ***Perf. 11***

2089 A1474 20c **dark brown** .60 .25
P# block of 4 3.50 —
Zip block of 4 1.90 —
Pane of 50 30.00
a. All color omitted —

On No. 2089a, an albino impression of the design is evident.

PERFORMING ARTS

John McCormack (1884-1945), Operatic Tenor — A1475

Designed by Jim Sharpe (US) and Ron Mercer (Ireland).

PHOTOGRAVURE
Plates of 200 in four panes of 50.

1984, June 6 **Tagged** ***Perf. 11***

2090 A1475 20c **multicolored** .40 .25
P# block of 4, 5# 2.00 —
Zip block of 4 1.65 —
Pane of 50 20.00

See Ireland No. 594.

ST. LAWRENCE SEAWAY, 25th ANNIV.

Aerial View of Seaway, Freighters A1476

Designed by Ernst Barenscher (Canada).

Printed by American Bank Note Company.

PHOTOGRAVURE
Plates of 200 in four panes of 50.

1984, June 26 **Tagged** ***Perf. 11***

2091 A1476 20c **multicolored** .40 .25
P# block of 4, 4#+A 1.75 —
Zip block of 4 1.65 —
Pane of 50 20.00
a. Tagging omitted —

WATERFOWL PRESERVATION ACT, 50th ANNIV.

"Mallards Dropping In" by Jay N. Darling A1477

Design adapted from Darling's work (No. RW1) by Donald M. McDowell.

ENGRAVED
Plates of 200 in four panes of 50.

1984, July 2 **Tagged** ***Perf. 11***

2092 A1477 20c **blue** .50 .25
P# block of 4 2.50 —
Zip block of 4 2.25 —
Pane of 50 25.00
a. Horiz. pair, imperf. vert. *275.00*

ROANOKE VOYAGES

The Elizabeth — A1478

Designed by Charles Lundgren.

Printed by American Bank Note Company.

PHOTOGRAVURE
Plates of 200 in four panes of 50.

1984, July 13 **Tagged** ***Perf. 11***

2093 A1478 20c **multicolored** .40 .25
P# block of 4, 5#+A 1.75 —
Zip block of 4 1.65 —
Pane of 50 20.00
Pair with full horiz. gutter btwn. —

LITERARY ARTS SERIES

Herman Melville (1819-1891), Author — A1479

Designed by Bradbury Thompson.

ENGRAVED
Plates of 200 in four panes of 50.

1984, Aug. 1 **Tagged** ***Perf. 11***

2094 A1479 20c **sage green** .40 .25
P# block of 4 1.75 —
Zip block of 4 1.65 —
Pane of 50 20.00
a. Tagging omitted 75.00 —

HORACE MOSES (1862-1947)

Horace Moses, Junior Achievement Founder — A1480

Designed by Dennis Lyall.

ENGRAVED (Combination Press)
Plates of 200 in panes of 50.

1984, Aug. 6 **Tagged** ***Perf. 11***

2095 A1480 20c **orange & dark brown** .40 .25
P# block of 6 3.00 —
P# block of 20, 1-2#, 1-2 copyright, 1-2 zip 10.00 —
Pane of 50 20.00

See Combination Press note after No. 1703.

SMOKEY BEAR

Smokey Bear — A1481

Designed by Rudolph Wendelin.

LITHOGRAPHED AND ENGRAVED
Plates of 200 in panes of 50.

1984, Aug. 13 **Tagged** ***Perf. 11***

2096 A1481 20c **multicolored** .40 .25
P# block of 4, 5# 2.25 —
Zip block of 4 1.65 —
Pane of 50 20.00
a. Horiz. pair, imperf. btwn. *175.00*
b. Vert. pair, imperf. btwn. *150.00*
c. Block of 4, imperf. btwn. vert. and horiz. *2,500.*
d. Horiz. pair, imperf. vert. *450.00*
e. Tagging omitted *275.00* —

ROBERTO CLEMENTE (1934-1972)

Clemente Wearing Pittsburgh Pirates Cap, Puerto Rican Flag — A1482

Designed by Juan Lopez-Bonilla.

PHOTOGRAVURE
Plates of 200 in panes of 50.

1984, Aug. 17	Tagged	*Perf. 11*	
2097 A1482 20c **multicolored**		1.00	.25
P# block of 4, 6#		5.00	—
Zip block of 4		4.25	—
Pane of 50		50.00	
a. Horiz. pair, imperf. vert.		*1,250.*	

DOGS

Beagle and Boston Terrier A1483

Chesapeake Bay Retriever and Cocker Spaniel A1484

Alaskan Malamute and Collie A1485

Black and Tan Coonhound and American Foxhound A1486

Designed by Roy Andersen.

PHOTOGRAVURE
Plates of 160 in panes of 40.

1984, Sept. 7	Tagged	*Perf. 11*	
2098 A1483 20c **multicolored**		.50	.25
2099 A1484 20c **multicolored**		.50	.25
2100 A1485 20c **multicolored**		.50	.25
2101 A1486 20c **multicolored**		.50	.25
a. Block of 4, #2098-2101		2.00	1.90
P# block of 4, 4#		3.00	—
Zip block of 4		2.10	—
Pane of 40		20.00	
b. As "a," imperf horiz.		*5,500.*	

CRIME PREVENTION

McGruff, the Crime Dog — A1487

Designed by Randall McDougall.

Printed by American Bank Note Company.

PHOTOGRAVURE
Plates of 200 in panes of 50.

1984, Sept. 26	Tagged	*Perf. 11*	
2102 A1487 20c **multicolored**		.40	.25
P# block of 4, 4#+A		2.00	—
Zip block of 4		1.65	—
Pane of 50		20.00	

HISPANIC AMERICANS

A1488

Designed by Robert McCall.

PHOTOGRAVURE
Plates of 160 in four panes of 40.

1984, Oct. 31	Tagged	*Perf. 11*	
2103 A1488 20c **multicolored**		.40	.25
P# block of 4, 6#		2.00	—
Zip block of 4		1.65	—
Pane of 40		16.00	
a. Vert. pair, imperf. horiz.		*1,250.*	

FAMILY UNITY

Stick Figures — A1489

Designed by Molly LaRue.

PHOTOGRAVURE AND ENGRAVED (Combination Press)
Plates of 230 in panes of 50.

1984, Oct. 1	Tagged	*Perf. 11*	
2104 A1489 20c **multicolored**		.40	.25
P# block of 20, 3-6#, 1-2 copyright, 1-2 zip		10.00	—
Pane of 50		20.00	
a. Horiz. pair, imperf. vert.		*325.00*	
b. Tagging omitted		*12.50*	
c. Vert. pair, imperf. btwn. and at bottom		—	
d. Horiz. pair, imperf. between		*900.00*	

See Combination Press note after No. 1703.
Used untagged imperfs exist from printer's waste.

ELEANOR ROOSEVELT (1884-1962)

A1490

Designed by Bradbury Thompson.

ENGRAVED
Plates of 192 in panes of 48.

1984, Oct. 11	Tagged	*Perf. 11*	
2105 A1490 20c **deep blue**		.40	.25
P# block of 4		2.00	—
Zip block of 4		1.65	—
Pane of 48		19.00	

NATION OF READERS

Abraham Lincoln Reading to Son, Tad — A1491

Design adapted from Anthony Berger daguerrotype by Bradbury Thompson.

ENGRAVED
Plates of 200 in panes of 50.

1984, Oct. 16	Tagged	*Perf. 11*	
2106 A1491 20c **brown & maroon**		.40	.25
P# block of 4		2.00	—
Zip block of 4		1.65	—
Pane of 50		20.00	

CHRISTMAS

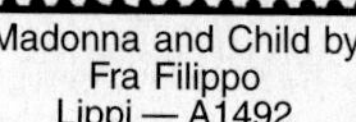
Madonna and Child by Fra Filippo Lippi — A1492

Santa Claus — A1493

Designed by Bradbury Thompson (No. 2107) and Danny La Boccetta (No. 2108).

PHOTOGRAVURE
Plates of 200 in panes of 50.

1984, Oct. 30	Tagged	*Perf. 11*	
2107 A1492 20c **multicolored**		.40	.25
P# block of 4, 5#		2.00	—
Zip block of 4		1.65	—
Pane of 50		20.00	
a. Imperf., pair		*1,400.*	
b. Tagging omitted		—	
2108 A1493 20c **multicolored**		.40	.25
P# block of 4, 5#		2.00	—
Zip block of 4		1.65	—
Pane of 50		20.00	
a. Horiz. pair, imperf. vert.		*750.00*	

No. 2108a is valued in the grade of fine.

VIETNAM VETERANS MEMORIAL

Memorial and Visitors — A1494

Designed by Paul Calle.

ENGRAVED
Plates of 160 in panes of 40.

1984, Nov. 10	Tagged	*Perf. 11*	
2109 A1494 20c **multicolored**		.50	.25
P# block of 4		3.00	—
Zip block of 4		2.10	—
Pane of 40		20.00	
a. Tagging omitted		*65.00*	

PERFORMING ARTS

Jerome Kern (1885-1945), Composer — A1495

Designed by Jim Sharpe.

Printed by the American Bank Note Company.

PHOTOGRAVURE
Plates of 200 in four panes of 50.

1985, Jan. 23 **Tagged** ***Perf. 11***

2110 A1495 22c **multicolored** .45 .25
P# block of 4, 5#+A 2.00 —
Zip block of 4 1.65 —
Pane of 100 22.50
a. Tagging omitted *12.50*

A1496

A1497

Designed by Bradbury Thompson.

PHOTOGRAVURE
Plates of 460 (20x23) in panes of 100.

1985, Feb. 1 **Tagged** ***Perf. 11***

2111 A1496 (22c) **green** .60 .25
P# block of 6 4.50 —
P# block of 20, 1-2 #, 1-2 Zip, 1-2 Copyright 17.50 —
Pane of 100 60.00
a. Vert. pair, imperf. 35.00
b. Vert. pair, imperf. horiz. *750.00*
c. Tagging omitted —

Counterfeits exist of No. 2111. See the Postal Counterfeits section of this catalog.

COIL STAMP
Perf. 10 Vert.

2112 A1496 (22c) **green** .60 .25
Pair 1.20 .25
P# strip of 3, #1, 2 3.00
P# strip of 5, #1, 2 4.00
P# single, #1, 2 — .50
a. Imperf., pair *45.00*
b. As "a," tagging omitted *100.00*
c. As No. 2112, tagging omitted *250.00* —

BOOKLET STAMP
ENGRAVED
Perf. 11 on 2 or 3 Sides

2113 A1497 (22c) **green** .70 .25
a. Booklet pane of 10 6.75 3.00
b. As "a," Horiz. imperf. btwn. *1,850.*

Two examples of No. 2113b are reported, both in unexploded booklet No. BK143a.

A1498

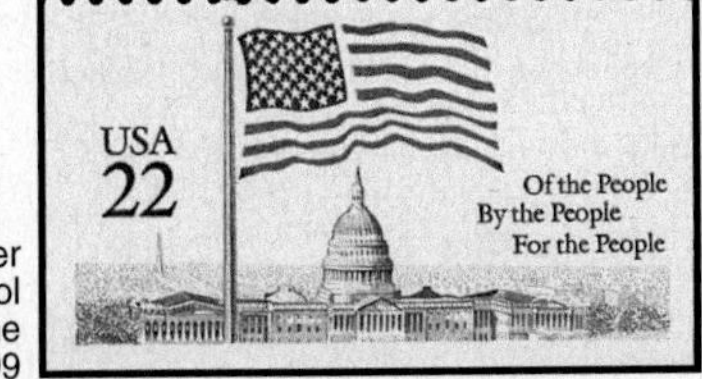

Flag Over Capitol Dome A1499

Designed by Frank Waslick.

ENGRAVED
Plates of 400 subjects in panes of 100.

1985, Mar. 29 **Tagged** ***Perf. 11***

2114 A1498 22c **blue, red & black** .45 .25
P# block of 4 2.10 —
Zip block of 4 1.85 —
Pair with full horizontal gutter *125.00*
Pane of 100 45.00
a. All color missing (EP) —
b. Tagging omitted — *25.00*

No. 2114a should be collected se-tenant with a normal or a partially printed stamp.

COIL STAMP
Perf. 10 Vert.

2115 A1498 22c **blue, red & black,** wide block tagging, 19mmx21.5mm (B press) .45 .25
Pair .90 .50
P# strip of 3, #2, 4, 6, 10 2.50
P# strip of 3, #13 5.50
P# strip of 3, #14 17.50
P# strip of 3, #15, 16, 21 2.25
P# strip of 5, #2, 4, 6, 10 3.00
P# strip of 5, #13 6.50
P# strip of 5, #14 25.00
P# strip of 5, #15, 16, 21 2.75
P# single, #2 — .50
P# single, #4 — .50
P# single, #6 — 5.50
P# single, #10 — .65
P# single, #13 — 8.00
P# single, #14 — 22.00
P# single, #15 — 1.50
P# single, #16 — 2.25
P# single, #21 — 2.25
a. Narrow block tagging, 17.5mmx21.5mm (C press) .40 .25
P# strip of 3, #1 3.75
P# strip of 3, #3 8.00
P# strip of 3, #5 2.00
P# strip of 3, #7 3.50
P# strip of 3, #8, 11-12, 17-20, 22 2.25
P# strip of 5, #1 6.00
P# strip of 5, #3 30.00
P# strip of 5, #5 3.00
P# strip of 5, #7 6.00
P# strip of 5, #8, 11-12, 17-20, 22 3.00
P# single, #1, 3, 5 — .70
P# single, #7-8 — .70
P# single, #11 — .70
P# single, #12 — .70
P# single, #17-18 — 2.00
P# single, #19 — .75
P# single, #20 — 1.75
P# single, #22 — .75
b. Wide and tall block tagging, 19.5mmx23mm (D press) .40 .25
P# strip of 3, #8 —
P# strip of 3, #18 *37.50*
P# strip of 3, #20 *55.00*
P# strip of 3, #22 *55.00*
P# strip of 5, #2 (B press) *225.00*
P# strip of 5, #8 *125.00*
P# strip of 5, #18 *55.00*
P# strip of 5, #20 *75.00*
P# strip of 5, #22 *150.00*
P# single, #2 (B press) *115.00*
P# single, #8 — *40.00*
P# single, #18 — *40.00*
P# single, #20 — *40.00*
P# single, #22 — *37.50*
c. Inscribed "T" at bottom, *May 23, 1987* .55 .40
P# strip of 3, #1 2.00
P# strip of 5, #1 3.00
P# single, #1 — 2.50
d. Black field of stars instead of blue — —
e. Tagging omitted 10.00
f. Imperf., pair, wide block tagging 10.00
g. Imperf., pair, narrow block tagging 10.00

No. 2115 is known with capitol in bluish black color, apparently from contaminated ink. Specialists often refer to this as "Erie blue."

No. 2115 plate number 2 exists with block tagging similar to that found on No. 2115b. Plate number 2 was used only on the B press and could not be used on either the C or D presses. The similar tagging is an anomaly, and specialists consider it to have been caused by excessive anvil roller pressure on the B press tagging mat, resulting in a tagging ink squeeze.

BOOKLET STAMP
Perf. 10 Horiz.

2116 A1499 22c **blue, red & black** .50 .25
a. Booklet pane of 5 2.50 1.25
Scored perforations 2.50 —

BOOKLET STAMPS

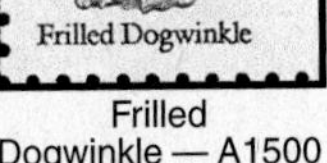

Frilled Dogwinkle — A1500

Reticulated Helmet — A1501

New England Neptune — A1502

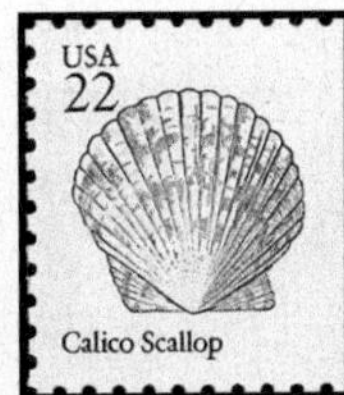

Calico Scallop — A1503

Lightning Whelk — A1504

Designed by Pete Cocci.

ENGRAVED

1985, Apr. 4 **Tagged** ***Perf. 10 on 2 or 3 Sides***

2117 A1500 22c **black & brown** .45 .25
a. Tagging omitted —
2118 A1501 22c **black & multi** .45 .25
2119 A1502 22c **black & brown** .45 .25
a. Tagging omitted —
2120 A1503 22c **black & violet** .45 .25
2121 A1504 22c **black & multi** .45 .25
a. Booklet pane of 10, 2 ea #2117-2121 4.50 3.00
b. As "a," violet omitted on both Nos. 2120 *400.00*
c. As "a," vert. imperf. between *350.00*
d. As "a," imperf. —
e. Strip of 5, Nos. 2117-2121 2.25 —

Eagle and Half Moon A1505

Type I

Type II

Designed by Young & Rubicam.

TYPE I: washed out, dull appearance most evident in the black of the body of the eagle, and the red in the background between the eagle's shoulder and the moon. "$10.75" appears splotchy or grainy (P# 11111).

TYPE II: brighter, more intense colors most evident in the black on the eagle's body, and red in the background. "$10.75" appears smoother, brighter, and less grainy (P# 22222).

PHOTOGRAVURE

Perf. 10 Vert. on 1 or 2 Sides

1985, Apr. 29		**Untagged**	
2122	A1505 $10.75 **multicolored,** type I	20.00	7.50
a.	Booklet pane of 3	60.00	—
b.	Type II, *June 19, 1989*	20.00	10.00
c.	As "b," booklet pane of 3	60.00	—

Coil Plate No. Strips of 3

Beginning with No. 2123, coil plate No. strips of 3 usually sell at the level of strips of 5 minus the face value of two stamps.

TRANSPORTATION ISSUE

School Bus 1920s — A1506

Buckboard 1880s — A1507

Star Route Truck 1910s — A1508

Tricycle 1880s — A1509

Tractor 1920s — A1510

Ambulance 1860s — A1511

Tow Truck 1920s — A1512

Oil Wagon 1890s — A1513

Stutz Bearcat 1933 — A1514

Stanley Steamer 1909 — A1515

Pushcart 1880s — A1516

Iceboat 1880s — A1517

Dog Sled 1920s — A1518

Bread Wagon 1880s — A1519

Designers: 3.4c, 17c, Lou Nolan. 4.9c, 8.5c, 14c, 25c, William H. Bond. 5.5c, David K. Stone. 6c, 8.3c, 10.1c, 12.5c. James Schleyer. 7.1c, 11c, 12c, Ken Dallison.

COIL STAMPS

ENGRAVED

1985-89	**Tagged**	***Perf. 10 Vert.***	
2123	A1506 3.4c **dark bluish green,** *June 8*	.30	.25
	Pair	.50	.50
	P# strip of 5, line, #1-2	.90	
	P# single, #1-2	—	.75
a.	Untagged (Bureau precancel, Non-profit Org. CAR-RT SORT)	.30	.25
	P# strip of 5, line, #1-2	2.75	
	P# single, #1-2	—	2.75
2124	A1507 4.9c **brown black,** *June 21*	.30	.25
	Pair	.50	.50
	P# strip of 5, line, #3-4	.90	
	P# single, #3-4	—	.65
a.	Untagged (Bureau precancel, Non-profit Org.)	.30	.25
	P# strip of 5, line, #1-6	1.25	
	P# single, #1-6	—	1.10
b.	Tagging omitted	—	
2125	A1508 5.5c **deep magenta,** *Nov. 1, 1986*	.30	.25
	Pair	.50	.50
	P# strip of 5, #1	1.35	
	P# single, #1	—	1.10
a.	Untagged (Bureau precancel, Non-profit Org. CAR-RT SORT)	.30	.25
	P# strip of 5, #1	1.30	
	P# strip of 5, #2	1.50	
	P# single, #1	—	1.10
	P# single, #2	—	1.75
b.	Tagging omitted		—

On No. 2125a, both vignette and the precancel inscription were printed from a single printing sleeve.

2126	A1509 6c **red brown,** *May 6*	.35	.25
	Pair	.70	.50
	P# strip of 5, #1	1.50	
	P# single, #1	—	1.00
a.	Untagged (Bureau precancel, Non-profit Org.)	.30	.25
	P# strip of 5, #1	1.50	
	P# strip of 5, #2	3.00	
	P# single, #1	—	1.00
	P# single, #2	—	2.50
b.	As "a," imperf., pair	*175.00*	
c.	Tagging omitted	—	
2127	A1510 7.1c **lake,** *Feb. 6, 1987*	.30	.25
	Pair	.50	.50
	P# strip of 5, #1	1.50	
	P# single, #1	—	1.40
a.	Untagged (Bureau precancel "Non-profit Org." in black), *Feb. 6, 1987*	.30	.25
	P# strip of 5, #1	1.75	
	P# single, #1	—	1.50
b.	Untagged (Bureau precancel "Non-profit 5-Digit Zip + 4" in black), *May 26, 1989*	.30	.25
	P# strip of 5, #1	1.40	
	P# single, #1	—	1.25
c.	As "a," black (precancel) omitted	—	

On Nos. 2127a and 2127b, both the vignette and the precancel inscription were printed from a single printing sleeve.

On No. 2127c, an albino impression of the precancel is present.

2128	A1511 8.3c **green,** *June 21*	.30	.25
	Pair	.50	.50
	P# strip of 5, line, #1-2	1.40	
	P# single, #1-2	—	1.00
a.	Untagged (Bureau precancel, Blk. Rt. CAR-RT SORT)	.30	.25
	P# strip of 5, line, #1-2	1.25	
	P# strip of 5, line, #3-4	2.00	
	P# single, #1-2	—	1.10
	P# single, #3-4	—	3.50

On No. 2231 "Ambulance 1860s" is 18mm long; on No. 2128, 18½mm long.

2129	A1512 8.5c **dark Prussian green,** *Jan. 24, 1987*	.30	.25
	Pair	.50	.50
	P# strip of 5, #1	1.90	
	P# single, #1	—	1.50
a.	Untagged (Bureau precancel, Non-profit Org.)	.30	.25
	P# strip of 5, #1	2.00	
	P# strip of 5, #2	5.75	
	P# single, #1	—	1.75
	P# single, #2	—	5.75
2130	A1513 10.1c **slate blue,** *Apr. 18*	.55	.25
	Pair	1.10	.50
	P# strip of 5, #1	2.50	
	P# single, #1	—	1.60
a.	Untagged (Bureau precancel "Bulk Rate Carrier Route Sort" in red), *June 27, 1988*	.30	.25
	P# strip of 5, #2-3	2.00	
	P# single, #2-3	—	1.50
	Untagged (Bureau precancel "Bulk Rate" and lines in black)	.30	.25
	P# strip of 5, #1-2	2.00	
	P# single, #1-2	—	1.60
b.	As "a," red precancel, imperf, pair	15.00	
	As "a," black precancel, imperf, pair	70.00	
2131	A1514 11c **dark green,** *June 11*	.30	.25
	Pair	.50	.50
	P# strip of 5, line, #1-4	1.40	
	P# single, #1-4	—	1.00
a.	Tagging omitted	*250.00*	
2132	A1515 12c **dark blue,** type I, *Apr. 2*	.35	.25
	Pair	.70	.50
	P# strip of 5, line, #1-2	2.25	
	P# single, #1-2	—	1.25
a.	Untagged, type I (Bureau precancel, PRESORTED FIRST-CLASS), *Apr. 2*	.30	.25
	P# strip of 5, line, #1-2	1.90	
	P# single, #1-2	—	1.50
b.	Untagged, type II, (Bureau precancel, PRESORTED FIRST-CLASS) *1987*	.40	.30
	P# strip of 5, no line, #1	12.50	
	P# single, #1	—	12.50
c.	Tagging omitted, type I, (not Bureau precanceled), *1987*	15.00	

Type II has "Stanley Steamer 1909" ⅓mm shorter (17⅔mm) than No. 2132 (18mm).

2133	A1516 12.5c **olive green,** *Apr. 18*	.35	.25
	Pair	.70	.50
	P# strip of 5, #1	2.50	
	P# strip of 5, #2	3.00	
	P# single, #1	—	2.00
	P# single, #2	—	2.75
a.	Untagged (Bureau precancel, Bulk Rate)	.30	.25

	P# strip of 5, #1	2.00	
	P# strip of 5, #2	2.50	
	P# single, #1	—	1.40
	P# single, #2	—	2.60
b.	As "a," imperf., pair	45.00	

All No. 2133 from plate 1 and some No. 2133a from plate 1 were printed with luminescent ink that is orange under long wave UV light.

2134 A1517	14c **sky blue,** type I, *Mar. 23*	.30	.25
	Pair	.60	.50
	P# strip of 5, line, #1-4	2.00	
	P# single, #1-4	—	1.50
a.	Imperf., pair	75.00	
b.	Type II, *Sept. 30, 1986*	.30	.25
	P# strip of 5, no line, #2	2.60	
	P# single, #2	—	2.40
c.	Tagging omitted, type I	35.00	—

Type II design is ¼mm narrower (17¼mm) than the original stamp (17½mm) and has block tagging. No. 2134 has overall tagging.

2135 A1518	17c **bright blue,** *Aug. 20, 1986*	.75	.25
	Pair	1.50	.50
	P# strip of 5, #2	5.50	
	P# single, #2	—	1.50
a.	Imperf., pair	*300.00*	
2136 A1519	25c **orange brown,** *Nov. 22, 1986*	.50	.25
	Pair	1.00	.50
	P# strip of 5, #1-5	3.00	
	P# single, #1	—	1.00
	P# single, #2-4	—	.55
	P# single, #5	—	2.25
a.	Imperf., pair	10.00	
b.	Pair, imperf. between	*525.00*	
c.	Tagging omitted	*50.00*	
d.	As "a," tagging omitted	—	
	Nos. 2123-2136 (14)	5.25	3.50

Precancellations on Nos. 2125a, 2127a do not have lines. Precancellation on No. 2129a is in red. See No. 2231.

BLACK HERITAGE SERIES

Mary McLeod Bethune (1875-1955), Educator — A1520

Designed by Jerry Pinkney from a photograph.

Printed by American Bank Note Company.

PHOTOGRAVURE

Plates of 200 in four panes of 50.

1985, Mar. 5 **Tagged** ***Perf. 11***

2137 A1520	22c **multicolored**	.60	.25
	P# block of 4, 6#+A	3.25	—
	Zip block of 4	2.50	—
	Pane of 50	30.00	
a.	Tagging omitted	—	—

AMERICAN FOLK ART SERIES
Duck Decoys

Broadbill A1521

Mallard A1522

Canvasback A1523

Redhead A1524

Designed by Stevan Dohanos.

Printed by American Bank Note Company.

PHOTOGRAVURE

Plates of 200 in four panes of 50.

1985, Mar. 22 **Tagged** ***Perf. 11***

2138 A1521	22c **multicolored**	.90	.25
2139 A1522	22c **multicolored**	.90	.25
2140 A1523	22c **multicolored**	.90	.25
2141 A1524	22c **multicolored**	.90	.25
a.	Block of 4, #2138-2141	3.60	2.75
	P# block of 4, 5#+A	4.00	—
	Zip block of 4	3.75	—
	Pane of 50	45.00	
b.	As "a," tagging omitted	—	

WINTER SPECIAL OLYMPICS

Ice Skater, Emblem, Skier — A1525

Designed by Jeff Carnell.

PHOTOGRAVURE

Plates of 160 in four panes of 40.

1985, Mar. 25 **Tagged** ***Perf. 11***

2142 A1525	22c **multicolored**	.50	.25
	P# block of 4, 6#	2.75	—
	Zip block of 4	2.10	—
	Pane of 40	25.00	
a.	Vert. pair, imperf. horiz.	*300.00*	

LOVE

A1526

Designed by Corita Kent.

PHOTOGRAVURE

Plates of 200 in four panes of 50.

1985, Apr. 17 **Tagged** ***Perf. 11***

2143 A1526	22c **multicolored**	.45	.25
	P# block of 4, 6#	2.00	—
	Zip block of 4	1.90	—
	Pane of 50	22.50	
a.	Imperf., pair	*800.00*	

RURAL ELECTRIFICATION ADMINISTRATION

REA Power Lines, Farmland A1527

Designed by Howard Koslow.

PHOTOGRAVURE & ENGRAVED (Combination Press)

Plates of 230 in panes of 50.

1985, May 11 **Tagged** ***Perf. 11***

2144 A1527	22c **multicolored**	.50	.25
	P# block of 20, 5-10 #, 1-2 Zip, 1-2 Copyright	16.00	—
	Pane of 50	25.00	
a.	Vert. pair, imperf between	—	

See Combination Press note after No. 1703.

AMERIPEX '86

US No. 134 — A1528

Designed by Richard Sheaff.

LITHOGRAPHED & ENGRAVED

Plates of 192 in four panes of 48

1985, May 25 **Tagged** ***Perf. 11***

2145 A1528	22c **multicolored**	.45	.25
	P# block of 4, 3#	2.10	—
	Zip block of 4	1.90	—
	Pane of 48	21.50	
a.	Red, black & blue (engr.) omitted	*110.00*	
b.	Red & black omitted	*1,250.*	
c.	Red omitted	*1,750.*	
d.	Black missing (PS)	450.00	

ABIGAIL ADAMS (1744-1818)

A1529

Designed by Bart Forbes.

PHOTOGRAVURE

Plates of 200 in four panes of 50.

1985, June 14 **Tagged** ***Perf. 11***

2146 A1529	22c **multicolored**	.45	.25
	P# block of 4, 4#	2.10	—
	Zip block of 4	1.90	—
	Pane of 50	22.50	
a.	Imperf., pair	*200.00*	

FREDERIC AUGUSTE BARTHOLDI (1834-1904)

Architect and Sculptor, Statue of Liberty A1530

Designed by Howard Paine from paintings by Jose Frappa and James Dean.

LITHOGRAPHED & ENGRAVED
Plates of 200 in four panes of 50.

1985, July 18 **Tagged** ***Perf. 11***

2147	A1530 22c **multicolored**	.45	.25
	P# block of 4, 5#	2.10	—
	Zip block of 4	1.90	—
	Pane of 50	22.50	

Examples of No. 2147 exist with most, but not all, of the engraved black omitted.

George Washington, Washington Monument — A1532

Sealed Envelopes — A1533

Designed by Thomas Szumowski (#2149) based on a portrait by Gilbert Stuart, and Richard Sheaff (#2150).

COIL STAMPS
PHOTOGRAVURE

1985 ***Perf. 10 Vertically***

2149	A1532 18c **multicolored,** low gloss gum, *Nov. 6*	.40	.25
	Pair	.80	.50
	P# strip of 5, #1112	2.75	
	P# strip of 5, #3333	3.00	
	P# single, #1112	—	2.00
	P# single, #3333	—	3.00
a.	Untagged (Bureau precanceled), low gloss gum	.35	.35
	P# strip of 5, #11121	4.00	
	P# strip of 5, #33333	2.75	
	P# single, #11121	—	4.00
	P# single, #33333	—	1.50
	Dull gum	.35	
	P# strip of 5, #33333	4.00	
	P# strip of 5, #43444	5.00	
	P# single, #43444	—	5.00
b.	Imperf., pair	*750.00*	
c.	As "a," imperf., pair	*575.00*	
d.	Tagging omitted (not Bureau precanceled)	75.00	—
e.	As "a," tagged (error), dull gum	2.00	1.75
	Pair	4.00	3.75
	P# strip of 5, #33333	*45.00*	
	P# single, #33333	—	*10.00*
	Low gloss gum	*2.00*	
	P# strip of 5, #33333	*150.00*	
	P# single, #33333	—	*35.00*
2150	A1533 21.1c **multicolored,** *Oct. 22*	.40	.25
	Pair	.80	.50
	P# strip of 5, #111111	3.00	
	P# strip of 5, #111121	3.25	
	P# single, #111111	—	2.25
	P# single, #111121	—	3.50
a.	Untagged (Bureau Precancel)	.40	.40
	Pair	.80	.80
	P# strip of 5, #111111	3.25	
	P# strip of 5, #111121	3.50	
	P# single, #111111	—	2.50
	P# single, #111121	—	2.75
b.	As "a," tagged (error)	.50	.50
	Pair	1.00	1.00
	P# strip of 5, #111111	3.25	
	P# strip of 5, #111121	4.25	
	P# single, #111111	—	*3.00*
	P# single, #111121	—	3.50
c.	Imperf., pair	—	

Precancellations on Nos. 2149a ("PRESORTED FIRST-CLASS"), 2150a and 2150b ("ZIP+4") do not have lines.

No. 2150b shows obvious tagging. All No. 2150a P#111121 and some P#111111 show a very faint block tagging due to contamination of a lacquer coating that was applied to the face of the stamps to keep the ink from smearing.

KOREAN WAR VETERANS

American Troops in Korea A1535

Designed by Richard Sheaff from a photograph by David D. Duncan.

ENGRAVED
Plates of 200 in four panes of 50.

1985, July 26 **Tagged** ***Perf. 11***

2152	A1535 22c **gray green & rose red**	.45	.25
	P# block of 4	2.50	—
	Zip block of 4	1.90	—
	Pane of 50	22.50	

SOCIAL SECURITY ACT, 50th ANNIV.

Men, Women, Children, Corinthian Columns A1536

Designed by Robert Brangwynne.

Printed by American Bank Note Company.

PHOTOGRAVURE
Plates of 200 in four panes of 50.

1985, Aug. 14 **Tagged** ***Perf. 11***

2153	A1536 22c **deep & light blue**	.45	.25
	P# block of 4, 2#+A	2.10	—
	Zip block of 4	1.90	—
	Pane of 50	22.50	

WORLD WAR I VETERANS

The Battle of Marne, France A1537

Designed by Richard Sheaff from Harvey Dunn's charcoal drawing.

ENGRAVED
Plates of 200 in four panes of 50.

1985, Aug. 26 **Tagged** ***Perf. 11***

2154	A1537 22c **gray green & rose red**	.45	.25
	P# block of 4	2.50	—
	Zip block of 4	1.90	—
	Pane of 50	22.50	
a.	Red missing (PS)	*300.00*	
b.	Tagging omitted	—	—

HORSES

Quarter Horse A1538

Morgan A1539

Saddlebred A1540

Appaloosa A1541

Designed by Roy Andersen.

PHOTOGRAVURE
Plates of 160 in four panes of 40.

1985, Sept. 25 **Tagged** ***Perf. 11***

2155	A1538 22c **multicolored**	1.10	.25
2156	A1539 22c **multicolored**	1.10	.25
2157	A1540 22c **multicolored**	1.10	.25
2158	A1541 22c **multicolored**	1.10	.25
a.	Block of 4, #2155-2158	4.40	4.00
	P# block of 4, 5#	6.00	—
	Zip block of 4	4.75	—
	Pane of 40	44.00	

PUBLIC EDUCATION IN AMERICA

Quill Pen, Apple, Spectacles, Penmanship Quiz — A1542

Designed by Uldis Purins.

Printed by American Bank Note Company

PHOTOGRAVURE
Plates of 200 in four panes of 50.

1985, Oct. 1 **Tagged** ***Perf. 11***

2159	A1542 22c **multicolored**	.45	.25
	P# block of 4, 5#+A	2.75	—
	Zip block of 4	1.85	—
	Pane of 50	22.50	
a.	Tagging omitted		—

INTERNATIONAL YOUTH YEAR

YMCA Youth Camping, Cent. A1543

Boy Scouts, 75th Anniv. A1544

Big Brothers / Big Sisters Federation, 40th Anniv. A1545

Camp Fire Inc., 75th Anniv. A1546

Designed by Dennis Luzak.

Printed by American Bank Note Company.

PHOTOGRAVURE

Plates of 200 in four panes of 50.

1985, Oct. 7	**Tagged**	***Perf. 11***	
2160	A1543 22c **multicolored**	.70	.25
2161	A1544 22c **multicolored**	.70	.25
2162	A1545 22c **multicolored**	.70	.25
2163	A1546 22c **multicolored**	.70	.25
a.	Block of 4, #2160-2163	3.00	2.25
	P# block of 4, 5#+A	4.00	—
	Zip block of 4	3.25	—
	Pane of 50	35.00	

HELP END HUNGER

Youths and Elderly Suffering from Malnutrition A1547

Designed by Jerry Pinkney.

Printed by the American Bank Note Company.

PHOTOGRAVURE

Plates of 200 in four panes of 50.

1985, Oct. 15	**Tagged**	***Perf. 11***	
2164	A1547 22c **multicolored**	.45	.25
	P# block of 4, 5#+A	2.25	—
	Zip block of 4	1.90	—
	Pane of 50	22.50	
a.	Tagging omitted		—

CHRISTMAS

Genoa Madonna, Enameled Terra-Cotta by Luca Della Robbia (1400-1482) — A1548

Poinsettia Plants A1549

Designed by Bradbury Thompson (No. 2165) and James Dean (No. 2166).

PHOTOGRAVURE

Plates of 200 in panes of 50.

1985, Oct. 30	**Tagged**	***Perf. 11***	
2165	A1548 22c **multicolored**	.45	.25
	P# block of 4, 4#	2.00	—
	Zip block of 4	1.90	—
	Pane of 50	22.50	
a.	Imperf., pair	*55.00*	
b.	Tagging omitted		—
2166	A1549 22c **multicolored**	.45	.25
	P# block of 4, 5#	2.00	—
	Zip block of 4	1.90	—
	Pane of 50	22.50	
	Vert. pair with full horiz. gutter between	—	
a.	Imperf., pair	*50.00*	

ARKANSAS STATEHOOD, 150th ANNIV.

Old State House, Little Rock — A1550

Designed by Roger Carlisle.

Printed by the American Bank Note Company

PHOTOGRAVURE

Plates of 200 in four panes of 50.

1986, Jan. 3	**Tagged**	***Perf. 11***	
2167	A1550 22c **multicolored**	.65	.25
	P# block of 4, 6#+A	3.25	—
	Zip block of 4	2.75	—
	Pane of 50	32.50	
a.	Vert. pair, imperf. horiz.	*500.00*	
b.	Tagging omitted		—

Marginal Inscriptions

Beginning with the Luis Munoz Marin issue a number of stamps include a descriptive inscription in the selvage.

GREAT AMERICANS ISSUE

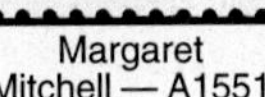

Margaret Mitchell — A1551

Mary Lyon — A1552

Designed by Ron Adair.

Printed by the Bureau of Engraving & Printing.

ENGRAVED

Panes of 100 (#2168-2193, 2195), Panes of 20 (#2194, 2196)

Perf. 11, 11½x11 (#2185), 11.2x11.1 (#2179)

1986-94		**Tagged**		
2168	A1551	1c **brownish vermilion,** large block tagging, *June 30*	.30	.25
		On cover		2.00
		P# block of 4	.50	—
		Zip block of 4	.50	—
		Pane of 100	18.00	
a.		Tagging omitted	*15.00*	
b.		1c **red brown**	.30	.30
		Pane of 100	30.00	
2169	A1552	2c **bright blue,** large block tagging, *Feb. 28, 1987*	.30	.25
		On cover		2.00
		P# block of 4	.50	—
		Zip block of 4	.50	—
		Pane of 100	20.00	
a.		Untagged	.40	.25
		P# block of 4	1.75	—
		Zip block of 4	1.60	—
		Pane of 100	40.00	
b.		Tagging omitted	—	—

The tagging omitted error No. 2169b appeared before No. 2169a was issued. Plate blocks from plate 1 are the error if untagged. No. 2169a is from plate 3. Other blocks and singles can be distinguished if se-tenant with tagged stamps. No. 2169a and 2169b also can be distinguished using a long wave ultraviolet light. The paper of No. 2169b will appear brownish, while the paper of No. 2169a appears almost white.

Paul Dudley White MD — A1553

Father Flanagan — A1554

Designed by Christopher Calle.

Printed by the Bureau of Engraving & Printing.

2170	A1553	3c **bright blue,** large block tagging, dull gum, *Sept. 15*	.30	.25
		On cover		2.00
		P# block of 4	.50	—
		Zip block of 4	.50	—
		Pane of 100	22.50	
a.		Untagged, dull gum, *1994*	.30	.25
		P# block of 4	1.00	—
		Zip block of 4	1.00	—
		Pane of 100	30.00	
		Shiny gum, *1994*	.35	.25
		P# block of 4	1.50	—
		Zip block of 4	1.40	—
		Pane of 100	35.00	
b.		Tagging omitted	*75.00*	—

No. 2170a with dull gum can be distinguished from No. 2170a with shiny gum, because the paper on the latter is significantly whiter in color.

The tagging omitted error No. 2170b appeared before No. 2170a was issued. Plate blocks from plates 2 and 3 are the error if untagged. No. 2170a is from plate 4. Other blocks and singles are indistiguishable, unless se-tenant with tagged stamps.

2171	A1554	4c **blue violet,** large block tagging, *July 14*	.30	.25
		On cover		4.00
		P# block of 4	.60	—
		Zip block of 4	.50	—
		Pane of 100	22.50	
a.		4c **grayish violet,** untagged	.25	.25
		P# block of 4	1.00	—
		Zip block of 4	1.00	—
		Pane of 100	22.50	
b.		4c **deep grayish blue,** untagged, *1993*	.35	.25
		P# block of 4	1.50	—
		Zip block of 4	1.40	—
		Pane of 100	35.00	
c.		As No. 2171, tagging omitted		—
d.		All color missing (EP)		—

No. 2171c was found on a USPS souvenir page with first day cancel. No. 2171a and 2171b were not available on the first day of issue.

No. 2171d has an albino impression, and it also may be collected with a fully or partially printed stamp.

Hugo L. Black — A1555

Louis Munoz Marin — A1556

Designers: No. 2172, Christopher Calle. No. 2173, Juan Maldonado.

Printed by the Bureau of Engraving & Printing.

2172	A1555	5c **dark olive green,** large block tagging, *Feb. 27*	.30	.25
		On cover		2.00
		P# block of 4	1.00	—
		Zip block of 4	1.00	—
		Pane of 100	22.50	
a.		As No. 2172, tagging omitted	*150.00*	—
b.		5c **light olive green,** large block tagging	.35	.25
		P# block of 4	1.50	—
		Zip block of 4	1.40	—
		Pane of 100	35.00	
2173	A1556	5c **carmine,** overall tagging, *Feb. 18, 1990*	.30	.25
		On cover		2.00
		P# block of 4	1.25	—
		P# zip block of 4	1.00	—
		Zip block of 4	1.00	—
		Pane of 100	22.50	
a.		Untagged, *1991*	.30	.25
		P# block of 4	1.00	—
		P# zip block of 4	1.00	—
		Zip block of 4	1.00	—
		Pane of 100	25.00	
b.		Tagging omitted	—	—

The tagging omitted error No. 2173b appeared before No. 2173a was issued. Plate blocks from plate 1 are the error if untagged. No. 2173a is from plate 2. Other blocks and singles are indistinguishable, unless se-tenant with tagged stamps.

Red Cloud — A1557

Julia Ward Howe — A1558

Designers: 10c, Robert Anderson. 14c, Ward Brackett.

Printed by the Bureau of Engraving & Printing.

2175 A1557 10c **lake,** large block tagging, dull gum, *Aug. 15, 1987* .30 .25
On cover 2.00
P# block of 4 1.10 —
Zip block of 4 1.00 —
Pane of 100 25.00
a. Overall tagging, dull gum, *1990* 1.35 .25
P# block of 4 11.00 —
Zip block of 4 5.50 —
Pane of 100 135.00
b. Tagging omitted *25.00*
c. Prephosphored coated paper with surface tagging showing a solid appearance, dull gum, *1991* 1.50 .25
P# block of 4 7.50 —
Zip block of 4 6.25 —
Pane of 100 150.00
d. Prephosphored uncoated paper with embedded tagging showing a mottled appearance, shiny gum, *1993* 1.50 .25
P# block of 4 7.50 —
Zip block of 4 6.25 —
Pane of 100 150.00
e. 10c **carmine,** prephosphored uncoated paper with embedded tagging showing a mottled appearance, shiny gum, *1994* .80 .25
P# block of 4 6.00 —
Zip block of 4 3.00 —
Pane of 100 80.00
f. As "c," all color omitted *125.00*

No. 2175f may be collected se-tenant with a partially printed stamp or longer vertical strip. Stamps not se-tenant with a partially printed stamp are identified by a light setoff on the gum side.

2176 A1558 14c **crimson,** large block tagging, *Feb. 12, 1987* .30 .25
On cover 2.00
P# block of 4 1.50 —
Zip block of 4 1.20 —
Pane of 100 30.00
a. Tagging omitted —

Buffalo Bill Cody — A1559

Belva Ann Lockwood — A1560

Designers: 15c, Jack Rosenthal. 17c, Christopher Calle.

Printed by the Bureau of Engraving & Printing.

2177 A1559 15c **claret,** large block tagging, *June 6, 1988* 1.00 .25
On cover 2.00
P# block of 4 12.00 —
Zip block of 4 4.25 —
Pane of 100 100.00
a. Overall tagging, *1990* .30 —
P# block of 4 3.25 —
Zip block of 4 1.20 —
Pane of 100 30.00
b. Prephosphored coated paper with surface tagging showing a solid appearance .60 —
P# block of 4 3.75 —
Zip block of 4 2.40 —
Pane of 100 60.00
c. Tagging omitted *15.00* —
d. All color omitted *200.00*

No. 2177d resulted from partially printed panes. It must be collected se-tenant with a partially printed stamp or in a longer horizontal strip showing error stamps plus partially/completely printed stamps.

2178 A1560 17c **dull blue green,** large block tagging, *June 18* .35 .25
On cover 2.00
P# block of 4 2.00 —
Zip block of 4 1.40 —
Pane of 100 35.00
Pair with full horizontal gutter between —
a. Tagging omitted *15.00*

Virginia Apgar — A1561

Chester Carlson — A1562

Designers: 20c, Robert Anderson. 21c, Susan Sanford.

Printed by: 20c, Banknote Corporation of America. 21c, Bureau of Engraving & Printing.

2179 A1561 20c **red brown,** prephosphored coated paper with surface tagging showing a grainy solid appearance, *Oct. 24, 1994* .40 .25
On cover 2.00
P# block of 4, 1#+B 2.00 —
Pane of 100 40.00
a. 20c **orange brown,** prephosphored coated paper with surface tagging showing a grainy solid appearance .75 .25
P# block of 4, 1#+B 4.00 —
Pane of 100 75.00
b. 20c **bright red brown,** prephosphored coated paper with surface tagging showing a grainy solid appearance 1.25 .25
P# block of 4, 1#+B 8.50 —
Pane of 100 125.00

2180 A1562 21c **blue violet,** large block tagging, *Oct. 21, 1988* .45 .25
On cover 4.00
P# block of 4 2.50 —
Zip block of 4 1.65 —
Pane of 100 45.00
a. Tagging omitted —

No. 2180 is known with worn tagging mats on which horizontal untagged areas have taggant giving the appearance of vertical band tagging.

Mary Cassatt — A1563

Jack London — A1564

Designers: 23c, Dennis Lyall. 25c, Richard Sparks.

Printed by the Bureau of Engraving & Printing.

2181 A1563 23c **purple,** large block tagging, dull gum, *Nov. 4, 1988* .45 .25
On cover 2.00
P# block of 4 2.50 —
Zip block of 4 1.90 —
Pane of 100 45.00
a. Overall tagging, dull gum .75 —
P# block of 4 6.50 —
Zip block of 4 3.25 —
Pane of 100 75.00
b. Prephosphored coated paper with surface tagging showing a solid appearance, dull gum 1.00 —
P# block of 4 6.50 —
Zip block of 4 4.25 —
Pane of 100 100.00
c. Prephosphored uncoated paper with embedded tagging showing a mottled appearance, shiny gum 1.50 .25
P# block of 4 8.50 —
Zip block of 4 6.25 —
Pane of 100 150.00
d. Tagging omitted *7.50*

2182 A1564 25c **blue,** large block tagging, *Jan. 11* .50 .25
On cover 2.00
International surface postcard 10.00
First-class Mexico letter 15.00
P# block of 4 2.75 —
Zip block of 4 2.00 —
Pane of 100 50.00
a. Booklet pane of 10, perf. 11¼, *May 3, 1988* 5.00 3.75
b. As #2182, tagging omitted — —
c. As "a," tagging omitted —
d. Horiz. pair, imperf between *750.00*
e. As "a," all color omitted on right stamps *1,250.*
f. As No. 2182 (sheet stamp), vert. pair, bottom stamp all color omitted —
g. As "a," tagging omitted on two stamps —
h. As "a," all color omitted on left stamps *1,250.*

No. 2182f may be collected se-tenant with a partially printed stamp or longer vertical strip.

Counterfeits exist of No. 2182. See the Postal Counterfeits section of this catalog.

See Nos. 2197, 2197a.

Sitting Bull — A1565

Earl Warren — A1566

Designers: 28c, Robert Anderson. 29c, Christopher Calle.

Printed by: No. 2183, Bureau of Engraving & Printing. No. 2184, Canadian Bank Note Co. for Stamp Venturers.

2183 A1565 28c **myrtle green,** large block tagging, *Sept. 14, 1989* .65 .35
On cover 5.00
International surface postcard 15.00
P# block of 4 3.75 —
Zip block of 4 2.60 —
Pane of 100 65.00

2184 A1566 29c **blue,** prephosphored uncoated paper with embedded tagging showing a mottled appearance, *Mar. 9, 1992* .70 .25
On cover 4.00
P# block of 4, #+S 4.00 —
Zip block of 4 3.00 —
Pane of 100 70.00

Thomas Jefferson — A1567

Dennis Chavez — A1568

Designed by Christopher Calle.

Printed by: No. 2185, Stamp Venturers. 2186, Canadian Bank Note Co. for Stamp Venturers.

2185 A1567 29c **indigo,** prephosphored coated paper with surface tagging showing a solid appearance, *Apr. 13, 1993* .65 .25
On cover 4.00
P# block of 4, 1#+S 3.50 —
Zip block of 4 2.70 —
Pane of 100 65.00

2186 A1568 35c **black,** prephosphored uncoated paper with embedded tagging showing a mottled appearance, *Apr. 3, 1991* .75 .25
On cover 4.00
Double-weight Mexco letter 15.00
International surface postcard 10.00
First-class Mexico postcard 8.00
P# block of 4, #+S 4.00 —
Zip block of 4 3.00 —
Pane of 100 75.00

Claire Chennault — A1569

Harvey Cushing MD — A1570

Designers: 40c, Christopher Calle. 45c, Bradbury Thompson.

Printed by: 40c, 45c, Bureau of Engraving & Printing.

2187 A1569 40c **dark blue,** overall tagging, dull gum, *Sept. 6, 1990* .85 .25
On cover 4.00
International surface postcard 15.00
International printed matter/packets 25.00
First-class Canada letter 8.00
International airmail postcard 10.00
First-class Canada postcard 8.00
P# block of 4 5.00 —
Zip block of 4 3.50 —
Pane of 100 85.00
a. Prephosphored coated paper with surface tagging, dull gum 1.25 .35
P# block of 4 6.50 —
Zip block of 4 5.25 —
Pane of 100 125.00
Low gloss gum, *1998* 1.25 .35
P# block of 4 6.50 —
Zip block of 4 5.25 —
Pane of 100 125.00
c. Prephosphored uncoated paper with embedded tagging showing a mottled appearance, shiny gum, *1994* 1.00 .25
P# block of 4 10.00 —
Zip block of 4 4.25 —
Pane of 100 100.00
d. Tagging omitted *75.00*

No. 2187a exists on two types of surface-tagged paper that exhibit either a solid appearance (dull gum) or a grainy solid appearance (low gloss gum).

2188 A1570 45c **bright blue,** large block tagging, *June 17, 1988* 1.00 .25
On cover 4.00
Double-weight first-class letter 5.00
International air letter 15.00

Double-weight first-class letter Mexico 15.00
Certificate of mailing 25.00
Single franking on aerogramme 15.00
P# block of 4 5.00 —
Zip block of 4 4.00 —
Pane of 100 100.00
a. 45c **blue,** overall tagging, *1990* 2.75 .25
P# block of 4 27.50 —
Zip block of 4 12.00 —
Pane of 100 275.00
b. Tagging omitted *17.50*

The blue on No. 2188a is noticeably lighter than on No. 2188. Color variety specialists, as well as tagging specialists, will want to consider it as a second variety of this stamp.

Almost all examples of No. 2188a are in the grade of fine or fine-very fine. Values are for stamps in the grade of fine-very fine.

Hubert H. Humphrey — A1571

John Harvard — A1572

Designers: 52c, John Berkey. 56c, Robert Anderson.

Printed by the Bureau of Engraving & Printing.

2189 A1571 52c **purple,** prephosphored coated paper with surface tagging showing a solid appearance, dull gum, *June 3, 1991* 1.10 .25
On cover 4.00
Double-weight first-class letter 5.00
Double-weight first-class letter Canada 10.00
P# block of 4 7.00 —
Zip block of 4 4.50 —
Pane of 100 110.00
a. Prephosphored uncoated paper with embedded tagging showing a mottled appearance, shiny gum, *1993* 1.25 —
P# block of 4 10.00 —
Zip block of 4 5.50 —
Pane of 100 125.00

Selvage inscriptions from the original printing of No. 2189 from plate 1 show the incorrect dates for Humphrey's vice-presidential term ("1964 to 1968"). Corrected plate 1 and plate 2 printings (No. 2189a) show the dates correctly as 1965 to 1969. Values for the two varieties of inscription blocks of 6 are approximately the same: $10 each.

2190 A1572 56c **scarlet,** large block tagging, *Sept. 3* 1.20 .25
On cover 8.00
P# block of 4 5.25 —
Zip block of 4 4.80 —
Pane of 100 120.00
a. Tagging omitted —

No. 2190 known with a "tagging spill" making stamp appear overall tagged.

H.H. Hap Arnold — A1573

Wendell Willkie — A1574

Designed by Christopher Calle.

Printed by the Bureau of Engraving & Printing.

2191 A1573 65c **dark blue,** large block tagging, *Nov. 5, 1988* 1.30 .25
On cover 8.00
P# block of 4 6.50 —
Zip block of 4 5.20 —
Pane of 100 130.00
a. Tagging omitted *22.50*

2192 A1574 75c **deep magenta,** prephosphored coated paper with surface tagging showing a solid appearance, dull gum, *Feb. 16, 1992* 1.75 .25
On cover 8.00
P# block of 4 8.00 —
Zip block of 4 7.25 —
Pane of 100 175.00
a. Prephosphored uncoated paper with embedded tagging showing a mottled appearance, shiny gum 1.90 —
P# block of 4 10.00 —
Zip block of 4 7.75 —
Pane of 100 190.00

Bernard Revel — A1575

Johns Hopkins — A1576

"Lipstick on Shirt Front" double gouge plate flaw

Designers: No. 2193, Tom Broad. No. 2194, Bradbury Thompson.

Printed by the Bureau of Engraving & Printing.

2193 A1575 $1 **dark Prussian green,** large block tagging, *Sept. 23* 3.00 .50
On cover 10.00
P# block of 4 13.00 —
Zip block of 4 12.00 —
Pane of 100 300.00
a. All color omitted —
b. Tagging omitted *75.00*

No. 2193a must be collected se-tenant vertically with partially printed stamps.

2194 A1576 $1 **intense deep blue,** large block tagging, dull gum, *June 7, 1989* 2.25 .50
On cover 5.00
P# block of 4 10.00 —
Pane of 20 48.00
Double gouge plate flaw ("Lipstick on Shirt Front"), (pos. 6 on one plate #1 pane) *375.00*
P# block of 4, UL, plate flaw at LL *425.00*
Pane of 20, plate flaw at pos. 6 *575.00*
b. $1 **deep blue,** overall tagging, dull gum, *1990* 2.50 .50
P# block of 4 13.00 —
Pane of 20 52.50
c. Tagging omitted *17.50*
d. $1 **dark blue,** prephosphored coated paper with surface tagging showing a solid appearance, dull gum, *1992* 2.50 .50
P# block of 4 13.00 —
Pane of 20 52.50
e. $1 **blue,** prephosphored uncoated paper with embedded tagging showing a mottled appearance, shiny gum, *1993* 2.75 .60
P# block of 4 14.00 —
Pane of 20 58.00
f. $1 **blue,** prephosphored coated paper with surface tagging showing a grainy solid appearance, low gloss gum, *1998* 2.75 .50
P# block of 4 14.00 —
Pane of 20 58.00

No. 2194 issued in pane of 20 (see No. 2196.)

The intense deep blue of No. 2194 is much deeper than the deep blue and dark blue of the other $1 varieties.

The "Lipstick on Shirt Front" flaw was discovered during production and the position was repaired. Very few have been found.

William Jennings Bryan — A1577

Bret Harte — A1578

Designers: $2, Tom Broad. $5, Arthur Lidov.

Printed by the Bureau of Engraving & Printing.

2195 A1577 $2 **bright violet,** large block tagging, *Mar. 19* 4.50 .50
On cover 10.00
First-class certified, return receipt 20.00
P# block of 4 20.00 —
Zip block of 4 17.00 —
Pane of 100 450.00
a. Tagging omitted *300.00 100.00*

No. 2195 is known with worn tagging mats on which horizontal untagged areas have taggant giving the appearance of vertical band tagging.

2196 A1578 $5 **copper red,** large block tagging, *Aug. 25, 1987* 9.00 1.00
On cover 10.00
Global Priority mail flat rate (small) 40.00
P# block of 4 42.50 —
Pane of 20 185.00
a. Tagging omitted *225.00* —
b. Prephosphored coated paper with surface tagging showing a solid appearance, *1992* 11.00 —
P# block of 4 45.00 —
Pane of 20 220.00
Nos. 2168-2196 (28) 34.25 8.60

Booklet Stamp

Perf. 10 on 2 or 3 Sides

2197 A1564 25c **blue,** large block tagging, *May 3, 1988* .55 .25
On cover 2.00
a. Booklet pane of 6 3.30 2.50
b. Tagging omitted 20.00
c. As "b," booklet pane of 6 150.00

UNITED STATES - SWEDEN STAMP COLLECTING

Handstamped Cover, Philatelic Memorabilia A1581

Boy Examining Stamp Collection A1582

No. 836 Under Magnifying Glass, Sweden Nos. 268, 271 — A1583

1986 Presidents Miniature Sheet on First Day Cover — A1584

Designed by Richard Sheaff and Eva Jern (No. 2200).

BOOKLET STAMPS
LITHOGRAPHED & ENGRAVED
Perf. 10 Vert. on 1 or 2 Sides

1986, Jan. 23 **Tagged**

2198	A1581 22c **multicolored**		.45	.25
2199	A1582 22c **multicolored**		.45	.25
2200	A1583 22c **multicolored**		.45	.25
2201	A1584 22c **multicolored**		.45	.25
	a.	Bklt. pane of 4, #2198-2201	2.00	1.75
	b.	As "a," black omitted on Nos. 2198, 2201	50.00	—
	c.	As "a," blue (litho.) omitted on Nos. 2198-2200	*1,500.*	
	d.	As "a," buff (litho.) omitted	—	
	e.	As "a," tagging omitted	—	

See Sweden Nos. 1585-1588.

LOVE ISSUE

A1585

Designed by Saul Mandel.

Plates of 200 in four panes of 50.
PHOTOGRAVURE

1986, Jan. 30 **Tagged** ***Perf. 11***

2202	A1585 22c **multicolored**	.55	.25
	P# block of 4, 5#	2.50	—
	Zip block of 4	2.25	—
	Pane of 50	27.50	
	Pair with full vert. gutter btwn.	200.00	
a.	Tagging omitted	*325.00*	

BLACK HERITAGE SERIES

Sojourner Truth (c. 1797-1883), Human Rights Activist — A1586

Designed by Jerry Pinkney.

Printed by American Bank Note Co.

Plates of 200 in four panes of 50
PHOTOGRAVURE

1986, Feb. 4 **Tagged** ***Perf. 11***

2203	A1586 22c **multicolored**	.55	.25
	P# block of 4, 6#+A	2.75	—
	Zip block of 4	2.25	—
	Pane of 50	27.50	
a.	Tagging omitted	—	

REPUBLIC OF TEXAS, 150th ANNIV.

San Jacinto, 1836, Texas State Flag and Silver Spur — A1587

Designed by Don Adair.

Printed by the American Bank Note Co.

Plates of 200 in four panes of 50.
PHOTOGRAVURE

1986, Mar. 2 **Tagged** ***Perf. 11***

2204	A1587 22c **dark blue, dark red & grayish black**	.50	.25
	P# block of 4, 3#+A	2.50	—
	Zip block of 4	2.25	—
	Pane of 50	25.00	
a.	Horiz. pair, imperf. vert.	*600.00*	
b.	Dark red omitted	*1,750.*	
c.	Dark blue omitted	*5,000.*	

FISH

Muskellunge — A1588

Atlantic Cod A1589

Largemouth Bass — A1590

Bluefin Tuna A1591

Catfish A1592

Designed by Chuck Ripper.

BOOKLET STAMPS
PHOTOGRAVURE
Perf. 10 Horiz. on 1 or 2 Sides

1986, Mar. 21 **Tagged**

2205	A1588 22c **multicolored**	.90	.25
2206	A1589 22c **multicolored**	.90	.25
2207	A1590 22c **multicolored**	.90	.25
2208	A1591 22c **multicolored**	.90	.25
2209	A1592 22c **multicolored**	.90	.25
a.	Bklt. pane of 5, #2205-2209	4.50	2.75

The magenta used to print this issue is extremely fugitive. Dangerous fakes purported to be magenta omitted exist. No genuine examples are known. Panes apparently lacking red must be certified, and examples presently with certificates should be recertified.

PUBLIC HOSPITALS

A1593

Designed by Uldis Purins.

Printed by the American Bank Note Co.

PHOTOGRAVURE
Plates of 200 in four panes of 50.

1986, Apr. 11 **Tagged** ***Perf. 11***

2210	A1593 22c **multicolored**	.45	.25
	P# block of 4, 5#+A	2.00	—
	Zip block of 4	1.90	—
	Pane of 50	22.50	
a.	Vert. pair, imperf. horiz.	*250.00*	
b.	Horiz. pair, imperf. vert.	*800.00*	

PERFORMING ARTS

Edward Kennedy "Duke" Ellington (1899-1974), Jazz Composer — A1594

Designed by Jim Sharpe.
Printed by the American Bank Note Co.

PHOTOGRAVURE
Plates of 200 in four panes of 50.

1986, Apr. 29 **Tagged** ***Perf. 11***

2211	A1594 22c **multicolored**	.45	.25
	P# block of 4, 6#+A	2.50	—
	Zip block of 4	1.90	—
	Pane of 50	22.50	
a.	Vert. pair, imperf. horiz.	*500.00*	

AMERIPEX '86 ISSUE

Miniature Sheets

A1599a

A1599b

A1599c

Presidents — A1599d

Illustrations reduced.

No. 2216: a, George Washington. b, John Adams. c, Thomas Jefferson. d, James Madison. e, James Monroe. f, John Quincy Adams. g, Andrew Jackson. h, Martin Van Buren. i, William H. Harrison.

No. 2217: a, John Tyler. b, James Knox Polk. c, Zachary Taylor. d, Millard Fillmore. e, Franklin Pierce. f, James Buchanan. g, Abraham Lincoln. h, Andrew Johnson. i, Ulysses S. Grant.

No. 2218: a, Rutherford B. Hayes. b, James A. Garfield. c, Chester A. Arthur. d, Grover Cleveland. e, Benjamin Harrison. f, William McKinley. g, Theodore Roosevelt. h, William H. Taft. i, Woodrow Wilson.

No. 2219: a, Warren G. Harding. b, Calvin Coolidge. c, Herbert Hoover. d, Franklin Delano Roosevelt. e, White House. f, Harry S. Truman. g, Dwight D. Eisenhower. h, John F. Kennedy. i, Lyndon B. Johnson.

Designed by Jerry Dadds.

LITHOGRAPHED & ENGRAVED

1986, May 22 **Tagged** ***Perf. 11***

2216 A1599a Pane of 9	6.50	4.00
a.-i. 22c, any single	.65	.40
j. Blue (engr.) omitted	*1,800.*	
k. Black inscription omitted	*1,000.*	
l. Imperf.	*10,500.*	
m. As "k," double impression of red	*1,700.*	
n. Blue omitted on b-c, e-f, i	—	
o. Tagging omitted on a, d, g	*225.00*	
p. Tagging omitted	—	
q. Double impression of red	*600.00*	
2217 A1599b Pane of 9	6.50	4.00
a-i. 22c, any single	.65	.40
j. Black inscription omitted	*1,500.*	
k. Tagging omitted	*225.00*	
2218 A1599c Pane of 9	6.50	4.00
a.-i. 22c, any single	.65	.40
j. Brown (engr.) omitted	—	
k. Black inscription omitted	*1,500.*	
l. Tagging omitted	*400.00*	
2219 A1599d Pane of 9	6.50	4.00
a.-i. 22c, any single	.65	.40
j. Blackish blue (engr.) inscription omitted on a-b, d-e, g-h	*2,250.*	
k. Tagging omitted on c, f, i	*2,750.*	
l. Blackish blue (engr.) omitted on all stamps	—	
m. Tagging omitted on a-b, d-e, g-h	—	
n. Tagging omitted on a, b, and i	—	
o. Tagging omitted on b-c, e-f, h-i	—	
Nos. 2216-2219 (4)	26.00	16.00

Issued in conjunction with AMERIPEX '86 Intl. Philatelic Exhibition, Chicago, IL May 22-June 1. Pane size: 120x207mm (pane size varied).

ARCTIC EXPLORERS

Elisha Kent Kane — A1600

Adolphus W. Greely A1601

Vilhjalmur Stefansson A1602

Robert E. Peary, Matthew Henson A1603

Designed by Dennis Lyall.
Printed by the American Bank Note Company

PHOTOGRAVURE

Plates of 200 in four panes of 50.

1986, May 28 **Tagged** ***Perf. 11***

2220 A1600 22c **multicolored**	.65	.25
2221 A1601 22c **multicolored**	.65	.25
2222 A1602 22c **multicolored**	.65	.25
2223 A1603 22c **multicolored**	.65	.25
a. Block of 4, #2220-2223	2.75	2.25
P# block of 4, 5#+A	4.50	—
Zip block of 4	3.00	—
Pane of 50	32.50	
b. As "a," black omitted	*3,500.*	
c. As "a," Nos. 2220, 2221 black omitted	*1,000.*	
d. As "a," Nos. 2222, 2223 black omitted	*1,000.*	

STATUE OF LIBERTY, 100th ANNIVERSARY

A1604

Designed by Howard Paine.

ENGRAVED

Plates of 200 in four panes of 50.

1986, July 4 **Tagged** ***Perf. 11***

2224	A1604 22c **scarlet & dark blue**		.45	.25
	P# block of 4		2.25	—
	Zip block of 4		1.65	—
	Pane of 50		22.50	
a.	Scarlet omitted		—	

On No. 2224a, virtually all of the dark blue also is omitted, so the error stamp should be collected as part of a transition strip. See France No. 2014.

> **Coil Plate No. Strips of 3**
> **Beginning with No. 2123, coil plate no. strips of 3 usually sell at the level of strips of 5 minus the face value of two stamps.**

TRANSPORTATION ISSUE

Types of 1982-85 and

A1604a — Omnibus 1880s

A1604b — Locomotive 1870s

Designers: 1c, 2c, David Stone.

COIL STAMPS
ENGRAVED

1986-90 **Tagged** ***Perf. 10 Vert.***

No.			
2225	A1604a 1c **violet,** large block tagging, dull gum, *Nov. 26*	.30	.25
	Pair	.30	.50
	P# strip of 5, #1, 2	.55	
	P# single, #1, 2	—	.40
a.	Prephosphored uncoated paper with embedded tagging showing a mottled appearance (error), shiny gum	3.00	.25
	Pair	6.00	.50
	P# strip of 5, #3	35.00	
	P# single, #3	—	35.00
b.	Untagged, dull gum	.30	.25
	Pair	.35	.50
	P# strip of 5, #2-3	.60	
	P# single, #2-3	—	.45
	Shiny gum	.30	
	P# strip of 5, #3	.70	
	Low gloss gum	.30	
	P# strip of 5, #3	2.50	
c.	Imperf., pair	*1,500.*	
d.	As No. 2225, tagging omitted (error), P# single, #1		—
2226	A1604b 2c **black,** dull gum, *Mar. 6, 1987*	.30	.25
	Pair	.30	.50
	P# strip of 5, #1	.40	
	P# single, #1	—	.35
a.	Untagged, dull gum	.30	.25
	Pair	.50	.50
	P# strip of 5, #2	1.00	
	P# single, #2	—	.45
	Shiny gum	.30	
	P# strip of 5, #2	2.00	

REDUCED SIZE

2228	A1285 4c **reddish brown,** large block tagging, *Aug.*	.30	.25
	Pair	.50	.50
	P# strip of 5, #1	1.10	
	P# single, #1	—	.85
a.	Overall tagging, *1990*	.70	.25
	Pair	1.40	.50
	P# strip of 5, #1	6.00	
	P# single, #1	—	5.75
b.	Imperf., pair	175.00	

Earliest known usage of No. 2228: Aug. 15, 1986.

On No. 2228 "Stagecoach 1890s" is 17¾mm long; on No. 1898A, 19½mm long.

Untagged

No.			
2231	A1511 8.3c **green** (Bureau precancel, Blk. Rt./CAR-RT/SORT), *Aug. 29*	.65	.25
	Pair	1.30	.50
	P# strip of 5, #1	3.75	
	P# strip of 5, #2	4.50	
	P# single, #1	—	3.00
	P# single, #2	—	4.50
	Nos. 2225-2231 (4)	1.55	1.00

On No. 2231 "Ambulance 1860s" is 18mm long; on No. 2128, 18⅛mm long.

Joint lines do not appear on Nos. 2225-2231.

AMERICAN FOLK ART SERIES
Navajo Art

A1605

A1606

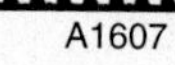

A1607

A1608

Designed by Derry Noyes.

LITHOGRAPHED & ENGRAVED

Plates of 200 in four panes of 50.

1986, Sept. 4 **Tagged** ***Perf. 11***

2235	A1605 22c **multicolored**	.80	.25
a.	Black (engr.) omitted	65.00	
2236	A1606 22c **multicolored**	.80	.25
a.	Black (engr.) omitted	65.00	
2237	A1607 22c **multicolored**	.80	.25
a.	Black (engr.) omitted	65.00	
2238	A1608 22c **multicolored**	.80	.25
a.	Black (engr.) omitted	65.00	
b.	Block of 4, #2235-2238	3.25	2.25
	P# block of 4, 5#	4.25	—
	Zip block of 4	3.50	—
	Pane of 50	40.00	
c.	As "b," black (engr.) omitted	*275.00*	

LITERARY ARTS SERIES

T.S. Eliot (1888-1965), Poet — A1609

Designed by Bradbury Thompson.

ENGRAVED

Plates of 200 in four panes of 50.

1986, Sept. 26 **Tagged** ***Perf. 11***

2239	A1609 22c **copper red**	.45	.25
	P# block of 4	2.25	—
	Zip block of 4	2.00	—
	Pane of 50	22.50	
a.	Tagging omitted		—

AMERICAN FOLK ART SERIES
Woodcarved Figurines

A1610

A1611

A1612

A1613

Designed by Bradbury Thompson.
Printed by the American Bank Note Company

PHOTOGRAVURE

Plates of 200 in four panes of 50.

1986, Oct. 1 **Tagged** ***Perf. 11***

2240	A1610 22c **multicolored**	.50	.25
2241	A1611 22c **multicolored**	.50	.25
2242	A1612 22c **multicolored**	.50	.25
2243	A1613 22c **multicolored**	.50	.25
a.	Block of 4, #2240-2243	2.00	1.50
	P# block of 4, 5#+A	3.75	—
	Zip block of 4	2.25	—
	Pane of 50	25.00	
b.	As "a," imperf. vert.	*750.00*	

CHRISTMAS

Madonna, National Gallery, by Perugino (c. 1450-1513)
A1614

Village Scene
A1615

Designed by Bradbury Thompson (#2244) & Dolli Tingle (#2245).

PHOTOGRAVURE

Panes of 100

1986, Oct. 24 **Tagged** ***Perf. 11***

2244	A1614 22c **multicolored**	.45	.25
	P# block of 4, 5#	2.10	—
	Zip block of 4	1.90	—
	Pane of 100	45.00	
a.	Imperf., pair	*400.00*	
2245	A1615 22c **multicolored**	.45	.25
	P# block of 4, 6#	2.10	—
	Zip block of 4	1.90	—
	Pane of 100	45.00	

MICHIGAN STATEHOOD, 150th ANNIV.

White Pine — A1616

Designed by Robert Wilbert.

PHOTOGRAVURE
Plates of 200 in four panes of 50.

1987, Jan. 26 **Tagged** ***Perf. 11***

2246	A1616 22c **multicolored**	.50	.25
	P# block of 4, 5#	2.25	—
	Zip block of 4	2.10	—
	Pane of 50	25.00	
	Pair with full vert. gutter between	—	

PAN AMERICAN GAMES

Indianapolis, Aug. 7-25

Runner in Full Stride A1617

Designed by Lon Busch.

PHOTOGRAVURE
Plates of 200 in four panes of 50.

1987, Jan. 29 **Tagged** ***Perf. 11***

2247	A1617 22c **multicolored**	.45	.25
	P# block of 4, 5#	2.10	—
	Zip block of 4	1.90	—
	Pane of 50	22.50	
a.	Silver omitted	*550.00*	

No. 2247a is valued in the grade of fine.

LOVE ISSUE

A1618

Designed by John Alcorn.

PHOTOGRAVURE
Panes of 100

1987, Jan. 30 **Tagged** ***Perf. 11½x11***

2248	A1618 22c **multicolored**	.45	.25
	P# block of 4, 5#	2.10	—
	Zip block of 4	1.90	—
	Pane of 100	45.00	
	Pair with full horiz. gutter between	*125.00*	

BLACK HERITAGE SERIES

Jean Baptiste Pointe du Sable (c. 1750-1818), Pioneer Trader, Founder of Chicago — A1619

Designed by Thomas Blackshear.

PHOTOGRAVURE
Plates of 200 in four panes of 50.

1987, Feb. 20 **Tagged** ***Perf. 11***

2249	A1619 22c **multicolored**	.40	.25
	P# block of 4, 5#	2.25	—
	Zip block of 4	2.00	—
	Pane of 50	20.00	
a.	Tagging omitted	*20.00*	

PERFORMING ARTS SERIES

Enrico Caruso (1873-1921), Opera Tenor — A1620

Designed by Jim Sharpe.
Printed by American Bank Note Co.

PHOTOGRAVURE
Plates of 200 in four panes of 50.

1987, Feb. 27 **Tagged** ***Perf. 11***

2250	A1620 22c **multicolored**	.45	.25
	P# block of 4, 4#+A	2.00	—
	Zip block of 4	1.90	—
	Pane of 50	22.50	
a.	Black omitted	*3,500.*	
b.	Tagging omitted	—	

GIRL SCOUTS, 75TH ANNIVERSARY

Fourteen Achievement Badges — A1621

Designed by Richard Sheaff.

LITHOGRAPHED & ENGRAVED
Plates of 200 in four panes of 50.

1987, Mar. 12 **Tagged** ***Perf. 11***

2251	A1621 22c **multicolored**	.45	.25
	P# block of 4, 6#	2.25	—
	Zip block of 4	1.90	—
	Pane of 50	22.50	
a.	All litho. colors omitted	*1,600.*	
b.	Red & black (engr.) omitted	*1,500.*	

All known examples of No. 2251a have been expertized and certificate must accompany purchase. The unique pane of No. 2251b has been expertized and a certificate exists for the pane of 50.

Coil Plate No. Strips of 3

Beginning with No. 2123, coil plate no. strips of 3 usually sell at the level of strips of 5 minus the face value of two stamps.

TRANSPORTATION ISSUE

Conestoga Wagon 1800s — A1622

Milk Wagon 1900s — A1623

Elevator 1900s — A1624

Carreta 1770s — A1625

Wheel Chair 1920s — A1626

Canal Boat 1880s — A1627

Patrol Wagon 1880s — A1628

Coal Car 1870s — A1629

Tugboat 1900s — A1630

Popcorn Wagon 1902 — A1631

Racing Car 1911 — A1632

Cable Car 1880s — A1633

Fire Engine 1900s — A1634

Railroad Mail Car 1920s — A1635

Tandem Bicycle 1890s — A1636

Designers: 3c, 7.6c, 13.2c, 15c, Richard Schlecht. 5c, 5.3c, 16.7c, Lou Nolan. 8.4c, 20.5c, 24.1c, Christopher Calle. 10c, William H. Bond. 13c, Joe Brockert. 17.5c, Tom Broad. 20c, Dan Romano. 21c, David Stone.

COIL STAMPS
ENGRAVED

1987-95 *Perf. 10 Vert.*

Tagged, Untagged (5.3c, 7.6c, 8.4c, 13c, 13.2c, 16.7c, 20.5c, 21c, 24.1c)

2252 A1622 3c **claret,** dull gum, *Feb. 29, 1988* .30 .25
Pair .35 .35
P# strip of 5, #1 .85
P# single, #1 — .60
a. Untagged, dull gum .30 .25
P# strip of 5, #2-3 1.35
P# single, #2 — 1.10
P# single, #3 — .90
Shiny gum, *1995* .30
P# strip of 5, #3 1.00
P# strip of 5, #5 7.00
P# strip of 5, #6 1.00
P# single, #3 1.00
P# single, #5 — 6.00
P# single, #6 — 1.10
Low gloss gum .40
P# strip of 5, #5 7.50
P# single, #5 6.00
b. As "a," imperf pair, shiny gum *1,350.*

The plate #5 on No. 2252a with low gloss gum is smaller than the #5 on No. 2252a with shiny gum. The smaller plate #5 represents a different printing sleeve (plate).

2253 A1623 5c **black,** *Sept. 25* .30 .25
Pair .50 .50
P# strip of 5, #1 .90
P# single, #1 — .65
2254 A1624 5.3c **black** (Bureau precancel "Nonprofit Carrier Route Sort" in red), *Sept. 16, 1988* .30 .25
Pair .50 .50
P# strip of 5, #1 1.40
P# single, #1 — .90
2255 A1625 7.6c **brown** (Bureau precancel "Nonprofit" in red), *Aug. 30, 1988* .30 .25
Pair .50 .50
P# strip of 5, #1-2 1.75
P# strip of 5, #3 3.25
P# single, #1-2 — 1.50
P# single, #3 — 4.00
2256 A1626 8.4c **deep claret** (Bureau precancel "Nonprofit" in red), *Aug. 12, 1988* .30 .25
Pair .50 .50
P# strip of 5, #1-2 1.75
P# strip of 5, #3 5.25
P# single, #1-2 — 1.00
P# single, #3 — 5.00
a. Imperf., pair *350.00*
2257 A1627 10c **blue,** large block tagging, dull gum, *Apr. 11* .40 .25
Pair .80 .50
P# strip of 5, #1 1.75
P# single, #1 — 1.00
a. Overall tagging, dull gum, *1993* 1.50 .25
Pair 3.00 .50
P# strip of 5, #1 9.00
P# single, #1 — 8.00
Shiny gum, *1994* .30 .25
Pair .50 .50
P# strip of 5, #4 3.25
P# single, #4 — 2.50
b. Prephosphored uncoated paper with embedded tagging showing a mottled appearance, shiny gum .30 .25
Pair .50 .50
P# strip of 5, #1, 2 3.00
P# strip of 5, #3, 4 3.75
P# single, #1, 2 — 2.90
P# single, #3, 4 — 2.90
c. Prephosphored coated paper with surface tagging showing a solid appearance, low gloss gum .30 .25
Pair .50 .50
P# strip of 5, #5 4.50
P# single, #5 — 4.00
d. Tagging omitted, shiny gum *15.00*
e. Imperf, pair, large block tagging *1,000.*
2258 A1628 13c **black** (Bureau precancel "Presorted First-Class" in red), *Oct. 29, 1988* .65 .25
Pair 1.30 .50
P# strip of 5, #1 3.50
P# single, #1 — 2.25
2259 A1629 13.2c **slate green** (Bureau precancel "Bulk Rate" in red), *July 19, 1988* .30 .25
Pair .50 .50
P# strip of 5, #1-2 2.50
P# single, #1-2 — 1.60
a. Imperf., pair 75.00
2260 A1630 15c **violet,** large block tagging, *July 12, 1988* .30 .25
Pair .60 .50
P# strip of 5, #1 2.00
P# strip of 5, #2 2.25
P# single, #1 — 1.00
P# single, #2 — 1.75
a. Overall tagging, *1990* .40 .30
Pair .80 .60
P# strip of 5, #2 3.00
P# single, #2 — 2.25
b. Tagging omitted *4.25*
c. As "a," imperf. pair *500.00*
2261 A1631 16.7c **rose** (Bureau precancel "Bulk Rate " in black), *July 7, 1988* .30 .30
Pair .60 .60
P# strip of 5, #1 2.25
P# strip of 5, #2 2.50
P# single, #1 — 1.60
P# single, #2 — 2.50
a. Imperf., pair *125.00*

All known examples of No. 2261a are miscut top to bottom.

2262 A1632 17.5c **dark violet,** *Sept. 25* .75 .25
Pair 1.50 .50
P# strip of 5, #1 3.50
P# single, #1 — 3.25
a. Untagged (Bureau Precancel "ZIP + 4 Presort" in red) .65 .30
Pair 1.30 .60
P# strip of 5, #1 4.00
P# single, #1 — 2.75
b. Imperf., pair *1,250.*
2263 A1633 20c **blue violet,** large block tagging, *Oct. 28, 1988* .35 .25
Pair .70 .50
P# strip of 5, #1-2 3.00
P# single, #1-2 — 1.75
a. Imperf., pair 50.00
b. Overall tagging, *1990* 1.00 .25
Pair 2.00 .50
P# strip of 5, #2 7.50
P# single, #2 — 5.75
2264 A1634 20.5c **rose** (Bureau precancel "ZIP + 4 Presort" in black), *Sept. 28, 1988* .75 .40
Pair 1.50 .80
P# strip of 5, #1 4.25
P# single, #1 — 3.00
2265 A1635 21c **olive green** (Bureau precancel "Presorted First-Class" in red), *Aug. 16, 1988* .50 .40
Pair 1.00 .80
P# strip of 5, #1-2 3.00
P# single, #1-2 — 2.50
a. Imperf., pair 35.00
2266 A1636 24.1c **deep ultra** (Bureau precancel ZIP + 4 in red), *Oct. 26, 1988* .80 .45
Pair 1.60 .90
P# strip of 5, #1 3.75
P# single, #1 — 2.25
Nos. 2252-2266 (15) 6.60 4.30

5.3c, 7.6c, 8.4c, 13.2c, 16.7c, 20.5c, 21c and 24.1c only available precanceled.

See Nos. 1897-1908, 2123-2136, 2225-2231, 2451-2468.

SPECIAL OCCASIONS

A1637

A1638

A1639

A1640

A1641

A1642

A1643

A1644

Designed by Oren Sherman.

BOOKLET STAMPS
PHOTOGRAVURE

1987, Apr. 20 Tagged ***Perf. 10 on 1, 2 or 3 Sides***

2267 A1637 22c **multicolored** .75 .25
2268 A1638 22c **multicolored** .90 .25
2269 A1639 22c **multicolored** .90 .25
2270 A1640 22c **multicolored** .90 .25
2271 A1641 22c **multicolored** .90 .25
2272 A1642 22c **multicolored** .75 .25
2273 A1643 22c **multicolored** 1.50 .25
2274 A1644 22c **multicolored** .90 .25
a. Bklt. pane of 10 (#2268-2271, 2273-2274, 2 each #2267, 2272) 9.00 5.00
Nos. 2267-2274 (8) 7.50 2.00

UNITED WAY, 100th ANNIV.

Six Profiles A1645

Designed by Jerry Pinkney.

LITHOGRAPHED & ENGRAVED

Plates of 200 in four panes of 50.

1987, Apr. 28 **Tagged** ***Perf. 11***

2275 A1645 22c **multicolored** .45 .25
P# block of 4, 6# 2.00 —
Zip block of 4 1.90 —
Pane of 50 22.50

A1646

A1647

A1648

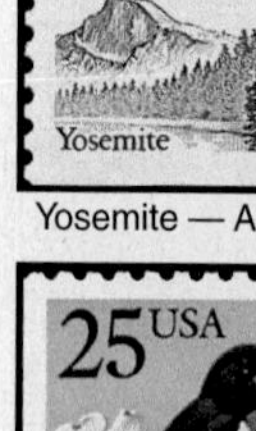

Yosemite — A1649

Pheasant — A1649a

Grosbeak — A1649b

Owl — A1649c

Honeybee — A1649d

Designs: Nos. 2276, 2278, 2280, Peter Cocci. Nos. 2277, 2279, 2282, Robert McCall. Nos. 2281, 2283-2285, Chuck Ripper.

PHOTOGRAVURE (Nos. 2276-2279)
Panes of 100

1987-88	**Tagged**	***Perf. 11***	
2276	A1646 22c **multicolored,** *May 9*	.45	.25
	P# block of 4, 4#	2.00	—
	Zip block of 4	1.90	—
	Pane of 100	45.00	
a.	Booklet pane of 20, *Nov. 30*	9.00	—
b.	As "a," vert. pair, imperf. btwn.	*1,450.*	
c.	As "a," miscut and inserted upside down into booklet cover, imperf between stamps and right selvage		—
d.	Yellow omitted		—

All documented examples of No. 2276d show significant misregistration of the red ink.

2277	A1647 (25c) **multi,** *Mar. 22, 1988*	.50	.25
	P# block of 4, 4#	2.25	—
	Zip block of 4	2.10	—
	Pane of 100	50.00	
a.	Tagging omitted	—	—
2278	A1648 25c **multi,** *May 6, 1988*	.50	.25
	P# block of 4, 4#	2.25	—
	Zip block of 4	2.10	—
	Pane of 100	50.00	
	Pair with full vert. gutter between	*125.00*	
a.	Tagging omitted	—	
	Nos. 2276-2278 (3)	1.45	.75

COIL STAMPS

Perf. 10 Vert.

2279	A1647 (25c) **multi,** *Mar. 22, 1988*	.50	.25
	Pair	1.00	.50
	P# strip of 5, #1111	3.00	
	P# strip of 5, #1211	3.25	
	P# strip of 5, #1222	3.00	
	P# strip of 5, #2222	3.25	
	P# single, #1111	—	.50
	P# single, #1211	—	1.10
	P# single, #1222	—	.90
	P# single, #2222	—	3.25
a.	Imperf., pair	60.00	—
b.	Tagging omitted		—

Engr.

2280	A1649 25c **multi,** large block tagging, *May 20, 1988*	.50	.25
	Pair	1.00	.50
	P# strip of 5, #1	3.50	
	P# strip of 5, #2-5	3.00	
	P# strip of 5, #7	3.50	
	P# strip of 5, #8	3.00	
	P# strip of 5, #9	6.00	
	P# single, #1	—	2.50
	P# single, #2-5	—	.75
	P# single, #7	—	1.75
	P# single, #8	—	.65
	P# single, #9	—	2.00
a.	Prephosphored uncoated paper with embedded tagging showing a mottled appearance *Feb. 14, 1989*	.45	.25
	P# strip of 5, #1	17.50	
	P# strip of 5, #2, 3	3.00	
	P# strip of 5, #5	5.25	
	P# strip of 5, #6	5.75	
	P# strip of 5, #7-11, 13-14	3.00	
	P# strip of 5, #15	4.25	
	P# single, #1	—	15.00
	P# single, #2	—	.60
	P# single, #3	—	.60
	P# single, #5	—	1.10
	P# single, #6	—	5.00
	P# single, #7-11, 13-14	—	.60
	P# single, #15	—	2.00
b.	Imperf., pair, large block tagging	25.00	
c.	Imperf., pair, prephosphored uncoated paper with embedded tagging showing a mottled appearance	10.00	
d.	Tagging omitted	*5.00*	
e.	Black trees	*90.00*	—
	P# strip of 5, #4, 5, 9	*700.00*	
f.	Pair, imperf. between	*375.00*	

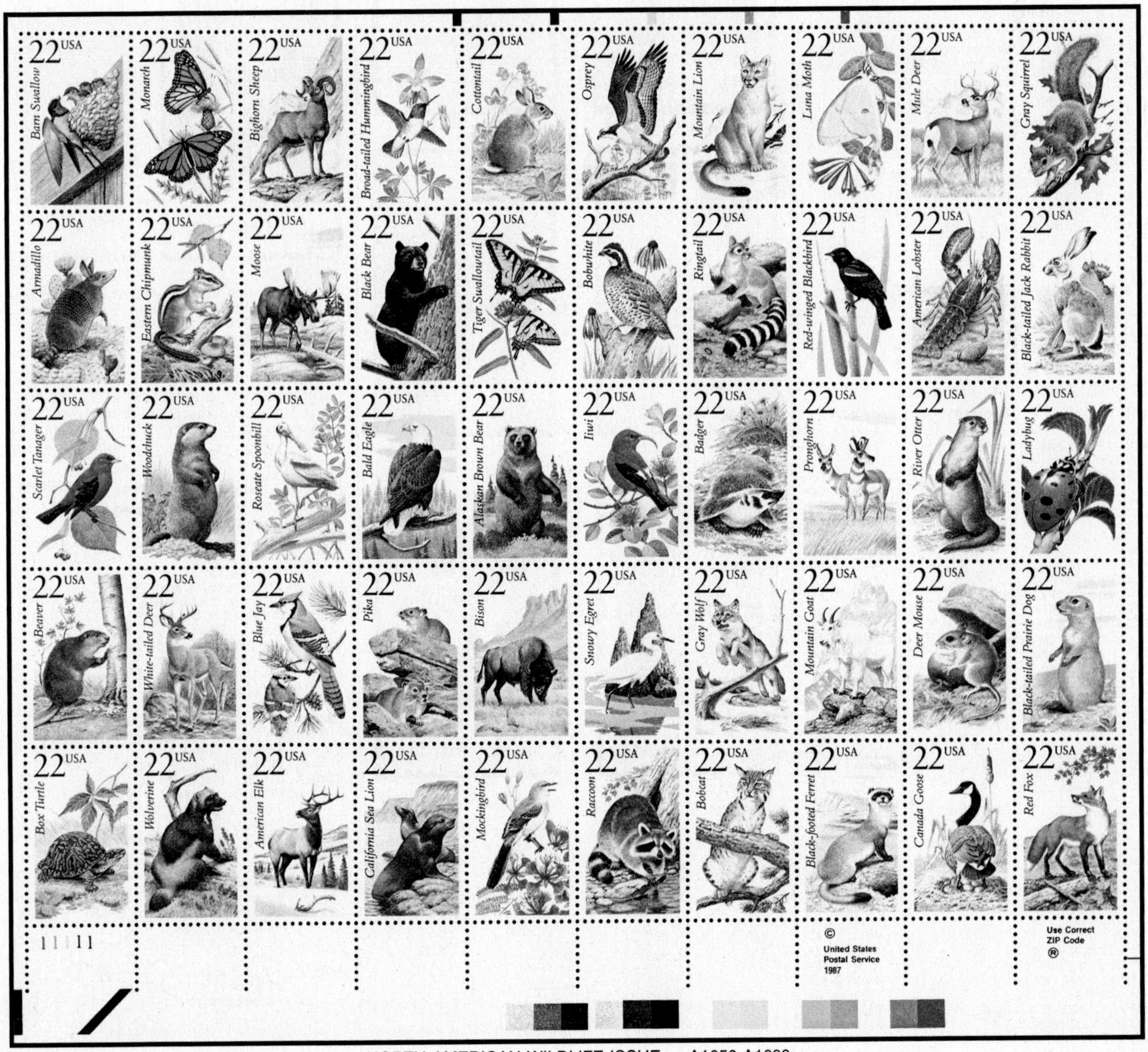

NORTH AMERICAN WILDLIFE ISSUE — A1650-A1699

Litho. & Engr.

2281	A1649d	25c **multi,** small block tagging *Sept. 2, 1988*	.50	.25
		Pair	1.00	.50
		P# strip of 5, #1	3.50	
		P# single, #1	—	.50
a.		As No. 2281, imperf. pair	45.00	
c.		Black (litho. - "25 USA") omitted	*500.00*	
d.		Pair, imperf. between	*600.00*	
e.		Yellow (litho.) omitted	*700.00*	
f.		Large block tagging	.45	.25
		Pair	.90	
		P# strip of 5, #1	3.50	
		P# strip of 5, #2	3.25	
		P# single, #1	—	.60
		P# single, #2	—	.50
g.		As "f," imperf, pair	45.00	
h.		As "f," tagging omitted	85.00	—
i.		As "f," black (engr. - details on bee) omitted	45.00	—
		Nos. 2279-2281 (3)	1.50	.75

No. 2281 from plate #1 is known with three types of "1" on the plate-numbered stamps. The original tall "1" was later shortened manually by removing the top of the "1," including the serif, so it would not penetrate the design. A short "1" with top serif also exists. Value of P# strip of 5 with tall "1," $17.50.

Beware of stamps with traces of the litho. black that are offered as No. 2281c.

Vertical pairs or blocks of No. 2281 and imperfs. with the engr. black missing are from printer's waste.

BOOKLET STAMPS

Printed by American Bank Note Co. (#2283)

PHOTOGRAVURE

Perf. 10 on 2 or 3 Sides

2282	A1647	(25c) **multi,** *Mar. 22, 1988*	.50	.25
a.		Booklet pane of 10	6.50	3.50
		Scored perforations	6.50	—

Perf. 11 on 2 or 3 Sides

2283	A1649a	25c **multi,** *Apr. 29, 1988*	.50	.25
a.		Booklet pane of 10	6.00	3.50
b.		25c multicolored, red removed from sky	4.50	.25
c.		As "b," bklt. pane of 10	45.00	—
d.		Vert. pair, imperf. btwn.	*275.00*	

Imperf. panes exist from printers waste, and a large number exist. No. 2283d resulted from a foldover. Non-foldover pairs and multiples are printer's waste.

Perf. 10 on 2 or 3 Sides

2284	A1649b	25c **multi,** *May 28, 1988*	.50	.25
2285	A1649c	25c **multi,** *May 28, 1988*	.50	.25
b.		Bklt. pane of 10, 5 each #2284-2285	5.00	3.50
d.		Pair, Nos. 2284-2285	1.10	.50
e.		As "d," tagging omitted	14.00	
f.		As "b," tagging omitted	*110.00*	
2285A	A1648	25c **multi,** *July 5, 1988*	.50	.25
c.		Booklet pane of 6	3.00	2.00
		Nos. 2282-2285A (5)	2.50	1.25

NORTH AMERICAN WILDLIFE

Illustration reduced.

Designed by Chuck Ripper.

PHOTOGRAVURE

Plates of 200 in four panes of 50.

1987, June 13		**Tagged**	***Perf. 11***	
2286	A1650	22c Barn swallow	1.00	.50
2287	A1651	22c Monarch butterfly	1.00	.50
2288	A1652	22c Bighorn sheep	1.00	.50
2289	A1653	22c Broad-tailed hummingbird	1.00	.50
2290	A1654	22c Cottontail	1.00	.50
2291	A1655	22c Osprey	1.00	.50
2292	A1656	22c Mountain lion	1.00	.50
2293	A1657	22c Luna moth	1.00	.50
2294	A1658	22c Mule deer	1.00	.50
2295	A1659	22c Gray squirrel	1.00	.50
2296	A1660	22c Armadillo	1.00	.50
2297	A1661	22c Eastern chipmunk	1.00	.50
2298	A1662	22c Moose	1.00	.50
2299	A1663	22c Black bear	1.00	.50
2300	A1664	22c Tiger swallowtail	1.00	.50
2301	A1665	22c Bobwhite	1.00	.50
2302	A1666	22c Ringtail	1.00	.50
2303	A1667	22c Red-winged blackbird	1.00	.50
2304	A1668	22c American lobster	1.00	.50
2305	A1669	22c Black-tailed jack rabbit	1.00	.50
2306	A1670	22c Scarlet tanager	1.00	.50
2307	A1671	22c Woodchuck	1.00	.50
2308	A1672	22c Roseate spoonbill	1.00	.50
2309	A1673	22c Bald eagle	1.00	.50
2310	A1674	22c Alaskan brown bear	1.00	.50
2311	A1675	22c Iiwi	1.00	.50
2312	A1676	22c Badger	1.00	.50
2313	A1677	22c Pronghorn	1.00	.50
2314	A1678	22c River otter	1.00	.50
2315	A1679	22c Ladybug	1.00	.50
2316	A1680	22c Beaver	1.00	.50
2317	A1681	22c White-tailed deer	1.00	.50
2318	A1682	22c Blue jay	1.00	.50
2319	A1683	22c Pika	1.00	.50
2320	A1684	22c Bison	1.00	.50
2321	A1685	22c Snowy egret	1.00	.50
2322	A1686	22c Gray wolf	1.00	.50
2323	A1687	22c Mountain goat	1.00	.50
2324	A1688	22c Deer mouse	1.00	.50
2325	A1689	22c Black-tailed prairie dog	1.00	.50
2326	A1690	22c Box turtle	1.00	.50
2327	A1691	22c Wolverine	1.00	.50
2328	A1692	22c American elk	1.00	.50
2329	A1693	22c California sea lion	1.00	.50
2330	A1694	22c Mockingbird	1.00	.50
2331	A1695	22c Raccoon	1.00	.50
2332	A1696	22c Bobcat	1.00	.50
2333	A1697	22c Black-footed ferret	1.00	.50
2334	A1698	22c Canada goose	1.00	.50
2335	A1699	22c Red fox	1.00	.50
a.		Pane of 50, #2286-2335	50.00	35.00
c.		Pane of 50, tagging omitted	—	
2286b-2335b		Any single, red omitted	*2,000.*	

RATIFICATION OF THE CONSTITUTION BICENTENNIAL

Delaware — A1700

Pennsylvania — A1701

New Jersey — A1702

Georgia — A1703

Connecticut A1704

Massachusetts A1705

Maryland — A1706

South Carolina — A1707

New Hampshire — A1708

Virginia — A1709

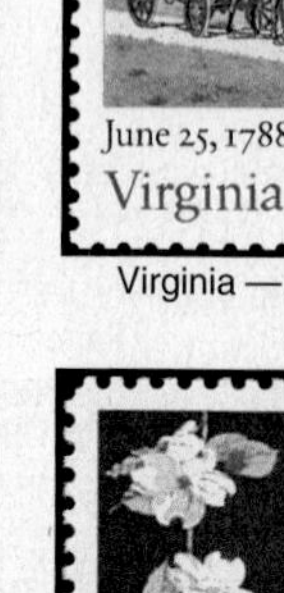

New York — A1710

North Carolina — A1711

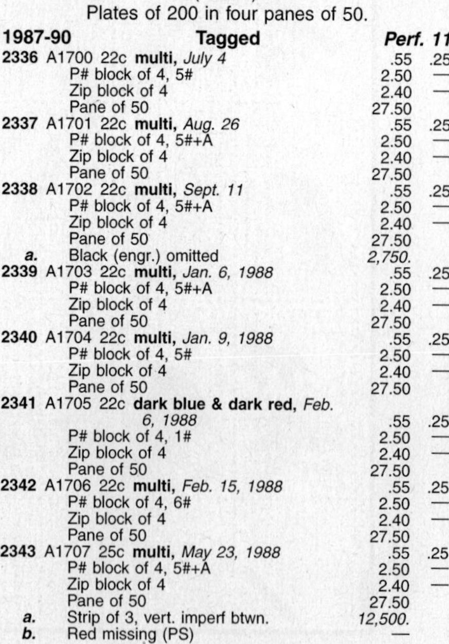

Rhode Island — A1712

Designers: Nos. 2336-2337, 2341 Richard Sheaff. No. 2338, Jim Lamb. No. 2339, Greg Harlin. No. 2340, Christopher Calle. No. 2342, Stephen Hustvedt. Nos. 2343, 2347, Bob Timberlake. No. 2344, Thomas Szumowski. No. 2345, Pierre Mion. No. 2346, Bradbury Thompson. No. 2348, Robert Brangwynne.

Printed by the Bureau of Engraving & Printing, J.W. Fergusson and Sons (Nos. 2337, 2338), American Bank Note Co. (Nos. 2339, 2343-2344, 2347).

LITHOGRAPHED & ENGRAVED, PHOTOGRAVURE (#2337-2339, 2343-2344, 2347), ENGRAVED (#2341).

Plates of 200 in four panes of 50.

1987-90		**Tagged**	***Perf. 11***	
2336	A1700	22c **multi,** *July 4*	.55	.25
		P# block of 4, 5#	2.50	—
		Zip block of 4	2.40	—
		Pane of 50	27.50	
2337	A1701	22c **multi,** *Aug. 26*	.55	.25
		P# block of 4, 5#+A	2.50	—
		Zip block of 4	2.40	—
		Pane of 50	27.50	
2338	A1702	22c **multi,** *Sept. 11*	.55	.25
		P# block of 4, 5#+A	2.50	—
		Zip block of 4	2.40	—
		Pane of 50	27.50	
a.		Black (engr.) omitted	*2,750.*	
2339	A1703	22c **multi,** *Jan. 6, 1988*	.55	.25
		P# block of 4, 5#+A	2.50	—
		Zip block of 4	2.40	—
		Pane of 50	27.50	
2340	A1704	22c **multi,** *Jan. 9, 1988*	.55	.25
		P# block of 4, 5#	2.50	—
		Zip block of 4	2.40	—
		Pane of 50	27.50	
2341	A1705	22c **dark blue & dark red,** *Feb. 6, 1988*	.55	.25
		P# block of 4, 1#	2.50	—
		Zip block of 4	2.40	—
		Pane of 50	27.50	
2342	A1706	22c **multi,** *Feb. 15, 1988*	.55	.25
		P# block of 4, 6#	2.50	—
		Zip block of 4	2.40	—
		Pane of 50	27.50	
2343	A1707	25c **multi,** *May 23, 1988*	.55	.25
		P# block of 4, 5#+A	2.50	—
		Zip block of 4	2.40	—
		Pane of 50	27.50	
a.		Strip of 3, vert. imperf btwn.	*12,500.*	
b.		Red missing (PS)	—	

2344 A1708 25c **multi,** *June 21, 1988* .55 .25
P# block of 4, 4#+A 2.50 —
Zip block of 4 2.40 —
Pane of 50 27.50
a. Red missing (PS) —
2345 A1709 25c **multi,** *June 25, 1988* .55 .25
P# block of 4, 5# 2.50 —
Zip block of 4 2.40 —
Pane of 50 27.50
2346 A1710 25c **multi,** *July 26, 1988* .55 .25
P# block of 4, 5# 2.50 —
Zip block of 4 2.40 —
Pane of 50 27.50
2347 A1711 25c **multi,** *Aug. 22, 1989* .55 .25
P# block of 4, 5#+A 2.50 —
Zip block of 4 2.40 —
Pane of 50 27.50
2348 A1712 25c **multi,** *May 29, 1990* .55 .25
P# block of 4, 7# 2.50 —
Zip block of 4 2.40 —
Pane of 50 27.50
Nos. 2336-2348 (13) 7.15 3.25

No. 2343b resulted either from a shifting of all colors or from a shift of both the perforations and the cutting of the pane.

US-MOROCCO DIPLOMATIC RELATIONS, 200th ANNIV.

Arabesque, Dar Batha Palace Door, Fez — A1713

Designed by Howard Paine.

LITHOGRAPHED & ENGRAVED
Plates of 200 in four panes of 50.

1987, July 17 **Tagged** ***Perf. 11***
2349 A1713 22c **scarlet & black** .50 .25
P# block of 4, 2# 2.10 —
Zip block of 4 2.00 —
Pane of 50 25.00
a. Black (engr.) omitted *180.00*

See Morocco No. 642.

LITERARY ARTS SERIES

William Faulkner (1897-1962), Novelist — A1714

Designed by Bradbury Thompson.

ENGRAVED
Plates of 200 in four panes of 50

1987, Aug. 3 **Tagged** ***Perf. 11***
2350 A1714 22c **bright green** .50 .25
P# block of 4 2.50 —
Zip block of 4 2.25 —
Pane of 50 25.00

Used untagged imperfs exist from printer's waste.

AMERICAN FOLK ART SERIES
Lacemaking

A1715

A1716

A1717

A1718

Designed by Libby Thiel.

LITHOGRAPHED & ENGRAVED
Plates of 160 in four panes of 40.

1987, Aug. 14 **Tagged** ***Perf. 11***
2351 A1715 22c **ultra & white** .45 .25
2352 A1716 22c **ultra & white** .45 .25
2353 A1717 22c **ultra & white** .45 .25
2354 A1718 22c **ultra & white** .45 .25
a. Block of 4, #2351-2354 1.90 1.90
P# block of 4, 4# 3.25 —
Zip block of 4 2.00 —
Pane of 40 18.00
b. As "a," white omitted *350.00*
c. Any single stamp, white omitted *90.00*

DRAFTING OF THE CONSTITUTION BICENTENNIAL
Excerpts from the Preamble

A1719

We the people of the United States, in order to form a more perfect Union...
Preamble, U.S. Constitution USA 22

A1720

Establish justice, insure domestic tranquility, provide for the common defense, promote the general welfare...
Preamble, U.S. Constitution USA 22

A1721

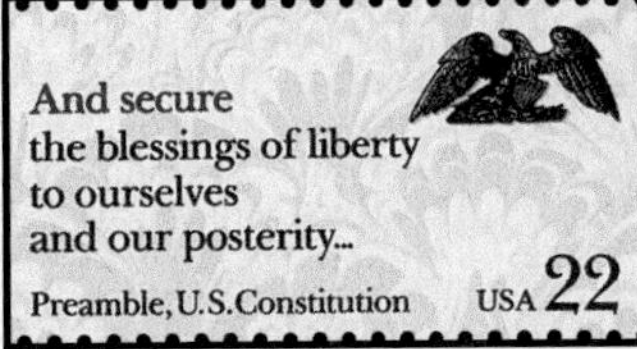

A1722

A1723

Designed by Bradbury Thompson.

BOOKLET STAMPS
PHOTOGRAVURE
Perf. 10 Horiz. on 1 or 2 Sides

1987, Aug. 28 **Tagged**
2355 A1719 22c **multicolored** .70 .25
a. Grayish green (background) omitted *400.00*
2356 A1720 22c **multicolored** .70 .25
a. Grayish green (background) omitted *400.00*
2357 A1721 22c **multicolored** .70 .25
a. Grayish green (background) omitted *400.00*
2358 A1722 22c **multicolored** .70 .25
a. Grayish green (background) omitted *400.00*
2359 A1723 22c **multicolored** .70 .25
a. Bklt. pane of 5, #2355-2359 3.50 2.25
b. Grayish green (background) omitted *400.00*

SIGNING OF THE CONSTITUTION

A1724

Designed by Howard Koslow.

LITHOGRAPHED & ENGRAVED
Plates of 200 in four panes of 50.

1987, Sept. 17 **Tagged** ***Perf. 11***
2360 A1724 22c **multicolored** .55 .25
P# block of 4, 6# 2.75 —
Zip block of 4 2.25 —
Pane of 50 27.50

CERTIFIED PUBLIC ACCOUNTING

A1725

Designed by Lou Nolan.

LITHOGRAPHED & ENGRAVED
Plates of 200 in four panes of 50.

1987, Sept. 21 **Tagged** ***Perf. 11***
2361 A1725 22c **multicolored** .70 .25
P# block of 4, 5# 3.50 —
Zip block of 4 3.00 —
Pane of 50 35.00
a. Black (engr.) omitted *425.00*

LOCOMOTIVES

Stourbridge Lion, 1829
A1726

Best Friend of Charleston, 1830 A1727

John Bull, 1831 A1728

Brother Jonathan, 1832 A1729

Gowan & Marx, 1839 A1730

Designed by Richard Leech.

BOOKLET STAMPS
LITHOGRAPHED & ENGRAVED
Perf. 10 Horiz. on 1 or 2 Sides

1987, Oct. 1		**Tagged**
2362 A1726 22c **multicolored**	.50	.25
a. Red (litho.) omitted		—
2363 A1727 22c **multicolored**	.50	.25
a. Red (litho.) omitted		—
2364 A1728 22c **multicolored**	.50	.25
a. Red (litho.) omitted		—
2365 A1729 22c **multicolored**	.50	.25
a. Red omitted	*1,000.*	*250.00*
2366 A1730 22c **multicolored**	.50	.25
a. Bklt. pane of 5, #2362-2366	2.50	2.00
b. As No. 2366, black (engr.) omitted (single)	—	
c. As No. 2366, blue omitted (single)		—

CHRISTMAS

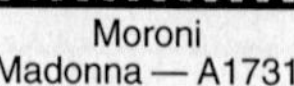

Moroni Madonna — A1731

Christmas Ornaments — A1732

Designed by Bradbury Thompson (No. 2367) and Jim Dean (No. 2368).

PHOTOGRAVURE
Plates of 800 in eight panes of 100.

1987, Oct. 23	**Tagged**	***Perf. 11***
2367 A1731 22c **multicolored**	.45	.25
P# block of 4, 6#	2.25	—
Zip block of 4	1.90	—
Pane of 100	45.00	
2368 A1732 22c **multicolored**	.45	.25
P# block of 4, 6#	2.10	—
Zip block of 4	1.90	—
Pane of 100	45.00	
Pair with full vert. gutter between	—	

1988 WINTER OLYMPICS, CALGARY

Skiing — A1733

Designed by Bart Forbes.

Printed by the American Bank Note Company

PHOTOGRAVURE
Plates of 200 in four panes of 50.

1988, Jan. 10	**Tagged**	***Perf. 11***
2369 A1733 22c **multicolored**	.50	.25
P# block of 4, 4#+A	3.00	—
Zip block of 4	2.10	—
Pane of 50	25.00	

AUSTRALIA BICENTENNIAL

Caricature of an Australian Koala and an American Bald Eagle — A1734

Designed by Roland Harvey.

PHOTOGRAVURE
Plates of 160 in four panes of 40.

1988, Jan. 26	**Tagged**	***Perf. 11***
2370 A1734 22c **multicolored**	.45	.25
P# block of 4, 5#	2.10	—
Zip block of 4	1.90	—
Pane of 40	18.00	

See Australia No. 1052.

BLACK HERITAGE SERIES

James Weldon Johnson (1871-1938), Author and Lyricist — A1735

Designed by Thomas Blackshear.

Printed by the American Bank Note Co.

PHOTOGRAVURE
Plates of 200 in four panes of 50.

1988, Feb. 2	**Tagged**	***Perf. 11***
2371 A1735 22c **multicolored**	.50	.25
P# block of 4, 5#+A	2.60	—
Zip block of 4	2.10	—
Pane of 50	25.00	
a. Tagging omitted		—

CATS

Siamese and Exotic Shorthair A1736

Abyssinian and Himalayan A1737

Maine Coon and Burmese A1738

American Shorthair and Persian A1739

Designed by John Dawson.

Printed by the American Bank Note Co.

PHOTOGRAVURE
Plates of 160 in four panes of 40.

1988, Feb. 5	**Tagged**	***Perf. 11***
2372 A1736 22c **multicolored**	.70	.25
2373 A1737 22c **multicolored**	.70	.25
2374 A1738 22c **multicolored**	.70	.25
2375 A1739 22c **multicolored**	.70	.25
a. Block of 4, #2372-2375	2.80	1.90
P# block of 4, 5#+A	4.00	—
Zip block of 4	3.00	—
Pane of 40	28.00	

AMERICAN SPORTS

Knute Rockne (1888-1931), Notre Dame football coach.

A1740

Designed by Peter Cocci and Thomas Hipschen.

LITHOGRAPHED & ENGRAVED

Plates of 200 in four panes of 50.

1988, Mar. 9	**Tagged**	*Perf. 11*	
2376 A1740 22c **multicolored**		.50	.25
P# block of 4, 7#		2.60	—
Zip block of 4		2.10	—
Pane of 50		25.00	

AMERICAN SPORTS

Francis Ouimet (1893-1967), 1st amateur golfer to win the US Open championship.

A1741

Designed by M. Gregory Rudd.
Printed by the American Bank Note Co.

PHOTOGRAVURE

Plates of 200 in four panes of 50.

1988, June 13	**Tagged**	*Perf. 11*	
2377 A1741 25c **multicolored**		.60	.25
P# block of 4, 5#+A		3.00	—
Zip block of 4		2.50	—
Pane of 50		30.00	

LOVE ISSUE (Roses)

A1742

A1743

Designed by Richard Sheaff.

PHOTOGRAVURE

Plates of 400 in four panes of 100 (25c).
Plates of 200 in four panes of 50 (45c).

1988	**Tagged**	*Perf. 11*	
2378 A1742 25c **multicolored,** *July 4*		.50	.25
P# block of 4, 5#		2.25	—
Zip block of 4		2.10	—
Pair with full horiz. gutter between		—	
Pane of 100		50.00	
a. Imperf., pair		*1,500.*	
2379 A1743 45c **multicolored,** *Aug, 8*		.85	.25
P# block of 4, 4#		3.75	—
Zip block of 4		3.50	—
Pane of 50		42.50	
a. Tagging omitted		—	

1988 SUMMER OLYMPICS, SEOUL

Gymnastic Rings — A1744

Designed by Bart Forbes.

PHOTOGRAVURE

Plates of 200 in four panes of 50

1988, Aug. 19	**Tagged**	*Perf. 11*	
2380 A1744 25c **multicolored**		.50	.25
P# block of 4, 5#		2.25	—
Zip block of 4		2.10	—
Pane of 50		25.00	

CLASSIC AUTOMOBILES

1928 Locomobile A1745

1929 Pierce-Arrow — A1746

1931 Cord A1747

1932 Packard A1748

1935 Duesenberg — A1749

Designed by Ken Dallison.

LITHOGRAPHED & ENGRAVED
BOOKLET STAMPS

Perf. 10 Horiz. on 1 or 2 Sides

1988, Aug. 25	**Tagged**	
2381 A1745 25c **multicolored**	.65	.25
2382 A1746 25c **multicolored**	.65	.25
2383 A1747 25c **multicolored**	.65	.25
2384 A1748 25c **multicolored**	.65	.25
2385 A1749 25c **multicolored**	.65	.25
a. Bklt. pane of 5, #2381-2385	3.25	2.50

ANTARCTIC EXPLORERS

Nathaniel Palmer (1799-1877) A1750

Lt. Charles Wilkes (1798-1877) A1751

Richard E. Byrd (1888-1957) A1752

Lincoln Ellsworth (1880-1951) A1753

Designed by Dennis Lyall.

Printed by the American Bank Note Co.

PHOTOGRAVURE

Plates of 200 in four panes of 50.

1988, Sept. 14	**Tagged**	*Perf. 11*	
2386 A1750 25c **multicolored**		.65	.25
2387 A1751 25c **multicolored**		.65	.25
2388 A1752 25c **multicolored**		.65	.25
2389 A1753 25c **multicolored**		.65	.25
a. Block of 4, #2386-2389		2.75	2.00
P# block of 4, 6#+A		4.50	—
Zip block of 4		3.00	—
Pane of 50		32.50	
b. As "a," black omitted		*600.00*	
c. As "a," imperf. horiz.		*1,500.*	

AMERICAN FOLK ART SERIES

Carousel Animals

Deer — A1754

Horse — A1755

Camel — A1756

Goat — A1757

Designed by Paul Calle.

LITHOGRAPHED & ENGRAVED

Plates of 200 in four panes of 50.

1988, Oct. 1	**Tagged**	*Perf. 11*	
2390 A1754 25c **multicolored**		.75	.25
2391 A1755 25c **multicolored**		.75	.25
2392 A1756 25c **multicolored**		.75	.25
2393 A1757 25c **multicolored**		.75	.25
a. Block of 4, #2390-2393		3.00	2.00
P# block of 4, 7#		4.00	—
Zip block of 4		3.25	—
Pane of 50		37.50	
b. As "a," red omitted		*800.00*	

EXPRESS MAIL RATE

Eagle and Moon — A1758

Designed by Ned Seidler.

LITHOGRAPHED & ENGRAVED
Panes of 20

1988, Oct. 4 **Tagged** *Perf. 11*

2394 A1758 $8.75 **multicolored**	16.00	8.00
P# block of 4, 7#	70.00	—
Pane of 20	320.00	

SPECIAL OCCASIONS

Happy Birthday A1759

Best Wishes A1760

Thinking of You A1761

Love You A1762

Designed by Harry Zelenko

Printed by the American Bank Note Co.

BOOKLET STAMPS
PHOTOGRAVURE

1988, Oct. 22 **Tagged** *Perf. 11 on 2 or 3 Sides*

2395 A1759 25c **multicolored**	.50	.25
2396 A1760 25c **multicolored**	.50	.25
a. Bklt. pane of 6, 3 #2395 + 3 #2396 with gutter between	3.50	3.25
2397 A1761 25c **multicolored**	.50	.25
2398 A1762 25c **multicolored**	.50	.25
a. Bklt. pane of 6, 3 #2397 + 3 #2398 with gutter between	3.50	3.25
b. As "a," imperf. horiz.	*2,250.*	
c. As "a," imperf.	—	
Nos. 2395-2398 (4)	2.00	1.00

CHRISTMAS

Madonna and Child, by Botticelli — A1763

One-horse Open Sleigh and Village Scene — A1764

"Missing Curlicue on Sleigh Runner" Cylinder Flaw

"Partially Missing Curlicue on Sleigh Runner" Cylinder Flaw

Designed by Bradbury Thompson (No. 2399) and Joan Landis (No. 2400).

LITHOGRAPHED & ENGRAVED (No. 2399),
PHOTOGRAVURE (No. 2400)
Plates of 300 in 6 Panes of 50

1988, Oct. 20 **Tagged** *Perf. 11½*

2399 A1763 25c **multicolored**	.50	.25
P# block of 4, 5+1#	2.25	—
Zip, copyright block of 4	2.10	—
Pane of 50	25.00	
Pair with full vert. gutter btwn.	—	
a. Gold omitted	25.00	

The pair with vert. gutter of No. 2399 also is misperfed through the stamps and the gutter.

2400 A1764 25c **multicolored**	.50	.25
P# block of 4, 5#	2.25	—
Zip, copyright block of 4	2.10	—
Pane of 50	25.00	
Pair with full vert. gutter btwn.	*225.00*	
Cylinder flaw (missing curlicue on sleigh runner, 11111UR19)	15.00	—
Cylinder flaw (partially missing curlicue on sleigh runner, 11111TopCenter46)	10.00	—

MONTANA STATEHOOD, 100th ANNIV.

C.M. Russell and Friends, by Charles M. Russell (1865-1926) A1765

Designed by Bradbury Thompson.

LITHOGRAPHED & ENGRAVED
Plates of 200 in four panes of 50.

1989, Jan. 15 **Tagged** *Perf. 11*

2401 A1765 25c **multicolored**	.55	.25
P# block of 4, 5#	2.75	—
Zip block of 4	2.25	—
Pane of 50	27.50	
a. Tagging omitted	—	—

Imperfs without gum exist from printer's waste.

BLACK HERITAGE SERIES

A. Philip Randolph (1889-1979), Labor and Civil Rights Leader — A1766

Designed by Thomas Blackshear.

PHOTOGRAVURE
Plates of 200 in four panes of 50.

1989, Feb. 3 **Tagged** *Perf. 11*

2402 A1766 25c **multicolored**	.50	.25
P# block of 4, 5#	2.50	—
Zip block of 4	2.10	—
Pane of 50	25.00	

NORTH DAKOTA STATEHOOD, 100th ANNIV.

Grain Elevator A1767

Designed by Wendell Minor.

Printed by the American Bank Note Co.

PHOTOGRAVURE
Plates of 200 in four panes of 50.

1989, Feb. 21 **Tagged** *Perf. 11*

2403 A1767 25c **multicolored**	.50	.25
P# block of 4, 4#+A	3.00	—
Zip block of 4	2.10	—
Pane of 50	25.00	

WASHINGTON STATEHOOD, 100th ANNIV.

Mt. Rainier — A1768

Designed by Howard Rogers.

Printed by the American Bank Note Co.

PHOTOGRAVURE
Plates of 200 in four panes of 50.

1989, Feb. 22 **Tagged** *Perf. 11*

2404 A1768 25c **multicolored**	.50	.25
P# block of 4, 4#+A	2.50	—
Zip block of 4	2.10	—
Pane of 50	25.00	

STEAMBOATS

Experiment, 1788-90 — A1769

Phoenix, 1809 A1770

New Orleans, 1812 A1771

Washington, 1816 — A1772

Walk in the Water, 1818 A1773

Designed by Richard Schlecht.

LITHOGRAPHED & ENGRAVED
BOOKLET STAMPS
Perf. 10 Horiz. on 1 or 2 Sides

1989, Mar. 3	**Tagged**		
2405 A1769 25c **multicolored**	.60	.25
2406 A1770 25c **multicolored**	.60	.25
2407 A1771 25c **multicolored**	.60	.25
2408 A1772 25c **multicolored**	.60	.25
2409 A1773 25c **multicolored**	.60	.25
a. Booklet pane of 5, #2405-2409	3.00	1.75
b. As "a," tagging omitted	—	—

WORLD STAMP EXPO '89

Nov. 17-Dec. 3. Washington, D.C.

No. 122 — A1774

Designed by Richard Sheaff.

LITHOGRAPHED & ENGRAVED
Plates of 200 in four panes of 50.

1989, Mar. 16 Tagged	*Perf. 11*	
2410 A1774 25c **grayish brn, blk & car rose**	.50	.25
P# block of 4, 4#	2.25	—
Zip block of 4	2.10	—
Pane of 50	25.00	

PERFORMING ARTS

Arturo Toscanini (1867-1957), Conductor — A1775

Designed by Jim Sharpe

Printed by the American Bank Note Co.

PHOTOGRAVURE
Plates of 200 in four panes of 50.

1989, Mar. 25 Tagged	*Perf. 11*	
2411 A1775 25c **multicolored**	.50	.25
P# block of 4, 5#+A	2.25	—
Zip block of 4	2.10	—
Pane of 50	25.00	

CONSTITUTION BICENTENNIAL SERIES

House of Representatives A1776

Senate A1777

Executive Branch — A1778

Supreme Court — A1779

Designed by Howard Koslow

LITHOGRAPHED & ENGRAVED
Plates of 200 in four panes of 50.

1989-90 Tagged	*Perf. 11*	
2412 A1776 25c **multi,** *Apr. 4, 1989*	.50	.25
P# block of 4, 4#	2.25	—
Zip block of 4	2.10	—
Pane of 50	25.00	
2413 A1777 25c **multi,** *Apr. 6, 1989*	.50	.25
P# block of 4, 4#	3.25	—
Zip block of 4	2.10	—
Pane of 50	25.00	
2414 A1778 25c **multi,** *Apr. 16, 1989*	.50	.25
P# block of 4, 4#	2.25	—
Zip block of 4	2.10	—
Pane of 50	25.00	
2415 A1779 25c **multi,** *Feb. 2, 1990*	.50	.25
P# block of 4, 4#	2.25	—
Zip block of 4	2.10	—
Pane of 50	25.00	
Nos. 2412-2415 (4)	2.00	1.00

SOUTH DAKOTA STATEHOOD, 100th ANNIV.

Pasque Flowers, Pioneer Woman and Sod House on Grasslands A1780

Designed by Marian Henjum.

Printed by the American Bank Note Co.

PHOTOGRAVURE
Plates of 200 in four panes of 50.

1989, May 3 Tagged	*Perf. 11*	
2416 A1780 25c **multicolored**	.60	.25
P# block of 4, 4#+A	3.00	—
Zip block of 4	2.50	—
Pane of 50	30.00	

Imperfs exist from printer's waste.

AMERICAN SPORTS

Lou Gehrig (1903-1941), New York Yankee Baseball Player — A1781

Designed by Bart Forbes.

Printed by the American Bank Note Co.

PHOTOGRAVURE
Plates of 200 in four panes of 50.

1989, June 10 Tagged	*Perf. 11*	
2417 A1781 25c **multicolored**	.60	.25
P# block of 4, 6#+A	3.00	—
Zip block of 4	2.50	—
Pane of 50	30.00	

LITERARY ARTS SERIES

Ernest Hemingway (1899-1961), 1954 Nobel Prize Winner for Literature — A1782

Designed by M. Gregory Rudd.

Printed by the American Bank Note Co.

PHOTOGRAVURE
Plates of 200 in four panes of 50.

1989, July 17 Tagged	*Perf. 11*	
2418 A1782 25c **multicolored**	.50	.25
P# block of 4, 5#+A	2.25	—
Zip block of 4	2.10	—
Pane of 50	25.00	
a. Vert. pair, imperf horiz.	*600.00*	

Imperforates on gummed stamp paper, including gutter pairs and blocks, are proofs from the ABNCo. archives. See No. 2418P in Proofs section.

MOON LANDING, 20TH ANNIVERSARY

Raising of the Flag on the Lunar Surface, July 20, 1969 — A1783

Designed by Christopher Calle.

LITHOGRAPHED & ENGRAVED
Panes of 20

1989, July 20 Tagged	*Perf. 11x11½*	
2419 A1783 $2.40 **multicolored**	4.75	2.00
P# block of 4, 6#	20.00	—
Pane of 20	100.00	—
a. Black (engr.) omitted	*1,350.*	
b. Imperf., pair	*375.00*	
c. Black (litho.) omitted	*1,500.*	
d. Tagging omitted		—

No. 2419 exists with a gray background instead of the normal dark blue. Some of these may have been caused by a chemical wiping of the blue plate. However, the same or extremely similar stamps can be produced by exposing normal stamps to sunlight or fluorescent light for varying time periods.

LETTER CARRIERS

A1784

Designed by Jack Davis.

Printed by the American Bank Note Co.

PHOTOGRAVURE
Plates of 160 in four panes of 40.

1989, Aug. 30 **Tagged** ***Perf. 11***

2420	A1784 25c **multicolored**	.50	.25
	P# block of 4, 5#+A	2.25	—
	Zip block of 4	2.10	—
	Pane of 40	20.00	

CONSTITUTION BICENTENNIAL

Bill of Rights — A1785

Designed by Lou Nolan.

LITHOGRAPHED & ENGRAVED
Plates of 200 in four panes of 50.

1989, Sept. 25 **Tagged** ***Perf. 11***

2421	A1785 25c **multicolored**	.50	.25
	P# block of 4	3.25	—
	Zip block of 4	2.10	—
	Pane of 50	25.00	
a.	Black (engr.) omitted	*225.00*	

PREHISTORIC ANIMALS

Tyrannosaurus Rex — A1786

Pteranodon A1787

Stegosaurus A1788

Brontosaurus A1789

Designed by John Gurche.

LITHOGRAPHED & ENGRAVED
Plates of 160 in four panes of 40.

1989, Oct. 1 **Tagged** ***Perf. 11***

2422	A1786 25c **multicolored**	.70	.25
a.	Black (engr.) omitted	80.00	—
2423	A1787 25c **multicolored**	.70	.25
a.	Black (engr.) omitted	80.00	
b.	Tagging omitted		—
2424	A1788 25c **multicolored**	.70	.25
a.	Black (engr.) omitted	80.00	—
2425	A1789 25c **multicolored**	.70	.25
a.	Black (engr.) omitted	80.00	
b.	Block of 4, #2422-2425	2.80	2.00
	P# block of 4, 6#	3.50	—
	Zip block of 4	3.00	—
	Pane of 40	28.00	
c.	As "b," black (engr.) omitted	*325.00*	

No. 2425c is valued in the grade of fine. Very fine blocks exist and sell for approximately $600.

PRE-COLUMBIAN AMERICA ISSUE

Southwest Carved Figure, A.D. 1150-1350 — A1790

Designed by Lon Busch.

Printed by the American Bank Note Company.

PHOTOGRAVURE
Plates of 200 in four panes of 50.

1989, Oct. 12 **Tagged** ***Perf. 11***

2426	A1790 25c **multicolored**	.60	.25
	P# block of 4, 6#+A	3.00	—
	Zip block of 4	2.50	—
	Pane of 50	30.00	
a.	Tagging omitted	—	—

See No. C121.

CHRISTMAS

Madonna and Child, by Carracci — A1791

Sleigh Full of Presents — A1792

Designed by Bradbury Thompson (#2427 & 2429) and Steven Dohanos (#2428).

Printed by the Bureau of Engraving and Printing (#2427 & 2429) and American Bank Note Company (#2428).

LITHOGRAPHED & ENGRAVED,
PHOTOGRAVURE (#2428-2429)
Sheets of 300 in six panes of 50.

1989, Oct. 19 **Tagged** ***Perf. 11¼***

2427	A1791 25c **multicolored**	.50	.25
	P# block of 4, 5#	2.25	—
	Zip, copyright block of 4	2.10	—
	Pane of 50	25.00	
	Pair with full horiz. gutter between	—	
a.	Booklet pane of 10	5.00	3.50
b.	Red (litho.) omitted	*300.00*	
c.	As "a," imperf.	—	

Perf. 11½

2428	A1792 25c **multicolored**	.50	.25
	P# block of 4, 5#+A	2.25	—
	Zip, copyright block of 4	2.10	—
	Pane of 50	25.00	
a.	Vert. pair, imperf. horiz.	*500.00*	

BOOKLET STAMP

Perf. 11½ on 2 or 3 Sides

2429	A1792 25c **multicolored**	.50	.25
a.	Booklet pane of 10	5.00	3.50
b.	Vert. pair, imperf. btwn. (from miscut bklt pane)	*500.00*	
c.	As "a," horiz. imperf. between	*2,250.*	
d.	As "a," red omitted	*3,250.*	
e.	Imperf., pair	*750.00*	

Marked differences exist between Nos. 2428 and 2429: No. 2429 was printed in four colors, No. 2428 in five colors. The runners on the sleigh in No. 2429 are twice as thick as those on No. 2428. On No. 2429 the package at the upper left in the sleigh has a red bow, whereas the same package in No. 2428 has a red and black bow; and the ribbon on the upper right package in No. 2429 is green, whereas the same ribbon in No. 2428 is black.

Eagle and Shield — A1793

Designed by Jay Haiden.

Printed by the American Bank Note Company.

PHOTOGRAVURE
BOOKLET STAMP

1989, Nov. 10 **Tagged** **Self-Adhesive** ***Die Cut***

2431	A1793 25c **multicolored** Ⓢ	.50	.25
a.	Booklet pane of 18	10.00	
b.	Vert. pair, die cutting omitted between	*325.00*	
c.	Die cutting omitted, pair	*200.00*	

Panes sold for $5.

Also available in strips of 18 with stamps spaced for use in affixing machines to service first day covers. Sold for $5.

No. 2431c will include part of the margins around the stamps.

Sold only in 15 test cities (Atlanta, Chicago, Cleveland, Columbus, OH, Dallas, Denver, Houston, Indianapolis, Kansas City, MO, Los Angeles, Miami, Milwaukee, Minneapolis, Phoenix, St. Louis) and through the philatelic agency.

Ⓢ: Adhesive residue sometimes remains on the back of examples of No. 2431 after soaking. See note after No. 1549.

WORLD STAMP EXPO '89
Washington, DC, Nov. 17-Dec. 3

A1794

Illustration reduced.

Designed by Richard Sheaff.

LITHOGRAPHED & ENGRAVED

1989, Nov. 17 **Tagged** ***Imperf.***

2433	A1794 Pane of 4	16.00	14.00
a.	90c like No. 122	4.00	3.00
b.	90c like 132TC4j	4.00	3.00
c.	90c like 132TC4i	4.00	3.00

d.	90c like 132TC4d	4.00	3.00
e.	As No. 2433, tagging omitted	—	
f.	Double impression of all 4 frames	—	

20th UPU CONGRESS
Traditional Mail Delivery

Stagecoach, c. 1850 — A1795

Paddlewheel Steamer — A1796

Biplane — A1797

Depot-hack Type Automobile — A1798

Designed by Mark Hess.

LITHOGRAPHED & ENGRAVED

Plates of 160 in four panes of 40.

1989, Nov. 19 **Tagged** ***Perf. 11***

2434	A1795 25c **multicolored**	.50	.25
2435	A1796 25c **multicolored**	.50	.25
2436	A1797 25c **multicolored**	.50	.25
2437	A1798 25c **multicolored**	.50	.25
a.	Block of 4, #2434-2437	2.00	1.75
	P# block of 4, 5#	3.75	—
	Zip block of 4	2.25	—
	Pane of 40	20.00	
b.	As "a," dark blue (engr.) omitted	*300.00*	
c.	As No. 2437a, tagging omitted	—	

No. 2437b is valued in the grade of fine. Very fine blocks exist and sell for approximately $450.

Souvenir Sheet

LITHOGRAPHED & ENGRAVED

1989, Nov. 28 **Tagged** ***Imperf.***

2438	Sheet of 4	5.00	3.75
a.	A1795 25c **multicolored**	1.25	.80
b.	A1796 25c **multicolored**	1.25	.80
c.	A1797 25c **multicolored**	1.25	.80
d.	A1798 25c **multicolored**	1.25	.80
e.	Dark blue & gray (engr.) omitted	*4,000.*	

20th Universal Postal Union Congress.

VALUES FOR HINGED STAMPS AFTER NO. 771

This catalogue does not value unused stamps after No. 771 in hinged condition. Hinged unused stamps from No. 772 to the present are worth considerably less than the values given for unused stamps, which are for never-hinged examples.

IDAHO STATEHOOD, 100th ANNIV.

Mountain Bluebird, Sawtooth Mountains — A1799

Designed by John Dawson.

Printed by the American Bank Note Company.

PHOTOGRAVURE

Plates of 200 in four panes of 50.

1990, Jan. 6 **Tagged** ***Perf. 11***

2439	A1799 25c **multicolored**	.55	.25
	P# block of 4, 5#+A	3.50	—
	Zip block of 4	2.25	—
	Pane of 50	27.50	

LOVE

A1800

Designed by Jayne Hertko.

Printed by the U.S. Banknote Company (#2440) and the Bureau of Engraving and Printing (#2441).

PHOTOGRAVURE

Plates of 200 in four panes of 50.

1990, Jan. 18 **Tagged** ***Perf. 12½x13***

2440	A1800 25c **multicolored**	.50	.25
	P# block of 4, 4#	2.25	—
	Zip, copyright block of 4	2.10	—
	Pane of 50	25.00	
a.	Imperf., pair	*550.00*	

BOOKLET STAMP

Perf. 11½ on 2 or 3 Sides

2441	A1800 25c **multicolored**	.50	.25
a.	Booklet pane of 10	5.00	3.50
b.	Bright pink omitted	*80.00*	
c.	As "a," bright pink omitted	*750.00*	
d.	As "a," tagging omitted	—	

No. 2441b may be obtained from booklet panes containing both normal and color-omitted stamps.

BLACK HERITAGE SERIES

Beach Umbrella — A1802

High Mountain Meadows, by Conrad Schwiering A1803

Ida B. Wells (1862-1931), Journalist — A1801

Designed by Thomas Blackshear.

Printed by American Bank Note Company.

PHOTOGRAVURE

Plates of 200 in four panes of 50.

1990, Feb. 1 **Tagged** ***Perf. 11***

2442	A1801 25c **multicolored**	.75	.25
	P# block of 4, 5#+A	3.75	—
	Zip block of 4	3.25	—
	Pane of 50	37.50	

Designed by Pierre Mion.

BOOKLET STAMP

PHOTOGRAVURE

1990, Feb. 3 **Tagged** ***Perf. 11 on 2 or 3 Sides***

2443	A1802 15c **multicolored**	.30	.25
a.	Booklet pane of 10	3.00	2.50
b.	Blue omitted	*100.00*	
c.	As "a," blue omitted	*900.00*	

WYOMING STATEHOOD, 100th ANNIV.

Designed by Jack Rosenthal.

LITHOGRAPHED & ENGRAVED

Plates of 200 in four panes of 50.

1990, Feb. 23 **Tagged** ***Perf. 11***

2444	A1803 25c **multicolored**	.80	.25
	P# block of 4, 5#	4.00	—
	Zip block of 4	3.25	—
	Pane of 50	40.00	
a.	Black (engr.) omitted	*900.00*	—

CLASSIC FILMS

Judy Garland and Toto (The Wizard of Oz) — A1804

Clark Gable & Vivien Leigh (Gone With the Wind) — A1805

Gary Cooper (Beau Geste) — A1806

John Wayne (Stagecoach) A1807

Designed by Thomas Blackshear.

Printed by the American Bank Note Company.

PHOTOGRAVURE
Plates of 160 in four panes of 40.

1990, Mar. 23 **Tagged** ***Perf. 11***

2445 A1804 25c **multicolored**	1.25	.25
2446 A1805 25c **multicolored**	1.25	.25
2447 A1806 25c **multicolored**	1.25	.25
2448 A1807 25c **multicolored**	1.25	.25
a. Block of 4, #2445-2448	5.00	3.50
P# block of 4, 5#+A	5.50	—
Zip block of 4	5.25	—
Pane of 40	50.00	

LITERARY ARTS SERIES

Marianne Moore (1887-1972), Poet — A1808

Designed by M. Gregory Rudd.

Printed by the American Bank Note Company.

PHOTOGRAVURE
Plates of 200 in four panes of 50.

1990, Apr. 18 **Tagged** ***Perf. 11***

2449 A1808 25c **multicolored**	.55	.25
P# block of 4, 3#+A	2.50	—
Zip block of 4	2.40	—
Pane of 50	27.50	
a. All colors missing (EP)	—	

No. 2449a must be collected se-tenant with a partially printed stamp or in longer horizontal strips with a partially printed stamp and normal stamps.

Coil Plate No. Strips of 3
Beginning with No. 2123, coil plate no. strips of 3 usually sell at the level of strips of 5 minus the face value of two stamps.

TRANSPORTATION ISSUE

Steam Carriage 1866 — A1810

Circus Wagon 1900s — A1811

A1811a

Canoe 1800s — A1812

Tractor Trailer 1930s — A1816

Cog Railway 1870s — A1822

Lunch Wagon 1890s — A1823

Ferryboat 1900s — A1825

Seaplane 1914 — A1827

Designers: 4c, 32c, Richard Schlecht. Nos. 2452, 2452B, 2452D, Susan Sanford. No. 2453, Paul Calle. 10c, David K. Stone. 20c, 23c, Robert Brangwynne. $1, Chuck Hodgson.

Printed by: Guilford Gravure for American Bank Note Co. (No. 2452B), J.W. Fergusson & Sons for Stamp Venturers (No. 2454), Stamp Venturers (No, 2452D), others by BEP.

COIL STAMPS
ENGRAVED, PHOTOGRAVURE (#2452B, 2452D, 2454, 2458)

1990-95 ***Perf. 9.8 Vert.***
Tagged, Untagged (Nos. 2452B, 2452D, 2453, 2454, 2457-2458)

2451 A1810 4c **claret,** *Jan. 25, 1991*	.30	.25
Pair	.50	.50
P# strip of 5, #1	.90	
P# single, #1	—	.65
a. Imperf., pair	*450.00*	
b. Untagged	.30	.25
Pair	.50	.50
P# strip of 5, #1	.90	
P# single, #1	—	.65
2452 A1811 5c **carmine,** dull gum, *Aug. 31*	.30	.25
Pair	.50	.50
P# strip of 5, #1	.90	
P# single, #1	—	.65
a. Untagged, dull gum	.30	.25
Pair	.50	.50
P# strip of 5, #1	2.50	
P# single, #1	—	2.25
Low gloss gum	.30	
Pair	.50	
P# strip of 5, #2	2.00	
P# single, #2	—	1.60
c. Imperf., pair	*350.00*	

No. 2452c is valued in the grade of fine.

2452B A1811 5c **carmine,** *Dec. 8, 1992*	.30	.25
Pair	.50	.50
P# strip of 5, #A1-A2	1.25	
P# single, #A1-A2	—	.90
f. Printed with luminescent ink	.40	.25
Pair	.80	.50
P# strip of 5, #A3	3.00	
P# single, #A3	—	2.00
2452D A1811a 5c **carmine,** low gloss gum, *Mar. 20, 1995*	.30	.25
Pair	.50	.50
P# strip of 5, #S1-S2	1.25	
P# single, #S1-S2	—	1.00
e. Imperf., pair	*115.00*	
g. Printed with luminescent ink, shiny gum	.30	.25
Pair	.50	.50
P# strip of 5, #S2	2.00	
P# single, #S2	—	1.60
Low gloss gum	.30	
P# strip of 5, #S3	2.00	
P# single, #S3	—	1.75
h. As "g," low gloss gum, imperf. pair	—	
2453 A1812 5c **brown** (Bureau precancel, Additional Nonprofit Postage Paid, in gray), *May 25, 1991*	.40	.25
Pair	.80	.50
P# strip of 5, #1-3	1.50	
P# single, #1-3	—	1.00
a. Imperf., pair	*225.00*	
b. Gray omitted		1,200.
2454 A1812 5c **red** (Bureau precancel, Additional Nonprofit Postage Paid, in gray), shiny gum, *Oct. 22, 1991*	.45	.25
Pair	.90	.50
P# strip of 5, #S11	1.25	
P# single, #S11	—	1.00
Low gloss gum	.65	
Pair	1.30	
P# strip of 5, #S11	4.00	
2457 A1816 10c **green** (Bureau precancel, Additional Presort Postage Paid, in gray), *May 25, 1991*	.45	.25
Pair	.90	.50
P# strip of 5, #1	2.25	
P# single, #1	—	1.40
a. Imperf., pair	*110.00*	
b. All color omitted	—	

No. 2457b must be accompanied by a 2012 certificate of authentication confirming that stamps are from the discovery coil roll that also contained normal and partially printed stamps.

2458 A1816 10c **green** (Bureau precancel, Additional Presort Postage Paid, in black), *May 25, 1994*	.55	.25
Pair	1.10	.50
P# strip of 5, #11, 22	3.50	
P# single, #11, 22	—	1.75
2463 A1822 20c **green,** *June 9, 1995*	.40	.25
Pair	.80	.50
P# strip of 5, #1-2	3.00	
P# single, #1-2	—	2.00
a. Imperf., pair	*75.00*	
2464 A1823 23c **dark blue,** prephosphored coated paper with surface tagging showing a solid appearance, dull gum, *Apr. 12, 1991*	.45	.25
Pair	.90	.50
P# strip of 5, #2-3	3.25	
P# single, #2-3	—	1.75
a. Prephosphored uncoated paper with embedded tagging showing a mottled appearance, dull gum, *1993*	1.20	.25
Pair	2.40	.50
P# strip of 5, #3	9.00	
Shiny gum, *1993*	.45	
Pair	.90	
P# strip of 5, #3	3.75	
P# strip of 5, #4	9.00	
P# strip of 5, #5	4.00	
P# single, #3		2.00
P# single, #4		8.00
P# single, #5	—	4.00
b. Imperf., pair, prephosphored coated paper	*100.00*	
c. Imperf., pair, prephosphored uncoated paper	*110.00*	
2466 A1825 32c **blue,** prephosphored uncoated paper with embedded tagging showing a mottled appearance, shiny gum, *June 2, 1995*	.80	.25
Pair	1.60	.50
P# strip of 5, #2	4.50	
P# strip of 5, #3	5.00	
P# strip of 5, #4	4.75	
P# strip of 5, #5	6.50	
P# single, #2, 3	—	2.25
P# single, #4	—	2.50
P# single, #5	—	3.50
Low gloss gum	1.10	
Pair	2.20	
P# strip of 5, #3	10.00	
P# strip of 5, #4	12.00	
P# strip of 5, #5	10.00	
P# single, #3	—	
P# single, #4	—	
P# single, #5	—	
a. Imperf., pair, shiny gum	*375.00*	
Low gloss gum	*475.00*	
b. 32c **bright blue,** prephosphored uncoated paper with embedded tagging showing a mottled appearance, low gloss gum	3.00	2.25
Pair	6.00	5.50
P# strip of 5, #5	90.00	
P# single, #5	—	90.00

Some specialists refer to No. 2466b as "Bronx blue," and it is considered to be an error of color.

2468 A1827 $1 **blue & scarlet,** overall tagging, dull gum, *Apr. 20*	2.25	.50
Pair	4.50	1.00
P# strip of 5, #1	12.50	
P# single, #1	—	5.00
a. Imperf., pair	*1,750.*	*1,150.*
b. Prephosphored uncoated paper with embedded tagging showing a mottled appearance, shiny gum, *1993*	2.50	.50
Pair	5.00	1.00
P# strip of 5, #3	13.00	
P# single, #3	—	5.00
c. Prephosphored coated paper with surface tagging showing a grainy solid appearance, low gloss gum, *1998*	3.00	.50
Pair	6.00	1.00

	Unused	Used
P# strip of 5, #3	16.00	
P# single, #3	—	10.00
Nos. 2451-2468 (12)	6.95	3.25

Some mint pairs of No. 2468 appear to be imperf. but have faint blind perforations on the gum. Beware of examples with the gum removed.

LIGHTHOUSES

Admiralty Head, WA — A1829

Cape Hatteras, NC — A1830

West Quoddy Head, ME — A1831

American Shoals, FL — A1832

Sandy Hook, NJ — A1833

Designed by Howard Koslow.

BOOKLET STAMPS

LITHOGRAPHED & ENGRAVED

Perf. 10 Vert. on 1 or 2 Sides

1990, Apr. 26 **Tagged**

2470 A1829 25c **multicolored**	1.50	.25
2471 A1830 25c **multicolored**	1.50	.25
2472 A1831 25c **multicolored**	1.50	.25
2473 A1832 25c **multicolored**	1.50	.25
2474 A1833 25c **multicolored**	1.50	.25
a. Bklt. pane of 5, #2470-2474	7.50	2.00
b. As "a," white ("USA 25") omitted	85.00	—

Perforations on Lighthouse booklet panes separate very easily. Careful handling is required.

FLAG 

A1834

Designed by Harry Zelenko.

Printed by Avery International Corp.

PHOTOGRAVURE

1990, May 18 Untagged Self-adhesive ***Die Cut***
Printed on Plastic

2475 A1834 25c **dark red & dark blue**	.55	.25
a. Pane of 12	6.60	

Sold only in panes of 12; peelable plastic backing inscribed in light ultramarine. Available for a test period of six months at 22 First National Bank automatic teller machines in Seattle.

Ⓢ: Adhesive residue sometimes remains on the back of examples of No. 2475 after soaking. See note after No. 1549.

FLORA AND FAUNA

American Kestrel — A1840

American Kestrel — A1841

Eastern Bluebird — A1842

Fawn — A1843

Cardinal — A1844

Pumpkinseed Sunfish — A1845

Bobcat A1846

Designers: 1c, 3c, 45c, Michael Matherly. 19c, Peter Cocci. 30c, Robert Giusti. $2, Chuck Ripper.

Printed by: No. 2476 and No. 2478, American Bank Note Co. No. 2477, No. 2479 and No. 2482, Bureau of Engraving & Printing. No. 2480, Stamp Venturers. No. 2481, Stamp Venturers (engraved) and The Press, Inc. (lithographed).

LITHOGRAPHED

Panes of 100

1990-95 Untagged (1c, 3c) ***Perf. 11, 11.2 (#2477)***

2476 A1840 1c **multicolored,** *June 22, 1991*	.30	.25
P# block of 4, 4#+A	.50	—
Zip block of 4	.50	—
Pane of 100	5.00	
a. Quadruple impression of black inscriptions and denomination	*850.00*	
b. Quintuple impression of black inscriptions and denomination	*1,500.*	
c. Triple impression of black inscriptions and denomination	—	

Other colors on Nos. 2476a, 2476b and 2476c are misregistered and the stamps are poorly centered.

2477 A1841 1c **multicolored,** shiny gum, *May 10, 1995*	.30	.25
P# block of 4, 4#	.50	—
Pane of 100	5.00	
Low gloss gum	.30	
P# block of 4, 4#	.50	
Pane of 100	5.00	
a. Tagged (error), shiny gum	—	
2478 A1842 3c **multicolored,** *June 22, 1991*	.30	.25
P# block of 4, 4#+A	.50	—
Zip block of 4	.50	—
Pane of 100	8.00	
a. Vert. pair, imperf horiz.	—	
b. Double impression of all colors except yellow	*200.00*	
c. Double impression of blue, triple impression of black	—	

Other colors on No. 2478c are misregistered and all kown examples have fine centering.

Imperforates on gummed stamp paper, plus imperforate and perforated gutter pairs and blocks (including imperforate and perforated gutter pairs and blocks of No. 2476 se-tenant with No. 2478), are proofs from the ABNCo. archives. See Nos. 2476P and 2478P in Proofs section.

See Nos. 3031, 3031A, 3044. Compare design A1842 with design A2336.

PHOTOGRAVURE

Plates of 400 in four panes of 100.

Tagged ***Perf. 11***

2479 A1843 19c **multicolored,** *Mar. 11, 1991*	.35	.25
P# block of 4, 5#	1.75	—
Zip block of 4	1.50	—
Pane of 100	35.00	
a. Tagging omitted	*10.00*	
b. Red omitted	*425.00*	
c. Imperf, pair	*900.00*	

On No. 2479b other colors are shifted.

2480 A1844 30c **multicolored,** *June 22, 1991*	.60	.25
P# block of 4, 4#+S	2.75	—
Zip block of 4	2.50	—
Pane of 100	60.00	

LITHOGRAPHED & ENGRAVED

Panes of 100

Perf. 11

2481 A1845 45c **multicolored,** *Dec. 2, 1992*	.90	.25
P# block of 4, 5#+S	4.25	—
Zip block of 4	3.75	—
Pane of 100	90.00	
a. Black (engr.) omitted	*300.00*	—

Panes of 20

2482 A1846 $2 **multicolored,** *June 1, 1990*	3.50	1.25
P# block of 4, 5#	14.00	—
Pane of 20	70.00	
a. Black (engr.) omitted	*200.00*	
b. Tagging omitted	22.50	
Nos. 2476-2482 (7)	6.25	2.75

Blue Jay — A1847

Wood Duck — A1848

African Violets — A1849

Peach — A1850

Pear — A1851

Red Squirrel — A1852

Rose — A1853

Pine Cone — A1854

Designed by Robert Giusti (#2483-2485), Ned Seidler (#2486-2488, 2493-2495A), Michael R. Matherly (#2489), Gyo Fujikawa (#2490), Paul Breeden (#2491), Gyo Fujikawa (#2492).

Printed by Stamp Venturers (#2483, 2492), Bureau of Engraving and Printing (#2484, 2487-2488), J.W. Fergusson & Sons for KCS Industries, Inc. (#2485), KCS Industries (#2486), Dittler Brothers, Inc. (#2489), Stamp Venturers (#2490), Banknote Corporation of America (#2491), Avery-Dennison (#2493-2495, 2495A).

PHOTOGRAVURE
BOOKLET STAMPS

1991-95 ***Perf. 10.9x9.8 on 2 or 3 Sides***
Tagged

2483 A1847 20c **multicolored,** *June 15, 1995* .50 .25
a. Booklet pane of 10 5.25 2.50
b. As "a," imperf —

Perf. 10 on 2 or 3 sides

2484 A1848 29c **black & multi,** overall tagging, *Apr. 12, 1991* .60 .25
a. Booklet pane of 10 6.00 3.75
b. Vert. pair, imperf. horiz. *175.00*
c. As "b," bklt. pane of 10 *875.00*
d. Prephosphored coated paper with surface tagging showing a solid appearance .60 .25
e. As "d," booklet pane of 10 6.00 3.75
f. Vert. pair, imperf between and with natural straight edge at top or bottom *175.00*
g. As "f," bklt. pane of 10 *875.00*

Perf. 11 on 2 or 3 Sides

2485 A1848 29c **red & multi,** *Apr. 12, 1991* .60 .25
a. Booklet pane of 10 6.00 4.00
b. Vert. pair, imperf. between *2,500.*
c. Imperf, pair *4,500.*

Perf. 10x11 on 2 or 3 Sides

2486 A1849 29c **multicolored,** *Oct. 8, 1993* .60 .25
a. Booklet pane of 10 6.00 4.00

Perf. 11x10 on 2 or 3 Sides

2487 A1850 32c **multicolored,** *July 8, 1995* .65 .25
2488 A1851 32c **multicolored,** *July 8, 1995* .65 .25
a. Booklet pane, 5 each #2487-2488 6.50 4.25
b. Pair, #2487-2488 1.30 .30

PHOTOGRAVURE, ENGRAVED (#2491)

1993-95 **Tagged** ***Die Cut***
Self-Adhesive
Booklet Stamps

2489 A1852 29c **multicolored,** *June 25* .60 .25
a. Booklet pane of 18 11.00
b. As "a," die cutting omitted —
2490 A1853 29c **red, green & black,** *Aug. 19* .60 .25
a. Booklet pane of 18 11.00

Nos. 2489-2490 also available in strips with stamps spaced for use in affixing machines to service first day covers. No plate numbers. Stamps removed from strips are virtually indistinguishable from booklet stamps. The stamps from strips have minutely rounded corners, whereas the corners of the booklet stamps are squared.

2491 A1854 29c **multicolored,** *Nov. 5* .60 .25
a. Booklet pane of 18 11.00
b. Horiz. pair, die cutting omitted between *175.00 125.00*
c. Coil with plate # B1 — 6.00
P# strip of 5, #B1 7.50

Stamps without plate number from coil strips are indistinguishable from booklet stamps once they are removed from the backing paper.

Serpentine Die Cut 11.3x11.7 on 2, 3 or 4 Sides

2492 A1853 32c **pink, green & black,** *June 2, 1995* .65 .25
a. Booklet pane of 20 + label 13.00
b. Booklet pane of 15 + label 9.75
c. Horiz. pair, die cutting omitted between —
d. As "a," 2 stamps and parts of 7 others printed on backing liner —
e. Booklet pane of 14 20.00
f. Booklet pane of 16 20.00
g. Coil with plate # S111 — 5.50
P# strip of 5, #S111 7.00
h. Vert. pair, die cutting omitted between (from No. 2492b) *400.00*
i. As "a," 6 pairs plus stamp and label die cutting omitted vert. btwn. (due to miscutting) *800.00*
j. As "f," with 2 vert. pairs at bottom die cutting omitted horiz., in full bklt. #BK178D —
k. As "a," horiz. die cutting omitted —

Nos. 2492, 2492a and 2492b exist on two types of surface-tagged paper that exhibit either a solid or a grainy solid appearance. Values are the same. Nos. 2492e, 2492f and 2492g have tagging with a solid appearance, while Nos. 2492c, 2492d and 2492h have tagging with a grainy solid appearance.

Stamps on plate # strips are separated on backing larger than the stamps. Stamps without plate # from coil strips are indistinguishable from interior position booklet stamps once they are removed from the backing paper.

For booklet panes containing No. 2492f with one stamp removed, see Nos. BK178B, BK178D-BK178E in Booklets section.

Serpentine Die Cut 8.8 on 2, 3 or 4 Sides

2493 A1850 32c **multicolored,** *July 8, 1995* .65 .25
2494 A1851 32c **multicolored,** *July 8, 1995* .65 .25
a. Booklet pane of 20, 10 each #2493-2494 + label 13.00
b. Pair, #2493-2494 1.30

c. As "b," die cutting omitted —

COIL STAMPS
Serpentine Die Cut 8.8 Vert.

2495 A1850 32c **multicolored,** *July 8, 1995* 2.00 .25
2495A A1851 32c **multicolored,** *July 8, 1995* 2.00 .25
b. Pair, #2495-2495A 4.00
P# strip of 5, 3 #2495A, 2 #2495, P#V11111 13.00
P# single, #V11111 — 6.75

See Nos. 3048-3049, 3053-3054.

Values for used self-adhesive stamps are for examples either on piece or off piece.

OLYMPIANS

Jesse Owens, 1936 — A1855

Ray Ewry, 1900-08 A1856

Hazel Wightman, 1924 — A1857

Eddie Eagan, 1920, 1932 — A1858

Helene Madison, 1932 — A1859

Designed by Bart Forbes.

Printed by the American Bank Note Company.

PHOTOGRAVURE
Panes of 35.

1990, July 6 **Tagged** ***Perf. 11***

2496 A1855 25c **multicolored** .60 .25
2497 A1856 25c **multicolored** .60 .25
2498 A1857 25c **multicolored** .60 .25
2499 A1858 25c **multicolored** .60 .25
2500 A1859 25c **multicolored** .60 .25
a. Strip of 5, #2496-2500 3.25 2.50
P# block of 10, 4#+A 8.00 —
Zip, inscription block of 10 6.50 —
Pane of 35 21.00
b. As "a," blue omitted 1,750.

Imperforates on gummed stamp paper, including gutter pairs, strips and blocks, are proofs from the ABNCo. archives. See No. 2500aP in Proofs section.

INDIAN HEADDRESSES

Assiniboin A1860

Cheyenne A1861

Comanche A1862

Flathead A1863

Shoshone A1864

Designed by Lunda Hoyle Gill.

LITHOGRAPHED & ENGRAVED
BOOKLET STAMPS

1990, Aug. 17 **Tagged** ***Perf. 11 on 2 or 3 Sides***

2501 A1860 25c **multicolored** .80 .25
2502 A1861 25c **multicolored** .80 .25
2503 A1862 25c **multicolored** .80 .25
a. Black (engr.) omitted *125.00* —
2504 A1863 25c **multicolored** .80 .25
a. Black (engr.) omitted *125.00* —
2505 A1864 25c **multicolored** .80 .25
a. Bklt. pane of 10, 2 each #2501-2505 8.00 6.00
b. As "a," black (engr.) omitted *2,500.*
c. Strip of 5, #2501-2505 4.00 2.50
d. As "a," horiz. imperf. between *2,250.*

At least one of the examples of No. 2505d that have been reported is actually split at the booklet fold and is a block of 4 and a block of 6.

MICRONESIA & MARSHALL ISLANDS

Canoe and Flag of the Federated States of Micronesia A1865

Stick Chart, Canoe and Flag of the Republic of the Marshall Islands
A1866

LITHOGRAPHED & ENGRAVED

Sheets of 200 in four panes of 50.

1990, Sept. 28 **Tagged** ***Perf. 11***

2506	A1865 25c **multicolored**	.50	.25
2507	A1866 25c **multicolored**	.50	.25
a.	Pair, #2506-2507	1.00	.75
	P# block of 4, 6#	2.75	—
	Zip block of 4	2.10	—
	Pane of 50	25.00	
b.	As "a," black (engr.) omitted	*1,400.*	

See Micronesia Nos. 124-126, Marshall Islands No. 381.

SEA CREATURES

Killer Whales
A1867

Northern Sea Lions — A1868

Sea Otter — A1869

Common Dolphin
A1870

Designed by Peter Cocci (Nos. 2508, 2511), Vladimir Beilin, USSR (Nos. 2509-2510).

LITHOGRAPHED & ENGRAVED

Sheets of 160 in four panes of 40.

1990, Oct. 3 **Tagged** ***Perf. 11***

2508	A1867 25c **multicolored**	.55	.25
2509	A1868 25c **multicolored**	.55	.25
2510	A1869 25c **multicolored**	.55	.25
2511	A1870 25c **multicolored**	.55	.25
a.	Block of 4, #2508-2511	2.25	1.90
	P# block of 4, 5#	2.75	—
	Zip block of 4	2.30	—
	Pane of 40	22.00	
b.	As "a," black (engr.) omitted	*250.00*	
c.	As "a," tagging omitted	—	

See Russia Nos. 5933-5936.

PRE-COLUMBIAN AMERICA ISSUE

Grand Canyon
A1871

Designed by Mark Hess.

Printed by the American Bank Note Company.

PHOTOGRAVURE

Plates of 200 in four panes of 50.

(3 panes of #2512, 1 pane of #C127)

1990, Oct. 12 **Tagged** ***Perf. 11***

2512	A1871 25c **multicolored**	.55	.25
	P# block of 4, 4#+A, UR, LL, LR	2.75	—
	Zip block of 4	2.25	—
	Pane of 50	27.50	

See No. C127.

DWIGHT D. EISENHOWER, BIRTH CENTENARY

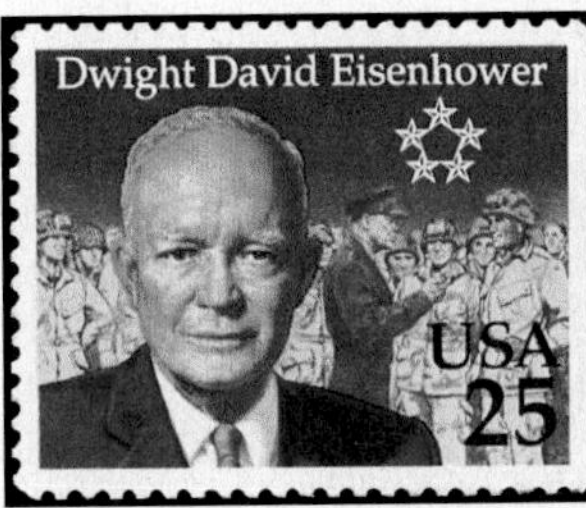

A1872

Designed by Ken Hodges.

Printed by the American Bank Note Company.

PHOTOGRAVURE

Plates of 160 in four panes of 40.

1990, Oct. 13 **Tagged** ***Perf. 11***

2513	A1872 25c **multicolored**	.80	.25
	P# block of 4, 5#+A	4.00	—
	P# block of 8, 5#+A and inscriptions	8.00	—
	Zip block of 4	3.75	—
	Pane of 40	32.00	

Imperforates on gummed stamp paper are proofs from the ABNCo. archives. See No. 2513P in Proofs section.

CHRISTMAS

Madonna & Child, by Antonello — A1873

Christmas Tree — A1874

Designed by Bradbury Thompson (#2514) and Libby Thiel (#2515-2516).

Printed by the Bureau of Engraving and Printing or the American Bank Note Company (#2515).

LITHOGRAPHED & ENGRAVED

Sheets of 300 in six panes of 50 (#2414-2415).

1990, Oct. 18 **Tagged** ***Perf. 11½x11½***

2514	A1873 25c **multicolored**, large block tagging	.50	.25
	P# block of 4, 5#	2.25	—
	Zip, copyright block of 4	2.10	—
	Pane of 50	25.00	
a.	Large block tagging over prephosphored coated paper with surface tagging showing a solid appearance	.50	.25
b.	As "a," bklt. pane of 10	5.00	3.25

PHOTOGRAVURE

Perf. 11

2515	A1874 25c **multicolored**	.50	.25
	P# block of 4, 4#+A	2.25	—
	Zip block of 4	2.10	—
	Pane of 50	25.00	
	Pair with full horiz. gutter btwn.	650.00	
a.	Vert. pair, imperf. horiz.	*500.00*	
b.	All colors missing (EP)	—	

No. 2515b must be collected se-tenant with normal and/or partially printed stamp(s).

BOOKLET STAMP

Perf. 11½x11 on 2 or 3 Sides

2516	A1874 25c **multicolored**	.60	.25
a.	Booklet pane of 10	6.00	3.25

Marked differences exist between Nos. 2515 and 2516. The background red on No. 2515 is even while that on No. 2516 is splotchy. The bands across the tree and "Greetings" are blue green on No. 2515 and yellow green on No. 2516.

A1875

A1876

Designed by Wallace Marosek (Nos. 2517-2520), Richard Sheaff (No. 2521).

Printed by U.S. Bank Note Company (No. 2517), Bureau of Engraving and Printing (No. 2518-2519), KCS Industries (No. 2520), American Bank Note Company (No. 2521).

PHOTOGRAVURE

Sheets of 100

1991, Jan. 22 **Tagged** ***Perf. 13***

2517	A1875 (29c) **yel, blk, red & yel grn**	.60	.25
	P# block of 4, 4#+U	2.75	—
	Zip block of 4	2.50	—
	Pane of 100	60.00	
a.	Imperf., pair	*1,000.*	
b.	Horiz. pair, imperf. vert.	*1,000.*	

See note after No. 2518.

Gutter pairs and blocks, and cross gutter blocks, all perforated, are proofs from the ABNCo. archives. See No. 2517P in Proofs section.

No. 2517a is usually collected as a vertical pair, though No. 2517 can be distinguished from the other "F" stamp issues.

COIL STAMP

Perf. 10 Vert.

2518	A1875 (29c) **yel, blk, dull red & dk yel grn**	.60	.25
	Pair	1.20	.25
	P# strip of 5, #1111	2.75	
	P# strip of 5, #1211	6.50	
	P# strip of 5, #1222	3.25	
	P# strip of 5, #2211	3.50	
	P# strip of 5, #2222	3.25	
	P# single, #1111	—	.50
	P# single, #1211	—	11.50
	P# single, #1222	—	.50
	P# single, #2211	—	3.00
	P# single, #2222	—	.50
a.	Imperf., pair	25.00	

"For U.S. addresses only" is 17½mm long on No. 2517, 16½mm long on No. 2518. Design of No. 2517 measures 21½x17½mm, No. 2518, 21x18mm.

BOOKLET STAMPS

Perf. 11 on 2 or 3 Sides

2519	A1875 (29c) **yel, blk, dull red & dk grn**	.60	.25
a.	Booklet pane of 10	6.50	4.50
2520	A1875 (29c) **pale yel, blk, red & brt grn**	1.50	.25
a.	Booklet pane of 10	15.00	4.50
b.	As "a," imperf. horiz.	—	
c.	Horiz. pair, imperf btwn., in error booklet pane of 12 stamps	*450.00*	
d.	Imperf. vert., pair	—	

No. 2519 has bullseye perforations that measure approximately 11.2. No. 2520 has less pronounced black lines in the leaf, which is a much brighter green than on No. 2519.

No. 2520c is from a paper foldover before perforating.

LITHOGRAPHED

Panes of 100

1991, Jan. 22 **Untagged** ***Perf. 11***

2521	A1876 (4c) **bister & carmine**	.30	.25
	P# block of 4, 2#	.60	—
	Zip block of 4	.50	—
	Pane of 100	12.00	
a.	Vert. pair, imperf. horiz.	70.00	
b.	Imperf., pair	60.00	

FLAG Ⓢ

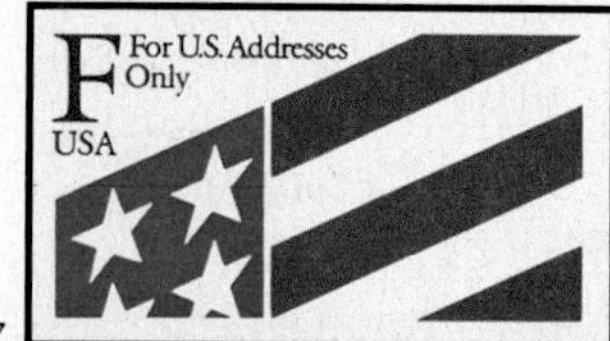

A1877

Designed by Harry Zelenko. Printed by Avery International Corp.

PHOTOGRAVURE

1991, Jan. 22 Untagged Self-Adhesive *Die Cut*
Printed on Plastic

2522 A1877 (29c) **blk, blue & dk red** .60 .25
a. Pane of 12 7.25

Sold only in panes of 12; peelable plastic backing inscribed in light ultramarine. Available during a test period at First National Bank automatic teller machines in Seattle.

Ⓢ: Adhesive residue sometimes remains on the back of examples of No. 2522 after soaking. See note after No. 1549.

Flag Over Mt. Rushmore — A1878

Designed by Clarence Holbert.

COIL STAMPS
ENGRAVED

1991, Mar. 29 Tagged *Perf. 10 Vert.*

2523 A1878 29c **blue, red & claret,** prephosphored uncoated paper with embedded tagging showing a mottled appearance .75 .25
Pair 1.50 .25
P# strip of 5, #1-7 4.00
P# strip of 5, #8 4.75
P# strip of 5, #9 5.25
P# single, #1 — .40
P# single, #2-4 — .50
P# single, #5 — 2.25
P# single, #6, 7 — .45
P# single, #8 — 2.50
P# single, #9 — 2.00
b. Imperf., pair 20.00
c. **blue, red & brown,** prephosphored uncoated paper with embedded tagging showing a mottled appearance 3.00 —
Pair 6.00
P# strip of 5, #1 *4,000.*
P# strip of 5, #7 *135.00*
P# single, #1 — *1,450.*
P# single, 7 — *120.00*
d. Prephosphored coated paper with surface tagging showing a solid appearance 5.00 —
Pair 10.00 —
P# strip of 5, #2 *1,500.*
P# strip of 5, #6 *225.00*
P# single, #2 — *200.00*
P# single, #6 — *150.00*

Specialists often call No. 2523c the "Toledo brown" variety, and No. 2523d "Lenz paper." It was from No. 2523d that it was discovered that "solid tagging" on prephosphored paper resulted from the application of taggant to coated paper.

COIL STAMP
PHOTOGRAVURE

Printed by American Bank Note Co.

1991, July 4 *Perf. 10 Vert.*

2523A A1878 29c **bl, red, lt brn, med brn & dk brn** .75 .25
Pair 1.50 .25
P# strip of 5, #A11111, A22211 4.25
P# single, #A11111, A22211 — 2.25
e. Medium brown omitted —

On No. 2523A, USA and 29 are not outlined in white and are farther from the bottom of the design.

A1879

Designed by Wallace Marosek.

Printed by U.S. Bank Note Co. (#2524), J.W. Fergusson & Sons for Stamp Venturers (#2525, 2526), J.W. Fergusson & Sons, Inc. for KCS Industries, Inc. (#2527).

PHOTOGRAVURE
Panes of 100

1991-92 Tagged *Perf. 11*

2524 A1879 29c **dull yel, blk, red & yel grn,** *Apr. 5, 1991* .60 .25
P# block of 4, 4#+U 2.75 —
Zip block of 4 2.50 —
Pane of 100 60.00

See note after No. 2527.

Perf. 13x12¾

2524A A1879 29c **dull yel, blk, red & yel grn,** *Apr. 5, 1991* 1.00 .25
P# block of 4, 4#+U 40.00 —
Zip block of 4 6.50 —
Pane of 100 100.00

COIL STAMPS
Rouletted 10 Vert.

2525 A1879 29c **pale yel, blk, red & yel grn,** *Aug. 16, 1991* .60 .25
Pair 1.20 .30
P# strip of 5, #S1111, S2222 4.00
P# single, #S1111, S2222 — .75

Perf. 10 Vert.

2526 A1879 29c **pale yel, blk, red & yel grn,** *Mar. 3, 1992* .80 .25
Pair 1.60 .30
P# strip of 5, #S2222 4.25
P# single, #S2222 — 2.25

BOOKLET STAMP
Perf. 11 on 2 or 3 Sides

2527 A1879 29c **pale yel, blk, red & bright grn,** *Apr. 5* .60 .25
a. Booklet pane of 10 6.00 3.50
b. Horiz. pair, imperf. between — —
c. Horiz. pair, imperf. vert. *150.00*
d. As "a," imperf. horiz. *750.00*
e. As "a," imperf. vert. *500.00*

Flower on Nos. 2524-2524A has grainy appearance, inscriptions look rougher.
No. 2527b resulted from a foldover.
The used example of No. 2527b is on a first day cover.

Flag, Olympic Rings — A1880

Designed by John Boyd.

Printed by KCS Industries, Inc.

BOOKLET STAMP
PHOTOGRAVURE

1991, Apr. 21 Tagged *Perf. 11 on 2 or 3 Sides*

2528 A1880 29c **multicolored** .60 .25
a. Booklet pane of 10 6.00 3.50
b. As "a," imperf. horiz. *2,750.*
c. Vert. pair, imperf. between, perfed at top and bottom *225.00*
d. Vert. strip of 3, top or bottom pair imperf. between —
e. Vert. pair, imperf. horiz. *650.00*
f. As "d," two pairs in #2528a with foldover —

No. 2528c comes from misperfed booklet panes. No. 2528d resulted from paper foldovers after normal perforating and before cutting into panes. Two No. 2528d are known. No. 2528e is valued in the grade of fine.

Fishing Boat — A1881

Type I

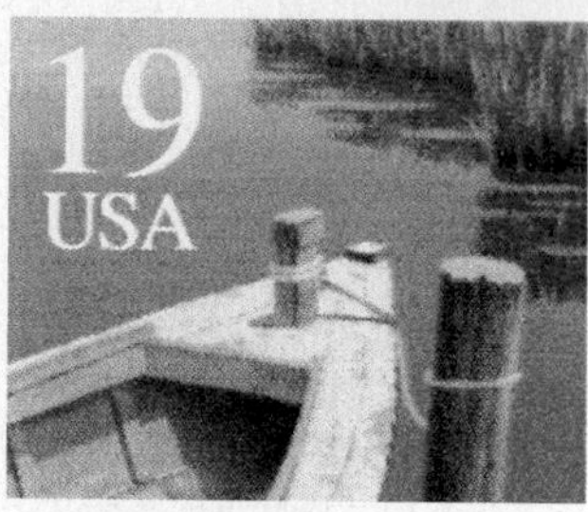

Type II

Designed by Pierre Mion.

Printed by: Multi-Color Corp. for American Bank Note Co (type I); Guilford Gravure (type II); J. W. Fergusson & Sons for Stamp Venturers (No. 2529C).

Type I: Vertical sides of "1" are jagged. Type II stamps are created by a finer dot pattern. Vertical sides of "1" are smooth.
Nos. 2529 and 2529a have two loops of rope tying boat to piling.

COIL STAMPS
PHOTOGRAVURE

1991, Aug. 8 Tagged *Perf. 9.8 Vert.*

2529 A1881 19c **multicolored,** type I .40 .25
Pair .80 .50
P# strip of 5, #A1111, A1212, A2424 3.00
P# strip of 5, #A1112 4.00
P# single, #A1111, A1212, A2424 — 2.25
P# single, #A1112 — 4.00
a. Type II, *1993* .40 .25
Pair .80 .50
P# strip of 5, #A5555, A5556, A6667, A7667, A7679, A7766, A7779 3.00
P# single, same # — 2.25
b. As "a," untagged, *1993* 1.00 .40
Pair 2.00 .80
P# strip of 5, #A5555 5.75
P# single, #A5555 — 4.25

Imperforates are from printer's waste. Also, No. 2529a, Plate #A7767 is known only from printer's waste.

1994, June 25 Tagged *Perf. 9.8 Vert.*

2529C A1881 19c **multicolored** .50 .25
Pair 1.00 .50
P# strip of 5, #S111 4.00
P# single, #S111 — 2.75

No. 2529C has one loop of rope tying boat to piling.

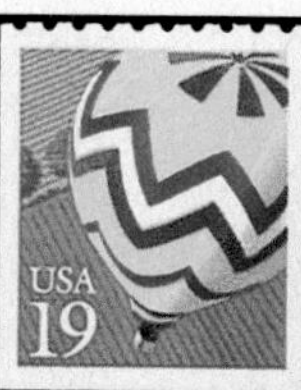

Balloon — A1882

BOOKLET STAMP

1991, May 17 Tagged *Perf. 10 on 2 or 3 Sides*

2530 A1882 19c **multicolored** .40 .25
a. Booklet pane of 10 4.00 2.75

Flags on Parade — A1883

Designed by Frank J. Waslick and Peter Cocci.

PHOTOGRAVURE
Panes of 100

1991, May 30 **Tagged** ***Perf. 11***

2531 A1883 29c **multicolored**, overall tagging .60 .25
P# block of 4, 4# 2.75 —
Zip block of 4 2.50 —
Pane of 100 60.00
b. Prephosphored coated paper with surface tagging showing a solid appearance .75 .25
P# block of 4, 4# 6.50 —
Zip block of 4 3.25 —
Pane of 100 75.00

Counterfeits exist of No. 2531. See the Postal Counterfeits section of this catalog.

Liberty Torch — A1884

Designed by Harry Zelenko.

Printed by Avery Dennison Co.

PHOTOGRAVURE

1991, June 25 **Tagged** ***Die Cut***

Self-Adhesive

2531A A1884 29c **black, gold & green**, prephosphored coated paper with surface tagging showing a solid appearance ⓢ .60 .25
b. Booklet pane of 18 11.00
c. Die cutting omitted, pair *1,000.*
d. Overall tagging, *1992* .60 .25
e. As "d," booklet pane of 18 11.00

Sold only in panes of 18; peelable paper backing inscribed in light blue. Available for consumer testing at First National Bank automatic teller machines in Seattle, WA.

ⓢ: Adhesive residue sometimes remains on the back of examples of No. 2531A after soaking. See note after No. 1549.

SWITZERLAND

Switzerland, 700th Anniv. A1887

Designed by Hans Hartman, Switzerland.

Printed by the American Bank Note Company.

PHOTOGRAVURE
Plates of 160 in four panes of 40

1991, Feb. 22 **Tagged** ***Perf. 11***

2532 A1887 50c **multicolored** 1.00 .25
P# block of 4, 5#+A 5.00 —
Zip block of 4 4.25 —
Pane of 50 50.00
a. Vert. pair, imperf. horiz. *1,400.*

See Switzerland No. 888.

Imperfs exist from printer's waste.

VERMONT STATEHOOD, 200th ANNIV.

A1888

Designed by Sabra Field.

Printed by the American Bank Note Company.

PHOTOGRAVURE
Plates of 200 in four panes of 50

1991, Mar. 1 **Tagged** ***Perf. 11***

2533 A1888 29c **multicolored** .80 .25
P# block of 4, 4#+A 4.00 —
Zip block of 4 3.50 —
Pane of 50 40.00

SAVINGS BONDS, 50TH ANNIVERSARY

A1889

Designed by Primo Angeli.

PHOTOGRAVURE
Plates of 200 in four panes of 50

1991, Apr. 30 **Tagged** ***Perf. 11***

2534 A1889 29c **multicolored** .60 .25
P# block of 4, 6# 2.75 —
Zip block of 4 2.50 —
Pane of 50 30.00
a. Tagging omitted —

LOVE

A1890

A1890a

Designed by Harry Zelenko (#2535-2535A).

Printed by U.S. Banknote Co. (#2535).

PHOTOGRAVURE
Panes of 50

1991, May 9 **Tagged** ***Perf. 12½x13***

2535 A1890 29c **multicolored** .60 .25
P# block of 4, 5#+U 2.75 —
Zip, copyright block of 4 2.50 —
Pane of 50 30.00
b. Imperf., pair *1,650.*

Perf. 11

2535A A1890a 29c **multicolored** 1.00 .25
P# block of 4, 5#+U 5.00 —
Zip, copyright block of 4 4.00 —
Pane of 50 50.00

A1890b

Designed by Harry Zelenko.

Printed by Bureau of Engraving and Printing.

BOOKLET STAMP

Perf. 11.1x11.3 on 2 or 3 Sides

2536 A1890b 29c **multicolored** .60 .25
a. Booklet pane of 10 6.00 3.50

"29" is closer to edge of design on No. 2536 than on No. 2535.

A1891

Designed by Nancy L. Krause.

Printed by American Bank Note Co.

Sheets of 200 in panes of 50

Perf. 11

2537 A1891 52c **multicolored** .90 .25
P# block of 4, 3#+A 4.50 —
Zip block of 4 4.00 —
Pane of 50 45.00

LITERARY ARTS SERIES

William Saroyan (1908-81), Author A1892

Designed by Ren Wicks.

Printed by J.W. Fergusson for American Bank Note Co.

PHOTOGRAVURE
Sheets of 200 in four panes of 50

1991, May 22 **Tagged** ***Perf. 11***

2538 A1892 29c **multicolored** .60 .25
P# block of 4, 5#+A 2.75 —
Zip block of 4 2.50 —
Pane of 50 30.00
a. All colors missing (EP) —
b. All colors except black missing (EP) 11,000.

No. 2538a must be collected se-tenant with a partially printed stamp. On No. 2538b, only part of the black is present; it is unique.

See Russia No. 6002.

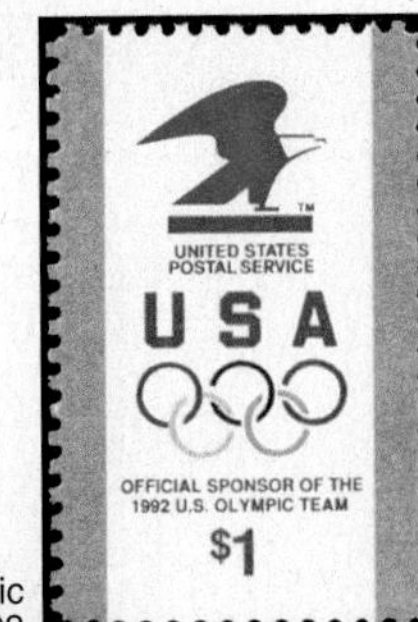

Eagle, Olympic Rings — A1893

Eagle — A1894

Eagle and Olympic Rings — A1895

Eagle in Flight — A1896

Futuristic Space Shuttle A1897

Space Shuttle Challenger A1898

Space Shuttle Endeavour — A1898a

Designed by: Terrence McCaffrey (Nos. 2539-2541), Timothy Knapp (No. 2542), Ken Hodges (No. 2543), Phil Jordan (Nos. 2544-2544A).

Printed by: J.W. Fergusson & Sons for Stamp Venturers (No. 2539); American Bank Note Co (Nos. 2540-2541); Jeffries Banknote Co. for the American Bank Note Co (No. 2542).

Nos. 2540, 2543-2544 for priority mail rate. Nos. 2541, 2544A for domestic express mail rate. No. 2542 for international express mail rate.
Nos. 2544-2544A printed by Ashton-Potter (USA) Ltd.

Sheet of 180 in nine panes of 20 (No. 2539)
Sheet of 120 in six panes of 20 (Nos. 2540-2542, 2544-2544A)
Pane of 40 (No. 2543)

PHOTOGRAVURE

Copyright information appears in the center of the top and bottom selvage.

1991, Sept. 29 **Tagged** ***Perf. 11***

2539	A1893 $1 **gold & multi**	2.00	.50
	P# block of 4, 6#+S	10.00	—
	Pane of 20	50.00	
a.	Black omitted		—

LITHOGRAPHED & ENGRAVED

1991, July 7 **Tagged** ***Perf. 11***

2540	A1894 $2.90 **multicolored**	6.00	1.50
	P# block of 4, 5#+A	24.00	—
	Pane of 20	120.00	
a.	Vert. pair, imperf horiz.	*900.00*	
b.	Black (engr.) omitted	*750.00*	

Imperforates on gummed stamp paper, including gutter pairs and blocks, are proofs from the ABNCo. archives. From the same source also come imperforate progressive proofs. See No. 2540P in Proofs section.

1991, June 16 **Untagged** ***Perf. 11***

2541	A1895 $9.95 **multicolored**	20.00	6.00
	P# block of 4, 5#+A	80.00	—
	Pane of 20	400.00	
a.	Imperf., pair	—	

No. 2541 exists imperf plus black (engr.) omitted from printer's waste.

1991, Aug. 31 **Untagged** ***Perf. 11***

2542	A1896 $14 **multicolored**	25.00	15.00
	P# block of 4, 5#+A	100.00	—
	Pane of 20	500.00	
a.	Red (engr. inscriptions) omitted	*750.00*	

No. 2542 exists imperf plus red omitted from printer's waste.

PHOTOGRAVURE

1993, June 3 **Tagged** ***Perf. 11x10¾***

2543	A1897 $2.90 **multicolored**	6.00	1.75
	P# block of 4, 6#	27.50	—
	Zip block of 4	25.00	—
	Pane of 40	240.00	
a.	Tagging omitted		—

Faked examples of No. 2543, unused and used, exist with red omitted due to bleaching.

1995, June 22 **Tagged** ***Perf. 11.2***

2544	A1898 $3 **multicolored,** dated "1995"	5.75	1.75
	P# block of 4, 5#+P	23.50	—
	Pane of 20	120.00	—
b.	Dated "1996"	5.75	1.75
	P# block of 4, 5#+P	23.50	—
	Pane of 20	120.00	—
c.	As "b," horiz. pair, imperf between	*1,000.*	
d.	As "b," imperf pair	*700.00*	

Imperf examples of No. 2544 with "1995" date are believed to be printer's waste.

1995, Aug. 4 **Tagged** ***Perf. 11***

2544A	A1898a $10.75 **multicolored**	20.00	9.00
	P# block of 4, 5#+P	82.50	—
	Pane of 20	425.00	—

No. 2544A was printed on paper embedded with red fibers.
Imperf examples of No. 2544A are believed to be printer's waste.

FISHING FLIES

Royal Wulff — A1899

Jock Scott — A1900

Apte Tarpon Fly — A1901

Lefty's Deceiver A1902

Muddler Minnow A1903

Designed by Chuck Ripper.

Printed by American Bank Note Co.

PHOTOGRAVURE
BOOKLET STAMPS

Perf. 11 Horiz. on 1 or 2 Sides

1991, May 31 **Tagged**

2545	A1899 29c **multicolored**	1.10	.25
a.	Black omitted	—	
b.	Horiz. pair, imperf. btwn., in #2549a with foldover	*2,400.*	
2546	A1900 29c **multicolored**	1.10	.25
a.	Black omitted	—	
2547	A1901 29c **multicolored**	1.10	.25
a.	Black omitted	—	
2548	A1902 29c **multicolored**	1.10	.25
2549	A1903 29c **multicolored**	1.10	.25
a.	Bklt. pane of 5, #2545-2549	5.50	3.00

Horiz. pairs, imperf vert., exist from printer's waste.
No. 2545b is unique and resulted from a foldover after perfing but before cutting. Both stamps are creased.

PERFORMING ARTS

Cole Porter (1891-1964), Composer — A1904

Designed by Jim Sharpe.

Printed by American Bank Note Co.

PHOTOGRAVURE
Panes of 50

1991, June 8 **Tagged** ***Perf. 11***

2550	A1904 29c **multicolored**	.60	.25
	P# block of 4, 5#+A	2.75	—
	Zip block of 4	2.50	—
	Pane of 50	30.00	
a.	Vert. pair, imperf. horiz.	*400.00*	

OPERATIONS DESERT SHIELD & DESERT STORM

S. W. Asia Service Medal — A1905

A1905a

Designed by Jack Williams.

Printed by J.W. Fergusson Co. for Stamp Venturers (No. 2551), Multi-Color Corp. for the American Bank Note Co. (No. 2552).

PHOTOGRAVURE
Panes of 50

1991, July 2	**Tagged**	***Perf. 11***	
2551 A1905 29c **multicolored**		.60	.25
	P# block of 4, 7#+S	2.75	—
	Zip block of 4	2.50	—
	Pane of 50	30.00	
a.	Vert. pair, imperf. horiz.	*600.00*	

No. 2551 is 21mm wide.

BOOKLET STAMP
Perf. 11 Vert. on 1 or 2 Sides

2552 A1905a 29c **multicolored**		.60	.25
a.	Booklet pane of 5	3.00	2.25

No. 2552 is 20½mm wide. Inscriptions are shorter than on No. 2551.
No. 2552 Vert. pairs, imperf horiz., are from printer's waste.

1992 SUMMER OLYMPICS, BARCELONA

Pole Vault — A1907

Discus A1908

Women's Sprints A1909

Javelin A1910

Women's Hurdles A1911

Designed by Joni Carter.

Printed by the American Bank Note Co.

PHOTOGRAVURE
Panes of 40

1991, July 12	**Tagged**	***Perf. 11***	
2553 A1907 29c **multicolored**		.60	.25
2554 A1908 29c **multicolored**		.60	.25
2555 A1909 29c **multicolored**		.60	.25
2556 A1910 29c **multicolored**		.60	.25
2557 A1911 29c **multicolored**		.60	.25
a.	Strip of 5, #2553-2557	3.00	2.25
	P# block of 10, 5#+A	8.00	—
	Zip block of 10	6.00	—
	Pane of 40	24.00	

NUMISMATICS

1858 Flying Eagle Cent, 1907 Standing Liberty Double Eagle, Series 1875 $1 Note, Series 1902 $10 National Currency Note — A1912

Designed by V. Jack Ruther.

LITHOGRAPHED & ENGRAVED
Sheets of 200 in four panes of 50

1991, Aug. 13	**Tagged**	***Perf. 11***	
2558 A1912 29c **multicolored**		.60	.25
	P# block of 4, 7#	2.75	—
	Zip block of 4	2.50	—
	Pane of 50	30.00	

WORLD WAR II

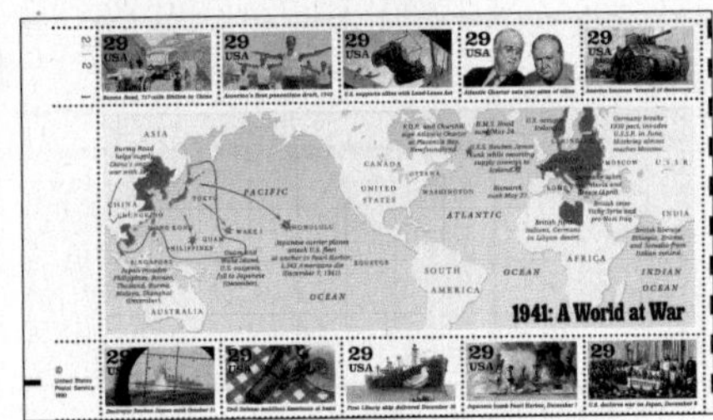

A1913

Illustration reduced.

Designed by William H. Bond.

Designs and events of 1941: a, Military vehicles (Burma Road, 717-mile lifeline to China). b, Recruits (America's first peacetime draft). c, Shipments for allies (U.S. supports allies with Lend-Lease Act). d, Franklin D. Roosevelt, Winston Churchill (Atlantic Charter sets war aims of allies). e, Tank (America becomes the "arsenal of democracy.") f, Sinking of Destoyer Reuben James, Oct. 31. g, Gas mask, helmet (Civil defense mobilizes Americans at home). h, Liberty Ship, sea gull (First Liberty ship delivered December 30). i, Sinking ships (Japanese bomb Pearl Harbor, December 7). j, Congress in session (U.S. declares war on Japan, December 8). Central label is the size of 15 stamps and shows world map, extent of axis control.

LITHOGRAPHED & ENGRAVED
Plates of eight subjects in four panes of 2 each

1991, Sept. 3	**Tagged**	***Perf. 11***	
2559 A1913 Block of 10		7.50	5.00
	Pane of 20	15.00	—
a.-j.	29c any single	.75	.45
k.	Black (engr.) omitted	*6,500.*	
l.	As "c," tagging omitted	—	

No. 2559 has selvage at left and right and either top or bottom.

BASKETBALL, 100TH ANNIVERSARY

Basketball, Hoop, Players' Arms — A1914

Designed by Lon Busch.

PHOTOGRAVURE
Sheets of 200 in four panes of 50

1991, Aug. 28	**Tagged**	***Perf. 11***	
2560 A1914 29c **multicolored**		.60	.25
	P# block of 4, 4#	3.50	—
	Zip block of 4	2.50	—
	Pane of 50	30.00	

DISTRICT OF COLUMBIA BICENTENNIAL

Capitol Building from Pennsylvania Avenue, Circa 1903 — A1915

Designed by Pierre Mion.

LITHOGRAPHED & ENGRAVED
Plates of 200 in four panes of 50

1991, Sept. 7	**Tagged**	***Perf. 11***	
2561 A1915 29c **multicolored**		.60	.25
	P# block of 4, 5#	2.75	—
	Zip block of 4	2.50	—
	Pane of 50	30.00	
a.	Black (engr.) omitted	*85.00*	

COMEDIANS

Stan Laurel (1890-1965) and Oliver Hardy (1892-1957) A1916

Edgar Bergen (1903-1978) and Charlie McCarthy A1917

Jack Benny (1894-1974) A1918

Fanny Brice (1891-1951) A1919

Bud Abbott (1895-1974) and Lou Costello (1908-1959) A1920

Designed by Al Hirschfeld.

LITHOGRAPHED & ENGRAVED
BOOKLET STAMPS

1991, Aug. 29	**Tagged**	***Perf. 11 on 2 or 3 Sides***	
2562 A1916 29c **multicolored**		1.00	.25
a.	Tagging omitted	—	
2563 A1917 29c **multicolored**		1.00	.25
2564 A1918 29c **multicolored**		1.00	.25
2565 A1919 29c **multicolored**		1.00	.25

2566	A1920 29c **multicolored**	1.00	.25
a.	Strip of 5, #2562-2566	5.00	2.25
b.	Bklt. pane of 10, 2 each #2562-2566	10.00	5.00
c.	As "b," scar & brt violet (engr.) omitted	*350.00*	

BLACK HERITAGE SERIES

Jan E. Matzeliger (1852-1889), Inventor — A1921

Designed by Higgins Bond.

Printed by J.W. Fergusson & Sons for the American Bank Note Co.

PHOTOGRAVURE

Plates of 200 in four panes of 50

1991, Sept. 15 Tagged *Perf. 11*

2567	A1921 29c **multicolored**	.60	.25
	P# block of 4, 6#+A	3.00	—
	Zip block of 4	2.50	—
	Pane of 50	30.00	
a.	Horiz. pair, imperf. vert.	*600.00*	
b.	Vert. pair, imperf. horiz.	*550.00*	
c.	Imperf., pair	*275.00*	

SPACE EXPLORATION

Mercury, Mariner 10 A1922

Venus, Mariner 2 A1923

Earth, Landsat A1924

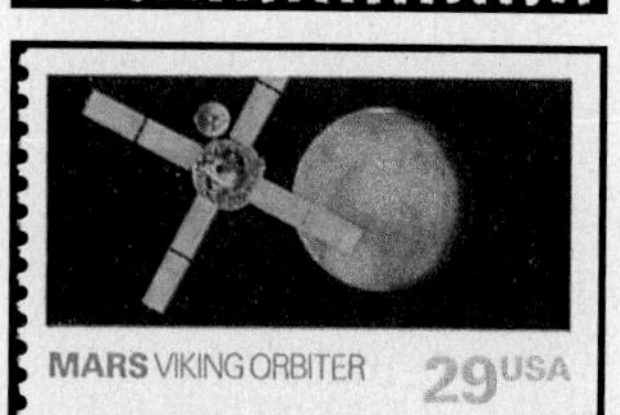

Moon, Lunar Orbiter A1925

Mars, Viking Orbiter A1926

Jupiter, Pioneer 11 A1927

Saturn, Voyager 2 A1928

Uranus, Voyager 2 A1929

Neptune, Voyager 2 A1930

Pluto — A1931

Designed by Ron Miller.

PHOTOGRAVURE

BOOKLET STAMPS

1991, Oct. 1 Tagged *Perf. 11 on 2 or 3 Sides*

2568	A1922 29c **multicolored**	.90	.25
2569	A1923 29c **multicolored**	.90	.25
2570	A1924 29c **multicolored**	.90	.25
2571	A1925 29c **multicolored**	.90	.25
2572	A1926 29c **multicolored**	.90	.25
2573	A1927 29c **multicolored**	.90	.25
2574	A1928 29c **multicolored**	.90	.25
2575	A1929 29c **multicolored**	.90	.25
2576	A1930 29c **multicolored**	.90	.25
2577	A1931 29c **multicolored**	.90	.25
a.	Bklt. pane of 10, #2568-2577	9.00	4.50

CHRISTMAS

Madonna and Child by Antoniazzo Romano — A1933

Santa Claus in Chimney — A1934

Santa Checking List — A1935

Santa with Present — A1936

Santa at Fireplace — A1937

Santa and Sleigh — A1938

Designed by Bradbury Thompson (#2578) and John Berkey (#2579-2585).

Printed by the Bureau of Engraving and Printing (#2578); J.W. Fergusson & Sons (#2579) and Multi-Color Corp. (#2580-2585) for the American Bank Note Co.

LITHOGRAPHED & ENGRAVED

Sheets of 300 in six panes of 50

1991, Oct. 17 Tagged *Perf. 11¼*

2578	A1933 (29c) **multicolored**	.60	.25
	P# block of 4, 5#	2.75	—
	Zip, copyright block of 4	2.50	—
	Pane of 50	30.00	
a.	Booklet pane of 10	6.00	3.25
b.	Red & black (engr.) omitted	*2,250.*	

PHOTOGRAVURE

Perf. 11

2579	A1934 (29c) **multicolored**	.60	.25
	P# block of 4, 3#+A	2.50	—
	Zip block of 4	2.25	—
	Pane of 50	30.00	
a.	Horiz. pair, imperf. vert.	175.00	
b.	Vert. pair, imperf. horiz.	*350.00*	

BOOKLET STAMPS

Size: 25x18½mm

Perf. 11 on 2 or 3 Sides

2580	A1934 (29c) **multicolored**, type I	2.00	.25
2581	A1934 (29c) **multicolored**, type II	2.00	.25
a.	Pair #2580-2581	4.00	.55
b.	Bklt. pane, 2 each, #2580-2581	8.00	1.25
2582	A1935 (29c) **multicolored**	.60	.25
a.	Bklt. pane of 4	2.40	1.25
2583	A1936 (29c) **multicolored**	.60	.25
a.	Bklt. pane of 4	2.40	1.25
2584	A1937 (29c) **multicolored**	.60	.25
a.	Bklt. pane of 4	2.40	1.25
2585	A1938 (29c) **multicolored**	.60	.25
a.	Bklt. pane of 4	2.40	1.25
	Nos. 2578-2585 (8)	7.60	2.00

The far left brick from the top row of the chimney is missing from Type II, No. 2581.

Imperfs of Nos. 2581, 2583-2585 are printer's waste.

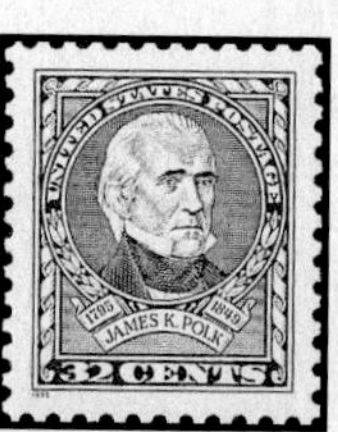

Pres. James K. Polk (1795-1849) A1939

"The Surrender of General Burgoyne at Saratoga," by John Trumbull A1942

Presidents George Washington and Andrew Jackson — A1944

Designed by John Thompson (No. 2587), based on painting by John Trumbull (No. 2590), Richard D. Sheaff (No. 2592).
Printed by Banknote Corporation of America (No. 2587), Stamp Venturers (Nos. 2590, 2592).

ENGRAVED

Sheets of 400 in four panes of 100 (No. 2587)
Sheets of 120 in six panes of 20 (Nos. 2590, 2592)

1994-95 Tagged *Perf. 11.2*

2587 A1939 32c **red brown,** *Nov. 2, 1995* .65 .25
P# block of 4, 1#+B 3.25 —
Pane of 100 65.00

Perf. 11.5

2590 A1942 $1 **blue,** *May 5, 1994* 1.90 .50
P# block of 4, 1#+S 7.60 —
Pane of 20 38.00 —
2592 A1944 $5 **slate green,** *Aug. 19, 1994* 8.00 2.50
P# block of 4, 1#+S 40.00 —
Pane of 20 160.00 —

Some plate blocks contain either inscription or plate position diagram.

Flag — A1946

Designed by Lou Nolan (#2593-2594).
Printed by Bureau of Engraving & Printing (#2593, #2593B), Stamp Venturers for KCS Industries (#2594).

BOOKLET STAMPS
PHOTOGRAVURE

1992, Sept. 8 Tagged *Perf. 10 on 2 or 3 Sides*

2593 A1946 29c **black & multi** .60 .25
a. Booklet pane of 10 6.00 4.25
d. Imperf, pair *500.00*

Perf. 11x10 on 2 or 3 Sides

2593B A1946 29c **black & multi,** shiny gum 2.50 .50
Low gloss gum 3.50
c. Bklt. pane of 10, shiny gum 30.00 7.50
Low gloss gum 40.00

1993, Apr. 8 (?) *Perf. 11x10 on 2 or 3 Sides*

2594 A1946 29c **red & multi** .65 .25
a. Booklet pane of 10 6.50 4.25

Denomination is red on #2594 and black on #2593 and 2593B.

Eagle and Shield — A1947

A1947a

A1947b

Designed by Jay Haiden.

Printed by Banknote Corporation of America (#2595), Dittler Brothers, Inc. (#2596), Stamp Venturers (#2597).

LITHOGRAPHED & ENGRAVED (#2595), PHOTOGRAVURE

1992, Sept. 25 Tagged *Die Cut*
Self-Adhesive

2595 A1947 29c **brown & multicolored** .75 .25
a. Bklt. pane of 17 + label 12.75
b. Die cutting omitted, pair *90.00*
c. Brown omitted *250.00*
d. As "a," die cutting omitted *725.00*
2596 A1947a 29c **blue green & multicolored** .75 .25
a. Bklt. pane of 17 + label 12.75
2597 A1947b 29c **red & multicolored** .75 .25
a. Bklt. pane of 17 + label 12.75

Plate No. and inscription reads down on No. 2595a and up on Nos. 2596a-2597a. Design is sharper and more finely detailed on Nos. 2595, 2597.
Nos. 2595a-2597a sold for $5 each.
Nos. 2595-2597 also available in strips with stamps spaced for use in affixing machines to service first day covers.

Eagle — A1950

Statue of Liberty — A1951

Designed by Richard Sheaff (#2598), Tom Engeman (#2599).
Printed by Dittler Brothers, Inc. (#2599), National Label Co. for 3M (#2598).

PHOTOGRAVURE

1994 Tagged *Die Cut*
Self-Adhesive

2598 A1950 29c **red, cream & blue,** *Feb. 4* .60 .25
a. Booklet pane of 18 11.00
b. Coil with P#111 — 5.00
P# strip of 5, #111 7.00
c. Die cutting omitted, pair *1,000.*
2599 A1951 29c **multicolored,** *June 24* .60 .25
a. Booklet pane of 18 11.00
b. Coil with P#D1111 — 5.00
P# strip of 5, #D1111 8.00

Except for No. 2599b with plate number, coil stamps of this issue are indistinguishable from booklet stamps once they are removed from the backing paper. For No. 2598b, however, the stamps from the coil strips have minutely rounded corners, whereas the corners of the booklet stamps are squared.
See Nos. 3122-3122E.

Scott values for used self-adhesive stamps are for examples either on piece or off piece.

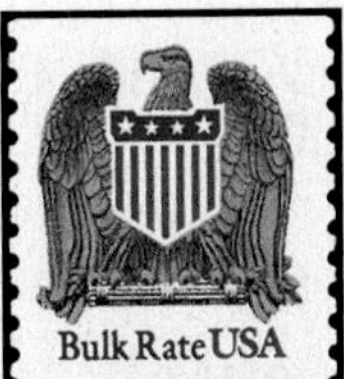

Eagle and Shield — A1956

Eagle and Shield — A1957

Flag — A1959

Flag — A1960

Flag Over White House — A1961

Designed by Chris Calle (#2602-2604), Terrence McCaffrey (#2605), Lon Busch (#2606-2608), V. Jack Ruther (29c).
Printed by Guildford Gravure, Inc. for the American Bank Note Co. (#2602, 2606), Bureau of Engraving and Printing (#2603, 2607), Stamp Venturers (#2604, 2608), American Bank Note Co. (#2605).

PHOTOGRAVURE
COIL STAMPS

1991-93 Untagged *Perf. 10 Vert.*

2602 A1956 (10c) **multi** (Bureau precancel, Bulk Rate, in blue), *Dec. 13* .30 .25
Pair .60 .50
P# strip of 5, #A11111, A11112, A21112, A21113, A22112, A22113, A33333, A43325, A43326, A43334, A43335, A53335, A54444, A54445, A77777, A88888 1.90
P# strip of 5, #A12213 5.00
P# strip of 5, #A34424, A34426, A43324, A88889 2.75
P# strip of 5, #A32333 *160.00*
P# strip of 5, #A33334 10.00
P# strip of 5, #A33335, A43426, A89999, A99998, A99999, A1010101010, A1011101011, A1011101012, A1110101010, A1110111010, A1111101010, A1111111010, A1411101010, A1411101011, A1412111110, A1412111111 2.25
P# strip of 5, #A1011101010 3.25
P# strip of 5, #A1211101010 3.00
P# strip of 5, #A1110101011 4.00
P# single, #A11111, A11112, A21112, A21113, A22112, A22113, A43324, A43325, A43326, A43334, A43335, A43426, A54444, A54445, A77777, A88888, A89999, A99998, A99999 — 1.75
P# single, #A12213 — 5.00
P# single, #A32333 — 175.00
P# single, #A33333, A33335, A34424, A34426 — 2.50
P# single, #A33334 — 45.00
P# single, #A53335, A88889, A1010101010, A1011101011, A1011101012, A1110101010, A1110111010, A1111101010, A1111111010, A1411101010, A1411101011, A1412111110, A1412111111 — 2.50
P# single, #A1011101010 — 3.00
P# single, #A1211101010 — 4.00
P# single, #A1110101011 — 7.00
a. Imperf., pair *3,500.*
2603 A1957 (10c) **org yel & multi,** shiny gum (Bureau precancel, Bulk Rate, in red), *May 29, 1993* .30 .25
Pair .60 .50
P# strip of 5, #11111, 22221, 22222 2.25
P# single, same — 1.75
Low gloss gum .25
Pair .50
P# strip of 5, #22222, 33333, 44444 3.00
P# strip of 5, #11111 15.00
P# single, #33333, 44444 — 2.00
a. Imperf., pair 20.00
b. Tagged (error), shiny gum 2.00 1.50
Pair 4.00 3.50
P# strip of 5, #11111, 22221 9.00
P# strip of 5, #22222 *400.00*
P# single, #11111, 22221 — 10.00
P# single, #22222 — *350.00*

All examples of Nos. 2603, 2603a and 2603b were printed with luminescent ink.
See No. 2907.

2604 A1957 (10c) **gold & multi,** low gloss gum (Bureau precancel, Bulk Rate, in red), *May 29, 1993* .30 .25
Pair .50 .50
P# strip of 5, #S11111 2.00
P# strip of 5, #S22222 1.75
P# single, #S11111 — 1.50
Shiny gum .50
Pair 1.00
P# strip of 5, #S22222 4.00
P# single, same — 1.50
2605 A1959 23c **multi** (Bureau precancel in blue), *Sept. 27* .45 .40
Pair .90 .80
P# strip of 5, #A111, A212, A222 3.00
P# strip of 5, #A112, A122, A333 3.25
P# single, #A111, A112, A122, A212, A222, A333 — 2.25
a. Imperf, pair —

Vertical pairs uncut between on gummed stamp paper are proofs from the ABNCo. archives. See No. 2605P in Proofs section.

2606 A1960 23c **multi** (Bureau precanceled), *July 21, 1992* .45 .40
Pair .90 .80
P# strip of 5, #A1111, A2222, A2232, A2233, A3333, A4364, A4443, A4444, A4453 3.50
P# single, same # — 2.50

"First-Class" is 9½mm long and "23" is 6mm long on No. 2606.

2607	A1960	23c **multi,** shiny gum (Bureau precanceled), *Oct. 9, 1992*	.45	.40
		Pair	.90	.80
		P# strip of 5, #1111	4.00	
		P# single, #1111	—	1.75
		Low gloss gum	.45	
		Pair	.90	
		P# strip of 5, #1111	4.00	
a.		Tagged (error), shiny gum	5.00	4.50
		Pair	10.00	9.00
		P# strip of 5, #1111	125.00	
		P# single, #1111	—	95.00
c.		Imperf., pair	65.00	

"First-Class" is 9mm long and "23" is 6½mm long on No. 2607.

2608	A1960	23c **vio bl, red & blk** (Bureau precanceled), *May 14, 1993*	.80	.40
		Pair	1.60	.80
		P# strip of 5, #S111	4.25	
		P# single, #S111	—	2.25

"First-Class" is 8½mm long and "23" is 6½mm long on No. 2608.

ENGRAVED
Tagged

2609	A1961	29c **blue & red,** *Apr. 23, 1992*	.60	.25
		Pair	1.20	.50
		P# strip of 5, #1-8	4.00	
		P# strip of 5, #9-16	4.50	
		P# strip of 5, #18	5.50	
		P# single, #1-4	—	.50
		P# single, #5	—	2.00
		P# single, #6-8	—	.50
		P# single, #9	—	2.25
		P# single, #10-16	—	.80
		P# single, #18	—	4.50
a.		Imperf., pair	15.00	*25.00*
b.		Pair, imperf. between	60.00	
c.		29c **Indigo blue & red**	*22.50*	—
		Pair	*45.00*	—
		Nos. 2602-2609 (8)	3.65	2.60

Beware of pairs with blind perfs sometimes offered as No. 2609b.

See Nos. 2907, 3270-3271.

WINTER OLYMPICS

Hockey
A1963

Figure Skating
A1964

Speed Skating
A1965

Skiing
A1966

Bobsledding
A1967

Designed by Lon Busch. Printed by J.W. Fergusson & Sons for Stamp Venturers.

PHOTOGRAVURE
Panes of 35

1992, Jan. 11		**Tagged**	***Perf. 11***	
2611	A1963	29c **multicolored**	.60	.25
2612	A1964	29c **multicolored**	.60	.25
2613	A1965	29c **multicolored**	.60	.25
2614	A1966	29c **multicolored**	.60	.25
2615	A1967	29c **multicolored**	.60	.25
a.		Strip of 5, #2611-2615	3.00	2.50
		P# block of 10, 4#+S	7.00	—
		Zip, copyright block of 15	9.00	—
		Pane of 35	21.00	

Inscriptions on six marginal tabs.

WORLD COLUMBIAN STAMP EXPO

Features detail from No. 129 — A1968

Designed by Richard Sheaff.

LITHOGRAPHED & ENGRAVED
Plates of 200 in four panes of 50

1992, Jan. 24		**Tagged**	***Perf. 11***	
2616	A1968	29c **multicolored**	.60	.25
		P# block of 4, 4#	3.00	—
		Zip block of 4	2.50	—
		Pane of 50	30.00	
a.		Tagging omitted	10.00	

BLACK HERITAGE SERIES

W.E.B. Du Bois (1868-1963), Civil Rights Leader — A1969

Designed by Higgins Bond.

LITHOGRAPHED & ENGRAVED
Plates of 200 in four panes of 50

1992, Jan. 31		**Tagged**	***Perf. 11***	
2617	A1969	29c **multicolored**	.60	.25
		P# block of 4, 7#	2.75	—
		Zip block of 4	2.50	—
		Pane of 50	30.00	

LOVE

Heart in Envelope — A1970

Designed by Uldis Purins. Printed by the U.S. Bank Note Co.

PHOTOGRAVURE
Panes of 50

1992, Feb. 6		**Tagged**	***Perf. 11***	
2618	A1970	29c **multicolored**	.60	.25
		P# block of 4, U+5#	2.75	—
		Zip, copyright block of 4	2.50	—
		Pane of 50	30.00	
a.		Horiz. pair, imperf. vert.	*300.00*	
b.		As "a," green omitted on right stamp	*1,250.*	

OLYMPIC BASEBALL

Baseball Players
A1971

Designed by Anthony DeLuz.

PHOTOGRAVURE
Plates of 200 in four panes of 50

1992, Apr. 3		**Tagged**	***Perf. 11***	
2619	A1971	29c **multicolored**	.60	.25
		P# block of 4, 5#	2.75	—
		Zip block of 4	2.50	—
		Pane of 50	30.00	

VOYAGES OF COLUMBUS

Seeking Queen Isabella's Support
A1972

Crossing the Atlantic
A1973

Approaching Land
A1974

Coming Ashore A1975

Designed by Richard Schlecht.

LITHOGRAPHED & ENGRAVED
Plates of 160 in four panes of 40

1992, Apr. 24 **Tagged** ***Perf. 11***

2620	A1972 29c **multicolored**		.65	.25
2621	A1973 29c **multicolored**		.65	.25
2622	A1974 29c **multicolored**		.65	.25
2623	A1975 29c **multicolored**		.65	.25
a.	Block of 4, #2620-2623		2.60	2.00
	P# block of 4, 5#		2.75	—
	Zip block of 4		2.60	—
	Pane of 40		26.00	

See Italy Nos. 1877-1880.

Souvenir Sheets

A1976

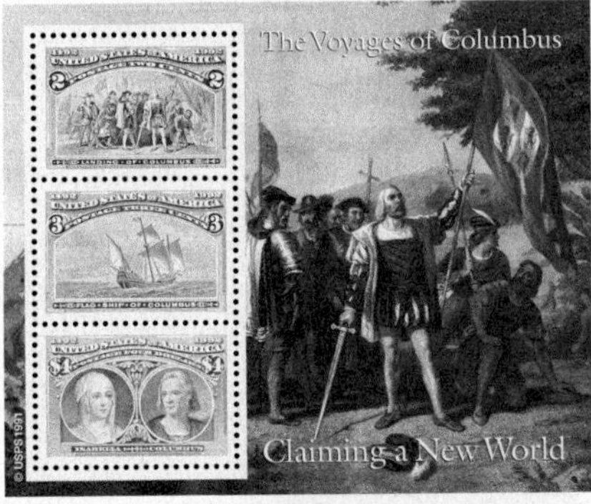
A1977

A1978

A1979

A1980

A1981

Illustrations reduced.

Designed by Richard Sheaff.

Printed by the American Bank Note Co. Margins on Nos. 2624a-2628c are lithographed. Nos. 2624a-2628c, 2629 are similar in design to Nos. 230-245 but are dated 1492-1992.

LITHOGRAPHED & ENGRAVED

1992, May 22 ***Perf. 10½***

Tagged (15c-$5), Untagged

2624	A1976	Pane of 3	2.35	1.50
a.	A71 1c	**deep blue**	.30	.25
b.	A74 4c	**ultramarine**	.30	.25
c.	A82 $1	**salmon**	1.75	1.00
d.		As No. 2624, tagging omitted on "c"	*800.00*	
2625	A1977	Pane of 3	7.50	5.00
a.	A72 2c	**brown violet**	.30	.25
b.	A73 3c	**green**	.30	.25
c.	A85 $4	**crimson lake**	7.00	4.00
2626	A1978	Pane of 3	1.80	1.25
a.	A75 5c	**chocolate**	.30	.25
b.	A80 30c	**orange brown**	.60	.30
c.	A81 50c	**slate blue**	.90	.50
d.		As No. 2626, tagging omitted on "c"	—	—
2627	A1979	Pane of 3	6.10	3.75
a.	A76 6c	**purple**	.30	.25
b.	A77 8c	**magenta**	.30	.25
c.	A84 $3	**yellow green**	5.50	3.00
2628	A1980	Pane of 3	4.30	3.00
a.	A78 10c	**black brown**	.30	.25
b.	A79 15c	**dark green**	.30	.25
c.	A83 $2	**brown red**	3.50	2.00
d.		As No. 2628, tagging omitted on "b"	*500.00*	
2629	A1981 $5	Pane of 1	8.75	6.00
a.	A86 $5	**black**, single stamp	8.50	5.00
		Nos. 2624-2629 (6)	30.80	20.50

See Italy Nos. 1883-1888, Portugal Nos. 1918-1923 and Spain Nos. 2677-2682.

Imperforate souvenir sheets on gummed stamp paper, singly or in pairs and blocks, are proofs from the ABNCo. archives. Additionally, one imperforate essay, with the background of No. 2622 combined with the stamps of No. 2620, is recorded. See Nos. 2624P-2629P in Proofs section.

NEW YORK STOCK EXCHANGE BICENTENNIAL

A1982

Designed by Richard Sheaff.

Printed by the Jeffries Bank Note Co. for the American Bank Note Co.

LITHOGRAPHED & ENGRAVED
Panes of 40

1992, May 17 **Tagged** ***Perf. 11***

2630	A1982 29c **green, red & black**	.60	.25
	P# block of 4, 3#+A	2.75	—
	Zip, Olympic block of 4	2.50	—
	Pane of 40	24.00	
a.	Black missing (EP)	*4,000.*	
b.	Black missing (CM)	*4,000.*	
c.	Center (black engr.) inverted	*17,000.*	
d.	Se-tenant pair, #2630b and #2630c	*22,500.*	

No. 2630a resulted from extraneous paper that blocked the black from appearing on the stamp paper. It is from a unique pane that contained four color-missing errors plus a fifth stamp missing half the black center.

No. 2630a must be collected se-tenant with a normal stamp or with a stamp with half of black engraving missing, or se-tenant with a normal stamp and an additional 2630a.

No. 2630b may be collected alone or se-tenant with No. 2630c.

Two panes, each containing 28 No. 2630c and 12 No. 2630b, have been documented.

SPACE ACCOMPLISHMENTS

Cosmonaut, US Space Shuttle — A1983

Astronaut, Russian Space Station, Russian Space Shuttle — A1984

Sputnik, Vostok, Apollo Command & Lunar Modules — A1985

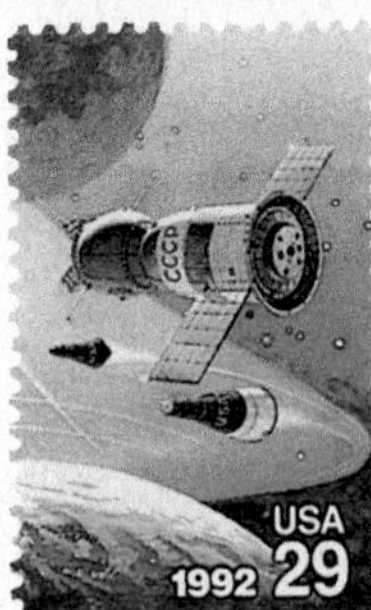
Soyuz, Mercury & Gemini Spacecraft — A1986

"Toaster Cord" Plate Flaw

Designed by Vladimir Beilin (Russia) and Robert T. McCall.

PHOTOGRAVURE

Plates of 200 in four panes of 50

1992, May 29 **Tagged** ***Perf. 11***

No.	Type	Description	Unused	Used
2631	A1983	29c **multicolored**	.60	.25
2632	A1984	29c **multicolored**	.60	.25
2633	A1985	29c **multicolored**	.60	.25
		Black line below space capsule, "Toaster Cord" plate flaw (plate 1111 LL 49 and LR 49)	4.50	2.50
2634	A1986	29c **multicolored**	.60	.25
a.		Block of 4, #2631-2634	2.40	2.00
		P# block of 4, 4#	3.25	—
		Zip block of 4	2.50	—
		Pane of 50	30.00	
b.		As "a," yellow omitted	*4,750.*	

The yellow color in Nos. 2631-2634 is easily removed by exposure to sunlight. Expertization of No. 2634b is essential. See Russia Nos. 6080-6083.

ALASKA HIGHWAY, 50th ANNIVERSARY

A1987

Designed by Byron Birdsall.

LITHOGRAPHED & ENGRAVED

Plates of 200 in four panes of 50

1992, May 30 **Tagged** ***Perf. 11***

No.	Type	Description	Unused	Used
2635	A1987	29c **multicolored**	.60	.25
		P# block of 4, 6#	2.75	—
		Zip block of 4	2.50	—
		Pane of 50	30.00	
a.		Black (engr.) omitted	*575.00*	—

Almost half the recorded No. 2635a errors are poorly centered. These sell for approximately $400.

KENTUCKY STATEHOOD BICENTENNIAL

A1988

Designed by Joseph Petro.

Printed by J.W. Fergusson & Sons for Stamp Venturers.

PHOTOGRAVURE

Plates of 200 in four panes of 50

1992, June 1 **Tagged** ***Perf. 11***

No.	Type	Description	Unused	Used
2636	A1988	29c **multicolored**	.60	.25
		P# block of 4, 5#+S	2.75	—
		Zip block of 4	2.50	—
		Pane of 50	30.00	
a.		Dark blue missing (EP)	—	
b.		Dark blue and red missing (EP)	—	
c.		All colors missing (EP)	—	

Nos. 2636a-2636c must be collected se-tenant with normal stamps.

SUMMER OLYMPICS

Soccer
A1989

Gymnastics
A1990

Volleyball
A1991

Boxing
A1992

Swimming
A1993

Designed by Richard Waldrep.

Printed by J.W. Fergusson & Sons for Stamp Venturers.

PHOTOGRAVURE

Panes of 35

1992, June 11 **Tagged** ***Perf. 11***

No.	Type	Description	Unused	Used
2637	A1989	29c **multicolored**	.60	.25
2638	A1990	29c **multicolored**	.60	.25
2639	A1991	29c **multicolored**	.60	.25
2640	A1992	29c **multicolored**	.60	.25
2641	A1993	29c **multicolored**	.60	.25
a.		Strip of 5, #2637-2641	3.00	2.50
		P# block of 10, 5#+S	6.50	—
		Zip, copyright block of 15	9.00	—
		Pane of 35	21.00	

Inscriptions on six marginal tabs.

HUMMINGBIRDS

Ruby-throated
A1994

Broad-billed
A1995

Costa's — A1996

Rufous — A1997

Calliope — A1998

Designed by Chuck Ripper.

Printed by Multi-Color Corp. for the American Bank Note Co.

PHOTOGRAVURE

BOOKLET STAMPS

Perf. 11 Vert. on 1 or 2 Sides

1992, June 15 **Tagged**

No.	Type	Description	Unused	Used
2642	A1994	29c **multicolored**	.60	.25
2643	A1995	29c **multicolored**	.60	.25
2644	A1996	29c **multicolored**	.60	.25
2645	A1997	29c **multicolored**	.60	.25
2646	A1998	29c **multicolored**	.60	.25
a.		Bklt. pane of 5, #2642-2646	3.00	2.50

Imperforate singles, booklet panes and pane multiples or varieties on gummed stamp paper are proofs from the ABNCo. archives. From the same source also come imperforate progressive proofs. See No. 2646aP in Proofs section.

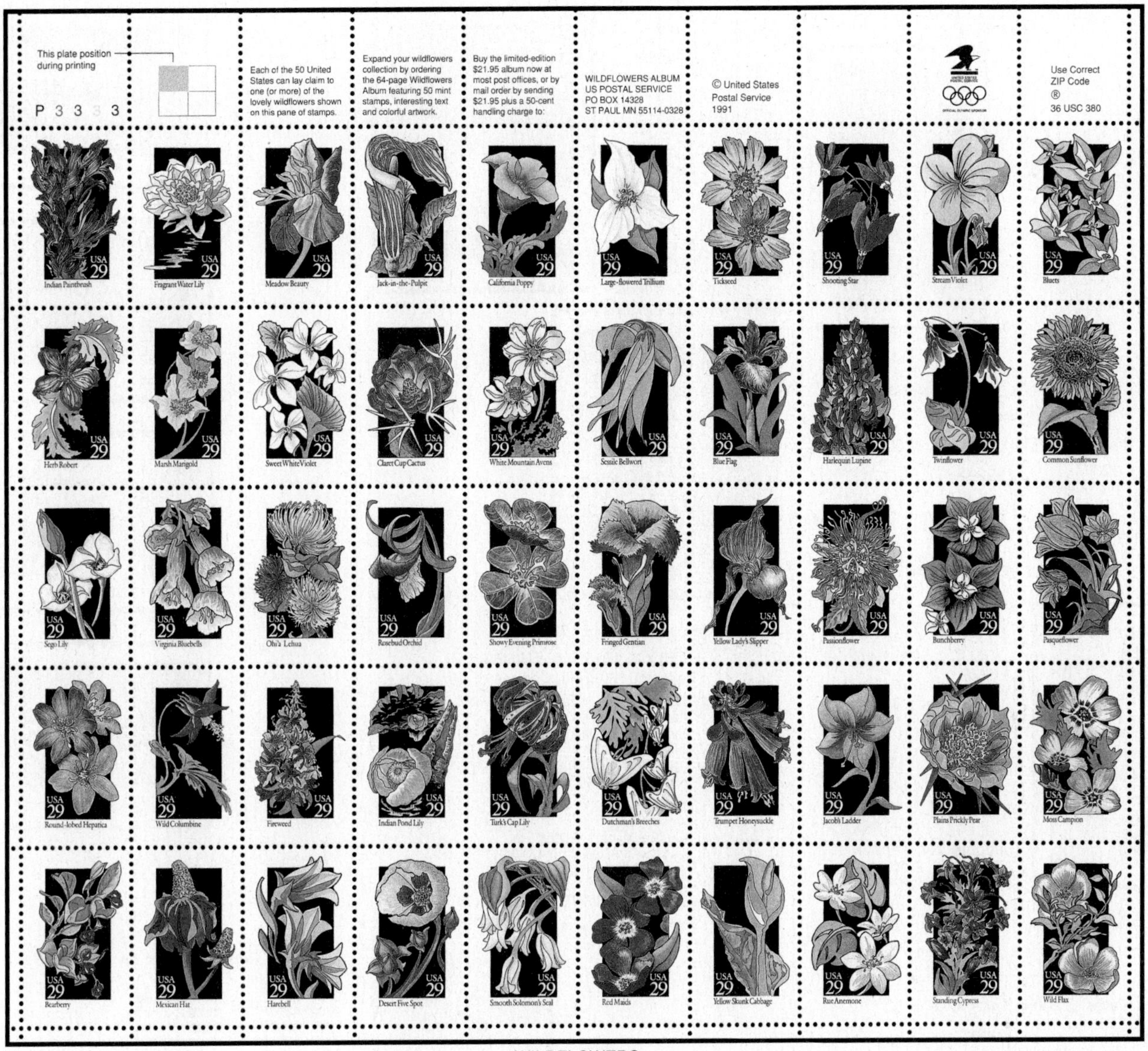

WILDFLOWERS
A1999-A2048

Illustration reduced.

Designed by Karen Mallary.

Printed by Ashton-Potter America, Inc.

LITHOGRAPHED

Plates of 300 in six panes of 50 and Plates of 200 in four panes of 50

1992, July 24 **Tagged** ***Perf. 11***

2647	A1999	29c	Indian paintbrush	.60	.60
2648	A2000	29c	Fragrant water lily	.60	.60
2649	A2001	29c	Meadow beauty	.60	.60
2650	A2002	29c	Jack-in-the-pulpit	.60	.60
2651	A2003	29c	California poppy	.60	.60
2652	A2004	29c	Large-flowered trillium	.60	.60
2653	A2005	29c	Tickseed	.60	.60
2654	A2006	29c	Shooting star	.60	.60
2655	A2007	29c	Stream violet	.60	.60
2656	A2008	29c	Bluets	.60	.60
2657	A2009	29c	Herb Robert	.60	.60
2658	A2010	29c	Marsh marigold	.60	.60
2659	A2011	29c	Sweet white violet	.60	.60
2660	A2012	29c	Claret cup cactus	.60	.60
2661	A2013	29c	White mountain avens	.60	.60
2662	A2014	29c	Sessile bellwort	.60	.60
2663	A2015	29c	Blue flag	.60	.60
2664	A2016	29c	Harlequin lupine	.60	.60
2665	A2017	29c	Twinflower	.60	.60
2666	A2018	29c	Common sunflower	.60	.60
2667	A2019	29c	Sego lily	.60	.60
2668	A2020	29c	Virginia bluebells	.60	.60
2669	A2021	29c	Ohi'a lehua	.60	.60
2670	A2022	29c	Rosebud orchid	.60	.60
2671	A2023	29c	Showy evening primrose	.60	.60
2672	A2024	29c	Fringed gentian	.60	.60
2673	A2025	29c	Yellow lady's slipper	.60	.60
2674	A2026	29c	Passionflower	.60	.60
2675	A2027	29c	Bunchberry	.60	.60
2676	A2028	29c	Pasqueflower	.60	.60
2677	A2029	29c	Round-lobed hepatica	.60	.60
2678	A2030	29c	Wild columbine	.60	.60
2679	A2031	29c	Fireweed	.60	.60
2680	A2032	29c	Indian pond lily	.60	.60
2681	A2033	29c	Turk's cap lily	.60	.60
2682	A2034	29c	Dutchman's breeches	.60	.60
2683	A2035	29c	Trumpet honeysuckle	.60	.60
2684	A2036	29c	Jacob's ladder	.60	.60
2685	A2037	29c	Plains prickly pear	.60	.60
2686	A2038	29c	Moss campion	.60	.60
2687	A2039	29c	Bearberry	.60	.60
2688	A2040	29c	Mexican hat	.60	.60
2689	A2041	29c	Harebell	.60	.60
2690	A2042	29c	Desert five spot	.60	.60
2691	A2043	29c	Smooth Solomon's seal	.60	.60
2692	A2044	29c	Red maids	.60	.60
2693	A2045	29c	Yellow skunk cabbage	.60	.60
2694	A2046	29c	Rue anemone	.60	.60
2695	A2047	29c	Standing cypress	.60	.60
2696	A2048	29c	Wild flax	.60	.60
a.			A1999-A2048 Pane of 50, #2647-2696	30.00	—

Sheet margin selvage contains a diagram of the plate layout with each pane's position shaded in gray.

WORLD WAR II

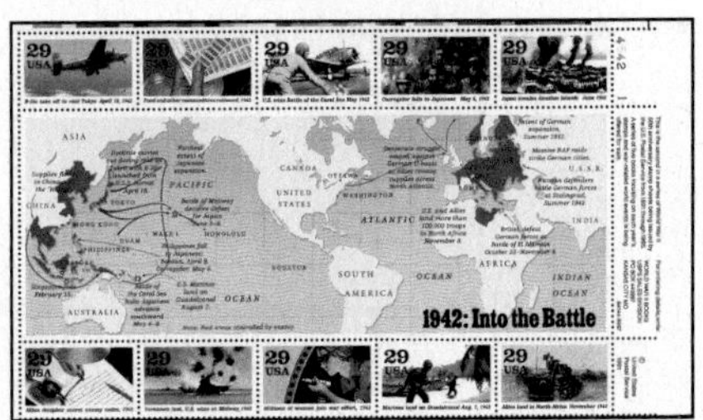

A2049

Illustration reduced.

Designed by William H. Bond.

No. 2697 — Events of 1942: a, B-25's take off to raid Tokyo, Apr. 18. b, Ration coupons (Food and other commodities rationed). c, Divebomber and deck crewman (US wins Battle of the Coral Sea, May). d, Prisoners of war (Corregidor falls to Japanese, May 6). e, Dutch Harbor buildings on fire (Japan invades Aleutian Islands, June). f, Headphones, coded message (Allies decipher secret enemy codes). g, Yorktown lost, U.S. wins at Midway. h, Woman with drill (Millions of women join war effort). i, Marines land on Guadalcanal, Aug. 7. j, Tank in desert (Allies land in North Africa, Nov.).

Central label is the size of 15 stamps and shows world map, extent of axis control.

LITHOGRAPHED & ENGRAVED

Plates of 80 in four panes of 20 each

1992, Aug. 17 **Tagged** ***Perf. 11***

2697	A2049	Block of 10	7.50	5.00
		Pane of 20	15.00	—
a.-j.		29c any single	.75	.30
k.		Red (litho.) omitted	*4,000.*	

No. 2697 has selvage at left and right and either top or bottom.

LITERARY ARTS SERIES

Dorothy Parker (1893-1967), Writer — A2050

Designed by Greg Rudd.

Printed by J.W. Fergusson & Sons for Stamp Venturers.

PHOTOGRAVURE

Plates of 200 in four panes of 50

1992, Aug. 22 **Tagged** ***Perf. 11***

2698 A2050 29c **multicolored**	.60	.25
P# block of 4, 5# + S	2.75	—
Zip block of 4	2.50	—
Pane of 50	30.00	

THEODORE VON KARMAN

Theodore Von Karman (1881-1963), Rocket Scientist — A2051

Designed by Chris Calle.

Printed by J.W. Fergusson & Sons for Stamp Venturers.

PHOTOGRAVURE

Plates of 200 in four panes of 50

1992, Aug. 31 **Tagged** ***Perf. 11***

2699 A2051 29c **multicolored**	.60	.25
P# block of 4, 4# + S	2.75	—
Zip block of 4	2.50	—
Pane of 50	30.00	

MINERALS

Azurite — A2052

Copper — A2053

Variscite — A2054

Wulfenite — A2055

Designed by Len Buckley.

LITHOGRAPHED & ENGRAVED

Sheets of 160 in four panes of 40.

1992, Sept. 17 **Tagged** ***Perf. 11***

2700 A2052 29c **multicolored**	.60	.25
2701 A2053 29c **multicolored**	.60	.25
2702 A2054 29c **multicolored**	.60	.25
2703 A2055 29c **multicolored**	.60	.25
a. Block or strip of 4, #2700-2703	2.40	2.00
P# block of 4, 6#	3.50	—
Zip block of 4	2.50	—
Pane of 40	24.00	
b. As "a," silver (litho.) omitted	*6,000.*	
d. As "a," silver omitted on two stamps	*900.00*	
e. As "a," tagging omitted	—	

JUAN RODRIGUEZ CABRILLO

Cabrillo (d. 1543), Ship, Map of San Diego Bay Area — A2056

Designed by Ren Wicks.

Printed by The Press and J.W. Fergusson & Sons for Stamp Venturers.

LITHOGRAPHED & ENGRAVED

Plates of 200 in four panes of 50

1992, Sept. 28 **Tagged** ***Perf. 11***

2704 A2056 29c **multicolored**	.60	.25
P# block of 4, 7# + 2 "S"s	3.50	—
Zip, Olympic block of 4	2.50	—
Pane of 50	30.00	
a. Black (engr.) omitted	*1,500.*	

WILD ANIMALS

Giraffe A2057

Giant Panda — A2058

Flamingo A2059

King Penguins A2060

White Bengal Tiger — A2061

Designed by Robert Giusti.

Printed by J.W. Fergusson & Sons for Stamp Venturers.

PHOTOGRAVURE

BOOKLET STAMPS

Perf. 11 Horiz. on 1 or 2 Sides

1992, Oct. 1 **Tagged**

2705 A2057 29c **multicolored**	.65	.25
2706 A2058 29c **multicolored**	.65	.25
2707 A2059 29c **multicolored**	.65	.25
2708 A2060 29c **multicolored**	.65	.25
2709 A2061 29c **multicolored**	.65	.25
a. Booklet pane of 5, #2705-2709	3.25	2.25
b. As "a," imperf.	*2,000.*	

CHRISTMAS

Madonna and Child, by Giovanni Bellini — A2062

Horse and Rider — A2063

Fire Pumper — A2064

Train Engine — A2065

Riverboat — A2066

Designed by Bradbury Thompson (#2710) and Lou Nolan (#2711-2719).

Printed by the Bureau of Engraving and Printing, Ashton-Potter America, Inc. (#2711-2714), the Multi-Color Corporation for American Bank Note Company (#2715-2718), and Avery Dennison (#2719).

LITHOGRAPHED & ENGRAVED

Sheets of 300 in six panes of 50 (#2710, 2714a)

1992 **Tagged** ***Perf. 11¼***

2710 A2062 29c **multicolored,** *Oct. 22* .60 .25
P# block of 4, 5# 2.75 —
Zip, copyright block of 4 2.50 —
Pane of 50 30.00
a. Booklet pane of 10 6.00 3.50

LITHOGRAPHED

Perf. 11¼x11

2711 A2063 29c **multicolored,** *Oct. 22* .75 .25
2712 A2064 29c **multicolored,** *Oct. 22* .75 .25
2713 A2065 29c **multicolored,** *Oct. 22* .75 .25
2714 A2066 29c **multicolored,** *Oct. 22* .75 .25
a. Block of 4, #2711-2714 3.00 1.10
P# block of 4, 5# + P 3.75 —
Zip, copyright block of 6 4.50 —
Pane of 50 37.50

Booklet Stamps

PHOTOGRAVURE

Perf. 11 on 2 or 3 Sides

2715 A2063 29c **multicolored,** *Oct. 22* .90 .25
2716 A2064 29c **multicolored,** *Oct. 22* .90 .25
2717 A2065 29c **multicolored,** *Oct. 22* .90 .25
2718 A2066 29c **multicolored,** *Oct. 22* .90 .25
a. Booklet pane of 4, #2715-2718 3.60 1.25

Imperforates and part-perforates on gummed stamp paper are proofs from the ABNCo. archives. From the same source come imperforates with Toys only and imperforates without denominations. See No. 2718aP in Proofs section.

Self-Adhesive

Die Cut

2719 A2065 29c **multicolored,** *Oct. 28* .65 .25
a. Booklet pane of 18 12.00

"Greetings" is 27mm long on Nos. 2711-2714, 25mm long on Nos. 2715-2718 and 21½mm long on No. 2719. Nos. 2715-2719 differ in color from Nos. 2711-2714.

CHINESE NEW YEAR

Year of the Rooster A2067

Designed by Clarence Lee.

Printed by the American Bank Note Co.

LITHOGRAPHED & ENGRAVED

Panes of 20

1992, Dec. 30 **Tagged** ***Perf. 11***

2720 A2067 29c **multicolored,** prephosphored uncoated paper with embedded tagging showing a mottled appearance, plus block tagging under the engraved portion of the design .60 .25
P# block of 4, 5#+A 2.50 —
Pane of 20 11.50 —
a. Prephosphored uncoated paper with embedded tagging showing a mottled appearance, plus block tagging on top of printed design 1.50 —
P# block of 4, 5#+A 7.50
Pane of 20 150.00
b. Prephosphored uncoated paper with embedded tagging showing a mottled appearance *125.00* —
Pane of 20 2,500.

See Nos. 3895j, 3997j.

AMERICAN MUSIC SERIES

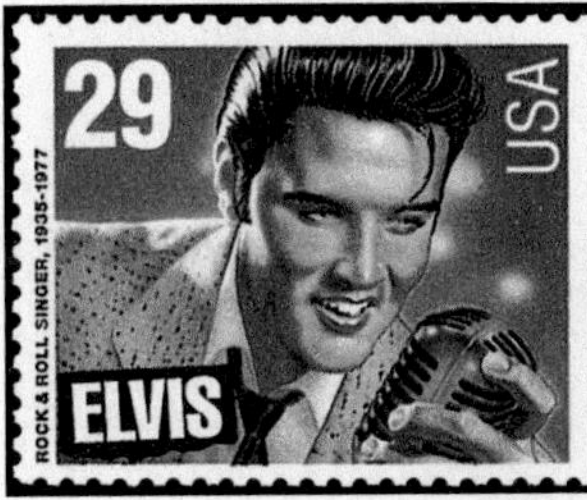

Elvis Presley A2068

Oklahoma! A2069

Hank Williams A2070

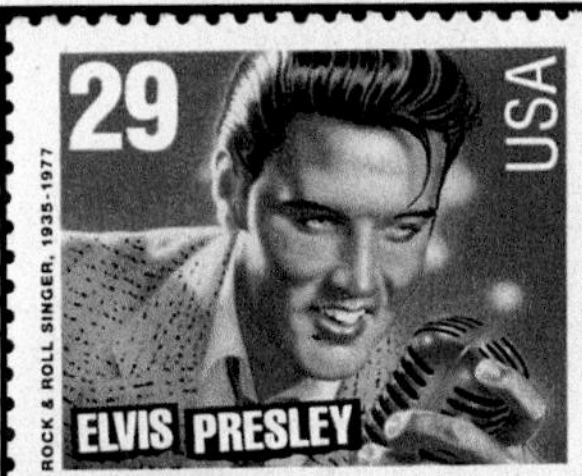

Elvis Presley A2071

Bill Haley — A2072

Clyde McPhatter A2073

Ritchie Valens A2074

Otis Redding A2075

Buddy Holly — A2076

Dinah Washington A2077

Designed by Mark Stutzman (#2721, 2724-2725, 2727, 2729, 2731-2732, 2734, 2736), Wilson McLean (#2722), Richard Waldrep (#2723), John Berkey (#2726, 2728, 2730, 2733, 2735, 2737).

Printed by the Bureau of Engraving and Printing (#2721), Stamp Venturers (#2722-2730), Multi-color Corp. for American Bank Note Co. (#2731-2737).

PHOTOGRAVURE

Panes of 40, Panes of 35 (#2724-2730)

1993 **Tagged** ***Perf. 11***

2721 A2068 29c **multicolored,** *Jan. 8* .60 .25
P# block of 4, 5# 2.75 —
Zip, copyright block of 4 2.50 —
Pane of 40 24.00
a. Imperf, pair —

Perf. 10

2722 A2069 29c **multicolored,** *Mar. 30* .60 .25
P# block of 4, 4#+S 3.25 —
Zip block of 4 2.50 —
Pane of 40 24.00
2723 A2070 29c **multicolored,** *June 9* .75 .25
P# block of 4, 6#+S 4.25 —
Zip block of 4 3.25 —
Pane of 40 30.00

Perf. 11.2x11.5

2723A A2070 29c **multicolored,** *June 9* 12.00 10.00
P# block of 4, 6#+S 95.00 —
Zip block of 4 65.00 —
Pane of 40 480.00

1993, June 16 ***Perf. 10***

2724 A2071 29c **multicolored** .70 .25
2725 A2072 29c **multicolored** .70 .25
2726 A2073 29c **multicolored** .70 .25
2727 A2074 29c **multicolored** .70 .25
2728 A2075 29c **multicolored** .70 .25
2729 A2076 29c **multicolored** .70 .25
2730 A2077 29c **multicolored** .70 .25
a. Vert. strip of 7, #2724-2730 5.50 3.00
Horiz. P# block of 10, 2 sets of 6P#+S, + top label 10.00 —
Vert. P# block of 8, 6#+S 7.75 —
Pane of 35 29.00 —

No. 2730a with Nos. 2724-2730 in numerical sequence cannot be obtained from the pane of 35.

Booklet Stamps

Perf. 11 Horiz. on 1 or 2 Sides

2731	A2071	29c **multicolored**	.65	.25
2732	A2072	29c **multicolored**	.65	.25
2733	A2073	29c **multicolored**	.65	.25
2734	A2074	29c **multicolored**	.65	.25
2735	A2075	29c **multicolored**	.65	.25
2736	A2076	29c **multicolored**	.65	.25
2737	A2077	29c **multicolored**	.65	.25
a.		Booklet pane, 2 #2731, 1 each #2732-2737	5.25	2.25
b.		Booklet pane, #2731, 2735-2737 + tab	2.60	1.50

Nos. 2731-2737 have smaller design sizes, brighter colors and shorter inscriptions than Nos. 2724-2730, as well as framelines around the designs and other subtle design differences.

No. 2737b without tab is indistinguishable from broken No. 2737a.

Imperforates of both No. 2737a and 2737b on gummed stamp paper are proofs from the ABNCo. archives. Perforated booklet pane multiples and varieties also exist from the same source. See Nos. 2737aP-2737bP in Proofs section.

See Nos. 2769, 2771, 2775 and designs A2112-A2117.

SPACE FANTASY

A2086

A2087

A2088

A2089

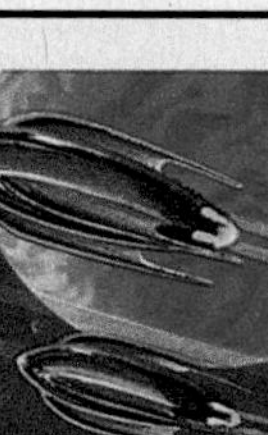

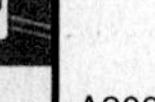

A2090

Designed by Stephen Hickman.

PHOTOGRAVURE
BOOKLET STAMPS

1993, Jan. 25		**Tagged**	***Perf. 11 Vert.***	
2741	A2086	29c **multicolored**	.60	.25
2742	A2087	29c **multicolored**	.60	.25
2743	A2088	29c **multicolored**	.60	.25
2744	A2089	29c **multicolored**	.60	.25
2745	A2090	29c **multicolored**	.60	.25
a.		Booklet pane of 5, #2741-2745	3.00	2.25

BLACK HERITAGE SERIES

Percy Lavon Julian (1899-1975), Chemist — A2091

Designed by Higgins Bond.

LITHOGRAPHED & ENGRAVED
Panes of 50

1993, Jan. 29		**Tagged**	***Perf. 11***	
2746	A2091	29c **multicolored**	.60	.25
		P# block of 4, 7#	2.75	—
		Zip block of 4	2.50	—
		Pane of 50	30.00	

OREGON TRAIL

A2092

Designed by Jack Rosenthal.

LITHOGRAPHED & ENGRAVED
Panes of 50

1993, Feb. 12		**Tagged**	***Perf. 11***	
2747	A2092	29c **multicolored**	.60	.25
		P# block of 4, 6#	3.00	—
		Zip block of 4	2.50	—
		Pane of 50	30.00	
a.		Tagging omitted	25.00	
b.		Blue omitted	*650.00*	

WORLD UNIVERSITY GAMES

A2093

Designed by David Buck.

PHOTOGRAVURE
Panes of 50

1993, Feb. 25		**Tagged**	***Perf. 11***	
2748	A2093	29c **multicolored**	.60	.25
		P# block of 4, 5#	2.75	—
		Zip block of 4	2.50	—
		Pane of 50	30.00	

GRACE KELLY (1929-1982)

Actress, Princess of Monaco — A2094

Designed by Czeslaw Slania.

Printed by Stamp Venturers.

ENGRAVED
Panes of 50

1993, Mar. 24		**Tagged**	***Perf. 11***	
2749	A2094	29c **deep ultra**	.60	.25
		P# block of 4, 1# +S	2.75	—
		Zip block of 4	2.50	—
		Pane of 50	30.00	

See Monaco No. 1851.

CIRCUS

Clown — A2095

Ringmaster — A2096

Trapeze Artist — A2097

Elephant — A2098

Designed by Steve McCracken.

Printed by Ashton Potter America.

LITHOGRAPHED
Panes of 40

1993, Apr. 6		**Tagged**	***Perf. 11***	
2750	A2095	29c **multicolored**	.60	.25
2751	A2096	29c **multicolored**	.60	.25
2752	A2097	29c **multicolored**	.60	.25
2753	A2098	29c **multicolored**	.60	.25
a.		Block of 4, #2750-2753	2.40	1.75
		P# block of 6, 5#+P	7.50	—
		Zip block of 6	3.75	—
		Pane of 40	24.00	

Plate and zip blocks of 6 and copyright blocks of 9 contain one #2753a with continuous design (complete spotlight).

CHEROKEE STRIP LAND RUN, CENTENNIAL

A2099

Designed by Harold T. Holden.

Printed by American Bank Note. Co.

LITHOGRAPHED & ENGRAVED
Panes of 20

1993, Apr. 17 **Tagged** ***Perf. 11***

2754 A2099 29c **multicolored**	.60	.25
P# block of 4, 5#+A	2.50	—
Pane of 20	12.50	—

Imperforates on gummed stamp paper, including gutter pairs and blocks, are proofs from the ABNCo. archives. From the same source also come perforated gutter pairs and blocks, plus imperforates missing the red text and black denomination and "USA." An approved die proof also is recorded. See No. 2754P in Proofs section.

DEAN ACHESON (1893-1971)

Secretary of State — A2100

Designed by Christopher Calle.

Printed by Stamp Venturers.

ENGRAVED
Sheets of 300 in six panes of 50

1993, Apr. 21 ***Perf. 11***

2755 A2100 29c **greenish gray**	.60	.25
P# block of 4, 1#+S	2.75	—
Zip block of 4	2.50	—
Pane of 50	30.00	

SPORTING HORSES

Steeplechase A2101

Thoroughbred Racing A2102

Harness Racing A2103

Polo — A2104

Designed by Michael Dudash.

Printed by Stamp Venturers.

LITHOGRAPHED & ENGRAVED
Panes of 40

1993, May 1 **Tagged** ***Perf. 11x11½***

2756 A2101 29c **multicolored**	.60	.25
2757 A2102 29c **multicolored**	.60	.25
2758 A2103 29c **multicolored**	.60	.25
2759 A2104 29c **multicolored**	.60	.25
a. Block of 4, #2756-2759	2.40	2.00
P# block of 4, 5#+S	2.75	—
Zip block of 4	2.50	—
Pane of 40	24.00	
b. As "a," black (engr.) omitted	*500.00*	

GARDEN FLOWERS

Hyacinth — A2105

Daffodil — A2106

Tulip — A2107

Iris — A2108

Lilac — A2109

Designed by Ned Seidler.

LITHOGRAPHED & ENGRAVED
BOOKLET STAMPS

1993, May 15 **Tagged** ***Perf. 11 Vert.***

2760 A2105 29c **multicolored**	.60	.25
2761 A2106 29c **multicolored**	.60	.25
2762 A2107 29c **multicolored**	.60	.25
2763 A2108 29c **multicolored**	.60	.25
2764 A2109 29c **multicolored**	.60	.25
a. Booklet pane of 5, #2760-2764	3.00	2.25
b. As "a," black (engr.) omitted	*135.00*	
c. As "a," imperf.	*700.00*	
d. As "a," tagging omitted	*650.00*	

WORLD WAR II

A2110

Illustration reduced.

Designed by William H. Bond.

Designs and events of 1943: a, Destroyers (Allied forces battle German U-boats). b, Military medics treat the wounded. c, Amphibious landing craft on beach (Sicily attacked by Allied forces, July). d, B-24s hit Ploesti refineries, August. e, V-mail delivers letters from home. f, PT boat (Italy invaded by Allies, Sept.). g, Nos. WS7, WS8, savings bonds, (Bonds and stamps help war effort). h, "Willie and Joe" keep spirits high. i, Banner in window (Gold Stars mark World War II losses). j, Marines assault Tarawa, Nov.

Central label is the size of 15 stamps and shows world map with extent of Axis control and Allied operations.

LITHOGRAPHED & ENGRAVED
Plates of 80 in four panes of 20 each

1993, May 31 **Tagged** ***Perf. 11***

2765 A2110 Block of 10	7.50	5.00
Pane of 20	15.00	—
a.-j. 29c any single	.75	.40
k. As No. 2765, tagging omitted on a.-e.	—	
l. As No. 2765, tagging omitted on f.-j.	—	—

No. 2765 has selvage at left and right and either top or bottom.

JOE LOUIS (1914-1981)

A2111

Designed by Thomas Blackshear.

LITHOGRAPHED & ENGRAVED
Plates of 200 in four panes of 50

1993, June 22 **Tagged** ***Perf. 11***

2766	A2111 29c **multicolored**	.60	.25
	P# block of 4, 5#	2.75	—
	Zip block of 4	2.50	—
	Pane of 50	30.00	

AMERICAN MUSIC SERIES
Oklahoma! Type and

Show Boat — A2112

Porgy & Bess — A2113

My Fair Lady — A2114

Designed by Wilson McLean.

Printed by Multi-Color Corp.

BOOKLET STAMPS
PHOTOGRAVURE
Perf. 11 Horiz. on 1 or 2 Sides

1993, July 14 **Tagged**

2767	A2112 29c **multicolored**	.60	.25
2768	A2113 29c **multicolored**	.60	.25
2769	A2069 29c **multicolored**	.60	.25
2770	A2114 29c **multicolored**	.60	.25
a.	Booklet pane of 4, #2767-2770	2.75	2.25

No. 2769 has smaller design size, brighter colors and shorter inscription than No. 2722, as well as a frameline around the design and other subtle design differences.

Imperforate booklet panes, singly or in multiples, on gummed stamp paper are proofs from the ABNCo. archives. From the same source come imperforate progressive proofs, plus imperforate proofs/essays showing slightly altered designs. See No. 2770aP in Proofs section.

AMERICAN MUSIC SERIES
Hank Williams Type and

Patsy Cline — A2115

The Carter Family A2116

Bob Wills — A2117

Designed by Richard Waldrep.

Printed by Stamp Venturers (#2771-2774) and American Bank Note Co. (#2775-2778).

PHOTOGRAVURE
Panes of 20

1993, Sept. 25 **Tagged** ***Perf. 10***

2771	A2070 29c **multicolored**	.75	.25
2772	A2115 29c **multicolored**	.75	.25
2773	A2116 29c **multicolored**	.75	.25
2774	A2117 29c **multicolored**	.75	.25
a.	Block or horiz. strip of 4, #2771-2774	3.00	1.75
	Horiz. P# block of 8, 2 sets of 6#+S + top label	6.50	—
	P# block of 4, 6#+S	3.25	—
	Pane of 20	16.00	—

Booklet Stamps
Perf. 11 Horiz. on one or two sides
With Black Frameline

2775	A2070 29c **multicolored**	.60	.25
2776	A2116 29c **multicolored**	.60	.25
2777	A2115 29c **multicolored**	.60	.25
2778	A2117 29c **multicolored**	.60	.25
a.	Booklet pane of 4, #2775-2778	2.50	2.00

Inscription at left measures 27½mm on No. 2723, 27mm on No. 2771 and 22mm on No. 2775. No. 2723 shows only two tuning keys on guitar, while No. 2771 shows those two and parts of two others.

Imperforate booklet panes on gummed stamp paper, singly or in multiples, are proofs from the ABNCo. archives. From the same source come panes perfed horiz. but uncut vertically, plus imperforate progressive proofs and other die proof varieties. See No. 2778aP in Proofs section.

NATIONAL POSTAL MUSEUM

Independence Hall, Benjamin Franklin, Printing Press, Colonial Post Rider — A2118

Pony Express Rider, Civil War Soldier, Concord Stagecoach A2119

JN-4H Biplane, Charles Lindbergh, Railway Mail Car, 1931 Model A Ford Mail Truck — A2120

California Gold Rush Miner's Letter, Nos. 39, 295, C3a, C13, Barcode and Circular Date Stamp A2121

Designed by Richard Schlecht.

Printed by American Bank Note Co.

LITHOGRAPHED AND ENGRAVED

1993, July 30 **Tagged** ***Perf. 11***

2779	A2118 29c **multicolored**	.60	.25
2780	A2119 29c **multicolored**	.60	.25
2781	A2120 29c **multicolored**	.60	.25
2782	A2121 29c **multicolored**	.60	.25
a.	Block or strip of 4, #2779-2782	2.40	2.00
	P# block of 4, 7#+A	2.50	—
	Pane of 20	12.50	—
b.	As "a," engr. maroon (USA/29) and black ("My dear...") omitted	*2,500.*	
c.	As "a," imperf	*2,500.*	

AMERICAN SIGN LANGUAGE

A2122

A2123

Designed by Chris Calle.

Printed by Stamp Venturers.

PHOTOGRAVURE

1993, Sept. 20 **Tagged** ***Perf. 11½***

2783	A2122 29c **multicolored**	.60	.25
2784	A2123 29c **multicolored**	.60	.25
a.	Pair, #2783-2784	1.20	.75
	P# block of 4, 4#+S	2.50	—
	Pane of 20	12.50	—

CLASSIC BOOKS

A2124

A2125

A2126

A2127

Designed by Jim Lamb.

Printed by American Bank Note Co.

Designs: No. 2785, Rebecca of Sunnybrook Farm, by Kate Douglas Wiggin. No. 2786, Little House on the Prairie, by Laura Ingalls Wilder. No. 2787, The Adventures of Huckleberry Finn, by Mark Twain. No. 2788, Little Women, by Louisa May Alcott.

LITHOGRAPHED & ENGRAVED
Panes of 40

1993, Oct. 23 Tagged *Perf. 11*

2785 A2124 29c **multicolored** .60 .25
2786 A2125 29c **multicolored** .60 .25
2787 A2126 29c **multicolored** .60 .25
2788 A2127 29c **multicolored** .60 .25
a. Block or horiz. strip of 4, #2785-2788 2.40 2.00
P# block of 4, 5#+A 5.00 —
Zip block of 4 2.50 —
Pane of 40 24.00

Imperforates on gummed stamp paper, including gutter pairs and blocks, are proofs from the ABNCo. archives. See No. 2788aP in Proofs section.

CHRISTMAS

Madonna and Child in a Landscape, by Giovanni Battista Cima — A2128

Jack-in-the-Box
A2129

Red-Nosed Reindeer
A2130

Snowman — A2131

Toy Soldier Blowing Horn — A2132

Designed by Bradbury Thompson (#2789-2790), Peter Good (#2791-2803).

Printed by Bureau of Engraving and Printing (#2789, 2791-2798), KCS Industries (#2790), Avery Dennison (#2799-2803).

LITHOGRAPHED & ENGRAVED
Panes of 50 (#2789, 2791-2794)

1993, Oct. 21 Tagged *Perf. 11*

2789 A2128 29c **multicolored** .60 .25
P# block of 4, 4# 2.75 —
Zip, copyright block of 4 2.50 —
Pane of 50 30.00

Booklet Stamp

Size: 18x25mm

Perf. 11½x11 on 2 or 3 Sides

2790 A2128 29c **multicolored** .60 .25
a. Booklet pane of 4 2.40 1.75
b. Imperf., pair —
c. As "a," imperf —

Nos. 2789-2790 have numerous design differences.

1993 *Perf. 11½*

PHOTOGRAVURE

2791 A2129 29c **multicolored,** *Oct. 21* .60 .25
2792 A2130 29c **multicolored,** *Oct. 21* .60 .25
2793 A2131 29c **multicolored,** *Oct. 21* .60 .25
2794 A2132 29c **multicolored,** *Oct. 21* .60 .25
a. Block or strip of 4, #2791-2794 2.40 2.00
P# block of 4, 6# 4.00 —
Zip, copyright block of 4 2.50 —
Pane of 50 30.00

Booklet Stamps

Size: 18x21mm

Perf. 11x10 on 2 or 3 Sides

2795 A2132 29c **multicolored,** *Oct. 21* .85 .25
2796 A2131 29c **multicolored,** *Oct. 21* .85 .25
2797 A2130 29c **multicolored,** *Oct. 21* .85 .25
2798 A2129 29c **multicolored,** *Oct. 21* .85 .25
a. Booklet pane, 3 each #2795-2796, 2 each #2797-2798 8.50 4.00
b. Booklet pane, 3 each #2797-2798, 2 each #2795-2796 8.50 4.00
c. Block of 4, #2795-2798 3.40 1.75

Self-Adhesive

Size: 19½x26½mm

Die Cut

2799 A2131 29c **multicolored,** *Oct. 28* .75 .25
a. Coil with plate # V1111111 — 6.00
b. Horiz. coil strip of 4, #2799-2802 3.00
P# strip of 5, 1 each #2799-2801, 2 #2802, P#V1111111 9.00
P# strip of 8, 2 each #2799-2802, P#V1111111 12.00
2800 A2132 29c **multicolored,** *Oct. 28* .75 .25
2801 A2129 29c **multicolored,** *Oct. 28* .75 .25
2802 A2130 29c **multicolored,** *Oct. 28* .75 .25
a. Booklet pane, 3 each #2799-2802 9.00
b. Block of 4, #2799-2802 3.00

Except for No. 2799a with plate number, coil stamps are indistinguishable from booklet stamps once they are removed from the backing paper.

Size: 17x20mm

2803 A2131 29c **multicolored,** *Oct. 28* ® .60 .25
a. Booklet pane of 18 11.00

Snowman on Nos. 2793, 2799 has three buttons and seven snowflakes beneath nose (placement differs on both stamps). No. 2796 has two buttons and five snowflakes beneath nose. No. 2803 has two orange buttons and four snowflakes beneath nose.

Adhesive residue may remain on some examples of No. 2803 after soaking. See note after No. 1549.

MARIANA ISLANDS

A2133

Designed by Herb Kane.

LITHOGRAPHED AND ENGRAVED

1993, Nov. 4 Tagged *Perf. 11*

2804 A2133 29c **multicolored** .60 .25
P# block of 4, 6# 3.25 —
Pane of 20 15.50 —

COLUMBUS' LANDING IN PUERTO RICO, 500th ANNIVERSARY

A2134

Designed by Richard Schlecht.

Printed by Stamp Venturers.

PHOTOGRAVURE
Panes of 50

1993, Nov. 19 Tagged *Perf. 11.2*

2805 A2134 29c **multicolored** .60 .25
P# block of 4, 5#+S 2.75 —
Zip block of 4 2.50 —
Pane of 50 30.00

AIDS AWARENESS

A2135

Designed by Tom Mann.
Printed by Stamp Venturers.

PHOTOGRAVURE
Panes of 50

1993, Dec. 1 Tagged *Perf. 11.2*

2806 A2135 29c **black & red** .60 .25
P# block of 4, 3#+S 2.75 —
Zip, copyright block of 6 2.50 —
Pane of 50 30.00
a. Perf. 11 vert. on 1 or 2 sides, from bklt. pane .70 .25
b. As "a," booklet pane of 5 3.50 2.00

WINTER OLYMPICS

Slalom — A2136

Luge — A2137

Ice Dancing — A2138

Cross-Country Skiing — A2139

Ice Hockey — A2140

Designed by Lon Busch.
Printed by Ashton-Potter.

LITHOGRAPHED
Sheets of 120 in six panes of 20

1994, Jan. 6 **Tagged** ***Perf. 11.2***

2807 A2136 29c **multicolored** .60 .25
2808 A2137 29c **multicolored** .60 .25
2809 A2138 29c **multicolored** .60 .25
2810 A2139 29c **multicolored** .60 .25
2811 A2140 29c **multicolored** .60 .25
a. Strip of 5, #2807-2811 3.00 2.50
Horiz. P# block of 10, 2 sets of 4#+P and inscriptions 6.50 —
Horiz. P# block of 10, 2 sets of 4#+P 6.00 —
Pane of 20 12.50 —

EDWARD R. MURROW, JOURNALIST (1908-65)

A2141

Designed by Chris Calle.

ENGRAVED
Panes of 50

1994, Jan. 21 **Tagged** ***Perf. 11.2***

2812 A2141 29c **brown** .60 .25
P# block of 4, 1# 3.50 —
Pane of 50 30.00

LOVE

A2142

A2143

A2144

Designed by Peter Good (#2813), Lon Busch (#2814-2815).

Printed by Banknote Corp. of America (#2813), American Banknote Co. (#2814) and Bureau of Engraving and Printing (#2814C, 2815).

Booklet Stamps
LITHOGRAPHED & ENGRAVED

1994 **Tagged** ***Die Cut***
Self-adhesive

2813 A2142 29c **multicolored,** *Jan. 27* .60 .25
a. Booklet pane of 18 11.00
b. Coil with plate # B1 — 5.00
P# strip of 5, #B1 7.00

Except for No. 2813b with plate number, coil stamps are indistinguishable from booklet stamps once they are removed from the backing paper.

PHOTOGRAVURE
Perf. 10.9x11.1 on 2 or 3 sides

2814 A2143 29c **multicolored,** *Feb. 14* .60 .25
a. Booklet pane of 10 6.00 3.50
b. Imperf, pair —
d. As "a," imperf. —

Horiz. pairs, imperf between, are printer's waste.

LITHOGRAPHED & ENGRAVED
Sheets of 300 in six panes of 50
Tagged
Perf. 11.1

2814C A2143 29c **multicolored,** *June 11* .70 .25
P# block of 4, 5# 3.00 —
Pane of 50 35.00

Size of No. 2814C is 20x28mm. No. 2814 is 18x24½mm.

PHOTOGRAVURE & ENGRAVED
Sheet of 300 in six panes of 50
Perf. 11.2

2815 A2144 52c **multicolored,** *Feb. 14* 1.00 .25
P# block of 4, 5# 5.00 —
P# block of 10, 2 sets of 5#, plate diagram, copyright and pane price inscriptions 11.00 —
Pane of 50 50.00

BLACK HERITAGE SERIES

Dr. Allison Davis (1902-83), Social Anthropologist, Educator — A2145

Designed by Chris Calle.

Printed by Stamp Venturers.

ENGRAVED

1994, Feb. 1 **Tagged** ***Perf. 11.2***

2816 A2145 29c **red brown & brown** .60 .25
P# block of 4, 1#+S 2.50 —
Pane of 20 12.50 —

CHINESE NEW YEAR

Year of the Dog — A2146

Designed by Clarence Lee.

Printed by J.W. Fergusson & Sons for Stamp Venturers.

PHOTOGRAVURE
Sheets of 180 in nine panes of 20

1994, Feb. 5 **Tagged** ***Perf. 11.2***

2817 A2146 29c **multicolored** .80 .25
P# block of 4, 4#+S 3.50 —
Pane of 20 17.50 —

See Nos. 3895k, 3997k.

BUFFALO SOLDIERS

A2147

Designed by Mort Kuntsler.

Printed by Stamp Venturers.

LITHOGRAPHED & ENGRAVED
Plates of 180 in nine panes of 20

1994, Apr. 22 **Tagged** ***Perf. 11.5x11.2***

2818 A2147 29c **multicolored** .60 .25
P# block of 4, 5#+S 2.50 —
Pane of 20 12.50 —
a. Double impression (second impression light) of red brown (engr. inscriptions) —

SILENT SCREEN STARS

Rudolph Valentino (1895-1926) — A2148

Clara Bow (1905-65) — A2149

Charlie Chaplin (1889-1977) — A2150

Lon Chaney (1883-1930) — A2151

John Gilbert (1895-1936) — A2152

Zasu Pitts (1898-1963) — A2153

Harold Lloyd (1894-1971) — A2154

Keystone Cops — A2155

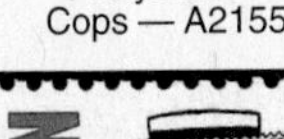

Theda Bara (1885-1955) — A2156

Buster Keaton (1895-1966) — A2157

Designed by Al Hirschfeld.

LITHOGRAPHED & ENGRAVED

Plates of 160 in four panes of 40

1994, Apr. 27 **Tagged** ***Perf. 11.2***

2819	A2148	29c	**red, black & bright violet**	1.10	.30
2820	A2149	29c	**red, black & bright violet**	1.10	.30
2821	A2150	29c	**red, black & bright violet**	1.10	.30
2822	A2151	29c	**red, black & bright violet**	1.10	.30
2823	A2152	29c	**red, black & bright violet**	1.10	.30
2824	A2153	29c	**red, black & bright violet**	1.10	.30
2825	A2154	29c	**red, black & bright violet**	1.10	.30
2826	A2155	29c	**red, black & bright violet**	1.10	.30
2827	A2156	29c	**red, black & bright violet**	1.10	.30
2828	A2157	29c	**red, black & bright violet**	1.10	.30
a.			Block of 10, #2819-2828	11.00	5.00
			P# block of 10, 4#, plate diagram and copyright inscription	12.00	—
			Half pane of 20	23.00	—
			Pane of 40	44.00	
b.			As "a," black (litho.) omitted	—	
c.			As "a," blk, red & brt vio (litho.) omitted	—	

GARDEN FLOWERS

Lily — A2158

Zinnia — A2159

Gladiola — A2160

Marigold — A2161

Rose — A2162

Designed by Ned Seidler.

LITHOGRAPHED & ENGRAVED

1994, Apr. 28 **Tagged** ***Perf. 10.9 Vert.***

Booklet Stamps

2829	A2158	29c	**multicolored**	.60	.25
2830	A2159	29c	**multicolored**	.60	.25
2831	A2160	29c	**multicolored**	.60	.25
2832	A2161	29c	**multicolored**	.60	.25
2833	A2162	29c	**multicolored**	.60	.25
a.			Booklet pane of 5, #2829-2833	3.00	2.25
b.			As "a," imperf	*400.00*	
c.			As "a," black (engr.) omitted	*125.00*	
d.			As "a," tagging omitted	—	

1994 WORLD CUP SOCCER CHAMPIONSHIPS

A2163

A2163a

A2164

A2165

Illustration reduced.

Designed by Michael Dudash.

Printed by J.W. Fergusson & Sons for Stamp Venturers. Design: 40c, Soccer player, diff.

PHOTOGRAVURE

Plates of 180 in nine panes of 20

1994, May 26 **Tagged** ***Perf. 11.1***

2834	A2163	29c	**multicolored**	.60	.25
			P# block of 4, 4#+S	2.50	—
			Pane of 20	12.50	—
2835	A2163a	40c	**multicolored**	.80	.25
			P# block of 4, 4#+S	3.20	—
			Pane of 20	16.00	—
2836	A2164	50c	**multicolored**	1.00	.25
			P# block of 4, 4#+S	4.00	—
			Pane of 20	20.00	—
			Nos. 2834-2836 (3)	2.40	.75

Souvenir Sheet

2837	A2165	Sheet of 3, #a.-c.	4.50	3.00

Nos. 2834-2836 are printed on phosphor-coated paper while Nos. 2837a (29c), 2837b (40c), 2837c (50c) are block tagged. No. 2837c has a portion of the yellow map in the LR corner.

Printer's waste exists for No. 2835, including imperf. pairs, imperf. pairs with gutter between, imperf. with all colors except black omitted, and imperf. with black omitted.

WORLD WAR II

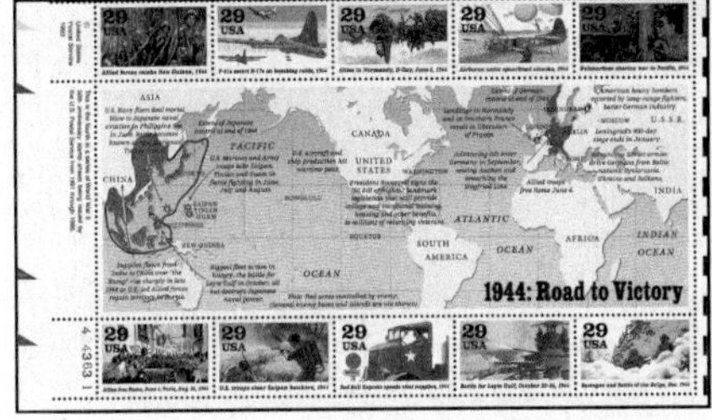

A2166

Illustration reduced.

Designed by William H. Bond.

Designs and events of 1944: a, Allied forces retake New Guinea. b, P-51s escort B-17s on bombing raids. c, Troops running from landing craft (Allies in Normandy, D-Day, June 6). d, Airborne units spearhead attacks. e, Officer at periscope (Submarines shorten war in Pacific). f, Parade (Allies free Rome, June 4; Paris, Aug. 25). g, Soldier firing flamethrower (US troops clear Saipan bunkers). h, Red Ball Express speeds vital supplies. i, Battleship firing main battery (Battle for Leyte Gulf, Oct. 23-26). j, Soldiers in snow (Bastogne and Battle of the Bulge, Dec.).

Central label is size of 15 stamps and shows world map with extent of Axis control and Allied operations.

LITHOGRAPHED & ENGRAVED

Plates of eight subjects in four panes of 2 each

1994, June 6 **Tagged** ***Perf. 10.9***

2838	A2166	Block of 10	17.00	10.00
		Pane of 20	34.00	—
a.-j.		29c any single	1.70	.50

No. 2838 has selvage at left and right and either top or bottom.

NORMAN ROCKWELL

A2167

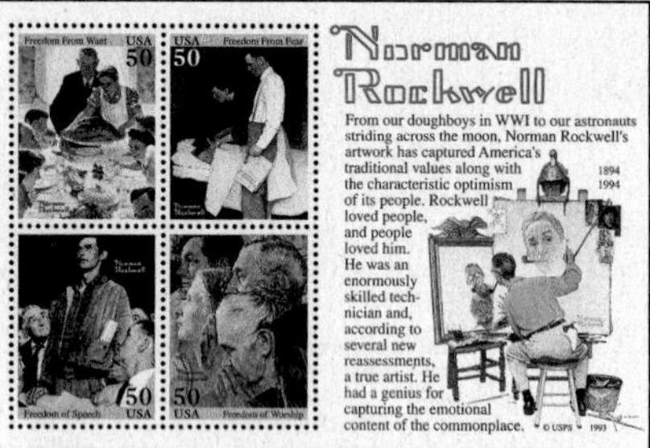

A2168

Illustration reduced.

Designed by Richard Sheaff based on Rockwell's works.

LITHOGRAPHED & ENGRAVED
Sheets of 200 in four panes of 50

1994, July 1 **Tagged** ***Perf. 10.9x11.1***

2839 A2167 29c **multicolored** .60 .25
P# block of 4, 5# 2.75 —
Pane of 50 30.00

Souvenir Sheet
LITHOGRAPHED

2840 A2168 Sheet of 4 4.50 2.75
a. 50c Freedom From Want 1.10 .65
b. 50c Freedom From Fear 1.10 .65
c. 50c Freedom of Speech 1.10 .65
d. 50c Freedom of Worship 1.10 .65

Panes of No. 2839 contain two plate blocks, one containing a plate position diagram.

Moon Landing, 25th Anniv.

A2169

A2170

Designed by Paul and Chris Calle.

Printed by Stamp Venturers (#2841) and Banknote Corp. of America (#2842).

Miniature Sheet
LITHOGRAPHED

1994, July 20 **Tagged** ***Perf. 11.2x11.1***

2841 A2169 29c Sheet of 12 10.50 —
a. Single stamp .85 .60

LITHOGRAPHED & ENGRAVED
Sheets of 120 in six panes of 20
Perf. 10.7x11.1

2842 A2170 $9.95 **multicolored** 20.00 16.00
P# block of 4, 5#+B 82.50 —
Pane of 20 400.00

LOCOMOTIVES

Hudson's General A2171

McQueen's Jupiter — A2172

Eddy's No. 242 — A2173

Ely's No. 10 — A2174

Buchanan's No. 999 — A2175

Designed by Richard Leech.

Printed by J.W. Ferguson & Sons for Stamp Venturers.

PHOTOGRAVURE

1994, July 28 **Tagged** ***Perf. 11 Horiz.***
Booklet Stamps

2843 A2171 29c **multicolored** .75 .25
2844 A2172 29c **multicolored** .75 .25
2845 A2173 29c **multicolored** .75 .25
2846 A2174 29c **multicolored** .75 .25
2847 A2175 29c **multicolored** .75 .25
a. Booklet pane of 5, #2843-2847 3.75 2.00
b. As "a," imperf. *2,500.*

GEORGE MEANY, LABOR LEADER (1894-1980)

A2176

Designed by Chris Calle.

ENGRAVED
Sheets of 200 in four panes of 50

1994, Aug. 16 **Tagged** ***Perf. 11.1x11***

2848 A2176 29c **blue** .60 .25
P# block of 4, 1# 2.50 —
Pane of 50 30.00

Panes of No. 2848 contain two plate blocks, one containing a plate position diagram.

AMERICAN MUSIC SERIES
Popular Singers

Al Jolson (1886-1950) A2177

Bing Crosby (1904-77) A2178

Ethel Waters (1896-1977) A2179

Nat "King" Cole (1919-65) A2180

Ethel Merman (1908-84) A2181

Jazz Singers

Bessie Smith (1894-1937) A2182

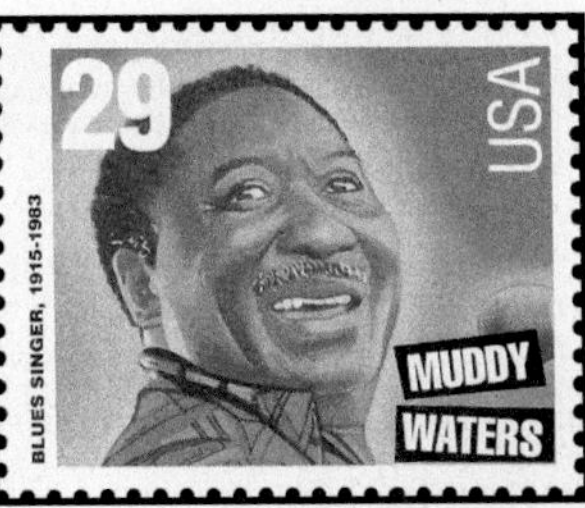

Muddy Waters (1915-83) A2183

Billie Holiday (1915-59) A2184

Robert Johnson (1911-38) A2185

Jimmy Rushing (1902-72) A2186

"Ma" Rainey (1886-1939) A2187

Mildred Bailey (1907-51) A2188

Howlin' Wolf (1910-76) A2189

Designed by Chris Payne (#2849-2853), Howard Koslow (#2854, 2856, 2858, 2860), Julian Allen (#2855, 2857, 2859, 2861).

Printed by J.W. Fergusson & Sons for Stamp Venturers (#2849-2853), Manhardt-Alexander for Ashton-Potter (USA) Ltd. (#2854-2861).

PHOTOGRAVURE

Plates of 180 in nine panes of 20, Plates of 210 in six panes of 35 (#2854-2861)

1994, Sept. 1 **Tagged** ***Perf. 10.1x10.2***

2849	A2177 29c **multicolored**	.85	.25
2850	A2178 29c **multicolored**	.85	.25
2851	A2179 29c **multicolored**	.85	.25
2852	A2180 29c **multicolored**	.85	.25
2853	A2181 29c **multicolored**	.85	.25
a.	Vert. strip of 5, #2849-2853	4.25	2.00
	Vert. P# block of 6, 6#+S	8.50	—
	Horiz. P# block of 12, 2 sets of 6#+S, + top label	16.50	—
	Pane of 20	23.50	—
b.	Pane of 20, imperf	*10,000.*	

Some plate blocks of 6 will contain plate position diagram and copyright inscription, others will contain pane price inscription.

1994, Sept. 17 ***Perf. 11x10.8***

LITHOGRAPHED

2854	A2182 29c **multicolored**	1.50	.25
2855	A2183 29c **multicolored**	1.50	.25
2856	A2184 29c **multicolored**	1.50	.25
2857	A2185 29c **multicolored**	1.50	.25
2858	A2186 29c **multicolored**	1.50	.25
2859	A2187 29c **multicolored**	1.50	.25
2860	A2188 29c **multicolored**	1.50	.25
2861	A2189 29c **multicolored**	1.50	.25
a.	Block of 10, #2854-2861 +2 additional stamps	15.00	4.50
	Vert. P# block of 10, 5#+P	16.00	—
	P# block of 10, 2 sets of 5#+P, + top label	17.00	—
	Pane of 35	55.00	—

Vertical plate blocks contain either pane price inscription or copyright inscription.

LITERARY ARTS SERIES

James Thurber (1894-1961) — A2190

Designed by Richard Sheaff based on drawing by James Thurber.

LITHOGRAPHED & ENGRAVED

Plates of 200 in four panes of 50

1994, Sept. 10 **Tagged** ***Perf. 11***

2862	A2190 29c **multicolored**	.60	.25
	P# block of 4, 2#	2.75	—
	Pane of 50	30.00	

Panes of No. 2862 contain two plate blocks, one containing a plate position diagram.

WONDERS OF THE SEA

Diver, Motorboat A2191

Diver, Ship — A2192

Diver, Ship's Wheel — A2193

Diver, Coral — A2194

Designed by Charles Lynn Bragg.

Printed by Barton Press for Banknote Corporation of America.

LITHOGRAPHED

Plates of 216 in nine panes of 24

1994, Oct. 3 **Tagged** ***Perf. 11x10.9***

2863	A2191 29c **multicolored**	.75	.25
2864	A2192 29c **multicolored**	.75	.25
2865	A2193 29c **multicolored**	.75	.25
2866	A2194 29c **multicolored**	.75	.25
a.	Block of 4, #2863-2866	3.00	1.50
	P# block of 4, 4#+B	3.25	—
	Pane of 24	19.00	—
b.	As "a," imperf	*350.00*	

CRANES

Black-Necked A2195

Whooping — A2196

Designed by Clarence Lee based on illustrations by Zhan Gengxi.

Printed by Barton Press for Banknote Corporation of America.

LITHOGRAPHED & ENGRAVED
Sheets of 120 in six panes of 20

1994, Oct. 9	**Tagged**	***Perf. 10.8x11***	
2867 A2195 29c **multicolored**		.70	.25
2868 A2196 29c **multicolored**		.70	.25
a. Pair, #2867-2868		1.40	.75
P# block of 4, 5#+B		3.00	—
Pane of 20		14.50	
b. As "a," black & magenta (engr.) omitted		*1,250.*	
c. As "a," double impression of engr. black (Birds' names and "USA") & magenta ("29")		*3,000.*	
d. As "a," double impression of engr. black ("USA") & magenta ("29")		*3,000.*	

See People's Republic of China Nos. 2528-2529.

Uncut Press Sheets

Typical Vertical Pair with Horizontal Gutter

Typical Horizontal Pair with Vertical Gutter

Cross Gutter Block of 8

Illustrations reduced.

Beginning with No. 2869, the U.S. Postal Service made available for sale uncut press sheets of selected commemorative and definitive issues. These sheets are noted in footnotes following each issue. These sheets generally contain cross-gutter blocks and pairs with gutters between (typical examples shown above) and sometimes other collectible pair or block formats. The cross-gutter blocks and the pairs with gutters between are valued in the footnotes. Other possible formats not noted sell for a premium, but they are not listed or valued herein.

See note before No. 4694 for uncut press sheets without die cutting (imperforates).

LEGENDS OF THE WEST

A2197

Illustration reduced.

g. Bill Pickett (1870-1932) (Revised)

Designed by Mark Hess.

Printed by J.W. Fergusson & Sons for Stamp Venturers.

Designs: a, Home on the Range. b, Buffalo Bill Cody (1846-1917). c, Jim Bridger (1804-81). d, Annie Oakley (1860-1926). e, Native American Culture. f, Chief Joseph (c. 1840-1904). h, Bat Masterson (1853-1921). i, John C. Fremont (1813-90). j, Wyatt Earp (1848-1929). k, Nellie Cashman (c. 1849-1925). l, Charles Goodnight (1826-1929). m, Geronimo (1823-1909). n, Kit Carson (1809-68). o, Wild Bill Hickok (1837-76). p, Western Wildlife. q, Jim Beckwourth (c. 1798-1866). r, Bill Tilghman (1854-1924). s, Sacagawea (c. 1787-1812). t, Overland Mail.

PHOTOGRAVURE
Sheets of 120 in six panes of 20

1994, Oct. 18	**Tagged**	***Perf. 10.1x10***	
2869 A2197 Pane of 20		15.00	10.00
a.-t. 29c any single		.75	.50
u. As No. 2869, a.-e. imperf. f.-j. part perf.			—

Uncut press sheets of No. 2869 were made available for sale. Values: cross-gutter block of 20, $27.50; pairs with gutters between, $2.50 each.

See note after No. 2868.

LEGENDS OF THE WEST (Recalled)

g. Bill Pickett (Recalled)

Nos. 2870b-2870d, 2870f-2870o, 2870q-2870s have a frameline around the vignette that is half the width of the frameline on similar stamps in No. 2869. Other design differences may exist.

PHOTOGRAVURE
Sheets of 120 in six panes of 20

1994	**Tagged**	***Perf. 10.1x10***	
2870 A2197 29c Pane of 20		125.00	—

150,000 panes of No. 2870 were made available through a drawing. Panes were delivered in an envelope. Value is for pane without envelope. Panes with envelopes sell for somewhat more.

CHRISTMAS

Madonna and Child, by Elisabetta Sirani — A2200

Stocking — A2201

Santa Claus — A2202

Cardinal in Snow — A2203

Designed by Bradbury Thompson (#2871), Lou Nolan (#2872), Harry Zelenko (#2873), Peter Good (#2874).

Printed by Bureau of Engraving and Printing (#2871), Ashton-Potter USA, Ltd. (#2872), Avery Dennison (#2873-2874).

LITHOGRAPHED & ENGRAVED
Sheets of 300 in six panes of 50

1994, Oct. 20	**Tagged**	***Perf. 11¼***	
2871 A2200 29c **multicolored,** shiny gum		.60	.25
P# block of 4, 5#		2.75	—
Pane of 50		30.00	
Low gloss gum		.60	
P# block of 4, 5#		2.75	
Pane of 50		30.00	

BOOKLET STAMP
Perf. 9¾x11

2871A A2200 29c **multicolored**		.60	.25
b. Booklet pane of 10		6.25	3.50
c. Imperf, pair		*350.00*	

LITHOGRAPHED

Sheets of 400 in eight panes of 50

Perf. 11¼

2872	A2201 29c **multicolored**	.60	.25
	P# block of 4, 5#+P	2.50	—
	Pane of 50	30.00	
a.	Booklet pane of 20	12.50	6.00
b.	Imperf., pair	—	
c.	Vert. pair, imperf. horiz.	—	
d.	Quadruple impression of black, triple impression of blue, double impressions of red and yellow, green normal	*900.00*	
e.	Vert. pair, imperf. between	*125.00*	
f.	As "a," imperf.	—	

Panes of Nos. 2871-2872 contain four plate blocks, one containing pane position diagram.

PHOTOGRAVURE

BOOKLET STAMPS

Self-Adhesive

Die Cut

2873	A2202 29c **multicolored**	.70	.25
a.	Booklet pane of 12	8.50	
b.	Coil with plate #V1111	—	5.75
	P# strip of 5, #V1111	7.25	

Except for No. 2873b with plate number, coil stamps are indistinguishable from booklet stamps once they are removed from the backing paper.

2874	A2203 29c **multicolored** ⓢ	.60	.25
a.	Booklet pane of 18	11.00	

ⓢ: Adhesive residue may adhere to the back of some examples of No. 2874 after soaking. See note after No. 1549.

BUREAU OF ENGRAVING & PRINTING

Souvenir Sheet

A2204

Double Impression of Brown Lettering Panel

Major Double Transfer

Minor Double Transfer

Illustration A2204 reduced.

Designed by Peter Cocci, using original die for Type A98.

LITHOGRAPHED & ENGRAVED

1994, Nov. 3 **Tagged** ***Perf. 11***

2875	A2204 $2 Pane of 4	16.00	13.50
a.	Single stamp	4.00	2.00
	Pane of 4 with major double transfer on right stamp	*65.00*	—
	Major double transfer, single stamp	—	—
	Pane of 4 with minor double transfer on right stamp	*22.50*	—
	Minor double transfer, single stamp	—	—
b.	Pane of 4 with double impression of the brown lettering panel	*1,000.*	—
c.	As "b," tagging omitted	*1,100.*	

The double impression is clear, but may be seen best in the scrolls at lower right. The major double transfer is most evident in the extra line at the bottom of the design. The minor double transfer is in the same area, but it is much less distinct.

CHINESE NEW YEAR

Year of the Boar — A2205

Designed by Clarence Lee. Printed by Stamp Venturers.

PHOTOGRAVURE

Panes of 20

1994, Dec. 30 **Tagged** ***Perf. 11.2x11.1***

2876	A2205 29c **multicolored**	.70	.25
	P# block of 4, 5#+S	3.00	—
	Pane of 20	15.00	—

See Nos. 3895l, 3997l.

A2206

A2206a

Type I

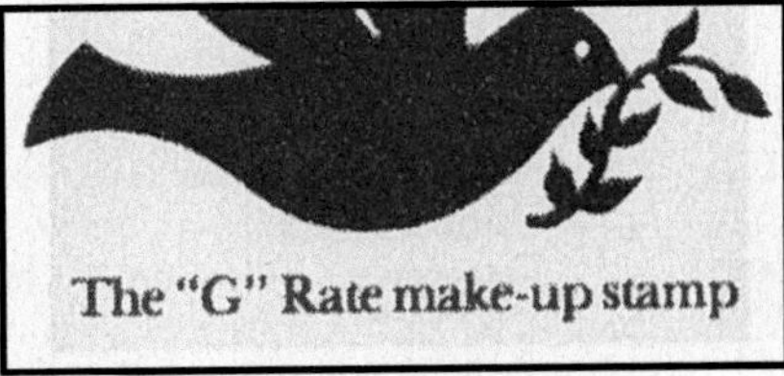

Type II

Inscriptions on No. 2877 are in a thin typeface. Those on No. 2878 are in heavy, bold type.

Designed by Richard D. Sheaff. Printed by American Bank Note Co. (#2877), Stamp Venturers (#2878).

LITHOGRAPHED

Sheets of 100

1994, Dec. 13 **Untagged** ***Perf. 11x10.8***

2877	A2206 (3c) **tan, bright blue & red,** type I	.30	.25
	P# block of 4, 3#+A	.50	—
	Zip block of 4	.30	—
	Pane of 100	8.00	
a.	Imperf., pair	*115.00*	
b.	Double impression of red	*175.00*	

No. 2877 imperf and with blue omitted is known from printer's waste.

Perf. 10.8x10.9

Untagged

2878	A2206a (3c) **tan, dark blue & red,** type II	.30	.25
	P# block of 4, 3#+S	.50	—
	Zip block of 4	.50	—
	Pane of 100	8.00	

A2207

A2207a

Designed by Lou Nolan (#2879-2892). Printed by Bureau of Engraving and Printing (#2879), Stamp Venturers (#2880).

PHOTOGRAVURE

Tagged

Perf. 11.2x11.1

2879	A2207 (20c) **black "G," yellow & multi**	.40	.25
	P# block of 4, 5#	7.50	—
	Zip block of 4	1.75	—
	Pane of 100	40.00	
a.	Imperf., pair	—	

Perf. 11x10.9

2880	A2207a (20c) **red "G," yellow & multi**	.75	.25
	P# block of 4, 5#+S	15.00	—
	Zip block of 4	3.25	—
	Pane of 100	75.00	

A2208

A2208a

Printed by Bureau of Engraving and Printing (#2881), Stamp Venturers (#2882).

Perf. 11.2x11.1

2881	A2208 (32c) **black "G" & multi**	1.25	.25
	P# block of 4, 4#	60.00	—
	Zip block of 4	5.50	—
	Pane of 100	125.00	
a.	Booklet pane of 10	12.50	5.00

Perf. 11x10.9

2882	A2208a (32c) **red "G" & multi**	.60	.25
	P# block of 4, 4#+S	4.00	—
	Zip block of 4	2.75	—
	Pane of 100	60.00	

Distance on #2882 from bottom of red G to top of flag immediately above is 13¾mm.

A2208b

A2208c

A2208d

No. 2885 Superimposed Over No. 2882

Printed by American Bank Note Co. (#2884), Bureau of Engraving and Printing (#2883), KCS Industries (#2885).

BOOKLET STAMPS

Perf. 10x9.9 on 2 or 3 Sides

2883 A2208b (32c) **black "G" & multi** .65 .25
a. Booklet pane of 10 6.50 3.75

Perf. 10.9 on 2 or 3 Sides

2884 A2208c (32c) **blue "G" & multi** .65 .25
a. Booklet pane of 10 6.50 3.75
b. As "a," imperf *4,500.*
c. Horiz. pair, imperf. btwn. due to miscut —
d. Horiz. pair, imperf. vert. —

Perf. 11x10.9 on 2 or 3 Sides

2885 A2208d (32c) **red "G" & multi** .90 .25
a. Booklet pane of 10 9.00 4.50
b. Horiz. pair, imperf vert. *750.00*
c. Horiz. pair, imperf. btwn., in #2885a with foldover —

Distance on #2885 from bottom of red G to top of flag immediately above is 13½mm. See note below #2882.

No. 2885c resulted from a paper foldover after perforating and before cutting into panes.

A2208e

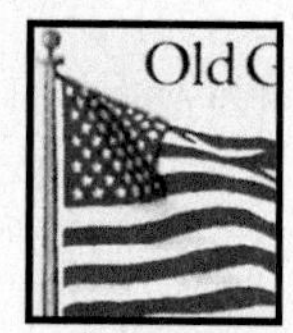

No. 2886

A2208f

No. 2887

Printed by Avery-Dennison.

Self-Adhesive ***Die Cut***

2886 A2208e (32c) **gray, blue, light blue, red & black** .70 .25
a. Booklet pane of 18 12.50
b. Coil with plate # V11111 — 9.50
P# strip of 5, same # 10.00

No. 2886 is printed on surface-tagged paper which is opaque, thicker and brighter than that of No. 2887 and has only a small number of blue shading dots in the white stripes immediately below the flag's blue field.

Except for No. 2886b with plate number, coil stamps are indistinguishable from booklet stamps once they are removed from the backing paper.

2887 A2208f (32c) **black, blue & red** ⓢ .70 .25
a. Booklet pane of 18 12.50

No. 2887 has noticeable blue shading in the white stripes immediately below the blue field and has overall tagging. The paper is translucent, thinner and duller than No. 2886.

ⓢ: Adhesive residue may remain on some examples of No. 2887 after soaking. See note after No. 1549.

A2209

A2209a

A2209b

A2209c

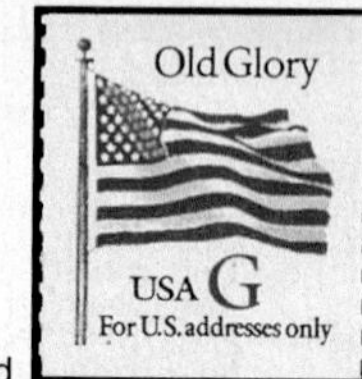

A2209d

Printed by American Bank Note Co. (#2890), Bureau of Engraving and Printing (#2889), Stamp Venturers (#2888, 2891-2892).

COIL STAMPS

Perf. 9.8 Vert.

2888 A2209 (25c) **black "G," blue & multi** .90 .50
Pair 1.80 1.00
P# strip of 5, #S11111 4.00
P# single, #S11111 2.50

2889 A2209a (32c) **black "G" & multi** 1.50 .25
Pair 3.00 .30
P# strip of 5, #1111, 2222 8.00
P# single, #1111, 2222 — 4.00
a. Imperf., pair *250.00*

2890 A2209b (32c) **blue "G" & multi** .65 .25
Pair 1.25 .50
P# strip of 5, #A1111, A1112, A1113, A1211, A1212, A1311, A1313, A1324, A2211, A2212, A2213, A2214, A3113, A3314, A3323, A3324, A3433, A3435, A3436, A4427, A5327, A5417, A5427 4.00
P# strip of 5, #A1222, A1314, A4426, A5437 4.25
P# strip of 5, #A1417, A2223 6.50
P# strip of 5, #A1433 6.00
P# strip of 5, #A2313 6.50
P# strip of 5, #A3114, A3315, A3423 6.50
P# strip of 5, #A3426 5.25
P# strip of 5, #A4435 *175.00*
P# single, #A1111, A1313, A2214, A3113, A3314, A3324, A4427, A5427 — 1.00
P# single, #A1212, A3323 — 3.00
P# single, #A2212, A3435 — 3.50
P# single, #A1112, A1311, A1324, A2213, A5327 — 2.50
P# single, #A1113, A5437 — 3.75
P# single, #A3315, A3423, A3426 4.75
P# single, #A1222, A2211, A3114 — 4.25
P# single, #A1211, A1314, A4426 4.00
P# single, #A1417, A1433 — 6.75
P# single, #A2223, A2313 — 6.00
P# single, #A3433, A3436 — 2.00
P# single, #A4435 — *190.00*
P# single, #A5417 3.00

2891 A2209c (32c) **red "G" & multi** .85 .25
Pair 1.70 .30
P# strip of 5, #S1111 4.25
P# single, #S1111 — 1.00

Rouletted 9.8 Vert.

2892 A2209d (32c) **red "G" & multi** .75 .25
Pair 1.50 .50
P# strip of 5, #S1111, S2222 4.75
P# single, #S1111, S2222 — 1.00

A2210

Designed by Lou Nolan. Printed by American Bank Note Co.

PHOTOGRAVURE

1995 **Untagged** ***Perf. 9.8 Vert.***

2893 A2210 (5c) **green & multi** .50 .25
Pair 1.00 .50
P# strip of 5, #A11111 3.00
P# strip of 5, #A21111 2.50
P# single, #A11111 3.00
P# single, #A21111 2.00

No. 2893 was only available through the Philatelic Fullfillment Center (and, for a short time, at the L'Enfant Plaza Philatelic Center in Washington, DC) after its announcement 1/12/95. Covers submitted for first day cancels received a 12/13/94 cancel, even though the stamps were not available on that date.

Flag Over Porch — A2212

Designed by Dave LaFleur. Printed by Stamp Venturers.

Sheets of 400 in four panes of 100

1995, May 19 **Tagged** ***Perf. 10.4***

2897 A2212 32c **multicolored,** .75 .25
P# block of 4, 5#+S 4.25 —
Pane of 100 75.00
a. Imperf., vert. pair 55.00

See Nos. 2913-2916, 2920-2921, 3133. For booklet see No. BK243.

Butte — A2217

A2217a

Designed by Tom Engeman (#2902-2904B).

Printed by J.W. Fergusson & Sons for Stamp Venturers (#2902), Stamp Venturers (#2902B).

COIL STAMPS

PHOTOGRAVURE

1995-97 ***Perf. 9.8 Vert.***

Untagged (Nos. 2902-2912B)

Self-Adhesive (#2902B)

2902 A2217 (5c) **yellow, red & blue,** *Mar. 10* .30 .25
Pair .50 .50
P# strip of 5, #S111, S222, S333 1.10
P# single, #S111, S222, S333 — .90
a. Imperf., pair 350.00

Serpentine Die Cut 11.5 Vert.

2902B A2217a (5c) **yellow, red & blue,** *June 15, 1996* .35 .25
Pair .70
P# strip of 5, #S111 1.75
P# single, #S111 — .80

Perf. 9.8 Vert.

Mountain — A2218

A2218a

A2218b

A2218c

Printed by Bureau of Engraving and Printing (#2903, 2904B), Stamp Venturers (#2904), Avery Dennison (#2904A).

Self-Adhesive (#2904A-2904B)

2903 A2218 (5c) **purple & multi,** *Mar. 16, 1996* .30 .25
Pair .50 .50
P# strip of 5, #11111 1.10
P# single, #11111 — .90
a. Tagged (error) 4.00 3.50
P# strip of 5, #11111 40.00
P# single, #11111 — 40.00

Letters of inscription "USA NONPROFIT ORG." outlined in purple on No. 2903. No. 2903 has purple "1996" at left bottom.

2904 A2218a (5c) **blue & multi,** *Mar. 16, 1996* .30 .25
Pair .50 .50
P# strip of 5, #S111 1.10
P# single, #S111 — 1.00
c. Imperf., pair 250.00

Letters of inscription have no outline on No. 2904. No. 2904 has blue "1996" at bottom left.

Serpentine Die Cut 11.2 Vert.

2904A A2218b (5c) **purple & multi,** *June 15, 1996* .40 .25
Pair .80
P# strip of 5, #V222222, V333323, V333342 4.00
P# strip of 5, #V333333 2.50
P# strip of 5, #V333343 3.00
P# single, #V222222, V333323, V333333, V333342 — 2.50

P# single, #V333343 4.50

Serpentine Die Cut 9.8 Vert.

2904B A2218c (5c) **purple & multi,** *Jan. 24, 1997* .25 .25
Pair .50
P# strip of 5, #1111 1.40
P# single, #1111 — 1.00

Letters of inscription outlined in purple on No. 2904B, not outlined on No. 2904A. No. 2904A has large purple "1996" at bottom left. No. 2904B has small purple "1997" at bottom left.

No. 2904B shows 10 "peaks" at left and 10 at right, or 9 "peaks" at left and 10 at right. The 9 "peaks" variety is extremely scarce. Values: mint $30, used $15; P# strip of 5, $2,500, used P# single $400.

Auto — A2220

A2220a

A2220b

Designed by Robert Brangwynne, Chris Calle (#2907). Printed by J.W. Fergusson & Sons for Stamp Venturers (#2905), Stamp Venturers (#2906-2907).

Self-Adhesive (#2906-2907)

Perf. 9.8 Vert.

2905 A2220 (10c) **black, red brown & brown,** small "1995" date, *Mar. 10* .30 .25
Pair .50 .50
P# strip of 5, #S111 2.00
P# single, #S111 — 1.25
a. Medium "1995" date .35 .25
Pair .70 .50
P# strip of 5, #S222 2.00
P# single, #S222 1.40
b. Large "1995" date, *1996* .60 .25
Pair 1.20 .50
P# strip of 5, #S333 3.00
P# single, #S333 — 1.50
c. As "b," brown omitted, P#S33 single *400.00*

Date on 2905 is approximately 1.9mm long, on No. 2905a 2mm long, and on No. 2905b 2.1mm long.

Serpentine Die Cut 11.5 Vert.

2906 A2220a (10c) **black, brown & red brown,** *June 15, 1996* .50 .25
Pair 1.00
P# strip of 5, #S111 2.40
P# single, #S111 — 2.00

2907 A2220b (10c) **gold & multi,** *May 21, 1996* .75 .25
Pair 1.50
P# strip of 5, #S11111 3.75
P# single, #S11111 — 2.50

Auto Tail Fin — A2223

A2223a

A2223b

Designed by Bill Nelson (#2908-2912B). Printed by J.W. Fergusson & Sons for Stamp Venturers (#2909), Bureau of Engraving and Printing (#2908), Stamp Venturers (#2910).

Self-Adhesive (#2910)

Perf. 9.8 Vert.

2908 A2223 (15c) **dark orange yellow & multi,** *Mar. 17* .30 .30
Pair .60 .60
P# strip of 5, #11111 2.00
P# single, #11111 — 1.60

No. 2908 has "1995" in blue and has dark, bold colors, heavy shading lines and heavily shaded chrome.

2909 A2223a (15c) **buff & multi,** *Mar. 17* .30 .30
Pair .60 .60
P# strip of 5, #S11111 2.00
P# single, #S11111 — 1.50

No. 2909 has "1995" in black and has shinier chrome, more subdued colors and finer details than No. 2908.

Serpentine Die Cut 11.5 Vert.

2910 A2223b (15c) **buff & multi,** *June 15, 1996* .30 .30
Pair .60
P# strip of 5, #S11111 2.00
P# single, #S11111 — 1.50

Juke Box — A2225

A2225a

A2225b

A2225c

Printed by J.W. Fergusson & Sons for Stamp Venturers (#2912), Bureau of Engraving and Printing (#2911, 2912B), Stamp Venturers (#2912A).

Perf. 9.8 Vert.

2911 A2225 (25c) **dark red, dark yellow green & multi,** *Mar. 17* .50 .50
Pair 1.00 1.00
P# strip of 5, #111111, 212222, 222222, 332222 3.50
P# single, #111111, 212222, 222222 — 2.25
P# single, #332222 — 2.75
a. Imperf, pair *400.00*

No. 2911 has dark, saturated colors and dark blue lines in the music selection board.
See No. 3132.

2912 A2225a (25c) **bright orange red, bright yellow green & multi,** *Mar. 17* .75 .50
Pair 1.50 1.00
P# strip of 5, #S11111, S22222 3.75
P# single, same # — 2.00

No. 2912 has bright colors, less shading and light blue lines in the music selection board.

Serpentine Die Cut 11.5 Vert.

2912A A2225b (25c) **bright orange red, bright yellow green & multi,** *June 15, 1996* .50 .50
Pair 1.00
P# strip of 5, #S11111, S22222 3.75
P# single, same # — 1.75

Serpentine Die Cut 9.8 Vert.

2912B A2225c (25c) **dark red, dark yellow green & multi,** *Jan. 24, 1997* .75 .50
Pair 1.50
P# strip of 5, #111111 4.00
P# strip of 5, #222222 4.25
P# single, #111111 — 1.50
P# single, #222222 — 3.50
c. Tagged (prephosphored coated paper, solid appearance) —
P# single, #222222 —

A2225d

A2225e

Designed by Dave LaFleur (#2913-2916).
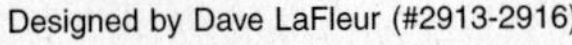

Printed by J.W. Fergusson & Sons for Stamp Venturers (#2914), Bureau of Engraving and Printing (#2913).

Tagged (Nos. 2913-2921)

Perf. 9.8 Vert.

2913 A2225d 32c **blue, tan, brown, red & light blue,** shiny gum, *May 19* .65 .25
Pair 1.30 .30
P# strip of 5, #11111, 22221 5.00
P# strip of 5, #22222 5.25
P# single, #11111, 22222 — 1.50
P# single, #22221 — 1.75
Low gloss gum .65
Pair 1.30
P# strip of 5, #11111 4.75
P# strip of 5, #22222 6.00
P# strip of 5, #33333, 34333, 44444, 45444, 66646, 77767, 78767, 91161, 99969 4.50
P# strip of 5, #22322 6.75
P# strip of 5, #66666 9.00
P# single, #22322 — 5.75
P# single, #33333, 44444, 45444, 66646, 77767 — 1.50
P# single, #34333 — 5.00
P# single, #66666 — 5.00
P# single, #78767, 91161, 99969 — 2.25
a. Imperf., pair 30.00

No. 2913 has pronounced light blue shading in the flag and red "1995" at left bottom. See No. 3133.

2914 A2225e 32c **blue, yellow brown, red & gray,** *May 19* .80 .25
Pair 1.60 .30
P# strip of 5, #S11111 4.50
P# single, #S11111 — 2.25

No. 2914 has pale gray shading in the flag and blue "1995" at left bottom.

A2225f

A2225g

Printed by Bureau of Engraving and Printing (#2915A), Avery Dennison (#2915).

Serpentine Die Cut 8.7 Vert.

Self-Adhesive (#2915-2915D)

2915 A2225f 32c **multicolored,** *Apr. 18* 1.25 .30
Pair 2.50
P# strip of 5, #V11111 9.00
P# single, #V11111 — 7.50

No. 2915 has blue "1995" at bottom left.

Serpentine Die Cut 9.8 Vert.

2915A A2225g 32c **dk blue, tan, brown, red & light blue,** *May 21, 1996* .65 .25
Pair 1.30
P# strip of 5, #11111, 22222, 23222, 33333, 44444, 45444, 55555, 66666, 88888, 99999, 11111A, 13231A, 13311A, 22222A, 33333A, 44444A, 55555A, 66666A, 77777A, 88888A 4.25
P# strip of 5, #78777 4.50
P# strip of 5, #78777A 30.00
P# strip of 5, #87888 20.00
P# strip of 5, #87898 8.00
P# strip of 5, #88898 *50.00*
P# strip of 5, #89878 *7.50*
P# strip of 5, #89888 14.00
P# strip of 5, #89898 8.00
P# strip of 5, #97898 9.00
P# strip of 5, #89899 *350.00*
P# strip of 5, #99899 10.00
P# strip of 5, #13211A 60.00
P# single, #11111, 22222, 23222, 33333, 44444, 45444, 55555, 66666, 88888, 99999, 11111A, 13231A, 13311A, 22222A, 33333A, 44444A, 55555A, 66666A, 77777A, 88888A — 1.00
P# single, #78777 — 1.00
P# single, #78777A 16.00
P# single, #87888 — *12.00*
P# single, #87898, 97898 — 4.00
P# single, #89878 2.00
P# single, #88898 — *75.00*
P# single, #89888 — 9.00
P# single, #89898 — 2.75
P# single, #89899 — 175.00
P# single, #99899 — 10.00
P# single, #13211A — *60.00*
h. Die cutting omitted, pair 32.50
i. Tan omitted —
j. Double die cutting 30.00

No. 2915A has red "1996" at left bottom.

Die cutting on No. 2915A shows either 10 serpentine "peaks" on each side, 11 "peaks" on the left side and 10 "peaks" on the right side, or 10 "peaks" on the left side and 11 "peaks" on the right side. The last configuration is considered by specialists to be an error, and it is rare. Value: $25 unused, $10 used.

Sky on No. 3133 shows color gradation at LR not on No. 2915A.

On No. 2915Ai all other colors except brown are severely shifted.

On No. 2915Aj, the second die cutting is a different gauge than the normal 9.8.

Plate number 99999 strips of No. 2915A are known with the brown plate number shifted one stamp to the right of the stamp with the other plate numbers. Such strips are scarce. Value of mint never hinged P# strip of 5 or 6, $1,500. Used examples are rare.

Examples of a self-adhesive Flag Over Porch coil stamp resembling Scott 2915C with a "1995" year date are test stamps and listed in that section of this catalog.

A2225h

A2225i

A2225j

Printed by Bureau of Engraving and Printing (#2915C-2915D), Stamp Venturers (#2915B).

Serpentine Die Cut 11.5 Vert.

2915B	A2225h 32c **dk blue, tan, brown, red & light blue,** *June 15, 1996*	1.00	*.90*
	Pair	2.00	
	P# strip of 5, #S11111	5.00	
	P# single, #S11111	—	2.75

Serpentine Die Cut 10.9 Vert.

2915C	A2225i 32c **dk blue, tan, brown, red & light blue,** *May 21, 1996*	3.50	.40
	Pair	7.00	
	P# strip of 5, #55555	25.00	
	P# strip of 5, #66666	20.00	
	P# single, #55555, 66666	—	3.50
	P# single, #88888		*3,000.*

Plate number 55555 strips of No. 2915C are known with the tan plate number shifted one stamp to the left of the stamp with the other plate numbers. Extremely scarce. Value of P# strip approximately $5,000.

Serpentine Die Cut 9.8 Vert.

2915D	A2225j 32c **dark blue, tan, brown, red & light blue,** *Jan. 24, 1997*	2.00	.90
	Pair	4.00	
	P# strip of 5, #11111	7.00	
	P# single, #11111	—	4.00

No. 2915D shows 9 "peaks" at left and 10 at right or 10 "peaks" at left and 10 at right.

Stamps on multiples of No. 2915A touch, and are on a peelable backing the same size as the stamps, while those of No. 2915D are separated on the peelable backing, which is larger than the stamps.

No. 2915D has red "1997" at left bottom; No. 2915A has red "1996" at left bottom.

Sky on No. 3133 shows color gradation at LR not on No. 2915D, and it has blue "1996" at left bottom.

A2225k

Printed by Bureau of Engraving and Printing (#2916).

BOOKLET STAMPS

Perf. 10.8x9.8 on 2 or 3 Adjacent Sides

2916	A2225k 32c **blue, tan, brown, red & light blue,** *May 19*	.65	.25
a.	Booklet pane of 10	6.50	3.25
b.	As "a," imperf.	*1,100.*	

Flag Over Field — A2230

Designed by Sabra Field. Printed by Avery Dennison.

Self-Adhesive (#2919-2921)

Die Cut

2919	A2230 32c **multicolored,** *Mar. 17* ⑤	.65	.25
a.	Booklet pane of 18	12.00	
b.	Vert. pair, die cutting omitted btwn.	—	

⑤: Adhesive may adhere to some examples of No. 2919 after soaking. See note after No. 1549.

A2230a

Large Date

Small Date

Printed by Avery Dennison.

Serpentine Die Cut 8.7 on 2, 3 or 4 Adjacent Sides

2920	A2230a 32c **multicolored,** dated blue "1995," *Apr. 18*	.65	.25
a.	Booklet pane of 20+label	13.00	
b.	Small date	6.00	.35
c.	As "b," booklet pane of 20+label	110.00	
f.	As No. 2920, pane of 15+label	9.75	
g.	As "a," partial pane of 10, 3 stamps and parts of 7 stamps printed on backing liner	—	
h.	As No. 2920, booklet pane of 15	*47.50*	
i.	As No. 2920, die cutting omitted, pair	—	
j.	Dark blue omitted (from No. 2920a)	*2,100.*	
k.	Vert. pair, die cutting missing btwn., three examples in No. 2920a with shift in die cutting (PS)	—	

Date on No. 2920 is nearly twice as large as date on No. 2920b. No. 2920f comes in various configurations.

No. 2920h is a pane of 16 with one stamp removed. The missing stamp is the lower right stamp in the pane or (more rarely) the upper left stamp. No. 2920h cannot be made from No. 2920f, a pane of 15 + label. The label is located in the sixth or seventh row of the pane and is die cut. If the label is removed, an impression of the die cutting appears on the backing paper.

A2230b

A2230c

Designed by Dave LaFleur (#2921). Printed by Bureau of Engraving and Printing (#2921).

Serpentine Die Cut 11.3 on 3 sides

2920D	A2230b 32c **multicolored,** dated blue "1996," *Jan. 20, 1996*	.80	.25
e.	Booklet pane of 10	8.00	
i.	As "e," die cutting omitted	—	

Serpentine Die Cut 9.8 on 2 or 3 Adjacent Sides

2921	A2230c 32c **dk bl, tan, brn, red & lt bl,** dated red 1996, *May 21, 1996*	.90	.25
a.	Booklet pane of 10, dated red "1996"	9.00	
b.	As No. 2921, dated red "1997," *Jan. 24, 1997*	1.20	.25
c.	As "a," dated red "1997"	12.00	
d.	Booklet pane of 5 + label, dated red "1997," *Jan. 24, 1997*	8.00	
e.	As "a," die cutting omitted	*200.00*	

Scott values for used self-adhesive stamps are for examples either on piece or off piece.

GREAT AMERICANS ISSUE

Milton S. Hershey — A2248

Cal Farley — A2249

Henry R. Luce — A2250

Lila and DeWitt Wallace — A2251

Ruth Benedict — A2253

Alice Hamilton, MD — A2255

Justin S. Morrill
A2256

Mary Breckinridge
A2257

Alice Paul — A2258

Designed by Dennis Lyall (#2933-2934), Richard Sheaff (#2935), Howard Paine (#2936, 2941-2942), Roy Andersen (#2938), Chris Calle (#2940, 2943).

Printed by Banknote Corporation of America (#2933-2935, 2940-2943), Ashton-Potter (USA) Ltd. (#2936), Bureau of Engraving & Printing (#2938).

ENGRAVED

Sheets of 400 in four panes of 100

Sheets of 160 in eight panes of 20 (#2935)

Sheets of 120 in six panes of 20 (#2936, 2941-2942)

1995-99 **Tagged**

Self-Adhesive (#2941-2942)

Perf. 11.2, Serpentine Die Cut 11.7x11.5 (#2941-2942)

2933 A2248 32c **brown,** prephosphored coated paper with surface tagging showing a solid appearance, *Sept. 13, 1995* .75 .25
On cover 4.00
P# block of 4, 1#+B 3.50 —
Pane of 100 75.00

2934 A2249 32c **green,** prephosphored coated paper with surface tagging showing a solid appearance, *Apr. 26, 1996* .75 .25
On cover 4.00
P# block of 4, 1#+B 3.50 —
Pane of 100 75.00

No. 2934 exists on two types of surface-tagged paper that exhibit either a solid or grainy solid appearance.

2935 A2250 32c **lake,** prephosphored coated paper with surface tagging showing a grainy solid appearance, *Apr. 3, 1998* .65 .35
On cover 4.00
P# block of 4, 1#+B 3.00 —
Pane of 20 14.75

2936 A2251 32c **gray blue,** prephosphored coated paper with surface tagging showing a solid appearance, *July 16, 1998* .65 .35
On cover 4.00
P# block of 4, 1#+P 3.00 —
Pane of 20 14.75 —
a. 32c **light blue** 2.00 .50
P# block of 4, 1#+P 9.00 —
Pane of 20 40.00 —

2938 A2253 46c **carmine,** prephosphored uncoated paper with embedded tagging showing a mottled appearance, *Oct. 20, 1995* .90 .30
On cover 5.00
P# block of 4, 1# 4.50 —
Pane of 100 90.00

Counterfeits exist of No. 2938. See the Postal Counterfeits section of this catalog.

2940 A2255 55c **green,** prephosphored coated paper with surface tagging showing a grainy solid appearance, *July 11, 1995* 1.15 .25
On cover 4.00
Certificate of mailing 30.00
Double-weight first-class letter 8.00
P# block of 4, 1#+B 6.00 —
Pane of 100 115.00
a. Imperf, pair —

2941 A2256 55c **black,** prephosphored coated paper with surface tagging showing a solid appearance, *July 17, 1999* 1.10 .25
On cover 4.00
P# block of 4, 1#+B 4.40
Pane of 20 22.00

2942 A2257 77c **blue,** prephosphored coated paper with surface tagging showing a solid appearance, *Nov. 9, 1998* 1.50 .40
On cover 4.00
Certificate of mailing 30.00
3-oz. first-class letter 8.00
P# block of 4, 1#+B 6.00
Pane of 20 30.00

2943 A2258 78c **bright violet,** prephosphored coated paper with surface tagging showing a solid appearance, *Aug. 18, 1995* 1.60 .25
On cover 4.00
P# block of 4, 1#+B 7.50 —
Pane of 100 160.00
a. 78c **dull violet,** prephosphored coated paper with surface tagging showing a grainy solid appearance 1.60 .25
P# block of 4, 1#+B 7.50 —
Pane of 100 160.00
b. 78c **pale violet,** prephosphored coated paper with surface tagging showing a grainy solid appearance 3.00 .30
P# block of 4, 1#+B 16.00 —
Pane of 100 300.00
Nos. 2933-2943 (9) 9.05 2.65

The pale violet ink on No. 2943b luminesces bright pink under long-wave ultraviolet light.

LOVE

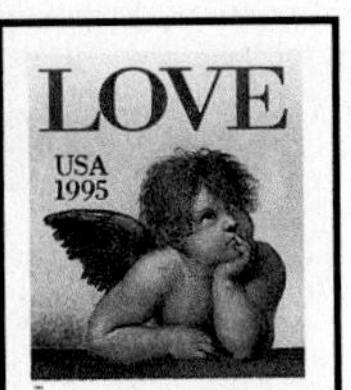

Cherub from Sistine Madonna, by Raphael
A2263 A2264

Designed by Terry McCaffrey.

Printed by the Bureau of Engraving and Printing (#2948) and Banknote Corp. of America (#2949).

LITHOGRAPHED & ENGRAVED

Sheets of 300 in six panes of 50

1995, Feb. 1 **Tagged** ***Perf. 11.2***

2948 A2263 (32c) **multicolored** .65 .25
P# block of 4, 5# 3.00 —
Pane of 50 33.00

Self-Adhesive

Die Cut

2949 A2264 (32c) **multicolored** .65 .25
a. Booklet pane of 20 + label 13.00
b. Red (engr.) omitted *100.00*
c. As "a," red (engr.) omitted *2,000.*
d. Red (engr.) missing (CM) —

No. 2949d must be collected se-tenant with a normal stamp. The error comes from the top row of three stamps of the booklet pane of 20 plus label.

See Nos. 2957-2960, 3030.

FLORIDA STATEHOOD

Florida Statehood, 150th Anniv.
A2265

Designed by Laura Smith.

Printed by Ashton-Potter (USA) Ltd.

LITHOGRAPHED

Sheets of 160 in eight panes of 20

1995, Mar. 3 **Tagged** ***Perf. 11.1***

2950 A2265 32c **multicolored** .65 .25
P# block of 4, 5#+P 3.00 —
Pane of 20 15.00 —

Imperf. examples of No. 2950 are believed to be printer's waste.

EARTH DAY

Earth Clean-Up
A2266

Solar Energy
A2267

Tree Planting
A2268

Beach Clean-Up
A2269

Designed by Christy Millard (#2951), Jennifer Michalove (#2952), Brian Hailes (#2953) and Melody Kiper (#2954).

Printed by Ashton-Potter (USA) Ltd.

LITHOGRAPHED

Sheets of 96 in six panes of 16

1995, Apr. 20 **Tagged** ***Perf. 11.1x11***

2951 A2266 32c **multicolored** .65 .25
2952 A2267 32c **multicolored** .65 .25
2953 A2268 32c **multicolored** .65 .25
2954 A2269 32c **multicolored** .65 .25
a. Block of 4, #2951-2954 2.60 1.75
P# block of 4, 5#+P 2.60 —
Horiz. P# block of 8, 2 sets of 5#+P, + top or bottom label 5.25 —
Pane of 16 10.50 —

RICHARD M. NIXON

37th President (1913-94)

A2270

Designed by Daniel Schwartz.

Printed by Barton Press and Bank Note Corp. of America.

LITHOGRAPHED & ENGRAVED

Sheets of 200 in four panes of 50

1995, Apr. 26 **Tagged** ***Perf. 11.2***

2955 A2270 32c **multicolored** .65 .25
P# block of 4, 5#+B 3.00 —
Pane of 50 33.00
a. Red (engr.) missing (CM) *800.00*

No. 2955 is known with red (engr. "Richard Nixon") inverted, and with red engr. omitted but only half the Nixon portrait present, both from printer's waste. No. 2955a shows a complete Nixon portrait.

BLACK HERITAGE SERIES

Bessie Coleman (d. 1926), Aviator

A2271

Designed by Chris Calle.

ENGRAVED

Sheets of 200 in four panes of 50

1995, Apr. 27 **Tagged** ***Perf. 11.2***

2956 A2271 32c **red & black**	.85	.25
P# block of 4, 1#	3.75	—
Pane of 50	42.00	

LOVE

A2272

A2273

Cherubs from Sistine Madonna, by Raphael — A2274

LOVE USA 32

A2272a

Designed by Terry McCaffrey.

Printed by Bureau of Engraving and Printing (#2957-2959), Bank Note Corp. of America (#2960).

LITHOGRAPHED & ENGRAVED

Sheets of 300 in six panes of 50

1995, May 12 **Tagged** ***Perf. 11.2***

2957 A2272 32c **multicolored**	.65	.25
P# block of 4, 5#	3.00	—
Copyright block of 6	4.25	—
Pane of 50	33.00	

Compare with No. 3030. For booklet see No. BK244.

2958 A2273 55c **multicolored**	1.10	.25
P# block of 4, 5#	5.50	—
Pane of 50	55.00	

BOOKLET STAMPS

Perf. 9.8x10.8

2959 A2272a 32c **multicolored**	.65	.25
a. Booklet pane of 10	6.50	3.25
b. Imperf, pair	*100.00*	
c. As "a," imperf.	*500.00*	

Self-Adhesive

Die Cut

2960 A2274 55c **multicolored**	1.10	.25
a. Booklet pane of 20 + label	22.50	

RECREATIONAL SPORTS

Volleyball A2275

Softball A2276

Bowling A2277

Tennis A2278

Golf — A2279

Designed by Don Weller.

Printed by Bank Note Corp. of America.

LITHOGRAPHED

Sheets of 120 in six panes of 20

1995, May 20 **Tagged** ***Perf. 11.2***

2961 A2275 32c **multicolored**	.65	.25
2962 A2276 32c **multicolored**	.65	.25
2963 A2277 32c **multicolored**	.65	.25
2964 A2278 32c **multicolored**	.65	.25
2965 A2279 32c **multicolored**	.65	.25
a. Vert. strip of 5, #2961-2965	3.25	2.00
P# block of 10, 2 sets of 4#+B	6.50	—
P# block of 8, 2 sets of 4#+B	5.50	—
Pane of 20	13.00	—
b. As "a," imperf	*1,750.*	
c. As "a," yellow omitted	*1,200.*	
d. As "a," yellow, blue & magenta omitted	*1,600.*	

PRISONERS OF WAR & MISSING IN ACTION

A2280

Designed by Carl Herrman.

Printed by Ashton-Potter (USA) Ltd.

LITHOGRAPHED

Sheets of 160 in eight panes of 20

1995, May 29 **Tagged** ***Perf. 11.2***

2966 A2280 32c **multicolored**	.65	.25
P# block of 4, 5#+P	2.50	—
Pane of 20	12.50	—

The five plate numbers do not include a sixth plate number for the plate that applied a transparent laquer "color."

LEGENDS OF HOLLYWOOD

Marilyn Monroe (1926-62) — A2281

Designed by Michael Deas.

Printed by Stamp Venturers.

PHOTOGRAVURE

Sheets of 120 in six panes of 20

1995, June 1 **Tagged** ***Perf. 11.1***

2967 A2281 32c **multicolored**	.80	.25
P# block of 4, 6#+S	5.00	—
Pane of 20	24.00	
a. Imperf., pair	*225.00*	
Pane of 20, imperf.	*3,250.*	

Perforations in corner of each stamp are star-shaped.

Uncut press sheets of No. 2967 were made available for sale. Values: cross-gutter block of 8, $55; pairs with gutters between, $5 each. See note after No. 2868.

TEXAS STATEHOOD

A2282

Designed by Laura Smith.

Printed by Sterling Sommer for Ashton-Potter (USA) Ltd.

LITHOGRAPHED

Sheets of 120 in six panes of 20

1995, June 16 **Tagged** ***Perf. 11.2***

2968 A2282 32c **multicolored**	.70	.25
P# block of 4, 6#+P	2.80	—
Pane of 20	14.00	—

GREAT LAKES LIGHTHOUSES

Split Rock, Lake Superior — A2283

St. Joseph, Lake Michigan — A2284

Spectacle Reef, Lake Huron — A2285

Marblehead, Lake Erie — A2286

Thirty Mile Point, Lake Ontario — A2287

Designed by Howard Koslow.
Printed by Stamp Venturers.

PHOTOGRAVURE
BOOKLET STAMPS

1995, June 17	Tagged	Perf. 11.2 Vert.	
2969 A2283 32c **multicolored**		.90	.30
2970 A2284 32c **multicolored**		.90	.30
2971 A2285 32c **multicolored**		.90	.30
2972 A2286 32c **multicolored**		.90	.30
2973 A2287 32c **multicolored**		.90	.30
a. Booklet pane of 5, #2969-2973		4.50	2.50
b. As "a," two vert. pairs imperf. horiz. of #2972 and 2973, in pane of 7+ stamps in cplt. bklt. #BK230 (due to foldover)		—	

U.N., 50th ANNIV.

A2288

Designed by Howard Paine.
Printed by Banknote Corp. of America.

ENGRAVED
Sheets of 180 in nine panes of 20

1995, June 26	Tagged	Perf. 11.2	
2974 A2288 32c **blue**		.65	.25
P# block of 4, 1#+B		2.60	—
Pane of 20		13.00	—

CIVIL WAR

A2289

Illustration reduced.

Designed by Mark Hess.

Printed by Stamp Venturers.

Designs: a, Monitor and Virginia. b, Robert E. Lee. c, Clara Barton. d, Ulysses S. Grant. e, Battle of Shiloh. f, Jefferson Davis. g, David Farragut. h, Frederick Douglass. i, Raphael Semmes. j, Abraham Lincoln. k, Harriet Tubman. l, Stand Watie. m, Joseph E. Johnston. n, Winfield Hancock. o, Mary Chesnut. p, Battle of Chancellorsville. q, William T. Sherman. r, Phoebe Pember. s, "Stonewall" Jackson. t, Battle of Gettysburg.

PHOTOGRAVURE
Sheets of 120 in six panes of 20

1995, June 29	Tagged	Perf. 10.1	
2975 A2289 Pane of 20		32.50	17.50
a.-t. 32c any single		1.50	.60
u. As No. 2975, a.-e. imperf, f.-j. part perf, others perf		800.00	
v. As No. 2975, k.-t. imperf, f.-j. part perf, others perf		1,250.	
w. As No. 2975, imperf		800.00	
x. Block of 9 (f.-h., k.-m., p.-r.) k.-l. & p.-q. imperf. vert.		800.00	
y. As No. 2975, a.-b. perf, c., f.-h. part perf, others imperf		800.00	
z. As No. 2975, o. and t. imperf, j., n. & s. part perf, others perf		—	
aa. As No. 2975, c.-e. imperf, b., g.-j. part perf, others perf		500.00	

Uncut press sheets of No. 2975 were made available for sale. Values: cross-gutter block of 20, $45; pairs with gutters between, $5.50 each. See note after No. 2868.

AMERICAN FOLK ART SERIES
Carousel Horses

A2290

A2291

A2292

A2293

Designed by Paul Calle.
Printed at Sterling Sommer for Ashton-Potter (USA) Ltd.

LITHOGRAPHED
Sheets of 160 in eight panes of 20

1995, July 21	Tagged	Perf. 11	
2976 A2290 32c **multicolored**		.65	.25
2977 A2291 32c **multicolored**		.65	.25
2978 A2292 32c **multicolored**		.65	.25
2979 A2293 32c **multicolored**		.65	.25
a. Block or strip of 4, #2976-2979		2.60	2.00
P# block of 4, 5#+P		2.60	—
Pane of 20		13.00	—

WOMAN SUFFRAGE

A2294

Designed by April Greiman.
Printed by Ashton-Potter (USA) Ltd.

LITHOGRAPHED & ENGRAVED
Sheets of 160 in four panes of 40

1995, Aug. 26	Tagged	Perf. 11.1x11	
2980 A2294 32c **multicolored**		.65	.25
P# block of 4, 5#+P		3.00	—
Pane of 40		26.00	
a. Black (engr.) omitted		275.00	
b. Imperf., pair		750.00	
c. Vert. pair, imperf between and at bottom		500.00	

No. 2980a is valued in the grade of fine. Very fine examples exist and sell for much more.

WORLD WAR II

A2295

Illustration reduced.

Designed by Bill Bond.

Designs and events of 1945: a, Marines raise flag on Iwo Jima. b, Fierce fighting frees Manila by March 3, 1945. c, Soldiers advancing (Okinawa, the last big battle). d, Destroyed bridge (US and Soviets link up at Elbe River). e, Allies liberate Holocaust survivors. f, Germany surrenders at Reims. g, Refugees (By 1945, World War II has uprooted millions). h, Truman announces Japan's surrender. i, Sailor kissing nurse (News of victory hits home). j, Hometowns honor their returning veterans.
Central label is size of 15 stamps and shows world map with extent of Axis control and Allied operations.

LITHOGRAPHED & ENGRAVED
Plates of eight subjects in four panes of 2 each

1995, Sept. 2	Tagged	Perf. 11.1	
2981 A2295 Block of 10		15.00	7.50
Pane of 20		30.00	—
a.-j. 32c any single		1.50	.50

No. 2981 has selvage at left and right and either top or bottom.

AMERICAN MUSIC SERIES

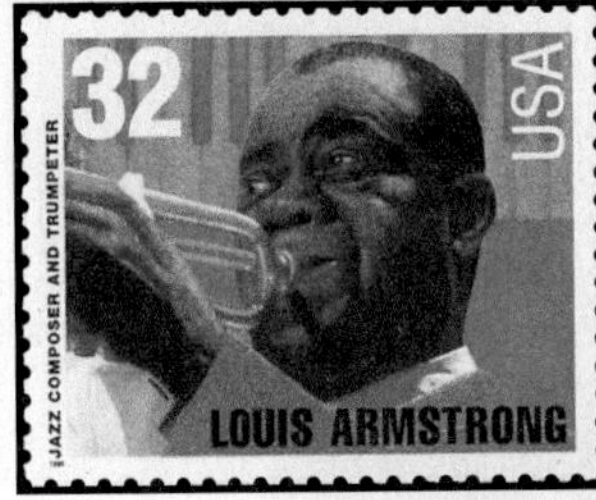

Louis Armstrong (1901-71) A2296

Coleman Hawkins (1904-69) A2297

A2297a

James P. Johnson (1894-1955) A2298

Jelly Roll Morton (1890-1941) A2299

Charlie Parker (1920-55) A2300

Eubie Blake (1883-1983) A2301

Charles Mingus (1922-79) A2302

Thelonious Monk (1917-82) A2303

John Coltrane (1926-67) A2304

Erroll Garner (1921-77) A2305

Designed by Dean Mitchell (#2982-2984, 2987, 2989, 2991-2992) and Thomas Blackshear (others).

Printed by Ashton-Potter (USA) Ltd. (#2982), Sterling Sommer for Ashton-Potter (USA) Ltd. (#2983-2992).

LITHOGRAPHED
Plates of 120 in six panes of 20

1995 Tagged *Perf. 11.1x11*

2982	A2296	32c **white denomination,** *Sept. 1*	.90	.25
		P# block of 4, 4#+P	3.60	—
		Pane of 20	18.00	—
a.		Imperf, pair	—	
2983	A2297	32c **multicolored,** *Sept. 16*	2.25	.30
2984	A2297a	32c **black denomination,** *Sept. 16*	2.25	.30
2985	A2298	32c **multicolored,** *Sept. 16*	2.25	.30
2986	A2299	32c **multicolored,** *Sept. 16*	2.25	.30
2987	A2300	32c **multicolored,** *Sept. 16*	2.25	.30
2988	A2301	32c **multicolored,** *Sept. 16*	2.25	.30
2989	A2302	32c **multicolored,** *Sept. 16*	2.25	.30
2990	A2303	32c **multicolored,** *Sept. 16*	2.25	.30
2991	A2304	32c **multicolored,** *Sept. 16*	2.25	.30
2992	A2305	32c **multicolored,** *Sept. 16*	2.25	.30
a.		Vert. block of 10, #2983-2992	23.00	7.50
		P# block of 10	23.00	—
		Pane of 20	46.00	—
b.		Pane of 20, dark blue (inscriptions) omitted	—	
c.		Imperf pair of Nos. 2991-2992	*5,000.*	

An imperf. block of Nos. 2983-2992 is believed to be printer's waste.

GARDEN FLOWERS

Aster A2306

Chrysanthemum A2307

Dahlia — A2308

Hydrangea — A2309

Rudbeckia — A2310

Designed by Ned Seidler.

LITHOGRAPHED & ENGRAVED
BOOKLET STAMPS

1995, Sept. 19 Tagged *Perf. 10.9 Vert.*

2993	A2306	32c **multicolored**	.65	.25
2994	A2307	32c **multicolored**	.65	.25
2995	A2308	32c **multicolored**	.65	.25
2996	A2309	32c **multicolored**	.65	.25
2997	A2310	32c **multicolored**	.65	.25
a.		Booklet pane of 5, #2993-2997	3.25	2.25
b.		As "a," imperf	*2,250.*	
c.		As "a," black (engr.) omitted	—	

EDDIE RICKENBACKER (1890-1973), AVIATOR

A2311

Small Date

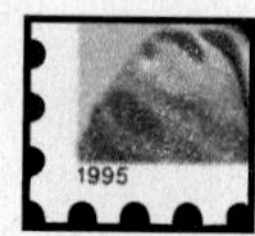
Large Date

Designed by Davis Meltzer.

PHOTOGRAVURE
Panes of 50

1995, Sept. 25 Tagged *Perf. 11¼*

2998	A2311	60c **multicolored,** small "1995" year date	1.40	.50
		P# block of 4, 5#	8.00	—
		Pane of 50	60.00	
a.		Large "1995" date, *Oct., 1999*	2.00	.50
		P# block of 4, 5#	17.50	—
		Pane of 50	100.00	

Date on No. 2998 is 1mm long, on No. 2998a 1½mm long.

REPUBLIC OF PALAU

A2312

Designed by Herb Kane.
Printed by Sterling Sommer for Ashton-Potter (USA) Ltd.

LITHOGRAPHED
Sheets of 200 in four panes of 50

1995, Sept. 29 Tagged *Perf. 11.1*

2999	A2312	32c **multicolored**	.65	.25
		P# block of 4, 5#+P	3.00	—
		Pane of 50	33.00	

See Palau Nos. 377-378.

COMIC STRIPS

A2313

Illustration reduced.

Designed by Carl Herrman.

Printed by Stamp Venturers.

Designs: a, The Yellow Kid. b, Katzenjammer Kids. c, Little Nemo in Slumberland. d, Bringing Up Father. e, Krazy Kat. f, Rube Goldberg's Inventions. g, Toonerville Folks. h, Gasoline Alley. i, Barney Google. j, Little Orphan Annie. k, Popeye. l, Blondie. m, Dick Tracy. n, Alley Oop. o, Nancy. p, Flash Gordon.

q, Li'l Abner. r, Terry and the Pirates. s, Prince Valiant. t, Brenda Starr, Reporter.

PHOTOGRAVURE

Sheets of 120 in six panes of 20

1995, Oct. 1 Tagged *Perf. 10.1*

3000	A2313 Pane of 20		13.00	10.00
a.-t.	32c any single		.65	.50
u.	As No. 3000, a.-h. imperf., i.-l. part perf		*3,250.*	
v.	As No. 3000, m.-t. imperf., i.-l. part perf		*3,250.*	
w.	As No. 3000, a.-l. imperf.,m.-t. imperf vert.		*3,250.*	
x.	As No. 3000, imperf		*4,250.*	

Inscriptions on back of each stamp describe the comic strip.

Uncut press sheets of No. 3000 were made available for sale. Values: cross-gutter block of 20, $35; pairs with gutters between, $3.75 each. See note after No. 2868.

U.S. NAVAL ACADEMY, 150th ANNIVERSARY

A2314

Designed by Dean Ellis. Printed by Sterling-Sommer for Aston-Potter (USA) Ltd.

LITHOGRAPHED

Sheets of 160 in eight panes of 20

1995, Oct. 10 Tagged *Perf. 10.9*

3001	A2314 32c **multicolored**	.65	.25
	P# block of 4, 5#+P	3.25	—
	Pane of 20	16.00	—

Imperf. examples of No. 3001 are believed to be printer's waste.

LITERARY ARTS SERIES

Tennessee Williams (1911-83) A2315

Designed by Michael Deas. Printed by Sterling-Sommer for Ashton-Potter (USA) Ltd.

LITHOGRAPHED

Sheets of 160 in eight panes of 20

1995, Oct. 13 Tagged *Perf. 11.1*

3002	A2315 32c **multicolored**	.65	.25
	P# block of 4, 5#+P	3.25	—
	Pane of 20	16.00	—

CHRISTMAS

Madonna and Child, by Giotto di Bondone — A2316

A2316a

Designed by Richard Sheaff (#3003).
Printed by Bureau of Engraving and Printing (#3003).

LITHOGRAPHED & ENGRAVED

Sheets of 300 in six panes of 50

1995 Tagged *Perf. 11.2*

3003	A2316 32c **multicolored,** *Oct. 19*	.65	.25
	P# block of 4, 5#	3.00	—
	Pane of 50	35.00	
c.	Black (engr., denomination) omitted	*200.00*	—
d.	Tagging omitted	75.00	—

BOOKLET STAMP

Perf. 9.8x10.9

3003A	A2316a 32c **multicolored,** *Oct. 19*	.65	.25
b.	Booklet pane of 10	6.50	4.00

Santa Claus Entering Chimney — A2317

Child Holding Jumping Jack — A2318

Child Holding Tree — A2319

Santa Claus Working on Sled — A2320

Designed by John Grossman & Laura Alders (#3004-3018).
Printed by Sterling-Sommer for Ashton-Potter (USA) Ltd.

LITHOGRAPHED

Sheets of 200 in four panes of 50

Perf. 11.25

3004	A2317 32c **multicolored,** *Sept. 30*	.70	.25
3005	A2318 32c **multicolored,** *Sept. 30*	.70	.25
3006	A2319 32c **multicolored,** *Sept. 30*	.70	.25
3007	A2320 32c **multicolored,** *Sept. 30*	.70	.25
a.	Block or strip of 4, #3004-3007	2.80	1.25
	P# block of 4, 4#+P	4.00	—
	Pane of 50	35.00	
b.	Booklet pane of 10, 3 each #3004-3005, 2 each #3006-3007	8.00	4.00
c.	Booklet pane of 10, 2 each #3004-3005, 3 each #3006-3007	8.00	4.00
d.	As "a," imperf	*325.00*	
e.	As "b," miscut and inserted upside down into booklet cover, with full bottom selvage	—	

A2317a

A2318a

A2319a

A2320a

Printed by Avery Dennison.

PHOTOGRAVURE

Self-Adhesive Stamps

Serpentine Die Cut 11.25 on 2, 3 or 4 sides

3008	A2320a 32c **multicolored,** *Sept. 30*	.95	.25
3009	A2318a 32c **multicolored,** *Sept. 30*	.95	.25
3010	A2317a 32c **multicolored,** *Sept. 30*	.95	.25
3011	A2319a 32c **multicolored,** *Sept. 30*	.95	.25
a.	Booklet pane of 20, 5 each #3008-3011 + label	19.00	
b.	Strip of 4, #3008-3011	3.80	

Midnight Angel — A2321

Children Sledding — A2322

Printed by Avery Dennison (#3013-3017), Banknote Corporation of America (#3012, 3018).

LITHOGRAPHED

Serpentine Die Cut 11.3x11.6 on 2, 3 or 4 sides

3012	A2321 32c **multicolored,** *Oct. 19*	.65	.25
a.	Booklet pane of 20 + label	13.00	
b.	Vert. pair, die cutting omitted between	—	
c.	Booklet pane of 15 + label, *1996*	12.00	
d.	Booklet pane of 15	*30.00*	

No. 3012a comes either with no die cutting in the label (1995 printing) or with the die cutting from the 1996 printing.

No. 3012d is a pane of 16 with one stamp removed. The missing stamp can be from either row 1, 2, 3, 7 or 8 of the pane. No. 3012d cannot be made from No. 3012c, a pane of 15 + label. The label is die cut. If the label is removed, an impression of the die cutting appears on the backing paper.

PHOTOGRAVURE

Die Cut

3013	A2322 32c **multicolored,** *Oct. 19* ⓢ	.65	.25
a.	Booklet pane of 18	12.00	
b.	As "a," tagging omitted	—	

ⓢ: Adhesive residue may adhere to the back of some examples of No. 3013 after soaking. See note after No. 1549.

A2317b

A2318b

A2319b

A2320b

Printed by Avery Dennison.

Self-Adhesive Coil Stamps

Serpentine Die Cut 11.2 Vert.

3014	A2320b 32c **multicolored,** *Sept. 30*	3.00	.30
3015	A2318b 32c **multicolored,** *Sept. 30*	3.00	.30
3016	A2317b 32c **multicolored,** *Sept. 30*	3.00	.30
3017	A2319b 32c **multicolored,** *Sept. 30*	3.00	.30
a.	Strip of 4, #3014-3017	12.00	
	P# strip of 5, 1 each #3014-3017 + 1 stamp, P#V1111	25.00	
	P# strip of 8, 2 each #3014-3017, P#V1111	35.00	
	P# single (#3017), #V1111	—	12.50

A2321a

Printed by Banknote Corporation of America.

LITHOGRAPHED

Serpentine Die Cut 11.6 Vert.

3018	A2321a 32c **multicolored,** *Oct. 19*	1.10	.30
	Pair	2.20	.60
	P# strip of 5, #B1111	8.00	
	P# single, #B1111	—	6.00

Nos. 3014-3018 were only available through the Philatelic Fullfillment Center in Kansas City.

Nos. 3005-3006 have "USA" printed in green. It is red on the self-adhesive stamps.

ANTIQUE AUTOMOBILES

1893 Duryea A2323

1894 Haynes A2324

1898 Columbia A2325

1899 Winton A2326

1901 White A2327

Designed by Ken Dallison.
Printed by Stamp Venturers.

PHOTOGRAVURE

Sheets of 200 in eight panes of 25

1995, Nov. 3 **Tagged** ***Perf. 10.1x11.1***

3019	A2323 32c **multicolored**	.90	.25
3020	A2324 32c **multicolored**	.90	.25
3021	A2325 32c **multicolored**	.90	.25
3022	A2326 32c **multicolored**	.90	.25
3023	A2327 32c **multicolored**	.90	.25
a.	Vert. or horiz. strip of 5, #3019-3023	4.50	2.00
	Vert. or Horiz. P# block of 10, 2 sets of 4#+S	10.00	—
	Pane of 25	24.00	—

Vert. and horiz. strips are all in different order.

UTAH STATEHOOD CENTENARY

Delicate Arch, Arches Natl. Park — A2328

Designed by McRay Magleby.
Printed by Sterling Sommer for Ashton-Potter (USA) Ltd.

LITHOGRAPHED

Sheets of 200 in four panes of 50

1996, Jan. 4 **Tagged** ***Perf. 11.1***

3024	A2328 32c **multicolored**	.75	.25
	P# block of 4, 5#+P	4.00	—
	Pane of 50	38.00	

For booklet see No. BK245.

GARDEN FLOWERS

Crocus — A2329

Winter Aconite — A2330

Pansy — A2331

Snowdrop — A2332

Anemone — A2333

Designed by Ned Seidler.

LITHOGRAPHED & ENGRAVED
BOOKLET STAMPS

1996, Jan. 19 **Tagged** ***Perf. 10.9 Vert.***

3025	A2329 32c **multicolored**	.65	.25
3026	A2330 32c **multicolored**	.65	.25
3027	A2331 32c **multicolored**	.65	.25
3028	A2332 32c **multicolored**	.65	.25
3029	A2333 32c **multicolored**	.65	.25
a.	Booklet pane of 5, #3025-3029	3.25	2.50
b.	As "a," imperf.	—	

LOVE

Cherub from Sistine Madonna, by Raphael — A2334

Designed by Terry McCaffrey.
Printed by Banknote Corporation of America.

LITHOGRAPHED & ENGRAVED
BOOKLET STAMP

Serpentine Die Cut 11.3x11.7

1996, Jan. 20 **Tagged**

Self-Adhesive

3030	A2334 32c **multicolored**	.65	.25
a.	Booklet pane of 20 + label	13.00	
b.	Booklet pane of 15 + label	9.75	
c.	Red (engr. "Love") omitted	*75.00*	
d.	Red (engr. "Love") missing (CM)	—	
e.	Double impression of red (engr. "Love")	*450.00*	
f.	Die cutting omitted, pair	*225.00*	
g.	As "a," stamps 1-5 double impression of red (engr. "LOVE")	*1,000.*	
h.	As "a," red (engr. "LOVE") omitted	*1,000.*	
i.	As "a," die cutting omitted	—	
j.	As "e," two examples in booklet pane of 20 (No. 3030a)	*1,000.*	
k.	As "d," three examples in booklet pane of 20 (No. 3030a)	*310.00*	

No. 3030d must be collected se-tenant with a stamp bearing the red engraving.

FLORA AND FAUNA SERIES

Kestrel, Blue Jay and Rose Types of 1993-95 and

A2334a

A2334b

Designed by Michael Matherly (#3031-3033).
Printed by Banknote Corporation of America (#3031A); Bureau of Engraving & Printing (#3031-3033).

LITHOGRAPHED

Sheets of 300 in six panes of 50 (#3031)
Sheets of 400 in eight panes of 50 (#3031A)

1996-2002 **Untagged** ***Serpentine Die Cut 10½***

Self-Adhesive (#3031, 3031A)

3031	A2334a 1c **multicolored,** *Nov. 19, 1999*	.30	.25
	P# block of 4, 4# or 4# + A, B or C	.50	
	Pane of 50	4.00	
c.	Die cutting omitted, pair	—	

Serpentine Die Cut 11¼

3031A	A2334b 1c **multicolored,** *Nov. 2000*	.30	.25
	P# block of 4, 6# + B	.50	
	Pane of 50	4.00	
b.	Die cutting omitted, pane of 50	*325.00*	

No. 3031A has blue inscription and year. See No. 2477.

Red-headed Woodpecker A2335

Eastern Bluebird A2336

Sheets of 400 in four panes of 100

Perf. 11

3032	A2335 2c **multicolored,** *Feb. 2*	.30	.25
	P# block of 4, 5#	.50	—
	Pane of 100	6.00	

3033 A2336 3c **multicolored,** *Apr. 3* .30 .25
P# block of 4, 5# .50 —
Pane of 100 8.00

Some plate blocks contain plate position diagram.

Red Fox — A2339

Designed by Derry Noyes.
Printed by Banknote Corporation of America.

Sheets of 120 in six panes of 20 (#3036)
Sheets of 200 in ten panes of 20 (#3036a)

Tagged

Serpentine Die Cut 11½x11¼

Self-Adhesive

3036 A2339 $1 **multicolored,** *Aug. 14, 1998* *10.00* *.50*
P# block of 4, 4#+B *40.00*
Pane of 20 *200.00*
a. Serpentine die cut 11¾x11, *2002* *11.00* *.50*
P# block of 4, 4#+B *44.00*
Pane of 20 *220.00*

The tagging of No. 3036 has a bright yellow-green appearance under shortwave ultraviolet light while that of No. 3036a appears light blue green. Nos. 3036 and 3036a are dated 1998 at left bottom.

A hidden 3-D image (a small fox) can be seen on Nos. 3036 and 3036a when they are viewed with a special "Stamp Decoder" lens sold by the USPS.

Beginning with Nos. 3036 and 3036a, hidden 3-D images can be seen on some stamps when they are viewed with a special "Stamp Decoder" lens sold by the USPS. Stamps with 3-D images are 3036-3036a, 3167, 3168-3172, 3178, 3206, 3230-3234, 3238-3242, 3261-3262, 3321-3324, 3472-3473, 3647-3648, 3651, 3771, 3787-3791, 3808-3811, 3838 and 3862.

A2339a

American
1996

Small Date

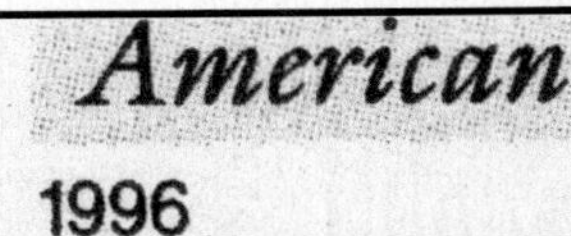

Large Date

Designed by Michael Matherly.
Printed by Bureau of Engraving & Printing.

COIL STAMPS

Untagged

Perf. 9¾ Vert.

3044 A2339a 1c **multicolored,** small date, *Jan. 20* .30 .25
Pair .30 .25
P# strip of 5, #1111 in black, yellow, blue, magenta order .65
P# single, same — .60
P# strip of 5, #1111 in black, blue, yellow, magenta order 3.00
P# single, same — 3.00
a. Large date .30 .25
Pair .30 .25
P# strip of 5, #1111, 2222, 3333, 4444 in yellow, magenta, blue, black order .70
P# single, same — .70

Date on No. 3044 is 1mm long, on No. 3044a 1.5mm long.

A2335a

Untagged

3045 A2335a 2c **multicolored,** *June 22, 1999* .30 .25
Pair .30 .25
P# strip of 5, #11111 .70 —
P# strip of 5, #22222 1.25
P# single, #11111 — .65
P# single, #22222 — .85

A2335b

A2335c

Printed by Stamp Venturers.

BOOKLET STAMPS

PHOTOGRAVURE

Serpentine Die Cut 10.4x10.8 on 3 Sides

Tagged

Self-Adhesive

3048 A2335b 20c **multicolored,** *Aug. 2, 1996* .40 .25
a. Booklet pane of 10 4.00
b. Booklet pane of 4 70.00
c. Booklet pane of 6 100.00

No. 3048 and 3048a exist on two types of surface-tagged paper that exhibit either a solid appearance (P# S1111) or a grainy solid appearance (P# S2222).

Nos. 3048b-3048c are from the vending machine booklet No. BK237 that has a glue strip at the top edge of the top pane, the peelable strip removed and the rouletting line 2mm lower than on No. 3048a on some booklets, when the panes are compared with bottoms aligned. Vending booklets with plate #S2222 always have gauge 8½ rouletting on booklet covers. Convertible booklets (No. 3048a) with plate #S2222 always have gauge 12½ rouletting on booklet covers. Vending booklets with plate #S1111 can have either 8½ or 12½ gauge rouletting on booklet cover, and it may be impossible to tell a vending booklet with 12½ gauge rouletting and plate #S1111 from a convertible booklet with peelable strip removed.

Serpentine Die Cut 11.3x11.7 on 2, 3 or 4 Sides

3049 A2335c 32c **yellow, orange, green & black,** *Oct. 24, 1996* .65 .25
a. Booklet pane of 20 + label 13.00
b. Booklet pane of 4, *Dec. 1996* 2.60
c. Booklet pane of 5 + label, *Dec. 1996* 3.50
P# single, #S1111 .85 *1.00*
d. Booklet pane of 6, *Dec. 1996* 4.00
Booklet pane of 6 containing P# single 6.00
P# single, #S1111 2.50 *1.00*

The plate # single in No. 3049c is on the lower left stamp. In No. 3049d it is the lower right stamp on the bottom pane of the booklet.

Ring-necked Pheasant — A2350

A2350a

A2350b

Designed by Terry McCaffrey (#3050-3051).
Printed by Avery Dennison.

Serpentine Die Cut 11.2 on 3 Sides

3050 A2350 20c **multicolored,** *July 31, 1998* .65 .25
a. Booklet pane of 10, all stamps upright 6.50
b. Serpentine die cut 11 3.25 .25
c. As "b," booklet pane of 10, all stamps upright 35.00

Serpentine Die Cut 10½x11 on 3 Sides

3051 A2350a 20c **multicolored,** *July 1999* 1.25 .25

Serpentine Die Cut 10.6x10.4 on 3 Sides

3051A A2350b 20c **multicolored** 7.00 .50
b. Booklet pane of 5, 4 #3051, 1 #3051A turned sideways at top 10.00
c. Booklet pane of 5, 4 #3051, 1 #3051A turned sideways at bottom 10.00

No. 3051 represents the eight upright stamps on the booklet panes Nos. 3051Ab and 3051Ac. The two stamps turned sideways on those panes are No. 3051A.

Specialists should note that 3051 can be either die cut 10.4 at top and 10.6 at bottom or 10.6 at top and 10.4 at bottom. These two varieties exist in equal numbers.

Coral Pink Rose — A2351

A2351a

Designed by Derry Noyes.
Printed by American Packaging Corp. for Sennett Security Products (#3052); Sennett Security Products (#3052E).

Serpentine Die Cut 11½x11¼ on 2, 3 or 4 Sides

3052 A2351 33c **multicolored,** *Aug. 13, 1999* .90 .25
a. Booklet pane of 4 3.60
b. Booklet pane of 5 + label 4.50
c. Booklet pane of 6 5.50
d. Booklet pane of 20 + label 17.50
j. Die cutting omitted, pair —
k. As "d," die cutting omitted *5,500.*

Serpentine Die Cut 10¾x10½ on 2 or 3 sides

3052E A2351a 33c **multi,** *Apr. 7, 2000* ⓢ .75 .25
f. Booklet pane of 20 15.00
g. Black ("33 USA," etc.) omitted 350.00
h. As "f," all 12 stamps on one side with black omitted —
i. Horiz. pair, die cutting missing between due to miscutting of the pane —
j. As "f," vert. die cutting missing between due to miscutting of the pane —

No. 3052Ef is a double-sided booklet pane with 12 stamps on one side and 8 stamps plus label on the other side.

See note after No. 1549.

A2351b

Printed by Stamp Venturers.

COIL STAMPS

Serpentine Die Cut 11½ Vert.

3053 A2351b 20c **multicolored,** *Aug. 2, 1996* .50 .25
Pair 1.00
P# strip of 5, #S1111 3.75
P# single, #S1111 — 1.00
a. Die cutting omitted, pair *2,100.*

A2351c

Printed by Bureau of Engraving and Printing.

LITHOGRAPHED
Serpentine Die Cut 9¾ Vert.
Tagged
Self-Adhesive

3054 A2351c 32c **yellow, magenta, black & green,** *Aug. 1, 1997* .65 .25
Pair 1.30
P# strip of 5, #1111, 1112, 1122, 2222, 2223, 2333, 3344, 4455, 5555, 5556, 5566, 5666, 6666, 7777 4.50
P# strip of 5, #2233, 3444 6.00
P# strip of 5, #6677, 6777, 8888 7.50
P# strip of 5, #5455 10.00
P# single, #1111, 1112, 1122, 4455, 5555, 5556, 5566, 5666, 6666, 7777 — 1.50
P# single, #2222, 2333 — 2.50
P# single, #2223, 8888 — 2.75
P# single, #2233, 3444 — 4.50
P# single, #3344, 5455, 6677 — 3.50
P# single, #6777 — 5.50
a. Die cutting omitted, pair *85.00*
b. Black, yellow & green omitted —
c. Black, yellow & green omitted, die cutting omitted, pair —
d. Black omitted *250.00*
e. Black omitted, die cutting omitted, pair *550.00*
f. All colors omitted, die cutting omitted —
g. Pair, die cutting omitted, containing one stamp each of "c" and "e" —

Nos. 3054b and 3054d also are miscut and with shifted die cuttings.
No. 3054f must be collected se-tenant with a partially printed stamp(s).

A2350c

Designed by Terry McCaffrey. Printed by Bureau of Engraving and Printing.

3055 A2350c 20c **multicolored,** *July, 31, 1998* .40 .25
Pair .80
P# strip of 5, P#1111, 2222 3.00
P# single, same — 1.25
a. Die cutting omitted, pair *125.00*

No. 3055a exists miscut. It is more common in this form and is valued thus.

BLACK HERITAGE SERIES

Ernest E. Just (1883-1941), Marine Biologist — A2358

Designed by Richard Sheaff.
Printed by Banknote Corporation of America.

LITHOGRAPHED
Sheets of 160 in eight panes of 20

1996, Feb. 1 **Tagged** ***Perf. 11.1***
3058 A2358 32c **gray & black** .65 .25
P# block of 4, 4#+B 2.60 —
Pane of 20 13.00 —

SMITHSONIAN INSTITUTION, 150TH ANNIVERSARY

A2359

Designed by Tom Engeman.
Printed by Ashton-Potter (USA) Ltd.

LITHOGRAPHED
Sheets of 160 in eight panes of 20

1996, Feb. 7 **Tagged** ***Perf. 11.1***
3059 A2359 32c **multicolored** .65 .25
P# block of 4, 4#+P 2.60 —
Pane of 20 13.00 —

CHINESE NEW YEAR

Year of the Rat — A2360

Designed by Clarence Lee.
Printed by Stamp Venturers.

PHOTOGRAVURE
Sheets of 180 in nine panes of 20

1996, Feb. 8 **Tagged** ***Perf. 11.1***
3060 A2360 32c **multicolored** .90 .25
P# block of 4, 4#+S 4.25 —
Pane of 20 19.00 —
a. Imperf., pair *550.00*

See Nos. 3895a, 3997a.

PIONEERS OF COMMUNICATION

Eadweard Muybridge (1830-1904), Photographer A2361

Ottmar Mergenthaler (1854-99), Inventor of Linotype A2362

Frederic E. Ives (1856-1937), Developer of Halftone Process A2363

William Dickson (1860-1935), Co-developer of Kinetoscope A2364

Designed by Fred Otnes.
Printed by Ashton-Potter USA.

LITHOGRAPHED
Sheets of 120 in six panes of 20

1996, Feb. 22 **Tagged** ***Perf. 11.1x11***
3061 A2361 32c **multicolored** .65 .25
3062 A2362 32c **multicolored** .65 .25
3063 A2363 32c **multicolored** .65 .25
3064 A2364 32c **multicolored** .65 .25
a. Block or strip of 4, #3061-3064 2.60 2.00
P# block of 4, 5#+P 2.60 —
Pane of 20 13.00 —

FULBRIGHT SCHOLARSHIPS, 50th ANNIVERSARY

A2365

Designed by Richard D. Sheaff.

LITHOGRAPHED & ENGRAVED
Sheets of 200 in four panes of 50

1996, Feb. 28 **Tagged** ***Perf. 11.1***
3065 A2365 32c **multicolored** .75 .25
P# block of 4, 5# 4.25 —
Pane of 50 38.00 —

For booklet see No. BK246.

JACQUELINE COCHRAN (1910-80), PILOT

A2366

Designed by Davis Meltzer.

LITHOGRAPHED & ENGRAVED
Sheets of 300 in six panes of 50

1996, Mar. 9 **Tagged** ***Perf. 11.1***
3066 A2366 50c **multicolored** 1.00 .40
P# block of 4, 5# 5.00 —
Pane of 50 50.00 —
a. Black (engr.) omitted 45.00

MARATHON

A2367

Designed by Michael Bartalos.

Printed by Banknote Corporation of America.

LITHOGRAPHED
Sheets of 160 in eight panes of 20

1996, Apr. 11 **Tagged** ***Perf. 11.1***
3067 A2367 32c **multicolored** .65 .25
P# block of 4, 4#+B 2.60 —
Pane of 20 13.00 —

1996 SUMMER OLYMPIC GAMES

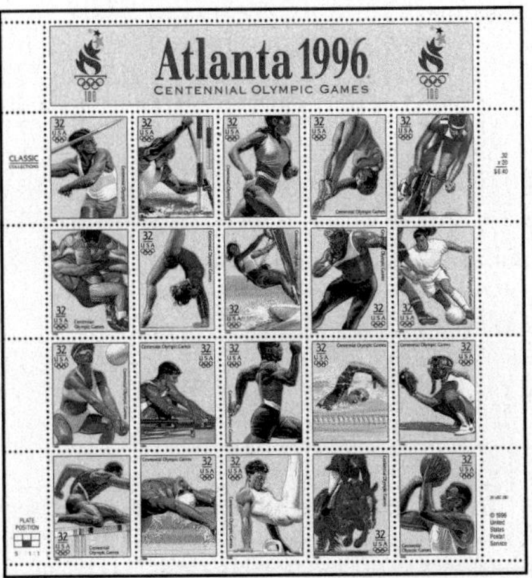

A2368

Illustration reduced.

Designed by Richard Waldrep. Printed by Stamp Venturers.

Designs: a, Decathlon (javelin). b, Men's canoeing. c, Women's running. d, Women's diving. e, Men's cycling. f, Freestyle wrestling. g, Women's gymnastics. h, Women's sailboarding. i, Men's shot put. j, Women's soccer. k, Beach volleyball. l, Men's rowing. m, Men's sprints. n, Women's swimming. o, Women's softball. p, Men's hurdles. q, Men's swimming. r, Men's gymnastics (pommel horse). s, Equestrian. t, Men's basketball.

PHOTOGRAVURE
Sheets of 120 in six panes of 20

1996, May 2 **Tagged** ***Perf. 10.1***

3068	A2368 Pane of 20	14.00	10.00
a.-t.	32c any single	.70	.50
u.	As No. 3068, imperf	*700.00*	
v.	As No. 3068, back inscriptions omitted on a., f., k. & p., incorrect back inscriptions on others	—	
w.	As No. 3068, e. imperf, d., i.-j. part perf, all others perf	*750.00*	

Inscription on back of each stamp describes the sport shown.
Uncut press sheets of No. 3068 were made available for sale. Values: cross-gutter block of 20, $45; pairs with gutters between, $4 each. See note after No. 2868.

GEORGIA O'KEEFFE (1887-1986)

A2369

Designed by Margaret Bauer. Printed by Stamp Venturers.

PHOTOGRAVURE
Sheets of 90 in six panes of 15

1996, May 23 **Tagged** ***Perf. 11.6x11.4***

3069	A2369 32c **multicolored**	.85	.25
	P# block of 4, 5#+S	5.00	—
	Pane of 15	15.00	9.00
a.	Imperf., pair	*110.00*	
	Pane of 15, imperf.	*675.00*	—

For booklet see No. BK247.

TENNESSEE STATEHOOD BICENTENNIAL

A2370

A2370a

Designed by Phil Jordan. Printed by Stamp Venturers.

PHOTOGRAVURE
Sheets of 200 in four panes of 50.

1996, May 31 **Tagged** ***Perf. 11.1***

3070	A2370 32c **multicolored**	.65	.25
a.	Imperf., pair	—	
	P# block of 4, 5#+S	3.00	—
	Pane of 50	32.00	—

One pane of 3070 containing 3069a is known. Some stamps on that pane have blind horizontal perforations.

For booklet see No. BK248.

Booklet Stamp
Self-Adhesive
Serpentine Die Cut 9.9x10.8

3071	A2370a 32c **multicolored**	.65	.30
a.	Booklet pane of 20, #S11111	13.00	
b.	Horiz. pair, die cutting omitted btwn.	*300.00*	—
c.	Die cutting omitted, pair	—	
d.	Horiz. pair, die cutting omitted vert.	—	—

AMERICAN INDIAN DANCES

Fancy — A2371

Butterfly — A2372

Traditional — A2373

Raven — A2374

Hoop — A2375

Designed by Keith Birdsong. Printed by Ashton-Potter (USA) Ltd.

LITHOGRAPHED
Sheets of 120 in six panes of 20.

1996, June 7 **Tagged** ***Perf. 11.1***

3072	A2371 32c **multicolored**	1.20	.25
3073	A2372 32c **multicolored**	1.20	.25
3074	A2373 32c **multicolored**	1.20	.25
3075	A2374 32c **multicolored**	1.20	.25
3076	A2375 32c **multicolored**	1.20	.25
a.	Strip of 5, #3072-3076	6.00	2.50
	P# block of 10, 4#+P	12.50	—
	Pane of 20	25.00	—

For booklet see No. BK249.

PREHISTORIC ANIMALS

Eohippus
A2376

Woolly Mammoth
A2377

Mastodon
A2378

Saber-tooth Cat — A2379

Designed by Davis Meltzer. Printed by Ashton-Potter (USA) Ltd.

LITHOGRAPHED
Sheets of 120 in six panes of 20

1996, June 8 **Tagged** ***Perf. 11.1x11***

3077	A2376 32c **multicolored**	.65	.25
3078	A2377 32c **multicolored**	.65	.25
3079	A2378 32c **multicolored**	.65	.25
3080	A2379 32c **multicolored**	.65	.25
a.	Block or strip of 4, #3077-3080	2.60	2.00
	P# block of 4, 4#+P	2.60	—
	Pane of 20	13.00	—

BREAST CANCER AWARENESS

A2380

Designed by Tom Mann. Printed by Ashton-Potter (USA) Ltd.

LITHOGRAPHED
Sheets of 120 in six panes of 20

1996, June 15 **Tagged** ***Perf. 11.1***

3081	A2380 32c **multicolored**	.65	.25
	P# block of 4, 5#+P	2.60	—
	Pane of 20	13.00	—

LEGENDS OF HOLLYWOOD

James Dean, (1931-55) — A2381

Designed by Michael Deas.

Printed by Stamp Venturers.

PHOTOGRAVURE
Sheets of 120 in six panes of 20.

1996, June 24 Tagged *Perf. 11.1*

3082	A2381 32c **multicolored**	.65	.25
	P# block of 4, 7#+S	4.25	—
	Pane of 20	20.00	10.00
a.	Imperf., pair	*100.00*	
	Pane of 20, imperf.	*1,250.*	—
b.	As "a," red (USA 32c) missing (CM) and tan (JAMES DEAN) omitted	—	
c.	As "a," tan (JAMES DEAN) omitted	—	
d.	As "a," top stamp red missing (CM) and tan (JAMES DEAN) omitted, bottom stamp tan omitted	—	
e.	As No. 3082 pane of 20, right two columns perf, left three columns imperf	*1,750.*	

Perforations in corner of each stamp are star-shaped. No. 3082 was also available on the first day of issue in at least 127 Warner Bros. Studio stores.

Uncut press sheets of No. 3082 were made available for sale. Values: cross-gutter block of 8, $35; pairs with gutters between, $4.25 each. See note after No. 2868.

For booklet see No. BK250.

Nos. 3082b-3082d come from the same error pane. The top row is No. 3082b; rows 2-4 are No. 3082c. No. 3082d is a vertical pair with one stamp from No. 3082b at top and one stamp from No. 3082c at bottom.

FOLK HEROES

A2382

A2383

A2384

A2385

Designed by David LaFleur.

Printed by Ashton-Potter (USA) Ltd.

LITHOGRAPHED
Sheets of 120 in six panes of 20

1996, July 11 Tagged *Perf. 11.1x11*

3083	A2382 32c **multicolored**	.65	.25
3084	A2383 32c **multicolored**	.65	.25
3085	A2384 32c **multicolored**	.65	.25
3086	A2385 32c **multicolored**	.65	.25
a.	Block or strip of 4, #3083-3086	2.60	2.00
	P# block of 4, 4#+P	2.60	—
	Pane of 20	13.00	—

For booklet see No. BK251.

CENTENNIAL OLYMPIC GAMES

Myron's Discobolus — A2386

Designed by Carl Herrman.

Printed by Ashton-Potter (USA) Ltd.

ENGRAVED
Sheets of 80 in four panes of 20

1996, July 19 Tagged *Perf. 11.1*

3087	A2386 32c **brown**	.75	.25
	P# block of 4, 1#+P	4.25	—
	Pane of 20	20.00	10.00

Sheet margin of the pane of 20 is lithographed.
For booklet see No. BK252.

IOWA STATEHOOD, 150TH ANNIVERSARY

Young Corn, by Grant Wood — A2387

A2387a

Designed by Carl Herrman.

Printed by Ashton-Potter (USA) Ltd. (#3088), Banknote Corporation of America (#3089)

LITHOGRAPHED
Sheets of 200 in four panes of 50

1996, Aug. 1 Tagged *Perf. 11.1*

3088	A2387 32c **multicolored**	.80	.25
	P# block of 4, 4#+P	3.75	—
	Pane of 50	40.00	—

For booklet see No. BK253.

BOOKLET STAMP
Self-Adhesive
Serpentine Die Cut 11.6x11.4

3089	A2387a 32c **multicolored**	.65	.30
a.	Booklet pane of 20	13.00	

RURAL FREE DELIVERY, CENT.

A2388

Designed by Richard Sheaff.

LITHOGRAPHED & ENGRAVED
Sheets of 120 in six panes of 20

1996, Aug. 7 Tagged *Perf. 11.2x11*

3090	A2388 32c **multicolored**	.80	.25
	P# block of 4, 5#	3.50	—
	Pane of 20	17.50	—

For booklet see No. BK254.

RIVERBOATS

Robt. E. Lee — A2389

Sylvan Dell — A2390

Far West — A2391

Rebecca Everingham A2392

Bailey Gatzert A2393

Designed by Dean Ellis.

Printed by Avery Dennison.

PHOTOGRAVURE
Sheets of 200 in 10 panes of 20
Serpentine Die Cut 11x11.1

1996, Aug. 22 Tagged

Self-Adhesive

3091	A2389 32c **multicolored**	.65	.40
3092	A2390 32c **multicolored**	.65	.40
3093	A2391 32c **multicolored**	.65	.40
3094	A2392 32c **multicolored**	.65	.40
3095	A2393 32c **multicolored**	.65	.40
a.	Vert. strip of 5, #3091-3095	3.25	
	P# block of 10, 5#+V	6.50	
	Pane of 20	13.00	
b.	Strip of 5, #3091-3095, with special die cutting, die cut 11 ¼	*45.00*	*45.00*
	P# block of 10, 5#+V	*90.00*	
	Pane of 20	*180.00*	

The serpentine die cutting runs through the peelable backing to which Nos. 3091-3095 are affixed. No. 3095a exists with stamps in different sequences.

On the long side of each stamp in No. 3095b, the die cutting is missing 3 "perforations" between the stamps, one near each end and one in the middle. This allows a complete strip to be removed from the backing paper for use on a first day cover. No. 3095b was also used to make Souvenir Page No. 1215.

For booklet see No. BK255.

AMERICAN MUSIC SERIES
Big Band Leaders

Count Basie — A2394

Tommy & Jimmy Dorsey A2395

Glenn Miller — A2396

Benny Goodman A2397

Songwriters

Harold Arlen — A2398

Johnny Mercer A2399

Dorothy Fields A2400

Hoagy Carmichael A2401

Designed by Bill Nelson (#3096-3099), Gregg Rudd (#3100-3103).
Printed by Ashton-Potter (USA) Ltd.

LITHOGRAPHED
Sheets of 120 in six panes of 20

1996, Sept. 11	**Tagged**	***Perf. 11.1x11***	
3096 A2394 32c **multicolored**		.75	.25
3097 A2395 32c **multicolored**		.75	.25
3098 A2396 32c **multicolored**		.75	.25
3099 A2397 32c **multicolored**		.75	.25
a. Block or strip of 4, #3096-3099		3.00	2.00
P# block of 4, 6#+P		4.00	—
P# block of 8, 2 sets of P# + top label		7.00	—
Pane of 20		19.00	—
3100 A2398 32c **multicolored**		.75	.25
3101 A2399 32c **multicolored**		.75	.25
3102 A2400 32c **multicolored**		.75	.25
3103 A2401 32c **multicolored**		.75	.25
a. Block or strip of 4, #3100-3103		3.00	2.00
P# block of 4, 6#+P		3.50	—
P# block of 8, 2 sets of P# + top label		5.75	—
Pane of 20		16.00	—

Imperf. examples of Nos. 3096-3099 are believed to be printer's waste.

LITERARY ARTS SERIES

F. Scott Fitzgerald (1896-1940) A2402

Designed by Michael Deas.

PHOTOGRAVURE
Sheets of 200 in four panes of 50

1996, Sept. 27	**Tagged**	***Perf. 11.1***	
3104 A2402 23c **multicolored**		.55	.25
P# block of 4, 4#		4.00	—
Pane of 50		29.00	—
Pair with full horiz. gutter between		—	

ENDANGERED SPECIES

A2403

Illustration reduced.
Designed by James Balog. Printed by Ashton-Potter (USA) Ltd.

Designs: a, Black-footed ferret. b, Thick-billed parrot. c, Hawaiian monk seal. d, American crocodile. e, Ocelot. f, Schaus swallowtail butterfly. g, Wyoming toad. h, Brown pelican. i, California condor. j, Gila trout. k, San Francisco garter snake. l, Woodland caribou. m, Florida panther. n, Piping plover. o, Florida manatee.

LITHOGRAPHED
Sheets of 90 in six panes of 15

1996, Oct. 2	**Tagged**	***Perf. 11.1x11***	
3105 A2403 Pane of 15		12.00	8.00
a.-o. 32c any single		.80	.50

See Mexico No. 1995. For booklet see No. BK256.

COMPUTER TECHNOLOGY

A2404

Designed by Nancy Skolos & Tom Wedell.
Printed by Ashton-Potter (USA) Ltd.

LITHOGRAPHED & ENGRAVED
Sheets of 160 in four panes of 40

1996, Oct. 8	**Tagged**	***Perf. 10.9x11.1***	
3106 A2404 32c **multicolored**		.65	.25
P# block of 4, 6#+P		3.00	—
Pane of 40		26.00	—

CHRISTMAS

Madonna and Child from Adoration of the Shepherds, by Paolo de Matteis — A2405

Family at Fireplace — A2406

Decorating Tree — A2407

Dreaming of Santa Claus — A2408

Holiday Shopping — A2409

Designed by Richard D. Sheaff (#3107), Julia Talcott (#3108-3111).
Printed by Bureau of Engraving and Printing (#3107), Ashton-Potter (USA) Ltd. (#3108-3111).

LITHOGRAPHED & ENGRAVED
Sheets of 300 in six panes of 50

1996	**Tagged**	***Perf. 11.1x11.2***	
3107 A2405 32c **multicolored,** *Nov. 1*		.65	.25
P# block of 4, 5#		3.00	—
Pane of 50		32.00	—
a. Black (engr.) omitted at bottom		*600.00*	

On No. 3107a, an albino impression of the lettering at bottom is present, but there is no trace of black ink.
For booklet see No. BK257.

LITHOGRAPHED

Perf. 11.3

3108 A2406 32c **multicolored,** *Oct. 8* .65 .25
3109 A2407 32c **multicolored,** *Oct. 8* .65 .25
3110 A2408 32c **multicolored,** *Oct. 8* .65 .25
3111 A2409 32c **multicolored,** *Oct. 8* .65 .25
a. Block or strip of 4, #3108-3111 2.60 1.75
P# block of 4, 4#+P 3.00 —
Pane of 50 32.00 —
b. Strip of 4, #3110-3111, 3108-3109, with #3109 imperf., #3108 imperf. at right *1,000.*
c. Strip of 4, #3108-3111, with #3111 imperf, #3110 imperf at right *1,000.*

A2405a

Designed by Richard D. Sheaff.
Printed by Bureau of Engraving and Printing.

BOOKLET STAMPS

Self-Adhesive

LITHOGRAPHED & ENGRAVED

Serpentine Die Cut 10 on 2, 3 or 4 Sides

3112 A2405a 32c **multicolored,** *Nov. 1* .75 .25
a. Booklet pane of 20 + label 15.00
b. Die cutting omitted, pair 40.00
c. As "a," die cutting omitted *400.00*
d. As "a," top seven stamps with black (engr.) missing (PS) —

No. 3112d is missing the black lettering at bottom due to a small upward shift of the horizontal perforations. This lettering is the only engraved black on the stamp.

A2406a

A2407a

A2408a

A2409a

Designed by Julia Talcott.
Printed by Banknote Corporation of America.

LITHOGRAPHED

Serpentine Die Cut 11.8x11.5 on 2, 3 or 4 Sides

3113 A2406a 32c **multicolored,** *Oct. 8* .65 .25
3114 A2407a 32c **multicolored,** *Oct. 8* .65 .25
3115 A2408a 32c **multicolored,** *Oct. 8* .65 .25
3116 A2409a 32c **multicolored,** *Oct. 8* .65 .25
a. Booklet pane of 20, 5 ea #3113-3116 13.00
b. Strip of 4, #3113-3116 2.60
c. As "a," die cutting omitted *1,250.*
d. As "b," die cutting omitted *500.00*
e. Block of 6, die cutting omitted *700.00*

Skaters — A2410

Designed by Julia Talcott.
Printed by Avery-Dennison.

PHOTOGRAVURE

Die Cut

3117 A2410 32c **multicolored,** *Oct. 8* .65 .25
a. Booklet pane of 18 12.00

HANUKKAH

A2411

Designed by Hannah Smotrich. Printed by Avery Dennison.

PHOTOGRAVURE

Sheets of 200 in 10 panes of 20

1996, Oct. 22 Tagged *Serpentine Die Cut 11.1*

Self-Adhesive

3118 A2411 32c **multicolored** .65 .25
P# block of 4, 5#+V 2.60
Pane of 20 13.00

Backing on No. 3118 is die cut with continuous vertical wavy lines. The 1997 reprint is die cut with two short vertical lines on each side of a semi-circle on the backing of each stamp.

See Nos. 3352, 3547, 3672, Israel No. 1289. For booklet see No. BK258.

CYCLING

Souvenir Sheet

A2412

Illustration reduced.
Designed by McRay Magleby.
Printed by Stamp Venturers.

PHOTOGRAVURE

1996, Nov. 1 Tagged *Perf. 11x11.1*

3119 A2412 Sheet of 2 2.75 2.00
a. 50c orange & multi 1.30 1.00
b. 50c blue green & multi 1.30 1.00

No. 3119 exists overprinted in gold and in silver for the Tour of China '96. This overprint is a private production. Value, set of 2 sheets $12.50.

CHINESE NEW YEAR

Year of the Ox — A2413

Designed by Clarence Lee.
Printed by Stamp Venturers.

PHOTOGRAVURE

Sheets of 180 in 9 panes of 20

1997, Jan. 5 Tagged *Perf. 11.2*

3120 A2413 32c **multicolored** .80 .25
P# block of 4, 4#+S 3.20 —
Pane of 20 16.00 —

See Nos. 3895b, 3997b.

BLACK HERITAGE SERIES

Brig. Gen. Benjamin O. Davis, Sr. (1880-1970) — A2414

Designed by Richard Sheaff.
Printed by Banknote Corp. of America.

LITHOGRAPHED

Sheets of 120 in six panes of 20

1997, Jan. 28 Tagged *Serpentine Die Cut 11.4*

Self-Adhesive

3121 A2414 32c **multicolored** .70 .25
P# block of 4, 4#+B 2.75
Pane of 20 14.00

A2414a

A2414b

Printed by Avery-Dennison.

PHOTOGRAVURE

Serpentine Die Cut 11 on 2, 3 or 4 Sides

1997, Feb. 1 Tagged

Self-Adhesive

3122 A2414a 32c **red, light blue, dark blue & yellow** .70 .25
a. Booklet pane of 20 + label 14.00
b. Booklet pane of 4 2.80
c. Booklet pane of 5 + label 3.75
P# single, #V1111 .95 1.00
d. Booklet pane of 6 4.25
Booklet pane of 6 containing P# single 6.00
P# single, #V1111 2.50 1.00
h. As "a," die cutting omitted —

The plate # single in No. 3122c is the lower left stamp and should be collected unused with the reorder label to its right to differentiate it from the plate # single in No. 3122d which is the lower left stamp in the bottom pane of the booklet and should be collected with a normal stamp adjoining it at right. In used condition, these plate # singles are indistinguishable.

Serpentine Die Cut 11.5x11.8 on 2, 3 or 4 Sides

1997 Tagged

Self-Adhesive

3122E A2414b 32c **red, light blue, dark blue & yellow** 1.50 .25
f. Booklet pane of 20 + label 40.00
g. Booklet pane of 6 9.00
Booklet pane of 6 containing P# single 13.50
P# single, #V1111 5.50 2.00

The plate # single in No. 3122Eg is the lower left stamp in the bottom pane of the booklet.

LOVE

Swans

A2415 A2416

Designed by Marvin Mattelson.
Printed by Banknote Corp. of America.

LITHOGRAPHED

Serpentine Die Cut 11.8x11.6 on 2, 3 or 4 Sides

1997, Feb. 4 **Tagged**

Self-Adhesive

3123	A2415 32c **multicolored**	.65	.25
a.	Booklet pane of 20 + label	13.00	
b.	Die cutting omitted, pair	*100.00*	
c.	As "a," die cutting omitted	*675.00*	
d.	As "a," black omitted	—	

Serpentine Die Cut 11.6x11.8 on 2, 3 or 4 Sides

3124	A2416 55c **multicolored**	1.10	.25
a.	Booklet pane of 20 + label	22.00	

HELPING CHILDREN LEARN

A2417

Designed by Chris Van Allsburg.
Printed by Avery-Dennison.

PHOTOGRAVURE

Sheets of 160 in eight panes of 20

Serpentine Die Cut 11.6x11.7

1997, Feb. 18 **Tagged**

Self-Adhesive

3125	A2417 32c **multicolored**	.65	.25
	P# block of 4, 4#+V	2.60	
	Pane of 20	13.00	

The die cut perforations of #3125 are fragile and separate easily.

MERIAN BOTANICAL PRINTS

Citron, Moth, Larvae, Pupa, Beetle
A2418

Flowering Pineapple, Cockroaches
A2419

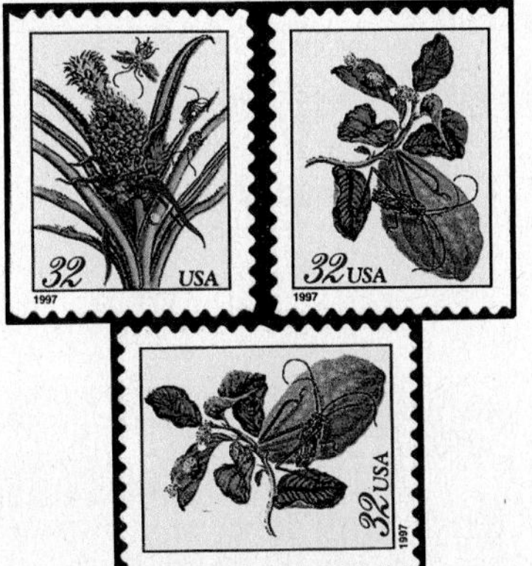

No. 3128 (r), No. 3129 (l), No. 3128a below

Designed by Phil Jordan based on works by Maria Sibylla Merian (1647-1717).
Printed by Stamp Venturers.

PHOTOGRAVURE

Serpentine Die Cut 10.9x10.2 on 2, 3 or 4 Sides

1997, Mar. 3 **Tagged**

Self-Adhesive

3126	A2418 32c **multicolored**	.65	.25
3127	A2419 32c **multicolored**	.65	.25
a.	Booklet pane, 10 ea #3126-3127 + label	13.00	
b.	Pair, #3126-3127	1.30	
c.	Vert. pair, die cutting omitted between	*350.00*	

Size: 18.5x24mm

Serpentine Die Cut 11.2x10.8 on 2 or 3 Sides

3128	A2418 32c **multicolored**	1.00	.25
a.	See footnote	2.50	.25
b.	Booklet pane, 2 ea #3128-3129, 1 #3128a	6.50	
3129	A2419 32c **multicolored**	1.00	.25
a.	See footnote	4.50	.35
b.	Booklet pane, 2 ea #3128-3129, 1 #3129a	8.50	
c.	Pair, #3128-3129	2.00	

Nos. 3128a-3129a are placed sideways on the pane and are serpentine die cut 11.2 on top and bottom, 10.8 on left side. One of the two No. 3128a per pane has a straight edge at left. The right side is 11.2 broken by a sloping die cut where the stamp meets the vertical die cutting of the two stamps above it. See illustration above.

PACIFIC 97

Sailing Ship — A2420

Stagecoach — A2421

Designed by Richard Sheaff.
Printed by Banknote Corporation of America.

ENGRAVED

Sheets of 96 in six panes of 16

1997, Mar. 13 **Tagged** ***Perf. 11.2***

3130	A2420 32c **blue**	.65	.30
3131	A2421 32c **red**	.65	.30
a.	Pair, #3130-3131	1.30	.75
	P# block of 4, 1#+B	2.60	—
	Pane of 16	10.50	7.50

Uncut press sheets of Nos. 3130-3131 were made available for sale. Values: cross-gutter block of 16 (8 #3131a), $30; pairs with gutters between, $7.50 each. See note after No. 2868.

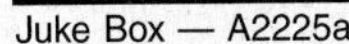

Juke Box — A2225a

Flag Over Porch — A2225b

Designed by Bill Nelson (#3132), Dave LaFleur (#3133).
Printed by Stamp Venturers.

PHOTOGRAVURE

COIL STAMPS

1997, Mar. 14 **Untagged** ***Imperf.***

Self-Adhesive

3132	A2225a (25c) **bright orange red, bright yellow green & multi**	1.50	.50
	Pair	3.00	
	P# strip of 5, #M11111	7.50	
	P#, single, #M11111		5.00

Tagged

Serpentine Die Cut 9.9 Vert.

3133	A2225b 32c **dark blue, tan, brown, red & light blue**	1.75	.25
	Pair	3.50	
	P# strip of 5, #M11111	9.00	
	P#, single, #M11111		4.00

Nos. 3132-3133 were issued without backing paper. No. 3132 has simulated perforations ending in black bars at the top and bottom edges of the stamp. Sky on No. 3133 shows color gradation at LR not on Nos. 2915A or 2915D, and it has blue "1996" at left bottom.

See Nos. 2897, 2913-2916, 2920-2921.

LITERARY ARTS SERIES

Thornton Wilder (1897-1975)
A2422

Designed by Phil Jordan.
Printed by Ashton-Potter (USA) Ltd.

LITHOGRAPHED

Sheets of 180 in nine panes of 20

1997, Apr. 17 **Tagged** ***Perf. 11.1***

3134	A2422 32c **multicolored**	.65	.25
	P# block of 4, 4#+P	2.60	—
	Pane of 20	13.00	—

RAOUL WALLENBERG (1912-47)

Wallenberg and Jewish Refugees
A2423

Designed by Howard Paine.
Printed by Sterling Sommer for Ashton-Potter (USA) Ltd.

LITHOGRAPHED

Sheets of 180 in nine panes of 20

1997, Apr. 24 **Tagged** ***Perf. 11.1***

3135	A2423 32c **multicolored**	.65	.25
	P# block of 4, 4#+P	2.60	—
	Pane of 20	13.00	—

DINOSAURS

A2424

Illustration reduced.
Designed by James Gurney.
Printed by Sterling Sommer for Ashton-Potter (USA) Ltd.

Designs: a, Ceratosaurus. b, Camptosaurus. c, Camarasaurus. d, Brachiosaurus. e, Goniopholis. f, Stegosaurus. g, Allosaurus. h, Opisthias. i, Edmontonia. j, Einiosaurus. k, Daspletosaurus. l, Palaeosaniwa. m, Corythosaurus. n, Ornithomimus. o, Parasaurolophus.

LITHOGRAPHED

1997, May 1 **Tagged** ***Perf. 11x11.1***

3136	A2424 Sheet of 15	10.00	8.00
a.-o.	32c any single	.65	.50
p.	As No. 3136, bottom 7 stamps imperf.	*2,500.*	
q.	As No. 3136, top 8 stamps imperf	*2,500.*	
r.	As No. 3136, all colors and tagging missing (EP)	—	

No. 3136r resulted from double sheeting in the sheet-fed press. It is properly gummed and perforated.

No. 3136 completely imperf. is believed to be printer's waste.

BUGS BUNNY

A2425

Designed by Warner Bros.
Printed by Avery Dennison.

PHOTOGRAVURE

1997, May 22 Tagged *Serpentine Die Cut 11*
Self-Adhesive

3137	Pane of 10 #3137a	6.75	
a.	A2425 32c single	.65	.25
b.	Pane of 9 #3137a	6.00	
c.	Pane of 1 #3137a	.65	

Die cutting on No. 3137 does not extend through the backing paper.

Nos. 3137b-3137c and 3138b-3138c are separated by a vertical line of microperforations that are absent on the uncut sheet of 60.

Uncut press sheets of No. 3137 were made available for sale. Values: top sheet of 60, $250; bottom sheet of 60 with P#, $450; cross-gutter block of 7, $200; pairs with gutters between, $30 each. See note after No. 2868.

3138	Pane of 10, #3138c, 9 #3138a	130.00	
a.	A2425 32c single	2.75	
b.	Pane of 9 #3138a	20.00	
c.	Pane of 1, no die cutting	100.00	

Die cutting on No. 3138b extends through the backing paper.

An untagged promotional piece similar to No. 3137c exists on the same backing paper as the pane, with the same design image, but without Bugs' signature and the single stamp. Replacing the stamp is an enlarged "32 / USA" in the same style as used on the stamp. This promotional piece was not valid for postage.

PACIFIC 97

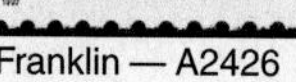

Franklin — A2426

Washington — A2427

Designed by Richard Sheaff. Selvage on Nos. 3139-3140 is lithographed.

LITHOGRAPHED & ENGRAVED

1997 Tagged *Perf. 10.5x10.4*

3139	Pane of 12, *May 29*	12.00	9.00
a.	A2426 50c single	1.00	.50
3140	Pane of 12, *May 30*	14.50	11.00
a.	A2427 60c single	1.20	.60

Nos. 3139-3140 were sold through June 8.

MARSHALL PLAN, 50TH ANNIV.

Gen. George C. Marshall, Map of Europe A2428

Designed by Richard Sheaff.
Printed by Stevens Security Press for Ashton-Potter (USA) Ltd.

LITHOGRAPHED & ENGRAVED
Sheets of 120 in six panes of 20

1997, June 4 Tagged *Perf. 11.1*

3141	A2428 32c **multicolored**	.65	.25
	P# block of 4, 5#+P	2.60	—
	Pane of 20	13.00	—

CLASSIC AMERICAN AIRCRAFT

A2429

Illustration reduced.
Designed by Phil Jordan.
Printed by Stamp Venturers.

Designs: a, Mustang. b, Model B. c, Cub. d, Vega. e, Alpha. f, B-10. g, Corsair. h, Stratojet. i, GeeBee. j, Staggerwing. k, Flying Fortress. l, Stearman. m, Constellation. n, Lightning. o, Peashooter. p, Tri-Motor. q, DC-3. r, 314 Clipper. s, Jenny. t, Wildcat.

PHOTOGRAVURE
Sheets of 120 in six panes of 20

1997, July 19 Tagged *Perf. 10.1*

3142	A2429 Pane of 20	13.00	10.00
a.-t.	32c any single	.65	.50

Inscriptions on back of each stamp describe the airplane.

Uncut press sheets of No. 3142 were made available for sale. Values: cross-gutter block of 20, $27.50; pairs with gutters between, $2.75 each. See note after No. 2868.

FOOTBALL COACHES

Bear Bryant A2430

Pop Warner A2431

Vince Lombardi A2432

George Halas A2433

Designed by Carl Herrman.
Printed by Sterling Sommer for Ashton-Potter (USA) Ltd.

LITHOGRAPHED
Sheets of 120 in six panes of 20

1997 Tagged *Perf. 11.2*

3143	A2430 32c **multicolored,** *July 25*	.65	.25
3144	A2431 32c **multicolored,** *July 25*	.65	.25
3145	A2432 32c **multicolored,** *July 25*	.65	.25
3146	A2433 32c **multicolored,** *July 25*	.65	.25
a.	Block or strip of 4, #3143-3146	2.60	1.50
	P# block of 4, 5#+P	2.60	1.75
	P# block of 8, 2 sets of P# + top label	5.25	—
	Pane of 20	13.00	

A2430a

A2431a

A2432a

A2433a

With Red Bar Above Coach's Name
Perf. 11

3147	A2432a 32c **multicolored,** *Aug. 5*	.65	.45
	P# block of 4, 4#+P	3.00	—
	Pane of 20	14.50	—
3148	A2430a 32c **multicolored,** *Aug. 7*	.65	.45
	P# block of 4, 4#+P	3.00	—
	Pane of 20	14.50	—
3149	A2431a 32c **multicolored,** *Aug. 8*	.65	.45
	P# block of 4, 4#+P	3.25	—
	Pane of 20	15.50	—
3150	A2433a 32c **multicolored,** *Aug. 16*	.65	.45
	P# block of 4, 4#+P	3.25	—
	Pane of 20	15.50	—

AMERICAN DOLLS

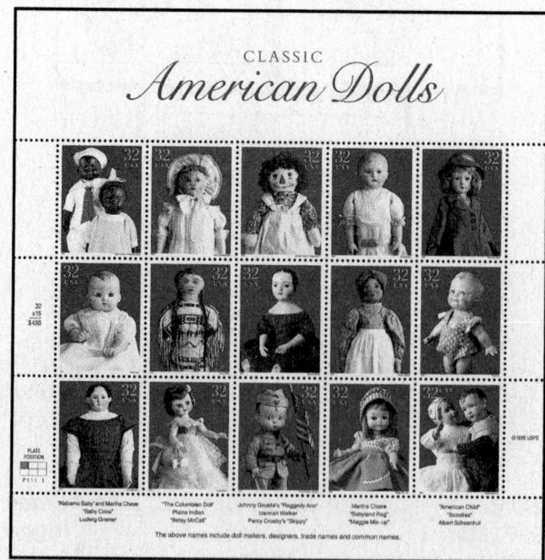

A2434

Illustration reduced.
Designed by Derry Noyes.
Printed by Sterling Sommer for Ashton-Potter (USA) Ltd.

Designs: a, "Alabama Baby," and doll by Martha Chase. b, "Columbian Doll." c, Johnny Gruelle's "Raggedy Ann." d, Doll by Martha Chase. e, "American Child." f, "Baby Coos." g, Plains Indian. h, Doll by Izannah Walker. i, "Babyland Rag." j, "Scootles." k, Doll by Ludwig Greiner. l, "Betsy McCall." m, Percy Crosby's "Skippy." n, "Maggie Mix-up." o, Dolls by Albert Schoenhut.

LITHOGRAPHED
Sheets of 90 in six panes of 15

1997, July 28	**Tagged**	***Perf. 10.9x11.1***	
3151	A2434 Pane of 15	13.50	—
a.-o.	32c any single	.90	.60

For booklet see No. BK266.

LEGENDS OF HOLLYWOOD
Humphrey Bogart (1899-1957).

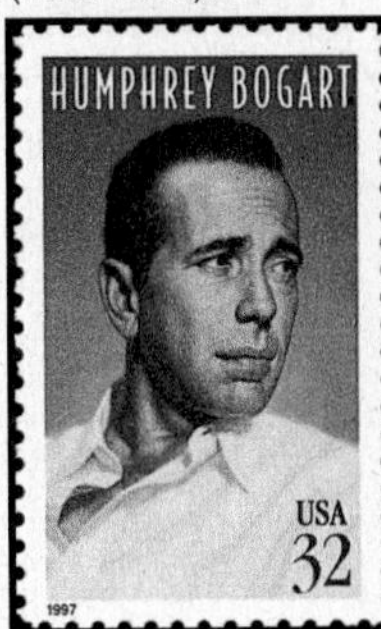

A2435

Designed by Carl Herrman.
Printed by Stamp Venturers.

PHOTOGRAVURE
Sheets of 120 in six panes of 20

1997, July 31	**Tagged**	***Perf. 11.1***	
3152 A2435 32c **multicolored**		.85	.25
P# block of 4, 5#+S		3.50	—
Pane of 20		17.50	—

Perforations in corner of each stamp are star-shaped.
Uncut press sheets of No. 3152 were made available for sale. Values: cross-gutter block of 8, $19; pairs with gutters between, $3 each. See note after No. 2868.
For booklet see No. BK267.

"THE STARS AND STRIPES FOREVER!"

A2436

Designed by Richard Sheaff.

Sheets of 300 in six panes of 50
PHOTOGRAVURE

1997, Aug. 21	**Tagged**	***Perf. 11.1***	
3153 A2436 32c **multicolored**		.65	.25
P# block of 4, 4#		3.00	—
Pane of 50		32.00	—

For booklet see No. BK268.

AMERICAN MUSIC SERIES
Opera Singers

Lily Pons — A2437

Richard Tucker A2438

Lawrence Tibbett A2439

Rosa Ponselle A2440

Designed by Howard Paine.
Printed by Ashton-Potter (USA) Ltd.

LITHOGRAPHED
Sheets of 120 in six panes of 20

1997, Sept. 10	**Tagged**	***Perf. 11***	
3154 A2437 32c **multicolored**		.75	.25
3155 A2438 32c **multicolored**		.75	.25
3156 A2439 32c **multicolored**		.75	.25
3157 A2440 32c **multicolored**		.75	.25
a. Block or strip of 4, #3154-3157		3.00	2.00
P# block of 4, 5#+P		3.00	—
P# block of 8, 2 sets of P# + top label		6.00	—
Pane of 20		15.00	—

AMERICAN MUSIC SERIES
Classical Composers & Conductors

Leopold Stokowski A2441

Arthur Fiedler A2442

George Szell — A2443

Eugene Ormandy A2444

Samuel Barber A2445

Ferde Grofé — A2446

Charles Ives — A2447

Louis Moreau Gottschalk A2448

Designed by Howard Paine.
Printed by Ashton-Potter (USA) Ltd.

LITHOGRAPHED
Sheets of 120 in six panes of 20

1997, Sept. 12	**Tagged**	***Perf. 11***	
3158 A2441 32c **multicolored**		1.50	.25
3159 A2442 32c **multicolored**		1.50	.25
3160 A2443 32c **multicolored**		1.50	.25
3161 A2444 32c **multicolored**		1.50	.25
3162 A2445 32c **multicolored**		1.50	.25
3163 A2446 32c **multicolored**		1.50	.25
3164 A2447 32c **multicolored**		1.50	.25
3165 A2448 32c **multicolored**		1.50	.25
a. Block of 8, #3158-3165		12.00	4.00
P# block of 8, 2 sets of 5P#+P + top label		14.00	—
Pane of 20		32.50	

PADRE FÉLIX VARELA (1788-1853)

A2449

Designed by Carl Herrman.

Printed by Sterling Sommer for Ashton-Potter (USA) Ltd.

LITHOGRAPHED

Sheets of 120 in six panes of 20

1997, Sept. 15 **Tagged** ***Perf. 11.2***

3166 A2449 32c **purple** .65 .25
P# block of 4, 1#+P 2.60 —
Pane of 20 13.00 —

DEPARTMENT OF THE AIR FORCE, 50TH ANNIV.

Thunderbirds Aerial Demonstration Squadron A2450

Designed by Phil Jordan.
Printed by Sterling Sommer for Ashton-Potter (USA) Ltd.

LITHOGRAPHED

Sheets of 180 in nine panes of 20

1997, Sept. 18 **Tagged** ***Perf. 11.2x11.1***

3167 A2450 32c **multicolored** .65 .25
P# block of 4, 4#+P 2.60 —
Pane of 20 13.00 —

A hidden 3-D image (USAF repeated) can be seen on the stamp when it is viewed with a special "Stamp Decoder" lens sold by the USPS.

CLASSIC MOVIE MONSTERS

Lon Chaney as The Phantom of the Opera — A2451

Bela Lugosi as Dracula — A2452

Boris Karloff as Frankenstein's Monster — A2453

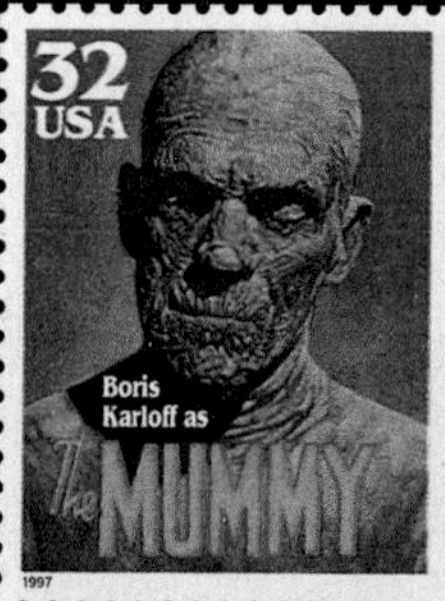

Boris Karloff as The Mummy — A2454

Lon Chaney, Jr. as The Wolf Man — A2455

Designed by Derry Noyes.
Printed by Stamp Venturers.

PHOTOGRAVURE

Sheets of 180 in nine panes of 20

1997, Sept. 30 **Tagged** ***Perf. 10.2***

3168 A2451 32c **multicolored** .75 .25
3169 A2452 32c **multicolored** .75 .25
3170 A2453 32c **multicolored** .75 .25
3171 A2454 32c **multicolored** .75 .25
3172 A2455 32c **multicolored** .75 .25
a. Strip of 5, #3168-3172 3.75 2.25
P# block of 10, 5#+S 7.50 —
Pane of 20 15.00 —

Plate blocks may contain top label.

For booklet see No. BK269.

Hidden 3-D images can be seen on these stamps when they are viewed with a special "Stamp Decoder" lens sold by the USPS. No. 3168, two masquerade masks; No. 3169, three flying bats; No. 3170, three electricity bolts; No. 3171, two Egyptian deities; No. 3172, two howling wolves.

Uncut press sheets of Nos. 3168-3172 were made available for sale. Values: cross-gutter block of 8, $20; pairs with gutters between, $2.75 each. See note after No. 2868.

FIRST SUPERSONIC FLIGHT, 50TH ANNIV.

A2456

Designed by Phil Jordan.
Printed by Banknote Corporation of America.

LITHOGRAPHED

Sheets of 180 in nine panes of 20

1997, Oct. 14 **Tagged** ***Serpentine Die Cut 11.4***

Self-Adhesive

3173 A2456 32c **multicolored** .65 .25
P# block of 4, 4#+B 2.60
Pane of 20 13.00

WOMEN IN MILITARY SERVICE

A2457

Designed by Derry Noyes.
Printed by Banknote Corporation of America.

LITHOGRAPHED

Sheets of 120 in six panes of 20

1997, Oct. 18 **Tagged** ***Perf. 11.1***

3174 A2457 32c **multicolored** .65 .25
P# block of 4, 6#+B 2.60 —
Pane of 20 13.00

KWANZAA

A2458

Designed by Synthia Saint James. Printed by Avery Dennison.

PHOTOGRAVURE

Sheets of 250 in five panes of 50

1997, Oct. 22 **Tagged** ***Serpentine Die Cut 11***

Self-Adhesive

3175 A2458 32c **multicolored** .65 .25
P# block of 4, 4#+V 3.00
Pane of 50 32.00 —

See Nos. 3368, 3548, 3673.

Uncut press sheets of No. 3175 were made available for sale. Values: horiz. pairs with vert. gutters between, $11 each. See note after No. 2868.

CHRISTMAS

Madonna and Child, by Sano di Pietro — A2459

Holly — A2460

Designed by Richard D. Sheaff (#3176), Howard Paine (#3177).

Printed by Bureau of Engraving and Printing (#3176), Banknote Corporation of America (#3177).

LITHOGRAPHED

Serpentine Die Cut 9.9 on 2, 3 or 4 Sides

1997 **Tagged**

Booklet Stamps

Self-Adhesive

3176 A2459 32c **multicolored,** *Oct. 27* .65 .25
a. Booklet pane of 20 + label 13.00

Serpentine Die Cut 11.2x11.6 on 2, 3 or 4 Sides

3177 A2460 32c **multicolored,** *Oct. 30* .65 .25
a. Booklet pane of 20 + label 13.00
b. Booklet pane of 4 2.60
c. Booklet pane of 5 + label 3.25
d. Booklet pane of 6 3.90

MARS PATHFINDER

Souvenir Sheet

Mars Rover Sojourner — A2461

Illustration reduced.

Designed by Terry McCaffrey. Printed by Stamp Venturers.

PHOTOGRAVURE

1997, Dec. 10 **Tagged** ***Perf. 11x11.1***

3178 A2461 $3 **multicolored** 6.00 4.00
a. $3, single stamp 5.50 3.00
b. Single souvenir sheet from sheet of 18 7.50 —
c. As No. 3178, imperf. —

The perforations at the bottom of the stamp contain the letters "USA." Vertical rouletting extends from the vertical perforations of the stamp to the bottom of the souvenir sheet.

Uncut press sheets of Nos. 3178 were made available for sale. Values: pane of 18 with perforations on one or two sides, $145; vert. pair with horiz. gutter between, $17.50. See note after No. 2868.

A hidden 3-D image (USPS and MARS PATHFINDER JULY 4, 1997 repeated) can be seen when viewed with a special "Stamp Decoder" lens sold by the USPS.

CHINESE NEW YEAR

Year of the Tiger — A2462

Designed by Clarence Lee. Printed by Stamp Venturers.

PHOTOGRAVURE

Sheets of 180 in nine panes of 20

1998, Jan. 5 **Tagged** ***Perf. 11.2***

3179 A2462 32c **multicolored**	.80	.25
P# block of 4, 4#+S	3.75	—
Pane of 20	18.00	

See Nos. 3895c, 3997c.

ALPINE SKIING

A2463

Designed by Michael Schwab.

Printed by Banknote Corporation of America.

LITHOGRAPHED

Sheets of 180 in nine panes of 20

1998, Jan. 22 **Tagged** ***Perf. 11.2***

3180 A2463 32c **multicolored**	.75	.25
P# block of 4, 6#+B	4.00	—
Pane of 20	19.00	

BLACK HERITAGE SERIES

Madam C.J. Walker (1867-1919), Entrepreneur.

A2464

Designed by Richard Sheaff. Printed by Banknote Corp. of America.

LITHOGRAPHED

Sheets of 180 in nine panes of 20

Serpentine Die Cut 11.6x11.3

1998, Jan. 28 **Tagged**

Self-Adhesive

3181 A2464 32c **sepia & black**	.70	.25
P# block of 4, 3#+B	3.00	
Pane of 20	15.00	

CELEBRATE THE CENTURY

1900s — A2465

No. 3182: a, Model T Ford. b, Theodore Roosevelt. c, Motion picture "The Great Train Robbery," 1903. d, Crayola Crayons introduced, 1903. e, St. Louis World's Fair, 1904. f, Design used on Hunt's Remedy stamp (#RS56), Pure Food & Drug Act, 1906. g, Wright Brothers first flight, Kitty Hawk, 1903. h, Boxing match shown in painting "Stag at Sharkey's," by George Bellows of the Ash Can School. i, Immigrants arrive. j, John Muir, preservationist. k, "Teddy" Bear created. l, W.E.B. Du Bois, social activist. m, Gibson Girl. n, First baseball World Series, 1903. o, Robie House, Chicago, designed by Frank Lloyd Wright.

1910s — A2466

No. 3183: a, Charlie Chaplin as the Little Tramp. b, Federal Reserve System created, 1913. c, George Washington Carver. d, Avant-garde art introduced at Armory Show, 1913. e, First transcontinental telephone line, 1914. f, Panama Canal opens, 1914. g, Jim Thorpe wins decathlon at Stockholm Olympics, 1912. h, Grand Canyon National Park, 1919. i, U.S. enters World War I. j, Boy Scouts started in 1910, Girl Scouts formed in 1912. k, Woodrow Wilson. l, First crossword puzzle published, 1913. m, Jack Dempsey wins heavyweight title, 1919. n, Construction toys. o, Child labor reform.

1920s — A2467

No. 3184: a, Babe Ruth. b, The Gatsby style. c, Prohibition enforced. d, Electric toy trains. e, 19th Amendment (woman voting). f, Emily Post's Etiquette. g, Margaret Mead, anthropologist. h, Flappers do the Charleston. i, Radio entertains America. j, Art Deco style (Chrysler Building). k, Jazz flourishes. l, Four Horsemen of Notre Dame. m, Lindbergh flies the Atlantic. n, American realism (Automat, by Edward Hopper). o, Stock Market crash, 1929.

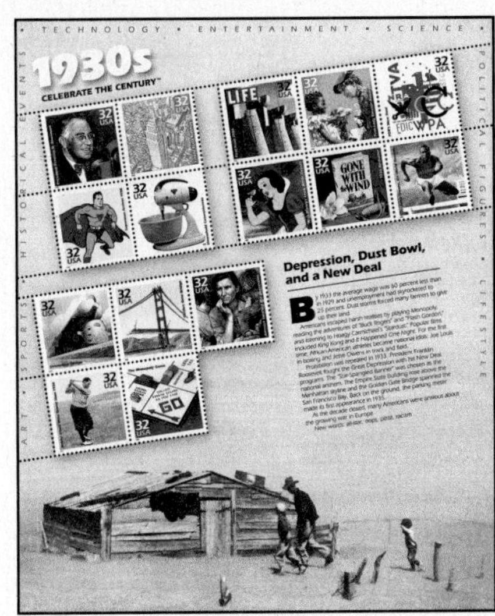

1930s — A2468

No. 3185: a, Franklin D. Roosevelt. b, The Empire State Building. c, 1st Issue of Life Magazine, 1936. d, Eleanor Roosevelt. e, FDR's New Deal. f, Superman arrives, 1938. g, Household conveniences. h, "Snow White and the Seven Dwarfs," 1937. i, "Gone with the Wind," 1936. j, Jesse Owens. k, Streamline design. l, Golden Gate Bridge. m, America survives the Depression. n, Bobby Jones wins golf Grand Slam, 1938. o, The Monopoly Game.

1940s — A2469

No. 3186: a, World War II. b, Antibiotics save lives. c, Jackie Robinson. d, Harry S Truman. e, Women support war effort. f, TV entertains America. g, Jitterbug sweeps nation. h, Jackson Pollock, Abstract Expressionism. i, GI Bill, 1944. j, Big Band Sound. k, Intl. style of architecture (UN Headquarters). l, Post-war baby boom. m, Slinky, 1945. n, "A Streecar Named Desire," 1947. o, Orson Welles' "Citizen Kane."

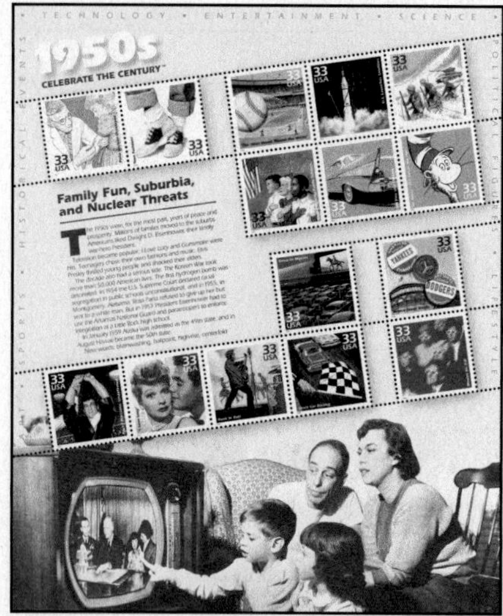

1950s — A2470

No. 3187: a, Polio vaccine developed. b, Teen fashions. c, The "Shot Heard 'Round the World." d, US launches satellites. e, Korean War. f, Desegregating public schools. g, Tail fins, chrome. h, Dr. Seuss' "The Cat in the Hat." i, Drive-in movies. j, World Series rivals. k, Rocky Marciano, undefeated boxer. l, "I Love Lucy." m, Rock 'n Roll. n, Stock car racing. o, Movies go 3-D.

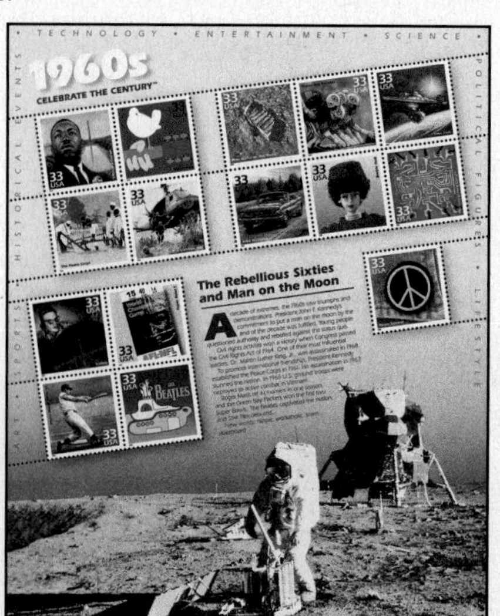

1960s — A2471

No. 3188: a, Martin Luther King, Jr., "I Have a Dream." b, Woodstock. c, Man walks on the moon. d, Green Bay Packers. e, Star Trek. f, The Peace Corps. g, Viet Nam War. h, Ford Mustang. i, Barbie Doll. j, Integrated circuit. k, Lasers. l, Super Bowl I. m, Peace symbol. n, Roger Maris, 61 in '61. o, The Beatles "Yellow Submarine."

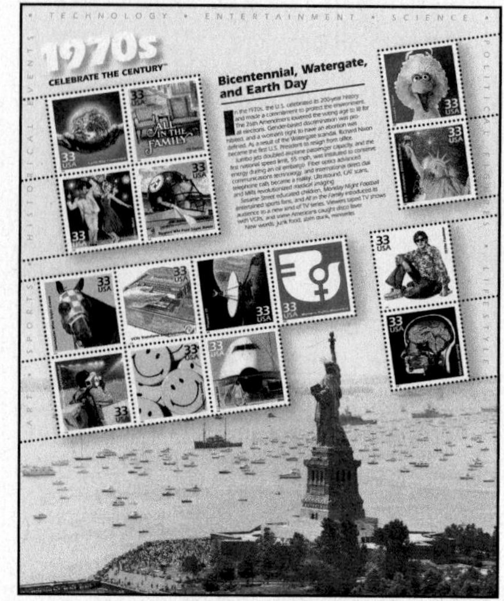

1970s — A2472

No. 3189: a, Earth Day celebrated. b, "All in the Family" television series. c, "Sesame Street" television series character, Big Bird. d, Disco music. e, Pittsburgh Steelers win four Super Bowls. f, US Celebrates 200th birthday. g, Secretariat wins Triple Crown. h, VCRs transform entertainment. i, Pioneer 10. j, Women's rights movement. k, 1970s fashions. l, "Monday Night Football." m, Smiley face buttons. n, Jumbo jets. o, Medical imaging.

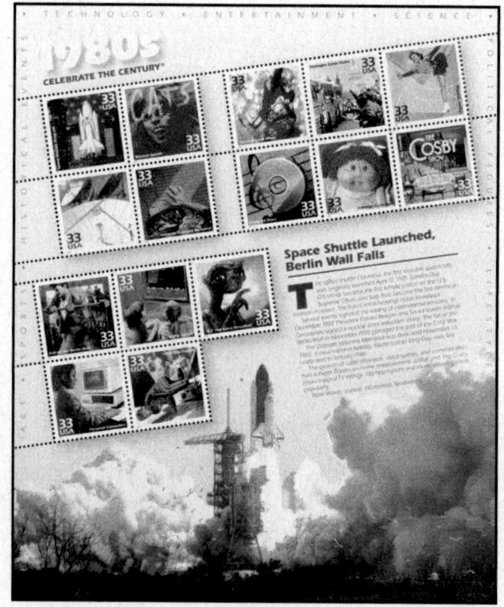

1980s — A2473

No. 3190: a, Space shuttle program. b, "Cats" Broadway show. c, San Francisco 49ers. d, Hostages in Iran come home. e, Figure skating. f, Cable TV. g, Vietnam Veterans Memorial. h, Compact discs. i, Cabbage Patch Kids. j, "The Cosby Show" television series. k, Fall of the Berlin Wall. l, Video games. m, "E. T. The Extra-Terrestrial" movie. n, Personal computers. o, Hip-hop culture.

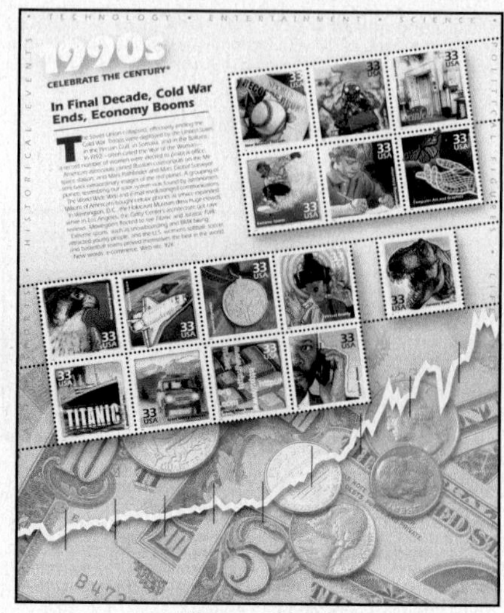

1990s — A2474

No. 3191: a, New baseball records. b, Gulf War. c, "Seinfeld" television series. d, Extreme sports. e, Improving education. f, Computer art and graphics. g, Recovering species. h, Return to space. i, Special Olympics. j, Virtual reality. k, Movie "Jurassic Park." l, Movie "Titanic." m, Sport utility vehicles. n, World Wide Web. o, Cellular phones.

All illustrations reduced.

Designed by Richard Waldrep (#3182), Dennis Lyall (#3183), Carl Herrman (#3184, 3188, 3190), Howard Paine (#3185-3187, 3189, 3191).

Printed by Ashton-Potter (USA) Ltd.

LITHOGRAPHED, ENGRAVED (#3182m, 3183f, 3184m, 3185b, 3186k, 3187a, 3188c, 3189h)

1998-2000		**Tagged**	***Perf. 11½***	
3182	A2465	Pane of 15, *Feb. 3, 1998*	10.00	8.50
a.-o.		32c any single	.75	.65
p.		Engr. red (No. 3182m, Gibson girl) omitted, in pane of 15	*3,000.*	
3183	A2466	Pane of 15, *Feb. 3, 1998*	10.00	8.50
a.-o.		32c any single	.75	.65
p.		Nos. 3183g, 3183 l-3183o imperf, in pane of 15	*7,000.*	
3184	A2467	Pane of 15, *May 28, 1998*	12.50	8.50
a.-o.		32c any single	.80	.65
3185	A2468	Pane of 15, *Sept. 10, 1998*	12.50	8.50
a.-o.		32c any single	.80	.65
3186	A2469	Pane of 15, *Feb. 18, 1999*	13.00	8.50
a.-o.		33c any single	.85	.65
p.		Tagging omitted on b-j and m-o	—	
q.		Tagging omitted on a-f, j-k, n-o	—	
3187	A2470	Pane of 15, *May 26, 1999*	13.00	8.50
a.-o.		33c any single	.85	.65
p.		Tagging omitted	—	
q.		Nos. "a" and "k" tagged, all others tagging omitted	—	
3188	A2471	Pane of 15, *Sept. 17, 1999*	13.00	8.50
a.-o.		33c any single	.85	.65
3189	A2472	Pane of 15, *Nov. 18, 1999*	13.00	8.50
a.-o.		33c any single	.85	.65
3190	A2473	Pane of 15, *Jan. 12, 2000*	13.00	8.50
a.-o.		33c any single	.85	.65
3191	A2474	Pane of 15, *May 2, 2000*	13.00	8.50
a.-o.		33c any single	.85	.65
		Nos. 3182-3191 (10)	123.00	85.00

Uncut press sheets of Nos. 3182-3191 were made available for sale. See note after No. 2868.

"REMEMBER THE MAINE"

A2475

Designed by Richard Sheaff.

LITHOGRAPHED & ENGRAVED
Sheets of 120 in six panes of 20

1998, Feb. 15		**Tagged**	***Perf. 11.2x11***	
3192	A2475	32c **red & black**	.70	.25
		P# block of 4, 2#	3.00	—
		Pane of 20	15.00	

FLOWERING TREES

Southern Magnolia — A2476

Blue Paloverde — A2477

Yellow Poplar — A2478

Prairie Crab Apple — A2479

Pacific Dogwood — A2480

Designed by Howard Paine.
Printed by Banknote Corporation of America.

LITHOGRAPHED
Sheets of 120 in six panes of 20

1998, Mar. 19 **Tagged** ***Die Cut Perf 11.3***

Self-Adhesive

3193	A2476 32c **multicolored**	2.00	.40
3194	A2477 32c **multicolored**	2.00	.40
3195	A2478 32c **multicolored**	2.00	.40
3196	A2479 32c **multicolored**	2.00	.40
3197	A2480 32c **multicolored**	2.00	.40
a.	Strip of 5, #3193-3197	10.00	
	P# block of 10, 2 sets of B+6#	20.00	
	Pane of 20	40.00	
b.	As "a," die cutting omitted	—	

ALEXANDER CALDER (1898-1976), SCULPTOR

Black Cascade, 13 Verticals, 1959 — A2481

Untitled, 1965 — A2482

Rearing Stallion, 1928 — A2483

Portrait of a Young Man, c. 1945 — A2484

Un Effet du Japonais, 1945 — A2485

Designed by Derry Noyes. Printed by Stamp Venturers.

PHOTOGRAVURE
Sheets of 120 in six panes of 20

1998, Mar. 25 **Tagged** ***Perf. 10.2***

3198	A2481 32c **multicolored**	.65	.25
3199	A2482 32c **multicolored**	.65	.25
3200	A2483 32c **multicolored**	.65	.25
3201	A2484 32c **multicolored**	.65	.25
3202	A2485 32c **multicolored**	.65	.25
a.	Strip of 5, #3198-3202	3.25	2.25
	P# block of 10, 2 sets of S+6#	7.00	—
	Pane of 20	14.00	—

Uncut press sheets of Nos. 3198-3202 were made available for sale. Values: cross-gutter block of 20, $37.50; pairs with gutters between, $4 each. See note after No. 2868.

CINCO DE MAYO

A2486

Designed by Carl Herrman.
Printed by Stamp Venturers.

PHOTOGRAVURE
Sheets of 180 in nine panes of 20
Serpentine Die Cut 11.7x10.9

1998, Apr. 16 **Tagged**

Self-Adhesive

3203	A2486 32c **multicolored**	.65	.25
	P# block of 4, 5#+S	2.60	
	Pane of 20	13.00	

See Mexico No. 2066. For 33c version, see No. 3309.

Uncut press sheets of No. 3203 were made available for sale. Values: cross-gutter block of 4, $15; pairs with gutters between, $2.50 each. See note after No. 2868.

SYLVESTER & TWEETY

A2487

Designed by Brenda Guttman.
Printed by Avery Dennison.

PHOTOGRAVURE

1998, Apr. 27 **Tagged** ***Serpentine Die Cut 11.1***

Self-Adhesive

3204	Pane of 10 #3204a	6.75	
a.	A2487 32c single	.65	.25
b.	Pane of 9 #3204a	6.00	
c.	Pane of 1 #3204a	.65	

Die cutting on No. 3204b does not extend through the backing paper. Pane with plate number comes from bottom uncut sheet of 60.

Uncut press sheets of No. 3204 were made available for sale. Values: top sheet of 60, $70; bottom sheet of 60 with P#, $110; cross-gutter block of 7, $45; pairs with gutters between, $10 each. See note after No. 2868.

3205	Pane of 10, #3205c, 9 #3205a	11.00	
a.	A2487 32c single	.90	
b.	Pane of 9 #3205a	*7.00*	
c.	Pane of 1, no die cutting	*3.00*	

Die cutting on #3205a extends through the backing paper.

Nos. 3204b-3204c and 3205b-3205c are separated by a vertical line of microperforations, which is absent on the uncut sheets of 60.

WISCONSIN STATEHOOD

A2488

Designed by Phil Jordan.
Printed by Sennett Security Products.

PHOTOGRAVURE
Sheets of 120 in six panes of 20
Serpentine Die Cut 10.8x10.9

1998, May 29 **Tagged**

Self-Adhesive

3206 A2488 32c **multicolored**	.65	.30
P# block of 4, 4#+S	3.00	
Pane of 20	15.00	

A hidden 3-D image (a badger) can be seen on this stamp when it is viewed with a special "Stamp Decoder" lens sold by the USPS.

Wetlands — A2489

A2489a

Diner — A2490

A2490a

Designer by Phil Jordan (#3207-3207A), Carl Herrman (#3208, 3208A).
Printed by Sennett Security Products (#3207, 3208), Bureau of Engraving and Printing (#3207A, 3208A).

PHOTOGRAVURE
COIL STAMPS

1998 **Untagged** ***Perf. 10 Vert.***

3207 A2489 (5c) **multicolored,** *June 5*	.30	.25
Pair	.30	.25
P# strip of 5, #S1111	1.25	
P#, single, #S1111	—	.75

Serpentine Die Cut 9.8 Vert.

Self-adhesive

Untagged

3207A A2489a (5c) **multicolored,** small date, *Dec.14*	.30	.25
Pair	.50	
P# strip of 5, #1111, 2222, 3333, 4444	1.40	
P# single, same #	—	.80
b. Large date	.30	.25
Pair	.60	
P# strip of 5, #5555, 6666	1.50	
P# single, same #	—	.80

Date on No. 3207A is approximately 1.4mm long, on No. 3207Ab approx. 1.6mm long.

Perf. 10 Vert.

Untagged

3208 A2490 (25c) **multicolored,** *June 5*	.50	.50
Pair	1.00	1.00
P# strip of 5, #S11111	3.50	
P#, single, #S11111	—	2.00

Serpentine Die Cut 9.8 Vert.

Self-Adhesive

Untagged

3208A A2490a (25c) **multicolored,** *Sept. 30*	.50	.50
Pair	1.00	
P# strip of 5, #11111, 22211, 22222, 33333, 44444, 55555	3.50	
P# single, same #	—	2.00

1898 TRANS-MISSISSIPPI STAMPS, CENT.

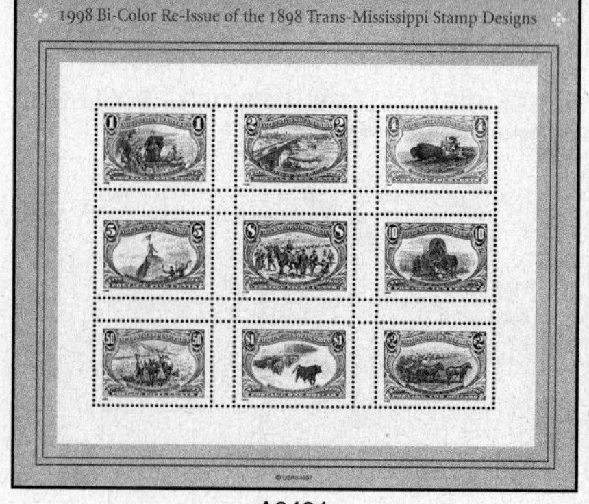

A2491

Illustration reduced.

Designed by Raymond Ostrander Smith (1898), Richard Sheaff (1998).
Printed by Banknote Corporation of America.

LITHOGRAPHED & ENGRAVED
Sheets of 54 in six panes of 9

1998, June 18 **Tagged** ***Perf. 12x12.4***

3209 A2491	Pane of 9	9.50	7.00
a.	A100 1c green & black	.30	.25
b.	A108 2c red brown & black	.30	.25
c.	A102 4c orange & black	.30	.25
d.	A103 5c blue & black	.30	.25
e.	A104 8c dark lilac & black	.30	.25
f.	A105 10c purple & black	.30	.25
g.	A106 50c green & black	1.25	.60
h.	A107 $1 red & black	2.50	1.25
i.	A101 $2 red brown & black	4.25	2.50

Vignettes on Nos. 3209b and 3209i are reversed in comparison to the original issue.

3210 A107	$1 Pane of 9 #3209h	22.50	—

Uncut press sheets of Nos. 3209-3210 were made available for sale. The press sheets have 3 panes of No. 3209 at left and 3 panes of No. 3210 at right. Values: cross-gutter block of 12, $60; pairs with gutters between, $10 each. See note after No. 2868.

BERLIN AIRLIFT, 50th ANNIV.

A2492

Designed by Bill Bond.
Printed by Banknote Corporation of America.

PHOTOGRAVURE
Sheets of 120 in six panes of 20

1998, June 26 **Tagged** ***Perf. 11.2***

3211 A2492 32c **multicolored**	.65	.25
P# block of 4, 4#+B	2.60	—
Pane of 20	13.00	—

AMERICAN MUSIC SERIES
Folk Singers

Huddie "Leadbelly" Ledbetter (1888-1949) A2493

Woody Guthrie (1912-67) A2494

Sonny Terry (1911-86) A2495

Josh White (1908-69) A2496

Designed by Howard Paine.
Printed by American Packaging Corp. for Sennett Security Products.

PHOTOGRAVURE
Sheets of 180 in nine panes of 20

1998, June 26 **Tagged** ***Perf. 10.1x10.2***

3212 A2493 32c **multicolored**	.90	.25
3213 A2494 32c **multicolored**	.90	.25
3214 A2495 32c **multicolored**	.90	.25
3215 A2496 32c **multicolored**	.90	.25
a. Block or strip of 4, #3212-3215	3.60	2.00
P# block of 4, 5#+S	4.25	—
P# block of 8, 2 sets of P# + top label	8.50	—
Pane of 20	21.00	—

AMERICAN MUSIC SERIES
Gospel Singers

Mahalia Jackson (1911-72) A2497

Roberta Martin (1917-69) A2498

Clara Ward (1924-73) A2499

Sister Rosetta Tharpe (1921-73) A2500

Designed by Howard Paine.
Printed by American Packaging Corp. for Sennett Security Products.

PHOTOGRAVURE
Sheets of 120 in six panes of 20

1998, July 15 **Tagged** ***Perf. 10.1x10.3***

3216	A2497 32c **multicolored**		1.00	.25
3217	A2498 32c **multicolored**		1.00	.25
3218	A2499 32c **multicolored**		1.00	.25
3219	A2500 32c **multicolored**		1.00	.25
a.	Block or strip of 4, #3216-3219		4.00	2.00
	P# block of 4, 6#+S		5.00	—
	P# block of 8, 2 sets of P# + top label		10.00	—
	Pane of 20		24.00	—

SPANISH SETTLEMENT OF THE SOUTHWEST

La Mision de San Miguel de San Gabriel, Espanola, NM — A2501

Designed by Richard Sheaff.
Printed by Banknote Corporation of America.

LITHOGRAPHED
Sheets of 180 in nine panes of 20

1998, July 11 **Tagged** ***Perf. 11.2***

3220	A2501 32c **multicolored**	.65	.25
	P# block of 4, 4#+B	2.60	—
	Pane of 20	13.00	—

LITERARY ARTS SERIES

Stephen Vincent Benét (1898-43) A2502

Designed by Carl Herrman.
Printed by Ashton-Potter (USA) Ltd.

LITHOGRAPHED
Sheets of 180 in nine panes of 20

1998, July 22 **Tagged** ***Perf. 11.2***

3221	A2502 32c **multicolored**	.65	.25
	P# block of 4, 4#+P	2.60	—
	Pane of 20	13.00	—

TROPICAL BIRDS

Antillean Euphonia A2503

Green-throated Carib — A2504

Crested Honeycreeper A2505

Cardinal Honeyeater A2506

Designed by Phil Jordan.
Printed by Banknote Corporation of America.

LITHOGRAPHED
Sheets of 180 in nine panes of 20

1998, July 29 **Tagged** ***Perf. 11.2***

3222	A2503 32c **multicolored**	.65	.25
3223	A2504 32c **multicolored**	.65	.25
3224	A2505 32c **multicolored**	.65	.25
3225	A2506 32c **multicolored**	.65	.25
a.	Block or strip of 4, #3222-3225	2.60	2.00
	P# block of 4, 4#+B	2.60	—
	Pane of 20	13.00	—

For booklet see No. BK272.

LEGENDS OF HOLLYWOOD

Alfred Hitchcock (1899-1980) — A2507

Designed by Richard Sheaff.
Printed at American Packaging Corp. for Sennett Security Products.

PHOTOGRAVURE
Sheets of 120 in six panes of 20

1998, Aug. 3 **Tagged** ***Perf. 11.1***

3226	A2507 32c **multicolored**	.75	.25
	P# block of 4, 4#+S	4.50	—
	Pane of 20	20.00	12.50

Perforations in corner of each stamp are star-shaped. Hitchcock's profile in the UL corner of each stamp is laser cut.

Uncut press sheets of No. 3226 were made available for sale. Values: cross-gutter block of 8, $20; pairs with gutters between, $3.50 each. See note after No. 2868.

ORGAN & TISSUE DONATION

A2508

Designed by Richard Sheaff. Printed by Avery Dennison.

PHOTOGRAVURE
Sheets of 160 in eight panes of 20

1998, Aug. 5 **Tagged** ***Serpentine Die Cut 11.7***
Self-Adhesive

3227	A2508 32c **multicolored**	.65	.25
	P# block of 4 5#+V	2.60	
	Pane of 20	13.00	

MODERN BICYCLE

A2509

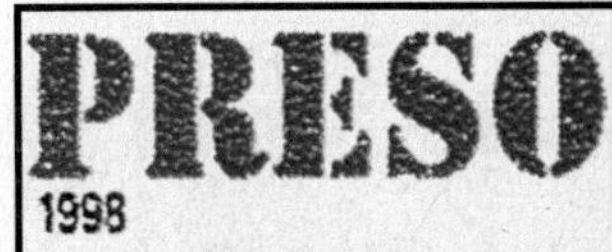

Small Date

Large Date

A2509a

Designed by Richard Sheaff. Printed by Bureau of Engraving and Printing (#3228), Sennett Security Printers (#3229).

PHOTOGRAVURE
COIL STAMP
Serpentine Die Cut 9.8 Vert.

1998, Aug. 14 **Untagged**
Self-Adhesive (#3228)

3228	A2509 (10c) **multicolored,** small "1998" year date	.30	.25
	Pair	.50	
	P# strip of 5, P#111, 221, 222, 333, 344, 444, 555	2.10	
	P# single, same #		1.90
a.	Large date	.35	.25
	Pair	.70	
	P# strip of 5, #666, 777, 888, 999	2.25	
	P# single, #666, 777, 888, 999	—	2.25

Date on No. 3228a is approximately 1½mm; on No. 3228 approximately 1mm.

Untagged
Perf. 9.9 Vert.

3229	A2509a (10c) **multicolored**	.30	.25
	Pair	.50	.50
	P# strip of 5, P#S111	1.75	
	P# single, same #	—	1.40

Date on No. 3229 is approximately 2mm wide.

BRIGHT EYES

Dog — A2510

Fish — A2511

Cat — A2512

Parakeet A2513

Hamster A2514

Designed by Carl Herrman. Printed at Guilford Gravure for Banknote Corp. of America.

PHOTOGRAVURE

Sheets of 180 in nine panes of 20

1998, Aug. 20 Tagged *Serpentine Die Cut 9.9*

Self-Adhesive

3230	A2510 32c **multicolored**		.75	.40
3231	A2511 32c **multicolored**		.75	.40
3232	A2512 32c **multicolored**		.75	.40
3233	A2513 32c **multicolored**		.75	.40
3234	A2514 32c **multicolored**		.75	.40
a.	Strip of 5, #3230-3234		3.75	
	P# block of 8, 2 sets of 6#+B		7.50	
	Pane of 20		15.00	

Hidden 3-D images can be seen on each stamp when viewed with a special "Stamp Decoder" lens sold by the USPS. No. 3230, bone and doghouse; No. 3231, eight bubbles; No. 3232, paw print and mouse; No. 3233, birdcage; No. 3234, exercise wheel.

Plate blocks may contain top label.

KLONDIKE GOLD RUSH, CENTENNIAL

A2515

Designed by Howard Paine. Printed at Sterling Sommer for Ashton Potter (USA) Ltd.

LITHOGRAPHED

Sheets of 180 in nine panes of 20

1998, Aug. 21 Tagged *Perf. 11.1*

3235	A2515 32c **multicolored**	.65	.25
	P# block of 4, 5#+P	2.60	—
	Pane of 20	13.00	—

AMERICAN ART

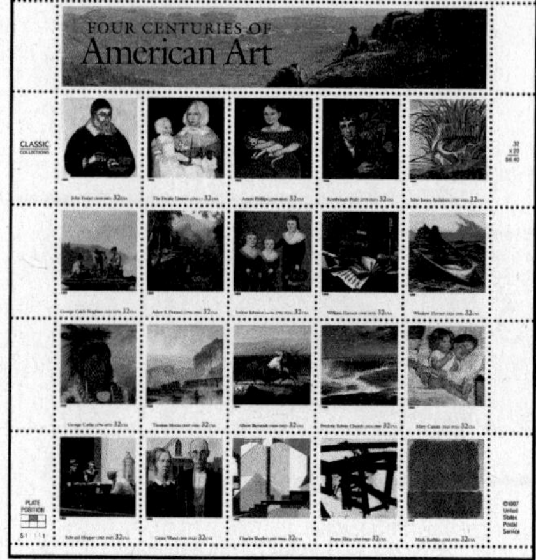

A2516

Illustration reduced.

Designed by Howard Paine. Printed by Sennett Security Products.

Paintings: a, "Portrait of Richard Mather," by John Foster. b, "Mrs. Elizabeth Freake and Baby Mary," by The Freake Limner. c, "Girl in Red Dress with Cat and Dog," by Ammi Phillips. d, "Rubens Peale with a Geranium," by Rembrandt Peale. e, "Long-billed Curlew, Numenius Longrostris," by John James Audubon. f, "Boatmen on the Missouri," by George Caleb Bingham. g, "Kindred Sprits," by Asher B. Durand. h, "The Westwood Children," by Joshua Johnson. i, "Music and Literature," by William Harnett. j, "The Fog Warning," by Winslow Homer. k, "The White Cloud, Head Chief of the Iowas," by George Catlin. l, "Cliffs of Green River," by Thomas Moran. m, "The Last of the Buffalo," by Alfred Bierstadt. n, "Niagara," by Frederic Edwin Church. o, "Breakfast in Bed," by Mary Cassatt. p, "Nighthawks," by Edward Hopper. q, "American Gothic," by Grant Wood. r, "Two Against the White," by Charles Sheeler. s, "Mahoning," by Franz Kline. t, "No. 12," by Mark Rothko.

PHOTOGRAVURE

Sheets of 120 stamps in six panes of 20

1998, Aug. 27 Tagged *Perf. 10.2*

3236	A2516 Pane of 20	18.00	10.00
a.-t.	32c any single	.90	.60

Inscriptions on the back of each stamp describe the painting and the artist.

Uncut press sheets of No. 3236 were made available for sale. Values: cross-gutter block of 20, $40; pairs with gutters between, $4 each. See note after No. 2868.

AMERICAN BALLET

A2517

Designed by Derry Noyes. Printed by Sterling Sommer for Ashton-Potter (USA) Ltd.

LITHOGRAPHED

Sheets of 120 in six panes of 20

1998, Sept. 16 Tagged *Perf. 10.9x11.1*

3237	A2517 32c **multicolored**	.65	.25
	P# block of 4, 4#+P	3.00	—
	Pane of 20	14.50	—

For booklet see No. BK273.

Uncut press sheets of No. 3237 were made available for sale. Values: cross-gutter block of 4, $17.50; pairs with gutters between, $3.25 each. See note after No. 2868.

SPACE DISCOVERY

A2518

A2519

A2520

A2521

A2522

Designed by Phil Jordan. Printed at American Packaging Corp. for Sennett Security Products.

PHOTOGRAVURE

Sheets of 180 in nine panes of 20

1998, Oct. 1 Tagged *Perf. 11.1*

3238	A2518 32c **multicolored**	.65	.25
3239	A2519 32c **multicolored**	.65	.25
3240	A2520 32c **multicolored**	.65	.25
3241	A2521 32c **multicolored**	.65	.25
3242	A2522 32c **multicolored**	.65	.25
a.	Strip of 5, #3238-3242	3.25	2.25
	P# block of 10, 2 sets of 5#+S	6.50	—
	Pane of 20	13.00	

Hidden 3-D images can be seen on each stamp when viewed with a special "Stamp Decoder" lens sold by the USPS. No. 3238, large spacecraft, small spacecraft and figure; No. 3239, small spacecraft; No. 3240, small spacecraft; No. 3241, small spacecraft; No. 3242, large spacecraft and small spacecraft.

Plate blocks may contain top label.

Uncut press sheets of Nos. 3238-3242 were made available for sale. Values: cross-gutter block of 10, $22.50; pairs with gutters between, $2.50 each. See note after No. 2868.

For booklet see No. BK274.

GIVING AND SHARING

A2523

Designed by Bob Dinetz.
Printed by Avery Dennison.

PHOTOGRAVURE
Sheets of 200 in 10 panes of 20

1998, Oct. 7 Tagged *Serpentine Die Cut 11.1*

Self-Adhesive

3243 A2523 32c **multicolored**		.65	.25
	P# block of 4, 4#+V	2.60	—
	Pane of 20	13.00	—

CHRISTMAS

Madonna and Child, Florence, 15th Cent. — A2524

Evergreen Wreath — A2525

Victorian Wreath — A2526

Chili Pepper Wreath — A2527

Tropical Wreath — A2528

Designed by Richard D. Sheaff (#3244), Lilian Dinihanian (#3245), George de Bruin (#3246), Chris Crinklaw (#3247), Micheale Thunin (#3248).
Printed by Bureau of Engraving and Printing (#3244), Banknote Corporation of America (#3245-3248).

LITHOGRAPHED

Serpentine Die Cut 10.1x9.9 on 2, 3 or 4 Sides

1998, Oct. 15 Tagged

Self-Adhesive

Booklet Stamps

3244 A2524 32c **multicolored**		.65	.25
a.	Booklet pane of 20 + label	13.00	
b.	Die cutting omitted, pair	—	

Size: 22x25mm

Serpentine Die Cut 11.3x11.7 on 2 or 3 Sides

3245 A2525 32c **multicolored**		3.25	.25
3246 A2526 32c **multicolored**		3.25	.25
3247 A2527 32c **multicolored**		3.25	.25
3248 A2528 32c **multicolored**		3.75	.25
a.	Booklet pane of 4, #3245-3248	13.00	
b.	Booklet pane of 5, #3245-3246, 3248, 2 #3247 + label	16.25	
c.	Booklet pane of 6, #3247-3248, 2 each #3245-3246	19.50	
d.	As "a," die cutting omitted	—	
e.	As "b," die cutting omitted	—	
f.	As "c," die cutting omitted	—	
g.	Block of 4, #3245-3248	13.00	

A2525a

A2526a

A2527a

A2528a

Designed by Lilian Dinihanian (#3249), George de Bruin (#3250), Chris Crinklaw (#3251), Micheale Thunin (#3252).
Printed byBanknote Corporation of America (#3249-3252).

Sheets of 160 in 8 panes of 20 (#3249-3252)

Size: 23x30mm

Serpentine Die Cut 11.4x11.5 on 2, 3, or 4 Sides

3249 A2525a 32c **multicolored**		1.35	.25
a.	Serp. die cut 11.7x11.6 on 2, 3, or 4 sides	1.75	.25
3250 A2526a 32c **multicolored**		1.35	.25
a.	Serp. die cut 11.7x11.6 on 3 or 4 sides	1.75	.25
3251 A2527a 32c **multicolored**		1.35	.25
a.	Serp. die cut 11.7x11.6 on 3 or 4 sides	1.75	.25
3252 A2528a 32c **multicolored + label**		1.35	.25
a.	Serp. die cut 11.7x11.6 on 2, 3, or 4 sides	1.75	.25
b.	Block or strip of 4, #3249-3252	5.40	
	P# block of 4, 6#+B	6.00	
	Pane of 20	27.00	
c.	Booklet pane of 20, 5 each #3249-3252 + label	30.00	
d.	Block or strip of 4, #3249a-3252a	7.00	
e.	Booklet pane of 20, 5 each #3249a-3252a + label	35.00	
f.	Block or strip of 4, #3249-3252, red ("Greetings 32 USA" and "1998") omitted on #3249, 3252	*625.00*	
g.	Block or strip of 4, #3249-3252, red ("Greetings 32 USA" and "1998") omitted on #3249, 3252; green (same) omitted on #3250, 3251	—	
h.	As "b," die cutting omitted	—	
i.	As "c," die cutting omitted	*4,500.*	

Dedicated printing plates were used to print the red and green denominations, salutations and dates. Red and green appearing in the wreaths come from other plates and, therefore, are not part of the color omissions.

Specialists will want to note that the "1998" date on the flat pane of 20 is about .1mm wider than the date on the corresponding booklet pane (No. 3252c). The measurements are approximately 1.3mm versus 1.2mm, respectively. Therefore, unused and used singles can be distinguished.

Weather Vane — A2529

A2529a

Designed by Terry McCaffrey.
Printed by Ashton Potter (USA) Ltd. (#3257), Banknote Corporation of America (#3258).

LITHOGRAPHED

Sheets of 400 in eight panes of 50 (#3257), Sheets of 300 in six panes of 50 (#3258)

1998 Untagged *Perf. 11.2*

3257 A2529 (1c) **multicolored** *Nov. 9*		.30	.25
	P# block of 4, 5# + P	.30	—
	Pane of 50	5.00	—
a.	Black omitted	125.00	
b.	Horiz. pair, imperf. vert. and at top	—	
3258 A2529a (1c) **multicolored,** *Nov. 9*		.30	.25
	P# block of 4, 5# + B	.30	—
	Pane of 50	5.00	—
a.	Black missing (PS)	—	

No. 3257 is 18mm high, has thin letters, white USA, and black 1998. No. 3258 is 17mm high, has thick letters, pale blue USA and blue 1998.

Uncle Sam — A2530

Uncle Sam's Hat — A2531

Designed by Richard Sheaff (#3259), Terry McCaffrey (#3260).
Printed by American Packaging Corp. for Sennett Security Products (#3259), Stamp Venturers (#3260).

PHOTOGRAVURE

Sheets of 160 in eight panes of 20 (#3259), Sheets of 400 in eight panes of 50 (#3260)

Tagged

Serpentine Die Cut 10.8

Self-Adhesive (#3259, 3261-3263, 3265-3269)

3259 A2530 22c **multicolored,** *Nov. 9*		.45	.25
a.	Die cut 10.8x10.5	2.50	.25
b.	Vert. pair, No. 3259 + 3259a	3.50	
	P# block of 4, 4# + S, all No. 3259	2.50	
	P# block of 4, top stamps No. 3259, bottom stamps No. 3259a	—	
	P# block of 4, top stamps No. 3259a, bottom stamps No. 3259	7.50	
	Pane of 20, all No. 3259	9.00	
	Pane of 20, row 1 No. 3259a, rows 2-4 No. 3259	—	
	Pane of 20, row 2 No. 3259a, rows 1, 3-4 No. 3259	35.00	
	Pane of 20, row 3 No. 3259a, rows 1-2, 4 No. 3259	22.50	
	Pane of 20, row 4 No. 3259a, rows 1-3 No. 3259	30.00	

See No. 3353.

Perf. 11.2

3260 A2531 (33c) **multicolored,** shiny gum, *Nov. 9*		.65	.25
	P# block of 4 4#+S	2.75	—
	Pane of 50	32.00	—
	Low-gloss gum	.65	.25
	P# block of 4 4#+S	2.75	—
	Pane of 50	32.00	—

Space Shuttle Landing A2532

Piggyback Space Shuttle A2533

Designed by Phil Jordan.
Printed by Banknote Corporation of America.

LITHOGRAPHED

Sheets of 120 in six panes of 20 (#3261-3262)

Serpentine Die Cut 11.5

3261 A2532 $3.20 **multicolored,** *Nov. 9*		6.00	1.50
	P# block of 4, 4#+B	24.00	
	Pane of 20	120.00	
3262 A2533 $11.75 **multicolored,** *Nov. 19*		22.50	10.00
	P# block of 4, 4#+B	90.00	
	Pane of 20	450.00	

Hidden 3-D images (ENTERPRISE/COLUMBIA/CHALLENGER/ATLANTIS/ENDEAVOR/DISCOVERY) can be seen on Nos. 3261 and 3262 when viewed with a special "Stamp Decoder" lens sold by the USPS.

A2530a

A2531a

A2531b

A2531c

Designed by Terry McCaffrey (#3264-3266), Richard Sheaff (#3263).
Printed by Bureau of Engraving and Printing.

COIL STAMPS

PHOTOGRAVURE

Serpentine Die Cut 9.9 Vert.

3263 A2530a	22c **multicolored,** *Nov. 9*	.45	.25
	Pair	.90	
	P# strip of 5, #1111	4.25	
	P# single, same #		1.75
a.	Die cutting omitted, pair	*600.00*	

See No. 3353.

Perf. 9.8 Vert.

3264 A2531a	(33c) **multicolored,** *Nov. 9*	.65	.25
	Pair	1.30	.50
	P# strip of 5, #1111, 3333, 3343, 3444	5.75	
	P# strip of 5, #3344	9.50	
	P# single, #1111, 3333, 3343, 3444		3.75
	P# single, #3344		4.50
a.	Imperf, pair	*325.00*	

On No. 3264, the black plate #1 of plate #1111 used in printing rolls of 100 places the plate digit "1" farther from the black printing in the vignette than does the black plate #1 of plate #1111 used in printing rolls of 3,000. These are referred to as "Low black 1" and "Hi black 1" and are used by plate number specialists to distinguish the different printings from plate #1111.

Serpentine Die Cut 9.9 Vert.

3265 A2531b	(33c) **multicolored,** *Nov. 9*	.80	.25
	Pair	1.60	
	P# strip of 5, #1111, 2222, 3333	6.00	
	P# strip of 5, #1131	8.50	
	P# single, #1111, 2222, 3333		1.50
	P# single, #1131		3.00
a.	Die cutting omitted, pair	65.00	—
b.	Red omitted	*300.00*	
c.	Black omitted	*1,400.*	
d.	Black omitted, die cutting omitted, pair	*700.00*	
e.	Red omitted, die cutting omitted, pair	*500.00*	
f.	Blue omitted	—	

Unused examples of No. 3265 are on backing paper the same size as the stamps. Corners of the stamp are 90 degree angles.

On No. 3265b, the blue and gray colors are shifted down and to the right.

On No. 3265f, the red is misregistered to right by 10½ stamps and gray by 3mm.

Serpentine Die Cut 9.9 Vert.

3266 A2531c	(33c) **multicolored,** *Nov. 9*	2.25	.25
	Pair	4.50	
	P# strip of 5, #1111	14.00	
	P# single, same #		4.00

Unused examples of No. 3266 are on backing paper larger than the stamps, and the stamps are spaced approximately 2mm. apart. Corners of stamps are rounded.

A2531d

A2531e

A2531f

Designed by Terry McCaffrey.
Printed by Bureau of Engraving and Printing (#3267), Avery Dennison (#3268-3269).

BOOKLET STAMPS

Serpentine Die Cut 9.9 on 2 or 3 Sides

3267 A2531d	(33c) **multicolored,** *Nov. 9*	.75	.25
a.	Booklet pane of 10	7.50	

Serpentine Die Cut 11¼ on 3 Sides (#3268, 3268a)

or 11 on 2, 3 or 4 sides (#3268b, 3268c)

3268 A2531e	(33c) **multicolored,** *Nov. 9*	.75	.25
a.	Booklet pane of 10	7.50	
b.	Serpentine die cut 11	.75	.25
c.	As "b," booklet pane of 20 + label	15.00	

Die Cut 8 on 2, 3 or 4 Sides

3269 A2531f	(33c) **multicolored,** *Nov. 9* ⓢ	.65	.25
a.	Booklet pane of 18	12.00	

ⓢ: Adhesive residue may remain on the backs of some examples of No. 3269 after soaking. See note after No. 1549.

Unused and used examples of an "H" nondenominated stamp inscribed "Postcard Rate" exist in the marketplace. There is no evidence that these stamps were ever officially issued. Values: unused $2,400; used $1,750.

A2534

A2534a

Small Date

Large Date

Designed by Chris Calle.

PHOTOGRAVURE

COIL STAMPS

1998, Dec. 14 **Untagged** ***Perf. 9.8 Vert.***

3270 A2534	(10c) **multicolored,** small date	.30	.25
	Pair	.50	—
	P# strip of 5, #11111	2.25	
	P# single, #11111		1.75
a.	Large date	.75	.25
	Pair	1.50	—
	P# strip of 5, #22222	7.00	—
	P# single, same #	—	5.00

Self-Adhesive

Serpentine Die Cut 9.9 Vert.

3271 A2534a	(10c) **multicolored,** small date	.30	.25
	Pair	.50	
	P# strip of 5, #11111, 22222	2.00	
	P# single, #11111, 22222		1.75
a.	Large date	1.00	.25
	Pair	2.00	
	P# strip of 5, #33333	5.25	
	P# single, #33333	—	5.00
b.	Tagged (error)	1.25	.75
	Pair	2.50	
	P# strip of 5, #11111	8.00	
	P# single, #11111	—	8.50

No. 3271 is known with eagle in red brown rather than the normal golden brown, apparently from contaminated ink. Values slightly higher than normal No. 3271.

Dates on Nos. 3270a and 3271a are approximately 1¾mm; on Nos. 3270-3271 approximately 1¼mm.

Compare to Nos. 2602-2604, 2907.

Scott values for used self-adhesive stamps are for examples either on piece or off piece.

CHINESE NEW YEAR

Year of the Rabbit A2535

Designed by Clarence Lee.
Printed at American Packaging Corp. for Sennett Security Printers.

PHOTOGRAVURE

Sheets of 180 in nine panes of 20

1999, Jan. 5 **Tagged** ***Perf. 11.2***

3272 A2535	33c **multicolored**	.80	.25
	P# block of 4, 4#+S	3.25	—
	Pane of 20	17.00	—

See Nos. 3895d, 3997d.

BLACK HERITAGE SERIES

Malcolm X (1925-65), Civil Rights Activist — A2536

Designed by Richard Sheaff. Printed by Banknote Corp. of America.

LITHOGRAPHED

Sheets of 180 in nine panes of 20

1999, Jan. 20 **Tagged** ***Serpentine Die Cut 11.4***

Self-Adhesive

3273 A2536	33c **multicolored**	1.00	.25
	P# block of 4, 3#+B	4.00	
	Pane of 20	20.00	

VICTORIAN LOVE

A2537

A2538

Designed by John Grossman, Holly Sudduth.
Printed by Avery Dennison.

PHOTOGRAVURE

1999, Jan. 28 **Tagged** ***Die Cut***

Booklet Stamp

Self-Adhesive

3274 A2537	33c **multicolored**	.65	.25
a.	Booklet pane of 20	13.00	
b.	Die cutting omitted, pair	*100.00*	
c.	As "a," die cutting omitted	*800.00*	

Sheets of 160 in eight panes of 20

3275 A2538	55c **multicolored**	1.10	.25
	P# block of 4, 7#+B	4.40	
	Pane of 20	22.00	

HOSPICE CARE

A2539

Designed by Phil Jordan.
Printed by Banknote Corp. of America.

LITHOGRAPHED
Sheets of 120 in six panes of 20

1999, Feb. 9 Tagged *Serpentine Die Cut 11.4*

3276	A2539 33c **multicolored**	.65	.25
	P# block of 4, 4#+B	2.80	
	Pane of 20	13.50	
a.	Horiz. pair, vert. die cutting omitted	*650.00*	

Flag and City — A2540

A2540a

Designed by Richard Sheaff.
Printed by Bureau of Engraving and Printing (#3277), Avery Dennison (#3278).

PHOTOGRAVURE
Sheets of 400 in four panes of 100 (#3277),
Sheets of 200 in 10 panes of 20 (#3278)

1999, Feb. 25 Tagged *Perf. 11.2*
Self-Adhesive (#3278, 3278F, 3279, 3281-3282)

3277	A2540 33c **multicolored**	.70	.25
	P# block of 4, 4#	60.00	—
	Pane of 100	125.00	—

No. 3277 has red date.

Serpentine Die Cut 11 on 2, 3 or 4 Sides

3278	A2540a 33c **multicolored**	.65	.25
	P# block of 4, 4#+V	5.00	
	Pane of 20	22.50	
a.	Booklet pane of 4	2.60	
b.	Booklet pane of 5 + label	3.25	
	P# single, #V1111, V1112, V1121, V1122, V1212, V2212	.80	1.00
c.	Booklet pane of 6	3.90	
d.	Booklet pane of 10	13.00	
e.	Booklet pane of 20 + label	17.00	
h.	As "e," die cutting omitted	—	
i.	Serpentine die cut 11¼	.90	.25
j.	As "i," booklet pane of 10	9.00	

No. 3278 has black date.
The plate # single in No. 3278b is the lower left stamp.

A2540b

A2540c

Printed by Bureau of Engraving and Printing (#3279), Avery Dennison (#3278F).

BOOKLET STAMPS

Serpentine Die Cut 11½x11¾ on 2, 3 or 4 Sides

3278F	A2540b 33c **multicolored**	1.40	.25
g.	Booklet pane of 20 + label	28.00	

No. 3278F has black date.

Serpentine Die Cut 9.8 on 2 or 3 Sides

3279	A2540c 33c **multicolored**	.85	.25
a.	Booklet pane of 10	8.50	

No. 3279 has red date.

A2540d

A2540e

A2540f

Printed by Bureau of Engraving and Printing.

COIL STAMPS

Perf. 9.9 Vert.

3280	A2540d 33c **multicolored,** small "1999" year date	.65	.25
	Pair	1.30	.50
	P# strip of 5, #1111, 2222	4.25	—
	P# single, same #		2.00
a.	Large date	2.00	.25
	Pair	4.00	.50
	P# strip of 5, #3333	11.00	—
	P# single, same #	—	6.50
b.	As No. 3280, imperf pair	*125.00*	*150.00*

Serpentine Die Cut 9.8 Vert.

Two types of No. 3281: Type I, Long vertical feature at left and right of tallest building consists of 3 separate lines; Type II, Same features consist of solid color.

3281	A2540e 33c **multicolored,** type I, large "1999" year date	.65	.25
	Pair	1.30	
	P# strip of 5, #6666, 7777, 8888, 9999, 1111A, 2222A, 3333A, 4444A, 5555A, 6666A, 7777A, 8888A, 1111B, 2222B	4.75	
	P# single, same #	—	.85
	P# single, 1111B, 2222B	—	1.50
a.	As No. 3281, die cutting omitted, pair	30.00	
b.	Light blue and yellow omitted	*275.00*	
c.	Small date, type II	.65	.25
	Pair	1.30	
	P# strip of 5, #1111, 2222, 3333, 3433, 4443, 4444, 5555	4.75	
	P# single, same #	—	.85
d.	Small date, type I	5.00	.30
	Pair	10.00	
	P# strip of 5, #9999A	40.00	
	P# single, same #		3.50
e.	As "c," die cutting omitted, pair	—	

Corners are square on No. 3281. Unused examples are on backing paper the same size as the stamps, and the stamps are adjoining.

Date on Nos. 3280a and 3281 is approximately 1¾mm; on Nos. 3280, 3281c and 3281d approximately 1¼mm.

Counterfeits exist of No. 3281. See the Postal Counterfeits section of this catalog.

3282	A2540f 33c **multicolored**	.65	.25
	Pair	1.30	
	P# strip of 5, #1111, 2222	4.25	
	P# single, same #		3.25

Corners are rounded on #3282. Unused examples are on backing paper larger than the stamps, and the stamps are spaced approximately 2mm. apart.

Flag and Chalkboard — A2541

Printed by Avery Dennison.

PHOTOGRAVURE

Serpentine Die Cut 7.9 on 2, 3 or 4 Sides

1999, Mar. 13 Tagged

Self-Adhesive

BOOKLET STAMP

3283	A2541 33c **multicolored**	.65	.25
a.	Booklet pane of 18	12.00	
b.	Die cutting omitted, pair	—	

IRISH IMMIGRATION

A2542

Designed by Howard Paine. Printed by Ashton-Potter (USA) Ltd.

LITHOGRAPHED
Sheets of 180 in nine panes of 20

1999, Feb. 26 Tagged *Perf. 11.2*

3286	A2542 33c **multicolored**	.65	.25
	P# block of 4, 4#+P	2.60	—
	Pane of 20	13.00	—

See Ireland No. 1168.

PERFORMING ARTS SERIES

Alfred Lunt (1892-1977), Lynn Fontanne (1887-1983), Actors

A2543

Designed by Carl Herrman. Printed by Sterling Sommer for Ashton-Potter (USA) Ltd.

LITHOGRAPHED
Sheets of 180 in nine panes of 20

1999, Mar. 2 Tagged *Perf. 11.2*

3287	A2543 33c **multicolored**	.65	.25
	P# block of 4, 4#+P	2.60	—
	Pane of 20	13.00	—

ARCTIC ANIMALS

Arctic Hare — A2544

Arctic Fox — A2545

Snowy Owl — A2546

Polar Bear — A2547

Gray Wolf — A2548

Designed by Derry Noyes. Printed by Banknote Corp. of America.

LITHOGRAPHED
Sheets of 90 in six panes of 15

1999, Mar. 12 **Tagged** ***Perf. 11***

3288 A2544 33c **multicolored** .85 .25
3289 A2545 33c **multicolored** .85 .25
3290 A2546 33c **multicolored** .85 .25
3291 A2547 33c **multicolored** .85 .25
3292 A2548 33c **multicolored** .85 .25
a. Strip of 5, #3288-3292 4.25 —
Pane of 15, 6#+B 13.00 —

While the normal definition of a plate block dictates a block of 10, this would require collectors to discard the decorative label and top row of stamps from the pane of 15. To avoid destroying the more collectible entire, we list the entire pane as the plate block.

SONORAN DESERT Ⓢ

A2549

Illustration reduced.

Designed by Ethel Kessler. Printed by Banknote Corporation of America.

Designs: a, Cactus wren, brittlebush, teddy bear cholla. b, Desert tortoise. c, White-winged dove, prickly pear. d, Gambel quail. e, Saguaro cactus. f, Desert mule deer. g, Desert cottontail, hedgehog cactus. h, Gila monster. i, Western diamondback rattlesnake, cactus mouse. j, Gila woodpecker.

LITHOGRAPHED
Sheets of 60 in six panes of 10
Serpentine Die Cut Perf 11.2

1999, Apr. 6 **Tagged**

Self-Adhesive

3293 A2549 Pane of 10 8.00
a.-j. 33c any single .80 .50

Uncut press sheets of No. 3293 were made available for sale. See note after No. 2868.
See note after No. 1549.

BERRIES

Blueberries
A2550

Raspberries
A2551

Strawberries
A2552

Blackberries
A2553

Designed by Howard Paine. Printed by Guilford Gravure for Banknote Corporation of America.

PHOTOGRAVURE
Serpentine Die Cut 11¼x11½ on 2, 3 or 4 Sides (Nos. 3294-3297), or 2 or 3 sides (Nos. 3294a-3297a)

1999, Apr. 10 **Tagged**

Self-Adhesive

3294 A2550 33c **multicolored** .85 .25
a. Dated "2000," *Mar. 15, 2000* 1.25 .25
3295 A2551 33c **multicolored** .85 .25
a. Dated "2000," *Mar. 15, 2000* 1.25 .25
3296 A2552 33c **multicolored** .85 .25
a. Dated "2000," *Mar. 15, 2000* 1.25 .25
3297 A2553 33c **multicolored** .85 .25
a. Dated "2000," *Mar. 15, 2000* 1.25 .25
b. Booklet pane of 20, 5 each #3294-3297 + label 17.50
c. Block or strip of 4, #3294-3297 3.50
d. Booklet pane of 20, 5 #3297e + label 25.00
e. Block of 4, #3294a-3297a 5.00

No. 3297d is a double-sided booklet pane, with 12 stamps on one side and eight stamps plus label on the other side.

A2550a

A2551a

A2552a

A2553a

Serpentine Die Cut 9½x10 on 2 or 3 Sides

3298 A2550a 33c **multicolored** 1.00 .25
3299 A2552a 33c **multicolored** 1.00 .25
3300 A2551a 33c **multicolored** 1.00 .25
3301 A2553a 33c **multicolored** 1.00 .25
a. Booklet pane of 4, #3298-3301 4.00
b. Booklet pane of 5, #3298, 3299, 3301, 2 #3300 + label 5.00
c. Booklet pane of 6, #3300, 3301, 2 #3298, 3299 6.00
d. Block of 4, #3298-3301 4.00

A2550b

A2551b

A2552b

A2553b

COIL STAMPS
Serpentine Die Cut 8.5 Vert.

3302 A2550b 33c **multicolored** 2.25 .25
3303 A2551b 33c **multicolored** 2.25 .25
3304 A2553b 33c **multicolored** 2.25 .25
3305 A2552b 33c **multicolored** 2.25 .25
a. Strip of 4, #3302-3305 9.00
P# strip of 5, 2 #3302, 1 ea #3303-3305, P#B1111, B1112, B2211, B2221, B2222 10.00
P# strip of 9, 2 ea #3302-3303, 3305, 3 #3304, same P# 22.50
P# single (#3304), same P# — 1.10

See Nos. 3404-3407.

DAFFY DUCK

A2554

Designed by Ed Wieczyk.
Printed by Avery Dennison.

PHOTOGRAVURE

1999, Apr. 16 **Tagged** ***Serpentine Die Cut 11.1***

Self-Adhesive

3306 Pane of 10 #3306a 6.75
a. A2554 33c single .65 .25
b. Pane of 9 #3306a 6.00
c. Pane of 1 #3306a .65

Nos. 3306b-3306c and 3307b-3307c are separated by a vertical line of microperforations, which is absent on the uncut sheet of 60.
Die cutting on No. 3306b does not extend through the backing paper.
Uncut press sheets of No. 3306 were made available for sale. Values: top sheet of 60, $40; bottom sheet of 60 with P#, $47.50; cross-gutter block of 7, $15; pairs with gutters between, $3 each. See note after No. 2868.

3307 Pane of 10, #3307c, 9 #3307a 13.00
a. A2554 33c single 1.10
b. Pane of 9 #3307a 10.00
c. Pane of 1, no die cutting 2.75
d. As "a," vert. pair, die cutting omitted btwn. pos. 6 and 9 (unique) *4,250.*

Die cutting on #3307b extends through the backing paper.

LITERARY ARTS SERIES

Ayn Rand (1905-82) — A2555

Designed by Phil Jordan.
Printed by Sterling Sommer for Ashton-Potter (USA) Ltd.

LITHOGRAPHED
Sheets of 180 in nine panes of 20

1999, Apr. 22 **Tagged** ***Perf. 11.2***

3308 A2555 33c **multicolored**	.65	.25
P# block of 4, 4#+P	2.60	—
Pane of 20	13.00	—

A2555a

Designed by Carl Herrman.
Printed by Banknote Corporation of America.

LITHOGRAPHED
Sheets of 160 in eight panes of 20
Serpentine Die Cut 11.6x11.3

1999, Apr. 27 **Tagged**

Self-Adhesive

3309 A2555a 33c **multicolored**	.70	.25
P# block of 4, 6#+B	3.00	
Pane of 20	15.00	

See No. 3203.

TROPICAL FLOWERS

Bird of Paradise A2556

Royal Poinciana A2557

Gloriosa Lily — A2558

Chinese Hibiscus A2559

Designed by Carl Herrman.
Printed by Sennett Security Products.

PHOTOGRAVURE
BOOKLET STAMPS
Serpentine Die Cut 10.9 on 2 or 1 Sides

1999, May 1 **Tagged**

Self-Adhesive

3310 A2556 33c **multicolored**	.65	.30
3311 A2557 33c **multicolored**	.65	.30
3312 A2558 33c **multicolored**	.65	.30
3313 A2559 33c **multicolored**	.65	.30
a. Block of 4, #3310-3313	2.60	
b. Booklet pane, 5 each #3313a	13.00	

No. 3313b is a double-sided booklet pane with 12 stamps on one side and 8 stamps plus label on the other side.

JOHN (1699-1777) & WILLIAM (1739-1823) BARTRAM, BOTANISTS

A2560

Designed by Phil Jordan. Printed by Banknote Corporation of America.

Design: 33c, Franklinia alatamaha, by William Bartram.

LITHOGRAPHED
Sheets of 180 in nine panes of 20

1999, May 18 **Tagged** ***Serpentine Die Cut 11½***

Self-Adhesive

3314 A2560 33c **multicolored**	.65	.25
P# block of 4, 4#+B	2.60	
Pane of 20	13.00	

PROSTATE CANCER AWARENESS

A2561

Designed by Michael Cronan. Printed by Avery Dennison.

PHOTOGRAVURE
Sheets of 200 in 10 panes of 20

1999, May 28 **Tagged** ***Serpentine Die Cut 11***

Self-Adhesive

3315 A2561 33c **multicolored**	.65	.25
P# block of 4, 5#+V	2.60	
Pane of 20	13.00	

CALIFORNIA GOLD RUSH, 150TH ANNIV.

A2562

Designed by Howard Paine. Printed by Ashton-Potter (USA) Ltd.

LITHOGRAPHED
Sheets of 180 in nine panes of 20

1999, June 18 **Tagged** ***Perf. 11¼***

3316 A2562 33c **multicolored**	.65	.25
P# block of 4, 5#+P	2.60	—
Pane of 20	13.00	—

AQUARIUM FISH Ⓢ

A2563

A2564

A2565

Reef Fish — A2566

Designed by Richard Sheaff. Printed by Banknote Corporation of America.

Designs: No. 3317, Yellow fish, red fish, cleaner shrimp. No. 3318, Fish, thermometer. No. 3319, Red fish, blue & yellow fish. No. 3320, Fish, heater/aerator.

LITHOGRAPHED
Sheets of 120 in six panes of 20

1999, June 24 **Tagged** ***Serpentine Die Cut 11½***

Self-Adhesive

3317 A2563 33c **multicolored,** block tagging	.65	.30
a. Overall tagging	15.00	*12.50*
3318 A2564 33c **multicolored,** block tagging	.65	.30
a. Overall tagging	15.00	*12.50*
3319 A2565 33c **multicolored,** block tagging	.65	.30
a. Overall tagging	15.00	*12.50*
3320 A2566 33c **multicolored,** block tagging	.65	.30
a. Overall tagging	15.00	*12.50*
b. Strip of 4, #3317-3320	2.60	
P# block of 8, 2 sets of 4#+B	5.20	
Pane of 20	13.00	

c.	Strip of 4, #3317a-3320a	50.00	
	P# block of 8, 2 sets of 4#+B	110.00	
	Pane of 20	275.00	

Plate blocks will have either top label or list of fish shown on bottom selvage.

Uncut press sheets of Nos. 3317-3320 were made available for sale. Values: cross-gutter block of 8, $60; pairs with gutters between, $8.25 each. Press sheets were printed with large block tagging. See note after No. 2868.

See note after No. 1549.

EXTREME SPORTS

Skateboarding — A2567

BMX Biking — A2568

Snowboarding — A2569

Inline Skating — A2570

Designed by Carl Herrman. Printed by Avery Dennison.

PHOTOGRAVURE

Sheets of 160 in eight panes of 20

1999, June 25 Tagged *Serpentine Die Cut 11*

Self-Adhesive

3321	A2567 33c **multicolored**	.75	.30
3322	A2568 33c **multicolored**	.75	.30
3323	A2569 33c **multicolored**	.75	.30
3324	A2570 33c **multicolored**	.75	.30
a.	Block or strip of 4, #3321-3324	3.00	
	P# block of 4, 4#+V	3.00	
	Pane of 20	15.00	

Uncut press sheets of Nos. 3321-3324 were made available for sale. Values: top sheet of 80, $62.50; bottom sheet of 80 with P#, $67.50; cross-gutter block of 8, $12.50; pairs with gutters between, $3 each. See note after No. 2868.

Hidden 3-D images can be seen on each of these stamps when viewed with a special "Stamp Decoder" lens sold by the USPS. No. 3321, GNARLY; No. 3322, RAD; No. 3323, SWEET; No. 3324, PHAT.

AMERICAN GLASS

Free-Blown Glass — A2571

Mold-Blown Glass — A2572

Pressed Glass — A2573

Art Glass — A2574

Designed by Richard Sheaff. Printed by Sterling Sommer for Ashton-Potter (USA) Ltd.

LITHOGRAPHED

Sheets of 90 in six panes of 15

1999, June 29 Tagged *Perf. 11*

3325	A2571 33c **multicolored**	1.90	.25
3326	A2572 33c **multicolored**	1.90	.25
3327	A2573 33c **multicolored**	1.90	.25
3328	A2574 33c **multicolored**	1.90	.25
a.	Strip or block of 4, #3325-3328	7.75	3.00
	Pane of 15, 4 each #3325, 3327-3328, 3 #3326	28.50	12.50

LEGENDS OF HOLLYWOOD

James Cagney (1899-1986) — A2575

Designed by Howard Paine.

Printed by Sennett Security Products.

PHOTOGRAVURE

Sheets of 120 in six panes of 20

1999, July 22 Tagged *Perf. 11*

3329	A2575 33c **multicolored**	.80	.25
	P# block of 4, 5#+S	4.75	—
	Pane of 20	22.00	—

Perforations in corner of each stamp are star-shaped.

Uncut press sheets of No. 3329 were made available for sale. Values: cross-gutter block of 8, $17.50; pairs with gutters between, $3.50. See note after No. 2868.

GEN. WILLIAM "BILLY" L. MITCHELL (1879-1936), AVIATION PIONEER

A2576

Designed by Phil Jordan.

Printed by Guilford Gravure for Banknote Corporation of America.

PHOTOGRAVURE

Sheets of 180 in nine panes of 20

1999, July 30 Tagged *Serpentine Die Cut 9¾x10*

Self-Adhesive

3330	A2576 55c **multicolored**	1.10	.30
	P# block of 4, 5#+B	4.40	
	Pane of 20	22.00	

HONORING THOSE WHO SERVED

A2577

Designed by Richard Sheaff and Uldis Purins. Printed by Avery Dennison.

PHOTOGRAVURE

Sheets of 200 in 10 panes of 20

1999, Aug. 16 Tagged *Serpentine Die Cut 11*

Self-Adhesive

3331	A2577 33c **black, blue & red**	.65	.25
	P# block of 4, 3#+V	2.60	
	Pane of 20	13.00	

UNIVERSAL POSTAL UNION

A2578

Designed by Gerald Gallo.

Printed by Sterling Sommer for Ashton-Potter (USA) Ltd.

LITHOGRAPHED

Sheets of 180 in nine panes of 20

1999, Aug. 25 Tagged *Perf. 11*

3332	A2578 45c **multicolored**	1.00	.45
	P# block of 4, 3#+P	4.50	—
	Pane of 20	22.00	—

FAMOUS TRAINS

Daylight A2579

Congressional A2580

20th Century Limited A2581

Hiawatha A2582

Super Chief — A2583

Designed by Howard Paine.
Printed by Ashton-Potter (USA) Ltd.

LITHOGRAPHED
Sheets of 120 in six panes of 20

1999, Aug. 26	**Tagged**	***Perf. 11***	
3333 A2579 33c **multicolored**		.75	.25
3334 A2580 33c **multicolored**		.75	.25
3335 A2581 33c **multicolored**		.75	.25
3336 A2582 33c **multicolored**		.75	.25
3337 A2583 33c **multicolored**		.75	.25
a. Strip of 5, #3333-3337		3.75	—
Pane of 20, 4 #3337a		15.00	—
P# block of 8, 2 sets of 4#+P		6.00	—

Stamps in No. 3337a are arranged in four different orders. Plate block may contain top label.

Uncut press sheets of Nos. 3333-3337 were made available for sale. Values: cross-gutter block of 8, $25; pairs with gutters between, $3.50 each. See note after No. 2868.

FREDERICK LAW OLMSTED (1822-1903), LANDSCAPE ARCHITECT

A2584

Designed by Ethel Kessler.
Printed by Ashton-Potter (USA) Ltd.

LITHOGRAPHED
Sheets of 120 in six panes of 20

1999, Sept. 12	**Tagged**	***Perf. 11***	
3338 A2584 33c **multicolored**		.65	.25
P# block of 4, 4#+P		2.60	—
Pane of 20		13.00	—

AMERICAN MUSIC SERIES
Hollywood Composers

Max Steiner (1888-1971) A2585

Dimitri Tiomkin (1894-1975) A2586

Bernard Herrmann (1911-75) A2587

Franz Waxman (1906-67) A2588

Alfred Newman (1907-70) A2589

Erich Wolfgang Korngold (1897-1957) A2590

Designed by Howard Paine.
Printed by Sterling Sommer for Ashton-Potter (USA) Ltd.

LITHOGRAPHED
Sheets of 120 in six panes of 20

1999, Sept. 16	**Tagged**	***Perf. 11***	
3339 A2585 33c **multicolored**		1.40	.25
3340 A2586 33c **multicolored**		1.40	.25
3341 A2587 33c **multicolored**		1.40	.25
3342 A2588 33c **multicolored**		1.40	.25
3343 A2589 33c **multicolored**		1.40	.25
3344 A2590 33c **multicolored**		1.40	.25
a. Block of 6, #3339-3344		8.50	4.50
P# block of 6, 5#+P		8.50	—
P# block of 8, 2 sets of 5#+P + top label		11.50	—
Pane of 20		28.50	—

AMERICAN MUSIC SERIES
Broadway Songwriters

Ira (1896-1983) & George (1898-1937) Gershwin A2591

Alan Jay Lerner (1918-86) & Frederick Loewe (1901-88) A2592

Lorenz Hart (1895-1943) A2593

Richard Rodgers (1902-79) & Oscar Hammerstein II (1895-1960) A2594

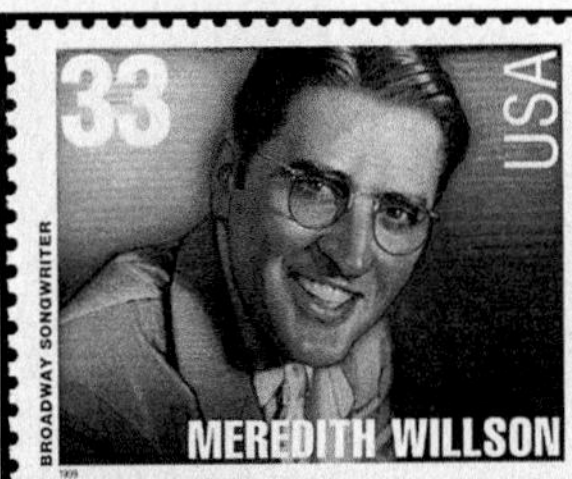

Meredith Willson (1902-84) A2595

Frank Loesser (1910-69) A2596

Designed by Howard Paine.
Printed by Sterling Sommer for Ashton-Potter (USA) Ltd.

LITHOGRAPHED
Sheets of 120 in six panes of 20

1999, Sept. 21	**Tagged**	***Perf. 11***	
3345 A2591 33c **multicolored**		1.25	.25
3346 A2592 33c **multicolored**		1.25	.25
3347 A2593 33c **multicolored**		1.25	.25
3348 A2594 33c **multicolored**		1.25	.25
3349 A2595 33c **multicolored**		1.25	.25
3350 A2596 33c **multicolored**		1.25	.25
a. Block of 6, #3345-3350		7.50	4.50
P# block of 6, 5#+P		7.50	—
P# block of 8, 2 sets of 5#+P + top label		10.00	—
Pane of 20		25.00	—

INSECTS & SPIDERS

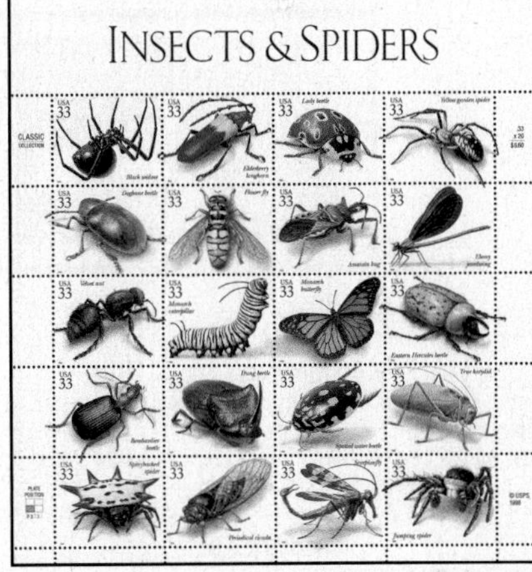

A2597

Illustration reduced.
Designed by Carl Herrman.
Printed by Ashton-Potter (USA) Ltd.

Designs: a, Black widow. b, Elderberry longhorn. c, Lady beetle. d, Yellow garden spider. e, Dogbane beetle. f, Flower fly. g, Assassin bug. h, Ebony jewelwing. i, Velvet ant. j, Monarch caterpillar. k, Monarch butterfly. l, Eastern Hercules beetle. m, Bombardier beetle. n, Dung beetle. o, Spotted water beetle. p, True katydid. q, Spinybacked spider. r, Periodical cicada. s, Scorpionfly. t, Jumping spider.

LITHOGRAPHED
Sheets of 80 in four panes of 20

1999, Oct. 1 **Tagged** ***Perf. 11***

3351	A2597	Pane of 20	14.00	10.00
a.-t.		33c any single	.70	.50

Uncut press sheets of No. 3351 were made available for sale. Values: cross-gutter block of 20, $30; pairs with gutters between, $2.50 each. See note after No. 2868.

Hanukkah — A2597a

Designed by Hannah Smotrich.
Printed by Avery Dennison.

PHOTOGRAVURE
Sheets of 200 in 10 panes of 20

1999, Oct. 8 **Tagged** ***Serpentine Die Cut 11***
Self-Adhesive

3352	A2597a	33c **multicolored**	.65	.25
		P# block of 4, 5#+V	2.60	
		Pane of 20	13.00	

See Nos. 3352, 3547, 3672, Israel No. 1289.

Uncle Sam — A2597b

Designed by Richard Sheaff.
Printed by Bureau of Engraving and Printing.

COIL STAMP
PHOTOGRAVURE

1999, Oct. 8 **Tagged** ***Perf. 9¾ Vert.***

3353	A2597b	22c **multicolored**	.45	.25
		Pair	.90	.50
		P# strip of 5, #1111	3.25	—
		P# single, same #	—	2.25

See Nos. 3259, 3263.

NATO, 50TH ANNIV.

A2598

Designed by Michael Cronan.
Printed by Ashton-Potter (USA) Ltd.

LITHOGRAPHED
Sheets of 180 in nine panes of 20

1999, Oct. 13 **Tagged** ***Perf. 11¼***

3354	A2598	33c **multicolored**	.65	.25
		P# block of 4, 4#+P	2.60	—
		Pane of 20	13.00	—

CHRISTMAS

Madonna and Child, by Bartolomeo Vivarini — A2599

Designed by Richard Sheaff (#3355).
Printed by Banknote Corp. of America.

LITHOGRAPHED
Serpentine Die Cut 11¼ on 2 or 3 sides

1999, Oct. 20 **Tagged**

Booklet Stamp
Self-Adhesive

3355	A2599	33c **multicolored**	.90	.25
a.		Booklet pane of 20	18.00	

Deer — A2600

A2260a

A2260b

A2260c

Designed by Tom Nikosey (#3356-3367).

Sheets of 120 in six panes of 20
Serpentine Die Cut 11¼

3356	A2600	33c **gold & red**	2.25	.25
3357	A2600a	33c **gold & blue**	2.25	.25
3358	A2600b	33c **gold & purple**	2.25	.25
3359	A2600c	33c **gold & green**	2.25	.25
a.		Block or strip of 4, #3356-3359	9.00	
		P# block of 4, 6#+B	9.00	
		Pane of 20	45.00	

A2600d

A2260e

A2260f

A2260g

Booklet Stamps
Serpentine Die Cut 11¼ on 2, 3 or 4 sides

3360	A2600d	33c **gold & red**	1.10	.25
3361	A2600e	33c **gold & blue**	1.10	.25
3362	A2600f	33c **gold & purple**	1.10	.25
3363	A2600g	33c **gold & green**	1.10	.25
a.		Booklet pane of 20, 5 each #3360-3363	22.50	
b.		Block or strip of 4, #3360-3363	4.40	
c.		As "b," die cutting omitted	*100.00*	
d.		As "a," die cutting omitted	*500.00*	

A2600h

A2260i

A2260j

A2260k

Size: 21x19mm
Serpentine Die Cut 11½x11¼ on 2 or 3 sides

3364	A2600h	33c **gold & red**	1.35	.25
3365	A2600i	33c **gold & blue**	1.35	.25
3366	A2600j	33c **gold & purple**	1.35	.25
3367	A2600k	33c **gold & green**	1.35	.25
a.		Booklet pane of 4, #3364-3367	5.50	
b.		Booklet pane of 5, #3364, 3366, 3367, 2 #3365 + label	7.00	
c.		Booklet pane of 6, #3365, 3367, 2 each #3364 & 3366	8.00	
d.		Block of 4, #3364-3367	5.50	

The frame on Nos. 3356-3359 is narrow and the space between it and the hoof is a hairline. The frame on Nos. 3360-3363 is much thicker, and the space between it and the hoof is wider.

Kwanzaa — A2600l

Designed by Synthia Saint James
Printed by Avery Dennison.

PHOTOGRAVURE
Sheets of 240 in 12 panes of 20

1999, Oct. 29 **Tagged** ***Serpentine Die Cut 11***
Self-Adhesive

3368	A2600l	33c **multicolored**	.65	.25
		P# block of 4, 4#+V	2.60	
		Pane of 20	13.00	

See Nos. 3175, 3548, 3673.

YEAR 2000

Baby New Year — A2601

Designed by Carl Herrman.

Printed by Banknote Corporation of America.

LITHOGRAPHED

Sheets of 120 in six panes of 20

1999, Dec. 27 Tagged *Serpentine Die Cut 11¼*

Self-Adhesive

3369	A2601 33c **multicolored**	.65	.25
	P# block of 4, 5#+B	3.00	
	Pane of 20	14.50	

CHINESE NEW YEAR

Year of the Dragon A2602

Designed by Clarence Lee.
Printed by Sterling Sommer.

LITHOGRAPHED

Sheets of 180 in nine panes of 20

2000, Jan. 6 Tagged *Perf. 11¼*

3370	A2602 33c **multicolored**	.80	.25
	P# block of 4, 4#+P	3.25	—
	Pane of 20	15.50	—

See Nos. 3895e, 3997e.

BLACK HERITAGE SERIES

Patricia Roberts Harris (1924-85), First Black Woman Cabinet Secretary — A2603

Designed by Richard Sheaff.
Printed by Ashton-Potter (USA) Ltd.

LITHOGRAPHED

Sheets of 180 in nine panes of 20

Serpentine Die Cut 11½x11¼

2000, Jan. 27 Tagged

Self-Adhesive

3371	A2603 33c **indigo**	.65	.25
	P# block of 4, 4#+P	2.75	
	Pane of 20	13.50	

SUBMARINES

S Class — A2604

Los Angeles Class A2605

Ohio Class — A2606

USS Holland A2607

Gato Class — A2608

Illustration of No. 3377 reduced.
Designed by Carl Herrman.
Printed by Banknote Corporation of America.

LITHOGRAPHED

Sheets of 180 in nine panes of 20

2000, Mar. 27 Tagged *Perf. 11*

3372	A2605 33c **multicolored,** with microprinted "USPS" at base of sail	.75	.25
	P# block of 4, 4#+B	3.00	—
	Pane of 20	15.00	—

BOOKLET STAMPS

3373	A2604 22c **multicolored**	.75	.75
3374	A2605 33c **multicolored,** no microprinting	1.00	1.00
3375	A2606 55c **multicolored**	1.50	1.25
3376	A2607 60c **multicolored**	1.75	1.50
3377	A2608 $3.20 **multicolored**	10.00	5.00
a.	Booklet pane of 5, #3373-3377	15.00	—

No. 3377a was issued with two types of text in the selvage.

PACIFIC COAST RAIN FOREST

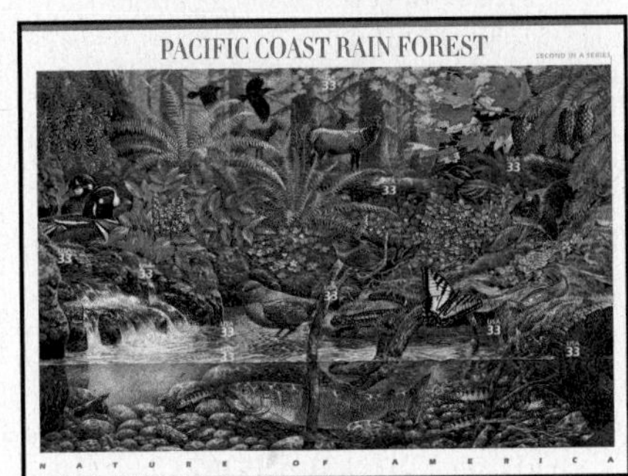

A2609

Illustration reduced.
Designed by Ethel Kessler.
Printed by Banknote Corporation of America.

Designs: a, Harlequin duck. b, Dwarf oregongrape, snail-eating ground beetle. c, American dipper, horiz. d, Cutthroat trout, horiz. e, Roosevelt elk. f, Winter wren. g, Pacific giant salamander, Rough-skinned newt. h, Western tiger swallowtail, horiz. i, Douglas squirrel, foliose lichen. j, Foliose lichen, banana slug.

LITHOGRAPHED

Sheets of 60 in six panes of 10

Serpentine Die Cut 11¼x11½, 11½ (horiz. stamps)

2000, Mar. 29 Tagged

Self-Adhesive

3378	A2609 Pane of 10	10.00	
a.-j.	33c any single	1.00	.50

Uncut press sheets of No. 3378 were made available for sale. See note after No. 2868.

LOUISE NEVELSON (1899-1988), SCULPTOR

Silent Music I — A2610

Royal Tide I — A2611

Black Chord — A2612

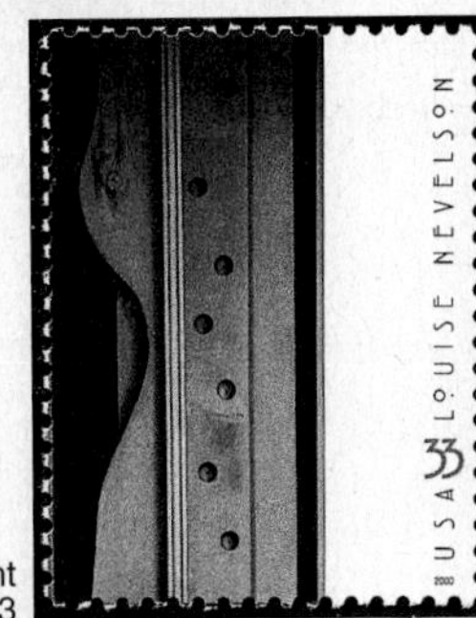

Nightsphere-Light A2613

Dawn's Wedding Chapel I — A2614

Designed by Ethel Kessler.
Printed by Ashton-Potter (USA) Ltd.

LITHOGRAPHED

Sheets of 80 in four panes of 20.

2000, Apr. 6 Tagged *Perf. 11x11¼*

3379	A2610 33c **multicolored**	.65	.25
3380	A2611 33c **multicolored**	.65	.25
3381	A2612 33c **multicolored**	.65	.25
3382	A2613 33c **multicolored**	.65	.25
3383	A2614 33c **multicolored**	.65	.25
a.	Strip of 5, #3379-3383	3.25	—
	P# block of 10, 4#+P	6.50	—
	Pane of 20	13.00	—

HUBBLE SPACE TELESCOPE IMAGES

Eagle Nebula — A2615

Ring Nebula — A2616

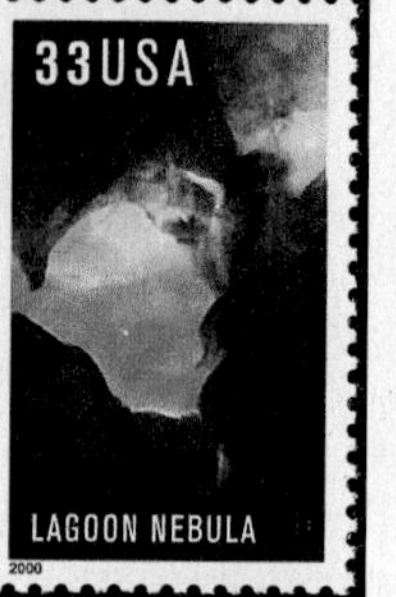

Lagoon Nebula — A2617

Egg Nebula — A2618

Galaxy NGC 1316 — A2619

Designed by Phil Jordan. Printed at American Packaging Corp. for Sennett Security Products.

PHOTOGRAVURE

Sheets of 120 in six panes of 20.

2000, Apr. 10 — Tagged — *Perf. 11*

3384 A2615 33c **multicolored**	.65	.25
3385 A2616 33c **multicolored**	.65	.25
3386 A2617 33c **multicolored**	.65	.25
3387 A2618 33c **multicolored**	.65	.25
3388 A2619 33c **multicolored**	.65	.25
a. Strip of 5, #3384-3388	3.25	2.00
P# block of 10, 6#+S	6.50	—
Pane of 20	13.00	—
b. As "a," imperf	*900.00*	
As "b," pane of 20	*4,500.*	

AMERICAN SAMOA

Samoan Double Canoe A2620

Designed by Howard Paine.
Printed by Ashton-Potter (USA) Ltd.

LITHOGRAPHED

Sheets of 120 in six panes of 20

2000, Apr. 17 — Tagged — *Perf. 11*

3389 A2620 33c **multicolored**	.85	.25
P# block of 4, 4#+P	4.25	—
Pane of 20	21.00	—

LIBRARY OF CONGRESS

Interior Dome and Arched Windows in Main Reading Room, Thomas Jefferson Building — A2621

Designed by Ethel Kessler.
Printed by Ashton-Potter (USA) Ltd.

LITHOGRAPHED

Sheets of 120 in six panes of 20

2000, Apr. 24 — Tagged — *Perf. 11*

3390 A2621 33c **multicolored**	.65	.25
P# block of 4, 5#+P	2.60	—
Pane of 20	13.00	—

ROAD RUNNER & WILE E. COYOTE

A2622

Designed by Ed Wleczyk, Warner Bros.
Printed by Banknote Corp. of America, Inc.

LITHOGRAPHED

2000, Apr. 26 — Tagged — *Serpentine Die Cut 11*

Self-Adhesive

3391 Pane of 10 #3391a	10.00	
a. A2622 33c single	.85	.25
b. Pane of 9 #3391a	8.00	
c. Pane of 1 #3391a	1.50	
d. All die cutting omitted, pane of 10	2,250.	

Die cutting on #3391b does not extend through the backing paper.

Uncut press sheets of No. 3391 were made available for sale. Values: top sheet of 60 with P# on reverse, $60; bottom sheet of 60 with P#, $62.50; cross-gutter block of 7, $17.50; pairs with gutters between, $3.50 each. See note after No. 2868.

3392 Pane of 10, #3392c, 9 #3392a	30.00	
a. A2622 33c single	2.75	
b. Pane of 9 #3392a	25.00	
c. Pane of 1, no die cutting	5.00	

Die cutting on #3392a extends through the backing paper. Used examples of No. 3392a are identical to those of No. 3391a.

Nos. 3391b-3391c and 3392b-3392c are separated by a vertical line of microperforations.

DISTINGUISHED SOLDIERS

Maj. Gen. John L. Hines (1868-1968) A2623

Gen. Omar N. Bradley (1893-1981) A2624

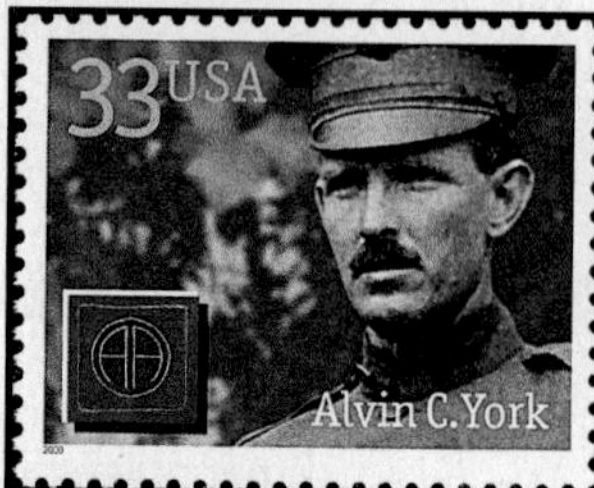

Sgt. Alvin C. York (1887-1964) A2625

Second Lt. Audie L. Murphy (1924-71) A2626

Designed by Phil Jordan.
Printed by Sterling Sommer for Ashton-Potter (USA) Ltd.

LITHOGRAPHED

Sheets of 120 in six panes of 20

2000, May 3 — Tagged — *Perf. 11*

3393 A2623 33c **multicolored**	.70	.25
3394 A2624 33c **multicolored**	.70	.25
3395 A2625 33c **multicolored**	.70	.25
3396 A2626 33c **multicolored**	.70	.25
a. Block or strip of 4, #3393-3396	2.80	1.50
P# block of 4, 4#+P	2.80	—
Pane of 20	14.00	—

SUMMER SPORTS

Runners A2627

Designed by Richard Sheaff.
Printed by Ashton-Potter (USA) Ltd.

LITHOGRAPHED

Sheets of 120 in six panes of 20

2000, May 5 — Tagged — *Perf. 11*

3397 A2627 33c **multicolored**	.65	.25
P# block of 4, 4#+P	2.60	—
Pane of 20	13.00	—

ADOPTION Ⓢ

Stick Figures — A2628

Designed by Greg Berger.
Printed by Banknote Corporation of America.

LITHOGRAPHED

Sheets of 120 in six panes of 20

2000, May 10 Tagged *Serpentine Die Cut 11½*

Self-Adhesive

3398 A2628 33c **multicolored**	.65	.25
P# block of 4, 5#+B	2.60	
Pane of 20	13.00	
a. Die cutting omitted, pair	*2,500.*	

See note after No. 1549.

YOUTH TEAM SPORTS

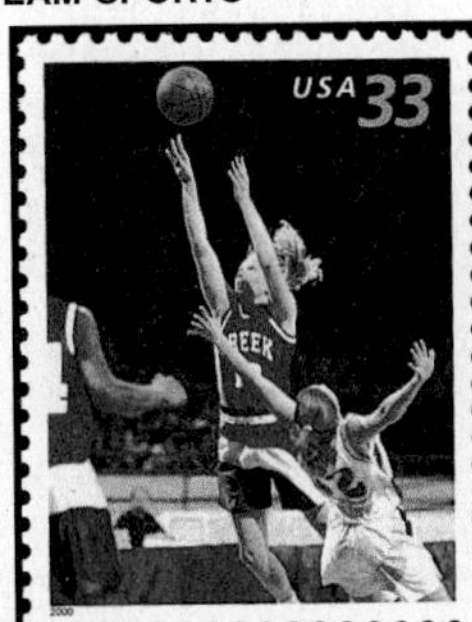

Basketball — A2629

Football — A2630

Soccer — A2631

Baseball — A2632

Designed by Derry Noyes.
Printed by Sterling Sommer for Ashton-Potter (USA) Ltd.

LITHOGRAPHED

Sheets of 120 in six panes of 20

2000, May 27 Tagged *Perf. 11*

3399 A2629 33c **multicolored**	.70	.25
3400 A2630 33c **multicolored**	.70	.25
3401 A2631 33c **multicolored**	.70	.25
3402 A2632 33c **multicolored**	.70	.25
a. Block or strip of 4, #3399-3402	2.80	1.75
P# block of 4, 4#+P	2.80	—
Pane of 20	14.00	—

THE STARS AND STRIPES

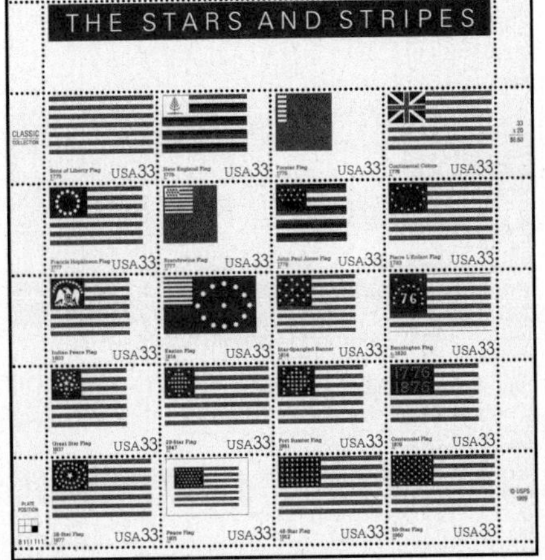

A2633

Illustration reduced.

Designed by Richard Sheaff.
Printed by Banknote Corp. of America.

Designs: a, Sons of Liberty Flag, 1775. b, New England Flag, 1775. c, Forster Flag, 1775. d, Continental Colors, 1776. e, Francis Hopkinson Flag, 1777. f, Brandywine Flag, 1777. g, John Paul Jones Flag, 1779. h, Pierre L'Enfant Flag, 1783. i, Indian Peace Flag, 1803. j, Easton Flag, 1814. k, Star-Spangled Banner, 1814. l, Bennington Flag, c. 1820. m, Great Star Flag, 1837. n, 29-Star Flag, 1847. o, Fort Sumter Flag, 1861. p, Centennial Flag, 1876. q, 38-Star Flag, 1877. r, Peace Flag, 1891. s, 48-Star Flag, 1912. t, 50-Star Flag, 1960.

LITHOGRAPHED

2000, June 14 Tagged *Perf. 10½x11*

3403 A2633 Pane of 20	15.00	11.00
a.-t. 33c any single	.75	.50

Inscriptions on the back of each stamp describe the flag.

Uncut press sheets of No. 3403 were made available for sale. Values: cross-gutter block of 20, $30; pairs with gutters between, $3.25 each. See note after No. 2868.

BERRIES

Blueberries — A2634

Strawberries — A2635

Blackberries — A2636

Raspberries — A2637

Designed by Howard Paine. Printed by Guilford Gravure.

See designs A2550-A2553.

PHOTOGRAVURE

COIL STAMPS

Serpentine Die Cut 8½ Horiz.

2000, June 16 Tagged

Self-Adhesive

3404 A2634 33c **multicolored**	3.50	.25
3405 A2635 33c **multicolored**	3.50	.25
3406 A2636 33c **multicolored**	3.50	.25
3407 A2637 33c **multicolored**	3.50	.25
a. Strip of 4, #3404-3407	15.00	
P# strip of 5, 2 #3404, 1 each #3405-3407, #G1111	30.00	
P# strip of 9, 2 each #3404-3405, 3407, 3 #3406, #G1111	45.00	
P# single (#3406), #G1111	—	1.25

Nos. 3404-3407 are linerless coils issued without backing paper. The adhesive is strong and can remove the ink from stamps in the roll.

LEGENDS OF BASEBALL

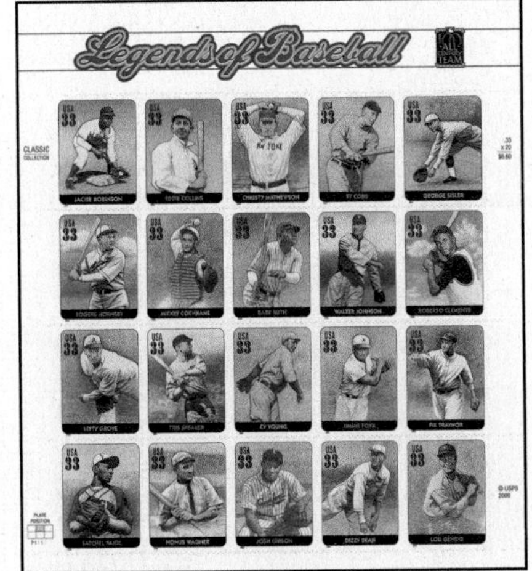

A2638

Illustration reduced.

Designed by Phil Jordan. Printed by Ashton-Potter (USA) Ltd.

Designs: a, Jackie Robinson. b, Eddie Collins. c, Christy Mathewson. d, Ty Cobb. e, George Sisler. f, Rogers Hornsby. g, Mickey Cochrane. h, Babe Ruth. i, Walter Johnson. j, Roberto Clemente. k, Lefty Grove. l, Tris Speaker. m, Cy Young. n, Jimmie Foxx. o, Pie Traynor. p, Satchel Paige. q, Honus Wagner. r, Josh Gibson. s, Dizzy Dean. t, Lou Gehrig.

LITHOGRAPHED

Sheets of 120 in six panes of 20

2000, July 6 Tagged *Serpentine Die Cut 11¼*

Self-Adhesive

3408 A2638 Pane of 20	15.00	
a.-t. 33c any single	.75	.50

Uncut press sheets of No. 3408 were made available for sale. Values: cross-gutter block of 20, $32.50; pairs with gutters between, $3 each. See note after No. 2868.

SPACE

Souvenir Sheets

Probing the Vastness of Space — A2639

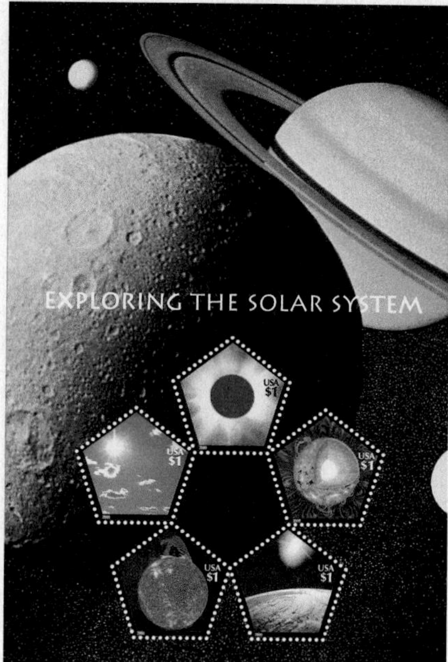

Exploring the Solar System — A2640

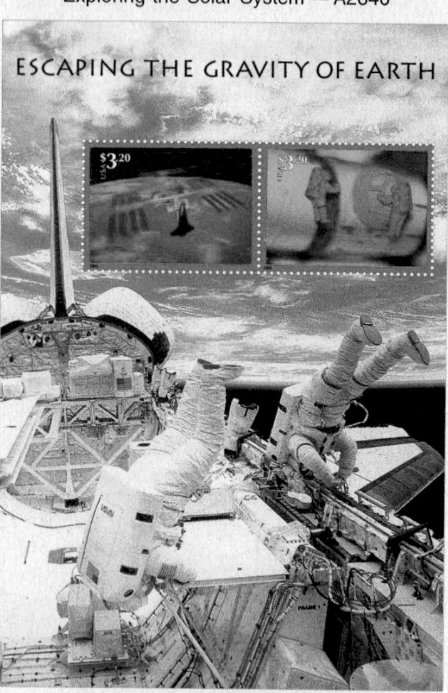

Escaping the Gravity of Earth — A2641

Space Achievement and Exploration — A2642

Landing on the Moon — A2643

Illustrations reduced.
Designed by Richard Sheaff. Printed by American Packaging Corporation for Sennett Security Products.

Designs: No. 3409: a, Hubble Space Telescope. b, Radio interferometer very large array, New Mexico. c, Optical and infrared telescopes, Keck Observatory, Hawaii. d, Optical telescopes, Cerro Tololo Observatory, Chile. e, Optical telescope, Mount Wilson Observatory, California. f, Radio telescope, Arecibo Observatory, Puerto Rico.
No. 3410: a, Sun and corona. b, Cross-section of sun. c, Sun and earth. d, Sun and solar flare. e, Sun and clouds.
No. 3411: a, Space Shuttle and Space Station. b, Astronauts working in space.

PHOTOGRAVURE

2000 **Tagged** ***Perf. 10½x11***

3409	A2639	Sheet of 6, *July 10*	15.00	7.00
a.-f.		60c any single	2.25	1.00

Perf. 10¾

3410	A2640	Sheet of 5 + label, *July 11*	17.50	10.00
a.-e.		$1 any single	3.00	1.75
f.		As No. 3410, imperf	*2,000.*	
g.		As No. 3410, with hologram from No. 3411b applied	*1,500.*	

Untagged

Photogravure with Hologram Affixed

Perf. 10½, 10¾ (#3412)

3411	A2641	Sheet of 2, *July 9*	22.50	10.00
a.-b.		$3.20 any single	10.00	4.00
c.		Hologram omitted on right stamp	—	
3412	A2642	**multicolored,** *July 7*	40.00	17.50
a.		$11.75 single	35.00	15.00
b.		Hologram omitted	—	
c.		Hologram omitted on No. 3412 in uncut sheet of 5 panes	—	
3413	A2643	**multicolored,** *July 8*	40.00	17.50
a.		$11.75 single	35.00	15.00
b.		Double hologram	*3,500.*	
c.		Double hologram on No. 3413 in uncut sheet of 5 panes	—	
d.		Hologram omitted on No. 3413 in uncut sheet of 5 panes	—	
		Nos. 3409-3413 (5)	135.00	62.00

The holograms on Nos. 3411-3413 scratch easily. Values are for examples with minimal scratches. Examples without scratches are worth more.

Warning: Soaking in water may affect holographic images.

Uncut press sheets containing Nos. 3409-3413 were made available for sale. Value, sheet of five panes, $140. See note after No. 2868.

STAMPIN' THE FUTURE CHILDREN'S STAMP DESIGN CONTEST WINNERS

By Zachary Canter A2644

By Sarah Lipsey A2645

By Morgan Hill — A2646

By Ashley Young A2647

Designed by Richard Sheaff. Printed by Ashton-Potter (USA) Ltd.

LITHOGRAPHED

Sheets of 120 in six panes of 20

2000, July 13 **Tagged** ***Serpentine Die Cut 11¼***

Self-Adhesive

3414	A2644 33c **multicolored**		.65	.30
3415	A2645 33c **multicolored**		.65	.30
3416	A2646 33c **multicolored**		.65	.30
3417	A2647 33c **multicolored**		.65	.30
a.		Horiz. strip of 4, #3414-3417	2.60	
		P# block of 8, 2 sets of 5#+P	5.25	
		Pane of 20	13.00	

Plate block may contain top label.

DISTINGUISHED AMERICANS

Gen. Joseph W. Stilwell (1883-1946) A2650

Wilma Rudolph (1940-94), Athlete A2652

Sen. Claude Pepper (1900-89) A2656

Sen. Margaret Chase Smith (1897-1995) A2657

James A. Michener (1907-97), Author — A2657a

Dr. Jonas Salk (1914-95), Polio Vaccine Pioneer — A2658

Harriet Beecher Stowe (1811-96), Author A2660

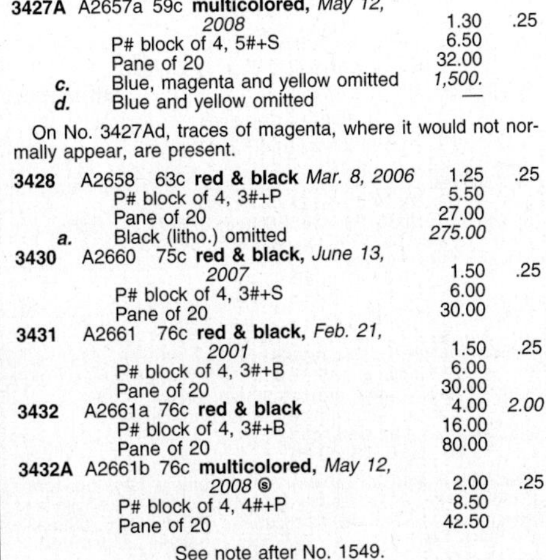

Sen. Hattie Caraway (1878-1950) A2661

A2661a

Edward Trudeau (1848-1915), Phthisiologist — A2661b

Mary Lasker (1900-94), Philanthropist — A2661c

Edna Ferber (1887-1968), Writer — A2662

Edna Ferber (With Curving Shoulder) — A2663

Dr. Albert Sabin (1906-93), Polio Vaccine Pioneer — A2664

Designed by: 10c, 23c, 33c, 58c, 59c, 63c, 75c, Nos. 3431-3432, 83c, 87c Richard Sheaff; No. 3432A, Howard E. Paine, 78c, Ethel Kessler.

Printed by Banknote Corporation of America (#3420-3433). Ashton-Potter (USA) Ltd. (#3422, 3427, 3428, 3432A, 3234B 3434). Banknote Corporation of America for Sennett Security Products, (#3427A, 3430).

LITHOGRAPHED & ENGRAVED, LITHOGRAPHED (#3427A, 3432A, 3432B)

Sheets of 120 in six panes of 20

Sheets of 300 in 15 panes of 20 (#3427A)

Perf. 11 (#3420, 3426), Serpentine Die Cut 11¼x10¾ (#3422, 3430, 3432B), 11¼x11 (#3427A, 3428, 3432A, 3435), 11 (#3427, 3431), 11½x11 (#3432), 11x11¾ (#3433), 11¼ (#3434)

2000-09 Tagged

Self-Adhesive (All Except #3420, 3426)

3420	A2650 10c **red & black,** *Aug. 24*	.30	.25
	P# block of 4, 3#+B	.80	—
	Pane of 20	4.00	—
a.	Imperf, pair	*300.00*	
3422	A2652 23c **red & black,** *July 14, 2004*	.45	.25
	P# block of 4, 2#+P	1.80	
	Pane of 20	9.00	
a.	Imperf, pair	*600.00*	
3426	A2656 33c **red & black,** *Sept. 7*	.65	.25
	P# block of 4, 3#+B	2.60	—
	Pane of 20	13.00	—
3427	A2657 58c **red & black,** *June 13, 2007*	1.25	.25
	P# block of 4, 3#+P	5.50	
	Pane of 20	27.00	
b.	Black (engr.) omitted	*200.00*	
3427A	A2657a 59c **multicolored,** *May 12, 2008*	1.30	.25
	P# block of 4, 5#+S	6.50	
	Pane of 20	32.00	
c.	Blue, magenta and yellow omitted	*1,500.*	
d.	Blue and yellow omitted	—	

On No. 3427Ad, traces of magenta, where it would not normally appear, are present.

3428	A2658 63c **red & black** *Mar. 8, 2006*	1.25	.25
	P# block of 4, 3#+P	5.50	
	Pane of 20	27.00	
a.	Black (litho.) omitted	*275.00*	
3430	A2660 75c **red & black,** *June 13, 2007*	1.50	.25
	P# block of 4, 3#+S	6.00	
	Pane of 20	30.00	
3431	A2661 76c **red & black,** *Feb. 21, 2001*	1.50	.25
	P# block of 4, 3#+B	6.00	
	Pane of 20	30.00	
3432	A2661a 76c **red & black**	4.00	*2.00*
	P# block of 4, 3#+B	16.00	
	Pane of 20	80.00	
3432A	A2661b 76c **multicolored,** *May 12, 2008* ⓢ	2.00	.25
	P# block of 4, 4#+P	8.50	
	Pane of 20	42.50	

See note after No. 1549.

3432B	A2661c 78c **multicolored,** *May 15, 2009*	1.60	.25
	P# block of 4, 4#+P	8.00	
	Pane of 20	38.50	
3433	A2662 83c **red & black,** *July 29, 2002*	1.70	.30
	P# block of 4, 3#+B1	7.00	
	Pane of 20	35.00	

The previously listed "Big Mouth" flaw on No. 3433 has been discovered to be not a constant plate flaw but rather the result of extraneous matter on the plate affecting a reported 15 panes before the matter fell off, or was removed from, the plate.

3434	A2663 83c **red & black,** *Aug. 2003*	1.60	.30
	P# block of 4, 3#+P	6.50	
	Pane of 20	32.50	
3435	A2664 87c **red & black,** *Mar. 8, 2006*	1.75	.30
	P# block of 4, 2#+S	7.00	
	Pane of 20	35.00	

A2652a

Designed by Richard Sheaff.

LITHOGRAPHED

BOOKLET STAMP

Serpentine Die Cut 11¼x10¾ on 3 Sides

Self-Adhesive

3436	A2652a 23c **red & black,** *July 14, 2004*	.45	.25
a.	Booklet pane of 4	1.80	
b.	Booklet pane of 6	2.70	
c.	As "a" & "b" in cplt booklet of 10 (No. BK279A), die cutting omitted and peel strip intact, P#P44	—	
d.	Booklet pane of 10	4.50	
e.	As "d," die cutting omitted	—	—

The backing on No. 3436b has a different product number (672900) than that found on the lower portion of No. 3436d (673000).

CALIFORNIA STATEHOOD, 150TH ANNIV.

Big Sur and Iceplant — A2668

Designed by Carl Herrman.
Printed by Avery Dennison.

PHOTOGRAVURE

Sheets of 200 in 10 panes of 20

2000, Sept. 8 Tagged *Serpentine Die Cut 11*

Self-Adhesive

3438	A2668 33c **multicolored**	1.00	.25
	P# block of 4, 5#+V	4.00	
	Pane of 20	20.00	

DEEP SEA CREATURES

Fanfin Anglerfish A2669

Sea Cucumber A2670

Fangtooth A2671

Amphipod A2672

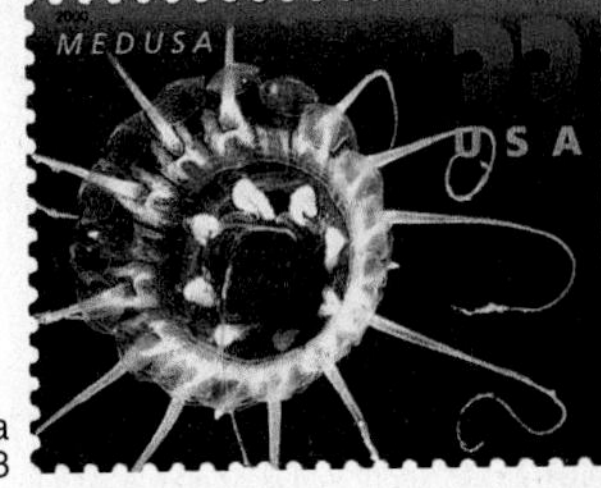

Medusa A2673

Designed by Ethel Kessler.
Printed by American Packaging Corp. for Sennett Security Products.

PHOTOGRAVURE

Sheets of 135 in nine panes of 15

2000, Oct. 2 Tagged *Perf. 10x10¼*

3439	A2669 33c **multicolored**	.75	.25
3440	A2670 33c **multicolored**	.75	.25
3441	A2671 33c **multicolored**	.75	.25
3442	A2672 33c **multicolored**	.75	.25
3443	A2673 33c **multicolored**	.75	.25
a.	Vert. strip of 5, #3439-3443	3.75	2.00
	Pane of 15, 4#+S	11.25	—

See note under No. 3292 regarding lack of plate block listing. Uncut press sheets of Nos. 3439-3443 were made available for sale. Values: cross-gutter block of 10, $20; pairs with gutters between, $3 each. See note after No. 2868.

LITERARY ARTS SERIES

Thomas Wolfe (1900-38), Novelist A2674

Designed by Phil Jordan.
Printed by Ashton-Potter (USA) Ltd.

LITHOGRAPHED
Sheets of 120 in six panes of 20

2000, Oct. 3 **Tagged** ***Perf. 11***

3444 A2674 33c **multicolored** .65 .25
P# block of 4, 5#+P 2.60 —
Pane of 20 13.00 —

WHITE HOUSE, 200TH ANNIV.

A2675

Designed by Derry Noyes.
Printed by Ashton-Potter (USA) Ltd.

LITHOGRAPHED
Sheets of 180 in nine panes of 20

2000, Oct. 18 **Tagged** ***Serpentine Die Cut 11¼***
Self-Adhesive

3445 A2675 33c **multicolored** 1.00 .25
P# block of 4, 4#+P 4.00
Pane of 20 20.00

LEGENDS OF HOLLYWOOD

Edward G. Robinson (1893-1973), Actor — A2676

Designed by Howard Paine.
Printed by American Packaging Corporation for Sennett Security Products.

PHOTOGRAVURE
Sheets of 120 in six panes of 20

2000, Oct. 24 **Tagged** ***Perf. 11***

3446 A2676 33c **multicolored** 1.60 .25
P# block of 4, 7#+S 7.50 —
Pane of 20 37.50 12.50

Perforations in corner of each stamp are star-shaped.

Uncut press sheets of No. 3446 were made available for sale. Values: cross-gutter block of 8, $32.50; pairs with gutters between, $5 each. See note after No. 2868.

New York Public Library Lion — A2677

Designed by Carl Herrman.
Printed by American Packaging Corporation for Sennett Security Products.

PHOTOGRAVURE
COIL STAMP
Serpentine Die Cut 11½ Vert.

2000, Nov. 9 **Untagged**
Self-Adhesive

3447 A2677 (10c) **multicolored**, "2000" year date .30 .25
Pair .40
P# strip of 5, #S11111, S22222, S33333, S44444, S66666, S77777 2.25
P# single, #S11111, S22222, S33333, S44444 — 1.50
P# single, #S66666 — 1.75
P# single, #S77777 — 1.90
a. "2003" year date .30 .25
Pair .40
P# strip of 5, #S55555 2.75
P# single, #S55555 — 2.00
b. As No. 3447, prephosphored coated paper with surface tagging showing a solid appearance (error) —
P# single, #S66666 —

No. 3447 also is known with extremely faint phosphor splotches. No. 3447b has full-strength tagging. Values with faint tagging: unused and used singles, $2; P# strip of 5, #S33333 and S44444 $10 each, #S77777 $25; P# single used, #S33333 and S44444 $20 each, #77777 $20.

See No. 3769.

Flag Over Farm — A2678

A2678a

A2678b

Designed by Richard Sheaff.
Printed by Sterling Sommer for Ashton-Potter (USA) Ltd. (#3448), Ashton-Potter (USA) Ltd. (#3449), Avery Dennison (#3450).

LITHOGRAPHED (#3448-3449), PHOTOGRAVURE (#3450)
Sheets of 120 in six panes of 20

2000, Dec. 15 **Tagged** ***Perf. 11¼***

3448 A2678 (34c) **multicolored** 1.00 .25
P# block of 4, 4# + P 10.00 —
Pane of 20 45.00 —

Self-Adhesive
Serpentine Die Cut 11¼

3449 A2678a (34c) **multicolored** 1.00 .25
P# block of 4, 4# + P 6.50
Pane of 20 30.00

Booklet Stamp
Self-Adhesive
Serpentine Die Cut 8 on 2, 3 or 4 Sides

3450 A2678b (34c) **multicolored** .85 .25
a. Booklet pane of 18 16.00
b. Die cutting omitted, pair —

A2679

Designed by Derry Noyes. Printed by Avery Dennison.

PHOTOGRAVURE
Serpentine Die Cut 11 on 2, 3 or 4 Sides

2000, Dec. 15 **Tagged**
Self-Adhesive
Booklet Stamp

3451 A2679 (34c) **multicolored** 1.10 .25
a. Booklet pane of 20 22.00
b. Booklet pane of 4 4.40
Booklet pane of 4 containing P# single 4.50
P# single, #V1111 1.50 .70
c. Booklet pane of 6 6.60
d. As "a," die cutting omitted —

The plate # single in No. 3451b is the lower right stamp of the right pane of 4 of the booklet.

Statue of Liberty — A2680

A2680a

Printed by Bureau of Engraving and Printing.

Coil Stamps
Perf. 9¾ Vert.

3452 A2680 (34c) **multicolored** 1.10 .25
Pair 2.20 .30
P# strip of 5, #1111 6.00 —
P# single, same # — 2.25

Serpentine Die Cut 10 Vert.
Self-Adhesive

3453 A2680a (34c) **multicolored**, small date .70 .25
Pair 1.40
P# strip of 5, #1111 6.50
P# single, same # — 1.50
a. Die cutting omitted, pair *300.00*
b. Large date .75 .25
Pair 1.50
P# strip of 5, #1111 7.25
P# single, same # — 1.50

The date on No. 3453 is 1.4mm long, on No. 3453b 1.55mm long and darker in color.

A2681

A2682

A2683

Flowers — A2684

Designed by Derry Noyes.
Printed by American Packaging Corporation for Sennett Security Products (#3454-3457), Guilford Gravure for Banknote Corporation of America, Inc. (#3462-3465).

PHOTOGRAVURE
Serpentine Die Cut 10½x10¾ on 2 or 3 Sides

2000, Dec. 15 **Tagged**
Booklet Stamps
Self-Adhesive

3454 A2681 (34c) **purple & multi** 1.10 .25
3455 A2682 (34c) **tan & multi** 1.10 .25
3456 A2683 (34c) **green & multi** 1.10 .25
3457 A2684 (34c) **red & multi** 1.10 .25
a. Block of 4, #3454-3457 4.40
b. Booklet pane of 4, #3454-3457 4.40
c. Booklet pane of 6, #3456, 3457, 2 each #3454-3455 7.00
d. Booklet pane of 6, #3454, 3455, 2 each #3456-3457 7.00
e. Booklet pane of 20, 5 each #3454-3457 + label 22.50

No. 3457e is a double-sided booklet pane, with 12 stamps on one side and eight stamps plus label on the other side.

A2681a

A2682a

A2683a

A2684a

Printed by American Packaging Corporation for Sennett Security Products.

Serpentine Die Cut 11½x11¾ on 2 or 3 Sides

3458	A2681a (34c) **purple & multi**		5.00	.25
3459	A2682a (34c) **tan & multi**		5.00	.25
3460	A2683a (34c) **green & multi**		5.00	.25
3461	A2684a (34c) **red & multi**		5.00	.25
a.	Block of 4, #3458-3461		20.00	
b.	Booklet pane of 20, 2 each #3461a, 3 each #3457a		55.00	
c.	Booklet pane of 20, 2 each #3457a, 3 each #3461a		90.00	

Nos. 3461b and 3461c are double-sided booklet panes, with 12 stamps on one side and eight stamps plus label on the other side.

A2681b

A2682b

A2683a

A2684b

Printed by Guilford Gravure for Banknote Corporation of America, Inc.

Coil Stamps

Serpentine Die Cut 8½ Vert.

3462	A2683b (34c) **green & multi**	4.50	.25
3463	A2684b (34c) **red & multi**	4.50	.25
3464	A2682b (34c) **tan & multi**	4.50	.25
3465	A2681b (34c) **purple & multi**	4.50	.25
a.	Strip of 4, #3462-3465	20.00	
	P# strip of 5, 2 #3462, 1 each #3463-3465, P#B1111	27.50	
	P# strip of 9, 2 each #3462-3463, 3465, 3 #3464, same P#	45.00	
	P# single (#3464)	—	1.25

Lettering on No. 3462 has black outline not found on No. 3456. Zeroes of "2000" are rounder on Nos. 3454-3457 than on Nos. 3462-3465.

Statue of Liberty — A2685

Designed by Derry Noyes.
Printed by Bureau of Engraving and Printing.

PHOTOGRAVURE

Serpentine Die Cut 9¾ Vert.

2001, Jan. 7 **Tagged**

Coil Stamp

Self-Adhesive

3466	A2685 34c **multicolored**	.70	.25
	Pair	1.40	
	P# strip of 5, #1111, 2222	5.00	
	P# single, same #	—	2.50

George Washington
A2686

American Buffalo
A2687

A2687a

Designed by Carl Herrman (#3467, 3468), Richard Sheaff (#3468A).
Printed by Sterling Sommer for Ashton-Potter (USA) Ltd. (#3467), Avery Dennison (#3468), Banknote Corporation of America (#3468A).

Sheets of 400 in four panes of 100 (#3467), Sheets of 200 in 10 panes of 20 (#3468), Sheets of 120 in six panes of 20 (#3468A)

Self-Adhesive (#3468-3468A)

2001 **Photo.** **Tagged** ***Perf. 11¼x11***

3467	A2687	21c **multicolored**, *Sept. 20*	.50	.25
		P# block of 4, 6#+P	27.50	—
		Pane of 100	75.00	—

Serpentine Die Cut 11

3468	A2687a	21c **multicolored**, *Feb. 22*	.50	.25
		P# block of 4, 4#+V	4.00	
		Pane of 20	18.00	

Litho.

Serpentine Die Cut 11¼x11¾

3468A	A2686	23c **green**, *Sept. 20*	.50	.25
		P# block of 4, 3#+B	3.00	
		Pane of 20	14.00	

Flag Over
Farm — A2688

A2688a

Designed by Richard Sheaff.
Printed by Ashton-Potter (USA) Ltd.

Sheets of 200 in two panes of 100 (#3469), Sheets of 120 in six panes of 20 (#3470)

Self-Adhesive (#3470)

Photo.

Perf. 11¼

3469	A2688	34c **multicolored**, *Feb. 7*	.75	.25
		P# block of 4, 4#+P	25.00	—
		Pane of 100	100.00	—

Serpentine Die Cut 11¼

3470	A2688a	34c **multicolored**, *Mar. 6*	1.00	.25
		P# block of 4, 4#+P	7.50	
		Pane of 20	34.00	

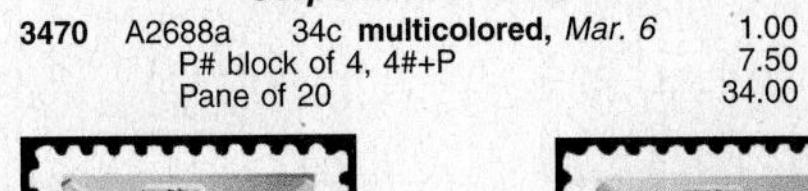

Eagle — A2696

A2696a

Designed by Carl Herrman.
Printed by American Packaging Corporation for Sennett Security Printers.

Sheets of 120 in six panes of 20 (#3471), Sheets of 160 in eight panes of 20 (#3471A)

Self-Adhesive (#3471-3471A)

Serpentine Die Cut 10¾

3471	A2696	55c **multicolored**, *Feb. 22*	1.10	.25
		P# block of 4, 5#+S	4.40	
		Pane of 20	22.00	
3471A	A2696a	57c **multicolored**, *Sept. 20*	1.10	.25
		P# block of 4, 5#+S	4.40	
		Pane of 20	22.00	

Capitol
Dome — A2697

Washington
Monument — A2698

Designed by Derry Noyes.
Printed by Banknote Corporation of America.

Sheets of 120 in six panes of 20

Serpentine Die Cut 11¼x11½

Litho.

Self-Adhesive (#3473)

3472	A2697	$3.50 **multicolored**, *Jan. 29*	7.00	2.00
		P# block of 4, 4#+B	28.00	
		Pane of 20	140.00	
a.		Die cutting omitted, pair	*500.00*	
3473	A2698	$12.25 **multicolored**, *Jan. 29*	22.50	10.00
		P# block of 4, 4#+B	90.00	
		Pane of 20	450.00	

Hidden images can be seen on Nos. 3472 and 3473 when viewed with a special "Stamp Decoder" lens sold by the USPS. No. 3472, PRIORITY MAIL; No. 3473, EXPRESS MAIL.

A2686a

A2687b

Designed by Carl Herrman (#3475), Richard Sheaff (#3475A).
Printed by Avery Dennison (#3475), Guilford Gravure, Inc. for Banknote Corporation of America (#3475A).

COIL STAMPS

Self-Adhesive (#3475-3475A, 3477-3481)

Photo.

Serpentine Die Cut 8½ Vert.

3475	A2687b	21c **multicolored**, *Feb. 22*	.50	.25
		Pair	1.00	.50
		P# strip of 5, #V1111, V2222	2.50	—
		P# single, same #	—	1.00
3475A	A2686a	23c **green**, *Sept. 20*	.75	.25
		Pair	1.50	
		P# strip of 5, #B11	3.25	
		P# single, same #	—	.85

Compare No. 3475A ("2001" date at lower left) with No. 3617 ("2002" date at lower left).

A2685a A2685b

Designed by Derry Noyes.
Printed by Bureau of Engraving and Printing.

Perf. 9¾ Vert.

3476 A2685a 34c **multicolored,** prephosphored coated paper, *Feb. 7* .90 .25
Pair 1.80 .50
P# strip of 5, #1111 5.50 —
P# single, #1111 — 2.75

No. 3476 exists on two types of surface-tagged paper that exhibit either a solid or a grainy solid appearance.

Serpentine Die Cut 9¾ Vert.

3477 A2685b 34c **multicolored,** *Feb. 7* .80 .25
Pair 1.60 .50
P# strip of 5, #1111, 2222, 3333, 4444, 5555, 6666 5.00 —
P# single, same # — 1.00
P# strip of 5, #7777 12.00
P# single, #7777 — 7.00
a. Die cutting omitted, pair *65.00*

No. 3477 has right angle corners and backing paper as high as the stamp. No. 3466 has rounded corners and is on backing paper larger than the stamp.

A2690 A2691

A2692 Flowers — A2693

Designed by Derry Noyes.
Printed by Guilford Gravure, Inc. for Banknote Corporation of America.

Serpentine Die Cut 8½ Vert.

3478 A2690 34c **green & multi,** *Feb. 7* 1.50 .25
3479 A2691 34c **red & multi,** *Feb. 7* 1.50 .25
3480 A2692 34c **tan & multi,** *Feb. 7* 1.50 .25
3481 A2693 34c **purple & multi,** *Feb. 7* 1.50 .25
a. Strip of 4, #3478-3481 6.00
P# strip of 5, 2 #3478, 1 each #3479-3481, P#B1111, B2111, B2122, B2211, B2222 10.00
P# strip of 9, 3 #3480, 2 each #3478-3479, 3481, P# B1111, B2111, B2122, B2211, B2222 15.00 —
P# single, (#3480), same # — 2.00

A2686b A2686c

Designed by Richard Sheaff.
Printed by Ashton-Potter (USA) Ltd.

BOOKLET STAMPS

Litho.

Self-Adhesive

Serpentine Die Cut 11¼x11 on 3 Sides

3482 A2686b 20c **dark carmine,** *Feb. 22* .55 .25
a. Booklet pane of 10 5.50
b. Booklet pane of 4 2.20
c. Booklet pane of 6 3.30

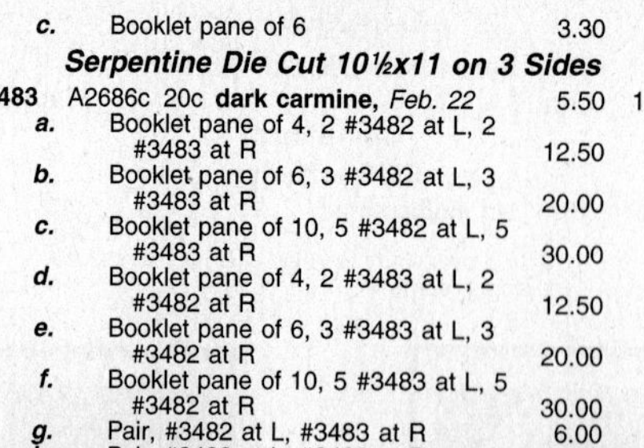

Serpentine Die Cut 10½x11 on 3 Sides

3483 A2686c 20c **dark carmine,** *Feb. 22* 5.50 1.25
a. Booklet pane of 4, 2 #3482 at L, 2 #3483 at R 12.50
b. Booklet pane of 6, 3 #3482 at L, 3 #3483 at R 20.00
c. Booklet pane of 10, 5 #3482 at L, 5 #3483 at R 30.00
d. Booklet pane of 4, 2 #3483 at L, 2 #3482 at R 12.50
e. Booklet pane of 6, 3 #3483 at L, 3 #3482 at R 20.00
f. Booklet pane of 10, 5 #3483 at L, 5 #3482 at R 30.00
g. Pair, #3482 at L, #3483 at R 6.00
h. Pair, #3483 at L, #3482 at R 6.00

A2687c A2687d

Designed by Carl Herrman.
Printed by Ashton-Potter (USA) Ltd.

Serpentine Die Cut 11¼ on 3 Sides

3484 A2687c 21c **multicolored,** *Sept. 20* .60 .25
b. Booklet pane of 4 2.40
c. Booklet pane of 6 3.60
d. Booklet pane of 10 6.00

Serpentine Die Cut 10½x11¼

3484A A2687d 21c **multicolored,** *Sept. 20* 5.50 1.50
e. Booklet pane of 4, 2 #3484 at L, 2 #3484A at R 12.50
f. Booklet pane of 6, 3 #3484 at L, 3 #3484A at R 20.00
g. Booklet pane of 10, 5 #3484 at L, 5 #3484A at R 30.00
h. Booklet pane of 4, 2 #3484A at L, 2 #3484 at R 12.50
i. Booklet pane of 6, 3 #3484A at L, 3 #3484 at R 20.00
j. Booklet pane of 10, 5 #3484A at L, 5 #3484 at R 30.00
k. Pair, #3484 at L, #3484A at R 6.00
l. Pair, #3484A at L, #3484 at R 6.00

Statue of Liberty — A2689

Designed by Derry Noyes.
Printed by Avery Dennison.

Photo.

Serpentine Die Cut 11 on 2, 3 or 4 Sides

3485 A2689 34c **multicolored,** *Feb. 7* .70 .25
a. Booklet pane of 10 7.00
b. Booklet pane of 20 14.00
c. Booklet pane of 4 3.00
Booklet pane of 4 containing P# single 4.00
P# single, #V1111, V1122, V2212, V2222 1.50 1.50
P# single, #V1112, V1121 — —
d. Booklet pane of 6 4.50
e. Die cutting omitted, pair (from No. 3485b) —
f. As "e," booklet pane of 20 —

The plate # single in No. 3485c is the lower right stamp of the right pane of 4 of the booklet.

A2690a A2691a

A2692a A2693a

Designed by Derry Noyes.
Printed by American Packaging Corporation for Sennett Security Printers.

Serpentine Die Cut 10½x10¾ on 2 or 3 Sides

3487 A2693a 34c **purple & multi,** *Feb. 7* .85 .25
3488 A2692a 34c **tan & multi,** *Feb. 7* .85 .25
3489 A2690a 34c **green & multi,** *Feb. 7* .85 .25
3490 A2691a 34c **red & multi,** *Feb. 7* .85 .25
a. Block of 4, #3487-3490 3.50
b. Booklet pane of 4, #3487-3490 3.50
c. Booklet pane of 6, #3489-3490, 2 each #3487-3488 5.00
d. Booklet pane of 6, #3487-3488, 2 each #3489-3490 5.00
e. Booklet pane of 20, 5 each #3490a + label 20.00

No. 3490e is a double-sided booklet pane, with 12 stamps on one side and eight stamps plus label on the other side.

Apple — A2694 A2694a

Orange — A2695 A2695a

Designed by Ned Seidler.
Printed by Banknote Corporation of America

Litho.

Serpentine Die Cut 11¼ on 2, 3 or 4 Sides

3491 A2694 34c **multicolored,** *Mar. 6* .70 .25
3492 A2695 34c **multicolored,** *Mar. 6* .70 .25
a. Pair, #3491-3492 1.40
b. Booklet pane, 10 each #3491-3492 14.00
c. As "a," black ("34 USA") omitted —
d. As "a," die cutting omitted *1,100.*
e. As "b," die cutting omitted *5,500.*
f. As "b," right four stamps yellow omitted *3,500.*

Serpentine Die Cut 11½x10¾ on 2 or 3 Sides

3493 A2694a 34c **multicolored,** *May* 1.05 .25
3494 A2695a 34c **multicolored,** *May* 1.05 .25
a. Pair, #3493-3494 2.10
b. Booklet pane, 2 each #3493-3494 4.20
Booklet pane, 2 each #3493-3494, containing P# single 5.50
P# single, #B1111 2.25 2.00
c. Booklet pane, 3 each #3493-3494, #3493 at UL 6.30
d. Booklet pane, 3 each #3493-3494, #3494 at UL 6.30

A2688b

Designed by Richard Sheaff.
Printed by Avery Dennison.

Serpentine Die Cut 8 on 2, 3, or 4 Sides

3495 A2688b 34c **multicolored,** *Dec. 17* 1.10 .25
a. Booklet pane of 18 18.00

See Nos. 3616-3619, 3819.

LOVE

Rose, Apr. 20, 1763 Love Letter by John Adams — A2699

Rose, Apr. 20, 1763 Love Letter by John Adams — A2700

A2700a

Rose, Aug. 11, 1763 Love Letter by Abigail Smith (Abigail Adams in 1764) — A2701

Designed by Lisa Catalone. Printed by Banknote Corporation of America, Inc.

LITHOGRAPHED

Sheets of 180 in nine panes of 20 (#3499)

Serpentine Die Cut 11¼ on 2, 3 or 4 Sides

2001 **Tagged**

Self-Adhesive

Booklet Stamps (Nos. 3496-3498)

3496 A2699 (34c) **multicolored,** *Jan. 19* 1.10 .25
- *a.* Booklet pane of 20 22.00
- *b.* Vert. pair, die cutting omitted between —

Serpentine Die Cut 11¼ on 2, 3 or 4 Sides

3497 A2700 34c **multicolored,** *Feb. 14* .90 .25
- *a.* Booklet pane of 20 18.00
- *b.* Vertical pair, die cutting omitted between —

Size: 18x21mm

Serpentine Die Cut 11½x10¾ on 2 or 3 Sides

3498 A2700a 34c **multicolored,** *Feb. 14* .85 .25
- *a.* Booklet pane of 4 3.50
  - Booklet pane of 4 containing P# single 5.50
  - P# single, #B1111 2.00 2.00
- *b.* Booklet pane of 6 5.10

Plate number single on No. 3498 is on the lower left stamp of the bottom pane of 4 of the booklet.

Serpentine Die Cut 11¼

3499 A2701 55c **multicolored,** *Feb. 14* 1.10 .25
- P# block of 4, 4#+B 4.50
- Pane of 20 22.50

See No. 3551.

CHINESE NEW YEAR

Year of the Snake — A2702

Designed by Clarence Lee. Printed by Sterling Sommer for Ashton-Potter (USA) Ltd.

LITHOGRAPHED

Sheets of 180 in nine panes of 20

2001, Jan. 20 **Tagged** ***Perf. 11¼***

3500 A2702 34c **multicolored** .75 .25
- P# block of 4, 5#+P 3.00 —
- Pane of 20 15.00 —

See Nos. 3895f, 3997f.

BLACK HERITAGE SERIES

Roy Wilkins (1901-81), Civil Rights Leader — A2703

Designed by Richard Sheaff. Printed by Ashton-Potter (USA) Ltd.

LITHOGRAPHED

Sheets of 180 in nine panes of 20

Serpentine Die Cut 11½x11¼

2001, Jan. 24 **Tagged**

Self-Adhesive

3501 A2703 34c **blue** .70 .25
- P# block of 4, 2#+P 2.80
- Pane of 20 14.00

AMERICAN ILLUSTRATORS

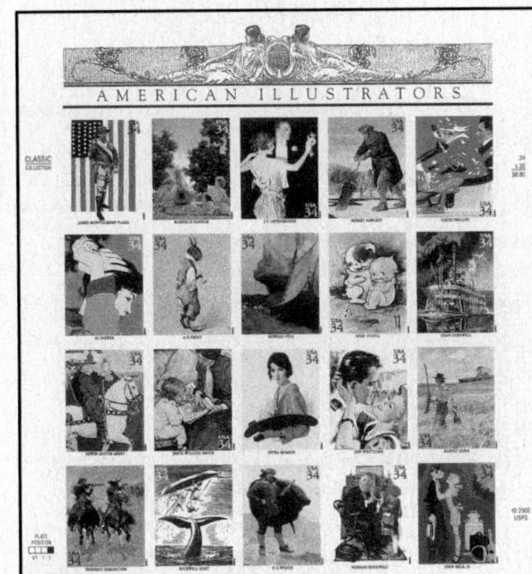
A2704

Illustration reduced.
Designed by Carl Herrman.
Printed by Avery Dennison.

No. 3502: a, Marine Corps poster "First in the Fight, Always Faithful," by James Montgomery Flagg. b, "Interlude (The Lute Players)," by Maxfield Parrish. c, Advertisement for Arrow Collars and Shirts, by J. C. Leyendecker. d, Advertisement for Carrier Corp. Refrigeration, by Robert Fawcett. e, Advertisement for Luxite Hosiery, by Coles Phillips. f, Illustration for correspondence school lesson, by Al Parker. g, "Br'er Rabbit," by A. B. Frost. h, "An Attack on a Galleon," by Howard Pyle. i, Kewpie and Kewpie Doodle Dog, by Rose O'Neill. j, Illustration for cover of True Magazine, by Dean Cornwell. k, "Galahad's Departure," by Edwin Austin Abbey. l, "The First Lesson," by Jessie Willcox Smith. m, Illustration for cover of McCall's Magazine, by Neysa McMein. n, "Back Home For Keeps," by Jon Whitcomb. o, "Something for Supper," by Harvey Dunn. p, "A Dash for the Timber," by Frederic Remington. q, Illustration for "Moby Dick," by Rockwell Kent. r, "Captain Bill Bones," by N. C. Wyeth. s, Illustration for cover of The Saturday Evening Post, by Norman Rockwell. t, "The Girl He Left Behind," by John Held, Jr.

PHOTOGRAVURE

Sheets of 80 in four panes of 20

2001, Feb. 1 **Tagged** ***Serpentine Die Cut 11¼***

Self-Adhesive

3502 A2704 Pane of 20 19.00
- *a.-t.* 34c any single .90 .60

Uncut press sheets of No. 3502 were made available for sale. Values: block of 20 diff. stamps with vert. gutter btwn. any 2 columns, $40; pairs with vert. gutters btwn., $4 each. See note after No. 2868.

DIABETES AWARENESS

A2705

Designed by Richard Sheaff. Printed by Ashton-Potter (USA) Ltd.

LITHOGRAPHED

Sheets of 180 in nine panes of 20

Serpentine Die Cut 11¼x11½

2001, Mar. 16 **Tagged**

Self-Adhesive

3503 A2705 34c **multicolored** .65 .25
- P# block of 4, 4#+P 2.60
- Pane of 20 13.00

NOBEL PRIZE CENTENARY

Alfred Nobel and Obverse of Medals A2706

Designed by Olof Baldursdottir of Sweden. Printed by De La Rue Security Printing.

LITHOGRAPHED & ENGRAVED

Sheets of 120 in six panes of 20

2001, Mar. 22 **Tagged** ***Perf. 11***

3504 A2706 34c **multicolored** .70 .25
- P# block of 4, 3#+S 2.80 —
- Pane of 20 14.00 —
- *a.* Imperf, pair *500.00*

See Sweden No. 2415.

PAN-AMERICAN EXPOSITION INVERT STAMPS, CENT.

A2707

Illustration reduced.

Designed by Richard Sheaff. Printed by Banknote Corporation of America.

No. 3505: Reproductions (dated 2001) of: a, #294a. b, #295a. c, #296a. d, Commemorative "cinderella" stamp depicting a buffalo.

LITHOGRAPHED (#3505d), ENGRAVED (others)

Sheets of 28 in four panes of 7

2001, Mar. 29 ***Perf. 12 (#3505d), 12½x12 (others)***

Tagged (#3505d), Untagged (others)

3505 A2707 Pane of 7, #3505a-3505c, 4 #3505d 10.00 7.00
- *a.* A109 1c **green & black** .75 .25
- *b.* A110 2c **carmine & black** .75 .25
- *c.* A111 4c **deep red brown & black** .75 .25
- *d.* 80c **red & blue** 1.90 .35
- *e.* As #3505, all colors except black (vignettes) missing on a.-c. (CM) *15,000.*

On No. 3505e, the green, carmine and deep red brown frames appear 4mm above Nos. 3505a-3505c on the pane.

Uncut press sheets of No. 3505 were made available for sale. Value: pane with vert. gutter, 80c stamps at left, Nos. 3505a-3505c at right, $22.50. See note after No. 2868.

GREAT PLAINS PRAIRIE Ⓢ

A2708

Illustration reduced.

Designed by Ethel Kessler. Printed by Ashton-Potter (USA) Ltd.

No. 3506 — Wildlife and flowers: a, Pronghorns, Canada geese. b, Burrowing owls, American buffalos. c, American buffalo, Black-tailed prairie dogs, wild alfalfa, horiz. d, Black-tailed prairie dog, American buffalos,. e, Painted lady butterfly, American buffalo, prairie coneflowers, prairie wild roses, horiz. f, Western meadowlark, camel cricket, prairie coneflowers, prairie wild roses. g, Badger, harvester ants. h, Eastern short-horned lizard, plains pocket gopher. i, Plains spadefoot, dung beetle, prairie wild roses, horiz. j, Two-striped grasshopper, Ord's kangaroo rat.

LITHOGRAPHED

Sheets of 60 in six panes of 10

2001, Apr. 19 Tagged *Serpentine Die Cut 10*

Self-Adhesive

3506 A2708 Pane of 10	10.00	
a.-j. 34c Any single	1.00	.50

Uncut press sheets of No. 3506 were made available for sale. See note after No. 2868.

See note after No. 1549.

PEANUTS COMIC STRIP

Snoopy A2709

Designed by Paige Braddock. Printed by Ashton-Potter (USA) Ltd.

LITHOGRAPHED

Sheets of 180 in nine panes of 20

Serpentine Die Cut 11¼x11½

2001, May 17 Tagged

Self-Adhesive

3507 A2709 34c **multicolored**	.80	.25
P# block of 4, 5#+P	3.50	
Pane of 20	17.50	

HONORING VETERANS

A2710

Designed by Carl Herrman. Printed by Ashton-Potter (USA) Ltd.

LITHOGRAPHED

Sheets of 180 in nine panes of 20

Serpentine Die Cut 11¼x11½

2001, May 23 Tagged

Self-Adhesive

3508 A2710 34c **multicolored**	.80	.25
P# block of 4, 4#+P	3.25	
Pane of 20	16.50	11.00

FRIDA KAHLO (1907-54), PAINTER

Self-portrait — A2711

Designed by Richard Sheaff. Printed by Sterling Sommer for Ashton-Potter (USA) Ltd..

LITHOGRAPHED

Sheets of 80 in four panes of 20

2001, June 21 Tagged *Perf. 11¼*

3509 A2711 34c **multicolored**	.70	.25
P# block of 4, 4#+P	3.25	—
Pane of 20	16.00	—

LEGENDARY PLAYING FIELDS

Ebbets Field — A2712

Tiger Stadium A2713

Crosley Field — A2714

Yankee Stadium A2715

Polo Grounds A2716

Forbes Field — A2717

Fenway Park — A2718

Comiskey Park — A2719

Shibe Park — A2720

Wrigley Field — A2721

Designed by Phil Jordan. Printed by Avery Dennison.

PHOTOGRAVURE

Sheets of 160 in eight panes of 20

Serpentine Die Cut 11¼x11½

2001, June 27 Tagged Self-Adhesive

3510 A2712 34c **multicolored**	.90	.60
3511 A2713 34c **multicolored**	.90	.60
3512 A2714 34c **multicolored**	.90	.60
3513 A2715 34c **multicolored**	.90	.60
3514 A2716 34c **multicolored**	.90	.60
3515 A2717 34c **multicolored**	.90	.60
3516 A2718 34c **multicolored**	.90	.60
3517 A2719 34c **multicolored**	.90	.60
3518 A2720 34c **multicolored**	.90	.60
3519 A2721 34c **multicolored**	.90	.60
a. Block of 10, #3510-3519	9.00	
P# block of 10, 4#+V	9.00	
Pane of 20	18.00	

Uncut press sheets of Nos. 3510-3519 were made available for sale. Values: cross-gutter block of 12, $27.50; pairs with gutters between, $3 each. See note after No. 2868.

ATLAS STATUE, NEW YORK CITY

A2722

Designed by Kevin Newman. Printed by Banknote Corporation of America.

PHOTOGRAVURE

COIL STAMP

Serpentine Die Cut 8½ Vert.

2001, June 29 Untagged

Self-Adhesive

3520 A2722 (10c) **multicolored**, dated "2001"	.30	.25
Pair	.40	
P# strip of 5, #B1111	2.25	
P# single, same #	—	1.40

No. 3520 is dated 2001. See No. 3770.

No. 3520 is known with extremely faint tagging, most likely from contamination in the paper-making process.

LEONARD BERNSTEIN (1918-90), CONDUCTOR

A2723

Designed by Howard Paine. Printed by Sterling Sommer for Ashton-Potter (USA) Ltd.

LITHOGRAPHED

Sheets of 180 in nine panes of 20

2001, July 10 Tagged *Perf. 11¼*

3521 A2723 34c **multicolored**	.70	.25
P# block of 4, 4#+P	2.80	—
Pane of 20	14.00	—

WOODY WAGON

A2724

Designed by Kevin Newman. Printed by American Packaging Corporation for Sennett Security Products.

PHOTOGRAVURE

COIL STAMP

Serpentine Die Cut 11½ Vert.

2001, Aug. 3 Untagged

Self-Adhesive

3522 A2724 (15c) **multicolored**	.30	.25
Pair	.60	
P# strip of 5, #S11111	2.75	
P# single, same #	—	2.00

LEGENDS OF HOLLYWOOD

Lucille Ball (1911-89) — A2725

Designed by Derry Noyes. Printed by Banknote Corporation of America.

LITHOGRAPHED

Sheets of 180 in nine panes of 20

2001, Aug. 6 Tagged *Serpentine Die Cut 11*

Self-Adhesive

3523 A2725 34c **multicolored**	1.00	.25
P# block of 4, 4#+B	5.00	
Pane of 20	24.00	13.00
a. Die cutting omitted, pair	*700.00*	
As "a," pane of 20	—	

Uncut press sheets of No. 3523 were made available for sale. Values: cross-gutter block of 8, $30; pairs with gutters between, $3.25 each. See note after No. 2868.

AMERICAN TREASURES SERIES
Amish Quilts

Diamond in the Square, c. 1920 — A2726

Lone Star, c. 1920 — A2727

Sunshine and Shadow, c. 1910 — A2728

Double Ninepatch Variation — A2729

Designed by Derry Noyes. Printed by Ashton-Potter (USA) Ltd.

LITHOGRAPHED

Sheets of 120 in six panes of 20

Serpentine Die Cut 11¼x11½

2001, Aug. 9 Tagged

Self-Adhesive

3524 A2726 34c **multicolored**	.70	.30
3525 A2727 34c **multicolored**	.70	.30
3526 A2728 34c **multicolored**	.70	.30
3527 A2729 34c **multicolored**	.70	.30
a. Block or strip of 4, #3524-3527	2.80	
P# block of 4, 5#+P	2.80	
Pane of 20	14.00	

CARNIVOROUS PLANTS

Venus Flytrap — A2730

Yellow Trumpet — A2731

Cobra Lily — A2732

English Sundew — A2733

Designed by Steve Buchanan. Printed by Avery Dennison.

PHOTOGRAVURE

Sheets of 160 in eight panes of 20

2001, Aug. 23 Tagged *Serpentine Die Cut 11½*

Self-Adhesive

3528 A2730 34c **multicolored**	.70	.25
3529 A2731 34c **multicolored**	.70	.25
3530 A2732 34c **multicolored**	.70	.25
3531 A2733 34c **multicolored**	.70	.25
a. Block or strip of 4, #3528-3531	2.80	
P# block of 4, 4#+V	2.80	
Pane of 20	14.00	

EID

"Eid Mubarak" — A2734

Designed by Mohamed Zakariya. Printed by Avery Dennison.

PHOTOGRAVURE

Sheets of 240 in 12 panes of 20

2001, Sept. 1 Tagged *Serpentine Die Cut 11¼*

Self-Adhesive

3532 A2734 34c **multicolored**	.70	.25
P# block of 4, 3#+V	2.80	
Pane of 20	14.00	

See Nos. 3674, 4117, 4202, 4351, 4416.

ENRICO FERMI (1901-54), PHYSICIST

A2735

Designed by Richard Sheaff. Printed by Sterling Sommer for Ashton-Potter (USA) Ltd.

LITHOGRAPHED

Sheets of 180 in nine panes of 20

2001, Sept. 29 **Tagged** *Perf. 11*

3533	A2735 34c **multicolored**	.70	.25
	P# block of 4, 4#+P	2.80	—
	Pane of 20	14.00	—

THAT'S ALL FOLKS!

Porky Pig at Mailbox — A2736

Designed by Ed Wleczyk, Warner Bros. Printed by Avery Dennison.

PHOTOGRAVURE

2001, Oct. 1 **Tagged** *Serpentine Die Cut 11*

Self-Adhesive

3534	Pane of 10 #3534a	7.00	
a.	A2736 34c single	.70	.25
b.	Pane of 9 #3534a	6.25	
c.	Pane of 1 #3534a	.70	

Die cutting on No. 3534b does not extend through the backing paper.

Uncut press sheets of No. 3534 were made available for sale. Values: sheet of 60 with no P#s, $50; sheet of 60 with P# on front and reverse, $55; cross-gutter block of 7, $17.50; pairs with gutters between, $4 each. See note after No. 2868.

3535	Pane of 10, #3535c, 9 #3535a	50.00	
a.	A2736 34c single	2.75	
b.	Pane of 9 #3535a	25.00	
c.	Pane of 1, no die cutting	25.00	

Die cutting on No. 3535a extends through backing paper.

Nos. 3534b-3534c and 3535b-3535c are separated by a vertical line of microperforations.

CHRISTMAS

Virgin and Child, by Lorenzo Costa — A2737

Designed by Richard Sheaff.
Printed by Guilford Gravure, Inc., for Banknote Corporation of America.

PHOTOGRAVURE

Serpentine Die Cut 11½ on 2, 3 or 4 Sides

2001, Oct. 10 **Tagged**

Self-Adhesive

Booklet Stamps (#3536, 3537a-3540a, 3537b, 3538b, 3539b, 3540e, 3541-3544)

3536	A2737 34c **multicolored**	.75	.25
a.	Booklet pane of 20	15.00	

A2738

A2739

A2740

19th Century Chromolithographs of Santa Claus — A2741

Printed by American Packaging Corporation for Sennett Security Products.

Sheets of 160 in eight panes of 20 (#3537-3540)

Serpentine Die Cut 10¾x11

Black Inscriptions

3537	A2738 34c **multicolored,** large date	.70	.25
a.	Small date (from booklet pane) ®	.90	.25
b.	Large date (from booklet pane)	2.00	.25
3538	A2739 34c **multicolored,** large date	.70	.25
a.	Small date (from booklet pane) ®	.90	.25
b.	Large date (from booklet pane)	2.00	.25
3539	A2740 34c **multicolored,** large date	.70	.25
a.	Small date (from booklet pane) ®	.90	.25
b.	Large date (from booklet pane)	2.00	.25
3540	A2741 34c **multicolored,** large date	.70	.25
a.	Small date (from booklet pane) ®	.90	.25
b.	Block or strip of 4, #3537-3540	2.80	
	P# block of 4, 4#+S	3.50	
	Pane of 20	17.00	
c.	Block of 4, small date, #3537a-3540a	3.60	
d.	Booklet pane of 20, 5 #3540c + label	18.00	
e.	Large date (from booklet pane)	2.00	.25
f.	Block of 4, large date, #3537b-3539b, 3540e	8.00	
g.	Booklet pane of 20, 5 #3540f + label	40.00	

Nos. 3540d and 3540g are double-sided booklet panes, with 12 stamps on one side and eight stamps plus label on the other side.

Numerals "3" and "4" are distinctly separate on Nos. 3537-3540, and touching or separated by a slight hairline on the booklet pane stamps.

Designs of booklet stamps Nos. 3537a-3539a and 3537b-3539b are slightly taller than Nos. 3537-3539. Nos. 3540a and 3540e measure the same as No. 3540.

See note after No. 1549

A2738a

A2739a

A2740a

A2741a

Printed by Avery Dennison.

Serpentine Die Cut 11 on 2 or 3 Sides

Size: 21x18½mm

Green and Red Inscriptions

3541	A2738a 34c **multicolored**	.90	.25
3542	A2739a 34c **multicolored**	.90	.25
3543	A2740a 34c **multicolored**	.90	.25
3544	A2741a 34c **multicolored**	.90	.25
a.	Block of 4, #3541-3544	3.60	
b.	Booklet pane of 4, #3541-3544	3.60	
c.	Booklet pane of 6, #3543-3544, 2 #3541-3542	5.40	
d.	Booklet pane of 6, #3541-3542, 2 #3543-3544	5.40	
	Nos. 3536-3544 (9)	7.15	2.25

JAMES MADISON (1751-1836)

Madison and His Home, Montpelier A2742

Designed by John Thompson.
Printed by Banknote Corporation of America.

LITHOGRAPHED & ENGRAVED

Sheets of 120 in six panes of 20

2001, Oct. 18 **Tagged** *Perf. 11x11¼*

3545	A2742 34c **green & black**	.70	.25
	P# block of 4, 2#+B	2.80	—
	Pane of 20	14.00	—

Uncut press sheets of No. 3545 were made available for sale. Values: cross-gutter block of 4, $10; pairs with gutters between, $3.50 each. See note after No. 2868.

THANKSGIVING

Cornucopia — A2743

Designed by Richard Sheaff.
Printed by Ashton-Potter (USA) Ltd.

LITHOGRAPHED

Sheets of 180 in nine panes of 20

2001, Oct. 19 **Tagged** *Serpentine Die Cut 11¼*

Self-Adhesive

3546	A2743 34c **multicolored**	.70	.25
	P# block of 4, 4#+P	2.80	
	Pane of 20	14.00	

Hanukkah — A2743a

Designed by Hannah Smotrich.
Printed by Avery Dennison.

PHOTOGRAVURE

Sheets of 200 in 10 panes of 20

2001, Oct. 21 **Tagged** *Serpentine Die Cut 11*

Self-Adhesive

3547	A2743a 34c **multicolored**	.70	.25
	P# block of 4, 5#+V	2.80	
	Pane of 20	14.00	

See Nos. 3118, 3352, 3672, Israel No. 1289.

Kwanzaa — A2743b

Designed by Synthia Saint James.
Printed by Avery Dennison.

PHOTOGRAVURE

Sheets of 240 in 12 panes of 20

2001, Oct. 21 **Tagged** *Serpentine Die Cut 11*

Self-Adhesive

3548	A2743b 34c **multicolored**	.70	.25
	P# block of 4, 4#+V	2.80	
	Pane of 20	14.00	

See Nos. 3175, 3368, 3673.

UNITED WE STAND

A2744

A2744a

Designed by Terry McCaffrey. Printed by Banknote Corporation of America (#3549), Bureau of Engraving and Printing (#3550).

LITHOGRAPHED
BOOKLET STAMPS

Serpentine Die Cut 11¼ on 2, 3, or 4 Sides

2001, Oct. 24 **Tagged**

Self-Adhesive

3549 A2744 34c **multicolored**	.75	.25
a. Booklet pane of 20	15.00	

PHOTOGRAVURE

Serpentine Die Cut 10½x10¾ on 2 or 3 Sides

2002, Jan. **Tagged**

Self-Adhesive

3549B A2744a 34c **multicolored**	.85	.25
c. Booklet pane of 4	3.40	
d. Booklet pane of 6	5.10	
e. Booklet pane of 20	18.00	

No. 3549Be is a double-sided booklet pane, with 12 stamps on one side and eight stamps plus label on the other side.

"First day covers" of No. 3549B are dated Oct. 24, 2001.

A2744b

A2744c

Printed by Bureau of Engraving and Printing (#3550).

COIL STAMPS
Self-Adhesive

Serpentine Die Cut 9¾ Vert.

2001, Oct. 24 **Tagged**

3550 A2744b 34c **multicolored,** perpendicular corners	1.25	.25
Pair	2.50	
P# strip of 5, #1111, 2222	5.50	
P# strip of 5, #3333	8.50	
P# single, #1111, 2222	—	1.00
P# single, #3333	—	3.00
3550A A2744c 34c **multicolored**	1.75	.25
Pair	3.50	
P# strip of 5, #1111	9.50	
P# single, same #	—	3.00

No. 3550 has right angle corners and backing paper as high as the stamp. No. 3550A has rounded corners, the backing paper larger than the stamp, and the stamps are spaced approximately 2mm apart.

Love Letters — A2744d

Designed by Lisa Catalone.
Printed by Banknote Corporation of America.

LITHOGRAPHED

Sheets of 160 in eight panes of 20

2001, Nov. 19 **Tagged** ***Serpentine Die Cut 11¼***

Self-Adhesive

3551 A2744d 57c **multicolored**	1.20	.25
P# block of 4, 4# + B	4.80	
Pane of 20	24.00	

See. No. 3499.

WINTER OLYMPICS

Ski Jumping A2745

Snowboarding A2746

Ice Hockey A2747

Figure Skating A2748

Designed by Jager Di Paola Kemp. Printed by American Packaging Corporation for Sennett Security Products.

PHOTOGRAVURE

Sheets of 180 in nine panes of 20

Serpentine Die Cut 11½x10¾

2002, Jan. 8 **Tagged**

Self-Adhesive

3552 A2745 34c **multicolored**	.70	.35
3553 A2746 34c **multicolored**	.70	.35
3554 A2747 34c **multicolored**	.70	.35
3555 A2748 34c **multicolored**	.70	.35
a. Block or strip of 4, #3552-3555	2.80	
P# block of 4, 6#+S (UL and UR only)	4.50	
Pane of 20	19.00	
b. Die cutting inverted, pane of 20	*100.00*	
c. Die cutting omitted, block of 4	*825.00*	
As "c," pane of 20	—	

Uncut press sheets of Nos. 3552-3555 were made available for sale. Values: cross-gutter block of 8, $25; pairs with gutters between, $3 each. See note after No. 2868.

MENTORING A CHILD

Child and Adult — A2749

Designed by Lance Hidy. Printed by American Packaging Corporation for Sennett Security Products.

PHOTOGRAVURE

Sheets of 120 in six panes of 20

Serpentine Die Cut 11x10¾

2002, Jan. 10 **Tagged**

Self-Adhesive

3556 A2749 34c **multicolored**	.70	.25
P# block of 4, 5#+S	2.80	
Pane of 20	14.00	

BLACK HERITAGE SERIES

Langston Hughes (1902-67), Writer — A2750

Designed by Richard Sheaff. Printed by Banknote Corporation of America.

LITHOGRAPHED

Sheets of 120 in six panes of 20

Serpentine Die Cut 10¼x10½

2002, Feb. 1 **Tagged**

Self-Adhesive

3557 A2750 34c **multicolored**	.70	.25
P# block of 4, 5#+B	3.00	
Pane of 20	15.00	
a. Die cutting omitted, pair	*725.00*	
As "a," pane of 20	—	

Beware of pairs/panes with extremely faint die cutting offered as imperf errors.

HAPPY BIRTHDAY

A2751

Designed by Harry Zelenko. Printed by Avery Dennison.

PHOTOGRAVURE

Sheets of 200 in 10 panes of 20

2002, Feb. 8 **Tagged** ***Serpentine Die Cut 11***

Self-Adhesive

3558 A2751 34c **multicolored**	.75	.25
P# block of 4, 4#+V	3.00	
Pane of 20	15.00	

See Nos. 3695, 4079.

CHINESE NEW YEAR

Year of the Horse A2752

Designed by Clarence Lee. Printed by Banknote Corporation of America.

LITHOGRAPHED

Sheets of 120 in six panes of 20

Serpentine Die Cut 10½x10¼

2002, Feb. 11 **Tagged**

Self-Adhesive

3559 A2752 34c **multicolored**	.75	.25
P# block of 4, 5#+B	3.00	
Pane of 20	15.00	
a. Horiz. pair, vert. die cutting omitted	*5,000.*	

See Nos. 3895g, 3997g.

U.S. MILITARY ACADEMY, BICENT.

Military Academy Coat of Arms — A2753

Designed by Derry Noyes. Printed by American Packaging Corp. for Sennett Security Products.

PHOTOGRAVURE
Sheets of 180 in nine panes of 20
Serpentine Die Cut 10½x11

2002, Mar. 16 **Tagged**

Self-Adhesive

3560 A2753 34c **multicolored**	.75	.25
P# block of 4, 6#+S	3.00	
Pane of 20	15.00	

GREETINGS FROM AMERICA

Illustration reduced.
Designed by Richard Sheaff. Printed by American Packaging Corp. for Sennett Security Products.

PHOTOGRAVURE
Sheets of 100 in two panes of 50

2002, Apr. 4 **Tagged** ***Serpentine Die Cut 10¾***

Self-Adhesive

3561 A2754 34c Alabama	.70	.60
3562 A2755 34c Alaska	.70	.60
3563 A2756 34c Arizona	.70	.60
3564 A2757 34c Arkansas	.70	.60
3565 A2758 34c California	.70	.60
3566 A2759 34c Colorado	.70	.60
3567 A2760 34c Connecticut	.70	.60
3568 A2761 34c Delaware	.70	.60
3569 A2762 34c Florida	.70	.60
3570 A2763 34c Georgia	.70	.60
3571 A2764 34c Hawaii	.70	.60
3572 A2765 34c Idaho	.70	.60
3573 A2766 34c Illinois	.70	.60
3574 A2767 34c Indiana	.70	.60
3575 A2768 34c Iowa	.70	.60
3576 A2769 34c Kansas	.70	.60
3577 A2770 34c Kentucky	.70	.60
3578 A2771 34c Louisiana	.70	.60
3579 A2772 34c Maine	.70	.60
3580 A2773 34c Maryland	.70	.60
3581 A2774 34c Massachusetts	.70	.60
3582 A2775 34c Michigan	.70	.60
3583 A2776 34c Minnesota	.70	.60
3584 A2777 34c Mississippi	.70	.60
3585 A2778 34c Missouri	.70	.60
3586 A2779 34c Montana	.70	.60
3587 A2780 34c Nebraska	.70	.60
3588 A2781 34c Nevada	.70	.60
3589 A2782 34c New Hampshire	.70	.60
3590 A2783 34c New Jersey	.70	.60
3591 A2784 34c New Mexico	.70	.60
3592 A2785 34c New York	.70	.60
3593 A2786 34c North Carolina	.70	.60
3594 A2787 34c North Dakota	.70	.60
3595 A2788 34c Ohio	.70	.60
3596 A2789 34c Oklahoma	.70	.60
3597 A2790 34c Oregon	.70	.60
3598 A2791 34c Pennsylvania	.70	.60
3599 A2792 34c Rhode Island	.70	.60
3600 A2793 34c South Carolina	.70	.60
3601 A2794 34c South Dakota	.70	.60
3602 A2795 34c Tennessee	.70	.60
3603 A2796 34c Texas	.70	.60
3604 A2797 34c Utah	.70	.60
3605 A2798 34c Vermont	.70	.60
3606 A2799 34c Virginia	.70	.60
3607 A2800 34c Washington	.70	.60
3608 A2801 34c West Virginia	.70	.60
3609 A2802 34c Wisconsin	.70	.60
3610 A2803 34c Wyoming	.70	.60
a. Pane of 50, #3561-3610	35.00	

See Nos. 3696-3745.

Uncut press sheets of Nos. 3561-3610 were made available for sale. Values: block of 50 diff. stamps with vert. gutter btwn. any 2 columns, $40; pairs with vert. gutters between, $3 each. See note after No. 2868.

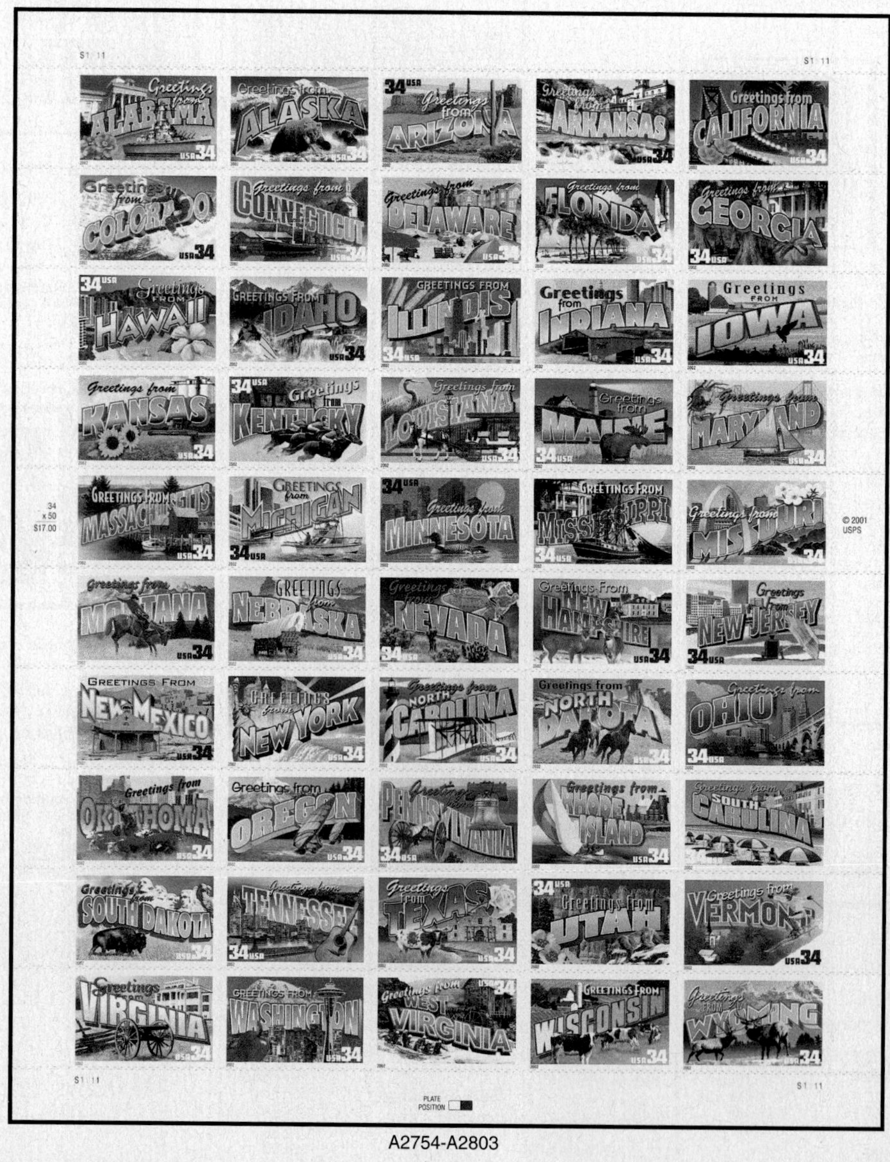

A2754-A2803

LONGLEAF PINE FOREST

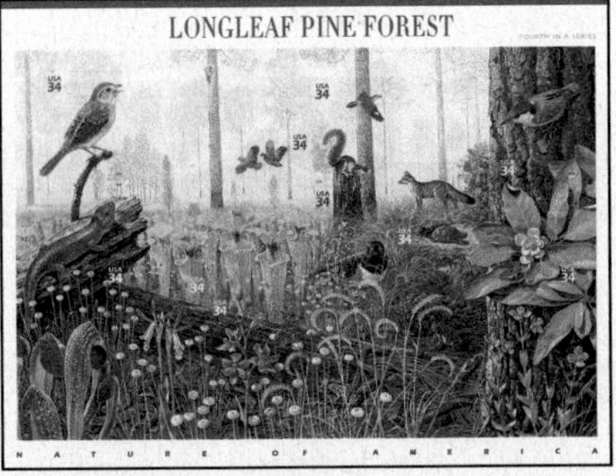

A2804

Illustration reduced.

Designed by Ethel Kessler. Printed by American Packaging Corp. for Sennett Security Products.

No. 3611 — Wildlife and flowers: a, Bachman's sparrow. b, Northern bobwhite, yellow pitcher plants. c, Fox squirrel, red-bellied woodpecker. d, Brown-headed nuthatch. e, Broadhead skink, yellow pitcher plants, pipeworts. f, Eastern towhee, yellow pitcher plants, Savannah meadow beauties, toothache grass. g, Gray fox, gopher tortoise, horiz. h, Blind click beetle, sweetbay, pine woods treefrog. i, Rosebud orchid, pipeworts, southern toad, yellow pitcher plants. j, Grass-pink orchid, yellow-sided skimmer, pipeworts, yellow pitcher plants, horiz.

PHOTOGRAVURE

Sheets of 90 in nine panes of 10

Serpentine Die Cut 10½x10¾, 10¾x10½

2002, Apr. 26 **Tagged**

Self-Adhesive

3611	A2804	Pane of 10	19.00	
a.-j.		34c Any single	1.90	.50
k.		As No. 3611, die cutting omitted	*2,500.*	

Uncut press sheets of No. 3611 were made available for sale. See note after No. 2868.

AMERICAN DESIGN SERIES

Toleware Coffeepot — A2805

Designed by Derry Noyes.

Printed by American Packaging Corp. for Sennett Security Products.

PHOTOGRAVURE

COIL STAMP

2002, May 31 **Untagged** ***Perf. 9¾ Vert.***

3612	A2805 5c **multicolored**	.30	.25
	Pair	.50	.50
	P# strip of 5, #S1111111	1.10	—
	P# single, #S1111111	—	.70
a.	Imperf, pair	1,200.	

No. 3612a is valued with disturbed gum. It is also known without gum and is valued only slightly less thus.

See Nos. 3756-3756A.

Star — A2806

Designed by Phil Jordan. Printed by Banknote Corporation of America.

LITHOGRAPHED

Sheets of 400 in eight panes of 50

2002, June 7 **Untagged** ***Serpentine Die Cut 11***

Self-Adhesive (#3613-3614)

Year at Lower Left

3613 A2806 3c **red, blue & black**	.30	.25
P# block of 4, 3#+B	.30	
Pane of 50	5.00	—
a. Die cutting omitted, pair	—	

A2806a

A2806b

PHOTOGRAVURE

Serpentine Die Cut 10

Year at Lower Right

Untagged

3614 A2806a 3c **red, blue & black**	.30	.25
P# block of 4, 3#+B	.30	
Pane of 50	5.00	—

Coil Stamp

Perf. 9¾ Vert.

Year at Lower Left

Untagged

3615 A2806b 3c **red, blue & black**	.30	.25
Pair	.30	.25
P# strip of 5, #S111	.90	—
P# single, same #	—	.70
a. Prephosphored coated paper with surface tagging showing a solid appearance (error)	.40	.25
Pair	.80	.50
P# strip of 5, #S111	8.00	—
P# single, same #	—	8.00

A2806c

A2806d

Designed by Richard Sheaff. Printed by Ashton-Potter (USA) Ltd. Avery Dennison (#3617).

LITHOGRAPHED, PHOTOGRAVURE (#3617)

Sheets of 400 in four panes of 100 (#3616)

2002, June 7 **Tagged** ***Perf. 11¼***

3616 A2806c 23c **green**	.50	.25
P# block of 4, 1#+P	25.00	—
Pane of 100	75.00	—

Self-Adhesive

Coil Stamp

Serpentine Die Cut 8½ Vert.

3617 A2806d 23c **gray green**	.45	.25
Pair	.90	
P# strip of 5, #V11, V13, V21, V22, V24, V35, V36, V45, V46	3.25	
P# single, same #	—	1.00
a. Die cutting omitted, pair	500.00	

Compare No. 3617 ("2002" date at lower left) with No. 3475A ("2001" date at lower left).

A2806e

A2806f

Printed by Ashton-Potter (USA) Ltd.

LITHOGRAPHED

Booklet Stamps

Serpentine Die Cut 11¼x11 on 3 Sides

3618 A2806e 23c **green**	.50	.25
a. Booklet pane of 4	2.00	
b. Booklet pane of 6	3.00	
c. Booklet pane of 10	5.00	
d. Nos. 3619c and 3619d, in bklt. of 10 (#BK289A), imperf. vert. btwn. on both panes	*1,100.*	

Serpentine Die Cut 10½x11 on 3 Sides

3619 A2806f 23c **green**	4.50	1.75
a. Booklet pane of 4, 2 #3619 at L, 2 #3618 at R	10.00	
b. Booklet pane of 6, 3 #3619 at L, 3 #3618 at R	15.00	
c. Booklet pane of 4, 2 #3618 at L, 2 #3619 at R	10.00	
d. Booklet pane of 6, 3 #3618 at L, 3 #3619 at R	15.00	
e. Booklet pane of 10, 5 #3619 at L, 5#3618 at R	27.50	
f. Booklet pane of 10, 5 #3618 at L, 5 #3619 at R	27.50	
g. Pair, #3619 at L, #3618 at R	5.00	
h. Pair, #3618 at L, #3619 at R	5.00	

See Nos. 3468A, 3475A, 3482-3483, 3819.

Flag — A2807

Designed by Terrence W. McCaffrey. Printed by Sterling Sommer for Ashton-Potter (USA) Ltd.

LITHOGRAPHED

Sheets of 400 in four panes of 100

2002, June 7 **Tagged** ***Perf. 11¼x11***

3620 A2807 (37c) **multicolored**	1.10	.25
P# block of 4, 4#+P	25.00	—
Pane of 100	130.00	—

A2807a

A2807b

Printed by Ashton-Potter (USA) Ltd. (#3621), Bureau of Engraving and Printing.

LITHOGRAPHED, PHOTOGRAVURE (#3622)

Sheets of 120 in six panes of 20 (#3621)

Self-Adhesive

Serpentine Die Cut 11¼x11

3621 A2807a (37c) **multicolored**	1.10	.25
P# block of 4, 4#+P	8.00	
Pane of 20	36.00	

Coil Stamp

Serpentine Die Cut 10 Vert.

3622 A2807b (37c) **multicolored**	1.10	.25
Pair	2.20	
P# strip of 5, #1111, 2222	7.00	
P# single, same #	—	1.00
a. Die cutting omitted, pair	*475.00*	
b. Yellow omitted		—

Counterfeits exist of No. 3622. See the Postal Counterfeits section of this catalog.

A2807c

A2807d

A2807e

Printed by Banknote Corporation of America (#3623), American Packaging Corporation for Sennett Security Products (#3624), Avery Dennison (#3625).

LITHOGRAPHED (#3623), PHOTOGRAVURE

Booklet Stamps

Serpentine Die Cut 11¼ on 2, 3 or 4 Sides

3623 A2807c (37c) **multicolored**	1.10	.25
a. Booklet pane of 20	22.00	

No. 3623 has "USPS" microprinted in the top red stripe of the flag.

Serpentine Die Cut 10½x10¾ on 2 or 3 Sides

3624	A2807d (37c) **multicolored**	1.10	.25
a.	Booklet pane of 4	4.40	
b.	Booklet pane of 6	6.60	
c.	Booklet pane of 20	22.00	

No. 3624 does not have a microprinted "USPS."

Serpentine Die Cut 8 on 2, 3 or 4 Sides

3625	A2807e (37c) **multicolored**	1.10	.25
a.	Booklet pane of 18	19.00	

Toy Mail Wagon — A2808

Toy Locomotive — A2809

Toy Taxicab — A2810

Toy Fire Pumper — A2811

Designed by Derry Noyes. Printed by Avery Dennison

PHOTOGRAVURE

Serpentine Die Cut 11 on 2, 3 or 4 Sides

2002, June 7 **Tagged**

Booklet Stamps

Self-Adhesive

3626	A2808 (37c) **multicolored**	1.10	.25
3627	A2809 (37c) **multicolored**	1.10	.25
3628	A2810 (37c) **multicolored**	1.10	.25
3629	A2811 (37c) **multicolored**	1.10	.25
a.	Block or strip of 4, #3626-3629	4.40	
b.	Booklet pane of 4, #3626-3629	4.40	
c.	Booklet pane of 6, #3627, 3629, 2 each #3626, 3628	6.60	
d.	Booklet pane of 6, #3626, 3628, 2 each #3627, 3629	6.60	
e.	Booklet pane of 20, 5 each #3626-3629	22.00	

Flag — A2812

A2812a

Designed by Terrence W. McCaffrey. Printed by Ashton-Potter (USA) Ltd.

LITHOGRAPHED

Sheets of 400 in four panes of 100

2002-05 **Tagged** ***Perf. 11¼***

3629F	A2812 37c **multicolored**, *Nov. 24, 2003*	.90	.25
	P# block of 4, 4#+P	25.00	—
	Pane of 100	110.00	—
g.	Imperf, pair	*100.00*	

No. 3629F has microprinted "USA" in top red stripe of flag.

Sheets of 120 in six panes of 20

Serpentine Die Cut 11¼x11

Self-Adhesive (#3630, 3632-3637)

3630	A2812a 37c **multicolored**, *June 7*	.90	.25
	P# block of 4, 4#+P	5.00	
	Pane of 20	23.50	

No. 3630 has microprinted "USA" in top red stripe of flag.

A2812b

A2812c

Printed by American Packaging Corporation for Sennett Security Products, Bureau of Engraving and Printing (#3632).

PHOTOGRAVURE

COIL STAMPS

Perf. 9¾ Vert.

3631	A2812b 37c **multicolored**, *June 7*	.75	.25
	Pair	1.50	—
	P# strip of 5, #S1111	5.25	—
	P# single, same #	—	2.00

No. 3631 is known printed with non-reactive yellow ink and also with luminescent yellow ink that makes the red flag stripes glow orange under long wave ultraviolet light.

Serpentine Die Cut 9¾ Vert.

3632	A2812c 37c **multicolored**, *June 7*	.75	.25
	Pair	1.50	
	P# strip of 5, #1111, 2222, 3333, 4444, 5555, 6666, 7777, 8888, 9999, 1111A, 2222A, 3333A, 4444A, 5555A, 6666A	5.00	
	P# single, same #	—	1.00
b.	Die cutting omitted, pair	55.00	55.00

On plate #s 1111 through 9999 and 5555A-6666A, the color laydown order of plate numbers is yellow, magenta, cyan, black. Plate #s 1111A through 4444A have a laydown order of cyan, magenta, yellow, black.

A2812d

A2812e

Printed by American Packaging Corporation for Sennett Security Products.

Serpentine Die Cut 10¼ Vert.

3632A	A2812d 37c **multicolored**, prephosphored coated paper, *Aug. 7, 2003*	.75	.25
	Pair	1.50	
	P# strip of 5, #S1111, S2222, S3333, S4444	5.25	
	P# single, #S1111, S2222, S3333, S4444	—	1.00
f.	Die cutting omitted, pair	*250.00*	
g.	Vert. pair, horiz. die-cut slits omitted	*750.00*	

No. 3632A lacks points of stars at margin at left top, and was printed in "logs" of adjacent coil rolls that are connected at the top or bottom, wherein each roll could be separated from an adjacent roll as needed.

No. 3632 has "2002" date at left bottom. No. 3632A has "2003" date at left bottom.

No. 3632A exists on two types of surface-tagged paper that exhibit either a solid or an uneven appearance. Value of plate #S4444 strip of 5 with solid tagging, $90; used plate #S4444 single with solid tagging, $60.

On No. 3632A, P# S3333 was printed with yellow ink that makes the red flag stripes glow orange under long wave ultraviolet light as well as with non-reactive yellow ink. P# S4444 was printed with and without luminescent yellow ink. Values the same.

Serpentine Die Cut 11¾ Vert.

3632C	A2812e 37c **multicolored**, prephosphored coated paper, *2004*	1.50	.25
	Pair	3.00	
	P# strip of 5, #S1111	8.50	
	P# single, #S1111	—	2.50
d.	Tagging omitted	—	

No. 3632C is the only 37c Flag coil stamp with a "2004" date at left bottom.

No. 3632C exists on two types of surface-tagged paper that exhibit either a solid or an uneven appearance. Values are the same.

A2812f

A2812g

A2812h

Printed by Ashton-Potter (USA) Ltd. (#3633B), Banknote Corporation of America (#3633), Guilford Gravure for Banknote Corporation of America (#3633A).

LITHOGRAPHED, PHOTOGRAVURE (#3633)

Serpentine Die Cut 8½ Vert.

3633	A2812f 37c **multicolored**, *June 7*	.75	.25
	Pair	1.50	
	P# strip of 5, #B1111	5.00	
	P# single, same #	—	1.75
3633A	A2812g 37c **multicolored** *April, 2003*	2.25	.25
	Pair	4.50	
	P# strip of 5 #B1111	12.50	
	P# single, same #	—	1.50

No. 3633A has right angle corners and backing paper as high as the stamp, and is dated "2003." No. 3633 is dated "2002," has rounded corners, the backing paper larger than the stamp, and the stamps are spaced approximately 2mm apart.

Serpentine Die Cut 9½ Vert.

3633B	A2812h 37c **multicolored** *June 7, 2005*	9.00	.25
	Pair	18.00	
	P# strip of 5, #P1111	50.00	
	P# single, #P1111	—	3.00

No. 3633B has microprinted "USA" in top red stripe of flag, and has "2005" date at bottom left.

A2812i

A2812j

A2812k

A2812l

Printed by American Packaging Corporation for Sennett Security Products (#3636), Banknote Corporation of America (#3635), Avery Dennison (#3634, 3634b, 3636D).

LITHOGRAPHED, PHOTOGRAVURE (#3634, 3636, 3636D)

Booklet Stamps

Serpentine Die Cut 11.1 on 3 Sides (#3634)

3634	A2812i 37c **multicolored**, large "2002" year date, *June 7*	.75	.25
a.	Booklet pane of 10	7.50	
b.	Small "2003," die cut 11, *Oct. 23, 2003*	.75	.25
c.	Booklet pane, 4 #3634b	3.00	
d.	Booklet pane, 6 #3634b	4.50	
e.	As #3634, die cut 11.3	1.00	.25
f.	As "e," booklet pane of 10	10.00	

Serpentine Die Cut 11.3 on 2, 3 or 4 Sides

3635	A2812j 37c **multicolored**, *June 7*	.75	.25
a.	Booklet pane of 20	15.00	
b.	Black omitted	*3,000.*	

No. 3635 has "USPS" microprinted in the top red flag stripe and has a small "2002" year date. Counterfeits exist of No. 3635. See the Postal Counterfeits section of this catalog.

Serpentine Die Cut 10½x10¾ on 2 or 3 Sides

3636	A2812k 37c **multicolored**, *June 7*	.75	.25
a.	Booklet pane of 4	3.00	
b.	Booklet pane of 6	4.50	
c.	Booklet pane of 20	15.00	
f.	As "c," 11 stamps and part of 12th stamp on reverse printed on backing liner, the 8 stamps on front side die cutting omitted	1,700.	

No. 3636c is a double-sided booklet pane, with 12 stamps on one side and eight stamps plus label on the other side.

Nos. 3636a and 3636b were issued on three types of prephosphored coated paper, with solid, grainy solid and uneven tagging characteristics. No. 3636c was issued on two types of prephosphored coated paper, with solid and uneven tagging.

Serpentine Die Cut 11¼x11 on 2 or 3 Sides

3636D	A2812l 37c **multicolored**, *July, 2004*	1.25	.25
e.	Booklet pane of 20	25.00	

No. 3636D lacks points of stars at margin at UL. No. 3636D is the only 37c Flag booklet stamp with a "2004" date at left bottom. No. 3636De is a double-sided booklet pane with 12 stamps on one side and eight stamps plus label on the other side.

A2812m

Printed by Avery Dennison.

LITHOGRAPHED

Serpentine Die Cut 8 on 2, 3 or 4 Sides

3637 A2812m 37c **multicolored,** *Feb. 4, 2003* .75 .25
a. Booklet pane of 18 13.50

Toy Locomotive — A2813

Toy Mail Wagon — A2814

Toy Fire Pumper — A2815

Toy Taxicab — A2816

Designed by Derry Noyes. Printed by Banknote Corporation of America.

PHOTOGRAVURE

2002-03 Tagged *Serpentine Die Cut 8½ Horiz.*

Self-Adhesive

Coil Stamps

3638 A2813 37c **multicolored,** *July 26* 1.50 .25
3639 A2814 37c **multicolored,** *July 26* 1.50 .25
3640 A2815 37c **multicolored,** *July 26* 1.50 .25
3641 A2816 37c **multicolored,** *July 26* 1.50 .25
a. Strip of 4, #3638-3641 6.00
P# strip of 5, 2 #3638, 1 each #3639-3641, #B11111, B12222 8.25
P# strip of 9, 2 each #3638-3639, 3641, 3 #3640, #B11111, B12222 14.00
P# single (#3640), #B11111, B12222 — 1.25

A2813a

A2814a

A2815a

A2816a

Printed by Avery Dennison.

Serpentine Die Cut 11 on 2, 3 or 4 Sides

Booklet Stamps

3642 A2814a 37c **multicolored,** "2002" year date, *July 26* .75 .25
a. Serpentine die cut 11x11¼ on 2 or 3 sides, dated "2003," *Sept. 3, 2003* .75 .25
3643 A2813a 37c **multicolored,** "2002" year date, *July 26* .75 .25
a. Serpentine die cut 11x11¼ on 2 or 3 sides, dated "2003," *Sept. 3, 2003* .75 .25
3644 A2816a 37c **multicolored,** "2002" year date, *July 26* .75 .25
a. Serpentine die cut 11x11¼ on 2 or 3 sides, dated "2003," *Sept. 3, 2003* .75 .25

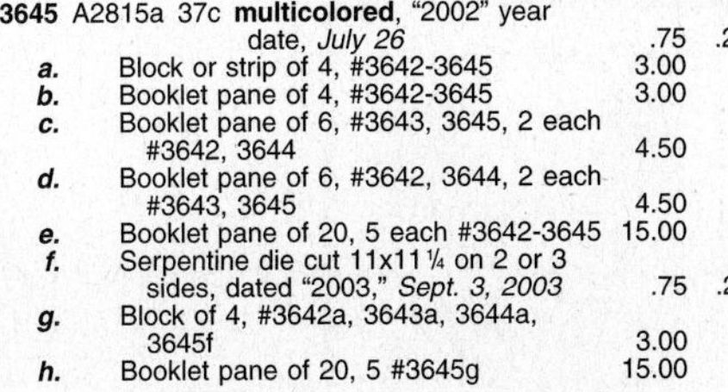
3645 A2815a 37c **multicolored,** "2002" year date, *July 26* .75 .25
a. Block or strip of 4, #3642-3645 3.00
b. Booklet pane of 4, #3642-3645 3.00
c. Booklet pane of 6, #3643, 3645, 2 each #3642, 3644 4.50
d. Booklet pane of 6, #3642, 3644, 2 each #3643, 3645 4.50
e. Booklet pane of 20, 5 each #3642-3645 15.00
f. Serpentine die cut 11x11¼ on 2 or 3 sides, dated "2003," *Sept. 3, 2003* .75 .25
g. Block of 4, #3642a, 3643a, 3644a, 3645f 3.00
h. Booklet pane of 20, 5 #3645g 15.00

No. 3645h is a double-sided booklet with 12 stamps on one side and 8 stamps plus label (booklet cover) on the other side. Nos. 3642a, 3643a, 3644a and 3645f have slightly narrower designs than Nos. 3642-3645.

Coverlet Eagle — A2817

Designed by Richard Sheaff. Printed by Ashton-Potter (USA) Ltd.

LITHOGRAPHED

Sheets of 120 in six panes of 20

Serpentine Die Cut 11x11¼

2002, July 12 Tagged

Self-Adhesive

3646 A2817 60c **multicolored** 1.25 .25
P# block of 4, 4#+P 5.00
Pane of 20 25.00

Jefferson Memorial A2818

A2818a

Capitol Dome — A2819

Designed by Derry Noyes. Printed by Banknote Corporation of America (#3647-3648), American Packaging Corporation for Sennett Security Printers (#3647A).

LITHOGRAPHED

Sheets of 180 in nine panes of 20

Serpentine Die Cut 11¼ (#3647, 3648), 11x10¾ (#3647A)

2002-03 Tagged

Self-Adhesive

3647 A2818 $3.85 **multicolored,** *July 30* 7.50 2.00
P# block of 4, 4#+B 30.00
Pane of 20 150.00
3647A A2818a $3.85 **multicolored,** *Nov. 2003* 9.00 2.00
P# block of 4, 5#+S 40.00
Pane of 20 195.00
3648 A2819 $13.65 **multicolored,** *July 30* 27.50 10.00
P# block of 4, 4#+B 110.00
Pane of 20 550.00

No. 3647 is dated 2002, and No. 3647A is dated 2003.

Hidden images can be seen on Nos. 3647-3648 when viewed with a special "Stamp Decoder" lens sold by the USPS. Nos. 3647-3647A, Jefferson's signature; No. 3648, a U.S. flag.

MASTERS OF AMERICAN PHOTOGRAPHY

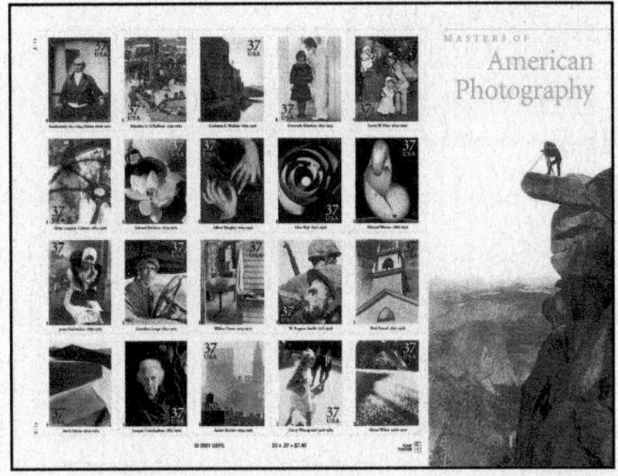

A2820

Illustration reduced.

Designed by Derry Noyes. Printed by American Packaging Corporation for Sennett Security Products.

No. 3649: a, Portrait of Daniel Webster, by Albert Sands Southworth and Josiah Johnson Hawes. b, Gen. Ulysses S. Grant and Officers, by Timothy H. O'Sullivan. c, "Cape Horn, Columbia River," by Carleton E. Watkins. d, "Blessed Art Thou Among Women," by Gertrude Käsebier. e, "Looking for Lost Luggage, Ellis Island," by Lewis W. Hine. f, "The Octopus," by Alvin Langdon Coburn. g, "Lotus, Mount Kisco, New York," by Edward Steichen. h, "Hands and Thimble," by Alfred Stieglitz. i, "Rayograph," by Man Ray. j, "Two Shells," by Edward Weston. k, "My Corsage," by James VanDerZee. l, "Ditched, Stalled, and Stranded, San Joaquin Valley, California," by Dorothea Lange. m, "Washroom and Dining Area of Floyd Burroughs' Home, Hale County, Alabama," by Walker Evans. n, "Frontline Soldier with Canteen, Saipan," by W. Eugene Smith. o, "Steeple," by Paul Strand. p, "Sand Dunes, Sunrise," by Ansel Adams. q, "Age and Its Symbols," by Imogen Cunningham. r, New York cityscape, by André Kertész. s, Photograph of pedestrians, by Garry Winogrand. t, "Bristol, Vermont," by Minor White.

PHOTOGRAVURE

Sheets of 120 in six panes of 20

Serpentine Die Cut 10½x10¾

2002, June 13 Tagged

Self-Adhesive

3649 A2820 Pane of 20 22.50
a.-t. 37c Any single 1.00 .50
u. As No. 3649, die cutting omitted —

Uncut press sheets of No. 3649 were made available for sale. Values: cross-gutter block of 20, $47.50; pairs with gutters between, $4 each. See note after No. 2868.

AMERICAN TREASURES SERIES

Scarlet and Louisiana Tanagers, by John James Audubon — A2821

Designed by Derry Noyes. Printed by American Pacakaging Corporation for Sennett Security Products.

PHOTOGRAVURE

Sheets of 120 in six panes of 20

2002, June 27 Tagged *Serpentine Die Cut 10¾*

Self-Adhesive

3650 A2821 37c **multicolored** 1.00 .25
P# block of 4, 7#+S 6.00
Pane of 20 27.50

HARRY HOUDINI (1874-1926), MAGICIAN

A2822

Designed by Richard Sheaff. Printed by Ashton-Potter (USA) Ltd.

LITHOGRAPHED
Sheets of 180 in nine panes of 20

2002, July 3 Tagged *Serpentine Die Cut 11¼*
Self-Adhesive

3651 A2822 37c **multicolored**	.75	.25
P# block of 4, 4#+P	3.00	—
Pane of 20	15.00	—

A hidden 3-D image (Houdini in chains) can be seen on this stamp when it is viewed with a special "Stamp Decoder" lens sold by the USPS.

ANDY WARHOL (1928-87), ARTIST

Self-Portrait — A2823

Designed by Richard Sheaff.
Printed by American Packaging Corporation for Sennett Security Products.

PHOTOGRAVURE
Sheets of 80 in four panes of 20
Serpentine Die Cut 10½x10¾
2002, Aug. 9 Tagged
Self-Adhesive

3652 A2823 37c **multicolored**	.75	.25
P# block of 4, 6#+S	4.00	
Pane of 20	19.00	

TEDDY BEARS, CENTENNIAL

Bruin Bear, c. 1907 — A2824

"Stick" Bear, 1920s — A2825

Gund Bear, c. 1948 — A2826

Ideal Bear, c. 1905 — A2827

Designed by Margaret Bauer.
Printed by American Packaging Corporation for Sennett Security Products.

PHOTOGRAVURE
Sheets of 120 in six panes of 20

2002, Aug. 15 Tagged *Serpentine Die Cut 10½*
Self-Adhesive

3653 A2824 37c **multicolored**	1.00	.30
3654 A2825 37c **multicolored**	1.00	.30
3655 A2826 37c **multicolored**	1.00	.30
3656 A2827 37c **multicolored**	1.00	.30
a. Block or vert. strip of 4, #3653-3656	4.00	
P# block of 4, 7#+S	5.00	
P# block of 10, 2 sets of P# + top label	15.00	
Pane of 20	27.50	

Uncut press sheets of Nos. 3653-3656 were made available for sale. Values: cross-gutter block of 8, $30; pairs with gutters between, $3.50 each. See note after No. 2868.

LOVE

A2828

A2829

Designed by Michael Osborne.
Printed by Banknote Corporation of America (#3657), Avery Dennison.

LITHOGRAPHED (#3657), PHOTOGRAVURE
Sheets of 200 in 10 panes of 20 (#3658)
Serpentine Die Cut 11 on 2, 3 or 4 Sides
2002, Aug. 16 Tagged
Booklet Stamp (#3657)
Self-Adhesive

3657 A2828 37c **multicolored**	.75	.25
a. Booklet pane of 20	15.00	
b. As "a," silver ("Love 37 USA") missing on top five stamps (CM)	*750.00*	
c. Strip of 5, silver ("Love 37 USA") omitted on one stamp	*1,000.*	

Serpentine Die Cut 11

3658 A2829 60c **multicolored**	1.25	.25
P# block of 4, 5#+V	5.00	
Pane of 20	25.00	

Beware of examples of No. 3658 with gold ink fraudulently removed.

LITERARY ARTS

Ogden Nash (1902-71), Poet — A2830

Designed by Carl T. Herrman.
Printed by Avery Dennison.

PHOTOGRAVURE
Sheets of 200 in 10 panes of 20

2002, Aug. 19 Tagged *Serpentine Die Cut 11*
Self-Adhesive

3659 A2830 37c **multicolored**	.75	.25
P# block of 4, 8#+V	3.00	
Pane of 20	15.00	

DUKE KAHANAMOKU (1890-1968), "FATHER OF SURFING" AND OLYMPIC SWIMMER

Kahanamoku and Surfers at Waikiki Beach — A2831

Designed by Carl T. Herrman.
Printed by Avery Dennison.

PHOTOGRAVURE
Sheets of 200 in 10 panes of 20
Serpentine Die Cut 11½x11¾
2002, Aug. 24 Tagged
Self-Adhesive

3660 A2831 37c **multicolored**	.75	.25
P# block of 4, 4#+V	3.00	
Pane of 20	15.00	

AMERICAN BATS

Red Bat — A2832

Leaf-nosed Bat — A2833

Spotted Bat — A2835

Pallid Bat — A2834

Designed by Phil Jordan.
Printed by American Packaging Corporation for Sennett Security Products.

PHOTOGRAVURE
Sheets of 120 in six panes of 20

2002, Sept. 13 Tagged *Serpentine Die Cut 10¾*
Self-Adhesive

3661 A2832 37c **multicolored**	.75	.30
3662 A2833 37c **multicolored**	.75	.30
3663 A2834 37c **multicolored**	.75	.30

3664 A2835 37c **multicolored** .75 .30
a. Block or strip of 4, #3661-3664 3.00
P# block of 4, 7#+S 3.25
P# block of 8, 2 sets of P# + top label 6.50
Pane of 20 16.00

WOMEN IN JOURNALISM

Nellie Bly (1864-1922) A2836

Ida M. Tarbell (1857-1944) A2837

Ethel L. Payne (1911-91) A2838

Marguerite Higgins (1920-66) A2839

Designed by Fred Otnes.
Printed by American Packaging Corporation for Sennett Security Products.

PHOTOGRAVURE
Sheets of 120 in six panes of 20
Serpentine Die Cut 11x10½
2002, Sept. 14 **Tagged**
Self-Adhesive

3665 A2836 37c **multicolored** 1.25 .35
3666 A2837 37c **multicolored** 1.25 .35
3667 A2838 37c **multicolored** 1.25 .35
3668 A2839 37c **multicolored** 1.25 .35
a. Block or horiz. strip of 4, #3665-3668 5.00
P# block of 4, 5#+S 5.25
P# block of 8, 2 sets of P# + top label 10.50
Pane of 20 25.00

IRVING BERLIN (1888-1989), COMPOSER

Berlin and Score of "God Bless America" — A2840

Designed by Greg Berger.
Printed by Avery Dennison.

PHOTOGRAVURE
Sheets of 200 in 10 panes of 20
2002, Sept. 15 **Tagged** ***Serpentine Die Cut 11***
Self-Adhesive

3669 A2840 37c **multicolored** .75 .25
P# block of 4, 4#+V 3.00
Pane of 20 15.00

NEUTER AND SPAY

Kitten — A2841

Puppy A2842

Designed by Derry Noyes. Printed by American Packaging Corporation for Sennett Security Products.

PHOTOGRAVURE
Sheets of 120 in six panes of 20
Serpentine Die Cut 10¾x10½
2002, Sept. 20 **Tagged**
Self-Adhesive

3670 A2841 37c **multicolored** 1.00 .25
3671 A2842 37c **multicolored** 1.00 .25
a. Horiz. or vert. pair, #3670-3671 2.00
P# block of 4, 5#+S 4.00
P# block of 8, 2 sets of P# + top label 8.00
Pane of 20 20.00

Hanukkah — A2842a

Designed by Hannah Smotrich.
Printed by Avery Dennison.

PHOTOGRAVURE
Sheets of 200 in 10 panes of 20
2002, Oct. 10 **Tagged** ***Serpentine Die Cut 11***
Self-Adhesive

3672 A2842a 37c **multicolored** .75 .25
P# block of 4, 5#+V 3.00
Pane of 20 15.00

See Nos. 3118, 3352, 3547, Israel No. 1289.

Kwanzaa — A2842b

Designed by Synthia Saint James.
Printed by Avery Dennison.

PHOTOGRAVURE
Sheets of 200 in 10 panes of 20
2002, Oct. 10 **Tagged** ***Serpentine Die Cut 11***
Self-Adhesive

3673 A2842b 37c **multicolored** .75 .25
P# block of 4, 4#+V 3.00
Pane of 20 15.00

See Nos. 3175, 3368, 3548.

Eid — A2842c

Designed by Mohamed Zakariya.
Printed by Avery Dennison.

PHOTOGRAVURE
Sheets of 240 in 12 panes of 20
2002, Oct. 10 **Tagged** ***Serpentine Die Cut 11***
Self-Adhesive

3674 A2842c 37c **multicolored** .75 .25
P# block of 4, 3#+V 3.00
Pane of 20 15.00

See Nos. 3532, 4117, 4202, 4351, 4416.

CHRISTMAS

Madonna and Child, by Jan Gossaert — A2843

Designed by Richard Sheaff.
Printed by Banknote Corporation of America.

LITHOGRAPHED
Serpentine Die Cut 11x11¼ on 2, 3 or 4 Sides
2002, Oct. 10 **Tagged**
Self-Adhesive
Booklet Stamp
Design size: 19x27mm

3675 A2843 37c **multicolored** .75 .25
a. Booklet pane of 20 15.00

Compare to No. 3820, which measures 19½x28mm.
See No. 3820.

CHRISTMAS

Snowman with Red and Green Plaid Scarf — A2844

Snowman with Blue Plaid Scarf — A2845

Snowman with Pipe — A2846

Snowman with Top Hat — A2847

Designed by Derry Noyes. Printed by Avery Dennison.

PHOTOGRAVURE
Sheets of 200 in 10 panes of 20
2002, Oct. 28 **Tagged** ***Serpentine Die Cut 11***
Self-Adhesive

3676 A2844 37c **multicolored** .90 .25
3677 A2845 37c **multicolored** .90 .25
3678 A2846 37c **multicolored** .90 .25

3679 A2847 37c **multicolored** .90 .25
a. Block or vert. strip of 4, #3676-3679 3.75
P# block of 4, 4#+V 4.25
Pane of 20 21.00

Snowman with Blue Plaid Scarf — A2848

Snowman with Pipe — A2849

Snowman with Top Hat — A2850

Snowman with Red and Green Plaid Scarf — A2851

Printed by Guilford Gravure.

COIL STAMPS

Serpentine Die Cut 8½ Vert.

3680 A2848 37c **multicolored** 3.25 .25
3681 A2849 37c **multicolored** 3.25 .25
3682 A2850 37c **multicolored** 3.25 .25
3683 A2851 37c **multicolored** 3.25 .25
a. Strip of 4, #3680-3683 13.00
P# strip of 5, 2 #3680, 1 each #3681-3683, #G1111, G1112 17.50
P# strip of 9, 2 each #3680, 3681, 3683, 3 #3682, same # 30.00
P# single (#3682), same # — 2.00

A2844a

A2845a

A2846a

A2847a

Printed by American Packaging Corp. for Sennett Security Products.

BOOKLET STAMPS

Serpentine Die Cut 10¾x11 on 2 or 3 Sides

3684 A2844a 37c **multicolored** 1.25 .25
3685 A2845a 37c **multicolored** 1.25 .25
3686 A2846a 37c **multicolored** 1.25 .25
3687 A2847a 37c **multicolored** 1.25 .25
a. Block of 4, #3684-3687 5.00
b. Booklet pane of 20, 5 #3687a + label 25.00

No. 3687b is a double-sided booklet pane with 12 stamps on one side and eight stamps plus label on the other side.

Colors of Nos. 3684-3687 are deeper and designs are slightly smaller than those found on Nos. 3676-3679.

A2848a

A2849a

A2850a

A2851a

Printed by Avery Dennison.

Serpentine Die Cut 11 on 2 or 3 Sides

3688 A2851a 37c **multicolored** 1.15 .25
3689 A2848a 37c **multicolored** 1.15 .25
3690 A2849a 37c **multicolored** 1.15 .25
3691 A2850a 37c **multicolored** 1.15 .25
a. Block of 4, #3688-3691 4.60
b. Booklet pane of 4, #3688-3691 4.60
c. Booklet pane of 6, #3690-3691, 2 each #3688-3689 7.00
d. Booklet pane of 6, #3688-3689, 2 each #3690-3691 7.00
Nos. 3676-3691 (16) 26.20 4.00

LEGENDS OF HOLLYWOOD

Cary Grant (1904-86), Actor — A2852

Designed by Carl Herrman. Printed by American Packaging Corporation for Sennett Security Products.

PHOTOGRAVURE

Sheets of 120 in six panes of 20

2002, Oct. 15 **Tagged** ***Serpentine Die Cut 10¾***

Self-Adhesive

3692 A2852 37c **multicolored** 1.25 .25
P# block of 4, 6#+S 5.00
Pane of 20 25.00

Uncut press sheets of No. 3692 were made available for sale. Values: cross-gutter block of 8, $27.50; pairs with gutters between, $4 each. See note after No. 2868.

Sea Coast — A2853

Designed by Tom Engeman.
Printed by Banknote Corporation Of America.

PHOTOGRAVURE

COIL STAMP

Serpentine Die Cut 8½ Vert.

2002, Oct. 21 **Tagged**

Self-Adhesive

3693 A2853 (5c) **multicolored**, dated "2002" .30 .25
Pair .50
P# strip of 5, #B111 1.30
P# single, #B111 — .90

See Nos. 3775, 3785, 3864, 3874-3875, 4348.

HAWAIIAN MISSIONARY STAMPS

A2854

Illustration reduced.
Designed by Richard Sheaff.
Printed by Banknote Corporation of America.

No. 3694: a, 2c stamp of 1851 (Hawaii Scott 1). b, 5c stamp of 1851 (Hawaii Scott 2) c, 13c stamp of 1851 (Hawaii Scott 3). d, 13c stamp of 1852 (Hawaii Scott 4).

LITHOGRAPHED

Sheets of 24 in six panes of 4

2002, Oct. 24 **Tagged** ***Perf. 11***

3694 A2854 Pane of 4 5.00 2.50
a.-d. 37c Any single 1.25 .50

Uncut press sheets of No. 3694 were made available for sale. See note after No. 2868.

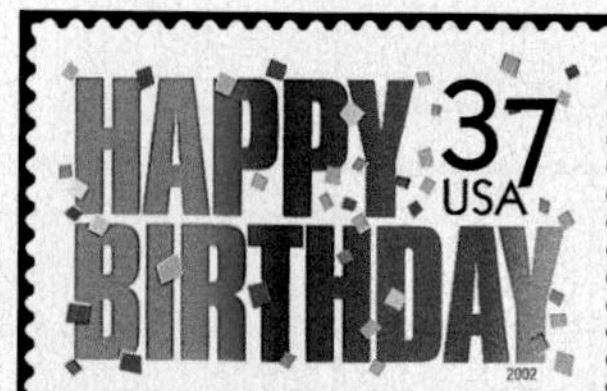

Happy Birthday — A2854a

Designed by Harry Zelenko. Printed by Avery Dennison.

PHOTOGRAVURE

Sheets of 200 in 10 panes of 20

2002, Oct. 25 **Tagged** ***Serpentine Die Cut 11***

Self-Adhesive

3695 A2854a 37c **multicolored** .75 .25
P# block of 4, 4#+V 3.00
Pane of 20 15.00

See Nos. 3558, 4079.

A2854b-A2854ay

Illustration Reduced

Designed by Richard Sheaff. Printed by American Packaging Corp. for Sennett Security Products.

PHOTOGRAVURE

Sheets of 100 in two panes of 50

2002, Oct. 25 Tagged *Serpentine Die Cut 10¾*

Self-Adhesive

3696	A2854b	37c	Alabama	.75	.60
3697	A2854c	37c	Alaska	.75	.60
3698	A2854d	37c	Arizona	.75	.60
3699	A2854e	37c	Arkansas	.75	.60
3700	A2854f	37c	California	.75	.60
3701	A2854g	37c	Colorado	.75	.60
3702	A2854h	37c	Connecticut	.75	.60
3703	A2854i	37c	Delaware	.75	.60
3704	A2854j	37c	Florida	.75	.60
3705	A2854k	37c	Georgia	.75	.60
3706	A2854l	37c	Hawaii	.75	.60
3707	A2854m	37c	Idaho	.75	.60
3708	A2854n	37c	Illinois	.75	.60
3709	A2854o	37c	Indiana	.75	.60
3710	A2854p	37c	Iowa	.75	.60
3711	A2854q	37c	Kansas	.75	.60
3712	A2854r	37c	Kentucky	.75	.60
3713	A2854s	37c	Louisiana	.75	.60
3714	A2854t	37c	Maine	.75	.60
3715	A2854u	37c	Maryland	.75	.60
3716	A2854v	37c	Massachusetts	.75	.60
3717	A2854w	37c	Michigan	.75	.60
3718	A2854x	37c	Minnesota	.75	.60
3719	A2854y	37c	Mississippi	.75	.60
3720	A2854z	37c	Missouri	.75	.60
3721	A2854aa	37c	Montana	.75	.60
3722	A2854ab	37c	Nebraska	.75	.60
3723	A2854ac	37c	Nevada	.75	.60
3724	A2854ad	37c	New Hampshire	.75	.60
3725	A2854ae	37c	New Jersey	.75	.60
3726	A2854af	37c	New Mexico	.75	.60
3727	A2854ag	37c	New York	.75	.60
3728	A2854ah	37c	North Carolina	.75	.60
3729	A2854ai	37c	North Dakota	.75	.60
3730	A2854aj	37c	Ohio	.75	.60
3731	A2854ak	37c	Oklahoma	.75	.60
3732	A2854al	37c	Oregon	.75	.60
3733	A2854am	37c	Pennsylvania	.75	.60
3734	A2854an	37c	Rhode Island	.75	.60
3735	A2854ao	37c	South Carolina	.75	.60
3736	A2854ap	37c	South Dakota	.75	.60
3737	A2854aq	37c	Tennessee	.75	.60
3738	A2854ar	37c	Texas	.75	.60
3739	A2854as	37c	Utah	.75	.60
3740	A2854at	37c	Vermont	.75	.60
3741	A2854au	37c	Virginia	.75	.60
3742	A2854av	37c	Washington	.75	.60
3743	A2854aw	37c	West Virginia	.75	.60
3744	A2854ax	37c	Wisconsin	.75	.60
3745	A2854ay	37c	Wyoming	.75	.60
a.			Pane of 50, #3696-3745	37.50	

See Nos. 3561-3610.

BLACK HERITAGE SERIES

Thurgood Marshall (1908-93), Supreme Court Justice — A2855

Designed by Richard Sheaff. Printed by Ashton-Potter (USA) Ltd.

LITHOGRAPHED

Sheets of 180 in nine panes of 20

2003, Jan. 7 Tagged *Serpentine Die Cut 11½*

Self-Adhesive

3746	A2855 37c **black & gray**	.75	.25
	P# block of 4, 3#+P	3.00	
	Pane of 20	15.00	

CHINESE NEW YEAR

Year of the Ram — A2856

Designed by Clarence Lee. Printed by Banknote Corporation of America.

LITHOGRAPHED

Sheets of 120 in six panes of 20

2003, Jan. 15 Tagged *Serpentine Die Cut 11½*

Self-Adhesive

3747	A2856 37c **multicolored**	.75	.25
	P# block of 4, 4#+B	3.00	
	Pane of 20	15.00	
a.	Tagging omitted	—	

See Nos. 3895h, 3997h.

LITERARY ARTS

Zora Neale Hurston (1891-1960), Writer
A2857

Designed by Howard E. Paine. Printed by American Packaging Corporation for Sennett Security Products.

PHOTOGRAVURE
Sheets of 120 in six panes of 20

2003, Jan. 24 Tagged *Serpentine Die Cut 10¾*
Self-Adhesive

3748 A2857 37c **multicolored** .90 .25
P# block of 4, 5#+S 3.60
Pane of 20 18.00

AMERICAN DESIGN SERIES

Tiffany Lamp — A2866

A2866a

Navajo Necklace — A2858

A2858a

A2858b A2858c

Designed by Derry Noyes. Printed by Ashton-Potter (USA) Ltd. (#3749, 3752), American Packaging Corp. for Sennett Security Products (#3751), Banknote Corporation of America for Sennett Security Products (#3749A, 3753), Avery Dennison (#3750).

LITHOGRAPHED, PHOTOGRAVURE (#3750, 3751)
Sheets of 300 in 15 panes of 20 (#3749A), Sheets of 280 in 14 panes of 20, Sheets of 240 in 12 panes of 20 (#3751, 3752), Sheets of 200 in 10 panes of 20 (#3749, 3753).
Self-Adhesive (#3749-3757)

2003-14 *Serpentine Die Cut 11¼x11*
Untagged (#3749-3756A, 3758-3762, 3763a)

3749 A2866 1c **multicolored,** *Mar. 16, 2007* .30 .25
P# block of 4, 6#+P .50
Pane of 20 3.00

3749A A2866a 1c **multicolored,** *Mar. 7, 2008* .30 .25
P# block of 4, 5#+S .50
Pane of 20 3.00

No. 3749A has "USPS" microprinted on a white field high on the lamp stand, just below the shade and is dated "2008." No. 3749 has "USPS" microprinted lower on the lamp stand and not on a white field and is dated "2007."

Serpentine Die Cut 11

3750 A2858 2c **multicolored,** *Aug. 20, 2004* .30 .25
P# block of 4, 5#+V .50
Pane of 20 3.00

A reprinting of No. 3750 shows the borders in a much brighter deep turquoise blue shade.

Serpentine Die Cut 11¼x11½

3751 A2858a 2c **multicolored,** *Dec. 8, 2005* 1.00 .25
P# block of 4, 6#+S 5.00
Pane of 20 21.50

Serpentine Die Cut 11¼x11
With "USPS" Microprinting

3752 A2858b 2c **multicolored,** *Dec. 8, 2005* .30 .25
P# block of 4, 5#+P .50
Pane of 20 3.00

Serpentine Die Cut 11¼x10¾

3753 A2858c 2c **multicolored,** *May 12, 2007* .30 .25
P# block of 4, 6#+S .50
Pane of 20 3.00

Silver Coffeepot — A2868

Printed by Banknote Corporation of America for Sennett Security Products.

LITHOGRAPHED
Sheets of 200 in 10 panes of 20.
Serpentine Die Cut 11¼x11

3754 A2868 3c **multicolored,** *Mar. 16, 2007* .30 .25
P# block of 4, 4#+S .50
Pane of 20 3.00

Microprinted "USPS" on No. 3752 is found on top silver appendage next to and below the middle turquoise stone on the right side of the necklace. Microprinting on No. 3753 is found on the top silver appendage next to and below the lower turquoise stone on the left side of the necklace. Nos. 3751 and 3752 are dated "2006." No. 3753 is dated "2007."

Chippendale Chair — A2859

Printed by Ashton-Potter (USA) Ltd.

LITHOGRAPHED
Sheets of 120 in six panes of 20 (#3755).
Serpentine Die Cut 10¾x10¼

3755 A2859 4c **multicolored,** *Mar. 5, 2004* .30 .25
P# block of 4, 4#+P .50
Pane of 20 3.00

A2858d

A2858e

Printed by American Packaging Corp. for Sennett Security Products (#3756), Banknote Corporation of America for Sennett Security Products (#3756A).

LITHOGRAPHED, PHOTOGRAVURE (#3756)
Sheets of 200 in 10 panes of 20 (#3756A), Sheets of 160 in eight panes of 20 (#3756).
Serpentine Die Cut 11¼x11¾

3756 A2858d 5c **multicolored,** *June 25, 2004* .30 .25
P# block of 4, 7#+S .50
Pane of 20 2.50

Serpentine Die Cut 11¼x10¾

3756A A2858e 5c **multicolored,** *Aug. 2008* .30 .25
P# block of 4, 7#+S .50
Pane of 20 3.00
b. Die cutting omitted, pair *400.00*

No. 3756A has microprinting on the lower part of the coffeepot handle and is dated "2007." No. 3756 has no microprinting and is dated "2004." Existence of No. 3756A was reported in Aug. 2008.

No. 3756A is known printed with non-reactive cream-colored background ink and also with luminescent cream-colored ink that glows orange under both shortwave and longwave ultraviolet light.

American Clock — A2860

Printed by Ashton-Potter (USA) Ltd.

LITHOGRAPHED
Sheets of 280 in 14 panes of 20, Sheets of 240 in 12 panes of 20.
Serpentine Die Cut 11¼x11
Tagged

3757 A2860 10c **multicolored,** prephosphored coated paper with surface tagging showing a solid appearance, plus block tagging on top of the printed design *Jan. 24* .30 .25
P# block of 4, 4#+P 1.00
Pane of 20 5.00
a. Die cutting omitted, pair —
b. 10c **multicolored,** overall tagging, *2013* .30 .25
P# block of 4, 4#+P 1.00
Pane of 20 5.00

No. 3757b was printed from plates P6666 and P7777.

A2866b

A2866c

Printed by American Packaging Corp. for Sennett Security Products (#3758), Banknote Corporation of America for Sennett Security Products (#3758A).

PHOTOGRAVURE
Perf. 9¾ Vert.
COIL STAMPS

3758 A2866b 1c **multicolored,** *Mar. 1* .30 .25
Pair .30 .25
P# strip of 5, #S11111 .60 —
P# single, #S11111 — .35

3758A A2866c 1c **multicolored,** *June 7, 2008* .30 .25
Pair .30 .25
P# strip of 5, #S11111 .80 —
P# single, #S11111 — .45

No. 3758A has microprinted "USPS" on lamp stand just below the lampshade and is dated "2008." No. 3758 lacks microprinting and is dated "2003."

A2858f

A2868a

Printed by Banknote Corporation of America for Sennett Security Products, American Packaging Corp. for Sennett Security Products (#3759).

3758B A2858f 2c **multicolored,** *Feb. 12, 2011* .30 .25
Pair .35 .40
P# strip of 5, #S111111 1.00 —
P# single, #S111111 — .50

3759 A2868a 3c **multicolored,** *Sept. 16, 2005* .30 .25
Pair .40 .40
P# strip of 5, #S1111 .80 —
P# single, #S1111 — .55
P# strip of 5, #S2222 2.00 —
P# single, #S2222 — 1.90

A2859a

A2859b

Printed by American Packaging Corp. for Sennett Security Products (#3761), Guildford Gravure for Ashton-Potter (USA) Ltd.

3761	A2859a 4c **multicolored,** dated "2007" at LL, *July 19, 2007*	.30	.25
	Pair	.40	.40
	P# strip of 5, #S1111	1.00	—
	P# single, #S1111	—	.90
3761A	A2859b 4c **multicolored,** dated "2013" at UL, *Jan. 2, 2014*	.30	.25
	Pair	.40	.40
	P# strip of 5, #P1111	1.35	—
	P# single, #P1111	—	1.25

On plate number singles, the plate number is at the lower right on No. 3761 and centered at bottom on No. 3761A.

A2860a

A2860b

Printed by American Packaging Corp. for Sennett Security Products (#3762), Banknote Corporation of America for Sennett Security Products.

LITHOGRAPHED, PHOTOGRAVURE (#3762)

3762	A2860a 10c **multicolored,** *Aug. 4, 2006*	.30	.25
	Pair	.50	.50
	P# strip of 5, #S1111	1.90	—
	P# single, #S1111	—	1.30
3763	A2860b 10c **multicolored** *July 15, 2008*	.30	.25
	Pair	.50	.50
	P# strip of 5, #S1111	2.50	—
	P# single, #S1111	—	2.00
a.	Untagged, *2013*	.30	.25
	Pair	.50	.50
	P# strip of 5, #S2222	3.00	—
	P# single, #S2222	—	3.00

Nos. 3763 and 3763a are dated "2008," have a microprinted "USPS" as the middle "I" in "VIII," and have network of beige dots on clock face. No. 3762 is dated "2006," lacks microprinting, and has network of gray dots on clock face.

This is an ongoing set. Numbers may change.
See No. 3612.

AMERICAN CULTURE SERIES

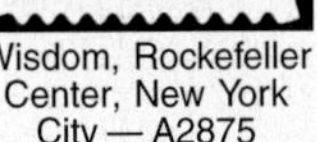
Wisdom, Rockefeller Center, New York City — A2875

A2875a

Designed by Carl Herrman. Printed by Ashton-Potter (USA) Ltd.

LITHOGRAPHED
Sheets of 120 in six panes of 20
Serpentine Die Cut 11¼x11

2003, Feb. 28 **Tagged**

Self-Adhesive

3766	A2875 $1 **multicolored**	2.00	.40
	P# block of 4, 5# + P	8.00	
	Pane of 20	40.00	
a.	A2875a Dated "2008" ⓢ	2.00	.40
	P# block of 4, 5# + P	8.00	
	Pane of 20	40.00	

See note after No. 1549.

New York Public Library Lion — A2875b

Designed by Carl Herrman. Printed by American Packaging Corporation for Sennett Security Products.

PHOTOGRAVURE
COIL STAMP

2003, Feb. 4 **Untagged** ***Perf. 9¾ Vert.***

3769	A2875b (10c) **multicolored**	.30	.25
	Pair	.50	.50
	P# strip of 5, #S11111	2.25	—
	P# single, #S11111	—	1.60

See No. 3447.

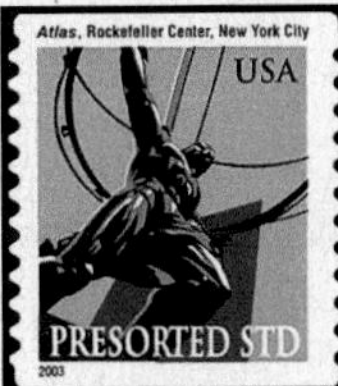

Atlas Statue — A2875c

Designed by Kevin Newman. Printed by Avery Dennison.

PHOTOGRAVURE

2003, Oct. **Untagged** ***Serpentine Die Cut 11 Vert.***

Coil Stamp

Self-Adhesive

3770	A2875c (10c) **multicolored**	.30	.25
	Pair	.50	
	P# strip of 5, #V11111, V11222, V12222, V21111, V21211, V22111, V22112, V22211, V23113, V32332, V33333, V33332	2.25	
	P# strip of 5, #V12111	*60.00*	
	P# strip of 5, #V22222	10.00	
	P# single, #V11111, V11222, V21111, V21211, V22111, V22112, V22211, V23113, V32332, V33332	—	2.00
	P# single, # V12111		*75.00*
	P# single, # V12222		*1.00*
	P# single, # V13222		*250.00*
	P# single, # V22222		8.50
	P# single, # V21113		*1,600.*
	P# single, # V33333		1.00
a.	Tagged, error		—
	P# single, # V21211		—

No. 3770 is dated 2003.

See No. 3520.

SPECIAL OLYMPICS

Athlete with Medal — A2879

Designed by Lance Hidy. Printed by Avery Dennison.

PHOTOGRAVURE
Sheets of 200 in 10 panes of 20

2003, Feb. 13 **Tagged** ***Serpentine Die Cut 11***

Self-Adhesive

3771	A2879 80c **multicolored**	1.60	.35
	P# block of 4, 6# + V	6.40	
	Pane of 20	32.00	

A hidden 3-D image (Special Olympics logo) can be seen on this stamp when it is viewed with a special "Stamp Decoder" lens sold by the USPS.

AMERICAN FILMMAKING: BEHIND THE SCENES

A2880

Illustration reduced.

Designed by Imaginary Forces. Printed by American Packaging Corporation for Sennett Security Products.

No. 3772: a, Screenwriting (segment of script from *Gone With the Wind*). b, Directing (John Cassavetes). c, Costume design (Edith Head). d, Music (Max Steiner working on score). e, Makeup (Jack Pierce working on Boris Karloff's makeup for *Frankenstein*). f, Art direction (Perry Ferguson working on sketch for *Citizen Kane*). g, Cinematography (Paul Hill, assistant cameraman for *Nagana*). h, Film editing (J. Watson Webb editing *The Razor's Edge*). i, Special effects (Mark Siegel working on model for *E.T. The Extra-Terrestrial*). j, Sound (Gary Summers works on control panel).

PHOTOGRAVURE
Sheets of 60 in six panes of 10
Serpentine Die Cut 11 Horiz.

2003, Feb. 25 **Tagged**

Self-Adhesive

3772	A2880 Pane of 10	12.00	
a.-j.	37c Any single	1.20	.50

Uncut press sheets of No. 3772 were made available for sale. Values: block of 10 with vert. gutter btwn., $15. See note after No. 2868.

OHIO STATEHOOD BICENTENNIAL

Aerial View of Farm Near Marietta — A2881

Designed by Phil Jordan. Printed by Banknote Corporation of America.

LITHOGRAPHED
Sheets of 120 in six panes of 20
Serpentine Die Cut 11¾x11½

2003, Mar. 1 **Tagged**

Self-Adhesive

3773	A2881 37c **multicolored**	.75	.25
	P# block of 4, 4# + B	3.00	
	Pane of 20	15.00	

PELICAN ISLAND NATIONAL WILDLIFE REFUGE, CENT.

Brown Pelican — A2882

Designed by Carl T. Herrman. Printed by Banknote Corporation of America.

LITHOGRAPHED
Sheets of 120 in six panes of 20
Serpentine Die Cut 12x11½

2003, Mar. 14 **Tagged**
Self-Adhesive

3774 A2882 37c **multicolored** .75 .25
P# block of 4, 4#+B 3.00
Pane of 20 15.00

Sea Coast — A2882a

Designed by Tom Engeman. Printed by Banknote Corporation of America.

PHOTOGRAVURE
COIL STAMP

2003, Mar. 19 **Untagged** ***Perf. 9¾ Vert.***

3775 A2882a (5c) **multicolored** .30 .25
Pair .50 —
P# strip of 5, #B111 1.30
P# single, #B111 .90

See No. 3864. No. 3775 has "2003" year date in blue, dots that run together in surf area, and a distinct small orange cloud. No. 3864 has "2004" year date in black, rows of distinctly separated dots in surf area, and the small orange cloud is indistinct.
See Nos. 3693, 3785, 3864, 3874-3875, 4348.

OLD GLORY

Uncle Sam on Bicycle with Liberty Flag, 20th Cent. — A2883

1888 Presidential Campaign Badge — A2884

1893 Silk Bookmark — A2885

Modern Hand Fan — A2886

Carving of Woman with Flag and Sword, 19th Cent. — A2887

Designed by Richard Sheaff. Printed by Ashton-Potter (USA) Ltd.

LITHOGRAPHED
BOOKLET STAMPS

2003, Apr. 3 **Tagged** ***Serpentine Die Cut 10x9¾***
Self-Adhesive

3776 A2883 37c **multicolored** .75 .50
3777 A2884 37c **multicolored** .75 .50
3778 A2885 37c **multicolored** .75 .50
3779 A2886 37c **multicolored** .75 .50
3780 A2887 37c **multicolored** .75 .50
a. Horiz. strip of 5, #3776-3780 3.75
b. Booklet pane, 2 #3780a 7.50

Nos. 3776-3780 were issued in booklets containing two No. 3780b, each with a different backing.

CESAR E. CHAVEZ (1927-93), LABOR ORGANIZER

A2888

Designed by Carl Herrman. Printed by Banknote Corporation of America.

LITHOGRAPHED
Sheets of 120 in six panes of 20
Serpentine Die Cut 11¾x11½

2003, Apr. 23 **Tagged**
Self-Adhesive

3781 A2888 37c **multicolored** .75 .25
P# block of 4, 4# + B 3.00
Pane of 20 15.00

LOUISIANA PURCHASE, BICENTENNIAL

English Translation of Treaty, Map of U.S., Treaty Signers — A2889

Designed by Richard Sheaff. Printed by American Packaging Corporation for Sennett Security Products

PHOTOGRAVURE
Sheets of 120 in six panes of 20

2003, Apr. 30 **Tagged** ***Serpentine Die Cut 10¾***
Self-Adhesive

3782 A2889 37c **multicolored** .95 .40
P# block of 4, 6# + S 4.00
Pane of 20 20.00

FIRST FLIGHT OF WRIGHT BROTHERS, CENT.

Orville Wright Piloting 1903 Wright Flyer — A2890

Designed by McRay Magleby. Printed by Avery Dennison.

PHOTOGRAVURE

2003, May 22 **Tagged** ***Serpentine Die Cut 11***
Self-Adhesive

3783 Pane of 10 9.00
a. A2890 37c single .90 .40
b. Pane of 9 #3783a 8.00
c. Pane of 1 #3783a .90

PURPLE HEART

A2891

A2891a

Designed by Carl Herrman. Printed by Banknote Corporation of America (#3784), Ashton-Potter (USA) Ltd. (#3784A).

LITHOGRAPHED
Sheets of 200 in 10 panes of 20 (#3784), Sheets of 120 in six panes of 20 (#3784A)

2003 **Tagged** ***Serpentine Die Cut 11¼x10¾***
Self-Adhesive

3784 A2891 37c **multicolored,** *May 30* .75 .25
P# block of 4, 4#+B 3.00
Pane of 20 15.00
b. Printed on back of backing paper —
d. Die cutting omitted, pair —

Serpentine Die Cut 10¾x10¼

3784A A2891a 37c **multicolored,** *Aug. 1* .75 .25
P# block of 4, 4#+P 3.00
Pane of 20 15.00
e. Die cutting omitted, pair 150.00
Pane of 20 *1,600.*

See Nos. 4032, 4164, 4263-4264, 4390.

Sea Coast — A2891b

Designed by Tom Engeman. Printed by J.W. Ferguson & Sons for Ashton-Potter (USA) Ltd.

COIL STAMP
PHOTOGRAVURE

2003, June **Untagged** ***Serpentine Die Cut 9½x10***
Self-Adhesive

3785 A2891b (5c) **multicolored** .30 .25
Pair .50
P# strip of 5, #P1111 1.40
P# single, same # — 1.00
a. Serp. die cut 9¼x10 .30 .25
Pair .50
P# strip of 5, #P2222 1.50
P# single, same # — 1.00
b. As "a," tagged (error) 3.25 2.50
P# strip of 5, #P2222 62.50
P# single, same # — 50.00

On No. 3785, the stamps are spaced on backing paper that is taller than the stamps.
One printing of No. 3785 has more of a scarlet shade in the sky than do other examples of Nos. 3785 and 3785a. Nos. 3785 and 3785a have black "2003" year date.
See Nos. 3693, 3775, 3864, 3874-3875, 4348.

LEGENDS OF HOLLYWOOD

Audrey Hepburn (1929-93), Actress — A2892

Designed by Michael J. Deas. Printed by American Packaging Corporation for Sennett Security Products.

PHOTOGRAVURE

Sheets of 120 in six panes of 20

2003, June 11 Tagged *Serpentine Die Cut 10¾*

Self-Adhesive

3786 A2892 37c **multicolored** 1.25 1.00
P# block of 4, 6#+S 6.00
Pane of 20 29.00

Uncut press sheets of No. 3786 were made available for sale. Values: cross-gutter block of 8, $27.50; pairs with gutters between, $4.25 each. See note after No. 2868.

SOUTHEASTERN LIGHTHOUSES

Old Cape Henry, Virginia — A2893

Cape Lookout, North Carolina — A2894

Morris Island, South Carolina — A2895

Tybee Island, Georgia — A2896

Hillsboro Inlet, Florida — A2897

Designed by Howard E. Paine. Printed by American Packaging Corporation for Sennett Security Products.

PHOTOGRAVURE

Sheets of 120 in six panes of 20

2003, June 13 Tagged *Serpentine Die Cut 10¾*

Self-Adhesive

3787 A2893 37c **multicolored** 1.10 .30
3788 A2894 37c **multicolored** 1.10 .30
a. Bottom of "USA" even with top of upper half-diamond of lighthouse (pos. 2) 4.00 2.50
3789 A2895 37c **multicolored** 1.10 .30
3790 A2896 37c **multicolored** 1.10 .30
3791 A2897 37c **multicolored** 1.10 .30
a. Strip of 5, #3787-3791 5.50
b. Strip of 5, #3787, 3788a, 3789-3791 9.50
P# block of 10, 2 sets of 6#+S 17.50
Pane of 20 37.00

Hidden 3-D images can be seen on Nos. 3787-3791 when viewed with a special "Stamp Decoder" lens sold by the USPS. No. 3787, 1792; No. 3788 and 3788a, 1859; No. 3789, 1876; No. 3790, 1867; No. 3791, 1907.

Eagle in Gold on Colored Background A2898

Colored Eagle on Gold Background A2899

A2898a

A2899a

A2898b

A2899b

A2898c

A2899c

A2898d

A2899d

Designed by Tom Engeman. Printed by American Packaging Corporation for Sennett Security Products.

PHOTOGRAVURE

COIL STAMPS

Dated "2003"

Serpentine Die Cut 11¾ Vert.

2003, June 26 Untagged

Self-Adhesive

3792 A2898 (25c) **gray & gold** .50 .25
a. Tagged —
3793 A2899 (25c) **gold & red** .50 .25
a. Tagged —
3794 A2898a (25c) **dull blue & gold** .50 .25
a. Tagged —
3795 A2899a (25c) **gold & Prussian blue** .50 .25
a. Tagged —
3796 A2898b (25c) **green & gold** .50 .25
a. Tagged —
3797 A2899b (25c) **gold & gray** .50 .25
a. Tagged —
3798 A2898c (25c) **Prussian blue & gold** .50 .25
a. Tagged —
3799 A2899c (25c) **gold & dull blue** .50 .25
a. Tagged —
3800 A2898d (25c) **red & gold** .50 .25
a. Tagged —
3801 A2899d (25c) **gold & green** .50 .25
a. Tagged —
b. Strip of 10, #3792-3801 5.00
P# strip of 11, 2 #3801, 1 each #3792-3800, #S1111111, S2222222, S3333333 8.00
P# strip of 21, 3 #3796, 2 each #3792-3795, 3797-3801, same # 16.00
P# single (#3796), #S1111111, S2222222 — 1.50
P# single (#3796), #S3333333 — 1.00
c. Strip of 10, #3792a-3801a —
P# strip of 11, 2 #3801a, 1 each #3792a-3800a, #S3333333 —
P# strip of 21, 3 #3796a, 2 each #3792a-3795a, 3797a-3801a, same # —
P# single (#3796a), same # — —

Dated "2005"

Serpentine Die Cut 11½ Vert.

2005, Aug. 5 Untagged

3792d A2898 (25c) **gray & gold** .50 .25
3793d A2899 (25c) **gold & red** .50 .25
3794d A2898 (25c) **dull blue & gold** .50 .25
3795d A2899 (25c) **gold & Prussian blue** .50 .25
3796d A2898 (25c) **green & gold** .50 .25
3797d A2899 (25c) **gold & gray** .50 .25
3798d A2898 (25c) **Prussian blue & gold** .50 .25
3799d A2899 (25c) **gold & dull blue** .50 .25
3800d A2898 (25c) **red & gold** .50 .25
3801d A2899 (25c) **gold & green** .50 .25
e. Strip of 10, #3792d-3801d 5.00
P# strip of 11, 2 #3801d, 1 each #3792d-3800d, P#S1111111 9.00
P# strip of 21, 3 #3796d, 2 each #3792d-3795d, 3797d-3800d, 3801d, P#S1111111 20.00
P# single (#3796d), #S1111111 3.25

See Nos. 3844-3853.

ARCTIC TUNDRA

A2900

Illustration reduced.

Designed by Ethel Kessler. Printed by Banknote Corporation of America.

No. 3802 — Wildlife and vegetation: a, Gyrfalcon. b, Gray wolf, vert. c, Common raven, vert. d, Musk oxen and caribou, vert. e, Grizzly bears, caribou. f, Caribou, willow ptarmigans. g, Arctic ground squirrel, vert. h, Willow ptarmigan, bearberry. i, Arctic grayling. j, Singing vole, thin-legged wolf spider, lingonberry, Labrador tea.

LITHOGRAPHED

Sheets of 80 in eight panes of 10

Serpentine Die Cut 10¾x10½, 10½x10¾

2003, July 2 Tagged

Self-Adhesive

3802 A2900 Pane of 10 8.50
a.-j. 37c Any single .85 .50

Uncut press sheets of No. 3802 were made available for sale. See note after No. 2868.

KOREAN WAR VETERANS MEMORIAL

Memorial in Snow — A2901

Designed by Richard Sheaff. Printed by Banknote Corporation of America.

LITHOGRAPHED
Sheets of 120 in six panes of 20
Serpentine Die Cut 11½x11¾

2003, July 27 **Tagged**

Self-Adhesive

3803	A2901 37c **multicolored**	.75	.25
	P# block of 4, 4#+B	3.00	
	Pane of 20	15.00	

MARY CASSATT PAINTINGS

Young Mother, 1888 — A2902

Children Playing on the Beach, 1884 — A2903

On a Balcony, 1878-79 — A2904

Child in a Straw Hat, c. 1886 — A2905

Designed by Derry Noyes. Printed by American Packaging Corporation for Sennett Security Products.

PHOTOGRAVURE
Serpentine Die Cut 10¾ on 2 or 3 Sides

2003, Aug. 7 **Tagged**

Self-Adhesive
Booklet Stamps

3804	A2902 37c **multicolored**	.75	.30
3805	A2903 37c **multicolored**	.75	.30
3806	A2904 37c **multicolored**	.75	.30
3807	A2905 37c **multicolored**	.75	.30
a.	Block of 4, #3804-3807	3.00	
b.	Booklet pane of 20, 5 #3807a	15.00	

No. 3807b is a double-sided booklet with 12 stamps on one side and 8 stamps plus label (booklet cover) on the other side.

EARLY FOOTBALL HEROES

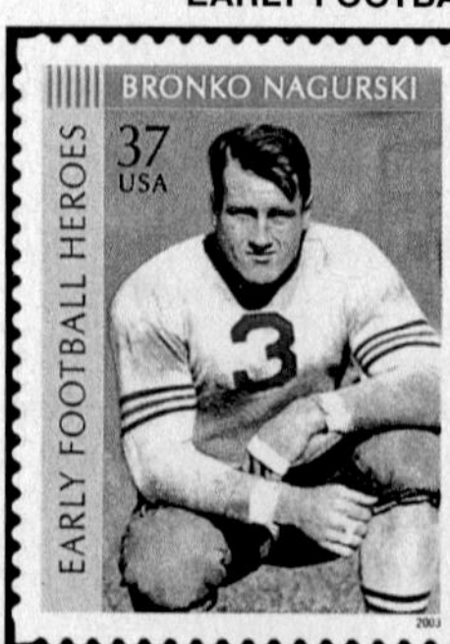

Bronko Nagurski (1908-90) — A2906

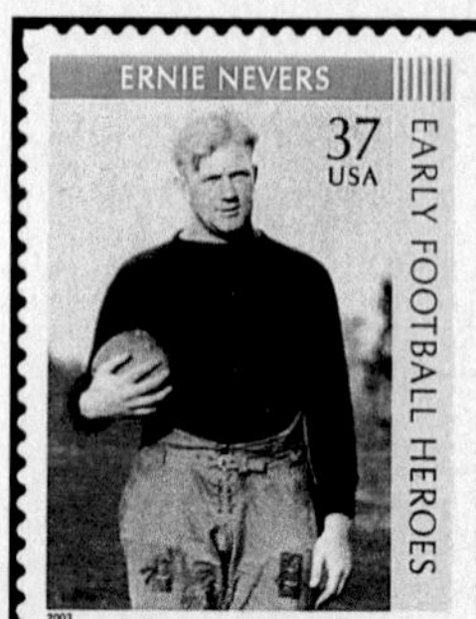

Ernie Nevers (1903-76) — A2907

Walter Camp (1859-1925) — A2908

Red Grange (1903-91) — A2909

Designed by Richard Sheaff. Printed by Avery Dennison.

PHOTOGRAVURE
Sheets of 200 in 10 panes of 20
Serpentine Die Cut 11½x11¾

2003, Aug. 8 **Tagged**

Self-Adhesive

3808	A2906 37c **multicolored**	.75	.35
3809	A2907 37c **multicolored**	.75	.35
3810	A2908 37c **multicolored**	.75	.35
3811	A2909 37c **multicolored**	.75	.35
a.	Block or strip of 4, #3808-3811	3.00	
	P# block of 4, 7#+V	3.00	
	Pane of 20	15.00	

Hidden 3-D images (a stylized football player) can be seen on Nos. 3808-3811 when viewed with a special "Stamp Decoder" lens sold by the USPS.

ROY ACUFF

Acuff (1903-92), Country Music Artist, and Fiddle — A2910

Designed by Richard Sheaff.
Printed by Avery Dennison.

PHOTOGRAVURE
Sheets of 200 in 10 panes of 20

2003, Sept. 13 **Tagged** ***Serpentine Die Cut 11***

Self-Adhesive

3812	A2910 37c **multicolored**	.75	.25
	P# block of 4, 4#+V	3.00	
	Pane of 20	15.00	

DISTRICT OF COLUMBIA

Map, National Mall, Row Houses and Cherry Blossoms — A2911

Designed by Greg Berger.
Printed by American Packaging Corporation for Sennett Security Products.

PHOTOGRAVURE
Sheets of 128 in eight panes of 16

2003, Sept. 23 **Tagged** ***Serpentine Die Cut 11***

Self-Adhesive

3813	A2911 37c **multicolored**	.80	.25
	P# block of 4, 8#+S	3.75	
	Pane of 16	18.00	

REPTILES AND AMPHIBIANS

Scarlet Kingsnake A2912

Blue-Spotted Salamander A2913

Reticulate Collared Lizard A2914

Ornate Chorus Frog — A2915

Ornate Box Turtle A2916

Designed by Steve Buchanan. Printed by Avery Dennison.

PHOTOGRAVURE
Sheets of 200 in 10 panes of 20

2003, Oct. 7 Tagged *Serpentine Die Cut 11*
Self-Adhesive

3814 A2912 37c **multicolored** .80 .40
3815 A2913 37c **multicolored** .80 .40
3816 A2914 37c **multicolored** .80 .40
3817 A2915 37c **multicolored** .80 .40
3818 A2916 37c **multicolored** .80 .40
a. Vert. strip of 5, #3814-3818 4.00
P# block of 10, 4#+V 8.00
Pane of 20 16.00

Washington — A2916a

Designed by Richard Sheaff. Printed by Avery Dennison.

PHOTOGRAVURE
Sheets of 200 in 10 panes of 20

2003, Oct. Tagged *Serpentine Die Cut 11*
Self-Adhesive

3819 A2916a 23c **gray green** 2.00 .25
P# block of 4, 2#+V 10.00
Pane of 20 50.00

See Nos. 3468A, 3475A, 3482-3483, 3616-3619.

Christmas — A2916b

Designed by Richard Sheaff. Printed by Ashton-Potter (USA) Ltd.

LITHOGRAPHED
Serpentine Die Cut 11¼ on 2 or 3 Sides
2003, Oct. 23 Tagged
Self-Adhesive
Booklet Stamp
Size: 19½x28mm

3820 A2916b 37c **multicolored** .75 .25
a. Booklet pane of 20 15.00
b. Die cutting omitted, pair —

See No. 3675.

No. 3820a is a double-sided booklet with 12 stamps on one side and 8 stamps plus label (booklet cover) on the other side. Compare to No. 3675, which measures 19x27mm.

CHRISTMAS

Reindeer with Pan Pipes — A2917

Santa Claus with Drum — A2918

Santa Claus with Trumpet — A2919

Reindeer with Horn — A2920

Reindeer with Pan Pipes — A2921

Santa Claus with Drum — A2922

Santa Claus with Trumpet — A2923

Reindeer with Horn — A2924

Designed by Ethel Kessler. Printed by American Packaging Corp. for Sennett Security Products.

PHOTOGRAVURE
Sheets of 160 in eight panes of 20
Serpentine Die Cut 11¾x11

2003, Oct. 23 Tagged
Self-Adhesive

3821 A2917 37c **multicolored** 1.00 .25
3822 A2918 37c **multicolored** 1.00 .25
3823 A2919 37c **multicolored** 1.00 .25
3824 A2920 37c **multicolored** 1.00 .25
a. Block or strip of 4, #3821-3824 4.00
P# block of 4, 4#+S 4.00
Pane of 20 20.00
b. Booklet pane of 20, 5 each #3821-3824 20.00

No. 3824b is a double-sided booklet with 12 stamps on one side and 8 stamps plus label (booklet cover) on the other side.

BOOKLET STAMPS
Serpentine Die Cut 10½x10¾ on 2 or 3 Sides

3825 A2921 37c **multicolored** 1.00 .25
3826 A2922 37c **multicolored** 1.00 .25
3827 A2923 37c **multicolored** 1.00 .25
3828 A2924 37c **multicolored** 1.00 .25
a. Block of 4, #3825-3828 4.00
b. Booklet pane of 4, #3825-3828 4.00
c. Booklet pane of 6, #3827-3828, 2 each #3825-3826 6.00
d. Booklet pane of 6, #3825-3826, 2 each #3827-3828 6.00

Snowy Egret — A2925

A2925a

A2925b

A2925c

Designed by Carl T. Herrman.
Printed by Avery Dennison (#3829), Ashton-Potter (USA) Ltd. (#3829A, 3830, 3830D).

COIL STAMPS
PHOTOGRAVURE

2003-04 Tagged *Serpentine Die Cut 8½ Vert.*
Self-Adhesive

3829 A2925 37c **multicolored,** *Oct. 24, 2003* .75 .25
Pair 1.50
P# strip of 5, #V1111, V2111, V3212, V3222 4.50
P# strip of 5, #V3221 250.00
P# single, #V1111, V2111, V3212, V3222 — 1.25
P# single, #V2121 *475.00*
P# single, #V3211 *400.00*
P# single, #V3221 — *115.00*
b. Black omitted — —

LITHOGRAPHED
Serpentine Die Cut 9½ Vert.

3829A A2925a 37c **multicolored,** *Mar. 2004* .85 .25
Pair 1.70
P# strip of 5, #P11111, P22222, P33333, P44444, P55555 6.00
P# single, same # — 1.75

Serpentine Die Cut 11½x11 on 2, 3 or 4 Sides
Booklet Stamps
PHOTOGRAVURE

3830 A2925b 37c **multicolored,** *Jan. 30, 2004* .75 .25
a. Booklet pane of 20 15.00
b. As "a," die cutting omitted *250.00*

With "USPS" Microprinted on Bird's Breast
Litho.

3830D A2925c 37c **multicolored,** *2004* *5.00* .25
e. Booklet pane of 20 *100.00*
f. Die cutting omitted, pair *150.00*
g. As "e," die cutting omitted *1,200.*

PACIFIC CORAL REEF

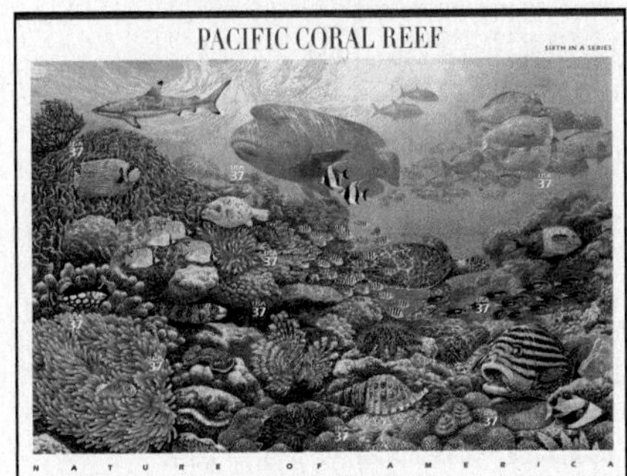

A2926

Illustration reduced.
Designed by Ethel Kessler. Printed by Avery Dennison.

No. 3831 — Marine life: a, Emperor angelfish, blue coral, mound coral, vert. b, Humphead wrasse, Moorish idol. c, Bumphead parrotfish, vert. d, Black-spotted puffer, threadfin butterflyfish, staghorn coral. e, Hawksbill turtle, palette surgeonfish. f, Pink anemonefish, magnificent sea anemone, vert. g, Snowflake moray eel, Spanish dancer. h, Lionfish, vert. i, Triton's trumpet. j, Oriental sweetlips, bluestreak cleaner wrasse, mushroom coral, vert.

PHOTOGRAVURE
Sheets of 80 in eight panes of 10

2004, Jan. 2 Tagged *Serpentine Die Cut 10¾*
Self-Adhesive

3831 A2926 Pane of 10 9.00
a.-j. 37c Any single .90 .40

Uncut press sheets of No. 3831 were made available for sale. See note after No. 2868.

CHINESE NEW YEAR

Year of the Monkey A2927

Designed by Clarence Lee. Printed by American Packaging Corporation for Sennett Security Products.

PHOTOGRAVURE
Sheets of 120 in six panes of 20

2004, Jan. 13 Tagged *Serpentine Die Cut 10¾*
Self-Adhesive

3832 A2927 37c **multicolored** .75 .25
P# block of 4, 4# + S 3.00
Pane of 20 15.00
a. Yellow omitted —

See Nos. 3895i, 3997i.

LOVE

Candy Hearts — A2928

Designed by Michael Osborne. Printed by Avery Dennison.

PHOTOGRAVURE
BOOKLET STAMP
Serpentine Die Cut 10¾ on 2, 3 or 4 Sides

2004, Jan. 14 Tagged
Self-Adhesive

3833 A2928 37c **multicolored** .75 .25
a. Booklet pane of 20 15.00

BLACK HERITAGE SERIES

Paul Robeson (1898-1976), Actor, Singer, Athlete and Activist — A2929

Designed by Richard Sheaff. Printed by American Packaging Corporation for Sennett Security Products.

PHOTOGRAVURE
Sheets of 120 in six panes of 20

2004, Jan. 20 Tagged *Serpentine Die Cut 10¾*
Self-Adhesive

3834 A2929 37c **multicolored** .85 .25
P# block of 4, 4# + S 3.40
Pane of 20 17.00

THEODOR SEUSS GEISEL (DR. SEUSS)

Dr. Seuss (1904-91), Children's Book Writer, and Book Characters A2930

Designed by Carl T. Herrman. Printed by American Packaging Corporation for Sennett Security Products.

PHOTOGRAVURE
Sheets of 180 in nine panes of 20
Serpentine Die Cut 10¾x10½

2004, Mar. 2 Tagged
Self-Adhesive

3835 A2930 37c **multicolored** .85 .25
P# block of 4, 6#+S 3.50
Pane of 20 17.50
a. Die cutting omitted, pair *1,400.*

FLOWERS

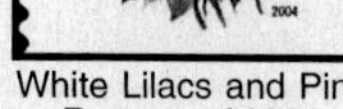

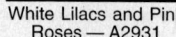

White Lilacs and Pink Roses — A2931

Five Varieties of Pink Roses — A2932

Designed by Richard Sheaff. Printed by Ashton-Potter (USA) Ltd. (#3836), American Packaging Corporation for Sennett Security Products.

LITHOGRAPHED (#3836), PHOTOGRAVURE
BOOKLET STAMP (#3836)
Sheets of 160 in eight panes of 20 (#3837)
Serpentine Die Cut 10¾ on 2, 3 or 4 Sides

2004, Mar. 4 Tagged
Self-Adhesive

3836 A2931 37c **multicolored** .75 .25
a. Booklet pane of 20 15.00

Serpentine Die Cut 11½x11

3837 A2932 60c **multicolored** 2.00 .25
P# block of 4, 5#+S 10.00
Pane of 20 45.00

UNITED STATES AIR FORCE ACADEMY, 50TH ANNIV.

Cadet Chapel A2933

Designed by Phil Jordan. Printed by American Packaging Corporation for Sennett Security Products.

PHOTOGRAVURE
Sheets of 120 in six panes of 20

2004, Apr. 1 Tagged *Serpentine Die Cut 10¾*
Self-Adhesive

3838 A2933 37c **multicolored** .75 .25
P# block of 4, 6# + S 3.00
Pane of 20 15.00

A hidden 3-D image (a stylized falcon) can be seen on this stamp when it is viewed with a special "Stamp Decoder" lens sold by the USPS.

HENRY MANCINI

Henry Mancini (1924-94), Composer, and Pink Panther A2934

Designed by Carl Herrman. Printed by American Packaging Corporation for Sennett Security Products.

PHOTOGRAVURE
Sheets of 120 in six panes of 20

2004, Apr. 13 Tagged *Serpentine Die Cut 10¾*
Self-Adhesive

3839 A2934 37c **multicolored** .75 .25
P# block of 4, 6#+S 3.00
Pane of 20 15.00

AMERICAN CHOREOGRAPHERS

Martha Graham (1893-1991) A2935

Alvin Ailey (1931-89), and Dancers A2936

Agnes de Mille (1909-93), and Dancers A2937

George Balanchine (1904-83), and Dancers A2938

Designed by Ethel Kessler. Printed by Ashton-Potter (USA) Ltd.

LITHOGRAPHED
Sheets of 120 in six panes of 20

2004, May 4 Tagged *Serpentine Die Cut 10¾*
Self-Adhesive

3840 A2935 37c **multicolored** .75 .35
3841 A2936 37c **multicolored** .75 .35
3842 A2937 37c **multicolored** .75 .35
3843 A2938 37c **multicolored** .75 .35
a. Horiz. strip of 4, #3840-3843 3.00
P# block of 8, 2 sets of P#, 6#+P 6.00
Pane of 20 15.00
b. Strip of 4, die cutting omitted *300.00*
Pane of 20 *1,750.*
c. Pane of 20 misprinted and miscut to show 5 #3843 and half of 5 #3842 at left, lower center plate position diagram at center, and 10 blank stamps at right. —
d. As "a," block tagging omitted 55.00

Normal tagging on Nos. 3840-3843 is prephosphored paper with additional block tagging on top of the printed designs.

Eagle

A2938a

A2938b

A2938c

A2938d

A2938e

A2938f

A2938g

A2938h

A2938i

A2938j

Designed by Tom Engeman. Printed by American Packaging Corporation for Sennett Security Products.

PHOTOGRAVURE

COIL STAMPS

2004, May 12 **Untagged** ***Perf. 9¾ Vert.***

3844	A2938a (25c) **gray & gold**	1.25	.25
3845	A2938b (25c) **gold & green**	1.25	.25
3846	A2938c (25c) **red & gold**	1.25	.25
3847	A2938d (25c) **gold & dull blue**	1.25	.25
3848	A2938e (25c) **Prussian blue & gold**	1.25	.25
3849	A2938f (25c) **gold & gray**	1.25	.50
3850	A2938g (25c) **green & gold**	1.25	.25
3851	A2938h (25c) **gold & Prussian blue**	1.25	.25
3852	A2938i (25c) **dull blue & gold**	1.25	.25
3853	A2938j (25c) **gold & red**	1.25	.25
a.	Strip of 10, #3844-3853	12.50	—
	P# strip of 11, 2 #3844, 1 each #3845-3853, #S1111111	16.50	—
	P# strip of 21, 3 #3849, 2 each #3844-3848, 3850-3853, #S1111111	33.00	—
	P# single (#3849), same #	—	.50

See Nos. 3792-3801, 3792d-3801d.

LEWIS & CLARK EXPEDITION, BICENTENNIAL

Meriwether Lewis (1774-1809) and William Clark (1770-1838) On Hill — A2939

Lewis — A2940

Clark — A2941

Designed by Michael J. Deas. Printed by Banknote Corporation of America for Sennett Security Products (#3854), Ashton-Potter (USA) Ltd.

LITHOGRAPHED & ENGRAVED

Sheets of 180 in nine panes of 20

2004, May 14 **Tagged** ***Serpentine Die Cut 10¾***

Self-Adhesive

3854	A2939 37c **green & multicolored**	1.10	.25
	P# block of 4, 6#+S	4.50	
	Pane of 20	22.50	

Uncut press sheets of No. 3854 were made available for sale. Values: cross-gutter block of 4, $18; pairs with gutters between, $3 each. See note after No. 2868.

Booklet Stamps

Serpentine Die Cut 10½x10¾

3855	A2940 37c **blue & multicolored** Ⓢ	.90	.45
3856	A2941 37c **red & multicolored** Ⓢ	.90	.45
a.	Horiz. or vert. pair, #3855-3856	1.80	
b.	Booklet pane, 5 each #3855-3856	9.00	

Nos. 3855-3856 were issued in booklets containing two No. 3856b, each with a different backing. The booklets sold for $8.95.

Ⓢ: Portrait ink can flake off during water soak. See note after No. 1549.

ISAMU NOGUCHI (1904-88), SCULPTOR

Akari 25N — A2942

Margaret La Farge Osborn — A2943

Black Sun — A2944

Mother and Child — A2945

Figure (Detail) — A2946

Designed by Derry Noyes. Printed by Ashton-Potter (USA) Ltd.

LITHOGRAPHED

Sheets of 120 in six panes of 20

Serpentine Die Cut 10½x10¾

2004, May 18 **Tagged**

Self-Adhesive

3857	A2942 37c **black**	.90	.40
3858	A2943 37c **black**	.90	.40
3859	A2944 37c **black**	.90	.40
3860	A2945 37c **black**	.90	.40
3861	A2946 37c **black**	.90	.40
a.	Horiz. strip of 5, #3857-3861	4.50	
	P# block of 6 (3 across x 2 down), 2#+P	6.00	
	P# block of 8, 2 sets of 2#+P + left label	8.00	
	Pane of 20	20.00	

Uncut press sheets of Nos. 3857-3861 were made available for sale. Values: cross-gutter block of 8, $25; pairs with gutters between, $3 each. See note after No. 2868.

NATIONAL WORLD WAR II MEMORIAL

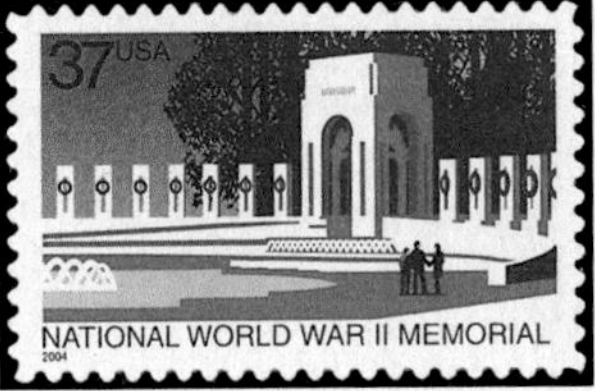

A2947

Designed by Howard E. Paine. Printed by Ashton-Potter (USA) Ltd.

LITHOGRAPHED

Sheets of 180 in nine panes of 20

2004, May 29 **Tagged** ***Serpentine Die Cut 10¾***

Self-Adhesive

3862	A2947 37c **multicolored**	.75	.25
	P# block of 4, 4#+P	3.00	
	Pane of 20	15.00	

A hidden 3-D image (a U.S. flag) can be seen on this stamp when it is viewed with a special "Stamp Decoder" lens sold by the USPS.

Scott values for used self-adhesive stamps are for examples either on piece or off piece.

OLYMPIC GAMES, ATHENS, GREECE Ⓢ

Stylized Runner A2948

Designed by Richard Sheaff. Printed by Ashton-Potter (USA) Ltd.

LITHOGRAPHED

Sheets of 120 in six panes of 20

2004, June 9 **Tagged** ***Serpentine Die Cut 10¾***

Self-Adhesive

3863	A2948 37c **multicolored**	.75	.25
	P# block of 4, 4#+P	3.00	
	Pane of 20	15.00	

Ⓢ: Ink cracks and flakes off during water soak. See note after No. 1549.

Sea Coast — A2948a

Designed by Tom Engeman. Printed by American Packaging Corp. for Sennett Security Products.

PHOTOGRAVURE
COIL STAMP

2004, June 11 **Untagged** ***Perf. 9¾ Vert.***

3864 A2948a (5c) **multicolored** .30 .25
Pair .50 —
P# strip of 5, #S1111 1.40 —
P# single, same # — 1.00

No. 3864 has "2004" year date in black, rows of distinctly separated dots in surf area, and the small orange cloud is indistinct. No. 3775 has "2003" year date in blue, dots that run together in surf area, and a distinct small orange cloud.

No. 3864 known with red ink that glows orange under long wave ultraviolet light. Values the same.

See Nos. 3693, 3775, 3785, 3874-3875, 4348.

THE ART OF DISNEY: FRIENDSHIP

Goofy, Mickey Mouse, Donald Duck — A2949

Bambi, Thumper — A2950

Mufasa, Simba — A2951

Jiminy Cricket, Pinocchio — A2952

Designed by David Pacheco. Printed by American Packaging Corporation for Banknote Corporation of America/Sennett Security Products.

LITHOGRAPHED
Sheets of 180 in nine panes of 20
Serpentine Die Cut 10½x10¾

2004, June 23 **Tagged**

Self-Adhesive

3865 A2949 37c **multicolored** 1.00 .30
3866 A2950 37c **multicolored** 1.00 .30
3867 A2951 37c **multicolored** 1.00 .30
3868 A2952 37c **multicolored** 1.00 .30
a. Block or vert. strip of 4, #3865-3868 4.00
P# block of 4, 4#+S 4.00
Pane of 20 20.00

U.S.S. CONSTELLATION

A2953

Designed by Howard E. Paine. Printed by Ashton-Potter (USA) Ltd.

ENGRAVED
Sheets of 180 in nine panes of 20

2004, June 30 **Tagged** ***Serpentine Die Cut 10½***

Self-Adhesive

3869 A2953 37c **brown** .75 .25
P# block of 4, 1#+P 3.00
Pane of 20 15.00

R. BUCKMINSTER FULLER (1895-1983), ENGINEER

Time Magazine Cover Depicting Fuller, by Boris Artzybasheff — A2954

Designed by Carl T. Herrman. Printed by Ashton-Potter (USA) Ltd.

LITHOGRAPHED
Sheets of 120 in six panes of 20
Serpentine Die Cut 10½x10¾

2004, July 12 **Tagged**

Self-Adhesive

3870 A2954 37c **multicolored** .75 .25
P# block of 4, 5#+P 3.00
Pane of 20 15.00

LITERARY ARTS

James Baldwin (1924-87), Writer A2955

Designed by Phil Jordan. Printed by Ashton-Potter (USA) Ltd.

LITHOGRAPHED
Sheets of 180 in nine panes of 20

2004, July 23 **Tagged** ***Serpentine Die Cut 10¾***

Self-Adhesive

3871 A2955 37c **multicolored** .75 .25
P# block of 4, 5#+P 3.00
Pane of 20 15.00
a. Die cutting omitted, pair *750.00*

AMERICAN TREASURES SERIES

Giant Magnolias on a Blue Velvet Cloth, by Martin Johnson Heade A2956

Designed by Derry Noyes. Printed by American Packaging Corporation for Sennett Security Products.

PHOTOGRAVURE
BOOKLET STAMP
Serpentine Die Cut 10¾ on 2 or 3 Sides

2004, Aug. 12 **Tagged**

Self-Adhesive

3872 A2956 37c **multicolored** .70 .25
a. Booklet pane of 20 15.00
b. Die cutting omitted, pair, in #3872a with foldover —

No. 3872a is a double-sided booklet pane with 12 stamps on one side and eight stamps plus label on the other side.

ART OF THE AMERICAN INDIAN

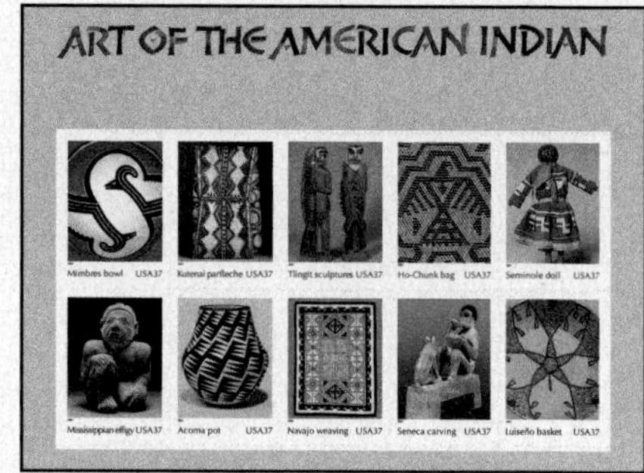

A2957

Illustration reduced.
Designed by Richard Sheaff. Printed by Avery Dennison.

No. 3873: a, Mimbres bowl. b, Kutenai parfleche. c, Tlingit sculptures. d, Ho-Chunk bag. e, Seminole doll. f, Mississippian effigy. g, Acoma pot. h, Navajo weaving. i, Seneca carving. j, Luiseño basket.

PHOTOGRAVURE
Serpentine Die Cut 10¾x11

2004, Aug. 21 **Tagged**

Self-Adhesive

3873 A2957 Pane of 10 25.00
a.-j. 37c Any single 2.50 .40

Sea Coast

A2957a

A2957b

A2957c

Designed by Tom Engeman.
Printed by Ashton-Potter (USA), Ltd. (#3874); American Packaging Corporation for Sennett Security Products (#3875).

LITHOGRAPHED
COIL STAMPS

2004-05 **Untagged** ***Serpentine Die Cut 10 Vert.***

Self-Adhesive

3874 A2957a (5c) **multicolored,** large "2003" year date .30 .25
Pair .50
P# strip of 5, #P2222 1.50
P# single, #P2222 — 1.10

a. A2957b Small "2003" year date, *2005* ⑤ .30 .25
Pair .50
P# strip of 5, #P3333, P4444, P5555, P6666, P7777, P8888, P9999 1.50
P# single, #P3333, P4444, P5555, P6666 — 1.10
P# single, #P7777, P8888, P9999 — .75

On Nos. 3874 and 3874a, the stamps are spaced on backing paper that is taller than the stamps.

On No. 3874 the color laydown order of plate numbers is cyan, magenta, yellow, black. On No. 3874a, the order is BCMY.

⑤: Later printings of No. 3874a do not respond to a water soak. See note after No. 1549.

Serpentine Die Cut 11½ Vert.

Untagged

3875 A2957c (5c) **multicolored**, "2004" year date .30 .25
Pair .50
P# strip of 5, #S1111 1.40
P# single, #S1111 — 1.10

On Nos. 3874, 3874a and 3875, the stamps are spaced on backing paper that is taller than the stamps.

No. 3875 exists with very faint traces of tagging.

See Nos. 3693, 3775, 3785, 3864, 4348.

LEGENDS OF HOLLYWOOD

John Wayne (1907-79), Actor — A2958

Designed by Derry Noyes.
Printed by American Packaging Corporation for Sennett Security Products.

PHOTOGRAVURE

Sheets of 120 in six panes of 20

2004, Sept. 9 Tagged *Serpentine Die Cut 10¾*

Self-Adhesive

3876 A2958 37c **multicolored** .85 .25
P# block of 4, 6#+S 3.50
Pane of 20 18.00

Uncut press sheets of No. 3876 were made available for sale. Values: cross-gutter block of 8, $27.50; pairs with gutters between, $3.50 each. See note after No. 2868.

SICKLE CELL DISEASE AWARENESS

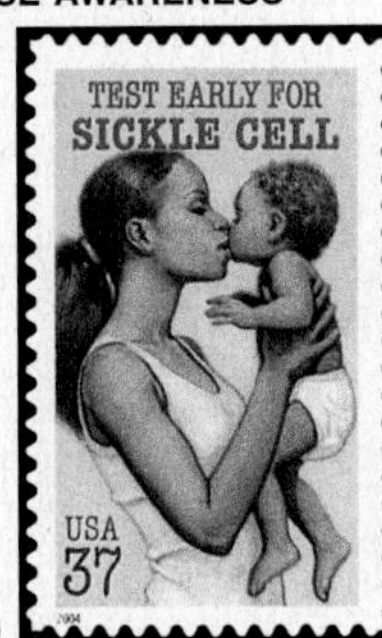

Mother and Child — A2959

Designed by Howard Paine. Printed by Avery Dennison.

PHOTOGRAVURE

Sheets of 200 in ten panes of 20

2004, Sept. 29 Tagged *Serpentine Die Cut 11*

Self-Adhesive

3877 A2959 37c **multicolored** .75 .25
P# block of 4, 6#+V 3.00
Pane of 20 15.00

CLOUDSCAPES

A2960

Illustration reduced.
Designed by Howard E. Paine. Printed by Avery Dennison.

No. 3878 — Clouds: a, Cirrus radiatus. b, Cirrostratus fibratus. c, Cirrocumulus undulatus. d, Cumulonimbus mammatus. e, Cumulonimbus incus. f, Altocumulus stratiformis. g, Altostratus translucidus. h, Altocumulus undulatus. i, Altocumulus castellanus. j, Altocumulus lenticularis. k, Stratocumulus undulatus. l, Stratus opacus. m, Cumulus humilis. n, Cumulus congestus. o, Cumulonimbus with tornado.

PHOTOGRAVURE

2004, Oct. 4 Tagged *Serpentine Die Cut 11*

Self-Adhesive

3878 A2960 Pane of 15 15.00
a.-o. 37c Any single 1.00 .50

CHRISTMAS

Madonna and Child, by Lorenzo Monaco — A2961

Designed by Richard Sheaff.
Printed by Ashton-Potter (USA), Ltd.

LITHOGRAPHED

BOOKLET STAMP

Serpentine Die Cut 10¾x11 on 2 or 3 Sides

2004, Oct. 14 Tagged

Self-Adhesive

3879 A2961 37c **multicolored** .75 .25
a. Booklet pane of 20 15.00
b. As "a," die cutting omitted —

No. 3879a is a double-sided booklet pane with 12 stamps on one side and eight stamps plus label that serves as a booklet cover on the other side.

HANUKKAH

Dreidel — A2962

Designed by Ethel Kessler.
Printed by Banknote Corporation of America for Sennett Security Products.

LITHOGRAPHED

Sheets of 300 in fifteen panes of 20

2004, Oct. 15 Tagged *Serpentine Die Cut 10¾*

Self-Adhesive

3880 A2962 37c **multicolored** .75 .25
P# block of 4, 4#+S 3.00
Pane of 20 15.00
a. Die cuts applied to wrong sides of stamp (hyphen-hole die cuts and wavy line on face, die cut 10¾ on reverse) — —

See Nos. 4118, 4219, 4372.

KWANZAA

People in Robes — A2963

Designed by Derry Noyes.
Printed by Ashton-Potter (USA), Ltd.

LITHOGRAPHED

Sheets of 160 in eight panes of 20

2004, Oct. 16 Tagged *Serpentine Die Cut 10¾*

Self-Adhesive

3881 A2963 37c **multicolored** .75 .25
P# block of 4, 6#+P 3.00
Pane of 20 15.00

See Nos. 4119, 4220, 4373.

Moss Hart (1904-61), Playwright A2964

Designed by Ethel Kessler.
Printed by Avery Dennison.

PHOTOGRAVURE

Sheets of 200 in ten panes of 20

2004, Oct. 25 Tagged *Serpentine Die Cut 11*

Self-Adhesive

3882 A2964 37c **multicolored** .75 .25
P# block of 4, 5#+V 3.00
Pane of 20 15.00

CHRISTMAS

Purple Santa Ornament — A2965

Green Santa Ornament — A2966

Blue Santa Ornament — A2967

Red Santa Ornament — A2968

Designed by Derry Noyes. Printed by American Packaging Corporation for Sennett Security Printers. (#3883-3890).

PHOTOGRAVURE

Sheets of 160 in eight panes of 20

Serpentine Die Cut 11½x11

2004, Nov. 16 Tagged

Self-Adhesive

3883 A2965 37c **purple & multicolored** 1.00 .25
3884 A2966 37c **green & multicolored** 1.00 .25
3885 A2967 37c **blue & multicolored** 1.00 .25
3886 A2968 37c **red & multicolored** 1.00 .25
a. Block or strip of 4, #3883-3886 4.00
P# block of 4, 4#+S 4.00
Pane of 20 20.00
b. Booklet pane of 20, 5 #3886a blocks 20.00

Purple Santa Ornament — A2969

Green Santa Ornament — A2970

Blue Santa Ornament — A2971

Red Santa Ornament — A2972

Booklet Stamps

Serpentine Die Cut 10½x10¾ on 2 or 3 Sides

3887	A2969 37c **purple & multicolored**	.90	.25
3888	A2970 37c **green & multicolored**	.90	.25
3889	A2971 37c **blue & multicolored**	.90	.25
3890	A2972 37c **red & multicolored**	.90	.25
a.	Block of 4, #3887-3890	3.60	
b.	Booklet pane of 4, #3887-3890	3.60	
c.	Booklet pane of 6, #3889-3890, 2 each #3887-3888	5.50	
d.	Booklet pane of 6, #3887-3888, 2 each #3889-3890	5.50	

A2969a

A2970a

A2971a

A2972a

Printed by Avery Dennison.

Serpentine Die Cut 8 on 2, 3 or 4 Sides

3891	A2970a 37c **green & multicolored**	2.00	.25
3892	A2969a 37c **purple & multicolored**	2.00	.25
3893	A2972a 37c **red & multicolored**	2.00	.25
3894	A2971a 37c **blue & multicolored**	2.00	.25
a.	Block of 4, #3891-3894	8.00	
b.	Booklet pane of 18, 6 each #3891, 3893, 3 each # 3892, 3894	36.00	
	Nos. 3883-3894 (12)	15.60	3.00

No. 3886b is a double-sided booklet with 12 stamps on one side and 8 stamps plus label that serves as a booklet cover on the other side.

The design of No. 3894b shows ornaments in a wooden box. The pattern of the wooden box dividers creates three types of each design. Rows 1 and 4 are Type 1, with a top horizontal strip of frame extending from edge to edge while the bottom strip of frame stops at the design's width. Rows 2 and 5 are Type 2, with both top and bottom strips of frame stopping at the design's width. Rows 3 and 6 are Type 3, with the top strip of frame stopping at design's width while the bottom strip of frame extends from edge to edge. Each variety is equally common.

Chinese New Year

A2972a

Designed by Clarence Lee. Printed by American Packaging Corporation for Sennett Security Products.

PHOTOGRAVURE

2005, Jan. 6 Tagged *Serpentine Die Cut 10¾*

Self-Adhesive

3895	A2972a Double sided pane of 24, 2 each #a-l	18.00	
a.	37c Rat	.75	.40
b.	37c Ox	.75	.40
c.	37c Tiger	.75	.40
d.	37c Rabbit	.75	.40
e.	37c Dragon	.75	.40
f.	37c Snake	.75	.40
g.	37c Horse	.75	.40
h.	37c Ram	.75	.40
i.	37c Monkey	.75	.40
j.	37c Rooster	.75	.40
k.	37c Dog	.75	.40
l.	37c Boar	.75	.40
m.	As No. 3895, die cutting missing on "a," "b," and "c" on reverse side (PS)	*900.00*	

No. 3895h has "2005" year date and is photogravure while No. 3747 has "2003" year date and is lithographed.

Stamps are on the right side of the front and on the left side of the reverse.

See Nos. 2720, 2817, 2876, 3060, 3120, 3179, 3272, 3370, 3500, 3559, 3747, 3832, 3997.

BLACK HERITAGE SERIES

Marian Anderson (1897-1993), Singer — A2973

Designed by Richard Sheaff. Printed by American Packaging Corporation for Sennett Security Products.

PHOTOGRAVURE

Sheets of 120 in six panes of 20

2005, Jan. 27 Tagged *Serpentine Die Cut 10¾*

Self-Adhesive

3896	A2973 37c **multicolored**	.85	.25
	P# block of 4, 4# + S	3.40	
	Pane of 20	17.00	

RONALD REAGAN

Ronald Reagan (1911-2004), 40th President — A2974

Designed by Howard E. Paine. Printed by American Packaging Corporation for Sennett Security Products.

PHOTOGRAVURE

Sheets of 120 in six panes of 20

2005, Feb. 9 Tagged *Serpentine Die Cut 10¾*

Self-Adhesive

3897	A2974 37c **multicolored**	.75	.25
	P# block of 4, 4#+S	3.00	
	Pane of 20	15.00	

The bottom center stamp (pos. 18) shows a small portion of the pane position diagram in the bottom margin, due to the too-high placement of the diagram in the selvage. There are three varieties of the portion appearing on the stamp, depending on the pane position on the press sheet.

Uncut press sheets of No. 3897 were made available for sale. Values: cross-gutter block of 4, $9.50; pairs with gutters between, $3 each. See note after No. 2868.

See No. 4078.

LOVE

Hand and Flower Bouquet — A2975

Designed by Derry Noyes. Printed by Avery Dennison.

PHOTOGRAVURE

BOOKLET STAMP

Serpentine Die Cut 10¾x11 on 2, 3 or 4 Sides

2005, Feb. 18 Tagged

Self-Adhesive

3898	A2975 37c **multicolored**	.75	.25
a.	Booklet pane of 20	15.00	

NORTHEAST DECIDUOUS FOREST

A2976

Illustration reduced.

Designed by Ethel Kessler. Printed by Avery Dennison.

No. 3899 — Wildlife: a, Eastern buckmoth, vert. b, Red-shouldered hawk. c, Eastern red bat. d, White-tailed deer. e, Black bear. f, Long-tailed weasel, vert. g, Wild turkey, vert. h, Ovenbird, vert. i, Red eft. j, Eastern chipmunk.

PHOTOGRAVURE

Sheets of 80 in eight panes of 10

2005, Mar. 3 Tagged *Serpentine Die Cut 10¾*

Self-Adhesive

3899	A2976 Pane of 10	8.50	
a.-j.	37c Any single	.85	.40

Uncut press sheets of No. 3899 were made available for sale. See note after No. 2868.

SPRING FLOWERS

Hyacinth — A2977

Daffodil — A2978

Tulip — A2979

Iris — A2980

Designed by Derry Noyes. Printed by Ashton-Potter (USA) Ltd.

LITHOGRAPHED
BOOKLET STAMPS

Serpentine Die Cut 10¾ on 2 or 3 Sides

2005, Mar. 15 **Tagged**

Self-Adhesive

3900	A2977 37c **multicolored**	.85	.30
3901	A2978 37c **multicolored**	.85	.30
3902	A2979 37c **multicolored**	.85	.30
3903	A2980 37c **multicolored**	.85	.30
a.	Block of 4, #3900-3903	3.40	
b.	Booklet pane of 20, 5 each #3900-3903	17.00	
c.	As "b," die cutting omitted on side with 8 stamps	—	

No. 3903b is a double-sided booklet with 12 stamps on one side and 8 stamps plus label (booklet cover) on the other side.

LITERARY ARTS

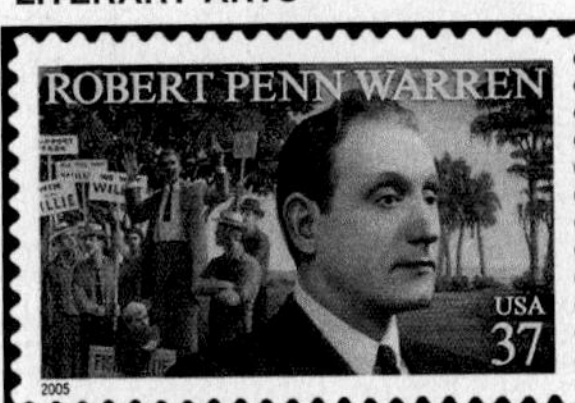

Robert Penn Warren (1905-89), Writer A2981

Designed by Carl Herrman. Printed by American Packaging Corporation for Sennett Security Products.

PHOTOGRAVURE
Sheets of 120 in six panes of 20

2005, Apr. 22 **Tagged** ***Serpentine Die Cut 10¾***

Self-Adhesive

3904	A2981 37c **multicolored**	.75	.25
	P# block of 4, 5#+S	3.00	
	Pane of 20	15.00	

EDGAR Y. "YIP" HARBURG

Harburg (1896-1981), Lyricist A2982

Designed by Ethel Kessler. Printed by Banknote Corporation of America for Sennett Security Products.

LITHOGRAPHED
Sheets of 120 in six panes of 20

2005, Apr. 28 **Tagged** ***Serpentine Die Cut 10¾***

Self-Adhesive

3905	A2982 37c **multicolored**	.75	.25
	P# block of 4, 4#+S	3.00	
	Pane of 20	15.00	

AMERICAN SCIENTISTS

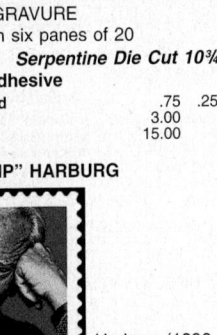

Barbara McClintock (1902-92), Geneticist A2983

Josiah Willard Gibbs (1839-1903), Thermodynamicist — A2984

John von Neumann (1903-57), Mathematician A2985

Richard Feynman (1918-88), Physicist A2986

Designed by Carl Herrman. Printed by Banknote Corporation of America for Sennett Security Products.

LITHOGRAPHED
Sheets of 180 in nine panes of 20

2005, May 4 **Tagged** ***Serpentine Die Cut 10¾***

Self-Adhesive

3906	A2983 37c **multicolored**	1.00	.35
3907	A2984 37c **multicolored**	1.00	.35
3908	A2985 37c **multicolored**	1.00	.35
a.	Vert. pair, die cutting omitted, #3906 & 3908	—	
3909	A2986 37c **multicolored**	1.00	.35
a.	Block or horiz. strip of 4, #3906-3909	4.00	
	P# block of 8, 2 sets of P# + top label, 5#+S	8.00	
	P# block of 4, 5#+S	4.00	
	Pane of 20	20.00	
b.	All colors omitted, tagging omitted, pane of 20	—	
c.	As "a," printing on back of stamps omitted	—	
d.	Vert. pair, die cutting omitted, #3907 & 3909	—	

On No. 3909b, the printing on the back of the pane and all die cutting is normal.

MODERN AMERICAN ARCHITECTURE

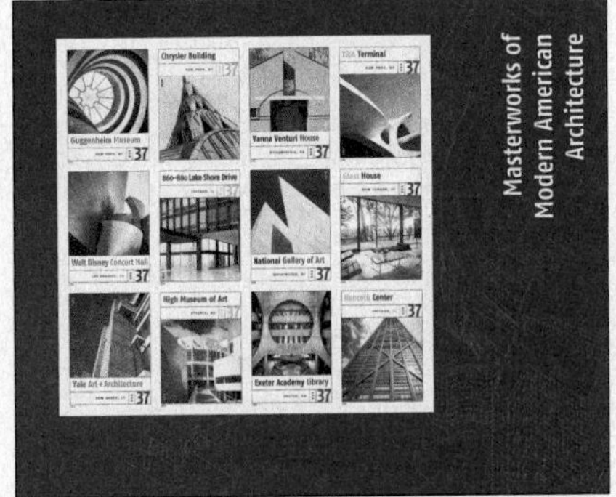

A2987

Illustration reduced.

Designed by Margaret Bauer. Printed by Ashton-Potter (USA) Ltd.

No. 3910 — Buildings: a, Guggenheim Museum, New York. b, Chrysler Building, New York. c, Vanna Venturi House, Philadelphia. d, TWA Terminal, New York. e, Walt Disney Concert Hall, Los Angeles. f, 860-880 Lake Shore Drive, Chicago. g, National Gallery of Art, Washington, DC. h, Glass House, New Canaan, CT. i, Yale Art and Architecture Building, New Haven, CT. j, High Museum of Art, Atlanta. k, Exeter Academy Library, Exeter, NH. l, Hancock Center, Chicago.

LITHOGRAPHED

Serpentine Die Cut 10¾x11

2005, May 19 **Tagged**

Self-Adhesive

3910	A2987 Pane of 12	11.00	
a.-l.	37c Any single	.90	.50
m.	As No. 3910, orange yellow omitted	*400.00*	—

No. 3910m exists on a first day cover.

LEGENDS OF HOLLYWOOD

Henry Fonda (1905-82), Actor — A2988

Designed by Derry Noyes. Printed by Ashton-Potter (USA) Ltd.

LITHOGRAPHED
Sheets of 180 in nine panes of 20

Serpentine Die Cut 11x10¾

2005, May 20 **Tagged**

Self-Adhesive

3911	A2988 37c **multicolored**	.90	.25
	P# block of 4, 5#+P	4.50	
	Pane of 20	22.00	

Uncut press sheets of No. 3911 were made available for sale. Values: cross-gutter block of 8, $22.50; pairs with gutters between, $3.50 each. See note after No. 2868.

THE ART OF DISNEY: CELEBRATION

Pluto, Mickey Mouse — A2989

Mad Hatter, Alice — A2990

Flounder, Ariel — A2991

Snow White, Dopey — A2992

Designed by David Pacheco. Printed by Banknote Corporation of America for Sennett Security Products.

LITHOGRAPHED
Sheets of 180 in nine panes of 20
Serpentine Die Cut 10½x10¾

2005, June 30 **Tagged**

Self-Adhesive

3912	A2989 37c **multicolored**	.85	.30
3913	A2990 37c **multicolored**	.85	.30
3914	A2991 37c **multicolored**	.85	.30
3915	A2992 37c **multicolored**	.85	.30
a.	Block or vert. strip of 4, #3912-3915	3.40	
	P# block of 4, 6#+S	3.40	
	P# block of 10, 2 sets of P# + top label	8.25	
	Pane of 20	17.00	
b.	Die cutting omitted, pane of 20	*5,500.*	*1,400.*
c.	Printed on backing paper, pane of 20	—	

On the unique used pane of No. 3915b, the outer selvage was removed by cutting.

ADVANCES IN AVIATION

Boeing 247 — A2993

Consolidated PBY Catalina A2994

Grumman F6F Hellcat A2995

Republic P-47 Thunderbolt A2996

Engineering and Research Corporation Ercoupe 415 — A2997

Lockheed P-80 Shooting Star — A2998

Consolidated B-24 Liberator A2999

Boeing B-29 Superfortress A3000

Beechcraft 35 Bonanza A3001

Northrop YB-49 Flying Wing — A3002

Designed by Phil Jordan. Printed by Ashton-Potter (USA) Ltd.

LITHOGRAPHED
Sheets of 180 in nine panes of 20
Serpentine Die Cut 10¾x10½

2005, July 29 **Tagged**

Self-Adhesive

3916	A2993 37c **multicolored**	.80	.40
3917	A2994 37c **multicolored**	.80	.40
3918	A2995 37c **multicolored**	.80	.40
3919	A2996 37c **multicolored**	.80	.40
3920	A2997 37c **multicolored**	.80	.40
3921	A2998 37c **multicolored**	.80	.40
3922	A2999 37c **multicolored**	.80	.40
3923	A3000 37c **multicolored**	.80	.40
3924	A3001 37c **multicolored**	.80	.40
3925	A3002 37c **multicolored**	.80	.40
a.	Block of 10, #3916-3925	8.00	
	P# block of 10, 7#+P	8.00	
	Pane of 20	16.00	
b.	As "a," tagging omitted	—	

No. 3925b currently is in a pane of 20 format. Only one pane is recorded.

RIO GRANDE BLANKETS

A3003

A3004

A3005

A3006

Designed by Derry Noyes. Printed by Ashton-Potter (USA) Ltd.

LITHOGRAPHED
BOOKLET STAMPS
Serpentine Die Cut 10¾ on 2 or 3 Sides

2005, July 30 **Tagged**

Self-Adhesive

3926	A3003 37c **multicolored**	.75	.30
3927	A3004 37c **multicolored**	.75	.30
3928	A3005 37c **multicolored**	.75	.30
3929	A3006 37c **multicolored**	.75	.30
a.	Block of 4, #3926-3929	3.00	
b.	Booklet pane, 5 each #3926-3929	15.00	

No. 3929b is a double-sided booklet with 12 stamps on one side and 8 stamps plus label (booklet cover) on the other side.

PRESIDENTIAL LIBRARIES ACT, 50th ANNIV.

Presidential Seal — A3007

Designed by Howard E. Paine. Printed by Banknote Corporation of America for Sennett Security Products.

LITHOGRAPHED
Sheets of 180 in nine panes of 20

2005, Aug. 4 **Tagged** ***Serpentine Die Cut 10¾***

Self-Adhesive

3930	A3007 37c **multicolored**	.80	.25
	P# block of 4, 3#+S	3.25	
	Pane of 20	16.50	

Uncut press sheets of No. 3930 were made available for sale. Values: cross-gutter block of 4, $9.50; pairs with gutters between, $3.50 each. See note after No. 2868.

SPORTY CARS OF THE 1950S

1953 Studebaker Starliner A3008

1954 Kaiser Darrin A3009

1953 Chevrolet Corvette A3010

1952 Nash Healey A3011

1955 Ford Thunderbird A3012

Designed by Art M. Fitzpatrick. Printed by Ashton-Potter (USA) Ltd.

LITHOGRAPHED
BOOKLET STAMPS

Serpentine Die Cut 10¾ on 2 or 3 Sides

2005, Aug. 20 **Tagged**

Self-Adhesive

3931	A3008 37c **multicolored**	1.60	.40
3932	A3009 37c **multicolored**	1.60	.40
3933	A3010 37c **multicolored**	1.60	.40
3934	A3011 37c **multicolored**	1.60	.40
3935	A3012 37c **multicolored**	1.60	.40
a.	Vert. strip of 5, #3931-3935	8.00	
b.	Booklet pane, 4 each #3931-3935	32.00	

Stamps in No. 3935a are not adjacent, as rows of selvage are between stamps one and two, and between stamps three and four.

No. 3935b is a double-sided booklet pane with 12 stamps on one side (2 each #3931, 3933, 3935, and 3 each #3932, 3934) and eight stamps (1 each #3932, 3934, and 2 each #3931, 3933, 3935) plus label on the other side.

ARTHUR ASHE

Arthur Ashe (1943-93), Tennis Player — A3013

Designed by Carl T. Herrman. Printed by Ashton-Potter (USA) Ltd.

LITHOGRAPHED
Sheets of 240 in twelve panes of 20

2005, Aug. 27 **Tagged** ***Serpentine Die Cut 10¾***

Self-Adhesive

3936	A3013 37c **multicolored**	.75	.25
	P# block of 4, 5#+P	3.00	
	Pane of 20	15.00	

TO FORM A MORE PERFECT UNION

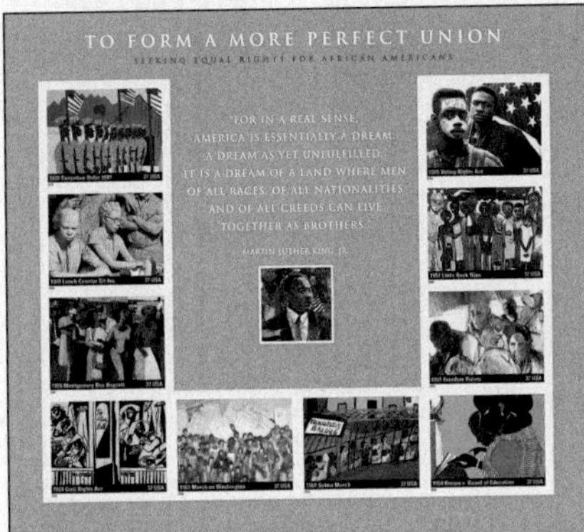

A3014

Illustration reduced.

Designed by Ethel Kessler. Printed by Ashton-Potter (USA) Ltd.

No. 3937 — Inscriptions and artwork: a, 1948 Executive Order 9981 (Training for War, by William H. Johnson). b, 1965 Voting Rights Act (Youths on the Selma March, 1965, photograph by Bruce Davidson). c, 1960 Lunch Counter Sit-ins (National Civil Rights Museum exhibits, by StudioEIS). d, 1957 Little Rock Nine (America Cares, by George Hunt). e, 1955 Montgomery Bus Boycott (Walking, by Charles Alston). f, 1961 Freedom Riders (Freedom Riders, by May Stevens). g, 1964 Civil Rights Act (Dixie Café, by Jacob Lawrence). h, 1963 March on Washington (March on Washington, by Alma Thomas). i, 1965 Selma March (Selma March, by Bernice Sims). j, 1954 Brown v. Board of Education (The Lamp, by Romare Bearden).

LITHOGRAPHED

Serpentine Die Cut 10¾x10½

2005, Aug. 30 **Tagged**

Self-Adhesive

3937	A3014 Pane of 10	11.00	
a.-j.	37c Any single	1.10	.40

CHILD HEALTH

Child and Doctor — A3015

Designed by Craig Frazier. Printed by Avery Dennison.

PHOTOGRAVURE
Sheets of 200 in ten panes of 20

Serpentine Die Cut 10½x11

2005, Sept. 7 **Tagged**

Self-Adhesive

3938	A3015 37c **multicolored**	.75	.25
	P# block of 4, 4#+V	3.00	
	Pane of 20	15.00	

LET'S DANCE

Merengue — A3016

Salsa — A3017

Cha Cha Cha — A3018

Mambo — A3019

Designed by Ethel Kessler. Printed by American Packaging Corporation for Sennett Security Products.

PHOTOGRAVURE
Sheets of 120 in six panes of 20

2005, Sept. 17 **Tagged** ***Serpentine Die Cut 10¾***

Self-Adhesive

3939	A3016 37c **multicolored**	1.00	.35
3940	A3017 37c **multicolored**	1.00	.35
3941	A3018 37c **multicolored**	1.00	.35
3942	A3019 37c **multicolored**	1.00	.35
a.	Vert. strip of 4, #3939-3942	4.00	
	P# block of 8, 8#+S	8.00	
	Pane of 20	20.00	

Stamps in the vertical strip are not adjacent as rows of selvage are between the stamps. The backing paper of stamps from the 2nd and 4th columns have Spanish inscriptions, while the other columns have English inscriptions.

GRETA GARBO

Garbo (1905-90), Actress — A3020

Designed by Carl T. Herrman. Printed by Banknote Corporation of America for Sennett Security Products.

ENGRAVED

Sheets of 120 in six panes of 20

2005, Sept. 23 Tagged *Serpentine Die Cut 10¾*

Self-Adhesive

3943 A3020 37c **black**		.75	.25
P# block of 4, 1#+S		3.00	
Pane of 20		15.00	

See Sweden No. 2517.

JIM HENSON AND THE MUPPETS

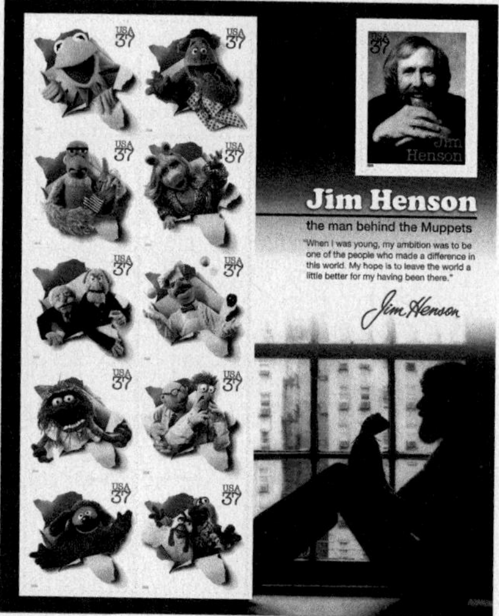

A3021

Illustration reduced.
Designed by Edward Eyth. Printed by Avery Dennison.

No. 3944: a, Kermit the Frog. b, Fozzie Bear. c, Sam the Eagle and flag. d, Miss Piggy. e, Statler and Waldorf. f, The Swedish Chef and fruit. g, Animal. h, Dr. Bunsen Honeydew and Beaker. i, Rowlf the Dog. j, The Great Gonzo and Camilla the Chicken. k, Jim Henson.

Nos. 3944a-3944j are 30x30mm; No. 3944k, 28x37mm.

PHOTOGRAVURE

Serpentine Die Cut 10½, 10½x10¾ (#3944k)

2005, Sept. 28 Tagged

Self-Adhesive

3944 A3021 Pane of 11		9.00	
a.-k. 37c Any single		.80	.50

CONSTELLATIONS Ⓢ

Leo — A3022

Orion — A3023

Lyra — A3024

Pegasus — A3025

Designed by McRay Magleby.
Printed by Ashton-Potter (USA) Ltd.

LITHOGRAPHED

Sheets of 240 in twelve panes of 20

2005, Oct. 3 Tagged *Serpentine Die Cut 10¾*

Self-Adhesive

3945 A3022 37c **multicolored**		.85	.35
3946 A3023 37c **multicolored**		.85	.35
3947 A3024 37c **multicolored**		.85	.35
3948 A3025 37c **multicolored**		.85	.35
a. Block or vert. strip of 4, #3945-3948		3.40	
P# block of 4, 6#+P		3.40	
P# block of 10, 2 sets of P# + top label		8.25	
Pane of 20		17.00	
b. As "a," die cutting omitted		750.00	

Ⓢ: Ink on Nos. 3945-3948 cracks and flakes off during water soak. See note after No. 1549.

CHRISTMAS COOKIES

Santa Claus — A3026

Snowmen — A3027

Angel — A3028

Elves — A3029

Designed by Derry Noyes.
Printed by Banknote Corporation of America for Sennett Security Products.

LITHOGRAPHED

Serpentine Die Cut 10¾x11

2005, Oct. 20 Tagged

Self-Adhesive

Design Size: 19x26mm

3949 A3026 37c **multicolored**		.85	.25
3950 A3027 37c **multicolored**		.85	.25
3951 A3028 37c **multicolored**		.85	.25
3952 A3029 37c **multicolored**		.85	.25
a. Block or vert. strip of 4, #3949-3952		3.50	
P# block of 4, 4#+S		3.50	
Pane of 20		17.50	

A3026a

A3027a

A3028a

A3029a

Printed by American Packaging Corporation for Sennett Security Products (#3953-3960).

PHOTOGRAVURE (#3953-3960)

Booklet Stamps

Serpentine Die Cut 10¾x11 on 2 or 3 Sides

Design Size: 19½x27mm

3953 A3026a 37c **multicolored**		1.00	.25
3954 A3027a 37c **multicolored**		1.00	.25
3955 A3028a 37c **multicolored**		1.00	.25
3956 A3029a 37c **multicolored**		1.00	.25
a. Block of 4, #3953-3956		4.00	
b. Booklet pane of 20, 5 #3956a		20.00	

Santa Claus — A3030

Snowmen — A3031

Angel — A3032

Elves — A3033

Serpentine Die Cut 10½x10¾

3957 A3030 37c **multicolored**		1.10	.25
3958 A3031 37c **multicolored**		1.10	.25
3959 A3032 37c **multicolored**		1.10	.25
3960 A3033 37c **multicolored**		1.10	.25
a. Block of 4, #3957-3960		4.50	
b. Booklet pane of 4, #3957-3960		4.50	
c. Booklet pane of 6, #3959-3960, 2 each #3957-3958		7.00	
d. Booklet pane of 6, #3957-3958, 2 each #3959-3960		7.00	

No. 3956b is a double-sided booklet pane with 12 stamps on one side and eight stamps plus label that serves as a booklet cover on the other side. Nos. 3949-3952 have a small "2005" year date, while Nos. 3953-3956 have a large year date. Other design differences caused by different cropping of the images can be found, with Nos. 3953-3956 showing slightly more design features on one or more sides.

DISTINGUISHED MARINES

Lt. Gen. John A. Lejeune (1867-1942), 2nd Infantry Division Insignia A3034

Lt. Gen. Lewis B. Puller (1898-1971), 1st Marine Division Insignia A3035

Sgt. John Basilone (1916-45), 5th Marine Division Insignia
A3036

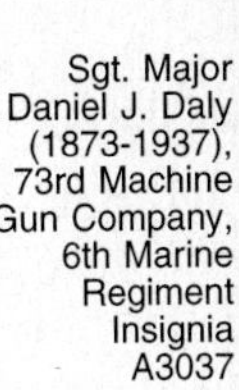
Sgt. Major Daniel J. Daly (1873-1937), 73rd Machine Gun Company, 6th Marine Regiment Insignia
A3037

Designed by Phil Jordan. Printed by Ashton-Potter (USA) Ltd.

LITHOGRAPHED
Sheets of 180 in nine panes of 20

Serpentine Die Cut 11x10½

2005, Nov. 10 **Tagged**

Self-Adhesive

3961 A3034 37c **multicolored** 1.00 .35
3962 A3035 37c **multicolored** 1.00 .35
3963 A3036 37c **multicolored** 1.00 .35
3964 A3037 37c **multicolored** 1.00 .35
a. Block or horiz. strip of 4, #3961-3964 4.00
P# block of 4, 6#+P 4.50
P# block of 8, 2 sets of P# + top panel 9.00
Pane of 20 23.00

Flag and Statue of Liberty — A3038

A3038a

Designed by Carl and Ann Purcell. Printed by Sterling Sommer, Inc. for Ashton-Potter (USA) Ltd. (#3965), Ashton-Potter (USA) Ltd. (#3966).

LITHOGRAPHED
Sheets of 400 in four panes of 100 (#3965), Sheets of 120 in six panes of 20 (#3966)

2005, Dec. 8 **Tagged** ***Perf. 11¼***

3965 A3038 (39c) **multicolored** 1.10 .25
P# block of 4, 4#+P 12.50 —
Pane of 100 120.00 —

Self-Adhesive (#3966, 3968-3975)

Serpentine Die Cut 11¼x10¾

3966 A3038a (39c) **multicolored** 1.10 .25
P# block of 4, 4#+P 4.00
Pane of 20 18.50
a. Booklet pane of 20 22.00
b. As "a," die cutting omitted 3,100.

A3038b

A3038c

A3038d

A3038e

Printed by Ashton-Potter (USA) Ltd. (#3970), American Packaging Corporation for Sennett Security Printers (#3967, 3969), Avery Dennison (#3968).

LITHOGRAPHED (#3970), PHOTOGRAVURE
COIL STAMPS

Perf. 9¾ Vert.

3967 A3038b (39c) **multicolored** 1.10 .25
Pair 2.20 —
P# strip of 5, #S1111 6.00 —
P# single, #S1111 2.00

Serpentine Die Cut 8½ Vert.

3968 A3038c (39c) **multicolored** 1.10 .25
Pair 2.20
P# strip of 5, #V1111 6.00
P# single, #V1111 1.50

Serpentine Die Cut 10¼ Vert.

3969 A3038d (39c) **multicolored** 1.50 .25
Pair 3.00
P# strip of 5, #S1111 8.00
P# single, #S1111 1.50

Serpentine Die Cut 9½ Vert.

3970 A3038e (39c) **multicolored** 3.50 .25
Pair 7.00
P# strip of 5, #P1111, P2222 20.00
P# single, #P1111, P2222 2.00

A3038f

A3038g

A3038h

A3038i

Printed by American Packaging Corporation for Sennett Security Printers (#3973), Avery Dennison (#3972, 3975), Banknote Corporation of America for Sennett Security Products (#3974).

LITHOGRAPHED (#3974), PHOTOGRAVURE
BOOKLET STAMPS

Serpentine Die Cut 11¼x10¾ on 2 or 3 Sides

3972 A3038f (39c) **multicolored** 1.10 .25
a. Booklet pane of 20 22.00

Serpentine Die Cut 10½x10¾ on 2 or 3 Sides

3973 A3038g (39c) **multicolored** 1.10 .25
a. Booklet pane of 20 22.00

On both Nos. 3972 and 3973, the sky immediately above the date is bright blue and extends from the left side to beyond the "6" in the date, the left arm of the star at the upper left barely touches the frame line and is without the "USPS" microprinting. They are distinguishable by the die cutting. Nos. 3872a and 3973a are double-sided booklet panes with 12 stamps on one side and eight stamps plus label that serves as a booklet cover on the other side.

No. 3973 was not available until January 2006.

Serpentine Die Cut 11¼x10¾ on 2 or 3 Sides

3974 A3038h (39c) **multicolored** 1.10 .25
a. Booklet pane of 4 4.40
b. Booklet pane of 6 6.60

Serpentine Die Cut 8 on 2, 3 or 4 Sides

3975 A3038i (39c) **multicolored** 1.10 .25
a. Booklet pane of 18 20.00
Nos. 3965-3975 (10) 13.80 2.50

Nos. 3965-3975 are dated "2006."

On No. 3966, the sky immediately above the date is bright blue and extends from the left side to beyond the "6" in the date, the left arm of the star at upper left is clear of the top frame, and "USPS" is microprinted on the top red flag stripe.

On No. 3974, the sky immediately above the date is dark blue and extends from the left side to the second "0" in the date, the left arm of the star at upper left touches the top frame, and lacks the microprinting found on No. 3966.

Nos. 3965 and 3970 also have "USPS" microprinted on the top red flag stripe.

Nos. 3966a and 3972a are double-sided booklet panes with 12 stamps on one side and eight stamps plus label that serves as a booklet cover on the other side. On No. 3966a, the stamps on one side are upside-down with relation to the stamps on the other side. On No. 3972a the stamps are all aligned the same on both sides.

LOVE

Birds — A3039

Designed by Craig Frazier. Printed by Avery Dennison.

PHOTOGRAVURE

Serpentine Die Cut 11 on 2, 3, or 4 Sides

2006, Jan. 3 **Tagged**

BOOKLET STAMP

Self-Adhesive

3976 A3039 (39c) **multicolored** 1.10 .25
a. Booklet pane of 20 22.00

See No. 4029.

Flag and Statue of Liberty — A3040

Designed by Carl and Ann Purcell. Printed by Ashton-Potter (USA) Ltd.

LITHOGRAPHED
Sheets of 120 in six panes of 20

2006 **Tagged** ***Serpentine Die Cut 11¼x10¾***

Self-Adhesive (#3978, 3980-3985)

3978 A3040 39c **multicolored**, *Apr. 8* .85 .25
P# block of 4, 4#+P 5.00
Pane of 20 24.00
a. Booklet pane of 10 8.50
b. Booklet pane of 20 17.00
c. As "b," die cutting omitted on side with 8 stamps —

No. 3978 has "USPS" microprinted on top red flag stripe.

No. 3978b is a double-sided booklet with 12 stamps on one side and 8 stamps plus label (booklet cover) on the other side.

A3040a

A3040b

A3040c

A3040d

A3040e

Printed by American Packaging Corporation for Sennett Security Products (#3979, 3982), Ashton-Potter (USA) Ltd. (#3981). Avery Dennison (#3980).

LITHOGRAPHED (#3981), PHOTOGRAVURE (#3979-3980, 3982-3983)
COIL STAMPS

Perf. 9¾ Vert.

3979 A3040a 39c **multicolored**, *Mar. 8* 1.00 .25
Pair 2.00 —
P# strip of 5, #S1111 5.25 —

P# single, #S1111 — 2.50

Serpentine Die Cut 11 Vert.

3980 A3040b 39c **multicolored,** overall tagging, *Jan. 9* ⓢ .80 .25
Pair 1.60
P# strip of 5, #V1111 5.25
P# single, #V1111 2.50
a. Prephosphored coated paper with surface tagging showing a solid appearance — —
Pair —
P# strip of 5, #V1111 —

No. 3980 has rounded corners and lacks microprinting. Unused examples are on backing paper taller than the stamp, and the stamps are spaced approximately 3mm apart.

See note after No. 1549.

Serpentine Die Cut 9½ Vert.

3981 A3040c 39c **multicolored,** *Apr. 8* 1.40 .25
Pair 2.80
P# strip of 5, #P1111 8.00
P# single, #P1111 1.75
a. Die cutting omitted, pair *150.00*

No. 3981 has "USPS" microprinted on top red flag stripe.

Counterfeits exist of No. 3981. See the Postal Counterfeits section of this catalog.

Serpentine Die Cut 10¼ Vert.

3982 A3040d 39c **multicolored,** *Apr. 8* 1.25 .25
Pair 2.50
P# strip of 5, #S1111 6.50
P# single, #S1111 1.75
a. Vert. pair, unslit between *500.00*

Counterfeits exist of No. 3982. See the Postal Counterfeits section of this catalog.

Serpentine Die Cut 8½ Vert.

3983 A3040e 39c **multicolored,** *Apr. 8* .80 .25
Pair 1.60
P# strip of 5, #V1111 5.25
P# single, #V1111 — 1.50

A3040f

Printed by Avery Dennison.

PHOTOGRAVURE
BOOKLET STAMP

Serpentine Die Cut 11¼x10¾ on 2 or 3 Sides

3985 A3040f 39c **multicolored,** *Apr. 8* .80 .25
a. Booklet pane of 20 16.00
b. Serpentine die cut 11.1 on 2 or 3 sides, *Nov. 8* .80 .25
c. Booklet pane of 4 #3985b 3.20
d. Booklet pane of 6 #3985b 4.80

Nos. 3983 and 3985 lack the microprinting found on Nos. 3978 and 3981. No. 3982 was not made available until June, despite the official first day of issue. No. 3983 was not made available until July and No. 3985 was not made available until August, despite the official first day of issue. No. 3985a is a double-sided booklet with 12 stamps on one side and 8 stamps plus label (booklet cover) on the other side.

CHILDREN'S BOOK ANIMALS

The Very Hungry Caterpillar, from *The Very Hungry Caterpillar,* by Eric Carle — A3041

Wilbur, from *Charlotte's Web,* by E. B. White — A3042

Fox in Socks, from *Fox in Socks,* by Dr. Seuss — A3043

Maisy, from *Maisy's ABC,* by Lucy Cousins — A3044

Wild Thing, from *Where the Wild Things Are,* by Maurice Sendak — A3045

Curious George, from *Curious George,* by Margaret and H. A. Rey — A3046

Olivia, from *Olivia,* by Ian Falconer — A3047

Frederick, from *Frederick,* by Leo Lionni — A3048

Designed by Derry Noyes. Printed by American Packaging Corporation for Sennett Security Products.

PHOTOGRAVURE
Sheets of 96 in six panes of 16

2006, Jan. 10 Tagged *Serpentine Die Cut 10¾*
Self-Adhesive

3987 A3041 39c **multicolored** .80 .40
3988 A3042 39c **multicolored** .80 .40
3989 A3043 39c **multicolored** .80 .40
3990 A3044 39c **multicolored** .80 .40
3991 A3045 39c **multicolored** .80 .40
3992 A3046 39c **multicolored** .80 .40
3993 A3047 39c **multicolored** .80 .40
3994 A3048 39c **multicolored** .80 .40
a. Block of 8, #3987-3994 6.50
P# block of 8, 9# + S 6.50
Pane of 16 13.00

Uncut press sheets of Nos. 3987-3994 were made available for sale. Values: cross-gutter block of 8, $17; pairs with gutters between, $2.25 each. See note after No. 2868.

See Great Britain Nos. 2340-2341.

2006 WINTER OLYMPICS, TURIN, ITALY

Skier — A3049

Designed by Derry Noyes. Printed by Banknote Corporation of America for Sennett Security Products.

LITHOGRAPHED
Sheets of 240 in twelve panes of 20

2006, Jan. 11 Tagged *Serpentine Die Cut 10¾*
Self-Adhesive

3995 A3049 39c **multicolored** .80 .25
P# block of 4, 4# + S 3.20
Pane of 20 16.00

BLACK HERITAGE SERIES

Hattie McDaniel (1895-1952), Actress — A3050

Designed by Ethel Kessler. Printed by Banknote Corporation of America for Sennett Security Products.

LITHOGRAPHED
Sheets of 240 in twelve panes of 20

2006, Jan. 25 Tagged *Serpentine Die Cut 10¾*
Self-Adhesive

3996 A3050 39c **multicolored** .80 .25
P# block of 4, 4# + S 3.20
Pane of 20 16.00

Chinese New Year

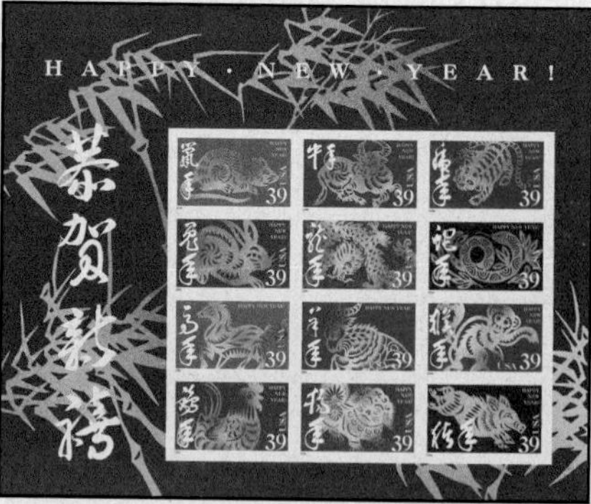

A3050a

Designed by Clarence Lee. Printed by Banknote Corporation of America for Sennett Security Products.

LITHOGRAPHED

2006, Jan. 29 **Tagged** ***Serpentine Die Cut 10¾***

Self-Adhesive

3997	A3050a Pane of 12	12.00	
a.	39c Rat	1.00	.50
b.	39c Ox	1.00	.50
c.	39c Tiger	1.00	.50
d.	39c Rabbit	1.00	.50
e.	39c Dragon	1.00	.50
f.	39c Snake	1.00	.50
g.	39c Horse	1.00	.50
h.	39c Ram	1.00	.50
i.	39c Monkey	1.00	.50
j.	39c Rooster	1.00	.50
k.	39c Dog	1.00	.50
l.	39c Boar	1.00	.50

See Nos. 2720, 2817, 2876, 3060, 3120, 3179, 3272, 3370, 3500, 3559, 3747, 3832, 3895.

WEDDING DOVES

Dove Facing Left — A3051

Dove Facing Right — A3052

Designed by Michael Osborne. Printed by Ashton-Potter (USA) Ltd.

LITHOGRAPHED
BOOKLET STAMPS

Serpentine Die Cut 10¾x11 on 2, 3 or 4 Sides

2006, Mar. 1 **Tagged**

Self-Adhesive

3998	A3051 39c **pale lilac**	.80	.25
a.	Booklet pane of 20	16.00	
b.	As "a," die cutting omitted	—	

Serpentine Die Cut 10¾x11

3999	A3052 63c **pale yellow green**	1.40	.50
a.	Booklet pane, 20 each #3998-3999	45.00	
b.	Horiz. pair, #3998-3999 with vertical gutter between	2.25	1.50

Common Buckeye Butterfly — A3053

A3053a

A3053b

Designed by Carl T. Herrman. Printed by Sterling Sommer, Inc. for Ashton-Potter (USA) Ltd. (#4000), Avery Dennison (#4001-4002).

LITHOGRAPHED (#4000), PHOTOGRAVURE (#4001-4002)

Sheets of 400 in four panes of 100 (#4000), Sheets of 280 in fourteen panes of 20 (#4001)

2006, Mar. 8 **Tagged** ***Perf. 11¼***

4000	A3053 24c **multicolored**	.50	.25
	P# block of 4, 4#+P	12.50	—
	Pane of 100	60.00	—

Self-Adhesive

Serpentine Die Cut 11

4001	A3053a 24c **multicolored**	.55	.25
	P# block of 4, 4#+V	3.00	
	Pane of 20	14.50	
a.	Serpentine die cut 10¾x11¼ on 3 sides (from booklet panes)	.50	.25
b.	Booklet pane of 10 #4001a	5.00	
c.	Booklet pane of 4 #4001a	2.00	
d.	Booklet pane of 6 #4001a	3.00	

Some panes of No. 4001 contain bottom-row stamps that are 1mm taller than the other stamps on the pane. This most likely was caused by a shift up by one row of the die cutting blade cylinder on a low percentage of sheets in the press run.

No. 4001b is a convertible booklet that was sold flat. It has a self-adhesive panel that covers the rouletting on the inside of the booklet cover. Nos. 4001c and 4001d are component panes of a vending machine booklet, which was sold pre-folded and sealed, and which does not have the self-adhesive panel covering the rouletting on the inside of the booklet cover.

COIL STAMP

Serpentine Die Cut 8½ Horiz.

4002	A3053b 24c **multicolored**	.50	.25
	Pair	1.00	
	P# strip of 5, #V1111	3.50	
	P# single, #V1111	—	1.75

CROPS OF THE AMERICAS

Chili Peppers — A3054

Beans — A3055

Sunflower and Seeds — A3056

Squashes — A3057

Corn — A3058

Designed by Phil Jordan. Printed by American Packaging Corporation for Sennett Security Products.

PHOTOGRAVURE

Serpentine Die Cut 10¼ Horiz.

2006, Mar. 16 **Tagged**

Self-Adhesive

Coil Stamps

4003	A3054 39c **multicolored**	2.40	.35
4004	A3055 39c **multicolored**	2.40	.35
4005	A3056 39c **multicolored**	2.40	.35
4006	A3057 39c **multicolored**	2.40	.35
4007	A3058 39c **multicolored**	2.40	.35
a.	Strip of 5, #4003-4007	12.00	
	P# strip of 5, #4003-4007, #S1111	15.00	—
	P# strip of 11, 3 #4005, 2 each #4003-4004, 4006-4007	27.50	
	P# single (#4005), #S1111	—	2.00

A3054a

A3055a

A3056a

A3057a

A3058a

Booklet Stamps

Serpentine Die Cut 10¾x10½ on 2 or 3 Sides

4008	A3058a 39c **multicolored**	1.25	.35
4009	A3057a 39c **multicolored**	1.25	.35
4010	A3056a 39c **multicolored**	1.25	.35
4011	A3055a 39c **multicolored**	1.25	.35
4012	A3054a 39c **multicolored**	1.25	.35
a.	Horiz. strip of 5, #4008-4012	6.25	
b.	Booklet pane, 4 each #4008-4012	25.00	

A3054b

A3055b

A3056b

A3057b

A3058b

Printed by Banknote Corporation of America for Sennett Security Products.

LITHOGRAPHED

Serpentine Die Cut 10¾x11¼ on 2 or 3 Sides

4013	A3054b 39c **multicolored**	1.50	.35
4014	A3058b 39c **multicolored**	1.50	.35
4015	A3057b 39c **multicolored**	1.50	.35
4016	A3056b 39c **multicolored**	1.50	.35
a.	Booklet pane of 4, #4013-4016	6.00	
4017	A3055b 39c **multicolored**	1.50	.35
a.	Horiz. strip of 5, #4013-4017	7.50	
b.	Booklet pane of 4, #4013-4015, 4017	6.00	
c.	Booklet pane of 6, #4013-4016, 2 #4017	9.00	
d.	Booklet pane of 6, #4013-4015, 4017, 2 #4016	9.00	

Stamps in Nos. 4012a and 4017a are not adjacent, as one or two rows of selvage is between stamps (or a blank space where selvage was removed by the manufacturer).

No. 4012b is a double-sided booklet with 12 stamps on one side and 8 stamps plus label (booklet cover) on the other side.

"USA" is at right of "39" on No. 4004, at left of "39" on Nos. 4011, 4017. Top of "USA" is aligned with top of "39" on No. 4013, with bottom of "39" on Nos. 4003, 4012.

The peelable selvage strips were removed by the manufacturer from 1 million of the 11 million vending booklets produced (containing Nos. 4017b, 4017c and 4017d).

X-PLANES

A3059

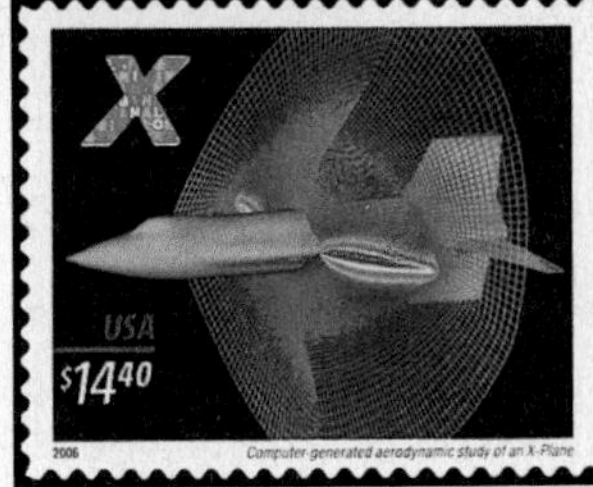

A3060

Designed by Phil Jordan. Printed by Banknote Corporation of America for Sennett Security Products.

LITHOGRAPHED WITH HOLOGRAM AFFIXED
Sheets of 120 in six panes of 20
Serpentine Die Cut 10¾x10½

2006, Mar. 17 Tagged Self-Adhesive

4018 A3059 $4.05 **multicolored** 8.00 5.00
P# block of 4, 4#+S 40.00
Pane of 20 160.00
a. Silver foil ("X") omitted —
4019 A3060 $14.40 **multicolored** 27.50 15.00
P# block of 4, 4#+S 110.00
Pane of 20 550.00

Beware of Nos. 4018 and 4019 with "X" hologram chemically removed. Certification is strongly recommended.

SUGAR RAY ROBINSON (1921-89), BOXER

A3061

Designed by Carl T. Herrman. Printed by Avery Dennison.

PHOTOGRAVURE
Sheets of 200 in ten panes of 20

2006, Apr. 7 Tagged *Serpentine Die Cut 11*
Self-Adhesive

4020 A3061 39c **red & blue** .80 .25
P# block of 4, 2#+V 3.20
Pane of 20 16.00

BENJAMIN FRANKLIN (1706-90)

Statesman A3062

Scientist A3063

Printer A3064

Postmaster A3065

Designed by Richard Sheaff. Printed by Avery Dennison.

PHOTOGRAVURE
Sheets of 200 in ten panes of 20
Serpentine Die Cut 11

2006, Apr. 7 Tagged Self-Adhesive

4021 A3062 39c **multicolored** 1.25 .35
4022 A3063 39c **multicolored** 1.25 .35
4023 A3064 39c **multicolored** 1.25 .35
4024 A3065 39c **multicolored** 1.25 .35
a. Block or horiz. strip of 4 5.00
P# block of 4, 4#+V 6.00
Pane of 20 29.00

THE ART OF DISNEY: ROMANCE

Mickey and Minnie Mouse — A3066

Cinderella and Prince Charming — A3067

Beauty and the Beast — A3068

Lady and Tramp — A3069

Designed by David Pacheco. Printed by Ashton-Potter (USA) Ltd.

LITHOGRAPHED
Sheets of 180 in nine panes of 20
Serpentine Die Cut 10½x10¾

2006, Apr. 21 Tagged
Self-Adhesive

4025 A3066 39c **multicolored** .80 .30
4026 A3067 39c **multicolored** .80 .30
4027 A3068 39c **multicolored** .80 .30
4028 A3069 39c **multicolored** .80 .30
a. Block or vert. strip of 4, #4025-4028 3.20
P# block of 4, 6#+P 3.50
Pane of 20 17.50

LOVE

Birds — A3070

Designed by Craig Frazier. Printed by Avery Dennison.

PHOTOGRAVURE
Serpentine Die Cut 11 on 2, 3 or 4 Sides

2006, May 1 Tagged
Self-Adhesive
Booklet Stamp

4029 A3070 39c **multicolored** .95 .25
a. Booklet pane of 20 19.00

See No. 3976.

LITERARY ARTS

Katherine Anne Porter (1890-1980), Author A3071

Designed by Derry Noyes. Printed by Banknote Corporation of America for Sennett Security Products.

LITHOGRAPHED
Sheets of 240 in twelve panes of 20

2006, May 15 Tagged *Serpentine Die Cut 10¾*
Self-Adhesive

4030 A3071 39c **multicolored** .80 .25
P# block of 4, 4#+S 3.20
Pane of 20 16.00

AMBER ALERT

Mother and Child — A3072

Designed by Derry Noyes. Printed by Avery Dennison.

PHOTOGRAVURE
Sheets of 160 in eight panes of 20

2006, May 25 Tagged *Serpentine Die Cut 10¾*
Self-Adhesive

4031 A3072 39c **multicolored** .80 .25
P# block of 4, 6#+V 3.20
Pane of 20 16.00

Purple Heart — A3072a

Designed by Carl T. Herrman. Printed by Ashton-Potter (USA) Ltd.

LITHOGRAPHED
Sheets of 120 in six panes of 20
Serpentine Die Cut 11¼x11

2006, May 26 Tagged
Self-Adhesive

4032 A3072a 39c **multicolored** .80 .25
P# block of 4, 4#+P 3.20
Pane of 20 16.00
a. Die cutting omitted, pair —

See Nos. 3784-3784A, 4164, 4263-4264, 4390.

WONDERS OF AMERICA

Illustration reduced.
Designed by Richard Sheaff. Printed by Avery Dennison.

Designs: No. 4033, American alligator, largest reptile. No. 4034, Moloka'i, highest sea cliffs. No. 4035, Saguaro, tallest cactus. No. 4036, Bering Glacier, largest glacier. No. 4037, Great Sand Dunes, tallest dunes. No. 4038, Chesapeake Bay, largest estuary. No. 4039, Cliff Palace, largest cliff dwelling. No. 4040, Crater Lake, deepest lake. No. 4041, American bison, largest land mammal. No. 4042, Off the Florida Keys, longest reef. No. 4043, Pacific Crest Trail, longest hiking trail. No. 4044, Gateway Arch, tallest man-made monument. No. 4045, Appalachians, oldest mountains. No. 4046, American lotus, largest flower. No. 4047, Lake Superior, largest lake. No. 4048, Pronghorn, fastest land animal. No. 4049, Bristlecone pines, oldest trees. No. 4050, Yosemite Falls, tallest waterfall. No. 4051, Great Basin, largest desert. No. 4052, Verrazano-Narrows Bridge, longest span. No. 4053, Mount Washington, windiest place. No. 4054, Grand Canyon, largest canyon. No. 4055, American bullfrog, largest frog. No. 4056, Oroville Dam, tallest dam. No. 4057, Peregrine falcon, fastest bird. No. 4058, Mississippi River Delta, largest delta. No. 4059, Steamboat, tallest geyser. No. 4060, Rainbow Bridge, largest natural bridge. No. 4061, White sturgeon, largest freshwater fish. No. 4062, Rocky Mountains, longest mountain chain. No. 4063, Coast redwoods, tallest trees. No. 4064, American beaver, largest rodent. No. 4065, Mississippi-Missouri, longest river system. No. 4066, Mount Wai'ale'ale, rainiest spot. No. 4067, Kilauea, most active volcano. No. 4068, Mammoth Cave, longest cave. No. 4069, Blue whale, loudest animal. No. 4070, Death Valley, hottest spot. No. 4071, Cornish-Windsor Bridge, longest covered bridge. No. 4072, Quaking aspen, largest plant.

PHOTOGRAVURE
Sheets of 80 in two panes of 40

2006, May 27 Tagged ***Serpentine Die Cut 10¾***
Self-Adhesive

4033 A3073 39c **multicolored** .80 .60
4034 A3074 39c **multicolored** .80 .60
4035 A3075 39c **multicolored** .80 .60
4036 A3076 39c **multicolored** .80 .60
4037 A3077 39c **multicolored** .80 .60
4038 A3078 39c **multicolored** .80 .60
4039 A3079 39c **multicolored** .80 .60
4040 A3080 39c **multicolored** .80 .60
4041 A3081 39c **multicolored** .80 .60
4042 A3082 39c **multicolored** .80 .60
4043 A3083 39c **multicolored** .80 .60
4044 A3084 39c **multicolored** .80 .60
4045 A3085 39c **multicolored** .80 .60
4046 A3086 39c **multicolored** .80 .60
4047 A3087 39c **multicolored** .80 .60
4048 A3088 39c **multicolored** .80 .60
4049 A3089 39c **multicolored** .80 .60
4050 A3090 39c **multicolored** .80 .60
4051 A3091 39c **multicolored** .80 .60
4052 A3092 39c **multicolored** .80 .60
4053 A3093 39c **multicolored** .80 .60
4054 A3094 39c **multicolored** .80 .60
4055 A3095 39c **multicolored** .80 .60
4056 A3096 39c **multicolored** .80 .60
4057 A3097 39c **multicolored** .80 .60
4058 A3098 39c **multicolored** .80 .60
4059 A3099 39c **multicolored** .80 .60
4060 A3100 39c **multicolored** .80 .60
4061 A3101 39c **multicolored** .80 .60
4062 A3102 39c **multicolored** .80 .60
4063 A3103 39c **multicolored** .80 .60
4064 A3104 39c **multicolored** .80 .60
4065 A3105 39c **multicolored** .80 .60
4066 A3106 39c **multicolored** .80 .60
4067 A3107 39c **multicolored** .80 .60
4068 A3108 39c **multicolored** .80 .60
4069 A3109 39c **multicolored** .80 .60
4070 A3110 39c **multicolored** .80 .60
4071 A3111 39c **multicolored** .80 .60
4072 A3112 39c **multicolored** .80 .60
a. Pane of 40, #4033-4072 32.00

Uncut press sheets of Nos. 4033-4072 were made available for sale. Values: block of 40 diff. stamps with horiz. gutter btwn. any two rows, $37.50; pairs with horiz. gutter btwn., $2.25 each.
See note after No. 2868.

EXPLORATION OF EAST COAST BY SAMUEL DE CHAMPLAIN, 400TH ANNIV.

Ship and Map — A3113

A3114

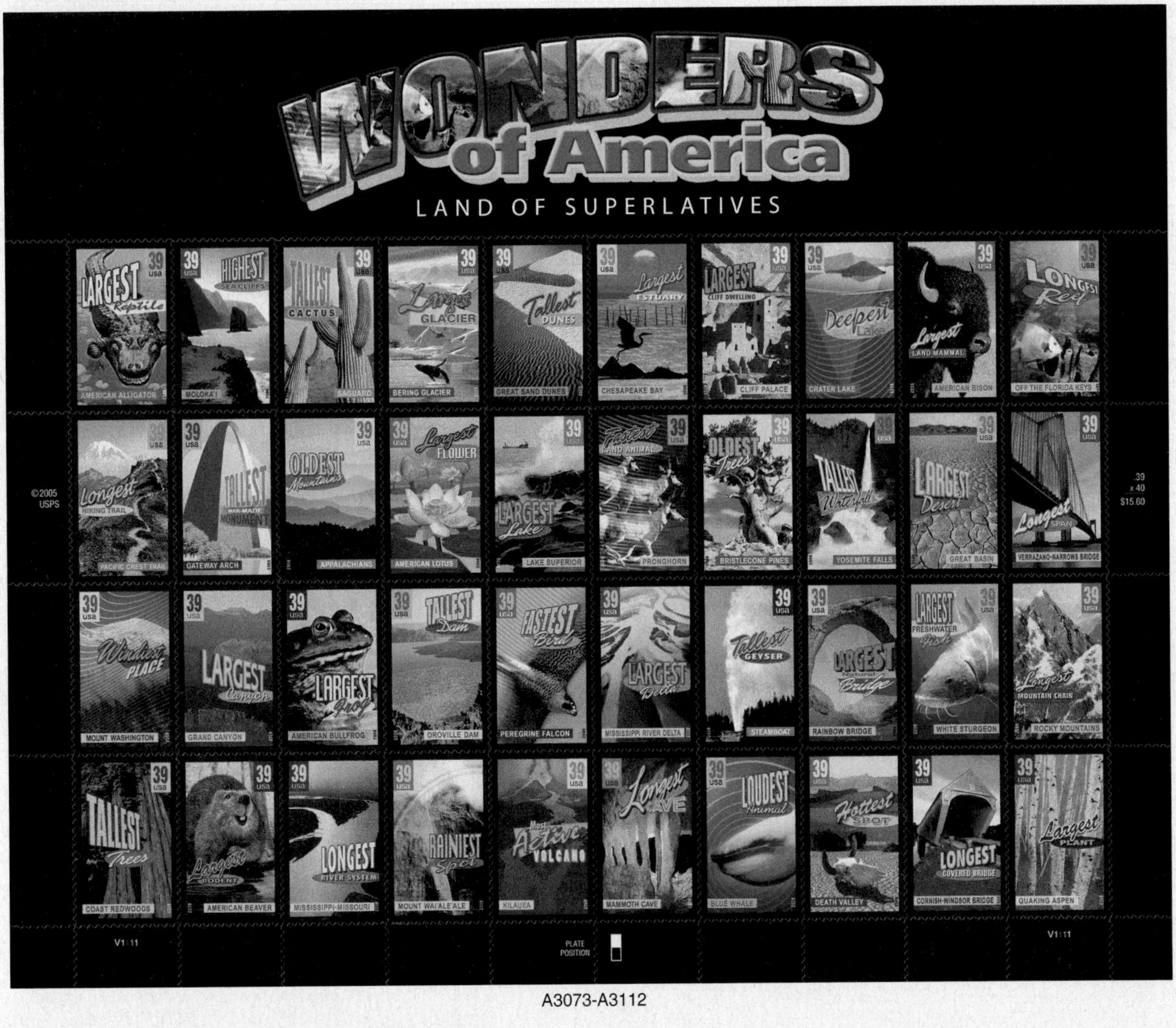

A3073-A3112

Illustration A3114 is reduced.

Designed by Rejean Myette and Francois Martin, Canada (#4073), Terrence W. McCaffrey and Francois Martin (#4074). Printed by Ashton-Potter (USA) Ltd.

LITHOGRAPHED & ENGRAVED

Sheets of 120 in six panes of 20 (#4073), Sheets of 24 in six panes of 4 (#4074)

2006, May 28 Tagged *Serpentine Die Cut 10¾*

Self-Adhesive (#4073)

4073 A3113 39c **multicolored** .85 .25
P# block of 4, 6#+P 3.75
Pane of 20 18.50

Souvenir Sheet

Perf. 11

4074 A3114 Pane of 4, 2 each #4074a, Canada #2156a 8.50 8.50
a. A3113 39c **multicolored** 2.00 .25

Washington 2006 World Philatelic Exhibition (#4074). Canada No. 2156, which was sold only by Canada Post, has a bar code in the lower left margin of the pane. No. 4074, which was sold only by the United States Postal Service for $1.75, lacks this bar code.

Uncut press sheets of No. 4074 were made available for sale. Values: cross-gutter block of 4 Canadian and 4 American stamps, $22.50; horiz. pair of Canadian and American stamps with vert. gutter btwn., $4. See note after No. 2868.

WASHINGTON 2006 WORLD PHILATELIC EXHIBITION

Souvenir Sheet

A3115

Illustration reduced.

Designed by Richard Sheaff. Printed by Banknote Corporation of America for Sennett Security Products.

LITHOGRAPHED (MARGIN) & ENGRAVED

Sheets of 18 in six panes of 3

2006, May 29 Tagged *Perf. 10¾x10½*

4075 A3115 Pane of 3 16.00 6.00
a. A174 $1 **violet brown** 2.00 .50
b. A175 $2 **deep blue** 4.00 1.00
c. A176 $5 **carmine & blue** 10.00 2.50

Uncut press sheets of No. 4075 were made available for sale. Values: cross-gutter block of 4 panes, $67.50; pairs of panes with gutters between, $35 each. See note after No. 2868.

DISTINGUISHED AMERICAN DIPLOMATS

Souvenir Sheet

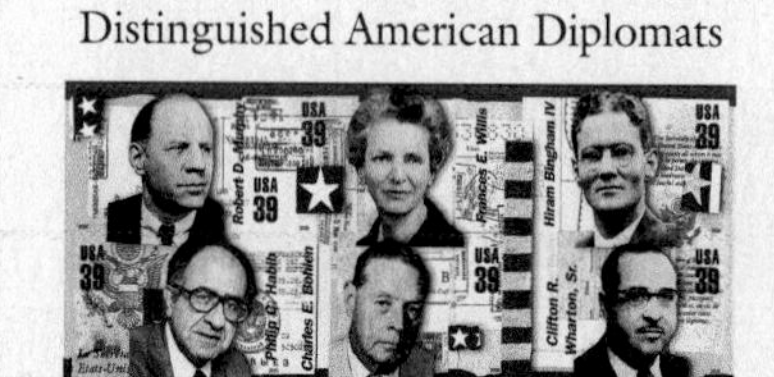

A3116

Illustration reduced.

Designed by Howard E. Paine. Printed by Avery Dennison.

No. 4076: a, Robert D. Murphy (1894-1978). b, Frances E. Willis (1899-1983). c, Hiram Bingham IV (1903-88). d, Philip C. Habib (1920-92). e, Charles E. Bohlen (1904-74). f, Clifton R. Wharton, Sr. (1899-1990).

Sheets of 90 in fifteen panes of 6

PHOTOGRAVURE

2006, May 29 Tagged *Serpentine Die Cut 10¾*

Self-Adhesive

4076 A3116 Pane of 6 6.00
a.-f. 39c any single 1.00 .40

Uncut press sheets of No. 4076 were made available for sale. Values: cross-gutter block of 6, $9; pairs with gutters between, $3 each. See note after No. 2868.

LEGENDS OF HOLLYWOOD

Judy Garland (1922-69), Actress — A3117

Designed by Ethel Kessler. Printed by Banknote Corporation of America for Sennett Security Products.

LITHOGRAPHED

Sheets of 120 in six panes of 20

2006, June 10 Tagged *Serpentine Die Cut 10¾*

Self-Adhesive

4077 A3117 39c **multicolored** 1.00 .25
P# block of 4, 4#+S 5.50
Pane of 20 24.00
a. Pair, die cutting omitted 750.00

Uncut press sheets of No. 4077 were made available for sale. Values: cross-gutter block of 8, $25; pairs with gutters between, $3.75 each. See note after No. 2868.

Ronald Reagan — A3117a

Designed by Howard E. Paine. Printed by American Packaging Corporation for Sennett Security Products.

PHOTOGRAVURE

Sheets of 120 in six panes of 20

2006, June 14 Tagged *Serpentine Die Cut 10¾*

Self-Adhesive

4078 A3117a 39c **multicolored** .90 .25
P# block of 4, 4#+S 3.60
Pane of 20 18.00

See No. 3897.

Happy Birthday — A3117b

Designed by Harry Zelenko. Printed by Avery Dennison.

PHOTOGRAVURE

Sheets of 200 in ten panes of 20

2006, June 23 Tagged *Serpentine Die Cut 11*

Self-Adhesive

4079 A3117b 39c **multicolored** .80 .25
P# block of 4, 4#+V 3.20
Pane of 20 16.00

See Nos. 3558, 3695.

BASEBALL SLUGGERS

Roy Campanella (1921-93) — A3118

Hank Greenberg (1911-86) — A3119

Mel Ott (1909-58) — A3120

Mickey Mantle (1931-95) — A3121

Designed by Phil Jordan. Printed by Avery Dennison.

PHOTOGRAVURE

Sheets of 120 in six panes of 20

2006, July 15 Tagged *Serpentine Die Cut 10¾*

Self-Adhesive

4080 A3118 39c **multicolored** .80 .30
4081 A3119 39c **multicolored** .80 .30
4082 A3120 39c **multicolored** .80 .30
4083 A3121 39c **multicolored** .80 .30
a. Block or vert. strip of 4, #4080-4083 3.20
P# block of 4, 6#+V 3.20
P# block of 10, 2 sets of P# + top label 8.00
Pane of 20 16.00

Uncut press sheets of Nos. 4080-4083 were made available for sale. Values: cross-gutter block of 8, $20; pairs with gutters between, $3.75 each. See note after No. 2868.

DC COMICS SUPERHEROES

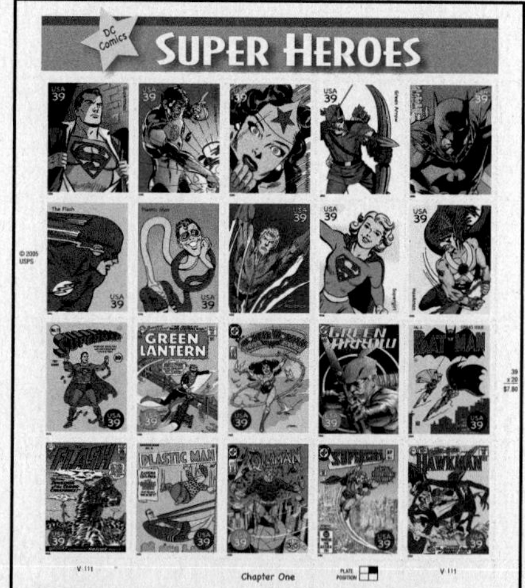

A3122

Illustration reduced.

Designed by Carl T. Herrman. Printed by Avery Dennison.

No. 4084: a, Superman. b, Green Lantern. c, Wonder Woman. d, Green Arrow. e, Batman. f, The Flash. g, Plastic Man. h, Aquaman. i, Supergirl. j, Hawkman. k, Cover of *Superman #11*. l, Cover of *Green Lantern #4*. m, Cover of *Wonder Woman #22 (Second Series)*. n, Cover of *Green Arrow #15*. o, Cover of *Batman #1*. p, Cover of *The Flash #111*. q, Cover of *Plastic Man #4*. r, Cover of *Aquaman #5 (of 5)*. s, Cover of *The Daring New Adventures of Supergirl #1*. t, Cover of *The Brave and the Bold Presents Hawkman #36*.

PHOTOGRAVURE

Sheets of 80 in four panes of 20

Serpentine Die Cut 10½x10¾

2006, July 20 **Tagged**

Self-Adhesive

4084	A3122	Pane of 20	16.00	
a.-t.		39c Any single	.80	.50
u.		As No. 4084, all inscriptions omitted on reverse	*2,000.*	

Uncut press sheets of No. 4084 were made available for sale. Values: cross-gutter block of 20, $25; pairs with gutters between, $3.50 each. See note after No. 2868.

MOTORCYCLES

1940 Indian Four — A3123

1918 Cleveland A3124

Generic "Chopper," c. 1970 — A3125

1965 Harley-Davidson Electra-Glide — A3126

Designed by Richard Sheaff. Printed by Avery Dennison.

PHOTOGRAVURE

Sheets of 160 in eight panes of 20

Serpentine Die Cut 10¾x10½

2006, Aug. 7 **Tagged**

Self-Adhesive

4085	A3123	39c	**multicolored**	1.00	.35
4086	A3124	39c	**multicolored**	1.00	.35
4087	A3125	39c	**multicolored**	1.00	.35
4088	A3126	39c	**multicolored**	1.00	.35
a.			Block or horiz. strip of 4, #4085-4088	4.00	
			P# block of 4, 5#+V	4.00	
			P# block of 8, 2 sets of P# + top label	8.00	
			Pane of 20	20.00	

AMERICAN TREASURES SERIES

Quilts of Gee's Bend, Alabama

Housetop Variation, by Mary Lee Bendolph — A3127

Pig in a Pen Medallion, by Minnie Sue Coleman — A3128

Nine Patch, by Ruth P. Mosely — A3129

Housetop Four Block Half Log Cabin Variation, by Lottie Mooney — A3130

Roman Stripes Variation, by Loretta Pettway — A3131

Chinese Coins Variation, by Arlonzia Pettway — A3132

Blocks and Strips, by Annie Mae Young — A3133

Medallion, by Loretta Pettway — A3134

Bars and String-pieced Columns, by Jessie T. Pettway — A3135

Medallion With Checkerboard Center, by Patty Ann Williams — A3136

Designed by Derry Noyes. Printed by American Packaging Corporation for Sennett Security Products.

PHOTOGRAVURE

BOOKLET STAMPS

Serpentine Die Cut 10¾ on 2 or 3 Sides

2006, Aug. 24 **Tagged**

Self-Adhesive

4089	A3127	39c	**multicolored**	1.10	.40
4090	A3128	39c	**multicolored**	1.10	.40
4091	A3129	39c	**multicolored**	1.10	.40
4092	A3130	39c	**multicolored**	1.10	.40
4093	A3131	39c	**multicolored**	1.10	.40
4094	A3132	39c	**multicolored**	1.10	.40
4095	A3133	39c	**multicolored**	1.10	.40
4096	A3134	39c	**multicolored**	1.10	.40
4097	A3135	39c	**multicolored**	1.10	.40
4098	A3136	39c	**multicolored**	1.10	.40
a.			Block of 10, #4089-4098	11.00	
b.			Booklet pane of 20, 2 each #4089-4098	22.50	

No. 4098b is a double-sided booklet pane with 12 stamps on one side (1 each #4090-4093, 4095-4098, and 2 each #4089, 4094) and eight stamps (1 each #4090-4093, 4095-4098) plus label (booklet cover) on the other side.

SOUTHERN FLORIDA WETLAND

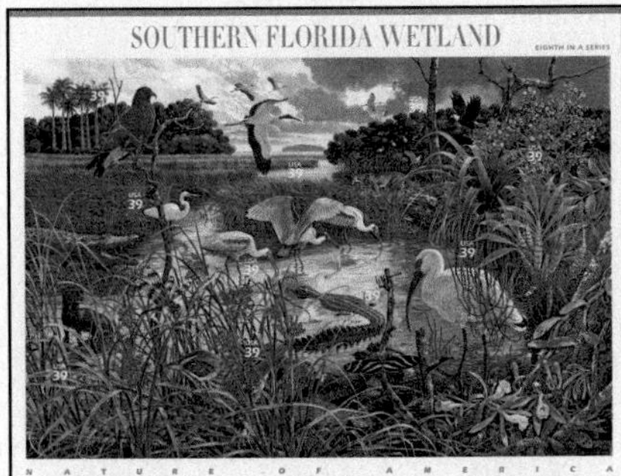

A3137

Illustration reduced.

Designed by Ethel Kessler. Printed by Avery Dennison.

No. 4099 — Wildlife: a, Snail kite. b, Wood storks. c, Florida panther. d, Bald eagle, horiz. e, American crocodile, horiz. f, Roseate spoonbills, horiz. g, Everglades mink. h, Cape Sable seaside sparrow, horiz. i, American alligator, horiz. j, White ibis.

PHOTOGRAVURE

Sheets of 80 in eight panes of 10

2006, Oct. 4 **Tagged** ***Serpentine Die Cut 10¾***

Self-Adhesive

4099	A3137	Pane of 10	9.00	
a.-j.		39c any single	.90	.40

Uncut press sheets of No. 4099 were made available for sale. Value: See note after No. 2868.

CHRISTMAS

Madonna and Child with Bird, by Ignacio Chacón — A3138

Snowflake — A3139

Snowflake — A3140

Snowflake — A3141

Snowflake — A3142

Designed by Michael Osborne (#4100), Richard Sheaff. Printed by Ashton-Potter (USA) Ltd. (#4100), Avery Dennison (#4113-4116).

LITHOGRAPHED

Sheets of 240 in twelve panes of 20 (#4101-4104)

Serpentine Die Cut 10¾x11 on 2 or 3 Sides

2006 **Tagged**

Self-Adhesive

Booklet Stamps (#4100, 4105-4116)

4100 A3138 39c **multicolored,** *Oct. 17* ⓢ .80 .25
a. Booklet pane of 20 16.00

ⓢ: The ink of No. 4100 cracks and flakes off during a water soak. See note after No. 1549.

Designed by Richard Sheaff.
Printed by Banknote Corporation of America for Sennett Security Products (#4101-4112).

Base of Denomination Higher Than Year Date

Serpentine Die Cut 11¼x11

4101 A3139 39c **multicolored,** *Oct. 5* .90 .25
4102 A3140 39c **multicolored,** *Oct. 5* .90 .25
4103 A3141 39c **multicolored,** *Oct. 5* .90 .25
4104 A3142 39c **multicolored,** *Oct. 5* .90 .25
a. Block or vert. strip of 4, #4101-4104 3.60
P# block of 4, 4#+S 3.60
Pane of 20 18.00

A3139a

A3140a

A3141a

A3142a

Base of Denominations Even With Year Date

Serpentine Die Cut 11¼x11½ on 2 or 3 Sides

4105 A3139a 39c **multicolored,** *Oct. 5* .90 .25
a. Red missing (PS) —
4106 A3140a 39c **multicolored,** *Oct. 5* .90 .25
a. Red missing (PS) —
4107 A3141a 39c **multicolored,** *Oct. 5* .90 .25
4108 A3142a 39c **multicolored,** *Oct. 5* .90 .25
a. Block of 4, #4105-4108 3.60
b. Booklet pane of 20, 5 #4108a 18.00
c. As "a," red ("USA") and green ("39") omitted —

A3139b

A3140b

A3141b

A3142b

Serpentine Die Cut 11¼x10¾ on 2 or 3 Sides

4109 A3139b 39c **multicolored,** *Oct. 5* 1.00 .25
4110 A3140b 39c **multicolored,** *Oct. 5* 1.00 .25
4111 A3141b 39c **multicolored,** *Oct. 5* 1.00 .25
4112 A3142b 39c **multicolored,** *Oct. 5* 1.00 .25
a. Block of 4, #4109-4112 4.00
b. Booklet pane of 4, #4109-4112 4.00
c. Booklet pane of 6, #4111-4112, 2 each #4109-4110 6.00
d. Booklet pane of 6, #4109-4110, 2 each #4111-4112 6.00

A3139c

A3140c

A3141c

A3142c

Printed by Avery Dennison (#4113-4116).

Serpentine Die Cut 8 on 2, 3 or 4 Sides

PHOTOGRAVURE

4113 A3139c 39c **multicolored,** *Oct. 5* 1.50 .35
a. Red and green missing (PS) —
4114 A3141c 39c **multicolored,** *Oct. 5* 1.50 .35
4115 A3140c 39c **multicolored,** *Oct. 5* 1.50 .35
4116 A3142c 39c **multicolored,** *Oct. 5* 1.50 .35
a. Block or strip of 4, #4113-4116 6.00
b. Booklet pane of 18, 4 each #4114, 4116, 5 each #4113, 4115 27.00
Nos. 4100-4116 (17) 18.00 4.65

No. 4108b is a double-sided booklet pane with 12 stamps on one side and eight stamps plus label that serves as a booklet cover on the other side. Snowflakes on Nos. 4101-4104 are slightly smaller than those on Nos. 4105-4116.

Eid — A3142a

Designed by Mohamed Zakariya. Printed by Avery Dennison.

PHOTOGRAVURE

Sheets of 240 in twelve panes of 20

2006, Oct. 6 **Tagged** ***Serpentine Die Cut 11***

Self-Adhesive

4117 A3142a 39c **multicolored** .80 .25
P# block of 4, 3#+V 3.50
Pane of 20 17.50

See Nos. 3532, 3674, 4202, 4351, 4416.

Hanukkah — A3142b

Designed by Ethel Kessler. Printed by Banknote Corporation of America for Sennett Security Products.

LITHOGRAPHED

Sheets of 240 in twelve panes of 20

2006, Oct. 6 **Tagged** ***Serpentine Die Cut 10¾x11***

Self-Adhesive

4118 A3142b 39c **multicolored** .80 .25
P# block of 4, 4#+S 3.20
Pane of 20 16.00
a. Die cutting omitted, pane of 20 —

See Nos. 3880, 4219, 4372.

Kwanzaa — A3142c

Designed by Derry Noyes. Printed by Ashton-Potter (USA) Ltd.

LITHOGRAPHED

Sheets of 160 in eight panes of 20

2006, Oct. 6 **Tagged** ***Serpentine Die Cut 11x10¾***

Self-Adhesive

4119 A3142c 39c **multicolored** .80 .25
P# block of 4, 6#+P 3.50
Pane of 20 17.50

See Nos. 3881, 4220, 4373.

BLACK HERITAGE SERIES

Ella Fitzgerald (1917-96), Singer — A3143

Designed by Ethel Kessler. Printed by Ashton-Potter (USA) Ltd.

LITHOGRAPHED

Sheets of 120 in six panes of 20

2007, Jan. 10 **Tagged** ***Serpentine Die Cut 11***

Self-Adhesive

4120 A3143 39c **multicolored** ⓢ .80 .25
P# block of 4, 6# + P 3.20
Pane of 20 16.00

ⓢ: Ink on No. 4120 cracks and flakes off during water soak. See note after No. 1549.

OKLAHOMA STATEHOOD, 100TH ANNIV.

Cimarron River — A3144

Designed by Phil Jordan. Printed by Ashton-Potter (USA) Ltd.

LITHOGRAPHED
Sheets of 120 in six panes of 20
2007, Jan. 11 Tagged *Serpentine Die Cut 11*
Self-Adhesive

4121 A3144 39c **multicolored** .80 .25
P# block of 4, 5# + P 3.20
Pane of 20 16.00

LOVE

Hershey's Kiss — A3145

Designed by Derry Noyes. Printed by Avery Dennison.

PHOTOGRAVURE
Serpentine Die Cut 10¾x11 on 2, 3 or 4 Sides
2007, Jan. 13 Tagged
BOOKLET STAMP
Self-Adhesive

4122 A3145 39c **multicolored** .80 .25
a. Booklet pane of 20 16.00

INTERNATIONAL POLAR YEAR Ⓢ
Souvenir Sheet

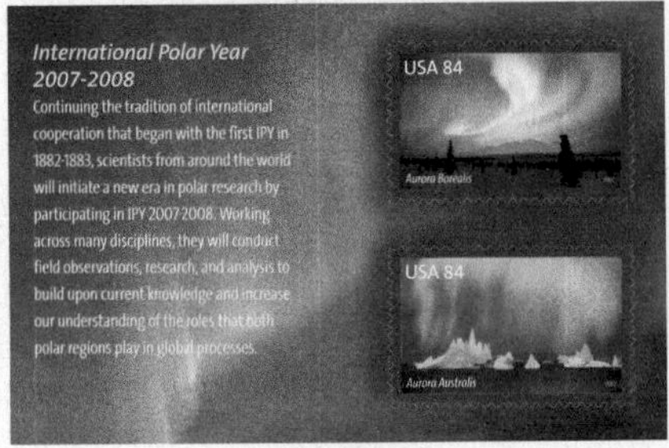

A3146

Illustration reduced.

Designed by Phil Jordan. Printed by Ashton-Potter (USA) Ltd.

No. 4123: a, Aurora borealis. b, Aurora australis.

LITHOGRAPHED
Sheets of 30 in fifteen panes of 2
2007, Feb. 21 Tagged *Serpentine Die Cut 10¾*
Self-Adhesive

4123 A3146 Pane of 2 4.00
a.-b. 84c Either single 2.00 .50

Ⓢ: Ink on Nos. 4123a and 4123b cracks and flakes off during water soak. See note after No. 1549.

Uncut press sheets of No. 4123 were made available for sale. Values: cross-gutter block of 4 stamps, $15; vert pair of stamps with horiz. gutter between, $4.50. See note after No. 2868.

LITERARY ARTS

Henry Wadsworth Longfellow (1807-82), Poet — A3147

Designed by Howard E. Paine. Printed by Ashton-Potter (USA) Ltd.

LITHOGRAPHED
Sheets of 120 in six panes of 20
2007, Mar. 15 Tagged *Serpentine Die Cut 10¾*
Self-Adhesive

4124 A3147 39c **multicolored** .80 .25
P# block of 4, 5#+P 3.20
Pane of 20 16.00

Beginning with No. 4125, the United States Postal Service began issuing "Forever" stamps that satisfy the domestic 1-ounce first-class letter rate and the 1-ounce international letter rate regardless of future rate increases. The denomination in parentheses in the catalogue listing represents the face value at the time of issue. The face value increases to the new letter rate whenever rates change.

"FOREVER" STAMP

Liberty Bell — A3148

Large Microprinting (#4125, 4128)

Small Microprinting (#4126)

Medium Microprinting (#4127)

Designed by Carl T. Herrman. Printed by Avery Dennison.

PHOTOGRAVURE
Serpentine Die Cut 11¼x10¾ on 2 or 3 Sides
2007-09 Tagged
Booklet Stamps
Self-Adhesive
Large Microprinting, Bell 16mm Wide

4125 A3148 (41c) **multicolored**, dated "2007," *Apr. 12* 1.25 .25
a. Booklet pane of 20 25.00
b. (42c) Dated "2008," *Aug. 22, 2008* Ⓢ 1.25 .25
c. Booklet pane of 20 #4125b 25.00
d. As "c," copper ("FOREVER") omitted *1,000.*
e. As "c," copper ("FOREVER") omitted on side with 12 stamps, copper splatters on side with 8 stamps —
f. (44c) Dated "2009," *Aug. 7, 2009* Ⓢ 1.25 .25
g. Booklet pane of 20 #4125f 25.00
h. As No. 4125, copper ("FOREVER") omitted —
On cover 500.00
i. As No. 4125, die cutting missing, horiz. pair (PS) —
j. As "b," copper ("FOREVER") omitted —

Counterfeits exist of No. 4125. See the Postal Counterfeits section of this catalog.

A3148a

Printed by Ashton-Potter (USA) Ltd. (#4126), Banknote Corporation of America for Sennett Security Products (#4127).

LITHOGRAPHED
Small Microprinting, Bell 16mm Wide

4126 A3148a (41c) **multicolored**, dated "2007," *April 12* 1.25 .25
a. Booklet pane of 20 25.00
b. (42c) Dated "2008," *Aug. 22, 2008* Ⓢ 1.25 .25
c. Booklet pane of 20 #4126b 25.00
d. (44c) Dated "2009" in copper, *Aug. 7, 2009* Ⓢ 1.25 .25
e. Booklet pane of 20 #4126d 25.00
f. As "b," copper ("FOREVER") omitted *1,400.*
g. As "c," die cutting omitted —

A3148b

Medium Microprinting, Bell 15mm Wide

4127 A3148b (41c) **multicolored**, dated "2007," prephosphored coated paper, *April 12* 1.25 .25
a. Booklet pane of 20 25.00
b. Booklet pane of 4 5.00
c. Booklet pane of 6 7.50
d. (42c) Dated "2008," *May 12, 2008* 1.25 .25
e. As "d," booklet pane of 20 25.00
f. (42c) Dated "2008," date in smaller type, *Oct. 25, 2008* 1.25 .25
g. As "f," booklet pane of 4 5.00
h. As "f," booklet pane of 6 7.50
i. (44c) Dated "2009" in copper, *May 15, 2009* 1.25 .25
j. As "i," booklet pane of 20 25.00
k. As "i," die cutting omitted, pair 300.00
l. As No. 4127, copper ("FOREVER") and "USA FIRST-CLASS" missing (PS) —
m. As "e," die cutting omitted *600.00*

A3148c

Printed by Avery Dennison.

PHOTOGRAVURE
Large Microprinting, Bell 16mm Wide
Serpentine Die Cut 8 on 2, 3 or 4 Sides

4128 A3148c (41c) **multicolored**, dated "2007", *April 12* Ⓢ 1.25 .25
a. Booklet pane of 18 22.50
b. (42c) Dated "2009" in black, *Feb. 24, 2009* Ⓢ 1.25 .25
c. As "b," booklet pane of 18 22.50
Nos. 4125-4128 (4) 5.00 1.00

Nos. 4125-4128 were sold for 41c on the day of issue and will be valid for the one ounce first class postage rate after any new rates go into effect. As of May 12, 2008, any "Forever" stamp (Nos. 4125-4128 and 4127d) in stock was sold for 42c. As of May 15, 2009, all "Forever" stamps in stock were sold for 44c, etc.

Nos. 4125a, 4125c, 4126a, 4126c, 4127a, 4127e and 4127j are double-sided booklet panes, with 12 stamps on one side and eight stamps plus a label that serves as a booklet cover on the other side.

No. 4127a and its varieties exist on two types of surface-tagged paper that exhibit either an uneven or solid appearance, as follows: tagging on No. 4127a appears uneven on both sides (most common), solid on both sides (value, $80), uneven on eight-stamp side and solid on 12-stamp side (extremely scarce), solid on eight stamp side and uneven on 12-stamp side (extremely scarce); tagging on No. 4127e appears solid on both sides, or solid on eight-stamp side and uneven on 12-stamp side (value, $25); tagging on No. 4127j appears solid.

Nos. 4127b and 4127c exist with rouletting on backing paper of either gauge 9½ or 13.

See No. 4437.

Ⓢ: Examples of No. 4128 with a shiny surface do not respond to a water soak. See note after No. 1549.

Flag — A3149

A3149a

Designed by Richard Sheaff. Printed by Ashton-Potter (USA) Ltd.

LITHOGRAPHED
Sheets of 400 in four panes of 100 (#4129), Sheets of 120 in six panes of 20 (#4130)
2007, Apr. 12 Tagged *Perf. 11¼*

4129 A3149 (41c) **multicolored** .90 .40
P# block of 4, 4#+P 18.00 —
Pane of 100 105.00 —

Self-Adhesive

Serpentine Die Cut 11¼x10¾

4130 A3149a (41c) **multicolored** 1.10 .25
P# block of 4, 4#+P 4.00
Pane of 20 20.00

A3149b A3149c

A3149d

A3149e

A3149f

Printed by Ashton-Potter (USA) Ltd. (#4132), Banknote Corporation of America for Sennett Security Products (#4131, 4133), Avery Dennison (#4134, 4135).

COIL STAMPS

Perf. 9¾ Vert.

4131 A3149b (41c) **multicolored** 1.10 .40
Pair 2.20 .80
P# strip of 5, #S1111 6.50 —
P# single, #S1111 — 2.75

Self-Adhesive (#4132-4135)
With Perpendicular Corners

Serpentine Die Cut 9½ Vert.

4132 A3149c (41c) **multicolored** 1.20 .25
Pair 2.40
P# strip of 5, #P1111 7.00
P# single, #P1111 — 1.75

Counterfeits exist of No. 4132. See the Postal Counterfeits section of this catalog.

Serpentine Die Cut 11 Vert.

4133 A3149d (41c) **multicolored** 1.20 .25
Pair 2.40
P# strip of 5, #S1111 7.00
P# single, #S1111 — 1.50
a. Die cutting omitted, pair *1,250.*

Counterfeits exist of No. 4133. See the Postal Counterfeits section of this catalog.

Serpentine Die Cut 8½ Vert.

PHOTOGRAVURE

4134 A3149e (41c) **multicolored,** overall tagging 1.10 .25
Pair 2.20
P# strip of 5, #V1111 5.75
P# single, #V1111 — 1.75
a. Prephosphored coated paper with surface tagging — —

With Rounded Corners

Serpentine Die Cut 11 Vert.

4135 A3149f (41c) **multicolored** 1.25 .75
Pair 2.50
P# strip of 5, #V1111 9.00
P# single, #V1111 — 2.25
Nos. 4129-4135 (7) 7.85 2.55

Nos. 4132-4134 are on backing paper as high as the stamp. No. 4135 is on backing paper that is larger than the stamp.

SETTLEMENT OF JAMESTOWN, 400TH ANNIV.

Ships Susan Constant, Godspeed and Discovery — A3150

Illustration reduced.

Designed by Richard Sheaff. Printed by Banknote Corporation of America for Sennett Security Products.

LITHOGRAPHED

Double-sided panes of 20 (19 on one side, 1 on other side)

Serpentine Die Cut 10½x10½x10¾

2007, May 11 **Tagged**

Self-Adhesive

4136 A3150 41c **multicolored** 1.10 .25
Pane of 20 22.00

WILDLIFE

Bighorn Sheep — A3151

Florida Panther — A3152

A3151a

A3152a

A3152b

A3152c

Designed by Carl T. Herrman. Printed by Ashton-Potter (USA) Ltd. (#4137, 4139), Avery Dennison (#4138, 4142), Banknote Corporation of America for Sennett Security Products (#4140, 4141).

LITHOGRAPHED, PHOTOGRAVURE (#4138, 4142)

Sheets of 400 in four panes of 100 (#4137), Sheets of 280 in fourteen panes of 20 (#4138), Sheets of 120 in six panes of 20 (#4139)

2007 **Tagged** ***Perf. 11¼x11***

4137 A3152 26c **multicolored,** *May 12* .60 .25
P# block of 4, 4#+P 15.00 —
Pane of 100 72.00 —

Self-Adhesive

Serpentine Die Cut 11

4138 A3151 17c **multicolored,** overall tagging, *May 14* .35 .25
P# block of 4, 4#+V 1.75
Pane of 20 9.00
a. Prephosphored paper .35 .25

Serpentine Die Cut 11¼x11

4139 A3152a 26c **multicolored,** *May 12* .55 .25
P# block of 4, 4#+P 2.25
Pane of 20 11.00

Coil Stamps

Serpentine Die Cut 11 Vert.

4140 A3151a 17c **multicolored,** *May 21* .35 .25
Pair .70
P# strip of 5, #S11111111 3.50
P# single, #S11111111 — 2.25

4141 A3152b 26c **multicolored,** prephosphored coated paper, *May 12* .75 .25
Pair 1.50
P# strip of 5, #S1111 4.50
P# single, #S1111 — 2.25
a. Die cutting omitted, pair *350.00*

No. 4140 and No. 4141 exist on two types of surface-tagged paper that exhibit either a solid or uneven appearance. Stamps with solid tagging are scarcer for No. 4141. Values: P# strip of 5, #S1111, $120; used P# single, $120.

Booklet Stamp

Serpentine Die Cut 11¼x11 on 3 Sides

4142 A3152c 26c **multicolored,** *May 12* .55 .25
a. Booklet pane of 10 5.50

Nos. 4137 and 4139 have microprinted "USPS" to the left and above the lower left whisker. No. 4140 has microprinted "USPS" on right horn. No. 4141 has microprinted "USPS" along the right edge of the stamp just above the panther. Nos. 4138 and 4142 lack microprinting.

PREMIERE OF MOVIE "STAR WARS," 30TH ANNIVERSARY

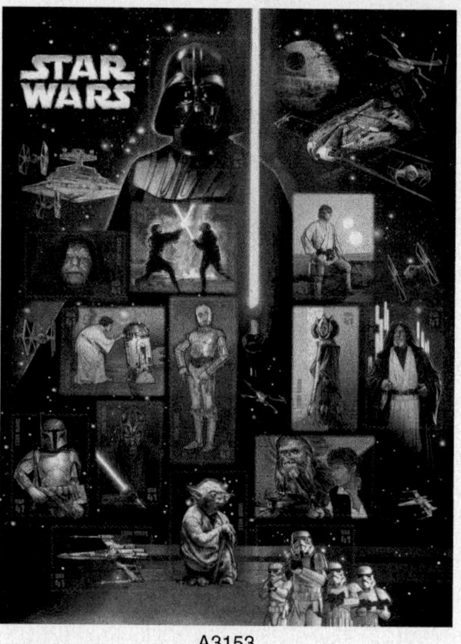

A3153

Illustration reduced.

Designed by Terrence McCaffrey and William J. Gicker, Jr. Printed by Banknote Corporation of America for Sennett Security Products.

No. 4143: a, Darth Vader (40x53mm). b, Millennium Falcon (47x25mm). c, Emperor Palpatine (41x26mm). d, Anakin Skywalker and Obi-Wan Kenobi (41x33mm). e, Luke Skywalker (31x41mm). f, Princess Leia and R2-D2 (41x33mm). g, C-3PO (21x65mm). h, Queen Padmé Amidala (26x48mm). i, Obi-Wan Kenobi (31x48mm). j, Boba Fett (32x40mm). k, Darth Maul (26x41mm). l, Chewbacca and Han Solo (48x31mm). m, X-wing Starfighter (41x26mm). n, Yoda (31x48mm). o, Stormtroopers (41x31mm).

LITHOGRAPHED

Sheets of 45 in three panes of 15

2007, May 25 **Tagged** ***Serpentine Die Cut 11***

Self-Adhesive

4143 A3153 Pane of 15 15.00
a.-o. 41c Any single 1.00 .50

Uncut press sheets of No. 4143 were made available for sale. Values: block of 15 with vert. gutter (6 stamps at left, 9 stamps at right), $18. See note after No. 2868.

PRESIDENTIAL AIRCRAFT

Air Force One — A3154

Marine One — A3155

Designed by Phil Jordan. Printed by Ashton-Potter (USA) Ltd. (#4144), Banknote Corporation of America for Sennett Security Products (#4145).

LITHOGRAPHED & ENGRAVED (#4144), LITHOGRAPHED (#4145)
Sheets of 120 in six panes of 20

2007, June 13 Tagged *Serpentine Die Cut 10¾*

Self-Adhesive

4144	A3154 $4.60 **multicolored**	9.25	5.00
	P# block of 4, 6#+P	37.50	
	Pane of 20	190.00	
a.	Black (engr.) omitted	*200.00*	
4145	A3155 $16.25 **multicolored**	30.00	16.00
	P# block of 4, 5#+S	120.00	
	Pane of 20	600.00	

PACIFIC LIGHTHOUSES

Diamond Head Lighthouse, Hawaii — A3156

Five Finger Lighthouse, Alaska — A3157

Grays Harbor Lighthouse, Washington — A3158

Umpqua River Lighthouse, Oregon — A3159

St. George Reef Lighthouse, California — A3160

Designed by Howard E. Paine. Printed by Avery Dennison.

PHOTOGRAVURE
Sheets of 160 in eight panes of 20

2007, June 21 Tagged *Serpentine Die Cut 11*

Self-Adhesive

4146	A3156 41c **multicolored**	1.20	.40
4147	A3157 41c **multicolored**	1.20	.40
4148	A3158 41c **multicolored**	1.20	.40
4149	A3159 41c **multicolored**	1.20	.40
4150	A3160 41c **multicolored**	1.20	.40
a.	Horiz. strip of 5, #4146-4150	6.00	
	P# block of 10, 5#+V	12.00	
	Pane of 20	24.00	

WEDDING HEARTS

Heart With Lilac Background — A3161

Heart With Pink Background — A3162

Designed by Carl T. Herrman. Printed by Ashton-Potter (USA) Ltd. (#4151), Avery Dennison (#4152).

LITHOGRAPHED (#4151), PHOTOGRAVURE (#4152)
BOOKLET STAMP (#4151)
Sheets of 240 in twelve panes of 20 (#4152)

Serpentine Die Cut 10¾ on 2, 3 or 4 Sides

2007, June 27 Tagged

Self-Adhesive

4151	A3161 41c **multicolored**	1.00	.25
a.	Booklet pane of 20	20.00	

Serpentine Die Cut 10¾x11

4152	A3162 58c **multicolored**	1.25	.25
	P# block of 4, 4#+V	5.00	
	Pane of 20	25.00	

POLLINATION

Purple Nightshade, Morrison's Bumblebee A3163

Hummingbird Trumpet, Calliope Hummingbird A3164

Saguaro, Lesser Long-nosed Bat — A3165

Prairie Ironweed, Southern Dogface Butterfly A3166

Designed by Steve Buchanan. Printed by Ashton-Potter (USA) Ltd.

No. 4153: Type I, Tip of bird wing is directly under center of "U" in "USA," straight edge at left. Type II, Tip of bird wing is directly under the right line of the "U" in "USA," straight edge at right.

No. 4154: Type I, Tip of bird wing is even with the top of denomination, straight edge at right. Type II, Tip of bird wing is well above denomination, straight edge at left.

No. 4155: Type I, Top of "USA" is even with the lower portion of the nearest unopened green saguaro flower bud, straight edge at left. Type II, Top of "USA" is even with the point where the flower and unopened green saguaro bud meet, straight edge at right.

No. 4156: Type I, Bottom of denomination is even with top point of the white triangle found between the bottom of the purple flower and the green leaf below it, straight edge at right. Type II, Bottom of denomination is even with the lower point of the white triangle found between the bottom of the purple flower and the green leaf below it, straight edge at left.

LITHOGRAPHED

Serpentine Die Cut 11 on 2, 3 or 4 Sides

2007, June 29 Tagged

Self-Adhesive

Booklet Stamps

4153	A3163 41c **multicolored,** Type I	.85	.30
a.	Type II	.85	.30
4154	A3164 41c **multicolored,** Type I	.85	.30
a.	Type II	.85	.30
4155	A3165 41c **multicolored,** Type I	.85	.30
a.	Type II	.85	.30
4156	A3166 41c **multicolored,** Type I	.85	.30
a.	Type II	.85	.30
b.	Block of 4, #4153-4156	3.40	
c.	Block of 4, #4153a-4156a	3.40	
d.	Booklet pane of 20, 3 each #4153-4156, 2 each #4153a-4156a	17.00	

No. 4156d is a double-sided booklet with 12 stamps (2 each #4153-4156, 1 each #4153a-4156a) on one side and 8 stamps plus label (booklet cover) on the other side.

Patriotic Banner — A3167

A3167a

Designed by Michael Osborne. Printed by Avery-Dennison (#4157), Banknote Corporation of America for Sennett Security Products (#4158).

PHOTOGRAVURE (#4157), LITHOGRAPHED (#4158)

Serpentine Die Cut 11 Vert.

2007, July 4 Untagged

Coil Stamps

Self-Adhesive

4157	A3167 (10c) **red, gold & blue** ⓢ	.30	.25
	Pair	.40	
	P# strip of 5, #V111, V222	2.25	
	P# strip of 5, V333	2.75	
	P# single, #V111, V222	—	1.40
	P# single, #V333		2.75

Later printings of No. 4157 do not respond to a water soak. See note after No. 1549.

Serpentine Die Cut 11¾ Vert.

4158	A3167a (10c) **red, gold & blue**	.30	.25
	Pair	.40	
	P# strip of 5, #S111	2.75	
	P# single, #S111	—	1.25

A later printing of No. 4158 shows the red and blue in somewhat darker shades.

See No. 4385.

MARVEL COMICS SUPERHEROES

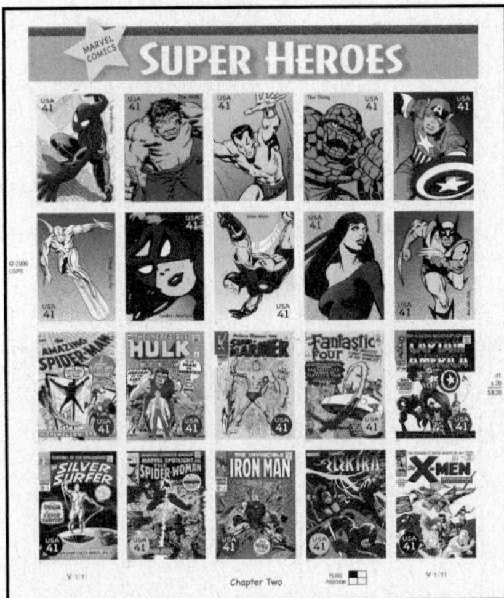

A3168

Illustration reduced.

Designed by Carl T. Herrman. Printed by Avery Dennison.

No. 4159: a, Spider-man. b, The Hulk. c, Sub-Mariner. d, The Thing. e, Captain America. f, Silver Surfer. g, Spider-Woman. h, Iron Man. i, Elektra. j, Wolverine. k, Cover of *The Amazing*

Spider-Man #1. l, Cover of *The Incredible Hulk #1.* m, Cover of *Sub-Mariner #1.* n, Cover of *The Fantastic Four #3.* o, Cover of *Captain America #100.* p, Cover of *The Silver Surfer #1.* q, Cover of *Marvel Spotlight on The Spider-Woman #32.* r, Cover of *Iron Man #1.* s, Cover of *Daredevil #176 Featuring Elektra.* t, Cover of *The X-Men #1.*

PHOTOGRAVURE
Sheets of 80 in four panes of 20
Serpentine Die Cut 10½x10¾

2007, July 26 **Tagged**

Self-Adhesive

4159 A3168 Pane of 20 20.00
a.-t. 41c Any single 1.00 .50

Uncut press sheets of No. 4159 were made available for sale. Values: cross-gutter block of 20, $30; pairs with gutters between, $3.25 each. See note after No. 2868.

VINTAGE MAHOGANY SPEEDBOATS Ⓢ

1915 Hutchinson — A3169

1954 Chris-Craft — A3170

1939 Hacker-Craft A3171

1931 Gar Wood — A3172

Designed by Carl T. Herrman. Printed by Ashton-Potter (USA) Ltd.

LITHOGRAPHED
Sheets of 72 in six panes of 12

2007, Aug. 4 **Tagged** ***Serpentine Die Cut 10½***

Self-Adhesive

4160 A3169 41c **multicolored** .85 .35
4161 A3170 41c **multicolored** .85 .35
4162 A3171 41c **multicolored** .85 .35
4163 A3172 41c **multicolored** .85 .35
a. Horiz. strip of 4, #4160-4163 3.40
P# block of 8, 4#+P 7.25
Pane of 12 10.50

See note after No. 1549.

Purple Heart — A3172a

Designed by Carl T. Herrman. Printed by Ashton-Potter (USA) Ltd.

LITHOGRAPHED
Sheets of 120 in six panes of 20
Serpentine Die Cut 11¼x10¾

2007, Aug. 7 **Tagged**

Self-Adhesive

4164 A3172a 41c **multicolored** Ⓢ .85 .25
P# block of 4, 4#+P 3.40
Pane of 20 17.00

See Nos. 3784-3784A, 4032, 4263-4264, 4390.
See note after No. 1549.

AMERICAN TREASURES SERIES

Magnolia and Irises, Stained Glass by Louis Comfort Tiffany — A3173

Designed by Derry Noyes. Printed by Ashton-Potter (USA) Ltd.

LITHOGRAPHED
BOOKLET STAMP
Serpentine Die Cut 10¾ on 2 or 3 Sides

2007, Aug. 9 **Tagged**

Self-Adhesive

4165 A3173 41c **multicolored** .85 .25
a. Booklet pane of 20 17.00

No. 4165a is a double-sided booklet pane with 12 stamps on one side and eight stamps plus label (booklet cover) on the other side.

FLOWERS

Iris — A3174

Dahlia — A3175

Magnolia — A3176

Red Gerbera Daisy — A3177

Coneflower — A3178

Tulip — A3179

Water Lily — A3180

Poppy — A3181

Chrysanthemum A3182

Orange Gerbera Daisy A3183

Designed by Carl T. Herrman. Printed by Ashton-Potter (USA) Ltd.

LITHOGRAPHED
Serpentine Die Cut 9½ Vert.

2007, Aug. 10 **Tagged**

COIL STAMPS Ⓢ

Self-Adhesive

4166 A3174 41c **multicolored** 2.00 .35
4167 A3175 41c **multicolored** 2.00 .35
4168 A3176 41c **multicolored** 2.00 .35
4169 A3177 41c **multicolored** 2.00 .35
4170 A3178 41c **multicolored** 2.00 .35
4171 A3179 41c **multicolored** 2.00 .35
4172 A3180 41c **multicolored** 2.00 .35
4173 A3181 41c **multicolored** 2.00 .35
4174 A3182 41c **multicolored** 2.00 .35
4175 A3183 41c **multicolored** 2.00 .35
a. Strip of 10, #4166-4175 20.00
P# strip of 11, 2 # 4175, 1 each #4166-4174, #P1111, P2222 25.00 —
P# single (#4170), same # — 2.00

Some later printings of Nos. 4166-4175 do not respond to a water soak. See note after No. 1549.

A3174a

A3175a

A3176a

A3177a

A3178a

A3179a

A3180a

A3181a

A3182a

A3183a

Printed by Avery Dennison.

PHOTOGRAVURE
BOOKLET STAMPS

Serpentine Die Cut 11¼x11½ on 2 or 3 Sides

4176 A3182a 41c **multicolored** 1.25 .35
4177 A3183a 41c **multicolored** 1.25 .35
4178 A3174a 41c **multicolored** 1.25 .35
4179 A3175a 41c **multicolored** 1.25 .35
4180 A3176a 41c **multicolored** 1.25 .35
4181 A3177a 41c **multicolored** 1.25 .35
4182 A3180a 41c **multicolored** 1.25 .35
4183 A3181a 41c **multicolored** 1.25 .35
4184 A3178a 41c **multicolored** 1.25 .35
4185 A3179a 41c **multicolored** 1.25 .35
a. Booklet pane of 20, 2 each #4176-4185 25.00
b. As "a," die cutting missing on Nos. 4178 & 4183 on side with 8 stamps (PS) *1,000.*

No. 4185a is a double-sided booklet pane with 12 stamps on one side (2 each #4176-4177, 1 each #4178-4185) and eight stamps (#4178-4185) plus label (booklet cover) on the other side.

Flag — A3184

A3184a

A3184b

A3184c

Designed by Richard Sheaff. Printed by Ashton-Potter (USA) Ltd. (#4186), Avery Dennison (#4188-4189), Banknote Corporation of America for Sennett Security Products (#4187).

LITHOGRAPHED

Serpentine Die Cut 9½ Vert.

2007, Aug. 15 **Tagged**

COIL STAMPS
Self-Adhesive
With "USPS" Microprinted on Right Side of Flagpole
With Perpendicular Corners

4186 A3184 41c **multicolored** 1.20 .25
Pair 2.40
P# strip of 5, #P11111 7.25
P# single, #P11111 — 2.00

With "USPS" Microprinted on Left Side of Flagpole

Serpentine Die Cut 11 Vert.

4187 A3184a 41c **multicolored,** prephosphored coated paper 1.20 .25
Pair 2.40
P# strip of 5, #S11111 7.50
P# single, #S11111 — 2.00

No. 4187 exists on two types of surface-tagged paper that exhibit either a solid or an uneven appearance.

No. 4186 was not sold to the public until October 2007 and No. 4187 was not sold to the public until November 2007.

Counterfeits exist of No. 4187. See the Postal Counterfeits section of this catalog.

PHOTOGRAVURE
Without "USPS" Microprinting on Flagpole

Serpentine Die Cut 8½ Vert.

4188 A3184b 41c **multicolored,** overall tagging .85 .25
Pair 1.70
P# strip of 5, #V11111 6.00
P# single, same # — 2.00
a. Prephosphored coated paper with surface tagging showing a solid appearance 1.00 .25
Pair 2.00
P# strip of 5, #V22222 6.50
P# single, #V22222 — 2.00
c. As "a," light blue ("41 USA") omitted, on cover —

Serpentine Die Cut 11 Vert.
With Rounded Corners

4189 A3184c 41c **multicolored** .85 .25
Pair 1.70
P# strip of 5, #V11111 6.00
P# single, #V11111 — 2.00

No. 4188 is on backing paper as high as the stamp. No. 4189 is on backing paper that is larger than the stamp.

A3184d

A3184e

Printed by Ashton-Potter (USA) Ltd. (#4190), Banknote Corporation of America for Sennett Security Products (#4191).

LITHOGRAPHED
BOOKLET STAMPS

Serpentine Die Cut 11¼x10¾ on 3 Sides
With "USPS" Microprinted on Right Side of Flagpole

4190 A3184d 41c **multicolored** .85 .25
a. Booklet pane of 10 8.50

With "USPS" Microprinted on Left Side of Flagpole

Serpentine Die Cut 11¼x10¾ on 2 or 3 Sides

4191 A3184e 41c **multicolored** .85 .25
a. Booklet pane of 20 17.00

The microprinting on Nos. 4190 and 4191 is under the ball of the flagpole. The flagpole is light gray on No. 4190 and dark gray on No. 4191. No. 4191a is a double-sided booklet with 12 stamps on one side of the peelable backing and 8 stamps plus label (booklet cover) on the other side.

THE ART OF DISNEY: MAGIC

Mickey Mouse — A3185

Peter Pan and Tinker Bell — A3186

Dumbo and Timothy Mouse — A3187

Aladdin and Genie — A3188

Designed by David Pacheco. Printed by Avery Dennison.

PHOTOGRAVURE
Sheets of 160 in eight panes of 20

Serpentine Die Cut 10½x10¾

2007, Aug. 16 **Tagged**

Self-Adhesive

4192 A3185 41c **multicolored** .85 .30
4193 A3186 41c **multicolored** .85 .30
4194 A3187 41c **multicolored** .85 .30
4195 A3188 41c **multicolored** .85 .30
a. Block or strip of 4, #4192-4195 3.40
P# block of 4, 6#+V 3.40
P# block of 10, 2 sets of P# + top label 8.50
Pane of 20 17.00

CELEBRATE

A3189

Designed by Ethel Kessler. Printed by Banknote Corporation of America for Sennett Security Products.

LITHOGRAPHED
Sheets of 160 in eight panes of 20

2007, Aug. 17 **Tagged** ***Serpentine Die Cut 10¾***

Self-Adhesive

4196 A3189 41c **multicolored** .85 .25
P# block of 4, 4#+S 3.40
Pane of 20 17.00

See Nos. 4335, 4407.

LEGENDS OF HOLLYWOOD

James Stewart (1908-97), Actor — A3190

Designed by Phil Jordan. Printed by Ashton-Potter (USA) Ltd.

LITHOGRAPHED
Sheets of 180 in nine panes of 20

2007, Aug. 17 Tagged *Serpentine Die Cut 10¾*
Self-Adhesive

4197 A3190 41c **multicolored** ⓢ 1.00 .25
P# block of 4, 4#+P 5.00
Pane of 20 20.00

ⓢ: Ink on No. 4197 cracks and flakes off during water soak. See note after No. 1549.

Uncut press sheets of No. 4197 were made available for sale. Values: cross-gutter block of 8, $24; pairs with gutters between, $3.25 each. See note after No. 2868.

ALPINE TUNDRA

A3191

Illustration reduced.

Designed by Ethel Kessler. Printed by Banknote Corporation of America for Sennett Security Products.

No. 4198 — Wildlife: a, Elk. b, Golden eagle, horiz. c, Yellow-bellied marmot. d, American pika. e, Bighorn sheep. f, Magdalena alpine butterfly. g, White-tailed ptarmigan. h, Rocky Mountain parnassian butterfly. i, Melissa arctic butterfly, horiz. j, Brown-capped rosy-finch, horiz.

PHOTOGRAVURE
Sheets of 80 in eight panes of 10

2007, Aug. 28 Tagged *Serpentine Die Cut 10¾*
Self-Adhesive

4198 A3191 Pane of 10 8.50
a.-j. 41c any single .85 .40

Uncut press sheets of Nos. 4198 were made available for sale. See note after No. 2868.

GERALD R. FORD ⓢ

Gerald R. Ford (1913-2006), 38th President — A3192

Designed by Ethel Kessler. Printed by Ashton-Potter (USA) Ltd.

LITHOGRAPHED
Sheets of 120 in six panes of 20

2007, Aug. 31 Tagged *Serpentine Die Cut 11*
Self-Adhesive

4199 A3192 41c **multicolored** .85 .25
P# block of 4, 5#+P 3.40
Pane of 20 17.00

Uncut press sheets of No. 4199 were made available for sale. Values: cross-gutter block of 4, $9; pairs with gutters between, $3 each. See note after No. 2868.

See note after No. 1549.

JURY DUTY ⓢ

Twelve Jurors — A3193

Designed by Carl T. Herrman. Printed by Ashton-Potter (USA) Ltd.

LITHOGRAPHED
Sheets of 120 in six panes of 20

2007, Sept. 12 Tagged *Serpentine Die Cut 10½*
Self-Adhesive

4200 A3193 41c **multicolored** .85 .25
P# block of 4, 5#+P 3.40
Pane of 20 17.00

See note after No. 1549.

MENDEZ v. WESTMINSTER, 60th ANNIV. ⓢ

A3194

Designed by Ethel Kessler. Printed by Ashton-Potter (USA) Ltd.

LITHOGRAPHED
Sheets of 120 in six panes of 20

2007, Sept. 14 Tagged *Serpentine Die Cut 11*
Self-Adhesive

4201 A3194 41c **multicolored** .85 .25
P# block of 4, 4#+P 3.40
Pane of 20 17.00

See note after No. 1549.

Eid — A3194a

Designed by Mohamed Zakariya. Printed by Avery Dennison.

PHOTOGRAVURE
Sheets of 240 in twelve panes of 20

2007, Sept. 28 Tagged *Serpentine Die Cut 11*
Self-Adhesive

4202 A3194a 41c **multicolored** .90 .25
P# block of 4, 3#+V 4.50
Pane of 20 22.00

See Nos. 3532, 3674, 4117, 4351, 4416.

AURORAS ⓢ

Aurora Borealis A3195

Aurora Australis A3196

Designed by Phil Jordan. Printed by Ashton-Potter (USA) Ltd.

LITHOGRAPHED
Sheets of 120 in six panes of 20

2007, Oct. 1 Tagged *Serpentine Die Cut 10¾*
Self-Adhesive

4203 A3195 41c **multicolored** 1.25 .30
4204 A3196 41c **multicolored** 1.25 .30
a. Horiz. or vert. pair, #4203-4204 2.50
P# block of 4, 5#+P 6.00
Pane of 20 29.00

See note after No. 1549.

YODA

A3197

Designed by Greg Breeding. Printed by Banknote Corporation of America for Sennett Security Products.

LITHOGRAPHED
Sheets of 120 in six panes of 20
Serpentine Die Cut 10½x10¾

2007, Oct. 25 Tagged
Self-Adhesive

4205 A3197 41c **multicolored** 1.00 .25
P# block of 4, 5#+S 4.00
Pane of 20 20.00

Uncut part press sheets of No. 4205 of 3 panes each (1x3) were made available for sale. Value: vertical pair with horizontal gutter, $3. See note after No. 2868.

CHRISTMAS

Madonna of the Carnation, by Bernardino Luini — A3198

Designed by Richard Sheaff.
Printed by Ashton-Potter (USA) Ltd.

LITHOGRAPHED
Serpentine Die Cut 10¾x11 on 2 or 3 Sides

2007, Oct. 25 Tagged
Self-Adhesive
Booklet Stamps (#4206, 4210b, 4211-4218)

4206 A3198 41c **multicolored** ⓢ .85 .25
a. Booklet pane of 20 17.00

No. 4206a is a double-sided booklet pane with 12 stamps on one side and eight stamps plus label that serves as a booklet cover on the other side.

Ink on No. 4206 cracks and flakes off during a water soak. See note after No. 1549.

Knit Reindeer — A3199

Knit Christmas Tree — A3200

Knit Snowman — A3201

Knit Bear — A3202

Designed by Carl T. Herrman.
Printed by Banknote Corporation of America for Sennett Security Products.

Sheets of 160 in eight panes of 20 (#4207-4210)
Serpentine Die Cut 10¾ on 2, 3 or 4 Sides

4207	A3199 41c **multicolored**, overall tagging	.85	.25
a.	Prephosphored coated paper with surface tagging showing an uneven appearance	.85	.25
4208	A3200 41c **multicolored**, overall tagging	.85	.25
a.	Prephosphored coated paper with surface tagging showing an uneven appearance	.85	.25
4209	A3201 41c **multicolored**, overall tagging	.85	.25
a.	Prephosphored coated paper with surface tagging showing an uneven appearance	.85	.25
4210	A3202 41c **multicolored**, overall tagging	.85	.25
a.	Prephosphored coated paper with surface tagging showing an uneven appearance	.85	.25
b.	Block or vert. strip of 4, #4207-4210	3.40	
	P# block of 4, 4#+S	3.40	
	Pane of 20	17.00	
c.	Block of 4, #4207a-4210a	3.40	
d.	Booklet pane of 20, 5 each #4207a-4210a	17.00	

No. 4210d is a double-sided booklet pane with 12 stamps on one side and eight stamps plus label that serves as a booklet cover on the other side.

Tagging on stamps from panes of 20 has a solid appearance; tagging on stamps from booklets has an uneven appearance.

Knit Reindeer — A3203

Knit Christmas Tree — A3204

Knit Snowman — A3205

Knit Bear — A3206

Serpentine Die Cut 11¼x11 on 2 or 3 Sides

4211	A3203 41c **multicolored**	1.25	.25
4212	A3204 41c **multicolored**	1.25	.25
4213	A3205 41c **multicolored**	1.25	.25
4214	A3206 41c **multicolored**	1.25	.25
a.	Block of 4, #4211-4214	5.00	
b.	Booklet pane of 4, #4211-4214	5.00	
c.	Booklet pane of 6, #4213-4214, 2 each #4211-4212	7.50	
d.	Booklet pane of 6, #4211-4212, 2 each #4213-4214	7.50	

A3203a

A3204a

A3205a

A3206a

Printed by Avery Dennison.

PHOTOGRAVURE
Serpentine Die Cut 8 on 2, 3 or 4 Sides

4215	A3203a 41c **multicolored** ⓢ	1.50	.25
4216	A3204a 41c **multicolored** ⓢ	1.50	.25
4217	A3205a 41c **multicolored** ⓢ	1.50	.25
4218	A3206a 41c **multicolored** ⓢ	1.50	.25
a.	Block or strip of 4, #4215-4218	6.00	
b.	Booklet pane of 18, 4 each #4215, 4218, 5 each #4216, 4217	27.00	
	Nos. 4206-4218 (13)	15.25	3.25

See note after No. 1549.

Hanukkah — A3206b

Designed by Ethel Kessler. Printed by Banknote Corporation of America for Sennett Security Products.

LITHOGRAPHED
Sheets of 160 in eight panes of 20
Serpentine Die Cut 10¾x11

2007, Oct. 26 Tagged
Self-Adhesive

4219	A3206b 41c **multicolored**	.85	.25
	P# block of 4, 4#+S	3.40	
	Pane of 20	17.00	

See Nos. 3880, 4118, 4372.

Kwanzaa — A3206c

Designed by Derry Noyes. Printed by Ashton-Potter (USA) Ltd.

LITHOGRAPHED
Sheets of 160 in eight panes of 20
Serpentine Die Cut 11x10¾

2007, Oct. 26 Tagged
Self-Adhesive

4220	A3206c 41c **multicolored** ⓢ	.85	.25
	P# block of 4, 6#+P	3.40	
	Pane of 20	17.00	

See Nos. 3881, 4119, 4373.
See note after No. 1549.

CHINESE NEW YEAR

Year of the Rat — A3207

Designed by Ethel Kessler. Printed by Avery Dennison

PHOTOGRAVURE
Sheets of 108 in nine panes of 12
Serpentine Die Cut 10¾

2008, Jan. 9 Tagged Self-Adhesive

4221	A3207 41c **multicolored**	.85	.25
	Pane of 12	10.50	

Uncut press sheets of No. 4221 were made available for sale. Values: cross-gutter block of 4, $9; pairs with gutters between, $2.25 each. See note after No. 2868.

BLACK HERITAGE SERIES

Charles W. Chesnutt (1858-1932), Writer — A3208

Designed by Howard E. Paine. Printed by Avery Dennison.

PHOTOGRAVURE
Sheets of 200 in ten panes of 20
Serpentine Die Cut 11

2008, Jan. 31 Tagged Self-Adhesive

4222	A3208 41c **multicolored**	.85	.25
	P# block of 4, 4# + V	3.40	
	Pane of 20	17.00	

LITERARY ARTS SERIES

Marjorie Kinnan Rawlings (1896-1953), Writer A3209

Designed by Carl T. Herrman. Printed by Avery Dennison.

PHOTOGRAVURE
Sheets of 200 in ten panes of 20

2008, Feb. 21 Tagged *Serpentine Die Cut 11*
Self-Adhesive

4223	A3209 41c **multicolored**	.85	.25
	P# block of 4, 4# + V	3.40	
	Pane of 20	17.00	

AMERICAN SCIENTISTS

Gerty Cori (1896-1957), Biochemist A3210

Linus Pauling (1901-94), Structural Chemist A3211

Edwin Hubble (1889-1953), Astronomer A3212

John Bardeen (1908-91), Theoretical Physicist A3213

Designed by Victor Stabin. Printed by Avery Dennison.

PHOTOGRAVURE

Sheets of 160 in eight panes of 20

2008, Mar. 6 Tagged *Serpentine Die Cut 11*

Self-Adhesive

4224 A3210 41c **multicolored**	1.00	.35
4225 A3211 41c **multicolored**	1.00	.35
4226 A3212 41c **multicolored**	1.00	.35
4227 A3213 41c **multicolored**	1.00	.35
a. Horiz. strip of 4, #4224-4227	4.00	
P# block of 8, 2 sets of 4# + V	8.00	
Pane of 20	20.00	

Plate block may contain top label.

Flag at Dusk — A3214

Flag at Night — A3215

Flag at Dawn — A3216

Flag at Midday — A3217

Designed by Phil Jordan. Printed by American Packaging Corporation for Sennett Security Products.

PHOTOGRAVURE

2008, Apr. 18 Tagged *Perf. 9¾ Vert.*

COIL STAMPS

4228 A3214 42c **multicolored**	2.50	.40
4229 A3215 42c **multicolored**	2.50	.40
4230 A3216 42c **multicolored**	2.50	.40
4231 A3217 42c **multicolored**	2.50	.40
a. Horiz. strip of 4, #4228-4231	10.00	1.60
P# strip of 5, 2 #4228, 1 each #4229-4231, #S1111111	15.00	—
P# strip of 9, 3 #4230, 2 each #4228-4229, 4230, P#S1111111	27.50	—
P# single, #S1111111 (#4230)	—	2.00

Counterfeits exist of Nos. 4228-4231. See the Postal Counterfeits section of this catalog.

A3214a

A3215a

A3216a

A3217a

Printed by Ashton-Potter (USA) Ltd.

LITHOGRAPHED (#4232-4239)

Self-Adhesive

With Perpendicular Corners

Serpentine Die Cut 9½ Vert.

4232 A3214a 42c **multicolored** Ⓢ	2.25	.25
4233 A3215a 42c **multicolored** Ⓢ	2.25	.25
4234 A3216a 42c **multicolored** Ⓢ	2.25	.25
4235 A3217 42c **multicolored** Ⓢ	2.25	.25
a. Horiz. strip of 4, #4232-4235	9.00	
P# strip of 5, 2 #4232, 1 each #4233-4235, #P1111	13.00	
P# strip of 9, 3 #4234, 2 each #4232-4233, 4235, P#P1111	21.50	
P# single, #P1111 (#4234)	—	2.00

Counterfeits exist of Nos. 4232-4235. See the Postal Counterfeits section of this catalog.

A3214b

A3215b

A3216b

A3217b

Printed by Banknote Corporation of America for Sennett Security Products.

Serpentine Die Cut 11 Vert.

4236 A3214b 42c **multicolored**	2.50	.25
4237 A3215b 42c **multicolored**	2.50	.25
4238 A3216b 42c **multicolored**	2.50	.25
4239 A3217b 42c **multicolored**	2.50	.25
a. Horiz. strip of 4, #4236-4239	10.00	
P# strip of 5, 2 #4236, 1 each #4237-4239, #S1111	16.00	
P# strip of 9, 3 #4238, 2 each #4236-4237, 4239, P#S1111	25.00	
P# single, #S1111 (#4238)	—	2.00

A3214c

A3215c

A3216c

A3217c

Printed by Avery Dennison (#4240-4247).

PHOTOGRAVURE

Serpentine Die Cut 8½ Vert.

4240 A3214c 42c **multicolored**	2.00	.25
4241 A3215c 42c **multicolored**	2.00	.25
4242 A3216c 42c **multicolored**	2.00	.25
4243 A3217c 42c **multicolored**	2.00	.25
a. Horiz. strip of 4, #4240-4243	8.00	
P# strip of 5, 2 #4240, 1 each #4241-4243, #V1111, V2222	12.50	
P# strip of 9, 3 #4242, 2 each #4240-4241, 4244, P#V1111, V2222	20.00	
P# single, same # (#4242)	—	2.00

A3214d

A3215d

A3216d

A3217d

Serpentine Die Cut 11 Vert.

With Rounded Corners

4244 A3214d 42c **multicolored**	1.25	.30
4245 A3215d 42c **multicolored**	1.25	.30
4246 A3216d 42c **multicolored**	1.25	.30
4247 A3217d 42c **multicolored**	1.25	.30
a. Horiz. strip of 4, #4244-4247	6.00	
P# strip of 5, 2 #4244, 1 each #4245-4247, #V1111, V2222	11.00	
P# strip of 9, 3 #4246, 2 each #4244-4245, 4247, P#V1111, V2222	17.00	
P# single, same # (#4246)	—	2.00
Nos. 4228-4247 (20)	42.00	5.80

Nos. 4232-4243 are on backing paper as high as the stamp. See note after No. 1549.

Nos. 4244-4247 are on backing paper that is larger than the stamp. Nos. 4232-4235 have "USPS" microprinted on the right side of a white flag stripe. Nos. 4236-4239 have "USPS" micorprinted on red flag stripes. On Nos. 4244-4247, the paper, vignette size and "2008" year date are slightly larger than those features on Nos. 4236-4239.

AMERICAN JOURNALISTS Ⓢ

Martha Gellhorn (1908-98) A3218

John Hersey (1914-93) A3219

George Polk (1913-48) A3220

Ruben Salazar (1928-70) A3221

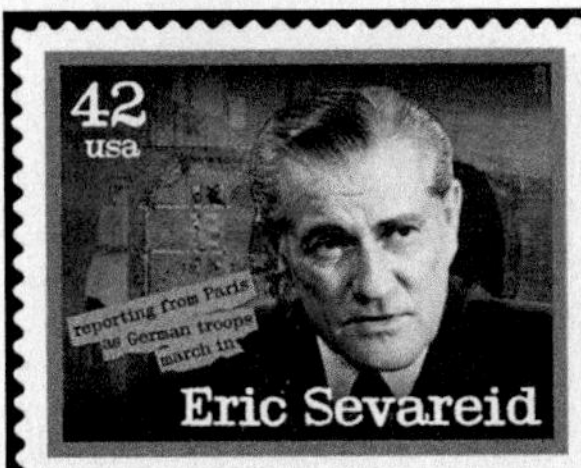

Eric Sevareid (1912-92) A3222

Designed by Howard E. Paine. Printed by Ashton-Potter (USA) Ltd.

LITHOGRAPHED
Sheets of 180 in nine panes of 20
Serpentine Die Cut 10¾x10½

2008, Apr. 22 **Tagged**

Self-Adhesive

4248 A3218 42c **multicolored** 1.40 .40
4249 A3219 42c **multicolored** 1.40 .40
4250 A3220 42c **multicolored** 1.40 .40
4251 A3221 42c **multicolored** 1.40 .40
4252 A3222 42c **multicolored** 1.40 .40
a. Vert. strip of 5, #4248-4252 7.00
P# block of 10, 2 sets of 4# + P 14.00
P# block of 8, 2 sets of 4# +P 12.50
Pane of 20 28.00

See note after No. 1549.

TROPICAL FRUIT

Pomegranate A3223

Star Fruit A3224

Kiwi — A3225

Papaya — A3226

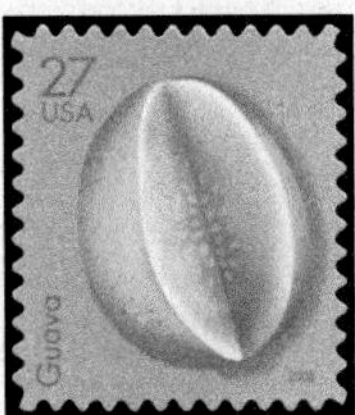

Guava — A3227

Designed by Ethel Kessler. Printed by Ashton-Potter (USA) Ltd.

LITHOGRAPHED
Serpentine Die Cut 11¼x10¾

2008, Apr. 25 **Tagged**

Self-Adhesive

4253 A3223 27c **multicolored** ⓢ 1.25 .25
4254 A3224 27c **multicolored** ⓢ 1.25 .25
4255 A3225 27c **multicolored** ⓢ 1.25 .25
4256 A3226 27c **multicolored** ⓢ 1.25 .25
4257 A3227 27c **multicolored** ⓢ 1.25 .25
a. Horiz. strip of 5, #4253-4257 6.25
P# block of 10, 2 sets of 4# + P 12.50
Pane of 20 25.00

See note after No. 1549.

A3223a

A3224a

A3225a

A3226a

A3227a

Printed by Avery Dennison.

PHOTOGRAVURE
COIL STAMPS
Serpentine Die Cut 8½ Vert.

4258 A3226a 27c **multicolored** 2.00 .25
4259 A3227a 27c **multicolored** 2.00 .25
4260 A3223a 27c **multicolored** 2.00 .25
4261 A3224a 27c **multicolored** 2.00 .25
4262 A3225a 27c **multicolored** 2.00 .25
a. Strip of 5, #4258-4262 10.00
P# strip of 5, #V1111111 12.00
P# strip of 11, 3 #4260, 2 each #4258-4259, 4261, 4262, #V1111111 24.00
P# single, #V1111111 (#4260) — 3.00
b. As No. 4262, light green ("27 USA," "Kiwi" and year date) omitted —
Nos. 4253-4262 (10) 16.25 2.50

Purple Heart

A3227b

A3227c

Designed by Carl T. Herrman. Printed by Ashton-Potter (USA) Ltd.

LITHOGRAPHED
Sheets of 400 in four panes of 100 (#4263), Sheets of 120 in six panes of 20 (#4264)

2008, Apr. 30 **Tagged** ***Perf. 11¼***

4263 A3227b 42c **multicolored** .90 .25
P# block of 4, 4#+P 35.00 —
Pane of 100 120.00 —

Self-Adhesive
Serpentine Die Cut 11¼x10¾

4264 A3227c 42c **multicolored** ⓢ .85 .25
P# block of 4, 4#+P 3.40
Pane of 20 17.00

See Nos. 4032, 4164, 4390.
See note after No. 1549.

FRANK SINATRA

Frank Sinatra (1915-98), Singer and Actor — A3228

Designed by Richard Sheaff. Printed by Ashton-Potter (USA) Ltd.

LITHOGRAPHED
Sheets of 120 in six panes of 20

2008, May 13 **Tagged** ***Serpentine Die Cut 10¾***

Self-Adhesive

4265 A3228 42c **multicolored** ⓢ .85 .25
P# block of 4, 4#+P 3.40
Pane of 20 17.00

See note after No. 1549.

Uncut press sheets of No. 4265 were made available for sale. Values: cross-gutter block of 4, $9; pairs with gutters between, $2.25 each. See note after No. 2868.

MINNESOTA STATEHOOD, 150th ANNIV. ⓢ

Bridge Over Mississippi River Near Winona — A3229

Designed by Ethel Kessler. Printed by Ashton-Potter (USA) Ltd.

LITHOGRAPHED
Sheets of 120 in six panes of 20

2008, May 17 **Tagged** ***Serpentine Die Cut 10¾***

Self-Adhesive

4266 A3229 42c **multicolored** .85 .25
P# block of 4, 4#+P 3.40
Pane of 20 17.00

See note after No. 1549.

WILDLIFE

Dragonfly — A3230

Designed by Carl T. Herrman. Printed by Banknote Corporation of America for Sennett Security Products.

LITHOGRAPHED
Sheets of 400 in twenty panes of 20
Serpentine Die Cut 11¼x11

2008, May 19 **Tagged**

Self-Adhesive

4267 A3230 62c **multicolored** 2.50 .25
P# block of 4, 4#+S 10.00
Pane of 20 50.00

AMERICAN LANDMARKS

Mount Rushmore A3231

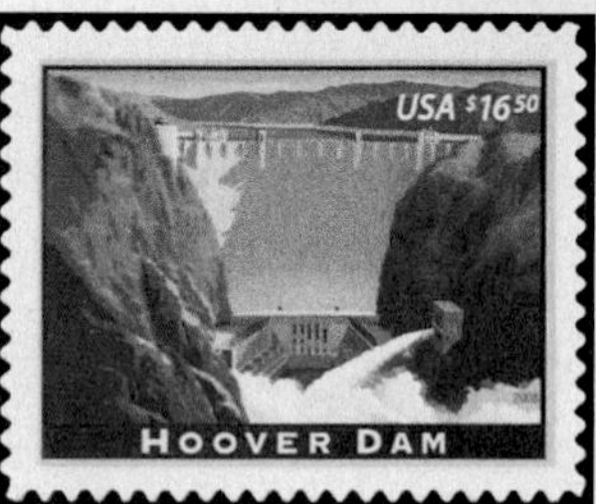

Hoover Dam — A3232

Designed by Carl T. Herrman. Printed by Ashton-Potter (USA) Ltd. (#4268), Banknote Corporation of America for Sennett Security Products (#4269).

LITHOGRAPHED

Sheets of 180 in nine panes of 20 (#4268), Sheets of 120 in six panes of 20 (#4269)

2008 Tagged ***Serpentine Die Cut 10¾x10½***

Self-Adhesive

4268	A3231	$4.80 **multicolored,** *June 6* Ⓢ	12.00	5.00
		P# block of 4, 4#+P	48.00	
		Pane of 20	240.00	
4269	A3232	$16.50 **multicolored,** *June 20*	35.00	17.00
		P# block of 4, 5#+S	140.00	
		Pane of 20	700.00	

See note after No. 1549.

LOVE

Man Carrying Heart — A3233

Designed by Ethel Kessler. Printed by Avery Dennison.

PHOTOGRAVURE

Serpentine Die Cut 10¾ on 2, 3, or 4 Sides

2008, June 10 Tagged

Booklet Stamp

Self-Adhesive

4270	A3233	42c **multicolored** Ⓢ	.95	.25
a.		Booklet pane of 20	19.00	

See note after No. 1549.

WEDDING HEARTS Ⓢ

Heart With Light Green Background — A3234

Heart With Buff Background — A3235

Designed by Carl T. Herrman. Printed by Ashton-Potter (USA) Ltd. (#4271), Avery Dennison (#4272).

LITHOGRAPHED (#4271), PHOTOGRAVURE (#4272)

BOOKLET STAMP (#4271)

Sheets of 240 in twelve panes of 20 (#4272)

Serpentine Die Cut 10¾ on 2, 3 or 4 Sides

2008, June 10 Tagged

Self-Adhesive

4271	A3234	42c **multicolored**	.90	.25
a.		Booklet pane of 20	18.00	

Serpentine Die Cut 10¾

4272	A3235	59c **multicolored**	1.25	.25
		P# block of 4, 3#+V	5.00	
		Pane of 20	25.00	

See note after No. 1549.

FLAGS OF OUR NATION

American Flag and Clouds A3236

Alabama Flag and Shrimp Boat A3237

Alaska Flag and Humpback Whale — A3238

American Samoa Flag and Island Peaks and Trees A3239

Arizona Flag and Saguaro Cacti A3240

Arkansas Flag and Wood Duck A3241

California Flag and Coast A3242

Colorado Flag and Mountain A3243

Connecticut Flag, Sailboats and Buoy — A3244

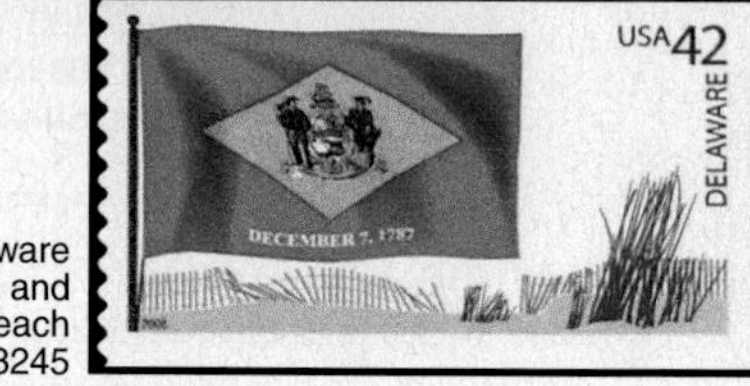

Delaware Flag and Beach A3245

Designed by Howard E. Paine. Printed by American Packaging Corp. for Sennett Security Products.

PHOTOGRAVURE

Serpentine Die Cut 11 Vert.

2008, June 14 Tagged

Self-Adhesive

Coil Stamps

4273	A3236	42c **multicolored**	1.00	.30
4274	A3237	42c **multicolored**	1.00	.30
4275	A3238	42c **multicolored**	1.00	.30
4276	A3239	42c **multicolored**	1.00	.30
4277	A3240	42c **multicolored**	1.00	.30
a.		Strip of 5, #4273-4277	5.00	
4278	A3241	42c **multicolored**	1.00	.30
4279	A3242	42c **multicolored**	1.00	.30
4280	A3243	42c **multicolored**	1.00	.30
4281	A3244	42c **multicolored**	1.00	.30
4282	A3245	42c **multicolored**	1.00	.30
a.		Strip of 5, #4278-4282	5.00	
b.		P # set of 10, #4277a + 4282a	10.00	
		P# strip of 11, #4273-4277, 4279-4282, 2 #4278, S#111111111	13.00	
		P# strip of 21, 3 #4273, 2 each #4274-4282, S#111111111	30.00	
		P# single (#4273), same #	—	2.75

No. 4273 always has a plate number. No. 4282b may be collected as one continuous strip, but the item will not fit in any standard album.

District of Columbia Flag and Cherry Tree A3246

Florida Flag and Anhinga A3247

Georgia Flag, Fence and Lamppost A3248

Guam Flag, Fish and Tropicbird
A3249

Hawaii Flag and Ohia Lehua Flowers
A3250

Idaho Flag and Rainbow Trout
A3251

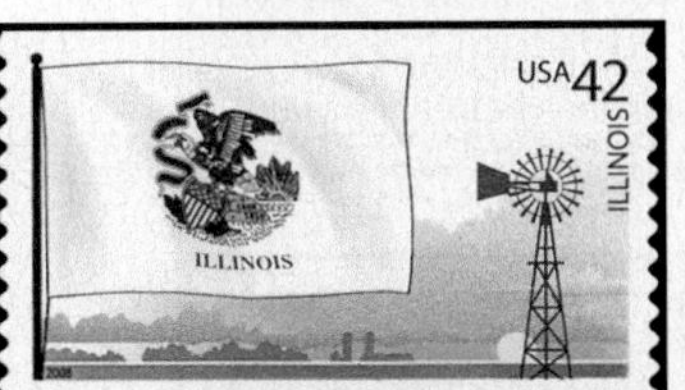

Illinois Flag and Windmill
A3252

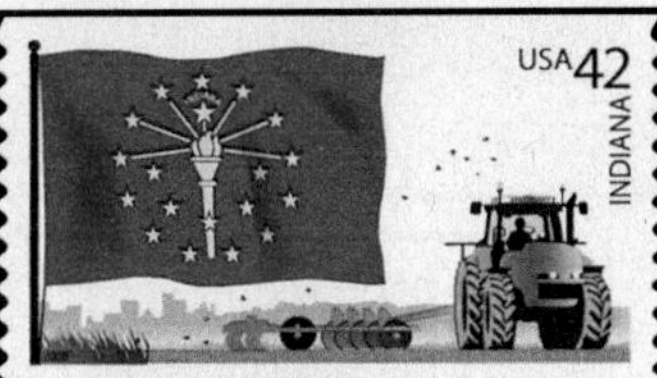

Indiana Flag and Tractor
A3253

Iowa Flag, Farm Field and Cornstalks — A3254

Kansas Flag and Farm Buildings
A3255

Designed by Howard E. Paine. Printed by American Packaging Corp. for Sennett Security Products.

PHOTOGRAVURE

Serpentine Die Cut 11 Vert.

2008, Sept. 2 **Tagged**

Self-Adhesive

Coil Stamps

4283	A3246 42c **multicolored**		1.00	.30
4284	A3247 42c **multicolored**		1.00	.30
4285	A3248 42c **multicolored**		1.00	.30
4286	A3249 42c **multicolored**		1.00	.30
4287	A3250 42c **multicolored**		1.00	.30
a.	Strip of 5, #4283-4287		5.00	
4288	A3251 42c **multicolored**		1.00	.30
4289	A3252 42c **multicolored**		1.00	.30
4290	A3253 42c **multicolored**		1.00	.30
4291	A3254 42c **multicolored**		1.00	.30
4292	A3255 42c **multicolored**		1.00	.30
a.	Strip of 5, #4288-4292		5.00	
b.	P # set of 10, #4287a + 4192a		10.00	
	P# strip of 11, #4283-4287, 4289-4292, 2 #4288, S#111111111		13.00	
	P# strip of 21, 3 #4283, 2 each #4284-4292, S#111111111		30.00	
	P# single (#4283), same #		—	2.75

No. 4283 always has a plate number. No. 4292b may be collected as one continuous strip, but the item will not fit in any standard album.

Kentucky Flag, Fence and Horses
A3256

Louisiana Flag and Brown Pelicans
A3257

Maine Flag and Moose
A3258

Maryland Flag and Red-winged Blackbird — A3259

Massachusetts Flag, Sea Birds and Sailboats — A3260

Michigan Flag and Great Lakes Ships
A3261

Minnesota Flag, Swans and Grain Elevator
A3262

Mississippi Flag and Black Bears
A3263

Missouri Flag and Paddle Wheeler
A3264

American Flag and Wheat
A3265

Designed by Howard E. Paine. Printed by American Packaging Corp. for Sennett Security Products.

PHOTOGRAVURE

2009, Aug. 6 Tagged *Serpentine Die Cut 11 Vert.*

Self-Adhesive

Coil Stamps

4293	A3256 44c **multicolored**		1.00	.30
4294	A3257 44c **multicolored**		1.00	.30
4295	A3258 44c **multicolored**		1.00	.30
4296	A3259 44c **multicolored**		1.00	.30
4297	A3260 44c **multicolored**		1.00	.30
a.	Strip of 5, #4293-4297		5.00	
4298	A3261 44c **multicolored**		1.00	.30
4299	A3262 44c **multicolored**		1.00	.30
4300	A3263 44c **multicolored**		1.00	.30
4301	A3264 44c **multicolored**		1.00	.30
4302	A3265 44c **multicolored**		1.00	.30
a.	Strip of 5, #4298-4302		5.00	
b.	P # set of 10, #4297a + 4302a		10.00	
	P# strip of 11, #4293-4297, 4299-4302, 2 #4298, P#S111111111		13.00	
	P# strip of 21, 3 #4293, 2 each #4294-4302, S#111111111		30.00	
	P# single (#4293), same #		—	2.75

No. 4293 always has a plate number. No. 4302b may be collected as one continuous strip, but the item will not fit in any standard album.

American Flag and Mountains
A3266

Montana Flag and Mountain Lion
A3267

Nebraska Flag and Central-pivot Irrigation System — A3268

Nevada Flag, Mountains and Ocotillos
A3269

New Hampshire Flag and Loon
A3270

New Jersey Flag and Sand Castle
A3271

New Mexico Flag, Mountains and Hot Air Balloons
A3272

New York Flag, Fireboats and City Skyline
A3273

North Carolina Flag, Great Blue Heron and Cape Hatteras Lighthouse — A3274

North Dakota Flag and Elk
A3275

Designed by Howard E. Paine. Printed by American Packaging Corp. for Sennett Security Products.

PHOTOGRAVURE

2010, Apr. 16 ***Serpentine Die Cut 11 Vert.***

Self-Adhesive

Coil Stamps

4303	A3266	44c	**multicolored**	1.00	.30
4304	A3267	44c	**multicolored**	1.00	.30
4305	A3268	44c	**multicolored**	1.00	.30
4306	A3269	44c	**multicolored**	1.00	.30
4307	A3270	44c	**multicolored**	1.00	.30
a.			Strip of 5, #4303-4307	5.00	
4308	A3271	44c	**multicolored**	1.00	.30
4309	A3272	44c	**multicolored**	1.00	.30
4310	A3273	44c	**multicolored**	1.00	.30
4311	A3274	44c	**multicolored**	1.00	.30
4312	A3275	44c	**multicolored**	1.00	.30
a.			Strip of 5, #4308-4312	5.00	
b.			P # set of 10, #4307a + 4312a	10.00	
			P# strip of 11, #4303-4307, 4309-4312, 2 #4308, P#S111111111	13.00	
			P# strip of 21, 3 #4303, 2 each #4304-4312, S#111111111	30.00	
			P# single (#4303), same #	—	2.75

No. 4303 always has a plate number. No. 4312b may be collected as one continuous strip, but the item will not fit in any standard album.

Northern Marianas Flag, Beach and Palm Trees
A3276

Ohio Flag, Butterfly, Milkweed Flowers and River
A3277

Oklahoma Flag and Oil Pumps
A3278

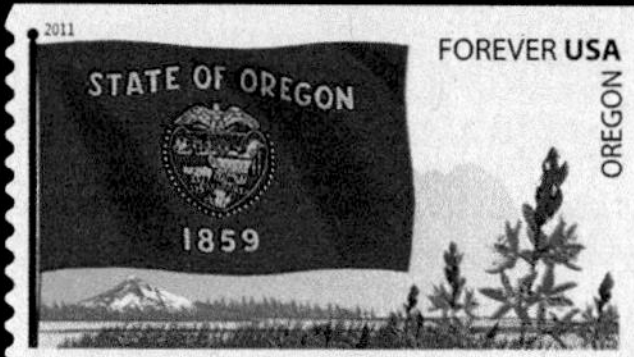

Oregon Flag, Mount Hood and Camas Lilies
A3279

Pennsylvania Flag and White-tailed Deer — A3280

Puerto Rico Flag and Puerto Rican Tody Bird
A3281

Rhode Island Flag and Sailboat
A3282

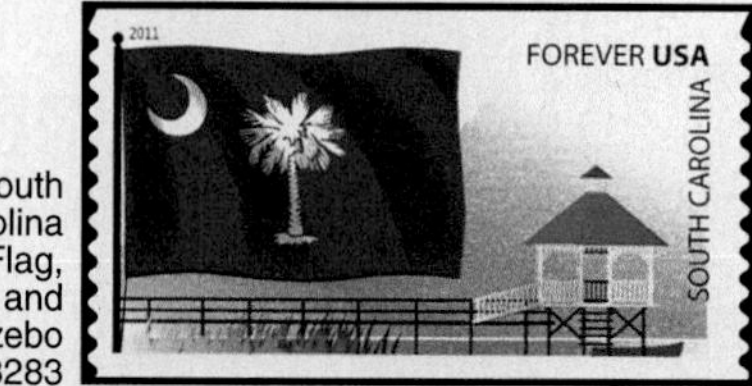

South Carolina Flag, Marsh and Gazebo
A3283

South Dakota Flag and Bison
A3284

Tennessee Flag and Scarlet Tanagers
A3285

Designed by Howard E. Paine. Printed by American Packaging Corp. for Sennett Security Products.

PHOTOGRAVURE

Serpentine Die Cut 11 Vert.

2011, Aug. 11 **Tagged**

Self-Adhesive

Coil Stamps

4313	A3276	(44c)	**multicolored**	1.50	.30
4314	A3277	(44c)	**multicolored**	1.50	.30
4315	A3278	(44c)	**multicolored**	1.50	.30
4316	A3279	(44c)	**multicolored**	1.50	.30
4317	A3280	(44c)	**multicolored**	1.50	.30
a.			Strip of 5, #4313-4317	7.50	
4318	A3281	(44c)	**multicolored**	1.50	.30
4319	A3282	(44c)	**multicolored**	1.50	.30
4320	A3283	(44c)	**multicolored**	1.50	.30
4321	A3284	(44c)	**multicolored**	1.50	.30
4322	A3285	(44c)	**multicolored**	1.50	.30
a.			Strip of 5, #4318-4322	7.50	
b.			P# set of 10, #4317a + 4322a	12.50	
			P# strip of 11, #4313-4317, 4319-4322, 2 #4318, P#S111111111	15.00	
			P# strip of 21, 3 #4313, 2 each #4314-4322, #S111111111	32.50	—
			P# single (#4313), same #	—	2.75

Alternating examples of the five examples of No. 4313 in the roll have a plate number. No. 4322b may be collected as one continuous strip, but the item will not fit in any standard album.

Texas Flag, Cotton Plant and Field
A3286

Utah Flag, Cactus and Rock Arch
A3287

Vermont Flag and Owls
A3288

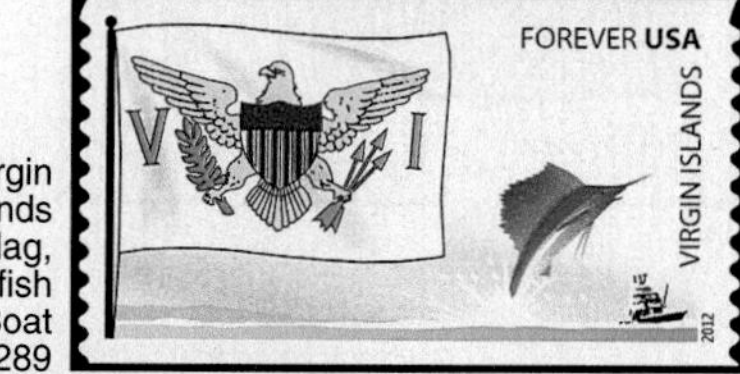

Virgin Islands Flag, Sailfish and Boat
A3289

Virginia Flag and Replicas of Ships that Carried Settlers to Jamestown — A3290

Washington Flag and Evergreen Forest — A3291

West Virginia Flag and Wild Turkeys A3292

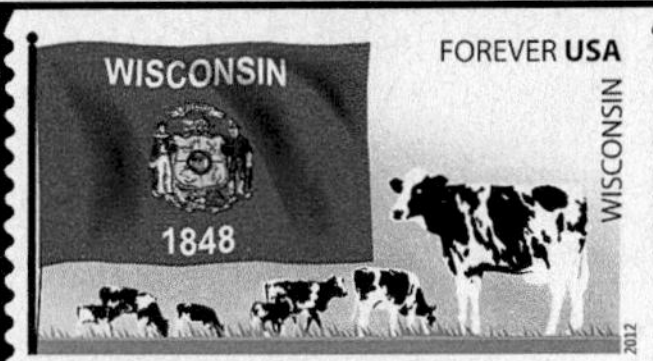

Wisconsin Flag and Dairy Cows A3293

Wyoming Flag and Bighorn Sheep A3294

American Flag and Fruited Plain A3295

Designed by Howard E. Paine. Printed by American Packaging Corp. for Sennett Security Products.

PHOTOGRAVURE

Serpentine Die Cut 11 Vert.

2012, Aug. 16 **Tagged**

Self-Adhesive

Coil Stamps

4323	A3286 (45c) **multicolored**		3.00	.30
4324	A3287 (45c) **multicolored**		3.00	.30
4325	A3288 (45c) **multicolored**		3.00	.30
4326	A3289 (45c) **multicolored**		3.00	.30
4327	A3290 (45c) **multicolored**		3.00	.30
a.	Strip of 5, #4323-4327		15.00	
4328	A3291 (45c) **multicolored**		3.00	.30
4329	A3292 (45c) **multicolored**		3.00	.30
4330	A3293 (45c) **multicolored**		3.00	.30
4331	A3294 (45c) **multicolored**		3.00	.30
4332	A3295 (45c) **multicolored**		3.00	.30
a.	Strip of 5, #4328-4332		15.00	
b.	P# set of 10, #4327a + 4332a		30.00	
	P# strip of 11, #4323-4327, 4329-4332, 2 #4328, P#S11111111		32.50	
	P# strip of 21, 3 #4323, 2 each #4324-4332, #S11111111		60.00	—
	P# single (#4323), same #		—	2.75

Alternating examples of the five examples of No. 4323 in the roll have a plate number. No. 4332b may be collected as one continuous strip, but the item will not fit in any standard album.

CHARLES (1907-78) AND RAY (1912-88) EAMES, DESIGNERS Ⓢ

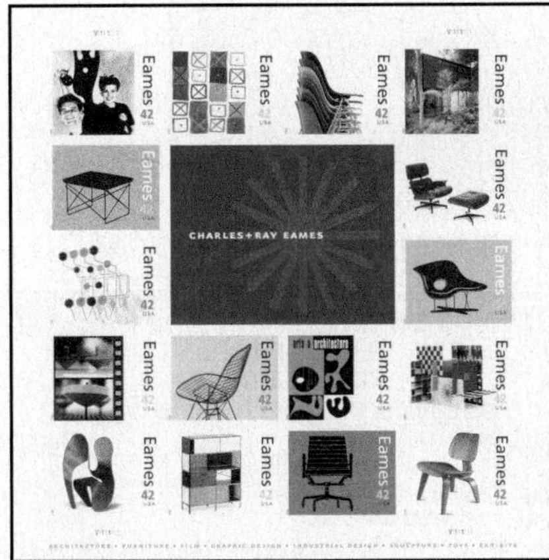

A3296

Illustration reduced.

Designed by Derry Noyes. Printed by Avery Dennison.

No. 4333: a, Christmas card depicting Charles and Ray Eames. b, "Crosspatch" fabric design. c, Stacking chairs. d, Case Study House #8, Pacific Palisades, CA. e, Wire-base table. f, Lounge chair and ottoman. g, Hang-it-all. h, La Chaise. i, Scene from film, "Tops." j, Wire mesh chair. k, Cover of May 1943 edition of *California Arts & Architecture* Magazine. l, House of Cards. m, Molded plywood sculpture. n, Eames Storage Unit. o, Aluminum group chair. p, Molded plywood chair.

PHOTOGRAVURE

Sheets of 160 in ten panes of 16

Serpentine Die Cut 10¾x10½

2008, June 17 **Tagged**

Self-Adhesive

4333	A3296 Pane of 16 + label	18.00	
a.-p.	42c Any single	1.10	.50

See note after No. 1549.

SUMMER OLYMPIC GAMES, BEIJING, CHINA

Gymnast A3297

Designed by Clarence Lee. Printed by Banknote Corporation of America for Sennett Security Products.

LITHOGRAPHED

Sheets of 180 in nine panes of 20

2008, June 19 **Tagged** ***Serpentine Die Cut 10¾***

Self-Adhesive

4334	A3297 42c **multicolored**	.85	.25
	P# block of 4, 6#+S	3.40	
	Pane of 20	17.00	

Celebrate — A3297a

Designed by Ethel Kessler. Printed by Banknote Corporation of America for Sennett Security Products.

LITHOGRAPHED

Sheets of 240 in twelve panes of 20

2008, July 10 **Tagged** ***Serpentine Die Cut 10¾***

Self-Adhesive

4335	A3297a 42c **multicolored**	.85	.25
	P# block of 4, 4# + S	3.40	
	Pane of 20	17.00	

See Nos 4196, 4407.

VINTAGE BLACK CINEMA Ⓢ

Poster for "Black and Tan" — A3298

Poster for "The Sport of the Gods" — A3299

Poster for "Prinsesse Tam-Tam" — A3300

Poster for "Caldonia" — A3301

Poster for "Hallelujah" — A3302

Designed by Carl T. Herrman. Printed by Ashton-Potter (USA) Ltd.

LITHOGRAPHED

Sheets of 120 in six panes of 20

2008, July 16 **Tagged** ***Serpentine Die Cut 10¾***

Self-Adhesive

4336	A3298 42c **multicolored**	.95	.45
4337	A3299 42c **multicolored**	.95	.45
4338	A3300 42c **multicolored**	.95	.45
4339	A3301 42c **multicolored**	.95	.45
4340	A3302 42c **multicolored**	.95	.45
a.	Horiz. strip of 5, #4336-4340	4.75	
	P# block of 10, 2 sets of 4# + P	9.50	
	Pane of 20	19.00	

Plate block may contain top label.

Uncut press sheets of Nos. 4336-4340 were made available for sale. Values: cross-gutter block of 8, $19; pairs with gutters between, $2.75 each. See note after No. 2868.

See note after No. 1549.

"TAKE ME OUT TO THE BALLGAME," CENT.

Baseball Players and First Six Notes of Song — A3303

Designed by Richard Sheaff. Printed by Avery Dennison.

PHOTOGRAVURE
Sheets of 200 in ten panes of 20

2008, July 16 Tagged *Serpentine Die Cut 11*

Self-Adhesive

4341 A3303 42c **multicolored** .85 .25
P# block of 4, 4# + V 3.40
Pane of 20 17.00

THE ART OF DISNEY: IMAGINATION Ⓢ

Pongo and Pup — A3304

Steamboat Willie — A3305

Princess Aurora, Flora, Fauna and Merryweather A3306

Mowgli and Baloo — A3307

Designed by David Pacheco. Printed by Avery Dennison.

PHOTOGRAVURE
Sheets of 160 in eight panes of 20

Serpentine Die Cut 10½x10¾

2008, Aug. 7 Tagged

Self-Adhesive

4342 A3304 42c **multicolored** .85 .30
4343 A3305 42c **multicolored** .85 .30
4344 A3306 42c **multicolored** .85 .30
4345 A3307 42c **multicolored** .85 .30
a. Block or strip of 4, #4342-4345 3.40
P# block of 4, 6#+V 3.40
P# block of 10, 2 sets of P# + top label 8.50
Pane of 20 17.00

See note after No. 1549.

AMERICAN TREASURES SERIES

Valley of the Yosemite, by Albert Bierstadt A3308

Designed by Derry Noyes. Printed by Banknote Corporation of America for Sennett Security Products.

LITHOGRAPHED
BOOKLET STAMP

Serpentine Die Cut 11 on 2 or 3 Sides

2008, Aug. 14 Tagged

Self-Adhesive

4346 A3308 42c **multicolored** .85 .25
a. Booklet pane of 20 17.00

No. 4346a is a double-sided booklet pane with 12 stamps on one side and eight stamps plus label (booklet cover) on the other side.

Sunflower — A3309

Designed by Derry Noyes. Printed by Ashton-Potter (USA) Ltd.

LITHOGRAPHED
BOOKLET STAMP

Serpentine Die Cut 11¼x10¾ on 2 or 3 Sides

2008, Aug. 15 Tagged

Self-Adhesive

4347 A3309 42c **multicolored** Ⓢ .85 .25
a. Booklet pane of 20 17.00

No. 4347a is a double-sided booklet pane with 12 stamps on one side and eight stamps plus label (booklet cover) on the other side.

See note after No. 1549.

Sea Coast — A3309a

Designed by Tom Engeman. Printed by Banknote Corporation of America for Sennett Security Products.

LITHOGRAPHED
COIL STAMP

2008, Sept. 5 Untagged *Perf. 9¾ Vert.*

4348 A3309a (5c) **multicolored** .30 .25
Pair .50 —
P# strip of 5, #S11111 1.50
P# single, #S11111 1.10

No. 4348 has "2008" year date in black, and microprinted "USPS" at the end of the purple rock to the right of the crashing wave.

See Nos. 3693, 3775, 3785, 3864, 3874-3875.

LATIN JAZZ Ⓢ

Musicians A3310

Designed by Richard Sheaff. Printed by Avery Dennison.

PHOTOGRAVURE
Sheets of 200 in ten panes of 20

Serpentine Die Cut 11x10¾

2008, Sept. 8 Tagged

Self-Adhesive

4349 A3310 42c **multicolored** .85 .25
P# block of 4, 4#+V 3.75
Pane of 20 19.00

See note after No. 1549.

LEGENDS OF HOLLYWOOD

Bette Davis (1908-89), Actress — A3311

Designed by Richard Sheaff. Printed by Ashton-Potter (USA) Ltd.

LITHOGRAPHED
Sheets of 180 in nine panes of 20

2008, Sept. 18 Tagged *Serpentine Die Cut 10¾*

Self-Adhesive

4350 A3311 42c **multicolored** Ⓢ 1.00 .25
P# block of 4, 4#+P 4.00
Pane of 20 20.00

Uncut press sheets of No. 4350 were made available for sale. Values: cross-gutter block of 8, $20; pairs with gutters between, $3 each. See note after No. 2868.

See note after No. 1549.

Eid — A3311a

Designed by Mohamed Zakariya. Printed by Avery Dennison.

PHOTOGRAVURE
Sheets of 240 in twelve panes of 20

2008, Sept. 23 Tagged *Serpentine Die Cut 11*

Self-Adhesive

4351 A3311a 42c **multicolored** .85 .25
P# block of 4, 3#+V 3.40
Pane of 20 17.00

See Nos. 3532, 3674, 4117, 4202, 4416.

GREAT LAKES DUNES

A3312

Illustration reduced.
Designed by Ethel Kessler. Printed by Avery Dennison.

No. 4352 — Wildlife: a, Vesper sparrow. b, Red fox, vert. c, Piping plover. d, Eastern hognose snake. e, Common mergansers. f, Spotted sandpiper, vert. g, Tiger beetle, vert. h, White-footed mouse, vert. i, Piping plover nestlings. j, Red admiral butterfly, vert.

PHOTOGRAVURE
Sheets of 80 in eight panes of 10

2008, Oct. 2 Tagged *Serpentine Die Cut 10¾*
Self-Adhesive

4352 A3312	Pane of 10	10.00	
a.-j.	42c Any single	1.00	.40

Uncut press sheets of No. 4352 were made available for sale.
See note after No. 2868.

AUTOMOBILES OF THE 1950s

1959 Cadillac Eldorado A3313

1957 Studebaker Golden Hawk A3314

1957 Pontiac Safari A3315

1957 Lincoln Premiere A3316

1957 Chrysler 300C A3317

Designed by Carl T. Herrman. Printed by Banknote Corporation of America for Sennett Security Products.

LITHOGRAPHED
Sheets of 180 in nine panes of 20

2008, Oct. 3 Tagged *Serpentine Die Cut 10¾*
Self-Adhesive

4353 A3313	42c **multicolored**	.85	.45
4354 A3314	42c **multicolored**	.85	.45
4355 A3315	42c **multicolored**	.85	.45
4356 A3316	42c **multicolored**	.85	.45
4357 A3317	42c **multicolored**	.85	.45
a.	Vert. strip of 5, #4353-4357	4.25	
	Vert. P# block of 10, 2 sets of 4# + S	8.50	
	Horiz. P# block of 8, 2 sets of 4# + S	7.00	
	Pane of 20	17.00	

ALZHEIMER'S DISEASE AWARENESS Ⓢ

A3318

Designed by Ethel Kessler. Printed by Avery Dennison.

PHOTOGRAVURE
Sheets of 240 in twelve panes of 20

2008, Oct. 17 Tagged *Serpentine Die Cut 10¾*
Self-Adhesive

4358 A3318	42c **multicolored**	.85	.25
	P# block of 4, 6#+V	3.50	
	Pane of 20	17.50	

See note after No. 1549.

CHRISTMAS

Virgin and Child with the Young John the Baptist, by Sandro Botticelli — A3319

Drummer Nutcracker — A3320

Santa Claus Nutcracker — A3321

King Nutcracker — A3322

Soldier Nutcracker — A3323

Designed by Richard Sheaff (#4359), Derry Noyes.
Printed by Ashton-Potter (USA) Ltd. (#4359), Banknote Corporation of America for Sennett Security Products (#4360-4367).

LITHOGRAPHED

Serpentine Die Cut 10¾x11 on 2 or 3 Sides
2008, Oct. 23 Tagged
Self-Adhesive
Booklet Stamps

4359 A3319	42c **multicolored** Ⓢ	.85	.25
a.	Booklet pane of 20	17.00	
b.	Die cutting omitted, pair	—	
4360 A3320	42c **multicolored**	1.00	.25
4361 A3321	42c **multicolored**	1.00	.25
4362 A3322	42c **multicolored**	1.00	.25
4363 A3323	42c **multicolored**	1.00	.25
a.	Block of 4, #4360-4363	4.00	
b.	Booklet pane of 20, 5 each #4360-4363	20.00	

No. 4359a is a double-sided booklet pane with 12 stamps on one side and eight stamps plus label that serves as a booklet cover on the other side. No. 4363b is a double-sided booklet pane with 12 stamps on one side (3 each of Nos. 4360-4363) and eight stamps (2 each of Nos. 4360-4363) plus label that serves as a booklet cover on the other side.
See note after No. 1549.

Drummer Nutcracker — A3324

Santa Claus Nutcracker — A3325

King Nutcracker — A3326

Soldier Nutcracker — A3327

Designed by Derry Noyes.
Printed by Banknote Corporation of America for Sennett Security Products.

Serpentine Die Cut 11¼x11 on 2 or 3 Sides

4364 A3324	42c **multicolored**	1.25	.25
4365 A3325	42c **multicolored**	1.25	.25
4366 A3326	42c **multicolored**	1.25	.25
4367 A3327	42c **multicolored**	1.25	.25
a.	Block of 4, #4364-4367	5.00	
b.	Booklet pane of 4, #4364-4367	5.00	
c.	Booklet pane of 6, #4366-4367, 2 each #4364-4365	7.50	
d.	Booklet pane of 6, #4364-4365, 2 each #4366-4367	7.50	

A3324a

A3325a

A3326a

A3327a

Designed by Derry Noyes.
Printed by Avery Dennison.

Serpentine Die Cut 8 on 2, 3 or 4 Sides

PHOTOGRAVURE

4368 A3324a	42c **multicolored** Ⓢ	1.25	.25
4369 A3325a	42c **multicolored** Ⓢ	1.25	.25
4370 A3326a	42c **multicolored** Ⓢ	1.25	.25
4371 A3327a	42c **multicolored** Ⓢ	1.25	.25
a.	Block or strip of 4, #4368-4371	5.00	
b.	Booklet pane of 18, 5 each #4368-4369, 4 each #4370-4371	22.50	
	Nos. 4359-4371 (13)	14.85	3.25

See note after No. 1549.

Hanukkah — A3327a

Designed by Ethel Kessler. Printed by Banknote Corporation of America for Sennett Security Products.

LITHOGRAPHED
Sheets of 240 in twelve panes of 20
Serpentine Die Cut 10¾x11

2008, Oct. 24 **Tagged**

Self-Adhesive

4372	A3327a 42c **multicolored**	.85	.25
	P# block of 4, 4#+S	3.40	
	Pane of 20	17.00	

See Nos. 3880, 4118, 4219.

Kwanzaa — A3327b

Designed by Derry Noyes. Printed by Ashton-Potter (USA) Ltd.

LITHOGRAPHED
Sheets of 160 in eight panes of 20
Serpentine Die Cut 11x10¾

2008, Oct. 24 **Tagged**

Self-Adhesive

4373	A3327b 42c **multicolored** Ⓢ	.85	.25
	P# block of 4, 6#+P	3.40	
	Pane of 20	17.00	

See note after No. 1549. See Nos. 3881, 4119, 4220.

ALASKA STATEHOOD, 50TH ANNIV.

Dogsledder Near Rainy Pass — A3328

Designed by Phil Jordan. Printed by Banknote Corporation of America for Sennett Security Products.

LITHOGRAPHED
Sheets of 180 in nine panes of 20

2009, Jan. 3 **Tagged** ***Serpentine Die Cut 10¾***

Self-Adhesive

4374	A3328 42c **multicolored**	.85	.25
	P# block of 4, 4#+S	3.40	
	Pane of 20	17.00	

CHINESE NEW YEAR

Year of the Ox — A3329

Designed by Ethel Kessler. Printed by Banknote Corporation of America for Sennett Security Products.

LITHOGRAPHED
Sheets of 108 in nine panes of 12

2009, Jan. 8 **Tagged** ***Serpentine Die Cut 10¾***

Self-Adhesive

4375	A3329 42c **multicolored**	.85	.25
	Pane of 12	10.50	

Uncut press sheets of No. 4375 were made available for sale. Values: cross-gutter block of 4, $9; pairs with gutters between, $2.25 each. See note after No. 2868.

OREGON STATEHOOD, 150TH ANNIV.

Pacific Coast of Oregon A3330

Designed by Derry Noyes. Printed by Banknote Corporation of America for Sennett Security Products.

LITHOGRAPHED
Sheets of 180 in nine panes of 20

2009, Jan. 14 **Tagged** ***Serpentine Die Cut 10¾***

Self-Adhesive

4376	A3330 42c **multicolored**	.85	.25
	P# block of 4, 5# + S	3.40	
	Pane of 20	17.00	

EDGAR ALLAN POE Ⓢ

Edgar Allan Poe (1809-49), Writer — A3331

Designed by Carl T. Herrman. Printed by Avery Dennison.

PHOTOGRAVURE
Sheets of 160 in eight panes of 20

2009, Jan. 16 **Tagged** ***Serpentine Die Cut 10¾***

Self-Adhesive

4377	A3331 42c **multicolored**	.90	.25
	P# block of 4, 5# + V	5.00	
	Pane of 20	23.50	

See note after No. 1549.

AMERICAN LANDMARKS

Redwood Forest A3332

Old Faithful A3333

Designed by Carl T. Herrman. Printed by Ashton-Potter (USA) Ltd.

LITHOGRAPHED
Sheets of 180 in nine panes of 20
Serpentine Die Cut 10¾x10½

2009, Jan. 16 **Tagged**

Self-Adhesive

4378	A3332 $4.95 **multicolored** Ⓢ	11.00	5.00
	P# block of 4, 4# + P	45.00	
	Pane of 20	220.00	
4379	A3333 $17.50 **multicolored** Ⓢ	40.00	20.00
	P# block of 4, 4# + P	160.00	
	Pane of 20	800.00	

See note after No. 1549.

ABRAHAM LINCOLN (1809-65), 16TH PRESIDENT
Ⓢ

Lincoln as Rail-splitter A3334

Lincoln as Lawyer A3335

Lincoln as Politician A3336

Lincoln as President A3337

Designed by Richard Sheaff. Printed by Ashton-Potter (USA) Ltd.

LITHOGRAPHED
Sheets of 120 in six panes of 20

2009, Feb. 9 **Tagged** ***Serpentine Die Cut 10¾***

Self-Adhesive

4380	A3334 42c **multicolored**	1.50	.35
4381	A3335 42c **multicolored**	1.50	.35
4382	A3336 42c **multicolored**	1.50	.35
4383	A3337 42c **multicolored**	1.50	.35
a.	Horiz. strip of 4, #4380-4383	6.00	
	P# block of 8, 2 sets of 4# + P	12.00	
	Pane of 20	28.00	

Uncut press sheets of Nos. 4380-4383 were made available for sale. Values: cross-gutter block of 8, $27.50; pairs with gutters between, $4 each. See note after No. 2868.

See note after No. 1549.

CIVIL RIGHTS PIONEERS Ⓢ

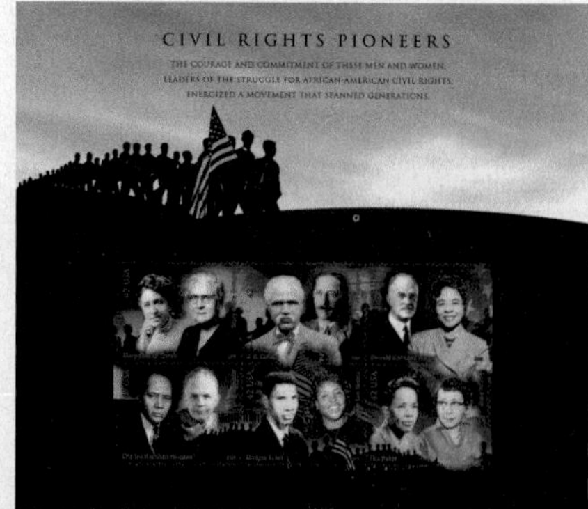

A3338

Illustration reduced.

Designed by Greg Berger. Printed by Avery Dennison.

No. 4384: a, Mary Church Terrell (1863-1954), writer, Mary White Ovington (1865-1951), journalist. b, J. R. Clifford (1848-1933), attorney, Joel Elias Spingarn (1875-1939), educator. c, Oswald Garrison Villard (1872-1949), co-founder of National Association for the Advancement of Colored People (NAACP), Daisy Gatson Bates (1914-99), mentor of black Little Rock Central High School students. d, Charles Hamilton Houston (1895-

1950), lawyer, Walter White (1893-1955), chief secretary of NAACP. e, Medgar Evers (1925-63), assassinated Mississippi NAACP field secretary, Fannie Lou Hamer (1917-77), voting rights activist. f, Ella Baker (1903-86), activist, Ruby Hurley (1909-80), NAACP Southeast Regional Director.

PHOTOGRAVURE

Sheets of 48 in eight panes of 6

2009, Feb. 21 Tagged *Serpentine Die Cut 10¾*

Self-Adhesive

4384 A3338 Pane of 6 9.00
a.-f. 42c Any single 1.50 .40

See note after No. 1549.

Patriotic Banner — A3338a

Designed by Michael Osborne. Printed by Banknote Corporation of America for Sennett Security Products.

LITHOGRAPHED
COIL STAMP

2009, Feb. 24 Untagged *Perf. 9¾ Vert.*

4385 A3338a (10c) **multicolored** .30 .25
Pair .40 —
P# strip of 5, #S111 2.50 —
P# single, #S111 — 2.10

See Nos. 4157-4158.

LITERARY ARTS

Richard Wright (1908-60), Author A3339

Designed by Carl T. Herrman. Printed by Ashton-Potter (USA) Ltd.

LITHOGRAPHED

Sheets of 120 in six panes of 20

2009, Apr. 9 Tagged *Serpentine Die Cut 10¾*

Self-Adhesive

4386 A3339 61c **multicolored** ⓢ 1.25 .25
P# block of 4, 6# + P 5.00
Pane of 20 25.00

See note after No. 1549.

WILDLIFE

Polar Bear — A3340

A3340a

Dolphin — A3341

Designed by Carl T. Herrman. Printed by Banknote Corporation of America for Sennett Security Products (#4387), Avery Dennison (#4388, 4389)

LITHOGRAPHED (#4387), PHOTOGRAVURE

Sheets of 300 in 15 panes of 20 or sheets of 200 in 10 panes of 20 (#4387)

Sheets of 280 in 14 panes of 20 (#4388)

2009 Tagged *Serpentine Die Cut 11¼x11*

Self-Adhesive

4387 A3340 28c **multicolored,** *Apr. 16* .75 .25
P# block of 4, 4# + S 3.00
Pane of 20 15.00
a. Die cutting omitted, pane of 20 *7,250.*

Serpentine Die Cut 11

4388 A3341 64c **multicolored,** *June 12* ⓢ 1.40 .25
P# block of 4, 5#+V 5.60
Pane of 20 28.00

COIL STAMP

Serpentine Die Cut 8½ Vert.

4389 A3340a 28c **multicolored,** *Apr. 16* ⓢ .60 .25
P# strip of 5, #V11111 4.25
P# single, #V11111 — 2.00

See note after No. 1549.

Purple Heart — A3341a

Designed by Carl T. Herrman. Printed by Ashton-Potter (USA) Ltd.

LITHOGRAPHED

Sheets of 120 in six panes of 20

Serpentine Die Cut 11¼x10¾

2009, Apr. 28 Tagged

Self-Adhesive

4390 A3341a 44c **multicolored** ⓢ .90 .25
P# block of 4, 4#+P 3.60
Pane of 20 18.00

See Nos. 3784-3784A, 4032, 4164, 4263-4264.

Counterfeits exist of No. 4390. See the Postal Counterfeits section of this catalog.

See note after No. 1549.

Flag — A3342

Designed by Terrence W. McCaffrey. Printed by Banknote Corporation of America for Sennett Security Products.

LITHOGRAPHED

2009 Tagged *Perf. 9¾ Vert.*

COIL STAMPS

4391 A3342 44c **multicolored,** *May 1* 1.00 1.00
Pair 2.00
P# strip of 5, #S111 6.25
P# single, #S111 — 3.50

A3342a

A3342b

A3342c

A3342d

Printed by Banknote Corporation of America for Sennett Security Products (#4392), Ashton-Potter (USA) Ltd. (#4393), Avery Dennison (#4394-4395).

Self-Adhesive

Serpentine Die Cut 11 Vert.

With Pointed Corners

4392 A3342a 44c **multicolored,** *May 8* 2.00 .25
Pair 4.00
P# strip of 5, #S111 12.50
P# single, #S111 — 2.50
a. Die cutting omitted, pair *350.00*

Counterfeits exist of No. 4392. See the Postal Counterfeits section of this catalog.

Serpentine Die Cut 9½ Vert.

Designed by Ashton-Potter (USA) Ltd.

4393 A3342b 44c **multicolored,** *May 8* ⓢ 1.50 .25
Pair 3.00
P# strip of 5, #P1111 8.00
P# single, #P1111 — 2.50

Counterfeits exist of No. 4393. See the Postal Counterfeits section of this catalog.

Serpentine Die Cut 8½ Vert.

PHOTOGRAVURE

Designed by Avery Dennison (#4394, 4395, 4396).

4394 A3342c 44c **multicolored,** *May 8* ⓢ 1.50 .25
Pair 3.00
P# strip of 5, #V1111 8.00
P# single, #V1111 — 2.50

Counterfeits exist of No. 4394. See the Postal Counterfeits section of this catalog.

Serpentine Die Cut 11 Vert.

With Rounded Corners

4395 A3342d 44c **multicolored,** *May 1* ⓢ 1.25 .25
Pair 2.50
P# strip of 5, #V1111 6.75
P# single, #V1111 — 2.00

A3342e

Printed by Avery Dennison.

BOOKLET STAMP

Serpentine Die Cut 11¼x10¾ on 3 Sides

4396 A3342e 44c **multicolored,** *June 5* ⓢ .90 .25
a. Booklet pane of 10 9.00

Nos. 4392-4394 are on backing paper as high as the stamp. No. 4395 is on backing paper that is taller than the stamp. No. 4393 has microprinted "USPS" on white stripe below the blue field.

See note after No. 1549.

WEDDINGS

Wedding Rings — A3343

Wedding Cake — A3344

Designed by Ethel Kessler. Printed by Banknote Corporation of America for Sennett Security Products (#4397), Avery Dennison (#4398)

LITHOGRAPHED, PHOTOGRAVURE (#4398)

Sheets of 160 in eight panes of 20, Sheets of 240 in twelve panes of 20 (#4398)

2009, May 1 Tagged *Serpentine Die Cut 10¾*

Self-Adhesive

4397 A3343 44c **multicolored** .90 .25
P# block of 4, 5#+S 3.60
Pane of 20 18.00
4398 A3344 61c **multicolored** ⓢ 1.40 .25
P# block of 4, 6#+V 5.60
Pane of 20 28.00

See Nos. 4521, 4602, 4735, 4867, 5000.

See note after No. 1549.

THE SIMPSONS TELEVISION SHOW, 20TH ANNIV.

Homer Simpson — A3345

Marge Simpson — A3346

Bart Simpson — A3347

Lisa Simpson — A3348

Maggie Simpson — A3349

Designed by Matt Groening. Printed by Banknote Corporation of America for Sennett Security Products.

LITHOGRAPHED
BOOKLET STAMPS

Serpentine Die Cut 10¾ on 2, 3 or 4 Sides

2009, May 7 **Tagged**

Self-Adhesive

4399	A3345 44c **multicolored**		1.15	.40
4400	A3346 44c **multicolored**		1.15	.40
4401	A3347 44c **multicolored**		1.15	.40
4402	A3348 44c **multicolored**		1.15	.40
4403	A3349 44c **multicolored**		1.15	.40
	a.	Horiz. strip of 5, #4399-4403	5.75	
	b.	Booklet pane of 20, 4 each #4399-4403	23.00	

LOVE

King of Hearts — A3350

Queen of Hearts — A3351

Designed by Jeanne Greco. Printed by Avery Dennison.

PHOTOGRAVURE
BOOKLET STAMPS

Serpentine Die Cut 10¾ on 2, 3 or 4 Sides

2009, May 8 **Tagged**

Self-Adhesive

4404	A3350 44c **multicolored** ⓢ		1.15	.25
4405	A3351 44c **multicolored** ⓢ		1.15	.25
	a.	Horiz. or vert. pair, #4404-4405	2.30	
	b.	Booklet pane of 20, 10 each #4404-4405	23.00	

See note after No. 1549.

BOB HOPE Ⓢ

Bob Hope (1903-2003), Actor, Comedian — A3352

Designed by Derry Noyes. Printed by Ashton-Potter (USA) Ltd.

LITHOGRAPHED
Sheets of 180 in nine panes of 20

2009, May 29 **Tagged** ***Serpentine Die Cut 10¾***

Self-Adhesive

4406 A3352 44c **multicolored**		1.00	.25
	P# block of 4, 4#+P	4.00	
	Pane of 20	20.00	

Uncut press sheets of No. 4406 were made available for sale. Values: cross-gutter block of 8, $20; pairs with gutters between, $2.50 each. See note after No. 2868.
See note after No. 1549.

Celebrate — A3352a

Designed by Ethel Kessler. Printed by Banknote Corporation of America for Sennett Security Products.

LITHOGRAPHED
Sheets of 240 in twelve panes of 20

2009, June 10 **Tagged** ***Serpentine Die Cut 10¾***

Self-Adhesive

4407	A3352a 44c **multicolored**		.90	.25
		P# block of 4, 4#+S	3.60	
		Pane of 20	18.00	
	a.	Die cutting omitted, pair	*175.00*	

See Nos. 4196, 4335.

BLACK HERITAGE

Anna Julia Cooper (c. 1858-1964), Educator — A3353

Designed by Ethel Kessler. Printed by Ashton-Potter (USA) Ltd.

LITHOGRAPHED
Sheets of 120 in six panes of 20

2009, June 11 **Tagged** ***Serpentine Die Cut 10¾***

Self-Adhesive

4408 A3353 44c **multicolored** ⓢ		.90	.25
	P# block of 4, 5#+P	3.60	
	Pane of 20	18.00	

See note after No. 1549.

GULF COAST LIGHTHOUSES Ⓢ

Matagorda Island Lighthouse, Texas — A3354

Sabine Pass Lighthouse, Louisiana — A3355

Biloxi Lighthouse, Mississippi — A3356

Sand Island Lighthouse, Alabama — A3357

Fort Jefferson Lighthouse, Florida — A3358

Designed by Howard E. Paine. Printed by Ashton-Potter (USA) Ltd.

LITHOGRAPHED
Sheets of 120 in six panes of 20

Serpentine Die Cut 11x10¾

2009, July 23 **Tagged**

Self-Adhesive

4409	A3354 44c **multicolored**		.90	.40
4410	A3355 44c **multicolored**		.90	.40
4411	A3356 44c **multicolored**		.90	.40
4412	A3357 44c **multicolored**		.90	.40
4413	A3358 44c **multicolored**		.90	.40
	a.	Horiz. strip of 5, #4409-4413	4.50	
		P# block of 10, 2 sets of 4#+P	10.00	
		Pane of 20	19.00	

Plate block may contain top label.
See note after No. 1549.

EARLY TV MEMORIES

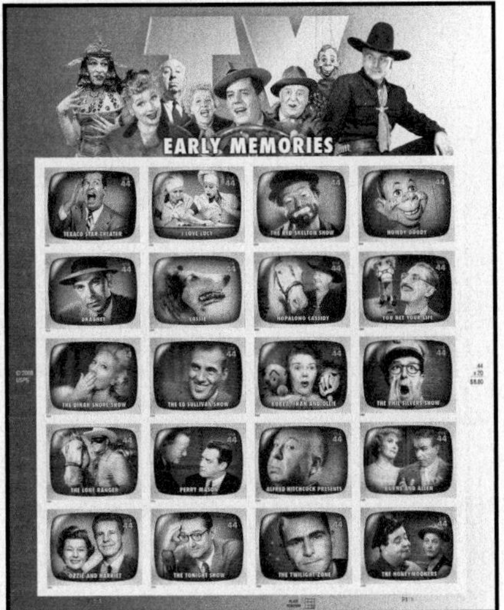

A3359

Illustration reduced.
Designed by Carl T. Herrman. Printed by Ashton-Potter (USA) Ltd.

No. 4414: a, Milton Berle in "Texaco Star Theater." b, Lucille Ball and Vivian Vance in "I Love Lucy." c, Red Skelton in "The Red Skelton Show." d, Marionette Howdy Doody in "Howdy Doody." e, Jack Webb in "Dragnet." f, Lassie in "Lassie." g, William Boyd and horse, Topper, in "Hopalong Cassidy." h, Groucho Marx in "You Bet Your Life." i, Dinah Shore in "The Dinah Shore Show." j, Ed Sullivan in "The Ed Sullivan Show." k, Fran Allison and puppets, Kukla and Ollie in "Kukla, Fran and Ollie." l, Phil Silvers in "The Phil Silvers Show." m, Clayton Moore and horse, Silver, in "The Lone Ranger." n, Raymond Burr and William Talman in "Perry Mason." o, Alfred Hitchcock in "Alfred Hitchcock Presents." p, George Burns and Gracie Allen in "Burns and Allen." q, Ozzie and Harriet Nelson in "Ozzie and Harriet." r, Steve Allen in "The Tonight Show." s, Rod Serling in "The Twilight Zone." t, Jackie Gleason and Art Carney in "The Honeymooners."

LITGHOGRAPHED
Sheets of 180 in nine panes of 20
Serpentine Die Cut 10¾x10½

2009, Aug. 11 **Tagged**

Self-Adhesive

4414 A3359 Pane of 20	20.00	
a.-t. 44c Any single	1.00	.50

Uncut press sheets of No. 4414 were made available for sale. Values: cross-gutter block of 20, $30; pairs with gutters between, $3.75 each. See note after No. 2868.
See note after No. 1549.

HAWAII STATEHOOD, 50TH ANNIV.

Surfer and Outrigger Canoe A3360

Designed by Phil Jordan. Printed by Avery Dennison.

PHOTOGRAVURE
Sheets of 200 in ten panes of 20

2009, Aug. 21 **Tagged** ***Serpentine Die Cut 11***

Self-Adhesive

4415 A3360 44c **multicolored**	1.25	.25
P# block of 4, 4#+V	7.00	
Pane of 20	28.00	

See note after No. 1549.

Eid — A3360a

Designed by Mohamed Zakariya. Printed by Avery Dennison.

PHOTOGRAVURE
Sheets of 240 in twelve panes of 20

2009, Sept. 3 **Tagged** ***Serpentine Die Cut 11***

Self-Adhesive

4416 A3360a 44c **multicolored** Ⓢ	.90	.25
P# block of 4, 3#+V	3.60	
Pane of 20	18.00	

See note after No. 1549.
See Nos. 3532, 3674, 4117, 4202, 4351.

THANKSGIVING DAY PARADE

Crowd, Street Sign, Bear Balloon A3361

Drum Major, Musicians A3362

Musicians, Balloon, Horse A3363

Cowboy, Turkey Balloon, Crowd, Television Cameraman A3364

Designed by Howard E. Paine. Printed by Avery Dennison.

PHOTOGRAVURE
Sheets of 200 in ten panes of 20
Serpentine Die Cut 11x10¾

2009, Sept. 9 **Tagged**

Self-Adhesive

4417 A3361 44c **multicolored**	.90	.35
4418 A3362 44c **multicolored**	.90	.35
4419 A3363 44c **multicolored**	.90	.35
4420 A3364 44c **multicolored**	.90	.35
a. Horiz. strip of 4, #4417-4420	3.60	
P# block of 8, 2 sets of 6#+V	8.75	
Pane of 20	19.00	

See note after No. 1549.

LEGENDS OF HOLLYWOOD

Gary Cooper (1901-61), Actor — A3365

Designed by Phil Jordan. Printed by Avery Dennison.

PHOTOGRAVURE
Sheets of 160 in eight panes of 20

2009, Sept. 10 **Tagged** ***Serpentine Die Cut 11***

Self-Adhesive

4421 A3365 44c **multicolored** Ⓢ	1.00	.25
P# block of 4, 4#+V	4.00	
Pane of 20	20.00	

Uncut press sheets of No. 4421 were made available for sale. Values: cross-gutter block of 8, $20; pairs with gutters between, $3 each. See note after No. 2868.
See note after No. 1549.

SUPREME COURT JUSTICES

Souvenir Sheet

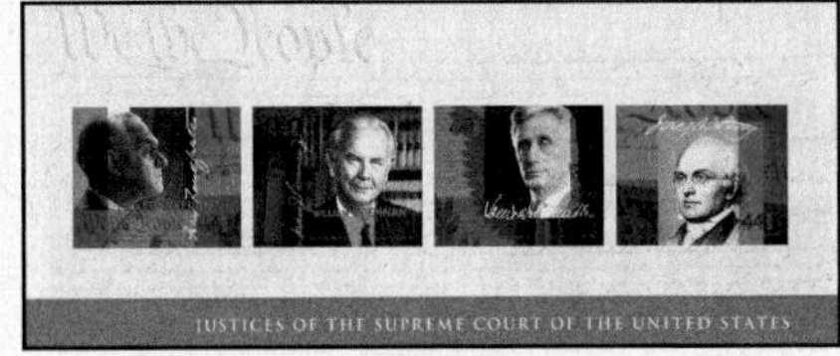

A3366

Illustration reduced.
Designed by Howard E. Paine. Printed by Avery Dennison.

No. 4422: a, Felix Frankfurter (1882-1965). b, William J. Brennan, Jr. (1906-97). c, Louis D. Brandeis (1856-1941). d, Joseph Story (1779-1845).

LITHOGRAPHED
Serpentine Die Cut 11x10½

2009, Sept. 22 **Tagged**

Self-Adhesive

4422 A3366 Pane of 4	4.00	
a.-d. 44c Any single	1.00	.30

See note after No. 1549.

KELP FOREST

A3367

Illustration reduced.
Designed by Ethel Kessler. Printed by Avery Dennison.

Wildlife: a, Brown pelican. b, Western gull, southern sea otters, red sea urchin. c, Harbor seal. d, Lion's mane nudibranch, vert. e, Yellowtail rockfish, white-spotted rose anemone. f, Vermilion rockfish. g, Copper rockfish. h, Pacific rock crab, jeweled top snail. i, Northern kelp crab, vert. j, Treefish, Monterey turban snail, brooding sea anemones.

PHOTOGRAVURE
Sheets of 80 in eight panes of 10

2009, Oct. 1 **Tagged** ***Serpentine Die Cut 10¾***

Self-Adhesive

4423 A3367 Pane of 10	14.00	
a.-j. 44c Any single	1.40	.40

Uncut press sheets of No. 4423 were made available for sale. See note after No. 2868.
See note after No. 1549.

CHRISTMAS

Madonna and Sleeping Child, by Sassoferrato (Giovanni Battista Salvi) — A3368

Reindeer — A3369

Snowman — A3370

Gingerbread Man — A3371

Toy Soldier — A3372

Reindeer — A3373

Snowman — A3374

Gingerbread Man — A3375

Toy Soldier — A3376

Designed by Carl T. Herrman (#4424), Richard Sheaff. Printed by Ashton-Potter (USA) Ltd. (#4424), Banknote Corporation of America for Sennett Security Products (#4425-4428), Avery Dennison (#4429-4432).

LITHOGRAPHED, PHOTOGRAVURE (#4429-4432)

Serpentine Die Cut 10¾x11 on 2 or 3 Sides

2009 **Tagged**

Self-Adhesive

Booklet Stamps

4424 A3368 44c **multicolored,** *Oct. 20* ⓢ .90 .25
a. Booklet pane of 20 18.00
4425 A3369 44c **multicolored,** *Oct. 8* 1.10 .25
4426 A3370 44c **multicolored,** *Oct. 8* 1.10 .25
4427 A3371 44c **multicolored,** *Oct. 8* 1.10 .25
4428 A3372 44c **multicolored,** *Oct. 8* 1.10 .25
a. Block of 4, #4425-4428 4.40
b. Booklet pane of 20, 5 each #4425-4428 22.00
c. As "b," die cutting omitted on side with 12 stamps —
d. As "b," die cutting omitted on side with 8 stamps —
e. As "a," die cutting omitted *375.00*

Serpentine Die Cut 8 on 2, 3 or 4 Sides

4429 A3373 44c **multicolored,** *Oct. 8* ⓢ 1.25 .25
4430 A3374 44c **multicolored,** *Oct. 8* ⓢ 1.25 .25
4431 A3375 44c **multicolored,** *Oct. 8* ⓢ 1.25 .25
4432 A3376 44c **multicolored,** *Oct. 8* ⓢ 1.25 .25
a. Block or strip of 4, #4429-4432 5.00
b. Booklet pane of 18, 5 each #4429, 4431, 4 each #4430, 4432 22.50
Nos. 4424-4432 (9) 10.30 2.25

No. 4424a is a double-sided booklet pane with 12 stamps on one side and eight stamps plus label that serves as a booklet cover on the other side. No. 4428b is a double-sided booklet pane with 12 stamps on one side (3 each of Nos. 4425-4428) and eight stamps (2 each of Nos. 4425-4428) plus label that serves as a booklet cover on the other side.

See note after No. 1549.

HANUKKAH

Menorah — A3377

Designed by Carl T. Herrman. Printed by Banknote Corporation of America for Sennett Security Products.

LITHOGRAPHED

Sheets of 200 in ten panes of 20

2009, Oct. 9 **Tagged** ***Serpentine Die Cut 10¾x11***

Self-Adhesive

4433 A3377 44c **multicolored** .90 .25
P# block of 4, 6#+S 3.60
Pane of 20 18.00

KWANZAA

Family — A3378

Designed by Carl T. Herrman. Printed by Ashton-Potter (USA) Ltd.

LITHOGRAPHED

Sheets of 160 in eight panes of 20

2009, Oct. 9 **Tagged** ***Serpentine Die Cut 10¾x11***

Self-Adhesive

4434 A3378 44c **multicolored** ⓢ .90 .25
P# block of 4, 4#+P 3.60
Pane of 20 18.00

See note after No. 1549.

CHINESE NEW YEAR

Year of the Tiger — A3379

Designed by Ethel Kessler. Printed by Avery Dennison.

PHOTOGRAVURE

Sheets of 108 in nine panes of 12

2010, Jan. 14 **Tagged** ***Serpentine Die Cut 11***

Self-Adhesive

4435 A3379 44c **multicolored** ⓢ 1.10 .25
Pane of 12 13.50

Uncut press sheets of No. 4435 were made available for sale. Values: cross-gutter block of 4, $10; pairs with gutters between, $2.50 each. See note after No. 2868.

See note after No. 1549.

2010 WINTER OLYMPICS, VANCOUVER ⓢ

Snowboarder — A3380

Designed by Howard E. Paine. Printed by Avery Dennison.

PHOTOGRAVURE

Sheets of 160 in eight panes of 20

2010, Jan. 22 **Tagged** ***Serpentine Die Cut 11***

Self-Adhesive

4436 A3380 44c **multicolored** .90 .25
P# block of 4, 6# + V 4.00
Pane of 20 20.00

See note after No. 1549.

"Forever" Liberty Bell — A3380a

Printed by Ashton-Potter (USA) Ltd.

Serpentine Die Cut 11¼x10¾ on 2, 3 or 4 Sides

2010, Feb. 3 **Self-Adhesive** **Litho.**

Booklet Stamp

Medium Microprinting, Bell 16mm Wide

Dated "2009" in Copper

4437 A3380a (44c) **multicolored** ⓢ 1.10 .25
a. Booklet pane of 18 20.00

On No. 4437, the "2009" date is smaller than that on No. 4127i, which has a 15mm wide bell. The bell on No. 4437 is also 17mm tall while No. 4127i is 16mm tall. The microprinted "Forever" is on a dotted background on No. 4437 and on a white background on No. 4127i.

See also Nos. 4125, 4128c.
See note after No. 1549.

AMERICAN LANDMARKS

Mackinac Bridge, Michigan A3381

Bixby Creek Bridge, California A3382

Designed by Carl T. Herrman. Printed by Avery Dennison.

PHOTOGRAVURE
Sheets of 200 in ten panes of 20
Serpentine Die Cut 10¾x10½

2010, Feb. 3 **Tagged**

Self-Adhesive

4438 A3381 $4.90 **multicolored** ⓢ	11.00	5.00
P# block of 4, 4# +V	45.00	
Pane of 20	220.00	
4439 A3382 $18.30 **multicolored** ⓢ	45.00	18.00
P# block of 4, 4# +V	180.00	
Pane of 20	900.00	

See note after No. 1549.

DISTINGUISHED SAILORS ⓢ

Admiral William S. Sims (1858-1936), Emblem of USS W.S. Sims — A3383

Admiral Arleigh A. Burke (1901-96), Emblem of USS Arleigh Burke A3384

Lieutenant Commander John McCloy (1876-1945), Emblem of USS McCloy A3385

Petty Officer 3rd Class Doris Miller (1919-43), Emblem of USS Miller A3386

Designed by Phil Jordan. Printed by Avery Dennison.

PHOTOGRAVURE
Sheets of 200 in ten panes of 20
Serpentine Die Cut 10¾x10½

2010, Feb. 4 **Tagged**

Self-Adhesive

4440 A3383 44c **multicolored**	.90	.40
4441 A3384 44c **multicolored**	.90	.40
4442 A3385 44c **multicolored**	.90	.40
4443 A3386 44c **multicolored**	.90	.40
a. Block or horiz. strip of 4, #4440-4443	3.60	
P# block of 4, 6# + V	4.00	
P# block of 8, 2 sets of 6# + V + top label	7.20	
Pane of 20	19.50	

See note after No. 1549.

ABSTRACT EXPRESSIONISTS ⓢ

A3387

Illustration reduced.

Designed by Ethel Kessler. Printed by Ashton-Potter (USA) Ltd.

No. 4444: a, The Golden Wall, by Hans Hofmann (30x30mm). b, Asheville, by Willem de Kooning (38x38mm). c, Orange and Yellow, by Mark Rothko (35x49mm). d, Convergence, by Jackson Pollock (63x43mm). e, The Liver Is the Cock's Comb, by Arshile Gorky (39x32mm). f, 1948-C, by Clyfford Still (35x49mm). g, Elegy to the Spanish Republic No. 34, by Robert Motherwell (54x49mm). h, La Grande Vallée 0, by Joan Mitchell (35x49mm). i, Romanesque Façade, by Adolph Gottlieb (35x49mm). j, Achilles, by Barnett Newman (35x49mm).

LITHOGRAPHED
Serpentine Die Cut 10¾x11, 10¾ (#4444a, 4444b, 4444e), 11x10¾ (#4444d)

2010, Mar. 11 **Tagged**

Self-Adhesive

4444 A3387 Pane of 10	12.50	
a.-j. 44c Any single	1.25	.40

See note after No. 1549.

BILL MAULDIN (1921-2003), CARTOONIST ⓢ

Mauldin and His Characters, Willie and Joe A3388

Designed by Terrence W. McCaffrey. Printed by Ashton-Potter (USA) Ltd.

LITHOGRAPHED
Sheets of 120 in six panes of 20

2010, Mar. 31 **Tagged** ***Serpentine Die Cut 10¾***

Self-Adhesive

4445 A3388 44c **multicolored**	.90	.25
P# block of 4, 4# + P	3.60	
Pane of 20	18.00	

See note after No. 1549.

COWBOYS OF THE SILVER SCREEN ⓢ

Roy Rogers (1911-98) — A3389

Tom Mix (1880-1940) — A3390

William S. Hart (1864-1946) — A3391

Gene Autry (1907-98) — A3392

Designed by Carl T. Herrman. Printed by Ashton-Potter (USA) Ltd.

LITHOGRAPHED
Sheets of 180 in nine panes of 20
Serpentine Die Cut 10½x10¾

2010, Apr. 17 **Tagged**

Self-Adhesive

4446 A3389 44c **multicolored**	1.25	.35
4447 A3390 44c **multicolored**	1.25	.35
4448 A3391 44c **multicolored**	1.25	.35
4449 A3392 44c **multicolored**	1.25	.35
a. Block or strip of 4, #4446-4449	5.00	
P# block of 4, 4# + P	5.00	
Pane of 20	25.00	

Uncut press sheets of Nos. 4446-4449 were made available for sale. Values: cross-gutter block of 8, $25; pairs with gutters between, $3.75 each. See note after No. 2868.

See note after No. 1549.

LOVE

Pansies in a Basket — A3393

Designed by Derry Noyes. Printed by Avery Dennison.

PHOTOGRAVURE
Sheets of 240 in twelve panes of 20

2010, Apr. 22 **Tagged** ***Serpentine Die Cut 10¾***

Self-Adhesive

4450 A3393 44c **multicolored** ⓢ	.90	.25
P# block of 4, 5# + V	3.60	
Pane of 20	18.00	

See note after No. 1549.

ANIMAL RESCUE

Wire-haired Jack Russell Terrier — A3394

Maltese — A3395

Calico — A3396

Yellow Labrador Retriever — A3397

Golden Retriever — A3398

Gray, White and Tan Cat — A3399

Black, White and Tan Cat — A3400

Australian Shepherd — A3401

Boston Terrier — A3402

Orange Tabby — A3403

Designed by Derry Noyes. Printed by Banknote Corporation of America for Sennett Security Products.

LITHOGRAPHED

Sheets of 160 in eight panes of 20

2010, Apr. 30 Tagged ***Serpentine Die Cut 10¾***

Self-Adhesive

4451	A3394 44c **multicolored**	1.50	.40
4452	A3395 44c **multicolored**	1.50	.40
4453	A3396 44c **multicolored**	1.50	.40
4454	A3397 44c **multicolored**	1.50	.40
4455	A3398 44c **multicolored**	1.50	.40
4456	A3399 44c **multicolored**	1.50	.40
4457	A3400 44c **multicolored**	1.50	.40
4458	A3401 44c **multicolored**	1.50	.40
4459	A3402 44c **multicolored**	1.50	.40
4460	A3403 44c **multicolored**	1.50	.40
a.	Block of 10, #4451-4460	15.00	
	P# block of 10, 8# + S	15.00	
	Pane of 20	30.00	

Uncut press sheets of Nos. 4451-4460 were made available for sale. Values: cross-gutter block of 10, $20; pairs with gutters between, $3.25 each. See note after No. 2868.

LEGENDS OF HOLLYWOOD

Katharine Hepburn (1907-2003), Actress — A3404

Designed by Derry Noyes. Printed by Avery Dennison.

PHOTOGRAVURE

Sheets of 80 in four panes of 20

2010, May 12 Tagged ***Serpentine Die Cut 10¾***

Self-Adhesive

4461	A3404 44c **black** Ⓢ	1.00	.25
	P# block of 4, 2#+V	4.25	
	Pane of 20	21.00	

Uncut press sheets of No. 4461 were made available for sale. Values: cross-gutter block of 8, $20; pairs with gutters between, $2.50 each. See note after No. 2868.

See note after No. 1549.

MONARCH BUTTERFLY Ⓢ

A3405

Designed by Derry Noyes. Printed by Avery Dennison.

PHOTOGRAVURE

Sheets of 200 in ten panes of 20

2010, May 17 Tagged ***Serpentine Die Cut 10½***

Self-Adhesive

4462	A3405 64c **multicolored**	1.50	.25
	P# block of 4, 6#+V	6.00	
	Pane of 20	30.00	

See note after No. 1549.

KATE SMITH Ⓢ

Kate Smith (1907-86), Singer — A3406

Designed by Ethel Kessler. Printed by Avery Dennison.

PHOTOGRAVURE

Sheets of 160 in eight panes of 20

2010, May 27 Tagged ***Serpentine Die Cut 11***

Self-Adhesive

4463	A3406 44c **multicolored**	.90	.25
	P# block of 4, 4#+V	3.60	
	Pane of 20	18.00	

See note after No. 1549.

BLACK HERITAGE

Oscar Micheaux (1884-1951), Film Director — A3407

Designed by Derry Noyes. Printed by Avery Dennison.

PHOTOGRAVURE

Sheets of 200 in ten panes of 20

2010, June 22 Tagged ***Serpentine Die Cut 11***

Self-Adhesive

4464	A3407 44c **multicolored** Ⓢ	.90	.25
	P# block of 4, 4#+V	3.60	
	Pane of 20	18.00	

See note after No. 1549.

NEGRO LEAGUES BASEBALL Ⓢ

Play at the Plate — A3408

Andrew "Rube" Foster (1879-1930), Founder of Negro National League A3409

Designed by Howard E. Paine. Printed by Avery Dennison.

PHOTOGRAVURE

Sheets of 200 in ten panes of 20

2010, July 15 Tagged ***Serpentine Die Cut 11***

Self-Adhesive

4465	A3408 44c **multicolored**	.90	.30
4466	A3409 44c **multicolored**	.90	.30
a.	Horiz. pair, #4465-4466	1.80	
	P# block of 4, 5#+V	3.60	
	Pane of 20	18.00	

See note after No. 1549.

SUNDAY FUNNIES

Beetle Bailey — A3410

Calvin and Hobbes — A3411

Archie — A3412

Garfield — A3413

Dennis the Menace — A3414

Designed by Ethel Kessler. Printed by Banknote Corporation of America for Sennett Security Products.

LITHOGRAPHED

Sheets of 180 in nine panes of 20

Serpentine Die Cut 10½x10¾

2010, July 16 **Tagged**

Self-Adhesive

4467 A3410 44c **multicolored** 1.00 .30
4468 A3411 44c **multicolored** 1.00 .30
4469 A3412 44c **multicolored** 1.00 .30
4470 A3413 44c **multicolored** 1.00 .30
4471 A3414 44c **multicolored** 1.00 .30
a. Horiz. strip of 5, #4467-4471 5.00
P# block of 10, 2 sets of 9#+S 10.00
Pane of 20 20.00

Uncut press sheets of Nos. 4467-4471 were made available for sale. Panes that are vertically adjacent are tete-beche in relation to each other. Values: cross-gutter block of 10 with or without top panel, $19; pairs with gutters between, $2.50 each. See note after No. 2868.

BOY SCOUTS OF AMERICA, CENTENNIAL Ⓢ

Boy Scouts — A3415

Designed by Derry Noyes. Printed by Avery Dennison.

PHOTOGRAVURE

Sheets of 160 in eight panes of 20

2010, July 27 **Tagged** ***Serpentine Die Cut 11***

Self-Adhesive

4472 A3415 44c **multicolored** .90 .25
P# block of 4, 6#+V 3.60
Pane of 20 18.00

See note after No. 1549.

AMERICAN TREASURES SERIES

Boys in a Pasture, by Winslow Homer (1836-1910) A3416

Designed by Derry Noyes. Printed by Banknote Corporation of America for Sennett Security Products.

PHOTOGRAVURE

Sheets of 180 in nine panes of 20

2010, Aug. 12 **Tagged** ***Serpentine Die Cut 10¾***

Self-Adhesive

4473 A3416 44c **multicolored** 1.00 .25
P# block of 4, 5#+S 4.00
Pane of 20 20.00

HAWAIIAN RAIN FOREST

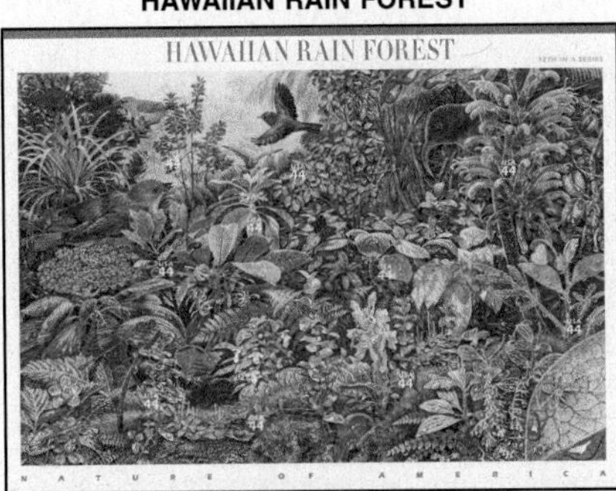

A3417

Designed by Ethel Kessler. Printed by Banknote Corporation of America for Sennett Security Products.

No. 4474: a, Hawaii 'amakihi, Hawaii 'elepaio, ohi'a lehua. b, 'Akepa, 'ope'ape'a, vert. c, 'I'iwi, haha. d, 'Oma'o, kanawao, 'ohelo kau la'au, vert. e, 'Oha, vert. f, Pulelehua butterfly, kolea lau nui, 'ilihia. g, Koele Mountain damselfly, 'akala, vert. h, 'Apapane, Hawaiian mint, vert. i, Jewel orchid, vert. j, Happyface spider, 'ala'ala wai nui, vert.

LITHOGRAPHED

Sheets of 80 in eight panes of 10

2010, Sept. 1 **Tagged** ***Serpentine Die Cut 10¾***

Self-Adhesive

4474 A3417 Pane of 10 10.00
a.-j. 44c Any single 1.00 .40

Uncut press sheets of No. 4474 were made available for sale. See note after No. 2868.

MOTHER TERESA Ⓢ

Mother Teresa (1910-97), Humanitarian, 1979 Nobel Peace Laureate — A3418

Designed by Derry Noyes. Printed by Avery Dennison.

PHOTOGRAVURE

Sheets of 200 in ten panes of 20

2010, Sept. 5 **Tagged** ***Serpentine Die Cut 11***

Self-Adhesive

4475 A3418 44c **multicolored** .90 .25
P# block of 4, 4#+V 3.60
Pane of 20 18.00

See note after No. 1549.

LITERARY ARTS

Julia de Burgos (1914-53), Poet — A3419

Designed by Howard E. Paine. Printed by Avery Dennison.

PHOTOGRAVURE

Sheets of 200 in ten panes of 20

2010, Sept. 14 **Tagged** ***Serpentine Die Cut 11***

Self-Adhesive

4476 A3419 44c **multicolored** ⓢ .90 .25
P# block of 4, 4#+V 3.60
Pane of 20 18.00

See note after No. 1549.

CHRISTMAS

Angel with Lute, Detail of Fresco by Melozzo da Forli — A3420

Designed by Terrence W. McCaffrey (#4477), Howard E. Paine

Printed by Avery Dennison (#4477), Banknote Corporation of America for Sennett Security Products (#4478-4481), Ashton-Potter (USA) Ltd. (#4482-4485).

PHOTOGRAVURE (#4477), LITHOGRAPHED

Sheets of 240 in twelve panes of 20 (#4477)

2010, Oct. 21 **Tagged** ***Serpentine Die Cut 10¾***

Self-Adhesive

4477 A3420 44c **multicolored** ⓢ 1.00 .25
P# block of 4, 5#+V 4.00
Pane of 20 20.00

Ponderosa Pine — A3421

Eastern Red Cedar — A3422

Balsam Fir — A3423

Blue Spruce — A3424

Designed by Howard E. Paine
Printed by Banknote Corporation of America for Sennett Security Products.

Booklet Stamps

Serpentine Die Cut 11 on 2 or 3 Sides

4478	A3421 (44c) **multicolored**	2.50	.25
4479	A3422 (44c) **multicolored**	2.50	.25
4480	A3423 (44c) **multicolored**	2.50	.25
4481	A3424 (44c) **multicolored**	2.50	.25
a.	Block of 4, #4478-4481	10.00	
b.	Booklet pane of 20, 5 each #4478-4481	50.00	
c.	As "a," die cutting omitted	—	*500.00*
d.	As "b," die cutting omitted on side with 12 stamps	*400.00*	
e.	As "b," die cutting omitted on side with 8 stamps	*450.00*	
f.	As "b," die cutting omitted on side with 12 stamps, die cutting omitted on bottom 4 stamps on side with 8 stamps	950.00	

Ponderosa Pine — A3425

Eastern Red Cedar — A3426

Balsam Fir — A3427

Blue Spruce — A3428

Printed by Ashton-Potter (USA) Ltd.

Serpentine Die Cut 11¼x10¾ on 2, 3 or 4 Sides

4482	A3425 (44c) **multicolored** Ⓢ	2.50	.25
4483	A3426 (44c) **multicolored** Ⓢ	2.50	.25
4484	A3427 (44c) **multicolored** Ⓢ	2.50	.25
4485	A3428 (44c) **multicolored** Ⓢ	2.50	.25
a.	Block or strip of 4, #4482-4485	10.00	
b.	Booklet pane of 18, 5 each #4482, 4484, 4 each #4483, 4485	45.00	
	Nos. 4477-4485 (9)	21.00	2.25

No. 4481b is a double-sided booklet pane with 12 stamps on one side (3 each of Nos. 4478-4481) and eight stamps (2 each of Nos. 4478-4481) plus label that serves as a booklet cover on the other side.

See note after No. 1549.

Replica of Statue of Liberty, Las Vegas — A3429

Flag — A3430

Designed by Terrence W. McCaffrey. Printed by Ashton-Potter (USA) Ltd.

LITHOGRAPHED (#4486-4489)

Serpentine Die Cut 9½ Vert.

2010, Dec. 1 **Tagged**

COIL STAMPS

Self-Adhesive

4486	A3429 (44c) **multicolored** Ⓢ	1.50	.25
4487	A3430 (44c) **multicolored** Ⓢ	1.50	.25
a.	Pair, #4486-4487	3.00	
	P# strip of 5, 3 #4487, 2 #4486	8.50	
	P# single (#4487), #P111111	—	2.00

A3429a

A3430a

Designed by Banknote Corporation of America for Sennett Security Products.

Serpentine Die Cut 11 Vert.

4488	A3429a (44c) **multicolored**	1.50	.25
a.	Vert. pair, horiz. unslit btwn.		—
4489	A3430a (44c) **multicolored**	1.50	.25
a.	Pair, #4488-4489	3.00	
	P# strip of 5, 3 #4489, 2 #4488	8.50	
	P# single (#4489), #S111111	—	2.00
b.	Block of 4 (one pair each from two different coil rolls), horiz. unslit btwn.	*900.00*	

A3429b

A3430b

PHOTOGRAVURE

Serpentine Die Cut 8½ Vert.

Designed by Avery Dennison.

4490	A3429b (44c) **multicolored** Ⓢ	1.50	.25
4491	A3430b (44c) **multicolored** Ⓢ	1.50	.25
a.	Pair, #4490-4491	3.00	
	P# strip of 5, 3 #4491, 2 #4490	8.50	
	P# single (#4491), #V111111	—	2.00
	Nos. 4486-4491 (6)	9.00	1.50

Microprinting reads "4evR" on Nos. 4486-4487, "4evr" on Nos. 4488-4489, and "4EVR" on Nos. 4490-4491. The microprinting is found above the Statue of Liberty's hair, and at the bottom of the lowest red stripe of the flag.

Counterfeits exist of Nos. 4488-4491. See the Postal Counterfeits section of this catalog.

See Nos. 4518-4519, 4559-4564.
See note after No. 1549.

CHINESE NEW YEAR

Year of the Rabbit A3431

Designed by Ethel Kessler. Printed by Avery Dennison.

PHOTOGRAVURE

Sheets of 108 in nine panes of 12

2011, Jan. 22 **Tagged** ***Serpentine Die Cut 11***

Self-Adhesive

4492	A3431 (44c) **multicolored** Ⓢ	1.25	.25
	Pane of 12	15.00	

Uncut press sheets of No. 4492 were made available for sale. Values: cross-gutter block of 4, $9; pairs with gutters between, $2.50 each. See note after No. 2868.

See note after No. 1549.

KANSAS STATEHOOD, 150TH ANNIV. Ⓢ

Windmill and Wind Turbines A3432

Designed by Howard E. Paine. Printed by Ashton-Potter (USA) Ltd.

LITHOGRAPHED

Sheets of 180 in nine panes of 20

2011, Jan. 27 **Tagged** ***Serpentine Die Cut 11***

Self-Adhesive

4493	A3432 (44c) **multicolored**	1.25	.25
	P# block of 4, 5# + P	5.00	
	Pane of 20	25.00	

See note after No. 1549.

PRES. RONALD REAGAN (1911-2004) Ⓢ

Pres. Ronald Reagan — A3433

Designed by Ethel Kessler. Printed by Avery Dennison.

PHOTOGRAVURE

Sheets of 200 in ten panes of 20

2011, Feb. 10 **Tagged** ***Serpentine Die Cut 10½***

Self-Adhesive

4494	A3433 (44c) **multicolored**	1.25	.25
	P# block of 4, 6#+V	5.00	
	Pane of 20	25.00	

Uncut press sheets of No. 4494 were made available for sale. Values: cross-gutter block of 4, $8; pairs with gutters between, $2.50 each. See note after No. 2868.

See note after No. 1549.

Art Deco Bird — A3434

Designed by Carl T. Herrman. Printed by Ashton-Potter (USA) Ltd.

LITHOGRAPHED

Serpentine Die Cut 10 Vert.

2011, Feb. 11 **Untagged**

COIL STAMP

Self-Adhesive

4495	A3434 (5c) **multicolored** Ⓢ	.30	.25
	Pair	.50	
	P# strip of 5, #P1111	1.25	
	P# strip of 5, #P2222	1.60	
	P# strip of 5, #P3333	2.50	
	P# single, #P1111	—	1.75
	P# single, #P2222, P3333	—	2.00

See note after No. 1549.

Quill and Inkwell — A3435

Designed by Craig Frazier. Printed by Banknote Corporation of America for Sennett Security Products.

LITHOGRAPHED

Serpentine Die Cut 11¾ Vert.

2011, Feb. 14 **Tagged**

COIL STAMP

Self-Adhesive

4496 A3435 44c **multicolored** .95 .25
Pair 1.90
P# strip of 5, #S11111 6.25
P# single, #S11111 — 2.00

LATIN MUSIC LEGENDS Ⓢ

Tito Puente (1923-2000) — A3436

Carmen Miranda (1909-55) — A3437

Selena (1971-95) — A3438

Carlos Gardel (1890-35) — A3439

Celia Cruz (1925-2003) — A3440

Designed by Ethel Kessler. Printed by Avery Dennison.

PHOTOGRAVURE

Sheets of 240 in twelve panes of 20

2011, Mar. 16 **Tagged** ***Serpentine Die Cut 10¾***

Self-Adhesive

4497 A3436 (44c) **multicolored** 1.25 .40
4498 A3437 (44c) **multicolored** 1.25 .40
4499 A3438 (44c) **multicolored** 1.25 .40
4500 A3439 (44c) **multicolored** 1.25 .40
4501 A3440 (44c) **multicolored** 1.25 .40
a. Horiz. strip of 5, #4497-4501 6.25
P# block of 10, 2 sets of 4#+V 12.50
Pane of 20 25.00

See note after No. 1549.

CELEBRATE

A3441

Designed by Phil Jordan. Printed by American Packaging Corporation for Sennett Security Products.

PHOTOGRAVURE

Sheets of 160 in eight panes of 20

Serpentine Die Cut 11x11½

2011, Mar. 25 **Tagged**

Self-Adhesive

4502 A3441 (44c) **multicolored** 1.25 .25
P# block of 4, 6#+S 5.00
Pane of 20 25.00

Compare with type A3855.

JAZZ Ⓢ

Musicians — A3442

Designed by Howard E. Paine. Printed by Avery Dennison.

PHOTOGRAVURE

Sheets of 200 in ten panes of 20

2011, Mar. 26 **Tagged** ***Serpentine Die Cut 10¾***

Self-Adhesive

4503 A3442 (44c) **multicolored** 1.25 .25
P# block of 4, 4#+V 5.00
Pane of 20 25.00

See note after No. 1549.

George Washington — A3443

Designed by Derry Noyes (#4504). Printed by Ashton-Potter (USA) Ltd. (#4504), Banknote Corporation of America for Sennett Security Products (#4518-4519).

LITHOGRAPHED (#4504, 4518-4519)

Sheets of 200 in ten panes of 20 (#4504).

2011 **Tagged** ***Serpentine Die Cut 11¼x10¾***

Self-Adhesive

4504 A3443 20c **multicolored,** *Apr. 11* Ⓢ .40 .25
P# block of 4, 5#+P 1.60
Pane of 20 8.00

Oregano — A3444

Flax — A3445

Foxglove — A3446

Lavender — A3447

Sage — A3448

Oveta Culp Hobby (1905-95), First Health, Education and Welfare Department Secretary — A3449

Designed by Phil Jordan (#4505-4510). Printed by Avery Dennison (#4505-4510).

PHOTOGRAVURE (#4505-4510)

Sheets of 420 in twenty-one panes of 20 (#4505-4509), Sheets of 240 in twelve panes of 20 (#4510).

Serpentine Die Cut 11

4505 A3444 29c **multicolored,** *Apr. 7* Ⓢ 1.50 .25
4506 A3445 29c **multicolored,** *Apr. 7* Ⓢ 1.50 .25
4507 A3446 29c **multicolored,** *Apr. 7* Ⓢ 1.50 .25
4508 A3447 29c **multicolored,** *Apr. 7* Ⓢ 1.50 .25
4509 A3448 29c **multicolored,** *Apr. 7* Ⓢ 1.50 .25
a. Horiz. strip of 5, #4505-4509 7.50
P# block of 10, 2 sets of 5#+V 15.00
Pane of 20 30.00
4510 A3449 84c **multicolored,** *Apr. 15* Ⓢ 1.75 .35
P# block of 4, 5#+V 7.00
Pane of 20 35.00

New River Gorge Bridge, West Virginia — A3450

Designed by Carl T. Herrman (#4511). Printed by Ashton-Potter (USA) Ltd. (#4511).

LITHOGRAPHED (#4511)

Sheets of 120 in six panes of 20 (#4511)

Serpentine Die Cut 10¾x10½

4511 A3450 $4.95 **multicolored,** *Apr. 11* Ⓢ 10.00 5.00
P# block of 4, 4#+P 40.00
Pane of 20 200.00
Nos. 4504-4511 (7) 17.90 6.50

A3450a

Designed by Derry Noyes (#4512). Printed by Ashton-Potter (USA) Ltd. (#4512).

LITHOGRAPHED (#4512)

Coil Stamps

Serpentine Die Cut 9½ Vert.

4512 A3450a 20c **multicolored,** *Apr. 11* Ⓢ .40 .25
Pair .80
P# strip of 5, #P11111, P22222 3.50
P# single, #P11111, P22222 — 2.50
a. Imperf., on cover —

No. 4512a is recorded only on a single cover bearing a strip of 9 and three strips of 10. The editors would welcome reports of unused examples.

A3450b

A3450c

A3450d

A3450e

A3450f

Designed by Phil Jordan (#4513-4517). Printed by Avery Dennison (4513-4517).

LITHOGRAPHED (#4512)

Serpentine Die Cut 8½ Vert.

4513	A3450b 29c **multicolored,** *Apr. 7* Ⓢ	2.00	.25
4514	A3450c 29c **multicolored,** *Apr. 7* Ⓢ	2.00	.25
4515	A3450d 29c **multicolored,** *Apr. 7* Ⓢ	2.00	.25
4516	A3450e 29c **multicolored,** *Apr. 7* Ⓢ	2.00	.25
4517	A3450f 29c **multicolored,** *Apr. 7* Ⓢ	2.00	.25
a.	Horiz. strip of 5, #4513-4517	10.00	
	P# strip of 5, #4513-4517, #V11111	12.00	
	P# strip of 11, 3 #4515, 2 each #4513-4514, 4516-4517, #V11111	22.00	
	P# single (#4515), #V11111	—	2.00
	Nos. 4512-4517 (6)	10.40	1.50

See note after No. 1549.

Statue of Liberty — A3450g

Flag — A3450h

Designed by Terrence W. McCaffrey.Printed by Banknote Corporation of America for Sennett Security Products (#4518-4519).

LITHOGRAPHED (#4518-4519)

Booklet Stamps

Thin Paper

Serpentine Die Cut 11¼x10¾ on 2, 3, or 4 Sides

4518	A3450g (44c) **multicolored,** *Apr. 8*	1.25	.25
4519	A3450h (44c) **multicolored,** *Apr. 8*	1.25	.25
a.	Pair, #4518-4519	2.50	
b.	Booklet pane of 18, 9 each #4518-4519	22.50	

Wedding Roses — A3450i

Wedding Cake With "USA" in Serifed Type — A3450j

Designed by Ethel Kessler. Printed by Banknote Corporation of America for Sennett Security Products (#4520). Printed by Avery Dennison (#4521).

LITHOGRAPHED (#4520), PHOTOGRAVURE (#4521)

Sheets of 200 in Ten Panes of 20 (#4520), Sheets of 120 in twelve panes of 20 (#4521)

2011 Tagged *Serpentine Die Cut 11*

Self-Adhesive

4520	A3450i (44c) **multicolored,** *Apr. 21*	5.00	.25
	P# block of 4, 5#+S	20.00	
	Pane of 20	100.00	
a.	Die cutting omitted, pair	*250.00*	
4521	A3450j 64c **multicolored,** *Apr. 11* Ⓢ	2.50	.25
	P# block of 4, 5#+V	10.00	
	Pane of 20	50.00	

Counterfeits exist of No. 4520. See the Postal Counterfeits section of this catalog.

See Nos. 4398, 4602, 4735, 4867, 5000.

See note after No. 1549.

CIVIL WAR SESQUICENTENNIAL

Battle of Fort Sumter — A3451

First Battle of Bull Run — A3452

Designed by Phil Jordan. Printed by Ashton-Potter (USA) Ltd.

LITHOGRAPHED

Double-sided sheets of 72 in six panes of 12 (60 on one side, 12 on other side)

2011, Apr. 12 Tagged *Serpentine Die Cut 11*

Self-Adhesive

4522	A3451 (44c) **multicolored** Ⓢ	1.25	.30
4523	A3452 (44c) **multicolored** Ⓢ	1.25	.30
a.	Pair, #4522-4523	2.50	
	Pane of 12	15.00	

Uncut press sheets of Nos. 4522-4523 were made available for sale. See note after No. 2868.

See note after No. 1549.

GO GREEN Ⓢ

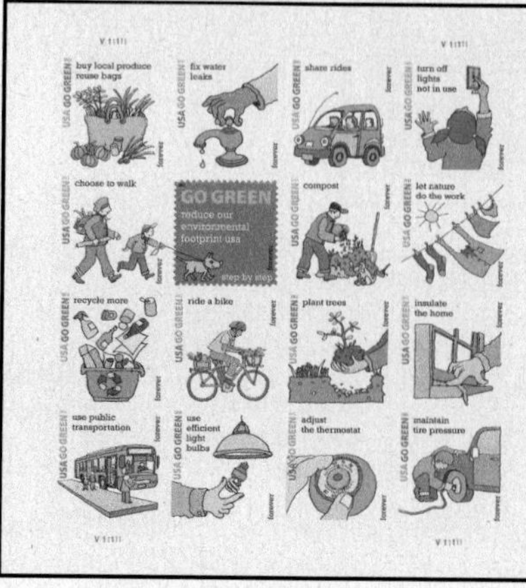

A3453

Illustration reduced.

Designed by Derry Noyes. Printed by Avery Dennison.

No. 4524 — Messages: a, Buy local produce, reuse bags. b, Fix water leaks. c, Share rides. d, Turn off lights not in use. e, Choose to walk. f, Go Green, reduce our environmental footprint step by step. g, Compost. h, Let nature do the work. i, Recycle more. j, Ride a bike. k, Plant trees. l, Insulate the home. m, Use public transportation. n, Use efficient light bulbs. o, Adjust the thermostat. p, Maintain tire pressure.

PHOTOGRAVURE

Sheets of 144 in nine panes of 16

2011, Apr. 14 Tagged *Serpentine Die Cut 10¾*

Self-Adhesive

4524	A3453 Pane of 16	20.00	
a.-p.	(44c) Any single	1.25	.50

Uncut press sheets of No. 4524 were made available for sale. Values: cross-gutter block of 16, $22.50; pairs with gutters between, $3.25 each. See note after No. 2868.

See note after No. 1549.

HELEN HAYES Ⓢ

Helen Hayes (1900-93), Actress — A3454

Designed by Howard E. Paine. Printed by Avery Dennison.

PHOTOGRAVURE

Sheets of 200 in ten panes of 20

2011, Apr. 25 Tagged *Serpentine Die Cut 11*

Self-Adhesive

4525	A3454 (44c) **multicolored**	1.25	.25
	P# block of 4, 5#+V	5.00	
	Pane of 20	25.00	

Uncut press sheets of No. 4525 were made available for sale. Values: cross-gutter block of 8, $20; pairs with gutters between, $2.50 each. See note after No. 2868.

See note after No. 1549.

LEGENDS OF HOLLYWOOD

Gregory Peck (1916-2003), Actor — A3455

Designed by Phil Jordan. Printed by Avery Dennison.

PHOTOGRAVURE

Sheets of 80 in four panes of 20

2011, Apr. 28 Tagged *Serpentine Die Cut 10¾*

Self-Adhesive

4526	A3455 (44c) **black** Ⓢ	1.25	.25
	P# block of 4, 4#+V	5.00	
	Pane of 20	25.00	

Uncut press sheets of No. 4526 were made available for sale. Values: cross-gutter block of 8, $20; pairs with gutters between, $2.50 each. See note after No. 2868.

See note after No. 1549.

SPACE FIRSTS

Alan B. Shepard, Jr. (1923-98), First American in Space A3456

Messenger, First Spacecraft to Orbit Mercury A3457

Designed by Phil Jordan. Printed by Banknote Corporation of America for Sennett Security Products.

LITHOGRAPHED

Sheets of 240 in twelve panes of 20

2011, May 4 Tagged *Serpentine Die Cut 11*

Self-Adhesive

4527	A3456 (44c) **multicolored**	1.25	.30
4528	A3457 (44c) **multicolored**	1.25	.30
a.	Horiz. pair, #4527-4528	2.50	
	P# block of 4, 6#+S	5.00	
	Pane of 20	25.00	

Uncut press sheets of Nos. 4527-4528 were made available for sale. Values: cross-gutter block of 4, $9; pairs with gutters between, $2.50 each. See note after No. 2868.

Purple Heart and Ribbon — A3458

Designed by Jennifer Arnold. Printed by Banknote Corporation of America for Sennett Security Products.

LITHOGRAPHED

Sheets of 80 in four panes of 20

Serpentine Die Cut 11¼x10¾

2011, May 5 Tagged

Self-Adhesive

4529	A3458 (44c) **multicolored**	1.25	.25
	P# block of 4, 8#+S	5.00	
	Pane of 20	25.00	

See Nos. 4529, 4704, 5035.

INDIANAPOLIS 500, CENT.

Ray Harroun Driving Marmon Wasp A3459

Designed by Phil Jordan. Printed by Banknote Corporation of America for Sennett Security Products.

LITHOGRAPHED

Sheets of 240 in 12 panes of 20

2011, May 20 Tagged *Serpentine Die Cut 10¾*

Self-Adhesive

4530	A3459 (44c) **multicolored**	1.25	.25
	P# block of 4, 6#+S	5.00	
	Pane of 20	25.00	

GARDEN OF LOVE Ⓢ

Pink Flower — A3460

Red Flower — A3461

Blue Flowers — A3462

Butterfly — A3463

Green Vine Leaves — A3464

Blue Flower — A3465

Doves — A3466

Orange Red Flowers — A3467

Strawberry — A3468

Yellow Orange Flowers — A3469

Designed by Derry Noyes. Printed by Avery Dennison.

PHOTOGRAVURE

Sheets of 240 in 12 panes of 20

2011, May 23 Tagged *Serpentine Die Cut 10¾*

Self-Adhesive

4531	A3460 (44c) **multicolored**	2.00	.40
4532	A3461 (44c) **multicolored**	2.00	.40
4533	A3462 (44c) **multicolored**	2.00	.40
4534	A3463 (44c) **multicolored**	2.00	.40
4535	A3464 (44c) **multicolored**	2.00	.40
4536	A3465 (44c) **multicolored**	2.00	.40
4537	A3466 (44c) **multicolored**	2.00	.40
4538	A3467 (44c) **multicolored**	2.00	.40
4539	A3468 (44c) **multicolored**	2.00	.40
4540	A3469 (44c) **multicolored**	2.00	.40
a.	Block of 10, #4531-4540	20.00	
	P# block of 10, 2 sets of 4#+V	20.00	
	Pane of 20	40.00	
	Nos. 4531-4540 (10)	20.00	4.00

The two blocks of 10 on the pane are separated by a gutter.

See note after No. 1549.

AMERICAN SCIENTISTS

Melvin Calvin (1911-97), Chemist A3470

Asa Gray (1810-88), Botanist A3471

Maria Goeppert Mayer (1906-72), Physicist A3472

Severo Ochoa (1905-93), Biochemist A3473

Designed by Greg Berger. Printed by Banknote Corporation of America for Sennett Security Products.

LITHOGRAPHED

Sheets of 240 in twelve panes of 20

2011, June 16 Tagged *Serpentine Die Cut 11*

Self-Adhesive

4541	A3470 (44c) **multicolored**	1.25	.50
4542	A3471 (44c) **multicolored**	1.25	.50
4543	A3472 (44c) **multicolored**	1.25	.50
4544	A3473 (44c) **multicolored**	1.25	.50
a.	Horiz. strip of 4, #4541-4544	5.00	
	P# block of 8, 2 sets of 8#+S	10.00	
	Pane of 20	25.00	
b.	Horiz. strip of 4, die cutting missing on backing paper (from misaligned die-cutting mat)	*375.00*	

LITERARY ARTS

Mark Twain (Samuel L. Clemens) (1835-1910), Writer A3474

Designed by Phil Jordan. Printed by Avery Dennison.

PHOTOGRAVURE

Sheets of 160 in eight panes of 20

2011, June 25 Tagged *Serpentine Die Cut 11*

Self-Adhesive

4545	A3474 (44c) **multicolored** Ⓢ	1.25	.25
	P# block of 4, 4#+V	5.00	
	Pane of 20	25.00	

See note after No. 1549.

PIONEERS OF AMERICAN INDUSTRIAL DESIGN

Ⓢ

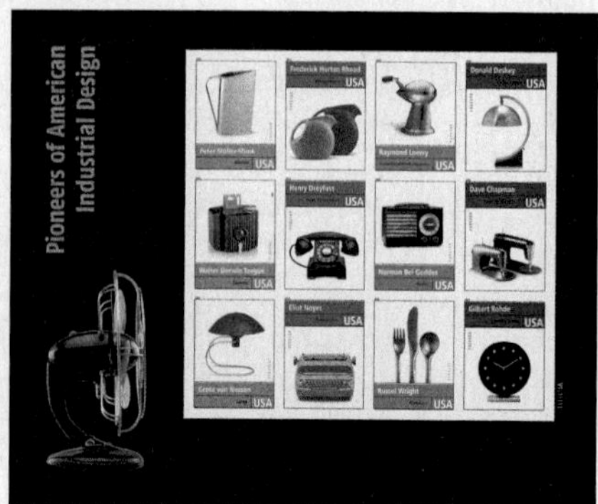

A3475

Designed by Derry Noyes. Printed by Avery Dennison.

No. 4546: a, "Normandie" pitcher, designed by Peter Müller-Munk (1904-67). b, Fiesta dinnerware, designed by Frederick Hurten Rhead (1880-1942). c, Streamlined pencil sharpener, designed by Raymond Loewy (1893-1986). d, Table lamp, designed by Donald Deskey (1894-1989). e, Kodak "Baby Brownie" camera, designed by Walter Dorwin Teague (1883-1960). f, Model 302 Bell telephone, designed by Henry Dreyfuss (1904-72). g, Emerson "Patriot" radio, designed by Norman Bel Geddes (1893-1958). h, Streamlined sewing machines, designed by Dave Chapman (1909-78). i, "Any-where" lamp, designed by Greta von Nessen (1900-74). j, IBM "Selectric" typewriter, designed by Eliot Noyes (1910-77). k, "Highlight/Pinch" flatware, designed by Russel Wright (1904-76). l, Herman Miller electric clock, designed by Gilbert Rohde (1894-1944).

PHOTOGRAVURE

2011, June 29 Tagged ***Serpentine Die Cut 10¾***
Self-Adhesive

4546 A3475 Pane of 12 15.00
a.-l. (44c) Any single 1.25 .50

See note after No. 1549.

OWNEY, THE POSTAL DOG Ⓢ

Owney, His Medals and Tags — A3476

Designed by Bill Bond. Printed by Avery Dennison.

PHOTOGRAVURE
Sheets of 200 in 10 panes of 20

2011, July 27 Tagged ***Serpentine Die Cut 11***
Self-Adhesive

4547 A3476 (44c) **multicolored** 1.50 .25
P# block of 4, 5#+V 6.00
Pane of 20 30.00

Uncut press sheets of No. 4547 were made available for sale. Values: cross-gutter block of 4, $10; pairs with gutters between, $2.50 each. See note after No. 2868.

See note after No. 1549.

U.S. MERCHANT MARINE Ⓢ

Clipper Ship — A3477

Auxiliary Steamship A3478

Liberty Ship — A3479

Container Ship — A3480

Designed by Carl T. Herrman. Printed by Avery Dennison.

PHOTOGRAVURE
Sheets of 240 in 12 panes of 20

2011, July 28 Tagged ***Serpentine Die Cut 11***
Self-Adhesive

4548 A3477 (44c) **multicolored** 1.25 .35
4549 A3478 (44c) **multicolored** 1.25 .35
4550 A3479 (44c) **multicolored** 1.25 .35
4551 A3480 (44c) **multicolored** 1.25 .35
a. Block or horiz. strip of 4, #4548-4551 5.00
P# block of 4, 6#+V 5.00
Pane of 20 25.00

See note after No. 1549.

EID

"Eid Mubarak" — A3481

Designed by Mohamed Zakariya. Printed by Avery Dennison.

PHOTOGRAVURE
Sheets of 240 in 12 panes of 20

2011, Aug. 12 Tagged ***Serpentine Die Cut 11¼***
Self-Adhesive

4552 A3481 (44c) **maroon, gray & gold** ® 1.25 .25
P# block of 4, 3#+V 5.00
Pane of 20 25.00

See note after No. 1549.

CHARACTERS FROM DISNEY-PIXAR FILMS

Send a Hello Ⓢ

Lightning McQueen and Mater from *Cars* — A3482

Remy the Rat and Linguini from *Ratatouille* — A3483

Buzz Lightyear and Aliens from *Toy Story* — A3484

Carl Fredricksen and Dug the Dog from *Up* — A3485

WALL-E from *WALL-E* — A3486

Designed by Terrence W. McCaffrey and William J. Gicker. Printed by Avery Dennison.

PHOTOGRAVURE
Sheets of 80 in four panes of 20

2011, Aug. 19 Tagged ***Serpentine Die Cut 10½***
Self-Adhesive

4553 A3482 (44c) **multicolored** 1.25 .40
4554 A3483 (44c) **multicolored** 1.25 .40
4555 A3484 (44c) **multicolored** 1.25 .40
4556 A3485 (44c) **multicolored** 1.25 .40
4557 A3486 (44c) **multicolored** 1.25 .40
a. Horiz. strip of 5, #4553-4557 6.25
P# block of 10, 4#+V 12.50
Pane of 20 25.00

Adjacent horizontal or vertical stamps have selvage between the stamps. Plate block may contain top label.

Uncut press sheets of Nos. 4553-4557 were made available for sale. Values: cross gutter block of 10 (four stamps from one side of the sheet and six stamps from the other side), $22.50; pairs with gutters between, $2.50. See note after No. 2868.

See note after No. 1549.

AMERICAN TREASURES SERIES

The Long Leg, by Edward Hopper (1882-1967) A3487

Designed by Derry Noyes. Printed by Avery Dennison.

PHOTOGRAVURE
Sheets of 200 in 10 panes of 20

2011, Aug. 24 Tagged ***Serpentine Die Cut 11***
Self-Adhesive

4558 A3487 (44c) **multicolored** ® 1.25 .25
P# block of 4, 5#+V 5.00
Pane of 20 25.00

See note after No. 1549.

A3487a

A3487b

A3487c

A3487d

A3487e

A3487f

Designed by Terrence W. McCaffrey. Printed by Ashton-Potter (USA) Ltd. (#4559-4560), Banknote Corporation of America for Sennett Security Products (#4561-4562), Avery Dennison (#4563-4564).

LITHOGRAPHED (#4559-4562), PHOTOGRAVURE

Serpentine Die Cut 11¼x11 on 2 or 3 Sides

2011, Sept. 14 **Tagged**

BOOKLET STAMPS

Self-Adhesive

4559	A3487a (44c) **multicolored** Ⓢ	1.50	.25
4560	A3487b (44c) **multicolored** Ⓢ	1.50	.25
a.	Pair, #4559-4560	3.00	
b.	Booklet pane of 20, 10 each #4559-4560	30.00	
4561	A3487c (44c) **multicolored**	1.50	.25
4562	A3487d (44c) **multicolored**	1.50	.25
a.	Pair, #4561-4562	3.00	
b.	Booklet pane of 20, 10 each #4561-4562	30.00	

Serpentine Die Cut 11¼x11½ on 2 or 3 Sides

4563	A3487e (44c) **multicolored** Ⓢ	1.25	.25
4564	A3487f (44c) **multicolored** Ⓢ	1.25	.25
a.	Pair, #4563-4564	2.50	
b.	Booklet pane of 20, 10 each #4563-4564	25.00	
	Nos. 4559-4564 (6)	8.50	1.50

Microprinting reads "4evR" on Nos. 4559-4560, "4evr" on Nos. 4561-4562, and "4EVR" on Nos. 4563-4564. The microprinting is found above the Statue of Liberty's hair, and at the bottom of the lowest red stripe of the flag. Nos. 4560b, 4562b and 4564b are double-sided booklet panes with 12 stamps one one side (6 each of types A3429-A3430) and 8 stamps (4 each of types A3429-A3430) on the other side. The paper used on Nos. 4561-4562 is thicker than that used on Nos. 4518-4519.

See note after No. 1549.

BLACK HERITAGE

Barbara Jordan (1936-96), Congresswoman — A3488

Designed by Richard Sheaff. Printed by Ashton-Potter (USA) Ltd.

LITHOGRAPHED

Sheets of 180 in nine panes of 20

2011, Sept. 16 **Tagged** ***Serpentine Die Cut 10¾***

Self-Adhesive

4565	A3488 (44c) **multicolored** Ⓢ	1.25	.25
	P# block of 4, 5#+P	5.00	
	Pane of 20	25.00	

See note after No. 1549.

ART OF ROMARE BEARDEN (1911-88) Ⓢ

Conjunction — A3489

Odysseus: Poseidon, The Sea God - Enemy of Odysseus — A3490

Prevalence of Ritual: Conjur Woman — A3491

Falling Star — A3492

Designed by Margaret Bauer. Printed by Avery Dennison.

PHOTOGRAVURE

Sheets of 128 in six panes of 16

2011, Sept. 28 **Tagged** ***Serpentine Die Cut 10¾***

Self-Adhesive

4566	A3489 (44c) **multicolored**	1.25	.40
4567	A3490 (44c) **multicolored**	1.25	.40
4568	A3491 (44c) **multicolored**	1.25	.40
4569	A3492 (44c) **multicolored**	1.25	.40
a.	Horiz. strip of 4, #4566-4569	5.00	
	P# block of 6 (#4567, 4569, 2 each #4566, 4568), 5#+V	7.50	
	Pane of 16	20.00	

See note after No. 1549.

CHRISTMAS

Madonna of the Candelabra, by Raphael — A3493

A3494

A3495

Ornaments

A3496 A3497

Designed by Richard Sheaff (#4570), William J. Gicker. Printed by Banknote Corporation of America for Sennett Security Products (#4570), Ashton-Potter (USA) Ltd. (#4571-4574).

LITHOGRAPHED

Serpentine Die Cut 10¾x 11 on 2 or 3 Sides

2011, Oct. 13 **Tagged**

Booklet Stamps

Self-Adhesive

4570	A3493 (44c) **multicolored**	1.25	.25
a.	Booklet pane of 20	25.00	

With "USPS" Microprinted on Collar of Ornament

4571	A3494 (44c) **multicolored** Ⓢ	1.50	.25
4572	A3495 (44c) **multicolored** Ⓢ	1.50	.25
4573	A3496 (44c) **multicolored** Ⓢ	1.50	.25
4574	A3497 (44c) **multicolored** Ⓢ	1.50	.25
a.	Block of 4, #4571-4574	6.00	
b.	Booklet pane of 20, 5 each #4571-4574	30.00	

See note after No. 1549.

A3497a A3497b

A3497c

A3497d

Designed by William J. Gicker.
Printed by Banknote Corporation of America for Sennett Security Products (#4575-4578).

Microprinted "USPS" in Places Other Than Collar of Ornament

4575	A3497a (44c) **multicolored**	1.50	.25
	Cylinder flaw ("USPS" microprinting doubled)	—	—
4576	A3497b (44c) **multicolored**	1.50	.25
	Cylinder flaw ("USPS" microprinting doubled)	—	—
4577	A3497c (44c) **multicolored**	1.50	.25
	Cylinder flaw ("USPS" microprinting doubled)	—	—
4578	A3497d (44c) **multicolored**	1.50	.25
	Cylinder flaw ("USPS" microprinting doubled)	—	—
a.	Block of 4, #4575-4578	6.00	
b.	Booklet pane of 20, 5 each #4575-4578	30.00	

A3498

A3499

Ornaments
A3500 A3501

Designed by William J. Gicker.
Printed by Banknote Corporation of America for Sennett Security Products (#4579-4582).

Serpentine Die Cut 11¼x11 on 2, 3 or 4 Sides

4579 A3498 (44c) **multicolored** 1.50 .25
4580 A3499 (44c) **multicolored** 1.50 .25
4581 A3500 (44c) **multicolored** 1.50 .25
4582 A3501 (44c) **multicolored** 1.50 .25
a. Block or strip of 4, #4579-4582 6.00
b. Booklet pane of 18, 5 each #4579, 4582, 4 each #4580-4581 27.50
Nos. 4570-4582 (13) 19.25 3.25

The microprinted "USPS" is to the left of the third stripe on Nos. 4575 and 4579, on the left side of the bottom ribbon of the ribbon cluster above the ornament collar on Nos. 4576 and 4578, below the bottom stripe near the bottom tip on No. 4577, on the vertical ribbon on No. 4580, on a curved ribbon above the collar on No. 4581, and on the left side of the ornament, below the collar, on No. 4582.

No. 4570a is a double-sided booklet with 12 stamps on one side and eight stamps plus a label that serves as a booklet cover on the other side. Nos. 4574b and 4578b are double sided booklets with 12 stamps (3 each of types A3494-A3497) on one side and eight stamps (2 each of types A3494-A3497) plus a label that serves as a booklet cover on the other side.

The cylinder flaw on Nos. 4575-4578 always appears on the four stamps to the left on the 12-stamp side of the booklet.

HANUKKAH

A3502

Designed by Suzanne Kleinwaks. Printed by Banknote Corporation of America for Sennett Security Products.

LITHOGRAPHED
Sheets of 200 in 10 panes of 20
Serpentine Die Cut 11x10¾

2011, Oct. 14 **Tagged**

Self-Adhesive

4583 A3502 (44c) **multicolored** 1.25 .25
P# block of 4, 5#+S 5.00
Pane of 20 25.00

KWANZAA

Family — A3503

Designed by Derry Noyes. Printed by Ashton-Potter (USA) Ltd.

LITHOGRAPHED
Sheets of 160 in eight panes of 20
Serpentine Die Cut 10¾x11

2011, Oct. 14 **Tagged**

Self-Adhesive

4584 A3503 (44c) **multicolored** Ⓢ 1.25 .25
P# block of 4, 4#+P 5.00
Pane of 20 25.00

See note after No. 1549.

EAGLE

A3504

A3504a

A3504b

A3504c

A3504d

A3504e

Designed by Ethel Kessler. Printed by Avery Dennison.

PHOTOGRAVURE
Serpentine Die Cut 11 Vert.

2012, Jan. 3 **Untagged**

Coil Stamps
Self-Adhesive
Color Behind "USA"

4585 A3504 (25c) **green** Ⓢ .50 .25
4586 A3504a (25c) **blue green** Ⓢ .50 .25
4587 A3504b (25c) **blue** Ⓢ .50 .25
4588 A3504c (25c) **red violet** Ⓢ .50 .25
4589 A3504d (25c) **brown orange** Ⓢ .50 .25
4590 A3504e (25c) **yellow orange** Ⓢ .50 .25
a. Strip of 6, #4585-4590 3.00
P# strip of 7, 2 #4585, 1 each #4586-4590, #V11111, V11112 5.00
P# strip of 13, 3 #4588, 2 each #4585-4587, 4589-4590, #V11111, V11112 9.00
P# single (#4588), #V11111, V11112 — 2.50

See note after No. 1549.
See Nos. 5013-5018.

NEW MEXICO STATEHOOD CENTENNIAL Ⓢ

Sanctuary II, Painting by Doug West — A3505

Designed by Richard Sheaff. Printed by Avery Dennison.

PHOTOGRAVURE
Sheets of 160 in eight panes of 20

2012, Jan. 6 **Tagged** ***Serpentine Die Cut 11***

Self-Adhesive

4591 A3505 (44c) **multicolored** 1.25 .25
P# block of 4, 4#+V 5.00
Pane of 20 25.00

See note after No. 1549.

ALOHA SHIRTS

Surfers and Palm Trees — A3506

Surfers — A3507

Bird of Paradise Flowers — A3508

Kilauea Volcano — A3509

Fossil Fish, Shells and Starfish — A3510

Designed by Carl T. Herrman. Printed by Avery Dennison (#4592-4596).

PHOTOGRAVURE
Sheets of 420 in 21 panes of 20

2012, Jan. 19 **Tagged** ***Serpentine Die Cut 11***

Self-Adhesive

4592 A3506 32c **multicolored** Ⓢ 2.00 .30
4593 A3507 32c **multicolored** Ⓢ 2.00 .30
4594 A3508 32c **multicolored** Ⓢ 2.00 .30
4595 A3509 32c **multicolored** Ⓢ 2.00 .30
4596 A3510 32c **multicolored** Ⓢ 2.00 .30
a. Horiz. strip of 5, #4592-4596 10.00
P# block of 10, 7#+V 20.00
Pane of 20 40.00

A3506a

A3507a

A3508a

A3509a

A3510a

Printed by Banknote Corporation of America for Sennett Security Products (#4597-4601).

LITHOGRAPHED
Coil Stamps
Serpentine Die Cut 11 Vert.

4597 A3510a 32c **multicolored** 2.00 .30
4598 A3506a 32c **multicolored** 2.00 .30
4599 A3507a 32c **multicolored** 2.00 .30
4600 A3508a 32c **multicolored** 2.00 .30

4601 A3509a 32c **multicolored** 2.00 .30
a. Strip of 5, #4597-4601 10.00
P# strip of 5, #4597-4601, #S1111111 12.00
P# strip of 11, 3 #4599, 2 each #4597-4598, 4600-4601, #S1111111 24.00
P# single (#4599), same # — 3.00
b. As "a," die cutting omitted 125.00
Nos. 4592-4601 (10) 20.00 3.00

On Nos. 4592-4596, the top of the shirt collars are all higher than the cross line of the "A" in "USA," and on Nos. 4597-4601, they are even with or slightly below the cross line.
See Nos. 4682-4686.
See note after No. 1549.

Wedding Cake — A3510b

Designed by Ethel Kessler. Printed by Banknote Corporation of America for Sennett Security Products.

LITHOGRAPHED
Sheets of 160 in eight panes of 20
2012, Jan. 20 Tagged ***Serpentine Die Cut 10¾***
Self-Adhesive

4602 A3510b 65c **multicolored** 2.50 .25
P# block of 4, 6#+S 10.00
Pane of 20 50.00

See Nos. 4398, 4521, 4735, 4867, 5000.

BALTIMORE CHECKERSPOT BUTTERFLY Ⓢ

A3511

Designed by Derry Noyes. Printed by Avery Dennison.

PHOTOGRAVURE
Sheets of 200 in 10 panes of 20
2012, Jan. 20 Tagged ***Serpentine Die Cut 10¾***
Self-Adhesive

4603 A3511 65c **multicolored** 1.50 .25
P# block of 4, 4#+V 7.00
Pane of 20 34.00

See note after No. 1549.

DOGS AT WORK Ⓢ

Seeing Eye Dog — A3512

Therapy Dog — A3513

Military Dog — A3514

Rescue Dog — A3515

Designed by Howard E. Paine. Printed by Avery Dennison.

PHOTOGRAVURE
Sheets of 240 in 12 panes of 20
2012, Jan. 20 Tagged ***Serpentine Die Cut 10¾***
Self-Adhesive

4604 A3512 65c **multicolored** 1.30 .30
4605 A3513 65c **multicolored** 1.30 .30
4606 A3514 65c **multicolored** 1.30 .30
4607 A3515 65c **multicolored** 1.30 .30
a. Block or vert. strip of 4, #4604-4607 5.20
P# block of 4, 4#+V 5.20
Pane of 20 26.00

See note after No. 1549.

BIRDS OF PREY Ⓢ

Northern Goshawk — A3516

Peregrine Falcon — A3517

Golden Eagle — A3518

Osprey — A3519

Northern Harrier — A3520

Designed by Howard E. Paine. Printed by Ashton-Potter (USA) Ltd.

LITHOGRAPHED
Sheets of 120 in six panes of 20
Serpentine Die Cut 11¼x10¾
2012, Jan. 20 Tagged
Self-Adhesive

4608 A3516 85c **multicolored** 1.75 .35
4609 A3517 85c **multicolored** 1.75 .35
4610 A3518 85c **multicolored** 1.75 .35
4611 A3519 85c **multicolored** 1.75 .35
4612 A3520 85c **multicolored** 1.75 .35
a. Horiz. strip of 5, #4608-4612 8.75
P# block of 10, 4#+P 17.50
Pane of 20 35.00

See note after No. 1549.

WEATHER VANES

Rooster With Perch — A3521

Cow — A3522

Eagle — A3523

Rooster Without Perch — A3524

Centaur — A3525

Designed by Derry Noyes. Printed by Banknote Corporation of America for Sennett Security Products.

LITHOGRAPHED
Serpentine Die Cut 11¾ Vert.
2012, Jan. 20 Tagged
Coil Stamps
Self-Adhesive

4613 A3521 45c **multicolored** 1.50 .30
4614 A3522 45c **multicolored** 1.50 .30
4615 A3523 45c **multicolored** 1.50 .30
4616 A3524 45c **multicolored** 1.50 .30
4617 A3525 45c **multicolored** 1.50 .30
a. Strip of 5, #4613-4617 7.50
P# strip of 5, #4613-4617, #S1111111 8.50
P# strip of 11, 3 #4615, 2 each #4613-4614, 4616-4617, #S1111111 17.50
P# single (#4615), same # — 2.75

BONSAI Ⓢ

Sierra Juniper — A3526

Black Pine — A3527

Banyan — A3528

Trident Maple — A3529

Azalea — A3530

Designed by Ethel Kessler. Printed by Ashton-Potter (USA) Ltd.

LITHOGRAPHED

Serpentine Die Cut 11x10¾ on 2 or 3 Sides

2012, Jan. 23 **Tagged**

Booklet Stamps
Self-Adhesive

4618	A3526 (45c) **multicolored**	2.00	.40
4619	A3527 (45c) **multicolored**	2.00	.40
4620	A3528 (45c) **multicolored**	2.00	.40
4621	A3529 (45c) **multicolored**	2.00	.40
4622	A3530 (45c) **multicolored**	2.00	.40
a.	Vert. strip of 5, #4618-4622	10.00	
b.	Booklet pane of 20, 4 each #4618-4622	40.00	

Stamps in No. 4622a are not adjacent, as rows of selvage are between stamps two and three, and between stamps four and five.

No. 4622b is a double-sided booklet with 12 stamps on one side (3 each #4618, 4621, 2 each #4619, 4620, 4622) and eight stamps (#4618, 4621, 2 each #4619, 4620, 4622) plus label that serves as a booklet cover on the other side.

Counterfeits exist of No. 4618-4622. See the Postal Counterfeits section of this catalog.

See note after No. 1549.

CHINESE NEW YEAR

Year of the Dragon A3531

Designed by Ethel Kessler. Printed by Avery Dennison.

PHOTOGRAVURE

Sheets of 108 in nine panes of 12

Serpentine Die Cut 11x10¾

2012, Jan. 23 **Tagged**

Self-Adhesive

4623	A3531 (45c) **multicolored** Ⓢ	1.25	.25
	Pane of 12	15.00	

Uncut press sheets of No. 4623 were made available for sale. Values: cross-gutter block of 4, $10; pairs with gutters between, $2.50 each. See note after No. 2868.

See note after No. 1549.

BLACK HERITAGE

John H. Johnson (1918-2005), Magazine Publisher — A3532

Designed by Howard E. Paine. Printed by Ashton-Potter (USA) Ltd.

LITHOGRAPHED

Sheets of 120 in six panes of 20

2012, Jan. 31 **Tagged** *Serpentine Die Cut 10¾*

Self-Adhesive

4624	A3532 (45c) **multicolored** Ⓢ	1.25	.25
	P# block of 4, 5#+P	5.00	
	Pane of 20	25.00	

Uncut press sheets of No. 4624 were made available for sale. Values: cross-gutter block of 4, $10; pairs with gutters between, $2.50 each. See note after No. 2868.

See note after No. 1549.

HEART HEALTH Ⓢ

Tree, Man, Sun and Apple — A3533

Designed by Derry Noyes. Printed by Avery Dennison.

PHOTOGRAVURE

Sheets of 200 in 10 panes of 20

2012, Feb. 9 **Tagged** *Serpentine Die Cut 11*

Self-Adhesive

4625	A3533 (45c) **multicolored**	1.25	.25
	P# block of 4, 6#+V	5.00	
	Pane of 20	25.00	

See note after No. 1549.

LOVE

Ribbons — A3534

Designed by Louise Fili. Printed by Banknote Corporation of America for Sennett Security Products.

LITHOGRAPHED

Sheets of 200 in 10 panes of 20

2012, Feb. 14 **Tagged** *Serpentine Die Cut 10¾*

Self-Adhesive

4626	A3534 (45c) **red**	1.25	.25
	P# block of 4, 2#+S	5.00	
	Pane of 20	25.00	
a.	Die cutting omitted, pair	*200.00*	

Postal Service officials declared on Feb. 2 that No. 4626 could be sold in post offices as of that date to make the stamp available to customers before St. Valentine's Day, but the first day ceremony for the stamp was held Feb. 14 in Colorado Springs, CO. Official first day covers have that date and city.

ARIZONA STATEHOOD CENTENNIAL Ⓢ

Cathedral Rock — A3535

Designed by Richard Sheaff. Printed by Avery Dennison.

PHOTOGRAVURE

Sheets of 200 in 10 panes of 20

2012, Feb. 14 **Tagged** *Serpentine Die Cut 11*

Self-Adhesive

4627	A3535 (45c) **multicolored**	1.25	.25
	P# block of 4, 5#+V	5.00	
	Pane of 20	25.00	

See note after No. 1549.

DANNY THOMAS

Thomas (1912-91), Comedian, and St. Jude's Children's Research Hospital, Memphis A3536

Designed by Greg Breeding. Printed by Banknote Corporation of America for Sennett Security Products.

LITHOGRAPHED

Sheets of 180 in nine panes of 20

Serpentine Die Cut 10¾x10½

2012, Feb. 16 **Tagged**

Self-Adhesive

4628	A3536 (45c) **multicolored**	1.25	.25
	P# block of 4, 5#+S	5.00	
	Pane of 20	25.00	

Flag and "Equality" — A3537

Flag and "Justice" — A3538

Flag and "Freedom" — A3539

Flag and "Liberty" — A3540

Designed by Howard E. Paine. Printed by Avery Dennison.

PHOTOGRAVURE

Serpentine Die Cut 8½ Vert.

2012, Feb. 22 **Tagged**

Coil Stamps
Self-Adhesive

4629	A3537 (45c) **multicolored** Ⓢ	1.50	.25
4630	A3538 (45c) **multicolored** Ⓢ	1.50	.25
4631	A3539 (45c) **multicolored** Ⓢ	1.50	.25
4632	A3540 (45c) **multicolored** Ⓢ	1.50	.25
a.	Strip of 4, #4629-4632	6.00	
	P# strip of 5, 2 #4629, 1 each #4630-4632, #V1111	8.50	
	P# strip of 9, 3# 4631, 2 each #4629-4630, 4632, #V1111	16.00	
	P# single, #V1111 (#4631)	—	2.75

Counterfeits exist of Nos. 4629-4632. See the Postal Counterfeits section of this catalog.

Flag and "Equality" — A3540a

Flag and "Justice" — A3540b

Flag and "Freedom" — A3540c

Flag and "Liberty" — A3540d

Printed by Ashton-Potter (USA) Ltd.

LITHOGRAPHED (#4633-4648)

Serpentine Die Cut 9½ Vert.

4633 A3540a (45c) **multi**, overall tagging Ⓢ 1.25 .25
- *a.* Prephosphored coated paper with surface tagging showing a solid appearance Ⓢ 1.25 .25

4634 A3540b (45c) **multi**, overall tagging Ⓢ 1.25 .25
- *a.* Prephosphored coated paper with surface tagging showing a solid appearance Ⓢ 1.25 .25

4635 A3540c (45c) **multi**, overall tagging Ⓢ 1.25 .25
- *a.* Prephosphored coated paper with surface tagging showing a solid appearance Ⓢ 1.25 .25

4636 A3540d (45c) **multi**, overall tagging Ⓢ 1.25 .25
- *a.* Prephosphored coated paper with surface tagging showing a solid appearance Ⓢ 1.25 .25
- *b.* Strip of 4, #4633-4636 5.00
  - P# strip of 5, 2 #4633, 1 each #4634-4636, #P1111 6.25
  - P# strip of 9, 3 #4635, 2 each #4633-4634, 4636, #P1111 11.50
  - P# single, #P1111 (#4635) — 2.75
- *c.* Strip of 4, #4633a-4636a 5.00
  - P# strip of 5, 2 #4633a, 1 each #4634a-4636a, #P2222 7.00
  - P# strip of 9, 3 #4635a, 2 each #4633a-4634a, 4636a, #P2222 12.50
  - P# single, #P2222 (#4635a) — 3.00

Nos. 4633-4636 were printed on nonphosphored paper with tagging applied after the stamps were printed.

Flag and "Equality" — A3540e

Flag and "Justice" — A3540f

Flag and "Freedom" — A3540g

Flag and "Liberty" — A3540h

Printed by Banknote Corporation of America for Sennett Security Products.

Serpentine Die Cut 11 Vert.

4637 A3540e (45c) **multicolored** 1.50 .25
4638 A3540f (45c) **multicolored** 1.50 .25
4639 A3540g (45c) **multicolored** 1.50 .25
4640 A3540h (45c) **multicolored** 1.50 .25
- *a.* Strip of 4, #4637-4640 6.00
  - P# strip of 5, 2 #4637, 1 each #4638-4640, #S11111, S22222 7.50
  - P# strip of 9, 3# 4639, 2 each #4637-4638, 4640, #S11111, S22222 13.50
  - P# single, #S11111, S22222 (#4639) — 2.75
- *b.* As "a," die cutting omitted *450.00*
  - *Nos. 4629-4640 (12)* 17.00 3.00

Counterfeits exist of Nos. 4637-4640. See the Postal Counterfeits section of this catalog.

Flag and "Freedom" — A3540i

Flag and "Liberty" — A3540j

Flag and "Equality" — A3540k

Flag and "Justice" — A3540l

Printed by Ashton-Potter (USA) Ltd.

Booklet Stamps
Colored Dots in Stars
18½mm From Lower Left to Lower Right Corners of Flag

Serpentine Die Cut 11¼x10¾ on 2 or 3 Sides

4641 A3540i (45c) **multi**, overall tagging Ⓢ 1.25 .25
- *a.* Prephosphored coated paper with surface tagging showing a solid appearance Ⓢ 1.25 .25

4642 A3540j (45c) **multi**, overall tagging Ⓢ 1.25 .25
- *a.* Prephosphored coated paper with surface tagging showing a solid appearance Ⓢ 1.25 .25

4643 A3540k (45c) **multi**, overall tagging Ⓢ 1.25 .25
- *a.* Prephosphored coated paper with surface tagging showing a solid appearance Ⓢ 1.25 .25

4644 A3540l (45c) **multi**, overall tagging Ⓢ 1.25 .25
- *a.* Prephosphored coated paper with surface tagging showing a solid appearance Ⓢ 1.25 .25
- *b.* Block of 4, #4641-4644 5.00
- *c.* Booklet pane of 20, 5 each #4641-4644 25.00
- *d.* Block of 4, #4641a-4644a 5.00
- *e.* Booklet pane of 20, 5 each #4641a-4644a 25.00

Flag and "Freedom" — A3540m

Flag and "Liberty" — A3540n

Flag and "Equality" — A3540o

Flag and "Justice" — A3540p

Printed by Banknote Corporation of America for Sennett Security Products.

Dark Dots Only in Stars
19mm from Lower Left to Lower Right Corners of Flag

4645 A3540m (45c) **multicolored** 1.50 .25
4646 A3540n (45c) **multicolored** 1.50 .25
4647 A3540o (45c) **multicolored** 1.50 .25
4648 A3540p (45c) **multicolored** 1.50 .25
- *a.* Block of 4, #4645-4648 6.00
- *b.* Booklet pane of 20, 5 each #4645-4648 30.00
  - *Nos. 4641-4648 (8)* 11.00 2.00

On Nos. 4641-4644, the blue canton of the flag is made up of blue and red inks. The paper is tagged over each block of 4, with no tagging on the paper between the blocks. The tagging is a dull yellow green under ultraviolet light. The tagging on Nos. 4641a-4644a is a bright yellow green under ultraviolet light. The words are slightly longer than those on Nos. 4645-4648.

On Nos. 4645-4648, the blue canton is made up of blue and dull blue inks. The paper is prephosphored with the tagging appearing bright yellow green under ultraviolet light. The words are slightly shorter than those on Nos. 4641-4644.

No. 4644c is a double-sided booklet with 12 stamps on one side (3 each #4641-4644) and eight stamps (2 each #4641-4644) plus label that serves as a booklet cover on the other side.

No. 4644e is a double-sided booklet with 12 stamps on one side (3 each #4641a-4644a) and eight stamps (2 each #4641a-4644a) plus label that serves as a booklet cover on the other side.

No. 4648b is a double-sided booklet with 12 stamps on one side (3 each #4645-4648) and eight stamps (2 each #4645-4648) plus label that serves as a booklet cover on the other side.

See Nos. 4673-4676.
See note after No. 1549.

AMERICAN LANDMARKS ISSUE

Sunshine Skyway Bridge, Florida A3541

Carmel Mission, Carmel, CA — A3542

Designed by Carl T. Hermann (#4649), Phil Jordan (#4650). Printed by Banknote Corporation of America for Sennett Security Products (#4649), Ashton-Potter (USA) Ltd. (#4650).

LITHOGRAPHED

Sheets of 180 in nine panes of 20 (#4649), Sheets of 60 in six panes of 10 (#4650)

Serpentine Die Cut 10¾x10½

2012, Feb. 28 **Tagged**

Self-Adhesive

4649 A3541 $5.15 **multicolored** 11.00 5.75
- P# block of 4, 5#+S 45.00
- Pane of 20 220.00

4650 A3542 $18.95 **multicolored** Ⓢ 42.50 19.00
- P# block of 4, 4#+P 170.00
- Pane of 10 425.00

See note after No. 1549.

CHERRY BLOSSOM CENTENNIAL Ⓢ

Cherry Blossoms and Washington Monument A3543

Cherry Blossoms and Jefferson Memorial A3544

Designed by Phil Jordan. Printed by Ashton-Potter (USA) Ltd.

LITHOGRAPHED

Sheets of 120 in six panes of 20

2012, Mar. 24 **Tagged** ***Serpentine Die Cut 10¾***

Self-Adhesive

4651 A3543 (45c) **multicolored** 1.25 .25
4652 A3544 (45c) **multicolored** 1.25 .25
- *a.* Horiz. pair, #4651-4652 2.50
  - P# block of 4, 5#+P 5.00
  - P# block of 8, 2 sets of 5#+P, + top label 10.00
  - Pane of 20 25.00

See Japan No. 3413.
See note after No. 1549.

AMERICAN TREASURES SERIES

Flowers, by William H. Johnson (1901-70) — A3545

Designed by Derry Noyes. Printed by Avery Dennison.

PHOTOGRAVURE

Sheets of 200 in 10 panes of 20

2012, Apr. 11 Tagged *Serpentine Die Cut 10¾*

Self-Adhesive

4653 A3545 (45c) **multicolored** ⓢ	1.25	.35
P# block of 4, 6#+V	5.00	
P# block of 10, 2 sets of 6#+V, + top label	12.50	
Pane of 20	25.00	

See note after No. 1549.

TWENTIETH CENTURY POETS ⓢ

Joseph Brodsky (1940-96) — A3546

Gwendolyn Brooks (1917-2000) — A3547

William Carlos Williams (1883-1963) — A3548

Robert Hayden (1913-80) — A3549

Sylvia Plath (1932-63) — A3550

Elizabeth Bishop (1911-79) — A3551

Wallace Stevens (1879-1955) — A3552

Denise Levertov (1923-97) — A3553

E. E. Cummings (1894-1962) — A3554

Theodore Roethke (1908-63) — A3555

Designed by Derry Noyes. Printed by Ashton-Potter (USA) Ltd.

LITHOGRAPHED

Sheets of 160 in eight panes of 20

Serpentine Die Cut 10¾x11

2012, Apr. 21 Tagged

Self-Adhesive

4654 A3546 (45c) **multicolored**	2.50	.50
4655 A3547 (45c) **multicolored**	2.50	.50
4656 A3548 (45c) **multicolored**	2.50	.50
4657 A3549 (45c) **multicolored**	2.50	.50
4658 A3550 (45c) **multicolored**	2.50	.50
4659 A3551 (45c) **multicolored**	2.50	.50
4660 A3552 (45c) **multicolored**	2.50	.50
4661 A3553 (45c) **multicolored**	2.50	.50
4662 A3554 (45c) **multicolored**	2.50	.50
4663 A3555 (45c) **multicolored**	2.50	.50
a. Block of 10, #4654-4663	25.00	
P# block of 10, 6#+P	25.00	
Pane of 20	50.00	
Nos. 4654-4663 (10)	25.00	5.00

See note after No. 1549.

CIVIL WAR SESQUICENTENNIAL

Battle of New Orleans — A3556

Battle of Antietam — A3557

Designed by Phil Jordan. Printed by Ashton-Potter (USA) Ltd.

LITHOGRAPHED

Double-sided sheets of 72 in six panes of 12 (60 on one side, 12 on other side)

2012, Apr. 24 Tagged *Serpentine Die Cut 11*

Self-Adhesive

4664 A3556 (45c) **multicolored** ⓢ	1.25	.30
4665 A3557 (45c) **multicolored** ⓢ	1.25	.30
a. Pair, #4664-4665	2.50	
Pane of 12	15.00	

Uncut press sheets of Nos. 4664-4665 were made available for sale. See note after No. 2868.

See note after No. 1549.

DISTINGUISHED AMERICANS

José Ferrer (1912-92), Actor — A3558

Designed by Antonio Alcala. Printed by Ashton-Potter (USA) Ltd.

LITHOGRAPHED

Sheets of 160 in eight panes of 20

Serpentine Die Cut 10¾x11

2012, Apr. 26 Tagged

Self-Adhesive

4666 A3558 (45c) **multicolored** ⓢ	1.25	.25
P# block of 4, 7#+P	5.00	
Pane of 20	25.00	

See note after No. 1549.

LOUISIANA STATEHOOD BICENTENNIAL ⓢ

Sunset Over Flat Lake — A3559

Designed by Phil Jordan. Printed by Avery Dennison.

PHOTOGRAVURE

Sheets of 160 in eight panes of 20

2012, Apr. 30 Tagged *Serpentine Die Cut 11*

Self-Adhesive

4667 A3559 (45c) **multicolored**	1.25	.25
P# block of 4, 5#+V	5.00	
Pane of 20	25.00	

See note after No. 1549.

GREAT FILM DIRECTORS ⓢ

John Ford (1894-1973), Scene From *The Searchers,* Starring John Wayne A3560

Frank Capra (1897-1991), Scene From *It Happened One Night,* Starring Clark Gable and Claudette Colbert A3561

Billy Wilder (1906-2002), Scene From *Some Like It Hot,* Starring Marilyn Monroe A3562

John Huston (1906-87), Scene From *The Maltese Falcon,* Starring Humphrey Bogart A3563

Designed by Derry Noyes. Printed by Avery Dennison.

PHOTOGRAVURE

Sheets of 200 in 10 panes of 20

2012, May 23 Tagged *Serpentine Die Cut 10¾*

Self-Adhesive

4668	A3560 (45c) **multicolored**		1.25	.40
4669	A3561 (45c) **multicolored**		1.25	.40
4670	A3562 (45c) **multicolored**		1.25	.40
4671	A3563 (45c) **multicolored**		1.25	.40
a.	Block or horiz. strip of 4, #4668-4671		5.00	
	P# block of 4, 5#+V		5.00	
	P# block of 8, 2 sets of 5#+V, + top label		5.00	
	Pane of 20		25.00	

See note after No. 1549.

WILDLIFE

Bobcat — A3564

A3564a

Designed by Carl T. Herrman. Printed by Ashton-Potter (USA) Ltd.

LITHOGRAPHED

Serpentine Die Cut 10 Vert.

2012, June 1 Untagged

Coil Stamp

Self-Adhesive

4672	A3564 1c **multicolored** Ⓢ		.30	.25
	Pair		.30	
	P# strip of 5, #P1111, P2222		.80	
	P# single, #P1111, P2222		—	.55
a.	A3564a Dated "2015," *Feb. 21, 2015*		.30	.25
	Pair		.30	
	P# strip of 5, #P1111		.75	
	P# single, #P1111		—	.60

Microprinting is on bobcat's ear on No. 4672 and on the bobcat's leg on No. 4672a.

See No. 4802. See note after No. 1549.

Flag and "Freedom" — A3564b

Flag and "Liberty" — A3564c

Flag and "Equality" — A3564d

Flag and "Justice" — A3564e

Designed by Howard E. Paine. Printed by Avery Dennison.

PHOTOGRAVURE

Serpentine Die Cut 11¼x10¾ on 3 Sides

2012, June 1 Tagged

Booklet Stamps

Self-Adhesive

Colored Dots in Stars

19¼mm From Lower Left to Lower Right Corners of Flag

4673	A3564b (45c) **multicolored** Ⓢ		1.25	.25
4674	A3564c (45c) **multicolored** Ⓢ		1.25	.25
4675	A3564d (45c) **multicolored** Ⓢ		1.25	.25
4676	A3564e (45c) **multicolored** Ⓢ		1.25	.25
a.	Block of 4, #4673-4676		5.00	
b.	Booklet pane of 10, 3 each #4673-4674, 2 each #4675-4676		12.50	

Nos. 4673 and No. 4675 have straight edge on left side only. Nos. 4674 and 4676 have straight edge on right side only. Nos. 4641-4648 each have a straight edge at top or bottom. The letters in the "USPS" microprinting on Nos. 4673-4676, found at the right side of the bottom white flag stripe, are printed in a distinct curve, with the tops of the middle letters, "SP," being below the tops of the outside letters, "U" and "S," and the letters can be difficult to distinguish against the shading on the stripe. The letters in the microprinting on Nos. 4641-4648, found in the same place on the stamp, are printed in a straight line, and are printed boldly, making them easily distinguishable from the shading. The lettering on Nos. 4673-4767 has a fuzzier, less distinct appearance under magnification than the lettering on Nos. 4641-4648, which is most evident in the year "2012."

See note after No. 1549.

CHARACTERS FROM DISNEY-PIXAR FILMS

Mail a Smile Ⓢ

Flik and Dot From *A Bug's Life* — A3565

Bob Parr and Dashiell Parr From *The Incredibles* — A3566

Nemo and Squirt From *Finding Nemo* — A3567

Jessie, Woody and Bullseye From *Toy Story 2* — A3568

Boo, Mike Wazowski and James P. "Sulley" Sullivan From *Monsters, Inc.* — A3569

Designed by William J. Gicker. Printed by Avery Dennison.

PHOTOGRAVURE

Sheets of 80 in four panes of 20

2012, June 1 Tagged *Serpentine Die Cut 10½*

Self-Adhesive

4677	A3565 (45c) **multicolored**		1.25	.40
4678	A3566 (45c) **multicolored**		1.25	.40
4679	A3567 (45c) **multicolored**		1.25	.40
4680	A3568 (45c) **multicolored**		1.25	.40
4681	A3569 (45c) **multicolored**		1.25	.40
a.	Horiz. strip of 5, #4677-4681		6.25	
	P# block of 10, 4#+V		12.50	
	Pane of 20		25.00	

Adjacent horizontal or vertical stamps have selvage between the stamps. Plate block may contain top label.

Uncut press sheets of Nos. 4677-4681 were made available for sale. Values: cross-gutter block of 10 (four stamps from one side of the sheet and six stamps from the other side), $25; pairs with gutters between, $2.50 each. See note after No. 2868.

See note after No. 1549.

ALOHA SHIRTS

A3569a

A3569b

A3569c

A3569d

A3569e

Designed by Carl T. Herrman. Printed by Ashton-Potter (USA) Ltd.

LITHOGRAPHED

Tagged

Serpentine Die Cut 11¼x10¾ on 3 Sides

2012, June 2

Booklet Stamps

Self-Adhesive

4682	A3569a 32c **multicolored** Ⓢ		8.50	.30
4683	A3569b 32c **multicolored** Ⓢ		8.50	.30
4684	A3569c 32c **multicolored** Ⓢ		8.50	.30
4685	A3569d 32c **multicolored** Ⓢ		8.50	.30
4686	A3569e 32c **multicolored** Ⓢ		8.50	.30
a.	Vert. strip of 5, #4682-4686		42.50	
b.	Booklet pane of 10, 2 each #4682-4686		85.00	

Stamps in No. 4686a are not adjacent, as a row of selvage is between stamps two and three.

See note after No. 1549.

See Nos. 4592-4601.

BICYCLING Ⓢ

Child on Bicycle with Training Wheels A3570

Commuter on Bicycle with Panniers A3571

Road Racer A3572

BMX Rider
A3573

Designed by Phil Jordan. Printed by Ashton-Potter (USA) Ltd.

LITHOGRAPHED

Sheets of 120 in six panes of 20

2012, June 7 Tagged *Serpentine Die Cut 10¾*

Self-Adhesive

4687	A3570 (45c) **multicolored**	1.25	.35
4688	A3571 (45c) **multicolored**	1.25	.35
4689	A3572 (45c) **multicolored**	1.25	.35
4690	A3573 (45c) **multicolored**	1.25	.35
a.	Horiz. strip of 4, #4687-4690	5.00	
	P# block of 8, 5#+P	10.00	
	Pane of 20	25.00	

Uncut press sheets of Nos. 4687-4690 were made available for sale. Values: cross-gutter block of 8, $12.50; pairs with gutters between, $2.50 each. See note after No. 2868.

See note after No. 1549.

GIRL SCOUTS OF AMERICA, CENT.

Girl Scouts — A3574

Designed by Derry Noyes. Printed by Banknote Corporation of America for Sennett Security Products.

LITHOGRAPHED

Sheets of 180 in nine panes of 20

2012, June 9 Tagged *Serpentine Die Cut 10¾*

Self-Adhesive

4691	A3574 (45c) **multicolored**	1.25	.25
	P# block of 4, 6#+S	5.00	
	Pane of 20	25.00	
a.	Die cutting omitted, pair	—	

Uncut press sheets of No. 4691 were made available for sale. Values: cross-gutter block of 4, $10; pairs with gutters between, $2.50 each. See note after No. 2868.

MUSICIANS Ⓢ

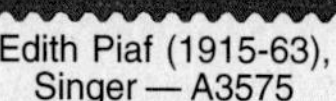

Edith Piaf (1915-63), Singer — A3575

Miles Davis (1926-91), Jazz Trumpet Player — A3576

Designed by Greg Breeding. Printed by Avery Dennison.

PHOTOGRAVURE

Sheets of 80 in four panes of 20

Serpentine Die Cut 10¾x11

2012, June 12 Tagged

Self-Adhesive

4692	A3575 (45c) **multicolored**	1.25	.30
4693	A3576 (45c) **multicolored**	1.25	.30
a.	Pair, #4692-4693	2.50	
	P# block of 5, 6#+V	6.25	
	P# block of 10, 6#+V, + top label	12.50	
	Pane of 20	25.00	

See France Nos. 4256-4257.

Uncut press sheets of Nos. 4692-4693 were made available for sale. Values: cross-gutter block of 10 (five stamps from each side of the sheet), $15; pairs with gutters between, $2.50 each. See note after No. 2868.

See note after No. 1549.

Imperforate Uncut Press Sheets

Beginning with Nos. 4694-4697, the U.S. Postal Service made available for sale imperforate uncut press sheets of selected commemorative and definitive issues. These sheets are noted in footnotes following each issue, and imperforate singles, small panes and booklets are listed and valued in the main listings. Imperforate pairs are valued at twice the value of imperforate singles. Like the perforated and die cut uncut press sheets, the imperforate uncut press sheets generally contain cross-gutter blocks and pairs with gutters between. Other collectible pair or block formats might also appear on selected sheets. The cross-gutter blocks, plus blocks and pairs with gutters between, are valued in the footnotes. The other possible formats not noted sell for a premium, but they are not listed or valued herein.

See note before No. 2869 for descriptions and illustrations of typical press-sheet multiples.

MAJOR LEAGUE BASEBALL ALL-STARS Ⓢ

Ted Williams (1918-2002) A3577

Larry Doby (1923-2003) A3578

Willie Stargell (1940-2001) A3579

Joe DiMaggio (1914-99) A3580

Designed by Phil Jordan. Printed by Avery Dennison.

PHOTOGRAVURE

Sheets of 120 in six panes of 20

Serpentine Die Cut 10¾x11

2012, July 20 Tagged

Self-Adhesive

4694	A3577 (45c) **multicolored**	1.25	.30
	P# block of 4, 5#+V	5.00	
	P# block of 8, 2 sets of 5#+V, + top panel	10.00	
	Pane of 20	25.00	
a.	Imperforate	2.50	—
	Pane of 20	50.00	
4695	A3578 (45c) **multicolored**	1.25	.30
	P# block of 4, 5#+V	5.00	
	P# block of 8, 2 sets of 5#+V, + top panel	10.00	
	Pane of 20	25.00	
a.	Imperforate	2.50	—
	Pane of 20	50.00	
4696	A3579 (45c) **multicolored**	1.25	.30
	P# block of 4, 5#+V	5.00	
	P# block of 8, 2 sets of 5#+V, + top panel	10.00	
	Pane of 20	25.00	
a.	Imperforate	2.50	—
	Pane of 20	50.00	
4697	A3580 (45c) **multicolored**	1.25	.30
	P# block of 4, 5#+V	5.00	
	P# block of 8, 2 sets of 5#+V, + top panel	10.00	
	Pane of 20	25.00	
a.	Imperforate	2.50	—
	Pane of 20	50.00	
b.	Horiz. strip or block of 4, #4694-4697	5.00	
	P# block of 4, 5#+V	5.00	
	P# block of 8, 2 sets of 5#+V, + top panel	10.00	
	Pane of 20, 5 each #4694-4697	25.00	
c.	Imperf. horiz. strip or block of 4, #4694a-4697a	14.00	—
	Pane of 20, 5 each #4694a-4697a	70.00	

Panes containing 20 of the same stamp were issued on July 21 in Boston, MA (for No. 4694), Cleveland, OH (for No. 4695), Pittsburgh, PA (for No. 4696) and New York, NY (for No. 4697). Imperforate uncut press sheets of these single stamps were also made available for sale on that day. Imperforate uncut press sheets containing the four different stamps were also made available for sale. These press sheets sold out prior to the day of issue. Values: cross-gutter block of 8 (from sheet containing all four stamps), $40; cross-gutter blocks of 4 (from sheets containing identical stamps), $15 each; pairs with gutters between, $6 each. See note after No. 4693.

See note after No. 1549.

INNOVATIVE CHOREOGRAPHERS

Isadora Duncan (1877-1927) — A3581

José Limón (1908-72) — A3582

Katherine Dunham (1909-2006) — A3583

Bob Fosse (1927-87) — A3584

Designed by Ethel Kessler. Printed by Banknote Corporation of America for Sennett Security Products.

LITHOGRAPHED

Sheets of 180 in nine panes of 20

Serpentine Die Cut 10¾x11

2012, July 28 Tagged

Self-Adhesive

4698	A3581 (45c) **multicolored**	1.25	.35
4699	A3582 (45c) **multicolored**	1.25	.35
4700	A3583 (45c) **multicolored**	1.25	.35
4701	A3584 (45c) **multicolored**	1.25	.35
a.	Vert. strip of 4, #4698-4701	5.00	
	P# block of 8, 2 sets of P#, 6#+S	10.00	
	Pane of 20	25.00	

Uncut press sheets of Nos. 4698-4701 were made available for sale. Values: cross-gutter block of 16, $24; pairs with gutters between, $2.50 each. Panes that are vertically adjacent are tete-beche in relation to each other. See note after No. 2868.

EDGAR RICE BURROUGHS

Edgar Rice Burroughs (1875-1950), Writer, and Tarzan — A3585

Designed by Phil Jordan. Printed by Banknote Corporation of America for Sennett Security Products.

LITHOGRAPHED

Sheets of 180 in nine panes of 20

2012, Aug. 17 Tagged *Serpentine Die Cut 10¾*

Self-Adhesive

4702	A3585 (45c) **multicolored**	1.25	.25
	P# block of 4, 6#+S	5.00	
	Pane of 20	25.00	

WAR OF 1812 BICENTENNIAL Ⓢ

Painting of U.S.S. Constitution, by Michele Felice Corné A3586

Designed by Greg Breeding. Printed by Avery Dennison.

PHOTOGRAVURE

Sheets of 100 in five panes of 20

Serpentine Die Cut 10¾x10½

2012, Aug. 18 Tagged

Self-Adhesive

4703	A3586 (45c) **multicolored**	1.75	.25
	Pane of 20	35.00	
a.	Imperforate	2.75	—
	Pane of 20	55.00	

Die-cut and imperforate uncut press sheets of No. 4703 were made available for sale. Values: pairs with gutters between, $4.25 each. See note after No. 2868.

See note after No. 1549.

Purple Heart and Ribbon

A3587

A3587a

Designed by Jennifer Arnold. Printed by Avery Dennison or CCL Label, Inc.

PHOTOGRAVURE

Sheets of 420 in 21 panes of 20

2012, Sept. 4 Tagged *Serpentine Die Cut 11*

Self-Adhesive

4704	A3587 (45c) **multicolored** Ⓢ	1.25	.25
	P# block of 4, 6#+V or C	5.00	
	Pane of 20	25.00	
a.	Imperforate	2.50	—
	Pane of 20	45.00	
b.	A3587a Dated "2014," *Oct. 11, 2014* Ⓢ	1.25	.25
	P# block of 4, 6#+C	5.00	
	Pane of 20	25.00	

Compare with Type A3458. See Nos. 4529, 5035.

Imperforate partial uncut press sheets of three vertical panes of No. 4704 were made available for sale. Values: vert. pair with horiz. gutter, $4.50. See note after No. 4693.

No. 4704b sold for 49c on day of issue.

See note after No. 1549.

LITERARY ARTS

O. Henry (William S. Porter) (1862-1910), New York City Buildings and Elevated Trains A3588

Designed by Ethel Kessler. Printed by Avery Dennison.

PHOTOGRAVURE

Sheets of 160 in eight panes of 20

2012, Sept. 11 Tagged *Serpentine Die Cut 11*

Self-Adhesive

4705	A3588 (45c) **multicolored** Ⓢ	1.25	.25
	P# block of 4, 5#+V	5.00	
	Pane of 20	25.00	

Uncut press sheets of No. 4705 were made available for sale. Values: cross-gutter block of 4, $10; pairs with gutters between, $2.50 each. See note after No. 2868.

See note after No. 1549.

Flags Type of 2012

Designed by Howard E. Paine. Printed by Ashton-Potter (USA) Ltd.

LITHOGRAPHED

Serpentine Die Cut 11¼x10¾ on 2, 3 or 4 Sides

2012, Sept. 22 Tagged

Booklet Stamps

Self-Adhesive

Colored Dots in Stars

18½mm From Lower Left to Lower Right Corners of Flag

Thin Paper

4706	A3539 (45c) **multicolored** Ⓢ	1.25	.25
4707	A3540 (45c) **multicolored** Ⓢ	1.25	.25
4708	A3537 (45c) **multicolored** Ⓢ	1.25	.25
4709	A3538 (45c) **multicolored** Ⓢ	1.25	.25
a.	Block or strip of 4, #4706-4709	5.00	
b.	Booklet pane of 18, 5 each #4706-4707, 4 each #4708-4709	25.00	
	Nos. 4706-4709 (4)	5.00	1.00

The overall-tagged paper used for Nos. 4706-4709 is glossier than that used on Nos. 4641-4644.The blue canton of the flag on Nos. 4706-4709 is made up of blue and red inks, similar to Nos. 4641-4644.

See note after No. 1549.

EARTHSCAPES

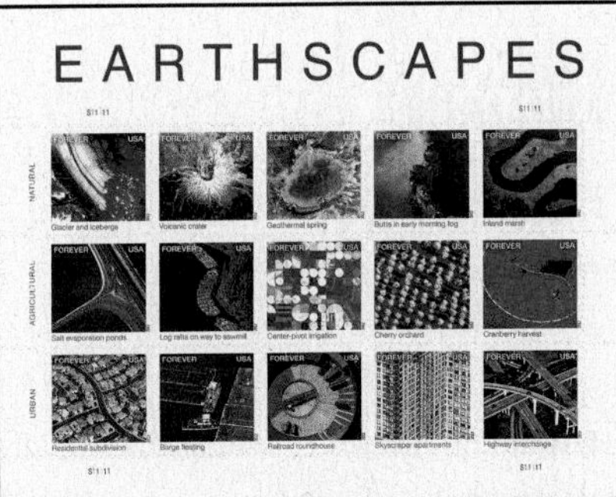

A3589

Designed by Howard E. Paine. Printed by Banknote Corporation of America for Sennett Security Products.

No. 4710: a, Glacier and icebergs. b, Volcanic crater. c, Geothermal spring. d, Butte in early morning fog. e, Inland marsh. f, Salt evaporation ponds. g, Log rafts on way to sawmill. h, Center-pivot irrigation. i, Cherry orchard. j, Cranberry harvest. k, Residential subdivision. l, Barge fleeting. m, Railroad roundhouse. n, Skyscraper apartments. o, Highway interchange.

LITHOGRAPHED

Sheets of 135 in nine panes of 15

2012, Oct. 1 Tagged *Serpentine Die Cut 10¾*

Self-Adhesive

4710	A3589 Pane of 15	33.00	
a.-o.	(45c) Any single	1.65	.50
p.	Imperforate pane of 15	75.00	

Imperforate uncut press sheets of No. 4710 were made available for sale. Values: pairs with gutters between, $8.50 each. Panes that are vertically adjacent are tete-beche in relation to each other. See note after No. 4693.

CHRISTMAS

Holy Family and Donkey — A3590

Reindeer in Flight, Moon — A3591

Santa Claus and Sleigh — A3592

Reindeer Over Roof — A3593

Snow-covered Buildings — A3594

Designed by Greg Breeding (#4711), Howard E. Paine.

Printed by Banknote Corporation of America for Sennett Security Products (#4711), Ashton-Potter (USA) Ltd. (#4712-4715).

LITHOGRAPHED

Serpentine Die Cut 11 on 2 or 3 Sides

2012 Tagged

Booklet Stamps

Self-Adhesive

4711	A3590 (45c) **multicolored,** "2012" year date, *Oct. 10*	1.25	.25
a.	Booklet pane of 20	25.00	
b.	Imperforate	1.75	—
c.	Imperforate booklet pane of 20	35.00	

Serpentine Die Cut 11x10¾ on 2 or 3 sides

4712	A3591 (45c) **multicolored,** *Oct. 13* Ⓢ	1.50	.25
4713	A3592 (45c) **multicolored,** *Oct. 13* Ⓢ	1.50	.25
4714	A3593 (45c) **multicolored,** *Oct. 13* Ⓢ	1.50	.25
4715	A3594 (45c) **multicolored,** *Oct. 13* Ⓢ	1.50	.25
a.	Block of 4, #4712-4715	6.00	
b.	Booklet pane of 20, 5 each #4712-4715	30.00	
c.	Imperforate block of 4	8.00	—
d.	Imperforate booklet pane of 20	40.00	
	Nos. 4711-4715 (5)	7.25	1.25

No. 4711a is a double-sided booklet with 12 stamps on one side and eight stamps plus a label that serves as a booklet cover on the other side. No. 4715b is a double-sided booklet with 12 stamps on one side (3 each of Nos. 4712-4715) and eight stamps (2 each of Nos. 4712-4715) plus a label that serves as a booklet cover on the other side.

Imperforate uncut press sheets of 10 booklet panes of Nos. 4711 and 4712-4715 were made available for sale, along with cut-down sheets containing three imperforate panes. Values: cross-gutter blocks of 4 of Nos. 4711 or 4712-4715 with marginal markings, $10 each; block of Nos. 4712-4715 with vert. gutter between, $10; pairs of Nos. 4711 or 4712-4715 with gutters between, $4.25 each. See note after No. 4693.

See note after No. 1549.

See No. 4813.

LADY BIRD JOHNSON Ⓢ

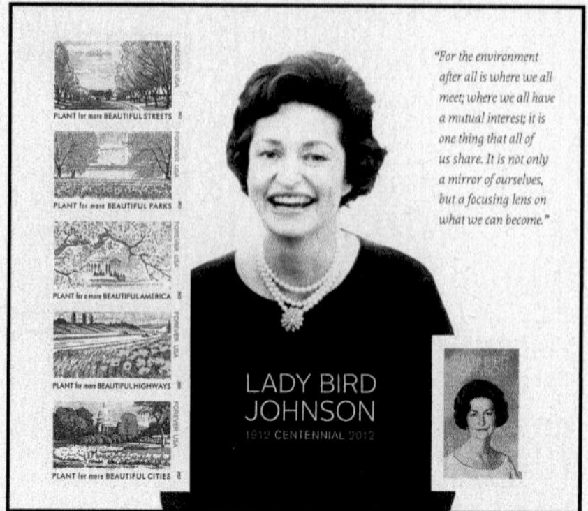

A3595

Designed by Antonio Alcalá. Printed by Ashton-Potter (USA) Ltd.

No. 4716: a, Blooming crab apples lining avenue (Plant for more Beautiful Streets). b, Washington Monument, Potomac River and daffodils (Plant for more Beautiful Parks). c, Jefferson Memorial, Tidal Basin and cherry blossoms (Plant for a more Beautiful America). d, Poppies and lupines along highway (Plant for more Beautiful Highways). e, Capitol, azaleas and tulips (Plant for more Beautiful Cities). f, Lady Bird Johnson (1912-2007), First Lady, vert.

LITHOGRAPHED

Sheets of 96 in 16 panes of six

2012, Nov. 30 Tagged *Serpentine Die Cut 10¾*

Self-Adhesive

4716	A3595	Pane of 6	9.00	
a.-f.		(45c) Any single	1.50	.40
g.		Imperforate pane of 6	25.00	

Imperforate uncut press sheets of No. 4716 were made available for sale. Values: vert. pairs with horiz. gutters, $6.50 each. See note after No. 4693.

See note after No. 1549.

WAVES OF COLOR

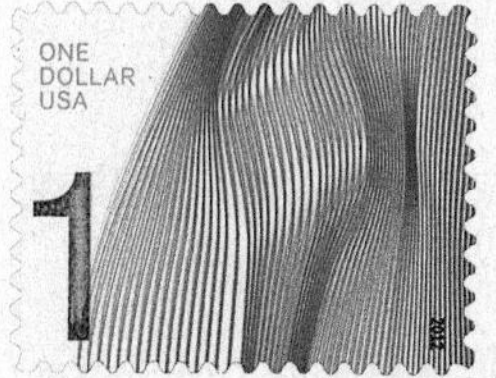

A3596

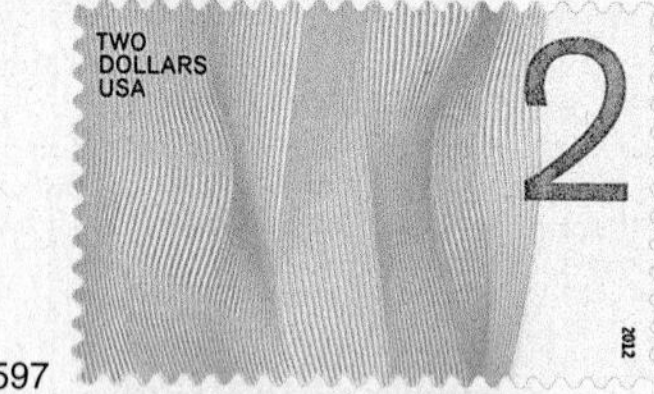

A3597

A3598

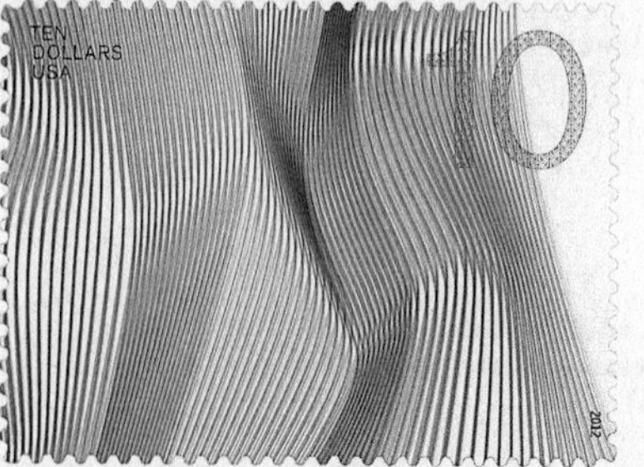

A3599

Designed by Antonio Alcalá. Printed by Ashton-Potter (USA) Ltd. (#4717-4718), Banknote Corporation of America for Sennett Security Products (#4719-4720).

LITHOGRAPHED & ENGRAVED

Sheets of 150 in 15 panes of 10 (#4717), Sheets of 120 in 12 panes of 10 (#4718, 4719), Sheets of 90 in nine panes of 10 (#4720)

Serpentine Die Cut 11, 10¾ (#4719)

2012, Dec. 1 Tagged

Self-Adhesive

4717	A3596	$1 **multicolored** Ⓢ	4.50	.50
		P# block of 4, 7#+P	18.00	
		Pane of 10	45.00	
4718	A3597	$2 **multicolored** Ⓢ	4.50	1.25
		P# block of 4, 7#+P	18.00	
		Pane of 10	45.00	
4719	A3598	$5 **multicolored**	8.75	2.50
		P# block of 4, 8#+S	35.00	
		Pane of 10	87.50	
4720	A3599	$10 **multicolored**	17.50	9.00
		P# block of 4, 8#+S	70.00	
		Pane of 10	175.00	
		Nos. 4717-4720 (4)	35.25	13.25

Adjacent horizontal or vertical stamps have selvage between the stamps. Plate blocks have sheet margins on the top or bottom and both sides.

See note after No. 1549.

EMANCIPATION PROCLAMATION, 150th ANNIV. Ⓢ

A3600

Designed by Gail Anderson. Printed by Avery Dennison.

PHOTOGRAVURE

Sheets of 200 in 10 panes of 20

2013, Jan. 1 Tagged *Serpentine Die Cut 11*

Self-Adhesive

4721	A3600	(45c) **multicolored**	1.25	.25
		P# block of 4, 4#+V	5.00	
		P# block of 8, 2 sets of 4#+V + side panel	10.00	
		Pane of 20	25.00	
a.		Imperforate	2.00	—
		Pane of 20	40.00	

Die cut and imperforate uncut press sheets of No. 4721 were made available for sale. Values: cross-gutter block of 4, $12.50; pairs with gutters between, $4.50 each. See note after No. 4693.

See note after No. 1549.

KALEIDOSCOPE FLOWERS

A3601

A3602

A3603

A3604

Designed by Antonio Alcalá. Printed by Banknote Corporation of America for Sennett Security Products.

LITHOGRAPHED

Serpentine Die Cut 11 Vert.

2013, Jan. 14 Tagged

Coil Stamps

Self-Adhesive

Color of Large Outer Leaves

4722	A3601	46c **yellow orange**	1.25	.25
4723	A3602	46c **yellow green**	1.25	.25
4724	A3603	46c **red violet**	1.25	.25
4725	A3604	46c **red**	1.25	.25
a.		Strip of 4, #4722-4725	5.00	
		P# strip of 5, 2 #4722, 1 each #4723-4725, #S11111	7.00	
		P# strip of 9, 3# 4724, 2 each #4722-4723, 4725, #S11111	12.50	
		P# single, #S1111 (#4724)	—	2.75
		Nos. 4722-4725 (4)	5.00	1.00

CHINESE NEW YEAR

Year of the Snake A3605

Designed by Ethel Kessler. Printed by Avery Dennison.

PHOTOGRAVURE

Sheets of 108 in nine panes of 12

2013, Jan. 16 Tagged *Serpentine Die Cut 11*

Self-Adhesive

4726	A3605	(45c) **multicolored** Ⓢ	1.25	.25
		Pane of 12	15.00	
a.		Imperforate	2.00	—
		Pane of 12	24.00	

Die cut and imperforate uncut press sheets of No. 4726 were made available for sale. Values: cross-gutter block of 4, $12.50; pairs with gutters between, $4.75 each. See note after No. 4693.

See note after No. 1549.

APPLES

Northern Spy Apple — A3606

Golden Delicious Apple — A3607

Granny Smith Apple — A3608

Baldwin Apple — A3609

Designed by Derry Noyes. Printed by Banknote Corporation of America for Sennett Security Products.

LITHOGRAPHED

Sheets of 200 in 10 panes of 20

Serpentine Die Cut 11¼x10¾

2013, Jan. 17 Tagged

Self-Adhesive

4727	A3606	33c **multicolored**	1.25	.25
4728	A3607	33c **multicolored**	1.25	.25
4729	A3608	33c **multicolored**	1.25	.25

4730 A3609 33c **multicolored** 1.25 .25
- *a.* Block or strip of 4, #4727-4730 5.00
  - P# block of 4, 5#+S 5.00
  - Pane of 20 25.00
- *b.* Imperforate block or strip of 4 6.50 —
  - Pane of 20 32.50

Die cut and imperforate uncut press sheets of Nos. 4727-4730 were made available for sale. Values: cross gutter-block of 8, $15; pairs with gutters between, $3 each. See note after No. 4693.

A3606a A3607a

A3608a A3609a

Coil Stamps

Serpentine Die Cut 11 Vert.

4731 A3609a 33c **multicolored** 1.50 .25
4732 A3606a 33c **multicolored** 1.50 .25
4733 A3607a 33c **multicolored** 1.50 .25
4734 A3608a 33c **multicolored** 1.50 .25
- *a.* Strip of 4, #4731-4734 6.00
  - P# strip of 5, 2 #4731, 1 each #4732-4734, #S11111 8.00
  - P# strip of 9, 3 #4733, 2 each #4731-4732, 4734, #S11111 15.00
  - P# single #S1111 (#4733) — 2.75
  - *Nos. 4727-4734 (8)* 11.00 2.00

Wedding Cake — A3609b

Designed by Ethel Kessler. Printed by Banknote Corporation of America for Sennett Security Products.

LITHOGRAPHED

Sheets of 200 in 10 panes of 20

2013, Jan. 18 Tagged *Serpentine Die Cut 10¾*

Self-Adhesive

4735 A3609b 66c **multicolored** 1.75 .25
- P# block of 4, 6#+S 7.00
- Pane of 20 35.00
- *a.* Imperforate 3.50 —
  - Pane of 20 70.00

Die cut and imperforate uncut press sheets of No. 4735 were made available for sale. Values: cross-gutter block of 4, $17.50; pairs with gutters between, $8.50 each. See note after No. 4693.

See Nos. 4398, 4521, 4602, 4867, 5000.

SPICEBUSH SWALLOWTAIL BUTTERFLY Ⓢ

A3610

Designed by Derry Noyes. Printed by Avery Dennison.

PHOTOGRAVURE

Sheets of 200 in 10 panes of 20

2013, Jan. 23 Tagged *Serpentine Die Cut 10¾*

Self-Adhesive

4736 A3610 66c **multicolored** 1.40 .25
- P# block of 4, 7#+V 5.60
- Pane of 20 28.00
- *a.* Imperforate 3.00 —
  - Pane of 20 60.00

Die cut and imperforate uncut press sheets of No. 4736 were made available for sale. Values: cross-gutter block of 4, $15; pairs with gutters between, $5.50 each. See note after No. 4693.

See note after No. 1549.

TUFTED PUFFINS Ⓢ

A3611

A3611a

Designed by Derry Noyes. Printed by Ashton-Potter (USA) Ltd.

LITHOGRAPHED

Sheets of 120 in six panes of 20

Serpentine Die Cut 11¼x10¾

2013, Jan. 23 Tagged

"2013" in Orange Red

Solid Color in "Tufted Puffins" and "86"

Self-Adhesive

4737 A3611 86c **multicolored** 1.80 .35
- P# block of 4, 5#+P 7.25
- Pane of 20 36.00
- *b.* Imperforate 4.00 —
  - Pane of 20 80.00

Die cut and imperforate uncut press sheets of No. 4737 were made available for sale. Values: cross-gutter block of 4, $22.50; pairs with gutters between, $9 each. See note after No. 4693.

"2013" in Black

With Dots in "Tufted Puffins" and "86"

4737A A3611a 86c **multicolored** Ⓢ 5.00 .35
- P# block of 4, 4#+P 20.00
- Pane of 20 100.00

See note after No. 1549.

AMERICAN LANDMARKS ISSUE

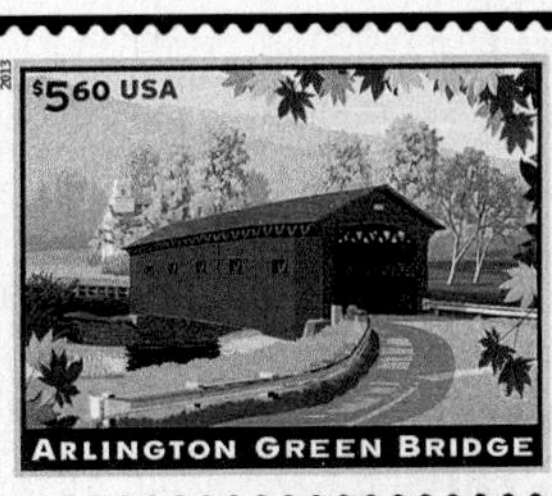

Arlington Green Bridge, Vermont A3612

Grand Central Terminal, New York City — A3613

Designed by Derry Noyes (#4738), Phil Jordan (#4739). Printed by Avery Dennison.

PHOTOGRAVURE

Sheets of 80 in eight panes of 10 (#4738), Sheets of 100 in ten panes of 10 (#4739)

2013 Tagged *Serpentine Die Cut 10¾x10½*

Self-Adhesive

4738 A3612 $5.60 **multicolored**, *Jan. 25* Ⓢ 11.00 6.25
- P# block of 4, 4#+V 44.00
- Pane of 10 110.00

4739 A3613 $19.95 **multicolored**, *Feb. 1* 40.00 21.00
- P# block of 4, 4#+V 160.00
- Pane of 10 400.00

See note after No. 1549.

Earth — A3614

Designed by Greg Breeding. Printed by Avery Dennison.

PHOTOGRAVURE

Sheets of 80 in four panes of 20

2013, Jan. 28 Tagged *Serpentine Die Cut*

Self-Adhesive

4740 A3614 ($1.10) **multicolored** Ⓢ 2.80 .50
- P# block of 4, 6#+V 11.20
- P# block of 8, 2 sets of 6#+V, + top label 22.40
- Pane of 20 56.00
- *a.* Imperforate 5.00 —
  - Pane of 20 100.00

Unused values are for stamps with surrounding selvage. Adjacent stamps are separated by rouletting.

Die cut and imperforate uncut press sheets of No. 4740 were made available for sale. Values: cross-gutter block of 4, $16.50; pairs with gutters between, $7 each. See note after No. 4693.

See note after No. 1549.

LOVE

Envelope With Wax Seal — A3615

Designed by Louise Fili. Printed by Avery Dennison.

PHOTOGRAVURE

Sheets of 120 in six panes of 20

2013, Jan. 30 Tagged *Serpentine Die Cut 10¾*

Self-Adhesive

4741 A3615 (46c) **multicolored** Ⓢ 1.25 .25
- P# block of 4, 5#+V 5.00
- Pane of 20 25.00
- *a.* Imperforate 2.00 —
  - Pane of 20 40.00

Die cut and imperforate uncut press sheets of No. 4741 were made available for sale. Values: cross-gutter block of 4, $11; pairs with gutters between, $4.50 each. See note after No. 4693.

See note after No. 1549.

ROSA PARKS Ⓢ

Parks (1913-2005), Civil Rights Pioneer — A3616

Designed by Derry Noyes. Printed by Avery Dennison.

PHOTOGRAVURE

Sheets of 200 in 10 panes of 20

2013, Feb. 4 Tagged *Serpentine Die Cut 10¾*

Self-Adhesive

4742 A3616 (46c) **multicolored** 1.25 .25
- P# block of 4, 5#+V 5.00
- P# block of 8, 2 sets of 5#+V + side panel 10.00
- Pane of 20 25.00
- *a.* Imperforate 2.00 —
  - Pane of 20 40.00

Die cut and imperforate uncut press sheets of No. 4742 were made available for sale. Values: cross-gutter block of 4, $12; pairs with gutters between, $5 each. See note after No. 4693.

See note after No. 1549.

MUSCLE CARS

1969 Dodge Charger Daytona A3617

1966 Pontiac GTO — A3618

1967 Ford Mustang Shelby GT 500 — A3619

1970 Chevrolet Chevelle SS — A3620

1970 Plymouth Hemi Barracuda A3621

Designed by Carl T. Herrman. Printed by Avery Dennison.

PHOTOGRAVURE

Sheets of 200 in 10 panes of 20

2013, Feb. 22 Tagged *Serpentine Die Cut 10¾*

Self-Adhesive

4743 A3617 (46c) **multicolored**		1.25	.30
4744 A3618 (46c) **multicolored**		1.25	.30
4745 A3619 (46c) **multicolored**		1.25	.30
4746 A3620 (46c) **multicolored**		1.25	.30
4747 A3621 (46c) **multicolored**		1.25	.30
a.	Vert. strip of 5, #4743-4747	6.25	
	Vert. P# block of 10, 5# + V	12.50	
	Horiz. P# block of 8, 2 sets of 5# + V	10.00	
	Pane of 20	25.00	
b.	Imperforate vert. strip of 5	10.00	—
	Pane of 20	40.00	
	Nos. 4743-4747 (5)	6.25	1.50

Die cut and imperforate uncut press sheets of Nos. 4743-4747 were made available for sale. Values: cross-gutter block of 10, $27.50; pairs with gutters between, $4.75 each. See note after No. 4693.

See note after No. 1549.

MODERN ART IN AMERICA

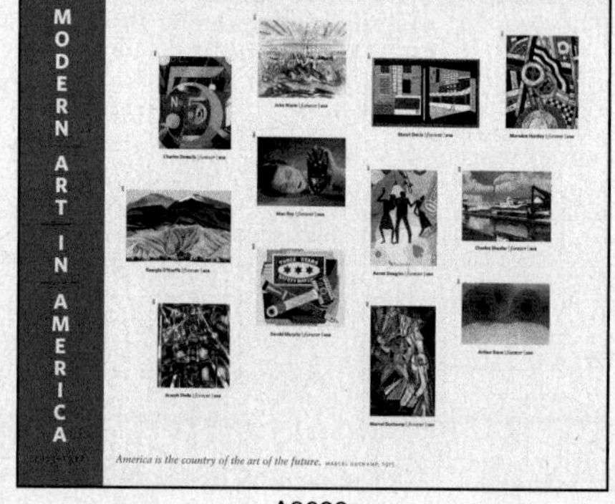

A3622

Designed by Margaret Bauer. Printed by Avery Dennison.

No. 4748: a, I Saw the Figure 5 in Gold, by Charles Demuth (37x51mm). b, Sunset, Maine Coast, by John Marin (43x43mm). c, House and Street, by Stuart Davis (51x41mm). d, Painting, Number 5, by Marsden Hartley (37x51mm). e, Black Mesa Landscape, New Mexico/Out Back of Marie's II, by Georgia O'Keeffe (51x41mm). f, Noire et Blanche, by Man Ray (43x41mm). g, The Prodigal Son, by Aaron Douglas (34x51mm). h, American Landscape, by Charles Sheeler (43x41mm). i, Brooklyn Bridge, by Joseph Stella (38x47mm). j, Razor, by Gerald Murphy (43x43mm). k, Nude Descending a Staircase, No. 2, by Marcel Duchamp (34x58mm). l, Fog Horns, by Arthur Dove (43x37mm).

PHOTOGRAVURE

Sheets of 48 in four panes of 12

2013, Mar. 7 Tagged *Serpentine Die Cut 10½*

Self-Adhesive

4748 A3622	Pane of 12	15.00	
a.-l.	(46c) Any single	1.25	.50
m.	Imperforate pane of 12	70.00	

Armory Show, cent.

Die cut and imperforate uncut press sheets of No. 4748 were made available for sale. See note after No. 4693.

See note after No. 1549.

Patriotic Star — A3623

Designed by Greg Breeding. Printed by Banknote Corporation of America for Sennett Security Products.

LITHOGRAPHED

Serpentine Die Cut 10¾ Vert.

2013, Mar. 19 Tagged

Coil Stamp

Self-Adhesive

4749 A3623 46c **multicolored**		1.25	.25
	Pair	2.50	
	P# strip of 5, #S111	6.50	
	P# single, #S111	—	2.75

LA FLORIDA

A3624 A3625 A3626 A3627

Designed by Ethel Kessler. Printed by Avery Dennison.

PHOTOGRAVURE

Sheets of 160 in 10 panes of 16

2013, Apr. 3 Tagged *Serpentine Die Cut 10½*

Self-Adhesive

4750 A3624 (46c) **multicolored**		1.25	.25
4751 A3625 (46c) **multicolored**		1.25	.25
4752 A3626 (46c) **multicolored**		1.25	.25
4753 A3627 (46c) **multicolored**		1.25	.25
a.	Block of 4, #4750-4753	5.00	
	P# block of 4, 9#+V	5.00	
	Pane of 16	20.00	
b.	Imperforate block of 4	10.00	—
	Pane of 16	40.00	
	Nos. 4750-4753 (4)	5.00	1.00

Naming of Florida, 500th anniv.

Die cut and imperforate uncut press sheets of Nos. 4750-4753 were made available for sale. Values: cross-gutter block of 4, $15; pairs with gutters between, $5.50 each. See note after No. 4693.

See note after No. 1549.

VINTAGE SEED PACKETS

Phlox — A3628

Calendula — A3629

Digitalis — A3630

Linum — A3631

Alyssum — A3632

Zinnias — A3633

Pinks — A3634

Cosmos — A3635

Aster — A3636

Primrose — A3637

Designed by Antonio Alcalá. Printed by Avery Dennison.

PHOTOGRAVURE

Serpentine Die Cut 10¾ on 2 or 3 Sides

2013, Apr. 5 **Tagged**

Booklet Stamps
Self-Adhesive

4754	A3628 (46c) **multicolored**	2.50	.25
4755	A3629 (46c) **multicolored**	2.50	.25
4756	A3630 (46c) **multicolored**	2.50	.25
4757	A3631 (46c) **multicolored**	2.50	.25
4758	A3632 (46c) **multicolored**	2.50	.25
4759	A3633 (46c) **multicolored**	2.50	.25
4760	A3634 (46c) **multicolored**	2.50	.25
4761	A3635 (46c) **multicolored**	2.50	.25
4762	A3636 (46c) **multicolored**	2.50	.25
4763	A3637 (46c) **multicolored**	2.50	.25
a.	Block of 10, #4754-4763	25.00	
b.	Booklet pane of 20, 2 each #4754-4763	50.00	
	Nos. 4754-4763 (10)	25.00	2.50

No. 4763b is a double-sided booklet pane with 12 stamps on one side (2 each #4754, 4759, 1 each #4755-4758, 4760-4763), and eight stamps (1 each #4755-4758, 4760-4763) plus label (booklet cover) on the other side.

See note after No. 1549.

WEDDING FLOWERS

Flowers — A3638

Flowers and "Yes I Do" — A3639

Designed by Michael Osborne. Printed by Banknote Corporation of America for Sennett Security Products (#4764), Ashton-Potter (USA) Ltd. (#4765).

LITHOGRAPHED

Sheets of 160 in eight panes of 20 (#4764), Sheets of 180 in nine panes of 20 (#4765)

2013, Apr. 11 **Tagged** ***Serpentine Die Cut 10¾***

Self-Adhesive

4764	A3638 (46c) **multicolored**	1.10	.25
	P# block of 4, 9#+S	4.40	
	Pane of 20	22.00	
a.	Dated "2014"	1.10	.25
	P# block of 4, 9#+S	4.40	
	Pane of 20	22.00	
b.	Imperforate	2.50	—
	Pane of 20	50.00	
4765	A3639 66c **multicolored** ®	1.40	.30
	P# block of 4, 4#+P	5.60	
	Pane of 20	28.00	
a.	Imperforate	3.00	—
	Pane of 20	60.00	

Die cut and imperforate uncut press sheets of Nos. 4764 and 4765 were made available for sale. Values: No. 4764 cross-gutter block of 4, $12; No. 4765 cross-gutter block of 4, $14; No. 4764 pairs with gutters between, $5.50 each; No. 4765 pairs with gutters between, $6.50 each. See note after No. 4693.

See note after No. 1549.

No. 4764a was issued 5/2/14, and sold for 49c on day of issue.

See Nos. 4881, 5001.

Flag in Autumn — A3640

Flag in Winter — A3641

Flag in Spring — A3642

Flag in Summer — A3643

Designed by Phil Jordan. Printed by Avery Dennison.

PHOTOGRAVURE

2013 **Tagged** ***Serpentine Die Cut 8½ Vert.***

Coil Stamps
Self-Adhesive

4766	A3640 (46c) **multicolored,** *May 3* ®	2.25	.25
4767	A3641 (46c) **multicolored,** *May 3* ®	2.25	.25
4768	A3642 (46c) **multicolored,** *May 3* ®	2.25	.25
4769	A3643 (46c) **multicolored,** *May 3* ®	2.25	.25
a.	Strip of 4, #4766-4769	9.00	
	P# strip of 5, 2 #4766, 1 each #4767-4769, #V1111	15.00	
	P# strip of 9, 3# 4768, 2 each #4766-4767, 4769, #V1111	20.00	
	P# single, #V1111 (#4768)	—	2.75

Flag in Autumn — A3640a

Flag in Winter — A3641a

Flag in Spring — A3642a

Flag in Summer — A3643a

Designed by Ashton-Potter (USA) Ltd.

LITHOGRAPHED (#4770-4785)

Serpentine Die Cut 9½ Vert.

4770	A3640a (46c) **multicolored,** *May 3* ®	2.25	.25
4771	A3641a (46c) **multicolored,** *May 3* ®	2.25	.25
4772	A3642a (46c) **multicolored,** *May 3* ®	2.25	.25
4773	A3643a (46c) **multicolored,** *May 3* ®	2.25	.25
a.	Strip of 4, #4770-4773	9.00	
	P# strip of 5, 2 #4770, 1 each #4771-4773, #P1111	15.00	
	P# strip of 9, 3 #4772, 2 each #4770-4771, 4773, #P1111	20.00	
	P# single, #P1111 (#4772)	—	2.75

Counterfeits exist of Nos. 4770-4773. See the Postal Counterfeits section of this catalog.

Flag in Winter — A3640b

Flag in Spring — A3641b

Flag in Summer — A3642b

Flag in Autumn — A3643b

Designed by Banknote Corporation of America for Sennett Security Products.

Serpentine Die Cut 11 Vert.

4774	A3641b (46c) **multicolored,** *May 3*	3.00	.25
4775	A3642b (46c) **multicolored,** *May 3*	3.00	.25
4776	A3643b (46c) **multicolored,** *May 3*	3.00	.25
4777	A3640b (46c) **multicolored,** *May 3*	3.00	.25
a.	Strip of 4, #4774-4777	12.00	
b.	Block of 28 (4x7), #4774-4777, with no horiz. slits	—	
	P# strip of 5, 2 #4774, 1 each #4775-4777, #S1111	17.50	
	P# strip of 9, 3 #4776, 2 each #4774-4775, 4777, #S1111	25.00	
	P# single, #S1111 (#4776)	—	2.75
	P# strip of 5, #S1111, seven strips (5x7) with no horiz. slits	—	
	P# strip of 9, #S1111, block of seven strips (9x7) with no horiz. slits	—	
c.	Block of 8 (4x2), #4774-4777, with no horiz. slits	800.00	
	Nos. 4766-4777 (12)	30.00	3.00

Nos. 4774-4777 were produced as "sticks" or "logs" of ten coil rolls of 100 with partial horizontal slits that allowed individual rolls to be snapped off for retail sale. Customers could buy an entire "log" if desired. No. 4777b has no horizontal slits and therefore is an error that can be collected as pairs or larger units of strips "imperf." horizontally.

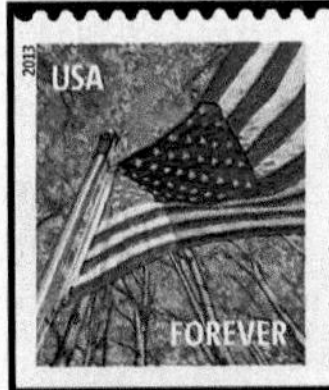
Flag in Autumn — A3640c

Flag in Winter — A3641c

Flag in Spring — A3642c

Flag in Summer — A3643c

Designed by Ashton-Potter (USA) Ltd.

Booklet Stamps
With Microprinted "USPS" at Lower Left Corner of Flag

Serpentine Die Cut 11¼x10¾ on 2 or 3 Sides

4778	A3642c (46c) **multicolored,** *May 17* ⓢ	1.25	.25
4779	A3643c (46c) **multicolored,** *May 17* ⓢ	1.25	.25
4780	A3640c (46c) **multicolored,** *May 17* ⓢ	1.25	.25
4781	A3641c (46c) **multicolored,** *May 17* ⓢ	1.25	.25
a.	Block of 4, #4778-4781	6.00	
b.	Booklet pane of 20, 5 each #4778-4781	30.00	

Flag in Autumn — A3640d

Flag in Winter — A3641d

Flag in Spring — A3642d

Flag in Summer — A3643d

Designed by Banknote Corporation of America for Sennett Security Products.

With Microprinted "USPS" Near Top of Pole or at Lower Left Corner Near Rope (#4783, 4783b)
Pre-phosphored Paper

4782	A3642d (46c) **multicolored,** *May 17*	1.25	.25
a.	Overall tagging, *Aug. 16*	1.25	.25
b.	As #4782, dated "2014," overall tagging, *Mar. 17, 2014*	1.25	.25
c.	Tagging omitted		—
4783	A3643d (46c) **multicolored,** *May 17*	1.25	.25
a.	Overall tagging, *Aug. 16*	1.25	.25
b.	As #4783, dated "2014," overall tagging, *Mar. 17, 2014*	1.25	.25
c.	Tagging omitted		—
4784	A3640d (46c) **multicolored,** *May 17*	1.25	.25
a.	Overall tagging, *Aug. 16*	1.25	.25
b.	As #4784, dated "2014," overall tagging, *Mar. 17, 2014*	1.25	.25
c.	Tagging omitted		—
4785	A3641d (46c) **multicolored,** *May 17*	1.25	.25
a.	Overall tagging, *Aug. 16*	1.25	.25
b.	As #4785, dated "2014," overall tagging, *Mar. 17, 2014*	1.25	.25
c.	Block of 4, #4782-4785	5.00	
d.	Booklet pane of 20, 5 each #4782-4785	25.00	
e.	Block of 4, #4782a, 4783a, 4784a, 4785a	5.00	
f.	Booklet pane of 10, 3 each #4782a, 4783a, 2 each #4784a, 4785a	12.50	
g.	Block of 4, #4782b, 4783b, 4784b, 4785b	5.00	
h.	Booklet pane of 20, 5 each #4782b, 4783b, 4784b, 4785b	25.00	
i.	As "h," die cutting omitted on side with 8 stamps and 3 pairs on side with 12 stamps	1,800.	
j.	Tagging omitted		—
	Nos. 4778-4785 (8)	10.00	2.00

No. 4781b is a double-sided booklet with 12 stamps on one side (3 each #4778-4781) and eight stamps (2 each #4778-4781) plus label that serves as a booklet cover on the other side.

No. 4785d is a double-sided booklet with 12 stamps on one side (3 each #4782-4785) and eight stamps (2 each #4782-4785) plus label that serves as a booklet cover on the other side.

A microprinted "USPS" is found on tree trunk to the left of the "F" in "Forever" on No. 4766, on tree trunk near lower left corner of flag on No. 4767, on white flag stripe at lower right on No. 4768, and on the top of the flagpole below the ball on No. 4769. Nos. 4770-4773 are microprinted "USPS" in the same places as on Nos. 4778-4781. Nos. 4774-4777 are microprinted "USPS" in the same places as on Nos. 4782-4785.

See Nos. 4796-4799.

All examples of No. 4782a will have straight edge on the left side only, left side and top, or left side and bottom. All examples of No. 4783a will have straight edge on the right side only, right side and top, or right side and bottom. No. 4784a has the straight edge on the left side of the stamp. No. 4785a has the straight edge on the right side of the stamp. One-sided straight-edged examples of Nos. 4784 and 4785 will have the straight edge on the bottom of the stamps. One-sided straight-edged examples of Nos. 4782 and 4783 will have the straight edge on the top of the stamps.

See note after No. 1549.

Nos. 4782b, 4783b, 4784b and 4785b each sold for 49c on day of issue.

MUSIC ICONS

Lydia Mendoza (1916-2007), Tejano Music Recording Artist — A3644

Designed by Patrick Donohue and Neal Ashby. Printed by Avery Dennison.

PHOTOGRAVURE
Sheets of 128 in eight panes of 16

2013, May 15 Tagged *Serpentine Die Cut 10¾*
Self-Adhesive

4786	A3644 (46c) **multicolored** ⓢ	1.25	.25
	Pane of 16	20.00	
a.	Imperforate	1.75	—
	Pane of 16	28.00	

Adjacent horizontal or vertical stamps have selvage between the stamps.

Die cut and imperforate uncut press sheets of No. 4786 were made available for sale. Values: cross-gutter block of 4, $11; pairs with gutters between, $4.50 each. See note after No. 4693.

See note after No. 1549.

CIVIL WAR SESQUICENTENNIAL

Battle of Vicksburg — A3645

Battle of Gettysburg — A3646

Designed by Phil Jordan. Printed by Ashton-Potter (USA) Ltd.

LITHOGRAPHED
Double-sided sheets of 72 in six panes of 12 (60 on one side, 12 on other side)

2013, May 23 Tagged *Serpentine Die Cut 11*
Self-Adhesive

4787	A3645 (46c) **multicolored** ⓢ	1.25	.30
4788	A3646 (46c) **multicolored** ⓢ	1.25	.30
a.	Pair, #4787-4788	2.50	
	Pane of 12	15.00	
b.	Imperforate pair, #4787-4788	5.50	—
	Imperforate pair with wide spacing	6.00	—
	Pane of 12	28.00	

Die cut and imperforate uncut press sheets of Nos. 4787-4788 were made available for sale. See note after No. 4693.

See note after No. 1549.

MUSIC ICONS

Johnny Cash (1932-2003), Country Music Recording Artist — A3647

Designed by Greg Breeding. Printed by Avery Dennison.

PHOTOGRAVURE
Sheets of 128 in eight panes of 16

2013, June 5 Tagged *Serpentine Die Cut 10¾*
Self-Adhesive

4789	A3647 (46c) **multicolored** ⓢ	1.25	.25
	Pane of 16	20.00	
a.	Imperforate	1.75	—
	Pane of 16	28.00	

Die cut and imperforate uncut press sheets of No. 4789 were made available for sale. Values: cross-gutter block of 4, $9; pairs with gutters between, $4.25 each. See note after No. 4693.

See note after No. 1549.

WEST VIRGINIA STATEHOOD, 150th ANNIV. ⓢ

Hills in Monongahela National Forest — A3648

Designed by Greg Breeding. Printed by Avery Dennison.

PHOTOGRAVURE
Sheets of 200 in 10 panes of 20

2013, June 20 Tagged *Serpentine Die Cut 11*
Self-Adhesive

4790	A3648 (46c) **multicolored**	1.25	.25
	P# block of 4, 4#+V	5.00	
	Pane of 20	25.00	
a.	Imperforate	1.75	—
	Pane of 20	35.00	

Die cut and imperforate uncut press sheets of No. 4790 were made available for sale. Values: cross-gutter block of 4, $9; pairs with gutters between, $4.25 each. See note after No. 4693.

See note after No. 1549.

NEW ENGLAND COASTAL LIGHTHOUSES

Portland Head Lighthouse, Maine — A3649

Portsmouth Harbor Lighthouse, New Hampshire — A3650

Boston Harbor Lighthouse, Massachusetts A3651

Point Judith Lighthouse, Rhode Island A3652

New London Harbor Lighthouse, Connecticut — A3653

Original

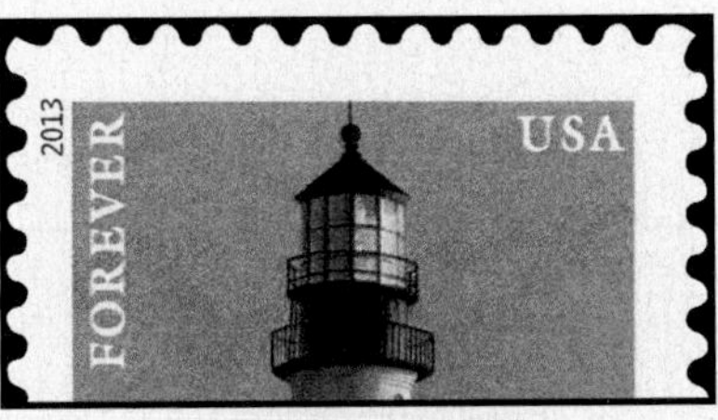

"FOREVER" and "USA" 1mm higher than original

Designed by Howard E. Paine. Printed by Banknote Corporation of America for Sennett Security Products.

LITHOGRAPHED

Sheets of 120 in six panes of 20

Serpentine Die Cut 11x10¾

2013, July 13 **Tagged**

Self-Adhesive

4791	A3649 (46c) **multicolored**	1.25	.40
a.	"FOREVER" and "USA" 1mm higher than normal (pos. 1)	2.00	1.00
b.	Horiz. strip of 5, #4791a, 4792-4795	6.50	
4792	A3650 (46c) **multicolored**	1.25	.40
4793	A3651 (46c) **multicolored**	1.25	.40
4794	A3652 (46c) **multicolored**	1.25	.40
4795	A3653 (46c) **multicolored**	1.25	.40
a.	Horiz. strip of 5, #4791-4795	6.25	
	P# block of 10, 2 sets of 4#+S	12.50	
	Pane of 20	25.00	
b.	Imperforate horiz. strip of 5	11.00	—
c.	Imperforate horiz. strip of 5, pos. 1 as No. 4791a	13.00	—
	Pane of 20	44.00	
	Nos. 4791-4795 (5)	6.25	2.00

Die cut and imperforate uncut press sheets of Nos. 4791-4795 were made available for sale. Values: cross gutter block of 10 (four stamps from one side of the sheet and six stamps from the other side), $22.50 each; vert. pair with horiz. gutter, $4 each; horiz. pair with vert. gutter, $4.25 each; horiz. strip of 5 without die cuts, $9. See note after No. 2868.

Flag Types of 2013

Designed by Phil Jordan. Printed by Avery Dennison.

PHOTOGRAVURE

Serpentine Die Cut 11¼x11½ on 2 or 3 Sides

2013, Aug. 8 **Tagged**

Booklet Stamps
Self-Adhesive

4796	A3653a (46c) **multicolored** ⓢ	1.50	.25
4797	A3653b (46c) **multicolored** ⓢ	1.50	.25
4798	A3653c (46c) **multicolored** ⓢ	1.50	.25
4799	A3653d (46c) **multicolored** ⓢ	1.50	.25
a.	Block of 4, #4796-4799	6.00	
b.	Booklet pane of 20, 5 each #4796-4799	30.00	
	Nos. 4796-4799 (4)	6.00	1.00

No. 4799b is a double-sided booklet with 12 stamps on one side (3 each #4796-4799) and eight stamps (2 each #4796-4799) plus label that serves as a booklet cover on the other side. Nos. 4796-4799 are microprinted "USPS" in the same places as Nos. 4766-4769.

See note after No. 1549.

EID

"Eid Mubarak" — A3654

Designed by Mohamed Zakariya. Printed by Ashton-Potter (USA) Ltd.

LITHOGRAPHED

Sheets of 160 in eight panes of 20

2013, Aug. 8 **Tagged** ***Serpentine Die Cut 11***

Self-Adhesive

4800	A3654 (46c) **dark green, gray & gold** ⓢ	1.25	.25
	P# block of 4, 3#+P	5.00	
	Pane of 20	25.00	
a.	Imperforate	2.00	—
	Pane of 20	40.00	

Imperforate uncut press sheets of No. 4800 were made available for sale. Values: cross-gutter block of 4, $10; pairs with gutters between, $4.50 each. See note after No. 4693.

See note after No. 1549.

BUILDING A NATION ⓢ

Airplane Mechanic, Photograph by Lewis Hine — A3655

Derrick Man on Empire State Building, Photograph by Lewis Hine — A3656

Millinery Apprentice, Photograph by Lewis Hine — A3657

Man on Hoisting Ball on Empire State Building, Photograph by Lewis Hine — A3658

Linotype Operator, Photograph by Lewis Hine — A3659

Welder on Empire State Building, Photograph by Lewis Hine — A3660

Coal Miner, by Anonymous Photographer A3661

Riveters on Empire State Building, Photograph by Lewis Hine — A3662

Powerhouse Mechanic, Photograph by Lewis Hine — A3663

Railroad Track Walker, Photograph by Lewis Hine — A3664

Textile Worker, Photograph by Lewis Hine — A3665

Man Guiding Beam on Empire State Building, Photograph by Lewis Hine — A3666

Designed by Derry Noyes. Printed by Avery Dennison.

PHOTOGRAVURE

Sheets of 60 in five panes of 12

Serpentine Die Cut 10½x10¾

2013, Aug. 8 **Tagged**

Self-Adhesive

4801	Pane of 12	15.00	
a.	A3655 (46c) **black & gray**	1.25	.50
b.	A3656 (46c) **black & gray**	1.25	.50
c.	A3657 (46c) **black & gray**	1.25	.50
d.	A3658 (46c) **black & gray**	1.25	.50
e.	A3659 (46c) **black & gray**	1.25	.50
f.	A3660 (46c) **black & gray**	1.25	.50
g.	A3661 (46c) **black & gray**	1.25	.50
h.	A3662 (46c) **black & gray**	1.25	.50
i.	A3663 (46c) **black & gray**	1.25	.50
j.	A3664 (46c) **black & gray**	1.25	.50
k.	A3665 (46c) **black & gray**	1.25	.50
l.	A3666 (46c) **black & gray**	1.25	.50
m.	Imperforate pane of 12	70.00	

No. 4801 was printed with five different sheet margins depicting coal miner from No. 4801g, man on hoisting ball on Empire State Building, man measuring bearings in large gearwheel, man on cable at Empire State Building, and woman welder. Value is for sheet with any margin. Value, set of 5 panes, $75.

Die cut and imperforate uncut press sheets of No. 4801 were made available for sale. Value, set of 5 individual imperforate panes of 12, $350. See note after No. 4693.

See note after No. 1549.

Wildlife

Bobcat — A3664a

Designed by Carl T. Herrman. Printed by Banknote Corporation of America for Sennett Security Products.

LITHOGRAPHED

2013, Aug. 9 **Untagged** ***Perf. 9¾ Vert.***

Coil Stamp

4802 A3664a 1c **multicolored**		.30	.25
	Pair	.30	.25
	P# strip of 5, #S111111	.60	
	P# single, #S111111	—	.50

See No. 4672.

BLACK HERITAGE

Althea Gibson (1927-2003), Tennis Player — A3667

Designed by Derry Noyes. Printed by Avery Dennison.

PHOTOGRAVURE

Sheets of 200 in 10 panes of 20

2013, Aug. 23 **Tagged** ***Serpentine Die Cut 11***

Self-Adhesive

4803 A3667 (46c) **multicolored** Ⓢ		1.25	.25
	P# block of 4, 4#+V	5.00	
	Pane of 20	25.00	
a.	Imperforate	1.75	—
	Pane of 20	35.00	

Die cut and imperforate uncut press sheets of No. 4803 were made available for sale. Values: cross-gutter block of 4, $9; pairs with gutters between, $4.25 each. See note after No. 4693.

See note after No. 1549.

MARCH ON WASHINGTON, 50th ANNIV.

Marchers and Washington Monument — A3668

Designed by Antonio Alcalá. Printed by Avery Dennison.

PHOTOGRAVURE

Sheets of 200 in 10 panes of 20

2013, Aug. 23 **Tagged** ***Serpentine Die Cut 10¾***

Self-Adhesive

4804 A3668 (46c) **multicolored** Ⓢ		1.25	.25
	P# block of 4, 5#+V	5.00	
	P# block of 8, 2 sets of 5#+V, + side panel	10.00	
	Pane of 20	25.00	
a.	Imperforate	1.75	—
	Pane of 20	35.00	

Die cut and imperforate uncut press sheets of No. 4804 were made available for sale. Values: cross-gutter block of 4, $9; pairs with gutters between, $4.25 each. See note after No. 4693.

See note after No. 1549.

WAR OF 1812 BICENTENNIAL

Painting of Battle of Lake Erie, by William Henry Powell A3669

Designed by Greg Breeding. Printed by Ashton-Potter (USA) Ltd.

LITHOGRAPHED

Sheets of 120 in six panes of 20

2013, Sept. 10 **Tagged** ***Serpentine Die Cut 10¾***

Self-Adhesive

4805 A3669 (46c) **multicolored** Ⓢ		1.25	.25
	Pane of 20	25.00	
a.	Imperforate	1.75	—
	Pane of 20	35.00	

Die-cut and imperforate uncut press sheets of No. 4805 were made available for sale. Values: cross-gutter block of 4, $9; pairs with gutters between, $4.25 each. See note after No. 4693.

See note after No. 1549.

INVERTED JENNY Ⓢ

Miniature Sheet

A3670

Designed by Antonio Alcalá. Printed by Banknote Corporation of America for Sennett Security Products.

LITHOGRAPHED & ENGRAVED

Sheets of 36 in six panes of 6

Serpentine Die Cut 10½x11¼

2013, Sept. 22 **Untagged**

Self-Adhesive

4806 A3670	Pane of 6	24.00	
a.	$2 Single stamp	4.00	1.25
b.	Imperforate pane of 6	72.50	—
c.	As "b," single stamp	12.00	—
d.	Pane of 6, airplane right-side up	*70,000.*	
e.	As "d," single stamp	*13,500.*	

No. 4806, along with a piece of white cardboard backing, was placed in a sealed envelope. The envelope, along with a piece of gray cardboard backing, was inside a sealed plastic outerwrap. One hundred panes were produced that contain the airplane right-side up. These panes were included in the same envelope and outerwrap and were distributed somewhat randomly. No returns or refunds were offered for any opened packages. Values for No. 4806 are for panes removed from the envelope.

A book containing an unused and a first-day canceled example of No. 4806, along with items that are termed "proofs" and "die wipes" sold for $200.

Die-cut and imperforate uncut press sheets of No. 4806 were made available for sale. Values: cross-gutter block of 4 with die cuts, $27.50; cross-gutter block of 4 without die cuts, $60; pairs with gutters between, die cut, $11 each; pairs with gutters between, without die cuts, $25 each. See note after No. 4693.

MUSIC ICONS

Ray Charles (1930-2004), Recording Artist — A3671

Designed by Ethel Kessler. Printed by Banknote Corporation of America for Sennett Security Products.

LITHOGRAPHED

Sheets of 144 in nine panes of 16

2013, Sept. 23 Tagged *Serpentine Die Cut 10½*

Self-Adhesive

4807 A3671 (46c) **multicolored** 1.25 .25
Pane of 16 20.00
a. Imperforate 1.75 —
Pane of 16 35.00

Adjacent horizontal or vertical stamps have selvage between the stamps.

Die cut and imperforate uncut press sheets of No. 4807 were made available for sale. Values: cross gutter block of 4, $9; pairs with gutters between, $4.25 each. See note after No. 4693.

SNOWFLAKES Ⓢ

A3672

A3673

A3674

A3675

A3676

Designed by Jennifer Arnold. Printed by CCL Label, Inc.

PHOTOGRAVURE

2013, Oct. 1 Tagged *Serpentine Die Cut 11 Vert.*

Coil Stamps

Self-Adhesive

4808 A3672 (10c) **light blue & multicolored** .30 .25
4809 A3673 (10c) **pale blue & multicolored** .30 .25
4810 A3674 (10c) **light blue & multicolored** .30 .25
4811 A3675 (10c) **pale blue & multicolored** .30 .25
4812 A3676 (10c) **lilac & multicolored** .30 .25
a. Strip of 5, #4808-4812 1.25
P# strip of 5, #4808-4812, #C11111111 2.50
P# strip of 11, 3 #4810, 2 each #4808-4809, 4811-4812, #C11111111 4.00
P# single (#4810), same # — 2.00
Nos. 4808-4812 (5) 1.50 1.25

See note after No. 1549.

Holy Family and Donkey Type of 2012 Dated "2013" and

Wreath — A3677

Virgin and Child, by Jan Gossaert — A3678

Poinsettia — A3679

Gingerbread House With Red Door — A3680

Gingerbread House With Blue Door — A3681

Gingerbread House With Green Door — A3682

Gingerbread House With Orange Door — A3683

Poinsettia — A3684

Designed by Greg Breeding (#4813), William J. Gicker (#4814), Richard Sheaff (#4815), Ethel Kessler (#4816, 4821), Derry Noyes (#4817-4820). Printed by Banknote Corporation of America for Sennett Security Products (#4813, 4815-4820), Ashton-Potter (USA) Ltd. (#4814), Avery Dennison (#4821).

LITHOGRAPHED, PHOTOGRAVURE (#4821)

Sheets of 200 in 10 panes of 20 (#4813), Sheets of 60 in six panes of 10 (#4814)

2013 Tagged *Serpentine Die Cut 11*

Self-Adhesive

4813 A3590 (46c) **multicolored,** "2013" year date, *Oct. 11* 1.25 .25
P# block of 4, 5#+S 5.00
Pane of 20 25.00
a. Imperforate 1.75 —
Pane of 20 35.00

Serpentine Die Cut

4814 A3677 ($1.10) **multicolored,** *Oct. 24* Ⓢ 2.80 .50
P# block of 4, 6#+P 11.20
Pane of 10 28.00
a. Imperforate 4.00 —
Pane of 10 40.00

Booklet Stamps

Serpentine Die Cut 11 on 2 or 3 Sides

4815 A3678 (46c) **multicolored,** *Oct. 11* 1.25 .25
a. Booklet pane of 20 25.00
b. Imperforate 1.75 —
c. Imperforate booklet pane of 20 35.00
4816 A3679 (46c) **multicolored,** *Oct. 10* 1.25 .25
a. Booklet pane of 20 25.00
b. Dated "2014" 1.25 .25
c. As #4816a, dated "2014" 25.00
d. Imperforate, dated "2013" 1.75 —
e. Imperforate booklet pane of 20 35.00
4817 A3680 (46c) **multicolored,** overall tagging on prephosphored paper, *Nov. 6* 1.25 .25
a. Strong overall tagging only 1.25 .25
4818 A3681 (46c) **multicolored,** overall tagging on prephosphored paper, *Nov. 6* 1.25 .25
a. Strong overall tagging only 1.25 .25

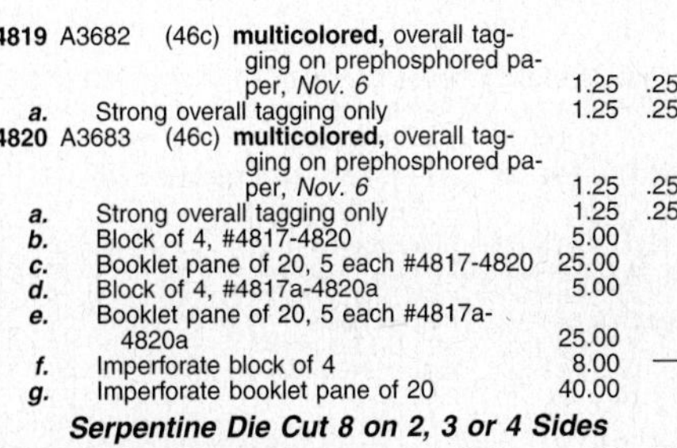

4819 A3682 (46c) **multicolored,** overall tagging on prephosphored paper, *Nov. 6* 1.25 .25
a. Strong overall tagging only 1.25 .25
4820 A3683 (46c) **multicolored,** overall tagging on prephosphored paper, *Nov. 6* 1.25 .25
a. Strong overall tagging only 1.25 .25
b. Block of 4, #4817-4820 5.00
c. Booklet pane of 20, 5 each #4817-4820 25.00
d. Block of 4, #4817a-4820a 5.00
e. Booklet pane of 20, 5 each #4817a-4820a 25.00
f. Imperforate block of 4 8.00 —
g. Imperforate booklet pane of 20 40.00

Serpentine Die Cut 8 on 2, 3 or 4 Sides

4821 A3684 (46c) **multicolored,** *Oct. 10* Ⓢ 1.25 .25
a. Booklet pane of 18 22.50
Nos. 4815-4821 (7) 8.75 1.75

Die cut and imperforate uncut press sheets of No. 4813 were made available for sale. Values: cross gutter block of 4, $9; pairs with gutters between, $4 each.

Die cut and imperforate uncut press sheets of No. 4814 were made available for sale. Values: cross gutter block of 4, $20; pairs with gutters between, $8.50 each.

Die cut and imperforate uncut press sheets of No. 4815 were made available for sale. Values for varieties from die cut press sheets: cross gutter block of 4 with booklet cover, imperf. within, $10; cross gutter block of 4, imperf. within, $10; vert. pair, imperf. between, $4; horiz. pair, imperf. between, $6. Values for varieties from imperforate press sheets: cross gutter block of 4 with booklet cover, $10; horiz. pair with booklet cover and gutter between, $6.

Die cut and imperforate uncut press sheets of No. 4816 were made available for sale. Values for varieties from die cut press sheets: cross gutter block of 4 with booklet cover, imperf. within, $10; cross gutter block of 4, imperf. within, $10; vert. pair, imperf. between, $4; horiz. pair, imperf. between, $6. Values for varieties from imperforate press sheets: cross gutter block of 4 with booklet cover, $10; horiz pair with booklet cover and gutter between, $6.

Die cut and imperforate uncut press sheets of No. 4817-4820 were made available for sale. Values for varieties from die cut press sheets: cross gutter block of 4 with booklet cover, imperf. within, $10: cross gutter block of 4, imperf. within, $10; vert. pair, imperf. between, $4; horiz. pair, imperf. between, $6. Values for varieties from imperforate press sheets: cross gutter block of 4 with booklet cover, $10; vert. pair with gutter between, $4; horiz. pair with booklet cover and gutter between, $6. See note after No. 4693.

See note after No. 1549.

Issued: No. 4816b, 8/21/14. No. 4816b sold for 49c on day of issue. Nos. 4815a, 4815c, 4816a, 4816c, 4816e, 4820c, 4820e, and 4820g are complete double-sided booklets. Eight stamps plus and the label that serves as a booklet cover are on one side of the peelable backing and 12 stamps are on the other side of the backing.

MEDALS OF HONOR

Navy Medal of Honor — A3685

A3685a

Army Medal of Honor — A3686

A3686a

Designed by Antonio Alcalá. Printed by Banknote Coporation of America for Sennett Security Products.

LITHOGRAPHED

Sheets of 60 in three panes of 20 (Panes are folded into a folio with 18 stamps on back side of folded pane and 2 stamps on the front side)

2013, Nov. 11 Tagged *Serpentine Die Cut 11*

Self-Adhesive

4822	A3685 (46c) **multicolored**	1.25	.30
a.	Dated "2014," *July 26, 2014*	1.25	.30
b.	A3685a Dated "2015," *May 25, 2015*	1.25	.30
4823	A3686 (46c) **multicolored**	1.25	.30
a.	Dated "2014," *July 26, 2014*	1.25	.30
b.	A3686a Dated "2015," *May 25, 2015*	1.25	.30
c.	Pair, #4822-4823	2.50	
	P# block of 4, 6#+S	5.00	
	Folio of 20	25.00	
d.	Pair, #4822a-4823a	2.50	
	Dated "2014," P# block of 4, 6#+S	5.00	
	Dated "2014," folio of 20	25.00	
e.	Pair, 4822b-4823b	2.50	
f.	Imperf. pair, #4822-4823	4.50	—
	Imperf. pair with wide margins	7.00	—
	Folio of 20	47.50	
g.	Imperf. pair, #4822a-4823a	4.50	—
	Imperf. pair with wide margins	7.00	—
	Folio of 20	47.50	

Die cut and imperforate uncut press sheets of Nos. 4822-4823 and 4822a-4823a were made available for sale. Values: vert. pairs with gutters between, $4.50 each. See note after No. 4693.

Nos. 4822a, 4822b, 4823a and 4823b sold for 49c on day of issue. Folios containing Nos. 4822a and 4823a have different images of Medal of Honor recipients, product numbers (on folio margins) and text on the paper backing than that found on the folios with Nos. 4822 and 4823. Nos. 4822b and 4823b were in a folio with No. 4988.

HANUKKAH

Menorah — A3687

Designed by Ethel Kessler. Printed by Ashton-Potter (USA) Ltd.

LITHOGRAPHED

Sheets of 160 in eight panes of 20

2013, Nov. 19 Tagged *Serpentine Die Cut 11*

Self-Adhesive

4824	A3687 (46c) **multicolored** ⓢ	1.25	.25
	P# block of 4, 5#+P	5.00	
	Pane of 20	25.00	
a.	Imperforate	1.75	—
	Pane of 20	35.00	

Postal Service officials declared on Nov. 8 that No. 4824 could be sold in post offices on Nov. 9, but the first day ceremony was held on Nov. 19 in New York, NY. Official first day covers have that date and city.

Imperforate uncut press sheets of No. 4824 were made available for sale. Values: cross gutter block of 4, $9; pairs with gutters between, $4.25 each. See note after No. 4693.

See note after No. 1549.

SCENES FROM HARRY POTTER MOVIES ⓢ

Harry Potter — A3688

Harry Potter and Ron Weasley A3689

Harry Potter, Ron Weasley, Hermione Granger A3690

Hermione Granger — A3691

Harry Potter and Fawkes the Phoenix A3692

Hedwig the Owl — A3693

Dobby the House Elf — A3694

Harry Potter and Buckbeak the Hippogriff A3695

Headmaster Albus Dumbledore — A3696

Professor Severus Snape A3697

Rubeus Hagrid A3698

Professor Minerva McGonagall — A3699

Harry Potter, Ron Weasley, Hermione Granger A3700

Luna Lovegood — A3701

Fred and George Weasley — A3702

Ginny Weasley A3703

Draco Malfoy — A3704

Harry Potter A3705

Lord Voldemort A3706

Bellatrix Lestrange — A3707

Designed by Greg Breeding. Printed by Ashton-Potter (USA) Ltd.

LITHOGRAPHED

2013, Nov. 19 Tagged ***Serpentine Die Cut 11***

Booklet Stamps
Self-Adhesive

4825 A3688 (46c) **multicolored** 2.00 .30
4826 A3689 (46c) **multicolored** 2.00 .30
4827 A3690 (46c) **multicolored** 2.00 .30
4828 A3691 (46c) **multicolored** 2.00 .30
a. Booklet pane of 4, #4825-4828, + central label 8.00
b. Imperf. booklet pane of 4 12.50 —
4829 A3692 (46c) **multicolored** 2.00 .30
4830 A3693 (46c) **multicolored** 2.00 .30
4831 A3694 (46c) **multicolored** 2.00 .30
4832 A3695 (46c) **multicolored** 2.00 .30
a. Booklet pane of 4, #4829-4832, + central label 8.00
b. Imperf. booklet pane of 4 12.50 —
4833 A3696 (46c) **multicolored** 2.00 .30
4834 A3697 (46c) **multicolored** 2.00 .30
4835 A3698 (46c) **multicolored** 2.00 .30
4836 A3699 (46c) **multicolored** 2.00 .30
a. Booklet pane of 4, #4833-4836, + central label 8.00
b. Imperf. booklet pane of 4 12.50 —
4837 A3700 (46c) **multicolored** 2.00 .30
4838 A3701 (46c) **multicolored** 2.00 .30
4839 A3702 (46c) **multicolored** 2.00 .30
4840 A3703 (46c) **multicolored** 2.00 .30
a. Booklet pane of 4, #4837-4840, + central label 8.00
b. Imperf. booklet pane of 4 12.50 —
4841 A3704 (46c) **multicolored** 2.00 .30
4842 A3705 (46c) **multicolored** 2.00 .30
4843 A3706 (46c) **multicolored** 2.00 .30
4844 A3707 (46c) **multicolored** 2.00 .30
a. Booklet pane of 4, #4841-4844, + central label 8.00
b. Imperf. booklet pane of 4 12.50 —
Nos. 4825-4844 (20) 40.00 6.00

Die cut and imperforate uncut press sheets of Nos. 4825-4844 were made available for sale. Values: imperforate singles, $3.50 each. See note after No. 4693.

See note after No. 1549.

KWANZAA

People, Candles and Book — A3708

Designed by Antonio Alcalá. Printed by Ashton-Potter (USA) Ltd.

LITHOGRAPHED
Sheets of 160 in 8 panes of 20

2013, Nov. 26 Tagged ***Serpentine Die Cut 11***

Self-Adhesive

4845 A3708 (46c) **multicolored** ⓢ 1.25 .25
P# block of 4, 6#+P 5.00
Pane of 20 25.00
a. Imperforate 1.75 —
Pane of 20 35.00

Imperforate uncut press sheets of No. 4845 were made available for sale. Values: cross gutter block of 4, $9; pairs with gutters between, $4.25 each. See note after No. 4693.

See note after No. 1549.

CHINESE NEW YEAR

Year of the Horse A3709

Designed by Ethel Kessler. Printed by CCL Label, Inc.

PHOTOGRAVURE
Sheets of 108 in nine panes of 12

2014, Jan. 15 Tagged ***Serpentine Die Cut 11***

Self-Adhesive

4846 A3709 (46c) **multicolored** ⓢ 1.25 .25
Pane of 12 15.00
a. Imperforate 2.00 —
Pane of 12 24.00

Die cut and imperforate uncut press sheets of No. 4846 were made available for sale. Values: cross gutter block of 4, $9; pairs with gutters between, $4.25 each. See note after No. 4693.

See note after No. 1549.

LOVE

Heart — A3710

Designed by Antonio Alcalá. Printed by CCL Label, Inc.

PHOTOGRAVURE
Sheets of 120 in six panes of 20

2014, Jan. 21 Tagged ***Serpentine Die Cut 10¾***

Self-Adhesive

4847 A3710 (46c) **multicolored** ⓢ 1.25 .25
P# block of 4, 3#+C 5.00
Pane of 20 25.00
a. Imperforate 2.00 —
Pane of 20 40.00

Die cut and imperforate uncut press sheets of No. 4847 were made available for sale. Values: cross gutter block of 4, $10; pairs with gutters between, $4.25 each. See note after No. 4693.

See note after No. 1549.

FERNS ⓢ

Fortune's Holly Fern — A3711

Soft Shield Fern — A3712

Autumn Fern — A3713

Goldie's Wood Fern — A3714

Painted Fern — A3715

Designed by Phil Jordan. Printed by CCL Label, Inc.

PHOTOGRAVURE

Serpentine Die Cut 11 Vert.

2014, Jan. 27 Tagged

Coil Stamps
Self-Adhesive

4848 A3711 49c **multicolored** 1.50 .25
4849 A3712 49c **multicolored** 1.50 .25
4850 A3713 49c **multicolored** 1.50 .25
4851 A3714 49c **multicolored** 1.50 .25
4852 A3715 49c **multicolored** 1.50 .25
a. Strip of 5, #4848-4852 7.50
P# strip of 5, #4848-4852, #C1111 10.50
P# strip of 11, 3# 4850, 2 each #4848-4849, 4851-4852, #C1111 18.00
P# single, #C1111 (#4850) — 3.00
Nos. 4848-4852 (5) 7.50 1.25

Fort McHenry Flag and Fireworks — A3716

A3716a

Designed by Phil Jordan. Printed by CCL Label, Inc.

PHOTOGRAVURE

Serpentine Die Cut 8½ Vert.

2014, Jan. 28 Tagged

Coil Stamps
Self-Adhesive

4853 A3716 (49c) **multicolored** ⓢ 1.25 .25
Pair 2.50
P# strip of 5, #C11111 7.50
P# single, #C11111 — 3.50

Designed by Ashton-Potter (USA) Ltd. (#4854-4855).

LITHOGRAPHED (#4854-4855)

Serpentine Die Cut 9½ Vert.

4854 A3716a (49c) **multicolored** ⓢ 1.25 .25
Pair 2.50
P# strip of 5, #P1111, P2222 7.50
P# single, #P1111, P2222 — 3.50
a. Die cutting omitted, pair 150.00

A3716b

Booklet Stamp

Serpentine Die Cut 11¼x10¾ on 2 or 3 Sides

4855 A3716b (49c) **multicolored** ⓢ 1.25 .25
a. Booklet pane of 20 25.00

No. 4855a is a double-sided booklet with 12 stamps on one side and eight stamps plus a label that serves as the booklet cover on the other side.

Nos. 4854 and 4855 each have a microprinted "USPS" on the right side of the lowest white stripe of the flag.

Counterfeits exist of No. 4854. See the Postal Counterfeits section of this catalog.

See note after No. 1549.

See Nos. 4868-4871.

BLACK HERITAGE

Shirley Chisholm (1924-2005), Congresswoman — A3717

Designed by Ethel Kessler. Printed by CCL Label, Inc.

PHOTOGRAVURE

Sheets of 200 in 10 panes of 20

2014, Jan. 31 Tagged *Serpentine Die Cut 11*

Self-Adhesive

4856 A3717 (49c) **multicolored** ⓢ		1.25	.25
	P# block of 4, 4#+C	5.00	
	Pane of 20	25.00	
a.	Imperforate	2.00	—
	Pane of 20	40.00	

Die cut and imperforate uncut press sheets of No. 4856 were made available for sale. Values: cross gutter block of 4, $10; pairs with gutters between, $4.25 each. See note after No. 4693.

See note after No. 1549.

WILDLIFE ISSUE

Hummingbird — A3718

A3718a

Designed by Carl T. Herrman. Printed by Ashton-Potter (USA) Ltd.

LITHOGRAPHED

Sheets of 200 in 10 panes of 20

Serpentine Die Cut 11¼x10¾

2014, Feb. 7 Tagged

Self-Adhesive

4857 A3718 34c **multicolored** ⓢ		.70	.25
	P# block of 4, 5#+P	2.80	
	Pane of 20	14.00	

Coil Stamp

Serpentine Die Cut 9½ Vert.

4858 A3718a 34c **multicolored,** prephosphored coated paper with surface tagging showing a solid appearance ⓢ		.70	.25
	Pair	1.40	
	P# strip of 5, #P11111	5.25	
	P# single #P11111	—	2.75
a.	Overall tagging	.70	.25
	Pair	1.40	
	P# strip of 5, #P22222	5.25	
	P# single #P22222	—	2.75
b.	As "a," die cutting omitted, pair	—	

See note after No. 1549.

GREAT SPANGLED FRITILLARY BUTTERFLY ⓢ

A3719

Designed by Derry Noyes. Printed by CCL Label, Inc.

PHOTOGRAVURE

Sheets of 200 in 10 panes of 20

2014, Feb. 10 Tagged *Serpentine Die Cut 10¾*

Self-Adhesive

4859 A3719 70c **multicolored**		1.50	.25
	P# block of 4, 7#+C	6.00	
	Pane of 20	30.00	
a.	Imperforate	3.25	—
	Pane of 20	65.00	

Die cut and imperforate uncut press sheets of No. 4859 were made available for sale. Values: cross gutter block of 4, $18; pairs with gutters between, $7.50 each. See note after No. 4693.

See note after No. 1549.

Statue of Abraham Lincoln in Lincoln Memorial — A3720

A3720a

Designed by Derry Noyes. Printed by CCL Label, Inc.

PHOTOGRAVURE

Sheets of 60 in three panes of 20

2014, Feb. 12 Tagged *Serpentine Die Cut 11*

Self-Adhesive

4860 A3720 21c **multicolored** ⓢ		.45	.25
	P# block of 4, 3#+C	1.80	
	Pane of 20	9.00	
a.	Imperforate	1.25	—
	Pane of 20	25.00	

Die cut and imperforate uncut press sheets of No. 4860 were made available for sale. Value: vert. pair with gutter between, $2.75. See note after No. 4693.

See note after No. 1549.

Coil Stamp

Serpentine Die Cut 8½ Vert.

4861 A3720a 21c **multicolored** ⓢ		.45	.25
	Pair	.90	
	P# strip of 5, #C111	3.75	
	P# single #C111	—	2.25

See note after No. 1549.

WINTER FLOWERS

Amaryllis — A3721

Cyclamen — A3722

Paperwhite — A3723

Christmas Cactus — A3724

Designed by Ethel Kessler. Printed by Banknote Corporation of America for Sennett Security Products.

LITHOGRAPHED

Serpentine Die Cut 11 on 2 or 3 Sides

2014, Feb. 14 Tagged

Booklet Stamps

Self-Adhesive

4862 A3721 (49c) **multicolored**		1.50	.30
4863 A3722 (49c) **multicolored**		1.50	.30
4864 A3723 (49c) **multicolored**		1.50	.30
4865 A3724 (49c) **multicolored**		1.50	.30
a.	Block of 4, #4862-4865	6.00	
b.	Booklet pane of 20, 5 each #4862-4865	30.00	
c.	Imperforate block of 4	7.00	—
d.	Imperforate booklet pane of 20	35.00	
	Nos. 4862-4865 (4)	6.00	1.20

Nos. 4865b and 4865d are double-sided booklet panes with 12 stamps on one side (3 each Nos. 4862-4865), and eight stamps (2 each Nos. 4862-4865) plus label (booklet cover) on the other side.

Die cut and imperforate uncut press sheets of No. 4862-4865 were made available for sale. Values for varieties from die cut press sheets: cross gutter block of 4 with booklet cover, imperf. within, $10; cross gutter block of 4, imperf. within, $10; vert. pair, imperf. between, $4; horiz. pair, imperf. between, $6. Values for varieties from imperforate press sheets: cross gutter block of 4 with booklet cover, $10; vert. pair with gutter between, $4; horiz. pair with booklet cover and gutter between, $6. See note after No. 4693.

LITERARY ARTS

Ralph Ellison (1913-94), Buildings in Harlem A3725

Designed by Ethel Kessler. Printed by CCL Label, Inc.

PHOTOGRAVURE

Sheets of 200 in 10 panes of 20

2014, Feb. 18 Tagged *Serpentine Die Cut 11*

Self-Adhesive

4866 A3725 91c **multicolored** ⓢ		1.90	.45
	P# block of 4, 5#+C	7.60	
	Pane of 20	38.00	
a.	Imperforate	4.00	—
	Pane of 20	80.00	

Die cut and imperforate uncut press sheets of No. 4866 were made available for sale. Values: cross-gutter block of 4, $22.50; pairs with gutters between, $10 each. See note after No. 4693.

See note after No. 1549.

Wedding Cake — A3725a

Designed by Ethel Kessler. Printed by Banknote Corporation of America for Sennett Security Products.

LITHOGRAPHED

Sheets of 200 in 10 panes of 20

2014, Feb. 22 Tagged *Serpentine Die Cut 10¾*

Self-Adhesive

4867 A3725a 70c **multicolored**		2.00	.25
	P# block of 4, 6#+S	8.00	
	Pane of 20	40.00	

See Nos. 4398, 4521, 4602, 4735, 5000.

A3725b

Designed by Phil Jordan. Printed by Banknote Corporation of America for Sennett Security Products.

LITHOGRAPHED
Coil Stamp
Self-Adhesive
With "USPS" Microprinted in Fireworks Above Flagpole

2014, Mar. 3 Tagged *Serpentine Die Cut 11 Vert.*

4868	A3725b (49c) **multicolored**	1.25	.25
	Pair	2.50	
	P# strip of 5, #S11111	7.00	
	P# single, #S11111	—	3.00
a.	Vert. strip of 3 (one single each from three different coil rolls), horiz. unslit between	60.00	
b.	Pair, die cutting omitted	—	

Counterfeits exist of No. 4868. See the Postal Counterfeits section of this catalog.

A3725c

A3725d

A3725e

Printed by CCL Label, Inc. (#4869), Banknote Corporation of America for Sennett Security Products (#4870-4871).

PHOTOGRAVURE (#4869), LITHOGRAPHED (#4870-4871)
Booklet Stamps
Without Microprinted "USPS"
Serpentine Die Cut 11¼x11½ on 2 or 3 Sides

4869	A3725c (49c) **multicolored** Ⓢ	1.25	.25
a.	Booklet pane of 20	25.00	

With "USPS" Microprinted in Fireworks Above Flagpole
Serpentine Die Cut 11¼x10¾ on 2 or 3 Sides

4870	A3725d (49c) **multicolored**	1.25	.25
a.	Booklet pane of 20	25.00	

The actual design images on Nos. 4855, 4869 and 4870 differ slightly in size. This is easiest seen by measuring the height of the flagpole: No. 4855 is 13mm, No. 4869 is 14mm, and No. 4870 is 12mm.

Thin Paper
Serpentine Die Cut 11¼x11 on 2, 3 or 4 Sides

4871	A3725e (49c) **multicolored**	1.25	.25
a.	Booklet pane of 18	25.00	

Nos. 4869a and 4870a are double-sided booklet panes with 12 stamps on one side and eight stamps plus a label that serves as the booklet cover on the other side.
See note after No. 1549.

AMERICAN LANDMARKS ISSUE

Verrazano-Narrows Bridge, New York — A3726

USS Arizona Memorial, Hawaii A3727

Designed by Phil Jordan. Printed by Ashton-Potter (USA) Ltd. (#4872), Banknote Corporation of America for Sennett Security Products (#4873).

LITHOGRAPHED
Sheets of 120 in 12 panes of 10 (#4872), Sheets of 30 in three panes of 10 (#4873)

2014 Tagged *Serpentine Die Cut 10¾x10½*
Self-Adhesive

4872	A3726 $5.60 **multicolored**, *Mar. 4* Ⓢ	11.00	6.25
	P# block of 4, 4#+P	44.00	
	Pane of 10	110.00	
4873	A3727 $19.99 **multicolored**, *Mar. 13*	40.00	21.00
	P# block of 4, 4#+S	160.00	
	Pane of 10	400.00	
a.	Imperforate	55.00	—
	Pane of 10	500.00	

Die cut and imperforate press sheets of No. 4873 were made available for sale. Value: horiz. pair with gutter between, $125. See note after No. 4693.
See note after No. 1549.

FERNS Ⓢ

Fortune's Holly Fern — A3728

Soft Shield Fern — A3729

Autumn Fern — A3730

Goldie's Wood Fern — A3731

Painted Fern — A3732

Designed by Phil Jordan. Printed by CCL Label, Inc.

PHOTOGRAVURE

2014, Mar. 6 Tagged *Serpentine Die Cut 11 Vert.*
Coil Stamps
Self-Adhesive

4874	A3728 (49c) **multicolored**	2.00	.25
4875	A3729 (49c) **multicolored**	2.00	.25
4876	A3730 (49c) **multicolored**	2.00	.25
4877	A3731 (49c) **multicolored**	2.00	.25
4878	A3732 (49c) **multicolored**	2.00	.25
a.	Strip of 5, #4874-4878	10.00	
	P# strip of 5, #4874-4878, #C1111	15.00	
	P# strip of 11, 3# 4876, 2 each #4874-4875, 4877-4878, #C1111	25.00	
	P# single, #C1111 (#4876)	—	3.00
	Nos. 4874-4878 (5)	10.00	1.25

See note after No. 1549.

DISTINGUISHED AMERICANS

C. Alfred "Chief" Anderson (1907-96), Aviator — A3733

Designed by Phil Jordan. Printed by Ashton-Potter (USA) Ltd.

LITHOGRAPHED
Sheets of 160 in eight panes of 20
Serpentine Die Cut 10¾x11

2014, Mar. 13 Tagged
Self-Adhesive

4879	A3733 70c **multicolored** Ⓢ	1.40	.30
	P# block of 4, 5#+P	5.60	
	Pane of 20	28.00	
a.	Imperforate	3.00	—
	Pane of 20	60.00	

Die cut and imperforate press sheets of No. 4879 were made available for sale. Values: cross gutter block of 4, $12; pairs with gutters between, $5 each. See note after No. 4693.
See note after No. 1549.

MUSIC ICONS

Jimi Hendrix (1942-70), Rock Guitarist — A3734

Designed by Greg Breeding. Printed by Banknote Corporation of America for Sennett Security Products.

PHOTOGRAVURE
Sheets of 144 in nine panes of 16

2014, Mar. 13 Tagged *Serpentine Die Cut 10½*
Self-Adhesive

4880	A3734 (49c) **multicolored**	1.25	.25
	Pane of 16	20.00	
a.	Imperforate	1.75	—
	Pane of 16	28.00	

Adjacent horizontal or vertical stamps have selvage between the stamps. Any stamp on the pane is rotated 90 degrees with respect to any adjacent stamp, so that any block of four has stamps oriented in each of the four directions.
Die cut and imperforate uncut press sheets of No. 4880 were made available for sale. Values: cross gutter block of 4, $9; pairs with gutters between, $4.25 each.
See No. 4765.
See note after Nos. 1549 and 4693.

Flowers and "Yes I Do" — A3734a

Designed by Michael Osborne. Printed by Ashton-Potter (USA) Ltd.

LITHOGRAPHED
Sheets of 180 in nine panes of 20

2014, Mar. 21 Tagged *Serpentine Die Cut 10¾*
Self-Adhesive

4881	A3734a 70c **multicolored** Ⓢ	1.40	.30
	P# block of 4, 4#+P	5.60	
	Pane of 20	28.00	

See note after No. 1549.
See Nos. 4765, 5001.

SONGBIRDS ⓢ

Western Meadowlark — A3735

Mountain Bluebird — A3736

Western Tanager — A3737

Painted Bunting — A3738

Baltimore Oriole — A3739

Evening Grosbeak — A3740

Scarlet Tanager — A3741

Rose-breasted Grosbeak — A3742

American Goldfinch — A3743

White-throated Sparrow — A3744

Designed by Derry Noyes. Printed by Ashton-Potter (USA) Ltd.

LITHOGRAPHED

Serpentine Die Cut 10¾ on 2 or 3 Sides

2014, Apr. 5 **Tagged**

Booklet Stamps
Self-Adhesive

4882	A3735 (49c)	**multicolored**	1.50	.40
4883	A3736 (49c)	**multicolored**	1.50	.40
4884	A3737 (49c)	**multicolored**	1.50	.40
4885	A3738 (49c)	**multicolored**	1.50	.40
4886	A3739 (49c)	**multicolored**	1.50	.40
4887	A3740 (49c)	**multicolored**	1.50	.40
4888	A3741 (49c)	**multicolored**	1.50	.40
4889	A3742 (49c)	**multicolored**	1.50	.40
4890	A3743 (49c)	**multicolored**	1.50	.40
4891	A3744 (49c)	**multicolored**	1.50	.40
a.	Block of 10, #4882-4891		15.00	
b.	Booklet pane of 20, 2 each #4882-4891		30.00	
c.	Imperforate block of 10		20.00	—
d.	Imperforate booklet pane of 20		40.00	
	Nos. 4882-4891 (10)		15.00	4.00

Nos. 4891b and 4891d are double-sided booklet panes with 12 stamps on one side (Nos. 4883-4886, 4888-4891, 2 each Nos. 4882, 4887) and eight stamps (Nos. 4883-4886, 4888-4891) plus label (booklet cover) on the other side.

Die cut and imperforate uncut press sheets of Nos. 4882-4891 were made available for sale. Values for varieties from die cut press sheets: cross gutter block of 4 with booklet cover, imperf. within, $10; cross gutter block of 4, imperf. within, $10; vert. pair, imperf. between, $4; horiz. pair, imperf. between, $6. Values for varieties from imperforate press sheets: cross gutter block of 4 with booklet cover, $10; vert. pair with gutter between, $4; horiz. pair with booklet cover and gutter between, $6. See note after No. 4693.

See note after No. 1549.

LEGENDS OF HOLLYWOOD

Charlton Heston (1923-2008), Actor — A3745

Designed by Greg Breeding. Printed by Ashton-Potter (USA) Ltd.

LITHOGRAPHED

Sheets of 180 in nine panes of 20

2014, Apr. 11 **Tagged** ***Serpentine Die Cut 11***

Self-Adhesive

4892	A3745 (49c) **multicolored** ⓢ	1.25	.25
	P# block of 4, 4#+P	5.00	
	Pane of 20	25.00	
a.	Imperforate	1.75	—
	Pane of 20	35.00	

Die cut and imperforate uncut press sheets of No. 4892 were made available for sale. Values: cross gutter block of 4, $9; pairs with gutters between, $4 each. See note after No. 4693.

See note after No. 1549.

Map of Sea Surface Temperatures A3746

Designed by William J. Gicker. Printed by Ashton-Potter (USA) Ltd.

LITHOGRAPHED

Sheets of 50 in five panes of 10

2014, Apr. 22 **Tagged** ***Serpentine Die Cut***

Self-Adhesive

4893	A3746 ($1.15) **multicolored** ⓢ	2.80	.50
	P# block of 4, 6#+P	11.20	
	Pane of 10	28.00	
a.	Imperforate	3.50	—
	Pane of 10	35.00	

Unused values are for stamps with surrounding selvage. Adjacent stamps are separated by rouletting.

Die cut and imperforate uncut press sheets of No. 4893 were made available for sale. Value: vert. pair with gutter between, $8. See note after No. 4693.

See note after No. 1549.

FLAGS ⓢ

Flag With 5 Full and 3 Partial Stars — A3747

Flag With 3 Full Stars — A3748

Flag With 4 Full and 2 Partial Stars — A3749

Flag With 2 Full and 2 Partial Stars — A3750

Designed by Ethel Kessler. Printed by CCL Label, Inc.

PHOTOGRAVURE

Serpentine Die Cut 11 Vert.

2014, Apr. 25 **Tagged**

Coil Stamps
Self-Adhesive

4894	A3747 (49c) **blue & red**	1.25	.25
4895	A3748 (49c) **blue & red**	1.25	.25
4896	A3749 (49c) **blue & red**	1.25	.25
4897	A3750 (49c) **blue & red**	1.25	.25
a.	Strip of 4, #4894-4897	5.00	
	P# strip of 5, #4895-4897, 2 #4894, #C11, C12	7.00	
	P# strip of 9, 3# 4896, 2 each #4894-4895, 4897, #C11, C12	12.00	
	P# single, #C11, C12 (#4896)	—	3.00
	Nos. 4894-4897 (4)	5.00	1.00

See note after No. 1549.

CIRCUS POSTERS

Barnum and Bailey Circus Poster With Clown — A3751

Sells-Floto Circus Poster — A3752

Ringling Bros. Barnum and Bailey Circus Poster With Dainty Miss Leitzel — A3753

Al G. Barnes Wild Animal Circus Poster — A3754

Ringling Bros. Shows Poster With Hillary Long — A3755

Barnum and Bailey Circus Poster With Tiger — A3756

Ringling Bros. Barnum and Bailey Circus Poster With Elephant — A3757

Carl Hagenbeck-Wallace Circus Poster — A3758

A3758a

Designed by Jennifer Arnold, Joe Brockert (#4905c). Printed by Banknote Coporation of America for Sennett Security Products.

LITHOGRAPHED, ENGRAVED (50c), SHEET MARGIN (#4905b) LITHOGRAPHED WITH FOIL APPLICATION

Sheets of 96 in six panes of 16

2014, May 5 ***Serpentine Die Cut 11***

Tagged, Untagged (No. 4905c)

Self-Adhesive

4898	A3751 (49c) **multicolored**	1.25	.45
4899	A3752 (49c) **multicolored**	1.25	.45
4900	A3753 (49c) **multicolored**	1.25	.45
4901	A3754 (49c) **multicolored**	1.25	.45
4902	A3755 (49c) **multicolored**	1.25	.45
4903	A3756 (49c) **multicolored**	1.25	.45
4904	A3757 (49c) **multicolored**	1.25	.45
4905	A3758 (49c) **multicolored**	1.25	.45
a.	Block of 8, #4898-4905	10.00	
	Pane of 16	20.00	
b.	Imperforate block of 8	16.00	—
	Pane of 16	32.00	
c.	A3758a Imperforate souvenir sheet of 3, #4905e, 2 #4905d, *Dec. 10*	9.00	—
d.	A1811 50c **red**, imperforate	2.25	—
e.	$1 **multicolored** (57x48mm stamp similar to #4898), imperforate	4.50	—
f.	As "c," gold omitted in sheet margin	—	
	Nos. 4898-4905 (8)	10.00	3.60

Die cut and imperforate uncut press sheets of Nos. 4898-4905 were made available for sale. Values: cross gutter block of 8, $22.50; block of 8 with horiz. gutter between, $17.50; pairs with gutters between, $4.25 each; No. 4905c in cross gutter block of 4, $40; pair of No. 4905c with horiz. gutter between, $17.50; pair of No. 4905c with wide horiz. gutter between, $20. See note after No. 4693.

No. 4905c was printed only in press sheets containing 12 souvenir sheets. No. 4905c has die cutting around the souvenir sheet margin, but values for unused examples are for souvenir sheets having the white press sheet margin surrounding the die cutting. Examples of No. 4905c with serpentine die cutting around the three stamps were sold only with the USPS 2014 Stamp Yearbook, which sold for $64.95. The souvenir sheets sold with the yearbook are punched out from the press sheets and lack the white press sheet margin.

HARVEY MILK

Harvey Milk (1930-78), Homosexual Rights Advocate and Politician — A3759

Designed by Antonio Alcalá. Printed by Banknote Corporation of America for Sennett Security Products.

LITHOGRAPHED

Sheets of 240 in 12 panes of 20

2014, May 22 Tagged ***Serpentine Die Cut 10¾***

Self-Adhesive

4906	A3759 (49c) **multicolored**	1.25	.25
	P# block of 4, 4#+S	5.00	
	Pane of 20	25.00	
a.	Imperforate	1.75	—
	Pane of 20	35.00	

Die cut and imperforate uncut press sheets of No. 4906 were made available for sale. Values: cross gutter block of 4, $9; pairs with gutters between, $4.25 each. See note after No. 4693.

NEVADA STATEHOOD, 150th ANNIV.

Fire Canyon A3760

Designed by Antonio Alcalá. Printed by Banknote Corporation of America for Sennett Security Products.

LITHOGRAPHED

Sheets of 240 in 12 panes of 20

2014, May 29 Tagged ***Serpentine Die Cut 10¾***

Self-Adhesive

4907	A3760 (49c) **multicolored**	1.25	.25
	P# block of 4, 6#+S	5.00	
	Pane of 20	25.00	
a.	Imperforate	1.75	—
	Pane of 20	35.00	

Die cut and imperforate uncut press sheets of No. 4907 were made available for sale. Values: cross gutter block of 4, $9; pairs with gutters between, $4.25 each. See note after No. 4693.

HOT RODS Ⓢ

Rear of 1932 Ford "Deuce" Roadster — A3761

Front of 1932 Ford "Deuce" Roadster — A3762

Designed by Derry Noyes. Printed by CCL Label, Inc.

PHOTOGRAVURE

Serpentine Die Cut 11¾x11¼ on 2 or 3 Sides

2014, June 6 Tagged

Booklet Stamps

Self-Adhesive

4908	A3761 (49c) **multicolored**	1.25	.25
4909	A3762 (49c) **multicolored**	1.25	.25
a.	Pair, #4908-4909	2.50	
b.	Booklet pane of 20, 10 each #4908-4909	25.00	
c.	Imperforate pair	4.00	—
d.	Imperforate booklet pane of 20	40.00	

Nos. 4909b and 4909d are double-sided booklet panes with 12 stamps on one side (6 each Nos. 4908-4909) and eight stamps (4 each Nos. 4908-4909) plus label (booklet cover) on the other side.

Die cut and imperforate uncut press sheets of Nos. 4908-4909 were made available for sale. Values for varieties from die cut press sheets: horiz. pair, imperf. between, $4.50. Values for varieties from imperforate press sheets: horiz. pair with booklet cover, $6. See note after No. 4693.

See note after No. 1549.

CIVIL WAR SESQUICENTENNIAL

Battle of Petersburg — A3763

Battle of Mobile Bay — A3764

Designed by Phil Jordan. Printed by Banknote Corporation of America for Sennett Security Products.

LITHOGRAPHED

Double-sided sheets of 72 in six panes of 12 (60 on one side, 12 on other side)

2014, July 30 Tagged *Serpentine Die Cut 11*

Self-Adhesive

4910 A3763 (49c) **multicolored**	1.25	.35
4911 A3764 (49c) **multicolored**	1.25	.35
a. Pair, #4910-4911	2.50	
Pane of 12	15.00	
b. Imperforate pair	5.00	—
Imperf. pair with wide spacing	7.00	
Pane of 12	32.00	

Die cut and imperforate uncut press sheets of Nos. 4910-4911 were made available for sale. Values: vert. pairs with gutters between, $4.50 each. See note after No. 4693.

FARMERS MARKETS Ⓢ

Breads — A3765

Fruits and Vegetables — A3766

Flowers — A3767

Plants — A3768

Designed by Greg Breeding. Printed by Ashton-Potter (USA) Ltd.

LITHOGRAPHED

Sheets of 100 in five panes of 20

2014, Aug. 7 Tagged *Serpentine Die Cut 10¾*

Self-Adhesive

4912 A3765 (49c) **multicolored**	1.25	.30
4913 A3766 (49c) **multicolored**	1.25	.30
4914 A3767 (49c) **multicolored**	1.25	.30
4915 A3768 (49c) **multicolored**	1.25	.30
a. Horiz. strip of 4, #4912-4915	5.00	
P# block of 8, 4#+P	10.00	
Pane of 20	25.00	
b. Imperf. horiz. strip of 4	9.00	—
Pane of 20	45.00	
Nos. 4912-4915 (4)	5.00	1.20

Die cut and imperforate uncut press sheets of Nos. 4912-4915 were made available for sale. Value: horiz. strip of 4 with vert. gutter between, $11. See note after No. 4693.

See note after No. 1549.

MUSIC ICONS

Janis Joplin (1943-70), Rock Singer — A3769

Designed by Antonio Alcalá. Printed by Ashton-Potter (USA) Ltd.

LITHOGRAPHED

Sheets of 144 in nine panes of 16

2014, Aug. 8 Tagged *Serpentine Die Cut 10½*

Self-Adhesive

4916 A3769 (49c) **multicolored** Ⓢ	1.25	.25
Pane of 16	20.00	
a. Imperforate	1.75	—
Pane of 16	28.00	

Die cut and imperforate uncut press sheets of No. 4916 were made available for sale. Values: cross gutter block of 4, $9; pairs with gutters between, $4.25 each. See note after No. 4693.

See note after No. 1549.

HUDSON RIVER SCHOOL PAINTINGS Ⓢ

Grand Canyon, by Thomas Moran (1837-1926) A3770

Summer Afternoon, by Asher B. Durand (1796-1886) A3771

Sunset, by Frederic Edwin Church (1826-1900) A3772

Distant View of Niagara Falls, by Thomas Cole (1801-48) A3773

Designed by Derry Noyes. Printed by CCL Label, Inc.

PHOTOGRAVURE

Serpentine Die Cut 10¾ on 2 or 3 Sides

2014, Aug. 21 Tagged

Booklet Stamps

Self-Adhesive

4917 A3770 (49c) **multicolored**	1.50	.30
4918 A3771 (49c) **multicolored**	1.50	.30
4919 A3772 (49c) **multicolored**	1.50	.30
4920 A3773 (49c) **multicolored**	1.50	.30
a. Block of 4, #4917-4920	6.00	
b. Booklet pane of 20, 5 each #4917-4920	30.00	
c. Imperforate block of 4	8.00	—
d. Imperforate booklet pane of 20	40.00	
Nos. 4917-4920 (4)	6.00	1.20

Nos. 4920b and 4920d are double-sided booklet panes with 12 stamps on one side (3 each Nos. 4917-4920), and eight stamps (2 each Nos. 4917-4920) plus label (booklet cover) on the other side.

Die cut and imperforate uncut press sheets of Nos. 4917-4920 were made available for sale. Values for varieties from die cut press sheets: block of 4, vert. imperf. between, $10. Values for varieties from imperforate press sheets: block of 4 with vert. gutter, $10. See note after No. 4693.

See note after No. 1549.

WAR OF 1812 BICENTENNIAL

Bombardment of Fort McHenry A3774

Designed by Greg Breeding. Printed by CCL Label, Inc.

PHOTOGRAVURE

Sheets of 100 in five panes of 20

Serpentine Die Cut 10¾x10½

2014, Sept. 13 Tagged

Self-Adhesive

4921 A3774 (49c) **multicolored** Ⓢ	1.25	.25
Pane of 20	25.00	
a. Imperforate	1.75	—
Pane of 20	35.00	

Die-cut and imperforate uncut press sheets of No. 4921 were made available for sale. Value, pair with gutter between, $4. See note after No. 4693.

See note after No. 1549.

CELEBRITY CHEFS Ⓢ

Edna Lewis (1916-2006) — A3775

Felipe Rojas-Lombardi (1946-91) — A3776

Joyce Chen (1917-94) — A3777

James Beard (1903-85) — A3778

Julia Child (1912-2004) — A3779

Designed by Greg Breeding. Printed by Ashton-Potter (USA) Ltd.

LITHOGRAPHED
Sheets of 180 in nine panes of 20
Serpentine Die Cut 11x10¾

2014, Sept. 26 **Tagged**

Self-Adhesive

4922	A3775 (49c) **multicolored**	1.25	.45
4923	A3776 (49c) **multicolored**	1.25	.45
4924	A3777 (49c) **multicolored**	1.25	.45
4925	A3778 (49c) **multicolored**	1.25	.45
4926	A3779 (49c) **multicolored**	1.25	.45
a.	Horiz. strip of 5, #4922-4926	6.25	
	P# block of 10, 2 sets of 5#+P	12.50	
	Pane of 20	25.00	
b.	Imperf. horiz. strip of 5	8.00	—
	Pane of 20	32.50	
	Nos. 4922-4926 (5)	6.25	2.25

The gray shading of the inner curve of the dinner plate shown in the margin of the pane continues into the white frames surrounding some of the stamps in the pane's outer rows and columns.

Die cut and imperforate uncut press sheets of Nos. 4922-4926 were made available for sale. Values: cross gutter block of 10, $22.50; pairs with gutters between, $4.25 each. See note after No. 4693.

See note after No. 1549.

AMERICAN LANDMARKS ISSUE

Glade Creek Grist Mill, West Virginia A3780

Designed by Derry Noyes. Printed by Ashton-Potter (USA) Ltd.

LITHOGRAPHED
Sheets of 60 in six panes of 10
Serpentine Die Cut 10¾x10½

2014, Sept. 29 **Tagged**

Self-Adhesive

4927	A3780 $5.75 **multicolored** Ⓢ	11.50	6.50
	P# block of 4, 4#+P	46.00	
	Pane of 10	115.00	
a.	Imperforate	15.00	—
	Pane of 10	150.00	

Die cut and imperforate press sheets of No. 4927 were made available for sale. Values: s cross gutter block of 4, $80; pairs with gutter between, $30 each. See note after No. 2868.

See note after No. 1549.

BATMAN

Bat Signal — A3781

Bat Signal — A3782

Bat Signal — A3783

Bat Signal — A3784

Batman — A3785

Batman and Bat Signal — A3786

Batman and Rope — A3787

Batman — A3788

Designed by Greg Breeding. Printed by Baknote Corporation of America for Sennett Security Products.

LITHOGRAPHED
Sheets of 180 in nine panes of 20

2014, Oct. 9 **Tagged** ***Serpentine Die Cut***

Self-Adhesive

4928	A3781 (49c) **multicolored**	2.50	.40
4929	A3782 (49c) **multicolored**	2.50	.40
4930	A3783 (49c) **multicolored**	2.50	.40
4931	A3784 (49c) **multicolored**	2.50	.40

Serpentine Die Cut 11x10¾

4932	A3785 (49c) **multicolored**	1.25	.40
4933	A3786 (49c) **multicolored**	1.25	.40
4934	A3787 (49c) **multicolored**	1.25	.40
4935	A3788 (49c) **multicolored**	1.25	.40
a.	Vert. block of 8, #4928-4935	15.00	
	Pane of 20, #4928-4931, 4 each #4932-4935	30.00	
b.	Imperf. vert. block of 8	20.00	—
	Pane of 20	40.00	
	Nos. 4928-4935 (8)	15.00	3.20

Die cut and imperforate press sheets of Nos. 4928-4935 were made available for sale. See note after No. 4693.

Silver Bells Wreath — A3789

Designed by Michael Owens and William J. Gicker. Printed by Banknote Corporation of America for Sennett Security Products.

LITHOGRAPHED
Sheets of 60 in six panes of 10

2014, Oct. 23 **Tagged** ***Serpentine Die Cut***

Self-Adhesive

4936	A3789 ($1.15) **multicolored**	2.50	.50
	P# block of 4, 5#+S	10.00	
	Pane of 10	25.00	
a.	Imperforate	4.00	—
	Pane of 10	40.00	

Unused values are for stamps with surrounding selvage. Adjacent stamps are separated by rouletting.

Die cut and imperforate uncut press sheets of No. 4936 were made available for sale. Values: cross gutter block of 4, $21; pairs with gutters between, $9.50 each. See note after No. 4693.

WINTER FUN Ⓢ

Skaters — A3790

Child Making Snowman — A3791

Cardinal — A3792

Child Making Snow Angel — A3793

Designed by Ethel Kessler. Printed by CCL Label, Inc.

PHOTOGRAVURE
Serpentine Die Cut 10¾x11 on 2 or 3 Sides

2014, Oct. 23 **Tagged**

Booklet Stamps
Self-Adhesive

4937	A3790 (49c) **multicolored**	1.25	.30
4938	A3791 (49c) **multicolored**	1.25	.30
4939	A3792 (49c) **multicolored**	1.25	.30
4940	A3793 (49c) **multicolored**	1.25	.30
a.	Block of 4, #4937-4940	5.00	
b.	Booklet pane of 20, 5 each #4937-4940	25.00	
c.	Imperforate block of 4	7.00	—
d.	Imperf. booklet pane of 20	35.00	

Skaters — A3794

Child Making Snowman — A3795

Cardinal — A3796

Child Making Snow Angel — A3797

Printed by Ashton-Potter (USA) Ltd.

LITHOGRAPHED
Serpentine Die Cut 11¼x11 on 2, 3 or 4 Sides

Thin Paper

4941	A3794 (49c) **multicolored**	4.00	.30
4942	A3795 (49c) **multicolored**	4.00	.30
4943	A3796 (49c) **multicolored**	4.00	.30
4944	A3797 (49c) **multicolored**	4.00	.30
a.	Block or strip of 4, #4941-4944	16.00	
b.	Booklet pane of 18, 5 each #4941-4942, 4 each #4943-4944	72.00	
	Nos. 4937-4944 (8)	21.00	2.40

Nos. 4940b and 4940d are double-sided booklet panes with 12 stamps on one side (3 each Nos. 4937-4940) and eight stamps (2 each Nos. 4937-4940) plus label (booklet cover) on the other side.

Die cut and imperforate uncut press sheets of Nos. 4937-4940 were made available for sale. Values for varieties from die cut press sheets: block of 4, horiz. imperf. between, $9. Values for varieties from imperforate sheets: block of 4 with horiz. gutter, $9. See note after No. 4693.

Counterfeits exist of No. 4937-4940. See the Postal Counterfeits section of this catalog.

See note after No. 1549.

CHRISTMAS

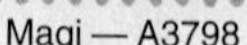
Magi — A3798

Rudolph, the Red-Nosed Reindeer — A3799

Hermey and Rudolph — A3800

Santa Claus — A3801

Bumble — A3802

Designed by Greg Breeding.
Printed by Banknote Corporation of America for Sennett Security Products (#4945), CCL Label, Inc. (#4946-4949).

LITHOGRAPHED (#4945), PHOTOGRAVURE

Serpentine Die Cut 10¾x11 on 2 or 3 Sides

2014 **Tagged**

Booklet Stamps
Self-Adhesive

4945	A3798 (49c) **multicolored,** *Nov. 19*	1.25	.25
a.	Booklet pane of 20	25.00	
b.	Imperforate	1.75	—
c.	Imperf. booklet pane of 20	35.00	

Serpentine Die Cut 11x10¾ on 2 or 3 sides

4946	A3799 (49c) **multicolored,** *Nov. 6* ⓢ	1.25	.30
4947	A3800 (49c) **multicolored,** *Nov. 6* ⓢ	1.25	.30
4948	A3801 (49c) **multicolored,** *Nov. 6* ⓢ	1.25	.30
4949	A3802 (49c) **multicolored,** *Nov. 6* ⓢ	1.25	.30
a.	Block of 4, #4946-4949	5.00	
b.	Booklet pane of 20, 5 each #4946-4949	25.00	
c.	Imperf. block of 4	7.50	—
d.	Imperf. booklet pane of 20	37.50	
	Nos. 4945-4949 (5)	6.25	1.45

Premiere of *Rudolph, the Red-Nosed Reindeer* animated television show, 50th anniv.

Nos. 4945a and 4945c are double-sided booklet panes with 12 stamps on one side and eight stamps plus a label that serves as a booklet cover on the other side. Nos. 4949b and 4949d are double-sided booklet panes with 12 stamps on one side (3 each of Nos. 4946-4949) and eight stamps (2 each of Nos. 4946-4949) plus a label that serves as a booklet cover on the other side.

Die cut and imperforate uncut press sheets of eight booklet panes of Nos. 4945 were made available for sale. Values for varieties from die cut press sheets: cross gutter block of 4 with booklet cover, imperf. within, $10; cross gutter block of 4, imperf. within, $10; vert. pair, imperf. between, $4; horiz. pair, imperf. between, $6. Values for varieties from imperforate press sheets: cross gutter block of 4 with booklet cover, $10; horiz. pair with booklet cover and gutter between, $6.

Die cut and imperforate uncut press sheets of Nos. 4946-4949 were made available for sale. Values for varieties from die cut press sheets: block of 4, vert. imperf. between, $8.50. Values for varieties from imperforate press sheets: block of 4, vert. gutter between, $8.50.

Counterfeits exist of No. 4946-4949. See the Postal Counterfeits section of this catalog.

See note after No. 4693.
See note after No. 1549.

WILT CHAMBERLAIN (1936-99), BASKETBALL PLAYER

Chamberlain in Philadelphia Warriors Uniform — A3803

Chamberlain in Los Angeles Lakers Uniform — A3804

Designed by Antonio Alcalá. Printed by Banknote Corporation of America for Sennett Security Products.

LITHOGRAPHED

Sheets of 144 in eight panes of 18

2014, Dec. 5 **Tagged** ***Serpentine Die Cut 11x10¾***

Self-Adhesive

4950	A3803 (49c) **multicolored**	1.25	.25
4951	A3804 (49c) **multicolored**	1.25	.25
a.	Pair, #4950-4951	2.50	
	P# block of 4, 4#+S	5.00	
	Pane of 18	25.00	
b.	Imperforate pair	3.50	—
	Pane of 18	35.00	

Die cut and imperforate uncut press sheets of Nos. 4950-4951 were made available for sale. Values: cross gutter block of 6, $9; pairs with gutters between, $4.25 each.

See note after No. 4693.

WAR OF 1812 BICENTENNIAL

Battle of New Orleans A3805

Designed by Greg Breeding. Printed by CCL Label, Inc.

PHOTOGRAVURE

Sheets of 100 in five panes of 20

Serpentine Die Cut 10¾x10½

2015, Jan. 8 **Tagged**

Self-Adhesive

4952	A3805 (49c) **multicolored** ⓢ	1.25	.25
	Pane of 20	25.00	
a.	Imperforate	1.75	—
	Pane of 20	35.00	

Die cut and imperforate uncut press sheets of No. 4952 were made available for sale. Value: vert. pair with gutter between, $4.25. See note after No. 4693.

See note after No. 1549.

PATRIOTIC WAVES Ⓢ

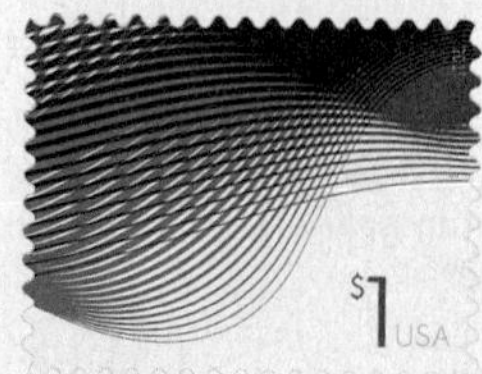

A3806

A3807

Designed by Michael Dyer. Printed by Ashton-Potter (USA) Ltd.

LITHOGRAPHED

Sheets of 140 in 14 panes of 10 (#4953), Sheets of 100 in 10 panes of 10 (#4954)

2015 **Tagged** ***Serpentine Die Cut 11***

Self-Adhesive

4953	A3806 $1 **multicolored,** *Jan. 12*	2.00	.50
	P# block of 4, 3#+P	8.00	
	Pane of 10	20.00	
a.	Imperforate	3.00	—
	Pane of 10	30.00	
4954	A3807 $2 **multicolored,** *Jan. 30*	4.00	1.00
	P# block of 4, 3#+P	16.00	
	Pane of 10	40.00	
a.	Imperforate	5.00	—
	Pane of 10	50.00	

Die-cut and imperforate uncut press sheets of No. 4953 were made available for sale. Values: cross gutter block of 4, $16.50; pairs with gutters between, $6.75 each.

Die-cut and imperforate uncut press sheets of No. 4954 were made available for sale. Values: cross gutter block of 4, $27.50; pairs with gutters between, $12.50 each. See note after No. 4693.

See note after No. 1549.

LOVE Ⓢ

A3808 A3809

Designed by Antonio Alcalá and Jessica Hische. Printed by CCL Label, Inc.

LITHOGRAPHED

Sheets of 120 in six panes of 20

2015, Jan. 22 **Tagged** ***Serpentine Die Cut 11***

Self-Adhesive

4955	A3808 (49c) **red**	1.25	.25
4956	A3809 (49c) **red & gray**	1.25	.25
a.	Pair, #4955-4956	2.50	
	P# block of 4, 2#+C	5.00	
	Pane of 20	25.00	
b.	Imperforate pair	3.50	—
	Pane of 20	35.00	

Die cut and imperforate uncut press sheets of Nos. 4955-4956 were made available for sale. Values: cross gutter block of 4, $9; pairs with gutters between, $4.25 each.

Counterfeits exist of Nos. 4955-4956. See the Postal Counterfeits section of this catalog.

See note after No. 4693. See note after No. 1549.

CHINESE NEW YEAR

Year of the Ram — A3810

Designed by Ethel Kessler. Printed by Banknote Corporation of America for Sennett Security Products.

LITHOGRAPHED

Sheets of 144 in 12 panes of 12

2015, Feb. 7 **Tagged** ***Serpentine Die Cut 11***

Self-Adhesive

4957	A3810 (49c) **multicolored**	1.25	.25
	Pane of 12	15.00	
a.	Imperforate	1.75	—
	Pane of 12	18.00	

Die cut and imperforate uncut press sheets of No. 4957 were made available for sale. Values: cross gutter block of 4, $9;

pairs with gutters between, $3.75 each. See note after No. 4693.

BLACK HERITAGE

Robert Robinson Taylor (1868-1942), Architect — A3811

Designed by Derry Noyes. Printed by Ashton-Potter (USA) Ltd.

LITHOGRAPHED
Sheets of 120 in six panes of 20

2015, Feb. 12 **Tagged** ***Serpentine Die Cut 11***
Self-Adhesive

4958	A3811 (49c) **multicolored** ⓢ	1.25	.25
	P# block of 4, 4#+P	5.00	
	Pane of 20	25.00	
a.	Imperforate	2.25	—
	Pane of 20	45.00	

Die cut and imperforate uncut press sheets of No. 4958 were made available for sale. Values: cross gutter block of 4, $9; pairs with gutters between, $4.25 each. See note after No. 4693.
See note after No. 1549.

FLOWERS

Rose and Heart — A3812

Tulip and Heart — A3813

Designed by Jeanne Greco. Printed by Banknote Corporation of America for Sennett Security Products.

ENGRAVED
Sheets of 240 in 12 panes of 20
Serpentine Die Cut 10¾x 11

2015, Feb. 14 **Tagged**
Self-Adhesive

4959	A3812 (49c) **red & black**	5.00	.25
	P# block of 4, 2#+S	20.00	
	Pane of 20	100.00	
a.	Imperforate	1.75	—
	Pane of 20	35.00	
b.	Tagging omitted	—	
4960	A3813 70c **black & red**	3.00	.30
	P# block of 4, 2#+S	12.00	
	Pane of 20	60.00	
a.	Imperforate	2.50	—
	Pane of 20	50.00	

Die cut and imperforate uncut press sheets of No. 4959 were made available for sale. Values: cross gutter block of 4, $9; pairs with gutters between, $4.25 each.
Counterfeits exist of No. 4959. See the Postal Counterfeits section of this catalog.
Die cut and imperforate uncut press sheets of No. 4960 were made available for sale. Values: cross gutter block of 4, $13.50; pairs with gutters between, $5.75 each.
See note after No. 4693.
See No. 5002.

FLAGS

Stripes at Left, Stars at Right — A3814

Stars and White Stripe — A3815

Stars at Left, Stripes at Right — A3816

Designed by Greg Breeding. Printed by Banknote Corporation of America for Sennett Security Products.

LITHOGRAPHED
Serpentine Die Cut 11 Vert.

2015, Feb. 27 **Tagged**
Coil Stamps
Self-Adhesive

4961	A3814 (10c) **multicolored**	.30	.25
4962	A3815 (10c) **multicolored**	.30	.25
4963	A3816 (10c) **multicolored**	.30	.25
a.	Strip of 3, #4961-4963	.75	
	P# strip of 5, #4962, 2 each #4961, 4963, #S111, B111	3.00	
	P# strip of 7, 3# 4962, 2 each #4961, 4963, #S111, B111	4.50	
	P# single, #S111, B111 (#4962)	—	2.25
	Nos. 4961-4963 (3)	.90	.75

WATER LILIES

Pale Pink Water Lily — A3817

Red Water Lily — A3818

Purple Water Lily — A3819

White Water Lily — A3820

Designed by Phil Jordan. Printed by Banknote Corporation of America for Sennett Security Products.

LITHOGRAPHED
Serpentine Die Cut 11x11¼ on 2 or 3 Sides

2015, Mar. 20 **Tagged**
Booklet Stamps
Self-Adhesive

4964	A3817 (49c) **multicolored**	1.50	.25
4965	A3818 (49c) **multicolored**	1.50	.25
4966	A3819 (49c) **multicolored**	1.50	.25
4967	A3820 (49c) **multicolored**	1.50	.25
a.	Block of 4, #4964-4967	6.00	
b.	Booklet pane of 20, 5 each #4964-4967	30.00	
c.	Imperf. block of 4	7.00	—
d.	Imperf. booklet pane of 20	35.00	
	Nos. 4964-4967 (4)	6.00	1.00

No. 4967b is known with the block of 4 at left on the 12-stamp side having no gum. Such booklets are rare and fragile.
Nos. 4967b and 4967d are double-sided booklet panes with 12 stamps on one side (3 each Nos. 4964-4967) and eight stamps (2 each Nos. 4964-4967) plus label (booklet cover) on the other side.
Die cut and imperforate uncut press sheets of Nos. 4964-4967 were made available for sale. Values for varieties from die cut press sheets: cross gutter block of 4 with booklet cover, imperf. within, $10; cross gutter block of 4, imperf. within, $10; block of 4, vert. imperf. between, $8.50; block of 4 with booklet cover, horiz. imperf. between, $10. Values for varieties from imperforate press sheets: cross gutter block of 4 with booklet cover, $10; block of 4 with booklet cover between, $10; block of 4 with vert. gutter between, $8.50. See note after No. 4693.

ART BY MARTIN RAMIREZ (1895-1963)

Untitled (Horse and Rider With Trees), 1954 — A3821

Untitled (Man Riding Donkey), c. 1960-63 — A3822

Untitled (Trains on Inclined Tracks), c. 1960-63 — A3823

Untitled (Deer), c. 1960-63 — A3824

Untitled (Tunnel with Cars and Buses), 1954 — A3825

Designed by Antonio Alcalá. Printed by Banknote Corporation of America for Sennett Security Products.

LITHOGRAPHED
Sheets of 240 in 12 panes of 20

2015, Mar. 26 **Tagged** ***Serpentine Die Cut 10¾***
Self-Adhesive

4968	A3821 (49c) **multicolored**	1.25	.40
4969	A3822 (49c) **multicolored**	1.25	.40
4970	A3823 (49c) **multicolored**	1.25	.40
4971	A3824 (49c) **multicolored**	1.25	.40
4972	A3825 (49c) **multicolored**	1.25	.40
a.	Vert. strip of 5, #4968-4972	6.25	
	P# block of 10, 5#+S	12.50	
	Pane of 20	25.00	
b.	Imperf. vert. strip of 5	7.50	—
	Pane of 20	30.00	

Die cut and imperforate uncut press sheets of Nos. 4968-4972 were made available for sale. Values: cross gutter block of 10, $22.50; pairs with gutters between, $3.75 each.
See note after No. 4693.

A3825a

A3825b

A3825c

A3825d

A3825e

Designed by Phil Jordan. Printed by Banknote Corporation of America for Sennett Security Products.

LITHOGRAPHED

Serpentine Die Cut 11 Vert.

2015, Mar. 27 **Tagged**

Coil Stamps
Self-Adhesive
With Microprinted "USPS"
Dated "2014"

4973	A3825a (49c) **multicolored**	1.25	.25
a.	Dated "2015"	1.25	.25
4974	A3825b (49c) **multicolored**	1.25	.25
a.	Dated "2015"	1.25	.25
4975	A3825c (49c) **multicolored**	1.25	.25
a.	Dated "2015"	1.25	.25
4976	A3825d (49c) **multicolored**	1.25	.25
a.	Dated "2015"	1.25	.25
4977	A3825e (49c) **multicolored**	1.25	.25
a.	Dated "2015"	1.25	.25
b.	Strip of 5, #4973-4977	5.50	
	P# strip of 5, #4973-4977, #S1111	7.00	
	P# strip of 11, 3# 4975, 2 each #4973-4974, 4976-4977, #S1111	13.00	
	P# single, #S1111 (#4975)	—	3.00
c.	Strip of 5, #4973a-4977a	5.50	
	P# strip of 5, #4973a-4977a, #S1111	7.00	
	P# strip of 11, 3# 4975a, 2 each #4973a-4974a, 4976a-4977a, #S1111	13.00	
	P# single, #S1111 (#4975a)	—	3.00
	Nos. 4973-4977 (5)	6.25	1.25

Nos. 4973a-4977a are from coil rolls containing 3,000 stamps. Nos. 4973-4977 are from coil rolls containing 10,000 stamps. Microprinted "USPS" is near the end of the upper left fern branch on No. 4973 and near the base of the fern's stem on Nos. 4974-4977. Nos. 4973a-4977a have same microprinting locations as Nos. 4973-4977. Nos. 4874-4878 lack microprinted "USPS."

FROM ME TO YOU Ⓢ

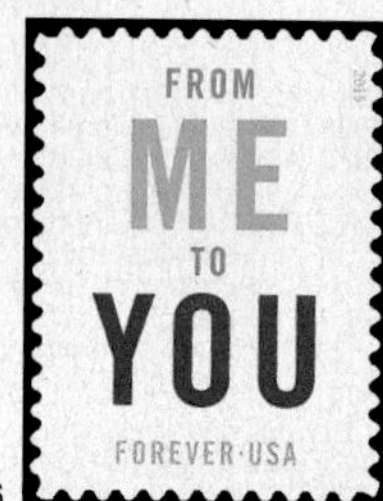

A3826

Designed by Michael Osborne. Printed by Ashton-Potter (USA) Ltd.

LITHOGRAPHED

Sheets of 120 in six panes of 20

2015, Apr. 1 **Tagged** ***Serpentine Die Cut 11***

Self-Adhesive

4978	A3826 (49c) **multicolored**	1.25	.25
	P# block of 10, 5#+P + top panel	12.50	
	Pane of 20 + 20 stickers	25.00	
a.	Imperforate	2.00	—
	Pane of 20 + 20 stickers	40.00	

Die cut and imperforate uncut press sheets of No. 4978 were made available for sale. Values: cross gutter block of 4, $11; pairs with gutters between, $4.25 each. See note after No. 4693.

See note after No. 1549.

MAYA ANGELOU (1928-2014), WRITER

Angelou and Quotation
A3827

Designed by Ethel Kessler. Printed by Banknote Corporation of America for Sennett Security Products.

LITHOGRAPHED

Sheets of 96 in eight panes of 12

2015, Apr. 7 **Tagged** ***Serpentine Die Cut 11***

Self-Adhesive

4979	A3827 (49c) **multicolored**	1.25	.25
	P# block of 4, 6#+S	5.00	
	Pane of 12	15.00	
a.	Imperforate	1.75	—
	Pane of 12	21.00	

The quotation on the stamp is not Angelou's but is similar to a quote by Joan Walsh Anglund.

Die cut and imperforate uncut press sheets of No. 4979 were made available for sale. Values: cross gutter block of 4, $9; pairs with gutters between, $4.25 each. See note after No. 4693.

CIVIL WAR SESQUICENTENNIAL

Battle of Five Forks — A3828

Surrender at Appomattox Court House — A3829

Designed by Phil Jordan. Printed by Banknote Corporation of America for Sennett Security Products.

LITHOGRAPHED

Double-sided sheets of 72 in six panes of 12 (60 on one side, 12 on other side)

2015, Apr. 9 **Tagged** ***Serpentine Die Cut 11***

Self-Adhesive

4980	A3828 (49c) **multicolored**	1.25	.30
4981	A3829 (49c) **multicolored**	1.25	.30
a.	Pair, #4980-4981	2.50	
	Pane of 12	15.00	
b.	Imperforate pair	*27.50*	—
	Imperforate pair with wide spacing	*37.50*	—
	Pane of 12	*175.00*	

Die cut and imperforate uncut press sheets of Nos. 4980-4981 were made available for sale. See note after No. 4693.

GIFTS OF FRIENDSHIP Ⓢ

Lincoln Memorial and Cherry Blossoms
A3830

U.S. Capitol and Dogwood Blossoms
A3831

Japanese Diet, Tokyo, and Cherry Blossoms
A3832

Clock Tower, Tokyo, and Dogwood Blossoms
A3833

Designed by William J. Gicker. Printed by Ashton-Potter (USA) Ltd.

LITHOGRAPHED

Sheets of 72 in six panes of 12

2015, Apr. 10 **Tagged** ***Serpentine Die Cut 11***

Self-Adhesive

4982	A3830 (49c) **multicolored**	1.25	.30
4983	A3831 (49c) **multicolored**	1.25	.30
a.	Horiz. pair, #4982-4983	2.50	
b.	Imperforate pair	4.50	—
4984	A3832 (49c) **multicolored**	5.00	.30
4985	A3833 (49c) **multicolored**	5.00	.30
a.	Horiz. pair, #4984-4985	10.00	
	Pane of 12 (#4984-4985, 5 each #4982-4983)	25.00	
b.	Imperforate pair	12.50	—
	Imperforate pane of 12	35.00	
	Nos. 4982-4985 (4)	12.50	1.20

Die cut and imperforate uncut press sheets of Nos. 4982-4985 were made available for sale. See note after No. 4693.

See note after No. 1549.

See Japan No. 3814

SPECIAL OLYMPICS WORLD GAMES

Emblem — A3834

Designed by Greg Breeding. Printed by Banknote Corporation of America for Sennett Security Products.

LITHOGRAPHED

Sheets of 80 in four panes of 20

2015, May 9 **Tagged** ***Serpentine Die Cut 10¾***

Self-Adhesive

4986	A3834 (49c) **multicolored**	1.25	.25
	P# block of 4, 6#+S	5.00	
	Pane of 20	25.00	
a.	Imperforate	1.75	—
	Pane of 20	35.00	

Die cut and imperforate uncut press sheets of No. 4986 were made available for sale. Values: horiz. pair with vert. gutter between, $3.75. See note after No. 4693.

HELP FIND MISSING CHILDREN

Forget-me-nots — A3835

Designed by Ethel Kessler. Printed by Ashton-Potter (USA) Ltd.

LITHOGRAPHED
Sheets of 120 in six panes of 20

2015, May 18 Tagged ***Serpentine Die Cut 10¾***
Self-Adhesive

4987 A3835 (49c) **multicolored** Ⓢ 1.25 .25
P# block of 4, 5#+P 5.00
Pane of 20 25.00
a. Imperforate 1.75 —
Pane of 20 35.00

Die cut and imperforate uncut press sheets of No. 4987 were made available for sale. Values: cross gutter block of 4, $9, pairs with gutters between, $4 each. See note after No. 4693.
See note after No. 1549.

MEDAL OF HONOR

Air Force Medal of Honor — A3836

Designed by Antonio Alcalá. Printed by Banknote Corporation of America for Sennett Security Products.

LITHOGRAPHED
Sheets of 72 in three panes of 24 (Panes are folded into a folio with 12 stamps on each side of the folded pane)

2015, May 25 Tagged ***Serpentine Die Cut 11***
Self-Adhesive

4988 A3836 (49c) **multicolored** 1.25 .25
a. Horiz. strip of 3, #4822b, 4823b, 4988 3.75
P# block of 6, 6#+S 7.50
Folio of 24 30.00
b. Imperforate strip of 3 6.00 —
Folio of 24 48.00

Die cut and imperforate uncut press sheets of Nos. 4988, 4822b and 4823b were made available for sale. Values: vert. pairs with horiz. gutters between, $4.50 each. See note after No. 4693.

WILDLIFE ISSUE

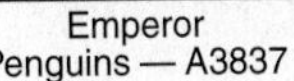
Emperor Penguins — A3837

A3837a

Designed by Carl T. Herrman. Printed by Banknote Corporation of America for Sennett Security Products.

LITHOGRAPHED
Sheets of 200 in ten panes of 20
Serpentine Die Cut 11¼x11

2015, June 1 Tagged
Self-Adhesive

4989 A3837 (22c) **multicolored** .50 .25
P# block of 4, 4#+S 2.00
Pane of 20 10.00
a. Imperforate 1.00 —
Pane of 20 20.00

Coil Stamp
Serpentine Die Cut 11 Vert.

4990 A3837a (22c) **multicolored** .50 .25
Pair 1.00
P# strip of 5, #S1111 3.50
P# single, #S1111 — 2.00

Die cut and imperforate uncut press sheets of No. 4989 were made available for sale. Values: cross gutter block of 4, $4.50; pairs with gutters between, $2 each. See note after No. 4693.

COASTAL BIRDS

Red Knot — A3838

King Eider — A3839

Spoonbill — A3840

Frigatebird — A3841

Designed by Greg Breeding. Printed by Banknote Corporation of America for Sennett Security Products.

LITHOGRAPHED
Sheets of 200 in ten panes of 20
Serpentine Die Cut 11¼x11

2015, June 1 Tagged
Self-Adhesive

4991 A3838 (35c) **multicolored** .90 .25
4992 A3839 (35c) **multicolored** .90 .25
4993 A3840 (35c) **multicolored** .90 .25
4994 A3841 (35c) **multicolored** .90 .25
a. Block or vert. strip of 4, #4991-4994 3.60
P# block of 4, 4#+S 3.60
Pane of 20 18.00
b. Imperforate block or vert. strip of 4 4.50 —
Pane of 20 22.50

Counterfeits exist of Nos. 4991-4994. See the Postal Counterfeits section of this catalog.

A3838a

A3839a

A3840a

A3841a

Printed by Ashton-Potter (USA) Ltd.

Coil Stamps
Serpentine Die Cut 9½ Vert.

4995 A3840a (35c) **multicolored** Ⓢ .90 .25
4996 A3841a (35c) **multicolored** Ⓢ .90 .25
4997 A3838a (35c) **multicolored** Ⓢ .90 .25
4998 A3839a (35c) **multicolored** Ⓢ .90 .25
a. Horiz. strip of 4, #4995-4998 3.60
P# strip of 5, #4996-4998, 2 #4995, #P1111 5.50
P# strip of 9, 2 each #4995-4996, 4998, 3 #4997, #P1111 9.25
P# single, #P1111 (#4997) — 2.75

Die cut and imperforate uncut press sheets of No. 4991-4994 were made available for sale. Values: cross gutter block of 8, $15; pairs with gutters between, $3.25 each. See note after No. 4693.
See note after No. 1549.

EASTERN TIGER SWALLOWTAIL BUTTERFLY

A3842

Designed by Derry Noyes. Printed by Ashton-Potter (USA) Ltd.

LITHOGRAPHED
Sheets of 120 in six panes of 20

2015, June 1 Tagged ***Serpentine Die Cut 10½***
Self-Adhesive

4999 A3842 (71c) **multicolored** Ⓢ 2.00 .25
P# block of 4, 5#+P 8.00
Pane of 20 40.00
a. Imperforate 2.50 —
Pane of 20 50.00

Die cut and imperforate uncut press sheets of No. 4999 were made available for sale. Values: cross gutter block of 4, $18, pairs with gutters between, $7.50 each. See note after No. 4693.
See note after No. 1549.

Wedding Cake — A3843

Designed by Ethel Kessler. Printed by Banknote Corporation of America for Sennett Security Products.

LITHOGRAPHED
Sheets of 160 in eight panes of 20

2015, June 1 Tagged ***Serpentine Die Cut 10¾***
Self-Adhesive

5000 A3843 (71c) **multicolored** 5.00 .25
P# block of 4, 6#+S 20.00
Pane of 20 100.00

See Nos. 4398, 4521, 4602, 4735, 4867.

Flowers and "Yes, I Do" — A3844

Designed by Michael Osborne. Printed by Ashton-Potter (USA), Ltd.

LITHOGRAPHED
Sheets of 120 in six panes of 20

2015, June 1 Tagged ***Serpentine Die Cut 10¾***
Self-Adhesive

5001 A3844 (71c) **multicolored** Ⓢ 5.00 .25
P# block of 4, 5#+P 20.00
Pane of 20 100.00

See note after No. 1549.
See Nos. 4765, 4881.

Tulip and Heart — A3845

Designed by Jeanne Greco. Printed by Banknote Corporation of America for Sennett Security Products.

ENGRAVED

Sheets of 240 in 12 panes of 20

2015, June 1 Tagged *Serpentine Die Cut 11*

Self-Adhesive

5002 A3845 (71c) **black & red** 6.00 .25
P# block of 4, 2#+S 24.00
Pane of 20 120.00

See No. 4960.

LITERARY ARTS

Flannery O'Connor (1925-64), Novelist A3846

Designed by Phil Jordan. Printed by Ashton-Potter (USA) Ltd.

LITHOGRAPHED

Sheets of 120 in six panes of 20

2015, June 5 Tagged *Serpentine Die Cut 10¾*

Self-Adhesive

5003 A3846 (93c) **multicolored** Ⓢ 2.20 .30
P# block of 4, 6#+P 8.80
Pane of 20 44.00
a. Imperforate 2.50 —
Pane of 20 50.00

Die cut and imperforate uncut press sheets of No. 5003 were made available for sale. Values: cross gutter block of 4, $18; pairs with gutters between, $7.50 each. See note after No. 4693.

See note after No. 1549.

SUMMER HARVEST Ⓢ

Watermelon — A3847

Sweet Corn — A3848

Cantaloupes — A3849

Tomatoes — A3850

Designed by Antonio Alcalá. Printed by Ashton-Potter (USA) Ltd.

LITHOGRAPHED

Serpentine Die Cut 11¼x10¾ on 2 or 3 Sides

2015, July 11 Tagged

Booklet Stamps

Self-Adhesive

5004 A3847 (49c) **multicolored** 1.50 .30
5005 A3848 (49c) **multicolored** 1.50 .30
5006 A3849 (49c) **multicolored** 1.50 .30
5007 A3850 (49c) **multicolored** 1.50 .30
a. Block of 4, #5004-5007 6.00
b. Booklet pane of 20, 5 each #5004-5007 30.00
c. As "a," imperforate 7.00 —
d. As "b," imperforate 35.00
Nos. 5004-5007 (4) 6.00 1.20

Nos. 5007b and 5007d are double-sided booklet panes with 12 stamps on one side (3 each Nos. 5004-5007), and eight stamps (2 each Nos. 5004-5007) plus label (booklet cover) on the other side.

Die cut and imperforate uncut press sheets of Nos. 5004-5007 were made available for sale. Values for varieties from die cut press sheets: cross gutter block of 4 with booklet cover, imperf. within, $10; cross gutter block of 4, imperf. within, $10; block of 4, horiz. imperf. between, $8; block of 4, vert. imperf. between, $8. Values for varieties from imperforate press sheets: cross gutter block of 4 with booklet cover, $10; block of 4 with horiz. gutter between, $8.50; block of 4 with vert. gutter between, $8.50. See note after No. 4693.

See note after No. 1549.

COAST GUARD

MH-65 Dolphin Helicopter and Cutter *Eagle* A3851

Designed by Phil Jordan. Printed by Banknote Corporation of America for Sennett Security Products.

LITHOGRAPHED

Sheets of 120 in six panes of 20

2015, Aug. 4 Tagged *Serpentine Die Cut 10¾*

Self-Adhesive

5008 A3851 (49c) **multicolored** 1.25 .25
P# block of 4, 4#+S 5.00
Pane of 20 25.00
a. Imperforate 1.75 —
Pane of 20 35.00

Die cut and imperforate uncut press sheets of No. 5008 were made available for sale. Values: cross gutter block of 4, $9; pairs with gutters between, $4 each. See note after No. 4693.

MUSIC ICONS

Elvis Presley (1935-77), Singer — A3852

Designed by Antonio Alcalá and Leslie Badani. Printed by Ashton-Potter (USA) Ltd.

LITHOGRAPHED

Sheets of 144 in nine panes of 16

2015, Aug. 12 Tagged *Serpentine Die Cut 10½*

Self-Adhesive

5009 A3852 (49c) **multicolored** Ⓢ 1.25 .25
Pane of 16 20.00
a. Imperforate 1.75 —
Pane of 16 28.00

Die cut and imperforate uncut press sheets of No. 5009 were made available for sale. Values: cross gutter block of 4, $9; pairs with gutters between, $4 each. See note after No. 4693.

See note after No. 1549.

2016 WORLD STAMP SHOW, NEW YORK CITY Ⓢ

Star — A3853

A3853a

Designed by Michael Dyer. Printed by Ashton-Potter (USA), Ltd.

LITHOGRAPHED

Sheets of 120 in six panes of 20

2015, Aug. 20 Tagged *Serpentine Die Cut 11*

Self-Adhesive

5010 A3853 (49c) **red** 1.25 .25
5011 A3853a (49c) **blue** 1.25 .25
a. Pair, #5010-5011 2.50
P# block of 4, 2#+P 5.00
Pane of 20 25.00
b. As "a," imperforate 4.00 —
Pane of 20 40.00

Die cut and imperforate uncut press sheets of Nos. 5010-5011 were made available for sale. Values: cross gutter block of 4, $12; pairs with gutters between, $4 each.

See note after No. 4693. See note after No. 1549.

LEGENDS OF HOLLYWOOD

Ingrid Bergman (1915-82), Actress — A3854

Designed by Ethel Kessler. Printed by Banknote Corporation of America for Sennett Security Products.

LITHOGRAPHED

Sheets of 180 in nine panes of 20

2015, Aug. 20 Tagged *Serpentine Die Cut 11*

Self-Adhesive

5012 A3854 (49c) **multicolored** 1.50 .25
P# block of 4, 4#+S 6.00
Pane of 20 30.00
a. Imperforate 1.75 —
Pane of 20 35.00

Die cut and imperforate uncut press sheets of No. 5012 were made available for sale. Values: cross gutter block of 4, $9; pairs with gutters between, $4 each. See note after No. 4693.

See Sweden Nos. 2756-2758.

Eagle

A3854a

A3854b

A3854c

A3854d

A3854e

A3854f

Designed by Ethel Kessler. Printed by Ashton-Potter (USA) Ltd.

LITHOGRAPHED

Serpentine Die Cut 10¼ Vert.

2015, Sept. 2 Untagged

Coil Stamps

Self-Adhesive

Color Behind "USA"

5013 A3854a (25c) **green** Ⓢ .50 .25
5014 A3854b (25c) **blue green** Ⓢ .50 .25
5015 A3854c (25c) **blue** Ⓢ .50 .25
5016 A3854d (25c) **red violet** Ⓢ .50 .25
5017 A3854e (25c) **orange** Ⓢ .50 .25
5018 A3854f (25c) **yellow orange** Ⓢ .50 .25
a. Strip of 6, #5013-5018 3.00
P# strip of 7, 2 #5013, 1 each #5014-5018, #P1111 5.00
P# strip of 13, 3 #5016, 2 each #5013-5015, 5017-5018, #P1111 9.00
P# single (#5016), #P1111 — 2.50
Nos. 5013-5018 (6) 3.00 1.50

Nos. 5013-5018 were printed using two offset plates on the same cylinder. One plate was 15 stamps high and the other 12 stamps high for a total circumference of 27. This was done to keep the plate numbers on the same design. However, it caused a three-stamp immediate repeat once every revolution. The end of the 15-high plate had the same color stamps as the first three on the 12-high plate.

See note after No. 1549.

See Nos. 4585-4590.

CELEBRATE

A3855

Designed by Phil Jordan. Printed by Banknote Corporation of America for Sennett Security Products.

LITHOGRAPHED

Sheets of 160 in eight panes of 20

2015, Sept. 9 Tagged *Serpentine Die Cut 10¾*

Self-Adhesive

5019 A3855 (49c) **multicolored**	1.25	.25
P# block of 4, 4#+S or 4#+B	5.00	
Pane of 20	25.00	

Compare with type A3441.

Counterfeits exist of No. 5019. See the Postal Counterfeits section of this catalog.

PAUL NEWMAN (1925-2008), ACTOR AND PHILANTHROPIST

A3856

Designed by Derry Noyes. Printed by Banknote Corporation of America for Sennett Security Products.

LITHOGRAPHED

Sheets of 120 in six panes of 20

2015, Sept. 18 Tagged *Serpentine Die Cut 10¾*

Self-Adhesive

5020 A3856 (49c) **multicolored**	1.25	.25
P# block of 4, 4#+S	5.00	
Pane of 20	25.00	
a. Imperforate	1.75	—
Pane of 20	35.00	

Die cut and imperforate uncut press sheets of No. 5020 were made available for sale. Values: horiz. pair with vert. gutter between, $3.75. See note after No. 4693.

CHRISTMAS

Charlie Brown Carrying Christmas Tree — A3857

Charlie Brown, Pigpen and Dirty Snowman — A3858

Snoopy, Lucy, Violet, Sally and Schroeder Skating — A3859

Characters, Dog House and Christmas Tree — A3860

Linus and Christmas Tree — A3861

Charlie Brown Looking in Mailbox — A3862

Charlie Brown and Linus Behind Brick Wall — A3863

Charlie Brown, Linus and Christmas Tree — A3864

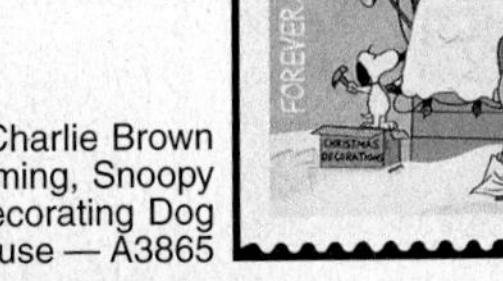

Charlie Brown Screaming, Snoopy Decorating Dog House — A3865

Charlie Brown Hanging Ornament on Christmas Tree — A3866

Designed by Antonio Alcalá. Printed by Banknote Corporation of America for Sennett Security Products.

LITHOGRAPHED

Serpentine Die Cut 10¾ on 2 or 3 Sides

2015, Oct. 1 Tagged

Booklet Stamps

Self-Adhesive

5021 A3857 (49c) **multicolored**	2.50	.40
5022 A3858 (49c) **multicolored**	2.50	.40
5023 A3859 (49c) **multicolored**	2.50	.40
5024 A3860 (49c) **multicolored**	2.50	.40
5025 A3861 (49c) **multicolored**	2.50	.40
5026 A3862 (49c) **multicolored**	2.50	.40
5027 A3863 (49c) **multicolored**	2.50	.40
5028 A3864 (49c) **multicolored**	2.50	.40
5029 A3865 (49c) **multicolored**	2.50	.40
5030 A3866 (49c) **multicolored**	2.50	.40
a. Block of 10, #5021-5030	25.00	
b. Booklet pane of 20, 2 each #5021-5030	50.00	
c. As "a," imperforate	17.50	—
d. As "b," imperforate	35.00	
Nos. 5021-5030 (10)	25.00	4.00

Premiere of *A Charlie Brown Christmas* animated television show, 50th anniv.

Nos. 5030b and 5030d are double-sided booklet panes with 12 stamps on one side (Nos. 5023-5030, 2 each Nos. 5021-5022) and eight stamps (Nos. 5023-5030) plus label (booklet cover) on the other side.

Die cut and imperforate uncut press sheets of Nos. 5021-5030 were made available for sale. Values for varieties from die cut press sheets: cross gutter block of 4 with booklet cover, imperf. within, $10; cross gutter block of 4, imperf. within, $10; horiz. pair, imperf. between, $4; vert. pair, imperf. between, $4. Values for varieties from imperforate press sheets: cross gutter block of 4 with booklet cover, $10; pair with horiz. gutter between, $4; pair with vert. gutter between, $4. See note after No. 4693.

GEOMETRIC SNOWFLAKES

A3867

A3868

A3869

A3870

Designed by Antonio Alcalá. Printed by Banknote Corporation of America for Sennett Security Products.

LITHOGRAPHED

Serpentine Die Cut 11¼x10¾ on 2 or 3 Sides

2015, Oct. 23 Tagged

Booklet Stamps

Self-Adhesive

Snowflake Colors

5031 A3867 (49c) **purple & lilac**	1.25	.30
5032 A3868 (49c) **dark blue & blue**	1.25	.30
5033 A3869 (49c) **dark green & green**	1.25	.30
5034 A3870 (49c) **crimson & pink**	1.25	.30
a. Block of 4, #5031-5034	5.00	
b. Booklet pane of 20, 5 each #5031-5034	25.00	
c. As "a," imperforate	7.00	—
d. As "b," imperforate	35.00	
Nos. 5031-5034 (4)	5.00	1.20

Nos. 5034b and 5034d are double-sided booklet panes with 12 stamps on one side (3 each Nos. 5031-5034), and eight stamps (2 each Nos. 5031-5034) plus label (booklet cover) on the other side.

Die cut and imperforate uncut press sheets of Nos. 5031-5034 were made available for sale. Values for varieties from die cut press sheets: cross gutter block of 4 with booket cover, imperf. within, $10; cross gutter block of 4, imperf. within, $10; block of 4 vert. imperf. between, $8.50; block of 4, horiz. imperf. between, $8.50. Values for varieties from imperforate press sheets: cross gutter block of 4 with booklet cover, $10; block of 4 with horiz. gutter between, $8.50; block of 4 with vert. gutter between, $8.50. See note after No. 4693.

Counterfeits exist of Nos. 5031-5034. See the Postal Counterfeits section of this catalog.

Purple Heart and Ribbon — A3870a

Designed by Jennifer Arnold. Printed by Banknote Corporation of America for Sennett Security Products.

LITHOGRAPHED

Sheets of 200 in 10 panes of 20

2015, Oct. Tagged *Serpentine Die Cut 11*

Self-Adhesive

With "USPS" Microprinted At Left of Ribbon

5035 A3870a (49c) **multicolored**	1.25	.25
P# block of 4, 6#+S or 6#+B	5.00	
Pane of 20	25.00	

See Nos. 4529, 4704.

LOVE

Quilled Paper Heart — A3871

Designed by Antonio Alcalá. Printed by Banknote Corporation of America for Sennett Security Products.

LITHOGRAPHED

Sheets of 200 in ten panes of 20

2016, Jan. 12 Tagged *Serpentine Die Cut 10¾*

Self-Adhesive

5036	A3871 (49c) **multicolored,** overall tagged	1.25	.25
	P# block of 4, 5#+S or 5#+B	5.00	
	Pane of 20	25.00	
a.	Imperforate	1.75	—
	Pane of 20	35.00	
b.	Die cutting omitted, P#B11111 block of 4	*100.00*	
c.	Prephosphored paper	1.25	.25
	P# block of 4, 5#+S or 5#+B	5.00	
	Pane of 20	25.00	

Die cut and imperforate uncut press sheets of No. 5036 were made available for sale. Values: cross gutter block of 4, $9; pairs with gutters between, $4 each. See note after No. 4693.

No. 5036b was printed from P#B11111 only and may also be collected in plate blocks of 6, half panes of 10 and full panes of 20. Pairs or other multiples without P#B11111 selvage attached cannot be distinguished from No. 5036a, which was printed only from P#S11111.

FRUIT

Albemarle Pippin Apples — A3872

Pinot Noir Grapes — A3873

Red Pears — A3874

Designed by Derry Noyes. Printed by Ashton-Potter (USA), Ltd. (Nos. 5037-5038), Banknote Corporation of America for Sennett Security Products (No. 5039).

LITHOGRAPHED

2016 Self-Adhesive *Serpentine Die Cut 10 Vert.*

Untagged

Coil Stamps

5037	A3872 1c **multicolored,** *Aug. 12*	.30	.25
	Pair	.30	
	P# strip of 5, #P111111	.60	
	P# single, #P111111	—	.50
5038	A3873 5c **multicolored,** *Feb. 19* Ⓢ	.30	.25
	Pair	.30	
	P# strip of 5, #P111111	1.00	
	P# single, #P111111	—	1.00

Serpentine Die Cut 10¾ Vert.

5039	A3874 10c **multicolored,** *Jan. 17*	.30	.25
	Pair	.40	
	P# strip of 5, #S111111, #B111111	3.00	
	P# single, #S111111, #B111111	—	2.50

See note after No. 1549.

See Nos. 5177-5178 for sheet versions of Nos. 5038-5039, also see No. 5201, 5256.

AMERICAN LANDMARKS ISSUE

La Cueva del Indio, Puerto Rico — A3875

Columbia River Gorge A3876

Designed by Greg Breeding (#5040), Phil Jordan (#5041). Printed by Ashton-Potter (USA) Ltd. (#5040), Banknote Corporation of America (#5041).

LITHOGRAPHED

Sheets of 60 in six panes of 10 (#5040), Sheets of 150 in 15 panes of 10 (#5041)

Serpentine Die Cut 10¾x10½

2016, Jan. 17 Tagged

Self-Adhesive

5040	A3875 $6.45 **multicolored** Ⓢ	17.50	7.50
	P# block of 4, 4#+P	60.00	
	Pane of 10	150.00	
a.	Imperforate	17.50	—
	Pane of 10	150.00	
5041	A3876 $22.95 **multicolored**	60.00	24.00
	P# block of 4, 4#+B	240.00	
	Pane of 10	600.00	
a.	Imperforate	*200.00*	—
	Pane of 10	*2,000.*	

Die cut and imperforate press sheets of No. 5040 were made available for sale. Value: cross gutter block of 4, $90; pairs with gutter between, $42.50.

Die cut and imperforate partial press sheets (containing 30 stamps) of No. 5041 were made available for sale. Value: vert. pair with horiz. gutter between, $290. See note after No. 4693.

See note after No. 1549.

BOTANICAL ART Ⓢ

Corn Lilies — A3877

Tulips — A3878

Tulips — A3879

Dahlias — A3880

Stocks — A3881

Roses — A3882

Japanese Irises — A3883

Tulips — A3884

Petunias — A3885

Jonquils — A3886

Designed by Ethel Kessler. Printed by Ashton-Potter (USA) Ltd.

LITHOGRAPHED

Serpentine Die Cut 10¾ on 2 or 3 Sides

2016, Jan. 29 Tagged

Booklet Stamps

Self-Adhesive

5042	A3877 (49c) **multicolored**	2.50	.40
5043	A3878 (49c) **multicolored**	2.50	.40
5044	A3879 (49c) **multicolored**	2.50	.40
5045	A3880 (49c) **multicolored**	2.50	.40
5046	A3881 (49c) **multicolored**	2.50	.40
5047	A3882 (49c) **multicolored**	2.50	.40
5048	A3883 (49c) **multicolored**	2.50	.40
5049	A3884 (49c) **multicolored**	2.50	.40
5050	A3885 (49c) **multicolored**	2.50	.40
5051	A3886 (49c) **multicolored**	2.50	.40
a.	Block of 10, #5042-5051	25.00	
b.	Booklet pane of 10, #5042-5051	25.00	
c.	Booklet pane of 20, 2 each #5042-5051	50.00	
d.	Imperforate block of 10	125.00	—
e.	Imperforate booklet pane of 20	225.00	
f.	As "c," horiz. die cutting missing between all stamps front and reverse	—	
	Nos. 5042-5051 (10)	25.00	4.00

Nos. 5051c and 5051e are double-sided booklet panes with 12 stamps on one side (Nos. 5042-5049, 2 each Nos. 5050-5051) and eight stamps (Nos. 5042-5049) plus label (booklet cover) on the other side.

No. 5051f resulted from a misregistration of the die cutting/pane cutting and the printed web. The horizontal rows are reversed from their normal positions, and horizontal die cutting appears at the top and bottom of the pane.

Die cut and imperforate uncut press sheets of Nos. 5042-5051 were made available for sale. Values for varieties from die cut press sheets: cross gutter block of 4 with booklet cover, imperf. within, $10; cross gutter block of 4, imperf. within, $10; vert. pair, imperf. between, $4; horiz. pair, imperf. between, $6. Values for varieties from imperforate press sheets: cross gutter block of 4 with booklet cover, $60; cross gutter block of 10, $250; pair with vert. gutter between, $20; horiz. pair with booklet cover and gutter between, $25. See note after No. 4693.

See note after No. 1549.

Flag — A3887

A3887a

Designed by Greg Breeding. Printed by Banknote Corporation of America for Sennett Security Products (#5052), Ashton-Potter (USA) Ltd. (#5053).

LITHOGRAPHED

Serpentine Die Cut 11 Vert.

2016, Jan. 29 **Tagged**

Coil Stamps

Self-Adhesive

Microprinted "USPS" To Right of Pole Under Flag

5052 A3887 (49c) **multicolored** 1.25 .25
Pair 2.50
P# strip of 5, #S11111, #B11111 7.50
P# single, #S11111, #B11111 — 2.50
a. Die cutting omitted, pair 200.00
b. As "a," grayish blue (inscription and date) omitted 200.00

Counterfeits exist of No. 5052. See the Postal Counterfeits section of this catalog.

Serpentine Die Cut 9½ Vert.

Microprinted "USPS" on Second White Flag Stripe

5053 A3887a (49c) **multicolored** ⓢ 1.25 .25
Pair 2.50
P# strip of 5, #P11111 7.50
P# single, #P11111 — 2.50
a. Tagging omitted —

Counterfeits exist of No. 5053. See the Postal Counterfeits section of this catalog.

A3887b

A3887c

Printed by Banknote Corporation of America for Sennett Security Products (#5054), Ashton-Potter (USA) Ltd. (#5055).

Booklet Stamps

Microprinted "USPS" To Right of Pole Under Flag

Serpentine Die Cut 11¼x10¾ on 2 or 3 Sides

5054 A3887b (49c) **multicolored** 1.25 .25
a. Booklet pane of 10 12.50
b. Booklet pane of 20 25.00
c. As "b," horiz. die cutting omitted on side with 12 stamps —

Microprinted "USPS" on Second White Flag Stripe

5055 A3887c (49c) **multicolored** ⓢ 1.25 .25
a. Booklet pane of 20 25.00

Nos. 5054b and 5055a are double-sided booklets with 12 stamps on one side and eight stamps plus a label that serves as the booklet cover on the other side.

See note after No. 1549.

BLACK HERITAGE

Richard Allen (1760-1831), Founder of African Methodist Episcopal Church — A3888

Designed by Greg Breeding. Printed by Ashton-Potter (USA) Ltd.

LITHOGRAPHED

Sheets of 120 in six panes of 20

2016, Feb. 2 **Tagged** ***Serpentine Die Cut 10¾***

Self-Adhesive

5056 A3888 (49c) **multicolored** ⓢ 1.25 .25
P# block of 4, 5#+P 5.00
Pane of 20 25.00
a. Imperforate 3.00 —
Pane of 20 60.00

Die cut and imperforate uncut press sheets of No. 5056 were made available for sale. Values: cross gutter block of 4, $18; pairs with gutters between, $7.25 each. See note after No. 4693.

See note after No. 1549.

CHINESE NEW YEAR

Year of the Monkey A3889

Designed by Ethel Kessler. Printed by Banknote Corporation of America for Sennett Security Products.

LITHOGRAPHED

Sheets of 144 in 12 panes of 12

2016, Feb. 5 **Tagged** ***Serpentine Die Cut 10¾***

Self-Adhesive

5057 A3889 (49c) **multicolored** 1.25 .25
Pane of 12 15.00
a. Imperforate 1.75 —
Pane of 12 21.00

Die cut and imperforate uncut partial press sheets (containing 72 stamps) of No. 5057 were made available for sale. Values: cross gutter block of 4, $9; pairs with gutters between, $3.75 each. See note after No. 4693.

Moon — A3890

Designed by Greg Breeding. Printed by Banknote Corporation of America.

LITHOGRAPHED

Sheets of 100 in ten panes of 10

2016, Feb. 22 **Tagged** ***Serpentine Die Cut***

Self-Adhesive

5058 A3890 ($1.20) **multicolored** 2.80 .50
P# block of 4, 6#+B 11.20
Pane of 10 28.00

Unused values are for stamps with surrounding selvage. Adjacent stamps are separated by rouletting.

Die cut uncut press sheets of No. 5058 were made available for sale. Values: cross gutter block of 4, $20; pairs with gutters between, $8.75 each. See note after No. 4693.

MUSIC ICONS

Sarah Vaughan (1924-90), Singer — A3891

Designed by Ethel Kessler. Printed by Ashton-Potter (USA) Ltd.

LITHOGRAPHED

Sheets of 144 in nine panes of 16

2016, Mar. 29 **Tagged** ***Serpentine Die Cut 10½***

Self-Adhesive

5059 A3891 (49c) **multicolored** ⓢ 1.25 .25
Pane of 16 20.00

Die cut uncut press sheets of No. 5059 were made available for sale. Values: cross gutter block of 4, $9; pairs with gutters between, $3.75 each. See note after No. 4693.

See note after No. 1549.

LEGENDS OF HOLLYWOOD

Shirley Temple (1928-2014), Actress and Diplomat — A3892

Designed by Ethel Kessler. Printed by Ashton-Potter (USA) Ltd.

LITHOGRAPHED

Sheets of 180 in nine panes of 20

2016, Apr. 18 **Tagged** ***Serpentine Die Cut 10¾***

Self-Adhesive

5060 A3892 (47c) **multicolored** ⓢ 2.00 .25
P# block of 4, 5#+P 8.00
Pane of 20 40.00

Die cut uncut press sheets of No. 5060 were made available for sale. Values: cross gutter block of 8, $9; pairs with gutters between, $4.25 each. See note after No. 4693.

See note after No. 1549.

"USA" and Star — A3893

Designed by Antonio Alcalá and Leslie Badani. Printed by Ashton-Potter (USA) Ltd.

LITHOGRAPHED

Serpentine Die Cut 10 Vert.

2016, Apr. 28 **Untagged**

COIL STAMP

Self-Adhesive

5061 A3893 (5c) **multicolored** ⓢ .30 .25
Pair .50
P# strip of 5, #P111 1.60
P# single, #P1111 — 1.25

See No. 5172. See note after No. 1549.

2016 WORLD STAMP SHOW, NEW YORK CITY

Star — A3894

A3894a

Designed by Michael Dyer. Printed by Banknote Corporation of America.

ENGRAVED

Sheets of 96 in four folios of 24

2016, May 28 **Tagged** ***Serpentine Die Cut 10¾***

Self-Adhesive

5062 A3894 (47c) **blue** 1.25 .25
5063 A3894a (47c) **red** 1.25 .25
a. Pair, #5062-5063 2.50
Folio of 24, 12 each #5062-5063 30.00

Die cut uncut press sheets of Nos. 5062-5063 were made available for sale. Values: cross gutter block of 4, $9; pairs with gutters between, $4.25 each.

See note after No. 4693.

REPEAL OF THE STAMP ACT, 250TH ANNIV.

Man Posting Notice of Repeal on Tree — A3895

Designed by Antonio Alcalá. Printed by Banknote Corporation of America.

LITHOGRAPHED
Sheets of 120 in 12 panes of 10

2016, May 29 Tagged *Serpentine Die Cut 10¾*
Self-Adhesive

5064 A3895 (47c) **multicolored**	1.25	.25
Pane of 10	12.50	

Die cut uncut press sheets of No. 5064 were made available for sale. Values: cross gutter block of 4, $9; pairs with gutters between, $4.25 each.
See note after No. 4693.

SERVICE CROSS MEDALS

Distinguished Service Cross — A3896

Navy Cross — A3897

Air Force Cross — A3898

Coast Guard Cross — A3899

Designed by Greg Breeding. Printed by Banknote Corporation of America.

LITHOGRAPHED
Sheets of 144 in 12 panes of 12

2016, May 30 Tagged *Serpentine Die Cut 10¾*
Self-Adhesive

5065 A3896 (47c) **multicolored**	1.25	.30
5066 A3897 (47c) **multicolored**	1.25	.30
5067 A3898 (47c) **multicolored**	1.25	.30
5068 A3899 (47c) **multicolored**	1.25	.30
a. Block or horiz. strip of 4, #5065-5068	5.00	
Pane of 12	15.00	
Nos. 5065-5068 (4)	5.00	1.20

Die cut uncut press sheets of Nos. 5065-5068 were made available for sale. Values: cross gutter block of 4, $9; pairs with gutters between, $4.25 each.
See note after No. 4693.

VIEWS OF OUR PLANETS Ⓢ

Mercury — A3900

Venus — A3901

Earth — A3902

Mars — A3903

Jupiter — A3904

Saturn — A3905

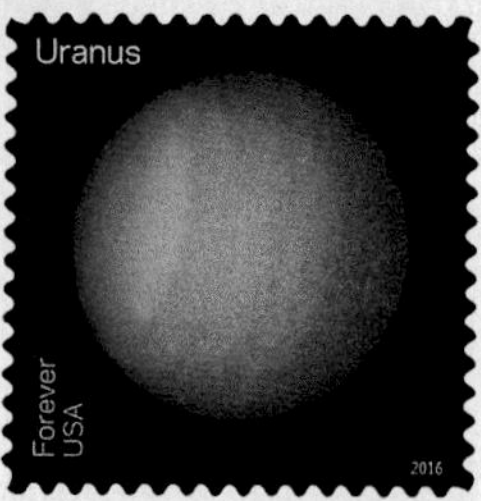

Uranus — A3906

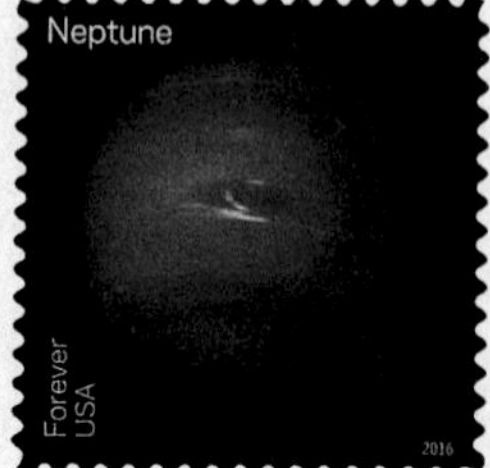

Neptune — A3907

Designed by Antonio Alcalá. Printed by Ashton-Potter (USA) Ltd.

LITHOGRAPHED
Sheets of 128 in eight panes of 16

2016, May 31 Tagged *Serpentine Die Cut 10½*
Self-Adhesive

5069 A3900 (47c) **multicolored**	2.00	.40
5070 A3901 (47c) **multicolored**	2.00	.40
5071 A3902 (47c) **multicolored**	2.00	.40
5072 A3903 (47c) **multicolored**	2.00	.40
5073 A3904 (47c) **multicolored**	2.00	.40
5074 A3905 (47c) **multicolored**	2.00	.40
5075 A3906 (47c) **multicolored**	2.00	.40
5076 A3907 (47c) **multicolored**	2.00	.40
a. Block of 8, #5069-5076	16.00	
P# block of 8, 5#+P	16.00	
Pane of 16	32.00	
Nos. 5069-5076 (8)	16.00	3.20

Die cut uncut press sheets of Nos. 5069-5076 were made available for sale. Values: cross gutter block of 8, $18; pairs with gutters between, $4.25 each. See note after No. 4693.
See note after No. 1549.

PLUTO EXPLORED Ⓢ

Pluto — A3908

New Horizons Probe — A3909

Designed by Antonio Alcalá. Printed by Ashton-Potter (USA) Ltd.

LITHOGRAPHED
Sheets of 56 in 14 panes of 4

2016, May 31 Tagged *Serpentine Die Cut 10½*
Self-Adhesive

5077 A3908 (47c) **multicolored**	1.25	.25
5078 A3909 (47c) **multicolored**	1.25	.25
a. Pair, #5077-5078	2.50	
Pane of 4, 2 each #5077-5078	5.00	

Die cut uncut press sheets of Nos. 5077-5078 were made available for sale. Values: cross gutter block of 4, $9; pairs with gutters between, $4.25 each. See note after No. 4693.
See note after No. 1549.

CLASSICS FOREVER

A3910

Designed by Antonio Alcalá. Printed by Banknote Corporation of America.

No. 5079: a, George Washington (redrawn type A16). b, Benjamin Franklin (redrawn type A5). c, Washington (redrawn type A17). d, Washington (redrawn type A19). e, Abraham Lincoln (redrawn type A33). f, Franklin (redrawn type A24).

LITHOGRAPHED & ENGRAVED
Sheets of 60 in 10 panes of six

2016, June 1 Tagged *Serpentine Die Cut 10¾*
Self-Adhesive

5079	A3910	Pane of 6	7.50	
a.		(47c) tan & black	1.25	.40
b.		(47c) tan & blue	1.25	.40
c.		(47c) tan & black	1.25	.40
d.		(47c) tan & blue	1.25	.40
e.		(47c) tan & black	1.25	.40
f.		(47c) tan & blue	1.25	.40

Die cut uncut press sheets of No. 5079 were made available for sale. Values: cross gutter block of 6, $12; pairs with gutters between, $4.25 each. See note after No. 4693.

NATIONAL PARK SERVICE, CENT.

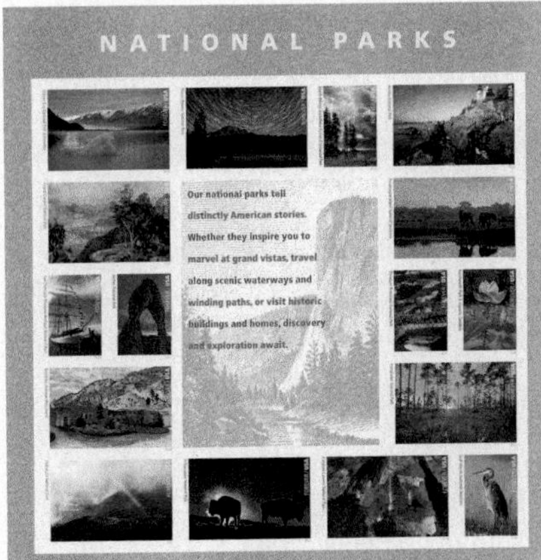

A3911

Designed by Ethel Kessler. Printed by Banknote Corporation of America.

No. 5080: a, Iceberg in Glacier Bay National Park and Preserve, Alaska (48x31mm). b, Mount Rainier National Park (48x31mm). c, *Scenery in the Grand Tetons,* painting by Albert Bierstadt, at Marsh-Billings-Rockefeller National Historic Park, Vermont (24x31mm). d, Bass Harbor Head Lighthouse, Acadia National Park, Maine (48x31mm). e, *The Grand Canyon of Arizona,* painting by Thomas Moran, at Grand Canyon National Park, Arizona (48x31mm). f, Horses at Assateague Island National Seashore, Virginia and Maryland (48x31mm). g, Ship *Balclutha,* at San Francisco Maritime National Historic Park, California (24x31mm). h, Stone arch at Arches National Park, Utah (24x31mm). i, Aerial view of Theodore Roosevelt National Park, North Dakota (24x31mm). j, Water lily at Kenilworth Park and Aquatic Gardens, Washington, D.C. (24x31mm). k, *Administration Building at Frijoles Canyon,* drawing by Helmuth Naumer, Sr., at Bandelier National Monument, New Mexico (48x31mm). l, Everglades National Park, Florida (48x31mm). m, Rainbow at Haleakala National Park, Hawaii (48x31mm). n, Bison at Yellowstone National Park, Idaho, Montana and Wyoming (48x31mm). o, Carlsbad Caverns National Park, New Mexico (48x31mm). p, Heron at Gulf Islands National Seashore, Florida and Mississippi (24x31mm).

LITHOGRAPHED
Sheets of 144 in nine panes of 16
Serpentine Die Cut 10½x10¾

2016, June 2 Self-Adhesive
Tagged

5080	A3911	Pane of 16 + label	20.00	
a.-p.		(47c) Any single	1.25	.50

Die cut uncut press sheets of No. 5080 were made available for sale. Values: pairs with gutters between, $4.25 each. See note after No. 4693.

COLORFUL CELEBRATIONS

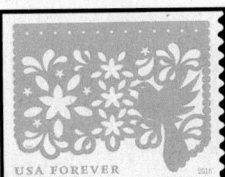

Bird and Flowers — A3912

Birds and Flowers — A3913

Flowers — A3914

Flowers — A3915

Flowers — A3916

Flowers — A3917

Birds and Flower — A3918

Bird and Flower — A3919

Flowers — A3920

Birds and Flower — A3921

Designed by Sally Anderson-Bruce. Printed by Banknote Corporation of America.

LITHOGRAPHED
Serpentine Die Cut 11 on 2 or 3 Sides

2016, June 3 Tagged
Booklet Stamps
Self-Adhesive

5081	A3912	(47c)	**light blue**	2.00	.40
5082	A3913	(47c)	**orange**	2.00	.40
5083	A3914	(47c)	**violet**	2.00	.40
5084	A3915	(47c)	**rose pink**	2.00	.40
5085	A3916	(47c)	**light blue**	2.00	.40
5086	A3917	(47c)	**orange**	2.00	.40
5087	A3918	(47c)	**violet**	2.00	.40
5088	A3919	(47c)	**rose pink**	2.00	.40
5089	A3920	(47c)	**rose pink**	2.00	.40
5090	A3921	(47c)	**violet**	2.00	.40
a.			Block of 10, #5081-5090	20.00	
b.			Booklet pane of 20, 2 each #5081-5090	40.00	
			Nos. 5081-5090 (10)	20.00	4.00

No. 5090b is a double-sided booklet pane with 12 stamps on one side (Nos. 5083-5090, 2 each Nos. 5081-5082) and eight stamps (Nos. 5083-5090) plus label (booklet cover) on the other side.

Die cut uncut press sheets of Nos. 5081-5090 were made available for sale. Values of varieties: cross gutter block of 4 with booklet cover, imperf. within, $10; cross gutter block of 4, imperf. within, $10; horiz. pair, imperf. between, $4. See note after No. 4693.

INDIANA STATEHOOD, 200th ANNIV. Ⓢ

Corn Field Near Milford
A3922

Designed by Derry Noyes. Printed by Ashton-Potter (USA) Ltd.

LITHOGRAPHED
Sheets of 120 in six panes of 20

2016, June 7 Tagged *Serpentine Die Cut 10¾*
Self-Adhesive

5091	A3922	(47c) **multicolored**	1.25	.25
		P# block of 4, 4#+P	5.00	
		Pane of 20	25.00	

Die cut uncut press sheets of No. 5091 were made available for sale. Values: cross gutter block of 4, $9; pairs with gutters between, $4.25 each. See note after No. 4693.

EID

"Eidukum Mubarak" — A3923

Designed by Mohamed Zakariya. Printed by Banknote Corporation of America.

LITHOGRAPHED
Sheets of 160 in eight panes of 20

2016, June 10 Tagged *Serpentine Die Cut 11*
Self-Adhesive

5092 A3923 (47c) **multicolored** 1.25 .25
P# block of 4, 3#+B 5.00
Pane of 20 25.00

Die cut uncut press sheets of No. 5092 were made available for sale. Values: cross gutter block of 4, $9; pairs with gutters between, $4.25 each. See note after No. 4693.

Counterfeits exist of No. 5092. See the Postal Counterfeits section of this catalog.

SODA FOUNTAIN FAVORITES

Ice Cream Cone — A3924

Egg Cream — A3925

Banana Split A3926

Root Beer Float — A3927

Hot Fudge Sundae — A3928

No. 5095 No. 5095a

Designed by Ethel Kessler. Printed by Banknote Corporation of America.

LITHOGRAPHED

2016, June 30 Tagged *Serpentine Die Cut 10¾*
Booklet Stamps
Self-Adhesive

5093 A3924 (47c) **multicolored** 1.50 .40
5094 A3925 (47c) **multicolored** 1.50 .40
5095 A3926 (47c) **multicolored** (long sloping die cut at bottom) 1.50 .40
a. Long sloping die cut at top 1.50 .40
5096 A3927 (47c) **multicolored** 1.50 .40
5097 A3928 (47c) **multicolored** 1.50 .40
a. Horiz. strip of 5, #5093-5097 7.50
b. Horiz. strip of 5, #5093-5094, 5095a, 5096-5097 7.50
c. Booklet pane of 20, 4 each #5093-5094, 5096-5097, 2 each #5095, 5095a 30.00
Nos. 5093-5097 (5) 7.50 2.00

Die cut uncut press sheets of Nos. 5093-5095 were made available for sale. Values: cross gutter block of 10 with booklet cover, $27.50; pairs with gutters between, $3.75 each. See note after No. 4693.

STAR QUILTS

A3929

A3930

Designed by Derry Noyes. Printed by Banknote Corporation of America.

LITHOGRAPHED

2016, July 6 Tagged *Serpentine Die Cut 11 Vert.*
Coil Stamps
Self-Adhesive

5098 A3929 (25c) **multicolored** .50 .25
5099 A3930 (25c) **multicolored** .50 .25
a. Pair, #5098-5099 1.00
P# strip of 5, 3 #5098, 2 #5099, #B11111 3.50
P# single, #B11111 (#5098) — 2.50
P# strip of 5, 2 #5098, 3 #5099, #B11111 10.00
P# single, #B11111 (#5099) — 5.00

JAIME ESCALANTE

Jaime Escalante (1930-2010), High School Calculus Teacher — A3931

Designed by Greg Breeding. Printed by Banknote Corporation of America.

LITHOGRAPHED
Sheets of 180 in nine panes of 20

2016, July 13 Tagged *Serpentine Die Cut 10¾*
Self-Adhesive

5100 A3931 (47c) **multicolored** 1.25 .25
P# block of 4, 6#+B 5.00
Pane of 20 25.00

Adjacent horizontal or vertical stamps have selvage between the stamps.

Die cut uncut press sheets of No. 5100 were made available for sale. Values: cross gutter block of 4, $9; pairs with gutters between, $4.25 each. See note after No. 4693.

PICKUP TRUCKS

1938 International Harvester D-2 — A3932

1953 Chevrolet — A3933

1948 Ford F-1 — A3934

1965 Ford F-100 — A3935

Designed by Antonio Alcalá. Printed by Banknote Corporation of America.

LITHOGRAPHED
Serpentine Die Cut 11 on 2 or 3 Sides

2016, July 15 Tagged
Booklet Stamps
Self-Adhesive

5101 A3932 (47c) **multicolored** 1.25 .30
5102 A3933 (47c) **multicolored** 1.25 .30
5103 A3934 (47c) **multicolored** 1.25 .30
5104 A3935 (47c) **multicolored** 1.25 .30
a. Block of 4, #5101-5104 5.00
b. Booklet pane of 20, 5 each #5101-5104 25.00
Nos. 5101-5104 (4) 5.00 1.20

No. 5104b is a double-sided booklet pane with 12 stamps on one side (3 each Nos. 5101-5104) and eight stamps (2 each Nos. 5101-5104) plus label (booklet cover) on the other side.

Die cut uncut press sheets of Nos. 5101-5104 were made available for sale. Values of varieties: cross gutter block of 4 with booklet cover, $10; cross gutter block of 4, imperf. within, $10; block of 4, vert. imperf. between, $8. See note after No. 4693.

LITERARY ARTS

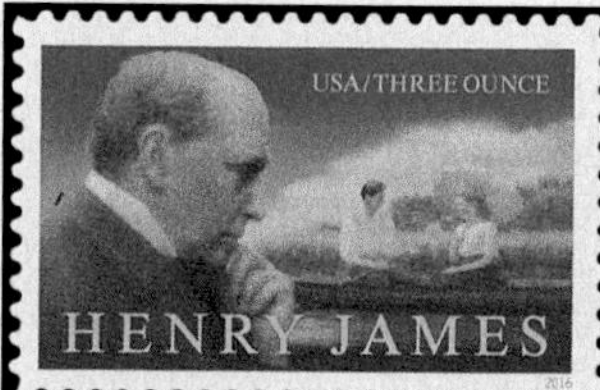

Henry James (1843-1916), Novelist A3936

Designed by Kate Sammons. Printed by Banknote Corporation of America.

LITHOGRAPHED
Sheets of 120 in six panes of 20

2016, July 31 Tagged *Serpentine Die Cut 11*
Self-Adhesive

5105 A3936 (89c) **multicolored** 2.20 .30
P# block of 4, 5#+B 8.80
Pane of 20 44.00

Die cut uncut press sheets of No. 5105 were made available for sale. Values: cross gutter block of 4, $18; pairs with gutters between, $7.50 each. See note after No. 4693.

PETS

Puppy — A3937

Betta Fish — A3938

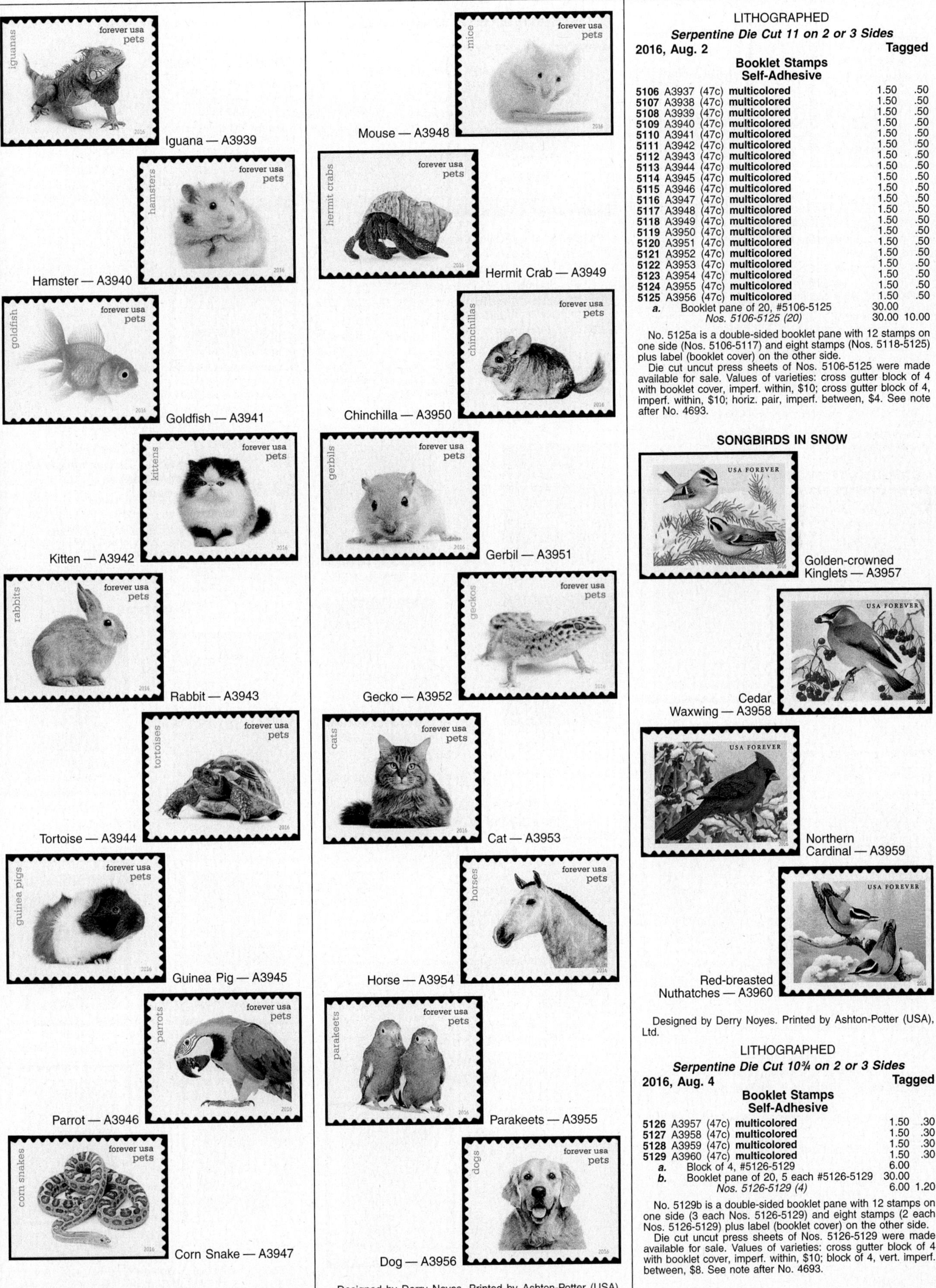

Iguana — A3939

Hamster — A3940

Goldfish — A3941

Kitten — A3942

Rabbit — A3943

Tortoise — A3944

Guinea Pig — A3945

Parrot — A3946

Corn Snake — A3947

Mouse — A3948

Hermit Crab — A3949

Chinchilla — A3950

Gerbil — A3951

Gecko — A3952

Cat — A3953

Horse — A3954

Parakeets — A3955

Dog — A3956

Designed by Derry Noyes. Printed by Ashton-Potter (USA), Ltd.

LITHOGRAPHED

Serpentine Die Cut 11 on 2 or 3 Sides

2016, Aug. 2 **Tagged**

Booklet Stamps
Self-Adhesive

5106	A3937 (47c)	**multicolored**	1.50	.50
5107	A3938 (47c)	**multicolored**	1.50	.50
5108	A3939 (47c)	**multicolored**	1.50	.50
5109	A3940 (47c)	**multicolored**	1.50	.50
5110	A3941 (47c)	**multicolored**	1.50	.50
5111	A3942 (47c)	**multicolored**	1.50	.50
5112	A3943 (47c)	**multicolored**	1.50	.50
5113	A3944 (47c)	**multicolored**	1.50	.50
5114	A3945 (47c)	**multicolored**	1.50	.50
5115	A3946 (47c)	**multicolored**	1.50	.50
5116	A3947 (47c)	**multicolored**	1.50	.50
5117	A3948 (47c)	**multicolored**	1.50	.50
5118	A3949 (47c)	**multicolored**	1.50	.50
5119	A3950 (47c)	**multicolored**	1.50	.50
5120	A3951 (47c)	**multicolored**	1.50	.50
5121	A3952 (47c)	**multicolored**	1.50	.50
5122	A3953 (47c)	**multicolored**	1.50	.50
5123	A3954 (47c)	**multicolored**	1.50	.50
5124	A3955 (47c)	**multicolored**	1.50	.50
5125	A3956 (47c)	**multicolored**	1.50	.50
a.	Booklet pane of 20, #5106-5125		30.00	
	Nos. 5106-5125 (20)		30.00	10.00

No. 5125a is a double-sided booklet pane with 12 stamps on one side (Nos. 5106-5117) and eight stamps (Nos. 5118-5125) plus label (booklet cover) on the other side.

Die cut uncut press sheets of Nos. 5106-5125 were made available for sale. Values of varieties: cross gutter block of 4 with booklet cover, imperf. within, $10; cross gutter block of 4, imperf. within, $10; horiz. pair, imperf. between, $4. See note after No. 4693.

SONGBIRDS IN SNOW

Golden-crowned Kinglets — A3957

Cedar Waxwing — A3958

Northern Cardinal — A3959

Red-breasted Nuthatches — A3960

Designed by Derry Noyes. Printed by Ashton-Potter (USA), Ltd.

LITHOGRAPHED

Serpentine Die Cut 10¾ on 2 or 3 Sides

2016, Aug. 4 **Tagged**

Booklet Stamps
Self-Adhesive

5126	A3957 (47c)	**multicolored**	1.50	.30
5127	A3958 (47c)	**multicolored**	1.50	.30
5128	A3959 (47c)	**multicolored**	1.50	.30
5129	A3960 (47c)	**multicolored**	1.50	.30
a.	Block of 4, #5126-5129		6.00	
b.	Booklet pane of 20, 5 each #5126-5129		30.00	
	Nos. 5126-5129 (4)		6.00	1.20

No. 5129b is a double-sided booklet pane with 12 stamps on one side (3 each Nos. 5126-5129) and eight stamps (2 each Nos. 5126-5129) plus label (booklet cover) on the other side.

Die cut uncut press sheets of Nos. 5126-5129 were made available for sale. Values of varieties: cross gutter block of 4 with booklet cover, imperf. within, $10; block of 4, vert. imperf. between, $8. See note after No. 4693.

PATRIOTIC SPIRAL

Stars — A3961

A3961a

Designed by Polygraph. Printed by Ashton-Potter (USA), Ltd.

LITHOGRAPHED

Serpentine Die Cut 10 Vert.

2016, Aug. 19 **Tagged**

Coil Stamp
Self-Adhesive

5130	A3961 (47c) **multicolored**	1.25	.25
	Pair	2.50	
	P# strip of 5, #P1111	7.50	
	P# single, #P1111	—	2.50
a.	Tagging omitted		—

Booklet Stamp

Serpentine Die Cut 11 on 2 or 3 Sides

5131	A3961a (47c) **multicolored**	1.25	.25
a.	Booklet pane of 10	12.50	

The discovery example of No. 5130a is on piece and canceled.

Counterfeits exist of No. 5131. See the Postal Counterfeits section of this catalog.

STAR TREK TELEVISION SHOW, 50TH ANNIV

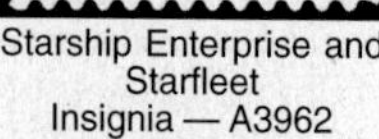

Starship Enterprise and Starfleet Insignia — A3962

Crewman in Transporter — A3963

Starship Enterprise and Planet — A3964

Starship Enterprise, Planet, Vulcan Hand Salute — A3965

Designed by The Heads of State. Printed by Ashton-Potter (USA), Ltd.

LITHOGRAPHED

Sheets of 120 in six panes of 20

2016, Sept. 2 **Tagged** ***Serpentine Die Cut 11***

Self-Adhesive

5132	A3962 (47c) **multicolored**	1.25	.30
5133	A3963 (47c) **multicolored**	1.25	.30
5134	A3964 (47c) **multicolored**	1.25	.30
5135	A3965 (47c) **multicolored**	1.25	.30
a.	Block or vert. strip of 4, #5132-5135	5.00	
	P# block of 4, 8#+P	5.00	
	Pane of 20	25.00	
	Nos. 5132-5135 (4)	5.00	1.20

Die cut uncut press sheets of No. 5132-5135 were made available for sale. Values: cross gutter block of 8, $18; pairs with gutters between, $4.25 each. See note after No. 4693.

EASTERN TAILED-BLUE BUTTERFLY

A3966

Designed by Derry Noyes. Printed by Ashton-Potter (USA) Ltd.

LITHOGRAPHED

Sheets of 120 in six panes of 20

2016, Sept. 24 **Tagged** ***Serpentine Die Cut 10½***

Self-Adhesive

5136	A3966 (68c) **multicolored**	2.00	.25
	P# block of 4, 4#+P	8.00	
	Pane of 20	40.00	

Die cut uncut press sheets of No. 5136 were made available for sale. Values: cross gutter block of 4, $18, pairs with gutters between, $7.50 each. See note after No. 4693.

JACK-O'-LANTERNS

Four Teeth — A3967

Five Teeth — A3968

Three Teeth — A3969

Nine Teeth — A3970

Designed by Derry Noyes. Printed by Banknote Corporation of America.

LITHOGRAPHED

Serpentine Die Cut 11x10¾ on 2 or 3 Sides

2016, Sept. 29 **Tagged**

Booklet Stamps
Self-Adhesive

5137	A3967 (47c) **multicolored**	1.25	.30
5138	A3968 (47c) **multicolored**	1.25	.30
5139	A3969 (47c) **multicolored**	1.25	.30
5140	A3970 (47c) **multicolored**	1.25	.30
a.	Block of 4, #5137-5140	5.00	
b.	Booklet pane of 20, 5 each #5137-5140	25.00	
	Nos. 5137-5140 (4)	5.00	1.20

No. 5140b is a double-sided booklet pane with 12 stamps on one side (3 each Nos. 5137-5140) and eight stamps (2 each Nos. 5137-5140) plus label (booklet cover) on the other side.

Die cut uncut press sheets of Nos. 5137-5140 were made available for sale. Values of varieties: cross gutter block of 4 with booklet cover, imperf. within, $10; cross gutter block of 4, imperf. within, $10; block of 4, vert. imperf.between, $8.50; block of 4, horiz. imperf. between, $7.50. See note after No. 4693.

KWANZAA

Woman, Fruits and Vegetables — A3971

Designed by Greg Breeding. Printed by Banknote Corporation of America.

LITHOGRAPHED

Sheets of 160 in eight panes of 20

2016, Oct. 1 **Tagged** ***Serpentine Die Cut 11***

Self-Adhesive

5141	A3971 (47c) **multicolored**	1.25	.25
	P# block of 4, 4#+B	5.00	
	Pane of 20	25.00	

Die cut uncut press sheets of No. 5141 were made available for sale. Values: cross gutter block of 4, $9; pairs with gutters between, $4.25 each. See note after No. 4693.

DIWALI

Diya — A3972

Designed by Greg Breeding. Printed by Ashton-Potter (USA) Ltd.

LITHOGRAPHED

Sheets of 160 in eight panes of 20

2016, Oct. 5 **Tagged** ***Serpentine Die Cut 11***

Self-Adhesive

5142	A3972 (47c) **multicolored**	1.25	.25
	P# block of 4, 4#+P	5.00	
	Pane of 20	25.00	

Die cut uncut press sheets of No. 5142 were made available for sale. Values: cross gutter block of 4, $9; pairs with gutters between, $4.25 each. See note after No. 4693.

Counterfeits exist of No. 5142. See the Postal Counterfeits section of this catalog.

CHRISTMAS

Madonna and Child, by a Follower of Fra Filippo Lippi and Peselino — A3973

Nativity — A3974

Candle in Window — A3975

Wreath in Window — A3976

Star in Window — A3977

Christmas Tree in Window — A3978

Designed by William J. Gicker (No. 5143), Greg Breeding (No. 5144), Ethel Kessler (Nos. 5145-5148). Printed by Ashton-Potter (USA) Ltd. (Nos. 5143-5144), Banknote Corporation of America (Nos. 5145-5148).

LITHOGRAPHED

Serpentine Die Cut 10¾x11 on 2 or 3 Sides

2016 **Tagged**

Booklet Stamps
Self-Adhesive

5143 A3973 (47c) **multicolored,** *Oct. 18* 1.25 .25
 a. Booklet pane of 20 25.00
5144 A3974 (47c) **multicolored,** *Nov. 3* 1.25 .25
 a. Booklet pane of 20 25.00
5145 A3975 (47c) **multicolored,** *Oct. 6* 1.25 .25
5146 A3976 (47c) **multicolored,** *Oct. 6* 1.25 .25
5147 A3977 (47c) **multicolored,** *Oct. 6* 1.25 .25
5148 A3978 (47c) **multicolored,** *Oct. 6* 1.25 .25
 a. Block of 4, #5145-5148 5.00
 b. Booklet pane of 20, 5 each #5145-5148 25.00
 Nos. 5143-5148 (6) 7.50 1.50

Nos. 5143a and 5144a are double-sided booklet panes with 12 stamps on one side and eight stamps plus label (booklet cover) on the other side. No. 5148b is a double-sided booklet pane with 12 stamps on one side (3 each Nos. 5145-5148) and eight stamps (2 each Nos. 5145-5148) plus label (booklet cover) on the other side.

Die cut uncut press sheets of Nos. 5143, 5144, and 5145-5148 were made available for sale. Values of varieties: cross gutter block of 4 with booklet cover, imperf. within, $10; cross gutter block of 4, imperf. within, $10; blocks of 4 (Nos. 5145-5148), imperf. vert. or horiz. between, $7.50 each; vert. pair, imperf. between, $4; horiz. pair, imperf. between, $6. See note after No. 4693.

Counterfeits exist of Nos. 5143, 5145-5148. See the Postal Counterfeits section of this catalog.

WONDER WOMAN, 75TH ANNIVERSARY

Modern Age Wonder Woman — A3979

Bronze Age Wonder Woman — A3980

Silver Age Wonder Woman — A3981

Golden Age Wonder Woman — A3982

Designed by Greg Breeding. Printed by Banknote Corporation of America.

LITHOGRAPHED

Sheets of 180 in nine panes of 20

2016, Oct. 7 **Tagged** ***Serpentine Die Cut 11***

Self-Adhesive

5149 A3979 (47c) **multicolored** 1.50 .30
5150 A3980 (47c) **multicolored** 1.50 .30
5151 A3981 (47c) **multicolored** 1.50 .30
5152 A3982 (47c) **multicolored** 1.50 .30
 a. Vert. strip of 4, #5149-5152 6.00
 P# block of 8, 4#+B 12.00
 Pane of 20 30.00
 Nos. 5149-5152 (4) 6.00 1.20

Die cut uncut press sheets of No. 5149-5152 were made available for sale. Values: cross gutter block of 8, $18; pairs with gutters between, $3.75 each. See note after No. 4693.

HANUKKAH

Menorah — A3983

Designed by Ethel Kessler. Printed by Banknote Corporation of America.

LITHOGRAPHED

Sheets of 160 in eight panes of 20

2016, Nov. 1 **Tagged** ***Serpentine Die Cut 11***

Self-Adhesive

5153 A3983 (47c) **multicolored** 1.25 .25
 P# block of 4, 5#+B 5.00
 Pane of 20 25.00

Die cut uncut press sheets of No. 5153 were made available for sale. Values: cross gutter block of 4, $9; pairs with gutters between, $4.25 each. See note after No. 4693.

CHINESE NEW YEAR

Year of the Rooster A3984

Designed by Ethel Kessler. Printed by Banknote Corporation of America.

LITHOGRAPHED

Sheets of 144 in 12 panes of 12

2017, Jan. 5 **Tagged** ***Serpentine Die Cut 10¾***

Self-Adhesive

5154 A3984 (47c) **multicolored** 1.25 .25
 Pane of 12 15.00

Die cut partial press sheets (containing 72 stamps) of No. 5154 were made available for sale. Values: cross gutter block of 4, $9; pairs with gutters between, $4.25 each. See note after No. 4693.

LOVE

Airplane and Skywriting — A3985

Designed by Louise Fili. Printed by Banknote Corporation of America.

LITHOGRAPHED

Sheets of 160 in eight panes of 20

2017, Jan. 7 **Tagged** ***Serpentine Die Cut 11x10¾***

Self-Adhesive

5155 A3985 (47c) **light blue** 1.25 .25
 P# block of 4, 1#+B 5.00
 Pane of 20 25.00

Die cut uncut press sheets of No. 5155 were made available for sale. Values: cross gutter block of 4, $9; pairs with gutters between, $4.25 each. See note after No. 4693.

Counterfeits exist of No. 5155. See the Postal Counterfeits section of this catalog.

AMERICAN LANDMARKS ISSUE

Lili'uokalani Gardens, Hilo, Hawaii A3986

Gateway Arch, St. Louis, Missouri A3987

Designed by Greg Breeding. Printed by Ashton-Potter (USA) Ltd.

LITHOGRAPHED

Sheets of 40 in 10 panes of 4 (#5156), Sheets of 20 in 5 panes of 4 (#5157)

Serpentine Die Cut 10¾x10½

2017, Jan. 22 **Tagged**

Self-Adhesive

5156 A3986 $6.65 **multicolored** ⓢ 17.50 7.75
 Pane of 4 70.00
5157 A3987 $23.75 **multicolored** ⓢ 65.00 25.00
 Pane of 4 260.00

Flag — A3988

A3988a

Designed by Greg Breeding. Printed by Banknote Corporation of America (#5158), Ashton-Potter (USA) Ltd. (#5159).

LITHOGRAPHED

Serpentine Die Cut 11 Vert.

2017, Jan. 27 **Tagged**

Coil Stamps
Self-Adhesive
Microprinted "USPS" On Right End of Fourth Red Stripe

5158 A3988 (49c) **multicolored** ⓢ 1.25 .25
 Pair 2.50
 P# strip of 5, #B1111 7.50
 P# single, #B1111 — 2.50
 a. Die cutting omitted, pair —
 b. Vert. pair, unslit between —

Counterfeits exist of No. 5158. See the Postal Counterfeits section of this catalog.

Serpentine Die Cut 9½ Vert.

Microprinted "USPS" on Right End of Second White Flag Stripe

5159 A3988a (49c) **multicolored** ⓢ 1.25 .25
 Pair 2.50
 P# strip of 5, #P1111 7.50
 P# single, #P1111 — 2.50

Counterfeits exist of No. 5159. See the Postal Counterfeits section of this catalog.

A3988b

A3988c

A3988d

Printed by Banknote Corporation of America (#5160), Ashton-Potter (USA) Ltd. (#5161-5162).

Booklet Stamps
Microprinted "USPS" on Right End of Fourth Red Stripe

Serpentine Die Cut 11¼x10¾ on 2 or 3 Sides

5160 A3988b (49c) **multicolored** ⓢ 1.25 .25
 a. Booklet pane of 10 12.50
 b. Booklet pane of 20 25.00

Microprinted "USPS" on Right End of Second White Flag Stripe

5161 A3988c (49c) **multicolored** ⓢ 1.25 .25
 a. Booklet pane of 20 25.00

Counterfeits exist of No. 5161. See the Postal Counterfeits section of this catalog.

Microprinted "USPS" on Left End of Second White Flag Stripe Near Blue Field
Thin Paper

Serpentine Die Cut 11¼x10¾ on 2, 3 or 4 Sides

5162 A3988d (49c) **multicolored** ⓢ 2.75 .25
a. Booklet pane of 18 50.00
Nos. 5160-5162 (3) 5.25 .75

Nos. 5160b and 5161a are double-sided booklets with 12 stamps on one side and eight stamps plus a label that serves as the booklet cover on the other side.

SHELLS

Queen Conch — A3989

Pacific Calico Scallop — A3990

Alphabet Cone — A3991

Zebra Nerite — A3992

Designed by Greg Breeding. Printed by Ashton-Potter (USA) Ltd.

LITHOGRAPHED
Sheets of 200 in ten panes of 20
Serpentine Die Cut 11¼x10¾

2017, Jan. 28 **Tagged**

Self-Adhesive

5163 A3989 (34c) **multicolored** ⓢ .90 .25
5164 A3990 (34c) **multicolored** ⓢ .90 .25
5165 A3991 (34c) **multicolored** ⓢ .90 .25
5166 A3992 (34c) **multicolored** ⓢ .90 .25
a. Horiz. or vert. strip of 4, #5163-5166 3.60
P# block of 8, 6#+P 7.20
Pane of 20 18.00
Nos. 5163-5166 (4) 3.60 1.00

A3989a

A3990a

A3991a

A3992a

Coil Stamps

Serpentine Die Cut 9¾ Vert.

5167 A3991a (34c) **multicolored** ⓢ .90 .25
5168 A3992a (34c) **multicolored** ⓢ .90 .25
5169 A3989a (34c) **multicolored** ⓢ .90 .25
5170 A3990a (34c) **multicolored** ⓢ .90 .25
a. Horiz. strip of 4, #5167-5170 3.60
P# strip of 5, #5168-5170, 2 #5167, #P111111 5.50
P# strip of 9, 2 each #5167-5168, 5170, 3 #5169, #P111111 9.25
P# single, #P111111 (#5169) — 2.75
Nos. 5167-5170 (4) 3.60 1.00

BLACK HERITAGE

Dorothy Height (1912-2010), President of National Council of Negro Women — A3993

Designed by Derry Noyes. Printed by Ashton-Potter (USA) Ltd.

LITHOGRAPHED
Sheets of 120 in six panes of 20

2017, Feb. 1 **Tagged** ***Serpentine Die Cut 11***

Self-Adhesive

5171 A3993 (49c) **multicolored** ⓢ 1.25 .25
P# block of 4, 4#+P 5.00
Pane of 20 25.00

Die cut uncut press sheets of No. 5171 were made available for sale. Values: cross gutter block of 4, $9; pairs with gutters between, $3.75 each. See note after No. 4693.

"USA" and Star With Blue Frame — A3994

Designed by Antonio Alcalá and Leslie Badani. Printed by Ashton-Potter (USA) Ltd.

LITHOGRAPHED
Serpentine Die Cut 10 Vert.

2017, Feb. 10 **Untagged**

COIL STAMP
Self-Adhesive

5172 A3994 (5c) **multicolored** ⓢ .30 .25
Pair .50
P# strip of 5, #P111 .85
P# single, #P111 — .50
a. Red omitted —

See note after No. 1549.
The discovery example of No. 5172a is on piece, uncanceled.

OSCAR DE LA RENTA ⓢ

Oscar de la Renta (1932-2014), Fashion Designer A3995

A3996

A3997

A3998

A3999

A4000

A4001

A4002

A4003

A4004

A4005

Designed by Derry Noyes. Printed by Ashton-Potter (USA) Ltd.

LITHOGRAPHED

Sheets of 99 in nine panes of 11

Serpentine Die Cut 11x10¾ (No. 5173a), 10¾x11

2017, Feb. 16 **Tagged**

Self-Adhesive

5173	Pane of 11	13.75	
a.	A3995 (49c) **multicolored**	1.25	.50
b.	A3996 (49c) **multicolored**	1.25	.50
c.	A3997 (49c) **multicolored**	1.25	.50
d.	A3998 (49c) **multicolored**	1.25	.50
e.	A3999 (49c) **multicolored**	1.25	.50
f.	A4000 (49c) **multicolored**	1.25	.50
g.	A4001 (49c) **multicolored**	1.25	.50
h.	A4002 (49c) **multicolored**	1.25	.50
i.	A4003 (49c) **multicolored**	1.25	.50
j.	A4004 (49c) **multicolored**	1.25	.50
k.	A4005 (49c) **multicolored**	1.25	.50

Die cut uncut press sheets of No. 5173 were made available for sale. See note after No. 4693.

See note after No. 1549.

People Wearing Uncle Sam Hats — A4006

Designed by Antonio Alcalá. Printed by Banknote Corporation of America.

LITHOGRAPHED

Sheets of 200 in 10 panes of 20

Serpentine Die Cut 11¼x11

2017, Feb. 18 **Tagged**

Self-Adhesive

5174 A4006 (21c) **multicolored** Ⓢ		.50	.25
	P# block of 4, 7#+B	2.00	
	Pane of 20	10.00	

See No. 5341. See note under No. 1549.

Counterfeits exist of No. 5174. See the Postal Counterfeits section of this catalog.

PRES. JOHN F. KENNEDY (1917-63) Ⓢ

Pres. John F. Kennedy — A4007

Designed by Derry Noyes. Printed by Banknote Corporation of America.

LITHOGRAPHED

Sheets of 96 in eight panes of 12

2017, Feb. 20 **Tagged** ***Serpentine Die Cut 10¾***

Self-Adhesive

5175 A4007 (49c) **brown**		1.25	.25
	P# block of 4, 2#+B	5.00	
	Pane of 12	15.00	

Die cut uncut press sheets of No. 5175 were made available for sale. Values: cross gutter block of 4, $9; pairs with gutters between, $3.75 each. See note after No. 4693.

See note after No. 1549.

Fruits

A4007a

A4007b

Designed by Derry Noyes. Printed by Ashton-Potter (USA) Ltd. (No. 5177); Banknote Corporation of America (No. 5178).

Designs: 5c, Pinot Noir Grapes. 10c, Red Pears.

LITHOGRAPHED

Sheets of 200 in 10 panes of 20

2017 ***Serpentine Die Cut 11¼x11***

Untagged (#5177), Tagged (#5178)

Self-Adhesive

5177 A4007a 5c **multicolored,** *Feb. 24* Ⓢ		.30	.25
	P# block of 4, 6#+P	.40	
	Pane of 20	2.00	

See Nos. 5038, 5039.

5178 A4007b 10c **multicolored,** *Mar. 23* Ⓢ		.30	.25
	P# block of 4, 6#+B	.80	
	Pane of 20	4.00	

See note after No. 1549.

See Nos. 5038-5039, 5201, 5256.

NEBRASKA STATEHOOD, 150th ANNIV. Ⓢ

Sandhill Cranes Flying Over Platte River A4008

Designed by Derry Noyes. Printed by Ashton-Potter (USA) Ltd.

LITHOGRAPHED

Sheets of 120 in six panes of 20

2017, Mar. 1 **Tagged** ***Serpentine Die Cut 10¾***

Self-Adhesive

5179 A4008 (49c) **multicolored**		1.25	.25
	P# block of 4, 4#+P	5.00	
	Pane of 20	25.00	

Die cut uncut press sheets of No. 5179 were made available for sale. Values: cross gutter block of 4, $9; pairs with gutters between, $3.75 each. See note after No. 4693.

See note after No. 1549.

WORKS PROGRESS ADMINISTRATION (WORK PROJECTS ADMINISTRATION) POSTERS Ⓢ

See America Welcome to Montana Poster — A4009

Work Pays America Poster — A4010

Field Day Poster — A4011

Discover Puerto Rico Poster — A4012

City of New York Municipal Airports Poster — A4013

Foreign Trade Zone Poster — A4014

Visit the Zoo Poster — A4015

Work with Care Poster — A4016

The National Parks Preserve Wild Life Poster — A4017

Hiking Poster — A4018

Designed by Antonio Alcalá. Printed by Ashton-Potter (USA) Ltd.

LITHOGRAPHED

Serpentine Die Cut 11 on 2 or 3 Sides

2017, Mar. 7 **Tagged**

Booklet Stamps
Self-Adhesive

5180	A4009 (49c) **multicolored**		1.50	.40
5181	A4010 (49c) **multicolored**		1.50	.40
5182	A4011 (49c) **multicolored**		1.50	.40
5183	A4012 (49c) **multicolored**		1.50	.40
5184	A4013 (49c) **multicolored**		1.50	.40
5185	A4014 (49c) **multicolored**		1.50	.40
5186	A4015 (49c) **multicolored**		1.50	.40
5187	A4016 (49c) **multicolored**		1.50	.40
5188	A4017 (49c) **multicolored**		1.50	.40
5189	A4018 (49c) **multicolored**		1.50	.40
a.	Block of 10, #5180-5189		15.00	
b.	Booklet pane of 20, 2 each #5180-5189		30.00	
	Nos. 5180-5189 (10)		15.00	4.00

No. 5189b is a double-sided booklet pane with 12 stamps on one side (Nos. 5181-5184, 5186-5189, 2 each Nos. 5180, 5185) and eight stamps (Nos. 5181-5184, 5186-5189) plus label (booklet cover) on the other side.

Die cut uncut press sheets of Nos. 5180-5189 were made available for sale. Values of varieties: cross gutter block of 4 with booklet cover, imperf. within, $10; cross gutter block of 4, imperf. within, $10; vert. pair, imperf. between, $4; horiz. pair imperf. between, $6. See note after No. 4693.

See note after No. 1549.

MISSISSIPPI STATEHOOD, 200th ANNIV. Ⓢ

Guitarist A4019

Designed by Greg Breeding. Printed by Ashton-Potter (USA) Ltd.

LITHOGRAPHED

Sheets of 120 in six panes of 20

2017, Mar. 31 **Tagged** ***Serpentine Die Cut 10¾***

Self-Adhesive

5190	A4019 (49c) **multicolored**	1.25	.25
	P# block of 4, 4#+P	5.00	
	Pane of 20	25.00	

Die cut uncut press sheets of No. 5190 were made available for sale. Values: cross gutter block of 4, $9; pairs with gutters between, $3.75 each. See note after No. 4693.

See note after No. 1549.

DISTINGUISHED AMERICANS

Robert Panara (1920-2014), Educator of the Deaf — A4020

Designed by Ethel Kessler. Printed by Banknote Corporation of America.

LITHOGRAPHED

Sheets of 120 in six panes of 20

2017, Apr. 11 **Tagged** ***Serpentine Die Cut 10¾***

Self-Adhesive

5191	A4020 (70c) **multicolored** Ⓢ	1.70	.25
	P# block of 4, 4#+B	6.80	
	Pane of 20	34.00	

Adjacent horizontal or vertical stamps have selvage between the stamps. See note after No. 1549.

DELICIOSO (LATIN AMERICAN DISHES) Ⓢ

Tamales — A4021

Flan — A4022

Sancocho — A4023

Empanadas — A4024

Chile Relleno — A4025

Ceviche — A4026

Designed by Antonio Alcalá. Printed by Banknote Corporation of America.

LITHOGRAPHED

Serpentine Die Cut 11 on 2 or 3 Sides

2017, Apr. 20 **Tagged**

Booklet Stamps
Self-Adhesive

5192	A4021 (49c) **multicolored**	1.25	.40
5193	A4022 (49c) **multicolored**	1.25	.40
5194	A4023 (49c) **multicolored**	1.25	.40
5195	A4024 (49c) **multicolored**	1.25	.40
5196	A4025 (49c) **multicolored**	1.25	.40
5197	A4026 (49c) **multicolored**	1.25	.40
a.	Block of 6, #5192-5197	7.50	
b.	Booklet pane of 20, 4 each #5192-5193, 3 each #5194-5197	25.00	
	Nos. 5192-5197 (6)	7.50	2.40

No. 5197b is a double-sided booklet pane with 12 stamps on one side (2 each Nos. 5192-5197) and eight stamps (Nos. 5194-5197, 2 each Nos. 5192-5193) plus label (booklet cover) on the other side.

Die cut uncut press sheets of Nos. 5192-5197 were made available for sale. Values of varieties: cross gutter block of 4 with booklet cover, imperf. within, $10; cross gutter block of 4, imperf. within, $10; vert. pair, imperf. between, $6; horiz. pair, imperf. between, $4. See note after No. 4693.

See note after No. 1549.

Echeveria A4027

Designed by Greg Breeding. Printed by Ashton-Potter (USA) Ltd.

LITHOGRAPHED

Sheets of 90 in nine panes of 10

2017, Apr. 28 **Tagged** ***Serpentine Die Cut***

Self-Adhesive

5198	A4027 ($1.15) **multicolored** Ⓢ	2.80	.50
	P# block of 4, 5#+P	11.20	
	Pane of 10	28.00	

Unused values are for stamps with surrounding selvage. Adjacent stamps are separated by rouletting.

CELEBRATION FLOWERS Ⓢ

Boutonniere — A4028

Corsage — A4029

Designed by Ethel Kessler. Printed by Banknote Corporation of America.

LITHOGRAPHED

Sheets of 200 in 10 panes of 20

2017, May 2 **Tagged** ***Serpentine Die Cut 10¾***

Self-Adhesive

5199	A4028 (49c) **multicolored** Ⓢ	1.25	.25
	P# block of 4, 5#+B	5.00	
	Pane of 20	25.00	
5200	A4029 (70c) **multicolored** Ⓢ	1.70	.25
	P# block of 4, 5#+B	6.80	
	Pane of 20	34.00	

See note after No. 1549.

Counterfeits exist of Nos. 5199-5200. See the Postal Counterfeits section of this catalog.

FRUIT

Strawberries — A4030

A4002

A4003

A4004

A4005

Designed by Derry Noyes. Printed by Ashton-Potter (USA) Ltd.

LITHOGRAPHED

Sheets of 99 in nine panes of 11

Serpentine Die Cut 11x10¾ (No. 5173a), 10¾x11

2017, Feb. 16 **Tagged**

Self-Adhesive

5173	Pane of 11	13.75	
a.	A3995 (49c) **multicolored**	1.25	.50
b.	A3996 (49c) **multicolored**	1.25	.50
c.	A3997 (49c) **multicolored**	1.25	.50
d.	A3998 (49c) **multicolored**	1.25	.50
e.	A3999 (49c) **multicolored**	1.25	.50
f.	A4000 (49c) **multicolored**	1.25	.50
g.	A4001 (49c) **multicolored**	1.25	.50
h.	A4002 (49c) **multicolored**	1.25	.50
i.	A4003 (49c) **multicolored**	1.25	.50
j.	A4004 (49c) **multicolored**	1.25	.50
k.	A4005 (49c) **multicolored**	1.25	.50

Die cut uncut press sheets of No. 5173 were made available for sale. See note after No. 4693.

See note after No. 1549.

People Wearing Uncle Sam Hats — A4006

Designed by Antonio Alcalá. Printed by Banknote Corporation of America.

LITHOGRAPHED

Sheets of 200 in 10 panes of 20

Serpentine Die Cut 11¼x11

2017, Feb. 18 **Tagged**

Self-Adhesive

5174	A4006 (21c) **multicolored** Ⓢ	.50	.25
	P# block of 4, 7#+B	2.00	
	Pane of 20	10.00	

See No. 5341. See note under No. 1549.

Counterfeits exist of No. 5174. See the Postal Counterfeits section of this catalog.

PRES. JOHN F. KENNEDY (1917-63) Ⓢ

Pres. John F. Kennedy — A4007

Designed by Derry Noyes. Printed by Banknote Corporation of America.

LITHOGRAPHED

Sheets of 96 in eight panes of 12

2017, Feb. 20 **Tagged** ***Serpentine Die Cut 10¾***

Self-Adhesive

5175	A4007 (49c) **brown**	1.25	.25
	P# block of 4, 2#+B	5.00	
	Pane of 12	15.00	

Die cut uncut press sheets of No. 5175 were made available for sale. Values: cross gutter block of 4, $9; pairs with gutters between, $3.75 each. See note after No. 4693.

See note after No. 1549.

Fruits

A4007a

A4007b

Designed by Derry Noyes. Printed by Ashton-Potter (USA) Ltd. (No. 5177); Banknote Corporation of America (No. 5178).

Designs: 5c, Pinot Noir Grapes. 10c, Red Pears.

LITHOGRAPHED

Sheets of 200 in 10 panes of 20

2017 ***Serpentine Die Cut 11¼x11***

Untagged (#5177), Tagged (#5178)

Self-Adhesive

5177	A4007a 5c **multicolored**, *Feb. 24* Ⓢ	.30	.25
	P# block of 4, 6#+P	.40	
	Pane of 20	2.00	

See Nos. 5038, 5039.

5178	A4007b 10c **multicolored**, *Mar. 23* Ⓢ	.30	.25
	P# block of 4, 6#+B	.80	
	Pane of 20	4.00	

See note after No. 1549.

See Nos. 5038-5039, 5201, 5256.

NEBRASKA STATEHOOD, 150th ANNIV. Ⓢ

Sandhill Cranes Flying Over Platte River A4008

Designed by Derry Noyes. Printed by Ashton-Potter (USA) Ltd.

LITHOGRAPHED

Sheets of 120 in six panes of 20

2017, Mar. 1 **Tagged** ***Serpentine Die Cut 10¾***

Self-Adhesive

5179	A4008 (49c) **multicolored**	1.25	.25
	P# block of 4, 4#+P	5.00	
	Pane of 20	25.00	

Die cut uncut press sheets of No. 5179 were made available for sale. Values: cross gutter block of 4, $9; pairs with gutters between, $3.75 each. See note after No. 4693.

See note after No. 1549.

WORKS PROGRESS ADMINISTRATION (WORK PROJECTS ADMINISTRATION) POSTERS Ⓢ

See America Welcome to Montana Poster — A4009

Work Pays America Poster — A4010

Field Day Poster — A4011

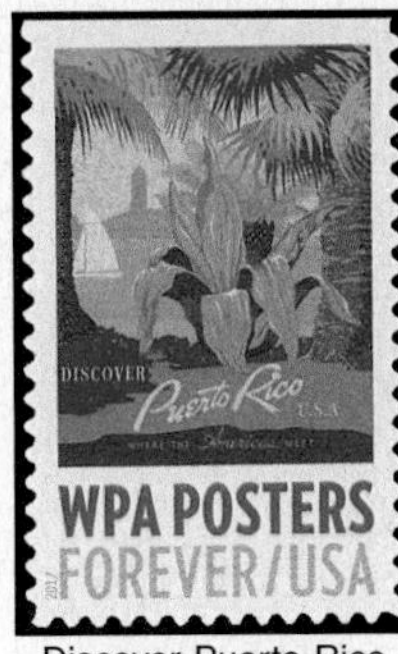

Discover Puerto Rico Poster — A4012

City of New York Municipal Airports Poster — A4013

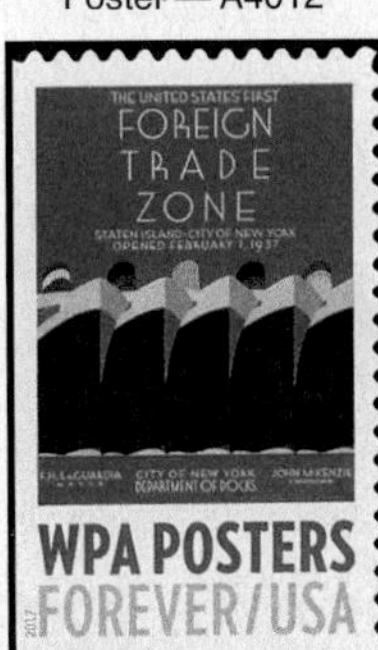

Foreign Trade Zone Poster — A4014

Visit the Zoo Poster — A4015

Work with Care Poster — A4016

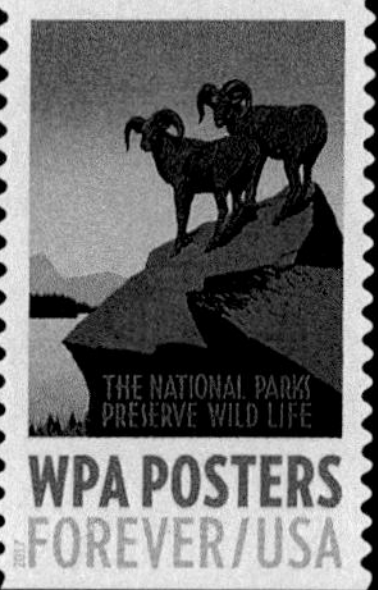

The National Parks Preserve Wild Life Poster — A4017

Hiking Poster — A4018

Designed by Antonio Alcalá. Printed by Ashton-Potter (USA) Ltd.

LITHOGRAPHED

Serpentine Die Cut 11 on 2 or 3 Sides

2017, Mar. 7 **Tagged**

Booklet Stamps
Self-Adhesive

5180	A4009 (49c) **multicolored**		1.50	.40
5181	A4010 (49c) **multicolored**		1.50	.40
5182	A4011 (49c) **multicolored**		1.50	.40
5183	A4012 (49c) **multicolored**		1.50	.40
5184	A4013 (49c) **multicolored**		1.50	.40
5185	A4014 (49c) **multicolored**		1.50	.40
5186	A4015 (49c) **multicolored**		1.50	.40
5187	A4016 (49c) **multicolored**		1.50	.40
5188	A4017 (49c) **multicolored**		1.50	.40
5189	A4018 (49c) **multicolored**		1.50	.40
a.	Block of 10, #5180-5189		15.00	
b.	Booklet pane of 20, 2 each #5180-5189		30.00	
	Nos. 5180-5189 (10)		15.00	4.00

No. 5189b is a double-sided booklet pane with 12 stamps on one side (Nos. 5181-5184, 5186-5189, 2 each Nos. 5180, 5185) and eight stamps (Nos. 5181-5184, 5186-5189) plus label (booklet cover) on the other side.

Die cut uncut press sheets of Nos. 5180-5189 were made available for sale. Values of varieties: cross gutter block of 4 with booklet cover, imperf. within, $10; cross gutter block of 4, imperf. within, $10; vert. pair, imperf. between, $4; horiz. pair imperf. between, $6. See note after No. 4693.

See note after No. 1549.

MISSISSIPPI STATEHOOD, 200th ANNIV. Ⓢ

Guitarist A4019

Designed by Greg Breeding. Printed by Ashton-Potter (USA) Ltd.

LITHOGRAPHED

Sheets of 120 in six panes of 20

2017, Mar. 31 **Tagged** ***Serpentine Die Cut 10¾***

Self-Adhesive

5190	A4019 (49c) **multicolored**	1.25	.25
	P# block of 4, 4#+P	5.00	
	Pane of 20	25.00	

Die cut uncut press sheets of No. 5190 were made available for sale. Values: cross gutter block of 4, $9; pairs with gutters between, $3.75 each. See note after No. 4693.

See note after No. 1549.

DISTINGUISHED AMERICANS

Robert Panara (1920-2014), Educator of the Deaf — A4020

Designed by Ethel Kessler. Printed by Banknote Corporation of America.

LITHOGRAPHED

Sheets of 120 in six panes of 20

2017, Apr. 11 **Tagged** ***Serpentine Die Cut 10¾***

Self-Adhesive

5191	A4020 (70c) **multicolored** Ⓢ	1.70	.25
	P# block of 4, 4#+B	6.80	
	Pane of 20	34.00	

Adjacent horizontal or vertical stamps have selvage between the stamps. See note after No. 1549.

DELICIOSO (LATIN AMERICAN DISHES) Ⓢ

Tamales — A4021

Flan — A4022

Sancocho — A4023

Empanadas — A4024

Chile Relleno — A4025

Ceviche — A4026

Designed by Antonio Alcalá. Printed by Banknote Corporation of America.

LITHOGRAPHED

Serpentine Die Cut 11 on 2 or 3 Sides

2017, Apr. 20 **Tagged**

Booklet Stamps
Self-Adhesive

5192	A4021 (49c) **multicolored**	1.25	.40
5193	A4022 (49c) **multicolored**	1.25	.40
5194	A4023 (49c) **multicolored**	1.25	.40
5195	A4024 (49c) **multicolored**	1.25	.40
5196	A4025 (49c) **multicolored**	1.25	.40
5197	A4026 (49c) **multicolored**	1.25	.40
a.	Block of 6, #5192-5197	7.50	
b.	Booklet pane of 20, 4 each #5192-5193, 3 each #5194-5197	25.00	
	Nos. 5192-5197 (6)	7.50	2.40

No. 5197b is a double-sided booklet pane with 12 stamps on one side (2 each Nos. 5192-5197) and eight stamps (Nos. 5194-5197, 2 each Nos. 5192-5193) plus label (booklet cover) on the other side.

Die cut uncut press sheets of Nos. 5192-5197 were made available for sale. Values of varieties: cross gutter block of 4 with booklet cover, imperf. within, $10; cross gutter block of 4, imperf. within, $10; vert. pair, imperf. between, $6; horiz. pair, imperf. between, $4. See note after No. 4693.

See note after No. 1549.

Echeveria A4027

Designed by Greg Breeding. Printed by Ashton-Potter (USA) Ltd.

LITHOGRAPHED

Sheets of 90 in nine panes of 10

2017, Apr. 28 **Tagged** ***Serpentine Die Cut***

Self-Adhesive

5198	A4027 ($1.15) **multicolored** Ⓢ	2.80	.50
	P# block of 4, 5#+P	11.20	
	Pane of 10	28.00	

Unused values are for stamps with surrounding selvage. Adjacent stamps are separated by rouletting.

CELEBRATION FLOWERS Ⓢ

Boutonniere — A4028

Corsage — A4029

Designed by Ethel Kessler. Printed by Banknote Corporation of America.

LITHOGRAPHED

Sheets of 200 in 10 panes of 20

2017, May 2 **Tagged** ***Serpentine Die Cut 10¾***

Self-Adhesive

5199	A4028 (49c) **multicolored** Ⓢ	1.25	.25
	P# block of 4, 5#+B	5.00	
	Pane of 20	25.00	
5200	A4029 (70c) **multicolored** Ⓢ	1.70	.25
	P# block of 4, 5#+B	6.80	
	Pane of 20	34.00	

See note after No. 1549.

Counterfeits exist of Nos. 5199-5200. See the Postal Counterfeits section of this catalog.

FRUIT

Strawberries — A4030

Designed by Derry Noyes. Printed by Ashton-Potter (USA), Ltd.

LITHOGRAPHED

Serpentine Die Cut 10 Vert.

2017, May 5 **Untagged**

Coil Stamps
Self-Adhesive

5201 A4030 3c **multicolored** ®	.25	.25
Pair	.25	
P# strip of 5, #P1111	1.25	
P# single, #P1111	—	.55

See note after No. 1549.

See Nos. 5038-5039, 5177-5178, 5256.

HENRY DAVID THOREAU Ⓢ

Henry David Thoreau (1817-62), Writer, and Sumac Leaves A4031

Designed by Greg Breeding. Printed by Banknote Corporation of America.

LITHOGRAPHED

Sheets of 180 in nine panes of 20

2017, May 23 **Tagged** ***Serpentine Die Cut 10¾***

Self-Adhesive

5202 A4031 (49c) **multicolored**	1.25	.25
P# block of 4, 4#+B	5.00	
Pane of 20	25.00	

Die cut uncut press sheets of No. 5202 were made available for sale. Values: cross gutter block of 4, $9; pairs with gutters between, $3.75 each. See note after No. 4693.

See note after No. 1549.

SPORTS BALLS Ⓢ

Football — A4032

Volleyball — A4033

Golf Ball — A4035

Baseball — A4036

Basketball — A4037

Tennis Ball — A4038

Kickball — A4039

Soccer Ball — A4034

Designed by Greg Breeding. Printed by Ashton-Potter (USA) Ltd.

LITHOGRAPHED & TYPOGRAPHED

Sheets of 128 in eight panes of 16

2017, June 14 **Tagged** ***Serpentine Die Cut***

Self-Adhesive

5203 A4032 (49c) **multicolored**	1.25	.40
5204 A4033 (49c) **multicolored**	1.25	.40
5205 A4034 (49c) **multicolored**	1.25	.40
5206 A4035 (49c) **multicolored**	1.25	.40
5207 A4036 (49c) **multicolored**	1.25	.40
5208 A4037 (49c) **multicolored**	1.25	.40
5209 A4038 (49c) **multicolored**	1.25	.40
5210 A4039 (49c) **multicolored**	1.25	.40
a. Block of 8, #5203-5210	10.00	
P# block of 8, 5#+P	10.00	
Pane of 16	20.00	
Nos. 5203-5210 (8)	10.00	3.20

The typographed printing imitates the texture of the ball.

Die cut uncut press sheets of Nos. 5203-5210 were made available for sale. Values: cross gutter block of 8, $18; pairs with gutters between, $3.75 each. See note after No. 4693.

Counterfeits exist of Nos. 5203-5210. See the Postal Counterfeits section of this catalog.

See note after No. 1549.

AUGUST 21, 2017, TOTAL SOLAR ECLIPSE Ⓢ

Total Solar Eclipse — A4040

Designed by Antonio Alcalá. Printed by Banknote Corporation of America.

LITHOGRAPHED

Sheets of 128 in eight panes of 16

2017, June 20 **Tagged** ***Serpentine Die Cut 10½***

Self-Adhesive

5211 A4040 (49c) **multicolored**	1.25	.25
P# block of 4, 5#+B	5.00	
Pane of 16	20.00	

The moon, directly in front of the sun, is covered with a circle of thermochromic ink, which when warmed, allows the moon and the corona of the sun around the moon to be seen.

Die cut uncut press sheets of No. 5202 were made available for sale. Values: cross gutter block of 4, $9; pairs with gutters between, $3.75 each. See note after No. 4693.

See note after No. 1549.

PAINTINGS BY ANDREW WYETH (1917-2009) Ⓢ

Wind from the Sea, 1947 A4041

Big Room, 1988 A4042

Christina's World, 1948 A4043

Alvaro and Christina, 1968 A4044

Frostbitten, 1962 A4045

Sailor's Valentine, 1985 A4046

Soaring, 1942-50 A4047

North Light, 1984 A4048

Spring Fed, 1967 A4049

The Carry, 2003 A4050

Young Bull, 1960 A4051

My Studio, 1974 A4052

Designed by Derry Noyes. Printed by Ashton-Potter (USA) Ltd.

LITHOGRAPHED
Sheets of 108 in nine panes of 12
Serpentine Die Cut 10¾x10½

2017, July 12 **Tagged**

Self-Adhesive

5212	Pane of 12	15.00	
a.	A4041 (49c) **multicolored**	1.25	.50
b.	A4042 (49c) **multicolored**	1.25	.50
c.	A4043 (49c) **multicolored**	1.25	.50
d.	A4044 (49c) **multicolored**	1.25	.50
e.	A4045 (49c) **multicolored**	1.25	.50
f.	A4046 (49c) **multicolored**	1.25	.50
g.	A4047 (49c) **multicolored**	1.25	.50
h.	A4048 (49c) **multicolored**	1.25	.50
i.	A4049 (49c) **multicolored**	1.25	.50
j.	A4050 (49c) **multicolored**	1.25	.50
k.	A4051 (49c) **multicolored**	1.25	.50
l.	A4052 (49c) **multicolored**	1.25	.50

Die cut uncut press sheets of No. 5212 were made available for sale. Values: cross gutter block of 12, $18; pairs with gutters between, $4.25 each. See note after No. 4693.

See note after No. 1549.

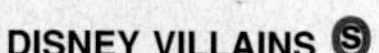

DISNEY VILLAINS Ⓢ

The Queen from *Snow White and the Seven Dwarfs* — A4053

Honest John from *Pinocchio* — A4054

Lady Tremaine from *Cinderella* — A4055

Queen of Hearts from *Alice in Wonderland* — A4056

Captain Hook from *Peter Pan* — A4057

Maleficent from *Sleeping Beauty* — A4058

Cruella De Vil from *One Hundred and One Dalmatians* — A4059

Ursula from *The Little Mermaid* — A4060

Gaston from *Beauty and the Beast* — A4061

Scar from *The Lion King* — A4062

Designed by Derry Noyes. Printed by Ashton-Potter (USA) Ltd.

LITHOGRAPHED

Sheets of 120 in six panes of 20

Serpentine Die Cut 10½x10¾

2017, July 15 **Tagged**

Self-Adhesive

5213	A4053	(49c) **multicolored**		1.25	.40
5214	A4054	(49c) **multicolored**		1.25	.40
5215	A4055	(49c) **multicolored**		1.25	.40
5216	A4056	(49c) **multicolored**		1.25	.40
5217	A4057	(49c) **multicolored**		1.25	.40
5218	A4058	(49c) **multicolored**		1.25	.40
5219	A4059	(49c) **multicolored**		1.25	.40
5220	A4060	(49c) **multicolored**		1.25	.40
5221	A4061	(49c) **multicolored**		1.25	.40
5222	A4062	(49c) **multicolored**		1.25	.40
a.		Block of 10, #5213-5222		12.50	
		P# block of 10, 2 sets of 5#+P		12.50	
		Pane of 20		25.00	
		Nos. 5213-5222 (10)		12.50	4.00

Die cut uncut press sheets of Nos. 5213-5222 were made available for sale. Values: cross gutter block of 10, $18; pairs with gutters between, $4.25 each. See note after No. 4693.

Counterfeits exist of Nos. 5213-5222. See the Postal Counterfeits section of this catalog.

See note after No. 1549.

SHARKS Ⓢ

Mako Shark A4063

Whale Shark A4064

Thresher Shark A4065

Hammerhead Shark A4066

Great White Shark A4067

Designed by Derry Noyes. Printed by Banknote Corporation of America.

LITHOGRAPHED

Sheets of 180 in nine panes of 20

2017, July 26 **Tagged** ***Serpentine Die Cut 10¾***

Self-Adhesive

5223	A4063	(49c) **multicolored**		1.25	.40
5224	A4064	(49c) **multicolored**		1.25	.40
5225	A4065	(49c) **multicolored**		1.25	.40
5226	A4066	(49c) **multicolored**		1.25	.40
5227	A4067	(49c) **multicolored**		1.25	.40
a.		Vert. strip of 5, #5223-5227		6.25	
		P# block of 10, 4#+B		12.50	
		Pane of 20		25.00	
		Nos. 5223-5227 (5)		6.25	2.00

Die cut uncut press sheets of Nos. 5223-5227 were made available for sale. Values: cross gutter block of 10, $18; pairs with gutters between, $4.25 each. See note after No. 4693.

Counterfeits exist of Nos. 5223-5227. See the Postal Counterfeits section of this catalog.

See note after No. 1549.

PROTECT POLLINATORS Ⓢ

Monarch Butterfly on Purple Coneflower A4068

Western Honeybee on Golden Ragwort A4069

Monarch Butterfly on Red Zinnia A4070

Western Honeybee on Purple New England Aster A4071

Monarch Butterfly on Goldenrod A4072

Designed by Derry Noyes. Printed by Ashton-Potter (USA) Ltd.

LITHOGRAPHED

Sheets of 180 in nine panes of 20

2017, Aug. 3 **Tagged** ***Serpentine Die Cut 10¾***

Self-Adhesive

5228	A4068	(49c) **multicolored**		1.25	.40
5229	A4069	(49c) **multicolored**		1.25	.40
5230	A4070	(49c) **multicolored**		1.25	.40
5231	A4071	(49c) **multicolored**		1.25	.40
5232	A4072	(49c) **multicolored**		1.25	.40
a.		Vert. strip of 5, #5228-5232		6.25	
		P# block of 10, 4#+P		12.50	
		Pane of 20		25.00	
		Nos. 5228-5232 (5)		6.25	2.00

Die cut uncut press sheets of Nos. 5228-5232 were made available for sale. Values: cross gutter block of 10, $18; pairs with gutters between, $4.25 each. See note after No. 4693.

See note after No. 1549.

FLOWERS FROM THE GARDEN Ⓢ

Red Camellias and Yellow Forsythia in Yellow Pitcher — A4073

White Peonies and Pink Tree Peonies in Clear Vase — A4074

Blue Hydrangeas in Blue Pot — A4075

Assorted Flowers in White Vase — A4076

Red Camellias and Yellow Forsythia in Yellow Pitcher — A4077

Assorted Flowers in White Vase — A4078

White Peonies and Pink Tree Peonies in Clear Vase — A4079

Blue Hydrangeas in Blue Pot — A4080

Designed by Derry Noyes. Printed by Banknote Corporation of America.

LITHOGRAPHED

Serpentine Die Cut 10¾ Vert.

2017, Aug. 16 **Tagged**

Coil Stamps
Self-Adhesive

5233 A4073 (49c) **multicolored** 1.25 .30
5234 A4074 (49c) **multicolored** 1.25 .30
5235 A4075 (49c) **multicolored** 1.25 .30
5236 A4076 (49c) **multicolored** 1.25 .30
a. Strip of 4, #5233-5236 5.00
P# strip of 5, #5234-5236, 2 #5233, #B1111 7.00
P# strip of 9, 3# 5235, 2 each #5233-5234, 5236, #B1111 12.00
P# single, #B1111 (#5235) — 3.00
Nos. 5233-5236 (4) 5.00 1.20

Booklet Stamps

Serpentine Die Cut 11 on 2 or 3 Sides

5237 A4077 (49c) **multicolored** 1.25 .30
5238 A4078 (49c) **multicolored** 1.25 .30
5239 A4079 (49c) **multicolored** 1.25 .30
5240 A4080 (49c) **multicolored** 1.25 .30
a. Block of 4, #5237-5240 5.00
b. Booklet pane of 20, 5 each #5237-5240 25.00
Nos. 5237-5240 (4) 5.00 1.20

No. 5240b is a double-sided booklet pane with 12 stamps on one side (3 each Nos. 5237-5240) and eight stamps (2 each Nos. 5237-5240) plus label (booklet cover) on the other side.

Die cut uncut press sheets of Nos. 5237-5240 were made available for sale. Values of varieties: cross gutter block of 4 with booklet cover, imperf. within, $10; cross gutter block of 4, imperf. within, $10; block of 4, horiz. imperf. between, $7.50; block of 4, vert. imperf. between, $8.50. See note after No. 4693.

See note after No. 1549.

FATHER THEODORE ("TED") HESBURGH

Hesburgh (1917-2015), President of University of Notre Dame — A4081

A4081a

Designed by Ethel Kessler. Printed by Ashton-Potter (USA) Ltd.

LITHOGRAPHED

Sheets of 120 in six panes of 20

2017, Sept. 1 **Tagged** ***Serpentine Die Cut 11***

Self-Adhesive

5241 A4081 (49c) **multicolored** ⓢ 1.25 .25
P# block of 4, 5#+P 5.00
Pane of 20 25.00

Coil Stamp

Serpentine Die Cut 9½ Horiz.

5242 A4081a (49c) **multicolored** ⓢ 1.25 .25
P# strip of 5, #P11111 7.00
P# single, #P11111 — 3.00

Die cut uncut press sheets of No. 5241 were made available for sale. Values: cross gutter block of 4, $9; pairs with gutters between, $3.75 each. See note after No. 4693. See note after No. 1549.

"THE SNOWY DAY," BY EZRA JACK KEATS ⓢ

Peter Making Snowball — A4082

Peter Sliding Down Mountain of Snow — A4083

Peter Making Snow Angel — A4084

Peter Leaving Footprints in Snow — A4085

Designed by Antonio Alcalá. Printed by Ashton-Potter (USA), Ltd.

LITHOGRAPHED

Serpentine Die Cut 10¾ on 2 or 3 Sides

2017, Oct. 4 **Tagged**

Booklet Stamps
Self-Adhesive

5243 A4082 (49c) **multicolored** 1.25 .30
5244 A4083 (49c) **multicolored** 1.25 .30
5245 A4084 (49c) **multicolored** 1.25 .30
5246 A4085 (49c) **multicolored** 1.25 .30
a. Block of 4, #5243-5246 5.00
b. Booklet pane of 20, 5 each #5243-5246 25.00
Nos. 5243-5246 (4) 5.00 1.20

No. 5246b is a double-sided booklet pane with 12 stamps on one side (3 each Nos. 5243-5246), and eight stamps (2 each Nos. 5243-5246) plus label (booklet cover) on the other side.

Die cut uncut press sheets of Nos. 5243-5246 were made available for sale. Values of varieties: cross gutter block of 4 with booklet cover, imperf. within, $10; cross gutter block of 4, imperf. within, $10; block of 4, horiz. imperf. between, $8.50; horiz. pair, imperf. between, $4. See note after No. 4693.

Counterfeits exist of No. 5243-5246. See the Postal Counterfeits section of this catalog.

CHRISTMAS CAROLS ⓢ

Christmas Lights, Cookies, and Line From "Deck the Halls" — A4086

Star of Bethlehem, Lamb, and Line From "Silent Night" — A4087

Snowflakes, Horse, and Line From "Jingle Bells" — A4088

Child, Santa Claus, and Line From "Jolly Old St. Nicholas" — A4089

Designed by Howard E. Paine. Printed by Banknote Corporation of America.

LITHOGRAPHED

Serpentine Die Cut 10¾ on 2 or 3 Sides

2017, Oct. 5 **Tagged**

Booklet Stamps
Self-Adhesive

5247 A4086 (49c) **multicolored** 1.25 .30
5248 A4087 (49c) **multicolored** 1.25 .30
5249 A4088 (49c) **multicolored** 1.25 .30
5250 A4089 (49c) **multicolored** 1.25 .30
a. Block of 4, #5247-5250 5.00
b. Booklet pane of 20, 5 each #5247-5250 25.00
Nos. 5247-5250 (4) 5.00 1.20

No. 5250b is a double-sided booklet pane with 12 stamps on one side (3 each Nos. 5247-5250), and eight stamps (2 each Nos. 5247-5250) plus label (booklet cover) on the other side.

Die cut uncut press sheets of Nos. 5247-5250 were made available for sale. Values of varieties: cross gutter block of 4 with booklet cover, imperf. within, $10; cross gutter block of 4, imperf. within, $10; block of 4, horiz. imperf. between, $8.50; block of 4, vert. imperf. between, $7.50. See note after No. 4693.

Counterfeits exist of Nos. 5247-5250. See the Postal Counterfeits section of this catalog.

NATIONAL MUSEUM OF AFRICAN AMERICAN HISTORY AND CULTURE ⓢ

Museum Building, Washington, D.C. — A4090

Designed by Antonio Alcalá. Printed by Banknote Corporation of America.

LITHOGRAPHED

Sheets of 180 in nine panes of 20

Serpentine Die Cut 10¾x10½

2017, Oct. 13 **Tagged**

Self-Adhesive

5251 A4090 (49c) **multicolored** 1.25 .25
P# block of 4, 4#+B 5.00
Pane of 20 25.00

Die cut uncut press sheets of No. 5251 were made available for sale. Values: cross gutter block of 4, $9; pairs with gutters between, $3.75 each. See note after No. 4693.

See note after No. 1549.

HISTORY OF ICE HOCKEY ⓢ

Player Wearing Helmet and Protective Gear — A4091

Player Wearing Hat and Scarf — A4092

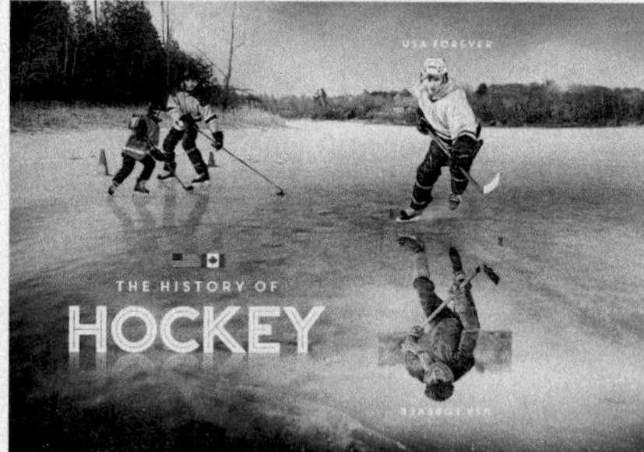

A4092a

Designed by Subplot Design, Inc. Printed by Ashton-Potter (USA), Ltd.

LITHOGRAPHED

Sheets of 120 in six panes of 20

2017, Oct. 20 **Tagged** ***Serpentine Die Cut 11***

Self-Adhesive

5252 A4091 (49c) **multicolored** 1.25 .25
a. As No. 5252, matte-finish stamp 1.25 .25
5253 A4092 (49c) **multicolored** 1.25 .25
a. As No. 5253, matte-finish stamp 1.25 .25
b. Vert. pair, #5252-5253 2.50

c. A4092a Souvenir sheet of 2, #5252a-5253a 2.50
P# block of 4, 4#+P 5.00
Pane of 20 25.00

On Nos. 5253b and 5253c, stamps are printed tete-beche. Stamps from No. 5253b have a glossier finish than those on No. 5253c. The matte finish on Nos. 5252a and 5253a is due to block tagging. Adjacent horizontal stamps have selvage between them.

Die cut uncut press sheets of No. 5252-5253 were made available for sale. Values: cross gutter block of 4, $9; pairs with gutters between, $3.75 each. See note after No. 4693.

See note after No. 1549.

See Canada Nos. 3039-3041.

CHINESE NEW YEAR Ⓢ

Year of the Dog — A4093

Designed by Ethel Kessler. Printed by Banknote Corporation of America.

LITHOGRAPHED

Sheets of 144 in 12 panes of 12

2018, Jan. 11 Tagged *Serpentine Die Cut 10¾*

Self-Adhesive

5254 A4093 (49c) **multicolored** 1.25 .25
Pane of 12 15.00

Die cut partial press sheets (containing 72 stamps) of No. 5254 were made available for sale. Values: cross gutter block of 4, $9; pairs with gutters between, $4.25 each. See note after No. 4693. See note after No. 1549.

LOVE Ⓢ

Flowers — A4094

Designed by Greg Breeding. Printed by Banknote Corporation of America.

LITHOGRAPHED

Sheets of 160 in eight panes of 20

Serpentine Die Cut 11x10¾

2018, Jan. 18 Tagged

Self-Adhesive

5255 A4094 (49c) **multicolored** 1.25 .25
P# block of 4, 5#+B 5.00
Pane of 20 25.00

Die cut uncut press sheets of No. 5255 were made available for sale. Values: cross gutter block of 4, $9; pairs with gutters between, $4.25 each. See note after No. 4693. See note after No. 1549.

Counterfeits exist of No. 5255. See the Postal Counterfeits section of this catalog.

FRUIT Ⓢ

Meyer Lemons — A4095

Designed by Derry Noyes. Printed by Banknote Corporation of America.

LITHOGRAPHED

Serpentine Die Cut 10¾ Vert.

2018, Jan. 19 Untagged

Coil Stamp

Self-Adhesive

5256 A4095 2c **multicolored** .30 .25
Pair .30
P# strip of 5, #B11111 1.25
P# single, #B11111 — .50

See note after No. 1549.

See Nos. 5038-5039, 5177-5178, 5201.

AMERICAN LANDMARKS ISSUE

Byodo-In Temple, Kaneohe, Hawaii A4096

Sleeping Bear Dunes, Michigan A4097

Designed by Greg Breeding. Printed by Ashton-Potter (USA) Ltd.

LITHOGRAPHED

Sheets of 48 in 12 panes of 4 (#5257), Sheets of 24 in six panes of 4 (#5258)

Serpentine Die Cut 10¾x10½

2018, Jan. 21 Tagged

Self-Adhesive

5257 A4096 $6.70 **multicolored** Ⓢ 15.00 7.75
Pane of 4 60.00
5258 A4097 $24.70 **multicolored** Ⓢ 60.00 25.00
Pane of 4 240.00

See note after No. 1549.

BLACK HERITAGE

Lena Horne (1917-2010), Singer — A4098

Designed by Ethel Kessler. Printed by Banknote Corporation of America.

LITHOGRAPHED

Sheets of 240 in 12 panes of 20

2018, Jan. 30 Tagged *Serpentine Die Cut 10¾*

Self-Adhesive

5259 A4098 (50c) **multicolored** Ⓢ 1.25 .25
P# block of 4, 5#+B 5.00
Pane of 20 25.00

Die cut partial press sheets (containing 120 stamps) of No. 5259 were made available for sale. Values: cross gutter block of 4, $9; pairs with gutters between, $3.75 each. See note after No. 4693. See note after No. 1549.

Flag — A4099

A4099a

Designed by Kit Hinrichs. Printed by Ashton-Potter (USA) Ltd. (#5260), Banknote Corporation of America (#5261).

LITHOGRAPHED

Serpentine Die Cut 9½ Vert.

2018, Feb. 9 Tagged

Coil Stamps

Self-Adhesive

Microprinted "USPS" at Left of Flag Fold on Fourth White Stripe

5260 A4099 (50c) **multicolored** Ⓢ 1.25 .25
Pair 2.50
P# strip of 5, #P111 7.50
P# single, #P111 — 2.50

Counterfeits exist of No. 5260. See the Postal Counterfeits section of this catalog.

Serpentine Die Cut 11 Vert.

Microprinted "USPS" at Right of Flag Fold on Fifth White Stripe

5261 A4099a (50c) **multicolored** Ⓢ 1.25 .25
Pair 2.50
P# strip of 5, #B111 7.50
P# single, #B111 — 2.50
a. Tagging omitted —

Counterfeits exist of No. 5261. See the Postal Counterfeits section of this catalog.

A4099b

A4099c

Printed by Ashton-Potter (USA) Ltd. (#5262), Banknote Corporation of America (#5263).

Booklet Stamps Microprinted "USPS" at Left of Flag Fold on Fourth Red Stripe

Serpentine Die Cut 11¼x10¾ on 2 or 3 Sides

5262 A4099b (50c) **multicolored** Ⓢ 1.25 .25
a. Booklet pane of 20 25.00

Counterfeits exist of No. 5262. See the Postal Counterfeits section of this catalog.

Microprinted "USPS" at Right of Flag Fold on Fifth White Stripe

5263 A4099c (50c) **multicolored** Ⓢ 1.25 .25
a. Booklet pane of 20 25.00

Nos. 5262a and 5263a are double-sided booklets with 12 stamps on one side and eight stamps plus a label that serves as the booklet cover on the other side.

See note after No. 1549.

Counterfeits exist of No. 5263. See the Postal Counterfeits section of this catalog.

BIOLUMINESCENT LIFE Ⓢ

Octopus A4100

Jellyfish A4101

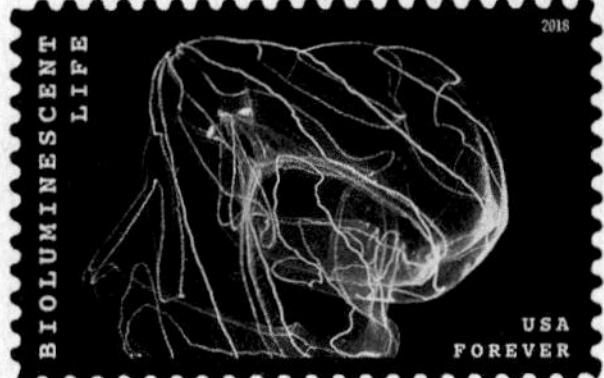

Comb Jelly — A4102

Mushrooms
A4103

Firefly
A4104

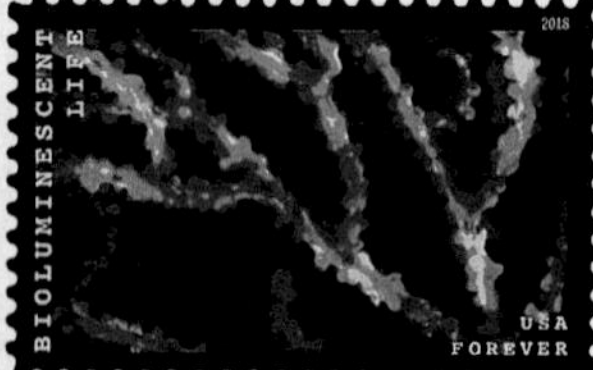

Bamboo
Coral — A4105

Marine Worm
A4106

Crown Jellyfish
A4107

Marine Worm
A4108

Sea
Pen — A4109

Designed by Derry Noyes. Printed by Banknote Corporation of America.

LITHOGRAPHED
Sheets of 180 in nine panes of 20

2018, Feb. 22 Tagged ***Serpentine Die Cut 11***
Self-Adhesive

5264 A4100 (50c) **multicolored**		1.25	.40
5265 A4101 (50c) **multicolored**		1.25	.40
5266 A4102 (50c) **multicolored**		1.25	.40
5267 A4103 (50c) **multicolored**		1.25	.40
5268 A4104 (50c) **multicolored**		1.25	.40
5269 A4105 (50c) **multicolored**		1.25	.40
5270 A4106 (50c) **multicolored**		1.25	.40
5271 A4107 (50c) **multicolored**		1.25	.40
5272 A4108 (50c) **multicolored**		1.25	.40
5273 A4109 (50c) **multicolored**		1.25	.40
a.	Block of 10, #5264-5273	12.50	
	Pane of 20	25.00	
	Nos. 5264-5273 (10)	12.50	4.00

Die cut uncut press sheets of Nos. 5264-5273 were made available for sale. Values: cross gutter block of 10, $18; pairs with gutters between, $4.25 each. See note after No. 4693.

See note after No. 1549.

ILLINOIS STATEHOOD, 200TH ANNIV.

Map of Illinois and Sun Rays — A4110

Designed by Michael Konetzka. Printed by Banknote Corporation of America.

LITHOGRAPHED
Sheets of 240 in 12 panes of 20

2018, Mar. 5 Tagged ***Serpentine Die Cut 11***
Self-Adhesive

5274 A4110 (50c) **multicolored** ⓢ		1.25	.25
	P# block of 4, 7#+B	5.00	
	Pane of 20	25.00	

Die cut partial press sheets (containing 120 stamps) of No. 5274 were made available for sale. Values: cross gutter block of 4, $9; pairs with gutters between, $3.75 each. See note after No. 4693. See note after No. 1549.

MISTER ROGERS

Fred Rogers (1928-2003), Host of Children's Television Show, *Mister Rogers*, and Puppet, King Friday XIII — A4111

Designed by Derry Noyes. Printed by Banknote Corporation of America.

LITHOGRAPHED
Sheets of 240 in 12 panes of 20

2018, Mar. 23 Tagged ***Serpentine Die Cut 11***
Self-Adhesive

5275 A4111 (50c) **multicolored** ⓢ		1.25	.25
	P# block of 4, 6#+B	5.00	
	Pane of 20	25.00	

Die cut partial press sheets (containing 120 stamps) of No. 5275 were made available for sale. Values: cross gutter block of 4, $9; pairs with gutters between, $3.75 each. See note after No. 4693. See note after No. 1549.

SCIENCE, TECHNOLOGY, ENGINEERING AND MATHEMATICS (STEM) EDUCATION

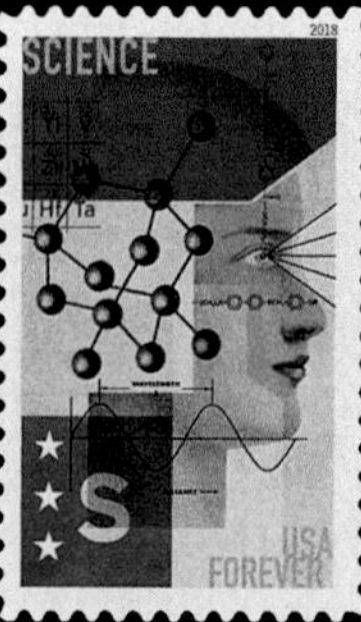

Head and Symbols of Science Education — A4112

Head and Symbols of Technology Education — A4113

Head and Symbols of Engineering Education — A4114

Head and Symbols of Mathematics Education — A4115

Designed by David Plunkert. Printed by Ashton-Potter (USA) Ltd.

LITHOGRAPHED
Sheets of 240 in 12 panes of 20

2018, Apr. 6 Tagged ***Serpentine Die Cut 11***
Self-Adhesive

5276 A4112 (50c) **multicolored** ⓢ		1.25	.30
5277 A4113 (50c) **multicolored** ⓢ		1.25	.30
5278 A4114 (50c) **multicolored** ⓢ		1.25	.30
5279 A4115 (50c) **multicolored** ⓢ		1.25	.30
a.	Vert. strip of 4, #5276-5279	5.00	
	P# block of 8, 4#+P	10.00	
	Pane of 20	25.00	
	Nos. 5276-5279 (4)	5.00	1.20

Die cut partial press sheets (containing 120 stamps) of Nos. 5276-5279 were made available for sale. Values: cross gutter block of 8, $18; pairs with gutters between, $3.75 each. See note after No. 4693. See note after No. 1549.

Peace Rose — A4116

Designed by Ethel Kessler. Printed by Ashton-Potter (USA) Ltd.

LITHOGRAPHED
Serpentine Die Cut 11¼x10¾ on 2 or 3 Sides
2018, Apr. 21 Tagged
Booklet Stamp
Self-Adhesive

5280 A4116 (50c) **multicolored** ⓢ		1.25	.25
a.	Booklet pane of 20	25.00	

No. 5280a is a double-sided booklet with 12 stamps on one side and eight stamps plus a label that serves as the booklet cover on the other side.
See note after No. 1549.

AIR MAIL, CENT.

Curtiss JN-4H "Jenny" Biplane
A4117

A4117a

Designed by Dan Gretta. Printed by Ashton-Potter (USA) Ltd.

ENGRAVED

Sheets of 120 in six panes of 20

2018 Tagged *Serpentine Die Cut 10¾*

Self-Adhesive

5281 A4117 (50c) **blue,** *May 1* ⓢ	1.25	.25
P# block of 4, 1#+P	5.00	
Pane of 20	25.00	
5282 A4117a (50c) **carmine lake,** *Aug. 11* ⓢ	1.25	.25
P# block of 4, 1#+P	5.00	
Pane of 20	25.00	

Die cut press sheets of Nos. 5281 and 5282 were each made available for sale. Values: cross gutter block of 4, $9; pairs with gutters between, $3.75 each. See note after No. 4693. See note after No. 1549.

SALLY RIDE

Sally Ride (1951-2012), First American Woman in Space, and Space Shuttle Launch — A4118

Designed by Ethel Kessler. Printed by Ashton-Potter (USA), Ltd.

LITHOGRAPHED

Sheets of 180 in nine panes of 20

Serpentine Die Cut 10½x10¾

2018, May 23 Tagged

Self-Adhesive

5283 A4118 (50c) **multicolored** ⓢ	1.25	.25
P# block of 4, 5#+P	5.00	
Pane of 20	25.00	

Die cut press sheets of No. 5283 were made available for sale. Values: cross gutter block of 4, $9; pairs with gutters between, $3.75 each. See note after No. 4693. See note after No. 1549.

FLAG ACT OF 1818, BICENT.

20-Star Flag — A4119

Designed by Kit Hinrichs. Printed by Ashton-Potter (USA) Ltd.

LITHOGRAPHED

Sheets of 120 in six panes of 20

2018, June 9 Tagged *Serpentine Die Cut 10¾*

Self-Adhesive

5284 A4119 (50c) **multicolored** ⓢ	1.25	.25
P# block of 4, 4#+P	5.00	
Pane of 20	25.00	

FROZEN TREATS ⓢ

A4120

A4121

A4122

A4123

A4124

A4125

A4126

A4127

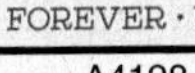

A4128

A4129

Designed by Leslie Baldani. Printed by Ashton-Potter (USA) Ltd.

LITHOGRAPHED

Serpentine Die Cut 11¼x10¾ on 2 or 3 Sides

2018, June 20 Tagged

Booklet Stamps

Self-Adhesive

5285 A4120 (50c) **multicolored**	1.25	.40
5286 A4121 (50c) **multicolored**	1.25	.40
5287 A4122 (50c) **multicolored**	1.25	.40
5288 A4123 (50c) **multicolored**	1.25	.40
5289 A4124 (50c) **multicolored**	1.25	.40
5290 A4125 (50c) **multicolored**	1.25	.40
5291 A4126 (50c) **multicolored**	1.25	.40
5292 A4127 (50c) **multicolored**	1.25	.40
5293 A4128 (50c) **multicolored**	1.25	.40
5294 A4129 (50c) **multicolored**	1.25	.40
a. Block of 10, #5285-5294	12.50	
b. Booklet pane of 20, 2 each #5285-5294	25.00	
Nos. 5285-5294 (10)	12.50	4.00

Nos. 5294b has a scratch-and-sniff coating with a fruity aroma, and is a double-sided booklet with 12 stamps on one side (Nos. 5286-5289, 5291-5294, 2 each Nos 5285, 5290), and eight stamps (Nos. 5286-5289, 5291-5294) plus a label that serves as the booklet cover on the other side.

Die cut uncut press sheets of Nos. 5285-5294 were made available for sale. Values: cross gutter block of 10 with booklet cover, $17; block of 10 with horiz. gutter between, $17. See note after No. 4693.

See note after No. 1549.

Counterfeits exist of No. 5285-5294. See the Postal Counterfeits section of this catalog.

STATUE OF FREEDOM ⓢ

Head of Statue of Freedom on U.S. Capitol Dome — A4130

A4130a

A4130b

Designed by Greg Breeding. Printed by Banknote Corporation of America.

LITHOGRAPHED & ENGRAVED

Sheets of 60 in six panes of 10 (#5295-5296), Sheets of 40 in 10 panes of 4 (#5297)

Serpentine Die Cut 10¾x10½

2018, June 27 Tagged

Self-Adhesive

5295 A4130 $1 **emer, reddsh pink & black**	2.00	.50
P# block of 4, 3#+B	8.00	
Pane of 10	20.00	
5296 A4130a $2 **indigo, reddsh pink & black**	4.00	1.00
P# block of 4, 3#+B	16.00	
Pane of 10	40.00	
5297 A4130b $5 **brick red, reddsh pink & black**	10.00	2.50
Pane of 4	40.00	
Nos. 5295-5297 (3)	16.00	4.00

Optically-variable ink was used for the numerals in the denominations.

O BEAUTIFUL ⓢ

Death Valley National Park, California and Nevada — A4131

Three Fingers Mountain, Washington — A4132

Double Rainbow Over Field, Kansas — A4133

Great Smoky Mountains National Park, North Carolina and Tennessee — A4134

Field of Wheat, Wisconsin — A4135

Plowed Wheat Fields, Palouse Hills, Washington — A4136

Grasslands Wildlife Management Area, Merced County, California — A4137

Field of Wheat, Montana — A4138

Yosemite National Park, California — A4139

Crater Lake National Park, Oregon — A4140

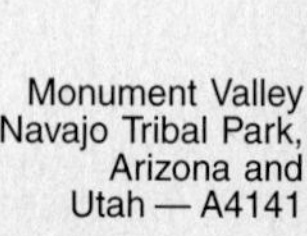

Monument Valley Navajo Tribal Park, Arizona and Utah — A4141

Maroon Bells, Colorado — A4142

Sunrise Near Orinda, California — A4143

Pigeon Point, Near Pescadero, California — A4144

Edna Valley, San Luis Obispo County, California — A4145

Livermore, California — A4146

Napali Coast State Wilderness Park, Hawaii — A4147

Lone Ranch Beach, Oregon — A4148

Canaveral National Seashore, Florida — A4149

Bailey Island, Maine — A4150

Designed by Ethel Kessler. Printed by Ashton-Potter (USA), Ltd.

LITHOGRAPHED

Sheets of 120 in six panes of 20

2018, July 4 **Tagged** ***Serpentine Die Cut 10½***

Self-Adhesive

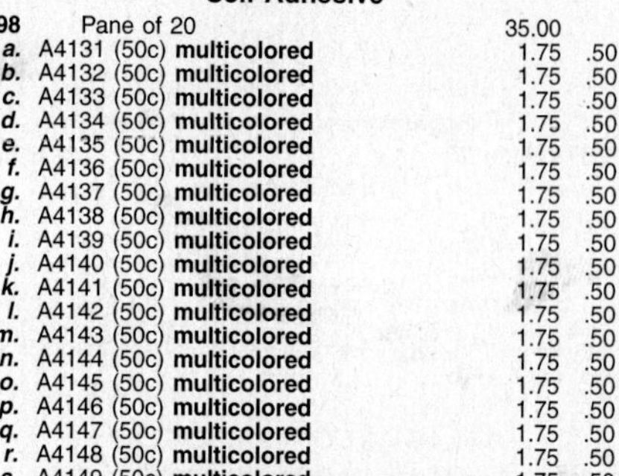

5298	Pane of 20	35.00	
a.	A4131 (50c) **multicolored**	1.75	.50
b.	A4132 (50c) **multicolored**	1.75	.50
c.	A4133 (50c) **multicolored**	1.75	.50
d.	A4134 (50c) **multicolored**	1.75	.50
e.	A4135 (50c) **multicolored**	1.75	.50
f.	A4136 (50c) **multicolored**	1.75	.50
g.	A4137 (50c) **multicolored**	1.75	.50
h.	A4138 (50c) **multicolored**	1.75	.50
i.	A4139 (50c) **multicolored**	1.75	.50
j.	A4140 (50c) **multicolored**	1.75	.50
k.	A4141 (50c) **multicolored**	1.75	.50
l.	A4142 (50c) **multicolored**	1.75	.50
m.	A4143 (50c) **multicolored**	1.75	.50
n.	A4144 (50c) **multicolored**	1.75	.50
o.	A4145 (50c) **multicolored**	1.75	.50
p.	A4146 (50c) **multicolored**	1.75	.50
q.	A4147 (50c) **multicolored**	1.75	.50
r.	A4148 (50c) **multicolored**	1.75	.50
s.	A4149 (50c) **multicolored**	1.75	.50
t.	A4150 (50c) **multicolored**	1.75	.50

Die cut uncut press sheets of Nos. 5298 were made available for sale. Values: cross gutter block of 20, $30; pairs with gutters between, $4.25 each.

See note after No. 4693. See note after No. 1549.

SCOOBY-DOO

Cartoon Character Scooby-Doo Watering Plant A4151

Designed by Greg Breeding. Printed by Ashton-Potter (USA), Ltd.

LITHOGRAPHED

Sheets of 72 in six panes of 12

Serpentine Die Cut 10¾x10½

2018, July 14 **Tagged**

Self-Adhesive

5299	A4151 (50c) **multicolored** ⓢ	1.25	.25
	P# block of 4, 5#+P	5.00	
	Pane of 12	15.00	

Die cut press sheets of No. 5299 were made available for sale. Values: cross gutter block of 4, $9; pairs with gutters between, $3.75 each. See note after No. 4693. See note after No. 1549.

Counterfeits exist of No. 5299. See the Postal Counterfeits section of this catalog.

WORLD WAR I, CENT.

Member of American Expeditionary Force Holding Flag — A4152

Designed by Greg Breeding. Printed by Ashton-Potter (USA), Ltd.

LITHOGRAPHED
Sheets of 120 in six panes of 20

2018, July 27 Tagged *Serpentine Die Cut 10¾*
Self-Adhesive

5300 A4152 (50c) **multicolored** Ⓢ	1.25	.25
P# block of 4, 7#+P	5.00	
Pane of 20	25.00	

Die cut press sheets of No. 5300 were made available for sale. Values: cross gutter block of 4, $9; pairs with gutters between, $3.75 each. See note after No. 4693. See note after No. 1549.

THE ART OF MAGIC Ⓢ

Rabbit in Hat — A4153

Fortune Teller and Crystal Ball — A4154

Levitating Woman and Hoop — A4155

Empty Bird Cage — A4156

Bird Emerging From Flower — A4157

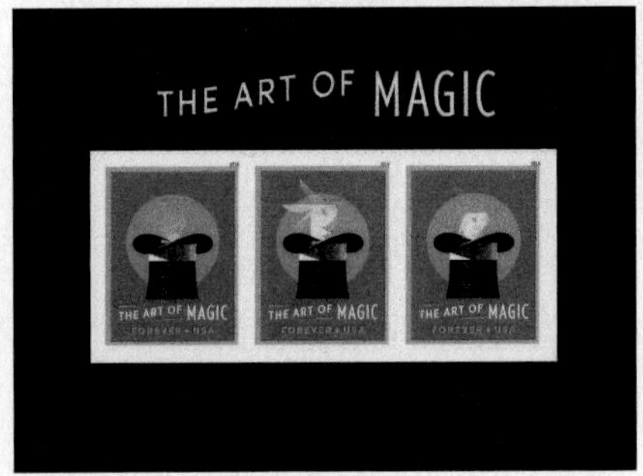

A4153a

Designed by Greg Breeding. Printed by Banknote Corporation of America.

LITHOGRAPHED (Nos. 5301-5305), TYPOGRAPHED WITH LENTICULAR LENS AFFIXED (No. 5306)
Sheets of 120 in six panes of 20 (Nos. 5301-5305)
Serpentine Die Cut 10½x10¾

2018, Aug. 7 Tagged
Self-Adhesive

5301 A4153 (50c) **multicolored**	1.25	.40
5302 A4154 (50c) **multicolored**	1.25	.40
5303 A4155 (50c) **multicolored**	1.25	.40
5304 A4156 (50c) **multicolored**	1.25	.40
5305 A4157 (50c) **multicolored**	1.25	.40
a. Horiz. strip of 5, #5301-5305	6.25	
P# block of 10, 9#+B	12.50	
Pane of 20	25.00	
Nos. 5301-5305 (5)	6.25	2.00

Souvenir Sheet

5306 A4153a Sheet of 3 #5306a	3.75	
a. (50c) Single stamp	1.25	.30
b. As No. 5306, die cutting omitted	*800.00*	

The printing method used on No. 5306a makes the rabbit in the vignette appear and disappear when the stamp is tilted. Die cut press sheets of No. 5301-5305 were made available for sale. Values: cross gutter block of 4, $9; pairs with gutters between, $3.75 each. See note after No. 4693. See note after No. 1549.

DRAGONS Ⓢ

Green Dragon and Castle — A4158

Purple Dragon and Castle — A4159

Black Dragon and Ship — A4160

Orange Dragon and Pagoda — A4161

Designed by Greg Breeding. Printed by Banknote Corporation of America.

LITHOGRAPHED WITH FOIL APPLICATION
Sheets of 64 in four panes of 16

2018, Aug. 9 Tagged *Serpentine Die Cut 10¾*
Self-Adhesive

5307 A4158 (50c) **multicolored**	1.25	.30
5308 A4159 (50c) **multicolored**	1.25	.30
5309 A4160 (50c) **multicolored**	1.25	.30
5310 A4161 (50c) **multicolored**	1.25	.30
a. Strip or block of 4, #5307-5310	5.00	
b. Horiz. strip of 4, #5307-5310, with die cutting missing (PS)	*400.00*	
P# block of 4, 4#+B	5.00	
Pane of 16	20.00	
Nos. 5307-5310 (4)	5.00	1.20

Die cut press sheets of Nos. 5307-5310 were made available for sale. Values: cross gutter block of 4, $9; pairs with gutters between, $3.75 each. See note after No. 4693. See note after No. 1549.

Poinsettia A4162

Designed by Greg Breeding. Printed by Banknote Corporation of America.

LITHOGRAPHED
Sheets of 60 in six panes of 10

2018, Aug. 26 Tagged *Serpentine Die Cut*
Self-Adhesive

5311 A4162 ($1.15) **multicolored** Ⓢ	2.80	.50
P# block of 4, 5#+B	11.20	
Pane of 10	28.00	

Unused values are for stamps with surrounding selvage. Adjacent stamps are separated by rouletting.

Counterfeits exist of No. 5311. See the Postal Counterfeits section of this catalog.

MUSIC ICONS

John Lennon (1940-80), Rock Musician — A4163

A4163a

A4163b

A4163c

Designed by Neal Ashby. Printed by Banknote Corporation of America.

LITHOGRAPHED
Sheets of 96 in six panes of 16

2018, Sept. 7 Tagged *Serpentine Die Cut 10¾*
Self-Adhesive
Color of Shoulders

5312 A4163 (50c) **red** Ⓢ 1.25 .30
5313 A4163a (50c) **red lilac** Ⓢ 1.25 .30
5314 A4163b (50c) **dark violet** Ⓢ 1.25 .30
5315 A4163c (50c) **blue** Ⓢ 1.25 .30
a. Vert. strip of 4, #5312-5315 5.00
Pane of 16 20.00
b. As "a," die cutting omitted —
Nos. 5312-5315 (4) 5.00 1.20

Adjacent horizontal or vertical stamps have selvage between the stamps.

Die cut press sheets of Nos. 5312-5315 were made available for sale. Values: cross gutter block of 8, $18; pairs with gutters between, $3.75 each. See note after No. 4693. See note after No. 1549.

FIRST RESPONDERS

Firefighter, Paramedic, and Law Enforcement Officer A4164

Designed by Antonio Alcalá. Printed by Ashton-Potter (USA), Ltd.

LITHOGRAPHED
Sheets of 120 in six panes of 20

2018, Sept. 13 Tagged *Serpentine Die Cut 11*
Self-Adhesive

5316 A4164 (50c) **multicolored** Ⓢ 1.25 .25
P# block of 4, 4#+P 5.00
Pane of 20 25.00

Die cut press sheets of No. 5316 were made available for sale. Values: cross gutter block of 4, $9; pairs with gutters between, $3.75 each. See note after No. 4693. See note after No. 1549.

BIRDS IN WINTER Ⓢ

Black-capped Chickadee — A4165

Northern Cardinal — A4166

Red-bellied Woodpecker — A4167

Blue Jay — A4168

Designed by Antonio Alcalá. Printed by Banknote Corporation of America.

LITHOGRAPHED
Serpentine Die Cut 10¾ on 2 or 3 Sides

2018, Sept. 22 Tagged
Booklet Stamps
Self-Adhesive

5317 A4165 (50c) **multicolored** 1.25 .30
5318 A4166 (50c) **multicolored** 1.25 .30
5319 A4167 (50c) **multicolored** 1.25 .30
5320 A4168 (50c) **multicolored** 1.25 .30
a. Block of 4, #5317-5320 5.00
b. Booklet pane of 20, 5 each #5317-5320 25.00
Nos. 5317-5320 (4) 5.00 1.20

No. 5320b is a double-sided booklet pane with 12 stamps on one side (3 each Nos. 5317-5320), and eight stamps (2 each Nos. 5317-5320) plus label (booklet cover) on the other side.

Die cut uncut press sheets of Nos. 5317-5320 were made available for sale. Values of varieties: cross gutter block of 4 with booklet cover, imperf. within, $10; cross gutter block of 4, imperf. within, $10; block of 4, horiz. imperf. between, $8.50; horiz. pair, imperf. between, $4. See note after No. 4693. See note after No. 1549.

HOT WHEELS TOY CARS, 50TH ANNIV. Ⓢ

Purple Passion A4169

Rocket-Bye-Baby — A4170

Rigor Motor A4171

Rodger Dodger A4172

Mach Speeder A4173

Twin Mill A4174

Bone Shaker A4175

HW40 A4176

Deora II A4177

Sharkruiser A4178

Designed by Greg Breeding. Printed by Banknote Corporation of America.

LITHOGRAPHED

Sheets of 160 in eight panes of 20

2018, Sept. 29 Tagged *Serpentine Die Cut 10¾*

Self-Adhesive

5321 A4169 (50c) **multicolored**			1.25	.40
5322 A4170 (50c) **multicolored**			1.25	.40
5323 A4171 (50c) **multicolored**			1.25	.40
5324 A4172 (50c) **multicolored**			1.25	.40
5325 A4173 (50c) **multicolored**			1.25	.40
5326 A4174 (50c) **multicolored**			1.25	.40
5327 A4175 (50c) **multicolored**			1.25	.40
5328 A4176 (50c) **multicolored**			1.25	.40
5329 A4177 (50c) **multicolored**			1.25	.40
5330 A4178 (50c) **multicolored**			1.25	.40
Pane of 20, 2 each #5321-5330, 2 sets of 5#+P			25.00	
Nos. 5321-5330 (10)			12.50	4.00

Die cut press sheets of No. 5321-5330 were made available for sale. Values: pairs with gutters between, $3.75 each. See note after No. 4693. See note after No. 1549.

Counterfeits exist of Nos. 5321-5330. See the Postal Counterfeits section of this catalog.

CHRISTMAS Ⓢ

Madonna and Child, by Bachiacca — A4179

Head of Santa Claus, by Haddon Sundblom — A4180

Santa Claus and Wreath, by Sundblom — A4181

Santa Claus and Book, by Sundblom — A4182

Santa Claus and Card, by Sundblom — A4183

Santa Claus and Book, by Sundblom — A4184

Designed by Greg Breeding. Printed by Banknote Corporation of America (No. 5331), Ashton-Potter (USA) Ltd. (Nos. 5332-5336).

LITHOGRAPHED

Serpentine Die Cut 10¾x11 on 2 or 3 Sides

2018 Tagged

Booklet Stamps

Self-Adhesive

5331 A4179 (50c) **multicolored**, *Oct. 3*		1.25	.25
a.	Booklet pane of 20	25.00	
5332 A4180 (50c) **multicolored**, *Oct. 11*		1.25	.30
5333 A4181 (50c) **multicolored**, *Oct. 11*		1.25	.30
5334 A4182 (50c) **multicolored**, *Oct. 11*		1.25	.30
5335 A4183 (50c) **multicolored**, *Oct. 11*		1.25	.30
a.	Block of 4, #5332-5335	5.00	
b.	Booklet pane of 20, 5 each #5332-5335	25.00	
c.	As "a," die cutting omitted	—	
	Nos. 5331-5335 (5)	6.25	1.45

Souvenir Sheet

Serpentine Die Cut 10¾

5336 A4184 (50c) **multicolored**, *Oct. 11*		1.25	.30
a.	Single stamp	1.25	.30

No. 5331a is a double-sided booklet panes with 12 stamps on one side and eight stamps plus label (booklet cover) on the other side. No. 5335b is a double-sided booklet pane with 12 stamps on one side (3 each Nos. 5332-5335) and eight stamps (2 each Nos. 5332-5335) plus label (booklet cover) on the other side.

Die cut uncut press sheets of Nos. 5331 and 5332-5335 were made available for sale. Values of varieties: cross gutter block of 4 with booklet cover, imperf. within, $10; cross gutter block of 4, imperf. within, $10; blocks of 4 (Nos. 5332-5335), imperf. vert. or horiz. between, $7.50 each; vert. pair, imperf. between, $4; horiz. pair, imperf. between, $6. See note after No. 4693. See note after No. 1549.

The three examples of No. 5335c are from a booklet pane missing the stamps on the 8-stamp side.

Counterfeits exist of No. 5332-5335. See the Postal Counterfeits section of this catalog.

KWANZAA Ⓢ

Family and Kinara — A4185

Designed by Derry Noyes. Printed by Banknote Corporation of America.

LITHOGRAPHED

Sheets of 120 in six panes of 20

2018, Oct. 10 Tagged *Serpentine Die Cut 10¾*

Self-Adhesive

5337 A4185 (50c) **multicolored**	1.25	.25
P# block of 4, 4#+B	5.00	
Pane of 20	25.00	

Die cut uncut press sheets of No. 5337 were made available for sale. Values: cross gutter block of 4, $9; pairs with gutters between, $4.25 each. See note after No. 4693. See note after No. 1549.

HANUKKAH Ⓢ

Menorah — A4186

Designed by Ethel Kessler. Printed by Banknote Corporation of America.

LITHOGRAPHED

Sheets of 120 in six panes of 20

2018, Oct. 16 Tagged *Serpentine Die Cut 10¾*

Self-Adhesive

5338 A4186 (50c) **multicolored**	1.25	.25
P# block of 4, 5#+B	5.00	
Pane of 20	25.00	

Die cut uncut press sheets of No. 5338 were made available for sale. Values: cross gutter block of 4, $9; pairs with gutters between, $4.25 each. See note after No. 4693. See note after No. 1549.

See Israel No. 2200.

LOVE Ⓢ

Hearts — A4187

Designed by Antonio Alcalá. Printed by Banknote Corporation of America.

LITHOGRAPHED

Sheets of 160 in eight panes of 20

Serpentine Die Cut 10¾x11

2019, Jan. 10 Tagged

Self-Adhesive

5339 A4187 (50c) **multicolored**	1.25	.25
P# block of 4, 5#+B	5.00	
Pane of 20	25.00	

Die cut uncut press sheets of No. 5339 were made available for sale. Values: cross gutter block of 4, $9; pairs with gutters between, $4.25 each. See note after No. 4693. See note after No. 1549.

Counterfeits exist of No. 5339. See the Postal Counterfeits section of this catalog.

CHINESE NEW YEAR Ⓢ

Year of the Boar — A4188

Designed by Ethel Kessler. Printed by Banknote Corporation of America.

LITHOGRAPHED

Sheets of 144 in 12 panes of 12

2019, Jan. 17 Tagged *Serpentine Die Cut 10¾*

Self-Adhesive

5340 A4188 (50c) **multicolored**	1.25	.25
Pane of 12	15.00	

Die cut partial press sheets (containing 72 stamps) of No. 5340 were made available for sale. Values: cross gutter block of 4, $9; pairs with gutters between, $4.25 each. See note after No. 4693. See note after No. 1549.

People Wearing Uncle Sam Hats — A4188a

Designed by Antonio Alcalá. Printed by Banknote Corporation of America.

LITHOGRAPHED

Serpentine Die Cut 11 Vert.

2019, Jan. 27 Tagged

Coil Stamp

Self-Adhesive

5341 A4188a (15c) **multicolored** Ⓢ	.30	.25
Pair	.60	
P# strip of 5, #B1111111	2.25	
P# single, #B1111111	—	.60

See note after No. 1549.

See No. 5174.

Flag — A4189

A4189a

Designed by Antonio Alcalá. Printed by Ashton-Potter (USA) Ltd. (#5342), Banknote Corporation of America. (#5343).

LITHOGRAPHED

Serpentine Die Cut 9½ Horiz.

2019, Jan. 27 Tagged

Coil Stamps

Self-Adhesive

Microprinted "USPS" at Lower Flag Grommet

5342 A4189 (55c) **multicolored** Ⓢ 1.25 .25
Pair 2.50
P# strip of 5, #P1111 7.75
P# single, #P1111 — 2.75

Counterfeits exist of No. 5342. See the Postal Counterfeits section of this catalog.

Serpentine Die Cut 11 Horiz.

Microprinted "USPS" to Right of Sixth Red Flag Stripe

5343 A4189a (55c) **multicolored** Ⓢ 1.25 .25
Pair 2.50
P# strip of 5, #B1111, #B2222 7.75
P# single, #B1111, #B2222 — 2.75
a. Die cutting omitted, pair — —

Used example of No. 5343 is single stamp on cover.
Counterfeits exist of No. 5343. See the Postal Counterfeits section of this catalog.

A4189b

A4189c

Printed by Ashton-Potter (USA) Ltd. (#5344), Banknote Corporation of America (#5345).

Booklet Stamps

Microprinted "USPS" at Upper Left Corner of Flag

Serpentine Die Cut 10¾x11¼ on 2 or 3 Sides

5344 A4189b (55c) **multicolored** Ⓢ 1.25 .25
a. Booklet pane of 20 25.00

Counterfeits exist of No. 5344. See the Postal Counterfeits section of this catalog.

Microprinted "USPS" to Right of Sixth Red Flag Stripe

5345 A4189c (55c) **multicolored** Ⓢ 1.25 .25
a. Booklet pane of 20 25.00

Nos. 5344a and 5345a are double-sided booklets with 12 stamps on one side and eight stamps plus a label that serves as the booklet cover on the other side.
See note after No. 1549.
Counterfeits exist of No. 5345. See the Postal Counterfeits section of this catalog.

CALIFORNIA DOGFACE BUTTERFLY Ⓢ

A4190

Designed by Derry Noyes. Printed by Banknote Corporation of America.

LITHOGRAPHED

Sheets of 120 in six panes of 20

2019, Jan. 27 Tagged *Serpentine Die Cut 10½*

Self-Adhesive

5346 A4190 (70c) **multicolored** 2.00 .25
P# block of 4, 6#+B 8.00
Pane of 20 40.00

See note after No. 1549.
Counterfeits exist of No. 5346. See the Postal Counterfeits section of this catalog.

AMERICAN LANDMARKS ISSUE

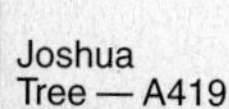
Joshua Tree — A4191

Bethesda Fountain, Central Park, New York City — A4192

Designed by Greg Breeding. Printed by Ashton-Potter (USA) Ltd.

LITHOGRAPHED

Sheets of 48 in 12 panes of 4 (#5347), Sheets of 24 in six panes of 4 (#5348)

Serpentine Die Cut 10¾x10½

2019, Jan. 27 Tagged

Self-Adhesive

5347 A4191 $7.35 **multicolored** Ⓢ 17.50 7.50
Pane of 4 70.00
5348 A4192 $25.50 **multicolored** Ⓢ 95.00 25.00
Pane of 4 380.00

See note after No. 1549.

BLACK HERITAGE

Gregory Hines (1946-2003), Tap Dancer — A4193

Designed by Derry Noyes. Printed by Ashton-Potter (USA) Ltd.

LITHOGRAPHED

Sheets of 240 in 12 panes of 20

2019, Jan. 28 Tagged *Serpentine Die Cut 10¾*

Self-Adhesive

5349 A4193 (55c) **multicolored** Ⓢ 1.25 .25
P# block of 4, 4#+P 5.00
Pane of 20 25.00

Die cut partial press sheets (containing 120 stamps) of No. 5349 were made available for sale. Values: cross gutter block of 4, $9; pairs with gutters between, $4 each. See note after No. 4693. See note after No. 1549.

CACTUS FLOWERS Ⓢ

Opuntia Engelmannii — A4194

Rebutia Minuscula — A4195

Echinocereus Dasyacanthus — A4196

Echinocereus Poselgeri — A4197

Echinocereus Coccineus — A4198

Pelecyphora Aselliformis — A4199

Parodia Microsperma — A4200

Echinocactus Horizonthalonius A4201

Thelocactus Heterochromus A4202

Parodia Scopa — A4203

Designed by Ethel Kessler. Printed by Banknote Corporation of America.

LITHOGRAPHED

Serpentine Die Cut 11 on 2 or 3 Sides

2019, Feb. 15 **Tagged**

Booklet Stamps
Self-Adhesive

5350 A4194 (55c) **multicolored**	2.50	.40
5351 A4195 (55c) **multicolored**	2.50	.40
5352 A4196 (55c) **multicolored**	2.50	.40
5353 A4197 (55c) **multicolored**	2.50	.40
5354 A4198 (55c) **multicolored**	2.50	.40
5355 A4199 (55c) **multicolored**	2.50	.40
5356 A4200 (55c) **multicolored**	2.50	.40
5357 A4201 (55c) **multicolored**	2.50	.40
5358 A4202 (55c) **multicolored**	2.50	.40
5359 A4203 (55c) **multicolored**	2.50	.40
a. Block of 10, #5350-5359	25.00	
b. Booklet pane of 20, 2 each #5350-5359	50.00	
Nos. 5350-5359 (10)	25.00	4.00

No. 5359b is a double-sided booklet pane with 12 stamps on one side (Nos. 5352-5359, 2 each Nos. 5350-5351), and eight stamps (Nos. 5352-5359) plus label (booklet cover) on the other side.

Die cut uncut press sheets of Nos. 5350-5359 were made available for sale. Values of varieties: cross gutter block of 4 with booklet cover, imperf. within, $11; cross gutter block of 4, imperf. within, $11; block of 4, horiz. imperf. between, $9; block of 4, vert. imperf. between, $8. See note after No. 4693. See note after No. 1549.

Counterfeits exist of Nos. 5350-5359. See the Postal Counterfeits section of this catalog.

ALABAMA STATEHOOD, BICENT. Ⓢ

Pulpit Rock, Cheaha State Park — A4204

Designed by Greg Breeding. Printed by Banknote Corporation of America.

LITHOGRAPHED

Sheets of 240 in 12 panes of 20

Serpentine Die Cut 11x10¾

2019, Feb. 23 **Tagged**

Self-Adhesive

5360 A4204 (55c) **multicolored**	1.25	.25
P# block of 4, 5#+B	5.00	
Pane of 20	25.00	

Die cut partial press sheets of No. 5360 (containing 120 stamps) were made available for sale. Values: cross gutter block of 4, $9; pairs with gutters between, $4 each. See note after No. 4693. See note after No. 1549.

Star Ribbon — A4205

A4205a

Designed by Aaron Draplin. Printed by Banknote Corporation of America.

LITHOGRAPHED

Sheets of 200 in 10 panes of 20

Serpentine Die Cut 11¼x10¾

2019, Mar. 22 **Tagged**

Self-Adhesive

5361 A4205 (55c) **multicolored** Ⓢ	1.25	.25
P# block of 4, 3#+B	5.00	
Pane of 20	25.00	

Counterfeits exist of No. 5361. See the Postal Counterfeits section of this catalog.

Coil Stamp

Serpentine Die Cut 10¾ Vert.

5362 A4205a (55c) **multicolored** Ⓢ	1.25	.25
Pair	5.00	
P# strip of 5, #B111	8.00	
P# single, #B111	—	2.50

See note after No. 1549.

CORAL REEFS Ⓢ

Elkhorn Coral and French Angelfish — A4206

Brain Coral and Spotted Moray Eel — A4207

Pillar Coral, Coney Grouper and Neon Gobies — A4208

Staghorn Coral and Blue-striped Grunts — A4209

Designed by Tyler Lang. Printed by Ashton-Potter (USA) Ltd.

LITHOGRAPHED

Sheets of 200 in 10 panes of 20

Serpentine Die Cut 11¼x10¾

2019, Mar. 29 **Tagged**

Self-Adhesive

5363 A4206 (35c) **multicolored**	.90	.25
5364 A4207 (35c) **multicolored**	.90	.25
5365 A4208 (35c) **multicolored**	.90	.25
5366 A4209 (35c) **multicolored**	.90	.25
a. Horiz. or vert. strip of 4, #5363-5366	3.60	
P# block of 8, 1 or 2 sets of 6#+P	7.20	
Pane of 20	18.00	
Nos. 5363-5366 (4)	3.60	1.00

Counterfeits exist of Nos. 5363-5366. See the Postal Counterfeits section of this catalog.

A4206a

A4207a

A4208a

A4209a

Coil Stamps

Serpentine Die Cut 9½ Vert.

5367 A4208a (35c) **multicolored**	.90	.25
a. Aqua ("POSTCARD") color omitted	—	—
5368 A4209a (35c) **multicolored**	.90	.25
a. Aqua ("POSTCARD") color omitted	—	
5369 A4206a (35c) **multicolored**	.90	.25
a. Aqua ("POSTCARD") color omitted	—	
5370 A4207a (35c) **multicolored**	.90	.25
a. Aqua ("POSTCARD") color omitted	—	—
b. Horiz. strip of 4, #5367-5370	3.60	
P# strip of 5, #5368-5370, 2 #5367, #P111111	5.50	
P# strip of 9, 2 each #5367-5368, 5370, 3 #5369, #P111111	10.00	
P# single, #P111111 (#5369)	—	3.00
c. Horiz. strip of 4, #5367a-5370a	—	
Nos. 5367-5370 (4)	3.60	1.00

MUSIC ICONS

Marvin Gaye (1939-84), Singer — A4210

Designed by Derry Noyes. Printed by Banknote Corporation of America.

LITHOGRAPHED

Sheets of 144 in nine panes of 16

2019, Apr. 2 **Tagged** ***Serpentine Die Cut 10½***

Self-Adhesive

5371 A4210 (55c) **multicolored** Ⓢ	1.25	.25
Pane of 16	20.00	

Die cut uncut press sheets of No. 5371 were made available for sale. Values: cross gutter block of 4, $9; pairs with gutters between, $4 each. See note after No. 4693.

See note after No. 1549.

POST OFFICE MURALS Ⓢ

Piggott, Arkansas Mural *Air Mail,* by Daniel Rhodes — A4211

Florence, Colorado Mural, *Antelope,* by Olive Rush — A4212

Rockville, Maryland Mural, *Sugarloaf Mountain,* by Judson Smith — A4213

Anadarko, Oklahoma Mural, *Kiowas Moving Camp,* by Stephen Mopope, James Auchiah, and Spencer Asah — A4214

Deming, New Mexico Mural, *Mountains and Yucca*, by Kenneth Miller Adams — A4215

Designed by Antonio Alcalá. Printed by Ashton-Potter (USA) Ltd.

LITHOGRAPHED
Sheets of 50 in five panes of 10
Serpentine Die Cut 11½x11

2019, Apr. 10 **Tagged**

Self-Adhesive

5372 A4211 (55c) **multicolored** 1.25 .40
5373 A4212 (55c) **multicolored** 1.25 .40
5374 A4213 (55c) **multicolored** 1.25 .40
5375 A4214 (55c) **multicolored** 1.25 .40
5376 A4215 (55c) **multicolored** 1.25 .40
a. Vert. strip of 5, #5372-5376 6.25
Pane of 10 12.50
Nos. 5372-5376 (5) 6.25 2.00

Die cut uncut press sheets of Nos. 5372-5376 were made available for sale. Values: cross gutter block of 10, $16; pairs with gutters between, $4 each. See note after No. 4693.
See note after No. 1549.

MAUREEN CONNOLLY BRINKER

Maureen "Little Mo" Connolly Brinker (1934-69), Tennis Player — A4216

Designed by Derry Noyes. Printed by Banknote Corporation of America.

LITHOGRAPHED
Sheets of 120 in six panes of 20

2019, Apr. 23 **Tagged** ***Serpentine Die Cut 10¾***

Self-Adhesive

5377 A4216 (55c) **multicolored** ⓢ 1.25 .25
P# block of 4, 4#+B 5.00
Pane of 20 25.00

Die cut press sheets of No. 5377 were made available for sale. Values: cross gutter block of 4, $9; pairs with gutters between, $4 each. See note after No. 4693. See note after No. 1549.

TRANSCONTINENTAL RAILROAD, 150th ANNIV. ⓢ

Jupiter Locomotive — A4217

Golden Spike — A4218

No. 119 Locomotive — A4219

Designed by Greg Breeding. Printed by Banknote Corporation of America.

LITHOGRAPHED WITH FOIL APPLICATION
Sheets of 72 in four panes of 18
Serpentine Die Cut 10¾x10½

2019, May 10 **Tagged**

Self-Adhesive

5378 A4217 (55c) **multicolored** 1.25 .30
5379 A4218 (55c) **multicolored** 1.25 .30
5380 A4219 (55c) **multicolored** 1.25 .30
a. Horiz. strip of 3, #5378-5380 3.75
P# block of 6, 4# + B 7.50
Pane of 18 22.50
Nos. 5378-5380 (3) 3.75 .90

Die cut uncut press sheets of Nos. 5378-5380 were made available for sale. Values: cross gutter block of 6, $10; pairs with gutters between, $4.25 each. See note after No. 4693.
A boxed set containing a pane of Nos. 5378-5380, imperforate panes of single-color progressive proofs in gold, cyan, magenta, yellow, and black, an imperforate proof pane with all colors except gold, a protective sleeve, a commemorative book, and a certificate of authenticity were sold together for $79.95.
See note after No. 1549.

WILD AND SCENIC RIVERS ⓢ

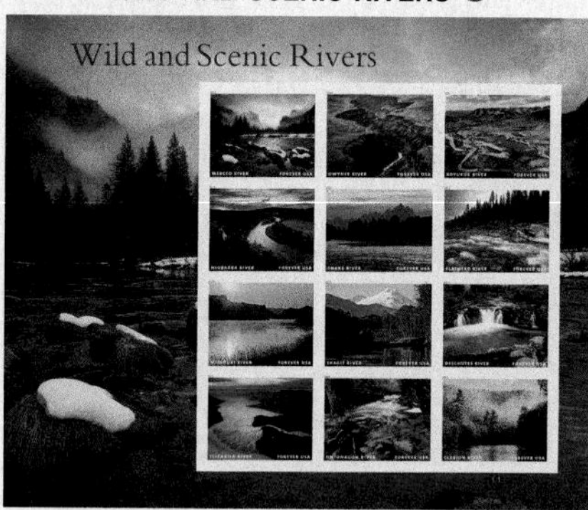

A4220

Designed by Derry Noyes. Printed by Banknote Corporation of America.

No. 5381: a, Merced River. b, Owyhee River. c, Koyukuk River. d, Niobrara River. e, Snake River. f, Flathead River. g, Missouri River. h, Skagit River. i, Deschutes River. j, Tlikakila River. k, Ontonagon River. l, Clarion River.

LITHOGRAPHED
Sheets of 108 in nine panes of 12
Serpentine Die Cut 10¾x10½

2019, May 21 **Tagged**

Self-Adhesive

5381 A4220 Pane of 12 15.00
a.-l. (55c) Any single 1.25 .50

Die cut uncut press sheets of No. 5381 were made available for sale. Values: pairs with gutters between, $4 each. See note after No. 4693. See note after No. 1549.

ART OF ELLSWORTH KELLY (1923-2015) ⓢ

Yellow White, 1961 — A4221

Colors for a Large Wall, 1951 — A4222

Blue Red Rocker, 1963 — A4223

Spectrum I, 1953 — A4224

South Ferry, 1956 — A4225

Blue Green, 1962 — A4226

Orange Red Relief (for Delphine Seyrig), 1990 — A4227

Meschers, 1951 — A4228

Red Blue, 1964 — A4229

Gaza, 1956 — A4230

Designed by Derry Noyes. Printed by Banknote Corporation of America.

LITHOGRAPHED

Sheets of 120 in six panes of 20

Serpentine Die Cut 10½x10¾

2019, May 31 **Tagged**

Self-Adhesive

5382 A4221 (55c) **multicolored** 1.25 .40
5383 A4222 (55c) **multicolored** 1.25 .40
5384 A4223 (55c) **multicolored** 1.25 .40
5385 A4224 (55c) **multicolored** 1.25 .40
5386 A4225 (55c) **multicolored** 1.25 .40
5387 A4226 (55c) **multicolored** 1.25 .40
5388 A4227 (55c) **multicolored** 1.25 .40
5389 A4228 (55c) **multicolored** 1.25 .40
5390 A4229 (55c) **multicolored** 1.25 .40
5391 A4230 (55c) **multicolored** 1.25 .40
a. Block of 10, #5382-5391 12.50
P# block of 10, 5# + B 12.50
Pane of 20 22.50
Nos. 5382-5391 (10) 12.50 4.00

Die cut uncut press sheets of Nos. 5382-5391 were made available for sale. Values: cross gutter block of 10, $18; pairs with gutters between, $4.25 each. See note after No. 4693. See note after No. 1549.

COMMISSIONING OF U.S.S. MISSOURI, 75th ANNIV.

U.S.S. Missouri — A4231

Designed by Greg Breeding. Printed by Banknote Corporation of America.

LITHOGRAPHED

Sheets of 180 in nine panes of 20

2019, June 11 **Tagged** ***Serpentine Die Cut 10¾***

Self-Adhesive

5392 A4231 (55c) **multicolored** Ⓢ 1.25 .25
P# block of 4, 5#+B 5.00
Pane of 20 25.00
a. Die cutting omitted, pair —

Die cut press sheets of No. 5392 were made available for sale. Values: cross gutter block of 4, $9; pairs with gutters between, $4 each. See note after No. 4693. See note after No. 1549.

Some panes that include No. 5392a might have blind die cut stamps as well.

GEORGE HERBERT WALKER BUSH

George Herbert Walker Bush (1924-2018), 41st President — A4232

Designed by Phil Jordan. Printed by Banknote Corporation of America.

LITHOGRAPHED

Sheets of 120 in six panes of 20

2019, June 12 **Tagged** ***Serpentine Die Cut 10¾***

Self-Adhesive

5393 A4232 (55c) **multicolored** Ⓢ 1.25 .25
P# block of 4, 5#+B 5.00
Pane of 20 25.00
a. Die cutting omitted, pair 500.00

Die cut press sheets of No. 5393 were made available for sale. Values: cross gutter block of 4, $9; pairs with gutters between, $4 each. See note after No. 4693. See note after No. 1549.

SESAME STREET CHILDREN'S TELEVISION SHOW, 50th ANNIV. Ⓢ

Muppet Characters — A4233

Designed by Derry Noyes. Printed by Ashton-Potter (USA) Ltd.

No. 5394: a, Big Bird. b, Ernie. c, Bert. d, Cookie Monster. e, Rosita. f, The Count. g, Oscar the Grouch. h, Abby Cadabby. i, Herry Monster. j, Julia. k, Guy Smiley. l, Snuffleupagus. m, Elmo. n, Telly. o, Grover. p, Zoe.

LITHOGRAPHED

Sheets of 160 in 10 panes of 16

2019, June 22 **Tagged** ***Serpentine Die Cut 10¾***

Self-Adhesive

5394 A4233 Pane of 16 20.00
a.-p. (55c) Any single 1.25 .50

Die cut uncut press sheets of No. 5394 were made available for sale. Values: pairs with gutters between, $4 each. See note after No. 4693. See note after No. 1549.

Counterfeits exist of No. 5394. See the Postal Counterfeits section of this catalog.

FROGS Ⓢ

Pacific Tree Frog — A4234

Northern Leopard Frog — A4235

American Green Tree Frog — A4236

Squirrel Tree Frog — A4237

Designed by William J. Gicker. Printed by Banknote Corporation of America.

LITHOGRAPHED

Serpentine Die Cut 11x10¾ on 2 or 3 Sides

2019, July 9 **Tagged**

Booklet Stamps

Self-Adhesive

5395 A4234 (55c) **multicolored** 1.25 .30
5396 A4235 (55c) **multicolored** 1.25 .30
5397 A4236 (55c) **multicolored** 1.25 .30

5398 A4237 (55c) **multicolored** 1.25 .30
a. Block of 4, #5395-5398 5.00
b. Booklet pane of 20, 5 each #5395-5398 25.00
Nos. 5395-5398 (4) 5.00 1.20

No. 5398b is a double-sided booklet pane with 12 stamps on one side (3 each Nos. 5395-5398), and eight stamps (2 each Nos. 5395-5398) plus label (booklet cover) on the other side.
See note after No. 1549.
Counterfeits exist of Nos. 5395-5398. See the Postal Counterfeits section of this catalog.

FIRST MOON LANDING, 50TH ANNIV. Ⓢ

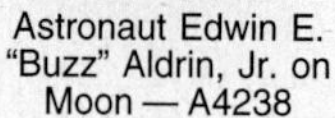
Astronaut Edwin E. "Buzz" Aldrin, Jr. on Moon — A4238

Moon with Landing Site Highlighted — A4239

Designed by Antonio Alcalá. Printed by Banknote Corporation of America.

LITHOGRAPHED
Sheets of 216 in nine panes of 24

2019, July 19 Tagged *Serpentine Die Cut 10¾*
Self-Adhesive

5399 A4238 (55c) **multicolored** 1.25 .25
5400 A4239 (55c) **multicolored** 1.25 .25
a. Pair, #5399-5400 2.50
P# block of 4, 4#+B 5.00
Pane of 24 30.00

Adjacent horizontal or vertical stamps have selvage between the stamps. Die cut press sheets of Noa. 5399-5400 were made available for sale. Values: cross gutter block of 4, $9; pairs with gutters between, $4 each. See note after No. 4693. See note after No. 1549.

STATE AND COUNTY FAIRS Ⓢ

Farmers Unloading Large Fruits and Vegetables — A4240

Girl and Farm Animals — A4241

Parents and Children — A4242

Child Buying Candy Apple — A4243

Designed by Antonio Alcalá. Printed by Banknote Corporation of America.

LITHOGRAPHED
Sheets of 180 in nine panes of 20
Serpentine Die Cut 10½x10¾

2019, July 25 Tagged
Self-Adhesive

5401 A4240 (55c) **multicolored** 1.25 .30
5402 A4241 (55c) **multicolored** 1.25 .30
5403 A4242 (55c) **multicolored** 1.25 .30
5404 A4243 (55c) **multicolored** 1.25 .30
a. Horiz. strip of 4, #5401-5404 5.00
P# block of 8, 2 sets of 4#+P 10.00
Pane of 20 25.00
Nos. 5401-5404 (4) 5.00 1.20

Adjacent vertical stamps have selvage between the stamps. Die cut press sheets of Nos. 5401-5404 were made available for sale. Values: cross gutter block of 8, $18; pairs with gutters between, $4 each. See note after No. 4693. See note after No. 1549.

MILITARY WORKING DOGS Ⓢ

German Shepherd A4244

Labrador Retriever — A4245

Belgian Malinois — A4246

Dutch Shepherd A4247

Designed by Greg Breeding. Printed by Banknote Corporation of America.

LITHOGRAPHED
Serpentine Die Cut 10¾x10½ (Nos. 5405, 5408), 10½x10¾ (Nos. 5406-5407)

2019, Aug. 1 Tagged
Booklet Stamps
Self-Adhesive

5405 A4244 (55c) **multicolored** 1.25 .30
5406 A4245 (55c) **multicolored** 1.25 .30
5407 A4246 (55c) **multicolored** 1.25 .30
5408 A4247 (55c) **multicolored** 1.25 .30
a. Block of 4, #5405-5408 5.00
b. Booklet pane of 20, 5 each #5405-5408 25.00
Nos. 5405-5408 (4) 5.00 1.20

Adjacent horizontal and vertical stamps have selvage between the stamps. No. 5408b is a double-sided booklet pane with 12 stamps on one side (3 each Nos. 5405-5408), and eight stamps (2 each Nos. 5405-5408) plus label (booklet cover) on the other side.
Die cut uncut press sheets of Nos. 5405-5408 were made available for sale. Values: cross gutter block of 12 with booklet cover, $27.50; pairs with gutters between, $4 each.
See note after No. 1549.
Counterfeits exist of Nos. 5405-5408. See the Postal Counterfeits section of this catalog.

WOODSTOCK MUSIC FESTIVAL, 50TH ANNIV.

Dove — A4248

Designed by Antonio Alcalá. Printed by Banknote Corporation of America.

TYPOGRAPHED
Sheets of 120 in six panes of 20

2019, Aug. 8 Tagged *Serpentine Die Cut 10¾*
Self-Adhesive

5409 A4248 (55c) **multicolored** Ⓢ 1.25 .25
P# block of 4, 3#+B 5.00
Pane of 20 25.00

Die cut press sheets of No. 5409 were made available for sale. Values: cross gutter block of 4, $9; pairs with gutters between, $4 each. See note after No. 4693. See note after No. 1549.

TYRANNOSAURUS REX Ⓢ

Juvenile Tyrannosaurus Rex, Egg, and Insect A4249

Adult Tyrannosaurus Rex — A4250

Young Adult Tyrannosaurus Rex and Juvenile Triceratops A4251

Juvenile Tyrannosaurus Rex Chasing Mammal A4252

Designed by Derry Noyes. Printed by Banknote Corporation of America.

TYPOGRAPHED WITH LENTICULAR LENS AFFIXED

Sheets of 96 in six panes of 16

Serpentine Die Cut 10¾x10½

2019, Aug. 29 **Tagged**

Self-Adhesive

5410 A4249 (55c) **multicolored**	1.25	.30
5411 A4250 (55c) **multicolored**	1.25	.30
5412 A4251 (55c) **multicolored**	1.25	.30
5413 A4252 (55c) **multicolored**	1.25	.30
a. Block of 4, #5410-5413	5.00	
P# block of 4, 4# + B	5.00	
Pane of 16	20.00	
Nos. 5410-5413 (4)	5.00	1.20

Adjacent stamps have selvage between them. Only Nos. 5411 and 5412 show movement in the design when viewed from different positions.

Die cut uncut press sheets of Nos. 5410-5413 were made available for sale. Values: cross gutter block of 4, $9; pairs with gutters between, $4 each. See note after No. 4693.

See note after No. 1549.

LITERARY ARTS

Walt Whitman (1819-92), Poet — A4253

Designed by Greg Breeding. Printed by Ashton-Potter (USA), Ltd.

LITHOGRAPHED

Sheets of 120 in six panes of 20

2019, Sept. 12 **Tagged** ***Serpentine Die Cut 10¾***

Self-Adhesive

5414 A4253 (85c) **multicolored** Ⓢ	2.20	.30
P# block of 4, 5#+P	8.80	
Pane of 20	44.00	

See note after No. 1549.

WINTER BERRIES Ⓢ

Winterberry — A4254

Juniper Berry — A4255

Beautyberry A4256

Soapberry A4257

Designed by Antonio Alcalá. Printed by Ashton-Potter (USA) Ltd.

LITHOGRAPHED

Serpentine Die Cut 11¼x10¾ on 2 or 3 Sides

2019, Sept. 17 **Tagged**

Booklet Stamps
Self-Adhesive

5415 A4254 (55c) **multicolored**	1.25	.30
5416 A4255 (55c) **multicolored**	1.25	.30
5417 A4256 (55c) **multicolored**	1.25	.30
5418 A4257 (55c) **multicolored**	1.25	.30
a. Block of 4, #5415-5418	5.00	
b. Booklet pane of 20, 5 each #5415-5418	25.00	
Nos. 5415-5418 (4)	5.00	1.20

No. 5418b is a double-sided booklet pane with 12 stamps on one side (3 each Nos. 5415-5418), and eight stamps (2 each Nos. 5415-5418) plus label (booklet cover) on the other side.

See note after No. 1549.

Counterfeits exist of Nos. 5415-5418. See the Postal Counterfeits section of this catalog.

Purple Heart and Ribbon With Frame — A4258

Designed by Bryan Duefrene. Printed by Banknote Corporation of America.

LITHOGRAPHED

Sheets of 200 in 10 panes of 20

Serpentine Die Cut 11¼x10¾

2019, Oct. 4 **Tagged**

Self-Adhesive

5419 A4258 (55c) **multicolored** Ⓢ	1.25	.25
P# block of 4, 6#+B	5.00	
Pane of 20	25.00	

See note after No. 1549.

Counterfeits exist of No. 5419. See the Postal Counterfeits section of this catalog.

SPOOKY SILHOUETTES Ⓢ

Cat and Raven — A4259

Ghosts — A4260

Spider and Web — A4261

Bats — A4262

Designed by Greg Breeding. Printed by Ashton-Potter (USA) Ltd.

TYPOGRAPHED WITH FOIL APPLICATION

Sheets of 160 in eight panes of 20

2019, Oct. 11 **Tagged** ***Serpentine Die Cut 10¾***

Self-Adhesive
Color of Foil

5420 A4259 (55c) **silver**	1.25	.30
5421 A4260 (55c) **orange**	1.25	.30
5422 A4261 (55c) **red**	1.25	.30
5423 A4262 (55c) **violet**	1.25	.30
a. Block of 4, #5420-5423	5.00	
P# block of 4, 6#+P	5.00	
Pane of 20	25.00	
Nos. 5420-5423 (4)	5.00	1.20

Die cut press sheets of Nos. 5420-5423 were made available for sale. Values: cross gutter block of 8, $18; pairs with gutters between, $4 each. See note after No. 4693. See note after No. 1549.

Counterfeits exist of Nos. 5420-5423. See the Postal Counterfeits section of this catalog.

CHRISTMAS WREATHS Ⓢ

Aspidistra Leaf Wreath — A4263

Wreath Made of Gilded Pine Cones and Magnolia Pods — A4264

Wreath Made of Gilded Hydrangea, Eucalyptus, Nandina and Ribbon — A4265

Wreath Made of Woodland Bush Ivy and Red Winterberry — A4266

Designed by Antonio Alcalá and Laura Dowling. Printed by Banknote Corporation of America.

LITHOGRAPHED

Serpentine Die Cut 11¼x10¾ on 2 or 3 Sides

2019, Oct. 25 **Tagged**

Booklet Stamps
Self-Adhesive

5424 A4263 (55c) **multicolored**	1.25	.30
5425 A4264 (55c) **multicolored**	1.25	.30
5426 A4265 (55c) **multicolored**	1.25	.30
5427 A4266 (55c) **multicolored**	1.25	.30
a. Block of 4, #5424-5427	5.00	
b. Booklet pane of 20, 5 each #5424-5427	25.00	
Nos. 5424-5427 (4)	5.00	1.20

No. 5427b is a double-sided booklet pane with 12 stamps on one side (3 each Nos. 5424-5427), and eight stamps (2 each Nos. 5424-5427) plus label (booklet cover) on the other side.

See note after No. 1549.

Counterfeits exist of Nos. 5424-5427. See the Postal Counterfeits section of this catalog.

CHINESE NEW YEAR Ⓢ

Year of the Rat — A4267

Designed by Antonio Alcalá. Printed by Banknote Corporation of America.

LITHOGRAPHED WITH FOIL APPLICATION

Sheets of 80 in four panes of 20

2020, Jan. 11 **Tagged** ***Serpentine Die Cut 10¾***

Self-Adhesive

5428 A4267 (55c) **multicolored**	1.25	.25
P# block of 4, 6#+B	5.00	
Pane of 20	25.00	

Die cut uncut press sheets of No. 5428 were made available for sale. Values: cross gutter block of 4, $9; pairs with gutters between, $4.25 each. See note after No. 4693. See note after No. 1549.

AMERICAN LANDMARKS ISSUE

Big Bend National Park, Texas A4268

Grand Island Ice Caves, Michigan A4269

Designed by Greg Breeding. Printed by Ashton-Potter (USA) Ltd.

LITHOGRAPHED
Sheets of 20 in five panes of 4
Serpentine Die Cut 10¾x10½

2020, Jan. 18 **Tagged**

Self-Adhesive

5429 A4268 $7.75 **multicolored** Ⓢ	15.50	7.75
Pane of 4	62.00	
5430 A4269 $26.35 **multicolored** Ⓢ	53.00	26.50
Pane of 4	215.00	

See note after No. 1549.

Counterfeits exist of No. 5430. See the Postal Counterfeits section of this catalog.

LOVE 

Hearts — A4270

Designed by Antonio Alcalá. Printed by Ashton-Potter (USA) Ltd.

LITHOGRAPHED
Sheets of 160 in eight panes of 20

2020, Jan. 23 **Tagged** ***Serpentine Die Cut 10¾***

Self-Adhesive

5431 A4270 (55c) **multicolored**	1.25	.25
P# block of 4, 4#+P	5.00	
Pane of 20	25.00	

Die cut uncut press sheets of No. 5431 were made available for sale. Values: cross gutter block of 4, $9; pairs with gutters between, $4.25 each. See note after No. 4693. See note after No. 1549.

Counterfeits exist of No. 5431. See the Postal Counterfeits section of this catalog.

BLACK HERITAGE

Gwen Ifill (1955-2016), Television Newscaster — A4271

Designed by Derry Noyes. Printed by Banknote Corporation of America.

LITHOGRAPHED
Sheets of 240 in 12 panes of 20

2020, Jan. 30 **Tagged** ***Serpentine Die Cut 10¾***

Self-Adhesive

5432 A4271 (55c) **multicolored** Ⓢ	1.25	.25
P# block of 4, 6#+B	5.00	
Pane of 20	25.00	

Die cut partial press sheets (containing 120 stamps) of No. 5432 were made available for sale. Values: cross gutter block of 4, $9; pairs with gutters between, $4 each. See note after No. 4693. See note after No. 1549.

Star and Stripes — A4272

Designed by Matt Pamer. Printed by Banknote Corporation of America.

LITHOGRAPHED
Serpentine Die Cut 10¾ Vert.

2020, Feb. 3 **Untagged**

COIL STAMP

Self-Adhesive

5433 A4272 (10c) **multicolored** Ⓢ	.30	.25
Pair	.50	
P# strip of 5, #B1111	3.00	
P# single, #B1111	—	2.25

See note after No. 1549.

CELEBRATE

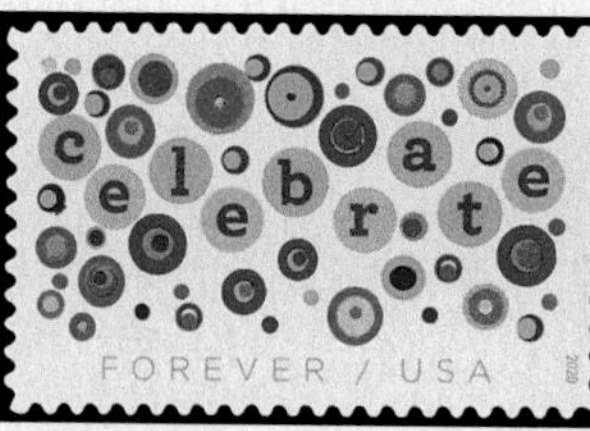

A4273

Designed by Antonio Alcalá. Printed by Banknote Corporation of America.

LITHOGRAPHED WITH FOIL APPLICATION
Sheets of 160 in eight panes of 20

2020, Feb. 14 **Tagged** ***Serpentine Die Cut 10¾***

Self-Adhesive

5434 A4273 (55c) **multicolored** Ⓢ	1.25	.25
P# block of 4, 5#+B	5.00	
Pane of 20	25.00	
a. Die cutting omitted, pair	—	

See note after No. 1549.

Counterfeits exist of No. 5434. See the Postal Counterfeits section of this catalog.

WILD ORCHIDS Ⓢ

Platanthera Grandiflora — A4274

Cyrtopodium Polyphyllum — A4275

Calopogon Tuberosus — A4276

Spiranthes Odorata — A4277

Triphora Trianthophoros A4278

Cypripedium Californicum A4279

Hexalectris Spicata — A4280

Cypripedium Reginae — A4281

Platanthera Leucophaea A4282

Triphora Trianthophoros A4283

Triphora Trianthophoros A4284

Cypripedium Californicum A4285

Hexalectris Spicata — A4286

Cypripedium Reginae — A4287

Spiranthes Odorata A4288

Platanthera Leucophaea A4289

Triphora Trianthophoros A4290

Platanthera Grandiflora A4291

Cyrtopodium Polyphyllum — A4292

Calopogon Tuberosus — A4293

Designed by Ethel Kessler. Printed by Banknote Corporation of America.

LITHOGRAPHED

Serpentine Die Cut 10¾ Vert.

2020, Feb. 21 **Tagged**

Coil Stamps

Self-Adhesive

5435 A4274 (55c) **multicolored** 1.25 .40
5436 A4275 (55c) **multicolored** 1.25 .40
5437 A4276 (55c) **multicolored** 1.25 .40
5438 A4277 (55c) **multicolored** 1.25 .40
5439 A4278 (55c) **multicolored** 1.25 .40
5440 A4279 (55c) **multicolored** 1.25 .40
5441 A4280 (55c) **multicolored** 1.25 .40
5442 A4281 (55c) **multicolored** 1.25 .40
5443 A4282 (55c) **multicolored** 1.25 .40
5444 A4283 (55c) **multicolored** 1.25 .40
a. Horiz. strip of 10, #5435-5444 12.50
P# strip of 10, #B1111 14.00
P# strip of 17, #5435-5437, 2 each #5438-5444, #B1111 22.00
P# single (#5443), #B1111 — 2.75
Nos. 5435-5444 (10) 12.50 4.00

Booklet Stamps

Serpentine Die Cut 10¾x11 on 2 or 3 Sides

5445 A4284 (55c) **multicolored** 1.25 .40
5446 A4285 (55c) **multicolored** 1.25 .40
5447 A4286 (55c) **multicolored** 1.25 .40
5448 A4287 (55c) **multicolored** 1.25 .40
5449 A4288 (55c) **multicolored** 1.25 .40
5450 A4289 (55c) **multicolored** 1.25 .40
5451 A4290 (55c) **multicolored** 1.25 .40
5452 A4291 (55c) **multicolored** 1.25 .40
5453 A4292 (55c) **multicolored** 1.25 .40
5454 A4293 (55c) **multicolored** 1.25 .40
a. Block of 10, #5445-5454 12.50
b. Booklet pane of 20, 2 each #5445-5454 25.00
Nos. 5445-5454 (10) 12.50 4.00

The plate number strip of 10 of Nos. 5435-5444 is a cut down version of the plate number strip of 17 (without the last seven stamps), so the stamp with the plate number appears on the ninth stamp in either strip.

Nos. 5454b is a double-sided booklet with 12 stamps on one side (Nos. 5446-5449, 5451-5454, 2 each Nos 5445, 5450), and eight stamps (Nos. 5446-5449, 5451-5454) plus a label that serves as the booklet cover on the other side.

See note after No. 1549.

Counterfeits exist of Nos. 5445-5454. See the Postal Counterfeits section of this catalog.

ARNOLD PALMER

Arnold Palmer (1929-2016), Professional Golfer — A4294

Designed by Antonio Alcalá. Printed by Ashton-Potter (USA) Ltd.

LITHOGRAPHED

Sheets of 240 in 12 panes of 20

2020, Mar. 4 **Tagged** ***Serpentine Die Cut 10¾***

Self-Adhesive

5455 A4294 (55c) **multicolored** Ⓢ 1.25 .25
P# block of 4, 4#+P 5.00
Pane of 20 25.00

Die cut partial press sheets (containing 120 stamps) of No. 5455 were made available for sale. Values: cross gutter block of 4, $9; pairs with gutters between, $4 each. See note after No. 4693. See note after No. 1549.

MAINE STATEHOOD BICENTENARY

Sea at Ogunquit, by Edward Hopper (1882-1967) A4295

Designed by Derry Noyes. Printed by Ashton-Potter (USA) Ltd.

LITHOGRAPHED

Sheets of 120 in six panes of 20

2020, Mar. 15 **Tagged** ***Serpentine Die Cut 10¾***

Self-Adhesive

5456 A4295 (55c) **multicolored** Ⓢ 1.25 .25
P# block of 4, 4#+P 5.00
Pane of 20 25.00

See note after No. 1549.

Boutonniere — A4296 Corsage — A4297

Designed by Ethel Kessler. Printed by Ashton-Potter (USA) Ltd.

LITHOGRAPHED

Sheets of 160 in eight panes of 20

2020, Apr. 2 **Tagged** ***Serpentine Die Cut 10¾x11***

Self-Adhesive

5457 A4296 (55c) **multicolored** Ⓢ 1.25 .25
P# block of 4, 5#+P 5.00
Pane of 20 25.00

Serpentine Die Cut 10¾x11

5458 A4297 (70c) **multicolored** Ⓢ 1.70 .25
P# block of 4, 5#+P 6.80
Pane of 20 34.00

See note after No. 1549.

Counterfeits exist of Nos. 5457-5458. See the Postal Counterfeits section of this catalog.

EARTH DAY, 50th ANNIV.

Stylized Globe — A4298

Designed by Antonio Alcalá. Printed by Banknote Corporation of America.

LITHOGRAPHED

Serpentine Die Cut 11x10¾ on 2 or 3 Sides

2020, Apr. 18 **Tagged**

Booklet Stamp

Self-Adhesive

5459 A4298 (55c) **multicolored** Ⓢ 1.25 .25
a. Booklet pane of 20 25.00

No. 5459a is a double-sided booklet with 12 stamps on one side and eight stamps plus a label that serves as the booklet cover on the other side.

See note after No. 1549.

Counterfeits exist of No. 5459. See the Postal Counterfeits section of this catalog.

Chrysanthemum A4299

Designed by Greg Breeding. Printed by Ashton-Potter (USA) Ltd.

LITHOGRAPHED

Sheets of 90 in nine panes of 10

2020, Apr. 24 **Tagged** ***Serpentine Die Cut***

Self-Adhesive

5460 A4299 ($1.20) **multicolored** Ⓢ 2.80 .50
P# block of 4, 6#+P 11.20
Pane of 10 28.00

Unused values are for stamps with surrounding selvage. Adjacent stamps are separated by rouletting. See note after No. 1549.

Counterfeits exist of No. 5460. See the Postal Counterfeits section of this catalog.

AMERICAN GARDENS Ⓢ

Brooklyn Botanic Garden, New York — A4300

Stan Hywet Hall and Gardens, Ohio — A4301

Dumbarton Oaks, District of Columbia A4302

Coastal Maine Botanical Gardens, Maine A4303

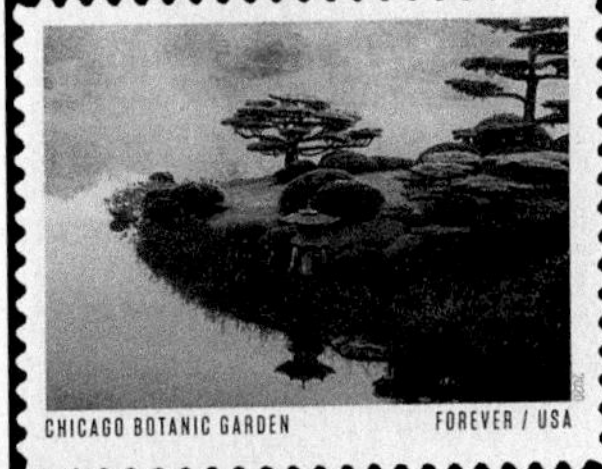

Chicago Botanic Garden, Illinois A4304

Winterthur Garden, Delaware A4305

Biltmore Estate Gardens, North Carolina A4306

Alfred B. Maclay Gardens State Park, Florida A4307

The Huntington Botanical Gardens, California A4308

Norfolk Botanical Garden, Virginia A4309

Designed by Ethel Kessler. Printed by Banknote Corporation of America.

LITHOGRAPHED

Sheets of 180 in nine panes of 20

Serpentine Die Cut 10¾x10½

2020, May 13 **Tagged**

Self-Adhesive

5461	A4300	(55c)	**multicolored**	1.25	.40
5462	A4301	(55c)	**multicolored**	1.25	.40
5463	A4302	(55c)	**multicolored**	1.25	.40
5464	A4303	(55c)	**multicolored**	1.25	.40
5465	A4304	(55c)	**multicolored**	1.25	.40
5466	A4305	(55c)	**multicolored**	1.25	.40
5467	A4306	(55c)	**multicolored**	1.25	.40
5468	A4307	(55c)	**multicolored**	1.25	.40
5469	A4308	(55c)	**multicolored**	1.25	.40
5470	A4309	(55c)	**multicolored**	1.25	.40
a.			Block of 10, #5461-5470	12.50	
			P# block of 10, 5# + B	12.50	
			Pane of 20	25.00	
			Nos. 5461-5470 (10)	12.50	4.00

Die cut uncut press sheets of Nos. 5461-5470 were made available for sale. Values: cross gutter block of 10, $18; pairs with gutters between, $4.25 each. See note after No. 4693.

See note after No. 1549.

VOICES OF THE HARLEM RENAISSANCE Ⓢ

Nella Larsen (1891-1964), Novelist — A4310

Arturo Schomburg (1874-1938), Historian — A4311

Anne Spencer (1882-1975), Poet — A4312

Alain Locke (1885-1954), Writer — A4313

Designed by Greg Breeding. Printed by Banknote Corporation of America.

LITHOGRAPHED

Sheets of 160 in eight panes of 20

2020, May 21 **Tagged** ***Serpentine Die Cut 10¾***

Self-Adhesive

5471	A4310	(55c)	**multicolored**	1.25	.30
5472	A4311	(55c)	**multicolored**	1.25	.30
5473	A4312	(55c)	**multicolored**	1.25	.30
5474	A4313	(55c)	**multicolored**	1.25	.30
a.			Horiz. or vert. strip of 4, #5471-5474	5.00	
			P# block of 8, 4# + B	10.00	
			Pane of 20	25.00	
			Nos. 5471-5474 (4)	5.00	1.20

Die cut uncut press sheets of Nos. 5471-5474 were made available for sale. Values: cross gutter block of 8, $16; pairs with gutters between, $4.25 each. See note after No. 4693.

See note after No. 1549.

ENJOY THE GREAT OUTDOORS Ⓢ

Child Building Sandcastle A4314

Canoeing A4315

Hiking A4316

Bicycling A4317

Cross-country Skiing A4318

Designed by Derry Noyes. Printed by Ashton-Potter (USA) Ltd.

LITHOGRAPHED

Sheets of 180 in nine panes of 20

2020, June 13 **Tagged** ***Serpentine Die Cut 10¾***

Self-Adhesive

5475	A4314	(55c)	**multicolored**	1.25	.40
5476	A4315	(55c)	**multicolored**	1.25	.40
5477	A4316	(55c)	**multicolored**	1.25	.40
5478	A4317	(55c)	**multicolored**	1.25	.40
5479	A4318	(55c)	**multicolored**	1.25	.40
a.			Vert. strip of 5, #5475-5479	6.25	
			P# block of 10, 4# + P	12.50	
			Pane of 20	25.00	
			Nos. 5475-5479 (5)	6.25	2.00

Die cut uncut press sheets of Nos. 5475-5479 were made available for sale. Values: cross gutter block of 10, $18; pairs with gutters between, $4.25 each. See note after No. 4693.

See note after No. 1549.

HIP HOP Ⓢ

MC With Microphone Rapping — A4319

B-Boy Dancing — A4320

Graffiti Art — A4321

DJ at Turntable — A4322

Designed by Antonio Alcalá. Printed by Ashton-Potter (USA) Ltd.

LITHOGRAPHED

Sheets of 240 in 12 panes of 20

2020, July 1 **Tagged** ***Serpentine Die Cut 10¾***

Self-Adhesive

5480	A4319	(55c)	**multicolored**	1.25	.30
5481	A4320	(55c)	**multicolored**	1.25	.30
5482	A4321	(55c)	**multicolored**	1.25	.30

5483 A4322 (55c) **multicolored** 1.25 .30
a. Block or vert. strip of 4, #5480-5483 5.00
P# block of 4, 5# + P 5.00
Pane of 20 25.00
Nos. 5480-5483 (4) 5.00 1.20

Die cut uncut partial press sheets (containing 120 stamps) of Nos. 5480-5483 were made available for sale. Values: cross gutter block of 8, $16; pairs with gutters between, $4.25 each. See note after No. 4693.

See note after No. 1549.

Counterfeits exist of Nos. 5480-5483. See the Postal Counterfeits section of this catalog.

FRUITS AND VEGETABLES Ⓢ

Red and Black Plums — A4323

Heirloom and Cherry Tomatoes — A4324

Carrots — A4325

Lemons — A4326

Blueberries — A4327

Red and Green Grapes — A4328

Lettuce — A4329

Strawberries — A4330

Eggplants — A4331

Figs — A4332

Designed by Derry Noyes. Printed by Banknote Corporation of America.

LITHOGRAPHED

Serpentine Die Cut 10¾x11 on 2 or 3 Sides

2020, July 17 **Tagged**

Booklet Stamps
Self-Adhesive

5484 A4323 (55c) **multicolored** 1.25 .40
5485 A4324 (55c) **multicolored** 1.25 .40
5486 A4325 (55c) **multicolored** 1.25 .40
5487 A4326 (55c) **multicolored** 1.25 .40
5488 A4327 (55c) **multicolored** 1.25 .40
5489 A4328 (55c) **multicolored** 1.25 .40
5490 A4329 (55c) **multicolored** 1.25 .40
5491 A4330 (55c) **multicolored** 1.25 .40
5492 A4331 (55c) **multicolored** 1.25 .40
5493 A4332 (55c) **multicolored** 1.25 .40
a. Block of 10, #5484-5493 12.50
b. Booklet pane of 20, 2 each #5484-5493 25.00
Nos. 5484-5493 (10) 12.50 4.00

Nos. 5493b is a double-sided booklet pane with 12 stamps on one side (Nos. 5485-5488, 5490-5493, 2 each Nos. 5484, 5489) and eight stamps (Nos. 5485-5488, 5490-5493) plus label (booklet cover) on the other side.

See note after No. 1549.

Counterfeits exist of Nos. 5484-5493. See the Postal Counterfeits section of this catalog.

BUGS BUNNY, 80th ANNIV. Ⓢ

Bugs Bunny as Barber, From *Rabbit of Seville,* 1950 — A4333

Bugs Bunny as Basketball Player, From *Space Jam,* 1996 — A4334

Bugs Bunny as Hollywood Celebrity, From *A Hare Grows in Manhattan,* 1947 — A4335

Bugs Bunny as Court Jester, From *Knighty Knight Bugs,* 1958 — A4336

Bugs Bunny as Brunhilde, From *What's Opera, Doc?,* 1957 — A4337

Bugs Bunny as Mermaid, From *Hare Ribbin',* 1944 — A4338

Bugs Bunny as Piano Player, From *Rhapsody Rabbit,* 1946 — A4339

Bugs Bunny as Super-Rabbit, From *Super-Rabbit,* 1943 — A4340

Bugs Bunny as Baseball Player, From *Baseball Bugs,* 1946 — A4341

Bugs Bunny as Soldier, From World War II Poster — A4342

Designed by Greg Breeding. Printed by Banknote Corporation of America.

LITHOGRAPHED

Sheets of 120 in six panes of 20

Serpentine Die Cut 10½x10¾

2020, July 27 **Tagged**

Self-Adhesive

5494 A4333 (55c) **multicolored**	1.25	.40
5495 A4334 (55c) **multicolored**	1.25	.40
5496 A4335 (55c) **multicolored**	1.25	.40
5497 A4336 (55c) **multicolored**	1.25	.40
5498 A4337 (55c) **multicolored**	1.25	.40
5499 A4338 (55c) **multicolored**	1.25	.40
5500 A4339 (55c) **multicolored**	1.25	.40
5501 A4340 (55c) **multicolored**	1.25	.40
5502 A4341 (55c) **multicolored**	1.25	.40
5503 A4342 (55c) **multicolored**	1.25	.40
a. Block of 10, #5494-5503	12.50	
P# block of 10, 2 sets of 4# + B	12.50	
Pane of 20	25.00	
Nos. 5494-5503 (10)	12.50	4.00

Die cut uncut press sheets of Nos. 5494-5503 were made available for sale. Values: cross gutter block of 10, $18; pairs with gutters between, $4.25 each. See note after No. 4693.

See note after No. 1549.

Counterfeits exist of Nos. 5494-5503. See the Postal Counterfeits section of this catalog.

WIRE SCULPTURES BY RUTH ASAWA (1926-2013) Ⓢ

Three Untitled Sculptures From 1958, 1978 and 1959 — A4343

Untitled Sculpture From 1959 — A4344

Untitled Sculpture From 1958 — A4345

Untitled Sculpture From 1955 — A4346

Untitled Sculpture From 1955 — A4347

Untitled Sculpture From 1980 — A4348

Untitled Sculpture From 1978 — A4349

Untitled Sculpture From 1952 — A4350

Untitled Sculpture From 1954 — A4351

Six Untitled Sculptures From Various Years — A4352

Designed by Ethel Kessler. Printed by Banknote Corporation of America.

LITHOGRAPHED

Sheets of 180 in nine panes of 20

2020, Aug. 13 **Tagged** ***Serpentine Die Cut 10¾***

Self-Adhesive

5504 A4343 (55c) **multicolored**	1.25	.40
5505 A4344 (55c) **multicolored**	1.25	.40
5506 A4345 (55c) **multicolored**	1.25	.40
5507 A4346 (55c) **multicolored**	1.25	.40
5508 A4347 (55c) **multicolored**	1.25	.40
5509 A4348 (55c) **multicolored**	1.25	.40
5510 A4349 (55c) **multicolored**	1.25	.40
5511 A4350 (55c) **multicolored**	1.25	.40
5512 A4351 (55c) **multicolored**	1.25	.40
5513 A4352 (55c) **multicolored**	1.25	.40
a. Block of 10, #5504-5513	12.50	
P# block of 10, 2 sets of 5# + B	12.50	
Pane of 20	22.00	
Nos. 5504-5513 (10)	12.50	4.00

Die cut uncut press sheets of Nos. 5504-5513 were made available for sale. Values: cross gutter block of 10, $18; pairs with gutters between, $4.25 each. See note after No. 4693.

See note after No. 1549.

INNOVATION Ⓢ

Computing — A4353

Biomedicine — A4354

Genome Sequencing — A4355

Robotics — A4356

Solar Technology — A4357

Designed by Antonio Alcalá. Printed by Banknote Corporation of America.

LITHOGRAPHED WITH FOIL APPLICATION

Sheets of 120 in six panes of 20

2020, Aug. 20 **Tagged** ***Serpentine Die Cut 10¾***

Self-Adhesive

5514 A4353 (55c) **multicolored**	1.25	.40
5515 A4354 (55c) **multicolored**	1.25	.40
5516 A4355 (55c) **multicolored**	1.25	.40
5517 A4356 (55c) **multicolored**	1.25	.40
5518 A4357 (55c) **multicolored**	1.25	.40
a. Horiz. strip of 5, #5514-5518	6.25	
P# block of 10, 2 sets of 5# + B	12.50	
Pane of 20	25.00	
Nos. 5514-5518 (5)	6.25	2.00

Die cut uncut press sheets of Nos. 5514-5518 were made available for sale. Values: cross gutter block of 10, $18; pairs with gutters between, $4.25 each. See note after No. 4693.

See note after No. 1549.

THANK YOU Ⓢ

A4358

A4359

A4360

A4361

Designed by Dana Tanamachi. Printed by Banknote Corporation of America.

TYPOGRAPHED WITH FOIL APPLICATION
Sheets of 160 in eight panes of 20

2020, Aug. 21 Tagged *Serpentine Die Cut 10¾*
Self-Adhesive

5519	A4358 (55c) **rose brown & gold**	1.25	.40
5520	A4359 (55c) **olive & gold**	1.25	.40
5521	A4360 (55c) **slate blue & gold**	1.25	.40
5522	A4361 (55c) **violet & gold**	1.25	.40
a.	Block of 4, #5519-5522	5.00	
	P# block of 4, 5# + B	5.00	
	Pane of 20	25.00	
	Nos. 5519-5522 (4)	5.00	1.60

Die cut uncut press sheets of Nos. 5519-5522 were made available for sale. Values: cross gutter block of 4, $9; pairs with gutters between, $4.25 each. See note after No. 4693.

See note after No. 1549.

Counterfeits exist of Nos. 5519-5522. See the Postal Counterfeits section of this catalog.

WOMAN SUFFRAGE CENTENARY

Suffragists Marching for Passage of 19th Amendment — A4362

Designed by Ethel Kessler. Printed by Banknote Corporation of America.

LITHOGRAPHED
Sheets of 120 in six panes of 20

2020, Aug. 22 Tagged *Serpentine Die Cut 10¾*
Self-Adhesive

5523	A4362 (55c) **multicolored** ⓢ	1.25	.25
	P# block of 4, 5#+B	5.00	
	Pane of 20	25.00	

Die cut uncut press sheets of No. 5523 were made available for sale. Values: cross gutter block of 4, $9; pairs with gutters between, $4.25 each. See note after No. 4693.

See note after No. 1549.

MAYFLOWER IN PLYMOUTH HARBOR, 400th ANNIV.

The Mayflower in Plymouth Harbor and Mayflower A4363

Designed by Greg Breeding. Printed by Ashton-Potter (USA) Ltd,

LITHOGRAPHED & ENGRAVED
Sheets of 80 in four panes of 20

2020, Sept. 17 Tagged *Serpentine Die Cut 10¾*
Self-Adhesive

5524	A4363 (55c) **multicolored** ⓢ	1.25	.25
	P# block of 4, 5#+P	5.00	
	Pane of 20	25.00	

Die cut uncut press sheets of No. 5524 were made available for sale. Values: cross gutter block of 4, $9; pairs with gutters between, $4.25 each. See note after No. 4693.

A pane of No. 5524, imperforate panes of single-color progressive proofs in cyan, magenta, yellow, and lithographed black, a commemorative book, and a numbered certificate were produced in a quantity of 2,500 and sold as a unit for $59.95.

See note after No. 1549.

CHRISTMAS ⓢ

Our Lady of Guápulo, by Unknown 18th Century Peruvian Artist — A4364

Ornament — A4365

Christmas Tree — A4366

Christmas Stocking — A4367

Reindeer — A4368

Designed by Greg Breeding (No. 5525), Antonio Alcalá (Nos. 5526-5529). Printed by Banknote Corporation of America.

LITHOGRAPHED
Serpentine Die Cut 10¾ on 2 or 3 Sides
2020 Tagged
Booklet Stamps
Self-Adhesive

5525	A4364 (55c) **multicolored,** *Oct. 20*	1.25	.25
a.	Booklet pane of 20	25.00	
5526	A4365 (55c) **multicolored,** *Sept. 24*	1.25	.30
5527	A4366 (55c) **multicolored,** *Sept. 24*	1.25	.30
5528	A4367 (55c) **multicolored,** *Sept. 24*	1.25	.30
5529	A4368 (55c) **multicolored,** *Sept. 24*	1.25	.30
a.	Block of 4, #5526-5529	5.00	
b.	Booklet pane of 20, 5 each #5526-5529	25.00	
	Nos. 5525-5529 (5)	6.25	1.45

No. 5525a is a double-sided booklet pane with 12 stamps on one side, and eight stamps plus label (booklet cover) on the other side.

No. 5529b is a double-sided booklet pane with 12 stamps on one side (3 each Nos. 5526-5529), and eight stamps (2 each Nos. 5526-5529) plus label (booklet cover) on the other side.

See note after No. 1549.

Counterfeits exist of Nos. 5525, 5526-5529. See the Postal Counterfeits section of this catalog.

HANUKKAH ⓢ

Children and Menorah — A4369

Designed by Ethel Kessler. Printed by Ashton-Potter (USA) Ltd.

LITHOGRAPHED
Sheets of 160 in eight panes of 20

2020, Oct. 6 Tagged *Serpentine Die Cut 10¾*
Self-Adhesive

5530	A4369 (55c) **multicolored**	1.25	.25
	P# block of 4, 5#+P	5.00	
	Pane of 20	25.00	

See note after No. 1549.

Counterfeits exist of No. 5530. See the Postal Counterfeits section of this catalog.

KWANZAA ⓢ

Woman and Kinara — A4370

Designed by Antonio Alcalá. Printed by Banknote Corporation of America.

LITHOGRAPHED
Sheets of 160 in eight panes of 20

2020, Oct. 13 Tagged *Serpentine Die Cut 10¾*
Self-Adhesive

5531	A4370 (55c) **multicolored**	1.25	.25
	P# block of 4, 4#+B	5.00	
	Pane of 20	25.00	

See note after No. 1549.

Counterfeits exist of No. 5531. See the Postal Counterfeits section of this catalog.

WINTER SCENES ⓢ

Two Deer, Photograph by Lisa Carter — A4371

Cardinal, Photograph by Gerald A. DeBoer — A4372

Snowy Morning at Sunrise, Photograph by Lisa Lacasse — A4373

Red Barn with Wreath, Photograph by Lisa Lacasse — A4374

Barred Owl, Photograph by Malachi Ives — A4375

Blue Jay, Photograph by Edgar Lee Espe — A4376

Mackenzie Barn, Woodstock, Vermont, Photograph by Lisa Lacasse — A4377

Rabbit, Photograph by Melani Wright — A4378

After the Snowfall, Photograph by Lisa Lacasse — A4379

Mike and Burt, the Belgian Draft Horses, Photograph by Lisa Lacasse — A4380

Designed by Derry Noyes. Printed by Ashton-Potter (USA) Ltd.

LITHOGRAPHED

Serpentine Die Cut 10¾ on 2 or 3 Sides

2020, Oct. 16 **Tagged**

Booklet Stamps

Self-Adhesive

5532	A4371 (55c) **multicolored**	1.25	.40
5533	A4372 (55c) **multicolored**	1.25	.40
5534	A4373 (55c) **multicolored**	1.25	.40
5535	A4374 (55c) **multicolored**	1.25	.40
5536	A4375 (55c) **multicolored**	1.25	.40
5537	A4376 (55c) **multicolored**	1.25	.40
5538	A4377 (55c) **multicolored**	1.25	.40
5539	A4378 (55c) **multicolored**	1.25	.40
5540	A4379 (55c) **multicolored**	1.25	.40
5541	A4380 (55c) **multicolored**	1.25	.40
a.	Block of 10, #5532-5541	12.50	
b.	Booklet pane of 20, 2 each #5532-5541	25.00	
	Nos. 5532-5541 (10)	12.50	4.00

Nos. 5541b is a double-sided booklet with 12 stamps on one side (Nos. 5533-5536, 5538-5541, 2 each Nos 5532, 5537), and eight stamps (Nos. 5533-5536, 5538-5541) plus a label that serves as the booklet cover on the other side.

See note after No. 1549.

Counterfeits exist of Nos. 5532-5541. See the Postal Counterfeits section of this catalog.

DRUG FREE USA

Star and Stripes — A4381

Designed by Greg Breeding. Printed by Ashton-Potter (USA) Ltd.

LITHOGRAPHED

Sheets of 120 in six panes of 20

2020, Oct. 27 **Tagged** ***Serpentine Die Cut 10¾***

Self-Adhesive

5542	A4381 (55c) **multicolored** ⓢ	1.25	.25
	P# block of 4, 5#+P	5.00	
	Pane of 20	25.00	

Die cut uncut press sheets of No. 5542 were made available for sale. Values: cross gutter block of 4, $9; pairs with gutters between, $4.25 each. See note after No. 4693.

See note after No. 1549.

Counterfeits exist of No. 5542. See the Postal Counterfeits section of this catalog.

LOVE ⓢ

A4382

Designed by Bailey Sullivan. Printed by Ashton-Potter (USA) Ltd.

LITHOGRAPHED

Sheets of 160 in eight panes of 20

2021, Jan. 14 **Tagged** ***Serpentine Die Cut 11***

Self-Adhesive

5543	A4382 (55c) **multicolored**	1.25	.25
	P# block of 4, 5#+P	5.00	
	Pane of 20	25.00	
a.	Imperforate	1.50	—
	Pane of 20	30.00	

BRUSH RABBIT

A4383

A4383a

Designed by Ethel Kessler. Printed by Ashton-Potter (USA) Ltd.

LITHOGRAPHED

Sheets of 200 in 10 panes of 20

Serpentine Die Cut 11¼x11

2021, Jan. 24 **Tagged**

Self-Adhesive

5544	A4383 (20c) **multicolored** ⓢ	.50	.25
	P# block of 4, 5#+P	2.00	
	Pane of 20	10.00	

Coil Stamp

Serpentine Die Cut 9½ Vert.

5545	A4383a (20c) **multicolored** ⓢ	.50	.25
	Pair	1.00	
	P# strip of 5, #P11111	2.75	
	P# single, #P11111	—	.40

See note after No. 1549.

BARNS ⓢ

Round Barn — A4384

Barn With Gambrel Roof, Windmill — A4385

Forebay Barn — A4386

Snow-covered Western Barn — A4387

Designed by Ashley Walton. Printed by Banknote Corporation of America.

LITHOGRAPHED

Sheets of 160 in eight panes of 20

Serpentine Die Cut 11x11¼

2021, Jan. 24 **Tagged**

Self-Adhesive

5546	A4384 (36c) **multicolored**	.90	.30
5547	A4385 (36c) **multicolored**	.90	.30
5548	A4386 (36c) **multicolored**	.90	.30
5549	A4387 (36c) **multicolored**	.90	.30
a.	Block or horiz. strip of 4, #5546-5549	3.60	
	P# block of 4, 4#+B	3.60	
	Pane of 20	18.00	
	Nos. 5546-5549 (4)	3.60	1.20

Counterfeits exist of Nos. 5546-5549. See the Postal Counterfeits section of this catalog.

Coil Stamps

Serpentine Die Cut 11 Horiz.

5550	A4385a (36c) **multicolored**	.90	.30
5551	A4387a (36c) **multicolored**	.90	.30
5552	A4386a (36c) **multicolored**	.90	.30
5553	A4384a (36c) **multicolored**	.90	.30
a.	Vert. strip of 4, #5550-5553	3.60	
	P# strip of 5, #5551-5553, 2 #5550, #B1111	5.75	
	P# strip of 9, 2 each #5550-5551, 5553, 3 #5552, #B1111	10.50	
	P# single, #B1111 (#5552)	—	3.00
	Nos. 5550-5553 (4)	3.60	1.20

See note after No. 1549.

AMERICAN LANDMARKS ISSUE

Castillo de San Marcos, St. Augustine, Florida A4388

Designed by Greg Breeding. Printed by Ashton-Potter (USA) Ltd.

LITHOGRAPHED

Sheets of 28 in seven panes of 4

Serpentine Die Cut 10¾x10½

2021, Jan. 24 **Tagged**

Self-Adhesive

5554	A4388 $7.95 **multicolored** ⓢ	16.00	8.00
	Pane of 4	64.00	

See note after No. 1549.

Counterfeits exist of No. 5554. See the Postal Counterfeits section of this catalog.

BLACK HERITAGE

August Wilson (1945-2005), Playwright — A4389

Designed by Ethel Kessler. Printed by Ashton-Potter (USA) Ltd.

LITHOGRAPHED

Sheets of 120 in six panes of 20

2021, Jan. 28 **Tagged** ***Serpentine Die Cut 11***

Self-Adhesive

5555	A4389 (55c) **multicolored** ⓢ	1.25	.25
	P# block of 4, 5#+P	5.00	
	Pane of 20	25.00	
a.	Imperforate	2.00	—
	Pane of 20	40.00	

Die cut and imperforate uncut press sheets of No. 5555 were made available for sale. Values for die cut cross gutter block of 4, $9; die cut pairs with gutters between, $4.25 each. See note after No. 4693.

See note after No. 1549.

CHINESE NEW YEAR

Year of the Ox — A4390

Designed by Antonio Alcalá. Printed by Banknote Corporation of America.

LITHOGRAPHED & TYPOGRAPHED WITH FOIL APPLICATION

Sheets of 80 in four panes of 20

2021, Feb. 2 Tagged ***Serpentine Die Cut 11***

Self-Adhesive

5556 A4390 (55c) **multicolored** ⓢ	1.25	.25
P# block of 4, 6#+B	5.00	
Pane of 20	25.00	
a. Imperforate	3.00	—
Pane of 20	60.00	

Die cut and imperforate uncut press sheets of No. 5556 were made available for sale. Values for die cut cross gutter block of 4, $9; die cut pairs with gutters between, $3.75 each. See note after No. 4693.

CHIEN-SHIUNG WU

Dr. Chien-Shiung Wu (1912-97), Nuclear Physicist — A4391

Designed by Ethel Kessler. Printed by Ashton-Potter (USA) Ltd.

LITHOGRAPHED

Sheets of 120 in six panes of 20

2021, Feb. 11 Tagged ***Serpentine Die Cut 11***

Self-Adhesive

5557 A4391 (55c) **multicolored** ⓢ	1.25	.25
P# block of 4, 4#+P	5.00	
Pane of 20	25.00	
a. Imperforate	*6.00*	—
Pane of 20	*120.00*	

Die cut and imperforate uncut press sheets of No. 5557 were made available for sale. Values for die cut cross gutter block of 4, $9; die cut pairs with gutters between, $4.25 each. See note after No. 4693.

See note after No. 1549.

GARDEN BEAUTY ⓢ

Pink Flowering Dogwood — A4392

Orange and Yellow Tulip — A4393

Allium — A4394

Pink Moth Orchid with Mottled Petals — A4395

Magenta Dahlia — A4396

Yellow Moth Orchid with Pink Center — A4397

Pink and White Sacred Lotus — A4398

White Asiatic Lily — A4399

Rose Pink and White Tulip — A4400

Pink American Lotus — A4401

Designed by Ethel Kessler. Printed by Banknote Corporation of America.

LITHOGRAPHED

Serpentine Die Cut 11 on 2 or 3 Sides

2021, Feb. 23 Tagged

Booklet Stamps

Self-Adhesive

5558 A4392 (55c) **multicolored**	1.25	.40
5559 A4393 (55c) **multicolored**	1.25	.40
5560 A4394 (55c) **multicolored**	1.25	.40
5561 A4395 (55c) **multicolored**	1.25	.40
5562 A4396 (55c) **multicolored**	1.25	.40
5563 A4397 (55c) **multicolored**	1.25	.40
5564 A4398 (55c) **multicolored**	1.25	.40
5565 A4399 (55c) **multicolored**	1.25	.40
5566 A4400 (55c) **multicolored**	1.25	.40
5567 A4401 (55c) **multicolored**	1.25	.40
a. Block of 10, #5558-5567	12.50	
b. Booklet pane of 20, 2 each #5558-5567	25.00	
Nos. 5558-5567 (10)	12.50	4.00

No. 5567b is a double-sided booklet pane with 12 stamps on one side (Nos. 5560-5567, 2 each Nos. 5558-5559), and eight stamps (Nos. 5560-5567) plus label (booklet cover) on the other side.

See note after No. 1549.

Counterfeits exist of Nos. 5558-5567. See the Postal Counterfeits section of this catalog.

COLORADO HAIRSTREAK BUTTERFLY ⓢ

A4402

Designed by Derry Noyes. Printed by Banknote Corporation of America.

LITHOGRAPHED

Sheets of 120 in six panes of 20

2021, Mar. 9 Tagged ***Serpentine Die Cut 10½***

Self-Adhesive

5568 A4402 (75c) **multicolored**	2.00	.25
P# block of 4, 5#+B	8.00	
Pane of 20	40.00	

See note after No. 1549.

Counterfeits exist of No. 5568. See the Postal Counterfeits section of this catalog.

ESPRESSO DRINKS ⓢ

Caffe Latte — A4403

Espresso — A4404

Caffe Mocha — A4405

Cappuccino — A4406

Designed by Greg Breeding. Printed by Ashton-Potter (USA) Ltd.

LITHOGRAPHED

Serpentine Die Cut 11¼x10¾ on 2 or 3 Sides

2021, Apr. 9 Tagged

Booklet Stamps

Self-Adhesive

5569 A4403 (55c) **multicolored**	1.25	.30
5570 A4404 (55c) **multicolored**	1.25	.30
5571 A4405 (55c) **multicolored**	1.25	.30
5572 A4406 (55c) **multicolored**	1.25	.30
a. Block of 4, #5569-5572	5.00	
b. Booklet pane of 20, 5 each #5569-5572	25.00	
Nos. 5569-5572 (4)	5.00	1.20

No. 5572b is a double-sided booklet pane with 12 stamps on one side (3 each Nos. 5569-5572), and eight stamps (2 each Nos. 5569-5572) plus label (booklet cover) on the other side.

See note after No. 1549.

Counterfeits exist of Nos. 5569-5572. See the Postal Counterfeits section of this catalog.

STAR WARS MOVIE DROIDS Ⓢ

IG-11 — A4407

R2-D2 — A4408

K-2SO — A4409

D-O — A4410

L3-37 — A4411

BB-8 — A4412

C-3PO — A4413

Gonk Droid — A4414

2-1B Droid — A4415

Chopper — A4416

Designed by Greg Breeding. Printed by Banknote Corporation of America.

LITHOGRAPHED & TYPOGRAPHED
Sheets of 80 in four panes of 20

2021, May 4 Tagged *Serpentine Die Cut 10¾*
Self-Adhesive

5573	A4407 (55c) **multicolored**	1.25	.40
a.	Imperforate	6.00	—
5574	A4408 (55c) **multicolored**	1.25	.40
a.	Imperforate	6.00	—
5575	A4409 (55c) **multicolored**	1.25	.40
a.	Imperforate	6.00	—
5576	A4410 (55c) **multicolored**	1.25	.40
a.	Imperforate	6.00	—
5577	A4411 (55c) **multicolored**	1.25	.40
a.	Imperforate	6.00	—
5578	A4412 (55c) **multicolored**	1.25	.40
a.	Imperforate	6.00	—
5579	A4413 (55c) **multicolored**	1.25	.40
a.	Imperforate	6.00	—
5580	A4414 (55c) **multicolored**	1.25	.40
a.	Imperforate	6.00	—
5581	A4415 (55c) **multicolored**	1.25	.40
a.	Imperforate	6.00	—
5582	A4416 (55c) **multicolored**	1.25	.40
a.	Imperforate	6.00	—
b.	Block of 10, #5573-5582	12.50	
c.	Imperforate block of 10, #5573a-5582a	60.00	
	P# block of 10, 2 sets of 5# + B	12.50	
	Pane of 20	25.00	
	Imperforate pane of 20	120.00	
	Nos. 5573-5582 (10)	12.50	4.00

Die cut and imperforate uncut press sheets of Nos. 5573-5582 were made available for sale. Values: cross gutter block of 10, $18; pairs with gutters between, $4.25 each. See note after No. 4693.

See note after No. 1549.

Counterfeits exist of Nos. 5573-5582. See the Postal Counterfeits section of this catalog.

HERITAGE BREEDS Ⓢ

Mulefoot Hog — A4417

Wyandotte Chicken — A4418

Milking Devon Cow — A4419

Narragansett Turkey — A4420

American Mammoth Jackstock Donkey — A4421

Cotton Patch Goose — A4422

San Clemente Island Goat — A4423

American Cream Draft Horse — A4424

Cayuga Duck — A4425

Barbados Blackbelly Sheep — A4426

Designed by Zack Bryant. Printed by Banknote Corporation of America.

LITHOGRAPHED & TYPOGRAPHED
Sheets of 80 in four panes of 20
Serpentine Die Cut 10½x10¾

2021, May 17 **Tagged**

Self-Adhesive

5583	A4417 (55c) **multicolored**	1.25	.40
a.	Imperforate	6.00	—
5584	A4418 (55c) **multicolored**	1.25	.40
a.	Imperforate	6.00	—
5585	A4419 (55c) **multicolored**	1.25	.40
a.	Imperforate	6.00	—
5586	A4420 (55c) **multicolored**	1.25	.40
a.	Imperforate	6.00	—
5587	A4421 (55c) **multicolored**	1.25	.40
a.	Imperforate	6.00	—
5588	A4422 (55c) **multicolored**	1.25	.40
a.	Imperforate	6.00	—
5589	A4423 (55c) **multicolored**	1.25	.40
a.	Imperforate	6.00	—
5590	A4424 (55c) **multicolored**	1.25	.40
a.	Imperforate	6.00	—
5591	A4425 (55c) **multicolored**	1.25	.40
a.	Imperforate	6.00	—
5592	A4426 (55c) **multicolored**	1.25	.40
a.	Imperforate	6.00	—
b.	Block of 10, #5583-5592	12.50	
c.	Imperforate block of 10, #5583a-5592a	60.00	
	P# block of 10, 2 sets of 6# + B	12.50	
	Pane of 20	25.00	
	Imperforate pane of 20	120.00	
	Nos. 5583-5592 (10)	12.50	4.00

Die cut and imperforate uncut press sheets of Nos. 5583-5592 were made available for sale. Values: die cut cross gutter block of 10, $18; die cut pairs with gutters between, $4.25 each. See note after No. 4693.

See note after No. 1549.

GO FOR BROKE

Japanese-American Soldier of World War II — A4427

Designed by Antonio Alcalá. Printed by Banknote Corporation of America.

LITHOGRAPHED & ENGRAVED
Sheets of 120 in six panes of 20

2021, June 3 **Tagged** ***Serpentine Die Cut 10¾***

Self-Adhesive

5593	A4427 (55c) **blue & red** Ⓢ	1.25	.25
	P# block of 4, 2#+B	5.00	
	Pane of 20	25.00	
a.	Imperforate	2.00	—
	Pane of 20	40.00	

Die cut and imperforate uncut press sheets of No. 5593 were made available for sale. Values for die cut cross gutter block of 4, $9; die cut pairs with gutters between, $4.25 each. See note after No. 4693.

See note after No. 1549.

PAINTINGS BY EMILIO SANCHEZ (1921-99) Ⓢ

Los Toldos, 1973
A4428

Ty's Place, 1976 — A4429

En el Souk, 1972
A4430

Untitled (Ventanita Entreabierta), 1981
A4431

Designed by Antonio Alcalá. Printed by Ashton-Potter (USA) Ltd.

LITHOGRAPHED
Sheets of 180 in nine panes of 20

2021, June 10 **Tagged** ***Serpentine Die Cut 10¾***

Self-Adhesive

5594	A4428 (55c) **multicolored**	1.25	.30
a.	Imperforate	2.00	—
5595	A4429 (55c) **multicolored**	1.25	.30
a.	Imperforate	2.00	—
5596	A4430 (55c) **multicolored**	1.25	.30
a.	Imperforate	2.00	—
5597	A4431 (55c) **multicolored**	1.25	.30
a.	Imperforate	2.00	—
b.	Horiz. or vert. stirip of 4, #5594-5597	5.00	
c.	Imperforate horiz. or vert. strip of 4, #5594a-5597a	8.00	
	P# block of 8, 2 sets of 5# + P	10.00	
	Pane of 20	25.00	
	Imperforate pane of 20	40.00	
	Nos. 5594-5597 (4)	5.00	1.20

Die cut and imperforate uncut press sheets of Nos. 5594-5597 were made available for sale. Values: die cut cross gutter block of 8, $16; die cut pairs with gutters between, $4.25 each. See note after No. 4693.

See note after No. 1549.

Counterfeits exist of Nos. 5594-5597. See the Postal Counterfeits section of this catalog.

SUN SCIENCE Ⓢ

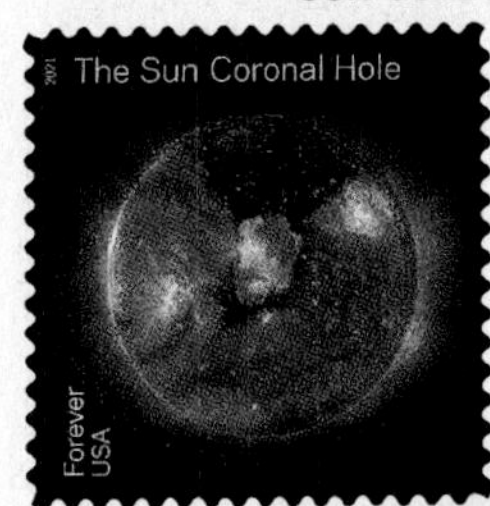

Coronal Hole — A4432

Coronal Loops — A4433

Solar Flare — A4434

Active Sun — A4435

Plasma Blast — A4436

Coronal Loops — A4437

Sunspots — A4438

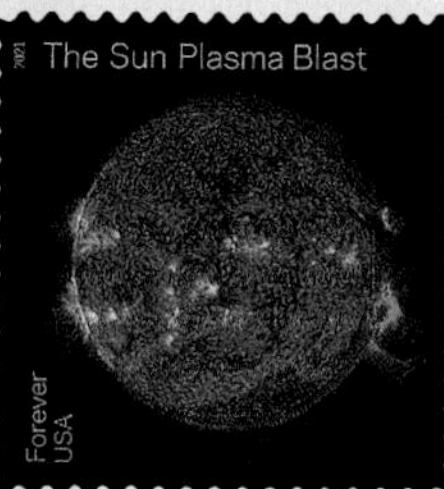

Plasma Blast — A4439

Solar Flare — A4440

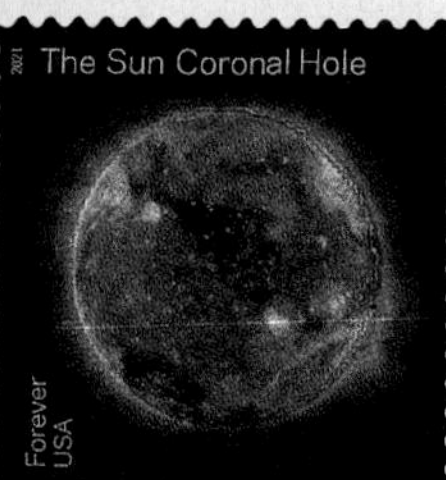

Coronal Hole — A4441

Designed by Antonio Alcalá. Printed by Banknote Corporation of America.

TYPOGRAPHED WITH FOIL APPLICATION
Sheets of 120 in six panes of 20
Serpentine Die Cut 10¾x10½

2021, June 18 **Tagged**
Self-Adhesive

5598 A4432 (55c) **multicolored**		1.25	.40
a.	Imperforate	5.00	—
5599 A4433 (55c) **multicolored**		1.25	.40
a.	Imperforate	5.00	—
5600 A4434 (55c) **multicolored**		1.25	.40
a.	Imperforate	5.00	—
5601 A4435 (55c) **multicolored**		1.25	.40
a.	Imperforate	5.00	—
5602 A4436 (55c) **multicolored**		1.25	.40
a.	Imperforate	5.00	—
5603 A4437 (55c) **multicolored**		1.25	.40
a.	Imperforate	5.00	—
5604 A4438 (55c) **multicolored**		1.25	.40
a.	Imperforate	5.00	—
5605 A4439 (55c) **multicolored**		1.25	.40
a.	Imperforate	5.00	—
5606 A4440 (55c) **multicolored**		1.25	.40
a.	Imperforate	5.00	—
5607 A4441 (55c) **multicolored**		1.25	.40
a.	Imperforate	5.00	—
b.	Block of 10, #5598-5607	12.50	
c.	Imperforate block of 10, #5598a-5607a	50.00	
	P# block of 10, 2 sets of 4# + B	12.50	
	Pane of 20	25.00	
	Imperforate pane of 20	100.00	
	Nos. 5598-5607 (10)	12.50	4.00

Die cut and imperforate uncut press sheets of Nos. 5598-5607 were made available for sale. Values: die cut cross gutter block of 8, $16; die cut pairs with gutters between, $4.25 each. See note after No. 4693.

See note after No. 1549.

YOGI BERRA

Lawrence Peter "Yogi" Berra (1925-2015), Baseball Player — A4442

Designed by Antonio Alcalá. Printed by Banknote Corporation of America.

LITHOGRAPHED & TYPOGRAPHED
Sheets of 120 in six panes of 20

2021, June 24 **Tagged** ***Serpentine Die Cut 10¾***
Self-Adhesive

5608 A4442 (55c) **multicolored** Ⓢ		1.25	.25
	P# block of 4, 7#+B	5.00	
	Pane of 20	25.00	
a.	Imperforate	2.00	—
	Pane of 20	40.00	

Die cut and imperforate uncut press sheets of No. 5608 were made available for sale. Values: die cut cross gutter block of 4, $9; die cut pairs with gutters between, $4.25 each. See note after No. 4693.

See note after No. 1549.

TAP DANCE Ⓢ

Max Pollak — A4443

Michela Marino Lerman — A4444

Derick Grant A4445

Dormeshia Sumbry-Edwards A4446

Ayodele Casel — A4447

Designed by Ethel Kessler. Printed by Ashton-Potter (USA) Ltd.

LITHOGRAPHED
Sheets of 240 in 12 panes of 20

2021, July 10 **Tagged** ***Serpentine Die Cut 11***
Color of "TAP"
Self-Adhesive

5609 A4443 (55c) **buff**		1.25	.40
a.	Imperforate	3.00	—
5610 A4444 (55c) **rose**		1.25	.40
a.	Imperforate	3.00	—
5611 A4445 (55c) **greenish blue**		1.25	.40
a.	Imperforate	3.00	—
5612 A4446 (55c) **light blue**		1.25	.40
a.	Imperforate	3.00	—
5613 A4447 (55c) **bister**		1.25	.40
a.	Imperforate	3.00	—
b.	Horiz. strip of 5, #5609-5613	5.50	
c.	Imperforate strip of 5, #5609a-5613a	15.00	
	P# block of 10, 2 sets of 4# + P	11.00	
	Pane of 20	22.00	
	Imperforate pane of 20	60.00	
	Nos. 5609-5613 (5)	6.25	2.00

Die cut and imperforate uncut press sheets of Nos. 5609-5613 (containing 120 stamps) were made available for sale. Values: die cut cross gutter block of 10, $18; die cut pairs with gutters between, $4.25 each. See note after No. 4693.

See note after No. 1549.

MYSTERY MESSAGE

"More Than Meets The Eye" — A4448

Designed by Antonio Alcalá. Printed by Banknote Corporation of America.

LITHOGRAPHED & TYPOGRAPHED
Sheets of 160 in eight panes of 20

2021, July 14 **Tagged** ***Serpentine Die Cut 10½***
Self-Adhesive

5614 A4448 (55c) **multicolored** Ⓢ		1.25	.25
	P# block of 4, 4#+B	5.00	
	Pane of 20	25.00	
a.	Imperforate	1.25	—
	Pane of 20	25.00	

Die cut and imperforate uncut press sheets of No. 5614 were made available for sale. Values: die cut cross gutter block of 4, $9; die cut pairs with gutters between, $4.25 each. See note after No. 4693.

See note after No. 1549.

Counterfeits exist of No. 5614. See the Postal Counterfeits section of this catalog.

WESTERN WEAR Ⓢ

Cowboy Hat, Snakes and Roses — A4449

Belt Buckle, Roses, Stars and Spurs — A4450

Cowboy Boot With Spur, Roses, Cacti and Star — A4451

Western Shirt, Roses, Cacti and Star — A4452

Designed by Greg Breeding. Printed by Ashton-Potter (USA) Ltd.

LITHOGRAPHED

Serpentine Die Cut 10¾ on 2 or 3 Sides

2021, July 23 **Tagged**

Booklet Stamps
Self-Adhesive

5615	A4449 (55c) **multicolored**	1.25	.30
5616	A4450 (55c) **multicolored**	1.25	.30
5617	A4451 (55c) **multicolored**	1.25	.30
5618	A4452 (55c) **multicolored**	1.25	.30
a.	Block of 4, #5615-5618	5.00	
b.	Booklet pane of 20, 5 each #5615-5618	25.00	
	Nos. 5615-5618 (4)	5.00	1.20

No. 5618b is a double-sided booklet pane with 12 stamps on one side (3 each Nos. 5615-5618), and eight stamps (2 each Nos. 5615-5618) plus label (booklet cover) on the other side.

See note after No. 1549.

Counterfeits exist of Nos. 5615-5618. See the Postal Counterfeits section of this catalog.

LITERARY ARTS

Ursula K. Le Guin (1929-2018), Science Fiction Novelist A4453

Designed by Antonio Alcalá. Printed by Ashton-Potter (USA), Ltd.

LITHOGRAPHED

Sheets of 120 in six panes of 20

2021, July 27 **Tagged** ***Serpentine Die Cut 10¾***

Self-Adhesive

5619	A4453 (95c) **multicolored** Ⓢ	2.20	.30
	P# block of 4, 4#+P	8.80	
	Pane of 20	44.00	

See note after No. 1549.

RAVEN STORY

Mythological Raven from Stories of Indigenous People of the Northern Northwest Coast A4454

Designed by Antonio Alcalá. Printed by Banknote Corporation of America.

TYPOGRAPHED WITH FOIL APPLICATION

Sheets of 120 in six panes of 20

2021, July 30 **Tagged** ***Serpentine Die Cut 10¾***

Self-Adhesive

5620	A4454 (55c) **multicolored** Ⓢ	1.25	.25
	P# block of 4, 2#+B	5.00	
	Pane of 20	25.00	
a.	Imperforate	*20.00*	—
	Pane of 20	*400.00*	

Die cut and imperforate uncut press sheets of No. 5620 were made available for sale. Values: die cut cross gutter block of 4, $9; die cut pairs with gutters between, $4.25 each. See note after No. 4693.

See note after No. 1549.

Counterfeits exist of No. 5620. See the Postal Counterfeits section of this catalog.

MID-ATLANTIC LIGHTHOUSES Ⓢ

Montauk Point Lighthouse, New York — A4455

Navesink Twin Lighthouses, New Jersey — A4456

Erie Harbor Lighthouse, Pennsylvania — A4457

Harbor of Refuge Lighthouse, Delaware — A4458

Thomas Point Shoal Lighthouse, Maryland — A4459

Designed by Greg Breeding. Printed by Banknote Corporation of America.

LITHOGRAPHED

Sheets of 240 in 12 panes of 20

2021, Aug. 6 **Tagged** ***Serpentine Die Cut 10¾***

Self-Adhesive

5621	A4455 (55c) **multicolored**	1.25	.40
a.	Imperforate	1.50	—
5622	A4456 (55c) **multicolored**	1.25	.40
a.	Imperforate	1.50	—
5623	A4457 (55c) **multicolored**	1.25	.40
a.	Imperforate	1.50	—
5624	A4458 (55c) **multicolored**	1.25	.40
a.	Imperforate	1.50	—
5625	A4459 (55c) **multicolored**	1.25	.40
a.	Imperforate	1.50	—
b.	Horiz. strip of 5, #5621-5625	6.25	
c.	Imperforate strip of 5, #5621a-5625a	7.50	
	P# block of 10, 2 sets of 4# + B	12.50	
	Pane of 20	25.00	
	Imperforate pane of 20	30.00	
	Nos. 5621-5625 (5)	6.25	2.00

Die cut and imperforate uncut press sheets of Nos. 5621-5625 (containing 120 stamps) were made available for sale. Values: die cut cross gutter block of 10, $18; die cut pairs with gutters between, $4.25 each. See note after No. 4693.

See note after No. 1549.

Counterfeits exist of Nos. 5621-5625. See the Postal Counterfeits section of this catalog.

MISSOURI STATEHOOD BICENTENARY

Bollinger Mill and Burfordville Covered Bridge A4460

Designed by Greg Breeding. Printed by Banknote Corporation of America.

LITHOGRAPHED

Sheets of 120 in six panes of 20

2021, Aug. 10 **Tagged** ***Serpentine Die Cut 10¾***

Self-Adhesive

5626	A4460 (55c) **multicolored** Ⓢ	1.25	.25
	P# block of 4, 4#+B	5.00	
	Pane of 20	25.00	
a.	Imperforate	1.25	—
	Pane of 20	25.00	

Die cut and imperforate uncut press sheets of No. 5626 were made available for sale. Values: die cut cross gutter block of 4, $9; die cut pairs with gutters between, $4.25 each. See note after No. 4693.

See note after No. 1549.

BACKYARD GAMES Ⓢ

Horseshoes — A4461

Bocce — A4462

Flying Disc — A4463

Croquet — A4464

Pick-up Baseball Variation — A4465

Tetherball — A4466

Badminton — A4467

Cornhole — A4468

Designed by Mike Ryan. Printed by Banknote Corporation of America.

LITHOGRAPHED

Sheets of 160 in 10 panes of 16

2021, Aug. 12 Tagged *Serpentine Die Cut 10¾*

Self-Adhesive

No.	Description	Unused	Used
5627	A4461 (55c) **multicolored**	1.25	.40
a.	Imperforate	2.00	—
5628	A4462 (55c) **multicolored**	1.25	.40
a.	Imperforate	2.00	—
5629	A4463 (55c) **multicolored**	1.25	.40
a.	Imperforate	2.00	—
5630	A4464 (55c) **multicolored**	1.25	.40
a.	Imperforate	2.00	—
5631	A4465 (55c) **multicolored**	1.25	.40
a.	Imperforate	2.00	—
5632	A4466 (55c) **multicolored**	1.25	.40
a.	Imperforate	2.00	—
5633	A4467 (55c) **multicolored**	1.25	.40
a.	Imperforate	2.00	—
5634	A4468 (55c) **multicolored**	1.25	.40
a.	Imperforate	2.00	—
b.	Block of 8, #5627-5634	10.00	
c.	Imperforate block of 8, #5627a-5634a	16.00	
	P# block of 8, 2 sets of 4# + B	10.00	
	Pane of 16	20.00	
	Imperforate pane of 20	32.00	
	Nos. 5627-5634 (8)	10.00	3.20

Die cut and imperforate uncut press sheets of Nos. 5627-5634 were made available for sale. Values: die cut cross gutter block of 8, $16; die cut pairs with gutters between, $4.25 each. See note after No. 4693.

See note after No. 1549.

Counterfeits exist of Nos. 5627-5634. See the Postal Counterfeits section of this catalog.

HAPPY BIRTHDAY

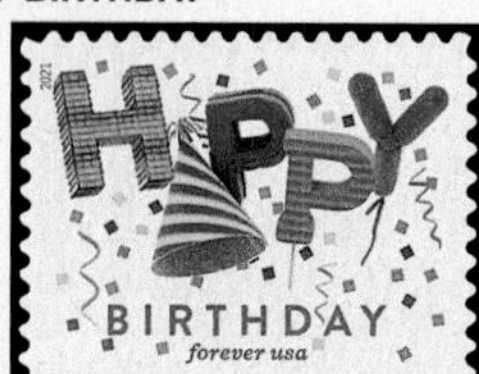

Birthday Hat, Confetti and Streamers — A4469

Designed by Lisa Catalone Castro. Printed by Ashton-Potter (USA) Ltd.

LITHOGRAPHED

Sheets of 160 in eight panes of 20

2021, Sept. 9 Tagged *Serpentine Die Cut 11*

Self-Adhesive

No.	Description	Unused	Used
5635	A4469 (58c) **multicolored** Ⓢ	1.25	.25
	P# block of 4, 4#+P	5.00	
	Pane of 20	25.00	

See note after No. 1549.

Counterfeits exist of No. 5635. See the Postal Counterfeits section of this catalog.

MESSAGE MONSTERS Ⓢ

Pink and Red Monster — A4470

Four-Armed Monster — A4471

Tentacled Monster — A4472

Red-Headed Monster — A4473

Designed by Antonio Alcalá. Printed by Banknote Corporation of America.

LITHOGRAPHED

Sheets of 60 in three panes of 20

Serpentine Die Cut 10½x10¾

2021, Sept. 24 Tagged

Self-Adhesive

No.	Description	Unused	Used
5636	A4470 (58c) **multicolored**	1.25	.30
a.	Imperforate	2.00	—
5637	A4471 (58c) **multicolored**	1.25	.30
a.	Imperforate	2.00	—
5638	A4472 (58c) **multicolored**	1.25	.30
a.	Imperforate	2.00	—
5639	A4473 (58c) **multicolored**	1.25	.30
a.	Imperforate	2.00	—
b.	Horiz. or vert. strip of 4, #5636-5639	5.00	
c.	Imperforate strip of 4 #5636a-5639a	8.00	
	P# block of 10, 2 sets of 4# + B	12.50	
	Pane of 20	25.00	
	Imperforate pane of 20	40.00	
	Nos. 5636-5639 (4)	5.00	1.20

The pane of 20 has 34 die cut stickers in the selvage. Die cut and imperforate uncut press sheets of Nos. 5636-5639 were made available for sale. Values: die cut gutter block of 8, $18; die cut pairs with gutters between, $4.25 each. See note after No. 4693.

See note after No. 1549.

Counterfeits exist of Nos. 5636-5639. See the Postal Counterfeits section of this catalog.

DAY OF THE DEAD Ⓢ

Girl's Skull With Bow — A4474

Man's Skull With Hat — A4475

Woman's Skull With Curled Hair — A4476

Boy's Skull — A4477

Designed by Luis Fitch. Printed by Banknote Corporation of America.

LITHOGRAPHED

Sheets of 160 in eight panes of 20

2021, Sept. 30 Tagged *Serpentine Die Cut 11*

Self-Adhesive

No.	Description	Unused	Used
5640	A4474 (58c) **multicolored**	1.25	.30
a.	Imperforate	1.75	—
5641	A4475 (58c) **multicolored**	1.25	.30
a.	Imperforate	1.75	—
5642	A4476 (58c) **multicolored**	1.25	.30
a.	Imperforate	1.75	—
5643	A4477 (58c) **multicolored**	1.25	.30
a.	Imperforate	1.75	—
b.	Horiz. strip of 4, #5640-5643	5.00	
c.	Imperforate strip of 4, #5640a-5643a	7.00	
	P# block of 8, 2 sets of 9# + B	10.00	
	Pane of 20	25.00	
	Imperforate pane of 20	35.00	
	Nos. 5640-5643 (4)	5.00	1.20

Die cut and imperforate uncut press sheets of Nos. 5640-5643 were made available for sale. Values: die cut cross gutter block of 8, $18; die cut pairs with gutters between, $4.25 each. See note after No. 4693.

See note after No. 1549.

Counterfeits exist of Nos. 5640-5643. See the Postal Counterfeits section of this catalog.

CHRISTMAS Ⓢ

Santa Claus on Roof — A4478

Santa Claus in Fireplace — A4479

Head of Santa Claus — A4480

Santa Claus, Sleigh and Reindeer in Flight — A4481

Designed by Greg Breeding. Printed by Ashton-Potter (USA) Ltd.

LITHOGRAPHED

Serpentine Die Cut 10¾x11 on 2 or 3 Sides

2021, Oct. 7 Tagged

Booklet Stamps

Self-Adhesive

No.	Description	Unused	Used
5644	A4478 (58c) **multicolored**	1.25	.30
5645	A4479 (58c) **multicolored**	1.25	.30
5646	A4480 (58c) **multicolored**	1.25	.30
5647	A4481 (58c) **multicolored**	1.25	.30
a.	Block of 4, #5644-5647	5.00	
b.	Booklet pane of 20, 5 each #5644-5647	25.00	
	Nos. 5644-5647 (4)	5.00	1.20

No. 5647b is a double-sided booklet pane with 12 stamps on one side (3 each Nos. 5644-5647), and eight stamps (2 each Nos. 5644-5647) plus label (booklet cover) on the other side.

See note after No. 1549.

Counterfeits exist of Nos. 5644-5647. See the Postal Counterfeits section of this catalog.

OTTERS IN SNOW Ⓢ

Otter in Water — A4482

Otter, Tail at Right — A4483

Otter, Tail at Left — A4484

Otter in Snow — A4485

Designed by Derry Noyes. Printed by Banknote Corporation of America.

LITHOGRAPHED

Serpentine Die Cut 10¾x11 on 2 or 3 Sides

2021, Oct. 12 Tagged

Booklet Stamps
Self-Adhesive

5648 A4482 (58c) **multicolored** 1.25 .30
5649 A4483 (58c) **multicolored** 1.25 .30
5650 A4484 (58c) **multicolored** 1.25 .30
5651 A4485 (58c) **multicolored** 1.25 .30
a. Block of 4, #5648-5651 5.00
b. Booklet pane of 20, 5 each #5648-5651 25.00
Nos. 5648-5651 (4) 5.00 1.20

No. 5651b is a double-sided booklet pane with 12 stamps on one side (3 each Nos. 5648-5651), and eight stamps (2 each Nos. 5648-5651) plus label (booklet cover) on the other side.
See note after No. 1549.
Counterfeits exist of Nos. 5648-5651. See the Postal Counterfeits section of this catalog.

FRUIT

Blueberries — A4486

Blueberries — A4486a

Designed by Derry Noyes. Printed by Banknote Corporation of America.

LITHOGRAPHED
Sheets of 120 in six panes of 20

Serpentine Die Cut 11¼x11

2022, Jan. 9 Untagged

Self-Adhesive

5652 A4486 4c **multicolored,** Ⓢ .30 .25
P# block of 4, 6#+B .35
Pane of 20 1.60

Coil Stamp

Serpentine Die Cut 10¾ Vert.

5653 A4486a 4c **multicolored** Ⓢ .30 .25
Pair .30
P# strip of 5, #B111111 .40
P# single, #B111111 — .50

See note after No. 1549.

Flags — A4487

Designed by Laura Stutzman. Printed by Banknote Corporation of America (#5654-5656, 5658). Ashton-Potter (USA) Ltd. (#5657, 5659).

LITHOGRAPHED

2022, Jan. 9 Tagged *Serpentine Die Cut 11¼x11*

Self-Adhesive

Microprinted "USPS" Above Lower Connector on Flagpole at Left

5654 A4487 (58c) **multicolored,** Ⓢ 1.25 .25
P# block of 4, 4#+B 5.00
Pane of 20 25.00

Coil Stamps
Stamps Not Adjacent on Coil Roll
Backing Paper Taller Than Stamp

Serpentine Die Cut 10¾ Vert.

5655 A4487a (58c) **multicolored** Ⓢ 1.25 .25
Pair 2.50
P# strip of 5, #B1111 8.50
P# single, #B1111 — 2.50

Serpentine Die Cut 11 Vert.

Stamps Adjacent on Coil Roll
Backing Paper Same Height as Stamp

5656 A4487b (58c) **multicolored** Ⓢ 1.25 .25
Pair 2.50
P# strip of 5, #B1111 8.50
P# single, #B1111 — 2.50

Microprinted "USPS" Above Lowest Blue Flag Field

Serpentine Die Cut 9½ Vert.

5657 A4487c (58c) **multicolored** Ⓢ 1.25 .25
Pair 2.50
P# strip of 5, #P1111 8.50
P# single, #P1111 — 2.50
Nos. 5655-5657 (3) 3.75 .75

Booklet Stamps
Microprinted "USPS" Above Lower Connector on Flagpole at Left

Serpentine Die Cut 11¼x10¾ on 2 or 3 Sides

5658 A4487d (58c) **multicolored** Ⓢ 1.25 .25
a. Booklet pane of 20 25.00

Microprinted "USPS" Above Lowest Blue Flag Field

5659 A4487e (58c) **multicolored** Ⓢ 1.25 .25
a. Booklet pane of 20 25.00

Nos. 5658a and 5659a are double-sided booklets with 12 stamps on one side and eight stamps plus a label that serves as the booklet cover on the other side.
See note after No. 1549.
Counterfeits exist of Nos. 5654, 5657, 5659. See the Postal Counterfeits section of this catalog.

LOVE Ⓢ

A4488

A4489

Designed by Bailey Sullivan. Printed by Banknote Corporation of America.

LITHOGRAPHED
Sheets of 320 in 16 panes of 20

2022, Jan. 14 Tagged *Serpentine Die Cut 11*

Self-Adhesive
Background Color

5660 A4488 (58c) **blue gray** 1.25 .25
a. Imperforate 1.25 —
5661 A4489 (58c) **pink** 1.25 .25
a. Imperforate 1.25 —
b. Horiz. or vert. pair, #5660-5661 2.50
c. Imperforate horiz. or vert. pair, #5660a-5661a 2.50
P# block of 4, 4# + B 5.00
Pane of 20 25.00
Imperforate pane of 20 25.00

Die cut and imperforate uncut press sheets of Nos. 5660-5661(containing 160 stamps) were made available for sale. Values: die cut cross gutter block of 4, $9; die cut pairs with gutters between, $4.25 each. See note after No. 4693.
See note after No. 1549.
Counterfeits exist of Nos. 5660-5661. See the Postal Counterfeits section of this catalog.

CHINESE NEW YEAR

Year of the Tiger — A4490

Designed by Antonio Alcalá. Printed by Banknote Corporation of America.

LITHOGRAPHED & TYPOGRAPHED WITH FOIL APPLICATION
Sheets of 80 in four panes of 20

2022, Jan. 20 Tagged *Serpentine Die Cut 11*

Self-Adhesive

5662 A4490 (58c) **multicolored** Ⓢ 1.25 .25
P# block of 4, 6#+B 5.00
Pane of 20 25.00
a. Imperforate 1.25 —
Pane of 20 25.00

Die cut and imperforate uncut press sheets of No. 5662 were made available for sale. Values: die cut cross gutter block of 4, $9; die cut pairs with gutters between, $4.25 each. See note after No. 4693.

BLACK HERITAGE

Edmonia Lewis (c. 1844-1907), Sculptor — A4491

Designed by Antonio Alcalá. Printed by Banknote Corporation of America.

LITHOGRAPHED
Sheets of 80 in four panes of 20

2022, Jan. 26 Tagged *Serpentine Die Cut 10¾*

Self-Adhesive

5663 A4491 (58c) **multicolored** Ⓢ 1.25 .25
P# block of 4, 5#+B 5.00
Pane of 20 25.00
a. Imperforate 1.25 —
Pane of 20 25.00

Die cut and imperforate uncut press sheets of No. 5663 were made available for sale. Values: die cut cross gutter block of 4, $9; die cut pairs with gutters between, $4.25 each. See note after No. 4693.
See note after No. 1549.

BUTTERFLY GARDEN FLOWERS

Cosmos — A4492

Scabiosas — A4493

Designed by Antonio Alcalá. Printed by Banknote Corporation of America.

LITHOGRAPHED

Serpentine Die Cut 10¾ Vert.

2022, Feb. 1 **Untagged**

Coil Stamps
Self-Adhesive

5664 A4492 (5c) **multicolored** Ⓢ	.30	.25
5665 A4493 (5c) **multicolored** Ⓢ	.30	.25
a. Pair, #5664-5665	.30	
P# strip of 5, 3 #5664, 2 #5665, #B1111	1.60	
P# single, #B1111 (#5664)	—	1.25

See note after No. 1549.

AMERICAN LANDMARKS ISSUE

Monument Valley, Utah — A4494

Palace of Fine Arts, San Francisco, California A4495

Designed by Greg Breeding. Printed by Ashton-Potter (USA) Ltd.

LITHOGRAPHED

Sheets of 96 in 24 panes of 4 (#5666), Sheets of 24 in six panes of 4 (#5667)

Serpentine Die Cut 10¾x10½

2022, Feb. 14 **Tagged**

Self-Adhesive

5666 A4494 $8.95 **multicolored** Ⓢ	18.00	8.00
Pane of 4	72.00	
5667 A4495 $26.95 **multicolored** Ⓢ	55.00	27.50
Pane of 4	220.00	

See note after No. 1549.

TITLE IX CIVIL RIGHTS LAW, 50TH ANNIV. Ⓢ

Runner — A4496

Swimmer — A4497

Gymnast — A4498

Soccer Player — A4499

Designed by Melinda Beck. Printed by Ashton-Potter (USA) Ltd.

LITHOGRAPHED

Sheets of 180 in nine panes of 20

2022, Mar. 3 **Tagged** ***Serpentine Die Cut 10¾***

Self-Adhesive

5668 A4496 (58c) **multicolored**	1.25	.30
a. Imperforate	1.25	—
5669 A4497 (58c) **multicolored**	1.25	.30
a. Imperforate	1.25	—
5670 A4498 (58c) **multicolored**	1.25	.30
a. Imperforate	1.25	—
5671 A4499 (58c) **multicolored**	1.25	.30
a. Imperforate	1.25	—
b. Block or vert. strip of 4, #5668-5671	5.00	
c. Imperforate block or vert. strip of 4 #5668a-5671a	5.00	
P# block of 4, 4# + P	5.00	
Pane of 20	25.00	
Imperforate pane of 20	25.00	
Nos. 5668-5671 (4)	5.00	1.20

Die cut and imperforate uncut press sheets of Nos. 5668-5671 were made available for sale. Values: die cut gutter block of 8, $18; die cut pairs with gutters between, $4.25 each. See note after No. 4693.

See note after No. 1549.

MOUNTAIN FLORA Ⓢ

Wood Lily — A4500

Alpine Buttercup — A4501

Woods' Rose A4502

Pasqueflower A4503

Pasqueflower A4504

Wood Lily A4505

Alpine Buttercup — A4506

Woods' Rose — A4507

Designed by Ethel Kessler. Printed by Ashton-Potter (USA) Ltd.

LITHOGRAPHED

Serpentine Die Cut 10 Vert.

2022, Mar. 14 **Tagged**

Coil Stamps
Self-Adhesive

5672 A4500 (58c) **multicolored**	1.25	.30
5673 A4501 (58c) **multicolored**	1.25	.30
5674 A4502 (58c) **multicolored**	1.25	.30
5675 A4503 (58c) **multicolored**	1.25	.30
a. Horiz. strip of 4, #5672-5675	5.00	
P# strip of 7, #5672, 2 each #5673-5675, #P1111	11.50	
P# strip of 9, 2 each #5672-5674, 3 #5675, #P1111	13.00	
P# single (#5675), #P1111	—	2.75
Nos. 5672-5675 (4)	5.00	1.20

Booklet Stamps

Serpentine Die Cut 10¾x11 on 2 or 3 Sides

5676 A4504 (58c) **multicolored**	1.25	.30
5677 A4505 (58c) **multicolored**	1.25	.30
5678 A4506 (58c) **multicolored**	1.25	.30
5679 A4507 (58c) **multicolored**	1.25	.30
a. Block of 4, #5676-5679	5.00	
b. Booklet pane of 20, 5 each #5676-5679	25.00	
Nos. 5676-5679 (4)	5.00	1.20

Nos. 5679b is a double-sided booklet with 12 stamps on one side (3 each Nos 5676-5679), and eight stamps (2 each Nos. 5676-5679) plus a label that serves as the booklet cover on the other side.

See note after No. 1549.

African Daisy — A4508

Designed by Greg Breeding. Printed by Ashton-Potter (USA) Ltd.

LITHOGRAPHED

Sheets of 90 in nine panes of 10

2022, Mar. 14 **Tagged** ***Serpentine Die Cut***

Self-Adhesive

5680 A4508 ($1.30) **multicolored** Ⓢ	2.60	.60
P# block of 4, 6#+P	10.40	
Pane of 10	26.00	

Unused values are for stamps with surrounding selvage. Adjacent stamps are separated by rouletting. See note after No. 1549.

Tulips — A4509

Sunflower Bouquet — A4510

Designed by Ethel Kessler. Printed by Banknote Corporation of America.

LITHOGRAPHED

Sheets of 160 in eight panes of 20

Serpentine Die Cut 11x10¾

2022, Mar. 24 **Tagged**

Self-Adhesive

5681 A4509 (58c) **multicolored** ⓢ 1.25 .25
P# block of 4, 6#+B 5.00
Pane of 20 25.00

Serpentine Die Cut 10¾x11

5682 A4510 (78c) **multicolored** ⓢ 1.60 .25
P# block of 4, 6#+B 6.40
Pane of 20 32.00

See note after No. 1549.

SHEL SILVERSTEIN (1930-99), CHILDREN'S BOOK WRITER

Boy Catching Apple, Illustration From *The Giving Tree,* by Silverstein — A4511

Designed by Derry Noyes. Printed by Ashton-Potter (USA) Ltd.

LITHOGRAPHED

Sheets of 240 in 12 panes of 20

2022, Apr. 8 **Tagged** ***Serpentine Die Cut 11***

Self-Adhesive

5683 A4511 (58c) **multicolored** ⓢ 1.25 .25
P# block of 4, 4#+P 5.00
Pane of 20 25.00
a. Imperforate — —
Pane of 20 —

Die cut and imperforate uncut press half sheets of No. 5683 were made available for sale. Values: die cut cross gutter block of 4, $9; die cut pairs with gutters between, $4.25 each. See note after No. 4693.

See note after No. 1549.

FLAGS ON BARNS ⓢ

Flag on Red Barn Near Well — A4512

Flag on White Barn in Winter — A4513

Flag on White Barn With Gambrel Roof — A4514

Flag on Barn Near Windmill — A4515

Designed by Stephanie Bower. Printed by Ashton-Potter (USA) Ltd..

LITHOGRAPHED

Serpentine Die Cut 10½ Vert.

2022, Apr. 14 **Untagged**

Coil Stamps

Self-Adhesive

5684 A4512 (10c) **multicolored** .30 .25
5685 A4513 (10c) **multicolored** .30 .25
5686 A4514 (10c) **multicolored** .30 .25
5687 A4515 (10c) **multicolored** .30 .25
a. Strip of 4, #5684-5687 1.20
P# strip of 5, #5685-5687, 2 #5684, #P11111 3.25
P# strip of 9, 3# 5686, 2 each #5684-5685, 5687, #P11111 5.00
P# single, #P11111 (#5686) — 2.25
Nos. 5684-5687 (4) 1.20 1.00

PAINTINGS BY GEORGE MORRISON (1919-2000) ⓢ

Sun and River, 1949 — A4516

Phenomena Against the Crimson: Lake Superior Landscape, 1985 — A4517

Lake Superior Landscape, 1981 — A4518

Spirit Path, New Day, Red Rock Variation: Lake Superior Landscape, 1990 — A4519

Untitled, 1995 — A4520

Designed by Antonio Alcalá. Printed by Ashton-Potter (USA) Ltd.

LITHOGRAPHED

Sheets of 180 in nine panes of 20

2022, Apr. 22 **Tagged** ***Serpentine Die Cut 10¾***

Self-Adhesive

5688 A4516 (58c) **multicolored** 1.25 .40
a. Imperforate — —
5689 A4517 (58c) **multicolored** 1.25 .40
a. Imperforate — —
5690 A4518 (58c) **multicolored** 1.25 .40
a. Imperforate — —
5691 A4519 (58c) **multicolored** 1.25 .40
a. Imperforate — —
5692 A4520 (58c) **multicolored** 1.25 .40
a. Imperforate — —
b. Vert. strip of 5, #5688-5692 6.25
c. Imperforate strip of 5, #5688a-5692a —
P# block of 10, 5# + P 12.50
Pane of 20 25.00
Imperforate pane of 20 —
Nos. 5688-5692 (5) 6.25 2.00

Die cut and imperforate uncut press sheets of Nos. 5688-5692 were made available for sale. Values: die cut gutter block of 10, $20; die cut pairs with gutters between, $4.25 each. See note after No. 4693.

See note after No. 1549.

EUGENIE CLARK (1922-2015), ICHTHYOLOGIST

Clark and Lemon Shark A4521

Designed by Amanda Phingbodhipakkiya. Printed by Banknote Corporation of America.

LITHOGRAPHED

Sheets of 120 in six panes of 20

2022, May 4 **Tagged** ***Serpentine Die Cut 10¾***

Self-Adhesive

5693 A4521 (58c) **multicolored** ⓢ 1.25 .25
P# block of 4, 4#+P 5.00
Pane of 20 25.00
a. Imperforate — —
Pane of 20 —

Die cut and imperforate uncut press sheets of No. 5693 were made available for sale. Values: die cut cross gutter block of 4, $9; die cut pairs with gutters between, $4.25 each. See note after No. 4693.

See note after No. 1549.

WOMEN'S ROWING ⓢ

Women Wearing Red Shirts, No Oar Splash A4522

Women Wearing Red Shirts, Oar Splash at Lower Left — A4523

Women Wearing Blue Shirts, Oar Splash at Center A4524

Women Wearing Blue Shirts, No Oar Splash A4525

Designed by Nancy Stahl. Printed by Ashton-Potter (USA) Ltd.

LITHOGRAPHED

Sheets of 180 in nine panes of 20

2022, May 13 Tagged *Serpentine Die Cut 10¾*

Self-Adhesive

5694	A4522 (58c) **multicolored**		1.25	.30
a.	Imperforate		—	—
5695	A4523 (58c) **multicolored**		1.25	.30
a.	Imperforate		—	—
b.	Horiz. pair, #5694-5695		2.50	
c.	Imperforate horiz. pair, #5694a-5695a		—	
5696	A4524 (58c) **multicolored**		1.25	.30
a.	Imperforate		—	—
5697	A4525 (58c) **multicolored**		1.25	.30
a.	Imperforate		—	—
b.	Horiz. pair, #5696-5697		2.50	
c.	Imperforate horiz. pair, #5696a-5697a		—	
	P# block of 8, 2 sets of 4# + P		8.80	
	Pane of 20, 3 #5694, 9 #5695, 6 #5696, 2 #5697		25.00	
	Imperforate pane of 20		—	
	Nos. 5694-5697 (4)		5.00	1.20

Die cut and imperforate uncut press sheets of Nos. 5694-5697 were made available for sale. Values: die cut pairs with gutters between, $4.25 each. See note after No. 4693.

See note after No. 1549.

MIGHTY MISSISSIPPI Ⓢ

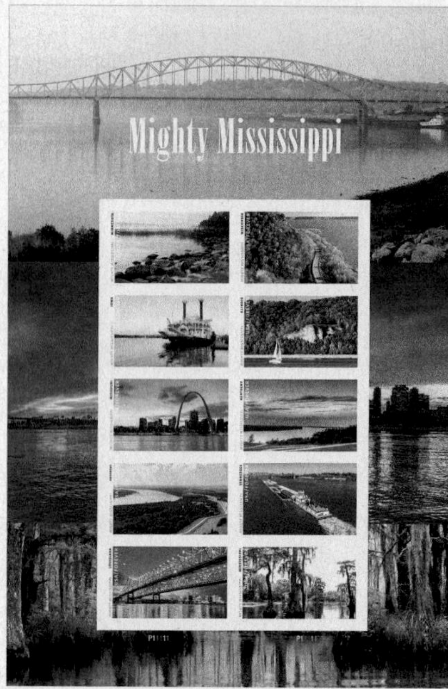

Views of the Mississippi River from States Along its Route — A4526

Designed by Ethel Kessler. Printed by Ashton-Potter (USA) Ltd.

No. 5698 — Photographs of: a, Headwaters of the Mississippi River, Lake Itasca, Minnesota. b, Great River Road, Wisconsin. c, Steamboat *American Queen*, Iowa. d, Sailboat and limestone cliff, Illinois. e, Gateway Arch and St. Louis skyline, Missouri. f, Mississippi River from Fort Jefferson Hill Park, Wickliffe, Kentucky. g, Curved levee and farmland, Arkansas. h, Towboat pushing barges near Memphis, Tennessee. i, Crescent City Connection Bridges, New Orleans, Louisiana. j, Cypress trees in bayou, Mississippi.

LITHOGRAPHED

Sheets of 120 in 12 panes of 10

2022, May 23 Tagged *Serpentine Die Cut 10¾*

Self-Adhesive

5698	A4526 Pane of 10	12.50	
a.-j.	(58c) Any single	1.25	.50
k.	As #5698, imperforate	—	—
l.	As #5698a, imperforate	—	—
m.	As #5698b, imperforate	—	—
n.	As #5698c, imperforate	—	—
o.	As #5698d, imperforate	—	—
p.	As #5698e, imperforate	—	—
q.	As #5698f, imperforate	—	—
r.	As #5698g, imperforate	—	—
s.	As #5698h, imperforate	—	—
t.	As #5698i, imperforate	—	—
u.	As #5698j, imperforate	—	—

Half sheets of die cut and imperforate uncut press sheets of No. 5698 were made available for sale. Values: pairs with gutters between, $4 each. See note after No. 4693. See note after No. 1549.

DISTINGUISHED AMERICANS

Katherine Graham (1917-2001), Publisher of the *Washington Post* — A4527

Designed by Derry Noyes. Printed by Banknote Corporation of America.

LITHOGRAPHED

Sheets of 160 in eight panes of 20

2022, June 14 Tagged *Serpentine Die Cut 10¾*

Self-Adhesive

5699	A4527 (78c) **multicolored** Ⓢ	1.60	.25
	P# block of 4, 5#+B	6.40	
	Pane of 20	32.00	

Adjacent horizontal or vertical stamps have selvage between the stamps. See note after No. 1549.

FLORAL GEOMETRY

A4528

A4529

Designed by Spaeth Hill Company. Printed by Banknote Corporation of America.

LITHOGRAPHED WITH FOIL APPLICATION

Sheets of 90 in nine panes of 10 (No. 5700), Sheets of 72 in 18 panes of four (No. 5701)

2022, June 20 Tagged *Serpentine Die Cut 10¾*

Self-Adhesive

5700	A4528 $2 **multicolored** Ⓢ	4.00	1.00
	P# block of 4, 4#+B	16.00	
	Pane of 10	40.00	
5701	A4529 $5 **multicolored** Ⓢ	10.00	2.50
	Pane of 4	40.00	

Adjacent horizontal or vertical stamps have selvage between the stamps. See note after No. 1549.

NANCY REAGAN (1921-2016), ACTRESS AND FIRST LADY

A4530

Designed by Greg Breeding. Printed by Banknote Corporation of America.

LITHOGRAPHED

Sheets of 120 in six panes of 20

2022, July 6 Tagged *Serpentine Die Cut 11*

Self-Adhesive

5702	A4530 (58c) **multicolored** Ⓢ	1.25	.25
	P# block of 4, 4#+B	5.00	
	Pane of 20	25.00	
a.	Imperforate	—	—
	Pane of 20	—	

Die cut and imperforate uncut press half sheets of No. 5702 were made available for sale. Values: die cut cross gutter block of 4, $9; die cut pairs with gutters between, $4.25 each. See note after No. 4693.

See note after No. 1549.

MARIACHI Ⓢ

Guitarist and Moon — A4531

Guitarist and Sun — A4532

Violinist and Sun — A4533

Bass Guitarist and Sun — A4534

Trumpet Player and Sun — A4535

Designed by Rafael López. Printed by Banknote Corporation of America.

LITHOGRAPHED

Sheets of 120 in six panes of 20

2022, July 15 Tagged *Serpentine Die Cut 10¾*

5703	A4531 (60c) **multicolored**	1.25	.40
a.	Imperforate	1.25	—
5704	A4532 (60c) **multicolored**	1.25	.40
a.	Imperforate	1.25	—
5705	A4533 (60c) **multicolored**	1.25	.40
a.	Imperforate	1.25	—
5706	A4534 (60c) **multicolored**	1.25	.40
a.	Imperforate	1.25	—
5707	A4535 (60c) **multicolored**	1.25	.40
a.	Imperforate	1.25	—
b.	Horiz. strip of 5, #5703-5707	6.25	
c.	Imperforate strip of 5, #5703a-5707a	6.25	
	P# block of 10, 2 sets of 4# + B	12/50	
	Pane of 20	25.00	
	Imperforate pane of 20	25.00	
	Nos. 5703-5707 (5)	6.25	2.00

Die cut and imperforate uncut press sheets of Nos. 5703-5707 were made available for sale. Values: die cut cross gutter block of 10, $18; die cut pairs with gutters between, $4.25 each. See note after No. 4693.

See note after No. 1549.

MUSIC ICONS

Pete Seeger (1919-2014), Folk Singer — A4536

Designed by Antonio Alcalá. Printed by Banknote Corporation of America.

LITHOGRAPHED

Sheets of 144 in nine panes of 16

2022, July 21 Tagged *Serpentine Die Cut 10½*

Self-Adhesive

5708	A4536 (60c) **multicolored** Ⓢ	1.25	.25
	Pane of 16	20.00	
a.	Imperforate	1.25	—
	Pane of 16	20.00	

Die cut and imperforate uncut press sheets of No. 5708 were made available for sale. Values: cross gutter block of 4, $9; pairs with gutters between, $4.25 each. See note after No. 4693.

See note after No. 1549.

BUZZ LIGHTYEAR Ⓢ

Head in Profile — A4537

Standing With Legs Visible — A4538

Running — A4539

Standing, Feet Not Visible — A4540

Designed by Greg Breeding. Printed by Ashton-Potter (USA) Ltd.

LITHOGRAPHED

Sheets of 180 in nine panes of 20

2022, Aug. 3 Tagged *Serpentine Die Cut 11*

5709	A4537 (60c) **multicolored**	1.25	.30
a.	Imperforate	1.25	—
5710	A4538 (60c) **multicolored**	1.25	.30
a.	Imperforate	1.25	—
5711	A4539 (60c) **multicolored**	1.25	.30
a.	Imperforate	1.25	—
5712	A4540 (60c) **multicolored**	1.25	.30
a.	Imperforate	1.25	—
b.	Vert. or horiz. strip of 4, #5709-5712	5.00	
c.	Imperforate vert. or horiz. strip of 4, #5709a-5712a	5.00	
	P# block of 8, 5# + P	10.00	
	Pane of 20	25.00	
	Imperforate pane of 20	25.00	
	Nos. 5709-5712 (4)	5.00	1.20

Die cut and imperforate uncut press sheets of Nos. 5708-5712 were made available for sale. Values: die cut cross gutter block of 8, $16; die cut pairs with gutters between, $4.25 each. See note after No. 4693.

See note after No. 1549.

NATIONAL MARINE SANCTUARIES Ⓢ

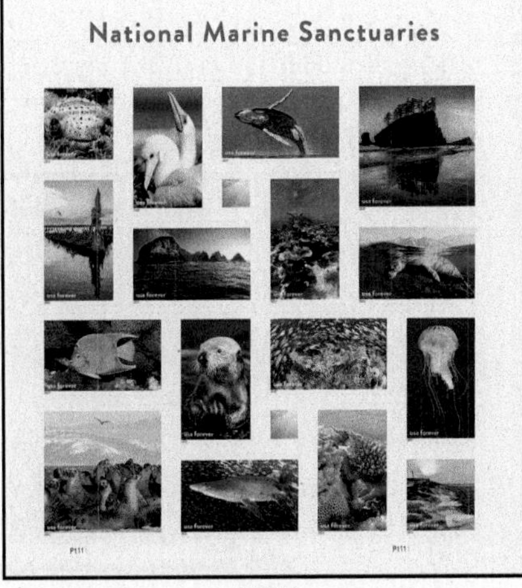

A4541

Designed by Greg Breeding. Printed by Ashton-Potter (USA) Ltd.

No. 5713: a, Balloon fish, Florida Keys National Marine Sanctuary (26x26mm). b, Red-footed boobies, Papahanaumokuakea Marine National Monument (26x41mm). c, Humpback whale, Stellwagen Bank National Marine Sanctuary (41x26mm). d, Sea stacks, Olympic Coast National Marine Sanctuary (41x41mm). e, Mallows Bay-Potomac River Marine Sanctuary at sunset (26x41mm). f, Farallon Islands, Greater Farallones National Marine Sanctuary (41x26mm). g, Elkhorn coral, Florida Keys National Marine Sanctuary (26x41mm). h, Hawaiian monk seal, Hawaiian Islands Humpback Whale National Marine Sanctuary (41x26mm). i, Queen angelfish, Flower Garden Banks National Marine Sanctuary (41x26mm). j, Sea otter, Monterey Bay National Marine Sanctuary (26x41mm). k, Young rockfish exploring reef, Cordell Bank National Marine Sanctuary (41x26mm). l, Atlantic sea nettle, Gray's Reef National Marine Sanctuary (26x41mm). m, Sea lions, Channel Islands National Marine Sanctuary (41x41mm). n, Sand tiger shark, Monitor National Marine Sanctuary (41x26mm). o, Corals and fish, Rose Atoll, National Marine Sanctuary of American Samoa (26x41mm). p, Ice on shoreline, Thunder Bay National Marine Sanctuary (26x26mm).

LITHOGRAPHED

Sheets of 96 in six panes of 16

2022, Aug. 5 Tagged *Serpentine Die Cut 11*

Self-Adhesive

5713	A4541 Pane of 16 + 2 labels	20.00	
a.-p.	(60c) Any single	1.25	.50
q.	As #5713, imperforate	20.00	—
r.	As #5713a, imperforate	1.25	—
s.	As #5713b, imperforate	1.25	—
t.	As #5713c, imperforate	1.25	—
u.	As #5713d, imperforate	1.25	—
v.	As #5713e, imperforate	1.25	—
w.	As #5713f, imperforate	1.25	—
x.	As #5713g, imperforate	1.25	—
y.	As #5713h, imperforate	1.25	—
z.	As #5713i, imperforate	1.25	—
aa.	As #5713j, imperforate	1.25	—
ab.	As #5713k, imperforate	1.25	—
ac.	As #5713l, imperforate	1.25	—
ad.	As #5713m, imperforate	1.25	—
ae.	As #5713n, imperforate	1.25	—
af.	As #5713o, imperforate	1.25	—
ag.	As #5713p, imperforate	1.25	—

Die cut and imperforate uncut press sheets of No. 5713 were made available for sale. Values: panes with gutters between, $40. See note after No. 4693. See note after No. 1549.

2022 END-OF-YEAR ISSUES

The USPS has announced that the following items will be released in late 2022. Dates, denominations and cities are tentative.

Elephants, Single (60c) forever stamp; double-sided convertible booklet pane of 20, *Aug. 12,* Hohenwald, TN.

Pony Cars, Five (60c) commemorative forever stamps: 1969 Ford Mustang Boss 302, 1970 Dodge Challenger R/T, 1969 Chevrolet Camaro Z/28, 1967 Mercury Cougar XR-7 GT, 1969 AMC Javelin SST; pane of 20, *Aug. 25,* Sacramento, CA.

James Webb Space Telescope, Single (60c) forever stamp; pane of 20, *Sept. 8,* Washington, D.C.

Holiday Elves, Four (60c) forever stamps; double-sided convertible booklet pane of 20, *Sept. 15,* North Pole, AK.

Christmas: Virgin and Child, Single (60c) forever stamp; double-sided convertible booklet pane of 20, *Sept. 22,* Boston, MA.

Charles M. Schulz, Ten (60c) commemorative forever stamps: Charlie Brown, Lucy van Pelt, Franklin, Sally Brown, Pig-Pen, Linus van Pelt, Snoopy and Woodstock, Schroeder; pane of 20, *Sept. 30,* Santa Rosa, CA.

Snowy Beauty, Ten (60c) forever stamps: camellia, winter aconite, crocus, hellebore, winterberry, pansy, plum blossom, grape hyacinth, daffodil, ranunculus; double-sided convertible booklet pane of 20, *Oct. 11,* Guilford, IN.

Kwanzaa, Single (60c) forever stamp; pane of 20, *Oct. 13,* St. Louis, MO.

Women Cryptologists of World War II, Single (60c) forever stamp; pane of 20, *Oct. 18,* Annapolis Junction, MD.

Hanukkah, Single (60c) forever stamp; pane of 20, *Oct. 20,* Chagrin Falls, OH.

Listings as of 1PM, Aug. 11, 2022.

SEMI-POSTAL STAMPS

The genesis of the U.S. semi-postal stamp program was a July 1997 bill passed by both houses of Congress that directed the USPS to issue a stamp to benefit breast-cancer research. On August 13, the President signed it into law. The surcharge was to be up to 25% of the current first-class rate.

BREAST CANCER RESEARCH

SP1

Designed by Ethel Kessler. Printed by Avery Dennison.

PHOTOGRAVURE

Sheets of 160 in eight panes of 20

1998, July 29 Tagged *Serpentine Die Cut 11*

Self-Adhesive

B1	SP1 (32c+8c) **multicolored**	1.00	.25
	P# block of 4, 6#+V	4.00	
	Pane of 20	20.00	

The 8c surtax was for cancer research. After the Jan. 10, 1999, first class postage rate changes, No. B1 became a 33c stamp with a 7c surtax; after Jan. 7, 2001, it became a 34c stamp with a 6c surtax. Effective Mar. 23, 2002, the stamp was sold for 45c, but the face value remained at 34c until June 30, 2002, at which time the face value rose to 37c. On Jan. 8, 2006, the face value rose to 39c, and on May 14, 2007, the face value rose to 41c and the stamp sold for 55c.

Sales of No. B1 were suspended Jan. 1, 2004, but resumed Feb. 2, 2004, after Congress extended the sales period through Dec. 31, 2005. Subsequently, the sales period was again extended, with the postage value matching changes in the first-class postage rates.

HEROES OF 2001

Firemen Atop World Trade Center Rubble — SP2

Designed by Derry Noyes. Printed by Ashton-Potter (USA) Ltd..

LITHOGRAPHED

Sheets of 120 in six panes of 20

2002, June 7 Tagged *Serpentine Die Cut 11¼*

Self-Adhesive

B2	SP2 (34c+11c) **multicolored**	.80	.35
	P# block of 4, 4#+P	3.25	
	Pane of 20	17.50	

The 11c surtax was for assistance to families of emergency relief personnel killed or permanently disabled in the line of duty in connection with the terrorist attacks of Sept. 11, 2001. No. B2 became a 37c stamp with an 8c surtax June 30, 2002.

STOP FAMILY VIOLENCE

SP3

Designed by Carl T. Herrman. Printed by Avery Dennison.

PHOTOGRAVURE

Sheets of 200 in 10 panes of 20

2003, Oct. 8 Tagged *Serpentine Die Cut 11*

Self-Adhesive

B3	SP3 (37c+8c) **multicolored**	.80	.45
	P# block of 4, 4#+V	3.25	
	Pane of 20	17.50	

The 8¢ surtax was for the U.S. Department of Health and Humans Services to support programs aimed at reducing domestic violence. On Jan. 8, 2006, the face value rose to 39¢. Sales were suspended Dec. 31, 2006.

SAVE VANISHING SPECIES Ⓢ

Amur Tiger Cub — SP4

Designed by Derry Noyes. Printed by Avery Dennison.

PHOTOGRAVURE

Sheets of 160 in eight panes of 20

2011, Sept. 20 Tagged *Serpentine Die Cut 10¾*

Self-Adhesive

B4	SP4 (44c+11c) **multicolored**	1.10	.50
	P# block of 4, 7#+V	4.40	
	Pane of 20	22.00	

The 11c surtax was for the Multinational Species Conservation Funds of the U.S. Fish and Wildlife Service. The stamp was sold for 55c when the first class franking value was at 45c and 46c, with the surtax being decreased in each instance. Sales of No. B4 were suspended on Jan. 1, 2014, but resumed in Oct. 2014, selling for 60c (49c franking value and 11c surtax) after Congress extended the sales period through Dec. 31, 2018.

See note after No. 1549.

Breast Cancer Awareness Type of 1998

Designed by Ethel Kessler. Printed by Banknote Corporation of America for Sennett Security Products.

LITHOGRAPHED

Sheets of 240 in 12 panes of 20

Design Size: 20x35mm

Serpentine Die Cut 11x10¾

2014, Sept. 30 Tagged

Dated 2014

Self-Adhesive

B5	SP1 (49c+11c) **multicolored**	1.10	.50
	P# block of 4, 6#+S or 6#+B	4.40	
	Pane of 20	22.00	
a.	Imperforate (from uncut press sheet)	2.25	—
	Pane of 20	45.00	
b.	Imperf., pair (error, see footnote)	—	

Die cut and imperforate uncut press sheets of No. B5 were made available for sale. Values: cross gutter block of 4, $12.50; pairs with gutters between, $5.50 each. See note after No. 4693.

Imperforates from imperforate uncut press sheets (No. B5a) do not have die cutting on either the front or the reverse. On the imperforate error (No. B5b), there is die cutting on the reverse.

ALZHEIMER'S DISEASE AWARENESS Ⓢ

SP5

Designed by Ethel Kessler. Printed by Banknote Corporation of America.

LITHOGRAPHED

Sheets of 120 in six panes of 20

Serpentine Die Cut 10½x10¾

2017, Nov. 30 Tagged

Self-Adhesive

B6	SP5 (49c+11c) **multicolored**	1.10	.60
	P# block of 4, 6#+B	4.40	
	Pane of 20	22.00	

The 11c surtax was for the National Institutes of Health.

See note after No. 1549.

HEALING POST-TRAUMATIC STRESS DISORDER

Plant Sprout and Fallen Leaves — SP6

Designed by Greg Breeding. Printed by Ashton-Potter (USA) Ltd.

LITHOGRAPHED

Sheets of 120 in six panes of 20

2019, Dec. 2 Tagged *Serpentine Die Cut 10¾*

Self-Adhesive

B7	SP6 (55c+10c) **multicolored**	1.10	.60
	P# block of 4, 4#+P	5.20	
	Pane of 20	26.00	

The 10c surtax was for the National Center for Post-traumatic Stress Disorder of the Department of Veterans Affairs to assist in treatment of those impacted by post-traumatic stress disorder.

AIR POST STAMPS

Air mail in the U. S. postal system developed in three stages: pioneer period (with many unofficial or semi-official flights before 1918), government flights and contract air mail (C.A.M.). Contract air mail began on February 15, 1926.

All C.A.M. contracts were canceled on February 19, 1934, and air mail was carried by Army planes for six months. After that the contract plan was resumed. Separate domestic airmail service was abolished Oct. 11, 1975.

See Domestic Air Mail Rates chart in introduction.

Curtiss Jenny — AP1

No. C3 first used on airplane mail service between Washington, Philadelphia and New York, on May 15, 1918, but was valid for ordinary postage. The rate of postage was 24 cents per ounce, which included immediate individual delivery.

Rate of postage was reduced to 16 cents for the first ounce and 6 cents for each additional ounce, which included 10 cents for immediate individual delivery, on July 15, 1918, by Postmaster General's order of June 26, 1918. No. C2 was first used for air mail in the tri-city service on July 15. Covers may be dated earlier than July 15, but they were held until the July 15 flight.

Rate of postage was reduced on December 15, 1918, by Postmaster General's order of November 30, 1918, to 6 cents per ounce. No. C1 was first used for air mail (same three-way service) on Dec. 16.

FLAT PLATE PRINTINGS

Plates of 100 subjects.

1918	**Unwmk.** **Engr.**		***Perf. 11***
C1	AP1 6c **orange,** *Dec. 10*	55.	30.
	pale orange	55.	30.
	Never hinged	110.	
	On cover		50.
	First flight cover, *Dec. 16*		2,000.
	Margin block of 4, arrow top or left	250.	150.
	Center line block	275.	160.
	P# block of 6, arrow	700.	—
	Never hinged	1,000.	
	Double transfer (#9155-14)	85.	47.50
C2	AP1 16c **green,** *July 11*	60.	35.
	dark green	60.	35.
	Never hinged	120.	
	On cover		55.
	First flight cover, *July 15*		800.
	Margin block of 4, arrow top or left	250.	180.
	Center line block	275.	200.
	P# block of 6, arrow	900.	—
	Never hinged	1,350.	
C3	AP1 24c **carmine rose & blue,** *May 14*	65.	35.
	dark carmine rose & blue	65.	35.
	Never hinged	130.	
	On cover		75.
	First flight cover, *May 15*		750.
	Margin block of 4, arrow top or left	275.	160.
	Margin block of 4, arrow bottom	300.	170.
	Margin block of 4, arrow right	325.	225.
	Center line block	350.	190.
	P# block of 4, red P# only	*750.*	—
	P# block of 12, two P#, arrow & two "TOP"	1,250.	—
	Never hinged	2,000.	
	P# block of 12, two P#, arrow & blue "TOP" only	*12,500.*	
	Never hinged	*16,500.*	
a.	Center inverted	*450,000.*	
	Never hinged	*850,000.*	
	Block of 4	*2,000,000.*	
	Block of 4 with horiz. guide line	*2,100,000.*	
	Corner margin block of 4 with siderographer's initials	*2,400,000.*	
	Center line block	*2,100,000.*	
	P# block of 4, blue P#	*5,000,000.*	
	Nos. C1-C3 (3)	180.00	100.00
	Nos. C1-C3, never hinged	360.00	

Plate Blocks

Scott values for plate blocks printed from flat plates are for very fine side and bottom positions. Top position plate blocks with full wide selvage sell for more.

Airplane Radiator and Wooden Propeller — AP2

Air Service Emblem — AP3

DeHavilland Biplane — AP4

Nos. C4-C6 were issued primarily for use in the new night-flying air mail service between New York and San Francisco, but valid for all purposes. Three zones were established; New York-Chicago, Chicago-Cheyenne, Cheyenne-San Francisco, and the rate of postage was 8 cents an ounce for each zone. Service was inaugurated on July 1, 1924.

These stamps were placed on sale at the Philatelic Agency at Washington on the dates indicated in the listings but were not issued to postmasters at that time.

Plates of 400 subjects in four panes of 100 each.

1923	**Unwmk.**		***Perf. 11***
C4	AP2 8c **dark green,** *Aug. 15*	17.50	15.00
	deep green	17.50	15.00
	Never hinged	35.00	
	On cover		25.00
	P# block of 6	240.00	—
	Never hinged	330.00	
	Double transfer	35.00	22.50
C5	AP3 16c **dark blue,** *Aug. 17*	60.00	30.00
	Never hinged	120.00	
	On cover		50.00
	P# block of 6	1,300.	—
	Never hinged	2,000.	
	Double transfer	110.00	45.00
C6	AP4 24c **carmine,** *Aug. 21*	65.00	30.00
	Never hinged	130.00	
	On cover		45.00
	P# block of 6	1,700.	—
	Never hinged	2,500.	
	Double transfer (Pl. 14841)	150.00	42.50
	Nos. C4-C6 (3)	142.50	75.00
	Nos. C4-C6, never hinged	285.00	

Map of United States and Two Mail Planes — AP5

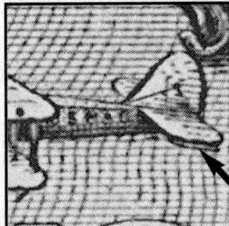

Double Transfer

The Act of Congress of February 2, 1925, created a rate of 10 cents per ounce for distances to 1000 miles, 15 cents per ounce for 1500 miles and 20 cents for more than 1500 miles on contract air mail routes.

Plates of 200 subjects in four panes of 50 each.

1926-27	**Unwmk.**		***Perf. 11***
C7	AP5 10c **dark blue,** *Feb. 13, 1926*	2.25	.35
	light blue	2.25	.35
	Never hinged	4.00	
	P# block of 6	32.50	—
	Never hinged	45.00	
	Double transfer (18246 UL 11)	20.00	1.25
C8	AP5 15c **olive brown,** *Sept. 18, 1926*	2.50	2.50
	light brown	2.50	2.50
	Never hinged	4.75	
	P# block of 6	32.50	—
	Never hinged	45.00	
C9	AP5 20c **yellow green,** *Jan. 25, 1927*	6.50	2.00
	green	6.50	2.00
	Never hinged	12.50	
	P# block of 6	70.00	—
	Never hinged	95.00	
	Nos. C7-C9 (3)	11.25	4.85
	Nos. C7-C9, never hinged	21.25	

Lindbergh's Plane "Spirit of St. Louis" and Flight Route — AP6

Double Impression

A tribute to Col. Charles A. Lindbergh, who made the first non-stop (and solo) flight from New York to Paris, May 20-21, 1927.

Plates of 200 subjects in four panes of 50 each.

1927, June 18	**Unwmk.**		***Perf. 11***
C10	AP6 10c **dark blue**	7.00	2.50
	Never hinged	12.50	
	P# block of 6	90.00	—
	Never hinged	130.00	
	Double transfer	11.00	3.25
a.	Booklet pane of 3, *May 26, 1928*	70.00	*65.00*
	Never hinged	115.00	
b.	Double impression		*16,500.*

No. C10b is unique.

Beacon on Rocky Mountains AP7

Issued to meet the new rate, effective August 1, of 5 cents per ounce.

Plates of 100 subjects in two panes of 50

1928, July 25	**Unwmk.**		***Perf. 11***
C11	AP7 5c **carmine and blue**	5.50	.85
	Never hinged	10.00	
	On cover, first day of 5c airmail rate, Aug. 1		3.00
	Margin block of 4, arrow, (line) right or left	25.00	4.50
	P# block of 6, two P# & red "TOP"	42.50	—
	Never hinged	57.50	
	P# block of 6, two P# & blue "TOP"	42.50	—
	Never hinged	57.50	
	P# block of 6, two P# & double "TOP"	110.00	—
	Never hinged	160.00	
	P# block of 6, two P# only (no "TOP")	200.00	—
	Never hinged	300.00	
	Recut frame line at left	8.00	1.50
	Double transfer	—	—
a.	Vert. pair, imperf. between	*7,000.*	
b.	Printed on "special" booklet paper, *1928* (see note before #551)	11.00	2.00
	Never hinged	20.00	
	On cover		6.00
	Block of 4	47.50	
	P# block of 6, two P#	125.00	
	Never hinged	175.00	
	P# block of 6, two P# & double top	—	

No. C11a is unique. It is torn and valued thus.

Winged Globe — AP8

Plates of 200 subjects in four panes of 50 each.

1930, Feb. 10 **Unwmk.** ***Perf. 11***

Stamp design: 46½x19mm

C12	AP8 5c **violet**	9.50	.50
	Never hinged	17.50	
	P# block of 6	130.00	—
	Never hinged	180.00	
	Double transfer (Pl. 20189)	19.00	1.25
a.	Horiz. pair, imperf. between	*4,500.*	

See Nos. C16-C17, C19.

GRAF ZEPPELIN ISSUE

Zeppelin Over Atlantic Ocean — AP9

Zeppelin Between Continents — AP10

Zeppelin Passing Globe — AP11

Issued for use on mail carried on the first Europe-Pan-America round trip flight of the Graf Zeppelin in May, 1930. They were withdrawn from sale June 30, 1930.

Plates of 200 subjects in four panes of 50 each.

1930, Apr. 19 **Unwmk.** ***Perf. 11***

C13	AP9 65c **green**	180.	160.
	Never hinged	250.	
	On cover or card		190.
	Block of 4	775.	750.
	P# block of 6	1,500.	—
	Never hinged	2,200.	
C14	AP10 $1.30 **brown**	375.	360.
	Never hinged	575.	
	On cover		390.
	Block of 4	1,600.	1,550.
	P# block of 6	3,600.	—
	Never hinged	5,000.	
C15	AP11 $2.60 **blue**	525.	550.
	Never hinged	850.	
	On cover		575.
	Block of 4	2,400.	2,400.
	P# block of 6	5,250.	—
	Never hinged	8,000.	
	Nos. C13-C15 (3)	1,080.	1,070.
	Nos. C13-C15, never hinged	1,675.	

ROTARY PRESS PRINTING

Plates of 200 subjects in four panes of 50 each.

1931-32 **Unwmk.** ***Perf. 10½x11***

Stamp design: 47½x19mm

C16	AP8 5c **violet**, *Aug. 19, 1931*	4.75	.60
	Never hinged	8.50	
	Block of 4	21.00	2.00
	P# block of 4	75.00	—
	Never hinged	95.00	

Issued to conform with new air mail rate of 8 cents per ounce which became effective July 6, 1932.

C17	AP8 8c **olive bister**, *Sept. 26, 1932*	2.25	.40
	Never hinged	3.75	
	Block of 4	10.00	2.00
	P# block of 4	27.50	—
	Never hinged	37.50	

CENTURY OF PROGRESS ISSUE

"Graf Zeppelin," Federal Building at Chicago Exposition and Hangar at Friedrichshafen — AP12

Issued in connection with the flight of the airship "Graf Zeppelin" in October, 1933, to Miami, Akron and Chicago and from the last city to Europe.

FLAT PLATE PRINTING

Plates of 200 subjects in four panes of 50 each.

1933, Oct. 2 **Unwmk.** ***Perf. 11***

C18	AP12 50c **green**	45.00	47.50
	Never hinged	75.00	
	On cover		80.00
	Block of 4	200.00	*275.00*
	P# block of 6	475.00	—
	Never hinged	600.00	

Catalogue values for unused stamps in this section, from this point to the end, are for Never Hinged items.

Type of 1930 Issue

ROTARY PRESS PRINTING

Issued to conform with new air mail rate of 6 cents per ounce which became effective July 1, 1934.

Plates of 200 subjects in four panes of 50 each.

1934, June 30 **Unwmk.** ***Perf. 10½x11***

C19	AP8 6c **dull orange**	3.50	.25
	On cover, first day of 6c airmail rate, July 1		10.00
	Block of 4	14.00	1.10
	P# block of 4	20.00	—
	Horiz. pair with full vert. gutter btwn.	*425.00*	
	Vert. pair with full horiz. gutter btwn.	*700.00*	

TRANSPACIFIC ISSUES

"China Clipper" over Pacific AP13

Issued to pay postage on mail transported by the Transpacific air mail service, inaugurated Nov. 22, 1935.

FLAT PLATE PRINTING

Plates of 200 subjects in four panes of 50 each.

1935, Nov. 22 **Unwmk.** ***Perf. 11***

C20	AP13 25c **blue**	1.40	1.00
	P# block of 6	20.00	—

"China Clipper" over Pacific — AP14

Issued primarily for use on the Transpacific service to China, but valid for all air mail purposes.

FLAT PLATE PRINTING

Plates of 200 subjects in four panes of 50 each.

1937, Feb. 15 **Unwmk.** ***Perf. 11***

C21	AP14 20c **green**	10.00	1.75
	dark green	10.00	1.75
	Block of 4	40.00	8.50
	P# block of 6	85.00	—
C22	AP14 50c **carmine**	10.00	5.00
	Block of 4	40.00	21.00
	P# block of 6	85.00	—

Wide full selvage top margin plate blocks of No. C22 are extremely scarce and sell for $3,000 or more in the grades of very fine and higher.

Eagle Holding Shield, Olive Branch and Arrows AP15

FLAT PLATE PRINTING

Frame plates of 100 subjects in two panes of 50 each separated by a 1½-inch wide vertical gutter with central guide line, and vignette plates of 50 subjects. Some plates were made of iron, then chromed; several of these carry an additional imprint, "E.I." (Electrolytic Iron).

1938, May 14 **Unwmk.** ***Perf. 11***

C23	AP15 6c **dark blue & carmine**	.70	.25
	Margin block of 4, bottom or side arrow	3.00	2.25
	P# block of 4, 2 P#	7.00	—
	Center line block	4.50	3.50
	Top P# block of 10, with two P#, arrow, two "TOP" and two registration markers	15.00	
a.	Vert. pair, imperf. horiz.	*300.00*	*300.00*
	On cover		1,750.
	Center line block	*1,100.*	
	P# block of 4, 2 P#	*1,750.*	
b.	Horiz. pair, imperf. vert.	*12,500.*	
	P# block of 4, 2 P#	*37,500.*	
c.	6c **ultramarine & carmine**	275.00	*2,000.*
	On cover		*2,250.*
	Center line block	*1,500.*	
	P# block of 4, 2 P#	*1,850.*	

Top plate number blocks of No. C23 are found both with and without top arrow.

The plate block of No. C23b is unique and never hinged; value is based on 1994 auction sale.

TRANSATLANTIC ISSUE

Winged Globe — AP16

Inauguration of Transatlantic air mail service.

FLAT PLATE PRINTING

Plates of 200 subjects in four panes of 50 each.

1939, May 16 **Unwmk.** ***Perf. 11***

C24	AP16 30c **dull blue**	11.00	1.50
	P# block of 6	110.00	—

Twin-Motored Transport Plane — AP17

ROTARY PRESS PRINTING

E. E. Plates of 200 subjects in four panes of 50 each.

1941-44 **Unwmk.** ***Perf. 11x10½***

C25	AP17 6c **carmine,** *June 25, 1941*	.25	.25
	P# block of 4	.60	—
	Pair with full vert. gutter btwn.	*225.00*	
	Pair with full horiz. gutter btwn.	—	
a.	Booklet pane of 3, *Mar. 18, 1943*	3.50	1.50
b.	Horiz. pair, imperf. between	*2,250.*	

Singles from No. C25a are imperf. at sides or at sides and bottom.

Value of No. C25b is for pair without blue crayon P. O. rejection mark on front. Very fine pairs with crayon mark sell for about $1,500.

C26	AP17 8c **olive green,** *Mar. 21, 1944*	.25	.25
	P# block of 4	1.10	—
	Pair with full horiz. gutter btwn.	*325.00*	
a.	All color omitted	—	

No. C26a has an albino impression and exists as a pair of stamps within a double-paper spliced strip of six stamps.

C27	AP17 10c **violet,** *Aug. 15, 1941*	1.10	.25
	P# block of 4	5.00	—
C28	AP17 15c **brown carmine,** *Aug. 19, 1941*	2.10	.35
	P# block of 4	9.00	—
C29	AP17 20c **bright green,** *Aug. 27, 1941*	2.10	.30
	P# block of 4	9.00	—
C30	AP17 30c **blue,** *Sept. 25, 1941*	2.10	.35
	P# block of 4	9.00	—

C31 AP17 50c **orange,** *Oct. 29, 1941* 11.00 3.25
P# block of 4 47.50 —
Nos. C25-C31 (7) 18.90 5.00

DC-4 Skymaster AP18

ROTARY PRESS PRINTING
E. E. Plates of 200 subjects in four panes of 50 each.

1946, Sept. 25 Unwmk. *Perf. 11x10½*
C32 AP18 5c **carmine** .25 .25
P# block of 4 .45 —
Pair with full vert. gutter btwn. —

DC-4 Skymaster — AP19

ROTARY PRESS PRINTING
E. E. Plates of 400 subjects in four panes of 100 each.

1947, Mar. 26 Unwmk. *Perf. 10½x11*
C33 AP19 5c **carmine** .25 .25
P# block of 4 .60 —

Pan American Union Building, Washington, D.C., and Martin 2-0-2 — AP20

Statue of Liberty, New York Skyline and Lockheed Constellation AP21

San Francisco-Oakland Bay Bridge and Boeing B377 Stratocruiser — AP22

Designed by Victor S. McCloskey, Jr., Leon Helguera and William K. Schrage.

ROTARY PRESS PRINTING
E. E. Plates of 200 subjects in four panes of 50 each.

1947 Unwmk. *Perf. 11x10½*
C34 AP20 10c **black,** *Aug. 30* .25 .25
P# block of 4 1.10 —
a. Dry printing .40 .25
P# block of 4 (#25613, 25614) 1.75 —
C35 AP21 15c **bright blue green,** *Aug. 20* .35 .25
blue green .35 .25
P# block of 4 1.50 —
Pair with full horiz. gutter btwn. *650.00*
a. Horiz. pair, imperf. between *1,500.*
b. Dry printing .55 .25
P# block of 4 (#25492 and up) 2.50 —
C36 AP22 25c **blue,** *July 30* .90 .25
P# block of 4 4.00 —
a. Dry printing 1.20 .25
P# block of 4 (#25615 and up) 5.25 —
Nos. C34-C36 (3) 1.50 .75

See note on wet and dry printings following No. 1029.

No. C35a is valued in the grade of fine.

Type of 1947
ROTARY PRESS COIL STAMP

1948, Jan. 15 Unwmk. *Perf. 10 Horizontally*
C37 AP19 5c **carmine** 1.00 .80
Pair 2.10 1.75
Joint line pair 10.00 3.00

NEW YORK CITY ISSUE

Map of Five Boroughs, Circular Band and Planes — AP23

50th anniv. of the consolidation of the five boroughs of New York City.

ROTARY PRESS PRINTING
E. E. Plates of 400 subjects in four panes of 100 each.

1948, July 31 Unwmk. *Perf. 11x10½*
C38 AP23 5c **bright carmine** .25 .25
P# block of 4 3.50 —

Type of 1947
ROTARY PRESS PRINTING
E. E. Plates of 400 subjects in four panes of 100 each.

1949 Unwmk. *Perf. 10½x11*
C39 AP19 6c **carmine,** *Jan. 18* .25 .25
P# block of 4 .50 —
Pair with full horiz. gutter btwn. *600.00*
a. Booklet pane of 6, *Nov. 18* 12.00 5.00
b. Dry printing .50 .25
P# block of 4 (#25340 and up) 2.25 —
c. As "a," dry printing 25.00 —

See note on wet and dry printings following No. 1029.

ALEXANDRIA BICENTENNIAL ISSUE

Home of John Carlyle, Alexandria Seal and Gadsby's Tavern AP24

200th anniv. of the founding of Alexandria, Va.

ROTARY PRESS PRINTING
E. E. Plates of 200 subjects in four panes of 50 each.

1949, May 11 Unwmk. *Perf. 11x10½*
C40 AP24 6c **carmine** .25 .25
P# block of 4 .55 —

Type of 1947
ROTARY PRESS COIL STAMP

1949, Aug. 25 Unwmk. *Perf. 10 Horizontally*
C41 AP19 6c **carmine** 3.00 .25
Pair 6.25 .25
Joint line pair 14.00 1.35

UNIVERSAL POSTAL UNION ISSUE

Post Office Department Building AP25

Globe and Doves Carrying Messages AP26

Boeing Stratocruiser and Globe — AP27

Universal Postal Union, 75th Anniv.

ROTARY PRESS PRINTING
E. E. Plates of 200 subjects in four panes of 50 each.

1949 Unwmk. *Perf. 11x10½*
C42 AP25 10c **violet,** *Nov. 18* .25 .25
P# block of 4 1.40 —
C43 AP26 15c **ultramarine,** *Oct. 7* .30 .25
P# block of 4 1.25 —
C44 AP27 25c **rose carmine,** *Nov. 30* .60 .40
P# block of 4 4.00 —
Nos. C42-C44 (3) 1.15 .90

WRIGHT BROTHERS ISSUE

Wilbur and Orville Wright and their Plane, 1903 — AP28

46th anniv. of the 1st successful flight in a motor-powered airplane, Dec. 17, 1903, at Kill Devil Hill near Kitty Hawk, NC, by Wilbur (1867-1912) and Orville Wright (1871-1948) of Dayton, OH. The plane flew 852 feet in 59 seconds.

ROTARY PRESS PRINTING
E. E. Plates of 200 subjects in four panes of 50 each.

1949, Dec. 17 Unwmk. *Perf. 11x10½*
C45 AP28 6c **magenta** .25 .25
P# block of 4 .70 —

Diamond Head, Honolulu, Hawaii AP29

ROTARY PRESS PRINTING
E. E. Plates of 200 subjects in four panes of 50 each.

1952, Mar. 26 Unwmk. *Perf. 11x10½*
C46 AP29 80c **bright red violet** 4.50 1.25
P# block of 4 19.00 —

POWERED FLIGHT, 50th ANNIV.

First Plane and Modern Plane — AP30

ROTARY PRESS PRINTING
E. E. Plates of 200 subjects in four panes of 50 each.

1953, May 29 Unwmk. *Perf. 11x10½*
C47 AP30 6c **carmine** .25 .25
P# block of 4 .55 —

Eagle in Flight — AP31

Issued primarily for use on domestic post cards.

ROTARY PRESS PRINTING

E. E. Plates of 400 subjects in four panes of 100 each.

1954, Sept. 3 **Unwmk.** ***Perf. 11x10½***

C48 AP31 4c **bright blue** .25 .25
P# block of 4 1.10 —

AIR FORCE, 50th ANNIV.

B-52 Stratofortress and F-104 Starfighters AP32

Designed by Alexander Nagy, Jr.

ROTARY PRESS PRINTING

E. E. Plates of 200 subjects in four panes of 50 each.

1957, Aug. 1 **Unwmk.** ***Perf. 11x10½***

C49 AP32 6c **ultra & blue** .25 .25
P# block of 4 .70 —

Type of 1954

Issued primarily for use on domestic post cards.

1958, July 31 **Unwmk.** ***Perf. 11x10½***

C50 AP31 5c **red** .25 .25
P# block of 4 1.00 —

Silhouette of Jet Airliner — AP33

Designed by William H. Buckley and Sam Marsh.

ROTARY PRESS PRINTING

E. E. Plates of 400 subjects in four panes of 100 each.

1958, July 31 **Unwmk.** ***Perf. 10½x11***

C51 AP33 7c **blue** .25 .25
P# block of 4 .60 —
a. Booklet pane of 6 6.50 5.00
b. Vert. pair, imperf. between (from booklet pane) *4,000.*

No. C51b resulted from a paper foldover after perforating and before cutting into panes. Two or three pairs are believed to exist.

ROTARY PRESS COIL STAMP

Perf. 10 Horizontally

C52 AP33 7c **blue** 2.00 .25
Pair 4.25 .40
Joint line pair 15.00 1.25
Small holes 7.50 —
Pair 15.00
Joint line pair 200.00 75.00

ALASKA STATEHOOD ISSUE

Big Dipper, North Star and Map of Alaska — AP34

Designed by Richard C. Lockwood.

ROTARY PRESS PRINTING

E. E. Plates of 200 subjects in four panes of 50 each.

1959, Jan. 3 **Unwmk.** ***Perf. 11x10½***

C53 AP34 7c **dark blue** .25 .25
P# block of 4 .80 —

BALLOON JUPITER ISSUE

Balloon and Crowd — AP35

Designed by Austin Briggs.

Centenary of the carrying of mail by the balloon Jupiter from Lafayette to Crawfordsville, Ind.

GIORI PRESS PRINTING

Plates of 200 subjects in four panes of 50 each.

1959, Aug. 17 **Unwmk.** ***Perf. 11***

C54 AP35 7c **dark blue & red** .30 .25
P# block of 4 1.60 —

HAWAII STATEHOOD ISSUE

Alii Warrior, Map of Hawaii and Star of Statehood AP36

Designed by Joseph Feher.

ROTARY PRESS PRINTING

E. E. Plates of 200 subjects in four panes of 50 each.

1959, Aug. 21 **Unwmk.** ***Perf. 11x10½***

C55 AP36 7c **rose red** .25 .25
P# block of 4 .85 —

PAN AMERICAN GAMES ISSUE

Runner Holding Torch — AP37

Designed by Suren Ermoyan.

3rd Pan American Games, Chicago, Aug. 27-Sept. 7, 1959.

GIORI PRESS PRINTING

Plates of 200 subjects in four panes of 50 each.

1959, Aug. 27 **Unwmk.** ***Perf. 11***

C56 AP37 10c **red, white & blue** .25 .25
P# block of 4 1.25 —

Liberty Bell — AP38

Statue of Liberty AP39

Abraham Lincoln AP40

GIORI PRESS PRINTING

Plates of 200 subjects in four panes of 50 each.

1959-66 **Unwmk.** ***Perf. 11***

C57 AP38 10c **black & green,** *June 10, 1960* 1.00 .70
P# block of 4 4.50 —
C58 AP39 15c **black & orange,** *Nov. 20, 1959* .35 .25
P# block of 4 1.50 —
C59 AP40 25c **black & maroon,** *Apr. 22, 1960* .50 .25
P# block of 4 2.00 —
a. Tagged, *Dec. 29, 1966* .60 .30
P# block of 4 2.50 —
Nos. C57-C59 (3) 1.85 1.20

See Luminescence data in Information for Collectors section.

Type of 1958

ROTARY PRESS PRINTING

E. E. Plates of 400 subjects in four panes of 100 each.

1960, Aug. 12 **Unwmk.** ***Perf. 10½x11***

C60 AP33 7c **carmine** .25 .25
P# block of 4 .60 —
Pair with full horiz. gutter btwn. 450.00
a. Booklet pane of 6, *Aug. 19* 7.00 6.00
b. Vert. pair, imperf between (from booklet pane) *5,500.*

No. C60b resulted from a paper foldover after perforating and before cutting into panes. Two pairs are known.

Type of 1958

ROTARY PRESS COIL STAMP

1960, Oct. 22 **Unwmk.** ***Perf. 10 Horizontally***

C61 AP33 7c **carmine** 4.00 .25
Pair 8.25 .55
Joint line pair 27.50 3.75

Type of 1959-60 and

Statue of Liberty AP41

GIORI PRESS PRINTING

Plates of 200 subjects in four panes of 50 each.

1961-67 **Unwmk.** ***Perf. 11***

C62 AP38 13c **black & red,** *June 28, 1961* .40 .25
P# block of 4 1.65 —
a. Tagged, *Feb. 15, 1967* .75 .50
P# block of 4 7.50 —
C63 AP41 15c **black & orange,** *Jan. 13, 1961* .30 .25
P# block of 4 1.25 —
a. Tagged, *Jan. 11, 1967* .35 .25
P# block of 4 1.50 —
b. As "a," horiz. pair, imperf. vert. *15,000.*
c. As "a," horiz. pair, imperf between and at left *2,750.*
d. All color omitted *100.00*

On No. C63d, there is a clear albino plate impression.

Jet Airliner over Capitol — AP42

Designed by Henry K. Bencsath.

ROTARY PRESS PRINTING

E.E. Plates of 400 subjects in four panes of 100 each.

1962, Dec. 5 Unwmk. *Perf. 10½x11*

C64 AP42 8c **carmine** .25 .25
P# block of 4 .65 —
a. Tagged, *Aug. 1, 1963* .25 .25
P# block of 4 .65 —
As "a," pair with full horiz. gutter between 650.00
b. Booklet pane of 5 + label 6.00 3.00
c. As "b," tagged, *1964* 1.75 .75

Nos. C64a and C64c were made by overprinting Nos. C64 and C64b with phosphorescent ink. No. C64a was first issued at Dayton, Ohio, for experiments in high speed mail sorting. The tagging is visible in shortwave ultraviolet light.

COIL STAMP; ROTARY PRESS

Perf. 10 Horizontally

C65 AP42 8c **carmine** .40 .25
Pair .80 .50
Joint line pair 4.00 .55
a. Tagged, *Sept. 1964* .35 .25
Pair .70 .50
Joint line pair 1.75 .60

Earliest documented use of C65a: Jan. 14, 1965.

MONTGOMERY BLAIR ISSUE

Montgomery Blair — AP43

Designed by Robert J. Jones

Montgomery Blair (1813-83), Postmaster General (1861-64), who called the 1st Intl. Postal Conf., Paris, 1863, forerunner of the UPU.

GIORI PRESS PRINTING

Plates of 200 subjects in four panes of 50 each.

1963, May 3 Unwmk. *Perf. 11*

C66 AP43 15c **dull red, dark brown & blue** .55 .50
P# block of 4 2.25 —

Bald Eagle — AP44

Designed by V. S. McCloskey, Jr.

Issued primarily for use on domestic post cards.

ROTARY PRESS PRINTING

E.E. Plates of 400 subjects in four panes of 100 each.

1963, July 12 Unwmk. *Perf. 11x10½*

C67 AP44 6c **red** .25 .25
P# block of 4 1.40 —
a. Tagged, *Feb. 15, 1967* 4.00 3.00
P# block of 4 100.00 —

AMELIA EARHART ISSUE

Amelia Earhart and Lockheed Electra — AP45

Designed by Robert J. Jones.

Amelia Earhart (1898-1937), 1st woman to fly across the Atlantic.

GIORI PRESS PRINTING

Plates of 200 subjects in four panes of 50 each.

1963, July 24 Unwmk. *Perf. 11*

C68 AP45 8c **carmine & maroon** .25 .25
P# block of 4 1.00 —

ROBERT H. GODDARD ISSUE

Robert H. Goddard, Atlas Rocket and Launching Tower, Cape Kennedy AP46

Designed by Robert J. Jones.

Dr. Robert H. Goddard (1882-1945), physicist and pioneer rocket researcher.

GIORI PRESS PRINTING

Plates of 200 subjects in four panes of 50 each.

1964, Oct. 5 Tagged *Perf. 11*

C69 AP46 8c **blue, red & bister** .35 .25
P# block of 4 1.60 —
Margin block of 4, Mr. Zip and "Use Zip Code" 1.65 —
a. Tagging omitted —

Luminescence

Air Post stamps issued after mid-1964 are tagged.

ALASKA PURCHASE ISSUE

Tlingit Totem, Southern Alaska — AP47

Designed by Willard R. Cox

Centenary of the Alaska Purchase. The totem pole shown is in the Alaska State Museum, Juneau.

GIORI PRESS PRINTING

Plates of 200 subjects in four panes of 50 each.

1967, Mar. 30 Unwmk. *Perf. 11*

C70 AP47 8c **brown** .25 .25
P# block of 4 1.20 —
Margin block of 4, Mr. Zip and "Use Zip Code" 1.05 —
a. Tagging omitted —

"Columbia Jays" by John James Audubon — AP48

GIORI PRESS PRINTING

Designed by Robert J. Jones.

Plates of 200 subjects in four panes of 50 each.

1967, Apr. 26 *Perf. 11*

C71 AP48 20c **multicolored** .75 .25
P# block of 4 3.25 —
Margin block of 4, Mr. Zip and "Use Zip Code" 3.10 —
a. Tagging omitted *12.50*

See note over No. 1241.

Fifty-Star Runway — AP49

ROTARY PRESS PRINTING

Designed by Jaan Born.

E. E. Plates of 400 subjects in four panes of 100 each.

1968, Jan. 5 Unwmk. *Perf. 11x10½*

C72 AP49 10c **carmine** .25 .25
P# block of 4 .90 —
Margin block of 4, "Use Zip Codes" 5.00 —
Vert. pair with full horiz. gutter between —
b. Booklet pane of 8 2.25 2.00
c. Booklet pane of 5 + label, *Jan. 6* 3.50 1.25
d. Vert. pair, imperf. btwn., in #C72b with foldover *5,000.*
e. Tagging omitted *12.50* —
f. As "b," tagging omitted — —
g. As "c," tagging omitted —

Red is the normal color of the tagging. Examples of No. C72b exist that have a mixture of the two tagging compounds.

No. C72d resulted from a paper foldover after perforating and before cutting into panes. Two pairs are recorded from different panes.

ROTARY PRESS COIL STAMP

Perf. 10 Vertically

C73 AP49 10c **carmine** .30 .25
Pair .65 .50
Joint line pair 1.75 .55
a. Imperf., pair *450.00*
Joint line pair *750.00*

$1 Airlift

This stamp, listed as No. 1341, was issued Apr. 4, 1968, to pay for airlift of parcels to and from U.S. ports to servicemen overseas and in Alaska, Hawaii and Puerto Rico.

It was "also valid for paying regular rates for other types of mail," the Post Office Department announced to the public in a philatelic release dated Mar. 10, 1968. The stamp is inscribed "U.S. Postage" and is untagged.

On Apr. 26, 1969, the P.O.D. stated in its Postal Manual (for postal employees) that this stamp "may be used toward paying the postage or fees for special services on *airmail* articles." On Jan. 1, 1970, the Department told postal employees through its Postal Bulletin that this $1 stamp "can only be used to pay the airlift fee or toward payment of postage or fees on *airmail* articles."

Some collectors prefer to consider No. 1341 an airmail stamp.

50th ANNIVERSARY OF AIR MAIL ISSUE

Curtiss Jenny — AP50

Designed by Hordur Karlsson.

50th anniv. of regularly scheduled air mail service.

LITHOGRAPHED, ENGRAVED (GIORI)

Plates of 200 subjects in four panes of 50 each.

1968, May 15 *Perf. 11*

C74 AP50 10c **blue, black & red** .25 .25
P# block of 4 1.30 —
Margin block of 4, Mr. Zip and "Use Zip Code" 1.05 —
b. Tagging omitted *8.00*

"USA" and Jet — AP51

Designed by John Larrecq.

LITHOGRAPHED, ENGRAVED (GIORI)

Plates of 200 subjects in four panes of 50 each.

1968, Nov. 22 ***Perf. 11***

C75 AP51 20c **red, blue & black** .35 .25
- P# block of 4 1.75 —
- Margin block of 4, Mr. Zip and "Use Zip Code" 1.50 —
- *a.* Tagging omitted *10.00*

See No. C81.

MOON LANDING ISSUE

First Man on the Moon AP52

Designed by Paul Calle.

Man's first landing on the moon July 20, 1969, by U.S. astronauts Neil A. Armstrong and Col. Edwin E. Aldrin, Jr., with Lieut. Col. Michael Collins piloting Apollo 11.

LITHOGRAPHED, ENGRAVED (GIORI)

Plates of 128 subjects in four panes of 32 each.

1969, Sept. 9 ***Perf. 11***

C76 AP52 10c **yellow, black, lt. blue, ultra., rose red & carmine** .25 .25
- P# block of 4 1.10 —
- Margin block of 4, Mr. Zip and "Use Zip Code" 1.05 —
- *a.* Rose red (litho.) omitted *500.00* —
- *b.* Tagging omitted *550.00* —

On No. C76a, the lithographed rose red is missing from the entire vignette-the dots on top of the yellow areas as well as the flag shoulder patch.

Silhouette of Delta Wing Plane — AP53

Silhouette of Jet Airliner — AP54

Winged Airmail Envelope — AP55

Statue of Liberty AP56

Designed by George Vander Sluis (9c, 11c), Nelson Gruppo (13c) and Robert J. Jones (17c).

ROTARY PRESS PRINTING

E. E. Plates of 400 subjects in four panes of 100 each.

1971-73 ***Perf. 10½x11***

C77 AP53 9c **red,** *May 15, 1971* .25 .25
- P# block of 4 .90 —
- Margin block of 4, "Use Zip Codes" .85 —
- *a.* Tagging omitted —

No. C77 issued primarily for use on domestic post cards.

Perf. 11x10½

C78 AP54 11c **carmine,** *May 7, 1971* .25 .25
- P# block of 4 .90 —
- Margin block of 4, "Use Zip Codes" .85 —
- Pair with full vert. gutter btwn. —
- *a.* Booklet pane of 4 + 2 labels 1.25 1.00
- *b.* Untagged (Bureau precanceled) .85 .85
- P# block of 4 27.50 —
- Margin block of 4, "Use Zip Codes" 13.75 —
- *c.* Tagging omitted (not Bureau precanceled) 7.50
- *d.* As "a," tagging omitted —

C79 AP55 13c **carmine,** *Nov. 16, 1973* .25 .25
- P# block of 4 1.10 —
- Margin block of 4, "Use Zip Codes" 1.05 —
- *a.* Booklet pane of 5 + label, *Dec. 27, 1973* 1.50 1.00
- *b.* Untagged (Bureau precanceled) .85 .85
- P# block of 4 20.00 —
- Margin block of 4, "Use Zip Codes" 9.50 —
- *c.* Green instead of red tagging (single from booklet pane) —
- *d.* Tagging omitted (not precanceled) 7.50 —

No. C78b Bureau precanceled "WASHINGTON D.C." (or "DC" - more valuable thus), No. C79b "WASHINGTON DC" only; both for use of Congressmen, but available to any permit holder.

Red is the normal color of the tagging. Examples also exist that have a mixture of the two tagging compounds.

GIORI PRESS PRINTING

Panes of 200 subjects in four panes of 50 each.

Perf. 11

C80 AP56 17c **bluish black, red, & dark green,** *July 13, 1971* .35 .25
- P# block of 4 1.60 —
- Margin block of 4, Mr. Zip and "Use Zip Code" 1.50 —
- *a.* Tagging omitted 12.50 —

"USA" & Jet Type of 1968

LITHOGRAPHED, ENGRAVED (GIORI)

Plates of 200 subjects in four panes of 50 each.

Perf. 11

C81 AP51 21c **red, blue & black,** *May 21, 1971* .40 .25
- P# block of 4 2.00 —
- Margin block of 4, Mr. Zip and "Use Zip Code" 1.75 —
- *a.* Tagging omitted *10.00*
- *b.* Black (engr.) missing (FO) *2,750.*

The two recorded examples of No. C81b are in a single full pane. Catalogue value is for both errors.

COIL STAMPS

ROTARY PRESS PRINTING

1971-73 ***Perf. 10 Vertically***

C82 AP54 11c **carmine,** *May 7, 1971* .25 .25
- Pair .50 .50
- Joint line pair .85 .60
- *a.* Imperf., pair *160.00*
- Joint line pair *350.00*
- *b.* Tagging omitted 10.00

C83 AP55 13c **carmine,** *Dec. 27, 1973* .30 .25
- Pair .60 .50
- Joint line pair 1.10 —
- *a.* Imperf., pair 60.00
- Joint line pair 145.00
- *b.* Tagging omitted —

NATIONAL PARKS CENTENNIAL ISSUE

City of Refuge, Hawaii

Kii Statue and Temple — AP57

Designed by Paul Rabut.

Centenary of national parks. This 11c honors the City of Refuge National Historical Park, established in 1961 at Honaunau, island of Hawaii.

LITHOGRAPHED, ENGRAVED (GIORI)

Plates of 200 subjects in four panes of 50 each.

1972, May 3 ***Perf. 11***

C84 AP57 11c **orange & multicolored** .25 .25
- P# block of 4 .90 —
- Margin block of 4, Mr. Zip and "Use Zip Code" .85 —
- *a.* Blue & green (litho.) omitted *425.00 900.00*
- *b.* Tagging omitted — —

OLYMPIC GAMES ISSUE

Skiing and Olympic Rings — AP58

Designed by Lance Wyman.

11th Winter Olympic Games, Sapporo, Japan, Feb. 3-13, and 20th Summer Olympic Games, Munich, Germany, Aug. 26-Sept. 11.

PHOTOGRAVURE (Andreotti)

Plates of 200 subjects in four panes of 50 each.

1972, Aug. 17 ***Perf. 11x10½***

C85 AP58 11c **black, blue, red, emerald & yellow** .25 .25
- P# block of 10, 5 P# 2.40 —
- Margin block of 4, "Use Zip Code" .85 —

ELECTRONICS PROGRESS ISSUE

De Forest Audions AP59

Designed by Walter and Naiad Einsel.

LITHOGRAPHED, ENGRAVED (GIORI)

Plates of 200 subjects in four panes of 50 each.

1973, July 10 ***Perf. 11***

C86 AP59 11c **vermilion, lilac, pale lilac, olive, brown, deep carmine & black** .30 .25
- P# block of 4 1.25 —
- Margin block of 4, Mr. Zip and "Use Zip Code" 1.20 —
- *a.* Vermilion & olive (litho.) omitted *550.00*
- *b.* Tagging omitted *60.00*
- *c.* Olive omitted *800.00*

Statue of Liberty AP60

Mt. Rushmore National Memorial AP61

Designed by Robert (Gene) Shehorn.

GIORI PRESS PRINTING

Panes of 200 subjects in four panes of 50 each.

1974 ***Perf. 11***

C87 AP60 18c **carmine, black & ultramarine,** *Jan. 11* .35 .30
- P# block of 4, 2# 1.50 —
- Margin block of 4, Mr. Zip and "Use Zip Code" 1.45 —
- *a.* Tagging omitted *22.50*

C88 AP61 26c **ultramarine, black & carmine,** *Jan. 2* .60 .25
- P# block of 4 2.30 —
- Margin block of 4, Mr. Zip and "Use Zip Code" 2.20 —
- Horiz. pair with full vert. gutter btwn. *1,600.*
- *a.* Tagging omitted *22.50*
- *b.* Yellow-green instead of orange-red tagging — —

Plane and Globes AP62

Plane, Globes and Flags — AP63

Designed by David G. Foote.

GIORI PRESS PRINTING

Panes of 200 subjects in four panes of 50 each.

1976, Jan. 2 *Perf. 11*

C89 AP62 25c **red, blue & black** .50 .25
P# block of 4 2.25 —
Margin block of 4, Mr. Zip and "Use Zip Code" 2.10 —
a. Tagging omitted *40.00* —
C90 AP63 31c **red, blue & black** .60 .25
P# block of 4 2.60 —
Margin block of 4, Mr. Zip and "Use Zip Code" 2.50 —
a. Tagging omitted *10.00*
b. All colors omitted —

On No. C90b, there is a colorless embossed image and a tagging ghost plane visible under UV light.

WRIGHT BROTHERS ISSUE

Orville and Wilbur Wright, and Flyer A — AP64

Wright Brothers, Flyer A and Shed — AP65

Designed by Ken Dallison.

75th anniv. of 1st powered flight, Kill Devil Hill, NC, Dec. 17, 1903.

LITHOGRAPHED, ENGRAVED (GIORI)

Plates of 400 subjects in four panes of 100 each.

1978, Sept. 23 *Perf. 11*

C91 AP64 31c **ultramarine & multicolored** .65 .30
C92 AP65 31c **ultramarine & multicolored** .65 .30
a. Vert. pair, #C91-C92 1.30 1.20
P# block of 4 2.75 —
Margin block of 4, "Use Correct Zip Code" 2.75 —
b. As "a," ultra. & black (engr.) omitted *475.00*
c. As "a," black (engr.) omitted *1,750.*
d. As "a," black, yellow, magenta, blue & brown (litho.) omitted *1,500.*

OCTAVE CHANUTE ISSUE

Chanute and Biplane Hang-glider — AP66

Biplane Hang-glider and Chanute — AP67

Designed by Ken Dallison.

Octave Chanute (1832-1910), civil engineer and aviation pioneer.

LITHOGRAPHED, ENGRAVED (GIORI)

Plates of 400 subjects in four panes of 100 each.

1979, Mar. 29 **Tagged** *Perf. 11*

C93 AP66 21c **blue & multicolored** .70 .35
C94 AP67 21c **blue & multicolored** .70 .35
a. Vert. pair, #C93-C94 1.40 1.20
P# block of 4 3.00 —
Margin block of 4, Mr. Zip 2.85 —
b. As "a," ultra & black (engr.) omitted *4,000.*

WILEY POST ISSUE

Wiley Post and "Winnie Mae" — AP68

NR-105-W, Post in Pressurized Suit, Portrait — AP69

Designed by Ken Dallison.

Wiley Post (1899-1935), first man to fly around the world alone and high-altitude flying pioneer.

LITHOGRAPHED, ENGRAVED (GIORI)

Plates of 400 subjects in four panes of 100 each.

1979, Nov. 20 **Tagged** *Perf. 11*

C95 AP68 25c **blue & multicolored** .90 .45
C96 AP69 25c **blue & multicolored** .90 .45
a. Vert. pair, #C95-C96 1.80 1.50
P# block of 4 4.75 —
Margin block of 4, Mr. Zip 3.75 —

OLYMPIC GAMES ISSUE

High Jump — AP70

Designed by Robert M. Cunningham.

22nd Olympic Games, Moscow, July 19-Aug. 3, 1980.

PHOTOGRAVURE

Plates of 200 subjects in four panes of 50 each.

1979, Nov. 1 **Tagged** *Perf. 11*

C97 AP70 31c **multicolored** .70 .30
P# block of 12, 6# 9.50 —
Zip block of 4 3.00 —

PHILIP MAZZEI (1730-1816)

Italian-born Political Writer — AP71

Designed by Sante Graziani

PHOTOGRAVURE

Plates of 200 subjects in four panes of 50 each.

1980, Oct. 13 **Tagged** *Perf. 11*

C98 AP71 40c **multicolored** .80 .25
P# block of 12, 6# 10.00 —
Zip block of 4 3.50 —
b. Imperf., pair *2,250.*
d. Tagging omitted *11.00*

1982 **Tagged** *Perf. 10½x11¼*

C98A AP71 40c **multicolored** 5.00 1.50
P# block of 12, 6# 80.00 —
c. Horiz. pair, imperf. vert. *3,250.*

BLANCHE STUART SCOTT (1886-1970)

First Woman Pilot — AP72

Designed by Paul Calle.

PHOTOGRAVURE

Plates of 200 subjects in four panes of 50.

1980, Dec. 30 **Tagged** *Perf. 11*

C99 AP72 28c **multicolored** .60 .25
P# block of 12, 6# 8.50 —
Zip block of 4 2.50 —
a. Imperf., pair *2,000.*

GLENN CURTISS (1878-1930)

Aviation Pioneer and Aircraft Designer AP73

Designed by Ken Dallison.

PHOTOGRAVURE

Plates of 200 subjects in four panes of 50.

1980, Dec. 30 **Tagged** *Perf. 11*

C100 AP73 35c **multicolored** .65 .25
P# block of 12, 6# 9.00 —
Zip block of 4 2.75 —
a. Light blue (background) omitted *2,000.*

SUMMER OLYMPICS 1984

Women's Gymnastics — AP74

Hurdles — AP75

Women's Basketball — AP76

Soccer — AP77

Designed by Robert Peak.

23rd Olympic Games, Los Angeles, July 28-Aug. 12, 1984.

PHOTOGRAVURE

Plates of 200 subjects in four panes of 50.

1983, June 17 **Tagged** *Perf. 11*

C101 AP74 28c **multicolored** 1.00 .30
C102 AP75 28c **multicolored** 1.00 .30
C103 AP76 28c **multicolored** 1.00 .30
C104 AP77 28c **multicolored** 1.00 .30
a. Block of 4, #C101-C104 4.25 2.50
P# block of 4, 4# 5.25 —
Zip block of 4 4.25 —
b. As "a," imperf. vert. *5,000.*

Shot Put — AP78

Men's Gymnastics AP79

Women's Swimming AP80

Weight Lifting — AP81

1983, Apr. 8	**Tagged**	***Perf. 11.2 Bullseye***	
C105 AP78 40c **multicolored**		.90	.40
a.	Perf. 11 line	1.00	.45
C106 AP79 40c **multicolored**		.90	.40
a.	Perf. 11 line	1.00	.45
C107 AP80 40c **multicolored**		.90	.40
a.	Perf. 11 line	1.00	.45
C108 AP81 40c **multicolored**		.90	.40
a.	Perf. 11 line	1.00	.45
b.	Block of 4, #C105-C108	4.25	3.00
	P# block of 4, 4#	5.00	—
	Zip block of 4	4.50	—
c.	Block of 4, #C105a-C108a	5.00	4.00
	P# block of 4, 4#	7.50	—
d.	Block of 4, imperf.	*650.00*	

Women's Fencing AP82

Cycling AP83

Women's Volleyball AP84

Pole Vaulting AP85

1983, Nov. 4	**Tagged**	***Perf. 11***	
C109 AP82 35c **multicolored**		.90	.55
C110 AP83 35c **multicolored**		.90	.55
C111 AP84 35c **multicolored**		.90	.55
C112 AP85 35c **multicolored**		.90	.55
a.	Block of 4, #C109-C112	4.00	3.25
	P# block of 4, 4#	6.00	—
	Zip block of 4	4.25	—

AVIATION PIONEERS

Alfred V. Verville (1890-1970), Inventor, Verville-Sperry R-3 Army Racer — AP86

Lawrence Sperry (1892-1923), Aircraft Designer, and Father Elmer (1860-1930), Designer and Pilot, 1st Seaplane AP87

Designed by Ken Dallison (No. C113) and Howard Koslow (No. C114)

PHOTOGRAVURE

Plates of 200 in four panes of 50
(2 panes each, No. C113 and No. C114)
Plates of 200 in four panes of 50 (No. C114)

1985, Feb. 13	**Tagged**	***Perf. 11***	
C113 AP86 33c **multicolored**		.65	.25
	P# block of 4, 5#, UL, LR	3.25	—
	Zip block of 4	2.90	—
a.	Imperf., pair	*500.00*	
C114 AP87 39c **multicolored**		.80	.25
	P# block of 4, 5#, UR, LL	3.75	—
	P# block of 4, 4#	3.75	—
	Zip block of 4	3.50	—
a.	Imperf., pair	*1,250.*	

Philatelic Foundation certificates issued prior to August 1994 for No. C114 with magenta missing have been rescinded. At this time no genuine magenta missing examples are known. The magenta color is very fugitive, fading rapidly when exposed to sunlight.

TRANSPACIFIC AIRMAIL

50th Anniversary

Martin M-130 China Clipper AP88

Designed by Chuck Hodgson.

PHOTOGRAVURE

Plates of 200 in four panes of 50

1985, Feb. 15	**Tagged**	***Perf. 11***	
C115 AP88 44c **multicolored**		.85	.25
	P# block of 4, 4#	4.00	—
	Zip block of 4	3.50	—
a.	Imperf., pair	*550.00*	

FR. JUNIPERO SERRA (1713-1784)

California Missionary

Outline Map of Southern California, Portrait, San Gabriel Mission AP89

Designed by Richard Schlecht from a Spanish stamp.

PHOTOGRAVURE

Plates of 200 in four panes of 50

1985, Aug. 22	**Tagged**	***Perf. 11***	
C116 AP89 44c **multicolored**		1.00	.35
	P# block of 4	7.00	—
	Zip block of 4	4.25	—
a.	Imperf., pair	*850.00*	

SETTLING OF NEW SWEDEN, 350th ANNIV.

Settler, Two Indians, Map of New Sweden, Swedish Ships "Kalmar Nyckel" and "Fogel Grip" — AP90

Designed by Goran Osterland based on an 18th century illustration from a Swedish book about the Colonies.

LITHOGRAPHED AND ENGRAVED

Plates of 200 in four panes of 50

1988, Mar. 29	**Tagged**	***Perf. 11***	
C117 AP90 44c **multicolored**		1.00	.25
	P# block of 4, 5#	6.50	—
	Zip block of 4	5.00	—

See Sweden No. 1672 and Finland No. 768.

SAMUEL P. LANGLEY (1834-1906)

Langley and Unmanned Aerodrome No. 5 — AP91

Designed by Ken Dallison.

LITHOGRAPHED AND ENGRAVED

Plates of 200 in four panes of 50

1988, May 14	**Tagged**	***Perf. 11***	
C118 AP91 45c **multicolored,** large block tagging		1.00	.25
	P# block of 4, 7#	5.00	—
	Zip block of 4	4.25	—
a.	Overall tagging	3.50	.50
	P# block of 4, 7#	45.00	—
	Zip block of 4	15.00	—

IGOR SIKORSKY (1889-1972)

Sikorsky and 1939 VS300 Helicopter AP92

Designed by Ren Wicks.

PHOTOGRAVURE AND ENGRAVED

Plates of 200 in four panes of 50

1988, June 23	**Tagged**	***Perf. 11***	
C119 AP92 36c **multicolored**		.70	.25
	P# block of 4, 6#	3.25	—
	Zip block of 4	3.10	—
a.	Red, dk blue & black (engraved) omitted	*900.00*	

Beware of examples with traces of engraved red offered as "red omitted" varieties.

FRENCH REVOLUTION BICENTENNIAL

Liberty, Equality and Fraternity — AP93

Designed by Richard Sheaff.

LITHOGRAPHED AND ENGRAVED
Plates of 120 in four panes of 30.

1989, July 14 Tagged *Perf. 11½x11*

C120	AP93 45c **multicolored**	.95	.25
	P# block of 4, 4#	4.75	—
	Zip block of 4	4.00	—

See France Nos. 2143-2145a.

PRE-COLUMBIAN AMERICA ISSUE

Southeast Carved Figure, 700-1430 A.D. — AP94

Designed by Lon Busch.

PHOTOGRAVURE
Plates of 200 in four panes of 50

1989, Oct. 12 *Perf. 11*

C121	AP94 45c **multicolored**	.90	.25
	P# block of 4, 4#	5.25	—
	Zip block of 4	3.75	—

20th UPU CONGRESS
Futuristic Mail Delivery

Spacecraft — AP95

Air-suspended Hover Car — AP96

Moon Rover — AP97

Space Shuttle — AP98

Designed by Ken Hodges.

LITHOGRAPHED & ENGRAVED
Plates of 160 in four panes of 40.

1989, Nov. 27 Tagged *Perf. 11*

C122	AP95 45c **multicolored**	1.00	.50
C123	AP96 45c **multicolored**	1.00	.50
C124	AP97 45c **multicolored**	1.00	.50
C125	AP98 45c **multicolored**	1.00	.50
a.	Block of 4, #C122-C125	4.00	3.00
	P# block of 4, 5#	5.00	—
	Zip block of 4	4.25	—
b.	As "a," light blue (engr.) omitted	*500.00*	
c.	As "a," tagging omitted	—	

Souvenir Sheet
LITHOGRAPHED & ENGRAVED

1989, Nov. 24 Tagged *Imperf.*

C126	Sheet of 4	5.00	4.00
a.	AP95 45c multicolored	1.25	.50
b.	AP96 45c multicolored	1.25	.50
c.	AP97 45c multicolored	1.25	.50
d.	AP98 45c multicolored	1.25	.50
e.	As No. C126, tagging omitted	*650.00*	

PRE-COLUMBIAN AMERICA ISSUE

Tropical Coast — AP99

Designed by Mark Hess.
Printed by the American Bank Note Company.

PHOTOGRAVURE
Plates of 200 in four panes of 50
(3 panes of #2512, 1 pane of #C127)

1990, Oct. 12 Tagged *Perf. 11*

C127	AP99 45c **multicolored**	.90	.25
	P# block of 4, 4#, UL only	7.00	—
	Zip block of 4	3.75	—
a.	Vert. pair, imperf. btwn. and at top	—	

No. C127a is the upper left pair in a pane of 50 with a paper foldover before perforating. The pair has diagonal perforations from rows other than the top and between perforations.

HARRIET QUIMBY, 1ST AMERICAN WOMAN PILOT

Quimby (1884-1912), Bleriot Airplane AP100

Designed by Howard Koslow. Printed by Stamp Venturers.

PHOTOGRAVURE
Panes of 200 in four panes of 50

1991, Apr. 27 Tagged *Perf. 11*

C128	AP100 50c **multicolored**, overall tagging	1.00	.25
	P# block of 4, #S1111	5.25	—
	Zip block of 4	4.25	—
a.	Vert. pair, imperf. horiz.	*800.00*	
b.	Perf. 11.2 bullseye, prephosphored uncoated paper (mottled tagging), *1993*	1.25	.25
	P# block of 4, #S2222	6.50	—
	Zip block of 6	5.00	—

WILLIAM T. PIPER, AIRCRAFT MANUFACTURER

Piper and Piper Cub — AP101

Designed by Ren Wicks.
Printed by J. W. Fergusson and Sons for American Bank Note Co.

PHOTOGRAVURE
Panes of 200 in four panes of 50

1991, May 17 Tagged *Perf. 11 Line*

C129	AP101 40c **multicolored,** shiny gum	.80	.25
	P# block of 4, 4#+A	3.75	—
	Zip block of 4	3.50	—

Blue sky is plainly visible all the way across stamp above Piper's head.
See No. C132.

ANTARCTIC TREATY, 30TH ANNIVERSARY

AP102

Designed by Howard Koslow. Printed by Stamp Venturers.

PHOTOGRAVURE
Sheets of 200 in four panes of 50

1991, June 21 Tagged *Perf. 11*

C130	AP102 50c **multicolored**	1.00	.35
	P# block of 4, 4#+S	5.00	—
	Zip block of 4	4.25	—

PRE-COLUMBIAN AMERICA ISSUE

Bering Land Bridge AP103

Designed by Richard Schlect.

PHOTOGRAVURE
Sheets of 200 in four panes of 50

1991, Oct. 12 Tagged *Perf. 11*

C131	AP103 50c **multicolored**	1.00	.35
	P# block of 4, 6#	5.25	—
	Zip block of 4	4.75	—

Piper Type of 1991

Printed by Stamp Venturers.

PHOTOGRAVURE
Sheets of 200 in four panes of 50

1993 Tagged *Perf. 11.2 Bullseye*

C132	AP101 40c **multicolored,** low gloss gum	3.50	.65
	P# block of 4, 4#+S	40.00	—
	Zip block of 4	16.00	—

Piper's hair touches top edge of design. No selvage inscriptions.

"All LC (Letters and Cards) mail receives First-Class Mail service in the United States, is dispatched by the fastest transportation available, and travels by airmail or priority service in the destination country. All LC mail should be marked 'AIRMAIL' or 'PAR AVION.'" (U.S. Postal Service, Pub. 51).

No. C133 listed below was issued to meet the LC rate to Canada and Mexico and is inscribed with the silhouette of a jet plane next to the denomination indicating the need for airmail service. This is unlike No. 2998, which met the LC rate to other countries, but contained no indication that it was intended for that use.

Future issues that meet a specific international airmail rate and contain the airplane silhouette will be treated by Scott as Air Post stamps. Stamps similar to No. 2998 will be listed in the Postage section.

SCENIC AMERICAN LANDSCAPES

Niagara Falls — AP104

Designed by Ethel Kessler. Printed by Avery Dennison.

PHOTOGRAVURE

Sheets of 200 in 10 panes of 20

1999, May 12 Tagged *Serpentine Die Cut 11*

Self-Adhesive

C133 AP104 48c **multicolored** 1.00 .25
P# block of 4, 5#+V 4.25
Pane of 20 30.00

Rio Grande AP105

Designed by Ethel Kessler. Printed by Avery Dennison.

PHOTOGRAVURE

Sheets of 200 in 10 panes of 20

1999, July 30 Tagged *Serpentine Die Cut 11*

Self-Adhesive

C134 AP105 40c **multicolored** .80 .60
P# block of 4, 5#+V 3.20
Pane of 20 16.00

Grand Canyon AP106

Designed by Ethel Kessler.
Printed by Banknote Corp. of America.

LITHOGRAPHED

Sheets of 180 in nine panes of 20

Serpentine Die Cut 11¼x11½

2000, Jan. 20 Tagged

Self-Adhesive

C135 AP106 60c **multicolored** 1.25 .25
P# block of 4, 4#+B 5.00
Pane of 20 25.00
a. Die cutting omitted, pair *1,250.*
b. Vert. pair, die cutting omitted horiz. —
c. Horiz. pair, die cutting omitted between —
d. Horiz. pair, die cutting omitted vert. —

Nine-Mile Prairie, Nebraska AP107

Designed by Ethel Kessler. Printed by Ashton-Potter (USA) Ltd.

LITHOGRAPHED

Sheets of 180 in nine panes of 20 .

Serpentine Die Cut 11¼x11½

2001, Mar. 6 Tagged

Self-Adhesive

C136 AP107 70c **multicolored** 1.40 .30
P# block of 4, 5#+P 5.60
Pane of 20 28.00

Mt. McKinley AP108

Designed by Ethel Kessler. Printed by Avery Dennison.

PHOTOGRAVURE

Sheets of 200 in ten panes of 20.

2001, Apr. 17 Tagged *Serpentine Die Cut 11*

Self-Adhesive

C137 AP108 80c **multicolored** 1.60 .35
P# block of 4, 5 #+V 6.40
Pane of 20 32.00

Acadia National Park — AP109

Designed by Ethel Kessler. Printed by Banknote Corporation of America, Banknote Corporation of America for Sennett Security Printers (No. C138b).

LITHOGRAPHED

Sheets of 180 in nine panes of 20 (#C138), Sheets of 120 in six panes of 20 (#C138a)

Serpentine Die Cut 11.25x11.5 (No. C138), 11.5x11.9 (No. C138a)

2001-05 Tagged

Self-Adhesive

C138 AP109 60c **multicolored**, prephosphored coated paper (solid tagging), *May 30, 2001* 1.25 .25
P# block of 4, 4# + B 5.00
Pane of 20 25.00
a. Overall tagging, dated "2001," *March 2003* 1.25 .25
P# block of 4, 4# + B 5.00
Pane of 20 25.00
b. As "a," with "2005" year date, *Jan. 2005* 1.25 .25
P# block of 4, 4#+S 6.00
Pane of 20 29.00
c. As "b," printed on back of backing paper —

Bryce Canyon National Park — AP110

Great Smoky Mountains National Park — AP111

Designed by Ethel Kessler. Printed by Banknote Corporation of America for Sennett Security Products (#C139), Ashton-Potter (USA) Ltd. (#C140), Avery Dennison (#C141).

LITHOGRAPHED, PHOTOGRAVURE (#C141)

Sheets of 180 in nine panes of 20 and sheets of 160 in eight panes of 20 (#C139), Sheets of 120 in six panes of 20 (#C140), Sheets of 200 in ten panes of 20 (#C141)

2006, Feb. 24 Tagged *Serpentine Die Cut 10¾*

Self-Adhesive

C139 AP110 63c **multicolored** 1.25 .25
P# block of 4, 5#+S 5.00
Pane of 20 25.00
a. Die cutting omitted, pair *450.00*

C140 AP111 75c **multicolored** 1.50 .35
P# block of 4, 5#+P 6.00
Pane of 20 30.00
a. Die cutting omitted, pair *500.00*

Two printings of No. C139 with different plate # order. Sheet of 180 has gray plate # first (and has glossier finish). Sheet of 160 has gray plate # last.

Yosemite National Park — AP112

Serpentine Die Cut 11

C141 AP112 84c **multicolored** 1.75 .35
P# block of 4, 5#+V 7.00
Pane of 20 35.00
Nos. C139-C141 (3) 4.50 .95

Okefenokee Swamp, Georgia and Florida AP113

Hagatña Bay, Guam AP114

Designed by Ethel Kessler. Printed by Ashton-Potter (USA) Ltd. (#C142), Avery Dennison (#C143).

LITHOGRAPHED (#C142), PHOTOGRAVURE (#C143)

Sheets of 120 in six panes of 20 (#C142), Sheets of 200 in ten panes of 20 (#C143)

2007, June 1 Tagged *Serpentine Die Cut 10¾*

Self-Adhesive

C142 AP113 69c **multicolored** 1.40 .30
P# block of 4, 5#+P 5.60
Pane of 20 28.00

Serpentine Die Cut 11

C143 AP114 90c **multicolored** 1.80 .40
P# block of 4, 5#+V 7.75
Pane of 20 38.00

13-Mile Woods, New Hampshire AP115

Trunk Bay, St. John, Virgin Islands AP116

Designed by Ethel Kessler. Printed by Banknote Corporation of America for Sennett Security Products (#C144), Avery Dennison (#C145).

LITHOGRAPHED (#C144), PHOTOGRAVURE (#C145)

Sheets of 180 in nine panes of 20 (#C144), Sheets of 200 in ten panes of 20 (#C145)

2008, May 16 Tagged *Serpentine Die Cut 10¾*

Self-Adhesive

C144 AP115 72c **multicolored** 1.50 .30
P# block of 4, 5#+S 6.50
Pane of 20 32.00

Serpentine Die Cut 11

C145 AP116 94c **multicolored** Ⓢ 1.90 .45
P# block of 4, 5#+V 8.00
Pane of 20 40.00

See note after No. 1549.

Zion National Park, Utah — AP117

Grand Teton National Park, Wyoming AP118

Designed by Ethel Kessler. Printed by Ashton-Potter (USA) Ltd. (#C146), Avery Dennison (#C147).

LITHOGRAPHED, PHOTOGRAVURE (#C147)

Sheets of 120 in six panes of 20 (#C146), Sheets of 200 in ten panes of 20 (#C147)

2009, June 28 Tagged *Serpentine Die Cut 10¾*

Self-Adhesive

C146 AP117 79c **multicolored** Ⓢ 1.75 .35
P# block of 4, 5#+P 7.00
Pane of 20 35.00

Serpentine Die Cut 11

C147 AP118 98c **multicolored** Ⓢ 2.00 .45
P# block of 4, 5#+V 8.00
Pane of 20 40.00

See note after No. 1549.

Voyageurs National Park, Minnesota AP119

Designed by Ethel Kessler. Printed by Ashton-Potter (USA) Ltd.

LITHOGRAPHED

Sheets of 180 in nine panes of 20

2011, Apr. 11 Tagged *Serpentine Die Cut 10¾*

Self-Adhesive

C148 AP119 80c **multicolored** Ⓢ 1.60 .25
P# block of 4, 5#+P 6.40
Pane of 20 32.00

See note after No. 1549.

Glacier National Park, Montana AP120

Amish Horse and Buggy on Road, Lancaster County, Pennsylvania AP121

Designed by Ethel Kessler. Printed by Ashton-Potter (USA) Ltd. (#C149), Banknote Corporation of America for Sennett Security Products (#C150).

LITHOGRAPHED

Sheets of 120 in six panes of 20 (#C149), Sheets of 240 in 12 panes of 20 (#C150)

2012 Tagged *Serpentine Die Cut 10¾*

Self-Adhesive

C149 AP120 85c **multi,** *Jan. 19* Ⓢ 1.75 .35
P# block of 4, 5#+P 7.00
Pane of 20 35.00

C150 AP121 $1.05 **multicolored,** *Jan. 20* 2.10 .45
P# block of 4, 5#+S 8.40
Pane of 20 42.50

a. Die cutting omitted on front, pair *500.00*

b. Silver (airplane silhouette) missing (PS) —

See note after No. 1549.

AIR POST SPECIAL DELIVERY STAMPS

Great Seal of United States APSD1

No. CE1 was issued for the prepayment of the air postage and the special delivery fee in one stamp. First day sale was at the American Air Mail Society Convention.

FLAT PLATE PRINTING

Plates of 200 subjects in four panes of 50 each.

1934, Aug. 30 Unwmk. *Perf. 11*

CE1 APSD1 16c **dark blue** .70 .80
blue .70 .80
Never hinged .90
P# block of 6 14.00 —
Never hinged 22.50
First day cover, Chicago *(40,171)* 25.00
First day cover, Washington, D.C., *Aug. 31* 15.00

For imperforate variety see No. 771.

Great Seal of United States APSD2

Type 1 - Thin red line with a thin blue line

Type 2 - Thick red line with a thin blue line

Type 3 - Thick red line with a dotted blue line

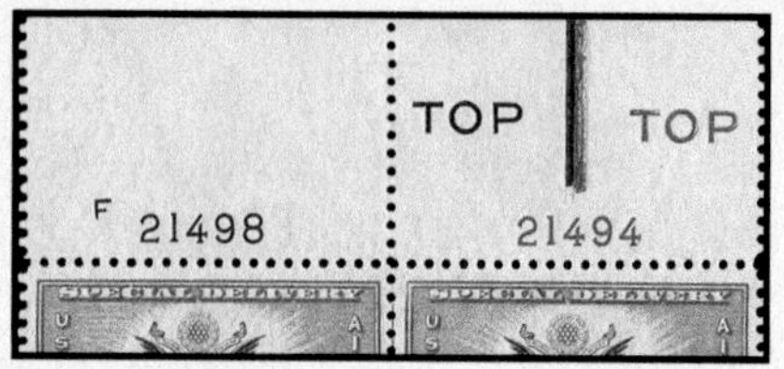

Type 4 - Thick red line with a thick blue line

Frame plates of 100 subjects in two panes of 50 each separated by a 1 ½ inch wide vertical gutter with central guide line, and vignette plates of 50 subjects.

The "seal" design for No. CE2 was from a new engraving, slightly smaller than that used for No. CE1.

Issued in panes of 50 each.

1936, Feb. 10

CE2 APSD2 16c **red & blue** .45 .35
- Never hinged .65
- Center line block 2.50 3.00
- Never hinged 3.60
- First day cover, Washington, D.C. *(72,981)* 20.00

Type 1 Marginal Markings, *Feb. 10, 1936*
- P# block of 4, 2#, two "TOP," thin red and thin blue registration markers 10.00 —
- Never hinged 14.00
- Bottom margin block of 4, thin red and thin blue registration markers below right stamp 2.00 2.00
- Left or right margin horizontal line block of 4 with thin red and thin blue registration markers, no red arrow 2.00 2.00

Type 2 Marginal Markings, *Aug. 1940*
- P# block of 4, 2#, two "TOP," thick red and thin blue registration markers 80.00 —
- Never hinged 115.00
- Bottom margin block of 4, thick red and thin blue registration markers below right stamp 10.00 10.00
- Left or right margin horizontal line block of 4 with thick red and thin blue registration markers, no red arrow 10.00 10.00

Type 3 Marginal Markings, *June 1941*
- P# block of 4, 2#, two "TOP," thick red and thin blue dotted registration markers 100.00 —
- Never hinged 145.00
- P# block of 10, 2#, two "TOP," thick red and thin blue dotted registration markers, thick red vertical inversion marker over stamps 1 & 5 110.00 —
- Never hinged 160.00
- Bottom margin arrow block of 4, thick red and thin blue dotted registration markers over center line 15.00 15.00
- Left or right margin horizontal line block of 4 with thick red and thin blue dotted registration markers, no red arrow 15.00 15.00

Type 4 Marginal Markings, *May 1942*
- P# block of 4, 2#, two "TOP," thick red and thick blue registration markers 15.00 —
- Never hinged 21.00
- P# block of 10, 2#, two "TOP," thick red and thick blue registration markers, thick red vertical inversion and thick blue horizontal inversion markers over stamps 1 & 5 25.00 —
- Never hinged 37.50
- Bottom margin arrow block of 4, thick red and thick blue registration markers over center line 3.00 3.00
- Left or right margin horizontal line block of 4, thick red and thick blue registration markers, no red arrow 3.00 3.00

a. Horiz. pair, imperf. vert. *4,250.*
- Never hinged *5,250.*
- P# block of 6, 2#, two "TOP," thick red and thick blue registration markers, thick red vertical and thick blue horizontal inversion markers over stamp 1 *60,000.*

The No. CE2a plate block is unique. Value represents sale in 2008.

Warning: Special care should be exercised when buying or selling type 3 printings. Some printers, when wiping a blue plate prior to printing, accidentally removed a portion of the blue ink from the blue registration marker. This exposed some of the blue dots that were used for type 3 printings, making a type 4 plate block appear to be a type 3 printing.

Three types of experimental versions of the type 1 plate block registration markers are known, often given the letters A, B, and C. Type 1A has 3 thin red lines and one thin blue line. type 1B has 2 thin red lines and one thin blue line, and type 1C has one long thin red line, one short thin red line and one thin blue line. These experimental markings are seldom seen and are worth much more than the values shown for type 1 plate blocks.

Quantities issued: #CE1, 9,215,750; #CE2, 72,517,850.

AIR POST SEMI-OFFICIAL STAMPS

Buffalo Balloon

This stamp was privately issued by John F. B. Lillard, a Nashville reporter. It was used on covers carried on a balloon ascension of June 18, 1877, which began at Nashville and landed at Gallatin, Tenn., and possibly on other flights. The balloon was owned and piloted by Samuel Archer King. The stamp was reported to have been engraved by (Mrs.?) J. H. Snively and printed in tete beche pairs from a single die. Lillard wrote that 300 were printed and 23 used.

Buffalo Balloon — APSO1

1877, June 18 **Typo.** ***Imperf.***

CL1 APSO1 5c **deep blue** *7,500.*
- Never hinged *10,000.*
- On cover with 3c #158 *150,000.*
- On cover with 1c #156 & 2c #178 *100,000.*

a. Tête bêche pair, vertical *22,500.*
- Never hinged *27,500.*

A black proof exists of No. CL1, value *$17,500.*

Rodgers Aerial Post

This stamp was privately issued by Calbraith Perry Rodgers' wife who acted as unofficial postmaster during her husband's cross-country airplane flight in 1911. Rodgers was competing for the $50,000 prize offered by William Randolph Hearst to whomever completed the trip within a 30-day period. Rodgers' flight was sponsored by the Armour meat-packing company, makers of the soft drink, Vin Fiz.

The stamp probably was first available in Texas about October 19. Recorded dated examples exist from Oct. 19 to Nov. 8.

Each of the thirteen known examples is trimmed close to the design on one or more sides.

APSO2

1911, Oct. ***Imperf.***

CL2 APSO2 25c **black** *55,000.*
- On postcard with 1c #374 *75,000.*
- Tied on cover with 1c #374 *115,000.*

No. CL2 is the first stamp in the world to picture an airplane.

There are six examples on postcard, not canceled; four on postcard, canceled; one on envelope, canceled; one on a piece of a postcard, not canceled; and one off cover with original gum.

COLOMBIA (SCADTA) CONSULAR OVERPRINTS

In July 1920, SCADTA was given authority by the Colombian government to operate exclusive airmail service in Colombia and to print its own postage stamps, while retaining all profits. Transportation in Colombia at this time was slow and difficult. This SCADTA airmail service enabled commerce to flourish.

Overprinted stamps were available at Colombian consulates, trade missions and agencies that were maintained by the SCADTA Company. These stamps paid the airmail service within Colombia once the mail arrived at a Colombian port.

Due to currency fluctuations between countries, two-letter overprints were applied by hand, and later by machine, denoting country of origin. The letters for the United States were "E.U." (Estados Unidos). For the SCADTA stamps used from countries other than the United States, see the Colombia listings in the *Scott Classic Specialized Catalogue of Stamps and Covers.*

The SCADTA system was extensively used throughout the world. In the United States, all mail that was sent singularly and not under separate cover was to have United States postage affixed for delivery to a Colombian port city post office and/or for delivery locally in Colombia. It was then processed and delivered to a ship destined for Colombia under normal international delivery agreements. Other mail was taken directly to ships by SCADTA agents, and on those no U.S. Stamps were required.

On Dec. 31, 1931, the Colombian government took over all airmail service in Colombia.

Values for unused stamps are for examples with no gum faults. Stamps with "tropicalized" gum sell at a substantial discount.

UNITED STATES DISPATCH FOR EXPEDITED AIR-MAIL SERVICE WITHIN COLOMBIA

Colombia (SCADTA) Consular Overprints Sociedad Colombo-Alemana de Transportes Aereos (S.C.A.D.T.A.)

Establishing an office in New York, the SCADTA Company sold the following two issues, each bearing the agent's signature, "G Mejia" (Gonzalo Mejia), in red ink, to designate use from the United States.

Colombia Nos. C14, C16 with ms "G Mejia" in red

Quantity printed of each value in parentheses.

1920, November

CLEU1	AP3 30c blk, *rose* (5,000)	100.00	350.00
	Never hinged	150.00	
	On cover		3,000.
CLEU2	AP3 50c green (1,000)	100.00	500.00
	Never hinged	150.00	
	On cover		7,000.
a.	Black signature		—

Two examples of No. CLEU2 on cover are known. Nos. CLEU1 and CLEU2 exist together on a unique cover.

E.U. or EU - STAMPS FOR USE IN THE UNITED STATES

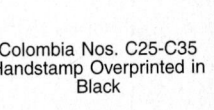

Colombia Nos. C25-C35 Handstamp Overprinted in Black

Letters 6½mm high

1921-23

CLEU3	AP4 5c org yel	20.00	15.00
	Never hinged	32.50	
	On cover		110.00
CLEU4	AP4 10c sl grn	20.00	15.00
	Never hinged	32.50	
	On cover		110.00
CLEU5	AP4 15c org brn	20.00	15.00
	Never hinged	32.50	
	On cover		165.00
CLEU6	AP4 20c red brown	20.00	15.00
	Never hinged	32.50	
	On cover		110.00
CLEU7	AP4 30c green	15.00	10.00
	Never hinged	27.50	
	On cover		165.00
CLEU8	AP4 50c blue	20.00	15.00
	Never hinged	32.50	
	On cover		225.00
CLEU9	AP4 60c vermilion	30.00	25.00
	Never hinged	47.50	
	On cover		325.00
CLEU10	AP5 1p gray black	35.00	30.00
	Never hinged	55.00	
	On cover		225.00
CLEU11	AP5 2p rose	75.00	70.00
	Never hinged	140.00	
	On cover		325.00
CLEU12	AP5 3p violet	100.00	100.00
	Never hinged	170.00	
	On cover		550.00
CLEU13	AP5 5p ol grn	425.00	400.00
	Never hinged	700.00	
	On cover		1,100.
	Nos. CLEU3-CLEU13 (11)	780.00	710.00
	Nos. CLEU3-CLEU13, never hinged	1,302.50	

Same Overprint in Violet on Colombia Nos. C25-C35

1921-23

CLEU14	AP4 5c org yel	15.00	17.50
	Never hinged	22.50	
	On cover		140.00
CLEU15	AP4 10c sl grn	12.50	17.50
	Never hinged	20.00	
	On cover		140.00
CLEU16	AP4 15c org brn	12.50	17.50
	Never hinged	20.00	
	On cover		225.00
CLEU17	AP4 20c red brown	12.50	17.50
	Never hinged	20.00	
	On cover		87.50
CLEU18	AP4 30c green	9.00	12.00
	Never hinged	14.00	
	On cover		140.00
a.	Double overprint	*750.00*	
b.	Double overprint, vert.	—	
CLEU19	AP4 50c blue	12.50	17.50
	Never hinged	20.00	
	On cover		165.00
CLEU20	AP4 60c vermilion	30.00	25.00
	Never hinged	45.00	
	On cover		225.00
CLEU21	AP5 1p gray black	27.50	37.50
	Never hinged	45.00	
	On cover		225.00
CLEU22	AP5 2p rose	62.50	72.50
	Never hinged	100.00	
	On cover		275.00
CLEU23	AP5 3p violet	112.50	125.00
	Never hinged	180.00	
	On cover		550.00
CLEU24	AP5 5p ol grn	375.00	400.00
	Never hinged	550.00	
	On cover		875.00
	Nos. CLEU14-CLEU24 (11)	681.50	759.50
	Nos. CLEU14-CLEU24, never hinged	1,036.50	

Same overprint in black on Colombia Nos. C38//51, CF1

No. CLEU29

No. CLEU32

1923

CLEU25	AP6 5c org yel	20.00	12.50
	Never hinged	32.50	
	On cover		110.00
CLEU26	AP6 10c green	20.00	12.50
	Never hinged	32.50	
	On cover		110.00
CLEU27	AP6 15c carmine	25.00	15.00
	Never hinged	32.50	
	On cover		110.00
CLEU28	AP6 20c gray	20.00	15.00
	Never hinged	32.50	
	On cover		110.00
CLEU29	AP6 30c blue	7.50	5.00
	Never hinged	11.00	
	On cover		82.50
CLEU30	AP6 50c green	20.00	10.00
	Never hinged	32.50	
	On cover		250.00
CLEU31	AP6 60c brown	20.00	10.00
	Never hinged	32.50	
	On cover		275.00
CLEU32	AP7 1p black	30.00	20.00
	Never hinged	45.00	
	On cover		275.00
CLEU33	AP7 2p red org	35.00	27.50
	Never hinged	50.00	
	On cover		325.00
CLEU34	AP7 3p violet	75.00	50.00
	Never hinged	110.00	
	On cover		450.00
CLEU35	AP7 5p ol grn	125.00	87.50
	Never hinged	190.00	
	On cover		775.00
CFLEU1	AP6 20c gray	125.00	37.50
	Never hinged	200.00	
	On cover		550.00
	Nos. CLEU25-CLEU35, CFLEU1 (12)	522.50	302.50
	Nos. CLEU25-CLEU35, CFLEU1, never hinged	801.00	

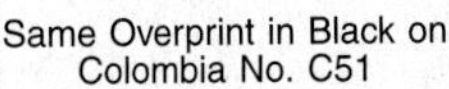

Same Overprint in Black on Colombia No. C51

1923

No.	Description	Unused	Used
CLEU36	AP6 30c on 20c gray (C)	*1,650.*	*600.00*
	On cover		*825.00*
a.	"60" instead of "30" at left, on cover		—

No. CLEU36a is unique.

Same Overprint in Violet on Colombia Nos. C38//C50, CF1

1923

No.	Description	Unused	Used
CLEU37	AP6 5c org yel	12.50	12.50
	Never hinged	17.50	
	On cover		75.00
CLEU38	AP6 10c green	12.50	12.50
	Never hinged	17.50	
	On cover		75.00
CLEU39	AP6 15c carmine	12.50	12.50
	Never hinged	17.50	
	On cover		75.00
CLEU40	AP6 20c gray	12.50	12.50
	Never hinged	17.50	
	On cover		75.00
CLEU41	AP6 30c blue	5.00	5.00
	Never hinged	7.50	
	On cover		75.00
CLEU42	AP6 50c green	10.00	10.00
	Never hinged	15.00	
	On cover		150.00
CLEU43	AP6 60c brown	10.00	10.00
	Never hinged	15.00	
	On cover		175.00
CLEU44	AP7 1p black	20.00	20.00
	Never hinged	30.00	
	On cover		175.00
CLEU45	AP7 2p red org	25.00	25.00
	Never hinged	35.00	
	On cover		200.00
CLEU46	AP7 3p violet	50.00	50.00
	Never hinged	75.00	
	On cover		350.00
CLEU47	AP7 5p ol grn	125.00	87.50
	Never hinged	175.00	
	On cover		600.00
CFLEU2	AP6 20c gray	75.00	50.00
	Never hinged	100.00	
	On cover		350.00
	Nos. CLEU37-CLEU47, CFLEU2 (12)	370.00	307.50
	Nos. CLEU37-CLEU47, CFLEU2, never hinged	522.50	

Same Overprint in Violet on Colombia No. C51

1923

No.	Description	Unused	Used
CLEU48	AP6 30c on 20c gray (C)	45.00	22.50
	Never hinged	90.00	
	On cover		250.00

Same Overprint in Red on Colombia No. C41

1923

No.	Description	Unused	Used
CLEU49	AP6 20c gray	60.00	*60.00*
	Never hinged	90.00	
	On cover		200.00

Colombia Nos. C38//C50, CF1 Lithograph Overprinted in Black, by the Reichsdruckerei, Berlin, Germany

No. CLEU50

No. CLEU58

Quantity printed of each value in parentheses.

Letters 10mm high

1923, June 4

No.	Description	Unused	Used
CLEU50	AP6 5c org yel (7500)	4.50	4.50
	Never hinged	7.50	
	On cover		75.00
CLEU51	AP6 10c green (15,000)	2.00	2.00
	Never hinged	3.00	
	On cover		75.00
CLEU52	AP6 15c carmine (11,600)	3.00	3.00
	Never hinged	4.00	
	On cover		75.00
CLEU53	AP6 20c gray (45,000)	6.00	6.00
	Never hinged	9.00	
	On cover		75.00
CLEU54	AP6 30c blue (170,000)	2.00	2.00
	Never hinged	3.00	
	On cover		50.00
CLEU55	AP6 50c green (5,000)	5.00	5.00
	Never hinged	7.50	
	On cover		125.00
CLEU56	AP6 60c brown (55,000)	2.75	2.75
	Never hinged	4.00	
	On cover		125.00
CLEU57	AP7 1p black (8,400)	6.75	6.00
	Never hinged	8.00	
	On cover		150.00
a.	Double impression of basic stamp		*1,250.*
CLEU58	AP7 2p red org (3,800)	17.50	17.50
	Never hinged	25.00	
	On cover		200.00
CLEU59	AP7 3p violet (3,200)	37.50	40.00
	Never hinged	50.00	
	On cover		300.00
CLEU60	AP7 5p ol grn (3,400)	55.00	55.00
	Never hinged	75.00	
	On cover		500.00

No.	Description	Unused	Used
CFLEU3	AP6 20c gray (2,000)	25.00	12.50
	Never hinged	75.00	
	On cover		250.00
	Nos. CLEU50-CLEU60, CFLEU3 (12)	167.00	156.25
	Nos. CLEU50-CLEU60, CFLEU3, never hinged	221.00	

Colombia Nos. C40, C42 Lithograph Overprinted in Black

Letters 10mm high

1928, Sept. 25

No.	Description	Unused	Used
CLEU61	AP6 15c carmine (1,500)	20.00	15.00
	Never hinged	50.00	
	On cover		200.00
a.	Inverted overprint	*400.00*	*300.00*
CLEU62	AP6 30c blue (49,000)	5.00	5.00
	Never hinged	10.00	
	On cover		35.00
a.	Inverted overprint	*450.00*	*450.00*
b.	Double overprint	*500.00*	*500.00*

Nos. CLEU61 and CLEU62 were lithograph overprinted in New York in a slightly different font by Fleming & Benedict for the New York agency. There were two printings of the 30c value, the first generally centered toward the top of the stamp, the second toward the bottom.

Nos. CLC68-CLC79, CLCF2 were sold abroad in the equivalent of U.S. gold dollars, thus eliminating the need to identify the various sales offices because of changes in rates of exchange. They were valid on mail sent to Colombia from outside its borders, and they were used from the United States in the same manner as the consular overprinted issues, which were still available and valid for use. Values for stamps on cover are for covers with United States postage as well as the Colombia gold dollar issues.

AP10

AP11

1929, June 1 **Wmk. 127** ***Perf. 14***

No.	Description	Unused	Used
CLC68	AP10 5c yellow org	7.00	*7.25*
	Never hinged	10.00	
	On cover		100.00
CLC69	AP10 10c red brown	1.50	*3.00*
	Never hinged	2.00	
	On cover		50.00
CLC70	AP10 15c deep green	1.50	*3.00*
	Never hinged	2.00	
	On cover		35.00
CLC71	AP10 20c carmine	1.50	*3.75*
	Never hinged	2.00	
	On cover		50.00
CLC72	AP10 25c violet blue	1.50	.85
	Never hinged	2.00	
	On cover		20.00
CLC73	AP10 30c gray blue	1.50	.95
	Never hinged	2.00	
	On cover		20.00
CLC74	AP10 50c dk olive grn	1.50	*1.90*
	Never hinged	2.00	
	On cover		35.00
CLC75	AP10 60c brown	3.00	*3.00*
	Never hinged	4.25	
	On cover		40.00
CLC76	AP11 1p blue	6.00	*7.25*
	Never hinged	8.00	
	On cover		60.00
CLC77	AP11 2p red orange	9.00	*10.00*
	Never hinged	13.00	
	On cover		75.00
CLC78	AP11 3p violet	110.00	100.00
	Never hinged	150.00	
	On cover		250.00
CLC79	AP11 5p olive green	125.00	*140.00*
	Never hinged	165.00	
	On cover		350.00
CLCF2	AP8 20c carmine	9.00	7.00
	Never hinged	13.50	
	On cover		125.00
	Nos. CLC68-CLC79, CLCF2 (13)	278.00	*287.95*
	Nos. CLC68-CLC79, CLCF2, never hinged	375.95	

Nos. CLC68-CLC79, CLCF2 unused are valued with fresh original gum. Stamps often are found with tropicalized gum or with no gum, and such examples sell for less.

On December 1, 1931, all airmail services were taken over from SCADTA by the government of Colombia.

R.F. OVERPRINTS

Authorized as a control mark by the United States Fleet Post Office during 1944-45 for the accommodation of and exclusive use by French naval personnel on airmail correspondence to the United States and Canada. All "R.F." (Republique Francaise) mail had to be posted on board French ships or at one of their western Mediterranean or northwest African naval bases and had to bear the return address, rank and/or serial number of a French officer or seaman. It also had to be reviewed by a censor.

All "R.F." overprints were handstamped by the French naval authorities after the stamps were affixed for mailing. The stamps had to be canceled by a special French naval cancellation. The status of unused stamps seems questionable; they are alleged to have been handstamped at a later date.

Several types of "R.F." overprints other than those illustrated are known, but their validity is doubtful.

United States No. C25 Handstamped in Black

a

b

c

d

e

f

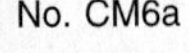

No. CM6a

g

h

i

j

k

l

1944-45		**Unwmk.**	*Perf. 11x10½*
CM1	AP17 (a)	6c **carmine,** on cover	325.00
CM2	AP17 (b)	6c **carmine,** on cover	550.00
CM3	AP17 (c)	6c **carmine,** on cover	500.00
a.		6c **carmine**, on cover, type "a" and type "c" overprints	—
CM4	AP17 (d)	6c **carmine,** on cover	500.00
CM5	AP17 (e)	6c **carmine,** on cover	600.00
CM6	AP17 (f)	6c **carmine,** on cover	500.00
a.		6c **carmine**, on cover, type "a" and type "f" overprints	—
CM7	AP17 (g)	6c **carmine,** on cover	600.00
CM8	AP17 (h)	6c **carmine,** on cover	600.00
CM9	AP17 (i)	6c **carmine,** on cover	750.00
CM10	AP17 (j)	6c **carmine,** on cover	—
CM11	AP17 (k)	6c **carmine,** on cover	—
CM12	AP17 (l)	6c **carmine,** on cover	—
a.		6c **carmine**, on cover, type "a" and type "l" overprints	—

Counterfeits of several types exist.

No. 907 is known with type "c" overprint; Nos. 804 and 928 with type "f"; No. C19 with type "e"; No. C25a (single) with type "c","d," "f," and "l"; No. C26 with type "a," "d" or "f."; and No. C28 with type "c." Type "i" exists in several very minor variations.

STAMPED ENVELOPES

Nos. UC3, UC4 or UC6 Handstamped in Black

1944-45			
UCM1	UC2 (a)	6c **orange,** entire	300.00
UCM2	UC2 (b)	6c **orange,** entire	500.00
a.		6c **orange**, entire, type "a" and type "b" overprints	*600.00*
UCM3	UC2 (d)	6c **orange,** entire	375.00
UCM3A	UC2 (e)	6c **orange,** entire	*1,450.*
UCM4	UC2 (f)	6c **orange,** entire	650.00
a.		6c **orange**, entire, type "a" and type "f" overprints	*750.00*
UCM5	UC2 (h)	6c **orange,** entire	—
UCM6	UC2 (i)	6c **orange,** entire	—
UCM7	UC2 (j)	6c **orange,** entire	*2,500.*
UCM8	UC2 (k)	6c **orange,** entire	—
UCM9	UC2 (l)	6c **orange,** entire	—

Values for Nos. UCM1-UCM9 reflect the scarcity of the actual overprint types. Use of No. UC6 envelopes was by far the most common. Overprints on Nos. UC3 or UC4 merit a premium.

SPECIAL DELIVERY STAMPS

Special Delivery service was instituted by the Act of Congress of March 3, 1885, and put into operation on October 1, 1885. The Act limited the service to free delivery offices and such others as served places with a population of 4,000 or more, and its privileges were thus operative in but 555 post offices. The Act of August 4, 1886, made the stamps and service available at all post offices and upon any article of mailable matter, beginning Oct. 1, 1886. To consume the supply of stamps of the first issue, Scott No. E2 was withheld until September 6, 1888.

A Special Delivery stamp, when affixed to any stamped letter or article of mailable matter, secured later delivery during daytime and evening at most post offices, so that the item did not have to wait until the next day for delivery.

Messenger Running SD1

ENGRAVED

Printed by the American Bank Note Co.

Plates of 100 subjects in two panes of 50 each

Flat Plate Printing

1885 **Unwmk.** ***Perf. 12***

E1	SD1 10c **blue**	575.00	80.00
	deep blue	575.00	80.00
	Never hinged	1,300.	
	On cover		225.00
	First day of service cover (Oct. 1)		*27,500.*
	Block of four	2,600.	
	P# block of 8, Impt. 495 or 496	*25,000.*	
	Margin strip of 4, same	6,500.	
	Double transfer at top	850.00	200.00

Earliest documented use: Sept. 29, 1885, on a cover delivered Oct. 1. There is also a Sept. 30 cover recorded, received for delivery at 7:00 a.m. Oct. 1.

Messenger Running SD2

1888, Sept. 6

E2	SD2 10c **blue**	500.00	45.00
	deep blue	500.00	45.00
	Never hinged	1,150.	
	On cover		135.00
	Block of four	2,100.	
	P# block of 8, Impt. 73 or 552	*17,500.*	
	Never hinged	*25,000.*	
	Margin strip of 4, same	5,250.	

Earliest documented use: Oct. 7, 1888.

See note above No. E3.

COLUMBIAN EXPOSITION ISSUE

Though not issued expressly for the Exposition, No. E3 is considered to be part of that issue. It was released in orange because No. E2 was easily confused with the 1c Columbian, No. 230.

From Jan. 24, 1893, until Jan. 5, 1894, the special delivery stamp was printed in orange; the issue in that color continued until May 19, 1894, when the stock on hand was exhausted. The stamp in blue was not issued from Jan. 24, 1893 to May 19, 1894. However, on Jan. 5, 1894, printing of the stamp in blue was resumed. Presumably it was reissued from May 19, 1894 until the appearance of No. E4 on Oct. 10, 1894. The emissions of the blue stamp of this design before Jan. 24, 1893 and after Jan. 5, 1894 are indistinguishable.

1893, Jan. 24

E3	SD2 10c **orange**	300.00	50.00
	deep orange	300.00	50.00
	Never hinged	650.00	
	On cover		200.00
	On cover, Columbian Expo. station machine canc.		1,250.
	On cover, Columbian Expo. station duplex handstamp cancel		1,500.
	Block of four	1,250.	
	P# block of 8, Impt. 73 or 552	*13,000.*	
	Never hinged	*16,500.*	
	Margin strip of 4, same	4,250.	
	Never hinged	*5,500.*	

Earliest documented use: Feb. 11, 1893.

Messenger Running SD3

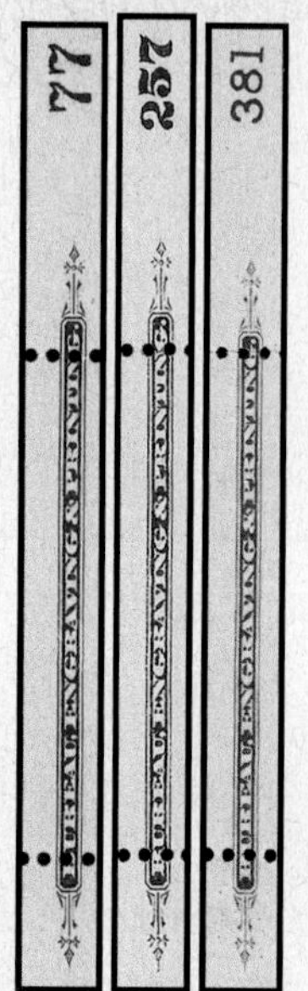

Type III Type VI Type VII

Printed by the Bureau of Engraving and Printing.

1894, Oct. 10

Line under "TEN CENTS"

E4	SD3 10c **blue**	875.00	110.00
	dark blue	875.00	110.00
	bright blue	1,100.	130.00
	Never hinged	2,000.	
	On cover		300.00
	Block of four	3,900.	
	Margin block of 4, arrow	4,000.	
	P#77 block of 6, T III Impt.	*21,000.*	
	Never hinged	*27,500.*	
	Margin strip of 3, same	5,350.	
	Never hinged	8,250.	
	Double transfer	—	—

Earliest documented use: Oct. 25, 1894.

Imperfs of No. E4 on stamp paper, currently listed as No. E4aP, may not be proofs, but it is also unlikely that they were regularly issued. They most likely are from printer's waste.

No. E5a

1895, Aug. 16 **Wmk. 191**

E5	SD3 10c **blue**	210.00	12.50
	dark blue	210.00	12.50
	deep blue	210.00	12.50
	Never hinged	475.00	
	On cover		25.00
	Block of four	900.00	
	Margin block of 4, arrow	925.00	
	P# block of 6, T III, VI or VII Impt.	*5,000.*	
	Never hinged	*7,000.*	
	Margin strip of 3, same	900.00	
	Never hinged	1,600.	
	Double transfer	—	80.00
	Line of color through "POSTAL DELIVERY," from bottom row of Plates 1257-1260	350.00	80.00
	Never hinged	700.00	
a.	Dots in curved frame above messenger (Pl. 882)	400.00	50.00
	Never hinged	800.00	
	P# block of 6, Impt.	*10,000.*	

Earliest documented use: Oct. 3, 1895.

See Die and Plate Proofs for imperf. on stamp paper.

Messenger on Bicycle — SD4

1902, Dec. 9

E6	SD4 10c **ultramarine**	230.00	10.00
	pale ultramarine	230.00	10.00
	dark ultramarine	250.00	10.00
	Never hinged	500.00	
	On cover		22.50
	Block of four	1,000.	
	Margin block of 4, arrow	1,050.	
	P# block of 6, T VII Impt.	*3,250.*	
	Never hinged	*4,750.*	
	Margin strip of 3, same	850.00	
	Never hinged	1,850.	
	P# block of 6, "09"	*3,000.*	
	Never hinged	*4,500.*	
	Margin strip of 3, same	825.00	
	Never hinged	1,800.	
	Double transfer	*260.00*	25.00
	Damaged transfer under "N" of "CENTS"	*260.00*	25.00
a.	10c **blue**	300.00	12.50
	Never hinged	750.00	
	On cover		65.00
	Block of four	1,300.	
	Margin block of 4, arrow	1,350.	
	P# block of 6, T VII Impt.	*4,250.*	
	Never hinged	*6,000.*	
	Margin strip of 3, same	1,100.	
	Never hinged	3,000.	
	Double transfer	—	—

Earliest documented use: Jan. 15, 1903.

No. E6 was re-issued in 1909 from new plates 5240, 5243-5245. After a few months use the Bureau added "09" to these plate numbers. The stamp can be identified only by plate number. The plate numbers without the "09" are scarcer and worth more.

Helmet of Mercury — SD5

Designed by Whitney Warren.

Plates of 280 subjects in four panes of 70 each

1908, Dec. 12

E7	SD5 10c **green**	65.00	50.00
	dark green	65.00	50.00
	yellowish green	65.00	50.00
	Never hinged	140.00	
	On cover		400.00
	Block of four	300.00	
	Margin strip of 3, P# and T V Impt.	300.00	
	Never hinged	500.00	
	P# block of 6, T V Impt.	*1,075.*	—
	Never hinged	*1,500.*	
	Double transfer	160.00	100.00

Earliest documented use: Dec. 14, 1908.

Plates of 200 subjects in four panes of 50 each

1911, Jan. Wmk. 190 ***Perf. 12***

E8 SD4 10c **ultramarine** 120.00 10.00
pale ultramarine 120.00 10.00
dark ultramarine 120.00 10.00
Never hinged 250.00
On cover 30.00
Block of four 500.00
P# block of 6, T VII Impt. *1,850.*
Never hinged *2,750.*
P# block of 6 *1,700.*
Never hinged *2,500.*
Top frame line missing (Pl. 5514) 160.00 22.50
Never hinged 350.00
b. 10c **violet blue** 160.00 14.00
Never hinged 350.00
On cover 25.00
Block of four 675.00
P# block of 6, T VII Impt. *2,100.*
Never hinged *3,250.*
P# block of 6 *1,900.*
Never hinged *2,750.*

Earliest documented use: Jan. 14, 1911.

1914, Sept. ***Perf. 10***

E9 SD4 10c **ultramarine** 190.00 12.00
pale ultramarine 190.00 12.00
Never hinged 425.00
On cover 65.00
Block of four 800.00
P# block of 6, T VII Impt. *4,000.* —
Never hinged *6,000.*
P# block of 6 *3,000.* —
Never hinged *4,500.*
P# block of 8, T VII Impt. (side) —
a. 10c **blue** 260.00 15.00
Never hinged 575.00
On cover 65.00
Block of four 1,150.
P# block of 6, T VII Impt. *5,000.* —
Never hinged *7,500.*
P# block of 6 *4,000.* —
Never hinged *6,000.*
P# block of 8, T VII Impt. (side) *6,500.*

Earliest documented use: Oct. 26, 1914.

1916, Oct. 19 Unwmk. ***Perf. 10***

E10 SD4 10c **pale ultramarine** 340.00 50.00
ultramarine 375.00 55.00
Never hinged 750.00
On cover 200.00
Block of four 1,500.
P# block of 6, T VII Impt. 5520 *5,500.* —
Never hinged *7,750.*
P# block of 6 *5,000.* —
Never hinged *7,250.*
a. 10c **blue** 400.00 55.00
Never hinged 800.00
On cover 110.00
Block of four 1,750.
P# block of 6, T VII Impt. 5520 *5,750.* —
P# block of 6 *5,000.* —

Earliest documented use: Nov. 1, 1916.

1917, May 2 Unwmk. ***Perf. 11***

E11 SD4 10c **ultramarine** 20.00 .75
pale ultramarine 20.00 .75
dark ultramarine 25.00 2.00
Never hinged 45.00
On cover 4.00
Block of four 85.00
P# block of 6, T VII Impt. 725.00 —
Never hinged 1,100.
P# block of 6 225.00 —
Never hinged 340.00
P# block of 8, T VII Impt. (side) —
b. 10c **gray violet** 35.00 3.00
Never hinged 75.00
On cover 4.00
Block of four 150.00
P# block of 6, T VII Impt. 850.00 —
Never hinged 1,300.
P# block of 6 325.00 —
Never hinged 475.00
P# block of 8, T VII Impt. (side) *2,500.*
c. 10c **blue** 100.00 5.00
Never hinged 210.00
On cover 30.00
Block of four 425.00
P# block of 6, T VII Impt. 2,100.
P# block of 6 725.00
P# block of 8, T VII Impt. (side) *2,850.*
d. Perf. 10 at left —

Earliest documented use: June 12, 1917.

The aniline ink used on some printings of No. E11 permeated the paper causing a pink tinge to appear on the back. Such stamps are called "pink backs." They are scarce and valued at approximately four times the value of the normal stamp.

Motorcycle Delivery SD6

1922, July 12 Unwmk. ***Perf. 11***

E12 SD6 10c **gray violet** 45.00 3.00
Never hinged 95.00
On cover 3.50
First day cover 500.00
P# block of 6 525.00 —
Never hinged 800.00
Double transfer — —
a. 10c **deep ultramarine** 55.00 3.50
Never hinged 130.00
On cover 5.00
P# block of 6 650.00 —
Never hinged 1,000.
Double transfer — —

Post Office Truck — SD7

FLAT PLATE PRINTING

1925 Unwmk. ***Perf. 11***

Issued to facilitate special delivery service for parcel post.

E13 SD6 15c **deep orange,** *Apr. 11, 1925* 40.00 3.75
Never hinged 75.00
On cover 55.00
First day cover 400.00
P# block of 6 450.00 —
Never hinged 700.00
Double transfer 47.50 4.00
a. Printed on "special" booklet paper, *1928* (see note before #551) 85.00 10.00
Never hinged 160.00
On cover 100.00
Block of 4 350.00
P# block of 6 *2,500.*
Never hinged *3,750.*
E14 SD7 20c **black,** *Apr. 25, 1925* 2.00 1.00
Never hinged 4.00
On cover 25.00
First day cover 175.00
P# block of 6 50.00
Never hinged 70.00

Motorcycle Type of 1922
ROTARY PRESS PRINTING

1927-31 Unwmk. ***Perf. 11x10½***

E15 SD6 10c **gray violet,** *Nov. 29, 1927* 1.25 .25
violet 1.25 .25
Never hinged 2.00
On cover .50
First day cover 130.00
First day cover, electric eye plate, *Sept. 8, 1941* 50.00
P# block of 4 6.50 —
Never hinged 10.50
Gashed plate 19280 LR 35 70.00 *75.00*
a. 10c **red lilac** .80 .25
Never hinged 1.40
b. 10c **gray lilac** .90 .25
Never hinged 1.60
c. Horiz. pair, imperf. btwn., red lilac shade *350.00*
Never hinged *575.00*
E16 SD6 15c **orange,** *Aug. 1931* .60 .25
Never hinged .90
On cover 1.50
First day cover, Washington, D.C., *Aug. 13, 1931* 125.00
P# block of 4 2.50 —
Never hinged 4.00

The Washington, D.C. Aug. 13, 1931 first day cover reflects the first day of sale at the philatelic agency. The actual earliest documented use of No. E16 is Aug. 6, 1931, at Easton, PA; value, $2,000.

Catalogue values for unused stamps in this section, from this point to the end, are for Never Hinged items.

ROTARY PRESS PRINTING
E. E. Plates of 200 subjects in four panes of 50 each.

1944-51 Unwmk. ***Perf. 11x10½***

E17 SD6 13c **blue,** *Oct. 30, 1944* .60 .25
First day cover 15.00
P# block of 4 2.75 —
E18 SD6 17c **orange yellow,** *Oct. 30, 1944* 3.50 2.50
On commercial cover 65.00
First day cover 20.00
First day cover, Nos. E17 & E18 45.00
P# block of 4 20.00 —
E19 SD7 20c **black,** *Nov. 30, 1951* 1.20 .25
First day cover 5.00
P# block of 4 5.00 —

Special Delivery Letter, Hand to Hand — SD8

ROTARY PRESS PRINTING
E.E. Plates of 200 subjects in four panes of 50 each

1954, Oct. 13 Unwmk. ***Perf. 11x10½***

E20 SD8 20c **deep blue** .40 .25
light blue .40 .25
First day cover, Boston *(194,043)* 3.00
P# block of 4 2.00 —

1957, Sept. 3

E21 SD8 30c **lake** .50 .25
First day cover, Indianapolis, Ind. *(111,451)* 2.25
P# block of 4 2.25 —

Arrows — SD9

Designed by Norman Ives.

GIORI PRESS PRINTING
Plates of 200 subjects in four panes of 50 each

1969, Nov. 21 Unwmk. ***Perf. 11***

E22 SD9 45c **red & blue** 1.20 .25
First day cover, New York, N.Y. 4.00
P# block of 4 5.00 —
Margin block of 4, Mr. Zip and "Use Zip Code" 4.90 —

1971, May 10 ***Perf. 11***

E23 SD9 60c **blue & red** 1.25 .25
First day cover, Phoenix, Ariz. *(129,562)* 3.50
P# block of 4 5.50 —
Margin block of 4, Mr. Zip and "Use Zip Code" 5.25 —

From 1885 to the present, special delivery stamps have not been and are not valid for the payment of postage of any description, nor for registry fees.

U.S. REGISTRY EXCHANGE LABELS (1883-1911)

Registry exchange labels resulted from the implementation of an 1882 Universal Postal Union resolution requiring that international registered mail matter bear a label or impression of a stamp with a capital letter "R" in Roman text. The United States Post Office Department opted for gummed labels which, for the most part, were produced through the joint efforts of the Government Printing Office (printing) and the Bureau of Engraving and Printing (gumming, perforating and distributing). The use of these labels by those post offices authorized to handle inbound and outbound foreign registered mail became effective Jan. 1, 1883, and stayed in effect, virtually unchanged, until Jan. 24, 1911. Such postal facilities were designated "exchange offices," and the labels have thus come to be known as "registry exchange labels" or simply "exchange labels."

During the time period these labels were in use, there were thirty-seven exchange offices that were authorized to use them. Labels are recorded from just twenty-eight of these offices.

Values shown are for complete registered covers with the most common franking. Although condition is always a factor in the determination of any philatelic item, it is somewhat less so with regard to many of the registry exchange label covers due to the small number available from many of the offices.

Numbers in parentheses following the office headings and catalog numbers represent the numbers of currently documented examples of the particular types of registry exchange labels.

Example of Cover Bearing Registry Exchange Label With the Narrow Roman Letter "R". — No. FX-NY1a(i)(i)

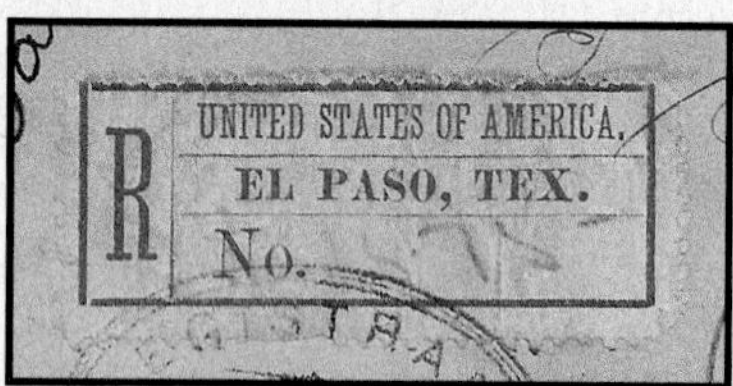

Roman "R"

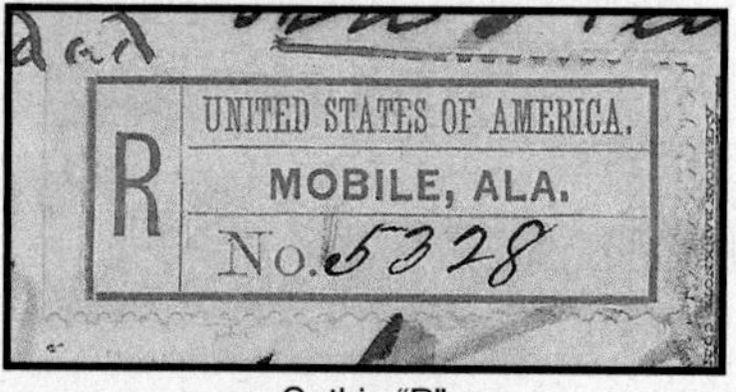

Gothic "R"

Baltimore, MD (11)

FX-BA2 Handstamped name (9) *1,500.*
FX-BA3 Manuscript name (2) *3,000.*

Boston, MA (102)

FX-BO1 Printed name (101) *150.*
FX-BO2 Handstamped name (1) *500.*

Brownsville, TX (1)

FX-BR2 Handstamped name *10,000.*

Cristobal, CZ (82)

FX-CZ1 Printed name (69) 400.
FX-CZ2 Handstamped name (12) 500.
FX-CZ4 Blank, no name (1) —

Douglas, AZ (3)

FX-DO2 Handstamped name *3,000.*

Eagle Pass, TX (8)

FX-EG2 Handstamped name (6) *2,000.*
FX-EG3 Manuscript name (2) *3,000.*

El Paso, TX (53)

FX-EP1 Printed name
a. Gothic letter "R" (14) *500.*
b. Narrow Roman letter "R" (29) *450.*
FX-EP2 Handstamped name
a. All capital letters (5) *600.*
b. Upper & lower case letters (1) *700.*
Used as official seals, on cover, unique *750.*
FX-EP4 Blank, no name (1) *700.*

Labels on two covers are torn and missing the letter "R." Sub-type unreported for one label.

Havana, Cuba (13)

FX-HA1 Printed name *2,000.*

Honolulu, HI (10)

FX-HO1 Printed name (8) *2,000.*
FX-HO2 Handstamped name (2) *3,000.*

Jacksonville, FL (8)

FX-JA2 Handstamped name (5) *2,500.*
FX-JA3 Manuscript name (1) *3,000.*
FX-JA4 Blank, no name (2) *2,000.*

Key West, FL (3)

FX-KW3 Manuscript name *1,500.*

Laredo, TX (28)

FX-LA1 Printed name 1,000.

Miami, FL (1)

FX-MA2 Handstamped name (1) *5,000.*

Mobile, AL (81)

FX-MO1 Printed name (62) 400.
FX-MO2 Handstamped name
a. Cursive letters (3) *1,000.*
b. Block letters (2) *1,000.*
FX-MO3 Manuscript name (6) *850.*

Sub-type unreported for eight labels.

Naco, AZ (4)

FX-NA2 Handstamped name
a. Cursive letters (2) *3,500.*
b. Block letters (2) *3,500.*

New Orleans, LA (47)

FX-NO1 Printed name (30) 600.
FX-NO4 Blank, no name (15) 525.

Sub-type unreported for two labels.

New York, NY

FX-NY1 Printed name
a(i)(i). "Exchange" label with narrow Roman letter "R" 2.5 mm in width, "United States of America." 25.5 mm in length 50.
a(i)(ii). "Exchange" label with narrow Roman letter "R" 3 mm in width, "United States of America." 26.5 mm in length 50.
a(ii). "Exchange" label with Gothic letter "R", "United States of America." 22 mm in length 150.
a(iii). "Exchange" label with Gothic letter "R", "United States of America." 28 mm in length 100.
Used as official seals, on cover 200.
Sheet of 50 *100.*
a(iv). "Exchange" label with narrow Gothic letter "R", "United States of America." 26 mm in length 100.
b(i). "City" in small letters followed by a period, Gothic letter "R," "United States of America." 28 mm in length 50.
b(ii). "City" in large letters followed by a period, Gothic letter "R," "United States of America." 27 mm in length 50.
b(iii). "City" in sans-serif letters, no period, narrow Roman letter "R" 250.
c. Printed name without "City" or "Exchange" *500.*
d. Printed name and "3d or 4th CLASS" *1,000.*
Used as official seals, on cover 200.
FX-NY4 Blank, no name 250.

Nogales, AZ (18)

FX-NOG1 Printed name (13) *1,000.*
FX-NOG2 Handstamped name (5) *1,300.*

Philadelphia, PA (20)

FX-PH1 Printed name
a. Name in sans-serif letters (2) *1,000.*
b. Name in serif letters (18) *400.*

St. Louis, MO (17)

FX-STL1 Printed name (14) *700.*
FX-STL2 Handstamped name (3) *1,200.*

San Antonio, TX (7)

FX-SA1 Printed name *2,000.*

San Diego, CA (2)

FX-SD3 Manuscript name (1) *4,500.*
FX-SD4 Blank, no name (1) *4,500.*

San Francisco, CA (239)

FX-SF1 Printed name
a. Name in sans-serif letters (210) 100.
b. Name in serif letters (29) 400.

San Juan, PR (11)

FX-SJ1 Printed name *2,000.*

Seattle, WA (35)

FX-SE1 Printed name
a. Gothic letter "R" (21) *500.*
b. Narrow Roman letter "R" (11) *800.*

Sub-type unreported for three labels.

Shanghai, China (57)

FX-SH1 Printed name
a. Gothic red letter "R" (24) *2,000.*
b. Narrow red Roman letter "R" (14) *2,000.*
c. Gothic black letter "R" (10) *4,000.*
d. Narrow black Roman letter "R" (9) *4,000.*

Nos. FX-SH1c and FX-SH1d were produced locally in China while awaiting arrival of red labels.

Tacoma, WA (15)

FX-TA1 Printed name *750.*

Tampa, FL (2)

FX-TP2 Handstamped name *2,000.*

A cover with a registry label bearing a manuscript "Tampa" (Florida) has been discovered. It is held in the collection of a historical society and is not available to collectors.

REGISTRATION STAMP

The Registry System for U.S. mail went into effect July 1, 1855, the fee being 5 cents. On June 30, 1863, the fee was increased to 20 cents.

On January 1, 1869, the fee was reduced to 15 cents and on January 1, 1874, to 8 cents. On July 1, 1875, the fee was increased to 10 cents. On January 1, 1893 the fee was again reduced to 8 cents and again it was increased to 10 cents on November 1, 1909.

Early registered covers with various stamps, rates and postal markings are of particular interest to collectors.

Registry stamps (10c ultramarine) were issued on December 1, 1911, to prepay registry fees (not postage), but ordinary stamps were valid for registry fees then as now. These special stamps were abolished May 28, 1913, by order of the Postmaster General, who permitted their use until supplies on hand were exhausted.

Eagle — RS1

ENGRAVED

1911, Dec. 1 **Wmk. 190** *Perf. 12*

F1 RS1 10c **ultramarine**	75.00	14.00
pale ultramarine	75.00	15.00
Never hinged	160.00	
On cover		85.00
Block of 4	375.00	*100.00*
P# block of 6, Impt. & "A"	*1,650.*	—
Never hinged	*2,500.*	
First day cover		*20,000.*

CERTIFIED MAIL STAMP

Certified Mail service began on June 6, 1955, in Washington, D.C., and the following day throughout the United States, for use on domestic first class mail for which no indemnity value is claimed, but for which proof of mailing and proof of delivery are available at less cost than registered mail. The mailer receives one receipt and the addressee signs another when the postman delivers the letter. The second receipt is kept on file at the post office for six months. The Certified Mail charge, originally 15 cents, is in addition to regular postage, whether surface mail, air mail, or special delivery.

Catalogue value for the unused stamp in this section is for a Never Hinged item.

Letter Carrier — CM1

ROTARY PRESS PRINTING

E. E. Plates of 200 subjects in four panes of 50

1955, June 6 **Unwmk.** *Perf. 10½x11*

FA1 CM1 15c **red**	.75	.75
P# block of 4	5.50	—
First day cover		10.00

POSTAGE DUE STAMPS

Postage due stamps were authorized by an act of Congress, approved March 3, 1879, and effective July 1, 1879. By law, postage due stamps were to be affixed by clerks to any piece of mailable matter to denote the amount collected from the addressee because of insufficient prepayment of postage.

Although the Post Office Department required postage to be prepaid beginning in 1855, there were many instances when full postage was not required, and postage due payment had to be collected in cash from the addressees. These instances included insufficiently prepaid letters, advertised letters, and unpaid ship letters and steamboat letters.

The reason for the appearance of postage due stamps may be summed up in one word: accountability. The 1880 *Report of the Postmaster General* noted that the former system of collecting postage due had one great weakness: "In securing the full returns of (the postage due collected in cash) the department was entirely dependent on the fidelity of the postmasters." Postage due stamps, affixed to underpaid mail as receipts for the underpayment collected, solved that problem by requiring postmasters to account for cash receipts that would balance any postage due stamps no longer in stock, in the same way that they had to account for regular postage stamp sales.

The last postage due stamps were printed in early November, 1985. With the advent of postage meters, the scrapping of the last Cottrell press in November 1985 (the last press capable of printing the current postage due stamps as designed), and finally new regulations requiring full prepayment of postage in all cases, postage due stamps became anachronistic, and their use ceased.

D1

Printed by the American Bank Note Co.

Plates of 200 subjects in two panes of 100 each.

1879 Unwmk. Engr. *Perf. 12*

J1	D1 1c **brown**	90.00	14.00
	pale brown	90.00	14.00
	deep brown	90.00	14.00
	Never hinged	260.00	
	Block of 4	400.00	75.00
	P# block of 10, Impt.	*1,700.*	

Earliest documented use: July 5, 1879.

J2	D1 2c **brown**	450.00	25.00
	pale brown	450.00	25.00
	Never hinged	1,050.	
	Block of 4	1,900.	—

Earliest documented use: July 27, 1879.

J3	D1 3c **brown**	100.00	6.00
	pale brown	100.00	6.00
	deep brown	100.00	6.00
	yellowish brown	*110.00*	7.00
	Never hinged	280.00	
	Block of 4	440.00	32.50
	P# block of 10, Impt.	*1,750.*	

Earliest documented use: June 18, 1879.

J4	D1 5c **brown**	800.00	70.00
	pale brown	800.00	70.00
	deep brown	800.00	70.00
	Never hinged	1,950.	
	Block of 4	3,400.	—

Earliest documented use: July 7, 1879.

J5	D1 10c **brown,** *Sept. 19*	925.00	70.00
	pale brown	925.00	70.00
	deep brown	925.00	70.00
	Never hinged	*2,500.*	
	Block of 4	4,000.	—
a.	Imperf., pair	*2,500.*	

Earliest documented use: Oct. 7, 1879.

J6	D1 30c **brown,** *Sept. 19*	400.00	65.00
	pale brown	400.00	65.00
	Never hinged	900.00	
	Block of 4	1,700.	—
	P# block of 10, Impt.	*5,000.*	
J7	D1 50c **brown,** *Sept. 19*	650.00	90.00
	pale brown	650.00	90.00
	Never hinged	1,600.	
	Block of 4	2,900.	—
	P# block of 10, Impt.	*12,000.*	
	Nos. J1-J7 (7)	3,415.	340.00

SPECIAL PRINTING

1879 Unwmk. *Perf. 12*

Soft porous paper

Printed by the American Bank Note Co.

J8	D1 1c deep brown *(9,420)*	*16,000.*	
	Never hinged	—	
	No gum	*6,500.*	
J9	D1 2c deep brown *(1,361)*	*15,000.*	
	No gum	*6,000.*	
J10	D1 3c deep brown *(436)*	*20,000.*	
	No gum	*8,000.*	
J11	D1 5c deep brown *(249)*	*13,000.*	
	No gum	*5,250.*	
J12	D1 10c deep brown *(174)*	*6,750.*	
	No gum	*2,900.*	
J13	D1 30c deep brown *(179)*	*7,000.*	
	No gum	*3,000.*	
J14	D1 50c deep brown *(179)*	*7,000.*	
	No gum	*3,000.*	

Identifying characteristics for the final 8,920 examples of No. J8 delivered to the Post Office are unknown, and it is likely that these were regular issue stamps (No. J1) that were then sold as special printings.

1884 Unwmk. *Perf. 12*

J15	D1 1c **red brown**	70.00	7.00
	pale red brown	70.00	7.00
	deep red brown	70.00	7.00
	Never hinged	190.00	
	Block of 4	325.00	45.00
	P# block of 10, Impt.	*1,400.*	
J16	D1 2c **red brown**	80.00	6.00
	pale red brown	80.00	6.00
	deep red brown	80.00	6.00
	Never hinged	225.00	
	Block of 4	360.00	37.50
	P# block of 10, Impt.	*1,550.*	
J17	D1 3c **red brown**	1,050.	350.00
	deep red brown	1,050.	350.00
	Never hinged	2,500.	
	Block of 4	4,750.	—
J18	D1 5c **red brown**	550.00	50.00
	pale red brown	550.00	50.00
	deep red brown	550.00	50.00
	Never hinged	1,300.	
	Block of 4	2,500.	—
J19	D1 10c **red brown**	550.00	35.00
	deep red brown	550.00	35.00
	Never hinged	1,300.	
	Block of 4	2,500.	—
	P# block of 10, Impt.	*25,000.*	
J20	D1 30c **red brown**	225.00	70.00
	deep red brown	225.00	70.00
	Never hinged	550.00	
	Block of 4	1,050.	450.00
	P# block of 10, Impt.	*3,500.*	
	Never hinged	*7,000.*	
J21	D1 50c **red brown**	1,800.	250.00
	Never hinged	3,750.	
	Block of 4	7,750.	—

1891 Unwmk. *Perf. 12*

J22	D1 1c **bright claret**	30.00	2.00
	light claret	30.00	2.00
	dark claret	30.00	2.00
	Never hinged	85.00	
	Block of 4	140.00	11.00
	P# block of 10, Impt.	*650.00*	
	Never hinged	*2,000.*	
J23	D1 2c **bright claret**	32.50	2.00
	light claret	32.50	2.00
	dark claret	32.50	2.00
	Never hinged	90.00	
	Block of 4	150.00	11.00
	P# block of 10, Impt.	*675.00*	
J24	D1 3c **bright claret**	67.50	16.00
	dark claret	67.50	16.00
	Never hinged	180.00	
	Block of 4	325.00	80.00
	P# block of 10, Impt.	*1,050.*	
	Never hinged	—	
J25	D1 5c **bright claret**	100.00	16.00
	light claret	100.00	16.00
	dark claret	100.00	16.00
	Never hinged	290.00	
	Block of 4	450.00	80.00
	P# block of 10, Impt.	*1,450.*	
J26	D1 10c **bright claret**	165.00	30.00
	light claret	165.00	30.00
	Never hinged	500.00	
	Block of 4	725.00	190.00
	P# block of 10, Impt.	*2,450.*	
J27	D1 30c **bright claret**	575.00	225.00
	Never hinged	1,700.	
	Block of 4	2,450.	—
	P# block of 10, Impt.	*8,250.*	
	Never hinged	*11,000.*	
J28	D1 50c **bright claret**	625.00	225.00
	dark claret	600.00	225.00
	Never hinged	1,750.	
	Block of 4	2,600.	—
	P# block of 10, Impt.	*10,000.*	
	Nos. J22-J28 (7)	1,595.	516.00

Nos. J22-J28 fluoresce orange under longwave ultraviolet light. Nos. J15-J21 do not.

See Die and Plate Proofs for imperfs. on stamp paper.

The color on Nos. J29-J44 will run when immersed in water. Extreme caution is advised.

D2

Printed by the Bureau of Engraving and Printing.

1894 Unwmk. *Perf. 12*

J29	D2 1c **vermilion,** *Aug. 14, 1894*	2,350.	750.
	pale vermilion	2,350.	750.
	Never hinged	*6,000.*	
	Block of 4	*10,500.*	*3,500.*
	P# strip of 3, Impt.	9,000.	
	P# block of 6, Impt.	*13,000.*	

Only one plate block of No. J29 exists in private hands. It has VG-F centering and small faults, and it is valued thus.

Earliest documented use: Nov. 15, 1894.

J30	D2 2c **vermilion,** *July 20, 1894*	775.	350.
	deep vermilion	775.	350.
	Never hinged	1,900.	
	Block of 4	3,500.	
	P# strip of 3, Impt.	3,250.	
	P# block of 6, Impt.	*6,750.*	
	Never hinged	*19,000.*	

Earliest documented use: July 31, 1894.

Nos. J29 and J30 fluoresce orange under longwave ultraviolet light. Nos. J31 and J32 do not.

1894-95

J31	D2 1c **deep claret**	72.50	12.00
	claret	72.50	12.00
	lake	72.50	12.00
	Never hinged	260.00	
	Block of 4	325.00	65.00
	P# strip of 3, Impt.	300.00	
	P# block of 6, Impt.	650.00	
	Never hinged	1,850.	
b.	Vertical pair, imperf. horiz.	—	

Earliest documented use: Oct. 6, 1894.

See Die and Plate Proofs for imperf. on stamp paper.

J32	D2 2c **deep claret**	62.50	10.00
	claret	62.50	10.00
	lake	62.50	10.00
	Never hinged	240.00	
	Block of 4	290.00	65.00
	P# strip of 3, Impt.	275.00	
	P# block of 6, Impt.	600.00	
	Never hinged	1,700.	

Earliest documented use: Oct. 30, 1894.

J33	D2 3c **deep claret,** *Apr. 27, 1895*	200.00	50.00
	lake	200.00	50.00
	Never hinged	575.00	
	Block of 4	875.00	—
	P# strip of 3, Impt.	850.00	
	P# block of 6, Impt.	2,650.	
	Never hinged	*4,750.*	
J34	D2 5c **deep claret,** *Apr. 27, 1895*	300.00	55.00
	claret	300.00	55.00
	Never hinged	850.00	
	Block of 4	1,300.	—

	P# strip of 3, Impt.	1,250.	
	P# block of 6, Impt.	3,250.	
	Never hinged	*7,750.*	

Earliest documented use: July 13, 1895.

J35	D2 10c **deep claret**, *Sept. 24, 1894*	350.00	40.00
	Never hinged	1,000.	
	Block of 4	1,550.	—
	P# strip of 3, Impt.	1,500.	
	P# block of 6, Impt.	4,000.	
	Never hinged	*7,500.*	
J36	D2 30c **deep claret**, *Apr. 27, 1895*	550.00	250.00
	claret	550.00	250.00
	Never hinged	1,250.	
	Block of 4	2,500.	—
	P# strip of 3, Impt.	2,250.	
	P# block of 6, Impt.	4,500.	
	Never hinged	8,750.	
a.	30c **carmine**	675.00	275.00
	Never hinged	1,600.	
	Block of 4	3,250.	—
	P# strip of 3, Impt.	3,250.	
	P# block of 6, Impt.	5,500.	
	Never hinged	*11,000.*	
b.	30c **pale rose**	450.00	200.00
	Never hinged	1,100.	
	Block of 4	2,000.	—
	P# strip of 3, Impt.	1,850.	
	P# block of 6, Impt.	4,000.	
	Never hinged	*8,500.*	
J37	D2 50c **deep claret**, *Apr. 27, 1895*	1,800.	800.00
	Never hinged	4,250.	
	Block of 4	8,000.	—
	P# strip of 3, Impt.	7,500.	
	P# block of 6, Impt.	*14,000.*	
a.	50c **pale rose**	1,600.	725.00
	Never hinged	3,750.	
	Block of 4	7,000.	—
	P# strip of 3, Impt.	6,500.	
	P# block of 6, Impt.	*12,000.*	

Shades are numerous in the 1894 and later issues.

Wmk. 191 Horizontally or Vertically

1895-97 ***Perf. 12***

J38	D2 1c **deep claret**, *Aug. 29, 1895*	13.50	1.00
	claret	13.50	1.00
	carmine	13.50	1.00
	lake	13.50	1.00
	Never hinged	40.00	
	Block of 4	57.50	8.50
	P# strip of 3, Impt.	60.00	
	Never hinged	175.00	
	P# block of 6, Impt.	270.00	
	Never hinged	450.00	
J39	D2 2c **deep claret**, *Sept. 14, 1895*	13.50	1.00
	claret	13.50	1.00
	carmine	13.50	1.00
	lake	13.50	1.00
	Never hinged	40.00	
	Block of 4	57.50	8.50
	P# strip of 3, Impt.	60.00	
	Never hinged	175.00	
	P# block of 6, Impt.	270.00	
	Never hinged	450.00	
	Double transfer	—	—

In October, 1895, the Postmaster at Jefferson, Iowa, surcharged a few 2 cent stamps with the words "Due I cent" in black on each side, subsequently dividing the stamps vertically and using each half as a 1 cent stamp. Twenty of these were used. Value, tied across cut, on cover, $6,000.

J40	D2 3c **deep claret**, *Oct. 30, 1895*	100.00	5.00
	claret	100.00	5.00
	rose red	100.00	5.00
	carmine	100.00	5.00
	Never hinged	225.00	
	Block of 4	425.00	27.50
	P# strip of 3, Impt.	425.00	
	Never hinged	1,000.	
	P# block of 6, Impt.	950.00	
	Never hinged	1,750.	
J41	D2 5c **deep claret**, *Oct. 15, 1895*	110.00	5.00
	claret	110.00	5.00
	carmine rose	100.00	5.00
	Never hinged	280.00	
	Block of 4	475.00	27.50
	P# strip of 3, Impt.	450.00	
	Never hinged	1,050.	
	P# block of 6, Impt.	1,000.	
	Never hinged	2,000.	
J42	D2 10c **deep claret**, *Sept. 14, 1895*	110.00	7.50
	claret	110.00	7.50
	carmine	110.00	7.50
	lake	110.00	7.50
	Never hinged	280.00	
	Block of 4	475.00	47.50
	P# strip of 3, Impt.	450.00	
	Never hinged	1,050.	
	P# block of 6, Impt.	1,000.	
	Never hinged	2,000.	
J43	D2 30c **deep claret**, *Aug. 21, 1897*	600.00	80.00
	claret	600.00	80.00
	Never hinged	1,500.	
	Block of 4	2,750.	475.00
	P# strip of 3, Impt.	2,500.	
	P# block of 6, Impt.	*6,000.*	
J44	D2 50c **deep claret**, *Mar. 17, 1896*	375.00	60.00
	claret	375.00	60.00
	Never hinged	925.00	
	Block of 4	1,700.	275.00
	P# strip of 3, Impt.	1,750.	
	P# block of 6, Impt.	*4,500.*	—
	Nos. J38-J44 (7)	1,322.	159.50

Plates of 400 subjects in four panes of 100.

1910-12 **Wmk. 190** ***Perf. 12***

J45	D2 1c **deep claret**, *Dec., 1910*	40.00	5.00
	Never hinged	115.00	
	Block of 4 (2 or 3mm spacing)	220.00	20.00
	P# block of 6, Impt. & star	575.00	
	Never hinged	950.00	
a.	1c **rose carmine**	35.00	5.00
	Never hinged	105.00	
	Block of 4 (2 or 3mm spacing)	180.00	20.00
	P# block of 6, Impt. & star	500.00	
	Never hinged	850.00	
J46	D2 2c **deep claret**, *Nov. 25, 1910*	40.00	2.00
	lake	40.00	2.00
	Never hinged	115.00	
	Block of 4 (2 or 3mm spacing)	220.00	7.50
	P# block of 6, Impt. & star	550.00	—
	Never hinged	925.00	
	P# block of 6	600.00	
	Never hinged	1,000.	
a.	2c **rose carmine**	35.00	2.00
	Never hinged	105.00	
	Block of 4 (2 or 3mm spacing)	180.00	7.50
	P# block of 6, Impt. & star	500.00	—
	Never hinged	850.00	
	P# block of 6	550.00	
	Never hinged	900.00	
	Double transfer	—	—
J47	D2 3c **deep claret**, *Aug. 31, 1910*	625.00	60.00
	lake	625.00	60.00
	Never hinged	1,600.	
	Block of 4 (2 or 3mm spacing)	2,750.	325.00
	P# block of 6, Impt. & star	6,000.	
	Never hinged	*11,500.*	
J48	D2 5c **deep claret**, *Aug. 31, 1910*	120.00	12.00
	Never hinged	275.00	
a.	5c **rose carmine**	120.00	12.00
	Never hinged	275.00	
	Block of 4 (2 or 3mm spacing)	500.00	60.00
	P# block of 6, Impt. & star	1,100.	
	Never hinged	*2,000.*	
J49	D2 10c **deep claret**, *Aug. 31, 1910*	125.00	20.00
	Never hinged	280.00	
	Block of 4 (2 or 3mm spacing)	550.00	120.00
	P# block of 6, Impt. & star	1,400.	
a.	10c **rose carmine**	125.00	20.00
	Never hinged	280.00	
J50	D2 50c **deep claret**, *Sept. 23, 1912*	1,100.	200.00
	Never hinged	2,900.	
	Block of 4 (2 or 3mm spacing)	4,750.	*1,150.*
	P# block of 6, Impt. & star	*9,500.*	
a.	50c **rose carmine**	1,150.	190.00
	Never hinged	*3,000.*	

1914 ***Perf. 10***

J52	D2 1c **carmine lake**	80.00	15.00
	deep carmine lake	80.00	15.00
	Never hinged	220.00	
	Block of 4 (2 or 3mm spacing)	360.00	80.00
	P# block of 6, Impt. & star	700.00	—
	Never hinged	1,700.	
a.	1c **dull rose**	85.00	15.00
	Never hinged	230.00	
	Block of 4 (2 or 3mm spacing)	375.00	85.00
	P# block of 6, Impt. & star	750.00	—
	Never hinged	1,750.	
J53	D2 2c **carmine lake**	62.50	1.00
	Never hinged	170.00	
	Block of 4	275.00	8.00
	P# block of 6	600.00	—
	Never hinged	1,200.	
a.	2c **dull rose**	67.50	2.00
	Never hinged	180.00	
	Block of 4		15.00
b.	2c **vermilion**	67.50	2.00
	Never hinged	180.00	
	Block of 4	300.00	14.00
	P# block of 6	625.00	—
	Never hinged	1,300.	
J54	D2 3c **carmine lake**	1,050.	75.00
	Never hinged	3,000.	
	Block of 4 (2 or 3mm spacing)	4,750.	—
	P# block of 6, Impt. & star	*9,000.*	—
a.	3c **dull rose**	1,000.	75.00
	Never hinged	2,900.	
	Block of 4 (2 or 3mm spacing)	4,500.	—
	P# block of 6, Impt. & star	*8,750.*	—
J55	D2 5c **carmine lake**	50.00	6.00
	Never hinged	140.00	
	Block of 4 (2 or 3mm spacing)	220.00	30.00
	P# block of 6, Impt. & star	425.00	—
	Never hinged	1,100.	
a.	5c **dull rose**	45.00	4.00
	carmine rose	45.00	4.00
	Never hinged	130.00	
	deep claret	—	—
	Block of 4 (2 or 3mm spacing)	200.00	20.00
	P# block of 6, Impt. & star	400.00	—
	Never hinged	1,050.	
J56	D2 10c **carmine lake**	75.00	4.00
	Never hinged	200.00	
	Block of 4 (2 or 3mm spacing)	340.00	22.50
	P# block of 6, Impt. & star	800.00	—
a.	10c **dull rose**	80.00	5.00
	carmine rose	80.00	5.00
	Never hinged	210.00	
	Block of 4 (2 or 3mm spacing)	360.00	25.00
	P# block of 6, Impt. & star	900.00	—
	Never hinged	1,650.	
J57	D2 30c **carmine lake**	225.00	55.00
	Never hinged	525.00	
	Block of 4 (2 or 3mm spacing)	1,000.	325.00
	P# block of 6, Impt. & star	2,750.	—
J58	D2 50c **carmine lake**	*11,500.*	1,700.
	Never hinged	*22,000.*	
	Precanceled		750.00
	Block of 4 (2 or 3mm spacing)	*50,000.*	*7,500.*
	P# block of 6, Impt. & star	*90,000.*	

No. J58 unused is valued in the grade of fine to very fine.

Only one plate block of No. J58 exists in private hands. It has full top selvage with perforations cutting into the design at top, and is valued thus.

No. J58, precanceled, was used at Buffalo (normal, inverted) and Chicago (normal, inverted, double, double inverted).

1916 **Unwmk.** ***Perf. 10***

J59	D2 1c **rose**	4,000.	750.00
	Never hinged	9,000.	
	Block of 4 (2 or 3mm spacing)	19,000.	*3,750.*
	P# block of 6, Impt. & star	*30,000.*	
	Experimental bureau precancel, New Orleans		*225.00*
J60	D2 2c **rose**	250.00	75.00
	Never hinged	625.00	
	Block of 4	1,100.	375.00
	P# block of 6	2,000.	—
	Experimental bureau precancel, New Orleans		30.00

1917 **Unwmk.** ***Perf. 11***

J61	D2 1c **carmine rose**	2.75	.25
	Never hinged	9.00	
	dull rose	5.00	.25
	Never hinged	15.00	
a.	1c **rose red**	2.75	.25
	Never hinged	9.00	
b.	1c **deep claret**	2.75	.25
	claret brown	2.75	.25
	Never hinged	9.00	
	Block of 4 (2 or 3mm spacing)	12.00	2.00
	Never hinged	42.50	
	P# block of 6, Impt. & star	150.00	—
	Never hinged	350.00	
	P# block of 6	45.00	—
	Never hinged	100.00	
c.	Vert. pair, imperf. horiz.	—	
J62	D2 2c **carmine rose**	2.75	.25
	Never hinged	9.00	
a.	2c **rose red**	2.75	.25
	Never hinged	9.00	
b.	2c **deep claret**	2.75	.25
	claret brown	2.75	1.10
	Never hinged	9.00	
	Block of 4	12.00	2.00
	Never hinged	42.50	
	P# block of 6	55.00	—
	Never hinged	125.00	
	Double transfer	—	—

J63	D2 3c **carmine rose**	13.50	.80
	Never hinged	35.00	
a.	3c **rose red**	13.50	.80
	Never hinged	35.00	
b.	3c **deep claret**	13.50	.80
	claret brown	13.50	.80
	Never hinged	35.00	
	Block of 4 (2 or 3mm spacing)	60.00	5.00
	Never hinged	155.00	
	P# block of 6, Impt. & star	150.00	—
	Never hinged	300.00	
	P# block of 6	125.00	—
	Never hinged	275.00	
J64	D2 5c **carmine**	11.00	.80
	carmine rose	11.00	.80
	Never hinged	32.50	
a.	5c **rose red**	11.00	.80
	Never hinged	32.50	
b.	5c **deep claret**	11.00	.80
	claret brown	11.00	.80
	Never hinged	32.50	
	Block of 4 (2 or 3mm spacing)	47.50	6.00
	Never hinged	140.00	
	P# block of 6, Impt. & star	125.00	—
	Never hinged	275.00	
	P# block of 6	105.00	—
	Never hinged	250.00	
J65	D2 10c **carmine rose**	22.50	1.00
	Never hinged	65.00	
a.	10c **rose red**	22.50	1.00
	Never hinged	65.00	
b.	10c **deep claret**	22.50	1.00
	claret brown	22.50	1.00
	Never hinged	65.00	
	Block of 4 (2 or 3mm spacing)	100.00	7.50
	Never hinged	300.00	
	P# block of 6, Impt. & star	220.00	—
	Never hinged	475.00	
	P# block of 6	240.00	—
	Never hinged	525.00	
	Double transfer	—	—
J66	D2 30c **carmine rose**	80.00	2.00
	Never hinged	220.00	
a.	30c **deep claret**	80.00	2.00
	claret brown	80.00	2.00
	Never hinged	220.00	
	Block of 4 (2 or 3mm spacing)	350.00	14.00
	Never hinged	950.00	
	P# block of 6, Impt. & star	700.00	—
	Never hinged	*1,500.*	
	P# block of 6	750.00	—
	Never hinged	*1,650.*	
b.	As "a," perf 10 at top, precanceled		*21,000.*

No. J66b is valued with small faults and fine centering, as the two recorded examples are in this condition and grade. One is precanceled St. Louis, Mo., and the other is precanceled Minneapolis, Minn.

J67	D2 50c **carmine rose**	140.00	1.00
	Never hinged	325.00	
a.	50c **rose red**	140.00	1.00
	Never hinged	325.00	
b.	50c **deep claret**	140.00	1.00
	claret brown	140.00	1.00
	Never hinged	325.00	
	Block of 4 (2 or 3mm spacing)	600.00	7.50
	Never hinged	1,400.	
	P# block of 6, Impt. & star	1,100.	—
	Never hinged	2,400.	
	P# block of 6	1,200.	—
	Nos. J61-J67, never hinged	695.50	

1925, Apr. 13

J68	D2 ½c **dull red**	1.00	.25
	Never hinged	1.75	
	Block of 4	4.00	1.50
	Never hinged	7.00	
	P# block of 6	12.50	—
	Never hinged	17.50	

D3

D4

1930 Unwmk. *Perf. 11*

Design measures 19x22mm

J69	D3 ½c **carmine**	4.25	1.90
	Never hinged	9.50	
	P# block of 6	50.00	—
	Never hinged	80.00	
J70	D3 1c **carmine**	2.75	.35
	Never hinged	6.25	
	P# block of 6	55.00	—
	Never hinged	100.00	
J71	D3 2c **carmine**	3.75	.35
	Never hinged	8.50	
	P# block of 6	50.00	—
	Never hinged	95.00	
J72	D3 3c **carmine**	20.00	2.75
	Never hinged	47.50	
	P# block of 6	300.00	—
	Never hinged	500.00	
J73	D3 5c **carmine**	18.00	5.00
	Never hinged	42.50	
	P# block of 6	300.00	—
	Never hinged	500.00	
J74	D3 10c **carmine**	42.50	2.00
	Never hinged	95.00	
	P# block of 6	550.00	—
	Never hinged	1,000.	
J75	D3 30c **carmine**	125.00	4.00
	Never hinged	275.00	
	P# block of 6	1,150.	—
	Never hinged	*2,250.*	
J76	D3 50c **carmine**	175.00	2.00
	Never hinged	375.00	
	P# block of 6	1,750.	—
	Never hinged	*3,250.*	

Design measures 22x19mm

J77	D4 $1 **carmine**	32.50	.35
	Never hinged	65.00	
	P# block of 6	250.00	—
	Never hinged	475.00	
a.	$1 **scarlet**	27.50	.35
	Never hinged	55.00	
	P# block of 6	275.00	—
	Never hinged	500.00	
J78	D4 $5 **dull carmine,** wet printing	37.50	.35
	Never hinged	85.00	
	P# block of 6	300.00	—
	Never hinged	600.00	
a.	**scarlet,** wet printing	32.50	.35
	Never hinged	70.00	
	P# block of 6	300.00	—
	Never hinged	600.00	
b.	$5 **scarlet,** dry printing	32.50	.35
	Never hinged	70.00	
	P# block of 6	260.00	—
	Never hinged	525.00	
	Nos. J69-J78, never hinged	1,009.	

See note on Wet and Dry Printings following No. 1029.

Type of 1930-31 Issue

Rotary Press Printing

Ordinary and Electric Eye Plates

Design measures 19x22½mm

1931 Unwmk. *Perf. 11x10½*

J79	D3 ½c **dull carmine**	1.25	.25
	Never hinged	1.80	
	P# block of 4	20.00	—
	Never hinged	30.00	
a.	½c **scarlet**	.90	.25
	Never hinged	1.30	
	P# block of 4	20.00	—
	Never hinged	30.00	—
J80	D3 1c **dull carmine,** wet printing	.40	.25
	Never hinged	.50	
	P# block of 4	1.75	—
	Never hinged	2.60	
a.	1c **scarlet,** wet printing	.25	.25
	Never hinged	.30	
	P# block of 4	1.75	—
	Never hinged	2.60	
	Pair with full vertical gutter between	—	
b.	1c **scarlet,** dry printing	.25	.25
	Never hinged	.30	
	P# block of 4 (#25635, 25636)	1.50	—
	Never hinged	2.25	
J81	D3 2c **dull carmine,** wet printing	.40	.25
	Never hinged	.50	
	P# block of 4	1.75	—
	Never hinged	2.60	
a.	2c **scarlet,** wet printing	.25	.25
	Never hinged	.30	
	P# block of 4	2.00	—
	Never hinged	3.00	
b.	2c **scarlet,** dry printing	.25	.25
	Never hinged	.30	
	P# block of 4 (#25637, 25638)	1.50	—
	Never hinged	2.25	
J82	D3 3c **dull carmine,** wet printing	.40	.25
	Never hinged	.50	
	P# block of 4	2.25	—
	Never hinged	3.40	
a.	3c **scarlet,** wet printing	.30	.25
	Never hinged	.45	
	P# block of 4	2.50	—
	Never hinged	3.75	
b.	3c **scarlet,** dry printing	.25	.25
	Never hinged	.40	
	P# block of 4 (#25641, 25642)	2.25	—
	Never hinged	3.40	
	Pair with full vert. gutter btwn., never hinged	400.00	
J83	D3 5c **dull carmine,** wet printing	.75	.25
	Never hinged	1.15	
	P# block of 4	4.00	—
	Never hinged	6.00	
a.	5c **scarlet,** wet printing	.50	.25
	Never hinged	.75	
	P# block of 4	3.50	—
	Never hinged	5.25	
b.	5c **scarlet,** dry printing	.40	.25
	Never hinged	.60	
	P# block of 4 (#25643, 25644)	3.00	—
	Never hinged	4.50	
J84	D3 10c **dull carmine,** wet printing	1.60	.25
	Never hinged	2.50	
	P# block of 4	8.25	—
	Never hinged	12.50	
a.	10c **scarlet,** wet printing	1.25	.25
	Never hinged	1.90	
	P# block of 4	7.00	—
	Never hinged	10.50	
b.	10c **scarlet,** dry printing	1.10	.25
	Never hinged	1.80	
	P# block of 4 (#25645, 25646)	6.50	—
	Never hinged	9.75	
J85	D3 30c **dull carmine**	12.50	.25
	Never hinged	20.00	
	P# block of 4	40.00	—
	Never hinged	67.50	
a.	30c **scarlet**	7.50	.25
	Never hinged	11.50	
	P# block of 4	35.00	—
	Never hinged	60.00	—
J86	D3 50c **dull carmine**	12.50	.25
	Never hinged	20.00	
	P# block of 4	57.50	—
	Never hinged	95.00	
a.	50c **scarlet**	9.00	.25
	Never hinged	15.00	
	P# block of 4	52.50	—
	Never hinged	85.00	—

Design measures 22½x19mm

1956 ***Perf. 10½x11***

J87	D4 $1 **scarlet**	30.00	.25
	Never hinged	52.50	
	P# block of 4	190.00	—
	Never hinged	290.00	
	Nos. J79-J87 (9)	59.80	2.25
	Nos. J79-J87, never hinged	99.45	

Catalogue values for unused stamps in this section, from this point to the end, are for Never Hinged items.

D5

Denominations added in black by rubber plates in an operation similar to precanceling.

Rotary Press Printing

1959, June 19 Unwmk. *Perf. 11x10½*

Denomination in Black

J88	D5 ½c **carmine rose**	1.50	1.10
	P# block of 4	120.00	—
J89	D5 1c **carmine rose,** shiny gum	.25	.25
	P# block of 4	.50	—
	Dull gum	.25	
	P# block of 4	6.50	
a.	Denomination omitted	150.00	
	P# block of 4	—	—
b.	Pair, one without "1 CENT"	350.00	
J90	D5 2c **carmine rose,** shiny gum	.25	.25
	P# block of 4	.55	—
	Wide spacing, pair	*120.00*	
	Dull gum	.40	
	P# block of 4	12.50	
J91	D5 3c **carmine rose,** shiny gum	.25	.25
	P# block of 4	.60	—
	Dull gum	.50	
	P# block of 4	17.50	
a.	Pair, one without "3 CENTS"	*550.00*	
J92	D5 4c **carmine rose**	.25	.25
	P# block of 4	1.10	—
	Wide spacing, pair	*190.00*	
	Dull gum	—	
	P# block of 4	—	
J93	D5 5c **carmine rose,** shiny gum	.25	.25
	P# block of 4	1.10	—
	Dull gum	.45	
	P# block of 4	8.00	
a.	Pair, one without "5 CENTS"	*1,500.*	
J94	D5 6c **carmine rose,** shiny gum	.25	.25
	P# block of 4	1.10	—
	Pair with full vertical gutter between	—	
	Dull gum	*70.00*	
	P# block of 4	*1,250.*	
a.	Pair, one without "6 CENTS"	*700.00*	
J95	D5 7c **carmine rose,** shiny gum	.25	.25
	P# block of 4	1.10	—
	Wide spacing, pair	*120.00*	
	Dull gum	*550.00*	
	P# block of 4	*3,500.*	
J96	D5 8c **carmine rose**	.25	.25
	P# block of 4	1.10	—
	Wide spacing, pair	*120.00*	
a.	Pair, one without "8 CENTS"	*750.00*	
J97	D5 10c **carmine rose,** shiny gum	.25	.25
	P# block of 4	1.10	—
	Wide spacing, pair	—	
	Dull gum	.35	
	P# block of 4	8.00	
J98	D5 30c **carmine rose,** shiny gum	.70	.25
	P# block of 4	3.25	—
	Dull gum	1.00	
	P# block of 4	16.00	
J99	D5 50c **carmine rose,** shiny gum	1.10	.25
	P# block of 4	5.00	—
	Dull gum	1.75	
	P# block of 4	22.50	

Straight Numeral Outlined in Black

J100	D5 $1 **carmine rose, shiny gum**	2.00	.25
	P# block of 4	8.50	—
	Dull gum	2.50	
	P# block of 4	22.50	

J101 D5	$5 **carmine rose**, shiny gum	9.00	.25
	P# block of 4	37.50	—
	Dull gum	11.00	
	P# block of 4	55.00	—
	Nos. J88-J101 (14)	16.55	4.35

All single stamps with denomination omitted are catalogued as No. J89a.

Rotary Press Printing

1978-85 Denomination in Black ***Perf. 11x10½***

J102 D5	11c **carmine rose,** *Jan. 3, 1978*	.25	.25
	P# block of 4	1.75	—
J103 D5	13c **carmine rose,** *Jan. 3, 1978*	.25	.25
	P# block of 4	1.75	—
J104 D5	17c **carmine rose,** *June 10, 1985*	.40	.35
	P# block of 4	22.50	—

U.S. POSTAL AGENCY IN CHINA

Postage stamps of the 1917-19 U.S. series (then current) were issued to the U.S. Postal Agency, Shanghai, China, surcharged at double the original value of the stamps.

These stamps were intended for sale at Shanghai at their surcharged value in local currency, valid for prepayment on mail despatched from the U.S. Postal Agency at Shanghai to addresses in the U.S.

Stamps were first issued May 24, 1919, and were placed on sale at Shanghai on July 1, 1919. These stamps were not issued to postmasters in the U.S. The Shanghai post office, according to the U.S.P.O. Bulletin, was closed in December 1922. The stamps were on sale at the Philatelic Agency in Washington, D.C. for a short time after that.

Italicized numbers in parentheses indicate quantities shipped to the postal agency in Shanghai and to the Washington Philatelic Agency. In the case of Nos. K17-K18, the numbers are the quantity locally overprinted. All Nos. K16a, K17 and K18 are believed to have been sold. The final disposition of remainders of the others is not known. Neither the records of the Shanghai Postal Agency nor the records of the Washington Philatelic Agency have been located at this time. Authority for quantities shipped is the research of Joseph M. Napp, who in turn benefitted by the research of Meyer Tuchinsky.

The cancellations of the China office included "U.S. Postal Agency Shanghai China", "U.S. Pos. Service Shanghai China" duplexes, and the Shanghai parcel post roller cancel. Used stamps are valued bearing legible cancels showing Chinese origin.

United States Stamps #498-499, 502-504, 506-510, 512, 514-518 Surcharged in Black or Red (Nos. K7, K16)

1919 **Unwmk.** ***Perf. 11***

No.	Description	Unused	Used
K1	A140 2c on 1c **green** (*355,000*)	22.50	*70.00*
	Never hinged	67.50	
	Block of 4	100.00	*375.00*
	P# block of 6	300.00	—
	Never hinged	600.00	
	Double transfer	40.00	
	Never hinged	105.00	
	Earliest documented use: July 2, 1919.		
K2	A140 4c on 2c **rose,** type I (*355,000*)	22.50	*70.00*
	Never hinged	67.50	
	Block of 4	100.00	*375.00*
	P# block of 6	300.00	—
	Never hinged	600.00	
	Earliest documented use: July 2, 1919.		
K3	A140 6c on 3c **violet,** type II, (*113,000*)	55.00	*140.00*
	Never hinged	140.00	
	Block of 4	240.00	*675.00*
	P# block of 6	675.00	—
	Never hinged	1,150.	
K4	A140 8c on 4c **brown** (*113,000*)	55.00	*140.00*
	Never hinged	140.00	
	Block of 4	240.00	*675.00*
	P# block of 6	675.00	—
	Never hinged	1,150.	
K5	A140 10c on 5c **blue** (*113,000*)	60.00	*140.00*
	Never hinged	160.00	
	Block of 4	260.00	*675.00*
	P# block of 6	600.00	
	Never hinged	1,100.	
K6	A140 12c on 6c **red orange** (*113,000*)	80.00	*210.00*
	Never hinged	210.00	
	Block of 4	360.00	*1,100.*
	P# block of 6	800.00	
	Never hinged	*1,500.*	
K7	A140 14c on 7c **black** (*113,000*)	82.50	*210.00*
	Never hinged	215.00	
	Block of 4	380.00	*1,100.*
	P# block of 6	1,050.	
	Never hinged	*1,650.*	
K8	A148 16c on 8c **olive bister** (*13,000*)	65.00	*160.00*
	Never hinged	170.00	
	Block of 4	280.00	*850.00*
	P# block of 6	625.00	
	Never hinged	1,150.	
a.	16c on 8c **olive green** (*100,000*)	55.00	*140.00*
	Never hinged	150.00	
	Block of 4	240.00	*750.00*
	P# block of 6	575.00	
	Never hinged	1,000.	
K9	A148 18c on 9c **salmon red** (*113,000*)	60.00	*175.00*
	Never hinged	150.00	
	Block of 4	260.00	*850.00*
	P# block of 6	700.00	
	Never hinged	1,200.	
K10	A148 20c on 10c **orange yellow** (*113,000*)	55.00	*140.00*
	Never hinged	140.00	
	Block of 4	240.00	*675.00*
	P# block of 6	725.00	
	Never hinged	1,300.	
K11	A148 24c on 12c **brown carmine** (*50,000*)	75.00	*160.00*
	Never hinged	190.00	
	Block of 4	325.00	*750.00*
	P# block of 6	1,000.	
	Never hinged	1,750.	
a.	24c on 12c **claret brown** (*8,000*)	110.00	*240.00*
	Never hinged	275.00	
	Block of 4	475.00	*1,150.*
	P# block of 6	1,200.	
	Never hinged	*2,100.*	
K12	A148 30c on 15c **gray** (*58,000*)	82.50	*230.00*
	Never hinged	200.00	
	Block of 4	360.00	—
	P# block of 6	1,150.	
	Never hinged	*2,000.*	
K13	A148 40c on 20c **deep ultramarine** (*58,000*)	120.00	*325.00*
	Never hinged	300.00	
	Block of 4	525.00	*1,800.*
	P# block of 6	1,300.	
	Never hinged	*2,250.*	
K14	A148 60c on 30c **orange red** (*58,000*)	110.00	*275.00*
	Never hinged	260.00	
	Block of 4	475.00	*1,500.*
	P# block of 6	1,050.	
	Never hinged	*1,800.*	
K15	A148 $1 on 50c **light violet** (*14,000*)	550.00	*1,000.*
	Never hinged	1,200.	
	Block of 4	2,400.	*6,250.*
	P# block of 6	*17,500.*	
K16	A148 $2 on $1 **violet brown** (*13,800*)	425.00	*750.00*
	Never hinged	925.00	
	Block of 4	1,900.	*4,900.*
	Margin block of 4, arrow, right or left	2,000.	
	P# block of 6	*7,000.*	
	Never hinged	*11,000.*	
a.	Double surcharge (*200*)	*10,500.*	*11,500.*
	Never hinged	*17,500.*	
	Block of 4	*45,000.*	
	Nos. K1-K16 (16)	1,920.	*4,195.*

Fake surcharges exist, but most are rather crudely made.

United States Stamps Nos. 498 and 528B Locally Surcharged

1922, July 3

No.	Description	Unused	Used
K17	A140 2c on 1c **green** (*10,000*)	100.00	*225.00*
	Never hinged	225.00	
	Block of 4	425.00	*1,050.*
	P# block of 6	850.00	
	Never hinged	1,750.	
K18	A140 4c on 2c **carmine,** type VII (*10,000*)	100.00	*225.00*
	Never hinged	225.00	
	Block of 4	425.00	*1,050.*
	P# block of 6	850.00	
	Never hinged	1,750.	
a.	"SHANGHAI" omitted	*7,500.*	
b.	"CHINA" only	*16,000.*	

OFFICIAL STAMPS

The original official stamps were authorized by Act of Congress, approved March 3, 1873, abolishing the franking privilege. Stamps for each executive government department were issued July 1, 1873.

Penalty franks were first authorized in 1877, and their expanded use after 1879 reduced the need for official stamps, the use of which was finally abolished on July 5, 1884.

DESIGNS. Stamps for departments other than the Post Office picture the same busts used in the regular postage issue: 1c Franklin, 2c Jackson, 3c Washington, 6c Lincoln, 7c Stanton, 10c Jefferson, 12c Clay, 15c Webster, 24c Scott, 30c Hamilton, and 90c Perry. William H. Seward appears on the $2, $5, $10 and $20.

Designs of the various denominations are not identical, but resemble those illustrated.

PLATES. Plates of 200 subjects in two panes of 100 were used for Post Office Department 1c, 3c, 6c; Treasury Department 1c, 2c, 3c, and War Department 2c, 3c. Plates of 10 subjects were used for State Department $2, $5, $10 and $20. Plates of 100 subjects were used for all other Official stamps up to No. O120.

CANCELLATIONS. Odd or Town cancellations on Departmental stamps are relatively much scarcer than those appearing on the general issues of the same period. Town cancellations, especially on the 1873 issue, are scarce. The "Kicking Mule" cancellation is found used on stamps of the War Department and has also been seen on some stamps of the other Departments. Black is usual.

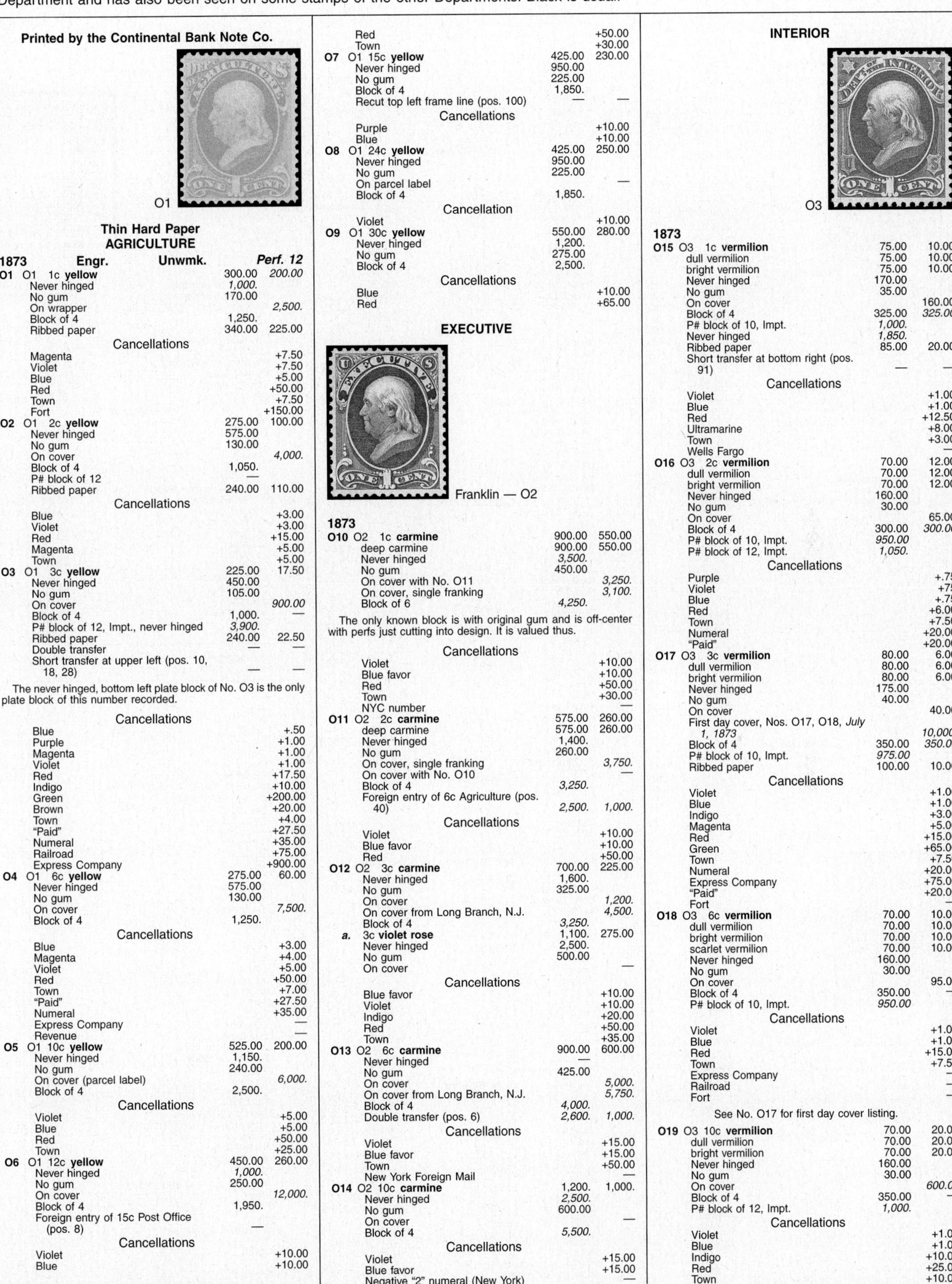

Printed by the Continental Bank Note Co.

O1

Thin Hard Paper

AGRICULTURE

1873 Engr. Unwmk. *Perf. 12*

O1 O1 1c **yellow**	300.00	*200.00*
Never hinged	*1,000.*	
No gum	170.00	
On wrapper		*2,500.*
Block of 4	1,250.	
Ribbed paper	340.00	225.00
Cancellations		
Magenta		+7.50
Violet		+7.50
Blue		+5.00
Red		+50.00
Town		+7.50
Fort		+150.00
O2 O1 2c **yellow**	275.00	100.00
Never hinged	575.00	
No gum	130.00	
On cover		*4,000.*
Block of 4	1,050.	
P# block of 12	—	
Ribbed paper	240.00	110.00
Cancellations		
Blue		+3.00
Violet		+3.00
Red		+15.00
Magenta		+5.00
Town		+5.00
O3 O1 3c **yellow**	225.00	17.50
Never hinged	450.00	
No gum	105.00	
On cover		*900.00*
Block of 4	1,000.	—
P# block of 12, Impt., never hinged	*3,900.*	
Ribbed paper	240.00	22.50
Double transfer	—	—
Short transfer at upper left (pos. 10, 18, 28)	—	—

The never hinged, bottom left plate block of No. O3 is the only plate block of this number recorded.

Cancellations		
Blue		+.50
Purple		+1.00
Magenta		+1.00
Violet		+1.00
Red		+17.50
Indigo		+10.00
Green		+200.00
Brown		+20.00
Town		+4.00
"Paid"		+27.50
Numeral		+35.00
Railroad		+75.00
Express Company		+900.00
O4 O1 6c **yellow**	275.00	60.00
Never hinged	575.00	
No gum	130.00	
On cover		*7,500.*
Block of 4	1,250.	
Cancellations		
Blue		+3.00
Magenta		+4.00
Violet		+5.00
Red		+50.00
Town		+7.00
"Paid"		+27.50
Numeral		+35.00
Express Company		—
Revenue		—
O5 O1 10c **yellow**	525.00	200.00
Never hinged	1,150.	
No gum	240.00	
On cover (parcel label)		*6,000.*
Block of 4	2,500.	
Cancellations		
Violet		+5.00
Blue		+5.00
Red		+50.00
Town		+25.00
O6 O1 12c **yellow**	450.00	260.00
Never hinged	*1,000.*	
No gum	250.00	
On cover		*12,000.*
Block of 4	1,950.	
Foreign entry of 15c Post Office (pos. 8)		—
Cancellations		
Violet		+10.00
Blue		+10.00
Red		+50.00
Town		+30.00
O7 O1 15c **yellow**	425.00	230.00
Never hinged	950.00	
No gum	225.00	
Block of 4	1,850.	
Recut top left frame line (pos. 100)	—	—
Cancellations		
Purple		+10.00
Blue		+10.00
O8 O1 24c **yellow**	425.00	250.00
Never hinged	950.00	
No gum	225.00	
On parcel label		—
Block of 4	1,850.	
Cancellation		
Violet		+10.00
O9 O1 30c **yellow**	550.00	280.00
Never hinged	1,200.	
No gum	275.00	
Block of 4	2,500.	
Cancellations		
Blue		+10.00
Red		+65.00

EXECUTIVE

Franklin — O2

1873

O10 O2 1c **carmine**	900.00	550.00
deep carmine	900.00	550.00
Never hinged	*3,500.*	
No gum	450.00	
On cover with No. O11		*3,250.*
On cover, single franking		*3,100.*
Block of 6	*4,250.*	

The only known block is with original gum and is off-center with perfs just cutting into design. It is valued thus.

Cancellations		
Violet		+10.00
Blue favor		+10.00
Red		+50.00
Town		+30.00
NYC number		—
O11 O2 2c **carmine**	575.00	260.00
deep carmine	575.00	260.00
Never hinged	1,400.	
No gum	260.00	
On cover, single franking		*3,750.*
On cover with No. O10		—
Block of 4	*3,250.*	
Foreign entry of 6c Agriculture (pos. 40)	*2,500.*	*1,000.*
Cancellations		
Violet		+10.00
Blue favor		+10.00
Red		+50.00
O12 O2 3c **carmine**	700.00	225.00
Never hinged	1,600.	
No gum	325.00	
On cover		*1,200.*
On cover from Long Branch, N.J.		*4,500.*
Block of 4	*3,250.*	
a. 3c **violet rose**	1,100.	275.00
Never hinged	2,500.	
No gum	500.00	
On cover		—
Cancellations		
Blue favor		+10.00
Violet		+10.00
Indigo		+20.00
Red		+50.00
Town		+35.00
O13 O2 6c **carmine**	900.00	600.00
Never hinged	—	
No gum	425.00	
On cover		*5,000.*
On cover from Long Branch, N.J.		*5,750.*
Block of 4	*4,000.*	
Double transfer (pos. 6)	*2,600.*	*1,000.*
Cancellations		
Violet		+15.00
Blue favor		+15.00
Town		+50.00
New York Foreign Mail		—
O14 O2 10c **carmine**	1,200.	1,000.
Never hinged	*2,500.*	
No gum	600.00	
On cover		—
Block of 4	*5,500.*	
Cancellations		
Violet		+15.00
Blue favor		+15.00
Negative "2" numeral (New York)		—

INTERIOR

O3

1873

O15 O3 1c **vermilion**	75.00	10.00
dull vermilion	75.00	10.00
bright vermilion	75.00	10.00
Never hinged	170.00	
No gum	35.00	
On cover		160.00
Block of 4	325.00	*325.00*
P# block of 10, Impt.	*1,000.*	
Never hinged	*1,850.*	
Ribbed paper	85.00	20.00
Short transfer at bottom right (pos. 91)	—	—
Cancellations		
Violet		+1.00
Blue		+1.00
Red		+12.50
Ultramarine		+8.00
Town		+3.00
Wells Fargo		—
O16 O3 2c **vermilion**	70.00	12.00
dull vermilion	70.00	12.00
bright vermilion	70.00	12.00
Never hinged	160.00	
No gum	30.00	
On cover		65.00
Block of 4	300.00	*300.00*
P# block of 10, Impt.	*950.00*	
P# block of 12, Impt.	*1,050.*	
Cancellations		
Purple		+.75
Violet		+75
Blue		+.75
Red		+6.00
Town		+7.50
Numeral		+20.00
"Paid"		+20.00
O17 O3 3c **vermilion**	80.00	6.00
dull vermilion	80.00	6.00
bright vermilion	80.00	6.00
Never hinged	175.00	
No gum	40.00	
On cover		40.00
First day cover, Nos. O17, O18, *July 1, 1873*		*10,000.*
Block of 4	350.00	*350.00*
P# block of 10, Impt.	*975.00*	
Ribbed paper	100.00	10.00
Cancellations		
Violet		+1.00
Blue		+1.00
Indigo		+3.00
Magenta		+5.00
Red		+15.00
Green		+65.00
Town		+7.50
Numeral		+20.00
Express Company		+75.00
"Paid"		+20.00
Fort		—
O18 O3 6c **vermilion**	70.00	10.00
dull vermilion	70.00	10.00
bright vermilion	70.00	10.00
scarlet vermilion	70.00	10.00
Never hinged	160.00	
No gum	30.00	
On cover		95.00
Block of 4	350.00	—
P# block of 10, Impt.	*950.00*	
Cancellations		
Violet		+1.00
Blue		+1.00
Red		+15.00
Town		+7.50
Express Company		—
Railroad		—
Fort		—

See No. O17 for first day cover listing.

O19 O3 10c **vermilion**	70.00	20.00
dull vermilion	70.00	20.00
bright vermilion	70.00	20.00
Never hinged	160.00	
No gum	30.00	
On cover		*600.00*
Block of 4	350.00	—
P# block of 12, Impt.	*1,000.*	
Cancellations		
Violet		+1.00
Blue		+1.00
Indigo		+10.00
Red		+25.00
Town		+10.00

Fort —
New York Foreign Mail +300.00
O20 O3 12c **vermilion** 90.00 12.00
bright vermilion 90.00 12.00
Never hinged 200.00
No gum 45.00
On cover *575.00*
Block of 4 400.00 500.00
P# block of 10, Impt. *1,150.*
Short transfer at right (pos. 6) — —

Cancellations
Violet +1.00
Magenta +1.00
Blue +1.00
Red +15.00
Brown +20.00
Town +7.50
Fort —
O21 O3 15c **vermilion** 200.00 25.00
bright vermilion 200.00 25.00
Never hinged 450.00
No gum 90.00
On cover *650.00*
Block of 4 900.00 —
P# block of 12, Impt. —
Double transfer of left side (pos. 37, 47, 57, and 67) 275.00 37.50

Cancellations
Blue +1.50
Violet +1.50
Town +5.00
O22 O3 24c **vermilion** 180.00 20.00
dull vermilion 180.00 20.00
bright vermilion 180.00 20.00
Never hinged 400.00
No gum 85.00
On cover *2,500.*
Block of 4 775.00 *2,000.*
P# block of 12, Impt. *2,500.*
a. Double impression —

Cancellations
Violet +1.50
Blue +1.50
Red +15.00
Town +5.00
O23 O3 30c **vermilion** 290.00 20.00
bright vermilion 290.00 20.00
Never hinged 625.00
No gum 130.00
On parcel label *6,000.*
Block of 4 1,250. —
P# block of 12, Impt. *4,250.*

Cancellations
Violet +2.00
Blue +2.00
Red +50.00
Town +7.50
O24 O3 90c **vermilion** 325.00 50.00
bright vermilion 325.00 50.00
Never hinged 700.00
No gum 140.00
On cover —
Block of 4 1,650. —
P# block of 12, Impt. *5,000.*
Double transfer 390.00
Major double transfer (Pos. 17) *600.00* *250.00*
Short transfer at right (Pos. 56) —
Silk paper —

Cancellations
Violet +4.00
Blue +4.00
Magenta +10.00
Red +50.00
Brown +60.00
Town +17.50

JUSTICE

O4

1873

O25 O4 1c **purple** 250.00 100.00
dark purple 250.00 100.00
Never hinged 550.00
No gum 120.00
On cover *1,750.*
On cover with No. O26 *4,000.*
Block of 4 1,100.
Double transfer — —

Cancellations
Violet +3.00
Blue +3.00
Indigo +5.00
Magenta +5.00
Red +20.00
Town +7.50
O26 O4 2c **purple** 310.00 110.00
light purple 310.00 110.00
Never hinged 700.00
No gum 135.00
On cover *1,500.*
Block of 4 1,400.
Short transfer at right side (pos. 3) — —

Cancellations
Violet +4.00
Blue +4.00
Ultramarine +10.00
Indigo +5.00
Magenta +5.00
Red +20.00
Town +20.00
O27 O4 3c **purple** 300.00 35.00
dark purple 300.00 35.00
bluish purple 300.00 35.00
Never hinged 700.00
No gum 135.00
On cover *575.00*
Block of 4 1,350.
Double transfer —

Cancellations
Violet +2.00
Magenta +2.00
Blue +2.00
Ultramarine +10.00
Indigo +5.00
Red +12.00
Green +100.00
Town +15.00
O28 O4 6c **purple** 310.00 45.00
light purple 310.00 45.00
bluish purple 310.00 45.00
Never hinged 700.00
No gum 135.00
On cover *1,200.*
Block of 4 1,400.

Cancellations
Violet +2.00
Blue +2.00
Indigo +5.00
Magenta +5.00
Red +15.00
Town +17.50
O29 O4 10c **purple** 310.00 100.00
bluish purple 310.00 100.00
Never hinged *1,250.*
No gum 135.00
On cover *4,000.*
Block of 4 1,400.
P# block of 10, Impt. *6,500.*
Double transfer — —

Cancellations
Violet +4.00
Blue +4.00
Magenta +5.00
Town +17.50
O30 O4 12c **purple** 260.00 75.00
dark purple 260.00 75.00
Never hinged *1,500.*
No gum 125.00
On cover *1,750.*
Block of 4 1,200.

Cancellations
Purple +2.00
Violet +2.00
Blue +2.00
Magenta +5.00
Red +35.00
Town +17.50
O31 O4 15c **purple** 500.00 200.00
Never hinged *1,500.*
No gum 240.00
On cover *1,250.*
Block of 4 *3,100.*
Double transfer — —

Cancellations
Violet +5.00
Blue +5.00
Indigo +5.00
Magenta +10.00
Red +35.00
Town +10.00

The block of 4 of No. O31 is unique. It is in the grade of fine and is valued thus.

O32 O4 24c **purple** 1,250. 425.00
Never hinged *4,250.*
No gum 600.00
On cover *8,000.*
Short transfer (pos. 98) — —

Cancellations
Violet +10.00
Blue +10.00
Magenta +10.00
Red +35.00
Town +40.00
O33 O4 30c **purple** 1,300. 350.00
Never hinged —
No gum 625.00
On cover with Nos. O27 & O28 *17,500.*
Block of 4 *7,500.*
Double transfer at top 1,400. 375.00

Cancellations
Purple +10.00
Violet +10.00
Blue +10.00
Magenta +10.00
Red +50.00
Town +40.00

The block of 4 of No. O33 is unique. It is in the grade of fine and is valued thus.

O34 O4 90c **purple** 1,900. 900.00
dark purple 1,900. 900.00
Never hinged *4,000.*
No gum 900.00
On cover with No. O33 *26,000.*
Pair —
Double plate scratch — —
Triple transfer at top — —

Cancellations
Purple +25.00
Violet +25.00
Blue +25.00
Magenta +25.00

No. O34 on cover is unique. The cover bears three No. O34 and four No. O33.

NAVY

O5

1873

O35 O5 1c **ultramarine** 160.00 50.00
dark ultramarine 160.00 50.00
Never hinged 350.00
No gum 75.00
On cover *750.00*
On cover with No. O36 *2,000.*
Block of 4 750.00
P# block of 12, Impt. *2,250.*
a. 1c **dull blue** 200.00 50.00
Never hinged 400.00
No gum 87.50

Cancellations
Violet +2.00
Blue +2.00
Indigo +5.00
Red +20.00
Town +7.50
Steamship +100.00
New York Foreign Mail —
O36 O5 2c **ultramarine** 160.00 25.00
dark ultramarine 160.00 25.00
Never hinged 350.00
No gum 75.00
On cover *500.00*
Block of 4 750.00
P# block of 12, Impt. *2,250.*
Double transfer — —
a. 2c **dull blue** 200.00 25.00
gray blue 200.00 25.00
Never hinged 400.00
No gum 87.50
Block of 4 825.00

The 2c deep green and the 2c black, both perforated and imperforate, are trial color proofs.

Cancellations
Violet +1.50
Blue +1.50
Indigo +5.00
Red +15.00
Green +75.00
Town +10.00
Steamship +100.00
New York Foreign Mail —
O37 O5 3c **ultramarine** 170.00 15.00
pale ultramarine 170.00 15.00
dark ultramarine 170.00 15.00
Never hinged *1,750.*
No gum 80.00
On cover *250.00*
Block of 4 775.00 *1,000.*
P# block of 12, Impt. *2,500.*
Double transfer — —
a. 3c **dull blue** 225.00 15.00
Never hinged 450.00
No gum 100.00

Cancellations
Violet +1.50
Blue +1.50
Indigo +5.00
Ultramarine +10.00
Magenta +5.00
Red +15.00
Town +5.00
Blue town +15.00
Steamship +75.00
O38 O5 6c **ultramarine** 150.00 25.00
bright ultramarine 150.00 25.00
Never hinged 450.00
No gum 70.00
On cover *750.00*
Block of 4 700.00 —
P# block of 12, Impt. *2,400.*
Vertical line through "N" of "Navy" 175.00 35.00
Double transfer — —
a. 6c **dull blue** 175.00 25.00
Never hinged 385.00
No gum 82.50

Cancellations
Violet +1.50
Purple +1.50
Blue +1.50
Magenta +10.00
Red +17.50
Green +100.00
Town +5.00
Steamship +100.00
New York Foreign Mail —

Cat.	Description	Unused	Used
O39	O5 7c **ultramarine**	700.00	230.00
	dark ultramarine	700.00	230.00
	Never hinged	1,600.	
	No gum	325.00	
	On cover		3,000.
	Block of 4	3,000.	
	Double transfer	—	—
a.	7c **dull blue**	750.00	230.00
	Never hinged	—	
	No gum	325.00	
	Cancellations		
	Blue		+10.00
	Violet		+10.00
	Magenta		+10.00
	Red		+45.00
	Town		+25.00
O40	O5 10c **ultramarine**	210.00	45.00
	dark ultramarine	210.00	45.00
	Never hinged	1,000.	
	No gum	95.00	
	On cover		6,500.
	Block of 4	1,000.	
	P# block of 12, Impt.	2,900.	
	Plate scratch (pos. 3)	325.00	—
	Ribbed paper	225.00	60.00
a.	10c **dull blue**	225.00	45.00
	Never hinged	1,000.	
	No gum	110.00	
	Cancellations		
	Violet		+2.00
	Blue		+2.00
	Brown		+20.00
	Red		+25.00
	Town		+10.00
	Steamship		+100.00
	New York Foreign Mail		—
O41	O5 12c **ultramarine**	240.00	45.00
	pale ultramarine	240.00	45.00
	dark ultramarine	240.00	45.00
	Never hinged	900.00	
	No gum	115.00	
	On cover		—
	Block of 4	1,100.	
	P# strip of 6, Impt.	—	
	Short transfer at lower right (pos. 10)	—	—
	Double transfer of left side (pos. 50)	400.00	250.00
	Cancellations		
	Violet		+2.50
	Magenta		+2.50
	Blue		+2.50
	Red		+25.00
	Town		+10.00
	Supplementary Mail		+80.00
	Steamship		+200.00
	New York Foreign Mail		+325.00
O42	O5 15c **ultramarine**	425.00	80.00
	dark ultramarine	425.00	80.00
	Never hinged	—	
	No gum	200.00	
	On cover		21,000.
	Block of 4	1,800.	
	P# strip of 6, Impt.	—	
	Short transfer at upper left (pos. 26)	—	
	Cancellations		
	Violet		+2.50
	Blue		+2.50
	Red		+35.00
	Yellow		—
	Town		+20.00
O43	O5 24c **ultramarine**	425.00	85.00
	dark ultramarine	425.00	85.00
	Never hinged	1,750.	
	No gum	200.00	
	On cover		30,000.
	Block of 4	2,000.	
	Recut at upper right (pos. 33, 92)	—	—
a.	24c **dull blue**	425.00	80.00
	Never hinged	1,350.	
	No gum	200.00	
	Cancellations		
	Violet		+5.00
	Magenta		+5.00
	Red		+50.00
	Blue		+5.00
	Green		+150.00
	Town		+40.00
	Steamship		+125.00
	New York Foreign Mail		—
O44	O5 30c **ultramarine**	350.00	50.00
	dark ultramarine	350.00	50.00
	Never hinged	3,000.	
	No gum	160.00	
	On cover		20,000.
	Block of 4	1,600.	3,000.
	Double transfer	375.00	55.00
	Cancellations		
	Blue		+4.00
	Red		+30.00
	Violet		+4.00
	Town		+20.00
	Supplementary Mail		+125.00
	Steamship		+150.00
	New York Foreign Mail		+400.00
O45	O5 90c **ultramarine**	1,050.	375.00
	Never hinged	6,000.	
	No gum	500.00	
	Block of 4	6,250.	
	Short transfer at upper left (pos. 1, 5)	—	—
a.	Double impression		20,000.
	Cancellations		
	Purple		+15.00
	Violet		+15.00
	Red		+75.00
	Town		+40.00

POST OFFICE

Stamps of the Post Office Department are often on paper with a gray surface. This is essentially a wiping problem, caused by an over-milled carbon black pigment that released acid and etched the plates. There is no premium for stamps on paper with a gray surface.

O6

1873

Cat.	Description	Unused	Used
O47	O6 1c **black**	25.00	12.00
	gray black	25.00	12.00
	Never hinged	60.00	
	No gum	12.00	
	On cover		75.00
	Block of 4	110.00	—
	P# block of 12, Impt.	400.00	
	Never hinged	550.00	
	Cancellations		
	Purple		+1.00
	Violet		+1.00
	Magenta		+1.00
	Blue		+1.00
	Red		+12.50
	Town		+3.50
O48	O6 2c **black**	30.00	10.00
	gray black	30.00	10.00
	Never hinged	75.00	
	No gum	14.00	
	On cover		175.00
	Block of 4	140.00	—
	P# block of 12, Impt.	475.00	
	Cancellations		
	Purple		+1.00
	Violet		+1.00
	Blue		+1.00
	Indigo		+5.00
	Magenta		+1.00
	Red		+12.50
	Town		+3.50
	Blue town		+7.50
	New York Foreign Mail		—
O49	O6 3c **black**	10.00	2.00
	gray black	10.00	2.00
	Never hinged	25.00	
	No gum	4.50	
	On cover		25.00
	Block of 4	45.00	—
	P# block of 12, Impt.	200.00	
	Never hinged	350.00	
	Cracked plate	—	—
	Double transfer at bottom	—	—
	Vertical ribbed paper	—	—
a.	Printed on both sides		7,500.
b.	Double paper	—	—
	Cancellations		
	Purple		+.75
	Violet		+.75
	Blue		+.75
	Indigo		+5.00
	Ultramarine		+1.50
	Magenta		+.75
	Red		+10.00
	Brown		+20.00
	Green		+60.00
	Numeral		+20.00
	Town		+1.50
	Railroad		+25.00
	"Paid"		+12.00
O50	O6 6c **black**	30.00	8.00
	gray black	30.00	8.00
	Never hinged	75.00	
	No gum	14.00	
	On cover		85.00
	Block of 4	150.00	—
	P# block of 14, Impt.	550.00	
	Vertical ribbed paper	—	12.50
	Double transfer of top frame (pos. 96L, 99L)	—	—
a.	Diagonal half used as 3c on cover		5,000.
b.	Double impression		3,000.
	Cancellations		
	Purple		+.75
	Violet		+.75
	Magenta		+.75
	Blue		+.75
	Indigo		+5.00
	Red		+12.00
	Brown		+20.00
	Numeral		+20.00
	Town		+2.50
	"Paid"		+15.00
O51	O6 10c **black**	140.00	55.00
	gray black	140.00	55.00
	Never hinged	325.00	
	No gum	65.00	
	On cover		400.00
	Block of 4	700.00	—
	P# block of 12, Impt.	1,950.	
	Cancellations		
	Violet		+3.50
	Red		+15.00
	Magenta		+3.50
	Blue		+3.50
	Town		+10.00
O52	O6 12c **black**	120.00	12.00
	gray black	120.00	12.00
	Never hinged	275.00	
	No gum	55.00	
	On cover		1,000.
	Block of 4	575.00	1,250.
	P# block of 12, Impt.	1,850.	
	Plate scratch above small "12"	—	—
	Cancellations		
	Purple		+1.00
	Magenta		+1.00
	Blue		+1.00
	Indigo		+5.00
	Red		+12.50
	Town		+4.00
O53	O6 15c **black**	140.00	20.00
	gray black	140.00	20.00
	Never hinged	325.00	
	No gum	65.00	
	On cover		5,000.
	Block of 4	675.00	—
	P# block of 10, Impt.	2,250.	
	Double transfer	—	—
	Cancellations		
	Violet		+1.50
	Magenta		+1.50
	Red		+20.00
	Blue		+1.50
	Town		+7.50
	New York Foreign Mail		—
O54	O6 24c **black**	225.00	25.00
	gray black	225.00	25.00
	Never hinged	500.00	
	No gum	105.00	
	Block of 4	900.00	—
	P# block of 12, Impt.	—	
a.	Double paper	—	—
	Cancellations		
	Violet		+1.50
	Blue		+1.50
	Red		+20.00
	Town		+7.50
	New York Foreign Mail		—
O55	O6 30c **black**	200.00	25.00
	gray black	200.00	25.00
	Never hinged	450.00	
	No gum	90.00	
	On cover		17,500.
	Block of 4	900.00	750.00
	P# block of 12, Impt.	2,900.	
	Cancellations		
	Purple		+1.50
	Blue		+1.50
	Red		+20.00
	Magenta		+1.50
	Town		+12.50
O56	O6 90c **black**	220.00	25.00
	gray black	220.00	25.00
	Never hinged	500.00	
	No gum	105.00	
	Block of 4	950.00	1,250.
	P# block of 12, Impt.	3,000.	
	Double transfer	—	—
	Silk paper	—	
a.	Double paper	—	—
	Cancellations		
	Purple		+1.50
	Magenta		+1.50
	Blue		+1.50
	Town		+6.50

STATE

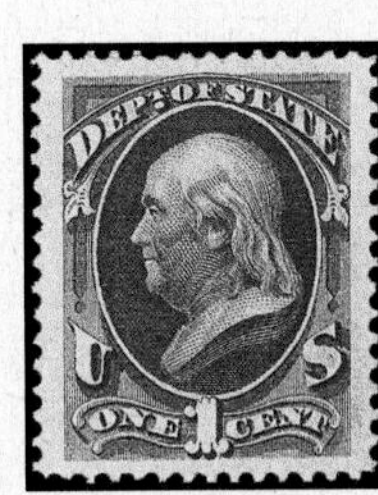

Franklin — O7

William H. Seward — O8

1873

Cat.	Description	Unused	Used
O57	O7 1c **dark green**	260.00	75.00
a.	dark yellow green	260.00	75.00
	Never hinged	575.00	
	No gum	125.00	
	On cover		—
	Block of 4	1,250.	
	Plate scratch at left (pos. 51)	—	—
	Cancellations		
	Violet		+2.00
	Blue favor		+2.00
	Red		+17.50
	Town		+7.50
O58	O7 2c **dark green**	310.00	100.00
a.	yellow green	310.00	100.00
	Never hinged	—	
	No gum	150.00	
	On cover		1,000.
	Double transfer at bottom (pos. 98)	600.00	—

Cancellations

Violet	+5.00
Blue favor	+5.00
Indigo	+5.00
Red	+50.00
Town	+25.00

O59 O7 3c **dark green**	220.00	25.00
a. yellow green	220.00	25.00
Never hinged	500.00	
No gum	105.00	
On cover		*600.00*
First day cover, *July 1, 1873*		—
Block of 4	1,100.	
Short transfer at right (pos. 85)		—
b. Double paper	—	—

Cancellations

Violet	+1.50
Blue favor	+1.50
Indigo	+1.50
Red	+10.00
Town	+6.50

O60 O7 6c **dark green**	250.00	30.00
a. yellow green	250.00	30.00
Never hinged	550.00	
No gum	120.00	
On cover		*800.00*
Block of 4	1,100.	
P# block of 12, Impt.	—	
Double transfer	—	—
Foreign entry of 1c Executive (pos. 11)	—	
Double transfer plus foreign entry of 1c Executive (pos. 1)	—	
Foreign entry of 6c Executive (pos. 21, 31, 41, 51, 71 ,81, 91)	—	*500.00*
Double transfer plus foreign entry of 6c Executive (pos. 61)	—	
Plate scratch in margin (pos. 26, right; 27, left)	*325.00*	*275.00*

Cancellations

Violet	+2.00
Blue favor	+10.00
Indigo	+2.00
Red	+20.00
Town	+17.50

O61 O7 7c **dark green**	290.00	65.00
a. yellow green	290.00	65.00
Never hinged	650.00	
No gum	140.00	
On cover		*1,000.*
Block of 4	1,500.	
Ribbed paper	310.00	70.00

Cancellations

Violet	+2.00
Blue favor	+2.00
Indigo	+2.00
Red	+25.00
Town	+10.00

O62 O7 10c **dark green**	250.00	55.00
a. yellow green	250.00	—
Never hinged	575.00	
No gum	120.00	
On cover		*2,000.*
Block of 4	1,150.	
P# block of 12, Impt.	—	
Short transfer (pos. 34)	275.00	67.50

Cancellations

Violet	+2.50
Blue favor	+2.50
Indigo	+2.50
Red	+35.00
Town	+25.00
New York Foreign Mail	+325.00

O63 O7 12c **dark green**	310.00	125.00
a. yellow green	—	—
Never hinged	700.00	
No gum	150.00	
On cover		*1,500.*
Block of 4	1,650.	

Cancellations

Violet	+5.00
Blue favor	+5.00
Red	+30.00
Town	+15.00

O64 O7 15c **dark green**	350.00	90.00
a. yellow green	350.00	90.00
Never hinged	775.00	
No gum	170.00	
On cover		*5,750.*
Block of 4	1,750.	
Short transfer at upper right		450.00
Plate scratch at lower left (pos. 91)	*450.00*	
Plate scratch in margin (pos. 95, right; 96, left)	—	
Damaged plate at left (pos. 63)	—	

Cancellations

Violet	+2.50
Blue favor	+2.50
Red	+30.00
Town	+30.00

O65 O7 24c **dark green**	550.00	230.00
a. yellow green	525.00	230.00
Never hinged	*1,200.*	
No gum	275.00	
On cover		*17,500.*
Block of 4	*3,100.*	
Short transfer at bottom left (pos. 10)	*600.00*	
Foreign entry of 90c Justice at top (pos. 76)	*850.00*	
Foreign entry of 90c Justice at bottom (pos. 66)	*750.00*	

Cancellations

Violet	+15.00
Blue favor	+15.00
Indigo	+15.00
Red	+85.00
Town	+55.00

O66 O7 30c **dark green**	525.00	180.00
a. yellow green	500.00	180.00
Never hinged	*1,150.*	
No gum	260.00	
On cover		*12,500.*
Block of 4	*4,500.*	

Cancellations

Violet	+5.00
Blue favor	+5.00
Indigo	+5.00
Red	+50.00
Town	+50.00
New York Foreign Mail	—

O67 O7 90c **dark green**	1,100.	325.00
a. yellow green	—	
Never hinged	*2,400.*	
No gum	525.00	
On parcel wrapper with either Nos. O60 and O66, or with 2 No. O62 and O66		*40,000.*

Cancellations

Violet	+15.00
Blue favor	+15.00
Red	+85.00
Red New York Foreign Mail	—
Town	+90.00

O68 O8 $2 **green & black**	1,800.	3,000.
a. yellow green & black	1,750.	3,000.
Never hinged	*3,750.*	
No gum	850.00	
On parcel label		*175,000.*
Block of 4	*19,000.*	
Ribbed paper		—

The No. O68 on parcel label/wrapper is unique. The item is from the U.S. State Dept. to Germany, and it also bears a single No. O62 and 17 No. O66.

Cancellations

Violet	+25.00
Blue favor	+25.00
Red	+175.00
Town	+125.00
Red New York Foreign Mail	+3,000.
Pen Cancel	*350.00*

O69 O8 $5 **green & black**	8,000.	*13,000.*
a. yellow green & black	7,500.	*13,000.*
Never hinged	—	
No gum	3,750.	
Irregular block of 6	*60,000.*	

Cancellations

Blue favor	+250.00
Red favor	+250.00
Pen Cancel	*2,000.*

O70 O8 $10 **green & black**	4,500.	*12,500.*
a. yellow green & black	4,500.	*12,500.*
Never hinged	10,500.	
No gum	2,500.	
Block of 4	*24,000.*	
P# sheet of 10, Impt.	*62,500.*	
Ribbed paper	—	

Cancellations

Blue favor	+200.00
Pen Cancel	*1,250.*

O71 O8 $20 **green & black**	5,000.	5,500.
a. yellow green & black	5,000.	5,500.
Never hinged	11,500.	
No gum	2,500.	
Block of 4	*27,000.*	
Block of 4, presentation pen cancel		*10,000.*
P# sheet of 10, Impt.	*70,000.*	

No. O71 used is valued with a blue or red handstamp favor cancel.

Cancellations

Blue favor	5,500.
Red favor	5,500.
Pen presentation	1,750.
Cork and manuscript	+15,000.

The design of Nos. O68 to O71 measures 25½x39½mm.

TREASURY

O9

1873

O72 O9 1c **brown**	120.00	10.00
dark brown	120.00	10.00
yellow brown	120.00	10.00
Never hinged	250.00	
No gum	55.00	
On cover		100.00
Block of 4	525.00	*325.00*
P# block of 10, Impt.	*2,100.*	
Never hinged	*4,000.*	
Double transfer	135.00	12.50

Cancellations

Purple	+1.00
Violet	+1.00
Magenta	+1.00
Blue	+1.00
Red	+10.00
Brown	+20.00
Green	+200.00
Town	+2.00
Blue town	+4.00
New York Foreign Mail	—

O73 O9 2c **brown**	125.00	8.00
dark brown	125.00	8.00
yellow brown	125.00	8.00
Never hinged	275.00	
No gum	57.50	
On cover		75.00
Block of 4	550.00	*325.00*
P# block of 14, Impt.	*2,000.*	
Double transfer	—	12.50
Plate scratch (pos. 3R)		—

Cancellations

Purple	+1.00
Violet	+1.00
Magenta	+1.00
Blue	+1.00
Indigo	+3.00
Red	+10.00
Town	+2.00
Blue town	+4.00
New York Foreign Mail	+275.00

O74 O9 3c **brown**	110.00	2.00
dark brown	110.00	2.00
yellow brown	110.00	2.00
Never hinged	230.00	
No gum	50.00	
On cover		100.00
First day cover, *July 1, 1873*		*11,000.*
Block of 4	475.00	*250.00*
P# block of 14, Impt.	*1,850.*	
Shaded circle outside of right frame line	—	—
Short transfer at bottom (pos. 36 R 29)	—	—
a. Double impression		*5,000.*
b. Double paper	—	

Cancellations

Purple	+.50
Violet	+.50
Blue	+.50
Indigo	+3.00
Ultramarine	+2.00
Magenta	+.50
Red	+3.50
Brown	+20.00
Green	+200.00
Town	+1.00
Railroad	+20.00
"Paid"	+10.00

O75 O9 6c **brown**	120.00	4.00
dark brown	120.00	4.00
yellow brown	120.00	4.00
Never hinged	250.00	
No gum	55.00	
On cover		75.00
On cover with 6c War #O86		*12,000.*
Block of 4	525.00	*500.00*
P# block of 12, Impt.	*1,900.*	
Never hinged	*3,500.*	
Dirty plate	120.00	6.00
Double transfer	—	—

Cancellations

Purple	+.50
Violet	+.50
Magenta	+.50
Blue	+.50
Indigo	+3.00
Ultramarine	+1.50
Red	+5.00
Green	+200.00
"Paid"	+20.00
Town	+1.50
New York Foreign Mail	—

O76 O9 7c **brown**	250.00	35.00
dark brown	250.00	35.00
yellow brown	250.00	35.00
Never hinged	550.00	
No gum	120.00	
On cover		750.00
Block of 4	1,100.	*1,000.*
P# block of 12, Impt.	—	

Cancellations

Purple	+2.00
Violet	+2.00
Blue	+2.00
Indigo	+3.00
Red	+30.00
Green	+200.00
Town	+7.50
Blue town	+12.50
New York Foreign Mail	—

O77 O9 10c **brown**	240.00	12.00
dark brown	240.00	12.00
yellow brown	240.00	12.00
Never hinged	525.00	
No gum	110.00	
On cover		*450.00*
Block of 4	1,075.	*325.00*
P# block of 12, Impt.	—	
Double transfer		—
a. Double paper	—	—

Cancellations

Purple	+1.00
Violet	+1.00
Blue	+1.00
Indigo	+3.00
Ultramarine	+4.00
Magenta	+1.00
Red	+12.00
Brown	+20.00
Green	+200.00

Town +4.00
Blue town +8.50
O78 O9 12c **brown** 350.00 10.00
dark brown 350.00 10.00
yellow brown 350.00 10.00
Never hinged 750.00
No gum 160.00
On cover 600.00
Block of 4 1,500. *325.00*

Cancellations

Purple +.50
Blue +.50
Ultramarine +10.00
Red +10.00
Green +200.00
Town +2.50
Railroad +20.00
O79 O9 15c **brown** 300.00 12.00
yellow brown 300.00 12.00
Never hinged 650.00
No gum 140.00
On cover *850.00*
Block of 4 1,400. *325.00*
P# block of 12, Impt. *4,250.*
Never hinged *6,000.*

Cancellations

Blue +1.00
Purple +1.00
Red +10.00
Green +200.00
Town +2.50
Blue town +7.50
Numeral +15.00
Steamship +100.00
O80 O9 24c **brown** 725.00 100.00
dark brown 725.00 100.00
yellow brown 725.00 100.00
Never hinged —
No gum 325.00
Block of 4 3,250. —
Block of 14 —
Double transfer at top 775.00 —
Short transfer at top (pos. 61) —

Cancellations

Violet +10.00
Blue +5.00
Ultramarine +10.00
Magenta +5.00
Red +30.00
Brown +20.00
Town +15.00
Blue town +25.00
New York Foreign Mail —
O81 O9 30c **brown** 400.00 12.00
dark brown 400.00 12.00
yellow brown 400.00 12.00
Never hinged —
No gum 180.00
On cover *5,000.*
Block of 4 1,750. *500.00*
Short transfer at left top (pos. 95) 450.00 25.00
Short transfer at right top (pos. 45) 450.00 25.00
Block of 4, one pos. 45 —
Short transfer across entire top (pos. 41) 450.00 25.00

Cancellations

Purple +1.00
Blue +1.00
Magenta +1.00
Red +12.00
Green +200.00
Town +3.50
Blue town +7.50
O82 O9 90c **brown** 475.00 17.50
dark brown 475.00 17.50
yellow brown 475.00 17.50
Never hinged 950.00
No gum 225.00
Block of 4 2,400. *375.00*
P# strip of 6, Impt. —
a. Double paper — —

Cancellations

Purple +1.00
Magenta +1.00
Blue +1.00
Red +30.00
Brown +7.50
Green +200.00
Town +3.50
Blue town +7.50

WAR

O10

1873

O83 O10 1c **rose** 240.00 15.00
rose red 240.00 15.00
Never hinged *850.00*
No gum 115.00
On cover 140.00
Block of 4 1,050.
Block of 10 —
P# block of 12, Impt. *3,250.*

Cancellations

Purple +1.00
Blue +1.00
Magenta +5.00
Red +15.00
Town +3.50
Fort +100.00
Numeral +12.50
"Paid" —
O84 O10 2c **rose** 260.00 15.00
rose red 260.00 15.00
Never hinged 1,200.0
No gum 125.00
On cover 70.00
Block of 4 1,100. —
P# block of 14, Impt. *3,750.*
Ribbed paper 275.00 17.50

Cancellations

Purple +1.50
Magenta +1.50
Blue +1.50
Red +15.00
Town +4.00
Fort +100.00
O85 O10 3c **rose** 275.00 5.00
rose red 275.00 5.00
Never hinged 650.00
No gum 135.00
On cover 50.00
Block of 4 1,150. *550.00*
P# block of 14, Impt. *3,750.*

Cancellations

Purple +1.00
Blue +1.00
Ultramarine +10.00
Magenta +1.00
Red +20.00
Green +35.00
Town +1.50
Fort +250.00
"Paid" +12.00
O86 O10 6c **rose** 675.00 12.50
pale rose 675.00 12.50
Never hinged 1,450.
No gum 325.00
On cover 60.00
On cover with 6c Treasury #O75 *12,000.*
Block of 4 *3,000.* —
P# block of 12, Impt. —

Cancellations

Purple +1.50
Blue +1.50
Indigo +3.00
Magenta +3.00
Red +15.00
Town +3.50
Blue town +6.50
Fort +100.00

Examples of Nos. O114-O117 which bear Continental Bank Note Co. imprints are often mistaken for/offered as Nos. O83-O86. If there are doubts, expert opinions should be requested.

O87 O10 7c **rose** 175.00 90.00
pale rose 175.00 90.00
rose red 175.00 90.00
Never hinged 600.00
No gum 90.00
On cover *2,000.*
Block of 4 725.00 *725.00*
P# block of 8, Impt. *1,500.*
P# block of 10, Impt. *2,250.*

Cancellations

Purple +2.50
Blue +3.50
Magenta +10.00
Red +25.00
Town +7.50
Fort +300.00
O88 O10 10c **rose** 140.00 25.00
rose red 140.00 25.00
Never hinged 375.00
No gum 65.00
On cover *2,000.*
Block of 4 600.00 *900.00*
P# block of 10, Impt. *2,000.*

All examples of No. O88 show a crack at lower left. It was on the original die.

Cancellations

Purple +1.00
Blue +1.00
Town +3.50
Fort +100.00
O89 O10 12c **rose** 275.00 12.00
Never hinged 700.00
No gum 130.00
On cover 450.00
Block of 4 1,250. *550.00*
P# block of 12, Impt. *3,850.*
Never hinged *7,750.*
Ribbed paper 300.00 20.00

Cancellations

Purple +1.00
Magenta +1.00
Blue +1.00
Indigo +5.00
Red +10.00
Town +3.00
Fort +100.00
O90 O10 15c **rose** 85.00 15.00
pale rose 85.00 15.00
rose red 85.00 15.00
Never hinged 260.00
No gum 40.00
On cover 3,250.
Block of 4 375.00 —
P# block of 12, Impt. *1,100.*
Ribbed paper 92.50 20.00
Short transfer at upper right (pos. 74) —

Cancellations

Purple +1.00
Blue +1.00
Ultramarine +10.00
Magenta +3.00
Red +10.00
Town +2.50
Fort +200.00
Express Company +1,000.
O91 O10 24c **rose** 85.00 12.00
pale rose 85.00 12.00
rose red 85.00 12.00
Never hinged 190.00
No gum 40.00
On cover *20,000.*
Block of 4 375.00 *2,250.*
P# block of 10, Impt. *1,300.*

Cancellations

Purple +1.00
Blue +1.00
Magenta +5.00
Town +2.50
Fort +100.00
O92 O10 30c **rose** 130.00 12.00
rose red 130.00 12.00
Never hinged 375.00
No gum 65.00
On cover *20,000.*
Block of 4 575.00 *350.00*
P# block of 12, Impt. *1,850.*
Ribbed paper 140.00 15.00

Cancellations

Purple +1.00
Magenta +1.00
Blue +1.00
Red +20.00
Town +2.50
Fort +100.00
O93 O10 90c **rose** 225.00 60.00
rose red 225.00 60.00
Never hinged 800.00
No gum 110.00
On parcel label *3,500.*
Block of 4 975.00 *2,000.*
P# block of 12, Impt. *3,750.*

Cancellations

Purple +2.00
Magenta +2.00
Blue +2.00
Red +20.00
Numeral +40.00
Town +7.50
Fort +125.00

The used block of 4 of No. O93 is unique. It has fine centering and is valued thus.

Printed by the American Bank Note Co.

The Continental Bank Note Co. was consolidated with the American Bank Note Co. on February 4, 1879. The American Bank Note Company used many plates of the Continental Bank Note Company to print the ordinary postage, Departmental and Newspaper stamps. Therefore, stamps bearing the Continental Company's imprint were not always its product.

1879 **Soft Porous Paper**

AGRICULTURE

O94 O1 1c **yellow** (issued without gum) 5,750.
Block of 4 *30,000.*
O95 O1 3c **yellow** 550.00 150.00
Never hinged 1,250.
No gum 260.00
Block of 4 2,750. *1,400.*
P# block of 12, Impt. *7,250.*

Cancellations

Purple +5.00
Blue +5.00
Town +30.00

Two examples of the O95 plate block of 6 with imprint exist, both contained in a unique pane of 100.

INTERIOR

O96 O3 1c **vermilion** 300.00 *400.00*
pale vermilion 300.00 *400.00*
Never hinged 550.00
No gum 150.00
Block of 4 1,450. —
P# block of 12, Impt. *4,500.*
Short transfer at lower right (pos. 91) 600.00

Cancellations

Purple +5.00
Blue +5.00
Town +15.00
O97 O3 2c **vermilion** 10.00 3.00
pale vermilion 10.00 3.00
scarlet vermilion 10.00 3.00
Never hinged 17.50
No gum 4.50
On cover 150.00
Block of 4 47.50 *250.00*
P# block of 10, Impt. *200.00*
Never hinged 300.00
P# block of 12, Impt. *225.00*

Cancellations

Purple +.50
Violet +.50
Blue +.50
Red +5.00
Town +1.50
Blue town +3.00

	Railroad		+40.00
	Fort		+100.00
O98	O3 3c **vermilion**	10.00	3.00
	pale vermilion	10.00	3.00
	Never hinged	22.50	
	No gum	4.50	
	On cover		30.00
	Block of 4	47.50	—
	P# block of 10, Impt.	*225.00*	
	Cancellations		
	Purple		+.50
	Violet		+.50
	Blue		+.50
	Red		+5.00
	Town		+1.50
	Blue town		+3.00
	Railroad		+40.00
	Numeral		+5.00
O99	O3 6c **vermilion**	10.00	*12.50*
	pale vermilion	10.00	*12.50*
	scarlet vermilion	10.00	*12.50*
	Never hinged	17.50	
	No gum	4.50	
	On cover		200.00
	Block of 4	47.50	—
	P# block of 12, Impt.	*250.00*	
	Cancellations		
	Purple		+.50
	Blue		+.50
	Red		+5.00
	Town		+1.50
	Fort		+100.00
O100	O3 10c **vermilion**	110.00	75.00
	pale vermilion	110.00	75.00
	Never hinged	250.00	
	No gum	55.00	
	On cover		*1,200.*
	Block of 4	500.00	
	P# block of 12, Impt.	*1,650.*	
	Cancellations		
	Purple		+5.00
	Blue		+5.00
	Town		+10.00
O101	O3 12c **vermilion**	230.00	115.00
	pale vermilion	230.00	115.00
	Never hinged	525.00	
	No gum	115.00	
	On cover		—
	Block of 4	1,075.	*1,000.*
	Block of 6		*1,500.*
	P# block of 12, Impt.	*2,900.*	
	Short transfer at lower right (pos. 6)	—	—
	Cancellation		
	Violet		+5.00
O102	O3 15c **pale vermilion**	400.00	500.00
	Never hinged	900.00	
	No gum	200.00	
	Block of 4	1,750.	
	P# block of 12, Impt.	—	
	On cover		*6,500.*
	Double transfer	450.00	—
	Cancellations		
	Purple		+5.00
	Blue		+5.00
O103	O3 24c **pale vermilion**	4,500.	*6,250.*
	Never hinged	10,000.	
	No gum	2,200.	
	Block of 4	*22,500.*	
	P# strip of 6, Impt.	—	
	Cancellation		
	Blue		—

JUSTICE

O106	O4 3c **bluish purple**	250.00	125.00
	deep bluish purple	250.00	125.00
	Never hinged	575.00	
	No gum	120.00	
	On cover		1,250.
	Block of 4	1,150.	
	Cancellations		
	Violet		+5.00
	Blue		+5.00
	Indigo		+5.00
	Ultramarine		+10.00
O107	O4 6c **bluish purple**	475.00	300.00
	Never hinged	1,050.	
	No gum	250.00	
	On cover		*1,000.*
	Block of 4	2,250.	
	Cancellations		
	Blue		+10.00
	Indigo		+5.00
	Town		+20.00

No. O107 on cover is unique, but the stamp is damaged. It is valued thus.

POST OFFICE

O108	O6 3c **black**	30.00	10.00
	gray black	30.00	10.00
	Never hinged	70.00	
	No gum	14.00	
	On cover		—
	Block of 4	130.00	—
	P# block of 14, Impt.	*475.00*	
	Cancellations		
	Purple		+1.00
	Violet		+1.00
	Blue		+1.00
	Indigo		+10.00
	Magenta		+1.00
	Red		+20.00
	Green		+40.00
	Town		+2.00
	"Paid"		+12.00

TREASURY

O109	O9 3c **brown**	80.00	10.00
	yellow brown	80.00	10.00
	Never hinged	175.00	
	No gum	35.00	
	On cover		110.00
	Block of 4	400.00	*900.00*
	P# block of 14, Impt.	*1,450.*	
	Cancellations		
	Purple		+1.50
	Blue		+1.50
	Indigo		+3.00
	Town		+2.00
	Numeral		+7.50
O110	O9 6c **brown**	200.00	50.00
	yellow brown	200.00	50.00
	dark brown	200.00	50.00
	Never hinged	450.00	
	No gum	90.00	
	On cover		300.00
	Block of 4	950.00	—
	P# block of 12, Impt.	*2,900.*	
	Cancellations		
	Purple		+6.00
	Magenta		+6.00
	Blue		+6.00
O111	O9 10c **brown**	275.00	80.00
	yellow brown	275.00	80.00
	dark brown	275.00	80.00
	Never hinged	650.00	
	No gum	130.00	
	On cover		*750.00*
	Block of 4	1,250.	—
	P# block of 12, Impt.	*4,500.*	
	Cancellations		
	Purple		+2.50
	Blue		+2.50
	Magenta		+5.00
	Town		+7.50
O112	O9 30c **brown**	2,400.	550.00
	Never hinged	—	
	No gum	1,200.	
	Block of 4	*12,000.*	
	Short transfer at right top	2,600.	
	Cancellations		
	Blue		+25.00
	Indigo		+25.00
	Town		+50.00
O113	O9 90c **brown**	10,000.	750.00
	dark brown	10,000.	750.00
	Never hinged	—	
	No gum	5,000.	
	Block of 4	*45,000.*	
	Cancellations		
	Purple		+25.00
	Blue		+25.00
	Town		+75.00

WAR

O114	O10 1c **rose red**	7.50	4.00
	rose	7.50	4.00
	dull rose red	7.50	4.00
	brown rose	7.50	4.00
	Never hinged	15.00	
	No gum	3.50	
	On cover		55.00
	Block of 4	32.50	—
	P# block of 12, Impt.	*150.00*	
	Never hinged	*220.00*	
	Cancellations		
	Purple		+.50
	Blue		+.50
	Town		+1.00
	Fort		+100.00
O115	O10 2c **rose red**	15.00	4.00
	dark rose red	15.00	4.00
	Never hinged	30.00	
	No gum	7.00	
	On cover		40.00
	Block of 4	65.00	—
	P# block of 12, Impt.	*200.00*	
	Never hinged	*325.00*	
	Cancellations		
	Purple		+.50
	Blue		+.50
	Magenta		+.50
	Green		+35.00
	Town		+2.00
	Fort		+100.00
O116	O10 3c **rose red**	10.00	2.00
	dull rose red	10.00	2.00
	Never hinged	20.00	
	No gum	3.25	
	On cover		35.00
	Block of 4	42.50	—
	P# block of 14, Impt.	*160.00*	
	Never hinged	*260.00*	
	Double transfer	14.00	6.00
	Plate flaw at upper left (32 R 11)	—	—
a.	Imperf., pair	*5,000.*	
b.	Double impression	*7,500.*	
	Cancellations		
	Purple		+.50
	Violet		+.50
	Blue		+.50
	Ultramarine		+5.00
	Magenta		+1.00
	Red		+5.00
	Town		+1.00
	Fort		+100.00
O117	O10 6c **rose red**	12.50	3.00
	dull rose red	12.50	3.00
	dull vermilion	—	—
	Never hinged	25.00	
	No gum	6.00	
	On cover		50.00
	Block of 4	52.50	—
	P# block of 12, Impt.	*190.00*	
	Cancellations		
	Purple		+.50
	Blue		+.50
	Magenta		+1.00
	Brown		+20.00
	Town		+1.00
	Fort		+100.00
	Numeral		+7.50
O118	O10 10c **rose red**	75.00	50.00
	dull rose red	75.00	50.00
	Never hinged	150.00	
	No gum	35.00	
	On cover		*1,800.*
	Block of 4	325.00	
	P# block of 10, Impt.	*950.00*	
	Cancellations		
	Violet		+3.00
	Town		+5.00
	Fort		+100.00
O119	O10 12c **rose red**	70.00	14.00
	dull rose red	70.00	14.00
	brown rose	70.00	14.00
	Never hinged	140.00	
	No gum	35.00	
	On cover		—
	Block of 4	300.00	—
	P# block of 10, Impt.	*775.00*	
	P# block of 12, Impt.	*950.00*	
	Cancellations		
	Purple		+1.00
	Violet		+1.00
	Red		+10.00
	Green		—
	Town		+2.50
	Fort		+150.00
O120	O10 30c **rose red**	225.00	100.00
	dull rose red	225.00	100.00
	Never hinged	500.00	
	No gum	110.00	
	Block of 4	975.00	—
	P# block of 10, Impt.	*3,500.*	
	Cancellations		
	Violet		+5.00
	Town		+10.00
	Fort		+125.00

SPECIAL PRINTINGS

Special printings of Official stamps were made in 1875 at the time the other Reprints, Re-issues and Special Printings were printed. They are ungummed. Though overprinted "SPECIMEN," these stamps are Special Printings, and they are not considered to be in the same category as the stamps listed in the Specimen section of this catalogue.

Although perforated, these stamps were sometimes (but not always) cut apart with scissors. As a result the perforations may be mutilated and the design damaged. Values are for very fine stamps with intact perforations.

Number sold indicated in parentheses.

All values exist imperforate.

The "SEPCIMEN" error appears once on some panes of 100. Blocks of 4 or larger with the "SEPCIMEN" error are rare and worth much more than the value of the individual stamps.

Printing flaws which resemble broken type (but are not) are commonly found on the SPECIMEN overprint on these and other overprinted stamps. The variety listed as a "small dotted i" is actually an "i"; it is not one of the printing flaws noted in the preceding sentence. All "small dotted 'i'" varieties are on ribbed paper from the second special printings. They occur in positions 7 and 26.

Printed by the Continental Bank Note Co.
Similar to Type D, without period, 11mm long
AGRICULTURE

Overprinted in Block Letters

Thin, hard white paper
Carmine Overprint

1875 *Perf. 12*

O1S	D 1c **yellow** (10,234)	32.50	
	Block of 4	*350.00*	
	P# block of 12, Impt.	*2,600.*	
a.	"Sepcimen" error	*2,500.*	
b.	Horiz. ribbed paper (10,000)	37.50	
	Block of 4	*425.00*	
	P# strip of 6, Impt.	*1,100.*	
c.	As "b," small dotted "i" in "Specimen"	500.00	
	Block of 4, one stamp small dotted "i"	750.00	

O2S D 2c **yellow** (4,192) 55.00
Block of 4 *625.00*
P# block of 8, Impt. —
a. "Sepcimen" error *3,000.*
Block of 4, one stamp "Sepcimen" error *7,250.*
O3S D 3c **yellow** (389) 400.00
a. "Sepcimen" error *19,000.*
O4S D 6c **yellow** (373) 400.00
a. "Sepcimen" error *22,500.*
O5S D 10c **yellow** (390) 400.00
P# strip of 5, Impt. —
a. "Sepcimen" error *19,000.*
O6S D 12c **yellow** (379) 400.00
a. "Sepcimen" error *15,000.*
O7S D 15c **yellow** (370) 400.00
a. "Sepcimen" error *12,500.*
O8S D 24c **yellow** (352) 400.00
a. "Sepcimen" error *12,500.*
O9S D 30c **yellow** (354) 400.00
a. "Sepcimen" error *13,500.*

EXECUTIVE
Blue Overprint

O10S D 1c **carmine** (10,000) 32.50
Block of 4 *350.00*
P# block of 14, Impt. *20,000.*
a. Horiz. ribbed paper (10,000) 40.00
Block of 4 *375.00*
P# strip of 7, Impt. *3,250.*
b. As "a," small dotted "i" in "Specimen" 500.00
O11S D 2c **carmine** (7,430) 55.00
Block of 4 550.00
P# strip of 6, Impt. *2,500.*
Foreign entry of 6c Agriculture (pos. 40) *2,250.*
O12S D 3c **carmine** (3,735) 67.50
Block of 4 —
O13S D 6c **carmine** (3,485) 67.50
Block of 4 —
O14S D 10c **carmine** (3,461) 67.50
Block of 4 —

INTERIOR
Blue Overprint

O15S D 1c **vermilion** (7,194) 60.00
Block of 4 *650.00*
P# block of 12, impt. *3,750.*
O16S D 2c **vermilion** (1,263) 140.00
Block of 4 1,600.
P# Block of 12, Impt. *7,500.*
a. "Sepcimen" error —

The existence of a genuine example of No. O16Sa has been questioned by specialists. The editors would like to see authenticated evidence of the existence of the single reported example.

O17S D 3c **vermilion** (88) *2,500.*
O18S D 6c **vermilion** (83) *2,500.*
O19S D 10c **vermilion** (82) *2,500.*
O20S D 12c **vermilion** (75) *2,500.*
O21S D 15c **vermilion** (78) *2,500.*
Double transfer at left *3,000.*
O22S D 24c **vermilion** (77) *2,500.*
O23S D 30c **vermilion** (75) *2,500.*
O24S D 90c **vermilion** (77) *2,500.*

JUSTICE
Blue Overprint

O25S D 1c **purple** (10,000) 32.50
Block of 4 *350.00*
P# block of 12, Impt. *3,250.*
a. "Sepcimen" error *2,500.*
b. Horiz. ribbed paper (9,729) 35.00
Block of 4 *550.00*
P# block of 12, Impt. *4,000.*
c. As "b," small dotted "i" in "Specimen" 500.00
P# block of 21, two stamps small dotted "i" *6,000.*
O26S D 2c **purple** (3,395) 55.00
Block of 4 650.00
P# block of 12, Impt. *5,500.*
a. "Sepcimen" error *3,500.*
Block of 4, one stamp "Sepcimen" error *9,750.*
O27S D 3c **purple** (178) 1,250.
Plate scratches —
a. "Sepcimen" error *11,000.*
O28S D 6c **purple** (163) 1,250.
O29S D 10c **purple** (163) 1,250.
O30S D 12c **purple** (154) 1,250.
a. "Sepcimen" error *19,000.*
O31S D 15c **purple** (157) 1,250.
a. "Sepcimen" error *25,000.*
O32S D 24c **purple** (150) 1,250.
a. "Sepcimen" error *20,000.*
O33S D 30c **purple** (150) 1,250.
a. "Sepcimen" error *15,000.*
O34S D 90c **purple** (152) 1,250.

NAVY
Carmine Overprint

O35S D 1c **ultramarine** (10,000) 35.00
Block of 4 *375.00*
P# strip of 6, Impt. *750.00*
a. "Sepcimen" error *2,750.*
Block of 4, one stamp "Sepcimen" error *6,250.*
b. Double "Specimen" overprint *1,900.*
O36S D 2c **ultramarine** (1,748) 75.00
Block of 4 *750.00*
P# strip of 6, Impt. *1,600.*
a. "Sepcimen" error *4,500.*
Block of 4, one stamp "Sepcimen" error *10,500.*
O37S D 3c **ultramarine** (126) 1,750.
O38S D 6c **ultramarine** (116) 1,750.
Vertical line through "N" of "Navy" *2,100.*
O39S D 7c **ultramarine** (501) 550.00
Block of 4 *5,000.*
P# strip of 5, Impt. *10,000.*
a. "Sepcimen" error *10,000.*
Block of 4, one stamp "Sepcimen" error *30,000.*
O40S D 10c **ultramarine** (112) 1,750.
a. "Sepcimen" error *17,500.*
O41S D 12c **ultramarine** (107) 1,750.
Double transfer at left side, pos. 50 —
a. "Sepcimen" error *21,000.*
O42S D 15c **ultramarine** (107) 1,750.
a. "Sepcimen" error *16,000.*
O43S D 24c **ultramarine** (106) 1,750.
a. "Sepcimen" error *15,000.*
O44S D 30c **ultramarine** (104) 1,750.
Double transfer —
a. "Sepcimen" error *17,500.*
O45S D 90c **ultramarine** (102) 1,750.

POST OFFICE
Carmine Overprint

O47S D 1c **black** (6,015) 45.00
Block of 4 *475.00*
P# block of 12, Impt. *4,500.*
P# block of 14, Impt. *4,750.*
a. "Sepcimen" error *3,250.*
Block of 4, one stamp "SEPCIMEN" error *7,000.*
b. Inverted overprint *2,500.*
O48S D 2c **black** (590) 325.00
Block of 4 *3,250.*
a. "Sepcimen" error *15,000.*
Block of 4, one stamp "Sepcimen" error *30,000.*
O49S D 3c **black** (91) 1,600.
a. "Sepcimen" error *37,500.*
O50S D 6c **black** (87) 1,600.
O51S D 10c **black** (177) 1,000.
a. "Sepcimen" error *15,000.*
O52S D 12c **black** (93) 1,600.
O53S D 15c **black** (82) 1,600.
a. "Sepcimen" error *26,000.*
O54S D 24c **black** (84) 1,600.
a. "Sepcimen" error *22,000.*
O55S D 30c **black** (81) 1,600.
O56S D 90c **black** (82) 1,600.
a. "Sepcimen" error *25,000.*

STATE
Carmine Overprint

O57S D 1c **bluish green** (10,000) 32.50
Block of 4 *250.00*
a. "Sepcimen" error *2,500.*
Block of 4, one stamp "Sepcimen" error *6,000.*
b. Horiz. ribbed paper (10,000) 35.00
Block of 4 *425.00*
c. As "b," small dotted "i" in "Specimen" 650.00
d. Double "Specimen" overprint *3,850.*
Block of 4 —
O58S D 2c **bluish green** (5,145) 90.00
Block of 4 *850.00*
Double transfer at bottom (pos. 98) *750.00*
a. "Sepcimen" error *2,500.*
Block of 4, one stamp "Sepcimen" error *17,500.*
O59S D 3c **bluish green** (793) 140.00
Block of 4 —
a. "Sepcimen" error *7,000.*
Block of 4, one stamp "Sepcimen" error *11,000.*
O60S D 6c **bluish green** (467) 350.00
Foreign entry of 6c Executive *600.00*
a. "Sepcimen" error *12,500.*
O61S D 7c **bluish green** (791) 175.00
Block of 4 *1,500.*
a. "Sepcimen" error *9,000.*
Block of 4, one stamp "Sepcimen" error *21,500.*
O62S D 10c **bluish green** (346) 550.00
Short transfer, pos. 34 *2,200.*
a. "Sepcimen" error *27,500.*
O63S D 12c **bluish green** (280) 550.00
a. "Sepcimen" error *19,000.*
O64S D 15c **bluish green** (257) 600.00
O65S D 24c **bluish green** (253) 600.00
a. "Sepcimen" error *25,000.*
O66S D 30c **bluish green** (249) 600.00
a. "Sepcimen" error *27,500.*
O67S D 90c **bluish green** (245) 600.00
a. "Sepcimen" error *27,500.*
O68S D $2 **green & black** (32) *15,000.*
O69S D $5 **green & black** (12) *67,500.*
O70S D $10 **green & black** (8) *100,000.*
O71S D $20 **green & black** (7) *145,000.*

TREASURY
Blue Overprint

O72S D 1c **dark brown** (2,185) 80.00
Block of 4 *975.00*
Double transfer —
O73S D 2c **dark brown** (309) 450.00
Block of 4 *3,250.*
P# block of 14, Impt. *17,500.*

The only two recorded plate blocks of No. O73S are contained in a unique left pane of 100 stamps.

O74S D 3c **dark brown** (84) 1,600.
O75S D 6c **dark brown** (85) 1,600.
O76S D 7c **dark brown** (198) 950.00
Block of 4 9,000.
P# block of 12, Impt. 30,000.

The only recorded plate block of No. O76S is contained in a half sheet of 50 stamps.

O77S D 10c **dark brown** (82) 1,600.
O78S D 12c **dark brown** (75) 1,600.
O79S D 15c **dark brown** (75) 1,600.
O80S D 24c **dark brown** (99) 1,600.
O81S D 30c **dark brown** (74) 1,600.
Short transfer at left top (pos. 95) (1) —
Short transfer at right top (pos. 45) (1) —
O82S D 90c **dark brown** (72) 1,650.

WAR
Blue Overprint

O83S D 1c **deep rose** (9,610) 35.00
Block of 4 *375.00*
P# strip of 6, Impt. *1,300.*
a. "Sepcimen" error *3,000.*
Block of 4, one stamp "Sepcimen" error *7,500.*
O84S D 2c **deep rose** (1,618) 125.00
Block of 4 *1,400.*
P# block of 12 *9,000.*
a. "Sepcimen" error *3,500.*
Block of 4, one stamp "Sepcimen" error *9,750.*
O85S D 3c **deep rose** (118) 1,400.
a. "Sepcimen" error *30,000.*
O86S D 6c **deep rose** (111) 1,400.
a. "Sepcimen" error *32,000.*
O87S D 7c **deep rose** (539) 425.00
Block of 4 *2,750.*
a. "Sepcimen" error *17,500.*
O88S D 10c **deep rose** (119) 1,400.
a. "Sepcimen" error *27,500.*
O89S D 12c **deep rose** (105) 1,400.
a. "Sepcimen" error *32,000.*
O90S D 15c **deep rose** (105) 1,400.
a. "Sepcimen" error *30,000.*
O91S D 24c **deep rose** (106) 1,400.
a. "Sepcimen" error *30,000.*
O92S D 30c **deep rose** (104) 1,400.
a. "Sepcimen" error *30,000.*
O93S D 90c **deep rose** (106) 1,400.
a. "Sepcimen" error *30,000.*

EXECUTIVE
Printed by the American Bank Note Co.
Soft Porous Paper

1881 **Blue Overprint**

O10xS D 1c **violet rose** (4,652) 95.00
Block of 4 *1,100.*
P# block of 14, Impt. *32,500.*

NAVY
Carmine Overprint

O35xS D 1c **gray blue** (4,182) 100.00
deep blue 100.00
Block of 4 *1,150.*
P# block of 12, Impt. *8,000.*
a. Double overprint 1,200.

STATE

O57xS D 1c **yellow green** (1,672) 180.00
Block of 4 *2,500.*
P# strip of 6, Impt. *3,000.*

OFFICIAL POSTAL SAVINGS MAIL

The Act of Congress, approved June 25, 1910, establishing postal savings depositories, provided:

"Sec. 2. That the Postmaster General is hereby directed to prepare and issue special stamps of the necessary denominations for use, in lieu of penalty or franked envelopes, in the transmittal of free mail resulting from the administration of this act."

The use of postal savings official stamps was discontinued by the Act of Congress, approved September 23, 1914. Postmasters were notified of the discontinuance in mid-October 1914. The unused stamps in the hands of postmasters were returned and destroyed.

O11

Printed by the Bureau of Engraving & Printing

1910-11 **Engr.** **Wmk. 191**

O121 O11 2c **black,** *Dec. 22, 1910* 17.50 2.00
Never hinged 40.00
On cover 12.50
Block of 4 (2mm spacing) 80.00 11.00
Block of 4 (3mm spacing) 77.50 10.00
P# block of 6, Impt. & Star 350.00
Double transfer 22.50 4.00
O122 O11 50c **dark green,** *Feb. 1, 1911* 175.00 60.00
Never hinged 425.00
On cover 225.00

	Block of 4 (2mm spacing)	675.00	300.00
	Block of 4 (3mm spacing)	650.00	300.00
	Margin block of 4, arrow	675.00	
	P# block of 6, Impt. & Star	2,400.	
	Never hinged	*3,500.*	
O123	O11 $1 **ultramarine,** *Feb. 1, 1911*	200.00	15.00
	Never hinged	450.00	
	On cover		110.00
	Block of 4 (2mm spacing)	850.00	75.00
	Block of 4 (3mm spacing)	825.00	75.00
	Margin block of 4, arrow	850.00	
	P# block of 6, Impt. & Star	2,400.	—

Wmk. 190

O124	O11 1c **dark violet,** *Mar. 27, 1911*	12.50	2.00
	Never hinged	27.50	
	On cover		15.00
	Block of 4 (2mm spacing)	55.00	9.00
	Block of 4 (3mm spacing)	52.50	8.50
	P# block of 6, Impt. & Star	190.00	—
	Never hinged	350.00	
O125	O11 2c **black**	65.00	7.00
	Never hinged	150.00	
	On cover		25.00
	Block of 4 (2mm spacing)	240.00	32.50
	Block of 4 (3mm spacing)	225.00	32.50
	P# block of 6, Impt. & Star	700.00	
	Double transfer	60.00	8.00
O126	O11 10c **carmine,** *Feb. 1, 1911*	20.00	2.00
	Never hinged	50.00	
	On cover		20.00
	Block of 4 (2mm spacing)	87.50	30.00
	Block of 4 (3mm spacing)	82.50	10.00
	P# block of 6, Impt. & Star	370.00	
	Double transfer	25.00	3.50

Catalogue values for unused stamps in this section, from this point to the end, are for Never Hinged items.

Catalogue values for used stamps are for regularly used examples, not for examples removed from first day covers.

From No. O127 onward, all official stamps are tagged unless noted.

OFFICIAL MAIL

O12

Designed by Bradbury Thompson.

Engraved

1983, Jan. 12-1985 Unwmk. *Perf. 11*

O127	O12 1c **red, blue & black**	.25	.25
	FDC, Washington, DC		1.00
	P# block of 4, UL or UR	.25	
O128	O12 4c **red, blue & black**	.25	.25
	FDC, Washington, DC		1.00
	P# block of 4, LR only	.40	
O129	O12 13c **red, blue & black**	.50	*15.00*
	FDC, Washington, DC		1.00
	P# block of 4, UR only	2.25	
O129A	O12 14c **red, blue & black,** *May 15, 1985*	.45	.50
	FDC, Washington, DC		1.00
	Zip-copyright block of 6	2.90	
O130	O12 17c **red, blue & black**	.55	.40
	FDC, Washington, DC		1.00
	P# block of 4, LL only	2.50	
O132	O12 $1 **red, blue & black**	2.25	1.00
	FDC, Washington, DC		2.25
	P# block of 4, UL only	10.00	
O133	O12 $5 **red, blue & black**	9.50	*20.00*
	FDC, Washington, DC		12.50
	P# block of 4, LL only	45.00	
	Nos. O127-O133 (7)	13.75	37.40

No. O129A does not have a "c" after the "14."

COIL STAMPS

Perf. 10 Vert.

O135	O12 20c **red, blue & black**	1.75	2.00
	FDC, Washington, DC		1.00
	Pair	3.50	4.00
	P# strip of 3, P# 1	7.00	
	P# strip of 5, P# 1	40.00	
	P# single, #1	—	12.50
a.	Imperf., pair	*750.00*	
b.	Tagging omitted	—	—
O136	O12 22c **red, blue & blk, low gloss gum,** *May 15, 1985*	1.00	*2.00*
	FDC, Washington, DC		1.00
	Pair	2.00	*4.00*
	Dull finish gum	*50.00*	
a.	Tagging omitted		—
b.	Imperf, pair		*1,750.*

Inscribed: Postal Card Rate D

1985, Feb. 4 *Perf. 11*

O138	O12 (14c) **red, blue & black**	5.00	*15.00*
	FDC, Washington, DC		1.00
	P# block of 4, LR only	27.50	—

Frame line completely around blue design — O13

Inscribed: No. O139, Domestic Letter Rate D; No. O140, Domestic Mail E.

COIL STAMPS

1985-88 Litho., Engr. (#O139) *Perf. 10 Vert.*

O138A	O13 15c **red, blue & blk,** *June 11, 1988*	.50	.50
	FDC, Corpus Christi, TX		1.25
	Pair	1.00	1.00
O138B	O13 20c **red, blue & blk,** *May 19, 1988*	.50	.30
	FDC, Washington		1.25
	Pair	1.00	.60
O139	O12 (22c) **red, blue & blk,** *Feb. 4*	5.25	*20.00*
	FDC, Washington, DC		1.00
	Pair	10.50	—
	P# strip of 3, P# 1	15.00	
	P# strip of 5, P# 1	30.00	
	P# single, #1	—	27.50
O140	O13 (25c) **red, blue & black,** *Mar. 22, 1988*	.75	*2.00*
	FDC, Washington		1.25
	Pair	1.50	—
O141	O13 25c **red, blue & blk,** *June 11, 1988*	.65	.50
	FDC, Corpus Christi, TX		1.25
	Pair	1.30	1.00
a.	Imperf., pair	*700.00*	—
	Nos. O138A-O141 (5)	7.65	*23.30*

First day cancellation was applied to 137,721 covers bearing Nos. O138A and O141.

Plates of 400 in four panes of 100.

1989, July 5 Litho. *Perf. 11*

O143	O13 1c **red, blue & black**	.25	.25
	FDC, Washington, DC		1.25

On No. O143, the denomination is shown as "1". See No. O154.

Type of 1985 and

O14

COIL STAMPS

1991 Litho. *Perf. 10 Vert.*

O144	O14 (29c) **red, blue & blk,** *Jan. 22*	.80	.50
	FDC, Washington, DC		1.25
	Pair	1.60	—
O145	O13 29c **red, blue & blk,** *May 24*	.70	.30
	FDC, Seattle, WA		1.25
	Pair	1.40	.60

Plates of 400 in four panes of 100.

1991-93 Litho. *Perf. 11*

O146	O13 4c **red, blue & blk,** *Apr. 6*	.25	.30
	FDC, Oklahoma City, OK		1.25
O146A	O13 10c **red, blue & black,** *Oct. 19, 1993*	.30	.30
	FDC, Washington, DC		1.25
O147	O13 19c **red, blue & blk,** *May 24*	.40	.50
	FDC, Seattle, WA		1.25
O148	O13 23c **red, blue & blk,** *May 24*	.50	.30
	FDC, Seattle, WA		1.25
	Horiz. pair with full vert. gutter between	—	
	Vert. pair with full horiz. gutter between	—	

See No. O156 for 23c with microscopic text below eagle. Imperfs of No. O148 are printer's waste.

Perf. 11¼

O151	O13 $1 **red, blue & black,** *Sept. 1993*	5.00	.75
	Nos. O146-O151 (5)	6.45	2.15

COIL STAMPS

Inscribed: No. O152, For U.S. addresses only G.

Perf. 9.8 Vert.

O152	O14 (32c) **red, blue & black,** *Dec. 13, 1994*	.65	.50
	FDC, Washington, DC		1.25
	Pair	1.30	—
O153	O13 32c **red, blue & black,** *May 9, 1995*	1.50	.50
	FDC, Washington, DC		1.25
	Pair	3.00	—

Nos. O146A, O151, O153 have a line of microscopic text below the eagle.

1995, May 9 Litho. Untagged *Perf. 11.2*

O154	O13 1c **red, blue & black**	.25	.50
	FDC, Washington, DC		1.25

Denomination on No. O154 has a cent sign. See No. O143.

O155	O13 20c **red, blue & black**	.55	.50
	FDC, Washington, DC		1.25
O156	O13 23c **red, blue & black**	.60	.50
	FDC, Washington, DC		1.25

COIL STAMP

1999, Oct. 8 Litho. *Perf. 9¾ Vert.*

O157	O13 33c **red, blue & black**	2.25	—
	FDC, Washington, DC		1.25
	Pair	4.50	—

Type of 1985

COIL STAMP

2001, Feb. 27 Litho. *Perf. 9¾ Vert.*

O158	O13 34c **red, blue & black**	2.25	.50
	FDC, Washington, DC		1.25
	Pair	4.50	—

Nos. O154-O158 have a line of microscopic text below the eagle.

Type of 1985

COIL STAMP

2002, Aug. 2 Photo. *Perf. 10 Vert.*

O159	O13 37c **red, blue & black**	.75	.50
	First day cover, Washington, DC		1.25
	First day cover, any other city		1.25
	Pair	1.50	—
	P# strip of 5, P#S111	8.00	—
	P# single, same #	—	7.00

Type of 1985

COIL STAMP

2006, Mar. 8 Photo. *Perf. 10 Vert.*

O160	O13 39c **red, blue & black**	1.00	*1.00*
	First day cover, Washington, DC		1.25
	First day cover, any other city		1.25
	Pair	1.60	—
	P# strip of 5, #S111	9.00	—
	P# single, #S111	—	6.00

Type of 1988

Designed by Bradbury Thompson. Printed by Sterling Sommer for Ashton-Potter (USA) Ltd.

Sheets of 240 in 12 panes of 20.

2006, Sept. 29 Litho. *Perf. 11¼*

O161	O13 $1 **red, blue & black**	5.00	*1.25*
	First day cover, Washington, DC		3.25
	First day cover, any other city		3.25
	Pane of 20	100.00	

No. O161 has a solid blue background. No. O151 has a background of crosshatched lines.

Type of 1985

COIL STAMP

2007, June 25 Litho. *Perf. 9¾*

O162	O13 41c **red, blue & black**	1.00	*1.00*
	First day cover, Kansas City, MO		2.10
	Pair	2.00	—
	P# strip of 5, #S111	9.50	—
	P# single, #S111	—	9.50

Nos. O159-O162 have solid blue backgrounds. Nos. O138A-O158 have a background of crosshatched lines.

Type of 1985

Designed by Bradbury Thompson. Printed by Banknote Corporation of America for Sennett Security Products.

Serpentine Die Cut 11½x10¾

2009, Feb. 24 Litho. Untagged

Self-Adhesive

O163	O13 1c **red, blue & black**	.25	*.40*
	First day cover, Washington, DC		2.10
	Pane of 20	1.00	

NEWSPAPER AND PERIODICAL STAMPS

First issued in September 1865 for prepayment of postage on bulk shipments of newspapers and periodicals. From 1875 on, the stamps were affixed to pages of receipt books, sometimes canceled, and retained by the post office.

Virtually all used stamps of Nos. PR1-PR4 are canceled by blue brush strokes and have faults such as tears, stains, creases, etc. All are rare. Most used stamps of Nos. PR9-PR32, PR57-PR79 and PR81-PR89 are pen canceled (or uncanceled), with many of Nos. PR9-PR32 also known canceled by a thick blue brush stroke or a handstamp cork or target cancellation. Used values for Nos. PR90-PR125 are for stamps with legible handstamp cancellations.

Discontinued on July 1, 1898.

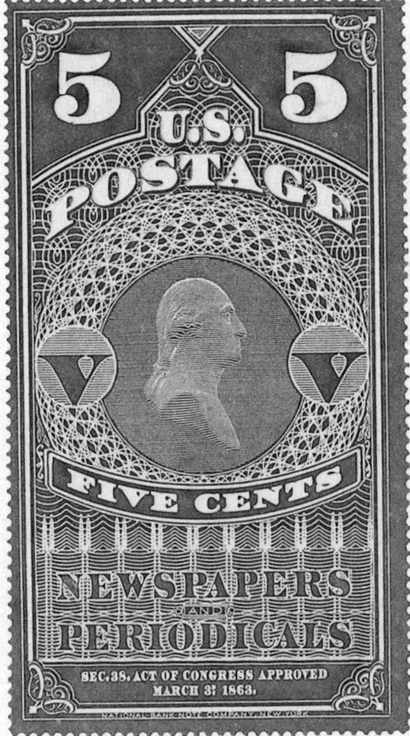

Washington — N1

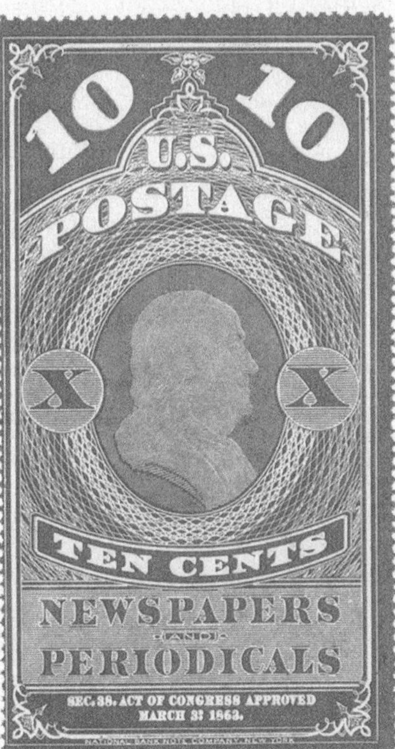

Franklin — N2

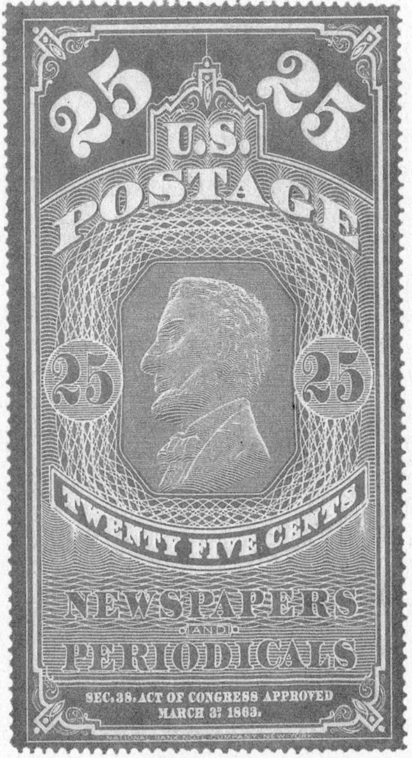

Lincoln — N3

Values for Nos. PR1-PR8 are for examples with perforations on all four sides. Examples with natural straight edges sell for somewhat less. Some panes were fully perforated, while others have natural straight edges either at top or bottom affecting five stamps in the pane of ten.

Printed by the National Bank Note Co.
Plates of 20 subjects in two panes of 10 each.
Thin hard paper, without gum
Size of design: 51x95mm

Typographed and Embossed

1865 **Unwmk.** *Perf. 12*

Colored Border

PR1	N1 5c **dark blue**	750.00	*2,000.*
	blue	750.00	*2,000.*
	Block of 4	3,750.	—
a.	5c **light blue**	1,350.	*4,250.*
PR2	N2 10c **blue green**	300.00	*2,250.*
a.	10c **green**	300.00	*2,250.*
	Block of 4	1,400.	—
b.	Pelure paper	400.00	*2,000.*
PR3	N3 25c **orange red**	400.00	*2,500.*
	Block of 4	1,700.	—
a.	25c **carmine red**	475.00	*2,500.*
	Block of 4	2,000.	—
b.	Pelure paper	500.00	

Nos. PR1-PR3 used are valued with faults.

White Border

Yellowish paper

PR4	N1 5c **light blue**	900.00	*5,000.*
	blue	900.00	—
	Block of 4	4,500.	
a.	5c **dark blue**	900.00	—
b.	Pelure paper	975.00	—

No. PR4 used is valued with faults.

REPRINTS of 1865 ISSUE

Printed by the Continental Bank Note Co. using the original National Bank Note Co. plates

1875 *Perf. 12*

Hard white paper, without gum

5c White Border, 10c and 25c Colored Border

PR5	N1 5c **dull blue** *(10,000)*	225.00
	dark blue	225.00
	Block of 4	1,000.
a.	Printed on both sides	*5,750.*
PR6	N2 10c **dark bluish green** *(7765)*	250.00
	deep green	250.00
	Block of 4	1,075.
a.	Printed on both sides	*4,250.*
PR7	N3 25c **dark carmine** *(6684)*	300.00
	dark carmine red	300.00
	Block of 4	1,350.
	Nos. PR5-PR7 (3)	775.00

750 examples of each value, which were remainders from the regular issue, were sold as reprints because of delays in obtaining Nos. PR5-PR7. These remainders cannot be distinguished from Nos. PR2-PR4, and are not included in the reprint quantities.

The Continental Bank Note Co. made another special printing from new plates, which did not have the colored border. These exist imperforate and perforated, but they were not regularly issued. Value, imperf. set $3,250.

On No. PR5, there is no thin line of color in the second white area on each side of the stamp. On No. PR8, there is often a thin line of color in this area, but not all examples of No. PR8 show this line (see illustration below). Expertization is based on color and paper.

#PR5

#PR8

Printed by the American Bank Note Co.
Soft porous paper, without gum

1881 **White Border**

PR8	N1 5c **dark blue** (5645)	750.
	Block of 4	3,500.

Statue of Freedom on Capitol Dome, by Thomas Crawford — N4

"Justice" — N5

Ceres — N6

"Victory" — N7

Clio — N8

Minerva — N9

Vesta — N10

"Peace" — N11

"Commerce" — N12

Hebe — N13

Indian Maiden — N14

Values for used examples of Nos. PR9-PR113 are for fine-very fine examples for denominations to $3, and fine for denominations of $5 or higher. Used examples of some Scott numbers might not exist without faults.

Printed by the Continental Bank Note Co.
Plates of 100 subjects in two panes of 50 each

Thin hard paper

Size of design: 24x35mm

1875, Jan. 1 Engr. *Perf. 12*

No.	Type	Description	Unused	Used
PR9	N4	2c **black**	350.00	45.00
		gray black	350.00	40.00
		greenish black	350.00	40.00
		No gum	140.00	
		Handstamp or blue brush cancel		125.00
		Block of 4	1,500.	250.00
PR10	N4	3c **black**	350.00	50.00
		gray black	350.00	45.00
		No gum	140.00	
		Handstamp or blue brush cancel		125.00
		Block of 4	1,500.	225.00
PR11	N4	4c **black**	350.00	45.00
		gray black	350.00	40.00
		greenish black	350.00	40.00
		No gum	140.00	
		Handstamp or blue brush cancel		125.00
		Block of 4	1,500.	
PR12	N4	6c **black**	350.00	50.00
		gray black	350.00	45.00
		greenish black	350.00	45.00
		No gum	140.00	
		Handstamp or blue brush cancel		125.00
		Block of 4	1,500.	
PR13	N4	8c **black**	350.00	75.00
		gray black	350.00	65.00
		greenish black	350.00	65.00
		No gum	140.00	
		Handstamp or blue brush cancel		200.00
PR14	N4	9c **black**	600.00	140.00
		gray black	600.00	125.00
		No gum	225.00	
		Handstamp or blue brush cancel		400.00
		Double transfer at top	650.00	140.00
PR15	N4	10c **black**	375.00	67.50
		gray black	375.00	60.00
		greenish black	375.00	60.00
		No gum	135.00	
		Handstamp or blue brush cancel		150.00
		Block of 4	1,700.	
PR16	N5	12c **rose**	800.00	110.00
		pale rose	800.00	100.00
		No gum	325.00	
		Handstamp or blue brush cancel		325.00
PR17	N5	24c **rose**	1,000.	175.00
		pale rose	1,000.	125.00
		No gum	400.00	
		Handstamp or blue brush cancel		375.00
		Paper with silk fibers	*2,000.*	—
PR18	N5	36c **rose**	1,000.	200.00
		pale rose	1,000.	150.00
		No gum	400.00	
		Handstamp or blue brush cancel		300.00
PR19	N5	48c **rose**	1,250.	500.00
		pale rose	1,250.	400.00
		No gum	450.00	
		Handstamp or blue brush cancel		600.00
		Horiz. ribbed paper		—
PR20	N5	60c **rose**	1,500.	125.00
		pale rose	1,500.	115.00
		No gum	550.00	
		Handstamp or blue brush cancel		225.00
PR21	N5	72c **rose**	1,500.	450.00
		pale rose	1,500.	375.00
		No gum	550.00	
		Handstamp or blue brush cancel		800.00
PR22	N5	84c **rose**	1,850.	450.00
		pale rose	1,850.	375.00
		No gum	650.00	
		Handstamp or blue brush cancel		1,350.
PR23	N5	96c **rose**	*2,250.*	300.00
		pale rose	*2,250.*	250.00
		No gum	875.00	
		Handstamp or blue brush cancel		1,000.
PR24	N6	$1.92 **dark brown**	*2,250.*	300.00
		No gum	825.00	
		Handstamp or blue brush cancel		850.00
PR25	N7	$3 **vermilion**	2,500.	600.00
		No gum	975.00	
		Handstamp or blue brush cancel		1,300.
PR26	N8	$6 **ultramarine**	*4,250.*	650.00
		dull ultramarine	*4,250.*	650.00
		No gum	1,700.	
		Handstamp or blue brush cancel		2,000.
PR27	N9	$9 **yellow orange**	4,500.	*2,400.*
		No gum	1,750.	
		Handstamp or blue brush cancel		—
PR28	N10	$12 **blue green**	4,750.	*1,250.*
		No gum	1,850.	
		Handstamp or blue brush cancel		—
PR29	N11	$24 **dark gray violet**	4,750.	*1,400.*
		No gum	1,850.	
		Handstamp or blue brush cancel		—
PR30	N12	$36 **brown rose**	*5,500.*	*1,600.*
		No gum	2,250.	
		Handstamp or blue brush cancel		—
PR31	N13	$48 **red brown**	*7,500.*	*1,800.*
		No gum	2,750.	
		Handstamp or blue brush cancel		—
PR32	N14	$60 **violet**	*7,000.*	*2,000.*
		No gum	2,600.	
		Handstamp or blue brush cancel		—

SPECIAL PRINTING of 1875 ISSUE

Printed by the Continental Bank Note Co.
Hard white paper, without gum

1875 *Perf. 12*

No.	Type	Description	Value
PR33	N4	2c **gray black** *(5,000)*	700.00
		Block of 4	3,250.
a.		Horizontally ribbed paper (10,000)	500.00
PR34	N4	3c **gray black** *(5,000)*	700.00
		Block of 4	3,250.
a.		Horizontally ribbed paper (1,952)	550.00
PR35	N4	4c **gray black** *(4451)*	700.00
		Block of 4	3,250.
		Horizontally ribbed paper	1,000.
PR36	N4	6c **gray black** *(2348)*	1,000.
PR37	N4	8c **gray black** *(1930)*	1,100.
PR38	N4	9c **gray black** *(1795)*	1,200.
PR39	N4	10c **gray black** *(1499)*	1,500.
PR40	N5	12c **pale rose** *(1313)*	1,600.
PR41	N5	24c **pale rose** *(411)*	2,250.
PR42	N5	36c **pale rose** *(330)*	3,000.
PR43	N5	48c **pale rose** *(268)*	4,000.
PR44	N5	60c **pale rose** *(222)*	4,750.
PR45	N5	72c **pale rose** *(174)*	4,500.
PR46	N5	84c **pale rose** *(164)*	5,750.
PR47	N5	96c **pale rose** *(141)*	*10,000.*
PR48	N6	$1.92 **dark brown** *(41)*	*22,500.*
PR49	N7	$3 **vermilion** *(20)*	*42,500.*
PR50	N8	$6 **ultramarine** *(14)*	*70,000.*
PR51	N9	$9 **yellow orange** *(4)*	*350,000.*
PR52	N10	$12 **blue green** *(5)*	*225,000.*
PR53	N11	$24 **dark gray violet** *(2)*	*500,000.*
PR54	N12	$36 **brown rose** *(2)*	*400,000.*
PR55	N13	$48 **red brown** *(1)*	—
PR56	N14	$60 **violet** *(1)*	—

Nos. PR50 and PR52 are valued in the grade of fine.

Although four examples of No. PR51 were sold, only one is currently documented.

Although two examples of No. PR53 were sold, only one is currently documented.

No. PR54 is valued in the grade of fine. Although two stamps were sold, only one is currently documented.

All values of this issue, Nos. PR33 to PR56, exist imperforate but were not regularly issued thus. Value, set $60,000.

Numbers in parentheses are quantities sold.

Printed by the American Bank Note Co.
Soft porous paper

1879 Unwmk. *Perf. 12*

No.	Type	Description	Unused	Used
PR57	N4	2c **black**	75.00	17.50
		gray black	75.00	17.50
		greenish black	75.00	17.50
		No gum	30.00	
		Handstamp cancel		50.00
		Block of 4	350.00	
		Double transfer at top	85.00	25.00
		Cracked plate	—	—
PR58	N4	3c **black**	85.00	22.50
		gray black	85.00	22.50
		intense black	85.00	22.50
		No gum	35.00	
		Handstamp cancel		75.00
		Block of 4	350.00	
		Double transfer at top	95.00	30.00
PR59	N4	4c **black**	85.00	22.50
		gray black	85.00	22.50
		intense black	85.00	22.50
		greenish black	85.00	22.50
		No gum	35.00	
		Handstamp cancel		75.00
		Block of 4	350.00	
		Double transfer at top	95.00	30.00
a.		Double paper	—	
PR60	N4	6c **black**	125.00	40.00
		gray black	125.00	40.00
		intense black	125.00	40.00
		greenish black	125.00	40.00
		No gum	50.00	
		Handstamp cancel		150.00
		Block of 4	600.00	
		Double transfer at top	140.00	50.00
PR61	N4	8c **black**	135.00	40.00
		gray black	135.00	40.00
		greenish black	135.00	40.00
		No gum	55.00	
		Handstamp cancel		150.00
		Block of 4	625.00	
		Double transfer at top	150.00	47.50
PR62	N4	10c **black**	135.00	40.00
		gray black	135.00	40.00
		greenish black	135.00	40.00
		No gum	55.00	
		Handstamp cancel		150.00
		Block of 4	625.00	
		Double transfer at top	150.00	
PR63	N5	12c **red**	500.00	140.00
		No gum	210.00	
		Handstamp cancel		350.00
		Block of 4	2,250.	
PR64	N5	24c **red**	500.00	140.00
		No gum	210.00	
		Handstamp cancel		350.00
		Block of 4	2,250.	
PR65	N5	36c **red**	1,000.	375.00
		No gum	475.00	
		Handstamp cancel		750.00
		Block of 4	4,500.	
PR66	N5	48c **red**	1,000.	350.00
		No gum	450.00	
		Handstamp cancel		750.00
PR67	N5	60c **red**	1,250.	325.00
		No gum	550.00	
		Handstamp cancel		700.00
		Block of 4	4,500.	
a.		Imperf., pair	*4,000.*	
PR68	N5	72c **red**	1,500.	475.00
		No gum	700.00	
		Handstamp cancel		1,000.
PR69	N5	84c **red**	1,250.	400.00
		No gum	575.00	
		Handstamp cancel		850.00
		Block of 4	—	
PR70	N5	96c **red**	1,500.	325.00
		No gum	700.00	
		Handstamp cancel		700.00
		Block of 4	6,750.	
PR71	N6	$1.92 **pale brown**	550.00	200.00
		brown	550.00	200.00
		No gum	225.00	
		Handstamp cancel		500.00
		Block of 4	2,500.	
		Cracked plate	600.00	
PR72	N7	$3 **red vermilion**	625.00	230.00
		No gum	250.00	
		Handstamp cancel		550.00
		Block of 4	2,850.	
PR73	N8	$6 **blue**	1,050.	350.00
		ultramarine	1,100.	350.00
		No gum	400.00	
		Handstamp cancel		1,250.
PR74	N9	$9 **orange**	800.00	260.00
		No gum	325.00	
		Handstamp cancel		750.00
PR75	N10	$12 **yellow green**	850.00	260.00
		No gum	325.00	
		Handstamp cancel		*5,000.*
PR76	N11	$24 **dark violet**	800.00	350.00
		No gum	300.00	
		Handstamp cancel		1,000.
PR77	N12	$36 **Indian red**	850.00	400.00
		No gum	350.00	
		Handstamp cancel		1,250.

No.	Type	Description	Unused	Used
PR78	N13	$48 **yellow brown**	900.00	525.00
		No gum	350.00	
		Handstamp cancel		*3,000.*
PR79	N14	$60 **purple**	850.00	450.00
		bright purple	850.00	450.00
		No gum	350.00	
		Handstamp cancel		1,250.

SPECIAL PRINTING of 1879 ISSUE

Printed by the American Bank Note Co.

Without gum

1883

No.	Type	Description	Unused	Used
PR80	N4	2c **intense black** (4,514)	1,750.	
		Block of 4	7,500.	

REGULAR ISSUE

Printed by the American Bank Note Co.

With gum

1885 Unwmk. *Perf. 12*

No.	Type	Description	Unused	Used
PR81	N4	1c **black**, *July 1, 1885*	95.00	14.00
		gray black	95.00	14.00
		intense black	95.00	14.00
		Never hinged	225.00	
		No gum	42.50	
		Handstamp cancel		35.00
		Block of 4	425.00	
		Block of 4, P#482, Impt.	650.00	
		Never hinged	1,000.	
		Double transfer at top	105.00	17.50
PR82	N5	12c **carmine**	200.00	35.00
		deep carmine	200.00	35.00
		rose carmine	200.00	35.00
		Never hinged	450.00	
		No gum	85.00	
		Handstamp cancel		105.00
		Block of 4	975.00	
		Plate crack (pos. 41)	*260.00*	
PR83	N5	24c **carmine**	225.00	35.00
		deep carmine	225.00	35.00
		rose carmine	225.00	35.00
		Never hinged	500.00	
		No gum	95.00	
		Handstamp cancel		200.00
		Block of 4	1,100.	
PR84	N5	36c **carmine**	350.00	65.00
		deep carmine	350.00	65.00
		rose carmine	350.00	65.00
		Never hinged	800.00	
		No gum	145.00	
		Handstamp cancel		250.00
		Block of 4	1,400.	
PR85	N5	48c **carmine**	425.00	85.00
		deep carmine	425.00	85.00
		Never hinged	975.00	
		No gum	180.00	
		Handstamp cancel		350.00
		Block of 4	1,850.	
PR86	N5	60c **carmine**	600.00	120.00
		deep carmine	600.00	120.00
		No gum	260.00	
		Handstamp cancel		*3,500.*
		Block of 4	2,750.	
PR87	N5	72c **carmine**	600.00	130.00
		deep carmine	600.00	130.00
		rose carmine	600.00	130.00
		No gum	260.00	
		Handstamp cancel		550.00
		Block of 4	2,750.	
PR88	N5	84c **carmine**	900.00	290.00
		rose carmine	900.00	290.00
		No gum	350.00	
		Handstamp cancel		850.00
		Block of 4	4,250.	
PR89	N5	96c **carmine**	750.00	225.00
		rose carmine	750.00	225.00
		Never hinged	2,250.	
		No gum	300.00	
		Handstamp cancel		800.00
		Block of 4	3,400.	

In early 1894, the Third Assistant Post Master General asked the American Bank Note Co., then the current printer of U. S. stamps, to provide the Bureau of Engraving and Printing with "examples" of their product. One submission featured a set of 25 imperforate and gummed sheets of Newspaper and Periodicals stamps which included both the current 1¢-$60 values (corresponding to Nos. PR57-PR79 and PR81) as well as a 9¢ value, a stamp that had only previously been printed by the Continental Bank Note Co. on hard paper (corresponding to No. PR14).

While the stamps were printed in sheets of 100, at some point they were divided in half, and one set of panes containing 50 stamps each was acquired by Hamilton F. Colman, a clerk in the General Land Office in Washington, D.C. Colman left five sets imperforate, and the balance, 45 sets, were privately perforated, and they were offered to the philatelic community.

The stamps generally have proof-like impressions and are printed on a fine wove paper that is almost completely devoid of the soft porous mesh paper found on Nos. PR57-PR71 and PR81. The stamps gauge 12, with sharp, clean perforations, and they have distinctly yellowish white, crackly gum. They are fairly often encountered with slightly blunted perforations on one or more sides, and will sell for somewhat less thus.

Values for individual perforated stamps, unused with hinged original gum, $200; mint never hinged, $300.

Printed by the Bureau of Engraving and Printing

1894 Unwmk. *Perf. 12*

Soft wove paper, with pale, whitish gum

No.	Type	Description	Unused	Used
PR90	N4	1c **intense black**	400.00	*5,000.*
		Never hinged	900.00	
		No gum	160.00	
		Block of 4	1,750.	
		Block of 4, P#482, Impt.	*3,000.*	
		Double transfer at top	425.00	
PR91	N4	2c **intense black**	450.00	—
		Never hinged	1,075.	
		No gum	190.00	
		Block of 4	2,000.	
		Double transfer at top	475.00	
PR92	N4	4c **intense black**	550.00	*13,500.*
		Never hinged	1,275.	
		No gum	210.00	
		Block of 4	2,450.	
PR93	N4	6c **intense black**	4,500.	
		Never hinged	*11,500.*	
		No gum	1,900.	
		Block of 4	—	
PR94	N4	10c **intense black**	1,400.	—
		Never hinged	*2,750.*	
		No gum	550.00	
		Block of 4	5,750.	
PR95	N5	12c **pink**	2,400.	*4,500.*
		Never hinged	*3,500.*	
		No gum	1,100.	
		Block of 4	12,000.	
PR96	N5	24c **pink**	3,750.	*8,000.*
		Never hinged	*8,500.*	
		No gum	1,850.	
		Block of 4	17,500.	
PR97	N5	36c **pink**	*50,000.*	
		Block of 4	—	
PR98	N5	60c **pink**	*40,000.*	*16,000.*
		Block of 4	—	
PR99	N5	96c **pink**	*50,000.*	—
PR100	N7	$3 **scarlet**	*50,000.*	
		Block of 4	—	
PR101	N8	$6 **pale blue**	*50,000.*	—
		No gum	*25,000.*	

The never hinged block of No. PR96 is in the fine grade, and it is valued thus.

Nos. PR90, PR95-PR98 used are valued with fine centering and small faults.

No. PR97 unused is valued in the grade of very good to fine. No. PR98 unused is valued in the grade of fine. Nos. PR99-PR100 unused are valued in the grade of fine-very fine.

Statue of Freedom — N15

N16

N17

N18

N19

N20

N21

N22

Size of designs: 1c-50c, 21x34mm; $2-$100, 24x35mm

1895, Feb. 1 Unwmk. *Perf. 12*

No.	Type	Description	Unused	Used
PR102	N15	1c **black**	230.00	*125.00*
		Never hinged	500.00	
		No gum	90.00	
		Block of 4	1,050.	*600.00*
		P# strip of 3, Impt., T IV	*1,000.*	
		P# block of 6, Impt., T IV	*1,850.*	
PR103	N15	2c **black**	230.00	*125.00*
		gray black	230.00	*125.00*
		Never hinged	500.00	
		No gum	90.00	
		Block of 4	1,050.	—
		P# strip of 3, Impt., T IV	*1,000.*	
		P# block of 6, Impt., T IV	*1,850.*	
		Double transfer at top	250.00	—
PR104	N15	5c **black**	300.00	*300.00*
		gray black	300.00	*300.00*
		Never hinged	650.00	
		No gum	125.00	
		Block of 4	1,350.	
		P# strip of 3, Impt., T IV	*1,300.*	
		P# strip of 4, Impt., T IV	*1,750.*	
		P# block of 6, Impt., T IV	*2,500.*	
PR105	N15	10c **black**	600.00	*600.00*
		Never hinged	1,300.	
		No gum	240.00	
		Block of 4	3,000.	
		P# strip of 3, Impt., T IV	*2,500.*	
		P# block of 6, Impt., T IV	4,750.	
PR106	N16	25c **carmine**	750.00	*650.00*
		Never hinged	1,650.	
		No gum	300.00	
		Block of 4	3,500.	
		P# strip of 3, Impt., T IV	*3,250.*	
		P# block of 6, Impt., T IV	6,250.	
PR107	N16	50c **carmine**	*2,750.*	*800.00*
		Never hinged	*6,250.*	
		No gum	*875.00*	
		Block of 4	*12,000.*	
		P# strip of 3, Impt., T IV	*11,500.*	
PR108	N17	$2 **scarlet**	2,250.	*1,100.*
		Never hinged	*5,000.*	
		No gum	850.00	
		P# strip of 3, Impt., T IV	*14,000.*	
PR109	N18	$5 **ultra**	2,250.	*1,750.*
		No gum	850.00	
		P# strip of 3, Impt., T IV	*14,000.*	
PR110	N19	$10 **green**	2,500.	*2,000.*
		No gum	900.00	
PR111	N20	$20 **slate**	3,250.	*2,500.*
		No gum	1,200.	
PR112	N21	$50 **dull rose**	2,750.	*950.00*
		Never hinged	*6,250.*	
		No gum	1,050.	
		P# strip of 3, Impt., T IV	*20,000.*	
PR113	N22	$100 **purple**	3,500.	*7,000.*
		No gum	1,400.	

Nos. PR102-PR113 were printed from plates with arrows in the top, bottom and side margins, but no guidelines between the stamps.

1895-97 Wmk. 191 *Perf. 12*

No.	Type	Description	Unused	Used
PR114	N15	1c **black**, *Jan. 11, 1896*	8.00	*25.00*
		gray black	8.00	*25.00*
		Never hinged	20.00	
		No gum	2.75	
		Block of 4	35.00	—
		P# strip of 3, Impt., T IV	50.00	
		P# block of 6, Impt., T IV	175.00	
PR115	N15	2c **black**, *Nov. 21, 1895*	8.00	*25.00*
		gray black	8.00	*25.00*
		Never hinged	20.00	
		No gum	2.75	
		Block of 4	35.00	—
		P# strip of 3, Impt., T IV	50.00	
		P# block of 6, Impt., T IV	175.00	
PR116	N15	5c **black**, *Feb. 12, 1896*	13.00	*40.00*
		gray black	13.00	*40.00*
		Never hinged	27.50	
		No gum	4.25	
		Block of 4	57.50	—
		P# strip of 3, Impt., T IV	90.00	
		P# block of 6, Impt., T IV	300.00	
PR117	N15	10c **black**, *Sept. 13, 1895*	13.00	*25.00*
		gray black	13.00	*25.00*
		Never hinged	27.50	
		No gum	4.25	
		Block of 4	57.50	—
		P# strip of 3, Impt., T IV	90.00	
		P# block of 6, Impt., T IV	325.00	
		P# block of 8, Impt., T IV	650.00	
		Never hinged	1,300.	

PR118	N16	25c **carmine,** *Oct. 11, 1895*	20.00	*65.00*
		lilac rose	20.00	*65.00*
		Never hinged	45.00	
		No gum	7.00	
		Block of 4	87.50	—
		P# strip of 3, Impt., T IV	125.00	
		P# block of 6, Impt., T IV	400.00	
PR119	N16	50c **carmine,** *Sept. 19, 1895*	25.00	*75.00*
		rose carmine	25.00	*75.00*
		lilac rose	25.00	*75.00*
		Never hinged	55.00	
		No gum	8.50	
		Block of 4	110.00	—
		P# strip of 3, Impt., T IV	165.00	
		P# block of 6, Impt., T IV	500.00	
		P# block of 8, Impt., T IV	800.00	
PR120	N17	$2 **scarlet,** *Jan. 23, 1897*	30.00	*110.00*
		scarlet vermilion	30.00	*110.00*
		Never hinged	75.00	
		No gum	10.00	
		Block of 4	130.00	—
		P# strip of 3, Impt., T IV	200.00	
		P# block of 6, Impt., T IV	650.00	
PR121	N18	$5 **dark blue,** *Jan. 16, 1896*	40.00	*175.00*
		Never hinged	100.00	
		No gum	13.50	
		Block of 4	200.00	
		P# strip of 3, Impt., T IV	260.00	
		P# block of 6, Impt., T IV	750.00	
	a.	$5 light blue	200.00	*500.00*
		Never hinged	500.00	
		No gum	67.50	
		Block of 4	*875.00*	*2,500.*
		P# strip of 3, Impt., T IV	900.00	
PR122	N19	$10 **green,** *Mar. 5, 1896*	42.50	*175.00*
		Never hinged	105.00	
		No gum	14.00	
		Block of 4	200.00	—
		P# strip of 3, Impt., T IV	275.00	
		P# block of 6, Impt., T IV	775.00	
		Never hinged	1,250.	
PR123	N20	$20 **slate,** *Jan. 27, 1896*	45.00	*200.00*
		Never hinged	110.00	
		No gum	15.00	
		Block of 4	210.00	—
		P# strip of 3, Impt., T IV	300.00	
		P# block of 6, Impt., T IV	800.00	
PR124	N21	$50 **dull rose,** *July 31, 1897*	75.00	*400.00*
		Never hinged	170.00	
		No gum	27.50	
		Block of 4	350.00	
		P# strip of 3, Impt., T IV	500.00	
		P# block of 6, Impt., T IV	1,250.	
		Never hinged	2,250.	
PR125	N22	$100 **purple,** *Jan. 23, 1896*	65.00	*300.00*
		Never hinged	150.00	
		No gum	22.50	
		Block of 4	300.00	
		P# strip of 3, Impt., T IV	450.00	
		P# block of 6, Impt., T IV	1,150.	
		Nos. PR114-PR125 (12)	384.50	*1,615.*
		Nos. PR114-PR125, never hinged	905.00	

Nos. PR114-PR125 were printed from the original plates with guide lines added in November 1895. Top and bottom plate strips and blocks of Nos. PR114-PR119 exist both with and without vertical guidelines. Those without guidelines sell for 4 to 5 time the values shown, which are for plate number strips and blocks with guidelines.

In 1899 the Government sold 26,989 sets of these stamps, but, as the stock of high values was not sufficient to make up the required number, an additional printing was made of the $5, $10, $20, $50 and $100. These are virtually indistinguishable from earlier printings.

POSTAL NOTE STAMPS

Postal note stamps were issued to supplement the regular money order service. They were a means of sending amounts under $1. One or two Postal note stamps, totaling 1c to 99c, were affixed to United States Postal Note cards that came in $0 to $10 denominations, and they were canceled by the clerk. The stamps were on the second of three parts, the one retained by the post office redeeming the Postal Note. They were discontinued March 31, 1951.

Catalogue Values for Unused Postal Note stamps are for Never Hinged items.

MO1

ROTARY PRESS PRINTING

1945, Feb. 1 **Unwmk.** ***Perf. 11x10½***

PN1	MO1	1c **black** (155950-155951)	.40	.35
PN2	MO1	2c **black** (156003-156004)	.40	.35
PN3	MO1	3c **black** (156062-156063)	.40	.35
PN4	MO1	4c **black** (155943, 156942-156943)	.45	.35
PN5	MO1	5c **black** (156261-156262)	.50	.35
PN6	MO1	6c **black** (156064-156065)	.70	.35
PN7	MO1	7c **black** (156075-156076)	.70	.35
PN8	MO1	8c **black** (156077-156078)	1.25	.40
PN9	MO1	9c **black** (156251-156252)	1.25	.40
PN10	MO1	10c **black** (156274-156275)	2.00	.40
PN11	MO1	20c **black** (156276-156277)	3.00	.40
PN12	MO1	30c **black** (156303-156304)	3.50	.40
PN13	MO1	40c **black** (156283-156284)	5.00	.45
PN14	MO1	50c **black** (156322-156323)	6.00	.45
PN15	MO1	60c **black** (156324-156325)	7.00	.45
PN16	MO1	70c **black** (156344-156345)	8.00	.50
PN17	MO1	80c **black** (156326-156327)	9.00	.50
PN18	MO1	90c **black** (156352-156353)	15.00	.50
		Nos. PN1-PN18 (18)	64.55	7.30

Blocks of four are valued at four times the unused single value, and plate number blocks of four are valued at approximately five to seven times the unused single value.

Postal note stamps exist on postal note cards with first day cancellation. Value, per card $25-$35. Value, cards with last day cancels, $35-$45. Value, single stamp on card canceled other than first day, $15-$25. For cards with multiple stamps, add $5-$10.

Numbers in parentheses are plate Nos.

PARCEL POST STAMPS

The Act of Congress approved Aug. 24, 1912, created postage rates on 4th class mail weighing 4 ounces or less at 1 cent per ounce or fraction. On mail over 4 ounces, the rate was by the pound. These rates were to be prepaid by distinctive postage stamps. Under this provision, the Post Office Department prepared 12 parcel post and 5 parcel post postage due stamps, usable only on parcel post packages starting Jan. 1, 1913. Other stamps were not usable on parcel post starting on that date.

Beginning on Nov. 27, 1912, the stamps were shipped to post offices offering parcel post service. Approximate shipping dates were: 1c, 2c, 5c, 25c, 1c due, 5c due, Nov. 27; 10c, 2c due, Dec. 9; 4c, 10c due, Dec. 12; 15c, 20c, 25c due, Dec. 16; 75c, Dec. 18. There was no prohibition on sale of the stamps prior to Jan. 1, 1913. Undoubtedly many were used on 4th class mail in Dec. 1912. Fourth class mail was expanded by adding former 2nd and 3rd class categories and was renamed "parcel post" effective Jan. 1, 1913. Normally 4th class (parcel post) mail did not receive a dated cancel unless a special service was involved. Small pieces, such as samples, are known with 1st class cancels.

With the approval of the Interstate Commerce Commission, the Postmaster General directed, in Order No. 7241 dated June 26, 1913, and effective July 1, 1913, that regular postage stamps should be valid on parcels. Parcel post stamps then became usable as regular stamps.

Parcel post and parcel post postage due stamps remained on sale, but no further printings were made. Remainders, consisting of 3,510,345 of the 75c, were destroyed in Sept. 1921.

The 20c was the first government-issued postage stamp of any country to show an airplane.

Post Office Clerk — PP1

City Carrier — PP2

Railway Postal Clerk — PP3

Rural Carrier — PP4

Mail Train and Mail Bag on Rack — PP5

Steamship "Kronprinz Wilhelm" and Mail Tender, New York — PP6

Automobile Service — PP7

Airplane Carrying Mail — PP8

Manufacturing (Steel Plant, South Chicago) — PP9

Dairying — PP10

Harvesting PP11

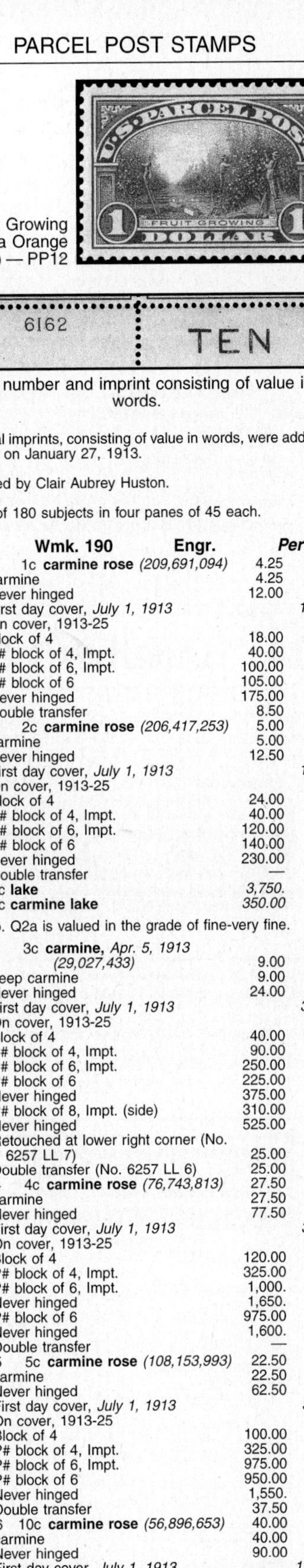

Fruit Growing (Florida Orange Grove) — PP12

Plate number and imprint consisting of value in words.

Marginal imprints, consisting of value in words, were added to the plates on January 27, 1913.

Designed by Clair Aubrey Huston.

Plates of 180 subjects in four panes of 45 each.

1913 Wmk. 190 Engr. *Perf. 12*

No.	Design	Description	Unused	Used
Q1	PP1	1c **carmine rose** *(209,691,094)*	4.25	1.60
		carmine	4.25	1.60
		Never hinged	12.00	
		First day cover, *July 1, 1913*		*1,500.*
		On cover, 1913-25		6.00
		Block of 4	18.00	8.00
		P# block of 4, Impt.	40.00	
		P# block of 6, Impt.	100.00	
		P# block of 6	105.00	
		Never hinged	175.00	
		Double transfer	8.50	3.50
Q2	PP2	2c **carmine rose** *(206,417,253)*	5.00	1.25
		carmine	5.00	1.25
		Never hinged	12.50	
		First day cover, *July 1, 1913*		*1,750.*
		On cover, 1913-25		5.75
		Block of 4	24.00	6.50
		P# block of 4, Impt.	40.00	
		P# block of 6, Impt.	120.00	
		P# block of 6	140.00	
		Never hinged	230.00	
		Double transfer	—	—
a.		2c **lake**	*3,750.*	
b.		2c **carmine lake**	*350.00*	

No. Q2a is valued in the grade of fine-very fine.

No.	Design	Description	Unused	Used
Q3	PP3	3c **carmine,** *Apr. 5, 1913 (29,027,433)*	9.00	6.00
		deep carmine	9.00	6.00
		Never hinged	24.00	
		First day cover, *July 1, 1913*		*3,500.*
		On cover, 1913-25		19.00
		Block of 4	40.00	35.00
		P# block of 4, Impt.	90.00	
		P# block of 6, Impt.	250.00	
		P# block of 6	225.00	
		Never hinged	375.00	
		P# block of 8, Impt. (side)	310.00	
		Never hinged	525.00	
		Retouched at lower right corner (No. 6257 LL 7)	25.00	14.50
		Double transfer (No. 6257 LL 6)	25.00	14.50
Q4	PP4	4c **carmine rose** *(76,743,813)*	27.50	3.00
		carmine	27.50	3.00
		Never hinged	77.50	
		First day cover, *July 1, 1913*		*3,500.*
		On cover, 1913-25		65.00
		Block of 4	120.00	17.50
		P# block of 4, Impt.	325.00	
		P# block of 6, Impt.	1,000.	
		Never hinged	1,650.	
		P# block of 6	975.00	
		Never hinged	1,600.	
		Double transfer	—	—
Q5	PP5	5c **carmine rose** *(108,153,993)*	22.50	2.25
		carmine	22.50	2.25
		Never hinged	62.50	
		First day cover, *July 1, 1913*		*3,500.*
		On cover, 1913-25		42.50
		Block of 4	100.00	14.00
		P# block of 4, Impt.	325.00	
		P# block of 6, Impt.	975.00	
		P# block of 6	950.00	
		Never hinged	1,550.	
		Double transfer	37.50	6.00
Q6	PP6	10c **carmine rose** *(56,896,653)*	40.00	3.00
		carmine	40.00	3.00
		Never hinged	90.00	
		First day cover, *July 1, 1913*		*12,500.*
		On cover, 1913-25		55.00
		Block of 4	190.00	25.00
		P# block of 4, Impt.	400.00	
		P# block of 6, Impt.	1,125.	
		P# block of 6	975.00	
		Never hinged	1,600.	
		Double transfer	—	—
Q7	PP7	15c **carmine rose** *(21,147,033)*	60.00	13.50
		carmine	60.00	13.50
		Never hinged	170.00	
		First day cover, *July 1, 1913*		—
		On cover, 1913-25		400.00
		Block of 4	280.00	90.00
		P# block of 4, Impt.	675.00	
		P# block of 6, Impt.	2,600.	
		P# block of 8, Impt.	3,100.	
		P# block of 6	2,300.	
		Never hinged	*3,700.*	
Q8	PP8	20c **carmine rose** *(17,142,393)*	110.00	25.00
		carmine	110.00	25.00
		Never hinged	260.00	
		On cover, 1913-25		850.00
		Block of 4	500.00	150.00
		P# block of 4, Impt.	1,250.	
		P# block of 6, Impt.	6,000.	
		P# block of 8, Impt. (side)	6,500.	
		P# block of 6	5,750.	
		Never hinged	*9,000.*	
Q9	PP9	25c **carmine rose** *(21,940,653)*	52.50	8.00
		carmine	52.50	8.00
		Never hinged	145.00	
		On cover, 1913-25		300.00
		Block of 4	250.00	55.00
		P# block of 6, Impt.	2,250.	
		P# block of 8, Impt. (side)	3,250.	
		P# block of 6	2,250.	
		Never hinged	*3,500.*	
Q10	PP10	50c **carmine rose,** *Mar. 15, 1913 (2,117,793)*	210.00	45.00
		carmine	210.00	45.00
		Never hinged	525.00	
		On cover, 1913-25		—
		Block of 4	950.00	300.00
		P# block of 4, Impt.	1,500.	
		Never hinged	2,500.	
		P# block of 6, Impt.	*17,500.*	
		Never hinged	*24,000.*	
Q11	PP11	75c **carmine rose** *(2,772,615)*	85.00	35.00
		carmine	85.00	35.00
		Never hinged	190.00	
		On cover, 1913-25		—
		Block of 4	400.00	225.00
		P# block of 6, Impt.	3,250.	
		P# block of 8, Impt. (side)	3,250.	
		Never hinged	*4,250.*	
		P# block of 6	2,500.	
		Never hinged	*3,750.*	
Q12	PP12	$1 **carmine rose,** *Jan. 3, 1913 (1,053,273)*	260.00	40.00
		carmine	.26000	40.00
		Never hinged	625.00	
		On cover, 1913-25		1,250.
		Block of 4	1,175.	225.00
		P# block of 6, Impt.	*20,000.*	
		Never hinged	*29,000.*	
		P# block of 8, Impt. (side)	*21,000.*	
		P# block of 6	*18,000.*	
		Never hinged	*27,500.*	
		Nos. Q1-Q12 (12)	885.75	183.60
		Nos. Q1-Q12, never hinged	2,273.	

The 1c, 2c, 4c, 5c, and 10c are known in parcel post usage postmarked Jan. 1, 1913.

PARCEL POST POSTAGE DUE STAMPS

See notes preceding Scott No. Q1. Parcel Post Postage Due stamps were allowed to be used as regular postage due stamps from July 1, 1913.

PPD1

Designed by Clair Aubrey Huston.

Plates of 180 subjects in four panes of 45

1913 **Wmk. 190** **Engr.** ***Perf. 12***

JQ1 PPD1 1c **dark green** (7,322,400)	8.00	4.00
yellowish green	8.00	4.00
Never hinged	22.50	
On cover, 1913-25		160.00
Block of 4	35.00	35.00
P# block of 6	450.00	
Never hinged	750.00	

Earliest documented use: Feb. 26, 1913.

JQ2 PPD1 2c **dark green** (3,132,000)	60.00	16.00
yellowish green	60.00	16.00
Never hinged	160.00	
On cover, 1913-25		225.00
Block of 4	260.00	140.00
P# block of 6	*3,000.*	
Never hinged	*4,850.*	

Earliest documented use: July 7, 1913.

JQ3 PPD1 5c **dark green** (5,840,100)	9.00	4.50
yellowish green	9.00	4.50
Never hinged	24.00	
On cover, 1913-25		200.00
Block of 4	40.00	35.00
P# block of 6	450.00	
Never hinged	775.00	

Earliest documented use: Jan. 15, 1913 (dated cancel on off-cover stamp).

JQ4 PPD1 10c **dark green** (2,124,540)	110.00	40.00
yellowish green	110.00	40.00
Never hinged	290.00	
On cover, 1913-25		650.00
Block of 4	500.00	375.00
P# block of 6	*7,500.*	
Never hinged	*10,500.*	

Earliest documented use: July 19, 1913.

JQ5 PPD1 25c **dark green** (2,117,700)	70.00	4.50
yellowish green	70.00	4.50
Never hinged	185.00	
On cover, 1913-25		—
Block of 4	325.00	35.00
P# block of 6	*3,500.*	
Never hinged	*6,000.*	

Earliest documented use: Aug. 30, 1913.

Nos. JQ1-JQ5 (5)	257.00	69.00
Nos. JQ1-JQ5, never hinged	642.50	

SPECIAL HANDLING STAMPS

The Postal Service Act, approved Feb. 28, 1925, provided for a special handling stamp of the 25-cent denomination for use on fourth-class mail matter, which would secure for such mail matter the expeditious handling accorded to mail matter of the first class.

PP13

FLAT PLATE PRINTING

Plates of 200 subjects in four panes of 50

1925-55 **Engr.** **Unwmk.** ***Perf. 11***

QE1 PP13 10c **yellow green,** wet printing, printed on "special" booklet paper, *1928* (see note before #551)	3.00	1.50
Never hinged	5.25	
First day cover, *June 25, 1928*		45.00
P# block of 6	27.50	
Never hinged	45.00	
a. 10c **green,** wet printing, *1940*	2.00	*1.00*
Never hinged	4.25	
P# block of 6	25.00	
Never hinged	40.00	
b. 10c **light green,** dry printing, *1955*	5.00	150.00
Never hinged	10.00	
P# block of 6	75.00	
Never hinged	125.00	

Earliest documented use: No. QE1b, Feb. 26, 1958 (dated cancel on off-cover stamp).

QE2 PP13 15c **yellow green,** wet printing, printed on "special" booklet paper, *1928* (see note before #551)	3.25	1.50
Never hinged	5.75	
First day cover, *June 25, 1928*		45.00
P# block of 6	32.50	
Never hinged	52.50	
a. 15c **green,** wet printing, *1940*	2.25	*.90*
Never hinged	4.75	
P# block of 6	30.00	
Never hinged	47.50	
b. 15c **light green,** dry printing, *1955*	5.00	150.00
Never hinged	10.00	
P# block of 6	80.00	
Never hinged	135.00	

Earliest documented use: No. QE2b, Aug. 1, 1957.

QE3 PP13 20c **yellow green,** wet printing, printed on "special" booklet paper, *1928* (see note before #551)	4.75	2.50
Never hinged	8.75	
First day cover, *June 25, 1928*		45.00
First day cover, Nos. QE1-QE3, *June 25, 1928*		350.00
P# block of 6	40.00	
Never hinged	65.00	
a. 20c **green,** wet printing, *1940*	3.75	*1.50*
Never hinged	7.75	
P# block of 6	37.50	
Never hinged	60.00	
b. 20c **light green,** dry printing, *1955*	7.50	150.00
Never hinged	15.00	
P# block of 6	85.00	
Never hinged	150.00	

"AT" joined at top

"TA" joined at top

Dot on second "T"

QE4 PP13 25c **deep green,** *April 11, 1925*	20.00	4.00
Never hinged	37.50	
P# block of 6	350.00	
Never hinged	525.00	
"A" and second "T" of "States" joined at top (Pl. 17103)	80.00	50.00
Never hinged	140.00	
"A" and second "T" of "States" and "T" and "A" of "Postage" joined at top (Pl. 17103)	125.00	125.00
Never hinged	210.00	
Dot on second "T" of "States" (17103 UR 40)	*1,250.*	*375.00*
First day cover		225.00
a. 25c **yellow green,** *1928*	16.50	*22.50*
Never hinged	30.00	
P# block of 6	250.00	
Never hinged	360.00	

Earliest documented use: No. QE4a, May 1928 dated cancel on off-cover stamp; Jan. 30, 1934 (on cover).

Nos. QE1-QE4 (4)	31.00	9.50
Nos. QE1-QE4, never hinged	57.25	

See note on Wet and Dry Printings following No. 1029.

POSTAL INSURANCE STAMPS

Postal insurance stamps were issued to pay insurance on parcels for loss or damage. The stamps come in a booklet of one which also carries instructions for use and a receipt form for use if there is a claim. The booklets were sold by vending machine. Values in unused column are for complete booklets. Values in used column are for used stamps. Booklet cover illustrations are reduced.

QI1 — PPI1

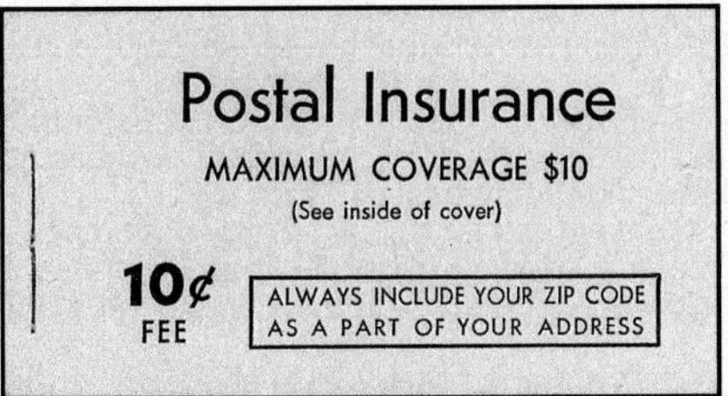

QI1 — PPIC1

1965, Aug. 19 **Typo.** ***Rouletted 9 at Top***

QI1 PPI1 (10c) **dark red** 140.00 —

No. QI1 paid insurance up to $10. It was sold at the Canoga Park, Calif., automatic post office, which opened Aug. 19, 1965. It was also sold at the Austin, Texas, post office beginning Oct. 28, 1965, and at the Wheaton, Maryland, post office beginning March 21, 1966. Sales of this booklet ceased on March 25, 1966. The "V" stands for "Vended."

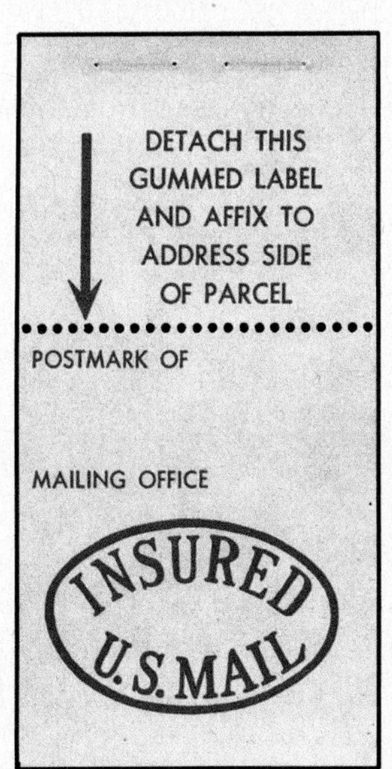

QI2 — PPI2

QI2 — PPIC2 Type I

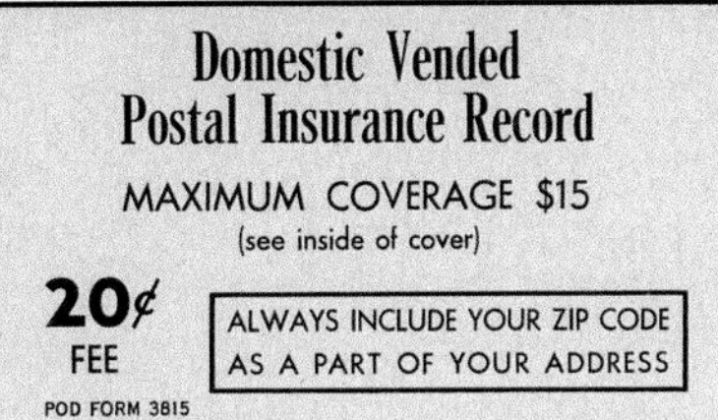

QI2 — PPIC2 Type II

1966, Mar. 26 **Litho.** ***Perf. 11 at Top***

QI2 PPI2 (20c) **red** 4.00 —

No. QI2 paid insurance up to $15. The rate increased from 20c to 25c on Apr. 18, 1976, and to 40c on July 18, 1976.

The QI2 booklet comes with two types of front covers, type I beginning "Vended..." and type II beginning "Domestic Vended...." There also are two types of back covers, the first with some white on black lettering, the second with all black on white lettering.

No 25c postal insurance stamps were printed. Existing examples of No. QI2 had 5c postage stamps added and the value on the cover was changed to 25c, usually by hand, but sometimes by handstamp or label. Twenty-cent stamps were added to make the 40c rate since new postal insurance stamps were not issued until 1977. Some 25c provisional booklets were further revalued to 40c by the addition of a 15c stamp. Each provisional booklet comes with both cover types.

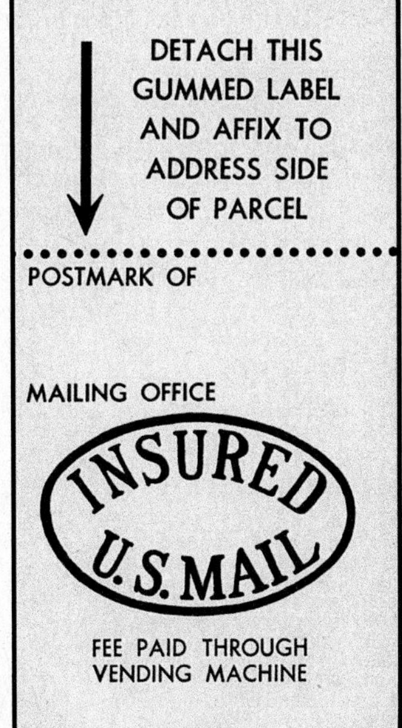

QI3 — PPI3

THIS PACKAGE CONTAINS ONE:
DOMESTIC
PARCEL POST
INSURANCE STAMP
($15 MAXIMUM COVERAGE PER PARCEL)
DEPOSIT 40¢ FEE TO PURCHASE

QI3 — PPIC3

"FEE PAID THROUGH VENDING MACHINE" Below "INSURED U.S. MAIL" Logo

1977, Aug. 28 **Litho.** ***Perf. 11 at Top***

QI3 PPI3 (40c) **black** 15.00 —

Available for use by Nov. 28, 1977 or earlier.

QI3 is often found misperfed with horizontal perforations running between "Postmark of" and "Mailing Office." This variety is relatively common and does not merit a large premium.

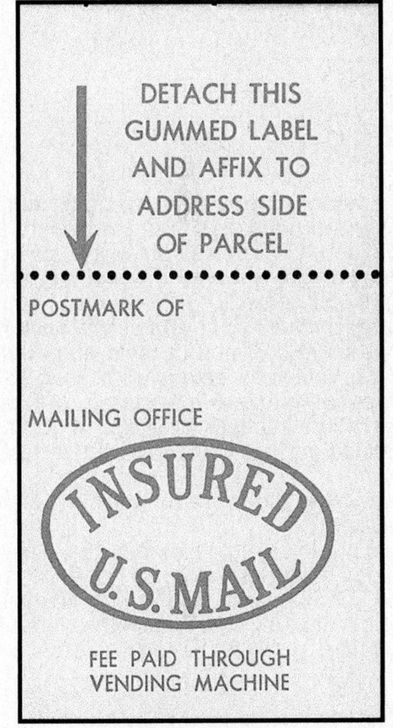

QI4 — PPI3

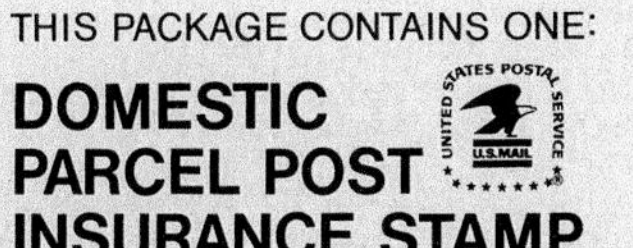

QI4 — PPIC4

1978, Nov. 20

QI4 PPI3 (50c) **green** 10.00 —

The rate increased to 50c on May 29, 1978. Examples of QI2 and QI3 exist revalued to 50c by the addition of stamps.

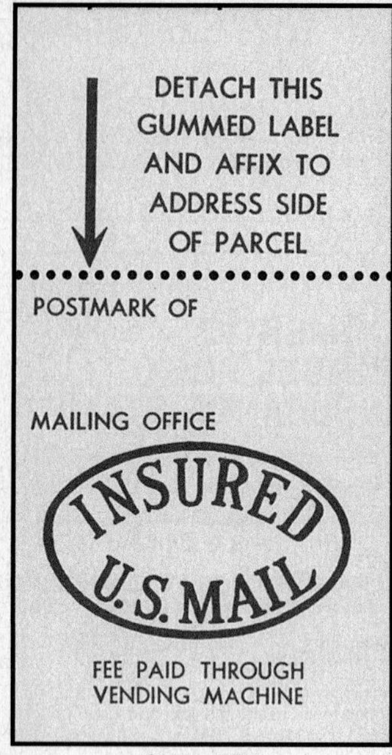

QI5 — PPI3

THIS PACKAGE CONTAINS ONE:
DOMESTIC
PARCEL POST
INSURANCE STAMP
($20 MAXIMUM COVERAGE PER PARCEL)
DEPOSIT 45c FEE TO PURCHASE

QI5 — PPIC5

1981, Sept. 1

QI5 PPI3 (45c) **red** 12.50 —

No. QI3 booklets exist revalued to 45c by the addition of a 5c stamp, and the QI4 booklet is known revalued to 45c on its cover.

FIRST DAY COVERS

All envelopes or cards are postmarked Washington, D.C., unless otherwise stated. Minors and sublistings without dates have the same date and city (if none is otherwise mentioned) as the previous listing. Minors and sublistings with dates differing from the previous listing are postmarked in Washington, D.C. unless otherwise stated.

Values are for first day covers in very fine condition, without tears, stains or smeared postmarks, and with sound stamps that have fresh color and are not badly off center.

Printed cachets on covers before Scott Nos. 772 and C20 sell at a substantial premium. Values for covers of Nos. 772-986 and C20-C45 are for those with the most common cachets and addressed. Unaddressed covers sell at a substantial premium and covers without cachet sell at a substantial discount. Values for covers from Scott 987 and C46 onward are for those with the most common cachets and unaddressed.

Values for 1st class rate stamps are for covers bearing single stamps. Blocks of 4 on first day covers usually sell for about 1½ times as much as singles; Plate number blocks of 4 at about 3 times; Plate number blocks of 6 at about 4 times; coil line pairs at about 3 times. Stamps with denominations less than the first class rate will have the proper multiple to make the rate if practical or additional postage. (See Nos. 899, 907-908, 930-931, etc.)

Dates given are those on which the stamps were first *officially* placed on sale. Many instances are known of stamps being sold in advance, contrary to regulations.

Numbers in parentheses are quantities stated to have received the first day cancel.

Listings from Scott Nos. 551 and C4 are for covers canceled at cities officially designated by the Post Office Department or Postal Service. Some tagged varieties and cities of special interest are exceptions.

Air post first day covers are listed following the Postage first day covers. Envelope, postal card and other first day covers are with the regular listings.

Quantities given for se-tenant issues include the multiple and any single or combination of singles (see No. 2375a).

1851-57

5A 1c **blue, type Ib,** *July 1, 1851,* Boston, Mass. *150,000.*
7 1c **blue, type II,** *July 1, 1851* *25,000.*
Same on printed circular *4,000.*
10 3c **orange brown,** *July 1, 1851,* any city *12,500.*

The No. 5A cover is unique. Value is based on 1996 auction sale. The No. 7 cover also is unique.

1861

64 3c **pink,** *Aug. 17, 1861,* Baltimore, Md. *22,000.*
64b 3c **rose pink,** *Aug. 17, 1861,* Baltimore, Md. *23,000.*

The Nos. 64 and 64b covers are each unique.

1883

210 2c **red brown,** *Oct. 1,* any city *2,000.*
210, 211 2c, 4c **blue green,** *Oct. 1,* New York, N.Y. *50,000.*

The Nos. 210, 211 cover is unique.

1890

219D 2c **lake,** *Feb. 22,* any city *35,000.*

COLUMBIAN EXPOSITION ISSUE

1893

230 1c **deep blue,** *Jan. 1,* any city *20,000.*
Jan. 2, any city *5,000.*
231 2c **brown violet,** *Jan. 1,* any city *20,000.*
Jan. 2, any city *4,000.*
232 3c **green,** *Jan. 1,* any city *20,000.*
Jan. 2, any city *7,000.*
230, 232 on one cover, *Jan. 2,* Boston, Mass. *8,250.*
233 4c **ultramarine,** *Jan. 1,* any city *20,000.*
Jan. 2, any city *14,000.*
234 5c **chocolate,** *Jan. 1,* any city *27,500.*
Jan. 2, any city *17,500.*
235 6c **purple,** *Jan. 2,* any city *22,500.*
237 10c **black brown,** *Jan. 1,* any city *32,500.*
Jan. 2, any city *27,500.*
242 $2 **brown red,** *Jan. 2,* any city *65,000.*

As Jan. 1, 1893, was a Sunday, specialists recognize both Jan. 1 and 2 as "first day."

TRANS-MISSISSIPPI EXPOSITION ISSUE

1898

285 1c **green,** *June 17,* any city *13,000.*
286 2c **copper red,** *June 17,* any city *8,000.*
Pittsburgh, Pa *15,000.*
287 4c **orange,** *June 17* *30,000.*
288 5c **dull blue,** *June 17,* any city *18,000.*
285, 287-288 on one cover *75,000.*
285-288 on one cover *75,000.*
289 8c **violet brown,** *June 17,* any city *22,500.*
290 10c **gray violet,** *June 17* *27,500.*
285-290, all 6 on one cover, *June 17* *75,000.*
291 50c **sage green,** *June 17,* any city *90,000.*
292 $1 **black,** *June 17,* any city *172,500.*

PAN AMERICAN EXPOSITION ISSUE

1901

294 1c **green & black,** *May 1,* any city *5,000.*
295 2c **carmine & black,** *May 1,* any city *2,750.*
297 5c **ultra. & blk.,** *May 1,* any city *37,500.*
294, 295, 297 on one cover, *May 1,* Boston, Mass. *17,500.*
294, 296, 297 on one cover, *May 1,* Boston, Mass. *16,000.*
295, 298 on one cover, *May 1,* Washington, D.C. *33,500.*
296, 298 on one cover, *May 1,* Boston, Mass. *27,500.*
297, 298 on one cover, *May 1,* Philadelphia, Pa. *27,500.*
294-299, complete set of 6 on one cover *May 1,* any city *30,000.*

LOUISIANA PURCHASE EXPOSITION ISSUE

1904

323 1c **green,** *Apr. 30,* any city *7,500.*
324 2c **carmine,** *Apr. 30,* any city *5,000.*
325 3c **violet,** *Apr. 30,* any city *20,000.*
326 5c **dark blue,** *Apr. 30,* any city *22,500.*
327 10c **red brown,** *Apr. 30,* any city *24,000.*
323-327, all 5 on one cover, *Apr. 30,* New York *65,000.*

The Nos. 323-327 combination cover is unique.

1907

328 1c **Jamestown,** *Apr. 26,* any city *12,500.*
329 2c **Jamestown,** *Apr. 26,* any city *15,000.*

1908

331a 1c **green,** booklet single, *Dec. 2,* Washington, D.C. *28,500.*
332a 2c **carmine,** booklet single, *Nov. 16,* Washington, D.C. *28,500.*

1909

367 2c **Lincoln,** *Feb. 12,* any city *500.*
On pictorial postcard, *Feb. 12,* Boston *650.*

Imperf

368 2c **Lincoln,** *Feb. 12,* any city *12,000.*

ALASKA-YUKON ISSUE

1909

370 2c **carmine**, *June 1*, any city *3,000.*
On Expo-related picture postcard, *June 1* *5,000.*

HUDSON-FULTON ISSUE

1909

372 2c **carmine**, *Sept. 25*, any city *950.*
On Expo-related picture postcard, *Sept. 25* *1,500.*

Imperf

373 2c **carmine**, *Sept. 25*, any city *8,000.*

PANAMA-PACIFIC ISSUE

1913

397 1c **green**, *Jan. 1*, any city *8,000.*
399 5c **blue**, *Jan. 1* *31,000.*
400 10c **orange yellow**, *Jan. 1* *10,000.*
397, 399 & 400, all 3 on one cover, San Francisco, Cal. —

The editors would like to see expertization of the above 3-stamp cover.

1916-22 **COIL STAMP**

497 10c **orange yellow**, *Jan. 31, 1922*, any city *6,000.*

1918-20 **OFFSET PRINTING**

526 2c **carmine**, type IV, *Mar. 15, 1920* *850.*

1919

537 3c **Victory**, *Mar. 3*, any city *900.*

1919 ***Perf. 11x10***

541 3c **violet**, type II, *June 14, 1919*, any city *9,000.*

REGULAR ISSUE

1920 ***Perf. 10x11***

542 1c **green**, *May 26* *1,750.*

1920

548 1c **Pilgrim**, *Dec. 21*, any city, pair *1,000.*
Plymouth, Mass. *5,000.*
549 2c **Pilgrim**, *Dec. 21*, any city *700.*
Plymouth, Mass. *5,000.*
550 5c **Pilgrim**, *Dec. 21*, any city *2,500.*
548-550, complete set of 3 on one cover, *Dec. 21*, any city *2,250.*
Washington, D.C. *3,000.*

1922-26 ***Perf. 11***

551 ½c **Hale**, *Apr. 4, 1925*, block of 4 20.00
New Haven, Conn. *25.00*
551 & 576 on one cover, *Apr. 4, 1925*, New Haven, Conn. *165.00*
552 1c **Franklin**, *Jan. 17, 1923*, pair 27.50
Philadelphia, Pa. *47.50*
553 1½c **Harding**, *Mar. 19, 1925*, pair 52.50
553, 582, 598 on one cover, *Mar. 19, 1925* *200.00*
554 2c **Washington**, *Jan. 15, 1923* 42.50
555 3c **Lincoln**, *Feb. 12, 1923* 40.00
Hodgenville, Ky. *350.00*
556 4c **Martha Washington**, *Jan. 15, 1923* 65.00
557 5c **Roosevelt**, *Oct. 27, 1922* *135.00*
New York, N.Y. *250.00*
Oyster Bay, N.Y. *2,000.*
558 6c **Garfield**, *Nov. 20, 1922* 235.00
559 7c **McKinley**, *May 1, 1923* 185.00
Niles, O. *275.00*
560 8c **Grant**, *May 1, 1923* 190.00
561 9c **Jefferson**, *Jan. 15, 1923* 190.00
562 10c **Monroe**, *Jan. 15, 1923* 190.00
554, 556, 561 & 562, all 4 stamps issued *Jan. 15* on one cover *3,500.*
563 11c **Hayes**, *Oct. 4, 1922* 650.00
Fremont, O. *3,750.*
564 12c **Cleveland**, *Mar. 20, 1923* 185.00
Boston, Mass. (Philatelic Exhibition) *200.00*
Caldwell, N.J. *230.00*
565 14c **American Indian**, *May 1, 1923* 400.00
Muskogee, Okla. *1,250.*
566 15c **Statue of Liberty**, *Nov. 11, 1922* 575.00
567 20c **Golden Gate**, *May 1, 1923* *600.00*
San Francisco, Cal. *2,000.*
559, 560, 565 & 567, all 4 stamps issued *May 1* on one cover *10,000.*
568 25c **Niagara Falls**, *Nov. 11, 1922* *650.00*
569 30c **American Buffalo**, *Mar. 20, 1923* *800.00*
570 50c **Arlington**, *Nov. 11, 1922* *1,500.*
571 $1 **Lincoln Memorial**, *Feb. 12, 1923* *7,000.*
Springfield, Ill. *7,500.*
572 $2 **U.S. Capitol**, *Mar. 20, 1923* *17,500.*
573 $5 **America**, *Mar. 20, 1923* *30,000.*

Imperf

576 1½c **Harding**, *Apr. 4, 1925* 42.50

Perf. 10

581 1c **Franklin**, *Oct. 17, 1923*, not precanceled *6,000.*
582 1½c **Harding**, *Mar. 19, 1925* 40.00
583a 2c **Washington booklet pane of 6**, *Aug. 27, 1926* *1,500.*
584 3c **Lincoln**, *Aug. 1, 1925* 55.00
585 4c **Martha Washington**, *Apr. 4, 1925*, not precanceled 50.00
586 5c **Roosevelt**, *Apr. 4, 1925*, not precanceled 60.00
587 6c **Garfield**, *Apr. 4, 1925*, not precanceled 60.00
585-587, all 3 stamps issued *April 4* on one cover *1,000.*
588 7c **McKinley**, *May 29, 1926* 60.00
589 8c **Grant**, *May 29, 1926* 70.00
590 9c **Jefferson**, *May 29, 1926* 77.50
588-590, all 3 stamps issued *May 29* on one cover —
591 10c **Monroe**, *June 8, 1925* 95.00

Perf. 10 Vertically

597 1c **Franklin**, *July 18, 1923* *600.00*
598 1½c **Harding**, *Mar. 19, 1925* 65.00
599 2c **Washington**, *Jan. 15, 1923* *1,750.*
600 3c **Lincoln**, *May 10, 1924* 85.00
602 5c **Roosevelt**, *Mar. 5, 1924* 95.00
603 10c **Monroe**, *Dec. 1, 1924* 110.00

No. 599 is known used on Jan. 10, 11 and 13, 1923 (one each day). Jan. 15 was the first day of sale in Washington, D. C.

Perf. 10 Horizontally

604 1c **Franklin**, *July 19, 1924* 100.00
605 1½c **Harding**, *May 9, 1925* 80.00
606 2c **Washington**, *Dec. 31, 1923* 150.00

1923

610 2c **Harding**, perf. 11, *Sept. 1* 37.50
Marion, O. 22.50
611 2c **Harding**, imperf., *Nov. 15* 90.00
612 2c **Harding**, perf. 10, *Sept. 12* 100.00

1924

614 1c **Huguenot-Walloon**, *May 1*, pair 30.00
Albany, N.Y 30.00
Allentown, Pa. 30.00
Charleston, S.C. 30.00
Jacksonville, Fla. 30.00
Lancaster, Pa. 30.00
Mayport, Fla. 30.00
New Rochelle, N.Y. 30.00
New York, N.Y. 30.00
Philadelphia, Pa. 30.00
Reading, Pa. 30.00
615 2c **Huguenot-Walloon**, *May 1* 45.00
Albany, N.Y. 45.00
Allentown, Pa. 45.00
Charleston, S.C. 45.00
Jacksonville, Fla. 45.00
Lancaster, Pa. 45.00
Mayport, Fla. 45.00
New Rochelle, N.Y. 45.00
New York, N.Y. 45.00
Philadelphia, Pa. 45.00
Reading, Pa. 45.00
616 5c **Huguenot-Walloon**, *May 1* 70.00
Albany, N.Y. 70.00
Allentown, Pa. 70.00
Charleston, S.C. 70.00
Jacksonville, Fla. 70.00
Lancaster, Pa. 70.00
Mayport, Fla. 70.00
New Rochelle, N.Y. 70.00
New York, N.Y. 70.00
Philadelphia, Pa. 70.00
Reading, Pa. 70.00
614-616 on one cover, any city listed above 150.00
614-616 on one cover, any other city 400.00

1925

617 1c **Lexington-Concord**, *Apr. 4*, pair 30.00
Boston, Mass. 30.00
Cambridge, Mass. 30.00
Concord, Mass. 30.00
Concord Junction, Mass. 30.00
Lexington, Mass. 30.00
618 2c **Lexington-Concord**, *Apr. 4* 40.00
Boston, Mass. 40.00
Cambridge, Mass. 40.00
Concord, Mass 40.00
Concord Junction, Mass. 40.00
Lexington, Mass. 42.50
619 5c **Lexington-Concord**, *Apr. 4* 75.00
Boston, Mass. 75.00
Cambridge, Mass. 75.00
Concord, Mass. 75.00
Concord Junction, Mass. 75.00
Lexington, Mass. 75.00
617-619 on one cover, Concord Junction or Lexington 175.00
Set of 3 on one cover, any other city 150.00

1925

620 2c **Norse-American**, *May 18* 20.00
Algona, Iowa 20.00
Benson, Minn. 20.00
Decorah, Iowa 20.00
Minneapolis, Minn. 20.00
Northfield, Minn. 20.00
St. Paul, Minn. 20.00
621 5c **Norse-American**, *May 18* 25.00
Algona, Iowa 25.00
Benson, Minn. 25.00
Decorah, Iowa 25.00
Minneapolis, Minn. 25.00
Northfield, Minn. 25.00
St. Paul, Minn. 25.00
620-621 on one cover, any city 50.00

1925-26

622 13c **Harrison**, *Jan. 11, 1926* 25.00
Indianapolis, Ind. 40.00
North Bend, Ohio *(500)* 200.00
623 17c **Wilson**, *Dec. 28, 1925* 15.00
New York, N.Y. 15.00
Princeton, N.J. 15.00
Staunton, Va. 30.00

1926

627 2c **Sesquicentennial**, *May 10* 15.00
Boston, Mass. 15.00
Philadelphia, Pa. 15.00
628 5c **Ericsson**, *May 29* 40.00
Chicago, Ill. 40.00
Minneapolis, Minn. 40.00
New York, N.Y. 40.00
629 2c **White Plains**, New York, N.Y., *Oct. 18* 9.00
New York, N.Y., Inter-Philatelic Exhibition Agency cancellation 9.00
White Plains, N.Y. 9.00
Washington, D.C., *Oct. 28* 5.00
630 2c Sheet of 25, *Oct. 18* 1,800.
Sheet of 25, *Oct. 28* 1,000.

1926-34 ***Imperf.***

631 1½c **Harding**, *Aug. 27, 1926*, pair 35.00

Perf. 11x10½

632 1c **Franklin**, *June 10, 1927*, pair 45.00
632a Booklet pane of 6, *Nov. 2, 1927* *4,000.*
633 1½c **Harding**, *May 17, 1927*, pair 45.00
634 2c **Washington**, *Dec. 10, 1926* 50.00
635 3c **Lincoln**, *Feb. 3, 1927* 50.00
635a 3c **bright violet**, *Feb. 7, 1934* 30.00
636 4c **Martha Washington**, *May 17, 1927* 50.00
637 5c **Roosevelt**, *Mar. 24, 1927* 50.00
638 6c **Garfield**, *July 27, 1927* 60.00
639 7c **McKinley**, *Mar. 24, 1927* 60.00
637, 639, both stamps issued *Mar. 24* 500.00
640 8c **Grant**, *June 10, 1927* 70.00
632, 640, both stamps issued *June 10* 350.00
641 9c **Jefferson**, *May 17, 1927* 75.00
633, 636, 641 all three stamps issued *May 17* 550.00
642 10c **Monroe**, *Feb. 3, 1927* 100.00

1927

643 2c **Vermont**, *Aug. 3* 6.00
Bennington, Vt. 6.00
644 2c **Burgoyne**, *Aug. 3* 12.50
Albany, N.Y. 12.50
Rome, N.Y. 12.50
Syracuse, N.Y. 12.50
Utica, N.Y. 12.50

1928

645 2c **Valley Forge**, *May 26* 4.00
Cleveland, O. 67.50
Lancaster, Pa. 4.00
Norristown, Pa. 4.00
Philadelphia, Pa. 4.00
Valley Forge, Pa. 4.00
West Chester, Pa. 4.00
Cleveland, Midwestern Philatelic Sta. cancellation 4.00
646 2c **Molly Pitcher**, *Oct. 20* 15.00
Freehold, N.J. 15.00
Red Bank, N.J. 15.00

1928

647 2c **Hawaii**, *Aug. 13* 15.00
Honolulu, Hawaii 17.50
648 5c **Hawaii**, *Aug. 13* 22.50
Honolulu, Hawaii 25.00
647-648 on one cover 40.00
649 2c **Aero Conf.**, *Dec. 12* 7.00
650 5c **Aero Conf.**, *Dec. 12* 10.00
649-650 on one cover 15.00

1929

651 2c **Clark**, Vincennes, Indiana, *Feb. 25* 6.00
Washington, *Feb. 26*, first day of sale by Philatelic Agency 3.00

Perf. 11x10½

653 ½c **olive brown**, *May 25*, block of four 27.50
654 2c **Electric Light**, perf. 11, Menlo Park, N.J., *June 5* 10.00
Washington, D.C., *June 6*, first day of sale by Philatelic Agency 4.00
655 2c **Electric Light**, perf. 11x10½, *June 11* 80.00
656 2c **Electric Light**, perf. 10 vert., *June 11* 90.00
657 2c **Sullivan**, Auburn, N.Y., *June 17* 4.00
Binghamton, N.Y. 4.00
Canajoharie, N.Y. 4.00
Canandaigua, N.Y. 4.00
Elmira, N.Y. 4.00
Geneseo, N.Y. 4.00
Geneva, N.Y. 4.00
Horseheads, N.Y. 4.00
Owego, N.Y. 4.00
Penn Yan, N.Y 4.00
Perry, N.Y. 4.00
Seneca Falls, N.Y. 4.00
Waterloo, N.Y. 4.00
Watkins Glen, N.Y. 4.00
Waverly, N.Y. 4.00
Washington, D.C., *June 18* 2.00

1929

658 1c **Kansas**, *May 1*, pair 55.00
Newton, Kan., *Apr. 15* 325.00
659 1½c **Kansas**, *May 1*, pair 62.50
Colby, Kan., *Apr. 16* —
660 2c **Kansas**, *May 1* 62.50
Colby, Kan., *Apr. 16* —
661 3c **Kansas**, *May 1* 65.00
Colby, Kan., *Apr. 16* 450.00

No.	Description	Value
662	4c **Kansas,** *May 1*	110.00
	Colby, Kan., *Apr. 16*	—
663	5c **Kansas,** *May 1*	110.00
	Colby, Kan., *Apr. 16*	—
664	6c **Kansas,** *May 1*	140.00
	Newton, Kan., *Apr. 15*	900.00
665	7c **Kansas,** *May 1*	140.00
	Colby, Kan., *Apr. 16*	—
666	8c **Kansas,** *May 1*	140.00
	Newton, Kan., *Apr. 15*	900.00
667	9c **Kansas,** *May 1*	165.00
	Colby, Kan., *Apr. 16*	—
668	10c **Kansas,** *May 1*	220.00
	Colby, Kan., *Apr. 16*	—
	658-668 on 1 cover, Washington, D.C., *May 1*	1,500.
669	1c **Nebraska,** *May 1,* pair	55.00
	Beatrice, Neb., *Apr. 15*	250.00
670	1½c **Nebraska,** *May 1,* pair	57.50
	Hartington, Neb., *Apr. 15*	400.00
671	2c **Nebraska,** *May 1*	62.50
	Auburn, Neb., *Apr. 15*	1,200.
	Beatrice, Neb., *Apr. 15*	—
	Hartington, Neb., *Apr. 15*	300.00
672	3c **Nebraska,** *May 1*	65.00
	Beatrice, Neb., *Apr. 15*	400.00
	Hartington, Neb., *Apr. 15*	400.00
673	4c **Nebraska,** *May 1*	110.00
	Beatrice, Neb., *Apr. 15*	400.00
	Hartington, Neb., *Apr. 15*	400.00
674	5c **Nebraska,** *May 1*	110.00
	Beatrice, Neb., *Apr. 15*	275.00
	Hartington, Neb., *Apr. 15*	275.00
675	6c **Nebraska,** *May 1*	140.00
	Auburn, Neb., *Apr. 17*	400.00
	Ravenna, Neb., *Apr. 17*	—
	Wahoo, Neb., *Apr. 17*	—
676	7c **Nebraska,** *May 1*	165.00
	Auburn, Neb., *Apr. 17*	400.00
677	8c **Nebraska,** *May 1*	140.00
	Humbolt, Neb., *Apr. 17*	250.00
	Pawnee City, Neb., *Apr. 17*	400.00
678	9c **Nebraska,** *May 1*	165.00
	Cambridge, Neb., *Apr. 17*	400.00
679	10c **Nebraska,** *May 1*	220.00
	Tecumseh, Neb., *Apr. 18*	—
	669-679 on 1 cover, Washington, D.C., *May 1*	*1,500.*
	658-679 on 1 cover, Washington, D.C., *May 1*	*5,000.*
680	2c **Fallen Timbers,** Erie, Pa., *Sept. 14*	3.50
	Maumee, O.	3.50
	Perrysburg, O.	3.50
	Toledo, O.	3.50
	Waterville, O.	3.50
	Washington, D.C., *Sept. 16*	2.00
681	2c **Ohio River,** Cairo, Ill., *Oct. 19*	3.50
	Cincinnati, O.	3.50
	Evansville, Ind.	3.50
	Homestead, Pa.	3.50
	Louisville, Ky.	3.50
	Pittsburgh, Pa.	3.50
	Wheeling, W. Va.	3.50
	Washington, D.C., *Oct. 21*	2.00

1930

No.	Description	Value
682	2c **Massachusetts Bay Colony,** Boston, Mass. *Apr. 8 (60,000)*	3.50
	Salem, Mass.	3.50
	Washington, D.C., *Apr. 11*	2.00
683	2c **Carolina-Charleston,** Charleston, S.C. *Apr. 10*	3.50
	Washington, D.C., *Apr. 11*	2.00

Perf. 11x10½

No.	Description	Value
684	1½c **Harding,** Marion, O., *Dec. 1,* pair	4.50
	Washington, D.C., *Dec. 2*	2.50
685	4c **Taft,** Cincinnati, O., *June 4*	6.00
	Washington, D.C., *June 5*	3.00

Perf. 10 Vertically

No.	Description	Value
686	1½c **Harding,** Marion, Ohio, *Dec. 1*	5.00
	Washington, D.C., *Dec. 2*	3.00
687	4c **Taft,** *Sept. 18*	20.00

Perf. 11

No.	Description	Value
688	2c **Braddock,** Braddock, Pa., *July 9*	4.00
	Washington, D.C., *July 10*	2.00
689	2c **Von Steuben,** New York, N.Y., *Sept. 17*	4.00
	Washington, D.C., *Sept. 18*	2.00

1931

No.	Description	Value
690	2c **Pulaski,** Brooklyn, N.Y., *Jan. 16*	4.00
	Buffalo, N.Y.	4.00
	Chicago, Ill.	4.00
	Cleveland, O.	4.00
	Detroit, Mich.	4.00
	Gary, Ind.	4.00
	Milwaukee, Wis.	4.00
	New York, N.Y.	4.00
	Pittsburgh, Pa.	4.00
	Savannah, Ga.	4.00
	South Bend, Ind.	4.00
	Toledo, O.	4.00
	Washington, D.C., *Jan. 17*	2.00

1931 ***Perf. 11x10½, 10½x11***

No.	Description	Value
692	11c **Hayes,** *Sept. 4*	100.
693	12c **Cleveland,** *Aug. 25*	100.
694	13c **Harrison,** *Sept. 4*	100.
695	14c **American Indian,** *Sept. 8*	100.
696	15c **Liberty,** *Aug. 27*	120.
697	17c **Wilson,** *July 25,* Brooklyn, N.Y.	*2,750.*
	Washington, D.C., *July 27*	400.
698	20c **Golden Gate,** *Sept. 8*	300.
699	25c **Niagara Falls,** *July 25,* Brooklyn, N.Y.	*2,000.*
	Washington, D.C., *July 27*	350.
	697, 699 on one cover, Brooklyn, *July 25*	*5,750.*
	697, 699 on one cover, Washington, *July 27*	*2,500.*
700	30c **American Buffalo,** *Sept. 8*	300.
701	50c **Arlington,** *Sept. 4*	400.
	Woolrich, Pa., *Sept. 4*	625.

1931

No.	Description	Value
702	2c **Red Cross,** *May 21*	3.50
	Dansville, N.Y.	3.50
703	2c **Yorktown,** *Oct. 19,* Wethersfield, Conn.	3.50
	Yorktown, Va.	3.50
	Washington, D.C., *Oct. 20*	2.00

WASHINGTON BICENTENNIAL ISSUE

1932

No.	Description	Value
704	½c *Jan. 1,* block of 4	10.00
705	1c *Jan. 1,* pair	10.00
706	1½c *Jan. 1,* pair	10.00
707	2c *Jan. 1*	10.00
708	3c *Jan. 1*	10.00
709	4c *Jan. 1*	10.00
710	5c *Jan. 1*	10.00
711	6c *Jan. 1*	10.00
712	7c *Jan. 1*	10.00
713	8c *Jan. 1*	10.00
714	9c *Jan. 1*	10.00
715	10c *Jan. 1*	10.00
	704-715, set of 12 on one cover, *Jan. 1*	110.00

1932

No.	Description	Value
716	2c **Olympic Winter Games,** *Jan. 25,* Lake Placid, N.Y.	6.00
	Washington, D.C., *Jan. 26*	1.50
717	2c **Arbor Day,** *Apr. 22,* Nebraska City, Neb.	4.00
	Washington, D.C., *Apr. 23*	1.50
	Adams, N.Y., *Apr. 23*	6.50
718	3c **Olympic Summer Games,** *June 15,* Los Angeles, Cal.	6.00
	Washington, D.C., *June 16*	2.75
719	5c **Olympic Summer Games,** *June 15,* Los Angeles, Cal.	8.00
	Washington, D.C., *June 16*	2.75
	718, 719 on one cover, Los Angeles, Cal.	10.00
	718, 719 on one cover, Washington, D.C.	4.50
720	3c **Washington,** *June 16*	7.50
720b	Booklet pane of 6, *July 25*	100.00
721	3c **Washington Coil,** Sideways, *June 24*	15.00
722	3c **Washington Coil,** Endways, *Oct. 12*	15.00
723	6c **Garfield Coil,** Sideways, *Aug. 18,* Los Angeles, Cal.	15.00
	Washington, D.C., *Aug. 19*	4.00
724	3c **William Penn,** *Oct. 24,* New Castle, Del.	3.25
	Chester, Pa.	3.25
	Philadelphia, Pa.	3.25
	Washington, D.C., *Oct. 25*	1.25
725	3c **Daniel Webster,** *Oct. 24,* Franklin, N.H.	3.25
	Exeter, N.H.	3.25
	Hanover, N.H.	3.25
	Washington, D.C., *Oct. 25*	1.25

1933

No.	Description	Value
726	3c **Gen. Oglethorpe,** *Feb. 12,* Savannah, Ga., *(200,000)*	3.25
	Washington, D.C., *Feb. 13*	1.50
727	3c **Peace Proclamation,** *Apr. 19,* Newburgh, N.Y. *(349,571)*	3.50
	Washington, D.C., *Apr. 20*	1.25
728	1c **Century of Progress,** *May 25,* Chicago, Ill., strip of 3	3.00
	Washington, D.C., *May 26*	1.00
729	3c **Century of Progress,** *May 25,* Chicago, Ill.	3.00
	Washington, D.C., *May 26*	1.00
	728, 729 on one cover	5.00

Covers mailed May 25, bearing Nos. 728 and 729 total 232,251.

No.	Description	Value
730	1c **American Philatelic Society,** sheet of 25, *Aug. 25,* Chicago, Ill.	100.00
730a	1c **A.P.S.,** imperf., *Aug. 25,* Chicago, Ill., strip of 3	3.25
	Washington, D.C., *Aug. 28*	1.25
731	3c **American Philatelic Society,** sheet of 25, *Aug. 25,* Chicago, Ill.	100.00
731a	3c **A.P.S.,** single, imperf., *Aug. 25,* Chicago, Ill.	3.25
	Washington, D.C., *Aug. 28*	1.25
	730a, 731a on one cover	5.50

Covers mailed Aug. 25 bearing Nos. 730, 730a, 731, 731a total 65,218.

No.	Description	Value
732	3c **National Recovery Administration,** *Aug. 15,(65,000)*	3.25
	Nira, Iowa, *Aug. 17*	2.50
733	3c **Byrd Antarctic,** *Oct. 9*	10.00
734	5c **Kosciuszko,** *Oct. 13,* Boston, Mass. *(23,025)*	4.50
	Buffalo, N.Y. *(14,981)*	5.50
	Chicago, Ill, *(26,306)*	4.50
	Detroit, Mich. *(17,792)*	5.25
	Pittsburgh, Pa. *(6,282)*	15.00
	Kosciusko, Miss. *(27,093)*	5.25
	St. Louis, Mo. *(17,872)*	5.25
	Washington, D.C., *Oct. 14*	1.60

1934

No.	Description	Value
735	3c **National Exhibition,** sheet of 6, Byrd imperf., *Feb. 10,* New York, N.Y.	40.00
	Washington, D.C., *Feb. 19*	27.50
735a	3c **National Exhibition,** single, imperf., New York, N.Y., *Feb. 10 (450,715)*	5.00
	Washington, D.C., *Feb. 19*	2.75
736	3c **Maryland Tercentenary,** *Mar. 23* St. Mary's City, Md. *(148,785)*	1.60
	Washington, D.C., *Mar. 24*	1.00
737	3c **Mothers of America,** perf. 11x10½, *May 2, any city*	1.60
738	3c **Mothers of America,** perf. 11, *May 2, any city*	1.60
	737, 738 on one cover	4.00

Covers mailed at Washington, May 2 bearing Nos. 737 and 738 total 183,359.

No.	Description	Value
739	3c **Wisconsin,** *July 7,* Green Bay, Wisc. *(130,000)*	1.10
	Washington, D.C., *July 9*	1.00
740	1c **Parks, Yosemite,** *July 16*	2.25
	Yosemite, Cal., *(60,000),* strip of 3	2.75
741	2c **Parks, Grand Canyon,** *July 24*	2.25
	Grand Canyon, Ariz., *(75,000),* pair	2.75
742	3c **Parks, Mt. Rainier,** *Aug. 3*	2.50
	Longmire, Wash., *(64,500)*	3.00
743	4c **Parks, Mesa Verde,** *Sept. 25*	2.25
	Mesa Verde, Colo., *(51,882)*	2.75
744	5c **Parks, Yellowstone,** *July 30*	2.25
	Yellowstone, Wyo., *(87,000)*	2.50
745	6c **Parks, Crater Lake,** *Sept. 5*	3.00
	Crater Lake, Ore., *(45,282)*	3.25
746	7c **Parks, Arcadia,** *Oct. 2*	3.00
	Bar Harbor, Maine *(51,312)*	3.25
747	8c **Parks, Zion,** *Sept. 18*	3.25
	Zion, Utah, *(43,650)*	3.75
748	9c **Parks, Glacier Park,** *Aug. 27*	3.50
	Glacier Park, Mont., *(52,626)*	3.75
749	10c **Parks, Smoky Mountains,** *Oct. 8*	6.00
	Sevierville, Tenn., *(39,000)*	7.50

Imperf

No.	Description	Value
750	3c **American Philatelic Society,** sheet of 6, *Aug. 28,* Atlantic City, N.J.	40.00
750a	3c **A.P.S.,** single, *Aug. 28,* Atlantic City, N.J. *(40,000)*	3.25
	Washington, D.C., *Sept. 4*	2.00
751	1c **Trans-Mississippi Philatelic Expo.,** sheet of 6, *Oct. 10,* Omaha, Neb.	35.00
751a	1c **Trans-Miss. Phil. Expo.,** Omaha. Neb., *Oct. 10 (125,000),* strip of 3	3.25
	Washington, D.C., Oct. 15	2.00

Nos. 752-771 issued Mar. 15

1935 **SPECIAL PRINTING**

No.	Description	Value
752	3c **Peace Commemoration**	5.00
753	3c **Byrd**	6.00
754	3c **Mothers of America**	6.00
755	3c **Wisconsin Tercentenary**	6.00
756	1c **Parks, Yosemite,** strip of 3	6.00
757	2c **Parks, Grand Canyon,** pair	6.00
758	3c **Parks, Mount Rainier**	6.00
759	4c **Parks, Mesa Verde**	6.50
760	5c **Parks, Yellowstone**	6.50
761	6c **Parks, Crater Lake**	6.50
762	7c **Parks, Acadia**	6.50
763	8c **Parks, Zion**	7.50
764	9c **Parks, Glacier Park**	7.50
765	10c **Parks, Smoky Mountains**	7.50
766a	1c **Century of Progress,** strip of 3	5.50
	Pane of 25	*250.00*
767a	3c **Century of Progress**	5.50
	Pane of 25	*250.00*
768a	3c **Byrd**	6.50
	Pane of 6	*250.00*
769a	1c **Parks, Yosemite,** strip of 3	4.00
	Pane of 6	*250.00*
770a	3c **Parks, Mount Rainier**	5.00
	Pane of 6	*250.00*
771	16c **Airmail Special Delivery**	12.50

Catalogue values from this point to No. 986 are for addressed covers with the most common cachets.

No.	Description	Value
772	3c **Connecticut Tercentenary,** *Apr. 26,* Hartford, Conn. *(217,800)*	15.00
	Washington, D.C., *Apr. 27*	2.25
773	3c **California Exposition,** *May 29,* San Diego, Cal. *(214,042)*	15.00
	Washington, D.C., *May 31*	1.50
774	3c **Boulder Dam,** *Sept. 30,* Boulder City, Nev. *(166,180)*	15.00
	Washington, D.C., *Oct. 1*	2.00
775	3c **Michigan Centenary,** *Nov. 1,* Lansing, Mich. *(176,962)*	15.00
	Washington, D.C., *Nov. 2*	1.50

1936

No.	Description	Value
776	3c **Texas Centennial,** *Mar. 2,* Gonzales, Texas *(319,150)*	20.00
	Washington, D.C., *Mar. 3*	2.00
777	3c **Rhode Island Tercentenary,** *May 4,* Providence, R.I. *(245,400)*	14.00
	Washington, D.C., *May 5*	2.25
778	**TIPEX** souvenir sheet, *May 9 (297,194) New York, N.Y.* (TIPEX cancellation)	14.00
	Washington, D.C., *May 11*	3.50
782	3c **Arkansas Centennial,** *June 15,* Little Rock, Ark. *(376,693)*	13.00
	Washington, D.C, *June 16*	1.25
783	3c **Oregon Territory Centennial,** *July 14,* Astoria, Ore. *(91,110)*	10.00
	Daniel, Wyo., *(67,013)*	10.00
	Lewiston, Ida., *(86,100)*	10.00
	Missoula, Mont., *(59,883)*	11.00
	Walla Walla, Wash., *(106,150)*	9.00
	Washington, D.C., *July 15*	1.25
784	3c **Susan B. Anthony,** *Aug. 26 (178,500)*	15.00

1936-37

No.	Description	Value
785	1c **Army,** *Dec. 15, 1936,* strip of 3	8.50
786	2c **Army,** *Jan. 15, 1937,* pair	8.50
787	3c **Army,** *Feb. 18, 1937*	8.50
788	4c **Army,** *Mar. 23, 1937*	8.50

789 5c **Army,** *May 26, 1937,* West Point, N.Y., *(160,000)* 8.50
Washington, D.C., *May 27* 4.50
790 1c **Navy,** *Dec. 15, 1936,* strip of 3 8.50
791 2c **Navy,** *Jan. 15, 1937,* pair 8.50
792 3c **Navy,** *Feb. 18, 1937* 8.50
793 4c **Navy,** *Mar. 23, 1937* 8.50
794 5c **Navy,** *May 26, 1937,* Annapolis, Md., *(202,806)* 8.50
Washington, D.C., *May 27* 4.50

Covers for #785 & 790 total 390,749; #786 & 791 total 292,570; #787 & 792 total 320,888; #788 & 793 total 331,000.

1937

795 3c **Ordinance of 1787,** *July 13* Marietta, Ohio *(130,531)* 9.00
New York, N.Y. *(125,134)* 9.00
Washington, D.C., *July 14* 1.25
796 5c **Virginia Dare,** *Aug. 18,* Manteo, N.C. *(226,730)* 11.00
797 10c **Souvenir Sheet,** *Aug. 26,* Asheville, N.C. *(164,215)* 11.00
798 3c **Constitution,** *Sept. 17,* Philadelphia, Pa. *(281,478)* 9.00
799 3c **Hawaii,** *Oct. 18,* Honolulu, Hawaii *(320,334)* 11.00
800 3c **Alaska,** *Nov. 12,* Juneau, Alaska *(230,370)* 10.00
801 3c **Puerto Rico,** *Nov. 25,* San Juan, P.R. *(244,054)* 10.00
802 3c **Virgin Islands,** *Dec. 15,* Charlotte Amalie, V.I. *(225,469)* 10.00

PRESIDENTIAL ISSUE

1938

803 ½c **Franklin,** *May 19,* Philadelphia, Pa. *(224,901),* block of 6 3.50
804 1c **G. Washington,** *Apr. 25 (124,037),* strip of 3 3.50
804b Booklet pane of 6, *Jan. 27, 1939* 12.50
805 1½c **M. Washington,** *May 5 (128,339),* pair 3.50
806 2c **J. Adams,** *June 3 (127,806),* pair 3.50
806b Booklet pane of 6, *Jan. 27, 1939* 15.00
807 3c **Jefferson,** *June 16 (118,097)* 3.50
807a Booklet pane of 6, *Jan. 27, 1939* 17.50
808 4c **Madison,** *July 1 (118,765)* 3.50
809 4½c **White House,** *July 11 (115,820)* 3.50
810 5c **Monroe,** *July 21 (98,282)* 3.50
811 6c **J.Q. Adams,** *July 28 (97,428)* 3.50
812 7c **Jackson,** *Aug. 4 (98,414)* 3.50
813 8c **Van Buren,** *Aug. 11 (94,857)* 3.50
814 9c **W.H. Harrison,** *Aug. 18 (91,229)* 3.50
815 10c **Tyler,** *Sept. 2 (83,707)* 3.50
816 11c **Polk,** *Sept. 8 (63,966)* 5.00
817 12c **Taylor,** *Sept. 14 (62,935)* 5.00
818 13c **Fillmore,** *Sept. 22 (58,965)* 5.00
819 14c **Pierce,** *Oct. 6 (49,819)* 5.00
820 15c **Buchanan,** *Oct. 13 (52,209)* 5.00
821 16c **Lincoln,** *Oct. 20 (59,566)* 7.50
822 17c **A. Johnson,** *Oct. 27 (55,024)* 6.00
823 18c **Grant,** *Nov. 3 (53,124)* 6.00
824 19c **Hayes,** *Nov. 10 (54,124)* 6.00
825 20c **Garfield,** *Nov. 10 (51,971)* 7.00
826 21c **Arthur,** *Nov. 22 (44,367)* 7.00
827 22c **Cleveland,** *Nov. 22 (44,358)* 8.00
828 24c **B. Harrison,** *Dec. 2 (46,592)* 8.00
829 25c **McKinley,** *Dec. 2 (45,691)* 8.00
830 30c **T. Roosevelt,** *Dec. 8 (43,528)* 9.00
831 50c **Taft,** *Dec. 8 (41,984)* 12.50
832 $1 **Wilson, purple & black,** *Aug. 29 (24,618)* 60.00
832c **red violet & black,** *Aug. 31, 1954 (20,202)* 30.00
833 $2 **Harding,** *Sept. 29 (19,895)* 120.00
834 $5 **Coolidge,** *Nov. 17 (15,615)* 200.00

1938

835 3c **Constitution,** *June 21,* Philadelphia, Pa. *(232,873)* 15.00
836 3c **Swedes and Finns,** *June 27,* Wilmington, Del. *(225,617)* 15.00
837 3c **Northwest Sesqui.,** *July 15,* Marietta, Ohio *(180,170)* 15.00
838 3c **Iowa,** *Aug. 24,* Des Moines, Iowa *(209,860)* 15.00

1939 **COIL STAMPS** ***Perf. 10 Vertically***

839 1c **G. Washington,** *Jan. 20,* strip of 3 5.00
840 1½c **M. Washington,** *Jan. 20,* pair 5.00
841 2c **J. Adams,** *Jan. 20,* pair 5.00
842 3c **Jefferson,** *Jan. 20* 5.00
843 4c **Madison,** *Jan. 20* 5.00
844 4½c **White House,** *Jan. 20* 5.00
845 5c **Monroe,** *Jan. 20* 5.00
846 6c **J.Q. Adams,** *Jan. 20* 6.50
847 10c **Tyler,** *Jan. 20* 9.00
839-847 on one cover, *Jan. 20* 45.00

Perf. 10 Horizontally

848 1c Strip of 3, *Jan. 27* 5.00
849 1½c Pair, *Jan. 27* 5.00
850 2c Pair, *Jan. 27* 5.00
851 3c *Jan. 27* 5.50
848-851 on one cover, *Jan. 27* 25.00

1939

852 3c **Golden Gate Expo,** *Feb. 18,* San Francisco, Cal. *(352,165)* 16.00
853 3c **N.Y. World's Fair,** *Apr. 1,* New York, N.Y. *(585,565)* 20.00
854 3c **Washington Inauguration,** *Apr. 30,* New York, N.Y. *(395,644)* 17.50
855 3c **Baseball Centennial,** *June 12,* Cooperstown, N.Y. *(398,199)* 35.00
856 3c **Panama Canal,** *Aug. 15,* U.S.S. Charleston, Canal Zone *(230,974)* 18.00
857 3c **Printing Tercentenary,** *Sept. 25,* New York, N.Y. *(295,270)* 15.00
858 3c **50th Statehood Anniversary,** Bismarck, N.D. *Nov. 2 (142,106)* 12.50
Pierre, S.D., *Nov. 2 (150,429)* 12.50
Helena, Mont., *Nov. 8 (130,273)* 12.50
Olympia, Wash., *Nov. 11 (150,429)* 12.50

FAMOUS AMERICAN ISSUE

1940

859 1c **Washington Irving,** *Jan. 29,* Tarrytown, N.Y. *(170,969),* strip of 3 4.50
860 2c **James Fenimore Cooper,** *Jan. 29,* Cooperstown, N.Y. *(154,836),* pair 3.00
861 3c **Ralph Waldo Emerson,** *Feb. 5,* Boston, Mass. *(185,148)* 3.00
862 5c **Louisa May Alcott,** *Feb. 5,* Concord, Mass. *(134,325)* 4.00
863 10c **Samuel L. Clemens,** *Feb. 13,* Hannibal, Mo. *(150,492)* 8.00
864 1c **Henry W. Longfellow,** *Feb. 16,* Portland, Me. *(160,508),* strip of 3 4.00
865 2c **John Greenleaf Whittier,** *Feb. 16,* Haverhill, Mass. *(148,423),* pair 3.00
866 3c **James Russell Lowell,** *Feb. 20,* Cambridge, Mass. *(148,735)* 3.00
867 5c **Walt Whitman,** *Feb. 20,* Camden, N.J. *(134,185)* 4.00
868 10c **James Whitcomb Riley,** *Feb. 24,* Greenfield, Ind. *(131,760)* 6.00
869 1c **Horace Mann,** *Mar. 14,* Boston, Mass. *(186,854),* strip of 3 3.00
870 2c **Mark Hopkins,** *Mar. 14,* Williamstown, Mass. *(140,286),* pair 3.00
871 3c **Charles W. Eliot,** *Mar. 28,* Cambridge, Mass. *(155,708)* 3.00
872 5c **Frances E. Willard,** *Mar. 28,* Evanston, Ill. *(140,483)* 4.00
873 10c **Booker T. Washington,** *Apr. 7,* Tuskegee Institute, Ala. *(163,507)* 10.00
874 1c **John James Audubon,** *Apr. 8,* St. Francisville, La. *(144,123),* strip of 3 4.00
875 2c **Dr. Crawford W. Long,** *Apr. 8,* Jefferson, Ga. *(158,128),* pair 3.00
876 3c **Luther Burbank,** *Apr. 17,* Santa Rosa, Cal. *(147,033)* 3.00
877 5c **Dr. Walter Reed,** *Apr. 17 (154,464)* 4.00
878 10c **Jane Addams,** *Apr. 26,* Chicago, Ill. *(132,375)* 6.00
879 1c **Stephen Collins Foster,** *May 3,* Bardstown, Ky. *(183,461),* strip of 3 3.00
880 2c **John Philip Sousa,** *May 3 (131,422),* pair 4.00
881 3c **Victor Herbert,** *May 13,* New York, N.Y. *(168,200)* 3.00
882 5c **Edward A. MacDowell,** *May 13,* Peterborough, N.H. *(135,155)* 4.00
883 10c **Ethelbert Nevin,** *June 10,* Pittsburgh, Pa. *(121,951)* 6.00
884 1c **Gilbert Stuart,** *Sept. 5,* Narragansett, R.I. *(131,965),* strip of 3 4.00
885 2c **James A. McNeill Whistler,** *Sept. 5,* Lowell, Mass. *(130,962),* pair 3.00
886 3c **Augustus Saint-Gaudens,** *Sept. 16,* New York, N.Y. *(138,200)* 3.00
887 5c **Daniel Chester French,** *Sept. 16,* Stockbridge, Mass. *(124,608)* 4.00
888 10c **Frederic Remington,** *Sept. 30,* Canton, N.Y. *(116,219)* 7.00
889 1c **Eli Whitney,** *Oct. 7,* Savannah, Ga. *(140,868),* strip of 3 4.00
890 2c **Samuel F.B. Morse,** *Oct. 7,* New York, N.Y. *(135,388),* pair 3.00
891 3c **Cyrus Hall McCormick,** *Oct. 14,* Lexington, Va. *(137,415)* 3.00
892 5c **Elias Howe,** *Oct. 14,* Spencer, Mass. *(126,334)* 4.00
893 10c **Alexander Graham Bell,** *Oct. 28,* Boston, Mass. *(125,372)* 10.00

1940

894 3c **Pony Express,** *Apr. 3,* St. Joseph, Mo. *(194,589)* 12.00
Sacramento, Cal. *(160,849)* 12.00
895 3c **Pan American Union,** *Apr. 14 (182,401)* 9.50
896 3c **Idaho Statehood,** *July 3,* Boise, Idaho *(156,429)* 9.50
897 3c **Wyoming Statehood,** *July 10* Cheyenne, Wyo. *(156,709)* 9.50
898 3c **Coronado Expedition,** *Sept. 7,* Albuquerque, N.M. *(161,012)* 9.50
899 1c **Defense,** *Oct. 16,* strip of 3 7.50
900 2c **Defense,** *Oct. 16,* pair 7.50
901 3c **Defense,** *Oct. 16* 7.50
899-901 on one cover 12.00

First day cancel was applied to 450,083 covers bearing one or more of Nos. 899-901.

902 3c **Thirteenth Amendment,** *Oct. 20,* World's Fair, N.Y. *(156,146)* 10.00

1941

903 3c **Vermont Statehood,** *Mar. 4,* Montpelier, Vt. *(182,423)* 10.00

MacArthur, W. Va.
Apr 15, 1942
First Day Cover

Covers exist with this cancellation. "First Day" refers to the first day of the new name of the town, previously known as Hollywood, W. Va.

1942

904 3c **Kentucky Statehood,** *June 1,* Frankfort, Ky. *(155,730)* 10.00
905 3c **"Win the War",** *July 4 (191,168)* 10.00
906 5c **Chinese Resistance,** *July 7,* Denver, Colo. *(168,746)* 20.00

1943-44

907 2c **Allied Nations,** *Jan. 14, 1943 (178,865),* pair 6.00
908 1c **Four Freedoms,** *Feb. 12, 1943 (193,800),* strip of 3 7.00
909 5c **Poland,** *June 22, 1943,* Chicago, Ill. *(88,170)* 10.00
Washington, D.C. *(136,002)* 5.00
910 5c **Czechoslovakia,** *July 12, 1943 (145,112)* 4.00
911 5c **Norway,** *July 27, 1943 (155,054)* 4.00
912 5c **Luxemborg,** *Aug. 10, 1943 (166,367)* 4.00
913 5c **Netherlands,** *Aug. 24, 1943 (148,763)* 4.00
914 5c **Belgium,** *Sept. 14, 1943 (154,220)* 4.00
915 5c **France,** *Sept. 28, 1943 (163,478)* 4.00
916 5c **Greece,** *Oct. 12, 1943 (166,553)* 4.00
917 5c **Yugoslavia,** *Oct. 26, 1943 (161,835)* 4.00
918 5c **Albania,** *Nov. 9, 1943 (162,275)* 4.00
919 5c **Austria,** *Nov. 23, 1943 (172,285)* 4.00
920 5c **Denmark,** *Dec. 7, 1943 (173,784)* 4.00
921 5c **Korea,** *Nov. 2, 1944 (192,860)* 5.00

1944

922 3c **Railroad,** *May 10,* Ogden, Utah *(151,324)* 10.00
Omaha, Neb. *(171,000)* 10.00
San Francisco, Cal. *(125,000)* 10.00
923 3c **Steamship,** *May 22,* Kings Point, N.Y. *(152,324)* 9.00
Savannah, Ga. *(181,472)* 9.00
924 3c **Telegraph,** *May 24 (141,907)* 9.00
Baltimore, Md. *(136,480)* 9.00
925 3c **Philippines,** *Sept. 27 (214,865)* 9.00
926 3c **Motion Picture,** *Oct. 31,* Hollywood, Cal. *(190,660)* 10.00
New York, N.Y. *(176,473)* 9.00

1945

927 3c **Florida,** *Mar. 3,* Tallahassee, Fla. *(228,435)* 9.00
928 5c **United Nations Conference,** *Apr. 25,* San Francisco, Cal. *(417,450)* 10.00
929 3c **Iwo Jima,** *July 11 (391,650)* 15.00

1945-46

930 1c **Roosevelt,** *July 26, 1945,* Hyde Park, N.Y. *(390,219),* strip of 3 5.00
931 2c **Roosevelt,** *Aug. 24, 1945,* Warm Springs, Ga. *(426,142),* pair 5.00
932 3c **Roosevelt,** *June 27, 1945 (391,650)* 5.00
933 5c **Roosevelt,** *Jan. 30, 1946 (466,766)* 5.00

1945

934 3c **Army,** *Sept. 28 (392,300)* 11.00
935 3c **Navy,** *Oct. 27,* Annapolis, Md. *(460,352)* 11.00
936 3c **Coast Guard,** *Nov. 10* New York, N.Y. *(405,280)* 11.00
937 3c **Alfred E. Smith,** *Nov. 26* New York, N.Y. *(424,950)* 3.00
938 3c **Texas,** *Dec. 29,* Austin, Tex. *(397,860)* 10.00

1946

939 3c **Merchant Marine,** *Feb. 26 (432,141)* 9.00
940 3c **Veterans of WWII,** *May 9 (492,786)* 12.00
941 3c **Tennessee,** *June 1, 1946,* Nashville, Tenn. *(463,512)* 4.00
942 3c **Iowa,** *Aug. 3,* Iowa City, Iowa *(517,505)* 4.00
943 3c **Smithsonian,** *Aug. 10 (402,448)* 4.00
944 3c **Kearny Expedition,** *Oct. 16,* Santa Fe, N.M. *(384,300)* 4.00

1947

945 3c **Thomas A. Edison,** *Feb. 11,* Milan, Ohio *(632,473)* 5.00
946 3c **Joseph Pulitzer,** *Apr. 10,* New York, N.Y. *(580,870)* 4.00
947 3c **Stamp Centenary,** *May 17,* New York, N.Y. *(712,873)* 4.00
948 5c and 10c **Centenary Exhibition Sheet,** *May 19,* New York, N.Y. *(502,175)* 4.50
949 3c **Doctors,** *June 9,* Atlantic City, N.J. *(508,016)* 10.00
950 3c **Utah,** *July 24,* Salt Lake City, Utah *(456,416)* 3.00
951 3c **"Constitution,"** *Oct. 21,* Boston, Mass. *(683,416)* 10.00
952 3c **Everglades Park,** *Dec. 5,* Florida City, Fla. *(466,647)* 3.00

1948

953 3c **Carver,** *Jan. 5,* Tuskegee Institute, Ala. *(402,179)* 3.00
954 3c **California Gold,** *Jan. 24,* Coloma, Calif. *(526,154)* 4.00
955 3c **Mississippi Territory,** *Apr. 7,* Natchez, Miss. *(434,804)* 2.00
956 3c **Four Chaplains,** *May 28 (459,070)* 10.00
957 3c **Wisconsin Centennial,** *May 29,* Madison, Wis. *(470,280)* 3.00
958 5c **Swedish Pioneers,** *June 4* Chicago, Ill. *(364,318)* 4.00
959 3c **Women's Progress,** *July 19,* Seneca Falls, N.Y. *(401,923)* 3.00
960 3c **William Allen White,** *July 31,* Emporia, Kans. *(385,648)* 2.50
961 3c **U.S.-Canada Friendship,** *Aug. 2,* Niagara Falls, N.Y. *(406,467)* 3.00
962 3c **Francis Scott Key,** *Aug. 9,* Frederick, Md. *(505,930)* 2.50
963 3c **Salute to Youth,** *Aug. 11 (347,070)* 2.50
964 3c **Oregon Territory Establishment,** *Aug. 14,* Oregon City, Ore. *(365,898)* 3.00

965 3c **Harlan Fiske Stone**, *Aug. 25*, Chesterfield, N.H. *(362,170)* 2.50
966 3c **Palomar Observatory**, *Aug. 30*, Palomar Mountain, Calif. *(401,365)* 5.00
967 3c **Clara Barton**, *Sept. 7*, Oxford, Mass. *(362,000)* 4.00
968 3c **Poultry Industry**, *Sept. 9*, New Haven, Conn. *(475,000)* 3.50
969 3c **Gold Star Mothers**, *Sept. 21 (386,064)* 2.00
970 3c **Fort Kearny**, *Sept. 22*, Minden, Neb. *(429,633)* 2.00
971 3c **Volunteer Firemen**, *Oct. 4*, Dover, Del. *(399,630)* 10.00
972 3c **Indian Centennial**, *Oct. 15*, Muskogee, Okla. *(459,528)* 3.50
973 3c **Rough Riders**, *Oct. 27*, Prescott, Ariz. *(399,198)* 2.50
974 3c **Juliette Low**, *Oct. 29*, Savannah, Ga. *(476,573)* 8.00
975 3c **Will Rogers**, *Nov. 4*, Claremore, Okla. *(450,350)* 3.00
976 3c **Fort Bliss**, *Nov. 5*, El Paso, Tex. *(421,000)* 5.00
977 3c **Moina Michael**, *Nov. 9*, Athens, Ga. *(374,090)* 2.50
978 3c **Gettysburg Address**, *Nov. 19*, Gettysburg, Pa. *(511,990)* 3.00
979 3c **American Turners Society**, *Nov. 20*, Cincinnati, Ohio *(434,090)* 2.00
980 3c **Joel Chandler Harris**, *Dec. 9*, Eatonton, Ga. *(426,199)* 2.25

1949

981 3c **Minnesota Territory**, *Mar. 3*, St. Paul, Minn. *(458,750)* 2.25
982 3c **Washington and Lee University**, *Apr. 12*, Lexington, Va. *(447,910)* 2.25
983 3c **Puerto Rico Election**, *Apr. 27*, San Juan, P.R. *(390,416)* 2.25
984 3c **Annapolis, Md.**, *May 23*, Annapolis, Md. *(441,802)* 3.00
985 3c **G.A.R.**, *Aug. 29*, Indianapolis, Ind. *(471,696)* 3.25
986 3c **Edgar Allan Poe**, *Oct. 7*, Richmond, Va. *(371,020)* 4.00

Catalogue values from this point to the end of the section are for unaddressed covers with the most common cachets.

1950

987 3c **American Bankers Assoc.**, *Jan. 3*, Saratoga Springs, N.Y. *(388,622)* 2.75
988 3c **Samuel Gompers**, *Jan. 27 (332,023)* 1.75

National Capital Sesquicentennial

989 3c **Freedom**, *Apr. 20 (371,743)* 1.50
990 3c **Executive**, *June 12 (376,789)* 1.50
991 3c **Judicial**, *Aug. 2 (324,007)* 1.50
992 3c **Legislative**, *Nov. 22 (352,215)* 1.50
993 3c **Railroad Engineers**, *Apr. 29*, Jackson, Tenn. *(420,830)* 4.00
994 3c **Kansas City Centenary**, *June 3*, Kansas City, Mo. *(405,390)* 1.50
995 3c **Boy Scouts**, *June 30*, Valley Forge, Pa. *(622,972)* 12.00
996 3c **Indiana Territory Sesquicentennial**, *July 4*, Vincennes, Ind. *(359,643)* 1.75
997 3c **California Statehood**, *Sept. 9*, Sacramento, Cal. *(391,919)* 2.50

1951

998 3c **United Confederate Veterans**, *May 30*, Norfolk, Va. *(374,235)* 3.00
999 3c **Nevada Centennial**, *July 14*, Genoa, Nev. *(336,890)* 1.50
1000 3c **Landing of Cadillac**, *July 24*, Detroit, Mich. *(323,094)* 1.50
1001 3c **Colorado Statehood**, *Aug. 1*, Minturn, Colo. *(311,568)* 1.50
1002 3c **American Chemical Society**, *Sept. 4*, New York, N.Y. *(436,419)* 1.75
1003 3c **Battle of Brooklyn**, *Dec. 10*, Brooklyn, N.Y. *(420,000)* 1.50

1952

1004 3c **Betsy Ross**, *Jan. 2*, Philadelphia, Pa. *(314,312)* 1.50
1005 3c **4-H Club**, *Jan. 15*, Springfield, Ohio *(383,290)* 3.25
1006 3c **B. & O. Railroad**, *Feb. 28*, Baltimore, Md. *(441,600)* 4.50
1007 3c **American Automobile Association**, *Mar. 4*, Chicago, Ill. *(520,123)* 1.75
1008 3c **NATO**, *Apr. 4 (313,518)* 1.50
1009 3c **Grand Coulee Dam**, *May 15*, Grand Coulee, Wash. *(341,680)* 1.50
1010 3c **Lafayette**, *June 13*, Georgetown, S.C. *(349,102)* 1.50
1011 3c **Mt. Rushmore Memorial**, *Aug. 11*, Keystone, S.D. *(337,027)* 1.50
1012 3c **Civil Engineers**, *Sept. 6*, Chicago, Ill. *(318,483)* 1.50
1013 3c **Service Women**, *Sept. 11 (308,062)* 2.00
1014 3c **Gutenberg Bible**, *Sept. 30 (387,078)* 1.50
1015 3c **Newspaper Boys**, *Oct. 4*, Philadelphia, Pa. *(626,000)* 1.50
1016 3c **Red Cross**, *Nov. 21*, New York, N.Y. *(439,252)* 2.50

1953

1017 3c **National Guard**, *Feb. 23 (387,618)* 2.00
1018 3c **Ohio Sesquicentennial**, *Mar. 2*, Chillicothe, Ohio *(407,983)* 1.50
1019 3c **Washington Territory**, *Mar. 2*, Olympia, Wash. *(344,047)* 1.50
1020 3c **Louisiana Purchase**, *Apr. 30*, St. Louis, Mo. *(425,600)* 1.50
1021 5c **Opening of Japan**, *July 14 (320,541)* 2.00
1022 3c **American Bar Association**, *Aug. 24*, Boston, Mass. *(410,036)* 8.00
1023 3c **Sagamore Hill**, *Sept. 14*, Oyster Bay, N.Y. *(379,750)* 1.50
1024 3c **Future Farmers**, *Oct. 13*, Kansas City, Mo. *(424,193)* 1.50
1025 3c **Trucking Industry**, *Oct. 27*, Los Angeles, Calif. *(875,021)* 1.50
1026 3c **Gen. G.S. Patton, Jr.**, *Nov. 11*, Fort Knox, Ky. *(342,600)* *5.00*
1027 3c **New York City**, *Nov. 20*, New York, N.Y. *(387,914)* 1.50
1028 3c **Gadsden Purchase**, *Dec. 30*, Tucson, Ariz. *(363,250)* 1.50

1954

1029 3c **Columbia University**, *Jan. 4*, New York, N.Y. *(550,745)* 1.50

LIBERTY ISSUE

1954-67

1030 ½c **Franklin**, *Oct. 20, 1955 (223,122)*, block of 6 1.00
1031 1c **Washington**, *Aug. 26, 1954*, Chicago, Ill. *(272,581)*, strip of 3 1.00
1031A 1¼c **Palace of Governors**, *June 17, 1960*, Santa Fe, N.M., strip of 3 1.00
1031A and 1054A on one cover 1.50

First day cancel was applied to 501,848 covers bearing one or more of Nos. 1031A, 1054A.

1032 1½c **Mt. Vernon**, *Feb. 22, 1956*, Mount Vernon, Va. *(270,109)*, pair 1.00
1033 2c **Jefferson**, *Sept. 15, 1954*, San Francisco, Cal. *(307,300)*, pair 1.00
1033a 2c **Jefferson** on Silkote paper, *Dec. 17, 1954*, Westbrook, Maine *10,000.*
1034 2½c **Bunker Hill**, *June 17, 1959*, Boston, Mass. *(315,060)*, pair 1.00
1035 3c **Statue of Liberty**, *June 24, 1954*, Albany, N.Y. *(340,001)* 1.00
1035a Booklet pane of 6, *June 30, 1954* 3.50
1035e 3c Tagged, *July 6, 1966* 40.00
1036 4c **Lincoln**, *Nov. 19, 1954*, New York, N.Y. *(374,064)* 1.50
1036b Booklet pane of 6, *July 31, 1958*, Wheeling, W. Va. *(135,825)* 4.00
1036e 4c Tagged, *Nov. 2, 1963* 65.00

No. 1036e was supposed to have been issued at Dayton Nov. 2, but a mix-up delayed its issuance there until Nov. 4. About 510 Covers received the Nov. 2 cancellation.

1037 4½c **Hermitage**, *Mar. 16, 1959*, Hermitage, Tenn. *(320,000)* 1.00
1038 5c **Monroe**, *Dec. 2, 1954*, Fredericksburg, Va. *(255,650)* 1.00
1039 6c **T. Roosevelt**, *Nov. 18, 1955*, New York, N.Y. *(257,551)* 1.00
1040 7c **Wilson**, *Jan. 10, 1956*, Staunton, Va. *(200,111)* 1.00
1041 8c **Statue of Liberty** (flat plate), *Apr. 9, 1954* 1.00
1041B 8c **Statue of Liberty** (rotary press), *Apr. 9, 1954* 1.00

First day cancellation was applied to 340,077 covers bearing one or more of Nos. 1041-1041B.

1042 8c **Statue of Liberty** (Giori press), *Mar. 22, 1958*, Cleveland, O. *(223,899)* 1.00
1043 9c **Alamo**, *June 14, 1956*, San Antonio, Texas *(207,086)* 2.00
1044 10c **Independence Hall**, *July 4, 1956*, Philadelphia, Pa., *(220,930)* 1.00
1044d 10c Tagged, *July 6, 1966* 40.00
1044A 11c **Statue of Liberty**, *June 15, 1961* *(238,905)* 1.25
1044Ac 11c Tagged, *Jan. 11, 1967* 40.00
1045 12c **B. Harrison**, *June 6, 1959*, Oxford, O. *(225,869)* 1.25
1045a 12c Tagged, *May 6, 1968* 40.00
1046 15c **Jay**, *Dec. 12, 1958 (205,680)* 1.25
1046a 15c Tagged, *July 6, 1966* 40.00
1047 20c **Monticello**, *Apr. 13, 1956*, Charlottesville, Va. *(147,860)* 1.25
1048 25c **Revere**, *Apr. 18, 1958*, Boston, Mass. *(196,530)* 1.25
1049 30c **Lee**, *Sept. 21, 1955*, Norfolk, Va. *(120,166)* 2.00
1050 40c **Marshall**, *Sept. 24, 1955*, Richmond, Va. *(113,972)* 2.00
1051 50c **Anthony**, *Aug. 25, 1955*, Louisville, Ky. *(110,220)* 6.00
1052 $1 **Henry**, *Oct. 7, 1955*, Joplin, Mo. *(80,191)* 15.00
1053 $5 **Hamilton**, *Mar. 19, 1956*, Paterson, N.J. *(34,272)* 50.00

1954-73 COIL STAMPS

1054 1c **Washington**, *Oct. 8, 1954*, Baltimore, Md. *(196,318)*, strip of 3 1.00
1054A 1¼c **Palace of Governors**, *June 17, 1960*, Santa Fe, N.M., strip of 3 1.00
1055 2c **Jefferson**, *Oct. 22, 1954*, St. Louis, Mo. *(162,050)*, pair 1.00
1055b 2c Tagged, *May 6, 1968*, pair, small holes 32.50
Large holes, pair or strip, *May 6, 1968* —
1056 2½c **Bunker Hill**, *Sept. 9, 1959*, Los Angeles, Calif. *(198,680)*, pair 2.00
1057 3c **Statue of Liberty**, *July 20, 1954* *(137,139)* 1.00
1058 4c **Lincoln**, *July 31, 1958*, Mandan, N.D. *(184,079)* 1.50
1059 4½c **Hermitage**, *May 1, 1959*, Denver, Colo. *(202,454)* 1.75
1059A 25c **Revere**, *Feb. 25, 1965*, Wheaton, Md. *(184,954)* 1.25
1059Ab 25c Tagged, *Apr. 3, 1973*, New York, N.Y. 40.00

1954

1060 3c **Nebraska Territory**, *May 7*, Nebraska City, Neb. *(401,015)* 1.00
1061 3c **Kansas Territory**, *May 31*, Fort Leavenworth, Kans. *(349,145)* 1.00
1062 3c **George Eastman**, *July 12*, Rochester, N.Y. *(630,448)* 1.00
1063 3c **Lewis & Clark Expedition**, *July 28*, Sioux City, Iowa *(371,557)* 2.00

1955

1064 3c **Pennsylvania Academy of the Fine Arts**, *Jan. 15*, Philadelphia, Pa. *(307,040)* 1.00
1065 3c **Land Grant Colleges**, *Feb. 12*, East Lansing, Mich. *(419,241)* 1.25
1066 8c **Rotary International**, *Feb. 23*, Chicago, Ill. *(350,625)* 3.00
1067 3c **Armed Forces Reserve**, *May 21* *(300,436)* 1.25
1068 3c **New Hampshire**, *June 21*, Franconia, N.H. *(330,630)* 2.00
1069 3c **Soo Locks**, *June 28*, Sault Sainte Marie, Mich. *(316,616)* 1.00
1070 3c **Atoms for Peace**, *July 28 (351,940)* 1.00
1071 3c **Fort Ticonderoga**, *Sept. 18*, Fort Ticonderoga, N.Y. *(342,946)* 1.50
1072 3c **Andrew W. Mellon**, *Dec. 20 (278,897)* 1.00

1956

1073 3c **Benjamin Franklin**, *Jan. 17*, Philadelphia, Pa. *(351,260)* 1.25
1074 3c **Booker T. Washington**, *Apr. 5*, Booker T. Washington Birthplace, Va. *(272,659)* 2.00
1075 11c **FIPEX Souvenir Sheet**, *Apr. 28*, New York, N.Y. *(429,327)* 5.00
1076 3c **FIPEX**, *Apr. 30*, New York, N.Y. *(526,090)* 1.00
1077 3c **Wildlife (Turkey)**, *May 5*, Fond du Lac, Wis. *(292,121)* 1.75
1078 3c **Wildlife (Antelope)**, *June 22*, Gunnison, Colo. *(294,731)* 1.75
1079 3c **Wildlife (Salmon)**, *Nov. 9*, Seattle, Wash. *(346,800)* 1.75
1080 3c **Pure Food and Drug Laws**, *June 27*, Washington, D.C. *(411,761)* 1.00
1081 3c **Wheatland**, *Aug. 5*, Lancaster, Pa. *(340,142)* 1.00
1082 3c **Labor Day**, *Sept. 3*, Camden, N.J. *(338,450)* 1.00
1083 3c **Nassau Hall**, *Sept. 22*, Princeton, N.J. *(350,756)* 1.00
1084 3c **Devils Tower**, *Sept. 24*, Devils Tower, Wyo. *(285,090)* 1.25
1085 3c **Children**, *Dec. 15 (305,125)* 1.00

1957

1086 3c **Alexander Hamilton**, *Jan. 11*, New York, N.Y. *(305,117)* 1.00
1087 3c **Polio**, *Jan. 15 (307,630)* 1.50
1088 3c **Coast & Geodetic Survey**, *Feb. 11*, Seattle, Wash. *(309,931)* 1.00
1089 3c **Architects**, *Feb. 23*, New York, N.Y. *(368,840)* 1.25
1090 3c **Steel Industry**, *May 22*, New York, N.Y. *(473,284)* 1.00
1091 3c **Naval Review**, *June 10*, U.S.S. Saratoga, Norfolk, Va. *(365,933)* 1.25
1092 3c **Oklahoma Statehood**, *June 14*, Oklahoma City, Okla. *(327,172)* 1.00
1093 3c **School Teachers**, *July 1*, Philadelphia, Pa. *(357,986)* 2.00
(Spelling error) Philadelpia 8.00
1094 4c **Flag**, *July 4 (523,879)* 1.00
1095 3c **Shipbuilding**, *Aug. 15*, Bath, Maine *(347,432)* 1.25
1096 8c **Ramon Magsaysay**, *Aug. 31 (334,558)* 2.00
1097 3c **Lafayette Bicentenary**, *Sept. 6*, Easton, Pa. *(260,421)* 1.00
Fayetteville, N.C. *(230,000)* 1.00
Louisville, Ky. *(207,856)* 1.00
1098 3c **Wildlife** (Whooping Cranes), *Nov. 22*, New York, N.Y. *(342,970)* 1.25
New Orleans, La. *(154,327)* 1.25
Corpus Christi, Tex. *(280,990)* 1.25
1099 3c **Religious Freedom**, *Dec. 27*, Flushing, N.Y. *(357,770)* 1.00

1958

1100 3c **Gardening-Horticulture**, *Mar. 15*, Ithaca, N.Y. *(451,292)* 1.00
1104 3c **Brussels Exhibition**, *Apr. 17*, Detroit, Mich. *(428,073)* 1.00
1105 3c **James Monroe**, *Apr. 28*, Montross, Va. *(326,988)* 1.00
1106 3c **Minnesota Statehood**, *May 11*, Saint Paul, Minn. *(475,552)* 1.00
1107 3c **International Geophysical Year**, *May 31*, Chicago, Ill. *(397,000)* 1.00
1108 3c **Gunston Hall**, *June 12*, Lorton, Va. *(349,801)* 1.00
1109 3c **Mackinac Bridge**, *June 25*, Mackinac Bridge, Mich. *(445,605)* 1.75

1110 4c **Simon Bolivar,** *July 24* 2.00
1111 8c **Simon Bolivar,** *July 24* 2.50
1110-1111 on one cover 2.00

First day cancellation was applied to 708, 777 covers bearing one or more of Nos. 1110-1111.

1112 4c **Atlantic Cable,** *Aug. 15,* New York, N.Y. *(365,072)* 1.00

1958-59

1113 1c **Lincoln Sesquicentennial,** *Feb. 12, 1959,* Hodgenville, Ky. *(379,862)* block of four 3.00
1114 3c **Lincoln Sesquicentennial,** *Feb. 27, 1959,* New York, N.Y. *(437,737)* 3.00
1115 4c **Lincoln-Douglas Debates,** *Aug. 27, 1958,* Freeport, Ill. *(373,063)* 3.00
1116 4c **Lincoln Sesquicentennial,** *May, 30, 1959 (894,887)* 3.00

1958

1117 4c **Lajos Kossuth,** *Sept. 19* 1.50
1118 8c **Lajos Kossuth,** *Sept. 19* 1.75
1117-1118 on one cover 3.00

First day cancellation was applied to 722,188 covers bearing one or more of Nos. 1117-1118.

1119 4c **Freedom of Press,** *Sept. 22,* Columbia, Mo. *(411,752)* 1.00
1120 4c **Overland Mail,** *Oct. 10,* San Francisco, Cal. *(352,760)* 1.00
1121 4c **Noah Webster,** *Oct. 16,* West Hartford, Conn. *(364,608)* 1.00
1122 4c **Forest Conservation,** *Oct. 27,* Tucson, Ariz. *(405,959)* 1.00
1123 4c **Fort Duquesne,** *Nov. 25,* Pittsburgh, Pa. *(421,764)* 1.00

1959

1124 4c **Oregon Statehood,** *Feb. 14,* Astoria, Ore. *(452,764)* 1.00
1125 4c **San Martin,** *Feb. 25* 1.75
1126 8c **San Martin,** *Feb. 25* 2.50
1125-1126 on one cover 3.00

First day cancellation was applied to 910,208 covers bearing one or more of No. 1125-1126.

1127 4c **NATO,** *Apr. 1 (361,040)* 1.25
1128 4c **Arctic Exploration,** *Apr. 6,* Cresson, Pa. *(397,770)* 1.00
1129 8c **World Trade,** *Apr. 20 (503,618)* 1.00
1130 4c **Silver Centennial,** *June 8,* Virginia City, Nev. *(337,233)* 1.00
1131 4c **St. Lawrence Seaway,** *June 26,* Massena, N.Y. *(543,211)* 1.25
1132 4c **Flag** (49 stars), *July 4,* Auburn, N.Y. *(523,773)* 1.00
1133 4c **Soil Conservation,** *Aug. 26,* Rapid City, S.D. *(400,613)* 1.00
1134 4c **Petroleum Industry,** *Aug. 27,* Titusville, Pa. *(801,859)* 2.00
1135 4c **Dental Health,** *Sept. 14,* New York, N.Y. *(649,813)* 4.00
1136 4c **Reuter,** *Sept. 29* 1.50
1137 8c **Reuter,** *Sept. 29* 1.75
1136-1137 on one cover 3.00

First day cancellation was applied to 1,207,933 covers bearing one or more of Nos. 1136-1137.

1138 4c **Dr. Ephraim McDowell,** *Dec. 3,* Danville, Ky. *(344,603)* 1.25

1960-61

1139 4c **Washington "Credo,"** *Jan. 20, 1960,* Mount Vernon, Va. *(438,335)* 1.25
1140 4c **Franklin "Credo,"** *Mar. 31, 1960,* Philadelphia, Pa. *(497,913)* 1.25
1141 4c **Jefferson "Credo,"** *May 18, 1960,* Charlottesville, Va. *(454,903)* 1.25
1142 4c **Francis Scott Key "Credo,"** *Sept. 14, 1960,* Baltimore, Md. *(501,129)* 1.25
1143 4c **Lincoln "Credo,"** *Nov. 19, 1960,* New York, N.Y. *(467,780)* 1.50
1144 4c **Patrick Henry "Credo,"** *Jan. 11, 1961,* Richmond, Va. *(415,252)* 1.25

1960

1145 4c **Boy Scouts,** *Feb. 8 (1,419,955)* 4.00
1146 4c **Olympic Winter Games,** *Feb. 18,* Olympic Valley, Calif. *(516,456)* 1.00
1147 4c **Masaryk,** *Mar. 7* 1.50
1148 8c **Masaryk,** *Mar. 7* 1.75
1147-1148 on one cover 3.00

First day cancellation was applied to 1,710,726 covers bearing one or more of Nos. 1147-1148.

1149 4c **World Refugee Year,** *Apr. 7 (413,298)* 1.00
1150 4c **Water Conservation,** *Apr. 18 (648,988)* 1.00
1151 4c **SEATO,** *May 31 (514,926)* 1.00
1152 4c **American Woman,** *June 2 (830,385)* 1.25
1153 4c **50-Star Flag,** *July 4,* Honolulu, Hawaii *(820,900)* 1.00
1154 4c **Pony Express Centennial,** *July 19,* Sacramento, Calif. *(520,223)* 1.75
1155 4c **Employ the Handicapped,** *Aug. 28,* New York, N.Y. *(439,638)* 1.50
1156 4c **World Forestry Congress,** *Aug. 29,* Seattle, Wash. *(350,848)* 1.00
1157 4c **Mexican Independence,** *Sept. 16,* Los Angeles, Calif. *(360,297)* 1.00
1158 4c **U.S.-Japan Treaty,** *Sept. 28 (545,150)* 2.00
1159 4c **Paderewski,** *Oct. 8* 1.50
1160 8c **Paderewski,** *Oct. 8* 1.75
1159-1160 on one cover 3.00

First day cancellation was applied to 1,057,438 covers bearing one or more of Nos. 1159-1160.

1161 4c **Robert A. Taft,** *Oct. 10,* Cincinnati, Ohio *(312,116)* 1.00
1162 4c **Wheels of Freedom,** *Oct. 15,* Detroit, Mich. *(380,551)* 1.00
1163 4c **Boys' Clubs,** *Oct. 18,* New York, N.Y. *(435,009)* 1.00
1164 4c **Automated P.O.,** *Oct. 20,* Providence, R.I. *(458,237)* 1.00
1165 4c **Mannerheim,** *Oct. 26* 1.25
1166 8c **Mannerheim,** *Oct. 26* 1.50
1165-1166 on one cover 3.00

First day cancellation was applied to 1,168,770 covers bearing one or more of Nos. 1165-1166.

1167 4c **Camp Fire Girls,** *Nov. 1,* New York, N.Y. *(324,944)* 3.00
1168 4c **Garibaldi,** *Nov. 2* 1.25
1169 8c **Garibaldi,** *Nov. 2* 1.50
1168-1169 on one cover 3.00

First day cancellation was applied to 1,001,490 covers bearing one or more of Nos. 1168-1169.

1170 4c **Senator George,** *Nov. 5,* Vienna, Ga. *(278,890)* 1.00
1171 4c **Andrew Carnegie,** *Nov. 25,* New York, N.Y. *(318,180)* 1.00
1172 4c **John Foster Dulles,** *Dec. 6 (400,055)* 1.00
1173 4c **Echo I,** *Dec. 15 (583,747)* 2.50

1961-65

1174 4c **Gandhi,** *Jan. 26, 1961* 1.50
1175 8c **Gandhi,** *Jan. 26, 1961* 2.00
1174-1175 on one cover 3.00

First day cancellation was applied to 1,013,515 covers bearing one or more of Nos. 1174-1175.

1176 4c **Range Conservation,** *Feb. 2, 1961,* Salt Lake City, Utah *(357,101)* 1.00
1177 4c **Horace Greeley,** *Feb. 3, 1961,* Chappaqua, N.Y. *(359,205)* 1.00
1178 4c **Fort Sumter,** *Apr. 12, 1961,* Charleston, S.C. *(602,599)* 4.00
1179 4c **Battle of Shiloh,** *Apr. 7, 1962,* Shiloh, Tenn. *(526,062)* 4.00
1180 5c **Battle of Gettysburg,** *July 1, 1963,* Gettysburg, Pa. *(600,205)* 4.00
1181 5c **Battle of Wilderness,** *May 5, 1964,* Fredericksburg, Va. *(450,904)* 4.00
1182 5c **Appomattox,** *Apr. 9, 1965,* Appomattox, Va. *(653,121)* 4.00

1961

1183 4c **Kansas Statehood,** *May 10,* Council Grove, Kansas *(480,561)* 1.00
1184 4c **Senator Norris,** *July 11 (482,875)* 1.00
1185 4c **Naval Aviation,** *Aug. 20,* San Diego, Calif. *(416,391)* 1.50
1186 4c **Workmen's Compensation,** *Sept. 4,* Milwaukee, Wis. *(410,236)* 1.00
1187 4c **Frederic Remington,** *Oct. 4 (723,443)* 1.25
1188 4c **China Republic,** *Oct. 10 (463,900)* 8.00
1189 4c **Naismith-Basketball,** *Nov. 6,* Springfield, Mass. *(479,917)* 7.50
1190 4c **Nursing,** *Dec. 28 (964,005)* 10.00

1962

1191 4c **New Mexico Statehood,** *Jan. 6,* Sante Fe, N.M. *(365,330)* 2.00
1192 4c **Arizona Statehood,** *Feb. 14,* Phoenix, Ariz. *(508,216)* 1.75
1193 4c **Project Mercury,** *Feb. 20,* Cape Canaveral, Fla. *(3,000,000)* 3.00
Any other city 5.00
1194 4c **Malaria Eradication,** *Mar. 30 (554,175)* 1.00
1195 4c **Charles Evans Hughes,** *Apr. 11 (544,424)* 1.00
1196 4c **Seattle World's Fair,** *Apr. 25,* Seattle, Wash. *(771,856)* 1.25
1197 4c **Louisiana Statehood,** *Apr. 30,* New Orleans, La. *(436,681)* 1.00
1198 4c **Homestead Act,** *May 20,* Beatrice, Nebr. *(487,450)* 1.00
1199 4c **Girl Scouts,** *July 24,* Burlington, Vt. *(634,347)* 5.00
1200 4c **Brien McMahon,** *July 28,* Norwalk, Conn. *(384,419)* 1.00
1201 4c **Apprenticeship,** *Aug. 31 (1,003,548)* 1.00
1202 4c **Sam Rayburn,** *Sept. 16,* Bonham, Texas *(401,042)* 1.50
1203 4c **Dag Hammarskjold,** *Oct. 23,* New York, N.Y. *(500,683)* 1.00

Experts believe that all examples of No. 1203a with a first-day cancel are believed to be backdated using examples of No. 1204.

1204 4c **Hammarskjold,** yellow inverted, *Nov. 16,* (about *75,000)* 5.00
1205 4c **Christmas,** *Nov. 1,* Pittsburgh, Pa. *(491,312)* 1.10
1206 4c **Higher Education,** *Nov. 14 (627,347)* 1.25
1207 4c **Winslow Homer,** *Dec. 15,* Gloucester, Mass. *(498,866)* 1.25

1963-66

1208 5c **Flag,** *Jan. 9, 1963 (696,185)* 1.00
1208a 5c Tagged, *Aug. 25, 1966* 30.00

REGULAR ISSUE

1962-66

1209 1c **Jackson,** *Mar. 22, 1963,* New York, N.Y. *(392,363),* block of 5 or 6 1.00
1209a 1c Tagged, *July 6, 1966,* block of 5 or 6 30.00
1213 5c **Washington,** *Nov. 23, 1962,* New York, N.Y. *(360,531)* 1.00
1213a Booklet pane of 5 + label, *Nov. 23, 1962,* New York, N.Y. *(111,452)* 4.00
1213b 5c Tagged, *Oct. 28, 1963,* Dayton, Ohio (about *15,000)* 30.00
1213c Booklet pane of 5 + label, tagged, *Oct. 28, 1963,* Dayton, Ohio 100.00
Washington, D.C. *(750)* 110.00
1214 8c **Pershing,** *Nov. 17, 1961,* New York, N.Y. *(321,031)* 1.25
1225 1c **Jackson,** Coil, *May 31, 1963,* Chicago, Ill. *(238,952),* pair and strip of 3 1.00
1225a 1c Coil, tagged, *July 6, 1966,* pair and strip of 3 30.00
1229 5c **Washington,** Coil, *Nov. 23, 1962,* New York, N.Y. *(184,627)* 1.00
1229a 5c Coil, tagged, *Oct. 28, 1963,* Dayton, Ohio (about *2,000)* 30.00

1963

1230 5c **Carolina Charter,** *Apr. 6,* Edenton, N.C. *(426,200)* 1.00
1231 5c **Food for Peace,** *June 4 (624,342)* 1.00
1232 5c **West Virginia Statehood,** *June 20,* Wheeling, W. Va. *(413,389)* 1.00
1233 5c **Emancipation Proclamation,** *Aug. 16,* Chicago, Ill, *(494,886)* 1.75
1234 5c **Alliance for Progress,** *Aug. 17 (528,095)* 1.00
1235 5c **Cordell Hull,** *Oct. 5* Carthage, Tenn. *(391,631)* 1.00
1236 5c **Eleanor Roosevelt,** *Oct. 11 (860,155)* 1.25
1237 5c **Science,** *Oct. 14 (504,503)* 1.25
1238 5c **City Mail Delivery,** *Oct. 26 (544,806)* 1.25
1239 5c **Red Cross,** *Oct. 29 (557,678)* 2.00
1240 5c **Christmas,** *Nov. 1,* Santa Claus, Ind. *(458,619)* 1.25
1240a 5c **Christmas,** tagged, *Nov. 2,* (about *500)* 60.00

Note below No. 1036b also applies to No. 1240a.

1241 5c **Audubon,** *Dec. 7,* Henderson, Ky. *(518,855)* 1.25

1964

1242 5c **Sam Houston,** *Jan. 10,* Houston, Tex. *(487,986)* 1.75
1243 5c **Charles Russell,** *Mar. 19,* Great Falls, Mont. *(658,745)* 1.25
1244 5c **N.Y. World's Fair,** *Apr. 22,* World's Fair, N.Y. *(1,656,346)* 3.00
1245 5c **John Muir,** *Apr. 29,* Martinez, Calif. *(446,925)* 1.50
1246 5c **John F. Kennedy,** *May 29,* Boston, Mass. *(2,003,096)* *3.00*
Any other city *5.00*
1247 5c **New Jersey Tercentenary,** *June 15,* Elizabeth, N.J. *(526,879)* 1.00
1248 5c **Nevada Statehood,** *July 22,* Carson City, Nev. *(584,973)* 1.00
1249 5c **Register & Vote,** *Aug. 1 (533,439)* 1.25
1250 5c **Shakespeare,** *Aug. 14,* Stratford, Conn. *(524,053)* 2.25
1251 5c **Drs. Mayo,** *Sept. 11,* Rochester, Minn. *(674,846)* 3.00
1252 5c **American Music,** *Oct. 15,* New York, N.Y. *(466,107)* 1.50
1253 5c **Homemakers,** *Oct. 26,* Honolulu, Hawaii *(435,392)* 1.00
1257b 5c **Christmas,** *Nov. 9,* Bethlehem, Pa. 3.00
1254-1257, any single 1.00
1257c 5c Tagged, *Nov. 10,* Dayton, O. 57.50
1254a-1257a, any single 30.00

First day cancellation was applied to 794,900 covers bearing Nos. 1254-1257 in singles or multiples and at Dayton to about 2,700 covers bearing Nos. 1254a-1257a in singles or multiples.

1258 5c **Verrazano-Narrows Bridge,** *Nov. 21,* Staten Island, N.Y. *(619,780)* 1.00
1259 5c **Fine Arts,** *Dec. 2 (558,046)* 1.00
1260 5c **Amateur Radio,** *Dec. 15,* Anchorage, Alaska *(452,255)* 5.00

1965

1261 5c **Battle of New Orleans,** *Jan. 8,* New Orleans, La. *(466,029)* 1.00
1262 5c **Physical Fitness-Sokol,** *Feb. 15 (864,848)* 1.25
1263 5c **Cancer Crusade,** *Apr. 1 (744,485)* 2.50
1264 5c **Churchill,** *May 13,* Fulton, Mo. *(773,580)* 3.00
1265 5c **Magna Carta,** *June 15,* Jamestown, Va. *(479,065)* 1.00
1266 5c **Intl. Cooperation Year,** *June 26,* San Francisco, Cal. *(402,925)* 1.00
1267 5c **Salvation Army,** *July 2,* New York, N.Y. *(634,228)* 3.00
1268 5c **Dante,** *July 17,* San Francisco, Cal. *(424,893)* 1.00
1269 5c **Herbert Hoover,** *Aug. 10,* West Branch, Iowa *(698,182)* 1.00
1270 5c **Robert Fulton,** *Aug. 19,* Clermont, N.Y. *(550,330)* 1.00
1271 5c **Florida Settlement,** *Aug. 28,* St. Augustine, Fla. *(465,000)* 1.00
1272 5c **Traffic Safety,** *Sept. 3,* Baltimore, Md. *(527,075)* 1.00
1273 5c **Copley,** *Sept. 17 (613,484)* 1.00

1274 11c **Intl. Telecommunication Union,** *Oct. 6 (332,818)* 1.10
1275 5c **Adlai Stevenson,** *Oct. 23,* Bloomington, Ill. *(755,656)* 1.00
1276 5c **Christmas,** *Nov. 2,* Silver Bell, Ariz. *(705,039)* 1.00
1276a 5c Tagged, *Nov. 15,* (about *300*) 50.00

PROMINENT AMERICANS ISSUE

1965-78

1278 1c **Jefferson,** *Jan. 12, 1968,* Jeffersonville, Ind., block of 5 or 6 1.00
1278a Booklet pane of 8, *Jan. 12, 1968,* Jeffersonville, Ind. 2.50
1278b Booklet pane of 4 + 2 labels, *May 10, 1971* 11.50

First day cancellation was applied to 655,680 covers bearing one or more of Nos. 1278, 1278a and 1299.

1279 1¼c **Gallatin,** *Jan. 30, 1967,* Gallatin, Mo. *(439,010)* 1.00
1280 2c **Wright,** *June 8, 1966,* Spring Green, Wis. *(460,427)* 1.00
1280a Booklet pane of 5 + label, *Jan. 8, 1968,* Buffalo, N.Y. *(147,244)* 3.50
1280c Booklet pane of 6, *May 7, 1971,* Spokane, Wash. 15.00
1281 3c **Parkman,** *Sept. 16, 1967,* Boston, Mass. *(518,355)* 1.00
1282 4c **Lincoln,** *Nov. 19, 1965,* New York, N.Y. *(445,629)* 1.50
1282a 4c Tagged, *Dec. 1, 1965,* Dayton, O. (about *2,000*) 32.50
Washington, D.C. *(1,200)* 32.50
1283 5c **Washington,** *Feb. 22, 1966* *(525,372)* 1.00
1283a 5c Tagged, *Feb. 23, 1966,* (about *900*) 26.00
Dayton, Ohio (about *200*) 75.00
1283B 5c **Washington,** Redrawn, *Nov. 17, 1967,* New York, N.Y. *(328,983)* 1.00
1284 6c **Roosevelt,** *Jan. 29, 1966,* Hyde Park, N.Y. *(448,631)* 1.00
1284a 6c Tagged, *Dec. 29, 1966* 35.00
1284b Booklet pane of 8, *Dec. 28, 1967* 2.75
1284c Booklet pane of 5 + label, *Jan. 9, 1968* 100.00
1285 8c **Einstein,** *Mar. 14, 1966,* Princeton, N.J. *(366,803)* 3.00
1285a 8c Tagged, *July 6, 1966* 35.00
1286 10c **Jackson,** *Mar. 15, 1967,* Hermitage, Tenn. *(255,945)* 1.00
1286A 12c **Ford,** *July 30, 1968,* Greenfield Village, Mich. *(342,850)* 2.00
1287 13c **Kennedy,** *May 29, 1967,* Brookline, Mass. *(391,195)* 2.00
1288 15c **Holmes,** type I, *Mar. 8, 1968* *(322,970)* 1.00
1288B 15c **Holmes,** from bklt., *June 14, 1978,* Boston, Mass. 1.00
1288Bc Booklet pane of 8 3.00

First day cancellation was applied to 387,119 covers bearing one or more of Nos. 1288B and 1305E.

1289 20c **Marshall,** *Oct. 24, 1967,* Lexington, Va. *(221,206)* 1.10
1289a 20c Tagged, *Apr. 3, 1973,* New York, N.Y. 35.00
1290 25c **Douglass,** *Feb. 14, 1967* *(213,730)* 2.50
1290a 25c Tagged, *Apr. 3, 1973,* New York, N.Y. 40.00
1291 30c **Dewey,** *Oct. 21, 1968,* Burlington, Vt. *(162,790)* 1.75
1291a 30c Tagged, *Apr. 3, 1973,* New York, N.Y. 40.00
1292 40c **Paine,** *Jan. 29, 1968,* Philadelphia, Pa. *(157,947)* 1.75
1292a 40c Tagged, *Apr. 3, 1973,* New York, N.Y. 40.00
1293 50c **Stone,** *Aug. 13, 1968,* Dorchester, Mass. *(140,410)* 2.50
1293a 50c Tagged, *Apr. 3, 1973,* New York, N.Y. 40.00
1294 $1 **O'Neill,** *Oct. 16, 1967,* New London, Conn. *(103,102)* 6.00
1294a $1 Tagged, *Apr. 3, 1973,* New York, N.Y. 52.50
1295 $5 **Moore,** *Dec. 3, 1966,* Smyrna, Del. *(41,130)* 40.00
1295a $5 Tagged, *Apr. 3, 1973,* New York, N.Y. 100.00

First day cancellation was applied to 17,533 covers bearing one or more of Nos. 1059b, 1289a, 1290a, 1291a, 1292a, 1293a, 1294a and 1295a.

COIL STAMPS

1297 3c **Parkman,** *Nov. 4, 1975,* Pendleton, Ore. *(166,798)* 1.00
1298 6c **Roosevelt,** Perf. 10 Horiz., *Dec. 28, 1967* 1.00

First day cancellation was applied to 312,330 covers bearing one or more of Nos. 1298 and 1284b.

1299 1c **Jefferson,** *Jan. 12, 1968,* Jeffersonville, Ind., pair and strip of 3 1.00
1303 4c **Lincoln,** *May 28, 1966,* Springfield, Ill. *(322,563)* 1.50
1304 5c **Washington,** *Sept. 8, 1966,* Cincinnati, O. *(245,400)* 1.00
1305 6c **Roosevelt,** Perf. 10 vert., *Feb. 28, 1968 (317,199)* 1.00
1305E 15c **Holmes,** type I, *June 14, 1978,* Boston, Mass. 1.00
1305C $1 **O'Neill,** *Jan. 12, 1973,* Hempstead, N.Y. *(121,217)* 4.00

1966

1306 5c **Migratory Bird Treaty,** *Mar. 16,* Pittsburgh, Pa. *(555,485)* 1.75
1307 5c **Humane Treatment of Animals,** *Apr. 9,* New York, N.Y. *(524,420)* 1.25
1308 5c **Indiana Statehood,** *Apr. 16,* Corydon, Ind. *(575,557)* 1.00
1309 5c **Circus,** *May 2,* Delavan, Wis. *(754,076)* 2.00
1310 5c **SIPEX,** *May 21 (637,802)* 1.00
1311 5c **SIPEX, souvenir sheet,** *May 23* *(700,882)* 1.10
1312 5c **Bill of Rights,** *July 1,* Miami Beach, Fla. *(562,920)* 1.75
1313 5c **Polish Millennium,** *July 30 (715,603)* 1.50
1314 5c **Natl. Park Service,** *Aug. 25,* Yellowstone National Park, Wyo. *(528,170)* 1.00
1314a 5c Tagged, *Aug. 26* 35.00
1315 5c **Marine Corps Reserve,** *Aug. 29* *(585,923)* 1.50
1315a 5c Tagged, *Aug. 29* 35.00
1316 5c **Gen. Fed. of Women's Clubs,** *Sept. 12,* New York, N.Y. *(383,334)* 1.25
1316a 5c Tagged, *Sept. 13* 35.00
1317 5c **Johnny Appleseed,** *Sept. 24,* Leominster, Mass. *(794,610)* 1.50
1317a 5c Tagged, *Sept. 26* 35.00
1318 5c **Beautification of America,** *Oct. 5* *(564,440)* 1.00
1318a 5c Tagged, *Oct. 5* 35.00
1319 5c **Great River Road,** *Oct. 21,* Baton Rouge, La. *(330,933)* 1.00
1319a 5c Tagged, *Oct. 22* 35.00
1320 5c **Savings Bond-Servicemen,** *Oct. 26,* Sioux City, Iowa *(444,421)* 1.00
1320a 5c Tagged, *Oct. 27* 35.00
1321 5c **Christmas,** *Nov. 1,* Christmas, Mich. *(537,650)* 1.00
1321a 5c Tagged, *Nov. 2* 35.00
1322 5c **Mary Cassatt,** *Nov. 17 (593,389)* 1.00
1322a 5c Tagged, *Nov. 17* 35.00

1967

1323 5c **National Grange,** *Apr. 17 (603,460)* 1.00
1324 5c **Canada Centenary,** *May 25,* Montreal, Canada *(711,795)* 1.00
1325 5c **Erie Canal,** *July 4,* Rome, N.Y. *(784,611)* 1.00
1326 5c **Search for Peace-Lions,** *July 5,* Chicago, Ill. *(393,197)* 1.00
1327 5c **Thoreau,** *July 12,* Concord, Mass. *(696,789)* 1.00
1328 5c **Nebraska Statehood,** *July 29,* Lincoln, Nebr. *(1,146,957)* 1.00
1329 5c **Voice of America,** *Aug. 1 (455,190)* 2.00
1330 5c **Davy Crockett,** *Aug. 17,* San Antonio, Tex. *(462,291)* 2.00
1332b 5c **Space Accomplishments,** *Sept. 29,* Kennedy Space Center, Fla. *(667,267)* 8.00
1331-1332, any single 3.25
1333 5c **Urban Planning,** *Oct. 2 (389,009)* 1.00
1334 5c **Finland Independence,** *Oct. 6,* Finland, Minn. *(408,532)* 1.00
1335 5c **Thomas Eakins,** *Nov. 2 (648,054)* 1.40
1336 5c **Christmas,** *Nov. 6,* Bethlehem, Ga. *(462,118)* 1.25
1337 5c **Mississippi Statehood,** *Dec. 11,* Natchez, Miss. *(379,612)* 1.00

1968-71

1338 6c **Flag** (Giori), *Jan. 24, 1968 (412,120)* 1.00
1338A 6c **Flag coil,** *May 30, 1969,* Chicago, Ill. *(248,434)* 1.00
1338D 6c **Flag** (Huck) *Aug. 7, 1970 (365,280)* 1.00
1338F 8c **Flag,** *May 10, 1971* 1.00
1338G 8c **Flag coil,** *May 10, 1971* 1.00

First day cancellation (May 10) was applied to 235,543 covers bearing one or more of Nos. 1338F-1338G.

1968

1339 6c **Illinois Statehood,** *Feb. 12,* Shawneetown, Ill. *(761,640)* 1.00
1340 6c **HemisFair**'68, *Mar. 30,* San Antonio, Tex. *(469,909)* 1.00
1341 $1 **Airlift,** *Apr. 4,* Seattle, Wash. *(105,088)* 7.00
1342 6c **Youth-Elks,** *May 1,* Chicago, Ill. *(354,711)* 1.00
1343 6c **Law and Order,** *May 17 (407,081)* 2.50
1344 6c **Register and Vote,** *June 27* *(355,685)* 1.00
1354a 6c **Historic Flag series of 10,** *July 4,* Pittsburgh, Pa. *(2,924,962)* 15.00
1345-1354, any single 3.00
1355 6c **Disney,** *Sept. 11,* Marceline, Mo. *(499,505)* 20.00
1356 6c **Marquette,** *Sept. 20,* Sault Ste. Marie, Mich. *(379,710)* 2.00
1357 6c **Daniel Boone,** *Sept. 26,* Frankfort, Ky. *(333,440)* 1.25
1358 6c **Arkansas River,** *Oct. 1,* Little Rock, Ark. *(358,025)* 1.00
1359 6c **Leif Erikson,** *Oct. 9,* Seattle, Wash. *(376,565)* 1.00
1360 6c **Cherokee Strip,** *Oct. 15,* Ponca, Okla. *(339,330)* 1.00
1361 6c **John Trumbull,** *Oct. 18,* New Haven, Conn. *(378,285)* 2.00
1362 6c **Waterfowl Conservation,** *Oct. 24,* Cleveland, Ohio, *(349,719)* 1.25
1363 6c **Christmas,** tagged, *Nov. 1 (739,055)* 1.25
1363a 6c Untagged, *Nov. 2* 10.00
1364 6c **American Indian,** *Nov. 4 (415,964)* 1.25

1969

1368a 6c **Beautification of America,** *Jan. 16* *(1,094,184)* 4.00
1365-1368, any single 1.00
1369 6c **American Legion,** *Mar. 15 (632,035)* 1.00
1370 6c **Grandma Moses,** *May 1 (367,880)* 1.50
1371 6c **Apollo 8,** *May 5,* Houston, Texas *(908,634)* 2.25
1372 6c **W.C. Handy,** *May 17,* Memphis, Tenn. *(398,216)* 2.25
1373 6c **California Bicentenary,** *July 16,* San Diego, Calif. *(530,210)* 1.00
1374 6c **J.W. Powell,** *Aug. 1,* Page, Ariz. *(434,433)* 1.00
1375 6c **Alabama Statehood,** *Aug. 2,* Huntsville, Ala. *(485,801)* 1.00
1379a 6c **Botanical Congress,** *Aug. 23,* Seattle, Wash. *(737,935)* 5.00
1376-1379, any single 1.50
1380 6c **Dartmouth Case,** *Sept. 22,* Hanover, N.H. *(416,327)* 1.00
1381 6c **Professional Baseball,** *Sept. 24,* Cincinnati, Ohio *(414,942)* 10.00
1382 6c **Intercollegiate Football,** *Sept. 26,* New Brunswick, N.J. *(414,860)* 6.00
1383 6c **Dwight D. Eisenhower,** *Oct. 14,*Abilene, Kans. *(1,009,560)* 1.00
1384 6c **Christmas,** *Nov. 3,* Christmas, Fla. *(555,500)* 1.25
1385 6c **Hope for Crippled,** *Nov. 20,* Columbus, Ohio *(342,676)* 1.25
1386 6c **William M. Harnett,** *Dec. 3,* Boston, Mass. *(408,860)* 1.00

1970-74

1390a 6c **Natural History,** *May 6, 1970,* New York, N.Y. *(834,260)* 4.00
1387-1390, any single 1.50
1391 6c **Maine Statehood,** *July 9, 1970,* Portland, Maine, *(472,165)* 2.75
1392 6c **Wildlife Conservation,** *July 20, 1970,* Custer, S.D. *(309,418)* 1.00
1393 6c **Eisenhower,** *Aug. 6, 1970* 1.00
1393a Booklet pane of 8 3.00
1393b Booklet pane of 5 + label 1.50

First day cancellations were applied to 823,540 covers bearing one or more of Nos. 1393 and 1401.

1393D 7c **Franklin,** *Oct. 20, 1972,* Philadelphia, Pa. *(309,276)* 1.00
1394 8c **Eisenhower** (multi), *May 10, 1971* 1.00
1395 8c **Eisenhower** (claret), *May 10, 1971* 1.00
1395a Booklet pane of 8 2.50
1395b Booklet pane of 6 2.50
1395c Booklet pane of 4 + 2 labels, *Jan. 28, 1972,* Casa Grande, Ariz. 2.25
1395d Booklet pane of 7 + label, *Jan. 28, 1972,* Casa Grande, Ariz. 2.25

First day cancellations were applied to 813,947 covers bearing one or more of Nos. 1394, 1395 and 1402. First day cancellations were applied to 181,601 covers bearing one or more of Nos. 1395c or 1395d.

1396 8c **Postal Service Emblem,** *July 1, 1971,* any city *(est. 16,300,000)* 1.00

First day cancels from over 16,000 different cities are known. Some are rare.

1397 14c **Fiorello H. LaGuardia,** *Apr. 24, 1972,* New York, N.Y. *(180,114)* 1.00
1398 16c **Ernie Pyle,** *May 7, 1971 (444,410)* 1.50
1399 18c **Elizabeth Blackwell,** *Jan. 23, 1974,* Geneva, N.Y. *(217,938)* 1.25
1400 21c **Amadeo Giannini,** *June 27, 1973,* San Mateo, Calif. *(282,520)* 1.50
1401 6c **Eisenhower coil,** *Aug. 6, 1970* 1.00
1402 8c **Eisenhower coil,** *May 10, 1971* 1.00

1970

1405 6c **Edgar Lee Masters,** *Aug. 22,* Petersburg Ill. *(372,804)* 1.00
1406 6c **Woman Suffrage,** *Aug. 26,* Adams, Mass. *(508,142)* 1.00
1407 6c **South Carolina Anniv.** *Sept. 12,* Charleston, S.C. *(533,000)* 1.00
1408 6c **Stone Mt. Memorial,** *Sept. 19,* Stone Mountain, Ga. *(558,546)* 1.00
1409 6c **Fort Snelling,** *Oct. 17,* Fort Snelling, Minn. *(497,611)* 1.00
1413a 6c **Anti-Pollution,** *Oct. 28,* San Clemente, Calif. *(1,033,147)* 4.00
1410-1413, any single 1.25
1414 6c **Christmas (Nativity),** *Nov. 5* 1.25
1414a 6c Precanceled, *Nov. 5* 7.50
1418b 6c **Christmas,** *Nov. 5* 5.50
1415-1418, any single 1.50
1414-1418 on one cover 8.50
1418c 6c Precanceled, *Nov. 5* 15.00
1415a-1418a, any single 5.00
1414a-1418a on one cover 30.00

First day cancellation was applied to 2,014,450 covers bearing one or more of Nos. 1414-1418 or 1414a-1418a.

1419 6c **United Nations,** *Nov. 20,* New York, N.Y. *(474,070)* 1.50
1420 6c **Pilgrims' Landing,** *Nov. 21,* Plymouth, Mass. *(629,850)* 1.00
1421 6c **Disabled Veterans,** *Nov. 24,* Cincinnati, Ohio, or Montgomery, Ala. 2.25
1422 6c **U.S. Servicemen,** *Nov. 24,* Cincinnati, Ohio, or Montgomery, Ala. 2.25
1422a 3.00

First day cancellation was applied to 476,610 covers at Cincinnati and 336,417 at Montgomery, each cover bearing one or more of Nos. 1421-1422.

1971

1423 6c **Wool Industry,** *Jan. 19,* Las Vegas, Nev. *(379,911)* 1.00
1424 6c **MacArthur,** *Jan. 26,* Norfolk, Va. *(720,035)* 2.50
1425 6c **Blood Donor,** *Mar. 12,* New York, N.Y. *(644,497)* 1.25
1426 8c **Missouri Sesquicentennial,** *May 8,* Independence, Mo. *(551,000)* 1.00
1430a 8c **Wildlife Conservation,** *June 12,* Avery Island, La. *(679,483)* 3.00
1427-1430, any single 1.25
1431 8c **Antarctic Treaty,** *June 23 (419,200)* 1.00
1432 8c **American Revolution Bicentennial,** *July 4 (434,930)* 1.00
1433 8c **John Sloan,** *Aug. 2,* Lock Haven, Pa. *(482,265)* 1.00
1435b 8c **Space Achievement Decade,** *Aug. 2,* Kennedy Space Center, Fla. *(1,403,644)* 2.50
Houston, Texas *(811,560)* 2.50
Huntsville, Ala. *(524,000)* 2.50
1434-1435, any single 1.25
1436 8c **Emily Dickinson,** *Aug. 28,* Amherst, Mass. *(498,180)* 1.00
1437 8c **San Juan,** *Sept. 12,* San Juan, P.R. *(501,668)* 1.00
1438 8c **Drug Abuse,** *Oct. 4,* Dallas, Texas *(425,330)* 1.25
1439 8c **CARE,** *Oct. 27,* New York, N.Y. *(402,121)* 1.00
1443a 8c **Historic Preservation,** *Oct. 29,* San Diego, Calif. *(783,242)* 3.00
1440-1443, any single 1.25
1444 8c **Christmas (religious),** *Nov. 10* 1.25
1445 8c **Christmas (secular),** *Nov. 10* 1.25
1444-1445 on one cover 1.50

First day cancellation was applied to 348,038 covers with No. 1444 and 580,062 with No. 1445.

1972

1446 8c **Sidney Lanier,** *Feb. 3,* Macon Ga. *(394,800)* 1.00
1447 8c **Peace Corps,** *Feb. 11 (453,660)* 1.00
1451a 2c **National Parks Centennial,** *Apr. 5,* Hatteras, N.C., block of 4 *(505,697)* 3.00
1448-1451, any single 1.00
1452 6c **National Parks,** *June 26,* Vienna, Va. *(403,396)* 1.00
1453 8c **National Parks,** *Mar. 1,* Yellowstone National Park, Wyo. 1.00
Washington, D.C. *(847,500)* 1.00
1454 15c **National Parks,** *July 28,* Mt. McKinley National Park, Alaska *(491,456)* 1.00
1455 8c **Family Planning,** *Mar. 18,* New York, N.Y. *(691,385)* 1.00
1459a 8c **Colonial Craftsmen** (Rev. Bicentennial), *July 4,* Williamsburg, Va. *(1,914,976)* 2.50
1456-1459, any single 1.00
1460 6c **Olympics,** *Aug. 17* 1.00
1461 8c **Winter Olympics,** *Aug. 17* 1.00
1462 15c **Olympics,** *Aug. 17* 1.00
1460-1462 and C85 on one cover 2.00

First day cancellation was applied to 971,536 covers bearing one or more of Nos. 1460-1462 and C85.

1463 8c **P.T.A.,** *Sept. 15,* San Francisco, Cal. *(523,454)* 1.00
1467a 8c **Wildlife,** *Sept. 20,* Warm Springs, Ore. *(733,778)* 3.00
1464-1467, any single 1.50
1468 8c **Mail Order,** *Sept. 27,* Chicago, Ill. *(759,666)* 1.50
1469 8c **Osteopathy,** *Oct. 9,* Miami, Fla. *(607,160)* 2.00
1470 8c **Tom Sawyer,** *Oct. 13,* Hannibal, Mo. *(459,013)* 2.50
1471 8c **Christmas (religious),** *Nov. 9* 1.00
1472 8c **Christmas (secular),** *Nov. 9* 1.00
1471-1472 on one cover 2.00

First day cancellation was applied to 713,821 covers bearing one or more of Nos. 1471-1472.

1473 8c **Pharmacy,** *Nov. 10,* Cincinnati, Ohio *(804,320)* 10.00
1474 8c **Stamp Collecting,** *Nov. 17,* New York, N.Y. *(434,680)* 1.25

1973

1475 8c **Love,** *Jan. 26,* Philadelphia, Pa. *(422,492)* 2.00
1476 8c **Pamphleteer** (Rev. Bicentennial), *Feb. 16,* Portland, Ore. *(431,784)* 1.00
1477 8c **Broadside** (Rev. Bicentennial), *Apr. 13,* Atlantic City, N.J. *(423,437)* 1.00
1478 8c **Post Rider** (Rev. Bicentennial), *June 22,* Rochester, N.Y. *(586,850)* 1.00
1479 8c **Drummer** (Rev. Bicentennial), *Sept. 28,* New Orleans, La. *(522,427)* 1.00
1483a 8c **Boston Tea Party** (Rev. Bicentennial), *July 4,* Boston, Mass. *(897,870)* 3.00
1480-1483, any single 1.00
1484 8c **George Gershwin,** *Feb. 28,* Beverly Hills, Calif. *(448,814)* 1.00
1485 8c **Robinson Jeffers,** *Aug. 13,* Carmel, Calif. *(394,261)* 1.00
1486 8c **Henry O. Tanner,** *Sept. 10,* Pittsburgh, Pa. *(424,065)* 2.50
1487 8c **Willa Cather,** *Sept. 20,* Red Cloud, Nebr. *(435,784)* 1.00
1488 8c **Nicolaus Copernicus,** *Apr. 23 (734,190)* 1.50
1498a 8c **Postal People,** *Apr. 30, any city* 5.00
1489-1498, any single 1.00

First day cancellation was applied at Boston to 1,205,212 covers bearing one or more of Nos. 1489-1498. Cancellations at other cities unrecorded.

1499 8c **Harry S Truman,** *May 8,* Independence, Mo. *(938,636)* 1.75
1500 6c **Electronics,** *July 10,* New York, N.Y. 1.00
1501 8c **Electronics,** *July 10,* New York, N.Y. 1.00
1502 15c **Electronics,** *July 10,* New York, N.Y. 1.00
1500-1502 and C86 on one cover 4.00

First day cancellation was applied to 1,197,700 covers bearing one or more of Nos. 1500-1502 and C86.

1503 8c **Lyndon B. Johnson,** *Aug. 27,* Austin, Texas *(701,490)* 1.00

1973-74

1504 8c **Angus Cattle,** *Oct. 5, 1973,* St. Joseph, Mo. *(521,427)* 1.00
1505 10c **Chautauqua,** *Aug. 6, 1974,* Chautauqua, N.Y. *(411,105)* 1.00
1506 10c **Wheat,** *Aug. 16, 1974,* Hillsboro, Kans. *(468,280)* 1.00
1507 8c **Christmas (religious),** *Nov. 7, 1973* 1.00
1508 8c **Christmas (secular),** *Nov. 7, 1973* 1.00
1507-1508 on one cover 1.10

First day cancellation was applied to 807,468 covers bearing one or both of Nos. 1507-1508.

1509 10c **Crossed Flags,** *Dec. 8, 1973,* San Francisco, Calif. 1.00

First day cancellation was applied to 341,528 covers bearing one or more of Nos. 1509 and 1519.

1510 10c **Jefferson Memorial,** *Dec. 14, 1973* 1.00
1510b Booklet pane of 5 + label 2.25
1510c Booklet pane of 8 2.50
1510d Booklet pane of 6, *Aug. 5, 1974,* Oakland, Calif. 3.00

First day cancellation was applied to 686,300 covers bearing one or more of Nos. 1510, 1510b, 1510c, 1520.

1511 10c **Zip Code,** *Jan. 4, 1974 (335,220)* 1.00
1518 6.3c **Bell Coil,** *Oct. 1, 1974 (221,141)* 1.00
1519 10c **Crossed Flags coil,** *Dec. 8, 1973,* San Francisco, Calif. 1.00
1520 10c **Jefferson Memorial coil,** *Dec. 14, 1973* 1.00

1974

1525 10c **Veterans of Foreign Wars,** *Mar. 11 (543,598)* 1.50
1526 10c **Robert Frost,** *Mar. 26,* Derry, N.H. *(500,425)* 1.00
1527 10c **EXPO '74,** *Apr. 18,* Spokane, Wash. *(565,548)* 1.00
1528 10c **Horse Racing,** *May 4,* Louisville, Ky. *(623,983)* 3.00
1529 10c **Skylab,** *May 14,* Houston, Tex. *(972,326)* 1.50
1537a 10c **UPU Centenary,** *June 6 (1,374,765)* 4.00
1530-1537, any single 1.00
1541a 10c **Mineral Heritage,** *June 13,* Lincoln, Neb. *(865,368)* 2.75
1538-1541, any single 1.00
1542 10c **Kentucky Settlement,** *June 15,* Harrodsburg, Ky. *(478,239)* 1.00
1546a 10c **Continental Congress** (Rev. Bicentennial), *July 4,* Philadelphia, Pa. *(2,124,957)* 2.75
1543-1546, any single 1.00
1547 10c **Energy Conservation,** *Sept. 23,* Detroit, Mich. *(587,210)* 1.00
1548 10c **Sleepy Hollow,** *Oct. 10,* North Tarrytown, N.Y. *(514,836)* 3.50
1549 10c **Retarded Children,** *Oct. 12,* Arlington Tex. *(412,882)* 1.00
1550 10c **Christmas (Religious),** *Oct. 23,* New York, N.Y. *(634,990)* 1.00
1551 10c **Christmas (Currier & Ives),** *Oct. 23,* New York, N.Y. *(634,990)* 1.00
1550-1551 on one cover 1.10
1552 10c **Christmas (Dove),** *Nov. 15,* New York, N.Y. *(477,410)* 1.50

1975

1553 10c **Benjamin West,** *Feb. 10,* Swarthmore, Pa. *(465,017)* 1.00
1554 10c **Paul L. Dunbar,** *May 1,* Dayton, Ohio *(397,347)* 1.50
1555 10c **D.W. Griffith,** *May 27,* Beverly Hills, Calif. *(424,167)* 1.00
1556 10c **Pioneer-Jupiter,** *Feb. 28,* Mountain View, Calif. *(594,896)* 1.25
1557 10c **Mariner 10,** *Apr. 4,* Pasadena, Calif. *(563,636)* 1.25
1558 10c **Collective Bargaining,** *Mar. 13 (412,329)* 1.00
1559 8c **Sybil Ludington** (Rev. Bicentennial), *Mar. 25,* Carmel, N.Y. *(394,550)* 1.00
1560 10c **Salem Poor** (Rev. Bicentennial, *Mar. 25,* Cambridge, Mass. *(415,565)* 1.50
1561 10c **Haym Salomon** (Rev. Bicentennial), *Mar. 25,* Chicago, Ill. *(442,630)* 1.00
1562 18c **Peter Francisco** (Rev. Bicentennial), *Mar. 25,* Greensboro, N.C. *(415,000)* 1.00
1563 10c **Lexington-Concord** (Rev. Bicentennial), *Apr. 19,* Lexington, Mass., or Concord, Mass, *(975,020)* 1.00
1564 10c **Bunker Hill** (Rev. Bicentennial), *June 17,* Charlestown, Mass. *(557,130)* 1.00
1568a 10c **Military Services** (Rev. Bicentennial), *July 4 (1,134,831)* 2.50
1565-1568, any single 1.00
1570a 10c **Apollo-Soyuz,** *July 15,* Kennedy Space Center, Fla. *(1,427,046)* 5.00
1569-1570, any single 3.00
1571 10c **International Women's Year,** *Aug. 26,* Seneca Falls, N.Y. *(476,769)* 1.00
1575a 10c **Postal Service Bicentenary,** *Sept. 3,* Philadelphia, Pa. *(969,999)* 2.50
1572-1575, any single 1.00
1576 10c **World Peace through Law,** *Sept. 29 (386,736)* 1.50
1578a 10c **Banking-Commerce,** *Oct. 6,* New York, N.Y. *(555,580)* 1.75
1577-1578, any single 1.00
1579 (10c) **Christmas (religious),** *Oct. 14* 1.00
1580 (10c) **Christmas (secular),** *Oct. 14* 1.00
1579-1580 on one cover 2.00

First day cancellation was applied to 730,079 covers bearing one or more of Nos. 1579-1580.

AMERICANA ISSUE

1975-79

1581 1c **Inkwell,** *Dec. 8, 1977,* St. Louis, Mo., multiple for 1st class rate 1.00
1582 2c **Speaker's Stand,** *Dec. 8, 1977,* St. Louis, Mo., multiple for 1st class rate 1.00
1584 3c **Ballot Box,** *Dec. 8, 1977,* St. Louis, Mo., multiple for 1st class rate 1.00
1585 4c **Books and Eyeglasses,** *Dec. 8, 1977,* St. Louis, Mo., multiple for 1st class rate 1.00

First day cancellation was applied to 530,033 covers bearing one or more of Nos. 1581-1582, 1584-1585.

1590 9c **Capitol Dome,** from bklt.,*Mar. 11, 1977,* New York, N.Y., plus postage for 1st class rate 1.00
1591 9c **Capitol Dome,** *Nov. 24, 1975 (190,117),* multiple for 1st class rate 1.00
1592 10c **Justice,** *Nov. 17, 1977,* New York, N.Y. *(359,050),* multiple for 1st class rate 1.00
1593 11c **Printing Press,** *Nov. 13, 1975,* Philadelphia, Pa. *(217,755),* multiple for 1st class rate 1.00
1594 12c **Torch,** *Apr. 8, 1981,* Dallas, TX, multiple for 1st class rate 1.00

First day cancellation was applied to 280,930 covers bearing one or more of Nos. 1594 and 1816.

1595 13c **Liberty Bell,** *Oct. 31, 1975,* Cleveland, Ohio *(256,734)* 1.00
1595a Booklet pane of 6 2.00
1595b Booklet pane of 7 + label 2.75
1595c Booklet pane of 8 2.50
1595d Booklet pane of 5 + label, *Apr. 2, 1976,* Liberty, Mo. 2.25
1596 13c **Eagle and Shield,** *Dec. 1, 1975,* Juneau, Alaska *(418,272)* 1.00
1597 15c **Flag,** *June 30, 1978,* Baltimore, Md. 1.00
1598 15c **Flag,** from bklt., *June 30, 1978,* Baltimore, Md. 1.00
1598a Booklet pane of 8 2.50

First day cancellation was applied to 315,359 covers bearing one or more of Nos. 1597, 1598, and 1618C.

1599 16c **Statue of Liberty,** *Mar. 31, 1978,* New York, N.Y. 1.00
1603 24c **Old North Church,** *Nov. 14, 1975,* Boston, Mass. *(208,973)* 1.00
1604 28c **Fort Nisqually,** *Aug. 11, 1978,* Tacoma, Wash. *(159,639)* 1.00
1605 29c **Sandy Hook Lighthouse,** *Apr. 14, 1978,* Atlantic City, N.J. *(193,476)* 1.50
1606 30c **Schoolhouse,** *Aug. 27, 1979,* Devils Lake, N.D. *(186,882)* 1.25
1608 50c **Betty Lamp,** *Sept. 11, 1979,* San Juan, P.R. *(159,540)* 1.50
1610 $1 **Rush Lamp,** *July 2, 1979,* San Francisco, Calif. *(255,575)* 3.00
1611 $2 **Kerosene Lamp,** *Nov. 16, 1978,* New York, N.Y. *(173,596)* 5.00
1612 $5 **Railroad Lantern,** *Aug. 23, 1979,* Boston, Mass. *(129,192)* 12.50

COIL STAMPS

1613 3.1c **Guitar,** *Oct. 25, 1979,* Shreveport, La. *(230,403)* 1.00
1614 7.7c **Saxhorns,** *Nov. 20, 1976,* New York, N.Y. *(285,290)* 1.00
1615 7.9c **Drum,** *Apr. 23, 1976,* Miami, Fla. *(193,270)* 1.00
1615C 8.4c **Piano,** *July 13, 1978,* Interlochen, Mich. *(200,392)* 1.00
1616 9c **Capitol Dome,** *Mar. 5, 1976,* Milwaukee, Wis. *(128,171)* 1.00
1617 10c **Justice,** *Nov. 4, 1977,* Tampa, Fla. *(184,954)* 1.00
1618 13c **Liberty Bell,** *Nov. 25, 1975,* Allentown, Pa. *(320,387)* 1.00
1618C 15c **Flag,** *June 30, 1978,* Baltimore, Md. 1.00
1619 16c **Statue of Liberty,** *Mar. 31, 1978,* New York, N.Y. 1.00

First day cancellation was applied to 376,338 covers bearing one or more of Nos. 1599 and 1619.

1975

1622 13c **13-Star Flag,** *Nov. 15,* Philadelphia, Pa. 1.00
1623 13c **Flag over Capitol,** *Mar. 11,* New York, N.Y. 1.50

1623a Booklet pane of 8, perf 11 (1 #1590 +7 #1623) 25.00
1623Bc Booklet pane of 8, perf. 10x9¾ (1 #1590A + 7 #1623B) 15.00

First day cancellation was applied to 242,208 covers bearing Nos. 1623, 1623a, 1623B or 1623Bc.

1625 13c **13-Star Flag coil,** *Nov. 15,* Philadelphia, PA 1.00

First day cancellation was applied to 362,959 covers bearing one or more of Nos. 1622 and 1625.

1976

1631a 13c **Spirit of '76,** *Jan. 1,* Pasadena, CA *(1,013,067)* 2.00
1629-1631, any single 1.25
1632 13c **Interphil '76,** *Jan. 17,* Philadelphia, Pa. *(519,902)* 1.00
1682a 13c **State Flags,** *Feb. 23* 27.50
1633-1682, any single 1.50
1683 13c **Telephone,** *Mar. 10,* Boston, Mass. *(662,515)* 1.00
1684 13c **Commercial Aviation,** *Mar. 19,* Chicago Ill. *(631,555)* 1.50
1685 13c **Chemistry,** *Apr. 6,* New York, N.Y. *(557,600)* 1.50

Bicentennial Souvenir Sheets of 5

1686 13c **Surrender of Cornwallis,** *May 29,* Philadelphia, Pa. 7.50
1687 18c **Declaration of Independence,** *May 29,* Philadelphia, Pa. 7.50
1688 24c **Declaration of Independence,** *May 29,* Philadelphia, Pa. 7.50
1689 31c **Washington at Valley Forge,** *May 29,* Philadelphia, Pa. 7.50

First day cancellation was applied to 879,890 covers bearing singles, multiples or complete sheets of Nos. 1686-1689.

1690 13c **Franklin,** *June 1,* Philadelphia, Pa. *(588,740)* 1.00
1694a 13c **Declaration of Independence,** *July 4,* Philadelphia, Pa. *(2,093,880)* 2.00
1691-1694, any single 1.00
1698a 13c **Olympic Games,** *July 16,* Lake Placid, N.Y. *(1,140,189)* 2.00
1695-1698, any single 1.00
1699 13c **Clara Maass,** *Aug. 18,* Belleville, N.J. *(646,506)* 2.50
1700 13c **Adolph S. Ochs,** *Sept. 18,* New York, N.Y. *(582,580)* 1.00
1701 13c **Christmas (religious),** *Oct. 27,* Boston, Mass. (540,050) 1.00
1702 13c **Christmas (secular),** *Oct. 27,* Boston, Mass. (181,410) 1.00
1703 13c **Christmas (secular),** block tagged, *Oct. 27,* Boston, Mass. (330,450) 1.00
1701 and 1702 or 1703 on one cover 1.25

1977

1704 13c **Washington at Princeton,** *Jan. 3,* Princeton, N.J. *(695,335)* 1.00
1705 13c **Sound Recording,** *Mar. 23 (632,216)* 1.25
1709a 13c **Pueblo Art,** *Apr. 13,* Santa Fe, N.M. *(1,194,554)* 2.00
1706-1709, any single 1.00
1710 13c **Lindbergh Flight,** *May 20,* Roosevelt Sta., N.Y. *(3,985,989)* 4.00
1711 13c **Colorado Statehood,** *May 21,* Denver, Colo. *(510,880)* 1.00
1715a 13c **Butterflies,** *June 6,* Indianapolis, Ind. *(1,218,278)* 2.00
1712-1715, any single 2.00
1716 13c **Lafayette's Landing,** *June 13,* Charleston, S.C. *(514,506)* 1.00
1720a 13c **Skilled Hands,** *July 4,* Cincinnati, Ohio *(1,263,568)* 2.00
1717-1720, any single 1.00
1721 13c **Peace Bridge,** *Aug. 4,* Buffalo, N.Y. *(512,995)* 1.00
1722 13c **Battle of Oriskany,** *Aug. 6,* Herkimer, N.Y. *(605,906)* 1.00
1724a 13c **Energy Conservation,** *Oct. 20 (410,299)* 1.50
1723-1724, any single 1.25
1725 13c **Alta California,** *Sept. 9,* San Jose, Calif. *(709,457)* 1.00
1726 13c **Articles of Confederation,** *Sept. 30,* York, Pa. *(605,455)* 1.00
1727 13c **Talking Pictures,** *Oct. 6,* Hollywood, Calif. *(570,195)* 1.50
1728 13c **Surrender at Saratoga** *Oct. 7,* Schuylerville, N.Y. *(557,529)* 1.00
1729 13c **Christmas (Valley Forge),** *Oct. 21,* Valley Forge, Pa. *(583,139)* 1.00
1730 13c **Christmas (mailbox),** *Oct. 21,* Omaha, Nebr. *(675,786)* 1.00

1978

1731 13c **Carl Sandburg,** *Jan. 6,* Galesburg, Ill. *(493,826)* 1.00
1733b 13c **Captain Cook,** *Jan. 20,* Honolulu, Hawaii, or Anchorage, Alaska 2.00
1732-1733, any single 1.50

First day cancellation was applied to 823,855 covers at Honolulu, and 672,804 at Anchorage, each cover bearing one or both of Nos. 1732-1733.

1734 13c **Indian Head Penny,** *Jan. 11,* Kansas City, Mo. *(512,426)* 1.50

REGULAR ISSUE

1978-80

1735 (15c) **"A" Eagle,** *May 22,* Memphis, Tenn. 1.00
1736 (15c) **"A" Eagle,** bklt. single *May 22,* Memphis, Tenn. 1.00
1736a Booklet pane of 8 2.50
1737 15c **Roses,** *July 11,* Shreveport, La. *(445,003)* 1.00
1737a Booklet pane of 8 2.50
1742a 15c **Windmills Booklet pane of 10,** *Feb. 7, 1980,* Lubbock, TX 3.50
1738-1742, any single 1.00
1743 15c **"A" Eagle coil,** *May 22,* Memphis, Tenn. 1.00

First day cancellation was applied to 689,049 covers bearing one or more of Nos. 1735, 1736 and 1743. First day cancellation was applied to 708,411 covers bearing one or more of Nos. 1738-1742a.

1978

1744 13c **Harriet Tubman,** *Feb. 1 (493,495)* 2.00
1748a 13c **American Quilts,** *Mar. 8,* Charleston, W.Va. 2.00
1745-1748, any single 1.00

First day cancellation was applied to 1,081,827 covers bearing one or more of Nos. 1745-1748.

1752a 13c **American Dance,** *Apr. 26,* New York, N.Y. *(1,626,493)* 2.00
1749-1752, any single 1.00
1753 13c **French Alliance,** *May 4,* York, Pa. *(705,240)* 1.00
1754 13c **Papanicolaou,** *May 18 (535,584)* 1.00
1755 13c **Jimmie Rodgers,** *May 24,* Meridian, Miss. *(599,287)* 1.00
1756 15c **George M. Cohan,** *July 3,* Providence, R.I. *(740,750)* 1.25
1757 **CAPEX** souv. sheet, *June 10,* Toronto, Canada *(1,994,067)* 2.75
1758 15c **Photography,** *June 26,* Las Vegas, Nev. *(684,987)* 1.00
1759 15c **Viking Missions,** *July 20,* Hampton, Va. *(805,051)* 1.00
1763a 15c **American Owls,** *Aug. 26,* Fairbanks, Alas. *(1,690,474)* 2.00
1760-1763, any single 1.25
1767a 15c **American Trees,** *Oct. 9,* Hot Springs National Park, Ark. *(1,139,100)* 2.00
1764-1767, any single 1.25
1768 15c **Christmas (Madonna),** *Oct. 18 (553,064)* 1.00
1769 15c **Christmas (Hobby Horse),** *Oct. 18,* Holly, Mich. *(603,008)* 1.00

1979-80

1770 15c **Robert Kennedy,** *Jan. 12 (624,582)* 2.00
1771 15c **Martin L. King,** *Jan. 13,* Atlanta, Ga. *(726,149)* 2.00
1772 15c **Year of Child,** *Feb. 15,* Philadelphia, Pa. *(716,782)* 1.00
1773 15c **John Steinbeck,** *Feb. 27,* Salinas, Calif. *(709,073)* 1.00
1774 15c **Albert Einstein,** *Mar. 4,* Princeton, N.J. *(641,423)* 3.50
1778a 15c **Toleware,** *Apr. 19,* Lancaster, Pa. *(1,581,962)* 2.00
1775-1778, any single 1.00
1782a 15c **American Architecture,** *June 4,* Kansas City, Mo. *(1,219,258)* 2.00
1779-1782, any single 1.00
1786a 15c **Endangered Flora,** *June 7,* Milwaukee, Wis. *(1,436,268)* 2.00
1783-1786, any single 1.00
1787 15c **Guide Dogs,** *June 15,* Morristown, N.J. *(588,826)* 1.25
1788 15c **Special Olympics,** *Aug. 9,* Brockport, N.Y. *(651,344)* 1.25
1789 15c **John Paul Jones,** *Sept. 23,* Annapolis, Md. 1.50
1789A 15c **John Paul Jones,** *Sept. 23,* Annapolis, Md. 1.50

Total for 1789 and 1789A is 587,018.

1790 10c **Olympic Javelin,** *Sept. 5,* Olympia, Wash. *(305,122)* 1.00
1794a 15c **Olympics 1980,** *Sept. 28,* Los Angeles, Calif. *(1,561,366)* 2.00
1791-1794, any single 1.25
1798b 15c **Winter Olympics,** *Feb. 1, 1980,* Lake Placid, N.Y. *(1,166,302)* 2.00
1795-1798, any single 1.25

1979

1799 15c **Christmas (Madonna),** *Oct. 18 (686,990)* 1.25
1800 15c **Christmas (Santa Claus),** *Oct. 18,* North Pole, Alaska *(511,829)* 1.25
1799-1800, both stamps issued *Oct. 18* 2.00
1801 15c **Will Rogers,** *Nov. 4,* Claremore, Okla. *(1,643,151)* 1.50
1802 15c **Viet Nam Veterans,** *Nov. 11,* Arlington, VA *(445,934)* *5.00*

1980

1803 15c **W.C. Fields,** *Jan. 29,* Beverly Hills, CA *(633,303)* 2.00
1804 15c **Benjamin Banneker,** *Feb. 15,* Annapolis, MD *(647,126)* 2.00
1810a 15c **Letter Writing,** *Feb. 25 (1,083,360)* 2.50
1805-1810, any single 1.00

1980-81 DEFINITIVES

1811 1c **Quill Pen,** coil, *Mar. 6, 1980,* New York, NY *(262,921)* 1.00
1813 3.5c **Violins,** coil, *June 23, 1980,* Williamsburg, PA 1.00

FD cancel was applied to 716,988 covers bearing Nos. 1813 or U590.

1816 12c **Torch,** coil, *Apr. 8, 1981,* Dallas, TX 1.00
1818 (18c) **"B" Eagle,** *Mar. 15, 1981,* San Francisco, CA 1.25

FD cancel was applied to 511,688 covers bearing one or more of Nos. 1818-1820, U592 or UX88.

1819 (18c) **"B" Eagle,** bklt. single, *Mar. 15, 1981,* San Francisco, CA 1.00
1819a Booklet pane of 8 3.00
1820 (18c) **"B" Eagle,** coil, *Mar. 15, 1981,* San Francisco, CA 1.00

1980

1821 15c **Frances Perkins,** *Apr. 10 (678,966)* 1.00
1822 15c **Dolley Madison,** *May 20 (331,048)* 1.00
1823 15c **Emily Bissell,** *May 31,* Wilmington, DE *(649,509)* 1.00
1824 15c **Helen Keller, Anne Sullivan,** *June 27,* Tuscumbia, AL *(713,061)* 1.25
1825 15c **Veterans Administration,** *July 21 (634,101)* 1.50
1826 15c **Bernardo de Galvez,** *July 23,* New Orleans, LA *(658,061)* 1.00
1830a 15c **Coral Reefs,** *Aug. 26,* Charlotte Amalie, VI *(1,195,126)* 2.00
1827-1830, any single 1.00
1831 15c **Organized Labor,** *Sept. 1 (759,973)* 1.00
1832 15c **Edith Wharton,** *Sept. 5,* New Haven, CT *(633,917)* 1.00
1833 15c **Education,** *Sept. 12,*Franklin, MA *(672,592)* 1.50
1837a 15c **Indian Masks,** *Sept. 25,* Spokane, WA *(2,195,136)* 2.00
1834-1837, any single 1.00
1841a 15c **Architecture,** *Oct. 9,* New York, NY *(2,164,721)* 1.75
1838-1841, any single 1.00
1842 15c **Christmas (Madonna),** *Oct. 31 (718,614)* 1.25
1843 15c **Christmas (Toys),** *Oct. 31,* Christmas, MI *(755,108)* 1.25

GREAT AMERICANS ISSUE

1980-85

1844 1c **Dorothea Dix,** *Sept. 23, 1983,* Hampden, ME *(164,140)* 1.00
1845 2c **Igor Stravinsky,** *Nov. 18, 1982,* New York, NY *(501,719)* 1.00
1846 3c **Henry Clay,** *July 13, 1983 (204,320)* 1.00
1847 4c **Carl Schurz,** *June 3, 1983,* Watertown, WI *(165,010)* 1.00
1848 5c **Pearl Buck,** *June 25, 1983,* Hillsboro, WV *(231,852)* 1.00
1849 6c **Walter Lippman,** *Sept. 19, 1985,* Minneapolis, MN *(371,990)* 1.00
1850 7c **Abraham Baldwin,** *Jan. 25, 1985,* Athens, GA *(402,285)* 1.25
1851 8c **Henry Knox,** *July 25, 1985,* Thomaston, ME *(315,937)* 1.00
1852 9c **Sylvanus Thayer,** *June 7, 1985,* Braintree, MA *(345,649)* 1.25
1853 10c **Richard Russell,** *May 31, 1984,* Winder, GA *(183,581)* 1.00
1854 11c **Alden Partridge,** *Feb. 12, 1985,* Northfield, VT *(442,311)* 1.25
1855 13c **Crazy Horse,** *Jan. 15, 1982,* Crazy Horse, SD 2.00
1856 14c **Sinclair Lewis,** *Mar. 21, 1985,* Sauk Centre, MN *(308,612)* 1.00
1857 17c **Rachel Carson,** *May 28, 1981,* Springdale, PA *(273,686)* 1.00
1858 18c **George Mason,** *May 7, 1981,* Gunston Hall, VA *(461,937)* 1.00
1859 19c **Sequoyah,** *Dec. 27, 1980,* Tahlequah, OK *(241,325)* 1.50
1860 20c **Ralph Bunche,** *Jan. 12, 1982,* New York, NY 1.75
1861 20c **Thomas H. Gallaudet,** *June 10, 1983,* West Hartford, CT *(261,336)* 1.25
1862 20c **Harry S Truman,** *Jan. 26, 1984 (267,631)* 1.50
1863 22c **John J. Audubon,** *Apr. 23, 1985,* New York, NY *(516,249)* 1.25
1864 30c **Frank Laubach,** *Sept. 2, 1984,* Benton, PA *(118,974)* 1.25
1865 35c **Charles Drew,** *June 3, 1981 (383,882)* 1.75
1866 37c **Robert Millikan,** *Jan. 26, 1982,* Pasadena, CA 1.25
1867 39c **Grenville Clark,** *Mar. 20, 1985,* Hanover, NH *(297,797)* 1.25
1868 40c **Lillian Gilbreth,** *Feb. 24, 1984,* Montclair, NJ *(110,588)* 1.50
1869 50c **Chester W. Nimitz,** *Feb. 22, 1985,* Fredericksburg, TX *(376,166)* 2.00

1981

1874 15c **Everett Dirksen,** *Jan. 4,* Pekin, IL *(665,755)* 1.00
1875 15c **Whitney M. Young,** *Jan. 30,* New York, NY *(963,870)* 1.75

1879a 18c **Flowers,** *Apr. 23,* Fort Valley, GA *(1,966,599)* 2.50
1876-1879, any single 1.00

DEFINITIVES

1889a 18c **Animals Booklet pane of 10,** *May 14,* Boise, ID 5.00
1880-1889, any single 1.00
1890 18c **Flag-Anthem (grain),** *Apr. 24,* Portland, ME 1.00
1891 18c **Flag-Anthem (sea),** *Apr. 24,* Portland, ME 1.50
1892 6c **Star Circle,** *Apr. 24,* Portland, ME 1.00
1893 18c **Flag-Anthem (mountain),** *Apr. 24,* Portland, ME 1.00
1893a Booklet pane of 8 (2 #1892, 6 #1893) 2.50

FDC cancel was applied to 691,526 covers bearing one or more of Nos. 1890-1893 & 1893a.

1894 20c **Flag-Court,** *Dec. 17* 1.00
1895 20c **Flag-Court,** coil, *Dec. 17* 1.00
1896 20c **Flag-Court,** perf. 11x10½, *Dec. 17 (185,543)* 1.00
1896a Booklet pane of 6 6.00
1896b Booklet pane of 10, *June 1, 1982* *10.00*

First day cancellations were applied to 598,169 covers bearing one or more of Nos. 1894-1896.

TRANSPORTATION ISSUE

1981-84

1897 1c **Omnibus,** *Aug. 19, 1983,* Arlington, VA *(109,463)* 1.00
1897A 2c **Locomotive,** *May 20, 1982,* Chicago, IL *(290,020)* 1.50
1898 3c **Handcar,** *Mar. 25, 1983,* Rochester, NY *(77,900)* 1.00
1898A 4c **Stagecoach,** *Aug. 19, 1982,* Milwaukee, WI *(152,940)* 1.00
1899 5c **Motorcycle,** *Oct. 10, 1983,* San Francisco, CA *(188,240)* 2.00
1900 5.2c **Sleigh,** *Mar. 21, 1983,* Memphis, TN *(141,979)* 1.00
1901 5.9c **Bicycle,** *Feb. 17, 1982,* Wheeling, WV *(814,419)* 1.75
1902 7.4c **Baby Buggy,** *Apr. 7, 1984,* San Diego, CA 1.00
1903 9.3c **Mail Wagon,** *Dec. 15, 1981,* Shreveport, LA *(199,645)* 1.00
1904 10.9c **Hansom,** *Mar. 26, 1982,* Chattanooga, TN 1.00
1905 11c **Railroad Caboose,** *Feb. 3, 1984,* Chicago, IL *(172,753)* 1.50
1906 17c **Electric Auto,** *June 25, 1981,* Greenfield Village, MI *(239,458)* 1.00
1907 18c **Surrey,** *May 18, 1981,* Notch, MO *(207,801)* 1.00
1908 20c **Fire Pumper,** *Dec. 10, 1981,* Alexandria, VA *(304,668)* 2.50
1909 $9.35 **Eagle,** *Aug. 12, 1983,* Kennedy Space Center, FL *(77,858)* 40.00
1909a Booklet pane of 3 *130.00*

1981

1910 18c **Red Cross,** *May 1 (874,972)* 2.00
1911 18c **Savings & Loan,** *May 8,* Chicago, IL *(740,910)* 1.00
1919a 18c **Space Achievement,** *May 21,* Kennedy Space Center, FL *(7,027,549)* 3.00
1912-1919, any single 1.00
1920 18c **Professional Management,** *June 18,* Philadelphia, PA *(713,096)* 1.00
1924a 18c **Wildlife Habitats,** *June 26,* Reno, NV *(2,327,609)* 2.50
1921-1924, any single 1.00
1925 18c **Year of Disabled,** *June 29,* Milford, MI *(714,244)* 1.00
1926 18c **Edna St. V. Millay,** *July 10,* Austerlitz, NY *(725,978)* 1.00
1927 18c **Alcoholism,** *Aug. 19 (874,972)* 3.00
1931a 18c **Architecture,** *Aug. 28,* New York, NY *(1,998,208)* 2.50
1928-1931, any single 1.00
1932 18c **Babe Zaharias,** *Sept. 22,* Pinehurst, NC 5.00
1933 18c **Bobby Jones,** *Sept. 22,* Pinehurst, NC 8.00
1932-1933, both stamps issued *Sept. 22,* Pinehurst, NC 10.00

First day cancel was applied to 1,231,543 covers bearing one or more of Nos. 1932-1933.

1934 18c **Frederic Remington,** *Oct. 9,* Oklahoma City, OK *(1,367,099)* 1.25
1935 18c **James Hoban,** *Oct. 13* 1.00
1936 20c **James Hoban,** *Oct. 13* 1.00
1935-1936, both stamps issued *Oct. 13* 3.00

FD cancel was applied to 635,012 covers bearing Nos. 1935-1936.

1938a 18c **Yorktown-Va. Capes Battle,** *Oct. 16,* Yorktown, VA *(1,098,278)* 1.50
1937-1938, any single 1.00
1939 (20c) **Christmas (Madonna),** *Oct. 28,* Chicago, IL *(481,395)* 1.00
1940 (20c) **Christmas (Teddy Bear),** *Oct. 28,* Christmas Valley, OR *(517,898)* 1.00
1941 20c **John Hanson,** *Nov. 5,* Frederick, MD *(605,616)* 1.00
1945a 20c **Desert Plants,** *Dec. 11,* Tucson, AZ *(1,770,187)* 2.50
1942-1945, any single 1.00

REGULAR ISSUE

1946 (20c) **"C" Eagle,** *Oct. 11,* Memphis, TN 1.00
1947 (20c) **"C" Eagle,** coil, *Oct. 11,* Memphis, TN 1.00
1948 (20c) **"C" Eagle,** bklt. single, *Oct. 11,* Memphis, TN 1.00
1948a Booklet pane of 10 *3.50*

First day cancellations were applied to 304,404 covers bearing one or more of Nos. 1946-1948.

1982

1949 20c **Bighorn,** *Jan. 8,* Bighorn, MT 1.25
1949a Booklet pane of 10 *6.00*
1950 20c **F.D. Roosevelt,** *Jan. 30,* Hyde Park, NY 1.00
1951 20c **Love,** *Feb. 1,* Boston, MA *(325,727)* 1.00
1952 20c **Washington,** *Feb. 22,* Mt. Vernon, VA 1.25
2002b 20c **Birds-Flowers,** perf 10½x11¼ *Apr. 14,* Washington, DC, or State Capital 30.00
1953-2002, any single 1.25
2002Ac 20c **Birds-Flowers,** perf 11¼x11 *Apr. 14,* Washington, DC, or State Capital —
1953A-2002A, any single —
2003 20c **U.S.-Netherlands,** *Apr. 20* 1.00
2004 20c **Library of Congress,** *Apr. 21* 1.00
2005 20c **Consumer Education,** *Apr. 27* 1.00
2009a 20c **Knoxville Fair,** *Apr. 29,* Knoxville, TN 2.50
2006-2009, any single 1.00
2010 20c **Horatio Alger,** *Apr. 30,* Willow Grove, PA 1.00
2011 20c **Aging,** *May 21,* Sun City, AZ *(510,677)* 1.00
2012 20c **Barrymores,** *June 8,* New York, NY 1.25
2013 20c **Dr. Mary Walker,** *June 10,* Oswego, NY 1.00
2014 20c **Peace Garden,** *June 30,* Dunseith, ND 1.00
2015 20c **America's Libraries,** *July 13,* Philadelphia, PA 1.00
2016 20c **Jackie Robinson,** *Aug. 2,* Cooperstown, NY 6.00
2017 20c **Touro Synagogue,** *Aug. 22,* Newport, RI *(517,264)* 2.00
2018 20c **Wolf Trap Farm Park,** *Sept. 1,* Vienna, VA *(704,361)* 1.00
2022a 20c **Architecture,** *Sept. 30 (1,552,567)* 2.50
2019-2022, any single 1.00
2023 20c **St. Francis,** *Oct. 7,* San Francisco, CA *(530,275)* 1.50
2024 20c **Ponce de Leon,** *Oct. 12,* San Juan, PR *(530,275)* 1.00
2025 13c **Puppy, Kitten,** *Nov. 3,* Danvers, MA *(239,219)* 1.25
2026 20c **Christmas (Madonna),** *Oct. 28 (462,982)* 1.00
2030a 20c **Christmas (Children),** *Oct. 28,* Snow, OK *(676,950)* 2.50
2027-2030, any single 1.00

1983

2031 20c **Science & Industry,** *Jan. 19,* Chicago, IL *(526,693)* 1.00
2035a 20c **Balloons,** *Mar. 31,* Albuquerque, NM or Washington, DC *(989,305)* 3.00
2032-2035, any single 1.00
2036 20c **U.S.-Sweden,** *Mar. 24,* Philadelphia, PA *(526,373)* 1.00
2037 20c **Civilian Conservation Corps.,** *Apr. 5,* Luray, VA *(483,824)* 1.00
2038 20c **Joseph Priestley,** *Apr. 13,* Northumberland, PA *(673,266)* 1.00
2039 20c **Voluntarism,** *Apr. 20 (574,708)* 1.00
2040 20c **U.S.-Germany,** *Apr. 29,* Germantown, PA *(611,109)* 1.00
2041 20c **Brooklyn Bridge,** *May 17,* Brooklyn, NY *(815,085)* 1.75
2042 20c **TVA,** *May 18,* Knoxville, TN *(837,588)* 1.00
2043 20c **Physical Fitness,** *May 14,* Houston, TX *(501,336)* 1.25
2044 20c **Scott Joplin,** *June 9,* Sedalia, MO *(472,667)* 1.75
2045 20c **Medal of Honor,** *June 7 (1,623,995)* 7.00
2046 20c **Babe Ruth,** *July 6,* Chicago, IL *(1,277,907)* 5.00
2047 20c **Nathaniel Hawthorne,** *July 8,* Salem, MA *(442,793)* 1.00
2051a 13c **Summer Olympics,** *July 28,* South Bend, IN *(909,332)* 2.50
2048-2051, any single 1.25
2052 20c **Treaty of Paris,** *Sept. 2 (651,208)* 1.00
2053 20c **Civil Service,** *Sept. 9 (422,206)* 1.00
2054 20c **Metropolitan Opera,** *Sept. 14,* New York, NY *(807,609)* 1.50
2058a 20c **American Inventors,** *Sept. 21 (1,006,516)* 2.50
2055-2058, any single 1.00
2062a 20c **Streetcars,** *Oct. 8,* Kennebunkport, ME *(1,116,909)* 2.50
2059-2062, any single 1.00
2063 20c **Christmas (Madonna),** *Oct. 28 (361,874)* 1.00
2064 20c **Christmas (Santa),** *Oct. 28,* Santa Claus, IN *(388,749)* 1.00
2065 20c **Martin Luther,** *Nov. 11 (463,777)* 1.50

1984

2066 20c **Alaska Statehood,** *Jan. 3,* Fairbanks, AK *(816,591)* 1.00
2070a 20c **Winter Olympics,** *Jan. 6,* Lake Placid, NY *(1,245,807)* 2.50
2067-2070, any single 1.00
2071 20c **Federal Deposit Ins. Corp.,** *Jan. 12 (536,329)* 1.00
2072 20c **Love,** *Jan. 31 (327,727)* 1.00
2073 20c **Carter Woodson,** *Feb. 1 (387,583)* 1.75
2074 20c **Soil & Water Conservation,** *Feb. 6,* Denver, CO *(426,101)* 1.00
2075 20c **Credit Union Act,** *Feb. 10,* Salem, MA *(523,583)* 1.00
2079a 20c **Orchids,** *Mar. 5,* Miami, FL *(1,063,237)* 2.50
2076-2079, any single 1.00
2080 20c **Hawaii Statehood,** *Mar. 12,* Honolulu, HI *(546,930)* 1.00
2081 20c **National Archives,** *Apr. 16 (414,415)* 1.00
2085a 20c **Olympics 1984,** *May 4,* Los Angeles, CA *(1,172,313)* 2.50
2082-2085, any single 1.25
2086 20c **Louisiana Exposition,** *May 11,* New Orleans, LA *(467,408)* 1.00
2087 20c **Health Research,** *May 17,* New York, NY *(845,007)* 1.00
2088 20c **Douglas Fairbanks,** *May 23,* Denver CO *(547,134)* 1.50
2089 20c **Jim Thorpe,** *May 24,* Shawnee, OK *(568,544)* 3.00
2090 20c **John McCormack,** *June 6,* Boston, MA *(464,117)* 1.00
2091 20c **St. Lawrence Seaway,** *June 26,* Massena, NY *(550,173)* 1.00
2092 20c **Waterfowl Preservation Act,** *July 2,* Des Moines, IA *(549,388)* 1.00
2093 20c **Roanoke Voyages,** *July 13,* Manteo, NC *(443,725)* 1.00
2094 20c **Herman Melville,** *Aug. 1,* New Bedford, MA *(378,293)* 2.00
2095 20c **Horace A. Moses,** *Aug. 6,* Bloomington, IN *(459,386)* 1.00
2096 20c **Smokey Bear,** *Aug. 13,* Capitan, NM *(506,833)* 5.00
2097 20c **Roberto Clemente,** *Aug. 17,* Carolina, PR *(547,387)* 9.00
2101a 20c **Dogs,** *Sept. 7,* New York, NY *(1,157,373)* 3.00
2098-2101, any single 1.50
2102 20c **Crime Prevention,** *Sept. 26 (427,564)* 1.25
2103 20c **Hispanic Americans,** *Oct. 31 (416,796)* 1.75
2104 20c **Family Unity,** *Oct. 1,* Shaker Heights, OH *(400,659)* 1.00
2105 20c **Eleanor Roosevelt,** *Oct. 11,* Hyde Park, NY *(479,919)* 1.25
2106 20c **Nation of Readers,** *Oct. 16 (437,559)* 1.00
2107 20c **Christmas (Madonna),** *Oct. 30 (386,385)* 1.00
2108 20c **Christmas (Santa),** *Oct. 30,* Jamaica, NY *(430,843)* 1.00
2109 20c **Vietnam Veterans' Memorial,** *Nov. 10 (434,489)* 5.00

1985

2110 22c **Jerome Kern,** *Jan. 23,* New York, NY (503,855) 1.00

REGULAR ISSUE

2111 (22c) **"D" Eagle,** *Feb. 1,* Los Angeles, CA 1.00
2112 (22c) **"D" Eagle, coil,** *Feb. 1,* Los Angeles, CA 1.00
2113 (22c) **"D" Eagle, bklt. single,** *Feb. 1,* Los Angeles, CA 1.00
2113a Booklet pane of 10 *7.50*

First Day cancel was applied to 513,027 covers bearing one or more of Nos. 2111-2113.

2114 22c **Flag over Capitol Dome,** *Mar. 29* 1.00
2115 22c **Flag over Capitol Dome,** coil, *Mar. 29* 1.00
2115c Inscribed "T" at bottom, *May 23, 1987,* Secaucus, NJ *1.00*

First Day Cancel was applied to 268,161 covers bearing one or more of Nos. 2114-2115.

2116 22c **Flag Over Capitol Dome,** bklt. single, *Mar. 29,* Waubeka, WI *(234,318)* 1.00
2116a Booklet pane of 5 3.50
2121a 22c **Seashells Booklet pane of 10,** *Apr. 4,* Boston, MA *(426,290)* *7.50*
2117-2121, any single 1.00
2122 $10.75 **Eagle and Half Moon,** type I, *Apr. 29,* San Francisco, CA *(93,154)* 50.00
2122a Booklet pane of 3 *125.00*
2122b Type II, *June 19, 1989* *350.00*
2122c Booklet pane of 3, type II *700.00*

TRANSPORTATION ISSUE

1985-87

2123 3.4c **School Bus,** *June 8, 1985,* Arlington, VA *(131,480)* 1.00
2124 4.9c **Buckboard,** *June 21, 1985,* Reno, NV 1.00
2125 5.5c **Star Route Truck,** *Nov. 1, 1986,* Fort Worth, TX *(136,021)* 1.00
2125a 5.5c **Star Route Truck,** untagged (Bureau precanceled), *Nov. 1, 1986,* Washington, DC 5.00

2126 6c **Tricycle,** *May 6, 1985,* Childs, MD *(151,494)* 1.25
2127 7.1c **Tractor,** *Feb. 6, 1987,* Sarasota, FL *(167,555)* 1.00
2127a 7.1c **Tractor,** "Non-profit Org." precancel in black, *Feb. 6, 1987,* Sarasota, FL 5.00
2127b 7.1c **Tractor,** "Non-profit 5-Digit Zip+4" precancel in black, untagged, *May 26, 1989,* Rosemont, IL *(202,804)* 1.00
2128 8.3c **Ambulance,** *June 21, 1986,* Reno, NV 1.00

First day cancel was applied to 338,765 covers bearing one or more of Nos. 2124 and 2128.

2129 8.5c **Tow Truck,** *Jan. 24, 1987,* Tucson, AZ *(224,285)* 1.25
2129a 8.5c **Tow Truck,** untagged (Bureau precancel) *Jan. 24, 1987,* Washington, DC 5.00
2130 10.1c **Oil Wagon,** *Apr. 18, 1985,* Oil Center, NM 1.25
2130a 10.1c "Bulk Rate Carrier Route Sort" precancel, *June 27, 1988 (136,428)* 1.25
2131 11c **Stutz Bearcat,** *June 11, 1985,* Baton Rouge, LA *(135,037)* 1.25
2132 12c **Stanley Steamer,** *Apr. 2, 1985,* Kingfield, ME *(173,998)* 1.25
2133 12.5c **Pushcart,** *Apr. 18, 1985,* Oil Center, NM 1.25

First day cancel was applied to 319,953 covers bearing one or more of Nos. 2130 and 2133.

2134 14c **Ice Boat,** *Mar. 23, 1985,* Rochester, NY *(324,710)* 1.25
2135 17c **Dog Sled,** *Aug. 20, 1986,* Anchorage, AK 1.75
2136 25c **Bread Wagon,** *Nov. 22, 1986,* Virginia Beach, VA *(151,950)* 1.25

1985

2137 22c **Mary McLeod Bethune,** *Mar. 5 (413,244)* 1.50
2141a 22c **Duck Decoys,** *Mar. 22,* Shelburne, VT *(932,249)* 2.50
2138-2141, any single 1.00
2142 22c **Winter Special Olympics,** *Mar. 25,* Park City, UT *(253,074)* 1.00
2143 22c **Love,** *Apr. 17,* Hollywood, CA *(283,072)* 1.00
2144 22c **Rural Electrification Administration,** *May 11,* Madison, SD *(472,895)* 1.00
2145 22c **AMERIPEX '86,** *May 25,* Rosemont, IL *(457,038)* 1.00
2146 22c **Abigail Adams,** *June 14,* Quincy, MA *(491,026)* 1.00
2147 22c **Frederic Auguste Bartholdi,** *July 18,* New York, NY *(594,896)* 1.00
2149 18c **George Washington, Washington Monument,** *Nov. 6 (376,238)* 1.00
2150 21.1c **Envelopes,** *Oct. 22 (119,941)* 1.00
2152 22c **Korean War Veterans,** *July 26 (391,754)* 3.00
2153 22c **Social Security Act,** *Aug. 14,* Baltimore, MD *(265,143)* 1.00
2154 22c **World War I Veterans,** *Aug. 26,* Milwaukee, WI 1.75
2158a 22c **Horses,** *Sept. 25,* Lexington, KY *(1,135,368)* 2.50
2155-2158, any single 1.50
2159 22c **Public Education in America,** *Oct. 1,* Boston, MA *(356,030)* 1.00
2163a 22c **International Youth Year,** *Oct. 7,* Chicago, IL *(1,202,541)* 2.50
2160, 2162-2163, any single 1.00
2161 2.00
2164 22c **Help End Hunger,** *Oct. 15 (299,485)* 1.00
2165 22c **Christmas (Madonna & Child),** *Oct. 30,* Detroit, MI 1.00
2166 22c **Christmas (Poinsettia),** *Oct. 30,* Nazareth, MI *(524,929)* 1.00

1986

2167 22c **Arkansas Statehood,** *Jan. 3,* Little Rock, AR *(364,729)* 1.00

GREAT AMERICANS ISSUE

1986-94

2168 1c **Margaret Mitchell,** *June 30, 1986,* Atlanta, GA *(316,764)* 2.00
2169 2c **Mary Lyon,** *Feb. 28, 1987,* South Hadley, MA *(349,831)* 1.00
2170 3c **Dr. Paul Dudley White,** *Sept. 15, 1986* 1.00
2171 4c **Father Flanagan,** *July 14, 1986,* Boys Town, NE *(367,883)* 1.25
2172 5c **Hugo Black,** *Feb. 27, 1986 (303,012)* 1.00
2173 5c **Luis Munoz Marin,** *Feb. 18, 1990,* San Juan, PR *(269,618)* 1.00
2175 10c **Red Cloud,** *Aug. 15, 1987,* Red Cloud, NE *(300,472)* 1.75
2176 14c **Julia Ward Howe,** *Feb. 12, 1987,* Boston, MA *(454,829)* 1.00
2177 15c **Buffalo Bill Cody,** *June 6, 1988* Cody, WY *(356,395)* 2.00
2178 17c **Belva Ann Lockwood,** *June 18, 1986,* Middleport, NY *(249,215)* 1.00
2179 20c **Virginia Apgar,** *Oct. 24, 1994,* Dallas, TX *(28,461)* 1.00
2180 21c **Chester Carlson,** *Oct. 21, 1988,* Rochester, NY *(288,073)* 1.00
2181 23c **Mary Cassatt,** *Nov. 4, 1988,* Philadelphia, PA *(322,537)* 1.00
2182 25c **Jack London,** *Jan. 11, 1986,* Glen Ellen, CA *(358,686)* 1.50
2182a Booklet pane of 10, *May 3, 1988,* San Francisco, CA 6.00
2183 28c **Sitting Bull,** *Sept. 14, 1989,* Rapid City, SD *(126,777)* 2.00
2184 29c **Earl Warren,** *Mar. 9, 1992 (175,517)* 1.25
2185 29c **Thomas Jefferson,** *Apr. 13, 1993,* Charlottesville, VA *(202,962)* 1.25
2186 35c **Dennis Chavez,** *Apr. 3, 1991,* Albuquerque, NM *(285,570)* 1.25
2187 40c **Claire Chennault,** *Sept. 6, 1990,* Monroe, LA *(186,761)* 2.00
2188 45c **Harvey Cushing,** *June 17, 1988,* Cleveland, OH *(135,140)* 1.25
2189 52c **Hubert Humphrey,** *June 3, 1991,* Minneapolis, MN *(93,391)* 1.40
2190 56c **John Harvard,** *Sept. 3, 1986,* Cambridge, MA 2.50
2191 65c **Hap Arnold,** *Nov. 5, 1988,* Gladwyne, PA *(129,829)* 2.50
2192 75c **Wendell Willkie,** *Feb. 18, 1992,* Bloomington, IN *(47,086)* 2.50
2193 $1 **Dr. Bernard Revel,** *Sept. 23, 1986,* New York, NY 5.00
2194 $1 **Johns Hopkins,** *June 7, 1989,* Baltimore, MD *(159,049)* 3.00
2195 $2 **William Jennings Bryan,** *Mar. 19, 1986,* Salem, IL *(123,430)* 6.00
2196 $5 **Bret Harte,** *Aug. 25, 1987,* Twain Harte, CA *(111,431)* 15.00
2197 25c **Jack London,** bklt. single, *May 3, 1988,* San Francisco, CA 1.00
2197a Booklet pane of 6 4.00

First day cancel was applied to 94,655 covers bearing one or more of Nos. 2183a, 2197, and 2197a.

1986

2201a 22c **Stamp Collecting Booklet pane of 4,** *Jan. 23,* State College, PA 4.00
2198-2201, any single 1.00

First day cancellation was applied to 675,924 covers bearing one or more of Nos. 2198-2201a.

2202 22c **Love,** *Jan. 30,* New York, NY 1.00
2203 22c **Sojourner Truth,** *Feb. 4,* New Paltz, NY *(342,985)* 1.75
2204 22c **Republic of Texas,** *Mar. 2,* San Antonio, TX *(380,450)* 1.75
2209a 22c **Fish Booklet pane of 5,** *Mar. 21,* Seattle, WA 5.00
2205-2209, any single 1.25

First day cancellation was applied to 988,184 covers bearing one or more of Nos. 2205-2209a.

2210 22c **Public Hospitals,** *Apr. 11,* New York, NY *(403,665)* 1.00
2211 22c **Duke Ellington,** *Apr. 29,* New York, NY *(397,894)* 2.25
2216 22c **Presidents Souvenir Sheet of 9 (Washington-Harrison),** *May 22,* Chicago, IL 4.50
2217 22c **Presidents Souvenir Sheet of 9 (Tyler-Grant),** *May 22,* Chicago, IL 4.50
2218 22c **Presidents Souvenir Sheet of 9 (Hayes-Wilson),** *May 22,* Chicago, IL 4.50
2219 22c **Presidents Souvenir Sheet of 9 (Harding-Johnson),** *May 22,* Chicago, IL 4.50
2216a-2219g, 2219i, any single 1.50
2219h 2.50

First day cancellation was applied to 9,009,599 covers bearing one or more of Nos. 2216-2219, 2216a-2219i.

2223a 22c **Polar Explorers,** *May 28,* North Pole, AK *(760,999)* 3.75
2220-2223, any single 1.25
2224 22c **Statue of Liberty,** *July 4,* New York, NY *(1,540,308)* 1.25

TRANSPORTATION ISSUE

1986-87

2225 1c **Omnibus,** *Nov. 26, 1986 (57,845)* 1.00
2226 2c **Locomotive,** *Mar. 6, 1987,* Milwaukee, WI *(169,484)* 1.50

1986

2238a 22c **Navajo Art,** *Sept. 4,* Window Rock, AZ *(1,102,520)* 2.00
2235-2238, any single 1.00
2239 22c **T.S. Eliot,** *Sept. 26,* St. Louis, MO *(304,764)* 1.00
2243a 22c **Woodcarved Figurines,** *Oct. 1 (629,399)* 2.00
2240-2243, any single 1.00
2244 22c **Christmas (Madonna),** *Oct. 24 (467,999)* 1.00
2245 22c **Christmas (Winter Village),** *Oct. 24,* Snow Hill, MD *(504,851)* 1.00

1987

2246 22c **Michigan Statehood Sesquicent.,** *Jan. 26,* Lansing, MI *(379,117)* 1.00
2247 22c **Pan American Games,** *Jan. 29,* Indianapolis, IN *(344,731)* 1.00
2248 22c **Love,** *Jan. 30,* San Francisco, CA *(333,329)* 1.00
2249 22c **Pointe du Sable,** *Feb. 20,* Chicago, IL *(313,054)* 1.50
2250 22c **Enrico Caruso,** *Feb. 27,* New York, NY *(389,834)* 1.25
2251 22c **Girl Scouts of America,** *Mar. 12 (556,391)* 3.00

TRANSPORTATION ISSUE

1987-88

2252 3c **Conestoga Wagon,** *Feb. 29, 1988,* Conestoga, PA *(155,203)* 1.00
2253 5c **Milk Wagon,** *Sept. 25, 1987,* Indianapolis, IN 1.00

First day cancel was applied to 162,571 covers bearing one or more of Nos. 2253 and 2262.

2254 5.3c **Elevator,** *Sept. 16, 1988,* New York, NY *(142,705)* 1.00
2255 7.6c **Carretta,** *Aug. 30, 1988,* San Jose, CA *(140,024)* 1.00
2256 8.4c **Wheelchair,** *Aug. 12, 1988,* Tucson, AZ *(136,337)* 1.00
2257 10c **Canal Boat,** *Apr. 11, 1987,* Buffalo, NY *(171,952)* 1.00
2258 13c **Police Patrol Wagon,** *Oct. 29, 1988,* Anaheim, CA *(132,928)* 1.50
2259 13.2c **Railway Coal Car,** *July 19, 1988,* Pittsburgh, PA *(123,965)* 1.00
2260 15c **Tugboat,** *July 12, 1988,* Long Beach, CA *(134,926)* 1.00
2261 16.7c **Popcorn Wagon,** *July 7, 1988,* Chicago, IL *(117,908)* 1.00
2262 17.5c **Racing Car,** *Sept. 25, 1987,* Indianapolis, IN 1.25
2263 20c **Cable Car,** *Oct. 28, 1988,* San Francisco, CA *(150,068)* 1.00
2264 20.5c **Fire Engine,** *Sept. 28, 1988,* San Angelo, TX *(123,043)* 1.75
2265 21c **Railway Mail Car,** *Aug. 16, 1988,* Santa Fe, NM *(124,430)* 1.00
2266 24.1c **Tandem Bicycle,** *Oct. 26, 1988,* Redmond, WA *(138,593)* 1.75

1987

2274a 22c **Special Occasions Booklet pane of 10,** *Apr. 20,* Atlanta, GA 5.00
2267-2274, any single 1.00

First day cancellation was applied to 1,588,129 covers bearing one or more of Nos. 2267-2274a.

2275 22c **United Way,** *Apr. 28 (556,391)* 1.00

1987-89

2276 22c **Flag and Fireworks,** *May 9, 1987* Denver, CO *(398,855)* 1.00
2276a Booklet pane of 20, *Nov. 30, 1987* 8.00
2277 (25c) **"E" Earth,** *Mar. 22, 1988* 1.25
2278 25c **Flag and Clouds,** *May 6, 1988,* Boxborough, MA *(131,265)* 1.25
2279 (25c) **"E" Earth,** coil, *Mar. 22, 1988* 1.25
2280 25c **Flag over Yosemite,** large block tagging, *May 20, 1988,* Yosemite, CA *(144,339)* 1.25
2280a 25c Prephosphored paper, *Feb. 14, 1989,* Yosemite, CA *(118,874)* 1.25
2281 25c **Honey Bee,** *Sept. 2, 1988,* Omaha, NE *(122,853)* 1.25
2282 (25c) **"E" Earth,** bklt. single, *Mar. 22, 1988* 1.25
2282a Booklet pane of 10 6.00

First day cancel was applied to 363,639 covers bearing one or more of Nos. 2277, 2279 and 2282.

2283 25c **Pheasant,** *Apr. 29, 1988,* Rapid City, SD *(167,053)* 1.25
2283a Booklet pane of 10 6.00
2285b 25c **Grosbeak & Owl, booklet pane of 10** *May 28, 1988,* Arlington, VA 6.00
2284-2285, any single 1.25

First day cancel was applied to 272,359 covers bearing one or more of Nos. 2284 and 2285.

2285A 25c **Flag and Clouds,** bklt. single, *July 5, 1988 (117,303)* 1.00
2285Ac Booklet pane of 6 4.00
2335a 22c **American Wildlife,** *June 13, 1987,* Toronto, Canada 50.00
2286-2335, any single 1.50

RATIFICATION OF THE CONSTITUTION

1987-90

2336 22c **Delaware,** *July 4, 1987,* Dover, DE *(505,770)* 1.50
2337 22c **Pennsylvania,** *Aug. 26, 1987,* Harrisburg, PA *(367,184)* 1.50
2338 22c **New Jersey,** *Sept. 11, 1987,* Trenton, NJ *(432,899)* 1.50
2339 22c **Georgia,** *Jan. 6, 1988,* Atlanta, GA *(467,804)* 1.50
2340 22c **Connecticut,** *Jan. 9, 1988,* Hartford, CT *(379,706)* 1.50
2341 22c **Massachusetts,** *Feb. 6, 1988,* Boston, MA *(412,616)* 1.50
2342 22c **Maryland,** *Feb. 15, 1988,* Annapolis, MD *(376,403)* 1.50
2343 25c **South Carolina,** *May 23, 1988,* Columbia, SC *(322,938)* 1.50
2344 25c **New Hampshire,** *June 21, 1988,* Concord, NH *(374,402)* 1.50
2345 25c **Virginia,** *June 25, 1988,* Williamsburg, VA *(474,079)* 1.50
2346 25c **New York,** *July 26, 1988,* Albany, NY *(385,793)* 1.50
2347 25c **North Carolina,** *Aug. 22, 1989,* Fayetteville, NC *(392,953)* 1.50
2348 25c **Rhode Island,** *May 29, 1990,* Pawtucket, RI *(305,566)* 1.50

1987

2349 22c **U.S.-Morocco Diplomatic Relations Bicent.**, *July 17 (372,814)* 1.00
2350 22c **William Faulkner**, *Aug. 3*, Oxford, MS *(480,024)* 1.00
2354a 22c **Lacemaking**, *Aug. 14*, Ypsilanti, MI 2.50
2351-2354, any single 1.00
2359a 22c **Drafting of Constitution Bicent. Booklet pane of 5**, *Aug. 28* 4.00
2355-2359, any single 1.25

First day cancellation was applied to 1,008,799 covers bearing one or more of Nos. 2355-2359a.

2360 22c **Signing of Constitution Bicent.**, *Sept. 17*, Philadelphia, PA *(719,975)* 1.25
2361 22c **Certified Public Accounting**, *Sept. 21*, New York, NY *(362,099)* 7.50
2366a 22c **Locomotives booklet pane of 5**, *Oct. 1*, Baltimore, MD 3.00
2362-2366, any single 1.25

First day cancellation was applied to 976,694 covers bearing one or more of Nos. 2362-2366a.

2367 22c **Christmas (Madonna)**, *Oct. 23 (320,406)* 1.25
2368 22c **Christmas (Ornaments)**, *Oct. 23*, Holiday-Anaheim, CA *(375,858)* 1.25

1988

2369 22c **Winter Olympics, Calgary**, *Jan. 10*, Anchorage, AK *(395,198)* 1.00
2370 22c **Australia Bicentennial**, *Jan. 26 (523,465)* 1.75
2371 22c **James Weldon Johnson**, *Feb. 2*, Nashville, TN *(465,282)* 1.75
2375a 22c **Cats**, *Feb. 5*, New York, NY *(872,734)* 4.50
2372-2375, any single 2.00
2376 22c **Knute Rockne**, *Mar. 9*, Notre Dame, IN *(404,311)* 4.00
2377 25c **Francis Ouimet**, *June 13*, Brookline, MA *(383,168)* 4.50
2378 25c **Love**, *July 4*, Pasadena, CA *(399,038)* 1.00
2379 45c **Love**, *Aug. 8*, Shreveport, LA *(121,808)* 1.25
2380 25c **Summer Olympics, Seoul**, *Aug. 19*, Colorado Springs, CO *(402,616)* 1.25
2385a 25c **Automobiles booklet pane of 5**, *Aug. 25*, Detroit, MI 4.00
2381-2385, any single 1.25

First day cancel was applied to 875,801 covers bearing one or more of Nos. 2381-2385a.

2389a 25c **Antarctic Explorers**, *Sept. 14 (720,537)* 3.00
2386-2389, any single 1.25
2393a 25c **Carousel Animals**, *Oct. 1*, Sandusky, OH *(856,380)* 4.00
2390-2393, any single 1.50
2394 $8.75 **Express Mail**, *Oct. 4*, Terre Haute, IN *(66,558)* 27.50
2396a 25c **Special Occasions (Happy Birthday, Best Wishes)**, *Oct. 22*, King of Prussia, PA 4.00
2395-2396, any single 1.25
2398a 25c **Special Occasions (Thinking of You, Love You)**, *Oct. 22*, King of Prussia, PA 4.00
2397-2398, any single 1.25

First day cancel was applied to 126,767 covers bearing one or more of Nos. 2395-2398, 2396a, 2398a.

2399 25c **Christmas (Madonna)**, *Oct. 20 (247,291)* 1.25
2400 25c **Christmas (Contemporary)**, *Oct. 20*, Berlin, NH *(412,213)* 1.25

1989

2401 25c **Montana**, *Jan. 15*, Helena, MT *(353,319)* 1.25
2402 25c **A. Philip Randolph**, *Feb. 3*, New York, NY *(363,174)* 1.75
2403 25c **North Dakota**, *Feb. 21*, Bismarck, ND *(306,003)* 1.00
2404 25c **Washington Statehood**, *Feb. 22*, Olympia, WA *(445,174)* 1.00
2409a 25c **Steamboats Booklet pane of 5**, *Mar. 3*, New Orleans, LA 3.00
2405-2409, any single 1.25

First day cancel was applied to 981,674 covers bearing one or more of Nos. 2405-2409a.

2410 25c **World Stamp Expo**, *Mar. 16*, New York, NY *(296,310)* 1.00
2411 25c **Arturo Toscanini**, *Mar. 25*, New York, NY *(309,441)* 1.00

BRANCHES OF GOVERNMENT

1989-90

2412 25c **House of Representatives**, *Apr. 4, 1989 (327,755)* 1.50
2413 25c **Senate**, *Apr. 6, 1989 (341,288)* 1.50
2414 25c **Executive Branch**, *Apr. 16, 1989* Mount Vernon, VA *(387,644)* 1.50
2415 25c **Supreme Court**, *Feb. 2, 1990 (233,056)* 1.50

1989

2416 25c **South Dakota**, *May 3*, Pierre, SD *(348,370)* 1.00
2417 25c **Lou Gehrig**, *June 10*, Cooperstown, NY *(694,227)* 4.00
2418 25c **Ernest Hemingway**, *July 17*, Key West, FL *(345,436)* 2.00
2419 $2.40 **Moon Landing**, *July 20 (208,982)* 7.50
2420 25c **Letter Carriers**, *Aug. 30*, Milwaukee, WI *(372,241)* 1.25
2421 25c **Bill of Rights**, *Sept. 25*, Philadelphia, PA *(900,384)* 1.00
2425a 25c **Dinosaurs**, *Oct. 1*, Orlando, FL *(871,634)* 3.00
2422-2425, any single 1.50
2426 25c **Southwest Carved Figure**, *Oct. 12*, San Juan, PR *(215,285)* 1.00
2427 25c **Christmas (Madonna)**, *Oct. 19 (395,321)* 1.00
2427a Booklet pane of 10 6.00
2428 25c **Christmas (Sleigh with Presents)**, *Oct. 19*, Westport, CT 1.00
2429 25c **Christmas (Sleigh with Presents) from bklt.**, *Oct. 19*, Westport, CT 1.00
2429a Booklet pane of 10 6.00

First day cancel was applied to 345,931 covers bearing one or more of Nos. 2428-2429a.

2431 25c **Eagle and Shield**, *Nov. 10*, Virginia Beach, VA 1.25
2433 90c **World Stamp Expo '89 Souvenir Sheet**, *Nov. 17 (281,725)* 7.00
2437a 25c **Classic Mail Transportation**, *Nov. 19 (916,389)* 2.50
2434-2437, any single 1.25
2438 25c **Classic Mail Transportation Souvenir Sheet**, *Nov. 28 (241,634)* 3.00

1990

2439 25c **Idaho Statehood**, *Jan. 6*, Boise, ID *(252,493)* 1.25
2440 25c **Love**, *Jan. 18*, Romance, AR 1.25
2441 25c **Love, from bklt.**, *Jan. 18*, Romance, AR 1.00
2441a Booklet pane of 10 6.00

First day cancel was applied to 257,788 covers bearing one or more of Nos. 2440-2441a.

2442 25c **Ida B. Wells**, *Feb. 1*, Chicago, IL *(229,226)* 2.00
2443 15c **Beach Umbrella**, *Feb. 3*, Sarasota, FL 1.25
2443a Booklet pane of 10 4.25

First day cancel was applied to 72,286 covers bearing one or more of Nos. 2443-2443a.

2444 25c **Wyoming Statehood**, *Feb. 23*, Cheyenne, WY *(317,654)* 1.00
2448a 25c **Classic Films**, *Mar. 23*, Hollywood, CA *(863,079)* *5.00*
2445-2448, any single *2.50*
2449 25c **Marianne Moore**, *Apr. 18*, Brooklyn, NY *(390,535)* 1.25

1990-95 **TRANSPORTATION COILS**

2451 4c **Steam Carriage**, *Jan. 25, 1991*, Tucson, AZ *(100,393)* 1.25
2452 5c **Circus Wagon**, engraved, *Aug. 31, 1990*, Syracuse, NY *(71,806)* 1.50
2452B 5c **Circus Wagon**, photogravure, *Dec. 8, 1992*, Cincinnati, OH 1.50
2452D 5c **Circus Wagon**, with cent sign, photogravure, *Mar. 20, 1995*, Kansas City MO *(20,835)* 2.00
2453 5c **Canoe**, engraved, *May 25, 1991*, Secaucus, NJ *(108,634)* 1.25
2454 5c **Canoe**, photogravure, *Oct. 22, 1991*, Secaucus, NJ 1.25
2457 10c **Tractor Trailer**, engr., *May 25, 1991*, Secaucus, NJ *(84,717)* 1.25
2458 10c **Tractor Trailer**, photo., *May 25, 1994*, Secaucus, NJ *(15,431)* 1.25
2463 20c **Cog Railway**, *June 9, 1995*, Dallas, TX *(28,883)* 1.25
2464 23c **Lunch Wagon**, *Apr. 12, 1991*, Columbus, OH *(115,830)* 1.25
2466 32c **Ferry Boat**, *June 2, 1995*, McLean VA 1.25

First day cancellation was applied to 59,100 covers bearing one or more of Nos. 2466, 2492.

2468 $1 **Seaplane**, *Apr. 20, 1990* Phoenix, AZ *(244,775)* 3.00

1990

2474a 25c **Lighthouses booklet pane of 5**, *Apr. 26* 5.00
2470-2474, any single 1.50

First day cancel was applied to 805,133 covers bearing one or more of Nos. 2470-2474a.

2475 25c **Flag**, *May 18*, Seattle, WA *(97,567)* 1.00

FLORA AND FAUNA ISSUE

1990-95

2476 1c **Kestrel**, *June 22*, Aurora, CO *(77,781)* 1.00
2477 1c **Kestrel, with cent sign**, *May 10, 1995* Aurora, CO *(21,767)* 1.00
2478 3c **Eastern Bluebird**, *June 22*, Aurora, CO *(76,149)* 1.00
2479 19c **Fawn**, *Mar. 11 (100,212)* 1.00
2480 30c **Cardinal**, *June 22*, Aurora, CO *(101,290)* 1.25
2481 45c **Pumpkinseed Sunfish**, *Dec. 2, 1992 (38,696)* 1.75
2482 $2 **Bobcat**, *June 1*, Arlington, VA *(49,660)* 5.00
2483 20c **Blue Jay**, booklet single, *June 15, 1995*, Kansas City MO 1.25

First day cancellation was applied to 16,847 covers bearing one or more of Nos. 2483, 2483a.

2484 29c **Wood Duck**, black denomination bklt. single, *Apr. 12*, Columbus, OH 1.00
2484a Booklet pane of 10 4.00
2485 29c **Wood Duck**, red denomination bklt. single, *Apr. 12*, Columbus, OH 1.00
2485a Booklet pane of 10 4.00

First day cancel was applied to 205,305 covers bearing one or more of Nos. 2484-2485, 2484a-2485a.

2486 29c **African Violet**, *Oct. 8, 1993*, Beaumont, TX 1.00
2486a Booklet pane of 10 4.00

First day cancellation was applied to 40,167 covers bearing one or more of Nos. 2486-2486a.

2487 32c **Peach**, booklet single, *July 8, 1995*, Reno NV 1.50
2488 32c **Pear**, booklet single, *July 8, 1995*, Reno NV 1.50

First day cancellation was applied to 71,086 covers bearing one or more of Nos. 2487-2488, 2488a, 2493-2495A.

2488a Booklet pane, 5 each #2488-2489 7.50
2489 29c **Red Squirrel**, self-adhesive, *June 25, 1993* Milwaukee, WI *(48,564)* 1.25
2490 29c **Red Rose**, self-adhesive, *Aug. 19, 1993* Houston, TX *(37,916)* 1.25
2491 29c **Pine Cone**, self-adhesive, *Nov. 5, 1993* Kansas City, MO *(110,924)* 1.25
2492 32c **Pink Rose**, self-adhesive, *June 2, 1995*, McLean VA 1.25

First day cancellation was applied to 59,100 covers bearing one or more of Nos. 2466, 2492.

2493 32c **Peach**, self-adhesive, *July 8, 1995*, Reno NV 1.25
2494 32c **Pear**, self-adhesive, *July 8, 1995*, Reno NV 1.25
2495 32c **Peach**, self-adhesive, serpentine die cut vert., *July 8, 1995*, Reno NV 1.25
2495A 32c **Pear**, self-adhesive, serpentine die cut vert., *July 8, 1995*, Reno NV 1.25

First day cancellation was applied to 71,086 covers bearing one or more of Nos. 2487-2488, 2488a, 2493-2495A.

1990

2500a 25c **Olympians**, *July 6*, Minneapolis, MN *(1,143,404)* 4.00
2496-2500, any single 1.25
2505a 25c **Indian Headdresses, booklet pane of 10** *Aug. 17*, Cody, WY 6.00
2501-2505, any single 1.25

First day cancel was applied to 979,580 covers bearing one or more of Nos. 2501-2505a.

2507a 25c **Micronesia, Marshall Islands**, *Sept. 28 (343,816)* 2.00
2506-2507, any single 1.25
2511a 25c **Sea Creatures**, *Oct. 3*, Baltimore, MD *(706,047)* 3.00
2508-2511, any single 1.25
2512 25c **Grand Canyon**, *Oct. 12*, Grand Canyon, AZ *(164,190)* 2.25
2513 25c **Dwight D. Eisenhower**, *Oct. 13*, Abilene, KS *(487,988)* 1.50
2514 25c **Christmas (traditional)**, *Oct. 18* 1.25
2514b Booklet pane of 10 6.00

First day cancel was applied to 378,383 covers bearing one or more of Nos. 2514-2514a.

2515 25c **Christmas (secular)**, *Oct. 18*, Evergreen, CO 1.25
2516 25c **Christmas (secular)**, *Oct. 18*, Evergreen, CO 1.00
2516a Booklet pane of 10 6.00

First day cancel was applied to 230,586 covers bearing one or more of Nos. 2515-2516a.

1991-94

2517 (29c) **"F" Flower**, *Jan. 22, 1991 (106,698)* 1.25
2518 (29c) **"F" Flower**, coil, *Jan. 22, 1991 (39,311)* 1.25
2519 (29c) **"F" Flower**, bklt. single (bullseye perf. 11.2), *Jan. 22, 1991* 1.00
2519a Booklet pane of 10 7.25
2520 (29c) **"F" Flower**, bklt. single (perf. 11), *Jan. 22, 1991* 1.25
2520a Booklet pane of 10 8.00

First day cancel was applied to 32,971 covers bearing one or more of Nos. 2519-2520, 2519a-2520a.

2521 (4c) **Makeup Stamp**, *Jan. 22, 1991 (51,987)* 1.25
2522 (29c) **"F" Flag**, *Jan. 22, 1991 (48,821)* 1.25
2523 29c **Flag over Mt. Rushmore**, engraved, *Mar. 29, 1991* Mt. Rushmore, SD *(233,793)* 1.25
2523A 29c **Flag over Mt. Rushmore**, photogravure, *July 4, 1991* Mt. Rushmore, SD *(80,662)* 1.25
2524 29c **Flower**, *Apr. 5, 1991*, Rochester, NY *(132,233)* 1.00
2525 29c **Flower**, roulette 10 coil, *Aug. 16, 1991*, Rochester, NY *(144,750)* 1.00

2526 29c **Flower,** perf. 10 coil, *Mar. 3, 1992,* Rochester, NY *(35,877)* 1.00
2527 29c **Flower,** bklt. single, *Apr. 5, 1991,* Rochester, NY 1.00
2527a Booklet pane of 10 4.00

First day cancel was applied to 16,975 covers bearing one or more of Nos. 2527-2527a.

2528 29c **Flag and Olympic Rings,** bklt. single, *Apr. 21, 1991,* Atlanta, GA 1.25
2528a Booklet pane of 10 5.00

First day cancel was applied to 319,488 covers bearing one or more of Nos. 2528-2528a.

2529 19c **Fishing Boat,** two loops, *Aug. 8, 1991 (82,698)* 1.50
2529C 19c **Fishing Boat,** one loop, *June 25, 1994,* Arlington, VA *(14,538)* 1.50
2530 19c **Balloon,** *May 17, 1991,* Denver, CO 1.25
2530a Booklet pane of 10 5.00

First day cancel was applied to 96,351 covers bearing one or more of Nos. 2530-2530a.

2531 29c **Flags on Parade,** *May 30, 1991,* Waterloo, NY *(104,046)* 1.00
2531A 29c **Liberty Torch,** *June 25, 1991,* New York, NY *(68,456)* 1.25

1991-95

2532 50c **Switzerland,** *Feb. 22,* Washington, DC *(316,047)* 1.40
2533 29c **Vermont,** *Mar. 1,* Bennington, VT *(308,105)* 1.50
2534 29c **Savings Bonds,** *Apr. 30,* Washington, DC *(341,955)* 1.25
2535 29c **Love,** *May 9,* Honolulu, HI *(336,132)* 1.25
2536 29c **Love,** bklt. single, *May 9,* Honolulu, HI 1.25
2536a Booklet pane of 10 5.00

First day cancel was applied to 43,336 covers bearing one or more of Nos. 2536-2536a.

2537 52c **Love,** *May 9,* Honolulu, HI *(90,438)* 1.25
2538 29c **William Saroyan,** *May 22,* Fresno, CA *(334,373)* 1.50
2539 $1 **Eagle & Olympic Rings,** *Sept. 29,* Orlando, FL *(69,241)* 2.25
2540 $2.90 **Eagle & Olympic Rings,** *July 7,* San Diego, CA *(79,555)* 5.50
2541 $9.95 **Eagle & Olympic Rings,** *June 16,* Sacramento, CA *(68,657)* 15.00
2542 $14 **Eagle,** *Aug. 31,* Hunt Valley, MD *(54,727)* 27.50
2543 $2.90 **Futuristic Space Shuttle,** *June 3, 1993,* Kennedy Space Center, FL *(36,359)* 6.00
2544 $3 **Space Shuttle Challenger,** *June 22, 1995* Anaheim CA *(16,502)* 6.00
2544A $10.75 **Space Shuttle Endeavour,** *Aug. 4, 1995* Irvine CA *(10,534)* 15.00

1991

2549a 29c **Fishing Flies booklet pane of 5,** *May 31,* Cuddebackville, NY *(1,045,726)* 3.00
2545-2549, any single 1.25
2550 29c **Cole Porter,** *June 8,* Peru, IN *(304,363)* 1.25
2551 29c **Desert Storm/ Desert Shield,** *July 2* 2.50
2552 29c **Desert Storm/ Desert Shield,** bklt. single, *July 2* 2.50
2552a Booklet pane of 5 5.00

First day cancel was applied to 860,455 covers bearing one or more of Nos. 2551-2552, 2552a.

2557a 29c **Summer Olympics,** *July 12,* Los Angeles, CA *(886,984)* 3.00
2553-2557, any single 1.25
2558 29c **Numismatics,** *Aug. 13,* Chicago, IL *(288,519)* 1.25
2559 29c **World War II block of 10,** *Sept. 3,* Phoenix, AZ *(1,832,967)* 7.00
2559a-2559j, any single 2.50
2560 29c **Basketball,** *Aug. 28,* Springfield, MA *(295,471)* 2.25
2561 29c **District of Columbia,** *Sept. 7 (299,989)* 1.25
2566a 29c **Comedians booklet pane of 10,** *Aug. 29,* Hollywood, CA 3.00
2562-2566, any single 1.25

First day cancel was applied to 954,293 covers bearing one or more of Nos. 2562-2566a.

2567 29c **Jan Matzeliger,** *Sept. 15,* Lynn, MA *(289,034)* 1.75
2577a 29c **Space Exploration booklet pane of 10,** *Oct. 1,* Pasadena, CA 5.00
2568-2577, any single 1.25

First day cancel was applied to 1,465,111 covers bearing one or more of Nos. 2568-2577a.

2578 (29c) **Christmas (religious),** *Oct. 17,* Houston, TX 1.25
2579 (29c) **Christmas (secular),** *Oct. 17,* Santa, ID *(169,750)* 1.25
2581b (29c) **Christmas booklet pane of 4,** *Oct. 17,* Santa, ID 2.50
2580-2581, any single 1.25
2582 (29c) **Christmas,** bklt. single, *Oct. 17,* Santa, ID 1.25
2582a Booklet pane of 4 2.50
2583 (29c) **Christmas,** bklt. single, *Oct. 17,* Santa, ID 1.25
2583a Booklet pane of 4 2.50
2584 (29c) **Christmas,** bklt. single, *Oct. 17,* Santa, ID 1.25
2584a Booklet pane of 4 2.50
2585 (29c) **Christmas,** bklt. single, *Oct. 17,* Santa, ID 1.25
2585a Booklet pane of 4 2.50

First day cancel was applied to 168,794 covers bearing one or more of Nos. 2580-2585, 2581b, 2582a, 2583a, 2584a and 2585a.

1991-95

2587 32c **James K. Polk,** *Nov. 2, 1995,* Columbia TN *(189,429)* 1.25
2590 $1 **Surrender of Gen. John Burgoyne,** *May 5, 1994,* New York, NY *(379,629)* 3.00
2592 $5 **Washington & Jackson,** *Aug. 19, 1994,* Pittsburgh, PA *(16,303)* *12.50*
2593 29c **Pledge of Allegiance,** black denomination, *Sept. 8, 1992,* Rome, NY 1.25
2593a Booklet pane of 10 5.00

First day cancel was applied to 61,464 covers bearing one or more of Nos. 2593-2593a.

2595 29c **Eagle & Shield,** brown denomination, *Sept. 25, 1992,* Dayton, OH 2.00
2596 29c **Eagle & Shield,** green denomination, *Sept. 25, 1992,* Dayton, OH 2.00
2597 29c **Eagle & Shield,** red denomination, *Sept. 25, 1992,* Dayton, OH 2.00

First day cancel was applied to 65,822 covers bearing one or more of Nos. 2595-2597.

2598 29c **Eagle,** *Feb. 4, 1994,* Sarasota, FL *(67,300)* 1.25
2599 29c **Statue of Liberty,** *June 24, 1994,* Haines City, FL *(39,810)* 1.25
2602 (10c) **Eagle & Shield,** Bulk Rate USA, *Dec. 13, 1991,* Kansas City, MO *(21,176)* 1.25
2603 (10c) **Eagle & Shield,** USA Bulk Rate, *May 29, 1993,* Secaucus, NJ 1.25
2604 (10c) **Eagle & Shield,** gold eagle, *May 29, 1993,* Secaucus, NJ 1.25

First day cancellation was applied to 36,444 covers bearing one or more of Nos. 2603-2604.

2605 23c **Flag,** *Sept. 27, 1991* 1.25
2606 23c **Reflected Flag,** *July 21, 1992,* Kansas City, MO *(35,673)* 1.25
2607 23c **Reflected Flag,** 7mm "23," *Oct. 9, 1992,* Kansas City, MO 1.25
2608 23c **Reflected Flag,** 8 ½mm "First Class" *May 14, 1993,* Denver, CO *(15,548)* 1.25
2609 29c **Flag over White House,** *Apr. 23, 1992 (56,505)* 1.25

1992

2615a 29c **Winter Olympics,** *Jan. 11,* Orlando, FL *(1,062,048)* 3.50
2611-2615, any single 1.25
2616 29c **World Columbian Stamp Expo,** *Jan. 24,* Rosemont, IL *(309,729)* 1.25
2617 29c **W.E.B. Du Bois,** *Jan. 31,* Atlanta, GA *(196,219)* 1.75
2618 29c **Love,** *Feb. 6,* Loveland, CO *(218,043)* 1.25
2619 29c **Olympic Baseball,** *Apr. 3,* Atlanta, GA *(105,996)* 2.00
2623a 29c **Voyages of Columbus,** *Apr. 24,* Christiansted, VI 2.75
2620-2623, any single 1.25

First day cancellation was applied to 509,270 covers bearing one or more of Nos. 2620-2623a.

2624 **First Sighting of Land Souvenir Sheet of 3,** *May 22,* Chicago, IL 3.50
2624a 1c 1.50
2624b 4c 1.50
2624c $1 2.50
2625 **Claiming a New World Souvenir Sheet of 3,** *May 22,* Chicago, IL 9.00
2625a 2c 1.50
2625b 3c 1.50
2625c $4 8.00
2626 **Seeking Royal Support Souvenir Sheet of 3,** *May 22,* Chicago, IL 3.00
2626a 5c 1.50
2626b 30c 1.50
2626c 50c 2.00
2627 **Royal Favor Restored Souvenir Sheet of 3,** *May 22,* Chicago, IL 7.50
2627a 6c 1.50
2627b 8c 1.50
2627c $3 7.50
2628 **Reporting Discoveries Souvenir Sheet of 3,** *May 22,* Chicago, IL 8.50
2628a 10c 1.50
2628b 15c 1.50
2628c $2 5.00
2629 $5 **Christopher Columbus Souvenir Sheet,** *May 22,* Chicago, IL 12.50

First day cancel was applied to 211,142 covers bearing one or more of Nos. 2624-2629.

2630 29c **New York Stock Exchange,** *May 17,* New York, NY *(261,897)* 3.00
2634a 29c **Space Accomplishments,** *May 29,* Chicago, IL 2.75
2631-2634, any single 1.50

First day cancel was applied to 277,853 covers bearing one or more of Nos. 2631-2634a.

2635 29c **Alaska Highway,** *May 30,* Fairbanks, AK *(186,791)* 1.25
2636 29c **Kentucky,** *June 1,* Danville, KY *(251,153)* 1.25
2641a 29c **Summer Olympics,** *June 11,* Baltimore, MD *(713,942)* 3.00
2637-2641, any single 1.25
2646a 29c **Hummingbirds booklet pane of 5,** *June 15* 3.00
2642-2646, any single 1.25

First day cancel was applied to 995,278 covers bearing one or more of Nos. 2642-2646a.

2696a 29c **Wildflowers,** *July 24,* Columbus, OH 30.00
2647-2696, any single 1.25

First day cancellation was applied to 3,693,972 covers bearing one or more of Nos. 2647-2696a.

2697 29c **World War II block of 10,** *Aug. 17,* Indianapolis, IN *(1,734,880)* 7.00
2697a-2697j, any single 2.50

First day cancellation was applied to 1,734,880 covers bearing one or more of Nos. 2697, 2697a-2697j.

2698 29c **Dorothy Parker,** *Aug. 22,* West End, NJ *(266,323)* 1.50
2699 29c **Theodore von Karman,** *Aug. 31 (256,986)* 1.50
2703a 29c **Minerals,** *Sept. 17* 2.75
2700-2703, any single 1.25

First day cancellation was applied to 681,416 covers bearing one or more of Nos. 2700-2703.

2704 29c **Juan Rodriguez Cabrillo,** *Sept. 28,* San Diego, CA *(290,720)* 1.25
2709a 29c **Wild Animals booklet pane of 5,** *Oct. 1,* New Orleans, LA 3.25
Any other city 4.00
2705-2709, any single 1.25

First day cancel was applied to 604,205 New Orleans covers bearing one or more of Nos. 2705-2709a.

2710 29c **Christmas (religious),** *Oct. 22* 1.25
2710a Booklet pane of 10 7.25

First day cancel was applied to 201,576 covers bearing one or more of Nos. 2710-2710a.

2714a 29c **Christmas (secular),** *Oct. 22,* Kansas City, MO 2.75
2711-2714, any single 1.25
2718a 29c **Christmas (secular) booklet pane of 4,** *Oct. 22,* Kansas City, MO 2.75
2715-2718, any single 1.25

First day cancel was applied to 461,937 covers bearing one or more of Nos. 2711-2714, 2715-2718 and 2718a.

2719 29c **Christmas (secular),** self-adhesive, *Oct. 28,* New York, NY *(48,873)* 1.25
2720 29c **Chinese New Year,** *Dec. 30,* San Francisco, CA *(138,238)* 2.25

1993

2721 29c **Elvis (Presley),** *Jan. 8,* Memphis, TN, AM cancellation, *(4,452,815)* 2.00
Any city, PM cancellation 3.00
2722 29c **Oklahoma!,** *Mar. 30,* Oklahoma City, OK *(283,837)* 1.25
2723 29c **Hank Williams,** perf 10, *June 9,* Nashville, TN 1.25
2723A 29c **Hank Williams,** perf 11.2x11.5, *June 9,* Nashville, TN —

First day cancel was applied to 311,106 covers bearing one or more of Nos. 2723-2723A.

2730a 29c **Rock & Roll/Rhythm & Blues Musicians,** *June 16,* Cleveland OH or Santa Monica CA 5.00
Any other city 5.00
2724-2730, any single 1.25
Any single, any other city 1.25

Value for No. 2730a is also for any se-tenant configuration of seven different stamps.

First day cancel was applied to 540,809 covers bearing one or more of Nos. 2724-2730a, 2731-2737b.

2737a 29c **Rock & Roll/Rhythm & Blues Musicians booklet pane of 8,** *June 16,* Cleveland, OH or Santa Monica CA 5.25
Any other city 5.25
2731-2737, any single 1.25
Any single, any other city 1.25
2737b 29c **Rock & Roll/Rhythm & Blues Musicians booklet pane of 4,** *June 16,* Cleveland, OH or Santa Monica CA 2.75
Any other city 2.75

For first day cancellation quantities, see No. 2730a.

2745a 29c **Space Fantasy booklet pane of 5,** *Jan. 25,* Huntsville, AL 3.25
2741-2745, any single 1.25

First day cancel was applied to 631,203 covers bearing one or more of Nos. 2741-2745a.

2746 29c **Percy Lavon Julian,** *Jan. 29,* Chicago, IL *(120,877)* 1.75
2747 29c **Oregon Trail,** *Feb. 12,* Salem, OR *(436,550)* 1.25

No. 2747 was also available on the first day of issue in 36 cities along the route of the Oregon Trail.

2748 29c **World University Games,** *Feb. 25,* Buffalo, NY *(157,563)* 1.50

2749 29c **Grace Kelly,** *Mar. 24,* Hollywood, CA *(263,913)* 3.50
2753a 29c **Circus,** *Apr. 6* 3.00
2750-2753, any single 1.50

First day cancel was applied to 676,927 covers bearing one or more of Nos. 2750-2753a.

2754 29c **Cherokee Strip Land Run,** *Apr. 17,* Enid, OK *(260,118)* 1.25
2755 29c **Dean Acheson,** *Apr. 21, (158,783)* 1.25
2759a 29c **Sporting Horses,** *May 1,* Louisville, KY 4.00
2756-2759, any single 2.00

First day cancel was applied to 448,059 covers bearing one or more of Nos. 2756-2759a.

2764a 29c **Garden Flowers booklet pane of 5,** *May 15,* Spokane, WA 3.00
2760-2764, any single 1.50

First day cancel was applied to 492,578 covers bearing one or more of Nos. 2760-2764a.

2765 29c **World War II block of 10,** *May 31,* 7.00
2765a-2765j, any single 2.50

First day cancel was applied to 543,511 covers bearing one or more of Nos. 2765, 2765a-2765j.

2766 29c **Joe Louis,** *June 22,* Detroit, MI *(229,272)* 3.00
2770a 29c **Broadway Musicals booklet pane of 4,** *July 14,* New York, NY 3.50
2767-2770, any single 1.25

First day cancel was applied to 308,231 covers bearing one or more of Nos. 2767-2770a.

2774a 29c **Country Music,** *Sept. 25,* Nashville, TN 3.00
2771-2774, any single 1.25
2778a 29c **Country Music booklet pane of 4,** *Sept. 25,* Nashville, TN 3.00
2775-2778, any single 1.25

First day cancel was applied to 362,904 covers bearing one or more of Nos. 2771-2774a, 2775-2778a.

2782a 29c **National Postal Museum,** *July 30* 2.75
2779-2782, any single 1.25

First day cancel was applied to 371,115 covers bearing one or more of Nos. 2779-2782a.

2784a 29c **Deafness/Sign Language,** *Sept. 20,* Burbank, CA 2.50
2783-2784, any single 1.50

First day cancel was applied to 112,350 covers bearing one or more of Nos. 2783-2784a.

2788a 29c **Classic Books,** *Oct. 23,* Louisville, KY 2.75
2785-2788, any single 1.25

First day cancel was applied to 269,457 covers bearing one or more of Nos. 2785-2788a.

2789 29c **Christmas (religious),** *Oct. 21,* Raleigh, NC 1.25
2790 29c **Christmas (religious),** booklet single, *Oct. 21,* Raleigh, NC 1.25
2790a Booklet pane of 4 2.50

First day cancellation was applied to 155,192 covers bearing one or more of Nos. 2789-2790a.

2794a 29c **Christmas (secular),** sheet stamps, *Oct. 21,* New York, NY 2.75
2791-2794, any single 1.25
2798a 29c **Christmas (secular) booklet pane of 10,** *Oct. 21,* New York, NY 6.50
2798b 29c **Christmas (secular) booklet pane of 10,** *Oct. 21,* New York, NY 6.50
2795-2798, any single 1.25
2799 29c **Christmas (snowman),** large self-adhesive, *Oct. 28,* New York, NY 1.25
2800 29c **Christmas (soldier),** self-adhesive, *Oct. 28,* New York, NY 1.25
2801 29c **Christmas (jack-in-the-box),** self-adhesive, *Oct. 28,* New York, NY 1.25
2802 29c **Christmas (reindeer),** self-adhesive, *Oct. 28,* New York, NY 1.25
2799-2802 on one cover 2.50
2803 29c **Christmas (snowman),** small self-adhesive, *Oct. 28,* New York, NY 1.25

First day cancel was applied to 384,262 covers bearing one or more of Nos. 2791-2794a, 2795-2798b, 2799-2803.

2804 29c **Mariana Islands,** *Nov. 4,* Saipan, MP *(157,410)* 1.25
2805 29c **Columbus' Landing in Puerto Rico,** *Nov. 19,* San Juan, PR *(222,845)* 1.25
2806 29c **AIDS Awareness,** *Dec. 1,* New York, NY 2.00
2806a Booklet single, perf. 11 vert. 2.00
2806b Booklet pane of 5 4.00

First day cancellation was applied to 209,200 covers bearing one or more of Nos. 2806-2806b.

1994

2811a 29c **Winter Olympics,** *Jan. 6,* Salt Lake City, UT 3.00
2807-2811, any single 1.25

First day cancellation was applied to 645,636 covers bearing one or more of Nos. 2807-2811a.

2812 29c **Edward R. Murrow,** *Jan. 21,* Pullman, WA *(154,638)* 1.25
2813 29c **Love,** self-adhesive, *Jan. 27,* Loveland, OH *(125,146)* 1.25
2814 29c **Love,** booklet single, *Feb. 14,* Niagara Falls, NY 1.25
2814a Booklet pane of 10 6.50
2814C 29c **Love,** *June 11,* Niagara Falls, NY *(42,109)* 1.25
2815 52c **Love,** *Feb. 14,* Niagara Falls, NY 1.50
2816 29c **Dr. Allison Davis,** *Feb. 1,* Williamstown, MA *(162,404)* 2.00
2817 29c **Chinese New Year,** *Feb. 5,* Pomona, CA *(148,492)* 2.00
2818 29c **Buffalo Soldiers,** *Apr. 22,* Dallas, TX *(107,223)* 3.00

No. 2818 was also available on the first day of issue in forts in Kansas, Texas and Arizona.

2828a 29c **Silent Screen Stars,** *Apr. 27,* San Francisco, CA 6.50
2819-2828, any single 2.00

First day cancellation was applied to 591,251 covers bearing one or more of Nos. 2819-2828a.

2833a 29c **Garden Flowers booklet pane of 5,** *Apr. 28,* Cincinnati, OH 3.25
2829-2833, any single 1.25

First day cancellation was applied to 153,069 covers bearing one or more of Nos. 2829-2833a.

2834 29c **World Cup Soccer,** *May 26,* New York, NY 2.00
2835 40c **World Cup Soccer,** *May 26,* New York, NY 2.00
2836 50c **World Cup Soccer,** *May 26,* New York, NY 2.00

First day cancellation was applied to 443,768 covers bearing one or more of Nos. 2834-2836.

2837 **World Cup Soccer souvenir sheet of 3,** *May 26,* New York, NY *(59,503)* 4.00
2838 29c **World War II block of 10,** *June 6,* USS Normandy 7.00
2838a-2838j, any single 2.50

No. 2838 was also available on the first day of issue in 13 other locations.
First day cancellation was applied to 744,267 covers bearing one or more of Nos. 2838, 2838a-2838j.

2839 29c **Norman Rockwell,** *July 1,* Stockbridge, MA *(232,076)* 1.50
2840 50c **Norman Rockwell Souvenir Sheet of 4,** *July 1,* Stockbridge, MA 4.00
2840a-2840d, any single 2.00

First day cancellation was applied to 19,734 covers bearing one or more of Nos. 2840-2840d.

2841 29c **Moon Landing Sheet of 12,** *July 20,* Washington, DC 6.50
2841a, single stamp 2.00

First day cancellation was applied to 303,707 covers bearing one or more of Nos. 2841-2841a.

2842 $9.95 **Moon Landing,** *July 20,* Washington, DC *(11,463)* 20.00
2847a 29c **Locomotives booklet pane of 5,** *July 28,* Chama, NM 7.00
2843-2847, any single 2.00

First day cancellation was applied to 169,016 covers bearing one or more of Nos. 2843-2847a.

2848 29c **George Meany,** *Aug. 16 (172,418)* 1.25
2853a 29c **American Music Series,** *Sept. 1,* New York, NY 4.50
2849-2853, any single 1.50

First day cancellation was applied to 156,049 covers bearing one or more of Nos. 2849-2853a.

2861a 29c **American Music Series,** *Sept. 17,* Greenville MS 6.00
2854-2861, any single 1.25

First day cancellation was applied to 483,737 covers bearing one or more of Nos. 2854-2861a.
Nos. 2854-2861 were available on the first day in 9 other cities.

2862 29c **James Thurber,** *Sept. 10,* Columbus OH *(39,064)* 1.25
2866a 29c **Wonders of the Sea,** *Oct. 3,* Honolulu HI 2.75
2863-2866, any single 1.25

First day cancellation was applied to 284,678 covers bearing one or more of Nos. 2863-2866a.

2868a 29c **Cranes,** *Oct. 9* 2.50
2867-2868, any single 1.25

First day cancellation was applied to 202,955 covers bearing one or more of Nos. 2867-2868a, 24,942 with the People's Republic of China stamps.

2869 29c **Legends of the West Pane of 20,** *Oct. 18,* Laramie WY *(429,680)* 15.00
Tucson, AZ *(220,417)* 15.00
Lawton, OK *(191,393)* 15.00
2869a-2869t, any single, any city 2.50

First day cancellation was applied to covers bearing one or more of Nos. 2869-2869t.

2871 29c **Christmas (religious),** perf 11¼, *Oct. 20 (155,192)* 1.25
2871A 29c **Christmas (religious),** perf 9¾x11, *Oct. 20 (155,192)* 1.25
2872 29c **Christmas (stocking),** *Oct. 20,* Harmony MN 1.25
2873 29c **Christmas (Santa Claus),** self-adhesive, *Oct. 20,* Harmony MN 1.25
2874 29c **Christmas (cardinal),** small self-adhesive, *Oct. 20,* Harmony MN 1.25

First day cancellation was applied to 132,005 covers bearing one or more of Nos. 2872, 2872a, 2873, 2874.

2875 $2 **Bureau of Printing and Engraving Souvenir sheet,** *Nov. 3,* New York, NY *(13,126)* 25.00
2875a $2 Single stamp 7.00
2876 29c **Chinese New Year (Boar),** *Dec. 30,* Sacramento CA 1.75
2877 (3c) **Dove, bright blue,** *Dec. 13* 1.25
2878 (3c) **Dove, dark blue,** *Dec. 13* 1.25
2879 (20c) **G, black,** *Dec. 13* 1.25
2880 (20c) **G, red,** *Dec. 13* 1.25
2881 (32c) **G, black,** *Dec. 13* 1.25
2881a Booklet pane of 10 6.75
2882 (32c) **G, red,** *Dec. 13* 1.25
2883 (32c) **G, black,** *Dec. 13* 1.25
2883a Booklet pane of 10 6.75
2884 (32c) **G, black,** *Dec. 13* 1.25
2884a Booklet pane of 10 6.75
2885 (32c) **G, red,** *Dec. 13* 1.25
2885a Booklet pane of 10 6.75
2886 (32c) **G, gray, blue, light blue, red & black,** self-adhesive, *Dec. 13* 1.25
2887 (32c) **G, black, blue & red,** self-adhesive, *Dec. 13* 1.25
2888 (25c) **G, black,** coil, *Dec. 13* 1.25
2889 (32c) **G, black,** coil, *Dec. 13* 1.25
2890 (32c) **G, blue,** coil, *Dec. 13* 1.25
2891 (32c) **G, red,** coil, *Dec. 13* 1.25
2892 (32c) **G, red,** rouletted coil, *Dec. 13* 1.25

Originally, No. 2893 (the 5c green Non-profit Presort G rate stamp) was only available through the Philatelic Fulfillment Center after their announcement 1/12/95. Requests for first day cancels received a 12/13/94 cancel, even though they were not available on that date. Value, $1.25.
First day cancellation was applied to 338,107 covers bearing one or more of Nos. 2877-2893(?), and U633-U634.

2897 32c **Flag Over Porch,** *May 19,* Denver CO 1.25

First day cancellation was applied to 66,609 covers bearing one or more of Nos. 2897, 2913-2914, 2916 and possibly, 2920.

1995-98

2902 (5c) **Butte,** coil, *Mar. 10,* State College PA 1.25

First day cancellation was applied to 80,003 covers bearing one or more of Nos. 2902, 2905, and U635-U636.

2902B (5c) **Butte,** self-adhesive coil, *June 15, 1996,* San Antonio TX 1.25

First day cancellation was applied to 87,400 covers bearing one or more of Nos. 2902B, 2904A, 2906, 2910, 2912A, 2915B.

2903 (5c) **Mountain,** purple & multi coil, *Mar. 16, 1996* San Jose CA 1.25
2904 (5c) **Mountain,** blue & multi coil, *Mar. 16,1996* San Jose CA 1.25

First day cancellation was applied to 28,064 covers bearing one or more of Nos. 2903-2904.

2904A (5c) **Mountain,** purple & multi self-adhesive coil, *June 15, 1996,* San Antonio TX 1.25

First day cancellation was applied to 87,400 covers bearing one or more of Nos. 2902B, 2904A, 2906, 2910, 2912A, 2915B.

2904B (5c) **Mountain,** purple & multi self-adhesive coil, inscription outlined, *Jan. 24, 1997,* Tucson, AZ 1.25
2905 (10c) **Auto,** coil, *Mar. 10,* State College PA 1.25
2906 (10c) **Auto,** self-adhesive coil, *June 15, 1996* San Antonio TX 1.25

First day cancellation was applied to 87,400 covers bearing one or more of Nos. 2902B, 2904A, 2906, 2910, 2912A, 2915B.

2907 (10c) **Eagle & Shield,** USA Bulk Rate self-adhesive coil, *May 21, 1996* 1.25

First day cancellation was applied to 54,102 covers bearing one or more of Nos. 2907, 2915A, 2915C, 2921.

2908 (15c) **Auto tail fin (dark orange yellow),** coil, *Mar. 17,* New York NY 1.25
2909 (15c) **Auto tail fin (buff),** coil, *Mar. 17,* New York, NY 1.25

First day cancellation was applied to 93,770 covers bearing one or more of Nos. 2908-2909, 2911-2912, 2919.

2910 (15c) **Auto tail fin (buff),** self-adhesive coil, *June 15, 1996,* San Antonio TX 1.25

First day cancellation was applied to 87,400 covers bearing one or more of Nos. 2902B, 2904A, 2906, 2910, 2915B.

2911 (25c) **Juke box,** coil, *Mar. 17,* New York NY 1.25
2912 (25c) **Juke box,** coil, *Mar. 17,* New York NY 1.25

First day cancellation was applied to 93,770 covers bearing one or more of Nos. 2908-2909, 2911-2912, 2919.

2912A (25c) **Juke box,** self-adhesive coil, bright orange red & multi, microperfs, *June 15, 1996,* New York NY 1.25

First day cancellation was applied to 87,400 covers bearing one or more of Nos. 2902B, 2904A, 2906, 2910, 2912A, 2915B.

2912B (25c) **Juke box,** self-adhesive coil, dark red & multi, *Jan. 24, 1997,* Tucson, AZ 1.25
2913 32c **Flag Over Porch,** coil, *May 19,* Denver CO 1.25
2914 32c **Flag Over Porch,** coil, *May 19,* Denver CO 1.25
2915 32c **Flag Over Porch,** self-adhesive, die cut 8.7 vert., *Apr. 18* 1.25

2915A 32c **Flag Over Porch,** self-adhesive, die cut 9.8 vert., 11 teeth, *May 21, 1996* 1.25
2915B 32c **Flag Over Porch,** self-adhesive die cut 11.5 vert., *June 15, 1996,* San Antonio TX 1.25

First day cancellation was applied to 87,400 covers bearing one or more of Nos. 2902B, 2904A, 2906, 2910, 2912A, 2915B.

2915C 32c **Flag Over Porch,** self-adhesive, die cut 10.9, *May 21, 1996* 2.00
2915D 32c **Flag Over Porch,** self-adhesive coil, self-adhesive die cut 9.8 vert., 9 teeth, *Jan. 24, 1997,* Tucson, AZ 1.25

First day cancellation was applied to 56,774 covers bearing one or more of Nos. 2904B, 2912B, 2915D and 2921b.

2916 32c **Flag Over Porch,** booklet single, *May 19,* Denver CO 1.25
2916a Booklet pane of 10 7.50
2919 32c **Flag Over Field,** self-adhesive, *Mar. 17,* New York NY 1.25

First day cancellation was applied to 93,770 covers bearing one or more of Nos. 2908-2909, 2911-2912, 2919.

2920 32c **Flag Over Porch,** self-adhesive, *Apr. 18* 1.25

First day cancellation was applied to 66,609 covers bearing one or more of Nos. 2897, 2913-2914, 2916 and possibly, 2920. First day cancellation was applied to 57,639 covers bearing one or more of Nos. 2920d, 3030, 3044.

2921 32c **Flag Over Porch,** self-adhesive, booklet stamp, die cut 9.8 on 2 or 3 sides, *May 21, 1996* 1.25

First day cancellation was applied to 54,102 covers bearing one or more of Nos. 2907, 2915A, 2915C, 2921.

GREAT AMERICANS ISSUE

2933 32c **Milton Hershey,** *Sept. 13,* Hershey PA *(121,228)* 1.25
2934 32c **Cal Farley,** *Apr. 26, 1996,* Amarillo TX *(109,440)* 1.25
2935 32c **Henry Luce,** *Apr. 3, 1998,* New York NY *(76,982)* 1.25
2936 32c **Wallace,** *July 16, 1998,* Pleasantville NY *(72,183)* 1.25
2938 46c **Ruth Benedict,** *Oct. 20,* Virginia Beach VA *(24,793)* 1.40
2940 55c **Alice Hamilton,** *July 11,* Boston MA *(24,225)* 1.40
2941 55c **Justin Morrill,** *July 17, 1999* Strafford VT *(19,699)* 1.40
2942 77c **Mary Breckinridge,** *Nov. 9, 1998* Troy, NY 1.75

First day cancellation was applied to 121,662 covers bearing one or more of Nos. 2942, 3257-3261, 3263-3269.

2943 78c **Alice Paul,** *Aug. 18,* Mount Laurel NJ *(25,071)* 1.75

1995

2948 (32c) **Love,** *Feb. 1,* Valentines VA 1.50
2949 (32c) **Love,** self-adhesive, *Feb. 1,* Valentines VA 1.50

First day cancellation was applied to 70,778 covers bearing one or more of Nos. 2948, 2949.

2950 32c **Florida Statehood,** *Mar. 3,* Tallahassee FL *(167,499)* 1.25
2954a 32c **Earth Day,** *Apr. 20* 2.75
2951-2954, any single 1.25

First day cancellation was applied to 328,893 covers bearing one or more of Nos. 2951-2954, 2954a.

2955 32c **Richard Nixon,** *Apr. 26,* Yorba Linda CA *(377,605)* 1.25
2956 32c **Bessie Coleman,** *Apr. 27,* Chicago IL *(299,834)* 2.00
2957 32c **Love,** *May 12,* Lakeville PA 1.25
2958 55c **Love,** *May 12,* Lakeville PA 1.25
2959 32c **Love,** booklet single, *May 12,* Lakeville PA 1.25
2959a Booklet pane of 10 7.50
2960 55c **Love,** self-adhesive, *May 12,* Lakeville PA 1.40

First day cancellation was applied to 273,350 covers bearing one or more of Nos. 2957-2959, 2959a, and U637.

2965a 32c **Recreational Sports,** *May 20,* Jupiter FL 3.25
2961-2965, any single 1.50

First day cancellation was applied to 909,807 covers bearing one or more of Nos. 2961-2965, 2965a.

2966 32c **Prisoners of War & Missing in Action,** *May 29 (231,857)* 3.00
2967 32c **Marilyn Monroe,** *June 1,* Universal City CA *(703,219)* 4.00
Any other city 2.00
2968 32c **Texas Statehood,** *June 16,* Austin TX *(177,550)* 1.75
2973a 32c **Great Lakes Lighthouses booklet pane of 5,** *June 17,* Cheboygan MI 5.00
2969-2973, any single 2.00

First day cancellation was applied to 626,055 covers bearing one or more of Nos. 2969-2973, 2973a.

2974 32c **UN, 50th Anniv.,** *June 26,* San Francisco CA *(160,383)* 1.50

2975 32c **Civil War pane of 20,** *June 29,* Gettysburg PA 16.00
Any other city 16.00
2975a-2975t, any single, Gettysburg PA 2.50
Any other city 2.00

First day cancellation was applied to 1,950,134 covers bearing one or more of Nos. 2975, 2975a-2975t, and UX200-UX219.

2979a 32c **Carousel Horses,** *July 21,* Lahaska PA 3.25
2976-2979, any single 1.25

First day cancellation was applied to 479,038 covers bearing one or more of Nos. 2976-2979, 2979a.

2980 32c **Woman Suffrage,** *Aug. 26 (196,581)* 1.25
2981 32c **World War II block of 10,** *Sept. 2,* Honolulu HI 7.00
2981a-2981j, any single 2.50

First day cancellation was applied to 1,562,094 covers bearing one or more of Nos. 2981, 2981a-2981j.

2982 32c **American Music Series,** *Sept. 1,* New Orleans LA *(258,996)* 1.75
2992a 32c **American Music Series,** *Sept. 16,* Monterey CA 6.50
2983-2992, any single 1.50

First day cancellation was applied to 629,956 covers bearing one or more of Nos. 2983-2992, 2992a.

2997a 32c **Garden Flowers booklet pane of 5,** *Sept. 19,* Encinitas CA 4.00
2993-2997, any single 1.25

First day cancellation was applied to 564,905 covers bearing one or more of Nos. 2993-2997, 2997a.

2998 60c **Eddie Rickenbacker,** *Sept. 25,* Columbus OH *(24,283)* 1.75
2999 32c **Republic of Palau,** *Sept. 29,* Agana GU *(157,377)* 1.25
3000 32c **Comic Strips Pane of 20,** *Oct. 1,* Boca Raton FL 13.00
3000a-3000t, any single 2.00

First day cancellation was applied to 1,362,990 covers bearing one or more of Nos. 3000, 3000a-3000t.

3001 32c **US Naval Academy,** *Oct. 10,* Annapolis, MD *(222,183)* 2.00
3002 32c **Tennessee Williams,** *Oct. 13,* Clarksdale MS *(209,812)* 1.25
3003 32c **Christmas, Madonna,** perf 11.2, *Oct. 19* 1.25
3003A 32c **Christmas, Madonna,** perf
3003Ab Booklet pane of 10 7.25

First day cancellation was applied to 223,301 covers bearing one or more of Nos. 3003, 3003A-3003Ab.

3007a 32c **Christmas (secular) sheet,** *Sept. 30,* North Pole NY 3.25
3004-3007, any single 1.25
3007b 32c Booklet pane of 10, 3 #3004, etc. 7.25
3007c 32c Booklet pane of 10, 2 #3004, etc. 7.25

First day cancellation was applied to 487,816 covers bearing one or more of Nos. 3004-3007, 3007a.

3008-3011 32c **Christmas (secular) self-adhesive booklet stamps,** *Sept. 30,* North Pole NY 3.25
3008-3011, any single 1.25
3012 32c **Angel,** *Oct. 19,* Christmas FL 1.25
3013 32c **Children sledding,** *Oct. 19,* Christmas FL 1.25

First day cancellation was applied to 77,675 covers bearing one or more of Nos. 3012, 3013, 3018.

3014-3017 32c **Self-adhesive coils,** *Sept. 30,* North Pole NY 2.50
3014-3017, any single 1.25
3018 32c **Self-adhesive coil,** *Oct. 19,* Christmas FL 1.25

First day cancellation was applied to 77,675 covers bearing one or more of Nos. 3012, 3013, 3018.

3023a 32c **Antique Automobiles,** *Nov. 3,* New York NY 3.00
3019-3023, any single 1.25

First day cancellation was applied to 757,003 covers bearing one or more of Nos. 3019-3023, 3023a.

1996

3024 32c **Utah Statehood Cent.,** *Jan. 4,* Salt Lake City UT *(207,089)* 1.25
3029a 32c **Garden Flowers booklet pane,** *Jan. 19,* Kennett Square PA 3.50
3025-3029, any single 1.25

First day cancellation was applied to 876,176 covers bearing one or more of Nos. 3025-3029, 3029a.

3030 32c **Love self-adhesive,** *Jan. 20,* New York NY 1.25

First day cancellation was applied to 57,639 covers bearing one or more of Nos. 2920d, 3030, 3044.

FLORA AND FAUNA ISSUE

1996-2000

3031 1c **Kestrel,** *Nov. 19, 1999,* New York, NY *(14,431)* 1.50
3032 2c **Red-headed woodpecker,** *Feb. 2,* Sarasota FL *(37,319)* 1.25
3033 3c **Eastern Bluebird,** *Apr. 3 (23,405)* 1.25
3036 $1 **Red Fox,** *Aug. 14, 1998* 5.00

First day cancellation was applied to 46,557 covers bearing one or more of Nos. 3228-3229, 3036.

3044 1c **American Kestrel, coil,** *Jan. 20,* New York NY 1.25

First day cancellation was applied to 57,639 covers bearing one or more of Nos. 2920d, 3030, 3044.

3045 2c **Red-Headed Woodpecker,** *June 22, 1999 (14,377)* 1.25
3048 20c **Blue Jay, booklet stamp, self-adhesive,** *Aug. 2,* St. Louis MO 1.25

First day cancellation was applied to 32,633 covers bearing one or more of Nos. 3048, 3053.

3049 32c **Yellow Rose, booklet stamp, self-adhesive,** *Oct. 24,* Pasadena, CA *(7,849)* 1.25
3050 20c **Ring-necked Pheasant, booklet stamp, self-adhesive,** *July 31, 1998* Somerset NJ 1.25

First day cancellation was applied to 32,220 covers bearing one or more of Nos. 3050, 3055.

3052 33c **Coral Pink Rose,** serpentine die cut 11½x11¼, *Aug. 13, 1999,* Indianapolis, IN 1.25
3052E 33c **Coral Pink Rose,** serpentine die cut 10¾x10½, *Apr. 7, 2000,* New York, NY *(18,199)* 1.25
3053 20c **Blue Jay, coil, self-adhesive,** *Aug. 2,* St. Louis MO 1.25
3054 32c **Yellow Rose, self-adhesive,** *Aug. 1, 1997,* Falls Church VA *(20,029)* 1.25
3055 20c **Ring-necked Pheasant,coil, self-adhesive,** *July 31, 1998* Somerset NJ 1.25

First day cancellation was applied to 32,220 covers bearing one or more of Nos. 3050, 3055.

1996

3058 32c **Ernest E. Just,** *Feb. 1 (191,360)* 1.75
3059 32c **Smithsonian, 150th anniv.,** *Feb. 7, (221,399)* 1.25
3060 32c **Chinese New Year,** *Feb. 8,* San Francisco CA *(237,451)* 1.75
3064a 32c **Pioneers of Communication,** *Feb. 22,* New York NY 2.50
3061-3064, any single 1.25

First day cancellation was applied to 567,205 covers bearing one or more of Nos. 3061-3064, 3064a.

3065 32c **Fulbright Scholarships,** *Feb. 28,* Fayetteville AR *(227,330)* 1.25
3066 50c **Jacqueline Cochran,** *Mar. 9,* Indio CA *(30,628)* 1.75
3067 32c **Marathon,** *Apr. 11,* Boston MA *(177,050)* 2.00
3068 32c **Olympics, pane of 20,** *May 2* 13.00
3068a-3068t, any single 1.25
Atlanta, GA —

Washington DC first day cancellation was applied to 1,807,316 covers bearing one or more of Nos. 3068, 3068a-3068t. Atlanta was also an official first day city, and covers postmarked there are scarce.

3069 32c **Georgia O'Keeffe,** *May 23,* Santa Fe NM *(200,522)* 1.50
3070 32c **Tennessee Statehood, Bicen.,** *May 31,* Knoxville, Memphis or Nashville TN 1.25
3071 32c **Tennessee, self-adhesive,** *May 31,* Knoxville, Memphis or Nashville TN 1.25

First day cancellation was applied to 217,281 covers bearing one or more of Nos. 3070-3071.

3076a 32c **American Indian Dances, strip of 5,** *June 7,* Oklahoma City OK 3.00
3072-3076, any single 1.25

First day cancellation was applied to 653,057 covers bearing one or more of Nos. 3072-3076, 3076a.

3080a 32c **Prehistoric Animals,** *June 8,* Toronto, Canada 2.75
3077-3080, any single 1.50

First day cancellation was applied to 485,929 covers bearing one or more of Nos. 3077-3080, 3080a.

3081 32c **Breast Cancer Awareness,** *June 15 (183,896)* 1.25
Any other city 1.25
3082 32c **James Dean,** *June 24,* Burbank CA *(263,593)* 3.00
3086a 32c **Folk Heroes,** *July 11,* Anaheim CA 2.75
3083-3086, any single 1.25

First day cancellation was applied to 739,706 covers bearing one or more of Nos. 3083-3086, 3086a.

3087 32c **Centennial Olympic Games,** *July 19,* Atlanta GA *(269,056)* 1.25
3088 32c **Iowa Statehood, 150th Anniv.,** *Aug. 1,* Dubuque IA 1.25

3089 32c **Iowa Statehood, self-adhesive** *Aug. 1,* Dubuque IA 1.25
3088, 3089, both stamps issued *Aug. 1,* Dubuque, IA 1.75

First day cancellation was applied to 215,181 covers bearing one or more of Nos. 3088-3089.

3090 32c **Rural Free Delivery,** *Aug. 7,* Charleston WV *(192,070)* 1.25
3091-3095 32c **Riverboats,** *Aug. 22,* Orlando FL 3.50
3091-3095, any single 1.25
3095b 32c **Riverboats, special die cutting,** *Aug. 22,* Orlando FL 3.50

First day cancellation was applied to 770,384 covers bearing one or more of Nos. 3091-3095, 3095b.

3099a 32c **Big Band Leaders,** *Sept. 11,* New York NY 3.25
3096-3099, any single 1.25

First day cancellation was applied to 1,235,166 covers bearing one or more of Nos. 3096-3103, 3099a, 3103a.

3103a 32c **Songwriters,** *Sept. 11,* New York NY 3.25
3100-3103, any single 1.25

First day cancellation was applied to 1,235,166 covers bearing one or more of Nos. 3096-3103, 3099a, 3103a.

3104 23c **F. Scott Fitzgerald,** *Sept. 27,* St. Paul MN *(150,783)* 1.25
3105 32c **Endangered Species,** *Oct. 2,* San Diego CA 7.50
3105a-3105o, any single 1.25

First day cancellation was applied to 941,442 covers bearing one or more of Nos. 3105, 3105a-3105o.

3106 32c **Computer Technology,** *Oct. 8,* Aberdeen Proving Ground MD *(153,688)* 1.75
3107 32c **Christmas Madonna,** *Nov. 1,* Richmond VA 1.25

First day cancellation was applied to 164,447 covers bearing one or more of Nos. 3107, 3112.

3111a 32c **Christmas (secular),** *Oct. 8,* North Pole AK 2.75
3108-3111, any single 1.25

First day cancellation was applied to 884,339 covers bearing one or more of Nos. 3108-3111, 3111a, 3113-3117.

3112 32c **As No. 3107, self-adhesive,** *Nov. 1,* Richmond VA 1.25
3113-3116 32c **Christmas (secular), self-adhesive,** *Oct. 8,* North Pole AK 3.25
3113-3116, any single 1.25
3117 32c **Skaters, self-adhesive,** *Oct. 8,* North Pole AK 1.25

First day cancellation was applied to 884,339 covers bearing one or more of Nos. 3108-3111, 3111a, 3113-3117.

3118 32c **Hanukkah,** *Oct. 22 (179,355)* 1.75
3119 50c **Cycling,** *Nov. 1,* New York NY 4.00
3119a-3119b, any single 2.00

First day cancellation was applied to 290,091 covers bearing one or more of Nos. 3119, 3119a-3119b.

1997

3120 32c **Chinese New Year,** *Jan. 5,* Honolulu *(233,638)* 2.00
3121 32c **Benjamin O. Davis, Sr.,** *Jan. 28 (166,527)* 2.00
3122 32c **Statue of Liberty, self-adhesive,** *Feb. 1,* San Diego CA *(40,003)* 1.25
3123 32c **Love, Swans, self-adhesive,** *Feb. 4,* Los Angeles CA 1.25
3124 55c **Love, Swans, self-adhesive,** *Feb. 4,* Los Angeles CA 1.50

First day cancellation was applied to 257,380 covers bearing one or more of Nos. 3123-3124.

3125 32c **Helping Children Learn, self-adhesive** *Feb. 18 (175,410)* 1.50
3126 32c **Merian Botanical Prints, Citron, etc., self-adhesive, die cut 10.9x10.2,** *Mar. 3* 1.25
3127 32c **Merian Botanical Prints, Pineapple, etc., self-adhesive, die cut 10.9x10.2,** *Mar. 3* 1.25
3128 32c **Merian Botanical Prints, Citron, etc., self-adhesive, die cut 11.2x10.8,** *Mar. 3* 1.25
3128a 32c **Merian Botanical Prints, Citron, etc., self-adhesive, die cut mixed perf,** *Mar. 3* 1.25
3129 32c **Merian Botanical Prints, Pineapple, etc., self-adhesive, die cut 11.2x10.8,** *Mar. 3* 1.25
3129a 32c **Merian Botanical Prints, Pineapple, etc., self-adhesive, die cut mixed perf,** *Mar. 3* 1.25

First day cancellation was applied to 336,897 covers bearing one or more of Nos. 3126-3129, 3128a-3129a.

3131a 32c **Pacific 97,** *Mar. 13,* New York NY 2.00
3130-3131, any single 1.50

First day cancellation was applied to 371,908 covers bearing one or more of Nos. 3130-3131, 3131a.

3132 (25c) **Juke Box, self-adhesive** *Mar. 14,* New York NY 1.25
3133 32c **Flag over Porch, Self-adhesive** *Mar. 14,* New York NY 1.25

First day cancellation was applied to 26,0820 covers bearing one or more of Nos. 3132-3133.

3134 32c **Thornton Wilder,** *Apr. 17,* Hamden CT *(157,299)* 1.25
3135 32c **Raoul Wallenberg,** *Apr. 24 (168,668)* 2.00
3136 32c **Dinosaurs, pane of 15** *May 1,* Grand Junction CO 7.50
3136a-3136o, any single 1.25

First day cancellation was applied to 1,782,1221 covers bearing one or more of Nos. 3136, 3136a-3136o.

3137a 32c **Bugs Bunny,** *May 22,* Burbank CA *(378,142)* 2.00
3139 50c **Pacific 97, Franklin, pane of 12** *May 29,* San Francisco CA 12.00
3139a, single 2.00
3140 60c **Pacific 97,, pane of 12,** *May 30,* San Francisco CA 12.00
3140a, single 2.00

First day cancellation was applied to 328,401 covers bearing one or more of Nos. 3139-3140, 3139a-3140b.

3141 32c **Marshall Plan,** *June 4,* Cambridge MA *(157,622)* 1.50
3142 32c **Classic American Aircraft,** *July 19,* Dayton OH 10.00
3142a-3142t, any single 1.25

First day cancellation was applied to 1,413,833 covers bearing one or more of Nos. 3142, 3142a-3142t.

3146a 32c **Football Coaches** *July 25,* Canton OH 3.00
3143-3146, any single 1.75

First day cancellation was applied to 586,946 covers bearing one or more of Nos. 3143-3146.

3147 32c **Vince Lombardi,** *Aug. 8,* Green Bay WI *(37,839)* 2.00
3148 32c **Bear Bryant,** *Aug. 5,* Tuscaloosa AL *(119,428)* 1.75
3149 32c **Pop Warner,** *Aug. 7,* Philadelphia PA *(23,858)* 1.75
3150 32c **George Halas,** *Aug. 16,* Chicago IL *(26,760)* 1.75
3151 32c **American Dolls,** *July 28,* Anaheim CA 8.00
3151a-3151o, any single 1.25

First day cancellation was applied to 831,359 covers bearing one or more of Nos. 3151, 3151a-3151o.

3152 32c **Humphrey Bogart,** *July 31,* Los Angeles CA *(220,254)* 2.50
3153 32c **"The Star and Stripes Forever,"** *Aug. 21,* Milwaukee WI *(36,666)* 1.25
3157a 32c **Opera Singers,** *Sept. 10,* New York NY 2.75
3154-3157, any single 1.25

First day cancellation was applied to 386,689 covers bearing one or more of Nos. 3154-3157.

3165a 32c **Classical Composers and Conductors,** *Sept. 12,* Cincinnati OH 5.25
3158-3165, any single 1.25

First day cancellation was applied to 424,344 covers bearing one or more of Nos. 3158-3165.

3166 32c **Padre Felix Varela,** *Sept. 15,* Miami FL *(120,079)* 1.25
3167 32c **Department of the Air Force,** *Sept. 18 (178,519)* 1.50
3172a 32c **Classic Movie Monsters,** *Sept. 30,* Universal City CA 3.75
3168-3172, any single 1.50

First day cancellation was applied to 476,993 covers bearing one or more of Nos. 3168-3172.

3173 32c **First Supersonic Flight,** *Oct. 14,* Edwards AFB CA *(173,778)* 1.50
3174 32c **Women in Military Service,** *Oct. 18 (106,121)* 2.00
3175 32c **Kwanzaa,** *Oct. 22,* Los Angeles CA *(92,489)* 1.75
3176 32c **Christmas Madonna,** *Oct. 27 (35,809)* 1.25
3177 32c **Holly,** *Oct. 30,* New York NY *(87,332)* 1.25
3178 $3 **Mars Pathfinder,** *Dec. 10* Pasadena CA *(11,699)* 9.00

1998

3179 32c **Chinese New Year,** *Jan. 5,* Seattle WA *(234,269)* 2.00
3180 32c **Alpine Skiing,** *Jan. 22,* Salt Lake City UT *(196,504)* 1.25
3181 32c **Madam C. J. Walker,** *Jan. 28,* Indianapolis IN *(146,348)* 1.75

CELEBRATE THE CENTURY ISSUE

1998-2000

3182 32c **1900s,** *Feb. 3 (11,699),* Washington DC 8.50
3182a-3182o, any single 1.50
3183 32c **1910s,** *Feb. 3,* Washington DC 8.50
3183a-3183o, any single 1.50

First day cancellation was applied to 3,896,387 covers bearing one or more of Nos. 3182-3182o, 3183-3183o.

3184 32c **1920s,** *May 28,* Chicago IL 8.50
3184a-3184o, any single 1.75

First day cancellation was applied to 1,057,909 covers bearing one or more of Nos. 3184-3184o.

3185 32c **1930s,** *Sept. 10,* Cleveland OH 8.50
3185a-3185o, any single 1.75

First day cancellation was applied to 999,017 covers bearing one or more of Nos. 3185-3185o.

3186 33c **1940s,** *Feb. 18, 1999,* Dobbins AFB GA 8.50
3186a-3186o, any single 1.75

First day cancellation was applied to 1,459,138 covers bearing one or more of Nos. 3186-3186o.

3187 33c **1950s,** *May 26, 1999,* Springfield MA 8.50
3187a-3187o, any single 1.75

First day cancellation was applied to 1,454,906 covers bearing one or more of Nos. 3187-3187o.

3188 33c **1960s,** *Sept. 17, 1999,* Green Bay, WI 8.50
3188a-3188o, any single 1.75

First day cancellation was applied to 1,252,243 covers bearing one or more of Nos. 3188-3188o.

3189 33c **1970s,** *Nov. 18, 1999,* New York, NY 8.50
3189a-3189o, any single 1.75

First day cancellation was applied to 894,084 covers bearing one or more of Nos. 3189-3189o.

3190 33c **1980s,** *Jan. 12, 2000,* Kennedy Space Center, Titusville FL 8.50
3190a-3190o, any single 1.75
3191 33c **1990s,** *May 2, 2000,* Escondido, CA 8.50
3191a-3191o, any single 1.75

First day cancellation was applied to 1,172,962 covers bearing one or more of Nos. 3191-3191o.

1998

3192 32c **"Remember the Maine,"** *Feb. 15,* Key West FL *(161,657)* 1.75
3193-3197 32c **Flowering Trees,** *Mar. 19,* New York NY 3.75
3193-3197, any single 1.50

First day cancellation was applied to 666,199 covers bearing one or more of Nos. 3193-3197.

3202a 32c **Alexander Calder,** *Mar. 25* 3.75
3198-3202, any single 1.50

First day cancellation was applied to 588,887 covers bearing one or more of Nos. 3198-3202, 3202a.

3203 32c **Cinco de Mayo,** *Apr. 16,* San Antonio TX *(144,443)* 1.25
3204a 32c **Sylvester & Tweety,** *Apr. 27,* New York NY *(213,839)* 1.25
3206 32c **Wisconsin Statehood,** *May 29,* Madison WI *(130,810)* 1.25

1998-99

3207 (5c) **Wetlands,** *June 5,* McLean VA 1.25
3207A (5c) **Wetlands, Serpentine die cut,** *Dec. 14* 1.25
3208 (25c) **Diner,** *June 5,* McLean VA 1.25

First day cancellation was applied to 35,333 covers bearing one or more of Nos. 3207, 3208; 13,378 covers bearing one of more of Nos. 3207A, 3270-3271.

3208A (25c) **Diner, Serpentine die cut,** *June 5 (13,984)* 1.25

1898 TRANS-MISSISSIPPI STAMPS, CENT. ISSUE

1998

3209 **Sheet of 9,** *June 18,* Anaheim CA 6.50
3209a 1c 1.50
3209b 2c 1.50
3209c 4c 1.50
3209d 5c 1.50
3209e 8c 1.50
3209f 10c 1.50
3209g 50c 2.00
3209h $1 2.50
3209i $2 4.50
3210 $1 **Sheet of 9,** *June 18,* Anaheim CA 15.00

First day cancellation was applied to 203,649 covers bearing one or more of Nos. 3209-3210, 3209a-3209i.

1998

3211 32c **Berlin Airlift,** *June 26,* Berlin, Germany *(137,894)* 1.50
3215a 32c **Folk Musicians,** *June 26* 3.25
3212-3215, any single 1.25

First day cancellation was applied to 341,015 covers bearing one or more of Nos. 3212-3215, 3215a.

3219a 32c **Gospel Music,** *July 15,* New Orleans LA 3.25
3216-3219, any single 1.25

First day cancellation was applied to 330,533 covers bearing one or more of Nos. 3216-3219, 3219a.

3220 32c **Spanish Settlement of the Southwest,** *July 11,* Española NM *(122,182)* 1.25
3221 32c **Stephen Vincent Benét,** *July 22,* Harpers Ferry WV *(107,412)* 1.25
3225a 32c **Tropical Birds,** *July 29,* Ponce PR 3.00
3222-3225, any single 1.25

First day cancellation was applied to 371,354 covers bearing one or more of Nos. 3222-3225, 3225a.

3226 32c **Alfred Hitchcock,** *Aug. 3,* Los Angeles CA *(140,628)* 2.00
3227 32c **Organ & Tissue Donation,** *Aug. 5,* Columbus OH *(110,601)* 1.25

3228 (10c) **Modern Bicycle, Serpentine die cut,** *Aug. 14* 1.25
3229 (10c) **Modern Bicycle,** *Aug. 14* 1.25

First day cancellation was applied to 46,557 covers bearing one or more of Nos. 3228-3229, 3036.

3230-3234 32c **Bright Eyes,** *Aug. 20,* Boston MA 3.25
3230-3234, any single 1.75

First day cancellation was applied to 394,280 covers bearing one or more of Nos. 3230-3234.

3235 32c **Klondike Gold Rush Cent.,** *Aug. 21,* Nome or Skagway AK *(123,559)* 1.50
3236 32c **American Art, pane of 20,** *Aug. 27,* Santa Clara CA 9.00
3236a-3236t, any single 1.25

First day cancellation was applied to 924,031 covers bearing one or more of Nos. 3236, 3236a-3236t.

3237 32c **American Ballet,** *Sept. 16,* New York NY *(133,034)* 1.25
3242a 32c **Space Discovery,** *Oct. 1,* Kennedy Space Center FL 3.75
3238-3242, any single 1.25

First day cancellation was applied to 399,807 covers bearing one or more of Nos. 3238-3242, 3242a.

3243 32c **Giving & Sharing,** *Oct. 7,* Atlanta GA *(124,051)* 1.25
3244 32c **Christmas, Madonna,** *Oct. 15 (105,835)* 1.25
3245-3248 32c **Christmas, Secular,** *Oct. 15,* Christmas MI 3.25
3245-3248, any single 1.25
3249-3252 32c **Christmas, Secular, size: 23x30mm,** *Oct. 15,* Christmas MI 3.00
3249-3252, any single 1.25

First day cancellation was applied to 328,199 covers bearing one or more of Nos. 3245-3252.

3257 (1c) **Weather Vane, white USA,** *Nov. 9,* Troy NY 1.25
3258 (1c) **Weather Vane, pale blue USA,** *Nov. 9,* Troy NY 1.25
3259 22c **Uncle Sam,** *Nov. 9,* Troy NY 1.25
3260 (33c) **Uncle Sam's Hat,** *Nov. 9,* Troy NY 1.25
3261 $3.20 **Space Shuttle Landing,** *Nov. 9,* 5.00
3262 $11.75 **Piggyback Space Shuttle,** *Nov. 19,* New York NY *(3,703)* 25.00
3263 22c **Uncle Sam, coil,** *Nov. 9,* Troy NY 1.25
3264 (33c) **Uncle Sam's Hat, coil,** *Nov. 9,* Troy NY 1.25
3265 (33c) **Uncle Sam's Hat, self-adhesive coil, die cut 9.9, round corners,** *Nov. 9,* Troy NY 1.25
3266 (33c) **Uncle Sam's Hat, self-adhesive coil, die cut 9.9, square corners,** *Nov. 9,* Troy NY 1.50
3267 (33c) **Uncle Sam's Hat, self-adhesive booklet single, die cut 9.9** *Nov. 9,* Troy NY 1.25
3268 (33c) **Uncle Sam's Hat, self-adhesive booklet single, die cut 11.2x11.1** *Nov. 9,* Troy NY 1.25
3269 (33c) **Uncle Sam's Hat, self-adhesive booklet single, die cut 8** *Nov. 9,* Troy NY 1.25

First day cancellation was applied to 121,662 covers bearing one or more of Nos. 2942, 3257-3261, 3263-3269.

3270 (10c) **Eagle & Shield, Presorted Std.,** *Dec. 14* 1.25
3271 (10c) **Eagle & Shield, Presorted Std., self-adhesive, Serpentine die cut,** *Dec. 14* 1.25

First day cancellation was applied to 13,378 covers bearing one of more of Nos. 3207A, 3270-3271.

1999

3272 33c **Chinese New Year,** *Jan. 5,* Los Angeles CA *(151,436)* 2.00
3273 33c **Malcolm X,** *Jan. 20,* New York NY *(107,226)* 2.00
3274 33c **Love,** *Jan. 28,* Loveland CO 1.25
3275 55c **Love,** *Jan. 28,* Loveland CO 1.50

First day cancellation was applied to 189,331 covers bearing one of more of Nos. 3274, 3275, UX300.

3276 33c **Hospice Care,** *Feb. 9,* Largo FL *(136,976)* 1.25
3277 33c **Flag & City,** *Feb. 25,* Orlando FL 1.25
3278 33c **Flag & City, self-adhesive, die cut 11.1** *Feb. 25,* Orlando FL 1.25
3279 33c **Flag & City, self-adhesive, die cut 9.8** *Feb. 25,* Orlando FL 1.25
3280 33c **Flag & City, coil, perf. 9.9 vert.** *Feb. 25,* Orlando FL 1.25
3281 33c **Flag & City, self-adhesive coil, die cut 9.8 vert, square corners,** *Feb. 25,* Orlando FL 1.25
3282 33c **Flag & City, self-adhesive coil, die cut 9.8 vert., round corners,** *Feb. 25,* Orlando FL 1.25

First day cancellation was applied to 88,569 covers bearing one of more of Nos. 3277-3282.

3283 33c **Flag & Blackboard, self-adhesive, die cut 7.9,** *Mar. 13 (26,067)* 1.25
3286 33c **Irish Immigration,** *Feb. 26,* Boston MA *(127,213)* 1.50
3287 33c **Lunt & Fontanne,** *Mar. 2,* New York NY *(120,423)* 1.25
3292a 33c **Arctic Animals,** *Mar. 12,* Barrow AK 3.25
3288-3292, any single 1.25

First day cancellation was applied to 476,863 covers bearing one of more of Nos. 3288-3292, 3292a.

3293 33c **Sonoran Desert, Pane of 10,** *Apr. 6,* Tucson AZ 6.75
3293a-3293j, any single 1.25

First day cancellation was applied to 410,985 covers bearing one of more of Nos. 3293-3293j.

3294-3297 33c **Christmas Berries, die cut 11.2x11.7** *Apr. 10,* Ponchatoula LA 3.25
3294-3297, any single 1.25
3297e, dated 2000, *Mar. 15, 2000,* Ponchatoula LA 3.25
3294a-3296a, 3297c, any single 1.25
3298-3301 33c **Christmas Berries, die cut 9.5x10** *Apr. 10,* Ponchatoula LA 3.25
3298-3301, any single 1.25
3302-3305 33c **Christmas Berries, die cut 8.5 vert.** *Apr. 10,* Ponchatoula LA 3.25
3302-3305, any single 1.25

First day cancellation was applied to 101,344 covers bearing one of more of Nos. 3294-3305.

3306a 33c **Daffy Duck,** *Apr. 16,* Los Angeles CA 1.50

First day cancellation was applied to 177,988 covers bearing one of more of Nos. 3306-3307c, UX304.

3308 33c **Ayn Rand,** *Apr. 22,* New York NY *(123,660)* 2.50
3309 33c **Cinco de Mayo,** *Apr. 27,* San Antonio TX *(20,904)* 1.25
3310-3313 33c **Tropical Flowers,** *May 1,* Honolulu HI 3.25
3310-3313, any single 1.25

First day cancellation was applied to 311,495 covers bearing one of more of Nos. 3310-3313, 3313a, 3313b.

3314 33c **Bartram,** *May 18,* Philadelphia PA *(110,381)* 1.25
3315 33c **Prostate Cancer Awareness,** *July 22,* Austin TX *(113,299)* 1.25
3316 33c **California Gold Rush,** *June 18,* Sacramento CA *(123,648)* 1.25
3317-3320 33c **Aquarium Fish,** *June 24,* Anaheim CA 3.25
3317-3320, any single 1.25

First day cancellation was applied to 301,719 covers bearing one of more of Nos. 3317-3320, 3320a-3320c.

3321-3324 33c **Extreme Sports,** *June 25,* San Francisco CA 3.00
3321-3324, any single 1.25

First day cancellation was applied to 278,068 covers bearing one of more of Nos. 3321-3324, 3324a.

3328a 33c **American Glass,** *June 29,* Corning NY 3.00
3325-3328, any single 1.25

First day cancellation was applied to 272,792 covers bearing one of more of Nos. 3325-3328, 3328a.

3329 33c **James Cagney,** *July 22,* Burbank CA *(135,867)* 2.50
3330 55c **"Billy" Mitchell,** *July 30,* Milwaukee WI 1.50

First day cancellation was applied to 42,144 covers bearing one of more of Nos. 3330, C134.

3331 33c **Honoring Those Who Served,** *Aug. 16,* Kansas City MO *(130,306)* 2.00
3332 45c **Universal Postal Union,** *Aug. 25,* Beijing, China (20,371) 1.25
3337a 33c **Famous Trains,** *Aug. 26,* Cleveland, OH 3.75
Any other city 3.75
#3333-3337, any single, Cleveland, OH 1.50
#3333-3337, any single, any other city 1.50

First day cancellation was applied to 518,446 covers bearing one of more of Nos. 3333-3337, 3337a, UX307-UX311a.

3338 33c **Frederick Law Olmsted,** *Sept. 12,* Boston, MA (109,735) 1.25
3344a 33c **Hollywood Composers,** *Sept. 16,* Los Angeles, CA 3.75
#3339-3344, any single, Los Angeles, CA 1.25

First day cancellation was applied to 287,407 covers bearing one of more of Nos. 3339-3344, 3344a.

3350a 33c **Broadway Songwriters,** *Sept. 21,* New York, NY 3.75
#3345-3350, any single, New York, NY 1.25

First day cancellation was applied to 284,840 covers bearing one of more of Nos. 3345-3350, 3350a.

3351 33c **Insects & Spiders,** *Oct. 1,* Indianapolis, IN 10.00
#3351a-3351t, any single 1.25

First day cancellation was applied to 773,590 covers bearing one of more of Nos. 3351-3351t.

3352 33c **Hanukkah,** *Oct. 8,* Washington, DC 1.50
3353 22c **Uncle Sam perforated coil,** *Oct. 8,* Washington, DC 1.25

First day cancellation was applied to 44,534 covers bearing one of more of Nos. 3352-3353, O157.

3354 33c **NATO,** *Oct. 13,* Brussels, Belgium *(110,415)* 1.50
3355 33c **Christmas Madonna,** *Oct. 20,* Washington, DC *(110,460)* 1.25
3356-3359 33c **Christmas Deer, narrow frame (sheet),** *Oct. 20,* Rudolph, WI 3.00
3356-3359, any single 1.25
3360-3363 33c **Christmas Deer, thick frame (booklet),** *Oct. 20,* Rudolph, WI 3.00
3360-3363, any single 1.25
3364-3367 33c **Christmas Deer, smaller size (booklet),** *Oct. 20,* Rudolph, WI 3.00
3364-3367, any single 1.25

First day cancellation was applied to 239,350 covers bearing one of more of Nos. 3356-3367, 3359a, 3363a, 3367a-3367c.

3368 33c **Kwanzaa,** *Oct. 29,* Los Angeles, CA *(20,493)* 1.75
3369 33c **Year 2000,** *Dec. 27,* Washington, DC *(145,928)* 1.25

2000

3370 33c **Chinese New Year,** *Jan. 6,* San Francisco, CA *(155,586)* 2.00
3371 33c **Patricia Roberts Harris,** *Jan. 27,* Washington, DC *(82,211)* 1.75
3372 33c **Los Angeles Class Submarine,** with microprinting, *Mar. 27,* Groton, CT 1.50
3373 22c **S Class Submarine,** *Mar. 27,* Groton, CT 1.50
3374 33c **Los Angeles Class Submarine,** no microprinting, *Mar. 27,* Groton, CT 1.50
3375 55c **Ohio Class Submarine,** *Mar. 27,* Groton, CT 1.75
3376 60c **USS Holland,** *Mar. 27,* Groton, CT 1.75
3377 $3.20 **Gato Class Submarine,** *Mar. 27,* Groton, CT 6.00
3377a, Booklet pane of 5, #3373-3377, either selvage 11.00

First day cancellation was applied to 265,226 covers bearing one of more of Nos. 3372-3377, 3377a.

3378 33c **Pacific Coast Rain Forest Pane of 10,** *Mar. 29,* Seattle, WA 6.75
3378a-3378j, any single 1.25

First day cancellation was applied to 435,549 covers bearing one of more of Nos. 3378-3378j.

3383a 33c **Louise Nevelson,** *Apr. 6,* New York, NY 3.25
3379-3383, any single 1.25

First day cancellation was applied to 389,200 covers bearing one of more of Nos. 3379-3383, 3383a.

3388a 33c **Hubble Space Telescope,** *Apr. 10,* Greenbelt, MD 3.25
3384-3388, any single 1.25

First day cancellation was applied to 411,449 covers bearing one of more of Nos. 3384-3388, 3388a.

3389 33c **American Samoa,** *Apr. 17,* Pago Pago, AS *(107,346_* 1.25
3390 33c **Library of Congress,** *Apr. 24,* Washington, DC *(115,679)* 1.50
3391a 33c **Road Runner & Wile E. Coyote,** *Apr. 26,* Phoenix, AZ 1.50

First day cancellation was applied to 154,903 covers bearing one of more of Nos. 3391-3392, 3391a-3391c, 3392a-3392c.

3396a 33c **Distinguished Soldiers,** *May 3,* Washington, DC 3.25
Any other city 3.25
3393-3396, any single, Washington, DC 1.75
Any other city 1.50

First day cancellation was applied to 322,278 covers bearing one of more of Nos. 3393-3396, 3396a.

3397 33c **Summer Sports,** *May 5,* Spokane, WA *(110,768)* 1.25
3398 33c **Adoption,** *May 10,* Beverly Hills, CA 1.25

First day cancellation was applied to 137,903 covers bearing one of more of Nos. 3398, UX315.

3402a 33c **Youth Team Sports,** *May 27,* Lake Buena Vista, FL 3.25
3399-3402, any single 1.25

First day cancellation was applied to 309,349 covers bearing one of more of Nos. 3399-3402, 3402a.

3403 33c **The Stars and Stripes, pane of 20,** *June 14,* Baltimore, MD 10.00
3403a-3403t, any single 1.25

First day cancellation was applied to 1,121,071 covers bearing one of more of Nos. 3403-3403t.

3404-3407 33c **Berries,** die cut 8½ horiz., *June 16,* Buffalo, NY 3.25
3404-3407, any single 1.25

First day cancellation was applied to 35,671 covers bearing one of more of Nos. 3404-3407, 3407a.

3408 33c **Legends of Baseball, pane of 20,** *July 6,* Atlanta, GA 10.00
3408a-3708t, any single 1.75

First day cancellation was applied to 1,214,413 covers bearing one of more of Nos. 3408-3408t.

3409 60c **Probing the Vastness of Space,** *July 10,* Anaheim, CA 6.00
3409a-3409f, any single 1.50

First day cancellation was applied to 296,252 covers bearing one of more of Nos. 3409-3409f.

3410 $1 **Exploring the Solar System,** *July 11,* Anaheim, CA 9.00
3410a-3410e, any single 2.00

First day cancellation was applied to 49,500 covers bearing one of more of Nos. 3410-3410e.

3411 $3.20 **Escaping the Gravity of Earth,** *July 9,* Anaheim, CA 9.50
3411a-3411b, any single 3.75

First day cancellation was applied to 22,321 covers bearing one of more of Nos. 3411-3411b.

3412 $11.75 **Space Achievement and Exploration,** *July 7,* Anaheim, CA *(12,070)* 17.50
3413 $11.75 **Landing on the Moon,** *July 8,* Anaheim, CA *(11,639)* 17.50
3414-3417 33c **Stampin' The Future,** *July 13,* Anaheim, CA 3.25
3414-3417, any single 1.25

First day cancellation was applied to 294,434 covers bearing one of more of Nos. 3414-3417, 3417a.

DISTINGUISHED AMERICANS ISSUE 2000-2009

3420 10c **Joseph W. Stilwell,** *Aug. 24,* Providence, RI *(21,669)* 1.50
3422 23c **Wilma Rudolph, litho. & engr.** *July 14, 2004,* Sacramento, CA 1.25
3426 33c **Claude Pepper,** *Sept. 7,* Washington, DC *(60,689)* 1.25
3427 58c **Margaret Chase Smith,** *June 13, 2007,* Washington, DC 2.40
3427A 59c **James A. Michener,** *May 12, 2008,* Washington, DC 2.40
3428 63c **Dr. Jonas Salk,** *Mar. 8,* Washington, DC 2.50
Any other city 2.50
3430 75c **Harriet Beecher Stowe,** *June 13, 2007* Washington, DC 2.75
3431 76c **Hattie Caraway,** *Feb. 21, 2001,* Little Rock, AR 1.75
3432A 76c **Edward Trudeau,** *May 12, 2008,* Washington, DC 2.75
3432B 78c **Mary Lasker,** *May 15, 2009,* Washington, DC 2.75
3433 83c **Edna Ferber,** *July 29, 2002,* Appleton, WI 1.75
3435 87c **Dr. Albert Sabin,** *Mar. 8,* Washington, DC 3.00
Any other city 3.00
3436 23c **Wilma Rudolph, litho. booklet stamp** *July 14, 2004,* Sacramento, CA 1.25
3438 33c **California Statehood,** *Sept. 8,* Sacramento, CA *(119,729)* 1.25
3443a 33c **Deep Sea Creatures,** *Oct. 2,* Monterey, CA 3.75
#3439-3443, any single 1.25

First day cancellation was applied to 385,406 covers bearing one of more of Nos. 3439-3443, 3443a.

3444 33c **Thomas Wolfe,** *Oct. 3,* Asheville, NC *(112,293)* 1.25
3445 33c **White House,** *Oct. 18,* Washington, DC *(135,844)* 1.25
3446 33c **Edward G. Robinson,** *Oct. 24,* Los Angeles, CA *(120,125)* 2.00
3447 (10c) **New York Public Library Lion,** *Nov. 9,* New York, NY *(18,477)* 1.25
3448 (34c) **Flag Over Farm, perf,** *Dec. 15,* Washington, DC 1.25
3449 (34c) **Flag Over Farm, litho. self-adhesive,** *Dec. 15,* Washington, DC 1.25
3450 (34c) **Flag Over Farm, photo. self-adhesive,** *Dec. 15,* Washington, DC 1.25
3451 (34c) **Statue of Liberty, booklet stamp,** *Dec. 15,* Washington, DC 1.25
3452 (34c) **Statue of Liberty perforated coil,** *Dec. 15,* Washington, DC 1.25
3453 (34c) **Statue of Liberty self-adhesive coil,** *Dec. 15,* Washington, DC 1.25
3454-3457 (34c) **Flowers, booklet stamps die cut 10¼x10¾,** *Dec. 15,* Washington, DC 3.25
3454-3457, any single 1.25
3458-3461 (34c) **Flowers, booklet stamps die cut 11½x11¾,** *Dec. 15,* Washington, DC 3.25
3458-3461, any single 1.25
3462-3465 (34c) **Flowers, coil stamps,** *Dec. 15,* Washington, DC 3.25
3462-3465, any single 1.25

First day cancellation was applied to 178,635 covers bearing one of more of Nos. 3448-3465, 3450a, 3451a-3451d, 3457a-3457e, 3461a-3461c, 3465a.

2001

3466 34c **Statue of Liberty coil (rounded corners),** *Jan. 7,* Washington, DC 1.25
3467 21c **American Buffalo, perforated sheet stamp,** *Sept. 20,* Washington, DC 1.25
3468 21c **American Buffalo, perforated sheet stamp,** *Feb. 22,* Wall, SD 1.25
3468A 23c **George Washington, sheet stamp,** *Sept. 20,* Washington, DC 1.25
3469 34c **Flag Over Farm, perforated sheet stamp,** *Feb. 7,* New York, NY 1.25
3470 34c **Flag Over Farm, self-adhesive sheet stamp,** *Mar. 6,* Lincoln, NE 1.25
3471 55c **Eagle,** *Feb. 22,* Wall, SD 1.50
3471A 57c **Eagle,** *Sept. 20,* Washington, DC 1.50
3472 $3.50 **Capitol Dome,** *Jan. 29,* Washington, DC 6.25
3473 $12.25 **Washington Monument,** *Jan. 29,* Washington, DC 15.00
3475 21c **American Buffalo coil stamp,** *Feb. 22,* Wall, SD 1.25
3475A 23c **George Washington, coil stamp,** *Sept. 20,* Washington, DC 1.25
3476 34c **Statue of Liberty, perforated coil stamp,** *Feb. 7,* New York, NY 1.25
3477 34c **Statue of Liberty coil stamp (right angle corners),** *Feb. 7,* New York, NY 1.25
3478-3481 34c **Flower coil stamps,** *Feb. 7,* New York, NY 3.25
3478-3481, any single 1.25

Serpentine Die Cut 11¼

3482 20c **George Washington booklet stamp,** *Feb. 22,* Wall, SD 1.25

Serpentine Die Cut 10½x11¼

3483 21c **George Washington booklet stamp,** *Feb. 22,* Wall, SD 1.25
3484 21c **American Buffalo, booklet stamp, serp. die cut 11¼,** *Sept. 20,* Washington, DC 1.25
3484A 21c **American Buffalo, booklet stamp, serp. die cut 10½x11¼,** *Sept. 20,* Washington, DC *1.25*
3485 34c **Statue of Liberty booklet stamp,** *Feb. 7,* New York, NY 1.25
3487-3490 34c **Flower booklet stamps,** *Feb. 7,* New York, NY 3.25
3487-3490, any single 1.25
3491-3492 34c **Apple & Orange booklet stamps,** *Feb. 7,* Lincoln, NE 2.25
3491-3492, any single 1.25
3495 34c **Flag Over Farm, booklet stamp,** *Dec. 17,* Washington, DC 1.25
3496 (34c) **Love Letter,** *Jan. 19,* Tucson, AZ 1.25
3497 34c **Love Letters,** *Feb. 14,* Lovejoy, GA 1.25

Serpentine Die Cut 11½x10¾

3498 34c **Love Letters, die cut 11½x10¾,** *Feb. 14,* Lovejoy, GA 1.25
3499 55c **Love Letter,** *Feb. 14,* Lovejoy, GA 1.50
3500 34c **Chinese New Year,** *Jan. 20,* Oakland, CA 1.75
3501 34c **Roy Wilkins,** *Jan. 24,* Minneapolis, MN 1.25
3502 34c **American Illustrators pane of 20,** *Feb. 1,* New York, NY 9.50
3502a-3502t, any single 1.25
3503 34c **Diabetes Awareness,** *Mar. 16,* Boston, MA 1.25
3504 34c **Nobel Prize Centenary,** *Mar. 22,* Washington, DC 1.50
3505 **Pan-American Inverts Pane,** *Mar. 29,* New York, NY 6.00
3505a 1c 1.25
3505b 2c 1.25
3505c 4c 1.25
3505d 80c 1.75
3506 34c **Great Plains Prairie Pane of 10,** *Apr. 19,* Lincoln, NE 7.00
3507 34c **Peanuts,** *May 17,* Santa Rosa, CA 1.50
3508 34c **Honoring Veterans,** *May 23,* Washington, DC 2.00
Any other city 1.25
3509 34c **Frida Kahlo,** *June 21,* Phoenix, AZ 1.25
3519a 34c **Legendary Playing Fields,** *June 27,* New York, NY, Boston, MA, Chicago, IL or Detroit, MI 6.50
3510-3519, any single, New York, NY, Boston, MA, Chicago, IL or Detroit, MI 1.50
3520 (10c) **Atlas Statue,** *June 29,* New York, NY 1.25
3521 34c **Leonard Bernstein,** *July 10,* New York, NY 1.25
3522 (15c) **Woody Wagon,** *Aug. 3,* Denver, CO 1.25
3523 34c **Lucille Ball,** *Aug. 6,* Los Angeles, CA 2.50
3527a 34c **Amish Quilts,** *Aug. 9,* Nappanee, IN 3.25
3524-3527, any single 1.25
3531a 34c **Carnivorous Plants,** *Aug. 23,* Des Plaines, IL 3.25
3528-3531, any single 1.25
3532 34c **Eid** *Sept. 1,* Des Plaines, IL 1.25
3533 34c **Enrico Fermi,** *Sept. 29,* Chicago, IL 1.25
3534a 34c **That's All Folks!,** *Oct. 1,* Beverly Hills, CA 1.25

First day cancellation was applied to 151,009 covers bearing one or more of Nos. 3534-3535, 3534a-3534c, 3535a-3535c.

3536 34c **Christmas, Madonna,** *Oct. 10,* Philadelphia, PA 1.25
3537-3540 34c **Christmas, Santas, black inscriptions, large date** *Oct. 10,* Santa Claus, IN 3.25
3537-3540, any single 1.25
3537a-3540a, small date (from booklet) 3.25
3537a-3540a, any single 1.25
3541-3544 34c **Christmas, Santas, green and red inscriptions,** *Oct. 10,* Santa Claus, IN 3.25
3541-3544, any single 1.25
3545 34c **James Madison,** *Oct. 18,* New York, NY 1.25
3546 34c **Thanksgiving,** *Oct. 19,* Dallas, TX 1.25
3547 34c **Hanukkah,** *Oct. 21,* New York, NY 1.25
3548 34c **Kwanzaa,** *Oct. 21,* New York, NY 1.25
3549 34c **United We Stand,** *Oct. 24,* Washington, DC 1.50

First day cancellation was applied to 451,053 covers bearing one or more of Nos. 3549, 3550, 3550A.

3549B 34c **United We Stand,** serpentine die cut 10½x10¾ booklet stamp *Oct. 24,* Washington, DC 1.50

Though No. 3549B was issued in Jan. 2002, first day covers received the Oct. 24, 2001 cancel.

Any other city in NY, NJ, CT, PA or DC metropolitan area 1.50
3550 34c **United We Stand coil, right angle corners,** *Oct. 24,* Washington, DC 1.50
Any other city in NY, NJ, CT, PA or DC metropolitan area 1.50
3550A 34c **United We Stand coil,** rounded corners, *Oct. 24,* Washington, DC 1.50
Any other city in NY, NJ, CT, PA or DC metropolitan area 1.25
3551 57c **Love Letters,** *Nov. 19,* Washington, DC 1.50

2002

3552-3555 34c **Winter Sports,** *Jan. 8,* Park City, UT 3.25
3552-3555, any single 1.25
3556 34c **Mentoring a Child,** *Jan. 10,* Annapolis, MD 1.25
3557 34c **Langston Hughes,** *Feb. 1,* New York, NY 1.25
3558 34c **Happy Birthday,** *Feb. 8,* Riverside, CA 1.25
3559 34c **Chinese New Year,** *Feb. 11,* New York, NY 1.50
3560 34c **U.S. Military Academy Bicent.,** *Mar. 16,* West Point, NY 2.00
3610a 34c **Greetings from America Pane,** *Apr. 4,* New York, NY 32.50
3561-3610, Any single, New York, NY 1.25
3610a, Any other city 32.50
3561-3610, Any single, any other city 1.50
3561-3610, any state capital 2.50
3611 34c **Longleaf Pine Forest Pane of 10,** *Apr. 26,* Tallahassee, FL 7.00
3611a-3611j, any single 1.25
3612 5c **Toleware Coffeepot,** *May 31,* McLean, VA 1.25
3613 3c **Litho. Star sheet stamp,** *June 7,* Washington, DC 1.25
Any other city 1.25
3614 3c **Photo. Star sheet stamp,** *June 7,* Washington, DC 1.25
Any other city 1.25
3615 3c **Star coil stamp,** *June 7,* Washington, DC 1.25
3616 23c **George Washington,** water-activated gum sheet stamp, *June 7,* Washington, DC 1.00
3617 23c **George Washington,** gray green coil stamp, *June 7,* Washington, DC 1.00
3618 23c **George Washington,** booklet stamp, serp. die cut 11¼ on 3 sides, *June 7,* Washington, DC 1.00
3620 (37c) **Flag,** water-activated gum sheet stamp, *June 7,* Washington, DC 1.25
Any other city 1.25
3621 (37c) **Flag,** self-adhesive sheet stamp, serp. die cut 11¼x11, *June 7,* Washington, DC 1.25
Any other city 1.25
3622 (37c) **Flag,** coil stamp, *June 7,* Washington, DC 1.25
Any other city 1.25

3623 (37c) **Flag,** booklet stamp, serp. die cut 11¼ on 2, 3 or 4 sides, *June 7,* Washington, DC 1.25
Any other city 1.25
3624 (37c) **Flag,** booklet stamp, serp. die cut 10½x10¾ on 2 or 3 sides, *June 7,* Washington, DC 1.25
Any other city 1.25
3625 (37c) **Flag,** booklet stamp, serp. die cut 8 on 2, 3 or 4 sides, *June 7,* Washington, DC 1.25
Any other city 1.25
3626-3629 (37c) **Antique Toys,** booklet stamps, *June 7,* Washington, DC 3.25
Any other city 3.25
3626-3629, any single 1.25
3626-3629, any single, any other city 1.25
3629F 37c **Flag,** perf. 11¼, *Nov. 24,* Washington, DC 1.25
3630 37c **Flag,** self-adhesive sheet stamp, serp. die cut 11¼x11, *June 7,* Washington, DC 1.25
Any other city 1.25
3631 37c **Flag,** water-activated gum coil stamp, *June 7,* Washington, DC 1.25
3632 37c **Flag,** self-adhesive coil stamp, serp. die cut 10 vert., *June 7,* Washington, DC 1.25
3632A 37c **Flag coil, lacking star points at top** *Aug. 7, 2003* Columbus, OH —
3633 37c **Flag,** self-adhesive coil stamp, serp. die cut 8½ vert., *June 7,* Washington, DC 1.25
3634 37c **Flag,** self-adhesive booklet stamps, serp. die cut 11 on 3 sides, *June 7,* Washington, DC 1.25
3635 37c **Flag,** booklet stamp, serp. die cut 11¼ on 2, 3 or 4 sides, *June 7,* Washington, DC 1.25
3636 37c **Flag,** booklet stamp, serp. die cut 10½x10¾ on 2 or 3 sides, *June 7,* Washington, DC 1.25
3637 37c **Flag,** booklet stamp, serp. die cut 8 on 2, 3 or 4 sides, *Feb. 4, 2003* Washington, DC 1.25
3638-3641 37c **Antique Toys coil stamps,** *July 26,* Rochester, NY 5.00
3638-3641, any single 1.25
3642-3645 37c **Antique Toys booklet stamps,** *July 26,* Rochester, NY 3.25
3642-3645, any single 1.25

2003

3642a-3645f 37c **Antique Toys,** booklet stamps, serp. die cut 11x11¼ on 2 or 3 sides, *Sept. 3,* Washington, DC 3.25
3642a-3645f, any single 1.25

2002

3646 60c **Coverlet Eagle,** *July 12,* Oak Brook, IL 1.50
3647 $3.85 **Jefferson Memorial,** *July 30,* Washington, DC 7.00
Any other city 7.00
3648 $13.65 **Capitol Dome,** *July 30,* Washington, DC 25.00
Any other city 25.00
3649 37c **Masters of American Photography,** *June 13,* San Diego, CA 10.00
3649a-3649t, any single 1.25
3650 37c **John James Audubon,** *June 27,* Santa Clara, CA 1.25
3651 37c **Harry Houdini,** *July 3,* New York, NY 1.75
3652 37c **Andy Warhol,** *Aug. 9,* Pittsburgh, PA 2.00
3653-3656 37c **Teddy Bears,** *Aug. 15,* Atlantic City, NJ 4.00
3653-3656, any single 1.25
3657 37c **Love,** *Aug. 16,* Atlantic City, NJ 1.25
3658 60c **Love,** *Aug. 16,* Atlantic City, NJ 1.50
3659 37c **Ogden Nash,** *Aug. 19,* Baltimore, MD 1.25
3660 37c **Duke Kahanamoku,** *Aug. 24,* Honolulu, HI 1.25
3661-3664 37c **American Bats,** *Sept. 13,* Austin, TX 3.25
3661-3664, any single 1.25
3665-3668 37c **Women in Journalism,** *Sept. 14,* Fort Worth, TX 3.25
3665-3668, any single 1.25
3669 37c **Irving Berlin,** *Sept. 15,* New York, NY 1.25
3670-3671 37c **Neuter and Spay,** *Sept. 20,* Washington, DC 2.25
Any other city 2.25
3670-3671, either single, Washington, DC 1.25
3670-3671, either single, any other city 1.25
3672 37c **Hanukkah,** *Oct. 10,* Washington, DC 1.25
3673 37c **Kwanzaa,** *Oct. 10,* Washington, DC 1.25
3674 37c **Eid,** *Oct. 10,* Washington, DC 1.25
3675 37c **Christmas Madonna,** design size 19x27mm, *Oct. 10,* Chicago, IL 1.25
3676-3679 37c **Christmas Snowmen,** serp. die cut 11 (sheet stamps), *Oct. 28,* Houghton, MI 3.25
3676-3679, any single 1.25
3680-3683 37c **Christmas Snowmen,** serp. die cut 8½ vert. (coil stamps), *Oct. 28,* Houghton, MI 3.25
3680-3683, any single 1.25
3684-3687 37c **Christmas Snowmen,** serp. die cut 10¾x11 on 2 or 3 sides (large booklet stamps), *Oct. 28,* Houghton, MI 3.25
3684-3687, any single 1.25
3688-3691 37c **Christmas Snowmen,** serp. die cut 11 on 2 or 3 sides (small booklet stamps), *Oct. 28,* Houghton, MI 3.25
3688-3691, any single 1.25
3692 37c **Cary Grant,** *Oct. 15,* Los Angeles, CA 2.00
3693 (5c) **Sea Coast,** *Oct. 21,* Washington, DC 1.25
3694 37c **Hawaiian Missionary Stamps sheet,** *Oct. 24,* New York, NY 4.00
3694a-3694d, any single 1.25
3695 37c **Happy Birthday,** *Oct. 25,* New York, NY 1.25
3745a 37c **Greetings From America,** *Oct. 25,* New York, NY 35.00
3696-3745, any single 1.25
3696-3745, any state capital 1.50

2003

3746 37c **Thurgood Marshall,** *Jan. 7,* Washington, DC 1.25
3747 37c **Chinese New Year,** *Jan. 15,* Chicago, IL 1.50
3748 37c **Zora Neale Hurston,** *Jan. 24,* Eatonville, FL 1.25

American Design Series 2003-14

3749 1c **Tiffany Lamp,** *Mar. 16, 2007,* New York, NY 2.00
3749A 1c **Tiffany Lamp,** *Mar. 7, 2008,* New York, NY 2.00
3750 2c **Navajo Necklace,** *Aug. 20, 2004,* Indianapolis, IN 1.25
3751 2c **Navajo Necklace,** photo., serpentine die cut 11¼x11½, *Dec. 8, 2005,* Washington, DC 2.00
Any other city 2.00
3752 2c **Navajo Necklace,** litho., serpentine die cut 11¼x11, *Dec. 8, 2005,* Washington, DC 2.00
Any other city 2.00
3753 2c **Navajo Necklace,** litho., serpentine die cut 11¼x10¾, microprinting at left, *May 12, 2007,* Washington, DC 2.00
3754 3c **Silver Coffeepot,** *Mar. 16, 2007,* New York, NY 2.00
3755 4c **Chippendale Chair,** *Mar. 5, 2004,* New York, NY 1.25
3756 5c **Toleware, serpentine die cut 11¼x11¾,** *June 25, 2004,* Santa Clara, CA 1.25
3757 10c **American Clock,** *Jan. 24, 2003,* Tucson, AZ 1.25
3758 1c **Tiffany Lamp Coil,** *Mar. 1, 2003,* Biloxi, MS 1.25
3758A 1c **Tiffany Lamp,** litho. coil stamp, *June 7, 2008,* McLean, VA 2.10
3758B 2c **Navajo Necklace coil,** *Feb. 12, 2011,* Charleston, SC 2.10
3759 3c **Silver Coffeepot Coil,** *Sept. 16, 2005,* Milwaukee, WI 2.00
3761 4c **Chippendale Chair coil,** *July 19, 2007,* Washington, DC 2.00
3761A 4c **Chippendale Chair coil,** dated "2013" at UL, *Jan. 2,* Kansas City, MO 2.25
3762 10c **American Clock Coil,** *Aug. 4, 2006,* Independence, OH 2.00
3763 10c **American Clock coil,** litho., *July 15, 2008,* Washington, DC 2.00

American Culture Series

3766 $1 **Wisdom,** *Feb. 28,* Biloxi, MS 2.50
3769 (10c) **New York Public Library Lion,** perf. 10 vert., *Feb. 4,* Washington, DC 1.25
3771 80c **Special Olympics,** *Feb. 13,* Chicago, IL 1.75
3772 37c **American Filmmaking: Behind the Scenes Pane of 10,** *Feb. 25,* Beverly Hills, CA 7.25
3772a-3772j, any single 1.25
3773 37c **Ohio Statehood Bicentennial,** *Mar. 1,* Chillicothe, OH 1.25
3774 37c **Pelican Island National Wildlife Refuge, Cent.,** *Mar. 14,* Sebastian, FL 1.25
3775 (5c) **Sea Coast,** perf. 9¾ vert. *Mar. 19,* Washington, DC 1.25
3776-3780 37c **Old Glory,** *Apr. 3,* New York, NY 4.00
3776-3780, any single 1.25
3781 37c **Cesar E. Chavez,** *Apr. 23,* Los Angeles, CA 1.25
3782 37c **Louisiana Purchase, Bicent.,** *Apr. 30,* New Orleans, LA 1.25
3783 37c **First Flight,** *May 22,* Dayton, OH or Kill Devil Hills, NC 1.25
3784 37c **Purple Heart,** *May 30,* Mount Vernon, VA 1.50
3784A 37c **Purple Heart, serpentine die cut 10¾x10¼,** *Aug. 1,* Somerset, NJ —
3786 37c **Audrey Hepburn,** *June 11,* Los Angeles, CA 2.00
3787-3791 37c **Southeastern Lighthouses,** *June 13,* Tybee Island, GA 4.00
3787, 3788a, 3789-3791, Tybee Island, GA 4.00
3787-3791, 3788a, any single 1.50
3792-3801 (25c) **Eagle coils,** *June 26,* Santa Clara, CA 6.00
3792-3801, any single 1.25
3792a-3801b (25c) **Eagle coil dated "2005",** *Aug. 5,* Grand Rapids, MI 6.00
3792a-3801b, any single 1.25
3802 37c **Arctic Tundra,** *July 2,* Fairbanks, AK 7.50
3802a-3802j, any single 1.25
3803 37c **Korean War Veterans Memorial,** *July 27,* Washington, DC 2.50
3804-3807 37c **Mary Cassatt booklet stamps,** *Aug. 7,* Columbus, OH 3.25
3804-3807, any single 1.25
3808-3811 37c **Early Football Heroes,** *Aug. 8,* South Bend, IN 3.25
3808-3811, any single 1.25
3812 37c **Roy Acuff,** *Sept. 13,* Nashville, TN 1.25
3813 37c **District of Columbia,** *Sept. 23,* Washington, DC 1.25
3814-3818 37c **Reptiles and Amphibians,** *Oct. 7,* San Diego, CA 4.00
3814-3818, any single, San Diego, CA 1.25
3820 37c **Christmas Madonna,** design size 19½x28mm, *Oct. 23,* New York, NY 1.25
3821-3824 37c **Christmas Music Makers (sheet stamps),** serp. die cut 11x11¼, *Oct. 23,* New York, NY 3.25
3821-3824, any single 1.25
3825-3828 37c **Christmas Music Makers (vending machine booklet stamps),** serp. die cut 11¾x11 on 3 sides, *Oct. 23,* New York, NY 3.25
3825-3828, any single 1.25
3829 37c **Snowy Egret coil,** *Oct. 24,* New York, NY 1.25

2004

3830 37c **Snowy Egret booklet stamp,** *Jan. 30,* Norfolk, VA 1.25
3831 37c **Pacific Coral Reef,** *Jan. 2,* Honolulu, HI 7.50
3831a-3831j, any single 1.25
3832 37c **Chinese New Year,** *Jan. 13,* San Francisco, CA 1.50
3833 37c **Love Candy Hearts,** *Jan. 14,* Revere, MA 1.25
3834 37c **Paul Robeson,** *Jan. 20,* Princeton, NJ 1.25
3835 37c **Theodor Seuss Geisel (Dr. Seuss),** *Mar. 2,* La Jolla, CA 1.25
3836 37c **Flowers,** *Mar. 4,* New York, NY 1.25
3837 60c **Flowers,** *Mar. 4,* New York, NY 1.50
3838 37c **U.S. Air Force Academy,** *Apr. 1,* Colorado Springs, CO 2.00
3839 37c **Henry Mancini,** *Apr. 13,* Los Angeles, CA 1.25
3840-3843 37c **American Choreographers,** *May 4,* Newark, NJ 3.25
3840-3843, any single 1.25
3844-3853 (25c) **Eagle coils,** perf. 9¾ vert. *May 12,* Washington, DC 6.00
3844-3853, any single 1.25
3854 37c **Lewis & Clark,** *May 14,* Astoria, OR 1.75
Atchison, KS 1.75
Great Falls, MT 1.75
Hartford, IL 1.75
Ilwaco, WA 1.75
Orofino, ID 1.75
Omaha, NE 1.75
Pierre, SD 1.75
Sioux City, IA 1.75
St. Charles, MO 1.75
Washburn, ND 1.75
3855-3856 37c **Lewis & Clark booklet stamps,** *May 14,* Astoria, OR 2.75
Atchison, KS 2.75
Great Falls, MT 2.75
Hartford, IL 2.75
Ilwaco, WA 2.75
Orofino, ID 2.75
Omaha, NE 2.75
Pierre, SD 2.75
Sioux City, IA 2.75
St. Charles, MO 2.75
Washburn, ND 2.75
3855-3856, any single, any of the aforementioned 11 cities 1.40
3857-3861 37c **Isamu Noguchi,** *May 18,* Long Island City, NY 4.00
3857-3861, any single 1.25
3862 37c **National World War II Memorial,** *May 29,* Washington, DC 2.00
Any other city 2.00
3863 37c **Summer Olympics,** *June 9,* Philadelphia, PA 1.25

3864 (5c) **Sea Coast coil with black 2004 date,** *June 11,* Washington, DC 1.25
3865-3868 37c **Disney Characters,** *June 23,* Anaheim, CA 3.25
3865-3868, any single 1.25
3869 37c **U.S.S. Constellation,** *June 30,* Baltimore, MD 1.25
3870 37c **R. Buckminster Fuller,** *July 12,* Stanford, CA 1.25
3871 37c **James Baldwin,** *July 23,* New York, NY 1.25
3872 37c **Martin Johnson Heade,** *Aug. 12,* Sacramento, CA 1.25
3873 37c **Art of the American Indian pane of 10,** *Aug. 21,* Santa Fe, NM 7.00
3873a-3873j, any single, Santa Fe, NM 1.25
3876 37c **John Wayne,** *Sept. 9,* Los Angeles, CA 2.50
3877 37c **Sickle Cell Disease,** *Sept. 29,* Atlanta, GA 1.25
3878 37c **Cloudscapes,** *Oct. 4,* Milton, MA 9.00
3878a-3878o any single 1.25
3879 37c **Christmas Madonna,** *Oct. 14,* New York, NY 1.25
3880 37c **Hanukkah,** *Oct. 15,* New York, NY 1.25
3881 37c **Kwanzaa,** *Oct. 16,* Chicago, IL 1.25
3882 37c **Moss Hart,** *Oct. 25,* New York, NY 1.25
3883-3886 37c **Christmas Santa Ornaments,** serpentine die cut 11½x11, *Nov. 16,* New York, NY 3.25
3883-3886, any single 1.25
3887-3890 37c **Christmas Santa Ornaments,** serpentine die cut 10¼x10¾ on 2 or 3 sides, *Nov. 16,* New York, NY 3.25
3887-3890, any single 1.25
3891-3894 37c **Christmas Santa Ornaments,** serpentine die cut 8 on 2, 3 or 4 sides, *Nov. 16,* New York, NY 3.25
3891-3894, any single 1.25

2005

3895 37c **Chinese New Year double-sided pane,** *Jan. 6,* Honolulu, HI 20.00
3895a-3895l, any single 1.25
3896 37c **Marian Anderson,** *Jan. 27,* Washington, DC 1.25
3897 37c **Ronald Reagan,** *Feb. 9,* Simi Valley, CA 2.00
Any other city 1.50
3898 37c **Love,** *Feb. 18,* Atlanta, GA 1.25
3899 37c **Northeast Deciduous Forest,** *Mar. 3,* New York, NY 7.50
3899a-3899j, any single 1.25
3900-3903 37c **Spring Flowers,** *Mar. 15,* Chicago, IL 3.25
3900-3903, any single 1.25
3904 37c **Robert Penn Warren,** *Apr. 22,* Guthrie, KY 1.25
3905 37c **Yip Harburg,** *Apr. 28,* New York, NY 1.25
3906-3909 37c **American Scientists,** *May 4,* New Haven, CT 3.25
3906-3909, any single 1.25
3910 37c **Modern American Architecture,** *May 19,* Las Vegas NV 9.00
Any other city 9.00
3910a-3910l, any single, Las Vegas, NV 1.25
3910a-3910l, any single, any other city 1.25
3911 37c **Henry Fonda,** *May 20,* Los Angeles, CA 1.50
3912-3915 37c **Disney Characters,** *June 30,* Anaheim, CA 3.25
3912-3915, any single 1.50
3916-3925 37c **Advances in Aviation,** *July 29,* Oshkosh, WI 7.50
3916-3925, Vienna, VA 7.50
3916-3925, any single, Oshkosh, WI 1.50
3916-3925, any single, Vienna, VA 1.50
3926-3929 37c **Rio Grande Blankets,** *July 30,* Santa Fe, NM 3.25
3926-3929, any single 1.25
3930 37c **Presidential Libraries Act, 50th Anniv.,** *Aug. 4,* Grand Rapids, MI 1.25
Abilene, KS 1.50
Ann Arbor, MI 1.25
Atlanta, GA 1.25
Austin, TX 1.25
Boston, MA 1.50
College Station, TX 1.25
Hyde Park, NY 1.25
Independence, MO 1.50
Little Rock, AR 1.25
Simi Valley, CA 1.50
West Branch, IA 1.25
Yorba Linda, CA 1.25
3931-3935 37c **Sporty Cars of the 1950s,** *Aug. 20,* Detroit, MI 6.00
3931-3935, any single 2.00
3936 37c **Arthur Ashe,** *Aug. 27,* Flushing, NY 2.00
3937 37c **To Form a More Perfect Union pane of 10,** *Aug. 30,* Washington, DC 8.75
Greensboro, NC 8.75
Jackson, MS 8.75
Little Rock, AR 8.75
Memphis, TN 8.75
Montgomery, AL 8.75
Selma, AL 8.75
Topeka, KS 8.75
Any other city 8.75
3937a-3937j, any single, Washington, DC 2.00
3937a-3937j, any single, Greensboro, NC 2.00
3937a-3937j, any single, Jackson, MS 2.00
3937a-3937j, any single, Little Rock, AR 2.00
3937a-3937j, any single, Memphis, TN 2.00
3937a-3937j, any single, Montgomery, AL 2.00
3937a-3937j, any single, Selma, AL 2.00
3937a-3937j, any single, Topeka, KS 2.00
3937a-3937j, any single, any other city 2.00
3938 37c **Child Health,** *Sept. 7,* Philadelphia, PA 2.00
Any other city 2.00
3939-3942 37c **Let's Dance,** *Sept. 17,* New York, NY 4.25
Miami, FL 4.25
3939-3942, any single, New York, NY 2.00
3939-3942, any single, Miami, FL 2.00
3943 37c **Greta Garbo,** *Sept. 23,* New York, NY 2.25
3944 37c **Jim Henson and the Muppets,** *Sept. 28,* North Hollywood, CA 9.25
3944a-3944k, any single 2.00
3945-3948 37c **Constellations,** *Oct. 3,* Bloomfield Hills, MI 4.25
3945-3948, any single 2.00
3949-3952 37c **Christmas Cookies,** serpentine die cut 10¾x11, *Oct. 20,* New York, NY 4.25
Minneapolis, MN 4.25
3949-3952, any single, New York, NY 2.00
3949-3952, any single, Minneapolis, MN 5.00
3953-3956 37c **Christmas Cookies,** convertible booklet stamps, serpentine die cut 10¾x11 on 2 or 3 sides, *Oct. 20,* New York, NY 4.25
Minneapolis, MN 4.25
3953-3956, any single, New York, NY 2.00
3953-3956, any single, Minneapolis, MN 2.00
3957-3960 37c **Christmas Cookies,** vending machine booklet stamps, serpentine die cut 10½x10¾, *Oct. 20,* New York, NY 4.25
Minneapolis, MN 4.25
3957-3960, any single, New York, NY 2.00
3957-3960, any single, Minneapolis, MN 2.00
3961-3964 37c **Distinguished Marines,** *Nov. 10,* Washington, DC 4.25
Oceanside, CA 4.25
Any other city 4.25
3961-3964, any single, Washington, DC 2.50
3961-3964, any single, Oceanside, CA 2.50
3961-3964, any single, any other city 2.00
3965 (39c) **Flag and Statue of Liberty,** perf. 11¼, *Dec. 8,* Washington, DC 2.00
Any other city 2.00
3966 (39c) **Flag and Statue of Liberty,** self-adhesive, serpentine die cut 11¼x11, *Dec. 8,* Washington, DC 2.00
Any other city 2.00
3967 (39c) **Flag and Statue of Liberty,** coil stamp, perf. 9¾ vert., *Dec. 8,* Washington, DC 2.00
Any other city 2.00
3968 (39c) **Flag and Statue of Liberty,** self-adhesive coil stamp, photo., serpentine die cut 8½ vert., *Dec. 8,* Washington, DC 2.00
Any other city 2.00
3969 (39c) **Flag and Statue of Liberty,** self-adhesive coil stamp, photo., serpentine die cut 10¼ vert., *Dec. 8,* Washington, DC 2.00
Any other city 2.00
3970 (39c) **Flag and Statue of Liberty,** self-adhesive coil stamp, litho., serpentine die cut 9½ vert., *Dec. 8,* Washington, DC 2.00
3972 (39c) **Flag and Statue of Liberty,** self-adhesive booklet stamp with bright blue spot over date, photo., serpentine die cut 11¼x10¾ on 2 or 3 sides, *Dec. 8,* Washington, DC 2.00
Any other city 2.00
3973 (39c) **Flag and Statue of Liberty,** self-adhesive booklet stamp, serpentine die cut 10¼x10¾, *Dec. 8,* Washington, DC 2.00
Any other city 2.00

Although No. 3973 has an issue date of Dec. 8, it was not known to have been available until January 2006.

3974 (39c) **Flag and Statue of Liberty,** self-adhesive booklet stamp with dark blue spot over date, litho., serpentine die cut 11¼x11 on 2 or 3 sides, *Dec. 8,* Washington, DC 2.00
Any other city 2.00
3975 (39c) **Flag and Statue of Liberty,** self-adhesive booklet stamp, photo., serpentine die cut 8 on 2, 3 or 4 sides, *Dec. 8,* Washington, DC 2.00
Any other city 2.00

2006

3976 (39c) **Birds,** self-adhesive booklet stamp, *Jan. 3,* Washington, DC 2.00
Any other city 2.00
3978 39c **Flag and Statue of Liberty,** self-adhesive, *Apr. 8,* Washington, DC 2.00
Any other city 2.00
3979 39c **Flag and Statue of Liberty,** coil stamp, perf. 10 vert. *Mar. 8,* Washington, DC 2.00
Any other city 2.00
3980 39c **Flag and Statue of Liberty,** self-adhesive coil stamp, serpentine die cut 11 vert. with rounded corners, *Jan. 9,* Washington, DC 2.00
Any other city 2.00
3981 39c **Flag and Statue of Liberty,** self-adhesive coil stamp, serpentine die cut 9½ vert., *Apr. 8,* Washington, DC 2.00
Any other city 2.00
3985b 39c **Flag and Statue of Liberty,** photo., serpentine die cut 11.1 on 2 or 3 sides, *Nov. 8,* Washington, DC 2.00
3987-3994 39c **Children's Book Animals,** *Jan. 10,* Findlay, OH 7.50
3987-3994, any single 2.00
3995 39c **2006 Winter Olympics,** *Jan. 11,* Colorado Springs, CO 2.00
3996 39c **Hattie McDaniel,** *Jan. 25,* Beverly Hills, CA 2.00
3997 39c **Chinese New Year pane,** *Jan. 29,* Washington, DC 10.50
3997a-3997l, any single 2.00
3998 39c **Wedding Dove,** *Mar. 1,* New York, NY 2.00
3999 63c **Wedding Dove,** *Mar. 1,* New York, NY 2.50
4000 24c **Common Buckeye Butterfly,** perf. 11¼, *Mar. 8,* Washington, DC 2.00
Any other city 2.00
4001 24c **Common Buckeye Butterfly,** self-adhesive, serpentine die cut 11, *Mar. 8,* Washington, DC 2.00
Any other city 2.00
4001a 24c **Common Buckeye Butterfly,** self-adhesive booklet pane stamp, serpentine die cut 10¾x11¼, *Mar. 8,* Washington, DC 2.00
Any other city 2.00
4002 24c **Common Buckeye Butterfly,** self-adhesive coil stamp, serpentine die cut 8½ horiz., *Mar. 8,* Washington, DC 2.00
Any other city 2.00
4003-4007 39c **Crops of the Americas,** self-adhesive coil stamps, *Mar. 16,* New York, NY 5.25
4003-4007, any single 2.00
4008-4012 39c **Crops of the Americas,** self-adhesive booklet stamps, serpentine die cut 10¾x10½ on 2 or 3 sides, *Mar. 16,* New York, NY 5.25
4008-4012, any single 2.00
4013-4017 39c **Crops of the Americas,** self-adhesive booklet stamps, serpentine die cut 10¾x11¼ on 2 or 3 sides, *Mar. 16,* New York, NY 5.25
4013-4017, any single 2.00
4018 $4.05 **X-Plane,** *Mar. 17,* New York, NY 8.00
Any other city 8.00
4019 $14.40 **X-Plane,** *Mar. 17,* New York, NY 27.50
Any other city 27.50
4020 39c **Sugar Ray Robinson,** *Apr. 7,* New York, NY 2.00
4021-4024 39c **Benjamin Franklin,** *Apr. 7,* Philadelphia, PA 4.50
4021-4024, any single 2.00
4025-4028 39c **Disney Characters,** *Apr. 21,* Orlando, FL 4.50
4025-4028, any single 2.00
4029 39c **Birds,** self-adhesive booklet stamp, *May 1,* Washington, DC 2.00
4030 39c **Katherine Anne Porter,** *May 15,* Kyle, TX 2.00
4031 39c **Amber Alert,** *May 25,* Arlington, TX 2.00
Washington, DC 2.00
4032 39c **Purple Heart,** *May 26,* Washington, DC 2.00
4072a 39c **Wonders of America,** *May 27,* Washington, DC 32.50
4033-4072, any single, Washington, DC 2.00
4072a, any other city 32.50
4033-4072, any single, any other city 2.75

4073 39c **Samuel de Champlain,** self-adhesive stamp, *May 28,* Washington, DC 2.00

Ticonderoga, NY 2.00

Annapolis Royal, Nova Scotia, Canada 2.00

4074 **Samuel de Champlain,** souvenir sheet, *May 28,* Washington, DC 4.75

Ticonderoga, NY 4.75

Annapolis Royal, Nova Scotia, Canada 4.75

4075 **Washington 2006 World Philatelic Exhibition,** souvenir sheet, *May 29,* Washington, DC 16.00

4075a $1 3.25

4075b $2 5.25

4075c $5 10.00

4076 39c **Distinguished American Diplomats,** souvenir sheet, *May 30,* Washington, DC 6.00

4076a-4076f, any single 2.00

4077 39c **Judy Garland,** *June 10,* New York, NY 2.50

4078 39c **Ronald Reagan,** *June 14,* Simi Valley, CA 2.00

4079 39c **Happy Birthday,** *June 23,* Santa Clara, CA 2.00

4080-4083 39c **Baseball Sluggers,** *July 15,* Bronx, NY 4.50

4080-4083, any single 2.50

4084 39c **DC Comics Superheroes,** *July 20,* San Diego, CA 16.00

4084a-4084t, any single 2.00

4085-4088 39c **Motorcycles,** *Aug. 7,* Sturgis, SD 4.50

4085-4088, any single, Sturgis, SD 2.00

4089-4098 39c **Quilts of Gee's Bend,** *Aug. 24,* Chicago, IL 8.00

4089-4098, any single, Chicago, IL 2.00

4099 39c **Southern Florida Wetland,** *Oct. 4,* Naples, FL 9.00

4099a-4099j, any single 2.00

4100 39c **Christmas Madonna,** *Oct. 17,* Denver, CO 2.00

4101-4104 39c **Christmas Snowflakes,** denominations higher than year date, serpentine die cut 11¼x11, *Oct. 5,* New York, NY 4.50

4101-4104, any single 2.00

4105-4108 39c **Christmas Snowflakes,** denominations even with year date, serpentine die cut 11¼x11½ on 2 or 3 sides, *Oct. 5,* New York, NY 4.50

4105-4108, any single 2.00

4109-4112 39c **Christmas Snowflakes,** denominations even with year date, serpentine die cut 11¼x11 on 2 or 3 sides, *Oct. 5,* New York, NY 4.50

4109-4112, any single 2.00

4113-4116 39c **Christmas Snowflakes,** denominations even with year date, serpentine die cut 8 on 2, 3 or 4 sides, *Oct. 5,* New York, NY 4.50

4113-4116, any single 2.00

4117 39c **Eid,** *Oct. 6,* New York, NY 2.00

4118 39c **Hanukkah,** *Oct. 6,* New York, NY 2.00

4119 39c **Kwanzaa,** *Oct. 6,* New York, NY 2.00

2007-09

4120 39c **Ella Fitzgerald,** *Jan. 10,* New York, NY 2.00

4121 39c **Oklahoma Statehood,** *Jan. 11,* Oklahoma City, OK 2.00

4122 39c **Love,** self-adhesive booklet stamp, *Jan. 13,* Hershey, PA 2.00

4123 84c **International Polar Year,** *Feb. 21,* Fairbanks, AK 4.75

4123a-4123b, either single 3.00

4124 39c **Henry Wadsworth Longfellow,** *Mar. 15,* New York, NY 2.00

4125 (41c) **Liberty Bell,** self-adhesive booklet stamp, large microprinting, 16mm bell, serpentine die cut 11¼x10¾, *Apr. 12,* Philadelphia, PA 2.10

4125b (42c) **Forever,** dated "2008," *Aug. 22, 2008,* Falls Church, VA 2.10

4125d (44c) **Forever,** dated "2009," *Aug. 7,* Pittsburgh, PA 2.10

4126 (41c) **Liberty Bell,** self-adhesive booklet stamp, small microprinting, 16mm bell, serpentine die cut 11¼x10¾, *Apr. 12,* Philadelphia, PA 2.10

4126b (42c) **Forever,** dated "2008," *Aug. 22, 2008,* Falls Church, VA 2.10

4126d (44c) **Forever,** dated "2009" in copper *Aug. 7,* Pittsburgh, PA 2.10

4127 (41c) **Liberty Bell,** self-adhesive booklet stamp, medium microprinting, 15mm bell, serpentine die cut 11¼x10¾, *Apr. 12,* Philadelphia, PA 2.10

4127d (42c) **Forever,** dated "2008," *May 12, 2008* Washington, DC 2.10

4127f (42c) **Forever,** small "2008" date, *Oct. 25, 2008,* New York, NY 2.10

4127i (44c) **Forever,** dated "2009" in copper, *May 15, 2009,* Washington, DC 2.10

4128 (41c) **Liberty Bell,** self-adhesive booklet stamp, large microprinting, 16mm bell, serpentine die cut 8, *Apr. 12,* Philadelphia, PA 2.10

4128b (42c) **Forever,** dated "2009," *Feb. 24,* Washington, DC 2.10

4129 (41c) **Flag,** perf. 11¼, *Apr. 12,* Washington, DC 2.10

4130 (41c) **Flag,** self-adhesive, serpentine die cut 11¼x10¾, *Apr. 12,* Washington, DC 2.10

4131 (41c) **Flag,** coil stamp, perf. 9¾ vert., *Apr. 12,* Washington, DC 2.10

4132 (41c) **Flag,** self-adhesive coil stamp, serpentine die cut 9½ vert., *Apr. 12,* Washington, DC 2.10

4133 (41c) **Flag,** self-adhesive coil stamp, serpentine die cut 11 vert., perpendicular corners, *Apr. 12,* Washington, DC 2.10

4134 (41c) **Flag,** self-adhesive coil stamp, serpentine die cut 8½ vert., *Apr. 12,* Washington, DC 2.10

4135 (41c) **Flag,** self-adhesive coil stamp, serpentine die cut 11 vert., rounded corners, *Apr. 12,* Washington, DC 2.10

4136 41c **Settlement of Jamestown,** *May 11,* Jamestown, VA 2.10

4137 26c **Florida Panther,** perf. 11¼x11 *May 12,* Washington, DC 2.10

4138 17c **Bighorn Sheep,** self-adhesive, serpentine die cut 11, *May 14,* Washington, DC 2.10

4139 26c **Florida Panther,** self-adhesive, serpentine die cut 11¼x11, *May 12,* Washington, DC 2.10

4140 17c **Bighorn Sheep,** self-adhesive coil, serpentine die cut 11 vert., *May 21,* Washington, DC 2.10

4141 26c **Florida Panther,** self-adhesive coil, serpentine die cut 11 vert., *May 12,* Washington, DC 2.10

4142 26c **Florida Panther,** self-adhesive booklet stamp, serpentine die cut 11¼x11 on 3 sides, *May 12,* Washington, DC 2.10

4143 39c **Star Wars,** *May 25,* Los Angeles, CA 12.50

4143a-4143o, any single 2.10

4144 $4.60 **Air Force One,** *June 13,* Washington, DC 10.00

4145 $16.25 **Marine One,** *June 13,* Washington, DC 32.50

4146-4150 41c **Pacific Lighthouses,** *June 21,* Westport, WA 5.50

4146-4150, any single 2.10

4151 41c **Wedding Heart,** *June 27,* Washington, DC 2.10

4152 58c **Wedding Heart,** *June 27,* Washington, DC 2.40

4153-4156 41c **Pollination,** type I, *June 29,* Washington, DC 4.50

4153-4156, type I, any single 2.10

4153a-4156a, type II 4.50

4153a-4156a, type II, any single 2.10

4157 (10c) **Patriotic Banner coil,** serpentine die cut 11 vert., *July 4,* Washington, DC 2.00

4158 (10c) **Patriotic Banner coil,** serpentine die cut 11½ vert., *July 4,* Washington, DC 2.00

4159 41c **Marvel Comics Superheroes,** *July 26,* San Diego, CA 17.00

4159a-4159t, any single 2.10

4160-4163 41c **Vintage Mahogany Speedboats,** *Aug. 4,* Clayton, NY 4.50

4160-4163, any single 2.50

4164 41c **Purple Heart,** *Aug. 7,* Washington, DC 2.10

4165 41c **Louis Comfort Tiffany,** *Aug. 9,* Portland, OR 2.10

4166-4175 41c **Flowers,** self-adhesive coil stamps, *Aug. 10,* Portland, OR 8.25

4166-4175, any single 2.10

4176-4185 41c **Flowers,** self-adhesive booklet stamps, *Aug. 10,* Portland, OR 8.25

4176-4185, any single 2.10

4186 41c **Flag,** self-adhesive coil stamp with microprinting on right side of flagpole, serpentine die cut 9½ vert., *Aug. 15,* Washington, DC 2.10

4187 41c **Flag,** self-adhesive coil stamp with microprinting on left side of flagpole, serpentine die cut 9½ vert., *Aug. 15,* Washington, DC 2.10

4188 41c **Flag,** self-adhesive coil stamp with perpendicular corners, serpentine die cut 8½ vert., *Aug. 15,* Washington, DC 2.10

4189 41c **Flag,** self-adhesive coil stamp with rounded corners, serpentine die cut 11 vert., *Aug. 15,* Washington, DC 2.10

4190 41c **Flag,** self-adhesive booklet stamp with microprinting on right side of flagpole, *Aug. 15,* Washington, DC 2.10

4191 41c **Flag,** self-adhesive booklet stamp with microprinting on left side of flagpole, *Aug. 15,* Washington, DC 2.10

4192-4195 41c **Disney Characters,** *Aug. 16,* Orlando, FL 4.50

4192-4195, any single 2.10

4196 41c **Celebrate,** *Aug. 17,* Stamford, CT 2.10

4197 41c **James Stewart,** *Aug. 17,* Universal City, CA 2.50

4198 41c **Alpine Tundra,** *Aug. 28,* Estes Park, CO 8.25

4198a-4198j, any single 2.10

4199 41c **Gerald R. Ford,** *Aug. 31,* Grand Rapids, MI 2.10

Rancho Mirage, CA 2.10

4200 41c **Jury Duty,** *Sept. 12,* New York, NY 2.10

4201 41c **Mendez v. Westminster,** *Sept. 14,* Santa Ana, CA 2.10

4202 41c **Eid,** *Sept. 28,* Washington, DC 2.10

4203-4204 41c **Auroras,** *Oct. 1,* Washington, DC 3.00

4203-4204, any single 2.10

4205 41c **Yoda,** *Oct. 25,* New York, NY 2.10

4206 41c **Christmas Madonna,** *Oct. 25,* New York, NY 2.10

4207-4210 41c **Christmas Knits,** serpentine die cut 10¾, *Oct. 25,* New York, NY 4.50

4207-4210, any single 2.10

4211-4214 41c **Christmas Knits,** serpentine die cut 11¼x11 on 2 or 3 sides, *Oct. 25,* New York, NY 4.50

4211-4214, any single 2.10

4215-4218 41c **Christmas Knits,** serpentine die cut 8 on 2, 3 or 4 sides, *Oct. 25,* New York, NY 4.50

4215-4218, any single 2.10

4219 41c **Hanukkah,** *Oct. 26,* New York, NY 2.10

4220 41c **Kwanzaa,** *Oct. 26,* New York, NY 2.10

2008

4221 41c **Chinese New Year,** *Jan. 9,* San Francisco, CA 2.50

4222 41c **Charles W. Chesnutt,** *Jan. 31,* Cleveland, OH 2.10

4223 41c **Marjorie Kinnan Rawlings,** *Feb. 21,* Hawthorne, FL 2.10

4224-4227 41c **American Scientists,** *Mar. 6,* New York, NY 4.50

4224-4227, any single 2.10

4228-4231 42c **Flags,** coil stamps, perf. 10 vert., *Apr. 18,* Washington, DC 4.75

4228-4231, any single 2.10

4232-4235 42c **Flags,** self-adhesive coil stamps, serpentine die cut 9½ vert., *Apr. 18,* Washington, DC 4.75

4232-4235, any single 2.10

4236-4239 42c **Flags,** self-adhesive coil stamps, serpentine die cut 11 vert. with perpendicular corners, *Apr. 18,* Washington, DC 4.75

4236-4239, any single 2.10

4240-4243 42c **Flags,** self-adhesive coil stamps, serpentine die cut 8½ vert., *Apr. 18,* Washington, DC 4.75

4240-4243, any single 2.10

4244-4247 42c **Flags,** self-adhesive coil stamps, serpentine die cut 11 vert. with rounded corners, *Apr. 18,* Washington, DC 4.75

4244-42471, any single 2.10

4248-4252 42c **American Journalists,** *Apr. 22,* Washington, DC 5.50

4248-4252, any single 2.10

4253-4257 27c **Tropical Fruit,** serpentine die cut 11¼x10¾, *Apr. 25,* Burlingame, CA 4.00

4253-4257, any single 1.75

4258-4262 27c **Tropical Fruit,** self-adhesive coil stamps, serpentine die cut 8½ vert., *Apr. 25,* Burlingame, CA 4.00

4258-4262, any single 1.75

4263 42c **Purple Heart,** perf. 11¼, *Apr. 30,* Washington, DC 2.10

4264 42c **Purple Heart,** self-adhesive, serpentine die cut 11¼x10¾, *Apr. 30,* Washington, DC 2.10

4265 42c **Frank Sinatra,** *May 13,* New York, NY 3.00

Las Vegas, NV 3.00

4266 42c **Minnesota Statehood, 150th Anniv.,** *May 17,* St. Paul, MN 2.10

4267 62c **Dragonfly,** *May 19,* Washington, DC 2.50

No.	Denom.	Description	Value
4268	$4.80	**Mount Rushmore,** *June 6,* McLean, VA	9.75
4269	$16.50	**Hoover Dam,** *June 20,* Washington, DC	33.00
4270	42c	**Love,** *June 10,* Washington, DC	2.10
4271	42c	**Wedding Heart,** *June 10,* Washington, DC	2.10
4272	59c	**Wedding Heart,** *June 10,* Washington, DC	2.40
4273-4282	42c	**Flags of Our Nation,** *June 14,* Washington, DC	8.50
		4273-4282, any single	2.10
4283-4292	42c	**Flags of Our Nation,** *Sept. 2,* Washington, DC	8.50
		4283-4292, any single	2.10
4293-4302	44c	**Flags of Our Nation,** *Aug. 6, 2009* Pittsburgh, PA	9.00
		4293-4302, any single	2.10
4303-4312	44c	**Flags of Our Nation,** *Apr. 16, 2010* New York, NY	9.00
		#4303-4312, any single	2.10
4313-4322	(44c)	**Flags of Our Nation,** *Aug. 11, 2011* Columbus, OH	9.00
		4313-4322, any single	2.10
4323-4332	(45c)	**Flags of Our Nation,** *Aug. 16, 2012* Sacramento, CA	9.00
		4323-4332, any single	2.10
4333	42c	**Charles and Ray Eames,** *June 17,* Santa Monica, CA	13.50
		4333a-4333p, any single	2.10
4334	42c	**Summer Olympics,** *June 19,* Philadelphia, PA	2.10
4335	42c	**Celebrate,** *July 10,* Washington, DC	2.10
4336-4340	42c	**Vintage Black Cinema,** *July 16,* Newark, NJ	5.50
		4336-4340, any single	2.10
4341	42c	**Take Me Out to the Ballgame, Cent.,** *July 16,* Washington, DC	2.50
4342-4345	42c	**Disney Characters,** *Aug. 7,* Anaheim, CA	4.75
		4342-4345, any single	2.10
4346	42c	**Albert Bierstadt,** *Aug. 14,* Hartford, CT	2.10
4347	42c	**Sunflower,** *Aug. 15,* Hartford, CT	2.10
4348	(5c)	**Sea Coast coil with 2008 date,** litho., *Sept. 5,* Washington, DC	2.10
4349	42c	**Latin Jazz,** *Sept. 8,* Washington, DC	2.10
4350	42c	**Bette Davis,** *Sept. 18,* Boston, MA	2.50
4351	42c	**Eid,** *Sept. 23,* Washington, DC	2.10
4352	42c	**Great Lakes Dunes,** *Oct. 2,* Empire, MI	8.50
		4352a-4352j, any single	2.10
4353-4357	42c	**Automobiles of the 1950s,** *Oct. 3,* Carlisle, PA	5.50
		4353-4357, any single	2.10
4358	42c	**Alzheimer's Disease Awareness,** *Oct. 17,* Morgantown, WV	2.10
4359	42c	**Christmas Madonna,** *Oct. 23,* New York, NY	2.10
4360-4363	42c	**Christmas Nutcrackers,** serpentine die cut 10¾x11 on 2 or 3 sides, *Oct. 23,* New York, NY	4.75
		4360-4363, any single	2.10
4364-4367	42c	**Christmas Nutcrackers,** serpentine die cut 11¼x11 on 2 or 3 sides, *Oct. 23,* New York, NY	4.75
		4364-4367, any single	2.10
4368-4371	42c	**Christmas Nutcrackers,** serpentine die cut 8 on 2, 3 or 4 sides, *Oct. 23,* New York, NY	4.75
		4368-4371, any single	2.10
4372	42c	**Hanukkah,** *Oct. 24,* New York, NY	2.10
4373	42c	**Kwanzaa,** *Oct. 24,* New York, NY	2.10

2009

No.	Denom.	Description	Value
4374	42c	**Alaska Statehood,** *Jan. 3,* Anchorage, AK	2.10
4375	42c	**Chinese New Year,** *Jan. 8,* New York, NY	2.50
4376	42c	**Oregon Statehood,** *Jan. 14,* Portland, OR	2.10
4377	42c	**Edgar Allan Poe,** *Jan. 16,* Richmond, VA	2.50
4378	$4.95	**Redwood Forest,** *Jan. 16,* San Diego, CA	10.00
4379	$17.50	**Old Faithful,** *Jan. 16,* San Diego, CA	35.00
4380-4383	42c	**Abraham Lincoln,** *Feb. 9,* Springfield, IL	5.00
		4380-4383, any single	2.50
4384	42c	**Civil Rights Pioneers,** *Feb. 21,* New York, NY	6.25
		4384a-4384f, any single	2.10
4385	(10c)	**Patriotic Banner coil,** perf. 9¾ vert., *Feb. 24,* Washington, DC	2.10
4386	61c	**Richard Wright,** *Apr. 9,* Chicago, IL	2.50
4387	28c	**Polar Bear,** serpentine die cut 11¼x11, *Apr. 16,* New York, NY	2.10
4388	64c	**Dolphin,** *June 12,* Washington, DC	3.00
4389	28c	**Polar Bear coil,** serpentine die cut 8½ vert., *Apr. 16,* New York, NY	2.10
4390	44c	**Purple Heart,** *Apr. 28,* Washington, DC	2.10
4391	44c	**Flag,** coil stamp, perf. 9¾ vert., *May 1,* Washington, DC	2.10
4392	44c	**Flag,** litho. self-adhesive coil stamp, serpentine die cut 11 vert. with perpendicular corners, *May 8,* Washington, DC	2.10
4393	44c	**Flag,** litho. self-adhesive coil stamp, serpentine die cut 9½ vert., *May 8,* Washington, DC	2.10
4394	44c	**Flag,** photo. self-adhesive coil stamp, serpentine die cut 8½ vert., *May 8,* Washington, DC	2.10
4395	44c	**Flag,** photo. self-adhesive coil stamp, serpentine die cut 11 vert. with rounded corners, *May 1,* Washington, DC	2.10
4396	44c	**Flag,** self-adhesive booklet stamp, serpentine die cut 11¼x10¾ on 3 sides, *June 5,* McLean, VA	2.10
4397	44c	**Wedding Rings,** *May 1,* Washington, DC	2.10
4398	61c	**Wedding Cake,** *May 1,* Washington, DC	2.50
4399-4403	44c	**The Simpsons,** *May 7,* Los Angeles, CA	5.75
		4399-4403, any single	2.10
4404-4405	44c	**Love (King and Queen of Hearts),** *May 8,* Washington, DC	3.00
		4404-4405, either single	2.10
4406	44c	**Bob Hope,** *May 29,* San Diego, CA	2.75
4407	44c	**Celebrate,** *June 10,* Washington, DC	2.10
4408	44c	**Anna Julia Cooper,** *June 11,* Washington, DC	2.10
4409-4413	44c	**Gulf Coast Lighthouses,** *July 23,* Biloxi, MS	5.75
		4409-4413, any single	2.10
4414	44c	**Early TV Memories,** *Aug. 11,* North Hollywood, CA	18.00
		4414a-4414t, any single	2.10
4415	44c	**Hawaii Statehood,** *Aug. 21,* Honolulu, HI	2.10
4416	44c	**Eid,** *Sept. 3,* Washington, DC	2.10
4417-4420	44c	**Thanksgiving Day Parade,** *Sept. 9,* New York, NY	4.75
		4417-4420, any single	2.10
4421	44c	**Gary Cooper,** *Sept. 10,* Los Angeles, CA	2.50
4422	44c	**Supreme Court Justices,** *Sept. 22,* Washington, DC	4.75
		4422a-4422d, any single	2.10
4423	44c	**Kelp Forest,** *Oct. 1,* Monterey, CA	9.00
		4423a-4423j, any single	2.10
4424	44c	**Christmas Madonna,** *Oct. 20,* San Simeon, CA	2.10
4425-4428	44c	**Christmas Winter Holidays,** serpentine die cut 10¾x11 on 2 or 3 sides, *Oct. 8,* New York, NY	4.75
		4425-4428, any single	2.10
4429-4432	44c	**Christmas Winter Holidays,** serpentine die cut 8 on 2, 3 or 4 sides, *Oct. 8,* New York, NY	4.75
		4429-4432, any single	2.10
4433	44c	**Hanukkah,** *Oct. 9,* New York, NY	2.10
4434	44c	**Kwanzaa,** *Oct. 9,* New York, NY	2.10

2010

No.	Denom.	Description	Value
4435	44c	**Chinese New Year,** *Jan. 14,* Los Angeles, CA	2.50
4436	44c	**2010 Winter Olympics,** *Jan. 22,* Park City, UT	2.10
4437	(44c)	**Forever,** serpentine die cut 11¼x10¾ on 2, 3, or 4 sides, medium microprinting, bell 16mm wide, dated "2009" in copper, *Feb. 3,* Washington, DC	2.10
4438	$4.90	**Mackinac Bridge,** *Feb. 3,* Mackinaw City, MI	10.00
4439	$18.30	**Bixby Creek Bridge,** *Feb. 3,* Washington, DC	37.50
4440-4443	44c	**Distinguished Sailors,** *Feb. 4,* Washington, DC	4.75
		4440-4443, any single	2.10
4444	44c	**Abstract Impressionists,** *Mar. 11,* Buffalo, NY	9.00
		4444a-4444j, any single	2.10
4445	44c	**Bill Mauldin,** *Mar. 31,* Santa Fe, NM	3.00
4446-4449	44c	**Cowboys of the Silver Screen,** *Apr. 17,* Oklahoma City, OK	4.75
		#4446-4449, any single	2.10
4450	44c	**Love,** *Apr. 22,* Kansas City, MO	2.10
4451-4460	44c	**Animal Rescue,** *Apr. 30,* North Hollywood, CA	9.00
		#4451-4460, any single	2.10
4461	44c	**Katharine Hepburn,** *May 12,* Old Saybrook, CT	2.50
4462	64c	**Monarch Butterfly,** *May 17,* New York, NY	3.00
4463	44c	**Kate Smith,** *May 27,* Washington, DC	2.10
4464	44c	**Oscar Micheaux,** *June 22,* New York, NY	2.10
4465-4466	44c	**Negro Leagues Baseball,** *July 15,* Kansas City, MO	3.00
		4465-4466, either single	2.10
4467-4471	44c	**Sunday Funnies,** *July 16,* Columbus, OH	5.75
		4467-4471, any single	2.10
4472	44c	**Scouting,** *July 27,* Fort A.P. Hill, VA	2.10
4473	44c	**Winslow Homer,** *Aug. 12,* Richmond, VA	2.10
4474	44c	**Hawaiian Rain Forest,** *Sept. 1,* Hawaii National Park, HI	9.00
		4474a-4474j, any single	2.10
4475	44c	**Mother Teresa,** *Sept. 5,* Washington, DC	2.50
4476	44c	**Julia de Burgos,** *Sept. 14,* San Juan, PR	2.10
4477	44c	**Christmas Angel With Lute,** *Oct. 21,* New York, NY	2.10
4478-4481	(44c)	**Christmas Evergreens,** serpentine die cut 11 on 2 or 3 sides, *Oct. 21,* New York, NY	4.75
		4478-4481, any single	2.10
4482-4485	(44c)	**Christmas Evergreens,** serpentine die cut 11¼x10¾ on 2, 3 or 4 sides, *Oct. 21,* New York, NY	4.75
		4482-4485, any single	2.10
4486	(44c)	**Statue of Liberty,** coil stamp, serpentine die cut 9½ vert., *Dec. 1,* Washington, DC	2.10
4487	(44c)	**Flag,** coil stamp, serpentine die cut 9½ vert., *Dec. 1,* Washington, DC	2.10
		4487a, pair	3.00
4488	(44c)	**Statue of Liberty,** coil stamp, serpentine die cut 11 vert., *Dec. 1,* Washington, DC	2.10
4489	(44c)	**Flag,** coil stamp, serpentine die cut 11 vert., *Dec. 1,* Washington, DC	2.10
		4489a, pair	3.00
4490	(44c)	**Statue of Liberty,** coil stamp, serpentine die cut 8½ vert., *Dec. 1,* Washington, DC	2.10
4491	(44c)	**Flag,** coil stamp, serpentine die cut 8½ vert., *Dec. 1,* Washington, DC	2.10
		4491a, pair	3.00

2011

No.	Denom.	Description	Value
4492	(44c)	**Chinese New Year,** *Jan. 22,* Morrow, GA	2.50
4493	(44c)	**Kansas Statehood,** *Jan. 27,* Topeka, KS	2.10
4494	(44c)	**Pres. Ronald Reagan,** *Feb. 10,* Simi Valley, CA	2.10
4495	(5c)	**Art Deco Bird coil,** *Feb. 11,* Charleston, SC	2.10
4496	44c	**Quill and Inkwell coil,** *Feb. 14,* Kansas City, MO	2.10
4497-4501	(44c)	**Latin Music Legends,** *Mar. 16,* Austin, TX	5.75
		4497-4501, any single	2.10
4502	(44c)	**Celebrate,**photo., *Mar. 25,* Cleveland, OH	2.10
4503	(44c)	**Jazz,** *Mar. 26,* New Orleans, LA	2.10
4504	20c	**George Washington,** *Apr. 11,* Washington, DC	2.10
4505-4509	29c	**Herbs,** *Apr. 7,* New York, NY	4.25
		4505-4509, any single	2.10
4510	84c	**Oveta Culp Hobby,** *Apr. 15,* Houston, TX	3.00
4511	$4.95	**New River Gorge Bridge,** *Apr. 11,* Fayetteville, WV	10.00
4512	20c	**George Washington coil stamp,** *Apr. 11,* Washington, DC	2.10
4513-4517	29c	**Herbs coil stamps,** *Apr. 7,* New York, NY	4.25
		4513-4517, any single	2.10
4518	(44c)	**Statue of Liberty booklet stamp,** serpentine die cut 11¼x 11 on 2, 3 or 4 sides, *Apr. 8,* New York, NY	2.10
4519	(44c)	**Flag booklet stamp,** serpentine die cut 11¼x 11 on 2, 3 or 4 sides, *Apr. 8,* New York, NY	2.10
		4519a, pair	3.00
4520	(44c)	**Wedding Roses,** *Apr. 21,* Washington, DC	2.10
4521	64c	**Wedding Cake,** *Apr. 11,* Washington, DC	2.50
4522-4523	(44c)	**Civil War Sesquicentennial,** *Apr. 12,* Charleston, SC	3.00
		4522-4523, any single	2.10
4524	(44c)	**Go Green,** *Apr. 14,* Washington, DC	14.50
		4524a-4524p, any single	2.10
4525	(44c)	**Helen Hayes,** *Apr. 25,* Washington, DC	2.10
4526	(44c)	**Gregory Peck,** *Apr. 28,* Beverly Hills, CA	2.10
4527-4528	(44c)	**Space Firsts,** *May 4,* Kennedy Space Center, FL	3.00
		4527-4528, either single	2.10
4529	(44c)	**Purple Heart,** *May 5,* San Diego, CA	2.10
4530	(44c)	**Indianapolis 500,** *May 20,* Indianapolis, IN	2.10
4531-4540	(44c)	**Garden of Love,** *May 23,* Crestwood, KY	9.00
		4531-4540, any single	2.10

4541-4544 (44c) **American Scientists,** *June 16,* St. Paul, MN 4.75
4541-4544, any single 2.10
4545 (44c) **Mark Twain,** *June 25,* Hannibal, MO 2.10
4546 (44c) **Pioneers of American Industrial Design,** *June 29,* New York, NY 12.00
4546a-4546l, any single 2.10
4547 (44c) **Owney, the Postal Dog,** *July 27,* Washington, DC 2.10
4548-4551 (44c) **U.S. Merchant Marine,** *July 28,* Great Neck, NY 4.75
4548-4551, any single 2.10
4552 (44c) **Eid,** *Aug. 12,* Columbus, OH 2.10
4553-4557 (44c) **Characters from Disney-Pixar Films (Send a Hello),** *Aug. 19,* Anaheim, CA 5.75
4553-4557, any single 2.10
4558 (44c) **Edward Hopper,** *Aug. 24,* Provincetown, MA 2.10
4559 (44c) **Statue of Liberty booklet stamp,** (Ashton-Potter printing), serpentine die cut 11¼x11 on 2 or 3 sides, microprinted "4evR," *Sept. 14,* Washington, DC 2.10
4560 (44c) **Flag booklet stamp,** (Ashton-Potter printing), serpentine die cut 11¼x11 on 2 or 3 sides, microprinted "4evR," *Sept. 14,* Washington, DC 2.10
4560a, pair 3.00
4561 (44c) **Statue of Liberty booklet stamp,** (Sennett printing), serpentine die cut 11¼x11 on 2 or 3 sides, microprinted "4evr," *Sept. 14,* Washington, DC 2.10
4562 (44c) **Flag booklet stamp,** (Sennett printing), serpentine die cut 11¼x11 on 2 or 3 sides, microprinted "4evr," *Sept. 14,* Washington, DC 2.10
4562a, pair 3.00
4563 (44c) **Statue of Liberty booklet stamp,** (Avery printing), serpentine die cut 11¼x11½ on 2 or 3 sides, microprinted "4EVR," *Sept. 14,* Washington, DC 2.10
4564 (44c) **Flag booklet stamp,** (Avery printing), serpentine die cut 11¼x11½ on 2 or 3 sides, microprinted "4EVR," *Sept. 14,* Washington, DC 2.10
4564a, pair 3.00
4565 (44c) **Barbara Jordan,** *Sept. 16,* Houston, TX 2.10
4566-4569 (44c) **Art of Romare Bearden,** *Sept. 28,* New York, NY 4.75
4566-4569, any single 2.10
4570 (44c) **Christmas Madonna,** *Oct. 13,* New York, NY 2.10
4571-4574 (44c) **Christmas Ornaments,** (Ashton-Potter printing), microprinted "USPS" on ornament collar, *Oct. 13,* New York, NY 4.75
4571-4574, any single 2.10
4575-4578 (44c) **Christmas Ornaments,** (Sennett double-sided booklet printing), microprinted "USPS" in various places, *Oct. 13,* New York, NY 4.75
4575-4578, any single 2.10
4579-4582 (44c) **Christmas Ornaments,** (Sennett ATM booklet printing), serpentine die cut 11¼x11 on 2, 3 or 4 sides, *Oct. 13,* New York, NY 4.75
4579-4582, any single 2.10
4583 (44c) **Hanukkah,** *Oct. 14,* New York, NY 2.10
4584 (44c) **Kwanzaa,** *Oct. 14,* New York, NY 2.10

2012

4585-4590 (25c) **Eagle coil stamps,** *Jan. 3,* Liberty, MO 4.25
4585-4590, any single 2.10
4591 (44c) **New Mexico Statehood,** *Jan. 6,* Santa Fe, NM 2.10
4592-4596 32c **Aloha Shirts,** serpentine die cut 11, *Jan. 19,* Honolulu, HI 4.50
4592-4596, any single 2.10
4597-4601 32c **Aloha Shirts coil stamps,** serpentine die cut 11 vert., *Jan. 19,* Honolulu, HI 4.50
4597-4601, any single 2.10
4602 65c **Wedding Cake,** *Jan. 20,* Alexandria, VA 2.50
4603 65c **Baltimore Checkerspot Butterfly,** *Jan. 20,* Baltimore, MD 2.50
4604-4607 65c **Dogs at Work,** *Jan. 20,* Merrifield, VA 6.50
4604-4607, any single 2.50
4608-4612 85c **Birds of Prey,** *Jan. 20,* Washington, DC 9.75
4608-4612, any single 3.00
4613-4617 45c **Weather Vane coil stamps,** *Jan. 20,* Shelburne, VT 5.75
4613-4617, any single 2.10
4618-4622 (45c) **Bonsai booklet stamps,** *Jan. 23,* Sacramento, CA 5.75
4618-4622, any single 2.10
4623 (45c) **Chinese New Year,** *Jan. 23,* San Francisco, CA 2.10
4624 (45c) **John H. Johnson,** *Jan. 31,* Chicago, IL 2.10
4625 (45c) **Heart Health,** *Feb. 9,* Washington, DC 2.10
4626 (45c) **Love,** *Feb. 14,* Colorado Springs, CO 2.10
Any other city, *Feb. 2* —

Postal Service officials declared on Feb. 2 that No. 4626 could be sold in post offices as of that date to make the stamp available to customers before St. Valentine's Day, but the first day ceremony for the stamp would still be held Feb. 14 in Colorado Springs, CO.

4627 (45c) **Arizona Statehood,** *Feb. 14,* Phoenix, AZ 2.10
4628 (45c) **Danny Thomas,** *Feb. 16,* Memphis, TN 2.10
4629-4632 (45c) **Flags coil stamps,** serpentine die cut 8½ vert., *Feb. 22,* Washington, DC 5.00
4629-4632, any single 2.10
4633-4636 (45c) **Flags coil stamps,** serpentine die cut 9½ vert., *Feb. 22,* Washington, DC 5.00
4633-4636, any single 2.10
4637-4640 (45c) **Flags coil stamps,** serpentine die cut 11 vert., *Feb. 22,* Washington, DC 5.00
4637-4640, any single 2.10
4641-4644 (45c) **Flags booklet stamps,** 18½mm from lower left to lower right corner of flag, *Feb. 22,* Washington, DC 5.00
4641-4644, any single 2.10
4645-4648 (45c) **Flags booklet stamps,** 19mm from lower left to lower right corner of flag, *Feb. 22,* Washington, DC 5.00
4645-4648, any single 2.10
4649 $5.15 **Sunshine Skyway Bridge,** *Feb. 28,* St. Petersburg, FL 10.50
4650 $18.95 **Carmel Mission,** *Feb. 28,* Carmel, CA 38.00
4651-4652 (45c) **Cherry Blossom Centennial,** *Mar. 24,* Washington, DC 3.00
4651-4652, any single 2.10
4653 (45c) **William H. Johnson,** *Apr. 11,* Baltimore, MD 2.10
4654-4663 (45c) **Twentieth Century Poets,** *Apr. 21,* Los Angeles, CA 9.00
4654-4663, any single 2.10
4664-4665 (45c) **Civil War Sesquicentennial,** *Apr. 24,* New Orleans, LA 3.00
4664-4665, any single 2.10
4666 (45c) **José Ferrer,** *Apr. 26,* New York, NY 2.10
4667 (45c) **Louisiana Statehood Bicentennial,** *Apr. 30,* Baton Rouge, LA 2.10
4668-4671 (45c) **Great Film Directors,** *May 23,* Silver Spring, MD 5.00
4668-4671, any single 2.10
4672 1c **Bobcat coil stamp,** *June 1,* San Marcos, TX 2.10
4672a 1c **Bobcat coil stamp,** dated "2015," *Feb. 21, 2015,* Mesa, AZ 2.25
4673-4676 (45c) **Flags booklet stamps,** photogravure, 19¼mm from lower left to lower right corner of flag, *June 1,* McLean, VA 5.00
4673-4676, any single 2.10
4677-4681 (45c) **Characters from Disney-Pixar Films (Mail a Smile),** *June 1,* Orlando, FL 5.75
4677-4681, any single 2.10
4682-4686 (32c) **Aloha Shirts booklet stamps,** *June 2,* McLean, VA 4.50
4682-4686, any single 2.10
4687-4690 (45c) **Bicycling,** *June 7,* Minneapolis, MN 5.00
4687-4690, any single 2.10
4691 (45c) **Girl Scouts of America,** *June 9,* Washington, DC 2.10
4692-4693 (45c) **Musicians (Edith Piaf and Miles Davis),** *June 12,* New York, NY 3.00
4692-4693, either single 2.10
4694-4697 (45c) **Major League Baseball All-Stars,** *July 20,* Cooperstown, NY 5.00
4694-4697, any single 2.10
4698-4701 (45c) **Innovative Choreographers,** *July 28,* Los Angeles, CA 5.00
4698-4701, any single 2.10
4702 (45c) **Edgar Rice Burroughs,** *Aug. 17,* Tarzana, CA 2.10
4703 (45c) **U.S.S. Constitution,** *Aug. 18,* Boston, MA 2.10
4704 (45c) **Purple Heart,** *Sept. 4,* Washington, DC 2.10
4704b (49c) **Purple Heart,** dated "2014," *Oct. 11,* Dover, DE 2.25
4705 (45c) **O. Henry,** *Sept. 11,* Greensboro, NC 2.10
4706-4709 (45c) **Flags ATM booklet stamps,** thin paper, *Sept. 22,* Humble, TX 5.00
4706-4709, any single 2.10
4710 (45c) **Earthscapes,** *Oct. 1,* Greenbelt, MD 13.50
4710a-4710o, any single 2.10
4711 (45c) **Christmas Holy Family,** *Oct. 10,* Washington, DC 2.10
4712-4715 (45c) **Christmas Santa and Sleigh,** *Oct. 13,* New York, NY 5.00
4712-4715, any single 2.10
4716 (45c) **Lady Bird Johnson,** *Nov. 30,* Austin, TX 6.75
4716a-4716f, any single 2.10
4717 $1 **Waves of Color,** *Dec. 1,* Orlando, FL 3.25
4718 $2 **Waves of Color,** *Dec. 1,* Orlando, FL 5.25
4719 $5 **Waves of Color,** *Dec. 1,* Orlando, FL 10.00
4720 $10 **Waves of Color,** *Dec. 1,* Orlando, FL 20.00

2013

4721 (45c) **Emancipation Proclamation, 150th Anniv.,** *Jan. 1,* Washington, DC 2.10
4722-4725 46c **Kaleidoscope Flowers,** *Jan. 14,* Kansas City, MO 5.00
4722-4725, any single 2.25
4726 (45c) **Chinese New Year,** *Jan. 16,* San Francisco, CA 2.10
4727-4730 33c **Apples,** serpentine die cut 11¼x10¾, *Jan. 17,* Yakima, WA 4.00
4727-4730, any single 2.10
4731-4734 33c **Apples coil stamps,** serpentine die cut 11 vert., *Jan. 17,* Yakima, WA 4.00
4731-4734, any single 2.10
4735 66c **Wedding Cake,** *Jan. 18,* Louisville, KY 2.60
4736 66c **Spicebush Swallowtail Butterfly,** *Jan. 23,* Pine Mountain, GA 2.60
4737 86c **Tufted Puffins,** *Jan. 23,* Seward, AK 3.00
4738 $5.60 **Arlington Green Bridge,** *Jan. 25,* Norcross, GA 11.50
4739 $19.95 **Grand Central Terminal,** *Feb. 1,* New York, NY 40.00
4740 ($1.10) **Earth (Global Forever),** *Jan. 28,* New York, NY 3.50
4741 (46c) **Love,** *Jan. 30,* Loveland, CO 2.25
4742 (46c) **Rosa Parks,** *Feb. 4,* Detroit or Dearborn, MI 2.25
4743-4747 (46c) **Muscle Cars,** *Feb. 22,* Daytona Beach, FL 6.00
4743-4747, any single 2.25
4748 (46c) **Modern Art in America,** *Mar. 7,* New York, NY 11.50
4748a-4748l, any single 2.25
4749 46c **Patriotic Star,** *Mar. 19,* San Francisco, CA 2.25
4750-4753 (46c) **La Florida,** *Apr. 3,* St. Augustine, FL 5.00
4750-4753, any single 2.25
4754-4763 (46c) **Vintage Seed Packets,** *Apr. 5,* Oaks, PA 9.25
4754-4763, any single 2.25
4764 (46c) **Flowers,** *Apr. 11,* New York, NY 2.25
4764a (49c) **Wedding Flowers, dated "2014,"** *May 2, 2014* Acton, MA 2.25
4765 66c **Flowers and "Yes I Do,"** *Apr. 11,* New York, NY 2.60
4766-4769 (46c) **Flags coil stamps,** serpentine die cut 8½ vert., *May 3,* Weston, MA 5.00
4766-4769, any single 2.25
4770-4773 (46c) **Flags coil stamps,** serpentine die cut 9½ vert., *May 3,* Weston, MA 5.00
4770-4773, any single 2.25
4774-4777 (46c) **Flags coil stamps,** serpentine die cut 11 vert., *May 3,* Weston, MA 5.00
4774-4777, any single 2.25
4778-4781 (46c) **Flags booklet stamps,** microprinting at lower left corner of flag, *May 17,* Rochester, NY 5.00
4778-4781, any single 2.25
4782-4785 (46c) **Flags booklet stamps,** microprinting at top of pole or lower left corner, *May 17,* Rochester, NY 5.00
4782-4785, any single 2.25
4782a-4785a **Flags booklet stamps,** overall tagging, *Aug. 16,* Independence, OH 5.25
4782a-4785a, any single 2.25
4782b-4785b **Flags booklet stamps,** dated "2014," *Mar. 17, 2014,* Liberty, MO 5.25
4782b-4785b, any single 2.25
4786 (46c) **Lydia Mendoza,** *May 15,* San Antonio, TX 2.25
4787-4788 (46c) **Civil War Sesquicentennial,** *May 23,* Vicksburg, MS or Gettysburg, PA 3.25
4787-4788, any single 2.25
4789 (46c) **Johnny Cash,** *June 5,* Nashville, TN 2.25
4790 (46c) **West Virginia Statehood,** *June 20,* Charleston, WV 2.25
4791-4795 (46c) **New England Coastal Lighthouses,** *July 13,* Portland, ME; New Castle, NH; Boston, MA; Narragansett, RI; and New London, CT 6.00
4791-4795, any single 2.25

4796-4799 (46c) **Flags booklet stamps,** serpentine die cut 11¼x11½ on 2 or 3 sides, *Aug. 8,* Milwaukee, WI 5.00
4796-4799, any single 2.25
4800 (46c) **Eid,** *Aug. 8,* Milwaukee, WI 2.25
4801 (46c) **Building a Nation,** *Aug. 8,* Washington, DC 11.00
4801a-4801l, any single 2.25
4802 1c **Bobcat coil stamp,** perf. 9¾ vert., *Aug. 9,* Milwaukee, WI 2.25
4803 (46c) **Althea Gibson,** *Aug. 23,* Flushing, NY 2.25
4804 (46c) **March on Washington, 50th Anniv.,** *Aug. 23,* Washington, DC 2.25
4805 (46c) **Battle of Lake Erie,** *Sept. 10,* Put-in-Bay, OH 2.25
4806 $2 **Inverted Jenny Pane of 6,** *Sept. 22,* Washington, DC 24.00
4806a, single stamp 5.25
4807 (46c) **Ray Charles,** *Sept. 23,* Atlanta, GA and Los Angeles, CA 2.25
4808-4812 (10c) **Snowflakes,** *Oct. 1,* Weston, MO 2.25
4808-4812, any single 2.25
4813 (46c) **Christmas - Holy Family,** *Oct. 11,* New York, NY 2.25
4814 ($1.10) **Christmas - Wreath,** *Oct. 24,* New York, NY 3.75
4815 (46c) **Christmas - Virgin and Child,** *Oct. 11,* New York, NY 2.25
4816 (46c) **Christmas - Poinsettia,** serpentine die cut 11 on 2 or 3 sides, *Oct. 10,* New York, NY 2.25
4816b (49c) **Poinsettia,** dated "2014," *Aug. 21, 2014* Hartford, CT 2.25
4817-4820 (46c) **Christmas - Gingerbread Houses,** *Nov. 6,* New York, NY 5.00
4817-4820, any single 2.25
4821 (46c) **Christmas - Poinsettia,** serpentine die cut 8 on 2, 3 or 4 sides, *Oct. 10,* New York, NY 2.75
4822-4823 (46c) **Medals of Honor,** *Nov. 11,* Washington, DC 3.00
4822-4823, any single 2.75
4823d (49c) **Medal of Honor,** dated "2014," *July 26,* Washington, DC 4.00
4822a-4823a, any single 3.00
4822b (49c) **Navy Medal of Honor,** dated "2015," *May 25,* Washington, DC 3.00
4823b (49c) **Army Medal of Honor,** dated "2015," *May 25,* Washington, DC 3.00
4824 (46c) **Hanukkah,** *Nov. 19,* New York, NY 2.75

Postal Service officials declared on Nov. 8 that No. 4824 could be sold in post offices on Nov. 9, but the first day ceremony was held on Nov. 19 in New York, NY. Official first day covers have that date and city.

4825-4844 (46c) **Harry Potter,** *Nov. 19,* Orlando, FL 20.00
4825-4844, any single 2.25
4845 (46c) **Kwanzaa,** *Nov. 26,* Philadelphia, PA 2.25

2014

4846 (46c) **Chinese New Year,** *Jan. 15,* San Francisco, CA 2.50
4847 (46c) **Love,** *Jan. 21,* New York, NY 2.25
4848-4852 49c **Ferns,** *Jan. 27,* Kansas City, MO 6.25
4848-4852, any single 2.25
4853 (49c) **Fort McHenry Flag and Fireworks coil stamp,** serpentine die cut 8½ vert., *Jan. 28,* Independence, MO 2.25
4854 (49c) **Fort McHenry Flag and Fireworks coil stamp,** serpentine die cut 9½ vert., *Jan. 28,* Independence, MO 2.25
4855 (49c) **Fort McHenry Flag and Fireworks booklet stamp,** serpentine die cut 11¼x10¾ on 2 or 3 sides, *Jan. 28,* Independence, MO 2.25
4856 (49c) **Shirley Chisholm,** *Jan. 31,* Brooklyn, NY 2.25
4857 34c **Hummingbird,** serpentine die cut 11¼x10¾, *Feb. 7,* Kansas City, MO 2.25
4858 34c **Hummingbird coil,** serpentine die cut 9½ vert., *Feb. 7,* Kansas City, MO 2.25
4859 70c **Great Spangled Fritillary Butterfly,** *Feb. 10,* Kansas City, MO 2.60
4860 21c **Abraham Lincoln,** serpentine die cut 11, *Feb. 12,* Springfield, IL 2.25
4861 21c **Abraham Lincoln coil,** serpentine die cut 8½ vert., *Feb. 12,* Springfield, IL 2.25
4862-4865 (49c) **Winter Flowers,** *Feb. 14,* Little Rock, AR 5.25
4862-4865, any single 2.25
4866 91c **Ralph Ellison,** *Feb. 18,* Kansas City, MO 3.00
4867 70c **Wedding Cake,** *Feb. 22,* Mesa, AZ 2.60
4868 (49c) **Fort McHenry Flag and Fireworks coil stamp,** serpentine die cut 11 vert., *Mar. 3,* Washington, DC 2.25
4869 (49c) **Fort McHenry Flag and Fireworks booklet stamp,** photo., serpentine die cut 11¼x11½ on 2 or 3 sides, without microprinted "USPS," *Mar. 3,* Washington, DC 2.25
4870 (49c) **Fort McHenry Flag and Fireworks booklet stamp,** litho., serpentine die cut 11¼x10¾ on 2 or 3 sides, microprinted "USPS" in fireworks, *Mar. 3,* Washington, DC 2.25
4871 (49c) **Fort McHenry Flag and Fireworks ATM booklet stamp,** litho., thin paper, serpentine die cut 11¼x11 on 2, 3 or 4 sides, microprinted "USPS" in fireworks, *Mar. 3,* Washington, DC 2.25
4872 $5.60 **Verrazano-Narrows Bridge,** *Mar. 4,* Brooklyn, NY 11.50
4873 $19.99 **USS Arizona Memorial,** *Mar. 13,* Honolulu, HI 40.00
4874-4878 (49c) **Ferns,** *Mar. 6,* Kansas City, MO 6.25
4874-4878, any single 2.25
4879 70c **C. Alfred "Chief" Anderson,** *Mar. 13,* Bryn Mawr, PA 2.60
4880 (49c) **Jimi Hendrix,** *Mar. 13,* Austin, TX 3.00
4881 70c **Flowers and "Yes I Do,"** *Mar. 21,* St. Louis, MO 2.60
4882-4891 (49c) **Songbirds,** *Apr. 5,* Dallas, TX 10.00
4882-4891, any single 2.25
4892 (49c) **Charlton Heston,** *Apr. 11,* Los Angeles, CA 2.25
4893 ($1.15) **Map of Sea Surface Temperatures,** *Apr. 22,* Washington, DC 3.50
4894-4897 (49c) **Flags,** *Apr. 25,* San Francisco, CA 5.25
4894-4897, any single 2.25
4898-4905 (49c) **Circus Posters,** *May 5,* Sarasota, FL 9.25
4898-4905, any single 2.25
4905c **Circus souvenir sheet,** *Dec. 10,* Baraboo, WI 5.00
4906 (49c) **Harvey Milk,** *May 22,* Washington, DC 2.25
4907 (49c) **Nevada Statehood, 150th Anniv.,** *May 29,* Las Vegas, NV 2.25
4908-4909 (49c) **Hot Rods,** *June 6,* York, PA 4.00
4908-4909, any single 2.25
4910-4911 (49c) **Civil War Sesquicentennial,** *July 30,* Petersburg, VA or Mobile, AL 3.25
4910-4911, any single 2.25
4912-4915 (49c) **Farmers Markets,** *Aug. 7,* Washington, DC 5.25
4912-4915, any single 2.25
4916 (49c) **Janis Joplin,** *Aug. 8,* San Francisco, CA 2.25
4917-4920 (49c) **Hudson River School Paintings,** *Aug. 21,* Hartford, CT 5.25
4917-4920, any single 2.25
4921 (49c) **Bombardment of Fort McHenry,** *Sept. 13,* Baltimore, MD 2.25
4922-4926 (49c) **Celebrity Chefs,** *Sept. 26,* Chicago, IL 6.25
4922-4926, any single 2.25
4927 $5.75 **Glade Creek Grist Mill,** *Sept. 29,* Danese, WV 11.50
4928-4935 (49c) **Batman,** *Oct. 9,* New York, NY 9.25
4928-4935, any single 2.25
4936 ($1.15) **Silver Bells Wreath,** *Oct. 23,* New York, NY 3.50
4937-4940 (49c) **Winter Fun,** serpentine die cut 10¾x11 on 2 or 3 sides, *Oct. 23,* New York, NY 5.25
4937-4940, any single 2.25
4941-4944 (49c) **Winter Fun,** serpentine die cut 11¼x11 on 2, 3 or 4 sides, *Oct. 23,* New York, NY 5.25
4941-4944, any single 2.25
4945 (49c) **Christmas - Magi,** *Nov. 19,* Washington, DC 2.25
4946-4949 (49c) **Christmas - Rudolph, the Red-Nosed Reindeer,** *Nov. 6,* Washington, DC 5.25
4946-4949, any single 2.25
4950-4951 (49c) **Wilt Chamberlain,** *Dec. 5,* Philadelphia, PA 3.25
4950-4951, any single 2.25

2015

4952 (49c) **Battle of New Orleans,** *Jan. 8,* Chalmette, LA 2.25
4953 $1 **Patriotic Waves,** *Jan. 12,* Kansas City, KS 4.00
4954 $2 **Patriotic Waves,** *Jan. 30,* Norcross, GA 6.00
4955-4956 (49c) **Love,** *Jan. 22,* Richmond, VA 3.25
4955-4956, any single 2.25
4957 (49c) **Chinese New Year,** *Feb. 7,* San Francisco, CA 2.25
4958 (49c) **Robert Robinson Taylor,** *Feb. 12,* Washington, DC 2.25
4959 (49c) **Rose and Heart,** *Feb. 14,* Riverside, CA 2.25
4960 70c **Tulip and Heart,** *Feb. 14,* Riverside, CA 2.60
4961-4963 (10c) **Flags,** *Feb. 27,* Grapevine, TX 2.25
4961-4963, any single 2.25
4964-4967 (49c) **Water Lilies,** *Mar. 20,* Cleveland, OH 5.25
4964-4967, any single 2.25
4968-4972 (49c) **Martín Ramírez,** *Mar. 26,* New York, NY 6.25
4968-4972, any single 2.25
4973-4977 (49c) **Ferns,** lithogruaphed coil stamps with microprinting dated 2014, *Mar. 27,* Kansas City, MO 6.25
4973-4977, any single 2.25
4973a-4977a (49c) **Ferns,** lithographed coil stamps with microprinting, dated "2015," *Mar. 27,* Kansas City, MO 6.25
4973a-4977a, any single 2.25
4978 (49c) **From Me to You,** *Apr. 1,* Washington, DC 2.25
4979 (49c) **Maya Angelou,** *Apr. 7,* Washington, DC 2.25
4980-4981 (49c) **Civil War Sesquicentennial,** *Apr. 9,* Appomattox, VA 3.25
4980-4981, any single 2.25
4982-4985 (49c) **Gifts of Friendship,** *Apr. 10,* Washington, DC 5.25
4982-4985, any single 2.25
4986 (49c) **Special Olympics World Games,** *May 9,* Irvine, CA 2.25
4987 (49c) **Help Find Missing Children,** *May 18,* Anaheim, CA 2.25
4988 (49c) **Air Force Medal of Honor,** *May 25,* Washington, DC 2.50
4988a, strip of 3 4.25
4989 (22c) **Emperor Penguins,** serpentine die cut 11¼x11, *June 1,* Kansas City, MO 2.25
4990 (22c) **Emperor Penguins coil,** serpentine die cut 11 vert., *June 1,* Kansas City, MO 2.25
4991-4994 (35c) **Coastal Birds,** serpentine die cut 11¼x11, *June 1,* Kansas City, MO 4.00
4991-4994, any single 2.25
4995-4998 (35c) **Coastal Birds coils,** serpentine die cut 9½ vert., *June 1,* Kansas City, MO 4.00
4995-4998, any single 2.25
4999 (71c) **Eastern Tiger Swallowtail Butterfly,** *June 1,* Kansas City, MO 2.75
5000 (71c) **Wedding Cake,** *June 1,* Kansas City, MO 2.75
5001 (71c) **Flowers and "Yes, I Do,"** *June 1,* Kansas City, MO 2.75
5002 (71c) **Tulip and Heart,** *June 1,* Kansas City, MO 2.75
5003 (93c) **Flannery O'Connor,** *June 5,* McLean, VA 3.25
5004-5007 (49c) **Summer Harvest,** *July 11,* Sacramento, CA 5.25
5004-5007, any single 2.25
5008 (49c) **Coast Guard,** *Aug. 4,* Washington, DC 2.25
5009 (49c) **Elvis Presley,** *Aug. 12,* Memphis, TN 3.00
5010-5011 (49c) **2016 World Stamp Show,** *Aug. 20,* Grand Rapids, MI 3.25
5010-5011, any single 2.25
5012 (49c) **Ingrid Bergman,** *Aug. 20,* Los Angeles, CA 2.25
5013-5018 (25c) **Eagle coil stamps,** serpentine die cut 10¼ vert., *Sept. 2,* Eagleville, MO 4.25
5013-5018, any single 2.25
5019 (49c) **Celebrate,** litho., *Sept. 9,* Kansas City, MO 2.25
5020 (49c) **Paul Newman,** *Sept. 18,* Cleveland, OH 2.25
5021-5030 (49c) **Christmas - A Charlie Brown Christmas,** *Oct. 1,* Santa Rosa, CA 10.00
5021-5030, any single 2.25
5031-5034 (49c) **Geometric Snowflakes,** *Oct. 23,* New York, NY 5.25
5031-5034, any single 2.25

2016

5036 (49c) **Love,** *Jan. 12,* Dallas, TX 2.25
5037 1c **Albemarle Pippin Apples,** *Aug. 12,* Kansas City, MO 2.25
5038 5c **Pinot Noir Grapes,** *Feb. 19,* Kansas City, MO 2.25
5039 10c **Red Pears,** *Jan. 17,* Washington, DC 2.25
5040 $6.45 **La Cueva del Indio,** *Jan. 17,* Washington, DC 13.00
5041 $22.95 **Columbia River Gorge,** *Jan. 17,* Washington, DC 46.00
5042-5051 (49c) **Botanical Art,** *Jan. 29,* Atlanta, GA 10.00
5042-5051, any single 2.25
5052 (49c) **Flag coil,** serpentine die cut 11 vert., *Jan. 29,* Washington, DC 2.25
5053 (49c) **Flag coil,** serpentine die cut 9½ vert., *Jan. 29,* Washington, DC 2.25

5054 (49c) **Flag booklet stamp,** microprinted "USPS" below flag, *Jan. 29,* Washington, DC 2.25
5055 (49c) **Flag booklet stamp,** microprinted "USPS" on second white stripe, *Jan. 29,* Washington, DC 2.25
5056 (49c) **Richard Allen,** *Feb. 2,* Philadelphia, PA 2.25
5057 (49c) **Chinese New Year,** *Feb. 5,* Jamaica, NY 2.25
5058 ($1.20) **Moon,** *Feb. 22,* Washington, DC 3.75
5059 (49c) **Sarah Vaughan,** *Mar. 29,* Newark, NJ 2.25
5060 (47c) **Shirley Temple,** *Apr. 18,* Los Angeles, CA 2.25
5061 (5c) **"USA" and Star,** *Apr. 28,* Dulles, VA 2.25
5062-5063 (47c) **2016 World Stamp Show,** *May 28,* New York, NY 3.25
5062-5063, any single 2.25
5064 (47c) **Repeal of the Stamp Act,** *May 29,* New York, NY 2.25
5065-5068 (47c) **Service Cross Medals,** *May 30,* New York, NY 5.00
5065-5068, any single 2.25
5069-5076 (47c) **Views of Our Planets,** *May 31,* New York, NY 8.75
5069-5076, any single 2.25
5077-5078 (47c) **Pluto Explored,** *May 31,* New York, NY 3.25
5077-5078, any single 2.25
5079 (47c) **Classics Forever,** *June 1,* New York, NY 7.00
5079a-5079f, any single 2.25
5080 (47c) **National Parks Service, Cent.,** *June 2,* New York, NY 15.00
5080a-5080p, any single 2.25
5081-5090 (47c) **Colorful Celebrations,** *June 3,* New York, NY 9.50
5081-5090, any single 2.25
5091 (47c) **Indiana Statehood,** *June 7,* Indianapolis, IN 2.25
5092 (47c) **Eid,** *June 10,* Dearborn, MI 2.25
5093-5097 (47c) **Soda Fountain Favorites,** *June 30,* Nashville, TN 6.00
5093-5097, 5095a, any single 2.25
5098-5099 (25c) **Star Quilts,** *July 6,* Washington, DC 2.25
5098-5099, any single 2.25
5100 (47c) **Jaime Escalante,** *July 13,* Washington, DC 2.25
5101-5104 (47c) **Pickup Trucks,** *July 15,* Syracuse, NY 5.00
5101-5104, any single 2.25
5105 (89c) **Henry James,** *July 31,* Dulles, VA 3.00
Cancel dated "Jul 31 31016" 3.00
5106-5125 (47c) **Pets,** *Aug. 2,* Las Vegas, NV 19.00
5106-5125, any single 2.25
5126-5129 (47c) **Songbirds in Snow,** *Aug. 4,* Portland, OR 5.00
5126-5129, any single 2.25
5130 (47c) **Patriotic Spiral coil stamp,** *Aug. 19,* Kansas City, MO 2.25
5131 (47c) **Patriotic Spiral booklet stamp,** *Aug. 19,* Kansas City, MO 2.25
5132-5135 (47c) **Star Trek,** *Sept. 2,* New York, NY 5.00
5132-5135, any single 2.25
5136 (68c) **Eastern Tailed-Blue Butterfly,** *Sept. 24,* Kansas City, MO 2.60
5137-5140 (47c) **Jack-o'-lanterns,** *Sept. 29,* Anoka, MN 5.00
5137-5140, any single 2.25
5141 (47c) **Kwanzaa,** *Oct. 1,* Charleston, SC 2.25
5142 (47c) **Diwali,** *Oct. 5,* New York, NY 2.25
5143 (47c) **Christmas - Madonna and Child,** *Oct. 18,* Washington, DC 2.25
5144 (47c) **Christmas - Nativity,** *Nov. 3,* Washington, DC 2.25
5145-5148 (47c) **Christmas - Holiday Windows,** *Oct. 6,* New York, NY 5.00
5145-5148, any single 2.25
5149-5152 (47c) **Wonder Woman,** *Oct. 7,* New York, NY 5.00
5149-5152, any single 2.25
5153 (47c) **Hanukkah,** *Nov. 1,* Boca Raton, FL 2.25

2017

5154 (47c) **Chinese New Year,** *Jan. 5,* Seattle, WA 2.25
5155 (47c) **Love,** *Jan. 7,* Chino, CA 2.25
5156 $6.65 **Lili'uokalani Gardens,** *Jan. 22,* Kansas City, MO 13.50
5157 $23.75 **Gateway Arch,** *Jan. 22,* Kansas City, MO 47.50
5158 (49c) **Flag coil,** serpentine die cut 11 vert., *Jan. 27,* Norcross, GA 2.25
5159 (49c) **Flag coil,** serpentine die cut 9½ vert., *Jan. 27,* Norcross, GA 2.25
5160 (49c) **Flag booklet stamp,** microprinted "USPS" on fourth red stripe, *Jan. 27,* Norcross, GA 2.25
5161 (49c) **Flag booklet stamp,** microprinted "USPS" at right of second white stripe, *Jan. 27,* Norcross, GA 2.25
5162 (49c) **Flag booklet stamp,** microprinted "USPS" at left of second white stripe, *Jan. 27,* Norcross, GA 2.25
5163-5166 (34c) **Shells,** serpentine die cut 11¼x10¾, *Jan. 28,* San Diego, CA 4.00
5163-5166, any single 2.25
5167-5170 (34c) **Shells coil stamps,** serpentine die cut 9¾ vert., *Jan. 28,* San Diego, CA 4.00
5167-5170, any single 2.25
5171 (49c) **Dorothy Height,** *Feb. 1,* Washington, DC 2.25
5172 (5c) **"USA" and Star With Blue Frame,** *Feb. 10,* Fort Lauderdale, FL 2.25
5173 (49c) **Oscar de la Renta,** *Feb. 16,* New York, NY 11.00
5173a-5173k, any single 2.25
5174 (21c) **People Wearing Uncle Sam Hats,** *Feb. 18,* Mesa, AZ 2.25
5175 (49c) **Pres. John F. Kennedy,** *Feb. 20,* Boston, MA 2.25
5177 5c **Pinot Noir Grapes,** serpentine die cut 11¼x11, *Feb. 24,* Grapevine, TX 2.25
5178 10c **Red Pears,** serpentine die cut 11¼x11, *Mar. 23,* Cleveland, OH 2.25
5179 (49c) **Nebraska Statehood,** *Mar. 1,* Lincoln, NE 2.25
5180-5189 (49c) **WPA Posters,** *Mar. 7,* Hyde Park, NY 10.00
5180-5189, any single 2.25
5190 (49c) **Mississippi Statehood,** *Mar. 31,* Gulfport, MS 2.25
5191 (70c) **Robert Panara,** *Apr.11,* Rochester, NY 2.60
5192-5197 (49c) **Delicioso (Latin American Dishes),** *Apr. 20,* Albuquerque, NM 7.25
5192-5197, any single 2.25
5198 ($1.15) **Echeveria,** *Apr. 28,* San Francisco, CA 3.50
5199 (49c) **Boutonniere,** *May 2,* St. Louis, MO 2.25
5200 (70c) **Corsage,** *May 2,* St. Louis, MO 2.60
5201 3c **Strawberries,** coil stamp, *May 5,* Acton, MA 2.25
5202 (49c) **Henry David Thoreau,** *May 23,* Concord, MA 2.25
5203-5210 (49c) **Sports Balls,** *June 14,* Hartford, WI 9.25
5203-5210, any single 2.25
5211 (49c) **Total Solar Eclipse,** *June 20,* Laramie, WY 2.25
5212 (49c) **Paintings by Andrew Wyeth,** *July 12,* Chadds Ford, PA 12.00
5212a-5212l, any single 2.25
5213-5222 (49c) **Disney Villains,** *July 15,* Anaheim, CA 10.00
5213-5222, any single 2.25
5223-5227 (49c) **Sharks,** *July 26,* Newport, KY 6.25
5223-5227, any single 2.25
5228-5232 (49c) **Protect Pollinators,** *Aug. 3,* Richmond, VA 6.25
5228-5232, any single 2.25
5233-5236 (49c) **Flowers from the Garden,** coil stamps, *Aug. 16,* Sioux Falls, SD 5.25
5233-5236, any single 2.25
5237-5240 (49c) **Flowers from the Garden,** booklet stamps, *Aug. 16,* Sioux Falls, SD 5.25
5237-5240, any single 2.25
5241 (49c) **Father Ted Hesburgh,** serpentine die cut 11, *Sept. 1,* Notre Dame, IN 2.25
5242 (49c) **Father Ted Hesburgh,** serpentine die cut 9½ horiz., *Sept. 1,* Notre Dame, IN 2.25
5243-5246 (49c) **"The Snowy Day,"** *Oct. 4,* Brooklyn, NY 5.25
5243-5246, any single 2.25
5247-5250 (49c) **Christmas Carols,** *Oct. 5,* New York, NY 5.25
5247-5250, any single 2.25
5251 (49c) **National Museum of African American History and Culture,** *Oct. 13,* Washington, DC 2.25
5252-5253 (49c) **History of Ice Hockey,** *Oct. 20,* Detroit, MI 3.25
5252-5253, any single 2.25
5253c Souvenir sheet of 2, #5252a-5253a 3.25

2018

5254 (49c) **Chinese New Year,** *Jan. 11,* Honolulu, HI 2.25
5255 (49c) **Love,** *Jan. 18,* Phoenix, AZ 2.25
5256 2c **Meyer Lemons,** coil stamp, *Jan. 19,* Kenner, LA 2.25
5257 $6.70 **Byodo-In Temple,** *Jan. 21,* Kansas City, MO 13.50
5258 $24.70 **Sleeping Bear Dunes,** *Jan. 21,* Kansas City, MO 50.00
5259 (50c) **Lena Horne,** *Jan. 30,* New York, NY 2.25
5260 (50c) **Flag coil,** serpentine die cut 9½ vert., *Feb. 9,* Fort Lauderdale, FL 2.25
5261 (50c) **Flag coil,** serpentine die cut 11 vert., *Feb. 9,* Fort Lauderdale, FL 2.25
5262 (50c) **Flag booklet stamp,** microprinted "USPS" at left of flag fold on fourth red stripe, *Feb. 9,* Fort Lauderdale, FL 2.25
5263 (50c) **Flag booklet stamp,** microprinted "USPS" at right of flag fold on fifth white stripe, *Feb. 9,* Fort Lauderdale, FL 2.25
5264-5273 (50c) **Bioluminescent Life,** *Feb. 22,* Fort Pierce, FL 10.00
5264-5273, any single 2.25
5274 (50c) **Illinois Statehood,** *Mar. 5,* Springfield, IL 2.25
5275 (50c) **Mister Rogers,** *Mar. 23,* Pittsburgh, PA 2.25
5276-5279 (50c) **STEM Education,** *Apr. 6,* Washington, DC 5.25
5276-5279, any single 2.25
5280 (50c) **Peace Rose,** *Apr. 21,* Shreveport, LA 2.25
5281 (50c) **Air Mail Centenary,** blue, *May 1,* Washington, DC 2.25
5282 (50c) **Air Mail Centenary,** carmine lake, *Aug. 11,* College Park, MD 2.25
5283 (50c) **Sally Ride,** *May 23,* La Jolla, CA 2.25
5284 (50c) **Flag Act of 1818, Bicent.,** *June 9,* Appleton, WI 2.25
5285-5294 (50c) **Frozen Treats,** *June 20,* Austin, TX 10.00
5285-5294, any single 2.25
5295 $1 **Statue of Freedom,** *June 27,* Bellefonte, PA 4.00
5296 $2 **Statue of Freedom,** *June 27,* Bellefonte, PA 10.00
5297 $5 **Statue of Freedom,** *June 27,* Bellefonte, PA 12.00
5298 (50c) **O Beautiful,** *July 4,* Colorado Springs, CO 20.00
5298a-5298t, any single 2.25
5299 (50c) **Scooby-Doo,** *July 14,* Bloomington, MN 2.25
5300 (50c) **World War I, Cent.,** *July 27,* Kansas City, MO 2.25
5301-5305 (50c) **The Art of Magic,** *Aug. 7,* Las Vegas, NV 6.25
5301-5305, any single 2.25
5306 (50c) **The Art of Magic,** sheet of 3, lenticular stamps, *Aug. 7,* Las Vegas, NV 4.25
5306a, single stamp 2.25
5307-5310 (50c) **Dragons,** *Aug. 9,* Columbus, OH 5.25
5307-5310, any single 2.25
5311 ($1.15) **Poinsettia,** *Aug. 26,* Kansas City, MO 3.50
5312-5315 (50c) **John Lennon,** *Sept. 7,* New York, NY 5.25
5312-5315, any single 2.25
5316 (50c) **First Responders,** *Sept. 13,* Missoula, MT 2.25
5317-5320 (50c) **Birds in Winter,** *Sept. 22,* Quechee, VT 5.25
5317-5320, any single 2.25
5321-5330 (50c) **Hot Wheels, 50th Anniv.,** *Sept. 29,* Fort Worth, TX 10.00
5321-5330, any single 2.25
5331 (50c) **Christmas - Madonna and Child,** *Oct. 3,* Santa Fe, NM 2.25
5332-5335 (50c) **Christmas - Santa Claus,** booklet pane stamps, *Oct. 11,* Pigeon Forge, TN 5.25
5332-5335, any single 2.25
5336 (50c) **Christmas - Santa Claus,** souvenir sheet, *Oct. 11,* Pigeon Forge, TN 2.25
5337 (50c) **Kwanzaa,** *Oct. 10,* Raleigh, NC 2.25
5338 (50c) **Hanukkah,** *Oct. 16,* Newport, RI 2.25

2019

5339 (50c) **Love,** *Jan. 10,* San Juan, PR 2.25

2019

5340 (50c) **Chinese New Year,** *Jan. 17,* Houston, TX 2.25
5341 (15c) **People Wearing Uncle Sam's Hats coil,** serpentine die cut 11 vert., *Jan. 27,* Kansas City, MO 2.25
5342 (55c) **Flag coil,** serpentine die cut 11 horiz., *Jan. 27,* Kansas City, MO 2.40
5343 (55c) **Flag coil,** serpentine die cut 9½ horiz., *Jan. 27,* Kansas City, MO 2.40
5344 (55c) **Flag booklet stamp,** microprinted "USPS" at upper left corner of flag, *Jan. 27,* Kansas City, MO 2.40
5345 (55c) **Flag booklet stamp,** microprinted "USPS" to right of sixth red flag stripe, *Jan. 27,* Kansas City, MO 2.40
5346 (70c) **California Dogface Butterfly,** *Jan. 27,* Kansas City, MO 2.60
5347 $7.35 **Joshua Tree,** *Jan. 27,* Kansas City, MO 15.00
5348 $25.50 **Bethesda Fountain,** *Jan. 27,* Kansas City, MO 51.00
5349 (55c) **Gregory Hines,** *Jan. 28,* New York, NY 2.40
5350-5359 (55c) **Cactus Flowers,** *Feb. 15,* Mesa, AZ 11.00
5350-5359, any single 2.40
5360 (55c) **Alabama Statehood,** *Feb. 23,* Huntsville, AL 2.40
5361 (55c) **Star Ribbon,** serpentine die cut 11¼x10¾, *Mar. 22,* Oakbrook Terrace, IL 2.40
5362 (55c) **Star Ribbon coil stamp,** serpentine die cut 10¾ vert., *Mar. 22,* Oakbrook Terrace, IL 2.40
5363-5366 (35c) **Coral Reefs,** serpentine die cut 11¼x10¾, *Mar. 29,* St. Louis, MO 4.00
5363-5366, any single 2.40

5367-5370 (35c) **Coral Reefs coil stamps,** serpentine die cut 9½ vert., *Mar. 29,* St. Louis, MO 4.00
5367-5370, any single 2.40
5371 (55c) **Marvin Gaye,** *Apr. 2,* Los Angeles, CA 2.40
5372-5376 (55c) **Post Office Murals,** *Apr. 10,* Piggott, AR 6.75
5372-5376, any single 2.40
5377 (55c) **Maureen "Little Mo" Connolly Brinker,** *Apr. 23,* Dallas, TX 2.40
5378-5380 (55c) **Transcontinental Railroad, 150th Anniv.,** *May 10,* Promontory Summit, UT 4.50
5378-5380, any single 2.40
5381 (55c) **Wild and Scenic Rivers,** *May 21,* Bend, OR 13.50
5381a-5381l, any single 2.40
5382-5391 (55c) **Art of Ellsworth Kelly,** *May 31,* Spencertown, NY 12.50
5382-5391, any single 2.40
5392 (55c) **U.S.S. Missouri,** *June 11,* Honolulu, HI 2.40
5393 (55c) **Pres. George Herbert Walker Bush,** *June 12,* College Station, TX 2.40
5394 (55c) **Sesame Street, 50th Anniv.,** *June 22,* Detroit, MI 18.00
5394a-5394p, any single 2.40
5395-5398 (55c) **Frogs,** *July 9,* Boise, ID 5.75
5395-5398, any single 2.40
5399-5400 (55c) **First Moon Landing, 50th Anniv.,** *July 19,* Cape Canaveral, FL 3.50
5399-5400, either single 2.40
5401-5404 (55c) **State and County Fairs,** *July 25,* Minot, ND 5.75
5401-5404, any single 2.40
5405-5408 (55c) **Military Working Dogs,** *Aug. 1,* Omaha, NE 5.75
5405-5408, any single 2.40
5409 (55c) **Woodstock Music Festival, 50th Anniv.,** *Aug. 8,* New York, NY 2.40
5410-5413 (55c) **Tyrannosaurus Rex,** *Aug. 29,* Washington, DC 5.75
5410-5413, any single 2.40
5414 (85c) **Walt Whitman,** *Sept. 12,* Huntington Station, NY 3.00
5415-5418 (55c) **Winter Berries,** *Sept. 17,* Tulsa, OK 5.75
5415-5418, any single 2.40
5419 (55c) **Purple Heart With Frame,** *Oct. 4,* Noblesville, IN 2.40
5420-5423 (55c) **Spooky Silhouettes,** *Oct. 11,* Milford, NH 5.75
5420-5423, any single 2.40
5424-5427 (55c) **Christmas Wreaths,** *Oct. 25,* Freeport, ME 5.75
5424-5427, any single 2.40

2020

5428 (55c) **Chinese New Year,** *Jan. 11,* Monterey Park, CA 2.40
5429 $7.75 **Big Bend National Park,** *Jan. 18,* Big Bend National Park, TX 15.50
5430 $26.35 **Grand Island Ice Caves,** *Jan. 18,* Munising, MI 53.00
5431 (55c) **Love,** *Jan. 23,* Memphis, TN 2.40
5432 (55c) **Gwen Ifill,** *Jan. 30,* Washington, DC 2.40
5433 (10c) **Star and Stripes,** *Feb. 3,* Kansas City, MO 2.40
5434 (55c) **Celebrate,** *Feb. 14,* Mesa, AZ 2.40
5435-5444 (55c) **Wild Orchid,** coil stamps, serpentine die cut 10¾ vert., *Feb. 21,* Coral Gables, FL 11.00
5435-5444, any single 2.40
5445-5454 (55c) **Wild Orchid,** booklet stamps, serpentine die cut 10¾x11 on 2 or 3 sides, *Feb. 21,* Coral Gables, FL 11.00
5445-5454, any single 2.40
5455 (55c) **Arnold Palmer,** *Mar. 4,* Orlando, FL 2.40
5456 (55c) **Maine Statehood Bicentenary,** *Mar. 15,* Augusta, ME 2.40
5457 (55c) **Boutonniere,** *Apr. 2,* Crestwood, KY 2.40
5458 (70c) **Corsage,** *Apr. 2,* Crestwood, KY 2.60
5459 (55c) **Earth Day, 50th Anniv.,** *Apr. 18,* Denver, CO 2.40
5460 ($1.15) **Chrysanthemum,** *Apr. 24,* Burlingame, CA 3.50
5461-5470 (55c) **American Gardens,** *May 13,* Winterthur, DE 12.50
5461-5470, any single 2.40
5471-5474 (55c) **Voices of the Harlem Renaissance,** *May 21,* New York, NY 5.75
5471-5474, any single 2.40
5475-5479 (55c) **Enjoy the Great Outdoors,** *June 13,* Incline Village, NV 6.75
5475-5479, any single 2.40
5480-5483 (55c) **Hip Hop,** *July 1,* New York, NY 5.75
5480-5483, any single 2.40
5484-5493 (55c) **Fruits and Vegetables,** *July 17,* Charleston, WV 12.50
5484-5493, any single 2.40
5494-5503 (55c) **Bugs Bunny, 80th Anniv.,** *July 27,* Burbank, CA 12.50
5494-5503, any single 2.40
5504-5513 (55c) **Wire Sculptures by Ruth Asawa,** *Aug. 13,* San Francisco, CA 12.50
5504-5513, any single 2.40
5514-5518 (55c) **Innovation,** *Aug. 20,* Bellefonte, PA 6.75
5514-5518, any single 2.40
5519-5522 (55c) **Thank You,** *Aug. 21,* Hartford, CT 5.75
5519-5522, any single 2.40
5523 (55c) **Woman Suffrage Centenary,** *Aug. 22,* Seneca Falls, NY 2.40
5524 (55c) **Mayflower in Plymouth Harbor,** *Sept. 17,* Plymouth, MA 2.40
5525 (55c) **Christmas Our Lady of Guápulo,** *Oct. 20,* New York, NY 2.40
5526-5529 (55c) **Christmas Holiday Delights,** *Sept. 24,* Frankenmuth, MI 5.75
5526-5529, any single 2.40
5530 (55c) **Hanukkah,** *Oct. 6,* New Rochelle, NY 2.40
5531 (55c) **Kwanzaa,** *Oct. 13,* Nashville, TN 2.40
5532-5541 (55c) **Winter Scenes,** *Oct. 16,* Winter Park, FL 12.50
5532-5541, any single 2.40
5542 (55c) **Drug Free USA,** *Oct. 27,* Arlington, VA 2.40

2021

5543 (55c) **Love,** *Jan. 14,* Loveland, CO 2.40
5544 (20c) **Brush Rabbit,** serpentine die cut 11¼x11, *Jan. 24,* Sacramento, CA 2.40
5545 (20c) **Brush Rabbit coil stamp,** serpentine die cut 9½ vert., *Jan. 24,* Sacramento, CA 2.40
5546-5549 (36c) **Barns,** serpentine die cut 11x11¼, *Jan. 24,* Barnesville, GA 4.25
5546-5549, any single 2.40
5550-5553 (36c) **Barns coil stamps,** serpentine die cut 11 horiz., *Jan. 24,* Barnesville, GA 4.25
5550-5553, any single 2.40
5554 $7.95 **Castillo de San Marcos,** *Jan. 24,* St. Augustine, FL 16.00
5555 (55c) **August Wilson,** *Jan. 28,* Pittsburgh, PA 2.40
5556 (55c) **Chinese New Year,** *Feb. 2,* Chicago, IL 2.40
5557 (55c) **Chien-Shiung Wu,** *Feb. 11,* New York, NY 2.40
5558-5567 (55c) **Garden Beauty,** *Feb. 23,* Bloomfield, IN 12.50
5558-5567, any single 2.40
5568 (75c) **Colorado Hairstreak Butterfly,** *Mar. 9,* Estes Park, CO 2.75
5569-5572 (55c) **Espresso Drinks,** *Apr. 9,* Seattle, WA 5.75
5569-5572, any single 2.40
5573-5582 (55c) **Star Wars Droids,** *May 4,* Nicasio, CA 12.50
5573-5582, any single 2.40
5583-5592 (55c) **Heritage Breeds,** *May 17,* Mount Vernon, VA 12.50
5583-5592, any single 2.40
5593 (55c) **Go For Broke,** *June 3,* Los Angeles, CA 2.40
5594-5597 (55c) **Paintings by Emilio Sanchez,** *June 10,* Miami, FL 5.75
5594-5597, any single 2.40
5598-5607 (55c) **Sun Science,** *June 18,* Greenbelt, MD 12.50
5598-5607, any single 2.40
5608 (55c) **Yogi Berra,** *June 24,* Little Falls, NJ 2.40
5609-5613 (55c) **Tap Dance,** *July 10,* New York, NY 6.75
5609-5613, any single 2.40
5614 (55c) **Mystery Message,** *July 14,* Washington, DC 2.40
5615-5618 (55c) **Western Wear,** *July 23,* Abilene, TX 5.75
5615-5618, any single 2.40
5619 (95c) **Ursula K. Le Guin,** *July 27,* Portland, OR 3.25
5620 (55c) **Raven Story,** *July 30,* Juneau, AK 2.40
5621-5625 (55c) **Mid-Atlantic Lighthouses,** *Aug. 6,* Highlands, NJ 6.75
5621-5625, any single 2.40
5626 (55c) **Missouri Statehood Bicentenary,** *Aug. 10,* Jefferson City, MO 2.40
5627-5634 (55c) **Backyard Games,** *Aug. 12,* Rosemont, IL 10.00
5627-5634, any single 2.40
5635 (58c) **Happy Birthday,** *Sept. 9,* Toast, NC 2.40
5636-5639 (58c) **Message Monsters,** *Sept. 24,* Topeka, KS 6.00
5636-5639, any single 2.40
5640-5643 (58c) **Day of the Dead,** *Sept. 30,* El Paso, TX 6.00
5640-5643, any single 2.40
5644-5647 (58c) **Christmas,** *Oct. 7,* Santa Claus, IN 6.00
5644-5647, any single 2.40
5648-5651 (58c) **Otters in Snow,** *Oct. 12,* Otter, MT 6.00
5648-5651, any single 2.40

2022

5652 4c **Blueberries,** serpentine die cut 11¼x11, *Jan. 9,* Blue Hill, ME 2.40
5653 4c **Blueberries coil,** serpentine die cut 10¾ vert., *Jan. 9,* Blue Hill, ME 2.40
5654 (58c) **Flags,** serpentine die cut 11¼x11, *Jan. 9,* Findlay, OH 2.40
5655 (58c) **Flags coil,** serpentine die cut 10¾ vert., *Jan. 9,* Findlay, OH 2.40
5656 (58c) **Flags coil,** serpentine die cut 11 vert., *Jan. 9,* Findlay, OH 2.40
5657 (58c) **Flags coil,** serpentine die cut 9½ vert., *Jan. 9,* Findlay, OH 2.40
5658 (58c) **Flags booklet stamp,** serpentine die cut 11¼x10¾ on 2 or 3 sides, microprinted "USPS" above lower connector on flagpole at left, *Jan. 9,* Findlay, OH 2.40
5659 (58c) **Flags booklet stamp,** serpentine die cut 11¼x10¾ on 2 or 3 sides, microprinted "USPS" above lowest blue flag field, *Jan. 9,* Findlay, OH 2.40
5660-5661 (58c) **Love,** *Jan. 14,* Romeo, MI 3.75
5660-5661, any single 2.40
5662 (58c) **Chinese New Year,** *Jan. 20,* New York, NY 2.40
5663 (58c) **Edmonia Lewis,** *Jan. 26,* Washington, DC 2.40
5664-5665 (5c) **Butterfly Garden Flowers,** *Feb. 1,* Pine Mountain, GA 2.40
5664-5665, any single 2.40
5666 $8.95 **Monument Valley,** *Feb. 14,* Monument Valley, UT 18.00
5667 $26.95 **Palace of Fine Arts,** *Feb. 14,* San Francisco, CA 54.00
5668-5671 (58c) **Title IX,** *Mar. 3,* Washington, DC 6.00
5668-5671, any single 2.40
5672-5675 (58c) **Mountain Flora,** coil stamps, serpentine die cut 10 vert., *Mar. 14,* Alpine, WY 6.00
5672-5675, any single 2.40
5676-5679 (58c) **Mountain Flora,** booklet stamps, serpentine die cut 10¾x11 on 2 or 3 sides, *Mar. 14,* Alpine, WY 6.00
5676-5679, any single 2.40
5680 ($1.30) **African Daisy,** *Mar. 14,* Kansas City, MO 4.00
5681 (58c) **Tulips,** *Mar. 24,* Mount Vernon, WA 2.40
5682 (78c) **Sunflower Bouquet,** *Mar. 24,* Lawrence, KS 2.75
5683 (58c) **Shel Silverstein,** *Apr. 8,* Chicago, IL 2.40
5684-5687 (10c) **Flags on Barns,** coil stamps, *Apr. 14,* Halifax, PA 2.50
5684-5687, any single 2.40
5688-5692 (58c) **Paintings by George Morrison,** *Apr. 22,* Grand Portage, MN 7.00
5688-5692, any single 2.40
5693 (58c) **Eugenie Clark,** *May 4,* Sarasota, FL 2.40
5694-5697 (58c) **Women's Rowing,** *May 13,* Philadelphia, PA 6.00
5694-5697, any single 2.40
5698 (58c) **Mighty Mississippi,** *May 23,* Memphis, TN 25.00
5698a-5698j, any single 2.40
5699 (78c) **Katherine Graham,** *June 14,* Washington, DC 2.75
5700 $2 **Floral Geometry,** *June 20,* Kansas City, MO 5.25
5701 $5 **Floral Geometry,** *June 20,* Kansas City, MO 10.00
5702 (58c) **Nancy Reagan,** *July 6,* Simi Valley, CA 2.40
5703-5707 (60c) **Mariachi,** *July 15,* Albuquerque, NM 7.25
5703-5707, any single 2.40
5708 (60c) **Pete Seeger,** *July 21,* Newport, RI 2.40
5709-5712 (60c) **Buzz Lightyear,** *Aug. 3,* Los Angeles, CA 6.00
5709-5712, any single 2.40
5713 (60c) **National Marine Sanctuaries,** *Aug. 5,* Santa Cruz, CA 20.00
5713a-5713p, any single 2.40

SEMI-POSTAL FIRST DAY COVERS

1998

B1 32c +8c **Breast Cancer,** *July 29,* Washington, DC (51,775) 2.00

2002

B2 (34c+11c) **Heroes of 2001,** *June 7,* New York, NY 3.50
Any other city 3.00

2003

B3 (37c+8c) **Stop Family Violence,** *Oct. 8,* Washington, DC 1.60
Any other city 1.60

2011

B4 (44c+11c) **Save Vanishing Wildlife,** *Sept. 20,* Washington, DC 2.40

2014

B5 (49c+11c) **Breast Cancer Awareness,** litho., *Sept. 30,* Sacramento, CA 2.40

2017

B6 (49c+11c) **Alzheimer's Disease Awareness,** *Nov. 30,* Baltimore, MD 2.40

2019

B7 (55c+10c) **Healing Post-traumatic Stress Disorder,** *Dec. 2,* Charlotte, NC 2.50

AIR POST FIRST DAY COVERS

1918

C1 6c **orange,** *Dec. 10* — *40,000.*

1923

C4 8c **dark green,** *Aug. 15* — 400.00
C5 16c **dark blue,** *Aug. 17* — 600.00
C6 24c **carmine,** *Aug. 21* — 750.00

1926-27

C7 10c **dark blue,** *Feb. 13, 1926* — 70.00
Chicago, Ill. — 85.00
Detroit, Mich. — 85.00
Cleveland, Ohio — 130.00
Dearborn, Mich. — 130.00
C8 15c **olive brown,** *Sept. 18, 1926* — 85.00
C9 20c **yellow green,** *Jan. 25, 1927* — 100.00
New York, N.Y. — 125.00
C10 10c **dark blue,** *June 18, 1927* — 25.00
St. Louis, Mo. — 25.00
Little Falls, Minn. — 35.00
Detroit, Mich. — 35.00
C10a Booklet pane of 3, *May 26, 1928* — 875.00
Cleveland Midwestern Philatelic Sta. cancel — 800.00
C10a & 645 on one cover, Washington, D.C. — 1,000.

1928-30

C11 5c **carmine & blue,** *July 25, 1928,* pair — 50.00
C12 5c **violet,** *Feb. 10, 1930* — 14.00
C13 65c **green,** *Apr. 19, 1930* — 1,000.
C14 $1.30 **brown,** *Apr. 19, 1930* — 900.00
C15 $2.60 **blue,** *Apr. 19, 1930* — 1,000.
C13-C15 on one cover — 10,000.

Values are for first day covers flown on Zeppelin flights with appropriate markings. Non-flown covers sell for less.

1931-33

C16 5c **violet,** *Aug. 19, 1931* — 175.00
C17 8c **olive bister,** *Sept. 26, 1932* — 15.00
C18 50c **green,** *Oct. 2, 1933,* New York, N.Y. *(3,500)* — 200.00
Akron, Ohio, *Oct. 4* — 300.00
Washington, D.C., *Oct. 5* — 275.00
Miami, Fla., *Oct. 6* — 150.00
Chicago, Ill., *Oct. 7* — 250.00

1934-37

C19 6c **dull orange,** *June 30, 1934,* Baltimore, Md. — *240.00*
New York, N.Y. — *1,000.*
Brooklyn, N.Y. — 1,500.
San Francisco, Calif. — 1,750.
Washington, D.C., *July 1* — 10.00

Catalogue values for Nos. C20-C45 are for addressed covers with the most common cachets.

C20 25c **blue,** *Nov. 22, 1935 (10,910)* — 40.00
San Francisco, Cal. *(15,000)* — 35.00
C21 20c **green,** *Feb. 15, 1937* — 45.00
C22 50c **carmine,** *Feb. 15, 1937* — 50.00
C21-C22 on one cover — 100.00

First day covers of Nos. C21 and C22 total 40,000.

1938-39

C23 6c **dark blue & carmine,** *May 14, 1938,* Dayton, Ohio *(116,443)* — 17.50
St. Petersburg, Fla. *(95,121)* — 17.50
Washington, D.C., *May 15* — 4.00
C24 30c **dull blue,** *May 16, 1939,* New York, N.Y. *(68,634)* — 50.00

1941-44

C25 6c **carmine,** *June 25, 1941 (99,986)* — 4.00
C25a Booklet pane of 3, *Mar. 18, 1943* — 22.50
C26 8c **olive green,** *Mar. 21, 1944 (147,484)* — 4.00
C27 10c **violet,** *Aug. 15, 1941,* Atlantic City, N.J. *(87,712)* — 6.00
C28 15c **brown carmine,** *Aug. 19, 1941,* Baltimore, Md. *(74,000)* — 8.00
C29 20c **bright green,** *Aug. 27, 1941,* Philadelphia, Pa. *(66,225)* — 10.00
C30 30c **blue,** *Sept. 25, 1941,* Kansas City, Mo. *(57,175)* — 17.50
C31 50c **orange,** *Oct. 29, 1941,* St. Louis, Mo. *(54,580)* — 35.00

1946-48

C32 5c **carmine,** *Sept. 25, 1946* — 2.00

First day covers of Nos. C32 & UC14 total 396,669.

C33 5c **carmine,** *Mar. 26, 1947 (342,634)* — 2.00
C34 10c **black,** *Aug. 30, 1947 (265,773)* — 2.00
C35 15c **bright blue green,** *Aug. 20, 1947,* New York, N.Y. *(230,338)* — 1.75
C36 25c **blue,** *July 30, 1947,* San Francisco, Cal. *(201,762)* — 2.25
C37 5c **carmine, coil,** *Jan. 15, 1948 (192,084)* — 1.75
C38 5c **New York City,** *July 31, 1948,* New York, N.Y. *(371,265)* — 1.75

1949

C39 6c **carmine,** *Jan. 18 (266,790)* — 1.50
C39a Booklet pane of 6, *Nov. 18, 1949,* New York, N.Y. — 8.00
C40 6c **Alexandria Bicentennial,** *May 11,* Alexandria, Va. *(386,717)* — 1.50
C41 6c **carmine coil,** *Aug. 25 (240,386)* — 1.25
C42 10c **U.P.U.,** *Nov. 18,* New Orleans, La. *(270,000)* — 1.75
C43 15c **U.P.U.,** *Oct. 7,* Chicago, Ill. *(246,833)* — 2.75
C44 25c **U.P.U.,** *Nov. 30,* Seattle, Wash. *(220,215)* — 3.75
C45 6c **Wright Brothers,** *Dec. 17,* Kitty Hawk, N.C. *(378,585)* — 2.75

Catalogue values from this point to the end of the section are for unaddressed covers with the most common cachets.

1952-59

C46 80c **Hawaii,** *Mar. 26, 1952,* Honolulu, Hawaii, *(89,864)* — 22.50
C47 6c **Powered Flight,** *May 29, 1953,* Dayton, Ohio *(359,050)* — 1.50
C48 4c **bright blue,** *Sept. 3, 1954,* Philadelphia, Pa. *(295,720)* — 1.00
C49 6c **Air Force,** *Aug. 1, 1957 (356,683)* — 3.00
C50 5c **red,** *July 31, 1958,* Colorado Springs, Colo. *(207,954)* — 1.00
C51 7c **blue,** *July 31, 1958,* Philadelphia, Pa. *(204,401)* — 1.00
C51a Booklet pane of 6, San Antonio, Tex. *(119,769)* — 9.00
C52 7c **blue coil,** *July 31, 1958,* Miami, Fla. *(181,603)* — 1.00
C53 7c **Alaska Statehood,** *Jan. 3, 1959,* Juneau, Alaska *(489,752)* — 2.00
C54 7c **Balloon Jupiter,** *Aug. 17, 1959,* Lafayette, Ind.*(383,556)* — 1.75
C55 7c **Hawaii Statehood,** *Aug. 21, 1959,* Honolulu, Hawaii *(533,464)* — 2.00
C56 10c **Pan American Games,** *Aug. 27, 1959,* Chicago, Ill. *(302,306)* — 1.00

1959-66

C57 10c **Liberty Bell,** *June 10, 1960,* Miami, Fla. *(246,509)* — 1.50
C58 15c **Statue of Liberty,** *Nov. 20, 1959,* New York, N.Y. *(259,412)* — 2.00
C59 25c **Abraham Lincoln,** *Apr. 22, 1960,* San Francisco, Cal. *(211,235)* — 1.75
C59a 25c Tagged, *Dec. 29, 1966 (about 3,000)* — 50.00
C60 7c **carmine,** *Aug. 12, 1960,* Arlington, Va. *(247,190)* — 1.00
C60a Booklet pane of 6, *Aug. 19, 1960,* St. Louis, Mo. *(143,363)* — 8.00
C61 7c **carmine coil,** *Oct. 22, 1960,* Atlantic City, N.J. *(197,995)* — 1.00

1961-67

C62 13c **Liberty Bell,** *June 28, 1961,* New York, N.Y. *(316,166)* — 1.00
C62a 13c Tagged, *Feb. 15, 1967* — 50.00
C63 15c **Redrawn Statue of Liberty,** *Jan. 13, 1961,* Buffalo, N.Y. *(192,976)* — 1.00
C63a 15c Tagged, *Jan. 11, 1967* — 50.00
C64 8c **carmine,** *Dec. 5, 1962 (288,355)* — 1.00
C64b Booklet pane of 5 + label *(146,835)* — 3.50
C64a 8c Tagged, *Aug. 1, 1963,* Dayton, Ohio *(262,720)* — 2.50
C65 8c **carmine coil,** *Dec. 5, 1962 (220,173)* — 1.00

1963-69

C66 15c **Montgomery Blair,** *May 3, 1963,* Silver Spring, Md. *(260,031)* — 2.00
C67 6c **Bald Eagle,** *July 12, 1963,* Boston, Mass. *(268,265)* — 1.00
C67a 6c Tagged, *Feb. 15, 1967* — 50.00
C68 8c **Amelia Earhart,** *July 24, 1963,* Atchison, Kan. *(437,996)* — 5.00
C69 8c **Robert H. Goddard,** *Oct. 5, 1964,* Roswell, N.M. *(421,020)* — 3.00
C70 8c **Alaska Purchase,** *Mar. 30, 1967,* Sitka, Alaska *(554,784)* — 1.50
C71 20c **Audubon,** *Apr. 26, 1967,* Audubon (Station of N.Y.C.), N.Y. *(227,930)* — 2.00
C72 10c **carmine,** *Jan. 5, 1968,* San Francisco, Cal. — 1.00
C72b Booklet pane of 8 — 3.75
C72c Booklet pane of 5 + label, slogan 4 *Jan. 6, 1968* — 125.00
With slogan 5 — 110.00
C73 10c **carmine coil,** *Jan. 5, 1968,* San Francisco, Cal. — 1.00
C74 10c **Air Mail Service,** *May 15, 1968 (521,084)* — 1.50
C75 20c **USA and Jet,** *Nov. 22, 1968,* New York, N.Y. *(276,244)* — 1.25
C76 10c **Moon Landing,** *Sept. 9, 1969 (8,743,070)* — 6.00

1971-73

C77 9c **red,** *May 15, 1971,* Kitty Hawk, N.C. — 1.00

First day cancellation was applied to 379,442 covers of Nos. C77 and UXC10.

C78 11c **carmine,** *May 7, 1971,* Spokane, Wash. — 1.00
C78a Booklet pane of 4 + 2 labels — 3.00
C79 13c **carmine,** *Nov. 16, 1973,* New York, N.Y. *(282,550)* — 1.00
C79a Booklet pane of 5 + label, *Dec. 27, 1973,* Chicago, Ill. — 3.00

First day cancellation was applied to 464,750 covers of Nos. C78, C78a and C82, and to 204,756 covers of Nos. C79a and C83.

C80 17c **Statue of Liberty,** *July 13, 1971,* Lakehurst, N.J. *(172,269)* — 1.50
C81 21c **USA and Jet,** *May 21, 1971 (293,140)* — 1.00
C82 11c **carmine coil,** *May 7, 1971,* Spokane, Wash. — 1.00
C83 13c **carmine coil,** *Dec. 27, 1973,* Chicago, Ill. — 1.00
C84 11c **National Parks Centennial,** *May 3, 1972,* Honaunau, Hawaii *(364,816)* — 1.00
C85 11c **Olympics,** *Aug. 17, 1972* — 1.00

First day cancellation was applied to 971,536 covers of Nos. 1460-1462 and C85.

C86 11c **Electronics,** *July 10, 1973,* New York, N.Y. — 1.00

First day cancellation was applied to 1,197,700 covers of Nos. 1500-1502 and C86.

1974-79

C87 18c **Statue of Liberty,** *Jan. 11, 1974,* Hempstead, N.Y. *(216,902)* — 1.25
C88 26c **Mt. Rushmore,** *Jan. 2, 1974,* Rapid City, S.D. *(210,470)* — 2.00
C89 25c **Plane and Globes,** *Jan. 2, 1976,* Honolulu, Hawaii — 1.00
C90 31c **Plane, Globes and Flag,** *Jan. 2, 1976,* Honolulu, Hawaii — 1.25
C92a 31c **Wright Brothers,** *Sept. 23, 1978,* Dayton, Ohio — 4.00
C91-C92, any single — 3.00
C94a 21c **Octave Chanute,** *Mar. 29, 1979,* Chanute, Kan. *(459,235)* — 4.00
C93-C94, any single — 3.00
C96a 25c **Wiley Post,** *Nov. 20, 1979,* Oklahoma City, Okla. — 4.00
C95-C96, any single — 3.00
C97 31c **Olympics,** *Nov. 1, 1979,* Colorado Springs, CO — 1.50

1980

C98 40c **Philip Mazzei,** *Oct. 13* — 1.50
C99 28c **Blanche Stuart Scott,** *Dec. 30,* Hammondsport, NY *(238,502)* — 2.00
C100 35c **Glenn Curtiss,** *Dec. 30,* Hammondsport, NY *(208,502)* — 1.50

1983

C104a 28c **Olympics,** *June 17,* San Antonio, TX *(901,028)* — 3.75
C101-C104, any single — 1.75
C108a 40c **Olympics,** *Apr. 8,* Los Angeles, CA *(1,001,657)* — 5.00
C105-C108, any single — 1.75
C112a 35c **Olympics,** *Nov. 4,* Colorado Springs, CO*(897,729)* — 4.50
C109-C112, any single — 1.75

1985

C113 33c **Alfred V. Verville,** *Feb. 13,* Garden City, NY — 1.50
C114 39c **Lawrence & Elmer Sperry,** *Feb. 13,* Garden City, NY — 1.50

First day cancel was applied to 429,290 covers bearing one more of Nos. C113-C114.

C115 44c **Transpacific Air Mail,** *Feb. 15,* San Francisco, CA *(269,229)* — 1.75

A total of 269,229 first day cancels were applied for Nos. C115 and UXC22.

C116 44c **Junipero Serra,** *Aug. 22,* San Diego, CA *(254,977)* — 2.00

1988

C117 44c **Settling of New Sweden,** *Mar. 29,* Wilmington, DE *(213,445)* — 1.50
C118 45c **Samuel P. Langley,** *May 14,* San Diego, CA — 1.50
C119 36c **Igor Sikorsky,** *June 23,* Stratford, CT *(162,986)* — 3.00

1989

C120 45c **French Revolution,** *July 14 (309,975)* — 1.50
C121 45c **Southeast Carved Figure,** *Oct. 12,* San Juan, PR *(93,569)* — 1.50
C125a 45c **Future Mail Transportation,** *Nov. 27 (765,479)* — 6.50
C122-C125, any single — 2.00
C126 45c **Future Mail Transportation Souvenir Sheet,** *Nov. 24 (257,826)* — 6.50

1990

C127 45c **Tropical Coast,** *Oct. 12,* Grand Canyon, AZ *(137,068)* — 1.50

1991

C128	50c	**Harriet Quimby,** *Apr. 27,* Plymouth, MI	2.00
C129	40c	**William T. Piper,** *May 17,* Denver, CO	2.00
C130	50c	**Antarctic Treaty,** *June 21*	2.00
C131	50c	**Bering Land Bridge,** *Oct. 12,* Anchorage, AK	2.00

1999

C133	48c	**Niagara Falls,** *May 12,* Niagara Falls, NY *(20,878)*	2.50
C134	40c	**Rio Grande,** *July 30,* Milwaukee, WI	2.50
		any other city	2.50

First day cancel was applied to 42,144 covers bearing one more of Nos. 3330, C134.

2000

C135	60c	**Grand Canyon,** *Jan. 20,* Grand Canyon, AZ *(64,282)*	3.00

2001

C136	70c	**Nine-mile Prairie,** *Mar. 6,* Lincoln, NE	2.50
C137	80c	**Mt. McKinley,** *Apr. 17,* Fairbanks, AK	3.00
C138	60c	**Acadia National Park,** *May 30,* Bar Harbor, ME	3.00

2006

C139	63c	**Bryce Canyon National Park,** *Feb. 24,* St. Louis, MO	3.00
		Any other city	3.00
C140	75c	**Great Smoky Mountains National Park,** *Feb. 24,* St. Louis, MO	3.00
		Any other city	3.00
C141	84c	**Yosemite National Park,** *Feb. 24,* St. Louis, MO	3.00
		Any other city	3.00

2007

C142	69c	**Okefenokee Swamp,** *June 1,* McLean, VA	3.00
C143	90c	**Hagatña Bay,** *June 1,* Barrigada, GU	3.00

2008

C144	72c	**13-Mile Woods, New Hampshire,** *May 16,* Rochester, NY	3.00
C145	94c	**Trunk Bay, St. John, Virgin Islands,** *May 16,* Rochester, NY	3.50
		St. John, VI	3.50

2009

C146	79c	**Zion National Park,** *June 28,* Washington, DC	3.50
C147	98c	**Grand Teton National Park,** *June 28,* Washington, DC	3.50

2011

C148	80c	**Voyageurs National Park,** *Apr. 11,* Washington, DC	3.00

2012

C149	85c	**Glacier National Park,** *Jan. 19,* Kalispell, MT	3.00
C150	$1.05	**Amish Buggy, Lancaster County, Pennsylvania,** *Jan. 20,* Lancaster, PA	4.00

BOOKLETS: PANES & COVERS

Most booklet panes issued before 1962 consist of a vertical block of 6 stamps perforated vertically through the center. The panes are perforated horizontally on all but the bottom edge and the top of the selvage tab. The selvage top, the two sides and the bottom are straight edged. Exceptions for panes issued before 1962 are the 1917 American Expeditionary Forces panes (30 stamps); Lindbergh and 6¢ 1943 air mails (3), and the Savings Stamps (10). Since 1962, panes have been issued with 3 to 20 stamps and various configurations. They have included one or more labels and two or more stamps se-tenant.

Flat plate booklet panes, with the exceptions noted above, were made from specially designed plates of 180 or 360 subjects. They are collected in plate positions. There are nine collectible positions on the 180-subject plate and 12 on the 360-subject plate.

Rotary booklet panes issued from 1926 to May 1978 (except for Nos. 1623a and 1623Bc) were made from specially designed plates of 180, 320, 360, and 400 subjects. They also are collected in plate positions. There are five collectible positions on the 360-subject plates which were printed before electric eye plates came into use, and 18 collectible positions on the Type II "new design" 360-subject rotary plates. There are 17 collectible positions in the rotary air mail 180-subject plate, and 21 collectible positions in the Type IV "modified design" 360-subject plate. There are 13 collectible positions on the 320-subject plates and 24 on the 400 subject plates. There are five collectible positions on Defense and War Savings 300-subject plates.

The generally accepted methods of designating pane positions as illustrated and explained hereafter are those suggested by George H. Beans in the May 1913 issue of "Everybody's Philatelist" and by B. H. Mosher in his monograph "Discovering U.S. Rotary Pane Varieties 1926-78." Some collectors seek all varieties possible, but the majority collect unused (A) panes and plate number (D) panes from flat plate issues, and plain panes and panes with electric eye bars and electric eye dashes, where available, from rotary plates.

Starting in 1977, BEP made two major changes in booklet production. Printing of panes was gradually moved from rotary plates to sleeves for modern high speed presses. Also, booklet production was transferred to Goebel booklet-forming machines. These changes virtually eliminated collectible pane positions for several years. However, beginning with No. BK156 (No. 2276a), BEP and other printers began placing printing process control marks in pane tabs. As a result, specialist booklet pane collectors actively resumed collecting pane positions. Collectible positions on these issues are not shown in this catalogue but can be found in the United States Stamp Society's Research Paper No. 2 "Folded Style Checklist," Michael O. Perry, editor. Also, because of the requirements of the Goebel machine, the subject size of printing plates or sleeves varied widely. For these reasons, plate layouts are not shown for each issue. The plate layout for No. 1288c and the sleeve layout for No. 1623a are shown as typical.

The following panes, issued after Mar. 11, 1977, were printed from pairs of rotary plates and assembled into booklets on the Goebel machine: Nos. 1288c, 1742a, 1819a, 1889a, and 1949a. One pane in 12 of those issues may have a join line along either long side of the pane, creating three collectible positions: no join line, join line top (or right) and join line bottom (or left). Except for Nos. 1736a and 2276a, all other booklet panes issued from Mar. 11, 1977 on were printed from intaglio sleeves, gravure cylinders, and/or offset plates.

At least one pane in every booklet produced on the BEP's Goebel machines contains two register marks in the tab: a cross register line (CRL) 1.5mm wide which runs across the width of the tab and a length register mark (LRM), typically 1.5x5mm, usually placed above the right hand (or top) stamp of the pane. Nos. 1623a and 1623Bc were regularly issued with the LRM over either stamp. Some examples of Nos. 1893a, 2121a and 3003Ab were issued with the LRM over the left stamp.

Starting with No. 1889a (except for No. 1948a), plate numbers (1 to 5 digits) were placed in the tab, normally over the left stamp. On booklets containing Nos. 1889a, 1949a and 2113a, the plate number is supposed to be on the top pane, the second pane not having a number. All subsequent multi-pane booklets have the plate number on each pane. Some multi-pane booklets contain panes with different plate numbers. The booklet value is determined by the top pane.

Most recent booklets have been printed by contractors other than the BEP so markings may differ or be absent.

Panes in all booklets assembled on the Goebel machine will be folded at least once. **Repeated handling of booklets with folded panes may cause the panes to fall apart.**

Booklet panes with tabs attached to the cover by adhesive instead of staples are valued on the basis of the tab intact. Minor damage on the back of the tab due to removal from the booklet does not affect the value. Some of these panes were furnished to first day cover processors unfolded and not pasted into covers. Around 1989, these panes were available to collectors through the Philatelic Agency.

All panes from 1967 to date are tagged, unless otherwise stated.

Dr. William R. Bush, Morton Dean Joyce, Robert E. Kitson, Richard F. Larkin, Dr. Robert Marks, Bruce H. Mosher, Michael O. Perry, the United States Stamp Society (formerly the Bureau Issues Association), and the Booklet Collectors Club helped the editors extensively in compiling the listings and preparing the illustrations of booklets, covers and plate layouts.

All illustrations in this section are reduced in size to a greater or lesser extent.

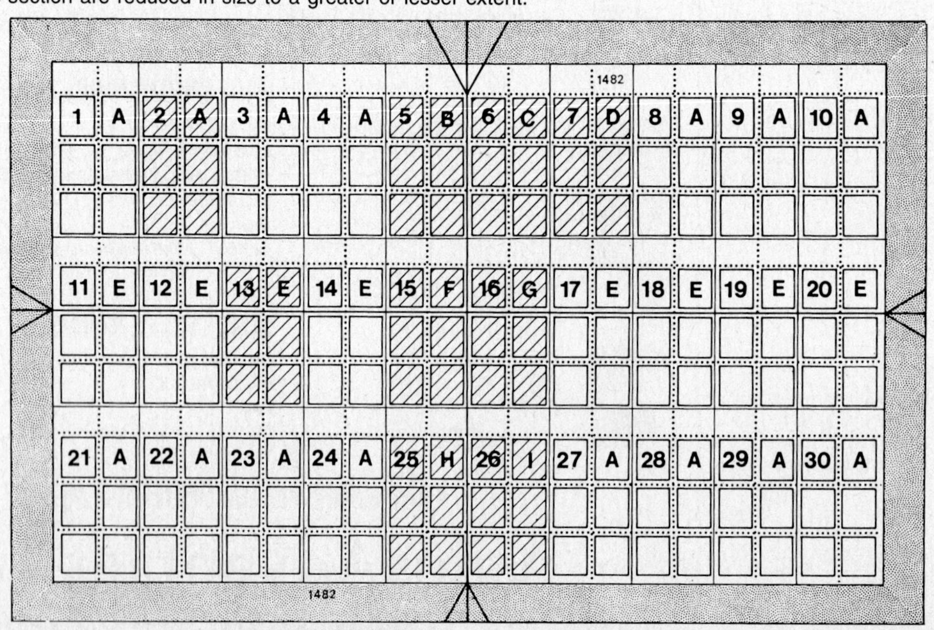

180-SUBJECT PLATE — 9 Collectible Positions

Beginning at upper left and reading from left to right, the panes are designated from 1 to 30. All positions not otherwise identifiable are designated by the letter A: Pane 1A, 2A, 3A, 4A, etc.

The identifiable positions are as follows:

A — The ordinary booklet pane without distinguishing features. Occurs in Position 1, 2, 3, 4, 8, 9, 10, 21, 22, 23, 24, 27, 28, 29, 30.
B — Split arrow and guide line at right. Occurs in Position 5 only.
C — Split arrow and guide line at left. Occurs in Position 6 only.
D — Plate number pane. Occurs in Position 7 only.
E — Guide line pane showing horizontal guide line between stamps 1-2 and 3-4 of the pane. Occurs in Positions 11, 12, 13, 14, 17, 18, 19, and 20.
F — Guide line through pane and at right. Occurs in Position 15 only.

G — Guide line through pane and at left. Occurs in Position 16 only.
H — Guide line at right. Occurs in Position 25 only.
I — Guide line at left. Occurs in Position 26 only.
Only positions B, F and H or C, G and I may be obtained from the same sheet, depending on whether the knife which separated the panes fell to right or left of the line. Side arrows, bottom arrows, or bottom plate numbers are seldom found because the margin of the sheets is usually cut off, as are the sides and bottom of each pane. In the illustrations, the dotted lines represent the rows of perforations, the unbroken lines represents the knife cut.

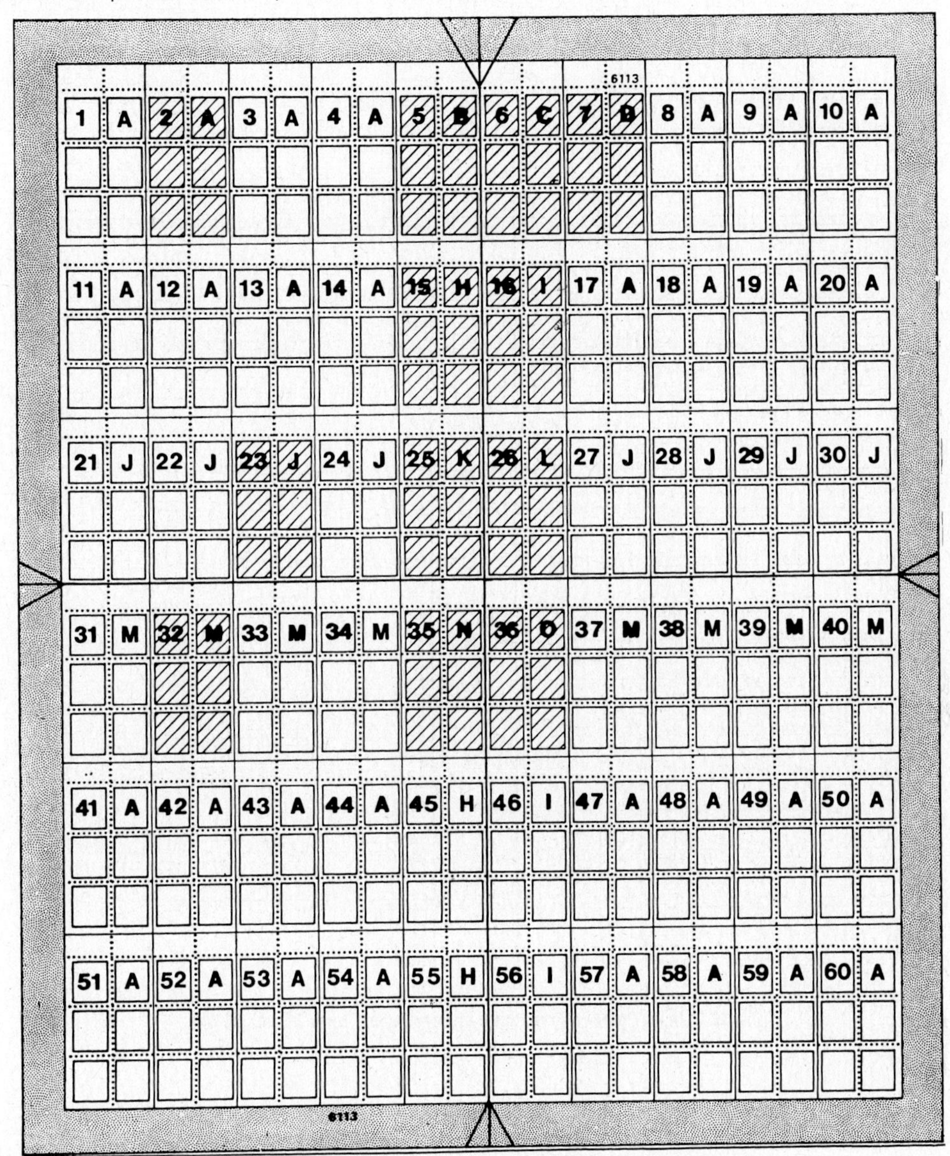

360-SUBJECT PLATE — 12 Collectible Positions

As with the 180-Subject Sheets, the position of the various panes is indicated by numbers beginning in the upper left corner with the No. 1 and reading from left to right to No. 60.

The identifiable positions are as follows:

A — The ordinary booklet pane without distinguishing features. Occurs in Positions 1, 2, 3, 4, 8, 9, 10, 11, 12, 13, 14, 17, 18, 19, 20, 41, 42, 43, 44, 47, 48, 49, 50, 51, 52, 53, 54, 57, 58, 59, and 60.
B — Split arrow and guide line at right. Occurs in Position 5 only.
C — Split arrow and guide line at left. Occurs in Position 6 only.
D — Plate number pane. Occurs in Position 7 only.
E, F, G — Do not occur in the 360-Subject Plate.
H — Guide line at right. Occurs in Positions 15, 45, and 55.
I — Guide line at left. Occurs in Positions 16, 46, and 56.
J — Guide line at bottom. Occurs in Positions 21, 22, 23, 24, 27, 28, 29 and 30.
K — Guide line at right and bottom. Occurs in Position 25 only.
L — Guide line at left and bottom. Occurs in Position 26 only.
M — Guide line at top. Occurs in Positions 31, 32, 33, 34, 37, 38, 39 and 40.
N — Guide line at top and right. Occurs in Position 35 only.
O — Guide line at top and left. Occurs in Position 36 only.

Only one each of Positions B or C, K, L, N or O; four positions of H or I, and eight or nine positions of J or M may be obtained from each 360 subject sheet, depending on whether the knife fell to the right or left, top or bottom of the guide lines.

Because the horizontal guide line appears so close to the bottom row of stamps on panes Nos. 21 to 30, Positions M, N, and O occur with great deal less frequency than Positions J, K and L.

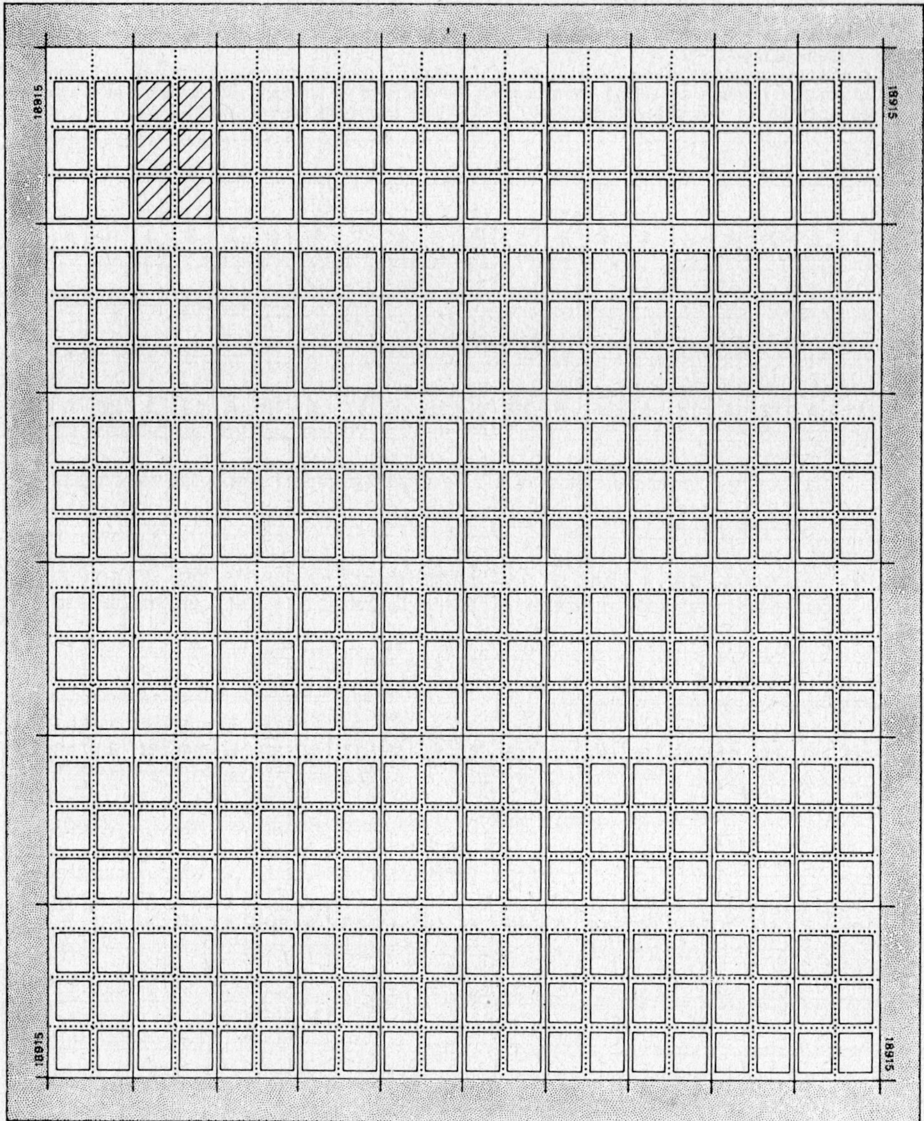

The 360-Subject Rotary Press Plate (before Electric Eye) Position A only

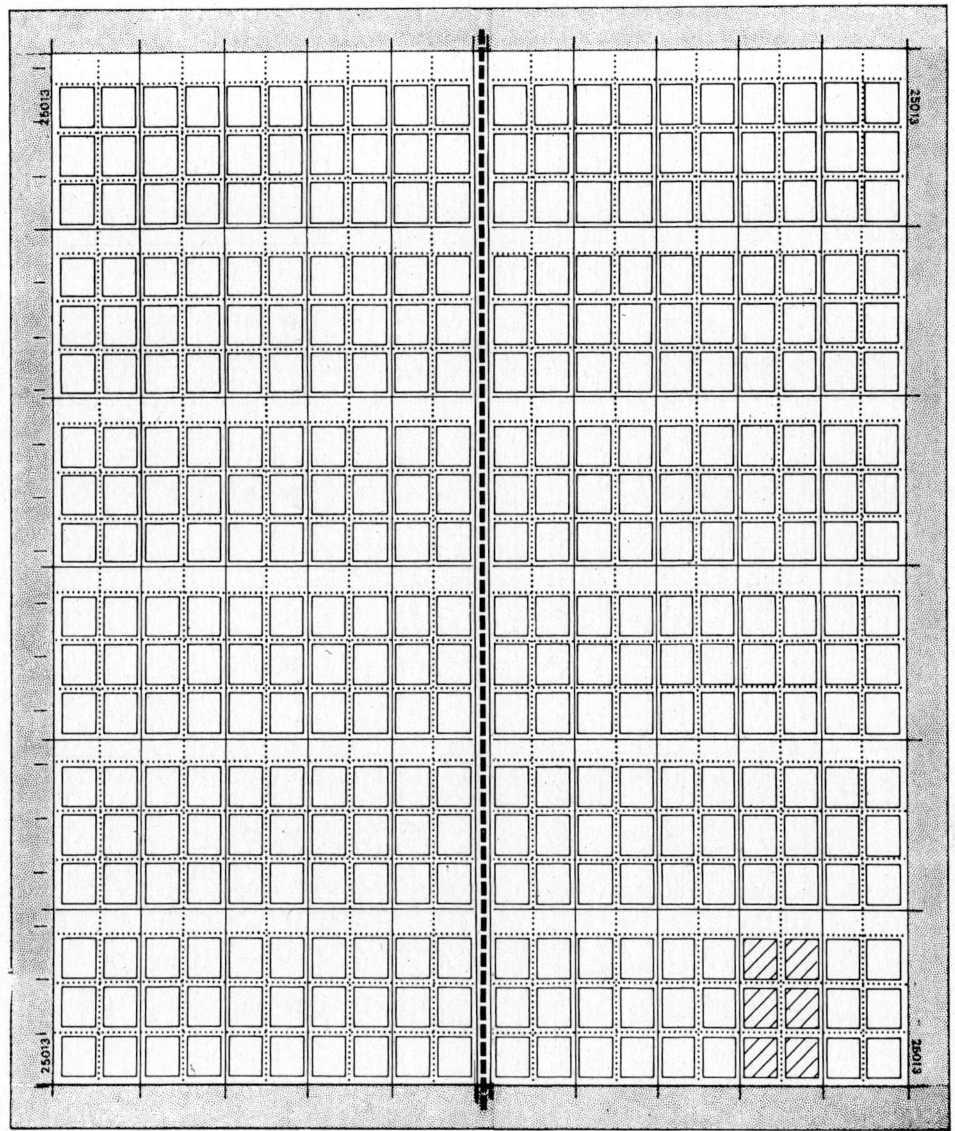

The 360-Subject Rotary Press Plate — Electric Eye

A modified design was put into use in 1956. The new plates have 20 frame bars instead of 17.

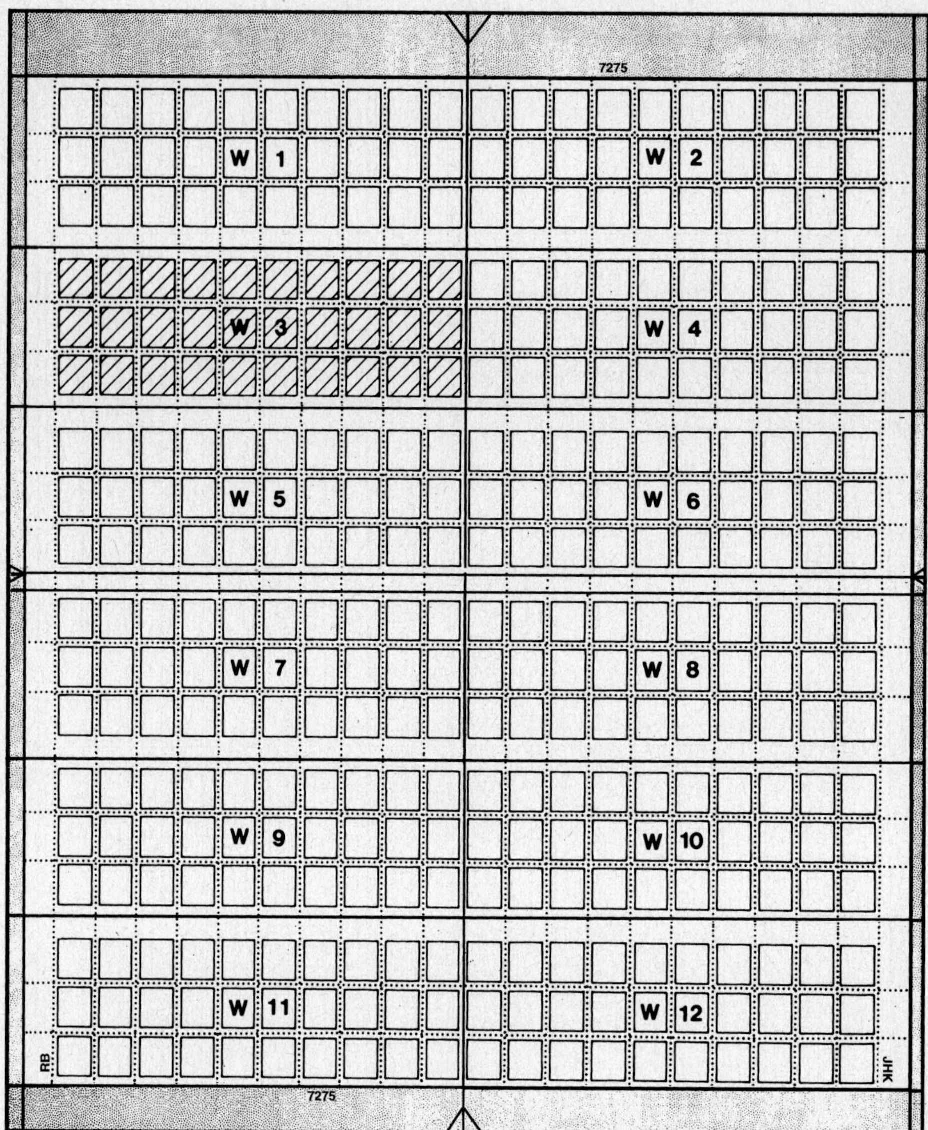

The A.E.F. Plate — 360-Subject Flat Plate — 8 Collectible Positions (See listings)

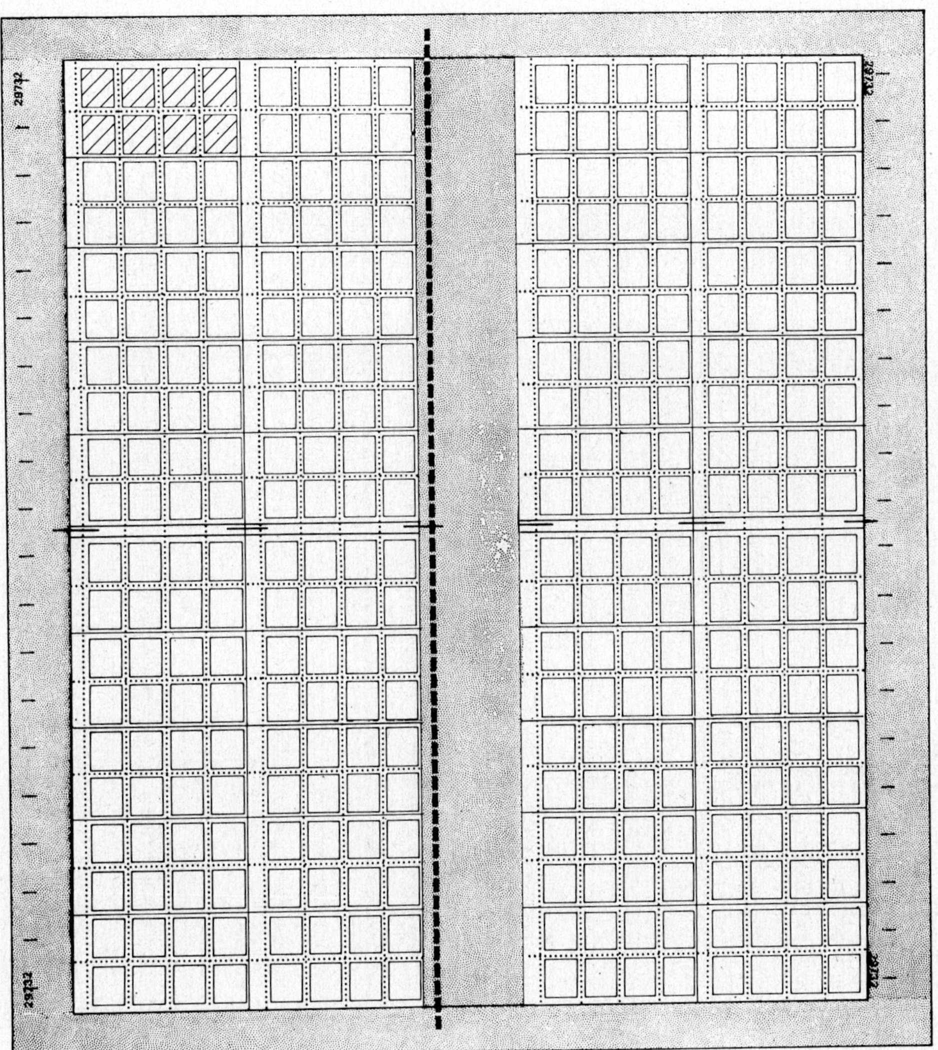

The 320-Subject Plate

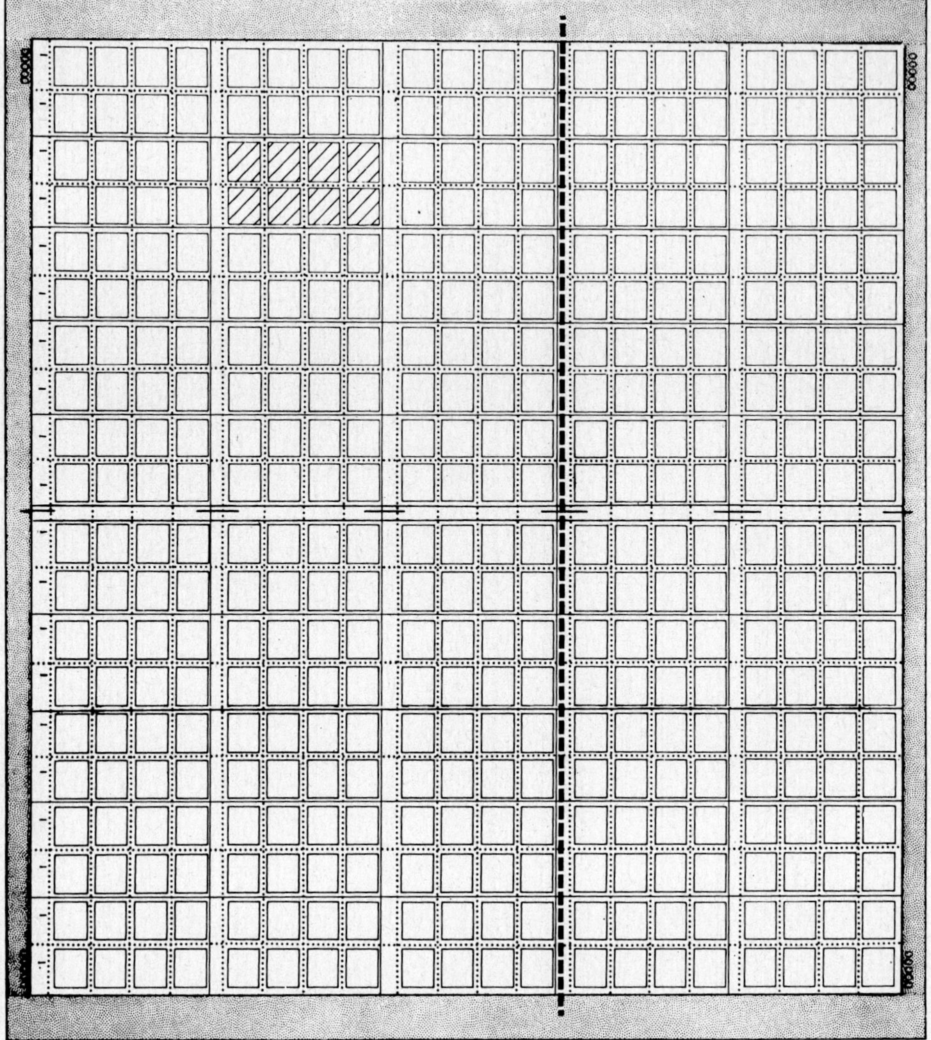

400-Subject Plate — The 300-Subject plate with double labels has the same layout.

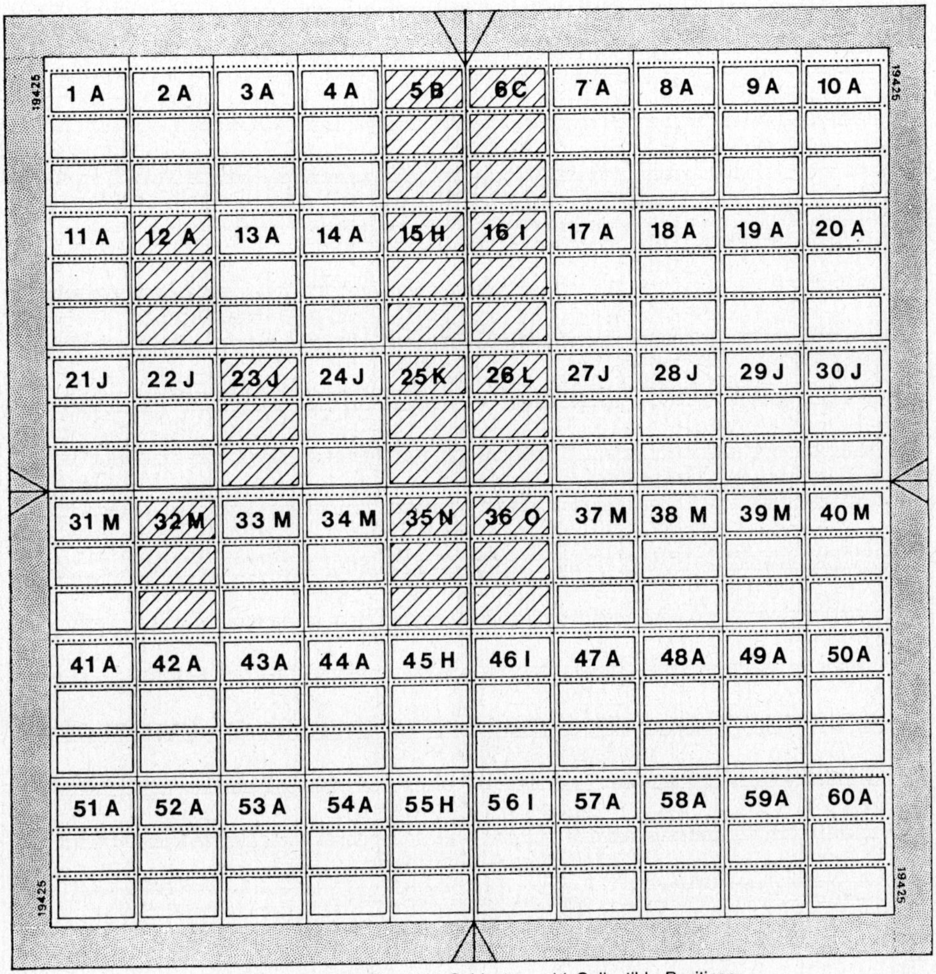

19425

1 A	2 A	3 A	4 A	5 B	6 C	7 A	8 A	9 A	10 A
11 A	12 A	13 A	14 A	15 H	16 I	17 A	18 A	19 A	20 A
21 J	22 J	23 J	24 J	25 K	26 L	27 J	28 J	29 J	30 J
31 M	32 M	33 M	34 M	35 N	36 O	37 M	38 M	39 M	40 M
41 A	42 A	43 A	44 A	45 H	46 I	47 A	48 A	49 A	50 A
51 A	52 A	53 A	54 A	55 H	56 I	57 A	58 A	59 A	60 A

19425

19425

19425

Lindbergh Booklet Plate-180 Subjects — 11 Collectible Positions

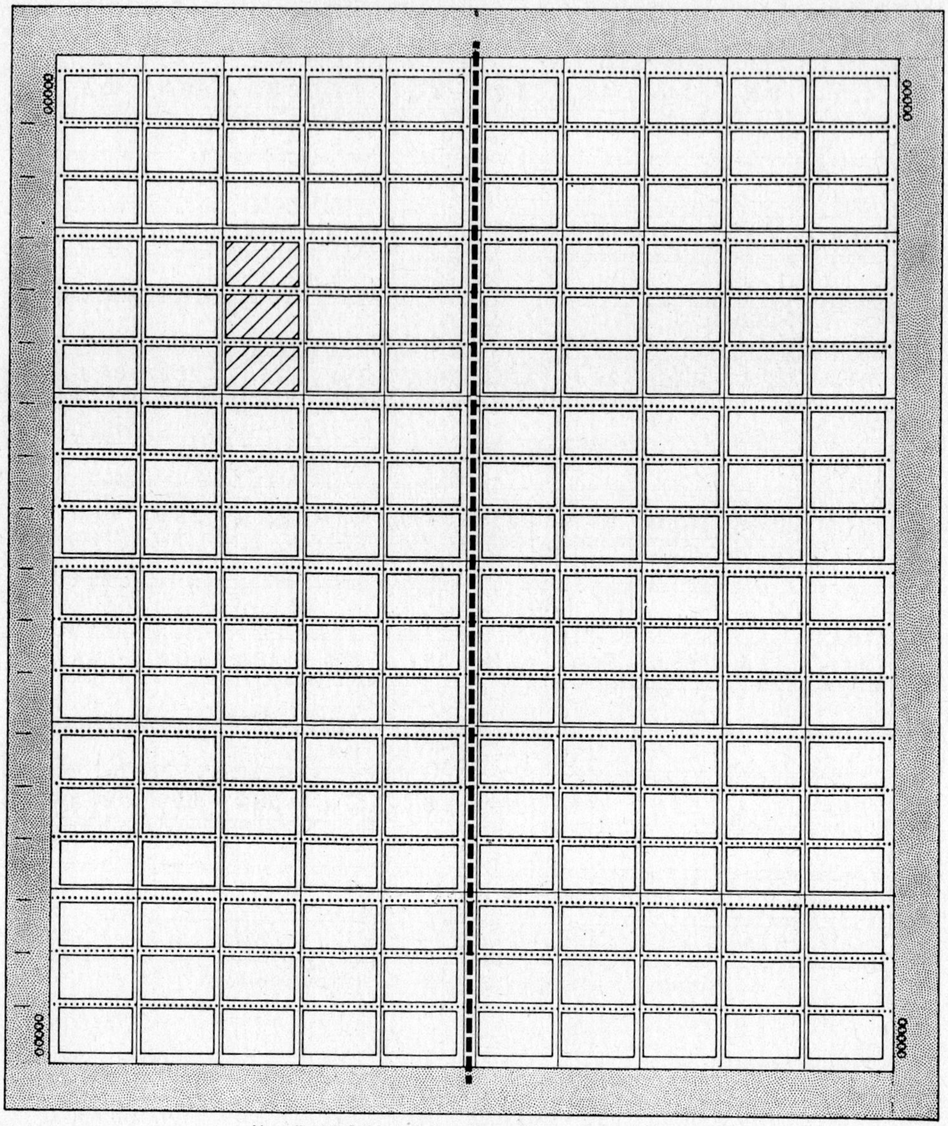

Airmail 180-Subject Rotary Press Plate — Electric Eye

Plate Sizes: No. 1288Bc to date.

Since 1978 numerous plate sizes from 78 to 1080 subjects have been used. Because plate size is not relevant to collecting these panes, we are not including this information in the catalogue.

BOOKLET PANES

Values for both unused and used booklet panes are for complete panes with selvage, and for panes of six unless otherwise stated. Panes in booklets are Never Hinged. Values for stapled booklets are for those with creasing along the lines of the staples. Values for booklets which were glued shut are for opened booklets without significant damage to the cover.

See other notes in the introduction to this section.

BOOKLET COVERS

Front covers of booklets of postage and airmail issues are illustrated and numbered.

Included are the Booklet Cover number (BC2A); and the catalogue numbers of the Booklet Panes (300b, 331a). The text of the inside and or back covers changes. Some modern issues have minor changes on the front covers also. When more than one combination of covers exists, the number of possible booklets is noted in parentheses after the booklet listing. Booklet covers that have no card stock color given are white.

USED BOOKLET PANES

Many early booklet panes are scarce to rare in used condition, and they are valued higher to much higher than the corresponding panes in unused condition. Such used panes are valued with contemporaneous cancellations, and it is strongly recommended that such panes be expertized by one of the competent expertizing bodies.

Washington — A88

Wmk. 191 Horizontally or Vertically

1900-03 *Perf. 12*

279Bj	A88 2c **red,** horizontal wmk., *Apr. 18*	500.	*3,000.*
	light red	500.	3,000.
	orange red, *1902*	500.	3,000.
	Never hinged	1,000.	
	With plate number (D)	1,350.	*6,000.*
	Never hinged	2,150.	
279Bk	A88 2c **red,** vertical watermark	500.	—
	orange red	750.	—
	Never hinged	1,000.	
	With plate number (D)	1,350.	*8,000.*
	Never hinged	2,150.	

360- (horiz. wmk.) and 180- (vert. wmk.) subject plates. All plate positions exist, except J, K, and L, due to the horizontal guide line being placed too far below stamps to appear on the upper panes.

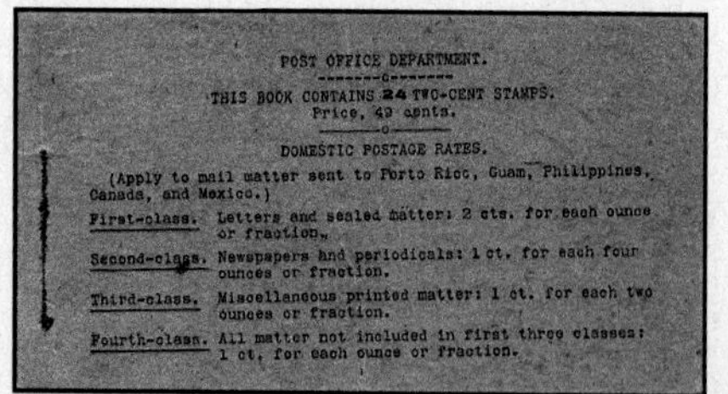

POST OFFICE DEPARTMENT.

THIS BOOK CONTAINS 24 TWO-CENT STAMPS.
Price, 49 cents.

DOMESTIC POSTAGE RATES.

(Apply to mail matter sent to Porto Rico, Guam, Philippines, Canada, and Mexico.)

First-class. Letters and sealed matter: 2 cts. for each ounce or fraction.

Second-class. Newspapers and periodicals: 1 ct. for each four ounces or fraction.

Third-class. Miscellaneous printed matter: 1 ct. for each two ounces or fraction.

Fourth-class. All matter not included in first three classes: 1 ct. for each ounce or fraction.

279Bj-279Bk — BC1

1900-03 **Text only cover**

25c booklet contains 2 panes of six 2c stamps.
49c booklet contains 4 panes of six 2c stamps.
97c booklet contains 8 panes of six 2c stamps.

Booklets sold for 1c more than the face value of the stamps.

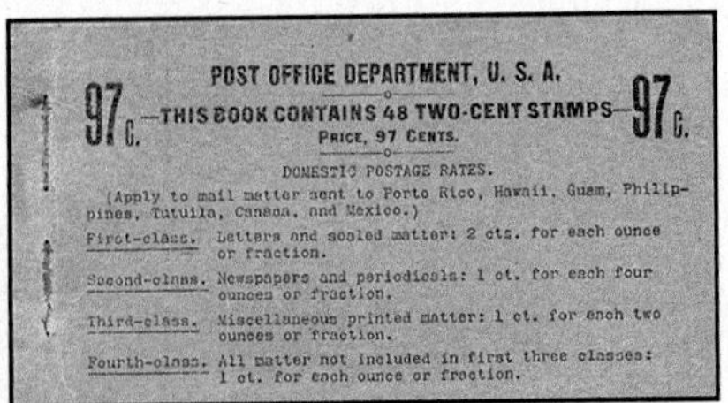

POST OFFICE DEPARTMENT, U. S. A.

97c. —THIS BOOK CONTAINS 48 TWO-CENT STAMPS— 97c.

PRICE, 97 CENTS.

DOMESTIC POSTAGE RATES.

(Apply to mail matter sent to Porto Rico, Hawaii, Guam, Philippines, Tutuila, Canada, and Mexico.)

First-class. Letters and sealed matter: 2 cts. for each ounce or fraction.

Second-class. Newspapers and periodicals: 1 ct. for each four ounces or fraction.

Third-class. Miscellaneous printed matter: 1 ct. for each two ounces or fraction.

Fourth-class. All matter not included in first three classes: 1 ct. for each ounce or fraction.

279Bj, 279Bk, 301c, 319, 332a — BC2B

1900-08

Text cover with price added in upper corners

25c booklets contain 4 panes of six 1c stamps or 2 panes of six 2c stamps.
49c booklet contains 4 panes of six 2c stamps.
97c booklet contains 8 panes of six 2c stamps.

Booklets

BK1	BC1	25c **black,** *cream*	*5,500.*
BK2	BC1	25c **black,** *buff*	*5,000.*
BK3	BC1	49c **green,** *cream*	*9,000.*
BK4	BC1	49c **black,** *buff*	—
BK5	BC1	97c **red,** *cream*	—
BK6	BC1	97c **black,** *gray*	—
BK7	BC2B	25c **black,** *cream* (3)	*6,000.*
BK8	BC2B	49c **black,** *buff* (3)	*5,000.*
BK9	BC2B	97c **black,** *gray* (3)	*12,500.*

Nos. BK1-BK6 and one type each of Nos. BK7-BK9 exist with specimen overprints handstamped on cover and individual stamps.

All covers of BK7-BK9 exist with "Philippines" overprint in 50mm or 48mm.

Franklin — A115

1903-07 **Wmk. 191 Vertically**

300b	A115	1c **blue green,** *Mar. 6, 1907*	600.	*11,500.*
		Never hinged	1,150.	
		With plate number (D)	1,200.	
		Never hinged	*2,250.*	
		With plate number 3472 over left stamp (D)	*8,750.*	
		Watermark horizontal	*2,000.*	

180-Subject Plates only. All plate positions exist.

POST OFFICE DEPARTMENT, U. S. A.

25c. —THIS BOOK CONTAINS 24 ONE-CENT STAMPS— 25c.

PRICE, 25 CENTS.

DOMESTIC POSTAGE RATES.

(Apply to Guam, Hawaii, Philippines, Porto Rico, Tutuila, Canal Zone, and to Canada, Cuba, Mexico, and the Republic of Panama.)

First-class. Letters and sealed matter: 2 cts. for each ounce or fraction. Postal cards and post cards 1 ct. each.

Second-class. Newspapers and periodicals: 1 ct. for each four ounces or fraction.

Third-class. Miscellaneous printed matter: 1 ct. for each two ounces or fraction.

Fourth-class. All matter not included in first three classes: 1 ct. for each ounce or fraction.

Special-delivery. A special-delivery stamp, in addition to postage, secures immediate delivery within the carrier-delivery limit of city free delivery and within one mile of any other United States post office.

300b, 331a, 332a — BC2A

1900-08

Text cover with price added in upper corners

25c booklets contain 4 panes of six 1c stamps or 2 panes of six 2c stamps.
49c booklet contains 4 panes of six 2c stamps.

Booklet

BK10	BC2A	25c **black,** *green* (6)	*6,000.*

Washington — A116

301c	A116	2c **carmine,** *Jan. 24, 1903*	500.	*6,000.*
		Never hinged	950.	
		With plate number (D)	1,500.	*8,000.*
		Never hinged	*2,500.*	

180-Subject Plates only. All plate positions exist.

Booklets

BK11	BC2B	25c **black,** *cream*	*3,000.*
BK12	BC2B	49c **black,** *buff*	*4,000.*
BK13	BC2B	97c **black,** *gray*	—

Washington — A129

1903 **Type I** **Wmk. 191 Vertically**

319g	A129	2c **carmine,** *Dec. 3, 1903*	125.00	*450.00*
		Never hinged	240.00	
		With plate number (D)	275.00	*750.00*
		Never hinged	500.00	
		With round marker (B)	*7,000.*	
		Wmk. horizontal	*3,000.*	
		Never hinged	*5,000.*	
		With Plate number (D)	*7,000.*	
319n	A129	2c **carmine rose**	275.00	*700.00*
		Never hinged	500.00	
		With plate number (D)	425.00	*1,000.*
		Never hinged	725.00	
319p	A129	2c **scarlet**	185.00	*625.00*
		Never hinged	350.00	
		With plate number (D)	350.00	*900.00*
		Never hinged	625.00	

Booklets (Carmine type I shades)

BK14	BC2B	25c **black,** *cream* (11)	850.00
BK15	BC2A	49c **black,** *buff* (11)	*1,150.*
BK16	BC2A	49c **black,** *pink*	*2,500.*
BK17	BC2B	97c **black,** *gray* (11)	*2,750.*

Type II

319Fh	A129	2c **carmine,** *1907*	900.00	—
		Never hinged	1,500.	
		With plate number (D)	1,500.	
		Never hinged	2,500.	
319Fl	A129	2c **scarlet**	—	
319Fq	A129	2c **lake**	300.00	*800.00*
		Never hinged	575.00	
		With plate number (D)	550.00	
		Never hinged	900.00	

180-Subject Plates only. All plate positions exist.

Booklets (Lake type II shades)

BK14A	BC2B	25c **black,** *cream*	*1,350.*
BK15A	BC2A	49c **black,** *buff*	*2,500.*
BK16A	BC2A	49c **black,** *pink*	*4,000.*
BK17A	BC2B	97c **black,** *gray*	*5,750.*
BK17b	BC2B	97c **black,** *gray,* carmine type II panes	*15,000.*

Values for type II booklets with carmine panes are much higher than the values for booklets with the lake shade panes.

Booklet Covers

When more than one combination of covers exists, the number of possible booklets is noted in parentheses after the booklet listing.

Franklin — A138

1908 **Wmk. 191 Vertically**

331a	A138	1c **green,** *Dec. 1908*	150.00	*700.00*
		Never hinged	300.00	
		With plate number (D)	225.00	
		Never hinged	450.00	

180- and 360-Subject Plates. All plate positions exist.

No. 331 exists in horizontal pair, imperforate between, a variety resulting from booklet experiments. Not regularly issued. Value, unused $3,750.

331a, 332a, 374a, 375a, 405b, 406a — BC3

1908-12 **Postrider**

25c booklet contains 4 panes of six 1c stamps.
25c booklet contains 2 panes of six 2c stamps.
49c booklet contains 4 panes of six 2c stamps.
97c booklet contains 8 panes of six 2c stamps.

Booklets

BK18 BC2A 25c **black,** *green* (3) *1,800.*
BK19 BC3 25c **black,** *green* *2,000.*

Washington — A139

332a A139 2c **carmine,** *Nov. 16, 1908* 135.00 *500.00*
Never hinged 240.00
With plate number (D) 175.00
Never hinged 310.00

180- and 360-Subject Plates. All plate positions exist.

Booklets

BK20 BC2A 25c **black,** *cream* (2) *1,250.*
BK21 BC2A 49c **black,** *buff* (2) *2,750.*
BK22 BC2A 49c **black,** *pink* *3,250.*
BK23 BC2B 97c **black,** *gray* (3) *3,000.*
BK24 BC3 25c **black,** *cream* *1,250.*
BK25 BC3 49c **black,** *pink* *2,500.*
BK26 BC3 97c **black,** *gray* *3,500.*

1910 **Wmk. 190 Vertically** ***Perf. 12***

374a A138 1c **green,** *Oct. 7, 1910* 225.00 *400.00*
Never hinged 375.00
With plate number (D) 300.00
Never hinged 475.00

360-Subject Plates only. All plate positions exist.

Booklet

BK27 BC3 25c **black,** *green* (2) *2,000.*

375a A139 2c **carmine,** *Nov. 30, 1910* 125.00 *300.00*
Never hinged 200.00
With plate number (D) 170.00
Never hinged 290.00

360-Subject Plates only. All plate positions exist.

Booklets

BK28 BC3 25c **black,** *cream* (2) *900.00*
BK29 BC3 49c **black,** *pink* (2) *2,500.*
BK30 BC3 97c **black,** *gray* (2) *3,000.*

375c A139 2c **lake,** with plate number (D) *10,000.*

Only one example of No. 375c is recorded, and it is position D with #5450 on upper right tab.

Washington — A140

1912 **Wmk. 190 Vertically**

405b A140 1c **green,** *Feb. 8, 1912* 65.00 *90.00*
Never hinged 110.00
With plate number (D) 80.00
Never hinged 140.00

360-Subject Plates only. All plate positions exist.

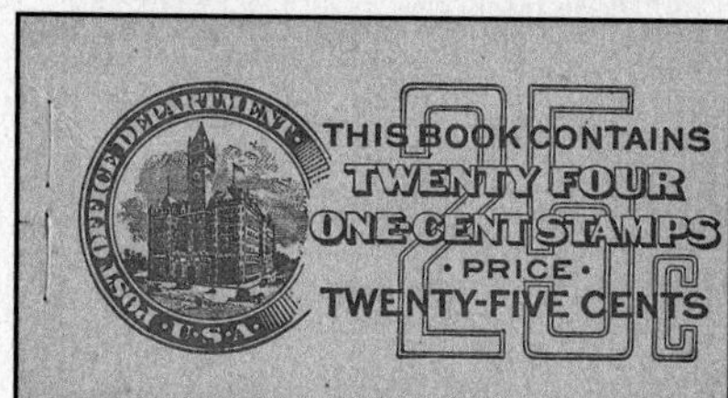

405b, 424d, 462a, 498e, 632a, 804b — BC4A

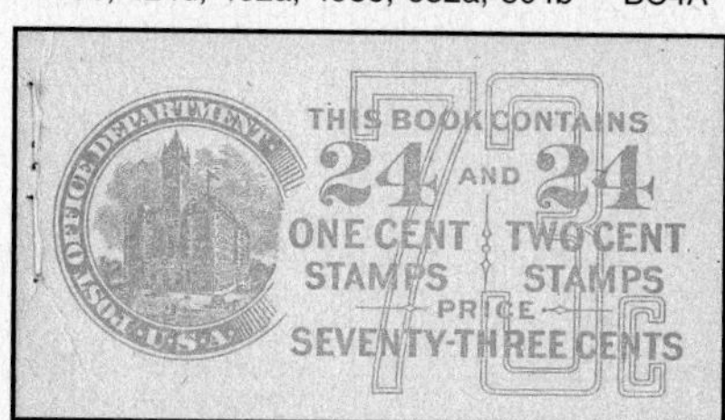

405b, 424d, 462a, 498e, 552a, 632a — BC4B

1912-39 **Washington P.O.**

Price of booklet in large numerals behind contents information

25c booklet contains 4 panes of six 1c stamps.
73c booklet contains 4 panes of six 1c stamps and 4 panes of six 2c stamps.
97c booklet contains 16 panes of six 1c stamps.

Ordinary Booklets

BK31 BC3 25c **black,** *green* (2) *1,000.*
BK32 BC4A 25c **green,** *green* (3) *1,250.*
BK33 BC4A 97c **green,** *lavender* *1,750.*

Combination Booklet

BK34 BC4B 73c **red,** 4 #405b + 4 #406a *3,000.*

Washington — A140

406a A140 2c **carmine,** *Feb. 8, 1912* 65.00 *90.00*
Never hinged 110.00
With plate number (D) 80.00 —
Never hinged 140.00

360-Subject Plates only. All plate positions exist.

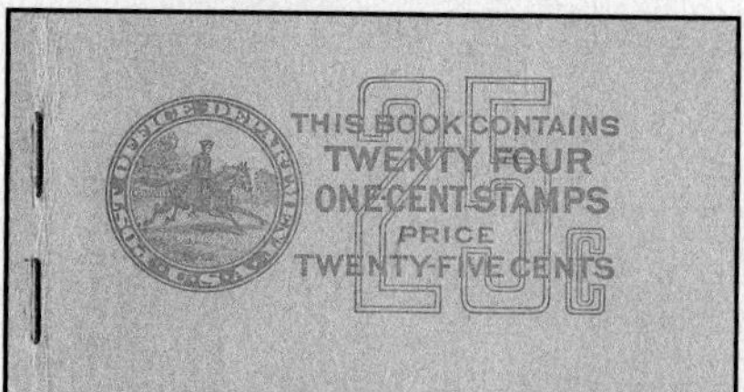

406a, 425e, 463a, 499e, 554c, 583a, 632a, 634d, 804b, 806b — BC5A

1912-39 **Small Postrider**

Large background numerals

25c booklets contain 4 panes of six 1c stamps or 2 panes of six 2c stamps.
49c booklet contains 4 panes of six 2c stamps.
97c booklets contain 16 panes of six 1c stamps or 8 panes of six 2c stamps.

Ordinary Booklets

BK35 BC3 25c **black,** *cream* (2) *825.00*
BK36 BC3 49c **black,** *pink* (2) *1,500.*
BK37 BC3 97c **black,** *gray* (2) 2,000.
BK38 BC5A 25c **red,** *buff* (3) *1,000.*
BK39 BC5A 49c **red,** *pink* (3) 1,750.
BK40 BC5A 97c **red,** *blue,* (3) 3,250.

Combination Booklet

See No. BK34.

Variety

BK35a As No. BK35, with 2 No. 406a and 3 Washburn Patent interleaving paper (embossed "Pat. Sept. 20, 1904" and with a washboard pattern throughout) *2,500.*

1914 **Wmk. 190 Vertically** ***Perf. 10***

424d A140 1c **green** 5.25 *7.50*
Never hinged 8.75
Double transfer, Plate 6363 — —
With plate number (D) 14.00
Never hinged 22.50
Cracked plate —

360-Subject Plates only. All plate positions exist.

Ordinary Booklets

BK41 BC4A 25c **green,** *green* (3) 300.00
BK42 BC4A 97c **green,** *lavender* (2) 140.00

Combination Booklet

BK43 BC4B 73c **red,** 4 #424d + 4 #425e (3) 300.00

425e A140 2c **carmine,** *Jan. 6, 1914* 17.50 *25.00*
Never hinged 30.00
With plate number (D) 42.50
Never hinged 70.00

360-Subject Plates only. All plate positions exist.

Ordinary Booklets

BK44 BC5A 25c **red,** *buff* (3) 500.00
BK45 BC5A 49c **red,** *pink* (3) 1,000.
BK46 BC5A 97c **red,** *blue* (3) 1,250.

Combination Booklet

See No. BK43.

1916 **Unwmk.** ***Perf. 10***

462a A140 1c **green,** *Oct. 15, 1916* 9.50 *12.50*
Never hinged 16.00
Cracked plate at right 250.00 —
Never hinged 350.00
Cracked plate at left 310.00

Never hinged	425.00	
With plate number (D)	25.00	
Never hinged	37.50	

360-Subject Plates only. All plate positions exist.

Ordinary Booklets

BK47 BC4A 25c **green,** *green* 650.00
BK48 BC4A 97c **green,** *lavender* 500.00

Combination Booklets

BK49 BC4B 73c **red,** 4 #462a + 4 #463a (2) 900.00

463a	A140 2c **carmine,** *Oct. 8, 1916*	110.00	*110.00*
	Never hinged	180.00	
	With plate number (D)	150.00	
	Never hinged	240.00	

360-Subject Plates only. All plate positions exist.

Ordinary Booklets

BK50 BC5A 25c **red,** *buff* *950.00*
BK51 BC5A 49c **red,** *pink* *1,500.*
BK52 BC5A 97c **red,** *blue* *2,750.*

Combination Booklets

See No. BK49.

1917-18 **Unwmk.** ***Perf. 11***

498e	A140 1c **green,** *Apr. 6, 1917*	2.50	*2.00*
	Never hinged	4.25	
	Double transfer	—	—
	With plate number (D)	6.00	*2.00*
	Never hinged	9.00	

360-Subject Plates only. All plate positions exist.

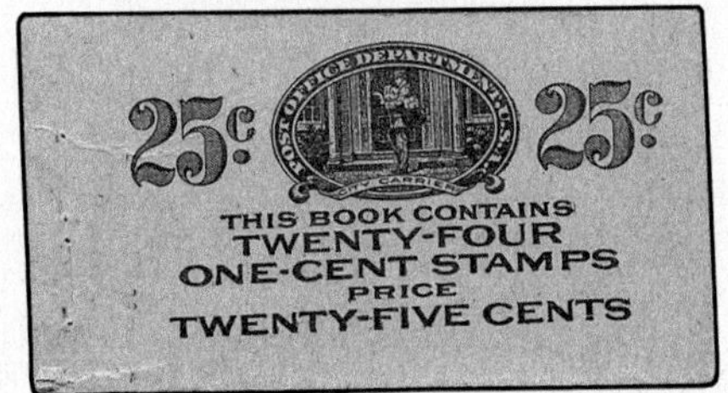

498e, 552a — BC6A

1917-23 **Oval designs**

25c booklet contains 4 panes of six 1c stamps.

Ordinary Booklets

BK53 BC4A 25c **green,** *green* (2) 300.00
BK54 BC4A 97c **green,** *lavender* (4) 85.00
BK55 BC6A 25c **green,** *green* (5) 110.00

Combination Booklets

BK56 BC4B 73c **red,** 4 #498e + 4 #499e (4) 75.00
BK57 BC4B 73c **red,** 4 #498e + 4 #554c (3) 100.00

Washington — A140

A.E.F. Panes of 30

1917, Aug.

498f	A140 1c **green** (pane of 30)	*1,050.*	*12,500.*
	Never hinged	*1,700.*	

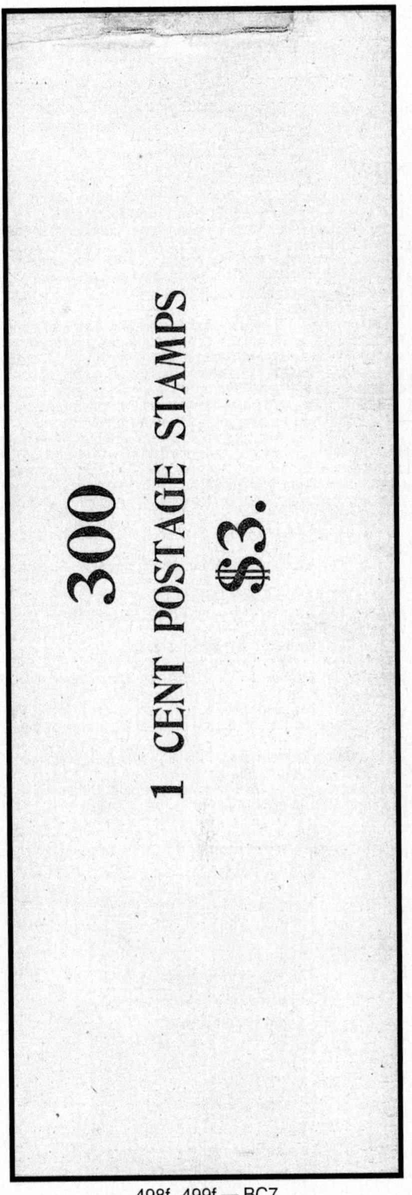

498f, 499f — BC7

A.E.F.

1917

$3 booklet contains 10 panes of thirty 1c stamps.
$6 booklet contains 10 panes of thirty 2c stamps.

Booklets sold for face value.

Booklet

BK64 BC7 $3 **black,** *green* *22,500.*

499e	A140 2c **rose,** type I, *Mar. 31, 1917*	4.00	*2.50*
	Never hinged	6.75	
	With plate number (D)	7.00	*2.25*
	Never hinged	10.00	

360-Subject Plates only. All plate positions exist.

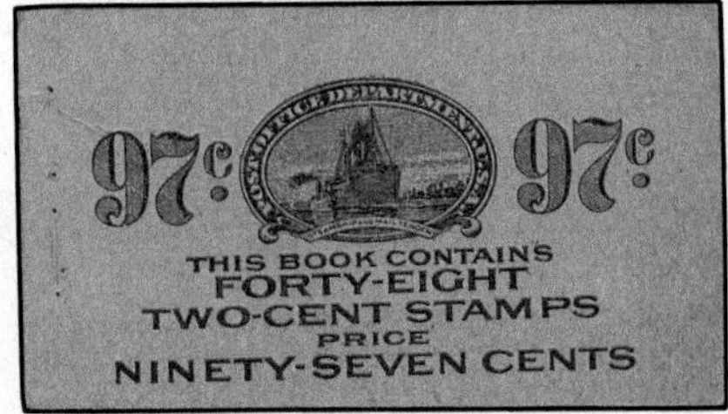

499e, 554c, 583a, 634d — BC6C

1917-27 **Oval designs**

97c booklet contains 8 panes of six 2c stamps.

Ordinary Booklets

BK58 BC5A 25c **red,** *buff* (5) 250.00
BK59 BC5A 49c **red,** *pink* (4) 400.00
BK60 BC5A 97c **red,** *blue* (3) 1,000.

BK61 BC6C 97c **red,** *blue* (2) 1,250.

Combination Booklets

See No. BK56.

499f A140 2c **rose,** (pane of 30) type I *20,000.* —
Never hinged *28,000.*

Booklet

BK65 BC7 $6 **black,** *pink*

No examples of No. BK65 are known. The number and description are provided only for specialist reference.

Nos. 498f and 499f were for use of the American Expeditionary Force in France.

They were printed from the ordinary 360-Subject Plates, the sheet being cut into 12 leaves of 30 stamps each in place of 60 leaves of 6 stamps each, and, of course, the lines of perforations changed accordingly.

The same system as used for designating plate positions on the ordinary booklet panes is used for designating the war booklet, only each war booklet pane is composed of 5 ordinary panes. Thus, No. W1 booklet pane would be composed of positions 1, 2, 3, 4, and 5 of an ordinary pane, etc.

The A. E. F. booklet panes were bound at side margins which accounts for side arrows sometimes being found on positions W5 and W6. As the top and bottom arrows were always removed when the sheets were cut, positions W1 and W2 cannot be distinguished from W7 and W8. Cutting may remove guidelines on these, but identification is possible by wide bottom margins. Positions W3 and W4 cannot be distinguished from W9 and W10.

There are thus just 8 collectible positions from the sheet as follows:

W1 or W7 Narrow top and wide bottom margins. Guide line at right.

W2 or W8 As W1, but guide line at left.

W3 or W9 Approximately equal top and bottom margins. Guide line at right.

W4 or W10 As W3, but guide line at left.

W5 Narrow bottom margin showing guideline very close to stamps. Wide top margin. Guide line at right. Pane with extra long tab may show part of split arrow at left.

W6 As W5, but guide line at left, split arrow at right. Guide line at left and at bottom. Arrow at lower right may or may not show.

W11 Narrow bottom and wide top margins. Guide line at right. Siderographer initials on left tab.

W12 Narrow bottom and wide top margins. Guide line at left. Finisher initials on right tab.

Washington — A140

501b A140 3c **violet,** type I, *Oct. 17, 1917* 75.00 *80.00*
Never hinged 125.00
With plate number (D) 105.00
Never hinged 160.00

360-Subject Plates only. All plate positions exist.

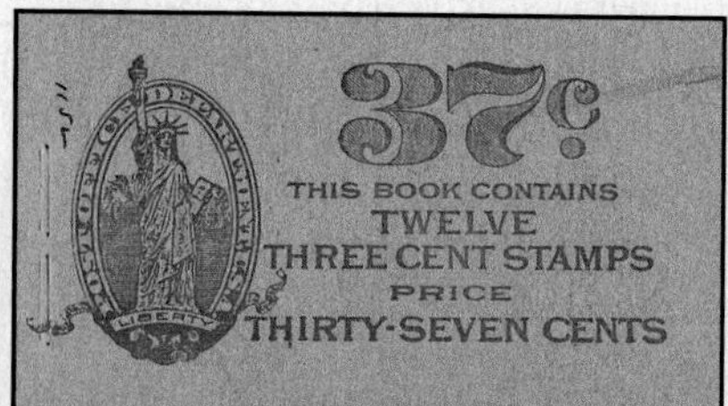

501b, 502b — BC6B

1917-18 **Oval designs**

37c booklet contains 2 panes of six 3c stamps.

Booklet

BK62 BC6B 37c **violet,** *sage* 500.00

502b A140 3c **violet,** type II, *Mar. 1918* 60.00 *75.00*
Never hinged 100.00
With plate number (D) 77.50
Never hinged 120.00

360-Subject Plates only. All plate positions exist.

Booklet

BK63 BC6B 37c **violet,** *sage* 225.00

Franklin — A155

1923 **Unwmk.** ***Perf. 11***

552a A155 1c **deep green,** *after Oct. 27, 1923* 7.50 *4.00*
Never hinged 12.50
With plate number (D) 13.00
Never hinged 21.00

360-Subject Plates only. All plate positions exist.

Ordinary Booklets

BK66 BC6A 25c **green,** *green* (2) 75.00
BK67 BC4A 97c **green,** *lavender* (3) *650.00*

Combination Booklet

BK68 BC4B 73c **red,** *buff,* 4 #552a + 4 #554c (3) 100.00

Washington — A157

554c A157 2c **carmine,** between Feb. 24 and Mar. 18, 1923 7.00 *3.00*
Never hinged 12.00
With plate number (D) 12.00
Never hinged 20.00

360-Subject Plates only. All plate positions exist.

Ordinary Booklets

BK69 BC5A 25c **red,** *buff* (3) *400.00*
BK70 BC5A 49c **red,** *pink* (3) 950.00
BK71 BC6C 97c **red,** *blue* (3) 1,500.

Combination Booklets

See Nos. BK57 and BK68.

ROTARY PRESS PRINTINGS

Two experimental plates were used to print No. 583a. At least one guide line pane (H) is known from these plates. The rest of rotary press booklet panes were printed from specially prepared plates of 360-subjects in arrangement as before, but without the guide lines and the plate numbers are at the sides instead of at the top as on the flat plates.

The only varieties possible are the ordinary pane (A) and partial plate numbers appearing at the right or left of the upper or lower stamps of a booklet pane when the trimming of the sheets is off center. The note applies to Nos. 583a, 632a, 634d, 720b, 804b, 806b and 807a, before Electric Eyes.

1926 ***Perf. 10***

583a A157 2c **carmine,** *Aug. 1926* 110.00 *150.00*
Never hinged 200.00
With guide line at right (H) *8,500.*

Only one example of No. 583a with guide line at right is recorded. Only the first two rotary plates laid out for booklets had guide lines.

Ordinary Booklets

BK72 BC5A 25c **red,** *buff* (3) *725.00*
BK73 BC5A 49c **red,** *pink* *1,000.*
BK74 BC6C 97c **red,** *blue* *2,250.*

1927 ***Perf. 11x10½***

632a A155 1c **green,** *Nov. 2, 1927* 5.00 *4.00*
Never hinged 8.00

Ordinary Booklets

BK75 BC5A 25c **green,** *green* (3) 65.00
BK76 BC4A 97c **green,** *lavender* 600.00
BK77 BC5A 97c **green,** *lavender* *2,750.*

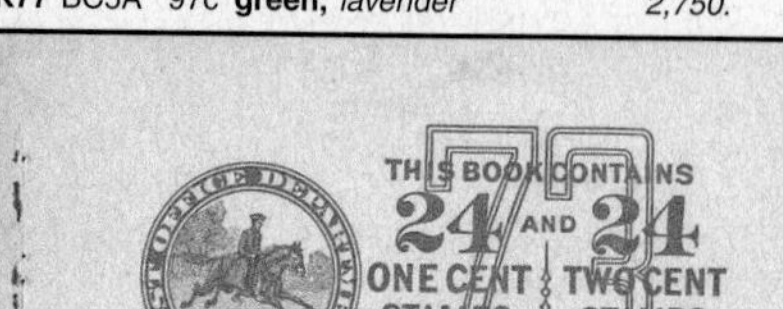

632a, 804b — BC5D

1927-39 **Small Postrider**

Large background numerals

73c booklet contains 4 panes of six 1c stamps and 4 panes of six 2c stamps.

Combination Booklets

BK78 BC4B 73c **red,** 4 #632a + 4 #634d —
BK79 BC5D 73c **red,** 4 #632a + 4 #634d (3) 85.00

634d A157 2c **carmine,** type I, *Feb. 25, 1927* 1.50 *1.50*
Never hinged 2.50

Ordinary Booklets

BK80 BC5A 25c **red,** *buff* (2) 10.00
a. With experimental cellophane interleaving *2,500.*
BK81 BC5A 49c **red,** *pink* (2) 14.00
BK82 BC5A 97c **red,** *blue* (3) 45.00
BK83 BC6C 97c **red,** *blue* 900.00

Combination Booklets

See Nos. BK78 and BK79.

56,000 booklets of BK80a were produced in 1928 using .00125 inch thick cellophane interleaving. Scarce, as few were saved.

Varieties

634e A157 2c **carmine lake,** type I *400.00* *1,000.*
Never hinged *750.00*

Booklet

BK82a BC5A As #BK82, with 8 panes of #634e *7,500.*

Washington — A226

1932

720b A226 3c **deep violet,** *July 25, 1932* 35.00 *12.50*
Never hinged 60.00

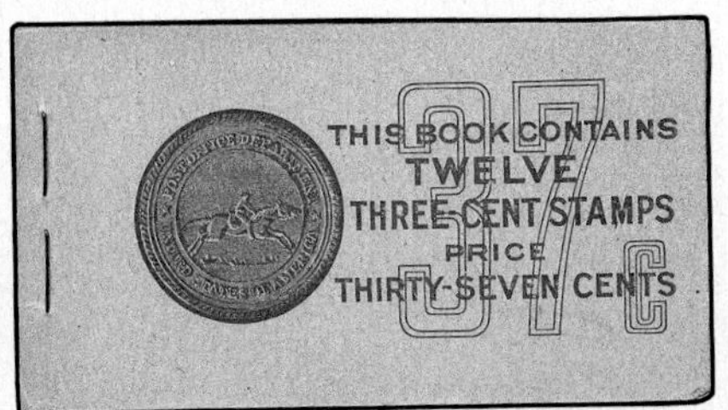

720b, 806b, 807a, 1035a — BC9A

1932-54 **Post Office Seal**

Large background numerals

25c booklet contains 2 panes of six 2c stamps.
37c booklet contains 2 panes of six 3c stamps.
49c booklet contains 4 panes of six 2c stamps.
73c booklets contain 4 panes of six 3c stamps or 4 panes of six 1c stamps and 4 panes of six 2c stamps.

Ordinary Booklets

BK84 BC9A 37c **violet,** *buff* (2) 125.00
a. With experimental cellophane interleaving *3,000.*
BK85 BC9A 73c **violet,** *pink* (2) 350.00

30,000 booklets of No. BK84a were made with .001 inch thick cellophane interleaving, similar to but thinner than the experimental interleaving used for No. BK80a. Poor handling qualities during booklet assembly plus higher cost prevented wider use. Placed on sale in Wash. D.C. post office in Sept., 1936. Extremely scarce, as few were saved.

Catalogue values for unused panes in this section, from this point to the end, are for Never Hinged items.

Washington — A276

In 1942 plates were changed to the Type II "new design" and the E. E. marks may appear at the right or left margins of panes of Nos. 804b, 806b and 807a. Panes printed from E. E. plates have 2½mm vertical gutter; those from pre-E. E. plates have 3mm vertical gutter.

1939-42 *Perf. 11x10½*

804b A276 1c 3mm vert. gutter, *Jan. 27, 1939* 4.00 *.85*

Ordinary Booklets

BK86 BC5A 25c **green,** *green* 70.00
BK87 BC5A 97c **green,** *lavender* *450.00*
BK88 BC4A 97c **green,** *lavender* —

Combination Booklet

BK89 BC5D 73c **red,** 4 #804b + 4 #806b 125.00

804b A276 1c 2½mm vert. gutter, *Apr. 14, 1942* 2.00 *.50*

Ordinary Booklets

BK90 BC5A 25c **green,** *green* 8.25
BK91 BC5A 97c **green,** *lavender* 450.00

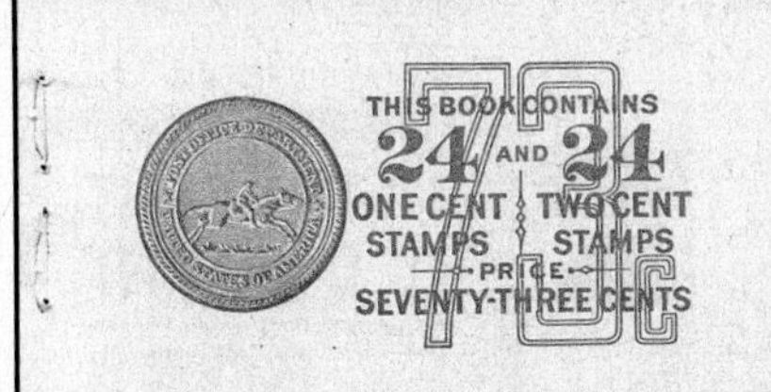

804b, 806b — BC9E

1939 **Post Office Seal**

Large background numerals

73c booklets contain 4 panes of six 3c stamps or 4 panes of six 1c stamps and 4 panes of six 2c stamps.

Combination Booklets

BK92 BC5D 73c **red,** 4 #804b + 4 #806b 32.50
BK93 BC9E 73c **red,** 4 #804b + 4 #806b 37.50

Adams — A278

806b A278 2c 3mm vert. gutter, *Jan. 27, 1939* 22.50 *2.50*

Ordinary Booklets

BK94 BC5A 97c **red,** *blue* *350.00*

Combination Booklet

See No. BK89.

806b A278 2c 2½mm vert. gutter, *Apr. 25, 1942* 5.50 *1.00*

Ordinary Booklets

BK95 BC5A 97c **red,** *blue* 1,250.
BK96 BC5A 25c **red,** *buff* 17.50
BK97 BC9A 25c **red,** *buff* 80.00
BK98 BC5A 49c **red,** *pink* 45.00
BK99 BC9A 49c **red,** *pink* 70.00

Combination Booklets

See Nos. BK92 and BK93.

Jefferson — A279

807a A279 3c 3mm vert. gutter, *Jan. 27, 1939* 30.00 *3.25*

Booklets

BK100 BC9A 37c **violet,** *buff* 85.00
BK101 BC9A 73c **violet,** *pink* *700.00*

807a A279 3c 2½mm vert. gutter, *Mar. 6, 1942* 8.50 *2.00*

Booklets

BK102 BC9A 37c **violet,** *buff* (3) 20.00
BK103 BC9A 73c **violet,** *pink* (3) 45.00

Variety

807d A279 As "a," imperf between vert. —

Statue of Liberty — A482

1954-58 *Perf. 11x10½*

1035a A482 3c pane of 6, *June 30, 1954* 3.50 *1.25*
1035d Dry printing 4.50 *1.50*

Booklets

BK104 BC9A 37c **violet,** *buff,* with #1035a 19.00
a. With #1035d 24.00
BK105 BC9A 73c **violet,** *pink,* with #1035a 21.00
a. With #1035d 26.00

Variety

1035b Horiz. pairs, imperf. btwn in #1035a with foldover (two pairs recorded in two full panes) or miscut (all three pairs in one full pane) *5,000.*

Lincoln — A483

1036b A483 4c pane of 6, *July 31, 1958* 2.75 *1.25*

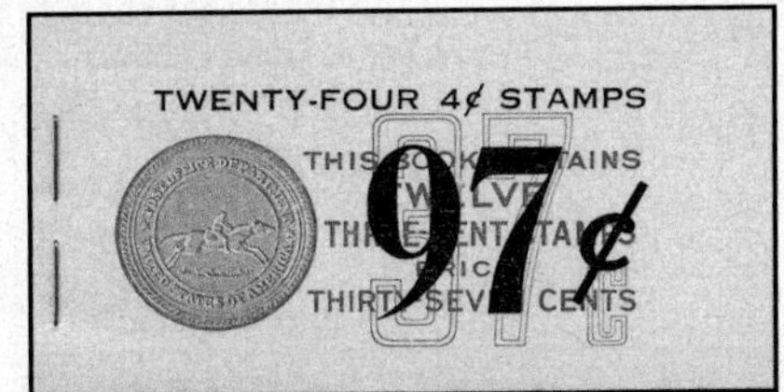

1036b — BC9F

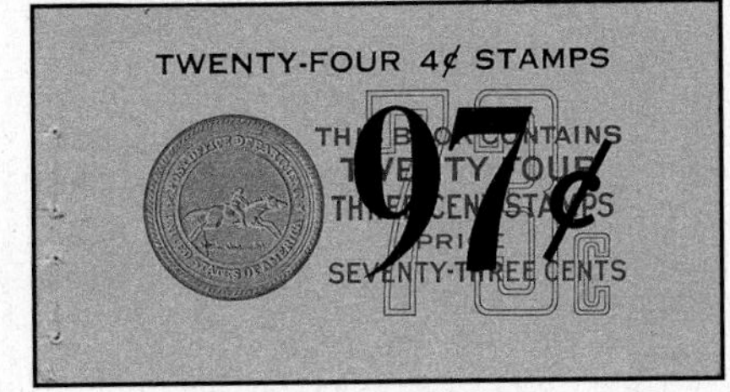

1036b — BC9G

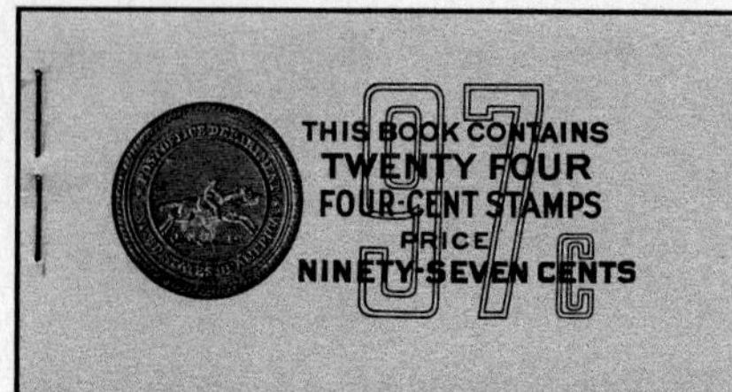

1036b — BC9H

1958

97c booklet contains 4 panes of six 4c stamps.

Booklets

BK106	BC9F	97c on 37c **violet,** *buff*	60.00
BK107	BC9G	97c on 73c **violet,** *pink*	30.00
BK108	BC9H	97c **blue,** *yellow*	150.00
BK109	BC9H	97c **blue,** *pink* (3)	17.50
a.		With experimental silicone interleaving	*150.00*

Variety

1036c	A483	As "b," imperf. horiz.	*10,000.*

Washington (Slogan 1) — A650

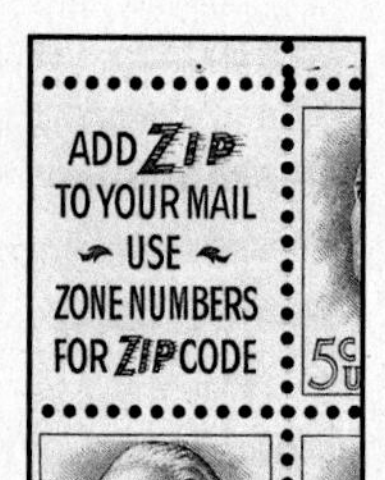

Slogan 2

Slogan 3

1962-64 *Perf. 11x10½*

Plate of 300 stamps, 60 labels

1213a	A650	5c pane of 5+label, slogan 1, *Nov. 23, 1962*	6.00	4.00
		With slogan 2, *1963*	16.00	7.00
		With slogan 3, *1964*	2.00	2.00

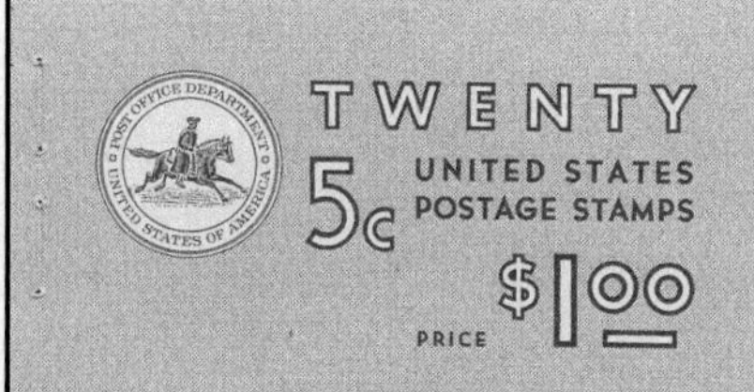

1213a — BC12A

1962-63 **Small Postrider**

$1 booklet contains 4 panes of five 5c stamps.

1213a, 1213c — BC13A

1963-64 **Mr. Zip**

$1 booklet contains 4 panes of five 5c stamps.

Booklets

BK110	BC12A	$1 **blue,** slogan 1	27.50
BK111	BC12A	$1 **blue,** slogan 2	110.00
BK112	BC13A	$1 **blue,** slogan 2	90.00
BK113	BC13A	$1 **blue,** slogan 3 (3)	13.50

1213c	A650	As No. 1213a, tagged, slogan 2, *Oct. 28, 1963*	60.00	*10.00*
		With slogan 3, *1964*	2.00	*1.50*

Booklets

BK114	BC13A	$1 **blue,** slogan 2	240.00
BK115	BC13A	$1 **blue,** slogan 3 (4)	6.00

Variety

1213d	A650	Horiz. pair, imperf. btwn., in #1213a with foldover or miscut	1,750.

Jefferson — A710

1967-78 *Perf. 11x10½*

1278a	A710	1c pane of 8, shiny gum, *Jan. 12, 1968*	1.00	.75
		Dull gum	1.75	

Combination Booklets

See Nos. BK116, BK117B, BK118 and BK119.

Variety

1278e	A710	As "a," dull gum, tagging omitted	*85.00*

An experimental moisture-resistant gum was used on 1,000,000 panes of No. 1278a and 4,000,000 of No. 1393a released in March, 1971. This dull finish gum shows no breaker ridges. The booklets lack interleaving. This gum was also used for Nos. 1395c, 1395d, 1288c and all engraved panes from No. 1510b on unless noted.

Jefferson — A710

1278b	A710	1c pane of 4+2 labels, slogans 5 & 4, *May 10, 1971*	.75	.60

Combination Booklet

See No. BK122.

Wright — A712

Slogan 4

Slogan 5

1280a	A712	2c pane of 5+label, slogan 4, *Jan. 8, 1968*	1.25	.80
		With slogan 5	1.25	.80

Combination Booklets

See Nos. BK117 and BK120.

1280c	A712	2c pane of 6, shiny gum, *May 7, 1971*	1.00	.75
		Dull gum	1.10	

Combination Booklets

See Nos. BK127 and BKC22.

The 1c and 6c panes of 8, Nos. 1278a and 1284b, were printed from 320-subject plates and from 400-subject plates, both with electric eye markings. The 2c and 6c panes of 5 stamps plus label, Nos. 1280a and 1284c, were printed from 360-subject plates.

Roosevelt — A716

Perf. 10½x11

1284b	A716	6c pane of 8, *Dec. 28, 1967*	1.50	1.00

1278a, 1284b, 1393a — BC14A

1967-70

$2 booklet contains 4 panes of eight 6c stamps and 1 pane of eight 1c stamps.

Combination Booklet

BK116 BC14A $2 **brown,** 4 #1284b (6c)+1 #1278a(1c)(2) 6.25

Variety

1284e A716 6c As "b," tagging omitted *90.00* —

Combination Booklet

BK116a BC14A As #BK116, with 4 #1284e (6c) + 1 #1278a (1c) *250.00*

Roosevelt — A716

1284c A716 6c pane of 5+label, slogan 4, *Jan. 9, 1968* 1.40 1.00
With slogan 5 1.40 1.00

1278a, 1280a, 1284c, 1393b, 1395b — BC15

1968-71

$1 booklets contain 2 panes of six 8c stamps and 1 pane of four 1c stamps, or 3 panes of five 6c stamps and 1 pane of five 2c stamps.

Combination Booklet

BK117 BC15 $1 **brown,** 3 #1284c (6c) + 1 #1280a (2c) (2) 5.50

No. BK117 contains panes with slogan 4, slogan 5 or combinations of 4 and 5.

Oliver Wendell Holmes — A720

1288Bc A720 15c pane of 8, *June 14, 1978* 2.80 1.75

1288Bc — BC23

1978

$3.60 booklet contains 3 panes of eight 15c stamps.

Booklet

BK117A BC23 $3.60 **red & light blue,** no P# 8.00

Varieties

1288Be A720 As "c," vert. imperf. btwn. *1,500.*
1288Bi A720 As "c," tagging omitted *80.00 50.00*

Eisenhower — A815

Plate of 400 subjects for No. 1393a.

1970 Tagged ***Perf. 11x10½***

1393a A815 6c pane of 8, shiny gum, *Aug. 6* 2.00 2.00
Dull gum 2.25

1278a, 1393a, 1395a — BC16

1970-71 **Eisenhower**

$2 booklet contains 4 panes of eight 6c stamps and 1 pane of eight 1c stamps.
$1.92 booklet contains 3 panes of eight 8c stamps.

Combination Booklets

BK117B BC14A $2 **blue,** 4 #1393a (6c) + 1 #1278a (1c) 11.00
BK118 BC16 $2 **blue,** 4 #1393a (6c) + 1 #1278a (1c) (2) 9.00
BK119 BC16 $2 **blue,** dull gum, 4 #1393a (6c) + 1 #1278a (1c) (2) 7.50

Varieties

1393h A815 6c As "a," tagging omitted, shiny gum *250.00* —
Dull gum 325.00

Eisenhower — A815

Plate of 300 stamps and 60 labels for No. 1393b.

1393b A815 6c pane of 5+label, slogan 4, *Aug. 6* 1.40 1.40
With slogan 5 1.40 1.40

Combination Booklet

BK120 BC15 $1 **blue,** 3 #1393b (6c) + 1 #1280a (2c) 5.00
BK120a BC15 $1 As #BK120, missing #1280a pane and with 4 panes of #1393b (error) —

No. BK120 contains panes with slogan 4, slogan 5 or combinations of 4 and 5.

Eisenhower — A815a

1971-72 **Shiny Gum** ***Perf. 11x10½***

1395a A815a 8c **deep claret,** pane of 8, *May 10, 1971* 2.00 2.00

Booklet

BK121 BC16 $1.92 **claret** (2) 6.00

Varieties

1395e A815a Vert. pair, imperf. btwn., in #1395a or #1395d with foldover *750.00*
1395f A815a As "a," tagging omitted — —

Eisenhower — A815a

1395b A815a 8c pane of 6, *May 10, 1971* 1.50 1.50

Combination Booklet

BK122 BC15 $1 **claret,** 2 #1395b (8c) + 1 #1278b (1c) (2) 4.00

Variety

1395g As "b," tagging omitted *80.00* —

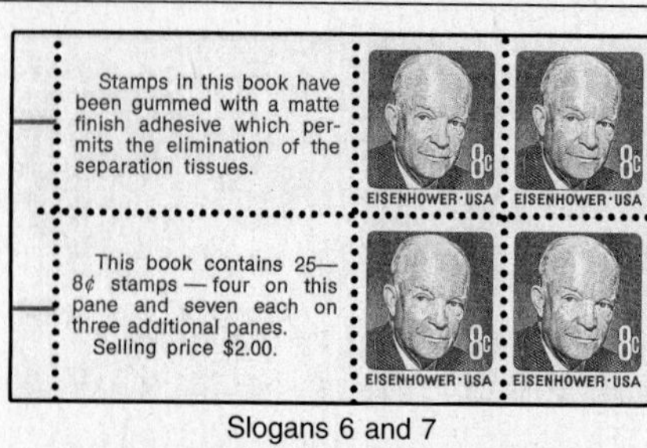

Slogans 6 and 7

Eisenhower — A815a

Dull Gum

1395c A815a 8c pane of 4 + 2 labels, slogans 6 and 7, *Jan. 28, 1972* 1.65 1.10
1395d A815a 8c pane of 7 + label, slogan 4, *Jan. 28, 1972* 1.90 1.90
With slogan 5 1.90 1.90

1395c, 1395d — BC17A

1972 **Postal Service Emblem**

$2 booklet contains 3 panes of seven 8c stamps and 1 pane of four 8c stamps.

Combination Booklet

BK123 BC17A $2 **claret,** *yellow,* 3 #1395d + 1 #1395c 6.75

No. BK123 exists with covers printed on both thin and thick card stock.

Varieties

1395h As "c," tagging omitted *55.00* —
1395i As "d," tagging omitted —

Plate of 400 subjects for No. 1395a. Plate of 360 subjects for No. 1395b. Plate of 300 subjects (200 stamps and 100 double-size labels) for No. 1395c. Plate of 400 subjects (350 stamps and 50 labels) for No. 1395d.

A pane of No. 1395d is known with a foldover resulting in a vertical pair of stamp and label, imperf between.

Booklet Covers

When more than one combination of covers exists, the number of possible booklets is noted in parentheses after the booklet listing.

Jefferson Memorial (Slogan 8) — A924

1973-74 ***Perf. 11x10½***

1510b A924 10c pane of 5 + label, slogan 8, *Dec. 14, 1973* 1.65 1.25

1510b — BC17B

1973 **Postal Service Emblem**

$1 booklet contains 2 panes of five 10c stamps.

Booklet

BK124 BC17B $1 **blue** 3.50

Jefferson Memorial — A924

1510c A924 10c pane of 8, *Dec. 14, 1973* 2.00 2.00

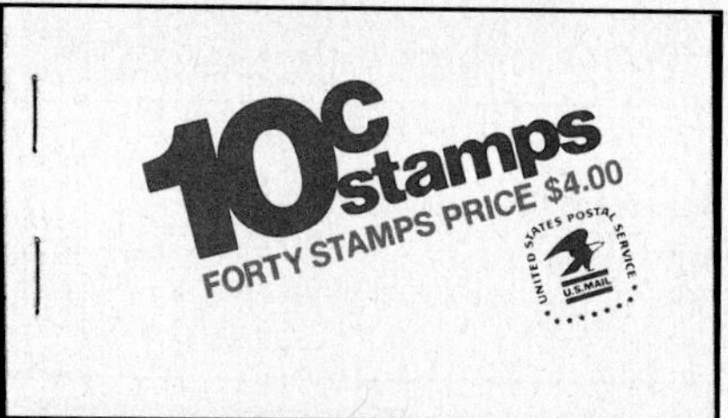

1510c — BC17C

1973 **Postal Service Emblem**

$4 booklet contains 5 panes of eight 10c stamps.

Booklet

BK125 BC17C $4 **red & blue** 10.00

No. BK125 exists with covers printed on both thin and thick card stock.

Jefferson Memorial — A924

1510d A924 10c pane of 6, *Aug. 5, 1974* 5.00 1.75
1510j As "d," tagging omitted —

1510d, C79a — BC17D

1974 **Postal Service Emblem**

$1.25 booklet contains 1 pane of five 13c stamps and 1 pane of six 10c stamps.

Combination Booklet

BK126 BC17D $1.25 **red & blue,** 1 #1510d (10c) + 1 #C79a (13c) 6.50

Varieties

1510f Vert. pair, imperf. btwn., in #1510c miscut or with foldover 475.00
1510h As "c," tagging omitted — —
1510i As "b," double booklet pane of 10 + stamps with 2 horiz. pairs imperf. btwn. + stamp and label imperf. btwn. (FO) *1,750.*

Liberty Bell — A998

1975-78 ***Perf. 11¼x10½***

1595a A998 13c pane of 6, *Oct. 31, 1975* 2.25 1.50

1595a, 1280c — BC19A

1975

90c booklet contains 1 pane of six 13c stamps and 1 pane of six 2c stamps.

Combination Booklet

BK127 BC19A 90c **red & blue,** 1 #1595a (13c) + 1 #1280c (2c) (2) 3.00

Variety

1595h As "a," miscut and inserted upside down into booklet cover, imperf below bottom stamps and with "tab" at bottom —

Liberty Bell — A998

1595b A998 13c pane of 7 + label, slogan 8, *Oct. 31, 1975* 2.25 1.50
1595c A998 13c pane of 8, *Oct. 31, 1975* 2.25 1.50
1595i As "b," tagging omitted —
1595j As "d," tagging omitted —

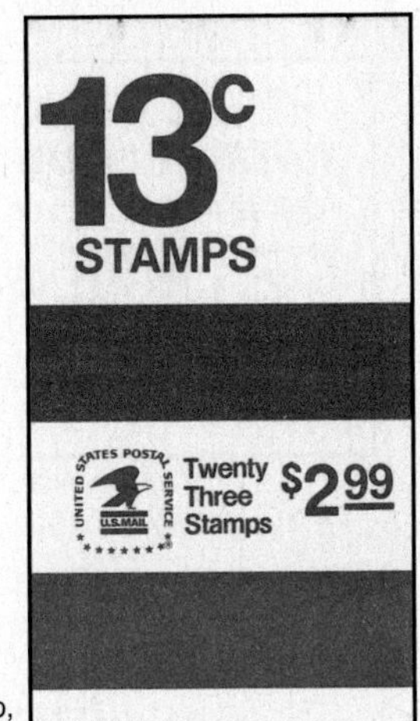

1595b, 1595c — BC19B

1975

$2.99 booklet contains 2 panes of eight 13c stamps and 1 pane of seven 13c stamps.

Combination Booklet

BK128 BC19B $2.99 **red & blue,** 2 #1595c (13c) + 1 #1595b (13c) (2) 7.50

No. BK128 exists with covers printed on both thin and thick card stock.

Variety

1595e Vert. pair, imperf. btwn., in #1595c with foldover *1,100.*

Liberty Bell (Slogan 9) — A998

1595d A998 13c pane of 5 + label, slogan 9, *Apr. 2, 1976* 1.75 1.25

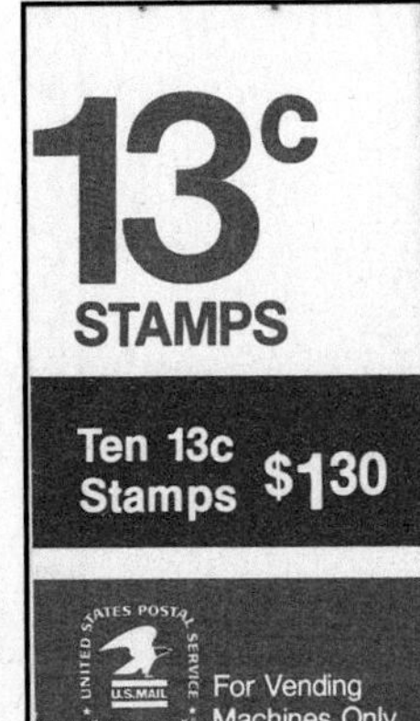

1595d — BC19C

1976

$1.30 booklet contains 2 panes of five 13c stamps.

Booklet

BK129 BC19C $1.30 **red & blue** 3.75

Variety

1595g Horiz. pair, imperf. btwn., in #1595d with foldover —

Fort McHenry Flag (15 Stars) — A1001

1977-78 ***Perf. 11x10½***

1598a A1001 15c pane of 8, *June 30, 1978* 3.75 1.50

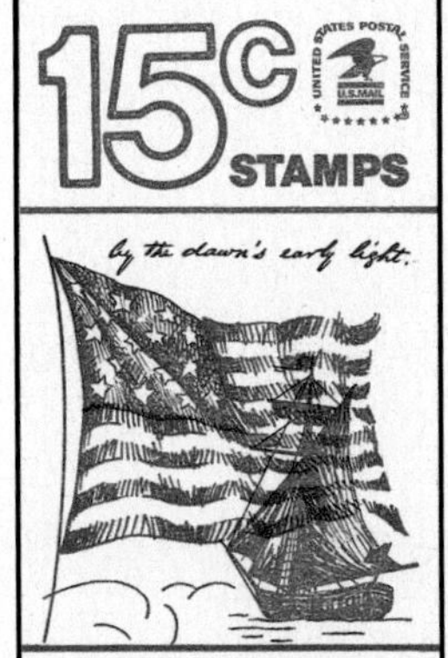

1598a — BC21

1978

$1.20 booklet contains 1 pane of eight 15c stamps.

Booklet

BK130 BC21 $1.20 **red & light blue,** no P# 3.75

1623a — A994, A1018a

The LRM can either above the 9c stamp, as shown, or above the 13c stamp.

1623a A1018a Pane of 8 (1 #1590 + 7 #1623), *Mar. 11, 1977* 2.25 2.00

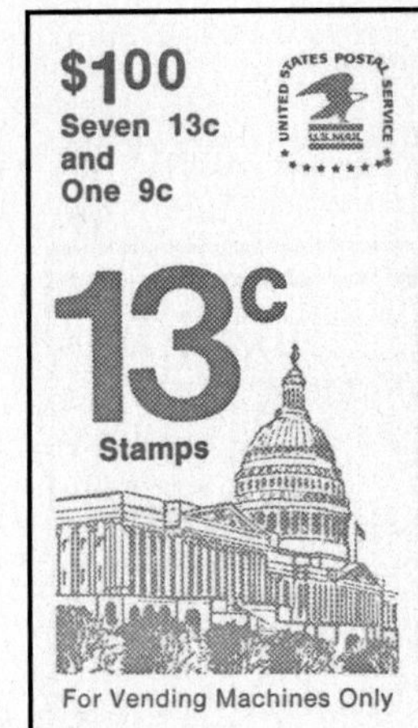

1623a — BC20

1977

$1 booklet contains 1 pane of one 9c stamp and seven 13c stamps.

Booklet

BK131 BC20 $1 **red & light blue,** no P# (3) 2.50

Variety

1623g As "a," tagging omitted —

Booklet

BK131a BC20 As #BK131, with #1623g —

Perf. 10x9¾

1623Bc A1018a Pane of 8 (1 #1590A + 7 #1623B), *Mar. 11, 1977* 15.00 15.00
Folded btwn. 2nd & 3rd rows *100.00* —

Normally produced panes were folded between the 1st and 2nd rows. The listed variety is from a special printing made to service first-day covers, and these were sold mint to collectors at the first-day site, and some were later sold at the Philatelic Agency.

Booklet

BK132 BC20 $1 **red & light blue,** no P# (2) 18.50

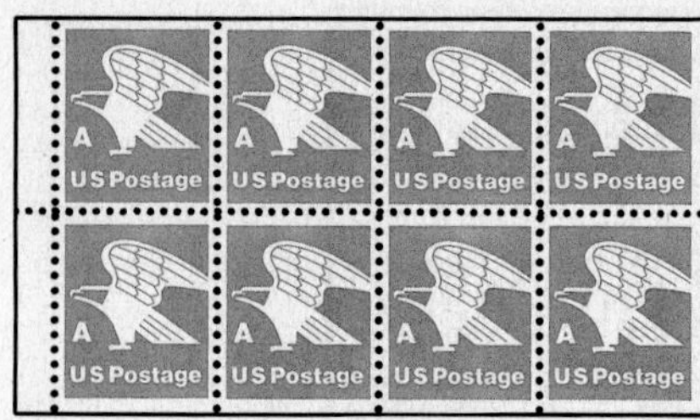

1736a — A1124

1978 **Tagged** ***Perf. 11x10½***

1736a A1124 A pane of 8, *May 22* 2.50 1.50

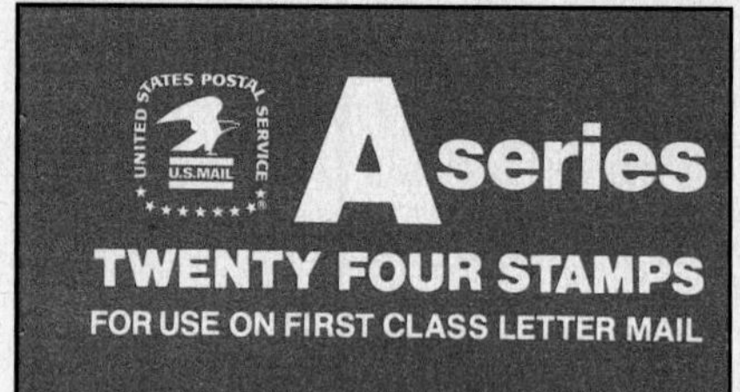

1736a — BC24

1978

$3.60 booklet contains 3 panes of eight A (15c) stamps.

Booklet

BK133 BC24 $3.60 **deep orange** 7.75

No. BK133 exists with covers printed on both thin and thick card stock.

Varieties

1736b As "a," tagging omitted —

1736c Vert. pair, imperf. btwn., in #1736a with foldover *1,000.*

1737a — A1126

Perf. 10

1737a A1126 15c pane of 8, *July 11* 2.50 2.00

1737a — BC22

1978

$2.40 booklet contains 2 panes of eight 15c stamps.

Booklet

BK134 BC22 $2.40 **rose red & yel grn,** no P# 5.25

Varieties

1737c As "a," imperf. *2,250.*

1737d As "a," tagging omitted *60.00*

Booklet

BK134a As #BK134, with 2 #1737c *4,000.*

Windmills — A1127-A1131

1980 ***Perf. 11***

1742a A1127 15c pane of 10, *Feb. 7* 3.50 3.00

1742a — BC25

1980

$3 booklet contains 2 panes of ten 15c stamps.

Booklet

BK135 BC25 $3 **light blue & dark blue,** *blue,* no P# 7.50

1819a — A1207

1981

1819a A1207 B pane of 8, *Mar. 15* 3.50 2.25

1819a — BC26

1981

$4.32 booklet contains 3 panes of eight B (18c) stamps.

Booklet

BK136 BC26 $4.32 **dull violet,** no P# 10.00

1889a — A1267-A1276

1889a A1267 18c pane of 10, *May 14* 5.00 5.00

1889a — BC28

1981

$3.60 booklet contains 2 panes of ten 18c stamps.

Booklet

BK137 BC28 $3.60 **gray & olive,** P#1-10 8.50
P#11-16 14.00

1893a — A1279-A1280

1893a A1279 Pane of 8 (2 #1892, 6 #1893), *Apr. 24* 3.00 2.50

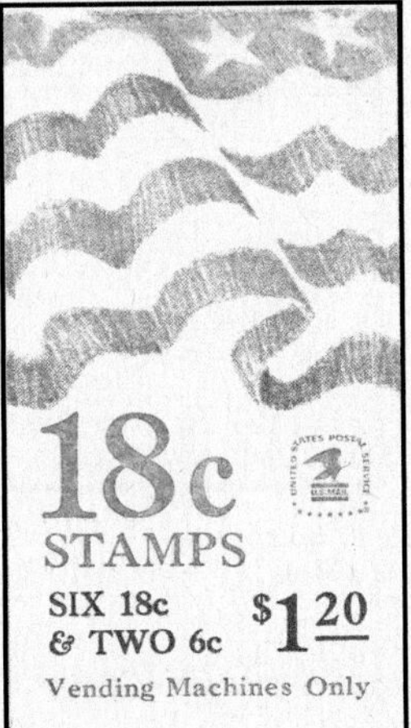

1893a — BC27

1981

$1.20 booklet contains 1 pane of two 6c and six 18c stamps.

Booklet

BK138 BC27 $1.20 **blue & red,** P#1 3.25

Varieties

1893b As "a," vert. imperf. btwn. 60.00
1893d As "a," tagging omitted *675.00*

Booklets

BK138a BC27 As #BK138, with #1893b 60.00
BK138b BC27 As #BK138, with #1893d *675.00*

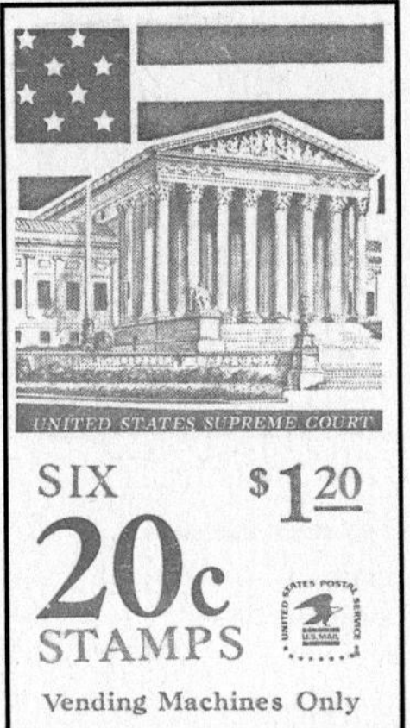
1896a — A1281

1981-83

1896a A1281 20c pane of 6, small block tagging, *Dec. 17, 1981* 3.00 2.25
Scored perforations 3.00 2.25

1896a — BC29

1982

$1.20 booklet contains 1 pane of six 20c stamps.

Booklet

BK139 BC29 $1.20 **blue & red,** P#1 (2) 3.00

1896b — A1281

1896b A1281 20c pane of 10, *June 1, 1982* 5.25 3.25
Scored perforations 7.50 5.00

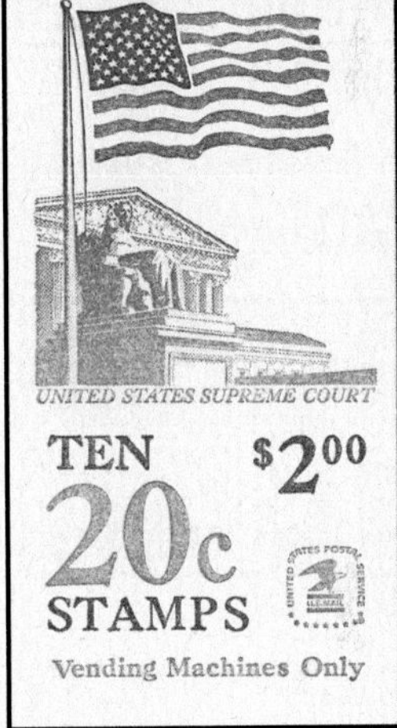

1896b — BC29A

1982

$2 booklet contains 1 pane of ten 20c stamps.

Booklet

BK140 BC29A $2 **blue & red,** P#1 (4) 5.00
P#4 47.50

Varieties

1896c As "b," tagging omitted — —
1896e A1281 20c pane of 10, large block tagging, *Nov. 17, 1983* 5.25 3.25
Scored perforations 5.25 3.25

1896b — BC29B

1983

$4 booklet contains 2 panes of ten 20c stamps.

Booklet

BK140A BC29B $4 **blue & red,** *Nov. 17, 1983,* P#2	10.50	
P#3	17.50	
P#4	*260.00*	

Variety

1896f	As "a," tagging omitted	—	—

The small block tagging is 16x18mm (Nos. 1896a-1896b). The large block tagging is 18x21mm (No. 1896e).

Booklet Covers

When more than one combination of covers exists, the number of possible booklets is noted in parentheses after the booklet listing.

1909a — A1296

1983

1909a A1296 $9.35 pane of 3, *Aug. 12*	57.50	—

3 STAMPS
NINE DOLLARS AND THIRTY-FIVE CENTS
FOR
$28.05

1909a — BC31

1983

$28.05 booklet contains 1 pane of three $9.35 stamps.

Booklet

BK140B BC31 28.05 **blue & red,** P#1111	57.50

1948a — A1333

1981

1948a A1333 C pane of 10, *Oct. 11*	4.50	3.25

1948a — BC26A

1981

$4 booklet contains 2 panes of ten C (20c) stamps.

Booklet

BK141 BC26A $4 **brown,** *blue,* no P#	9.50

1949a — A1334

1982

1949a A1334 20c pane of 10, type I, *Jan. 8*	5.00	2.50
1949d As "a," type II	14.00	—

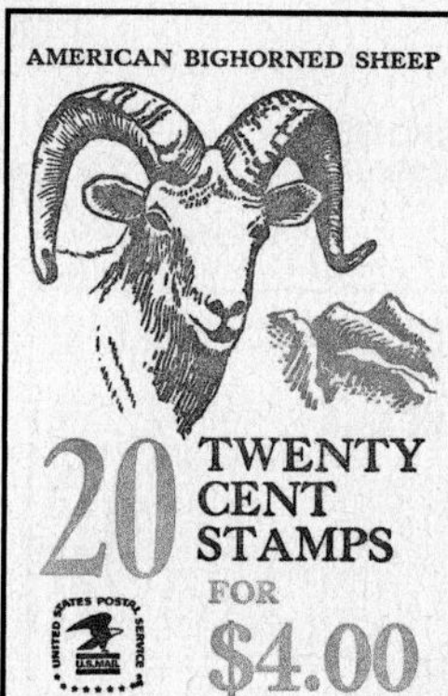

1949a — BC30

1982

$4 booklet contains 2 panes of ten 20c stamps.

Booklets

BK142 BC30 $4 **blue & yellow green,** P#1-6, 9-10	9.50
P#11, 12, 15	35.00
P#14	32.50
P#16	65.00
P#17-19	45.00
P#20, 22-23	80.00
P#24	67.50
P#21, 28, 29	*350.00*
P#25-26	*115.00*
a. Type II, P#34	25.00

Varieties

1949b	As "a," imperf. vert.	*90.00*	
1949f	As "a," tagging omitted	*55.00*	—

Booklets

BK142b	As #BK142, with 2 #1949b	*180.00*
BK142c	As #BK142, with 2 #1949f, P#4, 5, 6, 19	*100.00*

Stamps in No. 1949a are 18¾mm wide and have overall tagging. Stamps in No. 1949d are 18½mm wide and have block tagging.

Plate number does not always appear on top pane in Nos. BK142, BK142a. These booklets sell for more, except P#14 and 15.

Booklet cover BC30 comes in blue & yellow green and in blue & olive green. Both are equally common.

2113a — A1497

1985 *Perf. 11*

2113a A1497 D pane of 10 *Feb. 1*	6.75	3.00

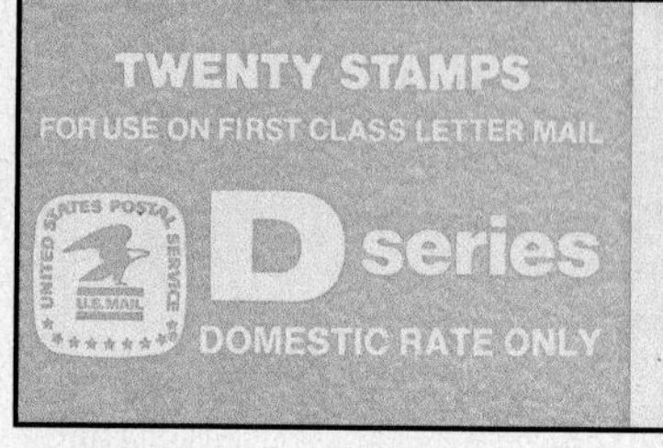

2113a BC26B

1985

$4.40 booklet contains 2 panes of ten D (22c) stamps.

Booklet

BK143 BC26B $4.40 **green,** P#1, 3, 4	13.50
P#2	*350.00*

Varieties

2113b	As "a," horiz. imperf. btwn.	*1,850.*
BK143a	As #BK143, both panes #2113b	*3,750.*

No. BK143 is known with no plate number on top pane and plate number 1, 2, 3 or 4 on bottom pane. These booklets sell for more except P#4. No. BK143 with P#1 or P#2 on bottom is rare; value, P#1 on bottom $1,000, P#2 on bottom $2,100.

2116a — A1499

Perf. 10 Horiz.

2116a A1499 22c pane of 5, *Mar. 29*	2.50	1.25
Scored perforations	2.50	—

2116a — BC33C

2116a — BC32

1985

$1.10 booklet contains one pane of five 22c stamps.
$2.20 booklet contains two panes of five 22c stamps.

Booklets

BK144 BC33C $1.10 **blue & red,** P#1, 3 (2) 2.75
BK145 BC32 $2.20 **blue & red,** P#1, 3 (2) 5.25

2121a — A1500-A1504

Perf. 10

2121a A1500 22c pane of 10, *Apr. 4* 4.50 3.00

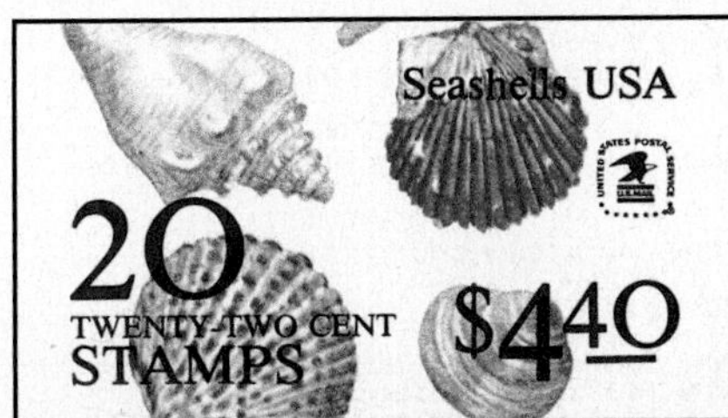

2121a — BC33A

Many different seashell configurations are possible on BC33A. Seven adjacent covers are necessary to show all 25 shells.

2121a — BC33B

1985

$4.40 booklet contains two panes of ten 22c stamps.

Booklets

BK146 BC33A $4.40 **multicolored,** P#1, 3 9.00
P#2 10.50
BK147 BC33B $4.40 **brown & blue,** P#1, 3, 5, 7, 10 9.00
P#6 17.50
P#8 10.00

Varieties

2121b As "a," violet omitted on both Nos. 2120 *400.00*
2121c As "a," vert. imperf. btwn. *350.00*
2121d As "a," imperf. —

2122a — A1505

1985-89 ***Perf. 10 Vert.***

2122a A1505 $10.75 type I, pane of 3, *Apr. 29, 1985* 60.00 —

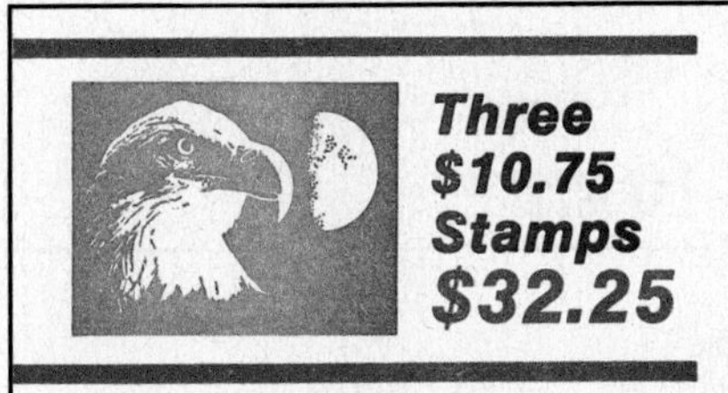

2122a — BC31A

1985

$32.25 booklet contains 1 pane of three $10.75 stamps.

Booklet

BK148 BC31A $32.25 **multicolored,** P#11111 65.00

Varieties

2122c A1505 $10.75 type II, pane of 3, *June 19, 1989* 60.00 —

2122c — BC31B

1989

$32.25 booklet contains 1 pane of three $10.75 stamps.

Booklet

BK149 BC31B 32.25 **blue & red,** P#22222 (2) 65.00

2182a — A1564

1988 ***Perf. 11***

2182a A1564 25c pane of 10, *May 3* 5.00 3.75

2182a — BC43

1988

$5 booklet contains two panes of ten 25c stamps.

Booklet

BK150 BC43 $5 **multicolored,** P#1-2 10.50

Varieties

2182c As "a," tagging omitted —
2182e As "a," all color omitted on right stamps *1,250.*
2182g As "a," tagging omitted on two stamps —

Booklets

BK150a BC43 As #BK150, both panes #2182c —
BK150b BC43 As #BK150, one pane #2182a, one pane #2182g —
BK150c BC43 As #BK150, both panes #2182g —

2197a — A1564

Perf. 10 on 2 or 3 Sides

2197a A1564 25c pane of 6, *May 3* 3.30 2.50

2197a — BC43A

2197a — BC43B

1988

$1.50 booklet contains one pane of six 25c stamps.
$3 booklet contains two panes of six 25c stamps.

Booklets

BK151	BC43A $1.50	**blue & brown,** P#1	3.30
BK152	BC43B $3	**brown & blue,** P#1	6.60

BK151 and BK152 exist with covers printed on both thin and thick card stock.

Variety

2197c A1564 25c As "a," tagging omitted 150.00

Booklet

BK151a BC43A As #BK151, with #2197c 160.00

2201a — A1581-A1584

1986

2201a A1581 22c pane of 4, *Jan. 23* 2.00 1.75

2201a — BC34

1986

$1.76 booklet contains 2 panes of four 22c stamps.

Booklet

BK153 BC34 $1.76 **purple & black,** P#1 4.00

Varieties

2201b	As "a," black omitted on Nos. 2198, 2201	50.00	—
2201c	As "a," blue (litho.) omitted on Nos. 2198-2200	*1,500.*	
2201d	As "a," buff (litho.) omitted	—	
2201e	As "a," tagging omitted	—	

Booklets

BK153a BC34	As #BK153, with 2 #2201b	100.00
BK153b BC34	As #BK153, with 2 #2201c	*3,250.*

2209a — A1588-A1592

2209a A1588 22c pane of 5, *Mar. 21* 4.50 2.75

2209a — BC35

1986

$2.20 booklet contains 2 panes of five 22c stamps.

Booklet

BK154 BC35 $2.20 **blue green and red,** P#11111, 22222 9.00

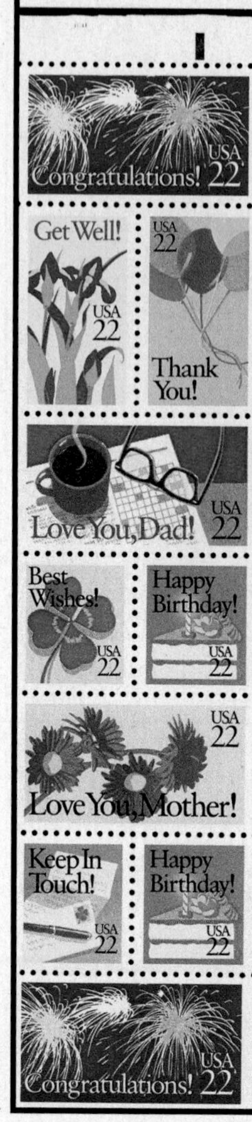

2274a — A1637-A1644

1987

2274a A1637 22c pane of 10, *Apr. 20* 9.00 5.00

FOR 22 CENTS, YOU CAN ADD ONE OF THESE GREETINGS TO A LETTER TO ANYONE IN THE UNITED STATES, CANADA OR MEXICO.
Get Well!
Thank You!
Best Wishes!
Keep in Touch!
Love You, Dad!
Happy Birthday!
Congratulations!
Love You, Mother!
10 TWENTY-TWO CENT U.S. POSTAGE STAMPS 2.20

2274a — BC36

1987

$2.20 booklet contains 1 pane of ten 22c stamps.

Booklet

BK155 BC36 $2.20 **blue & red,** P#111111, 222222 9.00

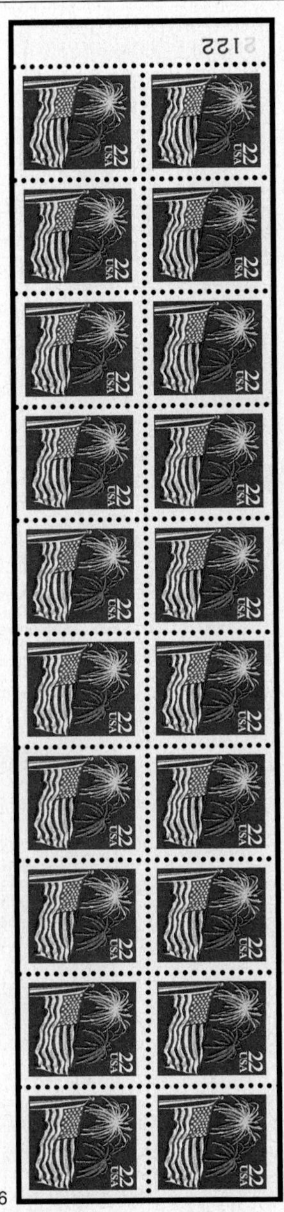
2276a — A1646

Perf. 11

2276a A1646 22c pane of 20, *Nov. 30* 9.00 —

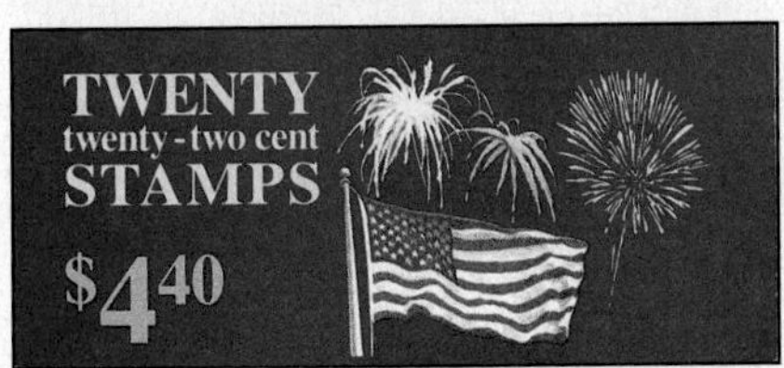

2276a — BC39

1987

$4.40 booklet contains one pane of twenty 22c stamps.

Booklet

BK156 BC39 $4.40 **multicolored,** no P# 9.00
P#1111, 2222 11.00
P#2122 17.50

Varieties

2276b As "a," vert. pair, imperf. between *1,450.*
2276c As "a," miscut and inserted upside down into booklet cover, imperf. between stamps and right selvage. —

No. 2276a was made from sheets of No. 2276 which had alternating rows of perforations removed and the right sheet margins trimmed off.

2282a — A1647

1988 *Perf. 10*

2282a A1647 E pane of 10, *Mar. 22* 6.50 3.50
Scored perforations 6.50 —

2282a — BC40

1988

$5 booklet contains two panes of ten E stamps.

Booklet

BK157 BC40 $5 **blue,** P#1111, 2222 13.00
P#2122 16.00

2283a — A1649a

Perf. 11

2283a A1649a 25c pane of 10, *Apr. 29* 6.00 3.50

2283a, 2283c — BC41

1988

$5 booklet contains two panes of ten 25c stamps.

Booklet

BK158 BC41 $5 **multicolored,** P#A1111 12.00

2283c — A1649a

Color Change

2283c A1649a 25c red removed from sky, pane of 10 45.00 —

Booklet

BK159 BC41 $5 **multicolored,** P#A3111, A3222 90.00

2285b — A1649b-A1649c

Perf. 10

2285b A1649b25c pane of 10, *May 28* 5.00 3.50

2285b — BC45

1988

$5 booklet contains two panes of ten 25c stamps.

Booklet

BK160 BC45 $5 **red & black,** P#1111, 1112, 1211, 1433, 1434, 1734, 2121, 2321, 3333, 5955 (2) 11.00
P#1133, 2111, 2122, 2221, 2222, 3133, 3233, 3412, 3413, 3422, 3521, 4642, 4644, 4911, 4941 (2) 17.50
P#1414 95.00
P#1634, 3512 50.00
P#3822 40.00
P#5453 150.00

No. BK160 exists with two cover types: one with one leaf at end of flowering branch, and one (shown) with two leaves. Two-leaf cover only contains panes with P# 1111, 1211, 2122 or 2222. One-leaf cover contains panes with all listed plate numbers.

Variety

2285f As "b," tagging omitted *110.00*

Booklet

BK160a As #BK160, with 2 #2285f *240.00*

2285Ac — A1648

2285Ac A1648 25c pane of 6, *July 5* 3.00 2.00

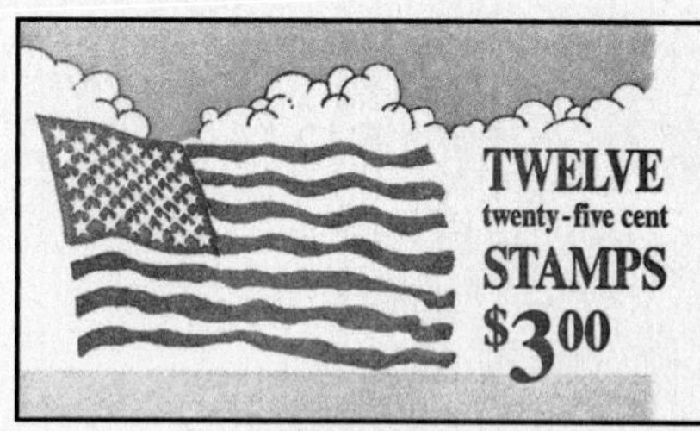

2285Ac — BC46

1988

$3 booklet contains two panes of six 25c stamps.

Booklet

BK161 BC46 $3 **blue & red,** P#1111 6.00

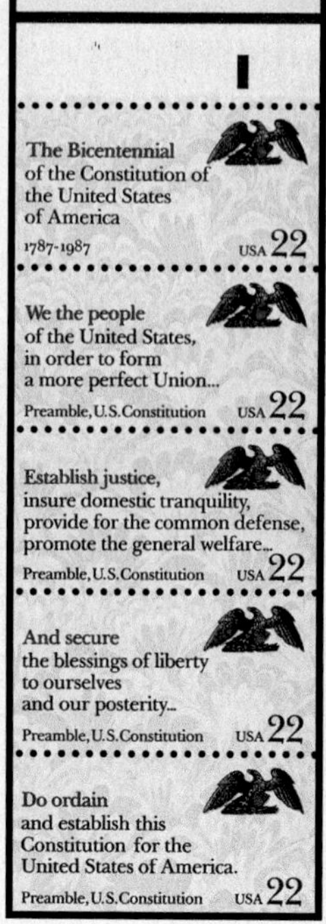

2359a — A1719-A1723

1987

2359a A1719 22c pane of 5, *Aug. 28* 3.50 2.25

2359a — BC37

1987

$4.40 booklet contains four panes of five 22c stamps.

Booklet

BK162 BC37 $4.40 **red & blue,** P#1111, 1112 14.00

2366a — A1726-A1730

2366a A1726 22c pane of 5, *Oct. 1* 2.50 2.00

2366a — BC38

1987

$4.40 booklet contains four panes of five 22c stamps.

Booklet

BK163 BC38 $4.40 **black & yellow,** P#1, 2 10.00

2385a — A1745-A1749

1988

2385a A1745 25c pane of 5, *Aug. 25* 3.25 2.50

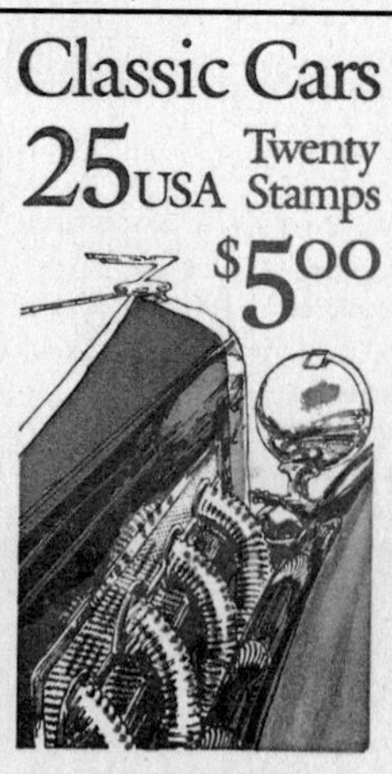

2385a — BC47

1988

$5 booklet contains four panes of five 25c stamps.

Booklet

BK164 BC47 $5 **black & red,** P#1 13.00

2396a — A1759-A1760

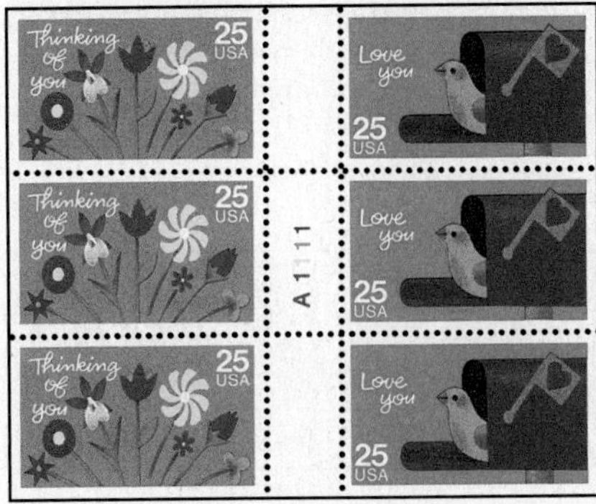

2398a — A1761-A1762

Perf. 11

2396a A1759 25c pane of 6, *Oct. 22* 3.50 3.25
2398a A1761 25c pane of 6, *Oct. 22* 3.50 3.25

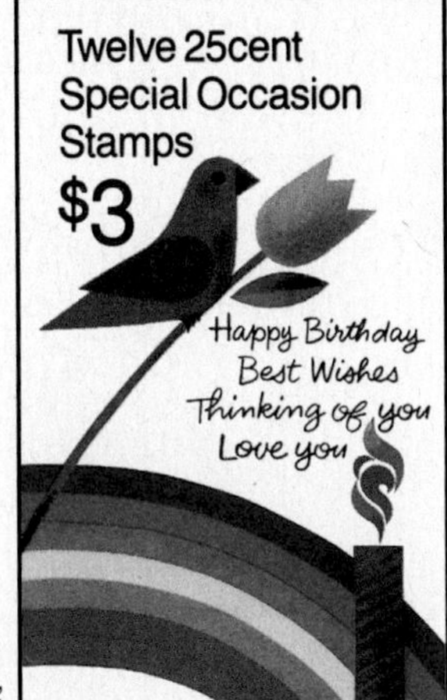

2396a, 2398a — BC48

1988

$3 booklet contains two panes of six 25c stamps.

Combination Booklet

BK165 BC48 $3 **multicolored,** 1 #2396a, 1 #2398a, P#A1111 (2) 7.00

Varieties

2398b As "a," imperf. horiz. 2,250.
2398c As "a," imperf —

One example of a mint, never-hinged and never-folded pane of No. 2396a is recorded. A second example of a never-folded pane of No. 2396a exists uncancelled, affixed to a USPS souvenir page. Examples of No. 2398a in mint, never-hinged, never-folded condition also are recorded (very scarce).

2409a — A1769-A1773

1989 ***Perf. 10***

2409a A1769 25c pane of 5, *Mar. 3* 3.00 1.75
Never folded pane, P#1 8.00
P#2 20.00

2409a — BC49

1989

$5 booklet contains four panes of five 25c stamps.

Booklet

BK166 BC49 $5 **blue & black,** P#1, 2 12.00

Variety

2409b As "a," tagging omitted — —

2427a — A1791

Perf. 11¼

2427a A1791 25c pane of 10, *Oct. 19* 5.00 3.50
Never folded pane, P#1 8.00

2427a — BC50

1989

$5 booklet contains two panes of ten 25c stamps.

Booklet

BK167 BC50 $5 **multicolored,** P#1 10.00

Variety

2427c As "a," imperf —

2429a — A1792

Perf. 11½

2429a A1792 25c pane of 10, *Oct. 19* 5.00 3.50
Never folded pane, P#1111 12.50

2429a — BC51

1989

$5 booklet contains two panes of ten 25c stamps.

Booklet

BK168 BC51 $5 **multicolored,** P#1111, 2111 10.00

Varieties

2429c As "a," horiz. imperf. between *2,250.*
2429d As "a," red omitted *3,250.*

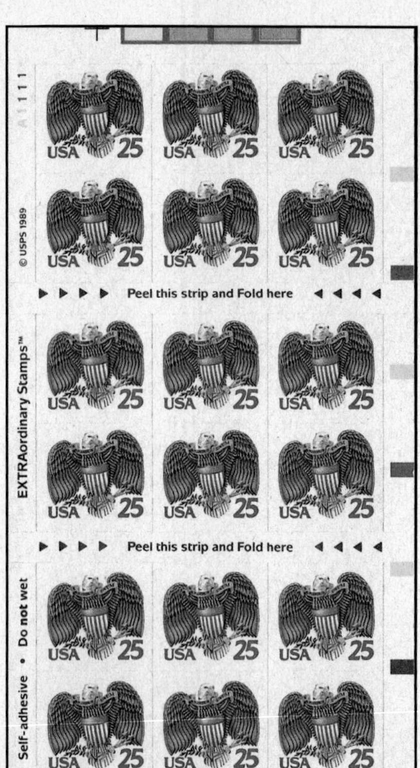

2431a — A1793

2431a — BC52

1989

$5 fold-it-yourself booklet contains eighteen self-adhesive 25c stamps.

Self-adhesive *Die cut*

2431a A1793 25c pane of 18, *Nov. 10,* P#A1111 10.00

By its nature, No. 2431a constitutes a complete booklet. Blue & red peelable paper backing is booklet cover (BC52). Sold for $5.

2441a — A1800

1990 *Perf. 11½*

2441a A1800 25c pane of 10, *Jan. 18* 5.00 3.50
Never folded pane, P#1211 20.00
2441d As "a," tagging omitted —

2441a — BC53

1990

$5 booklet contains two panes of ten 25c stamps.

Booklet

BK169 BC53 $5 **multicolored,** P#1211 10.50
P#2111 20.00
P#2211 27.50
P#2222 17.50

Variety

2441c As "a," bright pink omitted *950.00*

Panes exist containing both normal and bright pink omitted stamps. Value is less than that of No. 2441c.

2443a — A1802

Perf. 11

2443a A1802 15c pane of 10, *Feb. 3* 3.00 2.50
Never folded pane, P#111111 7.00

For Post Cards
USA 15
15USA Twenty Stamps
$3.00

2443a — BC54

1990

$3 booklet contains two panes of ten 15c stamps.

Booklet

BK170 BC54 $3 **multi,** P#111111 6.00
P#221111 9.00

Variety

2443c As "a," blue omitted *900.00*

2474a — A1829-A1833

Perf. 10

2474a A1829 25c pane of 5, *Apr. 26* 7.50 2.00
Never folded pane, P#1, 3, 5 9.50
P#2 11.50
P#4 52.50

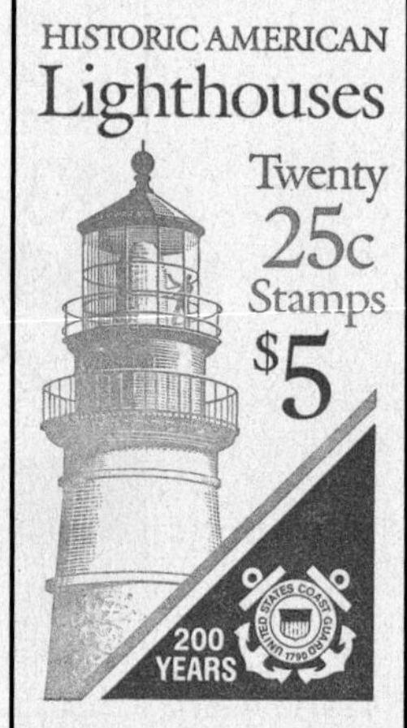

2474a — BC55

1990

$5 booklet contains four panes of five 25c stamps.

Booklet

BK171 BC55 $5 **blue & red,** P#1-5 (2) 30.00

Variety

2474b As "a," white omitted 85.00 —

Booklet

BK171a As #BK171, with 4 #2474b 350.00

Although often collected as a booklet pane, the 25¢ Flag ATM pane of 12 is not listed here because it does not have a removable selvage strip that allows it to be folded into a booklet. This pane is listed in the Postage section as No. 2475a.

2483a — A1847

1991-95

2483a A1847 20c **multicolored,** pane of 10, *June 15, 1995* 5.25 2.50
Never folded pane, P#S1111 6.25

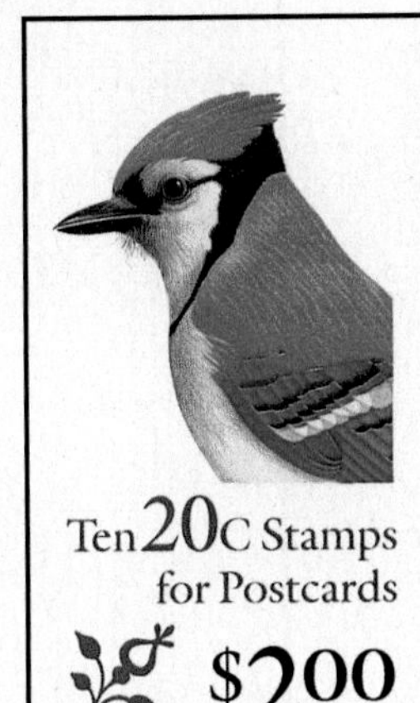

2483a — BC56

1995

$2 booklet contains one pane of 10 20c stamps.

Booklet

BK172 BC56 $2 **multicolored,** P#S1111 5.25

Variety

2483b As "a," imperf —

2484a — A1848

2484a A1848 29c **black & multi,** overall tagging, pane of 10, *Apr. 12, 1991* 6.00 3.75
Never folded pane, P#1111 9.00
2484e A1848 29c **black & multi,** prephosphored coated paper with surface tagging showing a solid appearance, pane of 10, *1992* 6.00 3.75

2484e — BC57

2484a, 2484e — BC57A

2485a — BC57B

1991-92

$2.90 booklet contains one pane of 10 29c stamps.
$5.80 booklet contains two panes of 10 29c stamps.

Booklets

BK173 BC57 $2.90 **black & green,** with No. 2484e, P#4444 6.25
BK174 BC57A $5.80 **black & red,** P#1111, 2222 12.00
P#1211 125.00
P#3222, 3333 18.00
BK174a As No. BK174, with 2 #2484e, P#2122, 2222, 3222, 3333 17.50
P#3221 95.00
P#3331 —
P#4444 15.00

Varieties

2484c As "a," imperf. horiz. *875.00*
2484g As "a," horiz. imperf. between and with natural straight edge at top or bottom *875.00*

Booklet

BK174b As #BK174, with 2 #2484g *1,750.*

2485a — A1848

2485a A1848 29c **red & multi,** pane of 10, *Apr. 12, 1991* 6.00 4.00
Never folded pane, P#K11111 11.00

Booklet

BK175 BC57B $5.80 **black & multi,** P#K11111 13.00

2486a — A1849

2486a A1849 29c pane of 10, *Oct. 8, 1993* 6.00 4.00
Never folded pane, P#K1111 6.50

AFRICAN VIOLET
Ten
29c Stamps
$2.90

2486a — BC58

2486a — BC58A

1993

$2.90 booklet contains one pane of 10 29c stamps.
$5.80 booklet contains two panes of 10 29c stamps.

Booklets

BK176 BC58 $2.90 **multicolored,** P#K1111 6.25
BK177 BC58A $5.80 **multicolored,** P#K1111 12.50

2488a — A1850-A1851

2488a A1850 32c **multicolored,** pane of 10, *July 8, 1995* 6.50 4.25
Never folded pane, P# 11111 7.25

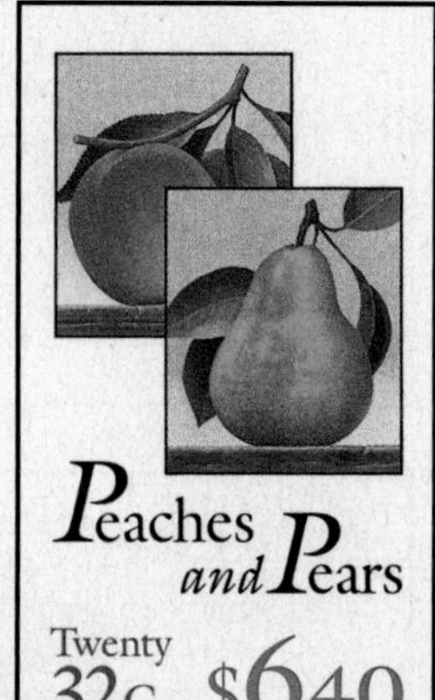

2488a — BC59

1995

$6.40 booklet contains two panes of 10 32c stamps.

Booklet

BK178 BC59 $6.40 **multicolored,** P#11111 13.00

2489a — A1852

2489a
BC60

1993

$5.22 fold-it-yourself booklet contains 18 self-adhesive 29c stamps.

Self-Adhesive ***Die Cut***

2489a A1852 29c pane of 18, *June 25, 1993,* P#D11111, D22211, D22221, D22222, D23133 11.00

By its nature, No. 2489a constitutes a complete booklet (BC60). The peelable backing serves as a booklet cover.

Variety

2489b As "a," die cutting omitted —

2490a —
A1853

Self-adhesive Stamps

USA 29

Eighteen 29c Stamps $5.22

2490a
BC61

1993

$5.22 fold-it-yourself booklet contains 18 self-adhesive 29c stamps.

Self-Adhesive ***Die Cut***

2490a A1853 29c pane of 18, *Aug. 19, 1993,* P#S111 11.00

By its nature, No. 2490a constitutes a complete booklet (BC61). The peelable backing, of which two types are known, serves as a booklet cover.

2491a —
A1854

Self-adhesive Stamps

Eighteen Stamps $5.22

2491a
BC61A

1993

$5.22 fold-it-yourself booklet contains 18 self-adhesive stamps.

Self-Adhesive *Die Cut*

2491a	A1854 29c pane of 18, *Nov. 5, 1993,* P#B3-11, 13-15	11.00
	P#B1	16.00
	P#B2, 12, 16	13.00

By its nature, No. 2491a constitutes a complete booklet (BC61A). The peelable backing serves as a booklet cover.

2492a — A1853

2492a
BC61B

1995

$6.40 fold-it-yourself booklet contains 20 self-adhesive 32c stamps.

Serpentine Die Cut 11.3x11.7 on 2, 3 or 4 Sides

Self-Adhesive

2492a	A1853 32c pane of 20 + label, *June 2, 1995,* P#S111, S112, S333, S444, S555	13.00
2492b	A1853 32c pane of 15 + label, *1996*	9.75
2492e	A1853 32c pane of 14, *1996*	20.00
2492f	A1853 32c pane of 16, *1996*	20.00

By its nature, No. 2492a is a complete booklet (BC61B). The peelable backing serves as a booklet cover.

Nos. 2492a and 2492b exist on two types of surface-tagged paper that exhibit either a solid or grainy solid appearance. Values are the same. Nos. 2492e and 2492f have only tagging with a solid appearance.

Nos. 2492a and 2492b come either with no die cutting on the label or with die cutting.

No. 2492e contains blocks of 4, 6 and 4 stamps. No. 2492f contains blocks of 6, 6 and 4 stamps. The blocks are on rouletted backing paper. The peel-a-way strips that were between the blocks have been removed to fold the pane.

Booklets

See note before No. BK243. For illustration of booklet cover BC126, see before No. BK243.

BK178A	BC126	$4.80	**blue,** No. 2492b (5)	10.00
BK178B	BC126	$4.80	**blue,** No. 2492f with bottom right stamp removed	37.50
BK178C	BC126	$9.60	**blue,** 2 #2492b, No P# (3) (grainy solid tagging only)	20.00
BK178D	BC126	$9.60	**blue,** 2 panes of #2492f ea with a stamp removed from either the top or bottom row, No P# (3)	42.50

Combination Booklets

See note before No. BK243.

BK178E	BC126	$9.60	**blue,** 1 ea #2492e, 2492f, no P# (3)	45.00
BK178F	BC126	$9.60	**blue,** #2492b, 2492f with bottom right stamp removed, no P#	*225.00*

No. BK178A was issued wrapped in cellophane and not wrapped in cellophane. The two cellophane-wrapped versions are scarcer.

No. BK178E was sold wrapped in cellophane with the contents of the booklet listed on a label. Three versions exist. No. 2492f is affixed to the booklet cover, and No. 2492e is loose.

The panes of #2492f with one stamp removed that are contained in Nos. BK178B, BK178D and BK178F cannot be made from No. 2492b, a pane of 15 + label. The label is located in the sixth or seventh row of the pane and is sometimes die cut. The panes with one stamp removed all have the stamp removed from the top or bottom row of the pane.

Nos. 2492a and 2492b exist on two types of surface-tagged paper that exhibit either a solid or grainy solid appearance. Values are the same. Nos. 2492e and 2492f have tagging with a solid appearance.

Varieties

2492d	As "a," 2 stamps and parts of 7 others printed on backing liner	—
2492i	As "a," 6 pairs plus stamp and label die cutting omitted vert. btwn. (due to miscutting)	*800.00*
2492j	As "f," with 2 vert. pairs at bottom die cutting omitted horiz., in full bklt. #BK178D	—

V1232 • Peel here to fold • Self-adhesive stamps • DO NOT WET

©USPS 1994 • Peel here to fold • Self-adhesive • DO NOT WET

TIME TO REORDER THIS BLOCK IS NOT VALID POSTAGE

2494a — A1850-A1851

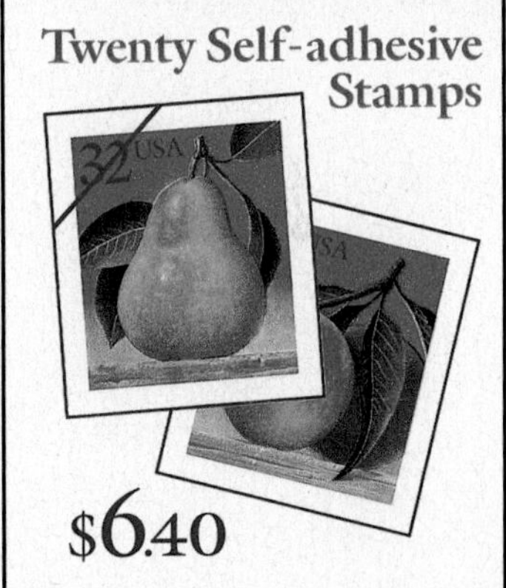

2494a
BC61C

1995

$6.40 fold-it-yourself booklet contains 20 self-adhesive 32c stamps.

Serpentine Die Cut 8.8

2494a	A1850 32c pane of 20+label, *July 8, 1995,* P# list 1	13.00
	P# list 2	18.00
	P#V33323	25.00
	P#V11232	—

By its nature, No. 2494a is a complete booklet (BC61C). The peelable backing serves as a booklet cover. It comes either with no die cutting on the label or with die cutting.

List 1 — P#V11111, V11122, V11132, V12132, V12211, V12221, V22212, V22222, V33142, V33243, V33333, V33343, V33353, V33363, V44424, V44434, V44454, V45434, V45464, V54365, V54565, V55365, V55565.

List 2 — P#V11131, V12131, V12232, V22221, V33143, V33453.

2505a — A1860-A1864

1990 ***Perf. 11***

2505a A1860 25c pane of 10, *Aug. 17* 8.00 6.00
Never folded pane, P#1-2 15.00

2505a — BC62

1990

$5 booklet contains two panes of 10 25c stamps.

Booklet

BK179 BC62 $5 **multicolored,** P#1, 2 18.00

Varieties

2505b As "a," black (engr.) omitted *2,500.*
2505d As "a," horiz. imperf. between *2,250.*

The one example of No. 2505d that has been reported is actually split at the booklet fold and is a block of 4 and a block of 6.

2514b — A1873

1990 ***Perf. 11½***

2514b A1873 25c pane of 10, *Oct. 18* 5.00 3.25
Never folded pane, P#1 11.00

2514a — BC63

1990

$5 booklet contains two panes of 10 25c stamps.

Booklet

BK180 BC63 $5 **multicolored,** P#1 10.00

2516a — A1874

1990 ***Perf. 11½x11***

2516a A1874 25c pane of 10, *Oct. 18* 6.00 3.25
Never folded pane, P#1211 10.00

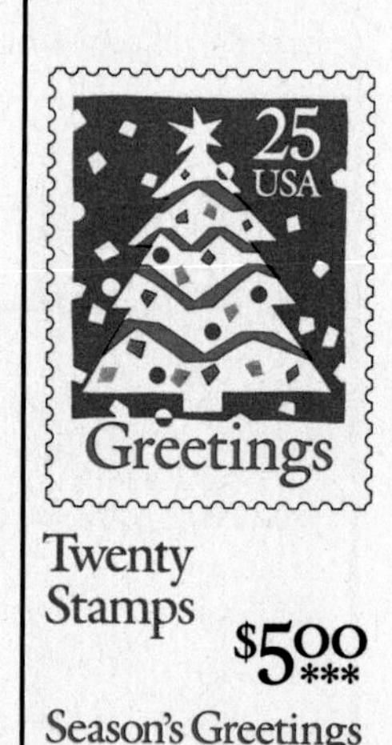

2516a — BC64

1990

$5 booklet contains two panes of 10 25c stamps.

Booklet

BK181 BC64 $5 **multicolored,** P#1211 12.00
P#1111 —

2519a — A1875

1991 ***Perf. 11.2 Bullseye***

2519a A1875 F pane of 10, *Jan. 22* 6.50 4.50

2519a, 2520a — BC65

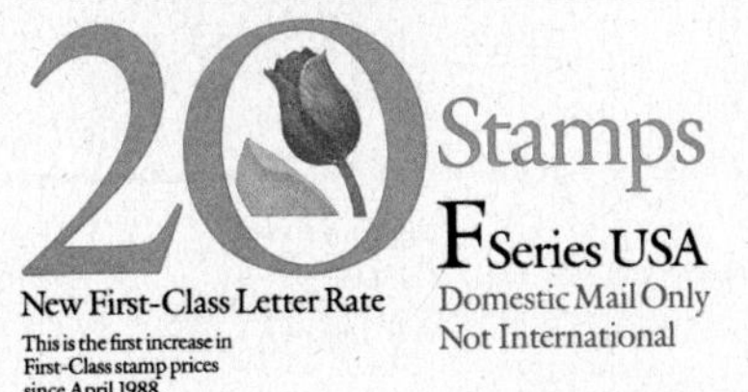

2519a, 2520a — BC65A

1991

$2.90 booklet contains one pane of 10 F stamps.
$5.80 booklet contains two panes of 10 F stamps.

Booklets

BK182 BC65 ($2.90) **yellow & multi,** P#2222 6.50

BK183 BC65A ($5.80) **grn, red & blk,** P#1111, 2121, 2222 13.00

P#1222, 2111, 2212 22.50

2520a — A1875

2520a A1875 F pane of 10, *Jan. 22* 15.00 4.50

Never folded pane, P#K1111 —

Booklet

BK184 BC65 ($2.90) like #BK182, **grn, red & blk,** P#K1111 15.00

Varieties

2520b As "a," imperf. horiz. —

2520c Horiz. pair, imperf between, in error booklet pane of 12 stamps *450.00*

No. 2520c is from a paper foldover before perforating.

Although often collected as a booklet pane, the nondenominated (29¢) F-rate Flag ATM pane of 12 is not listed here because it does not have a removable selvage strip that allows it to be folded into a booklet. This pane is listed in the Postage section as No. 2522a.

2527a — A1879

Perf. 11

2527a A1879 29c pane of 10, *Apr. 5* 6.00 3.50

Never folded pane, P#K1111 8.00

2527a — BC66

1991

$2.90 booklet contains one pane of 10 29c stamps.

Booklet

BK185 BC66 $5.80 **multicolored,** P#K1111, K2222, K3333 12.00

Varieties

2527d As "a," imperf horiz. *750.00*

2527e As "a," imperf vert. *500.00*

2528a — A1880

Perf. 11

2528a A1880 29c pane of 10, *Apr. 21* 6.00 3.50

Never folded pane 7.00

2528a — BC67

2528a — BC67A

1991

$2.90 booklet contains one pane of 10 29c stamps.

Booklets

BK186 BC67 $2.90 **black & multicolored,** P#K11111 6.00

BK186A BC67A $2.90 **red & multicolored,** P#K11111 (2) 6.75

Varieties

2528b As "a," imperf. horiz. *2,750.*

2528f As "d," two pairs, in #2528a with foldover —

Booklet Covers

When more than one combination of covers exists, the number of possible booklets is noted in parentheses after the booklet listing.

2530a — A1882

1991 ***Perf. 10***

2530a A1882 19c pane of 10, *May 17* 4.00 2.75
Never folded pane, P#1111 5.00

$3.80

2530a — BC68

1991

$3.80 booklet contains two panes of 10 19c stamps.

Booklet

BK187 BC68 $3.80 **black & blue,** P#1111, 2222 8.00
P#1222 32.50

2531Ab — A1884

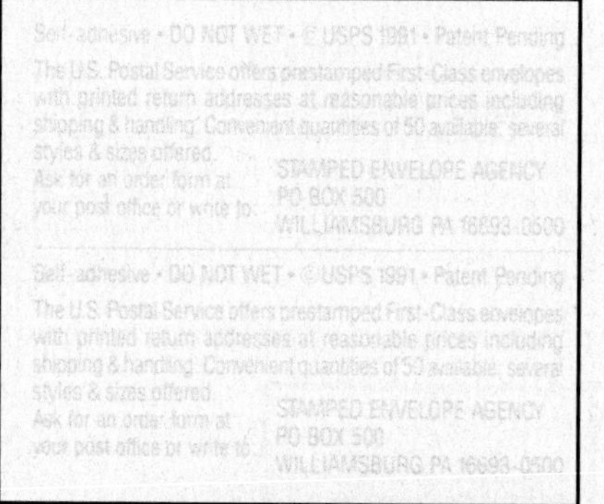

2531Ab — BC68A

Self-adhesive Stamps

Convenient: No Licking!

Strong Adhesive: Stays on Envelopes!

Easy to Use: No Tearing!

Eighteen Stamps

2531Ae — BC68B

1991-92

$5.22 fold-it-yourself booklet contains 18 self-adhesive 29c stamps.

Self-Adhesive ***Die Cut***

2531Ab A1884 29c pane of 18, prephosphored coated paper with surface tagging showing a solid appearance, *June 25,* no P# 11.00

By its nature, No. 2531Ab constitutes a complete booklet (BC68A). The peelable backing serves as a booklet cover.

Variety

2531Ae As "b," overall tagging (BC68B), *1992* 11.00

2536a — A1890

1991 ***Perf. 11***

2536a A1890 29c pane of 10, *May 9* 6.00 3.50
Never folded pane, P#1111, 1112 7.00

2536a — BC69

1991

$5.80 booklet contains two panes of 10 29c stamps.

Booklet

BK188 BC69 $5.80 **multicolored,** P#1111, 1112 12.00
P#1113, 1123, 2223 16.00
P#1212 42.50

2549a — A1899-A1903

Perf. 11

2549a A1899 29c pane of 5, *May 31* 5.50 3.00
Never folded pane, P#A23133, A23213 8.25
P#A11111, A22122, A22132, A33213 —
P#A23124 25.00
P#A32225, A33233 15.00

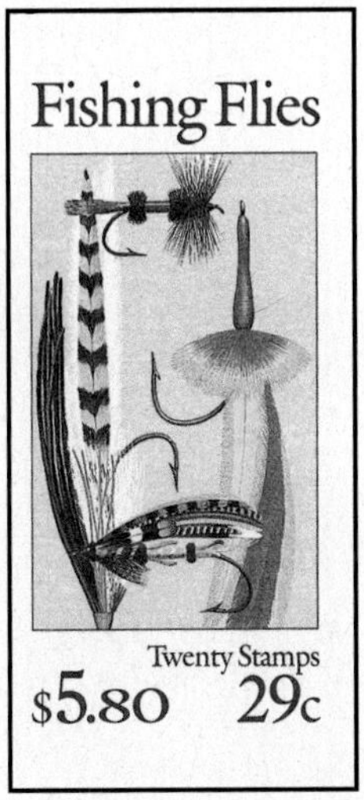

2549a — BC70

1991

$5.80 booklet contains four panes of 5 29c stamps.

Booklet

BK189 BC70 $5.80 **multicolored,** P#A22122, A23123, A23124, A33235, A44446, A45546, A45547 22.00
P#A11111, A22133, A23133, A23213 30.00
P#A22132, A32224, A32225, A33233 30.00
P#A31224 45.00

No. BK189 exists assembled from panes with different plate numbers.

P#33213 has yet to be found as top pane in booklets.

Variety

2545b Horiz. pair, imperf. between, in #2549a with foldover *2,400.*

2552a — A1905

2552a A1905 29c pane of 5, *July 2* 3.00 2.25
Never folded pane, P#A11121111 4.00

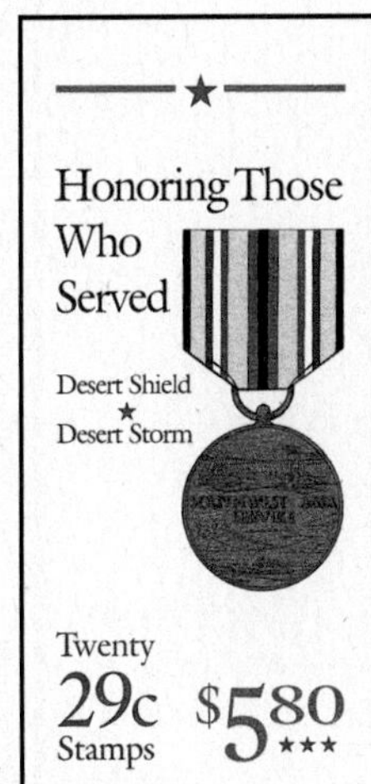

2552a — BC71

1991

$5.80 booklet contains four panes of 5 29c stamps.

Booklet

BK190 BC71 $5.80 **multicolored,** P#A11111111, A11121111 12.00

2566b — A1916-A1920

2566b A1916 29c pane of 10, *Aug. 29* 10.00 5.00
Never folded pane, P#1 12.00

2566a — BC72

1991

$5.80 booklet contains two panes of ten 29c stamps.

Booklet

BK191 BC72 $5.80 **scar, blk & brt vio,** P#1, 2 20.00

Varieties

2566c As "b," scar & brt violet (engr.) omitted *350.00*

2577a — A1922-A1931

2577a A1922 29c pane of 10, *Oct. 1* 9.00 4.50
Never folded pane, P#111111 11.00

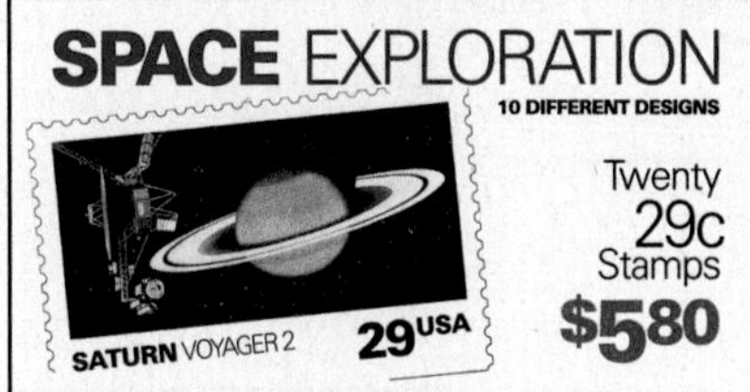

2577a — BC73

1991

$5.80 booklet contains two panes of 10 29c stamps.

Booklet

BK192 BC73 $5.80 **blue, black & red,** P#111111 18.00
P#111112 22.00

2578a — A1933

Perf. 11¼

2578a A1933 (29c) pane of 10, *Oct. 17* 6.00 3.25
Never folded pane, P#1 9.50

2578a — BC74

1991

($5.80) booklet contains two panes of 10 (29c) stamps.

Booklet

BK193 BC74 ($5.80) **multicolored,** P#1 12.00

2581b — A1934

2582a — A1935

2583a — A1936

2584a — A1937

2585a — A1938

2581b A1934 (29c) pane, 2 each, #2580, 2581, *Oct. 17* 8.00 1.25
Never bound pane, P#A11111 10.00
2582a A1935 (29c) pane of 4, *Oct. 17* 2.40 1.25
Never bound pane, P#A11111 4.00
2583a A1936 (29c) pane of 4, *Oct. 17* 2.40 1.25
Never bound pane, P#A11111 4.00
2584a A1937 (29c) pane of 4, *Oct. 17* 2.40 1.25
Never bound pane, P#A11111 4.00
2585a A1938 (29c) pane of 4, *Oct. 17* 2.40 1.25
Never bound pane, P#A11111 4.00

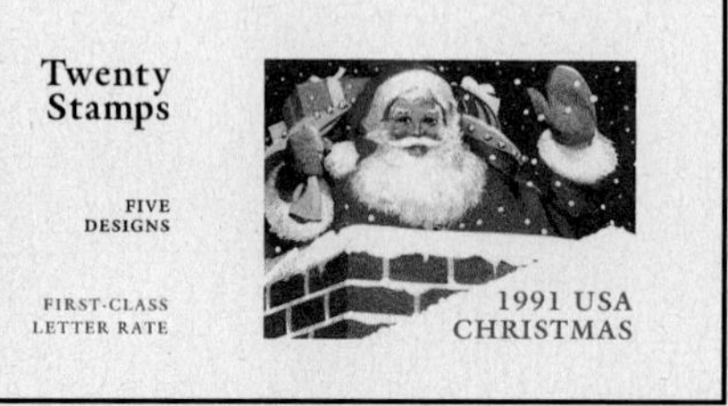

2581b, 2582a-2585a — BC75

1991

($5.80) booklet contains five panes of 4 (29c) stamps.

Combination Booklet

BK194 BC75 ($5.80) **multicolored,** 1 each #2581b, 2582a-2585a, P#A11111, A12111 16.00

Nos. 2581b-2585a are unfolded panes.
Imperf examples of Nos. 2582a-2585a are printer's waste.

2593a — A1946

1992-94 ***Perf. 10***

2593a A1946 29c **black & multi,** pane of 10, *Sept. 8* 6.00 4.25
Never folded pane, P#1111 7.00

2593a — BC76

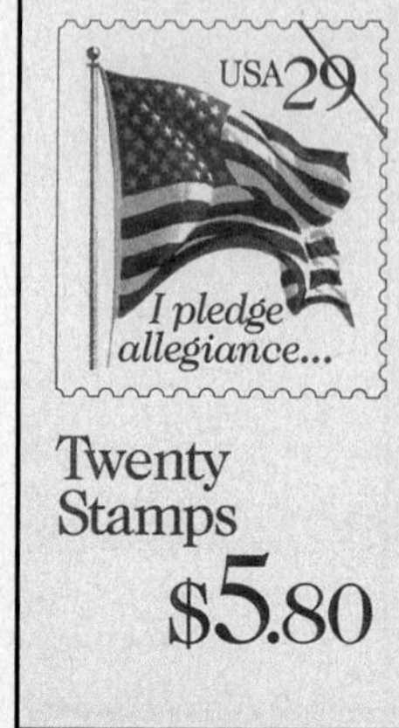

2593a — BC76A

1992

$2.90 booklet contains one pane of 10 29c stamps.
$5.80 booklet contains two panes of 10 29c stamps.

Booklets

BK195 BC76 $2.90 **blue & red,** P#1111 6.00
P#2222 11.00
BK196 BC76A $5.80 **blue & red,** P#1111 12.00
P#2222 20.00
P#1211, 2122 —

Perf. 11x10

2593Bc A1946 29c **black & multi,** pane of 10, shiny gum, *1993* 35.00 7.50
Low gloss gum 40.00

Booklet

BK197 BC76A $5.80 **blue & red,** shiny gum, P#1111, 1211, 2122, 2222, 2232, 3333 50.00
P#2232, low gloss gum 80.00
P#2333, low gloss gum —
P#2333, shiny gum —
P#3333, low gloss gum 175.00
P#4444, low gloss gum 140.00

2594a — A1946

2594a A1946 29c **red & multi,** pane of 10, *1993* 6.50 4.25
Never folded pane, P# K1111 7.50

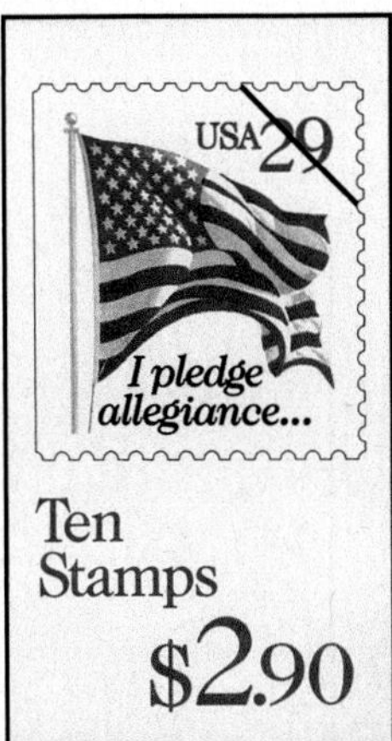

2594a — BC76B

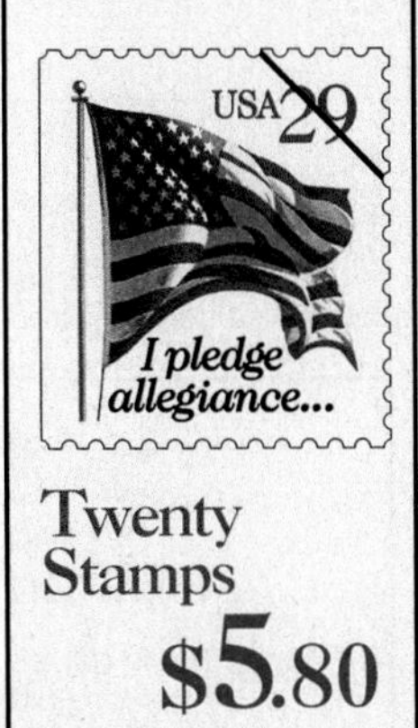

2594a — BC76C

1993-94

$2.90 booklet contains one pane of 10 29c stamps.
$5.80 booklet contains two panes of 10 29c stamps.

Booklet

BK198 BC76B $2.90 **black, red & blue,** P#K1111 — 6.00
BK199 BC76C $5.80 **multicolored,** *1994,* P#K1111 — 13.50

2595a — A1947

Self-adhesive Stamps
Convenient: No Licking!
Strong Adhesive: Stays on Envelopes!
Easy to Use: No Tearing!
USA 29
Seventeen 29 Cent Stamps

2595a — BC77

1992

$5 fold-it-yourself booklet contains 17 self-adhesive 29c stamps.

No. BC77 for Nos. 2595a, 2596a and 2597a differs in size and style of type as well as location of UPC labels.

Self-adhesive
Die Cut

2595a A1947 29c **brown & multi**, pane of 17 + label, *Sept. 25,* P#B1111-1, B1111-2, B2222-1, B2222-2, B3333-1, B3333-3, B3434-1, B3434-3, B4444-1 — 12.75
P#B4344-1, B4444-3 — 15.00
P#B4344-3 — *150.00*

Variety

2595d As "a," die cutting omitted — *725.00*
2596a A1947 29c **blue green & multi,** pane of 17 + label, *Sept. 25, 1992,* P#D11111, D21221, D22322, D32322, D32332, D43352, D43452, D43453, D54563, D54573, D65784 — 12.75
P#D54571, D54673, D61384 — 15.00
P#D32342, D42342 — 35.00
P#D54561 — 25.00
2597a A1947 29c **red & multi,** pane of 17 + label, *Sept. 25,* P#S1111 — 12.75

By their nature, Nos. 2595a-2597a constitute complete booklets (BC77). A peelable paper backing serves as a booklet cover for each. No. 2595a has a black and multicolored backing with serifed type. No. 2596a has a blue and multicolored backing, No. 2597a has a black and multicolored backing with unserifed type.

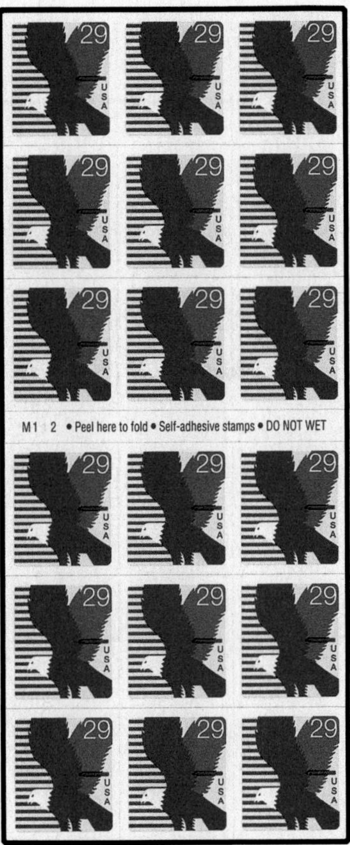

2598a — A1950

2598a BC78

1994

$5.22 fold-it-yourself booklet contains 18 self-adhesive 29c stamps.

Self-Adhesive — *Die Cut*

2598a A1950 29c pane of 18, *Feb. 4, 1994,* P#M111, M112 — 11.00

By its nature, No. 2598a constitutes a complete booklet (BC78). The peelable backing serves as a booklet cover.

2599a — A1951

Self-adhesive Stamps
USA 29
Eighteen Stamps $5.22

2599a — BC79

1994

$5.22 fold-it-yourself booklet contains 18 self-adhesive 29c stamps.

Self-Adhesive — *Die Cut*

2599a A1951 29c pane of 18, *June 24, 1994,* P#D1111, D1212 — 11.00

By its nature, No. 2599a constitutes a complete booklet (BC79). The peelable backing serves as a booklet cover.

2646a — A1994-A1998

1992

2646a A1994 29c pane of 5, *June 15* — 3.00 2.50
Never folded pane, P#A2212112, A2212122, A2222222 — 4.00
P#A1111111, A2212222 — 10.00

Imperforate panes are proofs.

2646a — BC80

1992

$5.80 booklet contains four panes of 5 29c stamps.

Booklet

BK201 BC80 $5.80 **multicolored,** P#A1111111, A2212112, A2212222, A2222222 12.00
P#A2212122 18.00

No. BK201 exists assembled from panes with different plate numbers.

2709a — A2057-A2061

2709a A2057 29c pane of 5, *Oct. 1* 3.25 2.25
Never folded pane, P#K1111 4.25

2709a — BC83

1992

$5.80 booklet contains four panes of 5 29c stamps.

Booklet

BK202 BC83 $5.80 **multicolored,** P#K1111 13.00

Variety

2709b As "a," imperf. *2,000.*

2710a — A2062

Perf. 11¼

2710a A2062 29c pane of 10, *Oct. 22* 6.00 3.50
Never folded pane, P#1 7.00

2710a — BC83A

1992

$5.80 booklet contains two panes of 10 29c stamps.

Booklet

BK202A BC83A $5.80 **multicolored,** P#1 12.00

2718a — A2063-A2066

2718a A2063 29c pane of 4, *Oct. 22* 3.60 1.25
Never bound pane, P#A111111, A222222 4.50
P#A112211 —

2718a — BC84

1992

$5.80 booklet contains five panes of 4 29c stamps.

Booklet

BK203 BC84 $5.80 **multi,** P#A111111, A112211, A222222 18.00

Imperfs and part-perfs of No. 2718a are proofs.

2719a — A2064

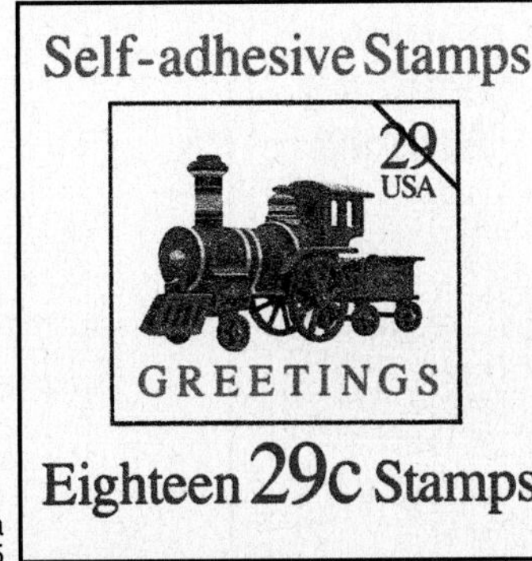

2719a
BC85

1992

$5.22 fold-it-yourself booklet contains 18 self-adhesive 29c stamps.

Self-Adhesive

Die Cut

2719a A2064 29c **multicolored,** pane of 18, *Oct. 29,* P#V11111 12.00

By its nature, No. 2719a constitutes a complete booklet (BC85). The peelable paper backing serves as a booklet cover.

2737a — A2071, A2075-A2077

Tab format on No. 2737a is similar to that shown for No. 2737b.

1993

2737a A2071 29c pane of 8, 2 #2731, 1 each #2732-2737, *June 16* 5.25 2.25
Never folded pane, P#A22222 8.00
P#A13113 —

2737b A2071 29c pane of 4, #2731, 2735-2737 + tab, *June 16* 2.60 1.50
Never folded pane, P#A22222 3.50
P#A13113 5.00

2737a, 2737b — BC86

1993

$5.80 booklet contains one pane of four 29c stamps and two panes of eight 29c stamps.

Combination Booklet

BK204 BC86 $5.80 **multicolored,** 2 #2737a + 1 #2737b, P#A11111, A22222 13.25
P#A13113, A44444 15.00

No. 2737b without tab is indistinguishable from broken No. 2737a.

Never folded panes of No. 2737a with P#A11111 or P#A22222 exist missing the bottom stamp (found in some USPS mint sets). This was the only source for the never folded pane with P#A11111, and such panes are scarce.

No. BK204 exists assembled from panes with different plate numbers.

Imperforate panes of Nos. 2737a and 2737b are proofs.

2745a — A2086-A2090

2745a A2086 29c pane of 5, *Jan. 25* 3.00 2.25
Never folded pane, P#1111, 1211 4.00
P#2222 6.50

Half of the printing of No. 2745a shows a part of No. 2745 on the left side of the selvage tab. Values, same.

2745a — BC89

1993

$5.80 booklet contains four panes of 5 29c stamps.

Booklet

BK207 BC89 $5.80 **multi,** P#1111, 1211, 2222 12.00

2764a — A2105-A2109

2764a A2105 29c pane of 5, *May 15* 3.00 2.25
Never folded pane, P#1 4.00

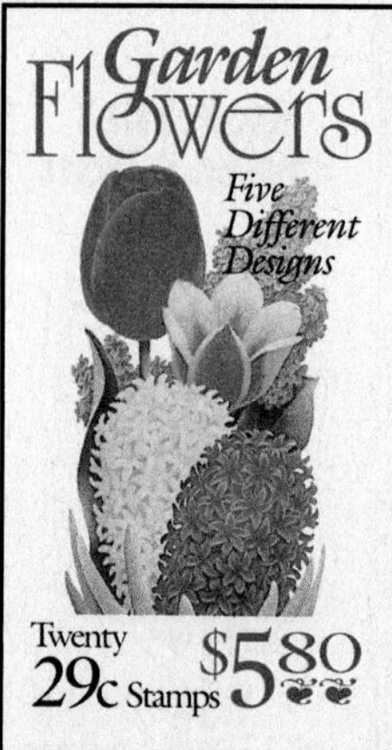

2764a — BC90

1993

$5.80 booklet contains four panes of 5 29c stamps.

Booklet

BK208 BC90 $5.80 **multicolored,** P#1, 2 12.00

Varieties

2764b	As "a," black (engr.) omitted	*135.00*
2764c	As "a," imperf.	*700.00*
2764d	As "a," tagging omitted	*650.00*

Booklet

BK208a As #BK208, with 4 #2764b *575.00*

2770a — A2069, A2112-A2114

2770a A2069 29c pane of 4, *July 14* 2.75 2.25
Never folded pane, P#A11111, A11121, A22222 3.75

Imperforate panes are proofs.

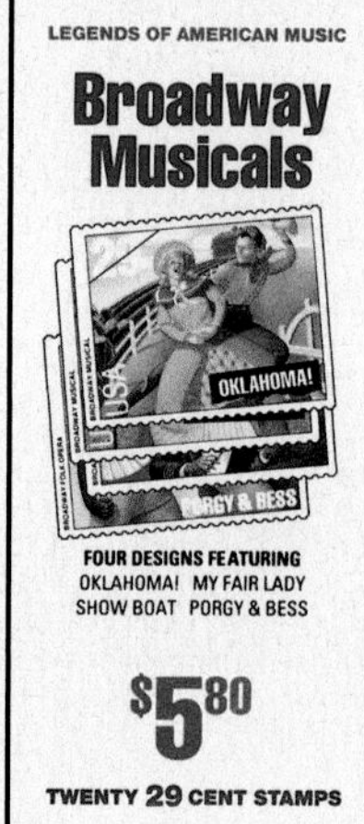

2770a — BC91

1993

$5.80 booklet contains five panes of 4 29c stamps.

Booklet

BK209 BC91 $5.80 **multicolored,** P#A11111, A11121, A22222, A23232, A23233 12.00

2778a — A2070, A2115-A2117

2778a A2070 29c pane of 4, *Sept. 25, 1993* 2.50 2.00
Never folded pane, P#A222222 3.50

Imperforate panes are proofs.

2778a — BC92

1993

$5.80 booklet contains five panes of 4 29c stamps.

Booklet

BK210 BC92 $5.80 **multicolored,** P#A111111, A222222, A333333, A422222 12.50
P#A333323 —

2790a — A2128

2790a A2128 29c pane of 4, *Oct. 21, 1993* 2.40 1.75
Never bound pane, P#K111111, K133333, K144444 3.50
P#K255555 *85.00*

2790a — BC93

1993

$5.80 booklet contains five panes of 4 29c stamps.

Booklet

BK211 BC93 $5.80 **multicolored,** P#K111111, K133333, K144444, K255555, K266666 12.00
P#K222222 35.00

No. BK211 exists assembled from panes with different plate numbers.

Variety

2790c As "a," imperf. —

2798a — A2129-A2132

2798a A2129 29c pane of 10, 3 each #2795-2796, 2 each #2797-2798, *Oct. 21, 1993* 8.50 4.00
Never folded pane, P#111111 10.00

2798b A2129 29c pane of 10, 3 each #2797-2798, 2 each #2795-2796, *Oct. 21, 1993* 8.50 4.00
Never folded pane, P#111111 10.00

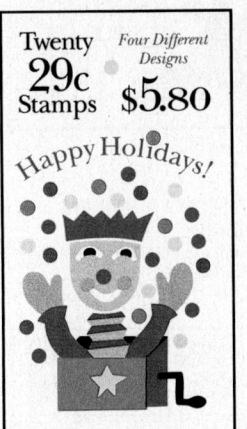

2798a — BC94

1993

$5.80 booklet contains two panes of 10 29c stamps.

Combination Booklet

BK212 BC94 $5.80 **multicolored,** 1 each #2798a, 2798b, P#111111, 222222 19.00

On No. 2798b the plate number appears close to the top row of perfs. Different selvage markings can be found there.

2802a — A2129-A2132

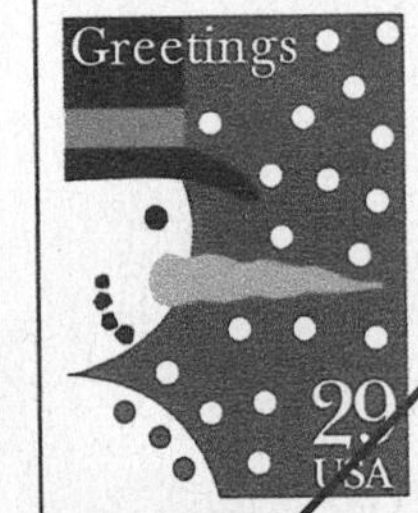

2802a — BC95

1993

$3.48 fold-it-yourself booklet contains 12 self-adhesive 29c stamps.

Self-Adhesive

Die Cut

2802a A2129 29c pane of 12, 3 each #2799-2802, *Oct. 28, 1993,* P#V1111111, V2221222, V2222112, V2222122, V2222221, V2222222 9.00
P#V3333333 10.50

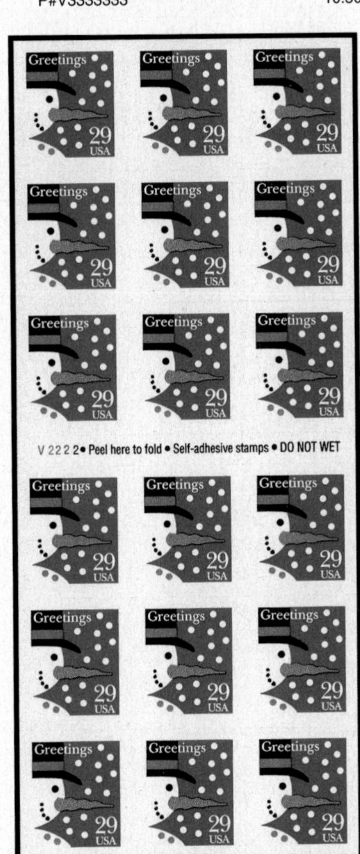

2803a — A2131

2803a BC96

1993

$5.22 fold-it-yourself booklet contains 18 self-adhesive 29c stamps.

2803a A2131 29c pane of 18, *Oct. 28, 1993,* P#V1111 11.00
P# V2222 13.00

By their nature, Nos. 2802a-2803a constitute complete booklets (BC95-BC96). The peelable backing serves as a booklet cover.

2806b — A2135

2806b A2135 29c pane of 5, *Dec. 1, 1993* 3.50 2.00
Never folded pane, P#K111 4.50

2806b — BC97

1993

$2.90 booklet contains two panes of 5 29c stamps.

Booklet

BK213 BC97 $2.90 **black & red,** P#K111 7.00

2813a — A2142

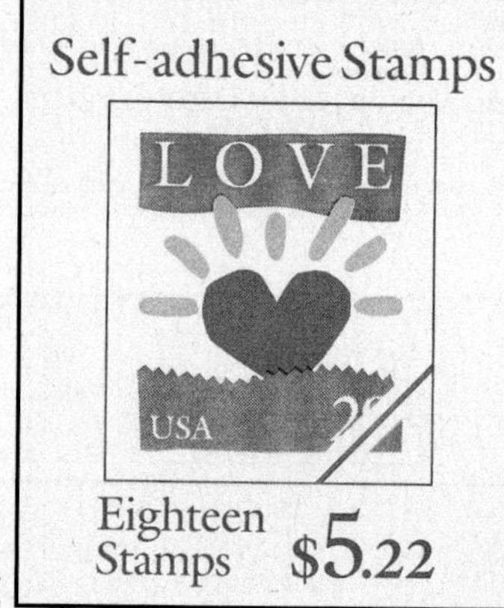

2813a BC98

1994

$5.22 fold-it-yourself booklet contains 18 self-adhesive 29c stamps.

Self-Adhesive ***Die Cut***

2813a A2142 29c pane of 18, *Jan. 27,* P#, see list 11.00
P#B111-5, B333-14 *50.00*
P#B444-7, B444-8, B444-9 14.00
P#B333-5, B333-7, B333-8 20.00
P#B334-11 *750.00*
P#B344-11 50.00
P#B434-10 100.00

By its nature, No. 2813a constitutes a complete booklet (BC98). The peelable backing serves as a booklet cover.

List — #B111-1, B111-2, B111-3, B111-4, B121-5, B221-5, B222-4, B222-5, B222-6, B333-9, B333-10, B333-11, B333-12, B333-17, B344-12, B344-13, B444-10, B444-13, B444-14, B444-15, B444-16, B444-17, B444-18, B444-19, B555-20, B555-21

2814a — A2143

2814a A2143 29c pane of 10, *Feb. 14, 1994* 6.00 3.50
Never folded pane, P#A11111 7.50

Variety

2814d As "a," imperf. —

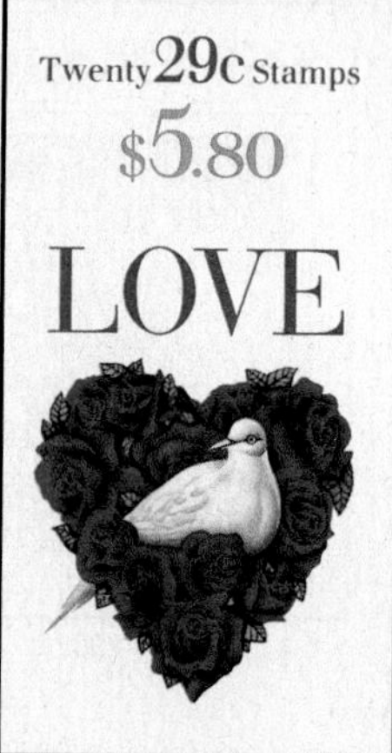

2814a — BC99

1994

$5.80 booklet contains two panes of 10 29c stamps.

Booklet

BK214 BC99 $5.80 **multicolored,** P#A11111, A11311, A12112, A21222, A22122, A22322 12.00
P#A12111, A12211, A12212, A21311 25.00
P#A22222 16.00

2833a — A2158-A2162

2833a A2158 29c pane of 5, *Apr. 28, 1994* 3.00 2.25
Never folded pane, P#2 3.50

2833a — BC100

1994

$5.80 booklet contains four panes of 5 29c stamps.

Booklet

BK215 BC100 $5.80 **multicolored,** P#1, 2 12.00

Varieties

2833b As "a," imperf *400.00*
2833c As "a," black (engr.) omitted *125.00*
2833d As "a," tagging omitted —

Booklets

BK215a As #BK215, with 4 #2833c *525.00*
BK215b As #BK215, with 3 #2833a, 1 #2833c —

2847a — A2171-A2175

2847a A2171 29c pane of 5, *July 28, 1994* 3.75 2.00
Never folded pane, P#S11111 4.50

2847a — BC101

1994

$5.80 booklet contains four panes of 5 29c stamps.

Booklet

BK216 BC101 $5.80 **multicolored,** P#S11111 15.00

Variety

2847b As "a," imperf *2,500.*

2871Ab — A2200

2871Ab A2200 29c pane of 10, *Oct. 20, 1994* 6.25 3.50
Never folded pane, P#1, 2 7.00

2871Ab — BC102

1994

$5.80 booklet contains two panes of 10 29c stamps.

Booklet

BK217 BC102 $5.80 **multicolored,** P#1, 2 12.50

2872a — A2201

2872a A2201 29c pane of 20, *Oct. 20, 1994* 12.50 6.00
Never folded pane, P#P11111, P22222, P44444 14.00
P#P33333 —

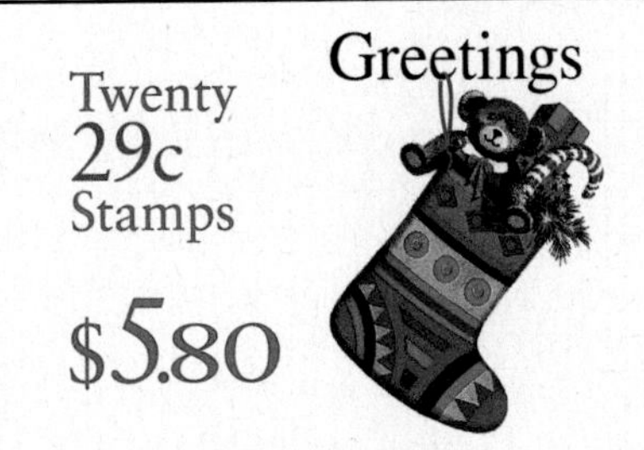

2872a — BC103

1994

$5.80 booklet contains one pane of 20 29c stamps.

Booklet

BK218 BC103 $5.80 **multicolored,** P#P11111, P22222, P33333, P44444 12.50

Variety

2872f As "a," imperf. —

2873a — A2202

2873a — BC104

1994

$3.48 fold-it-yourself booklet contains 12 self-adhesive 29c stamps.

2873a A2202 29c pane of 12, *Oct. 20, 1994,* P#V1111 8.50

By its nature, No. 2873a constitutes a complete booklet (BC104). The peelable backing serves as a booklet cover.

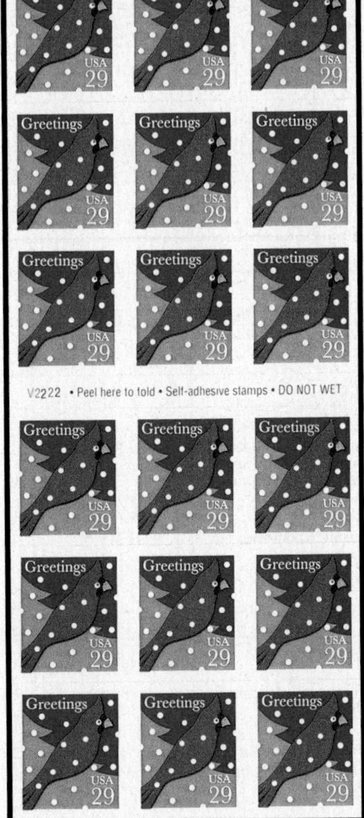

2874a — A2203

2874a
BC105

1994

$5.22 fold-it-yourself booklet contains 18 self-adhesive 29c stamps.

2874a A2203 29c pane of 18, *Oct. 20, 1994,* P#V1111, V2222 11.00

By its nature, No. 2874a constitutes a complete booklet (BC105). The peelable backing serves as a booklet cover.

2881a — A2208

1994 ***Perf. 11.2x11.1***

2881a A2208 (32c) **black "G" & multi,** pane of 10, *Dec. 13, 1994* 12.50 5.00

2881a, 2883a — BC106

2883a — BC106A

2884a — BC106B

2885a — BC106C

1994

($3.20) booklet contains one pane of 10 G stamps.
($6.40) booklet contains two panes of 10 G stamps.

No. BC106 was printed on both coated (BK219) and uncoated (BK220) paper. The coated paper has a shiny, uniform appearance, while the uncoated paper appears faded and washed out.

Booklet

BK219 BC106 ($3.20) **pale blue & red,** P#1111 12.50

Perf. 10x9.9

2883a A2208 (32c) **black "G" & multi,** pane of 10, *Dec. 13, 1994* 6.50 3.75

Booklets

BK220 BC106 ($3.20) **pale blue & red,** P#1111, 2222 6.50

BK221 BC106A ($6.40) **blue & red,** P#1111, 2222 13.00

Perf. 10.9

2884a A2208 (32c) **blue "G" & multi,** pane of 10, *Dec. 13, 1994* 6.50 3.75

Booklet

BK222 BC106B ($6.40) **blue "G" & multi,** P#A1111, A1211, A2222, A3333, A4444 13.00

No. BK222 exists with panes that have different plate numbers.

Variety

2884b As "a," imperf. *4,500.*

Perf. 11x10.9

2885a A2208 (32c) **red "G" & multi,** pane of 10, *Dec. 13, 1994* 9.00 4.50

Booklet

BK223 BC106C ($6.40) **red "G" & multi,** P#K1111 19.00

Variety

2885c Horiz. pair, imperf. btwn. in #2885a with foldover —

Booklet

BK223a As #BK223, with 2 #2885c —

2886a — A2208b

G Series
New First-Class Letter Rate
Eighteen Stamps
For Domestic Mail Only
Not for International Use

2886a, 2887a BC107

1994

($5.76) fold-it-yourself booklet contains 18 self-adhesive G stamps.

Self-Adhesive — *Die Cut*

2886a A2208b (32c) **gray, blue, light blue, red & black,** pane of 18, *Dec. 13, 1994,* P#V11111, V22222 12.50

2887a A2208c (32c) **black, blue & red,** pane of 18, *Dec. 13, 1994,* no P# 12.50

By their nature, Nos. 2886a and 2887a constitute complete booklets (BC107). The peelable backing serves as a booklet cover. The backing on No. 2886a contains a UPC symbol, while the backing on No. 2887a does not.

2916a — A2212

Perf. 10.8x9.8

2916a A2212 32c **blue, tan, brown, red & light blue,** pane of 10, *May 19, 1995* 6.50 3.25
Never folded pane, P#11111 7.25

Ten Stamps $3.20

2916a — BC108

1995

$3.20 booklet contains one pane of 10 32c stamps.
$6.40 booklet contains two panes of 10 32c stamps.

Booklets

BK225 BC108 $3.20 **blue & red,** P#11111, 22222, 33332 6.50
P#23222, 44444 —

BK226 BC108 $6.40 **multicolored,** P#11111, 22222, 33332, 44444 13.00
P#23222 17.50

Variety

2916b As "a," imperf. —

2919a — A2230

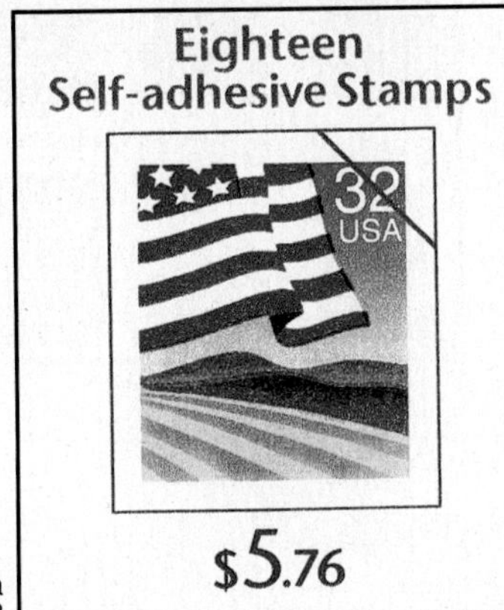

2919a
BC113

1995

$5.76 fold-it-yourself booklet contains 18 self-adhesive 32c stamps.

Self-Adhesive *Die Cut*

2919a A2230 32c pane of 18, *Mar. 17, 1995,* P#V1111 12.00
P#V1311 25.00
P#V1433, V2222, V2322 20.00
P#V2111 50.00

By its nature No. 2919a is a complete booklet (BC113). The peelable backing serves as a booklet cover.

2920a — A2212

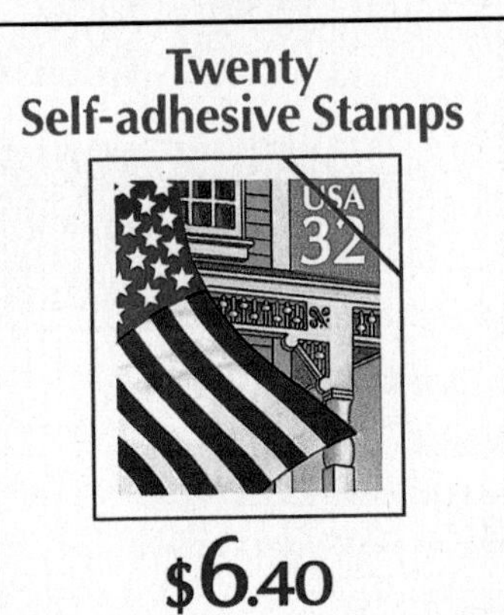

2920a
BC114

1995

$6.40 fold-it-yourself booklet contains 20 self-adhesive 32c stamps.

Serpentine Die Cut 8.7 on 2 or 3 Sides

Self-Adhesive

2920a A2212 32c pane of 20 + label, large date, *Apr. 18, 1995* (see List 1) 13.00
P#V23422 25.00
P#V23522 40.00
P#V57663 125.00

2920c A2212 32c pane of 20 + label, small date, *Apr. 18, 1995,* P#V11111 110.00

Varieties

2920g As "a," partial pane of 10, 3 stamps and parts of 7 stamps printed on backing liner —

2920k Vert. pair, die cutting missing btwn., three examples in No. 2920a with shift in die cutting (PS) —

By their nature Nos. 2920a, 2920c are complete booklets (BC114). The rouletted peelable backing, of which two versions are known on No. 2920a, serves as a booklet cover.

Date on No. 2920a is nearly twice as large as date on No. 2920c.

No. 2920a comes either with no die cutting on the label or with die cutting.

List 1 — P#V12211, V12212, V12312, V12321, V12322, V12331, V13322, V13831, V13834, V13836, V22211, V23322, V23432, V34743, V34745, V36743, V42556, V45554, V56663, V56665, V56763, V65976, V78989.

2920f — A2212

Serpentine Die Cut 8.7

Self-Adhesive

2920f A2212 32c pane of 15 + label 9.75
2920h A2212 32c pane of 15, see note, *1996* *47.50*

Booklets

BK226A BC126 $4.80 **blue,** 1 #2920f, no P# (4) 10.00
BK226B BC126 $4.80 **blue,** 1 #2920h, no P# (3) *67.50*
BK227 BC126 $9.60 **blue,** 2 #2920f (3) 20.00

No. 2920h is a pane of 16 with one stamp removed. The missing stamp is the lower right stamp in the pane or (more rarely) the upper left stamp. No. 2920h cannot be made from No. 2920f, a pane of 15 + label. The label is located in the sixth or seventh row of the pane and is die cut. If the label is removed, an impression of the die cutting appears on the backing paper.

Nos. BK226A-B and BK227 are makeshift vending machine booklets. See note before No. BK243.

For illustration of booklet cover BC126, see before No. BK243.

2920De — A2212

2920De — BC114a

Serpentine Die Cut 11.3

Self-Adhesive

2920De A2212 32c pane of 10, *Jan. 20, 1996* 8.00

By its nature No. 2920De is a complete booklet (BC114a). The rouletted peelable backing serves as a booklet cover.

Below is a list of known plate numbers. Some numbers are scarcer than the value indicated in the listing.

No. 2920De — P#V11111, V12111, V23222, V31121, V32111, V32121, V44322, V44333, V44444, V55555, V66666, V66886, V67886, V68886, V68896, V76989, V77666, V77668, V77766, V77776, V78698, V78886, V78896, V78898, V78986, V78989, V89999.

2921a — A2212

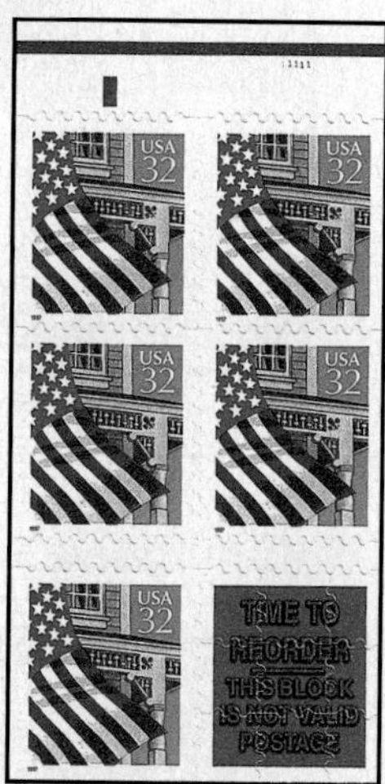

2921d — A2212

Serpentine Die Cut 9.8

Self-Adhesive

2921a A2212 32c pane of 10, dated red "1996," *May 21, 1996* 9.00

Never folded pane, P#21221, 22221, 22222 10.50

2921c A2212 32c pane of 10, dated red "1997," *Jan. 24, 1997* 12.00

Never folded pane, P#11111 14.00

2921d A2212 32c pane of 5 + label, dated red "1997," *Jan. 24, 1997* 8.00

Never folded pane, P#11111 9.50

Combination Booklet

BK227A BC108 $4.80 **multicolored,** 1 ea #2921c-2921d P#11111 20.00

No. BK227A is only source of No. 2921c with P# above right column of stamps and no length register marks or cross register lines on selvage tab. Some of the panes have color registration markings on the selvage tab. No. 2921d has no control markings - just the P# over the right column of stamps.

Booklets

BK228 BC108 $6.40 **blue, red & black,** 2 #2921a (5) 18.00

Known numbers for BK228: P#11111, 13111, 21221, 22221, 22222, 44434, 44444, 55555, 55556, 66666, 77777, 88788, 88888, 99999. Some numbers are scarcer than the value indicated in the listing.

No. BK228 is only source of No. 2921a, which has P# above left column of stamps and no length register marks or cross register lines in selvage tab.

BK228A BC108 $9.60 **multicolored,** 3 #2921c, P#11111 50.00

No. BK228A is only source of No. 2921c with P# above left column of stamps and length register marks and cross register lines on selvage tab.

Variety

2921e As "a," die cutting omitted *200.00*

Booklet

BK228b As #BK228, with 2 #2921e, P#11111, 13111 *400.00*

2949a — A2264

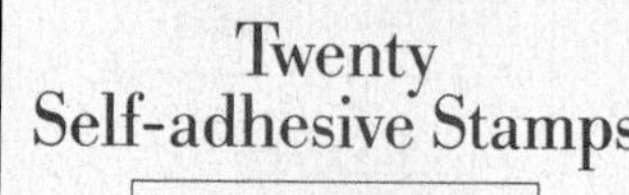

First-Class Letter Rate

For Domestic Mail Only / Not for International Use

2949a BC115

1995

($6.40) fold-it-yourself booklet contains 20 self-adhesive non-denominated 32c stamps.

Self-Adhesive ***Die Cut***

2949a A2264 (32c) pane of 20 + label, *Feb. 1, 1995,* P#B1111-1, B2222-1, B2222-2, B3333-2 13.00

By its nature, No. 2949a is a complete booklet (BC115). The peelable backing serves as a booklet cover.

Variety

2949c As "a," red (engr.) omitted *2,000.*

2959a — A2272

Perf. 9.8x10.8

2959a A2272 32c pane of 10, *May 12, 1995* 6.50 3.25
Never folded pane, P#1 6.75

2959a — BC116

1995

$6.40 booklet contains two panes of 10 32c stamps.

Booklet

BK229 BC116 $6.40 **multicolored,** P#1 13.00

Variety

2959c As "a," imperf. *500.00*

Booklet

BK229a As #BK229, with 2 #2959c *1,000.*

2960a — A2274

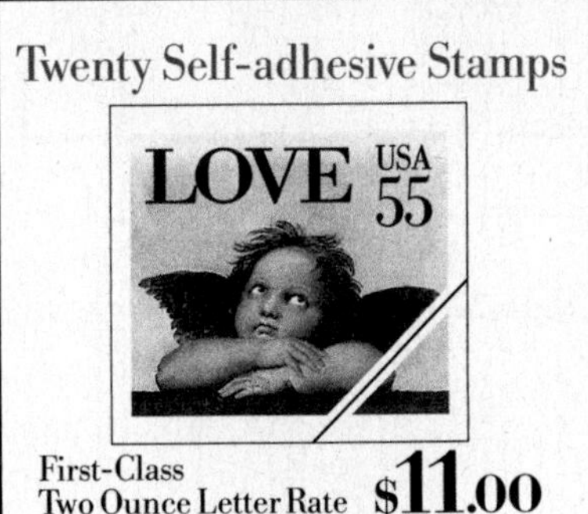

2960a — BC117

1995

$11 fold-it-yourself booklet contains 20 self-adhesive 55c stamps.

Self-Adhesive ***Die Cut***

2960a A2274 55c pane of 20 + label, *May 12, 1995,* P#B1111-1, B2222-1 22.50

By its nature, No. 2960a is a complete booklet (BC117). The peelable backing serves as a booklet cover. It comes either with no die cutting on the label or with die cutting.

2973a — A2283-A2287

2973a A2283 32c pane of 5, *June 17, 1995* 4.50 2.50
Never folded pane, P#S11111 5.00

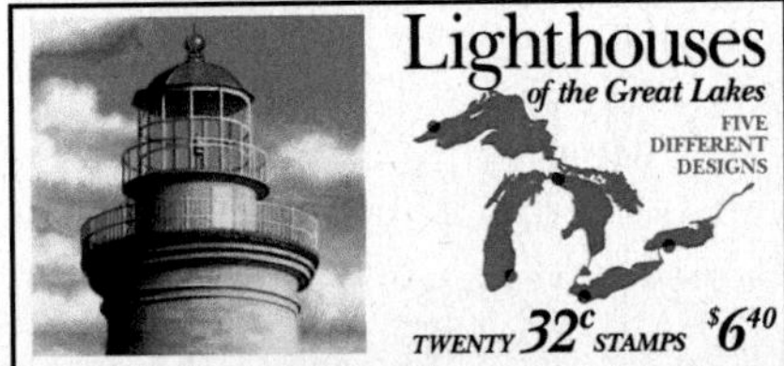

2973a — BC118

1995

$6.40 booklet contains four panes of 5 32c stamps.

Booklet

BK230 BC118 $6.40 **multicolored,** P#S11111 18.00

Variety

2973b As "a," 2 vert. pairs imperf. horiz. of #2972 and 2973, in pane of 7+ stamps in cplt. bklt. #BK230 (due to foldover) —

2997a — A2306-A2310

2997a A2306 32c pane of 5, *Sept. 19, 1995* 3.25 2.25
Never folded pane, P#2 4.25

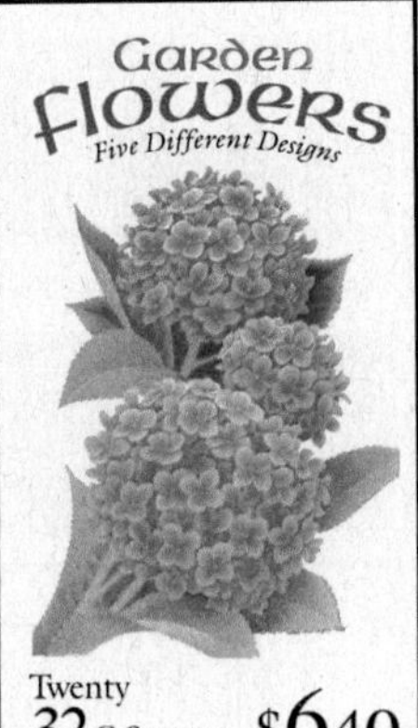

2997a — BC119

1995

$6.40 booklet contains four panes of 5 32c stamps.

Booklet

BK231 BC119 $6.40 **multicolored,** P#2 13.00

Variety

2997b As "a," imperf. *2,250.*

3003Ab — A2316

3003Ab A2316 32c pane of 10, *Oct. 19, 1995* 6.50 4.00
Never folded pane, P#1 7.50

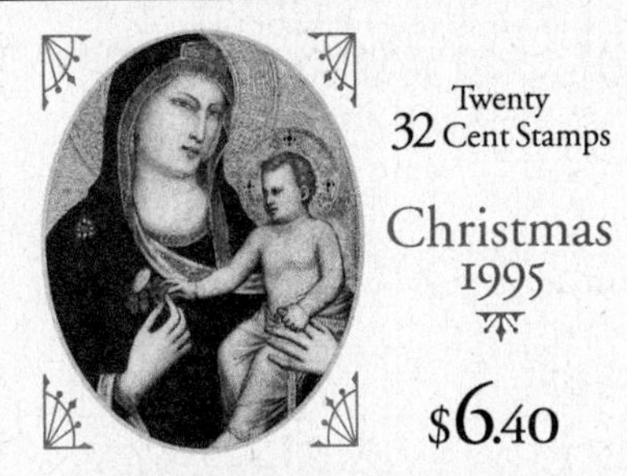

3003b — BC120

1995

$6.40 booklet contains two panes of 10 32c stamps.

Booklet

BK232 BC120 $6.40 **multicolored,** P#1 13.00

3007b — A2317-A2320

3007b A2317 32c pane of 10, 3 each #3004-3005, 2 each #3006-3007, *Sept. 30, 1995* 8.00 4.00
Never folded pane, P#P1111 9.00

3007c A2317 32c pane of 10, 2 each #3004-3005, 3 each #3006-3007, *Sept. 30, 1995* 8.00 4.00
Never folded pane, P#P1111 9.00

Variety

3007e As "b," miscut and inserted upside down into booklet cover, with full bottom selvage —

3007b-3007c — BC121

1995

$6.40 booklet contains two panes of 10 32c stamps

Combination Booklet

BK233 BC121 $6.40 **multicolored,** 1 each #3007b, 3007c, P#P1111, P2222 16.00

Tab at bottom (#3007e), in complete booklet with #3007c —

No. BK233 also is known with 2 panes of No. 3007b or 2 panes of No. 3007c.

3011a — A2317-A2320

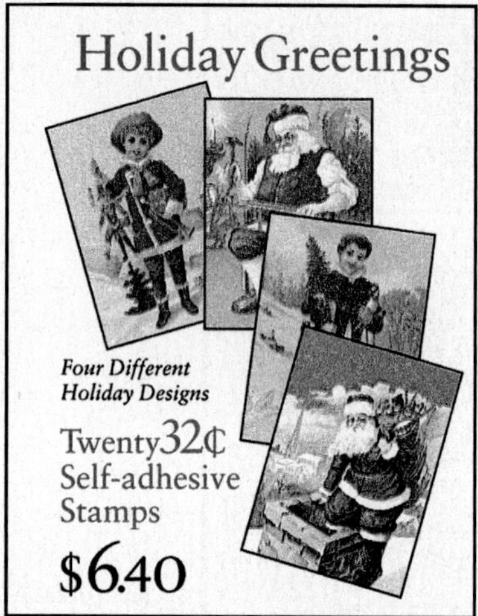

3011a — BC122

1995

$6.40 fold-it-yourself booklet contains 20 self-adhesive 32c stamps

Serpentine Die Cut

3011a A2317 32c pane of 20 +label, *Sept. 30, 1995,* P#V1111, V1211, V3233, V3333, V4444 19.00
P#V1212 26.00

By its nature, No. 3011a is a complete booklet (BC122). The peelable backing serves as a booklet cover.

3012a — A2321

3012a BC123

1995

$6.40 fold-it-yourself booklet contains 20 self-adhesive 32c stamps

Serpentine Die Cut

3012a A2321 32c pane of 20 + label, *Oct. 19, 1995,* P#B1111, B2222, B3333 13.00

By its nature, No. 3012a is a complete booklet (BC123). The peelable backing serves as a booklet cover.

No. 3012a comes either with no die cutting on the label (1995 printing) or with die cutting from the 1996 printing.

3012c A2321 32c pane of 15 + label, *1996,* no P# 12.00

3012d A2321 32c pane of 15, see note, *1996* *30.00*

Booklets

BK233A BC126 $4.80 **blue,** #3012c (2) 12.50

BK233B BC126 $4.80 **blue,** #3012d —

BK233C BC126 $9.60 **blue** 2 #3012c (3) 25.00

BK233D BC126 $9.60 **blue,** 2 #3012d, no P# (3) 70.00

f. As No. BK233D, but one pane is of 16 stamps (thus 31 stamps in the booklet) (error) —

Combination Booklet

BK233E BC126 $9.60 **blue,** 1 ea #3012c, 3012d (2) 75.00

No. 3012d is a pane of 16 with one stamp removed. The missing stamp can be from either row 1, 2, 3, 7 or 8. No. 3012d cannot be made from No. 3012c, a pane of 15 + label. The label is die cut. If the label is removed, an impression of the die cutting appears on the backing paper.

Nos. BK233A-E are makeshift vending machine booklets. See note before No. BK243.

For illustration of booklet cover BC126, see before No. BK243.

3013a — A2322

3013a BC124

1995

$5.76 fold-it-yourself booklet contains 18 self-adhesive 32c stamps

Die Cut

3013a A2322 32c Pane of 18, *Oct. 19, 1995,* P#V1111 12.00

Variety

3013b As "a," tagging omitted —

By its nature, No. 3013a is a complete booklet (BC124). The peelable backing serves as a booklet cover.

3029a — A2329-A2333

3029a A2329 32c pane of 5, *Jan. 19, 1996* 3.25 2.50
Never folded pane, P#P1 3.75

3029a — BC125

1996

$6.40 booklet contains four panes of 5 32c stamps

Booklet

BK234 BC125 $6.40 **multicolored,** P#1 13.00

Variety

3029b As "a," imperf. —

3030a — A2334

Serpentine Die Cut 11.3x11.7

3030a A2334 32c pane of 20+label, *Jan. 20, 1996* 13.00

By its nature, No. 3030a is a complete booklet (BC115). The peelable backing serves as a booklet cover.
P#B1111-1, B1111-2, B2222-1, B2222-2.

3030b A2334 32c pane of 15 + label, *1996* 9.75

Booklets

For illustration of booklet cover BC126, see before No. BK243.

BK235 BC126 $4.80 **blue,** #3030b (4) 10.00
BK236 BC126 $9.60 **blue,** 2 #3030b (3) 20.00

Varieties

3030g As "a," stamps 1-5 with double impression of red (engr. "LOVE") 1,000.
3030h As "a," red (engr. "LOVE") omitted 1,200.
3030i As "a," die cutting omitted —
3030j As "e," two examples in booklet pane of 20 (No. 3030a) *1,000.*

3048a — A1847

3048a-3048c — BC128

1996

$2.00 fold-it-yourself booklet contains 10 self-adhesive 20c stamps
$2.00 booklet contains 10 self-adhesive 20c stamps

Serpentine Die Cut 10.4x10.8

3048a A1847 20c pane of 10, *Aug. 2, 1996,* P#S1111, S2222 4.00

By is nature, No. 3048a is a complete booklet (BC128). The peelable backing serves as a booklet cover.

3048b, 3048c — A1847

3048b A1847 20c Booklet pane of 4 70.00
3048c A1847 20c Booklet pane of 6 100.00

No. 3048a exists on two types of surface-tagged paper that exhibit either a solid appearance (P# S1111) or a grainy solid appearance (P# S1111 and S2222).

Nos. 3048b-3048c are from the vending machine booklet No. BK237 that has a glue strip at the top edge of the top pane, the peelable strip removed and the rouletting line 2mm lower than on No. 3048a on some booklets, when the panes are compared with bottoms aligned. Vending booklets with plate #S2222 always have gauge 8½ rouletting on booklet covers. Convertible booklets (No. 3048a) with plate #S2222 always have gauge 12½ rouletting on booklet covers. Vending booklets with plate #S1111 can have either 8½ or 12½ gauge rouletting on booklet cover, and it may be impossible to tell a vending booklet with 12½ gauge rouletting and plate #S1111 from a convertible booklet with peelable strip removed.

Combination Booklet

BK237 BC128 $2 **multicolored,** 1 ea #3048b, 3048c, P#S1111, S2222 175.00

3049a — A1853

Serpentine Die Cut 11.3x11.7

3049a A1853 32c pane of 20 + label, *Oct. 24, 1996,* P#S1111, S2222 13.00

By its nature, No. 3049a is a complete booklet (BC61B). The peelable backing, of which three types are known, serves as a booklet cover.

3049b, 3049c, 3049d — A1853

3049b A1853 32c pane of 4, *Dec. 1996,* no P# 2.60
3049c A1853 32c pane of 5 + label, *Dec. 1996,* P#S1111 3.50
3049d A1853 32c pane of 6, *Dec. 1996,* without P# 4.00

3049b, 3049c, 3049d — BC129

1996

$4.80 booklet contains 15 self-adhesive 32c stamps
$9.60 booklet contains 30 self-adhesive 32c stamps

Combination Booklet

BK241 BC129 $4.80 **multicolored,** 1 ea #3049b-3049d, P#S1111 10.25

Booklet

BK242 BC129 $9.60 **multicolored,** 5 #3049d, P#S1111 20.00

The backing on Nos. BK241-BK242 is rouletted between each pane.

The plate # single in No. 3049c from No. BK241 is on the lower left stamp. In No. 3049d from BK242, P# single is the lower right stamp on the bottom pane of the booklet.

Variety

3049d Pane of 6 containing P# single 6.00

3050a, 3050c — A2350

3050a, 3050c, 3051Ab-3051Ac
BC130

1998

$2.00 fold-it-yourself booklet contains 10 self-adhesive 20c stamps
$2.00 booklet contains 10 self-adhesive 20c stamps

1998 ***Serpentine Die Cut 11.2***

3050a A2350 20c pane of 10, *July 31, 1998,* P#V1111, V2222, V2232, V3233 6.50
P#V2342, V2343, V3232 75.00

Serpentine Die Cut 11

3050c A2350 20c pane of 10, *July 31, 1998,* P#V2333, V2342, V2343, V3232, V3243, V3333 35.00
P#V2232, V2332 70.00

By their nature Nos. 3050a and 3050c are complete booklets (BC130). The peelable backing serves as a booklet cover. All stamps in Nos. 3050a and 3050c are upright.

3051Ab, 3051Ac — A2350

Serpentine Die Cut 10½x11 on 3 Sides (#3051), 10.6x10.4 on 3 sides (#3051A)

1999 **Self-Adhesive**

3051Ab A2350 20c pane, 4 #3051, 1 #3051A turned sideways at top, *July 1999* 10.00

3051Ac A2350 20c pane, 4 #3051, 1 #3051A turned sideways at bottom, *July 1999* 10.00

Booklet

BK242A BC130 $2.00 **multicolored,** #3051Ab, 3051Ac, P#V1111, *July 1999* 20.00

3052a-3052c — A2351

Serpentine Die Cut 11½x11¼

3052a	A2351	33c pane of 4, no P#	3.60
3052b	A2351	33c pane of 5 + label, no P#	4.50
3052c	A2351	33c pane of 6, P#S111	5.50

3052a-3052c — BC131A

1999

$4.95 booklet contains 15 self-adhesive 33c stamps + label

Combination Booklet

BK242B BC131A $4.95 **multicolored,** 1 each #3052a-3052c, P#S111, *Aug. 13, 1999* 13.75

No. BK242B has a self-adhesive strip on #3052b that adheres to the plastic-coated peelable backing of #3052a when the booklet is closed. When the booklet is opened, this strip is sticky and may adhere firmly to mounts, album pages, etc. Removal of this strip will damage the backing paper of #3052b.

Plate number for No. BK242B is on backing paper below bar code on No. 3052c.

3052d — A2351

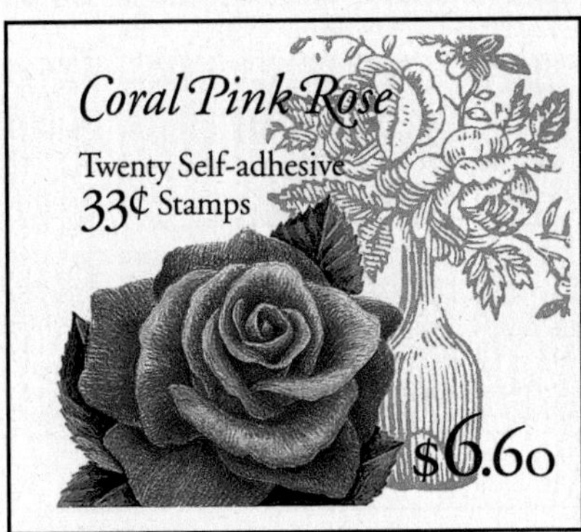

3052d — BC131

1999

$6.60 fold-it-yourself booklet contains 20 self-adhesive 33c stamps + label

3052d A2351 33c pane of 20 + label, P#S111, S222 17.50

No. 3052d is a complete booklet (BC131). The peelable backing serves as a booklet cover.

Variety

3052k As "d," die cutting omitted *5,500.*

3052Ef — A2351

Serpentine Die Cut 10¾x10½ on 2 or 3 Sides

2000

3052Ef A2351 33c pane of 20, *Apr. 7, 2000,* P#S111, S222, S333 15.00

By its nature, No. 3052Ef is a complete booklet. Eight stamps and the booklet cover (similar to BC131) are printed on one side of the peelable backing and twelve stamps plus P# appear on the other side of the backing.

Varieties

3052Eh As "f," all 12 stamps on one side with black ("33 USA," etc.) omitted —

3052Ej As "f," vert. die cutting missing between (PS) —

3071a — A2370

Twenty
Self-adhesive Stamps

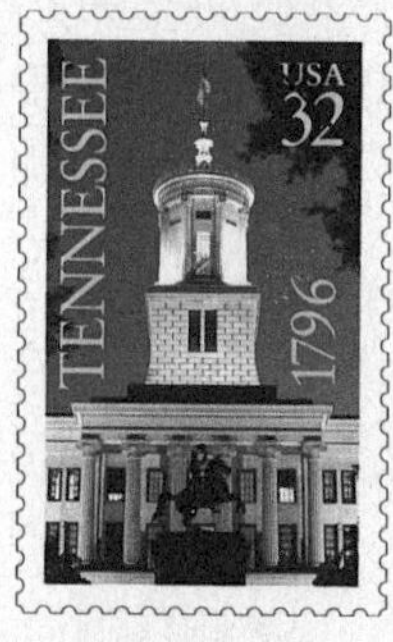

$6.40

3071a — BC127

1996

$6.40 fold-it-yourself booklet contains 20 self-adhesive 32c stamps

Serpentine Die Cut 9.9x10.8

3071a A2370 32c pane of 20, *May 31, 1996,* P#S11111 13.00

By its nature, No. 3071a is a complete booklet (BC127). The peelable backing serves as a booklet cover.

3089a — A2387

Twenty
Self-adhesive Stamps

$6.40

3089a — BC133

1996

$6.40 fold-it-yourself booklet contains 20 self-adhesive 32c stamps

Serpentine Die Cut 11.6x11.4

3089a A2387 32c pane of 20, *Aug. 1, 1996,* P#B1111 13.00

By its nature, No. 3089a is a complete booklet (BC133). The peelable backing serves as a booklet cover.

3112a — A2405

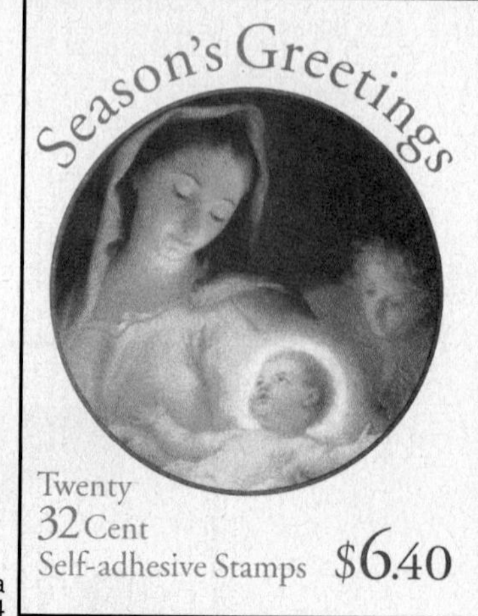

3112a
BC134

1996

$6.40 fold-it-yourself booklet contains 20 self-adhesive 32c stamps

Serpentine Die Cut 10 on 2, 3 or 4 Sides

3112a A2405 32c pane of 20 + label, *Nov. 1, 1996* 15.00

Variety

3112c As "a," die cutting omitted *400.00*

3112d As "a," top seven stamps with black (engr.) missing (PS) —

By its nature No. 3112a is a complete booklet (BC134). The peelable backing serves as a booklet cover.

No. 3112d is missing the black lettering at bottom due to a small upward shift of the horizontal perforations. This lettering is the only engraved black on the stamp.

Below is a list of known plate numbers. Some numbers may be scarcer than the value indicated in the listing.

P#1111-1, 1211-1, 2212-1, 2222-1, 2323-1, 3323-1, 3333-1, 3334-1, 4444-1, 5544-1, 5555-1, 5556-1, 5556-2, 5656-2, 6656-2, 6666-1, 6666-2, 6766-1, 7887-1, 7887-2, 7888-2, 7988-2.

3116a — A2406-2409

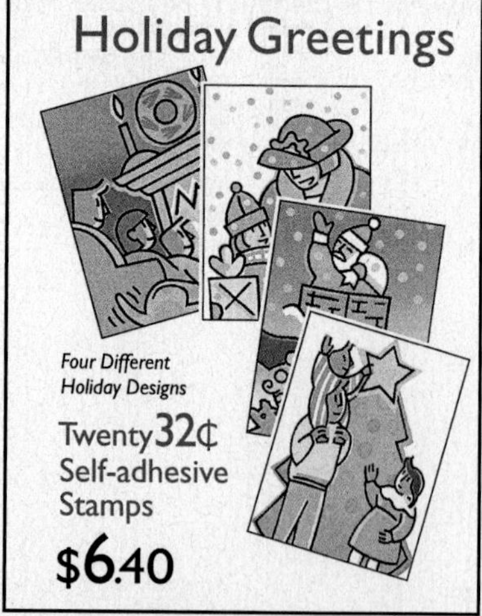

3116a — BC135

1996

$6.40 fold-it-yourself booklet contains 20 self-adhesive 32c stamps

Serpentine Die Cut 11.8x11.5 on 2, 3 or 4 Sides

3116a A2406 32c pane of 20 + label, *Oct. 8, 1996*, P#B1111, B2222, B3333 13.00

Variety

3116c As "a," die cutting omitted *1,250.*

By its nature No. 3116a is a complete booklet (BC135). The peelable backing serves as a booklet cover.

3117a — A2410

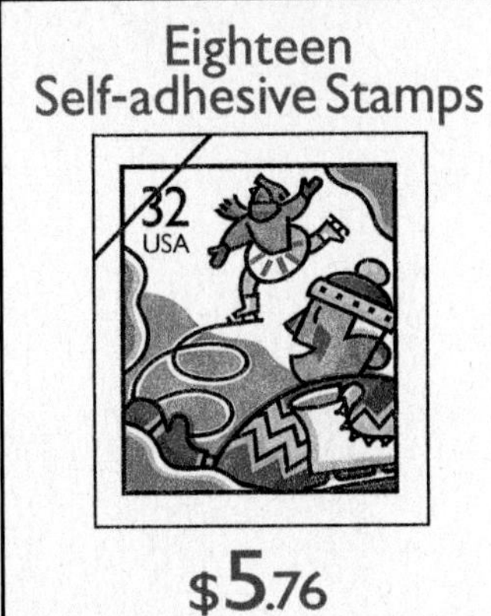

3117a BC136

1996

$5.76 fold-it-yourself booklet contains 18 self-adhesive 32c stamps

Die Cut

3117a A2410 32c pane of 18, *Oct. 8, 1996*, P#V1111, V2111 12.00

By its nature No. 3117a is a complete booklet (BC136). The peelable backing serves as a booklet cover.

MAKESHIFT VENDING MACHINE BOOKLETS

The booklets listed below were released in 1996 to meet the need for $4.80 and $9.60 vending machine booklets. The booklets consist of blocks of sheet stamps folded and affixed to a standard cover (BC126) with a spot of glue.

The cover varies from issue to issue in the line of text on the front that indicates the number of stamps contained in the booklet and in the four lines of text on the back that describe the contents of the booklet and list the booklet's item number. Due to the folding required to make stamps fit within the covers, the stamp blocks may easily fall apart when booklets are opened. Stamps may also easily detach from booklet cover.

Front

Back — BC126

1996

$4.80 booklet contains 15 32c stamps
$9.60 booklet contains 30 32c stamps

A number of different stamps have been sold in BC126. The text on the front and back changes to describe the contents of the booklet. The enclosed stamps are affixed to the cover with a spot of glue.

Booklets

BK243 BC126 $4.80 **blue,** 15 #2897 (32c Flag Over Porch) 11.50
BK244 BC126 $4.80 **blue,** 15 #2957 (32c Cherub/Love) 11.50
BK245 BC126 $4.80 **blue,** 15 #3024 (32c Utah) 13.00
BK246 BC126 $4.80 **blue,** 15 #3065 (32c Fulbright Scholarships) 11.50
BK247 BC126 $4.80 **blue,** 15 #3069 (32c Georgia O'Keeffe) 11.25
BK248 BC126 $4.80 **blue,** 15 #3070 (32c Tennessee) 11.50
BK249 BC126 $4.80 **blue,** 3 #3076a (32c Indian Dances) 12.00
BK250 BC126 $4.80 **blue,** 15 #3082 (32c James Dean) 13.50
BK251 BC126 $4.80 **blue,** 15 (#3083-3086) (32c Folk Heroes) 11.00
BK252 BC126 $4.80 **blue,** 15 #3087 (32c Olympic Centennial) 12.50
BK253 BC126 $4.80 **blue,** 15 #3088 (32c Iowa) 12.00
BK254 BC126 $9.60 **blue,** 30 #3090 (32c Rural Free Delivery) 25.00
BK255 BC126 $4.80 **blue,** 3 #3095a (32c Riverboats) 13.00
BK256 BC126 $4.80 **blue,** #3105a-3105o (32c Endangered Species) 12.00
BK257 BC126 $4.80 **blue,** 15 #3107 (32c Madonna Christmas) 11.00
BK258 BC126 $4.80 **blue,** 15 #3118 (32c Hanukkah) 11.00

The contents of #BK251 may vary.

See Nos. BK178A-BK178F, BK226A-BK226B, BK227, BK233A-BK233E, BK235-BK236, BK266-BK269, BK272-BK274, BK277-BK278.

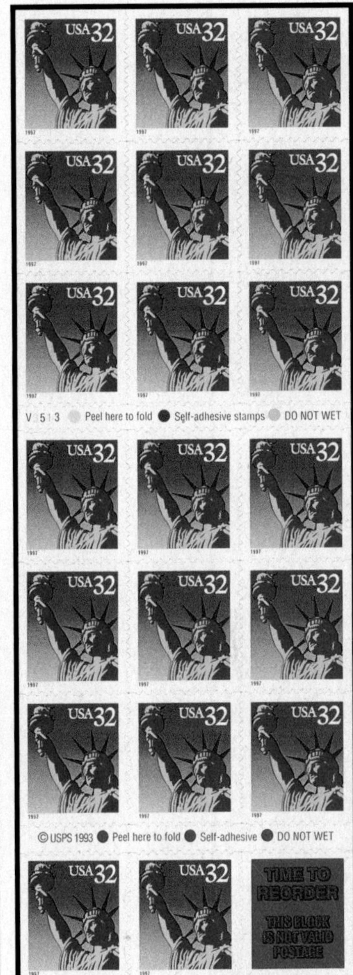

3122a — A1951

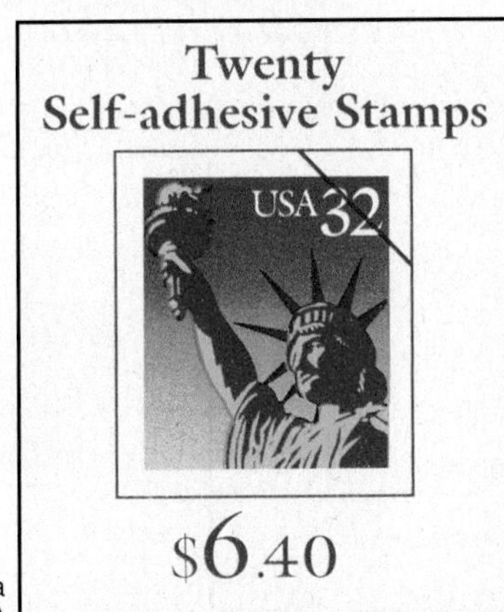

3122a BC79A

1997

$6.40 fold-it-yourself booklet contains 20 self-adhesive 32c stamps

Serpentine Die Cut 11

3122a A1951 32c pane of 20 + label, *Feb. 1,* P#V1111, V1211, V1311, V2122, V2222, V2311, V2331, V3233, V3333, V3513, V4532 14.00

Variety

3122h As "a," die cutting omitted —

By its nature, No. 3122a is a complete booklet (BC79A). The peelable backing, of which two versions are known, serves as a booklet cover.

3122b-3122d — A1951

3122b A1951 32c pane of 4, *Feb. 1,* no P# 2.80
3122c A1951 32c pane of 5 + label, *Feb. 1,* P#V1111 3.75
3122d A1951 32c pane of 6, *Feb. 1,* without P# 4.25

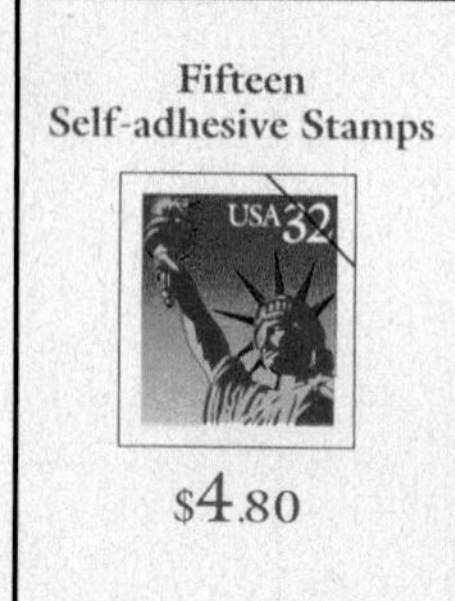

3122b-3122d — BC79B

1997

$4.80 booklet contains 15 self-adhesive 32c stamps
$9.60 booklet contains 30 self-adhesive 32c stamps

Combination Booklet

BK259 BC79B $4.80 **multicolored,** 1 ea #3122b-3122d, P#V1111 11.00

Booklet

BK260 BC79B $9.60 **multicolored,** 5 #3122d, P#V1111 23.00

The backing on Nos. BK259-BK260 is rouletted between each pane.

Variety

3122d pane of 6 containing P# single 6.00

The plate # single in No. 3122c is the lower left stamp and should be collected unused with the reorder label to its right to differentiate it from the plate # single in No. 3122d which is the lower left stamp in the bottom pane of the booklet and should be collected with a normal stamp adjoining it at right. In used condition, these plate # singles are indistinguishable.

Serpentine Die Cut 11.5x11.8 on 2, 3 or 4 Sides

3122Ef A1951 32c pane of 20 + label, P#V1211, V2122, V2222 40.00
P#V1111 60.00

By its nature, No. 3122Ef is a complete booklet (BC79A). The peelable backing, of which two versions are known, serves as a booklet cover.

3122Eg A1951 32c pane of 6, *1997,* without plate # single 9.00

Booklet

BK260A BC79B $9.60 **multicolored,** 5 #3122Eg, P#V1111 50.00

Variety

3122Eg pane of 6 containing P# single 13.50

The plate # single in No. 3122Eg from No. BK260A is the lower left stamp in the bottom pane of the booklet.

3123a — A2415

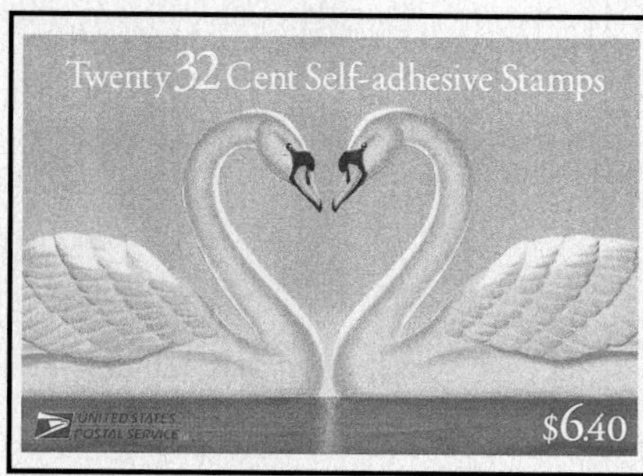

3123a — BC137

1997

$6.40 fold-it-yourself booklet contains 20 self-adhesive 32c stamps

Serpentine Die Cut 11.8x11.6 on 2, 3 or 4 Sides

3123a A2415 32c pane of 20 + label, *Feb. 4,* P#B1111, B2222, B3333, B4444, B5555, B6666, B7777 13.00

Varieties

3123c As "a," die cutting omitted *1,000.*
3123d As "a," black omitted —

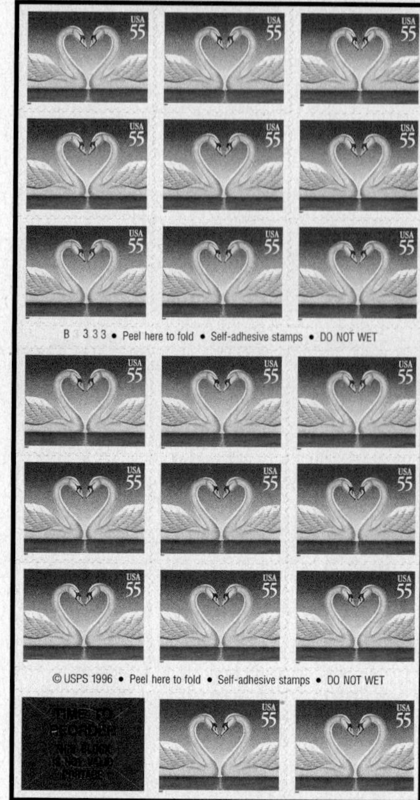

3124a — A2416

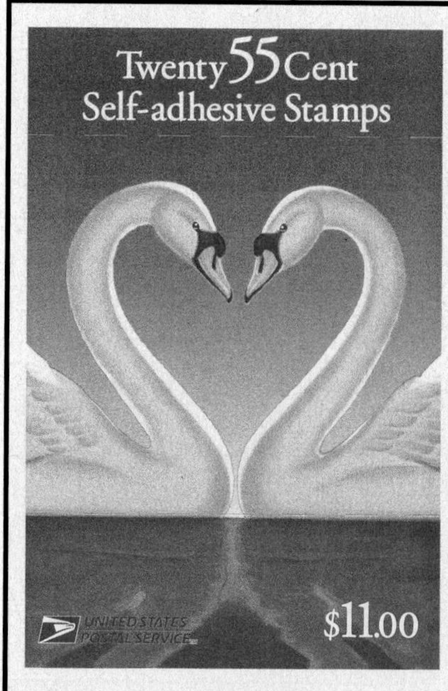

3124a — BC137A

1997

$11 fold-it-yourself booklet contains 20 self-adhesive 55c stamps

Serpentine Die Cut 11.6x11.8 on 2, 3 or 4 Sides

3124a A2416 55c pane of 20 + label, *Feb. 4,* P#B1111, B2222, B3333, B4444 22.00

By their nature, Nos. 3123a-3124a are complete booklets (BC137 and BC137A). The peelable backing serves as a booklet cover.

3127a — A2418-A2419

3127a
BC138

1997

$6.40 fold-it-yourself booklet contains 20 32c stamps

Serpentine Die Cut 10.9x10.2 on 2, 3 or 4 Sides

3127a A2418 32c pane of 20 + label, 10 ea #3126-3127, *Mar. 3,* P#S11111, S22222, S33333 13.00

By its nature, No. 3127a is a complete booklet (BC138). The peelable backing serves as a booklet cover.

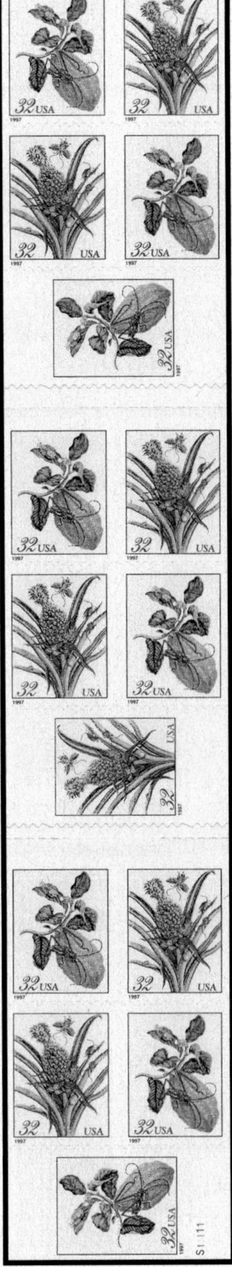

3128b, 3129b — A2418-A2419

3128b A2418 32c pane of 5, 2 ea #3128-3129, 1 #3128a, *Mar. 3,* no P# or P#S11111 6.50

3129b A2419 32c pane of 5, 2 ea #3128-3129, 1 #3129a, *Mar. 3,* no P# 8.50

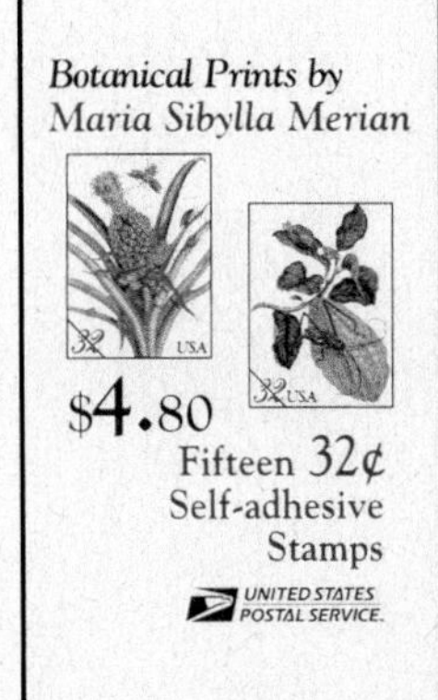

3128b, 3129b — BC138A

1997

$4.80 booklet contains 15 32c stamps

Combination Booklet

BK261 BC138A $4.80 2 #3128b, 1 #3129b, P#S11111 21.50

In No. BK261, No. 3128b at top has no plate #, while the No. 3128b at bottom has a plate # in the selvage.

3176a — A2459

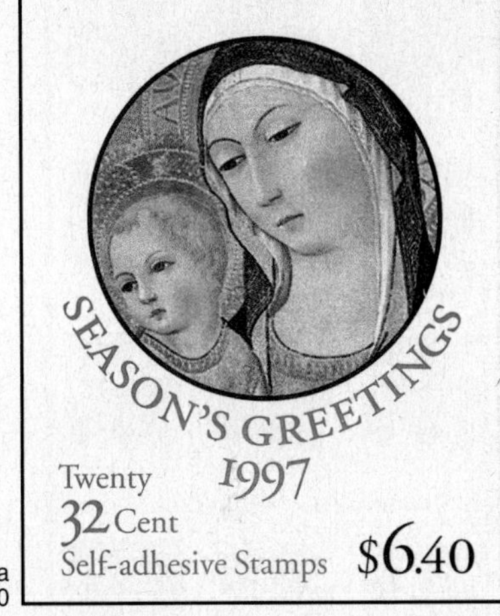

3176a
BC140

1997

$6.40 fold-it-yourself booklet contains 20 self-adhesive 32c stamps

Serpentine Die Cut 9.9 on 2, 3 or 4 Sides

1997, Oct. 27 **Tagged**

3176a A2459 32c pane of 20 + label, P#1111, 2222, 3333 13.00

By its nature, No. 3176a is a complete booklet (BC140). The peelable backing serves as a booklet cover.

3177a — A2460

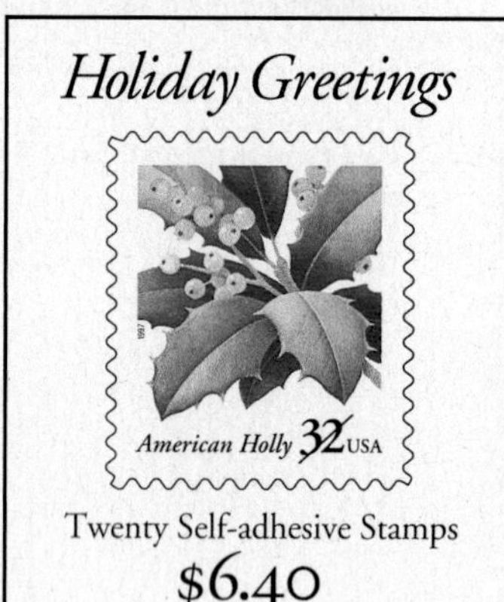

3177a BC141

1997

$6.40 fold-it-yourself booklet contains 20 self-adhesive 32c stamps

Serpentine Die Cut 11.2x11.6 on 2, 3 or 4 Sides

1997, Oct. 30 **Tagged**

Self-Adhesive

3177a	A2460	32c pane of 20 + label, P#B1111, B2222, B3333	13.00

By its nature No. 3177a is a complete booklet (BC141). The peelable backing serves as a booklet cover.

3177b-3177d — A2460

3177b	A2460	32c	Booklet pane of 4, no P#	2.60
3177c	A2460	32c	Booklet pane of 5 + label, no P#	3.25
3177d	A2460	32c	Booklet pane of 6, no P# or P#B1111	3.90

Holiday Greetings
American Holly 32USA
Fifteen Self-adhesive Stamps
$4.80

3177b-3177d — BC141A

1997

$4.80 booklet contains 15 self-adhesive 32c stamps

$9.60 booklet contains 30 self-adhesive 32c stamps

Combination Booklet

BK264	BC141A	$4.80	**black & green,** 1 ea #3177b-3177d, P#B1111	9.75

Booklet

BK265	BC141A	$9.60	**black & green,** 5 #3177d, P#B1111	20.00

Panes in Nos. BK264-BK265 are separated by rouletting between each pane.

MAKESHIFT VENDING MACHINE BOOKLETS

See note before No. BK243. For illustration of booklet cover BC126, see before No. BK243.

1997

BK266	BC126	$4.80	#3151a-3151o (32c Dolls)	11.00
BK267	BC126	$4.80	15 #3152 (32c Humphrey Bogart)	11.00
BK268	BC126	$4.80	15 #3153 (32c Stars & Stripes)	11.00
BK269	BC126	$4.80	3 ea #3168-3172 (32c Movie Monsters)	11.00

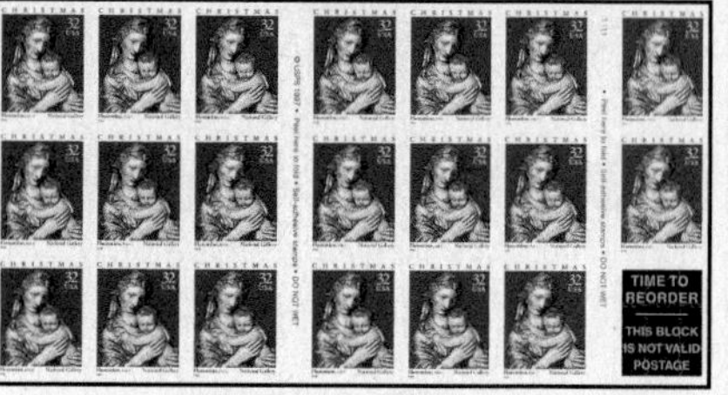

3244a — A2524

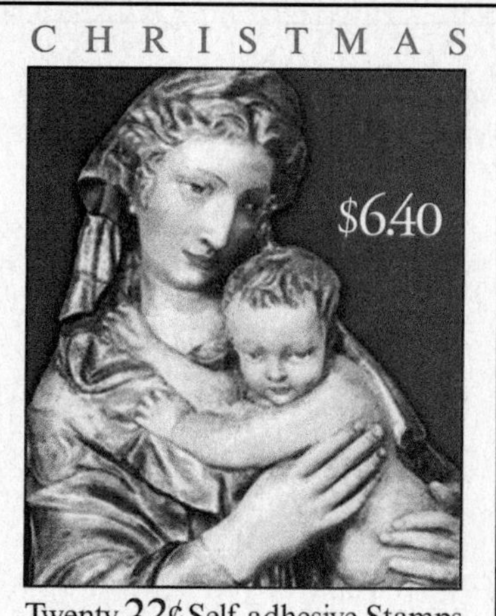

3244a — BC142

1998

$6.40 fold-it-yourself booklet contains 20 self-adhesive 32c stamps

Serpentine Die Cut 10.1x9.9 on 2, 3 or 4 Sides

1998, Oct. 15 **Tagged**

3244a	A2524	32c pane of 20 + label, P#11111, 22222, 33333	13.00

No. 3244a is a complete booklet (BC142). The peelable backing serves as a booklet cover.

3248a-3248c — A2525-A2528

Serpentine Die Cut 11.3x11.6 on 2, or 3 Sides

1998, Oct. 15 **Tagged**

3248a	A2525	32c pane of 4, #3245-3248, no P#	13.00
3248b	A2525	32c pane of 5, #3245-3246, 3248, 2 #3247 + label, no P#	16.25
3248c	A2525	32c pane of 6, #3247-3248, 2 each #3245-3246, P#B111111	19.50

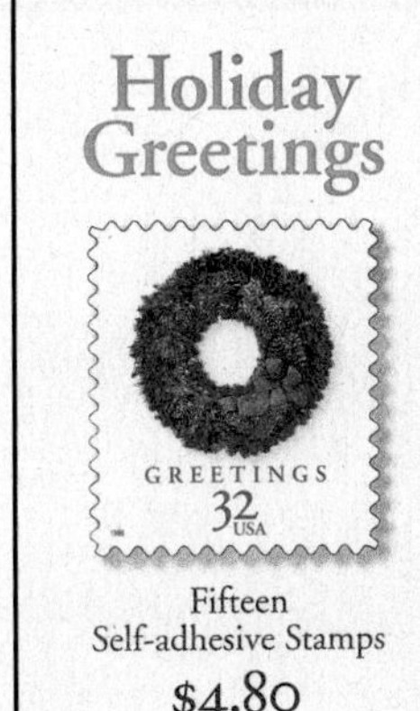

3248a-3248c — BC143

1998

$4.80 booklet contains 15 self-adhesive 32c stamps

Combination Booklet

BK270	BC143	$4.80	**multi,** 1 each #3248a-3248c, P#B111111	*50.00*

Varieties

3248d	A2525	32c As "a," die cutting omitted	—
3248e	A2525	32c As "b," die cutting omitted	—
3248f	A2525	32c As "c," die cutting omitted	—

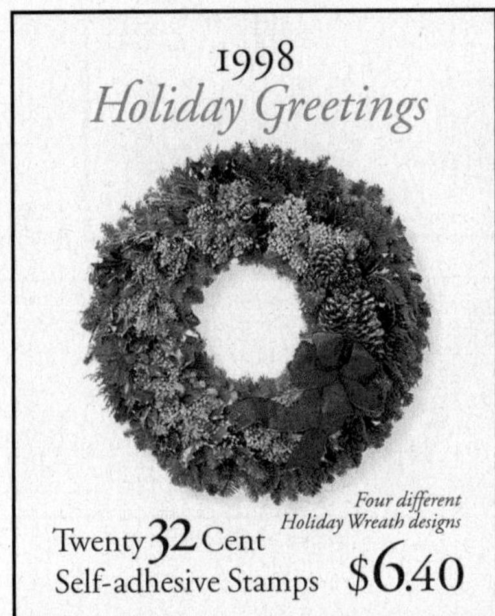

3252c, 3252e — BC143A

1998

$6.40 fold-it-yourself booklet contains 20 self-adhesive 32c stamps

Serpentine Die Cut 11.4x11.5 on 2, 3 or 4 Sides

3252c	A2525	32c pane of 20, 5 each #3249-3252 + label, P#B333333, B444444, B555555	30.00
		P#B222222	37.00

Serpentine Die Cut 11.7x11.6 on 2, 3 or 4 Sides

3252e	A2525	32c pane of 20, 5 each #3249a-3252a + label, P#B111111, B222222	35.00

Nos. 3252c and 3252e are complete booklets (BC143A). The peelable backing serves as a booklet cover.

Variety

3252i	As "c," die cutting omitted	*4,500.*

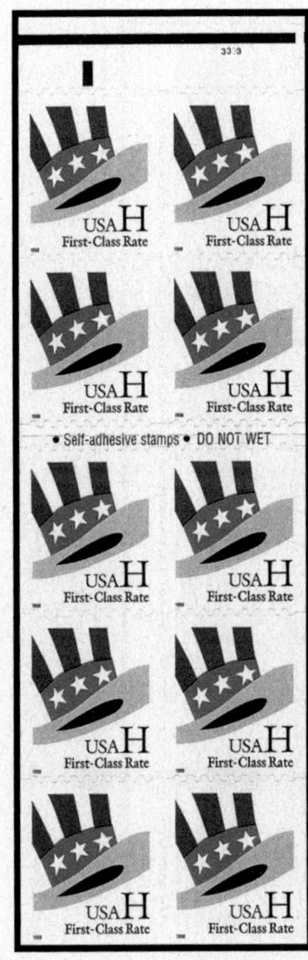

3267a — A2531

Serpentine Die Cut 9.9 on 2 or 3 Sides

1998, Nov. 9

3267a	A2531	(33c) pane of 10	7.50

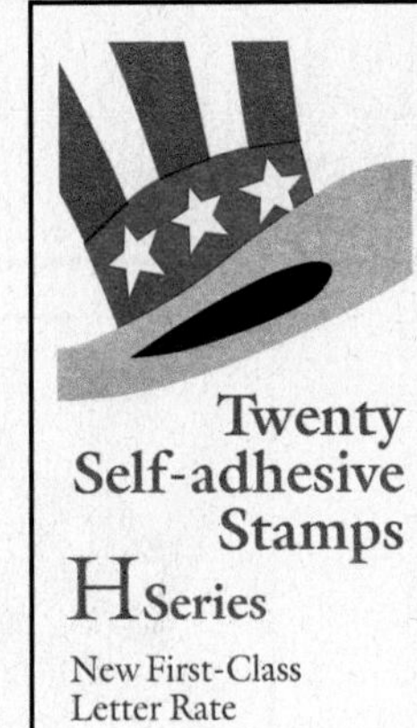

3267a, 3268a — BC144

1998

($6.60) booklet contains 20 self-adhesive (33c) stamps
($3.30) fold-it-yourself booklet (#3268a) contains 10 self-adhesive (33c) stamps

Booklet

BK271	BC144	($6.60)	**multi,** 2 #3267a, P#1111, 2222, 3333	15.00

3268c — A2531

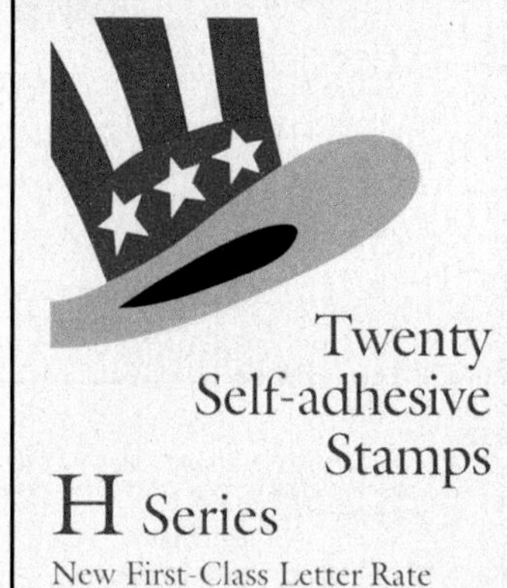

3268c BC144A

1998

($6.60) fold-it-yourself booklet contains 20 self-adhesive (33c) stamps

Die cut 11¼ on 3 sides (No. 3268a), 11 on 2, 3 or 4 Sides (No. 3268c)

3268a A2531 (33c) pane of 10, P#V1111, V1211, V2211, V2222 7.50
3268c A2531 (33c) pane of 20 + label, P#V1111, V1112, V1113, V1213, V2113, V2122, V2213, V2223 15.00
P# V1122 22.50
P# V1222, V2222 17.50

3269a — A2531

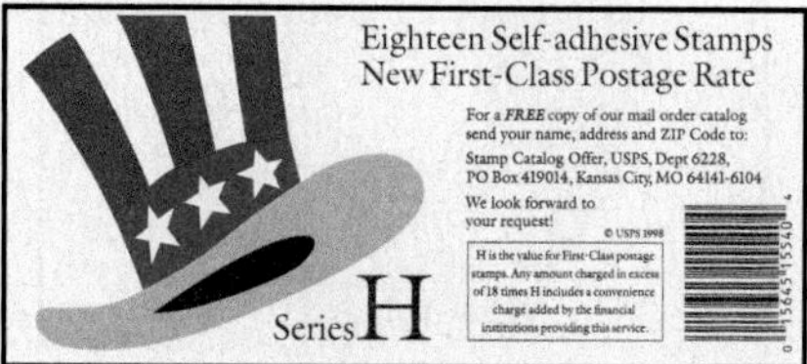

3269a — BC144B

1998

($5.94) fold-it-yourself booklet contains 18 self-adhesive (33c) stamps

Die Cut 8

3269a A2531 (33c) pane of 18, P#V1111 12.00

Nos. 3268a, 3268c, 3269a are complete booklets (BC144, BC144A, BC144B). The peelable backing serves as a booket cover.

MAKESHIFT VENDING MACHINE BOOKLETS

See note before No. BK243. For illustration of booklet cover BC126, see before No. BK243.

1998

BK272 BC126 $4.80 15 (#3222-3225) (32c Tropical Birds) 11.00
BK273 BC126 $4.80 15 #3237 (32c Ballet) 11.00
BK274 BC126 $4.80 3 #3242a (32c Space Discovery) 11.50

Configuration of stamps in #BK272 may vary.

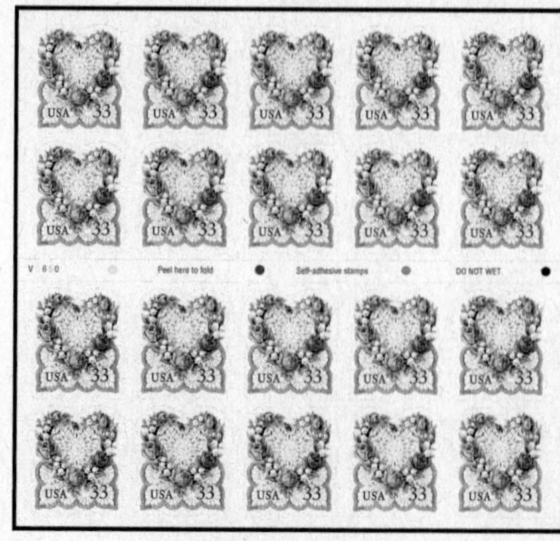

3274a — A2537

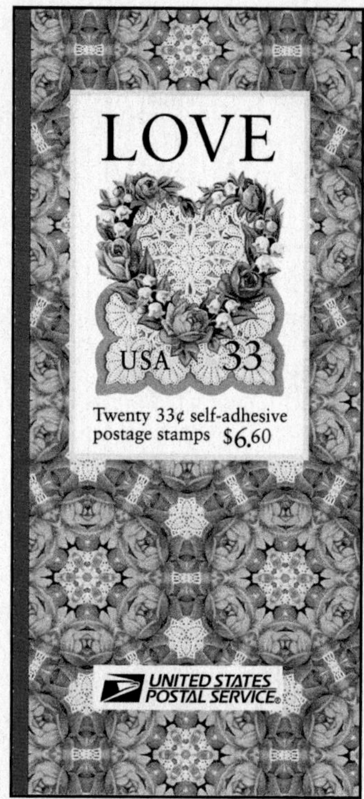

3274a BC145

1999

$6.60 Fold-it-yourself booklet contains 20 self-adhesive 33c stamps

Tagged ***Die Cut***

3274a A2537 33c pane of 20, *Jan. 28, 1999* 13.00

No. 3274a is a complete booklet (BC145). The peelable backing serves as a booklet cover.

Below is a list of known plate numbers. Some numbers are scarcer than the value indicated in the listing.

P#V1111, V1112, V1117, V1118, V1211, V1212, V1213, V1233, V1313, V1314, V1333, V1334, V1335, V2123, V2221, V2222, V2223, V2424, V2425, V2426, V2324, V3123, V3124, V3125, V3133, V3134, V3323, V3327, V3333, V3334, V3336, V4549, V5650.

Variety

3274c As "a," die cutting omitted *1,000.*

3278a-3278c — A2540

Serpentine Die Cut 11 on 2, 3 or 4 Sides

1999 **Tagged**

Self-Adhesive

3278a A2540 33c pane of 4, no P# 2.60
3278b A2540 33c pane of 5 + label, P#V1111, V1112, V1121, V1122, V1212, V2212 3.25
3278c A2540 33c pane of 6, no P# 3.90

City Flag
33 USA
Fifteen
Self-adhesive
Stamps
$4.95

3278a-3278c — BC146

1999

$4.95 booklet contains 15 self-adhesive 33c stamps

COMBINATION BOOKLET

BK275 BC146 $4.95 **multi,** 1 each #3278a-3278c, P#V1111, V1112, V1121, V1122, V1212, V2212 10.00

The plate # single in No. 3278b from No. BK275 is the lower left stamp in the bottom pane of the booklet.

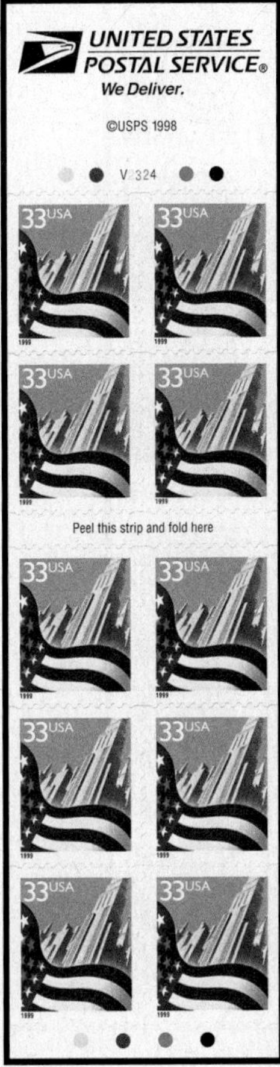

3278d, 3278j — A2540

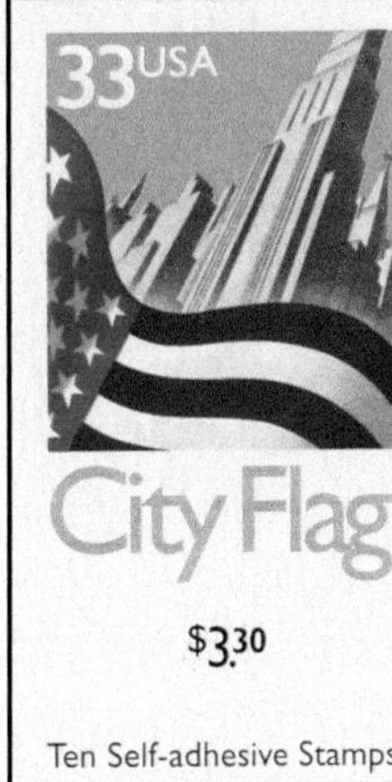

3278d — BC146A

1999

$3.30 Fold-it-yourself booklet contains 10 self-adhesive 33c stamps

3278d A2540 33c pane of 10, P#V1113, V2322, V2324, V3433, V3434, V3545 13.00
P#V1111 —
P#V1112 35.00
P#V2323 —

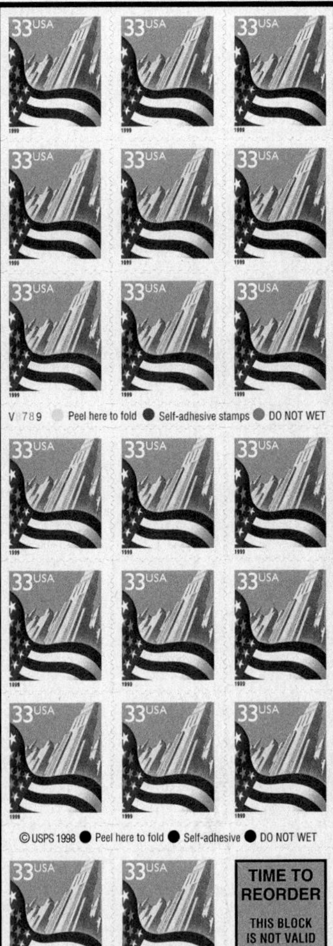

3278e, 3278Fg — A2540

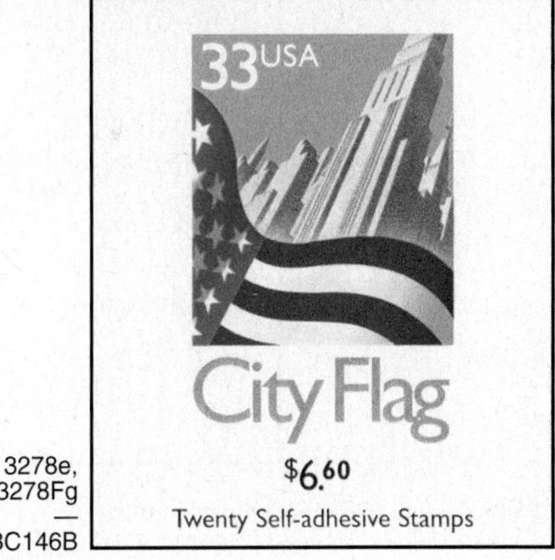

3278e, 3278Fg — BC146B

1999

$6.60 Fold-it-yourself booklet contains 20 self-adhesive 33c stamps

3278e A2540 33c pane of 20 + label, P#V1111, V1211, V2122, V2222, V2223, V3333, V4444 17.00
P#V8789 —

Nos. 3278d-3278e are complete booklets (BC146A, BC146B). The peelable backing serves as a booklet cover.

Variety

3278h As "e," die cutting omitted —

Serpentine Die Cut 11¼

3278j A2540 33c pane of 10, P#V2222 9.00
P#V1111, V1112 15.00
P#V1113, V2322 45.00
P#V3434 —

By its nature No. 3278j is a complete booklet. The peelable backing serves as a booklet cover and is similar to BC146A.

Serpentine Die Cut 11½x11¾ on 2, 3 or 4 Sides

3278Fg A2540 33c pane of 20 + label 28.00

No. 3278Fg is a complete booklet. The peelable backing serves as a booklet cover and is similar to BC146B.

Below is a list of known plate numbers. Some numbers are scarcer than the value indicated in the listing.

P# V1111, V1131, V2222, V2223, V2227, V2243, V2323, V2423, V2443, V3333, V4444, V5428, V5445, V5446, V5576, V5578, V6423, V6456, V6546, V6556, V6575, V6576, V7567, V7663, V7667, V7676, V8789.

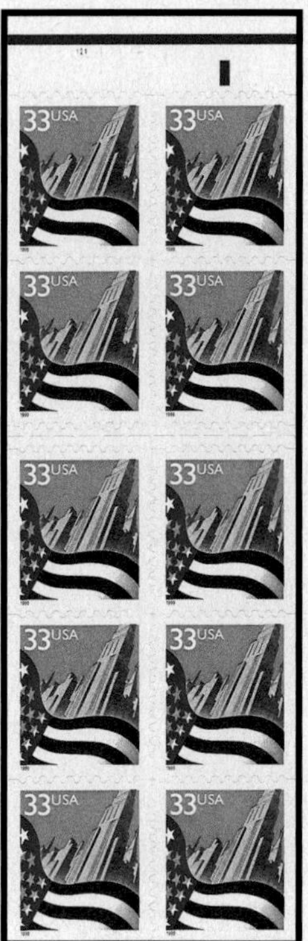

3279a — A2540

Serpentine Die Cut 9.8 on 2 or 3 Sides

3279a A2540 33c pane of 10 8.50

3279a — BC146C

1999

$6.60 Booklet contains 20 self-adhesive 33c stamps

BOOKLET

BK276 BC146C $6.60 **multi,** 2 #3279a, P#1111, 1121 17.00

3283a — A2541

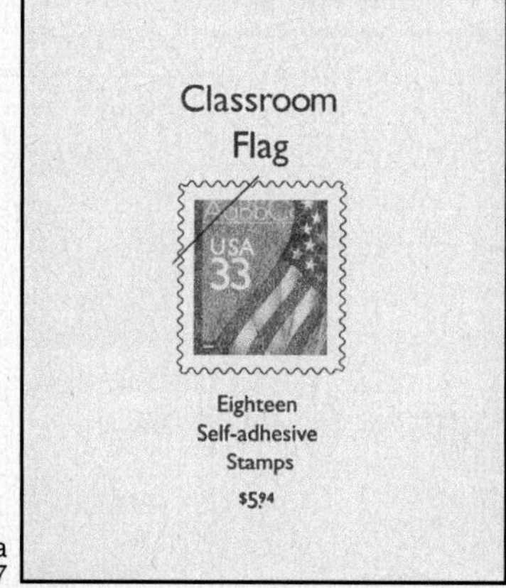

3283a BC147

1999

$5.94 fold-it-yourself booklet contains 18 self-adhesive 33c stamps

Serpentine Die Cut 7.9 on 2, 3 or 4 Sides

Tagged

3283a A2541 33c pane of 18, P#V1111 12.00

No. 3283a is a complete booklet (BC147). The peelable backing serves as a booklet cover.

3297b — A2550-A2553

3297b BC148

1999

$6.60 fold-it-yourself booklet contains 20 self-adhesive 33c stamps + label

Serpentine Die Cut 11¼x11½ on 2, 3 or 4 Sides

1999-2000 **Tagged**

Self-Adhesive

3297b A2550 33c pane of 20, 5 ea #3294-3297 + label 17.50

No. 3297b is a complete booklet (BC148). The peelable backing serves as a booklet cover.

P#B1111, B1112, B2211, B2222, B3331, B3332, B3333, B4444, B5555.

3297d, BC148A — A2550-A2553

Serpentine Die Cut 11¼x11½ on 2 or 3 Sides

3297d A2550 33c pane of 20, 5 #3297e + label, *Mar. 15, 2000,* P#B1111 25.00

By its nature, No. 3297d is a double-sided complete booklet. Eight stamps and the booklet cover (BC148A) plus P# are printed on one side of the peelable backing and 12 stamps are printed on the other side of the backing.

3301a-3301c — A2550-A2553

Serpentine Die Cut 9½x10 on 2 or 3 sides

3301a A2550 33c pane of 4, no P# 4.00
3301b A2550 33c pane of 5 + label, no P# 5.00
3301c A2550 33c pane of 6, P#B1111, B1112, B2212, B2222 6.00
P#B2221 —

3301a-3301c — BC148B

1999

$4.95 booklet contains 15 self-adhesive 33c stamps + label

COMBINATION BOOKLET

BK276A BC148B $4.95 **multicolored,** 1 each #3301a-3301c, P# see 3301c 17.00

3313b, BC149 — A2556-A2559

Serpentine Die Cut 10.9 on 2 or 3 Sides

1999 **Tagged**

3313b A2556 33c pane of 20, all P# (see below) except P#S22444 13.00
P#S22444 *2,500.*

By its nature, No. 3313b is a complete booklet. Eight stamps and the booklet cover (BC149) plus P# are printed on one side of the peelable backing and 12 stamps are printed on the other side of the backing.

P#S11111, S22222, S22244, S22344, S22444, S22452, S22462, S23222, S24222, S24224, S24242, S24244, S24422, S24442, S24444, S26462, S32323, S32333, S32444, S33333, S44444, S45552, S46654, S55452, S55552, S56462, S62544, S62562, S64452, S64544, S65544, S65552, S66462, S66544, S66552, S66562, S66652.

3355a, BC150 — A2599

1999, Oct. 20 ***Serpentine Die Cut 11¼***

Self-Adhesive

3355a A2599 33c pane of 20, P#B1111, B2222, B3333 18.00

No. 3355a is a complete booklet. Eight stamps and the booklet cover (BC150) plus P# are printed on one side of the peelable backing and 12 stamps are printed on the other side of the backing.

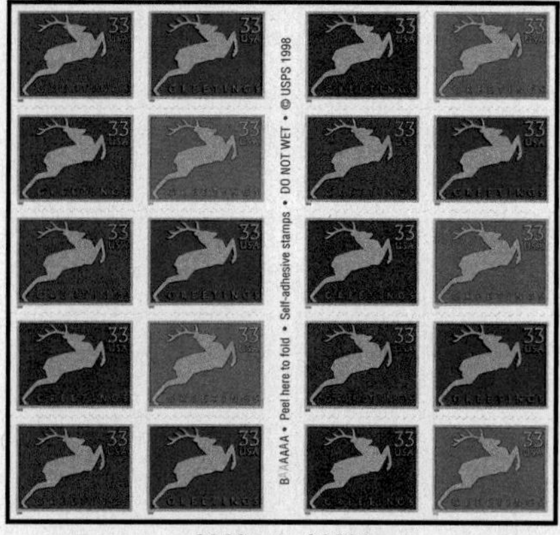

3363a — A2600

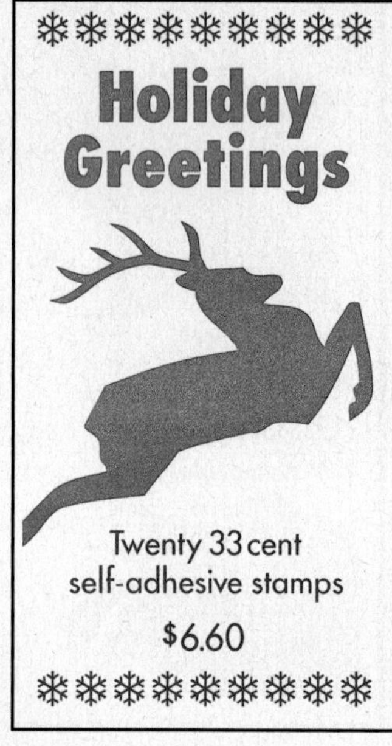

3363a
BC151

1999

$6.60 fold-it-yourself booklet contains 20 self-adhesive 33c stamps

1999, Oct. 20 *Serpentine Die Cut 11¼*

Self-Adhesive

3363a A2600 33c pane of 20, P#B111111, B222222, B333333, B444444, B555555, B666666, B777777, B888888, B999999, B000000, BAAAAAA, BBBBBBB 22.50

No. 3363a is a complete booklet (BC151). The peelable backing serves as a booklet cover.

Variety

3363d As "a," die cutting omitted *500.00*

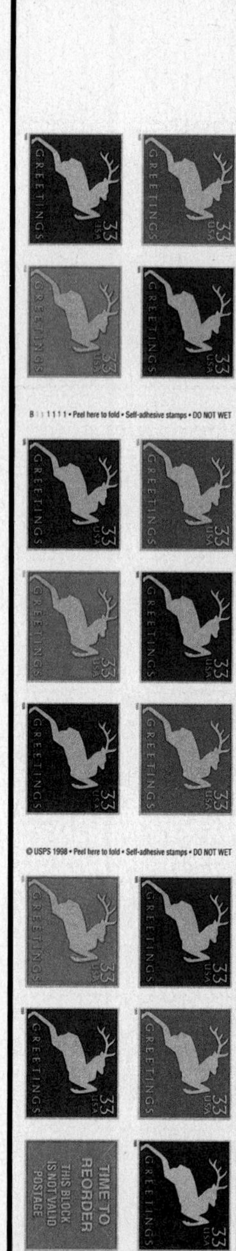

3367a-3367c — A2600

Serpentine Die Cut 11½x11¼ on 2 or 3 sides

Stamp Size: 21x19mm

3367a A2600 33c pane of 4, no P# 5.50
3367b A2600 33c pane of 5 + label, no P# 7.00
3367c A2600 33c pane of 6, P#B111111, B222222 8.00

3367a-3367c — BC152

1999

$4.95 fold-it-yourself booklet contains 15 self-adhesive 33c stamps

COMBINATION BOOKLET

BK276B BC152 $4.95 **green & gold,** 1 each #3367a-3367c, P# see 3367c 21.00

MAKESHIFT VENDING MACHINE BOOKLETS

See note before No. BK243. For illustration of booklet cover BC126, see before No. BK243.

1999

BK277 BC126 $4.95 4 each #3325, 3327-3328, 3 #3326 (33c American Glass) 11.00
BK278 BC126 $4.95 3 each #3333-3337 (33c Famous Trains) 11.00

3377a — A2604-A2608

THE DOLPHIN PIN

The U.S. Navy Submarine Force insignia is a pin featuring a pair of dolphins flanking a sub with its bow planes rigged for diving. The pin is gold plated for officers, silver plated for enlisted personnel. Training prepares submariners not only for day-to-day responsibilities such as navigation and depth control, but also for the most extreme situations, from floods and fires to fighting the enemy. Only after the ability to handle these difficult scenarios has been confirmed can a candidate finally wear the coveted "dolphins."

Selvage 1

THE SUBMARINE STAMPS
U.S. Navy Submarines
A Century of Service to America

USS *Holland,* the U.S. Navy's first submarine, was purchased in 1900.

S-class submarines were designed during WWI.

Gato class submarines played a key role in the destruction of Japanese maritime power in the Pacific during WWII.

Los Angeles class attack submarines, armed with "smart" torpedoes and cruise missiles, are nuclear powered.

Ohio class submarines–also nuclear powered–carry more than half of America's strategic weapons, making them a vital part of America's nuclear deterrence.

Selvage 2

2000, Mar. 27 *Perf. 11*

3377a pane of 5 with selvage 1 15.00 —
With selvage 2 15.00 —

3377a — BC153

2000

$9.80 booklet contains 2 panes of one 22c, 33c, 55c, 60c and $3.20 stamps and 6 leaves of text.

Booklet

BK279 BC153 $9.80 **multicolored,** no P# 30.00

No. BK279 contains one pane with selvage 1 and one pane with selvage 2.

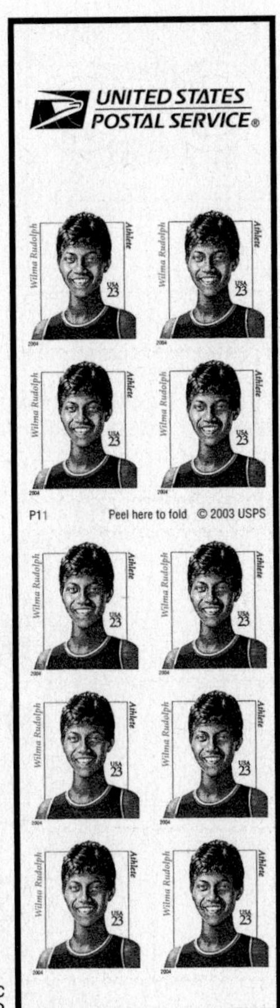

3436a, 3436b, 3436c — A2652

Serpentine Die Cut 11¼x10¾ on 3 Sides

2004, July 14 Self-Adhesive Litho.

3436a	A2652 23c	pane of 4, no P#	1.80
3436b	A2652 23c	pane of 6, no P#	2.70
3436c	A2652 23c	As "a" & "b" in cplt booklet of 10 (No. BK279A), die cutting omitted and peel strip intact, P#P44	—
3436d	A2652 23c	pane of 10, P#P11, P22	4.50

3436a, 3436b, 3436d — BC153A

2004

$2.30 booklet contains 10 self-adhesive 23c stamps

$2.30 fold-it-yourself booklet contains 10 self-adhesive 23c stamps

COMBINATION BOOKLET

BK279A BC153A $2.30 **multi,** #3436a-3436b, no P# 4.50

By its nature, No. 3436d is a complete booklet (BC153A). The peelable backing serves as a booklet cover. No. BK279A lacks the self-adhesive panel that covers the rouletting. The backing on No. 3436b has a different product code (672900) than that found on the lower portion of No. 3436c (673000).

Variety

3436e A2652 As "d," die cutting omitted —

3450a — A2678

3450a BC154

2000

$6.12 fold-it-yourself booklet contains 18 self-adhesive (34c) stamps

2000 ***Serpentine Die Cut 8 on 2, 3 or 4 Sides***

Self-Adhesive

3450a A2678 (34c) pane of 18, P#V1111, *Dec. 15* 16.00

No. 3450a is a complete booklet (BC154). The peelable backing serves as a booklet cover.

3451a — A2679

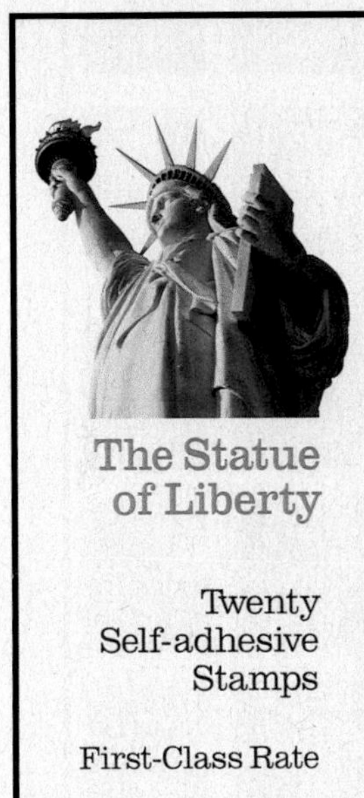

The Statue
of Liberty
Twenty
Self-adhesive
Stamps
First-Class Rate

3451a — BC155

2000

$6.80 fold-it-yourself booklet contains 20 self-adhesive (34c) stamps

Serpentine Die Cut 11 on 2, 3 or 4 Sides

2000, Dec. 15 Self-Adhesive

3451a A2679 (34c) pane of 20, P#V1111, V2222 22.00

No. 3451a is a complete booklet (BC155). The peelable backing serves as a booklet cover.

3451b-3451c — A2679

3451b A2679 (34c) pane of 4, without plate # 4.40
3451c A2679 (34c) pane of 6, no P# 6.60

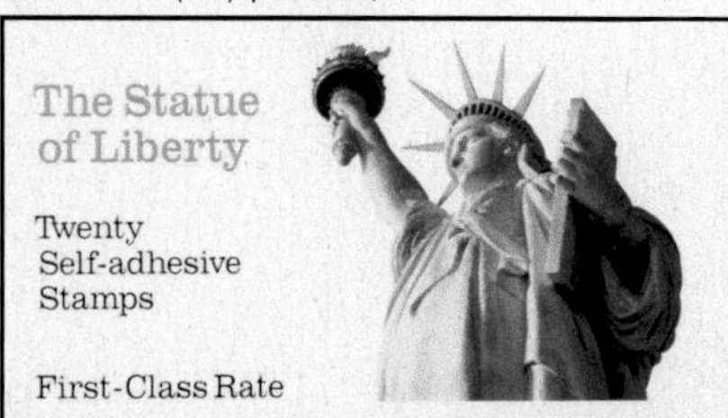

3451b, 3451c — BC156

2000

$6.80 booklet contains 20 self-adhesive (34c) stamps

COMBINATION BOOKLET

BK280 BC156 ($6.80) **multicolored,** 1 #3451b without P#, 1 #3451b with P#V1111, 2 #3451c 20.00

The plate # on No. 3451b from No. BK280 is on the lower right stamp of the right pane of 4 of the booklet.

Varieties

3451b pane of 4, containing P# single 4.50
3451d As "a," die cutting omitted —

3457b-3457d — A2681-A2684

Serpentine Die Cut 10½x10¾ on 2 or 3 Sides (#3454-3457), 11½x11¾ on 2 or 3 sides (#3458-3461)

2000 **Self-Adhesive**

3457b A2681 (34c) pane of 4, #3454-3457, *Dec. 15* 4.40
3457c A2681 (34c) pane of 6, #3456, 3457, 2 each #3454-3455, no P#, *Dec. 15* 7.00
3457d A2681 (34c) pane of 6, #3454, 3455, 2 each #3456-3457, no P#, *Dec. 15* 7.00

3457b-3457d — BC158

2000

$6.80 booklet contains 20 self-adhesive (34c) stamps

COMBINATION BOOKLET

BK281 BC158 ($6.80) **multicolored,** #3457c, 3457d, 2 #3457b, P#S1111 22.50

P# on No. BK281 is on the backing paper of the top pane of No. 3457b.

3457e, BC157 — A2681-A2684

3457e A2681 (34c) pane of 20, 5 each # 3454-3457, P#S1111, *Dec. 15* 22.50

No. 3457e is a complete booklet. Eight stamps and the booklet cover (BC157) are printed on one side of the peelable backing and 12 stamps plus P# are printed on the other side of the backing.

3461b A2681 pane of 20, 2 each #3461a, 3 each #3457a, #S1111, *Dec. 15* 55.00
3461c A2681 pane of 20, 2 each #3457a, 3 each #3461a, #S1111, *Dec. 15* 90.00

Nos. 3461b and 3461c are complete booklets. Two blocks of four with the same gauge die cutting and the booklet cover (BC157) are printed on one side of the peelable backing and three blocks of four with the other gauge die cutting plus P# are printed on the other side of the backing.

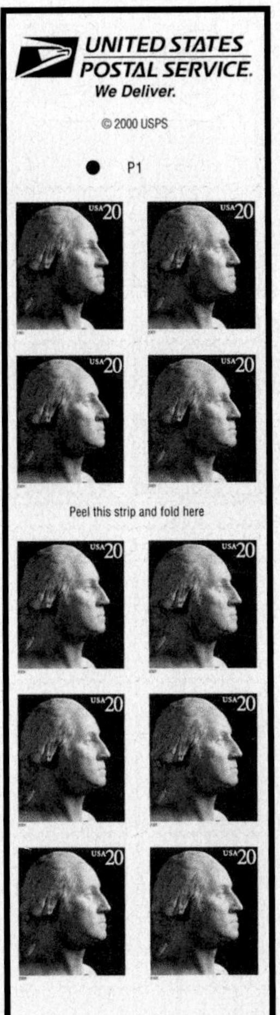

3482a, 3483c, 3483f — A2686

3482a, 3483c, 3483f — BC159

2001

$2 fold-it-yourself booklet contains 10 self-adhesive 20c stamps
$2 booklet contains 10 self-adhesive 20c stamps

Serpentine Die Cut 11¼x11 on 3 Sides

2001, Feb. 22 **Self-Adhesive**

3482a A2686 20c pane of 10, P#P1, P2, P3 5.50

3482b, 3483c — A2686

3482b A2686 20c pane of 4, P#P1, P2, P3 2.20
3482c A2686 20c pane of 6, no P# 3.30

COMBINATION BOOKLET

BK281A BC159 $2 **multicolored,** #3482b-3482c, P#P1, P2 5.50
P#P3 10.00

No. BK281A has slightly smaller cover (BC159) than No. 3482a and lacks self-adhesive panel that covers the rouletting.

3483a A2686 20c pane of 4, 2 #3482 at L, 2 #3483 at R, P#P1, P2, P3 12.50
3483b A2686 20c pane of 6, 3 #3482 at L, 3 #3483 at R, no P# 20.00
3483c A2686 20c pane of 10, 5 #3482 at L, 5 #3483 at R, P#P1, P2 30.00
P#P3 45.00
3483d A2686 20c pane of 4, 2 #3483 at L, 2 #3282 at R, P#P1, P2, P3 12.50
3483e A2686 20c pane of 6, 3 #3483 at L, 3 #3282 at R, no P# 20.00
3483f A2686 20c pane of 10, 5 #3483 at L, 5 #3282 at R, P#P1, P2 30.00
P#P3 45.00

Nos. 3482a, 3483c and 3483f are complete booklets (BC159) and include a self-adhesive panel that covers the rouletting. The peelable backing, which is slightly longer than that on Nos. BK282 and BK282A, serves as a booklet cover.

COMBINATION BOOKLETS

BK282 BC159 $2 **multicolored,** #3483a-3483b, P#P1, P2 32.50
P#P3 *55.00*
BK282A BC159 $2 **multicolored,** #3483d-3483e, P#P1, P2 32.50
P#P3 *55.00*

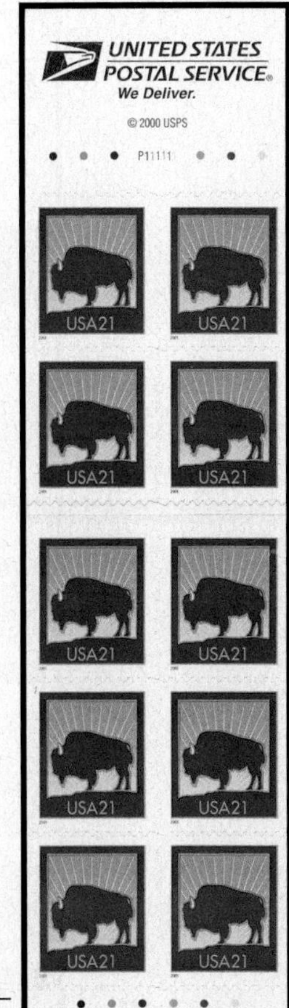

3484b, 3484c — A2687

3484d, 3484Ag, 3484Aj — BC159A

2001

$2.10 fold-it-yourself booklet contains 10 self-adhesive 21c stamps
$2.10 booklet contains 10 self-adhesive 21c stamps

Serpentine Die Cut 11¼ on 3 Sides

2001, Sept. 20 **Self-Adhesive**

3484b A2687 21c pane of 4, P#P111111, P333333, P444444 2.40
3484c A2687 21c pane of 6, no P# 3.60

COMBINATION BOOKLET

BK282B BC159A $2.10 **multi,** #3484b-3484c, P#P111111, P333333, P444444 6.00

3484d, 3484Ag, 3484Aj — A2687

3484d A2687 21c pane of 10, P#P111111, P222222, P333333, P444444, P555555 6.00

Serpentine Die Cut 10½x11¼ on 3 Sides

3484Ae A2687 21c pane of 4, 2 #3484 at L, 2# 3484A at R, P#P111111, P333333, P444444 12.50
3484Af A2687 21c pane of 6, 3 #3484 at L, 3# 3484A at R, no P# 20.00
3484Ag A2687 21c pane of 10, 5 #3484 at L, 5# 3484A at R, P#P111111, P222222, P333333, P444444 30.00
P#P555555 45.00
3484Ah A2687 21c pane of 4, 2 #3484A at L, 2# 3484 at R, P#P111111, P333333, P444444 12.50
3484Ai A2687 21c pane of 6, 3 #3484A at L, 3# 3484 at R, no P# 20.00
3484Aj A2687 21c pane of 10, 5 #3484A at L, 5# 3484 at R, P#P111111, P222222, P333333, P444444 30.00
P#P555555 45.00

COMBINATION BOOKLETS

BK282C BC159A $2.10 **multi,** #3484Ae-3484Af, P#P111111, P333333, P444444 32.50
BK282D BC159A $2.10 **multi,** #3484Ah-3484Ai, P#P111111, P333333, P444444 32.50

Nos. 3484d, 3484Ag and 3484Aj are complete booklets (BC159A). The peelable backing serves as a booklet cover. Nos. BK282B-BK282D lack self-adhesive panel that covers the rouletting. Nos. BK282B-BK282D have a small 662900 UPC code on cover back, while Nos. 3484d, 3484Ag and 3484Aj have a large 662800 UPC code on cover back.

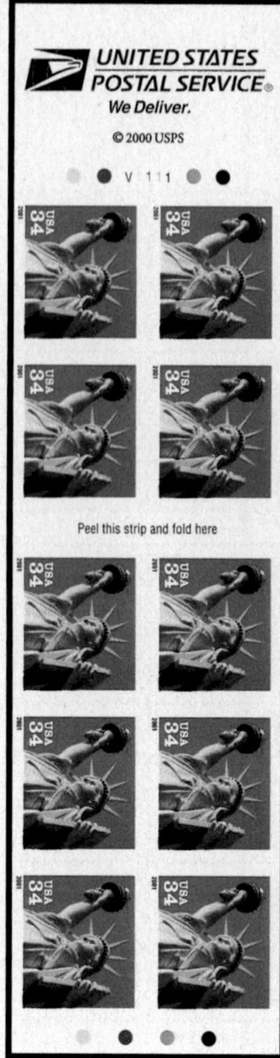

3485a — A2689

3485a — BC160

2001

$3.40 fold-it-yourself booklet contains 10 self-adhesive 34c stamps

2001, Feb. 7 ***Serpentine Die Cut 11 on 3 Sides***

Self-Adhesive

3485a A2689 34c pane of 10, P#V1111, V1221 7.00

3485b — A2689

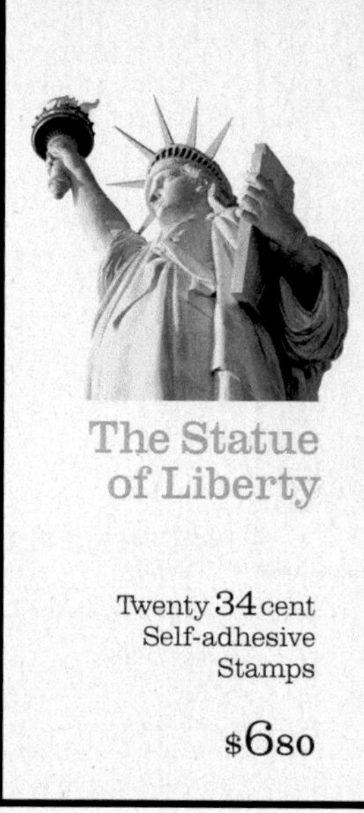

3485b — BC160B

2001

$6.80 fold-it-yourself booklet contains 20 self-adhesive 34c stamps

3485b A2689 34c pane of 20, P#V1111, V1211, V1221, V2111, V2112, V2121, V2122, V2212, V2222 14.00

Nos. 3485a-3485b are complete booklets (BC160 and BC160B). The peelable backing serves as a booklet cover.

Variety

3485f As "b," die cutting omitted —

3485c, 3485d — A2689

3485c A2689 34c pane of 4, without P# 3.00
3485d A2689 34c pane of 6, no P# 4.50

3485c, 3485d — BC160A

2001

$6.80 booklet contains 20 self-adhesive 34c stamps

COMBINATION BOOKLET

BK283 BC160A $6.80 **multicolored,** 1 #3485c with P#, 1 #3485c without P#, 2 3485d, P#V1111, V2212, V2222 16.00
P#V1112, V1121, V1122 —

The plate # on No. 3485c from No. BK283 is on the lower right stamp of the right pane of 4 of the booklet.

Variety

3485c Pane of 4 containing P#V1111, V1122, V2212, V2222 4.00
Pane of 4 containing P#V1112, V1121 —

3490b, 3490c, 3490d — A2690-A2693

Serpentine Die Cut 10½x 10¾ on 2 or 3 Sides

2001, Feb. 7 **Self-Adhesive**

3490b 34c pane of 4 3.50
3490c 34c pane of 6, #3489-3490, 2 each #3487-3488 5.00
3490d 34c pane of 6, #3487-3488, 2 each #3489-3490 5.00

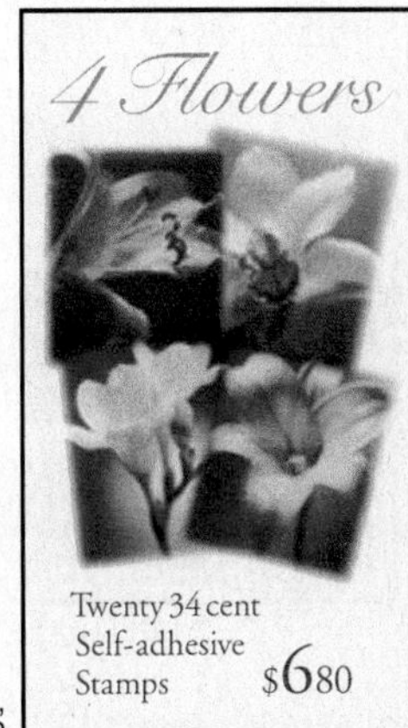

3490b, 3490c, 3490d — BC162

2001

$6.80 booklet contains 20 self-adhesive 34c stamps

COMBINATION BOOKLET

BK284 BC162 $6.80 **multicolored,** #3490c-3490d, 2 #3490b, P#S1111 17.50

P# on No. BK284 is on the backing paper of the bottom pane of No. 3490b.

3490e, BC161 — A2690-A2693

3490e 34c pane of 20, 5 #3490a, P#S1111, S2222 20.00

No. 3490e is a complete booklet with 12 stamps plus P# on one side and eight stamps plus booklet cover (BC161) on the other side. The peelable backing serves as a booklet cover.

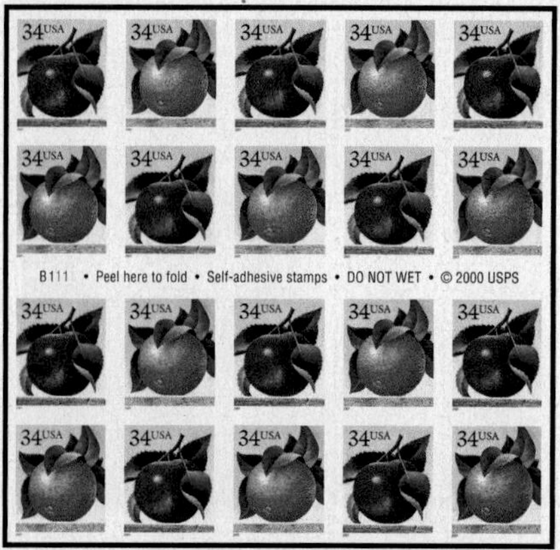

3492b — A2694-A2695

3492b — BC163

2001

$6.80 fold-it-yourself booklet contains 20 self-adhesive 34c stamps

Serpentine Die Cut 11¼ on 2, 3 or 4 sides

2001, Mar. 6 **Self-Adhesive**

3492b	34c pane of 20, 10 each #3491-3492, P# B1111, B2222, B3333, B4444, B5555, B6666, B7777	14.00

No. 3492b is a complete booklet (BC163). The peelable backing serves as a booklet cover.

Varieties

3492e	As "b," die cutting omitted	*5,500.*
3492f	As "b," right four stamps yellow omitted	*3,500.*

3494b, 3494c, 3494d — A2694-A2695

2001, May ***Serpentine Die Cut 11½x10¾***

Self-Adhesive

3494b	34c pane of 4, 2 each #3493-3494, without P#	4.20
3494c	34c pane of 6, 3 each #3493-3494, #3493 at UL, no P#	6.30
3494d	34c pane of 6, 3 each #3493-3494, #3494 at UL, no P#	6.30

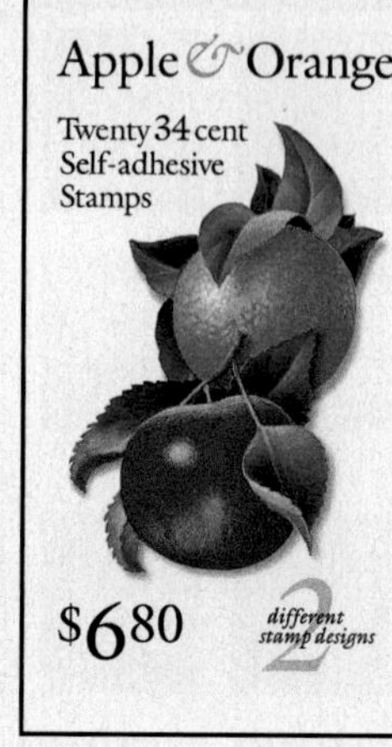

3494b, 3494c, 3494d — BC163A

2001

$6.80 booklet contains 20 self-adhesive 34c stamps

COMBINATION BOOKLET

BK284A	BC163A $6.80 **multi,** #3494c, 3494d, 2 #3494b, P#B1111	22.50

The plate # on No. 3494b from No. BK284A is on bottom left stamp in the bottom pane of the booklet.

Variety

3494b	Pane of 4 with P#B1111	5.50

3495a — A2688

3495a — BC163B

2001

$6.12 booklet contains 18 self-adhesive 34c stamps

Serpentine Die Cut 8 on 2, 3 or 4 Sides

2001, Dec. 17 **Self-Adhesive**

3495a 34c pane of 18, #V1111 18.00

Nos. 3495a is a complete booklet (BC163B). The peelable backing serves as a booklet cover.

3496a — A2699

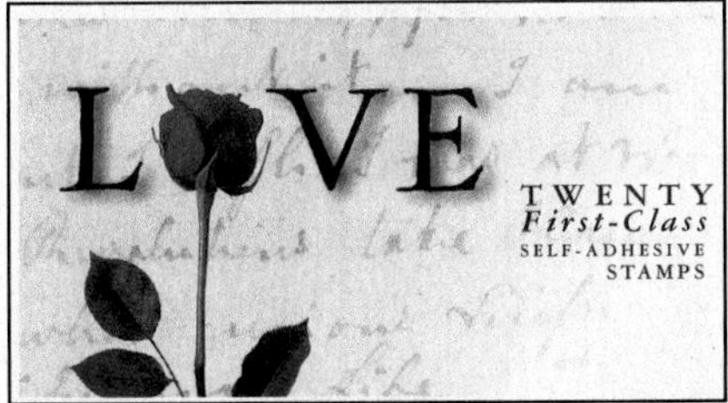

3496a — BC164

2001

$6.80 fold-it-yourself booklet contains 20 self-adhesive (34c) stamps

2001 ***Serpentine Die Cut 11¼ on 2, 3, or 4 Sides***

Self-Adhesive

3496a A2699 (34c) pane of 20, P#B1111, B2222, *Jan. 19* 22.00

No. 3496a is a complete booklet (BC164). The peelable backing serves as a booklet cover.

3497a — A2700

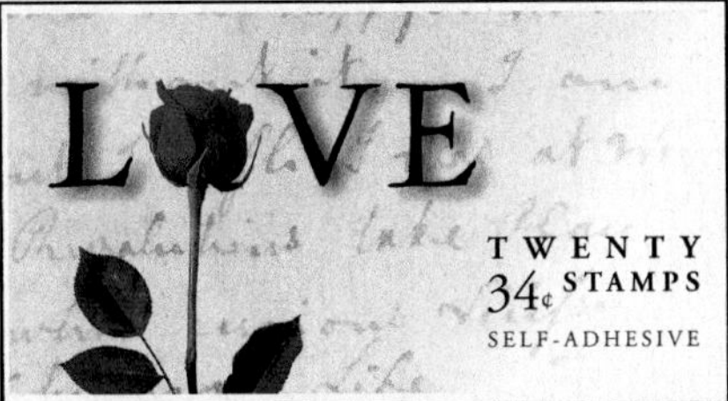

3497a — BC165

2001

$6.80 fold-it-yourself booklet contains 20 self-adhesive 34c stamps

2001 ***Serpentine Die Cut 11¼ on 2, 3 or 4 Sides***

Self-Adhesive

3497a A2700 34c pane of 20, P#B1111, B2222, B3333, B4444, B5555, *Feb. 14* 18.00

No. 3497a is a complete booklet (BC165). The peelable backing serves as a booklet cover.

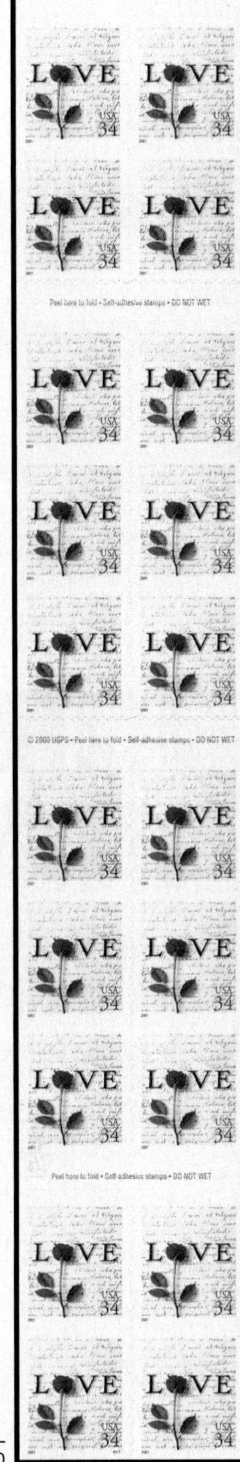

3498a, 3498b — A2700

Size: 18x21mm

Serpentine Die Cut 11½x10¾

3498a A2700 34c pane of 4, without P#, *Feb. 14* 3.50

3498b A2700 34c pane of 6, no P#, *Feb. 14* 5.10

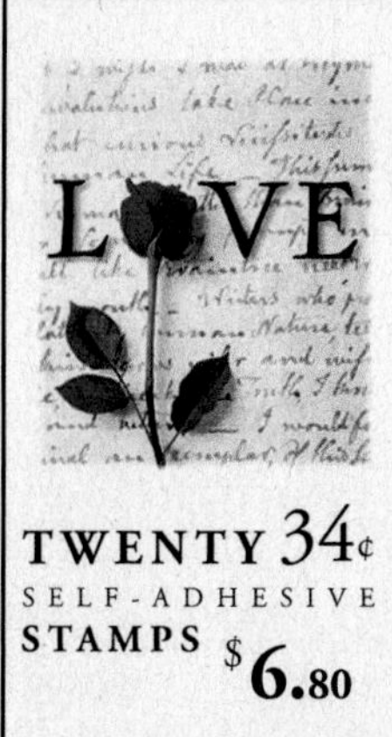

3498a,
3498b — BC166

2001

$6.80 booklet contains 20 self-adhesive 34c stamps

COMBINATION BOOKLET

BK285 BC166 $6.80 **multicolored,** 2 each #3498a-3498b, P#B1111 21.00

The plate # on No. 3498a from No. BK285 is on bottom left stamp in the bottom pane of the booklet.

Variety

3498a pane of 4, containing P#B1111 5.50

3536a — A2737

Seasons Greetings
Twenty 34 cent
First-Class
Self-adhesive
Stamps
$6.80

3536a — BC167

2001

$6.80 fold-it-yourself booklet contains 20 self-adhesive 34c stamps

Serpentine Die Cut 11½ on 2, 3 or 4 Sides

2001, Oct. 10 **Self-Adhesive**

3536a A2737 34c pane of 20, P#B1111 15.00

No. 3536a is a complete booklet (BC167). The peelable backing serves as a booklet cover.

3540d, 3540g, BC168 — A2738-A2741

Serpentine Die Cut 10¾x11 on 2 or 3 Sides

3540d A2738 34c pane of 20, small date, 5 #3540c + label, P#S1111 18.00

3540g A2738 34c pane of 20, large date, 5 #3540f + label, P#S3333, S4444 40.00

Nos. 3540d and 3540g are complete booklets with 12 stamps plus P# on one side and eight stamps plus booklet cover (BC168) on the other side. The peelable backing serves as a booklet cover.

3544b, 3544c, 3544d — A2738-A2741

Green Denomination

Stamp Size: 21x18½mm

Serpentine Die Cut 11 on 2 or 3 sides

3544b A2738 34c pane of 4, #3541-3544 3.60

3544c A2738 34c pane of 6, #3543-3544, 2 #3541-3542 5.40

3544d A2738 34c pane of 6, #3541-3542, 2 #3543-3544 5.40

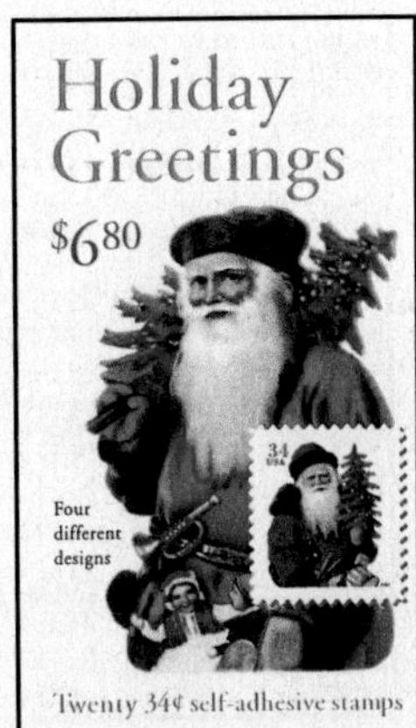

3544b, 3544c, 3544d — BC169

2001

$6.80 booklet contains 20 self-adhesive 34c stamps

COMBINATION BOOKLET

BK286 BC169 $6.80 **multi,** #3544c-3544d, 2 #3544b, P#V1111 18.00

P# on No. BK286 is on the backing paper of the bottom pane of No. 3544b.

3549a — A2744

3549a — BC170

2001

$6.80 booklet contains 20 self-adhesive 34c stamps

Serpentine Die Cut 11¼ on 2, 3 or 4 Sides

2001, Oct. 24 **Self-Adhesive**

3549a A2744 34c Pane of 20, P#B1111, B2222, B3333, B4444 15.00

No. 3549a is a complete booklet (BC170). The peelable backing serves as a booklet cover.

3549Bc, 3549Bd — A2744

Serpentine Die Cut 10½x10¾ on 2 or 3 Sides

2002, Jan. **Self-Adhesive**

3549Bc A2744 34c pane of 4 3.40
3549Bd A2744 34c pane of 6 5.10

3549Bc, 3549Bd — BC171

2002

$6.80 booklet contains 20 self-adhesive 34c stamps

COMBINATION BOOKLET

BK287 BC171 $6.80 **multi,** 2 each #3549Bc, 3549Bd, P#S1111 17.00

P# on No. BK287 is on the backing paper of the lower example of No. 3549Bd.

3549Be, BC172 — A2744

3549Be A2744 34c pane of 20, P#S1111 18.00

No. 3549Be is a complete booklet with 12 stamps plus P# on one side and eight stamps plus booklet cover (BC172) on the other side. The peelable backing serves as a booklet cover.

Washington Type of 2002

3618a, 3618b — A2686

Serpentine Die Cut 11¼x11 on 3 Sides

2002, June 7 **Self-Adhesive**

3618a A2686 23c pane of 4, P#P1, P2, P3 2.00
3618b A2686 23c pane of 6, no P# 3.00

George Washington
$2.30
Ten 23¢ self-adhesive stamps

3618c, 3619e, 3619f — BC173

2002

$2.30 booklet contains 10 self-adhesive 23c stamps

COMBINATION BOOKLET

BK288 BC173 $2.30 **multi,** #3618a-3618b, P#P1, P2, P4 5.00

No. BK288 has a 671800 UPC code on cover back, while No. 3618c has a 671000 UPC code on cover back.

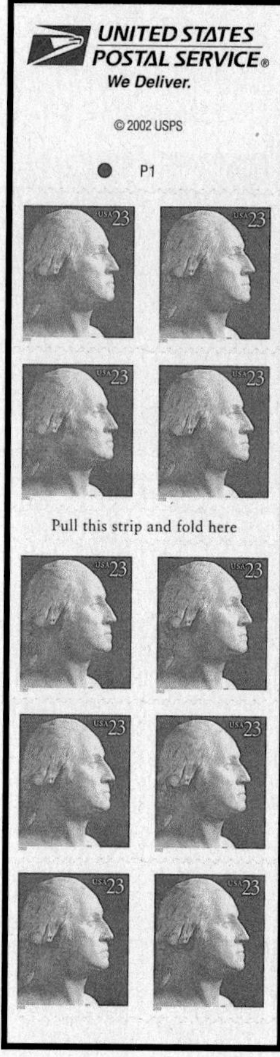

3618c — A2686

3618c A2686 23c pane of 10, P#P1, P2, P3 5.00

No. 3618c is a complete booklet and includes a self-adhesive panel that covers the rouletting. The peelable backing (BC173), which is slightly longer than on No. BK288, serves as a booklet cover.

Washington Type of 2002

Serpentine Die Cut 10½x11 on 3 Sides

2002, June 7 **Self-Adhesive**

3619a A2686 23c pane of 4, 2 #3619 at L, 2 #3618 at R, P#P1, P2, P3 10.00
3619b A2686 23c pane of 6, 3 #3619 at L, 3 #3618 at R, no P# 15.00
3619c A2686 23c pane of 4, 2 #3618 at L, 2 #3619 at R, P#P1, P2, P4 10.00
3619d A2686 23c pane of 6, 3 #3618 at L, 3 #3619 at R, no P# 15.00

COMBINATION BOOKLETS

BK289 BC173 $2.30 **multi,** #3619a-3619b, P#P1, P2, P4 25.00
BK289A BC173 $2.30 **multi,** #3619c-3619d, P#P1, P2, P4 25.00

Serpentine Die Cut 10½x11 on 3 Sides

Self-Adhesive

3619e A2686 23c pane of 10, 5 #3619 at L, 5 #3618 at R, P#P1, P2, P3 27.50
3619f A2686 23c pane of 10, 5 #3618 at L, 5 #3619 at R, P#P1, P2, P3 27.50

Nos. 3619e and 3619f are complete booklets and include a self-adhesive panel that covers the rouletting. The peelable backing (BC173), which is slightly longer than those on Nos. BK289 and BK289A, serves as a booklet cover.

Variety

3619i Nos. 3619c and 3619d in bklt. of 10 (#BK289A), imperf. vert. btwn. on both panes —

3623a — A2807

3623a — BC174

2002

$7.40 fold-it-yourself booklet contains 20 self-adhesive (37c) stamps

Serpentine Die Cut 11¼ on 2, 3 or 4 Sides

2002, June 7 **Self-Adhesive** **Litho.**

3623a A2807 (37c) pane of 20, P#B1111, B2222, B3333 22.00

No. 3623a is a complete booklet (BC174). The peelable backing serves as a booklet cover.

3624a, 3624b — A2807

Serpentine Die Cut 10½x10¾ on 2 or 3 Sides

2002, June 7 **Self-Adhesive** **Photo.**

3624a A2807 (37c) pane of 4, no P# 4.40
3624b A2807 (37c) pane of 6 6.60

3624a, 3624b — BC175

2002

$7.40 booklet contains 20 self-adhesive (37c) stamps

COMBINATION BOOKLET

BK290 BC175 ($7.40) **multi,** 2 each #3624a, 3624b, P#S11111 22.00

Plate number on No. BK290 is on the backing paper of the lower example of No. 3624b.

3624c, BC176 — A2807

Serpentine Die Cut 10½x10¾ on 2 or 3 Sides

3624c A2807 (37c) pane of 20, P#S1111 22.00

No. 3624c is a complete booklet with 12 stamps plus P# on one side and eight stamps plus booklet cover (BC176) on the other side. The peelable backing serves as a booklet cover.

3625a — A2807

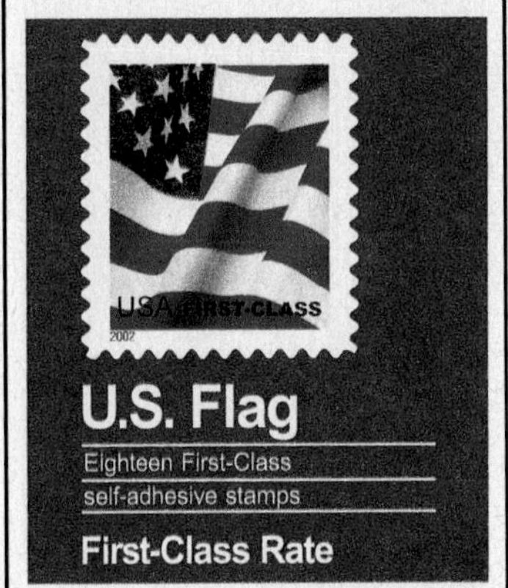

3625a BC177

2002

$6.66 fold-it-yourself booklet contains 18 self-adhesive (37c) stamps

Serpentine Die Cut 8 on 2, 3 or 4 Sides

2002, June 7 **Self-Adhesive** **Photo.**

3625a A2807 (37c) pane of 18, P#V1111 19.00

No. 3625a is a complete booklet (BC177). The peelable backing serves as a booklet cover.

3629b, 3629c, 3629d — A2808-A2811

Serpentine Die Cut 11 on 2 or 3 Sides

2002, June 7 **Self-Adhesive** **Photo.**

3629b A2808 (37c) pane of 4, #3626-3629, no P# 4.40
3629c A2808 (37c) pane of 6, #3627, 3629, 2 each #3626, 3628, no P# 6.60
3629d A2808 (37c) pane of 6, #3626, 3628, 2 each #3627, 3629, no P# 6.60

3629b, 3629c, 3629d — BC178

2002

$7.40 booklet contains 20 self-adhesive (37c) stamps

COMBINATION BOOKLET

BK291 BC178 ($7.40) **multi,** #3629c-3629d, 2 #3629b, no P# 22.00

3629e — A2808-A2811

3629e — BC179

2002

$7.40 fold-it-yourself booklet contains 20 self-adhesive (37c) stamps

Serpentine Die Cut 11 on 2, 3 or 4 Sides

3629e A2808 (37c) pane of 20, 5 each #3626-3629, P#V1111, V1112, V2222 22.00

No. 3629e is a complete booklet (BC179). The peelable backing serves as a booklet cover.

3634a — A2812

3634a — BC180

2002

$3.70 fold-it-yourself booklet contains 10 self-adhesive 37c stamps

Serpentine Die Cut 11.1 on 3 Sides

2002, June 7 **Self-Adhesive** **Photo.**

3634a A2812 37c pane of 10, P#V1111 7.50

No. 3634a is a complete booklet (BC180). The peelable backing serves as a booklet cover.

3634c, 3634d — A2812

Serpentine Die Cut 11 on 2 or 3 Sides

2003, Nov. Self-Adhesive Photo.

3634c A2812 37c pane of 4 #3634b, no P# 3.00
3634d A2812 37c pane of 6 #3634b 4.50

3634c, 3634d — BC180A

2002

$7.40 booklet contains 20 self-adhesive 37c stamps

COMBINATION BOOKLET

BK291A BC180A $7.40 **multi,** 2 each #3634c, 3634d, P#V1111 15.00

Plate number on No. BK291A is on the backing paper of the lower example of No. 3634d.

Serpentine Die Cut 11.3 on 3 Sides

2002(?) Self-Adhesive Photo.

3634f A2812 37c pane of 10, P#V1111 10.00

No. 3634f is a complete booklet (BC180). The peelable backing serves as a booklet cover.

3635a — A2812

3635a — BC181

2002

$7.40 fold-it-yourself booklet contains 20 self-adhesive 37c stamps

Serpentine Die Cut 11¼ on 2, 3 or 4 Sides

2002, June 7 Self-Adhesive Litho.

3635a A2812 37c pane of 20, P#B1111, B2222, B3333, B4444, B5555, B6666, B7777 15.00

No. 3635a is a complete booklet (BC181). The peelable backing serves as a booklet cover.

3636a, 3636b — A2812

Serpentine Die Cut 10½x10¾ on 2 or 3 Sides

2002, June 7 Self-Adhesive Photo.

3636a A2812 37c pane of 4, no P# 3.00
3636b A2812 37c pane of 6 4.50

3636a, 3636b — BC182

2002

$7.40 fold-it-yourself booklet contains 20 self-adhesive 37c stamps

COMBINATION BOOKLET

BK291B BC182 $7.40 **multi,** 2 each #3636a, 3636b, P#S11111 15.00

Plate number on No. BK291B is on the backing paper of the lower example of No. 3636b.

3636c, BC183 — A2812

Serpentine Die Cut 10½x10¾ on 2 or 3 Sides

2002, June 7 Self-Adhesive Photo.

3636c A2812 37c pane of 20, P#S1111, S2222, S3333, S4444, S5555, S6666 15.00

No. 3636c is a complete booklet with 12 stamps plus P# on one side and eight stamps plus booklet cover (BC183) on the other side. The peelable backing serves as a booklet cover.

Variety

3636f As "c," 11 stamps and part of 12th stamp on reverse printed on backing liner, the 8 stamps on front side imperf —

Serpentine Die Cut 11¼x11 on 2 or 3 Sides

2004, July Self-Adhesive Photo.

3636De A2812 37c pane of 20, P#V1111, V1112, V2222 25.00

No. 3636De is a complete booklet with 12 stamps plus P# on one side and eight stamps plus booklet cover (BC183) on the other side. The peelable backing serves as a booklet cover.

3637a — A2812

3637a—BC184

2003

$6.66 fold-it-yourself booklet contains 18 self-adhesive 37c stamps

Serpentine Die Cut 8 on 2, 3 or 4 Sides

2003, Feb. 4 Self-Adhesive Photo.

3637a A2812 37c pane of 18, #V1111 13.50

No. 3637a is a complete booklet (BC184). The peelable backing serves as a booklet cover.

3645b, 3645c, 3645d — A2813-A2816

Serpentine Die Cut 11 on 2 or 3 Sides

2002, July 26 Self-Adhesive Photo.

3645b A2813 37c pane of 4, #3642-3645, no P# 3.00
3645c A2813 37c pane of 6, #3643, 3645, 2 each #3642, 3644, no P# 4.50
3645d A2813 37c pane of 6, #3642, 3644, 2 each #3643, 3645, P#V1111 4.50

3645b, 3645c, 3645d — BC185

2002

$7.40 booklet contains 20 self-adhesive 37c stamps

COMBINATION BOOKLET

BK292 BC185 $7.40 **multi,** #3645c-3645d, 2 #3645b, P#V1111 15.00

Plate number on No. BK292 is on the backing paper of No. 3645d.

3645e — A2813-A2816

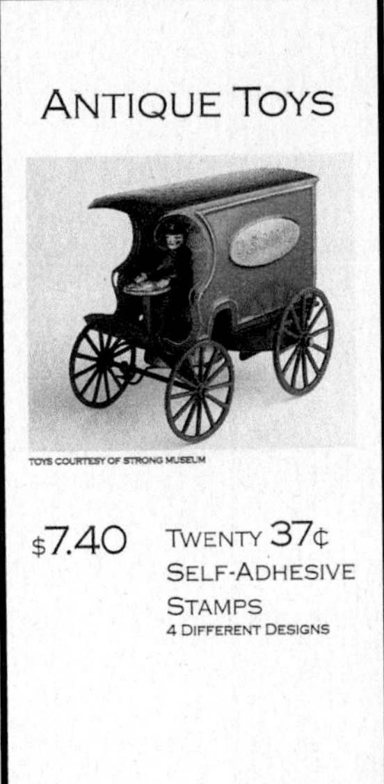

3645e — BC186

2002

$7.40 fold-it-yourself booklet contains 20 self-adhesive 37c stamps

Serpentine Die Cut 11 on 2, 3 or 4 Sides

3645e A2813 37c pane of 20, 5 each #3642-3645, P#V1111, V1112, V2221, V2222 15.00

No. 3645e is a complete booklet (BC186). The peelable backing serves as a booklet cover.

3645h, BC179A — A2813-A2816

Serpentine Die Cut 11x11¼ on 2 or 3 Sides

2003, Sept. 3 **Self-Adhesive** **Photo.**

3645h A2813 37c pane of 20, P#V1111, V1112, V2221, V2222 15.00

No. 3645h is a complete double-sided booklet. Eight stamps and the booklet cover (BC179A) are printed on one side of the peelable backing paper, and 12 stamps plus P# appear on the other side of the backing paper.

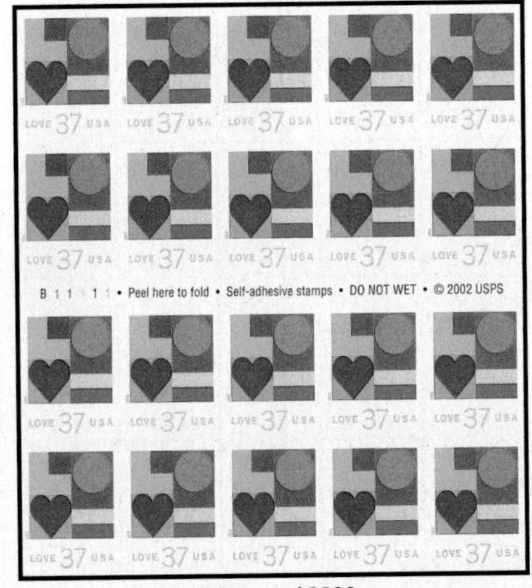

3657a — A2828

3657a — BC187

2002

$7.40 fold-it-yourself booklet contains 20 self-adhesive 37c stamps

Serpentine Die Cut 11 on 2, 3 or 4 Sides

2002, Aug. 16 **Self-Adhesive** **Litho.**

3657a A2828 37c pane of 20, P#B11111, B22222, B33333, B44444, B55555, B66666, B77777 15.00

No. 3657a is a complete booklet (BC187). The peelable backing serves as a booklet cover.

Variety

3657b As "a," silver ("Love 37 USA") missing on top five stamps (CM) *750.00*

3675a — A2843

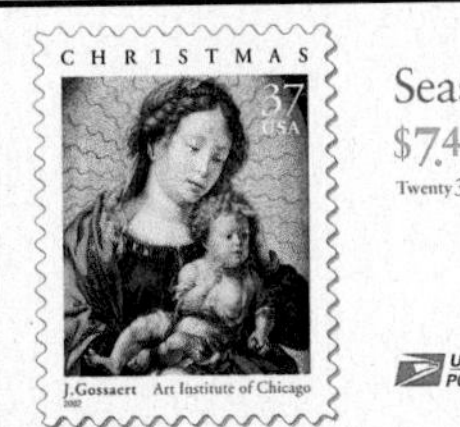

3675a — BC188

2002

$7.40 fold-it-yourself booklet contains 20 self-adhesive 37c stamps

Serpentine Die Cut 11x11¼ on 2, 3 or 4 Sides

2002, Oct. 10 **Self-Adhesive**

3675a A2843 37c pane of 20, P#B1111, B2222 15.00

No. 3675a is a complete booklet (BC188). The peelable backing serves as a booklet cover.

3687b, BC189 — A2844-A2847

Serpentine Die Cut 10¾ on 2 or 3 Sides

2002, Oct. 28 **Self-Adhesive**

3687b A2844 37c Pane of 20, P#S1111, S1113, S2222, S4444 25.00

No. 3687b is a complete booklet with 12 stamps plus P# on one side and eight stamps plus booklet cover (BC189) on the other side. The peelable backing serves as a booklet cover.

3691b, 3691c, 3691d — A2848-A2851

Serpentine Die Cut 11 on 2 or 3 Sides

3691b A2848 37c Pane of 4, #3688-3691 4.60
3691c A2848 37c Pane of 6, #3690-3691, 2 each #3688-3689, no P# 7.00
3691d A2848 37c Pane of 6, #3688-3689, 2 each #3690-3691 7.00

3691b, 3691c, 3691d — BC190

2002

$7.40 booklet contains 20 self-adhesive 37c stamps

COMBINATION BOOKLET

BK293 BC190 $7.40 **multi,** #3691c, 3691d, 2 #3691b, P#V1111 23.00

Plate number on No. BK293 is on the backing paper of the upper example of No. 3691b.

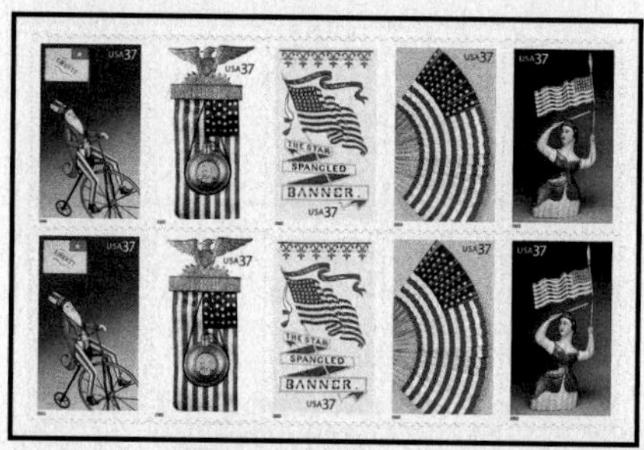

3780b — A2883-A2887

Backing 1

Backing 2

2003, Apr. 3 Litho. ***Serpentine Die Cut 10x9¾***

Self-Adhesive

3780b A2883 37c Pane of 2 #3780a with backing 1 7.50
With backing 2 7.50

3780b — BC191

2003

$7.40 booklet contains 20 self-adhesive stamps

Booklet

BK294 BC191 $7.40 **multi,** no P# 15.00

No. BK294 contains one No. 3780b with backing 1 and one No. 3780b with backing 2.

3807b, BC193 — A2902-A2905

Serpentine Die Cut 10¾ on 2 or 3 Sides

2003, Aug. 7 Self-Adhesive Photo.

3807b A2902 37c pane of 20, 5 #3807a, P#S11111 15.00

No. 3807b is a complete double-sided booklet. Eight stamps and the booklet cover (BC193) are printed on one side of the peelable backing paper and 12 stamps plus P# are printed on the other side of the backing paper.

3820a, BC194 — A2843

Serpentine Die Cut 11x11¼ on 2 or 3 Sides

2003, Oct. 23 Self-Adhesive

Size: 28x19½mm

3820a A2843 37c pane of 20, P#P1111, P2222, P3333, P4444 15.00

No. 3820a is a complete double-sided booklet. Eight stamps, P# and the booklet cover (BC194) are printed on one side of the peelable backing paper, and 12 stamps plus P# are printed on the other side of the backing paper.

On one version of this pane (shown), an incorrect bar code was printed over with white ink, mostly covering the incorrect code, and the correct bar code was then added. This version is much scarcer; value $30.

3824b, BC195 — A2917-A2920

Serpentine Die Cut 11¾x11 on 2 or 3 Sides

2003, Oct. 23 Self-Adhesive

3824b A2917 37c Pane of 20, 5 each #3821-3824, P#S1111, S2222 20.00

No. 3824b is a complete double-sided booklet. Eight stamps plus P# and the booklet cover (BC195) are printed on one side of the peelable backing paper, and 12 stamps plus P# are printed on the other side of the backing paper.

3828b, 3828c, 3828d — A2921-A2924

Serpentine Die Cut 10½x10¾ on 2 or 3 Sides

3828b A2921 37c Pane of 4, #3825-3828, no P# 4.00

3828c A2921 37c Pane of 6, #3827-3828, 2 each #3825-3828, no P# 6.00

3828d A2921 37c Pane of 6, #3825-3826, 2 each #3827-3828, P#S111111 6.00

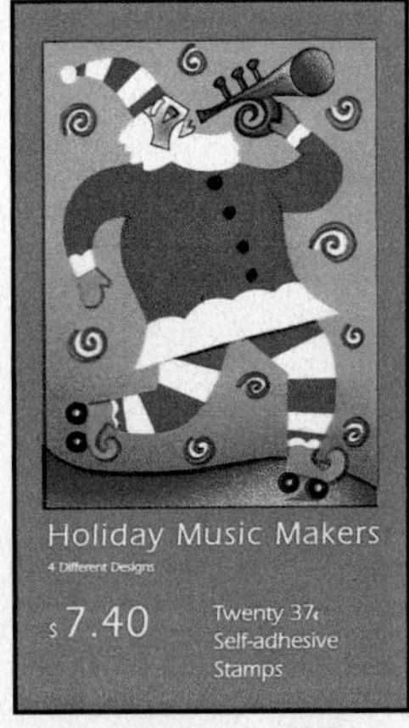

3828b, 3828c, 3828d — BC196

2003

$7.40 booklet contains 20 self-adhesive 37c stamps

COMBINATION BOOKLET

BK296 BC196 $7.40 **multi,** #3828c, 3828d, 2 each #3828b, P#S11111 21.00

Plate number on No. BK296 is printed on the backing paper of No. 3828d.

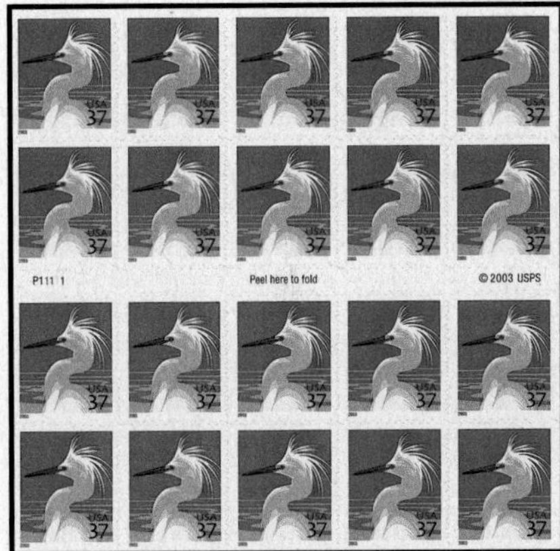

3830a — A2925

3830a — BC197

2004

$7.40 fold-it-yourself booklet contains 20 self-adhesive 37c stamps

Serpentine Die Cut 11½x11 on 2, 3 or 4 Sides

2004, Jan. 30 Self-Adhesive Litho.

3830a A2925 37c pane of 20, P#P11111, P22222 15.00

No. 3830a is a complete booklet (BC197). The peelable backing serves as a booklet cover.

Variety

3830b As "a," die cutting omitted —

Serpentine Die Cut 11½x11 on 2, 3 or 4 Sides

2005? Self-Adhesive Photo.

With "USPS" Microprinted on Bird's Breast

3830De A2925 37c pane of 20, P#P33333, P44444 *110.00*
P#P55555 —

No. 3830De is a complete booklet (BC197). The peelable backing serves as a booklet cover.

Variety

3830Dg As "e," die cutting omitted *1,200.*

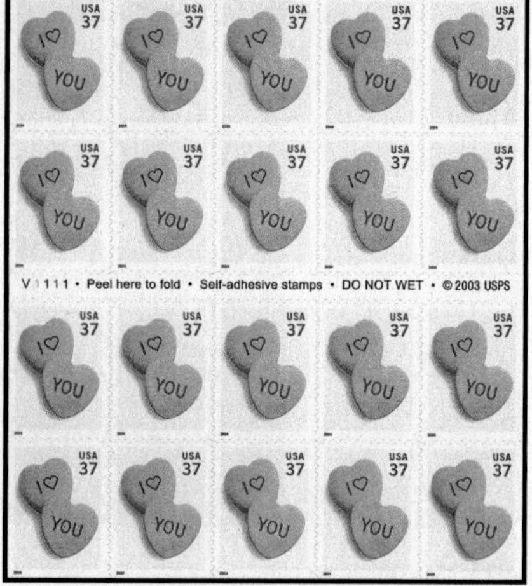

3833a — A2928

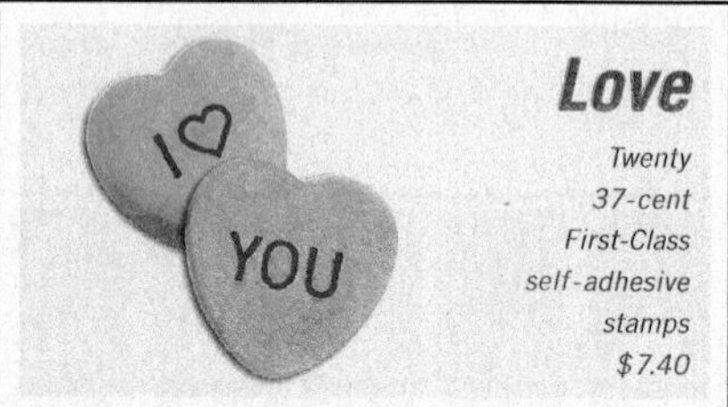

3833a — BC198

2004

$7.40 fold-it-yourself booklet contains 20 self-adhesive 37c stamps

Serpentine Die Cut 10¾ on 2, 3 or 4 Sides

2004, Jan. 14 Self-Adhesive Photo.

3833a A2928 37c pane of 20, P#V1111 15.00

No. 3833a is a complete booklet (BC198). The peelable backing serves as a booklet cover.

3836a — A2931

3836a — BC199

2004

$7.40 booklet contains 20 self-adhesive stamps

Serpentine Die Cut 10¾ on 2, 3 or 4 Sides

2004, Mar. 4 Self-Adhesive Litho.

3836a A2931 37c pane of 20, P#P11111, P22222, P33333, P44444, P55555, P66666, P77777, P88888 15.00

No. 3836a is a complete booklet (BC199). The peelable backing serves as a booklet cover.

3856b — A2940-A2941

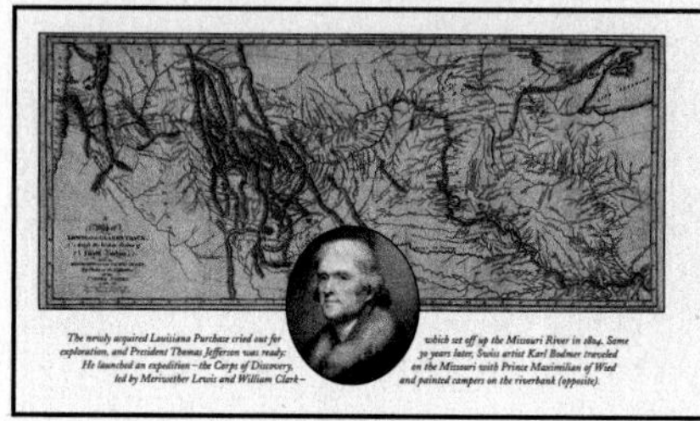

Backing 1

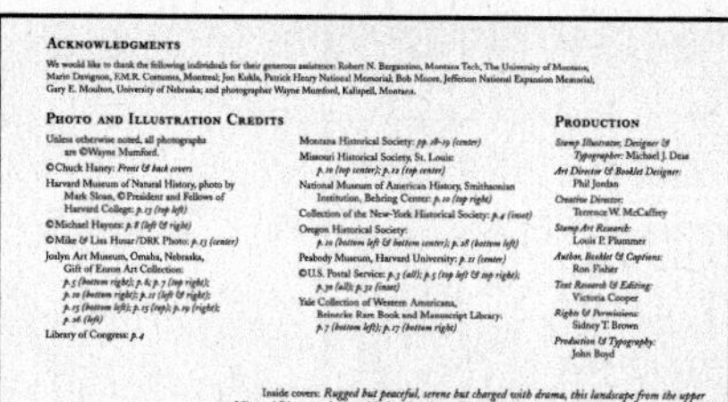

Backing 2

Serpentine Die Cut 10½x10¾

2004, May 14 Self-Adhesive Litho. & Engr.

3856b A2940 37c Pane, 5 each #3855-3856 with backing 1 9.00

With backing 2 9.00

3856b — BC200

2004

$8.95 booklet contains 20 self-adhesive stamps

Booklet

BK297 BC200 $8.95 **multi,** no P# 18.00

No. BK297 contains one No. 3856b with backing 1 and one No. 3856b with backing 2.

3872a, BC201 — A2956

Serpentine Die Cut 10¾ on 2 or 3 Sides

2004, Aug. 12 Self-Adhesive Photo.

3872a A2956 37c pane of 20, P#S1111 15.00

No. 3872a is a complete booklet with 12 stamps plus P# on one side and eight stamps plus booklet cover (BC201) on the other side. The peelable backing serves as a booklet cover.

Variety

3872b Die cutting omitted, pair, in #3872a with foldover —

3879a, BC202 — A2961

Serpentine Die Cut 10¾x11 on 2 or 3 Sides

2004, Oct. 14 Self-Adhesive Litho.

3879a A2961 37c pane of 20, P#P1111 15.00

No. 3879a is a complete booklet with 12 stamps plus P# on one side and eight stamps plus P# and a label that serves as a booklet cover (BC202) on the other side.

Variety

3879b As "a," die cutting omitted —

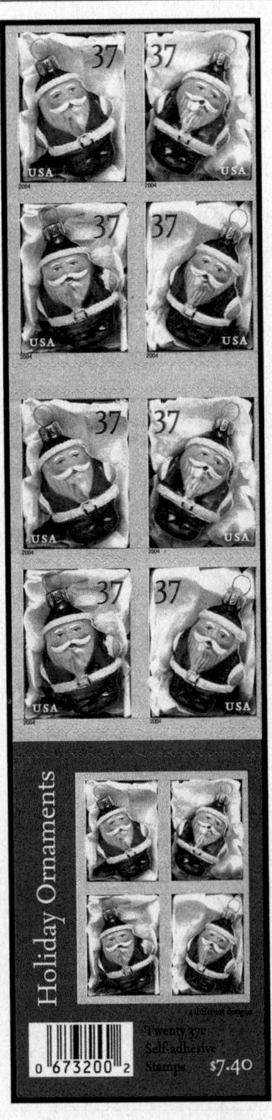

3886b, BC203
—A2965-A2968

Serpentine Die Cut 11½x11 on 2 or 3 Sides

2004, Nov. 16 Self-Adhesive Photo.

3886b A2965 37c pane of 20, 5 #3886a, P#S1111, S2222 20.00

No. 3886b is a complete double-sided booklet. Eight stamps and the booklet cover (BC203) are on one side of the peelable backing paper and 12 stamps plus P# are on the other side of the backing paper.

3890b, 3890c, 3890d
— A2969-A2972

Serpentine Die Cut 10½x10¾ on 2 or 3 Sides

3890b A2969 37c pane of 4 #3887-3890, no P# 3.60
3890c A2969 37c pane of 6 #3889-3890, 2 each #3887-3888, no P# 5.50
3890d A2969 37c pane of 6 #3887-3888, 2 each #3889-3890, P#S11111 5.50

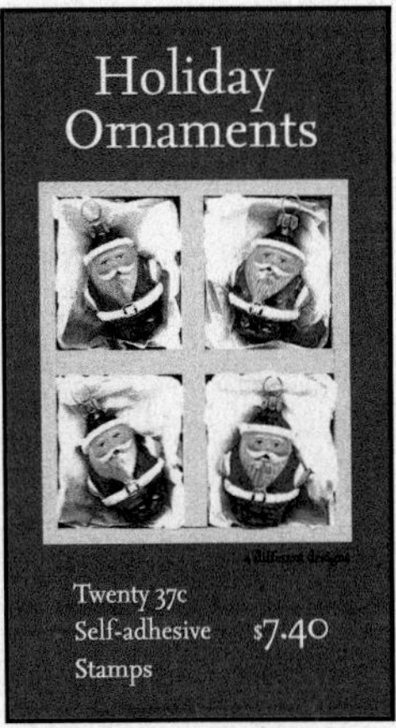

3890b, 3890c,
3890d — BC204

2004

$7.40 booklet contains 20 self-adhesive 37c stamps

COMBINATION BOOKLET

BK298 BC204 $7.40 **multi,** #3890c, 3890d, 2 #3890b, P#S11111 20.00

Plate number on No. BK298 is printed on the backing paper of No. 3890d.

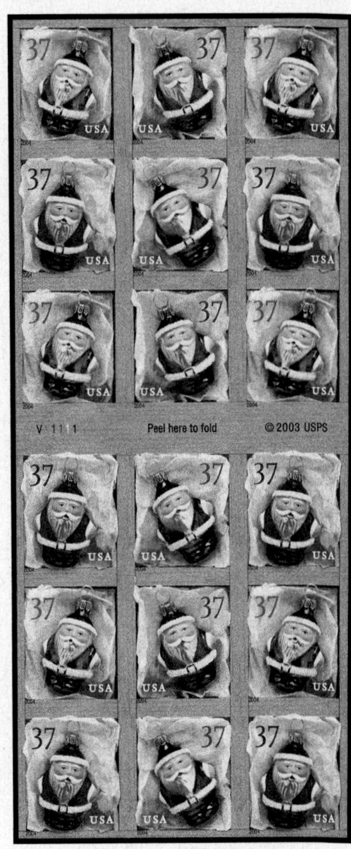

3894b — A2969-A2972

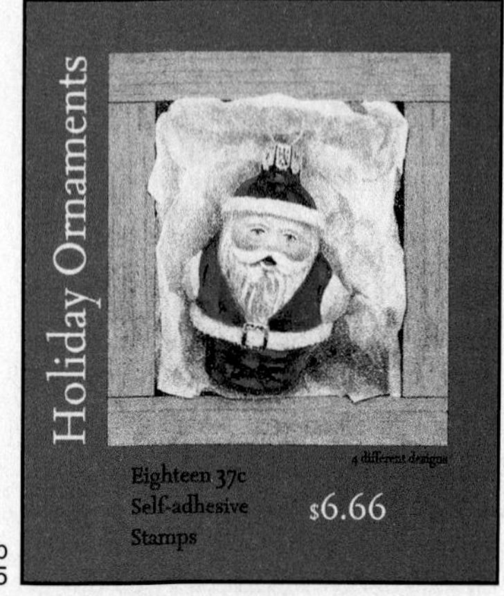

3894b
BC205

2004

$6.66 fold-it-yourself booklet contains 18 self-adhesive 37c stamps

Serpentine Die Cut 8 on 2, 3 or 4 Sides

3894b A2969 37c pane of 18, 6 each #3891, 3893, 3 each #3892, 3894, P#V11111 36.00

No. 3894b is a complete booklet (BC205). The peelable backing serves as a booklet cover.

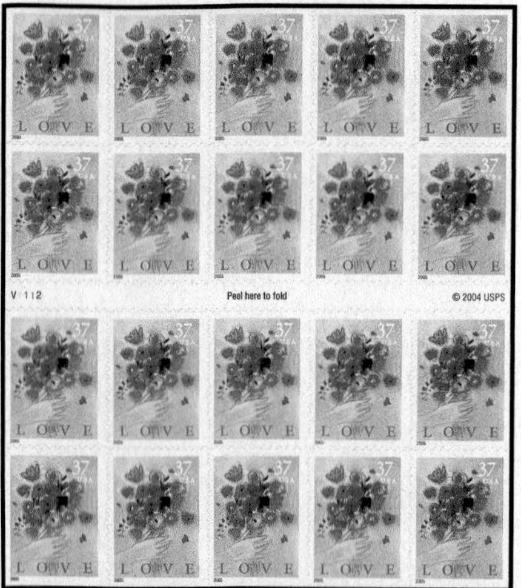

3898a — A2975

3898a — BC206

2005

$7.40 booklet contains 20 self-adhesive stamps

Serpentine Die Cut 10¾x11 on 2, 3 or 4 Sides

2005, Feb. 18 Self-Adhesive Photo.

3898a A2975 37c pane of 20, #V1111, V1112 15.00

No. 3898a is a complete booklet (BC206). The peelable backing serves as a booklet cover.

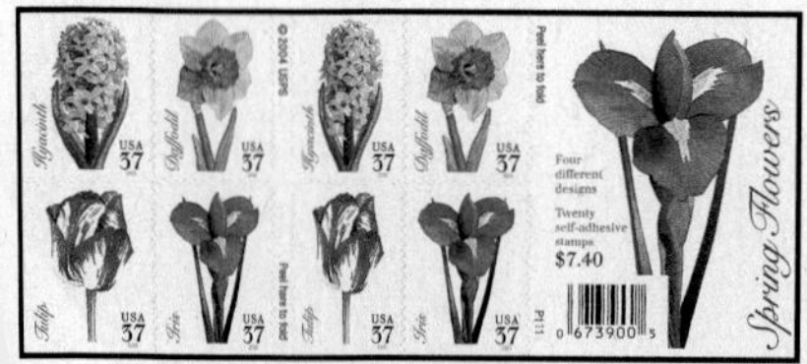

3903b, BC207 — A2977-A2980

Serpentine Die Cut 10¾ on 2 or 3 Sides

2005, Mar. 15 Self-Adhesive Litho.

3903b A2977 37c pane of 20, P#P1111 17.00
P#P2222 20.00

Variety

3903c As "b," die cutting omitted on side with eight stamps —

No. 3903b is a complete booklet with 12 stamps plus P# on one side and eight stamps plus P# and a label that serves as a booklet cover (BC207) on the other side.

3929b, BC208 — A3003-A3006

Serpentine Die Cut 10¾ on 2 or 3 Sides

2005, July 30 Self-Adhesive Litho.

3929b A3003 37c pane of 20, P#P1111 15.00

No. 3929b is a complete booklet with 12 stamps plus two P# on one side and eight stamps plus a label that serves as a booklet cover (BC208) on the other side.

3935b, BC209 — A3008-A3012

Serpentine Die Cut 10¾ on 2 or 3 Sides

2005, Aug. 20 Self-Adhesive Litho.

3935b A3008 37c pane of 20, P#P1111 32.00

No. 3935b is a complete booklet with 12 stamps (2 each #3931, 3933, 3935, and 3 each #3932, 3934) plus P# on one side and eight stamps (1 each #3932, 3934, and 2 each #3931, 3933, 3935) plus a label that serves as the booklet cover (BC209) on the other side.

3956b, BC210 — A3026-A3029

Serpentine Die Cut 10¾x11 on 2 or 3 Sides

2005, Oct. 20 Self-Adhesive Photo.

3956b A3026 37c pane of 20 #3956a, P#S1111 20.00

No. 3956b is a complete double-sided booklet. Eight stamps and the booklet cover (BC210) are on one side of the peelable backing paper and 12 stamps plus P# are on the other side of the backing.

3960b, 3960c, 3960d — A3030-A3033

Serpentine Die Cut 10½x10¾ on 2 or 3 Sides

3960b A3030 37c pane of 4 #3957-3960 4.50

3960c A3030 37c pane of 6 #3959-3960, 2 each #3957-3958, no P# 7.00

3960d A3030 37c pane of 6 #3957-3958, 2 each #3959-3960, no P# 7.00

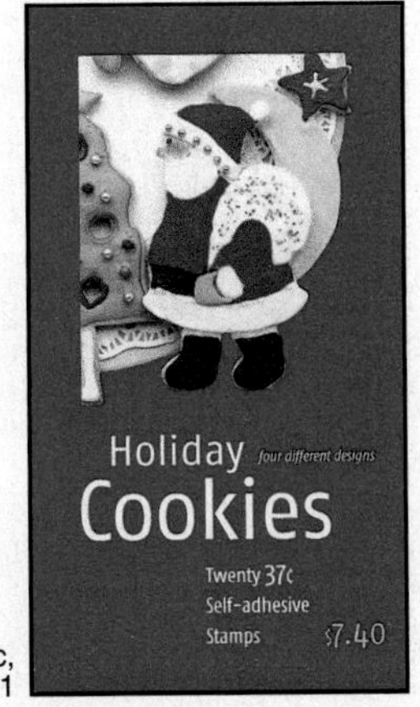

3960b, 3960c, 3960d — BC211

2005

$7.40 booklet contains 20 self-adhesive 37c stamps

COMBINATION BOOKLET

BK299 BC211 $7.40 **multi,** #3960c, 3960d, 2 #3960b, P#S1111 23.00

Plate number on No. BK299 is printed on the backing paper of the lower example of No. 3960b.

3966a, 3972a, 3973a, BC212 — A3038

Serpentine Die Cut 11¼x10¾ on 2 or 3 Sides

2005, Dec. 8 **Self-Adhesive** **Litho.**

3966a A3038 (39c) pane of 20, P#P1111 22.00

Variety

3966b As "a," die cutting omitted —

Photo.

Serpentine Die Cut 11¼x10¾ on 2 or 3 Sides

3972a A3038 (39c) pane of 20, P#V1111 22.00

Serpentine Die Cut 10½x10¾ on 2 or 3 Sides

3973a A3038 (39c) pane of 20, P#S1111 22.00

Nos. 3966a, 3972a and 3973a are complete double-sided booklets. Eight stamps and the booklet cover (BC212) are on one side of the peelable backing paper and 12 stamps plus P# are on the other side of the backing paper. On No. 3966a, the stamps on one side are upside-down with relation to the stamps on the other side. On Nos. 3972a and 3973a the stamps are all aligned the same on both sides.

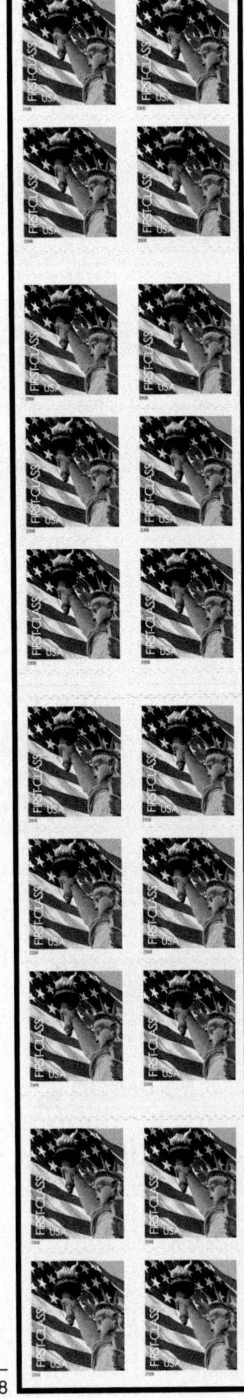

3974a, 3974b — A3038

Serpentine Die Cut 11¼x11 on 2 or 3 Sides

Litho.

3974a A3038 (39c) pane of 4 4.40
3974b A3038 (39c) pane of 6, no P# 6.60

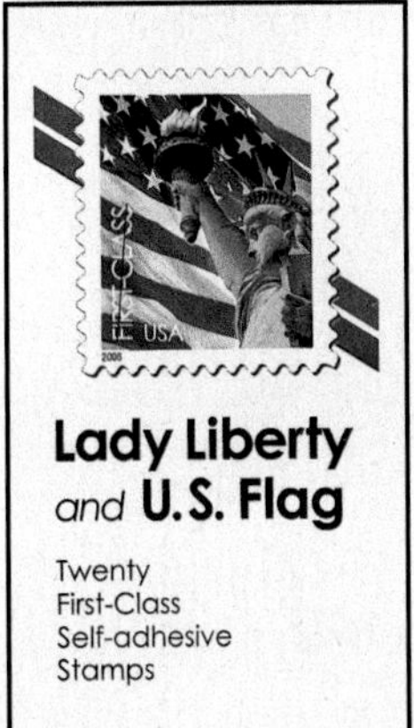

Lady Liberty
and U.S. Flag
Twenty
First-Class
Self-adhesive
Stamps

3974a, 3974b — BC213

2005

($7.80) booklet contains 20 self-adhesive (39c) stamps

COMBINATION BOOKLET

BK300 BC213 ($7.80) **multi,** 2 each #3974a, 3974b, P#S1111 22.00

Plate number on No. BK300 is printed on the backing paper of the upper example of No. 3974a.

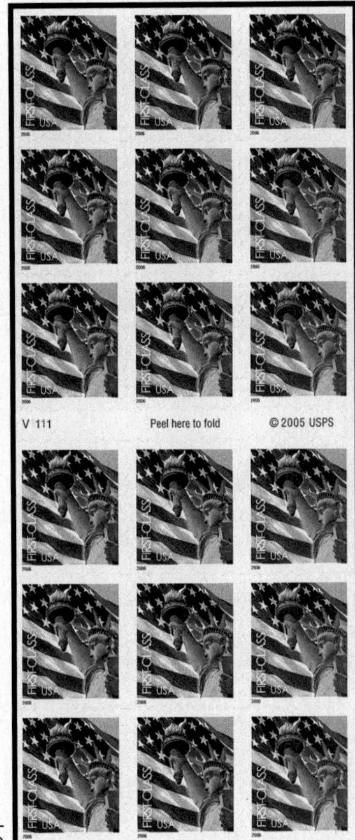

3975a — A3038

3975a
BC214

2005

($7.02) fold-it-yourself booklet contains 18 self-adhesive (39c) stamps

Serpentine Die Cut 8 on 2, 3 or 4 Sides

Photo.

3975a A3038 (39c) pane of 18, P#V1111 20.00

No. 3975a is a complete booklet (BC214). The peelable backing serves as a booklet cover.

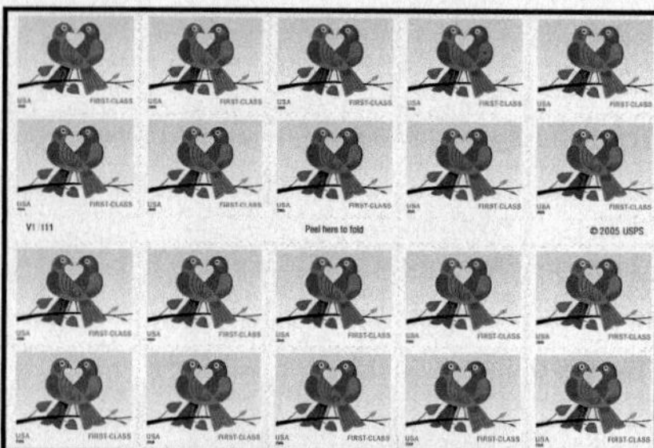

3976a — A3039

3976a — BC215

2006

($7.80) fold-it-yourself booklet contains 20 self-adhesive (39c) stamps

Serpentine Die Cut 11 on 2, 3 or 4 Sides

2006, Jan. 3 Self-Adhesive Photo.

3976a A3039 (39c) pane of 20, P#V11111 22.00

No. 3976a is a complete booklet (BC215). The peelable backing serves as a booklet cover.

3978a — A3040

Lady Liberty
and U.S. Flag
Ten 39¢
Self-adhesive
Stamps
$3.90

3978a — BC216

2006

$3.90 fold-it-yourself booklet contains 10 self-adhesive 39c stamps

Serpentine Die Cut 11¼x10¾ on 3 Sides

2006, Apr. 8 Self-Adhesive Litho.

3978a A3040 39c pane of 10, P#P1111, P2222 8.50

No. 3978a is a complete booklet (BC216). The peelable backing serves as a booklet cover.

3978b, 3985a, BC217 — A3040

Serpentine Die Cut 11¼x10¾ on 2 or 3 Sides

2006, Apr. 8 Self-Adhesive Litho.

3978b A3040 39c pane of 20, P#P1111 17.00

Variety

3978c As "b," die cutting omitted on the side with eight stamps —

No. 3978b is a complete booklet with 12 stamps plus P# on one side and eight stamps plus a label that serves as the booklet cover (BC217) on the other side.

Flag and Statue of Liberty (No. 3978b) Type of 2006

Serpentine Die Cut 11¼x10¾ on 2 or 3 Sides

2006, Apr. 8 Self-Adhesive Photo.

Without Microprinting

3985a A3040 39c pane of 20, #V1111 16.00

No. 3985a is a complete booklet with 12 stamps plus P# on one side and eight stamps plus a label that serves as the booklet cover (BC217) on the other side. The fonts of the UPC code on the booklet cover for No. 3985a differ from those used on No. 3978b.

3985c, 3985d — A3040

Serpentine Die Cut 11.1 on 2 or 3 Sides

2006, Nov. 8 **Self-Adhesive** **Photo.**

3985c A3040 39c pane of 4 3.20
3985d A3040 39c pane of 6, no P# 4.80

3985c, 3985d — BC216A

2006

$7.80 fold-it-yourself booklet contains 20 self-adhesive 39c stamps

COMBINATION BOOKLET

BK300A BC216A $7.80 **multi,** 2 each #3985c, 3985d P#V11111 16.00

Plate number on No. BK300A is printed on the backing paper of the lower example of No. 3985c.

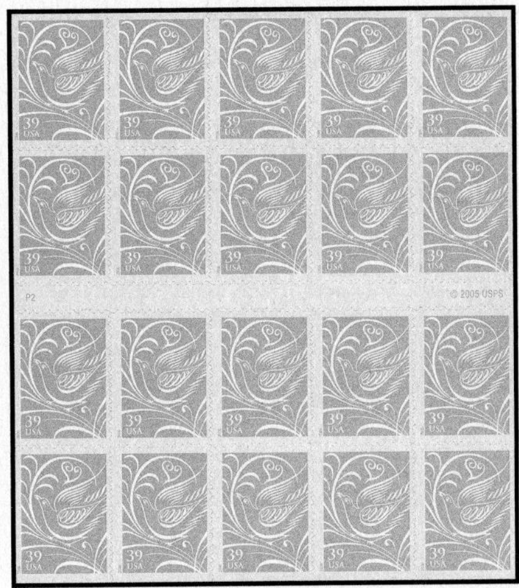

3998a — A3051

3998a — BC218

2006

$7.80 booklet contains 20 self-adhesive 39c stamps

Serpentine Die Cut 10¾x11 on 2, 3 or 4 Sides

2006, Mar. 1 **Self-Adhesive** **Litho.**

3998a A3051 39c pane of 20, #P1, P2 16.00

Variety

3998b As "a," die cutting omitted —

No. 3998a is a complete booklet (BC218). The peelable backing serves as a booklet cover.

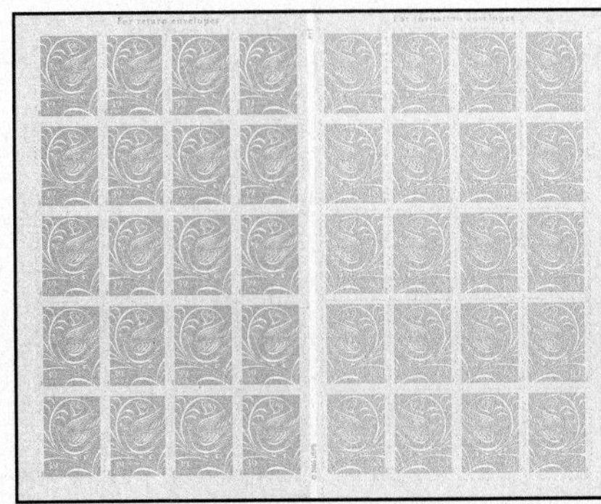

3999a — A3051-A3052

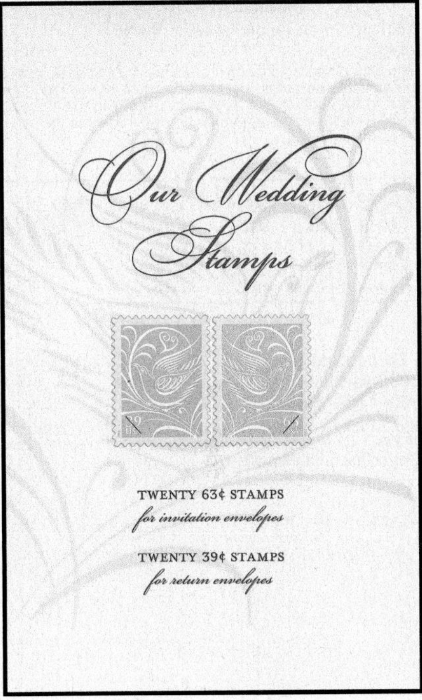

3999a — BC219

2006

$20.40 booklet contains 20 self-adhesive 39c stamps and 20 self-adhesive 63c stamps

Serpentine Die Cut 10¾x11

3999a Pane of 40 (20 each #3998-3999), #P11 45.00

No. 3999a is a complete booklet (BC219). The peelable backing serves as a booklet cover.

4001b — A3053

4001b — BC220

2006

$2.40 fold-it-yourself booklet contains 10 self-adhesive 24c stamps

Serpentine Die Cut 10¾x11¼

2006, Mar. 8 Self-Adhesive Photo.

4001b A3053 24c pane of 10 #4001a, P#V1111 5.00

No. 4001b is a complete booklet (BC220). The peelable backing paper serves as a booklet cover. No. 4001b was sold flat. It has a self-adhesive panel that covers the rouletting on the inside of the booklet cover that is not found in BK301. Three large cuts of rouletting separate the two halves of the booklet cover on No. 4001b.

4001c, 4001d — A3053

4001c A3053 24c pane of 4 #4001a, P#V1111 2.00
4001d A3053 24c pane of 6 #4001a, no P# 3.00

COMBINATION BOOKLET

BK301 BC220 $2.40 **multi,** #4001c, 4001d, P#V1111 5.00

No. BK301 was sold glued shut. When the booklet is opened, the self-adhesive panel found on the right side of No. 4001d sticks to the left side of 4001c, as shown in the illustration above. Fine rouletting separates the two halves of the booklet cover on No. BK301.

4012b, BC221 — A3054-A3058

Serpentine Die Cut 10¾x10½ on 2 or 3 Sides

2006, Mar. 16 Self-Adhesive Photo.

4012b A3054 39c pane of 20, P#S1111 25.00

No. 4012b is a complete booklet with 12 stamps plus P# on one side and eight stamps plus a label that serves as a booklet cover (BC221) on the other side.

4016a, 4017b, 4017c, 4017d — A3054-A3058

Serpentine Die Cut 10¾x11¼ on 2 or 3 Sides

Litho.

4016a A3054 39c pane of 4, #4013-4016, no P# 6.00
4017b A3054 39c pane of 4, #4013-4015, 4017, no P# 6.00
4017c A3054 39c pane of 6, #4013-4016, 2 #4017, no P# 9.00
4017d A3054 39c pane of 6, #4013-4015, 4017, 2 #4016, no P# 9.00

4016a, 4017b, 4017c, 4017d — BC222

2006

$7.80 booklet contains 20 self-adhesive 39c stamps

COMBINATION BOOKLET

BK302 BC222 $7.80 **multi,** #4016a, 4017b, 4017c, 4017d, no P# 30.00

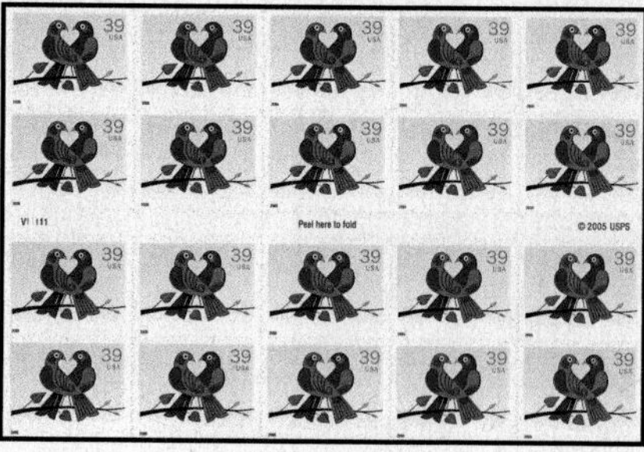

4029a — A3070

4029a — BC223

2006

$7.80 fold-it-yourself booklet contains 20 self-adhesive 39c stamps

Serpentine Die Cut 11 on 2, 3 or 4 Sides

2006, May 1 Self-Adhesive Photo.

4029a A3070 39c pane of 20, P#V11111 19.00

No. 4029a is a complete booklet (BC223). The peelable backing serves as a booklet cover.

4098b, BC224 — A3127-A3136

Serpentine Die Cut 10¾ on 2 or 3 Sides

2006, Aug. 24 Self-Adhesive Photo.

4098b A3127 39c pane of 20, P#S11111 22.50

No. 4098b is a complete booklet with 12 stamps (1 each #4090-4093, 4095-4098, and 2 each #4089, 4094) plus P# on one side and eight stamps (1 each #4090-4093, 4095-4098) plus a label that serves as the booklet cover (BC224) on the other side.

4100a, BC225 — A3138

Serpentine Die Cut 10¾x11 on 2 or 3 Sides

2006 **Self-Adhesive** **Litho.**

4100a A3138 39c pane of 20, P#P1111, *Oct. 17* 16.00

No. 4100a is a complete double-sided booklet with 12 stamps plus P# on one side of the peelable backing and eight stamps plus P# and the label that serves as a booklet cover (BC225) on the other side of the backing.

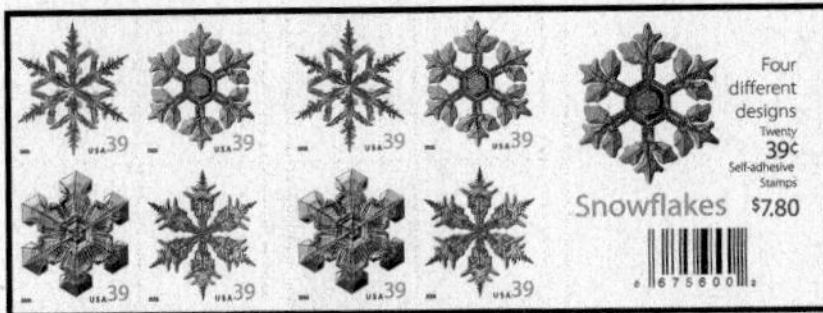

4108b, BC226 — A3139-A3142

Serpentine Die Cut 11¼x11½ on 2 or 3 Sides

4108b A3139 39c pane of 20, P#S1111, *Oct. 5* 18.00

No. 4108b is a complete double-sided booklet. Eight stamps and the label that serves as a booklet cover (BC226) are on one side of the peelable backing and 12 stamps plus P# are on the other side of the backing.

4112b, 4112c, 4112d — A3139-A3142

Serpentine Die Cut 11¼x10¾ on 2 or 3 Sides

4112b A3139 39c pane of 4, #4109-4112*Oct. 5* 4.00
4112c A3139 39c pane of 6, #4111-4112, 2 each #4109-4110, no P#, *Oct. 5* 6.00
4112d A3139 39c pane of 6, #4109-4110, 2 each #4111-4112, *Oct. 5* 6.00

Four different designs
Snowflakes
Twenty 39¢
Self-adhesive
Stamps
$7.80

4112b, 4112c, 4112d — BC227

2006

$7.80 booklet contains 20 self-adhesive 39c stamps

COMBINATION BOOKLET

BK303 BC227 $7.80 **multi,** #4112c, 4112d, 2 #4112b, P#S1111 20.00

Plate number on No. BK303 is printed on the backing paper of No. 4112d.

4116b — A3139-A3142

4116b BC228

2006

$7.02 fold-it-yourself booklet contains 18 self-adhesive 39c stamps

Serpentine Die Cut 8 on 2, 3 or 4 Sides

Photo.

4116b A3139 39c pane of 18, 4 each #4114, 4116, 5 each #4113, 4115, P#V1111, *Oct. 5* 27.00

No. 4116b is a complete booklet (BC228). The peelable backing serves as a booklet cover.

4122a — A3145

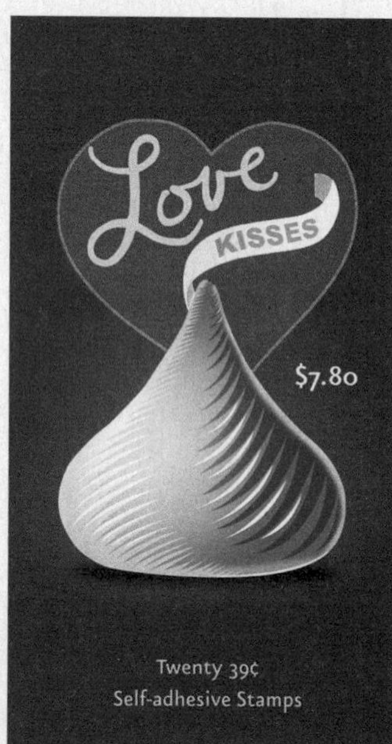

4122a BC229

2007

$7.80 fold-it-yourself booklet contains 20 self-adhesive 39c stamps

Serpentine Die Cut 10¾x11 on 2, 3 or 4 Sides

2007, Jan. 13 Self-Adhesive Photo.

4122a A3145 39c pane of 20 16.00

No. 4122a is a complete booklet (BC229). The peelable backing serves as a booklet cover. The plate number (V1111) is printed on the rear cover of the booklet.

4125a, 4125c, 4126a, 4126c, 4127a, 4127e, 4127j, BC230 — A3148

No. BC230 was printed by three different manufacturers with differences in the fonts used in the UPC code.

Serpentine Die Cut 11¼x10¾ on 2 or 3 Sides

2007, Apr. 12 Self-Adhesive Photo.

Large Microprinting, Bell 16mm Wide

4125a A3148 (41c) pane of 20, "2007" year date, P#V11111 22.00
4125c A3148 (42c) pane of 20 #4125b, "2008" year date, P#V11111 22.00
4125g A3148 (44c) pane of 20 #4125f, "2009" year date, P#V11111 22.00

Litho.

Small Microprinting, Bell 16mm Wide

4126a A3148 (41c) pane of 20, "2007" year date, P#P11111 22.00
4126c A3148 (42c) pane of 20 #4126b, "2008" year date, P#P11111 22.00
4126e A3148 (44c) pane of 20 #4126d, "2009" year date in copper, P#P11111 22.00

Medium Microprinting, Bell 15mm Wide

4127a A3148 (41c) pane of 20, P#S11111, "2007" year date 22.00
4127e A3148 (42c) pane of 20, P#S11111, "2008" year date 22.00
4127j A3148 (44c) pane of 20, P#S11111, "2009" year date in copper 22.00

Varieties

4125d As "c," copper ("FOREVER") omitted *1,000.*
4125e As "c," copper ("FOREVER") omitted on side with 12 stamps, copper splatters on side with 8 stamps —
4126g As "c," die cutting omitted —
4127m As "e," die cutting omitted *600.00*

Nos. 4125a, 4125c, 4125g, 4126a, 4126c, 4126e, 4127a, 4127e, and 4127j are complete double-sided booklets with 12 stamps plus P# on one side of the peelable backing and eight stamps and a label that serves as a booklet cover (BC230) on the other side of the backing. On Nos. 4125c and 4126c, the bar code number found on the booklet cover was changed to "06777005." On Nos. 4125g and 4126e, the bar code number found on the booklet cover was changed to "0678900."

No. 4127a and its varieties exist on two types of surface-tagged paper that exhibit either an uneven or solid appearance, as follows: tagging on No. 4127a appears uneven on both sides (most common), solid on both sides (value, $80), uneven on eight-stamp side and solid on 12-stamp side (extremely scarce); tagging on No. 4127e appears solid on both sides, or solid on eight-stamp side and uneven on 12-stamp side (value, $25); tagging on No. 4127j appears solid.

Issued: Nos. 4125f, 4126e, Aug. 7, 2009.

4127b, 4127c — A3148

Medium Microprinting, Bell 15mm Wide

4127b A3148 (41c) pane of 4 #4127 4.40
4127c A3148 (41c) pane of 6 #4127, no P# 6.60
4127g A3148 (42c) pane of 4 #4127f 4.40
4127h A3148 (42c) pane of 6 #4127f, no P# 6.60

Nos. 4127g and 4127h have a smaller "2008" date. The "2008" date on No. 4127e is the same size as the "2007" date on No. 4127a.

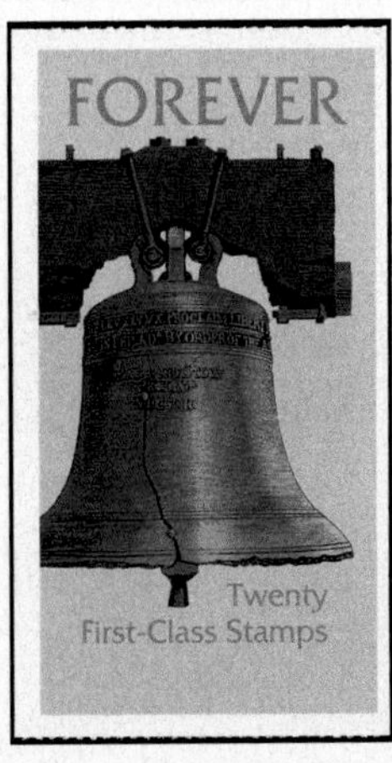

4127b, 4127c, 4127g, 4127h — BC231

2007

$8.20 booklet contains 20 self-adhesive (41c) stamps

COMBINATION BOOKLETS

BK304 BC231 ($8.20) **multi,** 2 each #4127b, 4127c, P#S11111 22.00

BK304a BC231 ($8.40) **multi,** 2 each #4127g, 4127h, P#S11111 22.00

Plate number on No. BK304 is printed on the backing of the lower example of No. 4127b. On No. BK304a, plate number appears on the backing of the lower example of No. 4127g.

Nos. 4127b and 4127c exist with rouletting on backing paper of either gauge 9½ or 13.

4128a — A3148

FOREVER 18 First-Class Stamps

4128a BC232

2007

$7.38 fold-it-yourself booklet contains 18 self-adhesive (41c) stamps

Serpentine Die Cut 8 on 2, 3 or 4 Sides

Large Microprinting, Bell 16mm Wide

Photo.

4128a A3148 (41c) pane of 18, "2007" year date ('07) 20.00

4128c A3148 (42c) pane of 18 #4128b, "2009" year date in black, P#V11111 ('09) 20.00

Nos. 4128a and 4128c are complete booklets (BC232). The peelable backing serves as a booklet cover.

Two versions of No. 4128a exist. The original issue has P#V11 on the backing paper, while a second printing has P#V22222 on the peelable strip on the front.

On No. 4128a, the bar code number on the booklet cover is "0-569900-1." On No. 4128c, the bar code number on the booklet cover was changed to "0-573300-2."

See No. 4437a.

4142a — A3152

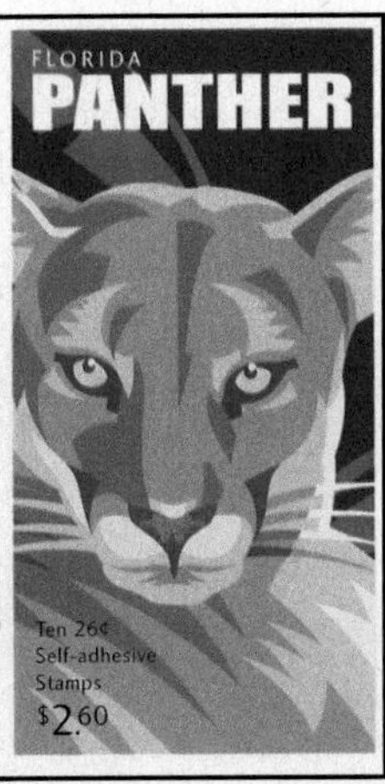

4142a — BC233

2007

$2.60 fold-it-yourself booklet contains 10 self-adhesive 26c stamps

Serpentine Die Cut 11¼x11 on 3 Sides

2007, May 12 **Self-Adhesive** **Photo.**

4142a A3152 26c pane of 10, P#V11111 5.50

No. 4142a is a complete booklet (BC233). The peelable backing serves as a booklet cover.

4151a — A3161

4151a — BC234

2007

$8.20 fold-it-yourself booklet contains 20 self-adhesive 41c stamps

Serpentine Die Cut 10¾ on 2, 3 or 4 Sides

2007, June 27 **Self-Adhesive** **Litho.**

4151a A3161 41c pane of 20 20.00

No. 4151a is a complete booklet (BC234). The peelable backing, which has a plate number (P11111), serves as a booklet cover.

4156d, BC235 — A3163-A3166

Serpentine Die Cut 11 on 2 or 3 Sides

2007, June 29 Self-Adhesive Litho.

4156d A3163 41c pane of 20, 3 each #4153-4156, 2 each #4153a-4156a, P#P1111 17.00

No. 4156d is a complete double-sided booklet with 12 stamps (2 each #4153-4156, 1 each 4153a-4156a) on one side of the peelable backing and eight stamps plus P# and the label that serves as a booklet cover (BC235) on the other side of the backing.

4165a, BC236 — A3173

Serpentine Die Cut 10¾ on 2 or 3 Sides

2007, Aug. 9 Self-Adhesive Litho.

4165a A3173 41c pane of 20, #P11111 17.00

No. 4165a is a complete double-sided booklet with 12 stamps on one side and eight stamps plus P# and a label that serves as the booklet cover (BC236) on the other side.

4185a, BC237 — A3174-A3183

Serpentine Die Cut 11¼x11½ on 2 or 3 Sides

2007, Aug. 10 Self-Adhesive Photo.

4185a 41c pane of 20, 2 each #4176-4185, P#V1111 25.00

Variety

4185b As "a," die cutting missing on Nos. 4178 and 4183 on side with eight stamps (PS) *1,000.*

No. 4185a is a complete double-sided booklet with 12 stamps (2 each #4176-4177, and 1 each #4178-4185) plus P# on one side and eight stamps (#4178-4185) plus a label (BC237) that serves as the booklet cover on the other side.

4190a—A3184

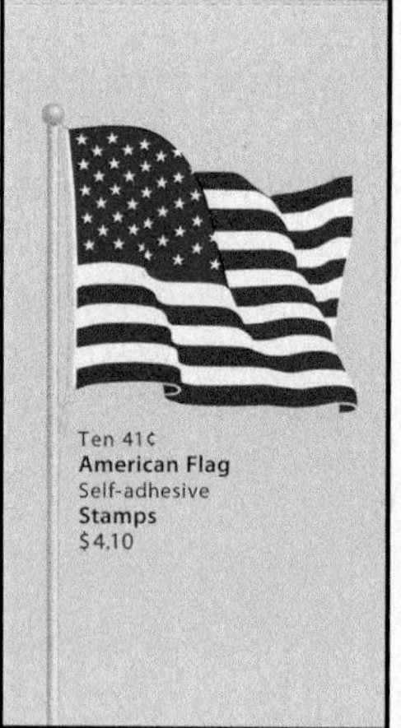

4190a — BC238

2007

$4.10 fold-it-yourself booklet contains 10 self-adhesive 41c stamps

Serpentine Die Cut 11¼x10¾ on 3 Sides

2007, Aug. 15 Self-Adhesive Litho.

With "USPS" Microprinted on Right Side of Flagpole

4190a 41c pane of 10, P#P11111 8.50

By its nature, No. 4190a is a complete booklet (BC238). The peelable backing serves as a booklet cover.

4191a, BC239 — A3184

Serpentine Die Cut 11¼x10¾ on 2 or 3 Sides

With "USPS" Microprinted on Left Side of Flagpole

4191a 41c pane of 20, P#S11111 17.00

No. 4191a is a complete double-sided booklet with 12 stamps plus P# on one side of the peelable backing and eight stamps plus a label (BC239) that serves as the booklet cover on the other side.

4206a, BC240 — A3198

Serpentine Die Cut 10¾x11 on 2 or 3 Sides

2007, Oct. 25 Self-Adhesive Litho.

4206a A3198 41c pane of 20, P#P1111 17.00

No. 4206a is a complete double-sided booklet with 12 stamps on one side of the peelable backing and eight stamps plus P# and the label that serves as a booklet cover (BC240) on the other side of the backing.

4210d, BC241 — A3199-A3202

Serpentine Die Cut 10¾ on 2 or 3 Sides

4210d 41c pane of 20, P#S1111 17.00

No. 4210d is a complete double-sided booklet. Eight stamps (two each #4207-4210) plus P# and the label that serves as a booklet cover (BC241) are on one side of the peelable backing and 12 stamps (three each #4207-4210) are on the other side of the backing.

4214b, 4214c, 4214d — A3203-A3206

Serpentine Die Cut 11¼x11 on 2 or 3 Sides

4214b 41c pane of 4, #4211-4214 5.00
4214c 41c pane of 6, #4213-4214, 2 each #4211-4212, no P# 7.50
4214d 41c pane of 6, #4211-4212, 2 each #42131-4214, no P# 7.50

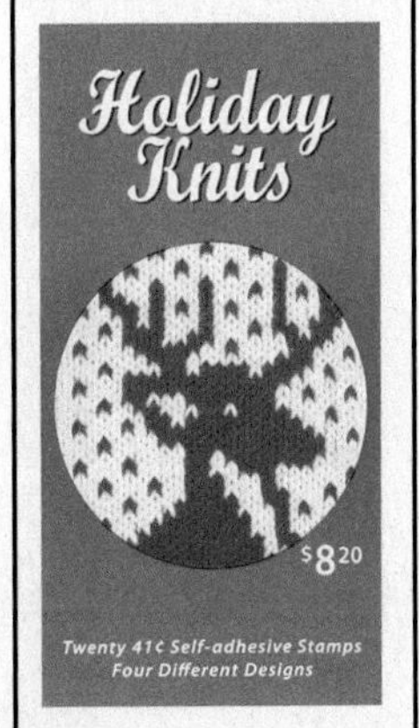

4214b, 4214c, 4214d — BC242

2007

$8.20 booklet contains 20 self-adhesive 41c stamps

COMBINATION BOOKLET

BK305 BC242 $8.20 **multi,** #4214c, 4214d, 2 #4214b, P#S1111 27.50

On No. BK305, plate number appears on the backing of the lower example of No. 4214b.

4218b — A3203-A3206

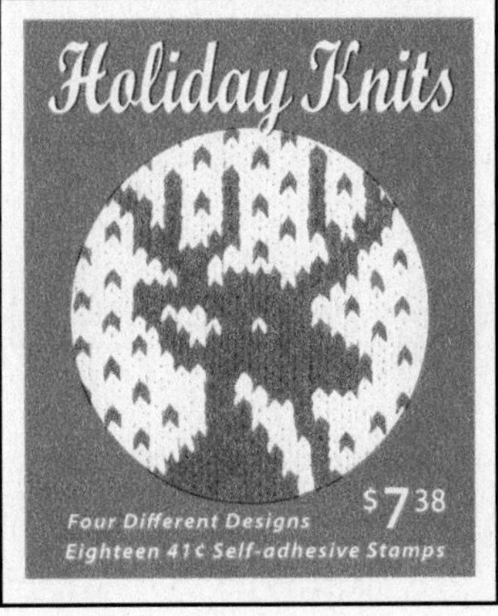

4218b BC243

2007

$7.38 fold-it-yourself booklet contains 18 self-adhesive 41c stamps

Serpentine Die Cut 8 on 2, 3 or 4 Sides

Photo.

4218b 41c pane of 18, 4 each #4215, 4218, 5 each #4216, 4217, P#V1111 27.00

No. 4218b is a complete booklet (BC243). The peelable backing serves as a booklet cover.

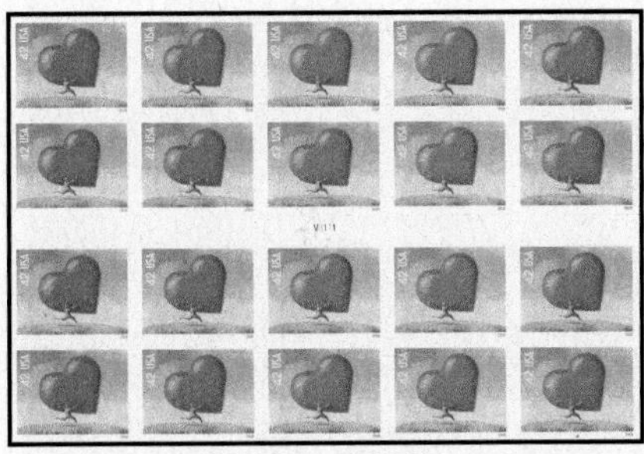

4270a — A3233

4270a — BC244

2008

$8.40 fold-it-yourself booklet contains 20 self-adhesive 42c stamps

Serpentine Die Cut 10¾ on 2, 3 or 4 Sides

2008, June 10 Self-Adhesive Photo.

4270a A3233 42c pane of 20, P#V1111 19.00

No. 4270a is a complete booklet (BC244). The peelable backing serves as a booklet cover.

4271a — A3234

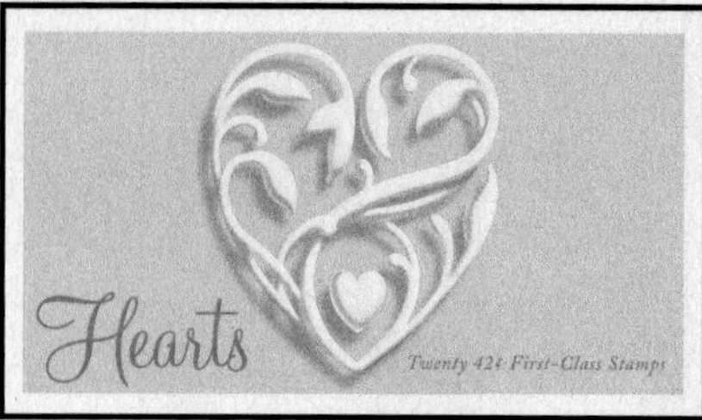

4271a — BC245

2008

$8.40 fold-it-yourself booklet contains 20 self-adhesive 42c stamps

Serpentine Die Cut 10¾ on 2, 3 or 4 Sides

2008, June 10 Self-Adhesive Litho.

4271a A3234 42c pane of 20 18.00

No. 4271a is a complete booklet (BC245). The peelable backing, which has a plate number (P1111), serves as a booklet cover.

4346a, BC246 — A3308

Serpentine Die Cut 11 on 2 or 3 Sides

2008, Aug. 14 Self-Adhesive Litho.

4346a A3308 42c pane of 20, P#S1111 17.00

No. 4346a is a complete booklet with 12 stamps plus P# on one side and eight stamps plus booklet cover (BC246) on the other side. The peelable backing serves as a booklet cover.

4347a, BC247 — A3309

Serpentine Die Cut 11¼x10¾ on 2 or 3 Sides

2008, Aug. 15 Self-Adhesive Litho.

4347a A3309 42c pane of 20, P#P1111 17.00

No. 4347a is a complete booklet with 12 stamps plus P# on one side and eight stamps plus booklet cover (BC247) on the other side. The peelable backing serves as a booklet cover.

4359a, BC248 — A3319

Serpentine Die Cut 10¾x11 on 2 or 3 Sides

2008, Oct. 23 Self-Adhesive Litho.

4359a A3319 42c pane of 20, P#P11111 17.00

No. 4359a is a complete double-sided booklet with 12 stamps on one side of the peelable backing and eight stamps plus P# and the label that serves as a booklet cover (BC248) on the other side of the backing.

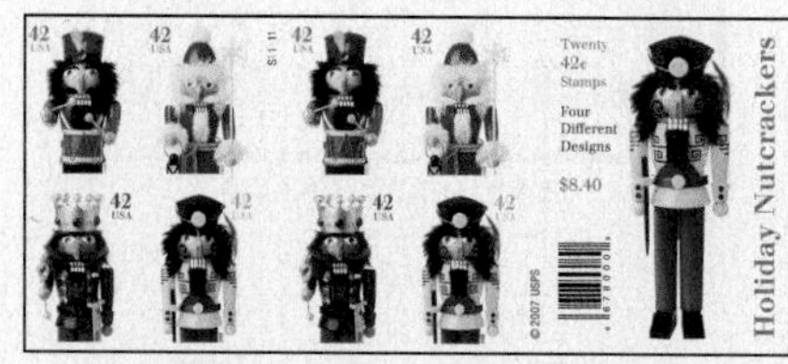

4363b, BC249 — A3320-A3323

Serpentine Die Cut 10¾x11 on 2 or 3 Sides

2008, Oct. 23 Self-Adhesive

4363b 42c pane of 20, P#S11111 20.00

No. 4363b is a complete double-sided booklet. Eight stamps (two each #4360-4363) plus P# and the label that serves as a booklet cover (BC249) are on one side of the peelable backing and 12 stamps (three each #4360-4363) are on the other side of the backing.

4367b, 4367c, 4367d — A3324-A3327

Serpentine Die Cut 11¼x11 on 2 or 3 Sides

2008, Oct. 23 Self-Adhesive

4367b 42c pane of 4, #4364-4367 5.00

4367c 42c pane of 6, #4366-4367, 2 each #4364-4365, no P# 7.50

4367d 42c pane of 6, #4364-4365, 2 each #4366-4367, no P# 7.50

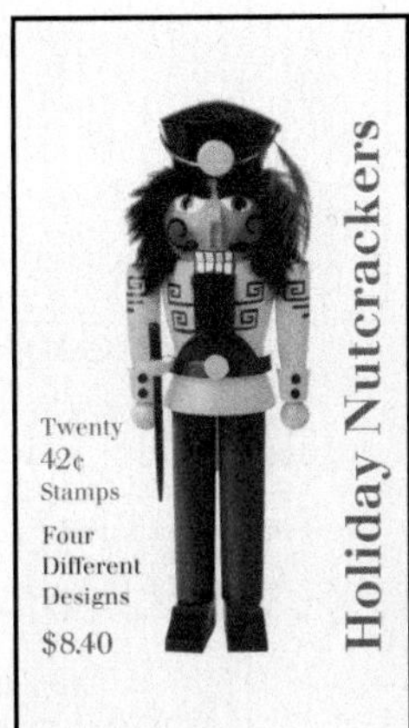

4367b, 4367c, 4367d — BC250

$8.40 booklet contains 20 self-adhesive 42c stamps

COMBINATION BOOKLET

BK306 BC250 $8.40 **multi,** #4367c, 4367d, 2 #4367b, P#S11111 25.00

On No. BK306, plate number appears on the backing of the lower example of No. 4367b.

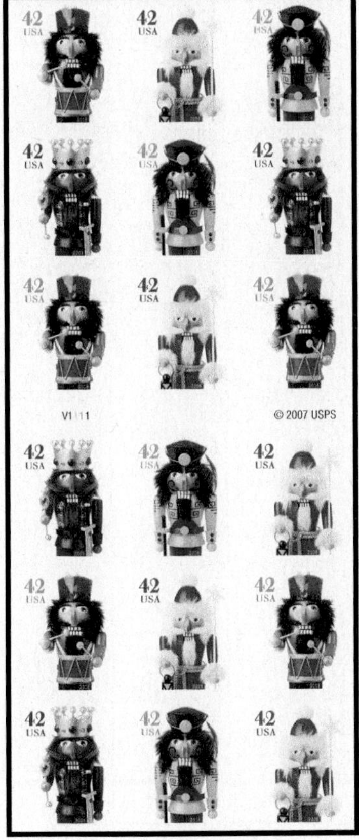
4371b — A3324-A3327

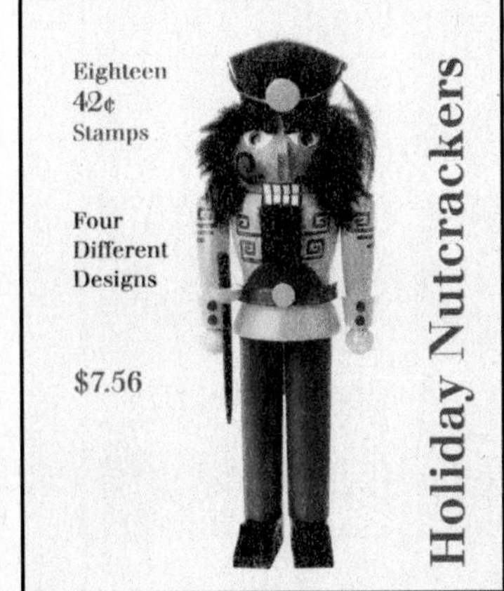

4371b BC251

2008

$7.56 fold-it-yourself booklet contains 18 self-adhesive 42c stamps

Serpentine Die Cut 8 on 2, 3 or 4 Sides

Photo.

4371b 42c pane of 18, 5 each #4368-4369, 4 each #4370-4371, P#V1111 22.50

No. 4371b is a complete booklet (BC251). The peelable backing serves as a booklet cover.

4396a—A3342

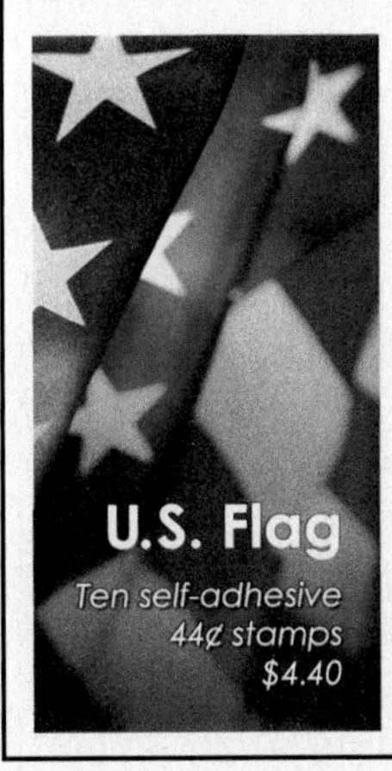

4396a — BC252

2009

$4.40 fold-it-yourself booklet contains 10 self-adhesive 44c stamps

Serpentine Die Cut 11¼x10¾ on 3 Sides

2009, June 5 **Self-Adhesive** **Photo.**

4396a A3342 44c pane of 10, #V1111 9.00

By its nature, No. 4396a is a complete booklet (BC252). The peelable backing serves as a booklet cover.

4403b — A3345-A3349

4403b — BC253

2009

$8.80 fold-it-yourself booklet contains 20 self-adhesive 44c stamps

Serpentine Die Cut 10¾ on 2, 3 or 4 Sides

2009, May 7 **Litho.**

4403b 44c pane of 20, 4 each #4399-4403, no P# (4) 23.00

No. 4403b is a complete booklet (BC253). The peelable backing, which has a plate number (S11111), serves as a booklet cover. The four different booklet covers show #4399 (shown above), #4400 and 4403, #4401, and #4402.

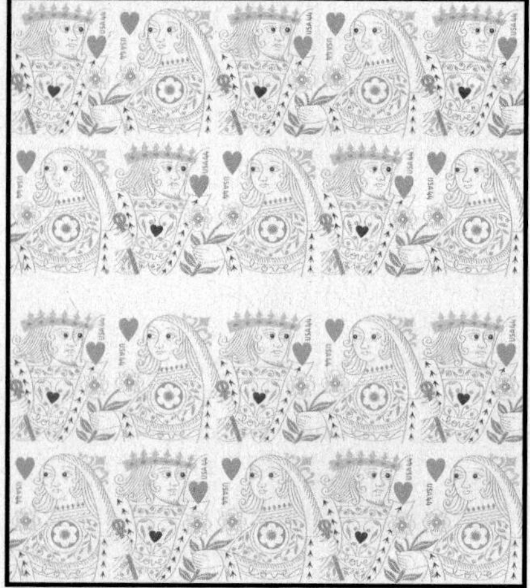
4405b — A3350-A3351

4405b — BC254

2009

$8.80 fold-it-yourself booklet contains 20 self-adhesive 44c stamps

Serpentine Die Cut 10¾ on 2, 3 or 4 Sides

2009, May 8 **Litho.**

4405b 44c pane of 20, 10 each #4404-4405 23.00

No. 4405b is a complete booklet (BC254). The peelable backing, which has a plate number (V11111), serves as a booklet cover.

4424a, BC255 — A3368

Serpentine Die Cut 10¾x11 on 2 or 3 Sides

2009, Oct. 20 **Self-Adhesive** **Litho.**

4424a A3368 44c pane of 20, P#P11111 18.00

No. 4424a is a complete double-sided booklet with 12 stamps on one side of the peelable backing and eight stamps plus P# and the label that serves as a booklet cover (BC255) on the other side of the backing.

4428b, BC256 — A3369-A3372

Serpentine Die Cut 10¾x11 on 2 or 3 Sides

2009, Oct. 8 **Self-Adhesive** **Litho.**

4428b 44c pane of 20, P#S1111 22.00

No. 4428b is a complete double-sided booklet. Eight stamps (two each #4425-4428) plus P# and the label that serves as a booklet cover (BC256) are on one side of the peelable backing and 12 stamps (three each #4425-4428) are on the other side of the backing.

Varieties

4428c As "b," die cutting omitted on side with 12 stamps —

4428d As "b," die cutting omitted on side with 8 stamps —

4432b — A3373-A3376

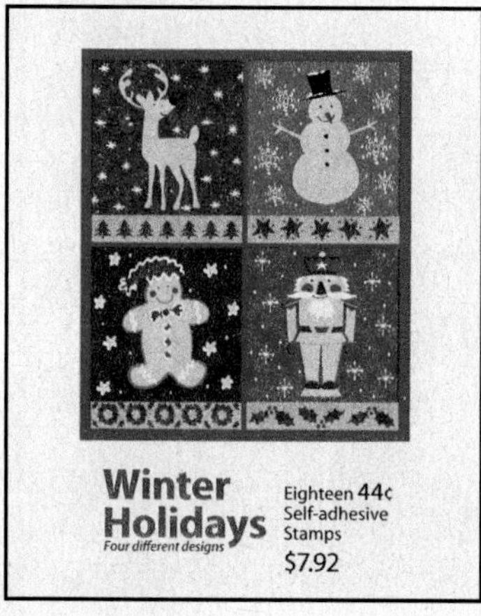

4432b
BC257

2009

$7.92 fold-it-yourself booklet contains 18 self-adhesive 44c stamps

Serpentine Die Cut 8 on 2, 3 or 4 Sides

2009, Oct. 8 **Photo.**

4432b 44c pane of 18, 5 each #4429, 4431, 4 each #4430, 4432, P#V1111 22.50

No. 4432b is a complete booklet (BC257). The peelable backing serves as a booklet cover.

"Forever" Liberty Bell Type of 2007

Serpentine Die Cut 11¼x10¾ on 2, 3 or 4 Sides

2010, Feb. 3 **Self-Adhesive** **Litho.**

Medium Microprinting, Bell 16mm Wide

Dated "2009" in Copper

4437a A3148 (44c) pane of 18 #4437, P#P11111 20.00

No. 4437a is a complete booklet (BC232). The peelable backing serves as a booklet cover. On No. 4437a, the bar code number found on the cover is "0-573300-2," the same as No. 4128c.

4481b, BC258 — A3421-A3424

Serpentine Die Cut 11 on 2 or 3 Sides

2010, Oct. 21 **Self-Adhesive** **Litho.**

4481b (44c) pane of 20, P#S11111 50.00

No. 4481b is a complete double-sided booklet. Eight stamps (two each #4478-4481) plus P# and the label that serves as a booklet cover (BC258) are on one side of the peelable backing and 12 stamps (three each #4478-4481) are on the other side of the backing.

Varieties

4481d As "b," die cutting omitted on side with 12 stamps *400.00*

4481e As "b," die cutting omitted on side with 8 stamps *450.00*

4481f As "b," die cutting omitted on side with 12 stamps, die cutting omitted on bottom 4 stamps on side with 8 stamps 950.00

4485b — A3425-A3428

4485b
BC259

2010

($7.92) fold-it-yourself booklet contains 18 self-adhesive (44c) stamps

Serpentine Die Cut 11¼x10¾ on 2, 3 or 4 Sides

2010, Oct. 21 **Litho.**

4485b (44c) pane of 18, 5 each #4482, 4484, 4 each #4483, 4485 P#P11111 45.00

No. 4485b is a complete booklet (BC259). The peelable backing serves as a booklet cover.

4519b — A3429-A3430

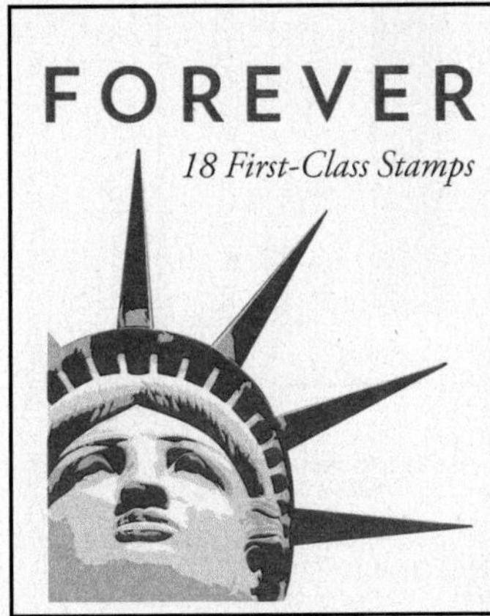

4519b BC260

2011

($7.92) fold-it-yourself booklet contains 18 self-adhesive (44c) stamps

Serpentine Die Cut 11¼x10¾ on 2, 3 or 4 Sides

2011, Apr. 8 **Litho.**

4519b (44c) pane of 18, 9 each #4518-4519, P#S111111 20.00

No. 4519b is a complete booklet (BC260). The peelable backing serves as a booklet cover.

4560b, BC261 — A3429-A3430

Serpentine Die Cut 11¼x11 on 2 or 3 Sides

2011, Sept. 14 **Self-Adhesive** **Litho.**

Stamps With Microprinting "4evR"

4560b (44c) pane of 20, P#P11111 30.00

No. 4560b is a complete double-sided booklet. Eight stamps (two each #4559-4560) plus P# and the label that serves as a booklet cover (BC261, with bar code number having a closed "4" and a small "2") are on one side of the peelable backing and 12 stamps (three each #4559-4560) are on the other side of the backing.

Stamps With Microprinting "4evr"

4562b (44c) pane of 20, P#S111111 30.00

No. 4562b is a complete double-sided booklet. Eight stamps (two each #4561-4562) plus P# and the label that serves as a booklet cover (BC261, with bar code number having a open "4" and a small "2") are on one side of the peelable backing and 12 stamps (three each #4561-4562) are on the other side of the backing.

Photo.

Serpentine Die Cut 11¼x11½ on 2 or 3 Sides

Stamps With Microprinting "4EVR"

4564b (44c) pane of 20, P#V11111 25.00

No. 4564b is a complete double-sided booklet. Eight stamps (two each #4563-4564) plus P# and the label that serves as a booklet cover (BC261, with bar code number having a open "4" and a large "2") are on one side of the peelable backing and 12 stamps (three each #4563-4564) are on the other side of the backing.

4570a, BC262 — A3493

Serpentine Die Cut 10¾x11 on 2 or 3 Sides

2011, Oct. 13 **Self-Adhesive** **Litho.**

4570a (44c) pane of 20, P#S11111 25.00

No. 4570a is a complete double-sided booklet. Eight stamps plus P# and the label that serves as a booklet cover (BC262) are on one side of the peelable backing and 12 stamps are on the other side of the backing.

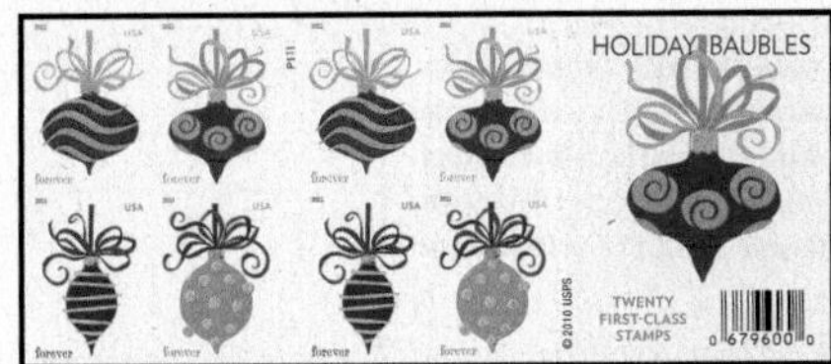

4574b, 4578b, BC263 — A3494-A3498

Serpentine Die Cut 10¾x11 on 2 or 3 Sides

2011, Oct. 13 **Self-Adhesive** **Litho.**

Stamps With Microprinted "USPS" on Ornament Collar

4574b (44c) pane of 20, P#P1111 30.00

Microprinted "USPS" in Places Other Than Collar of Ornament

4578b (44c) pane of 20, P#S11111 30.00

Nos. 4574b and 4578b are complete double-sided booklets. Eight stamps (two each types A3494-A3497) plus P# and the label that serves as a booklet cover (BC263) are on one side of the peelable backing and 12 stamps (three each types A3494-A3497) are on the other side of the backing.

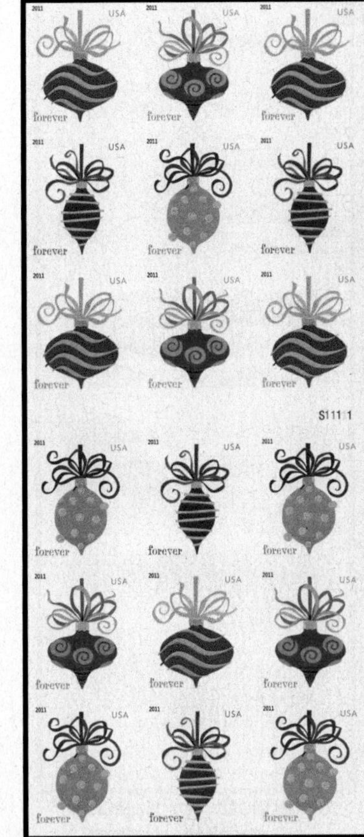

4582b — A3498-A3501

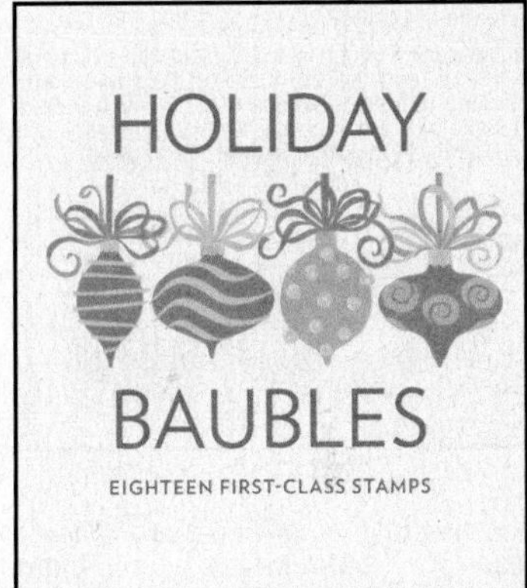

4582b BC264

2011

($7.92) fold-it-yourself booklet contains 18 self-adhesive (44c) stamps

Serpentine Die Cut 11¼x11 on 2, 3 or 4 Sides

2011, Oct. 13 **Litho.**

4582b (44c) pane of 18, 5 each #4579, 4582, 4 each #4580-4581, P#S11111 27.50

No. 4582b is a complete booklet (BC264). The peelable backing serves as a booklet cover.

4622b, BC265 — A3526-A3530

Serpentine Die Cut 11x10¾ on 2 or 3 Sides

2012, Jan. 23 Self-Adhesive Litho.

4622b (45c) pane of 20, P#P11111 40.00

No. 4622b is a complete double-sided booklet with 12 stamps (3 each #4618, 4621, 2 each #4619, 4620, 4622) on one side of the peelable backing and eight stamps (#4618, 4621, 2 each #4619, 4620, 4622) plus P# and the label that serves as a booklet cover (BC265) on the other side of the backing.

4644c, 4648b, BC266 — A3537-A3540

Serpentine Die Cut 11¼x10¾ on 2 or 3 Sides

2012, Feb. 22 Self-Adhesive Litho.

Colored Dots in Stars

18½mm From Lower Left to Lower Right Corner of Flag

4644c (45c) pane of 20, P#P1111 25.00

4644e (45c) pane of 20, P#P2222 25.00

Dark Dots Only in Stars

19mm From Lower Left to Lower Right Corners of Flag

4648b (45c) pane of 20, P#S11111, S22222 30.00

No. 4644c is a complete double-sided booklet with 12 stamps (3 each #4641-4644) on one side of the peelable backing and eight stamps (2 each #4641-4644) plus P# and the label that serves as a booklet cover (BC266) on the other side of the backing.

No. 4644e is a complete double-sided booklet with 12 stamps (3 each #4641a-4644a) on one side of the peelable backing and eight stamps (2 each #4641a-4644a) plus P# and the label that serves as a booklet cover (BC266) on the other side of the backing.

No. 4648b is a complete double-sided booklet with 12 stamps (3 each #4645-4648) on one side of the peelable backing and eight stamps (2 each #4645-4648) plus P# and the label that serves as a booklet cover (BC266) on the other side of the backing.

4676b—A3537-A3540

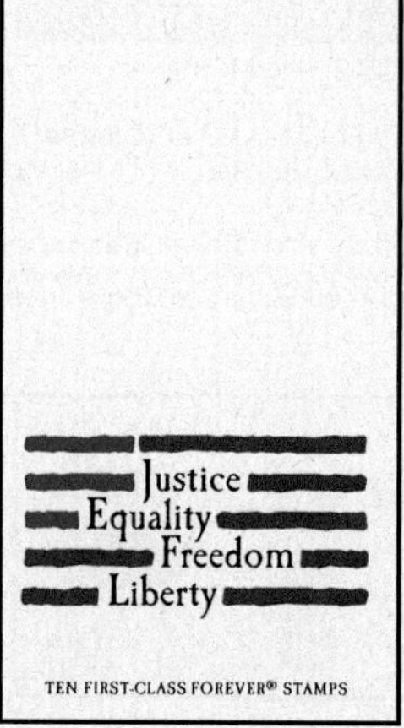

4676b — BC267

2012

$4.50 fold-it-yourself booklet contains 10 self-adhesive (45c) stamps

Serpentine Die Cut 11¼x10¾ on 3 Sides

2012, June 1 Self-Adhesive Photo.

Colored Dots in Stars

19¼mm From Lower Left to Lower Right Corners of Flag

4676b (45c) pane of 10, P#V1111 12.50

By its nature, No. 4676b is a complete booklet (BC267). The peelable backing serves as a booklet cover.

4686b—A3506-A3510

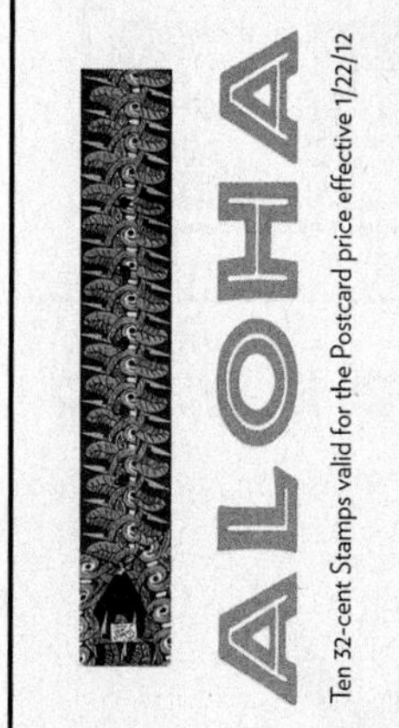

4686b — BC268

2012

$3.20 fold-it-yourself booklet contains 10 self-adhesive 32c stamps

Serpentine Die Cut 11¼x10¾ on 3 Sides

2012, June 2 Self-Adhesive Litho.

4686b 32c pane of 10, P#P11111 85.00

By its nature, No. 4686b is a complete booklet (BC268). The peelable backing serves as a booklet cover.

4709b — A3537-A3540

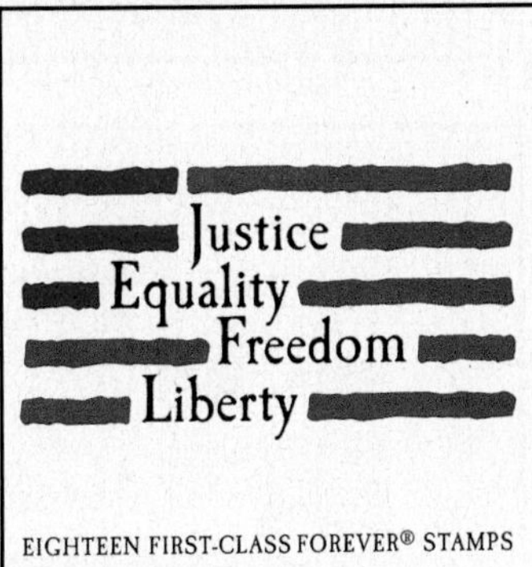

4709b BC269

2012

($8.10) fold-it-yourself booklet contains 18 self-adhesive (45c) stamps

Serpentine Die Cut 11¼x10¾ on 2, 3 or 4 Sides

2012, Sept. 22 **Litho.**

4709b (45c) pane of 18, 5 each #4706-4707, 4 each #4708-4709, P#P1111 25.00

No. 4709b is a complete booklet (BC269). The peelable backing serves as a booklet cover.

4711a, BC270 — A3590

Serpentine Die Cut 11 on 2 or 3 Sides

2012, Oct. 10 **Self-Adhesive** **Litho.**

4711a A3590 (45c) pane of 20, P#S11111 25.00
4711c A3590 (45c) imperf. pane of 20, P#S11111 35.00

No. 4711a is a complete double-sided booklet. Eight stamps plus P# and the label that serves as a booklet cover (BC270) are on one side of the peelable backing and 12 stamps are on the other side of the backing.

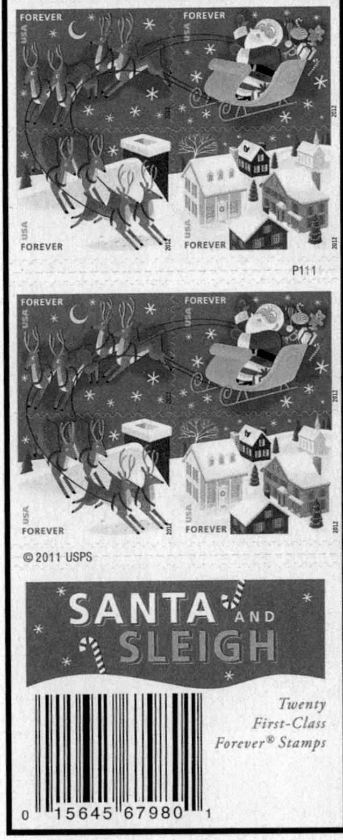

4715b, BC271 — A3591-A3594

Serpentine Die Cut 11x10¾ on 2 or 3 Sides

2012, Oct. 13 **Self-Adhesive** **Litho.**

4715b (45c) pane of 20, P#P1111 30.00
4715d (45c) imperf. pane of 20, P#P1111 40.00

No. 4715b is a complete double-sided booklet. Eight stamps (two each of Nos. 4712-4715) plus P# and the label that serves as a booklet cover (BC271) are on one side of the peelable backing and 12 stamps (three each of Nos. 4712-4715) are on the other side of the backing.

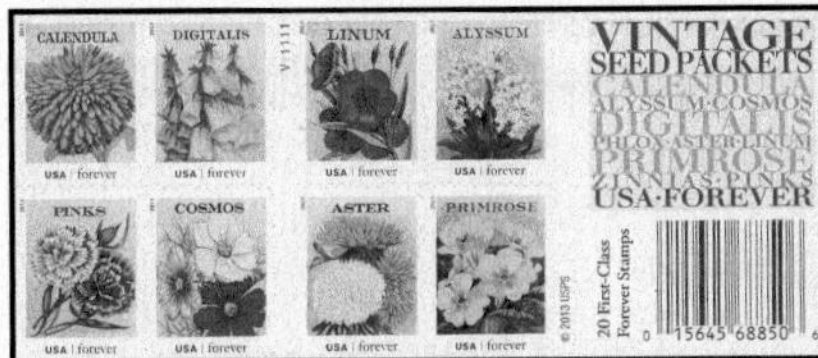

4763b, BC272 — A3628-A3637

Serpentine Die Cut 10¾ on 2 or 3 Sides

2013, Apr. 5 **Self-Adhesive** **Photo.**

4763b (46c) pane of 20, P#V11111 50.00

No. 4763b is a complete double-sided booklet. Eight stamps (1 each #4755-4758, 4760-4763) plus P# and the label that serves as a booklet cover (BC272) are on one side of the peelable backing and 12 stamps (2 each #4754, 4759, 1 each #4755-4758, 4760-4763) are on the other side of the backing.

4781b, 4785d, 4799b, BC273 — A3640-A3643

Serpentine Die Cut 11¼x10¾ on 2 or 3 Sides

2013, May 17 **Self-Adhesive** **Litho.**

Microprinted "USPS" at Lower Left Corner of Flag

4781b (46c) pane of 20, P#P1111 30.00

With Microprinted "USPS" Near Top of Pole or at Lower Left Corner Near Rope (#4783)

4785d (46c) pane of 20, P#S1111 25.00

No. 4781b is a complete double-sided booklet with 12 stamps (3 each #4778-4781) on one side of the peelable backing and eight stamps (2 each #4778-4781) plus P# and the label that serves as a booklet cover (BC273) on the other side of the backing.

No. 4785d is a complete double-sided booklet with 12 stamps (3 each #4782-4785) on one side of the peelable backing and eight stamps (2 each #4782-4785) plus P# and the label that serves as a booklet cover (BC273) on the other side of the backing.

Two types of BC273 exist. On No. 4781b, the diagonal and vertical lines of the "4" in the bar code touch, while on No. 4785d, they do not touch.

4785f—A3640-A3543

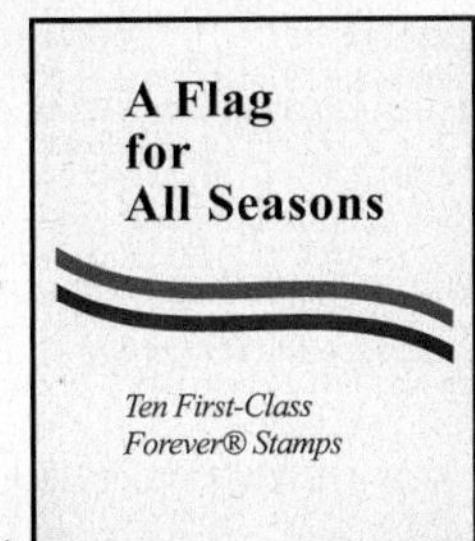

4785f — BC274

2013

$4.60 fold-it-yourself booklet contains 10 self-adhesive (46c) stamps

Serpentine Die Cut 11¼x10¾ on 3 Sides

2013, Aug. 16 **Self-Adhesive** **Photo.**

With Microprinted "USPS" Near Top of Pole or at Lower Left Corner Near Rope (#4783a)

4785f (46c) pane of 10, 3 each # 4782a, 4783a, 2 each #4784a, 4785a, P#S1111 12.50

By its nature, No. 4785f is a complete booklet (BC274). The peelable backing serves as a booklet cover.

Flags Type of 2013

Serpentine Die Cut 11¼x10¾ on 2 or 3 Sides

2014, Mar. 17 **Litho.**

With Microprinted "USPS" Near Top of Pole or at Lower Left Corner Near Rope (#4783)

Overall Tagging

4785h pane of 20, 5 each #4782b, 4783b, 4784b, 4785b (dated "2014"), P#S2222 25.00
4785i As "h," die cutting omitted on side with 8 stamps and 3 pairs on side with 12 stamps 1,800.

On day of issue, No. 4785h sold for $9.80, with individual stamps selling for 49c each.

Flags Type of 2013

Serpentine Die Cut 11¼x11½ on 2 or 3 Sides

2013, Aug. 8 Self-Adhesive Litho.

Microprinted "USPS" in Various Places

4799b (46c) pane of 20, P#V1111 30.00

No. 4799b is a complete double-sided booklet with 12 stamps (3 each #4796-4799) on one side of the peelable backing and eight stamps (2 each #4796-4799) plus P# and the label that serves as a booklet cover (BC273) on the other side of the backing.

BC273 on No. 4799b is like that found on No. 4785c.

4815a, BC275 — A3678

Serpentine Die Cut 11 on 2 or 3 Sides

2013, Oct. 11 Self-Adhesive Litho.

4815a A3678 (46c) pane of 20, P#S11111 25.00
4815c A3678 (46c) imperf. pane of 20, P#S11111 35.00

No. 4815a is a complete double-sided booklet. Eight stamps plus P# and the label that serves as a booklet cover (BC275) are on one side of the peelable backing and 12 stamps are on the other side of the backing.

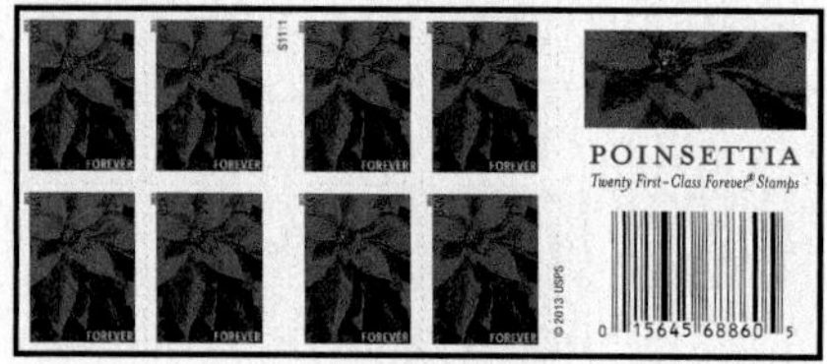

4816a, BC276 — A3679

Serpentine Die Cut 11 on 2 or 3 Sides

2013-14 Self-Adhesive Litho.

4816a A3679 (46c) pane of 20, P#S1111 25.00
4816c A3697 As #4816a, dated "2014," P#S2222 25.00
4816e A3697 As #4816a, imperf. 35.00

Issued: No. 4816a, 10/10/13; No. 4816c, 8/21/14.

No. 4816a and 4816c are complete double-sided booklets. Eight stamps plus P# and the label that serves as a booklet cover (BC276) are on one side of the peelable backing and 12 stamps are on the other side of the backing. The booklet cover on No. 4816c has a USPS emblem over a smaller bar code.

4820b, BC277 — A3680-A3683

Serpentine Die Cut 11 on 2 or 3 Sides

2013, Nov. 6 Self-Adhesive Litho.

4820c (46c) pane of 20, P#S1111 25.00
4820e (46c) pane of 20, P#S2222 —
4820g (46c) imperf. pane of 20, P#S1111 40.00

Nos. 4820c, 4820e and 4820g are complete double-sided booklets. Eight stamps plus P# and the label that serves as a booklet cover (BC277) are on one side of the peelable backing and 12 stamps are on the other side of the backing.

4821a — A3684

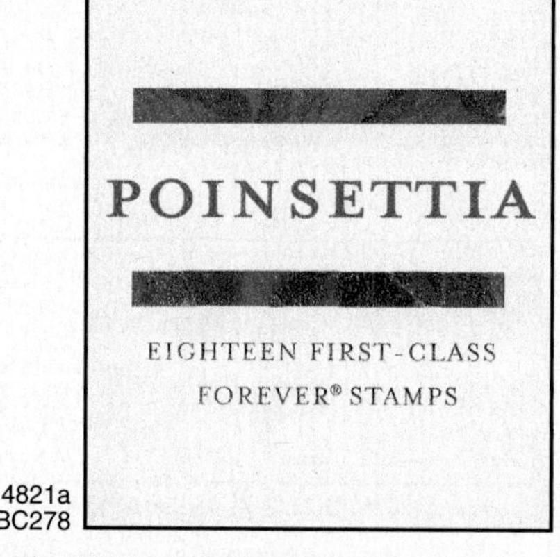

4821a BC278

($8.28) fold-it-yourself booklet contains 18 self-adhesive (46c) stamps

Serpentine Die Cut 8 on 2, 3 or 4 Sides

2013, Oct. 10 Self-Adhesive Photo.

4821a A3684 (46c) pane of 18, P#V1111 22.50

No. 4821a is a complete booklet (BC278). The peelable backing serves as a booklet cover.

4828a — A3688-A3691

4832a — A3692-A3695

4836a — A3696-A3699

4840a — A3700-A3703

4844a — A3704-A3707

2013, Nov. 19 Litho. *Serpentine Die Cut 11*
Self-Adhesive

4828a	(46c) pane of 4, #4825-4828, + central label, no P#	8.00	
4828b	(46c) imperf. pane of 4	12.50	—
4832a	(46c) pane of 4, #4829-4832, + central label, no P#	8.00	
4832b	(46c) imperf. pane of 4	12.50	—
4836a	(46c) pane of 4, #4833-4836, + central label, no P#	8.00	
4836b	(46c) imperf. pane of 4	12.50	—
4840a	(46c) pane of 4, #4837-4840, + central label, no P#	8.00	
4840b	(46c) imperf. pane of 4	12.50	—
4844a	(46c) pane of 4, #4841-4844, + central label, no P#	8.00	
4844b	(46c) imperf. pane of 4	12.50	—

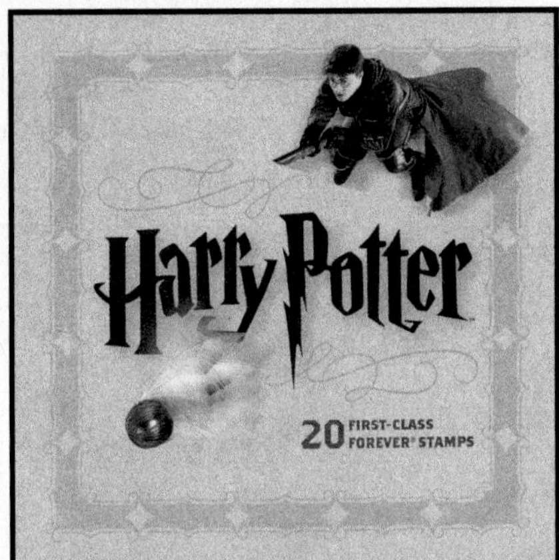

4828a, 4832a, 4836a, 4840a, 4844a — BC279

2013

$9.20 booklets contain 20 self-adhesive (46c) stamps

COMBINATION BOOKLETS

BK307	BC279	$9.20	**multi,** #4828a, 4832a, 4836a, 4840a, 4844a, no P#	40.00
BK307a	BC279	$9.20	**multi,** #4828b, 4832b, 4836b, 4840b, 4844b, no P#	62.50

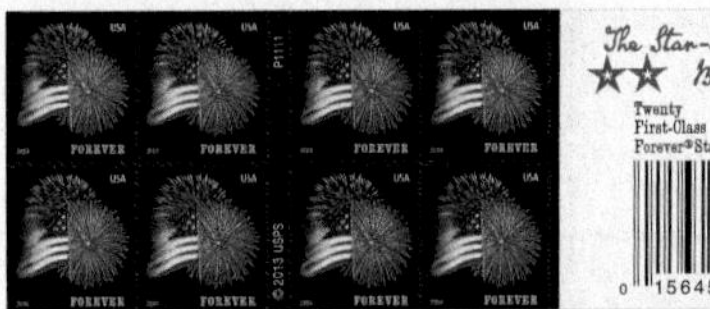

4855a, BC280 — A3716

Serpentine Die Cut 11¼x10¾ on 2 or 3 Sides
2014, Jan. 28 Self-Adhesive Litho.

4855a (49c) pane of 20, P#P1111, P2222 25.00

No. 4855a is a complete double-sided booklet with 12 stamps on one side of the peelable backing and eight stamps plus P# and the label that serves as a booklet cover (BC280) on the other side of the backing.

4865b, BC281 — A3721-A3724

Serpentine Die Cut 11 on 2 or 3 Sides
2014, Feb. 14 Self-Adhesive Litho.

4865b	(49c) pane of 20, 5 each #4862-4865, P#S11111	30.00
4865d	(49c) imperf. pane of 20	35.00

No. 4865b is a complete double-sided booklet. Eight stamps (2 each #4862-4865) plus P# and the label that serves as a booklet cover (BC281) are on one side of the peelable backing and 12 stamps (3 each #4862-4865) are on the other side of the backing.

Fort McHenry Flag and Fireworks Type of 2014 and

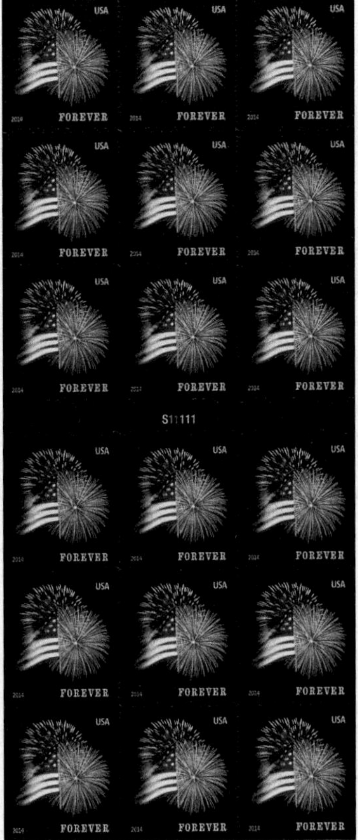

4871a — A3716

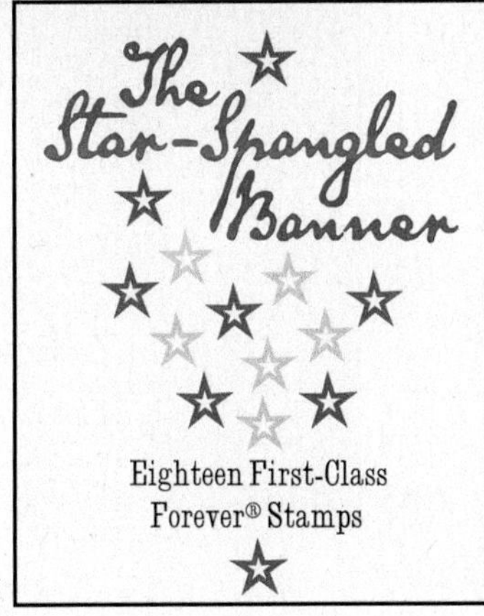

4871a BC282

2014

($8.82) fold-it-yourself booklet contains 18 self-adhesive (49c) stamps

Serpentine Die Cut 11¼x11½ on 2 or 3 Sides
2014, Mar. 3 Self-Adhesive Photo.
Without "USPS" Microprinting

4869a (49c) pane of 20, P#C1111 25.00

Litho.
Serpentine Die Cut 11¼x10¾ on 2 or 3 Sides
With "USPS" Microprinted in Fireworks Above Flagpole

4870a (49c) pane of 20, P#S11111 25.00

The actual design images on Nos. 4855, 4869 and 4870 differ slightly in size. This is easiest seen by measuring the height of the flagpole: No. 4855 is 13mm, No. 4869 is 14mm, and No. 4870 is 12mm.

Thin Paper
Serpentine Die Cut 11¼x11 on 2, 3, or 4 Sides

4871a (49c) pane of 18, P#S11111 25.00

Nos. 4869a and 4870a are complete double-sided booklets with 12 stamps on one side of the peelable backing and eight stamps plus P# and the label that serves as a booklet cover (BC280) on the other side of the backing.

No. 4871a is a complete booklet (BC282). The peelable backing serves as a booklet cover.

4891b, BC283 — A3735-A3744

Serpentine Die Cut 10¾ on 2 or 3 Sides
2014, Apr. 5 Self-Adhesive Litho.

4891b	(49c) pane of 20, P#P1111	30.00
4891d	(49c) imperf. pane of 20, P#P1111	40.00

No. 4891b is a complete double-sided booklet. Eight stamps (1 each #4883-4886, 4888-4891) plus P# and the label that serves as a booklet cover (BC283) are on one side of the peelable backing and 12 stamps (2 each #4882, 4887, 1 each #4883-4886, 4888-4891) are on the other side of the backing.

4909b, BC284 — A3761-A3762

Serpentine Die Cut 11¾x11¼ on 2 or 3 Sides
2014, June 6 Self-Adhesive Photo.

4909b	(49c) pane of 20, P#C1111	25.00
4909d	(49c) imperf. pane of 20, P#C1111	40.00

No. 4909b is a complete booklet with 12 stamps (6 each Nos. 4908-4909) on one side and 8 stamps (4 each Nos.4908-4909), plate number, and booklet cover (BC284) on the other side. The peelable backing serves as a booklet cover.

4920b, BC285 — A3770-A3773

Serpentine Die Cut 11¾ on 2 or 3 Sides

2014, Aug. 21 Self-Adhesive Photo.

4920b	(49c) pane of 20, P#C1111	22.00
4920d	(49c) imperf. pane of 20, P#C1111	30.00

No. 4920b is a complete booklet with 12 stamps (3 each Nos. 4917-4920) on one side and 8 stamps (2 each Nos. 4917-4920), plate number, and booklet cover (BC285) on the other side. The peelable backing serves as a booklet cover.

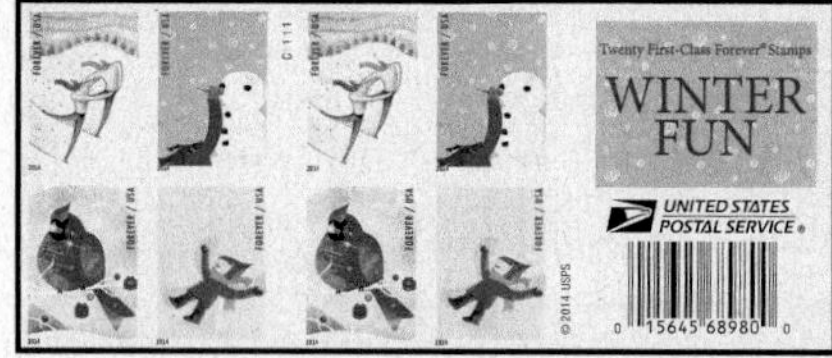

4940b, BC286 — A3790-A3793

Serpentine Die Cut 10¾x11 on 2 or 3 Sides

2014, Oct. 23 Self-Adhesive Photo.

4940b	(49c) pane of 20, P#C1111	25.00
4940d	(49c) imperf. pane of 20, P#C1111	35.00

No. 4940b is a complete double-sided booklet. Eight stamps (two each Nos. 4937-4940) plus P# and the label that serves as a booklet cover (BC286) are on one side of the peelable backing and 12 stamps (three each Nos. 4937-4940) are on the other side of the backing.

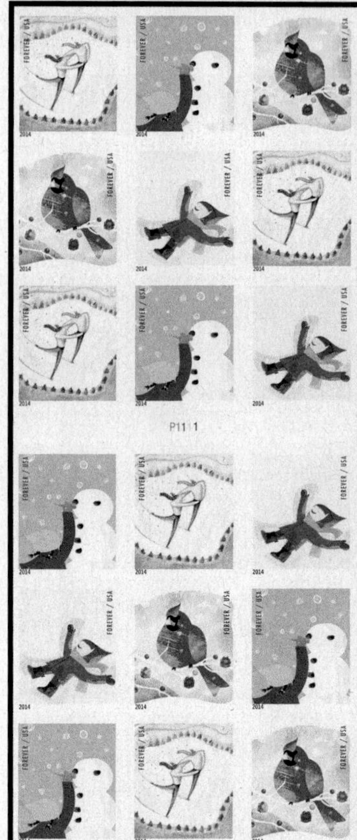

4944b — A3794-A3797

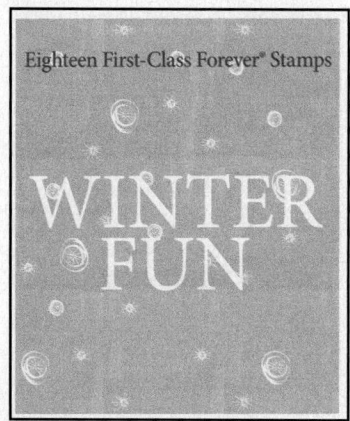

4944b
BC287

2014

($8.82) fold-it-yourself booklet contains 18 self-adhesive (49c) stamps

Serpentine Die Cut 11¼x11 on 2, 3 or 4 Sides

2014, Oct. 23 Litho.

4944b	(49c) pane of 18, 5 each #4941-4942, 4 each #4943-4944, P#P1111	72.00

No. 4944b is a complete booklet (BC287). The peelable backing serves as a booklet cover.

4945a, BC288 — A3798

Serpentine Die Cut 10¾x11 on 2 or 3 Sides

2014, Nov. 19 Self-Adhesive Litho.

4945a	A3798 (49c) pane of 20, P#S11111	25.00
4945c	A3798 (49c) imperf. pane of 20, P#S11111	35.00

No. 4945a is a complete double-sided booklet. Eight stamps plus P# and the label that serves as a booklet cover (BC288) are on one side of the peelable backing and 12 stamps are on the other side of the backing.

4949b, BC289 — A3799-A3802

Serpentine Die Cut 11x10¾ on 2 or 3 Sides

2014, Nov. 6 Self-Adhesive Photo.

4949b	(49c) pane of 20, P#C11111	25.00
4949d	(49c) imperf. pane of 20, P#C11111	37.50

No. 4949b is a complete double-sided booklet. Eight stamps (two each of Nos. 4946-4949) plus P# and the label that serves as a booklet cover (BC289) are on one side of the peelable backing and 12 stamps (three each of Nos. 4946-4949) are on the other side of the backing.

4967b, BC290 — A3817-A3820

Serpentine Die Cut 11x11¼ on 2 or 3 Sides

2015, Mar. 20 Self-Adhesive Litho.

4967b (49c) pane of 20, 5 each #4964-4967, P#S1111 30.00
4967d (49c) imperf. pane of 20, P#S1111 35.00

No. 4967b is a complete double-sided booklet. Eight stamps (2 each #4964-4967) plus P# and the label that serves as a booklet cover (BC290) are on one side of the peelable backing and 12 stamps (3 each #4964-4967) are on the other side of the backing.

No. 4967b is known with the block of 4 at left on the 12-stamp side having no gum. Such booklets are rare and fragile.

5007b, BC291 — A3847-A3850

Serpentine Die Cut 11¼x10¾ on 2 or 3 Sides

2015, July 11 Self-Adhesive Litho.

5007b (49c) pane of 20, P#P1111 30.00
5007d (49c) imperf. pane of 20, P#P1111 35.00

No. 5007b is a complete double-sided booklet with 12 stamps on one side of the peelable backing and eight stamps plus P# and the label that serves as a booklet cover (BC291) on the other side of the backing.

5030b, BC292 — A3857-A3866

Serpentine Die Cut 10¾ on 2 or 3 Sides

2015, Oct. 1 Self-Adhesive Litho.

5030b (49c) pane of 20, P#S1111 50.00
5030d (49c) imperf. pane of 20, P#S1111 35.00

No. 5030b is a complete booklet with 12 stamps (Nos. 5023-5030, 2 each Nos. 5021-5022) on one side and 8 stamps (Nos.5023-5030), plate number, and booklet cover (BC292) on the other side. The peelable backing serves as a booklet cover.

5034b, BC293 — A3867-A3870

Serpentine Die Cut 11¼x10¾ on 2 or 3 Sides

2015, Oct. 23 Self-Adhesive Litho.

5034b (49c) pane of 20, P#S11111 25.00
5034d (49c) imperf. pane of 20, P#S11111 35.00

No. 5034b is a complete booklet with 12 stamps (3 each Nos. 5031-5034) on one side and 8 stamps (2 each Nos.5031-5034), plate number, and booklet cover (BC293) on the other side. The peelable backing serves as a booklet cover.

5051b — A3877-A3886

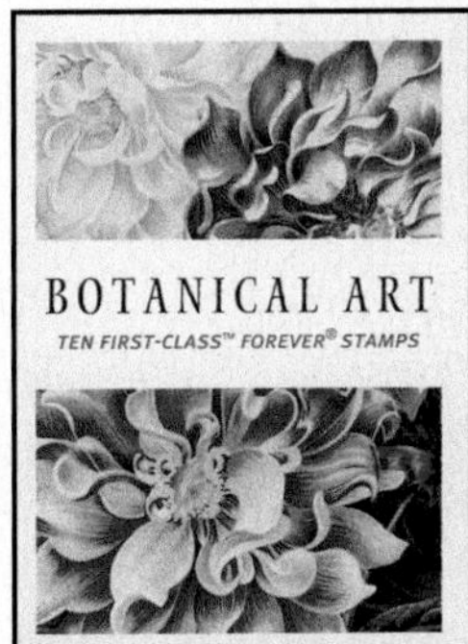

5051b — BC294

2016

$4.90 fold-it-yourself booklet contains 10 self-adhesive (49c) stamps

Serpentine Die Cut 10¾ on 2 or 3 Sides

2016, Jan. 29 Litho.

5051b (49c) pane of 10, #5042-5051, P#P1111 25.00

By its nature, No. 5051b is a complete booklet (BC294). The peelable backing serves as a booklet cover.

5051c, BC295 — A3877-A3886

Serpentine Die Cut 10¾ on 2 or 3 Sides

2016, Jan. 29 Self-Adhesive Litho.

5051c (49c) pane of 20, 2 each #5042-5051, P#P1111 50.00
5051e (49c) imperf. pane of 20, 2 each #5042-5051, P#P1111 225.00

No. 5051c is a complete double-sided booklet. Eight stamps (Nos. 5042-5049) plus P# and the label that serves as a booklet cover (BC295) are on one side of the peelable backing and 12 stamps (Nos. 5042-5049, 2 each Nos. 5050-5051) are on the other side of the backing.

5054a — A3887

5054a — BC296

2016

$4.90 fold-it-yourself booklet contains 10 self-adhesive (49c) stamps

Serpentine Die Cut 11¼x10¾ on 2 or 3 Sides

2016, Jan. 29 Litho.

5054a A3887 (49c) pane of 10, P#S11111 12.50

By its nature, No. 5054a is a complete booklet (BC296). The peelable backing serves as a booklet cover.

5054b, 5055a, BC297 — A3887

Serpentine Die Cut 11¼x10¾ on 2 or 3 Sides

2016, Jan. 29 Self-Adhesive Litho.

With Microprinted "USPS" to Right of Flagpole Under Flag

5054b A3887 (49c) pane of 20, P#S11111 25.00

With Microprinted "USPS" on Second White Flag Stripe

5055a A3887 (49c) Pane of 20, P#P1111 25.00

Nos. 5054b and 5055a are complete double-sided booklets. Eight stamps plus P# and the label that serves as a booklet cover (BC297) are on one side of the peelable backing and 12 stamps are on the other side of the backing. The booklet covers for Nos. 5054b and 5055a have different fonts in the numbers in the bar code.

5090b, BC298 — A3912-A3921

Serpentine Die Cut 11 on 2 or 3 Sides

2016, June 3 Self-Adhesive Litho.

5090b (47c) Pane of 20, P#B11111 40.00

No. 5090b is a complete booklet with 12 stamps (Nos. 5083-5090, 2 each Nos. 5081-5082) on one side and 8 stamps (Nos. 5083-5090), plate number, and booklet cover (BC298) on the other side. The peelable backing serves as a booklet cover.

5097c — A3924-A3928

5097c — BC299

2016

$9.40 fold-it-yourself booklet contains 20 self-adhesive (47c) stamps

2016, June 30 Litho. *Serpentine Die Cut 10¾*

5097c (47c) pane of 20, 4 each #5093-5094, 5096-5097, 2 each #5095, 5095a 30.00

No. 5097c is a complete booklet (BC299). The peelable backing, which has a plate number (B11111), serves as a booklet cover.

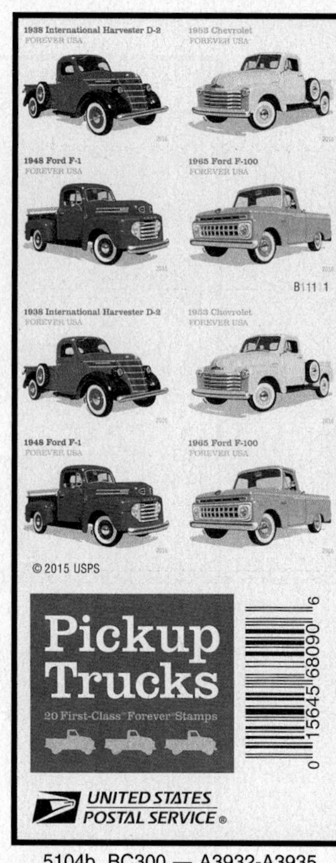

5104b, BC300 — A3932-A3935

Serpentine Die Cut 11 on 2 or 3 Sides

2016, July 15 Litho.

Self-Adhesive

5104b (47c) Pane of 20, P#B11111 25.00

No. 5104b is a complete booklet with 12 stamps (3 each Nos. 5101-5104) on one side and 8 stamps (2 each Nos. 5101-5104), plate number, and booklet cover (BC300) on the other side. The peelable backing serves as a booklet cover.

5125a, BC301 — A3937-A3956

Serpentine Die Cut 11 on 2 or 3 Sides

2016, Aug. 2 Self-Adhesive Litho.

5125a (47c) pane of 20, #5106-5125, P#P1111 30.00

No. 5125a is a complete double-sided booklet. Eight stamps (#5118-5125) plus P# and the label that serves as a booklet cover (BC301) are on one side of the peelable backing and 12 stamps (#5106-5117) are on the other side of the backing.

5129b, BC302 — A3957-A3960

Serpentine Die Cut 10¾ on 2 or 3 Sides

2016, Aug. 4 Self-Adhesive Litho.

5129b (47c) pane of 20, 5 each #5126-5129, P#P1111 30.00

No. 5129b is a complete double-sided booklet. Eight stamps (2 each #5126-5129) plus P# and the label that serves as a booklet cover (BC302) are on one side of the peelable backing and 12 stamps (3 each #5126-5129) are on the other side of the backing.

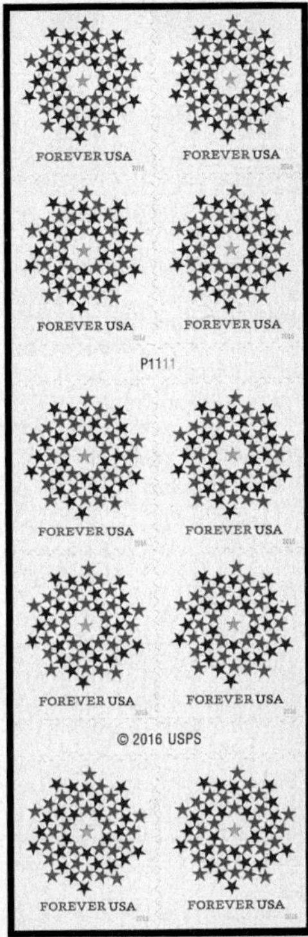

5131a — A3961

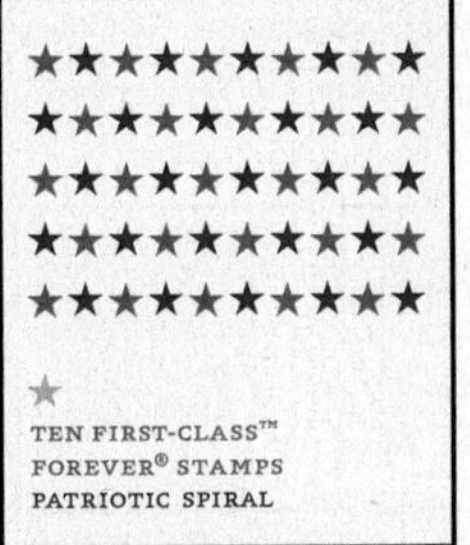

5131a — BC303

2016

$4.70 fold-it-yourself booklet contains 10 self-adhesive (47c) stamps

Serpentine Die Cut 11 on 2 or 3 Sides

2016, Aug. 19 Litho.

5131a A3961 (47c) pane of 10, P#P1111 12.50

By its nature, No. 5131a is a complete booklet (BC303). The peelable backing serves as a booklet cover.

5140b, BC304 — A3967-A3970

Serpentine Die Cut 11x10¾ on 2 or 3 Sides

2016, Sept. 29 Litho.

Self-Adhesive

5140b (47c) pane of 20, 5 each #5137-5140, P#B11111 25.00

No. 5140b is a complete double-sided booklet. Eight stamps (2 each #5137-5140) plus P# and the label that serves as a booklet cover (BC304) are on one side of the peelable backing and 12 stamps (3 each #5137-5140) are on the other side of the backing.

5143a, BC305 — A3973

5144a, BC306 — A3974

5148b, BC307 — A3975-A3978

Serpentine Die Cut 10¾x11 on 2 or 3 Sides

2016 Litho.

Self-Adhesive

5143a A3973 (47c) pane of 20, P#P11111, *Oct. 18* 25.00

5144a A3974 (47c) pane of 20, P#P11111, *Nov. 3* 25.00

5148b (47c) pane of 20, 5 each #5145-5148, P#B1111, *Oct. 7* 25.00

No. 5143a is a complete double-sided booklet. Eight stamps plus P# and the label that serves as a booklet cover (BC305) are on one side of the peelable backing and 12 stamps are on the other side of the backing. No. 5144a is a complete double-sided booklet. Eight stamps plus P# and the label that serves as a booklet cover (BC306) are on one side of the peelable backing and 12 stamps are on the other side of the backing. No. 5148b is a complete double-sided booklet. Eight stamps (2 each #5145-5148) plus P# and the label that serves as a booklet cover (BC307) are on one side of the peelable backing and 12 stamps (3 each #5145-5148) are on the other side of the backing.

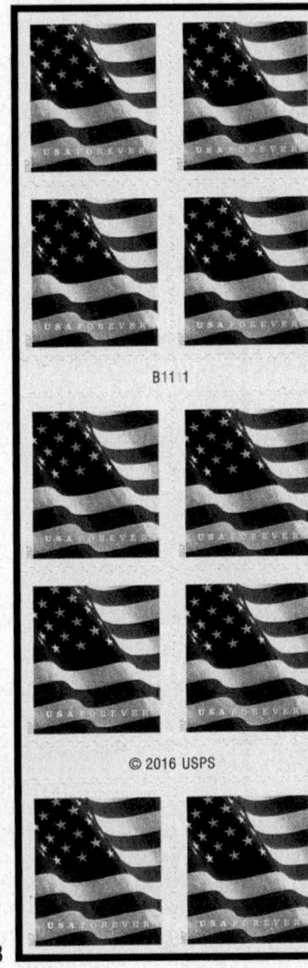

5160a — A3988

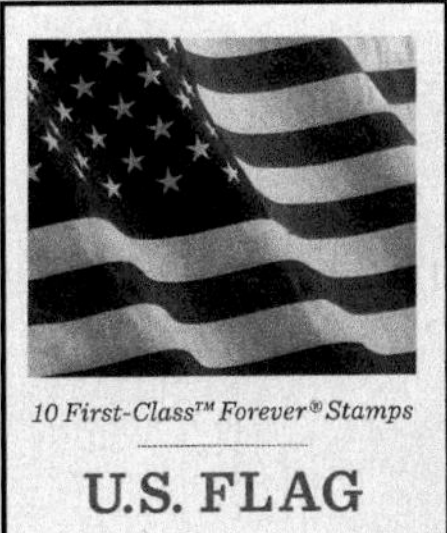

5160a — BC308

2017

$4.90 fold-it-yourself booklet contains 10 self-adhesive (49c) stamps

Serpentine Die Cut 11¼x10¾ on 2 or 3 Sides

2017, Jan. 27 Litho.

Microprinted "USPS" at Right on Fourth Red Stripe

5160a A3988 (49c) pane of 10, P#B1111 12.50

By its nature, No. 5160a is a complete booklet (BC308). The peelable backing serves as a booklet cover.

5160b, 5161a, BC309 — A3988

Serpentine Die Cut 11¼x10¾ on 2 or 3 Sides

2017, Jan. 27 Self-Adhesive Litho.

With Microprinted "USPS" at Right of Fourth Red Stripe

5160b (49c) pane of 20, P#B1111 25.00

With Microprinted "USPS" at Right on Second White Stripe

5161a (49c) pane of 20, P#P1111 25.00

Nos. 5160b and 5161a are complete double-sided booklets. Eight stamps plus P# and the label that serves as a booklet cover (BC309) are on one side of the peelable backing and 12 stamps are on the other side of the backing. The booklet covers for Nos. 5160b and 5161a have different fonts in the numbers in the bar code.

5162a — A3988

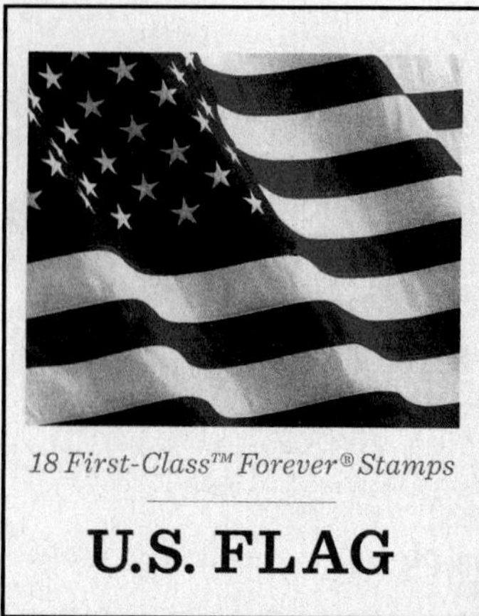

5162a
BC310

($8.82) fold-it-yourself booklet contains 18 self-adhesive (49c) stamps

Serpentine Die Cut 11¼x10¾ on 2, 3 or 4 Sides

2017, Jan. 27 Self-Adhesive Litho.

Microprinted "USPS" at Left on Second White Stripe

5162a A3988 (49c) pane of 18, P#P1111 50.00

No. 5162a is a complete booklet (BC310). The peelable backing serves as a booklet cover.

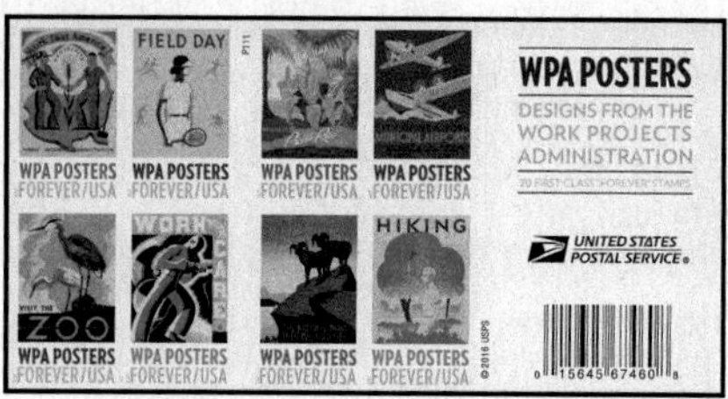

5189b, BC311 — A4009-A4018

Serpentine Die Cut 11 on 2 or 3 Sides

2017, Mar. 7 Self-Adhesive Litho.

5189b (49c) pane of 20, P#P1111 30.00

No. 5189b is a complete double-sided booklet. Eight stamps (1 each #5181-5184, 5186-5189) plus P# and the label that serves as a booklet cover (BC311) are on one side of the peelable backing and 12 stamps (2 each #5180, 5185, 1 each #5181-5184, 5186-5189) are on the other side of the backing.

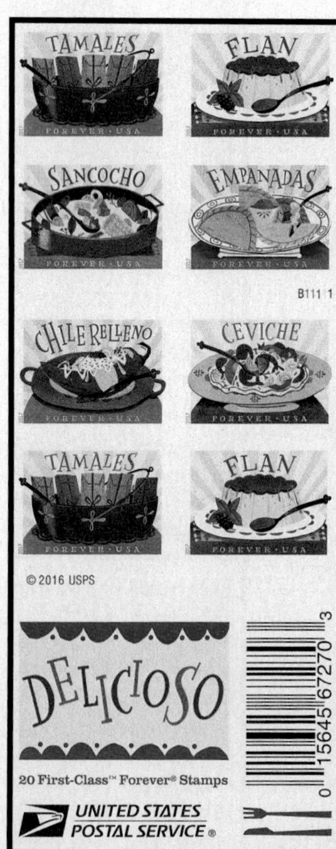

5197b, BC312 — A4021-A4026

Serpentine Die Cut 11 on 2 or 3 Sides

2017, Apr. 20 Self-Adhesive Litho.

5197b (49c) pane of 20, P#B11111 25.00

No. 5197b is a complete double-sided booklet. Eight stamps (1 each Nos. 5194-5197, 2 each Nos. 5192-5193) plus P# and the label that serves as a booklet cover (BC312) are on one side of the peelable backing and 12 stamps (2 each Nos. 5192-5197) are on the other side of the backing.

5240b, BC313 — A4077-A4080

Serpentine Die Cut 11 on 2 or 3 Sides

2017, Aug. 16 Self-Adhesive Litho.

5240b (49c) pane of 20, 5 each #5237-5240, P#B1111 25.00

No. 5240b is a complete double-sided booklet. Eight stamps (2 each Nos. 5237-5240) plus P# and the label that serves as a booklet cover (BC313) are on one side of the peelable backing and 12 stamps (3 each Nos. 5237-5240) are on the other side of the backing.

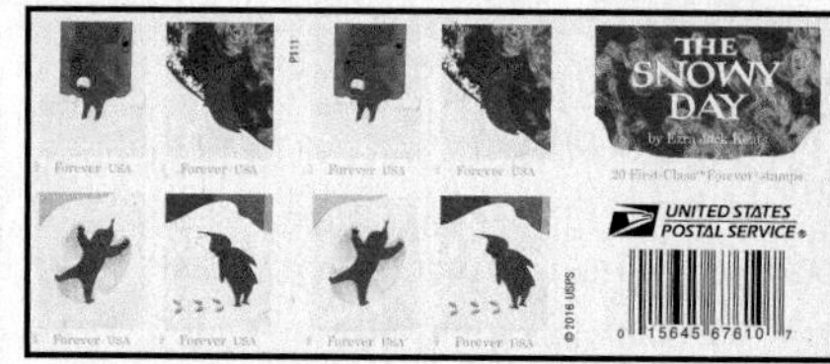

5246b, BC314 — A4082-A4085

Serpentine Die Cut 10¾ on 2 or 3 Sides

2017, Oct. 4 Self-Adhesive Litho.

5246b (49c) pane of 20, 5 each #5243-5246, P#P1111 25.00

No. 5246b is a complete double-sided booklet. Eight stamps (2 each Nos. 5243-5246) plus P# and the label that serves as a booklet cover (BC314) are on one side of the peelable backing and 12 stamps (3 each Nos. 5243-5246) are on the other side of the backing.

5250b, BC315 — A4086-A4089

Serpentine Die Cut 10¾ on 2 or 3 Sides

2017, Oct. 5 Self-Adhesive Litho.

5250b (49c) pane of 20, 5 each #5247-5250, P#B1111 25.00

No. 5250b is a complete double-sided booklet. Eight stamps (2 each Nos. 5247-5250) plus P# and the label that serves as a booklet cover (BC315) are on one side of the peelable backing and 12 stamps (3 each Nos. 5247-5250) are on the other side of the backing.

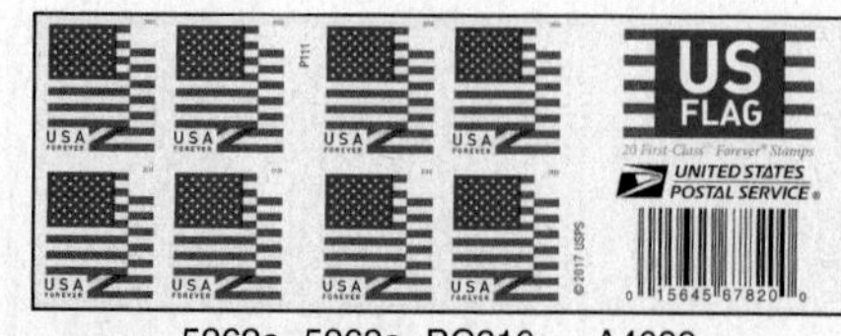

5262a, 5263a, BC316 — A4099

Serpentine Die Cut 11¼x10¾ on 2 or 3 Sides

2018, Feb. 9 Self-Adhesive Litho.

With Microprinted "USPS" at Left of Flag Fold on Fourth Red Stripe

5262a A4099 (50c) pane of 20, P#P111 25.00

With Microprinted "USPS" at Right of Flag Fold on Fifth White Stripe

5263a A4099 (50c) Pane of 20, P#B111 25.00

Nos. 5262a and 5263a are complete double-sided booklets. Eight stamps plus P# and the label that serves as a booklet cover (BC316) are on one side of the peelable backing and 12 stamps are on the other side of the backing. The booklet covers for Nos. 5262a and 5263a have different fonts in the numbers in the bar code.

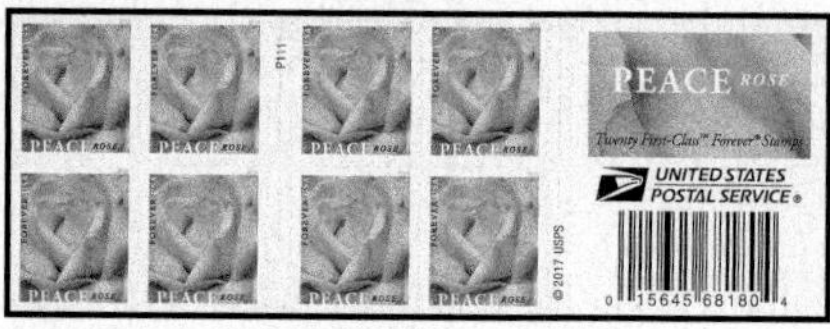

5280a, BC317 — A4116

Serpentine Die Cut 11¼x10¾ on 2 or 3 Sides

2018, Apr. 21 Self-Adhesive Litho.

5280a A4116 (50c) Pane of 20, P#P1111 25.00

No. 5280a is a complete double-sided booklet. Eight stamps plus P# and the label that serves as a booklet cover (BC317) are on one side of the peelable backing and 12 stamps are on the other side of the backing.

5294b, BC318 — A4120-A4129

Serpentine Die Cut 11¼x10¾ on 2 or 3 Sides

2018, June 20 Litho.

Self-Adhesive

5294b (50c) pane of 20, P#P1111 25.00

Nos. 5294b has a scratch-and-sniff coating with a fruity aroma, and is a double-sided booklet with 12 stamps on one side (Nos. 5286-5289, 5291-5294, 2 each Nos 5285, 5290), and eight stamps (Nos. 5286-5289, 5291-5294) plus a label that serves as the booklet cover (BC318) on the other side.

5320b, BC319 — A4165-A4168

Serpentine Die Cut 10¾ on 2 or 3 Sides

2018, Sept. 22 Self-Adhesive Litho.

5320b (50c) pane of 20, 5 each #5317-5320, P#B11111 25.00

No. 5320b is a complete double-sided booklet. Eight stamps (2 each Nos. 5317-5320) plus P# and the label that serves as a booklet cover (BC319) are on one side of the peelable backing and 12 stamps (3 each Nos. 5317-5320) are on the other side of the backing.

5331a, BC320 — A4179

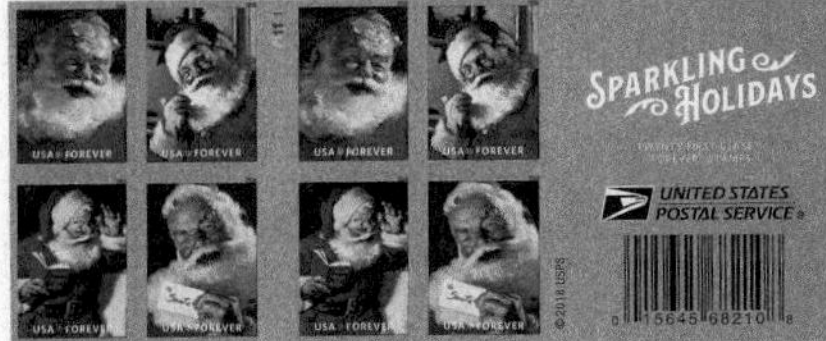
5335b, BC321 — A4180-A4183

Serpentine Die Cut 10¾x11 on 2 or 3 Sides

2018 Litho.

Self-Adhesive

5331a A4179 (50c) pane of 20, P#B11111, *Oct. 3* 25.00

5335b (50c) pane of 20, 5 each #5332-5335, P#P11111, *Oct. 11* 25.00

No. 5331a is a complete double-sided booklet. Eight stamps plus P# and the label that serves as a booklet cover (BC320) are on one side of the peelable backing and 12 stamps are on the other side of the backing.

No. 5335b is a complete double-sided booklet. Eight stamps (2 each Nos. 5332-5335) plus P# and the label that serves as a booklet cover (BC321) are on one side of the peelable backing and 12 stamps (3 each Nos. 5332-5335) are on the other side of the backing.

5344a, 5345a, BC322 — A4189

Serpentine Die Cut 10¾x11¼ on 2 or 3 Sides

2019, Jan. 27 Litho.

Self-Adhesive

Microprinted "USPS" at Upper Left Corner of Flag

5344a A4189 (55c) pane of 20, P#P1111, P2222 25.00

Microprinted "USPS" to Right of Sixth Red Flag Stripe

5345a A4189 (55c) pane of 20, P#B1111 25.00

Nos. 5344a and 5345a are complete booklets with 12 stamps on one side and 8 stamps, plate number, and booklet cover (BC322) on the other side. The peelable backing serves as a booklet cover. The booklet covers for Nos. 5344a and 5345a have different fonts for the numbers in the bar code.

5359b, BC323 — A4194-A4203

Serpentine Die Cut 11 on 2 or 3 Sides

2019, Feb. 15 Litho.

Self-Adhesive

5359b (55c) pane of 20, 2 each #5350-5359, P#B1111 50.00

No. 5359b is a complete double-sided booklet. Eight stamps (Nos. 5352-5359) plus P# and the label that serves as a booklet cover (BC323) are on one side of the peelable backing and 12 stamps (Nos. 5352-5359, 2 each Nos. 5350-5351) are on the other side of the backing.

5398b, BC324 — A4234-A4237

Serpentine Die Cut 11x10¾ on 2 or 3 Sides

2019, July 9 Litho.

Self-Adhesive

5398b (55c) pane of 20, 5 each #5395-5398, P#B11111 25.00

No. 5398b is a complete double-sided booklet. Eight stamps (2 each Nos. 5395-5398) plus P# and the label that serves as a booklet cover (BC324) are on one side of the peelable backing and 12 stamps (3 each Nos. 5395-5398) are on the other side of the backing.

5408b, BC325 — A4244-A4247

Serpentine Die Cut 10¾x10½ (Nos. 5405, 5408), 10½x10¾ (Nos. 5406-5407)

2019, Aug. 1 Litho.

Self-Adhesive

5408b (55c) pane of 20, 5 each #5405-5408, P#B1111 25.00

No. 5408b is a complete double-sided booklet. Eight stamps (2 each Nos. 5405-5408) plus P# and the label that serves as a booklet cover (BC325) are on one side of the peelable backing and 12 stamps (3 each Nos. 5405-5408) are on the other side of the backing.

5418b, BC326 — A4254-A4257

Serpentine Die Cut 11¼x10¾ on 2 or 3 Sides

2019, Sept. 17 Litho.

Self-Adhesive

5418b (55c) pane of 20, 5 each #5415-5418, P#P1111 25.00

No. 5418b is a complete double-sided booklet. Eight stamps (2 each Nos. 5415-5418) plus P# and the label that serves as a booklet cover (BC326) are on one side of the peelable backing and 12 stamps (3 each Nos. 5415-5418) are on the other side of the backing.

5427b, BC327 — A4263-A4266

Serpentine Die Cut 11¼x10¾ on 2 or 3 Sides

2019, Oct. 25 Litho.

Self-Adhesive

5427b (55c) pane of 20, 5 each #5424-5427, P#B11111 25.00

No. 5427b is a complete double-sided booklet. Eight stamps (2 each Nos. 5424-5427) plus P# and the label that serves as a booklet cover (BC327) are on one side of the peelable backing and 12 stamps (3 each Nos. 5424-5427) are on the other side of the backing.

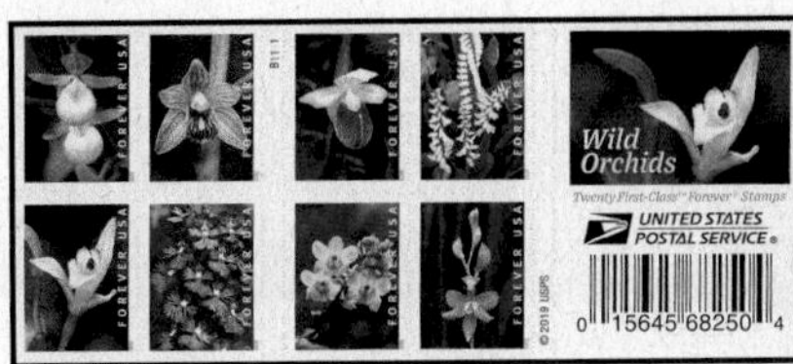
5454b, BC328 — A4284-A4293

Serpentine Die Cut 10¾x11 on 2 or 3 Sides

2020, Feb. 21 Litho.

Self-Adhesive

5454b (55c) pane of 20, 2 each #5445-5454, P#B1111 25.00

No. 5454b is a complete double-sided booklet. Eight stamps (Nos. 5446-5449, 5451-5454) plus P# and the label that serves as a booklet cover (BC328) are on one side of the peelable backing and 12 stamps (Nos. 5446-5449, 5451-5454, 2 each Nos. 5445, 5450) are on the other side of the backing.

5459a, BC329 — A4298

Serpentine Die Cut 11x10¾ on 2 or 3 Sides

2020, Apr. 18 Self-Adhesive Litho.

5459a A4298 (55c) Pane of 20, P#B1111 25.00

No. 5459a is a complete double-sided booklet. Eight stamps plus P# and the label that serves as a booklet cover (BC329) are on one side of the peelable backing and 12 stamps are on the other side of the backing.

5493b, BC330 — A4323-A4332

Serpentine Die Cut 10¾x11 on 2 or 3 Sides

2020, July 17 Self-Adhesive Litho.

5493b (55c) pane of 20, 2 each #5484-5493, P#B1111 25.00

No. 5493b is a complete double-sided booklet. Eight stamps (Nos. 5485-5488, 5490-5493) plus P# and the label that serves as a booklet cover (BC330) are on one side of the peelable backing and 12 stamps (Nos. 5485-5488, 5490-5493, 2 each Nos. 5484, 5489) are on the other side of the backing.

5525a, BC331 — A4364

Serpentine Die Cut 10¾ on 2 or 3 Sides

2020, Oct. 20 Litho.

Self-Adhesive

5525a A4364 (55c) pane of 20, P#B1111 25.00

No. 5525a is a complete double-sided booklet. Eight stamps plus P# and the label that serves as a booklet cover (BC331) are on one side of the peelable backing and 12 stamps are on the other side of the backing.

5529b, BC332 — A4365-A4368

Serpentine Die Cut 10¾ on 2 or 3 Sides

2020, Sept. 24 Litho.

Self-Adhesive

5529b (55c) pane of 20, 5 each #5526-5529, P#B1111 25.00

No. 5529b is a complete double-sided booklet. Eight stamps (2 each Nos. 5526-5529) plus P# and the label that serves as a booklet cover (BC332) are on one side of the peelable backing and 12 stamps (3 each Nos. 5526-5529) are on the other side of the backing.

5541b, BC333 — A4371-A4380

Serpentine Die Cut 10¾ on 2 or 3 Sides

2020, Oct. 16 Litho.

Self-Adhesive

5541b (55c) pane of 20, 5 each #5532-5541, P#P1111 25.00

No. 5541b is a complete double-sided booklet. Eight stamps (Nos. 5533-5536, 5538-5541) plus P# and the label that serves as a booklet cover (BC333) are on one side of the peelable backing and 12 stamps (Nos. 5533-5536, 5538-5541, 2 each Nos. 5532, 5537) are on the other side of the backing.

5567b, BC334 — A4392-A4401

Serpentine Die Cut 11 on 2 or 3 Sides

2021, Feb. 23 Litho.

Self-Adhesive

5567b (55c) pane of 20, 2 each #5558-5567, P#B1111 25.00

No. 5567b is a complete double-sided booklet. Eight stamps (Nos. 5560-5567) plus P# and the label that serves as a booklet cover (BC334) are on one side of the peelable backing and 12 stamps (Nos. 5560-5567, 2 each Nos. 5558-5559) are on the other side of the backing.

5572b, BC335 — A4403-A4406

Serpentine Die Cut 11¼x10¾ on 2 or 3 Sides

2021, Apr. 9 Litho.

Self-Adhesive

5572b (55c) pane of 20, 5 each #5569-5572, P#P1111 25.00

No. 5572b is a complete double-sided booklet. Eight stamps (2 each Nos. 5569-5572) plus P# and the label that serves as a booklet cover (BC335) are on one side of the peelable backing and 12 stamps (3 each Nos. 5569-5572) are on the other side of the backing.

5618b, BC336 — A4449-A4452

Serpentine Die Cut 10¾ on 2 or 3 Sides

2021, July 23 Litho.

Self-Adhesive

5618b (55c) pane of 20, 5 each #5615-5618, P#P1111 25.00

No. 5618b is a complete double-sided booklet. Eight stamps (2 each Nos. 5615-5618) plus P# and the label that serves as a booklet cover (BC336) are on one side of the peelable backing and 12 stamps (3 each Nos. 5615-5618) are on the other side of the backing.

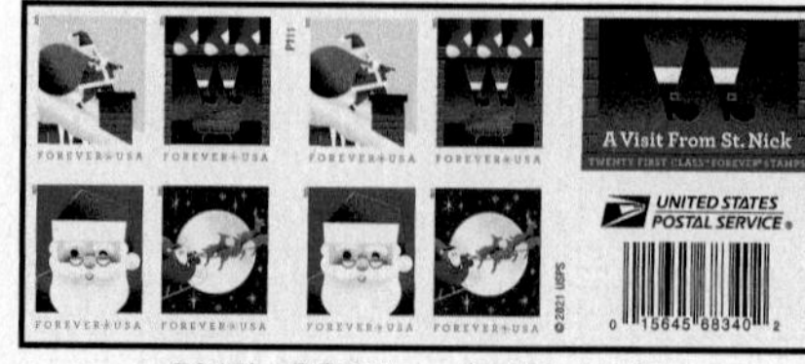

5647b, BC337 — A4478-A4481

Serpentine Die Cut 10¾x11 on 2 or 3 Sides

2021, Oct. 7 Litho.

Self-Adhesive

5647b (58c) pane of 20, 5 each #5644-5647, P#P1111 25.00

No. 5647b is a complete double-sided booklet. Eight stamps (2 each Nos. 5644-5647) plus P# and the label that serves as a booklet cover (BC337) are on one side of the peelable backing and 12 stamps (3 each Nos. 5644-5647) are on the other side of the backing.

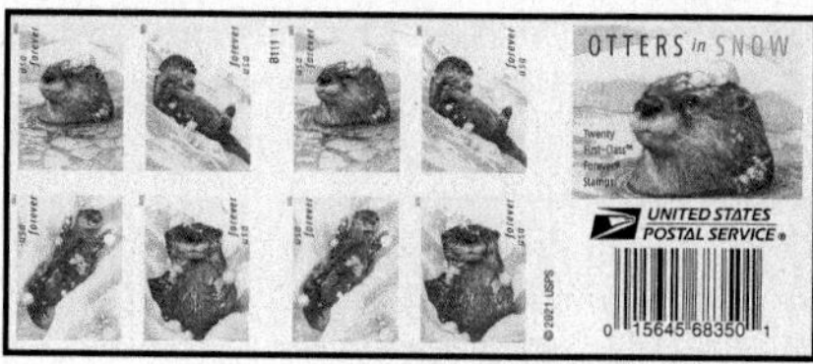

5651b, BC338 — A4482-A4485

Serpentine Die Cut 10¾x11 on 2 or 3 Sides

2021, Oct. 12 Litho.

Self-Adhesive

5651b (58c) pane of 20, 5 each #5648-5651, P#B11111 25.00

No. 5651b is a complete double-sided booklet. Eight stamps (2 each Nos. 5648-5651) plus P# and the label that serves as a booklet cover (BC338) are on one side of the peelable backing and 12 stamps (3 each Nos. 5648-5651) are on the other side of the backing.

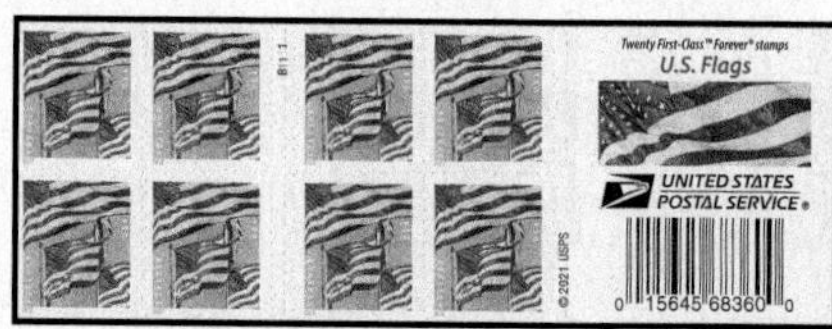

5658a, 5659a, BC339 — A4487

Serpentine Die Cut 11¼x10¾ on 2 or 3 Sides

2022, Jan. 9 Self-Adhesive Litho.

With Microprinted "USPS" Above Lower connector on Flagpole at Left

5658a A4487 (58c) pane of 20, P#B1111 25.00

With Microprinted "USPS" Above Lowest Blue Flag Field

5659a A4487 (58c) pane of 20, P#P1111 25.00

Nos. 5658a and 5659a are complete double-sided booklets. Eight stamps plus P# and the label that serves as a booklet cover (BC339) are on one side of the peelable backing and 12 stamps are on the other side of the backing. The booklet covers for Nos. 5658a and 5659a have different fonts in the numbers in the bar code.

5679b, BC340 — A4504-A4507

Serpentine Die Cut 10¾x11 on 2 or 3 Sides

2022, Mar. 14 **Litho.**

Self-Adhesive

5679b (58c) pane of 20, 5 each #5676-5679, P#P1111 25.00

No. 5679b is a complete double-sided booklet. Eight stamps (2 each Nos. 5676-5679) plus P# and the label that serves as a booklet cover (BC340) are on one side of the peelable backing and 12 stamps (3 each Nos. 5676-5679) are on the other side of the backing.

AIR POST BOOKLET PANES

C10a — AP6

FLAT PLATE PRINTING

1928 ***Perf. 11***

C10a	AP6	10c **dark blue,** *May 26*	70.00	*65.00*
		Never hinged	115.00	
		Tab at bottom, never hinged	*9,000.*	
		Tab at bottom, hinged	*7,500.*	

No. C10a was printed from specially designed 180-subject plates arranged exactly as a 360-subject plate-each pane of three occupying the relative position of a pane of six in a 360-subject plate. Plate numbers appear at the sides, therefore Position D does not exist except partially on panes which have been trimmed off center. All other plate positions common to a 360-subject plate are known.

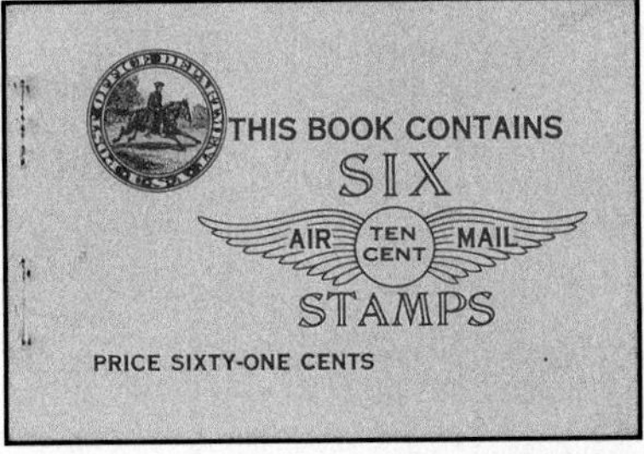

C10a BC8

1928 **Postrider and Wings**

61c booklet contains 2 panes of three 10c stamps.

Booklet

BKC1 BC8 61c **blue**	230.00	
Tab at bottom, one pane in complete booklet		*11,000.*

Catalogue values for unused panes in this section, from this point to the end, are for Never Hinged items.

C25a — AP17

ROTARY PRESS PRINTINGS

1943

C25a AP17 6c **carmine,** *Mar. 18* 3.50 1.50

180-Subject Plates Electric Eye Convertible.

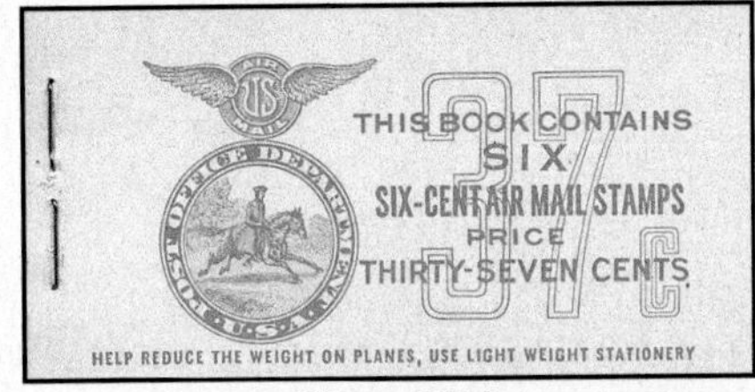

C25a — BC10

Large background numerals

1943 **Postrider and Wings**

37c booklet contains 2 panes of three 6c stamps.
73c booklet contains 4 panes of three 6c stamps.

Booklets

BKC2 BC10 37c **red**	8.00
BKC3 BC10 73c **red**	16.00

C39a — AP19

1949 ***Perf. 10½x11***

C39a	AP19	6c **carmine,** *Nov. 18*	12.00	5.00
C39c		Dry printing	25.00	—

C39a — BC11A

1949 **U.S. Airmail Wings**

The 73c and 85c booklets were the last sold for 1c over face value.

73c booklet contains 2 panes of six 6c stamps.

Booklets

BKC4 BC11A 73c **red,** with #C39a (3)	25.00
BKC4a BC11A 73c **red,** with #C39c	50.00

C51a — AP33

1958

C51a AP33 7c **blue,** *July 31* 6.50 5.00

C51a — BC11B

C51a, C60a — BC11C

1958-60 **U.S. Airmail Wings**

The 73c and 85c booklets were the last sold for 1c over face value.

85c booklet contains 2 panes of six 7c stamps.

Booklets

BKC5 BC11B 85c on 73c **red**	13.00
BKC6 BC11C 85c **blue**	13.00

1960

C60a AP33 7c **carmine,** *Aug. 19* 7.00 6.00

Booklets

BKC7 BC11C 85c **blue**	14.00
BKC8 BC11C 85c **red**	16.00

The different booklet slogan labels are illustrated with the regular-issue booklets in the Booklets section, beginning after No. 1036c.

C64b — AP42

1962-64

C64b AP42 8c **carmine,** pane of 5 + label, slogan 1, *Dec. 5, 1962*	6.00	3.00
With slogan 2, *1963*	45.00	5.00
With slogan 3, *1964*	12.00	2.50

For tagged variety, see No. C64c.

C64b, C64c — BC11D

C64b, C64c — BC11E

1962-64 **U.S. Airmail Wings**

80c booklet contains 2 panes of five 8c stamps.
$2 booklet contains 5 panes of five 8c stamps.

C64b, C64c — BC13B

1963-64 **Mr. Zip**

$2 booklet contains 5 panes of five 8c stamps.

Booklets (No. C64b)

BKC9 BC11D 80c **black,** *pink,* slogan 1 21.00
BKC10 BC11E $2 **red,** *pink,* slogan 1 32.50
BKC11 BC11D 80c **black,** *pink,* slogan 3 (2) 30.00
BKC12 BC11E $2 **red,** *pink,* slogan 2 275.00
BKC13 BC13B $2 **red,** *pink,* slogan 2 300.00
BKC14 BC13B $2 **red,** slogan 3 *3,500.*
BKC15 BC13B $2 **red,** *pink,* slogan 3 100.00

Fake examples of No. BKC14, such as booklets containing panes with extra staple holes, having obvious signs of being restapled and/or containing panes from two or more booklets, are known in the marketplace. Expertization by competent authorities is strongly recommended.

C64c AP42 As No. C64b, tagged, slogan 3, *1964* 1.75 .75
Plate of 360 subjects (300 stamps, 60 labels).

Booklets (No. C64c)

BKC16 BC11D 80c **black** (2) 65.00
BKC17 BC11D 80c **black,** *pink* *500.00*
BKC18 BC13B $2 **red,** *pink* *350.00*
BKC19 BC13B $2 **red** (3) 11.50

C72b — AP49

1968-73 ***Perf. 11x10½***

C72b AP49 10c **carmine,** pane of 8, *Jan. 5, 1968* 2.25 2.00

C72b — BC14B

1968

$4 booklet contains 5 panes of eight 10c stamps.

Booklet

BKC20 BC14B $4 **red** (2) 12.00

Varieties

C72d Vert. pair, imperf. btwn., in #C72b with foldover *5,250.* —
C72f As "b," tagging omitted — —

C72c — AP49

C72c AP49 10c **carmine,** pane of 5 + label, slogan 4, *Jan. 6, 1968* 3.50 1.25
With slogan 5 3.50 1.25
C72g As "c," tagging omitted, slogan 4 —
As "c," tagging omitted, slogan 5 —

C72c — BC15A

1968

$1 booklet contains 2 panes of five 10c stamps.

Booklet

BKC21 BC15A $1 **red** (2) 8.00

No. BKC21 normally is found with one pane each of slogans 4 and 5, and only very occasionally with two panes each of slogan 4 or slogan 5.

C78a — AP54

C78a AP54 11c **carmine,** pane of 4 + 2 labels, slogans 5 & 4, *May 7, 1971* 1.25 1.00
C78d As "a," tagging omitted —

C78a, 1280c — BC15B

1971

$1 booklet contains 2 panes of four 11c stamps and 1 pane of six 2c stamps.

Combination Booklet

BKC22 BC15B $1 **red,** 2 #C78a + 1 #1280c (2) 3.75

C79a — AP55

C79a AP55 13c **carmine,** pane of 5 + label, slogan 8, *Dec. 27, 1973* 1.50 1.00

C79a — BC18

1973

$1.30 booklet contains 2 panes of five 13c stamps.

Booklet

BKC23 BC18 $1.30 **blue & red** (2) 3.25

Combination Booklet

See No. BK126.

No. C72b, the 8-stamp pane, was printed from 320-subject plate and from 400-subject plate; No. C72c, C78a and C79a from 360-subject plates.

COMPUTER VENDED POSTAGE STAMPS

Unlike meters, except for the limits of the service requested, computer vended postage stamps are usable from any post office at any date.

Self-service user-interactive mailing system machines which vended computer-printed postage were in service and available to the general public at the Martin Luther King, Jr., Station of the Washington, DC, Post Office, and at the White Flint Mall in Kensington, MD, until May 7, 1990.

Machines were also available for use by delegates to the 20th Universal Postal Congress at the Washington Convention Center between Nov. 13 and Dec. 14, 1989. These machines, Washington Nos. 11 and 12, were not readily accessible by the general public.

A variety of services were available by using the machines, which could weigh items to be sent, determine postage rates through the connected computer, permit the customer to cancel the transaction or continue with it and generate a postage stamp, a label and a receipt. The stamps produced were valid only for domestic postage.

A tagged orange strip runs along the left side of the stamp. The requested mail service is in a double line box.

The denomination is in the upper box at right under "U.S. Postage." The date of the transaction is below the denomination. Next to the date is a number which indicates the item number within the transaction. The maximum number of items per transaction may be five.

Above the post office location is a box at right which gives the machine number, followed by the transaction or serial number. Stamps from the same transaction, which are generated and printed at the same time, will have the same transaction number, but different item numbers, even if different mail services are requested. Transaction numbers go back to 00001 every time the machine is reset. Below this is the weight of the item to be mailed.

Along with each stamp generated came an unattached label with one of three slogan types: "We Deliver. . .," used from September to November, "We Deliver. . . / United States Postal Service," used thereafter, and "Developed by / Technology Resource Department," used only on Machine 11 during its limited use.

Listings and values are for the basic denominations of the five postal services, though others are known or possible (45c, 65c, 85c for first class over 1 oz., $1.10 for certified first class, $3.25 for priority mail, $8.50 for express mail to post office boxes, parcel post weight and zone variations, etc.). Values for used copies are for those with a regular cancellation.

A total of 3,000 unused sets of five different service stamps and unused sets of two 25c (Nos. 02501-12500) first class stamps furnished to the Philatelic Agency have a first day date and serial numbers with the final three digits matching. First day dates Nos. 00101-02500 were sold over the counter at post offices.

Stamps were intended to be dispensed individually. The height of the stamps produced differs from machine to machine. Unsevered strips of stamps are known, as are unsevered strips of a slogan and one or more stamps. Printing varieties such as squeezes (more than one impression condensed on to one stamp) and stretches (impression stretched out so that a complete impression will not fit on the paper) also are known.

Issues starting with No. 31 will be explained with the listings.

CVP1

CVP2

1989, Aug. 23 **Tagged** ***Guillotined***

Self-Adhesive

Washington, DC, Machine 82

CVP1 CVP1 25c **First Class,** any date other than first day 6.00 —
a. First day dated, serial Nos. 12501-15500 5.00 —
b. First day dated, serial Nos. 00001-12500 5.00 —
On cover with first day cancel *150.00*
c. First day dated, over No. 27500 — —
On cover with first day cancel *150.00*

CVP2 CVP1 $1 **Third Class,** any date other than first day — —
a. First day dated, serial Nos. 24501-27500 — —
b. First day dated, over No. 27500 — —

CVP3 CVP2 $1.69 **Parcel Post,** any date other than first day — —
a. First day dated, serial Nos. 21501-24500 — —
b. First day dated, over No. 27500 — —

CVP4 CVP1 $2.40 **Priority Mail,** any date other than first day — —
a. First day dated, serial Nos. 18501-21500 — —
b. Priority Mail ($2.74), with bar code (CVP2) *100.00*
c. First day dated, over No. 27500 — —
On cover with first day cancel or verifying receipt *500.00*

CVP5 CVP1 $8.75 **Express Mail,** any date other than first day — —
a. First day dated, serial Nos. 15501-18500 — —
b. First day dated, over No. 27500 — —
On cover with first day cancel or verifying receipt —
Nos. 1a-5a (5) 82.50 —

Washington, DC, Machine 83

CVP6 CVP1 25c **First Class,** any date other than first day 6.00 —
a. First day dated, serial Nos. 12501-15500 5.00 —
b. First day dated, serial Nos. 00001-12500 5.00 —
On cover with first day cancel *150.00*
c. First day dated, over No. 27500 — —
On cover with first day cancel *150.00*

Error dates 11/17/90 and 11/18/90 exist.

CVP7 CVP1 $1 **Third Class,** any date other than first day — —
a. First day dated, serial Nos. 24501-27500 — —
b. First day dated, over No. 27500 — —

CVP8 CVP2 $1.69 **Parcel Post,** any date other than first day 15.00 —
a. First day dated, serial Nos. 21501-24500 — —
b. First day dated, over No. 27500 — —

CVP9 CVP1 $2.40 **Priority Mail,** any date other than first day — —
a. First day dated, serial Nos. 18501-21500 — —
b. First day dated, over No. 27500 — —
On cover with first day cancel or verifying receipt *500.00*

A Priority Mail $3.25 value also exists unused. A Priority Mail stamp exists on cover with error date 11/17/90 exists, and an unused stamp with error date 11/18/90 exists.

c. Priority Mail ($2.74), with bar code (CVP2) *100.00*

Error date 11/18/90 exists.

CVP10 CVP1 $8.75 **Express Mail,** any date other than first day — —
a. First day dated, serial Nos. 15501-18500 — —
b. First day dated, over No. 27500 — —
On cover with first day cancel or verifying receipt —
Nos. 6a-10a (5) 57.50 —

Error date 11/17/90 exists.

1989, Sept. 1

Kensington, MD, Machine 82

CVP11 CVP1 25c **First Class,** any date other than first day 6.00 —
a. First day dated, serial Nos. 12501-15500 5.00 —
b. First day dated, serial Nos. 00001-12500 5.00 —
On cover with first day cancel *100.00*
c. First day dated, over No. 27500 — —
On cover with first day cancel *100.00*

CVP12 CVP1 $1 **Third Class,** any date other than first day — —
a. First day dated, serial Nos. 24501-27500 — —
b. First day dated, over No. 27500 — —

CVP13 CVP2 $1.69 **Parcel Post,** any date other than first day — —
a. First day dated, serial Nos. 21501-24500 — —
b. First day dated, over No. 27500 — —

CVP14 CVP1 $2.40 **Priority Mail,** any date other than first day — —
a. First day dated, serial Nos. 18501-21500 — —
b. First day dated, over No. 27500 — —
c. Priority Mail ($2.74), with bar code (CVP2) *100.00*

CVP15 CVP1 $8.75 **Express Mail,** any date other than first day — —
a. First day dated, serial Nos. 15501-18500 — —
b. First day dated, over No. 27500 — —
Nos. 11a-15a (5) 57.50 —
Nos. 1b, 11b (2) 10.00 —

Kensington, MD, Machine 83

CVP16 CVP1 25c **First Class,** any date other than first day 6.00 —
a. First day dated, serial Nos. 12501-15500 5.00 —
b. First day dated, serial Nos. 00001-12500 5.00 —
c. First day dated, over No. 27500 — —
On cover with first day cancel *100.00*

CVP17 CVP1 $1 **Third Class,** any date other than first day — —
a. First day dated, serial Nos. 24501-27500 — —
b. First day dated, over No. 27500 — —

CVP18 CVP2 $1.69 **Parcel Post,** any date other than first day — *12.50*
a. First day dated, serial Nos. 21501-24500 — —
b. First day dated, over No. 27500 — —

CVP19 CVP1 $2.40 **Priority Mail,** any date other than first day — —
a. First day dated, serial Nos. 18501-21500 — —

b. First day dated, over No. 27500 — —
c. Priority Mail ($2.74), with bar code (CVP2) 100.00
CVP20 CVP1 $8.75 **Express Mail,** any date other than first day — —
a. First day dated, serial Nos. 15501-18500 — —
b. First day dated, over No. 27500 — —
Nos. 16a-20a (5) 57.50 —
Nos. 6b, 16b (2) 10.00 —

Unsevered pairs and single with advertising label exist for most, if not all, of the machine vended items from Kensington machine #83. Other combinations also exist.

1989, Nov. Washington, DC, Machine 11

CVP21 CVP1 25c **First Class** *150.00*
a. First Class, with bar code (CVP2) —

Stamps in CVP1 design with $1.10 denominations exist (certified first class) dated 11/20/89. Value, unused, $650. A 45c denomination exists unused (dated 11/22/89) on cover to Europe and on Certificate of Mailing.

CVP22 CVP1 $1 **Third Class** *500.00*
CVP23 CVP2 $1.69 **Parcel Post** *500.00*
CVP24 CVP1 $2.40 **Priority Mail** *500.00*
a. Priority Mail ($2.74), with bar code (CVP2) —
CVP25 CVP1 $8.75 **Express Mail** *500.00*

No. CVP21 dated Nov. 30 known on cover, Nos. CVP24-CVP25 known dated Dec. 2.

Washington, DC, Machine 12

CVP26 CVP1 25c **First Class** *200.00*

No. CVP26, dated 12/13/89 is known on cover. $1.10 Certified First Class stamps dated 11/20/89 exist on covers.

CVP27 CVP1 $1 **Third Class** *600.00*

A $1.40 Third Class stamp of type CVP2, dated Dec. 1 is known on a Dec. 2 cover.

CVP28 CVP2 $1.65 **Parcel Post** *600.00*
CVP29 CVP1 $2.40 **Priority Mail** *600.00*
a. Priority Mail ($2.74), with bar code (CVP2) —
CVP30 CVP1 $8.75 **Express Mail** *600.00*

Nos. CVP29-CVP30 known dated Dec. 1. An $8.50 Express Mail stamp, dated Dec. 2, exists on cover.

CVP3 — Type I

CVP3 — Type II

Denomination printed by ECA GARD Postage and Mailing Center machines.

COIL STAMPS

1992, Aug. 20 Engr. Tagged *Perf. 10 Horiz.*

CVP31 CVP3 29c **red & blue,** type I, prephosphored paper (solid tagging), dull gum .75 .25
Pair 1.50
P# strip of 5, P#1 8.00
P# single, #1 5.50
a. 29c Type I, prephosphored paper (mottled tagging), shiny gum .75 .25
Pair 1.50 —
P# strip of 5, P#1 8.00 —
P# single, #1 5.50
First day cover, Oklahoma City, OK 1.25
b. 32c Type II, prephosphored paper (solid tagging), dull gum, *Nov. 1994* .90 .40
Pair 1.80
P# strip of 5, P#1 35.00
P# single, #1 *30.00*
c. 32c Type II, prephosphored paper (mottled tagging), shiny gum 1.25 .40
Pair 2.50
P# strip of 5, P#1 12.00
P# single, #1 *15.00*

Types I and II differ in style of asterisk, period between dollar and cent figures and font used for figures, as shown in illustrations.

No. CVP31 was available at test sites in Arlington and Crystal City, VA, and in the Southern Maryland, Miami, Oklahoma City, Detroit and Santa Ana, CA, divisions. They were produced for use in ECA GARD Postage and Mailing Center (PMC) machines which can produce denominations from 1c through $99.99.

For Nos. CVP31-CVP31a, the 29c value is listed because it was the current first class rate and was the only value available through the USPS Philatelic Sales Division. The most common denomination available other than 29c is 1c (value 25c) because these were made in quantity, by collectors and dealers, between plate number strips. Later the machines were adjusted to provide only 19c and higher value stamps.

For Nos. CVP31b-CVP31c, the 32c value is listed because it was the first class rate in effect for the majority of the period the stamps were in use.

CVP4

Denominations printed by Unisys PMC machines.

1994, Feb. 19 Photo. Tagged *Perf. 9.9 Vert.*

CVP32 CVP4 29c **dark red & dark blue** .75 .35
Pair 1.50 —
P# strip of 5, #A11 8.50 —
P# single, #A11 5.00
First day cover, Merrifield, VA *(26,390)* 1.25

No. CVP32 was available at six test sites in northern Virginia. It was produced for use in machines which can produce values from 19c to $99.99. See note following No. CVP31.

For No. CVP32, the 29c value has been listed because it was the first class rate in effect at the time the stamp was issued.

1996, Jan. 26 Photo. Tagged *Perf. 9.9 Vert.*

CVP33 CVP4 32c **bright red & blue,** "1996" below design .75 .25
Pair 1.50 —
P# strip of 5, same, #11 8.50 —
P# single, #11 6.50

Letters in "USA" on No. CVP33 are thicker than on No. CVP32. Numerous other design differences exist in the moire pattern and in the bunting. No. CVP33 has "1996" in the lower left corner; No. CVP32 has no date.

For No. CVP33, the 32c value has been listed because it was the first class rate in effect at the time the stamp was issued.

CVP5

Illustration reduced.

1999, June Tagged *Die Cut*
Self-Adhesive

CVP34 CVP5 33c **black** *50.00* —
On cover *75.00*
a. "Priority Mail" under encryption at LL — —
b. "Express Mail" under encryption at LL — —

No. CVP34 was available from 15 NCR Automated Postal Center machines located in central Florida. Machines could produce values in any denomination required. The backing paper is taller and wider than the stamp.

Sales of No. CVP34 were discontinued in 2000 or 2001.

CVP6

Illustration reduced.

1999, May 7 Tagged *Die Cut*
Self-Adhesive
Size: 77½x39mm

Microprinting Above Red Orange Line

CVP35 CVP6 33c **black & red orange,** control numbers only at LL, round corners 20.00 —
Square corners 220.00 —
a. "Priority Mail" at LL, square corners 150.00 —
Round corners — —
b. "Priority Mail AS" and text string at LL, square corners 150.00 —
Round corners — —

No Microprinting Above Red Orange Line

CVP36 CVP6 33c **black & red orange,** control numbers only at LL, round corners 9.00 —
Square corners 250.00 —
a. "Priority Mail" at LL, square corners 125.00 —
Round corners — —
b. "Priority Mail AS" and text string at LL, square corners 125.00 —
Round corners — —

Size: 73½x42mm

CVP37 CVP6 33c **black & pink,** control numbers only at LL 3.75 —
a. "Priority Mail" at LL 5.00 —
b. "Priority Mail AS" and text string at LL 5.00 —

Nos. CVP35-CVP37 were available from 18 IBM Neopost machines located in central Florida, and at least one machine in the Washington, DC area (Merrifield, VA Automated Postal Center). The backing paper is taller than the stamp. Any denomination could be printed up to $99.99.

Simplypostage.com — CVP8

Serpentine Die Cut 8 at Right
2001 Self-Adhesive

Eagle and Stars Background

CVP39 CVP8 34c **black, blue & orange,** *2001* — —
On cover 75.00
Pane of 4 —
CVP40 CVP8 34c **black, blue & orange,** with control number at UL, *2001* — —
On cover 75.00
Pane of 4 —

Flag Background

CVP41 CVP8 34c **black, blue & orange,** with control number at UL, *2001* 50.00 —
On cover 150.00
Pane of 4 250.00
CVP42 CVP8 34c **black, blue & orange,** with control number at LL, *2001* 50.00 20.00
On cover 150.00
Pane of 4 250.00

Customers could print up to five panes of Nos. CVP39-CVP42 in each transaction. Panes were consecutively numbered identifying the total number of stamps and panes in each transaction.

Large Flag Design

The item shown was produced by Neopost. It was found that the large flag image hampered the barcode from being scanned. It is believed no examples were actually sold to the public. Five panes of four are believed to exist. Value, pane of 4, $300.

Neopostage.com — CVP9

Serpentine Die Cut 8¾ at Right
2002, June Self-Adhesive

CVP43 CVP9 21c **black, blue & orange,** 15.00
a. Booklet pane of 10 200.00
CVP44 CVP9 23c **black, blue & orange,** 10.00 —
On cover —
a. Booklet pane of 10 120.00
CVP45 CVP9 34c **black, blue & orange,** 20.00 —
On cover —
a. Booklet pane of 10 250.00
CVP46 CVP9 37c **black, blue & orange,** 12.50 —
On cover —
a. Booklet pane of 10 150.00

CVP47	CVP9	50c **black, blue & orange,**	15.00	—
		On cover		—
a.		Booklet pane of 10	180.00	
CVP47B	CVP9	57c **black, blue & orange,** *June 24, 2002*	—	
a.		Booklet pane of 10	—	
CVP48	CVP9	60c **black, blue & orange,**	14.00	—
		On cover		—
a.		Booklet pane of 10	160.00	
CVP49	CVP9	70c **black, blue & orange,**	16.00	—
		On cover		—
a.		Booklet pane of 10	200.00	
CVP50	CVP9	80c **black, blue & orange,**	18.00	—
		On cover		—
a.		Booklet pane of 10	200.00	
CVP51	CVP9	$3.50 **black, blue & orange,**	60.00	—
a.		Booklet pane of 1	—	
b.		Booklet pane of 2	—	
c.		Booklet pane of 5	—	
d.		Booklet pane of 10	700.00	
CVP52	CVP9	$3.85 **black, blue & orange,**	55.00	
a.		Booklet pane of 1	—	
b.		Booklet pane of 2	—	
c.		Booklet pane of 5	—	
d.		Booklet pane of 10	600.00	
CVP52E	CVP9	$12.45 **black, orange & blue,** *June 30, 2002*	—	
a.		Booklet pane of 1	—	
CVP53	CVP9	$13.65 **black, blue & orange,**	—	—
		On cover		—
a.		Booklet pane of 1	—	
b.		Booklet pane of 2	—	
c.		Booklet pane of 5	—	
d.		Booklet pane of 10	—	

Nos. CVP43-CVP53 were printed only with the stated values.

Denominations of 34c, 57c, $3.50 and perhaps others exist with a ICNOVA kiosk location designation. These were produced during pre-issue testing at a location not publicly accessible and are not considered to be valid postage. Stamps from the ICNOVA location have much smaller 2-D bar code squares. The denominations listed above come from other publicly accessible kiosk locations from June 20, 2002, forward. Official sales of these stamps began on June 20, 2002, or later for some denominations.

The 21c, 34c, 57c, $3.50 and $12.45 denominations were only sold from June 21 to June 29, 2002. They are all scarce, and some are rare. The 37c, $3.85 and $13.65 denominations were not sold until June 30, 2002, when the rate change took effect.

While the name on Nos. CVP39-CVP42 reads simplypostage.com and the name on Nos. CVP43-CVP53 reads neopostage.com, both were products of Neopost.

Earliest documented use: Nos. CVP43, CVP47, CVP51-CVP52, not known used; Nos. CVP44, CVP46, CVP48-CVP49, CVP53, 6/30; No. CVP45, 6/21; No. CVP50, 7/3.

CVP10

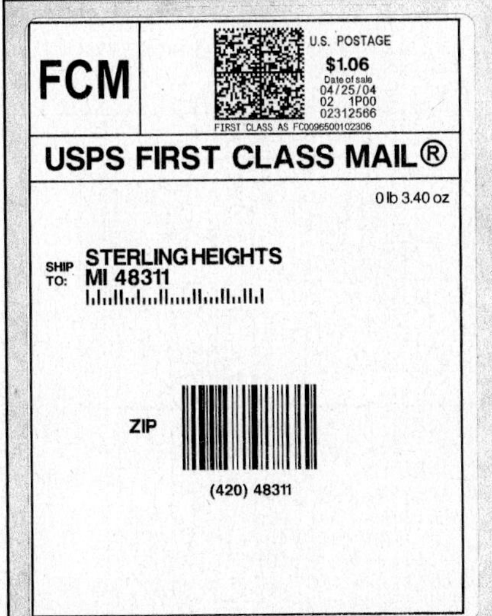

IBM Pitney Bowes — CVP11

Illustrations reduced.

2004, Apr. 14 Self-Adhesive *Die Cut*

CVP54	CVP10	37c **black & pink**	5.00	—
a.		"First Class Mail" under encryption at LL	2.50	—
b.		"Priority Mail" under encryption at LL	2.50	—
c.		"Parcel Post" under encryption at LL	2.50	—
d.		"International" under encryption at LL	2.50	—
CVP55	CVP11	37c **black,** "US Postage" under encryption at LL	5.00	—
a.		"First Class Mail" under encryption at LL	2.50	—
b.		"Priority Mail" under encryption at LL	2.50	—
c.		"Parcel Post" under encryption at LL	2.50	—
d.		"International" under encryption at LL	2.50	—

Nos. CVP54-CVP55 could be printed in any denomination up to $99.99. Catalogue values for Nos. CVP54-CVP54d and CVP55 are for stamps with low denominations. Stamps with denominations appropriate to the service described are valued correspondingly higher.

CVP12

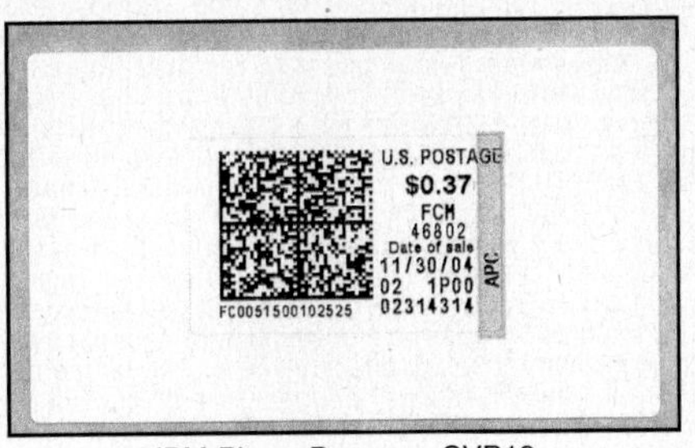

IBM Pitney Bowes — CVP13

Illustrations reduced.

2004, Nov. 19 Self-Adhesive *Die Cut*

CVP56	CVP12	37c **black & pink**	2.50	.45
CVP57	CVP13	37c **black & pink**	1.25	.45

Nos. CVP56-CVP57 could be printed in any denomination. No. CVP56 could be printed with three different rate inscriptions under the denomination. No. CVP57 could be printed with 18 different rate inscriptions and/or service indicators under the denomination, and with at least 27 different rate inscriptions and or/service indicators under the denomination on stamps with a four-digit code after the zip code.

Blank Under Denomination

"IM" and Numbers Under Encryption

CVP58	CVP13	60c **black & pink**	3.00	.50
CVP59	CVP13	80c **black & pink**	3.75	.50

"PM" and Numbers Under Encryption

CVP60	CVP13	$3.85 **black & pink**	15.00	.50

"EM" and Numbers Under Encryption

CVP61	CVP13	$13.65 **black & pink**	42.50	1.00

"IB" and Numbers Under Encryption

CVP62	CVP13	$1 **black & pink**	4.00	.25

Nos. CVP58-CVP61 could only be printed in denominations listed. No. CVP62 could be printed in any denomination above 99c. As of May 12, 2008, it was possible to create stamps with "IB" and numbers under encryption in any denomination. The computer software was later changed to once again only permit stamps of certain denominations to be created with "IB" and numbers under the encryption.

IBM Pitney Bowes Type of 2004

2006 Self-Adhesive *Die Cut*

Blank Under Denomination

"IM" and Numbers Under Encryption

CVP63	CVP13	48c **black & pink**	1.50	.40
CVP64	CVP13	63c **black & pink**	1.75	.50
CVP65	CVP13	84c **black & pink**	2.25	.50

"PM" and Numbers Under Encryption

CVP66	CVP13	$4.05 **black & pink**	11.00	.50
CVP66A	CVP13	$8.10 **black & pink**	30.00	1.00

"EM" and Numbers Under Encryption

CVP67	CVP13	$14.40 **black & pink**	32.50	1.00

Nos. CVP63-CVP67 could only be printed in denominations listed.

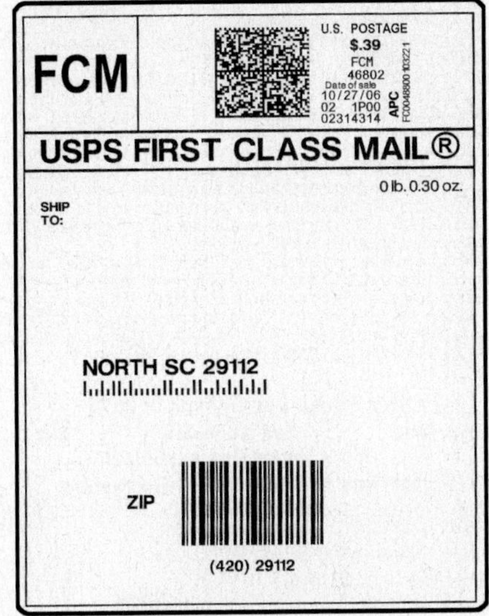

IBM Pitney Bowes — CVP14

Illustration reduced.

2006 Self-Adhesive *Die Cut*

No Inscription Under Encryption

Serial Number to Right of "APC"

"Ship To:" Above Destination City

CVP69	CVP14	39c **black**	2.25	.25

Nos. CVP69 could be printed in any denomination, with 14 different rate inscriptions and/or service indicators under the denomination on stamps having "Ship To:" at the left and no code below the weight, and at least 29 different rate inscriptions and/or service indicators under the denomination on stamps having a four-digit code at the right that is even with the words "Ship To:" and below the weight.

IBM Pitney Bowes Type of 2004

2006(?)-07 Self-Adhesive *Die Cut*

Blank Under Denomination

"IB" and Numbers Under Encryption

CVP70	CVP13	39c **black & pink**	1.00	.50
CVP71	CVP13	41c **black & pink**	1.75	.50
CVP72	CVP13	69c **black & pink**	2.50	.70

"IM" and Numbers Under Encryption

CVP73	CVP13	61c **black & pink**	2.25	.50
CVP74	CVP13	90c **black & pink**	3.50	.95

Nos. CVP70-CVP74 could only be printed in the denominations listed.

Nos. CVP71-CVP74 issued May, 2007. No. CVP70 was issued before the May rate change. As of May 12, 2008, it was possible to create stamps with "IB" and numbers under encryption in any denomination. The computer software was later changed to once again only permit stamps of certain denominations to be created with "IB" and numbers under the encryption. No. CVP70 was available for sale from Nov. 2006 to May 13, 2007. Nos. CVP71-CVP72 were available for sale from May 14, 2007 to May 11, 2008.

Pitney Bowes With Eagle at Right, One Code Number to Left of Sold Date — CVP15

Illustration reduced.

2006, Dec. **Self-Adhesive** ***Die Cut***

CVP75 CVP15 41c **black & pink,** no inscription below sold date — —
a. "Mailed From Zip Code ..." on bottom line 35.00 —
b. "Postcard" on bottom line 15.00 —
c. "First-Class Mail" on bottom line 15.00 —
d. "First-Class Mail Intl" on bottom line 15.00 —
e. "Priority" on bottom line 15.00 —
f. "Priority Envelope" on bottom line 15.00 —
g. "Priority Box" on bottom line 15.00 —
h. "Express Mail" on bottom line 30.00 —
i. "Express Envelope" on bottom line 30.00 —
j. "Parcel Post" on bottom line — —
k. "Priority Tube" on bottom line — —
l. "First Class" on bottom line 15.00 —

No. CVP75 was put into service at large companies and universities in Dec. 2006, with the majority of the machines not being available to the general public. Information about this stamp was not made available until 2007. Other rates and inscriptions might be available.

Nos. CVP75a could be printed in any denomination. Nos. CVP75b-CVP75f could be printed only in pre-programmed denominations based on the current rates for the service, or in any denominations at or above the minimum rates for the service. Values are for stamps with low denominations. A stamp with "Priority - Irregular Shape" on the bottom line has been reported to exist but has not been seen by the editors. Inscriptions generated by the software may vary from machine to machine depending on when the software was installed.

Two distinctly different colors of phosphor stripes on labels used in Mail & Go machines are known, with many Mail & Go adhesives appearing in both versions.

Private sector operators of Pitney Bowes "Mail & Go" machines are not bound to use only label paper supplied by Pitney Bowes. Competing label paper producers make and sell labels in the formats required for the machines that dispense Nos. CVP75 and CVP84. Thus, Nos. CVP75 and CVP84 without the Pitney Bowes logo on the reverse are not errors.

IBM Pitney Bowes Type of 2004

2008, May **Self-Adhesive** ***Die Cut***

Blank Under Denomination

"IM" and Numbers Under Encryption

CVP76 CVP13 94c **black & pink** 3.00 .60
CVP77 CVP13 $1.20 **black & pink** 3.75 1.25

Nos. CVP76-CVP77 could only be printed in the denominations listed.

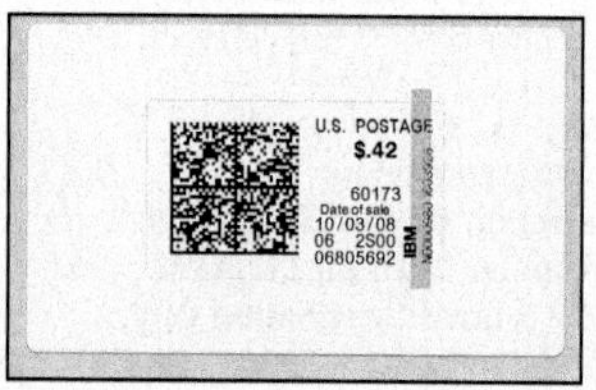

IBM — CVP16

Illustration reduced.

Die Cut With Rounded Corners

2008, June 4 **Self-Adhesive**

CVP78 CVP16 42c **black & pink** 4.25 —
a. Without "date of sale" inscription, *2009* — —

Die Cut With Perpendicular Corners

CVP79 CVP16 42c **black & pink** 4.25 —
a. Without "date of sale" inscription, *2009* — —

Nos. CVP78-CVP79 were made available during a pilot study to evaluate a new IBM kiosk at Schaumburg, IL. No. CVP78 could be printed in any denomination from 1c to $25. Each kiosk transaction was limited to $100. Individual panes with 6, 7, 8, 9 or 10 stamps could be purchased as long as the total face value of the pane did not exceed $100. The pane of 10 exists with the vertical pink tagging stripe along the left side of the stamps. The pane of 10 could only be bought with stamps denominated from 1c to $10. Stamps denominated from $10.01 to $16.66 could only be purchased in panes containing fewer than 10 stamps. Stamps denominated from $16.67 to $25 could only be purchased as a single stamp.

IBM Pitney Bowes Type of 2004

2009 **Self-Adhesive** ***Die Cut***

Blank Under Denomination

"IM" and Numbers Under Encryption

CVP80 CVP13 98c **black & pink** 2.00 .60
CVP81 CVP13 $1.24 **black & pink** 2.50 1.25

Nos. CVP80-CVP81 could only be printed in denominations listed.

IBM (Statue of Liberty) — CVP17

Illustration reduced.

Die Cut With Rounded Corners

2009, June 5 **Self-Adhesive**

CVP82 CVP17 44c **black & pink** 7.50 —
a. Without "date of sale" inscription, *2009* — —

Die Cut With Perpendicular Corners

CVP83 CVP17 44c **black & pink** 7.50 —
a. Without "date of sale" inscription, *2009* — —

No. CVP82 could be printed in any denomination from 1c to $25. Nos. CVP82-CVP83 were made available during a pilot study to evaluate a new IBM kiosk at Schaumburg, IL. The machine study at Schaumburg was scheduled to end on July 31, 2009. No. CVP82 was created for purchases of one to five individual stamps or any extra stamps beyond multiples of 10 ending in numerals 1 to 5.

INVERTS

Labels used to produce stamps in the dimensions of many items of CVP54 and similar later issues in this format were packaged in a fanfolded strip two labels wide and packaged in boxes that are stored in the machines from which the labels are fed to printers as purchases occur. Nothing prevents the labels from being fed in reverse, which results in inverted paper "errors." Such "inverts" (with phosphor stripe appearing on the opposite edge of the stamp than the intended edge) can be deliberately produced, and therefore are not listed.

SERVICE-INSCRIBED STAMPS

Listings of small label stamps from CVP84 reveal that various service-related abbreviations appear under the denominations of some stamps. From CVP84 onward (including the FOLD HERE varieties), all denominated stamps may be purchased that include service-specific indicators under the denominations (e.g., EXPRESS for a clearly identifiable service as well as abbreviations that are less clear such as EM HFPU FRB). When a machine asks a mailer if any postage is already affixed to an item, the mailer can indicate that all postage but one cent or more is affixed. A customer stating that almost all required postage is already affixed will result in the stamp vending machine dispensing a stamp with a service-specific indicator that has a face value as low as one cent. For this reason, listings no longer include small format vended stamps with service-specific indicators beyond No. CVP84, because the stamps can be produced to show any face value, use not being restricted to the class indicated, and all types may be used on any mail matter.

Flag
CVP18

Serpentine Die Cut 13¼x12½

2011, Oct. 18 **Self-Adhesive**

CVP84 CVP18 44c **multicolored,** date sold only on bottom line — —
a. Date sold and "Postcard" on bottom line — —
b. Date sold and "First-Class" on bottom line — —

No. CVP84 was issued in panes of 10. It was made available at Mail & Go postal stations in Super Target stores in the Dallas, TX area. Panes could be printed in any denomination from 29c to $9.99. Serpentine die cut 9 examples of No. CVP84 with dates earlier than Oct. 18 were produced at Pitney Bowes facilities. This serpentine die cut 9 sticker stock is not known to have been sent out for use in machines that were available for use by the general public. No. CVP84 was made available in 2013 with dozens of images other than the flag shown. These optional images are for various holidays and events, as well as social causes, such as support for breast cancer, education and recycling. One image, for bridal showers, has been made available in two different types.

Pitney Bowes With Eagle at Left — CVP18a

Pitney Bowes Without Eagle — CVP18b

Die Cut With Perpendicular Corners

2011, Oct. 18 **Self-Adhesive**

CVP84C CVP18a 46c **black & pink,** no inscription below sold date 5.00 —
d. CVP18b 46c With eagle emblem omitted — —
e. "Mailed From Zip Code ..." on bottom line — —
f. "Postcard" on bottom line 7.50 —
g. "First-Class Mail" on bottom line 5.00 —
h. "First-Class Mail Intl" on bottom line — —
i. "Priority Mail" on bottom line — —
j. "Priority Envelope" on bottom line — —
k. "Priority Box" on bottom line — —
l. "Priority Tube" on bottom line — —
m. "Priority - Irregular Shape" on bottom line — —
n. "Express Mail" on bottom line — —

No. CVP84C was made available at Mail & Go postal stations in Super Target stores in the Dallas, TX area, and presumably could be printed in any denomination.

In 2013, twelve Mail & Go machines vending No. CVP84C and the holiday and social cause designs noted under No. CVP84 were installed and operated at thirteen Rite Aid drug stores in central California along the Highway 1 corridor. The machines were installed by the LePages Company (a USPS-licensed manufacturer and wholesaler of USPS-brand mailing supplies). They were placed under the jurisdiction of the Oakland, CA region of the USPS throughout most of 2014-15. Postmasters in the towns supported the machines officially with Priority Mail containers, postal labels and daily mail collection. The locations were listed by the USPS in its online Internet database of self-service post office locations. The machines appear to have been removed between Oct. 2015 and Jan. 2016.

The stamps vended by these machines were officially approved by the USPS and are no different than stamps sold from the same models of machines installed at colleges and universities across the nation. Locations of about 40 other privately supported Mail & Go machines have been recorded. These other machines are installed and operated by Pitney Bowes employees who manage mail rooms the company operates under contracts. At those locations, the mail room staff takes the daily mail to the local post officce, and there is no USPS logistical support.

The USPS regulations classify Mail & Go machines as "third party kiosks." No. CVP84Cd is an error that Pitney Bowes technicians could not explain. It appeared for a short time on a machine in Illinois and at the U.S. Department of Defense Medical HQ facility mailroom in Annandale, Va., and other unidentified locations.

Thermal prints generated by vending machines with too little electrically generated heat tend to fade very quickly.

APC With Vertical Coding at Right of Date CVP19

Die Cut With Rounded Corners

2012, Apr. 12 **Self-Adhesive**

CVP85 CVP19 **black & pink** 1.50 —
a. Die cut with perpendicular corners, colored bar at left, "Fold Here" at center, 100x38mm — —

No. CVP85 has "APC" reading upwards at right. No. CVP78 has "IBM" reading upwards at right. No. CVP85 was available during a nationwide test of machines, and could be printed in any denomination from 1c to $99.99.

No. CVP85a was produced on label stock normally used for No. CVP87 when machines ran out of label stock to produce orders for Nos. CVP85, CVP85B, and varieties of CVP86.

APC With Vertical Coding At Left of Date — CVP19a

Die Cut With Rounded Corners

2012 **Self-Adhesive**

CVP85B CVP19a **black & pink** 2.00 —
c. Die cut with perpendicular corners, colored bar at left, "FOLD HERE" at center, 100x38mm 2.00 —

No. CVP85Bc was produced on label stock normally used for No. CVP87 when machines ran out of stock to produce orders for Nos. CVP85, CVP85B, and varieties of CVP86.

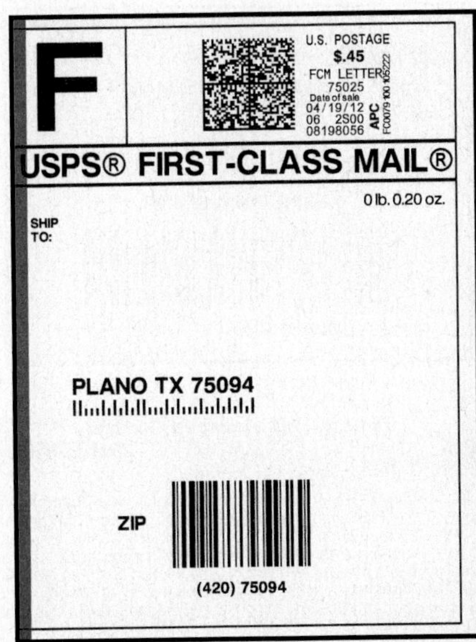

APC Variable Vignette Stamp CVP20

Die Cut With Rounded Corners

2012, Apr. 12 **Self-Adhesive**

CVP86 CVP20 (45c) **black & pink** 2.50 —
a. Die cut with perpendicular corners, colored bar at left, "Fold Here" at center, 100x38mm 3.00 —

No. CVP86 was available during a nationwide test of machines, and could be printed only as "Forever" stamps. The vignette portion of the stamp at left could be chosen from a gallery of six images (Mr. Zip, Heart, Flowers, Flag, Eagle, and Balloons and "Celebrate!", which is depicted). Values are for any vignette, or for any other vignette that may be programmed into the machine at a later date. Each vignette design could be purchased in a quantities ranging from 1 stamp to 100 stamps, but because a $1 minimum purchase was required, at least three examples of the first stamp chosen had to be purchased. A maximum of ten stamps could be printed on a sheet. Sales of stamps that are not in multiples of 10 were printed in strips, smaller-sized sheets containing an even number of stamps, or in sheets having one label inscribed "This Block Is Not Valid Postage" when the sheet contained an odd number of stamps.

No. CVP86a was produced on wide-label stock normally used for No. CVP87 when the small-label printer was defective or the machine had run out of small-label stock.

Examples of No. CVP86 without a printed image at left are the result of machines having their image-printing capability shut off so pre-printed label stock for producing No. CVP88 could be substituted for the blank label stock used for Nos. CVP85 and CVP86. See footnote under No. CVP88 for information about examples of No. CVP86 with date of purchase inscriptions to right of "Forever."

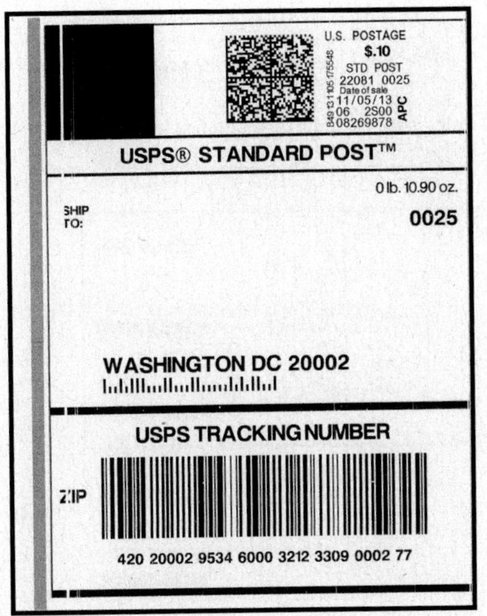

APC With Vertical Coding to Right of Date — CVP21

Die Cut With Perpendicular Corners

2012, Apr. 12 **Self-Adhesive**

CVP87 CVP21 **black & pink** — —

No. CVP87 was available during a nationwide test of machines, and could be printed in any denomination from 1c to $99.99. Stamps can be inscribed with a variety of different service inscriptions.

APC With Vertical Coding to Left of Date — CVP21a

Die Cut With Perpendicular Corners

2012 **Self-Adhesive**

CVP87A CVP21a **black & pink** — —

Labels of type CVP21a with postage indicia inscribed FCM LETTER below the denomination have only a bar code and the Zip code of the destination at the bottom third rather than a USPS TRACKING NUMBER. Labels for which a Certified Mail fee has been paid have a CERTIFIED MAIL bar code. Express Mail labels have POSTAL USE ONLY form at the bottom.

On Nov. 7, 2013, the USPS had distributed and had begun requiring the use of "signalling label" stock with a clear phosphor stripe. The clear stripe appears positioned vertically along the left margin of the labels. Labels with pink stripes along the right margin continued to be used until stocks were exhausted or labels with pre-printed vignettes were issued for use in some machines on Apr. 1, 2014 (CVP90-CVP91).

APC With Vertical Coding at Left of Date And Clear Phosphor Stripe Along Left Margin — CVP21b

Die Cut With Rounded Corners

2013, Nov. 7 **Self-Adhesive**

CVP87B CVP21b **black** 5.00 —
c. Die cut with perpendicular corners, colored bar at left, "Fold Here" at center, 100x38mm 8.50 —

The Scheduled Delivery and Expected Delivery inscriptions, date and times seen on Nos. CVP89B and CVP89C replaced "THIS BLOCK IS NOT VALID FOR POSTAGE" on labels normally found adjacent to Nos, CVP87B and CVP92A when sold for other than Priority Mail.

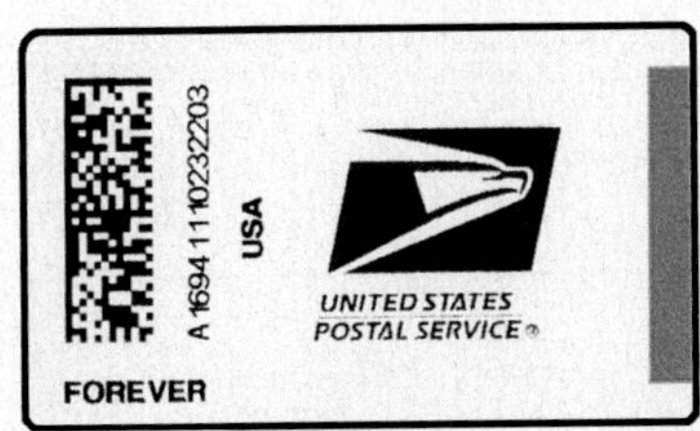

Mailbox CVP22

Die Cut With Rounded Corners

2012, Oct. 31 **Self-Adhesive**

CVP88 CVP22 (45c) **multicolored** 3.50 —

The mailbox vignette is preprinted on No. CVP88. This preprinted stock was placed in machines in November 2012 and was to be removed from machines on December 31, 2012. The earliest known date of sale is Nov. 10, 2012.

Examples of No. CVP88 with the mailbox design covered by images used for Nos. CVP85 and CVP86 were the result of machines having their blank label stock replaced with the preprinted label stock while the machine's image-printing capability was not shut off to accommodate the preprinted stock.

On No. CVP88, the number of the month and last two digits of the year in which the stamp was purchased, separated by an asterisk, appear to the right of "Forever." If the operator of the machine programmed it to sell No. CVP88 but failed to turn off the vignettes available as No. CVP86 and did not load the preprinted Christmas Mailbox label stock, the resulting vended product would be No. CVP86 with the month and year appearing to the right of "FOREVER."

Labels inscribed "This Block Is Not Valid For Postage" differ from similar labels created with No. CVP86. Various sizes of "Void" overprints on these labels exist.

USPS Emblem — CVP22a

Die Cut With Rounded Corners

2013, Oct. 31 **Self-Adhesive**

CVP88A CVP22a (46c) **black & pink** 3.00 —
b. Die cut with perpendicular corners, colored bar at left, "Fold Here" at center, 100x38mm 7.50 —

This design was first placed in a few machines in the Washington, DC and Merrifield, VA area on Oct. 31, 2013. Stamps vended with encoded dates prior to Nov. 7, 2013 were test stamps. On Nov. 6, 2013, the USPS declared the test to be successful and the image was released for general use as a fall-back design.

No. CVP88Ab was produced on wide-label stock normally used to produce No. CVP87 when the small-label printer was either defective or machines ran out of stock to produce orders for No. CVP88A. The earliest known sale date of No. CVP88Ab is Nov. 2, 2013.

Examples of CVP88A lacking the eagle vignette could be made if the machine had blank label stock in the feeder but was set to print on pre-printed labels such as No. CVP89. When the machine has pre-printed labels (starting with No. CVP89) in the feeder and is set to print on blank labels, the Eagle vignette will print on top of the preprinted image.

Reindeer — CVP23

Die Cut With Rounded Corners

2013, Nov. 7 **Self-Adhesive**

CVP89 CVP23 (46c) **multicolored** 3.00 2.00

The reindeer vignette is preprinted on No. CVP89. The issue date is the earliest documented sale date.

USPS Emblem With Clear Phosphor Stripe Along Left Margin — CVP23a

Die Cut With Rounded Corners

2014, Jan. 8 **Self-Adhesive**

CVP89A CVP23a (46c) **black** 3.00 —
d. (50c) Vertical serial number with no leading letter, *2018* 2.50 —

Examples of CVP89A lacking the eagle vignette could be made if the machine had blank label stock in the feeder but was set to print on pre-printed labels (starting with No. CVP89). When the machine has pre-printed labels (starting with No. CVP89) in the feeder and is set to print on blank labels, the Eagle vignette will print on top of the preprinted image. Examples known include 2018-generation stamps with serial number with no leading letter.

APC With Scheduled Delivery — CVP23b

Die Cut With Perpendicular Corners

2014, Jan. Self-Adhesive

CVP89B CVP23b **black & pink** — —

No. CVP89B is generated when the mailer answers a machine-system prompt with a "no" answer when asked if the full-length label (Type CVP21) will fit on the mailer's item. This is vended only when pre-printed labels are installed in the machine or the small-label printer is defective.

For selected mail service the USPS doesn't track, the field to the right of "FOLD HERE" remains blank (in effect creating No. CVP87Bc).

APC With Expected Delivery — CVP23c

Die Cut With Perpendicular Corners

2014, Jan. Self-Adhesive

CVP89C CVP23c **black & pink** — —

See note after No. CVP89B.

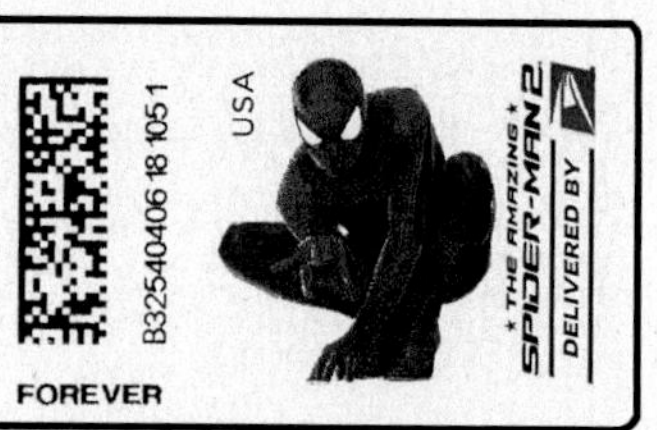

Spiderman — CVP24

Die Cut With Rounded Corners

2014, Apr. 1 Self-Adhesive

CVP90 CVP24 (49c) **multicolored** 3.00 1.25

The Spiderman vignette is preprinted on No. CVP90.

Flag CVP25

Die Cut With Rounded Corners

2014, Apr. 1 Self-Adhesive

CVP91 CVP25 (49c) **multicolored** 3.00 1.25

a. "FOREVER" (only) missing — —

b. (50c) With vertical serial number with no leading letter, *2018* 3.00 1.50

The flag vignette is preprinted on No. CVP91.

Examples of No. CVP91b exist with the USPS Eagle emblem (see illustration at design CVP23a) printed on top of the preprinted flag design label; value, $5. It is theoretically possible that blank labels without a preprinted flag or other preprinted design could be inserted in the new machine, and (likely) be printed without the operator having turned on the thermal-printed USPS logo that machines can produce on-site, leaving an indicia and value printed on a stamp without any pictorial element. Such varieties are products of local operator error that has occurred on all issues from No. CVP88 in 2013 and can be manufactured through illicit cooperation of postal officials.

Rudolph, the Red-Nosed Reindeer — CVP26

Die Cut With Rounded Corners

2014, Nov. 6 Self-Adhesive

CVP92 CVP26 (49c) **multicolored** 4.00 1.75

The Rudolph vignette is preprinted on No. CVP92.

From Nov. 14, 2014, Automated Postal Centers (APC) vending machines were renamed by the USPS to be Self Service Kiosks (SSK), and the machines were changed to issue stamps inscribed "SSK" rather than "APC."

SSK With Vertical Coding at Left of Date CVP27

Die Cut With Rounded Corners

2014, Nov. 14 Self-Adhesive

CVP93 CVP27 **black & pink** — —

a. **Black,** with vertical transparent stripe at left 1.00 —

No. CVP93 was available at machines that had not yet retired the pink-striped labels.

It was not intended by the USPS that indicia inscribed with SSK would be printed on pink-striped labels. The design was shifted to appear farther to the right, to insure the bar code would remain uncompromised and at a safe distance from the clear phosphor stripe on the newer labels. Almost all examples of this issue will have SSK appearing within the pink stripe.

Value of No. CVP93a is for 49c denomination, current at the time. Other denominations pro-rata.

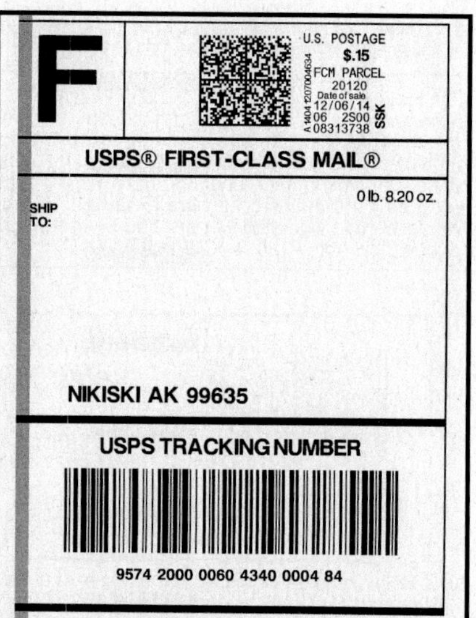

SSK With Vertical Coding to Left of Date — CVP28

Die Cut With Perpendicular Corners

2014, Nov. 14 Self-Adhesive

CVP94 CVP28 **black & pink** 2.50 —

a. Indicia at upper right with no leading letter, various service level indicators, *2018* 2.50 —

Like No. CVP87A, No. CVP94 exists in other denominations inscribed with various mail service inscriptions or with blackened square in place of letters such as "F," above.

SSK With Blank Area at Right of "Fold Here" — CVP29

Die Cut With Perpendicular Corners

2014, Nov. 14 Self-Adhesive

CVP95 CVP29 **black & pink** 5.00 —

a. **black,** vertical serial number with no leading letter, clear phosphor stripe, *2018* 5.00 —

See note below No. CVP89B.

SSK With "Expected Delivery" at Right of Dotted Line — CVP30

Die Cut With Perpendicular Corners

2014, Nov. 14 Self-Adhesive

CVP96 CVP30 **black & pink** — —

a. **black,** vertical serial number with no leading letter, various service level indicators, clear phosphor stripe, *2018* 3.00 —

See note below No. CVP89B.

SSK With "Scheduled Delivery" at Right of Dotted Line — CVP31

Die Cut With Perpendicular Corners

2014, Nov. 14 Self-Adhesive

CVP97 CVP31 **black & pink** — —

a. **black,** vertical serial number with no leading letter, various sevice level indicators, clear phosphor stripe, *2018* 3.00 —

See note below No. CVP89B.

Charlie Brown Looking in Mailbox — CVP32

Die Cut With Rounded Corners

2015, Oct. 20 Self-Adhesive

CVP98 CVP32 (49c) **multicolored** 4.00 1.00

The Charlie Brown vignette is preprinted on No. CVP98. Issue date is earliest recorded sale date. Post offices were authorized to place the labels in machines at the close of business on Oct. 20, which many did prior to the SSK system-wide date change that occurs daily prior to midnight.

mPOS — CVP33

Die Cut With Rounded Corners

2015 Self-Adhesive

CVP99 CVP33 **black** — —

No. CVP99 is generated by a mobile hand-held point-of-sale vending machine with integrated thermal postage printer and embedded credit/debit card acceptance processor. Possible denominations are limited to the postage prices applicable to each available pre-printed type of Priority and Express Mail flat rate envelopes and packages (rate determined by scanning the bar code on the package the customer needs). While this indicia is intended to be affixed to mail matter at the time it is presented, postage can be generated and sold in quantities to take away for later use. Labels are generated from vertical coils with blank labels.

Wreath in Window CVP34

Die Cut With Rounded Corners

2016, Oct. 27 **Self-Adhesive**

CVP100 CVP34 (47c) **multicolored** 3.00 1.00

The wreath in window vignette is preprinted on No. CVP100. Issue date is earliest recorded sale date.

Christmas Cookies — CVP35

Die Cut With Rounded Corners

2017, Oct. 17 **Self-Adhesive**

CVP101 CVP35 (49c) **multicolored** 3.00 1.00

a. On 2018-generation stamp with serial number with no leading letter — —

The Christmas cookies vignette is preprinted on No. CVP101. Issue date is earliest recorded sale date.

Flag CVP36

Die Cut With Rounded Corners

2018, Aug. 23 **Self-Adhesive**

CVP108 CVP36 (50c) **multicolored** 3.00 1.00

The flag vignette is preprinted on No. CVP108. Issue date is earliest recorded sale date.

Santa Claus CVP37

Die Cut With Rounded Corners

2018, Oct. 21 **Self-Adhesive**

CVP109 CVP37 (50c) **multicolored** 2.50 1.00

The Santa Claus vignette is preprinted on No. CVP109. Issue date is earliest recorded sale date.

Christmas Stocking — CVP38

Die Cut With Rounded Corners

2020, Nov. 16 **Self-Adhesive**

CVP110 CVP38 (55c) **multicolored** 2.50 1.00

The Christmas stocking vignette is preprinted on No. CVP110.

Santa Claus, Sleigh and Reindeer in Flight — CVP39

Die Cut With Rounded Corners

2021, Nov. **Self-Adhesive**

CVP111 CVP39 (58c) **multicolored** 2.50 1.00

The Santa Claus vignette is preprinted on No. CVP111.

MACHINE SET-UP AND TEST LABELS

Test labels were generated when machines were activated. They were not intended for public distribution.

Other samples, advertizing labels, proofs, etc. exist.

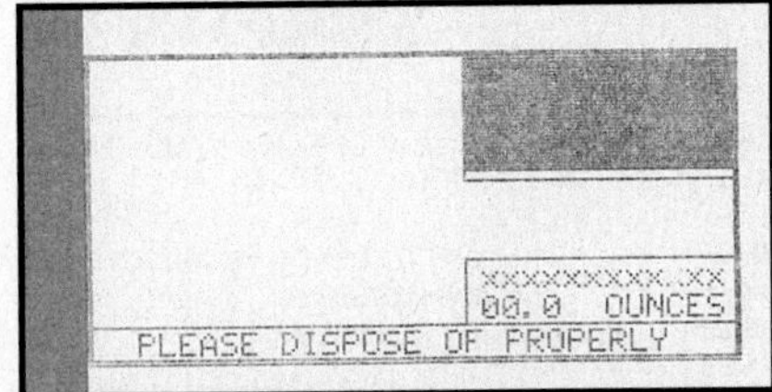

Autopost Test Label — CVPT1

Autopost Test Label with Bar Code — CVPT2

1989 **Self-Adhesive Tagged** ***Guillotined***

CVPT1 CVPT1 **black & orange** 100.00

CVPT2 CVPT2 **black & orange** —

APC Test Label — CVPT3

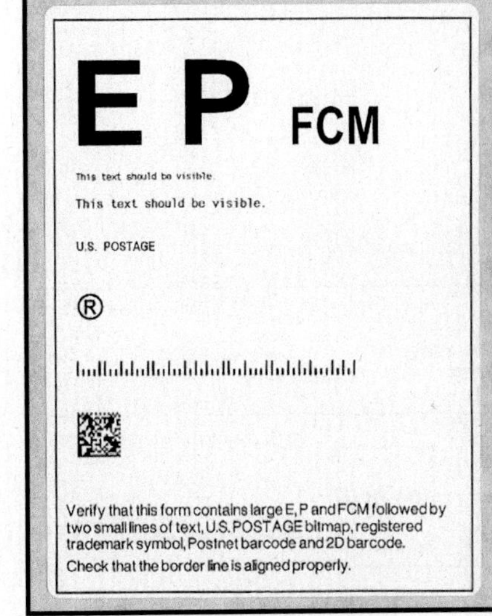

APC Test Label — CVPT4

2004, Apr. 14 **Self-Adhesive** ***Die Cut***

CVPT3 CVPT3 **black & pink** —

CVPT4 CVPT4 **black** —

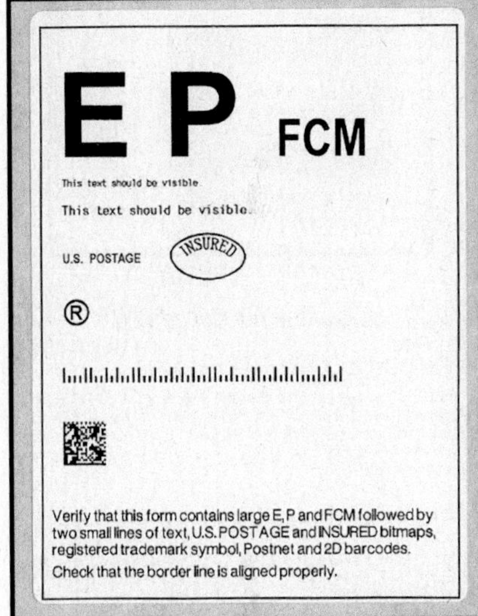

APC Test Label with "INSURED" in oval — CVPT5

APC Test Label with "APC" in Pink Bar — CVPT6

2004, Nov. 19 **Self-Adhesive** ***Die Cut***

CVPT5 CVPT5 **black** —

CVPT6 CVPT6 **black & pink** 30.00

APC Diagnostics Test Label — CVPT7

2004, Nov. 19 **Self-Adhesive** ***Die Cut***

CVPT7 CVPT7 **black & pink** 30.00

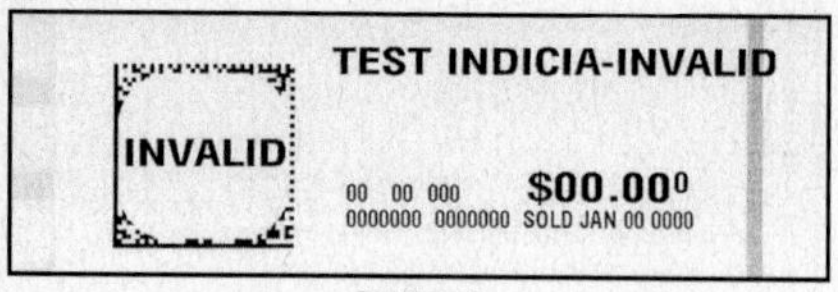

CVPT7A

Pitney Bowes "Mail & Go" Kiosks

Die Cut With Perpendicular Corners

2011, Oct. **Self-Adhesive**

CVPT7A CVPT7A **black & pink** 30.00 —

Flag — CVPT7B

Serpentine Die Cut 13¼x12½

2011, Oct. **Self-Adhesive**

CVPT7B CVPT7B **black & multicolored** 20.00 —

Theoretically, serpentine die cut 9 examples of No. CVPT7B could exist from set-up of machines used at the Pitney Bowes facilities in Connecticut, where die cut 9 paper labels are known to have been loaded. The editors have not seen an example of this label die cut 9.

APC Test Label With Vertical "VOID" at Right of Sale Date CVPT8

2012 ***Die Cut With Rounded Corners***

Self-Adhesive

CVPT8 CVPT8 **black & pink** 12.00

Compare with Nos. CVPT14 and CVPT20.

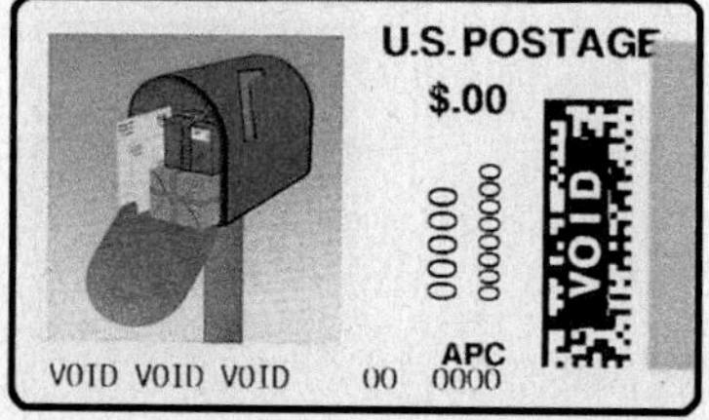

Mailbox — CVPT8A

2012, Nov. ***Die Cut With Rounded Corners***

Self-Adhesive

CVPT8A CVPT8A **black & multicolored** 12.00 —

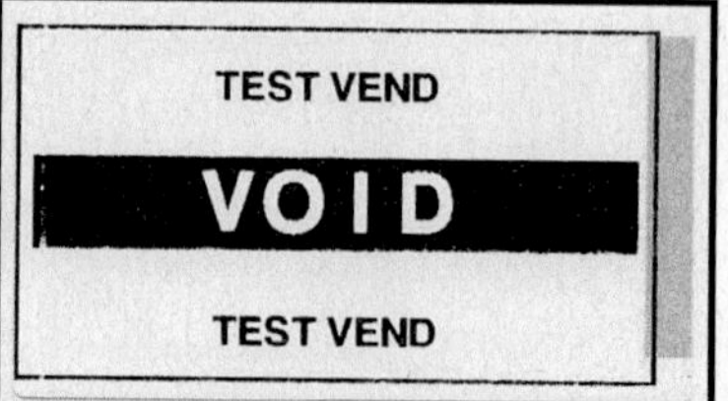

APC Test Vend Label for Setup to Use Thermal Vignettes — CVPT9

2013 ***Die Cut With Rounded Corners***

Self-Adhesive

CVPT9 CVPT9 **black & pink** 12.00

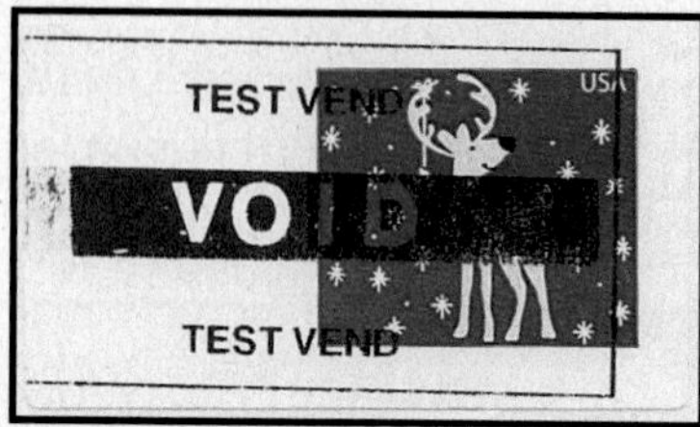

APC Test Vend Label for Setup to Use No. CVP89 — CVPT10

2013 ***Die Cut With Rounded Corners***

Self-Adhesive

CVPT10 CVPT10 **black & multicolored** 12.00

APC Test Vend Label for Setup to Use No. CVP89 — CVPT11

2013 ***Die Cut With Rounded Corners***

Self-Adhesive

CVPT11 CVPT11 **black & multicolored** 15.00

No. CVPT11 occasionally appears vertically se-tenant with No. CVPT10.

APC Diagnostics Test Label With Clear Phosphor Stripe Along Left Side for Setup to Use No. CVP89A — CVPT12

2013 ***Die Cut With Rounded Corners***

Self-Adhesive

CVPT12 CVPT12 **black** 10.00

APC Diagnostics Test Label For Pre-printed Label Setup — CVPT13

2013 ***Die Cut With Rounded Corners***

Self-Adhesive

CVPT13 CVPT13 **black & multicolored** 10.00

APC Test Vend Label With Vertical "VOID VOID VOID" to Left of Sale Date — CVPT14

2014 ***Die Cut With Rounded Corners***

Self-Adhesive

CVPT14 CVPT14 **black & pink** 10.00

Compare with Nos. CVPT8 and CVPT20.

APC Test Vend Label With "Fold Here," "VOID VOID VOID" at Right of Date — CVPT15

2012-14 ***Die Cut With Perpendicular Corners***

Self-Adhesive

CVPT15 CVPT15 **black & pink** 10.00

a. "VOID VOID VOID" vertically at left of date 10.00

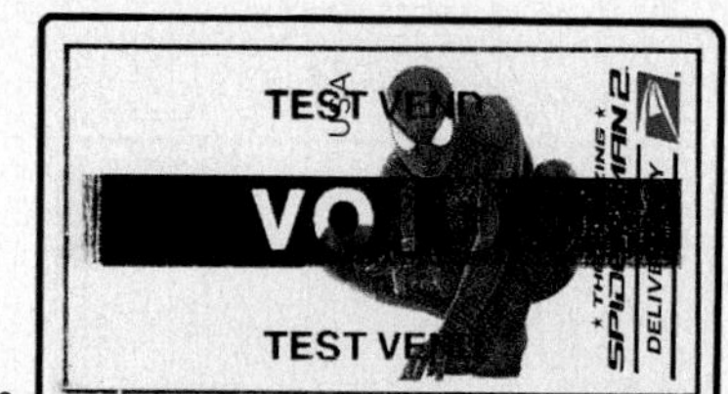

CVPT16

2014, Apr. 1 ***Die Cut With Rounded Corners***

Self-Adhesive

CVPT16 CVPT16 **black & multicolored** 12.00

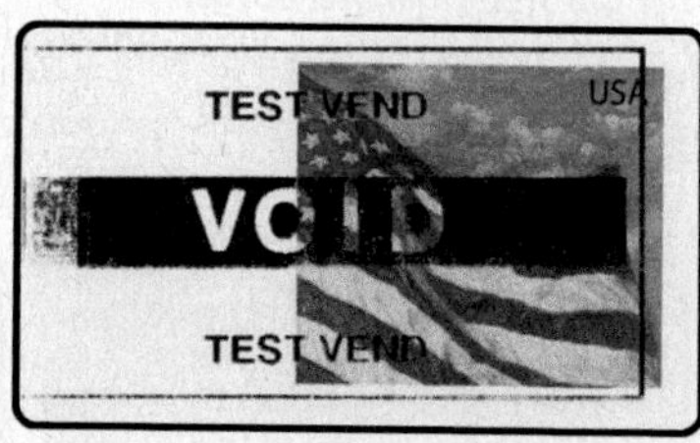

CVPT17

2014, Apr. 1 ***Die Cut With Rounded Corners***

Self-Adhesive

CVPT17 CVPT17 **black & multicolored** 12.00

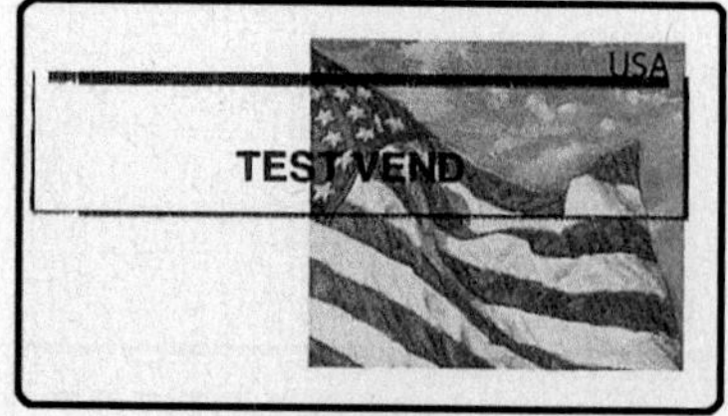

CVPT17A

2014 ***Die Cut With Rounded Corners***

Self-Adhesive

CVPT17A CVPT17A **black & multicolored** 8.50

No. CVPT17A occasionally appears vertically se-tenant with No. CVPT17.

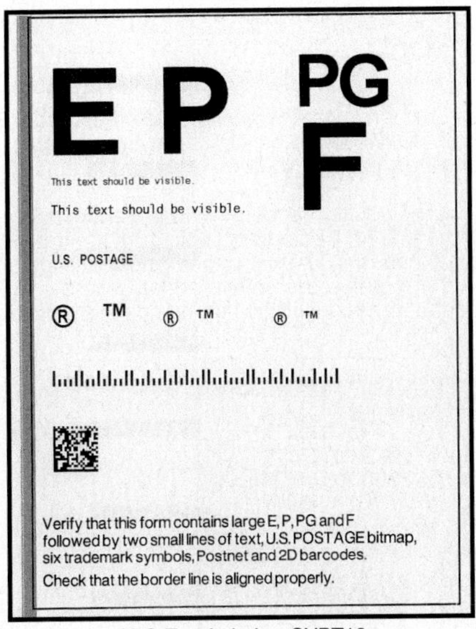

E P
PG
F
This text should be visible.
This text should be visible.
U.S. POSTAGE
® TM ® TM ® TM
Verify that this form contains large E, P, PG and F followed by two small lines of text, U.S. POSTAGE bitmap, six trademark symbols, Postnet and 2D barcodes.
Check that the border line is aligned properly.

APC Test Label — CVPT18

2014 ***Die Cut With Perpendicular Corners***
Self-Adhesive

CVPT18 CVPT18 **black & pink** —
a. **Black**, with rounded corners —

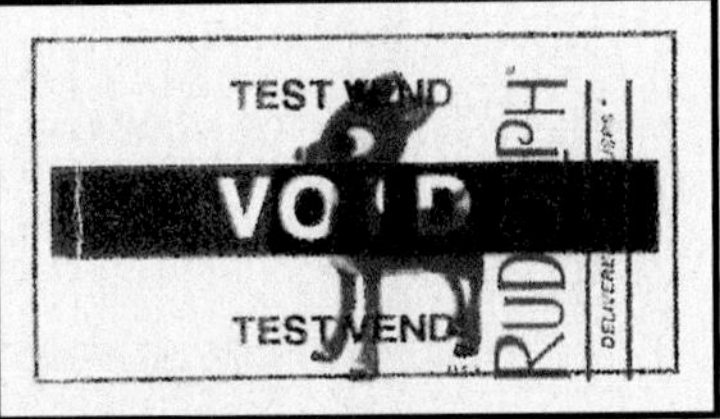

CVPT19

2014, Nov. 1 ***Die Cut With Rounded Corners***
Self-Adhesive

CVPT19 CVPT19 **black & multicolored** 15.00

SSK With "VOID VOID VOID" at Left of Sale Date — CVPT20

2014, Nov. ***Die Cut With Rounded Corners***
Self-Adhesive

CVPT20 CVPT20 **black** 8.50

Compare with Nos. CVPT8 and CVPT14.

SSK Test Vend Label With "Fold Here," "VOID VOID VOID" at Left of Date — CVPT21

2014, Nov. ***Die Cut With Perpendicular Corners***
Self-Adhesive

CVPT21 CVPT21 **black & pink** 5.00

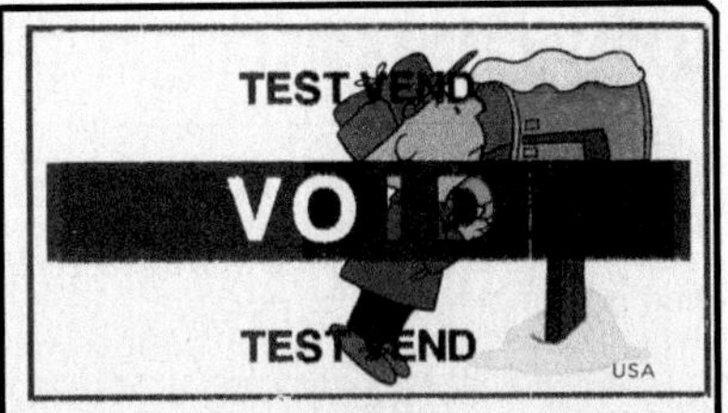

CVPT22

2015, Oct. 29 ***Die Cut With Rounded Corners***
Self-Adhesive

CVPT22 CVPT22 **black & multicolored** 5.00

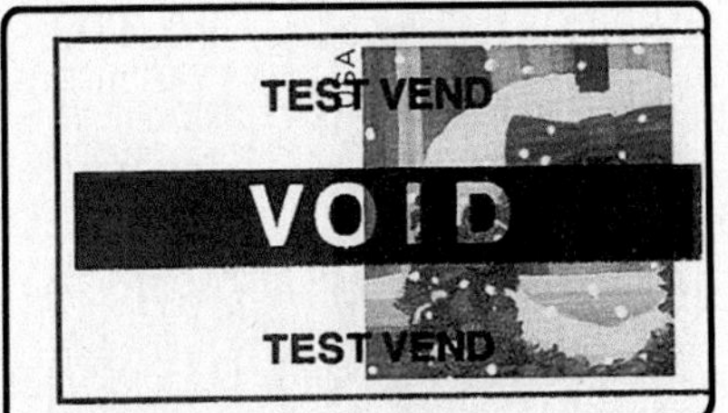

CVPT23

2016, Oct. 27 ***Die Cut With Rounded Corners***
Self-Adhesive

CVPT23 CVPT23 **black & multicolored** —

APC Diagnostics Test Label For Pre-printed Label Setup — CVPT24

2017, Oct. 17 ***Die Cut With Rounded Corners***
Self-Adhesive

CVPT24 CVPT24 **black & multicolored** —

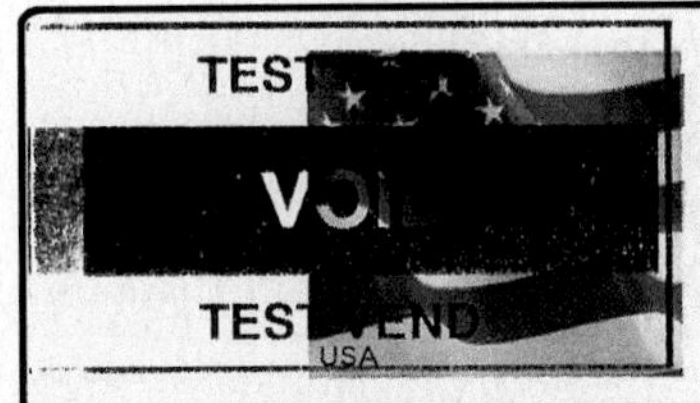

CVPT25

2018, Aug. 23 ***Die Cut With Rounded Corners***
Self-Adhesive

CVPT25 CVPT25 **black & multicolored** —

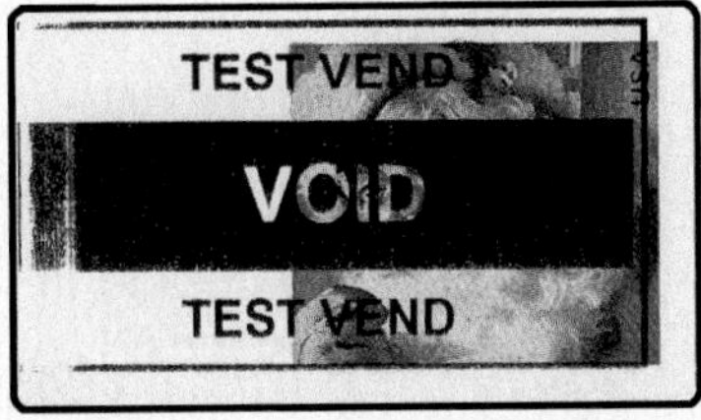

CVPT26

2018, Oct. 21 ***Die Cut With Rounded Corners***
Self-Adhesive

CVPT26 CVPT26 **black & multicolored** —

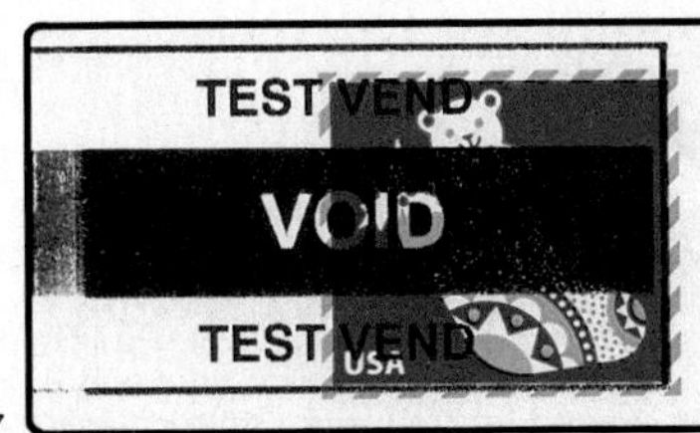

CVPT27

2020, Nov. 16 ***Die Cut With Rounded Corners***
Self-Adhesive

CVPT27 CVPT27 **black & multicolored** —

POSTAL CARDS

On July 5, 1990 the first of a number of "Postal Buddy" machines was placed in service at the Merrifield, VA post office. The machine printed out numerous items such as address labels (including monogram if you wished), fax labels, "penalty" cards, denominated postal cards, etc. Certain services were free, such as the penalty card mailed to your post office for change of address. The 15-cent denominated card cost 33-cents each and could be used to notify others of address change, meeting notices, customized messages, etc. Borders, messages, backs are different. The cards also came in sheets of 4.

These machines were tested in at least 30 locations in Virginia, including 16 post offices.

Denominated Postal Cards

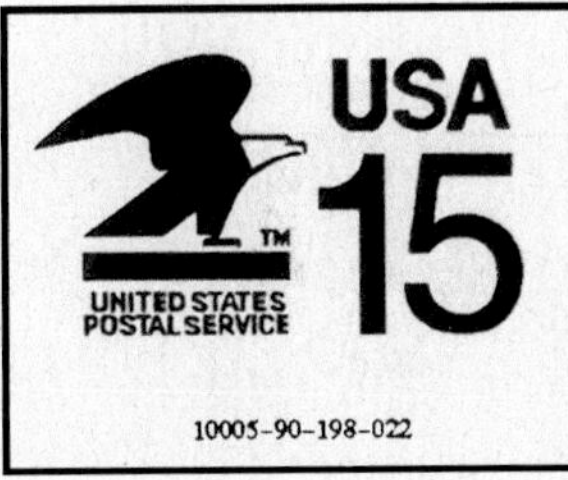

Number under design includes machine number, year, date (1 through 366) and transaction number.

1990, July 5

CVUX1 15c 6.00 *10.00*
First day cancel, Merrifield, VA *(6,500)* 5.00

1991, Feb. 3

CVUX2 19c 3.00 *8.00*
First day cancel, any location 35.00

Number under design includes ZIP Code of the originating machine (22203 in illustration), machine number (101), last digit of year, numbers of month and day (21203 for Dec. 3, 1992) and transaction number (041).

1992, Nov. 13

CVUX3 19c 6.00 *15.00*
First day dated, Reston or Chantilly, VA 25.00

A total of 171 machines were used, with 109 in the greater Washington, DC area (including locations in Virginia and Maryland), 59 in the greater San Diego area, and 3 in Denver. The machine numbers (011, 012, 021, 101, 111, 121, 131) when combined with the zip code created unique identification numbers for each machine.

No. 3 is known also on fluorescent paper. Two different designs on back known for each paper type.

The contract for Postal Buddy machines was canceled Sept. 16, 1993. After the contract was canceled, the Postal Buddy Corporation sold remaining stocks of card stock to the public with both reverse designs imprinted. By using this stock and a high quality copier, very dangerous counterfeits can be created. The duplication of numbers in the transaction line will be one indicator.

PERSONAL COMPUTER POSTAGE

Personal computer postage, approved by the US Postal Service, was created by subscribing to Stamps.com, an internet website. Customers ordered self-adhesive labels showing vignettes, but lacking any franking value. The franking value portion of the stamps could be printed at the customer's convenience at any computer with an internet connection, using the customer's access codes. Any postage printed would be charged against the customer's account. In 2005, Endicia.com began offering personal computer postage.

Stamps with major listings could be printed in any denomination up to $999.99. Stamps with minor listings could only be printed in denominations calculated by the weight of the piece being mailed. Denominations for minor listings can range from 23c to $133.20. Customers could print the franking value (encryption and text) of the stamps on whatever they put in their printer, be it envelopes, plain gummed labels or regular paper. These listings are limited to items on the self-adhesive labels shown that were produced for and sold by the companies that created the software that generates the franking value portion of the stamp. The labels of a particular company must have on it a franking value that is produced by that company's software that matches the label's dimensions.

Neopost

CVPA1

2000 — ***Serpentine Die Cut 8***

Self-Adhesive

1CVP1 CVPA1 33c **black, yellow & pink**	—	—
On cover		—
Pane of 10	—	—

Stamps.com

Flag and Star — CVPA1a

2002, July — ***Serpentine Die Cut 5¾ at Left***

"Stamps.com" in Lower Case Letters

Identification Code Below Zip Code

1CVP2 CVPA1a 37c **black, blue & orange,** no mail class inscribed	7.00	3.00
On cover		4.00
Sheet of 25	175.00	

Identification Code Above Zip Code

1CVP2A CVPA1a 37c **black, blue & orange**	4.00	3.00
On cover		3.50
Sheet of 25	100.00	
a. "First Class" below "US Postage"	2.75	2.00
b. "Priority" below "US Postage"	8.25	2.50
c. "Express" below "US Postage"	25.00	5.00
d. "Media Mail" below "US Postage"	7.75	2.50
e. "Parcel Post" below "US Postage"	7.75	2.50
f. "Bound Printed Matter" below "US Postage"	7.75	2.50
g. "BPM" below "US Postage"	7.75	2.50

See Nos. 1CVP9, 1CVP21.

No. 1CVP2 apparently could be printed in denominations up to and including 37c. The 37c denomination comes with "FIRST-CLASS" between the Zip code and the identification code.

Later versions of the Stamps.com software allow any denomination to be printed, as well as additional or different mail-class inscriptions, on any basic stamp except for No. 1CVP2.

Values for Nos. 1CVP2A and 1CVP3-1CVP42 are for items appropriate to the service described. Stamps with denominations far lower than those appropriate to the service are valued correspondingly lower.

The software changes allow Nos. 1CVP2A and 1CVP3-1CVP37 to be printed with the mail-class inscriptions described for Nos. 1CVP38f-1CVP38p.

Later software changes allow Nos. 1CVP2A, 1CVP3-1CVP42 and 1CVP51-1CVP58 to be printed with mail-class inscriptions "Library Mail," "Intl. First Class," "Intl Priority," "Intl Express," and "M-Bag" with any denomination.

Love — CVPA2

2002 — ***Serpentine Die Cut 5¾ at Left***

1CVP3 CVPA2 37c **black, blue & orange**	4.00	4.00
On cover		5.00
Sheet of 25	100.00	
a. "First Class" below "US Postage"	2.75	2.00
b. "Priority" below "US Postage"	8.25	2.50
c. "Express" below "US Postage"	25.00	5.00
d. "Media Mail" below "US Postage"	7.75	2.50
e. "Parcel Post" below "US Postage"	7.75	2.50
f. "Bound Printed Matter" below "US Postage"	7.75	2.50
g. "BPM" below "US Postage"	7.75	2.50

Statue of Liberty and Flag — CVPA3

Liberty Bell and Flag — CVPA4

Eagle and Flag — CVPA5

George Washington and Flag — CVPA6

Capitol Building and Flag — CVPA7

2003, June — ***Serpentine Die Cut 5¾ at Left***

1CVP4 CVPA3 37c **black, blue & orange**	3.50	2.00
On cover		3.00
a. "First Class" below "US Postage"	3.25	2.00
b. "Priority" below "US Postage"	8.00	1.00
c. "Express" below "US Postage"	25.00	3.00
d. "Media Mail" below "US Postage"	7.50	1.00
e. "Parcel Post" below "US Postage"	7.50	1.00
f. "Bound Printed Matter" below "US Postage"	7.50	1.00
g. "BPM" below "US Postage"	7.50	1.00
1CVP5 CVPA4 37c **black, blue & orange**	3.50	2.00
On cover		3.00
a. "First Class" below "US Postage"	3.25	2.00
b. "Priority" below "US Postage"	8.00	1.00
c. "Express" below "US Postage"	25.00	3.00
d. "Media Mail" below "US Postage"	7.50	1.00
e. "Parcel Post" below "US Postage"	7.50	1.00
f. "Bound Printed Matter" below "US Postage"	7.50	1.00
g. "BPM" below "US Postage"	7.50	1.00
1CVP6 CVPA5 37c **black, blue & orange**	3.50	2.00
On cover		3.00
a. "First Class" below "US Postage"	3.25	2.00
b. "Priority" below "US Postage"	8.00	1.00
c. "Express" below "US Postage"	25.00	3.00
d. "Media Mail" below "US Postage"	7.50	1.00
e. "Parcel Post" below "US Postage"	7.50	1.00
f. "Bound Printed Matter" below "US Postage"	7.50	1.00
g. "BPM" below "US Postage"	7.50	1.00

1CVP7 CVPA6 37c **black, blue & orange** 3.50 2.00
On cover 3.00
a. "First Class" below "US Postage" 3.25 .25
b. "Priority" below "US Postage" 8.00 1.00
c. "Express" below "US Postage" 25.00 3.00
d. "Media Mail" below "US Postage" 7.50 1.00
e. "Parcel Post" below "US Postage" 7.50 1.00
f. "Bound Printed Matter" below "US Postage" 7.50 1.00
g. "BPM" below "US Postage" 7.50 1.00
1CVP8 CVPA7 37c **black, blue & orange** 3.50 2.00
On cover 3.00
a. "First Class" below "US Postage" 3.25 .45
b. "Priority" below "US Postage" 8.00 1.00
c. "Express" below "US Postage" 25.00 3.00
d. "Media Mail" below "US Postage" 7.50 1.00
e. "Parcel Post" below "US Postage" 7.50 1.00
f. "Bound Printed Matter" below "US Postage" 7.50 1.00
g. "BPM" below "US Postage" 7.50 1.00
h. Strip of 5, #1CVP4-1CVP8 17.50

Flag and Star Type of 2002 Redrawn With "Stamps.com" in Upper Case Letters

2003, June ***Serpentine Die Cut 5¾ at Left***
Identification Code Above Zip Code

1CVP9 CVPA1a 37c **black, blue & orange, "US Postage" only** 3.00 1.50
On cover 2.50
Sheet of 25 75.00
a. "First Class" below "US Postage" 2.00 .45
b. "Priority" below "US Postage" 8.00 1.00
c. "Express" below "US Postage" 25.00 3.00
d. "Media Mail" below "US Postage" 7.50 1.00
e. "Parcel Post" below "US Postage" 7.50 1.00
f. "Bound Printed Matter" below "US Postage" 7.50 1.00
g. "BPM" below "US Postage" 7.50 1.00

Snowman — CVPA8

Snowflakes CVPA9

Holly — CVPA10

Dove — CVPA11

Gingerbread Man and Candy — CVPA12

2003, Dec. ***Serpentine Die Cut 4½ at Left***

1CVP10 CVPA8 37c **black, blue & orange** 3.00 1.50
On cover 2.50
a. "First Class" below "US Postage" 2.00 1.00
b. "Priority" below "US Postage" 8.00 1.00
c. "Express" below "US Postage" 25.00 3.00
d. "Media Mail" below "US Postage" 7.50 1.00
e. "Parcel Post" below "US Postage" 7.50 1.00
f. "Bound Printed Matter" below "US Postage" 7.50 1.00
g. "BPM" below "US Postage" 7.50 1.00
1CVP11 CVPA9 37c **black, blue & orange** 3.00 1.50
On cover 2.50
a. "First Class" below "US Postage" 2.00 1.00
b. "Priority" below "US Postage" 8.00 1.00
c. "Express" below "US Postage" 25.00 3.00
d. "Media Mail" below "US Postage" 7.50 1.00
e. "Parcel Post" below "US Postage" 7.50 1.00
f. "Bound Printed Matter" below "US Postage" 7.50 1.00
g. "BPM" below "US Postage" 7.50 1.00
1CVP12 CVPA10 37c **black, blue & orange** 3.00 1.50
On cover 2.50
a. "First Class" below "US Postage" 2.00 1.00
b. "Priority" below "US Postage" 8.00 1.00
c. "Express" below "US Postage" 25.00 3.00
d. "Media Mail" below "US Postage" 7.50 1.00
e. "Parcel Post" below "US Postage" 7.50 1.00
f. "Bound Printed Matter" below "US Postage" 7.50 1.00
g. "BPM" below "US Postage" 7.50 1.00
1CVP13 CVPA11 37c **black, blue & orange** 3.00 1.50
On cover 2.50
a. "First Class" below "US Postage" 2.00 1.00
b. "Priority" below "US Postage" 8.00 1.00
c. "Express" below "US Postage" 25.00 3.00
d. "Media Mail" below "US Postage" 7.50 1.00
e. "Parcel Post" below "US Postage" 7.50 1.00
f. "Bound Printed Matter" below "US Postage" 7.50 1.00
g. "BPM" below "US Postage" 7.50 1.00
1CVP14 CVPA12 37c **black, blue & orange** 3.00 1.50
On cover 2.50
a. "First Class" below "US Postage" 2.00 1.00
b. "Priority" below "US Postage" 8.00 1.00
c. "Express" below "US Postage" 25.00 3.00
d. "Media Mail" below "US Postage" 7.50 1.00
e. "Parcel Post" below "US Postage" 7.50 1.00
f. "Bound Printed Matter" below "US Postage" 7.50 1.00
g. "BPM" below "US Postage" 7.50 1.00
h. Strip of 5, #1CVP10-1CVP14 12.50

Mailbox — CVPA13

2004, Mar. ***Serpentine Die Cut 6½ at Left***

1CVP15 CVPA13 37c **black, blue & orange** 25.00 15.00
On cover 35.00
a. "First Class" below "US Postage" 25.00 15.00
b. "Priority" below "US Postage" — —
c. "Express" below "US Postage" — —
d. "Media Mail" below "US Postage" — —
e. "Parcel Post" below "US Postage" — —
f. "Bound Printed Matter" below "US Postage" — —
g. "BPM" below "US Postage" — —

Blank sheets of No. 1CVP15 were sent free of charge to those who responded to special Stamps.com promotions which offered a fixed amount of free postage as an enticement to new subscribers. The franking portion of the stamps could only be applied after subscribing.

George Washington CVPA14

Thomas Jefferson — CVPA15

Abraham Lincoln — CVPA16

Theodore Roosevelt — CVPA17

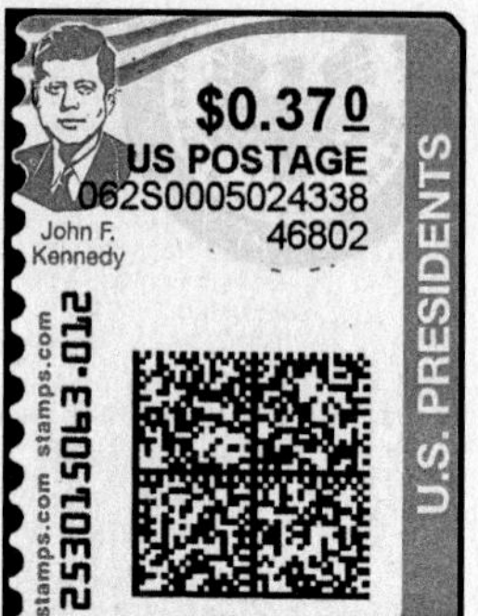

John F. Kennedy — CVPA18

2004, Apr.	*Serpentine Die Cut 6½ at Left*		
1CVP16	CVPA14 37c **black, blue & orange**	2.00	1.00
	On cover		2.50
a.	"First Class" below "US Postage"	1.10	.75
b.	"Priority" below "US Postage"	5.00	2.50
c.	"Express" below "US Postage"	20.00	5.00
d.	"Media Mail" below "US Postage"	5.00	2.50
e.	"Parcel Post" below "US Postage"	5.00	2.50
f.	"Bound Printed Matter" below "US Postage"	5.00	2.50
g.	"BPM" below "US Postage"	5.00	2.50
1CVP17	CVPA15 37c **black, blue & orange**	2.00	1.00
	On cover		2.50
a.	"First Class" below "US Postage"	1.10	.75
b.	"Priority" below "US Postage"	5.00	2.50
c.	"Express" below "US Postage"	20.00	5.00
d.	"Media Mail" below "US Postage"	5.00	2.50
e.	"Parcel Post" below "US Postage"	5.00	2.50
f.	"Bound Printed Matter" below "US Postage"	5.00	2.50
g.	"BPM" below "US Postage"	5.00	2.50
1CVP18	CVPA16 37c **black, blue & orange**	2.00	1.00
	On cover		2.50
a.	"First Class" below "US Postage"	1.10	.75
b.	"Priority" below "US Postage"	5.00	2.50
c.	"Express" below "US Postage"	20.00	5.00
d.	"Media Mail" below "US Postage"	5.00	2.50
e.	"Parcel Post" below "US Postage"	5.00	2.50
f.	"Bound Printed Matter" below "US Postage"	5.00	2.50
g.	"BPM" below "US Postage"	5.00	2.50
1CVP19	CVPA17 37c **black, blue & orange**	2.00	1.00
	On cover		2.50
a.	"First Class" below "US Postage"	1.10	.75
b.	"Priority" below "US Postage"	5.00	2.50
c.	"Express" below "US Postage"	20.00	5.00
d.	"Media Mail" below "US Postage"	5.00	2.50
e.	"Parcel Post" below "US Postage"	5.00	2.50
f.	"Bound Printed Matter" below "US Postage"	5.00	2.50
g.	"BPM" below "US Postage"	5.00	2.50
1CVP20	CVPA18 37c **black, blue & orange**	2.00	1.00
	On cover		2.50
a.	"First Class" below "US Postage"	1.10	.75
b.	"Priority" below "US Postage"	5.00	2.50
c.	"Express" below "US Postage"	20.00	5.00
d.	"Media Mail" below "US Postage"	5.00	2.50
e.	"Parcel Post" below "US Postage"	5.00	2.50
f.	"Bound Printed Matter" below "US Postage"	5.00	2.50
g.	"BPM" below "US Postage"	5.00	2.50
h.	Horiz. strip of 5, #1CVP16-1CVP20	10.00	

Flag and Star Type of 2002 Redrawn With Orange Stars and Text at Left

2004, Apr.	*Serpentine Die Cut 6½ at Left*		
	"Stamps.com" in Upper Case Letters		
	Identification Code Above Zip Code		
1CVP21	CVPA1a 37c **black, blue & orange**	2.00	1.00
	On cover		2.50
	Sheet of 25	50.00	
a.	"First Class" below "US Postage"	1.35	.75
b.	"Priority" below "US Postage"	6.00	2.50
c.	"Express" below "US Postage"	22.50	5.00
d.	"Media Mail" below "US Postage"	6.00	2.50
e.	"Parcel Post" below "US Postage"	6.00	2.50
f.	"Bound Printed Matter" below "US Postage"	6.00	2.50
g.	"BPM" below "US Postage"	6.00	2.50

Bicycling — CVPA19

Running — CVPA20

Swimming CVPA21

Boxing — CVPA22

Equestrian CVPA23

Basketball CVPA24

Judo — CVPA25

Soccer — CVPA26

Gymnastics CVPA27

Tennis — CVPA28

2004, Apr.	*Serpentine Die Cut 6½ at Left*		
1CVP22	CVPA19 37c **black, blue & orange**	3.00	2.00
	On cover		3.00
a.	"First Class" below "US Postage"	2.50	1.50
b.	"Priority" below "US Postage"	8.00	1.00
c.	"Express" below "US Postage"	25.00	3.00

No.	Description	Unused	Used
d.	"Media Mail" below "US Postage"	7.50	1.00
e.	"Parcel Post" below "US Postage"	7.50	1.00
f.	"Bound Printed Matter" below "US Postage"	7.50	1.00
g.	"BPM" below "US Postage"	7.50	1.00
1CVP23	CVPA20 37c **black, blue & orange**	3.00	2.00
	On cover		3.00
a.	"First Class" below "US Postage"	2.50	1.50
b.	"Priority" below "US Postage"	8.00	1.00
c.	"Express" below "US Postage"	25.00	3.00
d.	"Media Mail" below "US Postage"	7.50	1.00
e.	"Parcel Post" below "US Postage"	7.50	1.00
f.	"Bound Printed Matter" below "US Postage"	7.50	1.00
g.	"BPM" below "US Postage"	7.50	1.00
1CVP24	CVPA21 37c **black, blue & orange**	3.00	2.00
	On cover		3.00
a.	"First Class" below "US Postage"	2.50	1.50
b.	"Priority" below "US Postage"	8.00	1.00
c.	"Express" below "US Postage"	25.00	3.00
d.	"Media Mail" below "US Postage"	7.50	1.00
e.	"Parcel Post" below "US Postage"	7.50	1.00
f.	"Bound Printed Matter" below "US Postage"	7.50	1.00
g.	"BPM" below "US Postage"	7.50	1.00
1CVP25	CVPA22 37c **black, blue & orange**	3.00	2.00
	On cover		3.00
a.	"First Class" below "US Postage"	2.50	1.50
b.	"Priority" below "US Postage"	8.00	1.00
c.	"Express" below "US Postage"	25.00	3.00
d.	"Media Mail" below "US Postage"	7.50	1.00
e.	"Parcel Post" below "US Postage"	7.50	1.00
f.	"Bound Printed Matter" below "US Postage"	7.50	1.00
g.	"BPM" below "US Postage"	7.50	1.00
1CVP26	CVPA23 37c **black, blue & orange**	3.00	2.00
	On cover		3.00
a.	"First Class" below "US Postage"	2.50	1.50
b.	"Priority" below "US Postage"	8.00	1.00
c.	"Express" below "US Postage"	25.00	3.00
d.	"Media Mail" below "US Postage"	7.50	1.00
e.	"Parcel Post" below "US Postage"	7.50	1.00
f.	"Bound Printed Matter" below "US Postage"	7.50	1.00
g.	"BPM" below "US Postage"	7.50	1.00
h.	Horiz. strip of 5, #1CVP22-1CVP26	15.00	
1CVP27	CVPA24 37c **black, blue & orange**	3.00	2.00
	On cover		3.00
a.	"First Class" below "US Postage"	2.50	1.50
b.	"Priority" below "US Postage"	8.00	1.00
c.	"Express" below "US Postage"	25.00	3.00
d.	"Media Mail" below "US Postage"	7.50	1.00
e.	"Parcel Post" below "US Postage"	7.50	1.00
f.	"Bound Printed Matter" below "US Postage"	7.50	1.00
g.	"BPM" below "US Postage"	7.50	1.00
1CVP28	CVPA25 37c **black, blue & orange**	3.00	2.00
	On cover		3.00
a.	"First Class" below "US Postage"	2.50	1.50
b.	"Priority" below "US Postage"	8.00	1.00
c.	"Express" below "US Postage"	25.00	3.00
d.	"Media Mail" below "US Postage"	7.50	1.00
e.	"Parcel Post" below "US Postage"	7.50	1.00
f.	"Bound Printed Matter" below "US Postage"	7.50	1.00
g.	"BPM" below "US Postage"	7.50	1.00
1CVP29	CVPA26 37c **black, blue & orange**	3.00	2.00
	On cover		3.00
a.	"First Class" below "US Postage"	2.50	1.50
b.	"Priority" below "US Postage"	8.00	1.00
c.	"Express" below "US Postage"	25.00	3.00
d.	"Media Mail" below "US Postage"	7.50	1.00
e.	"Parcel Post" below "US Postage"	7.50	1.00
f.	"Bound Printed Matter" below "US Postage"	7.50	1.00
g.	"BPM" below "US Postage"	7.50	1.00
1CVP30	CVPA27 37c **black, blue & orange**	3.00	2.00
	On cover		3.00
a.	"First Class" below "US Postage"	2.50	1.50
b.	"Priority" below "US Postage"	8.00	1.00
c.	"Express" below "US Postage"	25.00	3.00
d.	"Media Mail" below "US Postage"	7.50	1.00
e.	"Parcel Post" below "US Postage"	7.50	1.00
f.	"Bound Printed Matter" below "US Postage"	7.50	1.00
g.	"BPM" below "US Postage"	7.50	1.00
1CVP31	CVPA28 37c **black, blue & orange**	3.00	2.00
	On cover		3.00
a.	"First Class" below "US Postage"	2.50	1.50
b.	"Priority" below "US Postage"	8.00	1.00
c.	"Express" below "US Postage"	25.00	3.00
d.	"Media Mail" below "US Postage"	7.50	1.00
e.	"Parcel Post" below "US Postage"	7.50	1.00
f.	"Bound Printed Matter" below "US Postage"	7.50	1.00
g.	"BPM" below "US Postage"	7.50	1.00
h.	Horiz. strip of 5, #1CVP27-1CVP31	15.00	

The item pictured above was produced by Stamps.com for a special promotional mailing of its own and was not made available unused to customers.

Leaning Tower of Pisa — CVPA29

Sphinx and Pyramids — CVPA30

Sydney Opera House — CVPA31

Mayan Pyramid — CVPA32

Asian Temple — CVPA33

2004, July ***Serpentine Die Cut 6½ at Left***

No.	Description	Unused	Used
1CVP32	CVPA29 37c **black, blue & orange**	3.00	2.00
	On cover		3.00
a.	"First Class" below "US Postage"	2.30	1.50
b.	"Priority" below "US Postage"	8.00	1.00
c.	"Express" below "US Postage"	25.00	3.00
d.	"Media Mail" below "US Postage"	7.50	1.00
e.	"Parcel Post" below "US Postage"	7.50	1.00
f.	"Bound Printed Matter" below "US Postage"	7.50	1.00
g.	"BPM" below "US Postage"	7.50	1.00
1CVP33	CVPA30 37c **black, blue & orange**	3.00	2.00
	On cover		3.00
a.	"First Class" below "US Postage"	2.30	1.50
b.	"Priority" below "US Postage"	8.00	1.00
c.	"Express" below "US Postage"	25.00	3.00
d.	"Media Mail" below "US Postage"	7.50	1.00
e.	"Parcel Post" below "US Postage"	7.50	1.00
f.	"Bound Printed Matter" below "US Postage"	7.50	1.00
g.	"BPM" below "US Postage"	7.50	1.00
1CVP34	CVPA31 37c **black, blue & orange**	3.00	2.00
	On cover		3.00
a.	"First Class" below "US Postage"	2.30	1.50
b.	"Priority" below "US Postage"	8.00	1.00
c.	"Express" below "US Postage"	25.00	3.00
d.	"Media Mail" below "US Postage"	7.50	1.00
e.	"Parcel Post" below "US Postage"	7.50	1.00
f.	"Bound Printed Matter" below "US Postage"	7.50	1.00
g.	"BPM" below "US Postage"	7.50	1.00
1CVP35	CVPA32 37c **black, blue & orange**	3.00	2.00
	On cover		3.00
a.	"First Class" below "US Postage"	2.30	1.50
b.	"Priority" below "US Postage"	8.00	1.00
c.	"Express" below "US Postage"	25.00	3.00
d.	"Media Mail" below "US Postage"	7.50	1.00
e.	"Parcel Post" below "US Postage"	7.50	1.00
f.	"Bound Printed Matter" below "US Postage"	7.50	1.00
g.	"BPM" below "US Postage"	7.50	1.00
1CVP36	CVPA33 37c **black, blue & orange**	3.00	2.00
	On cover		3.00
a.	"First Class" below "US Postage"	2.30	1.50
b.	"Priority" below "US Postage"	8.00	1.00
c.	"Express" below "US Postage"	25.00	3.00
d.	"Media Mail" below "US Postage"	7.50	1.00
e.	"Parcel Post" below "US Postage"	7.50	1.00
f.	"Bound Printed Matter" below "US Postage"	7.50	1.00
g.	"BPM" below "US Postage"	7.50	1.00
h.	Strip of 5, #1CVP32-1CVP36	15.00	

Computer and Letters — CVPA34

2005, Mar. ***Serpentine Die Cut 6½ at Left***

No.	Description	Unused	Used
1CVP37	CVPA34 37c **black, blue & orange**	25.00	15.00
	On cover		75.00
a.	"First Class" below "US Postage"	25.00	15.00
b.	"Priority" below "US Postage"	—	—
c.	"Express" below "US Postage"	—	—
d.	"Media Mail" below "US Postage"	—	—
e.	"Parcel Post" below "US Postage"	—	—
f.	"Bound Printed Matter" below "US Postage"	—	—
g.	"BPM" below "US Postage"	—	—

Blank sheets of No. 1CVP37 were sent free of charge to those who responded to special Stamps.com promotions which offered a fixed amount of free postage as an enticement to new subscribers. The franking portion of the stamps could only be applied after subscribing.

Logo — CVPA35

2005, Aug. ***Die Cut Perf. 6½ at Left***

1CVP38	CVPA35 37c **black, blue & orange**	1.00	.45
	On cover		2.50
a.	"Priority" below "US Postage"	8.00	1.00
b.	"Express" below "US Postage"	25.00	3.00
c.	"Media Mail" below "US Postage"	7.50	1.00
d.	"Parcel Post" below "US Postage"	7.50	1.00
e.	"BPM" below "US Postage"	7.50	1.00
f.	"Aerogramme" below "US Postage"	1.40	1.00
g.	"Intl Air Letter" below "US Postage"	1.25	1.00
h.	"Intl Eco Letter" (Economy Letter Mail) below "US Postage"	5.50	1.00
i.	"GXG" (Global Express Guaranteed) below "US Postage"	50.00	6.00
j.	"EMS" (Global Express Mail) below "US Postage"	32.50	4.00
k.	"GPM" (Global Priority Mail) below "US Postage"	8.00	1.00
l.	"Intl Air Parcel" (Air Parcel Post) below "US Postage"	26.00	3.00
m.	"Intl Eco Parcel" (Economy Parcel Post) below "US Postage"	32.50	4.00
n.	"M-Bag (Air)" below "US Postage"	35.00	5.00
o.	"M-Bag (Economy)" below "US Postage"	18.00	3.00
p.	"Mat for Blind" below "US Postage"	1.25	—
q.	"Library Mail"	5.00	1.00

Values for lettered varieties on Nos. 1CVP38 are based on the prices set as the minimum values for each service classification in the software available at the time the stamps were issued. In mid-December 2005, the software was changed to allow for a 1c minimum value for any of these lettered varieties.

In 2006, No. 1CVP38 was made available on a coil roll. Value, $1.40.

Snowman — CVPA36

Candy Cane — CVPA37

Dove — CVPA38

Stylized Christmas Tree and Window — CVPA39

2005, Nov. ***Die Cut Perf. 6 at Right***

1CVP39	CVPA36 37c **multicolored**	1.60	1.00
	On cover		2.50
a.	"Priority" below "US Postage"	8.00	1.00
b.	"Express" below "US Postage"	25.00	3.00
c.	"Media Mail" below "US Postage"	7.50	1.00
d.	"Parcel Post" below "US Postage"	7.50	1.00
e.	"BPM" below "US Postage"	7.50	1.00
f.	"Aerogramme" below "US Postage"	1.40	1.00
g.	"Intl Air Letter" below "US Postage"	1.25	1.00
h.	"Intl Eco Letter" (Economy Letter Mail) below "US Postage"	5.50	1.00
i.	"GXG" (Global Express Guaranteed) below "US Postage"	50.00	6.00
j.	"EMS" (Global Express Mail) below "US Postage"	32.50	4.00
k.	"GPM" (Global Priority Mail) below "US Postage"	8.00	1.00
l.	"Intl Air Parcel" (Air Parcel Post) below "US Postage"	26.00	3.00
m.	"Intl Eco Parcel" (Economy Parcel Post) below "US Postage"	32.50	4.00
n.	"M-Bag (Air)" below "US Postage"	35.00	5.00
o.	"M-Bag (Economy)" below "US Postage"	18.00	3.00
p.	"Mat for Blind" below "US Postage"	.25	—
1CVP40	CVPA37 37c **multicolored**	1.60	1.00
	On cover		2.50
a.	"Priority" below "US Postage"	8.00	1.00
b.	"Express" below "US Postage"	25.00	3.00
c.	"Media Mail" below "US Postage"	7.50	1.00
d.	"Parcel Post" below "US Postage"	7.50	1.00
e.	"BPM" below "US Postage"	7.50	1.00
f.	"Aerogramme" below "US Postage"	1.40	1.00
g.	"Intl Air Letter" below "US Postage"	1.25	1.00
h.	"Intl Eco Letter" (Economy Letter Mail) below "US Postage"	5.50	1.00
i.	"GXG" (Global Express Guaranteed) below "US Postage"	50.00	6.00
j.	"EMS" (Global Express Mail) below "US Postage"	32.50	4.00
k.	"GPM" (Global Priority Mail) below "US Postage"	8.00	1.00
l.	"Intl Air Parcel" (Air Parcel Post) below "US Postage"	26.00	3.00
m.	"Intl Eco Parcel" (Economy Parcel Post) below "US Postage"	32.50	4.00
n.	"M-Bag (Air)" below "US Postage"	35.00	5.00
o.	"M-Bag (Economy)" below "US Postage"	18.00	3.00
p.	"Mat for Blind" below "US Postage"	.45	—
1CVP41	CVPA38 37c **multicolored**	1.60	1.00
	On cover		2.50
a.	"Priority" below "US Postage"	8.00	1.00
b.	"Express" below "US Postage"	25.00	3.00
c.	"Media Mail" below "US Postage"	7.50	1.00
d.	"Parcel Post" below "US Postage"	7.50	1.00
e.	"BPM" below "US Postage"	7.50	1.00
f.	"Aerogramme" below "US Postage"	1.40	1.00
g.	"Intl Air Letter" below "US Postage"	1.25	1.00
h.	"Intl Eco Letter" (Economy Letter Mail) below "US Postage"	5.50	1.00
i.	"GXG" (Global Express Guaranteed) below "US Postage"	50.00	6.00
j.	"EMS" (Global Express Mail) below "US Postage"	32.50	4.00
k.	"GPM" (Global Priority Mail) below "US Postage"	8.00	1.00
l.	"Intl Air Parcel" (Air Parcel Post) below "US Postage"	26.00	3.00
m.	"Intl Eco Parcel" (Economy Parcel Post) below "US Postage"	32.50	4.00
n.	"M-Bag (Air)" below "US Postage"	35.00	5.00
o.	"M-Bag (Economy)" below "US Postage"	18.00	3.00
p.	"Mat for Blind" below "US Postage"	.45	—
1CVP42	CVPA39 37c **multicolored**	1.60	1.00
	On cover		2.50
a.	"Priority" below "US Postage"	8.00	1.00
b.	"Express" below "US Postage"	25.00	3.00
c.	"Media Mail" below "US Postage"	7.50	1.00
d.	"Parcel Post" below "US Postage"	7.50	1.00
e.	"BPM" below "US Postage"	7.50	1.00
f.	"Aerogramme" below "US Postage"	1.40	1.00
g.	"Intl Air Letter" below "US Postage"	1.25	1.00
h.	"Intl Eco Letter" (Economy Letter Mail) below "US Postage"	5.50	1.00
i.	"GXG" (Global Express Guaranteed) below "US Postage"	50.00	6.00
j.	"EMS" (Global Express Mail) below "US Postage"	32.50	4.00
k.	"GPM" (Global Priority Mail) below "US Postage"	8.00	1.00
l.	"Intl Air Parcel" (Air Parcel Post) below "US Postage"	26.00	3.00
m.	"Intl Eco Parcel" (Economy Parcel Post) below "US Postage"	32.50	4.00
n.	"M-Bag (Air)" below "US Postage"	35.00	5.00
o.	"M-Bag (Economy)" below "US Postage"	18.00	3.00
p.	"Mat for Blind" below "US Postage"	.45	—
q.	Vert. strip, 2 each #1CVP39-1CVP42	6.00	

Values for lettered varieties on Nos. 1CVP39-1CVP42 are based on the prices set as the minimum values for each service classification in the software available at the time the stamps were issued. In mid-December 2005, the software was changed to allow for a 1c minimum value for any of these lettered varieties.

Endicia.com

CVPA40

$0.24 0
US POSTAGE
POSTCARD
071V00566020
46860
000000146
endicia.com

CVPA41

2005-06 ***Serpentine Die Cut 10¼***

1CVP43	CVPA40 24c **black & bright rose**	10.00	4.00
a.	39c "First Class" under "US Postage"	2.00	.50
b.	63c "Intl. Mail" under "US Postage"	3.25	2.50
c.	$4.05 "Priority Mail" under "US Postage"	12.00	2.50

Coil Stamps

Serpentine Die Cut 10½x10¼ on 2 Sides

1CVP44	CVPA41 24c **black & pink**	11.00	4.00
a.	39c "First Class" under "US Postage"	2.25	.50
b.	63c "Intl. Mail" under "US Postage"	3.50	2.50
c.	$4.05 "Priority Mail" under "US Postage"	12.50	2.50

Issued: Nos. 1CVP43, Nov. 2005; Nos. 1CVP44, Jan. 2006.

Originally, face values of 2c, 52c, 63c, 87c, $1.11, $1.35, $1.59, $1.83, $2.07, $2.31, $2.55, $2.79, $3.03, and $3.27 could also be printed on stamps with the "First class" inscription. Additionally, an 84c face value could be printed on stamps with the "Intl. Mail" inscription, and a $8.10 face value could be printed on stamps with the "Priority Mail" inscription. Values for Nos. 1CVP43-1CVP44 are for stamps with the listed face values and mail-class inscription. Values for stamps with lower or higher face values are correspondingly lower or higher.

In 2007, software changes permitted Nos. 1CVP43 and 1CVP44 to be printed with mail class inscriptions "Media Mail," "BPM," "Parcel Post," "Library Mail," and "Express Mail," as well as any face value for any mail-class inscription.

Nos. 1CVP43 and 1CVP44 printed after the software changes are inscribed "First Class" under "US Postage" and sell for considerably less than the values shown. Stamps printed before the software changes are inscribed "Postcard" under "US Postage," as shown in the illustrations.

Stamps.com

Flag and Mount Rushmore — CVPA42

Flag and Eagle — CVPA43

Flag and Statue of Liberty — CVPA44

Flag and Liberty Bell — CVPA45

2006, Mar. ***Die Cut Perf. 6 at Right***

1CVP51	CVPA42 39c **multicolored**	1.25	1.00
	On cover		2.50
1CVP52	CVPA43 39c **multicolored**	1.25	1.00
	On cover		2.50
1CVP53	CVPA44 39c **multicolored**	1.25	1.00
	On cover		2.50
1CVP54	CVPA45 39c **multicolored**	1.25	1.00
	On cover		2.50
a.	Vert. strip of 8, 2 each #1CVP51-1CVP54	8.00	

Other service inscriptions with any possible face value can be printed on Nos. 1CVP51-1CVP54.

Stamps.com

Leaning Tower of Pisa — CVPA46

Taj Mahal — CVPA47

Eiffel Tower — CVPA48

Parthenon — CVPA49

2006 ***Die Cut Perf 6 at Right***

1CVP55	CVPA46 39c **multicolored**	1.25	1.00
	On cover		2.50

Serial Number Under Encryption APC

1CVP56	CVPA47 39c **multicolored**	1.25	1.00
	On cover		2.50
1CVP57	CVPA48 39c **multicolored**	1.25	1.00
	On cover		2.50
1CVP58	CVPA49 39c **multicolored**	1.25	1.00
	On cover		2.50
a.	Vert. strip, 2 each #1CVP55-1CVP58	8.00	

With the introduction of the new software in December 2005, any stamp could have any denomination 1c and above, and any service classification.

Pitney Bowes Stamp Expressions

CVPA50

Illustration reduced.

2006 ***Die Cut Perf. 6 Horiz.***

Inscribed "pitneybowes.com/se" at Right

1CVP59	CVPA50 39c **black** + label	1.35	.80
	On cover		4.00

The stamp and label are separated by vertical roulettes. Users could create their own label images on the Pitney Bowes Stamp Expressions website (which required approval of the image from Pitney Bowes before it could be used), or download various pre-approved label images from the website into their personal computers. Stamps could be printed without label images. Stamps were printed on rolls of tagged thermal paper from a device that could be operated without a direct connection to the personal computer. See No. 1CVT1.

Stamps.com

CVPA51

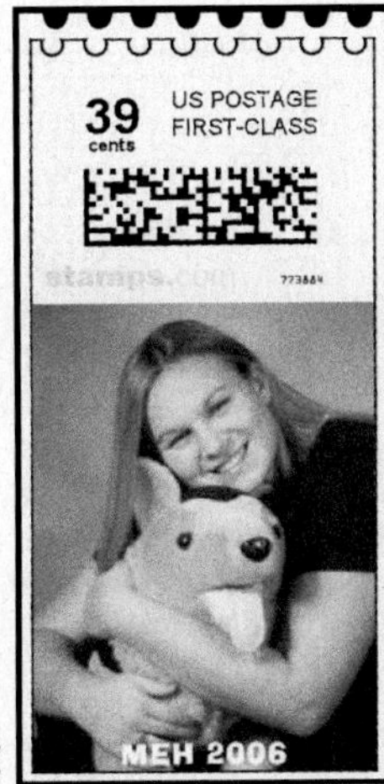

Personalizable Images — CVPA52

Illustration CVPA51 is reduced.

2006, Sept. ***Die Cut Perf. 6 at Right***

1CVP60	CVPA51 39c **multicolored**	1.50	.95
	On cover		4.50
a.	Numerals in denomination 2½mm high, thicker text	1.50	.95
	On cover		4.50

Perf. Die Cut Perf. 6 at Top

1CVP61	CVPA52 39c **multicolored**	1.50	.95
	On cover		4.50
a.	Numerals in denomination 2½mm high, thicker text	1.50	.95
	On cover		4.50

Users could requisition sheets of Nos. 1CVP60 and 1CVP61 with images of their choice from Stamps.com at $4.99 per sheet of 24. Priority and Express service classifications could also be printed on Nos. 1CVP60-1CVP61 with any denomination. Stamps exist with slightly larger die cutting (60x30mm and 30x60mm) in both squared and rounded corners. The denomination type shown on Nos. 1CVP60-1CVP61 can be placed on label types CVPA36-CVPA39, CVPA42-CVPA49, CVPA53-CVPA60 and any later stamps.com labels of this size.

Numerals in denomination are 3mm tall on Nos. 1CVP60-1CVP61. Serial numbers on Nos. 1CPVP60-1CVP61 lack periods and have small bank-check style numerals.

Autumn Leaves — CVPA53

Pumpkins — CVPA54

Basket of Apples, Sheaf of Wheat, Falling Leaves and Pumpkins — CVPA55

Leaves and Carved Pumpkin — CVPA56

2006 ***Die Cut Perf. 6 at Right***

1CVP62	CVPA53 39c **multicolored**	1.25	1.00
	On cover		2.50
1CVP63	CVPA54 39c **multicolored**	1.25	1.00
	On cover		2.50
1CVP64	CVPA55 39c **multicolored**	1.25	1.00
	On cover		2.50
1CVP65	CVPA56 39c **multicolored**	1.25	1.00
	On cover		2.50
a.	Vert. strip, 2 each #1CVP62-1CVP65	10.00	

See note after No. 1CVP58.

"Season's Greetings" — CVPA57

Christmas Trees — CVPA58

Snowman — CVPA59

Dove — CVPA60

2006 ***Die Cut Perf. 6 at Right***

1CVP66	CVPA57 39c **multicolored**	1.25	.45
	On cover		2.50
1CVP67	CVPA58 39c **multicolored**	1.25	.45
	On cover		2.50
1CVP68	CVPA59 39c **multicolored**	1.25	.45
	On cover		2.50
1CVP69	CVPA60 39c **multicolored**	1.25	.45
	On cover		2.50
a.	Vert. strip, 2 each #1CVP66-1CVP69	10.00	

See note after No. 1CVP58.

Flag — CVPA61

Statue of Liberty and Flag — CVPA62

Bald Eagle and Flag — CVPA63

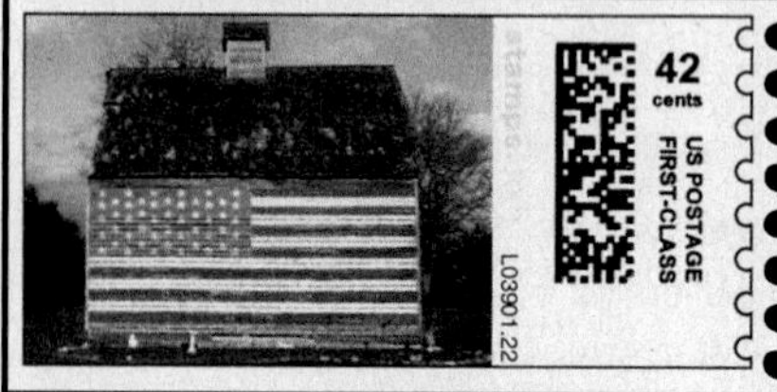

Flag Painted on Building — CVPA64

2008 ***Die Cut Perf. 5½ at Right***

Serial Number With Period, Large Letters and Numerals

1CVP70	CVPA61 42c **multicolored**	1.25	1.00
	On cover		2.50
1CVP71	CVPA62 42c **multicolored**	1.25	1.00
	On cover		2.50
1CVP72	CVPA63 42c **multicolored**	1.25	1.00
	On cover		2.50
1CVP73	CVPA64 42c **multicolored**	1.25	1.00
	On cover		2.50

On Nos. 1CVP70-1CVP105, and perhaps on other stamps, placement of the stamp serial number and the stamps.com logo might differ on various printings of the label stock. Descriptive text outside the frame might also vary or not be present on these various printings.

Autumn — CVPA65

Designs: No. 1CVP74, Oak leaves. No. 1CVP75, Pumpkin patch. No. 1CVP76, Autumn reflection. No. 1CVP77, Pumpkins and gourds.

2008 ***Die Cut Perf. 5½ at Right***

Serial Number With Period, Large Letters and Numerals

1CVP74	CVPA65 42c **multicolored**	2.00	1.00
	On cover		2.50
1CVP75	CVPA65 42c **multicolored**	2.00	1.00
	On cover		2.50
1CVP76	CVPA65 42c **multicolored**	2.00	1.00
	On cover		2.50
1CVP77	CVPA65 42c **multicolored**	2.00	1.00
	On cover		2.50

Flowers — CVPA66

Designs: No. 1CVP78, Sunflowers. No. 1CVP79, Daisies. No. 1CVP80, Sunflower sky. No. 1CVP81, Treasure flowers.

2008 ***Die Cut Perf. 5½ at Right***

Serial Number With Period, Large Letters and Numerals

1CVP78	CVPA66 42c **multicolored**	1.25	1.00
	On cover		2.50
1CVP79	CVPA66 42c **multicolored**	1.25	1.00
	On cover		2.50
1CVP80	CVPA66 42c **multicolored**	1.25	1.00
	On cover		2.50
1CVP81	CVPA66 42c **multicolored**	1.25	1.00
	On cover		2.50

Endangered Animals — CVPA67

Designs: No. 1CVP82, Bengal tiger. No. 1CVP83, Hawksbill turtle. No. 1CVP84, Panda. No. 1CVP85, African rhino.

2008 ***Die Cut Perf. 5½ at Right***

Serial Number With Period, Large Letters and Numerals

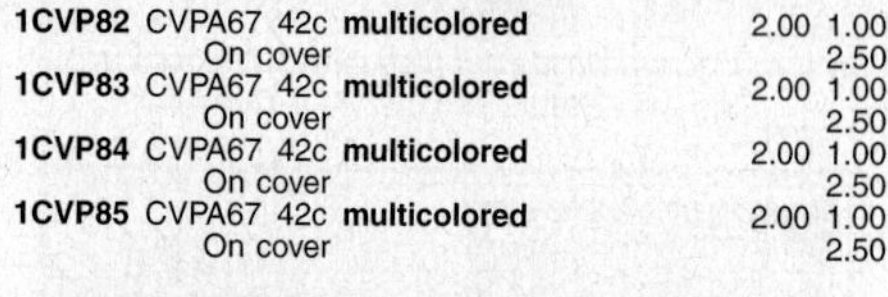

1CVP82	CVPA67 42c **multicolored**	2.00	1.00
	On cover		2.50
1CVP83	CVPA67 42c **multicolored**	2.00	1.00
	On cover		2.50
1CVP84	CVPA67 42c **multicolored**	2.00	1.00
	On cover		2.50
1CVP85	CVPA67 42c **multicolored**	2.00	1.00
	On cover		2.50

Parks — CVPA68

Designs: No. 1CVP86, Grand Canyon National Park, Arizona. No. 1CVP87, Yosemite National Park, California. No. 1CVP88, Niagara Falls. No. 1CVP89, Arches National Park, Utah.

2008 ***Die Cut Perf. 5½ at Right***

Serial Number With Period, Large Letters and Numerals

1CVP86	CVPA68 42c **multicolored**	1.25	1.00
	On cover		2.50
1CVP87	CVPA68 42c **multicolored**	1.25	1.00
	On cover		2.50
1CVP88	CVPA68 42c **multicolored**	1.25	1.00
	On cover		2.50
1CVP89	CVPA68 42c **multicolored**	1.25	1.00
	On cover		2.50

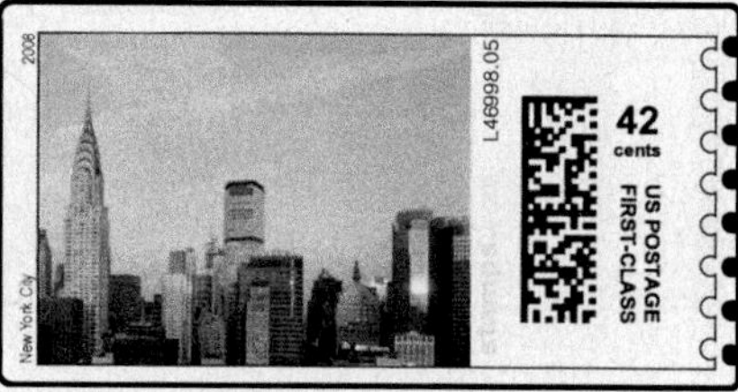

City Skylines — CVPA69

Designs: No. 1CVP90, New York City. No. 1CVP91, St. Louis. No. 1CVP92, Chicago. No. 1CVP93, San Francisco.

2008 ***Die Cut Perf. 5½ at Right***

Serial Number With Period, Large Letters and Numerals

1CVP90	CVPA69 42c **multicolored**	2.00	1.00
	On cover		2.50
1CVP91	CVPA69 42c **multicolored**	2.00	1.00
	On cover		2.50
1CVP92	CVPA69 42c **multicolored**	2.00	1.00
	On cover		2.50
1CVP93	CVPA69 42c **multicolored**	2.00	1.00
	On cover		2.50

Presidential Memorials — CVPA70

Designs: No. 1CVP94, Washington Monument. No. 1CVP95, Lincoln Memorial. No. 1CVP96, Jefferson Memorial. No. 1CVP97, Mount Rushmore.

2008 ***Die Cut Perf. 5½ at Right***

Serial Number With Period, Large Letters and Numerals

1CVP94 CVPA70 42c **multicolored**	1.25	1.00
On cover		2.50
1CVP95 CVPA70 42c **multicolored**	1.25	1.00
On cover		2.50
1CVP96 CVPA70 42c **multicolored**	1.25	1.00
On cover		2.50
1CVP97 CVPA70 42c **multicolored**	1.25	1.00
On cover		2.50

Christmas — CVPA71

Designs: No. 1CVP98, Ornament, "Happy Holidays." No. 1CVP99, Gingerbread men, "Season's Greetings." No. 1CVP100, Snowflake, "Happy Holidays." No. 1CVP101, Christmas tree, "Season's Greetings."

2008 ***Die Cut Perf. 5½ at Right***

Serial Number With Period, Large Letters and Numerals

Without Year or Text at Left

1CVP98 CVPA71 42c **multicolored**	2.00	1.00
On cover		2.50
1CVP99 CVPA71 42c **multicolored**	2.00	1.00
On cover		2.50
1CVP100 CVPA71 42c **multicolored**	2.00	1.00
On cover		2.50
1CVP101 CVPA71 42c **multicolored**	2.00	1.00
On cover		2.50

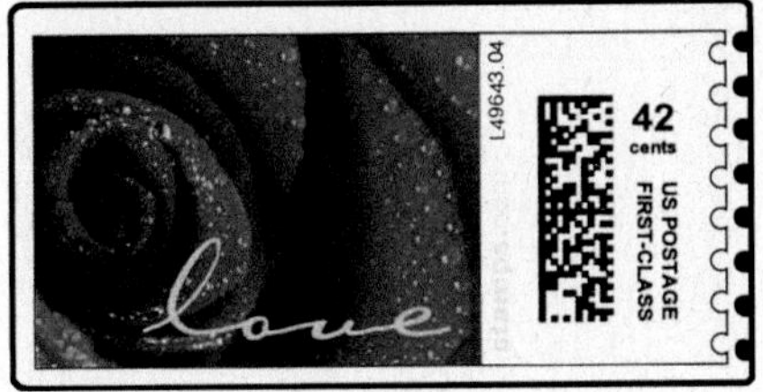

Love — CVPA72

"Love" and: No. 1CVP102, Rose. No. 1CVP103, Small hearts. No. 1CVP104, Large heart. No. 1CVP105, Hearts on curtain.

2009 ***Die Cut Perf. 5½ at Right***

Serial Number With Period, Large Letters and Numerals

Without Year or Text at Left

1CVP102 CVPA72 42c **multicolored**	1.25	1.00
On cover		2.50
1CVP103 CVPA72 42c **multicolored**	1.25	1.00
On cover		2.50
1CVP104 CVPA72 42c **multicolored**	1.25	1.00
On cover		2.50
1CVP105 CVPA72 42c **multicolored**	1.25	1.00
On cover		2.50

Wavy Lines — CVPA73

2009 ***Die Cut Perf 6½ at Right***

1CVP106 CVPA73 44c **multicolored**	1.25	.45
On cover		2.50

Software allowed for other inscriptions below "US Postage," including "Library Mail."

Endicia.com

CVPA74

Globe — CVPA74a

2009 ***Serpentine Die Cut 10¼x10½***

1CVP107 CVPA74 44c **orange & black,** with space between denomination and "US POSTAGE"	1.25	.45
On cover		2.50
1CVP107A CVPA74a 45c **orange & black,** with no space between denomination and "US POSTAGE"	—	—

Software allowed for six other inscriptions below "US Postage" (Priority Mail, Media Mail, Parcel Post, Library Mail, Express Mail and Intl Mail) and any face value for any mail-class inscription.

Stamps.com

Thank You For Your Business — CVPA75

Text: No. 1CVP108, On billboard. No. 1CVP109, And building. No. 1CVP110, On red background. No. 1CVP111, And two people shaking hands.

2009 ***Die Cut Perf. 5½ at Right***

Serial Number With Period, Large Letters and Numerals

Without Year or Text at Left

1CVP108 CVPA75 44c **multicolored**	1.25	1.00
On cover		2.50
1CVP109 CVPA75 44c **multicolored**	1.25	1.00
On cover		2.50
1CVP110 CVPA75 44c **multicolored**	1.25	1.00
On cover		2.50
1CVP111 CVPA75 44c **multicolored**	1.25	1.00
On cover		2.50

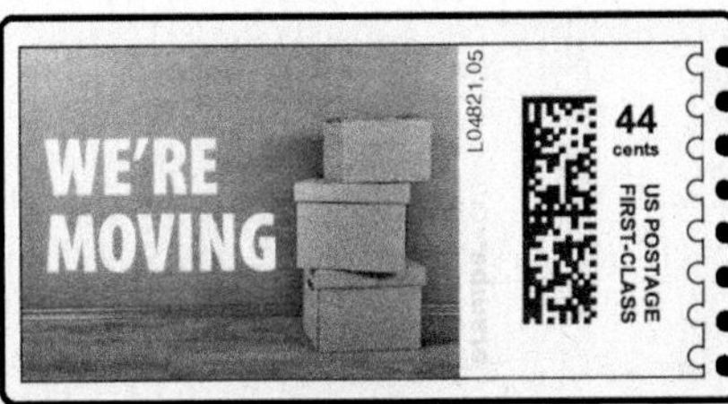

We're Moving — CVPA76

Text: No. 1CVP112, Stack of three boxes, green background. No. 1CVP113, Eleven boxes, orange background. No. 1CVP114, Four boxes, green background. No. 1CVP115, Four boxes, red background.

2009 ***Die Cut Perf. 5½ at Right***

Serial Number With Period, Large Letters and Numerals

Without Year or Text at Left

1CVP112 CVPA76 44c **multicolored**	1.25	1.00
On cover		2.50
1CVP113 CVPA76 44c **multicolored**	1.25	1.00
On cover		2.50
1CVP114 CVPA76 44c **multicolored**	1.25	1.00
On cover		2.50
1CVP115 CVPA76 44c **multicolored**	1.25	1.00
On cover		2.50

Special Invitation — CVPA77

Text: No. 1CVP116, And pen nib. No. 1CVP117, And circled "15" on calendar. No. 1CVP118, On card on envelope. No. 1CVP119, On wax seal.

2009 ***Die Cut Perf. 5½ at Right***

Serial Number With Period, Large Letters and Numerals

Without Year or Text at Left

1CVP116 CVPA77 44c **multicolored**	1.25	1.00
On cover		2.50
1CVP117 CVPA77 44c **multicolored**	1.25	1.00
On cover		2.50
1CVP118 CVPA77 44c **multicolored**	1.25	1.00
On cover		2.50
1CVP119 CVPA77 44c **multicolored**	1.25	1.00
On cover		2.50

US Flag — CVPA78

Flag: No. 1CVP120, On flagpole. No. 1CVP121, Behind Statue of Liberty. No. 1CVP122, Behind bald eagle. No. 1CVP123, On United States map.

2009 ***Die Cut Perf. 5½ at Right***

Serial Number With Period, Large Letters and Numerals

Without Year or Text at Left

1CVP120 CVPA78 44c **multicolored**	2.00	1.00
On cover		2.50
1CVP121 CVPA78 44c **multicolored**	2.00	1.00
On cover		2.50
1CVP122 CVPA78 44c **multicolored**	2.00	1.00
On cover		2.50
1CVP123 CVPA78 44c **multicolored**	2.00	1.00
On cover		2.50

Patriotic Symbols
CVPA79

Designs: No. 1CVP124, Statue of Liberty. No. 1CVP125, Flag. No. 1CVP126, Bald eagle.

2010 ***Die Cut Perf. 5½ Vert.***

1CVP124 CVPA79 44c **multicolored** 1.25 1.00
On cover 2.50
1CVP125 CVPA79 44c **multicolored** 1.25 1.00
On cover 2.50
1CVP126 CVPA79 44c **multicolored** 1.25 1.00
On cover 2.50

Jewish Symbols
CVPA80

Designs: No. 1CVP127, Menorah. No. 1CVP125, Dreidel. No. 1CVP126, Star of David.

2010 ***Die Cut Perf. 5½ Vert.***

1CVP127 CVPA80 44c **multicolored** 1.25 1.00
On cover 2.50
1CVP128 CVPA80 44c **multicolored** 1.25 1.00
On cover 2.50
1CVP129 CVPA80 44c **multicolored** 1.25 1.00
On cover 2.50

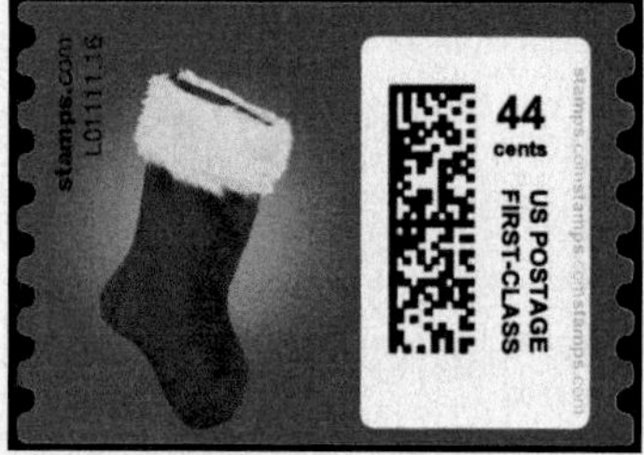

Christmas
CVPA81

Designs: No. 1CVP130, Christmas stocking. No. 1CVP131, Christmas tree. No. 1CVP132, Santa Claus.

2010 ***Die Cut Perf. 5½ Vert.***

1CVP130 CVPA81 44c **multicolored** 1.25 1.00
On cover 2.50
1CVP131 CVPA81 44c **multicolored** 1.25 1.00
On cover 2.50
1CVP132 CVPA81 44c **multicolored** 1.25 1.00
On cover 2.50

Valentine's Day — CVPA82

Designs: No. 1CVP133, Hearts. No. 1CVP134, Rose. No. 1CVP135, Candy hearts.

2011 ***Die Cut Perf. 5½ Vert.***

1CVP133 CVPA82 44c **multicolored** 2.00 1.00
On cover 2.50
1CVP134 CVPA82 44c **multicolored** 2.00 1.00
On cover 2.50
1CVP135 CVPA82 44c **multicolored** 2.00 1.00
On cover 2.50

Christian Symbols
CVPA83

Designs: No. 1CVP136, Cross. No. 1CVP137, Fish. No. 1CVP138, Rosary beads.

2011 ***Die Cut Perf. 5½ Vert.***

1CVP136 CVPA83 44c **multicolored** 1.25 1.00
On cover 2.50
1CVP137 CVPA83 44c **multicolored** 1.25 1.00
On cover 2.50
1CVP138 CVPA83 44c **multicolored** 1.25 1.00
On cover 2.50

OFFICAL STAMPS PRINTED TO ORDER

1CVPO1

1CVPO2

2002-06 ***Serpentine Die Cut 10.6***

Self-Adhesive

1CVPO1 1CVPO1 37c **blk, red & bluish gray** — —
On cover —
No denomination below vignette.

1CVPO2 1CVPO2 37c **blk, red & blue** — —
On cover —
Denomination below vignette.

1CVPO3 1CVPO2 39c **blk, red & blue** — —
On cover —
Denomination below vignette.

1CVPO5 1CVPO2 $4.05 **blk, red & blue** — —
On cover —
Denomination below vignette.

Endicia filled federal agency orders for stamps to be limited for use by government officials. Nos. 1CVPO1 and 1CVPO2 were printed in sheets of 10. 39c and 41c denominations are thought to exist.

COMPUTER VENDED POSTAGE TEST STAMPS

Pitney Bowes Stamp Expressions

CVT1

Illustration reduced.

2006 ***Die Cut Perf. 6 Horiz.***

Inscribed "pbstampexpressions.com" at Right

1CVT1 CVT1 39c **black** + label 5.00 —
On cover —

No. 1CVT1 were produced only by beta testers of the Pitney Bowes Stamp Expressions system, and as such were not available to normal subscribers to the system. Examples are known to have passed through the mail. Notes concerning No. 1CVP59 apply to No. 1CVT1.

NON-PERSONALIZABLE POSTAGE

These stamps, approved by the USPS, were non-personalizable stamps that could be purchased directly from private manufacturers, which shipped them to the customer. Other non-personalizable stamps have been created by a variety of companies, all sold at excessive amounts over face value as "collectibles". Such items are not listed here. Most items created that sold for excessive amounts over face value have vignettes that are licensed images, usually depicting sport team emblems or other sports-related themes, or celebrities.

Personalized postage stamps, first available in 2004, created by a variety of different companies, and heretofore listed with Scott numbers having a "2CVP" prefix, are no longer listed. Personalized stamps, though valid for postage, are not sold at any U.S. Postal Service post office. They are available only by on-line ordering through the company's website. Stamps are only available from the companies in full panes of 20. Each pane is sold at a significant premium above the stated face value to cover the costs of personalization, shipping and handling.

In recent years, there has been a steadily increasing number of private companies, either directly licensed by the USPS or created as spinoff companies of these licensees, creating distinctly different personalized stamps. None of the companies has issued fewer than seven stamps for each rate change, with one issuing as many as 42 different stamps. Because mailing rates set by the USPS are expected to change yearly, the collective output of distinctly different, rate-based stamps from these various companies likely will increase. There are no restrictions in place to prevent more firms from bringing personalized stamps to the marketplace, or to keep stamp producers from offering even more customer options. Some personalized stamps do not differ in any appreciable manner from some of the non-personalizable stamps sold as collectibles and not listed here.

NON-PERSONALIZABLE POSTAGE

Stamps.com

CVPC1

CVPC2

2007, May ***Die Cut***

Self-Adhesive

3CVP1 CVPC1 2c **black & gray green** 1.00 1.00
a. Inscribed "US Postag" — —

Die Cut Perf. 5¼ at Right

3CVP2 CVPC2 2c **multicolored** 1.00 1.00
a. Tagged *2.00 2.00*

2008 ***Die Cut***

Self-Adhesive

3CVP3 CVPC1 1c **black & gray** 1.00 1.00

No. 3CVP1 was printed in sheets of 40 stamps. Stamps with serial numbers ending in "06" are No. 3CVP1a. Sheets were sold for face value plus a shipping charge and were obtainable through the stamps.com website.

No. 3CVP2 was printed in sheets of 20. Full sheets were given free of charge to first-time stamps.com customers, but the full sheets were available for sale to other customers at face value plus a shipping charge through the stamps.com website.

Stamps.com Type of 2007

2019 ***Die Cut***

Self-Adhesive

3CVP4 CVPC1 5c **black & gray** 1.00 1.00

No. 3CVP4 was printed in sheets of 40 stamps that were sold for face value plus a shipping charge and were obtainable through the stamps.com website.

VENDING & AFFIXING MACHINE PERFORATIONS

Imperforate sheets of 400 were first issued in 1906 at the request of several makers of vending and affixing machines. The machine manufacturers made coils from the imperforate sheets and applied various perforations to suit the particular needs of their machines. These privately applied perforations were used for many years and form a chapter of postal history.

The Post Office Department had different arrangements with the various manufacturers of vending and affixing machines. Schermack and Mailometer coils were perforated in each city where those firms had customers. United States Automatic Vending Company perforated and coiled stamps for its machines under POD supervision in New York City, which were then returned for sale at any post office that had customers for them; in that respect, USAV coils can be regarded as semi-official. Farwell coils were perforated for the firm's use only on its Mailometer equipment, to avoid paying the coiling fee charged by Mailometer. Attleboro perforations were simply unusual separations punched into imperforate stamps by a philatelic publisher to create unusual perforation varieties for its customers. Covel perforations were applied to imperforate coil stamps supplied by the firm's purchasing agent, Alvin Filstrup (a stamp collector), as a convenience to use those stamps on mail from the company's sales staff, and on pre-stamped payment envelopes from customers, to its headquarters.

In 1927, the Post Office Department ceased supplying unfinished imperforate sheets to private firms, and required all users of proprietary perforations to configure their equipment to accept government coil stamps.

Unused values are for pairs, used values for singles. Used multiples are highly valued, with prices often equalling or exceeding those for unused pairs or strips. "On cover" values are for single stamps used commercially in the proper period when known that way. Several, primarily the Alaska-Yukon and Hudson-Fulton commemoratives, are known almost exclusively on covers from contemporaneous stamp collectors and stamp dealers. Virtually all are rare and highly prized by specialists.

The 2mm and 3mm spacings refer only to the 1908-10 issues. (See note following No. 330 in the Postage section.) Values for intermediate spacings would roughly correspond to the lower-valued of the two listed spacings. Guide line pairs of 1906-10 issues have 2mm spacing except the Alaska-Yukon and Hudson-Fulton issues, which have 3mm spacing. Scott Nos. 408-611 have 3mm spacing, except the "A" plates which have 2¾mm spacing and Scott No. 577, which has both 2¾mm and 3mm spacing. (All spacing measurements are approximate.)

Spacing on paste-up pairs is not a factor in valuing them. Because they were joined together by hand, many different spacings can occur, from less than 2mm to more than 3mm.

Perfins listed here are punched into the stamp just before being affixed to an envelope. The most common pattern consisted of a 7mm square made up of nine holes. Pins would be removed to create special perfins for each company using the machines. The catalogue value is for the most common perfin pattern on each stamp.

* — Many varieties are suspected or known to have been perforated for philatelic purposes and not actually used in machines. These are indicated by an asterisk before the number. Several of these privately applied perforation varieties exist in blocks, which were not produced in the regular course of business. They are valued at a premium over the multiple of the coil pairs contained, with an additional premium for plate numbers attached.

Counterfeits are prevalent, especially of items having a basic imperf. variety valued far lower than the vending machine coil.

The Vending and Affixing Machine Perforations Committee of the Bureau Issues Association (now the United States Stamp Society), William R. Weiss, Jr., Richard Champagne and Melvin Getlan compiled these listings.

The Attleboro Stamp Co.

See following U.S. Automatic Vending Company.

THE BRINKERHOFF COMPANY

Sedalia, Mo., Clinton, Iowa
Manufacturers of Vending Machines

Perforations Type I

Stamps were cut into strips and joined before being perforated.

Left Column = Unused Pair
Right Column = Used Single

On Issue of 1906-1908

No.	Description	Unused Pair	Used Single
314	1c **blue green**	220.00	35.00
	Guide line pair	400.00	
	Strip of 4	450.00	*150.00*
	Center line block of 4	*3,500.*	
320b	2c **scarlet**	250.00	35.00
	Guide line pair	500.00	
	Pasteup pair	375.00	
	Strip of 4	550.00	
* 320A	2c **lake**	180.00	30.00
	Guide line pair	360.00	
	Pasteup pair	260.00	
	Guide line strip of 4	750.00	

On Issue of 1908-09

No.	Description	Unused Pair	Used Single
* 343	1c **green**	135.00	25.00
	Guide line pair	325.00	
	Pasteup pair	250.00	
	Pasteup strip of 4	500.00	
* 344	2c **carmine**	115.00	25.00
	On cover		*2,250.*
	Guide line pair	225.00	
	Pasteup pair	200.00	
	Strip of 4	275.00	
	Guide line strip of 4	500.00	
* 345	3c **deep violet**	150.00	—
	Guide line pair	300.00	
	Strip of 4	400.00	
	Guide line strip of 4	600.00	
* 345a	3c Guide line pair, imperf. between	600.00	
* 346	4c **orange brown**	175.00	140.00
	Guide line pair	310.00	
	Pasteup pair	225.00	
	Pasteup strip of 4	600.00	
* 347	5c **blue**	500.00	90.00
	On cover		*5,000.*
	Guide line pair	900.00	

On Lincoln Issue of 1909

No.	Description	Unused Pair	Used Single
* 368	2c **carmine,** coiled endwise	185.00	*190.00*
	Guide line pair	500.00	575.00
	Strip of 4	500.00	
	Guide line strip of 4	700.00	

On Alaska-Yukon Issue of 1909

No.	Description	Unused Pair	Used Single
* 371	2c **carmine,** coiled sideways	*625.00*	—
	Guide line pair	*1,250.*	

On Issue of 1910

No.	Description	Unused Pair	Used Single
* 383	1c **green**	*900.00*	
	Guide line pair	*1,300.*	

On Issue of 1912

No.	Description	Unused Pair	Used Single
* 408	1c **green**	35.00	17.50
	On cover		*1,000.*
	Guide line pair	70.00	
	Pasteup pair	57.50	
	Strip of 4	100.00	
	Strip of 4, middle column with perforations omitted	150.00	
	Guide line strip of 4	200.00	
	Pasteup strip of 4	175.00	
* 409	2c **carmine**	35.00	17.50
	On cover		*2,000.*
	Guide line pair	70.00	
	Pasteup pair	57.50	
	Strip of 4	100.00	*100.00*
	Guide line strip of 4	200.00	
	Pasteup strip of 4	100.00	

Type IIa — One Knife Cut

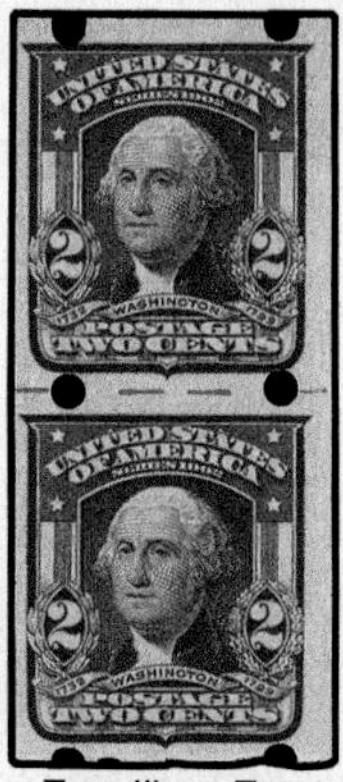

Type IIb — Two Knife Cuts

Perforations Type II, 2 Holes

The Type II items listed below are without knife cuts and did not pass through the vending machine. Types IIa and IIb (illustrated above) have knife cuts, applied by the vending machine, to help separate the stamps.

Left Column = Unused Pair
Right Column = Used Single

On Issue of 1906-08

No.	Description	Unused Pair	Used Single
314	1c **blue green**		
	* Type II	100.00	14.00
	On cover		*1,000.*
	Type IIa	90.00	14.00
	Guide line pair	175.00	
	* Type IIb	475.00	—
	Pasteup pair	1,150.	
320	2c **carmine**		
	* Type II	220.00	*70.00*
	On cover		*750.00*
	Guideline pair	400.00	
	Pasteup pair	375.00	
	Type IIa	45.00	14.00
	On cover		*600.00*
	Guide line pair	150.00	
320A	2c **lake**		
	* Type II	230.00	*70.00*
	On cover		*1,500.*
	Strip of 4	450.00	
	Guide line strip of 4	600.00	
	Pasteup strip of 4	550.00	
	Type IIa	95.00	14.50
	On cover		*800.00*
	Guide line pair	185.00	
	Pasteup pair	105.00	
	Strip of 4	450.00	
	Guide line strip of 4	700.00	
	* Type IIb	380.00	*80.00*

On Issue of 1908-09

No.	Description	Unused Pair	Used Single
343	1c **green**		
	* Type II	70.00	
	On cover		*750.00*
	Guide line pair	120.00	
	Type IIa	21.00	3.75
	On cover		750.00
	Pasteup pair	35.00	
	Type IIb	37.50	
	On cover		*1,500.*
	Pasteup pair	65.00	
	Pasteup strip of 4	250.00	
344	2c **carmine**		
	* Type II	80.00	
	On cover, pair		*750.00*
	Guide line pair	175.00	
	Pasteup pair	140.00	
	Strip of 4	200.00	
	Guide line strip of 4	400.00	
	Pasteup strip of 4	300.00	
	Type IIa	26.00	3.75
	On cover		*1,000.*
	Guide line pair	40.00	
	Strip of 4	200.00	
	Type IIb	30.00	7.00
	Guide line pair	80.00	
	Pasteup pair	65.00	
345	3c **deep violet**		
	* Type II	115.00	14.00
	Guide line pair	290.00	
	Pasteup pair	250.00	
	* Type IIa	95.00	14.00
	On cover		*1,750.*
	Guide line pair	190.00	
	Strip of 4	225.00	
	* Type IIb	340.00	
	Guide line pair	1,300.	
346	4c **orange brown**		
	* Type II	175.00	
	Guide line pair	300.00	
	Strip of 4	325.00	
	Guide line strip of 4	500.00	
	* Type IIa	160.00	*55.00*
	On cover		*1,500.*
	Guide line pair	260.00	
	Pasteup pair	220.00	
	Strip of 4	225.00	
	* Type IIb	175.00	*55.00*
	On cover		*1,500.*
	Strip of 4	275.00	
347	5c **blue**		
	* Type II	260.00	260.00
	Guide line pair	550.00	
	Strip of 4	550.00	
	Guide line strip of 4	1,100.	
	* Type IIa	170.00	*110.00*
	On cover		*3,250.*
	Pasteup pair	240.00	
	Strip of 4	250.00	
	* Type IIb	250.00	
	Pasteup pair	425.00	
	Strip of 4	325.00	

On Lincoln Issue of 1909

No.	Description	Unused Pair	Used Single
368	2c **carmine**		
	* Type II	85.00	—
	On cover		*1,250.*
	Guide line pair	175.00	
	Strip of 4	250.00	*100.00*
	Guide line strip of 4	400.00	
	Type IIa	80.00	16.00
	On cover		*1,250.*
	Guide line pair	350.00	
	Pasteup pair	300.00	
	Strip of 4	200.00	
	Guide line strip of 4	700.00	
	Pasteup strip of 4	500.00	
	Type IIb	240.00	25.00
	On cover		*2,000.*
	Guide line pair	800.00	
	Strip of 4	1,100.	

On Alaska-Yukon Issue of 1909

No.	Description	Unused Pair	Used Single
371	2c **carmine**		
	* Type II, coiled sideways	200.00	*110.00*
	On cover		*1,250.*
	Guide line pair	450.00	
	Pasteup pair	400.00	
	Strip of 4	425.00	
	Guide line strip of 4	875.00	
	Type IIa, coiled sideways	1,250.	*50.00*
	On cover		*900.00*
	Guide line pair	360.00	
	Pasteup pair	290.00	
	Guide line strip of 4	700.00	
371	2c **carmine**		
	Type II, coiled endwise	*975.00*	
	Guide line pair	*1,750.*	

On Hudson-Fulton Issue of 1909

No.	Description	Unused Pair	Used Single
373	2c **carmine**		
	* Type II, coiled sideways	*300.00*	
	Guide line pair	*650.00*	
	Pasteup pair	*650.00*	
	Pasteup strip of 4	1,500.	

On Issue of 1910

No.	Description	Unused Pair	Used Single
383	1c **green**		
	* Type II	40.00	
	Guide line pair	80.00	
	Strip of 4	100.00	50.00
	Guide line strip of 4	200.00	
	Type IIa	50.00	10.00
	On cover		*850.00*
	Type IIb	100.00	*55.00*
	On cover		*1,250.*
	Guide line pair	190.00	
	Pasteup pair	175.00	
384	2c **carmine**		
	* Type II	42.50	
	On cover		*950.00*
	Guide line pair	75.00	
	Pasteup pair	75.00	
	Guide line strip of 4	175.00	
	Pasteup strip of 4	170.00	
	Type IIa	130.00	
	On cover		*1,250.*
	Pasteup pair	200.00	
	Type IIb	70.00	10.00
	On cover		*1,800.*
	Guide line pair	200.00	
	Pasteup pair	145.00	
	Strip of 4	200.00	
	Pasteup strip of 4	300.00	
408	1c **green**		
	* Type II	105.00	—
	On cover		*1,000.*
	Guide line pair	175.00	
	Pasteup pair	130.00	
	Strip of 4	250.00	
	* Type IIa	130.00	
	Guide line pair	230.00	
	Strip of 4	300.00	
	Guide line strip of 4	550.00	
	Type IIb	27.50	6.00
	On cover		2,000.
	Guide line pair	52.50	
	Pasteup strip of 4	125.00	
409	2c **carmine**		
	* Type II	75.00	
	On cover		*1,000.*
	Guide line pair	700.00	
	Pasteup pair	145.00	
	Guide line strip of 4	350.00	
	Pasteup strip of 4	300.00	
	* Type IIa	300.00	—
	On cover		*1,000.*
	Guide line pair	525.00	
	Type IIb	35.00	6.00
	On cover		*750.00*
	Guide line pair	65.00	
	Strip of 4	100.00	
	Guide line strip of 4	200.00	

Covel Manufacturing Co.

See following the Attleboro Stamp Company.

THE FARWELL COMPANY

Chicago, Ill.

A wholesale dry goods firm using Schermack (Mailometer) affixing machines. In 1911 the Farwell Company began to make and perforate their own coils. These were sometimes wrongly called "Chambers" perforations.

Type A

Type B

Stamps were perforated in sheets, then cut into strips and coiled. Blocks exist.

The following listings are grouped according to the number of holes, further divided into two types of spacing, narrow and wide.

The type symbols (3A2) indicate 3 holes over 2 holes with narrow, type A, spacing between groups.

Types A and B occurred in different rows on the same sheet. Left margin or pasteup stamps sometimes show different perforation type on the two sides.

Commercial usages of Farwell perforations are generally, but not always, on printed Farwell Co. corner card covers.

Left Column=Unused Pair
Right Column=Used Single

Group 1, no spacing

On Issue of 1910

No.	Description	Unused Pair	Used Single
384	2c **carmine,** 7 holes		1,050.
	On cover		3,500.
	Unused pair, 2mm spacing	3,250.	
	Unused pair, 3mm spacing	3,250.	
384	2c **carmine,** 6 holes		2,750.
	On cover		5,000.
	Unused pair, 2mm spacing	5,000.	
	Unused pair, 3mm spacing	5,000.	

Group 2, two and three holes

On Issue of 1910

No.	Description	Unused Pair	Used Single
383	1c **green**		
	2B3 Unused pair, 2mm spacing	2,250.	250.00
	2B3 Unused pair, 3mm spacing	2,250.	
	3A2 Unused pair, 2mm spacing	2,250.	
	3A2 Strip of 4, 3mm spacing	3,000.	
	On cover		—
	Guide line pair	2,000.	
	3A2 Unused pair, 3mm spacing	2,400.	
384	2c **carmine**		
	2A3 Unused pair, 2mm spacing	340.00	250.00
	Guide line strip of 4	3,000.	
	On cover		1,300.
	Guide line pair	1,250.	
	2A3 Unused pair, 3mm spacing	600.00	
	Guide line pair	1,250.	
	Pasteup pair	1,000.	
	2B3 Unused pair, 2mm spacing	1,250.	275.00
	On cover		—
	2B3 Unused pair, 3mm spacing	1,350.	
	Pasteup pair	1,550.	
	3A2 Unused pair, 2mm spacing	550.00	250.00
	On cover		1,750.
	Guide line pair	925.00	
	Strip of 4	2,000.	
	3A2 Unused pair, 3mm spacing	600.00	
	3B2 Unused pair, 2mm spacing	475.00	375.00
	Guide line pair	2,500.	
	Strip of 4	1,250.	
	Guide line strip of 4	2,500.	
	3B2 Unused pair, 3mm spacing	1,250.	
	3B2 Used pair, 3mm spacing		500.00

Group 3, three and four holes

On Issue of 1910

No.	Description	Unused Pair	Used Single
383	1c **green**		
	3B4 Unused pair, 2mm spacing	380.00	250.00
	Pasteup pair	800.00	
	Strip of 4	1,500.	
	3B4 Unused pair, 3mm spacing	380.00	
	4B3 Unused pair, 2mm spacing	550.00	250.00
	4A3 Used single		375.00
	4B3 Unused pair, 3mm spacing	550.00	
	4B3 Strip of 4	1,150.	
384	2c **carmine**		
	3B4 Unused pair, 2mm spacing	925.00	290.00
	On cover		—
	Guide line pair	1,350.	
	3B4 Unused pair, 3mm spacing	925.00	
	Guide line strip of 4	1,900.	
	4B3 Unused pair, 2mm spacing	1,000.	450.00
	On cover		1,500.
	Guide line pair	2,000.	
	Guide line strip of 4	3,000.	
	4B3 Unused pair, 3mm spacing	1,650.	
	4A3 On cover		—

Group 4, four and four holes

On Issue of 1908-09

No.	Description	Unused Pair	Used Single
343	1c **green**		
	* A Unused pair, 2mm spacing	400.00	
	* B Unused pair, 2mm spacing	400.00	
	On cover		675.00
344	2c **carmine**		
	* A Unused pair, 2mm spacing	360.00	
	* A Unused pair, 3mm spacing	550.00	
	* B Unused pair, 2mm spacing	275.00	125.00
	* B Unused pair, 3mm spacing	275.00	

On Lincoln Issue of 1909

No.	Description	Unused Pair	Used Single
368	2c **carmine**		
	* A Unused pair, 2mm spacing	1,050.	
	* A Unused pair, 3mm spacing	1,050.	
	* B Unused pair, 2mm spacing	1,050.	
	* B Unused pair, 3mm spacing	1,050.	

On Issue of 1910

No.	Description	Unused Pair	Used Single
383	1c **green**		
	A Unused pair, 2mm spacing	85.00	75.00
	Guide line pair	190.00	
	Strip of 4	350.00	
	Guide line strip of 4	500.00	
	Strip of 4, both A and B spacings	1,250.	
	* B P# block of 6, Impt. and letter A, bot A and B spacings	2,600.	
	Block of 4, both A and B spacings	1,100.	
	A Unused pair, 3mm spacing	80.00	
	B Unused pair, 2mm spacing	85.00	—
	On cover		360.00
	Guide line pair	175.00	
	Strip of 4	400.00	
	Guide line strip of 4	650.00	
	B Unused pair, 3mm spacing	70.00	—
	B P# block of 6, Impt. and letter A	1,750.	—
384	2c **carmine**		
	A Unused pair, 2mm spacing	95.00	30.00
	Guide line pair	190.00	
	Guide line strip of 4	825.00	
	Block of 4, both A and B spacings	600.00	
	B P# block of 6, Impt. and star, both A and B spacings	2,000.	—
	A Unused pair, 3mm spacing	80.00	
	Block of 4, both A and B spacings	600.00	
	B Unused pair, 2mm spacing	90.00	22.50
	On cover		650.00
	Guide line pair	200.00	
	Pasteup pair	275.00	
	Guide line strip of 4	500.00	
	B Unused pair, 3mm spacing	85.00	
	Strip of 4	200.00	
	B P# block of 6, Impt. and star	1,500.	
	Block of 4, both A and B spacings	600.00	

On Issue of 1912

No.	Description	Unused Pair	Used Single
408	1c **green**		
	A Unused pair	47.50	3.25
	On cover		550.00
	Guide line pair	85.00	
	Strip of 4	150.00	
	Margin block of 4, arrow	600.00	
	Margin block of 4, arrow, both A and B spacings	700.00	
	P# block of 6, both A and B spacings	1,750.	
	Center line block of 4, both A and B spacings	1,000.	
	B Unused pair	47.50	3.25
	On cover		300.00
	Guide line pair	80.00	
	Strip of 4	200.00	
	Guide line strip of 4	300.00	
409	2c **carmine**		
	A Unused pair	47.50	3.25
	On cover		50.00
	Guide line pair	175.00	
	Guide line strip of 4	250.00	
	Strip of 4, both A and B spacings	400.00	
	Block of 4	300.00	
	Margin block of 4, arrow, both A and B spacings	700.00	
	Center line block of 4, both A and B spacings	1,000.	
	B Unused pair	47.50	3.25
	On cover		50.00
	Guide line pair	80.00	
	Strip of 4	200.00	
	Guide line strip of 4	300.00	

On Issue of 1916-17

No.	Description	Unused Pair	Used Single
482	2c **carmine**		
	A Unused pair	1,100.	75.00
	On cover		1,250.
	Guide line pair	1,500.	
	Pasteup pair	1,400.	
	B Unused pair	700.00	80.00
	On cover		1,250.
	Guide line pair	1,400.	
	Guide line strip of 4	3,250.	

Group 5, four and five holes

On Issue of 1910

No.	Description	Unused Pair	Used Single
383	1c **green**		
	4A5 Unused pair, 2mm spacing	1,150.	—
	Guide line pair	1,750.	
	Strip of 4	3,250.	
	Block of 4	1,300.	
	Strip of 4, type 4B4 in left margin and 4A5 elsewhere	1,900.	
	Block of 4, both types 4A4 and 4A5	1,500.	
	4A5 Unused pair, 3mm spacing	1,100.	
384	2c **carmine**		
	4A5 Unused pair, 2mm spacing	925.00	—
	Guide line pair	1,750.	
	Guide line strip of 4	5,000.	
	4A5 Unused pair, 3mm spacing	875.00	
	Pasteup pair	1,750.	
	Strip of 4	2,500.	
	Pasteup strip of 4	3,500.	
	Pasteup strip of 4, type 4B4 at pasteup joint and type 4A5 elsewhere	4,500.	
	Pair, both types 5A4 and 4B4 perforations	1,300.	

On Issue of 1912

No.	Description	Unused Pair	Used Single
408	1c **green**		
	4A5 Unused pair	1,900.	
	Guide line pair	3,250.	
	Guide line strip of 4	6,500.	
	* 5A4 Unused pair	1,900.	
	Guide line pair	3,250.	
409	2c **carmine**		
	* 4A5 Unused pair	2,250.	500.00
	Guide line or pasteup pair	3,250.	
	Guide line strip of 4	6,500.	
	* 5A4 Unused pair	1,900.	
	Guide line pair	3,850.	
	Pair, both types 4A5 and 4B4 perforations	1,650.	

INTERNATIONAL VENDING MACHINE CO.

Baltimore, Md.

Similar to the Government coin stamp #322, but approximately perf. 12½ with somewhat inconsistent spacing.

On Issue of 1906-08

320	2c **carmine,** unused pair	2,750.
320b	2c **scarlet,** unused pair	2,250.
	Strip of 4	1,000.

On Issue of 1908-09

343	1c **green,** unused pair	4,750.
344	2c **carmine,** unused pair	1,250.
345	3c **dp violet,** unused pair	4,000.
346	4c **org brown,** unused pair	—
347	5c **blue,** unused pair	6,500.

THE MAILOMETER COMPANY

Detroit, Mich.

Formerly the Schermack Mailing Machine Co., then Mail-om-eter Co., and later the Mail-O-Meter Co. Their round-hole perforations were developed in an attempt to get the Bureau of Engraving and Printing to adopt a larger perforation for coil stamps.

Perforations Type I

Used experimentally in Detroit and Chicago in August, 1909. Later used regularly in the St. Louis branch.

Two varieties exist: six holes 1.95mm in diameter spaced an average 1.2mm apart with an overall length of 17.7mm, and six holes 1.95mm in diameter spaced an average 1.15mm apart with an overall length of 17.45mm.

The 17.7mm length perfs are much scarcer than the 17.45mm length perfs and merit a 20% premium over the values shown.

To date, the vast majority of commercial covers are franked with the 17.7mm length perf. stamps.

Left Column=Unusued Pair
Right Column=Used Single

On Issue of 1906-08

No.	Description	Unused Pair	Used Single
* 320	2c **carmine,** unused pair	600.00	
	Strip of 4	1,250.	
* 320b	2c **scarlet,** unused pair	450.00	
	Strip of 4	1,000.	
* 320A	2c **lake,** unused pair	400.00	
	Guide line pair	1,000.	
	Strip of 4	850.00	
	Guide line strip of 4	2,500.	

On Issue of 1908-09

No.	Description	Unused Pair	Used Single
343	1c **green**		
	Unused pair, 2mm spacing	52.50	27.50
	On cover		850.00
	Guide line pair	80.00	
	Strip of 4	150.00	

No.	Item	Unused	Used
	Guide line strip of 4	200.00	
	Unused pair, 3mm spacing	57.50	
344	2c **carmine**		
	Unused pair, 2mm spacing	47.50	5.50
	On cover, St. Louis		*87.50*
	On cover, Detroit or Chicago		*2,100.*
	On cover, Washington, D.C.		*2,200.*
	Guide line pair	100.00	
	With perforated control mark, single		*110.00*
	Same, on cover		*500.00*
	Strip of 4	150.00	
	Guide line strip of 4	210.00	
	Unused pair, 3mm spacing	52.50	
345	3c **deep violet**		
	Unused pair, 2mm spacing	75.00	22.50
	Guide line pair	150.00	
	Strip of 4	200.00	*75.00*
	Guide line strip of 4	325.00	
	Unused pair, 3mm spacing	75.00	
346	4c **org brown**		
	Unused pair, 2mm spacing	150.00	45.00
	Guide line pair	290.00	
	Strip of 4	250.00	
	Guide line strip of 4	650.00	
	Unused pair, 3mm spacing	105.00	
347	5c **blue**		
	Unused pair, 2mm spacing	165.00	45.00
	Guide line pair	290.00	
	Guide line strip of 4	*950.00*	
	B margin strip of 4, P# & Impt. T V	*1,500.*	

On Lincoln Issue of 1909

No.	Item	Unused	Used
* 368	2c **carmine**		
	Unused pair, 2mm spacing	210.00	*120.00*
	Guide line pair	425.00	
	Guide line strip of 4	1,250.	
	Strip of 4, 2mm and 3mm spacings	500.00	
	Unused pair, 3mm spacing	150.00	
	Used pair		100.00
	Strip of 4	500.00	

On Alaska-Yukon Issue of 1909

No.	Item	Unused	Used
* 371	2c **carmine**		
	Unused pair	260.00	*120.00*
	Guide line pair	475.00	
	Guide line strip of 4	950.00	

On Hudson-Fulton Issue of 1909

No.	Item	Unused	Used
* 373	2c **carmine**		
	Unused pair	325.00	*110.00*
	Guide line pair	475.00	
	Pasteup pair	425.00	
	Pasteup strip of 4	850.00	

On Issue of 1910

No.	Item	Unused	Used
383	1c **green**		
	Unused pair, 2mm spacing	50.00	3.75
	On cover		—
	Guide line pair	90.00	
	Strip of 4	150.00	*75.00*
	Guide line strip of 4	300.00	
	Unused pair, 3mm spacing	45.00	

The recorded No. 383 2mm used strip of 4 is precanceled St. Louis.

No.	Item	Unused	Used
384	2c **carmine**		
	Unused pair, 2mm spacing	65.00	5.50
	On cover		150.00
	Guide line pair	115.00	
	Strip of 4	200.00	
	Guide line strip of 4	325.00	
	Unused pair, 3mm spacing	52.50	
	Block of 4	300.00	
	P# block of 6, Impt.	*875.00*	

On Issue of 1912

No.	Item	Unused	Used
* 408	1c **green**		
	Unused pair	29.00	5.00
	Guide line pair	55.00	
	Strip of 4	100.00	
* 409	2c **carmine**		
	Unused pair	29.00	5.00
	On cover		*525.00*
	Guide line pair	55.00	
	Strip of 4	125.00	
	Guide line strip of 4		*500.00*

Perforations Type II

Used experimentally: Chicago, 1909; Detroit, 1911. Perforation holes are 1.95mm in diameter, spacing between perforation holes is 1.15mm, length of seven perforation holes is 20.6mm.

On Issue of 1906-08

No.	Item	Unused	Used
* 320	2c **carmine,** unused pair	1,200.	
* 320b	2c **scarlet,** unused pair	1,300.	
	Guide line pair	1,650.	

On Issue of 1908-09

No.	Item	Unused	Used
343	1c **green**		
	Unused pair, 2mm spacing	80.00	16.50
	Guide line pair	165.00	
	Strip of 4	200.00	
	Unused pair, 3mm spacing	80.00	
344	2c **carmine**		
	Unused pair, 2mm spacing	95.00	16.50
	On cover		*5,750.*
	Guide line pair	190.00	
	Strip of 4	250.00	
	Unused pair, 3mm spacing	95.00	
* 345	3c **deep violet**		
	Unused pair, 2mm spacing	500.00	*75.00*
	Pasteup pair	525.00	
	Strip of 4	1,050.	
* 346	4c **org brown**		
	Unused pair, 2mm spacing	525.00	
	Unused pair, 3mm spacing	550.00	
	Strip of 4, 2mm and 3mm spacings	*1,750.*	
* 347	5c **blue,** unused pair, 2mm spacing	*1,500.*	

On Lincoln Issue of 1909

No.	Item	Unused	Used
* 368	2c **carmine**		
	Unused pair, 2mm spacing	1,200.	
	Unused pair, 3mm spacing	1,000.	

On Alaska-Yukon Issue of 1909

No.	Item	Unused	Used
* 371	2c **carmine,** unused pair	1,000.	

On Hudson-Fulton Issue of 1909

No.	Item	Unused	Used
* 373	2c **carmine**		
	Unused pair	1,000.	
	Guide line pair	1,250.	
	Pasteup pair	1,150.	
	Strip of 4	*2,250.*	

On Issue of 1910

No.	Item	Unused	Used
383	1c **green**		
	Unused pair, 2mm spacing	190.00	32.50
	Guide line pair	390.00	
	Pasteup pair	375.00	
	Unused pair, 3mm spacing	190.00	
	Strip of 4	500.00	
384	2c **carmine**		
	Unused pair, 2mm spacing	200.00	*65.00*
	On cover		*5,000.*
	Unused pair, 3mm spacing	190.00	

Perforations Type III

Used experimentally in Detroit in 1910. Perforation holes are 1.5mm in diameter, spacing between holes is 1.5mm.

On Issue of 1906-08

No.	Item	Unused	Used
* 320	2c **carmine,** unused pair	1,250.	
* 320b	2c **scarlet,** unused pair	1,250.	

On Issue of 1908-09

No.	Item	Unused	Used
343	1c **green**		
	Unused pair	220.00	
	Guide line pair	700.00	
	Strip of 4	450.00	
	Unused pair, 3mm spacing	220.00	
344	2c **carmine**		
	Unused pair	250.00	
	Guide line pair	575.00	
	Strip of 4	500.00	
	Unused pair, 3mm spacing	275.00	
	Pasteup pair	*525.00*	
	Pasteup strip of 4	*1,250.*	
* 345	3c **deep violet**		
	Unused pair	650.00	
	Guide line pair	1,000.	
	Pasteup pair	1,500.	
* 346	4c **org brown**		
	Unused pair	900.00	
	Pasteup pair	1,000.	
	Unused pair, 3mm spacing	850.00	
* 347	5c **blue,** unused pair	*1,300.*	
	Pasteup pair	*1,450.*	

On Lincoln Issue of 1909

No.	Item	Unused	Used
* 368	2c **carmine**		
	Unused pair, 2mm spacing	450.00	*110.00*
	Unused pair, 3mm spacing	400.00	
	Pasteup pair	800.00	

On Alaska-Yukon Issue of 1909

No.	Item	Unused	Used
* 371	2c **carmine,** unused pair	1,000.	

On Hudson-Fulton Issue of 1909

No.	Item	Unused	Used
* 373	2c **carmine**		
	Unused pair	875.00	
	Guide line pair	*2,000.*	
	Pasteup pair	1,300.	

Perforations Type IV

Used in St. Louis branch office.

Left Column = Unused Pair
Right Column = Used Single

On Issue of 1906-08

No.	Item	Unused	Used
* 320	2c **carmine,** unused pair	525.00	*85.00*
	Guide line pair	875.00	
	Pasteup pair	750.00	
* 320b	2c **scarlet,** unused pair	375.00	*70.00*
	Guide line pair	1,050.	

On Issue of 1908-09

No.	Item	Unused	Used
343	1c **green**		
	Unused pair, 2mm spacing	75.00	10.00
	Guide line pair	145.00	
	Pasteup pair	140.00	
	Pasteup strip of 4	325.00	
	Strip of 4, 2mm and 3mm spacings	200.00	
	Unused pair, 3mm spacing	65.00	
344	2c **carmine**		
	Unused pair, 2mm spacing	80.00	10.00
	On cover		—
	Guide line pair	140.00	
	Pasteup pair	130.00	
	Guide line strip of 4	350.00	
	Pasteup strip of 4	300.00	
	Strip of 4, 2mm and 3mm spacings	200.00	
	Block of 4	*450.00*	
	Unused pair, 3mm spacing	70.00	
345	3c **deep violet**		
	Unused pair, 2mm spacing	175.00	
	Guide line pair	325.00	
	Pasteup pair	300.00	
	Strip of 4		*100.00*
	Guide line strip of 4	850.00	
	Center line block of 4	*1,500.*	
346	4c **org brown**		
	Unused pair, 2mm spacing	300.00	
	Guide line pair	850.00	
	Unused pair, 3mm spacing	275.00	
347	5c **blue**		
	Unused pair, 2mm spacing	400.00	*60.00*
	Guide line pair	900.00	
	Strip of 4	850.00	
	Block of 4	*850.00*	
	P# block of 6, Impt.	*1,500.*	

On Lincoln Issue of 1909

No.	Item	Unused	Used
* 368	2c **carmine**		
	Unused pair, 2mm spacing	120.00	30.00
	Guide line pair	230.00	
	Pasteup pair	210.00	
	Strip of 4	300.00	
	Pasteup strip of 4	500.00	
	Unused pair, 3mm spacing	120.00	
	Block of 4	*1,250.*	

On Alaska-Yukon Issue of 1909

No.	Item	Unused	Used
* 371	2c **carmine**		
	Unused pair	500.00	
	Guide line pair	1,000.	
	Pasteup pair	1,000.	
	Block of 4	—	
	Center line block of 4	*1,600.*	

On Hudson-Fulton Issue of 1909

No.	Item	Unused	Used
* 373	2c **carmine**		
	Unused pair	500.00	
	On cover		—
	Guide line pair	950.00	
	Margin block of 4, arrow	*900.00*	
	P# block of 6, Impt.	*2,500.*	

On Issue of 1910

No.	Item	Unused	Used
383	1c **green**		
	Unused pair, 2mm spacing	16.50	2.50
	On cover		*250.00*
	Guide line pair	26.00	
	Pasteup pair	25.00	
	Strip of 4	100.00	*350.00*
	Guide line strip of 4	325.00	
	Pasteup strip of 4	250.00	
	Block of 4		*650.00*
	Margin block of 4, arrow, T or B	*500.00*	*1,500.*
	Unused pair, 3mm spacing	11.50	
	P# block of 6, Impt. and star	2,750.	
	Strip of 4		*100.00*
	Margin block of 4, arrow, L or R	*500.00*	

The recorded No. 383 3mm used strip of 4 is precanceled 2 lines and has some perforations omitted.

No.	Item	Unused	Used
384	2c **carmine**		
	Unused pair, 2mm spacing	29.00	1.40
	On cover		*100.00*
	Guide line pair	47.50	
	Guide line strip of 4	500.00	
	Strip of 4, 2mm and 3mm spacings	150.00	
	Unused pair, 3mm spacing	27.50	
	Strip of 4	125.00	
	Pasteup pair	45.00	
	Pasteup strip of 4	475.00	
	Block of 4	*300.00*	*200.00*
	P# block of 6, Impt. and star	*1,200.*	

On Issue of 1912

No.	Item	Unused	Used
408	1c **green**		
	Unused pair	8.25	1.40
	On cover		100.00
	Guide line pair	12.50	
	Pasteup pair	11.00	
	Strip of 4	40.00	
	Guide line strip of 4	200.00	
	Pasteup strip of 4	150.00	
	Block of 4	*250.00*	
	P# block of 6, Impt. and A	*950.00*	
409	2c **carmine**		
	Unused pair	9.25	.80
	On cover		40.00
	Guide line pair	16.50	
	Pasteup pair	15.50	
	Strip of 4	40.00	

	Guide line strip of 4	200.00	
	Pasteup strip of 4	150.00	
	Margin block of 4, arrow	250.00	

On Issue of 1916-17

481	1c **green**		650.00
	Precanceled (St. Louis), 2 types		850.00
482	2c **carmine**		
	Unused pair	140.00	75.00
	On cover		500.00
	Guide line pair	250.00	
	Pasteup pair	290.00	
	Strip of 4	325.00	
	Guide line strip of 4	650.00	
	Pasteup strip of 4	550.00	
	Block of 4	300.00	
483	3c **violet,** type I		
	Unused pair	190.00	225.00
	On cover		575.00
	Guide line pair	400.00	
	Pasteup pair	300.00	
	Pasteup strip of 4	800.00	

Perforations Type V

Perforation holes are 1.8 mm in diameter, spacing between perforation holes is 1.35mm, length of seven perforation holes is 20.7mm.

1911

On Issue of 1910

383	1c **green**		
	Single on cover		—
	Unused pair	100.00	
	Guide line pair	300.00	
	Strip of 4	600.00	
	Guide line strip of 4	1,000.	
384	2c **carmine**		1,500.
	Single on cover		3,000.
	Unused pair	—	
	Strip of 4	—	
	With perforated control mark, single		—

THE SCHERMACK COMPANY

Detroit, Mich.

These perforations were developed by the Schermack Mailing Machine Co. before it became the Mailometer Co. The Type III perforation was used in the company's affixing machines from 1908 through 1927 or 1928.

Perforations Type I. Eight Holes

Perforated in sheets, then cut into strips and coiled.

Left Column = Unused Pair
Right Column = Used Single

On Issue of 1906-08

314	1c **blue green**		
	Eight holes, unused pair	175.00	110.00
	Guide line pair	350.00	
	Strip of 4	500.00	
	Guide line strip of 4	750.00	
	Block of 4	800.00	
	Center line block of 4	1,500.	
	* Seven holes, unused pair	1,550.	
	Pasteup pair	2,600.	
	* Six holes, unused pair	1,050.	
	Guide line pair	3,250.	
320	2c **carmine**		
	Eight holes, unused pair	150.00	60.00
	On cover		4,500.
	Guide line pair	375.00	
	Pasteup pair	350.00	
	Strip of 4	400.00	
	Guide line strip of 4	750.00	
	Pasteup strip of 4	600.00	
	Block of 4	500.00	200.00
	Center line block of 4	1,500.	
	P# block of 6, Impt.	2,500.	
	Seven holes, unused pair	1,400.	325.00
	On cover		10,500.
	Guide line pair	2,500.	
	Pasteup pair	2,000.	
	Strip of 4	3,750.	
	Pasteup strip of 4, left pasteup stamp the 7-holes variety	5,750.	
	* Six holes, unused pair	1,250.	
	Guide line pair	2,600.	
* 320b	2c **scarlet**		
	* Six holes, guide line pair	2,250.	
* 320A	2c **lake**		
	* Eight holes, unused pair	400.00	120.00
	Strip of 4	900.00	
	P# block of 6, Impt.	2,750.	
	Block of 4	1,500.	
	* Seven holes, unused pair	1,000.	
	Guide line pair	2,600.	
	* Six holes, unused pair	2,250.	
	Guide line pair	3,750.	
* 315	5c **blue**		
	* Eight holes, unused pair	—	

On Issue of 1908-09

* 343	1c **green**		
	Unused pair, 2mm spacing	300.00	85.00
	Guide line pair	550.00	
	Guide line strip of 4	875.00	
	Unused pair, 3mm spacing	1,150.	
* 344	2c **carmine**		
	Unused pair, 2mm spacing	1,650.	1,900.
	Guide line pair	3,500.	1,900.
	Unused pair, 3mm spacing	—	
* 345	3c **deep violet**		
	Unused pair, 2mm spacing	2,500.	
	Guide line pair	3,000.	
* 346	4c **org brown**		
	Unused pair, 2mm spacing	825.00	
	Guide line pair	1,550.	
	Unused pair, 3mm spacing	—	
* 347	5c **blue**		
	Unused pair, 2mm spacing	825.00	
	Guide line pair	1,550.	

On Lincoln Issue of 1909

* 368	2c **carmine**		
	* Eight holes, unused pair, 2mm spacing	230.00	85.00
	Guide line pair	425.00	
	Strip of 4	600.00	
	Guide line strip of 4	1,000.	
	* Eight holes, unused pair, 3mm spacing	260.00	125.00
	Block of 4	1,000.	
	P# block of 6, Impt. and star	2,250.	
	* Seven holes, unused pair, 2mm spacing	1,350.	
	Guide line pair	2,750.	
	* Seven holes, unused pair, 3mm spacing	1,650.	
	* Six holes, unused pair, 2mm spacing	1,150.	
	Guide line pair	3,250.	
	* Six holes, unused pair, 3mm spacing	—	
	Guide line pair	1,750.	
	P# block of 6, Impt. and star	4,250.	

Perforations Type II

Cut into strips and joined before being perforated.

Left Column = Unused Pair
Right Column = Used Single

On Issue of 1906-08

314	1c **blue green**		
	* Unused pair	350.00	85.00
	On cover		2,250.
	Guide line pair	575.00	
	Strip of 4	700.00	
	Guide line strip of 4	1,400.	
320	2c **carmine**		
	* Unused pair	175.00	60.00
	Guide line pair	400.00	
	Guide line strip of 4	950.00	
*320A	2c **lake**		
	* Unused pair	300.00	110.00
	Guide line pair	725.00	
	Strip of 4	700.00	
*315	5c **blue**		
	* Unused pair	11,500.	4,000.
	Guide line pair	18,500.	

On Issue of 1908-09

* 343	1c **green**		
	Unused pair, 2mm spacing	1,600.	
	Guide line pair	2,500.	
	Unused pair, 3mm spacing	1,700.	
* 344	2c **carmine**		
	Unused pair, 2mm spacing	1,900.	
	Guide line pair	2,750.	
	Unused pair, 3mm spacing	2,500.	
* 345	3c **deep violet**		
	Unused pair, 2mm spacing	1,250.	
	Guide line pair	2,250.	
* 346	4c **org brown**		
	Unused pair, 2mm spacing	2,500.	
	Guide line pair	3,500.	
	Unused pair, 3mm spacing	—	
* 347	5c **blue**		
	Unused pair, 2mm spacing	1,750.	
	Guide line pair	3,000.	

On Lincoln Issue of 1909

* 368	2c **carmine**		
	Unused pair, 2mm spacing	175.00	70.00
	On cover		2,000.
	Guide line pair	400.00	
	Strip of 4	450.00	
	Guide line strip of 4	1,000.	
	Unused pair, 3mm spacing	155.00	

On Issue of 1910

* 383	1c **green**		
	Guide line or pasteup pair, 2mm spacing	250.00	
	Unused pair, 3mm spacing	250.00	
* 384	2c **carmine**		
	Unused pair, 2mm spacing	—	
	Unused pair, 3mm spacing	—	

The existence of genuine examples of Nos. 383-384 has been questioned.

Perforations Type III

Left Column = Unused Pair
Right Column = Used Single

On Issue of 1906-08

314	1c **blue green**		
	* Unused pair	12.50	2.50
	On cover		140.00
	Guide line pair	27.50	
	Pasteup pair	22.50	
	Strip of 4	50.00	100.00
	Guide line strip of 4	100.00	
	Pasteup strip of 4	75.00	
	With both type I (eight holes) and Type III perfs		—
	Block of 4	2,000.	
	With perforated control mark, on postcard		100.00
320	2c **carmine,** Type I		
	* Unused pair	19.00	6.00
	On cover		85.00
	Guide line pair	35.00	
	Pasteup pair	32.50	
	Strip of 4	50.00	100.00
	Guide line strip of 4	150.00	
	Pasteup strip of 4	75.00	
	Block of 4	950.00	
	With both type I (eight holes) and Type III perfs		—
* 320b	2c **scarlet,** Type I		
	* Unused pair	27.50	6.00
	On cover		—
	Guide line pair	47.50	
	Strip of 4	75.00	
	Guide line strip of 4	175.00	
320c	2c **carmine rose,** Type I, unused pair, 2mm spacing	65.00	
* 320A	2c **lake,** Type II		
	* Unused pair	27.50	3.00
	On cover		65.00
	Guide line pair	52.50	500.00
	Pasteup pair	47.50	
	Strip of 4	75.00	125.00
	Guide line strip of 4	175.00	
	Pasteup strip of 4	100.00	
	With perforated control mark, single		3,000.
	With both type I (eight holes) and Type III perfs		—
	Block of 4	350.00	
320Ad	2c **carmine,** Type II, single	135.00	—
	On cover		2,000.
	Pair	290.00	
	Guide line pair	500.00	6,000.
	Strip of 4	750.00	
	Guide line strip of 4	3,000.	
	Pasteup strip of 4	1,750.	
314A	4c **brown,** single	85,000.	45,000.
	On cover		140,000.
	Pair	200,000.	—
	Strip of 3		230,000.
	Guide line pair	250,000.	
315	5c **blue**		
	* Unused pair	7,000.	
	Strip of 4	17,000.	
	Block of 4	15,000.	

On Issue of 1908-09

343	1c **green**		
	Unused pair, 2mm spacing	6.25	1.40
	On cover		30.00
	Guide line pair	11.50	
	Pasteup pair	10.00	
	Strip of 4	25.00	
	Guide line strip of 4	50.00	
	Pasteup strip of 4	40.00	
	Block of 4	300.00	
	Unused pair, 3mm spacing	7.50	
	With perforated control mark, single		45.00
	Same, on cover		500.00

No.	Description	Unused	Used
344	2c **carmine**		
	Unused pair, 2mm spacing	6.50	1.40
	On cover		22.50
	Guide line pair	11.50	
	Pasteup pair	10.00	
	Strip of 4	25.00	
	Guide line strip of 4	50.00	
	Pasteup strip of 4	40.00	
	Block of 4		*50.00*
	Unused pair, 3mm spacing	7.50	
	With perforated control mark, single		45.00
	Same, on cover		*500.00*
	Block of 4	*300.00*	

Earliest documented use: Feb. 4, 1909.

No.	Description	Unused	Used
345	3c **deep violet**		
	Unused pair, 2mm spacing	27.50	14.00
	On cover		—
	Guide line pair	57.50	
	Pasteup pair	52.50	
	Strip of 4	75.00	
	Block of 4	200.00	
	Pasteup strip of 4	175.00	
	Margin block of 4, arrow	*300.00*	
	P# block of 6, Impt.	*4,250.*	
	Unused pair, 3mm spacing	*175.00*	
	With perforated control mark, single		*1,500.*
	Same, on cover		*8,000.*
346	4c **org brown**		
	Unused pair, 2mm spacing	40.00	19.00
	On cover		*2,500.*
	Guide line pair	62.50	
	Strip of 4	100.00	
	Guide line strip of 4	200.00	
	Margin block of 4, arrow	*400.00*	
	P# block of 6, Impt.	*2,750.*	
	Unused pair, 3mm spacing	25.00	
	With perforated control mark, single		*1,650.*
	Same, on cover		*10,000.*
347	5c **blue**		
	Unused pair, 2mm spacing	62.50	19.00
	On cover		*2,750.*
	Guide line pair	115.00	
	Strip of 4	200.00	
	Guide line strip of 4	400.00	
	Margin block of 4, arrow	*500.00*	
	P# block of 6, Impt.	*4,250.*	

On Lincoln Issue of 1909

No.	Description	Unused	Used
368	2c **carmine**		
	Unused pair, 2mm spacing	75.00	14.00
	On cover		*210.00*
	Guide line pair	150.00	*250.00*
	Pasteup pair	135.00	
	Guide line strip of 4	350.00	
	Pasteup strip of 4	300.00	
	Block of 4	200.00	
	Strip of 4, 2mm and 3mm spacings	225.00	*100.00*
	Unused pair, 3mm spacing	57.50	
	Block of 4	*300.00*	
	P# block of 6, Impt. and star	*1,250.*	

On Alaska-Yukon Issue of 1909

No.	Description	Unused	Used
* 371	2c **carmine**		
	Unused pair	100.00	
	On cover		*2,500.*
	Guide line pair	190.00	
	Pasteup pair	175.00	
	Strip of 4	225.00	
	Guide line strip of 4	475.00	
	Pasteup strip of 4	450.00	

On Hudson-Fulton Issue of 1909

No.	Description	Unused	Used
* 373	2c **carmine**		
	Unused pair	130.00	
	Guide line pair	230.00	
	Pasteup pair	210.00	
	Strip of 4	350.00	

On Issue of 1910

No.	Description	Unused	Used
383	1c **green**		
	Unused pair, 2mm spacing	5.25	1.40
	On cover		25.00
	Guide line pair	10.00	
	Pasteup pair	9.00	
	Guide line strip of 4	65.00	
	Pasteup strip of 4	60.00	
	Unused pair, 3mm spacing	3.75	
	With perforated control mark, single		*45.00*
	Same, on cover		*450.00*
	Strip of 4	25.00	

Earliest documented use: Feb. 8, 1911.

No.	Description	Unused	Used
384	2c **carmine**		
	Unused pair, 2mm spacing	11.50	1.40
	On cover		25.00
	Guide line pair	19.00	
	Strip of 4	30.00	
	Guide line strip of 4	75.00	
	Unused pair, 3mm spacing	9.00	
	With perforated control mark, single		*45.00*
	Same, on cover		*450.00*
	Strip of 4		*50.00*
	Block of 4	*300.00*	

On Issue of 1912

No.	Description	Unused	Used
408	1c **green**		
	Unused pair	2.60	.70
	On cover		25.00
	Guide line pair	5.25	
	Pasteup pair	5.00	
	Strip of 4	30.00	
	Guide line strip of 4	75.00	
	Pasteup strip of 4	60.00	*100.00*
	Block of 4	*150.00*	
	With perforated control mark, single		*52.50*
	Same, on cover		*380.00*
409	2c **carmine**		
	Unused pair	2.60	.55
	On cover		25.00
	Guide line pair	5.25	
	Pasteup pair	5.00	
	Strip of 4	25.00	*200.00*
	Guide line strip of 4	75.00	
	Pasteup strip of 4	60.00	
	Block of 4	*150.00*	
	Aniline ink ("pink back")	—	
	With perforated control mark, single		*52.50*
	Same, on cover		*380.00*
	Single stamp in pasteup with strip of three No. TD14a test stamps	*6,000.*	
	Guide line pair with both Schermack type III and 11.25-gauge perforations	**Guide line pair with both Schermack type III and 11.25-gauge perforations*	—*1,200.*

Earliest documented use: Mar. 13, 1912.

On Issue of 1916-17

No.	Description	Unused	Used
481	1c **green**		
	Unused pair	3.75	.45
	On cover		25.00
	Guide line pair	7.50	
	Pasteup pair	7.00	
	Strip of 4	30.00	
	Guide line strip of 4	75.00	
	Pasteup strip of 4	60.00	
	Margin block of 4, arrow		*50.00*
	Center line block of 4	*100.00*	
482	2c **carmine,** Type I		
	Unused pair	4.75	.65
	On cover		22.50
	Guide line pair	10.00	
	Pasteup pair	9.00	
	Strip of 4	25.00	*90.00*
	Guide line strip of 4	75.00	*50.00*
	Pasteup strip of 4	60.00	
	Aniline ink ("pink back")	—	
	Single stamp in pasteup with strip of 4 No. TD14a test stamps	*1,500.*	

Earliest documented use: Dec. 16, 1916.

No.	Description	Unused	Used
482A	2c **deep rose,** Type Ia, single	—	*55,000.*
	On cover		*70,000.*
	Pair		*147,500.*
483	3c **violet,** type I		
	Unused pair	12.50	3.00
	On cover		110.00
	Guide line pair	22.50	
	Pasteup pair	20.00	
	Strip of 4	40.00	
	Guide line strip of 4	100.00	
	Pasteup strip of 4	75.00	
	Block of 4	*290.00*	
	With perforated control mark, single		500.00
	On cover		*3,000.*

Earliest documented use: Nov. 2, 1917.

No.	Description	Unused	Used
484	3c **violet,** type II		
	Unused pair	19.00	5.00
	On cover		110.00
	Guide line pair	35.00	
	Pasteup pair	30.00	
	Strip of 4	40.00	
	Guide line strip of 4	100.00	
	Pasteup strip of 4	75.00	
	With perforated control mark, single		500.00
	On cover		*4,000.*

Earliest documented use: Apr. 5, 1918.

On Issue of 1918-20

No.	Description	Unused	Used
531	1c **green**		
	Unused pair	17.50	5.00
	On cover		120.00
	Guide line pair	35.00	
	Pasteup pair	30.00	
	Strip of 4	40.00	*50.00*
	Guide line strip of 4	100.00	
	Pasteup strip of 4	75.00	
532	2c **carmine,** Type IV		
	Unused pair	47.50	3.75
	On cover		85.00
	Guide line pair	90.00	
	Pasteup pair	85.00	
	Strip of 4	75.00	*100.00*
	Guide line strip of 4	250.00	
	Pasteup strip of 4	200.00	
	Pasteup strip of 4, left pair No. 532, right pair No. 482	*2,600.*	

Earliest documented use: Apr. 28, 1920.

No.	Description	Unused	Used
533	2c **carmine,** Type V		
	Unused pair	*425.00*	*50.00*
	On cover		*300.00*
	Guide line pair	*1,000.*	
	Pasteup pair	950.00	
	Guide line strip of 4	*2,500.*	
	Pasteup strip of 4	*2,000.*	
534	2c **carmine,** Type Va		
	Unused pair	30.00	2.50
	On cover		110.00
	Guide line pair	62.50	
	Pasteup pair	57.50	
	Strip of 4	100.00	*100.00*
	Guide line strip of 4	200.00	
	Pasteup strip of 4	150.00	
534A	2c **carmine,** Type VI		
	Unused pair	52.50	5.00
	On cover		85.00
	Guide line pair	105.00	
	Pasteup pair	95.00	
	Strip of 4	150.00	*80.00*
	Guide line strip of 4	350.00	
	Pasteup strip of 4	250.00	
	Pasteup strip of 6, left strip of 3 No. 482, right strip of 3 No. 534A	*2,750.*	

Earliest documented use: Aug. 31, 1920.

No.	Description	Unused	Used
534B	2c **carmine,** Type VII		
	Unused pair	*1,400.*	200.00
	On cover		*450.00*
	Guide line pair	*3,500.*	
	Pasteup pair	*2,750.*	
	Strip of 4	*3,250.*	
535	3c **violet,** Type IV		
	Unused pair	22.50	4.00
	On cover		85.00
	Guide line pair	47.50	
	Pasteup pair	42.50	
	Strip of 4	60.00	*100.00*
	Guide line strip of 4	200.00	275.00
	Pasteup strip of 4	150.00	
	Block of 4	*150.00*	

On Issue of 1923-26

No.	Description	Unused	Used
575	1c **green,** unused single	27.50	
	Unused pair	*230.00*	7.50
	On cover		*450.00*
	Guide line pair	*450.00*	
	Pasteup pair	425.00	
	Guide line strip of 4	1,750.	
	Pasteup strip of 4	1,250.	
	Margin block of 4, arrow	*300.00*	
	P# block of 6	*3,000.*	
	Precanceled	5.25	1.40
	On cover, precanceled		*130.00*
	Strip of 4		*50.00*

The reccorded No. 575 used strip of 4 is precanceled.

No.	Description	Unused	Used
576	1½c **yellow brown**		
	Unused pair	27.50	5.00
	On cover		*250.00*
	Guide line pair	47.50	
	Pasteup pair	42.50	
	Strip of 4	75.00	
	Guide line strip of 4	125.00	
	Pasteup strip of 4	90.00	
	Block of 4	*300.00*	
	Margin block of 4, arrow	400.00	
	Precanceled	5.25	1.10
	On cover, precanceled		*90.00*
577	2c **carmine**		
	Unused pair	32.50	1.40
	On cover		25.00
	Guide line pair	47.50	
	Pasteup pair	42.50	
	Strip of 4	65.00	*100.00*
	Guide line strip of 4	175.00	
	Pasteup strip of 4	150.00	
	Block of 4	*300.00*	
	P# block of 6	*4,500.*	

On Harding Issue of 1923

No.	Description	Unused	Used
611	2c **black**		
	Unused pair	110.00	19.00
	On cover		*6,000.*
	Guide line pair	190.00	
	Pasteup pair	175.00	
	Strip of 4	225.00	
	Guide line strip of 4	450.00	
	Pasteup strip of 4	400.00	
	Block of 4	250.00	150.00
	Margin block of 4, arrow	*350.00*	
	Center line block of 4	*1,750.*	
	P# block of 6	*3,000.*	

U.S. AUTOMATIC VENDING COMPANY

New York, N.Y.

Separations Type I

Cut into strips and joined before being perforated.
Two varieties exist: 15½ and 16mm between notches of the perforations.

Left Column = Unused Pair
Right Column = Used Single

On Issue of 1906-08
Coiled Endwise

No.	Description	Unused	Used
314	1c **blue green**	57.50	14.00
	On cover		*3,000.*
	Guide line pair	250.00	
	Pasteup pair	200.00	
	Strip of 4	150.00	
	Guide line strip of 4	450.00	
320	2c **carmine**	52.50	10.00
	On cover		*3,000.*
	Guide line pair	125.00	
	Pasteup pair	110.00	
	Strip of 4	150.00	
	Block of 4	500.00	
320b	2c **scarlet**	62.50	8.75
	On cover		*4,250.*
	Guide line pair	150.00	
* 320A	2c **lake**	105.00	10.00
	Guide line pair	230.00	
	Pasteup pair	210.00	
	Strip of 4	425.00	
	Guide line strip of 4	650.00	
	Pasteup strip of 4	550.00	
315	5c **blue**	1,100.	*2,250.*
	On cover		*12,500.*
	Guide line pair	*2,250.*	
	Pasteup pair	*1,900.*	
	Strip of 4	*2,500.*	
	Guide line strip of 4	*5,500.*	

On Issue of 1906-08
Coiled Endwise

No.	Description	Unused	Used
343	1c **green**	14.00	2.00
	On cover		130.00
	On postcard		60.00
	Guide line pair	27.50	
	Pasteup pair	25.00	
	Strip of 4	100.00	*100.00*
	Guide line strip of 4	125.00	

Earliest documented use: Jan. 4, 1909.

No.	Description	Unused	Used
344	2c **carmine**	11.50	2.00
	On cover		130.00
	Guide line pair	22.50	
	Pasteup pair	20.00	
	Strip of 4	50.00	*50.00*
	Guide line strip of 4	125.00	
	Pasteup strip of 4	100.00	
* 345	3c **deep violet**	40.00	11.00
	On cover		*675.00*
	Guide line pair	80.00	
	Pasteup pair	75.00	
	Strip of 4	100.00	
	Guide line strip of 4	*500.00*	
	Block of 4	*500.00*	
* 346	4c **orange brown**	62.50	12.00
	Guide line pair	135.00	
	Pasteup pair	120.00	
	Strip of 4	150.00	
	Guide line strip of 4	300.00	
	Block of 4	900.00	
347	5c **blue**	115.00	55.00
	On cover		*2,250.*
	On cover (pair) with No. 373 USAV Type II pair		*7,500.*
	Guide line pair	220.00	
	Pasteup pair	200.00	
	Strip of 4	250.00	
	Guide line strip of 4	500.00	
	Pasteup strip of 4	400.00	

On Lincoln Issue of 1909

No.	Description	Unused	Used
368	2c **carmine,** coiled endwise	47.50	8.75
	On cover		*2,250.*
	First day cover, *Feb. 12, 1909*		*7,500.*
	Guide line pair	90.00	325.00
	Pasteup pair	85.00	
	Strip of 4	150.00	
	Guide line strip of 4	300.00	
	Pasteup strip of 4	250.00	
	Block of 4	500.00	

On Alaska-Yukon Issue of 1909

No.	Description	Unused	Used
* 371	2c **carmine,** coiled sideways	100.00	16.00
	On cover		*625.00*
	Guide line pair	190.00	
	Strip of 4	225.00	
	Guide line strip of 4	500.00	
	Pasteup strip of 4	400.00	
	Type 1a, No T. and B. margins	175.00	21.00
	Type 1a, Guide line pair	290.00	
	Type 1a, Pasteup pair	275.00	

Type Ia stamps are a deep shade and have a misplaced position dot in the "S" of "Postage." Beware of trimmed copies of No. 371 type I.

On Issue of 1910

No.	Description	Unused	Used
383	1c **green**	7.50	3.00
	On cover		120.00
	On postcard		45.00
	Guide line pair	12.50	
	Pasteup pair	11.00	
	Strip of 4	50.00	
	Guide line strip of 4	125.00	
* 384	2c **carmine**	27.50	5.50
	Guide line pair	47.50	
	Pasteup pair	42.50	
	Guide line strip of 4	250.00	

No.	Description	Unused	Used
	On cover		—

On Issue of 1912

No.	Description	Unused	Used
* 408	1c **green**	12.50	2.50
	Guide line pair	22.50	
	Guide line strip of 4	100.00	
	Pasteup strip of 4	200.00	
* 409	2c **carmine**	16.50	5.00
	Guide line pair	27.50	
	Pasteup pair	25.00	
	Guide line strip of 4	200.00	
	Pasteup strip of 4	150.00	

Separations Type II

Similar to Type I but with notches farther apart and a longer slit. Cut into strips and joined before being perforated.

Left Column = Unused Pair
Right Column = Used Single

On Issue of 1906-08
Coiled Sideways

No.	Description	Unused	Used
* 314	1c **blue green**		
	* Unused pair	57.50	10.00
	On cover		—
	Guide line pair	95.00	
	Pasteup pair	90.00	
	Strip of 4	325.00	
	Guide line strip of 4	800.00	
* 320	2c **carmine**		
	* Unused pair	100.00	
	Guide line pair	145.00	
	Strip of 4	300.00	
* 320b	2c **scarlet**		
	* Unused pair	70.00	6.00
	Guide line pair	115.00	
	Strip of 4	350.00	
	Guide line strip of 4	750.00	
* 315	5c **blue**		
	* Unused pair	1,100.	
	Guide line pair	*2,500.*	

On Issue of 1908-09

No.	Description	Unused	Used
343	1c **green**		
	Unused pair, 2mm spacing	16.50	4.00
	On cover		*1,250.*
	Guide line pair	26.00	
	Pasteup pair	24.00	
344	2c **carmine**		
	Unused pair, 2mm spacing	19.00	
	On cover		*3,000.*
	Guide line pair	30.00	
	Strip of 4	100.00	
* 345	3c **deep violet**		
	Unused pair, 2mm spacing	72.50	
	Guide line pair	125.00	
	Unused pair, 3mm spacing	—	
* 346	4c **org brown**		
	Unused pair, 2mm spacing	110.00	
	Guide line pair	190.00	
	Unused pair, 3mm spacing	95.00	
* 347	5c **blue**		
	Unused pair, 2mm spacing	220.00	
	Guide line pair	350.00	

On Lincoln Issue of 1909

No.	Description	Unused	Used
368	2c **carmine**		
	Unused pair, 2mm spacing	120.00	27.50
	Guide line pair	220.00	
	Guide line strip of 4	600.00	
	Strip of 4, 2mm and 3mm spacings	250.00	
	Unused pair, 3mm spacing	110.00	

On Alaska-Yukon Issue of 1909

No.	Description	Unused	Used
* 371	2c **carmine**		
	Unused pair	95.00	50.00
	On cover		*650.00*
	Guide line pair	200.00	
	Pasteup pair	175.00	
	Guide line strip of 4	350.00	
	Pasteup strip of 4	300.00	

On Hudson-Fulton Issue of 1909

No.	Description	Unused	Used
* 373	2c **carmine**		
	Unused pair	100.00	*22.50*
	On cover		*2,750.*
	Guide line pair	190.00	*375.00*
	Pasteup pair	175.00	
	Strip of 4	400.00	
	Guide line strip of 4	500.00	
	Pasteup strip of 4	450.00	

See No. 347 USAV type I for combination cover.

On Issue of 1910

No.	Description	Unused	Used
383	1c **green**		
	Unused pair, 2mm spacing	19.00	
	On cover		*1,100.*
	Guide line pair	32.50	
	Unused pair, 3mm spacing	14.50	
384	2c **carmine**		
	Unused pair, 2mm spacing	27.50	
	On cover		*3,000.*
	Guide line pair	47.50	
	Guide line strip of 4	175.00	

No.	Description	Unused	Used
	Unused pair, 3mm spacing	19.00	

On Issue of 1912

No.	Description	Unused	Used
408	1c **green**		
	Unused pair	12.50	2.50
	On cover		*1,650.*
	Guide line pair	22.00	
	Strip of 4	50.00	
409	2c **carmine**		
	Unused pair	19.00	5.00
	Guide line pair	30.00	

Perforations Type III

Cut into strips and joined before being perforated.

Left Column = Unused Pair
Right Column = Used Single

On Issue of 1906-08

No.	Description	Unused	Used
* 314	1c **blue green**		
	* Unused pair	62.50	14.00
	Guide line pair	115.00	
* 320	2c **carmine**		
	* Unused pair	115.00	
* 320b	2c **scarlet**		
	* Unused pair	75.00	14.00
	Guide line pair	150.00	
	Strip of 4	150.00	
	Guide line strip of 4	600.00	
* 315	5c **blue**		
	* Unused pair	1,250.	
	Guide line or pasteup pair	*2,750.*	

On Issue of 1908-09

No.	Description	Unused	Used
343	1c **green**		
	Unused pair, 2mm spacing	35.00	6.50
	Guide line pair	57.50	
	Pasteup pair	52.50	
	Strip of 4	150.00	
	Pasteup strip of 4	225.00	
	Unused pair, 3mm spacing	32.50	
344	2c **carmine**		
	Unused pair, 2mm spacing	35.00	6.50
	Guide line pair	57.50	
	Unused pair, 3mm spacing	47.50	
* 345	3c **deep violet**		
	Unused pair, 2mm spacing	140.00	
	Guide line pair	240.00	
* 346	4c **org brown**		
	Unused pair, 2mm spacing	140.00	17.50
	Guide line pair	240.00	
	Strip of 4	300.00	
	Unused pair, 3mm spacing	125.00	
* 347	5c **blue**		
	Unused pair, 2mm spacing	180.00	
	Guide line pair	325.00	
	Strip of 4	350.00	

On Lincoln Issue of 1909

No.	Description	Unused	Used
* 368	2c **carmine**		
	Unused pair, 2mm spacing	80.00	21.00
	Guide line pair	145.00	
	Strip of 4	225.00	
	Guide line strip of 4	325.00	
	Unused pair, 3mm spacing	62.50	
	Experimental perf. 11.75	*4,250.*	
	Guide line pair	*7,500.*	

On Alaska-Yukon Issue of 1909

No.	Description	Unused	Used
* 371	2c **carmine**		
	Unused pair	115.00	22.50
	On cover front		*1,650.*
	Guide line pair	180.00	
	Pasteup pair	165.00	
	Strip of 4	*400.00*	
	Guide line strip of 4	350.00	

On Hudson-Fulton Issue of 1909

No.	Description	Unused	Used
* 373	2c **carmine**		
	Unused pair	125.00	22.50
	On cover		—
	Guide line pair	180.00	
	Pasteup pair	165.00	
	Strip of 4	225.00	
	Guide line strip of 4	350.00	

On Issue of 1910

No.	Description	Unused	Used
383	1c **green**		
	Unused pair, 2mm spacing	17.50	3.00
	Guide line pair	29.00	
	Pasteup pair	30.00	
	Strip of 4	100.00	*50.00*
	Pasteup strip of 4	175.00	
	Unused pair, 3mm spacing	15.00	
384	2c **carmine**		
	Unused pair, 2mm spacing	21.00	3.00
	Guide line pair	32.50	
	Strip of 4	100.00	
	Unused pair, 3mm spacing	17.50	

On Issue of 1912

No.	Description	Unused	Used
408	1c **green**		
	Unused pair	11.50	
	Guide line pair	19.00	
	Pasteup pair	20.00	
	Strip of 4	100.00	

	Guide line strip of 4	150.00
	Pasteup strip of 4	125.00
409	2c **carmine**	
	Unused pair	21.00
	Guide line pair	29.00
	Pasteup pair	27.50
	Strip of 4	125.00
	Guide line strip of 4	175.00
	Pasteup strip of 4	175.00

On 1914 Rotary Press Coil

459	2c **carmine**		
	Unused pair	*22,500.*	*10,000.*

This firm also produced coil strips of manila paper, folded so as to form small "pockets", each "pocket" containing one 1c stamp and two 2c stamps, usually imperforate but occasionally with either government or U.S.A.V. private perforations. The manila "pockets" were perforated type II, coiled sideways. They fit U.S.A.V. ticket vending machines. Multiples exist.

Values are for "pockets" with known combinations of stamps, listed by basic Scott Number. Other combinations exist, but are not listed due to the fact that the stamps may have been added at a later date.

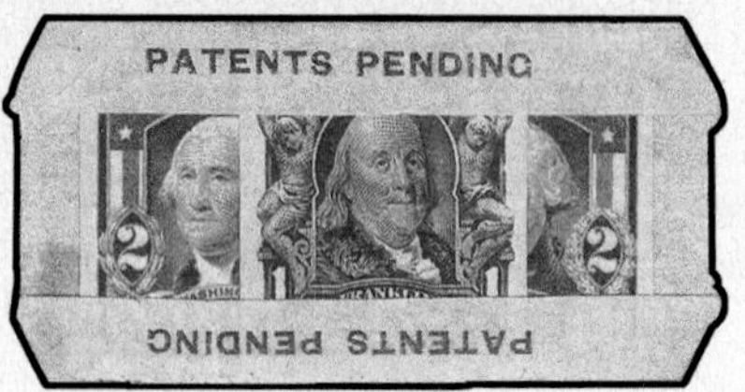

314 + 320b

Pocket Type 1 (1908)

("Patents Pending" on front in green at top and bottom, 3 serial numbers in red on reverse on the left)

Type 1-1	314 + 320	*4,250.*
Type 1-2	314 + 320b	*4,250.*

343 + 371

Pocket Type 2 (1909)

("Patent Applied For" handstamped in greenish blue at top of the pocket, 3 serial numbers in red on reverse on the left)

Type 2-1	343 + 371	1,750.
Type 2-2	343 + 372	1,000.
Type 2-3	343 (USAV type I) + 371	2,000.
Type 2-4	343 + 375	1,000.

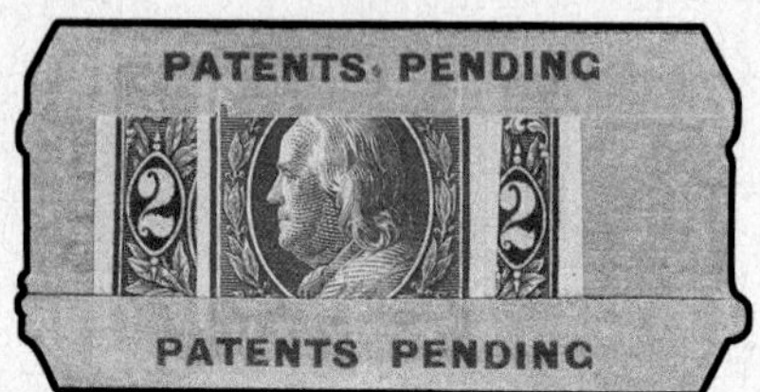

347 + 371

Pocket Type 3 (1909)

("Patents Pending" printed in red at top and bottom, 3 serial numbers printed in red on reverse on the right)

Type 3-1	343 + 371	1,000.
Type 3-1A	343 + 372	1,000.
Type 3-2	343 + 373	1,000.
Type 3-3	343 + 375	850.
Type 3-4	383 + 406	850.

343 + 344

Pocket Type 4 (1909)

(No printing on front, 3 serial numbers printed in red on reverse on the left)

Type 4-1	343 + 344	475.
Type 4-2	343 + 368	475.
Type 4-3	343 + 371	475.
Type 4-4	383 + 344	475.
Type 4-5	383 (USAV Type II) + 344	475.
Type 4-6	383 + 384	475.
Type 4-7	383 + 406	475.

THE ATTLEBORO STAMP COMPANY

Attleboro, Mass.

This Company used an affixing machine to stamp its newsletters during the summer and fall of 1909.

Nos. 343-344

No. 371

Right Column = Used Single
Left Column = Unused Pair

On Issue of 1908-09

343	1c **green**	*2,000.*	*1,000.*
	On Attleboro Philatelist wrapper		*4,000.*
	On cover		*7,500.*
	Guide line pair	*2,750.*	
	Pasteup pair	*2,500.*	
	Strip of 4	*3,750.*	
343a	1c Pair, imperf. between	*2,500.*	

No. 343a is unique.

344	2c **carmine**	*67,500.*	
	Pair, on Attleboro wrapper		*20,000.*

Both the unused and the used No. 344 pairs are unique.

On Alaska-Yukon Issue of 1909

371	2c **carmine,** coiled sidewise	*3,500.*	*1,350.*
	On wrapper or cover		*10,000.*
	Guide line pair	*7,000.*	*5,500.*
	Pasteup pair	*6,750.*	
	Strip of 4	*7,500.*	
	Pasteup strip of 4	*8,500.*	

COVEL MANUFACTURING COMPANY

Benton Harbor, Mich.

For the convenience of collectors, we list here the Covel coils that are avidly collected by specialists even though they were not dispensed by a vending or affixing machine.

From 1913 to 1920, this firm used a Rosback stroke perforator to apply gauge 11.75 perforations to imperforate coil stamps for use on company mail. The perforations resemble gauge 12 government perforations, so exact measurement (12-67 on a United States Specialist Gauge) is necessary, and expert certification is advisable (required for unused examples).

Stamps known to have Covel/Rosback perforations:
No. 314, vert. and horiz., used and on cover (unused pair value, $200; on cover value, $250); also known on cover in combination with No. 314 with Schermack Type III perfs. (value, $500).

No. 320, perf. horiz., used and on cover; perf. vert., unused (value of unused single with certification, $400).

No. 345, perf. vert., on cover (value, $1,000).

No. 408, perf. vert., unused, used, on cover (value, $300).

No. 481, on cover (value, $1,000).

No. 483, on cover (value, $500).

IMPERFORATE FLAT PLATE COIL STAMPS

The United States Post Office Department began issuing stamps finished and wound into coiled rolls in 1908, to firms that participated in a postage vending machine competition sponsored by Postmaster General George von L. Meyer. Entrants had the option of ordering the stamps coiled "sidewise" (wound horizontally) or "endwise" (wound vertically), with or without perforations, in rolls of 500 or 1,000 stamps. (Firms that preferred to manufacture their own coils by proprietary methods are listed in the Vending and Affixing Machine Perforations section of the catalogue.)

Except for being perforated or imperforate, all coil stamps manufactured by the Bureau of Engraving and Printing in 1908 and 1909 were produced by stripping printed sheets into ribbons 10- or 20-subjects long and manually pasting the strips together end to end, with a manila leader and trailer strip to form an outer wrapper and inner core for each roll. The 1908 orders were provided only to eight firms that participated in the original tests. In 1909, postmasters were authorized to accept orders for coil stamps from businesses. The forms for these special orders offered the choices of roll length, horizontal or vertical format, and perforated or imperforate. Buyers paid a premium above the face value of the stamps, 3¢ per roll of 500 and 6¢ per roll of 1,000, as a coiling fee.

By 1910, demand for coil stamps had grown to such an extent that the BEP installed a mechanized system called "Auto Wound," which pasted together sheets of stamps 10 subjects across, then slit and coiled them simultaneously. Perforated Auto-Wound coils required a coarser gauge than the 12-gauge sheet- and booklet-stamp standard, so a new gauge 8½ spacing became standard for perforated coils, while imperforate coils remained unchanged. Thus the coils listed in this section are counterparts to both versions of perforated coils, but for reasons of historical convenience, they have been numbered to match their imperforate sheet stamp counterparts, but with suffixes H or V to indicate horizontal and vertical formats, respectively.

In 1914, the BEP further streamlined coil stamp production with the web-fed Stickney rotary presses. The first rotary press stamp was an imperforate 2¢ George Washington coil stamp, Scott 459. The shift to rotary presses ended all flat-plate coil stamp production, both perforated and imperforate.

Imperforate coil stamps are often difficult or impossible to differentiate from sheet stamps, but many can be authenticated, especially as pairs or strips, and some bear authenticating marks of contemporaneous experts.

The numbers assigned below are those of the regularly issued imperforate sheet stamps to which "H" or "V" has been added to indicate that the stamps are coiled horizontally (side by side), or vertically (top to bottom).

Values for stamps on cover are for single stamps.

FLAT PLATE PRINTING

1908 Wmk. 191 *Imperf.*

314V A115 1c **blue green,** pair, never hinged	*18,500.*	—
Strip of 4	—	—
Guide line pair	—	
Guide line strip of 4	—	

The Philatelic Foundation has certified one unused No. 314V pair (with coil leader strip attached). The existence of any of the other listed items has been questioned by specialists. The editors would like to see certified evidence of the other listings.

314H A115 1c **blue green,** pair	*2,100.*	—
Never hinged	*3,750.*	
On cover		*1,300.*
Pair on cover		*2,000.*
Strip of 4	—	—
Never hinged	*8,000.*	
Guide line pair	*5,000.*	
Guide line strip of 4	8,000.	
Pasteup pair	*3,500.*	
Never hinged	*5,500.*	
Pasteup strip of 4	*5,000.*	
Never hinged	*8,000.*	

Earliest documented use: Mar. 9, 1908.

320V A129 2c **carmine,** pair	*1,650.*	—
On cover		*3,000.*
Strip of 4	—	—
Guide line pair	—	
Guide line strip of 4	—	

Earliest documented use: Apr. 9, 1908.

320H A129 2c **carmine,** pair	550.00	—
Strip of 4	—	—
Guide line pair	—	
Guide line strip of 4	—	

Earliest documented use: June 4, 1908.

1908-10 *Imperf.*

343V A138 1c **green,** pair	25.00	15.00
Never hinged	40.00	
On cover		20.00
Strip of 4	60.00	—
Never hinged	110.00	
Guide line pair	60.00	150.00
Never hinged	110.00	
Guide line strip of 4	110.00	
Never hinged	220.00	
Pasteup pair	50.00	
Never hinged	90.00	

Earliest documented use: Nov. 18, 1909.

343H A138 1c **green,** pair	50.00	30.00
Never hinged	80.00	
Strip of 4	120.00	—
Never hinged	200.00	
Guide line pair	100.00	100.00
Never hinged	180.00	
Guide line strip of 4	220.00	
Never hinged	400.00	
Pasteup pair	80.00	
Never hinged	150.00	
Pasteup strip of 4	150.00	
Never hinged	280.00	

344V A139 2c **carmine,** pair	30.00	30.00
Never hinged	50.00	
On cover		25.00
Strip of 4	70.00	—
Never hinged	130.00	
Guide line pair	60.00	—
Never hinged	110.00	
Guide line strip of 4	110.00	
Never hinged	200.00	
Pasteup pair	50.00	
Never hinged	90.00	
Pasteup strip of 4	80.00	
Never hinged	150.00	
Foreign entry, design of 1c	*2,500.*	*3,250.*
Never hinged	*4,500.*	

Earliest documented use: Oct. 13, 1909.

344H A139 2c **carmine,** pair (2mm spacing)	35.00	30.00
Never hinged	60.00	
On cover		*600.00*
Strip of 4	90.00	
Never hinged	160.00	
Guide line pair	90.00	
Never hinged	160.00	
Guide line strip of 4	150.00	
Never hinged	280.00	
Pasteup pair	75.00	
Never hinged	130.00	
Pair (3mm spacing)	40.00	—
Never hinged	70.00	
Strip of 4	100.00	
Never hinged	180.00	
Guide line pair	90.00	150.00
Never hinged	160.00	
Guide line strip of 4	160.00	
Never hinged	280.00	

Earliest documented use: March 23, 1909.

345V A140 3c **deep violet,** type I, single		—
Pair	—	

345H A140 3c **deep violet,** type I, pair	6,250.	

No. 345H was printed from star plates with 3mm spacing between stamps on the six outer rows at the left and right sides of each 400-subject press sheet, and 2mm spacing between stamps on the inner four rows on each side of the center guide lines. Earlier imperforate 3¢ stamps were issued only as uncut sheets, not as coils, and were printed from plates with 2mm horizontal spacing only. Stamps with 3mm spacing are coil stamps; stamps with 2mm spacing are either coil stamps or imperforate sheet stamps.

346V A140 4c **orange brown,** pair	170.00	
Never hinged	300.00	
On cover		—
Strip of 4	375.00	—
Never hinged	650.00	
Guide line pair	325.00	125.00
Never hinged	600.00	
Guide line strip of 4	550.00	
Never hinged	1,000.	
Pasteup pair	250.00	
Never hinged	400.00	
Pasteup strip of 4	450.00	
Never hinged	800.00	

Earliest documented use: Feb. 18, 1911.

347V A140 5c **blue,** pair	175.00	—
Never hinged	300.00	
On cover		—
Strip of 4	425.00	300.00
Never hinged	725.00	
Guide line pair	350.00	—
Never hinged	600.00	
Guide line strip of 4	600.00	
Never hinged	1,000.	
Pasteup pair	275.00	
Never hinged	450.00	
Pasteup strip of 4	500.00	
Never hinged	900.00	

Earliest documented use: April 17, 1909.

1909 *Imperf.*

368V A141 2c **carmine,** *Lincoln,* pair	180.00	—
Never hinged	280.00	
On cover		—
Strip of 4	450.00	—
Never hinged	750.00	
Guide line pair	360.00	—
Never hinged	650.00	
Guide line strip of 4	625.00	—
Never hinged	1,100.	
Pasteup pair	300.00	
Never hinged	500.00	
Pasteup strip of 4	450.00	
Never hinged	750.00	

Earliest documented use: Feb. 12, 1909.

368H A141 2c **carmine,** *Lincoln,* pair	250.00	—
Never hinged	425.00	
On cover		—
Strip of 4	600.00	
Never hinged	950.00	
Guide line pair	500.00	
Never hinged	800.00	
Guide line strip of 4	850.00	
Never hinged	1,300.	
Pasteup pair	400.00	
Never hinged	650.00	
Pasteup strip of 4	600.00	
Never hinged	900.00	

Earliest documented use: Dec. 9, 1909.

1910 Wmk. 190 *Imperf.*

383V A138 1c **green,** pair	12.00	—
Never hinged	20.00	
On cover		10.00
Strip of 4	27.50	—
Never hinged	45.00	
Guide line pair	25.00	—
Never hinged	40.00	
Guide line strip of 4	60.00	—
Never hinged	105.00	
Pasteup pair	20.00	
Never hinged	35.00	
Pasteup strip of 4	35.00	
Never hinged	60.00	
Double transfer	—	—

Earliest documented use: Mar. 24, 1911.

383H A138 1c **green,** pair (2mm spacing)	17.50	—
Never hinged	30.00	
Strip of 4	42.50	—
Never hinged	70.00	
Guide line pair	35.00	—
Never hinged	65.00	
Guide line strip of 4	65.00	—
Never hinged	115.00	
Pasteup pair	30.00	
Never hinged	50.00	
Pair (3mm spacing)	17.50	—
Never hinged	28.00	
Strip of 4	42.50	—
Never hinged	70.00	
Guide line pair	35.00	—
Never hinged	65.00	
Guide line strip of 4	65.00	—
Never hinged	115.00	

384V A139 2c **carmine,** pair	14.00	—
Never hinged	25.00	
On cover		10.00
Strip of 4	30.00	—
Never hinged	50.00	
Guide line pair	30.00	—
Never hinged	55.00	
Guide line strip of 4	55.00	—
Never hinged	90.00	
Pasteup pair	24.00	
Never hinged	40.00	
Pasteup strip of 4	35.00	
Never hinged	60.00	
Foreign entry, design of 1c	*1,500.*	—
Never hinged	2,500.	

Earliest documented use: Oct. 21, 1910.

384H A139 2c **carmine,** pair (2mm spacing)	27.50	—
Never hinged	45.00	
Strip of 4	70.00	
Never hinged	115.00	
Guide line pair	60.00	—
Guide line strip of 4	105.00	—
Pasteup pair	50.00	
Never hinged	90.00	
Pasteup strip of 4	80.00	
Never hinged	130.00	
Pair (3mm spacing)	25.00	—
Never hinged	40.00	
Strip of 4	70.00	—
Never hinged	110.00	
Guide line pair	55.00	—
Never hinged	90.00	
Guide line strip of 4	100.00	—
Never hinged	180.00	

Earliest documented use: Jan. 9, 1912.

1912 Wmk. 190 *Imperf.*

408V A140 1c **green,** pair	4.00	
Never hinged	7.00	
On cover		—
Strip of 4	9.00	
Never hinged	15.00	
Guide line pair	9.00	
Never hinged	15.00	
Guide line strip of 4	14.00	
Never hinged	25.00	
Pasteup pair	7.00	
Never hinged	12.00	
Pasteup strip of 4	11.00	
Never hinged	20.00	

Earliest documented use: May 17, 1912.

408H A140 1c **green,** pair	5.00	
Never hinged	8.00	
Strip of 4	12.00	
Never hinged	20.00	
Guide line pair	10.00	
Never hinged	17.50	
Guide line strip of 4	17.50	
Never hinged	25.00	
Pasteup pair	8.00	
Never hinged	14.00	
Pasteup strip of 4	—	

409V A140 2c **carmine,** pair	4.00	
Never hinged	7.00	
Strip of 4	9.00	
Never hinged	15.00	
Guide line pair	8.00	
Never hinged	15.00	
Guide line strip of 4	14.00	
Never hinged	26.00	
Pasteup pair	7.00	
Never hinged	11.00	
Pasteup strip of 4	11.00	
Never hinged	20.00	

Earliest documented use: May 29, 1912.

409H A140 2c **carmine,** pair	6.00	
Never hinged	10.00	
On cover		—

Strip of 4	14.00
Never hinged	22.50
Guide line pair	9.00
Never hinged	16.00
Guide line strip of 4	15.00
Never hinged	26.00

Pasteup pair	7.00
Never hinged	12.00
Pasteup strip of 4	12.00
Never hinged	22.00
Double transfer	7.00

Earliest documented use: Dec. 17, 1914.

COMMEMORATIVE STAMPS, QUANTITIES ISSUED

Quantities issued fall into four categories. First are stamps where reasonably accurate counts are made of the number of stamps sold.

Second are stamps where the counts are approximations of the number sold.

Third are stamps where the count is of quantities shipped to post offices and philatelic sales units, but no adjustments are made for returned or destroyed stamps.

Fourth are stamps for which the quantity printed is furnished but no other adjustments are made.

Occasionally more accurate figures are determined. In these cases the quantities here will be adjusted. For example, it is now known that while 2,000,000 sets of the Voyages of Columbus souvenir sheets were printed, the number sold was 1,185,170 sets.

Scott No.		Quantity
230		449,195,550
231		1,464,588,750
232		11,501,250
233		19,181,550
234		35,248,250
235		4,707,550
236		10,656,550
237		16,516,950
238		1,576,950
239		617,250
240		243,750
241		55,050
242		45,550
243		27,650
244		26,350
245		27,350
285		70,993,400
286		159,720,800
287		4,924,500
288		7,694,180
289		2,927,200
290		4,629,760
291		530,400
292		56,900
293		56,200
294		91,401,500
295		209,759,700
296		5,737,100
297		7,201,300
298		4,921,700
299		5,043,700
323		79,779,200
324		192,732,400
325		4,542,600
326		6,926,700
327		4,011,200
328		77,728,794
329		149,497,994
330		7,980,594
367		148,387,191
368		1,273,900
369		637,000
370		152,887,311
371		525,400
372		72,634,631
373		216,480
397 & 401		334,796,926
398 & 402		503,713,086
399 & 403		29,088,726
400 & 404		16,968,365
537		99,585,200
548		137,978,207
549		196,037,327
550		11,321,607
610		1,459,487,085
611		770,000
612		99,950,300
614		51,378,023
615		77,753,423
616		5,659,023
617		15,615,000
618		26,596,600
619		5,348,800
620		9,104,983
621		1,900,983
627		307,731,900
628		20,280,500
629		40,639,485
630	(sheet of 25)	107,398
643		39,974,900
644		25,628,450
645		101,330,328
646		9,779,896
647		5,519,897
648		1,459,897
649		51,342,273
650		10,319,700
651		16,684,674
654		31,679,200
655		210,119,474
656		133,530,000
657		51,451,880
658		13,390,000
659		8,240,000
660		87,410,000
661		2,540,000
662		2,290,000
663		2,700,000
664		1,450,000
665		1,320,000
666		1,530,000
667		1,130,000
668		2,860,000
669		8,220,000
670		8,990,000
671		73,220,000
672		2,110,000
673		1,600,000
674		1,860,000
675		980,000
676		850,000
677		1,480,000
678		530,000
679		1,890,000
680		29,338,274
681		32,680,900
682		74,000,774
683		25,215,574
688		25,609,470
689		66,487,000
690		96,559,400
702		99,074,600
703		25,006,400
704		87,969,700
705		1,265,555,100
706		304,926,800
707		4,222,198,300
708		456,198,500
709		151,201,300
710		170,565,100
711		111,739,400
712		83,257,400
713		96,506,100
714		75,709,200
715		147,216,000
716		51,102,800
717		100,869,300
718		168,885,300
719		52,376,100
724		49,949,000
725		49,538,500
726		61,719,200
727		73,382,400
728		348,266,800
729		480,239,300
730	(sheet of 25)	456,704
730a		11,417,600
731	(sheet of 25)	441,172
731a		11,029,300
732		1,978,707,300
733		5,735,944
734		45,137,700
735	(sheet of 6)	811,404
735a		4,868,424
736		46,258,300
737		193,239,100
738		15,432,200
739		64,525,400
740		84,896,350
741		74,400,200
742		95,089,000
743		19,178,650
744		30,980,100
745		16,923,350
746		15,988,250
747		15,288,700
748		17,472,600
749		18,874,300
750	(sheet of 6)	511,391
750a		3,068,346
751	(sheet of 6)	793,551
751a		4,761,306
752		3,274,556
753		2,040,760
754		2,389,288
755		2,294,948
756		3,217,636
757		2,746,640
758		2,168,088
759		1,822,684
760		1,724,576
761		1,647,696
762		1,682,948
763		1,638,644
764		1,625,244
765		1,644,900
766	(pane of 25)	98,712
766a		2,467,800
767	(pane of 25)	85,914
767a		2,147,850
768	(pane of 6)	267,200
768a		1,603,200
769	(pane of 6)	279,960
769a		1,679,760
770	(pane of 6)	215,920
770a		1,295,520
771		1,370,560
772		70,726,800
773		100,839,600
774		73,610,650
775		75,823,900
776		124,324,500
777		67,127,650
778	(sheet of 4)	2,809,039
778a		2,809,039
778b		2,809,039
778c		2,809,039
778d		2,809,039
782		72,992,650
783		74,407,450
784		269,522,200
785		105,196,150
786		93,848,500
787		87,741,150
788		35,794,150
789		36,839,250
790		104,773,450
791		92,054,550
792		93,291,650
793		34,552,950
794		36,819,050
795		84,825,250
796		25,040,400
797		5,277,445
798		99,882,300
799		78,454,450
800		77,004,200
801		81,292,450
802		76,474,550
835		73,043,650
836		58,654,368
837		65,939,500
838		47,064,300
852		114,439,600
853		101,699,550
854		72,764,550
855		81,369,600
856		67,813,350
857		71,394,750
858		66,835,000
859		56,348,320
860		53,177,110
861		53,260,270
862		22,104,950
863		13,201,270
864		51,603,580
865		52,100,510
866		51,666,580
867		22,207,780
868		11,835,530
869		52,471,160
870		52,366,440
871		51,636,270
872		20,729,030
873		14,125,580
874		59,409,000
875		57,888,600
876		58,273,180
877		23,779,000
878		15,112,580
879		57,322,790
880		58,281,580
881		56,398,790
882		21,147,000
883		13,328,000
884		54,389,510
885		53,636,580
886		55,313,230
887		21,720,580
888		13,600,580
889		47,599,580
890		53,766,510
891		54,193,580
892		20,264,580
893		13,726,580
894		46,497,400
895		47,700,000
896		50,618,150
897		50,034,400

898	60,943,700
902	44,389,550
903	54,574,550
904	63,558,400
906	21,272,800
907	1,671,564,200
908	1,227,334,200
909	19,999,646
910	19,999,646
911	19,999,646
912	19,999,646
913	19,999,646
914	19,999,646
915	19,999,646
916	14,999,646
917	14,999,646
918	14,999,646
919	14,999,646
920	14,999,646
921	14,999,646
922	61,303,000
923	61,001,450
924	60,605,000
925	50,129,350
926	53,479,400
927	61,617,350
928	75,500,000
929	137,321,000
930	128,140,000
931	67,255,000
932	133,870,000
933	76,455,400
934	128,357,750
935	138,863,000
936	111,616,700
937	308,587,700
938	170,640,000
939	135,927,000
940	260,339,100
941	132,274,500
942	132,430,000
943	139,209,500
944	114,684,450
945	156,540,510
946	120,450,600
947	127,104,300
948	10,299,600
949	132,902,000
950	131,968,000
951	131,488,000
952	122,362,000
953	121,548,000
954	131,109,500
955	122,650,500
956	121,953,500
957	115,250,000
958	64,198,500
959	117,642,500
960	77,649,600
961	113,474,500
962	120,868,500
963	77,800,500
964	52,214,000
965	53,959,100
966	61,120,010
967	57,823,000
968	52,975,000
969	77,149,000
970	58,332,000
971	56,228,000
972	57,832,000
973	53,875,000
974	63,834,000
975	67,162,200
976	64,561,000
977	64,079,500
978	63,388,000
979	62,285,000
980	57,492,610
981	99,190,000
982	104,790,000
983	108,805,000
984	107,340,000
985	117,020,000
986	122,633,000
987	130,960,000
988	128,478,000
989	132,090,000
990	130,050,000
991	131,350,000
992	129,980,000
993	122,315,000
994	122,170,000
995	131,635,000
996	121,860,000
997	121,120,000
998	119,120,000
999	112,125,000
1000	114,140,000
1001	114,490,000
1002	117,200,000
1003	116,130,000
1004	116,175,000
1005	115,945,000
1006	112,540,000
1007	117,415,000
1008	2,899,580,000
1009	114,540,000
1010	113,135,000
1011	116,255,000
1012	113,860,000
1013	124,260,000
1014	115,735,000
1015	115,430,000
1016	136,220,000
1017	114,894,600
1018	118,706,000
1019	114,190,000
1020	113,990,000
1021	89,289,600
1022	114,865,000
1023	115,780,000
1024	115,244,600
1025	123,709,600
1026	114,789,600
1027	115,759,600
1028	116,134,600
1029	118,540,000
1060	115,810,000
1061	113,603,700
1062	128,002,000
1063	116,078,150
1064	116,139,800
1065	120,484,800
1066	53,854,750
1067	176,075,000
1068	125,944,400
1069	122,284,600
1070	133,638,850
1071	118,664,600
1072	112,434,000
1073	129,384,550
1074	121,184,600
1075	2,900,731
1076	119,784,200
1077	123,159,400
1078	123,138,800
1079	109,275,000
1080	112,932,200
1081	125,475,000
1082	117,855,000
1083	122,100,000
1084	118,180,000
1085	100,975,000
1086	115,299,450
1087	186,949,627
1088	115,235,000
1089	106,647,500
1090	112,010,000
1091	118,470,000
1092	102,230,000
1093	102,410,000
1094	84,054,400
1095	126,266,000
1096	39,489,600
1097	122,990,000
1098	174,372,800
1099	114,365,000
1100	122,765,200
1104	113,660,200
1105	120,196,580
1106	120,805,200
1107	128,815,200
1108	108,415,200
1109	107,195,200
1110	115,745,280
1111	39,743,640
1112	114,570,200
1113	120,400,200
1114	91,160,200
1115	114,860,200
1116	126,500,000
1117	120,581,280
1118	44,064,576
1119	118,390,200
1120	125,770,200
1121	114,114,280
1122	156,600,200
1123	124,200,200
1124	120,740,200
1125	133,623,280
1126	45,569,088
1127	122,493,280
1128	131,260,200
1129	47,125,200
1130	123,105,000
1131	126,105,050
1132	209,170,000
1133	120,835,000
1134	115,715,000
1135	118,445,000
1136	111,685,000
1137	43,099,200
1138	115,444,000
1139	126,470,000
1140	124,560,000
1141	115,455,000
1142	122,060,000
1143	120,540,000
1144	113,075,000
1145	139,325,000
1146	124,445,000
1147	113,792,000
1148	44,215,200
1149	113,195,000
1150	121,805,000
1151	115,353,000
1152	111,080,000
1153	153,025,000
1154	119,665,000
1155	117,855,000
1156	118,185,000
1157	112,260,000
1158	125,010,000
1159	119,798,000
1160	42,696,000
1161	106,610,000
1162	109,695,000
1163	123,690,000
1164	123,970,000
1165	124,796,000
1166	42,076,800
1167	116,210,000
1168	126,252,000
1169	42,746,400
1170	124,117,000
1171	119,840,000
1172	117,187,000
1173	124,390,000
1174	112,966,000
1175	41,644,200
1176	110,850,000
1177	98,616,000
1178	101,125,000
1179	124,865,000
1180	79,905,000
1181	125,410,000
1182	112,845,000
1183	106,210,000
1184	110,810,000
1185	116,995,000
1186	121,015,000
1187	111,600,000
1188	110,620,000
1189	109,110,000
1190	145,350,000
1191	112,870,000
1192	121,820,000
1193	289,240,000
1194	120,155,000
1195	124,595,000
1196	147,310,000
1197	118,690,000
1198	122,730,000
1199	126,515,000
1200	130,960,000
1201	120,055,000
1202	120,715,000
1203	121,440,000
1204	40,270,000
1205	861,970,000
1206	120,035,000
1207	117,870,000
1230	129,945,000
1231	135,620,000
1232	137,540,000
1233	132,435,000
1234	135,520,000
1235	131,420,000
1236	133,170,000
1237	130,195,000
1238	128,450,000
1239	118,665,000
1240	1,291,250,000
1241	175,175,000
1242	125,995,000
1243	128,025,000
1244	145,700,000
1245	120,310,000
1246	511,750,000
1247	123,845,000
1248	122,825,000
1249	453,090,000
1250	123,245,000
1251	123,355,000
1252	126,970,000
1253	121,250,000
1254-1257	1,407,760,000
1258	120,005,000
1259	125,800,000
1260	122,230,000
1261	115,695,000
1262	115,095,000
1263	119,580,000
1264	125,180,000
1265	120,135,000
1266	115,405,000
1267	115,855,000
1268	115,340,000
1269	114,840,000
1270	116,140,000
1271	116,900,000
1272	114,085,000
1273	114,880,000
1274	26,995,000
1275	128,495,000
1276	1,139,930,000
1306	116,835,000
1307	117,470,000
1308	123,770,000
1309	131,270,000
1310	122,285,000
1311	14,680,000
1312	114,160,000
1313	128,475,000
1314	119,535,000
1315	125,110,000
1316	114,853,200
1317	124,290,000
1318	128,460,000
1319	127,585,000
1320	115,875,000
1321	1,173,547,420
1322	114,015,000
1323	121,105,000
1324	132,045,000
1325	118,780,000
1326	121,985,000
1327	111,850,000
1328	117,225,000
1329	111,515,000
1330	114,270,000
1331-1332	120,865,000
1333	110,675,000
1334	110,670,000
1335	113,825,000
1336	1,208,700,000
1337	113,330,000
1339	141,350,000
1340	144,345,000
1342	147,120,000
1343	130,125,000
1344	158,700,000
1345-1354	228,040,000
1355	153,015,000
1356	132,560,000
1357	130,385,000

1358	132,265,000
1359	128,710,000
1360	124,775,000
1361	128,295,000
1362	142,245,000
1363	1,410,580,000
1364	125,100,000
1365-1368	192,570,000
1369	145,770,000
1370	139,475,000
1371	187,165,000
1372	125,555,000
1373	144,425,000
1374	135,875,000
1375	151,110,000
1376-1379	159,195,000
1380	129,540,000
1381	130,925,000
1382	139,055,000
1383	150,611,200
1384	1,709,795,000
1385	127,545,000
1386	145,788,800
1387-1390	201,794,200
1391	171,850,000
1392	142,205,000
1405	137,660,000
1406	135,125,000
1407	135,895,000
1408	132,675,000
1409	134,795,000
1410-1413	161,600,000
1414-1414a	683,730,000
1415-1418,1415a-1418a	489,255,000
1419	127,610,000
1420	129,785,000
1421-1422	134,380,000
1423	136,305,000
1424	134,840,000
1425	130,975,000
1426	161,235,000
1427-1430	175,679,600
1431	138,700,000
1432	138,165,000
1433	152,125,000
1434-1435	176,295,000
1436	142,845,000
1437	148,755,000
1438	139,080,000
1439	130,755,000
1440-1443	170,208,000
1444	1,074,350,000
1445	979,540,000
1446	137,355,000
1447	150,400,000
1448-1451	172,730,000
1452	104,090,000
1453	164,096,000
1454	53,920,000
1455	153,025,000
1456-1459	201,890,000
1460	67,335,000
1461	179,675,000
1462	46,340,000
1463	180,155,000
1464-1467	198,364,800
1468	185,490,000
1469	162,335,000
1470	162,789,950
1471	1,003,475,000
1472	1,017,025,000
1473	165,895,000
1474	166,508,000
1475	320,055,000
1476	166,005,000
1477	163,050,000
1478	159,005,000
1479	147,295,000
1480-1483	196,275,000
1484	139,152,000
1485	128,048,000
1486	148,008,000
1487	139,608,000
1488	159,475,000
1489-1498	486,020,000
1499	157,052,800
1500	53,005,000
1501	159,775,000
1502	39,005,000
1503	152,624,000
1504	145,840,000
1505	151,335,000
1506	141,085,000
1507	885,160,000
1508	939,835,000
1525	143,930,000
1526	145,235,000
1527	135,052,000
1528	156,750,000
1529	164,670,000
1530-1537	190,156,800
1538-1541	167,212,800
1542	156,265,000
1543-1546	195,585,000
1547	148,850,000
1548	157,270,000
1549	150,245,000
1550	835,180,000
1551	882,520,000
1552	213,155,000
1553	159,995,000
1554	146,365,000
1555	148,805,000
1556	173,685,000
1557	158,600,000
1558	153,355,000
1559	63,205,000
1560	157,865,000
1561	166,810,000

1562	44,825,000
1563	144,028,000
1564	139,928,000
1565-1568	179,855,000
1569-1570	161,863,200
1571	145,640,000
1572-1575	168,655,000
1576	146,615,000
1577-1578	146,195,000
1579	739,430,000
1580	878,690,000
1629-1631	219,455,000
1632	157,825,000
1633-1682	436,005,000
1683	159,915,000
1684	159,060,000
1685	158,470,000
1686	1,990,000
1687	1,983,000
1688	1,953,000
1689	1,903,000
1690	164,890,000
1691-1694	208,035,000
1695-1698	185,715,000
1699	130,592,000
1700	158,322,800
1701	809,955,000
1702-1703	963,370,000
1704	150,328,000
1705	176,830,000
1706-1709	195,976,000
1710	208,820,000
1711	192,250,000
1712-1715	219,830,000
1716	159,852,000
1717-1720	188,310,000
1721	163,625,000
1722	156,296,000
1723-1724	158,678,000
1725	154,495,000
1726	168,050,000
1727	158,810,000
1728	153,736,000
1729	882,260,000
1730	921,530,000
1731	156,560,000
1732-1733	202,155,000
1744	156,525,000
1745-1748	165,182,400
1749-1752	157,598,400
1753	102,856,000
1754	152,270,000
1755	94,600,000
1756	151,570,000
1757	15,170,400
1758	161,228,000
1759	158,880,000
1760-1763	186,550,000
1764-1767	168,136,000
1768	963,120,000
1769	916,800,000
1770	159,297,600
1771	166,435,000
1772	162,535,000
1773	155,000,000
1774	157,310,000
1775-1778	174,096,000
1779-1782	164,793,600
1783-1786	163,055,000
1787	161,860,000
1788	165,775,000
1789	160,000,000
1790	67,195,000
1791-1794	186,905,000
1795-1798	208,295,000
1799	873,710,000
1800	931,880,000
1801	161,290,000
1802	172,740,000
1803	168,995,000
1804	160,000,000
1805-1810	232,134,000
1821	163,510,000
1822	256,620,000
1823	95,695,000
1824	153,975,000
1825	160,000,000
1826	103,850,000
1827-1830	204,715,000
1831	166,545,000
1832	163,310,000
1833	160,000,000
1834-1837	152,404,000
1838-1841	152,420,000
1842	692,500,000
1843	718,715,000
1874	160,155,000
1875	159,505,000
1876-1879	210,633,000
1910	165,175,000
1911	107,240,000
1912-1919	337,819,000
1920	99,420,000
1921-1924	178,930,000
1925	100,265,000
1926	99,615,000
1927	97,535,000
1928-1931	167,308,000
1932	101,625,000
1933	99,170,000
1934	101,155,000
1935	101,200,000
1936	167,360,000
1937-1938	162,420,000
1939	597,720,000
1940	792,600,000
1941	167,130,000
1942-1945	191,560,000
1950	163,939,200

1952	180,700,000
1953-2002	666,950,000
2003	109,245,000
2004	112,535,000
2006-2009	126,640,000
2010	107,605,000
2011	173,160,000
2012	107,285,000
2013	109,040,000
2014	183,270,000
2015	169,495,000
2016	164,235,000
2017	110,130,000
2018	110,995,000
2019-2022	165,340,000
2023	174,180,000
2024	110,261,000
2026	703,295,000
2027-2030	788,880,000
2031	118,555,000
2032-2035	226,128,000
2036	118,225,000
2037	114,290,000
2038	165,000,000
2039	120,430,000
2040	117,025,000
2041	181,700,000
2042	114,250,000
2043	111,775,000
2044	115,200,000
2045	108,820,000
2046	184,950,000
2047	110,925,000
2048-2051	395,424,000
2052	104,340,000
2053	114,725,000
2054	112,525,000
2055-2058	193,055,000
2059-2062	207,725,000
2063	715,975,000
2064	848,525,000
2065	165,000,000
2066	120,000,000
2067-2070	319,675,000
2071	103,975,000
2072	554,675,000
2073	120,000,000
2074	106,975,000
2075	107,325,000
2076-2079	306,912,000
2080	120,000,000
2081	108,000,000
2082-2085	313,350,000
2086	130,320,000
2087	120,000,000
2088	117,050,000
2089	115,725,000
2090	116,600,000
2091	120,000,000
2092	123,575,000
2093	120,000,000
2094	117,125,000
2095	117,225,000
2096	95,525,000
2097	119,125,000
2098-2101	216,260,000
2102	120,000,000
2103	108,140,000
2104	117,625,000
2105	112,896,000
2106	116,500,000
2107	751,300,000
2108	786,225,000
2109	105,300,000
2110	124,500,000
2137	120,000,000
2138-2141	300,000,000
2142	120,580,000
2143	729,700,000
2144	124,750,000
2145	203,496,000
2146	126,325,000
2147	130,000,000
2152	119,975,000
2153	120,000,000
2154	119,975,000
2155-2158	147,940,000
2159	120,000,000
2160-2163	130,000,000
2164	120,000,000
2165	759,200,000
2166	757,600,000
2198-2201	67,996,800
2202	947,450,000
2203	130,000,000
2204	136,500,000
2205-2209	219,990,000
2210	130,000,000
2211	130,000,000
2216	5,825,050
2217	5,825,050
2218	5,825,050
2219	5,825,050
2220-2223	130,000,000
2224	220,725,000
2235-2238	240,525,000
2239	131,700,000
2240-2243	240,000,000
2244	690,100,000
2245	882,150,000
2246	167,430,000
2247	166,555,000
2248	811,560,000
2249	142,905,000
2250	130,000,000
2251	149,980,000
2267-2274	610,425,000
2275	156,995,000
2286-2335	645,975,000

2336	166,725,000	2720	105,000,000	3066	314,175,000
2337	186,575,000	2721	517,000,000	3067	209,450,000
2338	184,325,000	2722	150,000,000	3068	16,207,500
2339	165,845,000	2723	152,000,000	3069	153,300,000
2340	155,170,000	2730a	14,285,715	3070	100,000,000
2341	102,100,000	2731	98,841,000	3071	60,120,000
2342	103,325,000	2732	32,947,000	3076a	27,850,000
2343	162,045,000	2733	32,947,000	3080a	22,218,000
2344	153,925,000	2734	32,947,000	3081	95,600,000
2345	160,425,000	2735	65,894,000	3082	300,000,000
2346	183,290,000	3736	65,894,000	3086a	23,681,250
2347	179,800,000	2737	65,894,000	3087	133,613,000
2348	164,130,000	2745a	140,000,000	3088	103,400,000
2349	157,475,000	2746	105,000,000	3089	60,000,000
2350	156,225,000	2747	110,000,000	3090	134,000,000
2351-2354	163,980,000	2748	110,000,000	3095a	32,000,000
2355-2359	584,340,000	2749	172,870,000	3099a	23,025,000
2360	168,995,000	2753a	65,625,000	3103a	23,025,000
2361	163,120,000	2754	110,000,000	3104	300,000,000
2362-2366	394,776,000	2755	115,870,000	3105	14,910,000
2367	528,790,000	2759a	40,000,000	3106	93,612,000
2368	978,340,000	2764a	199,784,500	3107	243,575,000
2369	158,870,000	2765	12,000,000	3111a	56,479,000
2370	145,560,000	2766	160,000,000	3112	847,750,000
2371	97,300,000	2770a	128,735,000	3116a	451,312,500
2372-2375	158,556,000	2774a	25,000,000	3117	495,504,000
2376	97,300,000	2778a	170,000,000	3118	103,520,000
2377	153,045,000	2782a	37,500,000	3120	106,000,000
2378	841,240,000	2784a	41,840,000	3121	112,000,000
2379	169,765,000	2788a	37,550,000	3123	1,660,000,000
2380	157,215,000	2804	88,300,000	3124	814,000,000
2381-2385	635,238,000	2805	105,000,000	3125	122,000,000
2386-2389	162,142,500	2806	100,000,000	3131a	65,000,000
2390-2393	305,015,000	2806a	250,000,000	3134	97,500,000
2395-2398	480,000,000	2811a	35,800,000	3135	96,000,000
2399	821,285,000	2812	150,500,000	3136	14,600,000
2400	1,030,850,000	2813	357,949,584	3137	37,800,000
2401	165,495,000	2814	830,000,000	3138	118,000
2402	151,675,000	2814C	300,000,000	3139	593,775
2403	163,000,000	2815	274,800,000	3140	592,849
2404	264,625,000	2816	155,500,000	3141	42,250,000
2405-2409	204,984,000	2817	105,000,000	3142	8,050,000
2410	103,835,000	2818	185,500,000	3146a	22,500,000
2411	152,250,000	2828a	18,600,000	3147	20,000,000
2412	138,760,000	2833a	166,000,000	3148	20,000,000
2413	137,985,000	2834	201,000,000	3149	10,000,000
2414	138,850,000	2835	300,000,000	3150	10,000,000
2415	150,545,000	2836	269,370,000	3151	7,000,000
2416	164,680,000	2837	60,000,000	3152	195,000,000
2417	262,755,000	2838	12,060,000	3153	323,000,000
2418	191,755,000	2839	209,000,000	3157a	21,500,000
2420	188,400,000	2840	20,000,000	3158-3161	12,900,000
2421	191,860,000	2841	12,958,000	3162-3165	8,600,000
2422-2425	406,988,000	2842	100,500,000	3166	22,250,000
2426	137,410,000	2847a	159,200,000	3167	45,250,000
2427	913,335,000	2848	150,500,000	3172a	36,250,000
2428	900,000,000	2853a	34,436,000	3173	173,000,000
2429	399,243,000	2854	24,986,000	3174	37,000,000
2433	2,017,225	2855	24,986,000	3175	133,000,000
2434-2437	163,824,000	2856	24,986,000	3176	882,500,000
2438	2,047,200	2857	19,988,800	3177	1,621,465,000
2439	173,000,000	2858	19,988,800	3178	15,000,000
2440	886,220,000	2859	19,988,800	3179	51,000,000
2441	995,178,000	2860	19,988,800	3180	80,000,000
2442	153,125,000	2861	19,988,800	3181	45,000,000
2444	169,495,000	2862	150,750,000	3182	12,533,000
2445-2448	176,808,000	2866a	56,475,000	3183	12,533,000
2449	150,000,000	2868a	77,748,000	3184	12,533,000
2470-2474	733,608,000	2869	20,000,000	3185	12,533,000
2496-2500	178,587,500	2870	150,186	3186	12,533,000
2501-2505	619,128,000	2871	518,500,000	3187	12,533,000
2506-2507	151,430,000	2872	602,500,000	3188	8,000,000
2508-2511	278,264,000	2873	236,997,600	3189	6,000,000
2512	143,995,000	2874	45,000,000	3190	6,000,000
2513	142,692,000	2875	5,000,000	3191	8,250,000
2517	728,919,000	2876	80,000,000	3192	30,000,000
2515	599,400,000	2948	214,700,000	3193-3197	250,000,000
2516	320,304,000	2949	1,220,970,000	3198-3202	80,000,000
2532	103,648,000	2950	94,500,000	3203	85,000,000
2533	179,990,000	2954a	50,000,000	3204	39,600,000
2534	150,560,000	2955	80,000,000	3205	650,000
2538	161,498,000	2956	97,000,000	3206	32,000,000
2545-2549	744,918,000	2957	315,000,000	3209	2,200,000
2550	149,848,000	2958	300,000,000	3210	2,200,000
2551	200,003,000	2965a	30,000,000	3211	30,000,000
2552	200,000,000	2966	125,000,000	3212-3215	45,000,000
2553-2557	170,025,600	2967	400,000,000	3216-3219	45,000,000
2558	150,310,000	2968	92,424,000	3220	46,300,000
2559	15,218,000	2973a	120,200,000	3221	30,000,000
2560	149,810,000	2974	60,000,0000	3222-3225	70,000,000
2561	149,260,000	2975	300,000,000	3226	65,000,000
2562-2566	699,978,000	2979a	62,500,000	3227	50,000,000
2567	148,973,000	2980	105,000,000	3230-3234	180,000,000
2577a	33,394,800	2981	10,000,000	3235	28,000,000
2615a	32,000,000	2982	150,000,000	3236	4.000.000
2616	148,665,000	2983-2992	15,000,000	3237	130,750,000
2617	149,990,000	2992	15,000,000	3238-3242	185,000,000
2618	835,000,000	2997a	200,000,000	3243	50,000,000
2619	160,000,000	2998	300,000,000	3244	925,200,000
2623a	40,005,000	2999	85,000,000	3245-3248	116,760,000
2624	1,185,170	3000	300,000,000	3249-3252	991,750,000
2625	1,185,170	3001	80,000,000	3272	51,000,000
2626	1,185,170	3002	80,000,000	3273	100,000,000
2627	1,185,170	3003	300,000,000	3274	1,000,000,000
2628	1,185,170	3007a	75,000,000	3275	
2629	1,185,170	3008	350,495,000	3276	100,000,000
2630	148,000,000	3009	350,495,000	3286	40,400,000
2634a	37,315,000	3010	350,495,000	3287	42,500,000
2635	146,610,000	3011	350,495,000	3288-3292	73,155,000
2636	160,000,000	3013	90,000,000	3293	10,000,000
2641a	32,000,000	3023a	30,000,000	3306	42,700,000
2646a	87,728,000	3024	120,000,000	3307	500,000
2696a	11,000,000	3029a	160,000,000	3308	42,500,000
2697	12,000,000	3030	2,550,000,000	3309	105,000,000
2698	105,000,000	3058	92,100,000	3310-3313	1,500,000,000
2699	142,500,000	3059	115,600,000	3314	145,375,000
2703a	36,831,000	3060	93,150,000	3315	78,100,000
2704	85,000,000	3064a	23,292,500	3316	89,270,000
2709a	80,000,000	3065	111,000,000	3317-3320	141,175,000

3321-3324	151,976,000
3325-3328	116,038,500
3329	75,500,000
3330	100,750,000
3331	101,800,000
3332	43,150,000
3333-3337	120,000,000
3338	42,500,000
3339-3344	42,500,000
3345-3350	42,500,000
3351	4,235,000
3352	65,000,000
3354	44,600,000
3355	1,555,560,000
3356-3359	116,500,000
3360-3363	1,785,060,000
3364-3367	118,125,000
3368	95,000,000
3369	120,000,000

Quantities for Nos. 3370-on, and for Nos. 3190, 3191 and 3236, are for quantities ordered.

3370	56,000,000
3371	150,000,000
3372	65,150,000
3373-3377	15,000,000
3378	10,000,000
3379-3383	55,000,000
3384-3388	105,350,000
3389	16,000,000
3390	55,000,000
3391	30,000,000
3392	236,000
3393-3396	55,000,000
3397	90,600,000
3398	200,000,000
3399-3402	88,000,000
3403	4,000,000
3408	11,250,000
3409	1,695,000
3410	1,695,000
3411	1,695,000
3412	1,695,000
3413	1,695,000
3413-3417	100,000,000
3438	53,000,000
3439-3443	85,000,000
3444	53,000,000
3445	125,000,000
3446	52,000,000
3496	500,000,000
3497	1,500,000,000
3498	80,000,000
3499	180,000,000
3500	55,000,000
3501	200,000,000
3502	125,000,000
3503	100,000,000
3504	35,000,000
3505	1,598,000
3506	8,960,000
3507	125,000,000
3508	200,000,000
3509	55,000,000
3510-3519	125,000,000
3521	55,000,000
3523	110,000,000
3524-3527	96,000,000
3528-3531	100,000,000
3532	75,000,000
3533	30,000,000
3534a	275,000,000
3535	236,000
3536	800,000,000
3537-3540	125,000,000
3537a-3540a	1,500,000,000
3541-3544	201,000,000
3545	32,000,000
3546	69,000,000
3547	49,000,000
3548	40,000,000
3551	100,000,000
3552-3555	80,000,000
3556	125,000,000
3557	120,000,000
3558	75,000,000
3559	70,000,000
3560	55,000,000
3561-3610	200,000,000
3611	7,000,000
3649	3,000,000
3650	70,000,000
3651	61,000,000
3652	61,000,000
3653-3656	200,000,000
3657	1,500,000,000
3658	150,000,000
3659	75,000,000
3660	62,800,000
3661-3664	111,000,000
3665-3668	61,000,000
3669	61,000,000
3670-3671	200,000,000
3672	35,000,000
3673	40,000,000
3674	35,000,000
3675	739,200,000
3676-3679	125,000,000
3680-3683	300,000,000
3684-3687	1,705,000,000
3688-3691	200,000,000
3692	80,000,000
3694	1,610,000
3695	50,000,000
3696-3745	200,000,000
3746	150,000,000
3747	70,000,000
3748	70,000,000
3771	60,000,000
3772	7,000,000
3773	50,000,000
3774	55,000,000
3776-3780	60,000,000
3781	75,000,000
3782	54,000,000
3783	85,000,000
3786	80,000,000
3787-3791	125,000,000
3802	6,000,000
3803	86,800,000
3804-3807	778,800,000
3808-3811	70,000,000
3812	52,000,000
3813	72,000,000
3814-3818	80,000,000
3820	700,000,000
3821-3824	1,875,000,000
3825-3828	200,990,000
3831	7,600,000
3832	80,000,000
3833	750,000,000
3834	130,000,000
3835	172,000,000
3836	750,000,000
3837	150,000,000
3838	60,000,000
3839	80,000,000
3840-3843	57,000,000
3854	62,200,000
3855-3856	20,000,000
3857-3861	57,000,000
3862	96,400,000
3863	71,800,000
3865-3868	284,000,000
3869	45,800,000
3870	60,000,000
3871	50,000,000
3872	794,000,000
3873	8,700,000
3876	100,000,000
3877	96,400,000
3878	8,336,000
3879	776,400,000
3881	60,000,000
3882	45,000,000
3883-3886	125,000,000
3887-3890	200,990,000
3891-3894	270,000,000
3895	4,500,000
3896	150,000,000
3897	170,000,000
3898	1,500,000,000
3899	5,600,000
3900-3903	790,000,000
3904	45,000,000
3905	40,000,000
3906-3909	50,000,000
3910	5,000,000
3911	65,000,000
3912-3915	215,000,000
3916-3925	110,000,000
3926-3929	420,000,000
3930	40,000,000
3931-3935	640,000,000
3936	75,000,000
3937	5,000,000
3938	65,000,000
3939-3942	70,000,000
3943	40,000,000
3944	21,000,000
3945-3948	70,000,000
3949-3952	200,000,000
3953-3956	800,000,000
3957-3960	100,000,000
3961-3964	60,000,000
3976	600,000,000
3987-3994	192,000,000
3995	60,000,000
3996	150,000,000
3997	5,000,000
3998-3999	200,000,000
4020	100,000,000
4021-4024	40,000,000
4025-4028	175,000,000
4029	400,000,000
4030	30,000,000
4031	80,000,000
4032	50,000,000
4033-4072	204,000,000
4073	40,000,000
4074	1,000,000
4075	3,000,000
4076	3,000,000
4077	75,000,000
4078	50,000,000
4079	60,000,000
4080-4083	200,000,000
4084	12,500,000
4085-4088	85,000,000
4089-4098	500,000,000
4099	5,000,000
4100	700,000,000
4101-4104	200,000,000
4105-4108	1,515,000,000
4109-4112	100,000,000
4113-4116	54,000,000
4117	35,000,000
4118	40,000,000
4119	40,000,000
4120	150,000,000
4121	25,000,000
4122	300,000,000
4123	2,000,000
4124	30,000,000
4136	60,000,000
4143	30,000,000
4146-4150	175,000,000
4151	500,000,000
4152	200,000,000
4153-4156	420,000,000
4153a-4156a	280,000,000
4159	12,500,000
4160-4163	36,000,000
4165	500,000,000
4192-4195	200,000,000
4196	60,000,000
4197	55,000,000
4198	5,000,000
4199	80,000,000
4200	40,000,000
4201	40,000,000
4202	40,000,000
4203-4204	80,000,000
4205	100,000,000
4206	700,000,000
4207-4210	1,700,000,000
4211-4214	80,900,000
4215-4218	88,200,000
4219	50,000,000
4220	50,000,000
4221	72,000,000
4222	125,000,000
4223	30,000,000
4224-4227	28,000,000
4228-4252	30,000,000
4265	120,000,000
4266	60,000,000
4270	750,000,000
4271	500,000,000
4272	100,000,000
4273-4282	500,000,000
4283-4292	500,000,000
4293-4302	500,000,000
4303-4312	500,000,000
4333-4322	250,000,000
4333	24,000,000
4334	40,000,000
4335	75,000,000
4336-4340	40,000,000
4341	75,000,000
4342-4345	125,000,000
4346	300,000,000
4349	30,000,000
4350	60,000,000
4351	25,000,000
4352	35,000,000
4353-4357	50,000,000
4358	65,000,000
4359	600,000,000
4360-4363	1,300,000,000
4368-4371	126,324,000
4372	40,000,000
4373	35,000,000
4374	30,000,000
4375	60,000,000
4376	30,000,000
4377	30,000,000
4380-4383	50,000,000
4384	24,000,000
4386	100,000,000
4397	300,000,000
4399-4403	1,000,000,000
4404-4405	500,000,000
4406	100,000,000
4407	100,000,000
4408	125,000,000
4409-4413	100,000,000
4414	50,000,000
4415	40,000,000
4416	20,000,000
4417-4420	40,000,000
4421	40,000,000
4422	8,000,000
4423	25,000,000
4424	600,000,000
4425-4428	1,300,000,000
4433	35,000,000
4434	30,000,000
4435	40,000,000
4436	45,000,000
4440-4443	25,000,000
4444	3,000,000
4445	20,000,000
4446-4449	40,000,000
4450	300,000,000
4451-4460	391,400,000
4461	50,000,000
4463	40,000,000
4464	80,000,000
4465-4466	80,000,000
4467-4471	85,000,000
4472	40,000,000
4473	40,000,000
4474	25,000,000
4475	60,000,000
4476	30,000,000
4477	300,000,000
4478-4481	2,000,000,000
4482-4485	157,080,000
4492	80,640,000
4493	50,000,000
4494	100,000,000
4497-4501	60,000,000
4502	100,000,000
4503	50,000,000
4520	300,000,000
4521	75,000,000
4522-4523	60,000,000
4524	160,000,000
4525	40,000,000
4526	40,000,000
4527-4528	60,000,000
4530	50,000,000
4531-4540	300,000,000
4541-4544	30,000,000
4545	50,000,000

4546	36,000,000
4547	60,000,000
4548-4551	60,000,000
4552	20,000,000
4553-4557	200,000,000
4558	60,000,000
4565	100,000,000
4566-4569	40,000,000
4570	600,000,000
4571-4574	600,000,000
4575-4578	900,000,000
4579-4582	252,000,000
4583	25,000,000
4584	35,000,000
4591	50,000,000
4618-4622	400,000,000
4623	72,000,000
4624	80,000,000
4625	50,000,000
4626	300,000,000
4627	40,000,000
4651-4652	150,000,000
4653	70,000,000
4654-4662	20,000,000
4664-4665	30,000,000
4666	20,000,000
4667	40,000,000
4668-4671	25,000,000
4677-4681	125,000,000
4687-4690	40,000,000
4691	40,000,000
4692-4693	30,000,000
4694-4697	80,000,000
4694	3,000,000
4695	3,000,000
4696	3,000,000
4697	3,000,000
4698-4701	25,000,000
4702	20,000,000
4703	25,000,000
4705	20,000,000
4710	39,999,990
4716	12,000,000
4721	55,000,000
4726	31,200,000
4741	311,000,000
4742	83,000,000
4743-4747	95,000,000
4748	23,400,000
4750-4753	92,000,000
4754-4763	400,000,000
4786	30,000,000
4787-4788	10,800,000
4789	60,000,000
4790	30,000,000
4791-4795	81,000,000
4801	30,000,000
4803	40,000,000
4804	59,000,000
4805	26,000,000
4806	13,200,000
4807	60,000,000
4822-4823	81,000,000
4825-4844	100,000,000
4846	17,600,400
4847	50,000,000
4856	33,500,000
4862-4865	500,000,000
4866	30,000,000
4880	60,000,000
4882-4891	400,000,000
4892	20,000,000
4898-4905	60,000,000
4905b	900,000
4906	30,000,000
4907	35,000,000
4908-4909	100,000,000
4910-4911	10,800,000
4912-4915	100,000,000
4916	50,000,000
4917-4920	100,000,000
4921	30,000,000
4922-4926	20,000,000
4928-4935	80,000,000
4950-4951	50,000,000
4952	30,000,000
4955-4956	200,000,000
4957	17,600,400
4958	30,000,000
4968-4972	20,000,000
4978	45,000,000
4979	80,000,004
4980-4981	10,800,000
4982-4985	80,000,004
4986	50,000,000
4987	60,000,000
4988	30,000,000

Figure for No. 4988 includes Nos. 4822b and 4822c.

5003	20,000,000
5008	15,000,000
5009	100,000,000
5010-5011	12,000,000
5012	20,000,000
5019	60,000,000
5020	12,000,000
5036	150,000,000
5056	30,000,000
5057	15,000,000
5059	25,000,000
5060	22,000,000
5062-5063	9,600,000
5064	12,000,000
5065-5068	20,400,000
5069-5076	40,000,000
5077-5078	15,000,000
5079	18,000,000
5080	100,000,000
5091	30,000,000
5092	15,000,000
5093-5097	50,000,000
5100	12,000,000
5105	20,000,000
5132-5135	80,000,000
5141	15,000,000
5142	30,000,000
5149-5152	60,000,000
5153	15,000,000
5154	15,000,000
5155	250,000,000
5171	35,000,000
5173	17,600,000
5175	84,000,000
5179	20,000,000
5180-5189	100,000,000
5190	25,000,000
5192-5197	200,000,000
5199	500,000,000
5200	50,000,000
5202	12,000,000
5203-5210	80,000,000
5211	60,000,000
5212	2,100,000
5213-5222	60,000,000
5223-5227	40,000,000
5228-5232	60,000,000
5241	15,000,000
5242	2,000,000
5251	15,000,000
5252-5253	15,000,000
5253c	500,000
5254	15,000,000
5259	35,000,000
5264-5273	40,000,000
5274	25,000,000
5275	12,000,000
5276-5279	15,000,000
5281	7,500,000
5282	20,000,000
5283	20,000,000
5284	20,000,000
5298	3,000,000
5299	252,000,000
5300	20,000,000
5301-5305	20,000,000
5306	1,500,000
5307-5310	30,000,000
5312-5315	40,000,000
5316	60,000,000
5321-5330	100,000,000
5340	20,100,000
5349	40,000,000
5360	25,000,000
5371	40,000,000
5372-5376	30,000,000
5377	20,000,000
5378-5380	50,400,000
5381	60,000,000
5382-5391	20,000,000
5392	20,000,000
5393	40,000,000
5394	3,875,000
5395-5398	200,000,000
5414	12,000,000
5420-5423	40,000,000
5428	24,000,000
5432	40,000,000
5434	300,000,000
5455	25,000,000
5456	20,000,000
5459	175,000,000
5461-5470	50,000,000
5471-5474	16,000,000
5475-5479	35,000,000
5480-5483	20,000,000
5494-5503	50,000,000
5504-5513	18,000,000
5514-5518	14,000,000
5519-5522	200,000,000
5523	30,000,000
5524	25,000,000
5526-5529	450,000,000
5530	15,000,000
5531	15,000,000
5532-5541	400,000,000
5525	200,000,000
5542	20,000,000
5543	200,000,000
5555	45,000,000
5556	24,000,000
5557	18,000,000
5558-5567	600,000,000
5569-5572	200,000,000
5573-5582	60,000,000
5583-5592	25,000,000
5593	20,000,000
5594-5597	18,000,000
5598-5607	30,000,000
5608	25,000,000
5609-5613	18,000,000
5614	20,000,000
5615-5618	175,000,000
5619	10,000,000
5620	18,000,000
5621-5625	40,000,000
5626	18,000,000
5627-5634	25,600,000
5635	50,000,000
5636-5369	18,000,000
5640-5343	35,000,000
5644-5647	400,000,000
5648-5651	300,000,000
5660-5661	150,000,000
5662	24,000,000
5663	35,000,000
5668-5671	30,000,000
5676-5679	500,000,000
5683	20,000,000
5688-5692	18,000,000
5693	18,000,000
5694-5697	18,000,000
5698	40,000,000
5702	18,000,000
5703-5707	18,000,000
5708	22,000,000

AIR POST STAMPS

Scott No.	Quantity
C1	3,395,854
C2	3,793,887
C3	2,134,888
C4	6,414,576
C5	5,309,275
C6	5,285,775
C7	42,092,800
C8	15,597,307
C9	17,616,350
C10	20,379,179
C11	106,887,675
C12	97,641,200
C13	93,536
C14	72,428
C15	61,296
C16	57,340,050
C17	76,648,803
C18	324,070
C19	302,205,100
C20	10,205,400
C21	12,794,600
C22	9,285,300
C23	349,946,500
C24	19,768,150
C25	4,746,527,700
C26	1,744,878,650
C27	67,117,400
C28	78,434,800
C29	42,359,850
C30	59,880,850
C31	11,160,600
C32	864,753,100
C33	971,903,700
C34	207,976,550
C35	756,186,350
C36	132,956,100
C37	33,244,500
C38	38,449,100
C39	5,070,095,200
C40	75,085,000
C41	260,307,500
C42	21,061,300
C43	36,613,100
C44	16,217,100
C45	80,405,000
C46	18,876,800
C47	78,415,000
C48	50,483,977
C49	63,185,000
C50	72,480,000
C51	1,326,960,000
C52	157,035,000
C53	90,055,200
C54	79,290,000
C55	84,815,000
C56	38,770,000
C57	39,960,000
C58	98,160,000
C59	
C60	1,289,460,000
C61	87,140,000
C62	
C63	
C64	
C65	
C66	42,245,000
C67	
C68	63,890,000
C69	62,255,000
C70	55,710,000
C71	50,000,000
C72	
C73	
C74	60,000,000
C75	
C76	152,364,800
C77	
C78	
C79	
C80	
C81	
C82	
C83	
C84	78,210,000
C85	96,240,000
C86	58,705,000
C87	
C88	
C89	
C90	
C91-C92	
C93-C94	
C95-C96	
C97	
C101-C104	165,000,000
C105-C108	165,000,000
C109-C112	175,000,000
C113	98,600,000
C114	110,475,000
C115	167,625,000
C116	45,700,000
C117	22,975,000
C118	201,150,000

C119	111,550,000	*C132*	100,000,000	*C142*	100,000,000
C120	38,532,000	*C133*	100,750,000	*C143*	100,000,000
C121	39,325,000	*C134*	100,750,000	*C144*	70,000,000
C122-C125	106,360,000	*C135*	100,800,00	*C145*	100,000,000
C126	1,944,000	*C136*	85,000,000	*C146*	40,000,000
C127	48,000,000	*C137*	85,000,000	*C147*	100,000,000
C128	250,000,000	*C138*	100,000,000	*C148*	40,000,000
C129	182,400,000	*C139*	145,000,000	*C149*	30,000,000
C130	113,000,000	*C140*	100,000,000	*C150*	60,000,000
C131	15,260,000	*C141*	100,000,000		

CARRIERS' STAMPS

The term "Carriers' Stamps" is applied to certain stamps of the United States used to defray delivery to a post office on letters going to another post office, and for collection and delivery in the same city (local letters handled only by the carrier department). A less common usage was for a collection fee from the addressee at the post office ("drop letters"). During the period when these were in use, the ordinary postage fee defrayed the carriage of mail matter from post office to post office only.

In many of the larger cities the private ("Local") posts delivered mail to the post office or to an addressee in the city direct for a fee of 1 or 2 cents (seldom more), and adhesive stamps were often employed to indicate payment. (See introduction to "Local Stamps" section.)

Carrier service dates back at least to 1689 when the postmaster of Boston was instructed "to receive all letters and deliver them at 1d." In 1794, the law allowed a penny post to collect 2 cents for the delivery of a letter. As these early fees were paid in cash, little evidence survives.

In 1851 the Federal Government, under the acts of 1825 and 1836, began to deliver letters in many cities and so issued Carriers' stamps for local delivery service. This Act of Congress of March 3, 1851, effective July 1, 1851 (succeeding Act of 1836), provided for the collecting and delivering of letters to the post office by carriers, "for which not exceeding 1 or 2 cents shall be charged."

Carriers' stamps were issued under the authority of, or derived from, the postmaster general. The "General Issues" (Nos. LO1-LO2) were general issues of which No. LO2 was valid for postage at face value, and No. LO1 at the value set upon sale, in any post office. They were issued under the direct authority of the postmaster general. The "City Carrier Department" were valid in the city in which they were issued either directly by or sanctioned by the local postmaster under authority derived from the postmaster general.

These "General" and "City Carrier Department" Carriers' stamps prepaid the fees of official letter carriers who were appointed by the postmaster general and were under heavy bond to the United States for the faithful performance of their duties. Some of the letter carriers received fixed salaries from the government. Others were paid from the fees received for the delivery and collection of letters carried by them. After discontinuance of carrier fees on June 30, 1863, all carriers of the United States Post Office were government employees, paid by salary at a yearly rate.

Some Carriers' stamps are often found on cover with the regular government stamps and have the official post office cancellation applied to them as well. Honour's City Express and the other Charleston, S.C., Carrier stamps almost always have the stamp uncanceled or canceled with pen, or less frequently pencil.

Unless indicated otherwise, values for Carriers' stamps on cover are for covers having the stamp tied by a handstamped cancellation. Carriers' stamps, either uncanceled or pen-canceled, **on covers to which they apparently belong**, also are valued where possible. For covers with stamps canceled by pen or pencil with initials or name of carrier, as sometimes seen on No. LO2 from Washington, and on Baltimore carrier stamps, the premium is 75% of the on-cover value.

All Carriers' stamps are imperforate and on wove paper, either white or colored through, unless otherwise stated.

Counterfeits exist of many Carriers' stamps.

GENERAL ISSUE CARRIER STAMPS

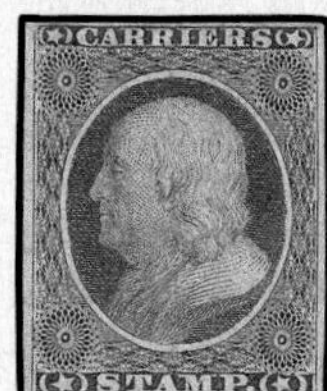

Franklin — OC1

Engraved and printed by Toppan, Carpenter, Casilear & Co. Plate of 200 subjects divided into two panes of 100 each, one left, one right

1851, Sept. Engr. Unwmk. *Imperf.*

LO1 OC1 (1c) **dull blue** (shades), *rose*	*7,000.*	*8,000.*
On cover from Philadelphia		*17,500.*
On cover from New York		*30,000.*
On cover from New Orleans with 3c #10 (a 2nd #LO1 removed)		*30,000.*
Pair	*18,000.*	*18,000.*
Strip of 3	*26,500.*	*26,000.*
Major plate crack	—	
Major plate crack, on cover		*50,000.*
Corner plate cracks (91L)	—	—
Double transfer	—	—
Double transfer, on cover		*30,000.*

Earliest documented use: Oct. 28, 1851.

Cancellations

Red star (Philadelphia)	*8,000.*
Blue town (Philadelphia)	+1,000.
Red town (New York)	+1,000.
Black town (New York), unique	+4,000.
Blue grid (New York)	—
Black grid (New York)	—
Black grid (New Orleans)	+6,000.
Green grid (New Orleans)	—

Of the entire issue of 310,000 stamps, 250,000 were sent to New York, 50,000 to New Orleans, 10,000 to Philadelphia. However, the quantity sent to each city is not indicative of proportionate use. More appear to have been used in Philadelphia than in the other two cities. The use in all three cities was notably limited.

No. LO1, major plate crack on cover, is unique. The double transfer on cover also is unique, as is the unused pair.

U.S.P.O. Despatch

Eagle — OC2

Engraved and printed by Toppan, Carpenter, Casilear & Co. Plate of 200 subjects divided into two panes of 100 each, one upper, one lower

1851, Nov. 17 Unwmk. *Imperf.*

LO2 OC2 1c **blue** (shades)	50.00	*80.00*
On cover, used alone		500.00
On cover, precanceled		600.00
On cover, pair or 2 singles		*1,500.*
On cover with 1c #9		*8,500.*
On cover with three 1c #9		*4,500.*
On cover with 3c #11		400.
On cover, tied, with 3c #11A		500.
On cover with 3c #25		—
On cover with 3c #26		*600.*
On cover with strip of 3, 3c #26		—
On cover with 5c #30A and 10c #32		*33,000.*
On cover, tied by town handstamp, with 3c #65 (Washington, D.C.)		*4,500.*
On 3c envelope #U1, #LO2 pen canceled		—
On 3c envelope #U2, tied by handstamp		—
On 3c envelope #U2, #LO2 pen canceled		—
On 3c envelope #U10, not canceled, with certicate		*500.00*
Pair	110.00	*400.00*
Pair on cover (Cincinnati)		*1,250.*
Block of 4	300.00	
Margin block of 8, imprint	*850.00*	
Double transfer	—	—
Double transfer on cover		—

Earliest documented use: Jan. 3, 1852.

Cancellations

Red star	*80.*
Philadelphia	+50.
Cincinnati	+200.
Black grid	—
Blue grid	+300.
Red grid	+300.
Black town	+5.
Blue town	+100.
Red town	+300.
Kensington, Pa. (red)	—
Kensington, Pa. red "3c"	—
Washington, D.C.	+1,000.
Blue squared target	—
Red squared target	—
Railroad	—
Black carrier (Type C32)	—
Red carrier (Type C32)	—
Carrier's initial, manuscript	—

Used principally in Philadelphia, Cincinnati, Washington, D.C., and Kensington, Pa.

GOVERNMENT REPRINTS

Printed by the Continental Bank Note Co. (first and second printings) and American Bank Note Co. (third printing).

First reprinting-10,000 stamps of each design, on May 19, 1875 (all sold).

Second reprinting-10,000 stamps of each design, on Dec. 22, 1875 (all sold).

Third reprinting of Franklin stamp - 1881 (2,110 sold).

Third reprinting of Eagle stamp - 1881 (9,680 sold).

The first reprinting of the Franklin stamp was on the rose paper of the original, obtained from Toppan, Carpenter, Casilear & Co. Two batches of ink were used, both darker than the original. The second reprinting was on rose paper using ink that fluoresces green. The third reprinting was on much thicker, paler paper in an indigo color. All of these differ under ultraviolet light. The design of the reprints is not as distinct as the original design and may appear a bit "muddy" in the lathework above the vignette.

The first two reprintings of 10,000 each of the Eagle stamp are on the same hard white paper used for special printings of the postage issue. Stamps from the second reprinting were printed with ink that fluoresces green. Stamps from the third reprinting are on thick wove paper using ink that does not fluoresce. Reprints may be differentiated from the originals under ultraviolet light by the whiteness of the paper. Nos. LO3-LO6 are ungummed, Nos. LO1-LO2 have brown gum. No. LO1 was printed on a somewhat yellowish paper.

Franklin Reprints

1875 *Imperf.*

LO3 OC1 (1c) **blue**, *rose*	60.
indigo, *rose*	80.
Block of 4	225.
Margin block of 4, imprint	—

Corner plate cracks (91L) 100.
Short transfer —

Perf. 12

LO4 OC1 (1c) **blue** *16,000.*
Pair *35,000.*

No. LO4 is valued in the grade of average to fine.

Eagle Reprints

Imperf.

LO5 OC2 1c **blue** 25.
Block of 4 125.
Margin block of 8, imprint & Pl.# —

Perf. 12

LO6 OC2 1c **blue** 175.
Block of 4 1,000.
Margin block of 8, imprint & Pl.# *12,500.*

No. LO6 is valued with the perfs cutting slightly into the design.

CITY CARRIER DEPARTMENT STAMPS

All are imperforate.

Baltimore, Md.

C1

1850-55 Typo. Settings of 10 (2x5) varieties

1LB1 C1 1c **red** (shades), *bluish* 180. 160.
On cover, tied by handstamp *1,000.*
On cover with 1c #9 —
On cover (tied) with 3c #11 *500.*
On cover (tied) with 3c #11A *500.*

1LB2 C1 1c **blue** (shades), *bluish* 200. 150.
On cover, tied *1,000.*
On cover (tied) with 3c #11 *500.*
On cover, uncanceled, with 3c #11A *225.*
a. Bluish laid paper — —

1LB3 C1 1c **blue** (shades) 160. 100.
On cover, tied by handstamp *1,500.*
On cover, tied by ms. *250.*
Block of 4 *1,000.*
a. Laid paper 200. 150.
On cover, tied by handstamp *1,000.*
b. Block of 14 containing three tete-beche gutter pairs (unique) *6,250.*

1LB4 C1 1c **green** — 1,000.
On cover, tied by handstamp *5,000.*
On cover, not tied *1,200.*
On cover with 1c #7, tied by handstamp *2,250.*
On cover, not tied, with 3c #10A *2,000.*
On cover with 3c #11, ms. tied —
On 3c envelope #U10 *3,500.*
Pair *5,000.*

1LB5 C1 1c **red** 2,250. 1,750.
On cover, tied by handstamp *4,500.*
On cover, not tied *3,000.*
On cover (tied) with 3c #10 or 10A *5,000.*

The No. 1LB4 pair is the unique multiple of this stamp.

Cancellations on Nos. 1LB1-1LB5:

Black grid —
Blue grid —
Black cross —
Black town —
Blue town +100.
Black numeral —
Blue numeral —
Black pen —

C2

1856 Typo.

1LB6 C2 1c **blue** (shades) 130. 90.
On cover 400.
On cover with 3c #11 or 11A *1,000.*
On cover with 3c #25 (both tied) *1,350.*
On cover with 3c #26 *1,250.*
On cover with 3c #26A —

1LB7 C2 1c **red** (shades) 130. 90.
On cover *300.*
On cover (tied) with 3c #25 *350.*
On cover (tied) with 3c #26 *350.*
On 3c envelope #U9, tied *300.*
On 3c envelope #U10, tied *350.*
Block of 4 *850.*

C3

The sheet consisted of at least four panes of 10 placed horizontally, the two center panes tete beche. This makes possible five horizontal tete beche gutter pairs.

Plate of 10 (2x5); 10 Varieties

1857 Typo.

1LB8 C3 1c **black** (shades) 65. 50.
On cover, tied by handstamp *125.*
On cover, tied by handstamp, to Germany *3,750.*
On cover (tied) with 3c #26 225.
On 3c envelope #U9, tied *225.*
On 3c envelope #U10 *225.*
On 3c envelope #U27, tied *250.*
Strip of 3 (not tied), on cover *4,000.*
Block of 4 275.
Pane of 10 *1,000.*
Tete beche gutter pair *650.*
a. "SENT," Pos. 7 100. 75.
On cover, tied by handstamp *175.*
On cover (tied) with 3c #26 *250.*
On 3c envelope #U9, tied *250.*
On 3c envelope #U10, tied *250.*
b. Short rays, Pos. 2 100. 75.
On cover (tied) with 3c #26 *600.*
c. "ONS," Pos. 5 — —
d. "ONS" and "SENTS," late state Pos. 7, on cover —

Cancellations

Black pen (or pencil) 20.00
Blue town +2.50
Black town +2.50
Black Steamship —

1LB9 C3 1c **red** (shades) 100. 90.
On cover *175.*
On cover (tied) with 3c #26 *300.*
On 3c envelope #U9 *325.*
On 3c envelope #U10 *325.*
Block of 6 *2,750.*
a. "SENT," Pos. 7 140. 110.
On cover (tied) with 3c #26 *500.*
b. Short rays, Pos. 2 140. 110.
c. As "b," double impression *800.*

The block of 6 of No. 1LB9 is the only recorded multiple of this stamp.

Cancellations on Nos. 1LB6-1LB7, 1LB9:

Black town —
Blue town —
Blue numeral —
Black pen —
Carrier's initial, manuscript +25.

Boston, Mass.

C6

Several Varieties

1849-50 Pelure Paper Typeset

3LB1 C6 1c **blue** 375. 180.
On cover, tied by handstamp 300.
On cover, uncanceled 150.
On cover with 5c #1 *4,500.*
On cover with two 5c #1 *8,750.*
On cover with 3c #10 *450.*
a. Wrong ornament at left *400.*
On cover, not tied, with certificate —

Cancellations

Red town —
Red grid —
Black ornate double oval —
Black "Penny Post Paid" in 3-bar circle —

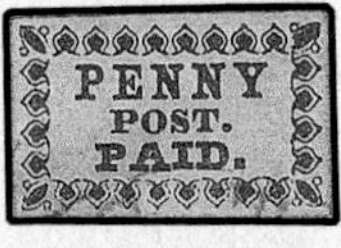

C7

Several Varieties

1851 Wove Paper Colored Through Typeset

3LB2 C7 1c **blue** (shades), *slate* 190. 100.
On cover 220.
On cover with 5c #1 *12,500.*
On cover with 3c #10 500.
On cover with 3c #11A 325.
On 3c envelope #U2, #U5 or #U9 350.
Tete beche gutter pair *600.*

Cancellations on Nos. 3LB2:

Black small fancy circle —
Black diamond grid +100.
Red town —
Black grid —
Black PAID —
Black crayon —
Red small fancy circle +50.
Red diamond grid +100.
Black railroad —
Black hollow star —
Black pencil —
Red crayon —
Black "Penny Post Paid" in 3-bar circle —
Red "Penny Post Paid" in 3-bar circle —

Charleston, S. C.

John H. Honour was appointed a letter carrier at Charleston, in 1849, and engaged his brother-in-law, E. J. Kingman, to assist him. They separated in 1851, dividing the carrier business of the city between them. At the same time Kingman was appointed a letter carrier. In March, 1858, Kingman retired, being replaced by Joseph G. Martin. In the summer of 1858, John F. Steinmeyer, Jr., was added to the carrier force. When Honour retired in 1860, John C. Beckman was appointed in his place.

Each of these carriers had stamps prepared. These stamps were sold by the carriers. The Federal Government apparently encouraged their use.

Honour's City Express

C8

1849 Typo. Wove Paper Colored Through

4LB1 C8 2c **black,** *brown rose* *10,000.*
Cut to shape *4,000.* *4,000.*
On cover, not canceled, with certificate *17,000.*
On cover, cut to shape, tied, with 10c #2 *40,000.*

4LB2 C8 2c **black,** *yellow,* cut to shape —
On cover, not tied, with certificate *12,500.*
On cover, cut to shape, uncanceled —
On cover, rectangular-cut, tied, with 10c #2 —

Cancellations on Nos. 4LB1-4LB2: Red grid, red town, red crayon.

No. 4LB1 unused is a unique uncanceled stamp on piece. The used cut-to-shape stamp is also unique. Additionally, each of the listed covers bearing No. 4LB1 is unique.

Four examples of No. 4LB2 are recorded, each listing above being unique.

4LB2A C8 2c **black,** *bluish gray,* on cover, cut to shape —

No. 4LB2A is unique.

C10

1854 Wove Paper Typeset

4LB3 C10 2c **black** *1,500.*
On cover, tied by pen cancel *3,000.*
On cover with 3c #11 or 11A, tied *4,000.*
On cover with 3c #11 or 11A, not tied *3,250.*

Cancellations

Black town —
Blue town —
Black pen —
Black pencil —
Brown "PAID" —
Initial "H" —

HONOUR'S CITY POST. 2 Cents.

C11

Several Varieties

1849-50 Typeset

Wove Paper Colored Through

4LB5 C11 2c **black,** *bluish,* pelure *750.* *500.*
On cover (not tied) *3,250.*
On cover with pair 5c #1b —
On cover with two 5c #1b —
On cover (tied) with 3c #11 or 11A *4,500.*
a. "Ceuts" *5,750.*

4LB7 C11 2c **black**, *yellow* 750. 1,000.
On cover, tied by handstamp *9,000.*
On cover, not canceled *2,000.*
a. "Ccnts," ms. tied on cover *14,500.*

No. 4LB5a is unique. It is without gum and is valued thus. No. 4LB7a also is unique.

The varieties of type C11 on bluish wove (thicker) paper and pink, pelure paper are not believed genuine.

Cancellation Nos. 4LB5, 4LB7:

Red town —
Black pen —
Red pen —
Red crayon —

C13

C14

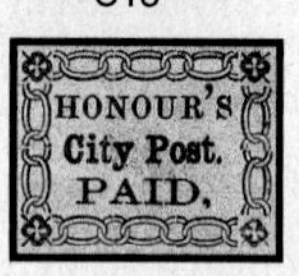
C15

Several varieties of each type

1851-58 **Typeset**

Wove Paper Colored Through

4LB8 C13 2c **black**, *bluish* 350. 175.
On cover, tied by handstamp *700.*
On cover, not tied *300.*
On cover with 10c #2 *5,500.*
On cover, tied, with 3c #10 *1,500.*
On cover, tied, with 3c #11 or 11A *1,500.*
On cover, tied, with 3c #26 *1,500.*
Pair *1,500.*
a. Period after "PAID" 500. 250.
On cover *650.*
On cover, ms. tied, with 5c #1, tied *19,000.*
On cover, ms. tied, with 3c #11 or 11A *750.*
b. "Cens" 700. 900.
On cover, ms. tied, with 3c #11 or 11A *3,250.*
c. "Conours" and "Bents" —

The No. 4LB8 with No. 2 combination cover is unique. It is a cover front only and is valued thus.

No. 4LB8a on cover with 5c No. 1 is unique.

4LB9 C13 2c **black**, *bluish*, pelure *850.* 950.
4LB10 C13 2c **black**, *pink*, pelure, on cover *7,000.*
4LB11 C14 (2c) **black**, *bluish* — 375.
On cover, tied by handstamp, with 3c #11 or 11A *7,750.*
On cover, ms. tied, with 3c #11 or 11A *3,000.*
On 3c envelope #U10, tied *1,500.*
On cover, tied, to foreign destination (Ireland), unique *25,000.*
4LB12 C14 (2c) **black**, *bluish*, pelure — —
4LB13 C15 (2c) **black**, *bluish* ('58) 750. 400.
On cover with 3c #11, Aiken, S.C. postmark, tied by handstamp (unique) *6,500.*
On cover with 3c #26, tied by pen cancel *4,500.*
On cover with 3c #26, tied by handstamp cancel *3,750.*
Horiz. pair *3,500.*
a. Comma after "PAID" *1,100.*
b. No period after "Post" *1,400.*

The pair of No. 4LB13 is the unique multiple of this stamp.

A 2c of design C13 exists on pink pelure paper. It is believed not to have been issued by the post, but to have been created later and perhaps accidentally.

Cancellations on Nos. 4LB8-4LB13

Black town —
Blue town —
Red town —
Black pen —
Black pencil —
Red crayon —
Brown cork initial "H"

Kingman's City Post

C16

C17

Several varieties of each

Wove Paper Colored Through

1851(?)-58(?) **Typeset**

4LB14 C16 2c **black**, *bluish* 1,400. 900.
Vert. pair, ms. tied, on Valentine cover *6,000.*
On cover with 3c #11 *7,000.*
On cover with 3c #26 *6,000.*
a. "Kingman's" erased *5,000.*

4LB15 C17 2c **black**, *bluish* 800. 800.
On cover —
Vertical pair —
Horiz. pair, not tied, on Valentine cover *8,750.*
Vertical strip of 3 uncanceled, on cover *22,500.*
a. "Kingman's" erased, on cover with 3c #11, tied by pen cancel (unique) *4,500.*

The No. 4LB14 pair on cover is the only recorded multiple of this stamp.

The 4LB15 pair and strip of 3 actually are uncanceled on covers and are valued thus. The horiz. pair on cover is ms. canceled.

Cancellations on Nos. 4LB14-4LB15: Black town, black pen.

Martin's City Post

C18

Several Varieties

1858 **Wove Paper Colored Through** **Typeset**

4LB16 C18 2c **black**, *bluish* *8,000.*

Beckman's City Post

C19

1860

4LB17 C19 2c **black**, on cover —

No. 4LB17 is unique. It is on cover with 3c No. 26, both tied by black circle townmark: "CHARLESTON, S.C. JUN 18, 1860".

Steinmeyer's City Post

C19a

C20

Several varieties of Type C19

Type C20 printed from plate of 10 (2x5) varieties

1859 **Wove Paper Colored Through** **Typeset**

4LB18 C19a 2c **black**, *bluish* *21,000.*
On cover, uncanceled —
4LB19 C20 2c **black**, *bluish* *4,500.* —
4LB20 C20 2c **black**, *pink* 200. —
Block of 4 850.
Sheet of 10 2,250.
4LB21 C20 2c **black**, *yellow* 200.
Block of 4 850.
Sheet of 10 *2,250.*

Sheets of 10 of Nos. 4LB20-4LB21 exist signed by J.F. Steinmeyer Jr. These sell for about 50% more than the unsigned sheets.

Two examples of No. 4LB18 are known on cover, both uncanceled.

Cancellation on Nos. 4LB19-4LB21: Black pen.

Cincinnati, Ohio

Williams' City Post

Organized by C. C. Williams, who was appointed and commissioned by the Postmaster General.

C20a

1854 **Wove Paper** **Litho.**

9LB1 C20a 2c **brown** — *4,000.*
On cover, tied by handstamp *13,500.*
On cover, tied by pen cancel *4,500.*
On cover with 1c #9 *7,500.*
Pair *6,000.*

Cancellations

Red squared target —
Black pen —
Blue company circle —

Frazer & Co.

Local stamps of designs L146-L147 were carrier stamps when used on cover between Feb. 3, 1848 and June 30, 1849.

Cleveland, Ohio

Bishop's City Post

Organized by Henry S. Bishop, "Penny Postman" who was appointed and commissioned by the Postmaster General.

C20b

C20c

1854 **Wove Paper** **Litho.**

10LB1 C20b **blue** *5,000.* *4,000.*
On cover, tied by handstamp *15,000.*
Pair on cover, canceled by pencil, with 3c #11, with certificate *7,500.*

Vertically Laid Paper

10LB2 C20c 2c **black**, *bluish* *4,000.* *6,000.*
On cover —
Pair —
Pair on cover, canceled by pencil, with 3c #11 *14,000.*

Cancellations on #10LB1-10LB2

Red town —
Red boxed numeral —
Black pencil —
Black pen —

No. 10LB2 unused is unique. It is cut in at bottom and without gum, and is valued thus.

Louisville, Ky.
Wharton's U.S.P.O. Despatch

Carrier Service was first established by the Louisville Post Office about 1854, with one carrier. David B. Wharton, appointed a carrier in 1856, issued an adhesive stamp in 1857, but as he was soon thereafter replaced in the service, it is believed that few, if any, of these stamps were used. Brown & McGill, carriers who succeeded Wharton, issued stamps in April, 1858.

C21

Sheet of 50 subjects in two panes of 25 (5x5) each, one upper, one lower

1857 **Lithographed by Robyn & Co.**

5LB1 C21 (2c) **bluish green** (shades) 125.
Block of 4 *650.*
Pane of 25 *3,250.*
Sheet of 50 *7,000.*

Brown & McGill's U. S. P. O. Despatch

C22

1858, Nov.-1860 **Litho. by Hart & Maypother**

5LB2 C22 (2c) **blue** (shades) 250. *750.*
On cover, not tied, with 3c #26 *750.*
On cover with 3c #26, tied by handstamp *6,250.*
Block of 4 *1,250.*

1858, Feb.-Aug.

5LB3 C22 (2c) **black** *4,500.* *15,000.*
On cover, not tied, with 3c #26 *17,500.*

The value for No. 5LB3 used refers to the finer of the two known used (canceled) examples; it is extremely fine and on a piece with a 3c #26.

Cancellations on Nos. 5LB2-5LB3: Blue town, black pencil.

New York, N. Y.

United States City Despatch Post

By an order made on August 1, 1842, the Postmaster General established a carrier service in New York known as the "United States City Despatch Post." Local delivery service had been authorized by the Act of Congress of July 2, 1836.

Greig's City Despatch Post was sold to the U. S. P. O. Department and on August 16, 1842, began operation as the "United States City Despatch Post" under the superintendence of Alexander M. Greig who was appointed a U. S. letter carrier for that purpose.

The Greig circular introducing this service stated that letter boxes had been placed throughout the city, that letters might be sent prepaid or collect, and that registry service was available for an extra 3 cents.

The City Despatch Post stamps were accepted for the service of the United States City Despatch Post. The stamps thus used bear the cancellation of the New York Post Office, usually "U.S." in an octagon which served to indicate that the carrier service was now a government operation (no longer a private local post) as well as a cancellation.

C23

Engraved and printed by Rawdon, Wright & Hatch.

Plate of 42 (6x7) subjects

Wove Paper Colored Through

1842		Engr.	
6LB1	C23 3c **black**, *grayish*	*2,000.*	
	On cover, tied by handstamp	*12,000.*	
	On cover, not tied	*10,000.*	
	On cover, not tied, with Aug. 16 (1842) cancel, First day of government carrier service	*100,000.*	

Cancellations

Red "U.S" in octagon	*2,000.*
Red circle "U.S. City Despatch Post"	—
Red town	—

Used examples that do not bear the official cancellation of the New York Post Office and unused examples are classed as Local stamps. See No. 40L1.

Some examples are canceled by a circular date stamp reading "U.S. CITY DESPATCH POST" or, infrequently, a New York town postmark. When canceled "FREE" in frame they were used as local stamps. See No. 40L1 in Locals section.

No. 6LB3 was the first stamp issued by authority of the U.S.P.O. Department. The 3c denomination included 1 cent in lieu of drop letter postage until June 30, 1845, and the maximum legal carrier fee of 2 cents. Service was discontinued late in November, 1846.

C24

Wove Paper (unsurfaced) Colored Through

Engraved plate of 50 in two panes of 25

1842-45			
6LB2	C24 3c **black**, *rosy buff*	*5,000.*	
6LB3	C24 3c **black**, *light blue*	*1,500.*	750.
	On cover, tied by handstamp		*2,500.*
	On cover, not tied		*1,000.*
	Pair	*5,000.*	
	Double transfer		*1,000.*
6LB4	C24 3c **black**, *green*	*11,500.*	
a.	3c **black**, *apple green*		—

Some authorities consider No. 6LB2 to be an essay, and No. 6LB4 a color changeling. No. 6LB2 unused is valued without gum.

Glazed Paper, Surface Colored

6LB5	C24 3c **black**, *blue green* (shades)	200.	175.
	On cover, tied by handstamp		600.
	Five on cover		*20,000.*
	On cover, tied by ink smear, with 5c #9X1d, also tied		*28,500.*
	Pair	—	400.
	Strip of 3		*650.*
	Strip of 4		800.
	Strip of 5		—
	Ribbed paper	—	—
	Double transfer		—
a.	Double impression		*1,500.*
	On cover		4,500.
b.	3c **black**, *blue*	650.	*300.*
	On cover		*750.*
	Strip of 3 + single on cover		*14,000.*
	Strip of 3	*2,500.*	—
	Block of 12	*40,000.*	—
	Ribbed paper	—	
c.	As "b," double impression		*1,000.*
d.	3c **black**, *green*	*1,250.*	750.
	black, *apple green*		*2,000.*
	Pair		*2,750.*
	On cover		*1,250.*
	Five examples on cover		*45,000.*
e.	As "d," double impression	—	
	On cover		—

Cancellations

Red curved PAID	—
Red "U.S City Despatch Post"	—
Red "U.S" in octagon	—
Red New York	—
Red double line circle "U.S. City Despatch Post"	—

No. 6LB5 also is known on cover front only with No. 9X1, to Europe.

6LB6	C24 3c **black**, *pink*, on cover front	*14,500.*

No. 6LB6 is unique.

No. 6LB5 Surcharged in Red

1846		
6LB7	C24 2c on 3c **black**, *bluish green*	*14,000.*
	On cover, not tied, with certificate	*70,000.*

The City Dispatch 2c red formerly listed as No. 6LB8 is now listed under Local Stamps as No. 160L1.

U.S. MAIL

C27

Issued by the Postmaster at New York, N.Y.

1849 Wove Paper, Colored Through — Typo.

6LB9	C27 1c **black**, *rose*	100.	100.
	On cover, tied by handstamp		*350.*
	On cover with 5c #1, both stamps tied		*2,000.*
	Pair	*250.*	
	Block of 4	*600.*	

1849-50 Glazed Surface Paper

6LB10	C27 1c **black**, *yellow*	100.	100.
	On cover, tied by handstamp		*350.*
	On cover with 5c #1, both stamps tied		*1,500.*
	Pair	*250.*	
	Block of 4	*600.*	
6LB11	C27 1c **black**, *buff*	100.	100.
	On cover		*250.*
	On cover, not tied, with 5c #1, with certificate		*3,000.*
a.	Pair, one stamp sideways	*2,850.*	

Cancellations on #6LB9-6LB11

Red town	—
Red grid	—
Red "PAID"	+50.
Black numeral in circle	—
Red "N.Y. U.S. CITY MAIL" in circle	+150.
Black pen	—
Black pencil	—

Philadelphia, Pa.

C28

Several Varieties

Thick Wove Paper Colored Through

1849-50		Typeset	
7LB1	C28 1c **black**, *rose* (with "L P")	450.	
	On cover, tied by handstamp		*3,500.*
	On cover, not canceled		*2,000.*
	On cover with 5c #1 or 1a		*6,000.*
7LB2	C28 1c **black**, *rose* (with "S")	*3,000.*	
	On cover, not canceled		*4,500.*
	On cover, not canceled, with 2 5c #1 (unique)		*7,000.*
7LB3	C28 1c **black**, *rose* (with "H")	275.	
	On cover, tied by handstamp		*3,250.*
	On cover, not canceled		*1,000.*
	On cover with 5c #1		*3,500.*
	On cover, not canceled, with 5c #1b		*2,750.*
7LB4	C28 1c **black**, *rose* (with "L S")	400.	*500.*
	On cover, not canceled		*2,000.*
	On cover, not canceled, with 5c #1 (unique)		*2,500.*
7LB5	C28 1c **black**, *rose* (with "J J")		*7,500.*
	On cover, not canceled, with 5c #1 (unique)		*60,000.*

The used No. 7LB5 also is unique and is an uncanceled stamp on a cover front.

C29

Several Varieties

7LB6	C29 1c **black**, *rose*	300.	250.
	On cover, tied by handstamp		*2,500.*
	On cover, uncanceled		*500.*
7LB7	C29 1c **black**, *blue*, glazed	*1,000.*	
	On cover, tied by handstamp		*6,500.*
	On cover, uncanceled		*1,250.*
	On cover, uncanceled, with 5c #1		*3,500.*
7LB8	C29 1c **black**, *vermilion*, glazed	*700.*	
	On cover, tied by handstamp		*1,500.*
	On cover, uncanceled		*900.*
	On cover, uncanceled, with 5c dark brown #1a		*12,500.*
	On cover, uncanceled, with 5c orange brown #1b		*21,000.*
7LB9	C29 1c **black**, *yellow*, glazed	*2,750.*	*2,250.*
	On cover, not canceled		*4,000.*
	On cover, uncanceled, with 3c #10		*2,000.*

Cancellations on Nos. 7LB1-7LB9: Normally these stamps were left uncanceled on the letter, but occasionally were accidentally tied by the Philadelphia town postmark which was normally struck in blue ink.

A 1c black on buff (unglazed) of type C29 is believed to be a color changeling.

C30

Settings of 25 (5x5) varieties (Five basic types)

1850-52		Litho.	
7LB11	C30 1c **gold**, *black*, glazed	175.	110.
	On cover, tied by handstamp		*550.*
	On cover, uncanceled		*325.*
	On cover (tied) with 5c #1		*3,500.*
	On cover (tied) with 3c #10		*800.*
	On cover (uncanceled) with 3c #10		*250.*
	On cover, not tied, with 3c #11		*250.*
	On cover, tied, with 3c #11A		*1,000.*
	Block of 19	*8,250.*	
7LB12	C30 1c **blue**	400.	275.
	On cover, tied by handstamp		*2,500.*
	On cover, not tied		*750.*
	On cover (tied) with 3c #10		*2,250.*
	On cover (tied) with 3c #11		*1,750.*
	Pair		1,600.
7LB13	C30 1c **black**	*750.*	550.
	On cover, tied by handstamp		*2,500.*
	On cover, uncanceled		*1,250.*
	On cover (tied) with 3c #10		—
	On cover (not tied) with 3c #11		*2,750.*
	On cover (tied) with 3c #11A		*3,250.*

Cancellations on #7LB11-7LB13

Red star	—
Red town	—
Blue town	—

C31

Handstamped

7LB14 C31 1c **blue,** *buff* 3,250.

No. 7LB14 was handstamped on coarse dark buff paper on which rectangles in the approximate size of the type C31 handstamp had been ruled in pencil. The stamps so produced were later cut out and show traces of the adjoining handstamp markings as well as parts of the penciled rectangle. Some uncanceled examples exist on covers.

1855(?)

7LB16 C31 1c **black** *5,000.*
On cover with strip of 3, 1c #9 25,000.
On cover with 3c 1851 stamp removed, tied by handstamp *7,000.*

C32

1856(?) **Handstamped**

7LB18 C32 1c **black** *1,250.* *2,000.*
Paper showing blue plate imprint *4,000.*
On cover (cut diamond-shaped) with pair 1c #7 and single 1c #9 —
On cover with strip of 3, 1c #7 *17,000.*
On cover with 3c #11 *9,500.*
On 3c envelope #U5 —
On 3c envelope #U10, not canceled *9,000.*

Cancellations on #7LB16, 7LB18

Black circled grid —
Black town —

Nos. 7LB16 and 7LB18 were handstamped on the sheet margins of U.S. 1851 1c stamps, cut out and used as adhesives. The paper therefore has some surface bluing, and some stamps show parts of the plate imprint.

Values are for stamps cut square unless otherwise mentioned.

ENVELOPES

Handstamps of types C31 and C32 were also used to make stamped envelopes and letter sheets or circulars. These same types were also used as postmarks or cancellations in the same period.

A handstamp similar to C32, but with "U. S. P. O. DESPATCH" in serif capitals, is believed to have been used only as a postmark.

Type C31 exists struck in blue or red, type C32 in blue, black or red. When found on cover, on various papers, struck alone, they are probably postmarks and not prepaid stamped envelopes. As such, these entire covers, depending upon the clarity of the handstamp and the general attractiveness of the letter are valued between $400 and $800.

When found on envelopes with the Carrier stamp canceled by a handstamp (such as type C31 struck in blue on a buff envelope canceled by the red solid star cancellation) they can be regarded as probably having been sold as prepaid envelopes. Value approximately $3,000.

P. O. PAID
1 Cent.

Labels of these designs are believed by most specialists not to be carrier stamps. Those seen are uncanceled, either off cover or affixed to stampless covers of the early 1850s. Some students believe they should be given carrier status.

St. Louis, Mo.

C36

C37

Illustrations enlarged to show details of the two types (note upper corners especially). Sizes of actual designs are 17 1/2x22mm.

1849 **White Wove Paper** **Litho.**
Two Types

8LB1 C36 2c **black** *7,000.* *3,000.*
8LB2 C37 2c **black** *6,000.* —

Cancellation on Nos. 8LB1-8LB2: Black town.

C38

1857 **Litho.**

8LB3 C38 2c **blue** *22,500.*
On cover, tied by handstamp *55,000.*
On Valentine cover, ms. cancel, not tied *35,000.*

The used example off cover is unique. Five covers are recorded.

Cancellations on No. 8LB3: Black boxed "1ct," "Paid" in arc, black pen.

LOCAL STAMPS

This listing of Local stamps includes stamps issued by Local Posts (city delivery), Independent Mail Routes and Services, Express Companies and other private posts which competed with, or supplemented, official services.

The Independent Mail Routes began using stamps early in 1844 and were put out of business by an Act of March, 1845, which became effective July 1, 1845. By this Act, the Government reduced the zones to two, reduced the rates to 5c and 10c and applied them to weight instead of the number of sheets of paper which composed a letter.

Most of the Local Posts still in business were forced to discontinue service by an Act of 1861, except Boyd's and Hussey's which were able to continue about 20 years longer because of the particular nature of their business. Other posts appeared illegally and sporadically after 1861 and were quickly suppressed.

City posts generally charged 1c to deliver a letter to the Post Office (usually the letter bore a government stamp as well) and 2c for intracity delivery (such letters naturally bore only local stamps). These usages are not catalogued separately because the value of a cover is determined as much by its attractiveness as its franking, rarity being the basic criterion.

Only a few Local Posts used special handstamps for canceling. The stamps frequently were left uncanceled, were canceled by pen, or less often by pencil. **Unless indicated otherwise, values for stamps on cover are for covers having the stamp tied by a handstamped cancellation, either private or governmental.** Local stamps, either uncanceled or pen canceled, **on covers to which they apparently belong**, also are valued where possible.

The absence of any specific cancellation listed indicates that no company handstamp is known so used, and that the canceling, if any, was done by pen, pencil or government handstamp. Local stamps used on letters directed out of town (and consequently bearing government stamps) sometimes, because of their position, are tied together with the government stamp by the cancellation used to cancel the latter.

Values for envelopes are for entires unless specifically mentioned.

All Local stamps are imperforate and on wove paper, either white or colored through, unless otherwise stated.

Counterfeits exist of many Local stamps, but most of these are crude reproductions and would deceive only the novice.

Adams & Co.'s Express, California

This post started in September, 1849, operating only on the Pacific Coast.

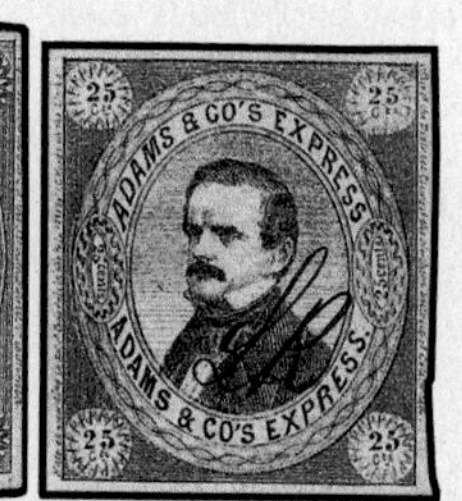

D. H. Haskell, Manager

L1 L2

Nos. 1L2-1L5 Printed in Sheets of 40 (8x5)

1854 **Litho.**

1L1 L1 25c **black,** *blue* *2,750.* —
On cover —
1L2 L2 25c **black** (initials in black) 75.00 —
Block of 4 375.00
Sheet of 40 —
a. Initials in red —
b. Without initials —

Cancellation (1L1-1L2): Black Express Co.

Nos. 1L1-1L2 were the earliest adhesive franks issued west of the Mississippi River.

No. 1L2 usually bear manuscript control markings "LR" for Louis Reed or less commonly "ICW" for Isaiah C. Wood.

Glazed Surface Cardboard

1L3 L2 25c **black,** *pink* 30.00
Block of 4 160.00
Sheet of 40 2,000.
Retouched flaw above LR "25" 100.00

No. 1L3 was probably never placed in use as a postage stamp.

Overprinted in red "Over our California lines only"

1L4 L2 25c **black** (with initials "LR" or "ICW") 750.00 —

L4

L5

1L5 L4 25c **black** (black surcharge) *4,000.* —
1L6 L5 25c **black** *3,000.*
Pair *7,500.*

The pair of No. 1L6 is unique.

NEWSPAPER STAMP

L6

1LP1 L6 **black,** *claret* — *2,000.*

Cancellation: Blue company oval.

ENVELOPES

L6a

L6b

Typo.

1LU1 L6a 25c **blue** (cut square) *15,000.*
1LU2 L6a 25c **black,** on U.S. #U9 — —
1LU3 L6b 50c **black,** on U.S. #U9 *2,500.* *2,500.*
1LU4 L6b 50c **black,** *buff* *15,000.*

Nos. 1LU2 and 1LU3 exist cut out and apparently used as adhesives.

Cancellation: Blue company oval.

Adams' City Express Post, New York, N.Y.

L7

L7a

L8

1850-51 **Typo.**

2L2 L7 2c **black,** *buff* *5,000.* *2,250.*
On cover, canceled, not tied, with certificate —
On cover, not canceled, with 5c #1 *3,000.*
2L3 L7a 1c **black,** *gray,* pelure paper — —
2L4 L8 2c **black,** *gray* *450.00* *450.00*
On cover, tied by handstamp *5,500.*
2L5 L8 2c **blue,** —
On cover, pen cancel *7,500.*

Nos. 2L3-2L4 were reprinted in black on white wove paper. Some students claim that a 1c in blue on white wove paper exists as originals.

Allen's City Dispatch, Chicago, Ill.

Established by Edwin Allen for intracity delivery of letters and circulars. The price of the stamps is believed to have been determined on a quantity basis. Uncanceled and canceled remainders were sold to collectors after suppression of the post in February, 1883.

L9

Sheet of 100 (10x10)

1882 **Typo.** ***Perf. 10***

3L1 L9 **pink** 7.50 *25.00*
On cover *900.00*
Block of 4 *40.00*
a. Horizontal pair, imperf. between —
3L2 L9 **black** 12.50 *100.00*
On cover, tied by handstamp *1,500.*
Block of 4 55.00
a. Horizontal pair, imperf. between —
3L3 L9 **red,** *yellow* .75 *20.00*
On cover, tied by handstamp *900.00*
Block of 4 *3.25*
a. Imperf., pair *150.00*
b. Horizontal pair, imperf. between —
3L4 L9 **blackish purple** 120.00

Cancellations: Violet company oval, violet "eagle."

American Express Co., New York, N.Y.

Believed by some researchers to have been established by Smith & Dobson in 1856, and short-lived.

L10

Typeset
Glazed Surface Paper

4L1 L10 2c **black,** *green* *9,000.*
a. Bottom ornament on right side turned sideways —

American Letter Mail Co.

Lysander Spooner established this independent mail line operating to and from New York, Philadelphia and Boston.

L12

L13

1844 **Sheet of 20 (5x4)** **Engr.**

5L1 L12 5c **black,** thin paper (2nd printing) 7.50 *35.00*
Thick paper (1st printing) 35.00 *50.00*
On cover, tied *750.00*
On cover, not tied *450.00*
Pair on cover *1,000.*
Pair on cover, tied by handstamp, with # 96L3a, ms. tied *10,000.*
Block of 4, thin paper 40.00
Sheet of 20, thin paper 225.00

No. 5L1 has been extensively reprinted in several colors, distinguishable by the rust marks on the plate, which were mostly removed from the margins and gutters between stamps but remain within the stamp designs. Cancellations: Red dotted star (2 types). Red "PAID," black brush, red brush.

Engr.

5L2 L13 **black,** *gray* 150.00 *250.00*
On cover, tied by handstamp *1,000.*
On cover, ms. tied *500.00*
On cover, not tied *350.00*
Pair on cover, tied by ms. 1,200.
Vertical strip of 4 *3,000.*
Block of 4 *4,000.*
5L3 L13 **blue,** *gray* *2,000.* *1,750.*
On cover, uncanceled, with certificate *11,000.*
On cover, not tied, with certificate *5,000.*
On cover, tied by ms. *10,000.*

Cancellations: Red "PAID," red company oval.

A. W. Auner's Despatch Post, Philadelphia, Pa.

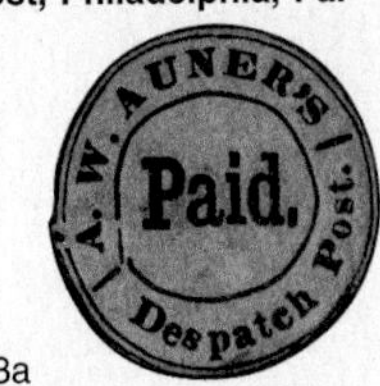

L13a

1851 **Cut to shape** **Typeset**

154L1 L13a **black,** *grayish* *9,000.*
On cover, not tied, with certificate *16,500.*

Nos. 154L1 unused and on cover are each unique.

Baker's City Express Post, Cincinnati, Ohio

L14

1849

6L1 L14 2c **black,** *pink* *2,250.*
On cover, uncanceled, with certificate *12,500.*

Bank & Insurance Delivery Office or City Post

See Hussey's Post.

Barnard's Cariboo Express, British Columbia

The adhesives were used on British Columbia mail and the post did not operate in the United States, so the formerly listed PAID and COLLECT types are omitted. This company had an arrangement with Wells, Fargo & Co. to exchange mail at San Francisco.

Barnard's City Letter Express, Boston, Mass.

Established by Moses Barnard

L19

1845

7L1 L19 **black,** *yellow,* glazed paper *1,250.* *1,000.*
On cover, not canceled *3,000.*
7L2 L19 **red** *1,000.*
On cover, ms. cancel, not tied, with certificate *5,000.*

No. 7L2 unused and on cover are each unique.

Barr's Penny Dispatch, Lancaster, Pa.

Established by Elias Barr.

L19a

L20

1855 **Five varieties of each** **Typeset**

8L1 L19a **red** 1,000. 1,000.
On cover, ms. tied *5,000.*
On cover, ms. cancel, not tied, with certificate *2,000.*
8L2 L20 **black,** *green* 300. 250.
On cover, uncanceled *900.*
On cover with 3c #11 —
Pair *750.*

Bayonne City Dispatch, Bayonne City, N.J.

Organized April 1, 1883, to carry mail, with three daily deliveries. Stamps sold at 80 cents per 100.

L21

1883 **Sheet of 10** **Electrotyped**

9L1 L21 1c **black** 200. 275.
On cover, tied by handstamp *750.*
On cover, tied by handstamp, with 1c #183 and 2c #206 *2,750.*
On cover with 3c #207 *1,600.*

Cancellation: Purple concentric circles.

ENVELOPE

1883, May 15 **Handstamped**

9LU1 L21 1c **purple,** *amber* 175. *1,000.*

Bentley's Dispatch, New York, N.Y.

Established by H. W. Bentley, who acquired Cornwell's Madison Square Post Office, operating until 1856, when the business was sold to Lockwood. Bentley's postmark was double circle handstamp.

L22

L22a

1856(?) **Glazed Surface Paper**

10L1 L22 **gold** *9,000.* *9,000.*
10L2 L22a **gold** *7,500.*
Pair *10,000.*

Two unused examples of No. 10L1 are known, while the used example is unique.

Cancellation: Black "PAID."

Berford & Co.'s Express, New York, N.Y.

Organized by Richard G. Berford and Loring L. Lombard. Carried letters, newspapers and packages by steamer to Panama and points on the West Coast, North and South America. Agencies in West Indies, West Coast of South America, Panama, Hawaii, etc.

L23

1851

11L1 L23 3c **black** *5,000.* *7,000.*
On cover, not canceled —
11L2 L23 6c **green** — —
On cover, tied *5,000.*
11L3 L23 10c **violet** *5,000.*
On cover, not canceled *5,000.*
Four cut to shape on cover *15,000.*
Pair —
a. Horiz. tete beche pair
On cover with normal pair *50,000.*
Two tete beche pair on cover *30,000.*
11L4 L23 25c **red** *17,000.*
On cover with #11L1 & 2 #11L2 *60,000.*

Values of cut to shape stamps are about half of those quoted.
No. 11L4 unused and on cover are each unique.
Cancellation: Red "B & Co. Paid" (sometimes impressed without ink). Dangerous counterfeits exist of Nos. 11L1-11L4.

Bicycle Mail Route, California

During the American Railway Union strike, Arthur C. Banta, Fresno agent for Victor bicycles, established this post to carry mail from Fresno to San Francisco and return, employing messengers on bicycles. The first trip was made from Fresno on July 6, 1894. Service was discontinued on July 18 when the strike ended. In all, 380 letters were carried. Stamps were used on covers with U.S. Government adhesive stamps and on stamped envelopes.

L24

Printed from single die. Sheet of six.
Error of spelling "SAN FRANSISCO"

1894 **Typo.** ***Rouletted 10***

12L1 L24 25c **green** 150. *200.*
On cover 2,750.
Block of 4 700.
Pane of 6 *1,750.*

L25

Retouched die. Spelling error corrected.

12L2 L25 25c **green** 30. 75.
On cover 1,500.
On cover with No. 220, both tied *2,000.*
Block of 4 125.
Pane of 6 250.
a. "Horiz." pair, imperf. "vert" 75.
As "a," pane of 6 —

ENVELOPES

12LU1 L25 25c **brown,** on 2c No. U311 200. *1,750.*
12LU2 L25 25c **brown,** on 2c No. U312 200. *1,750.*

Cancellation: Two black parallel bars 2mm apart.
Stamps and envelopes were reprinted from the defaced die.

Bigelow's Express, Boston, Mass.

Authorities consider items of this design to be express company labels rather than stamps.

Bishop's City Post, Cleveland, Ohio

See Carriers' Stamps, Nos. 10LB1-10LB2.

Blizzard Mail

Organized March, 1888, to carry mail to New York City during the interruption of U.S. mail by the Blizzard of 1888. Used March 12-16.

L27

1888, Mar. 12 **Quadrille Paper** **Typo.**

163L1 L27 5c **black** *3,750.*
a. "CETNS" instead of "CENTS" —
b. Tete beche pair —

D.O. Blood & Co., Philadelphia, Pa.
I. Philadelphia Despatch Post

Operated by Robertson & Co., predecessor of D.O. Blood & Co.

L28

Initialed "R & Co."

1843 **Cut to Shape** **Handstamped**

15L1 L28 3c **red,** *bluish* *1,500.*
On cover, not tied *5,000.*

1842

15L2 L28 3c **black** *1,500.*
On cover, not tied, with certificate *15,000.*

Cancellations on Nos. 15L1-15L2: Red "3," red pattern of segments.

L29

Initialed "R & Co"
With or without shading in background

1843 **Litho.**

15L3 L29 (3c) **black,** *grayish* 750.
On cover, tied by handstamp *12,500.*
On cover, tied by ms. cancel *5,000.*
On cover, not tied, with certificate *3,500.*
a. Double impression —

Cancellation on No. 15L3: Red "3"

The design shows a messenger stepping over the Merchants' Exchange Building, which then housed the Government Post Office, implying that the private post gave faster service.
See illustration L161 for similar design.

II. D.O. Blood & Co.

Formed by Daniel Otis Blood and Walter H. Blood in 1845. Successor to Philadelphia Despatch Post which issued Nos. 15L1-15L3.

L30

Initialed "Dob & Cos" or "D.O.B. & Co."

1845 **Shading in background**
15L4 L30 (3c) **black,** *grayish* 600.
On cover, tied by handstamp *7,000.*
On cover, not tied *1,500.*

L31

1845
15L5 L31 (2c) **black** 125. *250.*
On cover —
On cover, not tied, with certificate *800.*
On cover, not tied, with 5c #1 (unique) *9,500.*
Block of 4 *475.*
Pane of 12 *5,500.*

L32

1847
15L6 L32 (2c) **black** — 200.
On cover —
On cover, not tied, with certificate *1,250.*
On cover, not tied, with 5c #1 —

Cancellations on Nos. 15L4-15L6: Black dot pattern, black cross, red "PAID."
Dangerous counterfeits exist of Nos. 15L3-15L6.

L33

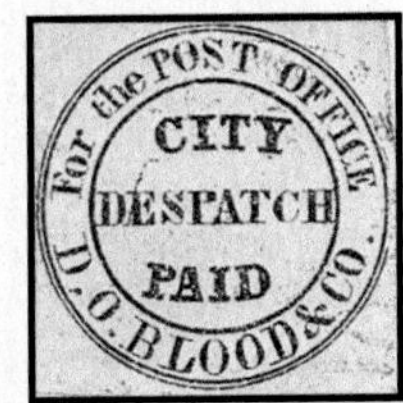
L34

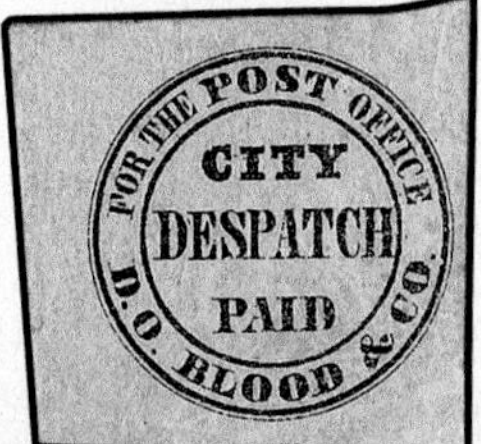
L35

1846-47
15L7 L33 (2c) **black** 175.00 350.00
On cover, tied by handstamp *1,750.*
On cover, cut to shape, tied by handstamp *1,100.*
On cover, not tied *750.00*
15L8 L34 (2c) **black** 110.00 75.00
On cover, tied by handstamp *950.00*
On cover, uncanceled *500.00*
On cover, uncanceled, with 5c #1 *2,000.*
On cover, tied by handstamp, with two 5c #1, tied by handstamps *25,000.*
On cover, tied by handstamp, with 3c #26A 500.00
15L9 L35 (2c) **black** 100.00 60.00
On cover, not tied *500.00*
On cover, tied by handstamp *1,500.*
On cover with 5c #1 or 1a *1,750.*
On cover, tied by handstamp, with 10c #2 *12,500.*
Block of 4 —

Values for Nos. 15L7-15L9 cut to shape are half of those quoted.
"On cover" listings of Nos. 15L7-15L9 are for stamps tied by government town postmarks, either Philadelphia, or rarely Baltimore.

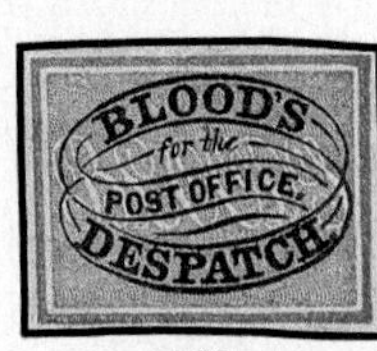
L36

L37

1848
15L10 L36 (2c) **black & blue** 350.00 *500.00*
On cover, tied by handstamp *2,250.*
On cover, not tied *1,750.*
On cover, not canceled *1,000.*
On cover, with 5c #1 —
Pair *1,300.*
On cover, with 10c #2 *1,500.*
15L11 L37 (2c) **black,** *pale green* 325.00 325.00
On cover, tied by handstamp *2,000.*
On cover, not tied *1,500.*

Cancellation: Black grid.

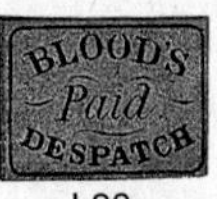
L38

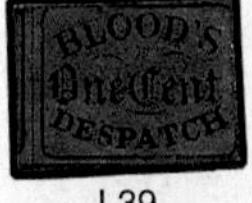
L39

L40

L41

1848-54
15L12 L38 (2c) **gold,** *black,* glazed *110.00* 100.00
On cover, tied by handstamp *500.00*
On cover, acid tied 200.00
On cover, uncanceled, with 5c #1 *2,000.*
15L13 L39 1c **bronze,** *black,* glazed ('50) 25.00 12.50
On cover, tied by handstamp *225.00*
On cover, acid tied 75.00
On cover, acid tied, with 5c #1 or 1b *2,000.*
On cover, acid tied, with pair of 5c #1b —
On cover, acid tied, with 10c #2 —
On cover with 10c #2, both tied *9,000.*
On cover, acid tied, with three 1c #7 *1,100.*
On cover, acid tied, with 3c #10 *1,000.*
On cover, acid tied, with 3c #10A *1,000.*
On cover, acid tied, with 3c #11 *1,000.*
On cover with 3c #11A, both tied *1,000.*
Block of 4 150.00
Pane of 24 *1,250.*
15L14 L40 (1c) **bronze,** *lilac* ('54) 4.25 2.50
On cover, tied by handstamp *200.00*
On cover, acid tied 30.00
On cover, acid tied, with 1c #9 *300.00*
On cover, acid tied, with 3c #11 *375.00*
On cover, tied by handstamp, with 3c #11 *400.00*
On cover, acid tied, with 3c #11A *300.00*
On cover, tied by handstamp, with 3c #11A *375.00*
On cover, acid tied, with 10c #14 *1,500.*
On cover, tied by handstamp, with 1c #24 and three 3c #26 *1,150.*
On cover, tied by handstamp, with 3c #26 *200.00*
On cover, acid tied, with 10c #32 —
On cover, acid tied, with 3c #64b *250.00*
On cover, acid tied, with 3c #65 *225.00*
Block of 4 50.00
Pane of 25 *750.00*
a. Laid paper — —
b. Tete beche pair —

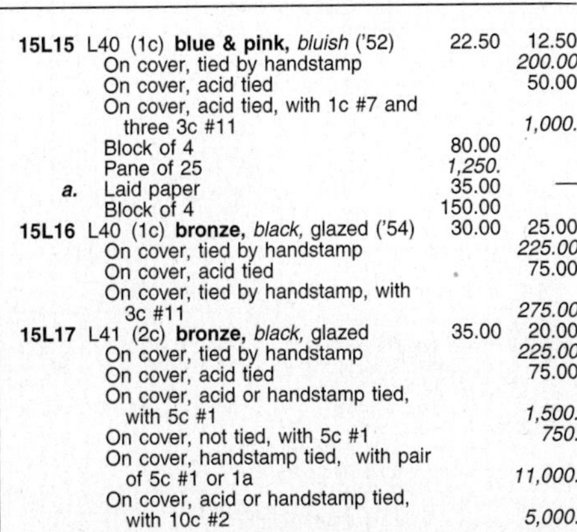
15L15 L40 (1c) **blue & pink,** *bluish* ('52) 22.50 12.50
On cover, tied by handstamp *200.00*
On cover, acid tied 50.00
On cover, acid tied, with 1c #7 and three 3c #11 *1,000.*
Block of 4 80.00
Pane of 25 *1,250.*
a. Laid paper 35.00 —
Block of 4 150.00
15L16 L40 (1c) **bronze,** *black,* glazed ('54) 30.00 25.00
On cover, tied by handstamp *225.00*
On cover, acid tied 75.00
On cover, tied by handstamp, with 3c #11 *275.00*
15L17 L41 (2c) **bronze,** *black,* glazed 35.00 20.00
On cover, tied by handstamp *225.00*
On cover, acid tied 75.00
On cover, acid or handstamp tied, with 5c #1 *1,500.*
On cover, not tied, with 5c #1 *750.*
On cover, handstamp tied, with pair of 5c #1 or 1a *11,000.*
On cover, acid or handstamp tied, with 10c #2 *5,000.*

D.O. Blood & Co. reduced the cost for mailing letters from 2c to 1c as of Jan. 8, 1849, in anticipation of the government carrier rate reduction. As a result, Nos. 15L12 and 15L17 could be purchased for 1c after this date.
Cancellations: Black grid (No. 15L12, 15L17). Nos. 15L13-15L16 were almost always canceled with an acid which discolored both stamp and cover.

III. Blood's Penny Post

Blood's Penny Post was acquired by the general manager, Charles Kochersperger, in 1855, when Daniel O. Blood died.

Henry Clay — L42

1858 **Engr. by Draper, Welsh & Co.**
15L18 L42 (1c) **black** 35.00 10.00
On cover 150.00
On cover, tied by handstamp, with 3c #11 *400.00*
On cover, not tied, with 1c #24 *900.00*
On cover, tied by handstamp, with 1c #24 and 3c #26 *2,000.*
On cover, tied by handstamp, with 3c #26 *350.00*
On 3c entire #U9 300.00
Block of 4 175.00

Cancellations: Black or red circular "Blood's Penny Post," black "1" in frame, red "1" in frame.

ENVELOPES

L42A

L43

L44

1848-60 **Embossed**
15LU1 L42A **albino embossing,** *white* —
15LU1A L42A **albino embossing,** *buff* — 4,000.
15LU1B L43 **red,** *white* 75.00 *100.00*
Used with 2 5c #1 (unique) —
a. **Pink,** *white* *100.00*
15LU2 L43 **red,** *buff* — 150.00
Used with 10c #2, #15LU2 an albino (unique) *2,250.*
15LU3 L44 **red,** *white* 75.00 160.00
15LU4 L44 **red,** *buff* 75.00 125.00

One example of No. 15LU1 is recorded, uncanceled, with the embossed stamp cut out and reattached. Two examples of No. 15LU1A are recorded, canceled by the "Blood's Despatch/28 So. Sixth" handstamp.

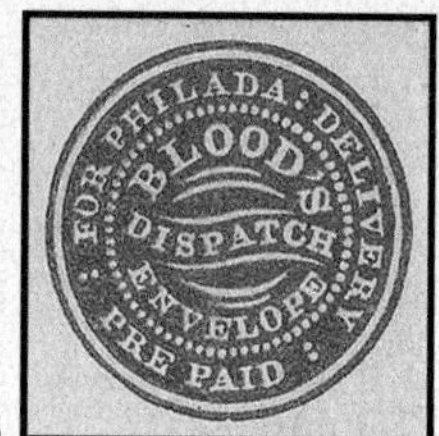

L45

15LU5 L45 **red,** *white*	35.00	75.00
Used with 3c #11		350.00
Used with 3c #26		*350.00*
15LU6 L45 **red,** *amber*	35.00	100.00
15LU6A L45 **red,** *buff*		*350.00*
Used with 10c #2 (unique)		*6,500.*
Used with three 1c #9		—
Used with 3c #11		—

Laid Paper

15LU7 L45 **red,** *white*	35.00	125.00
Used with acid tied #15L14		*200.00*
a. Impressed on US env. #U9		300.00
b. Impressed on US env. #U2		—
c. Impressed on US env. #U1		—
d. Impressed on US env. #U3		*500.00*
15LU8 L45 **red,** *amber*	35.00	125.00
Used with 3c No. 25		200.00
15LU9 L45 **red,** *buff*	35.00	250.00
Used with 3c No. 26A		—
15LU10 L45 **red,** *blue*		*6,500.*

Nos. 15LU1-15LU9 exist in several envelope sizes. No. 15LU6A exists in many shades, from buff to brown, as a result of various printings and changes over time.

Cancellations: Black grid (Nos. 15LU1-15LU4), black company circle (2 sizes and types). When on government envelope, the Blood stamp was often left uncanceled.

Bouton's Post, New York, N.Y.
I. Franklin City Despatch Post

Organized by John R. Bouton

L46

1847 Glazed Surface Paper Typo.

16L1 L46 (2c) **black,** *green*	*7,500.*	
a. "Bouton" in blk. ms. vert. at side	*7,000.*	
On cover, uncanceled		*7,500.*

II. Bouton's Manhattan Express

Acquired from William V. Barr

L47

1847 Typo.

17L1 L47 2c **black,** *pink*	*4,000.*	
Cut to shape	*900.*	
On cover, uncanceled		*4,500.*

III. Bouton's City Dispatch Post

(Sold to Swarts' in 1849.)

Corner Leaves — L48

Corner Dots — L49

Design: Zachary Taylor

1848 Litho.

18L1 L48 2c **black**	—	600.
On cover		*10,000.*
On cover with 5c #1		*27,500.*
On cover with 10c #2		*50,000.*
18L2 L49 2c **black,** *gray blue*	—	250.
On cover, tied by handstamp		800.
On cover tied by Swarts' handstamp		*1,150.*
On cover, tied by handstamp, with 5c #1, tied by red grid handstamp		*20,000.*
On cover with 10c #2		*5,000.*

Cancellations on Nos. 18L1-18L2: Red "PAID BOUTON."

The No. 18L2 with No. 2 combination cover is unique. It is a cover front only and is valued thus.

Boyce's City Express Post, New York, N.Y.

L50

Center background has 17 parallel lines

1852 Glazed Surface Paper Typo.

19L1 L50 2c **black,** *green*	*1,500.*	*1,000.*
Cut to shape	*850.00*	
On cover, tied by manuscript cancel		*4,000.*
On cover, uncanceled		*1,500.*

Boyd's City Express, New York, N.Y.

Boyd's City Express, as a post, was established by John T. Boyd, on June 17, 1844. In 1860 the post was briefly operated by John T. Boyd, Jr., under whose management No. 20L15 was issued.

For about six months in 1860 the post was suspended. It was then sold to William and Mary Blackham who resumed operation on Dec. 24, 1860.

The Blackham issues began with No. 20L16. Boyd's had arrangements to handle local delivery mail for Pomeroy, Letter Express, Brooklyn City Express Post, Staten Island Express Post and possibly others.

L51

Designs L51-L56, L59-L60 have a rectangular frame of fine lines surrounding the design.

1844 Glazed Surface Paper Litho.

20L1 L51 2c **black,** *green*		*1,000.*
On cover		*4,000.*
On cover, not tied, with #117L4		*7,000.*

Cancellation: Red "FREE."

L52

Plain background. Map on globe.

1844 Litho.

20L2 L52 2c **black,** *yellow green*		175.00
On cover		*450.00*

Cancellation: Red "FREE."

L53

Plain background. Only globe shaded.

1845 Engr.

20L3 L53 2c **black,** *bluish green*	—	250.00
On cover		*500.00*

Cancellation: Red "FREE."

L54

Inner oval frame of two thin lines. Netted background, showing but faintly on late impressions.

1845 Engr.

20L4 L54 2c **black,** *green*	—	15.00
On cover, tied by handstamp		250.00
On cover, not tied		75.00
On cover, tied, with 5c U.S. Postmaster Provisional #9X1		*30,000.*
On cover, tied, with 5c #1		*5,000.*
On cover, not tied, with 5c #1		*1,500.*
On cover, not tied, with two 5c #1		*12,500.*
Double transfer		35.00
a. Diagonal half used as 1c on cover		*2,300.*

Cancellations: Red "FREE." Black grid.

The 20L4 and 9X1 on cover is the only recorded usage of a local stamp and a Postmaster Provisional on full cover. Nos. 20L4 and 9X1 also are recorded on a rebacked cover front.

1848

20L5 L54 2c **gold,** *cream*	*600.00*	*600.00*
On cover, not tied		*1,750.*
On cover, cut to shape, not tied		*750.00*

Designs L54-L59 (except No. 20L23) were also obtainable die cut. An extra charge was made for such stamps. In general, genuine Boyd die-cuts sell for 75% of rectangular cut stamps. Stamps hand cut to shape are worth much less.

L55

No period after "CENTS." Inner oval frame has heavy inner line.

1848 Engr.

20L7 L55 2c **black,** *green* (glazed)	10.00	15.00
On cover, tied by handstamp		175.00
On cover, tied by handstamp, with 5c #1		*2,750.*
On cover with 3c #10		—
On cover, tied by handstamp, with 10c #2		17,000.
On cover, tied, with 3c #11		*275.00*
On cover, with 2c #28L5		—
Block of 4	40.00	
Partially erased transfer	—	
On cover		—
a. 2c **black,** *yellow green*		15.00
On cover		135.00

Cancellation: Black grid.

No. 20L7a is on unglazed surface-colored paper.

L56

Period after "CENTS." Inner frame as in L55. Each stamp is separated by rectangular dividing lines.

1852 Litho.

20L8 L56 2c **black,** *green*	—	35.00
On cover		*225.00*
On cover, tied by handstamp, with partial 3c #11A		—
20L9 L56 2c **gold,**	12.50	80.00
On cover, tied by handstamp		*750.00*
On cover with 3c #11		—
Block of 4	80.00	

Cancellations on Nos. 20L8-20L9: Black cork. Black "PAID J.T.B."

No. 20L8 was reprinted in 1862 on unglazed paper and about 1880 on unglazed paper. Neither of the reprints have rectangular dividing lines around the stamps.

L57

Period after "CENTS." Inner oval frame has heavy outer line. Eagle's tail pointed. Upper part of "2" open, with heavy downstroke at left shorter than one at right. "2C" closer than "T2."

1854

20L10 L57 2c **black,** *green* 32.50 25.00
On cover, tied by handstamp 200.00

Cancellation: Black "PAID J.T.B."

L58

Outer oval frame of three lines, outermost heavy. Solid background.

1855 Unglazed Paper Colored Through Typo.

20L11 L58 2c **black,** *olive green* *65.00* 90.00
On cover, tied by handstamp *350.00*

1856

20L12 L58 2c **brick red,** *white* 50.00 45.00
On cover, tied by handstamp *500.00*
20L13 L58 2c **dull orange,** *white* 50.00 45.00
On cover *400.00*
a. Printed on both sides —

Cancellation on Nos. 20L11-20L13: Black "PAID J.T.B."

Nos. 20L11-20L13 were reprinted in the 1880's for sale to collectors. They were printed from a new small plate of 25 on lighter weight paper and in colors of ink and paper lighter than the originals.

L59

Similar to No. 20L10, but eagle's tail square. Upper part of "2" closed (in well printed specimens) forming a symmetrical "o" with downstrokes equal. "T2" closer than "2C."

1857 Glazed Surface Paper Litho.

20L14 L59 2c **black,** *green* 12.50 *25.00*
On cover 90.00
On cover, tied by handstamp, with 3c #11 —
On cover, tied by handstamp, with 3c #11A —
On cover, tied by handstamp, with 3c #26 125.00
Pair on cover —
Block of 4 65.00
a. Serrate perf. —

The serrate perf. is probably of private origin.

No. 20L15 was made by altering the stone of No. 20L14, and many traces of the "S" of "CENTS" remain.

1860

20L15 L59 1c **black,** *green* 1.00 *50.00*
On cover, tied by handstamp *400.00*
Block of 4 7.50
a. "CENTS" instead of "CENT" — —
On cover *450.00*

Cancellation on Nos. 20L14-20L15: Black "PAID J.T.B."

L60

Center dots before "POST" and after "CENTS."

1861

20L16 L60 2c **black,** *red* 7.50 20.00
On cover, tied by handstamp 225.00
Block of 4 37.50
a. Tete beche pair 45.00
20L17 L60 1c **black,** *lilac* 12.50 17.50
On cover, tied by handstamp 250.00
On cover, tied by handstamp, with 3c #26 *200.00*
On cover, tied by handstamp, with 3c #65 *500.00*
Block of 4 50.00
a. "CENTS" instead of "CENT" 50.00 *75.00*
Two on cover (No. 20L17a) —
b. "1" inverted —
20L18 L60 1c **black,** *blue gray* 22.50 35.00
On cover, tied by handstamp *250.00*
On cover, tied by handstamp, with 3c #26 *225.00*
On cover, tied by handstamp, with 3c #65 *225.00*
Block of 4 90.00
a. "CENTS" instead of "CENT" 75.00 90.00
On cover 250.00
On cover, tied by handstamp, with 1c #24 and three 3c #26 *2,000.*
b. "1" inverted —

Cancellations on Nos. 20L16-20L18: Black or blue company oval, black company circle, black or blue "PAID" in circle.

1861

20L19 L60 2c **gold,** *250.00*
Block of 4 —
a. Tete beche pair —
20L20 L60 2c **gold,** *green* 20.00
Block of 4 —
a. Tete beche pair —
20L21 L60 2c **gold,** *dark blue* 12.50
On cover, tied by handstamp *150.00*
Block of 4 —
a. Tete beche pair *300.00*
20L22 L60 2c **gold,** *crimson* 25.00
Block of 4 —
a. Tete beche pair —

1866 Typo.

20L23 L58 2c **black,** *red* 7.50 25.00
On cover, tied by handstamp 250.00
Block of 4 37.50
a. Tete beche pair 55.00

Cancellations: Black company, black "PAID" in circle.

No. 20L23 was reprinted from a new stone on paper of normal color. See note after No. 20L13.

L61

No period or center dots.

1866 Typo.

20L24 L61 1c **black,** *lilac* *30.00* *65.00*
On cover, tied by handstamp *500.00*
Block of 4 —
20L25 L61 1c **black,** *blue* 6.00 *50.00*
On cover, tied by handstamp *500.00*
Block of 4 30.00

Cancellation on Nos. 20L24-20L25: Black company.

Reprints exist of Nos. 20L24 and 20L25. Originals of No. 20L24 are grayish black on glazed paper, while the reprints are deep black on unglazed paper. Reprints of No. 20L25 are identical to the originals, and it is customary to regard stamps with original gum as originals and those without gum as reprints.

Boyd's City Dispatch

(Change in Name)

L62

1874 Glazed Surface Paper Litho.

20L26 L62 2c **light blue** 35.00 40.00
On cover —
Block of 4 —

A unique sheet of 100 exists. It demonstrates 10 transfer types (2x5) repeated ten times to produce the printing stone. The same stone was modified to produce Nos. 20L30-20L36.

The 2c black on wove paper, type L62, is a cut-out from the Bank Notices Nos. 20LUX1, 20LUX2, or 20LUX3.

Surface Colored Paper

20L28 L62 2c **black,** *red* —
20L29 L62 2c **blue,** *red* *1,500.*

The adhesives of type L62 were made from the third state of the envelope die.

Nos. 20L28 and 20L29 are color trials, possibly used postally.

L63

1877 Litho.

20L30 L63 2c **lilac,** *roseate* —

Laid Paper

20L31 L63 2c **lilac,** *roseate* —

Wove Paper

Perf. 12½

20L32 L63 2c **lilac,** *roseate* 27.50 25.00
On cover *200.00*
a. 2c **lilac,** *grayish* 27.50 25.00

Laid Paper

20L33 L63 2c **lilac,** *roseate* 25.00
a. 2c **lilac,** *grayish* —

Glazed Surface Paper

20L34 L63 2c **brown,** *yellow* 35.00 35.00
On cover, tied by handstamp —
a. Imperf. horizontally —

L64

1877 Laid Paper *Perf. 11, 12, 12½*

20L35 L64 (1c) **violet,** *lilac* 15.00 17.50
On cover, tied by handstamp *450.00*
a. (1c) **red lilac,** *lilac* 27.50 27.50
b. (1c) **gray lilac,** *lilac* 17.50 17.50
c. Vert. pair, imperf. horiz. *400.00*
20L36 L64 (1c) **gray,** *roseate* 15.00 15.00
On cover, tied by handstamp *325.00*
a. (1c) **gray,** *grayish* 15.00

Cancellations on Nos. 20L30-20L36: Black "PAID" in circle. Purple company oval.

Boyd's Dispatch

(Change in Name)

Mercury Series — Type I — L65

Printed in sheets of 100.
Inner frame line at bottom broken below foot of Mercury.
Printed by C.O. Jones.

1878 Litho. Wove Paper *Imperf.*

20L37 L65 **black,** *pink* *400.00* *300.00*

Surface Colored Wove Paper

20L38 L65 **black,** *orange red* *750.00* *500.00*
20L39 L65 **black,** *crimson* *450.00* *300.00*

Laid Paper

20L40 L65 **black,** *salmon* *450.00*
20L41 L65 **black,** *lemon* *450.00* *400.00*
20L42 L65 **black,** *lilac pink* *450.00*

Nos. 20L37-20L42 are color trials, some of which may have been used postally.

Surface Colored Paper

Perf. 12

20L43 L65 **black,** *crimson* 60.00 50.00
On cover, tied by handstamp *300.00*
a. **black,** *dull brown red* 40.00 40.00
On cover, tied by handstamp *300.00*
20L43A L65 **black,** *orange red* 150.00 150.00
On cover, tied by handstamp *1,000.*

Cancellations on Nos. 20L37-20L43A: Black "PAID" in circle. Purple company oval.

Wove Paper

Perf. 11, 11½, 12, 12½ and Compound

20L44 L65 (1c) **black,** *pink* 1.50 2.50
On cover *200.00*
a. Horizontal pair, imperf. between — —

1879 *Perf. 11, 11½, 12*

20L45 L65 (1c) **black,** *blue* 10.00 15.00
On cover, tied by handstamp 200.00
20L46 L65 (1c) **blue,** *blue* 27.50 32.50
On cover, tied by handstamp *400.00*

1880 *Perf. 11, 12, 13½*

20L47 L65 (1c) **black,** *lavender* 8.00 20.00
On cover, tied by handstamp *300.00*
Block of 4 50.00
a. Horizontal pair, imperf. between *400.00*
20L48 L65 (1c) **blue,** *lavender* — —

1881 Laid Paper *Perf. 12, 12½, 14*

20L49 L65 (1c) **black,** *pink* *350.00*
On cover, tied by handstamp *600.00*

1880

20L50 L65 (1c) **black,** *lilac pink* 7.00 25.00
On cover, tied by handstamp *325.00*

Mercury Series — Type II — L65a

Printed by J. Gibson

No break in frame, the great toe raised, other toes touching line

1881 Wove Paper *Perf. 12, 16 & Compound.*

20L51 L65a (1c) **black,** *blue* 35.00 30.00
20L52 L65a (1c) **black,** *pink* 75.00 75.00
On cover, tied by handstamp *400.00*

Laid Paper

20L53 L65a (1c) **black,** *pink* 7.50 7.50
On cover, tied by handstamp 125.00
20L54 L65a (1c) **black,** *lilac pink* 12.50 10.00
On cover *200.00*

Mercury Series — Type III — L65b

Printed by the "Evening Post"

No break in frame, the great toe touching

Perf. 10, 11½, 12, 16 & Compound

1882 Wove Paper

20L55 L65b (1c) **black,** *blue* 4.00 10.00
On cover, tied by handstamp *225.00*
Pair on cover 225.00
20L56 L65b (1c) **black,** *pink* .40 *1.50*
On cover, tied by handstamp 100.00
Block of 4 2.00

Cancellations on Nos. 20L44-20L56: black or purple company ovals of various types, purple company circle, purple "SPECIAL," purple Maltese cross.

ENVELOPES

Boyd's City Post

Boyd's envelopes and cards (LU and LUX numbers) are valued as entires, cut squares are worth much less.

L66

Imprinted in upper right corner.
Used envelopes show Boyd's handstamps.

1864 Diagonally Laid Paper Embossed

20LU1 L66 **red** *175.00*
20LU2 L66 **red,** *amber* *90.00*
20LU3 L66 **red,** *yellow* — —
20LU4 L66 **blue** *175.00* —
20LU5 L66 **blue,** *amber* *175.00*
20LU6 L66 **blue,** *yellow* — —
20LU6A L66 **blue,** *blue* —

Several shades of red and blue.
No. 20LU6A is an indicium cut to shape. It is unique.

20LU7 L66 **deep blue,** *orange,* cut square *600.00*
Entire *5,500.*

Reprinted on pieces of white, fawn and oriental buff papers, vertically, horizontally or diagonally laid.

Wove Paper

20LU8 L66 **red,** *cream* *175.00*
20LU9 L66 **red,** *orange* — *2,500.*
20LU10 L66 **blue,** *cream* — —
20LU11 L66 **blue,** *orange* —
Impression at upper left *4,000.*
20LU11A L66 **blue,** *amber* — —

Boyd's City Dispatch

L67a

L67b

L67a. Lines and letters sharp and clear. Trefoils at sides pointed and blotchy, middle leaf at right long and thick at end.
L67b. Lines and letters thick and rough. Lobes of trefoils rounded and definitely outlined. Stamp impressed normally in upper right corner of envelope; L67b rarely in upper left.

1867 Diagonally Laid Paper Typo.

20LU12 L67 2c **red** (a) (b) — *800.00*
20LU13 L67 2c **red,** *amber* (b) — *300.00*
20LU14 L67 2c **red,** *cream* (b) — *300.00*
a. On horiz. laid paper —
b. Double impression, second impression in black, cut to shape —
20LU15 L67 2c **red,** *yellow* (a) (b) — *300.00*
20LU16 L67 2c **red,** *orange* (b) — *300.00*
a. Stamp impressed at upper left —

Wove Paper

20LU17 L67 2c **red** (a) (b) — *300.00*
20LU18 L67 2c **red,** *cream* (a) (b) — *300.00*
20LU19 L67 2c **red,** *yellow* (a) — —
20LU20 L67 2c **red,** *orange* (a) (b) — —
20LU21 L67 2c **red,** *blue* (a) (b) 500.00 *400.00*

Design as Type L62

First state of die, showing traces of old address

1874 Diagonally Laid Paper

20LU22 L62 2c **red,** *amber* *200.00*
20LU23 L62 2c **red,** *cream* — *200.00*

Wove Paper

20LU24 L62 2c **red,** *amber* *200.00*
20LU25 L62 2c **red,** *yellow* *200.00*

Second state of die, no traces of address

1875 Diagonally Laid Paper

20LU26 L62 2c **red,** *amber* *1,250.*
20LU27 L62 2c **red,** *cream* — *375.00*

Wove Paper

20LU28 L62 2c **red,** *amber* *450.00*

L68

1877 Laid Paper

20LU29 L68 2c **red,** *amber* *800.00*

Stamp usually impressed in upper left corner of envelope.

L69

1878 Diagonally Laid Paper

20LU30 L69 (1c) **red,** *amber* — *650.00*

Wove Paper

20LU31 L69 (1c) **red,** *cream* —
20LU32 L69 (1c) **red,** *yellow* —

Boyd's Dispatch

Mercury Series — Type IV — L70

Mercury Series-Type IV

Shading omitted in banner. No period after "Dispatch." Short line extends to left from great toe.

1878 Diagonally Laid Paper

20LU33 L70 **black** 40.00 *100.00*
20LU34 L70 **black,** *amber* *80.00*
20LU35 L70 **black,** *cream* 50.00 *100.00*
20LU36 L70 **red** *50.00*
20LU37 L70 **red,** *amber* 35.00 *45.00*
20LU38 L70 **red,** *cream* 35.00 *80.00*
20LU39 L70 **red,** *yellow green* —
20LU40 L70 **red,** *orange* *350.00*
20LU41 L70 **red,** *fawn* —

Wove Paper

20LU42 L70 **red** — *800.00*

Mercury Series — Type V — L71

Mercury Series-Type V

Colorless crosshatching lines in frame work. Very little shading on arms and legs.

1878 **Diagonally Laid Paper**

20LU43 L71 **red** — *450.00*
20LU44 L71 **red,** *cream* 25.00 *50.00*

Wove Paper

20LU44A L71 **red** *1,000.*

Boyd's Bank Notices

IMPORTERS' AND TRADERS' NATIONAL BANK OF NEW YORK

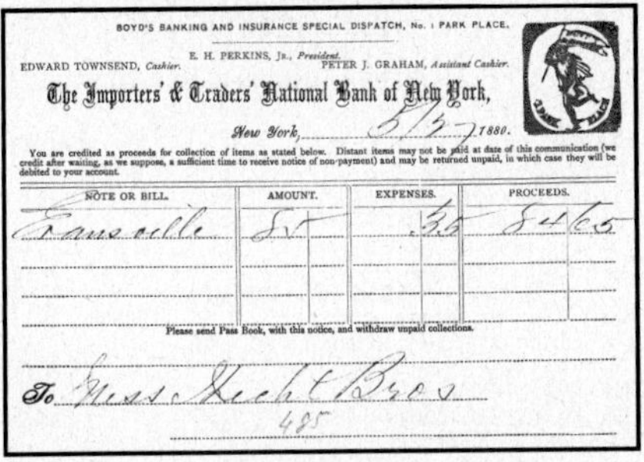
BOYD'S BANKING AND INSURANCE SPECIAL DISPATCH, No. 1 PARK PLACE.
E. H. PERKINS, Jr., *President.*
EDWARD TOWNSEND, *Cashier.* PETER J. GRAHAM, *Assistant Cashier.*
The Importers' & Traders' National Bank of New York,
New York, ...1880.
You are credited as proceeds for collection of items as stated below. Distant items may not be paid at date of this communication (we credit after waiting, as we suppose, a sufficient time to receive notice of non-payment) and may be returned unpaid, in which case they will be debited to your account.

NOTE OR BILL.	AMOUNT.	EXPENSES.	PROCEEDS.

Please send Pass Book, with this notice, and withdraw unpaid collections.
To ....

No. 20LUX9a

1874-83

Incomplete Year Date ("187 "), Card Stock

20LUX1 L62 (2c) **black,** 155x100mm *250.00*

Complete Year Date, Medium Wove Paper

20LUX2 L62 2c **black,** 157x104mm (1875) —
20LUX3 L62 2c **black,** 152x104mm (1876 *250.00*
20LUX4 L68 2c **black,** 154x105mm (1876) —
20LUX5 L68 2c **black,** 156x108mm (1877) *400.00*
20LUX6 L69 (1c) **black,** 156x108mm (1878) —
a. Four officers in masthead instead of three —
20LUX7 L70 (1c) **black,** 158x110mm (1879) *250.00*
20LUX8 L70 (1c) **black,** large year date and city, 158x110mm (1879) *250.00*
20LUX9 L70 (1c) **black,** 149x102mm (1880) *75.00* —
a. Three officers in masthead instead of four, 156x112mm *400.00*
20LUX10 L70 (1c) **black,** 149x102mm (1881) —
a. Four officers in masthead instead of three —
20LUX11 L71 (1c) **black,** 152x106mm (1883) —

Sizes of these cards may vary by up to two millimeters in either dimension from the measurements shown.

Nos. 20LUX5 and 20LUX9 exist on paper with a papermaker's watermark. Nos. 20LUX6, 20LUX9 and 20LUX10 may be found with either three or four bank officers listed in the masthead. The major number is the card that was issued first. No. 20LUX11 is known only unused, and may be a remainder that was printed but not used.

Values for Nos. 20LUX1-20LUX13 are for full covers. Cut squares sell for much less.

NATIONAL PARK BANK

1881 (?) **Medium Wove Paper**

20LUX12 L71 (1c) **black,** 122x63mm ('83) *300.00*

No postmarks or cancellations were used on Bank Notices. Boyd's sometimes added the recipient's address in pencil.

FLEISCHMANN'S MODEL BAKERY

1879 **Card Stock**

20LUX13 L69 (1c) **black,** 130x75mm *3,000.*

This card is imprinted "Fleischmann's Model Bakery."

Bradway's Despatch, Millville, N.J.

Operated by Isaac Bradway

L72

1857 **Typo.**

21L1 L72 **gold,** *lilac,* on cover, not tied, with certificate *7,500.*
On cover, not tied, with 3c #11, with certificate *12,000.*
On 3c U.S. envelope #U9,, not tied, with certificate *5,000.*

Brady & Co., New York, N.Y.

Operated by Abner S. Brady at 97 Duane St. Successor to Clark & Co.

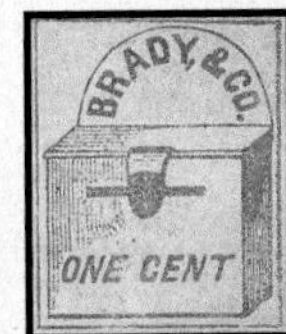

L73

1857 **Typo.**

22L1 L73 1c **red,** *yellow* *1,000.* *1,000.*
On cover, tied by company handstamp *22,000.*
On cover, tied by "PAID" handstamp *10,000.*

Cancellations: Blue boxed "PAID," blue company oval.

Reprints exist.

No. 22L1 tied on corner by company handstamp is unique. Three covers recorded with stamp tied by "PAID."

Brady & Co.'s Penny Post, Chicago, Ill.

L74

1860(?) **Litho.**

23L1 L74 1c **violet** *650.00* —

The authenticity of this stamp has not been fully established.

Brainard & Co.

Established by Charles H. Brainard in 1844, operating between New York, Albany and Troy, Exchanged mail with Hale & Co. by whom Brainard had been employed.

L75

1844 **Typo.**

24L1 L75 **black** *1,000.* *1,250.*
On cover, two stamps tied —
On cover, tied by pen cancel *2,500.*
On cover, not tied *2,000.*
On cover, cut to shape, not tied *1,750.*
24L2 L75 **blue** *1,000.* *1,250.*
On cover, not tied *4,500.*

Nos. 21L1-24L2 cut to shape are one half of values quoted.

Brigg's Despatch, Philadelphia, Pa.

Established by George W. Briggs

L76

1847

25L1 L76 (2c) **black,** *yellow buff* *1,000.*
On cover, not tied, with certificate *11,500.*
25L2 L76 (2c) **black,** *blue,* cut to shape *7,500.*

No. 25L2 is unique. It is on cover, manuscript "X" cancel, genuine, but Philatelic Foundation has declined to give an opinion as to whether the stamp originated on the cover.

L77

1848

25L4 L77 (2c) **gold,** *yellow,* glazed *5,500.*
On cover, not tied —
25L5 L77 (2c) **gold,** *black,* glazed *4,000.*
On cover —
25L6 L77 (2c) **gold,** *pink* —

No. 25L4 used and on cover are each unique.

Handstamps formerly illustrated as types L78 and L79 are included in the section "Local Handstamped Covers" at the end of the Local Stamp listings. They were used as postmarks and there is no evidence that any prepaid handstamped envelopes or letter sheets were ever sold.

Broadway Post Office, New York, N.Y.

Started by James C. Harriott in 1848. Sold to Dunham & Lockwood in 1855.

L80

1849(?) **Typo.**

26L1 L80 (1c) **gold,** *black,* glazed *1,000.* *1,250.*
Cut to shape 250.
On cover —
Pair (tied) on cover —

1851(?)

26L2 L80 (1c) **black** 250. *400.*
On cover *1,500.*
On cover, cut to shape, tied by handstamp *1,000.*
On cover with 3c #11 *2,750.*
Pair *1,000.* *1,000.*
Pair on part of cover *1,500.*
Block of 4 *2,250.*

Cancellation: Black oval "Broadway City Express Post-Office 2 Cts." Also know with red "Paid" cancel.

Bronson & Forbes' City Express Post, Chicago, Ill.

Operated by W.H. Bronson and G.F. Forbes.

L81

1856 **Typo.**

27L1 L81 **black,** *green* 600. *2,000.*
On cover, not tied —
On cover, tied by handstamp, with 3c #11 *4,000.*
27L2 L81 **black,** *lilac* *3,500.*

Cancellation: Black circle "Bronson & Forbes' City Express Post" (2 types).

No. 27L2 is unique.

Brooklyn City Express Post, Brooklyn, N.Y.

According to the foremost students of local stamps, when this concern was organized its main asset was the business of Kidder's City Express Post, of which Isaac C. Snedeker was the proprietor.

L82

L83

1855-64 **Glazed Surface Paper** **Typo.**

28L1 L82 1c **black,** *blue* (shades) 25.00 *80.00*
On cover, tied by handstamp *400.00*
Block of 4 125.00
a. Tete beche pair *80.00*

No.	Type	Description	Unused	Used
28L2	L82	1c **black,** *green*	20.00	50.00
		On cover, tied by handstamp		*350.00*
		On cover, tied by handstamp, with 3c #65		*1,250.*
		Block of 4	100.00	
a.		Tete beche pair	*125.00*	
28L3	L83	2c **black,** *crimson*	60.00	70.00
		On cover, tied by handstamp		*400.00*
		Block of 4	*300.00*	
28L4	L83	2c **black,** *pink*	17.50	*100.00*
		On cover, tied by handstamp		*550.00*
		On cover, tied by handstamp, with 3c #65		*1,750.*
		Block of 4	100.00	
a.		Tete beche pair	60.00	
28L5	L83	2c **black,** *dark blue*	50.00	*90.00*
		On cover, tied by handstamp		*500.00*
		On cover, tied by handstamp, with 3c #11		*500.00*
		On cover, tied, with 3c #26		*1,750.*
		Block of 4	*250.00*	

No. 28L5 has frame (dividing) lines around design.

No.	Type	Description	Unused	Used
28L6	L83	2c **black,** *orange*	—	—
		On cover		—
a.		Tete beche pair	—	

Unsurfaced Paper Colored Through

No.	Type	Description	Unused	Used
28L7	L83	2c **black,** *pink*	*300.00*	*750.00*

Cancellations: Black ring, red "PAID."

Reprints exist of Nos. 28L1-28L4, 28L6.

Browne & Co.'s City Post Office, Cincinnati, Ohio

Operated by John W.S. Browne

L84

L85

1852-55 **Litho.**

No.	Type	Description	Unused	Used
29L1	L84	1c **black** (Brown & Co.)	175.	150.
		On cover, tied by handstamp		*1,000.*
		On cover with 3c #11A		*2,750.*
		Pair	*450.*	
29L2	L85	2c **black** (Browne & Co.)	175.	175.
		On cover, tied by handstamp		*5,750.*
		On cover with 3c #11A		*4,500.*
		Pair	*575.*	

Cancellations: Black, blue or red circle "City Post*," red, bright blue or dull blue circle "Browne & Co. City Post Paid."

Browne's Easton Despatch, Easton, Pa.

Established by William J. Browne

L87

L88

1857 **Glazed Surface Paper** **Typeset**

No.	Type	Description	Unused	Used
30L1	L87	2c **black,** *red*	—	*5,000.*
30L2	L88	2c **black,** *red*	—	—

George Washington — L89

Wove Paper **Engr.**

No.	Type	Description	Unused	Used
30L3	L89	2c **black**	*750.*	*1,000.*
		Pair	*1,600.*	
		Block of 6	*5,750.*	

The No. 30L3 block of 6 is the only reported block of this stamp. Three pairs are reported.

The used value of No. 30L3 is for an example with pen cancel. There is one stamp with a handstamp cancel; value, $4,750.

Cancellation on No. 30L3: Black oval "Browne's Despatch Easton Pa."

Brown's City Post, New York, N.Y.

Established by stamp dealer William P. Brown for philatelic purposes.

L86

1877 **Glazed Surface Paper** **Typo.**

No.	Type	Description	Unused	Used
31L1	L86	1c **black,** *bright red*	200.00	*275.00*
		On cover, tied by handstamp		*2,250.*
31L2	L86	1c **black,** *yellow*	200.00	*275.00*
		On cover, tied by handstamp		*1,000.*
31L3	L86	1c **black,** *green*	200.00	*275.00*
		On cover, tied by handstamp		*1,000.*
31L4	L86	1c **black,** *violet*	200.00	*275.00*
		On cover, tied by handstamp		*2,250.*
31L5	L86	1c **black,** *vermilion*	200.00	*275.00*
		On cover, tied by handstamp		*500.00*

Cancellation: Black and purple circle "Brown's Despatch Paid."

Bury's City Post, New York, N.Y.

L90

No. 32L1

L91

1857 **Embossed without color**

No.	Type	Description	Unused	Used
32L1	L90	1c *blue*	*8,000.*	

Handstamped

No.	Type	Description	Unused	Used
32L2	L91	**black,** *blue*		—

Bush's Brooklyn City Express, Brooklyn, N.Y.

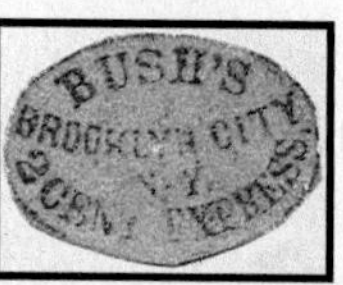

L91a

1848(?) **Cut to shape** **Handstamped**

No.	Type	Description	Unused	Used
157L1	L91a	2c **red,** *green,* glazed	*27,500.*	

No. 157L1 is unique. It is uncanceled on a large piece.

See Bush handstamp in Local Handstamped Covers section.

California City Letter Express Co., San Francisco, Calif.

Organized by J.W. Hoag, proprietor of the Contra-Costa Express, for local delivery. Known also as the California Letter Express Co.

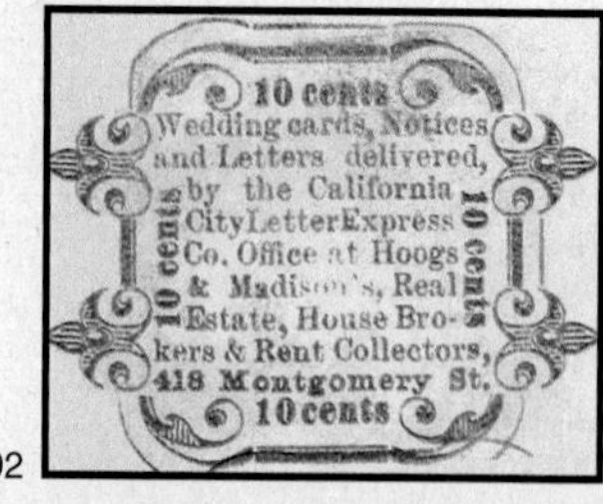

L92

L93

L93a

1862-66 **Typeset**

No.	Type	Description	Unused	Used
33L1	L92	10c **red**	*3,000.*	—
		On cover, not tied		*7,500.*
		On cover, not tied, with 10c #68, with certificate		*23,000.*
33L2	L92	10c **blue**		—
		On cover, not tied, with certificate		*16,500.*
33L3	L92	10c **green**	5,500.	
		On cover, uncanceled, with certificate		*18,000.*
33L4	L93	10c **red**	—	—
33L5	L93	10c **blue**		*14,000.*
33L6	L93	10c **green**	*19,000.*	
		On cover, not tied, with certificate		*31,000.*

No side ornaments, "Hoogs & Madison's" in one line

No.	Type	Description	Unused	Used
33L7	L93a	10c **red**		*1,200.*
		On cover, not tied, with certificate		*19,000.*
33L8	L93a	10c **blue**	*4,000.*	
		On cover, not tied, with 10c #68, with certificate		*50,000.*

Nos. 33L1 unused, 33L1 on cover with #68, 33L3 used, 33L3 on cover, 33L6 unused, 33L6 on (patriotic) cover, 33L7 used, 33L7 on cover, 33L8 unused and 33L8 on cover with #68 each are unique. The other varieties of Nos. 33L1-33L8 are all rare.

California Penny Post Co.

Established in 1855 by H. L. Goodwin and partners. At first confined its operations to San Francisco, Sacramento, Stockton and Marysville, but branches were soon established at Benicia, Coloma, Nevada, Grass Valley and Mokelumne Hill. Operation was principally that of a city delivery post, as it transported mail to the General Post Office and received mail for local delivery. Most of the business of this post was done by means of prepaid envelopes.

L94

L94b

L94a

L95

L95a

1855 **Litho.**

34L1 L94 2c **blue** 700. *750.*
On cover *20,000.*
Pair *3,000.*
34L1B L94b 2c **blue** —
34L1A L94a 3c **blue** *850.*
34L2 L95 5c **blue** *250.* *425.*
On cover *1,250.*
Block of 4 750.
34L3 L95a 10c **blue** 475. —
On cover *3,000.*
Pair *1,000.*

Cancellation: Blue circle "Penny Post Co."

Only one example of No. 34L1 on cover is recorded. The stamp is tied by manuscript cancel. Three examples of No. 34L1A are recorded, each uncanceled on cover.

L96

34L4 L96 5c **blue** *600.* *1,750.*
On cover *3,000.*
On cover, uncanceled, with 10c #14 *55,000.*
Strip of 3 *3,500.*

The strip of 3 of No. 34L4 has faults but is unique. Value is for strip in faulty condition.

ENVELOPES

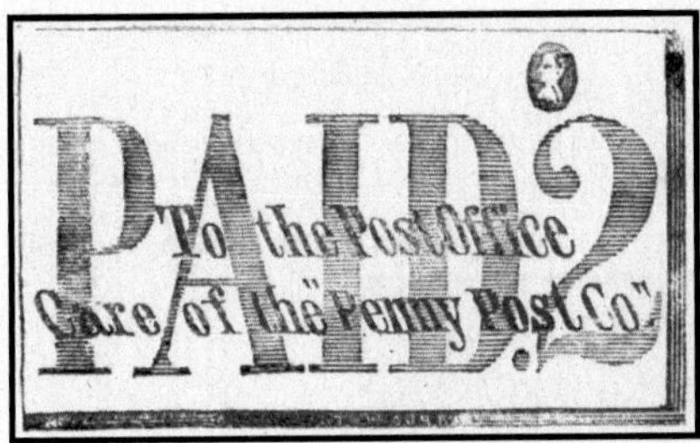

L97

1855-59

34LU1 L97 2c **black,** *white* 200. *900.*
With 1c #9 —
With 3c #11 *9,000.*
With 10c #14 *11,000.*
a. Impressed on 3c US env. #U10 250. *1,000.*
34LU2 L97 5c **blue,** *blue* 200. *900.*
34LU3 L97 5c **black,** *buff* 200. *900.*
a. Impressed on 3c US env. #U10 *1,500.*
34LU4 L97 7c **black,** *orange buff* —
a. Impressed on 3c US env. #U10 —

L98

34LU6 L98 7c **vermilion** on 3c US env. #U9 200.00 *1,000.*
34LU7 L98 7c **vermilion** on 3c US env. #U10 225.00 *1,750.*

L98A

34LU8 L98A 5c **black,** *white* 150. *1,200.*
34LU9 L98A 5c **black,** *buff* 150. *1,200.*
On cover, with 3c #11 *3,500.*
a. Impressed on 3c US env. #U10 *1,250.*
34LU10 L98A 7c **black,** *white* 150. *1,000.*
On cover, with 3c #11 —
a. Impressed on 3c US env. #U9 *1,750.*
34LU11 L98A 7c **black,** *buff* 150.00 *1,100.*
a. Impressed on 3c US env. #U10 *1,500.*
34LU11C L98A **black,** *buff,* "Collect Penny Postage" (no denomination) 250. *1,500.*
On cover, with 3c #11 —

L98B

34LU11B L98B 7c **black** on 3c US env. #U10 250. *1,400.*
34LU12 L98B 7c **black** on 3c US env. #U9 250. *4,500.*

L98C

34LU13 L98C 5c **black,** *buff* — —

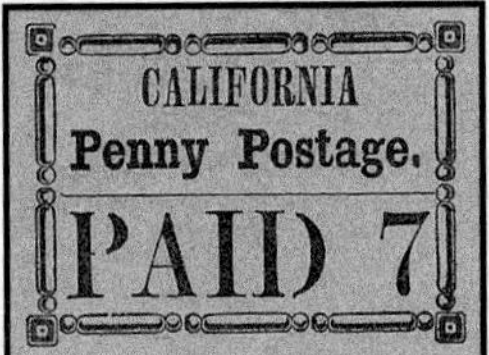

L98D

34LU13A L98D 5c **black,** *buff* —
34LU14 L98D 7c **black,** *buff* 300. *3,000.*
With 3c #11 *5,000.*
34LU15 L98D 7c **black** on 3c US env. #U9 350. *2,500.*
34LU16 L98D 7c **black** on 3c US env. #U10 — —

The non-government envelopes of types L97, L98A, L98C and L98D bear either 1c No. 9 or 3c No. 11 adhesives. These adhesives are normally canceled with the government postmark of the town of original mailing. Values are for covers of this kind. The U.S. adhesives are seldom canceled with the Penny Post cancellation. When they are, the cover sells for more.

At least eight different varieties of the 34LU14 are known with different printed instructions/addresses, some with room to add U.S. postage.

Carnes' City Letter Express, San Francisco, Calif.

Established by George A. Carnes, former P.O. clerk.

L99

1864 **Typo.**

35L1 L99 (5c) **rose** 175. 300.
On cover, tied *15,000.*
Block of 4 *750.*

Cancellations: Black dots. Blue dots. Blue "Paid." Blue oval "Wm. A. Frey."

See illustration L206

Overprinted in Blue

35L2 L99 10c **rose** 200.00

L100

1864 **Litho.**

35L3 L100 5c **bronze** 125.00
a. Tete beche pair 300.00
35L4 L100 5c **gold** 125.00
a. Tete beche pair 300.00
35L5 L100 5c **silver** 125.00
a. Tete beche pair 300.00
35L6 L100 5c **black** 125.00
a. Tete beche pair 300.00
35L7 L100 5c **blue** 100.00
a. Tete beche pair 250.00
35L8 L100 5c **red** 125.00
a. Tete beche pair 300.00

Printed in panes of 18 (3x6) from three settings of 6 (3x2), with the bottom setting inverted, creating three tete-beche pairs.

G. Carter's Despatch, Philadelphia, Pa.

Operated by George Carter

L101

1849-51

36L1 L101 2c **black** — 100.00
On cover, tied by pen cancel *225.00*
On cover, with 5c #1 —
On cover, with 5c #1, tied by handstamp *5,500.*
a. Vertically ribbed paper — 140.00
On cover, tied by pen cancel *300.00*

No. 36L1 exists on paper with a blue, red or maroon wash. The origin and status are unclear.

Cancellation: Black circle "Carter's Despatch."

ENVELOPE

L102

36LU1 L102 **blue,** *buff* *1,000.*
Cut to shape *150.*
On cover with 3c No. 10 *3,250.*
On cover with 3c No. 11 *1,750.*

Cheever & Towle, Boston, Mass.

Sold to George H. Barker in 1851

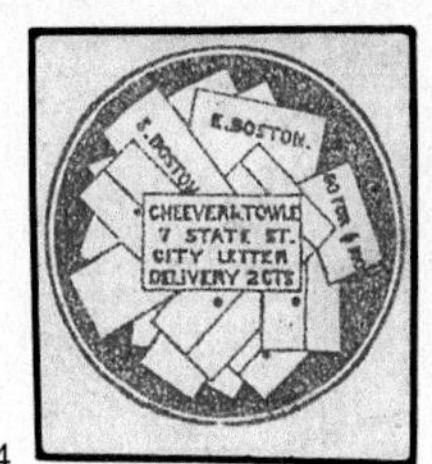

L104

1849(?)

37L1 L104 2c **blue** *600.* *350.*
Cut to shape 125.
On cover, tied by handstamp *7,000.*
On cover, not tied *1,500.*
On cover, not tied, cut to shape *500.*

Cancellation: Red oval "Towle's City Despatch Post 7 State Street."

Chestnut Street Line, Philadelphia, Pa.

The portrait almost certainly pictures Stephen Girard, a wealthy Philadelphian who died in 1836 and left his $6 million fortune to the city.

L104a

1856

169L1 L104a 1c **black,** *pink glazed* *17,500.*
On cover, with 3c #11 *25,000.*
169L2 L104a 1c **black,** *yellow glazed,* on cover, with 3c #11 *40,000.*

Only one each recorded of Nos. 169L1 used, 169L1 on cover, and 169L2 on cover.

Chicago Penny Post, Chicago, Ill.

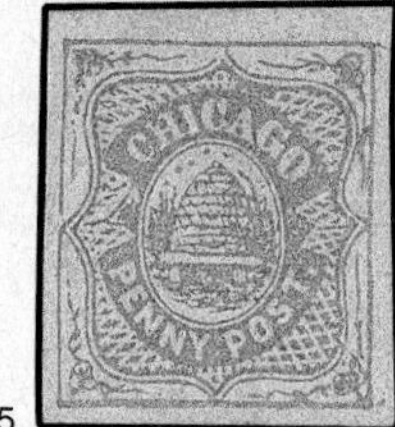

L105

1862 **Typo.**

38L1	L105 (1c) **orange brown**	800.	1,250.
	On cover, serrated perforations		*5,000.*

Reprints exist.

Cancellation: Black circle "Chicago Penny Post A. E. Cooke Sup't."

Cincinnati City Delivery, Cincinnati, Ohio

Operated by J. Staley, who also conducted the St. Louis City Delivery Co. He established the Cincinnati post in January, 1883. The government suppressed both posts after a few weeks. Of the 25,000 Cincinnati City Delivery stamps printed, about 5,000 were sold for postal use. The remainders, both canceled and uncanceled, were sold to collectors.

L106

1883 **Typo.** ***Perf. 11***

39L1	L106 (1c) **carmine**	2.50	*12.50*
	On cover		*300.00*
a.	Imperf., pair	—	—

Cancellation: Purple target.

City Despatch Post, New York, N.Y.

The City Despatch Post was started Feb. 1, 1842, by Alexander M. Greig and Henry T. Windsor. Greig's Post extended to 23rd St. Its operations were explained in a circular which throws light on the operations of all Local Posts:

New York City Despatch Post, Principal Office, 46 William Street.

"The necessity of a medium of communication by letter from one part of the city to another being universally admitted, and the Penny Post, lately existing having been relinquished, the opportunity has been embraced to reorganize it under an entirely new proprietory and management, and upon a much more comprehensive basis, by which Despatch, Punctuality and Security-those essential elements of success-may at once be attained, and the inconvenience now experienced be entirely removed."

"*** Branch Offices-Letter boxes are placed throughout every part of the city in conspicuous places; and all letters deposited therein not exceeding two ounces in weight, will be punctually delivered three times a day *** at three cents each."

"*** Post-Paid Letters.-Letters which the writers desire to send free, must have a free stamp affixed to them. An ornamental stamp has been prepared for this purpose *** 36 cents per dozen or 2 dolls. 50c per hundred. ***"

"No money must be put in boxes. All letters intended to be sent forward to the General Post Office for the inland mails must have a free stamp affixed to them."

"Unpaid Letters.-Letters not having a free stamp will be charged three cents, payable by the party to whom they are addressed, on delivery."

"Registry and Despatch.-A Registry will be kept for letters which it may be wished to place under special charge. Free stamps must be affixed for such letters for the ordinary postage, and three cents additional be paid (or an additional fee stamp be affixed), for the Registration."

NOTE: The word "Free," as used in this circular, should be read as "Prepaid." Likewise, the octagonal "FREE" cancellation should be taken to mean "Prepaid" (that is, "Free" of further charge).

The City Despatch Post was purchased by the United States Government and ceased to operate as a private carrier on August 15, 1842. It was replaced by the "United States City Despatch Post" which began operation on August 16, 1842, as a Government carrier.

No. 40L1 was issued by Alexander M. Greig; No. 40L2 and possibly No. 40L3 by Abraham Mead; Nos. 40L4-40L8 probably by Charles Cole.

L106a

Cancellation

This was the first adhesive stamp used in the United States. This stamp was also used as a carrier stamp. See No. 6LB1.

Plate of 42 (6x7) subjects

1842, Feb. 1

40L1	L106a 3c **black,** *grayish*	375.	350.
	On cover, tied by handstamp		*2,500.*
	On cover, not tied		*1,100.*
	First day cover		*25,000.*
	Pair	850.	
	Block of 4	2,000.	
	Sheet of 42	*32,500.*	

No. 40L1 was used until Aug. 16, 1842, the first day of operation of the U.S. City Despatch Post. The latest recorded No. 40L1 cover is dated Aug. 13, 1842.

Cancellations: Red framed "FREE" (see illustration above), red circle "City Despatch Post" (2 types).

Die reprints of No. 40L1 were made in 1892 on grayish white, orange, red and green surface-colored papers. It is believed that only four sets were made. Value, each reprint $500.

1846 **Glazed Surface Paper**

40L2	L106a 2c **black,** *green*	*200.00*	150.00
	On cover, tied by handstamp		*750.00*
	On cover, not tied		*400.00*
a.	With ms. "Cummings & Wright" overprint		*3,000.*
	On cover ("C&W" overprint)		—

1847

40L3	L106a 2c **black,** *pink*		*2,500.*
	On cover, not tied, with certificate		*9,000.*

Cancellations: Red framed "FREE," black framed "FREE," red circle "City Despatch Post."

L107

Similar to L106a with "CC" at sides.

1847-52

40L4	L107 2c **black,** *green glazed*	*1,500.*	200.
	On cover, tied by handstamp		*1,500.*
	On cover, not tied		*600.*
	Retouched plate ("Big Pupil" of right eye (Pos. 5 and 6))		—
	On cover		—
a.	"C" at right inverted		*4,000.*
b.	"C" at left sideways		—
	On cover, tied by handstamp		*1,000.*
c.	"C" at right only		—

Some students think No. 40L4c may have just a badly worn sideways "C" at left.

40L5	L107 2c **black,** *grayish*		900.
	On cover, tied by handstamp		*3,000.*
	On cover, not tied		*2,000.*
a.	"C" at right inverted		—
b.	"C" at left sideways		—
	On cover, tied		*4,250.*
	On cover, uncanceled		*1,250.*
c.	"C" in ms. between "Two" and "Cents"	*1,500.*	*1,000.*
	On cover, tied by handstamp		*5,000.*
	On cover, not tied		*1,500.*
d.	"C" at left sideways plus "C" in ms. between "Two" and "Cents"		*4,000.*
40L6	L107 2c **black,** *vermilion glazed*	450.	400.
	On cover, tied by handstamp		*1,500.*
	On cover, not tied		*600.*
a.	"C" at right inverted		—
b.	"C" at left sideways		*4,500.*
	On cover, tied by handstamp		5,250.
	On cover, not tied		*4,750.*
40L8	L107 2c **black,** *yellowish buff* ('52)	—	—
	On cover, not tied, with certificate		*15,000.*
a.	"C" at right inverted		*9,000.*
b.	"C" at left sideways		*9,000.*

Each of the No. 40L6b covers are unique as listed. An uncanceled example of No. 40L8 exists on cover.

Cancellations: Red framed "FREE," black framed "FREE," black "PAID," red "PAID," red circle company, black grid of 4 short parallel bars.

City Dispatch, New York, N.Y.

L107a

1846 **Typo.**

160L1	L107a 2c **red**	*3,000.*	*4,500.*
	On cover		—
	Vertical pair	*19,000.*	

The unique vertical pair is the only reported multiple of No. 160L1.

Cancellations: Red "PAID"; blue manuscript.

City Dispatch, Philadelphia, Pa.

Justice — L108

1860 **Thick to Thin Wove Paper** **Litho.**

41L1	L108 1c **black**	7.50	50.00
	On cover, tied by handstamp		*500.00*
	Block of 4	55.00	

Cancellations: Black circle "Penny Post Philada.," black circled grid of X's.

City Dispatch, St. Louis, Mo.

L109

Initials in black ms.

1851 **Litho.**

42L1	L109 2c **black,** *blue*		*40,000.*

No. 42L1 used is unique. A second example, on cover, is recorded.

City Dispatch Post Office, New Orleans, La.

Stamps sold at 5c each, or 30 for $1.

L110

1847 **Glazed Surface Paper** **Typeset**

43L1	L110 (5c) **black,** *green*	*6,000.*	
	On cover		—
43L2	L110 (5c) **black,** *pink*	*6,000.*	
	On cover, not canceled		—

City Express Post, Philadelphia, Pa.

L111

L112

184-(?) **Typeset**

44L1	L111 2c **black,** on cover, uncanceled, with certificate		*11,000.*
44L2	L112 (2c) **black,** *pink*	*10,000.*	
	On cover, uncanceled, with certificate		*20,000.*
44L3	L112 (2c) **red,** *yellow,* on cover, uncanceled		*30,000.*

One example recorded of Nos. 44L1 and 44L3. Six No. 44L2 recorded, five of these uncanceled on covers.

See illustration L8.

City Letter Express Mail, Newark, N.J.

Began business under the management of Augustus Peck at a time when there was no free city delivery in Newark.

L113

1856 **Litho.**
45L1 L113 1c **red** *350.00 500.00*
Cut to shape 100.00
On cover, not tied —
On cover, tied —
On cover, cut to shape, tied by handstamp, with 3c #11 *10,000.*
45L2 L113 2c **red,** on cover, cut to shape, uncanceled, with certificate *11,000.*

On No. 45L2, the inscription reads "City Letter/Express/City Delivery" in three lines across the top. The example on cover is unique.

City Mail Co., New York, N.Y.

There is evidence that Overton & Co. owned this post.

L114

1845
46L1 L114 (2c) **black,** *grayish* *1,500. 1,500.*
On cover, not tied, with certificate *8,000.*

Cancellation: Red "PAID."

City One Cent Dispatch, Baltimore, Md.

L115

1851
47L1 L115 1c **black,** *pink* (on cover) —

Clark & Co., New York, N.Y.

(See Brady & Co.)

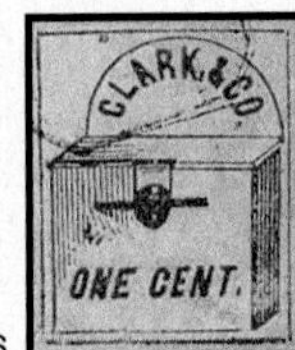

L116

1857 **Typo.**
48L1 L116 1c **red,** *yellow* 600. *900.*
On cover *2,500.*

Cancellation: Blue boxed "PAID."

Clark & Hall, St. Louis, Mo.

Established by William J. Clark and Charles F. Hall.

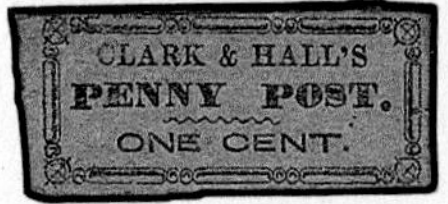

L117

1851 **Several varieties** **Typeset**
49L1 L117 1c **black,** *pink,* on cover, uncanceled, with certificate 19,000.

Clarke's Circular Express, New York, N.Y.

Established by Marion M. Clarke

George Washington — L118

Impression handstamped through inked ribbon
Cut squares from envelopes or wrappers

1865-68(?)
50LU1 L118 **blue,** wove paper *6,250.*
a. Diagonally laid paper *4,500.*
50LU2 L118 **black,** diag. laid paper *5,750.*

No. 50LU1 unused is unique.

Cancellation: Blue dated company circle.

Clinton's Penny Post, Philadelphia, Pa.

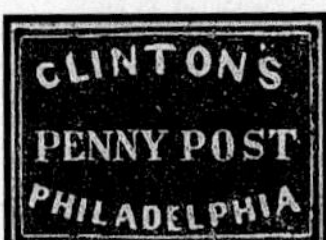

L118a

Typo.
161L1 L118a (1c) **black** *22,500.*

Cook's Dispatch, Baltimore, Md.

Established by Isaac Cook

L119

1853
51L1 L119 (1c) **green,** *white* *4,000. 3,000.*
Cut to shape *1,500.*
On cover —

Cancellation: Red straight-line "I cook."

Cornwell's Madison Square Post Office, New York, N.Y.

Established by Daniel H. Cornwell. Sold to H.W. Bentley.

L120

1856 **Typo.**
52L1 L120 (1c) **red,** *blue* *1,500.* —
On cover, tied by handstamp *10,000.*
52L2 L120 (1c) **reddish brown** 250. *600.*
brownish red 250. *600.*
On cover, tied by handstamp *10,000.*
Strip of 3 —

Five Types identified of Nos. 52L1 and 52L2.

Cancellation: Black oval "Cornwall's Madison Square Post Office." Covers also bear black boxed "Paid Swarts." The covers of Nos. 52L1 and 52L2 are each unique.

Cressman & Co.'s Penny Post, Philadelphia, Pa.

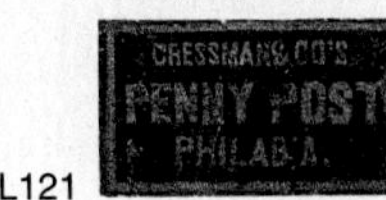

L121

1856 **Glazed Surface Paper**
53L1 L121 (1c) **gold,** *black* *350. 350.*
On cover, tied *1,500.*
Pair *1,200.*
53L2 L121 (1c) **gold,** *lilac,* on cover, acid tied *25,000.*

The vertical pair of No. 53L1 is unique. No. 53L2 also is unique.

Cancellation: Acid. (See D.O. Blood & Co. Nos. 15L13-15L16.)

Crosby's City Post, New York, N.Y.

Established by Oliver H. Crosby. Stamps printed by J.W. Scott & Co.

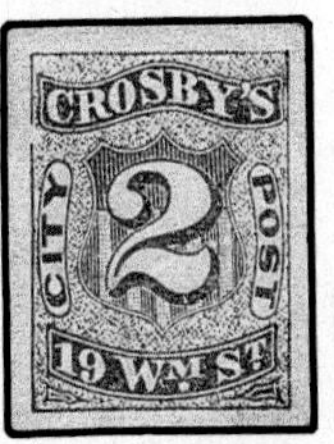

L123

Printed in sheets 25 (5x5), imprint at left.

1870 **Typo.**
54L1 L123 2c **carmine** (shades) 1.00 *50.00*
On cover, tied by handstamp *750.00*
Pair —
Sheet of 25 50.00

Cancellation: Black oval "Crosby's City Post."

Cummings' City Post, New York, N.Y.

Established by A. H. Cummings.

L124

1844 **Glazed Surface Paper** **Typo.**
55L1 L124 2c **black,** *rose* *1,000.*
On cover, tied, with certificate *5,000.*
On cover, not tied, with certificate —
55L2 L124 2c **black,** *green* *650.*
On cover *2,500.*
55L3 L124 2c **black,** *yellow* *750.*
On cover, tied by handstamp *2,000.*
On cover, not tied, with certificate *1,500.*

Cancellations: Red boxed "FREE," red boxed "PAID AHC," black cork (3 types).

L125

55L4 L125 2c **black,** *green* *750.00 750.00*
55L5 L125 2c **black,** *olive* *750.00 750.00*

L126

55L7 L126 2c **black,** *vermilion* *8,250.*
On cover, uncanceled, with certificate *22,000.*

As L124, but "Cummings" erased on cliche

55L8 L124 2c **black,** *vermilion* —

Nos. 55L7 on cover and 55L8 each are unique.

Cutting's Despatch Post, Buffalo, N.Y.

Established by Thomas S. Cutting

L127

Cut to shape

1847 **Glazed Surface Paper**
56L1 L127 2c **black,** *vermilion* —
On cover, cut to shape, uncanceled, with certificate *22,000.*

Davis's Penny Post, Baltimore, Md.

Established by William D. Davis and brother.

L128

1856 Several varieties Typeset

57L1 L128 (1c) **black,** *lilac* — *2,750.*
On cover, tied by handstamp — *12,500.*
a. "Pennq," pos. 2 — *8,250.* *8,250.*

Cancellation: Red company circle.

Deming's Penny Post, Frankford, Pa.

Established by Sidney Deming

L129

1854 Litho.

58L1 L129 (1c) **black,** *grayish* — *6,000.*
On cover, ms. tied, with 3c #11 (unique) — *7,500.*

Douglas' City Despatch, New York, N.Y.

Established by George H. Douglas

L130

L131

Printed in sheets of 25

1879 Typo. *Perf. 11*

59L1	L130 (1c) **pink**	10.00	*15.00*
	On cover		*300.00*
a.	Imperf.	30.00	—
59L2	L130 (2c) **blue**	10.00	*15.00*
	On cover, tied by handstamp		*500.00*
a.	Imperf.	50.00	—
b.	Printed on both sides, imperf.		—

Printed in sheets of 50 (10x5).

Perf. 11, 12 & Compound

59L3	L131 1c **vermilion**	15.00	*35.00*
	On cover		*325.00*
a.	Imperf.	1.00	—
59L4	L131 1c **orange**	25.00	*50.00*
	On cover, tied by handstamp		*600.00*
59L5	L131 1c **blue**	30.00	*50.00*
	On cover		*300.00*
a.	Imperf.	1.00	—
59L6	L131 1c **slate blue**	20.00	25.00
a.	Imperf.	7.50	—

Cancellations on Nos. 59L1-59L6: Ornate purple design, purple circular design composed of bars and wedges.

Imperforates are believed to be remainders sold by the printer.

Dupuy & Schenck, New York, N.Y.

Established by Henry J. Dupuy and Jacob H. Schenck, formerly carriers for City Despatch Post and U. S. City Despatch Post.

Beehive — L132

1846-47 Engr.

60L1	L132 (1c) **black,** glazed paper	175.	*300.*
	On cover, tied by handstamp		*1,750.*
	On cover, tied by ms.		*1,250.*
60L2	L132 (1c) **black,** *gray*	175.	*300.*
	On cover, tied by handstamp		*1,500.*
	On cover, tied by pen cancel		*1,000.*
	On cover, not tied		*450.*

Cancellation: Red "PAID."

Eagle City Post, Philadelphia, Pa.

Established by W. Stait, an employee of Adams' Express Co.

L133

Black manuscript "WS" on used examples

1847 Pelure Paper Typeset

61L1 L133 (2c) **black,** *grayish* — *14,000.* *10,000.*
Cut to shape, on cover — —

No. 61L1 unused is unique. Value reflects a 1997 auction sale.

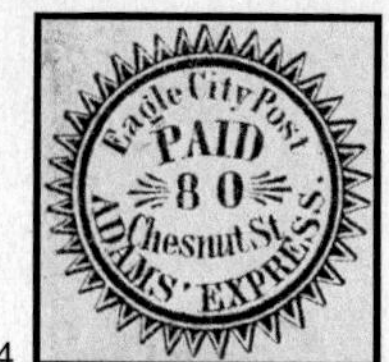

L134

Two types: 39 and 46 points around circle.

1846 Litho.

61L2	L134 (2c) **black**	125.00	*250.00*
	On cover, tied by handstamp		*1,500.*
	On cover, not tied		*1,000.*
	Block of 4	600.00	
a.	Tete beche pair	500.00	
	Block of 18, containing 4 tete beche pairs	*4,000.*	
	On cover, manuscript tied, with 5c #1		*17,500.*

Paper varies in thickness.

Five types identified of Nos. 61L3-61L4.

The No. 61L2 with No. 1 combination cover is unique.

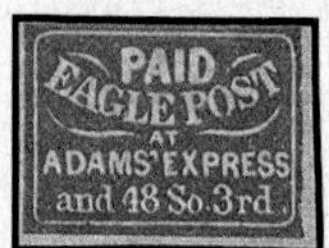

L135

1850

61L3	L135 (1c) **red,** *bluish*	225.00	225.00
	On cover, not tied, with certificate		*1,750.*
	Cracked plate		*350.00*
	On cover with 5c #1		—
61L4	L135 (1c) **blue,** *bluish*	175.00	250.00
	On cover, tied by handstamp		*6,500.*
	On cover, not tied		*400.00*
	Block of 4	*1,150.*	
	Cracked plate		*350.00*

Cancellations on Nos. 61L2-61L4: Red "PAID" in large box, red circular "Stait's at Adams Express."

East River Post Office, New York, N. Y.

Established by Jacob D. Clark and Henry Wilson in 1850, and sold to Sigmund Adler in 1852.

L136

1852 Typo.

62L1 L136 (1c) **black,** *rose* (on cover) — —

L137

1852-54 Litho.

62L3 L137 (1c) **black,** *green,* glazed — *1,000.* —
On cover, not tied — —

L138

1855

62L4	L138 (1c) **black,** *green,* glazed	250.00	250.00
	On cover		*800.00*
	On cover, not tied		*400.00*
	Vertical pair	*4,250.*	

The unique No. 62L4 pair is the only recorded multiple of any of the East River Post Office stamps.

Eighth Avenue Post Office, New York, N.Y.

L139

1852 Typo.

63L1 L139 **red,** on cover — *19,000.*

One example known, uncanceled on cover.

Empire City Dispatch, New York, N.Y.

Established by J. Bevan & Son and almost immediately suppressed by the Government.

L140

1881 Typo. Laid Paper *Perf. 12*

64L1	L140 **black,** *green*	4.00
	Block of 4	17.50
	Pane of 100	—
a.	Imperf., pair	40.00
	Block of 4	100.00
b.	Horiz. pair, imperf. btwn.	60.00
c.	Vert. pair, imperf. horiz.	40.00

No. 64L1 issued in panes of 100 (10x10) without marginal markings.

Essex Letter Express, New York, N.Y.

L141

1856 Glazed Surface Paper Typo.

65L1 L141 2c **black,** *red* — *1,250.*

Though uncanceled examples exist affixed to covers, some authorities doubt that No. 65L1 was placed in use.

Faunce's Penny Post, Atlantic City, N.J.

Established in 1884 by Ancil Faunce to provide local delivery of letters to and from the post office. Discontinued in 1887.

L141a

1885 Die cut

152L1 L141a (1c) **black,** *red* — 325. 350.
On cover — *1,500.*

Jabez Fearey & Co.'s Mustang Express, Newark, N.J.

Established by Jabez Fearey, Local Agent of the Pacific & Atlantic Telegraph Co.

L142

1887 (?) **Glazed Surface Paper** **Typeset**

66L1	L142 **black,** *red*		400.00	
	On cover			—

Some authorities consider this item to be an express company label rather than a stamp.

Fiske & Rice

Authorities consider items of this design to be express company labels rather than stamps.

Floyd's Penny Post, Chicago, Ill.

Established by John R. Floyd early in 1860, operated by him until June 20, 1861, then continued by Charles W. Mappa.

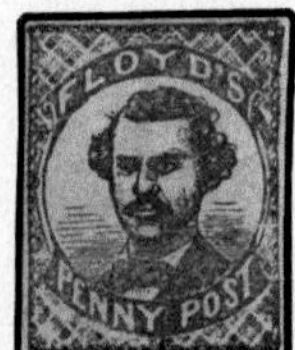

John R. Floyd — L144

1860 **Typo.**

68L1	L144 (1c) **blue** (shades)	—	125.
	On cover, tied by handstamp		1,000.
	On cover with 3c #26		2,750.
	On cover with 3c #65		1,500.
	Pair		275.
	Strip of 4		1,250.
68L2	L144 (1c) **brown**	500.	1,000.
	On cover		4,250.
68L3	L144 (1c) **green**	4,500.	3,250.
	On cover		—
	On 3c pink entire		20,000.

Cancellations: Black circle "Floyd's Penny Post Chicago," black circle "Floyd's Penny Post" and sunburst, black or blue oval "Floyd's Penny Post Chicago."

Franklin City Despatch Post, N.Y.

(See Bouton's Manhattan Express.)

Frazer & Co., Cincinnati, Ohio.

Established by Hiram Frazer. Stamps used while he was a Cincinnati letter carrier. Stamps of designs L146 and L147 were carrier stamps when used on cover between Feb, 3, 1848 and June 30, 1849.

L145

Cut to shape

1845 **Glazed Surface Paper**

69L1	L145 2c **black,** *green,* on cover, ms. tied		1,500.

L146

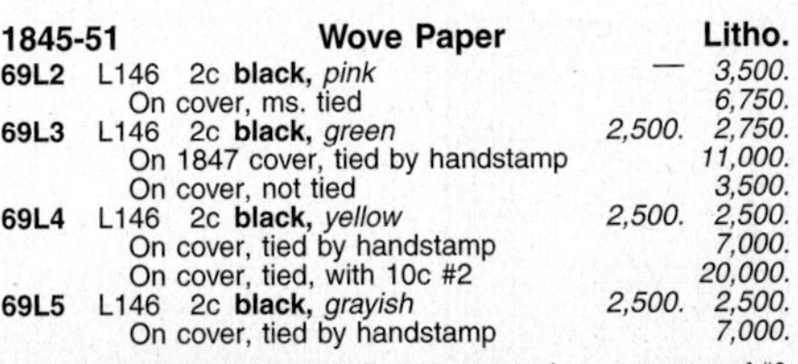

1845-51 **Wove Paper** **Litho.**

69L2	L146 2c **black,** *pink*	—	3,500.
	On cover, ms. tied		6,750.
69L3	L146 2c **black,** *green*	2,500.	2,750.
	On 1847 cover, tied by handstamp		11,000.
	On cover, not tied		3,500.
69L4	L146 2c **black,** *yellow*	2,500.	2,500.
	On cover, tied by handstamp		7,000.
	On cover, tied, with 10c #2		20,000.
69L5	L146 2c **black,** *grayish*	2,500.	2,500.
	On cover, tied by handstamp		7,000.

Three stamps of type L146 show manual ms. erasure of "& Co."

L147

1848-51

69L6	L147 2c **black,** *rose*	2,750.	
	On 1848 cover, not tied, with certificate		6,500.
69L7	L147 2c **black,** *blue* (shades)	3,500.	2,000.
69L8	L147 2c **black,** *yellow*	2,750.	
	On 1848 part-printed notice		7,500.

Hiram Frazer was a government letter carrier until June 5, 1849. Therefore, any usage before that date is a government-carrier usage, not a local-post usage.

Freeman & Co.'s Express, New York, N.Y.

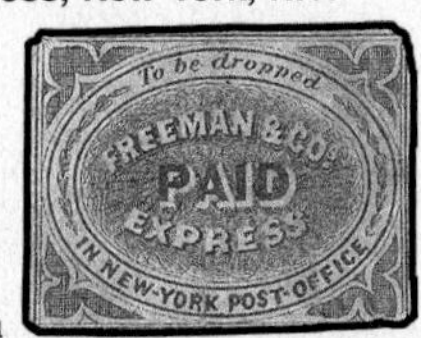

L147a

1855 (?) **Litho.**

164L1	L147a (25c) **blue**	3,500.	
	On cover, not tied, with certificate		—

Friend's Boarding School, Barnesville, Ohio.

(Barclay W. Stratton, Supt.)

On Nov. 6, 1877 the school committee decided to charge the students one cent for each letter carried to or from the post office, one and a half miles away. Adhesive labels were prepared and sold for one cent each. Their sale and use continued until 1884.

Type I — L147b

Type II — L147c

Type III — L147d

1877 **Typo.**

151L1	L147b (1c) **black,** type I	175.00	—
	On cover, uncanceled, affixed to front of cover		550.00
	On cover, uncanceled, affixed to back of cover		*400.00*
	On cover, used with 3c #147		2,400.
	On cover, used with 1c #156		2,400.
	On cover, used with 3c #158		2,000.
	On cover, used with 3c #184		2,250.
	On cover, used with 3c #207		2,400.
	On cover, used with 2c #210		2,400.

1881 **Typo.**

151L2	L147c (1c) **black,** type II	300.00	
	On cover, uncanceled, affixed to front of cover		600.00
	On cover, uncanceled, affixed to back of cover		*500.00*
	On cover, used with 3c #158		2,400.
	On cover, used with 3c #184		2,400.
	On cover, used with 3c #207		2,400.
	On cover, used with 2c #210		2,500.

1882 **Typo.**

151L3	L147d (1c) **black,** type III	300.00	
	On cover, uncanceled, affixed to front of cover		550.00
	On cover, uncanceled, affixed to back of cover		*450.00*
	On cover, used with 3c #158		2,400.
	On cover, used with 3c #184		2,400.
	On cover, used with 3c #207		2,500.
	On cover, used with 2c #210		2,250.

Nos. 151L1-151L3 were affixed to either the front or back of the envelope and left uncanceled.

Gahagan & Howe City Express, San Francisco, Calif.

Established by Dennis Gahagan and C. E. B. Howe, as successors to John C. Robinson, proprietor of the San Francisco Letter Express. Sold in 1865 to William E. Loomis, who later purchased the G. A. Carnes business. Loomis used the adhesive stamps and handstamps of these posts, changing the Carnes stamp by erasing his name.

L148

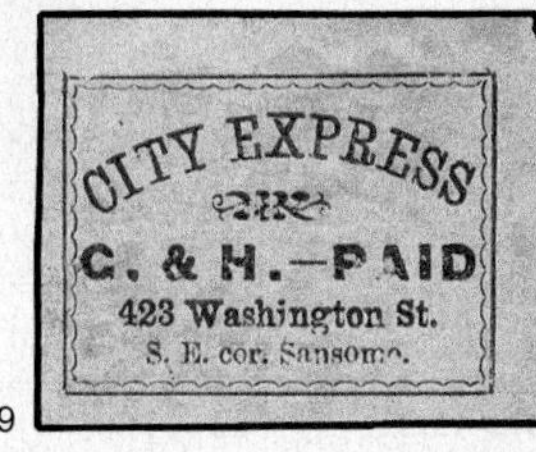

L149

1849-70 **Typeset**

70L1	L148 5c **light blue**	1,200.	800.
70L2	L149 (5c) **blue**	150.	400.
a.	Tete beche pair	450.	
	Sheet of 20, with 4 tete beche pairs		—

Sheets of No. 70L2 contain five vertical rows of 4, the first two rows being reversed against the others, making horizontal tete beche pairs with wide margins between. The pairs were not evenly locked up in the form. There are five different types of No. 70L2.

L150

70L3	L150 (5c) **black**	40.00	45.00
	Pair		100.00
	Strip of 3		175.00

No. 70L3 Overprinted

70L4	L150 10c **black**	1,500.	

Cancellations: Blue or black oval "Gahagan & Howe," blue or black oval "San Francisco Letter Express" and horseman (Robinson), blue or black oval "PAID" (Loomis).

Glen Haven Daily Mail, Glen Haven, N.Y.

Glen Haven was located at the head of Skaneateles Lake, Cayuga County, N.Y., until 1910 when the City of Syracuse, having purchased the land for reservoir purposes, razed all the buildings.

Glen Haven, by 1848, had become a famous Water Cure resort, with many sanitariums conducted there.

The hamlet had a large summer colony interested in dress reform under the leadership of Amelia Jenks Bloomer; also antislavery, and other reform movements.

A local post was established by the hotel and sanitarium managements for their guests' convenience to deliver mail to the U.S. post offices at Homer or Scott, N.Y. The local stamps were occasionally pen canceled. They are known tied to cover with the Homer or Scott town postmark when the local stamp was placed adjacent to the government stamp and received the cancellation accidentally. The local stamps are only known used in conjunction with government stamps.

L151

L152

1854-58 Several varieties of each Typeset

71L1 L151 1c **black,** *dark green* 1,000.
a. "Gien" instead of "Glen" *3,500.*
On cover, uncanceled, with 3c #26, with certificate *6,250.*

No. 71L1a unused (actually uncanceled on piece) and on cover with #26 each are unique.

Glazed Surface Paper

71L2 L152 1c **black,** *green* *500.* *500.*
On cover *2,000.*
On cover, tied by handstamp. with 3c #11 *3,750.*

Links at corners — L153

Varying ornaments at corners — L153a

Several varieties of each

Glazed Surface Paper

71L3 L153 1c **black,** *green* 200. *225.*
On cover *2,000.*
On cover, tied by handstamp, with 3c #11 *1,750.*
On cover, not tied, with 3c #11 *500.*
Pair 700.
71L4 L153a 1c **black,** *green* 300. 350.
On cover *1,000.*
On 3c entire #U9, tied by handstamp *1,650.*
On cover, tied by handstamp, with three 1c #7 *1,100.*
"Block" of 3 *900.00*

The strip of 3 of No. 71L4 is the only known multiple of any Glen Haven stamp. It has faults and is valued thus.

Gordon's City Express, New York, N. Y.

Established by Samuel B. Gordon

L154

1848-52 Typo. Surface Colored Paper

72L1 L154 2c **black,** *vermilion* *7,000.*
On cover, uncanceled, with certificate *15,000.*
72L2 L154 2c **black,** *green* 150. *175.*
On cover, tied by handstamp 950.

Glazed Surface Paper

72L3 L154 2c **black,** *green* 125. *200.*
On cover, not tied 650.

Cancellation: Small black or red "PAID."

Grafflin's Baltimore Despatch, Baltimore, Md.

Established by Joseph Grafflin; operated from Apr. 1, 1855, until June 30, 1863.

L155

Printed in sheets of 49

1856 Litho.

73L1 L155 1c **black** 200. *350.*
On cover, tied by handstamp *4,000.*
On cover, tied by handstamp, with 3c #11 *4,500.*
Block of 4 *1,050.*

Originals show traces of a fine horizontal line through tops of most of the letters in "BALTIMORE."

Guy's City Despatch, Philadelphia, Pa.

Established by F. A. Guy, who employed 8 carriers.

L156

Sheets of 25 (5x5)

1879 Typo. *Perf. 11, 12, 12½*

74L1 L156 (1c) **pink** 30.00 35.00
On cover, tied by handstamp 800.00
Block of 4 150.00
a. Imperf., pair —
74L2 L156 (1c) **blue** 45.00 60.00
On cover, tied by handstamp 1,500.
Block of 4 225.00
a. Imperf., pair —
b. (1c) **Ultramarine** *75.00* *100.00*

Cancellation: Purple company oval.

Guy's City Despatch was in operation from April to June, 1879. When Guy's was suppressed, the remainders were sold to a New York stamp dealer.

Hackney & Bolte Penny Post, Atlantic City, N.J.

Established in 1886 by Evan Hackney and Charles Bolte to provide delivery of mail to and from the post office. Discontinued in 1887.

L156a

Die cut

153L1 L156a (1c) **black,** *red* 250. 375.
On cover *1,500.*
On cover, tied by handstamp, with 2c #210 *4,500.*

Hale & Co.

Established by James W. Hale at New York, N.Y., to carry mail to points in New England, New York State, Philadelphia and Baltimore. Stamps sold at 6 cents each or "20 for $1.00."

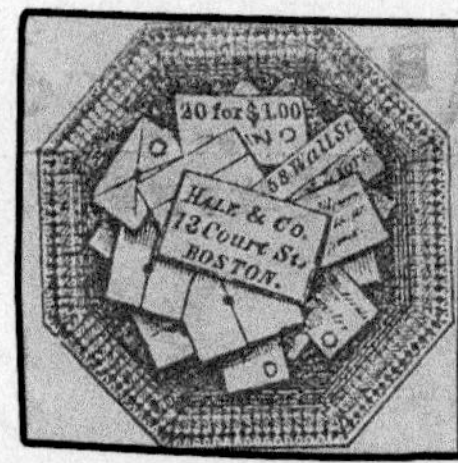

L157

L158

Pelure paper was used for initial printings, with medium wove paper used subsequently.

Printed in sheets of 20 (5x4)

1844 Typo.

75L1 L157 (6c) **light blue** (shades) 65.00 40.00
Cut to shape 17.50
On cover, tied by handstamp 500.00
Cut to shape on cover, tied by handstamp 200.00
Pair on cover, not tied *800.00*
Strip of 3 on cover, tied by handstamp *7,000.*
Strip of 3 on cover, not tied *2,750.*
a. Pelure paper —
75L2 L157 (6c) **red,** *bluish* *300.00* *300.00*
Cut to shape 75.00
On cover, tied by handstamp *2,500.*
On cover, tied by pencil cancel *1,500.*
On cover, not tied *500.00*
Cut to shape on cover, tied by handstamp *1,000.*
Pair on cover —
Ms. "23 State," cut to shape *1,900.*
On cover *4,500.*
a. Pelure paper —

Two covers recorded showing the manuscript change of address.

Nos. 75L1-75L2 Handstamped in Black or Red

75L3 L157 (6c) **red,** *bluish* (Bk), cut to shape *2,000.*
Pair, partly cut to shape *44,000.*
75L4 L157 (6c) **blue** (R), cut to shape *2,000.*

No. 75L3 single and pair each are unique.

No. 75L3 and 75L4 represent the first handstamped overprints in philately.

Same as Type L157 but street address omitted

75L5 L158 (6c) **blue** (shades) 40.00 20.00
Cut to shape 5.00
On cover, tied by handstamp 450.00
On cover, not tied 300.00
Cut to shape on cover, tied by handstamp 300.00
Pair on cover, tied by handstamp 900.00
Strip of 3 on cover, not tied —
Pair *500.00*
Block of 9 —
Block of 15 *9,500.*
Sheet of 20 (5x4) *17,000.*
Ms. "23 State St.," on cover, tied by handstamp *7,500.*

Cancellations on Nos. 75L1-75L5: Large red "PAID," red, black or blue oval "Hale & Co." (several types and cities), small red ornamental framed box (several types), red negative monogram "WE," magenta ms. "NB" (New Bedford).

The No. 75L5 sheet of 20 is unique.

Same as Type L158 Handstamped in Red "Office / 23 State St"

75L6 L158 (6c) **blue,** on cover —

No. 75L6 is unique.

Hall & Mills' Despatch Post, New York, N.Y.

Established by Gustavus A. Mills and A. C. Hall.

L159

Several Varieties

1847 Glazed Surface Paper Typeset

76L1 L159 (2c) **black,** *green* *300.* *300.*
On cover, tied by handstamp *2,500.*
On cover, tied, with 5c #1b (unique) *14,500.*

T.A. Hampton City Despatch, Philadelphia, Pa.

L159a

L159b

Several varieties of L159a.

1847	**Cut to shape**		**Typeset**
77L1	L159a (2c) **black**	*1,500.*	
	On cover, tied by handstamp		*14,000.*
	On cover, uncanceled, with certificate		*5,000.*
77L2	L159b **black**	*4,000.*	
	On cover		*13,000.*

Only one cover known with No. 77L1 tied by handstamp. Five or six covers are known with stamp uncanceled.

Two covers known with No. 77L2, each with stamp canceled, not tied. May 23 cover with certificate is valued above. Second cover is undated Valentine cover. The unused No. 77L2 is unique.

A handstamp similar to type L159b with denomination "2cts" or "3c" instead of "PAID." in center has been used as a postmark.

Hanford's Pony Express, New York, N.Y.

Established by John W. Hanford.

L160

1845	**Glazed Surface Paper**		**Typo.**
78L1	L160 2c **black,** *orange yellow* (shades)	400.	400.
	Cut to shape		60.
	On cover, tied by handstamp		*2,250.*
	On cover, not tied		*1,250.*

Cancellation: Small red "PAID."

The handstamp in black or red formerly listed as Nos. 78LU1-78LU6 is illustrated in the Local Handstamped Covers section. It was used as a postmark and there is no evidence that any prepaid handstamped envelopes or lettersheets were ever sold.

George S. Harris City Despatch Post, Philadelphia, Pa.

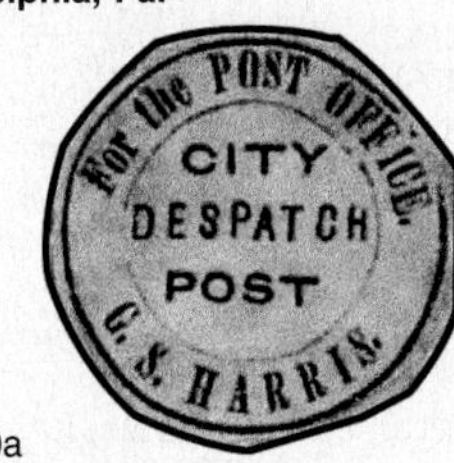

L160a

L160b

1847 (?)		**Litho. or Typo.**
79L1	L160a (2c) **black,** on cover	—
	Litho. or Typo.	
79L2	L160b **black,** on cover	*30,000.*

One example each known of Nos. 79L1-79L2, each uncanceled on cover, No. 79L2 with certificate.

Hartford, Conn. Mail Route

L161

Plate of 12 (6x2) varieties

1844	**Glazed Surface Paper**		**Engr.**
80L1	L161 (5c) **black,** *yellow*	*1,250.*	*2,000.*
	On cover, not canceled		*11,000.*
	On cover, not tied		*11,000.*
	Pair		5,000.
	Pair on cover, not canceled		*32,500.*
80L3	L161 **black,** *pink*		*3,500.*

Chemically affected examples of No. 80L1 appear as buff, and of No. 80L3 as salmon.

Cancellations are usually initials or words ("S," "W," "South," etc.) in black ms. This may indicate destination or routing.

Hill's Post, Boston, Mass.

Established by Oliver B. Hill

L162

1849		**Typo.**
81L1	L162 1c **black,** *rose,* on cover, tied by handstamp	*7,500.*
	On cover, canceled but not tied, with certificate	*6,500.*

Only one No. 81L1 tied to cover recorded. Six covers recorded bearing No. 80L1 not tied, all but one of those also uncanceled.

A. M. Hinkley's Express Co., New York, N.Y.

Organized by Abraham M. Hinkley, Hiram Dixon and Hiram M. Dixon, in 1855, and business transferred to the Metropolitan Errand & Carrier Express Co. in same year.

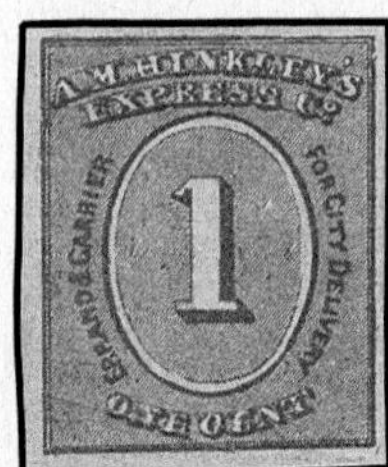

L163

Sheets of 64 (8x8)

1855			**Litho.**
82L1	L163 1c **red,** *bluish*	*650.00*	
	Block of 4	—	
a.	Tete-beche pair	—	

It is doubtful that No. 82L1 was ever placed in use.

Only one example of No. 82L1a is recorded. It is contained in a block of 16 of No. 82L1.

Reprints exist on white paper somewhat thicker than the originals.

Homan's Empire Express, New York, N.Y.

Established by Richard S. Homan

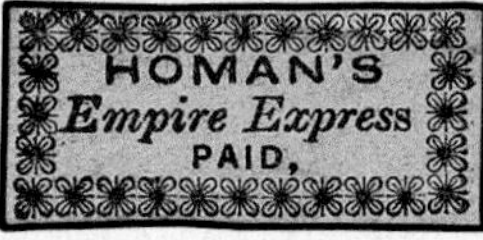

L164

1852	**Several varieties**		**Typeset**
83L1	L164 **black,** *yellow*	—	—
a.	"1" for "I" in "PAID"		*9,750.*

No. 83L1a is unique. It is affixed to a cover front, uncanceled, with certificate.

Hopedale Penny Post, Milford, Mass.

Hopedale was a large farm community southwest of Milford, Mass. The community meeting of Feb. 2, 1849, voted to arrange for regular transportation of mail to the nearest post office, which was at Milford, a mile and a half distant, at a charge of 1c a letter. A complete history of this community may be found in "The Hopedale Community," published in 1897.

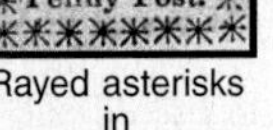

Rayed asterisks in corners — L165

Plain asterisks in corners — L166

Several varieties of Types L165-L166.

1849	**Glazed Surface Paper**		**Typeset**
84L1	L165 (1c) **black,** *pink*	*800.00*	*800.00*
	On cover with 3c #11, handstamp tied		*3,750.*
	On cover with 3c #11A, not canceled		*1,000.*
84L2	L166 (1c) **black,** *pink*	*1,000.*	*1,000.*

Types L165 and L166 probably were printed together in a single small plate.

L167

	Wove Paper		**Typo.**
84L3	L167 (1c) **black,** *yellow*	—	*2,400.*
	Cut to shape	*900.*	
	On cover		—
84L4	L167 (1c) **black,** *pink*	*600.*	*600.*
	Pair	*4,500.*	

The No. 84L4 pair is unique, defective at top. It is the only recorded multiple of any Hopedale Penny Post issue.

J. A. Howell's City Despatch, Philadelphia, Pa.

L167a

184?		**Typo.**
165L1	L167a **black**	—

Hoyt's Letter Express, Rochester, N.Y.

David Hoyt, agent at Rochester for the express company of Livingston, Wells & Pomeroy, operated a letter and package express by boats on the Genesee Canal between Dansville, N.Y., and Rochester, where connection was also made with Pomeroy's Letter Express.

L168

Several Varieties

1844	**Glazed Surface Paper**		**Typeset**
85L1	L168 (5c) **black,** *vermilion*	*4,000.*	—
	On cover, with #117L3, each ms. canceled, not tied		17,000.
a.	"Lettcr" instead of "Letter"		—
	Pair, #85L1, 85L1a, on cover front		—

Humboldt Express, Nevada

A branch of Langton's Pioneer Express, connecting with the main line of Pioneer Express at Carson City, Nevada, and making tri-weekly trips to adjacent points.

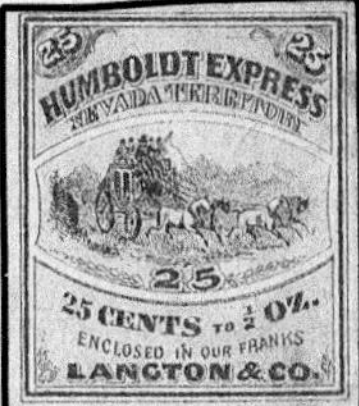

L169

1863 **Litho.**

86L1 L169 25c **brown** 1,750. 1,250.
Pair *2,750.*
On cover (U.S. Envelopes Nos. U34 or U35) *40,000.*
On cover with 3c #65 —

Cancellations: Blue oval "Langton's Pioneer Express Unionville." Red "Langton & Co."

Hussey's Post, New York, N.Y.

Established by George Hussey.
Reprints available for postage are so described.

L170

1856 **Litho.**

87L1 L170 (1c) **blue** 500. 500.
On cover, tied by handstamp *2,750.*
On cover, with U.S. 3c (#11) —

L171

1857

87L2 L171 (1c) **black** 300. 200.
On cover, tied by handstamp *1,850.*
87L3 L171 (1c) **red** 200.
On cover, tied by handstamp *750.*

Cancellation on Nos. 87L1-87L3: Black "FREE."

L172

1858

87L4 L172 1c **brown red** 45. *125.*
On cover, tied by handstamp *450.*
Pair on cover *1,000.*
87L5 L172 1c **black** *175.* —
On cover —
Block of 4 —
Strip of 7 —

Cancellation on Nos. 87L4-87L5: Black circle "1ct PAID HUSSEY 50 Wm. ST," date in center.

The No. 87L5 block of 4 and strip of 7 are unique.

L173

1858

87L6 L173 (1c) **black** 5.00 —
On cover —
87L7 L173 (1c) **rose red** 5.00 —
On cover —
Sheet of 46 *350.00*
87L8 L173 (1c) **red** 60.00 —
On cover —
Sheet of 46 —

Type L173 was printed in sheets of 46: 5 horizontal rows of 8, one row of 6 sideways at botton. Type L173 saw little, if any, commercial use and was probably issued mainly for collectors. Covers exist, many with apparently contemporaneous corner cards. On-cover stamps bear a black HUSSEY'S POST handstamp, but most if not all of Nos. 87L6-87L8 were canceled after the post ceased to operate.

L174

1858 **Typo.**

87L9 L174 (1c) **blue** 5.00

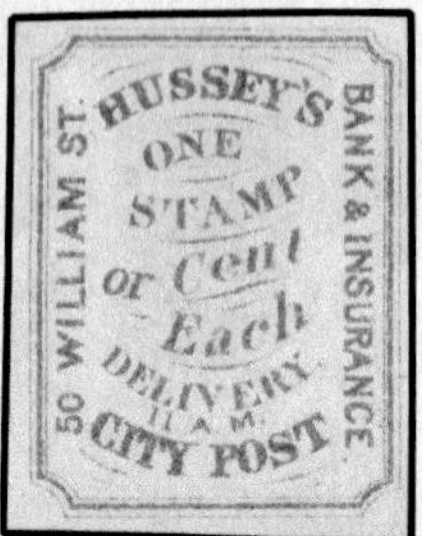

L175

1859 **Litho.**

87L10 L175 1c **rose red** 15.00 *40.00*
On cover, tied by handstamp *400.00*

No. 87L10 in orange red is not known to have been placed in use.

Cancellations: Black "FREE," black company circle "1 CT PAID HUSSEY 50 WM ST.," no date in center (smaller than cancel on Nos. 87L4-87L5).

87L11 L175 1c **lake** —
87L12 L175 1c **black** —

L176

1862

87L13 L176 1c **black** 25.00
87L14 L176 1c **blue** 15.00 *25.00*
On cover, tied by handstamp *600.00*
87L15 L176 1c **green** 20.00
On cover *450.00*
87L16 L176 1c **red** 30.00
87L17 L176 1c **red brown** 30.00
87L18 L176 1c **brown** 30.00
87L19 L176 1c **lake** —
87L20 L176 1c **purple** 30.00
87L21 L176 1c **yellow** 30.00

L177

Similar to L174 but has condensed "50" and shows a short flourish line over the "I" of "DELIVERY."

Printed in sheets of 49

1862

87L22 L177 (1c) **blue** 3.00 *25.00*
On cover —

L178

Similar to L171, but no dots in corners — L179

Printed in sheets of 30

1863

87L23 L178 (1c) **blue** 7.50
87L24 L179 (1c) **black** 5.00
Sheet of 30 225.00
87L25 L179 (1c) **red** 6.50
Sheet of 30 250.00
On cover with 6c #115 *12,500.*

See No. 87L52.

L180

87L26 L180 1c **brown red** 5.00 *25.00*
Block of 4 25.00
On cover, tied by handstamp *450.00*

A so-called "reprint" of No. 87L26, made for J. W. Scott, has a colored flaw extending diagonally upward from the "I" in "CITY."

Reprints of types L173, L174, L178, L179 and L180 were made in 1875-76 on thicker paper in approximately normal colors and were available for postage.

See No. 87L52

L182

1863

87L27 L182 1c **blue** 20.00
Cut to shape 12.50
On cover, tied by handstamp *500.00*
87L28 L182 1c **green** 27.50 —
Cut to shape 14.00
On cover, tied by handstamp *550.00*
87L29 L182 1c **yellow** 25.00 —
Cut to shape 12.50
On cover, tied by handstamp *500.00*
87L30 L182 1c **brown** 27.50
Cut to shape 14.00
87L31 L182 1c **red brown** 30.00
Cut to shape 15.00
87L32 L182 1c **red** 27.50
Cut to shape 14.00
87L33 L182 1c **black** 40.00
Cut to shape 20.00
87L34 L182 1c **violet** 40.00
Cut to shape 20.00
87L35 L182 2c **brown** 40.00 *75.00*
Cut to shape 20.00
On cover, tied by handstamp *650.00*

The 2c blue dated 1863 exists only as a counterfeit.

1865

87L38 L182 2c **blue** 35.00 *45.00*
On cover, tied by handstamp *475.00*

1867

87L39 L182 2c **blue** 45.00 40.00
On cover, tied by handstamp *450.00*

1868
87L40 L182 2c **blue** 40.00 *65.00*
On cover, tied by handstamp *500.00*

1869
87L41 L182 2c **blue** 45.00 *70.00*
On cover, tied by handstamp *500.00*

1871
87L42 L182 2c **blue** 40.00 *65.00*
On cover, tied by handstamp *750.00*

L183

1872 **Wove Paper**
87L43 L183 **black** 5.00 *20.00*
On cover, tied by handstamp *300.00*
Pair on cover, tied by handstamp *1,500.*
87L44 L183 **red lilac** 9.00 *40.00*
On cover, tied by handstamp *300.00*
87L45 L183 **blue** 6.00 *40.00*
On cover, tied by handstamp *300.00*
Pair on cover, tied by handstamp *750.00*
87L46 L183 **green** 10.00 *45.00*
On cover, tied by handstamp *300.00*

Sheets contain four panes of 28 each. Double periods after "A.M." on two stamps in two panes, and on four stamps in the other two panes.

Covers show postmark reading: "HUSSEY'S SPECIAL-MESSENGER EXPRESS-PAID-54 PINE ST."

L184

1872 **Thick Laid paper**
87L47 L184 **black** 10.00 *35.00*
On cover —
Block of 4 45.00
87L48 L184 **yellow** 17.50 *65.00*
87L49 L184 **red brown** 17.50 *50.00*
On cover *200.00*
87L50 L184 **red** 17.50 *40.00*
On cover —

L185

1873 **Thin Wove Paper**
87L51 L185 2c **black** 75.00 *150.00*
On cover, tied by handstamp *500.00*

A reprint of No. 87L51, believed to have been made for J. W. Scott, shows a 4mm break in the bottom frameline under "54."

Type of 1863

1875 **Thick Wove Paper**
87L52 L179 (1c) **blue** *750.00*

L186

L186 in imitation of L180, but no corner dots, "S" for "$," etc.

1875
87L53 L186 1c **black** 2.00

Some authorities believe Nos. 87L52-87L53 are imitations made from new stones. Attributed to J. W. Scott.

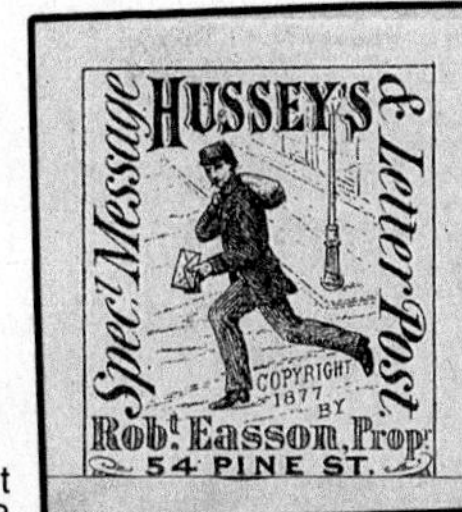

"Copyright 1877" — L188

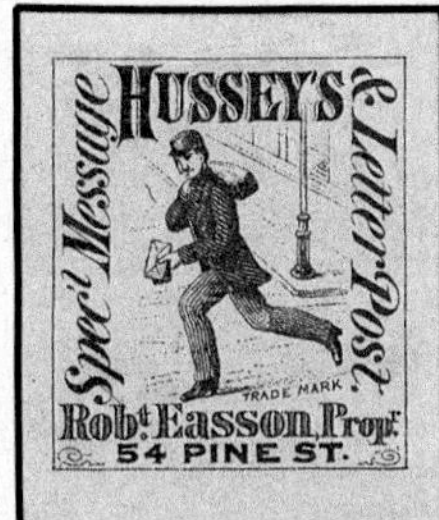

L188a

1877 **Thick Wove Paper**
87L55 L188 **black** *175.00* —
On cover, tied by handstamp *3,250.*

Error of design, used provisionally. Stamp was never copyrighted. Printed singly.

87L56 L188a **black** *350.00*

Thin Wove Paper

87L57 L188a **blue** *45.00*
87L58 L188a **rose** 30.00
On cover —

Perf. 12½

87L59 L188a **blue** 3.00 *10.00*
On cover *250.00*
a. Imperf. horizontally, pair —
87L60 L188a **rose** *3.00* 10.00
On cover *250.00*

"TRADE MARK" small — L189

"TRADE MARK" medium — L190

1878 **Wove Paper** ***Perf. 11, 11½, 11x12, 12***
87L61 L189 **blue** 15.00 *50.00*
On cover, tied by handstamp *150.00*
87L62 L189 **carmine** 12.50 *40.00*
On cover, tied by handstamp *200.00*
87L63 L189 **black** 100.00

Nos. 87L61-87L63 exist imperforate.

Perf. 11, 12, 12½, 14, 16 and Compound

87L64 L190 **blue** 5.00 *17.50*
On cover, tied by handstamp *200.00*
87L65 L190 **red** 5.00 *10.00*
On cover, tied by handstamp *150.00*
87L66 L190 **black** —

The existence of No. 87L66 either perforated or as an imperf reprint has been questioned by specialists. The editors would like to see authenticated evidence of its existence.

Nos. 87L64-87L65 imperf. are reprints.

"TRADE MARK" larger, touching "s" of "Easson." — L191

1879 ***Perf. 11, 12, and Compound***
87L67 L191 **blue** 3.00 *10.00*
On cover, tied by handstamp *300.00*

1880 ***Imperf.***
87L70 L191 **blue** 4.00 *50.00*
On cover, tied by handstamp *450.00*
87L71 L191 **red** 5.00 *75.00*
87L72 L191 **black** 4.00

The authenticity of Nos. 87L70-87L72 has not been fully established.

L192

Two types of L192:
I. Imprint "N. F. Seebeck, 97 Wall St. N. Y." is in lower tablet below "R Easson, etc."
II. Imprint in margin below stamp.

1880 **Glazed Surface Wove Paper** ***Perf. 12***
87L73 L192 **brown,** type I 10.00 *20.00*
On cover, tied by handstamp *250.00*
Block of 4 —
a. Type II 3.00 *5.00*
On cover, tied by handstamp *250.00*
b. Horiz. pair, imperf. between 50.00
c. Imperf., pair, type I 50.00
87L74 L192 **ultramarine,** type I 12.50 *25.00*
On cover, tied by handstamp *350.00*
a. Imperf., pair —
Imperf (single) on cover *135.00*
b. Deep blue, type II 40.00
87L75 L192 **red,** type II 1.50 *3.50*
On cover, tied by handstamp *175.00*
Block of 4 6.50
a. Imperf, single on cover *150.00*
b. Horiz. pair, imperf between —

1882 ***Perf. 16, 12x16***
87L76 L192 **brown,** type I 12.50 *30.00*
On cover, tied by handstamp *125.00*
87L77 L192 **ultramarine,** type I 10.00 *20.00*
On cover, tied by handstamp *125.00*

Cancellations: Violet 3-ring target, violet ornamental "T." Imperf. impressions of Type I in various colors, on horizontally laid paper, ungummed, are color trials.

SPECIAL DELIVERY STAMPS

L181

Typographed; Numerals Inserted Separately

1863 **Glazed Surface Paper**
87LE1 L181 5c **black,** *vermilion* 2.00 *17.50*
On cover, tied by handstamp *325.00*
87LE2 L181 10c **gold,** *green* 2.50 *20.00*
On cover, tied by handstamp *325.00*
87LE3 L181 15c **gold,** *black* 3.50 *27.50*
On cover, tied by handstamp *325.00*
On cover with 1c #87L10, tied by handstamps —
87LE4 L181 20c **black** 2.00 *17.50*
On cover, tied by handstamp *325.00*
87LE5 L181 25c **gold,** *blue* 4.00 *40.00*
On cover, tied by handstamp *325.00*
87LE6 L181 30c **black,** *vermilion* —
87LE7 L181 50c **black,** *green* —

Nos. 87LE1-87LE7 on cover show Hussey handstamp cancellations in various types.

Nos. 87LE4 and 87LE5 are on unglazed paper, the latter surface colored. Ten minor varieties of each value, except the 30c and 50c, which have the figures in manuscript. Printed in two panes of 10, certain values exist in horizontal cross-gutter tete beche pairs.

Originals of the 5c to 20c have large figures of value. The 25c has condensed figures with decimal point. Reprints exist with both large and condensed figures. Reprints of the 25c also exist with serifs on large figures.

Most of the Hussey adhesives are known on cover, tied with Hussey Express postmarks. Many of these were canceled after the post ceased to operate as a mail carrier. "On cover" values are for original stamps used while the post was operating.

LETTERSHEETS AND WRAPPERS (No. 87LUP2)

L192a

1856 Handstamped Inscribed: "82 Broadway"
87LUP1 L192a **black** — *500.*

L192b

1858 Inscribed: "50 William St. Basement"
87LUP2 L192b **black,** *manila* — *600.*
With 1c #87L3, tied by handstamp *1,250.*
87LUP3 L192b **black** — *650.*
With 1c #87L2, tied by handstamp *2,750.*
With 1c #87L3, tied by handstamp *1,750.*

Nos. 87LUP1 and 87LUP3 appear on papers of various colors.

Jefferson Market P. O., New York, N. Y.

Established by Godfrey Schmidt

L193

1850 Glazed Surface Paper Litho.
88L1 L193 (2c) **black,** *pink* *9,750.*
88L2 L193 (2c) **black,** *blue* —
On cover, tied by handstamp —
On cover, not tied *3,500.*

Four examples recorded of No. 88L1, all unused. Five No. 88L2 recorded, all on covers (two with stamp tied by handstamp).

Jenkins' Camden Dispatch, Camden, N. J.

Established by Samuel H. Jenkins and continued by William H. Jenkins.

George Washington — L194

There are two types of design L194.

1853-54 Litho.
89L1 L194 **black** (fine impression) (1854) *350.* *450.*
Block of 9 *7,500.*
On cover, not tied *900.*
On cover, tied by ms., with certificate *3,000.*

George Washington — L194a

Typo. from Woodcut
89L2 L194a **black,** *yellow* (coarse impression) (1853) *3,000.*
On cover, tied by ms., with certificate *6,500.*

L195

Typeset
89L3 L195 1c **black,** *grayish* (1853) —
On cover, tied by ms. *17,500.*

No. 89L3 was probably the first stamp issued by Jenkins. Each of the four known examples is of a different type. One exampled is unused; three are recorded on cover (one of which is uncanceled).

Johnson & Co.'s City Despatch Post, Baltimore, Md.

Operated by Ezekiel C. Johnson, letter carrier

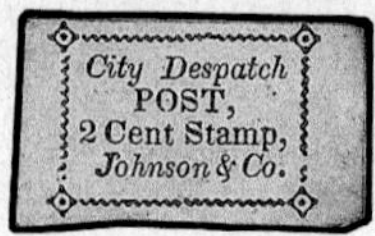

L196

1848 Typeset
90L1 L196 2c **black,** *lavender,* on cover, uncanceled *22,500.*

Two recorded examples of No. 90L1, each uncanceled on cover.

Jones' City Express, Brooklyn, N. Y.

George Washington — L197

1845 Glazed Surface Paper Engr.
91L1 L197 2c **black,** *pink* *1,000.* *1,500.*
On cover, not tied, with certificate *3,000.*

Cancellation: Red oval "Boyd's City Express Post."

Kellogg's Penny Post & City Despatch, Cleveland, Ohio

L198

1853 Typo.
92L1 L198 (1c) **vermilion** *1,750.*
On cover, tied by handstamp —
On cover, tied by handstamp, with 3c #11A, with certificate *10,000.*
On cover, not tied, with 3c #11, with certificate *7,500.*
On 3c entire #U2, tied by handstamp *6,000.*

Cancellation: Black grid.

Kidder's City Express Post, Brooklyn, N.Y.

In 1847, Henry A. Kidder took over the post of Walton & Co., and with the brothers Isaac C. Snedeker and George H. Snedeker increased its scope. In 1851, the business was sold to the Snedekers. It was operated under the old name until 1853 when the Brooklyn City Express Post was founded.

L199

Stamps bear black manuscript "I S" control in two styles.

1847 Glazed Surface Paper Typo.
93L1 L199 2c **black,** *blue* (shades) *750.* 500.
On cover, tied by handstamp *6,000.*
On cover, not tied *4,500.*
Block of 4 3,500.

Cancellation: Red "PAID."

Reprinted on green paper.

Kurtz Union Despatch Post, New York, N.Y.

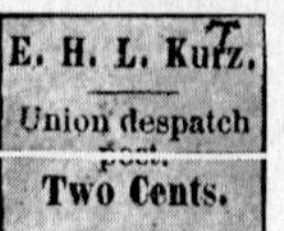

L200

Typeset; "T" in Black Ms.

1853 Glazed Surface Paper
94L1 L200 2c **black,** *green* *3,500.*

Langton & Co.

(See Humboldt Express.)

Ledger Dispatch, Brooklyn, N.Y.

Established by Edwin Pidgeon. Stamps reported to have been sold at 80 cents per 100. Suppressed after a few months.

L201

1882 Typo. *Rouletted 12 in color*
95L1 L201 **rose** (shades) 300. *600.*
Block of 4 *1,500.*

Letter Express

Established by Henry Wells. Carried mail for points in Western New York, Chicago, Detroit and Milwaukee.

L202

L203

1844 Glazed Surface Paper Typo.
96L1 L202 5c **black,** *pink* 300.00 200.00
On cover, tied by ms. cancel *1,000.*
On cover, not tied *500.00*
Pair on cover, tied by handstamp *3,500.*
Pair on cover, tied by ms. cancel *2,000.*
Pair on cover, not tied *1,000.*
Pair 700.00 450.00
Block of 10 *28,500.*
96L2 L202 5c **black,** *green* — 500.00
On cover, tied by ms. cancel *5,000.*
On cover, not tied *3,500.*
Pair *1,500.*
96L3 L203 10c **black,** *pink* — 500.00
On cover, tied by ms. cancel *2,000.*
On cover, not tied *1,500.*
On cover, not tied, with #117L1, not tied, with certificate *2,000.*
Pair *1,500.* *1,500.*
Pair on cover, uncanceled *5,000.*
Strip of 3 *9,250.*
a. Bisect on cover, tied by ms. cancel —
Bisect on cover, uncanceled *2,000.*

No. 96L3a was sold as a horizontal or vertical bisect. It is known used singly for 5c (rare), or as two bisects for 10c (extremely rare). Stamps are known almost exclusively tied with black ms. "X" covering the cut, and can be authenticated by experts.

The block of 10 of No. 96L1 is the only block recorded of any Letter Express issue. Value represents actual auction sale price in 1999.

L204

96L4	L204 10c **black,** *scarlet*	—	*2,500.*
	On cover, tied by ms. cancel, with certificate		*9,250.*
a.	Tete beche pair, one stamp a horiz. bisect, on piece		*8,750.*

Cancellations: Red large partly boxed "PAID," red boxed "Boyd's City Express Post."

Locomotive Express Post

L205

1847 (?) **Handstamped**

97L1	L205 **black,** uncancelled, on cover	—

No. 97L1 is unique.

Wm. E. Loomis Letter Express, San Francisco, Calif.

William E. Loomis established this post as the successor to the Gahagan & Howe City Express, which he bought in 1865. He continued to use the Gahagan & Howe stamps unchanged. Later Loomis bought Carnes' City Letter Express. He altered the Carnes stamp by erasing "CARNES" from the plate and adding the address below the oval: "S.E. cor. Sans'e & Wash'n."

L206

1868 **Typo.**

98L1	L206 (5c) **rose**	300.00	*650.00*
	On cover, tied by ms.		*4,250.*

Cancellation: Blue "PAID."

McGreely's Express, Alaska

Established in 1898 by S. C. Marcuse to carry letters and packages by motorboat between Dyea and Skagway, Alaska.

L208

1898 **Typo.** ***Perf. 14***

155L1	L208 25c **blue**	50.00	
	Block of 4	*250.00*	

The status of No. 155L1 is questioned.

McIntire's City Express Post, New York, N.Y.

Established by William H. McIntire

Mercury — L207

1859 **Litho.**

99L1	L207 2c **pink**	10.00	*100.00*
	Block of 4	75.00	
	On cover, tied by handstamp		*3,250.*
a.	Period after CENTS omitted	—	

Cancellation: Black oval "McIntire's City Express Post Paid."

McMillan's City Dispatch Post, Chicago, Ill.

L208a

1855 **Typeset**

100L1	L208a **black,** *rose*	*25,000.*

No. 100L1 is unique.

Mac & Co's Dispatch, Fallsington-Morrisville, Pa.

L208b

Typo.

166L1	L208b 1c **black,** on 3c entire #U1, uncanceled, with certificate	*17,500.*

No. 166L1 is unique.

Magic Letter Express, Richmond, Va.

Established by Evans, Porter & Co.

L209

L209a

1865 **Typo.**

101L1	L209 1c **black,** on cover, not tied by cancel		*40,000.*
101L2	L209a 2c **black,** *brown*		*14,000.*
101L3	L209a 5c **black,** *brown*	—	*8,000.*
	On cover		*24,000.*

Nos. 101L1-101L2 each are unique.

Mason's New Orleans City Express, New Orleans, La.

J. Mason, proprietor

L210

1850-51 **Typeset**

102L1	L210 ½c **black,** *blue* (value changed to "1" in black ms.)		*12,500.*
	On cover, tied		—
102L2	L210 2c **black,** *yellow*	—	*3,000.*
	On cover, tied by handstamp		*10,000.*

Cancellations: Red grid, small red circle "Mason's City Express."

Mearis' City Despatch Post, Baltimore, Md.

Established by Malcom W. Mearis

L211

L212

Black ms. initials "M W M" control on all stamps

1850-51 **Typeset**

103L1	L211 1c **black,** *gray*	—	—
	On cover, tied by handstamp		*22,000.*
103L2	L212 1c **black,** *gray*	—	
103L3	L212 2c **black,** *gray*	—	
	On cover, uncancelled, with certificate		*15,000.*
a.	Horiz. pair, #103L2-103L3	—	

Two types of No. 103L3.

L213

Two types of each.

103L4	L213 1c **black,** *gray*	—
103L5	L213 2c **black,** *gray*	—
a.	Horiz. pair, #103L4-103L5	—

L214

103L6	L214 1c **black,** *gray*	*11,000.*

No. 103L6 is unique; tied on small piece by handstamp.

All varieties of Nos. 103L1-103L6 contained in one plate.

L214a

103L7	L214a 2c **black,** *gray*	—

No. 103L7 is unique; tied on small piece by manuscript cancel.

All varieties of Nos. 103L1-103L7 are contained in one plate.

Menant & Co.'s Express, New Orleans, La.

L215

1853 (?) **Typo.**

104L1	L215 2c **dark red**	*15,000.*

Only four examples are known. Two have Philatelic Foundation Certificates. All four have faults, and the stamp is valued thus.

Reprints are fairly common and are orange red, not dark red.

Mercantile Library Association, New York, N.Y.

Stamps paid for special delivery service of books ordered from the library, and of forms especially provided to subscribers. The forms bore a government stamp on the outside, a library stamp inside.

L216

1870-75 **Litho.**

105L1 L216 5c **black,** *maroon* *250.* *350.*
105L2 L216 5c **black,** *yellow* *350.* *500.*
a. With delivery check attached at right *1,150.*
b. With order number on tab below stamp —
105L3 L216 5c **blue** *350.* *500.*
Pair, on delivery card, tied by handstamps *1,000.*
105L5 L216 6c **black,** *maroon* *2,250.* —
105L6 L216 10c **black,** *yellow* *500.* *750.*
On delivery card, tied by handstamp 1,000.

No. 105L5 is slightly larger than the 5c and 10c stamps.
The stamps "on delivery card" are affixed to cutouts from order blanks showing order number, title of book desired, and subscriber's name and address. When canceled, the stamps and order blanks show a dull blue double-lined oval inscribed "MERCANTILE LIBRARY ASSOCIATION" and date in center. The stamps are really more a form of receipt for a prepaid parcel delivery service than postage stamps.

POSTAL CARD

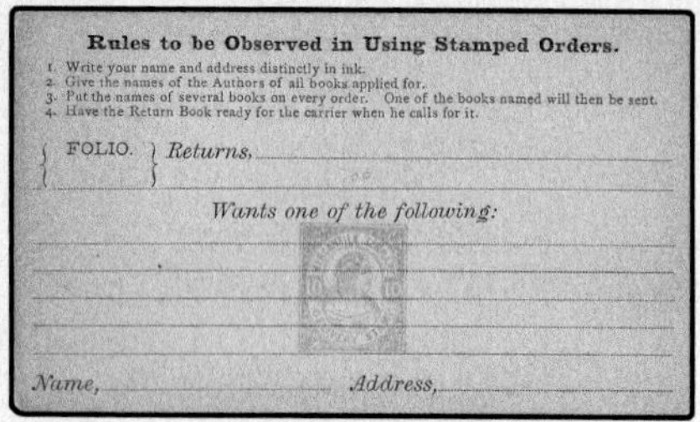
Rules to be Observed in Using Stamped Orders.

1. Write your name and address distinctly in ink.
2. Give the names of the Authors of all books applied for.
3. Put the names of several books on every order. One of the books named will then be sent.
4. Have the Return Book ready for the carrier when he calls for it.

FOLIO. *Returns,*

Wants one of the following:

Name, *Address,*

Printed on U.S. Postal Card, First Issue

105LUX1 L216a 10c **yellow** *2,500.*

No. 105LUX1 is unique.

Messenkope's Union Square Post Office, New York, N.Y.

Established by Charles F. Messenkope in 1849 and sold to Joseph E. Dunham in 1850.

L217

1849 **Glazed Surface Paper** **Litho.**

106L1 L217 (1c) **black,** *green* 90. 90.
On cover, tied by handstamp *500.*
Two singles on cover (2c rate), tied by handstamp *3,000.*
Pair on cover (2c rate), tied by handstamp *3,000.*
On cover, uncanceled, with 5c #1 *1,500.*
On cover, tied by handstamp, with 3c #10 *1,500.*
On cover, tied by handstamp, with 3c #11 *2,000.*
On cover with 3c #26 *1,000.*
Strip of 3 *400.*
106L2 L217 (2c) **black,** *pink* — —
On cover —

Some examples of No. 106L1 are found with "MESSENKOPES" crossed through in black ms. in an apparent attempt (by Dunham?) to obliterate it.
Cancellations: Red "PAID," red oval "DUNHAMS UNION SQUARE POST OFFICE," red grid of dots.

Metropolitan Errand and Carrier Express Co., New York, N.Y.

Organized Aug. 1, 1855, by Abraham M. Hinkley, Hiram Dixon, and others.

L218

L219

Printed in sheets of 100 (10x10), each stamp separated by thin ruled lines.

1855 **Thin to Medium Wove Paper** **Engr.**

107L1 L218 1c **red orange** (shades) 20.00 *25.00*
Cut to shape 5.00 *4.00*
On cover, tied by handstamp *600.00*
On cover, cut to shape, tied by handstamp *150.00*
On cover, cut to shape, tied by handstamp, with 3c #11 *900.00*
Pair 35.00
Pair on cover, tied by handstamp —
Pair on cover, uncanceled *1,000.*
Block of 4 *90.00*
107L2 L218 5c **red orange** 225.00
Cut to shape 60.00
107L3 L218 10c **red orange** 300.00
Cut to shape 60.00
107L4 L218 20c **red orange** 325.00
Cut to shape 60.00

Cancellations: Black, blue or green boxed "PAID."
The imprint "Baldwin, Bald & Cousland New York" appears in the bottom margin of the two stamps at the bottom right of the sheets.
Nos. 107L1-107L4 have been extensively reprinted in brown and in blue on paper much thicker than the originals.

ENVELOPE
Embossed
Wide Diagonally Laid Paper

107LU1 L219 2c **red,** *amber,* entire *125.00* —

No. 107LU1 has been reprinted on amber wove, diagonally laid or horizontally laid paper with narrow lines. The embossing is sharper than on the original.

Metropolitan Post Office, New York, N.Y.

Established by Lemuel Williams who later took William H. Laws as a partner.

L220

L221

L222

L223

Nos. 108L1-108L5 were issued die cut

1852-53 **Glazed Surface Paper** **Embossed**

108L1 L220 (2c) **red** (L. Williams) *550.* *550.*
On cover, tied by pencil, with certificate —
On cover, tied by blue ms., with two 3c #11 and strip of 3 12c #17 —
108L2 L221 (2c) **red** (address and name erased) *1,000.* *1,000.*
On cover, uncanceled, with certificate *5,500.*
108L3 L222 (2c) **red** *275.* *350.*
On cover, tied by handstamp *3,500.*
108L3A L222 (2c) **blue** *600.* *700.*
On cover, tied by handstamp *7,500.*
On cover, tied by handstamp, with 3c #11 *8,250.*

Wove Paper

108L4 L223 1c **red** 75. *90.*
On cover 300.
On cover, tied by handstamp, with 3c #11 *1,500.*
On cover, cut to shape, not tied, with 3c #11A *500.*
On 3c U.S. envelope #U9, tied by handstamp *1,500.*
108L5 L223 1c **blue** 600. *100.*
Cut to shape 400.
On cover 350.
On cover, cut to shape, tied by handstamp, with 3c #11 *300.*
On cover, tied by handstamp, with 3c #26 *700.*

Cancellations: Black circle "METROPOLITAN P. O.," black boxed "PAID W. H. LAWS," black smudge.

G. A. Mills' Despatch Post, New York, N.Y.

Established by Gustavus A. Mills at 6 Wall St., succeeding Hall & Mills.

L224

Several Varieties

1847 **Glazed Surface Paper** **Typeset**

109L1 L224 (2c) **black,** *green* *500.* *500.*
On cover, uncanceled, with 5c #1 *1,400.*
On cover, tied by handstamp *1,900.*
On cover, not tied, with 5c #1 *3,500.*
On cover with 10c #2 —

Moody's Penny Dispatch, Chicago, Ill.

Robert J. Moody, proprietor

"CHICAGO" 8mm — L225

Several Varieties

1856 **Glazed Surface Paper** **Typeset**

110L1 L225 (1c) **black,** *red,* *1,750.* *1,750.*
On cover, tied by handstamp, with 3c #11 *16,000.*
On cover with three 1c #9 (unique) *35,000.*
Vert. strip of 3 showing 3 varieties: period, colon, comma after "Dispatch" *18,000.* 6,000.
a. "CHICAGO" sans serif and 12½mm *2,750.*
b. "Henny" instead of "Penny," on cover, tied by handstamp, with 3c #11A (unique) *32,500.*

Cancellations: Blue circle "Moody's Despatch."
The vertical strip of 3, the cover with the three 1c stamps and No. 110L1b, are each unique.

Morton's Post, Philadelphia, Pa.

L225a

167L1 L225a 2c **black,** *grayish,* on cover, uncanceled, with certificate *14,000.*

No. 167L1 is unique.

New York City Express Post, New York, N.Y.

L226

Several varieties

1847 **Glazed Surface Paper** **Engr.**

111L1 L226 2c **black,** *green* *1,200.* *1,500.*
Cut to shape *400.* *450.*
On cover, not tied *1,750.*
On cover, tied by handstamp *4,000.*

On cover, cut to shape, tied by handstamp — 2,000.

Wove Paper

111L2 L226 2c **orange** — —
On cover — 8,000.

One Cent Despatch, Baltimore, Md., Washington, D.C.

Established by J.H. Wiley to deliver mail in Washington, Georgetown and Baltimore. Made as many as five deliveries daily at 1 cent if prepaid, or 2 cents payable on delivery.

Washington, D.C. — L227

Two types:
I. Courier's letter points to "O" of "ONE."
II. Letter points to "N" of "ONE."

Inscribed at bottom "Washington City"

1856 **Litho.**

112L1 L227 1c **violet** 225. 150.
On cover, tied by handstamp 750.
On cover, tied by handstamp, with 3c #11 1,500.
On cover, tied, with 10c #15 5,500.
On 3c entire #U1, tied by handstamp 750.
Horiz. pair, types I & II 1,250.

Baltimore, Maryland — L228

No name at bottom

112L2 L228 1c **red** 450. 250.
On cover, tied by handstamp 1,750.
On cover with 3c #11 2,250.

The No. 112L1 pair is the unique multiple of either One Cent Despatch stamp.
Cancellation on Nos. 112L1-112L2: Black circle "City Despatch."

Overton & Co.

Carried mail principally between New York and Boston; also to Albany. Stamps sold for 6c each, 20 for $1.

L229

1844-45

113L1 L229 (6c) **black,** *greenish* 400. 400.
On cover, tied by ms. 5,000.
On cover, not tied 2,250.
a. "FREE" printed below design 1,000.
On cover 4,000.
Pair on cover, not tied, with certificate 18,500.

Cancellation: Black "PAID." Red "Cd."
See also City Mail Co., No. 46L1.

Penny Express Co.

Little information is available on this post, but a sheet is known carrying the ms. initials of Henry Reed of the Holladay staff. The post was part of the Holladay Overland Mail and Express Co. system.

In 1866 in the West the "short-bit" or 10 cents was the smallest currency generally used. The word "penny" is believed to refer to the "half-bit" or 5 cents (nickel).

L230

Printed in sheets of 32 (8x4)

1866 **Litho.**

114L1 L230 5c **black** 400.00
Pair 850.00
a. Sheet of 32 initialed "HR," black ms., original gum 7,000.
114L2 L230 5c **blue** 15.00
Block of 4 65.00
Sheet of 32, no gum 650.00
114L3 L230 5c **red** 15.00
Block of 4 65.00
Sheet of 32, no gum 650.00

Nos. 114L1-114L3 lack gum and probably were never placed in use.

Philadelphia Despatch Post, Philadelphia, Pa.

(See D.O. Blood & Co.)

Pinkney's Express Post, New York, N.Y.

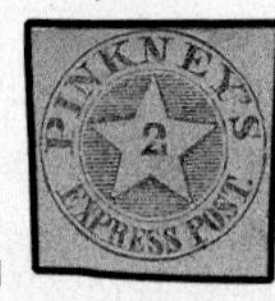

L231

1851 **Glazed Surface Paper** **Typo.**

115L1 L231 2c **black,** *green* 1,400.
Cut to shape 800.
On cover, tied by ms., with certificate 4,500.
On cover, uncanceled, with certificate 9,000.
On cover, uncanceled, cut to shape, with certificate 3,500.

On the cover with No. 115L1 tied, the stamp is faulty. It is valued thus.

Pips Daily Mail, Brooklyn, N.Y.

L232

1862 (?) **Litho.**

116L2 L232 1c **black,** *buff* 375. 2,250.
116L3 L232 1c **black,** *yellow* 600.
116L4 L232 1c **black,** *dark blue* 800.

Two types of Nos. 116L2-116L4: Type I, period after "Avenue;" Type II, comma after "Avenue."
No. 116L2 used is unique.

Pomeroy's Letter Express.

Established in 1844 by George E. Pomeroy. Carried mail principally to points in New York State. Connected with Letter Express for Western points.

L233

Engraved by John E. Gavit, Albany, N.Y.
(Seen as "GAVIT" in bottom part of stamp). Sheets of 40 (8x5).

Value Complete ("20 for $1")

1844 **Surface Colored Wove Paper**

117L1 L233 5c **black,** *greenish yellow, dull yellow* — 100.00
On cover, tied by ms. 1,000.
On cover, handstamp cancel 1,000.
Pair 375.00
Pair on cover 3,500.
Block of 4 —

Value Incomplete ("20 for $-")

117L2 L233 **black,** *greenish yellow, dull yellow* — 1,500.
On cover, tied by ms. 5,000.
On cover, handstamp cancel, not tied 4,500.
On cover, ms. cancel, not tied 3,500.
On cover, with No. 117L1 —

Value Complete ("20 for $1")

Thick Wove Paper

117L2A L233 5c **black,** *buff,* without gum —
117L2B L233 5c **black,** *yellow, buff tint on back,* without gum 5.00
Sheet of 40 300.00
117L2C L233 5c **black,** *yellow (colored through),* without gum 5.00
a. 5c **black,** orange yellow (colored through), with gum 10.00

No. 117L2A may be a proof impression. Nos. 117L2B-117L2Ca may be remainders or reprints.

Thin Bond Paper

117L3 L233 5c **blue (shades)** 150.00 500.00
On cover, not tied 2,000.
On cover, tied by pen cancel 2,500.
Pair on cover, not tied 6,000.
Block of 4 —
117L4 L233 5c **black** 5.00 150.00
On cover 1,500.
Pair on cover, red "Paid" cancel 7,500.
Strip of 4 on cover 5,000.
Block of 4 30.00
Sheet of 40, without gum 350.00
117L5 L233 5c **red (shades)** 5.00 300.00
On cover, not tied 3,500.
Strip of 3 on cover 8,500.
Block of 4 25.00
Sheet of 40 300.00
117L6 L233 5c **lake** — 750.00
On cover, tied by ms. 3,000.
Pair on cover —
On cover, handstamp cancel 6,000.
Block of 4 —

Cancellations: Large red partly boxed "PAID" (Nos. 117L1, 117L6), red "Cd" (Nos. 117L1-117L2, 117L4); stamps are considered "tied to cover" by this "Cd" when the impression shows through the letter paper.

Reprints/remainders of Nos. 117L1, 117L3, 117L4 and 117L5 are plentiful in unused condition, including multiples and sheets. They differ slightly from the original issue Nos. 117L1 and 117L2. Authentication of Nos. 117L1 and 117L2 unused is recommended. A 5c chocolate brown and a 5c bright yellow were prepared but not issued. No. 117L2 was never remaindered.

Thin Pelure Paper

117L7 L233 5c **deep blue (shades)** — —
Pair on cover, not tied 2,500.
117L8 L233 5c **black** — —
Pair — —
117L9 L233 5c **chocolate brown** — —

5c stamps on a medium, fibrous paper in orange, deep blue, black, red and brown exist. It is believed that stamps on this paper come from remainders of a printing that was prepared but never issued. They may also be reprints.

P. O. Paid, Philadelphia, Pa.

See note in Carriers' Stamps Section.

Price's City Express, New York, N.Y.

L235

1857-58 **Glazed Surface Paper** **Litho.**

119L1 L235 2c **black,** *vermilion* 275.
On cover, tied by handstamp 5,000.
On cover, ms. tied 900.
On cover, not tied, with certificate 750.
On cover, tied by handstamp, with 3c #26 —
119L2 L235 2c **black,** *green* 250.
Cut to shape 85.

L236

1858 **Sheets of 108 (12x9)**

119L3 L236 2c **black,** *green* 5.00 *150.00*
On cover —
Block of 4 27.50

Cancellation on #119L3: red oval "Price's/City Letter Exp/3 Everett House/Paid."

Price's Eighth Avenue Post Office, New York, N.Y.

Established by James Price at 350 Eighth Avenue, in 1854, and sold to Russell in the same year.

L237

1854 **Litho.**

120L1 L237 (2c) **red,** *bluish* *600.00*
On cover, uncanceled, with certificate *7,500.*

Priest's Despatch, Philadelphia, Pa.

Established by Solomon Priest

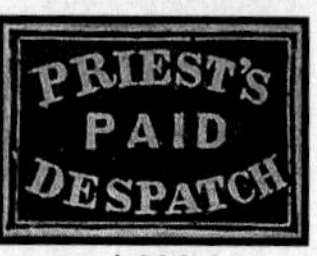

L238

L239

1851 **Glazed Surface Paper** **Typo.**

121L1 L238 (2c) **silver,** *vermilion* *2,250.* —
121L2 L238 (2c) **gold,** *dark blue* *500.*

Wove Paper

121L2A L238 (2c) **bronze,** *bluish* *500.* *1,000.*
121L3 L238 (2c) **black,** *yellow* *500.*
On cover, uncanceled, with 3c #11, with certificate *5,500.*
121L4 L238 (2c) **black,** *rose* *500.*
On cover, uncanceled, with certificate *2,000.*
121L5 L238 (2c) **black,** *blue* *1,000.*
121L6 L239 (2c) **black,** *yellow* *500.*
On cover, uncanceled, with certificate *1,500.*
On cover, uncanceled, with 3c #11, with certificate *4,500.*
121L7 L239 (2c) **black,** *blue* *750.*
On cover, uncanceled, with certificate *3,250.*
121L8 L239 (2c) **black,** *rose* *1,000.*
121L9 L239 (2c) **black,** *emerald,* uncanceled, on cover *6,500.*

No. 121L9 is believed to be unique.

Prince's Letter Dispatch, Portland, Maine

Established by J. H. Prince of Portland. Mail carried nightly by messenger travelling by steamer to Boston. Stamp engraved by Lowell of Lowell & Brett, Boston, his name appearing in the design below the steamship.

L240

Printed in sheets of 40 (5x8)

1861 **Litho.**

122L1 L240 **black** 7.50 *125.00*
On cover, tied by handstamp *5,000.*
On cover, uncanceled, with certificate —
On cover, tied by handstamp, with 3c #65 *8,000.*
On cover, tied by handstamp, with 3c #94 *5,000.*
Block of 4 40.00
Sheet of 40 550.00

Cancellations: Black, blue or red Boston datestamps, blue company serrated oval with 11 State St. or 9 Milk street addresses, black "Boston & Portland/Express/11 State Street, Boston/34 Exchange Street, Portland" framed ribbon-marker handstamp.

Private Post Office, San Francisco, Calif.
ENVELOPES

L241

Impressed on U.S. Envelopes, 1863-64 Issue

1864 **Typo.**

123LU1 L241 15c **blue,** *orange* (on US #U56) *600.00*
123LU2 L241 15c **blue,** *buff* (on US #U54) *600.00*
a. 15c **blue** (on US #U58) *700.00* *4,750.*
b. 15c **blue,** *buff* (on US #U59) *600.00*
123LU3 L241 25c **blue,** *buff* (on US #U54) *600.00*

Providence Despatch, Providence, R.I.

L242

1849 **Typeset**

124L1 L242 **black** *2,000.*

Public Letter Office, San Francisco, Calif.
ENVELOPES

L243

Impressed on U.S. Envelopes, 1863-64 Issue

1864 **Typeset**

125LU1 L243 **black** *400.00*
125LU2 L243 **blue** *400.00*
125LU3 L243 15c **blue** *450.00* *5,000.*
125LU4 L243 25c **blue** *450.00*

The Private Post Office of San Francisco changed its name to Public Post Office sometime in 1864. The office address was the same for both, 5 Kearny St.

Reed's City Despatch Post, San Francisco, Calif.

Pioneer San Francisco private post. Also serving Adams & Co. for city delivery.

L244

1853-54 **Glazed Surface Paper** **Litho.**

126L1 L244 **black,** *green,* on cover, tied by handstamp —
126L2 L244 **black,** *blue,* on cover, uncanceled *27,500.*

No. 126L1 is unique. Two No. 126L2 recorded, each uncanceled on cover.

Cancellation: Blue double-circle "Adams & Co. San Francisco."

Ricketts & Hall, Baltimore, Md.

L244a

1857 **Cut to shape** **Typo.**

127L1 L244a 1c **red,** *bluish* — *9,000.*
On cover —

Of the seven recorded examples of No. 127L1, three have been cut to shape removing the outer address circle, including the unique unused stamp. One of the three examples on cover has had the outer address circle removed.

Robison & Co., Brooklyn, N.Y.

L245

1855-56 **Typo.**

128L1 L245 1c **black,** *blue* *4,750.* *4,750.*
On cover, tied *7,000.*

Cancellation: Blue "PAID."

Roche's City Dispatch, Wilmington, Del.

L246

1850 **Glazed Surface Paper** **Typo.**

129L1 L246 (2c) **black,** *green* *2,250.*
Cut to shape *1,750.*
On cover, uncanceled, with certificate *8,250.*
On cover, cut to shape, uncanceled, with certificate *3,500.*

A black negative handstamp similar to type L246 served solely as a postmark and no evidence exists that any prepaid handstamped envelopes or lettersheets were ever sold.

Rogers' Penny Post, Newark, N.J.

Established by Alfred H. Rogers, bookseller, at 194 Broad St., Newark, N.J.

L246a

Cut to shape

1856 **Glazed Surface Paper** **Handstamped**

162L1 L246a (1c) **black,** *green* *30,000.*

No. 162L1 is unique. It is on a tiny piece. Value represents 2000 auction sale price.

See Rogers' handstamp in Local Handstamp Covers section.

Russell 8th Ave. Post Office, New York, N.Y.

(See Price's Eighth Avenue Post Office.)

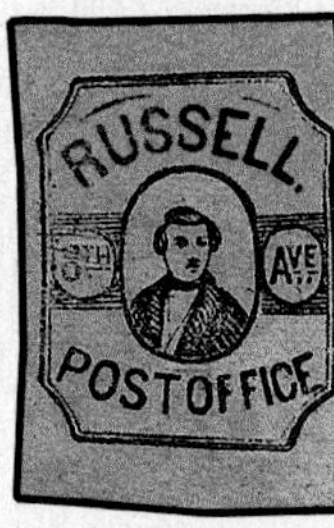

L247

1854-58 **Wood Engraving**

130L1 L247 (2c) **blue,** *rose* *600.* *500.*
On cover, uncanceled, with certificate —
On cover, tied by handstamp *27,500.*
On cover, tied with 3c #11 —
130L2 L247 (2c) **black,** *yellow* *750.* *650.*
On cover, tied *5,000.*
On cover, uncanceled, with 3c #11, with certificate *9,250.*
130L3 L247 (2c) **red,** *bluish* *900.* *750.*
On cover, tied by handstamp *8,250.*
On cover, not tied, with 3c #11, with certificate *5,750.*
130L4 L247 (2c) **blue green,** *green* *3,000.*

No. 130L4 used is unique. It is damaged and is valued thus.

St. Louis City Delivery Company, St. Louis, Mo.

(See Cincinnati City Delivery.)

L249

1883 **Typo.** ***Perf. 12***

131L1 L249 (1c) **red** 4.00 7.50
Block of 4 17.50
On cover, tied by handstamp *2,750.*
a. Imperf., pair —
b. Horiz. pair, imperf between *350.00*

Cancellation: Purple target.

Smith & Stephens' City Delivery, St. Louis, Mo.

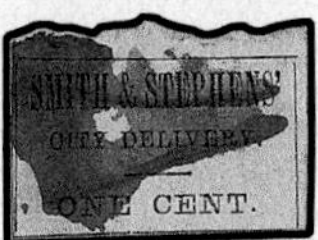

L284

Typeset

158L1 L284 1c **black,** *pale rose,* on cover, tied by ms. cancel 25,000.

No. 158L1 is unique.

Smith's City Express Post, New York, N.Y.

Successor to the American Express Co.

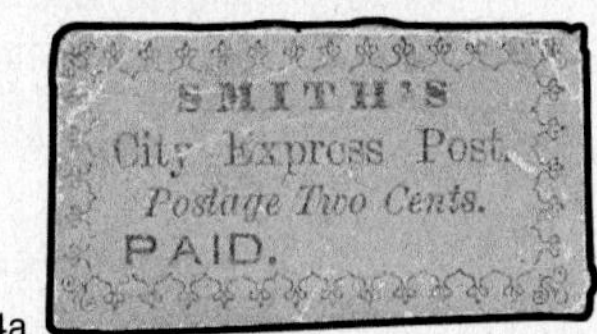

L284a

Typeset
Glazed Surface Paper

168L1 L284a 2c **black,** *green* —

Spaulding's Penny Post, Buffalo, N.Y.

L283

L283a

1848-49

156L1 L283 2c **vermilion** *25,000.*
156L2 L283a 2c **carmine** *25,000.*
On cover *12,000.*

Nos. 156L1 unused, 156L2 unused and 156L2 on cover each are unique.

A No. 156L1 on cover, uncanceled, was reported but has not been seen. The No. 156L2 stamp on cover shows light aging, and the value reflects auction sale in 2019.

Spence & Brown Express Post, Philadelphia, Pa.

L285

1847 (?) **Typeset**

159L1 L285 2c **black,** *bluish* *10,000. 11,500.*

One each recorded of No. 159L1 unused and used.

L286

1848 **Litho.**

159L2 L286 (2c) **black** *2,500.* —
On cover, tied by ms. *33,000.*
Block of 4 —

No. 159L2 on cover is unique.

Squier & Co. City Letter Dispatch, St. Louis, Mo. (Jordan & Co.)

This post began to operate as a local carrier on July 6, 1859 and was discontinued in the early part of 1860. Squier & Co. used imperforate stamps; their successors (Jordan & Co.) about Jan. 1 1860, used the roulettes.

L248

1859 **Litho.** ***Imperf.***

132L1 L248 1c **green** *150.* *175.*
On cover *1,500.*
On cover, tied by handstamp, with 3c #26 *4,000.*
On cover, tied by ms., with 3c #26 *1,000.*
On cover, uncanceled, with 3c #26 *600.*
Block of 4 *750.*

1860 ***Rouletted 19***

132L2 L248 1c **rose brown** *280.* *280.*
On cover *1,000.*
On cover, with 3c #26, each tied by handstamps (unique) *11,500.*
132L3 L248 1c **brownish purple** *280.* *280.*
On cover *1,000.*
132L4 L248 1c **green** *280.* *350.*
On cover *1,000.*
On cover, tied by handstamp, with 3c #26 *5,000.*

Cancellation: Black circle "Jordan's Penny Post Saint Louis."

Staten Island Express Post, Staten Island, N. Y.

Established by Hagadorn & Co., with office at Stapleton, Staten Island. Connected with Boyd for delivery in New York City.

L250

1849 **Typo.**

133L1 L250 3c **vermilion** *1,400.* *1,100.*
On cover, tied by ms. *4,750.*
On cover, not tied *3,500.*
On cover, uncanceled, with certificate *3,250.*
133L2 L250 6c **vermilion,** on cover —

Stringer & Morton's City Despatch, Baltimore, Md.

According to an advertisement in the Baltimore newspapers, dated October 19, 1850, this post aimed to emulate the successful posts of other cities, and divided the city into six districts, with a carrier in each district. Stamps were made available throughout the city.

L251

1850 **Glazed Surface Paper**

134L1 L251 (1c) **gold,** *black* *500.* —
On cover, uncanceled *650.*
On cover with pair if 5c #1 *7,500.*

Cancellation: Black circle "Baltimore City Despatch & Express Paid."

Sullivan's Dispatch Post, Cincinnati, Ohio

L252

1853 **Glazed Surface Paper** **Litho.**

135L1 L252 (2c) **black,** *green,* uncanceled, on cover —

Wove Paper

135L2 L252 (2c) **bluish black,** uncanceled, on magazine, with certificate *40,000.*
135L3 L252 (2c) **green** *60,000.*
On cover —

Nos. 135L1-135L2 are either die cut octagonally or cut round. They do not exist cut square.

Each listed Sullivan Post item is unique. Additionally, a second No. 135L2 on magazine is in the Smithsonian Institution collection.

Swarts' City Dispatch Post, New York, N.Y.

Established by Aaron Swarts, at Chatham Square, in 1847, becoming one of the largest local posts in the city.

The postmarks of Swarts' Post Office are often found on stampless covers, as this post carried large quantities of mail without using adhesive stamps.

Zachary Taylor
L253

George Washington
L254

1849-53 **Glazed Surface Paper** **Litho.**

136L1 L253 (2c) **black,** *light green* — *175.00*
On cover, tied by handstamp *450.00*
On cover, not tied *300.00*
On cover, tied, with 5c #1 *45,000.*
On cover with 3c #10 *450.00*
136L2 L253 (2c) **black,** *dark green* — 135.00
On cover, tied by handstamp *375.00*

Wove Paper

136L3 L253 (2c) **pink** — 35.00
On cover, tied by handstamp *500.00*
On cover with 5c #1 —
136L4 L253 (2c) **red** (shades) 20.00 20.00
On cover, tied by handstamp *600.00*
On cover, not tied *450.00*
On cover with 5c #1 *5,000.*
On cover, tied by handstamp cancel, with 1c #7 *8,500.*
On cover, tied by handstamp, with 3c #11 *650.00*
Block of 4 85.00
Sheet of 25 *600.00*

The 136L4 with No. 7 combination cover is unique.

136L5 L253 (2c) **pink,** *blue* 60.00
On cover, tied by handstamp *375.00*
136L6 L253 (2c) **red,** *blue* 60.00
On cover, tied by handstamp *400.00*
On cover, not tied, with 3c #10A, with certificate *850.00*
136L7 L253 (2c) **black,** *blue gray* 200.00 150.00
On cover, tied by handstamp *400.00*
On cover, uncanceled *225.00*
On cover, tied by "PAID" handstamp, with 10c #2, tied by grid *35,000.*
136L8 L253 (2c) **blue** 200.00
On cover, tied by handstamp *1,250.*
136L9 L254 (1c) **red** — 40.00
On cover, tied by handstamp *350.00*
On cover, tied by handstamp, with 3c #11 450.00
On cover, tied by handstamp, with 3c #11A 450.00
136L10 L254 (1c) **pink** — 30.00
On cover, tied by handstamp *250.00*
On cover, tied by handstamp, with 3c #11 *800.00*
On cover, tied by handstamp, with 3c #26 *350.00*
136L11 L254 (1c) **red,** *bluish* — 100.00
On cover *500.00*

136L12 L254 (1c) **pink,** *bluish* — 100.00
On cover *450.00*

Bouton's Stamp with Red ms. "Swarts" at Top

136L13 L49 2c **black,** *gray blue* *500.00 550.00*
On cover, tied by handstamp *1,500.*
On cover, not tied *600.00*

L255

Five minor varieties, the stamps in each vertical row being identical.

Printed in sheets of 25 (5x5)

136L14 L255 1c **blue** 15. 60.
On cover, tied by handstamp 175.
On cover, tied by handstamp, with 3c #11A *225.*
Block of 4 *65.*
a. Thin paper 8.00
Block of 4 35.
Sheet of 25 *225.00*
136L15 L255 1c **red** — *500.*
On cover, tied by handstamp *1,000.*
On cover, not tied, with 10c #2 *2,250.*
On cover with 3c #10 *1,650.*
On cover, tied by handstamp, with 3c #11A *4,000.*
136L16 L255 1c **red,** *bluish* — 135.
On cover, tied by handstamp *1,000.*
136L17 L255 1c **black,** on cover, tied by handstamp *17,500.*

Nos. 136L3-136L4, 136L9-136L10, 136L14-136L15 have been reprinted.

Cancellations: Red boxed "PAID" (mostly on Nos. 136L1-136L8, 136L13), black boxed "PAID SWARTS" (mostly on Nos. 136L9-136L12), black oval "Swarts Post Office Chatham Square" (Nos. 136L9-136L12), black oval "Swarts B Post Chatham Square," black grids (5-bar rectangle, 6-bar circle, solid star, hollow star, star in circle, etc). Other handstamp postmarks of the post have been found as cancellations. Government town postmarks exist on almost all Swarts stamps.

Teese & Co. Penny Post, Philadelphia, Pa.

L256

Printed in sheet of 200 divided into two panes of 100. Each pane includes setting of 20, repeated 5 times. Vertical or horizontal tete-beche pairs appear twice in each setting. Twenty varieties.

1852 Wove Paper Litho.

137L1 L256 (1c) **blue,** *bluish* 20.00 125.00
On cover, tied by handstamp *3,000.*
On cover, tied by handstamp, with 3c #11A *2,250.*
Block of 4 90.00
a. Tete beche pair 100.00

Telegraph Despatch P. O., Philadelphia, Pa.

L257

L257a

1848

138L1 L257 1c **black,** *yellowish* *2,750.*
On cover, tied by ms., with certificate *15,000.*
On cover, not tied, with certificate *5,500.*
138L2 L257a 2c **black,** *yellowish,* on cover, not tied, with 5c #1b *15,000.*

One example known of No. 138L2.

Third Avenue Post Office, New York, N.Y.

Established by S. Rothenheim, a former carrier for Boyd's City Express. All stamps were cut to shape by hand before being sold and exist only in that form.

L258

1855 Glazed Surface Paper Handstamped

139L1 L258 2c **black,** *green* *500. 500.*
On cover, uncanceled *1,250.*
On cover, uncanceled, with 3c #11, with certificate *1,600.*
139L1A L258 2c **blue,** *green,* on cover, uncanceled, with certificate *2,250.*
139L2 L258 2c **black,** *maroon* *3,250. 2,250.*

Unsurfaced Paper colored through

139L3 L258 2c **black,** *yellow* *2,250.*
On cover, uncanceled, with 3c #11, with certificate *3,000.*
139L4 L258 2c **black,** *blue* —
On cover, uncanceled, with 3c #11, with certificate *11,000.*
139L5 L258 2c **black,** *brown* *2,250.*
139L6 L258 2c **black,** *buff* *2,500.*
139L7 L258 2c **black,** *pink* *5,250.*
On cover, uncanceled, with 3c #11 *6,500.*
139L8 L258 2c **black,** *green* *4,150. 2,200.*

Nos. 139L1A, 139L2, 139L4 on cover, 139L7-139L8 unused and 139L8 used are each unique.

Cancellation on No. 139L1: Black "PAID."

Union Despatch, Chicago, Ill.

Established by William Stiles and his son, Edmund.

L258a

L258c

1855 *Irregular Rough Perf. 12½ to 15*

170L1 L258a 5c **brownish red** — —
170L3 L258c 20c **grayish green** — —

Union Post, New York, N.Y.

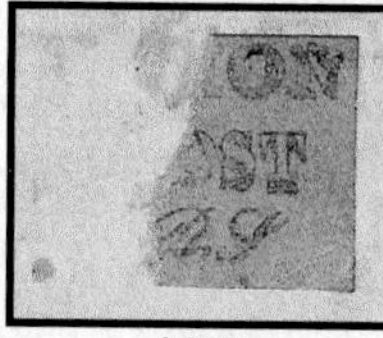
L259

Thick Glazed Surface Paper

1846 Handstamped

140L3 L259 **blue,** *green* ("UNOIN") *3,000.*
a. "UNION" spelled correctly, on cover —

The unique example of No. 140L3a is badly damaged, with only half the stamp still on the cover.

140L4 L259 **red,** *blue* ("UNION") *2,000.*
On cover —

Type L259 was used also as a postmark, usually struck in blue.

Union Square Post Office, New York, N.Y.

Established by Joseph E. Dunham about 1850. In 1851 Dunham acquired Messenkope's Union Square Post Office, operating the combined posts until 1854 or 1855. The business was sold in 1855 to Phineas C. Godfrey.

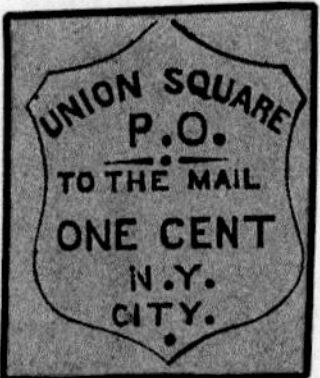

L259a

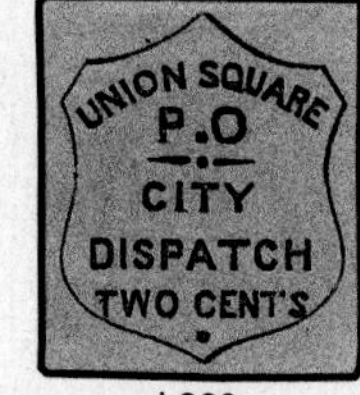

L260

Printed in sheets of 120 (6x20)

1852 Typo.

141L1 L259a 1c **black,** *dark green* 9.00 *45.00*
On cover, tied by handstamp *900.00*
On cover, tied by handstamp, with 3c #11A *1,250.*
On cover, not tied, with 3c #11A *750.00*
Block of 4 45.00
141L2 L259a 1c **black,** *light apple green* 40.00 *75.00*
On cover, tied by handstamp *700.00*
On cover, tied by handstamp, with 3c #11 *1,500.*
On cover, cut to shape, tied by handstamp, with 3c #11 *200.00*
141L3 L260 2c **black,** *rose* 3.50 *3,000.*
On cover *3,500.*
Block of 4 17.50

Used stamps must bear handstamp cancels.

Walton & Co.'s City Express, Brooklyn, N.Y.

Operated by Wellington Walton.

L261

1846 Glazed Surface Paper Litho.

142L1 L261 2c **black,** *pink* *700. 900.*
On cover, tied by ms. —
On cover, ms. cancel, not tied, with certificate *16,000.*
On cover, handstamp cancel, not tied —
On cover, cut to shape, tied by handstamp, with certificate *4,500.*
On cover, cut to shape, handstamp cancel, not tied, with certificate *6,000.*

Cancellations: Black "PAID / W. W." Black oblong quad (ties stamp "through" to cover).

Wells, Fargo and Co.

Wells, Fargo & Company entered the Western field about July 1, 1852, to engage in business on the Pacific Coast, and soon began to acquire other express businesses, eventually becoming the most important express company in its territory.

The Central Overland, California and Pikes Peak Express Company, inaugurated in 1860, was the pioneer Pony Express system and was developed to bring about quicker communication between the extreme portions of the United States. Via water the time was 28 to 30 days, with two monthly sailings, and by the overland route the time was 28 days. In 1860 the pioneer Pony Express carried letters only, reducing the time for the 2,100 miles (St. Joseph to San Francisco) to about 12 days. The postage rate was originally $5 the half-ounce.

About April 1, 1861, Wells, Fargo & Company became agents for the Central Overland, California and Pikes Peak Express Company and issued $2 red and $4 green stamps.

During the July 1 to Oct. 24, 1861, period of use of Nos. 143L3-143L6, Wells, Fargo & Co. was under contract with the U.S. government, so stamps used during this period are technically official issues authorized by Congress.

The rates were cut in half about July 1, 1861, and new stamps were issued: the $1 red, $2 green and $4 black, and the $1 garter design.

The revival of the Pony Express in 1862, known as the "Virginia City Pony" resulted in the appearance of the "cents" values, first rate.

Advertisement in the Placerville newspaper, Aug. 7, 1862: "Wells, Fargo & Co.'s Pony Express. On and after Monday, the 11th inst., we will run a Pony Express Daily between Sacramento and Virginia City, carrying letters and exchange papers, through from San Francisco in 24 hours, Sacramento in 15 hours and Placerville in 10 hours. Rates: All letters to be enclosed in our franks, and TEN CENTS PREPAID, in addition, for each letter weighing half an ounce or less, and ten cents for each additional half-ounce."

Wells, Fargo & Company used various handstamps to indicate mail transit. These are illustrated and described in the handbook, "Wells, Fargo & Co.'s Handstamps and Franks" by V. M. Berthold, published by Scott Stamp & Coin Co., Ltd. (out of print). The history of the Pony Express, a study of the stamps and reprints, and a survey of existing covers are covered in "The Pony Express," by M. C. Nathan and Winthrop S. Boggs, published by the Collectors Club, 22 E. 35th., New York, N.Y. 10016.

Wells Fargo stamps of types L262 and L264 were lithographed by Britton & Rey, San Francisco. Type L263 was printed by George F. Nesbitt, New York.

L262

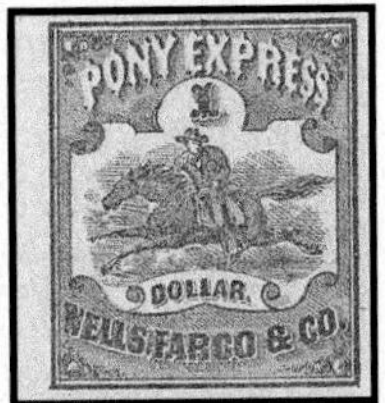

Front hoof missing

The $2 and $4 stamps were printed from plates of 20 (5x4), while the $1 was printed from a plate of 40 (8x5), and divided into two panes of 20 (4x5) each.

1861 (April to July 1) Litho.

143L1 L262 $2 **red** 275. *1,100.*
On US envelope #U10 —
On US envelope #U16 *12,500.*
On US envelope #U17 *12,500.*
On US envelope #U18 *12,500.*
On US envelope #U32 *15,000.*
On US envelope #U32 (patriotic cover) *100,000.*
On US envelope #U33 *32,500.*
On US envelope #U65 —
On cover, tied by "Running Pony" handstamp, with 5c #30A and 10c #35, to Prince Edward Island (unique) *350,000.*
143L2 L262 $4 **green** 850. *6,000.*
Block of 4 *20,000.*
On US envelope #U33 —

The No. 143L2 block is the only recorded $4 block.

1861 (July 1 to Nov.)

143L3 L262 $1 **red** 150. *900.*
Block of 4 *1,150.*
Sheet of 40 *12,000.*
On US envelope #U11 —
On US envelope #U15 *9,000.*
On US envelope #U17 *9,000.*
On US envelope #U32 *10,000.*
On US envelope #U33 *12,500.*
On US envelope #U35 *9,000.*
On US envelope #U40 *10,000.*
On US envelope #U41 *9,000.*
Front hoof missing (9R) *1,850.* *6,000.*
143L4 L262 $2 **green** 475. *4,500.*
Block of 4 *3,500.*
On US envelope #U41 *50,000.*
143L5 L262 $4 **black** 275. *12,500.*
Block of 4 *2,750.*
On cover to Wash., D.C., tied by handstamp *350,000.*

Cancellations: Blue, black or magenta express company.
Nos. 143L1-143L5 and 143L7-143L9 were reprinted in 1897. The reprints are retouched. Shades vary from originals. Originals and reprints are fully described in "The Pony Express," by M. C. Nathan and W. S. Boggs (Collectors Club).

L263

Printed in sheets of 20 (5x4). One example recorded with Nesbitt imprint (pos. 18).

1861 Thin Wove Paper

143L6 L263 $1 **blue** *1,250.* *1,250.*
Strip of 3 —
On 10c US env. #U40 *75,000.*
On 10c US env. #U40 with 10c #35, tied *185,000.*

No. 143L6 used only from east to west.
Most counterfeits have a horizontal line bisecting the shield. Some genuine stamps have a similar line drawn in with blue or red ink. Value for genuine with line, $900.

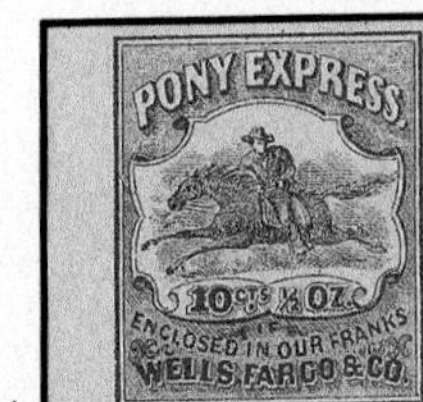

L264

Printed in sheets of 40 (8x5), four panes of 10, each pane 2x5.

1862-64

143L7 L264 10c **brown** (shades) 50. *175.*
Pair 125. *500.*
Block of 4 500.
On US envelope #U26 *6,500.*
On US envelope #U32 *4,000.*
On US envelope #U34 *6,000.*
On US envelope #U35 *5,500.*
On cover with 3c #65 —
143L8 L264 25c **blue** 75. *175.*
Pair 175.
Block of 4 500.
On plain cover *2,250.*
Strip of 3 on cover —
On US envelope #U10 —
On US envelope #U26 *2,000.*
On US envelope #U34 *4,750.*
On US envelope #U35 *4,500.*
143L9 L264 25c **red** 30. *100.*
Pair 80.
Block of 4 225.
Sheet of 40 *4,500.*
On US envelope #U9 —
On US envelope #U10 *8,000.*
On US envelope #U34 *8,000.*
On US envelope #U34 with 3c #65 *13,500.*
On US envelope #U35 *8,000.*
Pair on US envelope #U35 *9,000.*
On US envelope #U59 *3,750.*

Cancellations on Nos. 143L7-143L9: Blue or black express company, black town.

STEAMSHIP EXPRESS STAMP

L265

1860

143LP1 L265 **black** *1,250.* —
On cover, uncanceled, with certificate *6,000.*

No. 143LP1 was issued to pay the steamship express fee, plus the drop-rate fee for delivery at the New York City Post Office. The use on cover is unique.

NEWSPAPER STAMPS

L266

L267

L268

L269

L270

1861-70

143LP2 L266 **blue** *1,250.*
143LP3 L267 **blue** 20.00 *75.00*
Pair 100.00
Block of 4 —
Sheet of 50 —
a. Thin paper 40.00 *100.00*
143LP4 L268 **blue** 50.00

Rouletted 10

143LP5 L267 **blue** 25.00 *125.00*
On wrapper *1,500.*
Pair 55.00
Block of 4 125.00
a. Thin paper —
143LP6 L268 **blue** 22.50
a. Tete beche pair 350.00

Design L267 was printed in sheets of 50 (5x10).

1883-88 *Perf. 11, 12, 12½*

143LP7 L268 **blue** 12.50 *25.00*
143LP8 L269 **blue** 25.00 *35.00*
143LP9 L270 **blue** 3.50 *5.00*
Double transfer —
On wrapper *2,400.*
Strip of 3 on wrapper —
a. Vertical pair, imperf. between 125.00
b. Horiz. strip of 3, imperf. vert. between all stamps, natural straight edge at right *350.00*

FOR PUBLISHERS' USE

L271

1876 Typo.

143LP10 L271 **blue** 8.50 *25.00*
Pair 17.50 *60.00*
Block of 4 45.00
Sheet of 50 —
On wrapper *1,750.*
On wrapper with #143LP9 —

Cancellation: Blue company.

ENVELOPES

1862

143LU1 L264 10c **red** — *1,250.*
On US envelope #U34 *3,000.*
143LU2 L264 10c **blue** — —
On US envelope #U34 *9,500.*
143LU3 L264 25c **red** 700.00
On "Gould & Curry" overall advertising env. 700.00
On US envelope #U34 950.00

Westervelt's Post, Chester, N.Y.

Operated by Charles H. Westervelt. Rate was 1 cent for letters and 2 cents for packages carried to the post office. Local and government postage required prepayment.

L273

1863 (?) Several varieties Typeset

144L1 L273 (1c) **black,** *buff* 35.00 *100.00*
On cover *1,000.*
On cover, tied by handstamp, with 3c #65 *1,400.*
Sheet of 6 *675.00*
144L2 L273 **black,** *lavender* 40.00 75.00
On cover 2,000.

Indian Chief — L274

1864 (?) Six varieties Typeset

144L9 L274 (1c) **red,** *pink* 75.00 75.00
On cover *1,250.*
On cover, tied by handstamp, with 3c #65 *3,000.*

General U. S. Grant — L275

1865 **Six varieties** **Typo.**

144L29	L275	2c **black,** *yellow*	50.00	—
144L30	L275	2c **black,** *gray green*	50.00	—
144L40	L275	2c **red,** *pink*	50.00	—

All of the Westervelt stamps are believed to have a philatelic flavor, although it is possible that Nos. 144L1-144L2 were originally issued primarily for postal purposes. It is possible that Nos. 144L9, 144L29-144L30 and 144L40 were used in the regular course of business, particularly No. 144L9.

However, the large number of varieties on various colors of paper, which exist both as originals as well as contemporaneous and near-contemporaneous reprints, are believed to have been produced solely for sale to collectors. Design L275 was certainly issued primarily for sale to collectors. Many of the unlisted colors in all three types exist only as reprints. Forgeries of all three designs also exist.

L276

ENVELOPES

Impressed at top left

1865 **Typo.**

144LU1	L276	**red,** *white*	—	
144LU2	L276	**red brown,** *orange*	—	*300.00*
144LU3	L276	**black,** *bluish*	175.00	
144LU4	L276	**black,** *buff*	—	
144LU5	L276	**black,** *white*	—	

It is possible that Nos. 114LU1-144LU5 were corner cards and had no franking value.

Westtown, Westtown, Pa.

The Westtown School at Westtown, Pa., is the oldest of the secondary schools in America, managed by the Society of Friends. It was established in 1799. In 1853 the school authorities decided that all outgoing letters carried by stage should pay a fee of 2 cents. Prepaid stamps were placed on sale at the school. Stamps were usually affixed to the reverse of the letter sheets or envelopes.

At first, letters were usually mailed at West Chester, Pa. After March 4, 1859, letters were sent from Street Road Post Office, located at the railroad station. Later this became the Westtown Post Office. The larger stamp was the first used. The smaller stamp came into use about 1867.

L277 - Type I

L277 - Type II

L277 - Type III

L277 - Type IV

L277a - Type V

L277a - Type VI

L277a - Type VII

1853-67(?) **Litho.**

145L1	L277	(2c) **gold**	45.	—
		On front of cover, tied, with 3c #11		*3,000.*
		On front of cover, uncanceled, with 1c #9		*1,000.*
		On front of cover, uncanceled, with 3c #11		*150.*
		On front of cover, uncanceled, with 3c #26a		*200.*
145L2	L277a	(2c) **gold**	30.	—
		On cover		*400.*
		On cover, tied by handstamp, with 3c #158		*1,750.*
		Block of 4	*400.*	
		Block of 6	*1,000.*	
a.		Tete beche pair	*300.*	

No. 145L1 in red brown is a fake.

Whittelsey's Express, Chicago, Ill.

Operated by Edmund A. and Samuel M. Whittelsey

George Washington — L278

1857 **Typo.**

146L1	L278	2c **red**	*2,000.*	*6,500.*
		Block of 11	*20,000.*	

Cancellation: Blue oval "Whittelsey's Express."

Williams' City Post, Cincinnati, Ohio.

(See Carriers' Stamps, No. 9LB1.)

Wood & Co. City Despatch, Baltimore, Md.

Operated by W. Wood

L280

1856 **Typeset**

148L1	L280	(1c) **black,** *yellow,* on cover, ms. cancel, not tied, with certificate	*13,000.*
		On printed matter, tied by ms.	*7,500.*
		On 3c red entire #U10, tied by ms., with certificate	*14,500.*

W. Wyman, Boston, Mass.

Established to carry mail between Boston and New York

L281

1844 **Litho.**

149L1	L281	5c **black**	—	*750.00*
		On cover, tied by ms., Wyman handstamp		*3,250.*
		On cover, tied by ms., Overton handtsamp		*10,000.*
		On cover, not tied		*1,750.*

No. 149L1 may have been sold singly at 6 cents each.

Zieber's One Cent Dispatch, Pittsburgh, Pa.

L282

1851 **Typeset**

150L1	L282	1c **black,** *gray blue*		*20,000.*
		On cover, acid cancel, with 3c #10		—

No. 150L1 used and on cover are each unique.

Cancellation: Acid

For Local #151L1-151L3 see **Friend's Boarding School.**
For Local #152L1 see **Faunce's Penny Post.**
For Local #153L1 see **Hackney & Bolte Penny Post.**
For Local #154L1 see **A. W. Auner's Despatch Post.**
For Local #155L1 see **McGreely's Express.**
For Local #156L1-156L2 see **Spaulding's Penny Post.**
For Local #157L1 see **Bush's Brooklyn City Express.**
For Local #158L1 see **Smith & Stephens City Delivery.**
For Local #159L1-159L2 see **Spence & Brown Express Post.**
For Local #160L1 see **City Dispatch, New York City.**
For Local #161L1 see **Clinton's Penny Post.**
For Local #162L1 see **Rogers' Penny Post.**
For Local #163L1 see **Blizzard Mail.**
For Local #164L1 see **Freeman & Co.'s Express, New York City.**
For Local #165L1 see **J. A. Howell's City Despatch.**
For Local #166L1 see **Mac & Co's Dispatch.**
For Local #167L1 see **Morton's Post.**
For Local #168L1 see **Smith's City Express Post.**
For Local #169L1-169L2 see **Chestnut Street Line.**
For Local #170L1, 170L3 see **Union Despatch.**

LOCAL HANDSTAMPED COVERS

In 1835-1860 when private companies carried mail, many of them used handstamps on the covers they carried. Examples of these handstamps are shown on this and following pages.

Accessory Transit Co. of Nicaragua

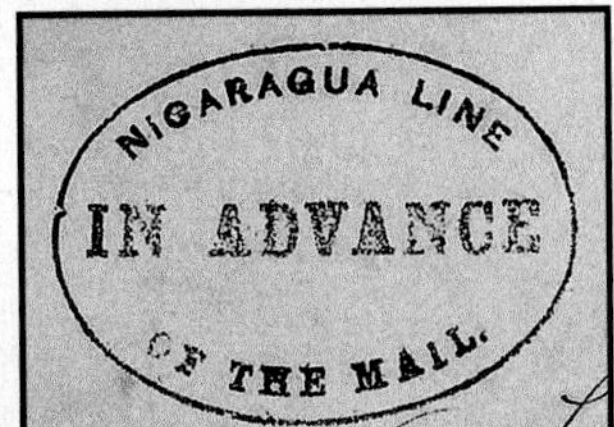

Blue or Black

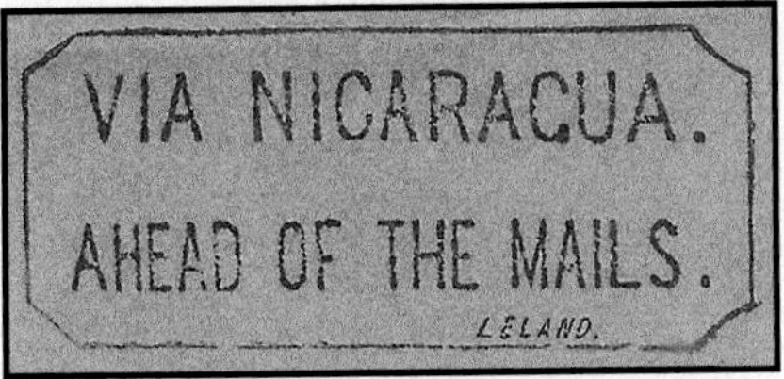

Red, Black or Blue

A sub-variety shows "Leland" below "MAILS" in lower right corner.

Red or Blue

1853

Barker's City Post, Boston, Mass.

Black

Also known with "34" instead of "10" Court Square.

1855-59

E. N. Barry's Despatch Post, New York, N.Y.

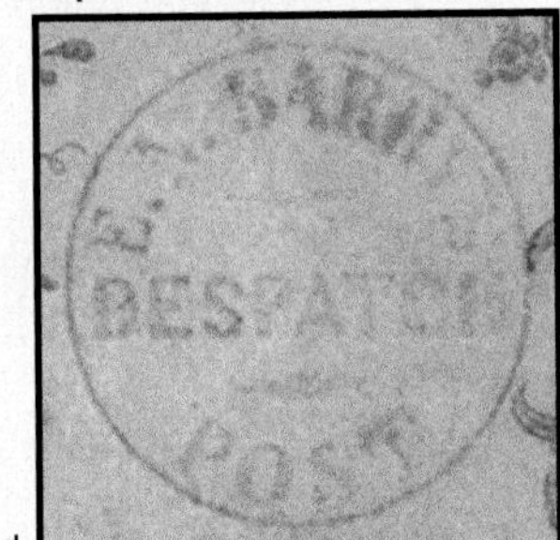

Black or Red

1852

Bates & Co., New Bedford, Mass.
(Agent for Hale & Co. at New Bedford)

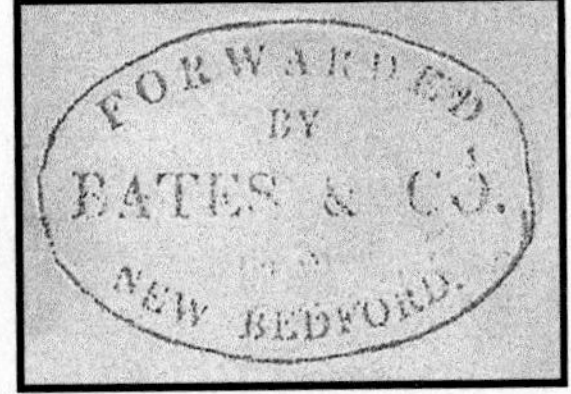

Red or Black

1845

Branch Post Office, New York, N. Y.
(Swarts' Chatham Square Post Office)

Red

1847

Brigg's Despatch, Philadelphia, Pa.

Black

1848

Bush's Brooklyn City Express, Brooklyn, N. Y.

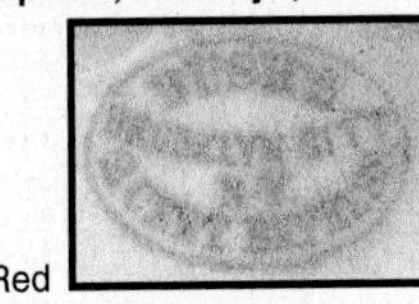

Red

1848

Cover shows red PAID.

Central Post Office, New York, N.Y.

Black

1856

Cover shows black PAID.

City Despatch Post, New York, N. Y.
(Used by Mead, successor to United States City Despatch Post.)

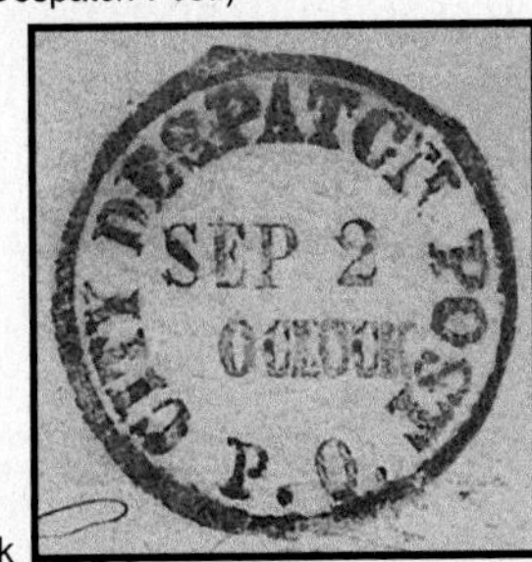

Black

1848

City Despatch Post, Baltimore, Md.

Red

1846-47

City Despatch & Express, Baltimore, Md.

Black

1850

Cole's City Despatch P. O., New York, N. Y.
(Used by Cole with some of the City Despatch Post stamps.)

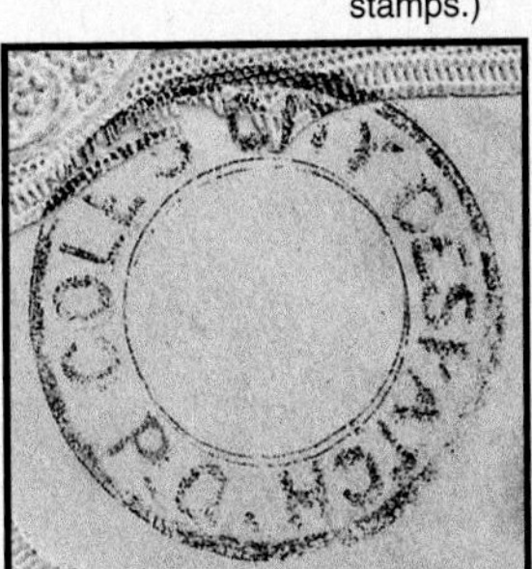

Black or Red

1848-50

Cumming's Express, New York, N.Y.

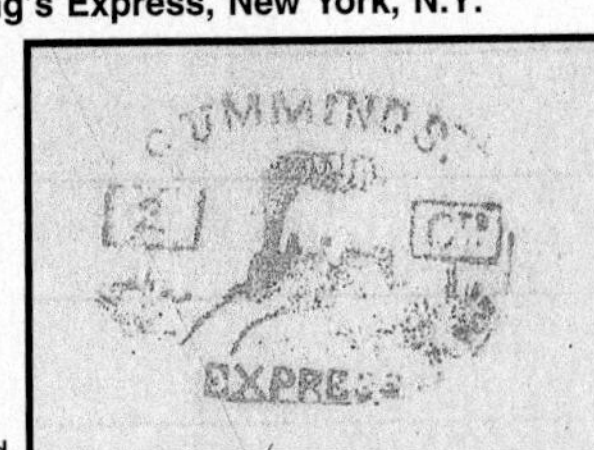

Red

1846

Dunhams Post Office, New York, N. Y.
(See Union Square Post Office).

Red

1848-52

Freeman & Coĉ‹¢s Express, Marysville, Calif.

Greenish Blue

1851

Gay, Kinsley & Co., Boston, Mass.
(A package express)

Red

Hanford's Pony Express Post, New York, N.Y.

Black or Red

1845-51

Hartford Penny Post, Hartford, Conn.

Black

1852-61

Hudson Street Post Office, New York, N. Y.

Red

1850

Cover shows red PAID.

Jones & Russell's Pikes Peak Express Co., Denver, Colo.

Black

1859-60

Kenyon's Letter Office, 91 Wall St., New York City

Red

1846-60

Langton & Bros. Express, French Corral

Blue

1849-53

Letter Express, San Francisco, Cal.
(See Gahagan & Howe, San Francisco, Cal.)

Blue

1865-66

Libbey & Co.'s City Post, Boston, Mass.

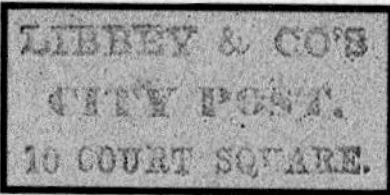

Black or Red

1852

Cover has 3c 1851 postmarked Boston, Mass.

Manhattan Express, New York, N. Y.
(W. V. Barr. See Bouton's Manhattan Express.)

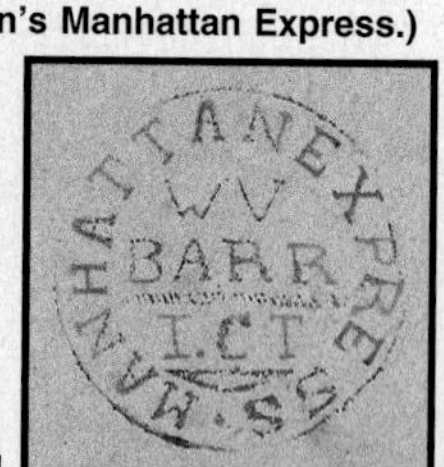

Red

1847

New York Penny Post, New York, N. Y.

Black or Red

1840-41

Also known with hour indicated.

Noisy Carriers, San Francisco, Cal.

Blue or Green

Blue

Black or Red

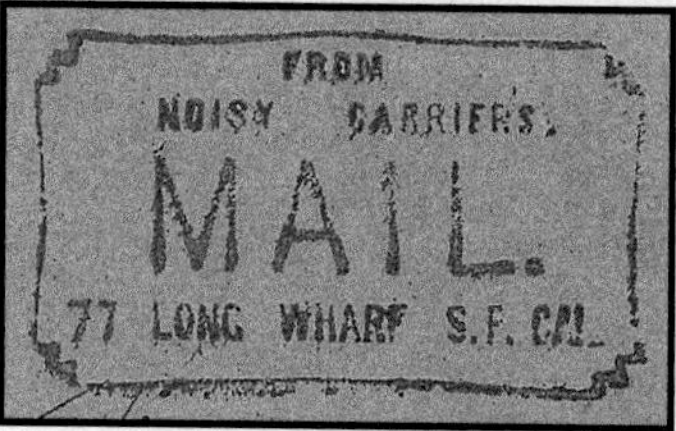

Black, Blue or Green

Black

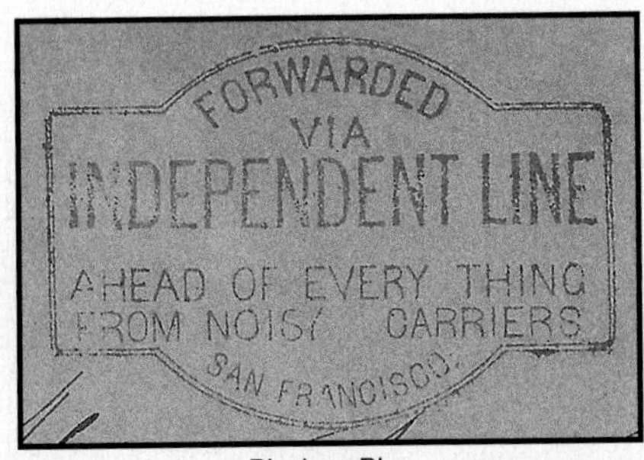

Black or Blue

1853-56

Northern Liberties News Rooms, Philadelphia, Pa.
(Actually a carrier marking mechanically applied.)

Black

Black

1835-36

Overton & Co.'s City Mail, New York, N. Y.

Red

1844-45

Pony Express

Blue or Red

1860

Blue (Enlarged)

1861

Black or Carmine

1860-61

Blue or Red

1853-56

from	
St. Joseph, Mo.	Black or Green
Denver City, K. T.	Black
Leavenworth City, K. T.	Black
San Francisco, Cal.	Blue

Black or Green

1860-61

Red

Blue

1860

Rogers' Penny Post, Newark, N. J.

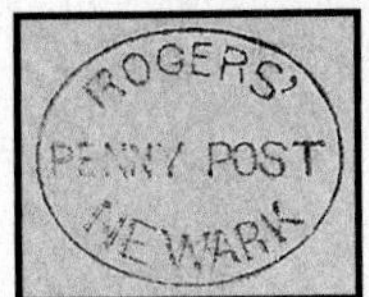

Black

1856

Spark's Post Office, New York, N. Y.

Red, Green, Blue or Black

1848

Spaulding's Penny Post, Buffalo, N. Y.

Black

1848

Spence & Brown Express Post, Philadelphia, Pa.

Black

1848

Stait's Despatch Post, Philadelphia, Pa. (Eagle City Post)

Red or Black

1850-51

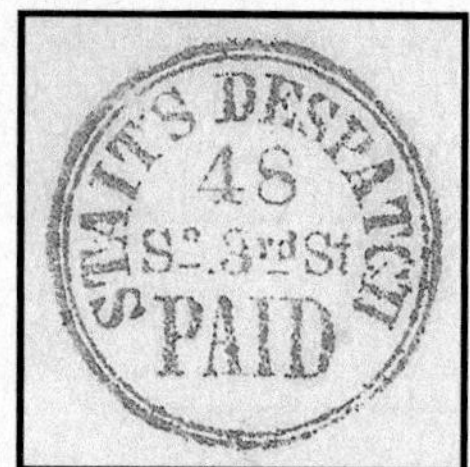

Red

1850-55

Stone's City Post, New York, N. Y.

Red

1858-59

J. W. Sullivan's Newspaper Office, San Francisco, Cal.

Black or Red

1854-55

Towle & Co. Letter Delivery, Boston, Mass.

Red

1847

Towle's City Dispatch Post, Boston, Mass.

Red

1849

Towle's City Post, Boston, Mass.

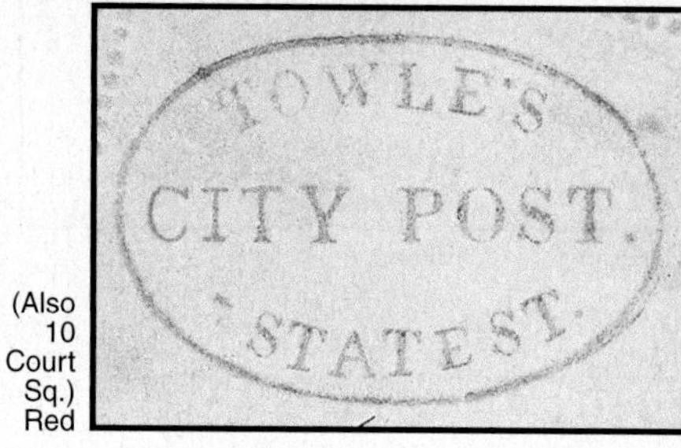

(Also 10 Court Sq.) Red

1849-50

Cover shows PAID.

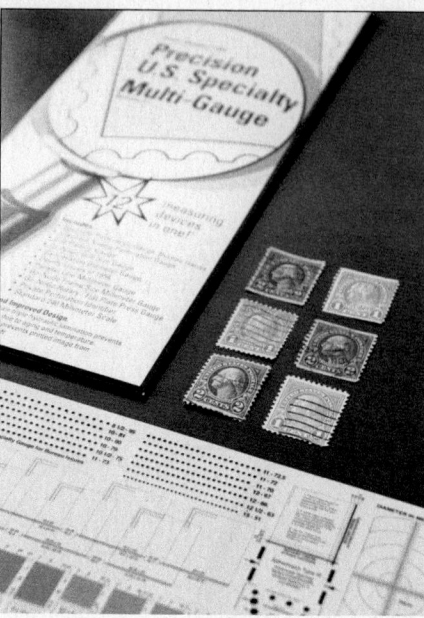

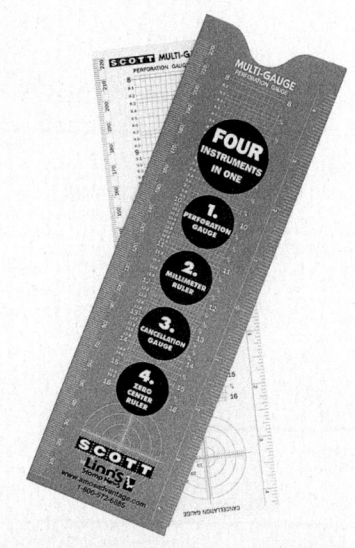

STAMPED ENVELOPES AND WRAPPERS

Fine-Very Fine

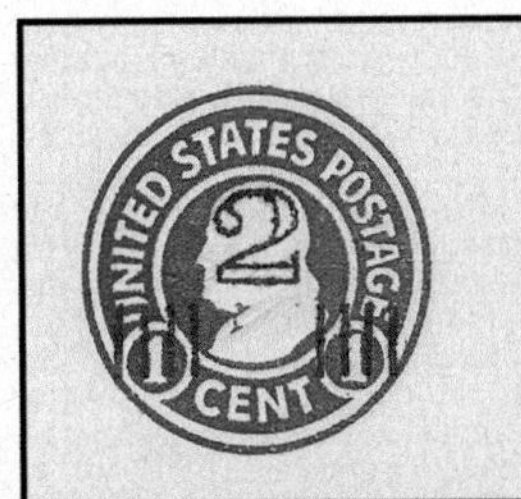

THE SCOTT CATALOGUE VALUES CUT SQUARES IN THIS GRADE

Very Fine

Extremely Fine

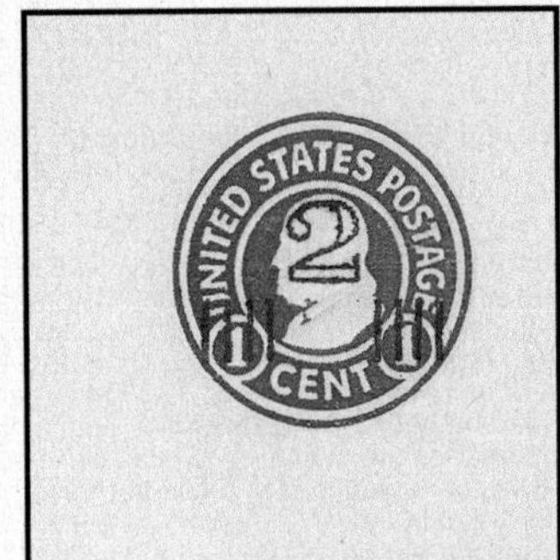

VALUES

Values for used envelopes are for examples used within the period of issue. Envelopes used much later sell at substantially reduced prices.

Unless otherwise noted, values for cut squares and most entires are for examples in the grade of very fine. Very fine cut squares will have the design well centered within moderately large margins. The margins on 20th century cut squares should be at least ¼ inch on the cut sides unless indicated otherwise. Cut squares of modern issues should show full tagging bars when they exist. An illustrated grading guide is shown above. These examples are computer-manipulated images made from single digitized master illustrations. Selected issues from both the 19th and 20th centuries are shown in the grades of fine-very fine, very fine and extremely fine. In addition to margin size, collectors are reminded that very fine cut squares (and entires) also will possess a fresh appearance and be free from defects.

Precanceled cut squares must include the entire precancellation. Values for unused entires are for those without printed or manuscript address, and for the most popular sizes. In a number of cases the larger envelopes are less expensive than the values shown here, for example, Nos. U348-U351. Values for letter sheets and wrappers are for folded entires. Unfolded examples sell for more.

"Full corner" cut squares include both back and side flaps. These items generally command a premium of 25% or more above the cut square values shown here, which are not for "full corners."

A plus sign (+) before a Catalogue number indicates that the item was not regularly issued and is not known used.

Envelopes are not available before the First day of issue so most cachets are applied after the envelope has been canceled. First day covers are valued uncacheted. First day covers prior to Nos. U532, UC18 and UO73 are addressed. Minimum values are $1 through 1986, and $1.25 after.

PRECANCELED CUT SQUARES

Precanceled envelopes do not normally receive another cancellation. Since the lack of a cancellation makes it impossible to distinguish between cut squares from used and unused envelopes, they are valued here as used only. Precanceled entires are valued mint and used since entires will show evidence of usage.

HISTORY

STAMPED ENVELOPES were first issued on July 1, 1853. They have always been made by private contractors, after public bidding, usually at four-year intervals. They have always been sold to the public at postage value plus cost of manufacture. They have appeared in many sizes and shapes, made of a variety of papers, with a number of modifications.

George F. Nesbitt & Co. made the government envelopes during the 1853-70 period. The Nesbitt seal or crest on the tip of the top flap was officially ordered discontinued July 7, 1853.

Watermarks in envelope paper, illustrated in this introduction, were mandatory from their first appearance in 1853. One important exception started in 1919 and lasted until the manila newspaper wrappers were discontinued in October 1934. The envelope contractor, due to inability to obtain watermarked Manila paper, was permitted to buy unwatermarked stock in the open market, a procedure that accounts for the wide range of shades and weights in this paper, including glazed and unglazed brown (kraft) paper. No. U615, and other unwatermarked envelopes that follow will be so noted in the listings. Diagonally laid paper has been used for some envelopes beginning with Scott U571.

A few stamped envelopes, in addition to the Manila items noted above, have been found without watermarks or with unauthorized watermarks. Such unusual watermarks or lack of watermarks are errors, bidders' samples or "specimen" envelopes, and most of them are quite rare.

Watermarks usually have been changed with every four-year contract, and thus serve to identify the envelope contractor, and since 1911, the manufacturer of the paper.

Envelope paper watermarks can be seen by spreading the envelope open and holding it against the light.

COLORS IN ENVELOPE PAPER

Stamped envelopes usually have been supplied in several colors and qualities of paper, some of which blend into each other and require study for identification. The following are the principal colors and their approximate years of use for stamped envelopes and wrappers:

Amber: 1870-1920 and 1929-1943; in two qualities; a pale yellow color; its intentional use in the Nesbitt series is doubtful.

Amber-Manila: 1886-98; same as Manila-amber.

Blue: 1874-1943; usually in two qualities; light and dark shades.

Buff: 1853-70; called cream, 1870-78; and oriental buff, 1886-1920; varies widely in shades.

Canary: 1873-78; another designation given to lemon.

Cream: 1870-78; see buff; second quality in 1c and 2c envelopes.

Fawn: 1874-86; very dark buff, almost light chocolate.

Lemon: 1873-78; Post Office official envelopes only, same as canary.

Manila: 1861-1934; second quality envelopes 1886-1928, and most wrappers; light and dark shades 1920-34; also kraft colored paper in later years.

Manila-Amber: 1886-98; amber shade of Manila quality.

Orange: 1861-83; second and third qualities only.

Oriental Buff: 1886-1920; see buff.

White: 1853-date; two qualities 1915-53; three qualities 1915-25; many shades including ivory, light gray, and bluish; far more common than any other color of paper. Envelopes that have no paper color given are white.

Laid paper was used almost exclusively from 1853 to 1915, but there were a few exceptions, mostly in the Manila papers. Wove paper has been the rule since 1915.

EMBOSSING AND PRINTING DIES

Until the modern era, stamped envelopes were always embossed, with the colorless areas slightly raised above the colored (or printed) flat background. While this process was not made mandatory in the original act, custom and tradition firmly established this policy. In 1977, No. U584 became the first envelope to have no embossing. Since 1977, most envelopes are not embossed. Embossing is an unusual procedure, seldom seen in other printed matter. Embossed impressions without color and those where lines are raised are not unusual. The method of making envelope embossings has few counterparts in the typographic industries, and hence is not well understood, even by stamp collectors.

Three types of dies are used, closely interrelated in their derivation, MASTER dies, HUB dies and WORKING (or PRINTING) dies. These types and the ways in which they are made, have undergone many changes with the years, and some of the earlier techniques are unrecorded and rather vague. No attempt will be made to describe other than the present day-methods. As an aid to clarity, the design illustrated herewith is the interlocked monogram "US," within a single circular border. Dies with curved faces for rotary printing are used extensively, as well as with straight faces for flat printing; only the latter will be described, since the basic principles are the same for both.

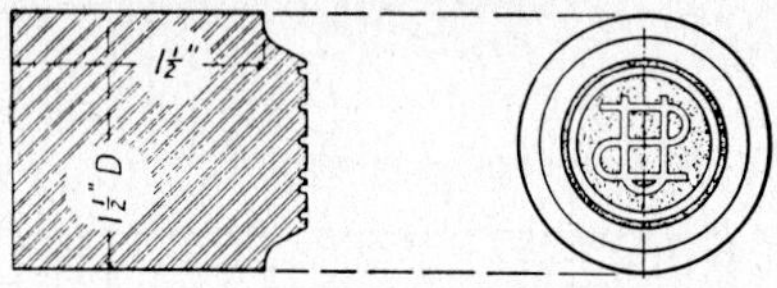

Figure 1

Master Die for Envelope Stamps

Colorless Lines are Recessed Below the Printing Surface.

It Reads Backward.

The MASTER die (Figure 1) is engraved on the squared end of a small soft steel cylinder, before hardening. The lines that are to remain colorless are cut or engraved into the face of this die, leaving the flat area of the face to carry the printing ink. The monogram is reversed, reading backward, as with any printing type or plate. Instead of engraving, a master die may be made by transfer under heavy pressure, usually for some modification in design, in which case it is called a sub-master or supplementary-master die. Sub-master dies are sometimes made without figures of value, when the balance of the design is as desired, and only the figures of value engraved by hand. Various other combinations of transfer and engraving are known, always resulting in a reversed design, with recessed lines and figures, from which proofs can be pulled, and which accurately represents the printing surface that is desired in the eventual working die. The soft steel of a master die, after engraving and transferring is completed, is hardened by heat treatments before it can be used for making hubs.

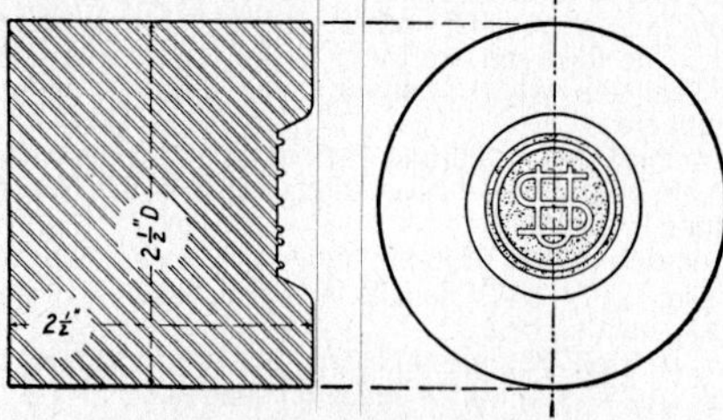

Figure 2

Hub Die for Envelope Stamps

Colorless Lines Protrude above the Surface.

The Monogram Reads Forward.

The HUB die (Figure 2), also called HOB die, is made from soft steel by transfer under pressure from the hardened master or sub-master die, which serves as a matrix or pattern. Since it is a transfer from the master die, the colorless lines protrude from the surface and it reads forward. This transfer impression of the hub die is made in a depression at the end of a sturdy cylinder, as it is subject to extremely hard service in making many working dies.

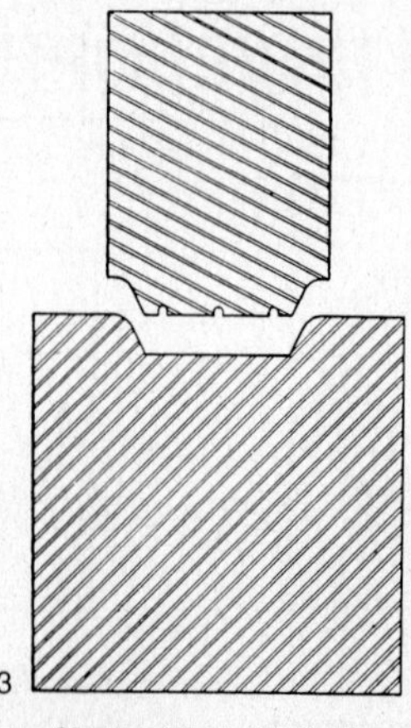

Figure 3

Pressure Transfer From Master Die to Hub Die

Above, Hardened Steel Master Die with Recessed Monogram.

Below, Soft Steel Hub Die Blank.

Figure 3 shows the relative position of the hardened steel master die as it enters the depression in the soft steel hub die blank. Some surplus metal may be squeezed out as the master die is forced into the hub blank, and require removal, leading to possible minor differences between the hub and master dies. At the completion of the pressure transfer the engraver may need to touch up the protruding surfaces to eliminate imperfections, to make letters and figures more symmetrical, and to improve the facial lines of the bust.

A hub die may be made by normal transfer, as above, the figures of value then ground off, and thus be ready for use in making a sub-master die without figures of value, and in which the figures of value may be engraved or punched. Since a hub die may be used to make a hundred or more working dies, it must be exceedingly sturdy and withstand terrific punishment without damage. Duplicate hub dies are frequently made from master dies, as stand-bys or reserves. After completion, hub dies are hardened. Hub dies cannot be engraved, nor can proof impressions be taken from them.

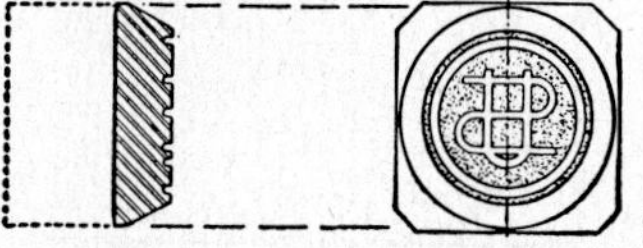

Figure 4

Working or Printing Die for Envelope Stamps

An exact Replica of the Master Die, except for size and shape of shank, which is designed for Printers} lock-up.

It Reads Backward.

The WORKING, or PRINTING, die (Figure 4) is like the type or plate that printers use, and may be thin to clamp to a base block, or type-high with square sides to lock in a printer's form. Its face reads backward, i.e., in reverse, and it is an exact replica of the master die as well as an exact matrix of the hub die.

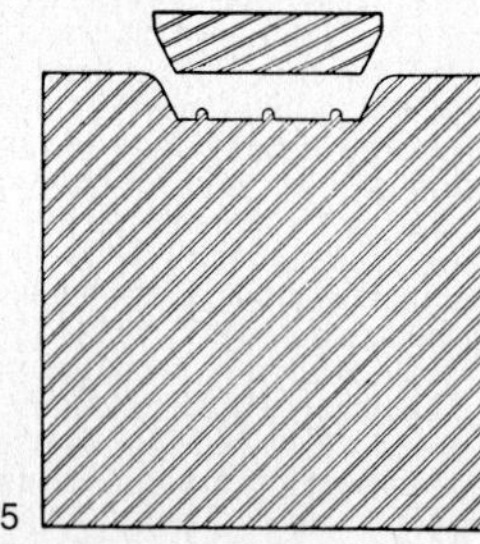

Figure 5

Pressure Transfer from Hub to Working Die

Above, Soft Steel Blank for Working Die.

Below, Hardened Steel Hub Die with Protruding Lines.

The process of pressure transfer is shown in Figure 5. where the soft steel blank of the working die is entering the depression on the top end of the hardened hub die, In fact the pressure transfer of working dies from hub dies closely resembles that of minting coins, and many of these envelope stamp dies are made at the United States Mint in Philadelphia.

In some cases even working dies may be made without figures of value, and the figures of value individually engraved thereon. This is known to be the case in Die B of the 6c orange airmail stamped envelope die, where the size and position of the "6" has eleven variations.

There are some known instances, as in the case of the 4c and 5c envelopes dies of 1903 and 1907, where the engraved master dies were used as printing dies, since the anticipated demand did not justify the expense of making hub dies.

While working envelope dies are heat treated to the hardest temper known, they do wear down eventually to a point where impressions deteriorate and are unsatisfactory, due to shallow recesses or to broken areas, and such dies are destroyed. In many cases these printing dies can be reworked, or deepened, by annealing the steel, touching up the lines or busts by hand engraving to restore the letters or renew the facial contour lines, and then rehardened for subsequent use. This recutting is the principal cause for minor die varieties in envelope stamps. When working dies are no longer useful, they are mutilated and eventually melted down into scrap metal.

The average "life" (in number of good impressions obtained) of a hardened steel working die, as used in envelope printing and embossing machines is around 30,000,000 on flat bed presses, and 43,000,000 on rotary presses. With a production of stamped envelopes of approximately 2 billion annually, 60 to 75 working dies are worn out each year, and require replacement with new dies or a reworking of old dies. Some 200 to 250 working dies can be in constant use, since most envelope printing presses are set up for a special size, type or value, and few can be operated continuously at maximum capacity.

Master and hub dies of obsolete envelope issues are kept in the vaults of the Bureau of Engraving and printing in Washington, as are the original dies of adhesive stamps, revenue paper, government securities and paper currency.

PRINTING ENVELOPE STAMPS

Embossed envelope stamps are not printed against a rigid flat platen, as is the normal printed page, but against a somewhat flexible or resilient platen or make-ready (Figure 6). This resilient platen is hard enough to produce a clear full impression from the ink on the face of the working die, and soft enough to push the paper into the uninked recesses that correspond to the engraved lines cut into the master die. The normal result is raised lines or embossments without ink or color, standing out in relief against an inked or colored background. The method differs from the usual embossing technique, where rigid dies are used on both sides of the paper, as in notarial seals. The use of the resilient platen in envelope embossing permits far higher operating speeds than can be obtained with rigid embossing dies, without the need of such accurate register between the printing surface and the platen.

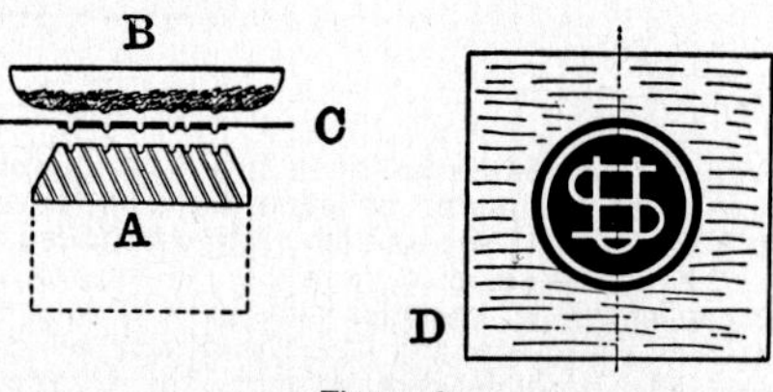

Figure 6

Printing Process for Embossed

A. Working Die, Carrying ink on its surface.

B. Resilient Platen, or Make-ready, Pushing Paper into uninked recesses, so that lines of Embossed Monogram receive no color.

C. Paper of Envelope Blank, after Printing and Embossing. Heavy line shows deposit of ink on surface of paper, but Embossed Lines are not inked.

D. Front view of Embossed impression.

When these recessed lines in a working die become filled with ink or other foreign material, the paper is not pushed in, the plugged area receives ink, and the corresponding colorless line does not appear on the stamp. This accounts for missing letters, lines or figures, and is a printing error, not a die variety.

An ALBINO impression is where two or more envelope blanks are fed into the printing press. The one adjacent to the printing die receives the color and the embossing, while the others are embossed only. Albinos are printing errors and are sometimes worth more than normal, inked impressions. Because of the nature of the printing process, many albinos were produced, and most collectors will not pay much, or any, premium for most of them. Albinos of earlier issues, canceled while current, are scarce.

Before January 1, 1965, stamped envelopes were printed by two processes: (1.) The rotary, with curved dies, on Huckins and Harris presses. (2.) The flat process, with straight dies, as illustrated, on the O'Connell-type press, which is a redesigned Hartford press. The flat bed presses include a gumming and folding attachment, while the rotary presses, running at higher speeds, require separate folding machines.

Different master dies in every denomination are required for Huckins, Harris and flat bed presses. This difference gives rise to most of the major die varieties in envelope stamps.

Web-fed equipment which converts paper from a roll into finished envelopes in a continuous operation has produced envelopes starting with Nos. U547 and UC37. Albino impressions do not occur on envelopes produced by web-fed equipment.

Some authorities claim that Scott U37, U48, U49, U110, U124, U125, U130, U133A, U137A, U137B, U137C, W138, U140A, U145, U162, U178A, U185, U220, U285, U286, U298, U299, UO3, UO32, UO38, UO45 and UO45A (with plus sign + before number), were not regularly issued and are not known to have been used.

Wrappers are listed with envelopes of corresponding design, and are numbered with the prefix "W" instead of "U."

ENVELOPE WATERMARKS

Watermark Illustrations 5, 6, 17 and 18 are condensed. Watermark 4 was intended for Official (Post Office Dept.) envelopes, but some leftover paper was also used for regular envelopes. Watermarks 9 and 10 (penalty) paper was never intended for public sale, but some manila/amber manila paper envelopes were released due to factory paper mixups. Watermarks 17-18 were the last laid paper watermarks; watermarks 19-21 the first wove paper watermarks. Beginning with No. U615, unwatermarked paper was used for some issues. Beginning with No. U625, unwatermarked paper was used for all issues.

Wmks. 1 (1853-70) & 2 (1870-78)

Wmk. 3 (1876)

Wmk. 4 (1877-82)

Wmk. 5 (1878-82)

Wmk. 6 (1882-86)

Wmks. 7 (1886-90) & 8 (1890-94)

Wmks. 9 (1886-87) & 10 (1886-99)

Wmk. 11 (1893)

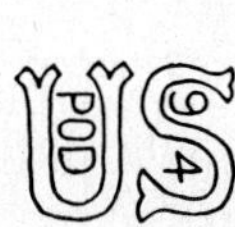

Wmks. 12 (1894-98) & 13 (1899-1902)

Wmks. 14 (1903-07) & 15 (1907-11)

Wmks. 15A (1907-11) & 16 (1911-15)

USSE US-SE

1911 1911

Wmks. 17 & 18 (1911-15)

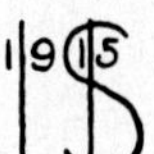
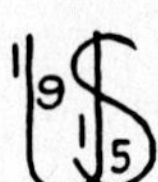

Wmk. 19, 20 & 21 (1915-19)

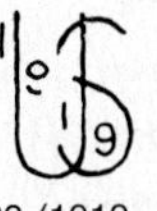

Wmks. 22 & 23 (1919-20)

Wmks. 24 & 25 (1921-24)

Wmks. 26 & 27 (1925-28)

Wmks. 28 & 28A (1929-32)

Wmks. 29, 30 & 30A (1929-32)

Wmks. 31, 32, 33 (1933-36)

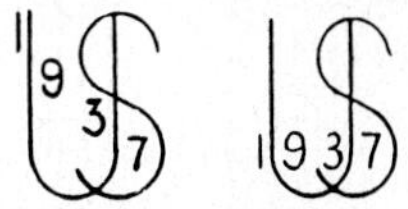

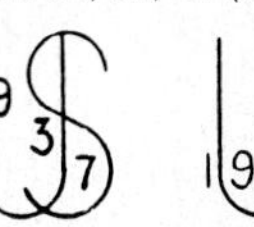

Wmks. 35 & 36 (1937-40)

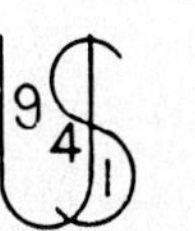

Wmks. 38 & 39 (1941-44)

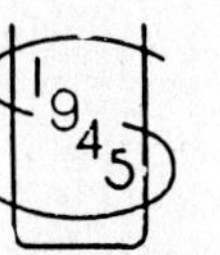
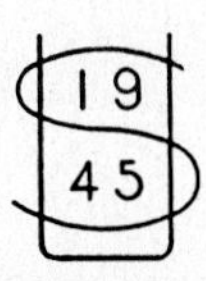

Wmks. 40 & 41 (1945-48)

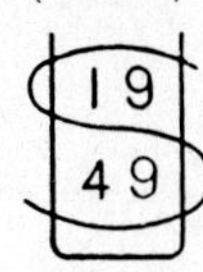

Wmks. 42 & 43 (1949-52)

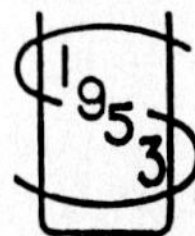

Wmks. 44 & 45 (1953-56)

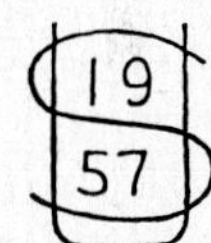

Wmk. 46 (1957-60)

☆USA USA☆

Wmks. 47 & 48 (1961-88)

Wmks. 49 & 50 (1965-92)

Letter Sheet (1886-94)

Official Envelopes (1991)

Washington — U1

"THREE" in short label with curved ends; 13mm wide at top. Twelve varieties.

U2

"THREE" in short label with straight ends; 15½mm wide at top. Three varieties.

U3

"THREE" in short label with octagonal ends. Two varieties.

U4

"THREE" in wide label with straight ends; 20mm wide at top.

U5

"THREE" in medium wide label with curved ends; 14½mm wide at top. Ten varieties. A sub-variety shows curved lines at either end of label omitted; both T's have longer cross stroke; R is smaller (20 varieties).

U6

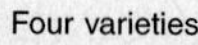

Four varieties.

U7

"TEN" in short label; 15½mm wide at top.

U8

"TEN" in wide label; 20mm wide at top.

Printed by George F. Nesbitt & Co., New York, N.Y.

1853-55

On Diagonally Laid Paper (Early printings of No. U1 on Horizontally Laid Paper)

U1	U1	3c **red**	350.00	35.00
		Entire	1,800.	60.00
U2	U1	3c **red,** *buff*	90.00	30.00
		Entire	850.00	40.00
U3	U2	3c **red**	950.00	50.00
		Entire	3,500.	120.00
U4	U2	3c **red,** *buff*	425.00	45.00
		Entire	4,500.	80.00
U5	U3	3c **red** ('54)	5,750.	500.00
		Entire	*26,000.*	800.00
U6	U3	3c **red,** *buff* ('54)	3,750.	100.00
		Entire	—	150.00
U7	U4	3c **red**	5,000.	150.00
		Entire	—	325.00
U8	U4	3c **red,** *buff*	*8,250.*	175.00
		Entire	—	325.00
U9	U5	3c **red** ('54)	40.00	4.00
		Entire	140.00	8.00
U10	U5	3c **red,** *buff* ('54)	20.00	4.00
		Entire	70.00	6.00
U11	U6	6c **red**	275.00	90.00
		Entire	350.00	175.00
U12	U6	6c **red,** *buff*	145.00	90.00
		Entire	350.00	200.00
U13	U6	6c **green**	260.00	150.00
		Entire	575.00	400.00
U14	U6	6c **green,** *buff*	200.00	125.00
		Entire	450.00	225.00
U15	U7	10c **green** ('55)	400.00	100.00
		Entire	675.00	175.00
U16	U7	10c **green,** *buff* ('55)	175.00	90.00
		Entire	425.00	175.00
a.		10c **pale green,** *buff*	135.00	70.00
		Entire	375.00	125.00
U17	U8	10c **green** ('55)	375.00	140.00
		Entire	675.00	225.00
a.		10c **pale green**	275.00	125.00
		Entire	675.00	200.00
U18	U8	10c **green,** *buff* ('55)	375.00	100.00
		Entire	625.00	190.00
a.		10c **pale green,** *buff*	350.00	100.00
		Entire	600.00	190.00

Earliest documented uses: No. U1, July 6, 1853; No. U2, July 12, 1853 (Nesbitt seal); No. U3, July 7, 1853 (Nesbitt seal); No. U4, July 7, 1853 (flap missing); No. U5, Feb. 18, 1854; No. U6, Feb. 24, 1854; No. U7, Oct. 6, 1853; No. U8, Nov. 9, 1853; No. U9, May 30, 1854; No. U10, Mar. 24, 1854; No. U11, Mar. 25, 1855; No. U12, Feb. 22, 1855; No. U13, Nov. 29, 1853; No. U14, Nov. 10, 1853; No. U15, Oct. 15, 1856; No. U16, May 15, 1857 (cut square), June 15, 1857 (entire); No. U16a, Dec. 19, 1856 (cut square), June 4, 1857 (entire); No. U17, no dates documented; No. U17a, Nov. 14, 1855; No. U18, June 1, 1855; No. U18a, Sept. 4, 1855.

Nos. U9, U10, U11, U12, U13, U14, U17, and U18 have been reprinted on white and buff papers, wove or vertically laid, and are not known entire. The originals are on diagonally laid paper. Value, set of 8 reprints on laid, $225. Reprints on wove sell for more.

The first printings of Nos. U1, U2, U3, U4 and U7 have G.F. Nesbitt crests printed on the envelope flaps. These sell for a premium. Such examples of Nos. U1-U4 with 1853 year-dated cancels sell for a very large premium.

No. U1 with watermark having a space between lines and on horizontally laid paper sells for a substantial premium.

Franklin — U9

Period after "POSTAGE." (Eleven varieties.)

Franklin — U10

Bust touches inner frame-line at front and back.

Franklin — U11

No period after "POSTAGE." (Two varieties.)

Washington — U12

Nine varieties of type U12.

Envelopes are on diagonally laid paper.
Wrappers on vertically or horizontally laid paper, or on unwatermarked wove paper (Nos. U21A, W22, W25)

Wrappers of the 1 cent denomination were authorized by an Act of Congress, February 27, 1861, and were issued in October, 1861. These were suspended in 1863, and their use resumed in June, 1864.

1860-61

W18B	U9	1c **blue** ('61)	*5,500.*	
		Entire	—	
U19	U9	1c **blue,** *buff*	35.00	12.50
		Entire	85.00	30.00
W20	U9	1c **blue,** *buff* ('61)	65.00	50.00
		Entire	120.00	75.00
W21	U9	1c **blue,** *manila* ('61)	55.00	45.00
		Entire	125.00	75.00
U21A	U9	1c **blue,** *orange*	*950.00*	*325.00*
		Entire	*1,800.*	
W22	U9	1c **blue,** *orange* ('61)	*3,000.*	
		Entire	*5,500.*	
U23	U10	1c **blue,** *orange*	500.00	350.00
		Entire	800.00	600.00
U24	U11	1c **blue,** *amber*	350.00	110.00
		Entire	675.00	300.00
W25	U11	1c **blue,** *manila* ('61)	*6,750.*	*1,500.*
		Entire	*20,000.*	*5,500.*
U26	U12	3c **red**	25.00	17.50
		Entire	55.00	32.50
U27	U12	3c **red,** *buff*	22.50	12.50
		Entire	45.00	22.50
U28	U12+U9	3c + 1c **red & blue**	250.00	225.00
		Entire	500.00	400.00
U29	U12+U9	3c + 1c **red & blue,** *buff*	250.00	250.00
		Entire	500.00	450.00
U30	U12	6c **red**	1,800.	1,500.
		Entire	*3,250.*	
U31	U12	6c **red,** *buff*	3,500.	1,450.
		Entire	*5,000.*	*15,000.*
U32	U12	10c **green**	1,250.	450.00
		Entire	*10,000.*	700.00
U33	U12	10c **green,** *buff*	1,250.	400.00
		Entire	*3,250.*	600.00

Nos. U26, U27, U30 to U33 have been reprinted on the same vertically laid paper as the reprints of the 1853-55 issue, and are not known entire. Value, Nos. U26-U27, $75 each; Nos. U30-U33, $75 each.

Washington — U13

17 varieties for Nos. U34-U35; 2 varieties for No. U36.

Washington — U14

Washington — U15

Washington — U16

Envelopes are on diagonally laid paper.

U36 and U45 come on vertically or horizontally laid paper. U36 appeared in August, 1861, and was withdrawn in 1864. Total issue 211,800.

1861

U34	U13	3c **pink**	27.50	5.00
		Entire	60.00	12.50
U35	U13	3c **pink,** *buff*	32.50	6.00
		Entire	62.50	12.00
U36	U13	3c **pink,** *blue* (Letter Sheet)	65.00	65.00
		Entire	230.00	*250.00*
+U37	U13	3c **pink,** *orange*	*2,750.*	
		Entire	*5,000.*	
U38	U14	6c **pink**	100.00	80.00
		Entire	200.00	190.00
U39	U14	6c **pink,** *buff*	60.00	60.00
		Entire	150.00	160.00
U40	U15	10c **yellow green**	40.00	30.00
		Entire	77.50	60.00
a.		10c **blue green**	40.00	30.00
		Entire	77.50	60.00
U41	U15	10c **yellow green,** *buff*	40.00	30.00
		Entire	77.50	70.00
a.		10c **blue green,** *buff*	40.00	30.00
		Entire	77.50	52.50
U42	U16	12c **red & brown,** *buff*	180.00	180.00
		Entire	475.00	*650.00*
a.		12c **lake & brown,** *buff*	*1,250.*	
U43	U16	20c **red & blue,** *buff*	250.00	225.00
		Entire	450.00	*1,250.*
U44	U16	24c **red & green,** *buff*	225.00	210.00
		Entire	625.00	*2,000.*
a.		24c **lake & green,** *salmon*	275.00	225.00
		Entire	750.00	*2,400.*
U45	U16	40c **black & red,** *buff*	325.00	400.00
		Entire	700.00	*4,500.*

Nos. U38 and U39 have been reprinted on the same papers as the reprints of the 1853-55 issue, and are not known entire. Value, set of 2 reprints, $60.

Jackson — U17

"U.S. POSTAGE" above. Downstroke and tail of "2" unite near the point (seven varieties).

Jackson — U18

"U.S. POSTAGE" above. The downstroke and tail of the "2" touch but do not merge.

Jackson — U19

"U.S. POST" above. Stamp 24-25mm wide (Sixteen varieties).

Jackson — U20

"U.S. POST" above. Stamp 25½-26¼mm wide. (Twenty-five varieties.)

Envelopes are on diagonally laid paper.
Wrappers on vertically or horizontally laid paper.

1863-64

U46	U17	2c **black,** *buff*	50.00	24.00
		Entire	80.00	37.50
W47	U17	2c **black,** *dark manila*	75.00	65.00
		Entire	120.00	90.00
+U48	U18	2c **black,** *buff*	*2,250.*	
		Entire	*4,500.*	
+U49	U18	2c **black,** *orange*	1,750.	
		Entire	4,000.	
U50	U19	2c **black,** *buff* ('64)	17.50	11.00
		Entire	40.00	21.00
W51	U19	2c **black,** *buff* ('64)	425.00	275.00
		Entire	650.00	600.00
U52	U19	2c **black,** *orange* ('64)	20.00	11.00
		Entire	37.50	18.00
W53	U19	2c **black,** *dark manila* ('64)	42.50	40.00
		Entire	175.00	140.00
U54	U20	2c **black,** *buff* ('64)	17.50	9.50
		Entire	37.50	16.00
W55	U20	2c **black,** *buff* ('64)	95.00	65.00
		Entire	160.00	120.00
U56	U20	2c **black,** *orange* ('64)	17.50	10.00
		Entire	32.50	16.00
W57	U20	2c **black,** *light manila* ('64)	22.50	14.00
		Entire	37.50	30.00

Washington — U21

79 varieties for Nos. U58-U61; 2 varieties for Nos. U63-U65.

Washington — U22

1864-65

U58	U21	3c **pink**	8.00	1.60
		Entire	20.00	3.25
U59	U21	3c **pink,** *buff*	7.50	1.25
		Entire	20.00	3.00
U60	U21	3c **brown** ('65)	60.00	40.00
		Entire	125.00	125.00
U61	U21	3c **brown,** *buff* ('65)	50.00	30.00
		Entire	115.00	95.00
U62	U21	6c **pink**	75.00	29.00
		Entire	160.00	85.00
U63	U21	6c **pink,** *buff*	35.00	27.50
		Entire	90.00	60.00
U64	U21	6c **purple** ('65)	50.00	26.00
		Entire	80.00	80.00
U65	U21	6c **purple,** *buff* ('65)	40.00	20.00
		Entire	70.00	80.00
U66	U22	9c **lemon,** *buff* ('65)	375.00	250.00
		Entire	575.00	*1,500.*
U67	U22	9c **orange,** *buff* ('65)	125.00	90.00
		Entire	210.00	300.00
a.		9c **orange yellow,** *buff*	150.00	90.00
		Entire	225.00	300.00
U68	U22	12c **brown,** *buff* ('65)	275.00	275.00
		Entire	600.00	*1,200.*
U69	U22	12c **red brown,** *buff* ('65)	125.00	55.00
		Entire	180.00	450.00
U70	U22	18c **red,** *buff* ('65)	70.00	95.00
		Entire	180.00	*800.00*
U71	U22	24c **blue,** *buff* ('65)	70.00	95.00
		Entire	200.00	*1,000.*
U72	U22	30c **green,** *buff* ('65)	80.00	80.00
		Entire	200.00	*2,200.*
a.		30c **yellow green,** *buff*	75.00	75.00
		Entire	200.00	*2,000.*
U73	U22	40c **rose,** *buff* ('65)	80.00	*250.00*
		Entire	340.00	*2,000.*

Nos. U60 and U61 issued on legal-size covers only.

Printed by George H. Reay, Brooklyn, N. Y.

The engravings in this issue are finely executed.

Franklin — U23

Bust points to the end of the "N" of "ONE."

Jackson — U24

Bust narrow at back. Small, thick figures of value.

Washington — U25

Queue projects below bust.

Lincoln — U26

Neck very long at the back.

Stanton — U27

Bust pointed at the back; figures "7" are normal.

Jefferson — U28

Queue forms straight line with the bust.

Clay — U29

Ear partly concealed by hair, mouth large, chin prominent.

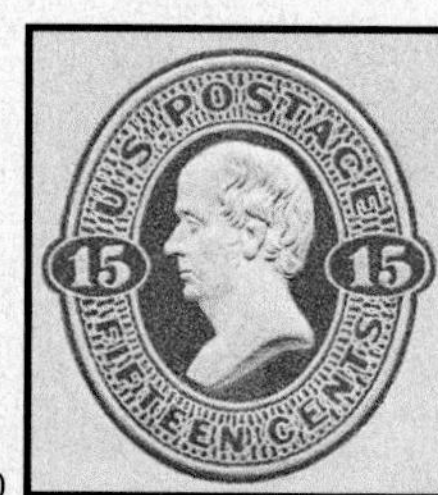

Webster — U30

Has side whiskers.

Scott — U31

Straggling locks of hair at top of head; ornaments around the inner oval end in squares.

Hamilton — U32

Back of bust very narrow, chin almost straight; labels containing figures of value are exactly parallel.

Perry — U33

Front of bust very narrow and pointed; inner lines of shields project very slightly beyond the oval.

1870-71

U74	U23 1c **blue**	32.50	30.00
	Entire	75.00	45.00
a.	1c **ultramarine**	60.00	35.00
	Entire	130.00	60.00
U75	U23 1c **blue,** *amber*	25.00	27.50
	Entire	55.00	40.00
a.	1c **ultramarine,** *amber*	55.00	30.00
	Entire	95.00	55.00
U76	U23 1c **blue,** *orange*	17.00	15.00
	Entire	35.00	22.50
W77	U23 1c **blue,** *manila*	35.00	35.00
	Entire	85.00	75.00
U78	U24 2c **brown**	35.00	16.00
	Entire	57.50	22.50
U79	U24 2c **brown,** *amber*	14.00	10.00
	Entire	40.00	17.50
U80	U24 2c **brown,** *orange*	8.00	6.50
	Entire	15.00	11.00
W81	U24 2c **brown,** *manila*	25.00	20.00
	Entire	60.00	57.50
U82	U25 3c **green**	7.00	1.00
	Entire	16.00	4.00
a.	3c **brown** (error), entire	*9,000.*	
U83	U25 3c **green,** *amber*	6.00	2.00
	Entire	17.50	5.00
U84	U25 3c **green,** *cream*	8.00	4.50
	Entire	16.00	10.00
U85	U26 6c **dark red**	17.50	16.00
	Entire	47.50	21.00
a.	6c **vermilion**	17.50	16.00
	Entire	50.00	20.00
U86	U26 6c **dark red,** *amber*	30.00	20.00
	Entire	55.00	40.00
a.	6c **vermilion,** *amber*	30.00	20.00
	Entire	75.00	30.00
U87	U26 6c **dark red,** *cream*	30.00	25.00
	Entire	70.00	40.00
a.	6c **vermilion,** *cream*	25.00	20.00
	Entire	70.00	40.00
U88	U27 7c **vermilion,** *amber* ('71)	55.00	175.00
	Entire	80.00	*900.00*
U89	U28 10c **olive black**	650.00	900.00
	Entire	900.00	1,200.
U90	U28 10c **olive black,** *amber*	625.00	800.00
	Entire	1,000.	1,400.
U91	U28 10c **brown**	82.50	70.00
	Entire	130.00	150.00
U92	U28 10c **brown,** *amber*	85.00	52.50
	Entire	120.00	200.00
a.	10c **dark brown,** *amber*	85.00	75.00
	Entire	120.00	125.00
U93	U29 12c **plum**	100.00	82.50
	Entire	225.00	*500.00*
U94	U29 12c **plum,** *amber*	110.00	100.00
	Entire	225.00	*750.00*
U95	U29 12c **plum,** *cream*	225.00	200.00
	Entire	300.00	

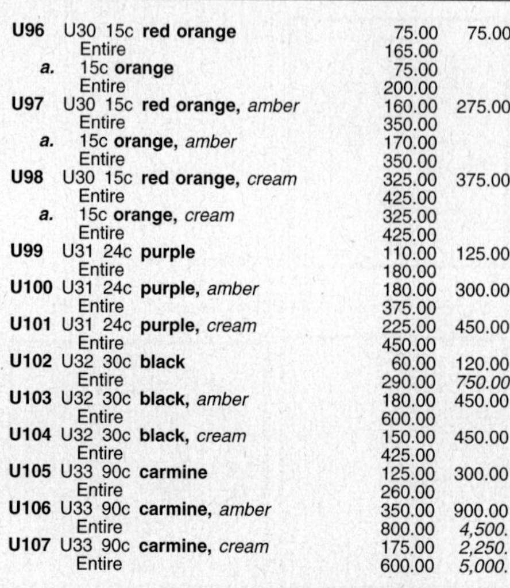

U96	U30 15c **red orange**	75.00	75.00
	Entire	165.00	
a.	15c **orange**	75.00	
	Entire	200.00	
U97	U30 15c **red orange,** *amber*	160.00	275.00
	Entire	350.00	
a.	15c **orange,** *amber*	170.00	
	Entire	350.00	
U98	U30 15c **red orange,** *cream*	325.00	375.00
	Entire	425.00	
a.	15c **orange,** *cream*	325.00	
	Entire	425.00	
U99	U31 24c **purple**	110.00	125.00
	Entire	180.00	
U100	U31 24c **purple,** *amber*	180.00	300.00
	Entire	375.00	
U101	U31 24c **purple,** *cream*	225.00	450.00
	Entire	450.00	
U102	U32 30c **black**	60.00	120.00
	Entire	290.00	*750.00*
U103	U32 30c **black,** *amber*	180.00	450.00
	Entire	600.00	
U104	U32 30c **black,** *cream*	150.00	450.00
	Entire	425.00	
U105	U33 90c **carmine**	125.00	300.00
	Entire	260.00	
U106	U33 90c **carmine,** *amber*	350.00	900.00
	Entire	800.00	*4,500.*
U107	U33 90c **carmine,** *cream*	175.00	*2,250.*
	Entire	600.00	*5,000.*

Printed by Plimpton Manufacturing Co.

U34

Bust forms an angle at the back near the frame. Lettering poorly executed. Distinct circle in "O" of "Postage."

U35

Lower part of bust points to the end of the "E" in "ONE." Head inclined downward.

U36

Bust narrow at back. Thin numerals. Head of "P" narrow. Bust broad at front, ending in sharp corners.

U37

Bust broad. Figures of value in long ovals.

U38

Similar to U37 but the figure "2" at the left touches the oval.

U39

Similar to U37 but the "O" of "TWO" has the center netted instead of plain and the "G" of "POSTAGE" and the "C" of "CENTS" have diagonal crossline.

U40

Bust broad: numerals in ovals short and thick.

U41

Similar to U40 but the ovals containing the numerals are much heavier. A diagonal line runs from the upper part of the "U" to the white frame-line.

U42

Similar to U40 but the middle stroke of "N" in "CENTS" is as thin as the vertical strokes.

U43

Bottom of bust cut almost semi-circularly.

U44

Thin lettering, long thin figures of value.

U45

Thick lettering, well-formed figures of value, queue does not project below bust.

U46

Top of head egg-shaped; knot of queue well marked and projects triangularly.

Taylor — U47

Die 1- Figures of value with thick, curved tops

Die 2- Figures of value with long, thin tops

U48

Neck short at back.

U49

Figures of value turned up at the ends.

U50

Very large head.

U51

Knot of queue stands out prominently.

U52

Ear prominent, chin receding.

U53

No side whiskers, forelock projects above head.

U54

Hair does not project; ornaments around the inner oval end in points.

U55

Back of bust rather broad, chin slopes considerably; labels containing figures of value are not exactly parallel.

U56

Front of bust sloping; inner lines of shields project considerably into the inner oval.

1874-86

No.	Description	Unused	Used
U108	U34 1c **dark blue**	175.00	60.00
	Entire	250.00	125.00
a.	1c **light blue**	175.00	60.00
	Entire	250.00	150.00
U109	U34 1c **dark blue,** *amber*	150.00	75.00
	Entire	200.00	140.00
+U110	U34 1c **dark blue,** *cream*	*1,000.*	
U111	U34 1c **dark blue,** *orange*	15.00	15.00
	Entire	40.00	25.00
a.	1c **light blue,** *orange*	12.50	12.50
	Entire	30.00	25.00
W112	U34 1c **dark blue,** *manila*	62.50	40.00
	Entire	105.00	90.00
U113	U35 1c **light blue**	2.25	1.00
	Entire	4.00	2.00
a.	1c **dark blue**	6.50	6.50
	Entire	27.50	20.00
U114	U35 1c **light blue,** *amber*	3.25	3.25
	Entire	8.25	6.00
a.	1c **dark blue,** *amber*	17.50	10.00
	Entire	30.00	20.00
U115	U35 1c **blue,** *cream*	4.25	4.25
	Entire	10.00	6.50
a.	1c **dark blue,** *cream*	17.50	8.50
	Entire	32.50	20.00
U116	U35 1c **light blue,** *orange*	.75	.40
	Entire	1.25	1.00
a.	1c **dark blue,** *orange*	4.00	2.50
	Entire	16.00	8.00
U117	U35 1c **light blue,** *blue* ('80)	6.50	5.00
	Entire	15.00	9.00
U118	U35 1c **light blue,** *fawn* ('79)	7.00	5.00
	Entire	17.00	12.00
U119	U35 1c **light blue,** *manila* ('86)	8.00	3.25
	Entire	17.00	5.00
W120	U35 1c **light blue,** *manila*	1.25	1.10
	Entire	2.75	1.75
a.	1c **dark blue,** *manila*	8.00	7.00
	Entire	16.00	15.00
U121	U35 1c **light blue,** *amber manila* ('86)	17.50	10.00
	Entire	29.00	25.00
U122	U36 2c **brown**	140.00	65.00
	Entire	175.00	100.00
U123	U36 2c **brown,** *amber*	67.50	40.00
	Entire	125.00	85.00
+U124	U36 2c **brown,** *cream*	*1,000.*	
+U125	U36 2c **brown,** *orange*	*18,000.*	
	Entire	*35,000.*	
W126	U36 2c **brown,** *manila*	125.00	85.00
	Entire	325.00	160.00
W127	U36 2c **vermilion,** *manila*	2,500.	500.00
	Entire	3,250.	*5,000.*
U128	U37 2c **brown**	60.00	35.00
	Entire	110.00	85.00
U129	U37 2c **brown,** *amber*	80.00	45.00
	Entire	125.00	77.50
+U130	U37 2c **brown,** *cream*	*35,000.*	
W131	U37 2c **brown,** *manila*	17.50	15.00
	Entire	29.00	26.00
U132	U38 2c **brown**	70.00	27.50
	Entire	120.00	80.00
U133	U38 2c **brown,** *amber*	325.00	70.00
	Entire	550.00	175.00
+U133A	U38 2c **brown,** *cream*	*70,000.*	
U134	U39 2c **brown**	800.00	160.00
	Entire	1,400.	300.00
U135	U39 2c **brown,** *amber*	425.00	150.00
	Entire	650.00	180.00
U136	U39 2c **brown,** *orange*	50.00	27.50
	Entire	80.00	37.50
W137	U39 2c **brown,** *manila*	75.00	40.00
	Entire	125.00	55.00
+U137A	U39 2c **vermilion**	*32,500.*	
+U137B	U39 2c **vermilion,** *amber*	*30,000.*	
	Entire	—	
+U137C	U39 2c **vermilion,** *orange*	*70,000.*	
+W138	U39 2c **vermilion,** *manila*	*25,000.*	
U139	U40 2c **brown** ('75)	57.50	37.50
	Entire	85.00	55.00
U140	U40 2c **brown,** *amber* ('75)	85.00	62.50
	Entire	130.00	85.00
+U140A	U40 2c **reddish brown,** *orange* ('75)	*17,500.*	
	Entire	*32,500.*	
W141	U40 2c **brown,** *manila* ('75)	32.50	25.00
	Entire	45.00	40.00
U142	U40 2c **vermilion** ('75)	8.00	5.00
	Entire	12.00	6.00
a.	2c **pink**	8.00	5.00
	Entire	16.00	9.00
U143	U40 2c **vermilion,** *amber* ('75)	9.00	5.00
	Entire	12.00	6.50
U144	U40 2c **vermilion,** *cream* ('75)	17.50	7.00
	Entire	25.00	12.50
+U145	U40 2c **vermilion,** *orange* ('75)	*35,000.*	
U146	U40 2c **vermilion,** *blue* ('80)	110.00	40.00
	Entire	*200.00*	140.00
U147	U40 2c **vermilion,** *fawn* ('75)	7.00	5.00
	Entire	15.00	7.00
W148	U40 2c **vermilion,** *manila* ('75)	4.00	3.50
	Entire	9.00	6.50
U149	U41 2c **vermilion** ('78)	45.00	25.00
	Entire	90.00	40.00
a.	2c **pink**	52.50	27.00
	Entire	90.00	42.50
U150	U41 2c **vermilion,** *amber* ('78)	45.00	15.00
	Entire	75.00	25.00
U151	U41 2c **vermilion,** *blue* ('80)	10.00	8.00
	Entire	25.00	25.00
a.	2c **pink,** *blue*	11.00	8.00
	Entire	17.50	12.50
U152	U41 2c **vermilion,** *fawn* ('78)	10.00	4.00
	Entire	17.50	9.00
U153	U42 2c **vermilion** ('76)	75.00	30.00
	Entire	115.00	45.00
U154	U42 2c **vermilion,** *amber* ('76)	300.00	90.00
	Entire	450.00	200.00
W155	U42 2c **vermilion,** *manila* ('76)	20.00	10.00
	Entire	45.00	20.00
U156	U43 2c **vermilion** ('81)	1,250.	175.00
	Entire	2,000.	*500.00*
U157	U43 2c **vermilion,** *amber* ('81)	*42,500.*	*27,500.*
	Entire	*60,000.*	
W158	U43 2c **vermilion,** *manila* ('81)	90.00	55.00
	Entire	200.00	200.00
U159	U44 3c **green**	35.00	10.00
	Entire	60.00	17.50
U160	U44 3c **green,** *amber*	35.00	10.00
	Entire	70.00	20.00
U161	U44 3c **green,** *cream*	35.00	12.00
	Entire	65.00	30.00
+U162	U44 3c **green,** *blue*	*75,000.*	
U163	U45 3c **green**	1.40	.30
	Entire	4.25	2.25
U164	U45 3c **green,** *amber*	1.50	.70
	Entire	4.25	2.00
U165	U45 3c **green,** *cream*	8.50	6.50
	Entire	19.00	11.00
U166	U45 3c **green,** *blue*	7.50	6.00
	Entire	17.00	11.00
U167	U45 3c **green,** *fawn* ('75)	4.75	3.50
	Entire	9.25	5.00
U168	U46 3c **green** ('81)	1,000.	80.00
	Entire	3,500.	275.00
U169	U46 3c **green,** *amber*	450.00	140.00
	Entire	700.00	300.00
U170	U46 3c **green,** *blue* ('81)	*11,500.*	*2,750.*
	Entire	*20,000.*	*4,250.*
U171	U46 3c **green,** *fawn* ('81)	*40,000.*	*2,750.*
	Entire		*14,000.*
U172	U47 5c **blue,** die 1 ('75)	10.00	10.00
	Entire	20.00	16.00
U173	U47 5c **blue,** die 1, *amber* ('75)	12.50	11.00
	Entire	21.00	17.00
U174	U47 5c **blue,** die 1, *cream* ('75)	95.00	45.00
	Entire	190.00	150.00
U175	U47 5c **blue,** die 1, *blue* ('75)	22.50	17.50
	Entire	40.00	35.00
U176	U47 5c **blue,** die 1, *fawn* ('75)	150.00	65.00
	Entire	325.00	
U177	U47 5c **blue,** die 2 ('75)	11.00	9.00
	Entire	18.00	18.00
U178	U47 5c **blue,** die 2, *amber* ('75)	8.00	8.00
	Entire	18.00	19.00
+U178A	U47 5c **blue,** die 2, *cream* ('76)	*10,000.*	
	Entire	*17,500.*	
U179	U47 5c **blue,** die 2, *blue* ('75)	20.00	12.50
	Entire	50.00	50.00
U180	U47 5c **blue,** die 2, *fawn* ('75)	125.00	50.00
	Entire	225.00	225.00
U181	U48 6c **red**	8.00	6.50
	Entire	15.00	12.50
a.	6c **vermilion**	8.00	6.50
	Entire	15.00	12.50
U182	U48 6c **red,** *amber*	12.50	6.50
	Entire	24.00	15.00
a.	6c **vermilion,** *amber*	12.50	6.50
	Entire	24.00	15.00
U183	U48 6c **red,** *cream*	50.00	17.50
	Entire	100.00	100.00
a.	6c **vermilion,** *cream*	45.00	15.00
	Entire	82.50	40.00
U184	U48 6c **red,** *fawn* ('75)	17.50	12.50
	Entire	32.50	50.00
+U185	U49 7c **vermilion**	*1,200.*	
U186	U49 7c **vermilion,** *amber*	125.00	75.00
	Entire	225.00	
U187	U50 10c **brown**	40.00	20.00
	Entire	65.00	
U188	U50 10c **brown,** *amber*	75.00	35.00
	Entire	170.00	
U189	U51 10c **chocolate** ('75)	6.00	4.00
	Entire	12.00	9.25
a.	10c **bister brown**	7.00	5.00
	Entire	12.50	10.50
b.	10c **yellow ocher**	*3,000.*	
	Entire	*5,250.*	
U190	U51 10c **chocolate,** *amber* ('75)	7.00	6.00
	Entire	13.00	14.00
a.	10c **bister brown,** *amber*	7.00	6.00
	Entire	13.00	14.00
b.	10c **yellow ocher,** *amber*	*3,000.*	
	Entire	*5,250.*	
U191	U51 10c **brown,** *oriental buff* ('86)	12.50	8.75
	Entire	20.00	15.00
U192	U51 10c **brown,** *blue* ('86)	12.50	8.00
	Entire	20.00	20.00
a.	10c **gray black,** *blue*	12.50	7.50
	Entire	30.00	20.00
b.	10c **red brown,** *blue*	12.50	7.50
	Entire	20.00	20.00
U193	U51 10c **brown,** *manila* ('86)	12.50	10.00
	Entire	22.50	25.00
a.	10c **red brown,** *manila*	12.50	10.00
	Entire	22.50	25.00
U194	U51 10c **brown,** *amber manila* ('86)	17.50	9.00
	Entire	30.00	30.00
a.	10c **red brown,** *amber manila*	17.50	9.00
	Entire	40.00	30.00
U195	U52 12c **plum**	250.00	100.00
	Entire	575.00	*1,000.*
U196	U52 12c **plum,** *amber*	200.00	160.00
	Entire	350.00	*1,000.*
U197	U52 12c **plum,** *cream*	450.00	130.00
	Entire	850.00	*2,200.*
U198	U53 15c **orange**	50.00	35.00
	Entire	100.00	100.00
U199	U53 15c **orange,** *amber*	140.00	130.00
	Entire	300.00	*2,000.*
U200	U53 15c **orange,** *cream*	550.00	300.00
	Entire	800.00	*2,000.*
U201	U54 24c **purple**	175.00	150.00
	Entire	260.00	*1,500.*
a.	Printed on both sides, one inverted and overlapping, cut to shape	450.00	
U202	U54 24c **purple,** *amber*	180.00	100.00
	Entire	375.00	*2,500.*
U203	U54 24c **purple,** *cream*	375.00	100.00
	Entire	750.00	
U204	U55 30c **black**	55.00	25.00
	Entire	90.00	200.00
U205	U55 30c **black,** *amber*	70.00	60.00
	Entire	130.00	*250.00*
U206	U55 30c **black,** *cream* ('75)	300.00	325.00
	Entire	600.00	
U207	U55 30c **black,** *oriental buff* ('81)	90.00	80.00
	Entire	160.00	
U208	U55 30c **black,** *blue* ('81)	90.00	80.00
	Entire	170.00	
U209	U55 30c **black,** *manila* ('81)	80.00	70.00
	Entire	190.00	
U210	U55 30c **black,** *amber manila* ('86)	190.00	100.00
	Entire	260.00	
U211	U56 90c **carmine** ('75)	80.00	75.00
	Entire	130.00	*500.00*
U212	U56 90c **carmine,** *amber* ('75)	175.00	250.00
	Entire	250.00	
U213	U56 90c **carmine,** *cream* ('75)	1,000.	
	Entire	2,000.	
U214	U56 90c **carmine,** *oriental buff* ('86)	140.00	250.00
	Entire	300.00	400.00
U215	U56 90c **carmine,** *blue* ('86)	160.00	250.00
	Entire	250.00	325.00
U216	U56 90c **carmine,** *manila* ('86)	120.00	225.00
	Entire	240.00	*700.00*
U217	U56 90c **carmine,** *amber manila* ('86)	140.00	200.00
	Entire	300.00	*700.00*

Note: No. U206 has watermark #2; No. U207 watermark #6 or #7. No U213 has watermark #2; No. U214 watermark #7. These envelopes cannot be positively identified except by the watermark.

U57

Single line under "POSTAGE."

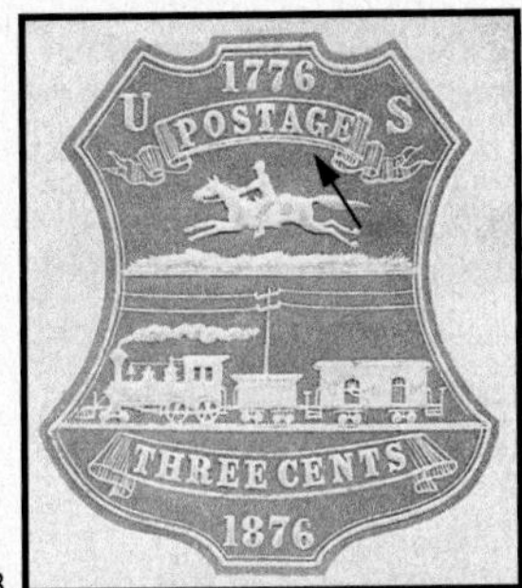

U58

Double line under "POSTAGE."

1876 Printed by Plimpton Manufacturing Co.

No.	Description	Unused	Used
U218	U57 3c **red**	30.00	25.00
	Entire	70.00	50.00
U219	U57 3c **green**	30.00	17.50
	Entire	60.00	40.00
+U220	U58 3c **red**	*27,500.*	
	Entire	*42,500.*	
U221	U58 3c **green**	30.00	25.00
	Entire	75.00	50.00

Used examples of Nos. U218-U221 with exposition cancels and/or typed addresses sell for a premium.

Garfield — U59

Printed by Plimpton Manufacturing Co. and Morgan Envelope Co.

1882-86

No.	Description	Unused	Used
U222	U59 5c **brown**	5.00	3.00
	Entire	10.00	7.50
U223	U59 5c **brown,** *amber*	5.25	3.50
	Entire	11.00	10.00
+U224	U59 5c **brown,** *oriental buff* ('86)	130.00	
	Entire	200.00	
+U225	U59 5c **brown,** *blue*	75.00	
	Entire	120.00	
U226	U59 5c **brown,** *fawn*	300.00	
	Entire	800.00	

Washington — U60

1883, October

No.	Description	Unused	Used
U227	U60 2c **red**	5.50	2.25
	Entire	11.00	4.00
a.	2c **brown** (error), entire	*3,000.*	
U228	U60 2c **red,** *amber*	6.50	2.75
	Entire	12.00	6.00
U229	U60 2c **red,** *blue*	8.00	5.00
	Entire	12.50	8.00
U230	U60 2c **red,** *fawn*	9.00	5.25
	Entire	14.00	7.00

Washington — U61

Wavy lines fine and clear.

1883, November **Four Wavy Lines in Oval**

No.	Description	Unused	Used
U231	U61 2c **red**	5.00	2.50
	Entire	9.50	4.00
U232	U61 2c **red,** *amber*	6.00	3.75
	Entire	11.00	5.75
U233	U61 2c **red,** *blue*	10.00	7.50
	Entire	12.00	10.00
U234	U61 2c **red,** *fawn*	7.50	4.75
	Entire	11.00	6.00
W235	U61 2c **red,** *manila*	18.00	6.25
	Entire	30.00	20.00

U62

Retouched die. Wavy lines thick and blurred.

1884, June

No.	Description	Unused	Used
U236	U62 2c **red**	15.00	4.00
	Entire	20.00	7.75
U237	U62 2c **red,** *amber*	20.00	10.00
	Entire	30.00	11.00
U238	U62 2c **red,** *blue*	29.00	12.00
	Entire	40.00	15.00
U239	U62 2c **red,** *fawn*	20.00	11.00
	Entire	22.50	12.50

U63

3½ links over left "2."

No.	Description	Unused	Used
U240	U63 2c **red**	90.00	45.00
	Entire	150.00	72.50
U241	U63 2c **red,** *amber*	550.00	300.00
	Entire	1,500.	750.00
U242	U63 2c **red,** *fawn*	*25,000.*	
	Entire	*47,500.*	

U64

2 links below right "2."

No.	Description	Unused	Used
U243	U64 2c **red**	110.00	75.00
	Entire	140.00	100.00
U244	U64 2c **red,** *amber*	250.00	100.00
	Entire	400.00	125.00
U245	U64 2c **red,** *blue*	275.00	125.00
	Entire	500.00	150.00
U246	U64 2c **red,** *fawn*	275.00	175.00
	Entire	525.00	200.00

U65

Round "O" in "TWO." White lines above "WO" of "TWO" joined to form thick white dash.

No.	Description	Unused	Used
U247	U65 2c **red**	1,500.	400.00
	Entire	2,500.	*800.00*
U248	U65 2c **red,** *amber*	2,500.	750.00
	Entire	5,000.	*2,500.*
U249	U65 2c **red,** *fawn*	750.	500.00
	Entire	1,250.	*750.00*

Jackson, Die 1 — U66

Die 1- Numeral at left is 2 ¾ mm wide

Die 2- Numeral at left is 3 ¼ mm wide

1883-86

No.	Description	Unused	Used
U250	U66 4c **green,** die 1	4.00	3.50
	Entire	6.50	6.00
U251	U66 4c **green,** die 1, *amber*	5.00	3.50
	Entire	7.50	8.00
U252	U66 4c **green,** die 1, *oriental buff* ('86)	13.00	9.00
	Entire	20.00	20.00
U253	U66 4c **green,** die 1, *blue* ('86)	11.00	6.50
	Entire	20.00	20.00
U254	U66 4c **green,** die 1, *manila* ('86)	16.00	7.50
	Entire	25.00	25.00
U255	U66 4c **green,** die 1, *amber manila* ('86)	22.50	10.00
	Entire	32.50	30.00
U256	U66 4c **green,** die 2	8.00	5.00
	Entire	17.50	10.00
U257	U66 4c **green,** die 2, *amber*	12.50	7.00
	Entire	22.50	20.00
U258	U66 4c **green,** die 2, *manila* ('86)	12.50	7.50
	Entire	22.50	18.00
U259	U66 4c **green,** die 2, *amber manila* ('86)	12.50	7.50
	Entire	22.50	18.00

1884, May

No.	Description	Unused	Used
U260	U61 2c **brown**	17.50	5.75
	Entire	20.00	9.00
U261	U61 2c **brown,** *amber*	17.50	6.50
	Entire	20.00	10.00
U262	U61 2c **brown,** *blue*	17.50	10.00
	Entire	26.00	14.00
U263	U61 2c **brown,** *fawn*	15.00	9.25
	Entire	20.00	12.50
W264	U61 2c **brown,** *manila*	15.00	11.50
	Entire	30.00	30.00

1884, June

Retouched Die

No.	Description	Unused	Used
U265	U62 2c **brown**	15.00	6.50
	Entire	25.00	12.00
U266	U62 2c **brown,** *amber*	60.00	40.00
	Entire	90.00	50.00
U267	U62 2c **brown,** *blue*	22.50	9.00
	Entire	30.00	15.00
U268	U62 2c **brown,** *fawn*	15.00	11.00
	Entire	21.00	15.00
W269	U62 2c **brown,** *manila*	25.00	15.00
	Entire	32.50	24.00

2 Links Below Right "2"

No.	Description	Unused	Used
U270	U64 2c **brown**	115.00	50.00
	Entire	150.00	110.00
U271	U64 2c **brown,** *amber*	425.00	125.00
	Entire	575.00	350.00

U272	U64 2c **brown,** *fawn*		7,000.	2,000.
	Entire		8,500.	4,000.

Round "O" in "Two"

U273	U65 2c **brown**	225.00	100.00
	Entire	375.00	190.00
U274	U65 2c **brown,** *amber*	225.00	100.00
	Entire	375.00	225.00
U275	U65 2c **brown,** *blue*		*10,000.*
	Entire		*47,500.*
U276	U65 2c **brown,** *fawn*	700.00	750.00
	Entire	1,200.	*1,200.*

Washington — U67

Extremity of bust below the queue forms a point.

U68

Extremity of bust is rounded. Similar to U61. Two wavy lines in oval.

1884-86

U277	U67 2c **brown**	.50	.25
	Entire	1.00	.40
a.	2c **brown lake,** die 1	22.50	21.00
	Entire	27.50	26.00
U278	U67 2c **brown,** *amber*	.65	.50
	Entire	1.75	1.00
a.	2c **brown lake,** *amber*	35.00	25.00
	Entire	42.50	32.50
U279	U67 2c **brown,** *oriental buff* ('86)	6.00	2.10
	Entire	9.00	9.00
U280	U67 2c **brown,** *blue*	3.00	2.10
	Entire	4.50	4.50
U281	U67 2c **brown,** *fawn*	3.75	2.40
	Entire	5.50	4.00
U282	U67 2c **brown,** *manila* ('86)	12.00	4.00
	Entire	17.50	12.00
W283	U67 2c **brown,** *manila*	8.00	5.00
	Entire	11.00	11.00
U284	U67 2c **brown,** *amber manila* ('86)	7.00	5.75
	Entire	15.00	12.00
+U285	U67 2c **red**	600.00	
	Entire	1,200.	
+U286	U67 2c **red,** *blue*	225.00	
	Entire	350.00	
W287	U67 2c **red,** *manila*	150.00	
	Entire	190.00	
U288	U68 2c **brown**	325.00	50.00
	Entire	700.00	150.00
U289	U68 2c **brown,** *amber*	20.00	13.00
	Entire	25.00	25.00
U290	U68 2c **brown,** *blue*	850.00	325.00
	Entire	1,600.	450.00
U291	U68 2c **brown,** *fawn*	25.00	25.00
	Entire	50.00	50.00
W292	U68 2c **brown,** *manila*	30.00	19.00
	Entire	35.00	30.00

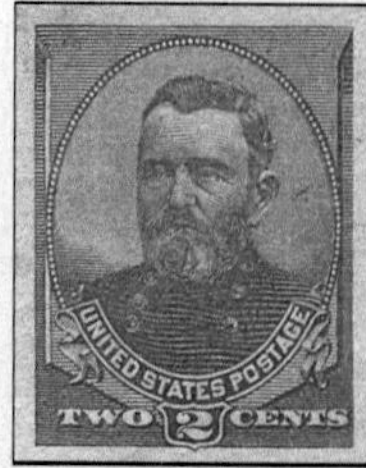

Gen. U.S. Grant — US1

Printed by American Bank Note Co.
Issued August 23, 1886. Withdrawn June 30, 1894.
Letter Sheet, 160x271mm

1886 **Creamy White Paper**

Stamp in upper right corner

U293	US1 2c **green,** entire	30.00	20.00

Perforation varieties:

83 perforations at top	30.00	20.00
42 perforations at top	150.00	100.00
33 perforations at top	45.00	20.00

All with 41 perforations at top

Inscribed: Series 1	30.00	20.00
Inscribed: Series 2	30.00	20.00
Inscribed: Series 3	30.00	20.00
Inscribed: Series 4	30.00	20.00
Inscribed: Series 5	30.00	20.00
Inscribed: Series 6	30.00	20.00
Inscribed: Series 7	30.00	20.00
No inscription, continuous side perforations	30.00	20.00
No inscription, interrupted side perforations	30.00	20.00

Earliest documented use: Aug. 23, 1886 (FDC).

Franklin — U69

Washington — U70

Bust points between third and fourth notches of inner oval "G" of "POSTAGE" has no bar.

U71

Bust points between second and third notches of inner oval; "G" of "POSTAGE" has a bar; ear is indicated by one heavy line; one vertical line at corner of mouth.

U72

Frame same as U71; upper part of head more rounded; ear indicated by two curved lines with two locks of hair in front; two vertical lines at corner of mouth.

Jackson — U73

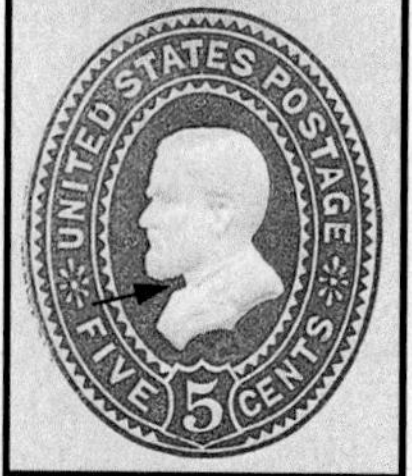
Grant — U74

There is a space between the beard and the collar of the coat. A button is on the collar.

U75

The collar touches the beard and there is no button.

Printed by Plimpton Manufacturing Co. and Morgan Envelope Co., Hartford, Conn.; James Purcell, Holyoke, Mass.

1887-94

U294	U69 1c **blue**	.55	.25
	Entire	1.00	.50
U295	U69 1c **dark blue** ('94)	6.50	2.50
	Entire	11.50	7.50
U296	U69 1c **blue,** *amber*	3.25	1.25
	Entire	5.50	3.50
U297	U69 1c **dark blue,** *amber* ('94)	40.00	22.50
	Entire	60.00	27.50
+U298	U69 1c **blue,** *oriental buff*	*7,000.*	—
	Entire	*12,000.*	
+U299	U69 1c **blue,** *blue*	*10,000.*	
	Entire	*18,000.*	
U300	U69 1c **blue,** *manila*	.65	.35
	Entire	1.25	.75
W301	U69 1c **blue,** *manila*	.45	.30
	Entire	1.25	.60
U302	U69 1c **dark blue,** *manila* ('94)	27.50	12.50
	Entire	35.00	20.00
W303	U69 1c **dark blue,** *manila* ('94)	12.50	10.00
	Entire	20.00	15.00
U304	U69 1c **blue,** *amber manila*	12.50	5.00
	Entire	17.50	10.00
U305	U70 2c **green**	15.00	10.00
	Entire	32.50	15.00
U306	U70 2c **green,** *amber*	40.00	17.50
	Entire	55.00	25.00
U307	U70 2c **green,** *oriental buff*	80.00	40.00
	Entire	120.00	70.00
U308	U70 2c **green,** *blue*	*12,500.*	4,250.
	Entire		*22,000.*
U309	U70 2c **green,** *manila*	*10,000.*	1,000.
	Entire	*22,500.*	1,200.
U310	U70 2c **green,** *amber manila*	*28,000.*	*4,000.*
	Entire	*28,000.*	*3,250.*
U311	U71 2c **green**	.30	.25
	Entire	.70	.25
a.	2c **dark green** ('94)	.45	.30
	Entire	1.00	.85
b.	Double impression, entire	375.00	
U312	U71 2c **green,** *amber*	.40	.25
	Entire	.75	.30
a.	Double impression	90.00	
b.	2c **dark green,** *amber* ('94)	.55	.35
	Entire	1.50	1.20
U313	U71 2c **green,** *oriental buff*	.55	.25
	Entire	1.10	.40
a.	2c **dark green,** *oriental buff* ('94)	2.00	1.00
	Entire	4.00	4.00
b.	Double impression	150.00	
U314	U71 2c **green,** *blue*	.60	.30
	Entire	1.20	.40
a.	2c **dark green** *blue* ('94)	.80	.40
	Entire	3.00	2.25
U315	U71 2c **green,** *manila*	2.00	.50
	Entire	3.00	1.00
a.	2c **dark green** *manila* ('94)	2.75	.75
	Entire	3.25	2.00
W316	U71 2c **green,** *manila*	3.50	2.50
	Entire	10.00	7.00
U317	U71 2c **green,** *amber manila*	2.50	1.90
	Entire	5.50	3.00
a.	2c **dark green,** *amber manila* ('94)	3.50	3.00
	Entire	7.00	4.00
U318	U72 2c **green**	110.00	12.50
	Entire	190.00	50.00
U319	U72 2c **green,** *amber*	160.00	27.50
	Entire	200.00	50.00
U320	U72 2c **green,** *oriental buff*	125.00	40.00
	Entire	240.00	70.00
U321	U72 2c **green,** *blue*	150.00	70.00
	Entire	250.00	90.00
U322	U72 2c **green,** *manila*	225.00	70.00
	Entire	300.00	110.00
U323	U72 2c **green,** *amber manila*	400.00	100.00
	Entire	700.00	300.00
U324	U73 4c **carmine**	3.25	2.00
	Entire	6.00	5.50
a.	4c **lake**	3.50	2.00
	Entire	7.00	3.75
b.	4c **scarlet** ('94)	3.50	2.00
	Entire	7.00	3.75
U325	U73 4c **carmine,** *amber*	3.50	3.50
	Entire	7.00	4.00
a.	4c **lake,** *amber*	3.50	3.50
	Entire	10.00	10.00
b.	4c **scarlet,** *amber* ('94)	4.00	3.75
	Entire	11.00	7.00
U326	U73 4c **carmine,** *oriental buff*	6.00	3.50
	Entire	14.00	14.00
a.	4c **lake,** *oriental buff*	7.00	3.50
	Entire	15.00	15.00

No.	Design	Description	Unused	Used
U327	U73	4c **carmine,** *blue*	5.50	4.00
		Entire	15.00	15.00
a.		4c **lake,** *blue*	6.00	4.00
		Entire	16.00	16.00
U328	U73	4c **carmine,** *manila*	8.00	7.00
		Entire	15.00	15.00
a.		4c **lake,** *manila*	8.00	6.00
		Entire	20.00	20.00
b.		4c **pink,** *manila*	15.00	10.00
		Entire	21.00	12.50
U329	U73	4c **carmine,** *amber manila*	6.00	3.25
		Entire	14.00	15.00
a.		4c **lake,** *amber manila*	6.00	3.25
		Entire	20.00	20.00
b.		4c **pink,** *amber manila*	15.00	10.00
		Entire	21.00	12.50
U330	U74	5c **blue**	3.75	4.00
		Entire	7.50	8.00
U331	U74	5c **blue,** *amber*	6.00	2.50
		Entire	11.00	14.00
a.		Double impression, entire	—	
U332	U74	5c **blue,** *oriental buff*	6.50	4.00
		Entire	16.00	18.00
U333	U74	5c **blue,** *blue*	7.00	6.00
		Entire	17.00	20.00
U334	U75	5c **blue** ('94)	20.00	12.50
		Entire	50.00	50.00
U335	U75	5c **blue,** *amber* ('94)	11.00	7.50
		Entire	22.00	40.00
U336	U55	30c **red brown**	40.00	45.00
		Entire	60.00	*600.00*
a.		30c **yellow brown**	40.00	45.00
		Entire	60.00	*600.00*
b.		30c **chocolate**	40.00	45.00
		Entire	60.00	*600.00*
U337	U55	30c **red brown,** *amber*	40.00	45.00
		Entire	60.00	*600.00*
a.		30c **yellow brown,** *amber*	40.00	45.00
		Entire	60.00	*600.00*
b.		30c **chocolate,** *amber*	40.00	45.00
		Entire	60.00	*600.00*
U338	U55	30c **red brown,** *oriental buff*	40.00	45.00
		Entire	60.00	*600.00*
a.		30c **yellow brown,** *oriental buff*	40.00	45.00
		Entire	60.00	*600.00*
U339	U55	30c **red brown,** *blue*	40.00	45.00
		Entire	60.00	*600.00*
a.		30c **yellow brown,** *blue*	40.00	45.00
		Entire	60.00	*600.00*
U340	U55	30c **red brown,** *manila*	40.00	45.00
		Entire	60.00	*600.00*
a.		30c **brown,** *manila*	40.00	45.00
		Entire	60.00	*600.00*
U341	U55	30c **red brown,** *amber manila*	40.00	45.00
		Entire	75.00	*600.00*
a.		30c **yellow brown,** *amber manila*	40.00	45.00
		Entire	75.00	*600.00*
U342	U56	90c **purple**	55.00	85.00
		Entire	100.00	*1,500.*
U343	U56	90c **purple,** *amber*	70.00	85.00
		Entire	120.00	*1,500.*
U344	U56	90c **purple,** *oriental buff*	75.00	85.00
		Entire	140.00	*1,500.*
U345	U56	90c **purple,** *blue*	75.00	85.00
		Entire	140.00	*1,500.*
U346	U56	90c **purple,** *manila*	80.00	85.00
		Entire	150.00	*1,500.*
U347	U56	90c **purple,** *amber manila*	80.00	85.00
		Entire	150.00	*1,500.*

Columbus and Liberty — U76

Four dies were used for the 1c, 2c and 5c:
1 — Meridian behind Columbus' head. Period after "CENTS" and "AMERICA" appears on 1c, 2c and 5c.
2 — No meridian. With periods. Appears on 1c, 2c and 5c.
3 — With meridian. No periods. Appears on 1c, 2c and 10c.
4 — No meridian. No periods. Appears on 2c.

1893

No.	Design	Description	Unused	Used
U348	U76	1c **deep blue**	2.00	1.25
		Entire	3.00	2.00
		Entire, Expo. station machine cancel		100.00
		Entire, Expo. station duplex hand-stamp cancel		250.00
U349	U76	2c **violet**	1.50	.50
		Entire	3.50	1.50
		Entire, Expo. station machine cancel		40.00
		Entire, Expo. station duplex hand-stamp cancel		85.00
a.		2c **dark slate** (error)	*1,500.*	
		Entire	*4,000.*	
U350	U76	5c **chocolate**	6.50	7.00
		Entire	15.00	12.00
		Entire, Expo. station machine cancel		150.00
		Entire, Expo. station duplex hand-stamp cancel		250.00
a.		5c **slate brown** (error)	*700.00*	*1,400.*
		Entire	*1,100.*	*1,500.*
U351	U76	10c **slate brown**	25.00	27.50
		Entire	75.00	75.00
		Entire, Expo. station machine cancel		250.00
		Entire, Expo. station duplex hand-stamp cancel		450.00

Franklin — U77

Bust points to fourth notch of inner circle.

Washington — U78

Bust points to first notch of inner oval and is only slightly concave below.

U79

Bust points to middle of second notch of inner oval and is quite hollow below. Queue has ribbon around it.

U80

Same as die 2, but hair flowing. No ribbon on queue.

Lincoln — U81

Bust pointed but not draped.

U82

Bust broad and draped.

U83

Head larger, inner oval has no notches.

Grant — U84

Similar to design of 1887-95 but smaller.

1899

No.	Design	Description	Unused	Used
U352	U77	1c **green**	2.75	.25
		Entire	4.75	.50
U353	U77	1c **green,** *amber*	5.00	1.50
		Entire	8.50	2.75
U354	U77	1c **green,** *oriental buff*	10.00	2.75
		Entire	20.00	5.00
U355	U77	1c **green,** *blue*	10.00	7.50
		Entire	19.00	12.50
U356	U77	1c **green,** *manila*	2.50	.95
		Entire	6.50	2.00
W357	U77	1c **green,** *manila*	2.75	1.10
		Entire	9.00	4.00
U358	U78	2c **carmine**	3.00	1.75
		Entire	8.00	5.00
U359	U78	2c **carmine,** *amber*	15.00	12.50
		Entire	27.50	21.00
U360	U78	2c **carmine,** *oriental buff*	17.50	11.00
		Entire	30.00	25.00
U361	U78	2c **carmine,** *blue*	55.00	35.00
		Entire	75.00	52.50
U362	U79	2c **carmine**	.35	.25
		Entire	.65	.30
a.		2c **dark lake**	30.00	30.00
		Entire	37.50	35.00
U363	U79	2c **carmine,** *amber*	1.75	.25
		Entire	2.75	.60
U364	U79	2c **carmine,** *oriental buff*	1.20	.25
		Entire	3.00	.60
U365	U79	2c **carmine,** *blue*	1.50	.55
		Entire	3.50	2.00
W366	U79	2c **carmine,** *manila*	9.00	3.25
		Entire	15.00	12.00
U367	U80	2c **carmine**	5.00	2.75
		Entire	10.00	6.75
U368	U80	2c **carmine,** *amber*	8.00	6.50
		Entire	16.00	15.00
U369	U80	2c **carmine,** *oriental buff*	17.50	12.50
		Entire	35.00	25.00
U370	U80	2c **carmine,** *blue*	11.00	10.00
		Entire	25.00	18.00
U371	U81	4c **brown**	15.00	12.50
		Entire	27.50	18.00
U372	U81	4c **brown,** *amber*	15.00	12.50
		Entire	30.00	24.00
U373	U82	4c **brown**	*6,500.*	1,000.
		Entire	*9,000.*	
U374	U83	4c **brown**	10.00	8.00
		Entire	26.00	15.00
U375	U83	4c **brown,** *amber*	60.00	25.00
		Entire	90.00	45.00
W376	U83	4c **brown,** *manila*	12.50	12.50
		Entire	35.00	45.00
U377	U84	5c **blue**	9.00	9.00
		Entire	16.00	16.00
U378	U84	5c **blue,** *amber*	10.00	10.00
		Entire	25.00	20.00

Franklin — U85

Washington — U86

"D" of "UNITED" contains vertical line at right that parallels the left vertical line. One short and two long vertical lines at the right of "CENTS."

Grant — U87

Lincoln — U88

Printed by Hartford Manufacturing Co., Hartford, Conn.

1903

U379	U85 1c **green**	.75	.25
	Entire	1.20	.35
U380	U85 1c **green,** *amber*	10.00	2.00
	Entire	20.00	7.00
U381	U85 1c **green,** *oriental buff*	12.50	2.50
	Entire	22.50	3.00
U382	U85 1c **green,** *blue*	15.00	2.50
	Entire	30.00	3.00
U383	U85 1c **green,** *manila*	3.50	.90
	Entire	5.00	1.25
W384	U85 1c **green,** *manila*	2.50	.40
	Entire	4.50	.80
a.	Double impression, entire letter sheet	*275.00*	
U385	U86 2c **carmine**	.40	.25
	Entire	.85	.35
a.	2c **pink**	2.00	1.50
	Entire	3.00	2.00
b.	2c **red**	2.00	1.50
	Entire	3.00	2.00
U386	U86 2c **carmine,** *amber*	2.00	.50
	Entire	3.50	.80
a.	2c **pink,** *amber*	5.50	3.00
	Entire	7.50	4.00
b.	2c **red,** *amber*	12.50	7.00
	Entire	20.00	10.00
U387	U86 2c **carmine,** *oriental buff*	2.00	.30
	Entire	3.25	.35
a.	2c **pink,** *oriental buff*	3.50	2.00
	Entire	5.00	3.00
b.	2c **red,** *oriental buff*	4.00	2.25
	Entire	5.50	3.25
U388	U86 2c **carmine,** *blue*	1.75	.50
	Entire	2.75	.60
a.	2c **pink,** *blue*	17.50	14.00
	Entire	30.00	18.00
b.	2c **red,** *blue*	17.50	14.00
	Entire	30.00	18.00
W389	U86 2c **carmine,** *manila*	15.00	9.00
	Entire	25.00	14.00
U390	U87 4c **chocolate**	17.50	11.00
	Entire	30.00	14.00
U391	U87 4c **chocolate,** *amber*	17.50	11.00
	Entire	32.50	14.00
W392	U87 4c **chocolate,** *manila*	20.00	12.50
	Entire	45.00	35.00
U393	U88 5c **blue**	15.00	11.00
	Entire	30.00	16.00
U394	U88 5c **blue,** *amber*	15.00	11.00
	Entire	30.00	18.00

U89

Re-cut die — "D" of "UNITED" is well rounded at right. The three lines at the right of "CENTS" and at the left of "TWO" are usually all short; the lettering is heavier and the ends of the ribbons slightly changed.

1904		**Re-cut Die**	
U395	U89 2c **carmine**	.75	.25
	Entire	1.75	.45
a.	2c pink	5.00	2.50
U396	U89 2c **carmine,** *amber*	7.50	1.00
	Entire	12.50	2.00
a.	2c pink, *amber*	8.50	3.00
U397	U89 2c **carmine,** *oriental buff*	5.00	1.10
	Entire	8.00	1.50
a.	2c pink, *oriental buff*	6.50	2.75
U398	U89 2c **carmine,** *blue*	3.75	.90
	Entire	5.50	1.40
a.	2c pink, *blue*	5.00	2.50
W399	U89 2c **carmine,** *manila*	12.50	8.00
	Entire	30.00	24.00
a.	2c pink, *manila*	25.00	17.50
	Entire	70.00	85.00
b.	Double impression, entire	*375.00*	

Franklin — U90

Die 1

Die 2

Die 3

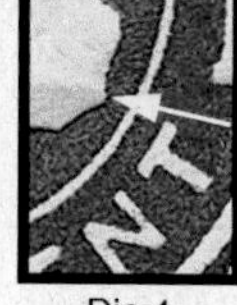

Die 4

Die 1 — Wide "D" in "UNITED."
Die 2 — Narrow "D" in "UNITED."
Die 3 — Wide "S-S" in "STATES" (1910).
Die 4 — Sharp angle at back of bust, "N" and "E" of "ONE" are parallel (1912).

Printed by Mercantile Corp. and Middle West Supply Co., Dayton, Ohio

1907-16

U400	U90 1c **green,** die 1, laid paper	.35	.25
	Entire	1.00	.75
	Wove paper	.35	.25
	Entire	2.00	2.00
a.	Die 2, laid paper	.85	.25
	Entire	1.50	.75
	Wove paper	.85	.25
	Entire	1.50	.75
b.	Die 3, laid paper	.85	.55
	Entire	1.50	1.50
	Wove paper	2.00	2.00
	Entire	6.50	8.00
c.	Die 4, laid paper	.85	.25
	Entire	1.50	1.00
	Wove paper	.85	.25
	Entire	1.50	1.00
U401	U90 1c **green,** *amber,* die 1, laid paper	2.00	.40
	Entire	3.00	2.50
	Wove paper	2.00	.40
	Entire	3.50	1.50
a.	Die 2, laid paper	2.50	1.00
	Entire	4.00	3.00
	Wove paper	3.00	2.50
	Entire	5.00	5.00
b.	Die 3, laid paper	3.25	3.00
	Entire	4.00	5.00
	Wove paper	75.00	50.00
	Entire	100.00	75.00
c.	Die 4, laid paper	2.00	1.00
	Entire	4.00	3.00
	Wove paper	2.00	.65
	Entire	3.00	2.50
U402	U90 1c **green,** *oriental buff,* die 1, laid paper	9.00	.75
	Entire	12.50	2.50
	Wove paper	9.00	.75
	Entire	12.50	2.50
a.	Die 2	12.50	1.50
	Entire	18.50	1.75
b.	Die 3, laid paper	14.00	1.50
	Entire	20.00	2.50
	Wove paper	1.00	.75
	Entire	2.50	3.00
c.	Die 4	3.50	.75
	Entire	4.50	2.50
U403	U90 1c **green,** *blue,* die 1, laid paper	9.00	.75
	Entire	12.50	2.25
	Wove paper	9.00	1.00
	Entire	12.50	4.00
a.	Die 2	12.50	3.00
	Entire	16.50	4.00
b.	Die 3	11.50	3.00
	Entire	17.50	7.00
c.	Die 4, laid paper	.75	.65
	Entire	1.00	1.50
	Wove paper	1.00	.75
	Entire	2.50	3.50
U404	U90 1c **green,** *manila,* die 1, laid paper	2.00	1.90
	Entire	3.75	4.50
	Wove paper	.75	1.00
	Entire	2.00	5.25
a.	Die 3	4.50	3.00
	Entire	7.00	4.50
W405	U90 1c **green,** *manila,* die 1, laid paper	.65	.25
	Entire	1.00	2.00
	Wove paper	1.00	1.00
	Entire	3.25	10.00
a.	Die 2	60.00	25.00
	Entire	90.00	30.00
b.	Die 3	11.00	4.00
	Entire	36.00	25.00
d.	Double impression, entire	*175.00*	

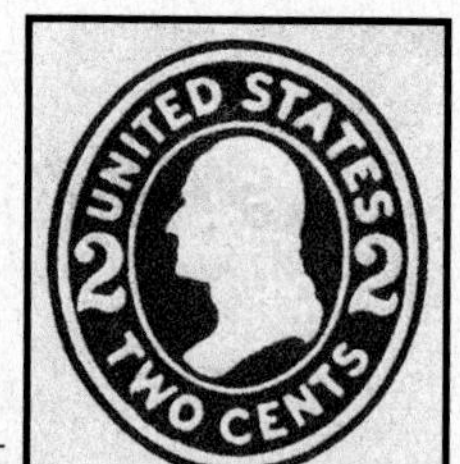

Washington — U91 — brown red

U91 Die 1 — carmine

U91 Die 2

U91 Die 3 — brown red

U91 Die 4

U91 Die 5

U91 Die 6

U91 Die 7

U91 Die 8

Die 1 — Oval "O" in "TWO" and "C" in "CENTS." Front of bust broad.
Die 2 — Similar to 1 but hair re-cut in two distinct locks at top of head.
Die 3 — Round "O" in "TWO" and "C" in "CENTS," coarse lettering.
Die 4 — Similar to 3 but lettering fine and clear, hair lines clearly embossed. Inner oval thin and clear.
Die 5 — All "S's" wide (1910).
Die 6 — Similar to 1 but front of bust narrow (1913).
Die 7 — Similar to 6 but upper corner of front of bust cut away (1916).
Die 8 — Similar to 7 but lower stroke of "S" in "CENTS" is a straight line. Hair as in Die 2 (1916).

U406	U91 2c **brown red,** die 1	.90	.25
	Entire	2.60	.30
a.	Die 2	40.00	7.00
	Entire	95.00	50.00
b.	Die 3	.80	.25
	Entire	2.50	1.00
U407	U91 2c **brown red,** *amber,* die 1	6.50	2.00
	Entire	9.00	6.00
a.	Die 2	350.00	65.00
	Entire	700.00	200.00
b.	Die 3	4.50	1.25
	Entire	7.00	6.00
U408	U91 2c **brown red,** *oriental buff,* die 1	8.75	1.50
	Entire	12.00	3.75
a.	Die 2	275.00	125.00
	Entire	500.00	300.00
b.	Die 3	7.50	2.50
	Entire	11.00	5.00

U409	U91 2c **brown red,** *blue,* die 1	5.75	2.00
	Entire	8.00	3.75
a.	Die 2	375.00	200.00
	Entire	550.00	500.00
b.	Die 3	5.75	1.75
	Entire	8.00	3.50
W410	U91 2c **brown red,** *manila,* die 1	35.00	35.00
	Entire	52.50	45.00
U411	U91 2c **carmine,** die 1, laid paper	.35	.25
	Entire	1.00	.75
	Wove paper	.55	.45
	Entire	1.50	1.00
a.	Die 2, laid paper	.75	.25
	Entire	2.00	1.50
	Wove paper	1.00	.55
	Entire	2.00	.50
b.	Die 3, laid paper	.75	.25
	Entire	2.00	1.00
	Wove paper	1.20	1.50
	Entire	4.00	7.00
c.	Die 4, laid paper	.65	.25
	Entire	1.00	.75
	Wove paper	.75	.25
	Entire	1.50	1.00
d.	Die 5, laid paper	.65	.30
	Entire	1.50	1.00
	Wove paper	1.00	1.00
	Entire	2.00	5.00
e.	Die 6, laid paper	.60	.25
	Entire	1.50	.75
	Wove paper	.60	.25
	Entire	1.00	.75
f.	Die 7, wove paper	3.00	3.00
	Entire	12.00	10.00
	Laid paper	75.00	25.00
	Entire	125.00	100.00
g.	Die 8	37.50	25.00
	Entire	52.50	30.00
h.	#U411 with added impression of #U400, entire	475.00	
i.	#U411 with added impression of #U416a, entire	475.00	
k.	As No. U411, double impression, entire	175.00	
U412	U91 2c **carmine,** *amber,* die 1, laid paper	.50	.25
	Entire	1.50	.75
	Wove paper	.50	.25
	Entire	1.50	.75
a.	Die 2, laid paper	1.00	.25
	Entire	3.50	4.00
	Wove paper	1.00	1.00
	Entire	2.50	15.00
b.	Die 3, laid paper	2.25	2.00
	Entire	3.00	5.00
	Wove paper	45.00	25.00
	Entire	75.00	60.00
c.	Die 4, laid paper	.55	.25
	Entire	1.50	.75
	Wove paper	1.00	1.00
	Entire	5.00	7.50
d.	Die 5	.90	.35
	Entire	1.50	.55
e.	Die 6, laid paper	.70	.25
	Entire	1.50	.75
	Wove paper	.60	.25
	Entire	1.00	.75
f.	Die 7, wove paper	35.00	25.00
	Entire	50.00	32.50
	Laid paper	125.00	100.00
	Entire	250.00	250.00
U413	U91 2c **carmine,** *oriental buff,* die 1, laid paper	.55	.25
	Entire	1.00	.75
	Wove paper	1.00	.25
	Entire	2.00	.75
a.	Die 2, laid paper	2.00	.45
	Entire	5.00	3.00
	Wove paper	7.00	10.00
	Entire	15.00	50.00
b.	Die 3	9.00	3.00
	Entire	15.00	5.50
c.	Die 4, laid paper	.55	1.00
	Entire	1.25	4.00
	Wove paper	1.00	1.00
	Entire	2.50	5.00
d.	Die 5	3.50	1.25
	Entire	5.00	3.25
e.	Die 6, laid paper	1.00	.70
	Entire	2.00	1.25
	Wove paper	1.20	1.00
	Entire	3.00	2.00
f.	Die 7	100.00	45.00
	Entire	135.00	62.50
g.	Die 8	25.00	17.50
	Entire	40.00	22.50
U414	U91 2c **carmine,** *blue,* die 1, laid paper	.55	.25
	Entire	1.30	.75
	Wove paper	.60	.25
	Entire	1.50	.75
a.	Die 2, laid paper	1.00	1.00
	Entire	5.00	2.50
	Wove paper	1.50	8.00
	Entire	6.50	30.00
b.	Die 3, laid paper	2.75	2.00
	Entire	4.00	6.50
	Wove paper	50.00	30.00
	Entire	75.00	50.00
c.	Die 4, laid paper	.50	.50
	Entire	1.00	3.50
	Wove paper	1.00	1.00
	Entire	2.50	10.00
d.	Die 5, laid paper	1.00	.45
	Entire	3.00	1.00
	Wove paper	70.00	40.00
	Entire	100.00	75.00
e.	Die 6, laid paper	.65	.30
	Entire	1.10	.75
	Wove paper	.55	.30
	Entire	1.50	.75
f.	Die 7	37.50	25.00
	Entire	50.00	35.00
g.	Die 8	37.50	25.00
	Entire	50.00	35.00
W415	U91 2c **carmine,** *manila,* die 1, laid paper	5.00	2.00
	Entire	8.00	*12.00*
	Wove paper	50.00	15.00
	Entire	70.00	75.00
a.	Die 2	5.50	1.25
	Entire	8.00	*20.00*
b.	Die 5	5.50	2.50
	Entire	8.00	*18.00*
c.	Die 7	120.00	97.50
	Entire	175.00	125.00

U90 4c Die 1

U90 4c Die 2

Die 1 — "F" close to (1mm) left "4."
Die 2 — "F" far from (1¾mm) left "4."

U416	U90 4c **black,** die 2, laid paper	2.00	1.50
	Entire	4.00	6.50
	Wove paper	30.00	20.00
	Entire	50.00	65.00
a.	Die 1, wove paper	1.50	2.00
	Entire	5.00	10.00
	Laid paper	7.50	4.00
	Entire	15.00	10.00
U417	U90 4c **black,** *amber,* die 2	7.50	2.50
	Entire	12.00	4.00
a.	Die 1, laid paper	.75	2.00
	Entire	1.50	20.00
	Wove paper	1.00	2.00
	Entire	2.50	10.00

Die 1 — Tall "F" in "FIVE"

Die 2 — Short "F" in "FIVE"

Die 1 — Tall "F" in "FIVE."
Die 2 — Short "F" in "FIVE."

U418	U91 5c **blue,** die 2, laid paper	1.50	1.50
	Entire	5.00	6.00
	Wove paper	.75	1.00
	Entire	2.00	5.00
a.	Die 1	7.00	2.25
	Entire	13.50	6.50
b.	5c **blue,** *buff,* die 2 (error)	*3,250.*	
c.	5c **blue,** *blue,* die 2 (error)	*3,000.*	
d.	As "c," die 1 (error), entire	*6,250.*	
U419	U91 5c **blue,** *amber,* die 2, laid paper	1.00	.75
	Entire	5.00	5.00
	Wove paper	3.00	1.50
	Entire	10.00	10.00
a.	Die 1	15.00	12.00
	Entire	25.00	14.00

On July 1, 1915 the use of laid paper was discontinued and wove paper was substituted. Nos. U400 to W405 and U411 to U419 exist on both papers: U406 to W410 come on laid only. Nos. U429 and U430 exist on laid paper.

Franklin — U92

Die 1

Die 2

Die 3

Die 4

Die 5

(The 1c and 4c dies are the same except for figures of value.)
Die 1 — UNITED nearer inner circle than outer circle.
Die 2 — Large U; large NT closely spaced.
Die 3 — Knob of hair at back of neck. Large NT widely spaced.
Die 4 — UNITED nearer outer circle than inner circle.
Die 5 — Narrow oval C, (also O and G).

Printed by Middle West Supply Co. and International Envelope Corp., Dayton, Ohio.

1915-32

U420	U92 1c **green,** die 1 ('17)	.25	.25
	Entire	.40	.25
a.	Die 2	100.00	55.00
	Entire, size 8	200.00	70.00
b.	Die 3	.35	.25
	Entire	.50	.25
c.	Die 4	.55	.40
	Entire	.80	.50
d.	Die 5	.45	.35
	Entire	.75	.45
U421	U92 1c **green,** *amber,*die 1 ('17)	.55	.30
	Entire	.80	.45
a.	Die 2	400.00	175.00
	Entire, size 8	750.00	300.00
b.	Die 3	1.40	.65
	Entire	2.00	.95
c.	Die 4	1.90	.85
	Entire	2.50	1.25
d.	Die 5	1.10	.55
	Entire	1.75	.80
U422	U92 1c **green,** *oriental buff,* die 1 ('17)	2.40	.90
	Entire	3.25	1.40
a.	Die 4	5.50	1.25
	Entire	8.00	2.75
U423	U92 1c **green,** *blue,* die 1 ('17)	.50	.35
	Entire	1.00	.50
a.	Die 3	.80	.45
	Entire	1.25	.70
b.	Die 4	1.40	.65
	Entire	2.50	.95
c.	Die 5	.85	.35
	Entire	1.60	.65
U424	U92 1c **grn,** *manila* (unglazed), die 1 ('16)	6.50	4.00
	Entire	8.00	5.00
W425	U92 1c **grn,** *manila* (unglazed), die 1 ('16)	.30	.25
	Entire	1.00	.25
a.	Die 3	175.00	125.00
	Entire	250.00	200.00
U426	U92 1c **green,** *brown* (glazed) , die 1 ('20)	45.00	16.00
	Entire	57.50	27.50
W427	U92 1c **green,** *brown* (glazed), die 1 ('20)	65.00	35.00
	Entire	80.00	*60.00*
a.	Printed on unglazed side	*400.00*	
	Entire	*750.00*	
b.	Unglazed on both sides		*150.00*
U428	U92 1c **green,** *brown* (unglazed), die 1 ('20)	12.50	7.50
	Entire	22.50	24.00
W428A	U92 1c **green,** *brown* (unglazed), die 1 ('20), entire		*3,000.*

All manila envelopes of circular dies are unwatermarked. Manila paper, including that of Nos. U424 and W425, exists in many shades.

Washington — U93

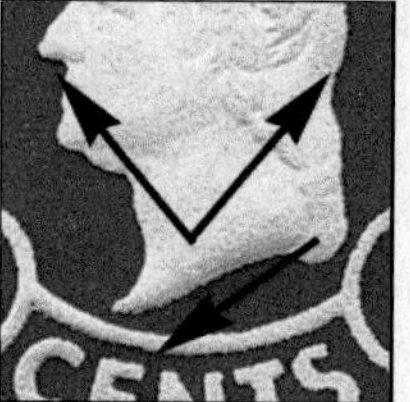
Die 1

Die 2

Die 3

Die 4

Die 5

Die 6

Die 7

Die 8

Die 9

(The 1½c, 2c, 3c, 5c, and 6c dies are the same except for figures of value.)
Die 1 — Letters broad. Numerals vertical. Large head (9¼mm). from tip of nose to back of neck. E closer to inner circle than N of cents.
Die 2 — Similar to 1; but U far from left circle.
Die 3 — Similar to 2; but all inner circles very thin (Rejected die).
Die 4 — Large head as in Die 1. C of CENTS close to circle. Baseline of right numeral "2" slants downward to right. Left numeral "2" is larger.
Die 5 — Small head (8¾mm) from tip of nose to back of neck. T and S of CENTS close at bottom.
Die 6 — Similar to 5; but T and S of CENTS far apart at bottom. Left numeral slopes to right.
Die 7 — Large head. Both numerals slope to right. Clean cut lettering. All letters T have short top strokes.
Die 8 — Similar to 7; but all letters T have long top strokes.
Die 9 — Narrow oval C (also O and G).

U429	U93 2c **carmine,** die 1, *Dec. 20, 1915*	.25	.25
	Entire	.40	.25
a.	Die 2	15.00	7.00
	Entire	25.00	10.00
b.	Die 3	40.00	50.00
	Entire	80.00	*200.00*
c.	Die 4	25.00	15.00
	Entire	40.00	20.00
d.	Die 5	.55	.35
	Entire	1.00	.45
e.	Die 6	.65	.30
	Entire	1.25	.60
f.	Die 7	.70	.25
	Entire	1.25	.75
g.	Die 8	.50	.25
	Entire	1.00	.50
h.	Die 9	.50	.25
	Entire	1.00	.45
i.	2c **green** (error), die 1, entire	*12,500.*	
j.	#U429 with added impression of #U420	600.00	
	Entire	1,000.	
k.	#U429 with added impression of #U416a, entire	*3,500.*	
l.	#U429 with added impression of #U400, entire	950.00	
m.	#U429, double impression, entire	1,500.	
n.	As "f," double impression, entire	*750.00*	
o.	As "e," triple impression	—	
p.	As "m," second impression on side flap, entire		*250.00*

Earliest documented use: Feb. 20, 1916.

U430	U93 2c **carmine,** *amber,* die 1 ('16)	.30	.25
	Entire	.50	.25
a.	Die 2	20.00	12.50
	Entire	30.00	15.00
b.	Die 4	50.00	25.00
	Entire	70.00	30.00
c.	Die 5	1.60	.35
	Entire	2.25	.60
d.	Die 6	1.25	.40
	Entire	2.25	.75
e.	Die 7	.75	.35
	Entire	1.75	.95
f.	Die 8	.70	.30
	Entire	1.10	.45
g.	Die 9	.65	.25
	Entire	1.10	.35
h.	As No. U430, with added impression of 4c black (#U416a), entire	*600.00*	
i.	As "g," with added impression of 2c car. die 1 on side flap, entire	—	
U431	U93 2c **carmine,** *oriental buff,* die 1 ('16)	2.25	.65
	Entire	4.75	1.40
a.	Die 2	180.00	75.00
	Entire	260.00	*250.00*
b.	Die 4	75.00	60.00
	Entire	100.00	75.00
c.	Die 5	3.50	2.00
	Entire	6.00	2.75

No.	Description	Unused	Used
d.	Die 6	3.50	2.00
	Entire	7.00	2.75
e.	Die 7	3.50	2.00
	Entire	6.00	3.25
U432	U93 2c **carmine,** *blue,* die 1 ('16)	.30	.25
	Entire	.60	.25
b.	Die 2	35.00	25.00
	Entire	50.00	35.00
c.	Die 3	130.00	90.00
	Entire	180.00	*400.00*
d.	Die 4	60.00	50.00
	Entire	90.00	55.00
e.	Die 5	1.10	.30
	Entire	2.00	.75
f.	Die 6	1.10	.40
	Entire	2.00	.60
g.	Die 7	.85	.35
	Entire	1.75	.65
h.	Die 8	.65	.25
	Entire	1.50	.50
i.	Die 9	1.00	.30
	Entire	2.75	.55
j.	2c purple (error), die 9	—	
k.	Double impression	650.00	
U432A	U93 2c **car,** *manila,* die 7, unwatermarked, entire	*50,000.*	
W433	U93 2c **carmine,** *manila,* die 1 ('16)	.25	.25
	Entire	.50	.30
W434	U93 2c **carmine,** *brown* (glazed) ('20), die 1	70.00	45.00
	Entire	95.00	55.00
W435	U93 2c **carmine,** *brown* (unglazed), die 1 ('20)	90.00	60.00
	Entire	115.00	*150.00*
U436	U93 3c **purple,** die 1 ('32)	.30	.25
	Entire	.55	.25
a.	3c **dark violet,** die 1 ('17)	.60	.25
	Entire	1.00	.25
b.	3c **dark violet,** die 5 ('17)	1.75	.75
	Entire	3.25	.90
c.	3c **dark violet,** die 6 ('17)	2.10	1.40
	Entire	3.25	1.50
d.	3c **dark violet,** die 7 ('17)	1.50	.95
	Entire	3.00	1.00
e.	3c **purple,** die 7 ('32)	.70	.30
	Entire	1.75	.75
f.	3c **purple,** die 9 ('32)	.45	.25
	Entire	.60	.30
g.	3c **carmine** (error), die 1	35.00	35.00
	Entire	60.00	*70.00*
h.	3c **carmine** (error), die 5	27.50	—
	Entire	50.00	—
i.	#U436 with added impression of #U420, entire	900.00	
j.	#U436 with added impression of #U429, entire	900.00	950.00
k.	As "f," double impression, preprinted, entire	*600.00*	
U437	U93 3c **purple,** *amber,* die 1 ('32)	.35	.25
	Entire	.60	.35
a.	3c **dark violet,** die 1 ('17)	5.50	1.25
	Entire	9.00	2.25
b.	3c **dark violet,** die 5 ('17)	8.50	2.50
	Entire	12.00	3.00
c.	3c **dark violet,** die 6 ('17)	8.50	2.50
	Entire	12.00	3.00
d.	3c **dark violet,** die 7 ('17)	8.50	2.25
	Entire	12.00	2.50
e.	3c **purple,** die 7 ('32)	.75	.25
	Entire	1.25	.50
f.	3c **purple,** die 9 ('32)	.55	.25
	Entire	1.00	.30
g.	3c **carmine** (error), die 5	375.00	400.00
	Entire	475.00	*750.00*
h.	3c **black** (error), die 1	190.00	—
	Entire	300.00	*375.00*
U438	U93 3c **dark violet,** *oriental buff,* die 1 ('17)	22.50	5.50
	Entire	32.50	21.00
a.	Die 5	22.50	5.50
	Entire	32.50	27.50
b.	Die 6	30.00	8.00
	Entire	45.00	35.00
c.	Die 7	30.00	10.00
	Entire	45.00	45.00

Earliest documented use: Nov. 2, 1917.

No.	Description	Unused	Used
U439	U93 3c **purple,** *blue,* die 1 ('32)	.35	.25
	Entire	.75	.25
a.	3c **dark violet,** die 1 ('17)	7.00	2.00
	Entire	14.00	6.00
b.	3c **dark violet,** die 5 ('17)	7.50	6.00
	Entire	15.00	7.50
c.	3c **dark violet,** die 6 ('17)	7.50	6.00
	Entire	15.00	7.50
d.	3c **dark violet,** die 7 ('17)	10.00	6.00
	Entire	17.50	7.50
e.	3c **purple,** die 7 ('32)	.75	.25
	Entire	1.50	.50
f.	3c **purple,** die 9 ('32)	.60	.25
	Entire	1.50	.45
g.	3c **carmine** (error), die 5	225.00	300.00
	Entire	400.00	*725.00*
U440	U92 4c **black,** die 1 ('18)	1.75	.60
	Entire	3.25	2.00
a.	With added impression of 2c carmine (#U429), die 1, entire	450.00	
U441	U92 4c **black,** *amber,* die 1 ('18)	3.00	.85
	Entire	5.00	2.00
a.	4c black, *amb,* with added impression of 2c car (#U429), die 1	175.00	
U442	U92 4c **black,** *blue,* die 1 ('21)	3.25	.85
	Entire	5.75	1.75
U443	U93 5c **blue,** die 1 ('18)	3.25	2.75
	Entire	5.75	3.25

Earliest documented use: Oct. 29, 1919.

No.	Description	Unused	Used
U444	U93 5c **blue,** *amber,* die 1 ('18)	4.00	1.60
	Entire	6.50	3.50
U445	U93 5c **blue,** *blue,* die 1 ('21)	3.25	3.25
	Entire	7.50	4.25

The following envelopes were officially issued June 16, 1932, in Washington, DC, and first day uses are known to exist: Nos. U436, U436e, U436f, U437 and U439. Nos. U437e, U437f, U439e and U439f presumably were issued at the same time, but first day uses have not yet been reported.

For 1½c and 6c see Nos. U481-W485, U529-U531.

Surcharged Envelopes

The provisional 2c surcharges of 1920-21 were made at central post offices with canceling machines using slugs provided by the Post Office Department.

Double or triple surcharge listings of 1920-25 are for examples with surcharge directly or partly upon the stamp.

Surcharged on 1874-1920 Envelopes indicated by Numbers in Parentheses

Type 1

1920-21 **Surcharged in Black**

No.	Description	Unused	Used
U446	U93 2c on 3c **dark vio** (U436a, die 1)	11.00	10.00
	Entire	22.50	12.50
a.	On No. U436b (die 5)	11.00	10.00
	Entire	22.50	12.50
b.	As U446, double surcharge	140.00	
	Entire	425.00	

Surcharged

Type 2

Rose Surcharge

No.	Description	Unused	Used
U447	U93 2c on 3c **dark vio** (U436a, die 1)	8.00	7.50
	Entire	16.00	10.00
b.	On No. U436c (die 6)	10.00	8.50
	Entire	25.00	10.00

Black Surcharge

No.	Description	Unused	Used
U447A	U92 2c on 1c **green** (U420, die 1) Entire	*3,000.*	
U447C	U93 2c on 2c **carmine** (U429, die 1)		—
U447D	U93 2c on 2c **carmine,** *amber* (U430, die 1)	12,000.	
U448	U93 2c on 3c **dark vio** (U436a, die 1)	2.75	2.00
	Entire	4.00	2.50
a.	On No. U436b (die 5)	2.75	2.00
	Entire	4.00	2.50
b.	On No. U436c (die 6)	3.50	2.00
	Entire	5.00	2.50
c.	On No. U436d (die 7)	2.75	2.00
	Entire	4.00	2.50
U449	U93 2c on 3c **dark violet,** *amber* (U437a, die 1)	6.50	6.00
	Entire	9.00	7.50
a.	On No. U437b (die 5)	13.00	7.50
	Entire	17.50	10.00
b.	On No. U437c (die 6)	9.50	6.00
	Entire	13.50	7.50
c.	On No. U437d (die 7)	8.50	6.50
	Entire	12.00	8.00
U450	U93 2c on 3c **dark violet,** *oriental buff* (U438, die 1)	12.50	15.00
	Entire	20.00	18.00
a.	On No. U438a (die 5)	15.00	15.00
	Entire	22.50	18.00
b.	On No. U438b (die 6)	15.00	15.00
	Entire	22.50	18.00
c.	On No. U438c (die 7)	130.00	90.00
	Entire	160.00	125.00
U451	U93 2c on 3c **dark violet,** *blue* (U439a, die 1)	11.00	10.50
	Entire	18.00	11.50
b.	On No. U439b (die 5)	11.00	10.50
	Entire	18.00	11.50
c.	On No. U439c (die 6)	11.00	10.50
	Entire	18.00	11.50
d.	On No. U439d (die 7)	22.50	22.50
	Entire	37.50	27.50

Type 2 exists in three city sub-types.

Surcharged

Type 3

Bars 2mm apart, 25 to 26mm in length from outer edges of end bars

No.	Description	Unused	Used
U451A	U90 2c on 1c **green** (U400, die 1)	*25,000.*	
	Entire	—	
U452	U92 2c on 1c **green** (U420, die 1)	1,750.	
	Entire	3,250.	
a.	On No. U420b (die 3)	3,000.	
	Entire	3,000.	
b.	As No. U452, double surcharge	3,750.	
	Entire	4,500.	
U453	U91 2c on 2c **car** (U411b, die 3)	3,500.	
	Entire	6,000.	
a.	On No. U411 (die 1)	3,250.	
	Entire	5,500.	
U453B	U91 2c on 2c **carmine,** *blue* (U414e, die 6)	1,250.	750.00
	Entire	2,250.	
U453C	U91 2c on 2c **carmine,** *oriental buff* (U413e, die 6)	1,400.	*750.00*
	Entire	2,000.	
d.	On No. U413 (die 1)	1,400.	
	Entire	1,750.	
U454	U93 2c on 2c **car** (U429e, die 6)	125.00	
	Entire	225.00	
a.	On No. U429 (die 1)	300.00	
	Entire	350.00	
b.	On No. U429d (die 5)	500.00	
	Entire	500.00	
c.	On No. U429f (die 7)	125.00	
	Entire	200.00	
U455	U93 2c on 2c **carmine,** *amber* (U430, die 1)	1,250.	
	Entire	2,000.	
a.	On No. U430d (die 6)	1,500.	
	Entire	2,500.	
b.	On No. U430e (die 7)	1,500.	
	Entire	2,000.	
U456	U93 2c on 2c **carmine,** *oriental buff* (U431a, die 2)	225.00	
	Entire	325.00	
a.	On No. U431c (die 5)	225.00	
	Entire	350.00	
b.	On No. U431e (die 7)	800.00	
	Entire	900.00	
c.	As No. U456, double surcharge	700.00	
U457	U93 2c on 2c **carmine,** *blue* (U432f, die 6)	325.00	
	Entire	350.00	
a.	On No. U432e (die 5)	275.00	
	Entire	475.00	
b.	On No. U432g (die 7)	650.00	
	Entire	800.00	
U458	U93 2c on 3c **dark vio** (U436a, die 1)	.50	.35
	Entire	.75	.45
a.	On No. U436b (die 5)	.50	.40
	Entire	.75	.50
b.	On No. U436c (die 6)	.50	.35
	Entire	.75	.45
c.	On No. U436d (die 7)	.50	.35
	Entire	.75	.45
d.	As #U458, double surcharge	25.00	7.50
	Entire	35.00	10.00
e.	As #U458, triple surcharge	90.00	
	Entire	150.00	
f.	As #U458, dbl. surch., 1 in **magenta**	90.00	
	Entire	150.00	
g.	As #U458, dbl. surch., types 2 & 3	140.00	
	Entire	190.00	
h.	As "a," double surcharge	27.50	15.00
	Entire	37.50	20.00
i.	As "a," triple surcharge	110.00	
	Entire	160.00	
j.	As "a," double surch., both **magenta**	110.00	
	Entire	150.00	
k.	As "b," double surcharge	25.00	8.00
	Entire	35.00	11.00
l.	As "c," double surcharge	25.00	8.00
	Entire	35.00	11.00
m.	As "c," triple surcharge	110.00	
	Entire	150.00	
n.	Double impression of indicia, single surcharge, entire	450.00	
U459	U93 2c on 3c **dark violet,** *amber* (U437c, die 6)	3.00	1.00
	Entire	4.50	1.75
a.	On No. U437a (die 1)	4.00	1.00
	Entire	5.50	1.75
b.	On No. U437b (die 5)	4.00	1.00
	Entire	5.50	1.75
c.	On No. U437d (die 7)	3.00	1.00
	Entire	5.50	1.75
d.	As #U459, double surcharge	35.00	
	Entire	50.00	
e.	As "a," double surcharge	35.00	
	Entire	50.00	
f.	As "b," double surcharge	35.00	
	Entire	50.00	
g.	As "b," double surcharge, types 2 & 3	125.00	
	Entire	175.00	

h.	As "c," double surcharge	35.00	
	Entire	50.00	
U460	U93 2c on 3c **dark violet,** *oriental buff* (U438a, die 5)	3.50	2.00
	Entire	4.50	2.50
a.	On No. U438 (die 1)	3.50	2.00
	Entire	4.50	2.50
b.	On No. U438b (die 6)	4.00	2.00
	Entire	5.50	2.50
c.	As #U460, double surcharge	20.00	
	Entire	30.00	
d.	As "a," double surcharge	20.00	
	Entire	30.00	
e.	As "b," double surcharge	20.00	
	Entire	30.00	
f.	As "b," triple surcharge	150.00	
	Entire	250.00	
U461	U93 2c on 3c **dark violet,** *blue* (U439a, die 1)	6.00	1.00
	Entire	8.25	1.50
a.	On No. U439b (die 5)	6.00	1.00
	Entire	8.25	1.50
b.	On No. U439c (die 6)	6.00	2.50
	Entire	8.25	3.50
c.	On No. U439d (die 7)	12.50	7.50
	Entire	17.50	15.00
d.	As #U461, double surcharge	17.50	
	Entire	40.00	30.00
e.	As "a," double surcharge	17.50	
	Entire	40.00	30.00
f.	As "b," double surcharge	17.50	
	Entire	40.00	30.00
g.	As "c," double surcharge	17.50	
	Entire	50.00	40.00
U462	U87 2c on 4c **chocolate** (U390)	475.00	260.00
	Entire	800.00	500.00
U463	U87 2c on 4c **chocolate,** *amber* (U391)	750.00	350.00
	Entire	1,000.	500.00
U463A	U90 2c on 4c **black** (U416, die 2)	800.00	400.00
	Entire	1,200.	
U464	U93 2c on 5c **blue** (U443)	850.00	
	Entire	1,250.	

Type 3 exists in 11 city sub-types.

Surcharged

Type 4

Bars 1 mm apart, 21 to 23 mm in length from outer edges of end bars

U465	U92 2c on 1c **green** (U420, die 1)	900.00	
	Entire	1,600.	
a.	On No. U420b (die 3)	1,100.	
	Entire	2,250.	
U466	U91 2c on 2c **car** (U411e, die 6), entire	22,500.	
U466A	U93 2c on 2c **carmine** (U429, die 1)	700.00	
	Entire	1,150.	
c.	On No. U429d (die 5)	900.00	
	Entire	1,000.	
d.	On No. U429e (die 6)	900.00	
	Entire	1,000.	
e.	On No. U429f (die 7)	750.00	
	Entire	750.00	
U466B	U93 2c on 2c **carmine,** *amber* (U430c)	*15,000.*	
	Entire	*22,500.*	
U466C	U93 2c on 2c **carmine,** *oriental buff* (U431), entire	*15,000.*	
U466D	U25 2c on 3c **green,** die 2 (U82)	*9,500.*	
U467	U45 2c on 3c **green,** die 2 (U163)	325.00	
	Entire	475.00	
U468	U93 2c on 3c **dark vio** (U436a, die 1)	.70	.45
	Entire	1.00	.75
a.	On No. U436b (die 5)	.70	.50
	Entire	1.00	.75
b.	On No. U436c (die 6)	.70	.50
	Entire	1.00	.75
c.	On No. U436d (die 7)	.70	.50
	Entire	1.00	.75
d.	As #U468, double surcharge	20.00	
	Entire	30.00	
e.	As #U468, triple surcharge	90.00	
	Entire	140.00	
f.	As #U468, dbl. surch., types 2 & 4	125.00	
	Entire	175.00	
g.	As "a," double surcharge	20.00	
	Entire	30.00	
h.	As "b," double surcharge	20.00	
	Entire	30.00	
i.	As "c," double surcharge	20.00	
	Entire	30.00	
j.	As "c," triple surcharge	100.00	
	Entire	150.00	
k.	As "c," inverted surcharge	75.00	
	Entire	125.00	
l.	2c on 3c **carmine** (error), (U436h)	600.00	
	Entire	1,400.	
m.	As #U468, triple surcharge, one inverted, entire		*700.00*
U469	U93 2c on 3c **dark violet,** *amber* (U437a, die 1)	3.75	2.25
	Entire	5.00	2.75
a.	On No. U437b (die 5)	3.75	2.25
	Entire	5.00	2.75
b.	On No. U437c (die 6)	3.75	2.25
	Entire	5.00	2.75
c.	On No. U437d (die 7)	3.75	2.25
	Entire	5.00	2.75
d.	As #U469, double surcharge	30.00	
	Entire	40.00	
e.	As "a," double surcharge	30.00	
	Entire	40.00	
f.	As "a," double surcharge, types 2 & 4	100.00	
	Entire	150.00	
g.	As "b," double surcharge	30.00	
	Entire	40.00	
h.	As "c," double surcharge	30.00	
	Entire	40.00	
U470	U93 2c on 3c **dark violet,** *oriental buff* (U438, die 1)	6.00	2.50
	Entire	10.00	5.00
a.	On No. U438a (die 5)	6.00	2.50
	Entire	10.00	6.00
b.	On No. U438b (die 6)	6.00	2.50
	Entire	10.00	6.00
c.	On No. U438c (die 7)	42.50	32.50
	Entire	70.00	70.00
d.	As #U470, double surcharge	25.00	
	Entire	35.00	
e.	As #U470, double surch., types 2 & 4	80.00	
	Entire	130.00	
f.	As "a," double surcharge	25.00	
	Entire	35.00	
g.	As "b," double surcharge	25.00	
	Entire	35.00	
U471	U93 2c on 3c **dark violet,** *blue* (U439a, die 1)	6.00	1.75
	Entire	12.50	3.50
a.	On No. U439b (die 5)	7.00	1.75
	Entire	13.00	6.00
b.	On No. U439c (die 6)	7.00	1.75
	Entire	13.00	3.50
c.	On No. U439d (die 7)	10.00	10.00
	Entire	35.00	30.00
d.	As #U471, double surcharge	25.00	
	Entire	40.00	
e.	As #U471, double surch., types 2 & 4	160.00	
	Entire	275.00	
f.	As "a," double surcharge	25.00	
	Entire	40.00	
g.	As "b," double surcharge	25.00	
	Entire	40.00	
U471A	U83 2c on 4c **brown,** (U374), entire	625.00	
U472	U87 2c on 4c **chocolate** (U390)	11.00	11.00
	Entire	25.00	16.00
a.	Double surcharge	150.00	
U473	U87 2c on 4c **chocolate,** *amber* (U391)	17.00	10.00
	Entire	27.50	13.50

Type 4 exists in 30 city sub-types.

Surcharged

Double Surcharge, Type 4 and 1c as above

U474	U93 2c on 1c on 3c **dark violet** (U436a, die 1)	175.	*500.*
	Entire	325.	*1,000.*
a.	On No. U436b (die 5)	200.	
	Entire	300.00	
b.	On No. U436d (die 7)	850.	
	Entire	1,000.	
U475	U93 2c on 1c on 3c **dark violet,** *amber* (U437a, die 1)	150.	
	Entire	300.	

Surcharged

U476	U93 2c on 3c **dark violet,** *amber* (U437a, die 1)	200.	
	Entire	325.	325.
a.	On No. U437c (die 6)	700.	
	Entire	1,000.	
b.	As #U476, double surcharge	—	

Surcharged at Duncan, OK.

Surcharged Type 6

U477	U93 2c on 3c **dark vio** (U436a, die 1)	120.	
	Entire	175.	
a.	On No. U436b (die 5)	250.	
	Entire	300.	
b.	On No. U436c (die 6)	250.	
	Entire	300.	
c.	On No. U436d (die 7)	250.	
	Entire	500.	
U478	U93 2c on 3c **dark violet,** *amber* (U437a, die 1)	250.	
	Entire	375.	

Surcharged at Frederick, OK, and other Oklahoma towns.

Handstamped Surcharged in Black or Violet

U479	U93 2c on 3c **dark violet** (Bk) (U436a, die 1)	240.	—
	Entire	525.	
a.	On No. U436b (die 5)	625.	
	Entire	950.	
b.	On No. U436d (die 7)	425.	
	Entire	450.	
U480	U93 2c on 3c **dark violet** (V) (U436d, die 7)	*4,500.*	
	Entire	*5,500.*	
a.	Double overprint		—

Expertization by competent authorities is required for Nos. U476-U480.

Surcharged at Daytona, FL (#U479) and Orlando Beach, FL (#U480).

Type of 1916-32 Issue

1925

U481	U93 1½c **brown,** die 1, *Mar. 19*	.25	.25
	Entire	.00	.25
	Entiro, 1st day cancel		60.00
a.	Die 8	.70	.25
	Entire	1.00	.50
b.	1½c purple, die 1 (error) ('34)	55.00	
	Entire	100.00	—
U482	U93 1½c **brown,** die 1, *amber*	.90	.40
	Entire	1.50	.60
a.	Die 8	1.75	.75
	Entire	2.25	.80
U483	U93 1½c **brown,** die 1, *blue*	1.60	.95
	Entire	2.50	1.25
a.	Die 8	2.40	1.25
	Entire	3.25	1.40
U484	U93 1½c **brown,** die 1, *manila*	5.00	3.00
	Entire	12.00	6.00
W485	U93 1½c **brown,** die 1, *manila*	.85	.25
	Entire	2.00	.45
a.	With added impression of #W433	120.00	—

The manufacture of newspaper wrappers was discontinued in 1934.

New rates on printed matter effective Apr. 15, 1925, resulted in revaluing some of the current envelopes.

Under the caption "Revaluation of Surplus Stocks of the 1 cent envelopes," W. Irving Glover, Third Assistant Postmaster-General, distributed through the Postal Bulletin a notice to postmasters authorizing the surcharging of envelopes under stipulated conditions.

Surcharging was permitted "at certain offices where the excessive quantities of 1 cent stamped envelopes remained in stock on April 15, 1925."

Envelopes were revalued by means of post office canceling machines equipped with special dies designed to imprint "1 ½" in the center of the embossed stamp and four vertical bars over the original numerals "1" in the lower corners.

Postmasters were notified that the revaluing dies would be available for use only in the International and "Universal" Model G machines and that the overprinting of surplus envelopes would be restricted to post offices having such canceling equipment available.

Envelopes of Preceding Issues Surcharged

Provisional surcharges exist for California cities Santa Rosa and Santa Ana. These were unauthorized but served postal duty. All are scarce. Expertization recommended.

1925

On Envelopes of 1887

No.	Type	Description	Unused	Used
U486	U71	1½c on 2c **green** (U311)	500.00	
		Entire	1,150.	
U487	U71	1½c on 2c **green,** *amber* (U312)	900.00	
		Entire	1,500.	

On Envelopes of 1899

No.	Type	Description	Unused	Used
U488	U77	1½c on 1c **green** (U352)	500.00	
		Entire	700.00	
U489	U77	1½c on 1c **green,** *amber* (U353)	110.00	60.
		Entire	200.00	90.

On Envelopes of 1907-16

No.	Type	Description	Unused	Used
U490	U90	1½c on 1c **green** (U400, die 1)	6.25	3.50
		Entire	10.00	5.50
a.		On No. U400a (die 2)	15.00	9.00
		Entire	20.00	12.00
b.		On No. U400b (die 3)	35.00	17.50
		Entire	50.00	22.50
c.		On No. U400c (die 4)	9.00	2.50
		Entire	13.00	4.00
U491	U90	1½c on 1c **green,** *amber* (U401c, die 4)	7.00	3.00
		Entire	12.00	8.50
a.		On No. U401 (die 1)	12.50	3.50
		Entire	17.50	8.50
b.		On No. U401a (die 2)	110.00	70.00
		Entire	140.00	140.00
c.		On No. U401b (die 3)	60.00	50.00
		Entire	100.00	100.00
U492	U90	1½c on 1c **green,** *oriental buff* (U402a, die 2)	500.00	150.00
		Entire	800.00	175.00
a.		On No. U402c (die 4)	700.00	250.00
		Entire	1,400.	300.00
U493	U90	1½c on 1c **grn,** *blue* (U403c, die 4)	100.00	65.00
		Entire	140.00	70.00
a.		On No. U403a (die 2)	100.00	67.50
		Entire	160.00	90.00
U494	U90	1½c on 1c **grn,** *manila* (U404, die 1)	250.00	100.00
		Entire	450.00	150.00
a.		On No. U404a (die 3)	950.00	
		Entire	950.00	

On Envelopes of 1916-20

No.	Type	Description	Unused	Used
U495	U92	1½c on 1c **green** (U420, die 1)	.80	.25
		Entire	1.10	.45
a.		On No. U420a (die 2)	80.00	52.50
		Entire	120.00	90.00
b.		On No. U420b (die 3)	2.10	.70
		Entire	3.00	.85
c.		On No. U420c (die 4)	2.10	.85
		Entire	3.00	1.15
d.		As #U495, double surcharge	10.00	3.00
		Entire	15.00	5.00
e.		As "b," double surcharge	10.00	3.00
		Entire	15.00	5.00
f.		As "c," double surcharge	10.00	3.00
		Entire	15.00	5.00
U496	U92	1½c on 1c **grn,** *amber* (U421, die 1)	15.00	12.50
		Entire	27.50	15.00
a.		On No. U421b (die 3)	725.00	
		Entire	1,500.	
b.		On No. U421c (die 4)	15.00	12.50
		Entire	27.50	15.00
U497	U92	1½c on 1c **green,** *oriental buff* (U422, die 1)	3.75	1.90
		Entire	7.00	2.25
a.		On No. U422b (die 4)	67.50	
		Entire	100.00	
U498	U92	1½c on 1c **grn,** *blue* (U423c, die 4)	1.40	.75
		Entire	2.25	1.00
a.		On No. U423 (die 1)	2.40	1.50
		Entire	4.25	2.00
b.		On No. U423b (die 3)	1.75	1.50
		Entire	3.25	2.00
U499	U92	1½c on 1c **green,** *manila* (U424)	8.00	6.00
		Entire	16.00	7.00
U500	U92	1½c on 1c **green,** *brown* (unglazed) (U428)	60.00	30.00
		Entire	85.00	35.00
U501	U92	1½c on 1c **green,** *brown* (glazed) (U426)	65.00	30.00
		Entire	90.00	35.00
U502	U93	1½c on 2c **carmine** (U429, die 1)	200.00	—
		Entire	450.00	—
a.		On No. U429d (die 5)	250.00	
		Entire	500.00	
b.		On No. U429f (die 7)	250.00	
		Entire	450.00	
c.		On No. U429e (die 6)	325.00	
		Entire	—	
d.		On No. U429g (die 8)	450.00	
U503	U93	1½c on 2c **carmine,** *oriental buff* (U431c, die 5)	200.00	—
		Entire	400.00	—
a.		Double surcharge	—	
b.		Double surcharge, one inverted	*700.00*	
U504	U93	1½c on 2c **car,** *blue* (U432, die 1)	300.00	—
		Entire	350.00	—
a.		On No. U432g (die 7)	300.00	
		Entire	450.00	
b.		As "a," double surcharge, entire	*350.00*	
c.		On No. U432f (die 6), entire	*400.00*	

On Envelopes of 1925

No.	Type	Description	Unused	Used
U505	U93	1½c on 1½c **brown** (U481, die 1)	300.00	
		Entire	550.00	
a.		On No. U481a (die 8)	400.00	
		Entire	500.00	
b.		As No. U505, double surcharge, entire	*2,000.*	
U506	U93	1½c on 1½c **brown,** *blue* (U483a, die 8)	200.00	
		Entire	550.00	
a.		On No. U483 (die 1)	300.00	

The paper of No. U500 is not glazed and appears to be the same as that used for the wrappers of 1920.

Type 8 exists in 20 city sub-types.

Surcharged

Black Surcharge

On Envelopes of 1887

No.	Type	Description	Unused	Used
U507	U69	1½c on 1c **blue** (U294)	1,750.	
		Entire	2,400.	
U507B	U69	1½c on 1c **blue,** *manila* (U300)	3,500.	
		Entire	3,500.	

On Envelope of 1899

No.	Type	Description	Unused	Used
U508	U77	1½c on 1c **green,** *amber* (U353)	55.00	
		Entire	90.00	

On Envelopes of 1903

No.	Type	Description	Unused	Used
U508A	U85	1½c on 1c **green** (U379)	2,750.	
		Entire	3,500.	
U509	U85	1½c on 1c **green,** *amber* (U380)	12.50	10.00
		Entire	27.50	*35.00*
a.		Double surcharge	75.00	
		Entire	100.00	
U509B	U85	1½c on 1c **green,** *oriental buff* (U381)	40.00	40.00
		Entire	60.00	50.00

On Envelopes of 1907-16

No.	Type	Description	Unused	Used
U510	U90	1½c on 1c **green** (U400, die 1)	2.75	1.25
		Entire	4.75	1.50
b.		On No. U400a (die 2)	9.00	4.00
		Entire	13.50	6.00
c.		On No. U400b (die 3)	37.50	8.00
		Entire	50.00	11.00
d.		On No. U400c (die 4)	3.50	1.25
		Entire	7.50	2.00
e.		As No. U510, double surcharge	25.00	
		Entire	50.00	
U511	U90	1½c on 1c **green,** *amber* (U401, die 1)	200.00	100.00
		Entire	325.00	150.00
U512	U90	1½c on 1c **green,** *oriental buff* (U402, die 1)	7.00	4.00
		Entire	14.00	6.50
a.		On No. U402c (die 4)	21.00	14.00
		Entire	30.00	17.00
U513	U90	1½c on 1c **grn,** *blue* (U403, die 1)	6.00	4.00
		Entire	9.50	5.00
a.		On No. U403c (die 4)	6.00	4.00
		Entire	9.50	5.00
U514	U90	1½c on 1c **green,** *manila* (U404, die 1)	30.00	9.00
		Entire	75.00	22.50
a.		On No. U404a (die 3)	77.50	40.00
		Entire	100.00	95.00

On Envelopes of 1916-20

No.	Type	Description	Unused	Used
U515	U92	1½c on 1c **green** (U420, die 1)	.40	.25
		Entire	.75	.30
a.		On No. U420a (die 2)	15.00	15.00
		Entire	30.00	20.00
b.		On No. U420b (die 3)	.40	.25
		Entire	.75	.30
c.		On No. U420c (die 4)	.40	.25
		Entire	.75	.30
d.		As #U515, double surcharge	10.00	
		Entire	15.00	
e.		As #U515, inverted surcharge	15.00	
		Entire	30.00	
f.		As #U515, triple surcharge	15.00	
		Entire	30.00	
g.		As #U515, dbl. surch., one invtd., entire	—	
h.		As "b," double surcharge	10.00	
		Entire	15.00	
i.		As "b," inverted surcharge	15.00	
		Entire	30.00	
j.		As "b," triple surcharge	25.00	
		Entire	40.00	
k.		As "c," double surcharge	10.00	
		Entire	15.00	
l.		As "c," inverted surcharge	15.00	
		Entire	30.00	
U516	U92	1½c on 1c **green,** *amber* (U421c, die 4)	50.00	27.50
		Entire	65.00	37.50
a.		On No. U421 (die 1)	55.00	32.50
		Entire	70.00	42.50
U517	U92	1½c on 1c **green,** *oriental buff* (U422, die 1)	6.25	1.25
		Entire	9.00	1.50
a.		On No. U422a (die 4)	7.25	1.50
		Entire	10.00	2.00
U518	U92	1½c on 1c **green,** *blue* (U423b, die 4)	5.00	1.50
		Entire	7.50	5.00
a.		On No. U423 (die 1)	8.25	4.50
		Entire	27.50	18.00
b.		On No. U423a (die 3)	27.50	7.50
		Entire	40.00	9.00
c.		As "a," double surcharge	30.00	
		Entire	42.50	
U519	U92	1½c on 1c **green,** *manila* (U424, die 1)	25.00	12.00
		Entire	42.50	15.00
a.		Double surcharge	100.00	
U520	U93	1½c on 2c **car** (U429, die 1)	300.00	—
		Entire	475.00	—
a.		On No. U429d (die 5)	275.00	
		Entire	450.00	
b.		On No. U429e (die 6)	275.00	
		Entire	475.00	
c.		On No. U429f (die 7)	275.00	
		Entire	450.00	
U520D	U93	1½c on 2c **car,** *amber* (U430c, die 5), entire	—	
U520E	U92	1½c on 4c **black** (U440, die 1), entire		—

Magenta Surcharge

No.	Type	Description	Unused	Used
U521	U92	1½c on 1c **green** (U420b, die 3), *Oct. 22, 1925*	4.25	3.50
		Entire	6.50	5.50
		Entire, 1st day cancel, Washington, D.C.		100.00
a.		Double surcharge	75.00	
		Entire	125.00	

Sesquicentennial Exposition Issue

150th anniversary of the Declaration of Independence.

Liberty Bell — U94

Die 1. The center bar of "E" of "postage" is shorter than top bar.

Die 2. The center bar of "E" of "postage" is of same length as top bar.

1926, July 27

No.	Type	Description	Unused	Used
U522	U94	2c **carmine,** die 1	1.00	.50
		Entire	1.50	.95
a.		Die 2	5.50	3.75
		Entire	10.00	5.50
		Entire, die 2, 1st day cancel, Washington, D.C.		32.50
		Entire, die 2, 1st day cancel, Philadelphia		27.50

Washington Bicentennial Issue

200th anniversary of the birth of George Washington.

Mount Vernon — U95

2c Die 1 — "S" of "Postage" normal.
2c Die 2 — "S" of "Postage" raised.

1932

U523	U95	1c **olive green,** *Jan. 1*	1.00	.80
		Entire	1.50	1.75
		Entire, 1st day cancel		18.00
U524	U95	1½c **chocolate,** *Jan. 1*	2.00	1.50
		Entire	2.75	2.50
		Entire, 1st day cancel		18.00
U525	U95	2c **carmine,** die 1, *Jan. 1*	.40	.25
		Entire	.50	.25
		Entire, 1st day cancel		16.00
a.		2c **carmine,** die 2	60.00	20.00
		Entire	80.00	27.50
b.		2c **carmine,** *blue,* die 1 (error) entire	*30,000.*	
U526	U95	3c **violet,** *June 16*	1.75	.35
		Entire	2.25	.40
		Entire, 1st day cancel		18.00
U527	U95	4c **black,** *Jan. 1*	15.00	17.50
		Entire	20.00	*35.00*
		Entire, 1st day cancel		30.00
U528	U95	5c **dark blue,** *Jan. 1*	3.50	3.50
		Entire	4.25	*20.00*
		Entire, 1st day cancel		20.00
		Nos. U523-U528 (6)	23.65	23.90

Type of 1916-32 Issue

1932, Aug. 18

U529	U93	6c **orange,** die 7	6.00	4.00
		Entire	9.50	7.50
		Entire, 1st day cancel, Los Angeles		20.00
U530	U93	6c **orange,** *amber,* die 7	10.00	10.00
		Entire	15.00	12.50
		Entire, 1st day cancel, Los Angeles		20.00
U531	U93	6c **orange,** *blue,* die 7	10.00	10.00
		Entire	15.00	12.50
		Entire, 1st day cancel		20.00

Franklin — U96

Die 1

Die 2

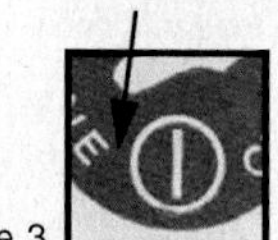

Die 3

Die 1 — Short (3½mm) and thick "I" in thick circle.
Die 2 — Tall (4½mm) and thin "1" in thin circle; upper and lower bars of E in ONE long and 1mm from circle.
Die 3 — As in Die 2, but E normal and 1½mm from circle.

Printed by International Envelope Corp.

1950

U532	U96	1c **green,** die 1, *Nov. 16*	5.00	1.75
		Entire	8.00	2.25
		Entire, 1st day cancel, NY, NY		1.00
a.		Die 2	6.50	3.00
		Entire	11.00	3.75
b.		Die 3	6.50	3.00
		Entire	11.00	3.75
		Precanceled, die 3		1.25
		Entire, precanceled, die 3	2.50	1.50

Washington — U97

Die 1

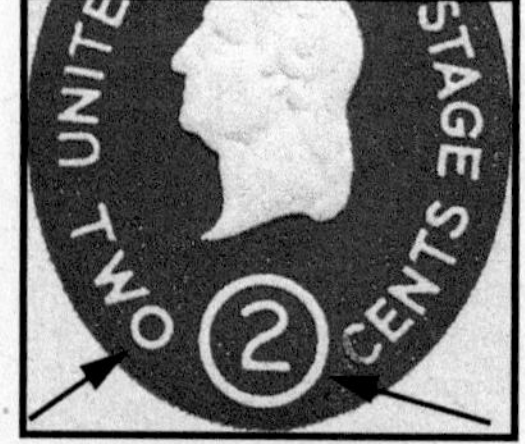

Die 2

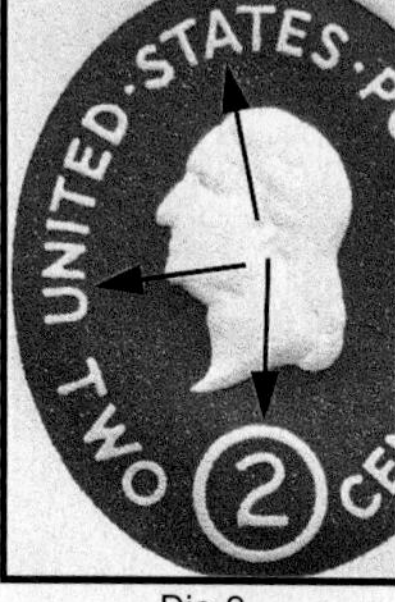

Die 3

Die 4

Die 1 — Thick "2" in thick circle; toe of "2" is acute angle.
Die 2 — Thin "2" in thin circle; toe of "2" is almost right angle; line through left stand of "N" in UNITED and stand of "E" in POSTAGE goes considerably below tip of chin; "N" of UNITED is tall; "O" of TWO is high.
Die 3 — Figure "2" as in Die 2. Short UN in UNITED thin crossbar in A of STATES.
Die 4 — Tall UN in UNITED; thick crossbar in A of STATES; otherwise like Die 3.

U533	U97	2c **carmine,** die 3	.70	.25
		Entire	1.20	.35
		Entire, precanceled, die 3	.30	.25
a.		Die 1, *Nov. 17*	.80	.30
		Entire	1.40	.45
		Entire, 1st day cancel, NY, NY		1.00
b.		Die 2	1.40	.85
		Entire	1.80	.95
c.		Die 4	1.30	.60
		Entire	1.50	.65
		Entire, precanceled	.40	.25

Die 1

Die 2

Die 3

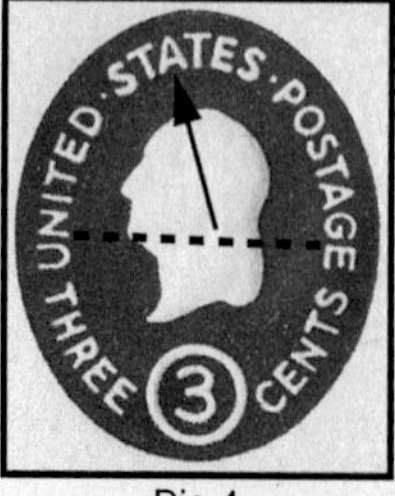

Die 4

Die 5

Die 1 — Thick and tall (4½mm) "3" in thick circle; long top bars and short stems in T's of STATES.
Die 2 — Thin and tall (4½mm) "3" in medium circle; short top bars and long stems in T's of STATES.
Die 3 — Thin and short (4mm) "3" in thin circle; lettering wider than Dies 1 and 2; line from left stand of N to stand of E is distinctly below tip of chin.
Die 4 — Figure and letters as in Die 3. Line hits tip of chin; short N in UNITED and thin crossbar in A of STATES.
Die 5 — Figure, letter and chin line as in Die 4; but tall N in UNITED and thick crossbar in A of STATES.

U534	U97	3c **dark violet,** die 4	.35	.25
		Entire	.45	.25
a.		Die 1, *Nov. 18*	1.90	.70
		Entire	2.40	1.20
		Entire, 1st day cancel, NY, NY		1.00
b.		Die 2, *Nov. 19*	.75	.50
		Entire	1.50	.55
		Entire, 1st day cancel, NY, NY		4.00
c.		Die 3	.55	.25
		Entire	1.00	.45
d.		Die 5	.75	.45
		Entire	1.20	.65
e.		As "c," double impression	*300.00*	

Washington — U98

1952

U535	U98	1½c **brown**	4.50	3.50
		Entire	5.50	4.25
		Precanceled		1.25
		Entire, precanceled	1.50	1.50

Die 1

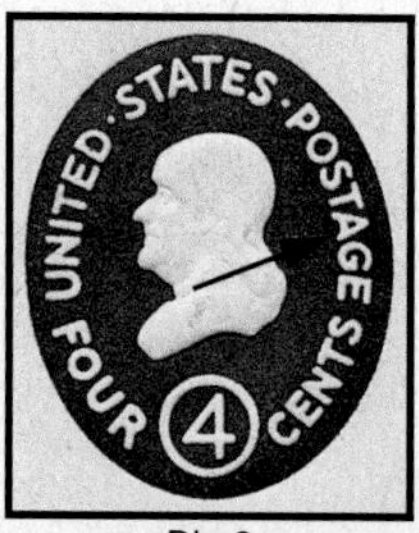

Die 2

Die 3

Die 1 — Head high in oval (2mm below T of STATES). Circle near (1mm) bottom of colored oval.
Die 2 — Head low in oval (3mm). Circle 1½mm from edge of oval. Right leg of A in POSTAGE shorter than left. Short leg on P.
Die 3 — Head centered in oval (2½mm). Circle as in Die 2. Legs of A of POSTAGE about equal. Long leg on P.

1958

U536	U96	4c **red violet,** die 1, *July 31*	.75	.25
		Entire	.95	.25
		Entire, 1st day cancel, Montpelier, Vt. *(163,746)*		1.00
a.		Die 2	.90	.25

	Entire	1.20	.25
b.	Die 3	.90	.25
	Entire	1.20	.25

Nos. U429, U429f, U429h, U533, U533a-U533c Surcharged in Red at Left of Stamp

1958

U537	U93 2c + 2c **carmine,** die 1	3.25	1.50
	Entire	4.25	*15.00*
a.	Die 7	10.00	7.00
	Entire	14.00	*15.00*
b.	Die 9	4.75	5.00
	Entire	7.00	15.00
U538	U97 2c + 2c **carmine,** die 1	.70	.80
	Entire	1.10	*1.25*
a.	Die 2	.90	1.00
	Entire	2.80	3.00
b.	Die 3	.70	.70
	Entire	1.90	*2.00*
c.	Die 4	.70	1.00
	Entire	1.40	*1.50*

Nos. U436a, U436e-U436f, U534, U534b-U534d Surcharged in Green at Left of Stamp

U539	U93 3c + 1c **purple,** die 1	12.50	9.00
	Entire	16.50	17.50
a.	Die 7	11.00	7.50
	Entire	14.00	17.50
b.	Die 9	17.50	15.00
	Entire	27.50	27.50
U540	U97 3c + 1c **dark violet,** die 3	.40	1.00
	Entire	.50	2.00
a.	Die 2	—	—
	Entire	*3,500.*	—
b.	Die 4	.65	1.00
	Entire	.80	*2.00*
c.	Die 5	.70	1.00
	Entire	.95	2.00

Earliest documented uses: Nos. U540b and U540c, both Aug. 1, 1958 (first day of new 4¢ letter rate).

Benjamin Franklin — U99

George Washington — U100

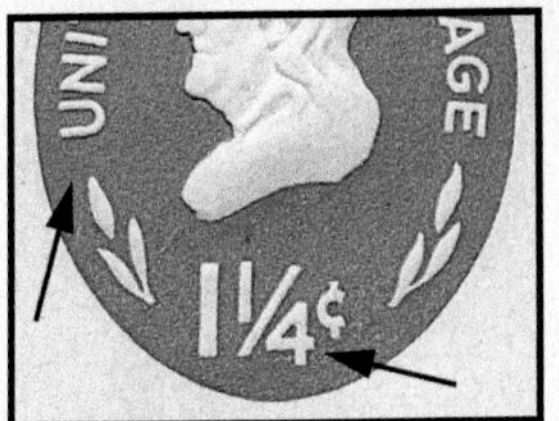

Die 1

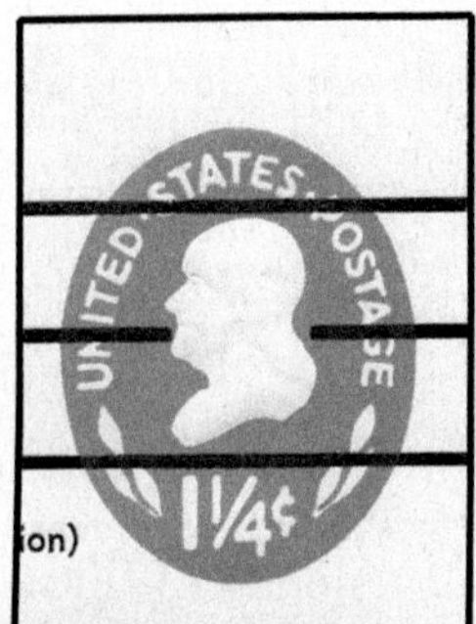

Die 2

Dies of 1¼c

Die 1 — The "4" is 3mm high. Upper leaf in left cluster is 2mm from "U."

Die 2 — The "4" is 3½mm high. Leaf clusters are larger. Upper leaf at left is 1mm from "U."

1960

U541	U99 1¼c **turquoise,** die 1, *June 25, 1960*	.65	.50
	Entire	.80	.55
	Entire, 1st day cancel, Birmingham, Ala. *(211,500)*		1.00
	Precanceled		.25
	Entire, precanceled	.45	.45
a.	Die 2, precanceled		1.25
	Entire, precanceled	1.75	1.75
U542	U100 2½c **dull blue,** *May 28, 1960*	.80	.50
	Entire	.90	.60
	Entire, 1st day cancel, Chicago, Ill. *(196,977)*		1.00
	Precanceled		.25
	Entire, precanceled	.75	.55

Precanceled cut squares

Precanceled envelopes do not normally receive another cancellation. Since the lack of a cancellation makes it impossible to distinguish between cut squares from used and unused envelopes, they are valued here as used only.

Pony Express Centennial Issue

Pony Express Rider — U101

Envelope White Outside, Blue Inside.

1960

U543	U101 4c **brown,** *July 19, 1960*	.55	.30
	Entire	.70	.40
	Entire, 1st day cancel, St. Joseph, Mo. *(407,160)*		1.00

Abraham Lincoln — U102

Die 1

Die 2

Die 3

Die 1 — Center bar of E of POSTAGE is above the middle. Center bar of E of STATES slants slightly upward. Nose sharper, more pointed. No offset ink specks inside envelope on back of die impression.

Die 2 — Center bar of E of POSTAGE in middle. P of POSTAGE has short stem. Ink specks on back of die impression.

Die 3 — FI of FIVE closer than Die 1 or 2. Second T of STATES seems taller than ES. Ink specks on back of die impression.

1962

U544	U102 5c **dark blue,** die 2, *Nov. 19, 1962*	.80	.25
	Entire	1.10	.30
	Entire, 1st day cancel, Springfield, Ill. *(163,258)*		1.50
a.	Die 1	.80	.25
	Entire	1.10	.30
b.	Die 3	.85	.35
	Entire	1.20	.40
c.	Die 2 with albino impression of 4c (#U536)	50.00	—
	Entire	120.00	
d.	Die 3 with albino impression of 4c (#U536), entire	*125.00*	—
e.	Die 3 on complete impression of 4c (#U536), cut square	*125.00*	

No. U536 Surcharged in Green at left of Stamp

Two types of surcharge:

Type I — "U.S. POSTAGE" 18½mm high. Serifs on cross of T both diagonal. Two lines of shading in C of CENT.

Type II — "U.S. POSTAGE" 17½mm high. Right serif on cross of T is vertical. Three shading lines in C.

1962

U545	U96 4c + 1c **red vio,** die 1, type I, *Nov. 1962*	1.25	1.10
	Entire	1.50	2.50
a.	Type II	1.25	1.10
	Entire	1.50	2.50

Values for used envelopes are for examples used within the period of issue. Envelopes used much later sell at substantially reduced prices.

New York World's Fair Issue

Issued to publicize the New York World's Fair, 1964-65.

Globe with Satellite Orbit — U103

1964

U546	U103 5c **maroon,** *Apr. 22, 1964*	.55	.40
	Entire	.70	2.00
	Entire, 1st day cancel World's Fair, N.Y. *(466,422)*		1.00

Liberty Bell — U104

Old Ironsides — U105

Eagle — U106

Head of Statue of Liberty — U107

Printed by the United States Envelope Company, Williamsburg, Pa. Designed (6c) by Howard C. Mildner and (others) by Robert J. Jones.

1965-69

U547 U104 1¼c **brown,** *Jan. 6, 1965* .50
Entire .90 2.00
Entire, 1st day cancel, Washington, D.C. 1.00
U548 U104 1⁴⁄₁₀c **brown,** *Mar. 26, 1968* .50
Entire 1.00 2.00
Entire, 1st day cancel, Springfield, Mass. *(134,832)* 1.00
U548A U104 1⁶⁄₁₀c **orange,** *June 16, 1969* .50
Entire 1.00 2.00
Entire, 1st day cancel, Washington, D.C. 1.00
b. 1⁶⁄₁₀c **brown (error), entire** *5,000.*
U549 U105 4c **bright blue,** *Jan. 6, 1965* .90 .25
Entire 1.00 .25
Entire, 1st day cancel, Washington, D.C. 1.00
U550 U106 5c **bright purple,** *Jan. 5, 1965* .75 .25
Entire .85 1.00
Entire, 1st day cancel, Williamsburg, Pa. *(246,496)* 1.00
a. Bar tagged, *Aug. 15, 1967* 3.00 1.00
Entire 5.00 5.00
Entire, tagged, 1st day cancel 3.50
b. orange-red (air post) instead of yellow-green tagging, entire *450.00*

Tagged

U551 U107 6c **light green,** *Jan. 4, 1968* .70 .25
Entire .80 .25
Entire, 1st day cancel, New York, N.Y. *(184,784)* 1.25
a. 6c **dark gray green,** entire 200.00 —

First day covers of the 1¼c and 4c total 451,960.

Nos. U549-U550 Surcharged in Red or Green at Left of Stamp

1968, Feb. 5

U552 U105 4c + 2c **bright blue** (R) 3.25 2.00
Entire 3.75 2.50
Entire, 1st day cancel 6.00
U553 U106 5c + 1c **bright purple** (G) 3.00 2.75
Entire 3.50 3.25
Entire, 1st day cancel 6.00
a. Tagged 3.00 2.75
Entire 4.00 3.25
Entire, 1st day cancel 6.00
b. With 2c surcharge type "b" (error) 400.00

Tagged

Envelopes from No. U554 onward are tagged, except for bulk-rate and non-profit envelopes, which are untagged. The tagging element is in the ink through No. 608 unless otherwise noted. From No. 611 on, envelopes have bar or block tagging unless otherwise noted.

Herman Melville Issue

Issued to honor Herman Melville (1819-1891), writer, and the whaling industry.

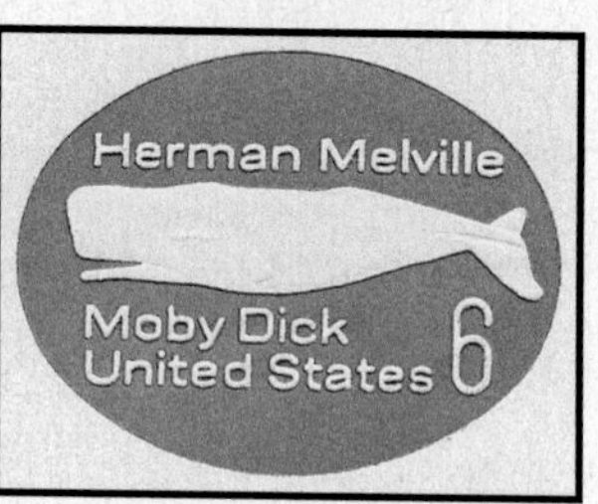

Moby Dick — U108

1970, Mar. 7

U554 U108 6c **blue** .50 .25
Entire .60 3.50
Entire, 1st day cancel, New Bedford, Mass. *(433,777)* 1.50

Youth Conference Issue

Issued to publicize the White House Conference on Youth, Estes Park, Colo., Apr. 18-22.

Conference Emblem Symbolic of Man's Expectant Soul and of Universal Brotherhood U109

Printed by United States Envelope Company, Williamsburg, Pa. Designed by Chermayeff and Geismar Associates.

1971, Feb. 24

U555 U109 6c **light blue** .70 1.00
Entire .80 4.00
Entire, 1st day cancel, Washington, D.C. *(264,559)* 1.00

Liberty Bell Type of 1965 and

Eagle — U110

Printed by the United States Envelope Co., Williamsburg, Pa. Designed (8c) by Bradbury Thompson.

1971

U556 U104 1⁷⁄₁₀c **deep lilac,** untagged, *May 10* .35
Entire .35 1.50
Entire, 1st day cancel, Baltimore, Md. *(150,767)* 1.00
U557 U110 8c **ultramarine,** *May 6* .40 .25
Entire .60 .40
Entire, 1st day cancel, Williamsburg, Pa. *(193,000)* 1.00

Nos. U551 and U555 Surcharged in Green at Left of Stamp

c

1971, May 16

U561 U107 6c + (2c) **light green** .90 1.25
Entire 1.00 2.50
Entire, 1st day cancel, Washington, D.C. 2.50
a. Inverted surcharge, entire *275.00*
U562 U109 6c + (2c) **light blue** 2.00 2.50
Entire 2.50 3.00
Entire, 1st day cancel, Washington, D.C. 3.00
a. Inverted surcharge printed on reverse, entire —

Bowling Issue

Issued as a salute to bowling and in connection with the 7th World Tournament of the International Bowling Federation, Milwaukee, Wis.

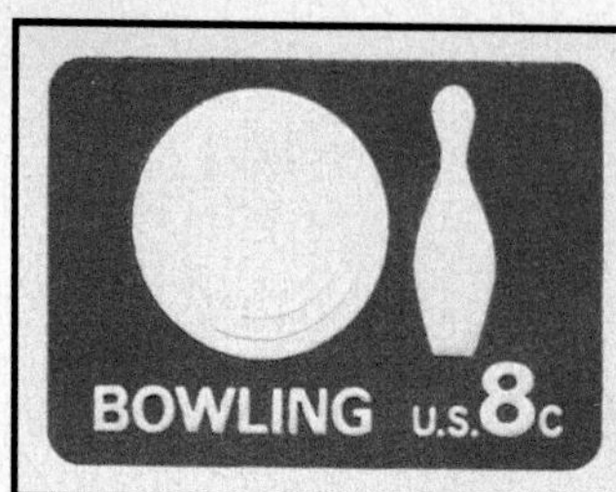

Bowling Ball and Pin — U111

Designed by George Giusti.

1971, Aug. 21

U563 U111 8c **rose red** .60 .25
Entire .70 2.00
Entire, 1st day cancel, Milwaukee, Wis. *(281,242)* 1.00

Aging Conference Issue

White House Conference on Aging, Washington, D.C., Nov. 28-Dec. 2, 1971.

Conference Symbol — U112

Designed by Thomas H. Geismar.

1971, Nov. 15

U564 U112 8c **light blue** .50 .25
Entire .75 4.00
Entire, 1st day cancel, Washington, D.C. *(125,000)* 1.00

International Transportation Exhibition Issue

U.S. International Transportation Exhibition, Dulles International Airport, Washington, D.C., May 27-June 4.

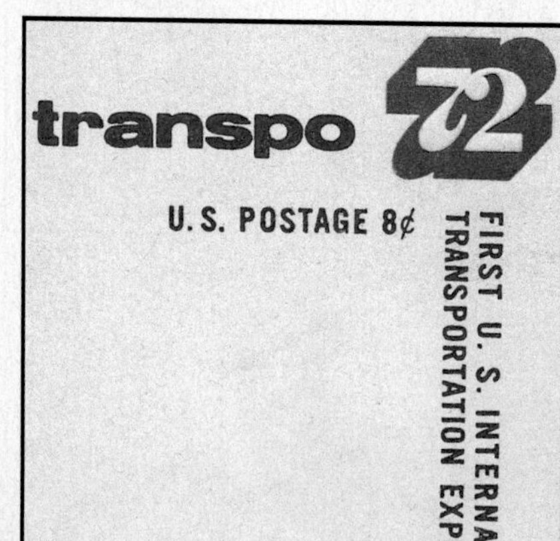

Transportation Exhibition Emblem — U113

Emblem designed by Toshihiki Sakow.

1972, May 2

U565 U113 8c **ultramarine & rose red** .50 .25
Entire .75 .60
Entire, 1st day cancel, Washington, D.C. 1.00

No. U557 Surcharged in Ultramarine at Left of Stamp

1973, Dec. 1

U566 U110 8c + 2c **brt. ultramarine** .40 1.25
Entire .75 2.50
Entire, 1st day cancel, Washington, D.C. 1.50

Liberty Bell — U114

1973, Dec. 5

U567 U114 10c **emerald** .40 .25
Entire .70 .35
Entire, 1st day cancel, Philadelphia, Pa. *(142,141)* 1.00

"Volunteer Yourself" — U115

Designed by Norman Ives.

1974, Aug. 23

Untagged

U568 U115 1 8/10c **blue green** .25
Entire 1.00 2.00
Entire, 1st day cancel, Cincinnati, Ohio 1.00

Tennis Centenary Issue

Centenary of tennis in the United States.

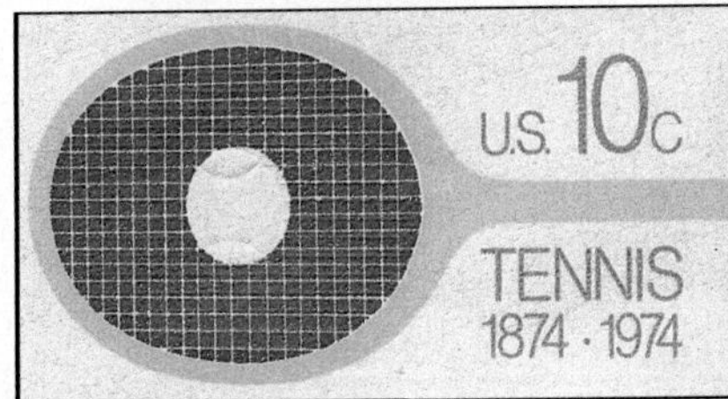

Tennis Racquet — U116

Designed by Donald Moss.

1974, Aug. 31 **Block Tagged**

U569 U116 10c **yellow, brt. blue & light green** .55 .25
Entire .80 2.00
Entire, 1st day cancel, Forest Hills, N.Y. *(245,000)* 1.25

Bicentennial Era Issue

The Seafaring Tradition — Compass Rose U118

The American Homemaker — Quilt Pattern — U119

The American Farmer — Sheaf of Wheat — U120

The American Doctor — Mortar — U121

The American Craftsman — Tools, c. 1750 — U122

Designs (in brown on left side of envelope): 10c, Norwegian sloop Restaurationen. No. U572, Spinning wheel. No. U573, Plow. No. U574, Colonial era medical instruments and bottle. No. U575, Shaker rocking chair.

Designed by Arthur Congdon.

1975-76 **Embossed** **Diagonally Laid Paper**

U571 U118 10c **brown & blue,** *light brown, Oct. 13, 1975* .30 .25
Entire .45 2.00
Entire, 1st day cancel, Minneapolis, Minn. *(255,304)* 1.00
a. Brown ("10c/USA," etc.) omitted, entire *125.00*

U572 U119 13c **brown & blue green,** *light brown, Feb. 2, 1976* .35 .25
Entire .55 2.00
Entire, 1st day cancel, Biloxi, Miss. *(196,647)* 1.00
a. Brown ("13c/USA," etc.) omitted, entire *125.00*

U573 U120 13c **brown & bright green,** *light brown, Mar. 15, 1976* .35 .25
Entire .55 2.00
Entire, 1st day cancel, New Orleans, La. *(214,563)* 1.00
a. Brown ("13c/USA," etc.) omitted, entire *125.00*

U574 U121 13c **brown & orange,** *light brown, June 30, 1976* .35 .25
Entire .55 2.00
Entire, 1st day cancel, Dallas, Texas 1.50
a. Brown ("13c/USA," etc.) omitted, entire *125.00*

U575 U122 13c **brown & carmine,** *lt. brown, Aug. 6, 1976* .35 .25
Entire .55 2.00
Entire, 1st day cancel, Hancock, Mass. 1.00
a. Brown ("13c/USA," etc.) omitted, entire *125.00*
Nos. U571-U575 (5) 1.70 1.25

Liberty Tree, Boston, 1646 U123

Designed by Leonard Everett Fisher.

1975, Nov. 8 **Embossed**

U576 U123 13c **orange brown** .30 .25
Entire .40 2.00
Entire, 1st day cancel, Memphis, Tenn. *(226,824)* 1.00

Star and Pinwheel — U124

U125

U126

Eagle — U127

Uncle Sam — U128

Designers: 2c, Rudolph de Harak. 2.1c, Norman Ives. 2.7c, Ann Sforza Clementino. 15c, George Mercer.

1976-78 **Embossed**

U577 U124 2c **red,** untagged, *Sept. 10, 1976* .25
Entire .70 1.50
Entire, 1st day cancel, Hempstead, N.Y. *(81,388)* 1.00
U578 U125 2.1c **green,** untagged, *June 3, 1977* .25
Entire .90 2.00
Entire, 1st day cancel, Houston, Tex. *(120,280)* 1.00
U579 U126 2.7c **green,** untagged, *July 5, 1978* .25
Entire 1.00 1.50
Entire, 1st day cancel, Raleigh, N.C. *(92,687)* 1.00
U580 U127 (15c) **orange,** *May 22, 1978* .40 .25
Entire .55 .75
Entire, 1st day cancel, Memphis, Tenn. 1.00
U581 U128 15c **red,** ink tagged, *June 3, 1978* .40 .25
Entire .55 .60
Entire, 1st day cancel, Williamsburg, Pa. *(176,000)* 1.00
a. Bar tagged *7.00* 7.00

For No. U581 with surcharge, see No. U586b.

Bicentennial Issue

Centennial Envelope, 1876 — U129

1976, Oct. 15 **Embossed**

U582 U129 13c **emerald** .35 .25
Entire .70 .40
Entire, 1st day cancel, Los Angeles, Cal. *(277,222)* 1.00

Golf Issue

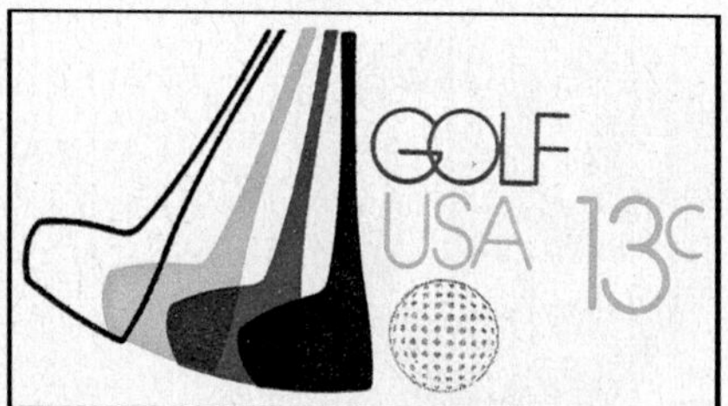

Golf Club in Motion and Golf Ball — U130

Designed by Guy Salvato.

1977, Apr. 7 **Photogravure and Embossed**

U583 U130 13c **black, blue & yellow green** .65 .25
Entire .75 3.00
Entire, 1st day cancel, Augusta, Ga. *(252,000)* 1.50
a. Black omitted, entire *500.00*
b. Black & blue omitted, entire *500.00*
c. Black, blue & yellow green omitted, entire *500.00*

On No. U583c, the embossing is present.

Energy Issue

Conservation and development of national resources.

"Conservation" U131

"Development" U132

Designed by Terrance W. McCaffrey.

1977, Oct. 20 **Photo.**

Bar Tagged

U584 U131 13c **black, red & yellow** .45 .25
Entire .55 2.00
Entire, 1st day cancel, Ridley Park, Pa. 1.00
a. Red, yellow & tagging omitted, entire *190.00*
b. Yellow & tagging omitted, entire *150.00*
c. Black omitted, entire *135.00*
d. Black & red omitted, entire *350.00*
U585 U132 13c **black, red & yellow** .45 .25
Entire .55 .25
Entire, 1st day cancel, Ridley Park, Pa. 1.00

First day cancellation applied to 353,515 of Nos. U584 and U585.

Olive Branch and Star — U133

Designed by George Mercer.

1978, July 28 **Embossed**

Black Surcharge

U586 U133 15c on 16c **blue** .40 .25
Entire .55 1.00
Entire, 1st day cancel, Williamsburg, Pa. *(193,153)* 1.00
a. Surcharge omitted, entire 225.00 1,000.
b. Surcharge on No. U581, entire 260.00
c. As "a," with surcharge printed on envelope flap 175.00 —
d. Surcharge inverted (in lower left corner), entire 200.00 —

Auto Racing Issue

Indianapolis 500 Racing Car — U134

Designed by Robert Peak.

1978, Sept. 2 **Embossed**

U587 U134 15c **red, blue & black** .45 .25
Entire .60 3.00
Entire, 1st day cancel, Ontario, Cal. *(209,147)* 1.75
a. Black omitted, entire 100.00
b. Black & blue omitted, entire *170.00*
c. Red & tagging omitted, entire 100.00
d. Red, blue & tagging omitted, entire *170.00*
e. Tagging bar inverted at LL, entire 100.00
f. Tagging bar on reverse, entire —

No. U576 Surcharged

1978, Nov. 28 **Embossed**

U588 U123 15c on 13c **orange brown** .40 .25
Entire .55 1.00
Entire, 1st day cancel, Williamsburg, Pa. *(137,500)* 1.00
a. Surcharge inverted (in lower left corner), entire 450.00

U135

1979, May 18 **Untagged** **Embossed**

U589 U135 3.1c **ultramarine** .35
Entire .55 2.50
Entire, 1st day cancel, Denver, Colo. *(117,575)* 1.00

Weaver Violins — U136

1980, June 23 **Untagged** **Embossed**

U590 U136 3.5c **purple** .35
Entire .35 1.50
Entire, 1st day cancel, Williamsburg, Pa. 1.00
a. 3.5c **violet**, tagged (in ink), error of color and tagging using ink intended for No. U592, entire *300.00 500.00*

U137

1982, Feb. 17 **Untagged** **Embossed**

U591 U137 5.9c **brown** .35
Entire .35 2.50
Entire, 1st day cancel, Wheeling, WV 1.00

Eagle — U138

1981, Mar. 15 **Embossed**

U592 U138 (18c) **violet** .45 .25
Entire .55 1.00
Entire, 1st day cancel, Memphis, TN *(179,171)* 1.00

U139

1981, Apr. 2 **Embossed**

U593 U139 18c **dark blue** .45 .25
Entire .55 4.00
Entire, 1st day cancel, Star City, IN *(160,439)* 1.00

Eagle — U140

1981, Oct. 11 **Embossed**

U594 U140 (20c) **brown** .45 .25
Entire .55 .60
Entire, 1st day cancel, Memphis, TN *(304,404)* 2.00

Veterinary Medicine Issue

Seal of Veterinarians U141

Design at left side of envelope shows 5 animals and bird in brown, "Veterinary Medicine" in gray.
Designed by Guy Salvato.

1979, July 24 **Embossed**

U595 U141 15c **brown & gray** .50 .25
Entire .90 3.00
Entire, 1st day cancel, Seattle, WA *(209,658)* 1.00
a. Gray omitted, entire *425.00*
b. Brown omitted, entire *500.00*
c. Gray & brown omitted, tagging omitted, entire *325.00*

On No. U595c, the embossing of the seal is present.

Olympic Games Issue

22nd Olympic Games, Moscow, July 19-Aug. 3, 1980.

U142

Design (multicolored on left side of envelope) shows two soccer players with ball.
Designed by Robert M. Cunningham.

1979, Dec. 10 **Embossed**

U596 U142 15c **red, green & black** .60 .25
Entire .70 2.00
Entire, 1st day cancel, East Rutherford, NJ *(179,336)* 1.00
a. Red & green omitted, tagging omitted, entire *150.00*
b. Black omitted, tagging omitted, entire *150.00*
c. Black & green omitted, entire *150.00*
d. Red omitted, tagging omitted, entire *325.00*
e. All colors omitted *250.00*
f. Tagging omitted, entire 125.00
g. Black omitted, tagged, entire —

No. U596c exists with a portion of the green present in the Olympics 1980 design at the lower left corner of the envelope.
On No. U596e, the blind embossing of "USA 15c" remains.

Highwheeler Bicycle — U143

Design (blue on left side of envelope) shows racing bicycle.
Designed by Robert Hallock.

1980, May 16 **Embossed**

U597 U143 15c **blue & rose claret** .40 .25
Entire .55 2.00
Entire, 1st day cancel, Baltimore, MD *(173,978)* 1.25
a. Blue ("15c USA") omitted, entire 100.00
b. As "a," tagging omitted 100.00

Yacht — U144

Designed by Cal Sachs.

1980, Sept. 15 **Embossed**

U598 U144 15c **blue & red** .40 .25
Entire .65 2.00
Entire, 1st day cancel, Newport, RI *(192,220)* 1.00

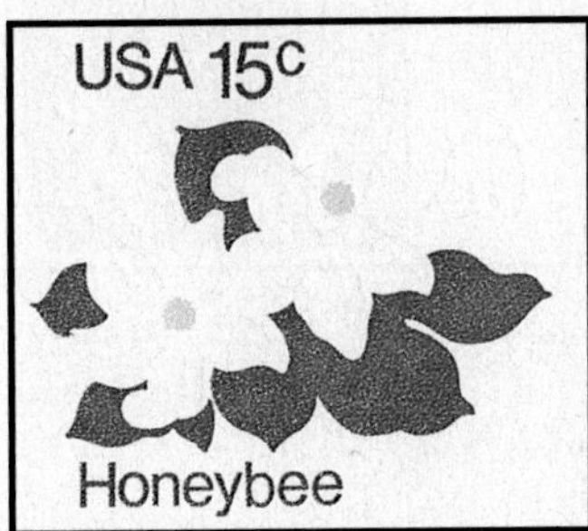

Italian Honeybee and Orange Blossoms U145

Bee and petals colorless embossed.
Designed by Jerry Pinkney.

1980, Oct. 10 **Photogravure and Embossed**

U599 U145 15c **brown, green & yellow** .35 .25
Entire .50 2.00
Entire, 1st day cancel, Paris, IL *(202,050)* 1.00
a. Brown ("USA 15c") omitted, entire *100.00*
b. Green omitted, entire *100.00*

No. U599b also has almost all of the brown color missing.

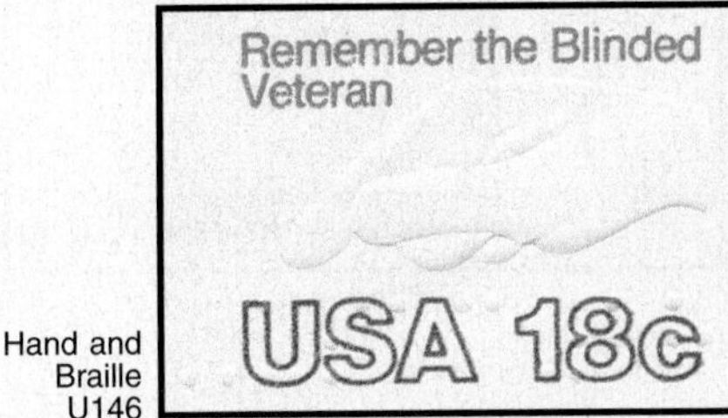

Hand and Braille U146

Hand and braille colorless embossed.
Designed by John Boyd.

1981, Aug. 13 **Embossed**

U600 U146 18c **blue & red** .45 .25
Entire .55 3.00
Entire, 1st day cancel, Arlington, VA *(175,966)* 1.00
a. Blue omitted, entire *300.00*
b. Red omitted, entire *210.00*

Capitol Dome — U147

1981, Nov. 13 **Embossed**

U601 U147 20c **deep magenta,** ink tagged .45 .25
Entire .55 .25
Entire, 1st day cancel, Los Angeles, CA 1.00
a. Bar tagged 4.50 1.50

U148

Designed by Bradbury Thompson.

1982, June 15 **Embossed**

U602 U148 20c **dark blue, black & magenta** .45 .25
Entire .55 2.00
Entire, 1st day cancel, Washington, DC *(163,905)* 1.00
a. Dark blue omitted, entire *175.00*
b. Dark blue & magenta omitted, entire *175.00*
c. All colors omitted, entire *175.00*

On No. 602c, the colorless embossed impression of the Great Seal is present.

U149

Designed by John Boyd.

1982, Aug. 6 **Embossed**

U603 U149 20c **purple & black** .75 .25
Entire 1.00 3.00
Entire, 1st day cancel, Washington, DC *(110,679)* 1.25
a. Black omitted, entire *80.00*
b. Purple omitted, entire *200.00*

U150

1983, Mar. 21 **Untagged** **Embossed**

U604 U150 5.2c **orange** .90
Entire .75 1.00
Entire, 1st day cancel, Memphis, TN *(141,979)* 1.00

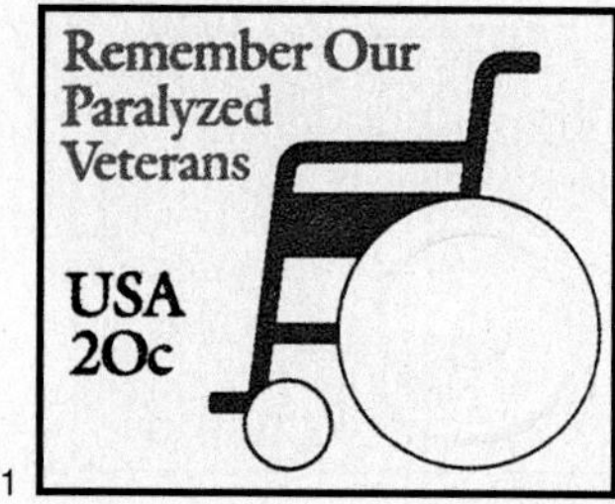

U151

1983, Aug. 3 **Embossed**

U605 U151 20c **red, blue & black**	.45	.25
Entire	.55	4.00
Entire, 1st day cancel, Portland, OR *(21,500)*		1.00
a. Red omitted, entire	*260.00*	
b. Blue omitted, entire	*260.00*	
c. Red & black omitted, entire	*125.00*	
d. Blue & black omitted, entire	*125.00*	
e. Black omitted, entire	*230.00*	

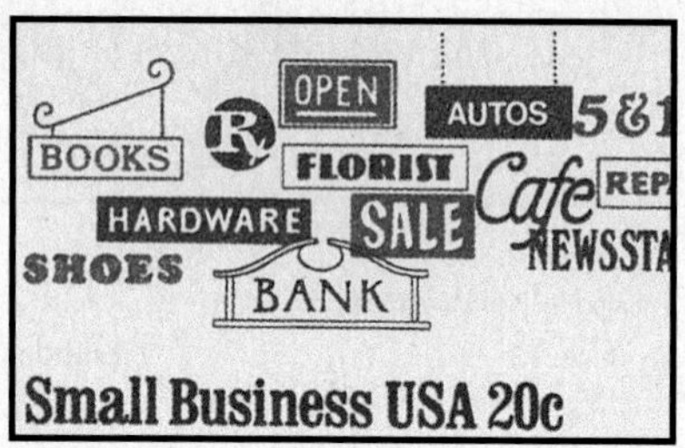

U152

Designed by Peter Spier and Pat Taylor.

Design shows storefronts at lower left. Stamp and design continue on back of envelope.

1984, May 7 **Photo.**

U606 U152 20c **multi**	.50	.25
Entire	.60	2.00
Entire, 1st day cancel, Washington, DC *(77,665)*		1.00

U153

Designed by Bradbury Thompson.

1985, Feb. 1 **Embossed**

U607 U153 (22c) **deep green**	.55	.30
Entire	.65	.40
Entire, 1st day cancel, Los Angeles, CA		1.00

American Buffalo U154

Designed by George Mercer.

1985, Feb. 25 **Embossed**

U608 U154 22c **violet brown**, ink tagged	.55	.25
Entire	.65	.25
Entire, 1st day cancel, Bison, SD *(105,271)*		1.00
a. Untagged, 3 precancel lines, unwatermarked, *Nov. 1, 1986*		.25
Entire	.60	.25
b. Bar tagged	2.00	1.00
Entire	10.00	1.25
c. As "b," tagging omitted	—	—

Original printings of No. U608 were printed with luminescent ink. later printings have a luminescent vertical bar to the left of the stamp.

Frigate U.S.S. Constitution — U155

Designed by Cal Sacks.

1985, May 3 **Untagged** **Embossed**

U609 U155 6c **green blue**		.35
Entire	.35	3.00
Entire, 1st day cancel, Boston, MA *(170,425)*		1.25

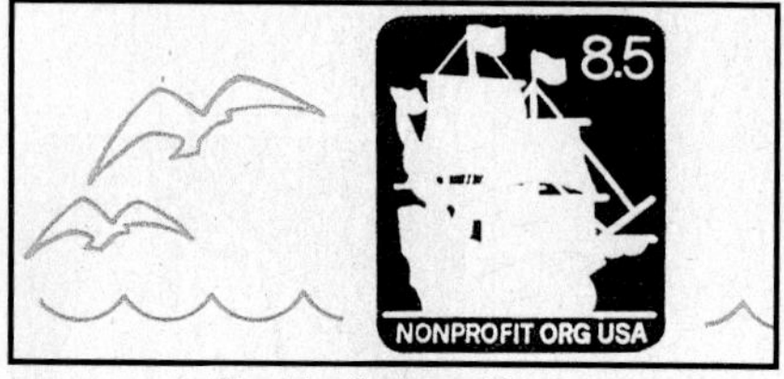

The Mayflower — U156

Designed by Robert Brangwynne.

1986, Dec. 4 **Untagged Precanceled** **Embossed**

U610 U156 8.5c **black & gray**		.65
Entire	.75	3.00
Entire, 1st day cancel, Plymouth, MA *(105,164)*		1.00

Stars U157

Designed by Joe Brockert.

1988, Mar. 26 **Typo. & Embossed**

U611 U157 25c **dark red & deep blue,** small block tagging	.60	.25
Entire	.70	.25
Entire, 1st day cancel, Star, MS *(29,393)*		1.25
a. Dark red (25) omitted, tagging omitted	50.00	—
Entire	60.00	—
b. Tagging omitted, entire	14.00	
c. Dark red (25) omitted, tagging not omitted	*60.00*	
d. Large block tagging	.60	.25
Entire	.70	.25

The tagging bar on No. U611 is 8x10mm. The tagging bar on No. U611d is 16x15mm.

U.S. Frigate Constellation — U158

Designed by Jerry Dadds.

1988, Apr. 12 **Untagged Precanceled** **Typo. & Embossed**

U612 U158 8.4c **black & bright blue**		.65
Entire	.75	4.00
Entire, 1st day cancel, Baltimore, MD *(41,420)*		1.25
a. Black omitted, entire	*500.00*	

Snowflake — U159

Designed by Randall McDougall. "Holiday Greetings!" inscribed in lower left.

1988, Sept. 8 **Typo.**

U613 U159 25c **dark red & green**	1.25	*20.00*
Entire	1.50	*40.00*
Entire, 1st day cancel, Snowflake, AZ *(32,601)*		1.25

Stars U160

Designed by Joe Brockert. "Philatelic Mail" and asterisks in dark red below vignette; continuous across envelope face and partly on reverse.

1989, Mar. 10 **Typo.**

U614 U160 25c **dark red & deep blue**	.50	.25
Entire	.60	.30
Entire, 1st day cancel, Cleveland, OH		1.25
a. Tagging omitted, entire		—
b. Red omitted, entire	125.00	

No. U614 was issued only in No. 9 size.

Stars — U161

Designed by Joe Brockert.

1989, July 10 **Typo.** **Unwmk.**

U615 U161 25c **dark red & deep blue**	.50	.25
Entire	.60	.30
Entire, 1st day cancel, Washington, DC *(33,461)*		1.25
a. Dark red omitted, entire	*425.00*	

Lined with a blue design to provide security for enclosures. Issued only in No. 9 size.

Love! U162

Designed by Tim Girvin.

1989, Sept. 22 **Litho. & Typo.** **Unwmk.**

U616 U162 25c **dark red & bright blue**	.50	.75
Entire	.60	3.00
Entire, 1st day cancel, McLean, VA *(69,498)*		1.25
a. Dark red and bright blue omitted, entire	150.00	
b. Bright blue omitted, entire	150.00	

No. U616 has light blue lines printed diagonally over the entire surface of the envelope. Issued only in No. 9 size.

Shuttle Docking at Space Station — U163

Designed by Richard Sheaff.

1989, Dec. 3 Typo. Unwmk.
Die Cut

U617 U163 25c **ultramarine**		.90	.60
Entire		1.00	2.00
Entire, 1st day cancel, Washington, DC			1.25
a. Ultramarine omitted, entire	*400.00*		

A hologram, visible through the die cut window to the right of "USA 25," is affixed to the inside of the envelope.
Available only in No. 9 size.
See Nos. U625, U639.

Vince Lombardi Trophy, Football Players — U164

Designed by Bruce Harman.

1990, Sept. 9 Typo. Unwmk. *Die Cut*

U618 U164 25c **vermilion**	.90	.60
Entire	1.00	2.00
Entire, 1st day cancel, Green Bay, WI *(54,589)*		1.25

A hologram, visible through the die cut window to the right of "USA 25," is affixed to the inside of the envelope.
Issued only in No. 10 size.

Star — U165

Designed by Richard Sheaff.

1991, Jan. 24 Typo. & Embossed Wmk.

U619 U165 29c **ultramarine & rose**		.60	.30
Entire		.70	.35
Entire, unwatermarked, *May 1, 1992*		.70	.35
Entire, 1st day cancel, Washington, DC *(33,025)*			1.25
a. Ultramarine omitted, entire	*300.00*		
b. Rose omitted, tagged, entire	*250.00*		
c. Rose omitted, tagging omitted, entire	*275.00*		
d. Tagging omitted, entire	—		

Unwatermarked envelopes are on recycled paper, were issued May 1, 1992, and have a "recycled" imprint under the flap.
See No. U623.

Birds — U166

Designed by Richard Sheaff
Stamp and design continue on back of envelope. Illustration reduced.

1991, May 3 Typo. Wmk.
Untagged, Precanceled

U620 U166 11.1c **blue & red**			.90
Entire		.55	4.00
Entire, 1st day cancel, Boxborough, MA *(20,720)*			1.25
Entire, unwatermarked, *May 1, 1992*		.60	.25
a. Blue omitted, entire	—		

Unwatermarked envelopes are on recycled paper, were issued May 1, 1992, and have a "recycled" imprint under the flap.

Love — U167

Designed by Salahattin Kanidinc.

1991, May 9 Litho. Unwmk.

U621 U167 29c **light blue, purple & bright rose**		.60	.60
Entire		.70	2.00
Entire, 1st day cancel, Honolulu, HI *(40,110)*			1.25
a. Bright rose omitted, entire	*200.00*		
b. Purple omitted, entire	*400.00*		

Envelopes on recycled paper were issued May 1, 1992, and have a "recycled" imprint under the flap. Envelopes on recycled paper show more gray in the paper, and "29/USA" is in a lighter shade of purple.

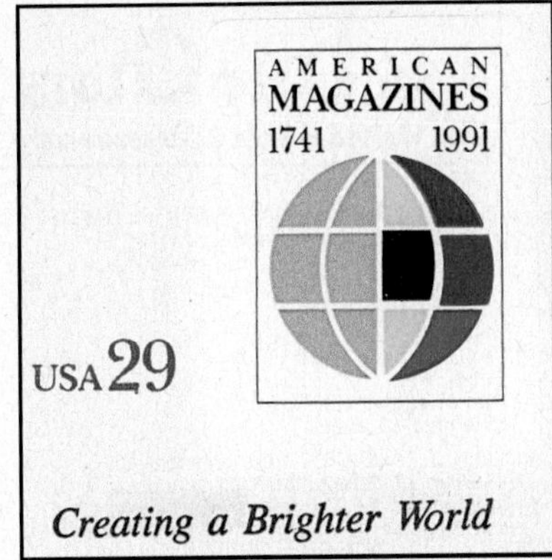

Magazine Industry, 250th Anniv. — U168

Designed by Bradbury Thompson.

1991, Oct. 7 Photo. & Typo. Unwmk.

U622 U168 29c **multicolored**	.70	1.00
Entire	.80	2.50
Entire, 1st day cancel, Naples, FL *(26,020)*		1.25

The photogravure vignette, visible through the die cut window to the right of "USA 29", is affixed to the inside of the envelope. Issued only in No. 10 size.

Star U169

Designed by Richard Sheaff.
Stamp and design continue on back of envelope.

1991, July 20 Typo. Unwmk.

U623 U169 29c **ultra & rose**		.60	.30
Entire		.70	1.00
Entire, 1st day cancel, Washington, DC *(16,038)*			1.25
a. Ultra omitted, entire	*350.00*		
b. Rose omitted, entire	*200.00*		

Lined with a blue design to provide security for enclosures. Envelopes on recycled paper were issued May 1, 1992, and have a "recycled" imprint under the flap. Issued only in No. 9 size. Value $1.50.

Country Geese U170

Designed by Marc Zaref.

1991, Nov. 8 Litho. & Typo. Wmk.

U624 U170 29c **blue gray & yellow**	.60	.60
Entire	.70	4.00
Entire, 1st day cancel, Virginia Beach, VA *(21,031)*		1.25
Entire, unwatermarked, *May 1, 1992*	1.00	.70

Unwatermarked envelopes are on recycled paper were issued May 1, 1992, and have a "recycled" imprint under the flap.

Space Shuttle Type of 1989

Designed by Richard Sheaff.

1992, Jan. 21 Typo. Unwmk. *Die Cut*

U625 U163 29c **yellow green**	.80	.50
Entire	1.00	3.50
Entire, 1st day cancel, Virginia Beach, VA *(37,646)*		1.25

A hologram, visible through the die cut window to the right of "USA 29," is affixed to the inside of the envelope. Examples on recycled paper were issued May 1, 1992 and have a "recycled" imprint under the flap. Issued only in No. 10 size. Value $1.25.

U171

Designed by Harry Zelenko.

1992, Apr. 10 Typo. & Litho. *Die Cut*

U626 U171 29c **multicolored**	.60	1.00
Entire	.70	4.00
Entire, 1st day cancel, Dodge City, KS *(34,258)*		1.25

The lithographed vignette, visible through the die cut window to the right of "USA 29," is affixed to the inside of the envelope. Issued only in the No. 10 size.

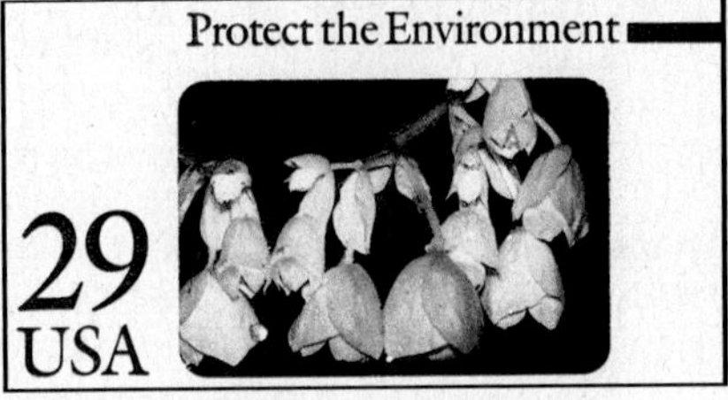

Hillebrandia — U172

Designed by Joseph Brockert. Illustration reduced.

1992, Apr. 22

U627 U172 29c **multicolored**	.65	1.00
Entire	.75	4.00
Entire, 1st day cancel, Chicago, IL *(29,432)*		1.25

The lithographed vignette, visible through the die cut window to the right of "29 USA," is affixed to the inside of the envelope.

Inscribed "Save the Rain Forests" in the lower left. Issued only in the No. 10 size.

Star — U173

Designed by Joseph Brockert.

1992, May 19 Typo. & Embossed Precanceled
Untagged

U628 U173 19.8c **red & blue** .40
Entire .60 *10.00*
Entire, 1st day cancel, Las Vegas, NV *(18,478)* 1.25

Issued only in No. 10 size.

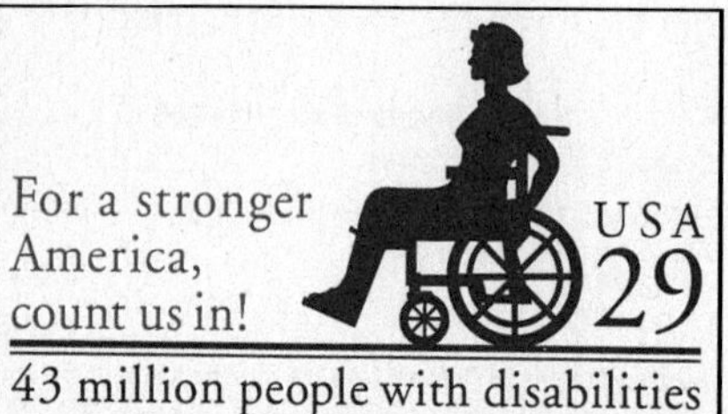

U174

Designed by Richard Sheaff. Illustration reduced.

1992, July 22 Typo.

U629 U174 29c **red & blue** .60 .30
Entire .70 2.00
Entire, 1st day cancel, Washington, DC *(28,218)* 1.25

U175

Designed by Nancy Krause. Illustration reduced.

1993, Oct. 2 Typo. & Litho. *Die Cut*

U630 U175 29c **multicolored** 1.10 1.10
Entire 1.25 3.00
Entire, 1st day cancel, King of Prussia, PA *(6,511)* 1.25

The lithographed vignette, visible through the die cut window to the right of "USA 29," is affixed to the inside of the envelope. Issued only in the No. 10 size.

U176

Designed by Richard Sheaff.

1994, Sept. 17 Typo. & Embossed

U631 U176 29c **brown & black** .70 1.25
Entire .80 3.00
Entire, 1st day cancel, Canton, OH *(28,977)* 1.25
a. Black ("29/USA") omitted, entire *325.00*

Issued only in No. 10 size.

Liberty Bell — U177

Designed by Richard Sheaff.

1995, Jan. 3 Typo. & Embossed

U632 U177 32c **greenish blue & blue** .65 .30
Entire .75 .40
Entire, 1st day cancel, Williamsburg, PA 1.25
a. Greenish blue omitted *120.00*
Entire *400.00*
b. Blue ("USA 32") omitted 90.00
Entire 200.00
c. All colors omitted, entire —

First day cancellation was applied to 54,102 of Nos. U632, UX198.

A colorless embossed design is present on No. U632c.

See No. U638.

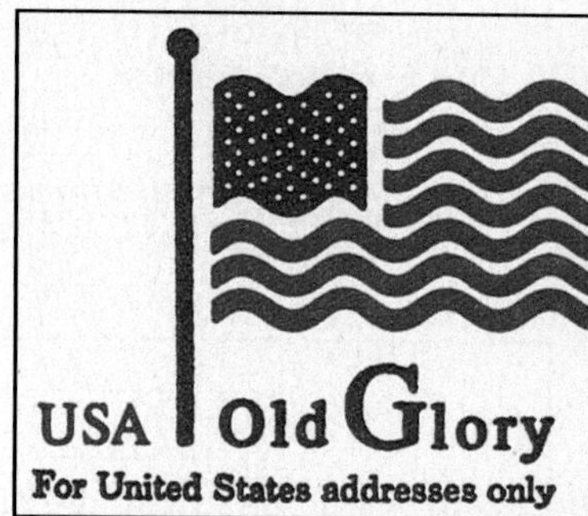

Design sizes: 49x38mm (#U633), 53x44mm (U634). Stamp and design continue on back of envelope.

1995 Typo.

U633 U178 (32c) **blue & red** 1.25 2.00
Entire, #6¾ 1.75 3.00
U634 U178 (32c) **blue & red** 1.25 2.00
Entire, #10 1.75 3.00
a. Red & tagging omitted, entire *325.00*
b. Blue omitted, entire *325.00*

Originally, Nos. U633-U634 were only available through the Philatelic Fullfillment Center after their announcement 1/12/95. Envelopes submitted for first day cancels received a 12/13/94 cancel, even though they were not available on that date.

U179

Design size: 58x25mm. Stamp and design continue on back of envelope.

Designed by Douglas Smith.

1995, Mar. 10 Typo.
Precanceled, Untagged

U635 U179 (5c) **green & red brown** .40
Entire .55 1.00
Entire, 1st day cancel, State College, PA 1.25

Graphic Eagle — U180

Designed by Uldis Purins.

1995, Mar. 10 Typo.
Precanceled, Untagged

U636 U180 (10c) **dark carmine & blue** 1.50
Entire .40 *10.00*
Entire, 1st day cancel, State College, PA 1.25

Issued only in No. 10 size.

Spiral Heart — U181

Designed by Uldis Purins.

1995, May 12 Typo.

U637 U181 32c **red,** *light blue* .65 .30
Entire .75 2.00
Entire, 1st day cancel, Lakeville, PA 1.25
a. Red omitted, entire *200.00*

On No. U637a, the red "RECYCLED" and recycling symbol appear on the bottom backflap.

Liberty Bell Type

1995, May 16 Typo.

U638 U177 32c **greenish blue & blue** .70 .30
Entire .80 .35
Entire, 1st day cancel, Washington, DC 1.25
a. Greenish blue omitted, entire *175.00*

No. U638 was printed on security paper and was issued only in No. 9 size.

Space Shuttle Type of 1989

Designed by Richard Sheaff.

1995, Sept. 22 Typo. *Die Cut*

U639 U163 32c **carmine rose** .75 .35
Entire .85 2.00
Entire, 1st day cancel, Milwaukee, WI 1.25

A hologram, visible through the die cut window to the right of "USA 32," is affixed to the inside of the envelope. No. U639 was issued only in No. 10 size.

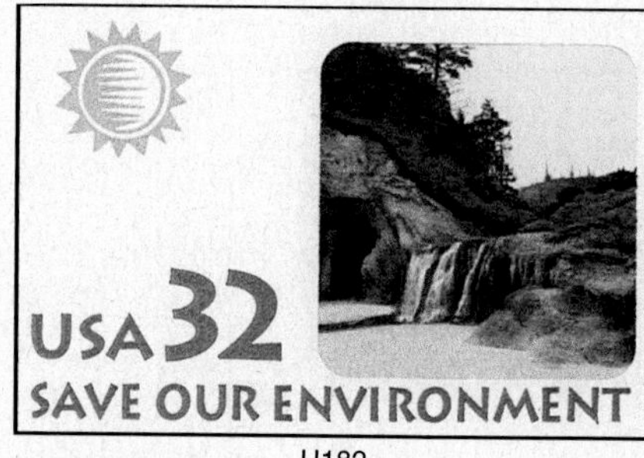

U182

Designed by Richard Sheaff.

1996, Apr. 20 Typo. & Litho. *Die Cut*

U640 U182 32c **multicolored** .70 .30
Entire .80 2.00
Entire, 1st day cancel, Chicago, IL *(9,921)* 1.25

The lithographed vignette, visible through the die cut window to the right of "USA 32c," is affixed to the inside of the envelope. Issued only in the No. 10 size.

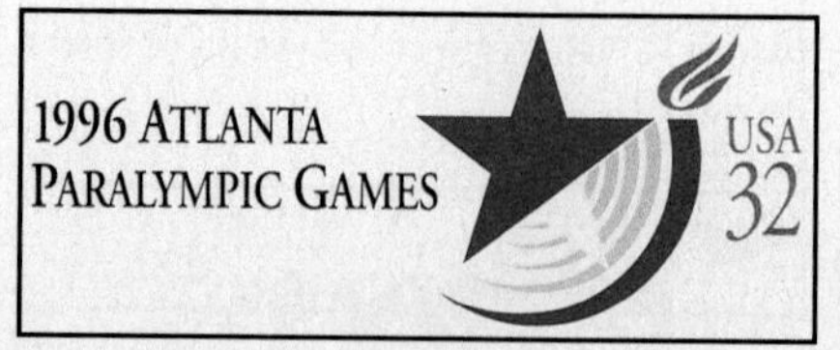

U183

Designed by Brad Copeland. Illustration reduced.

1996, May 2

U641 U183 32c **multicolored** .70 .30
Entire .80 3.00
Entire, 1st day cancel, Washington, DC 1.25
a. Blue & red omitted, entire *260.00*

b. Blue & gold omitted, entire *550.00*
c. Red omitted, entire *260.00*
d. Black & red omitted, entire *450.00*
e. Blue omitted, entire *300.00*

U184

U184a

Designed by Richard Sheaff.

1999, Jan. 11 **Typo. & Embossed**

U642 U184 33c **yellow, blue & red,** tagging bar to left of design 1.00 .30
Entire 1.50 .40
Entire, 1st day cancel, Washington, DC 1.25
a. Tagging bar to right of design 7.50 3.00
Entire 10.00 5.00
b. As "a," blue omitted, entire *200.00*
c. As "a," yellow omitted, entire *175.00*
d. As "a," yellow and blue omitted, entire *175.00*
e. As "a," blue and red omitted, entire *175.00*
f. As "a," all colors omitted, entire *175.00*
g. As No. U642, red omitted, entire *450.00*
h. As No. U642, yellow and red omitted, entire —
i. As No. U642, blue and red omitted, entire —
j. Tagging omitted —

Earliest documented use of No. U642a, 10/12/99.

On No. U642f, the distinctive tagging bar is present. Expertization is required.

1999, Jan. 11 **Typo.**

U643 U184a 33c **blue & red** 1.00 .30
Entire 1.50 .40
Entire, 1st day cancel, Washington, DC 1.25
a. Tagging bar to right of design 10.00 5.00
Entire 15.00 9.00

Issued only in No. 9 size.

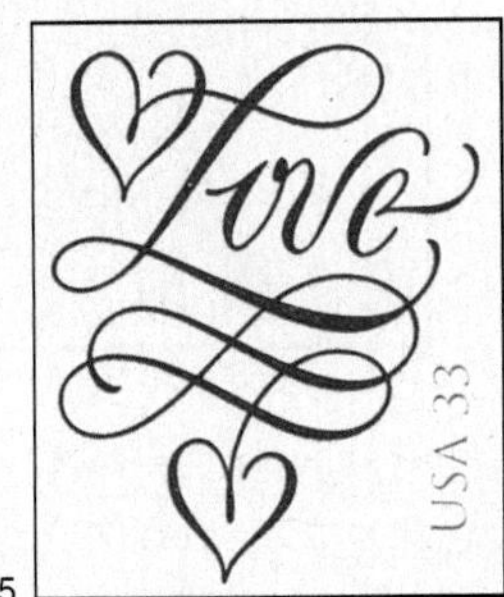

U185

Designed by Julian Waters.

1999, Jan. 28 **Litho.**

U644 U185 33c **violet** .65 .30
Entire .80 2.00
Entire, 1st day cancel, Loveland, CO 1.25
a. Tagging bar to right of design .65 .30
Entire .80 .40

Lincoln — U186

Designed by Richard Sheaff.

1999, June 5 **Typo. & Litho.**

U645 U186 33c **blue & black** .65 .30
Entire .80 .40
Entire, 1st day cancel, Springfield, IL 1.25

Eagle — U187

Designed by Michael Doret.

2001, Jan. 7 **Typo.**

U646 U187 34c **blue gray & gray** .70 .30
Entire .85 .40
Entire, 1st day cancel, Washington, DC 1.25
a. Blue gray omitted 175.00
Entire 225.00
b. Gray omitted —

Many color shades known.

All No. U646 were printed on recycled paper. It was also produced using a different blue-gray recycled paper starting in 2002, and valued much higher thus by specialists.

Lovebirds U188

Designed by Robert Brangwynne.

2001, Feb. 14 **Litho.**

U647 U188 34c **rose & dull violet** .70 .30
Entire .85 2.00
Entire, 1st day cancel, Lovejoy, GA 1.25

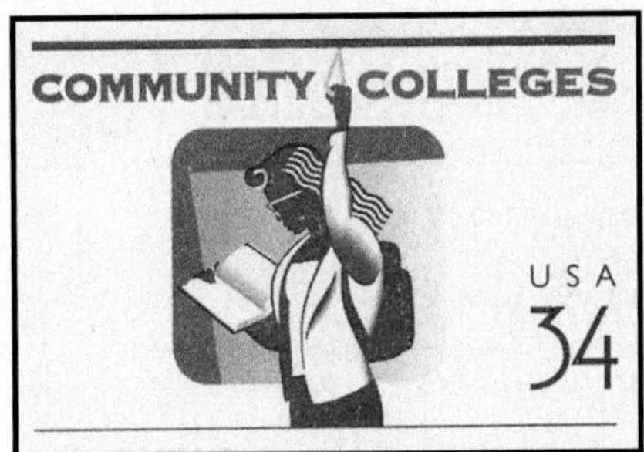

Community Colleges, Cent. — U189

Designed by Howard Paine.

2001, Feb. 20 **Typo.**

U648 U189 34c **dark blue & orange brown** .70 .30
Entire .85 2.00
Entire, 1st day cancel, Joliet, IL 1.25

Ribbon Star — U190

Designed by Terrence W. McCaffrey.

2002, June 7 **Typo.**

U649 U190 37c **red, blue & gray** .75 .35
Entire .90 .45
Entire, 1st day cancel, Washington, DC 1.25
Entire, 1st day cancel, any other city 1.25
a. Gray omitted, entire —
b. Blue and gray omitted, entire —

All No. U649 were printed on recycled paper. It was also produced using a different blue-gray recycled paper starting in 2002.

Type of 1995 Inscribed "USA / Presorted / Standard"

Designed by Uldis Purins.

2002, Aug. 8 **Typo.** **Untagged**

Precanceled

U650 U180 (10c) **dark carmine & blue** .25
Entire 1.75 *30.00*
Entire, 1st day cancel, Washington, DC 1.25

Issued only in No. 10 size.

Nurturing Love — U191

Designed by Craig Frazier.

2003, Jan. 25 **Typo.**

U651 U191 37c **olive green & yellow orange** .80 .35
Entire .95 3.00
Entire, 1st day cancel, Tucson, AZ 1.25
a. Tagging omitted, entire 60.00

Jefferson Memorial Type

Designed by Derry Noyes.

2003, Dec. 29 **Typo.**

U652 A2818 $3.85 **multicolored** 12.50 6.25
Entire 17.00 9.00
Entire, 1st day cancel, Washington, DC 5.75

On No. U652, the stamp indicia is printed on the flap of the envelope.

Disney Type of 2004

Designed by David Pacheco.

2004, June 23 **Letter Sheet** **Litho.**

U653 A2949 37c **multicolored** 2.50 2.25
Entire 2.50 2.50
Entire, 1st day cancel, Anaheim, CA 2.50
U654 A2950 37c **multicolored** 2.50 2.25
Entire 2.50 2.50
Entire, 1st day cancel, Anaheim, CA 2.50
U655 A2951 37c **multicolored** 2.50 2.25
Entire 2.50 2.50
Entire, 1st day cancel, Anaheim, CA 2.50
a. All color missing on reverse, entire —
U656 A2952 37c **multicolored** 2.50 2.25
Entire 2.50 2.50
Entire, 1st day cancel, Anaheim, CA 2.50
a. Booklet of 12 letter sheets, 3 each #U653-U656 30.00

No. U656a sold for $14.95.

White Lilacs and Pink Roses Type of 2004

Designed by Richard Sheaff.

2005, Mar. 3 **Letter Sheet** **Litho.**

U657 A2931 37c **multicolored** 3.00 2.50
First day cancel, New York, NY 2.50

No. U657 was sold in pads of 12 for $14.95.

Computer-generated Study of an X-Plane — U192

2006, Jan. 5 **Typo.** **Unwmk.**

U658 U192 $4.05 **multicolored** 10.00 9.00
Entire 12.00 10.00
Entire, 1st day cancel, Kansas City, MO 6.50

Benjamin Franklin — U193

Designed by Richard Sheaff.

2006, Jan. 9 **Typo.** **Unwmk.**

U659 U193 39c **blue green & black** .80 .40
Entire 1.00 .50
Entire, 1st day cancel, Washington, DC 1.25
Entire, 1st day cancel, any other city 1.25
a. All color omitted, entire —
b. Tagging omitted, entire 45.00

On No. 659a, the tagging bar and the blue green printing on the reverse are present.

Air Force One — U194

Designed by Phil Jordan.

2007, May 6 **Typo.** **Unwmk.**

U660 U194 $4.60 **multicolored** 12.50 10.00
Entire 15.00 12.50
Entire, 1st day cancel, Kansas City, MO 9.25

No. U660 was sold only in packs of 5, 10 or 25 envelopes.

Marine One — U195

Designed by Phil Jordan.

2007, May 6 **Typo.** **Unwmk.**

U661 U195 $16.25 **multicolored** 35.00 20.00
Entire 40.00 30.00
Entire, 1st day cancel, Kansas City, MO 33.00

No. U661 was sold only in packs of three envelopes, with each envelope having a different Star Wars character (Darth Vader, Yoda, or Obi-wan Kenobi) on the back of the envelope. Values for entires are for any envelope back.

Horses — U196

Illustration reduced. Designed by Tom Engeman.

2007, May 12 **Typo.** **Unwmk.**

U662 U196 41c **reddish brown & black** .85 .40
Entire 1.00 2.00
Entire, 1st day cancel, Washington, DC 2.10

Elk U197

Designed by Carl T. Herrman.

2008, May 2 **Typo.** **Unwmk.**

U663 U197 42c **green & black**, tagging bar 20mm tall, Ashton-Potter printing .85 .40
Entire, Ashton-Potter printing 1.00 2.00
Entire, 1st day cancel, Washington, DC 2.10
a. Tagging bar 26mm tall, Westvaco printing .85 .40
Entire, Westvaco printing 1.00 .50
Entire, 1st day cancel, Washington, DC 2.10
b. Tagging bar 19mm tall, *Aug. 16* .85 .40
Entire, Ashton-Potter litho. printing 1.00 .50
Entire, Ashton-Potter litho. printing, 1st day cancel, Hartford, CT 2.10

No. U663 was printed by National Envelope for Ashton-Potter (USA) Ltd. No. U663a was printed by Westvaco. Envelopes printed by Westvaco have copyright and recycled content text, found on the envelope's back, in black. These features are in green on Ashton-Potter envelopes. All Westvaco envelopes have pointed flaps, while the Ashton-Potter envelopes have flaps with curved ends.

No. U663b was printed by Ashton-Potter (USA) Ltd. The lithographed impressions of No. U663b are slightly sharper (some tree branches are slightly thinner and more distinct) than the typographed impressions on Nos. U663 and U663a, but because of the nature of the design are nonetheless difficult to distinguish without measuring the tagging bar. Entires of No. U663b have the recycling emblem on the back of the envelope at the right side of the paper content statement. On No. U663 the recycling emblem is in the lower left corner.

Mount Rushmore U198

Designed by Carl T. Herrman.

2008, May 12 **Typo.** **Unwmk.**

U664 U198 $4.80 **multicolored** 12.50 10.00
Entire 15.00 12.50
Entire, 1st day cancel, Kansas City, MO 9.75

No. U664 was sold only in packs of 5, 10 or 25 envelopes.

Sunflower Type of 2008

Designed by Derry Noyes.

Letter Sheet

2008, Aug. 15 **Litho.** **Unwmk.**

U665 A3309 42c **multicolored** 4.00 3.00
Entire, 1st day cancel, Hartford, CT 4.25

No. U665 was sold in packs of 10 for $14.95.

Redwood Forest Type of 2009

Designed by Carl T. Herrman.

2009, Jan. 16 **Typo.** **Unwmk.**

U666 A3332 $4.95 **multicolored** 10.00 7.50
Entire 10.00 7.50
Entire, 1st day cancel, Kansas City, MO 10.00

No. U666 was sold only in packs of 5.

Liberty Bell U199

Designed by Terrence W. McCaffrey.

2009-11 **Litho.** **Unwmk.**

U667 U199 (44c) **multicolored**, *May 11* .90 .90
Entire 1.10 2.00
Entire, 1st day cancel, Kansas City, MO 2.40
a. As #U667, typographed, *Aug. 18* .90 .45
Typographed, entire 1.10 .55
#U667a, entire, 1st day cancel, Kansas City, MO 2.40
b. As #U667, dated "2011," "FOREVER" multicolored (with color dots), *Jan. 3, 2011* .90 .90
Entire 1.10 1.10
Entire, 1st day cancel, Kansas City, MO 2.40
c. As #U667b, "FOREVER" in brown (solid color), *Jan. 3, 2011* .90 .90
Entire 1.10 1.10
Entire, 1st day cancel, Kansas City, MO 2.40

No. U667 had a franking value of 44c on the day of issue and will be valid for the one ounce first class postage rate after any new rates go into effect. The envelope was created primarily for customers desiring a printed return address on the envelope, and was not sold individually. Water-activated gum envelopes sold in boxes of 50 for $26.80 and boxes of 500 for $247. Self-adhesive envelopes sold in boxes of 50 for $31.80 and boxes of 500 for $262. A pack of 18 envelopes containing one example of each of the twelve different envelope styles of No. U667 and the six different self-adhesive envelope styles of No. U668 was sold for the convenience of collectors for $10.92. A similar package was sold in 2010, having examples of Nos. U667 and U668 with a "Cradle to Cradle" recycling emblem added on the backs fo the envelopes.

No. U667a was printed by National Envelope. The size of black dots on No. U667a are much larger than on No. U667, which is most noticeable on the bell fastenings. This also makes the appearance of the bell on No. U667a far grainier than No. U667. The text on the bell, particularly the Roman numeral date, is indistinct and difficult to read even under magnification on No. U667a, but sharper and easier to read on No. U667. The horizontal wood grain lines are distinct on the bell stock on No. U667, but No. U667a has no fine detail of the grain lines.

The typographed version (No. U667a) can also be distinguished from No. U667 by the position of the recycle logo on the back. On the litho. version it is to the right of the recycle text; on the typo. version it is to the left of the text.

Nos. U667 and U667a are dated "2009." The year date is found on the crown of the bell between the fastenings. No. U667b is available in No. 10 window and both regular and window No. 9 (security) and No. 6¾ envelope sizes. No. U667c is only found in the No. 10 regular envelope size only.

Nos. U667b and U667c were reprinted in June 2012 in the No. 10 size without the 'Cradle to Cradle' recycling logo on the back.

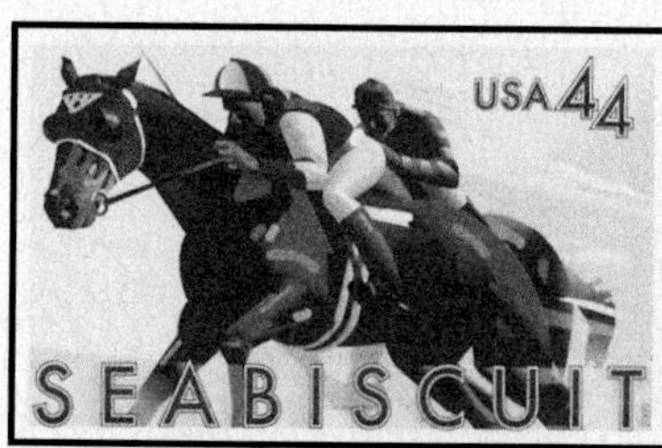

Racehorse Seabiscuit — U200

Designed by John Mattos. Printed by Ashton-Potter (USA) Ltd.

2009, May 11 **Litho.** **Unwmk.**

U668 U200 44c **multicolored** .90 .45
Entire 1.10 1.50
Entire, 1st day cancel, Kansas City, MO 2.40
a. As No. U668, typographed, *June 1* .90 .45
Typographed, entire 1.10 .55
Entire, 1st day cancel, Kansas City, MO 2.40
b. As No. U668, triple impression of black, entire —

No. U668 self-adhesive flap envelopes were not sold individually, but were sold in boxes and packs like No. U667.

No. U668a was printed by National Envelope. The screened blue dots cover the entire area between the "S" and the "C" on No. U668, but appear more random on No. U668a. The pattern of blue dots running towards the shoulder under the head and neck of the horse is long and distinct on No. U668, but barely noticeable, with only a few dots showing, on No. U668a.

See note under No. U667. The third paragraph of that note also applies to Nos. U668 and U668a.

Gulf Coast Lighthouses Type of 2009

Designed by Howard E. Paine.

2009, July 23 **Litho.**

U669 A3354 44c **multicolored** 3.75 3.00
Entire 3.75 3.75
Entire, 1st day cancel, Biloxi, MS 4.25
U670 A3355 44c **multicolored** 3.75 3.00
Entire 3.75 3.75
Entire, 1st day cancel, Biloxi, MS 4.25
U671 A3356 44c **multicolored** 3.75 3.00
Entire 3.75 3.75
Entire, 1st day cancel, Biloxi, MS 4.25
U672 A3357 44c **multicolored** 3.75 3.00
Entire 3.75 3.75
Entire, 1st day cancel, Biloxi, MS 4.25

U673 A3358 44c **multicolored** 3.75 3.00
Entire 3.75 3.75
Entire, 1st day cancel, Biloxi, MS 4.25
Nos. U669-U673 (5) 18.75 15.00

Pack of ten, containing two of each letter sheet, sold for $15.95.

Mackinac Bridge U201

Designed by Carl T. Herrman.

2010, Jan. 4 **Typo.** **Unwmk.**
U674 U201 $4.90 **multicolored** 12.50 10.00
Entire 15.00 12.50
Entire, first day cancel, Kansas City, MO 10.00

No. U674 was sold only in packs of 5.

New River Gorge Bridge, West Virginia U202

Designed by Carl T. Herrman.

2011, Jan. 3 **Typo.** **Unwmk.**
U675 U202 $4.95 **multicolored** 12.50 10.00
Entire 15.00 12.50
Entire, first day cancel, Kansas City, MO 10.00

No. U675 was sold only in packs of 5.

Sunshine Skyway Bridge, Florida U203

Designed by Carl T. Hermann.

2012, Jan. 3 **Typo.** **Unwmk.**
U676 U203 $5.15 **multicolored** 12.50 10.00
Entire 15.00 12.50
Entire, first day cancel, Liberty, MO 10.50

No. U676 was sold only in packs of 5.

Purple Martin U204

Designed by William J. Gicker.

2012, Jan. 23 **Litho.** **Unwmk.**

Design Size: 48x33mm

U677 U204 (45c) **multicolored** 1.50 .50
Entire 2.00 .55
Entire, first day cancel, Mulberry, FL 2.40

Design Size: 50x35mm

U678 U204 (45c) **multicolored** 1.50 .50
Entire 2.00 .55
Entire, first day cancel, Mulberry, FL 2.40

No. U677 was from No. 6¾ size envelopes only. No. U678 was from No. 9 and No. 10 size envelopes.

No. U678 was reprinted in June 2012 without the 'Cradle to Cradle' recycling logo on the back.

Arlington Green Bridge Type of 2013

Designed by Derry Noyes.

2013, Jan. 25 **Typo.** **Unwmk.**
U679 A3612 $5.60 **multicolored** 11.00 8.00
Entire 11.00 7.50
Entire, first day cancel, Norcross, GA 11.00

No. U679 was sold only in packs of 5.

Bank Swallows U205

Designed by William J. Gicker.

2013, Mar. 1 **Litho.** **Unwmk.**

Design Size: 38x35mm

U680 U205 (46c) **multicolored** 1.50 .50
Entire 2.00 2.00
Entire, first day cancel, Sacramento, CA 2.40

Design Size: 41x38mm

U681 U205 (46c) **multicolored** 1.50 .50
Entire 4.00 5.00
Entire, first day cancel, Sacramento, CA 2.40
a. Blurry microprinting —

No. U680 is from No. 6¾ size envelopes only. No. U681 is from No. 9 and No. 10 size envelopes.

Eagle, Shield and Flags — U206

Designed by Richard Sheaff.

2013, Aug. 9 **Litho.** **Unwmk.**
U682 U206 (46c) **multicolored** .95 .50
Entire 1.25 2.00
Entire, first day cancel, Milwaukee, WI 2.40
a. Double impression of magenta, entire —
b. Triple impression of light blue, entire —
c. Blurry microprinting 4.00 5.00
Entire — —

Verrazano-Narrows Bridge Type of 2014

Designed by Phil Jordan.

2014, Mar. 4 **Typo.** **Unwmk.**
U683 A3726 $5.60 **multicolored** 12.50 8.00
Entire 15.00 8.00
Entire, first day cancel, Brooklyn, NY 11.00

No. U683 was sold only in packs of 5, 10 or 25.

Poinsettia — U207

Snowflake — U208

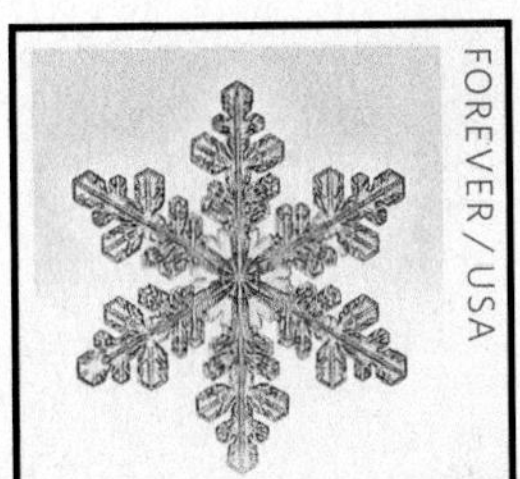

Snowflake — U209

Cardinal — U210

Child Making Snowman — U211

Designed by Ethel Kessler (Nos. U684, U687, U688), Jennifer Arnold (Nos. U685, U686).

2014, Oct. 1 **Litho.** **Unwmk.**
U684 U207 (49c) **multicolored** 2.50 1.50
Entire 3.00 3.00
Entire, first day cancel, Washington, DC 2.25
U685 U208 (49c) **multicolored** 2.50 1.50
Entire 3.00 3.00
Entire, first day cancel, Washington, DC 2.25
U686 U209 (49c) **multicolored** 2.50 1.50
Entire 3.00 3.00
Entire, first day cancel, Washington, DC 2.25
U687 U210 (49c) **multicolored** 2.50 1.50
Entire 3.00 3.00
Entire, first day cancel, Washington, DC 2.25
U688 U211 (49c) **multicolored** 2.50 1.50
Entire 3.00 3.00
Entire, first day cancel, Washington, DC 2.25
Nos. U684-U688 (5) 12.50 7.50

Packs of 10 No. U684 and 10 self-adhesive stickers sold for $9.95. Packs containing 5 each of Nos. U685 and U686 and 10 self-adhesive stickers sold for $9.95. Packs containing 5 each of Nos. U687 and U688 and 10 self-adhesive stickers sold for $9.95. Nos. U684-U688 were available only as No. 10 size envelopes.

Glade Creek Grist Mill Type of 2014

Designed by Derry Noyes.

2015, Jan. 12 Typo. Unwmk.

U689 A3780 $5.75 **multicolored** 11.50 8.25
Entire 11.50 8.25
Entire, first day cancel, Kansas City, MO 11.50

No. U689 was sold only in packs of 5.

Red Water Lily — U212

White Water Lily — U213

Designed by Phil Jordan.

2015, Apr. 17 Litho. Unwmk.

U690 U212 (49c) **multicolored** 2.50 1.75
Entire 3.00 4.00
Entire, first day cancel, New York, NY 3.25
U691 U213 (49c) **multicolored** 2.50 1.75
Entire 3.00 4.00
Entire, first day cancel, New York, NY 3.25

Nos. U690 and U691 were only sold in packets of 10 containing five of each envelope and 10 stickers for $9.95. Nos. U690 and U691 were only available in #10 size with self-adhesive flap.

Forget-me-nots — U214

Designed by Ethel Kessler.

2015, May 18 Litho. Unwmk.

U692 U214 (49c) **multicolored** 2.50 1.75
Entire 3.00 4.00
Entire, first day cancel, Anaheim, CA 3.25

No. U692 was sold only in packets of 10 + 10 stickers for $9.95. It was only available in #10 size with self-adhesive flap.

La Cueva del Indio Type of 2016

Designed by Greg Breeding.

2016, Jan. 17 Typo. Unwmk.

U693 A3875 $6.45 **multicolored** 13.00 9.50
Entire 13.00 9.50
Entire, first day cancel, Washington, DC 13.00

No. U693 was sold only in packs of 5.

Northern Cardinal U215

Designed by Derry Noyes.

2016, Nov. 3 Litho. Unwmk.

U694 U215 (47c) **multicolored** 1.75 1.75
Entire 2.00 4.00

No. U694 was sold only in packets of 12 + 12 stickers for $9.95. It was only available in #10 size with self-adhesive flap. Packets of No. U694 were sold in post offices in Ohio and Puerto Rico (and perhaps elsewhere) in late December, prior to the acknowledgment of the existence of the envelope by USPS Stamp Services. The packets were not offered for sale by USPS Stamp Fulfillment Services until Jan. 4, 2017. In late January, the packet was made available for direct order on the USPS Stamp Fulfillment Services website, which then noted that the day of issue was Jan. 8, 2017, even though the packets could be ordered on Jan. 4. The official first day of issue was announced as Nov. 3, 2016 in the Feb. 16, 2017 *Postal Bulletin*, but no indication was given that any first day cancels would be made available for this issue. The earliest documented use is postmarked Jan. 3, 2017.

Lili'uokalani Gardens Type of 2017

Designed by Greg Breeding.

2017, Jan. 22 Typo. Unwmk.

U695 A3986 $6.65 **multicolored** 13.50 9.75
Entire 13.50 9.75
Entire, first day cancel, Kansas City, MO 13.50

No. U695 was sold only in packs of 5.

Barn Swallows — U216

Designed by William J. Gicker.

2017, Mar. 3 Litho. Unwmk.

U696 U216 (49c) **multicolored** 1.25 .50
Entire 1.25 .60
Entire, first day cancel, Reno, NV 2.50
a. Blurry microprinting 4.00 5.00
Entire — —

Byodo-In Temple Type of 2018

Designed by Greg Breeding.

2018, Jan. 21 Typo. Unwmk.

U697 A4096 $6.70 **multicolored** 13.50 9.75
Entire 13.50 9.75
Entire, first day cancel, Kansas City, MO 13.50

No. U697 was sold only in packs of 5.

Joshua Tree Type of 2019

Designed by Greg Breeding.

2019, Jan. 27 Typo. Unwmk.

U698 A4191 $7.35 **multicolored** 15.00 10.00
Entire 15.00 10.00
Entire, first day cancel, Kansas City, MO 15.00

No. U698 was sold only in packs of 5 or 10.

Big Bend National Park Type of 2020

Designed by Greg Breeding.

2020, Jan. 18 Typo. Unwmk.

U699 A4268 $7.75 **multicolored** 15.50 10.50
Entire 15.50 10.50
Entire, first day cancel, Big Bend National Park, TX 15.50

No. U699 was sold only in packs of 5 or 10.

Flag and Stars — U217

Designed by Kit Hinrichs.

2020, June 15 Litho. Unwmk.

U700 U217 (55c) **multicolored** 1.40 .50
Entire 1.40 .60
Entire, first day cancel, Liberty, MO 2.60
a. Blurry microprinting —
Entire — —

Castillo de San Marcos Type of 2021

Designed by Greg Breeding.

2021, Jan. 24 Typo. Unwmk.

U701 A4388 $7.95 **multicolored** 16.00 11.00
Entire 16.00 11.00
Entire, first day cancel, St. Augustine, FL 16.00

No. U701 was sold only in packs of 5, 10 or 25.

AIR POST STAMPED ENVELOPES AND AIR LETTER SHEETS

All envelopes have carmine and blue borders, unless noted. There are seven types of borders:

Carmine Diamond in Upper Right Corner.

a — Diamonds measure 9 to 10mm paralled to edge of envelope and 11 to 12mm along oblique side (with top flap open). Sizes 5 and 13 only.

b — Like "a" except diamonds measure 7 to 8mm along oblique side (with top flap open). Sizes 5 and 13 only.

c — Diamonds measure 11 to 12mm parallel to edge of envelope. Size 8 only.

Blue Diamond in Upper Right Corner.

d — Lower points of top row of diamonds point to left. Size 8 only.

e — Lower points of top row of diamonds point to right. Size 8 only.

Diamonds Omitted in Upper Right Corner (1965 Onward)

f — Blue diamond above at left of stamp.

g — Red diamond above at left of stamp.

UC1

5c — Vertical rudder is not semi-circular but slopes down to the left. The tail of the plane projects into the G of POSTAGE. Border types a, b, c, d and e.

UC2

Die 2 (5c and 8c): Vertical rudder is semi-circular. The tail of the plane touches but does not project into the G of POSTAGE. Border types b, d, and e for the 5c; b and d for the 8c.

Die 2 (6c) — Same as UC2 except three types of numeral.
2a — The numeral "6" is 6½mm wide.
2b — The numeral "6" is 6mm wide.
2c — The numeral "6" is 5½mm wide.

Eleven working dies were used in printing the 6c. On each, the numeral "6" was engraved by hand, producing several variations in position, size and thickness.

Nos. UC1 and UC2 occur with varying size blue blobs, caused by a shallow printing die. They are not constant.

Border types b and d for dies 2a and 2b; also without border (June 1944 to Sept. 1945) for dies 2a, 2b and 2c.

Die 3 (6c): Vertical rudder leans forward. S closer to O than to T of POSTAGE. E of POSTAGE has short center bar. Border types b and d, also without border.

No. UC1 with 1933 and 1937 watermarks and No. UC2 with 1933 watermark were issued in Puerto Rico.

No. UC1 in blue black, with 1925 watermark #26 and border type a, is a proof.

1929-44

UC1 UC1 5c **blue**, *Jan. 12, 1929* 3.00 2.00
Entire, border a or b 4.50 2.25
Entire, border c, d or e 8.25 5.75
First day cancel, border a, entire 40.00
1933 wmk. #33, border d, entire *750.00 750.00*
1933 wmk. #33, border b, entire — —
1937 wmk. #36, border d, entire — *2,500.*

1937 wmk. #36, border b, entire — —
Bicolored border omitted, entire 1,200.
a. Orange and blue border, type b 375.00 *450.00*
UC2 UC2 5c **blue,** die 2 9.00 5.00
Entire, border b 12.00 6.50
Entire, border e 18.00 12.50
1929 wmk. #28, border d, entire — *1,500.*
1933 wmk. #33, border b, entire *650.00* —
1933 wmk. #33, border d, entire 325.00 —
UC3 UC2 6c **orange,** die 2a, *July 1, 1934* 1.25 .40
Entire, bicolored border 1.50 .60
Entire, without border 2.25 1.25
Entire, 1st day cancel 14.00
a. With added impression of 3c purple (#U436a), entire without border *4,000.*
b. Double impression of indicium, entire, with bicolored border —
UC4 UC2 6c **orange,** die 2b ('42) 3.00 2.00
Entire, without border 4.50 2.50
Entire, bicolored border, 1941 wmk. #39 60.00 22.00
UC5 UC2 6c **orange,** die 2c ('44) .70 .30
Entire, without border .95 .45
UC6 UC2 6c **orange,** die 3 ('42) 1.00 .35
Entire, bicolored border 1.50 .75
Entire, without border 2.50 .90
Entire, carmine of border omitted *4,000.*
a. 6c orange, *blue,* die 3 (error) Entire, without border *15,000.* *10,000.*
b. Double impression, entire *400.00*
UC7 UC2 8c **olive green,** die 2, *Sept. 26, 1932* 10.00 3.50
Entire, bicolored border 15.00 15.00
Entire, 1st day cancel 11.00

Surcharged in Black on Envelopes Indicated by Number in Parenthesis

1945
UC8 U93 6c on 2c **carmine** (U429, die 1) 1.25 .65
Entire 1.60 1.00
a. On U429f, die 7 2.25 1.50
Entire 3.00 2.00
b. On U429g, die 8 1.90 1.10
Entire 3.00 1.75
c. On U429h, die 9 8.00 7.50
Entire 15.00 11.00
d. 6c on 1c green (error) (U420) *1,750.*
Entire *2,500.*
e. 6c on 3c dk violet (error) (U436a) *2,000.*
Entire *4,000.*
f. 6c on 3c dk violet (error), *amber* (U437a) *3,000.*
Entire *3,500.*
g. 6c on 3c violet (error) (U526) *3,000.*
Entire *6,500.*
UC9 U95 6c on 2c **carmine** (U525) 40.00 35.00
Entire 80.00 45.00

Ten surcharge varieties are found on Nos. UC8-UC9.

Surcharged in Black on 6c Air Post Envelopes without borders

1946
UC10 UC2 5c on 6c **orange,** die 2a 2.75 1.50
Entire 5.50 2.50
First day of rate, *Oct. 1, 1946,* entire 100.00
a. Double surcharge 75.00
UC11 UC2 5c on 6c **orange,** die 2b 8.00 5.50
Entire 11.00 7.00
First day of rate, *Oct. 1, 1946,* entire 150.00
UC12 UC2 5c on 6c **orange,** die 2c .75 .50
Entire 1.25 .60
First day of rate, *Oct. 1, 1946,* entire 75.00
a. Double surcharge 75.00 *900.00*
UC13 UC2 5c on 6c **orange,** die 3 .70 .60
Entire .90 .75
First day of rate, *Oct. 1, 1946,* entire 75.00
a. Double surcharge 75.00 50.00
c. Double surcharge, one on reverse —
UC13B U93 5c on 6c (UC8a), entire —
First day of rate, *Oct. 1, 1946,* entire —

The 6c borderless envelopes and the revalued envelopes were issued primarily for use to and from members of the armed forces. The 5c rate came into effect Oct. 1, 1946.

Ten surcharge varieties are found on Nos. UC10-UC13.

DC-4 Skymaster UC3

Envelopes with borders types b and d.

Die 1 — The end of the wing at the right is a smooth curve. The juncture of the front end of the plane and the engine forms an acute angle. The first T of STATES and the E's of UNITED STATES lean to the left.

Die 2 — The end of the wing at the right is a straight line. The juncture of the front end of the plane and the engine is wide open. The first T of STATES and the E's of UNITED STATES lean to the right.

1946
UC14 UC3 5c **carmine,** die 1, *Sept. 25, 1946* .75 .25
Entire, bicolored border 1.00 .40
Entire, 1st day cancel 1.50
Entire, bicolored border omitted *2,500.*
UC15 UC3 5c **carmine,** die 2 .75 .25
Entire, bicolored border 1.00 .40

No. UC14, printed on flat bed press, measures 21½mm high. No. UC15, printed on rotary press, measures 22mm high. See No. UC18.

DC-4 Skymaster — UC4

1947-55 **Typographed, Without Embossing**
Letter Sheets for Foreign Postage

UC16 UC4 10c **bright red,** *pale blue,* "Air Letter" on face, 2-line inscription on back, entire 8.50 7.00
Entire, 1st day cancel, *Apr. 29, 1947* 2.00
Die cutting reversed, unfolded entire 150.00
e. Blue omitted, entire 400.00
f. Overlay omitted front & back, entire *100.00*
g. Overlay omitted from front only, entire *500.00*
UC16a UC4 10c **bright red,** *pale blue, Sept. 1951,* "Air Letter" on face, 4-line inscription on back, entire 17.50 10.00
Die cutting reversed, entire 400.00
b. 10c **chocolate,** *pale blue,* entire 450.00
UC16c UC4 10c **bright red,** *pale blue, Nov. 1953,* "Air Letter" and "Aerogramme" on face, 4-line inscription on back, entire 45.00 12.50
Die cutting reversed, entire 150.00
UC16d UC4 10c **bright red,** *pale blue, 1955,* "Air Letter" and "Aerogramme" on face, 3-line inscription on back, entire 9.00 8.00
Die cutting reversed, entire 100.00
Dark blue (inscriptions & border diamonds) omitted *2,000.*
Die cutting omitted, folded entire *90.00*

Printed on protective tinted paper containing colorless inscription.

UNITED STATES FOREIGN AIR MAIL multiple, repeated in parallel vertical or horizontal lines.

Postage Stamp Centenary Issue

Centenary of the first postage stamps issued by the United States Government.

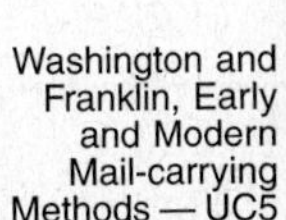
Washington and Franklin, Early and Modern Mail-carrying Methods — UC5

Two dies: Rotary, design measures 22¼mm high; and flat bed press, design 21¾mm high.

1947, May 21 **Embossed**
For Domestic Postage

UC17 UC5 5c **carmine** (rotary) .50 .30
Entire, bicolored border b .60 .40
Entire, 1st day cancel, NY, NY 1.75
a. Flat plate printing .50 .30
Entire .60 .40
Entire, 1st day cancel, NY, NY 1.25

Type of 1946

Type I: 6's lean to right.
Type II: 6's upright.

1950 , Sept. 22
UC18 UC3 6c **carmine,** type I .75 .25
Entire, bicolored border .85 .30
Entire, 1st day cancel, Philadelphia 1.00
a. Type II .90 .25
Entire 1.20 .30

Several other types differ slightly from the two listed.

Nos. UC14, UC15, UC18 Surcharged in Red Left of Stamp

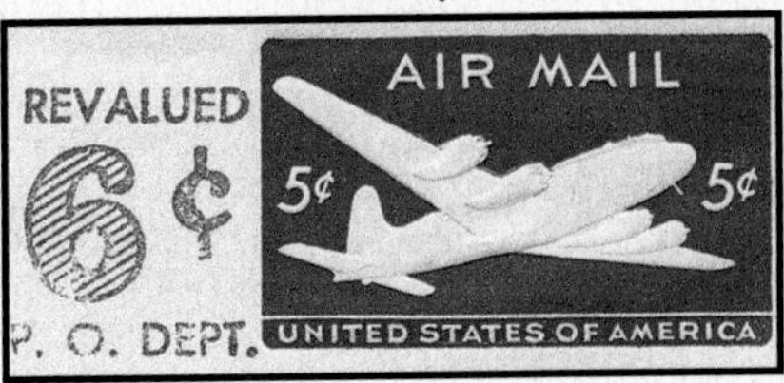

1951
UC19 UC3 6c on 5c **carmine,** die 1 .85 1.50
Entire 1.25 *1.75*
a. Surcharge inverted at lower left, entire —
UC20 UC3 6c on 5c **carmine,** die 2 .85 1.50
Entire 1.25 1.75
a. 6c on 6c **carmine** (error) entire *1,500.*
b. Double surcharge *975.00* —

To qualify as No. UC20b, both surcharges must be to the left of the indicia.

Nos. UC14-UC15 Surcharged in Red at Left of Stamp

1952
UC21 UC3 6c on 5c **carmine,** die 1 25.00 20.00
Entire 35.00 25.00
a. Double surcharge, entire *600.00*
UC22 UC3 6c on 5c **carmine,** die 2, *Aug. 29, 1952* 3.75 2.50
Entire 9.00 4.25
Entire, 1st day cancel, Norfolk, Va. 25.00
a. Double surcharge 250.00
b. Triple surcharge, entire 275.00

To qualify as Nos. UC22a or UC22b, all surcharges must be to the left of the indicia.

No. UC17 Surcharged in Red

UC23 UC5 6c on 5c **carmine** *850.*
Entire *1,250.*

The 6c on 4c black (No. U440) is believed to be a favor printing.

Fifth International Philatelic Exhibition Issue

FIPEX, the Fifth International Philatelic Exhibition, New York, N.Y., Apr. 28-May 6, 1956.

Eagle in Flight — UC6

1956, May 2

UC25 UC6 6c **red** .75 .50
Entire 1.00 .80
Entire, 1st day cancel, New York, N.Y. *(363,239)* 1.25

Two types exist, differing slightly in the clouds at top.

Skymaster Type of 1946

1958, July 31

UC26 UC3 7c **blue** .65 .50
Entire 1.00 .55
Entire, 1st day cancel, Dayton, O. *(143,428)* 1.00

Nos. UC3-UC5, UC18 and UC25 Surcharged in Green at Left of Stamp

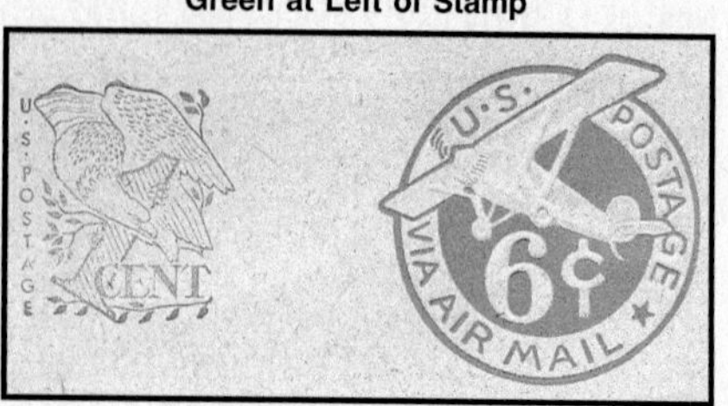

1958

UC27 UC2 6c + 1c **orange,** die 2a 250.00 *300.00*
Entire, without border 2.50 *600.00*
Entire, with border 8,000.
UC28 UC2 6c + 1c **orange,** die 2b 65.00 80.00
Entire, without border 100.00 *250.00*
UC29 UC2 6c + 1c **orange,** die 2c 30.00 55.00
Entire 165.00 110.00
UC30 UC3 6c + 1c **carmine,** type I 1.00 .50
Entire 1.25 .65
a. Type II 1.00 .50
Entire 1.25 .65
UC31 UC6 6c + 1c **red** 1.00 .50
Entire 1.40 .85

Jet Airliner — UC7

Type I: Back inscription in 3 lines.
Type II: Back inscription in 2 lines.

Letter Sheet for Foreign Postage

1958-59 Typographed, Without Embossing

UC32 UC7 10c **blue & red,** *blue,* II, *May, 1959,* entire 6.00 5.00
b. Red omitted, II, entire *625.00*
c. Blue omitted, II, entire *600.00*
UC32a UC7 10c **blue & red,** *blue,* I, *Sept. 12, 1958,* entire 10.00 5.00
Entire, 1st day cancel, St. Louis, Mo. *(92,400)* 1.25
Die cutting reversed, entire 75.00
d. Red omitted, I, entire *700.00*

Silhouette of Jet Airliner — UC8

1958, Nov. 21 Embossed

UC33 UC8 7c **blue** .60 .25
Entire .70 .30
Entire, 1st day cancel, New York, N.Y. *(208,980)* 1.00

1960, Aug. 18

UC34 UC8 7c **carmine** .60 .25
Entire .70 .30
Entire, 1st day cancel, Portland, Ore. *(196,851)* 1.00

Jet Airliner and Globe — UC9

Letter Sheet for Foreign Postage

Typographed, Without Embossing

1961, June 16

UC35 UC9 11c **red & blue,** *blue,* entire 3.00 3.50
Entire, 1st day cancel, Johnstown, Pa. *(163,460)* 1.00
Die cutting reversed, entire 35.00
a. Red omitted, entire *750.00*
b. Blue omitted, entire *950.00*

Jet Airliner — UC10

1962, Nov. 17 Embossed

UC36 UC10 8c **red** .55 .25
Entire .75 .30
Entire, 1st day cancel, Chantilly, Va. *(194,810)* 1.00

Jet Airliner — UC11

1965-67

UC37 UC11 8c **red,** *Jan. 7* .45 .25
Entire, border "f" .60 .30
Entire, border "g" *22.50*
Entire, 1st day cancel, Chicago, Ill. *(226,178)* 1.00
a. Tagged, *Aug. 15, 1967* 3.50 .30
Entire 6.00 .75
Tagged, 1st day cancel 3.50

No. UC37a has a 8x24mm panel at left of stamp that glows orange red under ultraviolet light.

Pres. John F. Kennedy and Jet Plane UC12

Letter Sheets for Foreign Postage

Typographed, Without Embossing

1965, May 29

UC38 UC12 11c **red & dark blue,** *blue,* entire 3.75 4.00
Entire, 1st day cancel, Boston, Mass. *(337,422)* 1.50
Die cutting reversed, entire 40.00

1967, May 29

UC39 UC12 13c **red & dark blue,** *blue,* entire 3.25 4.00
Entire, 1st day cancel, Chicago, Ill. *(211,387)* 1.50
Die cutting reversed, entire *100.00*
a. Red omitted, entire *600.00*
b. Dark blue omitted, entire *500.00*

Jet Liner — UC13

Designed by Robert J. Jones.

1968, Jan. 8 Tagged Embossed

UC40 UC13 10c **red** .50 .25
Entire .80 .25
Entire, 1st day cancel, Chicago, Ill. *(157,553)* 1.00

No. UC37 Surcharged in Red at Left of Stamp

1968, Feb. 5

UC41 UC11 8c + 2c **red** .65 .25
Entire 1.00 .50
Entire, 1st day cancel, Washington, D.C. 8.00

Tagging

Envelopes and Letter Sheets from No. UC42 onward are tagged unless otherwise noted.

Human Rights Year Issue

Issued for International Human Rights Year, and to commemorate the 20th anniversary of the United Nations' Declaration of Human Rights.

Globes and Flock of Birds — UC14

Printed by Acrovure Division of Union-Camp Corporation, Englewood, N.J. Designed by Antonio Frasconi.

Letter Sheet for Foreign Postage

1968, Dec. 3 Tagged Photo.

UC42 UC14 13c **gray, brown, orange & black,** *blue,* entire 8.00 7.50
Entire, 1st day cancel, Washington, D.C. *(145,898)* 1.25
Die cutting reversed, entire 75.00
a. Orange omitted, entire *800.00*
b. Brown omitted, entire *375.00*
c. Black omitted, entire *700.00*
d. Gray and black omitted, entire —
e. Tagging omitted, entire 150.00

No. UC42 has a luminescent panel ⅜x1 inch on the right globe. The panel glows orange red under ultraviolet light.

Jet Plane — UC15

Printed by United States Envelope Co., Williamsburg, Pa. Designed by Robert Geissmann.

1971, May 6 Embossed (Plane)

Center Circle Luminescent

UC43 UC15 11c **red & blue** .50 *1.75*
Entire .75 *2.00*
Entire, 1st day cancel, Williamsburg, Pa. *(187,000)* 1.00

Birds in Flight — UC16

Printed by Bureau of Engraving and Printing. Designed by Soren Noring.

Letter Sheet for Foreign Postage

1971 **Tagged** **Photo.**

UC44 UC16 15c **gray, red, white & blue,** *blue,* entire, *May 28* 1.50 *7.50*
Entire, 1st day cancel, Chicago, Ill. *(130,669)* 1.25
Die cutting reversed, entire 30.00
a. "AEROGRAMME" added to inscription, entire, *Dec. 13* 1.50 *7.50*
Entire, 1st day cancel, Philadelphia, Pa. 1.25
Die cutting reversed, entire 30.00
b. As #UC44, red omitted, entire *300.00*
c. As "a," red omitted, entire —

Folding instructions (2 steps) in capitals on No. C44; (4 steps) in upper and lower case on No. UC44a.

On Nos. UC44-UC44a the white rhomboid background of "USA postage 15c" is luminescent. No. UC44 is inscribed: "VIA AIR MAIL-PAR AVION". "postage 15c" is in gray. See No. UC46.

No. UC40 Surcharged in Green at Left of Stamp

1971, June 28 **Embossed**

UC45 UC13 10c + (1c) **red** 1.50 .75
Entire 2.50 *5.00*
Entire, 1st day cancel, Washington, D.C. 8.00

HOT AIR BALLOONING CHAMPIONSHIPS ISSUE

Hot Air Ballooning World Championships, Albuquerque, N.M., Feb. 10-17, 1973.

"usa" Type of 1971

Design: Three balloons and cloud at left in address section; no birds beside stamp. Inscribed "INTERNATIONAL HOT AIR BALLOONING." "postage 15c" in blue.

Printed by Bureau of Engraving and Printing. Designed by Soren Noring (vignette) and Esther Porter (balloons).

Letter Sheet for Foreign Postage

1973, Feb. 10 **Tagged** **Photo.**

UC46 UC16 15c **red, white & blue,** *blue,* entire 1.00 *7.50*
Entire, 1st day cancel, Albuquerque, N.M. *(210,000)* 1.00

Folding instructions as on No. UC44a. See notes after No. UC44.

Bird in Flight — UC17

1973, Dec. 1 **Luminescent Ink**

UC47 UC17 13c **rose red** .30 .25
Entire .40 .25
Entire, 1st day cancel, Memphis, Tenn. *(132,658)* 1.00

Beginning with No. UC48, all listings are letter sheets for foreign postage.

UC18

Printed by the Bureau of Engraving and Printing. Designed by Bill Hyde.

Letter Sheet for Foreign Postage.

1974, Jan. 4 **Tagged** **Photo.**

UC48 UC18 18c **red & blue,** *blue,* entire 1.00 *6.00*
Entire, 1st day cancel, Atlanta, Ga. *(119,615)* 1.00
Die cutting reversed, entire *40.00*
a. Red omitted, entire *200.00*

25TH ANNIVERSARY OF NATO ISSUE

UC19

Design: "NATO" and NATO emblem at left in address section. Printed by Bureau of Engraving and Printing. Designed by Soren Noring.

Letter Sheet for Foreign Postage

1974, Apr. 4 **Tagged** **Photo.**

UC49 UC19 18c **red & blue,** *blue,* entire 1.00 *6.00*
Entire, 1st day cancel, Washington, D.C. 1.00
Die cutting reversed, entire *100.00*

UC20

Printed by Bureau of Engraving and Printing. Designed by Robert Geissmann.

Letter Sheet for Foreign Postage

1976, Jan. 16 **Tagged** **Photo.**

UC50 UC20 22c **red & blue,** *blue,* entire 1.00 *6.00*
Entire, 1st day cancel, Tempe, Ariz. *(118,303)* 1.00
Die cutting reversed, entire 17.50
a. Red color missing due to foldover and die cutting —

UC22

Design (multicolored in bottom left corner) shows discus thrower.

Printed by Bureau of Engraving and Printing. Designed by Robert M. Cunningham.

"USA" — UC21

Printed by Bureau of Engraving and Printing. Designed by Soren Noring.

Letter Sheet for Foreign Postage

1978, Nov. 3 **Tagged** **Photo.**

UC51 UC21 22c **blue,** *blue,* entire 1.00 *3.00*
Entire, 1st day cancel, St. Petersburg, Fla. *(86,099)* 1.00
Die cutting reversed, entire 25.00

22nd OLYMPIC GAMES, MOSCOW, JULY 19-AUG. 3, 1980.

Letter Sheet for Foreign Postage

1979, Dec. 5 **Tagged** **Photo.**

UC52 UC22 22c **red, black & green,** *bluish,* entire 1.50 *6.00*
Entire, 1st day cancel, Bay Shore, N.Y. 1.00

"USA" — UC23

Design (brown on No. UC53, green and brown on No. UC54): lower left, Statue of Liberty. Inscribed "Tour the United States." Folding area shows tourist attractions.

Printed by Bureau of Engraving and Printing.

Designed by Frank J. Waslick.

Letter Sheet for Foreign Postage

1980, Dec. 29 **Tagged** **Photo.**

UC53 UC23 30c **blue, red & brown,** *blue,* entire .85 *6.00*
Entire, 1st day cancel, San Francisco, CA 1.25
Die cutting reversed, entire 20.00
a. Red (30) omitted, entire 70.00

1981, Sept. 21 **Tagged** **Photo.**

UC54 UC23 30c **yellow, magenta, blue & black,** *blue,* entire .65 *6.00*
Entire, 1st day cancel, Honolulu, HI 1.25
Die cutting reversed, entire 20.00

UC24

Design: "Made in USA . . . world's best buys!" on flap, ship, tractor in lower left. Reverse folding area shows chemicals, jet silhouette, wheat, typewriter and computer tape disks. Printed by Bureau of Engraving and Printing.

Designed by Frank J. Waslick.

Letter Sheet for Foreign Postage

1982, Sept. 16 **Tagged** **Photo.**

UC55 UC24 30c **multi,** *blue,* entire .80 *6.00*
Entire, 1st day cancel, Seattle, WA 1.25
Die cutting reversed, entire —

WORLD COMMUNICATIONS YEAR

World Map Showing Locations of Satellite Tracking Stations — UC25

Design: Reverse folding area shows satellite, tracking station.

Printed by Bureau of Engraving and Printing.

Designed by Esther Porter.

Letter Sheet for Foreign Postage

1983, Jan. 7 **Tagged** **Photo.**

UC56 UC25 30c **multi,** *blue,* entire .90 *8.00*
Entire, 1st day cancel, Anaheim, CA 1.25
Die cutting reversed, entire 25.00

1984 OLYMPICS

UC26

Indicia in black, multicolor design of woman equestrian at lower left with montage of competitive events on reverse folding area.
Printed by the Bureau of Engraving & Printing.
Designed by Bob Peak.

Letter Sheet for Foreign Postage

1983, Oct. 14 **Tagged** **Photo.**

UC57 UC26 30c **black & multi,** *light blue,* entire .85 *8.00*
Entire, 1st day cancel, Los Angeles, CA 1.25
Die cutting reversed, entire *45.00*

WEATHER SATELLITES, 25TH ANNIV.

Landsat Infrared and Thermal Mapping Bands UC27

Design: Landsat orbiting the earth at lower left with three Landsat photographs on reverse folding area. Inscribed: "Landsat views the Earth."
Printed by the Bureau of Engraving & Printing.
Designed by Esther Porter.

Letter Sheet for Foreign Postage

1985, Feb. 14 **Tagged** **Photo.**

UC58 UC27 36c **multi,** *blue,* entire 1.25 *12.50*
Entire, 1st day cancel, Goddard Flight Center, MD 1.40
Die cutting reversed, entire 30.00
a. Yellow omitted, entire — —

NATIONAL TOURISM WEEK

Urban Skyline — UC28

Design: Inscribed "Celebrate America" at lower left and "Travel. . . the perfect freedom" on folding area. Skier, Indian chief, cowboy, jazz trumpeter and pilgrims on reverse folding area.
Printed by the Bureau of Engraving & Printing.
Designed by Dennis Luzak.

Letter Sheet for Foreign Postage

1985, May 21 **Tagged** **Photo.**

UC59 UC28 36c **multi,** *blue,* entire 1.25 *12.50*
Entire, 1st day cancel, Washington, DC 1.40
Die cutting reversed, entire 25.00
a. Black omitted, entire *600.00* —

MARK TWAIN AND HALLEY'S COMET

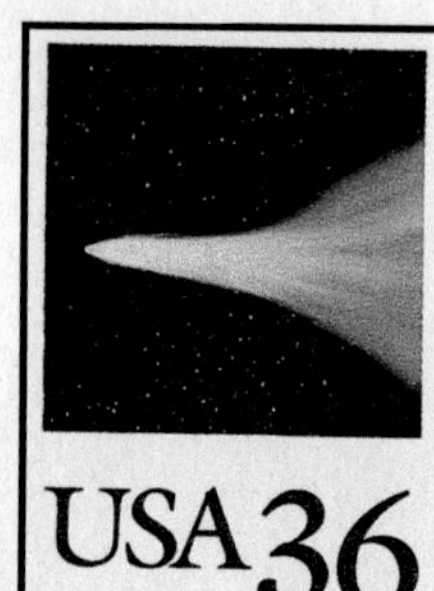

Comet Tail Viewed from Space — UC29

Design: Portrait of Twain at lower left and inscribed "I came in with Halley's Comet in 1835. It is coming again next year, and I expect to go out with it. It will be the greatest disappointment of my life if I don't go out with Halley's Comet." "1835 . Mark Twain . 1910 . Halley's Comet . 1985" and Twain, Huckleberry Finn, steamboat and comet on reverse folding areas.
Printed by the Bureau of Engraving & Printing.
Designed by Dennis Luzak.

Letter Sheet for Foreign Postage

1985, Dec. 4 **Tagged** **Photo.**

UC60 UC29 36c **multi,** entire 2.00 *12.50*
Entire, 1st day cancel, Hannibal, MO 2.00
Die cutting reversed, entire 25.00

UC30

Printed by the Bureau of Engraving & Printing.

Letter Sheet for Foreign Postage

1988, May 9 **Litho.** **Tagged**

UC61 UC30 39c **multi,** entire 1.25 *12.50*
Entire, 1st day cancel, Miami, FL *(27,446)* 1.60
a. Tagging bar to left of design ('89) 1.25 *1.50*

On No. UC61, the tagging bar is between "USA" and "39."

MONTGOMERY BLAIR, POSTMASTER GENERAL 1861-64

Blair and Pres. Abraham Lincoln — UC31

Design: Mail bags and "Free city delivery," "Railway mail service" and "Money order system" at lower left. Globe, locomotive, bust of Blair, UPU emblem and "The Paris conference of 1863, initiated by Postmaster General Blair, led, in 1874, to the founding of the Universal Postal Union" contained on reverse folding area.
Printed by the Bureau of Engraving & Printing.
Designed by Ned Seidler.

Letter Sheet for Foreign Postage

1989, Nov. 20 **Litho.** **Tagged**

UC62 UC31 39c **multicolored,** entire 1.40 *16.00*
Entire, 1st day cancel, Washington, DC 1.75
a. Double impression —
b. Triple impression —
c. Quadruple impression —

UC32

Designed by Bradbury Thompson.
Printed by the Bureau of Engraving and Printing.

Letter Sheet for Foreign Postage

1991, May 17 **Litho.** **Tagged**

UC63 UC32 45c **gray, red & blue,** *blue,* entire 1.40 *16.00*
a. White paper 1.00 *16.00*
Entire, 1st day cancel, Denver, CO *(19,941)* 1.40

Thaddeus Lowe (1832-1913), Balloonist — UC33

Designed by Davis Meltzer.
Printed by the Bureau of Engraving & Printing.

Letter Sheet for Foreign Postage

1995, Sept. 23 **Litho.** **Tagged**

UC64 UC33 50c **multicolored,** *blue,* entire 1.50 *20.00*
Entire, 1st day cancel, Tampa, FL 1.25

Voyageurs Natl. Park, Minnesota UC34

Designed by Phil Jordan.
Printed by Bureau of Engraving & Printing.

Letter Sheet for Foreign Postage

1999, May 15 **Litho.** **Tagged**

UC65 UC34 60c **multicolored,** *blue,* entire 1.75 *12.50*
Entire, 1st day cancel, Denver, CO 1.50

No. UC65 used is often found with additional postage affixed.

OFFICIAL ENVELOPES & WRAPPERS

By the Act of Congress, January 31, 1873, the franking privilege of officials was abolished as of July 1, 1873 and the Postmaster General was authorized to prepare official envelopes. At the same time official stamps were prepared for all Departments. Department envelopes became obsolete July 5, 1884. After that, government offices began to use franked envelopes of varied design. These indicate no denomination and lie beyond the scope of this Catalogue.

Post Office Department

UO1

Numeral 9mm high.

UO2

Numeral 9mm high.

UO3

Numeral 9½mm high.

Printed by George H. Reay, Brooklyn, N.Y.

1873

UO1	UO1	2c	**black,** *lemon*	25.00	10.00
	Entire			45.00	20.00
UO2	UO2	3c	**black,** *lemon*	12.50	6.50
	Entire			35.00	15.00
+UO3	UO2	3c	**black**	*17,500.*	
	Entire			*45,000.*	
UO4	UO3	6c	**black,** *lemon*	25.00	17.50
	Entire			40.00	30.00

The No. UO3 entire is unique. It has a tear through the stamp that has been professionally repaired. Value based on auction sale in 1999.

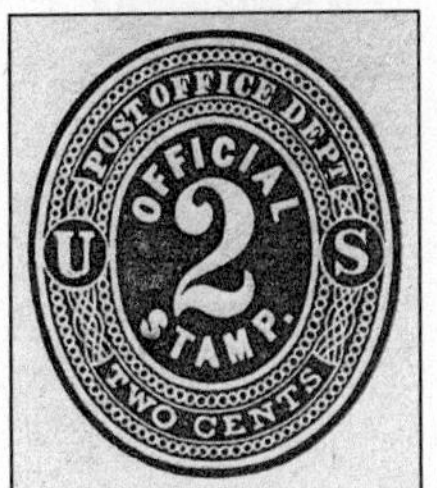

UO4

Numeral 9¼mm high.

UO5

Numeral 9¼mm high.

UO6

Numeral 10½mm high.

Printed by Plimpton Manufacturing Co., Hartford, Conn.

1874-79

UO5	UO4	2c	**black,** *lemon*	8.00	4.25
	Entire			17.50	8.00
UO6	UO4	2c	**black**	120.00	37.50
	Entire			175.00	57.50
UO7	UO5	3c	**black,** *lemon*	2.75	.75
	Entire			4.25	2.00
UO8	UO5	3c	**black**	1,750.	1,200.
	Entire			4,250.	
UO9	UO5	3c	**black,** *amber*	120.00	37.50
	Entire			175.00	60.00
UO10	UO5	3c	**black,** *blue*	—	
	Entire			*42,500.*	
UO11	UO5	3c	**blue,** *blue* ('75)	*20,000.*	
	Entire			*32,500.*	
UO12	UO6	6c	**black,** *lemon*	12.50	6.50
	Entire			22.50	12.50
UO13	UO6	6c	**black**	1,250.	1,750.
	Entire			3,750.	

Fakes exist of Nos. UO3, UO8 and UO13.

Postal Service

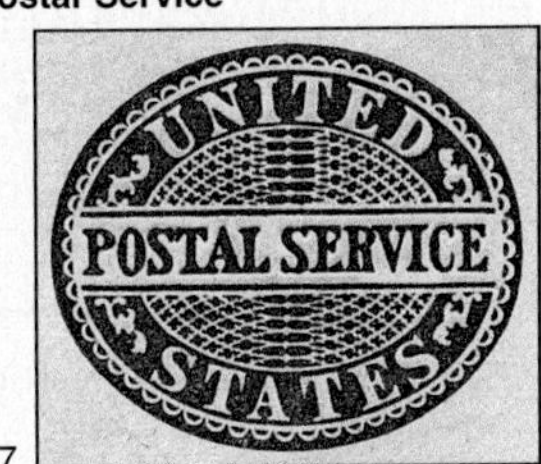

UO7

1877

UO14	UO7	**black**	6.00	4.50
	Entire		11.00	10.00
UO15	UO7	**black,** *amber*	125.00	42.50
	Entire		575.00	65.00
UO16	UO7	**blue,** *amber*	125.00	40.00
	Entire		575.00	65.00
UO17	UO7	**blue,** *blue*	7.50	6.75
	Entire		12.00	12.00

War Department

Franklin — UO8

Bust points to the end of "N" of "ONE".

Jackson — UO9

Bust narrow at the back.

Washington — UO10

Queue projects below the bust.

Lincoln — UO11

Neck very long at the back.

Jefferson — UO12

Queue forms straight line with bust.

Clay — UO13

Ear partly concealed by hair, mouth large, chin prominent.

Webster — UO14

Has side whiskers.

Scott — UO15

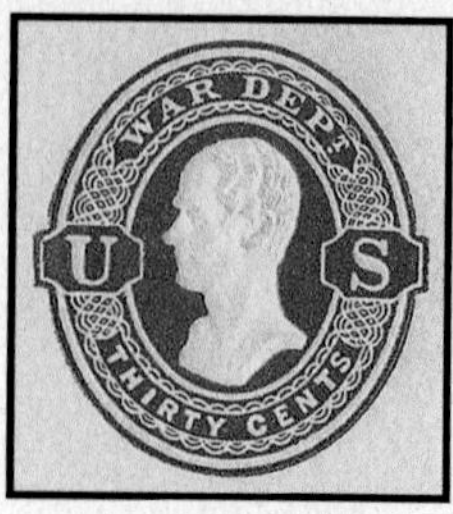

Hamilton — UO16

Back of bust very narrow; chin almost straight; the labels containing the letters "U S" are exactly parallel.

Printed by George H. Reay.

1873

UO18	UO8 1c **dark red**	350.00	200.00
	Entire	900.00	
WO18A	UO8 1c **dark red,** *manila,* entire		—
UO19	UO9 2c **dark red**	1,000.	—
	Entire	2,250.	*5,000.*
UO20	UO10 3c **dark red**	12.50	30.00
	Entire	17.50	70.00
UO21	UO10 3c **dark red,** *amber*	*27,500.*	
	Entire	*42,500.*	
UO22	UO10 3c **dark red,** *cream*	500.00	250.00
	Entire	850.00	400.00
UO23	UO11 6c **dark red**	250.00	100.00
	Entire	475.00	250.00
UO24	UO11 6c **dark red,** *cream*	4,000.	425.00
	Entire	6,500.	*3,500.*
UO25	UO12 10c **dark red**	*7,500.*	
	Entire	*22,500.*	
UO26	UO13 12c **dark red**	90.00	
	Entire	175.00	—
UO27	UO14 15c **dark red**	125.00	55.00
	Entire	210.00	*375.00*
UO28	UO15 24c **dark red**	100.00	40.00
	Entire	200.00	*1,500.*
UO29	UO16 30c **dark red**	250.00	150.00
	Entire	500.00	725.00

1873

UO30	UO8 1c **vermilion**	200.00	
	Entire	375.00	
WO31	UO8 1c **vermilion,** *manila*	17.50	14.00
	Entire	35.00	25.00
+UO32	UO9 2c **vermilion**	400.00	
	Entire	*22,500.*	
WO33	UO9 2c **vermilion,** *manila*	250.00	
	Entire	700.00	*1,000.*
UO34	UO10 3c **vermilion**	75.00	40.00
	Entire	150.00	150.00
UO35	UO10 3c **vermilion,** *amber*	85.00	40.00
	Entire	325.00	*400.00*
UO36	UO10 3c **vermilion,** *cream*	12.50	12.50
	Entire	37.50	26.00
UO37	UO11 6c **vermilion**	75.00	
	Entire	160.00	
+UO38	UO11 6c **vermilion,** *cream*	400.00	
	Entire	*22,500.*	
UO39	UO12 10c **vermilion**	300.00	
	Entire	650.00	
UO40	UO13 12c **vermilion**	130.00	
	Entire	200.00	
UO41	UO14 15c **vermilion**	200.00	
	Entire	4,000.	
UO42	UO15 24c **vermilion**	300.00	
	Entire	550.00	
UO43	UO16 30c **vermilion**	250.00	
	Entire	425.00	

UO17

Bottom serif on "S" is thick and short; bust at bottom below hair forms a sharp point.

UO18

Bottom serif on "S" is thick and short; front part of bust is rounded.

UO19

Bottom serif on "S" is short; queue does not project below bust.

UO20

Neck very short at the back.

UO21

Knot of queue stands out prominently.

UO22

Ear prominent, chin receding. No "dot" uner "T" of "Dept."

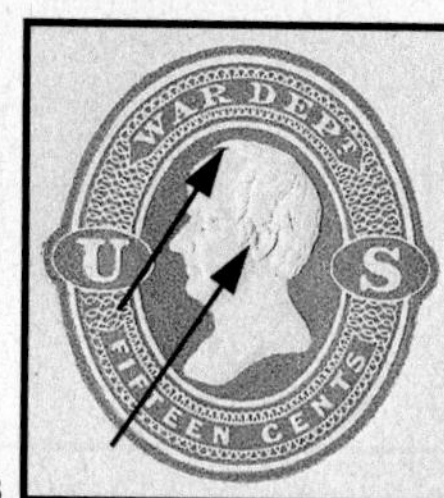

UO23

Has no side whiskers; forelock projects above head.

UO24

Back of bust rather broad; chin slopes considerably; the label containing letters "U S" are not exactly parallel.

Printed by Plimpton Manufacturing Co.

1875

UO44	UO17 1c **red**	175.00	85.00
	Entire	240.00	250.00
+UO45	UO17 1c **red,** *amber*	600.00	
+UO45A	UO17 1c **red,** *orange*	*32,500.*	
WO46	UO17 1c **red,** *manila*	4.50	2.75
	Entire	9.50	6.50
UO47	UO18 2c **red**	90.00	—
	Entire	150.00	
UO48	UO18 2c **red,** *amber*	12.50	17.50
	Entire	22.50	27.50
UO49	UO18 2c **red,** *orange*	12.50	17.50
	Entire	15.00	
WO50	UO18 2c **red,** *manila*	90.00	40.00
	Entire	200.00	—
UO51	UO19 3c **red**	11.00	10.00
	Entire	20.00	20.00
UO52	UO19 3c **red,** *amber*	12.50	10.00
	Entire	22.50	16.00
UO53	UO19 3c **red,** *cream*	5.00	3.75
	Entire	9.00	6.50
UO54	UO19 3c **red,** *blue*	3.00	2.00
	Entire	4.00	2.00
UO55	UO19 3c **red,** *fawn*	6.00	5.00
	Entire	11.00	4.00
UO56	UO20 6c **red**	45.00	30.00
	Entire	85.00	—
UO57	UO20 6c **red,** *amber*	65.00	40.00
	Entire	110.00	—
UO58	UO20 6c **red,** *cream*	175.00	85.00
	Entire	450.00	
UO59	UO21 10c **red**	180.00	80.00
	Entire	225.00	—
UO60	UO21 10c **red,** *amber*	650.00	
	Entire	1,150.	
UO61	UO22 12c **red**	25.00	25.00
	Entire	140.00	*250.00*
UO62	UO22 12c **red,** *amber*	400.00	
	Entire	650.00	
UO63	UO22 12c **red,** *cream*	450.00	
	Entire	700.00	
UO64	UO23 15c **red**	200.00	125.00
	Entire	300.00	—
UO65	UO23 15c **red,** *amber*	650.00	
	Entire	1,000.	
UO66	UO23 15c **red,** *cream*	525.00	
	Entire	850.00	
UO67	UO24 30c **red**	150.00	140.00
	Entire	210.00	—
UO68	UO24 30c **red,** *amber*	550.00	
	Entire	1,700.	
UO69	UO24 30c **red,** *cream*	675.00	
	Entire	1,100.	

POSTAL SAVINGS ENVELOPES

Issued under the Act of Congress, approved June 25, 1910, in lieu of penalty or franked envelopes. Unused remainders, after mid-October 1914, were overprinted with the Penalty Clause. Regular stamped envelopes, redeemed by the Government, were also overprinted for official use.

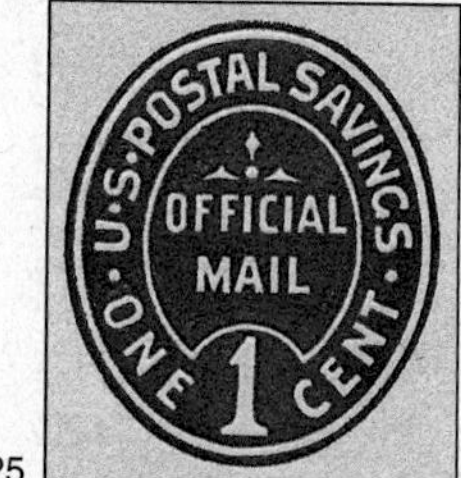

UO25

1911

UO70	UO25 1c **green**	75.00	25.00
	Entire	110.00	42.50
UO71	UO25 1c **green,** *oriental buff*	175.00	85.00
	Entire	275.00	100.00
UO72	UO25 2c **carmine**	12.50	4.00
	Entire	21.00	12.00
a.	2c **carmine,** *manila* (error)	*1,200.*	*1,000.*
	Entire	*1,800.*	*1,400.*

Tagged

Envelopes from No. UO73 onward are tagged unless otherwise noted.

OFFICIAL MAIL

Great Seal — UO26

1983, Jan. 12 **Typo. & Embossed**

UO73	UO26 20c **blue,** entire	1.00	*10.00*
	First day cancel, Washington, DC		1.00

UO27

1985, Feb. 26 **Typo. & Embossed**
UO74 UO27 22c **blue,** entire .90 *5.00*
First day cancel, Washington, DC 1.00

UO28

1987, Mar. 2 **Typo.**
UO75 UO28 22c **blue,** entire 1.50 *25.00*
First day cancel, Washington, DC 1.00
a. Tagging omitted —

Used exclusively to mail U.S. Savings Bonds.

UO29

1988, Mar. 22 **Typo.**
UO76 UO29 (25c) **black & blue,** entire 1.25 *15.00*
First day cancel, Washington, DC 1.25

Used exclusively to mail U.S. Savings Bonds.

UO30

UO31

1988, Apr. 11 **Typo. & Embossed**
UO77 UO30 25c **black & blue,** entire .85 *6.00*
First day cancel, Washington, DC 1.25
a. Denomination & lettering as on No. UO78, entire *5.00* *6.00*

Nos. UO77 and UO77a used to mail U.S. Savings Bonds and also occasionally used by the director of admissions at the U.S. Air Force Academy and by Air Force recruiting stations for intra-agency correspondence.

Typo.

UO78 UO31 25c **black & blue,** entire 1.00 *35.00*
First day cancel, Washington, DC *(12,017)* 1.25
a. Denomination & lettering as on No. UO77, entire 1.00 *35.00*

No. UO78 used to mail U.S. Savings Bonds. Also used by the Department of Agriculture.

First day cancellations applied to 12,017 of Nos. UO77, UO78.

Used Values

Postally used examples of Nos. UO79-UO94 seldom appear in the marketplace and thus cannot be valued with as much certainty as the editors would like. They must show evidence of postal usage. Clear cancels are valued even higher. The editors would like to have records of sales of examples of these used envelopes. If a value exists, it is based on a known transaction(s) or consultation with experts.

1990, Mar. 17 **Typo.**

Stars and "E Pluribus Unum" illegible. "Official" is 13mm, "USA" is 16mm long.

UO79 UO31 45c **black & blue,** entire 1.25 *80.00*
First day cancel, Springfield, VA *(5,956)* 1.50
UO80 UO31 65c **black & blue,** entire 1.75 *100.00*
First day cancel, Springfield, VA *(6,922)* 2.25

Used exclusively to mail U.S. passports.

UO32

Stars and "E Pluribus Unum" clear and sharply printed. "Official" is 14½mm, "USA" is 17mm long.

1990, Aug. 10 **Litho.**
UO81 UO32 45c **black & blue,** entire 1.25 *100.00*
First day cancel, Washington, DC *(7,160)* 1.50
UO82 UO32 65c **black & blue,** entire 1.75 *160.00*
First day cancel, Washington, DC *(6,759)* 2.25

Used exclusively to mail U.S. passports.

UO33

1991, Jan. 22 **Typo.** **Wmk.**
UO83 UO33 (29c) **black & blue,** entire 1.00 *20.00*
First day cancel, Washington, DC *(30,549)* 1.25

Used exclusively to mail U.S. Savings Bonds.

UO34

1991, Apr. 6 **Wmk.** **Litho. & Embossed**
UO84 UO34 29c **black & blue,** entire .70 *5.00*
First day cancel, Oklahoma City, OK *(27,841)* 1.25
a. Unwatermarked paper, entire *May 1, 1992* 7.50 *4.00*

No. UO84a has a "recycled" imprint under the flap.

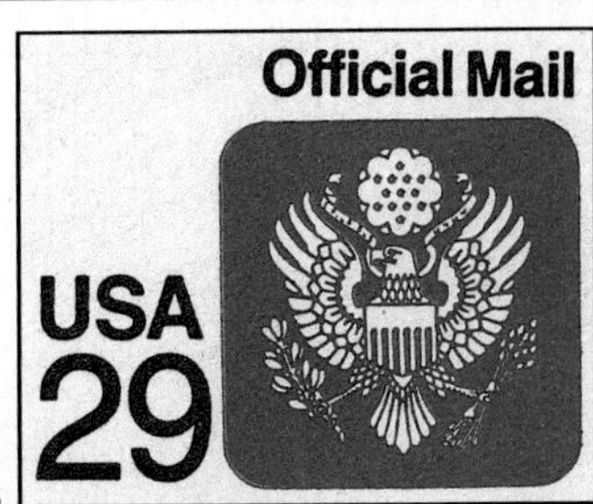

UO35

1991, Apr. 17 **Typo.** **Wmk.**
UO85 UO35 29c **black & blue,** entire .70 *20.00*
First day cancel, Washington, DC *(25,563)* 1.25
Entire, unwatermarked, *May 1, 1992* 75.00 *20.00*

Used exclusively to mail U.S. Savings Bonds. Unwatermarked envelopes on recycled paper were issued May 1, 1992, and have a "recycled" imprint under the flap. Value, unused $3., used $35.

Consular Service, Bicent. — UO36

Designed by Zebulon Rogers. Quotation from O. Henry on flap.

1992, July 10 **Litho.** **Unwmk.**
UO86 UO36 52c **blue & red,** entire 6.00 *20.00*
First day cancel, Washington, DC *(30,374)* 2.25
a. 52c blue & red, *blue-white,* entire 1.50 *20.00*
UO87 UO36 75c **blue & red,** entire 11.00 *30.00*
First day cancel, Washington, DC *(25,995)* 3.25
a. 75c blue & red, *blue-white,* entire 2.50 *30.00*

Used exclusively to mail U.S. passports.

Available only in 4⅜ inch x 8⅞ inch size with self-adhesive flap.

Original issues have "USPS copyright" on left under flap. Reissues (Nos. UO86a and UO87a) have it at right.

UO37

1995-99 **Typo. & Embossed** **Unwmk.**
UO88 UO37 32c **blue & red,** entire, *May 9, 1995* .90 *7.00*
First day cancel, Washington, DC 1.25
UO89 UO37 33c **blue & red,** entire, *Feb. 22, 1999* .90 *8.00*
First day cancel, Washington, DC 1.25

Type of 1995

2001, Feb. 27 **Typo. & Embossed** **Unwmk.**
UO90 UO37 34c **blue & red,** entire 1.00 *10.00*
First day cancel, Washington, DC 1.25

Type of 1995

2002, Aug. 2 **Typo. & Embossed** **Unwmk.**
UO91 UO37 37c **blue & red,** type I, entire 1.00 *15.00*
First day cancel, Washington, DC 1.25
First day cancel, any other city 1.25
a. Type II, entire, *Aug. 2, 2002* 1.00 *35.00*

Type I has 29x28mm blue panel, top of "USA" even with the bottom of the eagle's neck and is made with "100% recycled paper" as noted on reverse. Type II has a 27½x27½mm blue panel, top of "USA" even with the highest arrow, and has no mention of "100% recycled paper" on reverse.

Type of 1995

2006, Jan. 9 Typo. & Embossed Unwmk.

UO92 UO37 39c **blue & red, entire** 2.00 *12.50*
Entire, 1st day cancel, Washington, DC 1.25
Entire, 1st day cancel, any other city 1.25

Type of 1995

2007, May 12 Typo. & Embossed Unwmk.

UO93 UO37 41c **blue & red,** entire 2.00 *25.00*
Entire, 1st day cancel, Washington, DC 2.10

Type of 1995

2008, June 20 Typo. Unwmk.

UO94 UO37 42c **blue & red,** entire 2.00 *25.00*
Entire, 1st day cancel, Washington, DC 2.10

POSTAL CARDS

Values are for unused cards as sold by the Post Office, without printed or written address or message, and used cards with Post Office cancellation, when current. Used cards with postage added to meet higher rates sell for less. Used cards for international rates are for proper usage. Those used domestically sell for less.

The "Preprinted" values are for unused cards with printed or written address or message.

Starting with No. UX21, the Government Printing Office began printing the postal cards. Many outside firms produced cards starting October 1994 with Nos. UX178-UX197. The last GPO-produced cards were Nos. UX449 and UY45, January 9, 2006.

Nos. UX1-UX48 are typographed; others are lithographed (offset) unless otherwise stated.

Numerous printing varieties exist. Varieties of surcharged cards include (a) inverted surcharge at lower left, (b) double surcharge, one inverted at lower left, (c) surcharge in other abnormal positions, including back of card. Such surcharge varieties command a premium.

Colored cancellations sell for more than black in some instances. **All values are for entire cards.**

As of Jan. 1, 1999, postal cards were sold individually for 1¢ over face value. Starting on Jan. 7, 2001 they are sold for 2c over face value. On May 12, 2008, it increased to 3¢ over face value and from Jan. 27, 2013 to present it is 4¢ over face value.

See Computer Vended Postage section for "Postal Buddy" cards.

Since 1875 it has been possible to purchase some postal cards in sheets for multiple printing, hence pairs, strips and blocks are available. Some sheets have been cut up so that cards exist with stamp inverted, in center of card, two on one card, in another corner, etc. These are only curiosities and of minimal value.

Liberty — PC1

Wmk. Large "U S P O D" in Monogram, (90x60mm)

1873, May 12 Size: 130x76mm

UX1 PC1 1c **brown,** *buff* 375.00 25.00
Preprinted 70.00
First day of use cover, May 12, 1873, Springfield MA *12,500.*

The U.S. Postal Card Agency in Springfield, Mass. began distributing postal cards to post offices on May 12, 1873. The Springfield post office received its shipment that same day and immediately placed them on sale, so the one postal card post-marked May 12, 1873, from Springfield is the legitimate earliest documented use supported by Post Office Dept. records. Other cities began receiving the cards by train on May 13.

Wmk. Small "U S P O D" in Monogram, (53x36mm)

1873, July 6

UX3 PC1 1c **brown,** *buff* 75.00 3.50
Preprinted 22.50
a. Without watermark 775.00

The watermarks on Nos. UX1, UX3 and UX4 are found in normal position, inverted, reversed, and inverted and reversed. They are often dim, especially on No. UX4. Values listed are for clear watermarks.

No. UX3a is not known unused. Cards offered as such are either unwatermarked proofs, or have partial or vague watermarks. See No. UX65.

Liberty — PC2

Inscribed

WRITE THE ADDRESS ON THIS SIDE—THE MESSAGE ON THE OTHER

1875 Wmk. Small "U S P O D" in Monogram

UX4 PC2 1c **black,** *buff, Sept. 28* 3,500. 350.
Preprinted 700.

Unwmk.

UX5 PC2 1c **black,** *buff, Sept. 30* 75.00 .45
Preprinted 7.00

For other postal card of type PC2 see No. UX7.

Liberty — PC3

For International Use

1879, Dec. 1

UX6 PC3 2c **blue,** *buff* 35.00 25.00
Preprinted 11.50
a. 2c **dark blue,** *buff* 35.00 25.00
Preprinted 11.50

See Nos. UX13 and UX16.

Type of PC2, Inscribed

NOTHING BUT THE ADDRESS CAN BE PLACED ON THIS SIDE.

1881, Oct. 17 (?)

UX7 PC2 1c **black,** *buff* 70.00 .40
Preprinted 6.50
a. 23 teeth below "ONE CENT" 1,750. 65.00
Preprinted 225.00
b. Printed on both sides *1,200. 750.00*

Jefferson — PC4

1885, Aug. 24

UX8 PC4 1c **brown,** *buff* 55.00 1.25
Preprinted 10.00
c. 1c **dark chocolate,** *buff* 450.00 65.00
Preprinted 75.00
d. Double impression *5,500. 7,500.*
e. Double impression, one inverted *9,500.*
f. Printed on both sides —
g. "M" in double frame above "O" of "POSTAL" *1,250.*

Card was printed in many shades of brown ink. Earliest documented use: Aug. 29, 1885.

PC5

Head of Jefferson facing right, centered on card.

1886, Dec 1

UX9 PC5 1c **black,** *buff* 25.00 .55
Preprinted 1.75
a. 1c **black,** *dark buff* 75.00 5.00
Preprinted 20.00
b. Double impression *4,000. 1,500.*
c. Double impression, one inverted *10,000.*
d. **1c black,** *salmon pink* *900.00 3,250.*
e. Triple impression *4,500.*

No. UX9d was printed on spacer paper used for counting.

Grant — PC6

1891, Dec. 16 Size: 155x95mm

UX10 PC6 1c **black,** *buff* 47.50 1.75
Preprinted 7.50
a. Double impression, one inverted *3,500.*

Double impression, second impression inverted and quadruple split 3,250.
b. Double impression 1,750.
c. Triple impression, one inverted 7,000.
d. Quintuple impression, three inverted 6,500.

Two types exist of No. UX10.
Earliest documented use: Dec. 23, 1891.

Size: 117x75mm

UX11 PC6 1c **blue,** *grayish white* 22.50 3.00
Preprinted 5.00
b. Double impression, one inverted 8,000.

Cards printed in black instead of blue are invariably proofs.
Earliest documented use: Dec. 21, 1891.

PC7

Head of Jefferson facing left.
Small wreath and name below.

1894, Jan. 2 **Size: 140x89mm**

UX12 PC7 1c **black,** *buff* 45.00 .65
Preprinted 2.25
a. Double impression —

Two types exist of No. UX12: flat bed printing and rotary press printing.

For International Use
Type of PC3

1897, Jan. 25 **Size: 140x89mm**

UX13 PC3 2c **blue,** *cream* 200.00 85.00
Preprinted 85.00

Earliest documented use: Apr. 17, 1897.

PC8

Head same as PC7. Large wreath and name below.

1897, Dec. 1 **Size: 139x82mm**

UX14 PC8 1c **black,** *buff* 40.00 .45
Preprinted 2.75
a. Double impression, one inverted 7,000. 7,000.
Preprinted —
b. Printed both sides —
Preprinted 3,000.
c. Double impression — —
Preprinted —
d. **Black,** *salmon pink,* preprinted 1,500.

No. UX14d was printed on spacer paper used for counting.

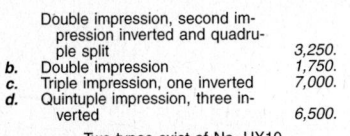

John Adams — PC9

1898 **Size: 126x74mm**

UX15 PC9 1c **black,** *buff, Mar. 31* 47.50 15.00
Preprinted 12.50

For International Use
Design same as PC3, without frame around card.
Size: 140x82mm

UX16 PC3 2c **black,** *buff* 15.00 *17.00*
Preprinted 5.00

McKinley — PC10

1902

UX17 PC10 1c **black,** *buff* 6,500.
Preprinted 2,500. 3,750.

Earliest documented use; May 27, 1902.

McKinley — PC11

1902

UX18 PC11 1c **black,** *buff* 17.50 .35
Preprinted 1.75
a. Double impression 7,500.
b. Black, dark buff — —
Preprinted —

Earliest documented use; July 14, 1902.

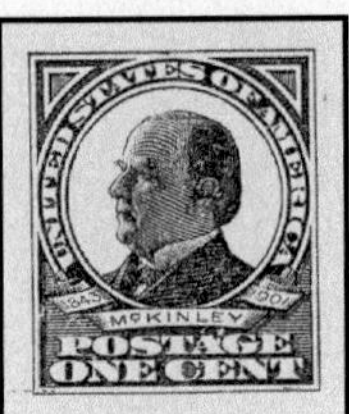

McKinley — PC12

1907

UX19 PC12 1c **black,** *buff* 45.00 .50
Preprinted 2.25

Earliest documented use: June 28, 1907.

Same design, correspondence space at left

1908, Jan. 2

UX20 PC12 1c **black,** *buff* 57.50 4.50
Preprinted 8.50

Two types exist of Nos. UX19-UX20.

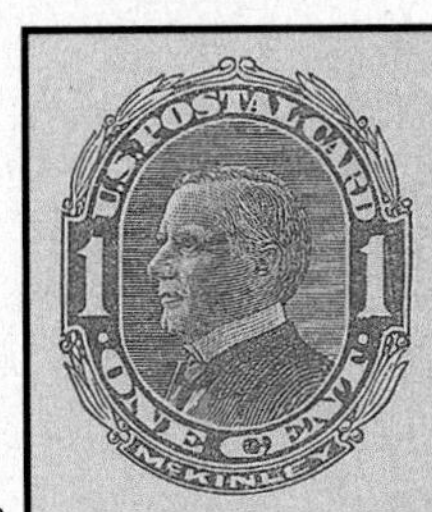

PC13

McKinley, background shaded.

1910 , Feb. 12

UX21 PC13 1c **blue,** *bluish* 90.00 13.00
Preprinted 17.50
a. 1c **bronze blue,** *bluish* 400.00 100.00
Preprinted 150.00
b. Double impression 1,600.
Preprinted 650.00
c. Triple impression 3,000.
Preprinted 1,500.
d. Double impression, one inverted —
e. Four arcs above and below "IS" of inscription to left of stamp impression are pointed 2,100. 600.00
Preprinted 900.00

Earliest documented use: Feb. 13, 1910.

A No. UX21 card exists with Philippines No. UX11 printed on the back.

PC14

Same design, white background.

1910, Apr. 13

UX22 PC14 1c **blue,** *bluish* 22.50 .45
Preprinted 2.00
a. Double impression 850.00
b. Triple impression 3,500. 3,250.
c. Triple impression, one inverted —
d. Quintuple impression 6,000.

See No. UX24.

PC15

Head of Lincoln, solid background.

1911, Jan. 21 **Size: 127x76mm**

UX23 PC15 1c **red,** *cream* 11.00 5.50
Preprinted 3.50
a. Triple impression —
b. Double impression 7,000.

See No. UX26.

Design same as PC14

1911, Aug. 10 **Size: 140x82mm**

UX24 PC14 1c **red,** *cream* 12.00 .35
Preprinted 1.25
a. Double impression 3,250.
b. Triple impression —

Cards with 1920 2-line surcharge are considered favor items.

Grant — PC16

For International Use

1911, Oct. 27 **Size: 140x82mm**

UX25 PC16 2c **red,** *cream* 1.50 *20.00*
Preprinted .65
a. Double impression 10,000.

For surcharge see No. UX36.

Design same as PC15

1913, July 29 **Size: 127x76mm**

UX26 PC15 1c **green,** *cream* 13.00 7.50
Preprinted 2.50

Jefferson — PC17

Die I — End of queue small, sloping sharply downward to right.

Die II (re-cut) — End of queue large and rounded.

1914-16 **Size: 140x82mm**

UX27	PC17 1c **green,** *buff,* die I, *June 4*	.25	.25
	Preprinted	.25	
a.	1c **green,** *cream*	5.00	.65
	Preprinted	1.25	
b.	Double impression	*2,500.*	*2,750.*
e.	Triple impression	*6,000.*	
f.	Quadruple impression	*6,500.*	

On gray, rough surfaced card

UX27C	PC17 1c **green,** die I, *Dec. 22, 1916*	*3,250.*	250.00
	Preprinted	*625.00*	
UX27D	PC17 1c **dark green,** die II, *1916*	*20,000.*	175.00
	Preprinted	550.00	

For surcharges see Nos. UX39 and UX41.

Lincoln — PC19

1917, Mar. 14 **Size: 127x76mm**

UX28	PC19 1c **green,** *cream*	.60	.30
	Preprinted	.30	
a.	1c **green,** *dark buff*	1.50	.60
	Preprinted	.50	
b.	Double impression	*3,500.*	*1,250.*
	Preprinted	*2,500.*	

No. UX28 was printed also on light buff and canary. See No. UX43. For surcharges see Nos. UX40 and UX42.

Jefferson — PC20

Die I — Rough, coarse impression. End of queue slopes sharply downward to right. Left basal ends of "2" form sharp points.

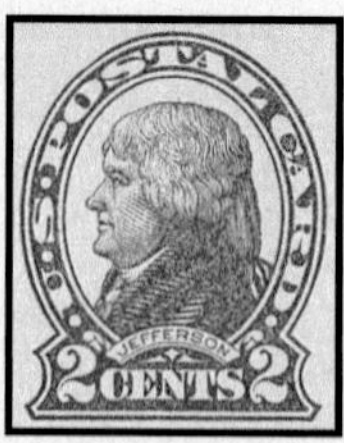

Jefferson — PC20a

Die II — Fine, clear impression. End of queue is almost horizontal at right. Left basal ends of "2" form balls.

1917-18 **Size: 140x82mm**

UX29	PC20 2c **red,** *buff,* die I, *Oct. 22*	42.50	2.10
	Preprinted	6.50	
a.	2c **lake,** *cream,* die I	50.00	4.00
	Preprinted	9.00	
c.	2c **vermilion,** *buff,* die I	850.00	165.00
	Preprinted	70.00	
UX30	PC20a 2c **red,** *cream,* die II, *Jan. 23, 1918*	30.00	1.60
	Preprinted	4.50	

2c Postal Cards of 1917-18 Revalued

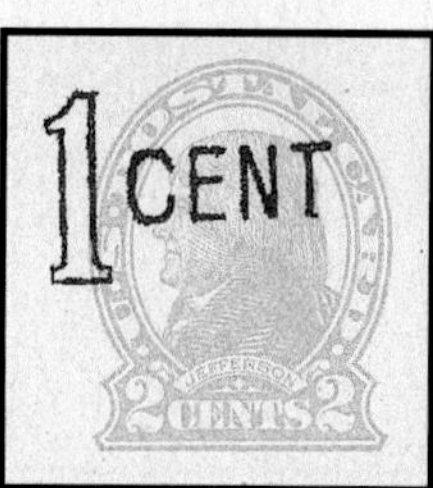

Surcharged in one line by canceling machine at Washington, DC

1920, Apr.

UX31	PC20a 1c on 2c **red,** *cream,* die II	*3,000.*	*4,000.*
	Preprinted	*2,250.*	

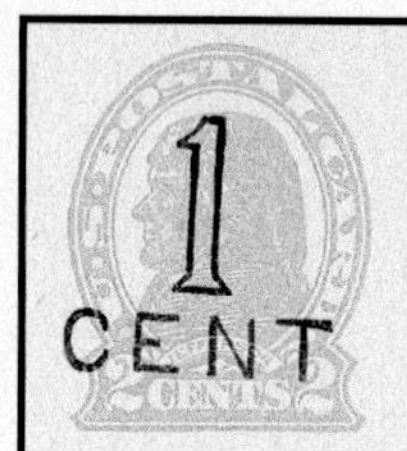

Surcharged in two lines by canceling machine (46 Types)

UX32	PC20 1c on 2c **red,** *buff,* die I	52.50	12.50
	Preprinted	15.00	
a.	1c on 2c **vermilion,** *buff*	150.00	60.00
	Preprinted	60.00	
b.	Double surcharge	150.00	100.00
	Preprinted	100.00	—
c.	Double surcharge, one inverted, both in normal position on stamp	—	—
	Preprinted	—	
d.	Double surcharge, one inverted at lower left	65.00	30.00
	Preprinted	30.00	
e.	Triple surcharge	—	—
	Preprinted	—	
f.	Inverted surcharge at lower left	65.00	30.00
	Preprinted	30.00	
UX33	PC20a 1c on 2c **red,** *cream,* die II	13.00	2.00
	Preprinted	2.50	
a.	Inverted surcharge, on stamp	150.00	*200.00*
	Preprinted	—	—
b.	Double surcharge	150.00	*175.00*
	Preprinted	50.00	
c.	Double surcharge, one inverted, both in normal position on stamp	350.00	
	Preprinted	—	
d.	Triple surcharge	375.00	
e.	Double surcharge, one inverted at lower left	30.00	25.00
	Preprinted	20.00	
f.	Inverted surcharge at lower left	30.00	30.00
	Preprinted	20.00	
g.	Triple surcharge, one inverted at lower left	—	—
	Preprinted	—	
h.	Double surcharge, one inverted on back	—	

Double and triple surcharges on Nos. UX32 and UX33 generally sell for less than above values if one or more of the surcharges is not on the stamp.

Surcharged in Two Lines by Press Printing

1920

UX34	PC20 1c on 2c **red,** *buff,* die I	700.00	52.50
	Preprinted	125.00	
a.	Double surcharge	1,000.	
UX35	PC20a 1c 2c **red,** *cream,* die II	225.00	37.50
	Preprinted	55.00	
a.	Double surcharge, one inverted at lower left	—	

Surcharges were prepared from (a) special dies fitting International and Universal post office canceling machines (Nos. UX31-UX33), and (b) printing press dies (Nos. UX34-UX35). There are 38 canceling machine types on Die I, and 44 on Die II. There are two printing press types of each die.

Editors would like to see an example of UX35a.

UX36	PC16 1c on 2c **red,** *cream* (#UX25)	*95,000.*

Unused examples of No. UX36 (New York surcharge) were probably made by favor. Used examples of No. UX36 (Los Angeles surcharge, three to four examples used in Long Beach are recorded) are unquestionably authentic. Surcharges on other numbers exist, but their validity is doubtful.

McKinley — PC21

For International Use

1926, Feb. 1

UX37	PC21 3c **red,** *buff*	4.50	*22.50*
	Preprinted	1.75	
	First day cancel, Washington, DC		200.00
a.	3c **red,** *yellow*	6.00	*22.50*
	Preprinted	1.75	
b.	Double impression	*5,000.*	
	Preprinted	*4,250.*	

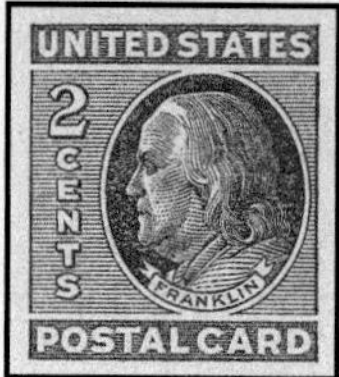

Franklin — PC22

1951, Nov. 16

UX38	PC22 2c **carmine rose,** *buff*	.35	.25
	Preprinted	.25	
	First day cancel		1.00
a.	Double impression	500.00	
b.	2c **carmine rose,** *dark buff,* (error)	700.00	
c.	2c **lake,** *buff,*	35.00	25.00
d.	Indicia omitted (inscriptions normal or partial)	*1,000.*	

No. UX38b was printed on spacer paper used for counting. For surcharge see No. UX47.

Nos. UX27 and UX28 Surcharged by Canceling Machine at Left of Stamp in Light Green

1952

UX39	PC17 2c on 1c **green,** *buff, Jan. 1*	.50	.35
	Preprinted	.25	
	First day cancel, any city		12.00
a.	Surcharged vertically, reading down	8.00	*10.00*
	Preprinted	3.00	
b.	Double surcharge	20.00	*25.00*
c.	Double surcharge, one inverted at lower left	20.00	25.00
d.	Inverted surcharge at lower left	12.00	12.00
e.	Triple surcharge	—	—
f.	Triple surcharge, one inverted at lower left	—	—
g.	Surcharge black (error)	*3,750.*	
h.	As "a," surcharge reading up	—	
UX40	PC19 2c on 1c **green,** *cream, Mar. 22*	.65	.45
	Preprinted	.40	
	First day cancel, Washington, D.C.		22.50
a.	Surcharged vertically, reading down	7.00	5.50
	Preprinted	4.00	
b.	Double surcharge	240.00	
c.	Double surcharge, one inverted at lower left	280.00	
d.	Inverted surcharge at lower left	180.00	

Nos. UX27 and UX28 With Similar Surcharge Typographed at Left of Stamp in Dark Green

1952

UX41	PC17 2c on 1c **green,** *buff*	5.00	2.00
	Preprinted	1.75	
a.	Inverted surcharge at lower left	85.00	125.00
	Preprinted	45.00	
b.	Double surcharge	—	—
	Preprinted	700.00	
c.	Vert. pair of cards, one with surcharge omitted	275.00	
UX42	PC19 2c on 1c **green,** *cream*	5.00	2.50
	Preprinted	3.00	
a.	Surcharged by offset lithography	5.00	2.50
b.	Surcharged on back	250.00	
c.	Double surcharge	—	

Type of 1917

1952, July 31 **Size: 127x76mm**

UX43 PC19 2c **carmine,** *buff* .30 *1.00*
Preprinted .25
First day cancel 1.00

Torch and Arm of Statue of Liberty — PC23

Fifth International Philatelic Exhibition (FIPEX), New York City, Apr. 28-May 6, 1956.

1956, May 4

UX44 PC23 2c **deep carmine & dark violet blue,** *buff* .25 *1.00*
First day cancel, New York, NY *(537,474)* 1.00
a. Dark violet blue omitted 525.00 *600.00*
b. Double impression of dark violet blue 40.00 —
c. Double impression of deep carmine 40.00 30.00
d. Double impression of deep carmine & dark violet blue *550.00*
e. Double impression of deep carmine, dark violet blue omitted *500.00*
f. 2c **rose pink & dark violet blue,** *buff* 100.00 75.00
g. As "f," dark violet blue omitted *750.00*
h. 2c **pink & dark violet blue,** *buff* *1,500.* *1,500.*
i. As "h," double impression of dark violet blue *1,500.*

Statue of Liberty — PC24

For International Use

1956, Nov. 16

UX45 PC24 4c **deep red & ultramarine,** *buff* 1.50 *110.00*
First day cancel, New York, NY *(129,841)* 1.00

See No. UY16.

Statue of Liberty — PC25

1958, Aug. 1

UX46 PC25 3c **bright violet,** *buff* .50 .25
First day cancel, Philadelphia, Pa. *(180,610)* 1.00
a. "N GOD WE TRUST" 12.00 *25.00*
First day cancel, Philadelphia, Pa. *175.00*
b. Double impression *1,000.*
c. Double impression one inverted *4,500.*
d. Precanceled with 3 printed purple lines, *1961* 4.25 2.50
e. Indicia omitted (inscription normal) *750.00*
f. 3c **purple,** *dark buff* (error) *900.00*

On No. UX46d, the precanceling lines are incorporated with the design. The earliest documented postmark on this experimental card is Oct. 31, 1961. UX46f was printed on spacer paper used for counting.

See No. UY17.

No. UX38 Surcharged by Canceling Machine at Left of Stamp in Black

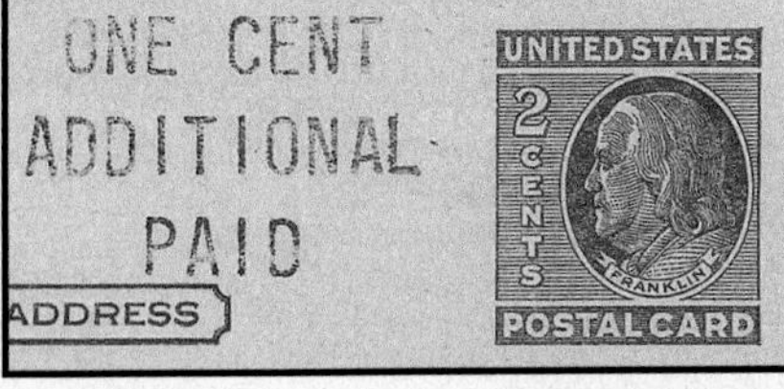

1958

UX47 PC22 2c + 1c **carmine rose,** *buff* 225.00 *900.00*
a. Surcharge inverted at lower left 500.00

The surcharge was applied to 750,000 cards for the use of the General Electric Co., Owensboro, Ky. A variety of the surcharge shows the D of PAID beneath the N of ADDITIONAL. All known examples of No. UX47 have a printed advertisement on the back and a small punch hole near lower left corner.

Used value is for commercially used card.

Lincoln PC26

Precanceled with 3 printed red violet lines

1962, Nov. 19

UX48 PC26 4c **reddish purple** .50 .25
First day cancel, Springfield, IL *(162,939)* 1.25
a. Tagged, *June 25, 1966* .60 .25
b. As No. UX48, inscription omitted *750.00*
First day cancel, Bellevue, OH 30.00

No. UX48a was printed with luminescent ink.
See note on Luminescence in "Information for Collectors."
See No. UY18.

Used values are for contemporaneous usage without additional postage applied. Used values for international-rate cards are for proper usage.

Map of Continental United States — PC27

Designed by Suren H. Ermoyan

For International Use

1963, Aug. 30

UX49 PC27 7c **blue & red** 4.00 *80.00*
First day cancel, New York, NY 1.00
a. Blue omitted *7,500.*

First day cancellation was applied to 270,464 of Nos. UX49 and UY19. See Nos. UX54, UX59, UY19-UY20.

Flags and Map of U.S. PC28

175th anniv. of the U.S. Customs Service.

Designed by Gerald N. Kurtz

Precanceled with 3 printed blue lines

1964, Feb. 22

UX50 PC28 4c **red & blue** .50 *1.00*
First day cancel, Washington, DC *(313,275)* 1.00
a. Blue omitted 550.00
b. Red omitted —
c. Double impression of red —

No. UX50c is unique and is a miscut foldunder card.

Americans "Moving Forward" (Street Scene) — PC29

Issued to publicize the need to strengthen the US Social Security system. Released in connection with the 15th conf. of the Intl. Social Security Association at Washington, DC.

Designed by Gerald N. Kurtz

Precanceled with a blue and 2 red printed lines

1964, Sept. 26

UX51 PC29 4c **dull blue & red** .40 *1.00*
First day cancel, Washington, D.C. *(293,650)* 1.00
a. Red omitted —
b. Dull blue omitted *625.00 625.00*

Coast Guard Flag — PC30

175th anniv. of the U.S. Coast Guard.

Designed by Muriel R. Chamberlain

Precanceled with 3 printed red lines

1965, Aug. 4

UX52 PC30 4c **blue & red** .30 *1.00*
First day cancel, Newburyport, Mass. *(338,225)* 1.25
a. Blue omitted *4,000.*

Crowd and Census Bureau Punch Card — PC31

Designed by Emilio Grossi

Precanceled with 3 bright blue printed lines

1965, Oct. 21

UX53 PC31 4c **bright blue & black** .30 *1.00*
First day cancel, Philadelphia, Pa. *(275,100)* 1.00

Map Type of 1963
For International Use

1967, Dec. 4

UX54 PC27 8c **blue & red** 4.50 *80.00*
First day cancel, Washington, DC 1.00

First day cancellation was applied to 268,077 of Nos. UX54 and UY20.

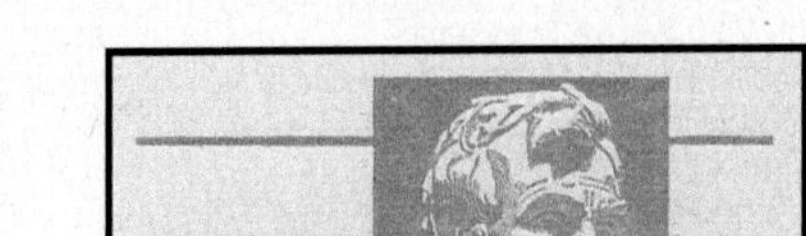

Lincoln PC33

Designed by Robert J. Jones

Precanceled with 3 printed green lines

1968, Jan. 4 **Luminescent Ink**

UX55 PC33 5c **emerald** .30 *.60*
First day cancel, Hodgenville, Ky. 1.25
a. Double impression 1,250.

First day cancellation was applied to 274,000 of Nos. UX55 and UY21.

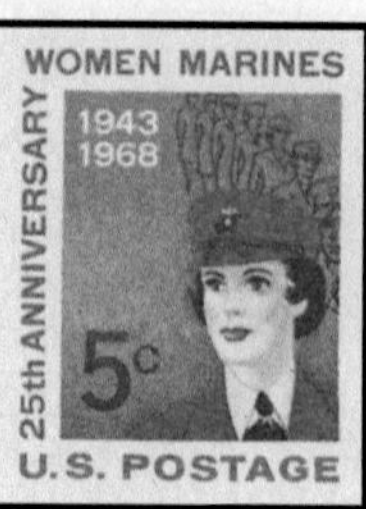

Woman Marine, 1968, and Marines of Earlier Wars — PC34

25th anniv. of the Women Marines.

Designed by Muriel R. Chamberlain

1968, July 26

UX56 PC34 5c **rose red & green** .35 *1.00*
First day cancel, San Francisco, Cal. *(203,714)* 1.25

Tagged

Postal cards from No. UX57 onward are either tagged or printed with luminescent ink unless otherwise noted.

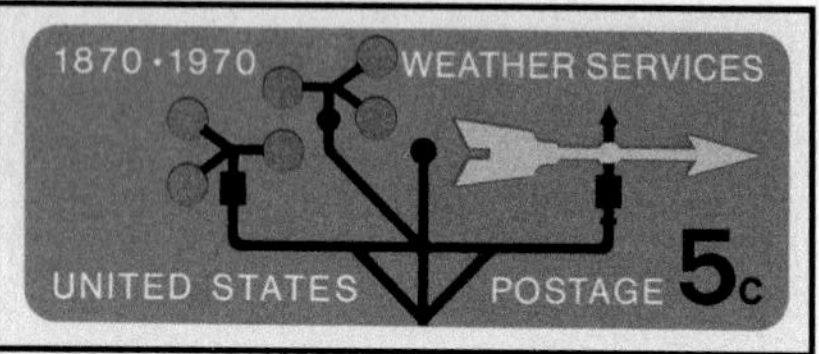

Weather Vane — PC35

Centenary of the Army's Signal Service, the Weather Services (Weather Bureau).

Designed by Robert Geissmann

1970, Sept. 1

UX57 PC35 5c **blue, yellow, red & black** .30 *1.00*
First day cancel, Fort Myer, Va. *(285,800)* 1.00
a. Yellow & black omitted *1,250.* *750.00*
Preprinted 300.00
b. Blue omitted *750.00* *5,000.*
c. Black omitted *1,250.* *850.00*
Preprinted 300.00

Paul Revere — PC36

Issued to honor Paul Revere, Revolutionary War patriot.

Designed by Howard C. Mildner after statue near Old North Church, Boston

Precanceled with 3 printed brown lines

1971, May 15

UX58 PC36 6c **brown** .30 *1.00*
First day cancel, Boston, Mass. 1.00
a. Double impression *3,250.*

First day cancellation was applied to 340,000 of Nos. UX58 and UY22.

Map Type of 1963

For International Use

1971, June 10

UX59 PC27 10c **blue & red** 4.50 *80.00*
First day cancel, New York, NY 1.00

First day cancellation was applied to 297,000 of Nos. UX59 and UXC11.

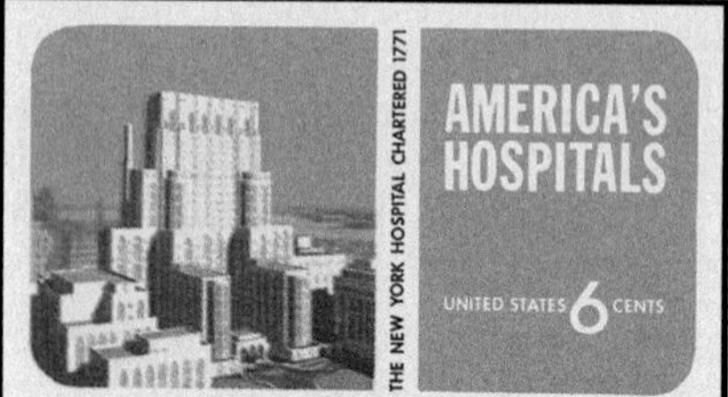

New York Hospital, New York City — PC37

Issued as a tribute to America's hospitals in connection with the 200th anniversary of New York Hospital.

Designed by Dean Ellis

1971, Sept. 16

UX60 PC37 6c **blue & multicolored** .30 *1.00*
First day cancel, New York, NY *(218,200)* 1.00
a. Blue & yellow omitted *1,000.*
b. Yellow omitted *500.00*
c. Red & black omitted 3,500.
d. Red omitted —
e. Tagging omitted 150.00
f. Black omitted *3,500.*

No. UX60f is significantly miscut, with only a small portion of the indicia present at the center top. The black vertical inscription line at the center is missing.

U.S.F. Constellation — PC38

Monument Valley — PC39

Gloucester, Mass. — PC40

Tourism Year of the Americas.

Designed by Melbourne Brindle

1972, June 29 **Size: 152½x108½mm**

UX61 PC38 6c **black,** U.S.F. Constellation, *buff* (Yosemite, Mt. Rushmore, Niagara Falls, Williamsburg on back) 1.00 *10.00*
First day cancel, any city 1.25
a. Address side blank *300.00*
b. Reverse blank *650.00* *750.00*
c. Tagging omitted 200.00

UX62 PC39 6c **black,** Monument Valley, *buff* (Monterey, Redwoods, Gloucester, U.S.F. Constellation on back) .50 *10.00*
First day cancel, any city 1.25
a. Black omitted on back *575.00*
b. Orange omitted on back —
c. Reverse blank 475.00
d. Tagging omitted 200.00

UX63 PC40 6c **black,** Gloucester, *buff* (Rodeo, Mississippi Riverboat, Grand Canyon, Monument Valley on back) .50 *6.00*
First day cancel, any city 1.25
a. Black inverted *1,500.*
b. Reverse blank 450.00
c. Tagging omitted 200.00
d. Back inverted to the front 800.00
e. Black and pale salmon omitted on back —
Nos. UX61-UX63,UXC12-UXC13 (4) 2.45 *26.50*

Nos. UX61-UX63, UXC12-UXC13 went on sale throughout the United States. They were sold as souvenirs without postal validity at Belgica Philatelic Exhibition in Brussels and were displayed at the American Embassies in Paris and Rome. This is reflected in the first day cancel.

Used value for No. UX61b is for a card that is canceled but unaddressed.

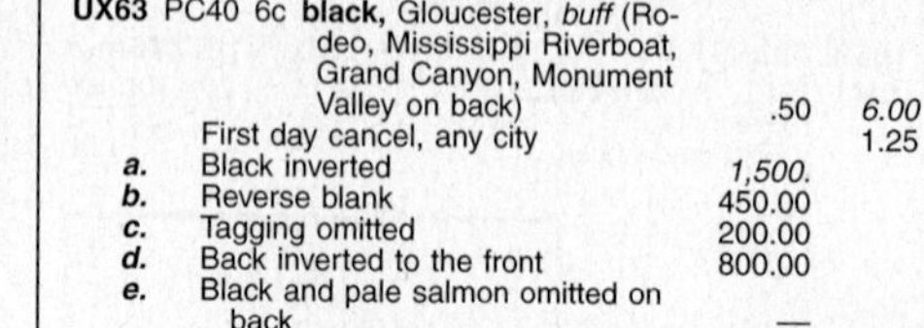

John Hanson — PC41

Designed by Thomas Kronen after statue by Richard Edwin Brooks in Maryland Capitol

Precanceled with 3 printed blue lines.

1972, Sept. 1

UX64 PC41 6c **gray blue** .50 *1.00*
First day cancel, Baltimore, MD 1.00
a. Coarse paper .75 *1.25*

Liberty Type of 1873

Centenary of first U.S. postal card.

1973, Sept. 14

UX65 PC1 6c **magenta** .25 *1.00*
First day cancel, Washington, D.C. *(289,950)* 1.00
a. Tagging omitted *500.00*
b. Tagging inverted at lower left *500.00*

Samuel Adams — PC42

Designed by Howard C. Mildner

Precanceled with 3 printed orange lines

1973, Dec. 16

UX66 PC42 8c **orange** .50 *1.00*
First day cancel, Boston, Mass. *(147,522)* 1.00
a. Coarse paper .75 *1.00*
b. Double impression *1,000.*
c. As "a," double impression *1,750.*

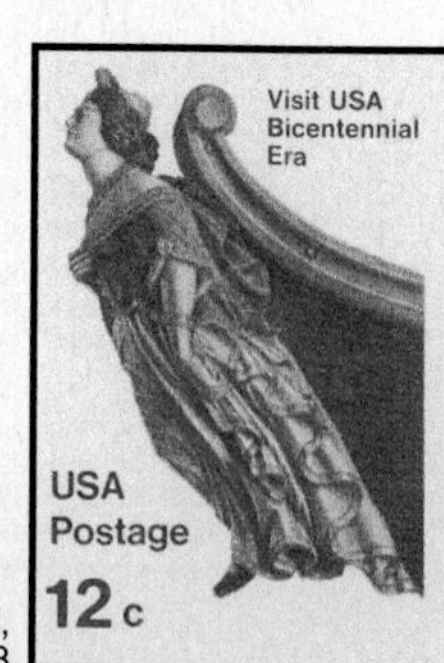

Ship's Figurehead, 1883 — PC43

Design is after a watercolor by Elizabeth Moutal of the oak figurehead by John Rogerson from the barque Edinburgh.

For International Use

1974, Jan. 4

UX67 PC43 12c **multicolored** .35 *50.00*
First day cancel, Miami, Fla. *(138,500)* 1.00
a. Yellow omitted *1,000.*
b. Tagging omitted *300.00*

Charles Thomson — PC44

John Witherspoon — PC45

Caesar Rodney — PC46

Designed by Howard C. Mildner

Precanceled with 3 printed emerald lines

1975-76

UX68 PC44 7c **emerald,** *Sept. 14, 1975* .30 *10.00*
First day cancel, Bryn Mawr, Pa. 1.00

Precanceled with 3 printed brown lines

UX69 PC45 9c **yellow brown,** *Nov. 10, 1975* .30 *1.00*
First day cancel, Princeton, N.J. 1.00

Precanceled with 3 printed blue lines

UX70 PC46 9c **blue,** *July 1, 1976* .30 *1.00*
First day cancel, Dover, Del. 1.00
a. Double impression *4,500.*

First day cancellation applied to 231,919 of Nos. UX68 and UY25; 254,239 of Nos. UX69 and UY26; 304,061 of Nos. UX70 and UY27.

Federal Court House, Galveston, Texas — PC47

The Court House, completed in 1861, is on the National Register of Historic Places.

Designed by Donald Moss

1977, July 20

UX71 PC47 9c **multicolored** .25 *1.00*
First day cancel, Galveston, Tex. *(245,535)* 1.00
a. Black Omitted *6,000.*
b. Tagging omitted 150.00

Nathan Hale — PC48

Designed by Howard C. Mildner

Precanceled with 3 printed green lines

1977, Oct. 14

UX72 PC48 9c **green** .25 *1.00*
First day cancel, Coventry, Conn. 1.00
a. Cent sign missing after "9" 125.00
b. Double impression *1,400.*

First day cancellation applied to 304,592 of Nos. UX72 and UY28.

Approximately 400 examples are recorded of No. UX72a. The variety also exists on fluorescent stock (18 recorded). Value thus is 7 times the listed value.

Cincinnati Music Hall — PC49

Centenary of Cincinnati Music Hall, Cincinnati, Ohio.

Designed by Clinton Orlemann

1978, May 12

UX73 PC49 10c **multicolored** .30 *1.00*
First day cancel, Cincinnati, O. *(300,000)* 1.75

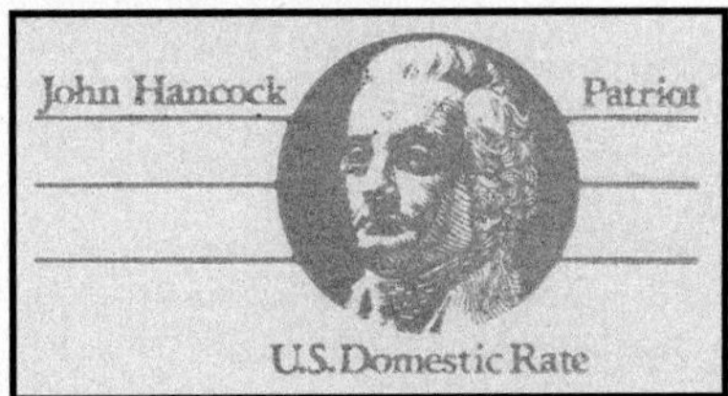

John Hancock — PC50

Designed by Howard Behrens

Precanceled with 3 printed brown orange lines.

1978

UX74 PC50 (10c) **orange brown,** *May 19* .30 *1.00*
First day cancel, Quincy, Mass. *(299,623)* 1.00

Inscribed "U.S. Postage 10¢"

UX75 PC50 10c **brown orange,** *June 20* .30 1.00
First day cancel, Quincy, Mass. *(187,120)* 1.00

Coast Guard Cutter Eagle — PC51

Designed by Carl G. Evers

For International Use

1978, Aug. 4

UX76 PC51 14c **multicolored** .40 *40.00*
First day cancel, Seattle, Wash. *(196,400)* 1.00

Molly Pitcher Firing Cannon at Monmouth — PC52

Bicentennial of Battle of Monmouth, June 28, 1778, and to honor Molly Pitcher (Mary Ludwig Hays).

Designed by David Blossom

1978, Sept. 8 **Litho.**

UX77 PC52 10c **multicolored** .30 *1.60*
First day cancel, Freehold, N.J. *(180,280)* 1.00

Clark and his Frontiersmen Approaching Fort Sackville — PC53

Bicentenary of capture of Fort Sackville from the British by George Rogers Clark.

Designed by David Blossom

1979, Feb. 23 **Litho.**

UX78 PC53 10c **multicolored** .30 *1.50*
First day cancel, Vincennes, Ind. 1.00
a. Yellow omitted —

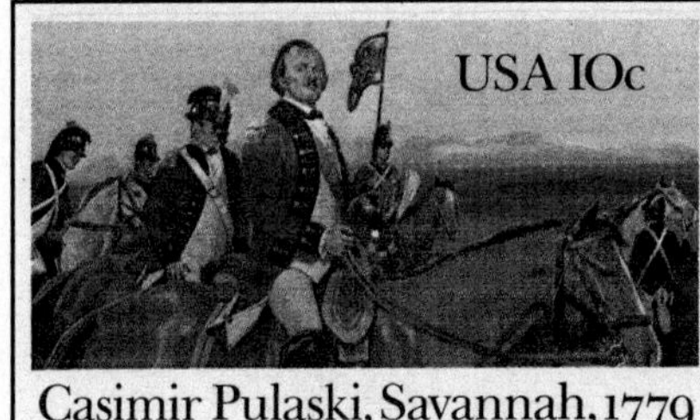

Gen. Casimir Pulaski — PC54

Bicentenary of the death of Gen. Casimir Pulaski (1748-1779), Polish nobleman who served in American Revolutionary Army.

Designed by David Blossom

1979, Oct. 11 **Litho.**

UX79 PC54 10c **multicolored** .30 *1.50*
First day cancel, Savannah. GA *(210,000)* 1.00

Olympic Games Issue

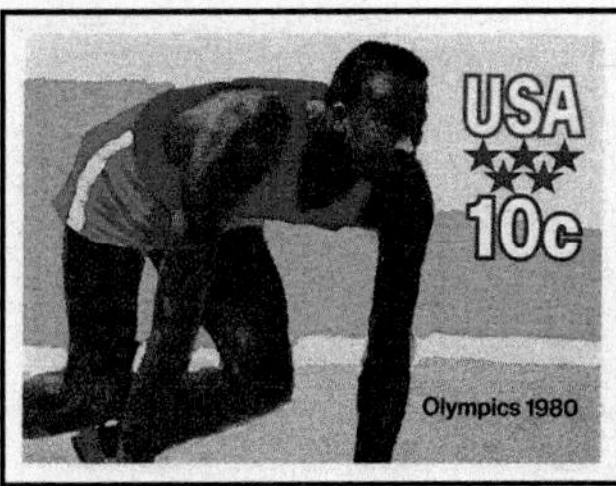

Sprinter PC55

22nd Olympic Games, Moscow, July 19-Aug. 3, 1980.

Designed by Robert M. Cunningham

1979, Sept. 17 **Litho.**

UX80 PC55 10c **multicolored** .60 *1.50*
First day cancel, Eugene, Ore. 1.00
a. Tagging omitted 200.00 *300.00*

Iolani Palace, Honolulu — PC56

Designed by Herb Kawainui Kane

1979, Oct. 1 **Litho.**
UX81 PC56 10c **multicolored** .30 *1.50*
First day cancel, Honolulu, HI *(242,804)* 1.00
a. Tagging omitted — —

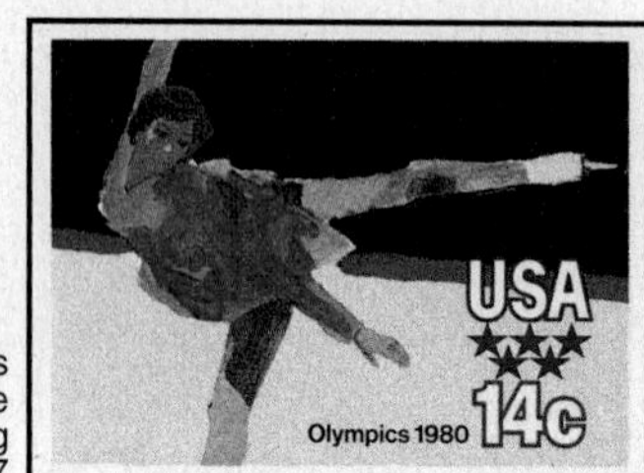

Women's Figure Skating PC57

13th Winter Olympic Games, Lake Placid, N.Y., Feb. 12-24.

Designed by Robert M. Cunningham

For International Use

1980, Jan. 15 **Litho.**
UX82 PC57 14c **multicolored** .60 *35.00*
a. Double impression of tagging bar, one at left *400.00*
First day cancel, Atlanta, GA *(160,977)* 1.00

Salt Lake Temple, Salt Lake City — PC58

1980, Apr. 5 **Litho.**
UX83 PC58 10c **multicolored** .25 *1.50*
First day cancel, Salt Lake City, UT *(325,260)* 1.00
a. Tagging omitted 300.00

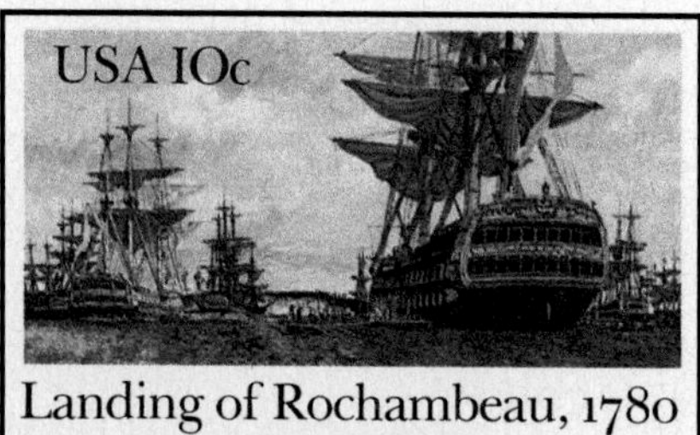

Rochambeau's Fleet — PC59

Count Jean-Baptiste de Rochambeau's landing at Newport, R.I. (American Revolution) bicentenary.

Designed by David Blossom

1980, July 11 **Litho.**
UX84 PC59 10c **multicolored** .25 *1.50*
First day cancel, Newport, R.I. *(180,567)* 1.00
a. Front normal, black & yellow on back *4,000.*
b. Magenta & blue omitted *3,000.*
Preprinting on reverse *1,500.*

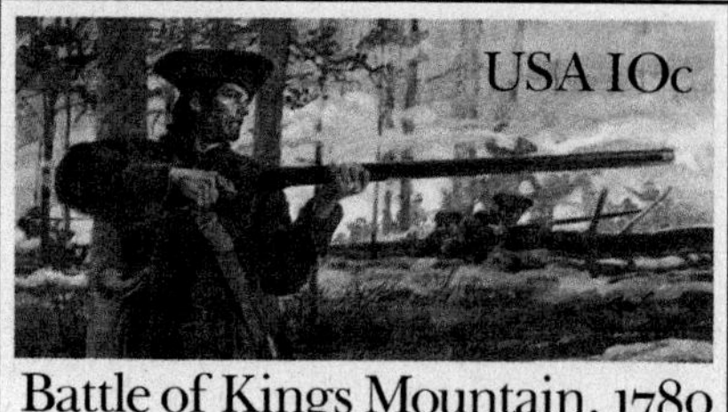

Whig Infantrymen — PC60

Bicentenary of the Battle of Kings Mountain (American Revolution).

Designed by David Blossom

1980, Oct. 7 **Litho.**
UX85 PC60 10c **multicolored** .25 *1.50*
First day cancel, Kings Mountain, NC *(136,130)* 1.00

Golden Hinde — PC61

300th anniv. of Sir Francis Drake's circumnavigation (1578-1580).

Designed by Charles J. Lundgren

For International Use

1980, Nov. 21
UX86 PC61 19c **multicolored** .75 *50.00*
First day cancel, San Rafael, CA *(290,547)* 1.00

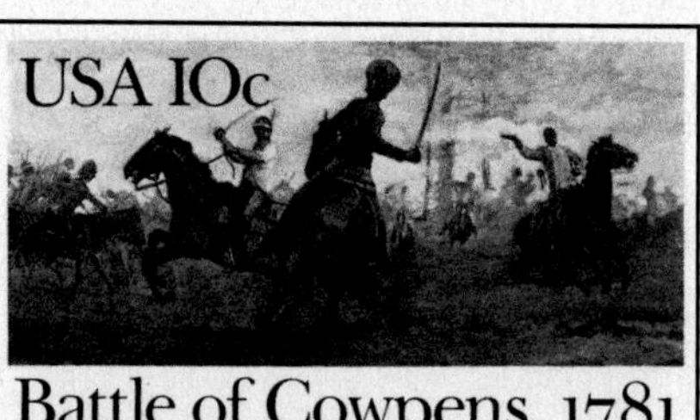

Cols. Washington and Tarleton — PC62

Bicentenary of the Battle of Cowpens (American Revolution).

Designed by David Blossom

1981, Jan. 17
UX87 PC62 10c **multicolored** .25 *25.00*
First day cancel, Cowpens, SC *(160,000)* 1.00

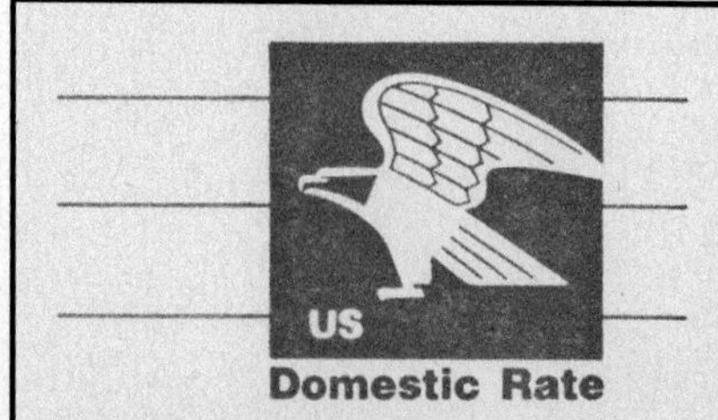

Eagle — PC63

Precanceled with 3 printed violet lines

1981, Mar. 15
UX88 PC63 (12c) **violet** .35 *.65*
First day cancel, Memphis, TN 1.00

See No. 1818, FDC section.

Isaiah Thomas — PC64

Designed by Chet Jezierski

1981, May 5 **Precanceled with 3 printed lines**
UX89 PC64 12c **light blue** .30 *.75*
First day cancel, Worcester, MA *(185,610)* 1.00

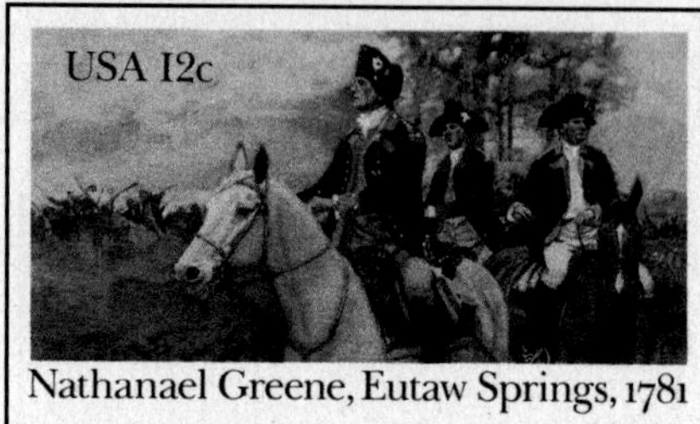

PC65

Bicentenary of the Battle at Eutaw Springs (American Revolution)

Designed by David Blossom

1981, Sept. 8 **Litho.**
UX90 PC65 12c **multicolored** .30 *25.00*
First day cancel, Eutaw Springs, SC *(115,755)* 1.00
a. Red & yellow omitted *2,900.*

PC66

Designed by David Blossom

1981, Sept. 23
UX91 PC66 12c **multicolored** .30 *30.00*
First day cancel, Saint Louis, MO 1.00

Robert Morris — PC67

1981 **Precanceled with 3 printed lines**
UX92 PC67 (13c) **pale org brn,** *Oct. 11* .30 *.60*
First day cancel, Memphis, TN 1.00

See No. 1946, FDC section.

Inscribed: U.S. Postage 13¢

UX93 PC67 13c **buff,** *Nov. 10* .30 *.60*
First day cancel, Philadelphia, PA 1.00
a. Buff omitted 500.00

On No. UX93a, the copyright symbol and "1981" in buff is present at the lower left corner of the card.

General Francis Marion (1732?-1795) — PC68

Designed by David Blossom

1982, Apr. 3 **Litho.**
UX94 PC68 13c **multicolored** .30 *1.00*
First day cancel, Marion, SC *(141,162)* 1.00

Rene Robert Cavelier, Sieur de la Salle (1643-1687) — PC69

Designed by David Blossom

1982, Apr. 7 **Litho.**
UX95 PC69 13c **multicolored** .30 *1.00*
First day cancel, New Orleans, LA 1.00

PC70

Designed by Melbourne Brindle

1982, June 18 **Litho.**
UX96 PC70 13c brown, red & cream, *buff* .30 *1.00*
First day cancel, Philadelphia, PA 1.00
a. Brown & cream omitted *1,000.*

PC71

Designed by Clint Orlemann

1982, Oct. 14 **Litho.**
UX97 PC71 13c **multicolored** .30 *1.00*
First day cancel, St. Louis, MO 1.00

Gen. Oglethorpe Meeting Chief Tomo-Chi-Chi of the Yamacraw — PC72

Designed by David Blossom

1983, Feb. 12 **Litho.**
UX98 PC72 13c **multicolored** .30 *1.00*
First day cancel, Savannah, GA *(165,750)* 1.00

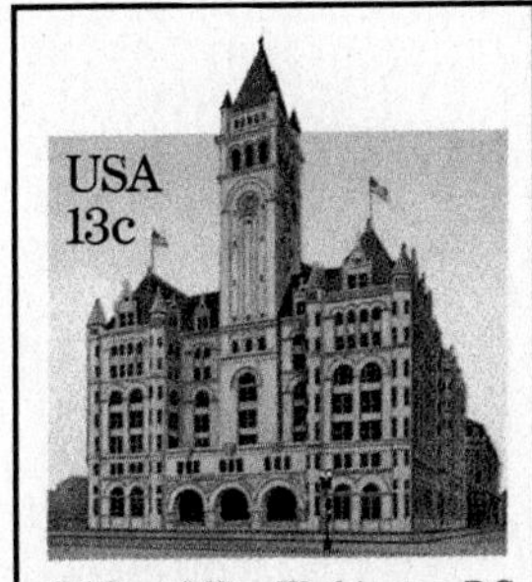

PC73

Designed by Walter Brooks

1983, Apr. 19 **Litho.**
UX99 PC73 13c **multicolored** .30 *1.00*
First day cancel, Washington, DC *(125,056)* 1.00

Olympics 84, Yachting — PC74

Designed by Bob Peak

1983, Aug. 5 **Litho.**
UX100 PC74 13c **multicolored** .30 *1.00*
First day cancel, Long Beach, CA *(132,232)* 1.00
a. Yellow & red omitted *5,500.* —
Preprinted *5,000.*

The Ark and the Dove — PC75

Designed by David Blossom

1984, Mar. 25 **Litho.**
UX101 PC75 13c **multicolored** .30 *1.00*
First day cancel, St. Clement's Island, MD *(131,222)* 1.00

Runner Carrying Olympic Torch — PC76

Designed by Robert Peak

1984, Apr. 30 **Litho.**
UX102 PC76 13c **multicolored** .30 *1.25*
First day cancel, Los Angeles, CA *(110,627)* 1.00
a. Black & yellow inverted 7,000.
b. Tagging omitted 350.00

Father Baraga and Indian Guide in Canoe — PC77

Designed by David Blossom

1984, June 29 **Litho.**
UX103 PC77 13c **multicolored** .30 *1.00*
First day cancel, Marquette, MI *(100,156)* 1.00

Dominguez Adobe at Rancho San Pedro — PC78

Designed by Earl Thollander

1984, Sept. 16 **Litho.**
UX104 PC78 13c **multicolored** .30 *1.00*
First day cancel, Compton, CA *(100,545)* 1.00
a. Black & blue omitted *1,500.*
b. Tagging omitted —

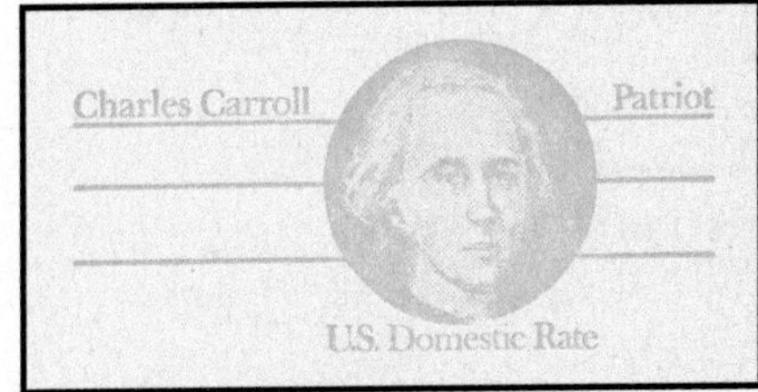

Charles Carroll (1737-1832) — PC79

Designed by Richard Sparks

1985 **Precanceled with 3 printed lines**
UX105 PC79 (14c) **blue green,** *Feb. 1* .45 *.65*
First day cancel, New Carrollton, MD *(135,642)* 1.00

Inscribed: USA 14

UX106 PC79 14c **blue green,** *Mar. 6* .45 *.55*
First day cancel, Annapolis, MD *(111,122)* 1.00

Clipper Flying Cloud — PC80

Designed by Richard Schlecht

For International Use

1985, Feb. 27 **Litho.**
UX107 PC80 25c **multicolored** .70 *35.00*
First day cancel, Salem, MA *(95,559)* 1.25

No. UX107 was sold by the USPS at CUP-PEX 87, Perth, Western Australia, with a cachet honoring CUP-PEX 87 and the America's Cup race. Value $2.

George Wythe (1726-1806) — PC81

Designed by Chet Jezierski from a portrait by John Fergusson.

Precanceled with 3 printed lines

1985, June 20
UX108 PC81 14c **bright apple green** .30 *.75*
First day cancel, Williamsburg, VA *(133,334)* 1.00
a. Indicia missing —

On No. UX108a, the left precancel, "George Wythe" and the copyright symbol are normal.

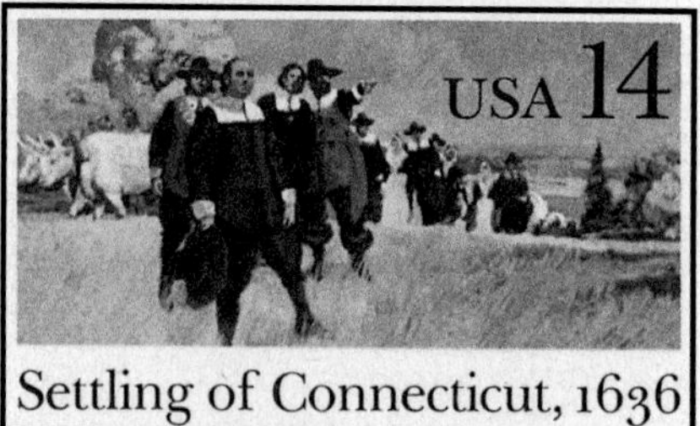

Arrival of Thomas Hooker and Hartford Congregation — PC82

Settlement of Connecticut, 350th Anniv.

Designed by David Blossom

1986, Apr. 18 **Litho.**
UX109 PC82 14c **multicolored** .30 *1.50*
First day cancel, Hartford, CT *(76,875)* 1.00

Stamp Collecting — PC83

Designed by Ray Ameijide

1986, May 23 **Litho.**
UX110 PC83 14c **multicolored** .30 *1.25*
First day cancel, Chicago, IL *(75,548)* 1.00

No. UX110 was sold by the USPS at "Najubria 86," in Germany, with a show cachet. Value: unused, $6; used, $20.

Francis Vigo (1747-1836) — PC84

Designed by David Blossom

1986, May 24 **Litho.**
UX111 PC84 14c **multicolored** .30 *1.25*
First day cancel, Vincennes, IN *(100,141)* 1.00

No. UX111 is a joint issue with an Italy 450-lira postal card of the same design.

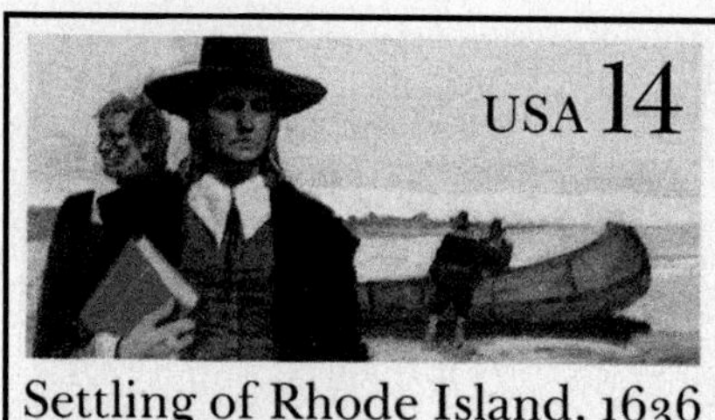

Roger Williams (1603-1683), Clergyman, Landing at Providence — PC85

Settling of Rhode Island, 350th Anniv.

Designed by David Blossom

1986, June 26 **Litho.**
UX112 PC85 14c **multicolored** .30 *1.50*
First day cancel, Providence, RI *(54,559)* 1.00

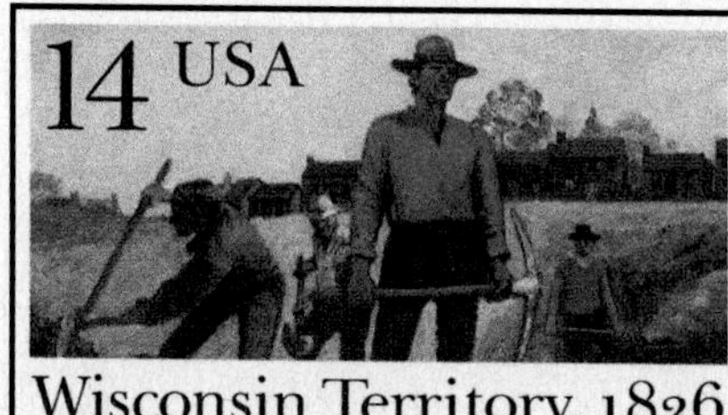

Miners, Shake Rag Street Housing — PC86

Wisconsin Territory Sesquicentennial.

Designed by David Blossom

1986, July 3 **Litho.**
UX113 PC86 14c **multicolored** .30 *1.00*
First day cancel, Mineral Point, WI *(41,224)* 1.00
a. Tagging omitted 200.00

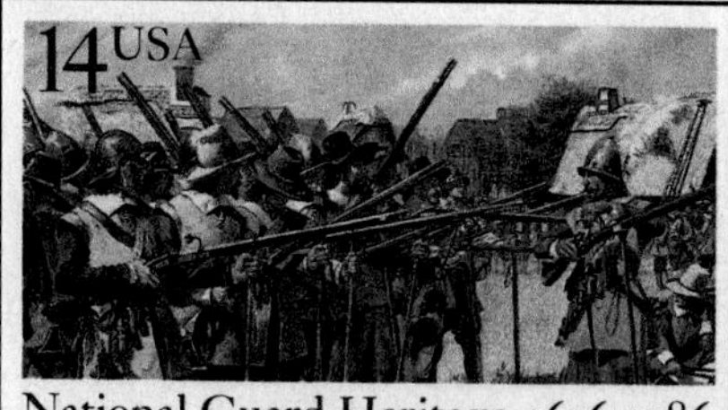

The First Muster, by Don Troiani — PC87

Designed by Bradbury Thompson

1986, Dec. 12 **Litho.**
UX114 PC87 14c **multicolored** .30 *1.25*
First day cancel, Boston, MA *(72,316)* 1.00
a. Tagging omitted —

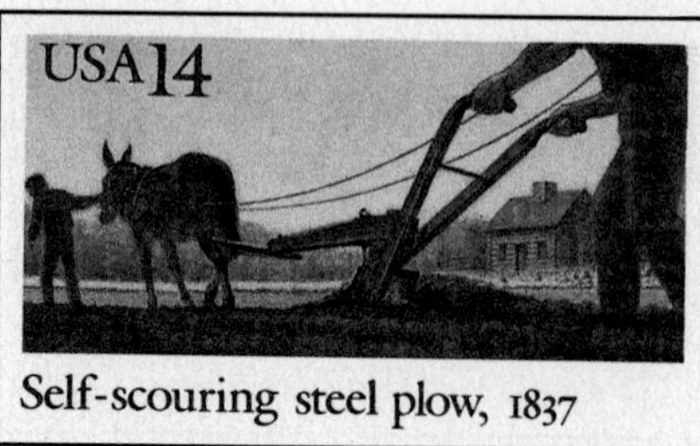

PC88

The self-scouring steel plow invented by blacksmith John Deere in 1837 pictured at lower left.

Designed by William H. Bond

1987, May 22 **Litho.**
UX115 PC88 14c **multicolored** .30 *1.25*
First day cancel, Moline, IL *(160,009)* 1.00

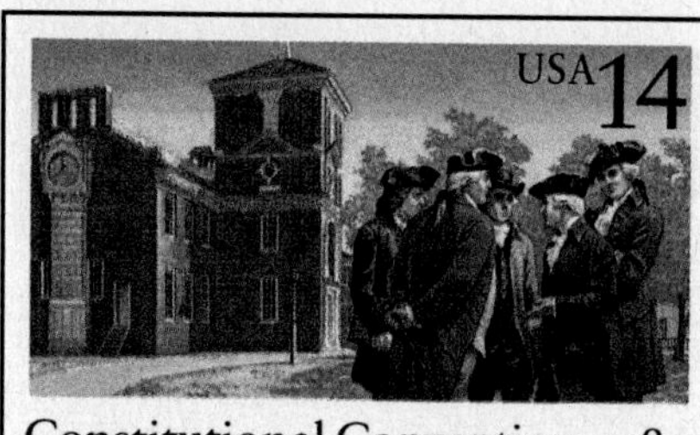

Convening of the Constitutional Convention, 1787 — PC89

George Mason, Gouverneur Morris, James Madison, Alexander Hamilton and Charles C. Pinckney are listed in the lower left corner of the card.

Designed by David K. Stone

1987, May 25 **Litho.**
UX116 PC89 14c **multicolored** .30 *1.00*
First day cancel, Philadelphia, PA *(138,207)* 1.00
a. Double black and blue, with first day cancel *650.00*

Stars and Stripes — PC90

Designed by Steven Dohanos

1987, June 14 **Litho.**
UX117 PC90 14c **black, blue & red** .30 *1.00*
First day cancel, Baltimore, MD 1.00
a. Double impression of tagging bar *250.00*

No. UX117 was sold by the USPS at Cologne, Germany, with a cachet for Philatelia '87. Value $2.

Take Pride in America — PC91

Designed by Lou Nolan

1987, Sept. 22 **Litho.**
UX118 PC91 14c **multicolored** .30 *1.25*
First day cancel, Jackson, WY *(47,281)* 1.00

Timberline Lodge, 50th Anniversary — PC92

Designed by Walter DuBois Richards

1987, Sept. 28 **Litho.**
UX119 PC92 14c **multicolored** .30 *1.25*
First day cancel, Timberline, OR *(63,595)* 1.25

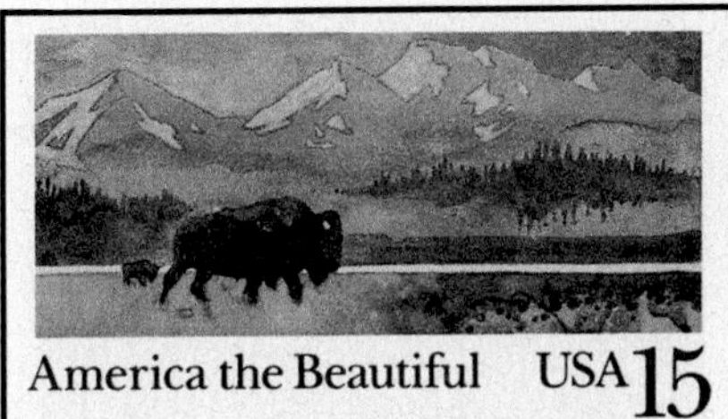

American Buffalo and Prairie — PC93

Designed by Bart Forbes

1988, Mar. 28 **Litho.**
UX120 PC93 15c **multicolored** .30 *.60*
First day cancel, Buffalo, WY *(52,075)* 1.00

a.	Black and tagging omitted	1,750.
b.	Printed on both sides	*350.00*
c.	Front normal, blue & black on back	*500.00*
d.	Black & magenta and tagging omitted	*1,000.*
e.	Black, yellow, blue & tagging omitted	*1,250.*
f.	Black, blue & tagging omitted	*1,750.*
g.	Black, magenta, yellow & tagging omitted	*1,750.*
h.	Double black impression	—
i.	Triple black impression	—
j.	Double black and blue impression	—
k.	Double magenta & blue, and triple black impression	—
l.	Magenta and tagging omitted	—

Tagged

Postal cards from No. UX57 onward are either tagged or printed with luminescent ink unless otherwise noted.

PC94

Inscribed: The President↔s Guest House, Washington, DC at lower left.

Designed by Pierre Mion

1988, May 4 **Litho.**
UX121 PC94 15c **multicolored** .30 *1.00*
First day cancel, Washington, DC *(52,188)* 1.00

Yorkshire, Squarerigged Packet — PC95

Inscribed: Yorkshire, Black Ball Line, Packet Ship, circa 1850 at lower left.

Designed by Richard Schlect

For International Use

1988, June 29 **Litho.**
UX122 PC95 28c **multicolored** .60 *30.00*
First day cancel, Mystic, CT *(46,505)* 1.00

a.	Black & blue omitted	*850.00*
b.	Black, blue, yellow & tagging omitted	*1,250.*
c.	Black, magenta & tagging omitted	*1,000.*
d.	Black, magenta, yellow & tagging omitted	*1,000.*
e.	Black & tagging omitted	*2,000.*

Harvesting Corn Fields — PC96

Iowa Territory Sesquicentennial.

Designed by Greg Hargreaves

1988, July 2 **Litho.**
UX123 PC96 15c **multicolored** .30 *1.00*
First day cancel, Burlington, IA *(45,565)* 1.00

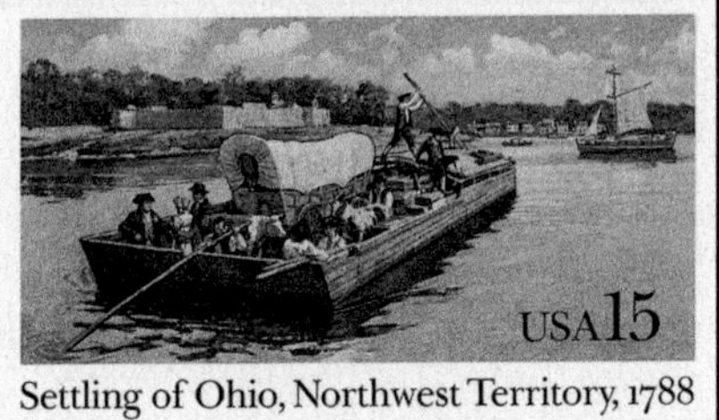

Flatboat Ferry Transporting Settlers Down the Ohio River — PC97

Bicentenary of the settlement of Ohio, the Northwest Territory. Design at lower left shows map of the eastern United States with Northwest Territory highlighted.

Designed by James M. Gurney and Susan Sanford

1988, July 15 **Litho.**
UX124 PC97 15c **multicolored** .30 *1.00*
First day cancel, Marietta, OH *(28,778)* 1.00

a.	Black, blue, yellow & tagging omitted	*1,150.*
b.	Black, magenta & tagging omitted	*750.00*
c.	Blue, black & tagging omitted	*900.00*
d.	Black & tagging omitted	*2,000.*
e.	Black, magenta, yellow & tagging omitted	*1,500.*

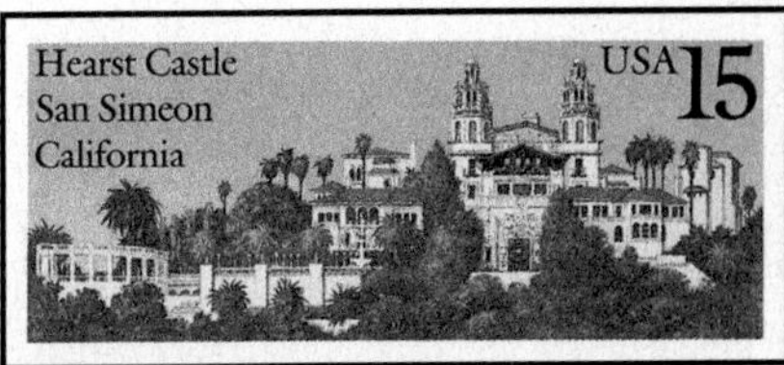

PC98

Designed by Robert Reynolds.
Image of zebra at lower left.

1988, Sept. 20 **Litho.**
UX125 PC98 15c **multicolored** .30 *1.00*
First day cancel, San Simeon, CA *(84,786)* 1.00

a.	Black, magenta & tagging omitted	*750.00*
b.	Black, blue, yellow & tagging omitted	*2,000.*
c.	Black, magenta, yellow & tagging omitted	*1,000.*
d.	Black & tagging omitted	*2,000.*
e.	Black, blue & tagging omitted	*1,000.*

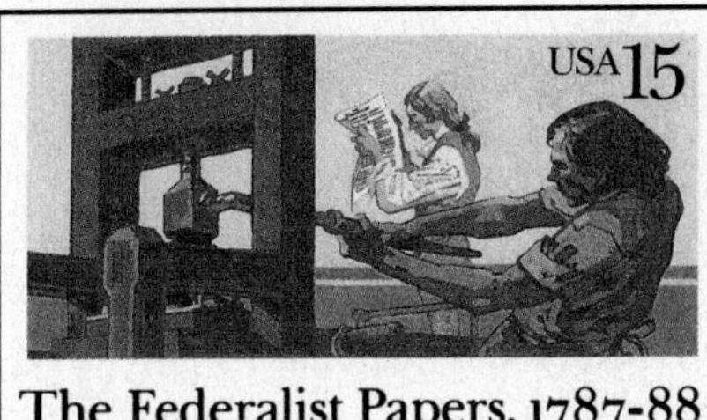

Pressman, New Yorker Reading Newspaper, 1787 — PC99

Designed by Roy Andersen.
Image of book at lower left.

1988, Oct. 27 **Litho.**
UX126 PC99 15c **multicolored** .30 *1.00*
First day cancel, New York, NY *(37,661)* 1.00

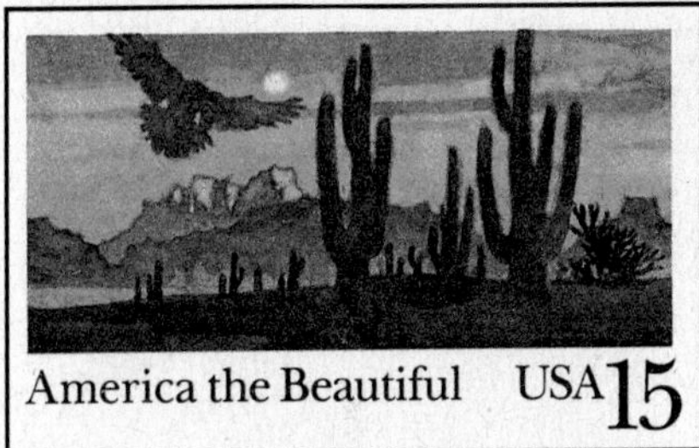

Red-tailed Hawk and Sonora Desert at Sunset — PC100

Designed by Bart Forbes

1989, Jan. 13 **Litho.**
UX127 PC100 15c **multicolored** .30 *1.00*
First day cancel, Tucson, AZ *(51,891)* 1.00

Healy Hall, Georgetown University — PC101

Designed by John Morrell. Inscription at lower left: "Healy Hall / Georgetown / Washington, DC / HISTORIC PRESERVATION."

1989, Jan. 23 **Litho.**
UX128 PC101 15c **multicolored** .30 *1.00*
First day cancel, Washington, DC *(54,897)* 1.00

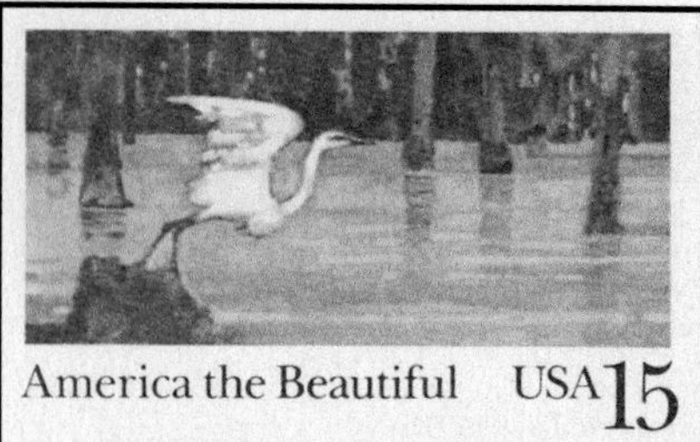

Great Blue Heron, Marsh — PC102

Designed by Bart Forbes

1989, Mar. 17 **Litho.**
UX129 PC102 15c **multicolored** .30 *1.00*
First day cancel, Okefenokee, GA *(58,208)* 1.25

Settling of Oklahoma — PC103

Designed by Bradbury Thompson.
Inscribed: First Land Run, 1889 Territory Established 1890 Cherokee Strip Run, 1893, at lower left.

1989, Apr. 22 **Litho.**
UX130 PC103 15c **multicolored** .30 *1.00*
First day cancel, Guthrie, OK *(68,689)* 1.00

Used values are for contemporaneous usage without additional postage applied. Used values for international-rate cards are for proper usage.

Canada Geese and Mountains — PC104

Designed by Bart Forbes

1989, May 5 **Litho.** **For Use to Canada**
UX131 PC104 21c **multicolored** .50 *35.00*
First day cancel, Denver, CO *(59,303)* 1.25

Seashore — PC105

Designed by Bart Forbes

1989, June 17 **Litho.**
UX132 PC105 15c **multicolored** .30 *1.25*
First day cancel, Cape Hatteras, NC *(67,073)* 1.25

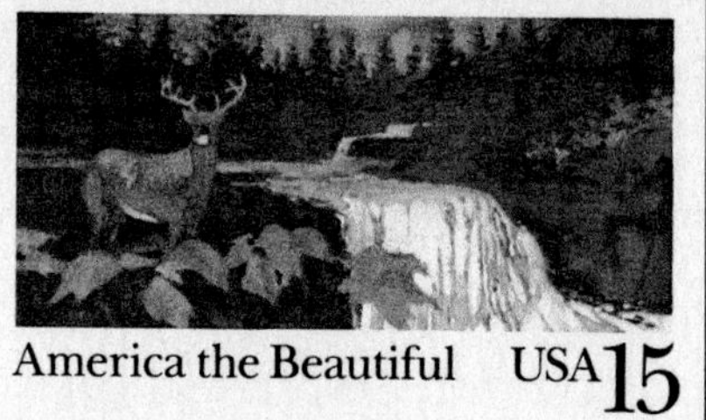

PC106

Designed by Bart Forbes

1989, Aug. 26 **Litho.**
UX133 PC106 15c **multicolored** .30 *1.25*
First day cancel, Cherokee, NC *(67,878)* 1.25

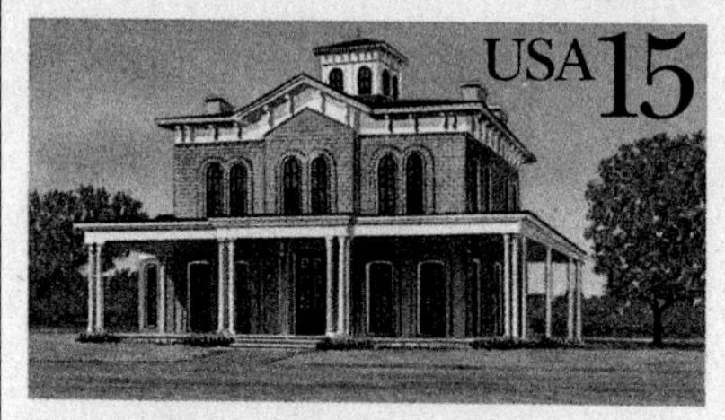

Jane Addams' Hull House Community Center 1889, Chicago — PC107

Designed by Michael Hagel.
Inscribed: Jane Adam↔s Hull House Chicago, 1889 Settlement House at lower left.

1989, Sept. 16 **Litho.**
UX134 PC107 15c **multicolored** .30 *1.25*
First day cancel, Chicago, IL *(53,773)* 1.00

Aerial View of Independence Hall, Philadelphia — PC108

Designed by Bart Forbes.
Inscribed: Philadelphia, Independence Hall at lower left.

1989, Sept. 25 **Litho.**
UX135 PC108 15c **multicolored** .30 *1.25*
First day cancel, Philadelphia, PA *(61,659)* 1.00

See No. UX139.

Inner Harbor, Baltimore — PC109

Designed by Bart Forbes.
Inscription at lower left: Baltimore, Inner Harbor.

1989, Oct. 7 **Litho.**
UX136 PC109 15c **multicolored** .30 *1.25*
First day cancel, Baltimore, MD *(58,746)* 1.00

See No. UX140.

59th Street Bridge, New York City — PC110

Designed by Bart Forbes.
Inscription at lower left: New York City, Manhattan Skyline

1989, Nov. 8 **Litho.**
UX137 PC110 15c **multicolored** .30 *1.25*
First day cancel, New York, NY *(48,044)* 1.00

See No. UX141.

West Face of the Capitol, Washington D.C. — PC111

Designed by Bart Forbes.
Inscription at lower left: Washington, United States Capitol.

1989, Nov. 26 **Litho.**
UX138 PC111 15c **multicolored** .30 *1.25*
First day cancel, Washington, DC 1.00

See No. UX142.

1989, Dec. 1 **Litho.**

Designed by Bart Forbes. Issued in sheets of 4 + 2 inscribed labels picturing 20th UPU Congress or World Stamp Expo '89 emblems, and rouletted 9½ on 2 or 3 sides.

UX139 PC108 15c **multicolored** 3.50 *5.00*
First day cancel, Washington, DC 1.00
UX140 PC109 15c **multicolored** 3.50 *5.00*
First day cancel, Washington, DC 1.00
UX141 PC110 15c **multicolored** 3.50 *5.00*
First day cancel, Washington, DC 1.00
UX142 PC111 15c **multicolored** 3.50 *5.00*
First day cancel, Washington, DC 1.00
a. Sheet of 4, #UX139-UX142 15.00
b. As "a," inverted rouletting —
Nos. UX139-UX142 (4) 14.00 20.00

Unlike Nos. UX135-UX138, Nos. UX139-UX142 do not contain inscription and copyright symbol at lower left. Order on sheet is Nos. UX140, UX139, UX142, UX141.

Most examples of No. UX142a and UX139 are bent at the upper right corner.

No. UX142a sheet size: 279x266mm.

The White House — PC112

Jefferson Memorial — PC113

Designed by Pierre Mion. Space for message at left.

1989 **Litho.**

UX143 PC112 15c **multicolored**, *Nov. 30* 1.50 *12.00*
First day cancel, Washington, DC 2.00
UX144 PC113 15c **multicolored**, *Dec. 2* 1.50 *12.00*
First day cancel, Washington, DC 2.00

Nos. UX143-UX144 sold for 50c each. Illustrations of the buildings without denominations are shown on the back of the card.

Rittenhouse Paper Mill, Germantown, PA — PC114

Designed by Harry Devlin.
Inscription at lower left: American Papermaking 1690-1990, Rittenhouse paper mill circa 1770, design of watermark, This watermark appears on the first paper made in the United States on this site in 1690.

1990, Mar. 13 **Litho.**

UX145 PC114 15c **multicolored** .30 *1.50*
First day cancel, New York, NY *(9,866)* 1.00

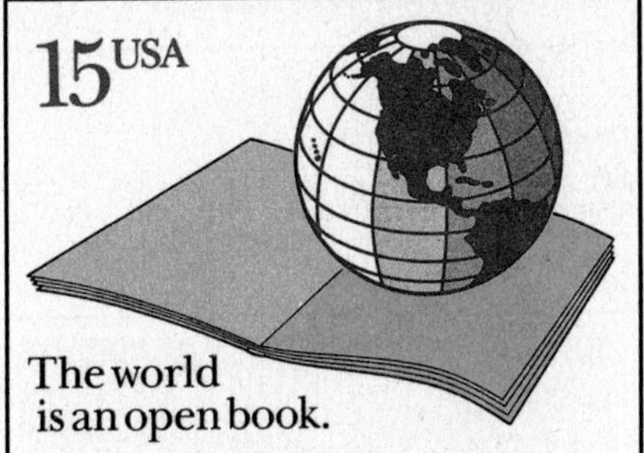

World Literacy Year — PC115

Designed by Joe Brockert.
Inscription at lower left: Literacy: a stronger future, a better world, and picture of a computer.

1990, Mar. 22 **Litho.**

UX146 PC115 15c **multicolored** .30 *1.00*
First day cancel, Washington, DC *(11,163)* 1.00

PC116

Designed by Bradbury Thompson. Inscription in upper left corner: "Fur Traders Descending the Missouri / George Caleb Bingham, 1845 / Metropolitan Museum of Art".

1990, May 4 **Litho.**

UX147 PC116 15c **multicolored** 1.50 *12.00*
First day cancel, St. Louis, MO *(13,632)* 2.00

No. UX147 sold for 50c and shows more of the painting without the denomination on the back.

PC117

Designed by Frank Constantino. Inscription at lower left: "HISTORIC PRESERVATION SERIES / Isaac Royall House, 1700s / Medford, Massachusetts / National Historic Landmark".

1990, June 16 **Litho.**

UX148 PC117 15c **multicolored** .30 *1.50*
First day cancel, Medford, MA *(21,708)* 1.00

Quadrangle, Stanford University — PC119

Designed by Jim M'Guinness.
Inscription at lower left: Stanford Centennial 1891-1991 Memorial Court The Quadrangle.

1990, Sept. 30 **Litho.**

UX150 PC119 15c **multicolored** .30 *1.50*
First day cancel, Stanford, CA *(28,430)* 1.00

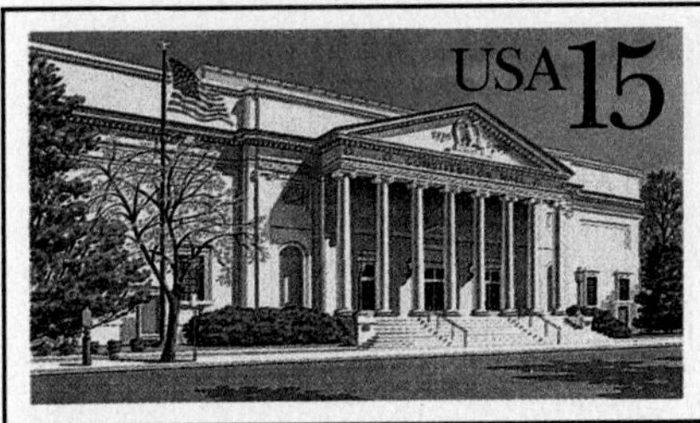

Constitution Hall, Washington, DC — PC120

Designed by Pierre Mion. Inscription at upper left: "Washington: Constitution Hall (at right)/ Memorial Continental Hall (reverse side) / Centennial, Daughters of the American Revolution".

1990, Oct. 11 **Litho.**

UX151 PC120 15c **multicolored** 1.50 *12.00*
First day cancel, Washington, DC *(33,254)* 2.00

No. UX151 sold for 50c.

Chicago Orchestra Hall — PC121

Designed by Michael Hagel. Inscription at lower left: "Chicago: Orchestra Hall / HISTORIC PRESERVATION / Chicago Symphony Orchestra / Centennial, 1891-1991".

1990, Oct. 19 **Litho.**

UX152 PC121 15c **multicolored** .30 *1.50*
First day cancel, Chicago, IL *(28,546)* 1.00

PC122

Designed by Richard Sheaff.

1991, Jan. 24 **Litho.**

UX153 PC122 19c **rose, ultramarine & black** .40 *1.00*
First day cancel, Washington, DC *(26,690)* 1.00

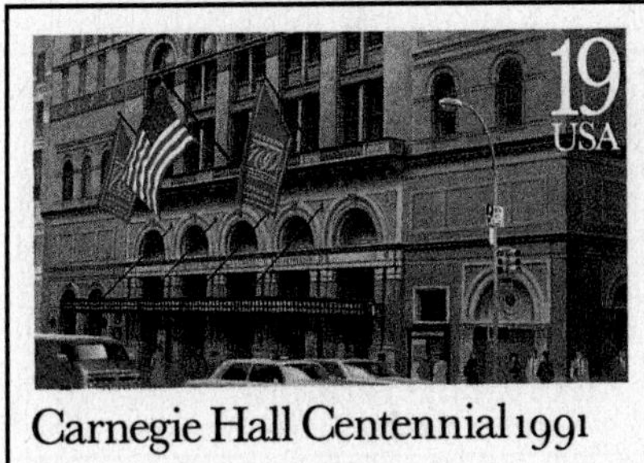

PC123

Designed by Howard Koslow.
Inscription at lower left: Old Red The University of Texas Medical Branch at Galveston.

1991, Apr. 1 **Litho.**

UX154 PC123 19c **multicolored** .40 *1.50*
First day cancel, New York, NY *(27,063)* 1.00

Old Red, University of Texas Medical Branch, Galveston, Cent. — PC124

Designed by Don Adair.

1991, June 14 **Litho.**

UX155 PC124 19c **multicolored** .40 *1.50*
First day cancel, Galveston, TX *(24,308)* 1.00

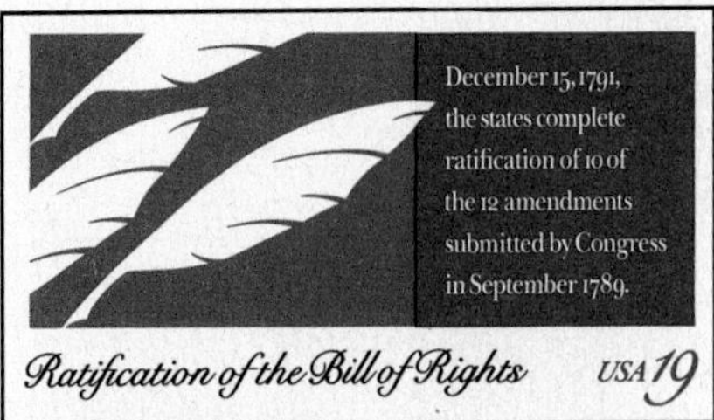

Ratification of the Bill of Rights, Bicent. — PC125

Designed by Mark Zaref.

1991, Sept. 25 **Litho.**

UX156 PC125 19c **red, blue & black** .40 *1.50*
First day cancel, Richmond, VA *(27,457)* 1.00

Main Building, University of Notre Dame PC126

Designed by Frank Costantino. Inscription at lower left: Notre Dame / Sesquicentennial / 1842-1992.

1991, Oct. 15 **Litho.**
UX157 PC126 19c **multicolored** .40 *1.50*
First day cancel, Notre Dame, IN *(34,325)* 1.00

Niagara Falls — PC127

Designed by Wendell Minor.

For Use to Canada & Mexico

1991, Aug. 21 **Litho.**
UX158 PC127 30c **multicolored** .75 *20.00*
First day cover, Niagara Falls, NY *(29,762)* 1.25

Tagged

Postal cards from No. UX57 onward are either tagged or printed with luminescent ink unless otherwise noted.

The Old Mill — PC128

Designed by Harry Devlin. Inscription at lower left: The Old Mill / University of Vermont / Bicentennial.

1991, Oct. 29 **Litho.**
UX159 PC128 19c **multicolored** .40 *1.50*
First day cancel, Burlington, VT *(23,965)* 1.00

Wadsworth Atheneum, Hartford, CT — PC129

Designed by Frank Costantino. Inscription at lower left: Wadsworth Atheneum / Hartford, Connecticut / 150th Anniversary / 1842-1992.

1992, Jan. 16 **Litho.**
UX160 PC129 19c **multicolored** .40 *1.50*
First day cancel, Hartford, CT *(41,499)* 1.00

Cobb Hall, University of Chicago — PC130

Designed by Michael P. Hagel. Inscription at lower left: Cobb Hall / The University of Chicago / Centennial Year, 1991-1992.

1992, Jan. 23 **Litho.**
UX161 PC130 19c **multicolored** .40 *1.50*
First day cancel, Chicago, IL *(27,150)* 1.00

Waller Hall, Willamette University — PC131

Designed by Bradbury Thompson. Inscription at lower left: Waller Hall / Salem, Oregon / Willamette University / Sesquicentennial / 1842-1992.

1992, Feb. 1 **Litho.**
UX162 PC131 19c **multicolored** .40 *1.50*
First day cancel, Salem, OR *(28,463)* 1.00

PC132

Designed by Dennis Simon. Space for message at left. Inscription at upper left: "At right: The Reliance, USA 1903 / Reverse: The Ranger, USA 1937."

1992, May 6 **Litho.**
UX163 PC132 19c **multicolored** 1.75 *12.00*
First day cancel, San Diego, CA *(19,944)* 2.00

No. UX163 sold for 50 cents.

PC133

Designed by Ken Hodges.

1992, May 9 **Litho.**
UX164 PC133 19c **multicolored** .40 *2.00*
First day cancel, Stevenson, WA *(32,344)* 1.00

Ellis Island Immigration Museum — PC134

Designed by Howard Koslow. Inscription at lower left: "Ellis Island / Centennial 1992."

1992, May 11 **Litho.**
UX165 PC134 19c **multicolored** .40 *1.50*
First day cancel, Ellis Island, NY *(38,482)* 1.00

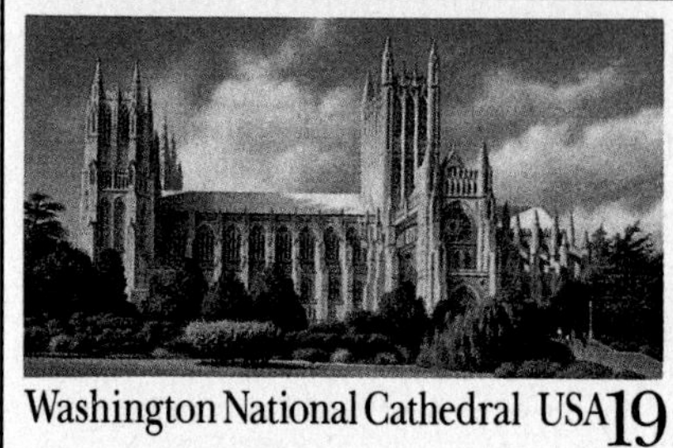

PC135

Designed by Howard Koslow.

1993, Jan. 6 **Litho.**
UX166 PC135 19c **multicolored** .40 *1.50*
First day cancel, Washington, DC *(8,315)* 1.00

PC136

Designed by Pierre Mion.

1993, Feb. 8 **Litho.**
UX167 PC136 19c **multicolored** .40 *1.50*
First day cancel, Williamsburg, VA *(9,758)* 1.00

Opening of Holocaust Memorial Museum — PC137

Designed by Tom Engeman. Space for message at left. Inscription at upper left: "Washington, DC: / United States / Holocaust Memorial Museum."

1993, Mar. 23 **Litho.**
UX168 PC137 19c **multicolored** 1.75 *3.00*
First day cancel, Washington, DC *(8,234)* 2.00

No. UX168 sold for 50c, and shows aerial view of museum on the back.

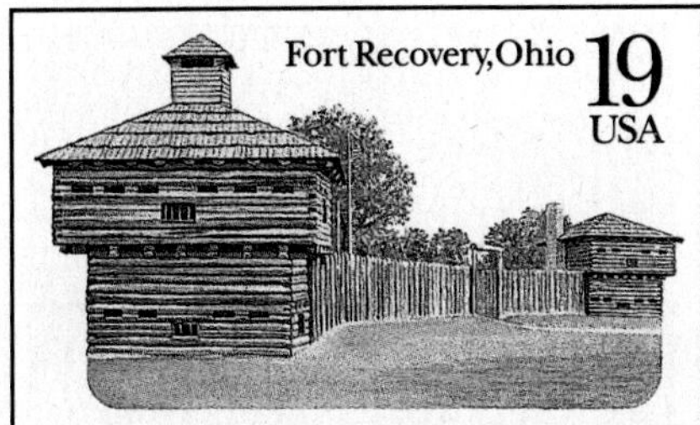

PC138

Designed by Michael Hagel.

1993, June 13 **Litho.**

UX169 PC138 19c **multicolored** .40 *1.25*
First day cancel, Fort Recovery, OH *(8,254)* 1.00

PC139

Designed by Robert Timberlake.

1993, Sept. 14 **Litho.**

UX170 PC139 19c **multicolored** .40 *1.25*
First day cancel, Chapel Hill, NC *(7,796)* 1.00

PC140

Designed by Frank Constantino.

1993, Sept. 17 **Litho.**

UX171 PC140 19c **multicolored** .40 *1.25*
First day cancel, Worcester, MA *(4,680)* 1.00

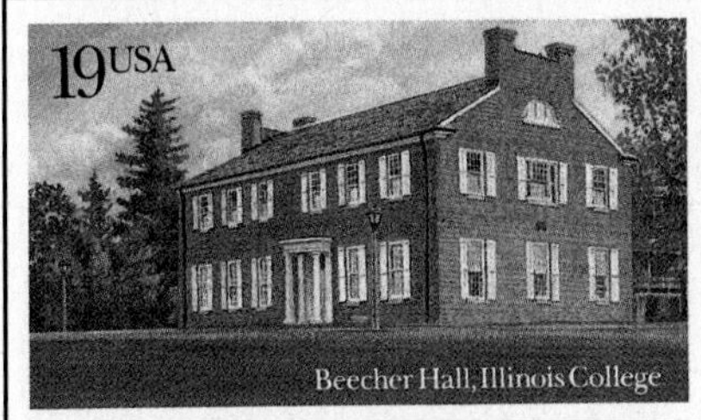

PC141

Designed by Michael Hagel.

1993, Oct. 9 **Litho.**

UX172 PC141 19c **multicolored** .40 *1.50*
First day cancel, Jacksonville, IL *(5,269)* 1.00

PC142

Designed by Harry Devlin.

1993, Oct. 14 **Litho.**

UX173 PC142 19c **multicolored** .40 *1.25*
First day cancel, Brunswick, ME *(33,750 est.)* 1.00

PC143

Designed by Michael Hagel.

1994, Feb. 12 **Litho.**

UX174 PC143 19c **multicolored** .40 *1.25*
First day cancel, Springfield, IL *(26,164)* 1.00

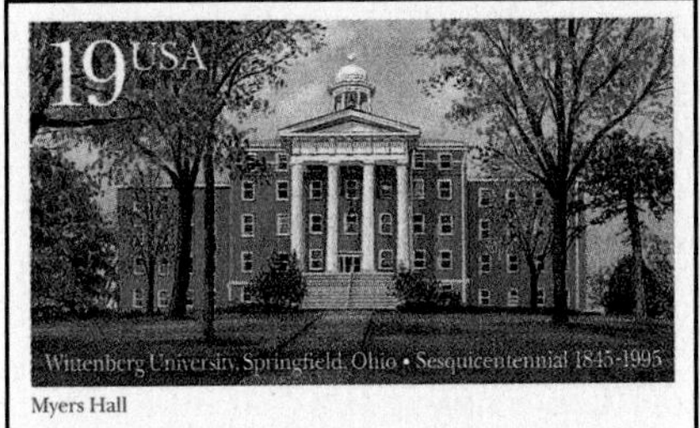

PC144

Designed by Michael Hagel.

1994, Mar. 11 **Litho.**

UX175 PC144 19c **multicolored** .40 *1.25*
First day cancel, Springfield, OH *(20,230)* 1.00

PC145

Designed by William Matthews.

1994, Aug. 11 **Litho.**

UX176 PC145 19c **multicolored** .40 *1.25*
First day cancel, Chinle, AZ *(19,826)* 1.00

St. Louis Union Station — PC146

Designed by Harry Devlin.

1994, Sept. 3 **Litho.**

UX177 PC146 19c **multicolored** .40 *1.25*
First day cancel, St. Louis, MO *(38,881)* 1.00

Legends of the West Type

Designed by Mark Hess.

1994, Oct. 18 **Litho.**

UX178	A2197	19c	Home on the Range	1.10	*3.00*
UX179	A2197	19c	Buffalo Bill	1.10	*3.00*
UX180	A2197	19c	Jim Bridger	1.10	*3.00*
UX181	A2197	19c	Annie Oakley	1.10	*3.00*
UX182	A2197	19c	Native American Culture	1.10	*3.00*
UX183	A2197	19c	Chief Joseph	1.10	*3.00*
UX184	A2197	19c	Bill Pickett (revised)	1.10	*3.00*
UX185	A2197	19c	Bat Masterson	1.10	*3.00*
UX186	A2197	19c	John Fremont	1.10	*3.00*
UX187	A2197	19c	Wyatt Earp	1.10	*3.00*
UX188	A2197	19c	Nellie Cashman	1.10	*3.00*
UX189	A2197	19c	Charles Goodnight	1.10	*3.00*
UX190	A2197	19c	Geronimo	1.10	*3.00*
UX191	A2197	19c	Kit Carson	1.10	*3.00*
UX192	A2197	19c	Wild Bill Hickok	1.10	*3.00*
UX193	A2197	19c	Western Wildlife	1.10	*3.00*
UX194	A2197	19c	Jim Beckwourth	1.10	*3.00*
UX195	A2197	19c	Bill Tilghman	1.10	*3.00*
UX196	A2197	19c	Sacagawea	1.10	*3.00*
UX197	A2197	19c	Overland Mail	1.10	*3.00*
			Nos. UX178-UX197 (20)	22.00	*60.00*
			First day cancel, #UX178-UX197, any card, Tucson, AZ, Lawton, OK or Laramie, WY *(10,000 USPS est.)*		1.50

Nos. UX178-UX197 sold in packages of 20 different for $7.95.
Imprinted stamp illustration without denomination on card back.

Red Barn — PC147

Designed by Wendell Minor.

1995, Jan. 3 **Litho.**

UX198 PC147 20c **multicolored** .40 *.75*
First day cancel, Williamsburg, PA 1.00

First day cancellation was applied to 54,102 of Nos. U632, UX198.

PC148

1995 **Litho.**

UX199 PC148 (20c) **black, blue & red** 3.00 *6.00*

No. UX199 was only available through the Philatelic Fullfillment Center after its announcement 1/12/95. Cards submitted for first day cancels received a 12/13/94 cancel, even though they were not available on that date. Value $1.00.

Civil War Types

Designed by Mark Hess.

1995, June 29		**Litho.**
UX200 A2289 20c Monitor & Virginia	1.75	*3.00*
UX201 A2289 20c Robert E. Lee	1.75	*3.00*
UX202 A2289 20c Clara Barton	1.75	*3.00*
UX203 A2289 20c Ulysses S. Grant	1.75	*3.00*
UX204 A2289 20c Battle of Shiloh	1.75	*3.00*
UX205 A2289 20c Jefferson Davis	1.75	*3.00*
UX206 A2289 20c David Farragut	1.75	*3.00*
UX207 A2289 20c Frederick Douglass	1.75	*3.00*
UX208 A2289 20c Raphael Semmes	1.75	*3.00*
UX209 A2289 20c Abraham Lincoln	1.75	*3.00*
UX210 A2289 20c Harriet Tubman	1.75	*3.00*
UX211 A2289 20c Stand Watie	1.75	*3.00*
UX212 A2289 20c Joseph E. Johnston	1.75	*3.00*
UX213 A2289 20c Winfield Hancock	1.75	*3.00*
UX214 A2289 20c Mary Chesnut	1.75	*3.00*
UX215 A2289 20c Battle of Chancellorsville	1.75	*3.00*
UX216 A2289 20c William T. Sherman	1.75	*3.00*
UX217 A2289 20c Phoebe Pember	1.75	*3.00*
UX218 A2289 20c Stonewall Jackson	1.75	*3.00*
UX219 A2289 20c Battle of Gettysburg	1.75	*3.00*
Nos. UX200-UX219 (20)	35.00	*60.00*
First day cancel, any card, Gettysburg, PA		1.50
First day cancel, any card, any other city		1.50

Nos. UX200-UX219 sold in packages of 20 different for $7.95.

Imprinted stamp illustration without denomination on card back.

PC148a

For International Use

1995, Aug. 24		**Litho.**
UX219A PC148a 50c **multicolored**	1.25	*12.50*
First day cancel, St. Louis, MO *(6,008)*		1.25

PC149

Designed by Richard Sheaff.

1995, Sept. 3		**Litho.**
UX220 PC149 20c **multicolored**	.40	*1.00*
First day cancel, Hunt Valley, MD *(5,281)*		1.00

Comic Strip Types

Designed by Carl Herrman.

1995, Oct. 1		**Litho.**
UX221 A2313 20c The Yellow Kid	2.50	*3.00*
UX222 A2313 20c Katzenjammer Kids	2.50	*3.00*
UX223 A2313 20c Little Nemo in Slumberland	2.50	*3.00*
UX224 A2313 20c Bringing Up Father	2.50	*3.00*
UX225 A2313 20c Krazy Kat	2.50	*3.00*
UX226 A2313 20c Rube Goldberg's Inventions	2.50	*3.00*
UX227 A2313 20c Toonerville Folks	2.50	*3.00*
UX228 A2313 20c Gasoline Alley	2.50	*3.00*
UX229 A2313 20c Barney Google	2.50	*3.00*
UX230 A2313 20c Little Orphan Annie	2.50	*3.00*
UX231 A2313 20c Popeye	2.50	*3.00*
UX232 A2313 20c Blondie	2.50	*3.00*
UX233 A2313 20c Dick Tracy	2.50	*3.00*
UX234 A2313 20c Alley Oop	2.50	*3.00*
UX235 A2313 20c Nancy	2.50	*3.00*
UX236 A2313 20c Flash Gordon	2.50	*3.00*
UX237 A2313 20c Li'l Abner	2.50	*3.00*
UX238 A2313 20c Terry and the Pirates	2.50	*3.00*

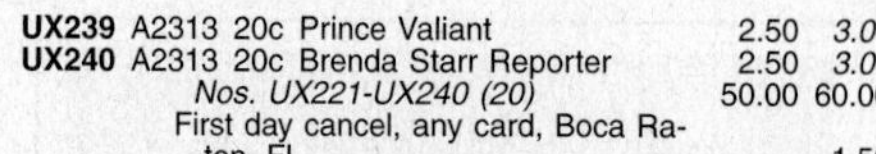

UX239 A2313 20c Prince Valiant	2.50	*3.00*
UX240 A2313 20c Brenda Starr Reporter	2.50	*3.00*
Nos. UX221-UX240 (20)	50.00	60.00
First day cancel, any card, Boca Raton, FL		1.50

Nos. UX221-UX240 sold in packages of 20 different for $7.95.

Imprinted stamp illustration without denomination on card back.

Winter Scene — PC150

1996, Feb. 23		**Litho.**
UX241 PC150 20c **multicolored**	.45	*1.00*
First day cancel, Watertown, NY *(11,764)*		1.00

Summer Olympics Type

Designed by Richard Waldrep.

1996, May 2 **Size: 150x108mm**		**Litho.**
UX242 A2368 20c Men's cycling	2.75	*3.00*
UX243 A2368 20c Women's diving	2.75	*3.00*
UX244 A2368 20c Women's running	2.75	*3.00*
UX245 A2368 20c Men's canoeing	2.75	*3.00*
a. Tagging omitted	—	
UX246 A2368 20c Decathlon (javelin)	2.75	*3.00*
a. Inverted impression of entire address side, men's cycling picture on reverse	*350.00*	
UX247 A2368 20c Women's soccer	2.75	*3.00*
UX248 A2368 20c Men's shot put	2.75	*3.00*
UX249 A2368 20c Women's sailboarding	2.75	*3.00*
UX250 A2368 20c Women's gymnastics	2.75	*3.00*
UX251 A2368 20c Freestyle wrestling	2.75	*3.00*
UX252 A2368 20c Women's softball	2.75	*3.00*
UX253 A2368 20c Women's swimming	2.75	*3.00*
UX254 A2368 20c Men's sprints	2.75	*3.00*
UX255 A2368 20c Men's rowing	2.75	*3.00*
UX256 A2368 20c Beach volleyball	2.75	*3.00*
UX257 A2368 20c Men's basketball	2.75	*3.00*
UX258 A2368 20c Equestrian	2.75	*3.00*
UX259 A2368 20c Men's gymnastics	2.75	*3.00*
UX260 A2368 20c Men's swimming	2.75	*3.00*
UX261 A2368 20c Men's hurdles	2.75	*3.00*
a. Booklet of 20 postal cards, #UX242-UX261	55.00	
First day cancel, any card, Washington, DC		1.50

First day cancels of Nos. UX242-UX261 were available as sets from the US Postal Service. Unused sets of Nos. UX242-UX261 were not available from the US Philatelic Fullfillment Center for several months after the "official" first day. No. UX261a sold for $12.95.

Imprinted stamp illustration without denomination on card back.

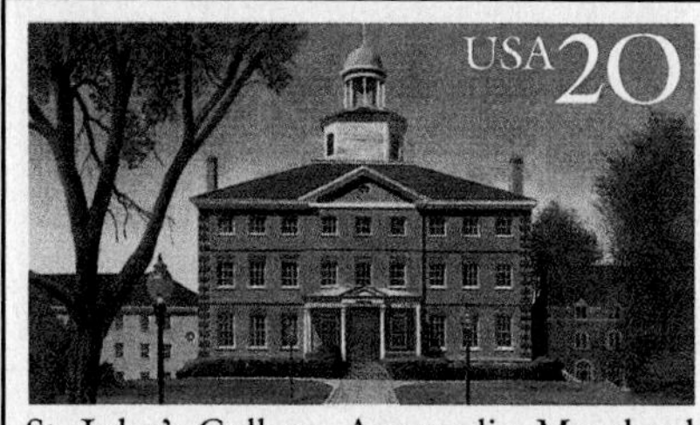

PC151

Designed by Harry Devlin.

1996, June 1		**Litho.**
UX262 PC151 20c **multicolored**	.50	*1.00*
First day cancel, Annapolis, MD *(8,793)*		1.00

PC152

Designed by Howard Koslow.

1996, Sept. 20		**Litho.**
UX263 PC152 20c **multicolored**	.50	*1.00*
First day cancel, Princeton, NJ *(11,621)*		1.00

Endangered Species Type

Designed by James Balog.

1996, Oct. 2		**Litho.**
UX264 A2403 20c Florida panther	3.75	3.00
UX265 A2403 20c Black-footed ferret	3.75	3.00
UX266 A2403 20c American crocodile	3.75	3.00
UX267 A2403 20c Piping plover	3.75	3.00
UX268 A2403 20c Gila trout	3.75	3.00
UX269 A2403 20c Florida manatee	3.75	3.00
UX270 A2403 20c Schaus swallowtail butterfly	3.75	3.00
UX271 A2403 20c Woodland caribou	3.75	3.00
UX272 A2403 20c Thick-billed parrot	3.75	3.00
UX273 A2403 20c San Francisco garter snake	3.75	3.00
UX274 A2403 20c Ocelot	3.75	3.00
UX275 A2403 20c Wyoming toad	3.75	3.00
UX276 A2403 20c California condor	3.75	3.00
UX277 A2403 20c Hawaiian monk seal	3.75	3.00
UX278 A2403 20c Brown pelican	3.75	3.00
a. Booklet of 15 cards, #UX264-UX278	57.50	
First day cancel, #UX264-UX278, any card, San Diego, CA *(5,000)*		1.75

Nos. UX264-UX278 were issued bound three-to-a-page in a souvenir booklet that was sold for $11.95.

Imprinted stamp illustration without denomination on card back.

Love (Swans) Type

Designed by Supon Design.

1997, Feb. 4		**Litho.**
UX279 A2415 20c multicolored	.80	*2.50*

Stamp Designs Depicted on Reverse of Card

Scott 2814	2.50	2.50
Scott 2815	2.50	2.50
Scott 3123	2.50	2.50
Scott 3124	2.50	2.50
Sheet of 4, #2814-2815, 3123-3124	10.00	
Scott 2202	7.50	3.50
Scott 2248	7.50	3.50
Scott 2440	7.50	3.50
Scott 2813	7.50	3.50
Sheet of 4, #2202, 2248, 2440, 2813	30.00	

No. UX279 was sold in sets of 3 sheets of 4 picture postal cards with 8 different designs for $6.95 (two sheets of #2814-2815, 3123-3124 and one sheet of #2202, 2248, 2440, 2813). The cards are separated by microperfs. The picture side of each card depicted a previously released Love stamp design without the inscriptions and value.

First day cancels were not available on Feb. 4. It was announced after Feb. 4 that collectors could purchase the cards and send them to the U.S.P.S. for First Day cancels. Value $1.50 each.

PC153

Designed by Howard Koslow.

1997, May 7		**Litho.**
UX280 PC153 20c **multicolored**	.50	*1.00*
First day cancel, New York, NY *(9,576)*		1.00

Bugs Bunny Type

Designed by Warner Bros.

1997, May 22 **Litho.**

UX281 A2425 20c **multicolored** 1.25 *2.00*
First day cancel, Burbank, CA 1.75
a. Booklet of 10 cards 12.50

No. UX281a sold for $5.95.

First day cancellations applied to 378,142 of Nos. UX281 and 3138.

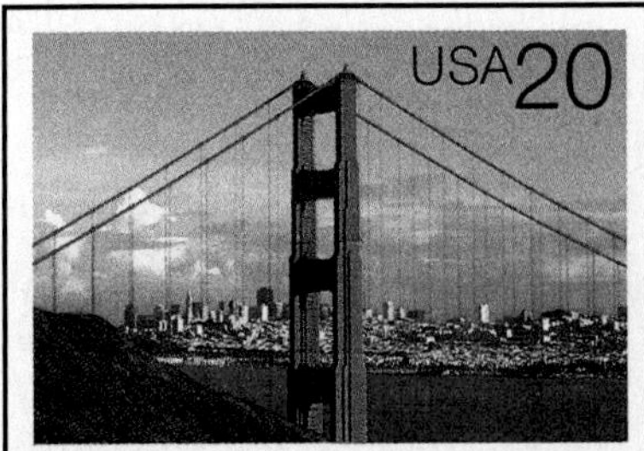

Golden Gate in Daylight — PC154

Golden Gate at Sunset — PC155

Designed by Carol Simowitz.

1997, June 2 **Litho.**

UX282 PC154 20c **multicolored,** *June 2* .40 *1.00*
First day cancel, San Francisco, CA 1.25

For International Use

UX283 PC155 50c **multicolored,** *June 3* 1.10 *15.00*
First day cancel, San Francisco, CA 2.00

First day cancellation was applied to 21,189 of Nos. UX282-UX283.

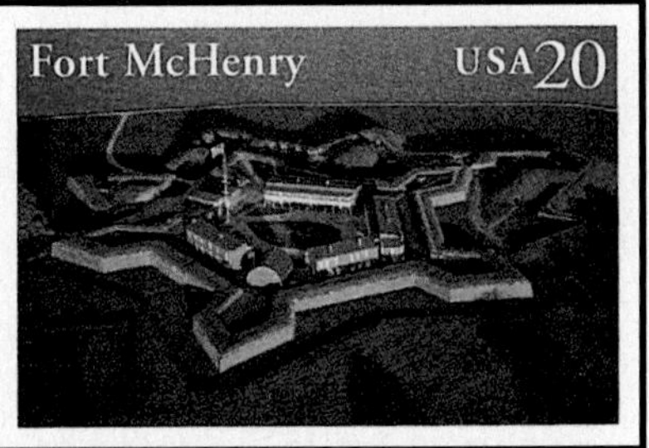

PC156

Designed by Richard Sheaff.

1997, Sept. 7 **Litho.**

UX284 PC156 20c **multicolored** .40 *1.00*
First day cancel, Baltimore, MD *(9,611)* 1.00

Similar to Classic Movie Monsters with 20c Denomination

Designed by Derry Noyes.

1997, Sept. 30 **Litho.**

UX285 A2451 20c Phantom of the Opera 1.60 *2.00*
UX286 A2452 20c Dracula 1.60 *2.00*
UX287 A2453 20c Frankenstein's Monster 1.60 *2.00*
UX288 A2454 20c The Mummy 1.60 *2.00*
UX289 A2455 20c The Wolf Man 1.60 *2.00*
a. Booklet of 20 cards, 4 each #UX285-UX289 32.00
First day cancel, #UX285-UX289, any card, Universal City, CA 1.75

Nos. UX285-UX289 were issued bound in a booklet of 20 cards containing four of each card. Booklet was sold in package for $5.95.

Imprinted stamp illustration without denomination on card back.

PC157

Designed by Howard Paine.

1998, Apr. 20 **Litho.**

UX290 PC157 20c **multicolored** .50 *1.00*
First day cancel, University, MS *(22,276)* 1.00

Similar to Sylvester & Tweety with 20c Denomination

Designed by Brenda Guttman.

1998, Apr. 27 **Litho.**

UX291 A2487 20c **multicolored** 1.40 *2.00*
First day cancel, New York, NY 1.75
a. Booklet of 10 cards 14.00

No. UX291a sold for $5.95.

First day cancellations applied to 231,839 of Nos. UX291, 3204 and 3205.

Imprinted stamp illustration without denomination on card back.

PC158

Designed by Phil Jordan.

1998, May 1 **Litho.**

UX292 PC158 20c **multicolored** .50 *1.00*
First day cancel, Philadelphia, PA *(13,853)* 1.00

Similar to Tropical Birds with 20c Denomination and No Inscription

Designed by Phil Jordan.

1998, July 29 **Litho.**

UX293 A2503 20c Antillean euphonia 1.25 *1.75*
UX294 A2504 20c Green-throated carib 1.25 *1.75*
UX295 A2505 20c Crested honeycreeper 1.25 *1.75*
UX296 A2506 20c Cardinal honeyeater 1.25 *1.75*
a. Booklet of 20 cards, 5 ea #UX293-UX296 25.00
First day cancel, #UX293-UX296, any card, Ponce PR 1.75

Nos. UX293-UX296 were issued bound in a booklet of 20 cards containing five of each card. Illustration of the stamp without denomination is shown on the back of each card. Booklet was sold in packages for $6.95.

Imprinted stamp illustration without denomination on card back.

American Ballet Type

Designed by Derry Noyes.

1998, Sept. 16 **Litho.**

UX297 A2517 20c **multicolored** 1.25 *1.50*
a. Booklet of 10 cards 12.50
First day cancel, New York, NY 1.75

No. UX297a was sold for $5.95.

Imprinted stamp illustration without denomination on card back.

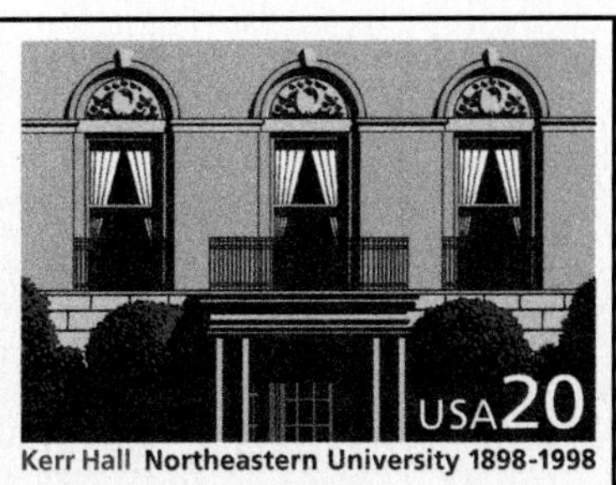

PC159

Designed by Richard Sheaff.

1998, Oct. 3 **Litho.**

UX298 PC159 20c **multicolored** .50 *1.00*
First day cancel, Boston, MA *(14,812)* 1.00

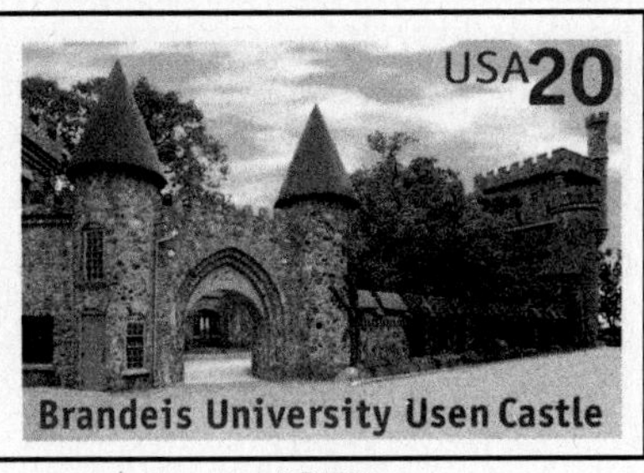

PC160

Designed by Richard Sheaff.

1998, Oct. 17 **Litho.**

UX299 PC160 20c **multicolored** .50 *1.00*
First day cancel, Waltham, MA *(14,137)* 1.00

Victorian Love Type

Designed by John Grossman, Holly Sudduth

1999, Jan. 28 **Litho.**

UX300 A2537 20c **multicolored** 1.25 *1.50*
First day cancel, Loveland, CO 1.00

No. UX300 was sold in packs containing 5 sheets of 4 cards for $6.95.

Imprinted stamp illustration without denomination on card back.

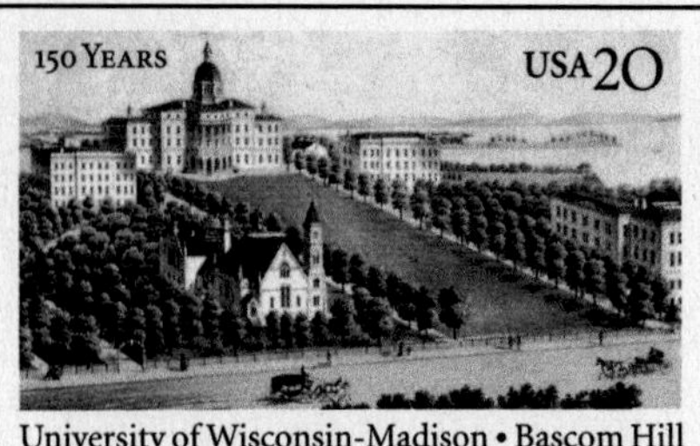

PC161

Designed by Carl Herrman.

1999, Feb. 5 **Litho.**

UX301 PC161 20c **multicolored** .50 *1.00*
First day cancel, Madison, WI *(12,582)* 1.00

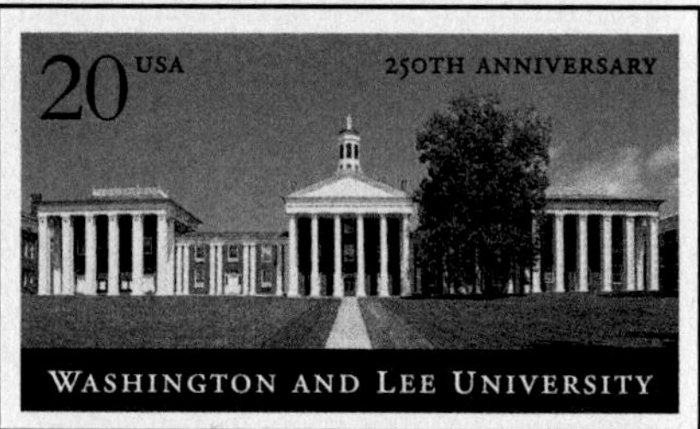

PC162

Designed by Derry Noyes.

1999, Feb. 11

UX302 PC162 20c **multicolored** .50 *1.00*
First day cancel, Lexington, VA *(17,556)* 1.00

PC163

Designed by Richard Sheaff.

1999, Mar. 11

UX303 PC163 20c **red & black** .50 *1.00*
First day cancel, Newport, RI *(13,649)* 1.00

Daffy Duck Type

Designed by Ed Wieczyk.

1999, Apr. 16 **Litho.**

UX304 A2554 20c **multicolored** 1.30 1.30
First day cancel, Los Angeles, CA 1.30
a. Booklet of 10 cards 13.00

No. UX304a sold for $6.95.

First day cancellation was applied to 177,988 of UX304, 3306 and 3307.

Imprinted stamp illustration without denomination on card back.

PC164

Designed by Richard Sheaff.

1999, May 14 **Litho.**

UX305 PC164 20c **multicolored** .50 *1.00*
First day cancel, Mount Vernon, VA *(14,642)* 1.00

Block Island Lighthouse — PC165

Designed by Derry Noyes.

1999, July 24 **Litho.**

UX306 PC165 20c **multicolored** .40 *1.00*
First day cancel, Block Island, RI *(12,694)* 1.25

Famous Trains Type

Designed by Howard Paine.

1999, Aug. 26 **Litho.**

UX307 A2583 20c Super Chief 1.50 *2.00*
UX308 A2582 20c Hiawatha 1.50 *2.00*
UX309 A2579 20c Daylight 1.50 *2.00*
UX310 A2580 20c Congressional 1.50 *2.00*
UX311 A2581 20c 20th Century Limited 1.50 *2.00*
a. Booklet of 20 cards, 4 ea #UX307-UX311 32.50
First day cancel, #UX307-UX311, any card, Cleveland, OH 1.75
First day cancel, #UX307-UX311, any card, any other city 1.75

Nos. UX307-UX311 were issued bound in a booklet of 20 cards containing four of each card. Booklet sold for $6.95.

Imprinted stamp illustration without denomination on card back.

PC166

Designed by Ethel Kessler.

2000, Feb. 28 **Litho.**

UX312 PC166 20c **multicolored** .40 *1.00*
First day cancel, Salt Lake City, UT *(14,230)* 1.00

PC167

Designed by Richard Sheaff.

2000, Mar. 18 **Litho.**

UX313 PC167 20c **multicolored** .40 *1.00*
First day cancel, Nashville, TN *(12,690)* 1.00
a. Double impression —

Road Runner & Wile E. Coyote Type

Designed by Ed Wleczyk, Warner Bros.

2000, Apr. 26 **Litho.**

UX314 A2622 20c **multicolored** 1.40 1.40
First day cancel, Phoenix, AZ 1.40
a. Booklet of 10 cards 14.00

No. UX314a sold for $6.95.

First day cancellation was applied to 154,903 of UX314 and 3391.

Imprinted stamp illustration without denomination on card back.

Adoption Type

Designed by Greg Berger.

2000, May 10 **Litho.**

UX315 A2628 20c **multicolored** 1.40 *1.50*
First day cancel, Beverly Hills, CA 1.40
a. Booklet of 10 cards 14.00

No. UX315a sold for $6.95. The design, without denominations, is shown on the back of the card.

First day cancellation was applied to 137,903 of UX315 and 3398.

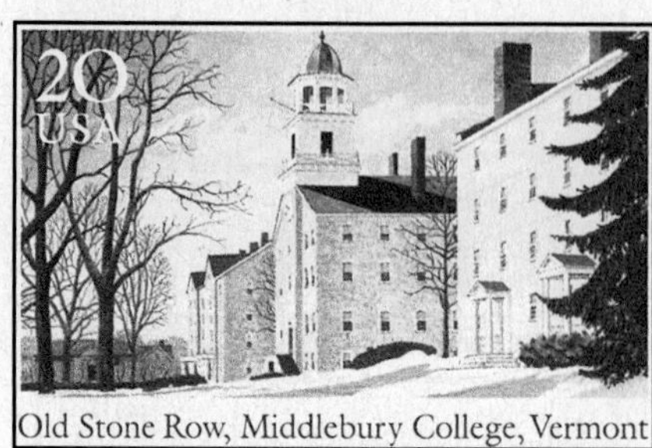

PC168

Designed by Howard Paine.

2000, May 19 **Litho.**

UX316 PC168 20c **multicolored** .40 *1.00*
First day cancel, Middlebury, VT *(13,586)* 1.00

Stars and Stripes Type

Designed by Richard Sheaff.

2000, June 14 **Litho.**

UX317 A2633 20c Sons of Liberty Flag, 1775 2.00 2.00
UX318 A2633 20c New England Flag, 1775 2.00 2.00
UX319 A2633 20c Forster Flag, 1775 2.00 2.00
UX320 A2633 20c Continental Colors, 1776 2.00 2.00
a. Sheet of 4 cards, #UX317-UX320 8.00
UX321 A2633 20c Francis Hopkinson Flag, 1777 2.00 2.00
UX322 A2633 20c Brandywine Flag, 1777 2.00 2.00
UX323 A2633 20c John Paul Jones Flag, 1779 2.00 2.00
UX324 A2633 20c Pierre L'Enfant Flag, 1783 2.00 2.00
a. Sheet of 4 cards, #UX321-UX324 8.00
UX325 A2633 20c Indian Peace Flag, 1803 2.00 2.00
UX326 A2633 20c Easton Flag, 1814 2.00 2.00
UX327 A2633 20c Star-Spangled Banner, 1814 2.00 2.00
UX328 A2633 20c Bennington Flag, c. 1820 2.00 2.00
a. Sheet of 4 cards, #UX325-UX328 8.00
UX329 A2633 20c Great Star Flag, 1837 2.00 2.00
UX330 A2633 20c 29-Star Flag, 1847 2.00 2.00
UX331 A2633 20c Fort Sumter Flag, 1861 2.00 2.00
UX332 A2633 20c Centennial Flag, 1876 2.00 2.00
a. Sheet of 4 cards, #UX329-UX332 8.00
UX333 A2633 20c 38-Star Flag, 1877 2.00 2.00
UX334 A2633 20c Peace Flag, 1891 2.00 2.00
UX335 A2633 20c 48-Star Flag, 1912 2.00 2.00
UX336 A2633 20c 50-Star Flag, 1960 2.00 2.00
a. Sheet of 4 cards, #UX333-UX336 8.00
First day cancel, any card, Baltimore, MD .90

Nos. UX320a, UX324a, UX328a, UX332a and UX336a were sold together in a package for $8.95. Microperforations are between individual cards on each sheet. Illustrations of the flags, without denominations, are shown on the back of the cards.

Legends of Baseball Type

Designed by Phil Jordan.

2000, July 6 **Litho.**

UX337 A2638 20c Jackie Robinson 1.50 1.50
UX338 A2638 20c Eddie Collins 1.50 1.50
UX339 A2638 20c Christy Mathewson 1.50 1.50
UX340 A2638 20c Ty Cobb 1.50 1.50
UX341 A2638 20c George Sisler 1.50 1.50
UX342 A2638 20c Rogers Hornsby 1.50 1.50
UX343 A2638 20c Mickey Cochrane 1.50 1.50
UX344 A2638 20c Babe Ruth 1.50 1.50
UX345 A2638 20c Walter Johnson 1.50 1.50
UX346 A2638 20c Roberto Clemente 1.50 1.50
UX347 A2638 20c Lefty Grove 1.50 1.50
UX348 A2638 20c Tris Speaker 1.50 1.50
UX349 A2638 20c Cy Young 1.50 1.50
UX350 A2638 20c Jimmie Foxx 1.50 1.50
UX351 A2638 20c Pie Traynor 1.50 1.50
UX352 A2638 20c Satchel Paige 1.50 1.50
UX353 A2638 20c Honus Wagner 1.50 1.50
UX354 A2638 20c Josh Gibson 1.50 1.50
UX355 A2638 20c Dizzy Dean 1.50 1.50
UX356 A2638 20c Lou Gehrig 1.50 1.50
a. Booklet of 20 cards, #UX337-UX356 30.00
First day cancel, any card, Atlanta, GA .90

No. UX356a sold for $8.95.

Imprinted stamp illustration without denomination on card back.

Christmas Deer Type of 1999

Designed by Tom Nikosey.

2000, Oct. 12 Litho. *Rouletted on 2 sides*

UX357	A2600 20c **gold & blue**	1.25	1.25
UX358	A2600 20c **gold & red**	1.25	1.25
UX359	A2600 20c **gold & purple**	1.25	1.25
UX360	A2600 20c **gold & green**	1.25	1.25
a.	Sheet of 4, #UX357-UX360	5.00	
	First day cancel, any card, Rudolph, WI		1.75

Nos. UX357-UX360 were sold in packs containing five No. UX360a for $8.95.

Imprinted stamp illustration without denomination on card back.

PC169

Designed by Derry Noyes.

2001, Mar. 30 Litho.

UX361	PC169 20c **multicolored**	.40	*1.00*
	First day cancel, New Haven, CT		1.00

PC170

Designed by Ethel Kessler.

2001, Apr. 26 Litho.

UX362	PC170 20c **multicolored**	.40	*1.00*
	First day cancel, Columbia, SC		1.00

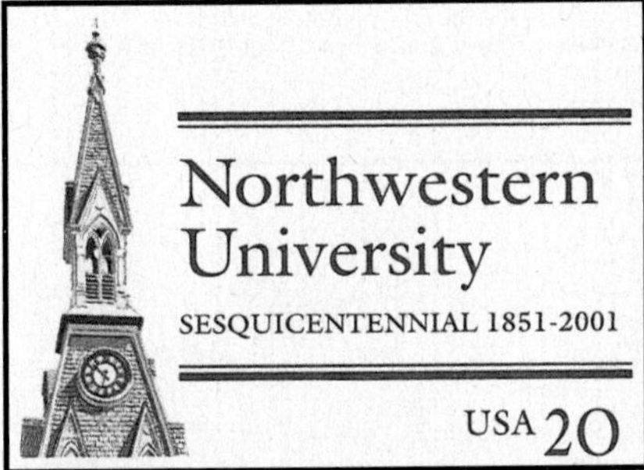

PC171

Designed by Howard Paine.

2001, Apr. 28 Litho.

UX363	PC171 20c **multicolored**	.40	*1.00*
	First day cancel, Evanston, IL		1.00

PC172

Designed by Richard Sheaff.

2001, May 1 Litho.

UX364	PC172 20c **multicolored**	.40	*1.00*
	First day cancel, Portland, OR		1.00

Legendary Playing Fields Type with 21c Denomination

Designed by Phil Jordan.

2001, June 27 Litho.

UX365	A2712 21c Ebbets Field	2.00	2.00
UX366	A2713 21c Tiger Stadium	2.00	2.00
UX367	A2714 21c Crosley Field	2.00	2.00
UX368	A2715 21c Yankee Stadium	2.00	2.00
UX369	A2716 21c Polo Grounds	2.00	2.00
UX370	A2717 21c Forbes Field	2.00	2.00
UX371	A2718 21c Fenway Park	2.00	2.00
UX372	A2719 21c Comiskey Park	2.00	2.00
UX373	A2720 21c Shibe Park	2.00	2.00
UX374	A2721 21c Wrigley Field	2.00	2.00
a.	Booklet of 10 cards, #UX365-UX374	22.50	
	First day cancel, any card, New York, NY, Boston, MA, Chicago, IL, or Detroit MI		1.00

No. UX374a sold for $6.95.

Imprinted stamp illustration without denomination on card back.

White Barn — PC173

Designed by Derry Noyes.

2001, Sept. 20 Litho.

UX375	PC173 21c **multicolored**	.45	*1.00*
	First day cancel, Washington, DC		1.00

That's All Folks! Type

Designed by Ed Wleczyk, Warner Bros.

2001, Oct. 1 Litho.

UX376	A2736 21c **multicolored**	1.50	1.50
	First day cancel, Beverly Hills, CA		1.50
a.	Booklet of 10 cards	15.00	

No. UX376a sold for $7.25.

Imprinted stamp illustration without denomination on card back.

Christmas Santas Type

Designed by Richard Sheaff.

2001, Oct. 10 Litho. *Rouletted on 2 Sides*

UX377	A2740 21c **multicolored**	1.25	1.25
UX378	A2741 21c **multicolored**	1.25	1.25
UX379	A2738 21c **multicolored**	1.25	1.25
UX380	A2739 21c **multicolored**	1.25	1.25
a.	Sheet of 4, #UX377-UX380	5.50	
	First day cancel, any card, Santa Claus, IN		1.25

Packages of 5 No. UX380a sold for $9.25.

Imprinted stamp illustration without denomination on card back.

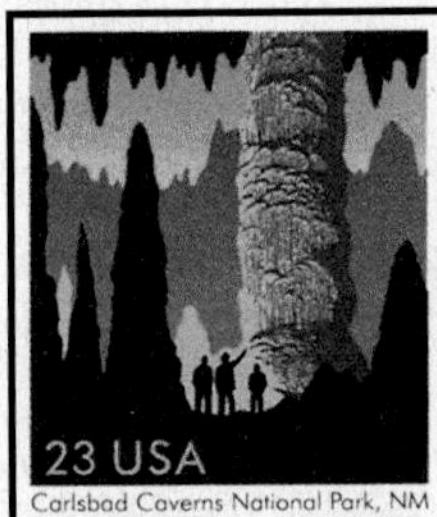

Carlsbad Caverns National Park — PC174

Designed by Carl Herrman.

2002, June 7 Litho.

UX381	PC174 23c **multicolored**	.50	*.75*
	First day cancel, Carlsbad, NM		1.00
	First day cancel, any other city		1.00

Teddy Bears Type

Designed by Margaret Bauer.

2002, Aug. 15 Litho. *Rouletted on 2 Sides*

UX382	A2827 23c Ideal Bear, c. 1905	1.25	1.25
UX383	A2826 23c Gund Bear, c. 1948	1.25	1.25
UX384	A2824 23c Bruin Bear, c. 1907	1.25	1.25
UX385	A2825 23c "Stick" Bear, 1920s	1.25	1.25
a.	Sheet of 4, #UX382-UX385	5.50	
	First day cancel, any card, Atlantic City, NJ		1.25

Packages of 5 No. UX385a sold for $9.25.

Imprinted stamp illustration without denomination on card back.

Christmas Snowmen Type

Designed by Derry Noyes.

2002, Oct. 28 Litho. *Rouletted on 2 Sides*

Design Size: 28x38mm

UX386	A2844 23c **multicolored**	1.25	1.25
UX387	A2845 23c **multicolored**	1.25	1.25
UX388	A2846 23c **multicolored**	1.25	1.25
UX389	A2847 23c **multicolored**	1.25	1.25
a.	Sheet of 4, #UX386-UX389	5.50	
	First day cancel, any card, Houghton, MI		1.00

Packages of 5 #UX389a sold for $9.75.

Photograph of family of snowmen similar to stamp illustrations on card back.

Old Glory Type

Designed by Richard Sheaff.

2003, Apr. 3 Litho. *Rouletted on 1 Side*

UX390	A2883 23c **multicolored**	1.25	1.25
UX391	A2884 23c **multicolored**	1.25	1.25
UX392	A2885 23c **multicolored**	1.25	1.25
UX393	A2886 23c **multicolored**	1.25	1.25
UX394	A2887 23c **multicolored**	1.25	1.25
a.	Booklet of 20 cards, 4 each #UX390-UX394	25.00	
	First day cancel, any card, New York, NY		1.00

No. UX394a sold for $9.75.

Imprinted stamp illustration without denomination on card back.

Southeastern Lighthouses Type

Designed by Howard E. Paine.

2003, June 13 Litho. *Rouletted on 1 Side*

UX395	A2893 23c **multicolored**	1.25	1.25
UX396	A2894 23c **multicolored**	1.25	1.25
UX397	A2895 23c **multicolored**	1.25	1.25
UX398	A2896 23c **multicolored**	1.25	1.25
UX399	A2897 23c **multicolored**	1.25	1.25
a.	Booklet of 20 cards, 4 each #UX395-UX399	25.00	
	First day cancel, any card, Tybee Island, GA		1.00

No. UX399a sold for $9.75.

Imprinted stamp illustration without denomination on card back.

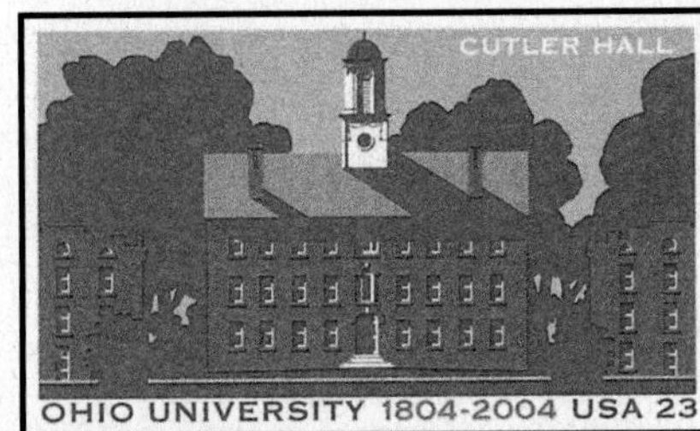

Ohio University, 200th Anniv. — PC175

Designed by Tom Engemann.

2003, Oct. 10 Litho.

UX400	PC175 23c **multicolored**	.50	*1.00*
	First day cancel, Athens, OH		1.00

Christmas Music Makers Type

Designed by Ethel Kessler.

2003, Oct. 23 Litho. *Rouletted on 2 Sides*

UX401	A2917 23c **multicolored**	1.10	1.10
UX402	A2918 23c **multicolored**	1.10	1.10
UX403	A2919 23c **multicolored**	1.10	1.10
UX404	A2920 23c **multicolored**	1.10	1.10
a.	Sheet of 4, #UX401-UX404	4.50	
	First day cancel, any card, New York, NY		1.00

Packages of 5 #UX404a sold for $9.75.

Imprinted stamp illustration without denomination on card back.

Columbia University, 250th Anniv. — PC176

Designed by Tom Engeman.

2004, Mar. 25 **Litho.**
UX405 PC176 23c **multicolored** .50 *1.00*
First day cancel, New York, NY 1.00

Harriton House, Bryn Mawr, PA, Bicent. PC177

Designed by Carl T. Herrman.

2004, June 10 **Litho.**
UX406 PC177 23c **multicolored** .50 *1.00*
First day cancel, Bryn Mawr, PA 1.00

Disney: Friendship Type of 2004

Designed by David Pacheco.

2004, June 23 **Litho.**
UX407 A2950 23c **multicolored** 1.50 1.25
UX408 A2951 23c **multicolored** 1.50 1.25
UX409 A2949 23c **multicolored** 1.50 1.25
UX410 A2952 23c **multicolored** 1.50 1.25
a. Booklet of 20 cards, 5 each #UX407-UX410 30.00
First day cancel, any card, Anaheim, CA 1.00

No. UX410a sold for $9.75.

Imprinted stamp illustration without denomination on card back.

Art of the American Indian Type of 2003

Designed by Richard Sheaff.

2004, Aug. 21 **Litho.** ***Rouletted on 1 Side***
UX411 A2957 23c Mimbres bowl 1.25 1.25
UX412 A2957 23c Kutenai parfleche 1.25 1.25
UX413 A2957 23c Tlingit sculptures 1.25 1.25
UX414 A2957 23c Ho-Chunk bag 1.25 1.25
UX415 A2957 23c Seminole doll 1.25 1.25
UX416 A2957 23c Mississippian effigy 1.25 1.25
UX417 A2957 23c Acoma pot 1.25 1.25
UX418 A2957 23c Navajo weaving 1.25 1.25
UX419 A2957 23c Seneca carving 1.25 1.25
UX420 A2957 23c Luiseño basket 1.25 1.25
a. Booklet of 20 cards, 2 each #UX411-UX420 25.00
First day cancel, any card, Santa Fe, NM 1.00

No. UX420a sold for $9.75.

Imprinted stamp illustration without denomination on card back.

Cloudscapes Type

Designed by Howard E. Paine.

2004, Oct. 4 **Litho.** ***Rouletted at Left***
UX421 A2960 23c Cirrus radiatus 1.60 *2.50*
UX422 A2960 23c Cirrostratus fibratus 1.60 *2.50*
UX423 A2960 23c Cirrocumulus undulatus 1.10 *1.50*
UX424 A2960 23c Cumulonimbus mammatus 1.10 *1.50*
UX425 A2960 23c Cumulonimbus incus 1.60 *2.50*
UX426 A2960 23c Altocumulus stratiformis 1.10 *1.50*
UX427 A2960 23c Altostratus translucidus 1.60 *2.50*
UX428 A2960 23c Altocumulus undulatus 1.10 *1.50*
UX429 A2960 23c Altocumulus castellanus 1.60 *2.50*
UX430 A2960 23c Altocumulus lenticularis 1.10 *1.50*
UX431 A2960 23c Stratocumulus undulatus 1.60 *2.50*
UX432 A2960 23c Stratus opacus 1.60 *2.50*
UX433 A2960 23c Cumulus humilis 1.60 *2.50*
UX434 A2960 23c Cumulus congestus 1.60 *2.50*
UX435 A2960 23c Cumulonimbus with tornado 1.60 *2.50*
a. Booklet of 20, #UX421-UX422, UX425, UX427, UX429, UX431-UX435, 2 each #UX423-UX424, UX426, UX428, UX430 27.00
First day cancel, any card, Milton, MA 1.00

No. UX435a sold for $9.75.

Imprinted stamp illustration without denomination on card back.

Disney: Celebration Type of 2005

Designed by David Pacheco.

2005, June 30 **Litho.**
UX436 A2989 23c **multicolored** 1.25 1.10
UX437 A2990 23c **multicolored** 1.25 1.10
UX438 A2991 23c **multicolored** 1.25 1.10
UX439 A2992 23c **multicolored** 1.25 1.10
a. Booklet of 20 cards, 5 each #UX436-UX439 25.00
First day cancel, any card, Anaheim, CA 1.00

No. UX439a sold for $9.75.

Imprinted stamp illustration without denomination on card back.

Sporty Cars Type of 2005

Designed by Art M. Fitzpatrick.

2005, Aug. 20 **Litho.** ***Rouletted at Left***
UX440 A3012 23c 1955 Ford Thunderbird 1.25 1.00
UX441 A3011 23c 1952 Nash Healey 1.25 1.00
UX442 A3010 23c 1953 Chevrolet Corvette 1.25 1.00
UX443 A3008 23c 1953 Studebaker Starliner 1.25 1.00
UX444 A3009 23c 1954 Kaiser Darrin 1.25 1.00
a. Booklet of 20 cards, 4 each #UX440-UX444 25.00
First day cancel, any card, Detroit, MI 1.75

No. UX444a sold for $9.75.

Imprinted stamp illustration without denomination on card back.

Let's Dance Type

Designed by Ethel Kessler.

2005, Sept. 17 **Litho.** ***Rouletted at Left***
UX445 A3018 23c Cha cha cha 1.25 1.00
UX446 A3019 23c Mambo 1.25 1.00
UX447 A3017 23c Salsa 1.25 1.00
UX448 A3016 23c Merengue 1.25 1.00
a. Booklet of 20, 5 each #UX445-UX448 25.00
First day cancel, any card, New York, NY 1.75
First day cancel, any card, Miami, FL 1.75

No. UX448a sold for $9.75.

Imprinted stamp illustration without denomination on card back.

USA 24
Pike Expedition, November 1806, Rocky Mountains

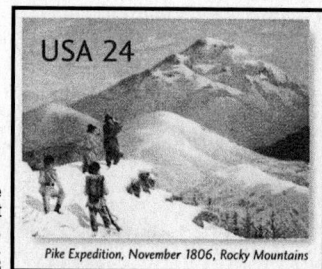

Zebulon Pike Expedition at Pikes Peak, Bicent. PC178

Designed by Carl Herrman.

2006, Jan. 9 **Litho.**
UX449 PC178 24c **multicolored** .55 *1.00*
First day cancel, Washington, DC 1.75
First day cancel, any other city 1.75

Disney: Romance Type of 2006

Designed by David Pacheco.

2006, Apr. 21 **Litho.** ***Rouletted at Left***
UX450 A3066 24c **multicolored** 1.25 1.00
UX451 A3067 24c **multicolored** 1.25 1.00
UX452 A3069 24c **multicolored** 1.25 1.00
UX453 A3068 24c **multicolored** 1.25 1.00
a. Booklet of 20, 5 each #UX450-UX453 25.00
First day cancel, any card, Orlando, FL 1.75

No. UX453a sold for $9.75.

Imprinted stamp illustration without denomination on card back.

Baseball Sluggers Type of 2006

Designed by Phil Jordan.

2006, July 15 **Litho.** ***Rouletted at Left***
UX454 A3121 24c Mickey Mantle 1.25 1.25
UX455 A3118 24c Roy Campanella 1.25 1.25
UX456 A3119 24c Hank Greenberg 1.25 1.25
UX457 A3120 24c Mel Ott 1.25 1.25
a. Booklet of 20 cards, 5 each #UX454-UX457 25.00
First day cancel, any card, Bronx, NY 1.75

No. UX457a sold for $9.95.

Imprinted stamp illustration without denomination on card back.

DC Comics Superheroes Type of 2006

Designed by Carl T. Herrman.

2006, July 20 **Litho.** ***Rouletted at Left***
UX458 A3122 24c Superman cover 1.50 1.50
UX459 A3122 24c Superman 1.50 1.50
UX460 A3122 24c Batman cover 1.50 1.50
UX461 A3122 24c Batman 1.50 1.50
UX462 A3122 24c Wonder Woman cover 1.50 1.50
UX463 A3122 24c Wonder Woman 1.50 1.50
UX464 A3122 24c Green Lantern cover 1.50 1.50
UX465 A3122 24c Green Lantern 1.50 1.50
UX466 A3122 24c Green Arrow cover 1.50 1.50
UX467 A3122 24c Green Arrow 1.50 1.50
UX468 A3122 24c The Flash cover 1.50 1.50
UX469 A3122 24c The Flash 1.50 1.50
UX470 A3122 24c Plastic Man cover 1.50 1.50
UX471 A3122 24c Plastic Man 1.50 1.50
UX472 A3122 24c Aquaman cover 1.50 1.50
UX473 A3122 24c Aquaman 1.50 1.50
UX474 A3122 24c Supergirl cover 1.50 1.50
UX475 A3122 24c Supergirl 1.50 1.50
UX476 A3122 24c Hawkman cover 1.50 1.50
UX477 A3122 24c Hawkman 1.50 1.50
a. Booklet of 20 cards, #UX458-UX477 30.00
First day cancel, any card, San Diego, CA 1.75

No. UX477a sold for $9.95.

Imprinted stamp illustration without denomination on card back.

Southern Florida Wetland Type of 2006

Designed by Ethel Kessler.

2006, Oct. 4 **Litho.** ***Rouletted on 1 Side***
UX478 A3137 39c Snail kite 4.50 4.00
UX479 A3137 39c Cape Sable seaside sparrow 4.50 4.00
a. Sheet of 2, #UX478-UX479 9.00
UX480 A3137 39c Wood storks 4.50 4.00
UX481 A3137 39c Florida panther 4.50 4.00
a. Sheet of 2, #UX480-UX481 9.00
UX482 A3137 39c Bald eagle 4.50 4.00
UX483 A3137 39c White ibis 4.50 4.00
a. Sheet of 2, #UX482-UX483 9.00
UX484 A3137 39c American crocodile 4.50 4.00
UX485 A3137 39c Everglades mink 4.50 4.00
a. Sheet of 2, #UX484-UX485 9.00
UX486 A3137 39c Roseate spoonbills 4.50 4.00
UX487 A3137 39c American alligator 4.50 4.00
a. Sheet of 2, #UX486-UX487 9.00
First day cancel, any card, Naples, FL 2.00
Nos. UX478-UX487 (10) 45.00 40.00

Packet of 10 cards sold for $7.95.

Imprinted stamp illustration without denomination on card back.

Pineapple — PC179

Designed by Ethel Kessler.

2007, May 12 **Litho.**
UX488 PC179 26c **multicolored** .60 *1.00*
First day cancel, Washington, DC 1.75

Star Wars Type of 2007

Designed by Terrence McCaffrey and William J. Gicker, Jr.

2007, May 27 **Litho.** ***Rouletted at Left***
UX489 A3153 26c Darth Vader 1.75 1.75
UX490 A3153 26c Luke Skywalker 1.75 1.75
UX491 A3153 26c C-3PO 1.75 1.75
UX492 A3153 26c Queen Padmé Amidala 1.75 1.75
UX493 A3153 26c Millennium Falcon 1.75 1.75
UX494 A3153 26c Emperor Palpatine 1.75 1.75
UX495 A3153 26c Anakin Skywalker and Obi-Wan Kenobi 1.75 1.75
UX496 A3153 26c Obi-Wan Kenobi 1.75 1.75
UX497 A3153 26c Boba Fett 1.75 1.75
UX498 A3153 26c Darth Maul 1.75 1.75
UX499 A3153 26c Yoda 1.75 1.75
UX500 A3153 26c Princess Leia and R2-D2 1.75 1.75
UX501 A3153 26c Chewbacca and Han Solo 1.75 1.75
UX502 A3153 26c X-wing Starfighter 1.75 1.75

UX503 A3153 26c Stormtroopers 1.75 1.75
a. Booklet of 15, #UX489-UX503 26.00
First day cancel, any card, Los Angeles, CA 3.00

No. UX503a sold for $12.95.

Imprinted stamp illustration without denomination on card back.

Pacific Lighthouses Type of 2007

Designed by Howard E. Paine.

2007, June 21 **Litho.** ***Rouletted at Left***
UX504 A3158 26c Grays Harbor Lighthouse 1.25 1.25
UX505 A3157 26c Five Finger Lighthouse 1.25 1.25
UX506 A3159 26c Umpqua River Lighthouse 1.25 1.25
UX507 A3156 26c Diamond Head Lighthouse 1.25 1.25
UX508 A3160 26c St. George Reef Lighthouse 1.25 1.25
a. Booklet of 20, 4 each #UX504-UX508 26.00
First day cancel, any card, Westport, WA 2.50

No. UX503a sold for $12.95.

Imprinted stamp illustration without denomination on card back.

Marvel Comics Superheroes Type of 2006

Designed by Carl T. Herrman.

2007, July 26 **Litho.** ***Rouletted at Left***
UX509 A3168 26c Spider-Man 1.25 1.25
UX510 A3168 26c The Hulk 1.25 1.25
UX511 A3168 26c Sub-Mariner 1.25 1.25
UX512 A3168 26c The Thing 1.25 1.25
UX513 A3168 26c Captain America 1.25 1.25
UX514 A3168 26c Silver Surfer 1.25 1.25
UX515 A3168 26c Spider-Woman 1.25 1.25
UX516 A3168 26c Iron Man 1.25 1.25
UX517 A3168 26c Elektra 1.25 1.25
UX518 A3168 26c Wolverine 1.25 1.25
UX519 A3168 26c Spider-Man cover 1.25 1.25
UX520 A3168 26c Incredible Hulk cover 1.25 1.25
UX521 A3168 26c Sub-Mariner cover 1.25 1.25
UX522 A3168 26c Fantastic Four cover 1.25 1.25
UX523 A3168 26c Captain America cover 1.25 1.25
UX524 A3168 26c Silver Surfer cover 1.25 1.25
UX525 A3168 26c Spider-Woman cover 1.25 1.25
UX526 A3168 26c Iron Man cover 1.25 1.25
UX527 A3168 26c Elektra cover 1.25 1.25
UX528 A3168 26c X-Men cover 1.25 1.25
a. Booklet of 20 cards, #UX509-UX528 26.00
First day cancel, any card, San Diego, CA 1.75

No. UX528a sold for $12.95.

Imprinted stamp illustration without denomination on card back.

Disney: Magic Type of 2007

Designed by David Pacheco.

2007, Aug. 16 **Litho.** ***Rouletted at Left***
UX529 A3185 26c Mickey Mouse 1.25 1.25
UX530 A3186 26c Peter Pan and Tinker Bell 1.25 1.25
UX531 A3187 26c Dumbo and Timothy Mouse 1.25 1.25
UX532 A3188 26c Aladdin and Genie 1.25 1.25
a. Booklet of 20, 5 each #UX529-UX532 26.00
First day cancel, any card, Orlando, FL 2.50

No. UX503a sold for $12.95.

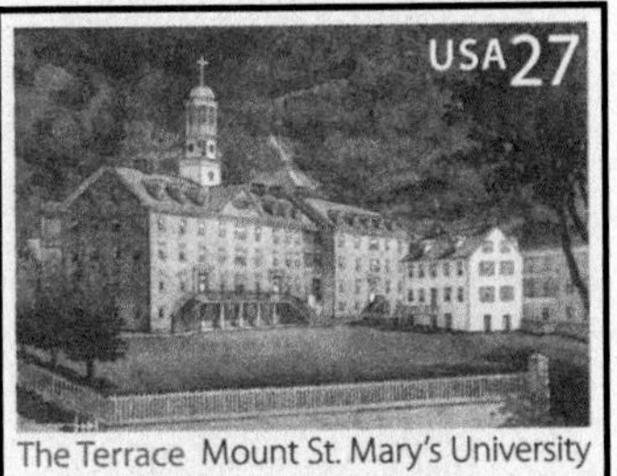

Mount St. Mary's University, Bicent. PC180

Designed by Richard Sheaff.

2008, Apr. 26 **Litho.**
UX533 PC180 27c **multicolored** .60 *1.00*
First day cancel, Emmitsburg, MD 1.75

Corinthian Column From Capitol Building — PC181

Designed by Gerald Gallo.

2008, May 12 **Litho.**
UX534 PC181 27c **multicolored** .60 *1.00*
First day cancel, Washington, DC 1.75

Disney: Imagination Type of 2008

Designed by David Pacheco.

2008, Aug. 7 **Litho.** ***Rouletted at Left***
UX535 A3305 27c Steamboat Willie 1.40 1.40
UX536 A3304 27c Pongo and Pup 1.40 1.40
UX537 A3306 27c Princess Aurora, Flora, Fauna, Merryweather 1.40 1.40
UX538 A3307 27c Mowgli and Baloo 1.40 1.40
a. Booklet of 20, 5 each #UX535-UX538 28.00
First day cancel, any card, Anaheim, CA 2.60

No. UX538a sold for $13.95.

Imprinted stamp illustration without denomination on card back.

Great Lakes Dunes Type of 2008

Designed by Ethel Kessler.

2008, Oct. 2 **Litho.** ***Rouletted on 1 Side***
UX539 A3312 42c Vesper sparrow 1.90 1.90
UX540 A3312 42c Piping plover 1.90 1.90
a. Sheet of 2, #UX539-UX540 4.00
UX541 A3312 42c Eastern hognose snake 1.90 1.90
UX542 A3312 42c Common mergansers 1.90 1.90
a. Sheet of 2, #UX541-UX542 4.00
UX543 A3312 42c Piping plover nestlings 1.90 1.90
UX544 A3312 42c Red fox 1.90 1.90
a. Sheet of 2, #UX543-UX544 4.00
UX545 A3312 42c Tiger beetle 1.90 1.90
UX546 A3312 42c White-footed mouse 1.90 1.90
a. Sheet of 2, #UX545-UX546 4.00
UX547 A3312 42c Spotted sandpiper 1.90 1.90
UX548 A3312 42c Red admiral butterfly 1.90 1.90
a. Sheet of 2, #UX547-UX548 4.00
First day cancel, any card, Empire, MI 3.00
Nos. UX539-UX548 (10) 19.00 19.00

Packet of 10 cards sold for $8.95.

Imprinted stamp illustration without denomination on card back.

Automobiles of the 1950s Type of 2008

Designed by Carl T. Herrman.

2008, Oct. 3 **Litho.** ***Rouletted at Left***
UX549 A3316 27c 1957 Lincoln Premiere 1.40 1.40
UX550 A3317 27c 1957 Chrysler 300C 1.40 1.40
UX551 A3313 27c 1959 Cadillac Eldorado 1.40 1.40
UX552 A3314 27c 1957 Studebaker Golden Hawk 1.40 1.40
UX553 A3315 27c 1957 Pontiac Safari 1.40 1.40
a. Booklet of 20, 4 each #UX549-UX553 28.00
First day cancel, any card, Carlisle, PA 2.60

No. UX553a sold for $13.95.

Imprinted stamp illustration without denomination on card back.

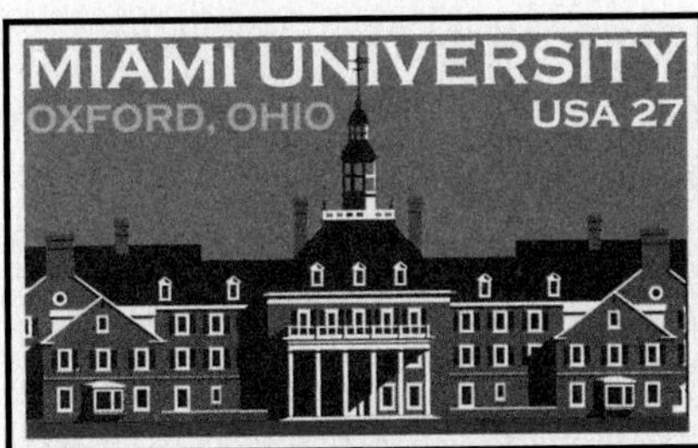

Miami University (Oxford, Ohio), Bicent. — PC182

Designed by Howard E. Paine

2009, Feb. 17 **Litho.**
UX554 PC182 27c **multicolored** .60 *1.00*
First day cancel, Oxford, OH 1.75

White, Orange and White Koi — PC183

Black, Red and White Koi — PC184

Designed by Ethel Kessler.

2009, Apr. 17 **Litho.**
UX555 PC183 28c **multicolored** .65 *1.00*
First day cancel, New York, NY 1.90
UX556 PC184 28c **multicolored** .65 *1.00*
First day cancel, New York, NY 1.90
a. Pair, #UX555-UX556 1.50

Nos. UX555 and UX556 were also printed in uncut sheets of 40 cards (20 of each) on a rougher stock and having a background dot pattern that differs from the cut cards. Nos. UX555 and UX556 were sold in 2010 with a "Cradle to Cradle" recycling emblem added to the front of the card.

The Simpsons Type of 2009

Designed by Matt Groening.

2009, May 7 **Litho.** ***Rouletted at Left***
UX557 A3345 28c Homer Simpson 1.50 1.50
UX558 A3346 28c Marge Simpson 1.50 1.50
UX559 A3347 28c Bart Simpson 1.50 1.50
UX560 A3348 28c Lisa Simpson 1.50 1.50
UX561 A3349 28c Maggie Simpson 1.50 1.50
a. Booklet of 20, 4 each #UX557-UX561 30.00
First day cancel, any card, Los Angeles, CA 2.75

No. UX561a sold for $14.95.

Imprinted stamp illustration without denomination on card back.

Gulf Coast Lighthouses Type of 2009

Designed by Howard E. Paine.

2009, July 23 **Litho.** ***Rouletted at Left***
UX562 A3354 28c Matagorda Island Lighthouse 1.50 1.50
UX563 A3355 28c Sabine Pass Lighthouse 1.50 1.50
UX564 A3356 28c Biloxi Lighthouse 1.50 1.50
UX565 A3357 28c Sand Island Lighthouse 1.50 1.50
UX566 A3358 28c Fort Jefferson Lighthouse 1.50 1.50
a. Booklet of 20, 4 each #UX562-UX566 30.00
First day cancel, any card, Biloxi, MS 2.75

No. UX566a sold for $14.95.

Imprinted stamp illustration without denomination on card back.

Early TV Memories Type of 2009

Designed by Carl T. Herrman.

2009, Aug. 11 **Litho.** ***Rouletted at Left***
UX567 A3359 28c Alfred Hitchcock Presents 1.50 1.50
UX568 A3359 28c Burns and Allen 1.50 1.50
UX569 A3359 28c The Dinah Shore Show 1.50 1.50
UX570 A3359 28c Dragnet 1.50 1.50
UX571 A3359 28c The Ed Sullivan Show 1.50 1.50
UX572 A3359 28c The Honeymooners 1.50 1.50
UX573 A3359 28c Hopalong Cassidy 1.50 1.50
UX574 A3359 28c Howdy Doody 1.50 1.50
UX575 A3359 28c I Love Lucy 1.50 1.50
UX576 A3359 28c Kukla, Fran and Ollie 1.50 1.50
a. With Dragnet picture on back *550.00*
UX577 A3359 28c Lassie 1.50 1.50
a. With Ed Sullivan picture on back —
UX578 A3359 28c The Lone Ranger 1.50 1.50
UX579 A3359 28c Ozzie and Harriet 1.50 1.50
UX580 A3359 28c Perry Mason 1.50 1.50
UX581 A3359 28c The Phil Silvers Show 1.50 1.50
UX582 A3359 28c The Red Skelton Show 1.50 1.50
UX583 A3359 28c Texaco Star Theater 1.50 1.50
UX584 A3359 28c The Tonight Show 1.50 1.50
UX585 A3359 28c The Twilight Zone 1.50 1.50
UX586 A3359 28c You Bet Your Life 1.50 1.50
a. Booklet of 20, #UX567-UX586 30.00
First day cancel, any card, North Hollywood, CA 2.75

No. UX586a sold for $14.95.

Imprinted stamp illustration without denomination on card back.

Kelp Forest Type of 2009

Designed by Ethel Kessler.

2009, Oct. 1 **Litho.** ***Rouletted on 1 Side***
UX587 A3367 44c Western gull, southern sea otters, red sea urchin 1.90 1.90
UX588 A3367 44c Lion's mane nudibranch 1.90 1.90
a. Sheet of 2, #UX587-UX588 4.00
UX589 A3367 44c Northern kelp crab 1.90 1.90
UX590 A3367 44c Vermilion rockfish 1.90 1.90
a. Sheet of 2, #UX589-UX590 4.00
UX591 A3367 44c Yellowtail rockfish, white-spotted rose anemone 1.90 1.90

UX592 A3367 44c Pacific rock crab, jeweled top snail 1.90 1.90
a. Sheet of 2, #UX591-UX592 4.00
UX593 A3367 44c Harbor seal 1.90 1.90
UX594 A3367 44c Brown pelican 1.90 1.90
a. Sheet of 2, #UX593-UX594 4.00
UX595 A3367 44c Treefish, Monterey turban snail, brooding sea anemones 1.90 1.90
UX596 A3367 44c Copper rockfish 1.90 1.90
a. Sheet of 2, #UX595-UX596 4.00
First day cancel, any card, Monterey, CA 3.00

Packet of 10 cards sold for $8.95.
Stamp pane illustration without denominations on card back.

Cowboys of the Silver Screen Type of 2010

Designed by Carl T. Herrman.

2010, Apr. 17 **Litho.**
UX597 A3389 28c Roy Rogers 1.50 1.50
UX598 A3390 28c Tom Mix 1.50 1.50
UX599 A3391 28c William S. Hart 1.50 1.50
UX600 A3392 28c Gene Autry 1.50 1.50
a. Booklet of 20, 5 each #UX597-UX600 30.00
First day cancel, any card, Oklahoma City, OK 2.75

No. UX600a sold for $14.95.
Imprinted stamp illustration without denomination on card back.

National Parks Types of Air Post and Air Post Postal Cards of 1999-2009

Designed by Journey Group, Inc.

2010, Apr. 20 **Litho.**
UX601 AP109 28c Acadia 1.50 1.50
UX602 APC23 28c Badlands 1.50 1.50
UX603 AP110 28c Bryce Canyon 1.50 1.50
UX604 AP106 28c Grand Canyon 1.50 1.50
UX605 AP111 28c Great Smoky Mountains 1.50 1.50
UX606 AP108 28c Mount McKinley 1.50 1.50
UX607 APC22 28c Mount Rainier 1.50 1.50
UX608 AP116 28c St. John, Virgin Islands 1.50 1.50
UX609 AP112 28c Yosemite 1.50 1.50
UX610 AP117 28c Zion 1.50 1.50
a. Booklet of 20, 2 each #UX601-UX610 30.00
First day cancel, any card, Washington, DC 2.75

No. UX610a sold for $14.95.
Imprinted stamp illustration without denomination on card back.

Hawaiian Rain Forest Type of 2010

Designed by Ethel Kessler.

2010, Sept. 1 **Litho.** ***Rouletted on 1 Side***
UX611 A3417 44c 'Apapane, Hawaiian mint 1.90 1.90
UX612 A3417 44c Pulelehua butterfly, kolea lau nui, 'ilihia 1.90 1.90
a. Sheet of 2, #UX611-UX612 4.00
UX613 A3417 44c Hawaii 'amakihi, Hawaii 'elepaio, ohi'a lehua 1.90 1.90
UX614 A3417 44c Happyface spider, 'ala'ala wai nui 1.90 1.90
a. Sheet of 2, #UX613-UX614 4.00
UX615 A3417 44c 'I'iwi, haha 1.90 1.90
UX616 A3417 44c 'Akepa, 'ope'ape'a 1.90 1.90
a. Sheet of 2, #UX615-UX616 4.00
UX617 A3417 44c Koele Mountain damselfly, 'akala 1.90 1.90
UX618 A3417 44c Jewel orchid 1.90 1.90
a. Sheet of 2, #UX617-UX618 4.00
UX619 A3417 44c 'Oma'o, 'ohelo kau la'au 1.90 1.90
UX620 A3417 44c 'Oha 1.90 1.90
a. Sheet of 2, #UX619-UX620 4.00
First day cancel, any card, Hawaii National Park, HI 3.00
Nos. UX611-UX620 (10) 19.00 19.00

Packet of 10 cards sold for $8.95.
Entire stamp pane illustration without denominations on card back.

Common Terns — PC185

Designed by Chuck Ripper.

2011, Apr. 7 **Litho.**
UX621 PC185 29c **multicolored** .65 *1.00*
First day cancel, New York, NY 1.90

Characters From Disney-Pixar Films (Send a Hello) Type of 2011

Designed by Terrence W. McCaffrey and William J. Gicker.

2011, Aug. 19 **Litho.** ***Rouletted at Left***
UX622 A3484 29c Toy Story 1.50 1.50
UX623 A3482 29c Cars 1.50 1.50
UX624 A3485 29c Up 1.50 1.50
UX625 A3483 29c Ratatouille 1.50 1.50
UX626 A3486 29c WALL-E 1.50 1.50
a. Booklet of 20, 4 each #UX622-UX626 30.00
First day cancel, any card, Anaheim, CA 2.75

No. UX626a sold for $14.95.
Imprinted stamp illustration without denomination on card back.

Sailboat — PC186

Designed by Derry Noyes.

2012, Jan. 22 **Litho.**
UX627 PC186 (32c) **multicolored** .70 .70
First day cancel, Oyster Bay, NY 1.90

Characters From Disney-Pixar Films (Mail a Smile) Type of 2012

Designed by William J. Gicker.

2012, June 1 **Litho.** ***Rouletted at Left***
UX628 A3565 (32c) A Bug's Life 1.60 1.60
UX629 A3567 (32c) Finding Nemo 1.60 1.60
UX630 A3566 (32c) The Incredibles 1.60 1.60
UX631 A3569 (32c) Monsters, Inc. 1.60 1.60
UX632 A3568 (32c) Toy Story 2 1.60 1.60
a. Booklet of 20, 4 each #UX628-UX632 32.00
First day cancel, any card, Orlando, FL 3.00

No. UX632a sold for $15.95.
Imprinted stamp illustration without denomination on card back.

Sailboat Type of 2012

Designed by Derry Noyes.

2012, June 22 **Litho.** ***Microperforated on 2 Sides***
Size of Card:140x108mm
UX633 PC186 (32c) **multicolored** 1.50 .75
a. Sheet of 4 6.00
First day cancel, Lancaster, PA 1.90

No. UX633 was sold only in packages of 10 sheets that sold for $14.10.

Scenic American Landscapes Types of Air Post of 1999-2012 Inscribed "Forever"

Designed by Journey Group, Inc.

2012, June 23 **Litho.** ***Rouletted at Left***
UX634 AP115 (32c) 13-Mile Woods, NH 1.60 1.60
UX635 AP120 (32c) Glacier National Park, MT 1.60 1.60
UX636 AP117 (32c) Grand Teton National Park, WY 1.60 1.60
UX637 AP114 (32c) Hagatña Bay, Guam 1.60 1.60
UX638 AP121 (32c) Lancaster County, PA 1.60 1.60
UX639 AP104 (32c) Niagara Falls, NY 1.60 1.60
UX640 AP107 (32c) Nine-Mile Prairie, NE 1.60 1.60
UX641 AP113 (32c) Okefenokee Swamp, GA and FL 1.60 1.60
UX642 AP105 (32c) Rio Grande, TX 1.60 1.60
UX643 AP119 (32c) Voyageurs National Park, MN 1.60 1.60
a. Booklet of 20, 2 each #UX634-UX643 32.00
First day cancel, any card, Lancaster, PA 3.00

No. UX643a sold for $15.95.
Imprinted stamp illustration without denomination on card back.

Deer — PC187

Designed by Ethel Kessler.

2013, Mar. 8 **Litho.**
UX644 PC187 (33c) **multicolored** .75 .75
First day cancel, Middleburg, VA 2.00

Tree — PC188

Designed by Ethel Kessler.

2014, Mar. 28 **Litho.**
UX645 PC188 (34c) **multicolored** .80 .80
First day cancel, New York, NY 2.00

Flowers and Bee — PC189

Designed by Ethel Kessler.

2015, July 31 **Litho.**
UX646 PC189 (35c) **multicolored** .80 .80
First day cancel, Clackamas, OR 2.00

Tecophilaea Cyanocrocus (Azulillo) — PC190

Designed by Ethel Kessler.

2017, Aug. 11 **Litho.**
UX647 PC190 (34c) **multicolored** .80 .80
First day cancel, Independence, OH 2.00

Mallard Duck PC191

Designed by Ethel Kessler.

2021, June 1 **Litho.**
UX648 PC191 (36c) **multicolored** .80 .80
First day cancel, Fargo, ND 2.00

PAID REPLY POSTAL CARDS

These are sold to the public as two unsevered cards, one for message and one for reply. These are listed first as unsevered cards and then as severed cards. Values are for:

Unused cards (both unsevered and severed) without printed or written address or message.

Unsevered cards sell for a premium if never folded.

Used unsevered cards, Message Card with Post Office cancellation and Reply Card uncanceled (from 1968 value is for a single used severed card); and used severed cards with cancellation when current.

Used values for International Paid Reply Cards are for proper usage. Those domestically used or with postage added sell for less than the unused value.

"Preprinted," unused cards (both unsevered and severed) with printed or written address or message. Used value applies after 1952.

First day cancel values are for cards without cachets.

PM1

PR1

Frame around card.

1892, Oct. 25 **Size: 140x89mm**

UY1	PM1+PR1 1c +1c **black,** *buff,* unsevered	40.00	9.00
	Preprinted	15.00	
a.	Message card printed on both sides, reply card blank	250.00	*750.00*
b.	Message card blank, reply card printed on both sides	300.00	
c.	Cards joined at bottom	200.00	100.00
	Preprinted	100.00	
m.	PM1 Message card detached	6.00	1.75
	Preprinted	3.00	
r.	PR1 Reply card detached	6.00	1.75
	Preprinted	3.00	

PM2

PR2

Frame around card.

1893, Mar. 1 **For International Use**

UY2	PM2+PR2 2c +2c **blue,** *buff,* unsevered	22.50	20.00
	Preprinted	12.50	
a.	2c+2c **dark blue,** *grayish white,* unsevered	22.50	20.00
	Preprinted	12.50	
b.	Message card printed on both sides, reply card blank	500.00	
c.	Message card blank, reply card printed on both sides	—	
d.	Message card normal, reply card blank	300.00	
m.	PM2 Message card detached	5.00	*6.00*
	Preprinted	2.50	
r.	PR2 Reply card detached	5.00	*6.00*
	Preprinted	2.50	

For other postal cards of types PM2 and PR2 see No. UY11.

PM3

PR3

No frame around card.

1898, Sept.

Size: 140x82mm

UY3	PM3+PR3 1c +1c **black,** *buff,* unsevered	67.50	12.50
	Preprinted	12.50	
a.	Message card normal, reply card blank	400.00	
b.	Message card printed on both sides, reply card blank	450.00	
c.	Message card blank, reply card printed on both sides	450.00	
d.	Message card without "Detach annexed card/for answer"	250.00	150.00

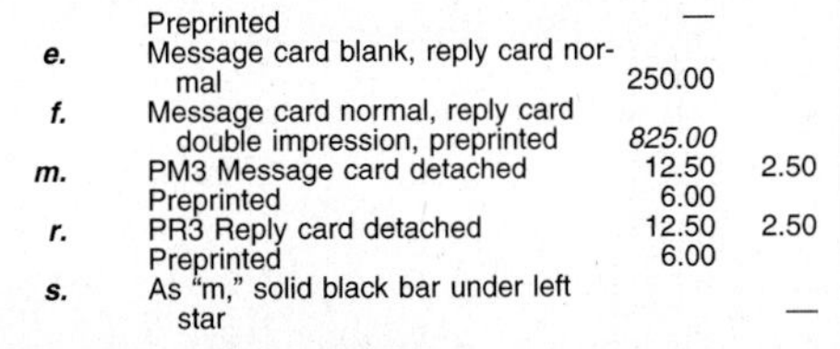

	Preprinted	—	
e.	Message card blank, reply card normal	250.00	
f.	Message card normal, reply card double impression, preprinted	*825.00*	
m.	PM3 Message card detached	12.50	2.50
	Preprinted	6.00	
r.	PR3 Reply card detached	12.50	2.50
	Preprinted	6.00	
s.	As "m," solid black bar under left star		—

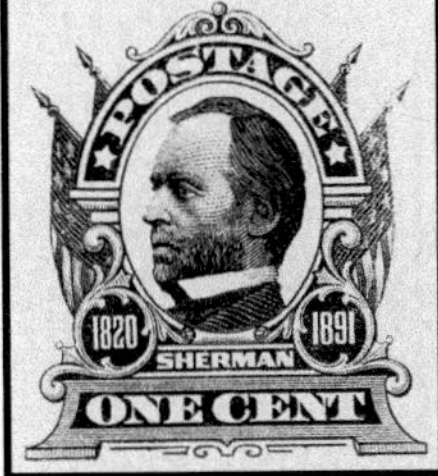

PM4

PR4

No frame around card.

1904, Mar, 31

UY4	PM4+PR4 1c +1c **black,** *buff,* unsevered	57.50	6.50
	Preprinted	10.00	
a.	Message card normal, reply card blank	275.00	
b.	Message card printed on both sides, reply card blank	*950.00*	
c.	Message card blank, reply card normal	275.00	
d.	Message card blank, reply card printed on both sides	*750.00*	175.00
	Preprinted	200.00	
m.	PM4 Message card detached	9.00	1.10
	Preprinted	4.00	
r.	PR4 Reply card detached	9.00	1.10
	Preprinted	4.00	

George Washington — PM5

Martha Washington — PR5

Double frame line around instructions

1910, Sept. 14

UY5	PM5+PR5 1c +1c **blue,** unsevered	175.00	25.00
	Preprinted	40.00	
a.	Message card normal, reply card blank	*425.00*	*750.00*
m.	PM5 Message card detached	15.00	3.75
	Preprinted	9.00	
r.	PR5 Reply card detached	15.00	3.75
	Preprinted	9.00	

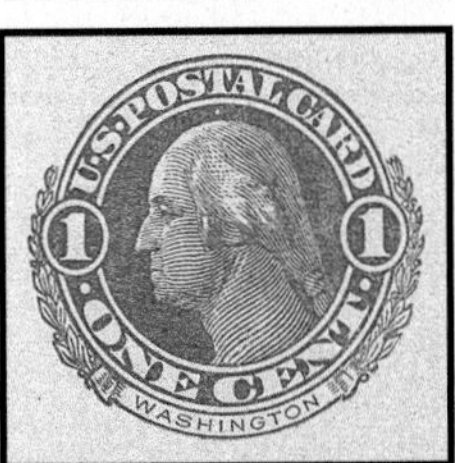

PM6

PR6

1911, Oct. 27

UY6	PM6+PR6 1c +1c **green,** *cream,* unsevered	175.00	25.00
	Preprinted	60.00	
a.	Message card normal, reply card blank	*1,500.*	
m.	PM6 Message card detached	22.50	6.50
	Preprinted	12.50	
r.	PR6 Reply card detached	22.50	6.50
	Preprinted	12.50	

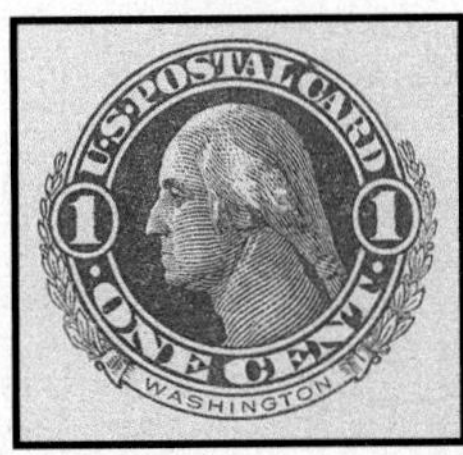

PM7

PR7

Single frame line around instructions

1915, Sept. 18

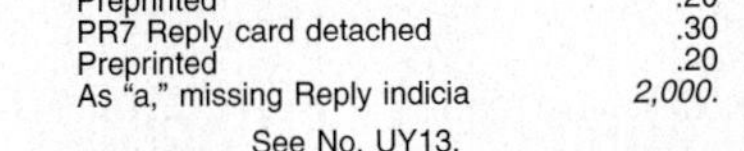

UY7	PM7+PR7 1c +1c **green,** *cream,* unsevered	1.50	.50
	Preprinted	.60	
a.	1c+1c **dark green,** *buff,* unsevered	1.50	.50
	Preprinted	.60	
b.	Message card normal, reply card blank	*1,500.*	
m.	PM7 Message card detached	.30	.25
	Preprinted	.20	
r.	PR7 Reply card detached	.30	.25
	Preprinted	.20	
s.	As "a," missing Reply indicia	*2,000.*	

See No. UY13.

PM8

PR8

No frame around card.

1918, Aug. 2

UY8	PM8+PR8 2c +2c **red,** *buff,* unsevered	90.00	40.00
	Preprinted	30.00	
m.	PM8 Message card detached	20.00	7.50
	Preprinted	10.00	
r.	PR8 Reply card detached	20.00	7.50
	Preprinted	10.00	

No. UY8 Surcharged in Black

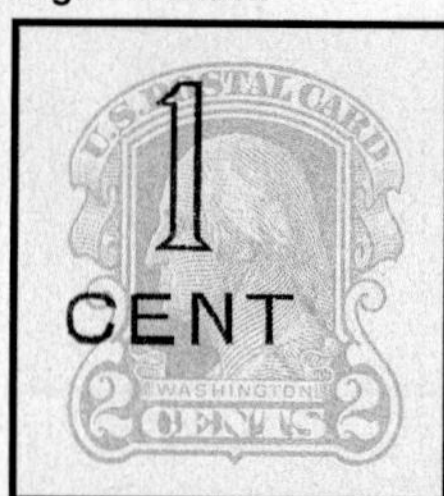

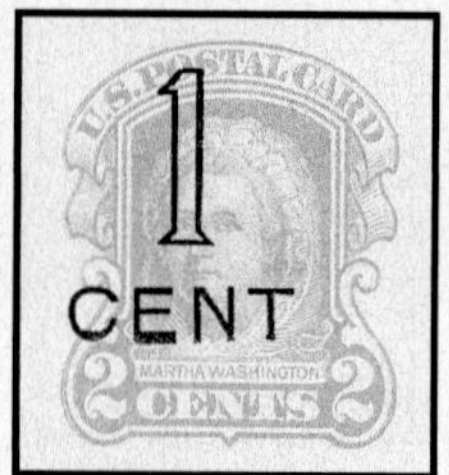

Fifteen canceling machine types

1920, Apr.

UY9 PM8+PR8 1c on 2c+1c on 2c **red,** *buff,* unsevered 20.00 11.00
Preprinted 10.00
a. Message card normal, reply card no surcharge 85.00 —
Preprinted —
b. Message card normal, reply card double surcharge 85.00 —
Preprinted —
c. Message card double surcharge, reply card normal 85.00 —
Preprinted —
d. Message card no surcharge, reply card normal 85.00 —
Preprinted —
e. Message card no surcharge, reply card double surcharge 85.00
m. PM8 Message card detached 5.00 4.00
Preprinted 3.00
r. PR8 Reply card detached 5.00 4.00
Preprinted 3.00
s. As "r," double surcharge *350.00*

One press printed type

UY10 PM8+PR8 1c on 2c+1c on 2c **red,** *buff,* unsevered 450.00 200.00
Preprinted 150.00
a. Message card no surcharge, reply card normal *1,100.* —
Preprinted —
b. Surcharge double on message card, reply card normal *950.00*
m. PM8 Message card detached 75.00 45.00
Preprinted 40.00
r. PR8 Reply card detached 75.00 45.00
Preprinted 40.00

PM11

PR11

1924, Mar. 18 **For International Use**

Size: 139x89mm

UY11 PM11+PR11 2c +2c **red,** *cream,* unsevered 2.50 *50.00*
Preprinted 1.50
m. PM11 Message card detached .50 *14.00*
Preprinted .40
r. PR11 Reply card detached .50 *20.00*
Preprinted .40

PM12

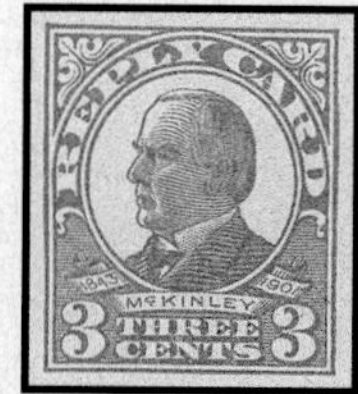

PR12

For International Use

1926, Feb. 1

UY12 PM12+PR12 3c +3c **red orange,** *buff,* unsevered 12.00 *27.50*
Preprinted 6.00
a. 3c +3c **red,** *yellow,* unsevered 12.00 *27.50*
Preprinted 6.00
First day cancel —
m. PM9 Message card detached 3.00 *7.50*
Preprinted 1.50
r. PR9 Reply card detached 3.00 *10.00*
Preprinted 1.50

PM13

PR13

Single frame line around instructions

1951, Dec. 29

UY13 PM13+PR13 2c +2c **carmine,** *buff,* unsevered 1.40 *2.25*
Preprinted .65
First day cancel, Washington, D.C. 1.25
m. PM13 Message card detached .35 *1.00*
Preprinted .25
r. PR13 Reply card detached .35 *1.00*
Preprinted .25

No. UY7a Surcharged by Canceling Machine in Emerald

1952, Jan. 1

UY14 PM5+PR5 2c on 1c+2c on 1c **dk green,** *buff,* unsevered 1.25 *2.25*
Preprinted .50
a. Surcharge vertical at left of stamps 14.00 7.50
Preprinted 7.50
b. Surcharge horizontal at left of stamps 15.00 12.50
Preprinted 8.50
c. Inverted surcharge horizontal at left of stamps 140.00 90.00
Preprinted 75.00
d. Message card normal, reply card no surcharge 40.00 40.00
Preprinted —
e. Message card normal, reply card double surcharge 40.00 40.00
Preprinted —
f. Message card no surcharge, reply card normal 40.00 40.00
Preprinted —
g. Message card double surcharge, reply card normal 40.00 40.00
Preprinted —
h. Both cards, dbl. surch. 50.00 50.00
Preprinted —
i. As No. UY14, reply card surcharge missing, message card with second surcharge on reverse 70.00
m. PM5 Message card detached .40 *1.00*
Preprinted .30
r. PR5 Reply card detached .40 *1.00*
Preprinted .30

No. UY7a Surcharged (horizontal) Typographed at Left of Stamp in Dark Green

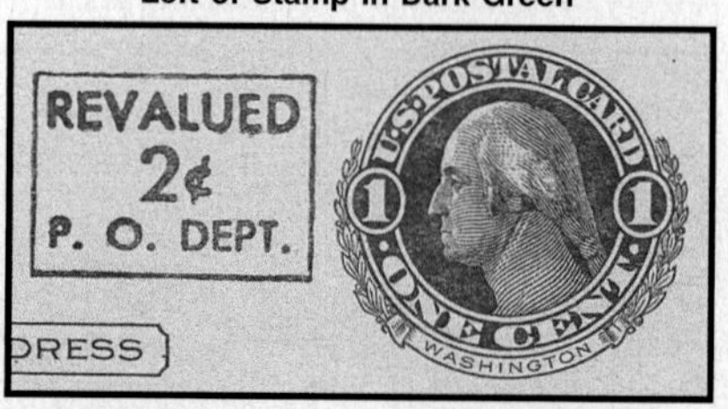

1952

UY15 PM5+PR5 2c on 1c+2c on 1c **dk green,** *buff,* unsevered 115.00 45.00
Preprinted 35.00
a. Surcharge on message card only 175.00
b. Message side normal, reply side no surcharge —
m. PM5 Message card detached 17.50 10.00
Preprinted 9.00
r. PR5 Reply card detached 17.50 10.00
Preprinted 9.00

On No. UY15a, the surcharge also appears on blank side of card.

Liberty Type
For International Use

1956, Nov. 16

UY16 PC24 4c +4c **brt scarlet & dark violet blue,** *buff,* unsevered 1.25 *90.00*
First day cancel, New York, N. Y. *(127,874)* 1.00
a. Message card printed on both halves 125.00 —
b. Reply card printed on both halves 125.00 —
c. Double scarlet on reply side 200.00 —
First day cancel 350.00
d. Double scarlet on message side 200.00
e. Double violet blue on message side —
f. Double violet blue on both sides —
g. Message side blank, reply side normal —
m. Message card detached .40 *40.00*
r. Reply card detached .40 *40.00*

Liberty Type of 1956

1958, July 31

UY17 PC25 3c +3c **bright violet,** *buff,* unsevered 3.50 *2.00*
First day cancel, Boise, Idaho *(136,768)* 1.00
a. One card blank 750.00
Preprinted 500.00
b. Double impression on one card, preprinted *1,000.*

Both halves of No. UY17 are identical, inscribed as No. UX46, "This side of card is for address."

Lincoln Type
Precanceled with 3 printed red violet lines

1962, Nov. 19

UY18 PC26 4c +4c **reddish purple,** unsevered 3.50 *2.50*
First day cancel, Springfield, Ill. *(107,746)* 1.00
a. Tagged, *Mar. 7, 1967* 6.50 3.00
First day cancel, Dayton, OH 30.00

Both halves of No. UY18 are identical, inscribed as No. UX48, "This side of card is for address."
No. UY18a was printed with luminescent ink.

Map Type

1963, Aug. 30 **For International Use**

UY19 PC27 7c +7c **blue & red,** unsevered 2.50 *80.00*
First day cancel, New York 1.00
a. Message card normal, reply card blank 400.00 100.00
b. Message card blank, reply card normal 400.00 —
c. Additional message card printed on back of reply card *750.00*
d. Double red on message side —
e. Double red & blue on message side *500.00*
m. Message card detached .85 *35.00*
r. Reply card detached .85 *35.00*
s. Double impression of blue on message side 350.00
t. Double impression of blue on reply side *500.00*

Message card inscribed "Postal Card With Paid Reply" in English and French. Reply card inscribed "Reply Postal Card Carte Postale Réponse."

Map Type of 1963

1967, Dec. 4 **For International Use**

UY20 PC27 8c +8c **blue & red,** unsevered 2.50 *80.00*
First day cancel, Washington, D.C. 1.00
m. Message card detached .85 *35.00*
r. Reply card detached .85 *35.00*
s. Message card normal, reply card blank *750.00*

Message card inscribed "Postal Card With Paid Reply" in English and French. Reply card inscribed "Reply Postal Card Carte Postale Résponse."

Tagged

Paid Reply Postal cards from No. UY21 onward are either tagged or printed with luminescent ink unless otherwise noted.

Lincoln Type

1968, Jan. 4

UY21 PC33 5c +5c **emerald,** unsevered 1.25 *2.00*
First day cancel, Hodgenville, Ky. 1.50
a. Printed on one side only *800.00*

Paul Revere Type

1971, May 15

Precanceled with 3 printed brown lines.

UY22 PC36 6c +6c **brown,** unsevered .85 *2.00*
First day cancel, Boston, Mass. 1.00

John Hanson Type

1972, Sept. 1

Precanceled with 3 printed blue lines.

UY23 PC41 6c +6c **gray blue,** unsevered 1.00 *2.00*
First day cancel, Baltimore, Md. 1.00

Samuel Adams Type

1973, Dec. 16

Precanceled with 3 printed orange lines

UY24 PC42 8c +8c **orange,** unsevered .75 *2.00*
First day cancel, Boston, Mass. *(105,369)* 1.00
a. Coarse paper 1.25 *2.00*
b. Printed on one side only *800.00*
Preprinted 700.00
c. As "a," printed on one side only 500.00

Thomson, Witherspoon, Rodney, Hale & Hancock Types

1975-78

Precanceled with 3 printed emerald lines

UY25 PC44 7c +7c **green,** unsevered, *Sept. 14, 1975* .75 *8.00*
First day cancel, Bryn Mawr, Pa. 1.00

Precanceled with 3 printed yellow brown lines

UY26 PC45 9c +9c **yellow brown,** unsevered, *Nov. 10, 1975* .75 *2.00*
First day cancel, Princeton, N.J. 1.00

Precanceled with 3 printed blue lines

UY27 PC46 9c +9c **gray blue,** unsevered, *July 1, 1976* 1.00 *2.00*
First day cancel, Dover, Del. 1.00

Precanceled with 3 printed green lines

UY28 PC48 9c +9c **green,** unsevered, *Oct. 14, 1977* 1.00 *2.00*
First day cancel, Coventry, Conn. 1.00

Inscribed "U.S. Domestic Rate"

Precanceled with 3 printed brown orange lines

UY29 PC50 (10c +10c) **brown orange,** unsevered, *May 19, 1978* 7.50 *9.00*
First day cancel, Quincy, Mass. 1.75

Precanceled with 3 printed brown orange lines

UY30 PC50 10c +10c **brown orange,** unsevered, *June 20, 1978* 1.00 *2.00*
First day cancel, Quincy, Mass. 1.00
a. One card "Domestic Rate," other "Postage 10¢" —
b. Printed on one side only *700.00*
Nos. UY25-UY30 (6) 12.00

Eagle Type

Inscribed "U. S. Domestic Rate"

1981, Mar. 15

Precanceled with 3 printed violet lines

UY31 PC63 (12c +12) **reddish purple,** unsevered 1.00 *2.00*
First day cancel, Memphis, TN 1.00

Isaiah Thomas Type

1981, May 5 **Precanceled with 3 printed lines**

UY32 PC64 12c +12c **light blue,** unsevered 5.00 *2.00*
First day cancel, Worcester, MA 1.00
a. Small die on one side 3.00 —

Morris Type

Inscribed "U.S. Domestic Rate"

1981 **Precanceled with 3 printed lines**

UY33 PC67 (13c +13c) **pale org brn,** *Oct. 11,* unsevered 1.50 *2.00*
First day cancel, Memphis, TN 1.25

Inscribed "U.S. Postage 13¢"

UY34 PC67 13c +13c **pale org brn,** *Nov. 10,* unsevered .85 .25
First day cancel, Philadelphia, PA 1.25
a. Message card normal, reply card blank 350.00
b. Extra copyright symbol and "USPS 1981" on back of reply card 45.00

Charles Carroll Type

Inscribed: U.S. Domestic Rate

1985 **Precanceled with 3 printed lines**

UY35 PC79 (14c +14c) **blue green,** *Feb. 1,* unsevered 3.00 *2.00*
First day cancel, New Carrollton, MD 1.25

Inscribed: USA

UY36 PC79 14c +14c **blue green,** *Mar. 6,* unsevered 1.00 *2.00*
First day cancel, Annapolis, MD 1.25
a. One card blank *5,000.*

George Wythe Type

Precanceled with 3 printed lines

1985, June 20

UY37 PC81 14c +14c **bright apple green,** unsevered .75 *2.00*
First day cancel, Williamsburg, VA 1.25
a. One card blank, preprinted 275.00

Flag Type

1987, Sept. 1

UY38 PC90 14c +14c **black, blue & red,** unsevered .75 *2.00*
First day cancel, Washington, DC *(22,314)* 1.25

America the Beautiful Type

1988, July 11

UY39 PC93 15c +15c **multicolored,** unsevered .75 *1.50*
First day cancel, Buffalo, WY *(24,338)* 1.25

Flag Type

1991, Mar. 27

UY40 PC122 19c +19c **red, blue & black,** unsevered .80 *1.50*
First day cancel, Washington, DC *(25,562)* 1.25
a. One card blank *650.00*

Red Barn Type

1995, Feb. 1 **Litho.**

UY41 PC147 20c +20c **multi,** unsevered .80 *1.50*
First day cancel, Williamsburg, PA 1.50
a. One card blank —

Block Island Lighthouse Type

1999, Nov. 10 **Litho.**

UY42 PC165 20c +20c **multi,** unsevered .85 *1.50*
First day cancel, Block Island, RI 1.75

White Barn Type

2001, Sept. 20 **Litho.**

UY43 PC173 21c +21c **multi,** unsevered .90 *1.50*
First day cancel, Washington, DC 1.50

Carlsbad Caverns Type

2002, June 7 **Litho.**

UY44 PC174 23c+23c **multi,** unsevered 1.00 *1.25*
First day cancel, Carlsbad, NM 1.50
First day cancel, any other city 1.50

Pikes Peak Type of 2006

2006, Jan. 9 **Litho.**

UY45 PC178 24c+24c **multicolored,** unsevered 1.10 *1.25*
First day cancel, Washington, DC 1.50
First day cancel, any other city 1.50

Pineapple Type of 2007

2007, May 12 **Litho.**

UY46 PC179 26c+26c **multicolored,** unsevered 1.25 *1.40*
First day cancel, Washington, DC 2.40

Corinthian Column Type of 2008

2008, May 12 **Litho.**

UY47 PC181 27c+27c **multicolored,** unsevered 1.25 *1.40*
First day cancel, Washington, DC 2.40

Koi Types of 2009

2009, Apr. 17 **Litho.**

UY48 PC183+PC184 28c+28c **multicolored,** unsevered 1.25 *1.40*
First day cancel, New York, NY 2.40
m. PC183 Card detached .60 .60
r. PC184 Card detached .60 .60

Common Terns Type of 2011

2011, Apr. 7 **Litho.**

UY49 PC185 29c+29c **multicolored,** unsevered 1.40 *1.60*
First day cancel, New York, NY 4.00

Sailboat Type of 2012

2012, Jan. 22 **Litho.**

UY50 PC186 (32c)+(32c) **multicolored,** unsevered 1.40 *1.60*
First day cancel, Oyster Bay, NY 4.00

Deer Type of 2013

2013, Mar. 8 **Litho.**

UY51 PC187 (33c)+(33c) **multicolored,** unsevered 1.50 *1.75*
First day cancel, Middleburg, VA 4.00

Tree Type of 2014

2014, Mar. 28 **Litho.**

UY52 PC188 (34c)+(34c) **multicolored,** unsevered 1.60 *1.90*
First day cancel, New York, NY 4.00

Flowers and Bee Type of 2015

2015, July 31 **Litho.**

UY53 PC189 (35c)+(35c) **multicolored,** unsevered 1.60 *1.90*
First day cancel, Clackamas, OR 4.00

Tecophilaea Cyanocrocus (Azulillo) Type of 2017

2017, Aug.11 **Litho.**

UY54 PC190 (34c)+(34c) **multicolored,** unsevered 1.60 *1.90*
First day cancel, Independence, OH 4.00

Mallard Duck Type of 2021

2021, June 1 **Litho.**

UY55 PC191 (36c)+(36c) 1.60 *1.90*
First day cancel, Fargo, ND 4.00

AIR POST POSTAL CARDS

Eagle in Flight — APC1

1949, Jan.10 **Typo.**

UXC1 APC1 4c **red orange,** *buff* .60 *.75*
Preprinted .35
First day cancel, Washington, D.C. *(236,620)* 3.00
a. 4c **deep red,** *buff* *475.00* *450.00*
First day cancel, Washington, D.C. *250.00*

Expertization is recommended for No. UXC1a.

Type of Air Post Stamp, 1954

1958, July 31

UXC2 AP31 5c **red,** *buff* 2.00 .75
First day cancel, Wichita, Kans. *(156,474)* 1.00

Type of 1958 Redrawn

1960, June 18 **Lithographed (Offset)**

UXC3 AP31 5c **red,** *buff,* bicolored border 6.50 4.50
First day cancel, Minneapolis, Minn. *(228,500)* 1.50
a. Red omitted *1,500.*
b. Two lozenges at left double printed, red over blue 200.00

Size of stamp of No. UXC3: 18½x21mm; on No. UXC2: 19x22mm. White cloud around eagle enlarged and finer detail of design on No. UXC3. Inscription "AIR MAIL-POSTAL CARD" has been omitted and blue and red border added on No. UXC3.

Bald Eagle — APC2

Precanceled with 3 printed red lines

1963, Feb. 15
UXC4 APC2 6c **red,** bicolored border 1.10 *2.50*
First day cancel, Maitland, Fla. *(216,203)* 1.50

Emblem of Commerce Department's Travel Service — APC3

Issued at the Sixth International Philatelic Exhibition (SIPEX), Washington, D.C., May 21-30.

1966, May 27 **For International Use**
UXC5 APC3 11c **blue & red** .65 *40.00*
First day cancel, Washington, D.C. *(272,813)* 1.00

Four photographs at left on address side show: Mt. Rainier, New York skyline, Indian on horseback and Miami Beach. The card has blue and red border.

See Nos. UXC8, UXC11.

Virgin Islands and Territorial Flag — APC4

50th anniv. of the purchase of the Virgin Islands.

Designed by Burt Pringle

1967, Mar. 31 **Litho.**
UXC6 APC4 6c **multicolored** .75 *12.50*
First day cancel, Charlotte Amalie, V. I. *(346,906)* 1.00
a. Red & yellow omitted *1,700.*
b. Orange red (instead of red) 6.00

The orange red in No. UXC6b is most easily seen in the two lines at the bottom of the card.

Borah Peak, Lost River Range, Idaho, and Scout Emblem — APC5

12th Boy Scout World Jamboree, Farragut State Park, Idaho, Aug. 1-9.

Designed by Stevan Dohanos

1967, Aug. 4 **Litho.**
UXC7 APC5 6c **blue, yellow, black & red** .75 *15.00*
First day cancel, Farragut State Park, ID *(471,585)* 1.00
a. Blue omitted —
b. Blue & black omitted *11,000.*
c. Red & yellow omitted *11,000.*

Travel Service Type of 1966

Issued in connection with the American Air Mail Society Convention, Detroit, Mich.

1967, Sept. 8 **For International Use**
UXC8 APC3 13c **blue & red** 1.50 *45.00*
First day cancel, Detroit, Mich. *(178,189)* 1.00

Stylized Eagle APC6

Designed by Muriel R. Chamberlain

Precanceled with 3 printed red lines

1968, Mar. 1
UXC9 APC6 8c **blue & red** .75 *2.50*
First day cancel, New York, N.Y. *(179,923)* 1.00
a. Tagged, *Mar. 19, 1969* 2.50 3.00
Tagged, first day cancel 15.00
b. **Blue & pale pink**, tagged *1,250.*

No. UXC9a is known with tagging omitted. It can be distinguished from No. UXC9, as No. UXC9a was printed on fluorescent stock. Believed to be unique. Value $2,500.

Tagged
Air Post Postal Cards from No. UXC10 onward are either tagged or printed with luminescent ink unless otherwise noted.

Precanceled with 3 printed blue lines

1971, May 15
UXC10 APC6 9c **red & blue** .50 *1.25*
First day cancel, Kitty Hawk, N.C. 1.00

Travel Service Type of 1966
For International Use

1971, June 10
UXC11 APC3 15c **blue & red** 1.75 *55.00*
First day cancel, New York, N.Y. 1.00

Grand Canyon APC7

Niagara Falls APC8

Tourism Year of the Americas 1972.

Designed by Melbourne Brindle

1972, June 29 **Size: 152½x108½mm** **Litho.**
UXC12 APC7 9c **black,** Grand Canyon, *buff* (Statue of Liberty, Hawaii, Alaska, San Francisco on back) .75 *60.00*
First day cancel, any city 1.50
a. Red and blue lozenges omitted *3,500.*
b. Red lozenges omitted —
c. Tagging omitted 2,250.

For International Use

UXC13 APC8 15c **black,** Niagara Falls, *buff* (Mt. Vernon, Washington, D.C., Lincoln, Liberty Bell on back) .75 *75.00*
First day cancel, any city 1.50
a. Address side blank *1,500.*

b. Double blue lozenges *6,000.*
c. Tagging omitted *2,250.*
d. Red and blue lozenges omitted —

See note after No. UX63.

Stylized Eagle — APC9

Eagle Weather Vane — APC10

Designed by David G. Foote (11c) & Stevan Dohanos (18c)

1974, Jan. 4 **Litho.**
UXC14 APC9 11c **ultramarine & red** 1.10 *25.00*
First day cancel, State College, Pa. *(160,500)* 1.00
a. Double tagging *500.00*
b. Tagging omitted *500.00*
c. Tagging inverted *400.00*

For International Use

UXC15 APC10 18c **multicolored** 1.10 *32.50*
First day cancel, Miami, Fla. *(132,114)* 1.00
a. Tagging omitted 350.00
b. Black and yellow omitted *7,500.*

All following issues are for international use.

Angel Gabriel Weather Vane — APC11

Designed by Stevan Dohanos

1975, Dec. 17 **Litho.**
UXC16 APC11 21c **multicolored** .85 *40.00*
First day cancel, Kitty Hawk, N.C. 1.00
a. Blue & red omitted *7,500.*
b. Tagging omitted 250.00 —

Curtiss (JN4H) Jenny — APC12

Designed by Keith Ferris

1978, Sept. 16 **Litho.**
UXC17 APC12 21c **multicolored** 1.00 *40.00*
First day cancel, San Diego, Cal. *(174,886)* 1.25

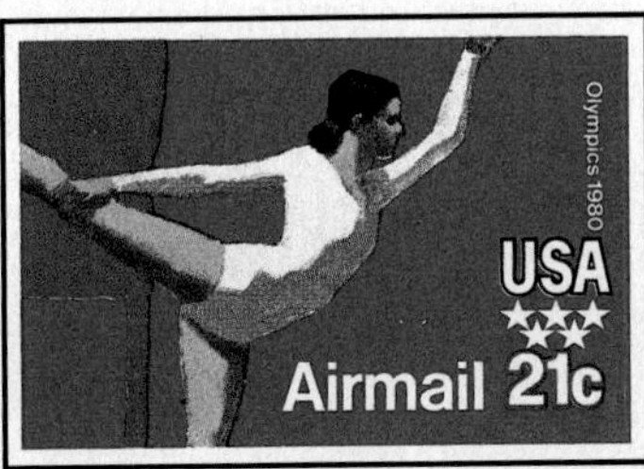

Gymnast APC13

22nd Olympic Games, Moscow, July 19-Aug. 3, 1980.

Designed by Robert M. Cunningham

1979, Dec. 1 **Litho.**
UXC18 APC13 21c **multicolored** 1.25 *40.00*
First day cancel, Fort Worth, Tex. 1.00

Pangborn, Herndon and Miss Veedol — APC14

First non-stop transpacific flight by Clyde Pangborn and Hugh Herndon, Jr., 50th anniv.

Designed by Ken Dallison

1981, Jan. 2 **Litho.**
UXC19 APC14 28c **multicolored** 1.00 *30.00*
First day cancel, Wenatchee, WA 1.25
a. Tagging omitted —

Gliders — APC15

Designed by Robert E. Cunningham

1982, Mar. 5 **Litho.**
UXC20 APC15 28c **magenta, yellow, blue & black** 1.00 *35.00*
First day cancel, Houston, TX *(106,932)* 1.25

Speedskater — APC16

Designed by Robert Peak

1983, Dec. 29 **Litho.**
UXC21 APC16 28c **multicolored** 1.00 *30.00*
First day cancel, Milwaukee, WI *(108,397)* 1.25
a. Red, pink, magenta, yellow, double impression, one inverted *4,250.*

No. UXC21a also exhibits a dramatic color shift.

Martin M-130 China Clipper Seaplane — APC17

Designed by Chuck Hodgson

1985, Feb. 15 **Litho.**
UXC22 APC17 33c **multicolored** 1.00 *30.00*
First day cancel, San Francisco, CA 1.50

First day cancellation was applied to 269,229 of Nos. UXC22 and C115.

Chicago Skyline — APC18

AMERIPEX '86, Chicago, May 22-June 1.

Designed by Ray Ameijide

1986, Feb. 1 **Litho.**
UXC23 APC18 33c **multicolored** 1.00 *30.00*
First day cancel, Chicago, IL *(84,480)* 1.25

No. UXC23 was sold at Sudposta '87 by the U.S.P.S. with a show cachet.

DC-3 — APC19

Designed by Chuck Hodgson

1988, May 14 **Litho.**
UXC24 APC19 36c **multicolored** .85 *30.00*
First day cancel, San Diego, CA 1.25

No. UXC24 was sold at SYDPEX '88 by the USPS with a cachet for Australia's bicentennial and SYDPEX '88.
First day cancellations applied to 167,575 of Nos. UXC24 and C118.

Yankee Clipper — APC20

Designed by Chuck Hodgson.

1991, June 28 **Litho.**
UXC25 APC20 40c **multicolored** .90 *30.00*
First day cancel, Flushing, NY *(24,865)* 1.50

Mt. Rainier — APC22

Designed by Ethel Kessler.

1999, May 15 **Litho.**
UXC27 APC22 55c **multicolored** 1.25 *30.00*
First day cancel, Denver, CO 1.50

First day cancellation was applied to 19,658 of Nos. UXC27 and UC65.
See note before No. C133.

Badlands Natl. Park, South Dakota — APC23

Designed by Ethel Kessler.

2001, Feb. 22 **Litho.**
UXC28 APC23 70c **multicolored** 1.40 *20.00*
First day cancel, Wall, SD 1.50

OFFICIAL POSTAL CARDS

PO1

1913, July **Size: 126x76mm**
UZ1 PO1 1c **black** 700.00 500.00

All No. UZ1 cards have printed address and printed form on message side.

Used values are for contemporaneous usage without additional postage applied.

Great Seal — PO2

1983-85
UZ2 PO2 13c **blue,** *Jan. 12* .75 *100.00*
First day cancel, Washington, DC 1.00
UZ3 PO2 14c **blue,** *Feb. 26, 1985* .80 *90.00*
First day cancel, Washington, DC *(62,396)* 1.25

Official postal cards from No. UZ4 onward are tagged unless otherwise noted.

PO3

Designed by Bradbury Thompson

1988, June 10 **Litho.**
UZ4 PO3 15c **multicolored** .80 *75.00*
First day cancel, New York *(133,498)* 1.25

PO4

Designed by Bradbury Thompson

1991, May 24 **Litho.**
UZ5 PO4 19c **multicolored** .80 *75.00*
First day cancel, Seattle, WA *(23,097)* 1.25

PO5

1995, May 9 **Litho.**
UZ6 PO5 20c **multicolored** .90 *75.00*
First day cancel, Washington, DC 1.25

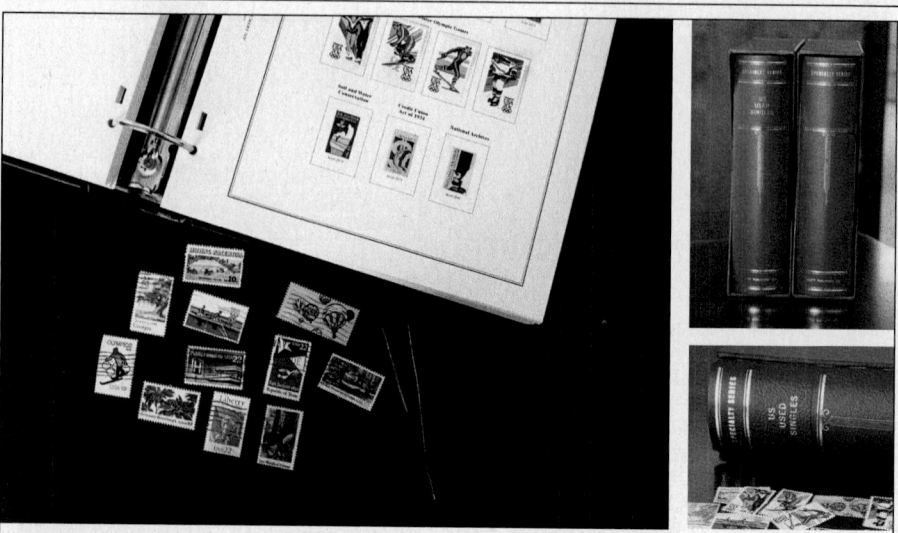

REVENUE STAMPS

The Commissioner of Internal Revenue advertised for bids for revenue stamps in August 1862, and the contract was awarded to Butler & Carpenter of Philadelphia.

Nos. R1-R102 were used to pay taxes on documents and proprietary articles including playing cards. Until December 25, 1862, the law stated that a stamp could be used only for payment of the tax upon the particular instrument or article specified on its face. After that date, stamps, except the Proprietary, could be used indiscriminately.

Most stamps of the first issue appeared in the latter part of 1862 or early in 1863. The 5c and 10c Proprietary were issued in the fall of 1864, and the 6c Proprietary on April 13, 1871.

Plate numbers and imprints are usually found at the bottom of the plate on all denominations except 25c and $1 to $3.50. On these it is nearly always at the left of the plate. The imprint reads "Engraved by Butler & Carpenter, Philadelphia" or "Jos. R. Carpenter."

Plates were of various sizes: 1c and 2c, 210 subjects (14x15); 3c to 20c, 170 subjects (17x10); 25c to 30c, 102 subjects (17x6); 50c to 70c, 85 subjects (17x5); $1 to $1.90, 90 subjects (15x6); $2 to $10, 72 subjects (12x6); $15 to $50, 54 subjects (9x6); $200, 8 subjects (2x4). No. R132, one subject.

The paper varies, the first employed being thin, hard and brittle until September, 1869, from which time it acquired a softer texture and varied from medium to very thick. Early printings of some revenue stamps occur on paper which appears to have laid lines. Some are found on experimental silk paper, first employed about August, 1870.

Some of the stamps were in use eight years and were printed several times. Many color variations occurred, particularly if unstable pigments were used and the color was intended to be purple or violet, such as the 4c Proprietary, 30c and $2.50 stamps. Before 1868 dull colors predominate on these and the early red stamps. In later printings of the 4c Proprietary, 30c and $2.50 stamps, red predominates in the mixture and on the dollar values of red is brighter. The early $1.90 stamp is dull purple, imperforate or perforated. In a later printing, perforated only, the purple is darker.

In the first issue, canceling usually was done with pen and ink and all values quoted are for stamps canceled in that way. Handstamped cancellations as a rule sell for more than pen. Printed and stencil cancellations are scarce and command much higher prices. Herringbone, punched or other types of cancellation which break the surface of the paper adversely affect prices.

Many, but not all, of the pre-1898 revenue stamps exist unused with original gum. These are not valued in the listings, but they sell for more than used examples in the marketplace. Uncanceled first through third revenue stamps without gum are generally not considered unused by the marketplace because the vast majority have been soaked or sweated from documents.

1862-72 revenue stamps from the first three issues were often used on large folded documents. As a result, multiples (blocks and strips of four or more) are not often found in sound condition. In addition, part perforate pairs of all but the most common varieties generally are off center. Catalogue values of the noted multiples are for items in fine condition or for very fine appearing examples with small faults. Examples of such multiples in a true very fine grade without any faults are scarce to rare and will sell for substantially more than catalogue value.

Where a stamp is known in a given form or variety but insufficient information is available on which to base a value, its existence is indicated by a dash.

Part perforate stamps are understood to be imperforate horizontally unless otherwise stated.

Part perforate stamps with an asterisk (*) after the value exist imperforate horizontally or vertically. As a general rule, part perforate first issue revenues that are imperforate vertically are considerably scarcer than their imperforate horizontally counterparts.

Part perforate PAIRS should be imperforate between the stamps as well as imperforate at opposite ends. See illustration **Type A** under "Information For Collectors-Perforations."

All imperforate or part perforate stamps listed are known in pairs or larger multiples. Certain unlisted varieties of this nature exist as singles and specialists believe them genuine. Exceptions are Nos. R11a, R13a, R22a, R30b, R51b, R60b, R80a, R112b, and R115b, which have not been reported in multiples but are regarded as legitimate by most students. Authenticated imperforate errors from later issues that exist only as singles include No. R728.

With respect to plate varieties (double transfers, cracked plates, scratched plates, etc.), there can be numerous types of each for a given stamp, ranging from minute to extremely dramatic, and with great differences in scarcity and value. Unless specifically named (e.g., T5, T7, T13) or described (e.g., complete double transfer, doubling of shields at top), the values given are generally for the most common type.

Documentary revenue stamps were no longer required after December 31, 1967.

First Issue

R1

George Washington — R2

Old Paper

1862-71 **Engr.** ***Perf. 12***

R1 R1 1c **Express, red**
- *a.* Imperf. 125.00
  - Pair 300.00
  - Block of 4 800.00
  - Short transfer, No. 156 250.00
- *b.* Part perf. 75.00*
  - Pair 250.00
  - Block of 4 750.00
  - Short transfer, No. 156 150.00
- *c.* Perf. 1.50
  - Pair 3.25
  - Block of 4 12.50
  - Double transfer 45.00
  - Short transfer, No. 156 85.00
  - Foreign entry of 2c, pos. 28 —
  - Foreign entry of 2c, pos. 66 —
- *d.* As No. R1c, silk paper *450.00*
- *e.* As No. R1c, vertical pair, imperf. between *200.00*

R2 R1 1c **Playing Cards, red**
- *a.* Imperf. 4,500.
  - Pair *8,500.*
  - Cracked plate —
- *b.* Part perf. 2,500.
  - Pair *5,000.*
- *c.* Perf. 250.00
  - Pair 550.00
  - Block of 4 1,200.
  - Cracked plate 350.00
  - Scratched plate —

R3 R1 1c **Proprietary, red**
- *a.* Imperf. 1,800.
  - Pair *3,500.*
- *b.* Part perf. 350.00*
  - Pair 800.00
  - Block of 4 *3,000.*
- *c.* Perf. .50
  - Pair 1.25
  - Block of 4 3.25
- *d.* As No. R3c, silk paper 75.00
  - Pair 145.00
  - Block of 4 *375.00*

R4 R1 1c **Telegraph, red**
- *a.* Imperf. 1,000.
  - Pair 3,000.
- *c.* Perf. 20.00
  - Pair 45.00
  - Block of 4 110.00
  - Scratched plate 50.00
  - Double transfer in bottom scroll —

Double transfer (T5)

R5 R2 2c **Bank Check, blue**
- *a.* Imperf. 1.50
  - Pair 19.00
  - Block of 4 190.00
  - Major double transfer (T5) 150.00
  - Minor double transfer 20.00
  - Privately rouletted —
- *b.* Part perf. 5.50*
  - Pair 17.00
  - Block of 4 140.00
  - Major double transfer (T5) 300.00
  - Cracked plate 22.50
- *c.* Perf. .50
  - Pair 2.00
  - Block of 4 8.00
  - Major double transfer (T5) 75.00
  - Minor double transfer 10.00
  - Scratched plate 15.00
- *e.* As No. R5c, Double impression *1,500.*
- *f.* As No. R5c, pair imperf between 500.00

R6 R2 2c **Bank Check, orange**
- *b.* Part perf. 60.00*
  - Pair —
- *c.* Perf. .45
  - Pair .90
  - Block of 4 2.50
  - Major double transfer (T5) 350.00
  - Minor double transfer (T5) 8.00
- *d.* As No. R6c, silk paper 275.00
- *e.* As No. R6c, **orange,** *green* 1,000.
- *f.* As No. R6c, half used as 1c on document 250.00

Double transfer (T7)

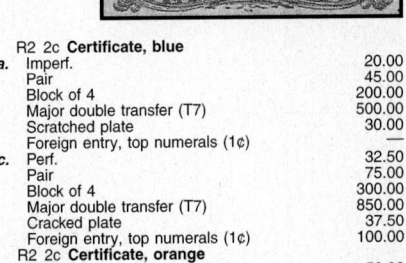

R7 R2 2c **Certificate, blue**
- *a.* Imperf. 20.00
  - Pair 45.00
  - Block of 4 200.00
  - Major double transfer (T7) 500.00
  - Scratched plate 30.00
  - Foreign entry, top numerals (1¢) —
- *c.* Perf. 32.50
  - Pair 75.00
  - Block of 4 300.00
  - Major double transfer (T7) 850.00
  - Cracked plate 37.50
  - Foreign entry, top numerals (1¢) 100.00

R8 R2 2c **Certificate, orange**
- *c.* Perf. 50.00
  - Pair 200.00
  - Block of 4 *850.00*
  - Major double transfer (T7) 800.00
  - Foreign entry, top numerals (1¢) —

R9 R2 2c **Express, blue**
- *a.* Imperf. 15.00
  - Pair 50.00
  - Block of 4 200.00
  - Double transfer 60.00
- *b.* Part perf. 35.00*
  - Pair 140.00
  - Block of 4 350.00
  - Double transfer at bottom, pos.47 75.00
- *c.* Perf. .40
  - Pair 1.25
  - Block of 4 6.50
  - Double transfer 17.50
  - Cracked plate, pos. 62 20.00
  - Foreign entry of 1c, pos. 68 *300.00*

R10 R2 2c **Express, orange**
- *b.* Part perf. *3,250.*
- *c.* Perf. 14.00
  - Pair 30.00

Block of 4 62.50
Double transfer 24.00
Cracked plate, pos. 62 —
Foreign entry of 1c, pos. 68 —
d. As No. R10c, silk paper 500.00

R11 R2 2c **Playing Cards, blue**
a. Imperf. *1,750.*
b. Part perf. 325.00
Pair 850.00
c. Perf. 4.50
Pair 13.00
Block of 4 50.00
Scratched plate, position 210 30.00

R12 R2 2c **Playing Cards, org**
c. Perf. 55.00
Pair *500.00*

Double transfer (T13)

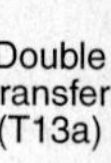

Double transfer (T13a)

R13 R2 2c **Proprietary, blue**
a. Imperf. 2,000.
b. Part perf. 250.
Pair 700.
Block of 4 *2,500.*
c. Perf. .40
Pair .90
Block of 4 5.00
Double transfer (T13) 150.00
T13a double transfer, pos. 147: top and bottom elements 250.00
T13a double transfer, pos. 133: bottom elements only 100.00
T13a double transfer, pos. 161: top elements only 100.00
Double transfer covering entire stamp 750.00
Short transfer at upper right —
Cracked plate 25.00
d. As No. R13c, silk paper 350.00
Double transfer (T13a) 500.00
e. **ultramarine** 400.00
Pair 750.00
Block of 4 —
Double transfer (T13) —
Complete double transfer (T13a) *1,250.*
f. As No. R13c, horiz. half used as 1c on document —

R14 R2 2c **Proprietary, orange**
c. Perf. 70.00
Pair 350.00
Block of 4 —
Double transfer (T13) 350.00
Complete double transfer (T13a) 700.00

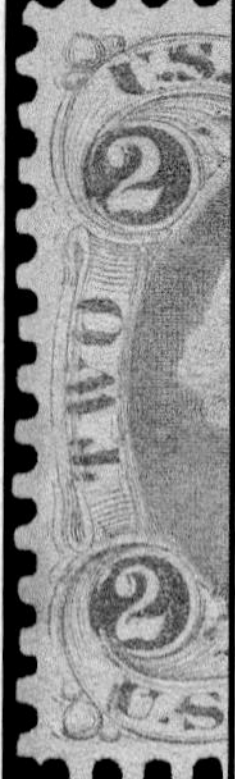
Double transfer (T15)

Double transfer (T15a)

R15 R2 2c **U.S. Internal Revenue, orange** ('64)
c. Perf. .25
Pair .60
Block of 4 2.00
Double transfer (T15) 65.00
Complete double transfer (T15a) 50.00
Complete double transfer, pos. 145 150.00
Double transfer 12.00
Triple transfer 40.00
Cracked plate 10.00
d. As No. R15c, silk paper 1.00
Pair 2.25
e. As No. R15c, **orange,** *green* *2,500.*
f. As No. R15c, half used as 1c on document *250.00*

Examples of No. R15e should be expertized. No. R15e is valued in fine condition.

R3

R16 R3 3c **Foreign Exchange, green**
b. Part perf. 1,750.*
Pair *3,500.*
c. Perf. 5.00
Pair 12.00
Block of 4 75.00
Double transfer at top, position 11 —
Gouged plate ("bruised chin"), positions 18, 19, 20, 21 —
d. As No. R16c, silk paper 250.00

R17 R3 3c **Playing Cards, green** ('63)
a. Imperf. *27,500.*
Pair *75,000.*
c. Perf. 200.00
Pair 450.00
Block of 4 *1,000.*

R18 R3 3c **Proprietary, green**
b. Part perf. 1,250.
Pair *3,000.*
Block of 4 *8,500.*
c. Perf. 9.00
Pair 20.00
Block of 4 45.00
Double transfer in numerals 12.50
Double transfer, 4 value ovals shifted north 175.00
Double transfer, 4 value ovals shifted west 125.00
Cracked plate 20.00
d. As No. R18c, silk paper 300.00
Pair 750.00
e. As No. R18c, double impression *1,750.*
f. As No. R18c, printed on both sides *4,000.*

R19 R3 3c **Telegraph, green**
a. Imperf. 100.00
Pair 500.00
Block of 4 1,200.
Privately perforated, sewing machine perf. *700.00*
b. Part perf. 30.00
Pair 82.50
Block of 4 500.00
c. Perf. 3.00
Pair 8.75
Block of 4 80.00

R20 R3 4c **Inland Exchange, brown** ('63)
c. Perf. 2.25
Pair 5.25
Block of 4 22.50
Double transfer at top, position 78 15.00
Plate scratches through "U.S." at top —
d. As No. R20c, silk paper 190.00

R21 R3 4c **Playing Cards, slate** ('63)
c. Perf. 700.00
Pair *1,600.*
Block of 4 *3,500.*

R22 R3 4c **Proprietary, purple**
a. Imperf. —
b. Part perf. 500.00
Pair 1,600.
Block of 4 4,400.
c. Perf. 8.50
Pair 20.00
Block of 4 55.00
Double transfer at top 19.00
Double transfer at bottom 13.50
Plate gash in lower left numeral, position 88 —
d. As No. R22c, silk paper 350.00
Pair *600.00*
Block of 4 —

There are shade and color variations of Nos. R21-R22. See foreword of "Revenue Stamps" section.

R23 R3 5c **Agreement, red**
c. Perf. .50
Pair 1.00
Block of 4 2.10
Double transfer in numerals, pos. 82 25.00
Double transfer across top, pos. 160, late state 75.00
d. As No. R23c, silk paper 4.50
Pair 8.00
Block of 4 22.50
e. As No. R23c, half used as 2c on document *2,500.*

R24 R3 5c **Certificate, red**
a. Imperf. 4.00
Pair 35.00
Block of 4 350.00
b. Part perf. 15.00
Pair 150.00
Block of 4 400.00
c. Perf. .50
Pair 1.25
Block of 4 3.00
Double transfer in upper label 10.00
Double transfer throughout 200.00
Triple transfer, position 121 35.00
Scratched plate, position 170 —
d. As No. R24c, silk paper 1.10
Pair 2.50
Block of 4 10.00
Complete double transfer —
e. As No. R24c, half used as 2c on document —
f. As No. R24d, impression of No. R3 on back *3,000.*

R25 R3 5c **Express, red**
a. Imperf. 8.00
Pair 30.00
Block of 4 350.00
b. Part perf. 8.00*
Pair 100.00
Block of 4 300.00
c. Perf. .40
Pair .90
Block of 4 2.25
Double transfer, position 75 15.00

R26 R3 5c **Foreign Exchange, red**
b. Part perf. *2,500.*
Pair —
c. Perf. .50
Pair 1.25
Block of 4 15.00
Double transfer at top 20.00
Double transfer at bottom 10.00
d. As No. R26c, silk paper 850.00

R27 R3 5c **Inland Exchange, red**
a. Imperf. 10.00
Pair 37.50
Block of 4 120.00
Double transfer at top 77.50
Cracked plate 95.00
Privately rouletted —
b. Part perf. 6.75
Pair 42.50
Block of 4 110.00
Double transfer at top 47.50
Cracked plate 90.00
c. Perf. .60
Pair 1.30
Block of 4 3.00
Double transfer at top 27.50
Double transfer at bottom —
Double transfer at left and right 60.00
Cracked plate 32.50
d. As No. R27c, silk paper 17.50
Pair 50.00
e. As No. R27c, double impression *3,500.*

R28 R3 5c **Playing Cards, red** ('63)
c. Perf. 40.00
Pair 90.00
Block of 4 200.00
d. As No. R28c, silk paper *1,000.*
e. Double impression *2,000.*

R29 R3 5c **Proprietary, red** ('64)
c. Perf. 30.00
Pair 70.00
Block of 4 350.00
Scratched plate 45.00
d. As No. R29c, silk paper 400.00

R30 R3 6c **Inland Exchange, orange** ('63)
b. Part perf. (imperf. vert.), on document —
c. Perf. 2.25
Pair 18.50
Block of 4 100.00
Scratched plate, position 19 15.00
Double transfer at top —
d. As No. R30c, silk paper 350.00

R31 R3 6c **Proprietary, orange** ('71)
c. Perf. *1,800.*

Nearly all examples of No. R31 are faulty or repaired and poorly centered. The catalogue value is for a fine centered stamp with minor faults which do not detract from its appearance.

R32 R3 10c **Bill of Lading, blue**
a. Imperf. 90.00
Pair 300.00
Block of 4 1,000.
b. Part perf. 600.00*
Pair 2,500.
c. Perf. 1.75
Pair 4.00
Block of 4 10.00
Double transfer, positions 33 and 143 —
Tool gouge, position 151 —
e. As No. R32c, half used as 5c on document *300.00*

R33 R3 10c **Certificate, blue**
a. Imperf. 400.00
Pair 850.00
Block of 4 *3,000.*
Cracked plate —
b. Part perf. 850.00*
Pair 2,000.
Block of 4 —
c. Perf. .35
Pair .75
Block of 4 2.25
Double transfer at right, position 93 15.00
Cracked plate 15.00
Scratched plate —
d. As No. R33c, silk paper 6.00
Pair 17.50
Block of 4 90.00
e. As No. R33c, half used as 5c on document *300.00*

R34 R3 10c **Contract, blue**
b. Part perf. 700.00*
Pair 1,800.
Block of 4 —
be. As No. R34b, **ultramarine** 1,000.
c. Perf. .50
Pair 1.25
Block of 4 4.75
Complete double transfer 70.00
ce. As No. R34c, **ultramarine** 1.00
Pair 2.50
Block of 4 17.50
d. As No. R34c, silk paper 4.25
Pair 11.00
Block of 4 70.00
f. As No. R34c, half used as 5c on document *300.00*

R35 R3 10c **Foreign Exchange, blue**
- *c.* Perf. 14.00
  - Pair 30.00
  - Block of 4 92.50
- *d.* As No. R35c, silk paper —
- *e.* As No. R35c, **ultramarine** 20.00
  - Pair 60.00
  - Block of 4 180.00

R36 R3 10c **Inland Exchange, blue**
- *a.* Imperf. 500.00
  - Pair 2,000.
  - Block of 4 *4,500.*
- *b.* Part perf. 4.50*
  - Pair 15.00
  - Block of 4 80.00
- *c.* Perf. .30
  - Pair .60
  - Block of 4 1.75
  - Double transfer at right —
  - Scratched plate —
- *d.* As No. R36c, silk paper 125.00
  - Pair 275.00
  - Block of 4 —
- *e.* As No. R36c, half used as 5c on document *300.00*

R37 R3 10c **Power of Attorney, blue**
- *a.* Imperf. 1,000.
  - Pair 2,500.
  - Block of 4 *6,250.*
- *b.* Part perf. 30.00
  - Pair 100.00
  - Block of 4 300.00
- *be.* As No. R37b, half used as 5c on document —
- *c.* Perf. 1.00
  - Pair 2.25
  - Block of 4 8.00
  - Scrathed plate —
- *ce.* As No. R37c, half used as 5c on document *300.00*

R38 R3 10c **Proprietary, blue** ('64)
- *c.* Perf. 19.00
  - Pair 45.00
  - Block of 4 110.00

R39 R3 15c **Foreign Exchange, brown** ('63)
- *c.* Perf. 35.00
  - Pair 95.00
  - Block of 4 300.00
- *e.* Double impression *1,750.*

R40 R3 15c **Inland Exchange, brown**
- *a.* Imperf. 45.00
  - Pair 200.00
  - Block of 4 750.00
  - Cracked plate 60.00
  - Double transfer at top, pos. 68 100.00
- *b.* Part perf. 14.00
  - Pair 50.00
  - Block of 4 600.00
  - Cracked plate 37.50
- *c.* Perf. 2.00
  - Pair 5.00
  - Block of 4 12.00
  - Double transfer at top, position 68 20.00
  - Cracked plate, position 11 14.00
- *e.* As No. R40b, double impression *2,250.*
- *f.* As No. R40c, double impression *1,000.*

R41 R3 20c **Foreign Exchange, red**
- *a.* Imperf. 100.00
  - Pair 350.00
  - Block of 4 1,000.
- *c.* Perf. 80.00
  - Pair 200.00
  - Block of 4 450.00
  - Double transfer *200.00*
- *d.* As No. R41c, silk paper 650.00
  - Double transfer —

R42 R3 20c **Inland Exchange, red**
- *a.* Imperf. 17.00
  - Pair 50.00
  - Block of 4 600.00
- *b.* Part perf. 22.50
  - Pair 60.00
  - Block of 4 300.00
- *c.* Perf. .45
  - Pair 1.00
  - Block of 4 14.00
- *d.* As No. R42c, silk paper —
- *e.* As No. R42c, half used as 5c on document *300.00*

R4

R5

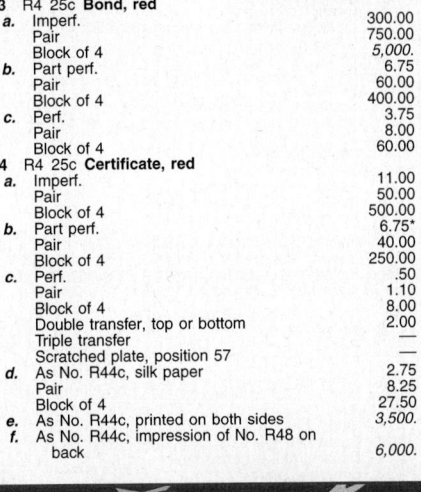

R43 R4 25c **Bond, red**
- *a.* Imperf. 300.00
  - Pair 750.00
  - Block of 4 *5,000.*
- *b.* Part perf. 6.75
  - Pair 60.00
  - Block of 4 400.00
- *c.* Perf. 3.75
  - Pair 8.00
  - Block of 4 60.00

R44 R4 25c **Certificate, red**
- *a.* Imperf. 11.00
  - Pair 50.00
  - Block of 4 500.00
- *b.* Part perf. 6.75*
  - Pair 40.00
  - Block of 4 250.00
- *c.* Perf. .50
  - Pair 1.10
  - Block of 4 8.00
  - Double transfer, top or bottom 2.00
  - Triple transfer —
  - Scratched plate, position 57 —
- *d.* As No. R44c, silk paper 2.75
  - Pair 8.25
  - Block of 4 27.50
- *e.* As No. R44c, printed on both sides *3,500.*
- *f.* As No. R44c, impression of No. R48 on back *6,000.*

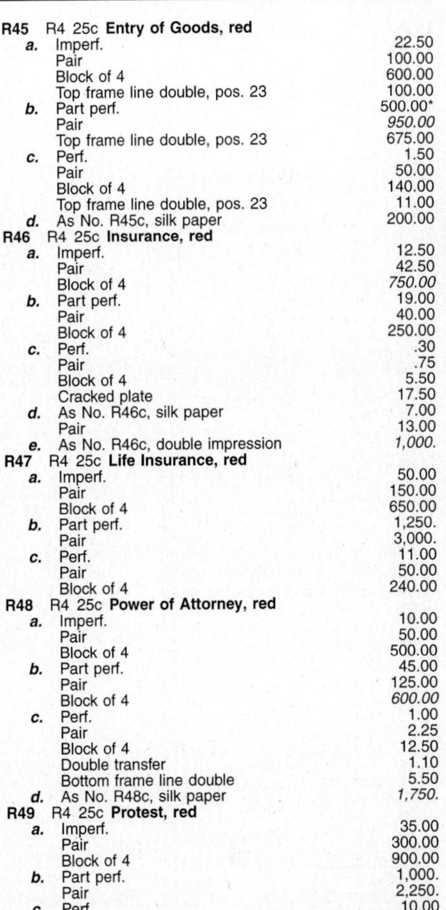

R45 R4 25c **Entry of Goods, red**
- *a.* Imperf. 22.50
  - Pair 100.00
  - Block of 4 600.00
  - Top frame line double, pos. 23 100.00
- *b.* Part perf. 500.00*
  - Pair *950.00*
  - Top frame line double, pos. 23 675.00
- *c.* Perf. 1.50
  - Pair 50.00
  - Block of 4 140.00
  - Top frame line double, pos. 23 11.00
- *d.* As No. R45c, silk paper 200.00

R46 R4 25c **Insurance, red**
- *a.* Imperf. 12.50
  - Pair 42.50
  - Block of 4 *750.00*
- *b.* Part perf. 19.00
  - Pair 40.00
  - Block of 4 250.00
- *c.* Perf. .30
  - Pair .75
  - Block of 4 5.50
  - Cracked plate 17.50
- *d.* As No. R46c, silk paper 7.00
  - Pair 13.00
- *e.* As No. R46c, double impression *1,000.*

R47 R4 25c **Life Insurance, red**
- *a.* Imperf. 50.00
  - Pair 150.00
  - Block of 4 650.00
- *b.* Part perf. 1,250.
  - Pair 3,000.
- *c.* Perf. 11.00
  - Pair 50.00
  - Block of 4 240.00

R48 R4 25c **Power of Attorney, red**
- *a.* Imperf. 10.00
  - Pair 50.00
  - Block of 4 500.00
- *b.* Part perf. 45.00
  - Pair 125.00
  - Block of 4 *600.00*
- *c.* Perf. 1.00
  - Pair 2.25
  - Block of 4 12.50
  - Double transfer 1.10
  - Bottom frame line double 5.50
- *d.* As No. R48c, silk paper *1,750.*

R49 R4 25c **Protest, red**
- *a.* Imperf. 35.00
  - Pair 300.00
  - Block of 4 900.00
- *b.* Part perf. 1,000.
  - Pair 2,250.
- *c.* Perf. 10.00
  - Pair 29.00
  - Block of 4 115.00

R50	R4 25c **Warehouse Receipt, red**	
a.	Imperf.	55.00
	Pair	250.00
	Block of 4	*1,500.*
b.	Part perf.	1,300.
	Pair	2,900.
c.	Perf.	45.00
	Pair	100.00
	Block of 4	325.00
R51	R4 30c **Foreign Exchange, lilac**	
a.	Imperf.	200.00
	Pair	650.00
	Block of 4	*5,000.*
b.	Part perf.	*11,000.*
c.	Perf.	60.00
	Pair	225.00
	Block of 4	—
	Double transfer	100.00
	Top frame line double	85.00
d.	As No. R51c, silk paper	*675.00*
R52	R4 30c **Inland Exchange, lilac**	
a.	Imperf.	75.00
	Pair	350.00
	Block of 4	1,000.
b.	Part perf.	90.00
	Pair	425.00
	Block of 4	—
c.	Perf.	8.50
	Pair	40.00
	Block of 4	140.00
	Double transfer	30.00
d.	As No. R52c, silk paper	*1,750.*

There are shade and color variations of Nos. R51-R52. See foreword of "Revenue Stamps" section.

R53	R4 40c **Inland Exchange, brown**	
a.	Imperf.	*2,500.*
	Pair	*5,750.*
b.	Part perf.	9.00
	Pair	50.00
	Block of 4	210.00
	Double transfer	50.00
c.	Perf.	8.00
	Pair	18.00
	Block of 4	275.00
	Double transfer	30.00
d.	As No. R53c, silk paper	550.00
f.	As No. R53c, double impression	*2,000.*
R54	R5 50c **Conveyance, blue**	
a.	Imperf.	20.00
	Pair	100.00
	Block of 4	700.00
b.	Part perf.	3.50
	Pair	45.00
	Block of 4	160.00
c.	Perf.	.35
	Pair	.70
	Block of 4	2.50
	Double transfer	6.00
	Cracked plate	15.00
	Scratched plate at bottom, pos. 52	15.00
ce.	As No. R54c, **ultramarine**	.50
	Pair	1.25
	Block of 4	10.00
d.	As No. R54c, silk paper, **blue**	3.00
	Pair	6.50
	Powder blue	10.00
de.	As No. R54d, **ultramarine**	—
R55	R5 50c **Entry of Goods, blue**	
b.	Part perf.	17.50
	Pair	300.00
	Block of 4	650.00
c.	Perf.	.60
	Pair	2.00
	Block of 4	25.00
	Double transfer, position 20	14.00
	Scratched plate, position 76	20.00
d.	As No. R55c, silk paper	150.00
	Pair	275.00
R56	R5 50c **Foreign Exchange, blue**	
a.	Imperf.	75.00
	Pair	400.00
b.	Part perf.	125.00*
	Pair	600.00
c.	Perf.	7.50
	Pair	42.50
	Block of 4	140.00
	Double transfer at left	11.00
e.	As No. R56c, double impression	*1,000.*
f.	As No. R56c, half used as 25c on document	*350.00*
R57	R5 50c **Lease, blue**	
a.	Imperf.	35.00
	Pair	200.00
	Block of 4	*1,000.*
b.	Part perf.	250.00
	Pair	600.00
	Block of 4	1,400.
c.	Perf.	10.00
	Pair	67.50
	Block of 4	225.00
R58	R5 50c **Life Insurance, blue**	
a.	Imperf.	45.00
	Pair	160.00
	Block of 4	1,000.
	Double transfer	47.50
b.	Part perf.	200.00
c.	Perf.	1.75
	Pair	10.00
	Block of 4	50.00
	Double transfer at top, position 10 and 13	20.00
e.	As No. R58c, double impression	*1,100.*

Cracked Plate (C59)

R59	R5 50c **Mortgage, blue**	
a.	Imperf.	22.50
	Pair	100.00
	Block of 4	500.00
	Scratched plate, diagonal, positions 26, 42, 43	35.00
b.	Part perf.	5.00
	Pair	225.00
	Block of 4	500.00
	Cracked plate, positions 64 and 81	37.50
	Scratched plate, diagonal, positions 26, 42, 43	25.00
c.	Perf.	.70
	Pair	2.00
	Block of 4	7.50
	Cracked plate, positions 64 and 81	12.50
	Scratched plate, diagonal, positions 26, 42, 43	12.50
	Double transfer	3.50
	Tool gouge, position 63	40.00
d.	As No. R59c, silk paper	—
e.	As No. R59a, double impression	—
f.	As No. R59c, double impression	—

The plate crack listed for Nos. R59b and R59c crosses positions 64 and 81. The illustrated crack (C59) is position 64. Value is for a single. The scratch listed for Nos. R59a, R59b and R59c crosses positions 26, 42 and 43. Value is for a single.

R60	R5 50c **Original Process, blue**	
a.	Imperf.	5.50
	Pair	77.50
	Block of 4	*1,200.*
b.	Part perf.	*5,000.*
c.	Perf.	1.00
	Pair	2.75
	Block of 4	7.50
	Double transfer at top and left, position 28	12.00
	Double transfer at bottom	8.00
	Scratched plate	10.00
d.	As No. R60c, silk paper	7.50
	Pair	22.50
	Block of 4	150.00
e.	As No. R60c, half used as 25c on document	*5,000.*
R61	R5 50c **Passage Ticket, blue**	
a.	Imperf.	140.00
	Pair	400.00
	Block of 4	*1,250.*
b.	Part perf.	750.00*
	Pair	1,650.
c.	Perf.	2.25
	Pair	12.50
	Block of 4	225.00
	Scratched plate, position 9	25.00
R62	R5 50c **Probate of Will, blue**	
a.	Imperf.	55.00
	Pair	250.00
	Block of 4	1,000.
b.	Part perf.	250.00
	Pair	825.00
	Block of 4	1,650.
	Scratched plate	300.00
c.	Perf.	22.50
	Pair	50.00
	Block of 4	350.00
R63	R5 50c **Surety Bond, blue**	
a.	Imperf.	400.00
	Pair	*1,500.*
b.	Part perf.	2.75
	Pair	15.00
	Block of 4	100.00
c.	Perf.	.30
	Pair	1.75
	Block of 4	10.00
e.	As No. R63c, **ultramarine**	.75
	Pair	5.50
	Block of 4	55.00
R64	R5 60c **Inland Exchange, orange**	
a.	Imperf.	120.00
	Pair	500.00
	Block of 4	*1,200.*
b.	Part perf.	90.00
	Pair	300.00
	Block of 4	600.00
c.	Perf.	9.00
	Pair	20.00
	Block of 4	100.00
d.	As No. R64c, silk paper	85.00
	Pair	190.00
R65	R5 70c **Foreign Exchange, green**	
a.	Imperf.	750.00
	Pair	3,000.
b.	Part perf.	200.00
	Pair	950.00
	Block of 4	*2,000.*
	Scratched plate at bottom, pos. 52	250.00
c.	Perf.	14.00
	Pair	40.00
	Block of 4	250.00
	Scratched plate at bottom, pos. 52	30.00
	Double transfer at top	—
d.	As No. R65c, silk paper	75.00
	Pair	175.00

Pairs and blocks of No. R65b are valued in the grade of fine.

R6

R7

R66	R6 $1 **Conveyance, red**	
a.	Imperf.	27.50
	Pair	90.00
	Block of 4	750.00
	Double transfer	35.00
	Right frame line double	90.00
	Top frame line double	125.00
b.	Part perf.	*4,500.*
	Pair	*11,000.*
c.	Perf.	27.50
	Pair	75.00
	Block of 4	160.00
	Double transfer	37.50
	Right frame line double, position 60	77.50
	Top frame line double, position 6	60.00
d.	As No. R66c, silk paper	200.00
R67	R6 $1 **Entry of Goods, red**	
a.	Imperf.	50.00
	Pair	150.00
	Block of 4	750.00
c.	Perf.	2.75
	Pair	6.50
	Block of 4	55.00
	Scratched plate, position 43	15.00
d.	As No. R67c, silk paper	180.00
R68	R6 $1 **Foreign Exchange, red**	
a.	Imperf.	125.00
	Pair	300.00
	Block of 4	*1,600.*
	Left frame line double, pos. 80	180.00
c.	Perf.	.75
	Pair	1.75
	Block of 4	11.00
	Double transfer, pos. 79	20.00
	Recut frame lines at upper left	6.00
	Left frame line double, pos. 80	19.00
	Recut shield at upper left	40.00
d.	As No. R68c, silk paper	150.00
e.	As No. R68d, half used as 50c on document	*300.00*
R69	R6 $1 **Inland Exchange, red**	
a.	Imperf.	17.00
	Pair	75.00
	Block of 4	950.00
	Double transfer of top shields, position 29	110.00
b.	Part perf.	*6,000.**
	Pair	*12,500.*
c.	Perf.	.70
	Pair	2.00
	Block of 4	9.50
	Double transfer at bottom	4.25
	Double transfer of top shields, position 29	21.00
d.	As No. R69c, silk paper	6.00
	Pair	9.00
	Block of 4	35.00
e.	As No. R69c, horiz. pair, imperf. vert.	—
f.	As No. R69c, half used as 50c on document	*300.00*

No. R69e is an error from a pane of stamps that was intended to be issued fully perforated. It can be differentiated from No. R69b by the color, paper and date of cancel. Expertization is strongly recommended and some specialists doubt the existence of No. R69b.

R70	R6 $1 **Lease, red**	
a.	Imperf.	50.00
	Pair	200.00
	Block of 4	800.00
	Double transfer at bottom	80.00
	Double transfer at top, pos. 17	—
c.	Perf.	4.50
	Pair	12.00
	Block of 4	80.00
	Double transfer at bottom	11.00
	Cracked plate	26.00
	Double transfer at top, pos. 17	—
e.	As No. R70c, half used as 50c on document	*500.00*
R71	R6 $1 **Life Insurance, red**	
a.	Imperf.	300.00
	Pair	650.00
	Block of 4	*1,400.*
	Right frame line double	500.00
c.	Perf.	10.00
	Pair	25.00
	Block of 4	60.00

Right frame line double, pos. 46 50.00
d. As No. R71c, silk paper *1,000.*
e. As No. R71c, half used as 50c on document *1,000.*

R72 R6 $1 **Manifest, red**
a. Imperf. 47.50
Pair 150.00
Block of 4 800.00
c. Perf. 40.00
Pair 85.00
Block of 4 210.00
e. As No. R72c, half used as 50c on document *300.00*

R73 R6 $1 **Mortgage, red**
a. Imperf. 27.50
Pair 100.00
Block of 4 800.00
Double transfer at left 45.00
Bottom frame line double, position 13 60.00
c. Perf. 300.00
Pair 650.00
Block of 4 1,400.
Double transfer at left 350.00
Bottom frame line double, position 13 450.00

R74 R6 $1 **Passage Ticket, red**
a. Imperf. 350.00
Pair 750.00
Block of 4 *1,600.*
c. Perf. 350.00
Pair 750.00
Block of 4 1,750.

R75 R6 $1 **Power of Attorney, red**
a. Imperf. 100.00
Pair 250.00
Block of 4 700.00
c. Perf. 2.75
Pair 6.00
Block of 4 26.00
Double transfer 9.50
Recut 11.50
e. As No. R75c, half used as 50c on document —

R76 R6 $1 **Probate of Will, red**
a. Imperf. 100.00
Pair 350.00
Block of 4 *1,000.*
Right frame line double 160.00
Double transfer at top 225.00
c. Perf. 55.00
Pair 125.00
Block of 4 325.00
Right frame line double 75.00

R77 R7 $1.30 **Foreign Exchange, orange** ('63)
a. Imperf. *11,000.*
c. Perf. 120.00
Pair 400.00
Block of 4 —
Double transfer —

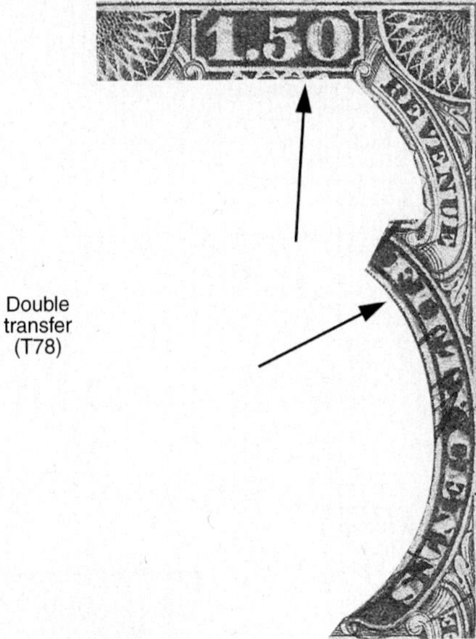

Double transfer (T78)

R78 R7 $1.50 **Inland Exchange, blue**
a. Imperf. 32.50
Pair 200.00
Block of 4 800.00
Bottom frame line double —
c. Perf. 7.00
Pair 75.00
Block of 4 400.00
Double transfer (T78) 13.50
Top and bottom frame lines doubled —
Cracked plate —

R79 R7 $1.60 **Foreign Exchange, green** ('63)
a. Imperf. 1,400.
Pair *8,000.*
c. Perf. 180.00
Pair 500.00

R80 R7 $1.90 **Foreign Exchange, purple** ('63)
a. Imperf. *12,500.*
c. Perf. 200.00
Pair 500.00
Block of 4 1,200.
d. As No. R80c, silk paper 650.00

There are many shade and color variations of No. R80. See foreword of "Revenue Stamps" section.

R8

R81 R8 $2 **Conveyance, red**
a. Imperf. 250.00
Pair 700.00
Block of 4 1,800.
b. Part perf. 5,500.
Pair *8,500.*
c. Perf. 4.00
Pair 10.00
Block of 4 65.00
Cracked plate, position 17 32.50
Scratched plate, position 9 —
d. As No. R81c, silk paper 40.00
Pair 90.00
Block of 4 200.00
e. As No. R81c, half used as $1 on document *600.00*

R82 R8 $2 **Mortgage, red**
a. Imperf. 200.00
Pair 600.00
Block of 4 1,300.
c. Perf. 7.00
Pair 16.00
Block of 4 60.00
Double transfer at upper left, pos. 7, 27, 62-64 25.00
Cracked plate, position 8 —
Scratched plate, position 2 —
Plate erosion, pos. 43 20.00
d. As No. R82c, silk paper 60.00
Pair 125.00
e. As No. R82c, half used as $1 on document *900.00*

R83 R8 $2 **Probate of Will, red** ('63)
a. Imperf. *5,500.*
Pair *16,000.*
c. Perf. 90.00
Pair 200.00
Block of 4 425.00
Double transfer 90.00
e. As No. R83c, half used as $1 on document *750.00*

R84 R8 $2.50 **Inland Exchange, purple** ('63)
a. Imperf. *10,000.*
Pair *45,000.*
c. Perf. 22.50
Pair 50.00
Block of 4 600.00
d. As No. R84c, silk paper 40.00
Pair 90.00
Block of 4 425.00
e. As No. R84c, double impression *2,000.*

There are many shade and color variations of Nos. R84c and R84d. See foreword of "Revenues Stamps" section.

R85 R8 $3 **Charter Party, green**
a. Imperf. 250.00
Pair 450.00
Block of 4 *8,000.*
c. Perf. 11.00
Pair 65.00
Block of 4 300.00
Double transfer at top 25.00
Double transfer at bottom 12.00
Scratched plate, position 44 —
d. As No. R85c, silk paper 175.00
Pair 275.00
e. As No. R85c, printed on both sides *7,000.*
f. As No. R85c, half used as $1.50 on document —
g. As No. R85c, impression of No. RS208 on back *17,000.*

R86 R8 $3 **Manifest, green**
a. Imperf. 250.00
Pair 600.00
Block of 4 *7,000.*
c. Perf. 55.00
Pair 125.00
Block of 4 300.00
Double transfer 210.00

R87 R8 $3.50 **Inland Exchange, blue** ('63)
a. Imperf. *8,500.*
Pair *40,000.*
c. Perf. 70.00
Pair 180.00
Block of 4 450.00
e. As No. R87c, printed on both sides *4,000.*

The $3.50 has stars in upper corners.

R9

R10

R88 R9 $5 **Charter Party, red**
a. Imperf. 350.00
Pair 750.00
Block of 4 *1,600.*
Right frame line double 425.00
Top frame line double 425.00
c. Perf. 10.00
Pair 65.00
Block of 4 200.00
Right frame line double 70.00
Top frame line double 60.00
d. As No. R88c, silk paper 170.00

R89 R9 $5 **Conveyance, red**
a. Imperf. 50.00
Pair 200.00
Block of 4 *1,000.*

c.	Perf.	11.00
	Pair	24.00
	Block of 4	110.00
d.	As No. R89c, silk paper	160.00
	Pair	350.00
R90	R9 $5 **Manifest, red**	
a.	Imperf.	250.00
	Pair	600.00
	Block of 4	*1,300.*
	Left frame line double	325.00
c.	Perf.	120.00
	Pair	300.00
	Block of 4	650.00
	Left frame line double	175.00
R91	R9 $5 **Mortgage, red**	
a.	Imperf.	200.00
	Pair	900.00
	Block of 4	—
c.	Perf.	25.00
	Pair	87.50
	Block of 4	1,200.
R92	R9 $5 **Probate of Will, red**	
a.	Imperf.	750.00
	Pair	1,800.
	Block of 4	*4,000.*
c.	Perf.	27.50
	Pair	100.00
	Block of 4	375.00
R93	R9 $10 **Charter Party, green**	
a.	Imperf.	900.00
	Pair	*1,900.*
	Block of 4	—
c.	Perf.	37.50
	Pair	100.00
	Block of 4	450.00
	Double transfer	85.00
R94	R9 $10 **Conveyance, green**	
a.	Imperf.	175.00
	Pair	450.00
	Block of 4	1,200.
	Double transfer at top	225.00
	Top frame line double	—
c.	Perf.	77.50
	Pair	200.00
	Block of 4	700.00
	Double transfer at top	125.00
	Right frame line double, position 71	150.00
	Top frame line double	—
R95	R9 $10 **Mortgage, green**	
a.	Imperf.	800.00
	Pair	2,500.
	Block of 4	*12,000.*
	Top frame line double	900.00
c.	Perf.	40.00
	Pair	120.00
	Block of 4	—
	Top frame line double	55.00
R96	R9 $10 **Probate of Will, green**	
a.	Imperf.	*3,500.*
	Pair	*12,000.*
	Double transfer, pos. 27	—
c.	Perf.	45.00
	Pair	100.00
	Block of 4	400.00
	Double transfer at top, pos. 27	90.00
R97	R10 $15 **Mortgage, blue**	
a.	Imperf.	4,500.
	Pair	*10,000.*
	Block of 4	*25,000.*
c.	Perf.	300.00
	Pair	700.00
	Block of 4	*4,000.*
e.	As No. R97c, **ultramarine**	500.00
	Pair	1,200.
	Block of 4	*5,000.*
f.	As No. R97c, **milky blue**	525.00
	Pair	1,900.
R98	R10 $20 **Conveyance, orange**	
a.	Imperf.	150.00
	Pair	450.00
	Block of 4	2,000.
c.	Perf.	110.00
	Pair	300.00
	Block of 4	1,000.
d.	As No. R98c, silk paper	175.00
	Pair	350.00
R99	R10 $20 **Probate of Will, orange**	
a.	Imperf.	2,500.
	Pair	*8,000.*
	Block of 4	*18,000.*
c.	Perf.	3,000.
	Pair	*6,500.*
	Block of 4	*18,000.*
R100	R10 $25 **Mortgage, red** ('63)	
a.	Imperf.	3,250.
	Pair	*8,000.*
	Block of 4	*25,000.*
c.	Perf.	250.00
	Pair	600.00
	Block of 4	*1,800.*
	Scratched plate	—
d.	As No. R100c, silk paper	300.00
e.	As No. R100c, horiz. pair, imperf. between	*6,000.*
R101	R10 $50 **U.S. Internal Revenue, green** ('63)	
a.	Imperf.	325.00
	Pair	750.00
	Block of 4	4,000.
c.	Perf.	210.00
	Pair	450.00
	Block of 4	1,000.
	Cracked plate	250.00

R11

Illustration reduced.

R102	R11 $200 **U.S. Int. Rev., green & red** ('64)	
a.	Imperf.	2,500.
	Pair	*5,500.*
	Block of 4	*15,000.*
c.	Perf.	750.00
	Pair	2,250.
	Block of 4	*5,000.*

DOCUMENTARY STAMPS
Second Issue

After release of the First Issue revenue stamps, the Bureau of Internal Revenue received many reports of fraudulent cleaning and re-use. The Bureau ordered a Second Issue with new designs and colors, using a patented "chameleon" paper which is usually violet or pinkish, with silk fibers.

While designs are different from those of the first issue, stamp sizes and make up of the plates are the same as for corresponding denominations.

R12

R12a

George Washington

Engraved and printed by Jos. R. Carpenter, Philadelphia.
Various Frames and Numeral Arrangements

1871 ***Perf. 12***

R103	R12 1c **blue & black**	100.00
	Cut cancel	40.00
	Pair	220.00
	Block of 4	475.00
a.	Inverted center	*2,000.*
	Cut cancel	*750.00*
	Pair	*3,500.*
	Block of 4	—
R104	R12 2c **blue & black**	2.75
	Cut cancel	.30
	Pair	6.25
	Block of 4	40.00
a.	Inverted center	*6,000.*
	Cut cancel	*3,500.*
R105	R12a 3c **blue & black**	75.00
	Cut cancel	30.00
	Pair	160.00
	Block of 4	350.00
R106	R12a 4c **blue & black**	160.00
	Cut cancel	65.00
	Pair	340.00
	Block of 4	725.00
a.	Half used as 2c on document	*1,000.*
R107	R12a 5c **blue & black**	2.00
	Cut cancel	.50
	Pair	6.00
	Block of 4	22.50
a.	Inverted center	*5,000.*
	Cut cancel	*2,500.*
b.	Half used as 2c on document	*1,000.*
R108	R12a 6c **blue & black**	300.00
	Cut cancel	100.00
	Pair	625.00
	Block of 4	1,400.
R109	R12a 10c **blue & black**	1.50
	Cut cancel	.30
	Pair	9.50
	Block of 4	25.00
	Double transfer	—
a.	Inverted center	*2,500.*
	Cut cancel	*1,250.*
	Pair	*5,250.*
b.	Double impression of center	—
c.	Half used as 5c on document	*300.00*

No. R109a is valued in the grade of fine.

R110	R12a 15c **blue & black**	100.00
	Cut cancel	35.00
	Pair	210.00
	Block of 4	450.00
R111	R12a 20c **blue & black**	10.00
	Cut cancel	4.00
	Pair	22.50
	Block of 4	87.50
a.	Inverted center	*8,000.*
	Cut cancel	*4,000.*
	Pair	*17,000.*

No. R111a is valued in the grade of fine and with small faults, as almost all examples have faults.

R13

R13a

R112	R13 25c **blue & black**	1.50
	Cut cancel	.30
	Pair	3.25
	Block of 4	11.00
	Double transfer, position 57	50.00
a.	Inverted center	*13,000.*
	Cut cancel	*6,500.*
b.	Imperf.	—
c.	Privately rouletted, sewing machine perfs	160.00
	Cut cancel	80.00
	Pair	375.00
	Block of 4	1,750.
d.	Privately perforated 8	750.00
R113	R13 30c **blue & black**	175.00
	Cut cancel	70.00
	Pair	370.00
	Block of 4	825.00
	Double transfer in stars	250.00
R114	R13 40c **blue & black**	150.00
	Cut cancel	50.00
	Pair	325.00
R115	R13a 50c **blue & black**	1.40
	Cut cancel	.35
	Pair	3.00
	Block of 4	9.25
	Double transfer	20.00
a.	Inverted center	1,050.
	Cut cancel	650.00
	Pair	*2,750.*
	Punch cancel	275.00
	Pair	575.00
b.	Imperf.	*800.00*
c.	Privately perforated, sewing machine perfs	500.00
	Pair	1,200.
	Block of 4	*2,250.*
d.	Privately perforated 8-9	—
R116	R13a 60c **blue & black**	250.00
	Cut cancel	80.00
	Pair	550.00
	Foreign entry, design of 70c	500.00
R117	R13a 70c **blue & black**	100.00
	Cut cancel	35.00
	Pair	210.00
a.	Inverted center	*4,000.*
	Cut cancel	*1,750.*

R13b

R118	R13b $1 **blue & black**	10.00
	Cut cancel	2.25
	Pair	22.50
	Block of 4	55.00
a.	Inverted center	*6,000.*
	Cut cancel	*1,500.*

	Punch cancel	*1,150.*
b.	Half used as 50c on document	*1,000.*
R119	R13b $1.30 **blue & black**	750.00
	Cut cancel	175.00
	Pair	1,650.
R120	R13b $1.50 **blue & black**	22.50
	Cut cancel	9.00
	Pair	65.00
	Block of 4	—
	Foreign entry, design of $1	750.00
a.	Privately perforated sewing machine perfs	*3,500.*
	Cut cancel	*2,500.*
	Pair	—
R121	R13b $1.60 **blue & black**	750.00
	Cut cancel	325.00
	Pair	1,650.
R122	R13b $1.90 **blue & black**	500.00
	Cut cancel	150.00
	Pair	1,100.
	Block of 4	—

R13c

R123	R13c $2 **blue & black**	25.00
	Cut cancel	10.00
	Pair	55.00
	Block of 4	350.00
	Double transfer at top	45.00
R124	R13c $2.50 **blue & black**	60.00
	Cut cancel	30.00
	Pair	130.00
	Block of 4	750.00
R125	R13c $3 **blue & black**	75.00
	Cut cancel	35.00
	Pair	170.00
	Block of 4	600.00
	Double transfer	—
R126	R13c $3.50 **blue & black**	500.00
	Cut cancel	250.00
	Pair	1,100.

R13d

R127	R13d $5 **blue & black**	40.00
	Cut cancel	15.00
	Pair	110.00
	Block of 4	500.00
a.	Inverted center	*3,000.*
	Cut cancel	*1,500.*
	Punch cancel	*1,100.*
R128	R13d $10 **blue & black**	260.00
	Cut cancel	90.00
	Pair	550.00
	Block of 4	*1,200.*

R13e

R129	R13e $20 **blue & black**	800.00
	Cut cancel	275.00
	Pair	2,000.
	Block of 4	*9,000.*
R130	R13e $25 **blue & black**	750.00
	Cut cancel	275.00
	Pair	2,000.
R131	R13e $50 **blue & black**	900.00
	Cut cancel	325.00
	Pair	2,400.

R13f

R132	R13f $200 **red, blue & black**	*8,500.*
	Cut cancel	*3,500.*

Printed in sheets of one.

R13g

R133 R13g $500 **red orange, green & black** *17,500.*
Cut cancel *8,500.*

Printed in sheets of one.

Value for No. R133 is for a very fine appearing example with a light circular cut cancel or with minor flaws.

Inverted Centers: Fraudulently produced inverted centers exist, some excellently made.

Confusion resulting from the fact that all 1c through $50 denominations of the Second Issue were uniform in color, caused the ordering of a new printing with values in distinctive colors.

Plates used were those of the preceding issue.

Third Issue

Engraved and printed by Jos. R. Carpenter, Philadelphia.
Various Frames and Numeral Arrangements.
Violet "Chameleon" Paper with Silk Fibers.

1871-72 ***Perf. 12***

R134 R12 1c **claret & black** ('72) 65.00
Cut cancel 30.00
Pair 140.00
Block of 4 425.00

R135 R12 2c **orange & black** .40
Cut cancel .25
Pair .80
Block of 4 1.75
Double transfer —
a. 2c vermilion & black (error) *900.00*
b. Inverted center 425.00
Cut cancel 300.00
Pair *1,850.*
Block of 4 4,250.
c. Imperf., pair —
Block of 4 —
d. As No. R135, double impression of frame *2,500.*
e. As No. R135, frame printed on both sides *1,800.*
f. As No. R135, double impression of center *150.00*

R136 R12a 4c **brown & black** ('72) 110.00
Cut cancel 45.00
Pair 250.00

R137 R12a 5c **orange & black** .35
Cut cancel .25
Pair .75
Block of 4 1.60
Scratched plate —
a. Inverted center *6,500.*
Cut cancel *3,750.*
"Block" of 3 *15,000.*
b. Half used as 2c on document *1,000.*

No. R137a is valued in the grade of fine.

R138 R12a 6c **orange & black** ('72) 125.00
Cut cancel 50.00
Pair 275.00
Block of 4 1,100.

R139 R12a 15c **brown & black** ('72) 27.50
Cut cancel 10.00
Pair 65.00
Block of 4 200.00
a. Inverted center *16,000.*
Cut cancel *9,000.*
Pair 15,000.

The used pair of No. R139a is unique. It has average centering and has manuscript and waffle-iron grid cancels. Value reflects 2011 auction sale price.

R140 R13 30c **orange & black** ('72) 50.00
Cut cancel 15.00
Pair 110.00
Block of 4 350.00
Double transfer in Washington's hair —
Double transfer in stars *80.00*
a. Inverted center *3,500.*
Cut cancel *1,750.*

R141 R13 40c **brown & black** ('72) 110.00
Cut cancel 35.00
Pair 240.00
Block of 4 525.00

R142 R13a 60c **orange & black** ('72) 140.00
Cut cancel 55.00
Pair 350.00
Block of 4 750.00
Foreign entry, design of 70c 300.00

R143 R13a 70c **green & black** ('72) 90.00
Cut cancel 30.00
Pair 220.00
Block of 4 500.00

R144 R13b $1 **green & black** ('72) 3.00
Cut cancel .80
Pair 10.00
Block of 4 80.00
a. Inverted center *12,500.*
Cut cancel *10,000.*
Block of 4, on document *85,000.*

No. R144a is valued in the grade of fine.

R145 R13c $2 **vermilion & black** ('72) 65.00
Cut cancel 25.00
Pair 120.00
Block of 4 375.00
Double transfer at top 70.00

R146 R13c $2.50 **claret & black** ('72) 125.00
Cut cancel 35.00
Pair 240.00
Block of 4 525.00
a. Inverted center *25,000.*
Cut cancel *17,000.*

R147 R13c $3 **green & black** ('72) 125.00
Cut cancel 35.00
Pair 240.00
Block of 4 525.00
Double transfer —

R148 R13d $5 **vermilion & black** ('72) 50.00
Cut cancel 20.00
Pair 110.00
Block of 4 240.00

R149 R13d $10 **green & black** ('72) 400.00
Cut cancel 85.00
Pair 900.00
Block of 4 2,100.

R150 R13e $20 **orange & black** ('72) 900.00
Cut cancel 350.00
Pair 1,800.
Block of 4 *5,000.*
a. $20 vermilion & black (error) 1,250.
Cut cancel 700.00

See note on Inverted Centers after No. R133.

1874 ***Perf. 12***

R151 R12 2c **orange & black,** *green* .25
Cut cancel .25
Pair .50
Block of 4 1.00
a. Inverted center 800.00
Cut cancel 375.00
Pair 1,750.

Liberty — R14

1875-78 ***Perf. 12***

R152 R14 2c **blue,** *blue*

		Unused	Used
a.	silk paper	3.00	.45
	Pair	6.00	.90
	Block of 4	14.00	1.90
	Double transfer in bottom letters	—	20.00
	Twisted transfer of upper right frame		6.00
b.	Wmk. 191R ('78)	2.00	.35
	Pair	4.00	.70
	Block of 4	12.00	2.10
	Double transfer	—	20.00
	Twisted transfer of upper right frame		6.00
c.	Wmk. 191R, rouletted 6	125.00	32.50
	Pair	200.00	125.00
	"L" shaped strip of 3		600.00
d.	As "a," vert. pair, imperf. horiz.		525.00
e.	As "b," imperf., pair		*350.00*
f.	As "b," vert. pair, imperf. horiz.		350.00

The watermarked paper came into use in 1878. The rouletted stamps probably were introduced in 1881.

Nos. 279, 267a, 267, 279Bg, 279B, 272-274 Overprinted in Red or Blue

a — Rectangular Periods

a — Square Periods

b

b — Small Period after "I"

Overprint "a" exists in two (or possibly more) settings, with upright rectangular periods or with altered right leg of "R" and square periods (pos. 10, 20, 30, 40, 50, 60, 70, 80, 90, 100), both illustrated. Overprint "b" has 4 stamps with small period following the "I" in each pane of 100 (pos. 41, 46, 91 & 96).

1898 **Wmk. 191** ***Perf. 12***

For Nos. R153-R160, values in the first column are for unused examples, values in the second column are for used.

			Unused	Used
R153	A87(a)	1c **deep grn,** red overprint	5.00	2.75
		Block of 4	29.00	12.00
		P# strip of 3, Impt.	35.00	
		P# block of 6, Impt.	110.00	
R154	A87(b)	1c **green,** red overprint	.35	.35
		Block of 4	1.50	1.50
		P# strip of 3, Impt.	10.50	
		P# block of 6, Impt.	57.50	
	a.	Overprint inverted	45.00	30.00
		Block of 4	175.00	—
		P# strip of 3, Impt.	190.00	
		P# block of 6, Impt.	450.00	
	b.	Overprint on back instead of face, inverted	*4,000.*	
	c.	Pair, one without overprint	*10,000.*	
		Vert. strip of 3 containing No. R154c at top and No. R154b at bottom	—	
	d.	Half used as ½c on document		*750.00*
R155	A88(b)	2c **pink,** type III, blue overprint, *July 1, 1898*	.30	.25
		Block of 4	1.25	1.10
		P# strip of 3, Impt.	11.50	
		P# block of 6, Impt.	55.00	
		Dot in "S" of "CENTS"	1.10	
		P# strip of 3, Impt.	18.00	
	b.	2c **carmine,** type III, blue overprint, *July 1, 1898*	.35	.25
		Block of 4	1.40	1.10
		P# strip of 3, Impt.	13.00	
		P# block of 6, Impt.	57.50	
		Dot in "S" of "CENTS"	1.40	
		P# strip of 3, Impt.	24.00	
	c.	As No. R155, overprint inverted, *July 1898*	10.00	7.50
		Block of 4	27.50	20.00
		P# strip of 3, Impt.	65.00	
		P# block of 6, Impt.	160.00	
	d.	Vertical pair, one without overprint	*1,750.*	
	e.	Horiz. pair, one without overprint	—	
	f.	As No. R155, overprint on back instead of face, inverted	350.00	
	i.	Double ovt., one split		*850.00*

NOTE: Old No. R155 is now Nos. R155b, R155Ag; old No. R155a is Nos. R155c, R155Ah; old No. R155b is Nos. R155d, R155e; old No. R155c is No. R155f.

			Unused	Used
R155A	A88(b)	2c **pink,** type IV, blue overprint *July 1, 1898*	.25	.25
		Block of 4	1.25	1.10
		P# strip of 3, Impt.	10.50	
		P# block of 6, Impt.	52.50	
	g.	2c **carmine,** type IV, blue overprint, *July 1, 1898*	.25	.25
		Block of 4	1.40	1.10
		P# strip of 3, Impt.	11.50	
		P# block of 6, Impt.	55.00	
	h.	As No. R155A, overprint inverted, *July 1898*	2.75	2.00
		Block of 4	13.00	9.25
		P# strip of 3, Impt.	32.50	
		P# block of 6, Impt.	77.50	

Handstamped Type "b" or Type "c" in Magenta

c

No.	Description	Unused	Used
R156	A93(b) 8c **violet brown**		*5,250.*
R157	A94(b) 10c **dark green**		*4,000.*
	Block of 6		—
a.	As No. R157, handstamped type "c"	—	—
R158	A95(b) 15c **dark blue**		*6,250.*
	Pair		—

Nos. R156-R158 were emergency provisionals, privately prepared, not officially issued.

Privately Prepared Provisionals

No. 285 Overprinted in Red

1898 Wmk. 191 *Perf. 12*

No.	Description	Unused	Used
R158A	A100 1c **dark yellow green**	*15,000.*	*12,500.*

No. R158A is valued in sound condition and in the grade of fine to very fine. Most examples have faults, and such examples sell for less.

No. 285 Ovptd. "I.R./P.I.D. & Son" in Red

No.	Description	Unused	Used
R158B	A100 1c **dark yellow green**	*25,000.*	*30,000.*

No. R158B is valued with small faults as each of the four recorded examples have faults.

Nos. R158A-R158B were overprinted with federal government permission by the Purvis Printing Co. upon order of Capt. L. H. Chapman of the Chapman Steamboat Line. Both the Chapman Line and P. I. Daprix & Son operated freight-carrying steamboats on the Erie Canal. The Chapman Line touched at Syracuse, Utica, Little Falls and Fort Plain; the Daprix boat ran between Utica and Rome. Overprintings of 250 of each stamp were made.

Dr. Kilmer & Co. provisional overprints and St. Louis provisional proprietary stamps are listed under "Private Die Medicine Stamps," Nos. RS307-RS315 and RS320-395.

Newspaper Stamp No. PR121 Surcharged in Red

1898 *Perf. 12*

No.	Description	Unused	Used
R159	N18 $5 **dark blue,** surcharge reading down	550.00	325.00
	Block of 4	2,300.	1,400.
	P# strip of 3, Impt.	*2,400.*	
R160	N18 $5 **dark blue,** surcharge reading up	150.00	140.00
	Block of 4	625.00	*750.00*
	P# strip of 3, Impt.	2,000.	*750.00*

Battleship—R15

There are two styles of rouletting for the proprietary and documentary stamps of the 1898 issue, an ordinary rouletting 5½ and one by which small rectangles of the paper are cut out, usually called hyphen-hole perforation 7. Several stamps are known with an apparent roulette 14 caused by slippage of a hyphen-hole 7 rouletting wheel.

1898 Wmk. 191R *Rouletted 5½*

No.	Description	Unused	Used
R161	R15 ½c **orange**	5.00	*25.00*
	Block of 4	22.50	*160.00*
	P# block of 6	300.00	
R162	R15 ½c **dark gray**	.30	.25
	Block of 4	1.60	1.10
	P# block of 6	225.00	
	Double transfer		7.75
a.	Vert. pair, imperf. horiz.	125.00	
R163	R15 1c **pale blue**	.25	.25
	Block of 4	1.00	1.00
	P# block of 6	40.00	
	Double transfer	10.00	
a.	Vert. pair, imperf. horiz.	8.00	
b.	Imperf., pair	*600.00*	
R164	R15 2c **car rose**	.30	.30
	Block of 4	1.50	1.50
	P# block of 6	50.00	
	Double transfer	1.10	.30
a.	Vert. pair, imperf. horiz.	125.00	
b.	Imperf., pair	400.00	
c.	Horiz. pair, imperf. vert.	375.00	
R165	R15 3c **dark blue**	3.50	.35
	Block of 4	14.00	1.40
	P# block of 6	425.00	
	Double transfer	—	
R166	R15 4c **pale rose**	2.50	.35
	Block of 4	11.50	1.40
	P# block of 6	425.00	
a.	Vert. pair, imperf. horiz.	250.00	
R167	R15 5c **lilac**	.65	.35
	Block of 4	3.25	1.25
	P# block of 6	275.00	
a.	Pair, imperf. horiz. or vert.	350.00	175.00
b.	Horiz. pair, imperf. btwn.		*650.00*
R168	R15 10c **dark brown**	2.00	.25
	Block of 4	12.00	1.25
	P# block of 6	350.00	
a.	Vert. pair, imperf. horiz.	40.00	35.00
b.	Horiz. pair, imperf. vert.	—	
R169	R15 25c **pur brown**	7.50	.50
	Block of 4	32.50	2.25
	P# block of 6	750.00	
	Double transfer	—	
R170	R15 40c **blue lilac**	125.00	1.50
	Block of 4	600.00	52.50
	P# block of 6	—	
	Cut cancel		.35
R171	R15 50c **slate violet**	35.00	.25
	Block of 4	150.00	2.25
	P# block of 6	850.00	
a.	Imperf., pair	*450.00*	
b.	Horiz. pair, imperf. btwn.		*550.00*
R172	R15 80c **bister**	125.00	.50
	Block of 4	600.00	32.50
	P# block of 6	—	
	Cut cancel		.25

Numerous double transfers exist on this issue.

Hyphen Hole Perf. 7

No.	Description	Unused	Used
R163p	1c	.30	.25
	Block of 4	1.60	1.50
	P# block of 6	50.00	
R164p	2c	.35	.25
	Block of 4	2.75	1.10
	P# block of 6	60.00	
R165p	3c	40.00	1.40
	Block of 4	170.00	6.25
	P# block of 6	750.00	
R166p	4c	17.50	1.60
	Block of 4	75.00	7.75
	P# block of 6	—	
R167p	5c	17.50	.35
	Block of 4	75.00	1.60
	P# block of 6	450.00	
R168p	10c	10.00	.25
	Block of 4	42.50	1.25
	P# block of 6	450.00	
R169p	25c	20.00	.50
	Block of 4	85.00	1.75
	P# block of 6	—	
R170p	40c	210.00	35.00
	Block of 4	1,000.	225.00
	P# block of 6	—	
	Cut cancel		12.50
R171p	50c	75.00	1.00
	Block of 4	350.00	6.75
	P# block of 6	—	
b.	Horiz. pair, imperf. btwn.	—	*250.00*
R172p	80c	250.00	60.00
	Block of 4	1,250.	240.00
	P# block of 6	—	
	Cut cancellation		20.00

Commerce — R16

1898 *Rouletted 5½*

No.	Description	Unused	Used
R173	R16 $1 **dark green**	35.00	.25
	Block of 4	140.00	1.00
	Cut cancel		.25
a.	Vert. pair, imperf. horiz.	800.00	
b.	Horiz. pair, imperf. vert.	—	325.00
p.	Hyphen hole perf. 7	37.50	2.00
	Block of 4		10.00
	Cut cancel		.75
R174	R16 $3 **dark brown**	65.00	1.25
	Block of 4	—	6.00
	Cut cancel		.30
a.	Horiz. pair, imperf. vert.		500.00
p.	Hyphen hole perf. 7	110.00	3.50
	Block of 4		15.00
	Cut cancel		.40
R175	R16 $5 **orange red**	115.00	2.00
	Block of 4	—	10.00
	Cut cancel		.30
R176	R16 $10 **black**	190.00	3.50
	Block of 4		17.00
	Cut cancel		.65
a.	Horiz. pair, imperf. vert.		—
R177	R16 $30 **red**	750.00	175.00
	Block of 4		700.00
	Cut cancel		47.50
R178	R16 $50 **gray brown**	400.00	7.00
	Block of 4		32.50
	Cut cancel		2.50

See Nos. R182-R183.

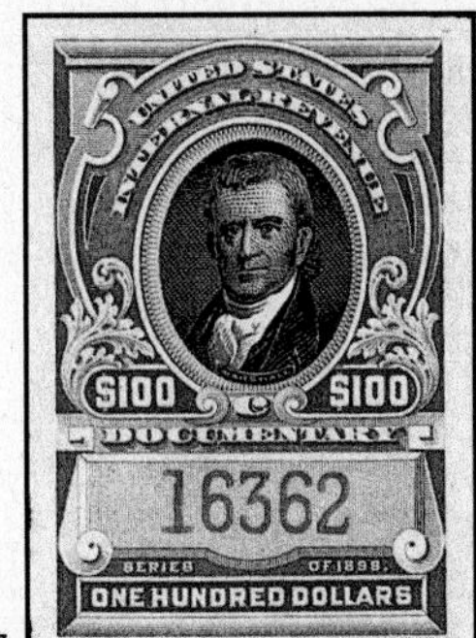

John Marshall — R17

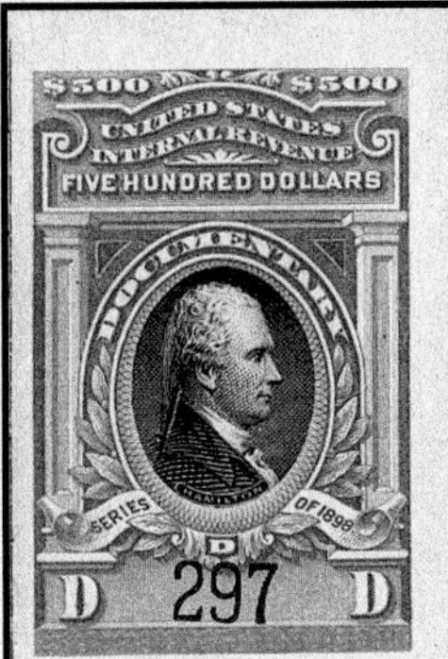

Alexander Hamilton — R18

James Madison — R19

Various Portraits in Various Frames, Each Inscribed "Series of 1898"

1899 ***Imperf.***

Without Gum

No.	Description	Unused	Used
R179	R17 $100 **yellow brown & black**	400.00	40.00
	Cut cancel		22.50
	Vertical strip of 4	—	190.00
	Vertical strip of 4, cut cancel		95.00
R180	R18 $500 **carmine lake & black**	2,500.	1,000.
	Cut cancel		350.00
	Vertical strip of 4	—	3,500.
	Vertical strip of 4, cut cancel		1,500.
R181	R19 $1000 **green & black**	1,750.	350.00
	Cut cancel		150.00
	Vertical strip of 4	—	1,650.
	Vertical strip of 4, cut cancel		600.00

1900 ***Hyphen-hole perf. 7***

Allegorical Figure of Commerce

No.	Description	Unused	Used
R182	R16 $1 **carmine**	60.00	.55
	Cut cancel		.30
	Block of 4	230.00	2.50
	Block of 4, cut cancel		1.25
R183	R16 $3 **lake** (fugitive ink)	400.00	60.00
	Cut cancel		10.00
	Block of 4	1,500.	290.00
	Block of 4, cut cancel		45.00

Warning: The ink on No. R183 will run in water.

Surcharged in Black with Open Numerals of Value

No.	Description	Unused	Used
R184	R16 $1 **gray**	50.00	.40
	Cut cancel		.30
	Block of 4	—	1.75
	Block of 4, cut cancel		1.25
a.	Horiz. pair, imperf. vert	—	
b.	Surcharge omitted	140.00	
	Surcharge omitted, cut cancel		82.50
R185	R16 $2 **gray**	50.00	.40
	Cut cancel		.25
	Block of 4	190.00	1.60
	Block of 4, cut cancel		1.10
R186	R16 $3 **gray**	200.00	15.00
	Cut cancel		6.00
	Block of 4	—	67.50
	Block of 4, cut cancel		25.00
R187	R16 $5 **gray**	110.00	11.00
	Cut cancel		1.60
	Block of 4	—	47.50
	Block of 4, cut cancel		8.00
R188	R16 $10 **gray**	275.00	25.00
	Cut cancel		4.50
	Block of 4	—	110.00
	Block of 4, cut cancel		19.00
R189	R16 $50 **gray**	2,750.	575.00
	Cut cancel		140.00
	Block of 4		2,750.
	Block of 4, cut cancel		625.00

Surcharged in Black with Ornamental Numerals of Value

Warning: If Nos. R190-R194 are soaked, the center part of the surcharged numeral may wash off. Before the surcharging, a square of soluble varnish was applied to the middle of some stamps.

1902

No.	Description	Unused	Used
R190	R16 $1 **green**	70.00	3.50
	Cut cancel		.30
	Block of 4	—	15.00
	Block of 4, cut cancel		1.25
a.	Inverted surcharge		*190.00*
R191	R16 $2 **green**	70.00	2.50
	Cut cancel		.45
	Block of 4	—	11.00
	Block of 4, cut cancel		1.90
a.	Surcharged as No. R185	150.00	90.00
b.	Surcharged as No. R185, in violet	*2,000.*	—
c.	As "a," double surcharge	*150.00*	
d.	As "a," triple surcharge	*2,500.*	
e.	Pair, Nos. R191c and R191d	*5,000.*	
R192	R16 $5 **green**	325.00	42.50
	Cut cancel		5.00
	Block of 4	—	175.00
	Block of 4, cut cancel		25.00
a.	Surcharge omitted	400.00	
b.	Pair, one without surcharge	*700.00*	
R193	R16 $10 **green**	525.00	225.00
	Cut cancel		80.00
	Block of 4		950.00
	Block of 4, cut cancel		350.00
R194	R16 $50 **green**	3,000.	1,250.
	Cut cancel		500.00
	Block of 4	—	—
	Block of 4, cut cancel		1,500.

R20

Inscribed "Series of 1914"

1914 **Wmk. 190** **Offset Printing** ***Perf. 10***

No.	Description	Unused	Used
R195	R20 ½c **rose**	16.00	5.00
	Block of 4	67.50	21.00
R196	R20 1c **rose**	3.50	.30
	Block of 4	15.00	1.25
R197	R20 2c **rose**	5.00	.30
	Block of 4	21.50	1.25
	Double impression	—	
R198	R20 3c **rose**	125.00	40.00
	Block of 4	525.00	175.00
R199	R20 4c **rose**	35.00	2.50
	Block of 4	150.00	11.50
	Recut U. L. corner	*325.00*	
R200	R20 5c **rose**	12.00	.40
	Block of 4	50.00	1.75
R201	R20 10c **rose**	10.00	.25
	Block of 4	42.50	1.25
R202	R20 25c **rose**	60.00	.60
	Block of 4	260.00	2.50
R203	R20 40c **rose**	40.00	3.00
	Block of 4	175.00	13.00
R204	R20 50c **rose**	15.00	.35
	Block of 4	62.50	1.50
R205	R20 80c **rose**	250.00	17.00
	Block of 4	1,050.	72.50
	Nos. R195-R205 (11)	571.50	69.70

Wmk. 191R

No.	Description	Unused	Used
R206	R20 ½c **rose**	1.60	.50
	Block of 4	7.00	2.50
R207	R20 1c **rose**	.25	.25
	Block of 4	1.00	1.00
	Double impression	*300.00*	—
R208	R20 2c **rose**	.30	.25
	Block of 4	1.25	1.10
R209	R20 3c **rose**	1.50	.25
	Block of 4	6.50	1.10
R210	R20 4c **rose**	4.50	.50
	Block of 4	21.00	2.25
R211	R20 5c **rose**	2.00	.35
	Block of 4	9.00	1.50
R212	R20 10c **rose**	.80	.25
	Block of 4	3.75	1.00
R213	R20 25c **rose**	10.00	1.50
	Block of 4	42.50	7.00
R214	R20 40c **rose**	150.00	15.00
	Cut cancel		.50
	Block of 4	700.00	65.00
R215	R20 50c **rose**	35.00	.40
	Cut cancel		.25
	Block of 4	160.00	1.75
R216	R20 80c **rose**	225.00	35.00
	Cut cancel		1.25
	Block of 4	950.00	250.00
	Nos. R206-R216 (11)	430.95	54.25

Liberty — R21

Inscribed "Series 1914"

Engr.

No.	Description	Unused	Used
R217	R21 $1 **green**	100.00	.55
	Cut cancel		.25
	Block of 4	—	3.00
	Block of 4, cut cancel		1.10
a.	$1 **yellow green**	85.00	.25
R218	R21 $2 **carmine**	175.00	1.00
	Cut cancel		.25
	Block of 4	625.00	4.50
	Block of 4, cut cancel		1.00
R219	R21 $3 **purple**	200.00	5.00
	Cut cancel		.80
	Block of 4	800.00	27.50
	Block of 4, cut cancel		3.25
R220	R21 $5 **blue**	140.00	4.50
	Cut cancel		.65
	Block of 4	500.00	19.00
	Block of 4, cut cancel		3.25
R221	R21 $10 **yellow orange**	400.00	7.50
	Cut cancel		1.10
	Block of 4	—	35.00
	Block of 4, cut cancel		5.00
R222	R21 $30 **vermilion**	1,000.	21.00
	Cut cancel		2.25
	Block of 4	—	90.00
	Block of 4, cut cancel		11.50
R223	R21 $50 **violet**	2,000.	1,250.
	Cut cancel		600.00
	Block of 4		*6,000.*

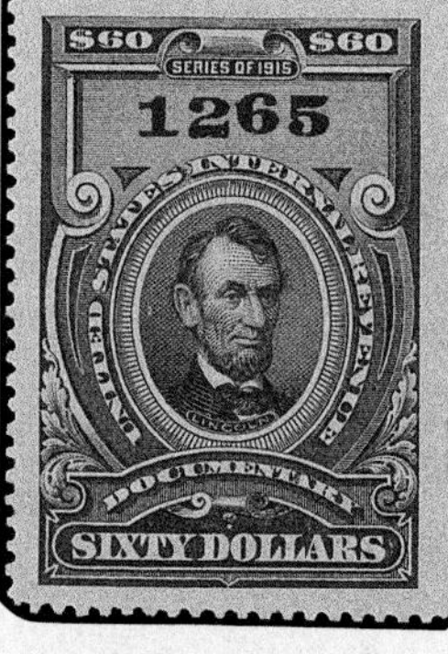

Portrait Types of 1899 Inscribed "Series of 1915" (#R224), or "Series of 1914"

1914-15 **Without Gum** ***Perf. 12***

No.	Description	Unused	Used
R224	R19 $60 **brown** *(Lincoln)*	300.	150.00
	Vertical strip of 4		800.00
	Cut cancel		70.00
	Vertical strip of 4, cut cancel		325.00
R225	R17 $100 **green** *(Washington)*	90.	45.00
	Vertical strip of 4		190.00
	Cut cancel		16.00
	Vertical strip of 4, cut cancel		70.00
R226	R18 $500 **blue** *(Hamilton)*	13,000.	650.00
	Cut cancel		275.00
	Vertical strip of 4, cut cancel		1,150.
R227	R19 $1000 **orange** *(Madison)*	—	750.00
	Cut cancel		325.00
	Vert. strip of 4, cut cancel		1,400.

The stamps of types R17, R18 and R19 in this and subsequent issues were issued in vertical strips of 4 which are imperforate at the top, bottom and right side; therefore, single stamps are always imperforate on one or two sides.

R22

Two types of design R22 are known.
Type I — With dot in centers of periods before and after "CENTS."
Type II — Without such dots.
First printings were done by commercial companies, later printings by the Bureau of Engraving and Printing.

1917 Offset Printing Wmk. 191R *Perf. 11*

		Unused	Used
R228	R22 1c **carmine rose**	.35	.25
	Block of 4	1.50	1.00
	Double impression	20.00	4.00
R229	R22 2c **carmine rose**	.25	.25
	Block of 4	1.10	1.00
	Double impression	20.00	5.00
R230	R22 3c **carmine rose**	1.75	.40
	Block of 4	7.25	1.75
	Double impression	—	—
R231	R22 4c **carmine rose**	.75	.25
	Block of 4	3.50	1.10
	Double impression	—	—
R232	R22 5c **carmine rose**	.30	.25
	Block of 4	1.25	1.00
R233	R22 8c **carmine rose**	3.00	.35
	Block of 4	13.50	1.60
R234	R22 10c **carmine rose**	.40	.25
	Block of 4	1.90	1.00
	Double impression		5.25
R235	R22 20c **carmine rose**	.75	.25
	Block of 4	3.50	1.10
	Double impression		—
R236	R22 25c **carmine rose**	1.75	.25
	Block of 4	7.50	1.10
	Double impression	—	—
R237	R22 40c **carmine rose**	2.25	.50
	Block of 4	10.50	2.25
	Double impression	8.00	5.00
R238	R22 50c **carmine rose**	2.50	.25
	Block of 4	10.50	1.00
	Double impression	—	—
R239	R22 80c **carmine rose**	9.00	.35
	Block of 4	40.00	1.50
	Double impression	42.50	—
	Nos. R228-R239 (12)	23.05	3.60

No. R234 is known used provisionally as a playing card revenue stamp in August 1932 with a "P.J.W.Co." (P.J. Wenger Co) and date cancellation. Value for this use, authenticated, $400.

Liberty Type of 1914 without "Series 1914"

1917-33 Engr.

		Unused	Used
R240	R21 $1 **yellow green**	15.00	.30
	Block of 4	55.00	1.25
a.	$1 green	9.50	.25
R241	R21 $2 **rose**	25.00	.25
	Block of 4	85.00	1.10
R242	R21 $3 **violet**	90.00	1.50
	Cut cancel		.30
	Block of 4	—	6.50
R243	R21 $4 **yellow brown** ('33)	60.00	2.00
	Cut cancel		.30
	Block of 4	—	10.00
	Block of 4, cut cancel		1.40
R244	R21 $5 **dark blue**	40.00	.35
	Cut cancel		.25
	Block of 4	—	1.50
R245	R21 $10 **orange**	90.00	1.40
	Cut cancel		.30
	Block of 4	—	7.00
	Block of 4, cut cancel		1.25

Portrait Types of 1899 without "Series of" and Date

1917 Without Gum *Perf. 12*

		Unused	Used
R246	R17 $30 **deep orange, green numerals** *(Grant)*	65.00	13.00
	Cut cancel		2.25
	Vertical strip of 4		—
	Vert. strip of 4, cut cancel		3.50
a.	As "b," imperf. pair		*1,000.*
b.	Numerals in blue	150.00	3.50
	Cut cancel		1.50
R247	R19 $60 **brown** *(Lincoln)*	75.00	8.00
	Cut cancel		.85
	Vertical strip of 4		—
	Vert. strip of 4, cut cancel		5.00
R248	R17 $100 **green** *(Washington)*	55.00	2.00
	Cut cancel		.50
	Vertical strip of 4		—
	Vert. strip of 4, cut cancel		3.00
R249	R18 $500 **blue, red numerals** *(Hamilton)*	350.00	50.00
	Cut cancel		15.00
	Vertical strip of 4		*250.00*
	Vert. strip of 4, cut cancel		70.00
	Double transfer	—	85.00
a.	Numerals in orange	425.00	65.00
	Cut cancel		20.00
	Vert. strip of 4		—
	Vert. strip of 4, cut cancel		—
	Double transfer	—	—
	Vert. strip of 4, bottom stamp double transfer	—	—
R250	R19 $1000 **orange** *(Madison)*	200.00	20.00
	Cut cancel		7.50
	Vertical strip of 4		100.00
	Vert. strip of 4, cut cancel		35.00
a.	Imperf., pair		*2,000.*

See note after No. R227.

1928-29 Offset Printing *Perf. 10*

		Unused	Used
R251	R22 1c **carmine rose**	2.10	1.60
	Block of 4	9.50	7.50
R252	R22 2c **carmine rose**	.60	.30
	Block of 4	3.00	1.50
R253	R22 4c **carmine rose**	7.00	4.00
	Block of 4	32.50	19.00
R254	R22 5c **carmine rose**	1.75	.55
	Block of 4	8.50	2.50
R255	R22 10c **carmine rose**	2.75	1.25
	Block of 4	13.00	5.50
R256	R22 20c **carmine rose**	6.00	4.50
	Block of 4	27.50	20.00
	Double impression		—

Engr.

		Unused	Used
R257	R21 $1 **green**	200.00	45.00
	Block of 4	—	—
	Cut cancel		5.00
R258	R21 $2 **rose**	90.00	5.00
	Block of 4	—	20.00
R259	R21 $10 **orange**	325.00	75.00
	Block of 4	—	—
	Cut cancel		30.00

1929 Offset Printing *Perf. 11x10*

		Unused	Used
R260	R22 2c **carmine rose** ('30)	3.00	2.75
	Block of 4	13.00	12.00
	Double impression	—	—
R261	R22 5c **carmine rose** ('30)	2.00	1.90
	Block of 4	10.00	8.75
R262	R22 10c **carmine rose**	9.25	6.75
	Block of 4	45.00	32.50
R263	R22 20c **carmine rose**	15.00	8.25
	Block of 4	70.00	42.50

Types of 1917-33 Overprinted in Black

SERIES 1940

1940 Wmk. 191R Offset Printing *Perf. 11*

		Unused	Used
R264	R22 1c **rose pink**	3.75	2.40
	Cut cancel		.35
	Perf. initial		.25
R265	R22 2c **rose pink**	5.00	2.25
	Cut cancel		.45
	Perf. initial		.35
R266	R22 3c **rose pink**	11.00	5.00
	Cut cancel		.90
	Perf. initial		.55
R267	R22 4c **rose pink**	5.00	.80
	Cut cancel		.30
	Perf. initial		.25
R268	R22 5c **rose pink**	5.00	1.25
	Cut cancel		.35
	Perf. initial		.25
R269	R22 8c **rose pink**	22.50	17.00
	Cut cancel		3.50
	Perf. initial		2.50
R270	R22 10c **rose pink**	2.50	.65
	Cut cancel		.25
	Perf. initial		.25
R271	R22 20c **rose pink**	3.25	.80
	Cut cancel		.30
	Perf. initial		.25
R272	R22 25c **rose pink**	8.00	1.50
	Cut cancel		.30
	Perf. initial		.25
R273	R22 40c **rose pink**	6.75	.90
	Cut cancel		.25
	Perf. initial		.25
R274	R22 50c **rose pink**	11.00	.55
	Cut cancel		.25
	Perf. initial		.25
R275	R22 80c **rose pink**	14.00	1.75
	Cut cancel		.35
	Perf. initial		.25

Engr.

		Unused	Used
R276	R21 $1 **green**	80.00	1.25
	Cut cancel		.35
	Perf. initial		.25
R277	R21 $2 **rose**	80.00	2.00
	Cut cancel		.35
	Perf. initial		.25
R278	R21 $3 **violet**	115.00	37.50
	Cut cancel		4.25
	Perf. initial		2.00
b.	Vert. pair, imperf. horiz.		*750.00*

Only one example of No. R278b is recorded. It is thinned and is valued thus.

		Unused	Used
R279	R21 $4 **yellow brown**	210.00	35.00
	Cut cancel		5.50
	Perf. initial		2.10
R280	R21 $5 **dark blue**	100.00	20.00
	Cut cancel		1.60
	Perf. initial		.75
R281	R21 $10 **orange**	275.00	50.00
	Cut cancel		4.25
	Perf. initial		.75

Types of 1917 Handstamped "Series 1940" like R264-R281

1940 Wmk. 191R *Perf. 12*
Without Gum

		Unused	Used
R282	R17 $30 **vermilion** (B, G)		1,250.
	Cut cancel		650.
	Perf. initial		350.
a.	With black 2-line handstamp in larger type		*25,000.*
b.	Green handstamp, 3-hole punch cancel		—
R283	R19 $60 **brown** (B, G)		2,400.
	Cut cancel		1,500.
	Perf. initial		800.
a.	As #R282a, cut cancel		*12,500.*
b.	Green handstamp, 3-hole punch cancel		—
R284	R17 $100 **green** (B)		4,500.
	Cut cancel		2,500.
	Perf. initial		1,500.
R285	R18 $500 **blue** (V)		3,000.
	Cut cancel		1,400.
	Perf. initial		1,000.
	Double transfer		—
a.	As #R282a	*3,250.*	*4,000.*
	Cut cancel		*2,650.*
	Double transfer	—	—
b.	Blue handstamp, double transfer	—	
R286	R19 $1000 **orange** (B, G)		1,250.
	Cut cancel		600.
	Perf. initial		400.
b.	Double overprint, cut cancel		—

Types of 1917 Handstamped with black 2-line "Series 1941" in larger type.

1941

		Unused	Used
R287	R17 $30 vermilion		*35,000.*
R287A	R19 $60 brown		35,000.

Alexander Hamilton — R23

Levi Woodbury — R24

Overprinted in Black 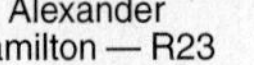

Various Portraits: 2c, Oliver Wolcott, Jr. 3c, Samuel Dexter. 4c, Albert Gallatin. 5c. G. W. Campbell. 8c, Alexander Dallas. 10c, William H. Crawford. 20c, Richard Rush. 25c, S. D. Ingham. 40c. Louis McLane. 50c, William J. Duane. 80c, Roger B. Taney. $2, Thomas Ewing. $3, Walter Forward. $4, J. C. Spencer. $5, G. M. Bibb. $10, R. J. Walker. $20, William M. Meredith.

The "sensitive ink" varieties are in a bluish-purple overprint showing minute flecks of gold.

1940 Engr. Wmk. 191R *Perf. 11*
Plates of 400 subjects, issued in panes of 100

		Unused	Used
R288	R23 1c **carmine**	5.75	4.50
	Cut cancel		1.75
	Perf. initial		.90
	Sensitive ink	9.00	4.25
a.	Imperf, pair, without gum	*250.00*	
	Block of 4	*500.00*	
R289	R23 2c **carmine**	8.50	4.00
	Cut cancel		1.75
	Perf. initial		1.00
	Sensitive ink	9.00	4.25
a.	Imperf, pair, without gum	*250.00*	
	Block of 4	*500.00*	
R290	R23 3c **carmine**	30.00	12.00
	Cut cancel		4.00
	Perf. initial		2.75
	Sensitive ink	32.50	9.25
a.	Imperf, pair, without gum	*250.00*	
	Block of 4	*500.00*	
R291	R23 4c **carmine**	62.50	27.50
	Cut cancel		5.25
	Perf. initial		4.25
a.	Imperf, pair, without gum	*250.00*	
	Block of 4	*500.00*	
R292	R23 5c **carmine**	4.75	.80
	Cut cancel		.35
	Perf. initial		.30
a.	Imperf, pair, without gum	*250.00*	
	Block of 4	*500.00*	
R293	R23 8c **carmine**	85.00	60.00
	Cut cancel		18.00
	Perf. initial		13.00
a.	Imperf, pair, without gum	*250.00*	
	Block of 4	*500.00*	
R294	R23 10c **carmine**	4.25	.60
	Cut cancel		.30
	Perf. initial		.25
a.	Imperf, pair, without gum	*250.00*	
	Block of 4	*500.00*	

No.	Description	Unused	Used
R295	R23 20c **carmine**	5.50	4.25
	Cut cancel		1.25
	Perf. initial		.85
a.	Imperf, pair, without gum	*250.00*	
	Block of 4	*500.00*	
R296	R23 25c **carmine**	5.00	.75
	Cut cancel		.35
	Perf. initial		.25
a.	Imperf, pair, without gum	*250.00*	
	Block of 4	*500.00*	
R297	R23 40c **carmine**	75.00	30.00
	Cut cancel		6.50
	Perf. initial		2.75
a.	Imperf, pair, without gum	*250.00*	
	Block of 4	*500.00*	
R298	R23 50c **carmine**	8.00	.60
	Cut cancel		.30
	Perf. initial		.25
a.	Imperf, pair, without gum	*250.00*	
	Block of 4	*500.00*	
R299	R23 80c **carmine**	200.00	110.00
	Cut cancel		29.00
	Perf. initial		20.00
a.	Imperf, pair, without gum	*475.00*	
	Block of 4	*1,400.*	

Plates of 200 subjects, issued in panes of 50

No.	Description	Unused	Used
R300	R24 $1 **carmine**	50.00	.60
	Cut cancel		.25
	Perf. initial		.25
	Sensitive ink	65.00	21.00
a.	Imperf, pair, without gum	*250.00*	
	Block of 4	*550.00*	
R301	R24 $2 **carmine**	100.00	.90
	Cut cancel		.25
	Perf. initial		.25
	Sensitive ink	110.00	10.50
a.	Imperf, pair, without gum	—	
R302	R24 $3 **carmine**	190.00	95.00
	Cut cancel		11.50
	Perf. initial		8.00
	Sensitive ink	250.00	100.00
a.	Imperf, pair, without gum	*1,400.*	
	Block of 4	*3,000.*	
R303	R24 $4 **carmine**	150.00	50.00
	Cut cancel		9.00
	Perf. initial		2.00
a.	Imperf, pair, without gum	—	
R304	R24 $5 **carmine**	85.00	3.00
	Cut cancel		.75
	Perf. initial		.35
a.	Imperf, pair, without gum	—	
R305	R24 $10 **carmine**	150.00	10.00
	Cut cancel		1.25
	Perf. initial		.50
R305A	R24 $20 **carmine**	*3,000.*	1,750.
	Cut cancel		600.00
	Perf. initial		450.00
b.	Imperf, pair, without gum	*700.00*	
	Block of 4	*1,500.*	

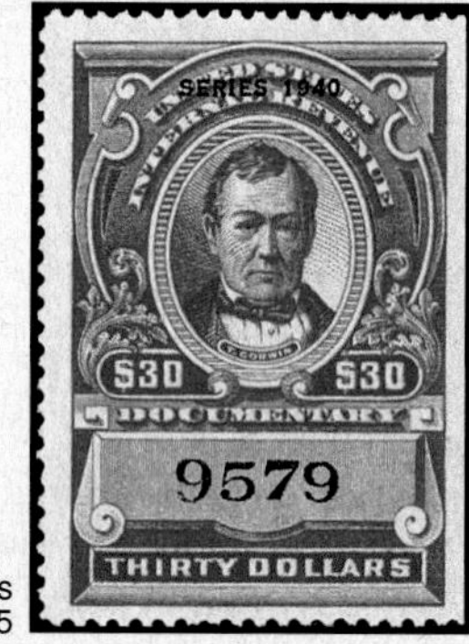

Thomas Corwin — R25

Various Frames and Portraits: $50, James Guthrie. $60, Howell Cobb. $100, P. F. Thomas. $500, J. A. Dix, $1,000, S. P. Chase.

Plates of 16 subjects, issued in strips of 4

Without Gum *Perf. 12*

No.	Description	Unused	Used
R306	R25 $30 **carmine**	350.00	75.00
	Cut cancel		20.00
	Perf. initial		13.50
R306A	R25 $50 **carmine**	—	*8,500.*
	Cut cancel		*3,000.*
	Perf. initial		900.00
R307	R25 $60 **carmine**	450.00	100.00
	Cut cancel		45.00
	Perf. initial		22.50
a.	Vert. pair, imperf. btwn.	*2,750.*	*1,500.*
R308	R25 $100 **carmine**	375.00	100.00
	Cut cancel		45.00
	Perf. initial		15.00
R309	R25 $500 **carmine**	—	5,000.
	Cut cancel		2,250.
	Perf. initial		800.00
R310	R25 $1000 **carmine**	—	
	Cut cancel		400.00
	Perf. initial		200.00

The $30 to $1,000 denominations in this and following similar issues, and the $2,500, $5,000 and $10,000 stamps of 1952-58 have straight edges on one or two sides. They were issued without gum through No. R723.

Editors would like to see a used uncut example of No. R310.

Nos. R288-R310 Overprinted

SERIES 1941

1941 **Wmk. 191R** *Perf. 11*

No.	Description	Unused	Used
R311	R23 1c **carmine**	5.00	2.75
	Cut cancel		.85
	Perf. initial		.75
R312	R23 2c **carmine**	5.25	1.10
	Cut cancel		.55
	Perf. initial		.45
R313	R23 3c **carmine**	10.00	4.25
	Cut cancel		1.75
	Perf. initial		1.10
R314	R23 4c **carmine**	7.50	1.75
	Cut cancel		.40
	Perf. initial		.25
R315	R23 5c **carmine**	1.50	.40
	Cut cancel		.30
	Perf. initial		.30
R316	R23 8c **carmine**	21.00	8.50
	Cut cancel		3.75
	Perf. initial		2.75
R317	R23 10c **carmine**	2.00	.35
	Cut cancel		.30
	Perf. initial		.25
R318	R23 20c **carmine**	4.75	.65
	Cut cancel		.40
	Perf. initial		.30
R319	R23 25c **carmine**	2.40	.65
	Cut cancel		.30
	Perf. initial		.25
R320	R23 40c **carmine**	16.00	3.25
	Cut cancel		1.10
	Perf. initial		.65
R321	R23 50c **carmine**	3.50	.30
	Cut cancel		.25
	Perf. initial		.25
R322	R23 80c **carmine**	65.00	12.00
	Cut cancel		3.75
	Perf. initial		2.75
R323	R24 $1 **carmine**	15.00	.30
	Cut cancel		.25
	Perf. initial		.25
R324	R24 $2 **carmine**	20.00	.50
	Cut cancel		.30
	Perf. initial		.25
R325	R24 $3 **carmine**	32.50	3.50
	Cut cancel		.40
	Perf. initial		.30
R326	R24 $4 **carmine**	47.50	27.50
	Cut cancel		1.10
	Perf. initial		.80
R327	R24 $5 **carmine**	60.00	1.10
	Cut cancel		.30
	Perf. initial		.25
R328	R24 $10 **carmine**	100.00	6.00
	Cut cancel		.30
	Perf. initial		.25
R329	R24 $20 **carmine**	850.00	500.00
	Cut cancel		75.00
	Perf. initial		50.00

Without Gum *Perf. 12*

No.	Description	Unused	Used
R330	R25 $30 **carmine**	275.00	55.00
	Cut cancel		17.50
	Perf. initial		11.50
R331	R25 $50 **carmine**	1,500.	1,000.
	Cut cancel		500.00
	Perf. initial		250.00
R332	R25 $60 **carmine**	275.00	87.50
	Cut cancel		27.50
	Perf. initial		13.50
R333	R25 $100 **carmine**	140.00	37.50
	Cut cancel		7.75
	Perf. initial		5.00
R334	R25 $500 **carmine**	—	375.00
	Cut cancel		200.00
	Perf. initial		75.00
R335	R25 $1000 **carmine**	1,500.	225.00
	Cut cancel		60.00
	Perf. initial		30.00

Nos. R288-R310 Overprinted

SERIES 1942

1942 **Wmk. 191R** *Perf. 11*

No.	Description	Unused	Used
R336	R23 1c **carmine**	2.00	.60
	Cut cancel		.30
	Perf. initial		.25
R337	R23 2c **carmine**	2.00	.60
	Cut cancel		.30
	Perf. initial		.25
R338	R23 3c **carmine**	2.00	.80
	Cut cancel		.35
	Perf. initial		.25
R339	R23 4c **carmine**	3.00	1.10
	Cut cancel		.30
	Perf. initial		.25
R340	R23 5c **carmine**	.60	.35
	Cut cancel		.25
	Perf. initial		.25
R341	R23 8c **carmine**	9.50	4.75
	Cut cancel		1.40
	Perf. initial		1.10
R342	R23 10c **carmine**	1.75	.35
	Cut cancel		.25
	Perf. initial		.25
R343	R23 20c **carmine**	4.50	.60
	Cut cancel		.30
	Perf. initial		.25
R344	R23 25c **carmine**	3.00	.55
	Cut cancel		.30
	Perf. initial		.25
R345	R23 40c **carmine**	6.50	1.75
	Cut cancel		.55
	Perf. initial		.35
R346	R23 50c **carmine**	4.00	.35
	Cut cancel		.25
	Perf. initial		.25
R347	R23 80c **carmine**	27.50	13.00
	Cut cancel		3.00
	Perf. initial		2.00
R348	R24 $1 **carmine**	12.50	.25
	Cut cancel		.25
	Perf. initial		.25
R349	R24 $2 **carmine**	15.00	.30
	Cut cancel		.25
	Perf. initial		.25
R350	R24 $3 **carmine**	27.50	3.25
	Cut cancel		.45
	Perf. initial		.25
R351	R24 $4 **carmine**	35.00	7.50
	Cut cancel		.55
	Perf. initial		.30
R352	R24 $5 **carmine**	37.50	1.50
	Cut cancel		.25
	Perf. initial		.25
R353	R24 $10 **carmine**	85.00	3.75
	Cut cancel		.40
	Perf. initial		.25
R354	R24 $20 **carmine**	300.00	45.00
	Cut cancel		20.00
	Perf. initial		11.50
a.	Imperf., perf. initials		—

Without Gum *Perf. 12*

No.	Description	Unused	Used
R355	R25 $30 **carmine**	125.00	42.50
	Cut cancel		15.00
	Perf. initial		7.00
R356	R25 $50 **carmine**	2,250.	1,400.
	Cut cancel		375.00
	Perf. initial		190.00
R357	R25 $60 **carmine**	*5,000.*	1,500.
	Cut cancel		450.00
	Perf. initial		190.00
R358	R25 $100 **carmine**	325.00	175.00
	Cut cancel		100.00
	Perf. initial		75.00
R359	R25 $500 **carmine**	*2,000.*	275.00
	Cut cancel		160.00
	Perf. initial		87.50
R360	R25 $1000 **carmine**	6,500.	175.00
	Cut cancel		70.00
	Perf. initial		55.00

Nos. R288-R310 Overprinted

1943 **Wmk. 191R** *Perf. 11*

No.	Description	Unused	Used
R361	R23 1c **carmine**	.80	.65
	Cut cancel		.30
	Perf. initial		.25
R362	R23 2c **carmine**	.65	.55
	Cut cancel		.30
	Perf. initial		.25
R363	R23 3c **carmine**	3.75	3.50
	Cut cancel		.70
	Perf. initial		.40
R364	R23 4c **carmine**	1.60	1.50
	Cut cancel		.40
	Perf. initial		.35
R365	R23 5c **carmine**	.70	.45
	Cut cancel		.30
	Perf. initial		.25
R366	R23 8c **carmine**	6.00	4.00
	Cut cancel		1.90
	Perf. initial		1.25
R367	R23 10c **carmine**	.85	.30
	Cut cancel		.25
	Perf. initial		.25
R368	R23 20c **carmine**	2.50	.80
	Cut cancel		.40
	Perf. initial		.35
R369	R23 25c **carmine**	2.75	.50
	Cut cancel		.30
	Perf. initial		.30
R370	R23 40c **carmine**	7.50	4.00
	Cut cancel		1.75
	Perf. initial		.90
R371	R23 50c **carmine**	2.00	.30
	Cut cancel		.25
	Perf. initial		.25
R372	R23 80c **carmine**	27.50	8.00
	Cut cancel		3.00
	Perf. initial		1.50
R373	R24 $1 **carmine**	9.00	.35
	Cut cancel		.25
	Perf. initial		.25
R374	R24 $2 **carmine**	18.00	.35
	Cut cancel		.25
	Perf. initial		.25

		Unused	Used
R375	R24 $3 **carmine**	30.00	3.00
	Cut cancel		.45
	Perf. initial		.30
R376	R24 $4 **carmine**	55.00	10.00
	Cut cancel		1.50
	Perf. initial		1.00
R377	R24 $5 **carmine**	52.50	.75
	Cut cancel		.40
	Perf. initial		.25
R378	R24 $10 **carmine**	85.00	5.00
	Cut cancel		1.75
	Perf. initial		.70
R379	R24 $20 **carmine**	350.00	60.00
	Cut cancel		10.00
	Perf. initial		5.50

Without Gum ***Perf. 12***

R380	R25 $30 **carmine**	225.00	25.00
	Cut cancel		7.50
	Perf. initial		6.00
R381	R25 $50 **carmine**	250.00	75.00
	Cut cancel		15.00
	Perf. initial		6.00
R382	R25 $60 **carmine**	375.00	125.00
	Cut cancel		42.50
	Perf. initial		14.00
R383	R25 $100 **carmine**	50.00	22.50
	Cut cancel		6.75
	Perf. initial		4.25
R384	R25 $500 **carmine**	*800.00*	325.00
	Cut cancel		125.00
	Perf. initial		87.50
R385	R25 $1000 **carmine**	*800.00*	200.00
	Cut cancel		60.00
	Perf. initial		40.00

Nos. R288-R310 Overprinted

1944 **Wmk. 191R** ***Perf. 11***

R386	R23 1c **carmine**	.50	.45
	Cut cancel		.25
	Perf. initial		.25
R387	R23 2c **carmine**	.65	.55
	Cut cancel		.30
	Perf. initial		.25
R388	R23 3c **carmine**	.65	.40
	Cut cancel		.30
	Perf. initial		.25
R389	R23 4c **carmine**	.75	.65
	Cut cancel		.30
	Perf. initial		.25
R390	R23 5c **carmine**	.40	.25
	Cut cancel		.25
	Perf. initial		.25
R391	R23 8c **carmine**	2.25	1.75
	Cut cancel		.50
	Perf. initial		.45
R392	R23 10c **carmine**	.50	.25
	Cut cancel		.25
	Perf. initial		.25
R393	R23 20c **carmine**	1.10	.35
	Cut cancel		.25
	Perf. initial		.25
R394	R23 25c **carmine**	2.00	.30
	Cut cancel		.25
	Perf. initial		.25
R395	R23 40c **carmine**	3.75	.80
	Cut cancel		.40
	Perf. initial		.30
R396	R23 50c **carmine**	4.00	.35
	Cut cancel		.30
	Perf. initial		.30
R397	R23 80c **carmine**	21.00	5.50
	Cut cancel		1.75
	Perf. initial		.90
R398	R24 $1 **carmine**	10.00	.30
	Cut cancel		.25
	Perf. initial		.25
R399	R24 $2 **carmine**	15.00	.45
	Cut cancel		.35
	Perf. initial		.25
R400	R24 $3 **carmine**	25.00	2.40
	Cut cancel		.55
	Perf. initial		.25
R401	R24 $4 **carmine**	32.50	11.50
	Cut cancel		1.40
	Perf. initial		1.10
R402	R24 $5 **carmine**	32.50	.50
	Cut cancel		.35
	Perf. initial		.30
R403	R24 $10 **carmine**	65.00	1.60
	Cut cancel		.40
	Perf. initial		.30
R404	R24 $20 **carmine**	275.00	19.00
	Cut cancel		4.00
	Perf. initial		2.50

Without Gum ***Perf. 12***

R405	R25 $30 **carmine**	110.00	35.00
	Cut cancel		9.00
	Perf. initial		7.00
R406	R25 $50 **carmine**	50.00	22.50
	Cut cancel		7.00
	Perf. initial		4.75
R407	R25 $60 **carmine**	350.00	75.00
	Cut cancel		29.00
	Perf. initial		10.50
R408	R25 $100 **carmine**	70.00	12.50
	Cut cancel		5.25
	Perf. initial		3.25
R409	R25 $500 **carmine**	—	*3,250.*
	Cut cancel		1,750.
	Perf. initial		1,250.
R410	R25 $1000 **carmine**	*4,000.*	500.00
	Cut cancel		200.00
	Perf. initial		125.00

Nos. R288-R310 Overprinted

1945 **Wmk. 191R** ***Perf. 11***

R411	R23 1c **carmine**	.40	.30
	Cut cancel		.25
	Perf. initial		.25
R412	R23 2c **carmine**	.40	.30
	Cut cancel		.25
	Perf. initial		.25
R413	R23 3c **carmine**	.75	.50
	Cut cancel		.30
	Perf. initial		.25
R414	R23 4c **carmine**	.45	.35
	Cut cancel		.30
	Perf. initial		.25
R415	R23 5c **carmine**	.45	.30
	Cut cancel		.25
	Perf. initial		.25
R416	R23 8c **carmine**	6.25	2.75
	Cut cancel		.75
	Perf. initial		.40
R417	R23 10c **carmine**	1.25	.25
	Cut cancel		.25
	Perf. initial		.25
R418	R23 20c **carmine**	8.00	1.50
	Cut cancel		.60
	Perf. initial		.35
R419	R23 25c **carmine**	1.75	.30
	Cut cancel		.25
	Perf. initial		.25
R420	R23 40c **carmine**	9.00	1.25
	Cut cancel		.55
	Perf. initial		.40
R421	R23 50c **carmine**	4.00	.25
	Cut cancel		.25
	Perf. initial		.25
R422	R23 80c **carmine**	26.00	14.00
	Cut cancel		4.00
	Perf. initial		2.75
R423	R24 $1 **carmine**	13.50	.30
	Cut cancel		.25
	Perf. initial		.25
R424	R24 $2 **carmine**	13.50	.40
	Cut cancel		.25
	Perf. initial		.25
R425	R24 $3 **carmine**	27.50	3.00
	Cut cancel		1.00
	Perf. initial		.75
R426	R24 $4 **carmine**	35.00	4.25
	Cut cancel		.70
	Perf. initial		.45
R427	R24 $5 **carmine**	35.00	.50
	Cut cancel		.30
	Perf. initial		.25
R428	R24 $10 **carmine**	65.00	2.50
	Cut cancel		.40
	Perf. initial		.30
R429	R24 $20 **carmine**	200.00	16.00
	Cut cancel		3.75
	Perf. initial		3.00

Without Gum ***Perf. 12***

R430	R25 $30 **carmine**	250.00	40.00
	Cut cancel		10.00
	Perf. initial		5.75
R431	R25 $50 **carmine**	230.00	45.00
	Cut cancel		20.00
	Perf. initial		12.00
R432	R25 $60 **carmine**	450.00	80.00
	Cut cancel		32.50
	Perf. initial		14.00
R433	R25 $100 **carmine**	50.00	20.00
	Cut cancel		9.00
	Perf. initial		5.50
R434	R25 $500 **carmine**	750.00	325.00
	Cut cancel		125.00
	Perf. initial		75.00
R435	R25 $1000 **carmine**	500.00	125.00
	Cut cancel		45.00
	Perf. initial		25.00

Nos. R288-R310 Overprinted

Series 1946

1946 **Wmk. 191R** ***Perf. 11***

R436	R23 1c **carmine**	.30	.30
	Cut cancel		.25
	Perf. initial		.25
R437	R23 2c **carmine**	.45	.35
	Cut cancel		.25
	Perf. initial		.25
R438	R23 3c **carmine**	.55	.40
	Cut cancel		.30
	Perf. initial		.25
R439	R23 4c **carmine**	.80	.65
	Cut cancel		.30
	Perf. initial		.25
R440	R23 5c **carmine**	.45	.30
	Cut cancel		.25
	Perf. initial		.25
R441	R23 8c **carmine**	2.50	2.00
	Cut cancel		.40
	Perf. initial		.35
R442	R23 10c **carmine**	1.10	.30
	Cut cancel		.25
	Perf. initial		.25
R443	R23 20c **carmine**	1.75	.50
	Cut cancel		.30
	Perf. initial		.25
R444	R23 25c **carmine**	6.00	.35
	Cut cancel		.25
	Perf. initial		.25
R445	R23 40c **carmine**	4.50	.85
	Cut cancel		.40
	Perf. initial		.25
R446	R23 50c **carmine**	6.00	.30
	Cut cancel		.25
	Perf. initial		.25
R447	R23 80c **carmine**	17.50	5.00
	Cut cancel		.75
	Perf. initial		.50
R448	R24 $1 **carmine**	16.00	.30
	Cut cancel		.25
	Perf. initial		.25
R449	R24 $2 **carmine**	19.00	.30
	Cut cancel		.25
	Perf. initial		.25
R450	R24 $3 **carmine**	27.50	5.00
	Cut cancel		.90
	Perf. initial		.40
R451	R24 $4 **carmine**	60.00	20.00
	Cut cancel		3.75
	Perf. initial		2.00
R452	R24 $5 **carmine**	40.00	.50
	Cut cancel		.30
	Perf. initial		.25
R453	R24 $10 **carmine**	72.50	1.75
	Cut cancel		.40
	Perf. initial		.30
R454	R24 $20 **carmine**	200.00	16.00
	Cut cancel		3.50
	Perf. initial		1.60

Without Gum ***Perf. 12***

R455	R25 $30 **carmine**	75.00	17.50
	Cut cancel		5.25
	Perf. initial		3.25
R456	R25 $50 **carmine**	65.00	12.50
	Cut cancel		5.00
	Perf. initial		2.75
R457	R25 $60 **carmine**	110.00	22.50
	Cut cancel		14.00
	Perf. initial		7.75
R458	R25 $100 **carmine**	90.00	12.50
	Cut cancel		4.25
	Perf. initial		3.00
R459	R25 $500 **carmine**	*1,750.*	150.00
	Cut cancel		47.50
	Perf. initial		26.00
R460	R25 $1000 **carmine**	*750.00*	160.00
	Cut cancel		37.50
	Perf. initial		18.00

Nos. R288-R310 Overprinted

Series 1947

1947 **Wmk. 191R** ***Perf. 11***

R461	R23 1c **carmine**	.85	.55
	Cut cancel		.30
	Perf. initial		.25
R462	R23 2c **carmine**	.75	.55
	Cut cancel		.30
	Perf. initial		.25
R463	R23 3c **carmine**	.85	.55
	Cut cancel		.30
	Perf. initial		.25
R464	R23 4c **carmine**	.90	.75
	Cut cancel		.30
	Perf. initial		.25
R465	R23 5c **carmine**	.55	.40
	Cut cancel		.30
	Perf. initial		.25
R466	R23 8c **carmine**	1.75	.80
	Cut cancel		.30
	Perf. initial		.25

No.	Type	Description	Unused	Used
R467	R23	10c **carmine**	1.40	.30
		Cut cancel		.25
		Perf. initial		.25
R468	R23	20c **carmine**	2.25	.55
		Cut cancel		.30
		Perf. initial		.25
R469	R23	25c **carmine**	3.00	.70
		Cut cancel		.30
		Perf. initial		.25
R470	R23	40c **carmine**	5.50	1.10
		Cut cancel		.35
		Perf. initial		.25
R471	R23	50c **carmine**	3.75	.40
		Cut cancel		.30
		Perf. initial		.25
R472	R23	80c **carmine**	12.00	8.00
		Cut cancel		.85
		Perf. initial		.35
R473	R24	$1 **carmine**	8.25	.35
		Cut cancel		.30
		Perf. initial		.25
R474	R24	$2 **carmine**	14.00	.65
		Cut cancel		.30
		Perf. initial		.25
R475	R24	$3 **carmine**	17.50	6.00
		Cut cancel		1.25
		Perf. initial		.90
R476	R24	$4 **carmine**	19.00	5.00
		Cut cancel		.55
		Perf. initial		.40
R477	R24	$5 **carmine**	27.50	.60
		Cut cancel		.30
		Perf. initial		.25
R478	R24	$10 **carmine**	67.50	3.00
		Cut cancel		.80
		Perf. initial		.30
R479	R24	$20 **carmine**	110.00	14.00
		Cut cancel		1.40
		Perf. initial		.90

Without Gum ***Perf. 12***

No.	Type	Description	Unused	Used
R480	R25	$30 **carmine**	180.00	27.50
		Cut cancel		6.00
		Perf. initial		2.75
R481	R25	$50 **carmine**	150.00	17.50
		Cut cancel		5.50
		Perf. initial		3.25
R482	R25	$60 **carmine**	250.00	60.00
		Cut cancel		25.00
		Perf. initial		9.25
R483	R25	$100 **carmine**	85.00	15.00
		Cut cancel		6.00
		Perf. initial		2.10
R484	R25	$500 **carmine**	*900.00*	250.00
		Cut cancel		67.50
		Perf. initial		50.00
R485	R25	$1000 **carmine**	*550.00*	100.00
		Cut cancel		40.00
		Perf. initial		24.00

Nos. R288-R310 Overprinted

1948 **Wmk. 191R** ***Perf. 11***

No.	Type	Description	Unused	Used
R486	R23	1c **carmine**	.35	.30
		Cut cancel		.25
		Perf. initial		.25
R487	R23	2c **carmine**	.50	.45
		Cut cancel		.30
		Perf. initial		.25
R488	R23	3c **carmine**	.60	.40
		Cut cancel		.30
		Perf. initial		.25
R489	R23	4c **carmine**	.55	.40
		Cut cancel		.30
		Perf. initial		.25
R490	R23	5c **carmine**	.50	.25
		Cut cancel		.25
		Perf. initial		.25
R491	R23	8c **carmine**	1.00	.50
		Cut cancel		.30
		Perf. initial		.30
R492	R23	10c **carmine**	1.00	.25
		Cut cancel		.25
		Perf. initial		.25
R493	R23	20c **carmine**	2.50	.40
		Cut cancel		.30
		Perf. initial		.25
R494	R23	25c **carmine**	2.25	.30
		Cut cancel		.25
		Perf. initial		.25
R495	R23	40c **carmine**	7.00	1.75
		Cut cancel		.35
		Perf. initial		.25
R496	R23	50c **carmine**	2.50	.30
		Cut cancel		.25
		Perf. initial		.25
R497	R23	80c **carmine**	12.00	8.00
		Cut cancel		3.25
		Perf. initial		.80
R498	R24	$1 **carmine**	10.50	.30
		Cut cancel		.25
		Perf. initial		.25
R499	R24	$2 **carmine**	18.00	.40
		Cut cancel		.30
		Perf. initial		.25
R500	R24	$3 **carmine**	24.00	3.50
		Cut cancel		.60
		Perf. initial		.40
R501	R24	$4 **carmine**	35.00	4.00
		Cut cancel		1.00
		Perf. initial		.70
R502	R24	$5 **carmine**	30.00	.50
		Cut cancel		.35
		Perf. initial		.25
R503	R24	$10 **carmine**	70.00	1.50
		Cut cancel		.40
		Perf. initial		.30
a.		Pair, one dated "1946"		—
R504	R24	$20 **carmine**	400.00	18.00
		Cut cancel		5.00
		Perf. initial		2.25

Without Gum ***Perf. 12***

No.	Type	Description	Unused	Used
R505	R25	$30 **carmine**	150.00	35.00
		Cut cancel		7.00
		Perf. initial		4.00
R506	R25	$50 **carmine**	180.00	27.50
		Cut cancel		12.00
		Perf. initial		3.75
a.		Vert. pair, imperf. btwn.	*2,500.*	
R507	R25	$60 **carmine**	300.00	75.00
		Cut cancel		25.00
		Perf. initial		8.00
a.		Vert. pair, imperf. btwn.	*4,250.*	
R508	R25	$100 **carmine**	140.00	20.00
		Cut cancel		6.00
		Perf. initial		4.00
a.		Vert. pair, imperf. btwn.	*2,000.*	

No. R508a is known as four used singles, all four positions from a single pane of four, clearly imperf. horiz. before being separated.

No.	Type	Description	Unused	Used
R509	R25	$500 **carmine**	1,500.	200.00
		Cut cancel		75.00
		Perf. initial		45.00
R510	R25	$1000 **carmine**	450.00	125.00
		Cut cancel		50.00
		Perf. initial		25.00

Nos. R288-R310 Overprinted

Series 1949

1949 **Wmk. 191R** ***Perf. 11***

No.	Type	Description	Unused	Used
R511	R23	1c **carmine**	.40	.35
		Cut cancel		.30
		Perf. initial		.25
R512	R23	2c **carmine**	.75	.45
		Cut cancel		.30
		Perf. initial		.25
R513	R23	3c **carmine**	.60	.50
		Cut cancel		.30
		Perf. initial		.25
R514	R23	4c **carmine**	.80	.60
		Cut cancel		.30
		Perf. initial		.25
R515	R23	5c **carmine**	.55	.30
		Cut cancel		.25
		Perf. initial		.25
R516	R23	8c **carmine**	1.00	.70
		Cut cancel		.30
		Perf. initial		.25
R517	R23	10c **carmine**	.60	.35
		Cut cancel		.30
		Perf. initial		.25
R518	R23	20c **carmine**	1.75	.75
		Cut cancel		.40
		Perf. initial		.30
R519	R23	25c **carmine**	2.25	.85
		Cut cancel		.35
		Perf. initial		.30
R520	R23	40c **carmine**	6.50	2.75
		Cut cancel		.55
		Perf. initial		.40
R521	R23	50c **carmine**	5.00	.40
		Cut cancel		.30
		Perf. initial		.25
R522	R23	80c **carmine**	15.00	7.50
		Cut cancel		2.00
		Perf. initial		.90
R523	R24	$1 **carmine**	13.50	.85
		Cut cancel		.40
		Perf. initial		.30
R524	R24	$2 **carmine**	17.00	2.50
		Cut cancel		.50
		Perf. initial		.35
R525	R24	$3 **carmine**	27.50	8.00
		Cut cancel		3.00
		Perf. initial		1.10
R526	R24	$4 **carmine**	30.00	8.00
		Cut cancel		3.50
		Perf. initial		1.90
R527	R24	$5 **carmine**	32.50	4.25
		Cut cancel		.75
		Perf. initial		.50
R528	R24	$10 **carmine**	72.50	5.25
		Cut cancel		1.10
		Perf. initial		.90
R529	R24	$20 **carmine**	150.00	15.00
		Cut cancel		2.50
		Perf. initial		1.60

Without Gum ***Perf. 12***

No.	Type	Description	Unused	Used
R530	R25	$30 **carmine**	200.00	35.00
		Cut cancel		8.00
		Perf. initial		4.25
R531	R25	$50 **carmine**	210.00	60.00
		Cut cancel		16.00
		Perf. initial		7.50
R532	R25	$60 **carmine**	350.00	70.00
		Cut cancel		27.50
		Perf. initial		11.50
R533	R25	$100 **carmine**	100.00	21.00
		Cut cancel		4.50
		Perf. initial		2.75
R534	R25	$500 **carmine**	*1,250.*	260.00
		Cut cancel		125.00
		Perf. initial		57.50
R535	R25	$1000 **carmine**	*1,000.*	160.00
		Cut cancel		47.50
		Perf. initial		22.50

Nos. R288-R310 Overprinted

Series 1950

1950 **Wmk. 191R** ***Perf. 11***

No.	Type	Description	Unused	Used
R536	R23	1c **carmine**	.40	.25
		Cut cancel		.25
		Perf. initial		.25
R537	R23	2c **carmine**	.40	.35
		Cut cancel		.30
		Perf. initial		.25
R538	R23	3c **carmine**	.50	.40
		Cut cancel		.30
		Perf. initial		.25
R539	R23	4c **carmine**	.70	.50
		Cut cancel		.30
		Perf. initial		.25
R540	R23	5c **carmine**	.45	.35
		Cut cancel		.30
		Perf. initial		.25
R541	R23	8c **carmine**	1.75	.80
		Cut cancel		.30
		Perf. initial		.25
R542	R23	10c **carmine**	.80	.30
		Cut cancel		.25
		Perf. initial		.25
R543	R23	20c **carmine**	1.40	.45
		Cut cancel		.35
		Perf. initial		.30
R544	R23	25c **carmine**	2.00	.45
		Cut cancel		.35
		Perf. initial		.30
R545	R23	40c **carmine**	6.00	2.10
		Cut cancel		.50
		Perf. initial		.30
R546	R23	50c **carmine**	8.00	.35
		Cut cancel		.30
		Perf. initial		.25
R547	R23	80c **carmine**	15.00	8.50
		Cut cancel		1.00
		Perf. initial		.60
R548	R24	$1 **carmine**	15.00	.40
		Cut cancel		.30
		Perf. initial		.25
R549	R24	$2 **carmine**	17.50	2.75
		Cut cancel		.45
		Perf. initial		.25
R550	R24	$3 **carmine**	20.00	6.00
		Cut cancel		1.40
		Perf. initial		.80
R551	R24	$4 **carmine**	27.50	7.50
		Cut cancel		2.75
		Perf. initial		1.40
R552	R24	$5 **carmine**	35.00	1.00
		Cut cancel		.35
		Perf. initial		.25
R553	R24	$10 **carmine**	70.00	10.00
		Cut cancel		1.00
		Perf. initial		.65
R554	R24	$20 **carmine**	150.00	15.00
		Cut cancel		3.50
		Perf. initial		2.10

Without Gum ***Perf. 12***

No.	Type	Description	Unused	Used
R555	R25	$30 **carmine**	150.00	70.00
		Cut cancel		17.50
		Perf. initial		10.50
R556	R25	$50 **carmine**	125.00	22.50
		Cut cancel		11.00
		Perf. initial		6.50
a.		Vert. pair, imperf. horiz.		—
R557	R25	$60 **carmine**	260.00	75.00
		Cut cancel		25.00
		Perf. initial		9.75
R558	R25	$100 **carmine**	100.00	22.50
		Cut cancel		6.00
		Perf. initial		3.25
R559	R25	$500 **carmine**	*1,250.*	125.00
		Cut cancel		55.00
		Perf. initial		32.50
R560	R25	$1000 **carmine**	*900.00*	95.00
		Cut cancel		30.00
		Perf. initial		19.00

Nos. R288-R310 Overprinted

Series 1951

1951 **Wmk. 191R** ***Perf. 11***

No.	Type	Description	Unused	Used
R561	R23	1c **carmine**	.30	.25
		Cut cancel		.25
		Perf. initial		.25

R562 R23 2c **carmine** .30 .35
Cut cancel .25
Perf. initial .25
R563 R23 3c **carmine** .30 .35
Cut cancel .25
Perf. initial .25
R564 R23 4c **carmine** .30 .35
Cut cancel .25
Perf. initial .25
R565 R23 5c **carmine** .30 .35
Cut cancel .25
Perf. initial .25
R566 R23 8c **carmine** 1.25 .45
Cut cancel .25
Perf. initial .25
R567 R23 10c **carmine** .30 .35
Cut cancel .25
Perf. initial .25
R568 R23 20c **carmine** .30 .55
Cut cancel .30
Perf. initial .25
R569 R23 25c **carmine** .30 .50
Cut cancel .30
Perf. initial .25
R570 R23 40c **carmine** 3.75 1.60
Cut cancel .55
Perf. initial .35
R571 R23 50c **carmine** 3.00 .60
Cut cancel .30
Perf. initial .25
R572 R23 80c **carmine** 10.00 3.25
Cut cancel 2.00
Perf. initial 1.00
R573 R24 $1 **carmine** 16.00 .30
Cut cancel .25
Perf. initial .25
R574 R24 $2 **carmine** 21.00 .55
Cut cancel .35
Perf. initial .30
R575 R24 $3 **carmine** 16.00 4.00
Cut cancel 2.10
Perf. initial 1.25
R576 R24 $4 **carmine** 20.00 12.50
Cut cancel 4.00
Perf. initial 2.25
R577 R24 $5 **carmine** 10.00 .70
Cut cancel .35
Perf. initial .25
R578 R24 $10 **carmine** 18.00 2.50
Cut cancel 1.25
Perf. initial .90
R579 R24 $20 **carmine** 55.00 16.00
Cut cancel 5.00
Perf. initial 3.25

Without Gum *Perf. 12*

R580 R25 $30 **carmine** 150.00 25.00
Cut cancel 7.50
Perf. initial 5.00
a. Imperf., pair *2,500.* *2,000.*
R581 R25 $50 **carmine** 300.00 45.00
Cut cancel 12.50
Perf. initial 7.50
R582 R25 $60 **carmine** 375.00 75.00
Cut cancel 25.00
Perf. initial 16.00
R583 R25 $100 **carmine** 90.00 25.00
Cut cancel 7.50
Perf. initial 5.00
R584 R25 $500 **carmine** *900.00* 175.00
Cut cancel 75.00
Perf. initial 35.00
R585 R25 $1000 **carmine** *750.00* 150.00
Cut cancel 55.00
Perf. initial 40.00

No. R583 is known imperf horizontally. It exists as a reconstructed used vertical strip of 4 that was separated into single stamps.

Documentary Stamps and Types of 1940 Overprinted in Black

Series 1952

Designs: 55c, $1.10, $1.65, $2.20, $2.75, $3.30, L. J. Gage; $2500, William Windom; $5000, C. J. Folger; $10,000, W. Q. Gresham.

1952 Wmk. 191R *Perf. 11*

R586 R23 1c **carmine** .35 .30
Cut cancel .25
Perf. initial .25
R587 R23 2c **carmine** .50 .35
Cut cancel .25
Perf. initial .25
R588 R23 3c **carmine** .40 .35
Cut cancel .30
Perf. initial .25
R589 R23 4c **carmine** .45 .30
Cut cancel .25
Perf. initial .25
R590 R23 5c **carmine** .35 .30
Cut cancel .25
Perf. initial .25
R591 R23 8c **carmine** .90 .60
Cut cancel .30
Perf. initial .25
R592 R23 10c **carmine** .50 .30
Cut cancel .25
Perf. initial .25
R593 R23 20c **carmine** 1.25 .40
Cut cancel .30
Perf. initial .25
R594 R23 25c **carmine** 2.50 .45
Cut cancel .30
Perf. initial .30
R595 R23 40c **carmine** 6.00 1.75
Cut cancel .55
Perf. initial .45
R596 R23 50c **carmine** 3.50 .30
Cut cancel .25
Perf. initial .25
R597 R23 55c **carmine** .60 15.00
Cut cancel 2.00
Perf. initial 1.10
R598 R23 80c **carmine** 19.00 4.00
Cut cancel .80
Perf. initial .75
R599 R24 $1 **carmine** 7.00 1.50
Cut cancel .75
Perf. initial .40
R600 R24 $1.10 **carmine** 25.00 30.00
Cut cancel 14.00
Perf. initial 6.25
R601 R24 $1.65 **carmine** 175.00 62.50
Cut cancel 37.50
Perf. initial 21.00
R602 R24 $2 **carmine** 17.00 .90
Cut cancel .30
Perf. initial .25
R603 R24 $2.20 **carmine** 160.00 70.00
Cut cancel 35.00
Perf. initial 16.00
R604 R24 $2.75 **carmine** 190.00 70.00
Cut cancel 35.00
Perf. initial 16.00
R605 R24 $3 **carmine** 32.50 6.00
Cut cancel 1.60
Perf. initial 1.40
a. Horiz. pair, imperf. btwn. *1,300.*
R606 R24 $3.30 **carmine** 225.00 90.00
Cut cancel 50.00
Perf. initial 25.00
R607 R24 $4 **carmine** 37.50 6.00
Cut cancel 2.10
Perf. initial 1.60
R608 R24 $5 **carmine** 32.50 1.25
Cut cancel .50
Perf. initial .40
R609 R24 $10 **carmine** 60.00 1.25
Cut cancel .50
Perf. initial .35
R610 R24 $20 **carmine** 92.50 16.00
Cut cancel 4.50
Perf. initial 3.00

Without Gum *Perf. 12*

R611 R25 $30 **carmine** 90.00 27.50
Cut cancel 6.00
Perf. initial 4.25
R612 R25 $50 **carmine** 95.00 35.00
Cut cancel 9.00
Perf. initial 5.50
R613 R25 $60 **carmine** 600.00 70.00
Cut cancel 19.00
Perf. initial 10.50
R614 R25 $100 **carmine** 110.00 10.00
Cut cancel 4.00
Perf. initial 2.10
R615 R25 $500 **carmine** *750.00* 160.00
Cut cancel 100.00
Perf. initial 40.00
R616 R25 $1000 **carmine** *325.00* 75.00
Cut cancel 20.00
Perf. initial 12.50
R617 R25 $2500 **carmine** *1,250.* 275.00
Cut cancel 175.00
Perf. initial 125.00
R618 R25 $5000 **carmine** — *5,000.*
Cut cancel 1,900.
Perf. initial 1,500.
R619 R25 $10,000 **carmine** *1,750.* *1,400.*
Cut cancel 1,200.
Perf. initial 1,100.

Documentary Stamps and Types of 1940 Overprinted in Black

Series 1953

1953 Wmk. 191R *Perf. 11*

R620 R23 1c **carmine** .40 .35
Cut cancel .25
Perf. initial .25
R621 R23 2c **carmine** .40 .30
Cut cancel .25
Perf. initial .25
R622 R23 3c **carmine** .45 .35
Cut cancel .25
Perf. initial .25
R623 R23 4c **carmine** .60 .45
Cut cancel .30
Perf. initial .25
R624 R23 5c **carmine** .50 .30
Cut cancel .25
Perf. initial .25
a. Vert. pair, imperf. horiz. *1,150.*
R625 R23 8c **carmine** 1.10 .85
Cut cancel .30
Perf. initial .25
R626 R23 10c **carmine** .65 .35
Cut cancel .25
Perf. initial .25
R627 R23 20c **carmine** 1.50 .50
Cut cancel .30
Perf. initial .25
R628 R23 25c **carmine** 1.75 .65
Cut cancel .35
Perf. initial .25
R629 R23 40c **carmine** 2.50 .90
Cut cancel .50
Perf. initial .35
R630 R23 50c **carmine** 3.00 .35
Cut cancel .25
Perf. initial .25
R631 R23 55c **carmine** 7.00 2.00
Cut cancel .80
Perf. initial .55
a. Horiz. pair, imperf. vert. *550.00*
R632 R23 80c **carmine** 10.00 2.10
Cut cancel 1.50
Perf. initial 1.40
R633 R24 $1 **carmine** 5.25 .35
Cut cancel .25
Perf. initial .25
R634 R24 $1.10 **carmine** 12.00 2.50
Cut cancel 2.10
Perf. initial 1.60
a. Horiz. pair, imperf. vert. *700.00*
b. Imperf. pair *850.00*
R635 R24 $1.65 **carmine** 12.00 4.50
Cut cancel 3.25
Perf. initial 2.10
R636 R24 $2 **carmine** 9.00 .75
Cut cancel .35
Perf. initial .25
R637 R24 $2.20 **carmine** 20.00 6.00
Cut cancel 2.75
Perf. initial 2.10
R638 R24 $2.75 **carmine** 1.75 7.00
Cut cancel 3.75
Perf. initial 2.75
R639 R24 $3 **carmine** 17.00 4.00
Cut cancel 1.75
Perf. initial 1.40
R640 R24 $3.30 **carmine** 50.00 17.50
Cut cancel 10.00
Perf. initial 5.00
R641 R24 $4 **carmine** 40.00 15.00
Cut cancel 4.00
Perf. initial 3.25
R642 R24 $5 **carmine** 27.50 1.25
Cut cancel .55
Perf. initial .35
R643 R24 $10 **carmine** 60.00 2.25
Cut cancel 1.10
Perf. initial .90
R644 R24 $20 **carmine** 140.00 22.50
Cut cancel 4.50
Perf. initial 2.40

Without Gum *Perf. 12*

R645 R25 $30 **carmine** 175.00 40.00
Cut cancel 8.00
Perf. initial 4.25
R646 R25 $50 **carmine** 175.00 50.00
Cut cancel 15.00
Perf. initial 6.25
R647 R25 $60 **carmine** 1,000. 425.00
Cut cancel 170.00
Perf. initial 75.00
With complete receipt tab *2,000.*
R648 R25 $100 **carmine** 70.00 15.00
Cut cancel 5.75
Perf. initial 3.75
R649 R25 $500 **carmine** *3,500.* 175.00
Cut cancel 70.00
Perf. initial 29.00
R650 R25 $1000 **carmine** 800.00 80.00
Cut cancel 27.50
Perf. initial 16.00
R651 R25 $2500 **carmine** 2,000. 1,750.
Cut cancel 575.00
Perf. initial 375.00
R652 R25 $5000 **carmine** — *7,500.*
Cut cancel *3,750.*
Perf. initial *2,500.*
R653 R25 $10,000 **carmine** — *4,250.*
Cut cancel 1,250.
Perf. initial 750.00

In 1955, the BEP began printing flat plate documentary stamps Nos. R654-R681 using the dry-printing method. This method used paper with a 5-10% moisture content versus the 15-35% moisture content for the wet printing. The dry-printed stamps from the same plates are .25-.75mm larger than the wet-printed examples. Four sub-varieties are known: (1) wet printing with ridged yellow gum, (2) wet printing with smooth yellow gum, (3) dry printing with smooth yellow gum, and (4) dry printing with smooth white gum.

Types of 1940

Without Overprint

1954 Wmk. 191R *Perf. 11*

R654 R23 1c **carmine** .25 .25
Cut cancel .25
Perf. initial .25
a. Horiz. pair, imperf. vert. *1,500.*
R655 R23 2c **carmine** .25 .30
Cut cancel .25
Perf. initial .25
R656 R23 3c **carmine** .25 .30
Cut cancel .25
Perf. initial .25
R657 R23 4c **carmine** .25 .30
Cut cancel .25
Perf. initial .25
R658 R23 5c **carmine** .25 .25
Cut cancel .25
Perf. initial .25
a. Vert. pair, imperf. horiz. —
R659 R23 8c **carmine** .25 .25
Cut cancel .25
Perf. initial .25

No.	Description	Unused	Used
R660	R23 10c **carmine**	.25	.25
	Cut cancel		.25
	Perf. initial		.25
R661	R23 20c **carmine**	.30	.40
	Cut cancel		.30
	Perf. initial		.25
R662	R23 25c **carmine**	.35	.45
	Cut cancel		.30
	Perf. initial		.25
R663	R23 40c **carmine**	.75	.60
	Cut cancel		.45
	Perf. initial		.35
R664	R23 50c **carmine**	1.00	.25
	Cut cancel		.25
	Perf. initial		.25
a.	Horiz. pair, imperf. vert.	900.00	
R665	R23 55c **carmine**	.90	1.25
	Cut cancel		.55
	Perf. initial		.45
R666	R23 80c **carmine**	1.50	1.90
	Cut cancel		1.25
	Perf. initial		1.10
R667	R24 $1 **carmine**	.90	.35
	Cut cancel		.30
	Perf. initial		.25
R668	R24 $1.10 **carmine**	2.00	2.50
	Cut cancel		1.60
	Perf. initial		1.10
R669	R24 $1.65 **carmine**	25.00	25.00
	Cut cancel		3.75
	Perf. initial		.75
R670	R24 $2 **carmine**	1.00	.45
	Cut cancel		.25
	Perf. initial		.25
R671	R24 $2.20 **carmine**	2.25	3.75
	Cut cancel		2.75
	Perf. initial		1.60
R672	R24 $2.75 **carmine**	25.00	55.00
	Cut cancel		30.00
	Perf. initial		17.50
R673	R24 $3 **carmine**	2.00	2.00
	Cut cancel		.90
	Perf. initial		.55
R674	R24 $3.30 **carmine**	3.50	5.00
	Cut cancel		3.25
	Perf. initial		2.10
R675	R24 $4 **carmine**	2.75	4.00
	Cut cancel		2.10
	Perf. initial		1.60
R676	R24 $5 **carmine**	3.25	.50
	Cut cancel		.35
	Perf. initial		.25
R677	R24 $10 **carmine**	5.00	1.50
	Cut cancel		.85
	Perf. initial		.70
R678	R24 $20 **carmine**	10.00	6.50
	Cut cancel		3.25
	Perf. initial		1.90

Documentary Stamps & Type of 1940 Ovptd. in Black

1954 Wmk. 191R *Perf. 12*

Without Gum

No.	Description	Unused	Used
R679	R25 $30 **carmine**	55.00	17.50
	Cut cancel		5.25
	Perf. initial		3.50
	With complete receipt tab	55.00	
a.	Booklet pane of 4	*225.00*	
	Complete booklet, 10 #R679a	*2,250.*	
R680	R25 $50 **carmine**	55.00	29.00
	Cut cancel		10.00
	Perf. initial		6.25
	With complete receipt tab	55.00	
a.	Booklet pane of 4	*225.00*	
	Complete booklet, 10 #R680a	*2,250.*	
R681	R25 $60 **carmine**	55.00	30.00
	Cut cancel		13.00
	Perf. initial		9.25
	With complete receipt tab	55.00	
a.	Booklet pane of 4	*225.00*	
	Complete booklet, 10 #R681a	*2,250.*	
R682	R25 $100 **carmine**	55.00	7.50
	Cut cancel		5.25
	Perf. initial		4.00
	With complete receipt tab	55.00	
a.	Booklet pane of 4	*225.00*	
	Complete booklet, 10 #R682a	*2,250.*	
R683	R25 $500 **carmine**	*150.00*	87.50
	Cut cancel		30.00
	Perf. initial		25.00
	With complete receipt tab	150.00	
a.	Booklet pane of 4	*600.00*	
	Complete booklet, 2 #R683a	*1,200.*	
R684	R25 $1000 **carmine**	200.00	90.00
	Cut cancel		21.00
	Perf. initial		17.00
	With complete receipt tab	*300.00*	

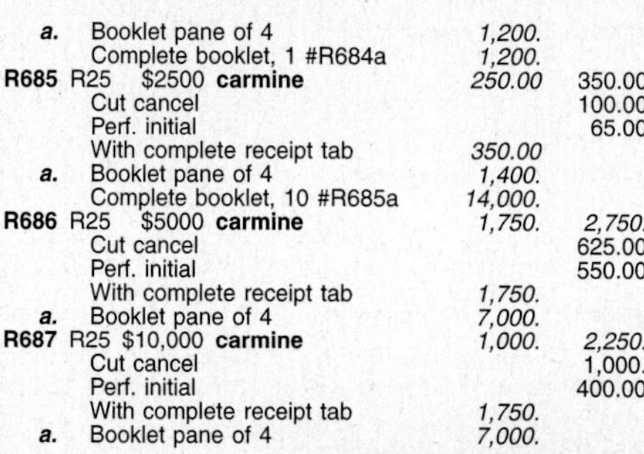

No.	Description	Unused	Used
a.	Booklet pane of 4	*1,200.*	
	Complete booklet, 1 #R684a	*1,200.*	
R685	R25 $2500 **carmine**	*250.00*	350.00
	Cut cancel		100.00
	Perf. initial		65.00
	With complete receipt tab	*350.00*	
a.	Booklet pane of 4	*1,400.*	
	Complete booklet, 10 #R685a	*14,000.*	
R686	R25 $5000 **carmine**	*1,750.*	*2,750.*
	Cut cancel		625.00
	Perf. initial		550.00
	With complete receipt tab	*1,750.*	
a.	Booklet pane of 4	*7,000.*	
R687	R25 $10,000 **carmine**	*1,000.*	*2,250.*
	Cut cancel		1,000.
	Perf. initial		400.00
	With complete receipt tab	*1,750.*	
a.	Booklet pane of 4	*7,000.*	

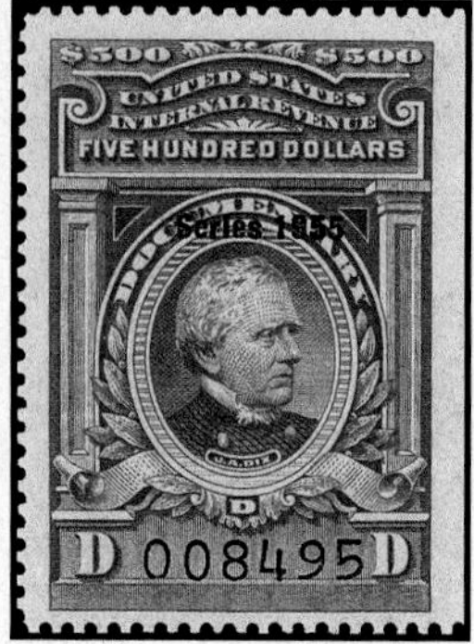

Documentary Stamps and Type of 1940 Overprinted in Black

1955 Wmk. 191R *Perf. 12*

Without Gum

No.	Description	Unused	Used
R688	R25 $30 **carmine**	110.00	17.50
	Cut cancel		7.00
	Perf. initial		3.75
R689	R25 $50 **carmine**	125.00	30.00
	Cut cancel		11.00
	Perf. initial		7.00
R690	R25 $60 **carmine**	200.00	45.00
	Cut cancel		17.50
	Perf. initial		5.25
R691	R25 $100 **carmine**	160.00	20.00
	Cut cancel		6.00
	Perf. initial		4.00
R692	R25 $500 **carmine**	1,250.	200.00
	Cut cancel		75.00
	Perf. initial		35.00
R693	R25 $1000 **carmine**	*1,800.*	80.00
	Cut cancel		22.50
	Perf. initial		15.00
R694	R25 $2500 **carmine**	*1,250.*	275.00
	Cut cancel		125.00
	Perf. initial		75.00
R695	R25 $5000 **carmine**	*4,000.*	*2,000.*
	Cut cancel		800.00
	Perf. initial		550.00
R696	R25 $10,000 **carmine**	—	1,250.
	Cut cancel		750.00
	Perf. initial		275.00

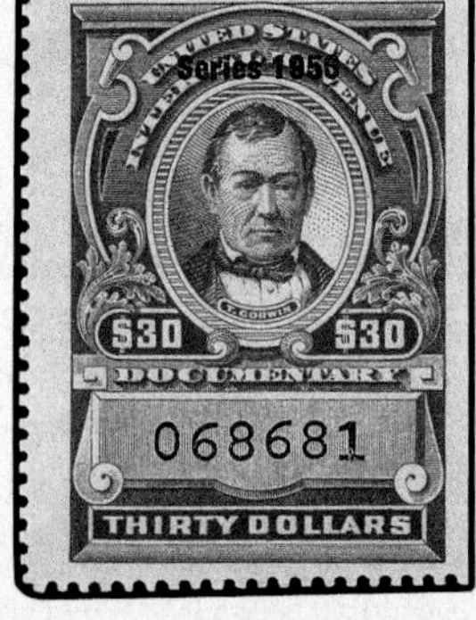

Documentary Stamps and Type of 1940 Overprinted

1956 Wmk. 191R Without Gum *Perf. 12*

No.	Description	Unused	Used
R697	R25 $30 **carmine**	180.00	20.00
	Cut cancel		10.00
	Perf. initial		4.75
R698	R25 $50 **carmine**	300.00	27.50
	Cut cancel		15.00
	Perf. initial		6.50
R699	R25 $60 **carmine**	250.00	60.00
	Cut cancel		20.00
	Perf. initial		7.50
R700	R25 $100 **carmine**	125.00	15.00
	Cut cancel		6.00
	Perf. initial		5.00
R701	R25 $500 **carmine**	*1,500.*	150.00
	Cut cancel		35.00
	Perf. initial		22.50
R702	R25 $1000 **carmine**	*1,750.*	100.00
	Cut cancel		25.00
	Perf. initial		13.00
R703	R25 $2500 **carmine**	—	750.00
	Cut cancel		290.00
	Perf. initial		170.00
R704	R25 $5000 **carmine**	—	2,000.
	Cut cancel		800.00
	Perf. initial		500.00
R705	R25 $10,000 **carmine**	—	750.00
	Cut cancel		240.00
	Perf. initial		150.00

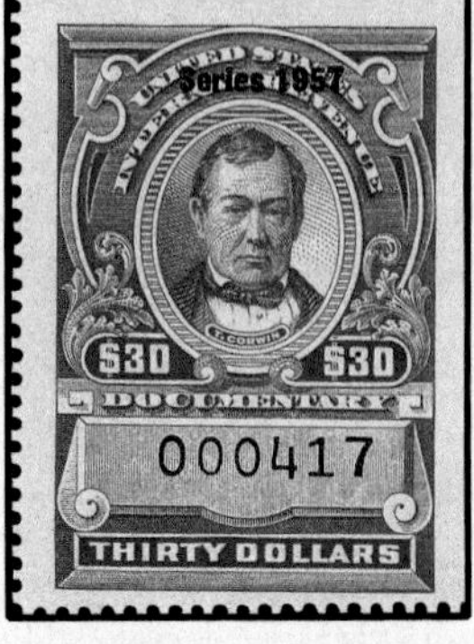

Documentary Stamps and Type of 1940 Overprinted

1957 Wmk. 191R *Perf. 12*

Without Gum

No.	Description	Unused	Used
R706	R25 $30 **carmine**	275.00	60.00
	Cut cancel		15.00
	Perf. initial		6.75
R707	R25 $50 **carmine**	160.00	47.50
	Cut cancel		14.00
	Perf. initial		5.75
R708	R25 $60 **carmine**	*1,500.*	400.00
	Cut cancel		140.00
	Perf. initial		57.50
R709	R25 $100 **carmine**	140.00	20.00
	Cut cancel		9.00
	Perf. initial		4.50
R710	R25 $500 **carmine**	900.00	200.00
	Cut cancel		70.00
	Perf. initial		37.50
R711	R25 $1000 **carmine**	*4,000.*	100.00
	Cut cancel		35.00
	Perf. initial		21.00
R712	R25 $2500 **carmine**	—	1,200.
	Cut cancel		450.00
	Perf. initial		300.00
R713	R25 $5000 **carmine**	*4,250.*	1,800.
	Cut cancel		1,000.
	Perf. initial		450.00
R714	R25 $10,000 **carmine**	—	650.00
	Cut cancel		225.00
	Perf. initial		175.00

Documentary Stamps and Type of 1940 Overprinted in Black

1958 Wmk. 191R *Perf. 12*

Without Gum

No.	Description	Unused	Used
R715	R25 $30 **carmine**	140.00	27.50
	Cut cancel		17.50
	Perf. initial		8.25
R716	R25 $50 **carmine**	190.00	35.00
	Cut cancel		17.00
	Perf. initial		6.75
R717	R25 $60 **carmine**	210.00	42.50
	Cut cancel		20.00
	Perf. initial		10.50
R718	R25 $100 **carmine**	225.00	15.00
	Cut cancel		6.50
	Perf. initial		2.10
a.	Vert. pair, imperf. between horiz.	2,500.	
R719	R25 $500 **carmine**	600.00	125.00
	Cut cancel		50.00
	Perf. initial		25.00
R720	R25 $1000 **carmine**	*2,750.*	90.00
	Cut cancel		45.00
	Perf. initial		35.00
R721	R25 $2500 **carmine**	—	1,500.
	Cut cancel		775.00
	Perf. initial		500.00
R722	R25 $5000 **carmine**	—	*4,250.*
	Cut cancel		2,700.
	Perf. initial		2,250.

No.	Description	Unused	Used
R723	R25 $10,000 **carmine**	—	2,750.
	Cut cancel		1,900.
	Perf. initial		1,000.

Documentary Stamps and Type of 1940 Without Overprint

1958 **Wmk. 191R** ***Perf. 12***

With Gum

No.	Description	Unused	Used
R724	R25 $30 **carmine**	11.00	7.00
	Cut cancel		6.00
	Perf. initial		4.25
	With complete receipt tab	14.00	
a.	Booklet pane of 4	*57.50*	
	Complete booklet, 10 #R724a	*575.00*	
b.	Vert. pair, imperf. horiz.	*3,000.*	
R725	R25 $50 **carmine**	12.00	7.00
	Cut cancel		4.00
	Perf. initial		3.25
	With complete receipt tab	15.00	
a.	Booklet pane of 4	*60.00*	
	Complete booklet, 10 #R725a	*600.00*	
b.	Vert. pair, imperf. horiz.		*3,500.*
R726	R25 $60 **carmine**	17.50	21.00
	Cut cancel		11.00
	Perf. initial		5.50
	With complete receipt tab	22.00	
a.	Booklet pane of 4	*90.00*	
	Complete booklet, 10 #R726a	*900.00*	
R727	R25 $100 **carmine**	13.00	4.75
	Cut cancel		3.25
	Perf. initial		2.00
	With complete receipt tab	16.00	
a.	Booklet pane of 4	*65.00*	
	Complete booklet, 10 #R727a	*650.00*	
R728	R25 $500 **carmine**	17.50	26.00
	Cut cancel		10.50
	Perf. initial		7.75
	With complete receipt tab	22.00	
a.	Booklet pane of 4	*90.00*	
	Complete booklet, 10 #R728a	*900.00*	
R729	R25 $1000 **carmine**	16.00	21.00
	Cut cancel		10.50
	Perf. initial		7.75
	With complete receipt tab	20.00	
a.	Booklet pane of 4	*80.00*	
	Complete booklet, 10 #R729a	*800.00*	
b.	Vert. pair, imperf. horiz.		*1,750.*
c.	Vert. pair, imperf. btwn.	*1,500.*	
R730	R25 $2500 **carmine**	*125.00*	175.00
	Cut cancel		90.00
	Perf. initial		55.00
	With complete receipt tab	—	
a.	Booklet pane of 4	*600.00*	
	Complete booklet, 10 #R730a	—	
R731	R25 $5000 **carmine**	200.00	175.00
	Cut cancel		90.00
	Perf. initial		65.00
	With complete receipt tab	—	
a.	Booklet pane of 4	*850.00*	
	Complete booklet, 10 #R731a	—	
R732	R25 $10,000 **carmine**	*200.00*	140.00
	Cut cancel		55.00
	Perf. initial		25.00
	With complete receipt tab	—	
a.	Booklet pane of 4	*850.00*	
	Complete booklet, 10 #R732a	—	

Internal Revenue Building, Washington, D.C. — R26

Centenary of the Internal Revenue Service.

Giori Press Printing

1962, July 2 **Unwmk.** ***Perf. 11***

No.	Description	Unused	Used
R733	R26 10c **violet blue & bright green**	1.00	.40
	Never hinged	1.25	
	Cut cancel		.25
	Perf. initial		.25
	P# block of 4	15.00	
	Cross gutter block of 4	*2,500.*	
	Horiz. pair with vert. gutter	*200.00*	
	Vert. pair with horiz. gutter	*400.00*	

1963 **"Established 1862" Removed**

No.	Description	Unused	Used
R734	R26 10c **violet blue & bright green**	3.00	.70
	Never hinged	5.00	
	Cut cancel		.25
	Perf. initial		.25
	P# block of 4	30.00	

Documentary revenue stamps were no longer required after Dec. 31, 1967.

PROPRIETARY STAMPS

Stamps for use on proprietary articles were included in the first general issue of 1862-71. They are R3, R13, R14, R18, R22, R29, R31 and R38.

Several varieties of "violet" paper were used in printing Nos. RB1-RB10. One is grayish with a slight greenish tinge, called "intermediate" paper by specialists. It should not be confused with the "green" paper, which is truly green.

All values prior to 1898 are for used examples. Printed cancellations on proprietary stamps command sizable premiums.

George Washington — RB1

RB1a

Engraved and printed by Jos. R. Carpenter, Philadelphia.

Various Frame Designs

1871-74 **Engr.** ***Perf. 12***

No.	Description	Value
RB1	RB1 1c **green & black**	
a.	Violet paper ('71)	8.00
	Pair	17.00
	Block of 4	37.50
b.	Green paper ('74)	14.00
	Pair	35.00
	Block of 4	85.00
c.	As "a," Imperf.	80.00
	Imperf., pair	175.00
	Imperf., block of 4	475.00
d.	As "a." Inverted center	*5,250.*
RB2	RB1 2c **green & black**	
a.	Violet paper ('71)	8.75
	Pair	19.00
	Block of 4	42.50
	Double transfer	30.00
b.	Green paper ('74)	30.00
	Pair	67.50
	Block of 4	160.00
	Double transfer	90.00
c.	As "a," Invtd. center	*40,000.*
d.	As "b," Invtd. center	*8,000.*
e.	As "b," vert. half used as 1c on document	—

Only three examples recorded of the inverted center on violet paper, No. RB2c. Value is for example with very good to fine centering and very small faults.

RB2d is valued with fine centering and small faults.

No.	Description	Value
RB3	RB1a 3c **green & black**	
a.	Violet paper ('71)	32.50
	Pair	75.00
	Block of 4	160.00
	Double transfer	—
b.	Green paper ('74)	67.50
	Pair	150.00
	Block of 4	325.00
c.	As "a," privately perforated, sewing machine perfs	800.00
d.	As "a," inverted center	*14,000.*

No. RB3d is valued with small faults because all of the 8 recorded examples have faults.

No.	Description	Value
RB4	RB1a 4c **green & black**	
a.	Violet paper ('71)	16.00
	Pair	37.50
	Block of 4	100.00
	Double transfer	—
b.	Green paper ('74)	25.00
	Pair	60.00
	Block of 4	130.00
c.	As "a." inverted center	*15,000.*
d.	As "b," vert. half used as 2c on document	—

No. RB4c is valued with small faults as all seven of the recorded examples have faults.

No.	Description	Value
RB5	RB1a 5c **green & black**	
a.	Violet paper ('71)	175.00
	Pair	360.00
	Block of 4	750.00
b.	Green paper ('74)	250.00
	Pair	525.00
	Block of 4	1,075.
c.	As "a," inverted center	*155,000.*

No. RB5c is unique. Value represents price realized in 2000 auction sale.

No.	Description	Value
RB6	RB1a 6c **green & black**	
a.	Violet paper ('71)	57.50
	Pair	125.00
	Block of 4	350.00
	Double transfer	—
b.	Green paper ('74)	140.00
	Pair	325.00
	Block of 4	725.00
RB7	RB1a 10c **green & black** ('73)	
a.	Violet paper ('71)	300.00
	Pair	700.00
	Block of 4	—
	Double transfer	—
b.	Green paper ('74)	65.00
	Pair	150.00
	Block of 4	350.00

See note on Inverted Centers after No. R133.

RB1b

No.	Description	Value
RB8	RB1b 50c **green & black ('73)**	
a.	Violet paper ('71)	1,000.
	Pair	*2,250.*
b.	Green paper ('74)	850.00
RB9	RB1b $1 **green & black** ('73)	
a.	Violet paper ('71)	*3,500.*
	Pair	—
b.	Green paper ('74)	*12,500.*

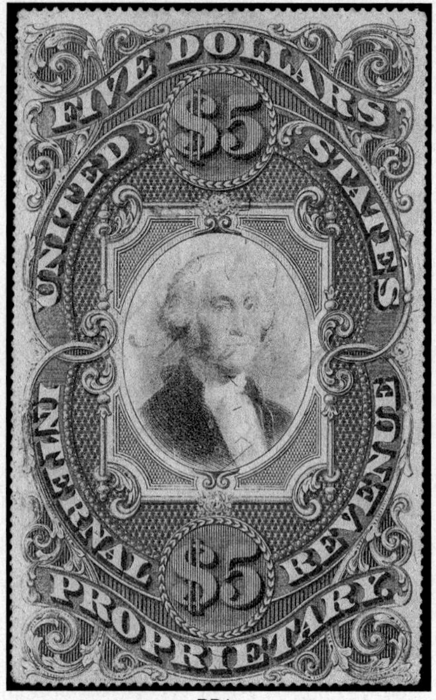
RB1c

RB10 RB1c $5 **green & black** ('73)
a. Violet paper ('71) *11,000.*
Pair *26,000.*
b. Green paper ('74) *75,000.*

No. RB10b is valued with small faults.

When the Carpenter contract expired Aug. 31, 1875, the proprietary stamps remaining unissued were delivered to the Bureau of Internal Revenue. Until the taxes expired, June 30, 1883, the B.I.R. issued 34,315 of the 50c, 6,585 of the $1 and 2,109 of the $5, Nos. RB8-RB10. No. RB19, the 10c blue, replaced No. RB7b, the 10c on green paper, after 336,000 stamps were issued, exhausting the supply in 1881.

George Washington — RB2

RB2a

Plates prepared and printed by both the National Bank Note Co. and the Bureau of Engraving and Printing. No. RB11, and possibly others, also printed by the American Bank Note Co. All silk paper printings were by National, plus early printings of Nos. RB11b-RB14b, RB16b, RB17b. All rouletted stamps printed by the BEP plus Nos. RB15b, RB18b, RB19b. Otherwise, which company printed the stamps can be told only by guide lines (BEP) or full marginal inscriptions. ABN used National plates with A.B. Co. added on the second stamp to the left of the National inscription.

1875-81 ***Perf. 12***

RB11 RB2 1c **green**
a. Silk paper 2.25
Pair 5.00
Block of 4 12.50
Double transfer —
b. Wmk 191R .50
Pair 1.25
Block of 4 3.00
c. Rouletted 6 200.00
Pair 400.00
Block of 4 925.00
d. As No. RB11b, vert. pair, imperf btwn. *400.00*

RB12 RB2 2c **brown**
a. Silk paper 3.25
Pair 7.00
Block of 4 65.00
b. Wmk 191R 2.00
Pair 4.50
Block of 4 11.00
c. Rouletted 6 225.00
Pair 400.00
Block of 4 950.00

RB13 RB2a 3c **orange**
a. Silk paper 14.00
Pair 30.00
Block of 4 70.00
b. Wmk 191R 4.00
Pair 9.00
Block of 4 21.00
c. Rouletted 6 160.00

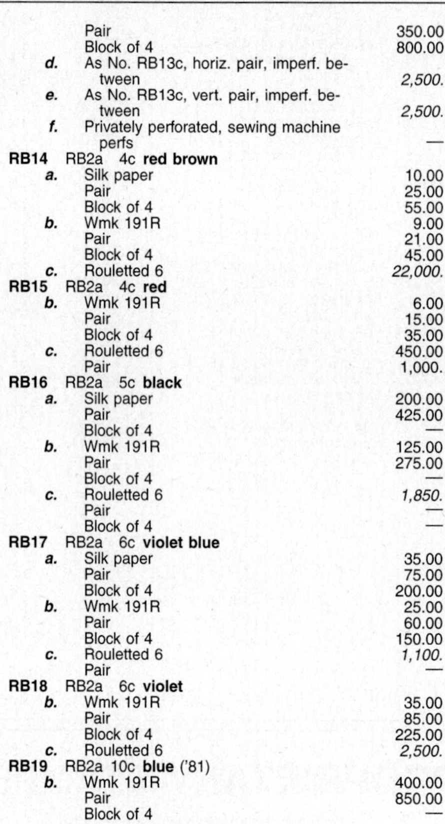
Pair 350.00
Block of 4 800.00
d. As No. RB13c, horiz. pair, imperf. between *2,500.*
e. As No. RB13c, vert. pair, imperf. between *2,500.*
f. Privately perforated, sewing machine perfs —

RB14 RB2a 4c **red brown**
a. Silk paper 10.00
Pair 25.00
Block of 4 55.00
b. Wmk 191R 9.00
Pair 21.00
Block of 4 45.00
c. Rouletted 6 *22,000.*

RB15 RB2a 4c **red**
b. Wmk 191R 6.00
Pair 15.00
Block of 4 35.00
c. Rouletted 6 450.00
Pair 1,000.

RB16 RB2a 5c **black**
a. Silk paper 200.00
Pair 425.00
Block of 4 —
b. Wmk 191R 125.00
Pair 275.00
Block of 4 —
c. Rouletted 6 *1,850.*
Pair —
Block of 4 —

RB17 RB2a 6c **violet blue**
a. Silk paper 35.00
Pair 75.00
Block of 4 200.00
b. Wmk 191R 25.00
Pair 60.00
Block of 4 150.00
c. Rouletted 6 *1,100.*
Pair —

RB18 RB2a 6c **violet**
b. Wmk 191R 35.00
Pair 85.00
Block of 4 225.00
c. Rouletted 6 *2,500.*

RB19 RB2a 10c **blue** ('81)
b. Wmk 191R 400.00
Pair 850.00
Block of 4 —

Many fraudulent roulettes exist.

Battleship — RB3

Inscribed "Series of 1898." and "Proprietary."
See note on rouletting preceding No. R161.

1898	Wmk. 191R	Engr.	*Rouletted 5½*	
RB20	RB3 ⅛c **yellow green**		.25	.25
	Block of 4		1.00	1.00
	P# block of 6		125.00	
	Double transfer		—	
a.	Vert. pair, imperf. horiz.		—	
b.	Vert. pair, imperf. btwn.		*1,100.*	
RB21	RB3 ¼c **brown**		.25	.25
a.	¼c **red brown**		.25	.25
b.	¼c **yellow brown**		.25	.25
c.	¼c **orange brown**		.25	.25
d.	¼c **bister**		.25	.25
	Block of 4		1.00	1.00
	P# block of 6		110.00	
	Double transfer		—	—
e.	Vert. pair, imperf. horiz.		—	—
f.	Printed on both sides		—	
RB22	RB3 ⅜c **deep orange**		.30	.30
	Block of 4		1.40	1.90
	P# block of 6		200.00	
a.	Horiz. pair, imperf. vert.		12.50	
b.	Vert. pair, imperf. horiz.		—	
RB23	RB3 ⅝c **deep ultra**		.25	.25
	Block of 4		1.25	1.10
	P# block of 6		75.00	
	Double transfer		1.50	
a.	Vert. pair, imperf. horiz.		85.00	—
b.	Horiz. pair, imperf. btwn.		*450.00*	*400.00*
RB24	RB3 1c **dark green**		2.25	.50
	Block of 4		11.00	2.25
	P# block of 6		250.00	
a.	Vert. pair, imperf. horiz.		*600.00*	
RB25	RB3 1¼c **violet**		.35	.25
	Block of 4		1.50	1.00
	P# block of 6		200.00	
a.	1¼c **brown violet**		.25	.25
b.	Vert. pair, imperf. btwn.		—	
RB26	RB3 1⅞c **dull blue**		15.00	2.00
	Block of 4		65.00	—
	P# block of 6		800.00	
	Double transfer		—	
RB27	RB3 2c **violet brown**		1.40	.35
	Block of 4		6.75	—
	P# block of 6		450.00	
	Double transfer			—
a.	Horiz. pair, imperf. vert.		60.00	
RB28	RB3 2½c **lake**		5.00	.35
	Block of 4		25.00	1.50
	P# block of 6		250.00	
a.	Vert. pair, imperf. horiz.		400.00	
RB29	RB3 3¾c **olive gray**		42.50	15.00
	Block of 4		210.00	—
	P# block of 6		—	
RB30	RB3 4c **purple**		16.00	1.50
	Block of 4		75.00	7.50
	P# block of 6		750.00	
	Double transfer		—	
RB31	RB3 5c **brown orange**		15.00	1.50
	Block of 4		70.00	7.00
	P# block of 6		*1,500.*	
a.	Vert. pair, imperf. horiz.		—	*400.00*
b.	Horiz. pair, imperf. vert.		—	*750.00*
	Nos. RB20-RB31 (12)		98.55	22.50

Hyphen Hole Perf. 7

RB20p	⅛c	.30	.25
	Block of 4	1.00	1.00
	P# block of 6	125.00	
RB21p	¼c	.25	.25
b.	¼c **yellow brown**	.25	.25
c.	¼c **orange brown**	.25	.25
	Block of 4	.55	1.00
d.	¼c **bister**	.25	.25
	P# block of 6	125.00	
RB22p	⅜c	.50	.35
	Block of 4	2.25	—
	P# block of 6	200.00	
RB23p	⅝c	.30	.25
	Block of 4	1.50	1.25
	P# block of 6	100.00	
RB24p	1c	30.00	15.00
	Block of 4	140.00	67.50
	P# block of 6	550.00	
RB25p	1¼c	.30	.30
	Block of 4	1.40	1.25
	P# block of 6	250.00	
a.	1¼c brown violet	.25	.25
RB26p	1⅞c	40.00	9.00
	Block of 4	200.00	—
	P# block of 6	1,250.	
RB27p	2c	10.00	1.00
	Block of 4	45.00	—
	P# block of 6	*550.00*	
RB28p	2½c	7.50	.40
	Block of 4	40.00	—
	P# block of 6	375.00	
RB29p	3¾c	100.00	27.50
	Block of 4	500.00	140.00
	P# block of 6	—	
RB30p	4c	70.00	22.50
	Block of 4	350.00	100.00
	P# block of 6	—	
RB31p	5c	85.00	25.00
	Block of 4	425.00	190.00
	P# block of 6	*1,500.*	

See note after No. RS315 regarding St. Louis Provisional Labels of 1898.

RB4

Inscribed "Series of 1914"

1914	Offset Printing	Wmk. 190	*Perf. 10*
RB32	RB4 ⅛c **black**	.25	.35
	Block of 4	1.25	1.60
RB33	RB4 ¼c **black**	4.00	1.50
	Block of 4	18.00	
RB34	RB4 ⅜c **black**	.35	.35
	Block of 4	1.50	1.50
RB35	RB4 ⅝c **black**	10.00	3.00
	Block of 4	45.00	
RB36	RB4 1¼c **black**	7.50	1.75
	Block of 4	35.00	
RB37	RB4 1⅞c **black**	80.00	22.50
	Block of 4	350.00	
RB38	RB4 2½c **black**	19.00	3.50
	Block of 4	80.00	15.00
RB39	RB4 3⅛c **black**	230.00	67.50
	Block of 4	950.00	
RB40	RB4 3¾c **black**	75.00	27.50
	Block of 4	400.00	
RB41	RB4 4c **black**	110.00	45.00
	Block of 4	550.00	
RB42	RB4 4⅜c **black**	*3,000.*	—
	Block of 4	*13,000.*	
RB43	RB4 5c **black**	200.00	110.00
	Block of 4	—	
	Nos. RB32-RB41,RB43 (11)	736.10	282.95

Wmk. 191R

RB44	RB4 ⅛c **black**	.35	.30
	Block of 4	1.50	1.50
RB45	RB4 ¼c **black**	.25	.25
	Block of 4	1.25	1.10
	Double impression	30.00	
RB46	RB4 ⅜c **black**	.75	.45
	Block of 4	3.50	2.00
RB47	RB4 ½c **black**	4.25	3.75
	Block of 4	17.50	
RB48	RB4 ⅝c **black**	.30	.25
	Block of 4	1.50	1.10
RB49	RB4 1c **black**	5.50	5.50
	Block of 4	25.00	25.00
RB50	RB4 1¼c **black**	.65	.40
	Block of 4	3.00	1.75
RB51	RB4 1½c **black**	4.25	3.00
	Block of 4	17.50	14.00

RB52	RB4 1⅞c **black**	1.35	.90
	Block of 4	6.00	4.00
RB53	RB4 2c **black**	7.50	6.00
	Block of 4	32.50	
RB54	RB4 2½c **black**	2.00	1.40
	Block of 4	9.00	7.50
RB55	RB4 3c **black**	6.00	4.00
	Block of 4	27.50	
RB56	RB4 3⅛c **black**	10.00	5.00
	Block of 4	42.50	
RB57	RB4 3¾c **black**	22.50	11.00
	Block of 4	92.50	
RB58	RB4 4c **black**	.50	.30
	Block of 4	2.25	1.50
RB59	RB4 4⅜c **black**	22.50	11.00
	Block of 4	92.50	
RB60	RB4 5c **black**	6.00	3.75
	Block of 4	26.00	
RB61	RB4 6c **black**	90.00	52.50
	Block of 4	425.00	
RB62	RB4 8c **black**	30.00	16.00
	Block of 4	130.00	
RB63	RB4 10c **black**	20.00	11.00
	Block of 4	97.50	
RB64	RB4 20c **black**	40.00	24.00
	Block of 4	175.00	
	Nos. RB44-RB64 (21)	274.65	160.75

RB5

1919 Offset Printing *Perf. 11*

RB65	RB5 1c **dark blue**	.25	.25
	Block of 4	1.25	1.10
	Double impression	30.00	20.00
RB66	RB5 2c **dark blue**	.35	.25
	Block of 4	1.50	1.10
	Double impression	70.00	
RB67	RB5 3c **dark blue**	1.50	.75
	Block of 4	6.00	3.50
	Double impression	70.00	—
RB68	RB5 4c **dark blue**	2.25	.75
	Block of 4	10.00	
RB69	RB5 5c **dark blue**	3.00	1.25
	Block of 4	13.50	5.75
RB70	RB5 8c **dark blue**	27.50	20.00
	Block of 4	120.00	
RB71	RB5 10c **dark blue**	12.50	5.00
	Block of 4	57.50	25.00
RB72	RB5 20c **dark blue**	20.00	7.50
	Block of 4	100.00	
RB73	RB5 40c **dark blue**	75.00	25.00
	Block of 4	350.00	
	Nos. RB65-RB73 (9)	142.35	60.75

FUTURE DELIVERY STAMPS

Issued to facilitate the collection of a tax upon each sale, agreement of sale or agreement to sell any products or merchandise at any exchange or board of trade, or other similar place for future delivery.

Documentary Stamps of 1917 Overprinted in Black or Red

Type I

1918-34 Wmk. 191R Offset Printing *Perf. 11*

Overprint Horizontal (Lines 8mm apart)

Left Value — Unused With Gum

Right Value — Used

RC1	R22 2c **carmine rose**	8.75	.25
	Block of 4	37.50	1.10
RC2	R22 3c **carmine rose** ('34)	47.50	37.50
	Cut cancel		20.00
RC3	R22 4c **carmine rose**	17.50	.25
	Cut cancel		.25
	Block of 4	80.00	1.10
b.	Double impression of stamp		10.00
RC3A	R22 5c **carmine rose** ('33)	100.00	7.50
	Block of 4	—	37.50
RC4	R22 10c **carmine rose**	24.00	.35
	Block of 4	110.00	1.50
a.	Double overprint	—	5.25
b.	"FUTURE" omitted	—	*500.00*
c.	"DELIVERY FUTURE"		37.50
RC5	R22 20c **carmine rose**	40.00	.25
	Cut cancel		.25
	Block of 4	200.00	1.10
a.	Double overprint		21.00
RC6	R22 25c **carmine rose**	85.00	.60
	Cut cancel		.30
	Block of 4	390.00	3.00
	Block of 4, cut cancel		1.50
RC7	R22 40c **carmine rose**	110.00	1.25
	Cut cancel		.35
	Block of 4	480.00	5.75
	Block of 4, cut cancel		1.50
RC8	R22 50c **carmine rose**	27.50	.35
	Cut cancel		.25
	Block of 4	130.00	1.50
a.	"DELIVERY" omitted	—	*110.00*
RC9	R22 80c **carmine rose**	190.00	15.00
	Cut cancel		4.00
	Block of 4	900.00	70.00
	Block of 4, cut cancel		16.00
a.	Double overprint		37.50
	Double overprint, cut cancel		6.25

Engr.

Overprint Vertical, Reading Up (Lines 2mm apart)

RC10	R21 $1 **green** (R)	75.00	.35
	Cut cancel		.25
	Block of 4	320.00	1.60
a.	Overprint reading down		*450.00*
b.	Black overprint		—
	Cut cancel		125.00
RC11	R21 $2 **rose**	85.00	.45
	Cut cancel		.25
	Block of 4	390.00	2.00
RC12	R21 $3 **violet** (R)	270.00	3.50
	Cut cancel		.30
	Block of 4	—	16.00
	Block of 4, cut cancel		1.50
a.	Overprint reading down	—	52.50
RC13	R21 $5 **dark blue** (R)	150.00	.60
	Cut cancel		.25
	Block of 4	—	2.75
	Block of 4, cut cancel		1.10
RC14	R21 $10 **orange**	180.00	1.35
	Cut cancel		.30
	Block of 4	800.00	5.00
	Block of 4, cut cancel		1.40
a.	"DELIVERY FUTURE"		*110.00*
RC15	R21 $20 **olive bister**	450.00	9.00
	Cut cancel		.80
	Perf initial		.35
	Block of 4		47.50
	Block of 4, cut cancel		3.50

Overprint Horizontal (Lines 11⅔mm apart)

Perf. 12

Without Gum

RC16	R17 $30 **vermilion,** green numerals	150.00	5.50
	Cut cancel		1.75
	Perf initial		1.25
	Vertical strip of 4		30.00
	Vertical strip of 4, cut cancel		8.25
a.	Numerals in blue	160.00	4.75
	Cut cancel		2.00
	Perf initial		1.50
b.	Imperf., blue numerals		*175.00*
RC17	R19 $50 **olive green** *(Cleveland)*	125.00	3.00
	Cut cancel		.90
	Vertical strip of 4		15.00
	Vertical strip of 4, cut cancel		3.50
a.	$50 olive bister	125.00	2.75
	Cut cancel		.25
	Perf initial		.50
RC18	R19 $60 **brown**	160.00	9.00
	Cut cancel		1.20
	Perf initial		.80
	Vertical strip of 4		40.00
	Vertical strip of 4, cut cancel		5.75
a.	Vert. pair, imperf. horiz.		*950.00*
RC19	R17 $100 **yellow green** ('34)	260.00	37.50
	Cut cancel		9.00
	Perf initial		7.00
	Vertical strip of 4	—	*200.00*
	Vertical strip of 4, cut cancel		37.50
RC20	R18 $500 **blue,** red numerals (R)	325.00	25.00
	Cut cancel		9.00
	Perf initial		7.50
	Vertical strip of 4		125.00
	Vertical strip of 4, cut cancel		45.00
	Double transfer		40.00
	Vert. strip of 4, bottom stamp double transfer	—	150.00
a.	Numerals in orange	—	70.00
	Cut cancel		20.00
	Perf initial		15.00
	Vert. strip of 4		300.00
	Vert. strip of 4, cut cancel		100.00
	Double transfer	—	100.00
	Vert. strip of 4, bottom stamp double transfer	—	350.00
RC21	R19 $1000 **orange**	230.00	7.50
	Cut cancel		2.00
	Perf initial		1.50
	Vertical strip of 4		32.50
	Vertical strip of 4, cut cancel		9.00
a.	Vert. pair, imperf. horiz.		*1,350.*

See note after No. R227.

1923-24 Offset Printing *Perf. 11*

Overprint Horizontal (Lines 2mm apart)

RC22	R22 1c **carmine rose**	1.25	.25
	Block of 4	6.00	1.25
RC23	R22 80c **carmine rose**	200.00	3.50
	Cut cancel		.70
	Block of 4	—	18.00
	Block of 4, cut cancel		3.50

Type II

1925-34 Engr.

RC25	R21 $1 **green** (R)	100.00	2.00
	Cut cancel		.45
	Block of 4	—	8.00
	Block of 4, cut cancel		1.50
RC26	R21 $10 **orange** (Bk) ('34)	260.00	29.00
	Cut cancel		18.00
	Perf initial		11.50

Overprint Type I

1928-29 Offset Printing *Perf. 10*

RC27	R22 10c **carmine rose**		*5,000.*
RC28	R22 20c **carmine rose**		*5,000.*

STOCK TRANSFER STAMPS

Issued to facilitate the collection of a tax on all sales or agreements to sell, or memoranda of sales or delivery of, or transfers of legal title to shares or certificates of stock.

Documentary Stamps of 1917 Overprinted in Black or Red

1918-22 Offset Printing Wmk. 191R *Perf. 11*

Overprint Horizontal (Lines 8mm apart)

RD1	R22	1c **carmine rose**	1.00	.25
		Block of 4	4.25	1.10
a.		Double overprint	—	—
RD2	R22	2c **carmine rose**	.25	.25
		Block of 4	1.10	1.10
a.		Double overprint	—	15.00
		Double overprint, cut cancel		7.50
		Double impression of stamp	—	
RD3	R22	4c **carmine rose**	.25	.25
		Block of 4	1.25	1.10
a.		Double overprint	—	4.25
		Double overprint, cut cancel		2.10
b.		"STOCK" omitted		10.50
d.		Ovpt. lines 10mm apart	—	
		Double impression of stamp		6.00
RD4	R22	5c **carmine rose**	.30	.25
		Block of 4	1.40	1.10
a.		Ovpt. lines 7mm apart		—
RD5	R22	10c **carmine rose**	.30	.25
		Block of 4	1.40	1.10
a.		Double overprint	—	5.25
		Double overprint, cut cancel		2.75
b.		"STOCK" omitted		—
		Double impression of stamp		—
RD6	R22	20c **carmine rose**	.55	.25
		Perf initial		.25
		Block of 4	2.25	1.10
a.		Double overprint		6.25
b.		"STOCK" double		—
		Double impression of stamp		6.00
RD7	R22	25c **carmine rose**	2.25	.30
		Cut cancel		.25
		Block of 4	10.50	1.30
RD8	R22	40c **carmine rose** ('22)	2.25	.25
		Block of 4	10.50	1.10
RD9	R22	50c **carmine rose**	.80	.25
		Block of 4	3.75	1.10
a.		Double overprint	—	
		Double impression of stamp		—
RD10	R22	80c **carmine rose**	10.00	.45
		Cut cancel		.25
		Block of 4	45.00	2.00

Engr.

Overprint Vertical, Reading Up (Lines 2mm apart)

RD11	R21	$1 **green** (R)	225.00	40.00
		Cut cancel		10.00
		Block of 4	—	—
		Block of 4, cut cancel		15.00
a.		Overprint reading down	300.00	60.00
		Overprint reading down, cut cancel		20.00
RD12	R21	$1 **green** (Bk)	3.00	.30
		Block of 4	13.00	1.40
a.		Pair, one without overprint	—	*180.00*
b.		Overprinted on back instead of face, inverted	—	*150.00*
c.		Overprint reading down	—	7.50
d.		$1 yellow green	3.00	.25
RD13	R21	$2 **rose**	3.00	.25
		Perf initial		.25
		Block of 4	13.00	1.10
a.		Overprint reading down		11.50
		Overprint reading down, cut cancel		1.50
b.		Vert. pair, imperf. horiz.	*800.00*	
RD14	R21	$3 **violet** (R)	35.00	6.00
		Cut cancel		.30
		Perf initial		.25
		Block of 4	160.00	
		Block of 4, cut cancel		1.50
RD15	R21	$4 **yellow brown**	15.00	.30
		Cut cancel		.25
		Block of 4	65.00	1.30
RD16	R21	$5 **dark blue** (R)	10.00	.30
		Cut cancel		.25
		Block of 4	42.50	1.30
		Block of 4, cut cancel		.25
a.		Overprint reading down	42.50	1.35
		Overprint reading down, cut cancel		.25
RD17	R21	$10 **orange**	37.50	.45
		Cut cancel		.25
		Block of 4	150.00	2.00
		Block of 4, cut cancel		.40
RD18	R21	$20 **olive bister** ('21)	150.00	18.00
		Cut cancel		4.50
		Perf initial		2.25
		Block of 4	650.00	82.50
		Block of 4, cut cancel		25.00
a.		Overprint reading down		—

Shifted overprints on the $2, and $10 result in "TRANSFER STOCK," "TRANSFER" omitted, and possibly other varieties.

Overprint Horizontal (Lines 11½mm apart)

1918 Without Gum *Perf. 12*

RD19	R17	$30 **vermilion,** green numerals	55.00	6.50
		Cut cancel		2.25
		Perf initial		1.25
		Vertical strip of 4		29.00
		Vertical strip of 4, cut cancel		10.00
a.		Numerals in blue	200.00	75.00
RD20	R19	$50 **olive green** *(Cleveland)*	160.00	70.00
		Cut cancel		27.50
		Perf initial		25.00
		Vertical strip of 4		300.00
		Vertical strip of 4, cut cancel		120.00
RD21	R19	$60 **brown**	350.00	30.00
		Cut cancel		12.00
		Perf initial		7.25
		Vertical strip of 4		100.00
		Vertical strip of 4, cut cancel		47.50
RD22	R17	$100 **green**	50.00	7.50
		Cut cancel		3.00
		Perf initial		2.25
		Vertical strip of 4		32.50
		Vertical strip of 4, cut cancel		13.00
RD23	R18	$500 **blue** (R)	625.00	160.00
		Cut cancel		75.00
		Perf initial		55.00
		Vertical strip of 4		—
		Vertical strip of 4, cut cancel		325.00
		Double transfer	*900.00*	250.00
a.		Numerals in orange		175.00
		Numerals in orange, double transfer		300.00
RD24	R19	$1,000 **orange**	500.00	110.00
		Cut cancel		35.00
		Perf initial		22.50
		Vertical strip of 4		400.00
		Vertical strip of 4, cut cancel		160.00

See note after No. R227.

1928 Offset Printing *Perf. 10*

Overprint Horizontal (Lines 8mm apart)

RD25	R22	2c **carmine rose**	5.50	.30
		Block of 4	24.00	1.40
RD26	R22	4c **carmine rose**	5.50	.30
		Block of 4	24.00	1.40
RD27	R22	10c **carmine rose**	5.50	.30
		Block of 4	24.00	1.40
a.		Inverted overprint		*1,400.*
b.		Ovpt. lines 9½mm apart		—
RD28	R22	20c **carmine rose**	6.50	.35
		Perf initial		.25
		Block of 4	29.00	1.50
		Double impression of stamp		—
RD29	R22	50c **carmine rose**	10.00	.50
		Block of 4	47.50	2.25

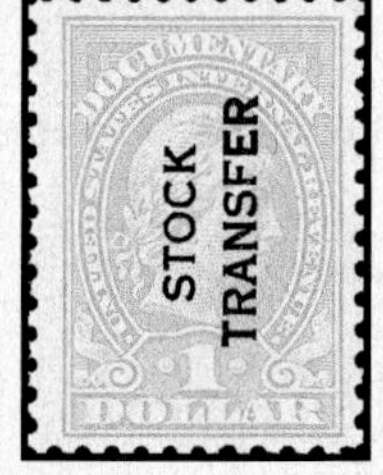

Engr.

Overprint Vertical, Reading Up (Lines 2mm apart)

RD30	R21	$1 **green**	60.00	.35
		Cut cancel		.25
		Block of 4	—	1.60
a.		$1 yellow green	60.00	.50
RD31	R21	$2 **carmine rose**	55.00	.35
		Perf initial		.25
		Block of 4	—	1.50
a.		Pair, one without overprint	*225.00*	*190.00*
RD32	R21	$10 **orange**	60.00	.50
		Cut cancel		.25
		Perf initial		.25
		Block of 4	—	2.25
		Perf. 11 at top or bottom		—

Overprinted Horizontally in Black

1920 Offset Printing *Perf. 11*

RD33	R22	2c **carmine rose**	12.50	1.00
		Block of 4	60.00	4.25
RD34	R22	10c **carmine rose**	3.00	.35
		Block of 4	14.00	1.50
b.		Inverted overprint	*2,250.*	*1,250.*
RD35	R22	20c **carmine rose**	5.75	.25
		Block of 4	26.00	1.10
a.		Horiz. pair, one without overprint	950.00	
d.		Inverted overprint (perf. initials)		—
RD36	R22	50c **carmine rose**	5.00	.30
		Block of 4	24.00	1.25

Shifted overprints on the 10c, 20c and 50c result in "TRANSFER STOCK," "TRANFSER" omitted, "STOCK" omitted, pairs, and other varieties.

Engr.

RD37	R21	$1 **green**	85.00	17.50
		Cut cancel		3.25
		Block of 4	375.00	80.00
		Block of 4, cut cancel		15.00
RD38	R21	$2 **rose**	100.00	17.50
		Cut cancel		3.25
		Block of 4	425.00	80.00
		Block of 4, cut cancel		15.00

Offset Printing

Perf. 10

RD39	R22	2c **carmine rose**	13.00	1.10
		Block of 4	67.50	5.00
		Double impression of stamp	—	
RD40	R22	10c **carmine rose**	5.25	.55
		Block of 4	26.00	2.50
RD41	R22	20c **carmine rose**	6.00	.25
		Cut cancel		.25
		Block of 4	30.00	1.10

Documentary Stamps of 1917-33 Overprinted in Black

1940 Offset Printing Wmk. 191R *Perf. 11*

RD42	R22	1c **rose pink**	4.50	.65
		Cut cancel		.25
		Perf. initial		.25
a.		"Series 1940" inverted (pos. 31LR)	*1,000.*	600.00
		Pair, one normal, one inverted		1,100.
		Cut cancel		125.00

No. RD42a always comes with a natural straight edge at left.

RD43	R22	2c **rose pink**	6.00	.65
		Cut cancel		.25
		Perf. initial		.25
RD45	R22	4c **rose pink**	7.50	.35
		Cut cancel		.25
		Perf. initial		.25
RD46	R22	5c **rose pink**	8.00	.25
		Cut cancel		.25
		Perf. initial		.25
RD48	R22	10c **rose pink**	14.00	.35
		Cut cancel		.25
		Perf. initial		.25
RD49	R22	20c **rose pink**	17.00	.35
		Cut cancel		.25
		Perf. initial		.25
RD50	R22	25c **rose pink**	17.00	1.10
		Cut cancel		.35
		Perf. initial		.25
RD51	R22	40c **rose pink**	11.00	1.00
		Cut cancel		.35
		Perf. initial		.25
RD52	R22	50c **rose pink**	12.50	.35
		Cut cancel		.25
		Perf. initial		.25
RD53	R22	80c **rose pink**	280.00	110.00
		Cut cancel		60.00
		Perf. initial		30.00

Engr.

RD54	R21	$1 **green**	50.00	.60
		Cut cancel		.35
		Perf. initial		.25
RD55	R21	$2 **rose**	55.00	1.00
		Cut cancel		.40
		Perf. initial		.25
RD56	R21	$3 **violet**	350.00	18.00
		Cut cancel		.75
		Perf. initial		.50
RD57	R21	$4 **yellow brown**	125.00	1.60
		Cut cancel		.50
		Perf. initial		.30
RD58	R21	$5 **dark blue**	100.00	2.00
		Cut cancel		.55
		Perf. initial		.35
RD59	R21	$10 **orange**	275.00	10.00
		Cut cancel		1.10
		Perf. initial		.75
RD60	R21	$20 **olive bister**	500.00	150.00
		Cut cancel		25.00
		Perf. initial		11.50

Nos. RD19-RD24 Handstamped in Blue "Series 1940"

1940 **Wmk. 191R** *Perf. 12*

Without Gum

RD61 R17 $30 **vermilion** *2,000.* 1,500.
Cut cancel 650.
Perf. initial 400.
RD62 R19 $50 **olive green** *2,500.* *2,500.*
Cut cancel 1,250.
Perf. initial 400.
a. Double ovpt., perf. initial *1,400.*
RD63 R19 $60 **brown** *5,500.* *3,000.*
Cut cancel 1,000.
Perf. initial 500.
RD64 R17 $100 **green** *5,000.* 850.00
Cut cancel 350.
Perf. initial 110.
RD65 R18 $500 **blue** 4,250.
Cut cancel 1,600.
Perf. initial 950.
Double transfer *3,750.*
a. With black 2-line handstamp in larger type —
RD66 R19 $1,000 **orange**
Cut cancel *5,000.*
Perf. initial 3,000.

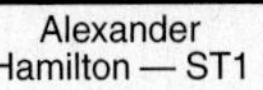
Alexander Hamilton — ST1

Levi Woodbury — ST2

Overprinted in Black

SERIES 1940

Same Portraits as Nos. R288-R310.

1940 **Engr.** **Wmk. 191R** *Perf. 11*

RD67 ST1 1c **bright green** 17.50 3.25
Cut cancel .65
Perf. initial .40
a. Imperf, pair, without gum *250.00*
RD68 ST1 2c **bright green** 10.00 1.75
Cut cancel .30
Perf. initial .30
a. Imperf, pair, without gum *250.00*
RD70 ST1 4c **bright green** 19.00 4.50
Cut cancel .65
Perf. initial .35
a. Imperf, pair, without gum *250.00*
RD71 ST1 5c **bright green** 12.00 1.75
Cut cancel .25
Perf. initial .25
a. Imperf, pair, without gum *250.00*
b. Without overprint, cut cancel *850.00*
RD73 ST1 10c **bright green** 16.00 2.10
Cut cancel .25
Perf. initial .25
a. Imperf, pair, without gum *250.00*
RD74 ST1 20c **bright green** 19.00 2.40
Cut cancel .25
Perf. initial .25
a. Imperf, pair, without gum *250.00*
RD75 ST1 25c **bright green** 60.00 10.50
Cut cancel .90
Perf. initial .45
a. Imperf, pair, without gum *250.00*
RD76 ST1 40c **bright green** 125.00 50.00
Cut cancel 3.50
Perf. initial 1.25
a. Imperf, pair, without gum *250.00*
RD77 ST1 50c **bright green** 16.00 2.10
Cut cancel .45
Perf. initial .30
a. Imperf, pair, without gum *250.00*
RD78 ST1 80c **bright green** 180.00 75.00
Cut cancel 27.50
Perf. initial 3.50
a. Imperf, pair, without gum *250.00*
RD79 ST2 $1 **bright green** 75.00 4.25
Cut cancel .55
Perf. initial .30
a. Without overprint, perf. initial *750.00*
RD80 ST2 $2 **bright green** 75.00 12.00
Cut cancel .75
Perf. initial .30
a. Imperf, pair, without gum *250.00*
RD81 ST2 $3 **bright green** 110.00 15.00
Cut cancel .90
Perf. initial .25
a. Imperf, pair, without gum *250.00*
RD82 ST2 $4 **bright green** 1,000. 300.00
Cut cancel 110.00
Perf. initial 50.00
a. Imperf, pair, without gum *250.00*
RD83 ST2 $5 **bright green** 110.00 16.00
Cut cancel 2.00
Perf. initial .30
a. Imperf, pair, without gum *250.00*
RD84 ST2 $10 **bright green** 250.00 60.00
Cut cancel 6.50
Perf. initial 3.25
a. Imperf, pair, without gum *250.00*
RD85 ST2 $20 **bright green** 1,250. 125.00
Cut cancel 15.00
Perf. initial 5.75
a. Imperf, pair, without gum *250.00*

Nos. RD67-RD85 exist imperforate, without overprint. Value, set of pairs, $750.

Thomas Corwin — ST3

Overprinted "SERIES 1940"

Various frames and portraits as Nos. R306-R310.

Without Gum *Perf. 12*

RD86 ST3 $30 **bright green** *6,000.* 200.00
Cut cancel 100.00
Perf. initial 37.50
RD87 ST3 $50 **bright green** 3,250. 900.00
Cut cancel 500.00
Perf. initial 92.50
RD88 ST3 $60 **bright green** *5,000.* *2,250.*
Cut cancel 850.00
Perf. initial 160.00
RD89 ST3 $100 **bright green** *3,000.* 450.00
Cut cancel 150.00
Perf. initial 67.50
RD90 ST3 $500 **bright green** —
Cut cancel *3,000.*
Perf. initial *2,000.*
RD91 ST3 $1,000 **bright green** *4,000.*
Cut cancel *3,000.*
Perf. initial *1,750.*

Nos. RD86-RD91 exist as unfinished imperforates with complete receipt tabs, without overprints or serial numbers. Known in singles, pairs (Nos. RD86-RD88 and Nos. RD90-RD91, value $300 per pair; No. RD89, value $150 per pair), panes of four with plate number, uncut sheets of four panes (with two plate numbers), cross gutter blocks of eight, and blocks of four with vertical gutter between and plate number.

Stock Transfer Stamps and Type of 1940 Overprinted in Black

SERIES 1941

1941 **Wmk. 191R** *Perf. 11*

RD92 ST1 1c **bright green** .80 .55
Cut cancel .25
Perf. initial .25
RD93 ST1 2c **bright green** .60 .30
Cut cancel .25
Perf. initial .25
RD95 ST1 4c **bright green** .65 .25
Cut cancel .25
Perf. initial .25
RD96 ST1 5c **bright green** .60 .25
Cut cancel .25
Perf. initial .25
RD98 ST1 10c **bright green** 1.10 .25
Cut cancel .25
Perf. initial .25
RD99 ST1 20c **bright green** 2.40 .30
Cut cancel .25
Perf. initial .25
RD100 ST1 25c **bright green** 2.40 .45
Cut cancel .30
Perf. initial .30
RD101 ST1 40c **bright green** 3.75 .75
Cut cancel .30
Perf. initial .25
RD102 ST1 50c **bright green** 5.00 .35
Cut cancel .25
Perf. initial .25
RD103 ST1 80c **bright green** 35.00 10.00
Cut cancel .80
Perf. initial .60
RD104 ST2 $1 **bright green** 25.00 .25
Cut cancel .25
Perf. initial .25
RD105 ST2 $2 **bright green** 27.50 .30
Cut cancel .25
Perf. initial .25
RD106 ST2 $3 **bright green** 40.00 1.50
Cut cancel .35
Perf. initial .25
RD107 ST2 $4 **bright green** 65.00 8.50
Cut cancel .60
Perf. initial .30
RD108 ST2 $5 **bright green** 65.00 .65
Cut cancel .30
Perf. initial .25
RD109 ST2 $10 **bright green** 140.00 5.50
Cut cancel 1.00
Perf. initial .25
RD110 ST2 $20 **bright green** 500.00 110.00
Cut cancel 25.00
Perf. initial 5.00

Perf. 12

Without Gum

RD111 ST3 $30 **bright green** 2,250. 500.00
Cut cancel 110.00
Perf. initial 40.00
RD112 ST3 $50 **bright green** 1,250. 750.00
Cut cancel 175.00
Perf. initial 70.00
RD113 ST3 $60 **bright green** *2,500.* 1,000.
Cut cancel 275.00
Perf. initial 175.00
RD114 ST3 $100 **bright green** 500.00 210.00
Cut cancel 65.00
Perf. initial 45.00
RD115 ST3 $500 **bright green** 4,000. *3,500.*
Cut cancel 2,500.
Perf. initial 1,200.
RD116 ST3 $1,000 **bright green** — *4,000.*
Cut cancel 1,500.
Perf. initial 1,000.

Stock Transfer Stamps and Type of 1940 Overprinted in Black

SERIES 1942

1942 **Wmk. 191R** *Perf. 11*

RD117 ST1 1c **bright green** .75 .30
Cut cancel .25
Perf. initial .25
RD118 ST1 2c **bright green** .65 .35
Cut cancel .25
Perf. initial .25
RD119 ST1 4c **bright green** 3.50 1.10
Cut cancel .55
Perf. initial .45
RD120 ST1 5c **bright green** .70 .25
Cut cancel .25
Perf. initial .25
a. Overprint inverted *1,000.*
Cut cancel *700.00*
Perf. initial *350.00*
RD121 ST1 10c **bright green** 2.25 .25
Cut cancel .25
Perf. initial .25
RD122 ST1 20c **bright green** 2.75 .25
Cut cancel .25
Perf. initial .25
RD123 ST1 25c **bright green** 2.50 .25
Cut cancel .25
Perf. initial .25
RD124 ST1 40c **bright green** 5.75 .40
Cut cancel .25
Perf. initial .25
RD125 ST1 50c **bright green** 6.50 .25
Cut cancel .25
Perf. initial .25
RD126 ST1 80c **bright green** 30.00 6.00
Cut cancel 1.50
Perf. initial .35
RD127 ST2 $1 **bright green** 27.50 .40
Cut cancel .25
Perf. initial .25
RD128 ST2 $2 **bright green** 45.00 .40
Cut cancel .25
Perf. initial .25
RD129 ST2 $3 **bright green** 50.00 1.10
Cut cancel .30
Perf. initial .25
RD130 ST2 $4 **bright green** 65.00 24.00
Cut cancel .65
Perf. initial .25
RD131 ST2 $5 **bright green** 60.00 .40
Cut cancel .25
Perf. initial .25
a. Double overprint, perf. initial *2,500.*
RD132 ST2 $10 **bright green** 125.00 9.50
Cut cancel 2.00
Perf. initial 1.10
RD133 ST2 $20 **bright green** 350.00 65.00
Cut cancel 15.00
Perf. initial 5.00

Perf. 12

Without Gum

RD134 ST3 $30 **bright green** 900.00 175.00
Cut cancel 65.00
Perf. initial 30.00
RD135 ST3 $50 **bright green** 950.00 400.00
Cut cancel 55.00
Perf. initial 27.50
RD136 ST3 $60 **bright green** 2,500. 350.00
Cut cancel 150.00
Perf. initial 62.50
RD137 ST3 $100 **bright green** *900.00* 110.00
Cut cancel 35.00
Perf. initial 21.00
RD138 ST3 $500 **bright green** *15,000.*
Cut cancel *10,000.*
Perf. initial *8,500.*
RD139 ST3 $1,000 **bright green** — 2,750.
Cut cancel 850.00
Perf. initial 300.00

Stock Transfer Stamps and Type of 1940 Overprinted in Black

SERIES 1943

1943 **Wmk. 191R** ***Perf. 11***

RD140	ST1 1c **bright green**	.55	.30
	Cut cancel		.25
	Perf. initial		.25
RD141	ST1 2c **bright green**	.60	.40
	Cut cancel		.25
	Perf. initial		.25
RD142	ST1 4c **bright green**	2.10	.25
	Cut cancel		.25
	Perf. initial		.25
RD143	ST1 5c **bright green**	.60	.25
	Cut cancel		.25
	Perf. initial		.25
RD144	ST1 10c **bright green**	1.50	.25
	Cut cancel		.25
	Perf. initial		.25
RD145	ST1 20c **bright green**	2.25	.25
	Cut cancel		.25
	Perf. initial		.25
RD146	ST1 25c **bright green**	6.75	.35
	Cut cancel		.25
	Perf. initial		.25
RD147	ST1 40c **bright green**	6.25	.30
	Cut cancel		.25
	Perf. initial		.25
RD148	ST1 50c **bright green**	5.75	.30
	Cut cancel		.25
	Perf. initial		.25
RD149	ST1 80c **bright green**	35.00	7.50
	Cut cancel		2.50
	Perf. initial		1.25
RD150	ST2 $1 **bright green**	27.50	.25
	Cut cancel		.25
	Perf. initial		.25
RD151	ST2 $2 **bright green**	30.00	.50
	Cut cancel		.25
	Perf. initial		.25
RD152	ST2 $3 **bright green**	35.00	2.50
	Cut cancel		.45
	Perf. initial		.30
RD153	ST2 $4 **bright green**	85.00	30.00
	Cut cancel		5.00
	Perf. initial		3.00
RD154	ST2 $5 **bright green**	90.00	.60
	Cut cancel		.30
	Perf. initial		.25
RD155	ST2 $10 **bright green**	140.00	7.50
	Cut cancel		1.50
	Perf. initial		.45
RD156	ST2 $20 **bright green**	450.00	90.00
	Cut cancel		45.00
	Perf. initial		10.00

Perf. 12

Without Gum

RD157	ST3 $30 **bright green**	2,500.	750.00
	Cut cancel		100.00
	Perf. initial		32.50
RD158	ST3 $50 **bright green**	2,500.	450.00
	Cut cancel		50.00
	Perf. initial		20.00
RD159	ST3 $60 **bright green**	*4,000.*	*2,750.*
	Cut cancel		1,000.
	Perf. initial		200.00
RD160	ST3 $100 **bright green**	225.00	90.00
	Cut cancel		30.00
	Perf. initial		20.00
RD161	ST3 $500 **bright green**	—	2,250.
	Cut cancel		1,100.
	Perf. initial		450.00
RD162	ST3 $1,000 **bright green**	2,500.	2,000.
	Cut cancel		500.00
	Perf. initial		200.00

Stock Transfer Stamps and Type of 1940 Overprinted in Black

Series 1944

1944 **Wmk. 191R** ***Perf. 11***

RD163	ST1 1c **bright green**	.90	.75
	Cut cancel		.35
	Perf. initial		.25
RD164	ST1 2c **bright green**	.70	.25
	Cut cancel		.25
	Perf. initial		.25
RD165	ST1 4c **bright green**	.70	.35
	Cut cancel		.25
	Perf. initial		.25
RD166	ST1 5c **bright green**	.65	.25
	Cut cancel		.25
	Perf. initial		.25
RD167	ST1 10c **bright green**	1.00	.30
	Cut cancel		.25
	Perf. initial		.25
RD168	ST1 20c **bright green**	2.25	.25
	Cut cancel		.25
	Perf. initial		.25
RD169	ST1 25c **bright green**	3.25	.90
	Cut cancel		.25
	Perf. initial		.25
RD170	ST1 40c **bright green**	17.50	8.00
	Cut cancel		3.25
	Perf. initial		1.75
RD171	ST1 50c **bright green**	5.50	.30
	Cut cancel		.25
	Perf. initial		.25
RD172	ST1 80c **bright green**	17.50	6.25
	Cut cancel		2.75
	Perf. initial		1.75
RD173	ST2 $1 **bright green**	17.50	.50
	Cut cancel		.30
	Perf. initial		.25
RD174	ST2 $2 **bright green**	60.00	.75
	Cut cancel		.35
	Perf. initial		.25
RD175	ST2 $3 **bright green**	55.00	2.00
	Cut cancel		.35
	Perf. initial		.25
RD176	ST2 $4 **bright green**	95.00	17.50
	Cut cancel		1.75
	Perf. initial		.75
RD177	ST2 $5 **bright green**	65.00	3.50
	Cut cancel		.40
	Perf. initial		.25
RD178	ST2 $10 **bright green**	150.00	7.25
	Cut cancel		1.00
	Perf. initial		.45
RD179	ST2 $20 **bright green**	425.00	25.00
	Cut cancel		9.00
	Perf. initial		5.50

Perf. 12

Without Gum

Designs: $2,500, William Windom. $5,000, C. J. Folger. $10,000, W. Q. Gresham.

RD180	ST3 $30 **bright green**	850.00	125.00
	Cut cancel		50.00
	Perf. initial		22.50
RD181	ST3 $50 **bright green**	1,000.	150.00
	Cut cancel		30.00
	Perf. initial		17.50
RD182	ST3 $60 **bright green**	*4,750.*	750.00
	Cut cancel		125.00
	Perf. initial		70.00
RD183	ST3 $100 **bright green**	3,250.	100.00
	Cut cancel		35.00
	Perf. initial		17.50
RD184	ST3 $500 **bright green**	*2,500.*	*2,250.*
	Cut cancel		1,750.
	Perf. initial		650.00
RD185	ST3 $1,000 **bright green**	*3,000.*	2,500.
	Cut cancel		1,500.
	Perf. initial		400.00
RD185A	ST3 $2,500 **bright green**		—
RD185B	ST3 $5,000 **bright green**, perf. initial		*65,000.*
RD185C	ST3 $10,000 **bright green**, cut cancel		*45,000.*
	Perf. initial		*35,000.*

Nos. RD185A-R185C exist as unfinished imperforates with complete receipt tabs, without overprints or serial numbers. Known in singles, pairs, panes of four with plate number, uncut sheets of four panes (with two plate numbers), cross gutter blocks of eight, and blocks of four with vertical gutter between and plate number. Value, pairs $450 each.

Stock Transfer Stamps and Type of 1940 Overprinted in Black

Series 1945

1945 **Wmk. 191R** ***Perf. 11***

RD186	ST1 1c **bright green**	.45	.25
	Cut cancel		.25
	Perf. initial		.25
RD187	ST1 2c **bright green**	.45	.35
	Cut cancel		.25
	Perf. initial		.25
RD188	ST1 4c **bright green**	.50	.35
	Cut cancel		.25
	Perf. initial		.25
RD189	ST1 5c **bright green**	.45	.25
	Cut cancel		.25
	Perf. initial		.25
RD190	ST1 10c **bright green**	1.25	.35
	Cut cancel		.25
	Perf. initial		.25
RD191	ST1 20c **bright green**	2.25	.45
	Cut cancel		.25
	Perf. initial		.25
RD192	ST1 25c **bright green**	3.50	.40
	Cut cancel		.30
	Perf. initial		.25
RD193	ST1 40c **bright green**	5.00	.25
	Cut cancel		.25
	Perf. initial		.25
RD194	ST1 50c **bright green**	11.00	.45
	Cut cancel		.30
	Perf. initial		.25
RD195	ST1 80c **bright green**	17.50	4.75
	Cut cancel		1.00
	Perf. initial		.70
RD196	ST2 $1 **bright green**	20.00	.30
	Cut cancel		.25
	Perf. initial		.25
RD197	ST2 $2 **bright green**	37.50	.90
	Cut cancel		.30
	Perf. initial		.25
RD198	ST2 $3 **bright green**	65.00	1.75
	Cut cancel		.50
	Perf. initial		.25
RD199	ST2 $4 **bright green**	65.00	4.25
	Cut cancel		1.10
	Perf. initial		.65
RD200	ST2 $5 **bright green**	40.00	1.00
	Cut cancel		.30
	Perf. initial		.25
RD201	ST2 $10 **bright green**	95.00	12.00
	Cut cancel		1.50
	Perf. initial		1.00
RD202	ST2 $20 **bright green**	375.00	25.00
	Cut cancel		5.00
	Perf. initial		1.40

Perf. 12

Without Gum

RD203	ST3 $30 **bright green**	300.00	90.00
	Cut cancel		40.00
	Perf. initial		22.50
RD204	ST3 $50 **bright green**	275.00	70.00
	Cut cancel		12.50
	Perf. initial		8.00
RD205	ST3 $60 **bright green**	1,750.	500.00
	Cut cancel		200.00
	Perf. initial		55.00
RD206	ST3 $100 **bright green**	600.00	75.00
	Cut cancel		20.00
	Perf. initial		10.50
RD207	ST3 $500 **bright green**	—	1,400.
	Cut cancel		800.00
	Perf. initial		450.00
RD208	ST3 $1,000 **bright green**	*3,250.*	2,250.
	Cut cancel		1,050.
	Perf. initial		500.00
RD208A	ST3 $2,500 **bright green**		
	Cut cancel		*25,000.*
	Perf. initial		*17,500.*
RD208B	ST3 $5,000 **bright green**		
	Cut cancel		*45,000.*
RD208C	ST3 $10,000 **bright green**		
	Cut cancel		*45,000.*

Stock Transfer Stamps and Type of 1940 Overprinted in Black

Series 1946

1946 **Wmk. 191R** ***Perf. 11***

RD209	ST1 1c **bright green**	.50	.35
	Cut cancel		.25
	Perf. initial		.25
a.	Pair, one dated "1945"	*850.00*	
RD210	ST1 2c **bright green**	.50	.25
	Cut cancel		.25
	Perf. initial		.25
RD211	ST1 4c **bright green**	.50	.25
	Cut cancel		.25
	Perf. initial		.25
RD212	ST1 5c **bright green**	.55	.25
	Cut cancel		.25
	Perf. initial		.25
RD213	ST1 10c **bright green**	1.25	.25
	Cut cancel		.25
	Perf. initial		.25
RD214	ST1 20c **bright green**	2.50	.30
	Cut cancel		.25
	Perf. initial		.25
RD215	ST1 25c **bright green**	3.00	.40
	Cut cancel		.30
	Perf. initial		.25
RD216	ST1 40c **bright green**	6.50	1.25
	Cut cancel		.40
	Perf. initial		.25
RD217	ST1 50c **bright green**	6.75	.25
	Cut cancel		.25
	Perf. initial		.25
RD218	ST1 80c **bright green**	24.00	9.50
	Cut cancel		3.25
	Perf. initial		1.60
RD219	ST2 $1 **bright green**	17.50	.90
	Cut cancel		.35
	Perf. initial		.25
RD220	ST2 $2 **bright green**	19.00	1.00
	Cut cancel		.40
	Perf. initial		.25
RD221	ST2 $3 **bright green**	35.00	2.25
	Cut cancel		.45
	Perf. initial		.25
RD222	ST2 $4 **bright green**	35.00	9.00
	Cut cancel		3.50
	Perf. initial		1.25
RD223	ST2 $5 **bright green**	60.00	2.25
	Cut cancel		.35
	Perf. initial		.25
RD224	ST2 $10 **bright green**	100.00	4.25
	Cut cancel		1.25
	Perf. initial		.35
RD225	ST2 $20 **bright green**	550.00	75.00
	Cut cancel		16.00
	Perf. initial		8.75

Without Gum ***Perf. 12***

RD226	ST3 $30 **bright green**	350.00	62.50
	Cut cancel		25.00
	Perf. initial		18.00
RD227	ST3 $50 **bright green**	450.00	75.00
	Cut cancel		27.50
	Perf. initial		15.00
RD228	ST3 $60 **bright green**	1,250.	250.00
	Cut cancel		60.00
	Perf. initial		20.00
RD229	ST3 $100 **bright green**	225.00	90.00
	Cut cancel		27.50
	Perf. initial		17.00
RD230	ST3 $500 **bright green**	*2,500.*	350.00
	Cut cancel		125.00
	Perf. initial		90.00
RD231	ST3 $1,000 **bright green**	2,000.	300.00
	Cut cancel		200.00
	Perf. initial		95.00
RD232	ST3 $2,500 **bright green**		*25,000.*
	Cut cancel		*15,000.*
	Perf. initial		*12,500.*

RD233 ST3 $5,000 **bright green**		
Cut cancel		*17,500.*
Perf. initial		*7,500.*
RD234 ST3 $10,000 **bright green**		
Cut cancel		*22,500.*

Stock Transfer Stamps and Type of 1940 Overprinted in Black

Series 1947

1947 **Wmk. 191R**		*Perf. 11*
RD235 ST1 1c **bright green**	2.75	.90
Cut cancel		.35
Perf. initial		.25
RD236 ST1 2c **bright green**	2.75	.90
Cut cancel		.35
Perf. initial		.25
RD237 ST1 4c **bright green**	2.00	.70
Cut cancel		.35
Perf. initial		.25
RD238 ST1 5c **bright green**	2.00	.60
Cut cancel		.35
Perf. initial		.25
RD239 ST1 10c **bright green**	2.00	.90
Cut cancel		.35
Perf. initial		.25
RD240 ST1 20c **bright green**	3.75	.90
Cut cancel		.30
Perf. initial		.25
RD241 ST1 25c **bright green**	6.00	.90
Cut cancel		.35
Perf. initial		.25
RD242 ST1 40c **bright green**	6.00	1.40
Cut cancel		.35
Perf. initial		.25
RD243 ST1 50c **bright green**	7.50	.35
Cut cancel		.25
Perf. initial		.25
RD244 ST1 80c **bright green**	32.50	14.00
Cut cancel		5.50
Perf. initial		3.75
RD245 ST2 $1 **bright green**	25.00	1.00
Cut cancel		.35
Perf. initial		.25
RD246 ST2 $2 **bright green**	35.00	1.25
Cut cancel		.35
Perf. initial		.25
RD247 ST2 $3 **bright green**	50.00	2.50
Cut cancel		.60
Perf. initial		.35
RD248 ST2 $4 **bright green**	70.00	9.50
Cut cancel		1.60
Perf. initial		.90
RD249 ST2 $5 **bright green**	50.00	3.25
Cut cancel		.65
Perf. initial		.35
RD250 ST2 $10 **bright green**	225.00	11.00
Cut cancel		3.25
Perf. initial		2.25
RD251 ST2 $20 **bright green**	300.00	50.00
Cut cancel		12.50
Perf. initial		6.75

Without Gum		*Perf. 12*
RD252 ST3 $30 **bright green**	2,000.	85.00
Cut cancel		25.00
Perf. initial		13.00
RD253 ST3 $50 **bright green**	1,500.	325.00
Cut cancel		90.00
Perf. initial		25.00
RD254 ST3 $60 **bright green**	2,750.	250.00
Cut cancel		80.00
Perf. initial		50.00
RD255 ST3 $100 **bright green**	175.00	70.00
Cut cancel		22.50
Perf. initial		17.00
RD256 ST3 $500 **bright green**	2,500.	850.00
Cut cancel		400.00
Perf. initial		175.00
RD257 ST3 $1,000 **bright green**	2,750.	140.00
Cut cancel		75.00
Perf. initial		40.00
RD258 ST3 $2,500 **bright green**	*3,000.*	
Cut cancel		400.00
Perf. initial		350.00
RD259 ST3 $5,000 **bright green**	2,500.	
Cut cancel		600.00
Perf. initial		500.00
RD260 ST3 $10,000 **bright green**		—
Cut cancel		75.00
Perf. initial		—
a. Vert. pair, imperf. horiz., cut cancel		—

Stock Transfer Stamps and Type of 1940 Overprinted in Black

Series 1948

1948 **Wmk. 191R**		*Perf. 11*
RD261 ST1 1c **bright green**	.45	.35
Cut cancel		.25
Perf. initial		.25
RD262 ST1 2c **bright green**	.45	.35
Cut cancel		.25
Perf. initial		.25
RD263 ST1 4c **bright green**	.80	.45
Cut cancel		.30
Perf. initial		.25
RD264 ST1 5c **bright green**	.45	.25
Cut cancel		.25
Perf. initial		.25
RD265 ST1 10c **bright green**	.55	.35
Cut cancel		.25
Perf. initial		.25
RD266 ST1 20c **bright green**	1.60	.40
Cut cancel		.25
Perf. initial		.25
RD267 ST1 25c **bright green**	1.90	.55
Cut cancel		.30
Perf. initial		.25
RD268 ST1 40c **bright green**	5.00	1.00
Cut cancel		.35
Perf. initial		.25
RD269 ST1 50c **bright green**	7.00	.45
Cut cancel		.25
Perf. initial		.25
RD270 ST1 80c **bright green**	30.00	9.50
Cut cancel		3.50
Perf. initial		2.25
RD271 ST2 $1 **bright green**	17.50	.50
Cut cancel		.30
Perf. initial		.20
RD272 ST2 $2 **bright green**	35.00	1.00
Cut cancel		.30
Perf. initial		.25
RD273 ST2 $3 **bright green**	60.00	10.00
Cut cancel		3.00
Perf. initial		1.60
RD274 ST2 $4 **bright green**	70.00	20.00
Cut cancel		3.75
Perf. initial		2.25
RD275 ST2 $5 **bright green**	80.00	5.00
Cut cancel		.50
Perf. initial		.25
RD276 ST2 $10 **bright green**	90.00	7.25
Cut cancel		1.00
Perf. initial		.75
RD277 ST2 $20 **bright green**	400.00	30.00
Cut cancel		10.00
Perf. initial		4.75

Perf. 12 **Without Gum**		
RD278 ST3 $30 **bright green**	350.00	100.00
Cut cancel		35.00
Perf. initial		18.00
RD279 ST3 $50 **bright green**	400.00	95.00
Cut cancel		32.50
Perf. initial		16.00
RD280 ST3 $60 **bright green**	2,000.	350.00
Cut cancel		75.00
Perf. initial		27.50
RD281 ST3 $100 **bright green**	175.00	30.00
Cut cancel		10.00
Perf. initial		7.00
RD282 ST3 $500 **bright green**	2,500.	375.00
Cut cancel		200.00
Perf. initial		52.50
RD283 ST3 $1,000 **bright green**	2,500.	125.00
Cut cancel		80.00
Perf. initial		40.00
RD284 ST3 $2,500 **bright green**	2,500.	1,750.
Cut cancel		600.00
Perf. initial		225.00
RD285 ST3 $5,000 **bright green**	2,500.	1,750.
Cut cancel		600.00
Perf. initial		225.00
RD286 ST3 $10,000 **bright green**		
Cut cancel		75.00
Perf. initial		—

Stock Transfer Stamps and Type of 1940 Overprinted in Black

Series 1949

1949 **Wmk. 191R**		*Perf. 11*
RD287 ST1 1c **bright green**	2.25	.70
Cut cancel		.35
Perf. initial		.25
RD288 ST1 2c **bright green**	2.25	.75
Cut cancel		.35
Perf. initial		.25
RD289 ST1 4c **bright green**	2.50	.75
Cut cancel		.35
Perf. initial		.25
RD290 ST1 5c **bright green**	3.00	.75
Cut cancel		.35
Perf. initial		.25
RD291 ST1 10c **bright green**	7.50	1.00
Cut cancel		.35
Perf. initial		.25
RD292 ST1 20c **bright green**	12.00	1.00
Cut cancel		.35
Perf. initial		.25
RD293 ST1 25c **bright green**	13.00	1.25
Cut cancel		.40
Perf. initial		.25
RD294 ST1 40c **bright green**	30.00	3.25
Cut cancel		.50
Perf. initial		.30
RD295 ST1 50c **bright green**	35.00	.45
Cut cancel		.35
Perf. initial		.25
RD296 ST1 80c **bright green**	45.00	10.00
Cut cancel		4.25
Perf. initial		3.00
RD297 ST2 $1 **bright green**	32.50	1.00
Cut cancel		.35
Perf. initial		.25
RD298 ST2 $2 **bright green**	60.00	1.75
Cut cancel		.50
Perf. initial		.30
RD299 ST2 $3 **bright green**	110.00	10.00
Cut cancel		2.25
Perf. initial		1.10
RD300 ST2 $4 **bright green**	110.00	20.00
Cut cancel		3.00
Perf. initial		1.75
RD301 ST2 $5 **bright green**	85.00	3.00
Cut cancel		.30
Perf. initial		.25
RD302 ST2 $10 **bright green**	150.00	12.50
Cut cancel		3.75
Perf. initial		2.00
RD303 ST2 $20 **bright green**	325.00	22.50
Cut cancel		10.00
Perf. initial		6.25

Perf. 12 **Without Gum**		
RD304 ST3 $30 **bright green**	3,000.	150.00
Cut cancel		45.00
Perf. initial		18.00
RD305 ST3 $50 **bright green**	2,250.	300.00
Cut cancel		75.00
Perf. initial		27.50
RD306 ST3 $60 **bright green**	2,500.	400.00
Cut cancel		175.00
Perf. initial		75.00
RD307 ST3 $100 **bright green**	225.00	70.00
Cut cancel		35.00
Perf. initial		18.00
RD308 ST3 $500 **bright green**	*1,500.*	300.00
Cut cancel		65.00
Perf. initial		35.00
RD309 ST3 $1,000 **bright green**	*1,500.*	85.00
Cut cancel		52.50
Perf. initial		32.50
RD310 ST3 $2,500 **bright green**		
Cut cancel		*750.00*
Perf. initial		600.00
RD311 ST3 $5,000 **bright green**		
Cut cancel		*675.00*
Perf. initial		*600.00*
RD312 ST3 $10,000 **bright green**		475.00
Cut cancel		45.00
Perf. initial		—
a. Pair, one without ovpt., cut cancel		*8,000.*

No. RD312a is unique.

Stock Transfer Stamps and Type of 1940 Overprinted in Black

Series 1950

1950 **Wmk. 191R**		*Perf. 11*
RD313 ST1 1c **bright green**	.80	.40
Cut cancel		.30
Perf. initial		.25
RD314 ST1 2c **bright green**	.70	.35
Cut cancel		.25
Perf. initial		.25
RD315 ST1 4c **bright green**	.65	.40
Cut cancel		.25
Perf. initial		.25
RD316 ST1 5c **bright green**	.75	.25
Cut cancel		.25
Perf. initial		.25
RD317 ST1 10c **bright green**	3.25	.30
Cut cancel		.25
Perf. initial		.25
RD318 ST1 20c **bright green**	5.00	.80
Cut cancel		.35
Perf. initial		.25
RD319 ST1 25c **bright green**	10.00	1.00
Cut cancel		.25
Perf. initial		.25
RD320 ST1 40c **bright green**	15.00	1.50
Cut cancel		.35
Perf. initial		.25
RD321 ST1 50c **bright green**	19.00	.50
Cut cancel		.30
Perf. initial		.25
RD322 ST1 80c **bright green**	27.50	7.25
Cut cancel		2.40
Perf. initial		1.50
RD323 ST2 $1 **bright green**	27.50	.55
Cut cancel		.25
Perf. initial		.25
RD324 ST2 $2 **bright green**	40.00	1.25
Cut cancel		.35
Perf. initial		.25
RD325 ST2 $3 **bright green**	70.00	8.50
Cut cancel		1.25
Perf. initial		1.00
RD326 ST2 $4 **bright green**	85.00	20.00
Cut cancel		7.50
Perf. initial		5.00
RD327 ST2 $5 **bright green**	70.00	3.25
Cut cancel		.45
Perf. initial		.25
RD328 ST2 $10 **bright green**	210.00	12.50
Cut cancel		2.25
Perf. initial		1.00
RD329 ST2 $20 **bright green**	300.00	60.00
Cut cancel		40.00
Perf. initial		10.00

Perf. 12 **Without Gum**		
RD330 ST3 $30 **bright green**	600.00	250.00
Cut cancel		75.00
Perf. initial		22.50
RD331 ST3 $50 **bright green**	800.00	225.00
Cut cancel		85.00
Perf. initial		35.00
RD332 ST3 $60 **bright green**	1,000.	250.00
Cut cancel		125.00
Perf. initial		60.00

No.	Type	Denom.	Color	Unused	Used
RD333	ST3	$100	**bright green**	150.00	55.00
	Cut cancel				30.00
	Perf. initial				15.00
a.	Vert. pair, imperf. btwn.			2,000.	*1,750.*
RD334	ST3	$500	**bright green**	—	350.00
	Cut cancel				160.00
	Perf. initial				95.00
RD335	ST3	$1,000	**bright green**	275.00	85.00
	Cut cancel				35.00
	Perf. initial				22.50
RD336	ST3	$2,500	**bright green**	5,500.	2,500.
	Cut cancel				1,250.
	Perf. initial				900.00
RD337	ST3	$5,000	**bright green**	5,500.	2,500.
	Cut cancel				900.00
	Perf. initial				750.00
RD338	ST3	$10,000	**bright green**	5,500.	1,500.
	Cut cancel				125.00
	Perf. initial				100.00

Stock Transfer Stamps and Type of 1940 Overprinted in Black

Series 1951

1951 Wmk. 191R *Perf. 11*

No.	Type	Denom.	Color	Unused	Used
RD339	ST1	1c	**bright green**	3.00	.75
	Cut cancel				.40
	Perf. initial				.25
RD340	ST1	2c	**bright green**	2.50	.50
	Cut cancel				.30
	Perf. initial				.25
RD341	ST1	4c	**bright green**	3.00	.75
	Cut cancel				.35
	Perf. initial				.25
RD342	ST1	5c	**bright green**	2.25	.55
	Cut cancel				.25
	Perf. initial				.25
RD343	ST1	10c	**bright green**	3.00	.35
	Cut cancel				.25
	Perf. initial				.25
RD344	ST1	20c	**bright green**	10.00	1.25
	Cut cancel				.35
	Perf. initial				.25
RD345	ST1	25c	**bright green**	12.00	1.50
	Cut cancel				.35
	Perf. initial				.25
RD346	ST1	40c	**bright green**	50.00	12.50
	Cut cancel				4.00
	Perf. initial				2.00
RD347	ST1	50c	**bright green**	20.00	1.50
	Cut cancel				.30
	Perf. initial				.25
RD348	ST1	80c	**bright green**	40.00	14.00
	Cut cancel				5.25
	Perf. initial				2.25
RD349	ST2	$1	**bright green**	40.00	1.25
	Cut cancel				.35
	Perf. initial				.25
RD350	ST2	$2	**bright green**	55.00	1.75
	Cut cancel				.35
	Perf. initial				.25
RD351	ST2	$3	**bright green**	70.00	14.00
	Cut cancel				4.50
	Perf. initial				2.00
RD352	ST2	$4	**bright green**	350.00	25.00
	Cut cancel				10.00
	Perf. initial				2.25
RD353	ST2	$5	**bright green**	90.00	4.00
	Cut cancel				.35
	Perf. initial				.25
RD354	ST2	$10	**bright green**	170.00	11.00
	Cut cancel				3.00
	Perf. initial				1.75
RD355	ST2	$20	**bright green**	400.00	35.00
	Cut cancel				10.00
	Perf. initial				5.75

Perf. 12

Without Gum

No.	Type	Denom.	Color	Unused	Used
RD356	ST3	$30	**bright green**	*2,500.*	200.00
	Cut cancel				55.00
	Perf. initial				25.00
RD357	ST3	$50	**bright green**	*2,500.*	250.00
	Cut cancel				32.50
	Perf. initial				20.00
RD358	ST3	$60	**bright green**	*2,500.*	*1,600.*
	Cut cancel				800.00
	Perf. initial				450.00
RD359	ST3	$100	**bright green**	250.00	100.00
	Cut cancel				35.00
	Perf. initial				15.00
RD360	ST3	$500	**bright green**	*2,500.*	550.00
	Cut cancel				210.00
	Perf. initial				125.00
RD361	ST3	$1,000	**bright green**	275.00	125.00
	Cut cancel				80.00
	Perf. initial				57.50
RD362	ST3	$2,500	**bright green**		*4,250.*
	Cut cancel				2,500.
	Perf. initial				2,000.
RD363	ST3	$5,000	**bright green**	—	*3,250.*
	Cut cancel				1,400.
	Perf. initial				1,000.
RD364	ST3	$10,000	**bright green**	*2,000.*	250.00
	Cut cancel				150.00
	Perf. initial				75.00

Stock Transfer Stamps and Type of 1940 Overprinted in Black

1952 Wmk. 191R *Perf. 11*

No.	Type	Denom.	Color	Unused	Used
RD365	ST1	1c	**bright green**	42.50	27.50
	Cut cancel				7.00
	Perf. initial				3.00
RD366	ST1	10c	**bright green**	45.00	27.50
	Cut cancel				7.00
	Perf. initial				3.00
RD367	ST1	20c	**bright green**	400.00	—
	Cut cancel				—
	Perf. initial				—
RD368	ST1	25c	**bright green**	550.00	—
	Cut cancel				—
	Perf. initial				—
RD369	ST1	40c	**bright green**	140.00	55.00
	Cut cancel				18.00
	Perf. initial				12.00
RD370	ST2	$4	**bright green**	*1,500.*	1,250.
	Perf. initial				—
RD371	ST2	$10	**bright green**	*3,500.*	—
	Cut cancel				—
	Perf. initial				—
RD372	ST2	$20	**bright green**	*6,000.*	—
	Cut cancel				—
	Perf. initial				—

Stock Transfer Stamps were discontinued in 1952.

CORDIALS, WINES, ETC. STAMPS

RE1

Inscribed "Series of 1914"

1914 Wmk. 190 Offset Printing *Perf. 10*

No.	Type	Denom.	Color	Unused	Used
RE1	RE1	¼c	**green**	1.25	.60
RE2	RE1	½c	**green**	.60	.55
RE3	RE1	1c	**green**	.65	.35
RE4	RE1	1½c	**green**	3.25	1.90
RE5	RE1	2c	**green**	5.25	4.25
RE6	RE1	3c	**green**	4.25	1.60
RE7	RE1	4c	**green**	3.25	1.90
RE8	RE1	5c	**green**	1.75	1.00
RE9	RE1	6c	**green**	9.50	4.00
a.	Double impression				—
RE10	RE1	8c	**green**	7.25	1.90
RE11	RE1	10c	**green**	4.50	3.75
RE12	RE1	20c	**green**	6.00	2.40
RE13	RE1	24c	**green**	19.00	10.00
RE14	RE1	40c	**green**	4.50	.90

RE1a

Without Gum *Imperf.*

No.	Type	Denom.	Color	Unused	Used
RE15	RE1a	$2	**green**	12.50	.25
a.	Double impression				175.00

1914 Wmk. 191R *Perf. 10*

No.	Type	Denom.	Color	Unused	Used
RE16	RE1	¼c	**green**	8.50	6.50
RE17	RE1	½c	**green**	7.50	4.00
RE18	RE1	1c	**green**	.30	.25
RE19	RE1	1½c	**green**	110.00	60.00
RE20	RE1	2c	**green**	.30	.25
a.	Double impression				—
RE21	RE1	3c	**green**	3.75	2.50
RE22	RE1	4c	**green**	1.25	1.10
RE23	RE1	5c	**green**	20.00	13.00
a.	Double impression				—
RE24	RE1	6c	**green**	.90	.40
RE25	RE1	8c	**green**	2.75	.65
RE26	RE1	10c	**green**	.90	.35
RE27	RE1	20c	**green**	1.10	.55
RE28	RE1	24c	**green**	17.50	1.00
RE29	RE1	40c	**green**	45.00	14.00

Imperf

Without Gum

No.	Type	Denom.	Color	Unused	Used
RE30	RE1a	$2	**green**	65.00	3.75

Perf. 11

No.	Type	Denom.	Color	Unused	Used
RE31	RE1	2c	**green**	160.00	140.00

WINE STAMPS

Issued Without Gum

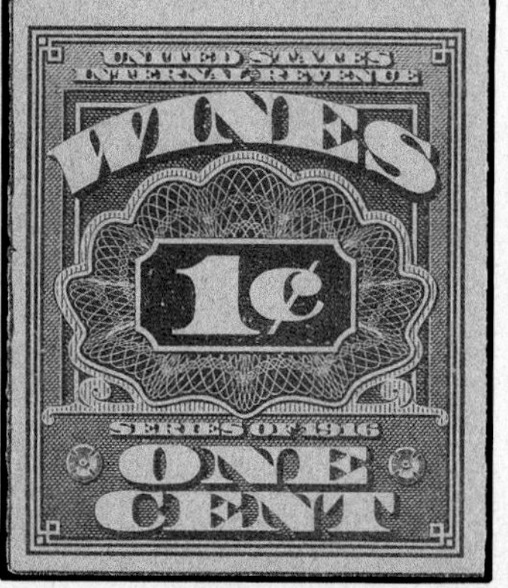

RE2

Inscribed: "Series of 1916"

1916 Wmk. 191R Offset Printing *Rouletted 3½*

Plates of 100 subjects

No.	Type	Denom.	Color	Unused	Used
RE32	RE2	1c	**green**	.50	.45
a.	Double impression			200.00	
RE33	RE2	3c	**green**	6.50	5.25
RE34	RE2	4c	**green**	.40	.50
a.	Double impression				—
RE35	RE2	6c	**green**	2.75	1.10
RE36	RE2	7½c	**green**	7.75	4.25
RE37	RE2	10c	**green**	1.50	.45
RE38	RE2	12c	**green**	5.25	4.75
RE39	RE2	15c	**green**	1.75	1.90
RE40	RE2	18c	**green**	30.00	32.50
RE41	RE2	20c	**green**	.35	.30
RE42	RE2	24c	**green**	6.00	4.00
a.	Double impression			200.00	
RE43	RE2	30c	**green**	3.50	3.75
a.	Double impression				—
RE44	RE2	36c	**green**	30.00	18.00
RE45	RE2	50c	**green**	1.00	.50

RE46	RE2	60c	**green**	7.00	3.00
RE47	RE2	72c	**green**	40.00	37.50
RE48	RE2	80c	**green**	1.50	.90
RE49	RE2	$1.20	**green**	9.00	7.25
RE50	RE2	$1.44	**green**	13.00	3.75
RE51	RE2	$1.60	**green**	35.00	30.00
RE52	RE2	$2	**green**	1.75	1.60

For rouletted 7 see Nos. RE60-RE80, RE102-RE105.

RE3

Engr.

Plates of 50 subjects

RE53	RE3	$4	**green**	1.10	.30
RE54	RE3	$4.80	**green**	4.50	4.00
RE55	RE3	$9.60	**green**	1.60	.45

Nos. RE32-RE55 exist in many shades. Size variations of 1c-$2 are believed due to offset printing. For rouletted 7 see Nos. RE81-RE83, RE106-RE107.

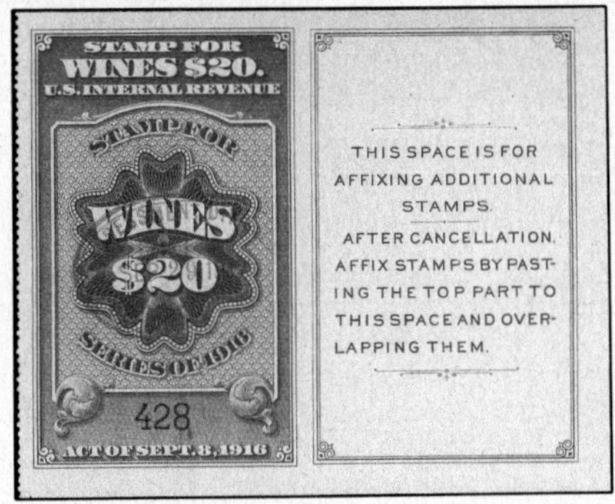

RE4

Illustration reduced.

Plates of 6 subjects

Perf. 12 at left

RE56	RE4	$20	**green**	150.00	60.00
RE57	RE4	$40	**green**	325.00	70.00
RE58	RE4	$50	**green**	100.00	57.50
RE59	RE4	$100	**green**	400.00	225.00

Stamps of design RE4 have an adjoining tablet at right for affixing additional stamps. Values are for examples with the tablets attached. Examples with the tablets removed sell for much less. Used stamps with additional stamps have been recorded on the $20 and sell for about three times the value given; the $50 has also been recorded with additional stamps and these sell for about ten or more times the value given. See Nos. RE107A-RE107D.

Same designs as Issue of 1916

1933 Wmk. 191R Offset Printing *Rouletted 7*

RE60	RE2	1c	**light green**	3.25	.50
a.	Double impression				—
RE61	RE2	3c	**light green**	7.50	2.75
RE62	RE2	4c	**light green**	2.25	.55
RE63	RE2	6c	**light green**	13.00	7.50
RE64	RE2	7½c	**light green**	6.75	1.40
RE65	RE2	10c	**light green**	2.75	.25
a.	Double impression				—
RE66	RE2	12c	**light green**	13.00	6.00
RE67	RE2	15c	**light green**	5.00	.40
RE69	RE2	20c	**light green**	7.50	.25
a.	Double impression				—
RE70	RE2	24c	**light green**	5.75	.25
a.	Double impression			—	*160.00*
RE71	RE2	30c	**light green**	6.00	.25
a.	Double impression				—
RE72	RE2	36c	**light green**	14.00	1.25
RE73	RE2	50c	**light green**	4.75	.30
RE74	RE2	60c	**light green**	10.00	.25
RE75	RE2	72c	**light green**	17.50	.40
RE76	RE2	80c	**light green**	17.50	.40
RE77	RE2	$1.20	**light green**	17.00	1.75
RE78	RE2	$1.44	**light green**	35.00	5.25
RE79	RE2	$1.60	**light green**	—	275.00
RE80	RE2	$2	**light green**	40.00	4.50

Engr.

RE81	RE3	$4	**light green**	50.00	8.75
RE82	RE3	$4.80	**light green**	55.00	17.50
RE83	RE3	$9.60	**light green**	210.00	100.00

RE5

Inscribed: "Series of 1934"

Plates of 200 and 224 subjects

Offset Printing

1934-40 Wmk. 191R *Rouletted 7*

Issued With and Without Gum

RE83A	RE5	⅕c	**green** ('40)	.75	.25
RE84	RE5	½c	**green**	.55	.65
RE85	RE5	1c	**green**	.70	.25
RE86	RE5	1¼c	**green**	1.10	1.00
RE87	RE5	1½c	**green**	7.50	*8.75*
RE88	RE5	2c	**green**	2.25	1.00
RE89	RE5	2½c	**green**	2.00	.70
RE90	RE5	3c	**green**	5.25	4.25
RE91	RE5	4c	**green**	3.00	.30
RE92	RE5	5c	**green**	.70	.25
RE93	RE5	6c	**green**	2.00	.60
RE94	RE5	7½c	**green**	3.25	.25
RE95	RE5	10c	**green**	.50	.70
RE96	RE5	12c	**green**	2.10	.25
RE96A	RE5	14⅖c	**green** ('40)	230.00	3.50
b.	Imperf, pair, without gum			*5,000.*	
RE97	RE5	15c	**green**	.90	.25
RE98	RE5	18c	**green**	1.75	.25
RE99	RE5	20c	**green**	1.40	.25
RE100	RE5	24c	**green**	2.75	.25
RE101	RE5	30c	**green**	2.00	.25

Nos. RE83A-RE101 unused are valued without gum. Examples with gum sell for substantially more.

Nos. RE83A, RE86, RE96A were printed from plates of 200 only and all were issued without gum.

No. RE96Ab was printed but not delivered to the Internal Revenue Service for use.

Plates of 100 subjects

Issued Without Gum

RE102	RE2	40c	**green**	4.75	.25
RE102A	RE2	43⅕c	**green** ('40)	35.00	2.75
RE103	RE2	48c	**green**	45.00	4.00
RE104	RE2	$1	**green**	29.00	11.50
RE105	RE2	$1.50	**green**	45.00	17.00
	Perforated initials				5.75

Engr.

Plates of 50 subjects.

RE106	RE3	$2.50	**green**	52.50	18.00
	Perforated initials				9.00
RE107	RE3	$5	**green**	45.00	7.50
	Perforated initials				3.25

Stamps of types RE5 and RE2 overprinted "Rectified Spirits / Puerto Rico" are listed under Puerto Rico.

Nos. RE102-RE204 issued without gum.

Inscribed: "Series of 1916"

Plates of 6 subjects

1934 *Perf. 12 at left*

RE107A	RE4	$20	**yellow green**		2,500.
RE107B	RE4	$40	**yellow green**		*12,000.*

Perf. 12 At Left

RE107C	RE4	$50	**yellow green**		*10,000.*
RE107D	RE4	$100	**yellow green**		*1,000.*

Perf. 12½ At Left

RE107E	RE4	$50	**yellow green**	—	*5,000.*
RE107F	RE4	$100	**yellow green**	*1,750.*	500.00

The serial numbers of Nos. RE107A-RE107F are much thinner than on Nos. RE56-RE59. Only No. RE107F has been recorded used with additional examples of No. RE107F and these sell for three times the value given. See valuing note after No. RE59.

RE6

Offset Printing

Inscribed "Series of 1941"

1942 Wmk. 191R *Rouletted 7*

RE108	RE6	⅕c	**green & black**	.35	*.55*
RE109	RE6	¼c	**green & black**	.90	*2.50*
RE110	RE6	½c	**green & black**	1.10	*2.10*
a.	Horiz. pair, imperf. vertically			200.00	
RE111	RE6	1c	**green & black**	.45	*1.25*
RE112	RE6	2c	**green & black**	2.25	*5.25*
RE113	RE6	3c	**green & black**	2.25	*4.50*
RE114	RE6	3½c	**green & black**	—	*17,500.*
RE115	RE6	3¾c	**green & black**	4.25	*7.25*
RE116	RE6	4c	**green & black**	1.00	*3.25*
RE117	RE6	5c	**green & black**	1.25	*2.40*
RE118	RE6	6c	**green & black**	1.50	*2.75*
RE119	RE6	7c	**green & black**	2.75	*5.50*
RE120	RE6	7½c	**green & black**	4.00	*6.00*
RE121	RE6	8c	**green & black**	2.00	*4.25*
RE122	RE6	9c	**green & black**	6.00	*9.50*
RE123	RE6	10c	**green & black**	2.00	1.10
RE124	RE6	11¼c	**green & black**	2.25	*6.00*
RE125	RE6	12c	**green & black**	3.00	*6.00*
RE126	RE6	14c	**green & black**	15.00	*26.00*
RE127	RE6	15c	**green & black**	2.25	*3.00*
a.	Horiz. pair, imperf. vertically				*1,500.*
RE128	RE6	16c	**green & black**	5.00	*9.00*
RE129	RE6	19⅕c	**green & black**	250.00	7.75
RE130	RE6	20c	**green & black**	2.75	2.10
RE131	RE6	24c	**green & black**	2.00	.25
RE132	RE6	28c	**green & black**	*5,000.*	*2,500.*
RE133	RE6	30c	**green & black**	.55	.25
RE134	RE6	32c	**green & black**	210.00	7.50
RE135	RE6	36c	**green & black**	1.25	.25
RE136	RE6	40c	**green & black**	1.00	.25
RE137	RE6	45c	**green & black**	3.25	.25
RE138	RE6	48c	**green & black**	8.00	9.25
RE139	RE6	50c	**green & black**	3.50	7.50
RE140	RE6	60c	**green & black**	1.60	.25
RE141	RE6	72c	**green & black**	4.75	1.50
RE142	RE6	80c	**green & black**	*300.00*	10.50
RE143	RE6	84c	**green & black**	—	90.00
RE144	RE6	90c	**green & black**	9.00	.25
RE145	RE6	96c	**green & black**	5.50	.30

See Nos. RE182D-RE194.

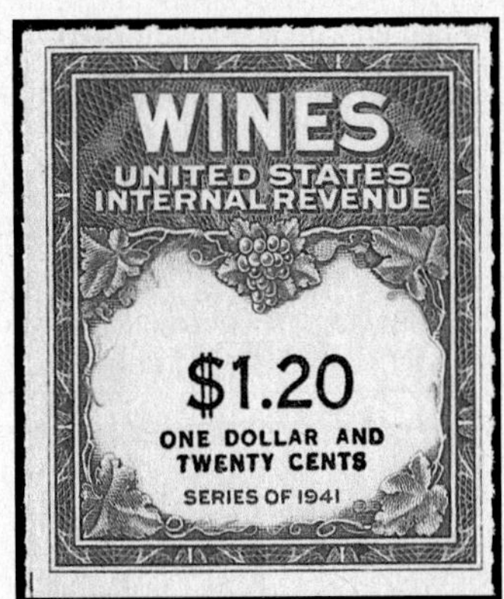

Denomination Spelled Out in Two Lines — RE7

1942 Engraved, Offset (denominations)

RE146	RE7	$1.20	**yel grn & blk**	3.50	.25
RE147	RE7	$1.44	**yel grn & blk**	.70	.30
a.	Denomination missing (FO)			*2,750.*	*2,750.*
	Pair, one with denomination missing (FO)			—	—
b.	First line small letters, second line larger letters			3,000.	*4,500.*
RE148	RE7	$1.50	**yel grn & blk**	150.00	67.50
RE149	RE7	$1.60	**yel grn & blk**	3.50	1.40
RE150	RE7	$1.68	**yel grn & blk**	120.00	50.00
	Perforated initials				35.00
RE151	RE7	$1.80	**yel grn & blk**	1.00	.25
a.	Pair, one with denomination missing (FO)			*5,000.*	

No. RE151a may be collected as a vertical pair or a horizontal pair.

RE152	RE7	$1.92	**yel grn & blk**	35.00	*72.50*
RE153	RE7	$2.40	**yel grn & blk**	4.75	1.25
RE154	RE7	$3	**yel grn & blk**	35.00	*42.50*
RE155	RE7	$3.36	**yel grn & blk**	92.50	29.00
RE156	RE7	$3.60	**yel grn & blk**	*200.00*	10.00
RE157	RE7	$4	**yel grn & blk**	32.50	5.25
RE158	RE7	$4.80	**yel grn & blk**	*175.00*	3.75
RE159	RE7	$5	**yel grn & blk**	17.50	10.50
RE159A	RE7	$7.14	**yel grn & blk**	*150.00*	
RE160	RE7	$7.20	**yel grn & blk**	7.00	.50
RE161	RE7	$10	**yel grn & blk**	240.00	200.00
RE162	RE7	$20	**yel grn & blk**	130.00	77.50
RE163	RE7	$50	**yel grn & blk**	125.00	77.50
	Perforated initials				21.00
RE164	RE7	$100	**yel grn & blk**	375.00	30.00
	Perforated initials				21.00
RE165	RE7	$200	**yel grn & blk**	190.00	24.00
	Perforated initials				8.75
RE165A	RE7	$300	**yel grn & blk**	*150.00*	
RE165B	RE7	$400	**yel grn & blk**	*8,000.*	*22,500.*
RE166	RE7	$500	**yel grn & blk**	*250.00*	150.00
	Perforated initials				35.00
RE167	RE7	$600	**yel grn & blk**	*200.00*	125.00
RE167A	RE7	$700	**yel grn & blk**	*150.00*	
RE167B	RE7	$800	**yel grn & blk**	*150.00*	

RE168 RE7 $900 **yel grn & blk** *2,500.* *4,000.*
Perforated initials *1,500.*
RE169 RE7 $1,000 **yel grn & blk** *250.00* 250.00
RE170 RE7 $2,000 **yel grn & blk** *3,000.* *3,000.*
RE171 RE7 $3,000 **yel grn & blk** 200.00 *225.00*
RE172 RE7 $4,000 **yel grn & blk** *1,000.* 1,000.

Denomination Repeated, Spelled Out in One Line

1949

RE173 RE7 $1 **yellow green & black** 1.75 1.60
RE174 RE7 $2 **yellow green & black** 3.75 2.10
RE175 RE7 $4 **yellow green & black** 1,000. 600.00
Perforated initials 175.00
RE176 RE7 $5 **yellow green & black** *100.00* 82.50
RE177 RE7 $6 **yellow green & black** 700.00 700.00
RE178 RE7 $7 **yellow green & black** *100.00* 47.50
RE179 RE7 $8 **yellow green & black** 1,250. 600.00
Perforated initials 85.00
RE179A RE7 $9 **yel grn & blk** *150.00*
RE180 RE7 $10 **yellow green & black** 4.00 *5.25*
Perforated initials 2.10
RE180A RE7 $12 **yel grn & blk** *150.00*
RE181 RE7 $20 **yellow green & black** 25.00 5.25
Perforated initials 1.90
RE182 RE7 $30 **yellow green & black** *2,000.* 1,250.
RE182A RE7 $40 **yel grn & blk** *150.00*
RE182B RE7 $60 **yel grn & blk** *150.00*
RE182C RE7 $70 **yel grn & blk** *150.00*
RE182D RE7 $80 **yel grn & blk** *150.00*
RE182E RE7 $90 **yel grn & blk** *150.00*

The $90 denomination, No. RE182E, was printed but was not delivered to the Internal Revenue Service for use.

Types of 1942-49

1951-54 **Offset Printing**

RE182F RE6 1 7/10c **green & black** *32,500.* *25,000.*
RE183 RE6 3 2/5c **green & black** 20.00 *52.50*
RE183A RE6 6 7/10c **green & black** *150.00*
RE184 RE6 8 ½c **green & black** 6.00 *20.00*
RE184A RE6 10 1/5c **green & black** *150.00*
RE185 RE6 13 2/5c **green & black** 27.50 *82.50*
RE186 RE6 17c **green & black** 6.00 *15.00*
RE187 RE6 20 2/5c **green & black** 110.00 62.50
RE188 RE6 33 ½c **green & black** 35.00 *92.50*
RE189 RE6 38 ¼c **green & black** 150.00 90.00
RE190 RE6 40 4/5c **green & black** 1.40 .80
RE191 RE6 51c **green & black** 1.50 1.40
RE192 RE6 67c **green & black** 4.75 4.25
RE193 RE6 68c **green & black** 1.00 .70
RE194 RE6 80 2/5c **green & black** 175.00 110.00

The 6 7/10c and 10 1/5c denominations, Nos. RE183A and RE184A, were printed but were not delivered to the Internal Revenue Service for use.

Engr.

Denomination Spelled Out in Two Lines in Small Letters

Two types of $1.60 4/5:

I — The "4" slants sharply. Loop of "5" almost closes to form oval. Each numeral 2mm high.

II — The "4" is less slanted. Loop of "5" more open and nearly circular. Each numeral 2 ½mm high.

RE195 RE7 $1.50 ¾ **yel grn & blk** 17.50 *47.50*
RE196 RE7 $1.60 4/5 **yel grn & blk** (I) 1.60 1.00
a. "DOLLLAR" 75.00 25.00
Perforated initials 20.00
b. As "a," horiz. pair, one with denomination missing *6,250.*
c. Type II 1,000. 250.00
d. First line larger letters, second line small letters *15,000.* *5,000.*
RE197 RE7 $1.88 3/10 **yel grn & blk** 240.00 85.00
Perforated initials 35.00

Denomination Spelled Out in Two Lines in Slightly Larger Letters Same as Nos. RE146-RE172

RE198 RE7 $1.60 4/5 **yel grn & blk** (II) 35.00 6.25
b. Type I ('53) 75.00 25.00
RE199 RE7 $2.01 **yel grn & blk** 1.25 1.00
RE200 RE7 $2.68 **yel grn & blk** 1.25 1.40
RE201 RE7 $4.08 **yel grn & blk** 50.00 35.00
RE202 RE7 $5.76 **yel grn & blk** 275.00 225.00
RE203 RE7 $8.16 **yel grn & blk** 6.50 7.00
RE204 RE7 $9.60 **yel grn & blk** *4,500.* *7,500.*

No. RE196d unused is unique.

Wine stamps were discontinued on Dec. 31, 1954.

BEER STAMPS

Basic stamps were printed by the Bureau of Engraving and Printing, unless otherwise noted.

All stamps are imperforate, unless otherwise noted.

Values for Nos. REA1-REA13 are for stamps with small faults, due to the fragile nature of the thin paper. Used values for Nos. REA14-REA199 are for canceled stamps with small faults.

All examples of Nos. REA1-REA13 contain a circular pattern of 31 perforations in the design, 27 or 28 ½mm in diameter, often poorly punched.

Values for cut squares of Nos. REA1-REA13 are for margins clear of the design. Die cut and cut to shape stamps are valued for margins clear to slightly cutting into the design.

Eric Jackson, Michael Aldrich, Henry Tolman II and Thomas W. Priester helped the editors extensively in compiling the listings.

An excellent study of beer stamps by Frank Applegate appeared in *Weekly Philatelic Gossip* from Oct. 1-Nov. 26, 1927.

A List of the Beer Stamps of the United States of America by Ernest R. Vanderhoof appeared in the *American Philatelist* in June 1934. This was reprinted in pamphlet form.

United States Beer Stamps by Thomas W. Priester, published in 1979, comprised an illustrated and priced catalogue, illustrations of all known provisional surcharges, background notes on the stamps and tax laws, and a census of over 27,500 stamps. The catalogue and census sections were updated in the 1990 edition.

Printed by the Treasury Department. Tax rate $1 per barrel (bbl.).

12 ½c = ⅛ barrel
16 2/3c = 1/6 barrel
25c = ¼ barrel
33 1/3c = ⅓ barrel
50c = ½ barrel
$1 = 1 barrel
$2 = 1 hogshead
$5 = 5 barrels
$10 = 10 barrels
$25 = 25 barrels

1866 **Engr.**

REA1 12 ½c **orange** 450. 750.
Cut to shape 125.
a. Die cut 750. 325.
b. Silk paper *2,250.*
REA2 16 2/3c **dark green** 200. 450.
Cut to shape 30.
a. Die cut 85.
REA3 25c **blue** 75. 150.
Cut to shape 25.
a. Die cut 50.
b. Silk paper *4,500.*
Double transfer —

REA4 50c **orange brown** 35. 50.
Printed cancellation, "A.S. 1869" 200.
Cut to shape 10.
a. Die cut 200.
REA5 $1 **black** 500. 275.
Cut to shape 75.
a. Die cut 300.
REA6 $2 **red** 1,500. 1,600.
Cut to shape 200.
a. Die cut 1,000.

Printed by the Treasury Department. See individual rates before No. REA1.

1867 **Engr.**

REA7 12 ½c **orange** *3,250.* 2,000.
Cut to shape 1,000.
a. Die cut 1,000. 1,500.
REA8 16 2/3c **dark green** *3,500.* *2,600.*
Cut to shape 550.
a. Die cut *2,000.*
REA9 25c **blue** 250. 300.
Cut to shape 50.
a. Die cut 450.

REA10 33 1/3c **violet brown** *5,500.*
Cut to shape *2,750.*
b. Silk paper *3,500.*
c. 33 1/3c **ocher red,** cut to shape *3,500.*
d. 33 1/3c **ocher red,** die cut *14,500.*
REA11 50c **orange brown** 75. 125.
Printed cancellation, "A.S. 1869" 425.
Cut to shape 35.
a. Die cut 150.
REA12 $1 **black** 2,500.
Cut to shape 400.
a. Die cut 1,250.
REA13 $2 **red** *4,000.* *1,350.*
Cut to shape 1,250. 500.
a. Die cut *1,500.*

See individual rates before No. REA1.

Silk Paper

1870 **Engr.** **Lilac Security Lines**

REA14 12 ½c **brown** *1,000.* 350.
a. Yellow security lines 2,500. 2,000.

REA15	16⅔c **yellow orange**		450.
	a. Yellow security lines		1,100.
	b. Gray-green and yellow security lines		2,500.
	c. 16⅔c **yellow ocher,** lilac security lines		2,000.
REA16	25c **green**		125.
	a. Yellow security lines		225.
	b. Gray-green & yellow security lines	2,500.	
REA17	50c **red**	400.	125.
	a. Yellow security lines	2,500.	1,250.
	b. Gray-green and yellow security lines	2,250.	2,000.
	c. 50c **brick red,** lilac security lines		1,500.
	d. 50c **brick red,** yellow security lines		3,250.
REA18	$1 **blue**	3,000.	1,500.
	a. Yellow security lines	1,500.	500.
	b. Gray-green and yellow security lines		2,500.
REA19	$2 **black**	2,000.	950.
	a. Yellow security lines		4,500.
	b. Gray-green and yellow security lines		5,000.

The security lines were printed across the center of the stamp where the cancel was to be placed.

Andrew Jackson

Designs: 16⅔c, Abraham Lincoln. 25c, Daniel Webster. 33⅓c, David G. Farragut. 50c, William T. Sherman. $1, Hugh McCulloch. $2, Alexander Hamilton.
Centers printed by the Bureau of Engraving and Printing. Frames printed by the National Bank Co.
See individual rates before No. REA1.

1871 **Engr.**

Centers, Plate Letters and Position Numbers in Black

REA20	12½c **blue,** white silk paper		125.
	a. Pinkish gray silk paper		200.
	b. Gray silk paper		65.
	c. Green silk paper		200.
REA21	16⅔c **vermilion,** white silk paper		400.
	a. Pinkish gray silk paper		500.
	b. Gray silk paper		425.
	c. Green silk paper		425.
REA22	25c **green,** white silk paper		25.
	a. Pinkish gray silk paper		125.
	b. Gray silk paper		50.
	c. Green silk paper		30.
REA23	33⅓c **orange,** green silk paper		4,500.
	b. Gray silk paper		11,000.
REA24	33⅓c **violet brown,** white silk paper		12,500.
REA25	50c **brown,** gray silk paper		20.
	a. Pinkish gray silk paper		60.
	c. Green silk paper		75.
REA26	50c **red,** white silk paper		55.
REA27	$1 **yellow orange,** white silk paper	250.	350.
	a. Pinkish gray silk paper		1,100.
	b. Gray silk paper		150.
REA28	$1 **scarlet,** gray silk paper		200.
	a. Pinkish gray silk paper		800.
	c. Green silk paper	1,500.	500.
REA29	$2 **red brown,** white silk paper		300.
	a. Pinkish gray silk paper		1,900.
	b. Gray silk paper		700.
	c. Green silk paper	2,000.	1,000.

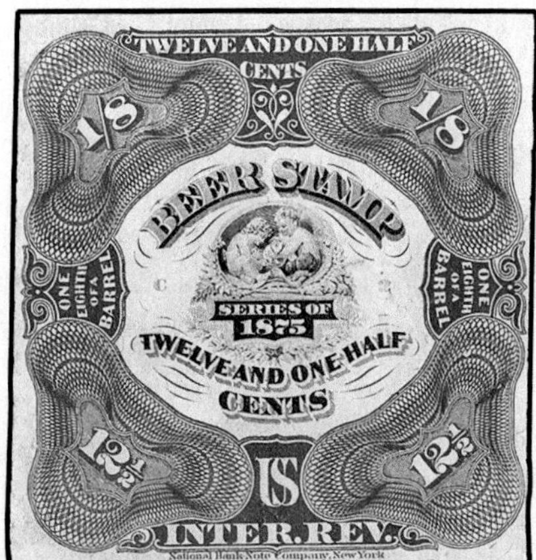

Bacchus Serving the First Fermented Brew to Man

Printed by the National Bank Note Co. See individual rates before No. REA1.

1875 **Typo. & Engr.**

Center in Black

REA30	12½c **blue**		25.00
REA31	16⅔c **red brown**		150.00
REA32	25c **green**		40.00
	a. Inverted center		55,000.
REA33	33⅓c **violet**	3,000.	1,250.
REA34	50c **orange**	100.00	100.00
REA35	$1 **red**	225.00	225.00
REA36	$2 **brown**	1,500.	750.00
	a. Inverted center		55,000.

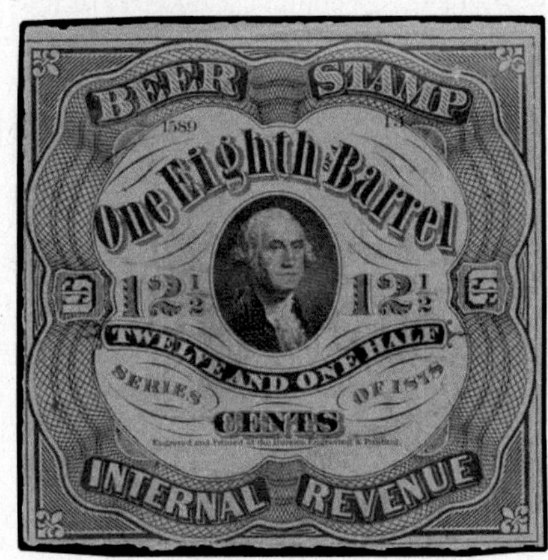

Designs: 12½c, Washington. 16⅔c, Corwin. 25c, Benton. 33⅓c, Thomas. 50c, Jefferson. $1, Johnson. $2, Wright.
Stamps on pale green paper have short greenish blue fibers. Plate designations for center consist of plate letter or number at left and position number at right.
See individual rates before No. REA1.

1878 **Typo. & Engr.** **Wmk. USIR**

Center, Plate Letters and Position Numbers in Black

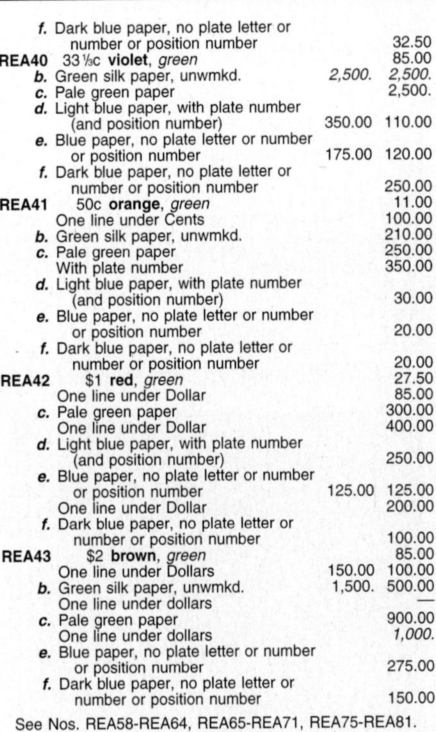

REA37	12½c **blue,** *green*		7.50
	b. Green silk paper, unwmkd.		1,250.
	c. Pale green paper		200.00
	With plate number and position number		1,250.
	d. Light blue paper, with plate number (and position number)		35.00
	e. Blue paper, no plate letter or number or position number		30.00
	f. Dark blue paper, no plate letter or number or position number		50.00
REA38	16⅔c **light brown,** *green*		7.50
	One line under Cents		75.00
	b. Green silk paper, unwmkd., one line under Cents	250.00	140.00
	c. Pale green paper		75.00
	With plate number		750.00
	d. Light blue paper, with plate number (and position number)		40.00
	e. Blue paper, no plate letter or number or position number		150.00
	With plate number 1979		250.00
	f. Dark blue paper, no plate letter or number or position number		75.00
REA39	25c **green,** *green*		5.00
	a. Inverted center		57,500.
	b. Green silk paper, unwmkd.		200.00
	c. Pale green paper		100.00
	With plate number		35.00
	d. Light blue paper, with plate number (and position number)		7.50
	e. Blue paper, no plate letter or number or position number		30.00
	f. Dark blue paper, no plate letter or number or position number		32.50
REA40	33⅓c **violet,** *green*		85.00
	b. Green silk paper, unwmkd.	2,500.	2,500.
	c. Pale green paper		2,500.
	d. Light blue paper, with plate number (and position number)	350.00	110.00
	e. Blue paper, no plate letter or number or position number	175.00	120.00
	f. Dark blue paper, no plate letter or number or position number		250.00
REA41	50c **orange,** *green*		11.00
	One line under Cents		100.00
	b. Green silk paper, unwmkd.		210.00
	c. Pale green paper		250.00
	With plate number		350.00
	d. Light blue paper, with plate number (and position number)		30.00
	e. Blue paper, no plate letter or number or position number		20.00
	f. Dark blue paper, no plate letter or number or position number		20.00
REA42	$1 **red,** *green*		27.50
	One line under Dollar		85.00
	c. Pale green paper		300.00
	One line under Dollar		400.00
	d. Light blue paper, with plate number (and position number)		250.00
	e. Blue paper, no plate letter or number or position number	125.00	125.00
	One line under Dollar		200.00
	f. Dark blue paper, no plate letter or number or position number		100.00
REA43	$2 **brown,** *green*		85.00
	One line under Dollars	150.00	100.00
	b. Green silk paper, unwmkd.	1,500.	500.00
	One line under dollars		—
	c. Pale green paper		900.00
	One line under dollars		1,000.
	e. Blue paper, no plate letter or number or position number		275.00
	f. Dark blue paper, no plate letter or number or position number		150.00

See Nos. REA58-REA64, REA65-REA71, REA75-REA81.

Stamps of 1878 Surcharged in Various Ways

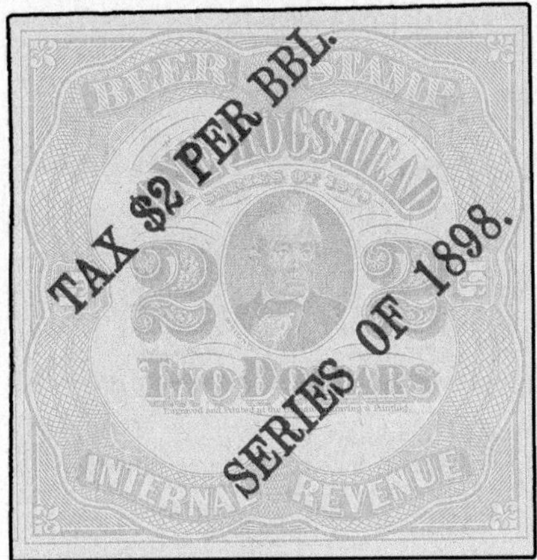

Type B

Four general surcharge types:
A — Bureau of Engraving and Printing surcharge "TAX $2 PER BBL./SERIES OF 1898" printed diagonally in red, letters 4¼mm high.
B — same, but letters 5½mm high.
C — handstamped provisional surcharge with similiar wording in 1-3 lines, more than 30 styles.
D — printed provisional 2-line surcharges, horizontal in various colors.
Tax rate $2 per bbl.

25c = ⅛ barrel	$1 = ½ barrel
33⅓c = ⅙ barrel	$2 = 1 barrel
50c = ¼ barrel	$4 = 1 hogshead
66⅔c = ⅓ barrel	

1898 **Type A**

REA44	(25c) on 12½c #REA37f		400.00
	a. Type C surcharge		325.00
	b. Type D surcharge		1,500.
REA45	(33⅓c) on 16⅔c #REA38e		100.00
	a. on #REA38f		200.00
	b. As "a," type C surcharge		350.00
	c. As "a," type D surcharge	750.00	500.00
	d. on #REA38d		800.00
	e. As "c," double impression of surcharge		—
REA46	(50c) on 25c #REA39f		90.00
	a. Type C surcharge		150.00
	b. Type D surcharge		2,250.
	c. on #REA39e		1,750.
	d. on #REA39, type C surcharge		5,750.
REA47	(66⅔c) on 33⅓c #REA40, plate B		1,500.
REA48	($1) on 50c #REA41f		35.00
	a. Type C surcharge		375.00
	b. Type D surcharge		750.00
REA49	($2) on $1 #REA42f		125.00
	a. Type C surcharge		1,500.
	b. Type D surcharge		1,750.
	c. on #REA42e, type C surcharge		2,250.

REA50	($4) on $2 #REA43f	*1,500.*	500.00
a.	Type C surcharge		700.00
b.	Type D surcharge		*3,000.*
c.	on #REA43e, type C surcharge		*4,000.*

Type B

REA51	(25c) on 12½c #REA37f		95.00
a.	on #REA37e	225.00	225.00
b.	As "a," type C surcharge		*7,250.*
REA52	(33⅓c) on 16⅔c #REA38d	2,000.	1,250.
a.	on #REA38f	*1,100.*	*1,500.*
b.	on #REA38e	*1,100.*	*1,500.*
REA53	(50c) on 25c #REA39f		25.00
a.	on #REA39e		25.00
REA54	(66⅔c) on 33⅓c #REA40f		*9,500.*
a.	Type D surcharge		*9,000.*
b.	On #REA40, plate B, dark blue paper		*6,000.*
REA55	($1) on 50c #REA41f		12.50
REA56	($2) on $1 #REA42f		50.00
REA57	($4) on $2 #REA43f	1,000.	500.00

Counterfeit type C and D overprints exist.

Designs: 25c, Washington. 33⅓c, Corwin. 50c, Benton. 66⅔c, Thomas. $1, Jefferson. $2, Johnson. $4, Wright.
See individual rates before No. REA44.

1898 Typo. & Engr. Wmk. USIR

Center in Black, Dark Blue Paper

REA58	25c **blue**	110.
REA59	33⅓c **brown**	85.
REA60	50c **green**	25.
REA61	66⅔c **violet**	*12,500.*
REA62	$1 **yellow**	20.
REA63	$2 **red**	25.
REA64	$4 **dark brown**	225.

Used values for 1901-51 issues are for stamps canceled by perforated company name (or abbreviation) and date.

Designs: 20c, Washington. 26⅔c, Corwin. 40c, Benton. 53⅓c, Thomas. 80c, Jefferson. $1.60, Johnson. $3.20, Wright.
Tax rate $1.60 per bbl.

20c = ⅛ barrel
26⅔c = ⅙ barrel
40c = ¼ barrel
53⅓c = ⅓ barrel
80c = ½ barrel
$1.60 = 1 barrel
$3.20 = 1 hogshead

Engr. (center) & Typo. (frame)

1901 Wmk. USIR

Dark Blue Paper

REA65	20c **blue**		75.
REA66	26⅔c **yellow orange**		75.
REA67	40c **green**		17.50
REA68	53⅓c **violet**	*8,500.*	*7,000.*
REA69	80c **brown**		17.50
REA70	$1.60 **red**		75.
REA71	$3.20 **dark brown**		1,250.

Stamps of 1901 Provisionally Surcharged by Bureau of Engraving & Printing Diagonally in Red "TAX $1 PER BBL./SERIES OF 1902"

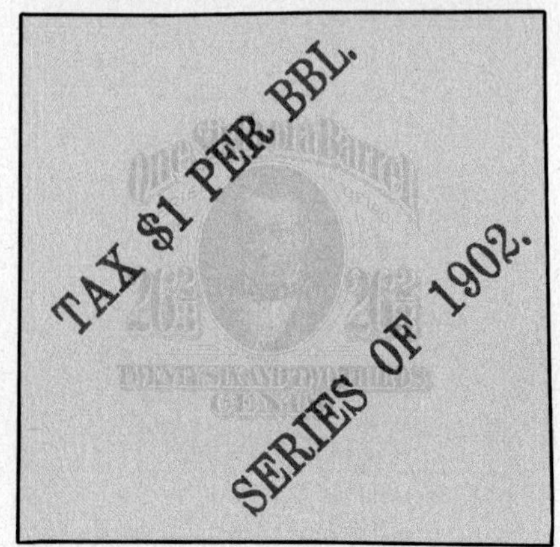

1902

REA72	(16⅔c) on 26⅔c #REA66		150.
REA73	(33⅓c) on 53⅓c #REA68		*5,250.*
REA74	($2) on $3.20 #REA71	*1,500.*	1,000.

Designs: 12½c, Washington. 16⅔c, Corwin. 25c, Benton. 33⅓c, Thomas. 50c, Jefferson. $1, Johnson. $2, Wright.
Stamps on pale green paper have short greenish blue fibers.
See individual rates before No. REA1.

1902 Typo. & Engr. Wmk. USIR

Center in Black

REA75	12½c **blue**		
a.	Dark blue paper		75.00
b.	Pale green paper		350.00
c.	Light blue paper		110.00
d.	Bright blue paper		50.00
REA76	16⅔c **yellow orange**		
a.	Dark blue paper		250.00
b.	Pale green paper		350.00
c.	Light blue paper	225.00	225.00
d.	Bright blue paper		400.00
REA77	25c **green**		
a.	Dark blue paper		25.00
b.	Pale green paper		85.00
c.	Light blue paper		25.00
d.	Bright blue paper		30.00
REA78	33⅓c **violet**		
a.	Dark blue paper		500.00
c.	Light blue paper		750.00
d.	Bright blue paper		1,000.
REA79	50c **brown**		
a.	Dark blue paper		20.00
b.	Pale green paper		30.00
c.	Light blue paper		25.00
d.	Bright blue paper		20.00
REA80	$1 **red**		
a.	Dark blue paper		125.00
b.	Pale green paper	400.00	325.00
c.	Light blue paper		75.00
d.	Bright blue paper		75.00
REA81	$2 **dark brown**		
a.	Dark blue paper		1,250.
b.	Pale green paper		900.00
c.	Light blue paper		575.00
d.	Bright blue paper		725.00

For surcharges see Nos. REA99A, REA100A, REA100Ab, REA141.

In the 1911-33 issues, the 5-25 barrel sizes were generally available only as center cutouts of the stamp. Values for these are for cutout portions that show enough of the denomination (or surcharge) to identify the item.

See individual rates before No. REA1.

1909-11 Engr. Wmk. USIR

Paper of Various Shades of Blue

REA82	12½c **black**		500.00
REA83	16⅔c **black**	200.00	90.00
REA84	25c **black**	550.00	450.00
REA85	33⅓c **black**		*20,000.*
REA86	50c **black**	55.00	6.00
REA87	$1 **black**	1,000.	750.00
REA88	$2 **black**	*10,000.*	*8,000.*

Center Cutout Only

REA89	$5 **black,** *1911*		*150.00*
REA90	$10 **black,** *1911*		*250.00*
REA91	$25 **black,** *1911*		*250.00*

For surcharges see Nos. REA97, REA99-REA100, REA103-REA105, REA128.

1910 Engr. Wmk. USIR

Paper of Various Shades of Blue

REA92	12½c **red brown**	75.00
REA93	25c **green**	10.00
REA94	$1 **carmine**	110.00
REA95	$2 **orange**	125.00

For surcharges see Nos. REA96, REA98, REA101-REA102, REA126.

1914 Provisional Issue

Stamps of of 1902-11 With Printed Provisional BEP Diagonal Surcharge "EMERGENCY/TAX/UNDER ACT OF 1914" in Red, Black or Yellow, or Handstamped Surcharge of Value Spelled Out in Full and Separate "Roscoe Irwin" Handstamped Facsimile Signature

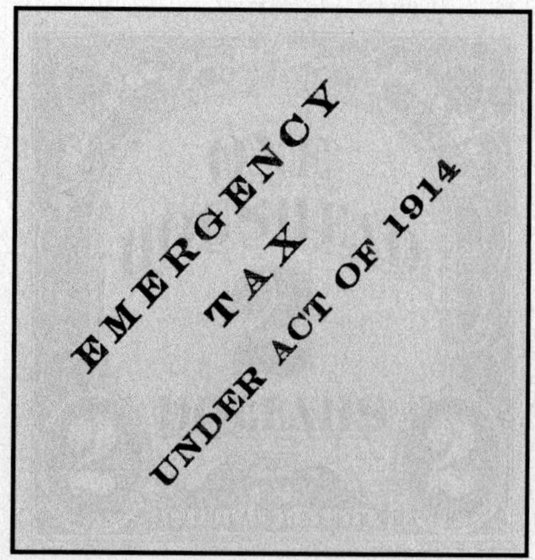

Tax rate $1.50 per bbl.

18¾c = ⅛ barrel		$1.50	= 1 barrel
25c = ⅙ barrel		3	= 1 hogshead
37½c = ¼ barrel		$7.5	= 5 barrels
50c = ⅓ barrel		$15	= 10 barrels
75c = ½ barrel		$37.50	= 25 barrels

1914 **Entire Stamps**

REA96	(18¾c) on 12½ #REA92		65.00
REA97	(25c) on 16⅔c #REA83		60.00
REA98	(37½c) on 25c #REA93		7.50
	a. 37½c handstamped; 50mm signature		750.00
REA99	(50c) on 33⅓c #REA85		225.00
REA99A	(50c) on 33⅓c #REA78d	*1,750.*	900.00
REA100	(75c) on 50c #REA86		7.50
	c. 75c handstamped on #REA86; 50mm signature		175.00
	d. As "c," 65mm signature		350.00
REA100A	(75c) On 50c #REA79c		1,000.
	b. (75c) On 50c #REA79b		*11,500.*
REA101	($1.50) on $1 #REA94		50.00
	a. $1.50 handstamped; 50mm signature		*2,000.*
	b. As "a," 65mm signature		*9,000.*
REA102	($3.00) on $2 #REA95		75.00
	a. $3 handstamped; 76mm signature		*2,750.*

Center Cutout Only

REA103	($7.50) on $5 #REA89		17.50
REA104	($15) on $10 #REA90		160.00
REA105	($37.50) on $25 #REA91		225.00

For surcharges see Nos. REA119, REA123, REA133, REA140, REA140A.

See individual rates before No. REA96.

1914 **Engr.** **Wmk. USIR**

Paper of Various Shades of Blue

Entire Stamp

REA106	18¾c **red brown**		85.00
REA107	25c **black**		175.00
	a. 25c **violet blue**	*3,500.*	*2,500.*
REA108	37½c **green**		17.50
	a. 37½c **black**		*32,500.*
REA108B	50c **black**		—
REA109	75c **black**		6.00
REA110	$1.50 **red orange**		30.00
REA111	$3 **orange**		200.00

Center Cutout Only

REA112	$7.50 **black**		10.00
REA113	$15 **black**		15.00
REA114	$37.50 **black**		7.50

For surcharges see Nos. REA118, REA120, REA120a, REA121, REA124-REA125, REA127, REA129-REA131, REA134, REA134a, REA137, REA144, REA146-REA149.

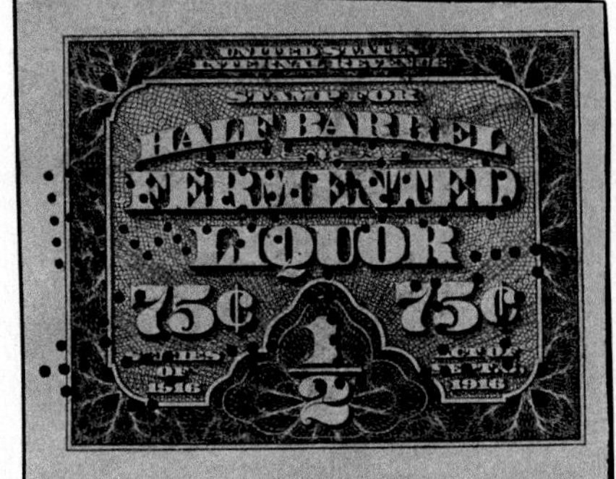

See individual rates before No. REA96.

1916 **Engr.** **Wmk. USIR**

Paper of Various Shades of Greenish Blue

Entire Stamp

REA115	37½c **green**		110.00
REA116	75c **black**		45.00

For surcharges see Nos. REA122, REA124, REA138. Surcharge also exists in manuscript on No. REA115.

Stamps of 1914-16 Provisionally Surcharged Types A, B & C

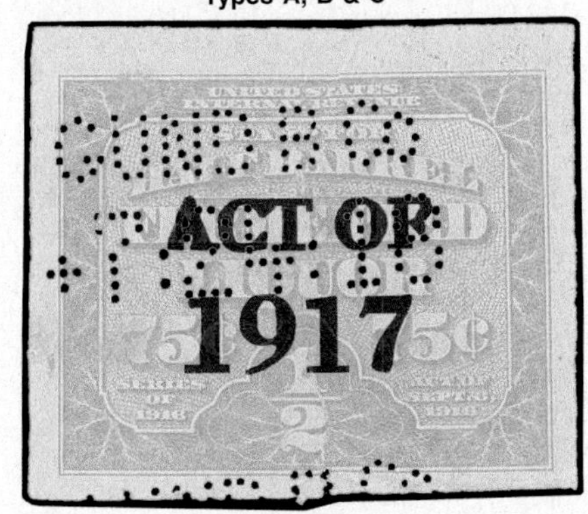

Type C

Surcharge types:

A — "ACT OF 1917" handstamped in 1-3 lines in more than 30 styles.

B — "ACT OF 1917" locally printed horizontally in black or red.

C — "ACT OF 1917" printed in black or red by BEP, horizontally on ⅛ bbl-1 hhd and reading down on 5-25 bbl.

Surcharge also exists in manuscript on some values. Tax rate $3 per bbl.

37½c = ⅛ barrel	$3 = 1 barrel
50c = ⅙ barrel	$6 = 1 hogshead
75c = ¼ barrel	$15 = 5 barrels
$1 = ⅓ barrel	$30 = 10 barrels
$1.50 = ½ barrel	$75 = 25 barrels

1917 **Type A Surcharge**

Entire Stamp

REA117	(37½c) on #REA96		*27,500.*
REA118	(37½c) on #REA106		325.00
	b. Type B surcharge		*15,000.*
	c. Type C surcharge	500.00	500.00
	d. As No. REA118, double surcharge		—
REA119	(50c) on #REA97		150.00
REA120	(50c) on #REA107a	1,000.	600.00
	a. On #REA107	500.00	500.00
REA120B	(75c) on #REA98		*25,000.*
REA121	(75c) on #REA108		140.00
REA122	(75c) on #REA115		60.00
	b. Type B surcharge		10,000.
	c. Type C surcharge		100.00
REA123	($1) on #REA99		175.00
REA124	($1.50) on #REA116		75.00
	b. Type B surcharge		*10,000.*
	c. Type C surcharge	45.00	7.50
	d. As "c," inverted surcharge	1,750.	
	e. As No. REA124, double surcharge		—

$1.50 surcharge exists in manuscript on No. REA109. Value, $1,250.

REA125	($3) on #REA110	100.00	100.00
	c. Type C surcharge		40.00
REA126	($6) on #REA102		*5,000.*
REA127	($6) on #REA111	1,000.	500.00

Center Cutout Only

REA128	($15) on #REA103		500.00
REA129	($15) on #REA112, entire stamp, type C surcharge	6,000.	
REA130	($30) on #REA113		100.00
	c. Type C surcharge		45.00
REA131	($75) on #REA114		225.00
	c. Type C surcharge		12.50

For surcharges see Nos. REA132, REA132a, REA135-REA136, REA139-REA139b, REA142-REA143, REA145, REA150-REA151.

Stamps of 1914-17 Provisionally Surcharged "ACT OF 1918" or "Revenue Act of 1918" With Rubber Stamp in Various Colors in More Than 20 Styles

A subtype has the incorrect date of 1919 due to the effective date of the act (at least five styles).

Tax rate $6 per bbl.

75c = ⅛ barrel	$6 = 1 barrel
$1 = ⅙ barrel	$12 = 1 hogshead
$1.50 = ¼ barrel	$30 = 5 barrels
$2 = ⅓ barrel	$60 = 10 barrels
$3 = ½ barrel	$150 = 25 barrels

1918 **Entire Stamp**

REA132	(75c) on #REA118	900.	600.
	a. On #REA118c	1,000.	1,750.
REA133	($1) on #REA97	*3,500.*	*3,000.*
REA134	($1) on #REA107	2,500.	
	a. On #REA107a	10,000.	

Exists with additional overprint "Non-Intoxicating, containing not to/exceed 2¾% of Alcohol by weight." Value, *$1,750.*

REA135	($1) on #REA119	8,000.	
REA136	($1) on #REA120		*2,500.*
REA137	($1.50) on #REA108	*2,000.*	1,100.
	a. Surcharge dated "1919"		3,500.
REA138	($1.50) on #REA115	*3,000.*	1,250.
REA139	($1.50) on #REA122c		75.
	a. Surcharge dated "1919"	350.	60.
	b. On #REA122	1,600.	1,600.
REA140	($2) on #REA99	2,000.	1,250.
REA140A	($2) on #REA99A	1,500.	
REA141	($2) on #REA99A	*5,000.*	*5,000.*

No. REA141 bears additional 1917 provisional surcharge, as well as the 1914 surcharge, but was not issued in that form without 1918 surcharge.

REA142	($2) on #REA123	*27,500.*	
REA143	($3) on #REA124c	175.	75.
	a. Surcharge dated "1919"	750.	600.
REA144	($6) on #REA110	*2,000.*	1,000.
REA145	($6) on #REA125c		50.
	a. Surcharge dated "1919"	750.	500.
REA146	($12) on #REA111	*2,000.*	1,000.
REA147	($12) on #REA111		75.

No. REA147 bears additional 1917 Type C provisional surcharge but was not issued in that form without 1918 surcharge.

Center Cutout Only

REA148	($30) on #REA112		85.
REA149	($60) on #REA113		85.
REA150	($60) on #REA130c		350.
	a. Entire stamp	5,000.	
REA151	($150) on #REA131c		45.
	a. Entire stamp	8,000.	

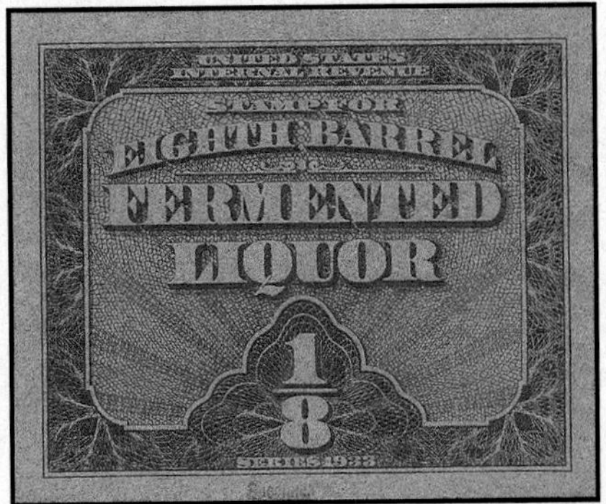

REA152-REA158

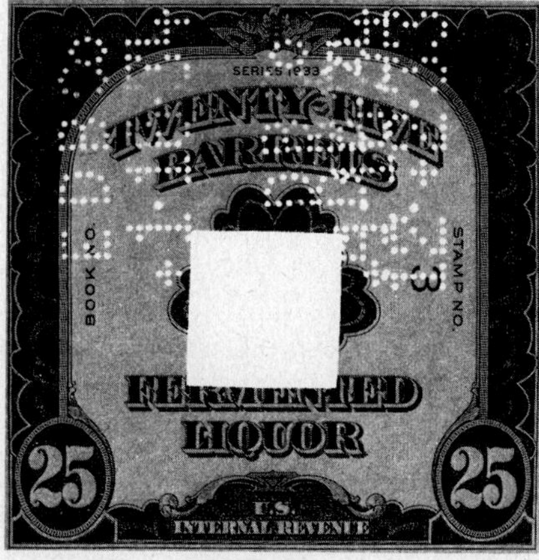

REA159-REA161

Tax rate $5 per barrel through Jan. 11, 1934. $6 rate also effective Dec. 5, 1933. Provisional handstamp "Surcharged $6.00 Rate" in 1-3 lines (seven styles).

Type A
Entire Stamp

1933 Engr. Wmk. USIR

Paper of Various Shades of Greenish Blue to Blue

REA152	⅛ bbl., **violet red**		17.50
a.	Provisional surcharge, $6 rate		4,500.
REA153	⅙ bbl., **purple**		700.00
REA154	¼ bbl., **green**		8.00
a.	Provisional surcharge, $6 rate		—
REA155	⅓ bbl., **brown orange**		2,750.
REA156	½ bbl., **orange**	70.00	5.00
a.	Provisional surcharge, $6 rate		*1,750.*
REA157	1 bbl., **blue**		25.00
a.	Provisional surcharge, $6 rate		*3,000.*
REA158	1 hhd., **black**		*9,000.*
REA159	5 bbl., **black,** center cut-out only		250.00
REA160	10 bbl., **black**, with cut-out center, rouletted 7 at left		*7,500.*
a.	Center cutout only		250.00
REA161	25 bbl., **black**, with cut-out center, rouletted 7 at left		7,500.
a.	Center cutout only		250.00

Center cutout portions of Nos. REA159-REA161 are on greenish blue paper. See Nos. REA177-REA178A for examples on bright blue paper.

Nos. REA152-REA159, REA161 Surcharged in Black

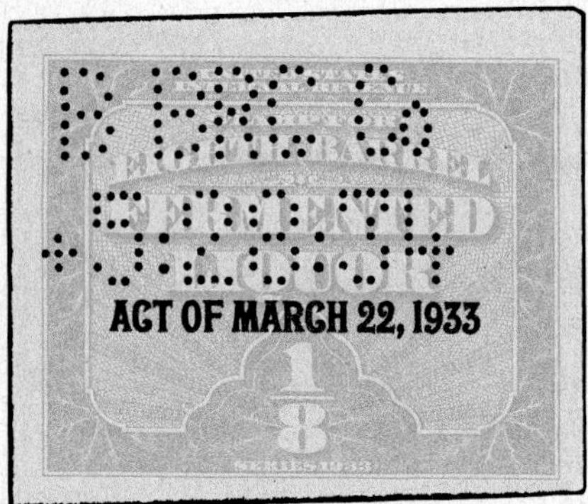

Type B

A — additional provisional handstamped surcharge.
B — additional manuscript and handstamped surcharges.
Tax rate same as Nos. REA152-REA161.

1933 Engr. Wmk. USIR

Entire Stamp

REA162	⅛ bbl., **violet red**		10.00
REA163	⅙ bbl., **purple**		175.00
REA164	¼ bbl., **green**		15.00
a.	With 1918 provisional handstamped surcharge, $6 rate		*2,250.*
b.	Type A surcharge, $6 rate		*4,500.*
REA165	⅓ bbl., **brown orange**		*6,000.*
REA166	½ bbl., **orange**		15.00
a.	Type A surcharge, $6 rate		*3,250.*
b.	Type B surcharge, $6 rate		*5,000.*
REA167	1 bbl., **blue**		25.00
REA168	1 hhd., **black**		*11,000.*
REA169	5 bbl., **black**		*4,500.*
a.	Center cutout only		500.00
REA170	25 bbl., **black,** center cutout only		450.00

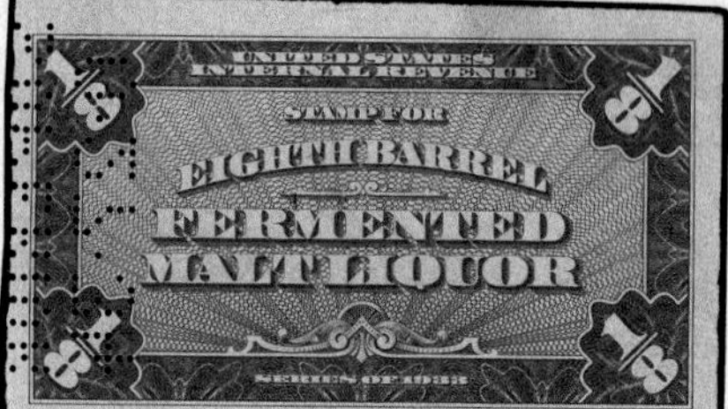

REA171-REA176

REA177-REA178A

Tax rate same as previous issue. Provisional handstamp reads "SOLD AT $5.00 RATE" or "$5.00 RATE."

1933 Engr. Wmk. USIR

Entire Stamp

REA171	⅛ bbl., **violet red**		35.00
REA172	⅙ bbl., **purple**		500.00
REA173	¼ bbl., **green**	75.00	8.00
a.	Provisional surcharge, $5 rate		*17,500.*
REA174	½ bbl., **brown orange**	100.00	5.00
a.	Provisional surcharge, $5 rate		*1,500.*
REA175	1 bbl., **blue**		110.00
REA176	1 hhd., **black**		*9,000.*

Bright Blue Paper

REA177	5 bbl., **black**		*2,000.*
a.	Entire stamp with cut-out center		7.50
b.	Center cutout only		1.00
REA178	10 bbl., **black**	800.00	500.00
b.	Entire stamp with cut-out center		10.00
c.	Center cutout only		1.00
REA178A	25 bbl., **black**		500.00
b.	Entire stamp with cut-out center		4.50
c.	Center cutout only		1.00
d.	Rouletted 7 at left		—

For surcharge see Nos. REA180B, REA199.

Nos. REA173-REA174 with BEP Printed Surcharge, "Act of March 22, 1933"

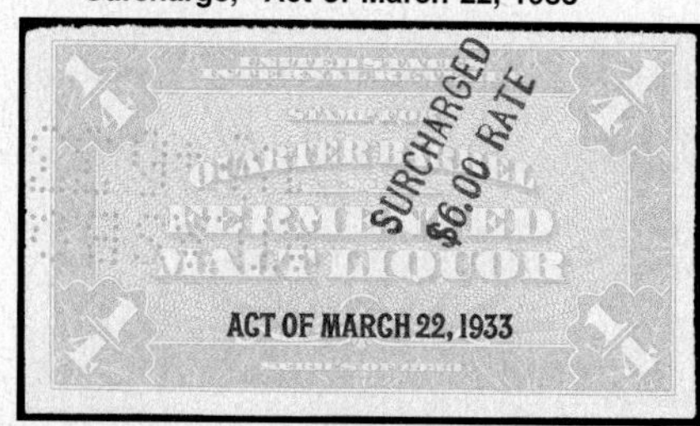

Additional provisional handstamped surcharge, $6 rate as previous issue.

1933-40 Entire Stamp

REA179	¼ bbl., **green**		27.50
a.	Handstamped "Surcharged $6 rate," *1940*		2,750.
REA180	½ bbl., **brown orange**		12.50
a.	Handstamped "Surcharged $6 rate," *1940*		3,250.

No. REA178 with handstamp surcharge, "Value increased under Revenue Act of 1940."

1940 Entire Stamp

REA180B	10 bbl., **black**		—

REA181-REA187

REA188-REA189

Tax rates $5 per bbl; $6 from July 1, 1940; $7 from Nov. 1, 1942; $8 from Apr. 1, 1944.

1934-45 Engr. Wmk. USIR

With Black Control Numbers

REA181	⅛ bbl., **violet red**	140.00	7.50
a.	With cutout center		2.00
b.	Ovptd. "NOT LESS THAN 3⅝ GALLONS," uncut		—
REA182	⅙ bbl., **purple**		150.00
a.	With cutout center		100.00
b.	Ovptd. "NOT LESS THAN 4⅚ GALLONS," uncut		—
REA183	¼ bbl., **green**		4.00
a.	With cutout center		2.50
b.	Ovptd. "NOT LESS THAN 7¼ GALLONS," uncut		—
REA184	⅓ bbl., **brown orange**	—	*25,000.*
REA185	½ bbl., **orange**		3.00
a.	With cutout center		2.00
REA186	1 bbl., **blue**		7.50
a.	With cutout center		7.50
REA187	1 hhd., **black**, with cutout center	—	500.00
REA188	100 bbl., **carmine**, *1942*		200.00
a.	With cutout center		10.00
REA189	500 bbl., **dark brown**, with cut-out center, *1945*		500.00

Most values also exist as center cutout portions only.

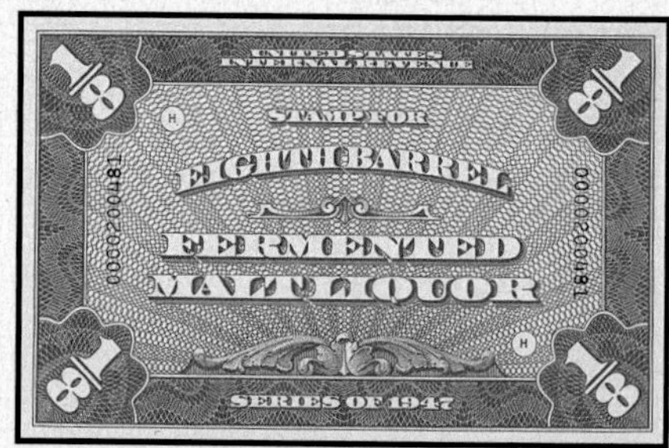

REA190-REA193

REA194-REA198

Tax rates $8 per bbl, $9 from Nov. 1, 1951.

1947	Black Control Numbers		Litho.
REA190	⅛ bbl., **carmine**	125.00	60.00
a.	With cutout center		15.00
REA190B	⅛ bbl., **purple**	225.00	
REA191	¼ bbl., **green**	100.00	20.00
a.	With cutout center		22.50
REA192	½ bbl., **orange**	30.00	10.00
a.	With cutout center		12.50
REA193	1 bbl., **blue**	100.00	150.00
a.	With cutout center		15.00

Blue Paper

REA194	5 bbl., **black**	80.00	200.00
a.	With cutout center		12.50
REA195	10 bbl., **black**	125.00	300.00
a.	With cutout center		27.50
REA196	25 bbl., **black**	*1,100.*	*3,200.*
a.	With cutout center		*3,000.*

White Paper

REA197	100 bbl., **carmine**	125.00	250.00
a.	With cutout center		10.00
REA198	500 bbl., **dark brown**	550.00	600.00
a.	With cutout center		60.00

All values except No. REA190B also exist as center cutouts only.

No. REA190B was not officially issued.

No. REA178A Provisionally Handstamp Surcharged in Black or Purple

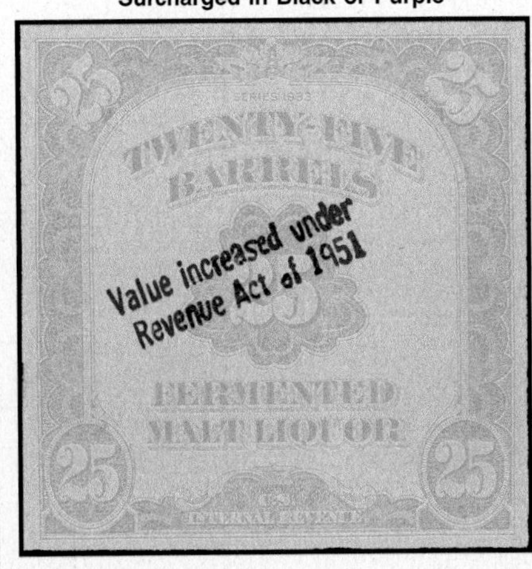

Tax rate $9 per bbl.

1951

REA199 ($225) on 25 bbl., #REA178A, uncut *25,000.*

Also exists as center cutout only, showing portion of handstamped surcharge. Value, $150.

FERMENTED FRUIT JUICE STAMPS

Fermented fruit juice stamps were issued pending the ratification of the Repeal Amendment (Dec. 5, 1933) that made full-strength beer and wine legal again.

Congress, as a temporary measure, redefined intoxicating beverages by changing the legal definition from .5% to 3.2%, thus permitting the sale of 3.2 beer and wine beginning in early May 1933.

Regular wine stamps were available to pay the Internal Revenue taxes. However, these Fermented Fruit Juice stamps were authorized for placement on individual bottles or containers of fermented fruit juice. Use was discontinued Dec. 4, 1933.

Stamps are valued in the grade of very fine. Most stamps are found in average to fine condition. Unused stamps are valued with original gum.

REF1

Plates of 220 subjects in two panes of 110.

1933	Wmk. USIR		Engr.	*Perf. 11*
REF1	REF1	4 oz **gray**		200.00
REF3	REF1	8 oz **light green**	175.00	150.00
REF4	REF1	12 oz **light blue**	25.00	11.00
REF5	REF1	13 oz **olive green**		200.00
REF6	REF1	16 oz **lavender**	700.00	550.00
REF7	REF1	24 oz **orange**	650.00	450.00
REF8	REF1	29 oz **brown**	500.00	400.00
REF9	REF1	32 oz **red**	225.00	200.00

A dark blue 7-ounce stamp was issued, but the only recorded examples currently are in the National Postal Museum collection.

No. REF4 stamps normally are canceled "H. B. Co." (Hoffman Beverage Company) or "M. D. C." (Mission Dry Corporation). Specialists collect them by date (H. B. Co. and M. D. C.) and control number (M. D. C.). Identifiable cancels from other companies are scarce and sell for premiums from 50% to 250% more than the used value shown for No. REF4.

Earliest documented use: May 27, 1933 (No. REF4).

Beer Stamp No. REA154 Overprinted in Red

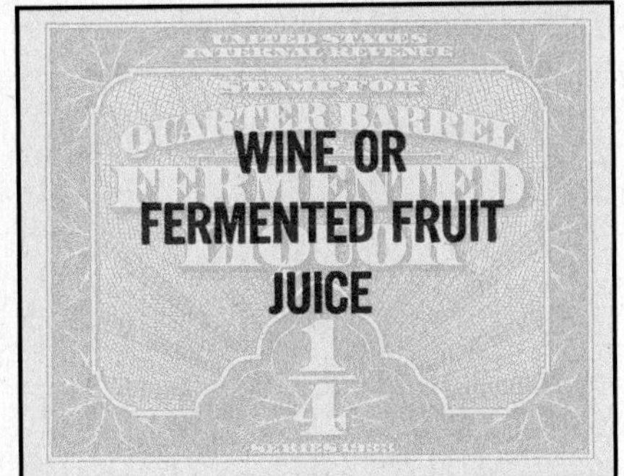

1933	Engr.		*Imperf.*
REF10	¼ bbl., **green,** *blue*	*40,000.*	

The ½ barrel and 1 barrel beer stamps, Nos. REA156-REA157, also were issued with this overprint, but no examples are currently recorded.

PLAYING CARDS

Stamps for use on packs of playing cards were included in the first general issue of 1862-71. They are Nos. R2, R11, R12, R17, R21 and R28. The tax on playing cards was repealed effective June 22, 1965.

"ON HAND . . ." — RF1

"ACT OF . . ." — RF2

1894 **Engr.** **Unwmk.** ***Rouletted 5½***

RF1 RF1 2c **lake** 1.50 1.50
P# block of 6, Impt. T I 200.00
a. Horizontal pair, imperf. between *600.00* *500.00*
b. Horiz. pair, imperf. vert. —

RF2 RF2 2c **ultramarine** 30.00 4.00
P# block of 6, Impt. T I 350.00
a. 2c **blue** 35.00 4.00
P# block of 6, Impt. T I 450.00
b. Imperf., pair 600.00
c. Imperf. horizontally 160.00 160.00
d. Rouletted 12½ 100.00 100.00
e. Imperf. horizontally, rouletted 12½ vertically, pair 225.00 225.00

No vertical pairs of No. RF2e are known. Pairs will be horizontal. Singles are valued at 50% of the pair value.

Nos. RF2 and RF3 are known with an apparent roulette 11 (No. RF2) and hyphen-hole 14 (No. RF3) caused by slippage of the perforator.

Roulettted 5½, 7; Hyphen Hole 7

1896-99 **Wmk. 191R**

RF3 RF2 2c **blue** 20.00 .65
a. 2c **ultramarine** ('99) 15.00 2.00
b. Imperf., pair 125.00

No. RF3 surcharged " VIRGIN / ISLANDS / 4 CTS" are listed under Danish West Indies.

1902 ***Perf. 12***

RF4 RF2 2c **deep blue** — 65.00

No. RF4 is known with cancel date "1899" but that is due to the use of an old canceling plate. The stamp was first used in 1902.

Stamp of 1899 Surcharged in Rose

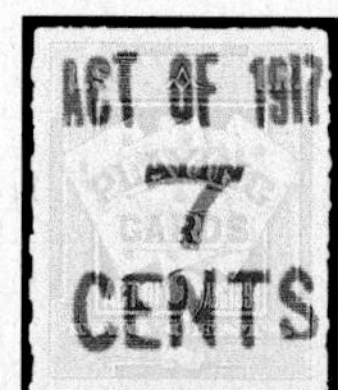

1917 **Wmk. 191R** ***Rouletted 7***

RF5 RF2 7c on 2c **ultramarine** *750.00* 700.00
a. Inverted surcharge *2,000.*

The surcharge on No. RF5 was handstamped at the Internal Revenue Office in New York City. Different handstamps were used at other Internal Revenue Offices as well, values $400 to $750.

Surcharged in Black

1917

RF6 RF2 (7c) on 2c **blue** 85.00
a. Inverted surcharge 65.00

The "17" indicated that the 7 cent tax had been paid according to the Act of 1917.

Used by N. Y. Consolidated Card Co.

Cancellations are in red.

Surcharged in Black

RF7 RF2 7c on 2c **blue** 1,100.
a. Inverted surcharge 550.00

Used by Standard Playing Card Co.

The surcharges on Nos. RF7-RF10, RF13, RF15, RF18 were applied by the manufacturers, together with their initials, dates, etc., thus forming a combination of surcharge and precancellation. The surcharge on No. RF16 was made by the Bureau of Engraving and Printing. After it appeared the use of some combinations was continued but only as cancellations.

Surcharged Vertically Reading Up in Red or Violet

RF8 RF2 7c on 2c **blue** 1,750.
a. Double surcharge 3,000.
b. Reading down 2,750.

Used by Russell Playing Card Co. (red surcharge/cancellation) and Standard Playing Card Co. of Chicago (violet surcharge/cancellation).

Surcharged Vertically, Reading Up in Black, Violet or Red

RF9 RF2 7c on 2c **blue** 10.00
a. Double surcharge (violet) 100.00
b. Numeral omitted (black) 90.00
c. Surcharge reading down 15.00
d. As "c," numeral omitted (black) 77.50
e. As "c," double surcharge (violet) *300.00*
f. Double surcharge, one down (red) *325.00*
g. Surcharge and "A.D." in violet *400.00*
h. Surcharge and "A.D." in red, "U.S.P.C. Co." in black *1,500.*
i. Surcharge and "A.D." in red reading up, "U.S.P.C. Co." in black reading down *2,500.*
j. As "g," reading down *2,500.*
k. Double surcharge (black) *1,100.*
l. Double surcharge (red) *2,500.*
m. Double surcharge and "A.D.," both reading down (red) —
n. Double surcharge and "U.S. P.C. Co.," both reading down (black) *2,750.*
o. Violet surcharge reading down on #RF4 (perf. 12) *4,500.*

"A.D." (Andrew Dougherty Co.) printed in red, "S. P. C. Co." (Standard Playing Card Co.) printed in violet, "U.S.P.C. Co." printed in black. The first two became divisions of United States Playing Card Co.

See No. RF13.

Surcharged in Carmine

RF10 RF2 7c on 2c **blue** 85.00
a. Inverted surcharge 60.00
b. Double surcharge 1,250.
c. Double surcharge, inverted 550.00
d. Triple surcharge *3,000.*

Used by Russell Playing Card Co.

RF3

1918 **Size: 21x40mm** ***Imperf.***

RF11 RF3 **blue** 55.00 32.50
Block of 4 200.00 150.00

Private Roulette 14

RF12 RF3 **blue** 400.
a. Rouletted 13 in red *2,250.*
b. Rouletted 6½ 750.
c. Perf. 12 horiz., imperf. vert. 300.
d. Perf. 12 on 4 sides *1,250.*

Nos. RF11-RF12 served as 7c stamps when used before April 1, 1919, and as 8c stamps when used after that date.

No. RF11 is known handstamped "7" or "8," or both "7" and "8," as well as "Act of 1918" in black or magenta, either by the user to indicate the value when applied to the pack or by the IRS district offices at the time of sale.

No. RF12 was used by N. Y. Consolidated Card Co., Nos. RF12a, RF12b were used by Russell Playing Card Co., Nos. RF12, RF12c, RF12d were used by Logan Printing House.

Surcharged like No. RF9 (but somewhat smaller) in Violet, Red or Black

Private Roulette 9½

RF13 RF3 7c **blue** 55.00
a. Inverted surcharge 60.00
b. Double surcharge *1,750.*
c. Double surcharge, inverted *1,750.*
d. Surcharge omitted —

No. RF13b exists with a red surcharge used only by Andrew Dougherty Co and with a black surcharge used only by U.S. Playing Card Co. No. RF13c is a black surcharge, and it was used only by U.S. Playing Card Co.

See No. RF9.

Stamp of 1899 Surcharged in Magenta or Rose

No. RF14

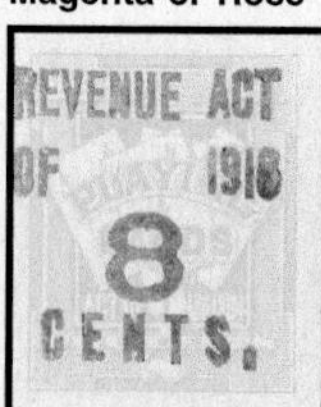

Black Handstamp, See Footnote

1919 *Rouletted 7*

RF14	RF2	8c on 2c **ultramarine**	175.00	
a.		Double surcharge	1,100.	
b.		Inverted surcharge	2,750.	

The surcharge on No. RF14 was handstamped at the Internal Revenue Office in New York City. A handstamp in black is known, and it often was applied inverted (see illustration). Value, $1,000.

Exists in pair, one double surcharge, also in pair, one with inverted surcharge.

Inverted Surcharge in Carmine

RF15	RF2	8c on 2c **blue**	650.00	
a.		Double surcharge	*2,000.*	

No. RF15 is surcharged only with large "8c" inverted, and overprinted with date and initials (also inverted). No. RF16 is often found with additional impression of large "8c," as on No. RF15, but in this usage the large "8c" is a cancellation.

Used by Russell Playing Card Co.

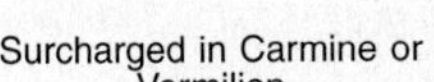
Surcharged in Carmine or Vermilion

RF16	RF2	8c on 2c **blue**	275.00	1.50
a.		Inverted surcharge		*3,000.*

See note after No. RF15.

RF4

1922 **Size: 19x22mm** *Rouletted 7*

RF17	RF4	(8c) **blue**	35.00	1.50
		Block of 4	140.00	—

No. RF17, rouletted 7 and perforated 11, surcharged " VIRGIN / ISLANDS / 4 cts." are listed under Danish West Indies.

Surcharged in Carmine, Blue or Black

RF18	RF4	8c on (8c) **blue**	100.00	
a.		Inverted surcharge	100.00	

Used by Pyramid Playing Card Co.

RF5

1924 *Rouletted 7*

RF19	RF5	10c **blue**	30.00	.60
		Block of 4	120.00	

ROTARY PRESS COIL STAMP

1926 *Perf. 10 Vertically*

RF20	RF5	10c **blue**		.30
		Pair		3.25
		Joint line pair		6.50

No. RF20 exists only precanceled. **Bureau precancels:** 11 different.

FLAT PLATE PRINTING

1927 *Perf. 11*

RF21	RF5	10c **blue**	50.00	7.50
		Block of 4	175.00	

1929 *Perf. 10*

RF22	RF5	10c **blue**	35.00	5.50
		Block of 4	125.00	—

RF6

ROTARY PRESS COIL STAMP

1929 *Perf. 10 Horizontally*

RF23	RF6	10c **light blue**		.25
		Pair		2.50
		Joint line pair		5.00

No. RF23 exists only precanceled. **Bureau precancels:** 16 different.

FLAT PLATE PRINTING

1930 *Perf. 10*

RF24	RF6	10c **blue**	30.00	2.00
		Block of 4	110.00	11.00
a.		Horiz. pair, imperf. vert.	175.00	

1931 *Perf. 11*

RF25	RF6	10c **blue**	30.00	2.00
		Block of 4	110.00	—

No. R234 is known used provisionally as a playing card revenue stamp Aug. 6 and 8, 1932. Value for this use, authenticated, $400.

RF7

ROTARY PRESS COIL STAMP

1940 **Wmk. 191R** *Perf. 10 Vertically*

RF26	RF7	**blue,** wet printing	—	.45
		Pair		2.25
		Joint line pair		4.50

Unwmk.

RF26A	RF7	**blue,** dry printing	35.00	.40
		Pair	55.00	

See note after No. 1029.

Bureau precancels: 11 different (3 of No. RF26, 8 of No. RF26A).

RF8

ROTARY PRESS COIL STAMP

1940 **Wmk. 191R** *Perf. 10 Horizontally*

RF27	RF8	**blue,** wet printing	3.00	.25
		Pair	7.50	
		Joint line pair	12.50	

Unwmk.

RF27A	RF8	**blue,** dry printing		3.25

Bureau precancels: 10 different (8 of No. RF27, 2 of No. RF27A).

FLAT PLATE PRINTING

Wmk. 191R *Perf. 11*

RF28	RF8	**blue,** wet printing	5.25	.80
		Block of 4	26.00	—
a.		Dry printing	10.00	7.50

ROTARY PRESS PRINTING

Unwmk.

RF28B	RF8	**blue,** dry printing		12.50
		Block of 4		—

Wmk. 191R *Perf. 10x11*

RF29	RF8	**blue**	200.00	92.50
		Block of 4	900.00	—
a.		Imperforate (P.C. Co.)		*2,000.*

SILVER TAX STAMPS

The Silver Purchase Act of 1934 imposed a 50 per cent tax on the net profit realized on a transfer of silver bullion occurring after May 15, 1934. The tax was paid by affixing stamps to the transfer memorandum. Congress authorized the Silver Tax stamps on June 19, 1934. They were discontinued after June 4, 1963.

Documentary Stamps of 1917 Overprinted

1934 Offset Printing Wmk. 191R *Perf. 11*

RG1	R22	1c **carmine rose**	2.00	.95
RG2	R22	2c **carmine rose**	2.10	.65
		Double impression of stamp	—	
RG3	R22	3c **carmine rose**	2.40	.80
RG4	R22	4c **carmine rose**	2.50	1.60
RG5	R22	5c **carmine rose**	4.00	1.40
RG6	R22	8c **carmine rose**	5.50	3.25
RG7	R22	10c **carmine rose**	5.75	3.00
RG8	R22	20c **carmine rose**	8.25	3.75
RG9	R22	25c **carmine rose**	7.50	4.25
RG10	R22	40c **carmine rose**	8.75	6.00
RG11	R22	50c **carmine rose**	12.00	7.50
RG12	R22	80c **carmine rose**	22.50	12.00

Engr.

RG13	R21	$1 **green**	45.00	16.00
RG14	R21	$2 **rose**	52.50	25.00
RG15	R21	$3 **violet**	95.00	35.00
RG16	R21	$4 **yellow brown**	100.00	40.00
RG17	R21	$5 **dark blue**	85.00	25.00
RG18	R21	$10 **orange**	100.00	27.50

Perf. 12

Without Gum

RG19	R17	$30 **vermilion**	1,100.	75.00
		Cut cancel		20.00
RG20	R19	$60 **brown**	1,250.	90.00
		Cut cancel		27.50
		Vertical strip of 4		400.00
RG21	R17	$100 **green**	900.00	50.00
		Vertical strip of 4		210.00
RG22	R18	$500 **blue**	1,000.	400.00
		Cut cancel		125.00
		Vertical strip of 4		—
RG23	R19	$1000 **orange**	—	125.00
		Cut cancel		60.00
		Vertical strip of 4		—

See note after No. R227.

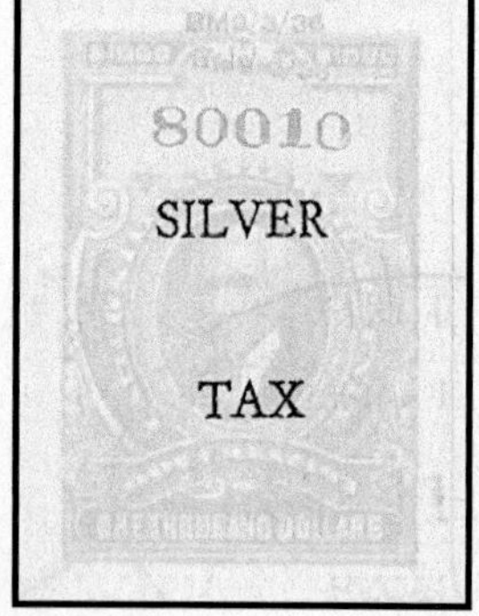

Same Overprint, spacing 11mm between words

1936 Without Gum *Perf. 12*

RG26	R17	$100 **green**	1,250.	125.00
		Vertical strip of 4		—
RG27	R19	$1000 **orange**		2,250.

Documentary Stamps of 1917 Handstamped in Violet, Large Block Letters, in Two Lines

1939 Wmk. 191R Offset Printing *Perf. 10*

RG28	R22	1c **rose pink**	*17,500.*

Perf. 11

RG29	R22	3c **rose pink**	*17,500.*
RG30	R22	5c **rose pink**	*17,500.*
RG31	R22	10c **rose pink**	*17,500.*
RG32	R22	80c **rose pink**	*17,500.*

Other handstamps exist on various values. One has letters 4mm high, 2mm wide with "SILVER" and "TAX" applied in separate operations. Denominations with this overprint are the 1c, 2c, 5c, 10c, $2 and $5. Another has "Silver Tax" in two lines in a box, but it is believed this handstamp was privately applied. Denominations with this overprint are the 5c, 40c, $4 and $10.

Overprint Typewritten in Black ($2, $3) or Red ($5)

1934-35 Engr. *Perf. 11*

RG34	R21	$2 **carmine**	*10,000.*
RG35	R21	$3 **violet**	*10,000.*
RG36	R21	$5 **dark blue**	*10,000.*

Nos. RG35 and RG36 are unique.

Typewritten overprints also exist on 2c, 3c, 4c, 20c and 50c.

Type of Documentary Stamps 1917, Overprinted in Black

1940 Offset Printing *Perf. 11*

RG37	R22	1c **rose pink**	30.00	—
RG38	R22	2c **rose pink**	30.00	—
RG39	R22	3c **rose pink**	30.00	—
RG40	R22	4c **rose pink**	35.00	—
RG41	R22	5c **rose pink**	22.50	—
RG42	R22	8c **rose pink**	35.00	—
RG43	R22	10c **rose pink**	30.00	—
RG44	R22	20c **rose pink**	35.00	—
RG45	R22	25c **rose pink**	30.00	—
RG46	R22	40c **rose pink**	52.50	—
RG47	R22	50c **rose pink**	52.50	—
RG48	R22	80c **rose pink**	52.50	—

Engr.

RG49	R21	$1 **green**	350.00	—
RG50	R21	$2 **rose**	500.00	—
RG51	R21	$3 **violet**	600.00	—
RG52	R21	$4 **yellow brown**	900.00	—
RG53	R21	$5 **dark blue**	1,100.	—
RG54	R21	$10 **orange**	1,500.	—

Nos. RG19-RG20, RG26 Handstamped in Blue

1940 Without Gum *Perf. 12*

RG55	R17	$30 **vermilion**	—	*7,000.*
a.		Double "Series 1940" overprint		—
RG56	R19	$60 **brown**	—	*17,500.*
RG57	R17	$100 **green**	—	*6,000.*

Nos. R274, R278, R280, R281, R308 Handstamped in Black "Silver Tax"

1940 *Perf. 11*

RG57A	R22	50c **rose pink**	*3,600.*
RG57B	R21	$3 **violet**	*3,600.*
RG57C	R21	$5 **dark blue**	*3,600.*
RG57D	R21	$10 **orange**	*2,450.*
RG57E	R17	$100 **carmine**	*3,600.*

Additional denominations bearing the provisional "Silver Tax" handstamp might exist.

Alexander Hamilton — RG1

Levi Woodbury — RG2

Thomas Corwin — RG3

Overprinted in Black **SERIES 1941**

1941 Wmk. 191R Engr. *Perf. 11*

RG58	RG1	1c **gray**	10.00	2.40
a.		Imperf, pair, without gum	*75.00*	
RG59	RG1	2c **gray** *(Oliver Wolcott, Jr.)*	10.00	3.00
a.		Imperf, pair, without gum	*75.00*	
RG60	RG1	3c **gray** *(Samuel Dexter)*	10.00	3.00
a.		Imperf, pair, without gum	*75.00*	
RG61	RG1	4c **gray** *(Albert Gallatin)*	10.00	5.25
a.		Imperf, pair, without gum	*75.00*	
RG62	RG1	5c **gray** *(G.W. Campbell)*	15.00	9.25
a.		Imperf, pair, without gum	*75.00*	
RG63	RG1	8c **gray** *(A.J. Dallas)*	15.00	—
a.		Imperf, pair, without gum	*75.00*	
RG64	RG1	10c **gray** *(Wm. H. Crawford)*	17.50	8.50
a.		Imperf, pair, without gum	*75.00*	
RG65	RG1	20c **gray** *(Richard Rush)*	30.00	7.75
a.		Imperf, pair, without gum	*75.00*	
RG66	RG1	25c **gray** *(S.D. Ingham)*	35.00	—
a.		Imperf, pair, without gum	*75.00*	
RG67	RG1	40c **gray** *(Louis McLane)*	60.00	37.50
a.		Imperf, pair, without gum	*75.00*	
RG68	RG1	50c **gray** *(Wm. J. Duane)*	60.00	32.50
a.		Imperf, pair, without gum	*75.00*	
RG69	RG1	80c **gray** *(Roger B. Taney)*	100.00	32.50
a.		Imperf, pair, without gum	*125.00*	
RG70	RG2	$1 **gray**	150.00	50.00
a.		Imperf, pair, without gum	*600.00*	
RG71	RG2	$2 **gray** *(Thomas Ewing)*	350.00	75.00
a.		Imperf, pair, without gum	*600.00*	
RG72	RG2	$3 **gray** *(Walter Forward)*	375.00	100.00
a.		Imperf, pair, without gum	*600.00*	
RG73	RG2	$4 **gray** *(J.C. Spencer)*	425.00	95.00
a.		Imperf, pair, without gum	*600.00*	
RG74	RG2	$5 **gray** *(G.M. Bibb)*	325.00	100.00
a.		Imperf, pair, without gum	*600.00*	
RG75	RG2	$10 **gray** *(R.J. Walker)*	750.00	125.00
a.		Imperf, pair, without gum	*650.00*	
RG76	RG2	$20 **gray** *(Wm. M. Meredith)*	1,600.	300.00
a.		Imperf, pair, without gum	*2,000.*	

Perf. 12

Without Gum

RG77	RG3	$30 **gray**	*5,000.*	750.
		Cut cancel		175.
RG78	RG3	$50 **gray** *(James Guthrie)*	*3,500.*	*4,250.*
RG79	RG3	$60 **gray** *(Howell Cobb)*	*3,500.*	750.
		Cut cancel		175.
RG80	RG3	$100 **gray** *(P.F. Thomas)*	*7,500.*	700.
		Cut cancel		175.
		Vertical strip of 4		—
RG81	RG3	$500 **gray** *(J.A. Dix)*		*32,500.*
RG82	RG3	$1000 **gray** *(S.P. Chase)*	*5,000.*	*2,750.*
		Cut cancel		*1,750.*

Nos. RG58-RG82 Overprinted Instead:

1942 **Wmk. 191R** ***Perf. 11***

No.	Type	Value	Unused	Used
RG83	RG1	1c **gray**	3.25	—
RG84	RG1	2c **gray**	3.25	—
RG85	RG1	3c **gray**	3.25	—
RG86	RG1	4c **gray**	3.25	—
RG87	RG1	5c **gray**	3.25	—
RG88	RG1	8c **gray**	8.00	—
RG89	RG1	10c **gray**	8.00	—
RG90	RG1	20c **gray**	15.00	—
RG91	RG1	25c **gray**	26.00	—
RG92	RG1	40c **gray**	35.00	—
RG93	RG1	50c **gray**	40.00	—
RG94	RG1	80c **gray**	100.00	—
RG95	RG2	$1 **gray**	150.00	72.50
a.		Overprint "SERIES 5942"	*2,000.*	
RG96	RG2	$2 **gray**	160.00	72.50
a.		Overprint "SERIES 5942"	1,350.	
		Block of 4, one stamp ovptd. "SERIES 5942"	*2,000.*	
RG97	RG2	$3 **gray**	300.00	140.00
a.		Overprint "SERIES 5942"	1,450.	
RG98	RG2	$4 **gray**	350.00	140.00
a.		Overprint "SERIES 5942"	*2,500.*	
RG99	RG2	$5 **gray**	300.00	175.00
a.		Overprint "SERIES 5942"	*2,000.*	
RG100	RG2	$10 **gray**	1,000.	700.00
RG101	RG2	$20 **gray**	1,250.	
a.		Overprint "SERIES 5942"	*10,000.*	

Perf. 12

Without Gum

No.	Type	Value	Unused	Used
RG102	RG3	$30 **gray**	*7,500.*	*4,500.*
		Cut cancel		*3,500.*
RG103	RG3	$50 **gray**	*40,000.*	—
RG104	RG3	$60 **gray**	*7,500.*	*2,250.*
		Cut cancel		1,000.
RG105	RG3	$100 **gray**		3,500.
		Cut cancel		950.
RG106	RG3	$500 **gray**		*6,000.*
		Cut cancel		*4,000.*
RG107	RG3	$1000 **gray**	*15,000.*	*8,500.*
		Cut cancel		*4,500.*

Silver Purchase Stamps of 1941 without Overprint

1944 **Wmk. 191R** ***Perf. 11***

No.	Type	Value	Unused	Used
RG108	RG1	1c **gray**	1.00	.30
RG109	RG1	2c **gray**	1.00	.65
RG110	RG1	3c **gray**	1.40	1.00
RG111	RG1	4c **gray**	1.60	1.25
RG112	RG1	5c **gray**	3.25	2.75
RG113	RG1	8c **gray**	5.00	2.75
RG114	RG1	10c **gray**	6.50	3.25
RG115	RG1	20c **gray**	10.00	5.50
RG116	RG1	25c **gray**	16.00	6.00
RG117	RG1	40c **gray**	24.00	11.50
RG118	RG1	50c **gray**	25.00	14.00
RG119	RG1	80c **gray**	32.50	20.00
RG120	RG2	$1 **gray**	67.50	21.00
RG121	RG2	$2 **gray**	95.00	47.50
RG122	RG2	$3 **gray**	125.00	37.50
RG123	RG2	$4 **gray**	150.00	85.00
RG124	RG2	$5 **gray**	150.00	47.50
RG125	RG2	$10 **gray**	225.00	35.00
		Cut cancel		19.00
RG126	RG2	$20 **gray**	900.00	550.00
		Cut cancel		275.00

Perf. 12

Without Gum

No.	Type	Value	Unused	Used
RG127	RG3	$30 **gray**	750.00	175.00
		Cut cancel		80.00
		Vertical strip of 4		—
a.		Booklet pane of 4	*7,250.*	
RG128	RG3	$50 **gray**	1,500.	700.00
		Cut cancel		350.00
		Vertical strip of 4		—
a.		Booklet pane of 4	*13,000.*	
RG129	RG3	$60 **gray**	*4,250.*	575.00
		Cut cancel		275.00
RG130	RG3	$100 **gray**	*2,000.*	35.00
		Cut cancel		15.00
		Vertical strip of 4		—
RG131	RG3	$500 **gray**	1,200.	500.00
		Cut cancel		250.00
		With complete receipt tab	*1,500.*	
a.		Booklet pane of 4	*6,500.*	
		Complete booklet, 2 #RG131a	*13,500.*	
RG132	RG3	$1000 **gray**	900.00	160.00
		Cut cancel		80.00
		Vertical strip of 4		—
		With complete receipt tab	1,000.	
a.		Booklet pane of 4	—	
		Complete booklet, 1 #RG132a	*5,000.*	

CIGARETTE TUBES STAMPS

These stamps were for a tax on the hollow tubes of cigarette paper, with or without thin cardboard mouthpieces attached. They were sold in packages so buyers could add loose tobacco to make cigarettes.

Documentary Stamp of 1917 Overprinted

1919 **Offset Printing** **Wmk. 191R** ***Perf. 11***

No.	Type	Value	Unused	Used
RH1	R22	1c **carmine rose**	1.25	.75
		Block of 4	5.50	3.00
		On package		60.00
		Pair on package		75.00
		P# block of 8	175.00	
a.		Without period	35.00	15.00
		On package		100.00
		Block of 4, one stamp #RH1a	70.00	

1929 ***Perf. 10***

No.	Type	Value	Unused	Used
RH2	R22	1c **carmine rose**	75.00	11.00
		On package		80.00

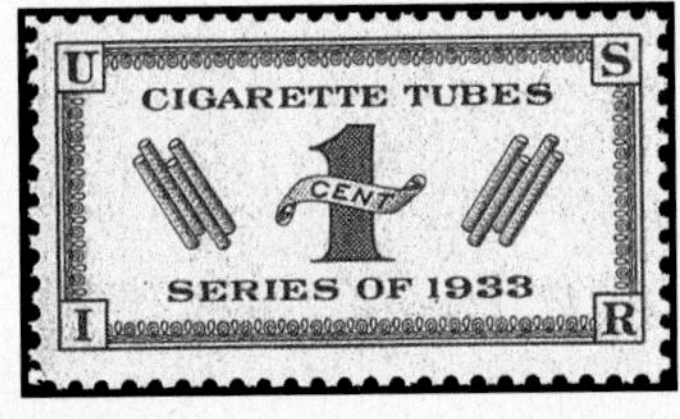

RH1

1933 **Without Gum** **Wmk. 191R** ***Perf. 11***

No.	Type	Value	Unused	Used
RH3	RH1	1c **rose** (shades)	5.00	2.50
		Block of 4	22.50	12.50
		On package		45.00
RH4	RH1	2c **rose** (shades)	30.00	7.50
		Pair		17.50
		Block of 4		50.00
		On package		110.00

Cigarette tube on-package values for Nos. RH1 and RH3 are for fine undamaged stamps affixed to a full package of Himyar Tobacco cigarette tubes manufactured by the Axton-Fisher Tobacco Co. Opened packages containing no cigarette tubes sell for 50 to 100 percent less. No. RH1 pairs are unseparated stamps. The listing for No. RH1 pair on package is not on a Himyar package.

Specialists have questioned whether No. RH1a is known on packages. The editors would like to see evidence of the existence of these listings.

RH2

1945 **Wmk. 191R** ***Perf. 11***

No.	Type	Value	Unused	Used
RH5	RH2	10c **rose**		—

POTATO TAX STAMPS

These stamps were required by the Potato Act of 1935, an amendment to the Agricultural Adjustment Act that became effective Dec. 1, 1935.

Potato growers were given allotments for which they were provided Tax Exempt Potato stamps. Growers exceeding their allotments would have paid for the excess with Tax Paid Potato stamps at the rate of ¾ cent per pound.

On Jan. 6, 1936, the U. S. Supreme Court declared the Agricultural Adjustment Act unconstitutional. Officially the Potato Act was in effect until Feb. 10, 1936, when it was repealed by Congress but, in essence, the law was ignored once the Supreme Court ruling was issued.

Because of the Act's short life, Tax Paid stamps were never used.

Young Woman from *The Bouquet* — RI1

Tax Paid Potatoes

1935 **Engr.** **Wmk. 191R** ***Perf. 11***

No.	Type	Denom.	Color	Unused
RI1	RI1	¾c	**carmine rose**	1.00
RI2	RI1	1½c	**black brown**	1.00
RI3	RI1	2¼c	**yellow green**	1.00
RI4	RI1	3c	**light violet**	1.00
RI5	RI1	3¾c	**olive bister**	1.25
RI6	RI1	7½c	**orange brown**	4.00
RI7	RI1	11¼c	**deep orange**	5.00
RI8	RI1	18¾c	**violet brown**	12.50
RI9	RI1	37½c	**red orange**	15.00
RI10	RI1	75c	**blue**	17.50
RI11	RI1	93¾c	**rose lake**	21.00
RI12	RI1	$1.12½	**green**	40.00
RI13	RI1	$1.50	**yellow brown**	40.00
		Nos. RI1-RI13 (13)		160.25

RI2

Tax Exempt Potatoes

1935 **Engr.** **Unwmk.** ***Perf. 11x10½***

No.	Type	Description	Unused	Used
RI14	RI2	2 lb **black brown**	2.00	*37.50*
a.		Booklet pane of 12	16.00	*375.00*
		Provisional booklet of 24, purple on pink cover	35.00	
		Provisional booklet of 96, purple on buff cover	100.00	
		Provisional booklet of 192, purple on white cover	250.00	
		Definitive booklet of 96, black on buff cover	100.00	
		Definitive booklet of 192, black on white cover	200.00	
RI15	RI2	5 lb **black brown**	25.00	
a.		Booklet pane of 12	*750.00*	
		Provisional booklet of 192, purple on white cover	*5,000.*	
		Provisional booklet of 24, purple on pink cover	*1,000.*	
RI16	RI2	10 lb **black brown**	35.00	
a.		Booklet pane of 12	*550.00*	
		Provisional booklet of 192, purple on white cover	*5,000.*	
RI17	RI2	25 lb **black brown**	*400.00*	
		No gum	125.00	
a.		Booklet pane of 12	*5,000.*	
		No gum	2,000.	
		Provisional booklet of 24, purple on pink cover, with stamps stuck down, badly disturbed gum	*5,500.*	
RI18	RI2	50 lb **black brown**	1.50	*50.00*
a.		Booklet pane of 12	30.00	
		Provisional booklet of 24, purple on pink cover	50.00	
		Provisional booklet of 96, purple on buff cover	150.00	
		Provisional booklet of 192, purple on white cover	300.00	
		Definitive booklet of 96, black on buff cover	100.00	
		Definitive booklet of 192, black on white cover	150.00	
		Nos. RI14-RI16,RI18 (4)	*63.50*	

The booklet panes are arranged 4x3 with a tab at top. Edges are imperforate at left, right and bottom, yielding four stamps fully perforated, six stamps imperf. on one side and two stamps imperf. on two sides per pane. Values for single stamps are for examples perforated on all four sides. Stamps with straight edges generally sell for less.

These stamps were printed from 360-subject rotary booklet plates and cut into 30 panes of 12. The panes were stapled into booklets of 24 (2 panes, pink covers), 96 (8 panes, buff covers) and 196 (16 panes, white covers), with handstamped covers (provisionals) and later with covers printed with the Dept. of Agriculture seal in the center (definitives). Both types of cover were prepared by the Bureau of Engraving and Printing.

Values for booklets are for examples containing panes that have very good to fine centering, because the overwhelming majority of booklets are in this grade. It should be noted that Scott values for individual panes (listed above) are for very fine panes. For this reason, individual panes are valued higher than the per-pane value of panes in booklets. For example, a pane of No. RI14a is valued at $14, but the No. RI14 definitive booklet of 96 (8 panes) is valued at $100, or $12.50 per pane, which is a little more than what a collector would pay for an individual very good to fine pane. Booklets containing very fine panes will command a premium over the values given.

One No. RI17 192-stamp booklet exists, from which some panes have been removed, but no complete 192-stamp booklet is known to exist.

A 100 lb Tax Exempt stamp was printed, but all are believed to have been destroyed.

TOBACCO SALE TAX STAMPS

These stamps were required to pay the tax on the sale of tobacco in excess of quotas set by the Secretary of Agriculture. The tax was 25 per cent of the price for which the excess tobacco was sold. It was intended to affect tobacco harvested after June 28, 1934 and sold before May 1, 1936. The tax was stopped when the Agricultural Adjustment Act was declared unconstitutional by the Supreme Court on Jan. 6, 1936.

Values for unused stamps are for examples with original gum.

Stamps and Types of 1917 Documentary Issue Overprinted

1934 **Offset Printing** **Wmk. 191R** ***Perf. 11***

No.	Type	Denom.	Color	Unused	Used
RJ1	R22	1c	**carmine rose**	.30	.25
RJ2	R22	2c	**carmine rose**	.40	.25
RJ3	R22	5c	**carmine rose**	1.25	.50
RJ4	R22	10c	**carmine rose**	1.60	.45
a.		Inverted overprint		15.00	*22.50*
RJ5	R22	25c	**carmine rose**	4.75	2.00
RJ6	R22	50c	**carmine rose**	7.50	2.00

Engr.

No.	Type	Denom.	Color	Unused	Used
RJ7	R21	$1	**green**	15.00	2.00
RJ8	R21	$2	**rose**	35.00	2.25
RJ9	R21	$5	**dark blue**	40.00	4.25
RJ10	R21	$10	**orange**	50.00	11.00
RJ11	R21	$20	**olive bister**	125.00	12.50
		Nos. RJ1-RJ11 (11)		280.80	37.45

On No. RJ11 the overprint is vertical, reading up.

The right serif on the "T" of "TOBACCO" exists both normal and split. Both varieties exist within the same sheet, and the quantities of each type are approximately equal.

No. RJ2 is known with a counterfeit inverted overprint.

NARCOTIC TAX STAMPS

The Revenue Act of 1918 imposed a tax of 1 cent per ounce or fraction thereof on opium, coca leaves and their derivatives. The tax was paid by affixing Narcotic stamps to the drug containers. The tax lasted from Feb. 25, 1919, through Apr. 30, 1971.

Members of the American Revenue Association helped compile the listings in this section.

Documentary Stamps of 1917 Handstamped "NARCOTIC," "Narcotic," "NARCOTICS" or "ACT/NARCOTIC/1918" in Magenta, Black, Blue, Violet or Red

RJA22

RJA25

1919 Wmk. 191R Offset Printing *Perf. 11*

RJA9 R22	1c **carmine rose**		3.00	1.90
RJA10 R22	2c **carmine rose**		6.00	4.00
RJA11 R22	3c **carmine rose**		35.00	37.50
RJA12 R22	4c **carmine rose**		13.00	10.00
RJA13 R22	5c **carmine rose**		20.00	16.00
RJA14 R22	8c **carmine rose**		16.00	12.50
RJA15 R22	10c **carmine rose**		52.50	20.00
RJA17 R22	25c **carmine rose**		47.50	32.50
RJA18 R22	40c **carmine rose**		*150.00*	*150.00*
RJA19 R22	50c **carmine rose**		—	*22.50*
RJA20 R22	80c **carmine rose**		*150.00*	*150.00*

Engr.

RJA21 R21	$1 **green**	200.00	125.00
RJA22 R21	$2 **rose**		*2,400.*
RJA23 R21	$3 **violet**		*3,000.*
RJA24 R21	$5 **dark blue**		*2,000.*
RJA25 R21	$10 **orange**		*2,000.*

Drug manufacturer cancels have enabled experts to identify conclusively the origin of only eight of the handstamped overprints. Four of these read simply "Narcotic." A 3-line handstamp, "Act / Narcotic / 1918," was used in Seattle; "Narcotics" in Kansas City, Missouri. Perhaps as many as 20 other styles and sizes have been recorded, although these occur only on mint stamps. Most or all of these mints stamps appear to be philatelic fantasies.

Many fake overprints exist.

No. R228 Overprinted in Black

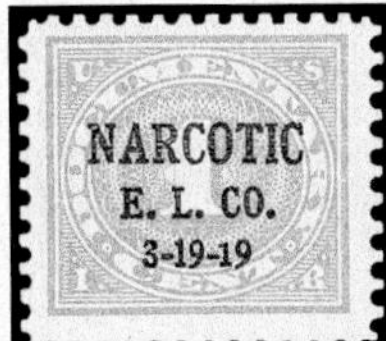

1919 Wmk. 191R *Perf. 11*
"NARCOTIC" 14½mm wide

RJA26 R22	1c **carmine rose**	*3,750.*

Overprinted by Eli Lilly Co., Indianapolis, for that firm's use.

No. R228 Overprinted in Black

1919 Wmk. 191R *Perf. 11*
"NARCOTIC" 14½mm wide

RJA27 R22	1c **carmine rose**	*6,500.*
RJA27A R22	2c **carmine rose**	*7,500.*

Overprinted by John Wyeth & Brother, Philadelphia, for that firm's use.

The overprints on Nos. RJA27 and RJA27A are often mistaken for a cancellation used on the government-issued stamps Nos. RJA33-RJA40, with the latter having the "NARCOTICS" overprint measuring 17.5mm.

Nos. R228, R231-R232 Handstamped in Blue

1919 Wmk. 191R *Perf. 11*

RJA28 R22	1c **carmine rose**	*1,250.*
RJA28A R22	4c **carmine rose**	*1,500.*
RJA29 R22	5c **carmine rose**	—
RJA29A R22	25c **carmine rose**	—
RJA29B R21	$1 **green** (violet handstamp)	—

The handstamp was applied by the Powers-Weightmann-Rosengarten Co., Philadelphia, for that firm's use.

Proprietary Stamps of 1919 Handstamped "NARCOTIC" in Blue

1919 Wmk. 191R Offset Printing *Perf. 11*

RJA30 RB5	1c **dark blue**	—	—
RJA31 RB5	2c **dark blue**	—	
RJA32 RB5	4c **dark blue**	—	

No. RB65 is known with "Narcotic" applied in red ms.

The editors would like to see authenticated evidence of the existence of Nos. RJA30-RJA32.

Documentary Stamps of 1917 Overprinted in Black, "Narcotic" 17½mm wide

1919 Wmk. 191R Offset Printing *Perf. 11*

RJA33 R22	1c **carmine rose** *(6,900,000)*	1.25	.80
RJA34 R22	2c **carmine rose** *(3,650,000)*	2.50	1.10
RJA35 R22	3c **carmine rose** *(388,400)*	40.00	21.00
RJA36 R22	4c **carmine rose** *(2,400,000)*	6.00	4.75
RJA37 R22	5c **carmine rose** *(2,400,000)*	15.00	10.50
RJA38 R22	8c **carmine rose** *(1,200,000)*	25.00	18.00
RJA39 R22	10c **carmine rose** *(3,400,000)*	3.75	2.75
RJA40 R22	25c **carmine rose** *(700,000)*	25.00	16.00

Overprint Reading Up

Engr.

RJA41 R21	$1 **green** *(270,000)*	47.50	20.00

The overprint on Nos. RJA33-RJA41 was produced by the Bureau of Engraving & Printing. Fake overprints exist on Nos. RJA33-RJA41. In the genuine the C's are not slanted.

NT1

NT2

1919-64 Offset Printing Wmk. 191R *Imperf.*

RJA42a NT1	1c **violet**		5.25
RJA43a NT2	1c **violet**		.55
RJA44a NT2	2c **violet**		1.40

Rouletted 7

RJA42b NT1	1c **violet**	1.25	.30
d.	1c **purple**		7.50
RJA43b NT2	1c **violet**		.30
d.	1c **purple**		5.25
e.	Double impression		—
RJA44b NT2	2c **violet**		.55
d.	2c **purple**		5.25
RJA45b NT2	3c **violet**		175.00

The purple shade, Nos. RJA42d, RJA43d and RJA44d, is a distinctive shade with a decidedly reddish cast to it that arose because of the unavailability during WWII of inks previously used. All authenticated purple stamps were used from 1944 to 1947.

NT3

NT4

Imperf

RJA46a NT3	1c **violet**		2.75
RJA47a NT3	2c **violet**		1.60
RJA48a NT3	3c **violet**	*750.00*	*750.00*
RJA49a NT3	4c **violet** ('42)		—
RJA50a NT3	5c **violet**		42.50
RJA52a NT3	8c **violet**		75.00
RJA53a NT3	9c **violet** ('53)		67.50
RJA54a NT3	10c **violet**		32.50
RJA55a NT3	16c **violet**		52.50
RJA56a NT3	18c **violet** ('61)		110.00
RJA57a NT3	19c **violet** ('61)		125.00
RJA58a NT3	20c **violet**		375.00

Nos. RJA47a-RJA58a have "CENTS" below the value.

Rouletted 7

RJA46b NT3	1c **violet**		.75
d.	1c **purple**		9.00
RJA47b NT3	2c **violet**		.75
d.	2c **purple**		8.25
RJA49b NT3	4c **violet**		11.00
d.	4c **purple**		30.00
RJA50b NT3	5c **violet**	10.00	4.00
d.	5c **purple**		13.00
RJA51b NT3	6c **violet**		1.00
d.	6c **purple**		9.25
RJA52b NT3	8c **violet**		4.25
d.	8c **purple**		26.00
RJA53b NT3	9c **violet**		21.00
RJA54b NT3	10c **violet**		.55
d.	10c **purple**		7.00

RJA55b	NT3	16c **violet**	10.00	4.00
d.		16c **purple**		14.50
RJA56b	NT3	18c **violet**		12.50
RJA57b	NT3	19c **violet**	50.00	26.00
RJA58b	NT3	20c **violet**	250.00	350.00

Nos. RJA47b-RJA58b have "CENTS" below the value.

Multiple type differences for the large Narcotic Tax stamps

RJA59 Type I-II

RJA59 Type I — Outline of left "1" without a distinctive line at top-left side of numeral; scrollwork at lower right of left "1" has one distinct short line extending upward with a large break between scroll lines; outline of right "1" without a distinctive line at left side of numeral.

RJA59 Type II — Outline of left "1" with a distinctive line at top left side of numeral; scrollwork at lower right of left "1" has two distinct short lines extending upward with a small break between scroll lines; outline of right "1" with a distinctive line at left side of numeral.

RJA60 Type I-II

RJA60 Type I — Scrollwork at right of left "2" has a continuous line below large scroll; scrollwork at lower right of left "2" has one short line and one long line extending upward; spike at 4 o'clock of circle enclosing left "2" is short; scrollwork at upper left of right "2" contains three distinct lines; scrollwork to left of right "2" has a break; scrollwork at lower right of right "2" has two distinct lines extending upward; spike at 4 o'clock of circle enclosing right "2" is short.

RJA60 Type II — Scrollwork at right of left "2" has a broken line below large scroll; scrollwork at lower right of left "2" has one short line and two long lines extending upward; spike at 4 o'clock of circle enclosing left "2" is long; scrollwork at upper left of right "2" contains four distinct lines; scrollwork to left of right "2" is continuous; scrollwork at lower right of right "2" has three distinct lines extending upward; spike at 4 o'clock of circle enclosing right "2" is long.

RJA62 Type I-II

RJA62 Type I — Spike at 4 o'clock of circle enclosing left "5" is short; scrollwork at upper left of right "5" contains three distinct lines; spike at 4 o'clock of circle enclosing right "5" is short.

RJA62 Type II — Spike at 4 o'clock of circle enclosing left "5" is long; scrollwork at upper left of right "5" contains four distinct lines; spike at 4 o'clock of circle enclosing right "5" is long.

RJA63 Type I-II

RJA63 Type I — Spike at 4 o'clock of circle enclosing left "6" is short; scrollwork at left of right "6" has a large gap between the lines; scrollwork at far right of right "6" does not extend at left to below the ball above it.

Type II — Spike at 4 o'clock of circle enclosing left "6" is long; scrollwork at left of right "6" has a narrow gap between the lines; scrollwork at far right of right "6" extends at left to below the ball above it.

RJA64 Type I-II

RJA64 Type I — Scrollwork at lower right of left "8" has one short line and one long line extending upward; spike at 4 o'clock of circle enclosing left "8" is short; scrollwork at upper left of right "8" contains three distinct lines; spike at 4 o'clock of circle enclosing right "8" is short; scrollwork at far right of right "8" does not extend at left to below the ball above it.

RJA64 Type II — Scrollwork at lower right of left "8" has three distinct lines extending upward; spike at 4 o'clock of circle enclosing left "8" is long; scrollwork at upper left of right "8" contains four distinct lines; spike at 4 o'clock of circle enclosing right "8" is long; scrollwork at far right of right "8" extends at left to below the ball above it.

RJA66 Type I-II

RJA66 Type I — Scrollwork at far right of right "10" does not extend at left to below the ball above it.

RJA66 Type II — Scrollwork at far right of right "10" extends at left to below the ball above it.

RJA67 Type I-III

RJA67 Type I — Spike at 4 o'clock of circle enclosing left "16" is short; scrollwork at upper left of right "16" contains three distinct lines; scrollwork at right of right "16" has a break.

RJA67 Type II — Spike at 4 o'clock of circle enclosing left "16" is short; scrollwork at upper left of right "16" contains three distinct lines; scrollwork at right of right "16" is continuous.

RJA67 Type III — Spike at 4 o'clock of circle enclosing left "16" is long; scrollwork at upper left of right "16" contains four distinct lines; scrollwork at right of right "16" is continuous.

RJA71 Type I-II

RJA71 Type I — Scrollwork at right of right "25" has a break.

RJA71 Type II — Scrollwork at right of right "25" is continuous.

RJA72 Type I-II

RJA72 Type I — Scrollwork at lower right of left "40" has a large break with an additional line; scrollwork at right of right "40" has a break.

RJA72 Type II — Scrollwork at lower right of left "40" has a small break without an additional line; scrollwork at right of right "40" is continuous.

RJA73 Type I-II

RJA73 Type I — Scrollwork at lower right of left "1" has one short line and one long line extending upward; scrollwork to left of right "1" has a break; curled scrollwork to left and right of right "1" has thin green line; scrollwork at lower right of right "1" has two distinct lines extending upward; scrollwork at far right of right "1" does not extend at left to below the ball above it.

RJA73 Type II — Scrollwork at lower right of left "1" has two short lines and one long line extending upward; scrollwork to left of right "1" is continuous; curled scrollwork to left and right of right "1" has thick green line; scrollwork at lower right of right "1" has one distinct line extending upward; scrollwork at far right of right "1" extends at left to below the ball above it.

RJA74 Type I-II

RJA74 Type I — Scrollwork at far right of right "1.28" does not extend at left to below the ball above it.

RJA74 Type II — Scrollwork at far right of right "1.28" extends at left to below the ball above it.

Imperf

RJA59Ea	NT4	1c **violet**, type II		47.50
RJA60Ea	NT4	2c **violet**, type II		50.00
RJA61a	NT4	3c **violet**	55.00	52.50
RJA63Ea	NT4	6c **violet**, type II		62.50
RJA65a	NT4	9c **violet** ('61)	60.00	35.00
RJA66Ea	NT4	10c **violet**, type II		17.50
RJA67Ea	NT4	16c **violet**, type II		16.00
RJA67Fa	NT4	16c **violet**, type III		25.00
RJA68a	NT4	18c **violet** ('61)	*250.00*	250.00
RJA69a	NT4	19c **violet**	25.00	16.00
RJA70a	NT4	20c **violet**	*200.00*	325.00
RJA72a	NT4	40c **violet**, type I		1,000.
RJA74a	NT4	$1.28 **green**, type I		32.50
RJA74Ea	NT4	$1.28 **green**, type II		32.50
c.		As "RJA74Ea," measuring ¾ inch by 8 inches with wide side margins		*200.00*

On Nos. RJA60Ea-RJA74a the value tablet is solid.

Rouletted 7

RJA59b	NT4	1c **violet**, type I		10.50
c.		Rouletted 3½	10.00	5.00
RJA59Eb	NT4	1c **violet**, type II	11.00	10.50
RJA60b	NT4	2c **violet**, type I	27.50	20.00
RJA60Eb	NT4	2c **violet**, type II	35.00	20.00
RJA61b	NT4	3c **violet**	350.00	350.00
RJA62b	NT4	5c **violet**, type I	35.00	26.00
RJA62Eb	NT4	5c **violet**, type II	35.00	26.00
RJA63b	NT4	6c **violet**, type I	30.00	25.00
RJA63Eb	NT4	6c **violet**, type II	30.00	
RJA64b	NT4	8c **violet**, type I	65.00	50.00
RJA64Eb	NT4	8c **violet**, type II	65.00	50.00
RJA65b	NT4	9c **violet**		21.00
RJA66b	NT4	10c **violet**, type I	25.00	17.50
RJA66Eb	NT4	10c **violet**, type II	25.00	17.50
RJA67b	NT4	16c **violet**, type I	27.50	20.00
RJA67Eb	NT4	16c **violet**, type II		20.00
RJA67Fb	NT4	16c **violet**, type III	27.50	20.00
RJA68b	NT4	18c **violet**		425.00
RJA69b	NT4	19c **violet**		190.00
RJA70b	NT4	20c **violet**		240.00
RJA71b	NT4	25c **violet**, type I		21.00
c.		Rouletted 3½	9.00	4.25
RJA71Eb	NT4	25c **violet**, type II	57.50	21.00
d.		25c **purple**		—
RJA72b	NT4	40c **violet**, type I		*4,000.*
c.		Rouletted 3½	80.00	67.50
RJA73b	NT4	$1 **green**, type I	17.50	1.60
RJA73Eb	NT4	$1 **green**, type II	17.50	1.60
d.		$1 **violet** (error), type II		*2,000.*
RJA74b	NT4	$1.28 **green**, type I	25.00	10.50
RJA74Eb	NT4	$1.28 **green**, type II		10.50
d.		As "RJA74Eb," measuring ¾ inch by 8 inches with wide side margins	*100.00*	*100.00*

On Nos. RJA60b-RJA74b the value tablet is solid.

1963(?)-70 **Offset Printing** ***Imperf.***
Unwatermarked

No.	Type	Description	Unused	Used
RJA75a	NT1	1c **violet**		7.75
RJA76a	NT2	1c **violet**		1.10
RJA77a	NT2	2c **violet**		5.25
RJA79a	NT3	1c **violet**		5.25
RJA80a	NT3	2c **violet**	175.00	
RJA82a	NT3	5c **violet**		72.50
RJA83a	NT3	6c **violet**		—
RJA85a	NT3	9c **violet**		—
RJA86a	NT3	10c **violet**		—
RJA87a	NT3	16c **violet**		150.00
RJA88a	NT3	18c **violet**		—

Nos. RJA80a-RJA88a have "CENTS" below the value.

Rouletted 7

No.	Type	Description	Unused	Used
RJA75b	NT1	1c **violet**	2.10	
RJA76b	NT2	1c **violet**		1.10
RJA77b	NT2	2c **violet**	2.10	
RJA78b	NT2	3c **violet**	*100.00*	175.00
RJA79b	NT3	1c **violet**		2.10
RJA80b	NT3	2c **violet**	3.00	2.00
RJA81b	NT3	4c **violet**		10.00
RJA83b	NT3	6c **violet**	22.50	
RJA84b	NT3	8c **violet**		5.25
RJA85b	NT3	9c **violet**	60.00	50.00
RJA86b	NT3	10c **violet**	22.50	
RJA87b	NT3	16c **violet**		4.25
RJA88b	NT3	18c **violet**	52.50	
RJA89b	NT3	20c **violet**	325.00	

Nos. RJA80b-RJA89b have "CENTS" below the value.

Imperf

No.	Type	Description	Unused	Used
RJA91a	NT4	1c **violet**, type II		67.50
RJA93a	NT4	3c **violet**		85.00
RJA94a	NT4	6c **violet**, type II		100.00
RJA96a	NT4	10c **violet**, type II		*1,500.*
RJA97a	NT4	16c **violet**, type III		40.00
RJA98a	NT4	19c **violet**		25.00
RJA99a	NT4	20c **violet**		*2,500.*
RJA101a	NT4	40c **violet**, type II		*1,000.*
RJA104a	NT4	$4 **green** ('70)	*1,000.*	*1,000.*

On Nos. RJA93a-RJA104a the value tablet is solid.

Rouletted 7

No.	Type	Description	Unused	Used
RJA91b	NT4	1c **violet**, type II	15.00	15.00
RJA92b	NT4	2c **violet**, type II	80.00	
RJA93b	NT4	3c **violet**	120.00	*160.00*
RJA94b	NT4	6c **violet**, type II	80.00	
RJA94Cb	NT4	8c **violet**, type II	175.00	175.00
RJA95b	NT4	9c **violet**	130.00	50.00
RJA96b	NT4	10c **violet**, type II	70.00	
RJA97b	NT4	16c **violet**, type III	50.00	21.00
RJA98b	NT4	19c **violet**	*350.00*	400.00
RJA99b	NT4	20c **violet**	*425.00*	
RJA100b	NT4	25c **violet**, type II	200.00	250.00
RJA102b	NT4	$1 **green**, type II	37.50	
RJA103b	NT4	$1.28 **green**, type II	60.00	
d.		As "RJA103b," measuring ¾ inch by 8 inches with wide side margins	125.00	

On Nos. RJA92b-RJA103b the value tablet is solid.

NT5

Denomination added in black by rubber plate in an operation similar to precanceling.

1963 **Engr.** **Unwmk.** ***Imperf.***

No.	Type	Description	Unused	Used
RJA105	NT5	1c **violet**, type 2	90.00	85.00
a.		Type 1	*140.00*	*140.00*
b.		Type 3	*50.00*	

Printed in sheets of 144 in six columns of 24 stamps. The majority of the stamps have block markings in all four corners of the margin (type 1), and many fewer have block margins only in the two left corners (type 2). A third scarcer type has dashes in the left two corners (Type 3). Despite the printing totals, type 2 is the most common of the three varieties and, therefore, is listed as the major number.

Nos. RJA105, RJA105a, and RJA105b were issued in vertical coil strips.

Denomination on Stamp Plate

1964 **Offset Printing** ***Imperf.***

No.	Type	Description	Unused	Used
RJA106	NT5	1c **violet**	90.00	5.25

RJA106 was issued in sheet of 80 stamps.

MARIHUANA TAX STAMPS

Act of Congress, 1937, to enforce uniform regulation of cannabis.

Nos. R240, R244, R245
Overprinted

Issued with gum. Unused values are for stamps that are never hinged.

1937 **Engr.** ***Perf. 11***

No.	Type	Description	Unused	Used
RJM1	R21	$1 **yellow green**	*400.*	*15,000.*
		On document		—
		P# block of 6	*3,000.*	
a.		Imperf, pair	*900.*	
RJM2	R21	$5 **blue**	*475.*	
		P# block of 6	*4,000.*	
a.		Imperf, pair	*900.*	
RJM3	R21	$10 **yellow orange**	*425.*	
		P# block of 6	*3,750.*	
a.		Imperf, pair	*900.*	

Same overprint on No. R248

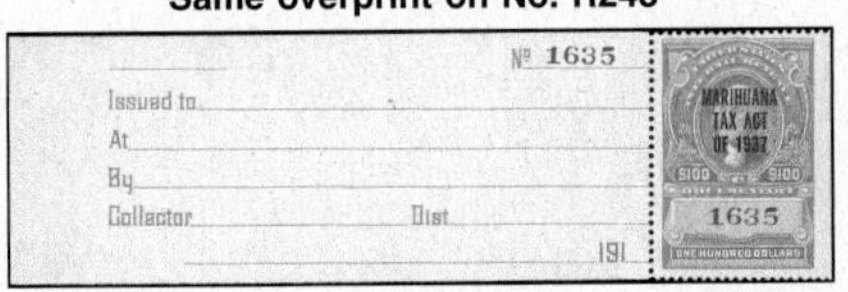

Illustration reduced.

Without Gum ***Perf. 12***
Control Number in Red

No.	Type	Description	Unused	Used
RJM4	R17	$100 **green,** with complete receipt tab	*750.*	
a.		Booklet pane of 4	*3,500.*	
		Complete booklet, 4 #RJM4a	*15,000.*	

Nos. R300, R304, R305
Without Date Inscription
Overprinted

1962 ***Perf. 11***

No.	Type	Description	Unused	Used
RJM5	R24	$1 **carmine**	*425.*	
RJM6	R24	$5 **carmine**	*425.*	
RJM7	R24	$10 **carmine**	*425.*	

No. R306A Without Date Inscription Overprinted

Issued to
At
By
Director located at
19

Illustration reduced.

No.	Type	Description	Unused	Used
RJM8	R25	$50 **carmine,** with complete receipt tab, no serial #	*1,400.*	
a.		Booklet pane of 4	*5,750.*	

CONSULAR SERVICE FEE STAMPS

Act of Congress, April 5, 1906, effective June 1, 1906, provided that every consular officer should be provided with special adhesive stamps printed in denominations determined by the Department of State.

Every document for which a fee was prescribed had to have attached a stamp or stamps representing the amount collected, and such stamps were used to show payment of these prescribed fees.

These stamps were usually affixed close to the signature, or at the lower left corner of the document. If no document was issued, the stamp or stamps were attached to a receipt for the amount of the fee and canceled either with pen and ink or rubber stamp showing the date of cancellation and bearing the initials of the canceling officer or name of the Consular Office. Stamps with embossed cancels sell for somewhat less. These stamps were not sold to the public uncanceled. Their use was discontinued Sept. 30, 1955.

Bisect uses may be on full documents or partial documents, which sell for only slightly less. Some bisects may only be found on partial documents.

CSF1

1906 **Unwmk.** **Engr.** ***Perf. 12***

RK1 CSF1 25c **dark green** 120.00
RK2 CSF1 50c **carmine** 150.00
RK3 CSF1 $1 **dark violet** 12.50
a. Diagonal half used as 50c with 2 #RK3, paying $2.50 fee, on document *325.00*
RK4 CSF1 $2 **brown** 6.75
RK5 CSF1 $2.50 **dark blue** 2.00
RK6 CSF1 $5 **brown red** 42.50
a. Horizontal or diagonal half used as $2.50, on document *250.00*
RK7 CSF1 $10 **orange** 140.00
a. Diagonal half used as $5, on partial document —

Perf. 10

RK8 CSF1 25c **dark green** 120.00
RK9 CSF1 50c **carmine** 150.00
RK10 CSF1 $1 **dark violet** 750.00
RK11 CSF1 $2 **brown** 175.00
a. Diagonal half used as $1, on document —
RK12 CSF1 $2.50 **dark blue** 32.50
RK13 CSF1 $5 **brown red** 500.00

Perf. 11

RK14 CSF1 25c **dark green** 140.00
RK15 CSF1 50c **carmine** 225.00
RK16 CSF1 $1 **dark violet** 2.25
reddish violet *2.25*
a. Diagonal half used as 50c, on document *425.00*
RK17 CSF1 $2 **brown** 2.50
RK18 CSF1 $2.50 **dark blue** 1.10
RK19 CSF1 $5 **brown red** 5.00
a. Diagonal half used as $2.50, on document 50.00
RK20 CSF1 $9 **gray** 35.00
RK21 CSF1 $10 **orange** 65.00
a. Diagonal half used as $5, on document 110.00

CSF2

1924 ***Perf. 11***

RK22 CSF2 $1 **violet** 160.00
RK23 CSF2 $2 **brown** 210.00
RK24 CSF2 $2.50 **blue** 30.00
RK25 CSF2 $5 **brown red** 140.00
RK26 CSF2 $9 **gray** 600.00
Nos. RK22-RK26 (5) 1,140.

CSF3

1925-52 ***Perf. 10***

RK27 CSF3 $1 **violet** 47.50
RK28 CSF3 $2 **brown** 125.00
RK29 CSF3 $2.50 **ultramarine** 3.00
RK30 CSF3 $5 **carmine** 27.50
RK31 CSF3 $9 **gray** 75.00

Perf. 11

RK32 CSF3 25c **green** ('37) 160.00
RK33 CSF3 50c **orange** ('34) 160.00
RK34 CSF3 $1 **deep violet** 4.00
violet 4.00
lilac 4.00
a. Diagonal half used as 50c, on document —
RK35 CSF3 $2 **brown** 5.75
RK36 CSF3 $2.50 **blue** .60
a. $2.50 ultramarine .55
RK37 CSF3 $5 **carmine** 3.50
RK38 CSF3 $9 **gray** 35.00
RK39 CSF3 $10 **blue gray** ('37) 175.00
RK40 CSF3 $20 **violet** ('52) 210.00
Nos. RK27-RK40 (14) 1,032.

Consular Fee

The "Consular Fee stamp" on revenue stamped paper (previously listed as No. RN-Y1 but since deleted) was found to be nothing more than an illustration. Two identical examples are known.

CUSTOMS FEE STAMPS

New York Custom House

Issued to indicate the collection of miscellaneous customs fees. Use was discontinued on February 28, 1918. The stamps were not utilized in the collection of customs duties.

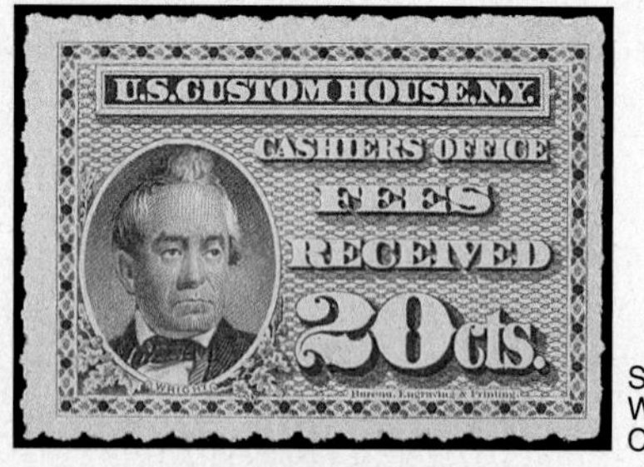

Silas Wright
CF1

Size: 48x34mm

1887 **Engr.** ***Rouletted 5½***

RL1 CF1 20c **dull rose** 150.00 2.00
a. 20c **red,** perf. 10 *7,500.*
b. Vert. half used as 10c, on document *250.00*
c. 20c **red,** rouletted 7 *500.00*
RL2 CF1 30c **orange** 190.00 3.00
RL3 CF1 40c **green** 210.00 5.00
RL4 CF1 50c **dark blue** 185.00 6.00
RL5 CF1 60c **red violet** 160.00 3.00
RL6 CF1 70c **brown violet** 170.00 35.00
RL7 CF1 80c **brown** 240.00 95.00
RL8 CF1 90c **black** 290.00 100.00
Nos. RL1-RL8 (8) 1,595. 249.00

Each of these stamps has its own distinctive background.

EMBOSSED REVENUE STAMPED PAPER

Some of the American colonies of Great Britain used embossed stamps in raising revenue, as Britain had done from 1694. The British government also imposed stamp taxes on the colonies, and in the early 19th century the U.S. government and some of the states enacted similar taxes.

Under one statute or another, these stamps were required on such documents as promissory notes, bills of exchange, insurance policies, bills of lading, bonds, protests, powers of attorney, stock certificates, letters patent, writs, conveyances, leases, mortgages, charter parties, commissions and liquor licenses.

A few of these stamps were printed, but most were colorless impressions resembling a notary public's seal.

The scant literature of these stamps includes E.B. Sterling's revenue catalogue of 1888, *The Stamps that Caused the American Revolution: The Stamps of the British Stamp Act for America,* by Adolph Koeppel, published in 1976 by the Town of North Hempstead (New York) American Revolution Bicentennial Commission, *New Discovery from British Archives on the 1765 Tax Stamps for America,* edited by Adolph Koeppel and published in 1962 by the American Revenue Association, *First Federal Issue 1798-1801 U.S. Embossed Revenue Stamped Paper,* by W.V. Combs, published in 1979 by the American Philatelic Society, *Second Federal Issue, 1801-1802,* by W.V. Combs, published in 1988 by the American Revenue Association, and *Third Federal Issue, 1814-1817,* by W.V. Combs, published in 1993 by the American Revenue Association.

Values are for stamps of clear impression on entire documents of the most common usage in good condition. The document may be folded. Unusual or rare usages may sell for much more. Parts of documents, cut squares or poor impressions sell for much less.

Colin MacR. Makepeace originally compiled the listings in this section.

INCLUDING COLONIAL EMBOSSED REVENUES

I. COLONIAL ISSUES

A. MASSACHUSETTS

Act of January 8, 1755

In effect May 1, 1755-April 30, 1757

ERP1

ERP2

ERP3

ERP4

Die 2 — ERP2

Typo.

RM1	ERP1	½p **red**	*2,500.*

Embossed

RM2	ERP2	2p	400.
RM3	ERP3	3p	160.
RM4	ERP4	4p	700.

A second die of ERP2 with no fin on the under side of the codfish has been seen. There were at least two dies of the ½p.

B. NEW YORK

Act of December 1, 1756

In effect January 1, 1757-December 31, 1760

ERP9

Typo.

RM9	ERP9	½p **red**	*1,600.*

Embossed

RM10	ERP9	1p	1,750.
RM11	ERP9	2p	450.
RM12	ERP9	3p	550.
RM13	ERP9	4p	550.

II. BRITISH REVENUES FOR USE IN AMERICA

Act of March 22, 1765

In effect November 1, 1765-May 1, 1766.

A. ALMANAC STAMPS

ERP15

Engr.

RM15	ERP15	2p **red**	
RM16	ERP15	4p **red**	*400.00*
RM17	ERP15	8p **red**	

Proofs of all of these stamps printed in the issued color are known. Full size facsimile reproductions in the color of the originals were made about 1876 of the proof sheets of the 8p stamp, Plates 1 and 2, Dies 1 to 50 inclusive.

B. PAMPHLETS AND NEWSPAPER STAMPS

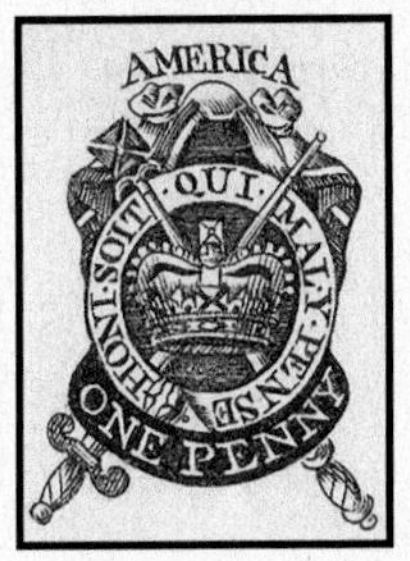

ERP18

Engr.

RM18	ERP18	½p **red,** on newspaper	*2,000.*
RM19	ERP18	1p **red**	—
RM20	ERP18	2p **red**	

Proofs of all of these stamps printed in the issued color are known. Full size facsimile reproductions in the color of the originals were made about 1876 of the proof sheets of the 1p stamp, Plates 3 and 4, Dies 51 to 100 inclusive.

C. GENERAL ISSUE

ERP24

ERP25

ERP26 ERP27

ERP28

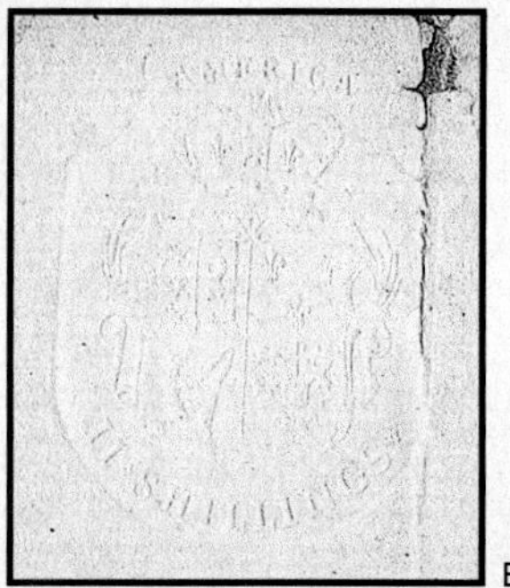
ERP29

ERP30

ERP31

ERP33

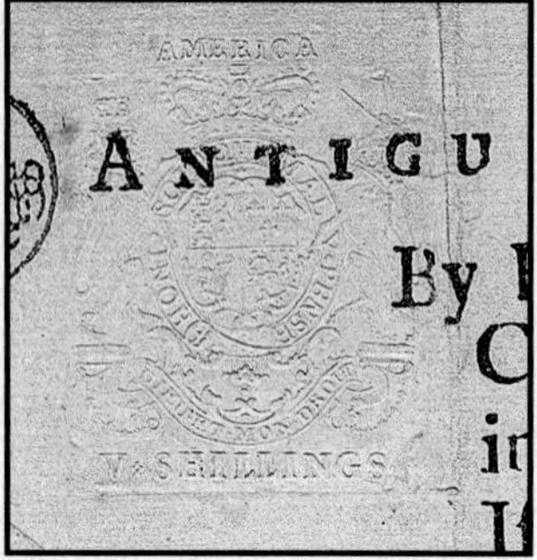

ERP34

ERP35

Embossed

RM24	ERP24	3p	*3,000.*
RM25	ERP25	4p	*22,500.*
RM26	ERP26	6p	*4,500.*
RM27	ERP27	1sh	*17,000.*
RM28	ERP28	1sh6p	*2,000.*
RM29	ERP29	2sh	*4,500.*
RM30	ERP30	2sh3p	*2,250.*
RM31	ERP31	2sh6p	*4,000.*
a.	Not on document		450.
RM33	ERP33	4sh	*2,500.*
RM34	ERP34	5sh	*3,750.*
RM35	ERP35	10sh	*8,000.*

Proofs exist of similar 1sh, 1sh6p and 2sh6p stamps inscribed "AMERICA CONT.& c."

Various Similar Designs

RM36	£1	
RM37	£2	—
RM38	£3	—
RM39	£4	
RM40	£6	—
RM41	£10	—

The £1 to £10 denominations probably exist only as proofs.

D. PLAYING CARDS STAMP

Type similar to EP29, with Arms of George III Encircled by Garter.

RM42	3sh W. India	9,000.
RM43	1sh	—

All of these were embossed without color and most of them were embossed directly on the document except the 2sh 6p which was general embossed on a rectangular piece of bluish or brownish stiff paper or cardboard only slightly larger than the stamp which was attached to the document by a small piece of metal. Three dies exist of the 3p; two of the 4p, 6p, 1sh, 1sh 6p, 2sh and 2sh 3p.

All of these stamps have the word "America" somewhere in the design and this is the feature which distinguishes them from the other British revenues. The stamps of the general issue are occasionally found with a design of a British revenue stamp struck over the American design, as a number of them were afterwards re-struck and used elsewhere as British revenues.

These stamps are sometimes called the "Teaparty" or "Tax on Tea" stamps. This, however, is a misnomer, as the act under which these stamps were issued laid no tax on tea. The tax on tea was levied by an act passed two years later, and the duties imposed by that act were not collected by stamps.

It must be remembered that these stamps were issued under an act applicable to all of the British colonies in America which included many which are not now part of the United States. Examples have been seen which were used in Quebec, Nova Scotia and in the West Indies. So great was the popular clamor against taxation by a body in which the colonists had no representation that ships bringing the stamps from England were not allowed to land them in some of the colonies, the stamps were destroyed in others, and in practically all of those which are now a part of the United States the "Stamp Masters" who were to administer the act were forced to resign and to take oath that they would never carry out the duties of the offices. Notwithstanding the very general feeling about these stamps there is evidence that a very small number of them were actually used on ships' documents for one vessel clearing from New York and for a very small number of vessels clearing from the Savannah River. Florida was at this time under British authority and the only known examples of these stamps used in what is now the United States, a 4p (#RM25), a 1sh (#RM27), and two examples of the 5sh (#RM34) were used there.

III. ISSUES OF THE UNITED STATES

A. FIRST FEDERAL ISSUE

Act of July 6, 1797

In effect July 1, 1798-February 28, 1801

RM142

RM228

The distinguishing feature of the stamps of this issue is the name of a state in the design. These stamps were issued by the Federal Government, however, and not by the states. The design, with the exception of the name of the state, was the same for each denomination; but different denominations had the shield and the eagle in different positions. The design of only one denomination of these stamps is illustrated.

In addition to the eagle and shield design on the values from four cents to ten dollars there are two other stamps for each state, similar in design to one another, one of which is illustrated above at right. All of these stamps are embossed without color.

Values are for clearly impressed examples.

RM45	4c	Connecticut	45.00
RM46	10c	Connecticut	125.00
RM47	20c	Connecticut	300.00
RM48	25c	Connecticut	45.00
RM49	30c	Connecticut	*2,750.*
RM50	50c	Connecticut	135.00
RM51	75c	Connecticut	*1,800.*
RM52	$1	Connecticut	*1,500.*
RM53	$2	Connecticut	*4,800.*
RM54	$4	Connecticut	*1,250.*
RM58	4c	Delaware	350.00
RM59	10c	Delaware	350.00
RM60	20c	Delaware	650.00
RM61	25c	Delaware	450.00
RM62	30c	Delaware	—
RM63	50c	Delaware	500.00
RM64	75c	Delaware	900.00
RM65	$1	Delaware	—
RM71	4c	Georgia	250.00
RM72	10c	Georgia	250.00
RM73	20c	Georgia	*1,550.*
RM74	25c	Georgia	250.00
RM75	30c	Georgia	*3,000.*
RM76	50c	Georgia	1,250.
RM77	75c	Georgia	*2,250.*
RM78	$1	Georgia	*2,400.*
RM84	4c	Kentucky	20.00
RM85	10c	Kentucky	100.00
RM86	20c	Kentucky	250.00
RM87	25c	Kentucky	40.00
RM88	30c	Kentucky	300.00
RM89	50c	Kentucky	60.00
RM90	75c	Kentucky	125.00
RM91	$1	Kentucky	*7,500.*
RM97	4c	Maryland	75.00
RM98	10c	Maryland	50.00
RM99	20c	Maryland	800.00
RM100	25c	Maryland	75.00
RM101	30c	Maryland	600.00
RM102	50c	Maryland	125.00
RM103	75c	Maryland	100.00
RM104	$1	Maryland	*2,500.*
RM106	$4	Maryland	—
RM110	4c	Massachusetts	20.00
RM111	10c	Massachusetts	40.00
RM112	20c	Massachusetts	85.00
RM113	25c	Massachusetts	50.00
RM114	30c	Massachusetts	500.00
RM115	50c	Massachusetts	100.00
RM116	75c	Massachusetts	900.00
RM117	$1	Massachusetts	400.00
RM123	4c	New Hampshire	30.00
RM124	10c	New Hampshire	30.00
RM125	20c	New Hampshire	750.00
RM126	25c	New Hampshire	70.00
RM127	30c	New Hampshire	425.00
RM128	50c	New Hampshire	80.00
RM129	75c	New Hampshire	80.00
RM130	$1	New Hampshire	*3,000.*
RM136	4c	New Jersey	450.00
RM137	10c	New Jersey	150.00
RM138	20c	New Jersey	*2,000.*
RM139	25c	New Jersey	110.00
RM140	30c	New Jersey	750.00
RM141	50c	New Jersey	175.00
RM142	75c	New Jersey	*2,000.*
RM143	$1	New Jersey	—
RM147	$10	New Jersey	*4,500.*
RM149	4c	New York	35.00
RM150	10c	New York	20.00
RM151	20c	New York	60.00
RM152	25c	New York	50.00
RM153	30c	New York	25.00
RM154	50c	New York	30.00
RM155	75c	New York	50.00
RM156	$1	New York	250.00
RM157	$2	New York	—
RM159	$5	New York	*3,500.*
RM160	$10	New York	*12,000.*
RM162	4c	North Carolina	50.00
RM163	10c	North Carolina	50.00
RM164	20c	North Carolina	950.00
RM165	25c	North Carolina	55.00
RM166	30c	North Carolina	3,500.
RM167	50c	North Carolina	175.00
RM168	75c	North Carolina	450.00
RM169	$1	North Carolina	*3,750.*
RM175	4c	Pennsylvania	27.50
RM176	10c	Pennsylvania	17.50

RM177	20c Pennsylvania	25.00
RM178	25c Pennsylvania	15.00
RM179	30c Pennsylvania	27.50
RM180	50c Pennsylvania	22.50
RM181	75c Pennsylvania	70.00
RM182	$1 Pennsylvania	350.00
RM184	$4 Pennsylvania	13,000.
RM187	Pennsylvania, "Ten cents per centum"	—
RM188	4c Rhode Island	35.00
RM189	10c Rhode Island	50.00
RM190	20c Rhode Island	200.00
RM191	25c Rhode Island	65.00
RM192	30c Rhode Island	2,250.
RM193	50c Rhode Island	150.00
RM194	75c Rhode Island	*1,500.*
RM195	$1 Rhode Island	*1,250.*
RM201	4c South Carolina	65.00
RM202	10c South Carolina	130.00
RM203	20c South Carolina	350.00
RM204	25c South Carolina	125.00
RM205	30c South Carolina	—
RM206	50c South Carolina	140.00
RM207	75c South Carolina	*4,000.*
RM208	$1 South Carolina	*5,000.*
RM211	$5 South Carolina	—
RM214	4c Tennessee	500.00
RM215	10c Tennessee	240.00
RM216	20c Tennessee	—
RM217	25c Tennessee	300.00
RM218	30c Tennessee	—
RM219	50c Tennessee	*1,250.*
RM220	75c Tennessee	*2,500.*
RM221	$1 Tennessee	—
RM227	4c Vermont	75.00
RM228	10c Vermont	35.00
RM229	20c Vermont	350.00
RM230	25c Vermont	100.00
RM231	30c Vermont	*1,350.*
RM232	50c Vermont	130.00
RM233	75c Vermont	*3,000.*
RM234	$1 Vermont	*2,500.*
RM238	$10 Vermont	—
RM240	4c Virginia	15.00
RM241	10c Virginia	15.00
RM242	20c Virginia	125.00
RM243	25c Virginia	20.00
RM244	30c Virginia	500.00
RM245	50c Virginia	25.00
RM246	75c Virginia	50.00
RM247	$1 Virginia	*2,000.*

The Act called for a $2, $4, $5 and $10 stamp for each state; only the listed ones have been seen.

The Act also called for a "Ten cents per centum" and a "Six mills per dollar" stamp for each state, none of which has been seen except No. RM187.

A press and a set of dies, one die for each denomination, were prepared and sent to each state where it was the duty of the Supervisors of the Revenue to stamp all documents presented to them upon payment of the proper tax. The Supervisors were also to have on hand for sale blank paper stamped with the different rates of duty to be sold to the public upon which the purchaser would later write or print the proper type of instrument corresponding with the value of the stamp impressed thereon. So far as is now known there was no distinctive watermark for the paper sold by the government. The Vermont set of dies is in the Vermont Historical Society at Montpelier.

B. SECOND FEDERAL ISSUE

Act of April 23, 1800

In effect March 1, 1801-June 30, 1802

No. RM266 Counter Stamp

No. RM266

Government watermark in italics; laid paper

RM260a	4c	15.00
RM261a	10c	20.00
RM262a	20c	65.00
RM263a	25c	15.00
RM264a	30c	75.00
RM265a	50c	65.00
RM266a	75c	30.00
RM267a	$1	250.00

Government watermark in roman; wove paper

RM260b	4c	15.00
RM261b	10c	20.00
RM262b	20c	75.00
RM263b	25c	15.00
RM264b	30c	75.00
RM265b	50c	45.00
RM266b	75c	50.00
RM267b	$1	225.00
RM271b	$10	*3,250.*

No Government watermark

RM260c	4c	50.00
RM261c	10c	50.00
RM262c	20c	85.00
RM263c	25c	17.50
RM264c	30c	400.00
RM265c	50c	85.00
RM266c	75c	100.00
RM267c	$1	200.00
RM269c	$4	*500.00*

The distinguishing feature of the stamps of this issue is the counter stamp, the left stamp shown in the illustration, which usually appears on a document below the other stamp. In the right stamp the design of the eagle and the shield are similar to their design in the same denomination of the First Federal Issue but the name of the state is omitted and the denomination appears below instead of above the eagle and the shield. All of these stamps were embossed without color.

All the paper which was furnished by the government contained the watermark vertically along the edge of the sheet, "GEN STAMP OFFICE," either in Roman capitals on wove paper or in italic capitals on laid paper. The wove paper also had in the center of each half sheet either the watermark "W. Y. & Co." or "Delaware." William Young & Co. who owned the Delaware Mills made the government paper. The laid paper omitted the watermark "Delaware." The two stamps were separately impressed. The design of the eagle and shield differed in each value.

All the stamping was done in Washington, the right stamp being put on in the General Stamp Office and the left one or counter stamp in the office of the Commissioner of the Revenue as a check on the stamping done in the General Stamp Office. The "Com. Rev. C. S." in the design of the counter stamp stands for "Commissioner of the Revenue, Counter Stamp."

The Second Federal issue was intended to include $2 and $5 stamps, but these denominations have not been seen.

C. THIRD FEDERAL ISSUE

Act of August 2, 1813

In effect January 1, 1814-December 31, 1817

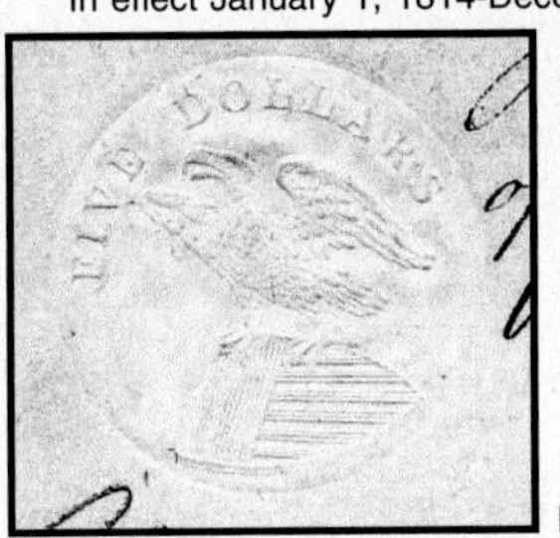

No. RM286

Watermarked

RM275a	5c	10.00
RM276a	10c	10.00
RM277a	25c	15.00
RM278a	50c	10.00
RM279a	75c	13.00
RM280a	$1	14.50
RM281a	$1.50	22.50
RM282a	$2	45.00
RM283a	$2.50	40.00
RM284a	$3.50	240.00
RM286a	$5	250.00

Unwmk.

RM275b	5c	15.00
RM276b	10c	10.00
RM277b	25c	15.00
RM278b	50c	10.00
RM279b	75c	17.50
RM280b	$1	30.00
RM281b	$1.50	100.00
RM282b	$2	100.00
RM283b	$2.50	160.00
RM284b	$3.50	150.00
RM285b	$4	*550.00*
RM286b	$5	*250.00*

The distinguishing features of the stamps of this issue are the absence of the name of a state in the design and the absence of the counter stamp. Different values show different positions of the eagle.

All stamps of this issue were embossed without color at Washington. The paper with the watermark "Stamp U. S." was sold by the government. Unwatermarked paper may be either wove or laid.

IV. ISSUES BY VARIOUS STATES

DELAWARE

Act of June 19, 1793

In effect October 1, 1793-February 7, 1794

ERP50

ERP51

ERP53

RM291	ERP50	5c	*6,500.*
RM292	ERP51	20c	*6,500.*
RM293	ERP53	50c	—

In some cases a reddish ink was used in impressing the stamp and in other cases the impressions are colorless.

Besides the denominations listed, 3c, 33c, and $1 stamps were called for by the taxing act. Stamps of these denominations have not been seen.

VIRGINIA

Act of February 20, 1813

In effect May 1, 1813-April 30, 1815

Act of December 21, 1814

In effect May 1, 1815-February 27, 1816

ERP60

ERP61

RM305	ERP61	4c	
a.	Die cut		17.50
b.	On document		100.00
RM306	ERP60	6c	
a.	Die cut		17.50
b.	On document		300.00
RM307	ERP61	10c	
b.	On document		500.00
RM308	ERP60	12c	
a.	Die cut		25.00
b.	On document		300.00
RM309	ERP61	20c	
a.	Die cut		60.00
b.	On document		500.00
RM310	ERP61	25c	
a.	Die cut		17.50
b.	On document		275.00
RM311	ERP61	37c	
a.	Die cut		17.50
b.	On document		*1,000.*
RM312	ERP61	45c	
a.	Die cut		60.00
b.	On document		*1,250.*
RM313	ERP61	50c	
a.	Die cut		17.50
b.	On document		500.00

RM314	ERP61	70c	
	a.	Die cut	40.00
	b.	On document	*1,000.*
RM315	ERP61	75c	
	a.	Die cut	17.50
	b.	On document	*750.00*
RM316	ERP61	95c	
	a.	Die cut	40.00
	b.	On document	*1,000.*
RM317	ERP61	100c	
	a.	Die cut	60.00
	b.	On document	*750.00*
RM318	ERP61	120c	
	b.	On document	*1,000.*
RM319	ERP61	125c	
	a.	Die cut	125.00
	b.	On document	*1,000.*
RM323	ERP60	175c	
	a.	Die cut	17.50
RM325	ERP61	200c	
	a.	Die cut	17.50
	b.	On document	475.00

All of these stamps are colorless impressions and with some exceptions as noted below those issued under the 1813 Act cannot be distinguished from those issued under the 1814 Act. The 10c, 20c, 45c, 70c, 95c, 120c, 145c, 150c, 170c and 190c were issued only under the 1813 Act, the 6c, 12c, and 37c only under the 1814 Act.

No. RM311 has the large lettering of EP60 but the 37 is to the left and the XXXVII to the right as in EP61. The design of the dogwood branch and berries is similar but not identical in all values.

When the tax on the document exceeded "two hundred cents," two or more stamps were impressed or attached to the document. For instance a document has been seen with 45c and 200c to make up the $2.45 rate, and another with 75c and 200c.

Since both the Virginia and the Third Federal Acts to some extent taxed the same kind of document, and since during the period from Jan. 1, 1814 to Feb. 27, 1816, both Acts were in effect in Virginia, some instruments have both stamps on them.

The circular die cut Virginia stamps about 29mm in diameter were cut out of previously stamped paper which after the Act was repealed, was presented for redemption at the office of the Auditor of Public Accounts. They were threaded on fine twine and until about 1940 preserved in his office as required by law. Watermarked die cut Virginia stamps are all cut out of Third Federal watermarked paper.

Not seen yet, the 145c, 150c, and 170c stamps were called for by the 1813 Act, and 195c by both the 1813 and 1814 Acts.

MARYLAND

1. Act of February 11, 1818
In effect May 1, 1818-March 7, 1819

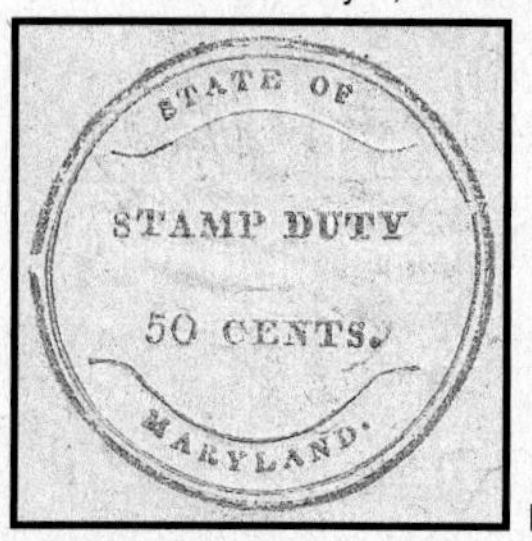

ERP70

RM362	ERP70	30c **red,** printed	400.
		Sheet of 4	*2,000.*
RM363	ERP70	50c **red,** printed	—

The Act called for five other denominations, none of which has been seen. The Act imposing this tax was held unconstitutional by the United States Supreme Court in the case of McCulloch vs. Maryland.

2. Act of March 10, 1845
In effect May 10, 1845-March 10, 1856

ERP71

RM370	ERP71	10c	15.00
RM371	ERP71	15c	14.00
RM372	ERP71	25c	14.00
RM373	ERP71	50c	16.00
RM374	ERP71	75c	40.00
RM375	ERP71	$1	16.00
RM376	ERP71	$1.50	35.00
RM377	ERP71	$2	60.00
RM378	ERP71	$2.50	20.00
RM379	ERP71	$3.50	60.00
RM380	ERP71	$4	100.00
RM381	ERP71	$5.50	60.00
RM382	ERP71	$6	75.00

Nos. RM370-RM382 are embossed without color with a similar design for each value. They vary in size from 20mm in diameter for the 10c to 33mm for the $6.

V. FEDERAL LICENSES TO SELL LIQUOR, ETC.

1. Act of June 5, 1794
In effect September 30, 1794-June 30, 1802

ERP80

RM400	ERP80	$5	600.00

Provisionals are in existence using the second issue Connecticut Supervisors' stamp with the words "Five Dollars" written or printed over it or the second issue of the New Hampshire Supervisors' stamp without the words "Five Dollars."

2. Act of August 2, 1813
In effect January 1, 1814-December 31, 1817

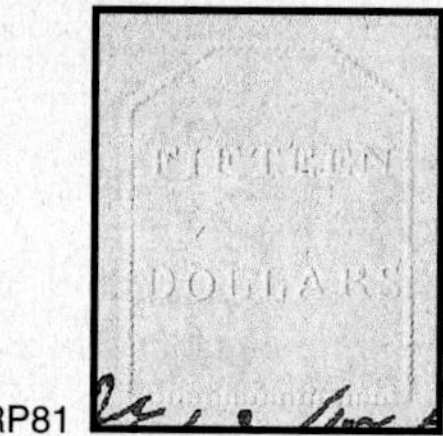

ERP81

RM451	ERP81	$10	750.00
RM452	ERP81	$12	775.00
RM453	ERP81	$15	425.00
RM454	ERP81	$18	900.00
RM455	ERP81	$20	*4,250.*
RM456	ERP81	$22.50	700.00
RM457	ERP81	$25	600.00
RM458	ERP81	$30	*4,000.*
RM459	ERP81	$37.50	550.00

The Act of December 23, 1814, increased the basic rates of $10, $12, $15, $20 and $25 by 50 per cent, effective February 1, 1815. This increase applied to the unexpired portions of the year so far as licenses then in effect were concerned and these licenses were required to be brought in and to have the payment of the additional tax endorsed on them.

VI. FEDERAL LICENSES TO WORK A STILL

Act of July 24, 1813
In effect January 1, 1814-December 31, 1817

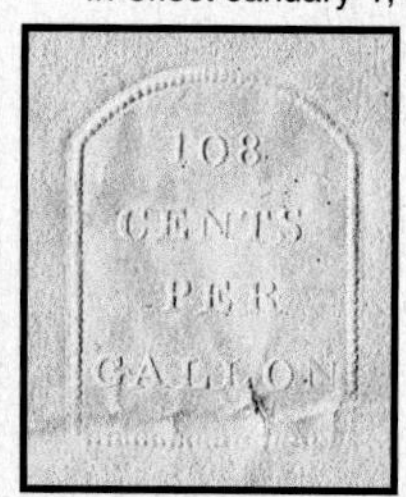

(Embossed) — ERP82

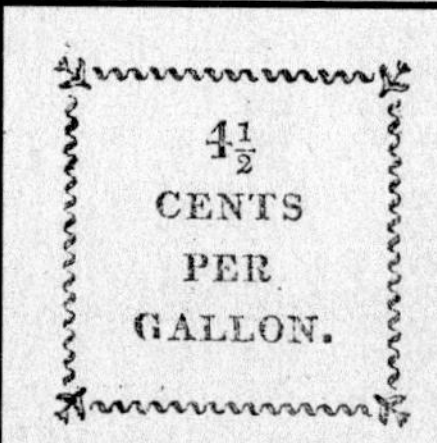

(Printed) — ERP83

RM466	4½c		
	b. ERP83	Printed	*2,000.*
RM468	9c		
	a. ERP82	Embossed	*1,500.*
	b. ERP83	Printed	*1,800.*
RM471	18c		
	a. ERP82	Embossed	—
	b. ERP83	Printed	*1,400.*
RM472	21c		
	a. ERP82	Embossed	—
RM475	32c		
	a. ERP82	Embossed	*1,000.*
RM477	36c		
	b. ERP83	Printed	*2,100.*
RM478	42c		
	b. ERP83	Embossed	*1,750.*
RM480	52c		
	a. ERP82	Embossed	*2,000.*
RM484	70c		
	a. ERP82	Embossed	*2,100.*
RM488	$1.08		
	a. ERP82	Embossed	*2,000.*

The statute under which these were issued provided for additional rates of 2½c, 5c, 10c, 16c, 25c, 26c, 35c, 42c, 50c, 54c, 60c, 64c, 84c, $1.04, $1.05, $1.20, $1.35, $1.40, $2.10, $2.16 and $2.70 per gallon of the capacity of the still. Stamps of these denominations have not been seen.

VII. SUPERVISORS' AND CUSTOM HOUSE SEALS

1. Seals came into use on required certificates, as follows: April 1, 1791, imported tea; July 1, 1791, domestic and imported distilled spirits; July 1, 1792 imported wine.

Check Letter Shown in Left Field — ERP90

RM501	ERP90	B	South Carolina	40.00
RM503	ERP90	D	Virginia	*1,350.*
RM505	ERP90	F	Delaware	—
RM506	ERP90	G	Pennsylvania	90.00
RM508	ERP90	I	New York	22.50
RM509	ERP90	K	Connecticut	30.00
RM510	ERP90	L	Rhode Island	90.00
RM511	ERP90	M	Massachusetts	22.50
RM512	ERP90	N	New Hampshire	700.00
RM514	ERP90	P	Kentucky	1,000.

Use of RM501-RM514 on domestic distilled spirits shows payment of the tax that was being resisted in the Whiskey Rebellion. All such reported uses are from New York and the New England States and are quite scarce. Nos. RM501-RM514 were removed from service in late 1799. In Connecticut and Massachusetts, they were passed on to the Collector of Customs in those states for use beginning July 1, 1802.

2. Use from October 2, 1799

ERP91

RM552	ERP91	North Carolina	500.00
RM553	ERP91	Virginia	900.00
RM554	ERP91	Maryland	200.00
RM556	ERP91	Pennsylvania	250.00
RM558	ERP91	New York	15.00
RM559	ERP91	Connecticut	30.00
RM560	ERP91	Rhode Island	35.00
RM561	ERP91	Massachusetts	25.00
RM562	ERP91	New Hampshire	90.00

Nos. RM552-RM562 were necessitated by excessive wear on Nos. RM501-RM514.

3. Custom House Seals

ERP92

RM575	ERP92	Custom House, Philadelphia	50.00
RM576	ERP92	Custom House, Perth Amboy, N.J.	250.00
RM577	ERP92	Custom House, Port of Noblesboro, District of Maine	250.00

The Philadelphia Customs House Seal came into use in 1802 and was used on import documents for distilled spirits, tea and wine. It functioned in the way that the Supervisor's Seals functioned in other states. When the Perth Amboy Customs House

Seal came into use is not known, but there are recorded examples from the 1820s.

The editors would like to hear from those having other Customs House Seals used on import documents.

REVENUE STAMPED PAPER

These stamps were printed in various denominations and designs on a variety of financial documents, including checks, drafts, receipts, specie clerk statements, insurance policies, bonds and stock certificates.

They were authorized by Act of Congress of July 1, 1862, effective October 1, 1862, although regular delivery of stamped paper did not begin until July 1, 1865. The 2-cent tax on receipts ended Oct. 1, 1870. The 2-cent tax on checks and sight drafts ended July 1, 1883. All other taxes ended Oct. 1, 1872. The use of stamped paper was revived by the War Revenue Act of 1898, approved June 13, 1898. Type X was used July 1, 1898 through June 30, 1902.

Most of these stamps were typographed; some, types H, I and J, were engraved. They were printed by private firms under supervision of government representatives from dies loaned by the Bureau of Internal Revenue. Types A-F, P-W were printed by the American Phototype Co., New York (1865-75); type G, Graphic Co., New York (1875-83); types H-L, Joseph R. Carpenter, Philadelphia (1866-75); types M-N, A. Trochsler, Boston (1873-75); type O, Morey and Sherwood, Chicago (1874). Type X was printed by numerous regional printers under contract with the government.

Samples of these stamps are known for types B-G, P and Q with a section of the design removed and replaced by the word "Sample." Types G, P-Q, U-W exist with a redemption clause added by typography or rubber stamp. Redeemed type X's have a 5mm punched hole.

Multiples or single impressions on various plain papers are usually considered proofs or printers' waste.

For further information see "Handbook for United States Revenue Stamped Paper," published (1979) by the American Revenue Association.

Illustration size varies, with actual size quoted for each type.

Values for types A-O are for clear impressions on plain entire checks and receipts. Attractive documents with vignettes sell for more. The value of individual examples is also affected by the place of use. For example, territorial usage generally sells for more than a similar item from New York City.

Values for types P-W are for stamps on documents with attractive engravings, usually stock certificates, bonds and insurance policies.

Examples on plain documents and cut squares sell for less.

Type A

Size: 22x25mm

RN-A1	2c **black**	90.	75.
	a. Printed on both sides		30.
RN-A2	2c **orange**		160.
RN-A3	2c **gray**		*2,000.*
RN-A4	2c **blue**		*8,000.*
RN-A5	2c **brown**		*5,000.*
RN-A8	2c **purple**		*2,000.*
RN-A9	2c **green**		*1,350.*
	a. Inverted		—

No. RN-A4 is unique. The unique example of No. RN-A9a is on a partial document. The catalogue value for RN-A8 is for an impression on William Moller & Son stationery; a second more violet shade is on Carter, Kirkland & Co. receipts. Value of latter is $3,250.

Same Type with 1 Entire and 53 or 56 Partial Impressions in Vertical Format ("Tapeworm")
Left Col. — Full Document
Right Col. — Strip with Bank Names

RN-A10	2c **orange**, 1 full plus 56 partial impressions	675.	100.
	Cut square (full strip without bank names)		45.
RN-A11	2c **orange**, 1 full plus 53 partial impressions	*1,100.*	250.

Nos. RN-A10 and RN-A11 were used by the Mechanics' National Bank of New York on a bank specie clerk's statement. It was designed so that the full stamp or one of the repeated bottom segments fell on each line opposite the name of a bank.

The three additional banks were added at the bottom of the form. No. RN-A11 must show white space below the "First National Bank" line.

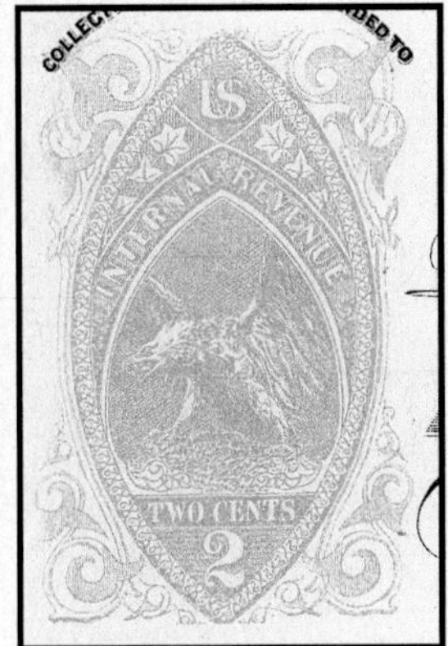

Eagle Type B

Size: 31x48mm

RN-B1	2c **orange**	5.00	3.00
	yellow orange	5.00	3.00
	deep orange	5.00	3.00
	a. Printed on both sides	200.00	20.00
	b. Double impression	350.00	
	c. Printed on back		—
	d. With 10 centimes blue French handstamp, right	400.00	
	e. Inverted		*600.00*

The unique example of No. RN-B1e is on a partial document.

All examples of the previously-listed "yellow" have some red in them.

RN-B2	2c **black**		40.00
RN-B3	2c **blue**		40.00
	light blue		40.00
RN-B4	2c **brown**	125.00	40.00
RN-B5	2c **bronze**		40.00
RN-B6	2c **green** (shades)	110.00	15.00
RN-B10	2c **red** (shades)	200.00	22.50
RN-B11	2c **purple**		125.00
RN-B13	2c **violet** (shades)	125.00	40.00
	a. 2c **violet brown**		45.00

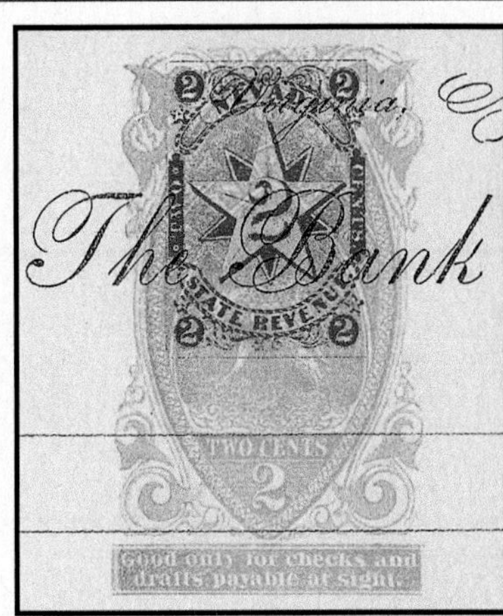

"Good only for checks and drafts payable at sight." in Rectangular Tablet at Base

RN-B16	2c **orange**	45.00	12.50
	a. With 2c orange red Nevada	325.00	250.00

"Good only for checks and drafts payable at sight." in Octagonal Tablet at Base

RN-B17	2c **orange**	42.50	10.00
	a. Tablet inverted		1,750.
	b. With 2c orange red Nevada		35.00
	c. With 2c green Nevada		35.00
	d. With 2c dull violet Nevada		*1,500.*
	e. With 2c brownish violet Nevada		*2,500.*

"Good when issued for the payment of money." in Octagonal Tablet at Base

RN-B20	2c **orange**	70.00	15.00
	a. Printed on both sides	30.00	10.00
	b. As "a," one stamp inverted		*1,500.*
	c. Tablet inverted		*4,000.*

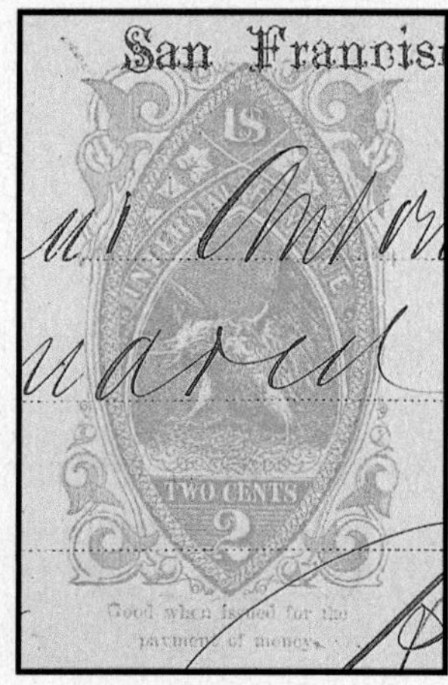

"Good when issued for the payment of money" in two lines at base in orange

RN-B23 2c **orange** 900.00

"Good when the amount does not exceed $100." in Octagonal Tablet at Base

RN-B24 2c **orange** 200.00 50.00

Washington Type C

Size: 108x49mm

RN-C1 2c **orange** 7.00 4.00
red orange 7.00 4.00
yellow orange 7.00 4.00
salmon 8.00 4.00
brown orange 8.00 4.00
a. "Good when used..." vert. at left black *2,250.*

All examples of the previously-listed "yellow" have some red in them.

RN-C2 2c **brown** 30.00 12.00
a. 2c **buff** 30.00 12.00
RN-C5 2c **pale red** (shades) 50.00 25.00
RN-C8 2c **green** —

"Good only for Sight Draft" in two lines in color of stamp

RN-C9 2c **orange,** legend at lower right 85.00 50.00
RN-C11 2c **brown,** legend at lower left 110.00
RN-C13 2c **orange,** legend at lower left 45.00 20.00

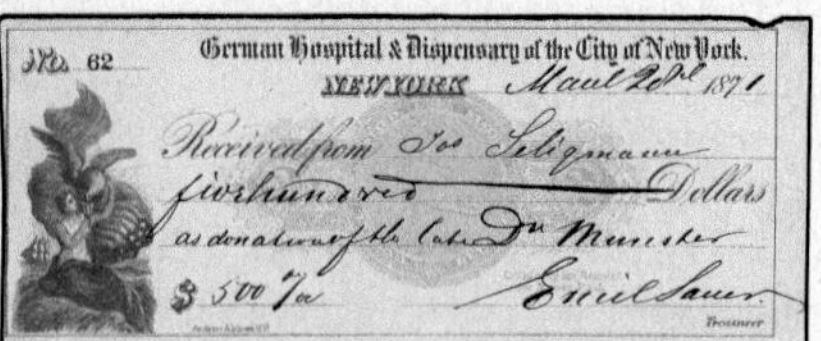

"Good only for Receipt for Money Paid" in two lines in color of stamp

RN-C15 2c **orange,** legend at lower right *2,500.* *1,750.*
RN-C16 2c **orange,** legend at lower left 350.00

"Good when issued for the payment of money" in one line at base in color of stamp

RN-C17 2c **orange** (shades) 575.00

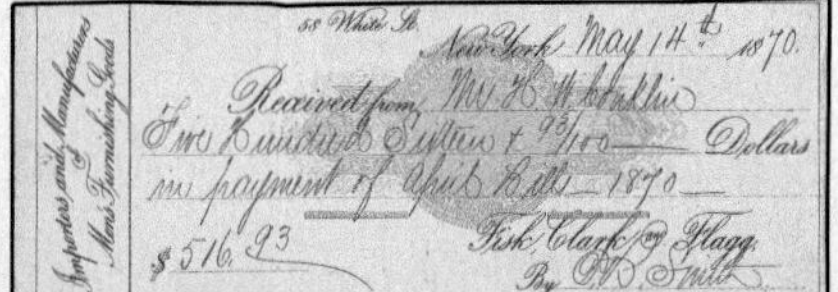

"Good when issued for the/Payment of Money" in two tablets at lower left and right

RN-C19 2c **orange** 550.00
a. Printed on both sides 35.00

"Good/only for Bank/Check" in 3-part Band

RN-C21 2c **orange** 60.00 12.50
salmon 12.50
yellow orange 20.00
a. Inverted 750.00
b. With 2c red orange Nevada 140.00 65.00
c. Printed on back *2,900.*
RN-C22 2c **brown** 300.00 25.00
a. Printed on back 1,800.

"Good when the amount does not exceed $100" in tablet at lower right

RN-C26 2c **orange** 200.00

Franklin Type D

Size: 80x43mm

RN-D1 2c **orange** (shades) 10.00 4.00
a. Double impression —
b. Printed on back 700.00 400.00
c. Inverted 475.00

All examples of the previously-listed "yellow" have some red in them and are included in the "shades."

RN-D3 2c **brown** *3,000.* *500.00*
RN-D4 2c **buff** (shades) 9.00 5.00
RN-D5 2c **red** *2,000.*

"Good only for/Bank Check" in panels within circles at left and right

RN-D7 2c **orange** 25.00 10.00
a. Printed on back 2,100.

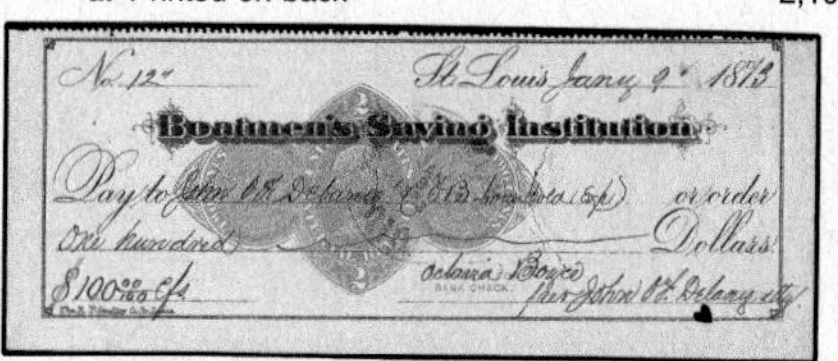

"Good only for/Bank Check" in two lines at lower right in color of stamp

RN-D8 2c **orange** 850.00

"Good only for Sight Draft" in two lines at lower left in color of stamp

RN-D9 2c **orange** 175.00 75.00

Franklin Type E

Size: 28x50mm

RN-E2 2c **brown** *1,200.*
RN-E4 2c **orange** 12.50 5.00
Broken die, lower right or left 40.00 20.00
a. Double impression *925.00*

"Good only for sight draft" in two lines at base in orange

RN-E5 2c **orange** 75.00 37.50

"Good only for Bank / Check" in two lines at base in orange

RN-E6 2c **orange** —

"Good only for / Bank Check" in colorless letters in two lines above and below portrait

RN-E7 2c **orange** 75.00 17.50
a. Double impression —

Franklin Type F

Size: 56x34mm

RN-F1 2c **orange** 10.00 5.00
a. Inverted —

All examples of the previously-listed "yellow" have some red in them

Liberty Type G

Size: 80x48mm

RN-G1 2c **orange** 6.00 4.00
a. Printed on back 65.00 40.00
b. Printed on back, inverted 125.00 50.00

All examples of the previously-listed "yellow" have some red in them.

Imprint: "Graphic Co., New York" at left and right in minute type

RN-G3 2c **orange** 100.00 100.00

Eagle Type H

Size: 32x50mm

RN-H3	2c **orange**	15.00	5.00
	a. Inverted		—
	b. Double impression		600.00
	c. "Good when used for payment of money," black		*750.00*
	d. "Good when used as a receipt for payment of money," black		*750.00*
	e. As "d," upward at left		*1,600.*
	f. As "d," legend in red		*1,500.*
	g. "Good when used as a receipt for the payment of money," black		*400.00*
	h. As "g," inverted legend		*7,500.*
	i. As "g," legend in two lines		*700.00*
	j. As "g," legend in violet		*700.00*
	k. As "g," legend in yellow		*2,000.*
	l. "Good only when used as a receipt for the payment of moneys," black		*750.00*

"Good for check or sight draft only" at left and right in color of stamp

RN-H5	2c **orange**		

Experts claim that No. RN-H5 exists only as a proof.

"Good for bank check or sight draft only" in black

RN-H6	2c **orange**		150.00

Type I

Design R2 of 1862-72 adhesive revenues "BANK CHECK"

Size: 20x23mm

RN-I1	2c **orange**		225.00

"U.S. INTER. REV."

RN-I2	2c **orange**	650.00	350.00

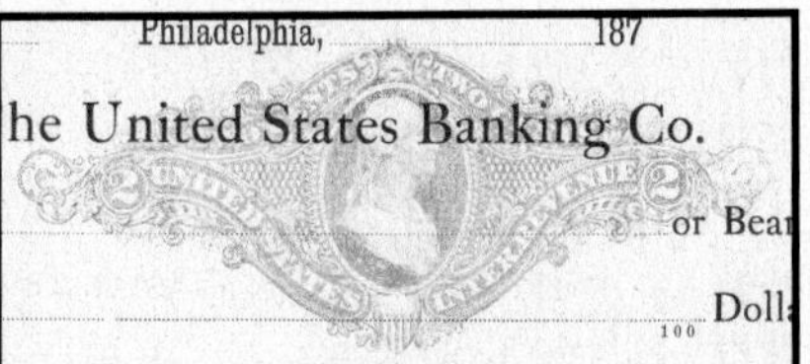

Washington Type J

Size: 100x40mm

Background of medallion crosshatched, filling oval except for bust

RN-J4	2c **orange**	20.00	10.00
	pale orange	20.00	10.00
	deep orange	50.00	12.50
	a. Double impression		*500.00*
	b. "Good only for . . ." added vertically at left in red orange		750.00
RN-J5	2c **red**	50.00	13.00
	a. Double impression		—

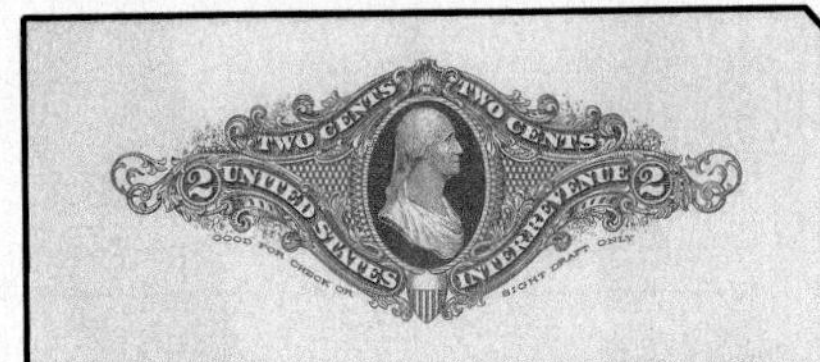

"Good for check or sight draft only" curved, below

RN-J9	2c **red**	—	*2,000.*

Background shaded below bust and at left.

RN-J11	2c **orange**	60.00	15.00
	a. Double impression, 203x72mm		

Washington Type K

Size: 84x38mm

RN-K1	2c **blue**		—
RN-K4	2c **gray**	45.00	15.00
	pale gray	45.00	10.00
RN-K5	2c **brown**	160.00	125.00
RN-K6	2c **orange**	15.00	7.50
RN-K8	2c **red** (shades)	575.00	350.00
RN-K11	2c **olive**	175.00	175.00
	pale olive		110.00

Washington Type L

Size: 50x33mm

RN-L1	2c **blue** (shades)	175.00	—
RN-L2	2c **turquoise**	250.00	200.00
RN-L3	2c **gray**	35.00	20.00
	pale gray	35.00	20.00
RN-L4	2c **green**	900.00	600.00
	light green	600.00	400.00
RN-L5	2c **orange**	15.00	10.00
RN-L6	2c **olive**		55.00
	gray olive		30.00
RN-L10	2c **red**	15.00	10.00
	a. 2c **violet red**	15.00	10.00
RN-L13	2c **brown**	—	275.00

Washington Type M

Size: 68x37mm

RN-M2	2c **orange**	50.00	10.00
	a. Printed on back, inverted		*1,600.*

All examples of the previously-listed "yellow" have some red in them.

RN-M3	2c **green**		475.00
RN-M4	2c **gray**		1,250.

Eagle, Numeral and Monitor Type N

Size: 107x48mm

RN-N3	2c **orange**	60.00	15.00
	a. Printed on back	300.00	225.00
	b. Inverted		900.00
RN-N4	2c **light brown**		150.00

Liberty Type O

Size: 75x35mm

RN-O2	2c **orange**	1,750.	600.

Values for types P-W

are for stamps on documents with attractive engravings, usually stock certificates, bonds and insurance policies. Examples on plain documents sell for less.

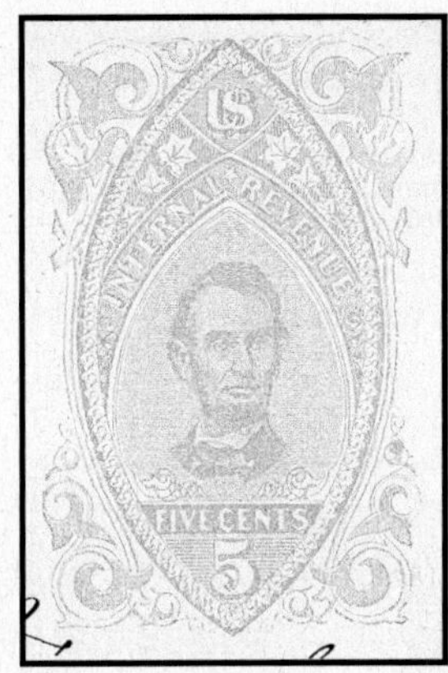

Lincoln Type P

Size: 32x49mm

RN-P2	5c **brown**		350.00
	Cut square		90.00
RN-P3	5c **green**		—
RN-P4	5c **pink**		—
RN-P5	5c **orange**	50.00	45.00
	Cut square		8.00

All examples of the previously listed "yellow" have some orange in them.

RN-P6	5c **red** (shades)	—	210.00
	Cut square		40.00

No. RN-P3 only exists in combination with a 25c green or 50c green. No. RN-P4 is unique and only exists in combination with a $1 pink. See Nos. RN-T2, RN-V1, RN-W6.

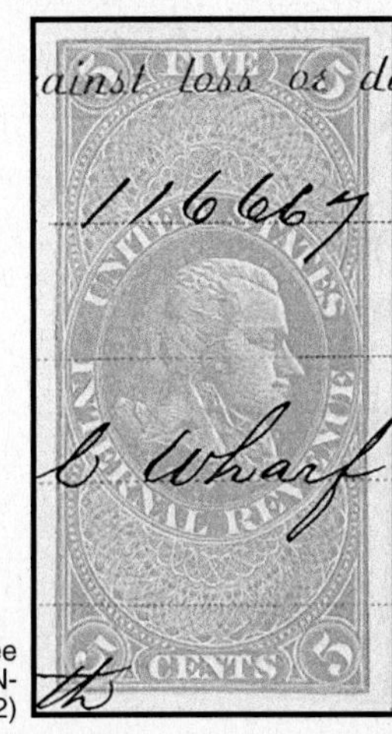

Madison Type Q (See note before No. RN-P2)

Size: 28x56mm

RN-Q1	5c **orange**	175.	150.
	Cut square		20.
	brownish orange	175.	150.
RN-Q2	5c **brown**		*2,750.*
	Cut square		500.

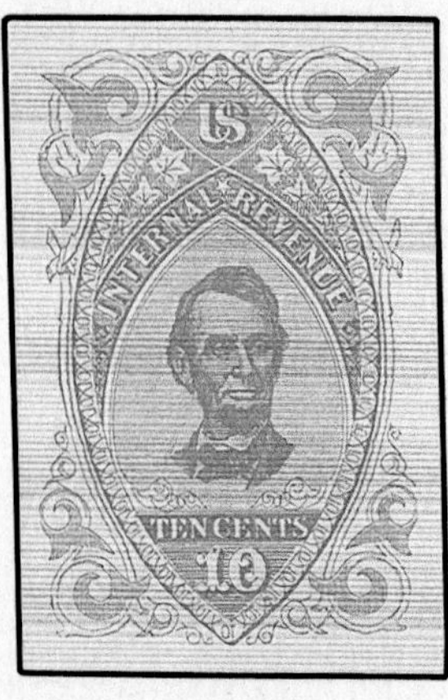

Type R, Frame as Type B, Lincoln in Center

Size: 32x49mm

RN-R1	10c **brown**		*2,500.*
RN-R2	10c **pale red**	—	675.
	Cut square		100.
RN-R3	10c **orange**		500.
	Cut square		50.

"Good when the premium does not exceed $10" in tablet at base

RN-R6	10c **orange**	—	400.
	Cut square		50.

Motto Without Tablet

RN-R7	10c **orange**		
	Cut square		500.

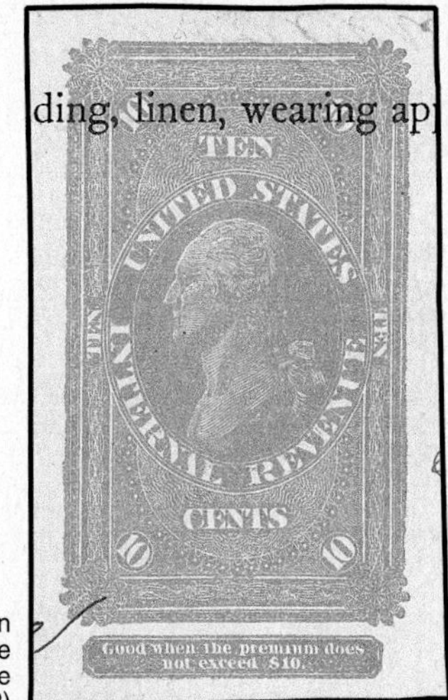

Washington Type S (See note before No. RN-P2)

Size: 33x54mm

RN-S1	10c **orange**		*3,750.*

"Good when the premium does not exceed $10" in tablet at base

RN-S2	10c **orange**		*4,750.*
	Cut square		500.

Eagle Type T (See note before No. RN-P2)

For type T design with Lincoln in center see type V, Nos. RN-V1 to RN-V10.

Size: 33x40mm

RN-T1	25c **black**	—	
	Cut square		—
RN-T2	25c **green**		*7,500.*
RN-T3	25c **red**	175.00	*100.00*
	Cut square		9.00

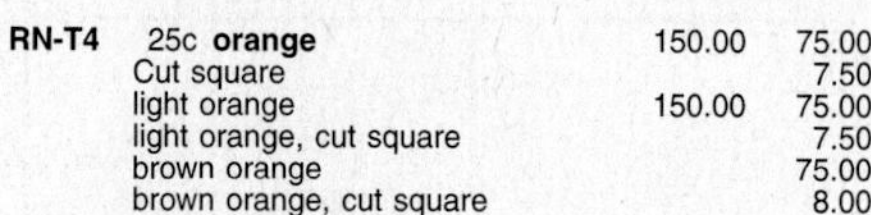

RN-T4	25c **orange**	150.00	75.00
	Cut square		7.50
	light orange	150.00	75.00
	light orange, cut square		7.50
	brown orange		75.00
	brown orange, cut square		8.00

No. RN-T2 includes No. RN-P3, and a 25c green, type T, obliterating a No. RN-V4.

"Good when the premium does not exceed $50" in tablet at base

RN-T6	25c **orange**	450.	350.
	Cut square		50.
RN-T7	25c **orange,** motto without tablet		1,500.
	Cut square		400.

"Good when the amount insured shall not exceed $1000" in tablet at base

RN-T8	25c **deep orange**	800.	700.
	Cut square		75.
RN-T9	25c **orange,** motto without tablet		
	Cut square		600.

Franklin Type U (See note before No. RN-P2)

Size: 126x65mm

RN-U1	25c **orange**	35.00	35.00
	Cut square		5.00
RN-U2	25c **brown**	45.00	35.00
	Cut square		5.00

"Good when the premium does not exceed $50" in tablet at lower right

RN-U3	25c **red**		*8,000.*
RN-U4	25c **orange**		*2,500.*
	Cut square		400.

Tablet at lower left

RN-U5	25c **red**	800.	
	Cut square		250.
RN-U6	25c **orange**	500.	450.
	Cut square		65.

All examples of the previously-listed "yellow" have some red in them.

Tablet at base

RN-U7	25c **brown**		*1,750.*
	Cut square		300.
RN-U9	25c **orange**		*1,000.*
	Cut square		400.

Lincoln Type V

Size: 32x41mm

RN-V1	50c **green**		175.00
	Cut square		52.50
RN-V2	50c **brown**	—	400.00
	Cut square		125.00
RN-V4	50c **orange**	175.00	90.00
	Cut square		17.50
	deep orange	175.00	90.00
	deep orange, cut square		17.50
RN-V5	50c **red**	700.00	
	Cut square		250.00

No. RN-V1 includes a 50c green, type V, and a No. RN-P3, obliterating a No. RN-W2.

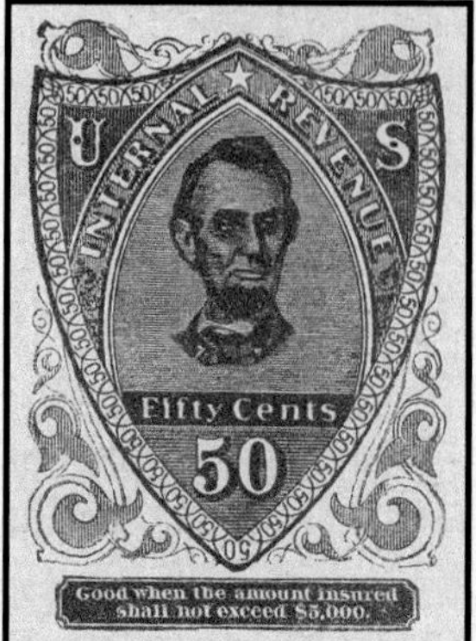

"Good when the amount insured shall not exceed $5000" in tablet at base

RN-V6	50c **orange**	450.00	400.00
	Cut square		65.00
RN-V9	50c **red**		—
	Cut square		550.00

Motto Without Tablet

RN-V10	50c **orange**		
	Cut square		600.00

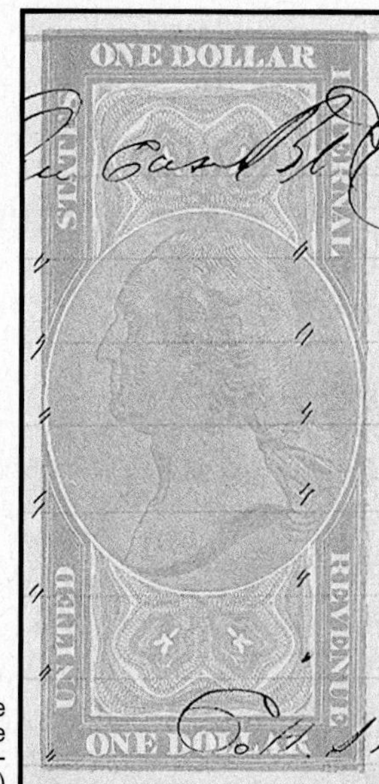

Washington Type W (See note before No. RN-P2)

Size: 34x73mm

RN-W2	$1 **orange** (shades)	150.00	85.00
	Cut square		15.00
RN-W5	$1 **brown**		*4,500.*
RN-W6	$1 **pink**		*3,750.*

The former light brown is now included with the orange shades.

No. RN-W6 used with No. RN-P4 is unique. Two examples of No. RN-W6 exist used alone.

SPANISH-AMERICAN WAR SERIES

Many of these stamps were used for parlor car tax and often were torn in two or more parts.

Liberty Type X

1898 **Size: 68x38mm**

RN-X1	1c **rose**	800.00	—
	Partial		65.00
	dark red, partial		65.00
RN-X4	1c **orange**	165.00	
a.	On pullman ticket	600.00	—
	Partial		25.00
b.	As "a," printed on back		
	As "a," printed on back, partial		65.00

No.	Description	Unused	Used
RN-X5	1c **green**	65.00	30.00
	Partial		25.00
a.	On parlor car ticket	65.00	15.00
b.	On pullman ticket	500.00	
	On pullman ticket, partial		15.00
RN-X6	2c **yellow**	2.00	1.00
	pale olive		*900.00*
RN-X7	2c **orange**	3.00	2.00
	pale orange	3.00	2.00
a.	Printed on back only	500.00	500.00
c.	Printed on front and back	—	*2,500.*
d.	Vertical		85.00
e.	Double impression		—
f.	On pullman ticket	1,000.	200.00
g.	Inverted		750.00

No. RN-X1 exists only as a four-part unused pullman ticket, used as an unsevered auditor's and passenger's parts of the four-part ticket, or partial as a used half of a two-part ticket. Nos. RN-X4a and RN-X5b exist as unused two-part tickets and as used half portions. No. RN-X7f exists as an unused four-part ticket and as a used two-piece portion with nearly complete stamp design.

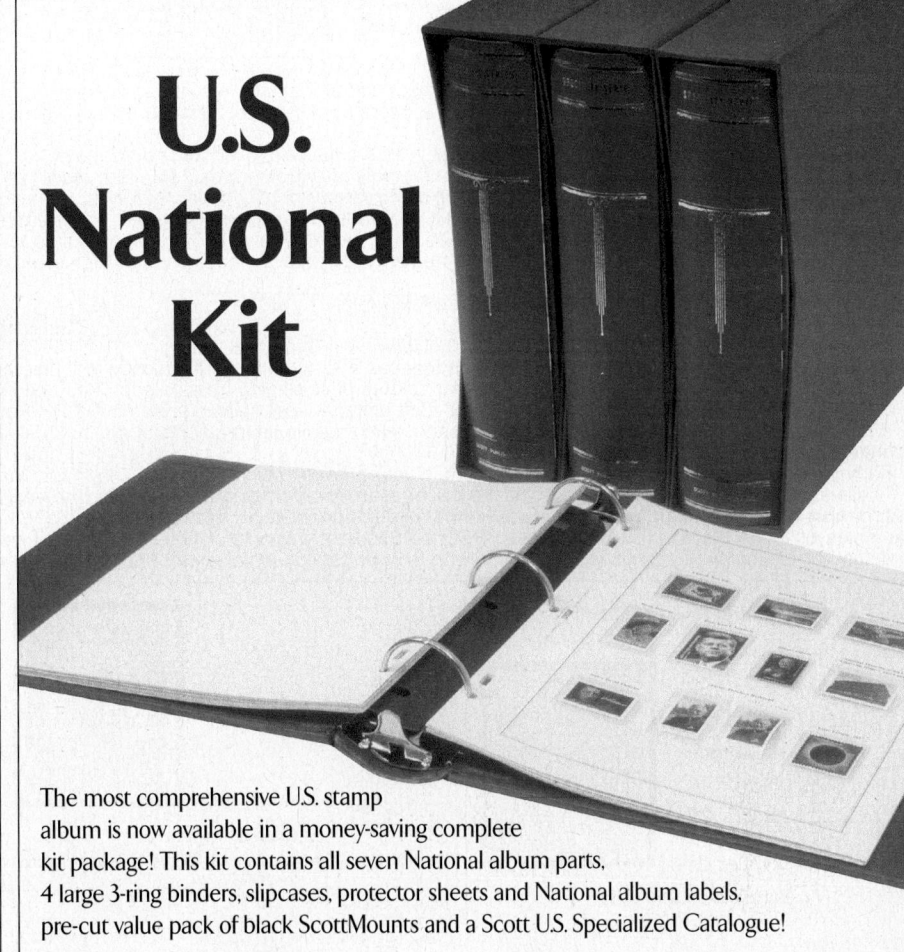

PRIVATE DIE PROPRIETARY STAMPS

The extraordinary demands of the Civil War upon the Federal Treasury resulted in Congress devising and passing the Revenue Act of 1862. The Government provided revenue stamps to be affixed to boxes or packages of matches, and to proprietary medicines, perfumery, playing cards — as well as to documents, etc.

But manufacturers were permitted, at their expense, to have dies engraved and plates made for their exclusive use. Many were only too willing to do this because a discount or premium of from 5% to 10% was allowed on orders from the die which often made it possible for them to undersell their competitors. Also, the considerable advertising value of the stamps could not be overlooked. These are now known as Private Die Proprietary stamps.

The face value of the stamp used on matches was determined by the number, i.e., 1c for each 100 matches or fraction thereof. Medicines and perfumery were taxed at the rate of 1c for each 25 cents of the retail value or fraction thereof up to $1 and 2c for each 50 cents or fraction above that amount. Playing cards were first taxed at the same rate but subsequently the tax was 5c for a deck of 52 cards and 10c for a greater number of cards or double decks.

The stamp tax was repealed on March 3, 1883, effective July 1, 1883.

The various papers were:

a. Old paper, 1862-71. First Issue. Hard and brittle varying from thick to thin.
b. Silk paper, 1871-77. Second Issue. Soft and porous with threads of silk, mostly red, blue and black, up to ¼inch in length.
c. Pink paper, 1877-78. Third Issue. Soft paper colored pink ranging from pale to deep shades.
d. Watermarked paper, 1878-83. Fourth Issue. Soft porous paper showing part of "USIR." Roulettes on watermarked paper are rouletted 6.
e. Experimental silk paper. Medium smooth paper, containing minute fragments of silk threads either blue alone or blue and red (infrequent), widely scattered, sometimes but a single fiber on a stamp.

Early printings of some private die revenue stamps are on paper which appears to have laid lines.

These stamps were usually torn in opening the box or container. **Values quoted are for fine-veryfine examples that may be somewhat faulty but reasonably attractive, with the faults usually not readily apparent on the face.** Nos. RS278-RS306 are valued in the grade of very fine. Sound examples of these stamps (other than Nos. RS278-RS306) at a grade of fine-very fine can sell for 50% to 300% more than catalogue value. Outstanding examples of stamps in this section with a lower catalogue value can bring many multiples of catalogue value.

PRIVATE DIE MATCH STAMPS

A

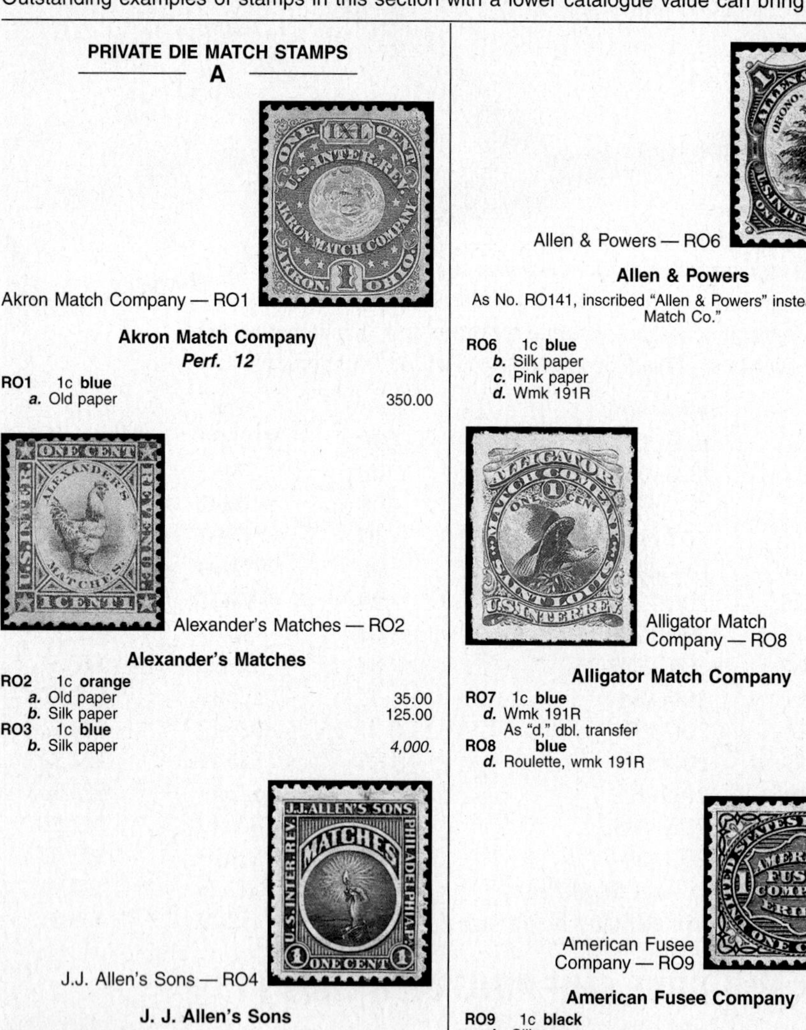

Akron Match Company — RO1

Akron Match Company
Perf. 12

RO1 1c **blue**
a. Old paper 350.00

Alexander's Matches — RO2

Alexander's Matches

RO2 1c **orange**
a. Old paper 35.00
b. Silk paper 125.00
RO3 1c **blue**
b. Silk paper *4,000.*

J.J. Allen's Sons — RO4

J. J. Allen's Sons

RO4 1c **blue**
d. Wmk. 191R 16.00

Thos. Allen — RO5

Thos. Allen

RO5 1c **green**
a. Old paper 175.00

Allen & Powers — RO6

Allen & Powers

As No. RO141, inscribed "Allen & Powers" instead of "Orono Match Co."

RO6 1c **blue**
b. Silk paper 7.75
c. Pink paper 35.00
d. Wmk 191R 11.00

Alligator Match Company — RO8

Alligator Match Company

RO7 1c **blue**
d. Wmk 191R 24.00
As "d," dbl. transfer —
RO8 **blue**
d. Roulette, wmk 191R 140.00

American Fusee Company — RO9

American Fusee Company

RO9 1c **black**
b. Silk paper 10.00
c. Pink paper 11.00
As "c," dbl. transfer 125.00
d. Wmk 191R 10.00
As "d," dbl. transfer —

American Match Company — RO10

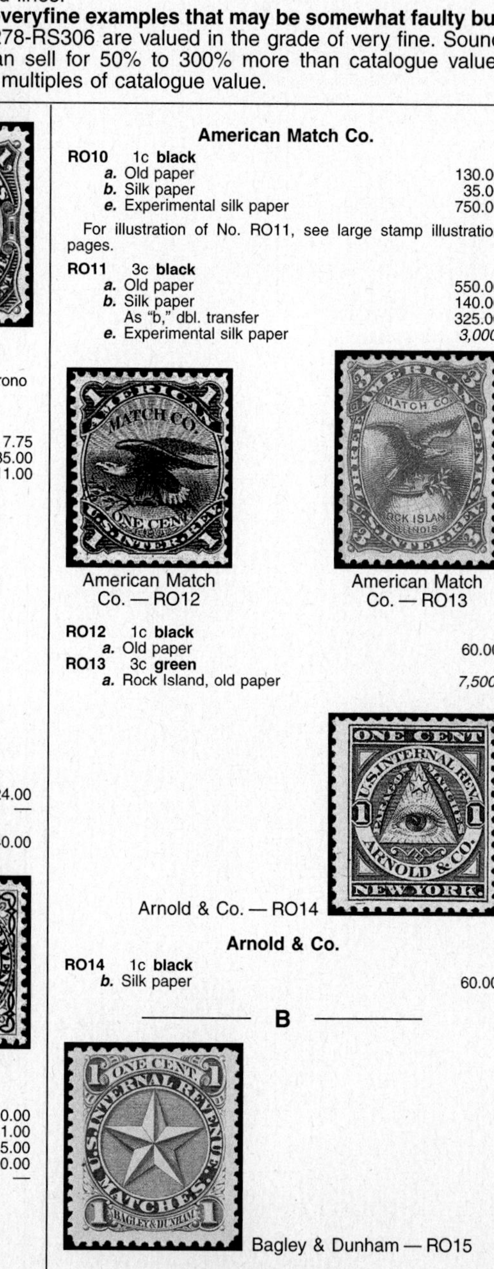

American Match Co.

RO10 1c **black**
a. Old paper 130.00
b. Silk paper 35.00
e. Experimental silk paper 750.00

For illustration of No. RO11, see large stamp illustration pages.

RO11 3c **black**
a. Old paper 550.00
b. Silk paper 140.00
As "b," dbl. transfer 325.00
e. Experimental silk paper *3,000.*

American Match Co. — RO12

American Match Co. — RO13

RO12 1c **black**
a. Old paper 60.00
RO13 3c **green**
a. Rock Island, old paper *7,500.*

Arnold & Co. — RO14

Arnold & Co.

RO14 1c **black**
b. Silk paper 60.00

B

Bagley & Dunham — RO15

Bagley & Dunham

RO15 **green**
d. Wmk 191R 32.50

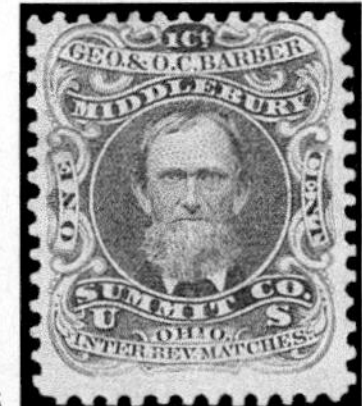
Geo. & O. C. Barber — RO16

Geo. & O. C. Barber

As No. RO17, inscribed "Geo. & O. C. Barber" instead of "Barber Match Co."

RO16 **blue**
a. Old paper 72.50

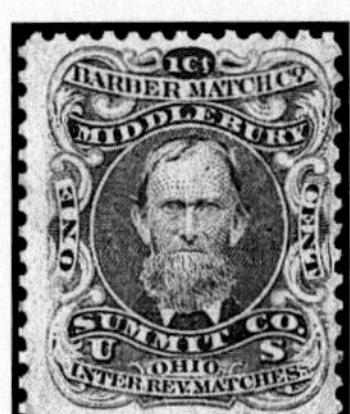
Barber Match Co. — RO17

Barber Match Co.

RO17 1c **blue**
a. Old paper 25.00
As "a," dbl. transfer 85.00
b. Silk paper 1.25
As "b," dbl. transfer 37.50
c. Pink paper 20.00
As "b," dbl. transfer 85.00
d. Wmk 191R 1.75
As "d," dbl. transfer 35.00
e. Experimental silk paper 175.00
u. **Ultra,** old paper 600.00
RO18 1c **blue**
d. Roulette, wmk 191R 5,000.
RO19 3c **black**
a. Old paper 200.00
b. Silk paper 140.00
e. Experimental silk paper *1,000.*

Barber & Peckham — RO20

Barber & Peckham

RO20 1c **blue**
a. Old paper 67.50

For illustration of No. RO21, see large stamp illustration pages.

RO21 3c **black**
a. Old paper 300.00

Bauer & Beudel — RO22

Bauer & Beudel

RO22 1c **blue**
a. Old paper 72.50
b. Silk paper 250.00
u. **Ultra,** old paper 325.00

A.B. & S. (A. Beecher & Son) — RO23

A. B. & S. (A. Beecher & Son)

As No. RO175, inscribed "A. B. & S." instead of "C. B. C. S." in the four corners.

RO23 1c **orange**
a. Old paper 17.00
As "a," dbl. transfer —
b. Silk paper 67.50
As "b," dbl. transfer —
e. Experimental silk paper 175.00
As "e," dbl. transfer 225.00

RO24

B. Bendel & Co. — RO25

Illustration reduced.

B. Bendel & Co.

RO24 1c **brown**
b. Silk paper 2.75
As "b," dbl. transfer —
d. Wmk. 191R 750.00
RO25 12c **brown**
b. Silk paper 500.00

H. Bendel — RO26

H. Bendel

Nos. RO26-RO27 are RO24-RO25 altered to read "H. Bendel doing business as B. Bendel & Co."

RO26 1c **brown**
b. Silk paper 5.00
c. Pink paper 2.50
d. Wmk. 191R 2.00
RO27 12c **brown**
b. Silk paper 550.00

H. & M. Bentz — RO28

H. & M. Bentz

RO28 1c **blue**
a. Old paper 42.50

Bent & Lea — RO29

Bent & Lea

RO29 1c **black**
a. Old paper 40.00
As "a," dbl. transfer at left 125.00
e. Experimental silk paper 50.00
As "e," dbl. transfer 900.00

B. J. & Co. — RO30

B. J. & Co. (Barber, Jones & Co.)

As No. RO100 with "B. J. & Co." added above eagle.

RO30 1c **green**
b. Silk paper 140.00
As "b," dbl. transfer 175.00

Bock, Schneider & Co. — RO31

Bock, Schneider & Co.

RO31 1c **black**
b. Silk paper 20.00

Wm. Bond & Co. — RO32/RO33

Wm. Bond & Co.

RO32 4c **black**
b. Silk paper 275.00
RO33 4c **green**
b. Silk paper 175.00
c. Pink paper 200.00
d. Wmk. 191R 18.00

Bousfield & Poole — RO34/RO35

Bousfield & Poole

RO34 1c **lilac**
a. Old paper 275.00
As "a," dbl. transfer 300.00
RO35 1c **black**
a. Old paper 18.00
As "a," dbl. transfer 70.00
b. Silk paper 15.00
As "b," dbl. transfer 90.00
e. Experimental silk paper 90.00

For illustration of Nos. RO36-RO37, see large stamp illustration pages.

RO36 3c **lilac**
a. Old paper 3,000.
RO37 3c **black**
a. Old paper 200.00
b. Silk paper 150.00
As "b," dbl. transfer 175.00
e. Experimental silk paper 2,000.

Barber & Peckham – RO21

Bousfield & Poole – RO37

Byam, Carlton & Co. – RO51

American Match Co. RO11

Byam, Carlton & Co. – RO52

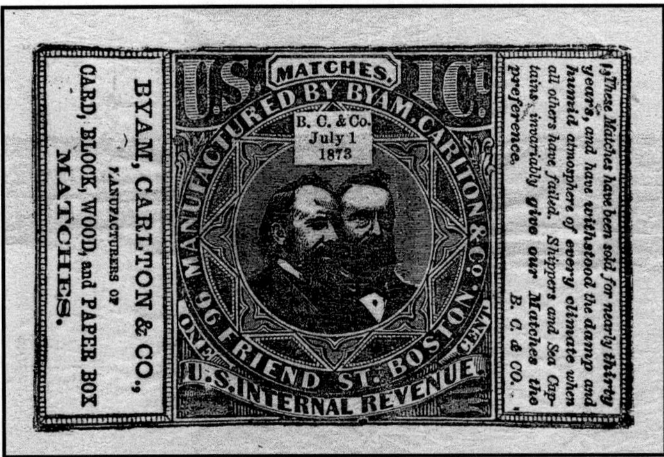

Byam, Carlton & Co. – RO54

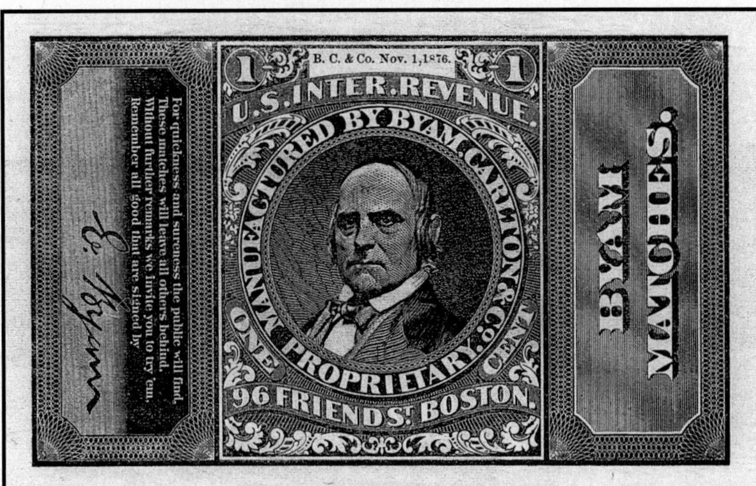

Byam, Carlton & Co. – RO55

Byam, Carlton & Co. – RO56

Wm. Gates – RO90

Boutell & Maynard — RO38

Boutell & Maynard

RO38 1c **black**
b. Silk paper 300.00

Bowers & Dunham — RO39

Bowers & Dunham

As No. RO15, inscribed "Bowers & Dunham" instead of "Bagley & Dunham."

RO39 1c **green**
d. Wmk 191R 275.00
RO40 1c **blue**
d. Wmk 191R 95.00

B. & N. (Brocket & Newton) — RO41

B. & N. (Brocket & Newton)

RO41 1c **lake**
b. Die I, silk paper 45.00
RO42 1c **lake**
b. Die II, silk paper 8.25

The initials "B. & N." measure 5¼mm across the top on Die I, and 4¾mm on Die II.

RO43

Brown & Durling

RO43 1c **black**
a. Old paper 2,500.
RO44 1c **green**
a. Old paper 82.50

L. W. Buck & Co. — RO45

L. W. Buck & Co.

RO45 1c **black**
a. Old paper *3,000.*
e. Experimental silk paper 2,000.

D. Burhans & Co. — RO46

D. Burhans & Co.

RO46 1c **black**
a. Old paper 200.00
As "a," dbl. transfer 275.00
b. Silk paper *10,000.*
e. Experimental silk paper 1,100.

Charles Busch — RO47

Charles Busch

RO47 1c **black**
d. Wmk 191R 35.00

Byam, Carlton & Co. — RO48

Byam, Carlton & Co.

RO48 1c **black**
a. Imperf., old paper *6,500.*

2 heads to left, 41x75mm.

Byam, Carlton & Co. — RO49

RO49 1c **black,** 19x23mm
a. Old paper 27.50
b. Silk paper 7.75
d. Wmk 191R 2.00
As "d," dbl. transfer 140.00
e. Experimental silk paper 140.00
i. As "d," Vert. pair, imperf. horiz. 140.00
RO50 1c **black**
a. Old paper 2,000.

2 heads to left, buff wrapper, 131x99mm.

For illustrations of Nos. RO51, RO52, RO54, RO55 and RO56, see large stamp illustration pages.

RO51 1c **black**
a. Old paper 275.00

As #RO50, 131x89mm.

RO52 1c **black**
a. Old paper 70.00

1 head to right, white wrapper, 94x54mm.

RO53 1c **black**
a. Old paper 175.00

As #RO52, buff wrapper.

RO54 1c **black**
a. Old paper 11.00
h. Right block reading up 60.00

2 heads to right, buff wrapper, 81x50mm

RO55 1c **black**
a. Old paper 35.00

1 head to left, white wrapper, 94x56mm.

RO56 1c **black**
a. Old paper 10.00

As #RO50, 95x57mm.

C

Cannon Match Co. — RO57

Cannon Match Co.

As No. RO68, "Cannon Match Co." instead of "W. D. Curtis."

RO57 1c **green**
c. Pink paper 55.00

Cardinal Match Co. — RO58

Cardinal Match Co.

RO58 1c **lake**
d. Wmk 191R 32.50

As No. RO41, "F.E.C." instead of "B. & N." — RO59

F. E. C. (Frank E. Clark)

RO59 1c **lake**
a. Old paper 110.00
b. Silk paper 110.00
e. Experimental silk paper 150.00

Chicago Match Co. — RO60

Chicago Match Co.

RO60 3c **black**
a. Old paper 1,000.

Henry A. Clark — RO61

Henry A. Clark

RO61 1c **green**
b. Silk paper 110.00

Jas. L. Clark — RO62/RO63

Jas. L. Clark

RO62 1c **green**
b. Silk paper 2.75
c. Pink paper 27.50
d. Wmk 191R 1.75
As "d," dbl. transfer 67.50
RO63 1c **green**
d. Rouletted, wmk 191R 2,000.

Clark Match Co. — RO64

The Clark Match Co.

RO64 1c **lake**
b. Silk paper 10.00

Cramer & Kemp — RO65/RO66

Cramer & Kemp

RO65 1c **black**
a. Old paper 72.50
RO66 1c **blue**
a. Old paper 125.00
b. Silk paper 7.75
e. Experimental silk paper *1,500.*
u. **Ultra,** old paper 750.00

Crown Match Co. — RO67

Crown Match Co.

RO67 1c **black**
b. Silk paper 25.00

W. D. Curtis Matches — RO68

W. D. Curtis Matches

RO68 1c **green**
a. Old paper 160.00
b. Silk paper 140.00
e. Experimental silk paper 1,000.

D

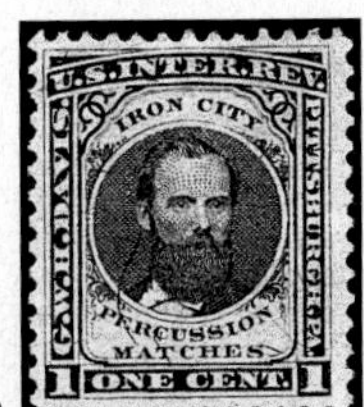
G. W. H. Davis — RO69/RO70

G. W. H. Davis

RO69 1c **black**
b. Silk paper 52.50
RO70 1c **carmine**
d. Wmk 191R 125.00

W.E. Doolittle — RO71

W. E. Doolittle

RO71 1c **blue**
a. Old paper 550.00

E. P. Dunham — RO72

E. P. Dunham

RO72 1c **green**
d. Wmk 191R 90.00

E

Jas. Eaton — RO73

Jas. Eaton — RO74

Jas. Eaton

RO73 1c **black**
a. Old paper 55.00
b. Silk paper 1.50
c. Pink paper 20.00
d. Wmk 191R 1.75
e. Experimental silk paper 225.00
RO74 1c **black**
d. Wmk 191R, rouletted 72.50

E.B. Eddy — RO75

E.B. Eddy — RO75A

E. B. Eddy

RO75 1c **carmine**
d. Wmk 191R, Die I 25.00
RO75A 1c **carmine**
d. Wmk 191R, Die II 40.00

Die II shows eagle strongly recut; ribbon across bottom is narrower; color is deeper.

Aug. Eichele — RO76

Aug. Eichele

RO76 1c **black**
a. Old paper 160.00

P. Eichele & Co. — RO77

P. Eichele & Co.

As No. RO78, "P. Eichele & Co." at top.

RO77 1c **blue**
a. Old paper 67.50
b. Silk paper 8.25
e. Experimental silk paper 225.00
u. **Ultra,** old paper 1,750.

Eichele & Co. — RO78/RO79

Eichele & Co.

RO78 1c **blue**
b. Silk paper 5.00
c. Pink paper 20.00
d. Wmk 191R 4.50
RO79 1c **blue**
d. Wmk 191R, rouletted 500.00

J.W. Eisenhart's — RO80

J. W. Eisenhart's Matches

RO80 1c **blue**
b. Silk paper 55.00
c. Pink paper 125.00
d. Wmk 191R 42.50

Excelsior Match Co.—RO81/RO82

Excelsior Match Co.

RO81 1c **black**
b. Silk paper, Watertown, NY 110.00
RO82 1c **black**
b. Silk paper, Syracuse, NY 10.00
c. Pink paper 20.00
d. Wmk 191R 10.00
As "d," dbl. transfer 52.50

Excelsior Match, Baltimore — RO83

Excelsior Match, Baltimore, Md.

RO83	1c **blue**	
a.	Old paper	95.00
b.	Silk paper	125.00
u.	**Ultra,** old paper	1,250.

F

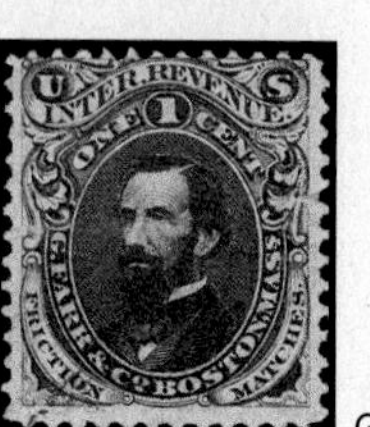
G. Farr & Co. — RO84

G. Farr & Co.

RO84	1c **black**	
a.	Old paper	140.00

L. Frank — RO85

L. Frank

RO85	1c **brown**	
b.	Silk paper	110.00

G

Gardner, Beer & Co. — RO86

Gardner, Beer & Co.

RO86	1c **black**	
c.	Pink paper	300.00

Wm. Gates — RO88

Wm. Gates

RO87	1c **black**	
a.	Old paper, Die I	9.00
b.	Silk paper, Die I	6.00
RO88	1c **black**	
a.	Old paper, Die II	50.00
b.	Silk paper, Die II	5.50
	As "b," dbl. transfer	35.00
e.	Experimental silk paper	1,250.

The shirt collar is colorless in Die I and shaded in Die II. The colorless circle surrounding the portrait appears about twice as wide on Die I as it does on Die II.

RO89	3c **black**	
a.	Old paper	60.00
	As "a," dbl. transfer	92.50
b.	Silk paper	52.50
	As "b," dbl. transfer	90.00
d.	Wmk 191R	
	As "d," dbl. transfer	—
e.	Experimental silk paper	225.00
	As "e," dbl. transfer	—

For illustration of Nos. RO90-RO91, see large stamp illustration pages.

RO90	6c **black**	
a.	Old paper	200.00
RO91	3c **black**	
b.	Silk paper, 3 1c stamps	160.00

William Gates' Sons — RO92

William Gates' Sons

The 1c is as No. RO87, 3c as No. RO91, "William Gates' Sons" replaces "Wm. Gates."

For illustration of No. RO94, see large stamp illustration pages.

RO92	1c **black**	
b.	Silk paper	35.00
c.	Pink paper	11.00
d.	Wmk 191R	2.25
RO93	1c **black**	
d.	Wmk 191R, rouletted	*3,250.*
RO94	3c **black**	
b.	Silk paper, 3 1c stamps	140.00
c.	Pink paper	200.00
d.	Wmk 191R	95.00

A. Goldback & Co. — RO95

A. Goldback & Co.

RO95	1c **green**	
b.	Silk paper	55.00

A. Goldback — RO96

A. Goldback

As No. RO95, "A. Goldback" instead of "A. Goldback & Co."

RO96	1c **green**	
b.	Silk paper	200.00
c.	Pink paper	15,000.

T. Gorman & Bro. — RO97

T. Gorman & Bro.

As No. RO99, "T. Gorman & Bro." instead of "Thomas Gorman."

RO97	1c **black**	
a.	Old paper	1,100.
	As "a," dbl. transfer	—
RO98	1c **green**	
a.	Old paper	35.00
	As "a," dbl. transfer	—
b.	Silk paper	40.00

Thomas Gorman

RO99	1c **green**	
b.	Silk paper	4.50
c.	Pink paper	40.00
d.	Wmk 191R	82.50

Greenleaf & Co. — RO100

Greenleaf & Co. — RO101/RO102

Greenleaf & Co.

RO100	1c **green**	
a.	Old paper	100.00
b.	Silk paper	125.00
e.	Experimental silk paper	1,500.
RO101	3c **carmine**	95.00
a.	Old paper	95.00
b.	Silk paper	175.00
e.	Experimental silk paper	1,250.
RO102	5c **orange**	
a.	Old paper	175.00
b.	Silk paper	4,500.
e.	Experimental silk paper	1,250.

Griggs & Goodwill — RO103/RO104

Griggs & Goodwill

RO103	1c **black**	
b.	Silk paper	60.00
RO104	1c **green**	
b.	Silk paper	35.00
	As "b," dbl. transfer	160.00

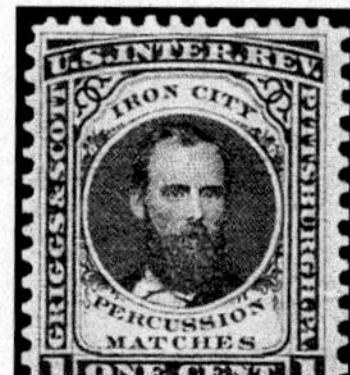
As No. RO69, inscribed "Griggs & Scott" instead of "G. W. H. Davis." — RO105

Griggs & Scott

RO105	1c **black**	
a.	Old paper	12.00
b.	Silk paper	42.50
e.	Experimental silk paper	80.00

H

Charles S. Hale — RO106

Charles S. Hale

RO106	1c **green**	
c.	Pink paper	300.00

Henning & Bonhack — RO107

Henning & Bonhack

RO107	1c **blue**	
a.	Old paper	500.00

W. E. Henry & Co. — RO108

W. E. Henry & Co.

RO108 1c **red**
d. Wmk 191R 35.00
RO109 1c **black**
d. Wmk 191R 17.00

J. G. Hotchkiss — RO110

The J. G. Hotchkiss Match Co.

RO110 1c **green**
b. Silk paper 17.00
c. Pink paper 50.00
d. Wmk 191R 12.00

B. & H. D. Howard

RO111 1c **lake**
a. Old paper 125.00
RO112 1c **blue**
a. Old paper 12.00
u. **Ultra,** old paper 1,000.

L. G. Hunt — RO113

L. G. Hunt

RO113 1c **black**
a. Old paper 850.00
b. Silk paper 1,650.
e. Experimental silk paper 750.00

D. F. Hutchinson Jr. — RO114

D. F. Hutchinson Jr.

RO114 1c **lake**
d. Wmk 191R 22.50

I

As No. RO116, "Ives Matches" instead of "P. T. Ives." — RO115

Ives Matches

RO115 1c **blue**
a. Old paper 7.75
As "a," dbl. transfer —
b. Silk paper 6.75
u. **Ultra,** old paper 950.00

P. T. Ives — RO116/RO117

P. T. Ives

For illustration of No. RO118, see large stamp illustration pages.

RO116 1c **blue**
b. Silk paper 7.75
c. Pink paper 45.00
d. Wmk 191R 5.00
RO117 1c **blue**
d. Wmk 191R, rouletted 650.00
RO118 8c **blue**
a. Old paper 240.00
e. Experimental silk paper *2,500.*
u. **Ultra,** old paper *3,250.*

Ives & Judd — RO119

Ives & Judd

RO119 1c **green**
b. Silk paper 27.50
c. Pink paper 60.00
d. Wmk 191R 160.00

Ives & Judd Match Co. — RO120

The Ives & Judd Match Co.

RO120 1c **green**
d. Wmk 191R 140.00
As "d," dbl. transfer 325.00

J

Jock & Wildner — RO120A

Jock & Wildner

RO120A 1c **red brown**
a. Old paper, imperf. *9,000.*

Some specialists believe No. RO120A was not officially issued. Three examples are recorded.

K

Kirby & Sons — RO121

Kirby & Sons

RO121 1c **green**
b. Silk paper 77.50

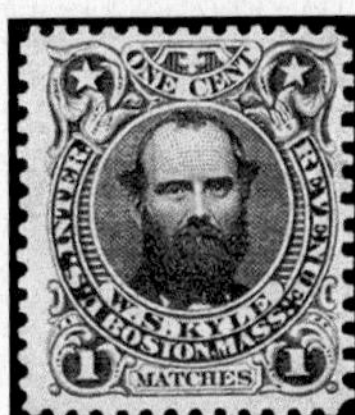
W. S. Kyle — RO122

W. S. Kyle

RO122 1c **black**
a. Old paper 22.50
As "d," dbl. transfer 82.50
b. Silk paper 17.00
e. Experimental silk paper *2,500.*

L

Lacour's Matches — RO123

Lacour's Matches

RO123 1c **black**
a. Old paper 20.00
As "a,"dbl. transfer 110.00
b. Silk paper 60.00
e. Experimental silk paper 200.00

Leeds, Robinson & Co. — RO124

Leeds, Robinson & Co.

RO124 1c **green**
d. Wmk 191R 82.50

H. Leigh — RO125

H. Leigh

RO125 1c **blue**
d. Wmk 191R 11.00

Leigh & Palmer — RO126

Leigh & Palmer

As No. RO125, "Leigh & Palmer" replaces "H. Leigh."

RO126	1c **black**	
	b. Silk paper	25.00
	c. Pink paper	77.50
	d. Wmk 191R	47.50

John Loehr — RO127

John Loehr

RO127	1c **blue**	
	b. Silk paper	27.50

As No. RO127, "Joseph" replaces "John." — RO128

Joseph Loehr

RO128	1c **blue**	
	b. Silk paper	3.50
	c. Pink paper	22.50
	d. Wmk 191R	5.50

M

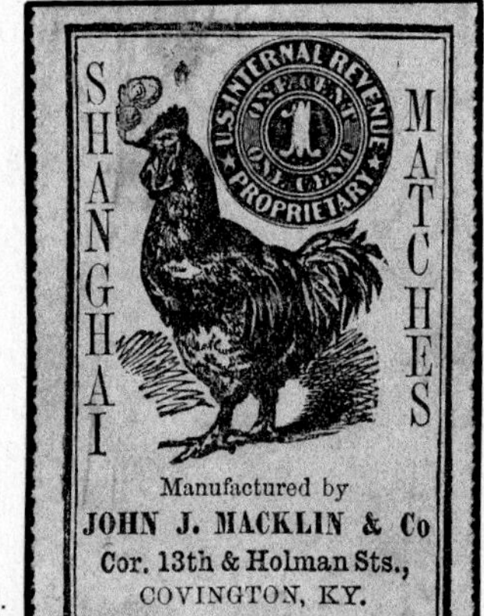

John J. Macklin & Co. — RO129

John J. Macklin & Co.

RO129	1c **black**	
	a. Old paper, rouletted	*10,000.*
	f. Thin buff paper, rouletted	*20,000.*

F. Mansfield & Co. — RO130

F. Mansfield & Co.

RO130	1c **blue**	
	b. Silk paper	7.25
	c. Pink paper	15.00
	d. Wmk 191R	14.00

Maryland Match Co. — RO131

Maryland Match Co.

RO131	1c **blue**	
	b. Silk paper	140.00
	d. Wmk 191R	*42,500.*

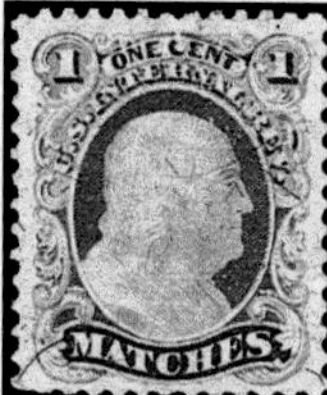

"Matches" — RO132

"Matches"

RO132	1c **blue**	
	a. Old paper	7.75
	As "a," dbl. transfer	110.00
	b. Silk paper	5.50
	e. Experimental silk paper	160.00
	u. **Ultra,** old paper	*2,000.*

See Nos. RO168-RO169.

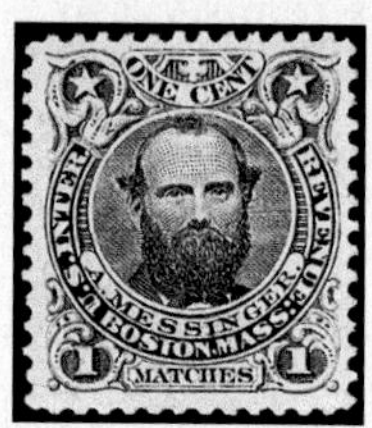

A. Messinger — RO133

A. Messinger

RO133	1c **black**	
	b. Silk paper	4.50
	c. Pink paper	20.00
	d. Wmk 191R	4.00

N

National Match Co. — RO134

National Match Co.

RO134	1c **blue**	
	d. Wmk 191R	77.50

Newbauer & Co. (N. & C.) follows No. RO139.

National Union Match Co. items are bogus.

F. P. Newton — RO135

F. P. Newton

RO135	1c **lake**	
	b. Silk paper	3.50
	c. Pink paper	17.50
	d. Wmk 191R	4.50

See No. RO64 for another "The Clark Match Co." design.

New York Match Co. — RO136

New York Match Co. — RO137

New York Match Co.

No. RO136 is as No. RO22, "New York Match Co." instead of "Bauer & Beudel."

RO136	1c **blue**	
	a. Old paper, Shield	1,000.
	b. Silk paper	9.00

No. RO137 is as No. RO111, "New York Match Co." instead of "B. & H. D. Howard."

RO137	1c **vermilion**	
	a. Old paper, Eagle	100.00
	b. Silk paper	11,000.
	e. Experimental silk paper	500.00
	As "e," dbl. transfer	625.00

New York Match Co. — RO139

RO138	1c **green,** 22x60mm	
	a. Old paper	60.00
	b. Silk paper	11.00
	e. Experimental silk paper	110.00
RO139	5c **blue,** 22x60mm	
	b. Silk paper	1,000.

N. & C. — RO140

N. & C. (Newbauer & Co.)

RO140	4c **green**	
	b. Silk paper	5.50
	c. Pink paper	140.00
	d. Wmk 191R	6.75
	i. As "b," imperf., pair, unused	*1,000.*

O

Orono Match Co. — RO141

Orono Match Co.

RO141	1c **blue**	
	a. Old paper	40.00
	b. Silk paper	40.00
	e. Experimental silk paper	1,750.
	u. **Ultra,** old paper	1,500.

P

Park City Match Co. — RO142

Park City Match Co.

RO142	1c **green**	
	a. Old paper	55.00
	b. Silk paper	52.50
	e. Experimental silk paper	2,500.
RO143	3c **orange**	
	a. Old paper	60.00
	e. Experimental silk paper	—

Penn Match Co. Limited — RO144

Penn Match Co. Limited

RO144	1c **blue**	
	d. Wmk 191R	50.00

Pierce Match Co. — RO145

Pierce Match Co.

RO145	1c **green**	
	a. Old paper	4,000.

P. M. Co. (Portland M. Co.) — RO146

P. M. Co. (Portland M. Co.)

RO146	1c **black**	
	a. Old paper	27.50

Portland Match Co.

RO147	1c **black**	
	a. Old paper, wrapper	110.00

The value of No. RO147 applies to the most common date (Dec. 1866); all others are much rarer.

V.R. Powell — RO148

V.R. Powell—RO149-RO151

V. R. Powell

RO148	1c **blue**	
	a. Old paper	10.00
	As "a," dbl. transfer	110.00
	b. Silk paper	12.00
	e. Experimental silk paper	175.00
	u. **Ultra,** old paper	1,000.
RO149	1c **black**	
	a. Old paper	*7,000.*

Buff wrapper, uncut.

RO150	1c **black**	
	a. Old paper	4,000.

Buff wrapper, cut to shape.

RO151	1c **black**	
	a. Old paper	4,500.

White wrapper, cut to shape.

R

Reading Match Company

RO152	1c **black**	
	d. Wmk 191R	10.00

Reed & Thompson — RO153

Reed & Thompson

RO153	1c **black**	
	d. Wmk 191R	22.50

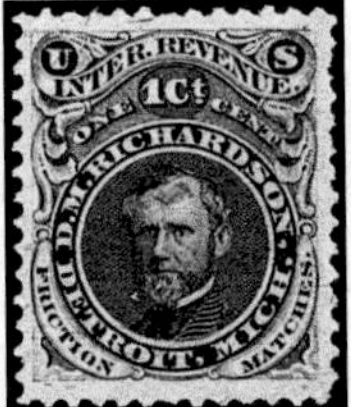

D.M. Richardson RO155

D.M. Richardson RO156

D. M. Richardson

RO154	1c **red**	
	a. Old paper	175.00
RO155	1c **black**	
	a. Old paper	4.00
	b. Silk paper	3.25
	As "b," dbl. transfer	80.00
	e. Experimental silk paper	75.00
RO156	3c **vermilion**	
	a. Old paper	190.00
RO157	3c **blue**	
	a. Old paper	7.75
	b. Silk paper	5.00
	As "b," dbl. transfer	30.00
	e. Experimental silk paper	200.00

RO158

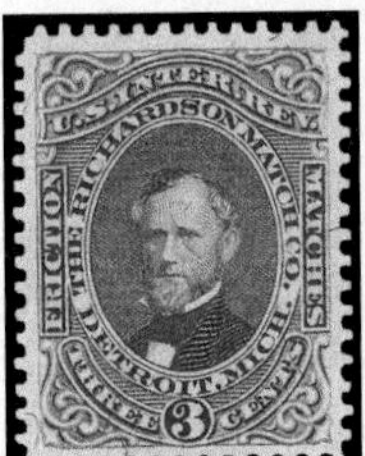

The Richardson Match Co. — RO159

The Richardson Match Co.

The 1c is as No. RO154, 3c as No. RO156, inscribed "The Richardson Match Co." instead of "D. M. Richardson."

RO158	1c **black**	
	b. Silk paper	2.25
	c. Pink paper	6.75
	d. Wmk 191R	9.00
RO159	3c **blue**	
	b. Silk paper	95.00

H. & W. Roeber — RO160

H. & W. Roeber

RO160	1c **blue**	
	a. Old paper	8.00
	As "a," dbl. transfer	200.00
	b. Silk paper	3.00
	e. Experimental silk paper	*1,750.*
	u. **Ultra,** old paper	*1,500.*

William Roeber — RO161

William Roeber

As No. RO160, "William Roeber" instead of "H. & W. Roeber."

RO161	1c **blue**	
	b. Silk paper	2.75
	c. Pink paper	9.00
	d. Wmk 191R	4.00
RO162	1c **blue**	
	d. Wmk 191R, rouletted	125.00

E. T. Russell — RO163

E. T. Russell

RO163	1c **black**	
	a. Old paper	10.00
	b. Silk paper	20.00
	e. Experimental silk paper	*150.00*

R. C. & W. (Ryder, Crouse & Welch) — RO164

R. C. & W. (Ryder, Crouse & Welch)

RO164	1c **lake**	
	d. Wmk 191R	110.00

S

San Francisco Match Co. — RO165

Illustration reduced.

San Francisco Match Company

RO165	12c **blue**	
	b. Silk paper	675.00

Schmitt & Schmittdiel — RO166/RO167

Wm. Gates – RO91

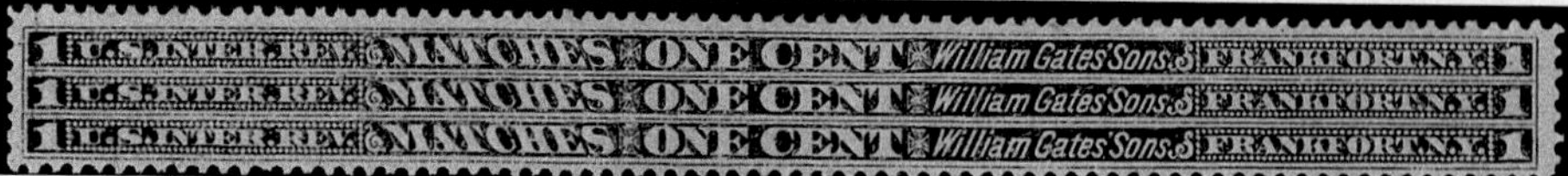

William Gates' Sons – RO94

P.T. Ives – RO118

J.C. Ayer & Co. – RS4

Barham Pile Cure Co. – RS14

D.S. Barnes
RS15

D.S. Barnes
RS16

D.S. Barnes
RS17

Demas
Barnes RS23

T.H. Barr & Co. – RS27

Demas Barnes & Co. – RS24

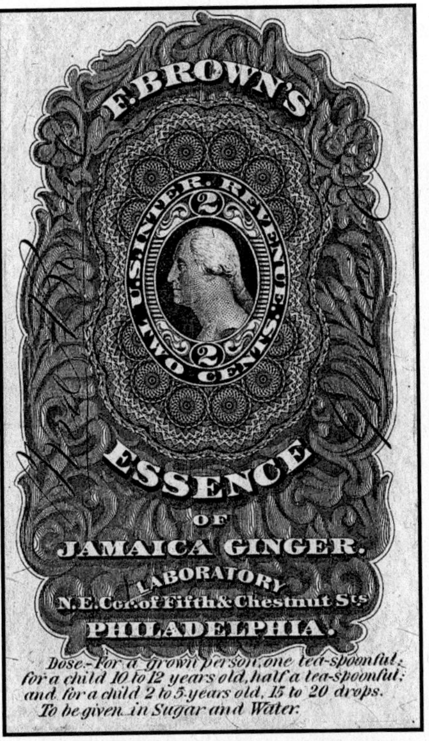

Fred Brown Co. – RS37

John I. Brown & Son – RS39

Dr. John Bull RS42

J.W. Campion & Co. – RS47

Dr. A.W. Chase, Son & Co. – RS55

Cannon & Co. – RS49

Cook & Bernheimer – RS61

Oliver Crook & Co. – RS65

Jeremiah Curtis & Son – RS67

Curtis & Brown – RS72

Dalley's Galvanic Horse Salve – RS73

Dalley's Magical Pain Extractor – RS74

Schmitt & Schmittdiel

RO166 1c **vermilion**
b. Silk paper 5.50
c. Pink paper 100.00
d. Wmk 191R 5.50
RO167 3c **blue**
b. Silk paper 67.50

E. K. Smith — RO168/RO169

E. K. Smith

RO168 1c **blue**
b. Silk paper 14.00
c. Pink paper 55.00
d. Wmk 191R 20.00
RO169 1c **blue**
d. Wmk 191R, rouletted *7,000.*

See No. RO132.

Standard Match Co. — RO170

The Standard Match Company

RO170 1c **black**
d. Wmk 191R 35.00

H. Stanton — RO171

H. Stanton

RO171 1c **black**
a. Old paper 17.00
b. Silk paper 11.00
c. Pink paper 22.50
d. Wmk 191R 10.00
e. Experimental silk paper 125.00

Star Match — RO172

Star Match

RO172 1c **black**
a. Old paper 5.50
b. Silk paper 1.10
As "b," dbl. transfer —
c. Pink paper 2.00
d. Wmk 191R 1.25
As "d," dbl. transfer 20.00
e. Experimental silk paper 85.00

Swift & Courtney — RO173

Swift & Courtney

As No. RO174, "Swift & Courtney" in one line.

RO173 1c **blue**
a. Old paper 3.50
b. Silk paper 3.50
As "b," dbl. transfer —
e. Experimental silk paper 47.50
u. **Ultra,** old paper 110.00

Swift & Courtney & Beecher Co.— RO174

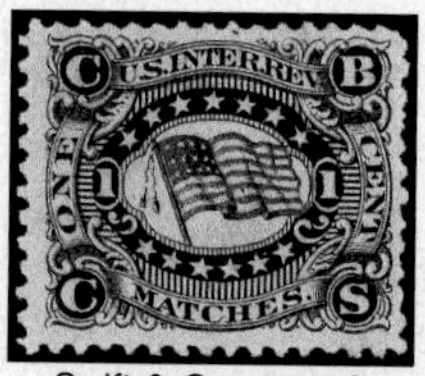

Swift & Courtney & Beecher — RO175

Swift & Courtney & Beecher Co.

RO174 1c **blue**
b. Silk paper 3.50
c. Pink paper 5.50
d. Wmk 191R 2.25
As "d," dbl. transfer —
RO175 1c **black**
d. Wmk 191R 110.00

T

Trenton Match Co. — RO176

Trenton Match Co.

RO176 1c **blue**
d. Wmk 191R 12.00

E. R. T. (E. R. Tyler) — RO177

E. R. T. (E. R. Tyler)

As No. RO119, inscribed "E. R. T." instead of "Ives & Judd."

RO177 1c **green**
a. Old paper 17.00
b. Silk paper 4.50
As "b," dbl. transfer —
e. Experimental silk paper 200.00

U

Alex Underwood & Co. — RO178

Alex. Underwood & Co.

RO178 1c **green**
a. Old paper 110.00
b. Silk paper 160.00
e. Experimental silk paper *2,250.*

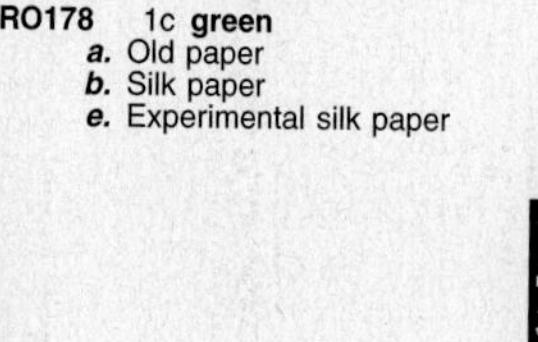

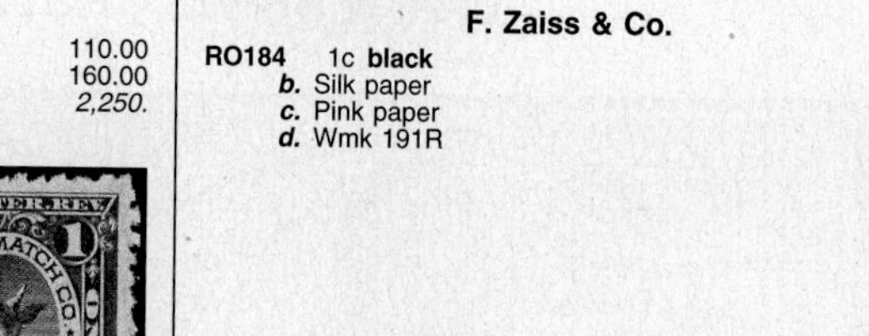

Union Match Co. — RO179

Union Match Co.

RO179 1c **black**
d. Wmk 191R 55.00

U.S.M. Co. — RO180

U. S. M. Co. (Universal Safety Match Co.)

RO180 1c **black**
a. Old paper 4.50
b. Silk paper 30.00
e. Experimental silk paper 110.00

W

Washington Match Co. — RO181

Washington Match Co.

RO181 1c **black**
b. Silk paper 50.00

Wilmington Parlor Match Co. — RO182

Wilmington Parlor Match Co.

RO182 1c **black**
a. Old paper 175.00
b. Silk paper *11,500.*
e. Experimental silk paper 500.00

Wise & Co. — RO183

Wise & Co.

RO183 1c **black**
a. Old paper 2,000.

Z

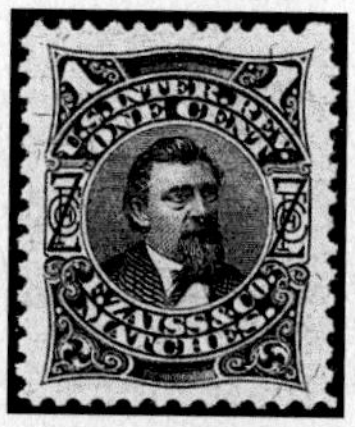

F. Zaiss & Co. — RO184

F. Zaiss & Co.

RO184 1c **black**
b. Silk paper 2.25
c. Pink paper 9.00
d. Wmk 191R 2.75

Zisemann, Griesheim & Co. — RO185

RO185 1c **green**
a. Old paper 3,000.
RO186 1c **blue**
a. Old paper 160.00
b. Silk paper 25.00
u. **Ultra,** old paper 3,000.

PRIVATE DIE CANNED FRUIT STAMP

T. Kensett & Co. — RP1

T. Kensett & Co.

RP1 1c **green**
a. Old paper 2,500.

Virtually all examples of No. RP1a are faulty to some degree, with many being extremely faulty.

PRIVATE DIE MEDICINE STAMPS

A

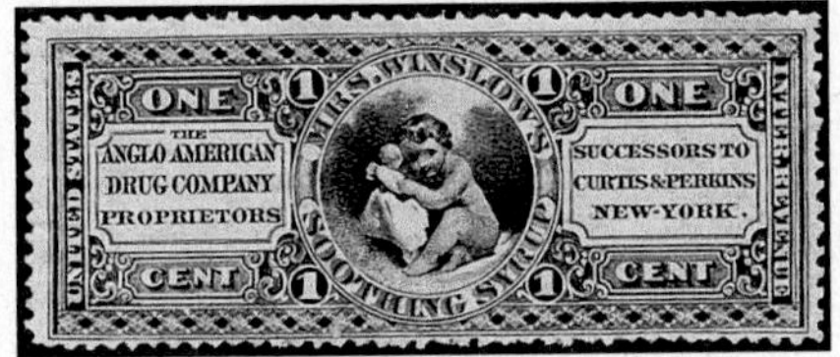

Anglo American Drug Co. — RS1

Anglo American Drug Co.

RS1 1c **black**
d. Wmk 191R 75.00

J. C. Ayer & Co.

For illustration of No. RS4, see large stamp illustration pages.

RS2 1c **brn car**
a. Old paper, imperf. *22,500.*
RS3 1c **green**
a. Old paper, imperf. *25,000.*
RS4 1c **black,** imperf.
a. Old paper, Type I 275.00
b. Silk paper, Type I 250.00
d. Wmk 191R, Type I 95.00
e. Experimental silk paper, Type I —
f. Old paper, Type 2 225.00
g. Silk paper, Type 2 200.00
As "g", dbl. transfer —
h. Pink paper, Type 2 *2,250.*
i. Wmk 191R, Type 2 77.50

Type I: long, full-pointed "y" in "Ayers"; Type 2: short, truncated "y" in "Ayers".

RS5 1c **blue**
a. Old paper, imperf. *22,500.*
RS6 1c **orange**
a. Old paper, imperf. *22,500.*
RS6F 1c **red**
a. Old paper, imperf. *22,500.*
RS7 1c **gray lilac**
a. Old paper, imperf. *22,500.*

J.C. Ayer & Co. — RS8, RS9, RS11/RS13

J.C. Ayer & Co. RS10

RS8 4c **red**
a. Old paper, die cut *12,500.*
RS9 4c **blue**
a. Old paper, die cut 10.50
b. Silk paper 10.50
d. Wmk 191R 10.50
e. Experimental silk paper *2,000.*
u. **Ultra,** old paper *1,500.*
RS10 4c **blue**
a. Old paper, imperf. 450.00
b. Silk paper 450.00
d. Wmk 191R 350.00
RS11 4c **purple**
a. Old paper, die cut *22,500.*
RS12 4c **green**
a. Old paper, die cut *17,500.*
RS13 4c **vermilion**
a. Old paper, die cut *17,500.*

The 4c in black was printed and sent to Ayer & Co. It may exist but has not been seen by collectors.

B

Barham Pile Cure Co.

For illustration of No. RS14, see large stamp illustration pages.

RS14 4c **green**
d. Wmk lozenges 90.00

D. S. Barnes

The 1c, 2c and 4c are about 184mm, 242mm and 304mm tall. The products mentioned differ. "D. S. Barnes" is in manscript.
For illustration of No. RS16 and RS17, see large stamp illustration pages.

RS15 1c **vermilion**
a. Old paper 750.00
RS16 2c **vermilion**
a. Old paper 675.00
RS17 4c **vermilion**
a. Old paper 1,400.
RS18 1c **black**
a. Old paper 30.00
RS19 2c **black**
a. Old paper 60.00
RS20 4c **black**
a. Old paper 82.50

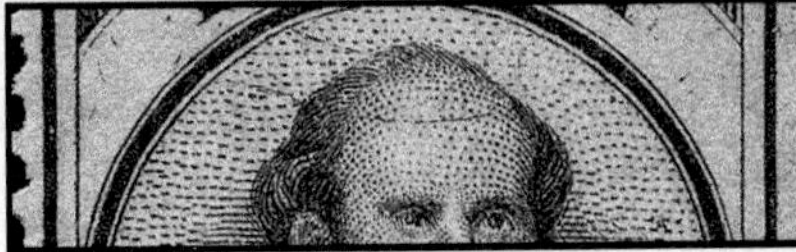

RS22 Foreign entry

Demas Barnes

Same as above but with "Demas Barnes" in serifed letters.

For illustration of No. RS23, see large stamp illustration pages.

RS21 1c **black**
a. Old paper 27.50
RS22 2c **black**
a. Old paper 75.00
As "a," foreign entry of 1c (No. RS15 or RS21), old paper *2,750.*
RS23 4c **black**
a. Old paper 35.00

Demas Barnes & Co.

For illustration of No. RS24, see large stamp illustration pages.

RS24 1c **black**
a. Old paper 20.00
b. Silk paper 675.00
e. Experimental silk paper *5,000.*
RS25 2c **black**
a. Old paper 20.00
b. Silk paper 500.00
e. Experimental silk paper 1,250.
RS26 4c **black**
a. Old paper 20.00

T. H. Barr & Co.

For illustration of No. RS27, see large stamp illustration pages.

RS27 4c **black**
a. Old paper 30.00
As "a," dbl. transfer 225.00
e. Experimental silk paper 450.00

Barry's — RS28/RS29

Barry's

RS28 2c **green**
a. Old paper, Tricopherous 12.00
b. Silk paper 22.50
RS29 2c **green**
b. Silk paper, Proprietary 6.75
As "b," dbl. transfer *1,000.*
c. Pink paper 275.00
d. Wmk 191R 6.00

D. M. Bennett — RS30

D. M. Bennett

RS30 1c **lake**
a. Old paper 20.00
e. Experimental silk paper 4,000.

W. T. Blow — RS31

W. T. Blow

RS31 1c **green**
a. Old paper 325.00
b. Silk paper 77.50
c. Pink paper 450.00
d. Wmk 191R 95.00
e. Experimental silk paper 1,900.

B. Brandreth — RS33

R. Brandreth — RS35

B. Brandreth

RS32 1c **black**
a. Old paper, perf. 1,750.
b. Silk paper 1,750.
RS33 1c **black**
a. Old paper, imperf. 2.75
b. Silk paper 1.75
e. Experimental silk paper 42.50

Nos. RS32-RS33 inscribed "United States Certificate of Genuineness" around vignette.

RS34 1c **black,** 41x50mm
b. Silk paper, imperf. 300.00

L. Pills – RS90

Reuben P. Hall & Co. – RS94

(Dr.) S.B. Hartman & Co. – RS99

The Father Mathew Temperance & Manufacturing Company – RS85

(Dr.) S.B. Hartman & Co. – RS100

John F. Henry RS114

Hiscox & Co. RS123

Herrick's Pills RS117

The Home Bitters Co. – RS128

Hostetter & Smith – RS132

S.D. Howe – RS134

S.D. Howe – RS137

T.J. Husband – RS140

James A. Jackson & Co. – RS143

Dr. D. Jayne & Son – RS144

Dr. Jas. C. Kerr – RS159

Jacob Lippman & Bro. – RS163

Lyon Manufg. Co. – RS167

T.W. Marsden – RS175

T.W. Marsden – RS176

Mercado & Seully – RS177

Mette & Kanne – RS180

J.B. Kelly & Co.
RS153

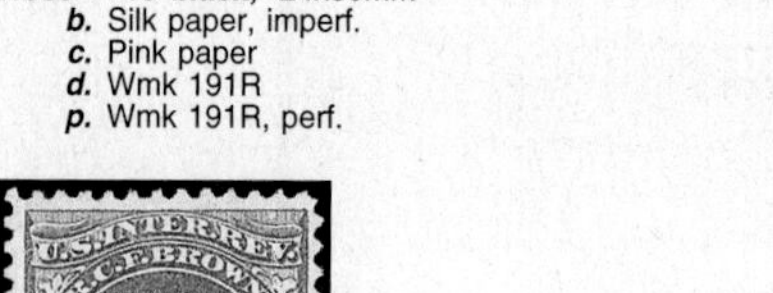

RS35 1c **black,** 24x30mm
b. Silk paper, imperf. 2.00
c. Pink paper 11.00
d. Wmk 191R 2.25
p. Wmk 191R, perf. *2,000.*

Dr. C.F. Brown — RS36

Dr. C. F. Brown

RS36 1c **greenish blue**
a. Old paper 650.00
b. Silk paper 87.50
d. Wmk 191R 100.00

Fred Brown Co.

For illustration of No. RS37, see large stamp illustration pages.

RS37 2c **black**
a. Old paper, imperf., Die I 140.00
b. Silk paper 47.50
c. Pink paper 3,750.
d. Wmk 191R 40.00
e. Experimental silk paper *1,500.*
RS38 2c **black**
b. Silk paper, imperf., Die II 82.50

Die I has "E" of "Fred" incomplete. Die II shows recutting in the "E" of "Fred" and "Genuine."

John I. Brown & Son.

For illustration of No. RS39, see large stamp illustration pages.

RS39 1c **black**
a. Old paper 11.00
b. Silk paper 45.00
d. Wmk 191R 10.00
RS40 2c **green**
a. Old paper 11.00
As "a," dbl. transfer —
b. Silk paper 20.00
c. Pink paper 400.00
d. Wmk 191R 400.00
e. Experimental silk paper *1,750.*
RS41 4c **brown**
a. Old paper 550.00
b. Silk paper 140.00
d. Wmk 191R 2,000.

Dr. John Bull

For illustration of No. RS42, see large stamp illustration pages.

RS42 1c **black**
a. Old paper 210.00
b. Silk paper 22.50
c. Pink paper 825.00
d. Wmk 191R 22.50
e. Experimental silk paper 1,100.
RS43 4c **blue**
a. Old paper 225.00
b. Silk paper 13.50
c. Pink paper 600.00
d. Wmk 191R 12.00
e. Experimental silk paper *1,750.*
u. **Ultra,** old paper *2,750.*

J. S. Burdsal & Co.

"J. S. Burdsal & Co./Sole Proprietors" added under United States Proprietary Medicine Co. design, as on Nos. RS245-RS247.

RS44 1c **black**
b. White silk paper, wrapper 60.00
d. Wmk 191R, white paper, wrapper 40.00
RS45 1c **black**
b. Orange silk paper, wrapper *12,500.*
d. Wmk 191R, orange paper, wrapper 4,000.
RS45A 1c **black**
b. Yellow silk paper, wrapper 7,500.

Joseph Burnett & Co. — RS46

Joseph Burnett & Co.

RS46 4c **black**
a. Old paper 125.00
b. Silk paper 16.00
c. Pink paper 550.00
d. Wmk 191R 7.75

C

J. W. Campion & Co.

For illustration of No. RS47, see large stamp illustration pages.

RS47 4c **black,** imperf.
b. Silk paper 550.00
d. Wmk 191R 425.00
p. As "d," pair, perf. horiz. 2,750.
RS48 4c **black**
b. Die cut, silk paper 160.00
c. Pink paper 550.00
d. Wmk 191R 125.00

Cannon & Co.

For illustration of No. RS49, see large stamp illustration pages.

RS49 4c **green**
b. Silk paper 150.00
c. Pink paper 325.00
d. Wmk 191R 90.00

The Centaur Co. — RS50/RS52

The Centaur Co.

RS50 1c **vermilion**
c. Pink paper 72.50
d. Wmk 191R 11.00
RS51 2c **black**
c. Pink paper 16.00
d. Wmk 191R 4.00
RS52 4c **black**
d. Wmk 191R 67.50

Dr. A. W. Chase, Son & Co.

For illustration of No. RS55, see large stamp illustration pages.

RS53 1c **black**
b. Silk paper 160.00
d. Wmk 191R 10,000.
RS54 2c **black**
b. Silk paper 160.00
RS55 4c **black**
b. Silk paper 300.00

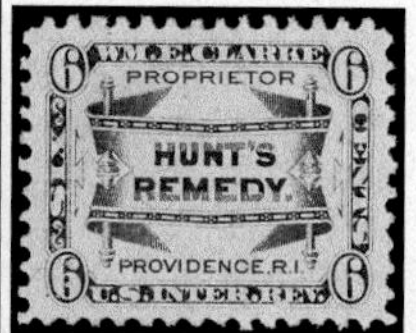

Wm. E. Clarke
RS56 RS57

Wm. E Clarke

RS56 3c **blue**
d. Wmk 191R 350.00
RS57 6c **black**
d. Wmk 191R 100.00

R. C. & C. S. Clark — RS58

R. C. & C. S. Clark

RS58 4c **black**
b. Silk paper 20.00
d. Wmk 191R 27.50

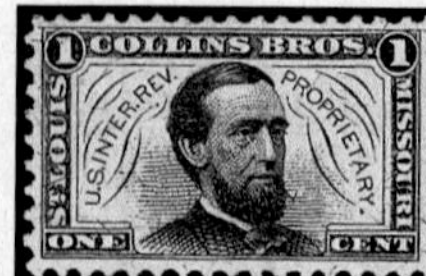

Collins Bros. — RS59

Collins Bros.

RS59 1c **black**
a. Old paper 29.00
b. Silk paper 1,000.
e. Experimental silk paper *2,500.*

W. H. Comstock — RS60

W. H. Comstock

RS60 1c **black**
d. Wmk 191R 5.50

Cook & Bernheimer

For illustration of No. RS61, see large stamp illustration pages.

RS61 4c **blue**
d. Wmk 191R 140.00

Charles N. Crittenton — RS62/RS64

Charles N. Crittenton

RS62 1c **black**
b. Silk paper 11.00
RS63 1c **blue**
c. Pink paper 14.00
d. Wmk 191R 7.25
RS64 2c **black**
b. Silk paper 95.00
c. Pink paper 55.00
d. Wmk 191R 5.50

Oliver Crook & Co.

For illustration of No. RS65, see large stamp illustration pages.

RS65 4c **black**
a. Old paper 750.00
b. Silk paper 27.50
e. Experimental silk paper 150.00

Jeremiah Curtis & Son

For illustration of No. RS67, see large stamp illustration pages.

RS66 1c **black**
a. Old paper, die I, small "1s." 140.00
RS67 1c **black**
d. Wmk 191R, die II, large "1s." 125.00
RS68 2c **black**
a. Old paper 11.00
b. Silk paper 11.00
As "b," dbl. transfer *1,300.*
c. Pink paper 175.00
d. Wmk 191R 400.00

Die II numerals nearly fill the circles.

Curtis & Brown RS69

Curtis & Brown

RS69 1c **black**
- *a.* Old paper 6.25
- *b.* Silk paper 4.50
- *e.* Experimental silk paper *6,000.*

RS70 2c **black**
- *b.* Silk paper 200.00

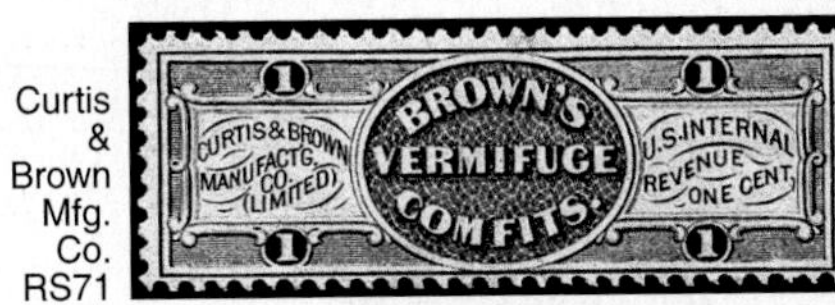

Curtis & Brown Mfg. Co. RS71

Curtis & Brown Mfg. Co.

These are identical to RS69-RS70 with "Mfg. Co. Limtd." instead of the right hand "TWO CENTS."

For illustration of No. RS72, see large stamp illustration pages.

RS71 1c **black**
- *c.* Pink paper 275.00
- *d.* Wmk 191R 10.00

RS72 2c **black**
- *b.* Silk paper 2,450.
- *d.* Wmk 191R *1,750.*

D

Dalley's Galvanic Horse Salve

For illustration of No. RS73, see large stamp illustration pages.

RS73 2c **green**
- *a.* Old paper 250.00
- *b.* Silk paper 275.00
- *d.* Wmk 191R 325.00

Dalley's Magical Pain Extractor

For illustration of No. RS74, see large stamp illustration pages.

RS74 1c **black**
- *a.* Old paper 16.00
- *b.* Silk paper 12.00
- *d.* Wmk 191R 9.25
- *ah.* As "a," $100 625.00
- *dh.* As "d," $100 20.00

Denomination on Nos. RS74ah and RS74dh reads "$100" in error, instead of "$1.00."

Perry Davis & Son — RS75/RS81

Perry Davis & Son

RS75 1c **blue**
- *a.* Old paper 10.00
- *b.* Silk paper 4.00
- *c.* Pink paper 400.00
- *d.* Wmk 191R 3.00
- *e.* Experimental silk paper 450.00
- *u.* **Ultra,** old paper *2,250.*

RS76 2c **brown red**
- *a.* Old paper 300.00

RS77 2c **black**
- *a.* Old paper 90.00

RS78 2c **dull purple**
- *b.* Silk paper 11.00

RS78A 2c **slate**
- *b.* Silk paper 14.00
- *d.* Wmk 191R 7.25

RS79 2c **dull red**
- *b.* Silk paper 100.00

RS80 2c **brown**
- *b.* Silk paper *10,500.*

RS81 4c **brown**
- *a.* Old paper 14.50
- *b.* Silk paper 4.50
- *d.* Wmk 191R 3.25

P.H. Drake & Co. — RS82/RS83

Illustration reduced.

P. H. Drake & Co.

RS82 2c **black**
- *a.* Old paper *4,500.*

RS83 4c **black**
- *a.* Old paper 67.50
- *b.* Silk paper 77.50
- *e.* Experimental silk paper 275.00

F

B. A. Fahnestock — RS84

Illustration reduced.

B. A. Fahnestock

RS84 1c **lake,** imperf.
- *a.* Old paper 175.00
- *b.* Silk paper 140.00

The Father Mathew Temperance & Manufacturing Company

For illustration of No. RS85, see large stamp illustration pages.

RS85 4c **black**
- *d.* Wmk 191R 17.50

A. H. Flanders, M.D. — RS87

A. H. Flanders, M. D.

RS86 1c **green,** perf.
- *b.* Silk paper 16.00
- *d.* Wmk 191R 14.50

RS87 1c **green,** part perf.
- *a.* Old paper 27.50
- *b.* Silk paper 2.25
- *c.* Pink paper 45.00
- *d.* Wmk 191R 3.25

Fleming Bros. — RS88/RS90

Fleming Bros.
Vermifuge

RS88 1c **black,** imperf.
- *a.* Old paper 16.00
- *b.* Silk paper 25.00
- *d.* Wmk 191R 70.00
- *e.* Experimental silk paper 350.00

L. Pills

For illustration of No. RS90, see large stamp illustration pages.

RS89 1c **black,** imperf.
- *a.* Old paper *7,000.*

RS90 1c **blue,** imperf.
- *a.* Old paper 7.75
- *b.* Silk paper 9.00
- As "b," dbl. transfer 77.50
- *d.* Wmk 191R 11.00
- As "d," dbl. transfer 77.50
- *e.* Experimental silk paper *2,000.*
- *u.* **Ultra,** old paper 3,500.

Seth W. Fowle & Son — RS91

Seth W. Fowle & Son, J. P. Dinsmore

RS91 4c **black**
- *a.* Old paper 22.50
- *b.* Silk paper 3.25
- *d.* Wmk 191R 3.25

G

G. G. Green — RS92/RS93

G. G. Green

RS92 3c **black**
- *d.* Wmk 191R 7.75
- *h.* As "d," tete beche pair *2,500.*

RS93 3c **black,** rouletted
- *d.* Wmk 191R 300.00

H

Reuben P. Hall & Co.

For illustration of No. RS94, see large stamp illustration pages.

RS94 4c **black**
- *a.* Old paper 22.50
- *b.* Silk paper 22.50
- *d.* Wmk 191R 25.00
- *e.* Experimental silk paper *2,500.*

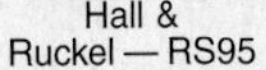

Hall & Ruckel — RS95

Hall & Ruckel — RS96

Hall & Ruckel as agents for Xavier Bazin — RS95h/RS96h

Hall & Ruckel

RS95 1c **green**
- *a.* Old paper 2.00
- *b.* Silk paper 2.00
- *c.* Pink paper 35.00
- *d.* Wmk 191R 2.00
- *e.* Experimental silk paper 35.00
- *h.* Handstamped "X.B." (Xavier Bazin) and obliteration, wmk 191R 30.00

RS96 3c **black**
- *a.* Old paper 3.50
- *b.* Silk paper 3.25
- *c.* Pink paper 67.50
- *d.* Wmk 191R 3.25
- *h.* Handstamped "X.B." (Xavier Bazin) and obliteration, wmk 191R 60.00

Dr. Harter & Co. — RS97

Dr. Harter & Co.

RS97 1c **black**
- *a.* Old paper 27.50
- *b.* Silk paper 18.00
- *e.* Experimental silk paper *5,000.*

Mishler Herb Bitters Co. – RS181

Moody, Michel & Co. – RS182

Morehead's – RS186

New York Pharmacal Association
RS187

Dr. M. Perl & Co. – RS188

Bennett Pieters & Co. – RS191

Bennett Pieters & Co. – RS192

R. V.
Pierce
RS190

Radway & Co. – RS193

M., P.J. & H.M. Sands – RS209

Scheetz's Celebrated Bitter Cordial – RS210

Schenck's Mandrake Pills – RS212

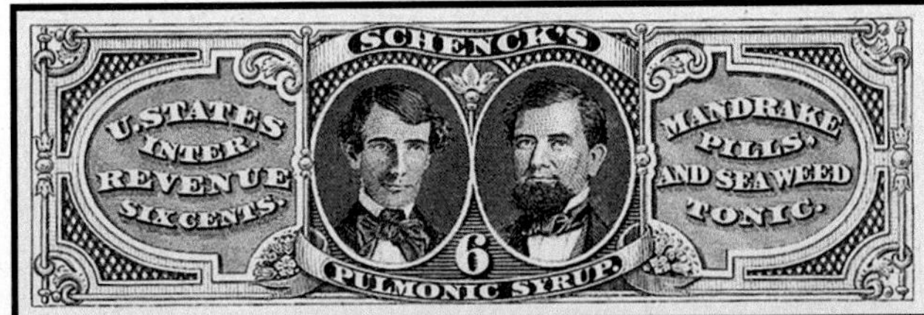

Schenck's Pulmonic Syrup – RS213

J.E. Schwartz & Co. – RS215

Dr. D.H. Seelye & Co. – RS222

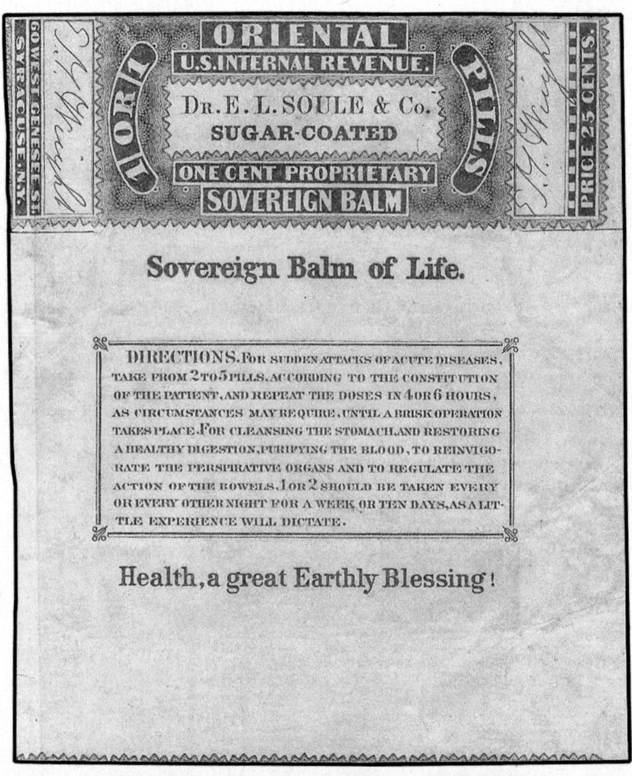

Dr. E.L. Soule & Co. – RS227

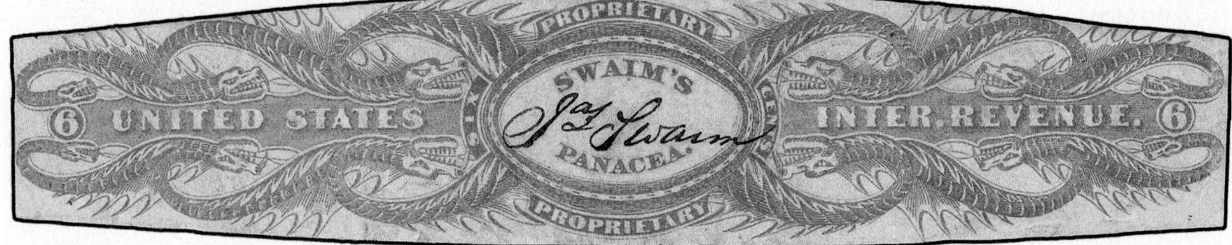

Jas. Swaim RS231

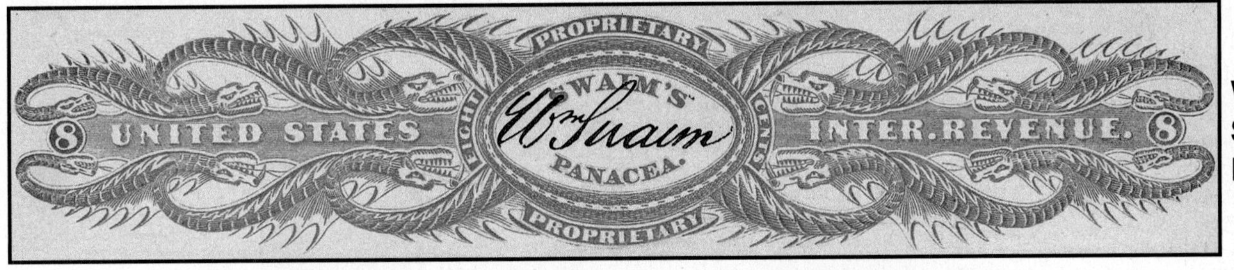

Wm. Swaim RS234

George Tallcot RS240

United States Proprietary Medicine Co. – RS243

S.R. Van Duzer – RS249

Dr. Harter — RS98

Dr. Harter's

As No. RS97, inscribed "Dr. Harter" instead of "Dr. Harter & Co."

RS98 1c **black**
b. Silk paper 4.50
c. Pink paper 17.50
d. Wmk 191R 5.50
f. Dbl. impression, silk paper *4,500.*

(Dr.) S. B. Hartman & Co.

For illustrations of Nos. RS99 and RS100, see large stamp illustration pages.

RS99 4c **black**
a. Old paper 2,500.
b. Silk paper 87.50
c. Pink paper 1,750.
d. Wmk 191R 1,750.
RS100 6c **black**
a. Old paper 1,000.
b. Silk paper 400.00

E. T. Hazeltine — RS101/RS103

E. T. Hazeltine

RS101 1c **black**
d. Wmk 191R 21.00
RS102 2c **blue**
b. Silk paper 42.50
RS103 4c **black**
a. Old paper 1,000.
b. Silk paper 27.50
d. Wmk 191R 20.00
e. Experimental silk paper 3,750.
i. Imperf, pair, old paper *3,000.*

E. H. (Edward Heaton) — RS105

E. H. (Edward Heaton)

RS104 3c **black**
d. Wmk 191R 55.00
RS105 3c **brown**
d. Wmk 191R 20.00

Helmbold's — RS106/RS109

Helmbold's

RS106 2c **blue**
a. Old paper 2.00
As "a," dbl. transfer —
b. Silk paper 400.00
RS107 3c **green**
a. Old paper 55.00
b. Silk paper 40.00
RS108 4c **black**
a. Old paper 5.00
As "a," dbl. transfer 300.00
b. Silk paper 225.00
e. Experimental silk paper *2,500.*

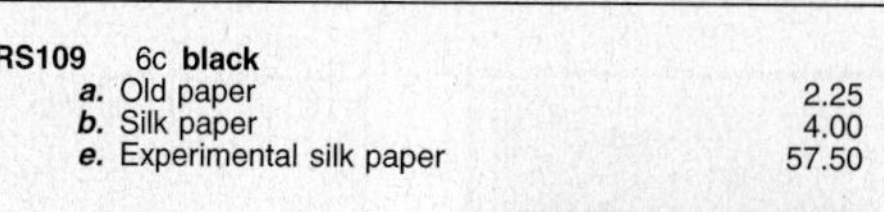

RS109 6c **black**
a. Old paper 2.25
b. Silk paper 4.00
e. Experimental silk paper 57.50

A.L. Helmbold's — RS110

A. L. Helmbold's

Same as "Helmbold's" but inscribed "A. L. Helmbold's."

RS110 2c **blue**
b. Silk paper 140.00
c. Pink paper 500.00
d. Wmk 191R 110.00
RS111 4c **black**
b. Silk paper 30.00
c. Pink paper 300.00
d. Wmk 191R 11.00

John F. Henry — RS112

Illustration reduced.

John F. Henry

RS112 2c **violet**
a. Old paper 900.00
RS113 4c **bister**
a. Old paper 2,100.

For illustration of No. RS114, see large stamp illustration pages.

RS114 1c **black**
a. Old paper 67.50
b. Silk paper 1.10
c. Pink paper 15.00
d. Wmk 191R 1.75
e. Experimental silk paper 500.00

Horiz. pairs imperf between were issued of No. RS114d. All known pairs were originally separated, and some have been matched and rejoined. Three rejoined pairs are reported.

RS115 2c **blue**
a. Old paper 40.00
b. Silk paper 7.25
c. Pink paper 160.00
d. Wmk 191R 6.75
u. **Ultra,** old paper *2,000.*
RS116 4c **red**
a. Old paper 200.00
b. Silk paper 1.75
c. Pink paper 40.00
d. Wmk 191R 2.75
e. Experimental silk paper 225.00

Herrick's Pills

For illustration of No. RS117, see large stamp illustration pages.

RS117 1c **black**
a. Old paper 100.00
b. Silk paper 45.00
c. Pink paper 160.00
d. Wmk 191R 50.00
e. Experimental silk paper 275.00
i. Imperf, pair, old paper *3,000.*

No. RS117i is valued in sound condition. Most pairs are faulty and sell for much less.

Herrick's Pills & Plasters — RS118

Herrick's Pills & Plasters

RS118 1c **red**
a. Old paper 2.75
b. Silk paper 5.50
c. Pink paper 82.50
d. Wmk 191R 2.75
e. Experimental silk paper 3,000.

J.E. Hetherington — RS120

J. E. Hetherington

RS119 1c **black**
d. Wmk 191R 20.00
RS120 2c **black**
d. Wmk 191R 725.00
RS121 3c **black**
d. Wmk 191R 25.00
i. Imperf, pair 2,250.

Hiscox & Co.

For illustration of No. RS123, see large stamp illustration pages.

RS122 2c **black**
d. Wmk 191R 17.00
RS123 4c **black**
b. Silk paper 125.00
c. Pink paper 525.00
d. Wmk 191R 1,750.

Holloway's Pills and Ointment — RS124/RS125

Holloway's Pills and Ointment

RS124 1c **blue**
a. Old paper, perf. 11.00
RS125 1c **blue**
a. Old paper, imperf. 750.00

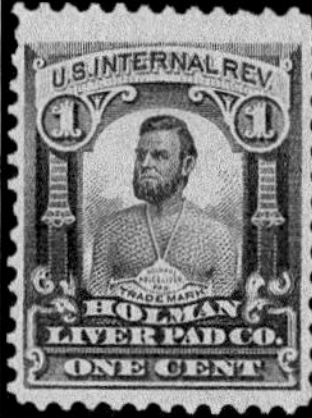

Holman Liver Pad Co. — RS126/RS127

Holman Liver Pad Co.

RS126 1c **green**
d. Wmk 191R 22.50
RS127 4c **green**
d. Wmk 191R 11.00

The Home Bitters Co.

For illustration of No. RS128, see large stamp illustration pages.

RS128 2c **blue**
d. Wmk 191R 250.00
As "d," dbl. transfer —
RS129 3c **green**
b. Silk paper 125.00
c. Pink paper 175.00
d. Wmk 191R 110.00
RS130 4c **green**
b. Silk paper 250.00
d. Wmk 191R 400.00

Hop Bitters Co. — RS131

Hop Bitters Co.

RS131 4c **black**
d. Wmk 191R 7.75

Hostetter & Smith

For illustration of No. RS132, see large stamp illustration pages.

RS132 4c **black**
a. Old paper, imperf. 82.50
As "a," dbl. transfer —
b. Silk paper 45.00
As "b," dbl. transfer 55.00
c. Pink paper 110.00
As "c," dbl. transfer 125.00
d. Wmk 191R 35.00
As "d," dbl. transfer 42.50
e. Experimental silk paper 3,000.
RS133 6c **black**
a. Old paper, imperf. 100.00
e. Experimental silk paper 1,500.

S. D. Howe

For illustration of No. RS137, see large stamp illustration pages.

RS134 4c **black,** Duponco's Pills
a. Old paper 140.00
b. Silk paper 500.00
RS135 4c **red,** Duponco's Pills
b. Silk paper 475.00
RS136 4c **green,** Duponco's Pills
b. Silk paper 475.00

Nos. RS135b and RS136b were never used.

RS137 4c **blue,** Arabian Milk
b. Silk paper 10.00
d. Wmk 191R 175.00

C.E. Hull & Co. — RS138

C. E. Hull & Co.

RS138 1c **black**
a. Old paper 400.00
b. Silk paper 6.25
c. Pink paper 60.00
d. Wmk 191R 6.25
e. Experimental silk paper —

T. J. Husband

For illustration of No. RS140, see large stamp illustration pages.

RS139 2c **violet**
a. Old paper, imperf. 2,500.
RS140 2c **vermilion**
a. Old paper, imperf. 17.00
b. Silk paper 11.00
d. Wmk 191R 10.00

Hutchings & Hillyer — RS141

Hutchings & Hillyer

RS141 4c **green**
a. Old paper, imperf. 22.50
b. Silk paper 35.00
e. Experimental silk paper 250.00

I

H. A. Ingham & Co. — RS142

H. A. Ingham & Co.

RS142 1c **black**
d. Wmk 191R 60.00

J

James A. Jackson & Co.

For illustration of No. RS143, see large stamp illustration pages.

RS143 4c **green**
a. Old paper 2,250.
b. Silk paper 400.00
As "b," dbl. transfer —

Dr. D. Jayne & Son

For illustration of No. RS149, see large stamp illustration pages.

RS144 1c **blue,** imperf.
a. Old paper 20,000.
ap. As "a," perf 1,500.
b. Silk paper 3,500.
bp. As "b," perf. *3,500.*
d. Wmk 191R 600.00
dp. As "d," perf *6,500.*
RS145 2c **black,** imperf.
a. Old paper *10,000.*
ap. As "a," perf *4,000.*
b. Silk paper 2,250.
d. Wmk 191R 1,400.
dp. As "d," perf —
RS146 4c **green,** imperf.
a. Old paper *5,500.*
ap. As "a," perf *6,000.*
b. Silk paper 2,250.
c. Pink paper 1,500.
d. Wmk 191R 650.00
dp. As "d," perf —
RS146F 4c **red,** imperf.
a. Old paper *7,000.*
RS146G 4c **orange,** imperf.
a. Old paper *15,000.*
ap. As "a," perf. and die cut *10,000.*
h. As "a," die cut *16,000.*
RS147 1c **blue,** die cut
a. Old paper 6.75
ap. As "a," perf & die cut *250.00*
As No. RS147ap, horiz. laid paper 62.50
b. Silk paper 5.50
bp. As "b," perf & die cut *275.00*
c. Pink paper 400.00
cp. As "c," perf & die cut *275.00*
d. Wmk 191R 5.50
dp. As "d," perf & die cut *1,500.*
e. Experimental silk paper *2,000.*
RS148 2c **black,** die cut
a. Old paper 11.00
As "a," dbl. transfer 60.00
ap. As "a," perf & die cut *45.00*
b. Silk paper 9.00
As "b," dbl. transfer 60.00
bp. As "b," perf & die cut *250.00*
c. Pink paper 110.00
As "c," dbl. transfer 125.00
cp. As "c," perf & die cut *900.00*
d. Wmk 191R 5.50
As "d," dbl. transfer 100.00
e. Experimental silk paper 210.00
RS149 4c **green,** die cut
a. Old paper 7.75
ap. As "a," perf & die cut 50.00
Vert. laid paper 40.00
b. Silk paper 5.50
As "b," dbl. transfer —
bp. As "b," perf & die cut *240.00*
c. Pink paper 100.00
d. Wmk 191R 9.25
dp. As "d," perf & die cut *1,750.*
e. Experimental silk paper 190.00

I. S. Johnson & Co. — RS150

I. S. Johnson & Co.

RS150 1c **vermilion**
b. Silk paper 1.50
As "b," dbl. transfer 22.50
c. Pink paper 16.00
As "c," dbl. transfer 60.00
d. Wmk 191R 1.00
As "d," dbl. transfer 27.50

Johnston Holloway & Co. — RS151/RS152

Johnston Holloway & Co.

RS151 1c **black**
b. Silk paper 4.00
d. Wmk 191R 3.00
RS152 2c **green**
b. Silk paper 4.00
d. Wmk 191R 3.25

K

J. B. Kelly & Co.

For illustration of No. RS153, see large stamp illustration pages.

RS153 4c **black,** imperf.
a. Old paper 3,500.
e. Experimental silk paper 4,000.

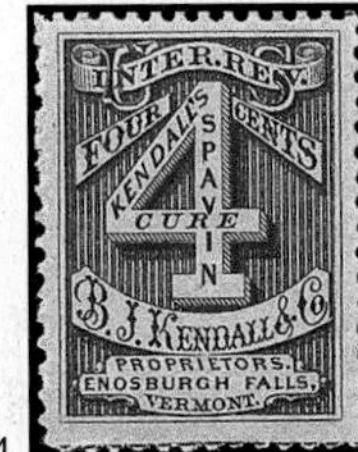

B. J. Kendall & Co. — RS154

B. J. Kendall & Co.

RS154 4c **blue**
d. Wmk 191R 35.00

Dr. Kennedy — RS155 Dr. Kennedy — RS156

Dr. Kennedy

RS155 2c **green**
a. Old paper 60.00
b. Silk paper 9.00
c. Pink paper 40.00
d. Wmk 191R 6.75
As "d," dbl. transfer —
e. Experimental silk paper *5,000.*
RS156 6c **black**
b. Silk paper 9.00
c. Pink paper 82.50
d. Wmk 191R 9.00

Kennedy & Co. RS157

Kennedy & Co.

RS157 2c **black**
b. Silk paper 7.75
c. Pink paper 110.00
d. Wmk 191R 9.25

K & Co. (Kennedy & Co.)

RS158 1c **green**
d. Wmk 191R 8.25

Dr. Jas. C. Kerr

For illustration of No. RS159, see large stamp illustration pages.

RS159 4c **blue**
a. Old paper *8,750.*
b. Silk paper 350.00
d. Wmk 191R 200.00
RS160 6c **black**
a. Old paper 1,000.

L

Lawrence & Martin

RS161 4c **black**
d. Wmk 191R 50.00

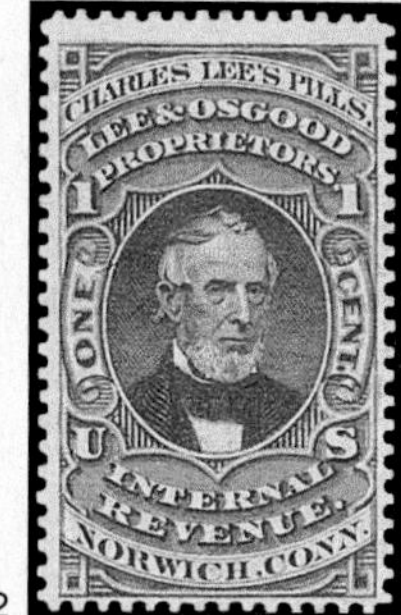
Lee & Osgood — RS162

Lee & Osgood

RS162 1c **blue**
a. Old paper 16.00
b. Silk paper 22.50
d. Wmk 191R 17.00

Jacob Lippman & Bro.

For illustration of No. RS163, see large stamp illustration pages.

RS163 4c **blue**
a. Old paper 2,000.
b. Silk paper 2,500.
e. Experimental silk paper 3,750.

Alvah Littlefield — RS165

Alvah Littlefield

RS164 1c **black**
a. Old paper 2.25
b. Silk paper 1.25
As "b," dbl. transfer 82.50
d. Wmk 191R 22.50
e. Experimental silk paper 400.00
As "e," horiz. laid paper *1,500.*
As "e," dbl. transfer 450.00
RS165 4c **green**
a. Old paper 2,000.
b. Silk paper 250.00

Prof. Low — RS166

Prof. Low

RS166 1c **black**
b. Silk paper 3.50
As "b," dbl. transfer —
c. Pink paper 20.00
As "c," dbl. transfer 60.00
d. Wmk 191R 3.50
As "d," dbl. transfer 45.00

Lyon Manufg. Co.

As No. RS24, inscribed "Lyon Manufg. Co." instead of "Demas Barnes & Co."

For illustration of No. RS167, see large stamp illustration pages.

RS167 1c **black**
b. Silk paper 22.50
c. Pink paper 400.00
d. Wmk 191R 16.00
RS168 2c **black**
b. Silk paper 10.00
c. Pink paper 200.00
d. Wmk 191R 10.00
i. Vert. pair, imperf btwn., wmk 191R 2,250.

M

J. McCullough

As No. RS134, inscribed "J. McCullough" instead of "S. D. Howe."

RS169 4c **black**
b. Silk paper 140.00
d. Wmk 191R 125.00

J. H. McLean — RS170

Dr. J. H. McLean

RS170 1c **black**
a. Old paper 2.75
As "a," dbl. transfer 55.00
b. Silk paper 1.75
As "b," dbl. transfer 72.50
c. Pink paper 17.00
As "c," dbl. transfer —
d. Wmk 191R 1.75
As "d," dbl. transfer 40.00
e. Experimental silk paper 140.00
i. As "a," vert. pair, imperf horiz. —

Manhattan Medicine Co. — RS171/RS172

Manhattan Medicine Co.

RS171 1c **violet**
d. Wmk 191R 75.00
u. As "d," **purple** 100.00
RS172 2c **black**
b. Silk paper 30.00
c. Pink paper 42.50
d. Wmk 191R 16.00

Mansfield & Higbee — RS173

Mansfield & Higbee

As No. RS174, inscribed "Mansfield & Higbee Memphis, Tenn."

RS173 1c **blue**
b. Silk paper 18.00
i. As "b," pair, imperf btwn. 250.00
j. As "b," block of 4, imperf btwn. 275.00

S. Mansfield & Co. — RS174

S. Mansfield & Co.

RS174 1c **blue**
b. Silk paper 30.00
bi. As "b," pair, imperf. btwn. 300.00
bj. As "b," block of 4, imperf. within 500.00
c. Pink paper 300.00
ci. As "c," pair, imperf. btwn. 750.00
cj. As "c," block of 4, imperf. within 1,000.
d. Wmk 191R 17.00
di. As "d," pair, imperf. btwn. 400.00
dj. As "d," block of 4, imperf. within 275.00

Nos. RS173-RS174 are perf on 4 sides. The "i." and "j." varieties served as 2c or 4c stamps. Straight-edged stamps from severed pairs or blocks are worth much less.

T. W. Marsden

For illustrations of Nos. RS175-RS176, see large stamp illustration pages.

RS175 2c **blue**
a. Old paper *11,500.*
RS176 4c **black**
a. Old paper 525.00

Mercado & Seully

For illustration of No. RS177, see large stamp illustration pages.

RS177 2c **black,** imprf.
a. Old paper *7,500.*

Merchant's Gargling Oil — RS178/RS179

Merchant's Gargling Oil

RS178 1c **black**
a. Old paper 275.00
b. Silk paper 45.00
c. Pink paper 1,750.
d. Wmk 191R 35.00
e. Experimental silk paper *3,250.*
RS179 2c **green**
a. Old paper 275.00
b. Silk paper 35.00
As "b," foreign entry *3,250.*
c. Pink paper 1,500.
d. Wmk 191R 27.50
As "d," foreign entry *3,750.*
e. Experimental silk paper 3,250.

Foreign entry is over design of No. RO11.

Mette & Kanne

For illustration of No. RS180, see large stamp illustration pages.

RS180 3c **black**
d. Wmk 191R 400.00

Mishler Herb Bitters Co.

For illustration of No. RS181, see large stamp illustration pages.

RS181 4c **black**
d. Wmk 191R 150.00
p. As "d," imperf at ends 1,500.

Moody, Michel & Co.

For illustration of No. RS182, see large stamp illustration pages.

RS182 4c **black,** imperf.
b. Silk paper 200.00

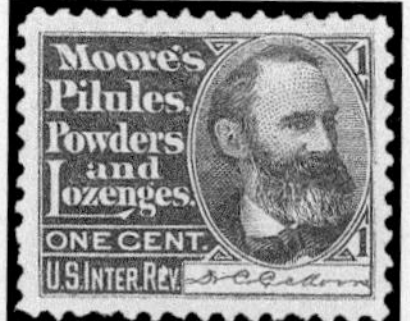
RS183

Dr. C. C. Moore — RS184

Dr. C. C. Moore

RS183 1c **vermilion,** Pilules
d. Wmk 191R 6.75

United States Proprietary Medicine Co. – RS247

World's Dispensary Medical Association RS272

World's Dispensary Medical Association RS273

Dr. J. Walker – RS253

West India Manufacturing Co. – RS264

Hostetter Co. – RS285

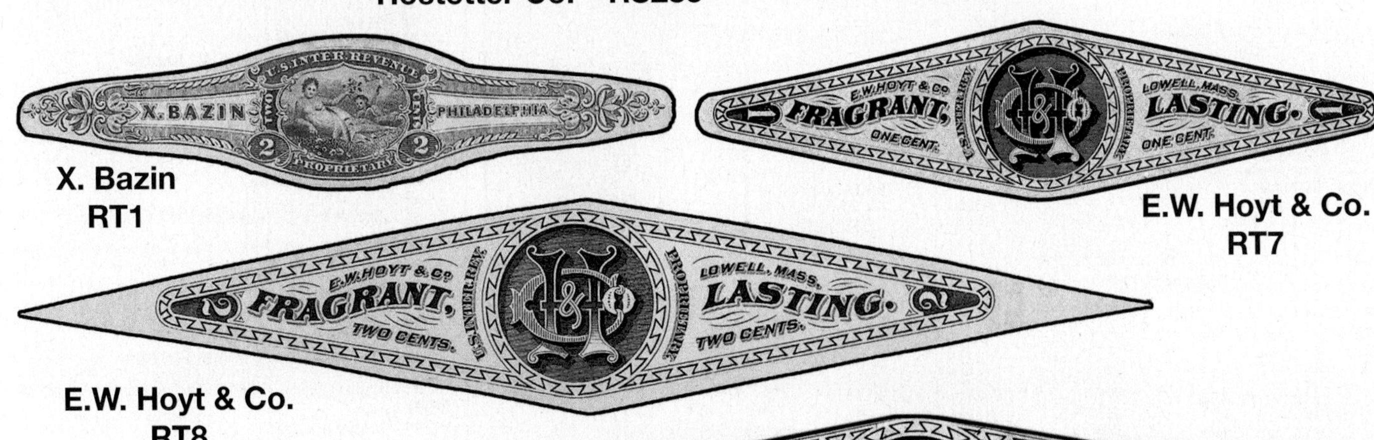

X. Bazin RT1

E.W. Hoyt & Co. RT7

E.W. Hoyt & Co. RT8

E.W. Hoyt & Co. – RT11

RS184 2c **black,** Sure Cure
- ***b.*** Silk paper 82.50
- ***c.*** Pink paper *17,500.*
- ***d.*** Wmk 191R 30.00

Morehead's

For illustration of No. RS186, see large stamp illustration pages.

RS185 1c **black,** Magnetic Plaster
- ***a.*** Old paper 30.00
- ***e.*** Experimental silk paper *2,500.*

RS186 4c **black,** Neurodyne
- ***a.*** Old paper *4,500.*

N

New York Pharmacal Association

For illustration of No. RS187, see large stamp illustration pages.

RS187 4c **black**
- ***b.*** Silk paper 17.00
- ***c.*** Pink paper 40.00
- ***d.*** Wmk 191R 11.00

P

Dr. M. Perl & Co.

For illustration of No. RS188, see large stamp illustration pages.

RS188 6c **black,** cut to shape
- ***a.*** Old paper 1,650.

All known examples of No. RS188a are faulty or defective.

R. V. Pierce — RS189/RS190

R. V. Pierce

For illustration of No. RS190, see large stamp illustration pages.

RS189 1c **green**
- ***b.*** Silk paper 25.00
- ***c.*** Pink paper 200.00
- ***d.*** Wmk 191R 27.50

RS190 2c **black**
- ***a.*** Old paper 30.00
- ***b.*** Silk paper 8.25
- As "b," dbl. transfer —
- ***c.*** Pink paper 35.00
- ***d.*** Wmk 191R 7.75
- ***e.*** Experimental silk paper 160.00

Bennett Pieters & Co.

For illustration of No. RS191, see large stamp illustration pages.

RS191 4c **black**
- ***a.*** Old paper 650.00
- ***b.*** Silk paper *5,500.*
- ***e.*** Experimental silk paper *6,000.*

RS192 6c **black**
- ***a.*** Old paper 1,600.
- ***i.*** As "a," imperf *3,000.*

R

Radway & Co.

For illustration of No. RS193, see large stamp illustration pages.

RS193 2c **black**
- ***a.*** Old paper 5.00
- ***b.*** Silk paper 3.25
- As "b," dbl. transfer 72.50
- ***c.*** Pink paper 12.00
- As "c," dbl. transfer 110.00
- ***d.*** Wmk 191R 5.50
- As "d," dbl. transfer 82.50
- ***e.*** Experimental silk paper 90.00

D. Ransom & Co. — RS194

D. Ransom & Co.

RS194 1c **blue**
- ***a.*** Old paper 5.00
- ***b.*** Silk paper 3.00
- As "b," dbl. transfer —
- ***e.*** Experimental silk paper 175.00

RS195 2c **black**
- ***a.*** Old paper 27.50
- ***b.*** Silk paper 35.00
- ***e.*** Experimental silk paper 175.00

D. Ransom, Son & Co. — RS197

D. Ransom, Son & Co.

As Nos. RS194-RS195 with "Son" added.

RS196 1c **blue**
- ***b.*** Silk paper 4.50
- As "b," dbl. transfer —
- ***c.*** Pink paper 17.00
- ***d.*** Wmk 191R 6.75

RS197 2c **black**
- ***b.*** Silk paper 18.00
- ***c.*** Pink paper 82.50
- ***d.*** Wmk 191R 11.00

Redding's Russia Salve — RS198

Redding's Russia Salve

RS198 1c **black**
- ***b.*** Silk paper 9.00
- As "b," dbl. transfer 150.00
- ***d.*** Wmk 191R 9.00

Ring's Vegetable Ambrosia — RS199/RS200

Ring's Vegetable Ambrosia

RS199 2c **blue**
- ***b.*** Silk paper, imperf. 4,000.
- ***p.*** As "b," perf. *14,500.*

RS200 4c **black,** imperf.
- ***a.*** Old paper 5,500.
- ***b.*** Silk paper 5,500.

No. RS199p is unique.

Ring's Vegetable Ambrosia — RS201/RS202

Ring's Vegetable Ambrosia — RS203

RS201 2c **blue,** die cut
- ***b.*** Silk paper 25.00

RS202 4c **black,** die cut
- ***a.*** Old paper 17.00
- ***b.*** Silk paper 17.00
- ***d.*** Wmk 191R 25.00
- ***e.*** Experimental silk paper 175.00

RS203 4c **black,** perf.
- ***b.*** Silk paper 2,000.
- ***bk.*** As "b," perf & die cut *4,500.*
- ***bp.*** As "b," part perf. 3,750.
- ***d.*** Wmk 191R 2,750.
- ***dk.*** As "d," perf & die cut *5,000.*
- ***dp.*** As "d," part perf. —

J. B. Rose & Co. — RS204/RS205

J. B. Rose & Co.

RS204 2c **black**
- ***b.*** Silk paper 6.75
- As "b," dbl. transfer 160.00
- ***c.*** Pink paper 35.00
- As "c," dbl. transfer 225.00

RS205 4c **black**
- ***a.*** Old paper *8,500.*
- ***b.*** Silk paper 160.00
- As "b," dbl. transfer 230.00

Rumford Chemical Works

RS206 2c **green**
- ***d.*** Wmk 191R 5.00

RS207 2c **green,** imperf.
- ***d.*** Wmk 191R 27.50

S

A. B. & D. Sands

RS208 1c **green**
- ***a.*** Old paper 11.00
- ***b.*** Silk paper 22.50
- ***e.*** Experimental silk paper 110.00

M., P. J. & H. M. Sands

The #RS208 die was altered to make #RS209.

For illustration of No. RS209, see large stamp illustration pages.

RS209 2c **green**
- ***b.*** Silk paper 20.00
- ***c.*** Pink paper 125.00
- ***d.*** Wmk 191R 17.00

Scheetz's Celebrated Bitter Cordial

For illustration of No. RS210, see large stamp illustration pages.

RS210 4c **black,** perf.
- ***b.*** Silk paper 1,000.

RS211 4c **black,** imperf.
- ***b.*** Silk paper *8,000.*

Schenck's Mandrake Pills

For illustration of No. RS212, see large stamp illustration pages.

RS212 1c **green,** imperf.
- ***a.*** Old paper 5.50
- ***b.*** Silk paper 11.00
- As "b," dbl. transfer 100.00
- ***c.*** Pink paper 125.00
- ***d.*** Wmk 191R 5.50
- As "d," dbl. transfer 250.00
- ***p.*** As "d," perf. *4,000.*
- ***e.*** Experimental silk paper *1,750.*

Schenck's Pulmonic Syrup

For illustration of No. RS213, see large stamp illustration pages.

RS213 6c **black,** imperf.
a. Old paper 8.25
p. As "a," perf. 240.00
b. Silk paper 5.50
As "b," dbl. transfer 62.50
c. Pink paper 110.00
d. Wmk 191R 200.00
As "d," dbl. transfer —
e. Experimental silk paper 800.00

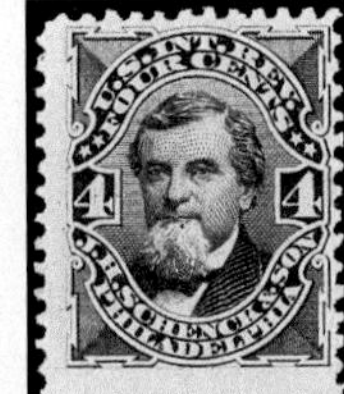

J. H. Schenck & Son — RS214

J. H. Schenck & Son

RS214 4c **black**
d. Wmk 191R 11.00

J. E. Schwartz & Co.

As No. RS84, inscribed "J. E. Schwartz & Co." instead of "B. A. Fahnestock."
For illustration of No. RS215, see large stamp illustration pages.

RS215 1c **lake,** imperf.
b. Silk paper 160.00
c. Pink paper 1,500.
d. Wmk 191R 125.00

"A. L. Scovill" follows No. RS219.

Seabury & Johnson — RS216

Seabury & Johnson — RS218

Illustration reduced.

Seabury & Johnson

RS216 1c **black**
d. Wmk 191R 82.50
RS217 1c **black**
d. Wmk 191R, printed obliteration over "porous" 5.50
h. "Porous" obliterated by pen 5.50
RS218 1c **lake**
d. Wmk 191R *3,250.*

"Dr. D. H. Seelye & Co." follows No. RS221

Dr. S. Brown Sigesmond — RS219

Dr. S. Brown Sigesmond

RS219 4c **blue**
d. Wmk 191R 125.00

A. L. Scovill & Co. — RS220/RS221

A. L. Scovill & Co.

RS220 1c **black**
a. Old paper 2.00
As "a," dbl. transfer —
b. Silk paper 2.75
As "b," dbl. transfer 500.00
e. Experimental silk paper 77.50
r. As "b," printed on both sides *2,500.*
RS221 4c **green**
a. Old paper 2.25
b. Silk paper 5.50
e. Experimental silk paper 350.00

Dr. D. H. Seelye & Co.

For illustration of No. RS222, see large stamp illustration pages.

RS222 8c **black,** imperf.
a. Old paper 27.50

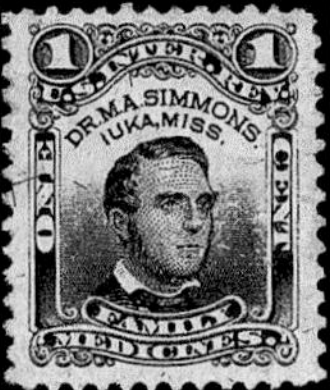

Dr. M. A. Simmons — RS223

Dr. M. A. Simmons

RS223 1c **black,** Iuka, Miss.
b. Silk paper 125.00
d. Wmk 191R *14,000.*
RS224 1c **black,** St. Louis, Mo.
d. Wmk 191R 125.00

S. N. Smith & Co.

As No. RS65, inscribed "S. N. Smith & Co." instead of "Oliver Crook & Co."
For illustration of No. RS225, see large stamp illustration pages.

RS225 4c **black**
b. Silk paper 55.00
d. Wmk 191R 55.00

Dr. E. L. Soule & Co.

For illustration of No. RS227, see large stamp illustration pages.

N.Y. Wrapper

RS226 1c **blue**
a. Old paper 82.50
As "a," foreign entry *1,750.*

Syracuse Wrapper

RS227 1c **blue**
a. Old paper 82.50
As "a," foreign entry *2,000.*
b. Silk paper 40.00
As "b," foreign entry *1,500.*
e. Experimental silk paper *3,000.*
u. **Ultra,** old paper 975.00
As "u," foreign entry —

For Nos. RS226, RS227, the foreign entry is the design of No. RT1 (pos. 1).

H. R. Stevens — RS228/RS229

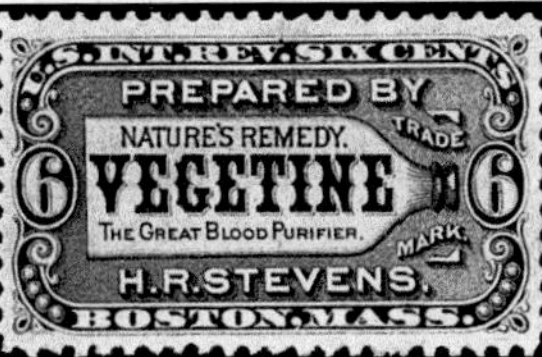

H.R. Stevens RS230

H. R. Stevens

RS228 1c **brown**
d. Wmk 191R 18.00
RS229 2c **chocolate**
d. Wmk 191R 6.75
RS230 6c **black**
c. Pink paper 125.00
d. Wmk 191R 6.75

Jas. Swaim

For illustration of No. RS231, see large stamp illustration pages.

RS231 6c **orange,** die cut
a. Old paper *6,500.*
f. As "a," without signature *20,000.*

Manuscript signature.

RS232 8c **orange,** imperf.
a. Old paper *3,000.*
ah. As "a," manuscript signature *10,000.*
bh. Manuscript signature, silk paper *10,000.*
RS233 8c **orange,** die cut
a. Old paper 400.00
ah. As "a," manuscript signature 4,500.
bh. Manuscript signature, silk paper *7,500.*
e. Experimental silk paper *3,000.*

Wm. Swaim

For illustration of No. RS234, see large stamp illustration pages.

RS234 8c **orange,** imperf.
a. Old paper *20,000.*
ak. As "a," without signature *20,000.*
b. Silk paper *6,000.*
bk. As "b," without signature *20,000.*
d. Wmk 191R 2,600.

No. RS234d is found with signature "Suaim" or "Swaim." Also, No. RS234b is found with a period under the raised "m" of "Wm" and the right leg of "w" of "Swaim" retouched, both by pen.

RS235 8c **orange,** die cut
a. Old paper *2,500.*
b. Silk paper 210.00
bh. As "b," manuscript signature *25,000.*
bk. As "b," inverted signature *18,000.*
d. Wmk 191R 250.00

No. RS235bh is unique.

Dr. G. W. Swett — RS237

Illustration reduced.

Dr. G. W. Swett

RS236 4c **black,** die cut
a. Old paper 18.00
RS237 4c **green,** perf.
b. Silk paper 250.00
d. Wmk 191R *2,750.*
RS238 4c **green,** perf. & cie cut
b. Silk paper 450.00
d. Wmk 191R *3,250.*

T

George Tallcot

For illustration of No. RS240, see large stamp illustration pages.

RS239 2c **vermilion**
d. Wmk 191R 17.00
RS240 4c **black**
b. Silk paper 95.00
c. Pink paper *14,000.*
d. Wmk 191R 22.50

Tarrant & Co. — RS241

Tarrant & Company

RS241 4c **red**
b. Silk paper 3.25
c. Pink paper 100.00
d. Wmk 191R 2.25

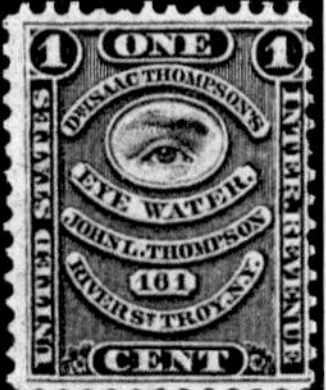

John L. Thompson — RS242

John L. Thompson

RS242 1c **black**
a. Old paper 6.75
As "a," dbl. transfer —
b. Silk paper 8.25
d. Wmk 191R 6.75
e. Experimental silk paper 160.00

U

United States Proprietary Medicine Co.

For illustration of No. RS243, see large stamp illustration pages.

RS243 4c **black**
a. Old paper 50.00
b. Silk paper 125.00
e. Experimental silk paper 450.00
RS244 6c **black**
a. Old paper *2,500.*
e. Experimental silk paper *24,000.*

No. RS244e is unique.

U. S. Proprietary Medicine Co. Wrappers

For illustration of No. RS247, see large stamp illustration pages.

RS245 1c **black,** *white*
a. Old paper 50.00
b. Silk paper 50.00
e. Experimental silk paper *1,250.*
RS246 1c **black,** *yel*
a. Old paper 140.00
b. Silk paper 250.00
RS247 1c **black,** *org*
a. Old paper 1,500.
b. Silk paper *7,000.*
RS248 1c **black,** *org red*
a. Old paper *3,500.*
b. Silk paper *10,000.*

V

S. R. Van Duzer

For illustration of No. RS249, see large stamp illustration pages.

RS249 4c **black**
a. Old paper 45.00
b. Silk paper 40.00
d. Wmk 191R 210.00
RS250 6c **black**
d. Wmk 191R 82.50

A. Vogeler & Co. — RS251

A. Vogeler & Co.

RS251 1c **black**
b. Silk paper 1.75
d. Wmk 191R 2.25

Vogeler, Meyer & Co. — RS252

Vogeler, Meyer & Co.

RS252 1c **vermilion**
c. Pink paper 4.50
d. Wmk 191R 1.50

W

Dr. J. Walker

For illustration of No. RS253, see large stamp illustration pages.

RS253 4c **black**
a. Old paper 45.00
b. Silk paper 25.00
As "b," dbl. transfer 55.00
d. Wmk 191R 22.50
As "d," dbl. transfer 45.00
e. Experimental silk paper *1,500.*

H. H. Warner & Co. — RS254/RS255

H. H. W. & Co. (H. H. Warner & Co.)

RS254 1c **brown**
d. Wmk 191R 6.75
RS255 6c **brown,** 19x26mm
d. Wmk 191R 90.00
RS256 2c **brown,** 88x11mm
d. Wmk 191R 35.00
RS257 4c **brown,** 95x18mm
d. Wmk 191R 35.00
RS258 6c **brown**
d. Wmk 191R 8.25
As "d," dbl. transfer 90.00

Weeks & Potter — RS259

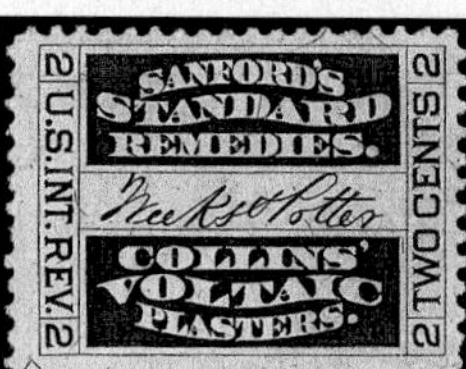

Weeks & Potter—RS260/RS261

Weeks & Potter—RS262

Weeks & Potter

RS259 1c **black**
b. Silk paper 7.75
d. Wmk 191R 6.00
RS260 2c **black**
b. Silk paper 110.00
RS261 4c **black**
b. Silk paper 30.00
c. Pink paper 30.00
d. Wmk 191R 7.75
RS262 2c **red**
c. Pink paper 40.00
d. Wmk 191R 7.75

Wells, Richardson & Co. — RS263

Wells, Richardson & Co.

RS263 4c **black**
d. Wmk 191R 30.00

West India Manufacturing Co.

For illustration of No. RS264, see large stamp illustration pages.

RS264 4c **black,** die I
b. Silk paper 300.00
c. Pink paper 400.00
d. Wmk 191R 750.00
RS264A 4c **black,** die II
d. Wmk 191R 675.00

Die II shows evidence of retouching, particularly in the central disk.

Edward Wilder — RS265/RS269

Edward Wilder

RS265 1c **green,** imperf.
a. Old paper *1,750.*
b. Silk paper 325.00
d. Wmk 191R 325.00
e. Experimental silk paper *7,500.*
RS266 1c **green,** die cut
a. Old paper 55.00
b. Silk paper 50.00
d. Wmk 191R 25.00
e. Experimental silk paper 1,100.
RS266A 4c **vermilion,** imperf
e. Experimental silk paper *16,000.*
RS267 4c **vermilion,** die cut
a. Old paper 200.00
b. Silk paper *2,250.*
e. Experimental silk paper 500.00
RS268 4c **lake,** imperf.
b. Silk paper 275.00
d. Wmk 191R 2,250.
RS269 4c **lake,** die cut
a. Old paper *2,500.*
b. Silk paper 14.00
d. Wmk 191R 14.00

No. RS266Ae is unique.

Rev. E.A. Wilson — RS270

Rev. E. A. Wilson

RS270 12c **blue**
b. Silk paper 80.00
d. Wmk 191R 550.00

Thos. E. Wilson, M.D. — RS271

Thos. E. Wilson, M. D.

RS271 4c **black**
a. Old paper *25,000.*

No. RS271a is unique.

World's Dispensary Medical Assocn.

For illustration of No. RS273, see large stamp illustration pages.

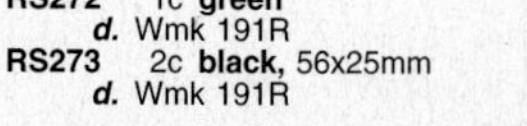

RS272 1c **green**
d. Wmk 191R 27.50
RS273 2c **black,** 56x25mm
d. Wmk 191R 9.00

Wright's Indian Vegetable Pills — RS274

Wright's Indian Vegetable Pills

RS274 1c **green**
a. Old paper 2.25
b. Silk paper 1.75
c. Pink paper 40.00
d. Wmk 191R 3.50
As "d," dbl. transfer —
e. Experimental silk paper 200.00

Z

J.H. Zeilin & Co. — RS275/RS277

J.H. Zeilin & Co.

RS275 2c **red**
b. Silk paper 1,100.
RS276 2c **green**
b. Silk paper, perf. 45.00
d. Wmk 191R —
RS277 2c **green**
a. Old paper, imperf. 450.00
b. Silk paper 8.25
c. Pink paper 140.00
d. Wmk 191R 5.50

1898-1900

See rouletting note preceding No. R161.
Left value = Unused
Right value = Used

The Antikamnia Chemical Co. — RS278

The Antikamnia Chemical Co.

RS278 2½c **carmine**
p. Hyphen hole perf. 7 4.00 4.00

Fernet Branca (Branca Bros.) — RS279

Fernet Branca (Branca Bros.)

RS279 4c **black**
r. Rouletted 5½ 9.50 9.50
p. Hyphen hole perf. 7 9.50 9.50

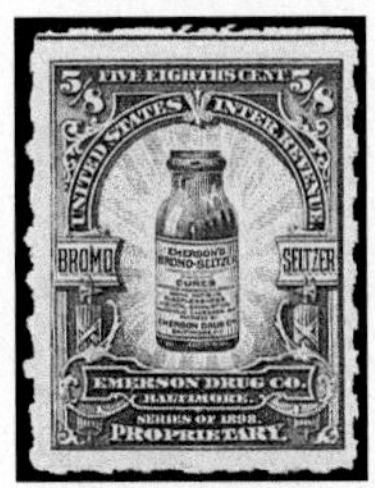

Emerson Drug Co. — RS281

Emerson Drug Co.

RS280 ⅛c **carmine**
p. Hyphen hole perf. 7 7.00 3.00
RS281 ⅝c **green**
p. Hyphen hole perf. 7 7.00 3.50
RS282 1¼c **violet brown**
p. Hyphen hole perf. 7 9.00 7.00
RS283 2½c **brown orange**
p. Hyphen hole perf. 7 8.50 5.00

Chas. H. Fletcher — RS284

Chas. H. Fletcher

RS284 1¼c **black**
r. Rouletted 5½ .60 .60
p. Hyphen hole perf. 7 .60 .60

Hostetter Co.

For illustration of No. RS285, see large stamp illustration pages.

RS285 2½c **black,** imperf .60 .60

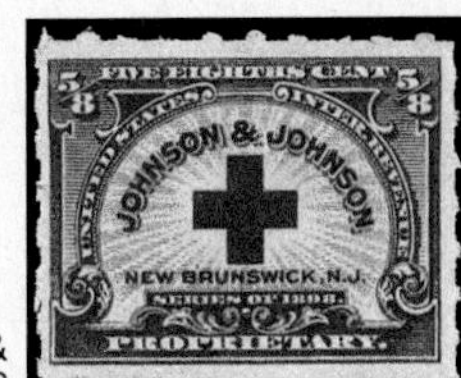

Johnson & Johnson — RS286

Johnson & Johnson

RS286 ⅝c **carmine**
r. Rouletted 5½ .50 .50
p. Hyphen hole perf. 7 .50 .50

Lanman & Kemp — RS287

Lanman & Kemp

RS287 ⅝c **green**
r. Rouletted 5½ 8.50 6.00
p. Hyphen hole perf. 7 11.00 4.50
RS288 1¼c **brown**
r. Rouletted 5½ 11.00 6.50
p. Hyphen hole perf. 7 16.00 12.00
RS289 1⅞c **blue**
r. Rouletted 5½ 11.00 8.00
p. Hyphen hole perf. 7 21.00 11.00

J. Ellwood Lee Co. — RS290

J. Ellwood Lee Co.

RS290 ⅛c **dk blue**
p. Hyphen hole perf. 7 3.25 3.00
RS291 ⅝c **carmine**
p. Hyphen hole perf. 7 2.75 2.00
RS292 1¼c **dk green**
p. Hyphen hole perf. 7 2.25 2.00
RS293 2½c **orange**
p. Hyphen hole perf. 7 2.75 2.50
RS294 5c **chocolate**
p. Hyphen hole perf. 7 3.00 2.75

Charles Marchand — RS295

Charles Marchand

RS295 ⅝c **black**
r. Rouletted 5½ 8.50 8.50
p. Hyphen hole perf. 7 9.00 9.00

RS296 1¼c **black**
r. Rouletted 5½ 1.75 1.75
p. Hyphen hole perf. 7 1.75 1.75
RS297 1⅞c **black**
r. Rouletted 5½ 2.50 2.50
p. Hyphen hole perf. 7 3.00 3.00
RS298 2½c **black**
r. Rouletted 5½ 3.00 3.00
p. Hyphen hole perf. 7 3.00 3.00
RS299 3⅛c **black**
r. Rouletted 5½ 8.50 8.50
p. Hyphen hole perf. 7 8.50 8.50
RS300 4⅜c **black**
r. Rouletted 5½ 16.00 16.00
p. Hyphen hole perf. 7 16.00 16.00
RS301 7½c **black**
r. Rouletted 5½ 11.00 11.00
p. Hyphen hole perf. 7 11.00 11.00

Od Chem. Co. — RS302

Od Chem. Co.

RS302 2½c **carmine**
p. Hyphen hole perf. 7 — 2.50

The Piso Company — RS303

The Piso Company (E. T. Hazeltine)

RS303 ⅝c **blue**
r. Rouletted 5½ .50 .50
p. Hyphen hole perf. 7 .50 .50

Radway & Co. — RS304

Radway & Co.

RS304 ⅝c **blue**
r. Rouletted 5½ 1.25 1.25
p. Hyphen hole perf. 7 1.25 1.25

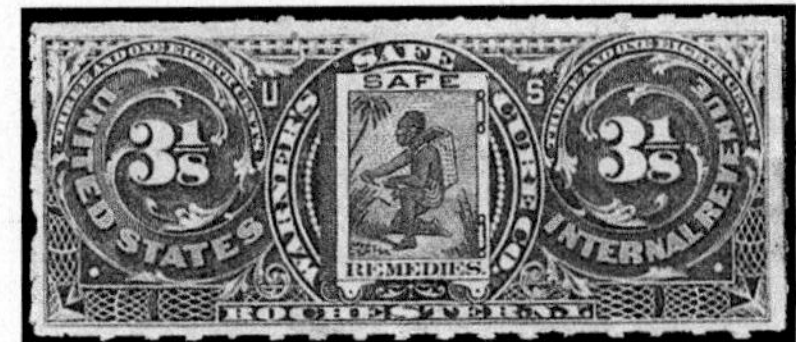

Warner's Safe Cure Co. — RS305

Warner's Safe Cure Co.

RS305 3⅛c **brown**
r. Rouletted 5½ 1.25 1.25
p. Hyphen hole perf. 7 1.25 1.25

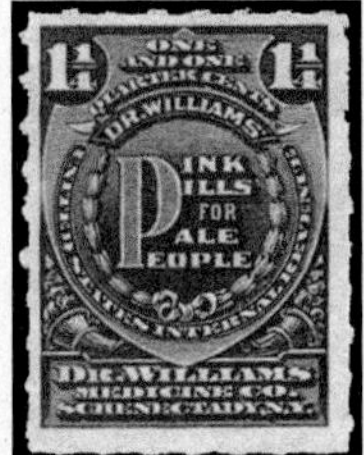

Dr. Williams Medicine Co. — RS306

Dr. Williams Medicine Co.

RS306 1¼c **pink**
p. Hyphen hole perf. 7 3.50 3.50

DR. KILMER & CO., PROVISIONAL PROPRIETARY STAMPS

Postage Stamps of 1895, 1897-1903, Nos. 267a, 279, 279Bg and 268, Precancel Overprinted in Black:

a

Overprint "a," Large "I.R." Dated July 5, 1898.

1898	**Wmk. 191**	***Perf. 12***
RS307	A87 1c **deep green**	175.00
a.	Red (trial) plus black ovpts.	*2,500.*
RS308	A88 2c **pink,** type III	160.00
RS308A	A88 2c **pink,** type IV	175.00
b.	Dark blue (trial) ovpt.	*2,500.*
RS309	A89 3c **purple**	160.00
a.	Red (trial) ovpt.	—
b.	Inverted ovpt.	*1,500.*

The trial overprint in dark blue on the 2c stamp is known used on July 5.

b

Overprint "b," Small "I.R.," "Dr. K. & Co." with Serifs Dated July 6, 7, 9, 11 to 14, 1898

RS310	A87 1c **deep green**	140.00
RS311	A88 2c **pink,** type III	150.00
RS311A	A88 2c **pink,** type IV	77.50
RS312	A89 3c **purple**	67.50
a.	Inverted ovpt.	*1,500.*

c

Overprint "c," Small "I.R.," "Dr. K. & Co." without Serifs Dated July 7, 9, 11 to 14, 1898

RS313	A87 1c **deep green**	150.00
RS314	A88 2c **pink,** type III	150.00
RS314A	A88 2c **pink,** type IV	100.00
RS315	A89 3c **purple**	125.00
a.	Inverted ovpt.	*2,500.*

Nos. RS307a, RS308Ab and RS309a were all overprinted on July 5, the first day of overprinting. Though called "trials," there is every reason to believe they were used in the regular course of business, as they represented money spent by Dr. Kilmer & Co. and there was no reason not to use them. Four examples are recorded of No. RS307a, three of No. RS308Ab and one of No. RS309a. For the inverted overprints, four examples are recorded of No. RS309b, 16 of No. RS312a and three of No. RS315a. Forgeries exist of No. RS312a, all dated July 6. The height of "I.R." is shorter on the forgeries, and the periods after these letters are circular rather than diamond shaped. Many varieties of the Kilmer overprints exist. For the complete listing see "The Case of Dr. Kilmer's," by Morton Dean Joyce, 1954 (also serialized in "The Bureau Specialist," Mar.-Nov. 1957).

ST. LOUIS PROVISIONAL PROPRIETARY STAMPS

U.S. "Battleship" revenue stamps (Nos. RB20-RB31) not being available to meet the July 1, 1898, effective date of new taxes on proprietary medicines, eleven proprietary drug companies (10 in St. Louis, Missouri, and one in Macon, Georgia) struck agreements with local collectors of internal revenue to print their own revenue stamps for temporary use and pay their taxes by sworn returns until the government-issued stamps were available. Even though one company that used such stamps was from Macon, Georgia, these stamps are commonly referred to as the St. Louis Provisionals.

The Antikamnia Chemical Co. — RS320/RS321

The Antikamnia Chemical Co. — RS323

1898		***Imperf.***
	Antikamnia Chemical Co., St. Louis	
RS320	1/8c **black,** *yellow*	2,750.
RS321	2 1/2c **black**	500.00
RS323	no value **black,** *yellow*	750.00

No. RS323 was for use on free samples not subject to tax.

Fairchild Chemical Laboratory Co. — RS325

Fairchild Chemical Laboratory Co., St. Louis

Imperf

RS325	5/8c **black**	*25,000.*

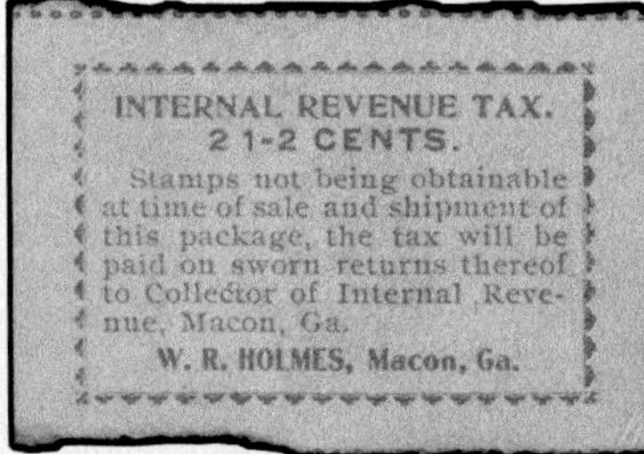

W.R. Holmes — RS330

W.R. Holmes, Macon, Georgia

Rouletted 9½ Horiz. in Green, Imperf Vert.

RS330	2 1/2c **green**	*25,000.*

Lambert Pharmacal Co. — RS335

Lambert Pharmacal Co., St. Louis

Imperf

RS335	2 1/2c **red**	1,000.

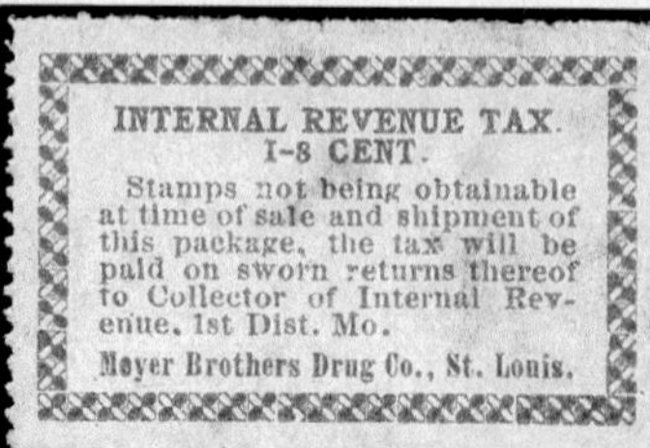

Meyer Brothers Drug Co. — RS340/RS350

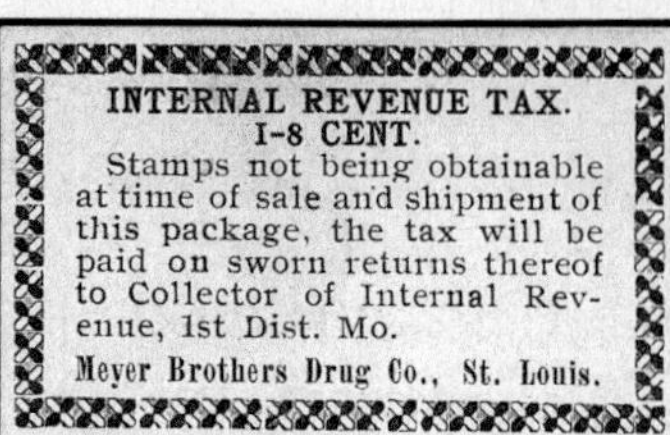

Meyer Brothers Drug Co. — RS351/RS361

Meyer Brothers Drug Co., St. Louis

These stamps were printed on at least three distinct papers: white, buff and rough manila.

Rouletted 9½ Horiz. in Green, Perf 12 and/or Imperf Vert.

RS340a	1/8c **green,** white paper	*17,500.*
RS343b	5/8c **green,** buff paper	*17,500.*
RS345c	1 1/4c **green,** rough manila paper	*25,000.*
RS348c	5c **green,** rough manila paper	*25,000.*
RS349a	7 7/8c **green,** white paper	*25,000.*
RS350b	11 1/4c **green,** buff paper	*25,000.*

Imperf

RS351a	1/8c **black,** white paper	125.00
RS352a	1/4c **black,** white paper	125.00
RS353a	3/8c **black,** white paper	125.00
RS354a	5/8c **black,** white paper	125.00
RS355a	1c **black,** white paper	125.00
RS357a	2c **black,** white paper	125.00
RS358a	3c **black,** white paper	125.00
RS359a	4c **black,** white paper	125.00
RS360a	5c **black,** white paper	125.00
RS361a	11 1/4c **black,** white paper	125.00

John T. Milliken & Co. — RS365/RS366

John T. Milliken & Co., St. Louis

Imperf

RS365	1/8c **black**	1,250.
RS366	5/8c **black**	1,250.

Phenique Chemical Co. — RS370/RS377

Phenique Chemical Co., St. Louis

These stamps were printed on two distinct papers: yellow and buff.

Imperf

RS370b	1/8c **black,** buff paper	*25,000.*
RS371a	1/4c **black,** yellow paper	*17,500.*
RS372a	5/8c **black,** yellow paper	*12,500.*
RS372b	5/8c **black,** buff paper	*25,000.*
RS374a	1 7/8c **black,** yellow paper	*25,000.*
RS375a	2 1/2c **black,** yellow paper	*25,000.*
RS376b	3 1/8c **black,** buff paper	*25,000.*
RS377b	3 3/4c **black,** buff paper	*25,000.*

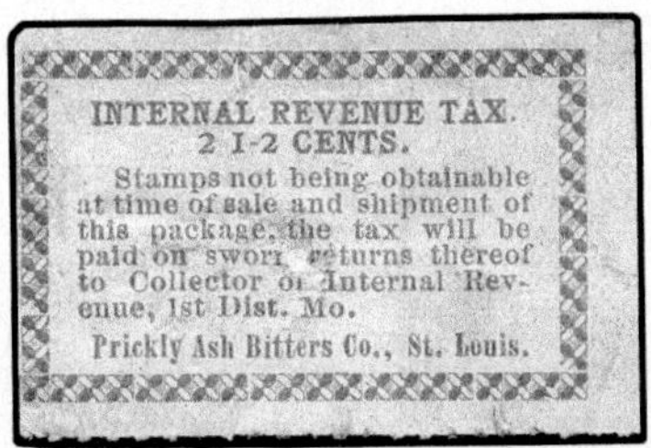

Prickly Ash Bitters Co. — RS381

Prickly Ash Bitters Co., St. Louis

Rouletted 9½ Horiz. in Green, Imperf Vert.

RS381	2½c **green**	*12,500.*

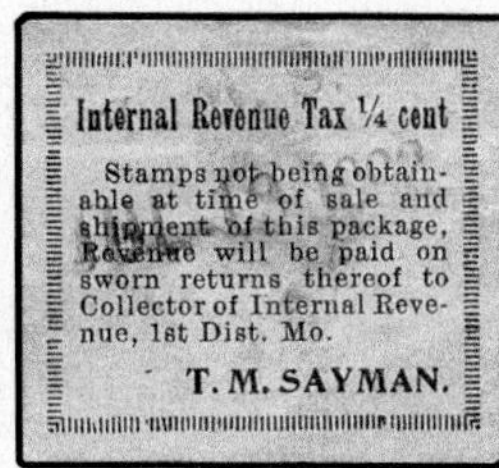

T.M. Sayman — RS385/RS387

T.M. Sayman, St. Louis

Imperf

RS385	¼c **dark blue**	*25,000.*
RS386	⅝c **dark blue**	*17,500.*
RS387	1¼c **dark blue**	*25,000.*

Van Dyke Bitters Co. — RS390

Van Dyke Bitters Co., St. Louis

Imperf

RS390	2½ **blue,** *bluish glazed*	5,500.

Internal Revenue Tax 2 1-2 Cents.
Stamps not being obtainable at time of sale and shipment of this package, will be paid on sworn returns thereof to Collector of Internal Revenue, 1st Dist. Mo.
Walker Phar. Co.

Walker Pharmacal Co. — RS395

Walker Pharmacal Co., St. Louis

Imperf

RS395	2½ **black**	*25,000.*

PRIVATE DIE PERFUMERY STAMPS

X. Bazin

For illustration of No. RT1, see large stamp illustration pages.

RT1	2c **blue,** die cut	
a.	Old paper	1,400.

This stamp was never placed in use.

RT2

Corning & Tappan — RT3/RT4

Corning & Tappan

RT2	1c **black,** imperf.	
d.	Wmk 191R	2,250.
h.	Die cut, 19mm diameter	125.00
k.	Die cut, 21mm diameter	175.00
RT3	1c **black,** perf.	
d.	Wmk 191R	800.00
RT4	1c **blue,** perf.	
d.	Wmk 191R	4.50

Fetridge & Co. — RT5

Illustration reduced.

Fetridge & Co.

RT5	2c **vermilion,** cut to shape	
a.	Old paper	150.00

E. W. Hoyt & Co.

For illustrations of Nos. RT7, RT8 and RT11, see large stamp illustration pages.

RT6	1c **black,** imperf.	
b.	Silk paper	*4,000.*
c.	Pink paper	3,500.
d.	Wmk 191R	160.00
RT7	1c **black,** die cut	
b.	Silk paper	37.50
c.	Pink paper	37.50
d.	Wmk 191R	18.00
RT8	2c **black,** imperf.	
d.	Wmk 191R	900.00
RT9	2c **black,** die cut	
d.	Wmk 191R	100.00
RT10	4c **black,** imperf.	
b.	Silk paper	2,250.
c.	Pink paper	300.00
d.	Wmk 191R	1,750.
RT11	4c **black,** die cut	
b.	Silk paper	125.00
c.	Pink paper	80.00
d.	Wmk 191R	80.00

The 2c is larger than the 1c, 4c larger than the 2c.

Kidder & Laird — RT12

Kidder & Laird

RT12	1c **vermilion**	
d.	Wmk 191R	17.00
RT13	2c **vermilion**	
d.	Wmk 191R	17.00

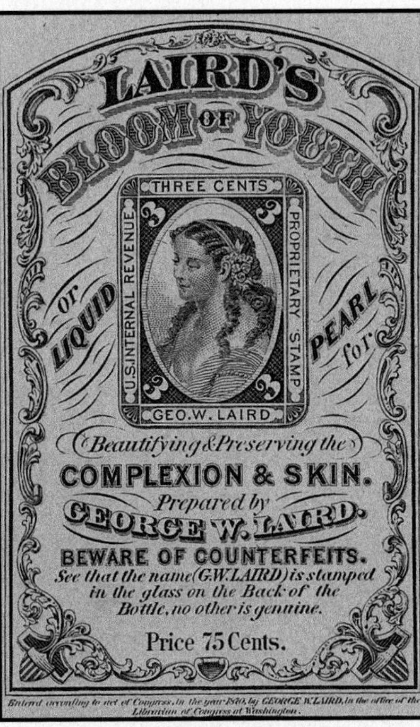

George W. Laird — RT14/RT15

George W. Laird

RT14	3c **black,** imperf.	
b.	Silk paper	800.00
	As "b," dbl. transfer	1,750.
c.	Pink paper	1,000.
	As "c," dbl. transfer	2,250.
d.	Wmk 191R	800.00
	As "d," dbl. transfer	2,500.
ap.	Perf, old paper	*3,250.*
	As "ap," Dbl. transfer	*5,500.*
bp.	Perf, silk paper	*9,000.*
RT15	3c **black,** die cut	
a.	Old paper, die cut	3,000.
ap.	As "a," perf & die cut	1,250.
b.	Silk paper	110.00
	As "b," dbl. transfer	250.00
bp.	As "b," perf & die cut	*1,500.*
c.	Pink paper	4,000.
	As "c," dbl. transfer	6,500.
d.	Wmk 191R	110.00
	As "d," dbl. transfer	325.00
e.	Experimental silk paper	*3,000.*
	Double transfer	*3,500.*

Lanman & Kemp — RT16/RT18

Lanman & Kemp

RT16	1c **black**	
b.	Silk paper	8.25
	As "b," dbl. transfer	—
c.	Pink paper	950.00
d.	Wmk 191R	8.25
RT17	2c **brown**	
b.	Silk paper	35.00
d.	Wmk 191R	11.00
RT18	3c **green**	
b.	Silk paper	9.00
	As "b," dbl. transfer	175.00
d.	Wmk 191R	9.00
	As "d," dbl. transfer	77.50

Tetlow's Perfumery — RT19

Tetlow's Perfumery

RT19	1c **vermilion**	
d.	Wmk 191R	3.75

C. B. Woodworth & Son — RT20/RT21

C. B. Woodworth & Son

RT20	1c **green**	
b.	Silk paper	6.00
	As "b," dbl. transfer	67.50
c.	Pink paper	20.00
	As "c," dbl. transfer	82.50
d.	Wmk 191R	7.75
	As "d," dbl. transfer	67.50
RT21	2c **blue**	
b.	Silk paper	180.00
c.	Pink paper	*4,000.*
d.	Wmk 191R	10.00

R. & G. A. Wright — RT22/RT25

R. & G. A. Wright

RT22	1c **blue**	
a.	Old paper	6.75
b.	Silk paper	9.00
d.	Wmk 191R	67.50
e.	Experimental silk paper	125.00

RT23 2c **black**
a. Old paper 13.00
b. Silk paper 25.00
d. Wmk 191R 600.00
RT24 3c **lake**
a. Old paper 35.00
b. Silk paper 125.00
d. Wmk 191R 525.00
RT25 4c **green**
a. Old paper 110.00
b. Silk paper 160.00
d. Wmk 191R 750.00

Young, Ladd & Coffin — RT26/RT33

Young, Ladd & Coffin

RT26 1c **green**, imperf.
b. Silk paper 110.00
c. Pink paper 100.00
d. Wmk 191R 110.00
RT27 1c **green**, perf.
b. Silk paper 25.00
c. Pink paper 17.00
d. Wmk 191R 17.00
RT28 2c **blue**, imperf.
b. Silk paper 150.00
c. Pink paper 130.00
d. Wmk 191R 90.00
RT29 2c **blue**, perf.
b. Silk paper 60.00
c. Pink paper 110.00
d. Wmk 191R 17.00
RT30 3c **vermilion**, imperf.
b. Silk paper 130.00
c. Pink paper 150.00
d. Wmk 191R 95.00
RT31 3c **vermilion**, perf.
b. Silk paper 40.00
c. Pink paper 8.25
d. Wmk 191R 7.75
RT32 4c **brown**, imperf.
b. Silk paper *9,500.*
c. Pink paper 160.00
d. Wmk 191R 110.00
RT33 4c **brown**, perf.
b. Silk paper 45.00
c. Pink paper 14.00
d. Wmk 191R 5.50

PRIVATE DIE PLAYING CARD STAMPS

RU1

Caterson Brotz & Co.

RU1 5c **brown**
d. Wmk 191R *12,000.*

This stamp was never placed in use. Value is for an unused stamp with perfs trimmed off. Three examples are recorded: one fully perfed, two with perfs trimmed off.

A. Dougherty — RU2/RU6

A. Dougherty — RU5

A. Dougherty

RU2 2c **orange**
a. Old paper 175.00
RU3 4c **black**
a. Old paper 75.00
RU4 5c **blue,** 20x26mm
a. Old paper 4.00
b. Silk paper 7.50
As "b," dbl. transfer *1,000.*
c. Pink paper 17.50
e. Experimental silk paper *1,500.*
As "e," inverted dbl. transfer —
u. **Ultra,** old paper *1,750.*

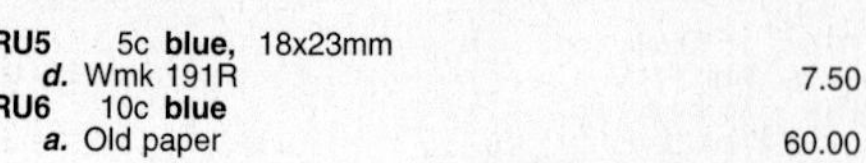

RU5 5c **blue,** 18x23mm
d. Wmk 191R 7.50
RU6 10c **blue**
a. Old paper 60.00

The 2c, 4c and 5c have numerals in all four corners.

Eagle Card Co. — RU7

Eagle Card Co.

RU7 5c **black**
d. Wmk 191R 150.00

Goodall — RU8

Goodall (London, New York)

As No. RU13, "London Goodall New York" replaces both "American Playing Cards" and "Victor E. Mauger and Petrie New York."

RU8 5c **black**
a. Old paper 175.00
b. Silk paper 10.00
e. Experimental silk paper 2,750.

Samuel Hart & Co. — RU9

Samuel Hart & Co.

RU9 5c **black**
a. Old paper 9.00
b. Silk paper 9.00
e. Experimental silk paper 2,750.

Lawrence & Cohen — RU10/RU11

Lawrence & Cohen

RU10 2c **blue**
a. Old paper 150.00
RU11 5c **green**
a. Old paper 10.00
b. Silk paper 12.50
e. Experimental silk paper 165.00

Jn. J. Levy — RU12

Jn. J. Levy

RU12 5c **black**
a. Old paper 40.00
b. Silk paper 45.00
e. Experimental silk paper 140.00

Victor E. Mauger & Petrie — RU13

Victor E. Mauger and Petrie

RU13 5c **blue**
b. Silk paper 6.00
c. Pink paper 7.00
d. Wmk 191R 5.00

New York Consolidated Card Co. — RU14

New York Consolidated Card Co.

RU14 5c **black**
b. Silk paper 7.50
c. Pink paper 27.50
d. Wmk 191R 7.00

Paper Fabrique — RU15

Paper Fabrique Company

RU15 5c **black**
b. Silk paper 15.00
c. Pink paper 30.00
d. Wmk 191R 15.00

Russell, Morgan & Co. — RU16

Russell, Morgan & Co.

RU16 5c **black**
d. Wmk 191R 30.00

MOTOR VEHICLE USE REVENUE STAMPS

When affixed to a motor vehicle, the stamp permitted use of that vehicle for a stated period. The purchase month is shown in parentheses, and the denomination corresponds to the month in which the stamp is purchased, in relation to when the stamp expired. Thus, a stamp purchased in June expired that month, and the denomination is the lowest of the all the denominations in that year's set. A stamp purchased in July was good through the following June, and thus has the highest denomination in its set, and so on. Sales of motor vehicle use stamps ceased in June 1946.

Unused stamps are valued with gum on the face. Stamps without gum sell for reduced prices. Stamps with car details on the reverse are used, whether they have gum on the face or not.

RV1

1942 Wmk. 191R OFFSET PRINTING *Perf. 11*

With Gum on Back

RV1	RV1	$2.09	**light green** *(February)*	1.75	.50

With Gum on Face

Inscriptions on Back

RV2	RV1	$1.67	**light green** *(March)*	32.50	8.50
RV3	RV1	$1.25	**light green** *(April)*	25.00	7.50
RV4	RV1	84c	**light green** *(May)*	27.50	7.25
RV5	RV1	42c	**light green** *(June)*	27.50	7.25

With Gum and Control Number on Face

Inscriptions on Back

RV6	RV1	$5	**rose red** *(July)*	3.25	1.50
RV7	RV1	$4.59	**rose red** *(August)*	60.00	13.00
RV8	RV1	$4.17	**rose red** *(September)*	65.00	16.00
RV9	RV1	$3.75	**rose red** *(October)*	60.00	12.50
RV10	RV1	$3.34	**rose red** *(November)*	60.00	12.50
RV11	RV1	$2.92	**rose red** *(December)*	60.00	12.50
			Nos. RV1-RV11 (11)	422.50	99.00

1943

RV12	RV1	$2.50	**rose red** *(January)*	67.50	16.00
RV13	RV1	$2.09	**rose red** *(February)*	45.00	11.00
RV14	RV1	$1.67	**rose red** *(March)*	40.00	12.50
RV15	RV1	$1.25	**rose red** *(April)*	40.00	9.00
RV16	RV1	84c	**rose red** *(May)*	40.00	9.00
RV17	RV1	42c	**rose red** *(June)*	40.00	10.00
RV18	RV1	$5	**yellow** *(July)*	3.75	1.00
RV19	RV1	$4.59	**yellow** *(August)*	70.00	17.00
RV20	RV1	$4.17	**yellow** *(September)*	87.50	21.00
RV21	RV1	$3.75	**yellow** *(October)*	87.50	21.00
RV22	RV1	$3.34	**yellow** *(November)*	100.00	22.00
RV23	RV1	$2.92	**yellow** *(December)*	120.00	25.00
			Nos. RV12-RV23 (12)	741.25	174.50

1944

RV24	RV1	$2.50	**yellow** *(January)*	140.00	25.00
RV25	RV1	$2.09	**yellow** *(February)*	80.00	19.00
RV26	RV1	$1.67	**yellow** *(March)*	67.50	16.00
RV27	RV1	$1.25	**yellow** *(April)*	67.50	17.00
RV28	RV1	84c	**yellow** *(May)*	60.00	16.00
RV29	RV1	42c	**yellow** *(June)*	60.00	16.00

Gum on Face

Control Number and Inscriptions on Back

RV30	RV1	$5	**violet** *(July)*	2.40	1.75
RV31	RV1	$4.59	**violet** *(August)*	100.00	21.00
RV32	RV1	$4.17	**violet** *(September)*	75.00	19.00
RV33	RV1	$3.75	**violet** *(October)*	75.00	19.00
RV34	RV1	$3.34	**violet** *(November)*	67.50	12.50
RV35	RV1	$2.92	**violet** *(December)*	67.50	12.50
			Nos. RV24-RV35 (12)	862.40	194.75

1945

RV36	RV1	$2.50	**violet** *(January)*	60.00	12.00
RV37	RV1	$2.09	**violet** *(February)*	52.50	12.00
RV38	RV1	$1.67	**violet** *(March)*	52.50	10.50
RV39	RV1	$1.25	**violet** *(April)*	52.50	10.50
RV40	RV1	84c	**violet** *(May)*	42.50	9.00
RV41	RV1	42c	**violet** *(June)*	30.00	7.25

Daniel Manning — RV2

Gum on Face

Control Number and Inscriptions on Back

1945 Wmk. 191R Offset Printing *Perf. 11*

Bright Blue Green & Yellow Green

RV42	RV2	$5	*(July)*	3.25	1.00
RV43	RV2	$4.59	*(August)*	75.00	19.00
RV44	RV2	$4.17	*(Sept.)*	75.00	19.50
RV45	RV2	$3.75	*(October)*	67.50	12.50
RV46	RV2	$3.34	*(November)*	55.00	12.00
RV47	RV2	$2.92	*(December)*	50.00	9.00
			Nos. RV36-RV47 (12)	615.75	134.25

1946

Bright Blue Green & Yellow Green

RV48	RV2	$2.50	*(January)*	52.50	12.50
RV49	RV2	$2.09	*(February)*	52.50	12.00
RV50	RV2	$1.67	*(March)*	42.50	9.00
RV51	RV2	$1.25	*(April)*	32.50	9.00
RV52	RV2	84c	*(May)*	32.50	9.00
RV53	RV2	42c	*(June)*	25.00	1.20
			Nos. RV48-RV53 (6)	237.50	52.70

BOATING STAMPS

Required on applications for the certificate of number for motorboats of more than 10 horsepower, starting April 1, 1960. The pictorial upper part of the $3 stamp was attached to the temporary certificate and kept by the boat owner. The lower part (stub), showing number only, was affixed to the application and sent by the post office to the U.S. Coast Guard, which issued permanent certificates. The $3 fee was for three years. The $1 stamp covered charges for reissue of a lost or destroyed certificate of number. These stamps were used in the 12 states and the District of Columbia that had not passed laws in conformity with the Boating Act of 1958.

Catalogue value for unused stamps in this section are for Never Hinged items.

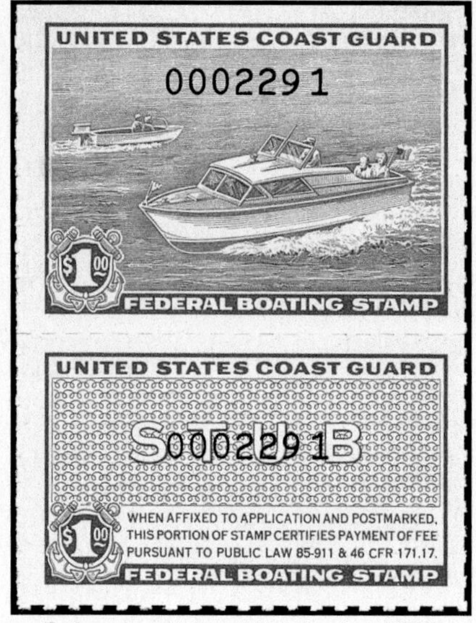

Outboard and Inboard Motorboats — RVB1

Offset Printing, Number Typographed

1960, Apr. 1 **Unwmk.** ***Rouletted***

RVB1	RVB1	$1 **rose red, black number**	40.00	*775.00*
		P# block of 4	160.00	
		On license		—
RVB2	RVB1	$3 **blue, red number**	50.00	35.00
		P# block of 4	200.00	
		On license		55.00
		First day license		*550.00*

Nos. RVB1 and RVB2 unused stamp values are for MNH complete two-part stamps. Used values are for stamps, without the stubs, bearing a complete cancel dated between April 1, 1960, and January 31, 1964. On-license values are for clean licenses with undamaged stamps and a complete cancel. A license fold can be expected. Mute oval cancels are usually favor cancels.

CAMP STAMPS

The Camp Stamp program of the Department of Agriculture's National Forest Service was introduced in 1985. The public was offered the option of prepaying their recreation fees through the purchase of camp stamps. The fees varied but were typically $3 to $4.

The stamps were supplied in rolls with the backing roulettted 9 horizontally. The letter preceding the serial number indicated the face value and printer (A-D, Denver; E-J, Washington). The stamps were designed so that any attempt to remove them from the fee envelope would cause them to come apart.

The program ended in the summer of 1988. The envelopes containing the stamps were destroyed by the National Forerst Service after use. No used examples have been reported.

Catalogue value for unused stamps in this section are for Never Hinged items.

National Forest Service Logo — RVC1

Printed in Denver, CO.

1985 **Typo.** ***Die Cut***

Self-Adhesive, Coated Paper

RVC1	RVC1	50c **black,** *pink,* "A"	*400.00*
a.		Serifed letter "A," serial number with comma	*400.00*
RVC2	RVC1	$1 **black,** *red,* "B"	*500.00*
a.		Serifed letter "B," serial number with comma	*400.00*
RVC3	RVC1	$2 **black,** *yellow,* "C"	*525.00*
a.		Serifed letter "C," serial number with comma	*400.00*
RVC4	RVC1	$3 **black,** *green,* "D"	*525.00*
a.		Serifed letter "D," serial number with comma	*400.00*

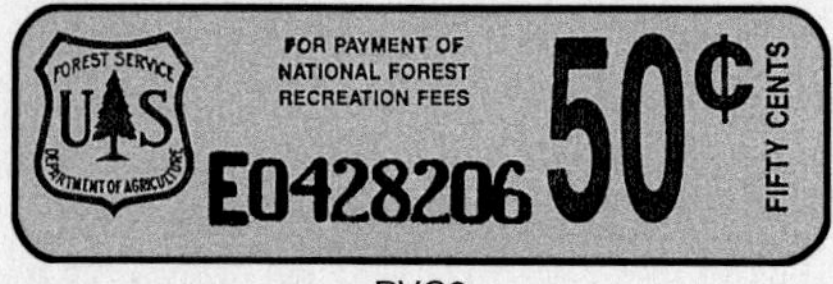

RVC2

Printed by the Government Printing Office, Washington, DC (?).

1986 **Typo.** ***Die Cut***

Self-Adhesive, Coated Paper

RVC5	RVC2	50c **black,** *pink,* "E"	*950.00*
RVC6	RVC2	$1 **black,** *red,* "F"	*975.00*
RVC7	RVC2	$2 **black,** *yellow,* "G"	*950.00*
RVC8	RVC2	$3 **black,** *green,* "H"	550.00
a.		Serial number omitted	—
RVC9	RVC2	$5 **black,** *silver,* "I"	*2,000.*
RVC10	RVC2	$10 **black,** *bronze,* "J"	*2,750.*

NATIONAL PARK SERVICE GOLDEN EAGLE PASS STAMP

Issued by the National Park Service of the Department of the Interior for use as a $25 annual Golden Eagle Pass for entry to national parks nationwide. The pass was valid January 1 through December 31, 1988. Printed as a perforated souvenir sheet of seven, only the two right stamps were applied to the license. The Golden Eagle Pass stamp is usually collected as a complete souvenir sheet that bears a serial number at the top. The mint souvenir sheet was tipped into the National Park Service license brochure that included the souvenir sheet and the pass to which the stamps were to be affixed. Most dealers sell the mint stamp in this original issue configuration. Six different first day covers, one with each artist's stamp design and bearing a complete souvenir sheet (without selvage), canceled at the post office serving the park shown on the cachet and stamp, were produced. Each is signed by the artist. Problems with the issue format caused the stamp program to be terminated after 1988. National Park stamps, in a similar format but with a $10 face value, were issued for nine more years from 1989 to 1997 as part of the National Park Foundation's Arts for the Parks program. While all ten stamps often are collected as a series, the $10 stamps are not federal revenue stamps.

No. RVP1 is tipped onto the brochure; thus there will be some gum disturbance in the top selvage. Stamps are values as never hinged.

RVP1

1987, Dec. 10 **Unwmk.** ***Perf. 12½***

RVP1	RVP1 $25 **multicolored,** souvenir sheet of 7	65.00	25.00
	On license		50.00
	First day cover		100.00
a.	Tipped into issue brochure with license		75.00
b.	Specimen (marked "sample")		150.00

TRAILER PERMIT STAMPS

Issued by the National Park Service of the Department of the Interior. Required to be affixed to "License to Operate Motor Vehicle" starting July 1, 1939, when a house trailer was attached to a motor vehicle entering a national park or national monument.

Issued to rangers in booklets of 50 (five 2x5 panes).

Use was continued at least until 1952.

Unused stamps may have a ranger's handwritten control number. The $1 stamp on license have been found only used for the large parks in the western United States.

Trailer and Automobile
RVT1

1939 **Unwmk.** **Offset Printing** ***Perf. 11***

RVT1	RVT1 50c **bright blue**	*5,000.*	—
	On license		*4,500.*
RVT2	RVT1 $1 **carmine**	*1,500.*	600.00
	On license		*800.00*

Earliest documented use: May 14,1939 (No. RVT2).

DISTILLED SPIRITS EXCISE TAX STAMPS

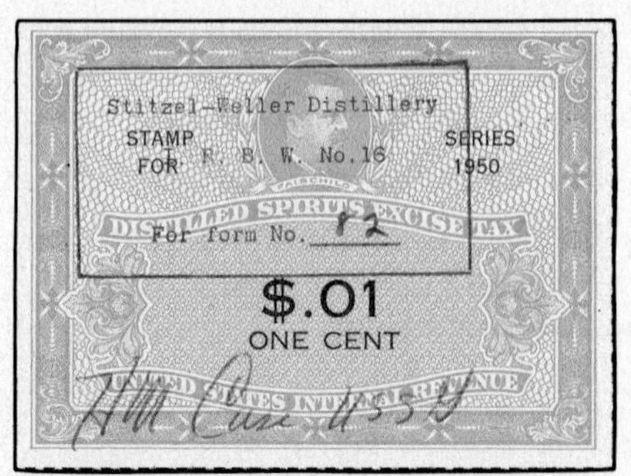

Charles S. Fairchild, Secretary of Treasury 1887-89 — DS1

Actual size: 89½x63½mm

Inscribed "STAMP FOR SERIES 1950"

1950 Wmk. 191R Offset Printing ***Rouletted 7***

Left Value — Unused
Right Value — Used

No.	Design	Denomination & color	Unused	Used
RX1	DS1	1c **yellow green & black**	50.00	27.50
		Punched cancel		21.00
RX2	DS1	3c **yellow green & black**	140.00	100.00
		Punched cancel		92.50
RX3	DS1	5c **yellow green & black**	27.50	20.00
		Punched cancel		17.50
RX4	DS1	10c **yellow green & black**	25.00	17.50
		Punched cancel		15.00
RX5	DS1	25c **yellow green & black**	40.00	11.00
		Punched cancel		9.00
RX6	DS1	50c **yellow green & black**	25.00	11.00
		Punched cancel		8.00
RX7	DS1	$1 **yellow green & black**	30.00	3.00
		Punched cancel		1.75
RX8	DS1	$3 **yellow green & black**	40.00	20.00
		Punched cancel		15.00
RX9	DS1	$5 **yellow green & black**	30.00	6.50
		Punched cancel		4.50
RX10	DS1	$10 **yellow green & black**	15.00	3.00
		Punched cancel		1.75
RX11	DS1	$25 **yellow green & black**	25.00	12.50
		Punched cancel		9.25
RX12	DS1	$50 **yellow green & black**	25.00	8.75
		Punched cancel		5.00
RX13	DS1	$100 **yellow green & black**	15.00	4.00
		Punched cancel		3.00
RX14	DS1	$300 **yellow green & black**	45.00	25.00
		Punched cancel		21.00
RX15	DS1	$500 **yellow green & black**	30.00	15.00
		Punched cancel		10.00
RX16	DS1	$1,000 **yellow green & black**	25.00	11.00
		Punched cancel		8.00
RX17	DS1	$1,500 **yellow green & black**	70.00	50.00
		Punched cancel		40.00
RX18	DS1	$2,000 **yellow green & black**	12.50	5.00
		Punched cancel		4.00
RX19	DS1	$3,000 **yellow green & black**	35.00	25.00
		Punched cancel		15.00
RX20	DS1	$5,000 **yellow green & black**	35.00	25.00
		Punched cancel		17.50
RX21	DS1	$10,000 **yellow green & black**	45.00	27.50
		Punched cancel		22.50
RX22	DS1	$20,000 **yellow green & black**	55.00	35.00
		Punched cancel		30.00
RX23	DS1	$30,000 **yellow green & black**	90.00	70.00
		Punched cancel		50.00
RX24	DS1	$40,000 **yellow green & black**	750.00	950.00
		Punched cancel		600.00
RX25	DS1	$50,000 **yellow green & black**	200.00	95.00
		Punched cancel		75.00

Inscription "STAMP FOR SERIES 1950" Omitted

1952

Left Value — Unused
Right Value — Used

No.	Design	Denomination & color	Unused	Used
RX27	DS1	3c **yellow green & black**	*750.00*	
RX28	DS1	5c **yellow green & black**	250.00	
		Punched cancel		40.00
RX29	DS1	10c **yellow green & black**	35.00	90.00
		Punched cancel		5.00
RX30	DS1	25c **yellow green & black**	45.00	90.00
		Punched cancel		15.00
RX31	DS1	50c **yellow green & black**	45.00	90.00
		Punched cancel		15.00
RX32	DS1	$1 **yellow green & black**	30.00	90.00
		Punched cancel		2.50
RX33	DS1	$3 **yellow green & black**	55.00	90.00
		Punched cancel		22.50
RX34	DS1	$5 **yellow green & black**	55.00	90.00
		Punched cancel		25.00
RX35	DS1	$10 **yellow green & black**	30.00	90.00
		Punched cancel		2.50
RX36	DS1	$25 **yellow green & black**	40.00	90.00
		Punched cancel		10.00
RX37	DS1	$50 **yellow green & black**	90.00	90.00
		Punched cancel		25.00
RX38	DS1	$100 **yellow green & black**	30.00	90.00
		Punched cancel		2.50
RX39	DS1	$300 **yellow green & black**	40.00	90.00
		Punched cancel		7.50
RX40	DS1	$500 **yellow green & black**	350.00	
		Punched cancel		30.00
RX41	DS1	$1,000 **yellow green & black**	140.00	75.00
		Punched cancel		6.00
RX42	DS1	$1,500 **yellow green & black**	*750.00*	
RX43	DS1	$2,000 **yellow green & black**	550.00	
		Punched cancel		75.00
RX44	DS1	$3,000 **yellow green & black**	750.00	
		Punched cancel		700.00
RX45	DS1	$5,000 **yellow green & black**	500.00	
		Punched cancel		50.00
RX46	DS1	$10,000 **yellow green & black**	550.00	
		Punched cancel		90.00

Five other denominations with "Stamp for Series 1950" omitted were prepared but are not known to have been put into use: 1c, $20,000, $30,000, $40,000 and $50,000.

Stamps listed as used have staple holes.

Distilled Spirits Excise Tax stamps were discontinued in 1959.

FIREARMS TRANSFER TAX STAMPS

Used on transfer tax documents for tax paid transfers of National Firearms Act weapons. Prior to 1968, transfers of NFA weapons were processed by the Alcohol, Tobacco and Firearms division of the Internal Revenue Service. Current examples of firearms transfer stamps are not available for sale to collectors because of the possibility of fraudulent misuse.

Documentary Stamp of 1917 Overprinted Vertically in Black. Reading Up

1938 Engr. Wmk. 191R ***Perf. 11***
Without Gum

No.	Design	Denomination & color	Unused	Used
RY1	R21	$1 **green**	600.00	—
		On license		—

Type I — RY1

Eagle, Shield and Stars from U.S. Seal

Two types of $200:

I — Serial number with serifs, not preceded by zeros. Tips of 6 lines project into left margin.

II — Gothic serial number preceded by zeros. Five line tips in left margin.

Size: 28x42mm
Without Gum

1934 Wmk. 191R ***Perf. 12***

No.	Design	Denomination & color	Unused	Used
RY2	RY1	$200 **dark blue & red,** type I, #1-1600	2,500.	1,500.
		On license		*1,750.*

Issued in vertical strips of 4, with tab at left, which are imperforate at top, bottom and right side.

See Nos. RY4, RY6-RY8.

RY2

1939 Size: 28x33½mm ***Perf. 11***

No.	Design	Denomination & color	Unused	Used
RY3	RY2	$1 **green**	85.00	35.00
		On license		—

See No. RY5.

Type II — RY3

1966 Wmk. 191R ***Perf. 12***
Size: 29x43mm

No.	Design	Denomination & color	Unused	Used
RY4	RY3	$200 **dull blue & red,** type II, #1601(?) - #3000(?)	750.00	700.00
		On license		750.00

No. RY4 has a clear impression and is printed on white paper. No. RY2 has a "muddy" impression in much darker blue ink and is printed on off-white paper.

1960, July 1 Size: 29x34mm ***Perf. 11***

No.	Design	Denomination & color	Unused	Used
RY5	RY2	$5 **red**	85.00	45.00
		On license		200.00

No. RY5 was issued in sheets of 50 (10x5) with straight edge on four sides of sheet.

The watermark is hard to see on many examples of #RY4-RY5.

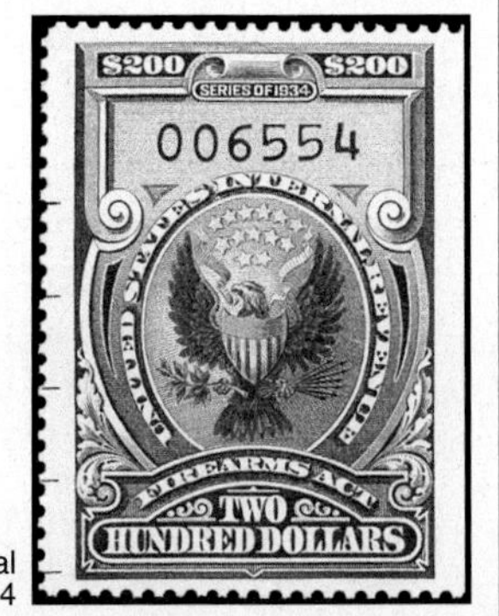
Gothis Serial Numbers — RY4

1974(?) **Unwmk.** *Perf. 12*
Size: 29x43mm

RY6	RY4 $200 **dull blue & red**, type II, #3001-up		275.00	110.00
	On license			125.00
a.	Booklet pane of 4		*1,100.*	

Panes of 32

1990(?) **Litho.** **Without Gum** *Imperf.*

RY7	RY1 $200 **dull blue**		*900.00*
	On license		*1,150.*

1990 *Perf. 12½*

RY8	RY1 $200 **dull blue**	350.00	80.00
	On license		150.00
RY9	RY2 $5 **red,** *1994*	450.00	150.00
	On license		225.00

Nos. RY7 and RY8 do not have a printed serial number or the tabs at left.

WARNING: Nos. RY7-RY9 are usually taped or glued to the transfer of title documents. The glue used is NOT water soluble. Attempts to soak the stamps may result in damage.

A certificate is recommended for No. RY7.

2001(?) *Serpentine Die Cut 11.5*
Self-Adhesive

RY10	RY2 $5 **dull red**		125.00
	On license		*250.00*

RY5

2012(?) **Litho.** *Serpentine Die Cut 11*
Self-Adhesive

RY11	RY5 $200 **dull blue**	—	200.00
	On license		225.00

2014 **Photo.** *Serpentine Die Cut 6.3*
Self-Adhesive

RY12	RY5 $200 **dull blue**		175.00
	On license		200.00

2020(?) **Photo.** *Serpentine Die Cut 7.8*
Self-Adhesive

RY13	RY5 $200 **dull blue**		—
	On license		—

RECTIFICATION TAX STAMPS

Used to indicate payment of the tax on distilled spirits that were condensed and purified for additional blending through repeated distillations.

RZ1

Actual size: 89½x64mm

1946 **Offset Printing** **Wmk. 191R** *Rouletted 7*

RZ1	RZ1	1c **blue & black**	6.75	4.00
		Punched cancel		2.00
RZ2	RZ1	3c **blue & black**	22.50	8.00
		Punched cancel		7.50
RZ3	RZ1	5c **blue & black**	12.50	2.50
		Punched cancel		1.25
RZ4	RZ1	10c **blue & black**	12.50	3.00
		Punched cancel		1.25
RZ5	RZ1	25c **blue & black**	12.50	3.00
		Punched cancel		2.00
RZ6	RZ1	50c **blue & black**	17.50	5.00
		Punched cancel		3.50
RZ7	RZ1	$1 **blue & black**	17.50	4.00
		Punched cancel		2.50
RZ8	RZ1	$3 **blue & black**	90.00	18.00
		Punched cancel		9.00
RZ9	RZ1	$5 **blue & black**	30.00	10.00
		Punched cancel		6.00
RZ10	RZ1	$10 **blue & black**	22.50	3.00
		Punched cancel		1.25
RZ11	RZ1	$25 **blue & black**	90.00	10.00
		Punched cancel		3.00
RZ12	RZ1	$50 **blue & black**	90.00	7.50
		Punched cancel		3.00
RZ13	RZ1	$100 **blue & black**	*175.00*	9.50
		Punched cancel		3.50
RZ14	RZ1	$300 **blue & black**	*220.00*	10.00
		Punched cancel		7.50
RZ15	RZ1	$500 **blue & black**	*240.00*	10.00
		Punched cancel		7.00
RZ16	RZ1	$1000 **blue & black**	*240.00*	18.00
		Punched cancel		15.00
RZ17	RZ1	$1500 **blue & black**	*260.00*	60.00
		Punched cancel		45.00
RZ18	RZ1	$2000 **blue & black**	*260.00*	80.00
		Punched cancel		60.00

Stamps listed as used have staple holes.

HUNTING PERMIT STAMPS

Authorized by an Act of Congress, approved March 16, 1934, to license hunters. Receipts go to maintain waterfowl life in the United States. Sales to collectors were made legal June 15, 1935.

No. RW1 used is valued with handstamp or manuscript cancel, though technically it was against postal regulations to deface the stamp or to apply a postal cancellation. Beginning with No. RW2, the used values are for stamps with signatures.

Nos. RW1-RW12 were issued in panes of 28, of which 10 stamps have a straight edge on one or two sides. Such examples sell for 20%-30% less than the values shown.

Plate number blocks of six have selvage on two sides. Values for plate blocks of Nos. RW1-RW25 are for bottom plate blocks or top plate blocks with narrow selvage. Top margin plate blocks with wide untrimmed selvage sell for approximately 20%-25% more than the values shown.

Hunting permit stamps are valid from July 1 - June 30. Stamps have been made available prior to the date of validity, and stamps are sold through the philatelic agency after the period of validity has passed.

All hunting permit stamps through No. RW68A were printed by the Bureau of Engraving & Printing.

Catalogue values for all unused stamps in this section are for stamps with never-hinged original gum. Minor natural gum skips and bends are normal on Nos. RW1-RW20. No-gum stamps are without signature or other cancel.

Catalogue values for all unused stamps in this section are for stamps with never-hinged original gum. Hinged examples from No. RW13 to present usually sell for 40%-60% of the values of never-hinged examples. Minor natural gum skips and bends are normal on Nos. RW1-RW20. No-gum stamps are without signature or other cancel.

Nos. RW1-RW12 were issued in panes of 28, of which 10 stamps have a straight edge on one or two sides. Such examples sell for 20%-30% less than the values shown.

Department of Agriculture

Various Designs Inscribed

"U. S. Department of Agriculture"

Mallards Alighting — HP1

Engraved: Flat Plate Printing
Issued in panes of 28 subjects.

1934 **Unwmk.** ***Perf. 11***

Inscribed "Void after June 30, 1935"

RW1 HP1 $1 **blue**	775.	175.
Hinged	300.	
No gum	175.	
P# block of 6	14,500.	

Used value is for stamp with handstamp or manuscript cancel.

It is almost certain that examples of No. RW1 offered as imperforate vertical pairs or as vertical pairs imperforate horizontally are from printer's waste. Additionally, it is almost certain that all imperforate vertical pairs are pairs imperforate horizontally that have had the vertical perforations trimmed off. No horizontal imperforate pairs are known. All recorded pairs are vertical, with narrow side margins. Most examples exist without gum and with faults. Some pairs have gum on the front (which in some cases appears to have been removed).

The stamps imperforate horizontally are recorded as a unique vertical block of eight, with the other recorded varieties being the manufactured imperforate vertical pairs.

Canvasbacks Taking to Flight — HP2

1935 **Inscribed "Void after June 30, 1936"**

RW2 HP2 $1 **rose lake**	700.	160.
deep rose lake	—	
Hinged	375.	
No gum	175.	
P# block of 6	12,500.	
P# block of 6, deep rose lake	—	

Canada Geese in Flight — HP3

1936 **Inscribed "Void after June 30, 1937"**

RW3 HP3 $1 **brown black**	325.	100.
Hinged	150.	
No gum	90.	
P# block of 6	3,500.	

Scaup Ducks Taking to Flight — HP4

1937 **Inscribed "Void after June 30, 1938"**

RW4 HP4 $1 **light green**	300.	65.
Hinged	140.	
No gum	85.	
P# block of 6	3,250.	

Pintail Drake and Hen Alighting — HP5

1938 **Inscribed "Void after June 30, 1939"**

RW5 HP5 $1 **light violet**	425.	75.
Hinged	200.	
No gum	85.	
P# block of 6	4,500.	

Department of the Interior

Various Designs Inscribed

"U. S. Department of the Interior"

Green-winged Teal — HP6

1939 **Inscribed "Void after June 30, 1940"**

RW6 HP6 $1 **chocolate**	250.	50.
Hinged	115.	
No gum	60.	
P# block of 6	2,500.	

Black Mallards — HP7

1940 **Inscribed "Void after June 30, 1941"**

RW7 HP7 $1 **sepia**	250.	50.
Hinged	115.	
No gum	60.	
P# block of 6	2,500.	

Family of Ruddy Ducks — HP8

1941 **Inscribed "Void after June 30, 1942"**

RW8 HP8 $1 **brown carmine**	225.	50.
Hinged	95.	
No gum	45.	
P# block of 6	2,500.	

Baldpates — HP9

1942 **Inscribed "Void after June 30, 1943"**

RW9 HP9 $1 **violet brown**	225.	45.
Hinged	95.	
No gum	45.	
P# block of 6	2,500.	

Wood Ducks — HP10

1943 **Inscribed "Void After June 30, 1944"**

RW10 HP10 $1 **deep rose**	120.	35.
Hinged	55.	
No gum	35.	
P# block of 6	700.	

Hawaiian Nene Geese — HP31

1964 **Inscribed "Void after June 30, 1965"**

RW31 HP31 $3 **multicolored** 100.00 12.50
No gum 35.00
P# block of 6 1,950.

Three Canvasback Drakes — HP32

1965 **Inscribed "Void after June 30, 1966"**

RW32 HP32 $3 **multicolored** 100.00 12.50
No gum 40.00
P# block of 4 450.00

Whistling Swans — HP33

1966 **Inscribed "Void after June 30, 1967"**

RW33 HP33 $3 **multicolored** 100.00 12.50
No gum 40.00
P# block of 4 500.00

Old Squaw Ducks — HP34

1967 **Inscribed "Void after June 30, 1968"**

RW34 HP34 $3 **multicolored** 100.00 12.50
No gum 40.00
P# block of 4 550.00

Hooded Mergansers — HP35

1968 **Inscribed "Void after June 30, 1969"**

RW35 HP35 $3 **multicolored** 65.00 12.50
No gum 20.00
P# block of 4 300.00
a. Back inscription omitted —

White-winged Scoters — HP36

1969 **Inscribed "Void after June 30, 1970"**

RW36 HP36 $3 **multicolored** 65.00 8.00
No gum 20.00
P# block of 4 275.00

Ross's Geese — HP37

1970 **Engraved & Lithographed**
Inscribed "Void after June 30, 1971"

RW37 HP37 $3 **multicolored** 65.00 8.00
No gum 20.00
P# block of 4 280.00

Three Cinnamon Teal — HP38

1971 **Inscribed "Void after June 30, 1972"**

RW38 HP38 $3 **multicolored** 42.50 8.00
No gum 15.00
P# block of 4 180.00

Emperor Geese — HP39

1972 **Inscribed "Void after June 30, 1973"**

RW39 HP39 $5 **multicolored** 30.00 6.00
No gum 8.00
P# block of 4 125.00

Steller's Eiders — HP40

1973 **Inscribed "Void after June 30, 1974"**

RW40 HP40 $5 **multicolored** 18.00 6.00
No gum 7.00
P# block of 4 75.00

Wood Ducks — HP41

RW41a

1974 **Inscribed "Void after June 30, 1975"**

RW41 HP41 $5 **multicolored** 18.00 5.00
No gum 6.00
P# block of 4 72.50
a. Back inscription missing, but printed vertically on face of stamp and selvage, from foldover *4,750.*

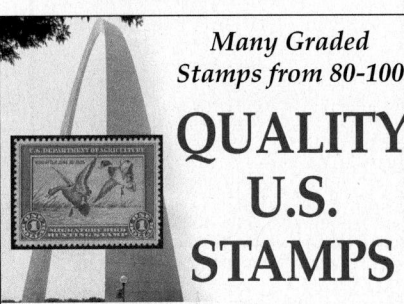

Canvasback Ducks and Decoy — HP42

1975 **Inscribed "Void after June 30, 1976"**

RW42 HP42 $5 **multicolored** 15.00 5.00
No gum 7.00
P# block of 4 65.00

Family of Canada Geese — HP43

1976 **Engr.**

Inscribed "Void after June 30, 1977"

RW43 HP43 $5 **green & black** 12.50 5.00
No gum 7.00
P# block of 4 50.00

Pair of Ross's Geese — HP44

1977 **Litho. & Engr.**

Inscribed "Void after June 30, 1978"

RW44 HP44 $5 **multicolored** 10.00 5.00
No gum 7.00
P# block of 4 50.00

Hooded Merganser Drake — HP45

1978 **Inscribed "Void after June 30, 1979"**

RW45 HP45 $5 **multicolored** 10.00 5.00
No gum 7.00
P# block of 4 40.00

Green-winged Teal — HP46

1979 **Inscribed "Void after June 30, 1980"**

RW46 HP46 $7.50 **multicolored** 12.50 6.00
No gum 8.00
P# block of 4 50.00

Mallards — HP47

1980 **Inscribed "Void after June 30, 1981"**

RW47 HP47 $7.50 **multicolored** 12.50 6.00
No gum 8.00
P# block of 4 55.00

Ruddy Ducks — HP48

1981 **Inscribed "Void after June 30, 1982"**

RW48 HP48 $7.50 **multicolored** 12.50 6.00
No gum 8.00
P# block of 4 50.00

Canvasbacks — HP49

1982 **Inscribed "Void after June 30, 1983"**

RW49 HP49 $7.50 **multicolored** 15.00 7.00
No gum 9.00
P# block of 4 60.00
a. Orange and violet omitted *10,000.*

A certificate from a recognized expertization committee is required for No. RW49a.

Pintails — HP50

1983 **Inscribed "Void after June 30, 1984"**

RW50 HP50 $7.50 **multicolored** 15.00 7.00
No gum 7.00
P# block of 4 60.00

Widgeons — HP51

1984 **Inscribed "Void after June 30, 1985"**

RW51 HP51 $7.50 **multicolored** 12.50 7.00
No gum 7.00
P# block of 4 50.00

See Special Printings section that follows.

Cinnamon Teal — HP52

1985 **Inscribed "Void after June 30, 1986"**

RW52 HP52 $7.50 **multicolored** 15.00 8.00
No gum 7.00
P# block of 4 60.00
a. Light blue (litho.) omitted *20,000.*

The omitted color on No. RW52a coincides with a double paper splice affecting the top row of five stamps from the sheet and top ⅓ of stamps in the second row. There is also a color changeling of the brownish red ducks and their reflections in the water to yellow and yellow orange, respectively, on the error stamps. This error currently exists as three vertical strips of 6 (top stamp the error) and a plate number block of 12 (2x6, top two stamps the error).

Fulvous Whistling Duck — HP53

1986 **Inscribed "Void after June 30, 1987"**

RW53 HP53 $7.50 **multicolored** 15.00 8.00
No gum 9.00
P# block of 4 60.00
a. Black omitted *1,450.*

Redheads — HP54

1987 *Perf. 11½x11*

Inscribed "Void after June 30, 1988"

RW54	HP54	$10 **multicolored**	17.50	8.00
		No gum	8.00	
		P# block of 4	70.00	

Snow Goose — HP55

1988 **Inscribed "Void after June 30, 1989"**

RW55	HP55	$10 **multicolored**	17.50	8.00
		No gum	8.00	
		P# block of 4	70.00	

Lesser Scaup — HP56

1989 **Inscribed "Void after June 30, 1990"**

RW56	HP56	$12.50 **multicolored**	21.50	8.00
		No gum	9.00	
		P# block of 4	85.00	

Black Bellied Whistling Duck — HP57

1990 **Inscribed "Void after June 30, 1991"**

RW57	HP57	$12.50 **multicolored**	20.00	8.00
		No gum	9.00	
		P# block of 4	85.00	
	a.	Back inscription omitted	*300.00*	

The back inscription is normally on top of the gum so beware of examples with gum removed offered as No. RW57a. Full original gum must be intact on No. RW57a. Used examples of No. RW57a cannot exist.

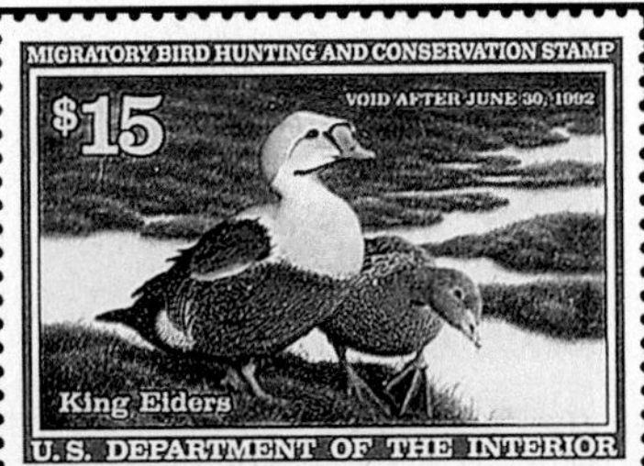

King Eiders HP58

1991 **Inscribed "Void after June 30, 1992"**

RW58	HP58	$15 **multicolored**	30.00	8.00
		No gum	15.00	
		P# block of 4	120.00	
	a.	Black (engr.) omitted	*20,000.*	

Spectacled Eider — HP59

1992 **Inscribed "Void after June 30, 1993"**

RW59	HP59	$15 **multicolored**	30.00	10.00
		No gum	15.00	
		P# block of 4	125.00	

Canvasbacks — HP60

1993 **Inscribed "Void after June 30, 1994"**

RW60	HP60	$15 **multicolored**	27.50	9.00
		No gum	15.00	
		P# block of 4	125.00	
	a.	Black (engr.) omitted	*1,750.*	*1,500.*

Red-breasted Mergansers — HP61

1994 *Perf. 11¼x11*

Inscribed "Void after June 30, 1995"

RW61	HP61	$15 **multicolored**	27.50	10.00
		No gum	15.00	
		P# block of 4	125.00	

Mallards — HP62

1995 **Inscribed "Void after June 30, 1996"**

RW62	HP62	$15 **multicolored**	32.50	12.00
		No gum	15.00	
		P# block of 4	135.00	

Surf Scoters — HP63

1996 **Inscribed "Void after June 30, 1997"**

RW63	HP63	$15 **multicolored**	32.50	12.00
		No gum	12.50	
		P# block of 4	130.00	

Canada Goose — HP64

"Long breast feather" plate flaw

"Short breast feather" plate flaw

1997 **Inscribed "Void after June 30, 1998"**

RW64	HP64 $15 **multicolored**	27.50	12.00
	No gum	15.00	
	P# block of 4	120.00	
	"Long breast feather" plate flaw, pos. 28	85.00	—
	In pair with normal stamp	175.00	
	"Short breast feather" plate flaw, pos. 28	65.00	—
	In pair with normal stamp	110.00	

Barrow's Goldeneye — HP65

1998 *Perf. 11¼*

Inscribed "Void after June 30, 1999"

RW65	HP65 $15 **multicolored**	45.00	22.50
	No gum	22.50	
	P# block of 4	180.00	

Self-Adhesive

Die Cut Perf. 10

RW65A	HP65 $15 **multicolored**	30.00	15.00
	No gum	15.00	

Nos. RW65 and later issues were sold in panes of 30 (RW65 and RW66) or 20 (RW67 and later issues), with four plate numbers per pane. The self-adhesives starting with No. RW65A were sold in panes of 1. The self-adhesives are valued unused as complete panes and used as single stamps.

Greater Scaup — HP66

1999 *Perf. 11¼*

Inscribed "Void after June 30, 2000"

RW66	HP66 $15 **multicolored**	40.00	20.00
	No gum	22.50	
	P# block of 4	175.00	

Self-Adhesive

Die Cut Perf. 10

RW66A	HP66 $15 **multicolored**	30.00	12.00
	No gum	15.00	

Mottled Duck — HP67

2000 *Perf. 11¼*

Inscribed "Void after June 30, 2001"

RW67	HP67 $15 **multicolored**	35.00	15.00
	No gum	17.50	
	P# block of 4	135.00	

Self-Adhesive

Die Cut Perf. 10

RW67A	HP67 $15 **multicolored**	30.00	14.00
	No gum	17.50	

Northern Pintail — HP68

2001 *Perf. 11¼*

Inscribed "Void after June 30, 2002"

RW68	HP68 $15 **multicolored**	35.00	18.00
	No gum	17.50	
	P# block of 4	150.00	

Self-Adhesive

Die Cut Perf. 10

RW68A	HP68 $15 **multicolored**	30.00	14.00
	No gum	15.00	

Black Scoters — HP69

Printed by Banknote Corporation of America.

2002 *Perf. 11¼*

Inscribed "Void after June 30, 2003"

RW69	HP69 $15 **multicolored**	35.00	16.00
	No gum	17.50	
	P# block of 4	125.00	

Self-Adhesive

Serpentine Die Cut 11x10¾

RW69A	HP69 $15 **multicolored**	30.00	12.00
	No gum	15.00	

Snow Geese — HP70

Printed by Ashton-Potter (USA) Ltd.

2003 *Perf. 11*

Inscribed "Void after June 30, 2004"

RW70	HP70 $15 **multicolored**	35.00	16.00
	No gum	17.50	
	P# block of 4	125.00	
b.	Imperf, pair	*5,000.*	
c.	Back inscription omitted	*4,500.*	

Self-Adhesive

Serpentine Die Cut 11x10¾

RW70A	HP70 $15 **multicolored**	30.00	12.00
	No gum	15.00	

Redheads — HP71

Printed by Banknote Corporation of America for Sennett Security Products.

2004 *Perf. 11*

Inscribed "Void after June 30, 2005"

RW71	HP71 $15 **multicolored**	35.00	16.00
	No gum	17.00	
	P# block of 4	125.00	

Self-Adhesive

Serpentine Die Cut 11x10¾

RW71A	HP71 $15 **multicolored**	30.00	12.00
	No gum	15.00	

Hooded Mergansers — HP72

Printed by Banknote Corporation of America for Sennett Security Products.

Two types of RW72: I, No framelines at top, right or bottom (from left two panes of the press sheet); II, Gray framelines at top, right and bottom (from right two panes of the press sheet).

2005 **Litho. & Engr.** *Perf. 11*

Inscribed "Void after June 30, 2006"

RW72	HP72 $15 **multicolored,** type I	30.00	16.00
	No gum	16.00	
	P# block of 4	120.00	
b.	Souvenir sheet of 1	*1,950.*	
c.	Type II	30.00	16.00
	No gum	16.00	
	P# block of 4	100.00	
d.	As "b," without artist's signature (error)	*3,250.*	

No. RW72b sold for $20. 1,000 No. RW72b were issued. Approximately 750 were signed by the artist in black, value $1,950 as shown. Approximately 150 were signed in blue ink, value $2,500. Approximately 100 were signed in gold ink, value $3,000. Most examples of No. RW72b are in the grade of F-VF. Catalogue values are for Very Fine examples.

The Duck Stamp Office never announced the existence of No. RW72b to the public through a press release or a website announcement during the time the sheet was on sale, apparently because it was not clear beforehand that the souvenir sheet could be produced successfully and on time. No. RW72b sold out before a public announcement of the item's existence could be made.

Self-Adhesive

Litho. & Debossed

Serpentine Die Cut 11x10¾

RW72A	HP72 $15 **multicolored**	27.50	11.00
	No gum	15.00	

One hundred press sheets containing four panes of 20 of No. RW72 and one hundred press sheets containing 18 of No. RW72A were offered for sale by the U.S. Fish and Wildlife Service at a premium above face value.

Ross's Goose — HP73

Printed by Banknote Corporation of America for Sennett Security Products

2006 **Litho. & Engr.** ***Perf. 11***

Inscribed "Void after June 30, 2007"

RW73	HP73 $15 **multicolored**	25.00	11.00
	No gum	15.00	
	P# block of 4	110.00	
b.	Souvenir sheet of 1	95.00	—
c.	As "b," without artist's signature (error)	*2,500.*	

No. RW73b sold for $25. All examples of No. RW73b have a black signature of the artist on a designated line in the sheet margin. Ten thousand were issued.

The sheet margin has a line designated for the signature of the engraver, Piotr Naszarkowski, but no sheets were sold with his signature. Naszarkowski signed approximately 2,500 sheets during three days at the Washington 2006 World Philatelic Exhibition, and he signed another 2,500 or more after the conclusion of the exhibition. Value $150.

Self-Adhesive

Serpentine Die Cut 11x10¾

RW73A	HP73 $15 **multicolored**	25.00	11.00
	No gum	15.00	

Two hundred fifty press sheets containing four panes of 20 of No. RW73 and two hundred fifty press sheets containing 18 of No. RW73A were offered for sale by the U.S. Fish and Wildlife Service.

Ring-necked Ducks — HP74

Printed by Banknote Corporation of America for Sennett Security Products.

2007 **Litho.** ***Perf. 11***

Inscribed "Void after June 30, 2008"

RW74	HP74 $15 **multicolored**	35.00	11.00
	No gum	16.00	
	P# block of 4	130.00	
b.	Souvenir sheet of 1	140.00	
c.	As "b", without artist's signature (error)	*2,750.*	

No. RW74b sold for $25 plus a shipping fee. The artist signed No. RW74b on a designated line in the sheet margin. Ten thousand were issued. There is no back inscription on No. RW74b.

Self-Adhesive

Serpentine Die Cut 11x10¾

RW74A	HP74 $15 **multicolored**	27.50	11.00
	No gum	15.00	

Five hundred press sheets containing four panes of 20 of No. RW74 and 500 press sheets containing 18 of No. RW74A were offered for sale by the Fish and Wildlife Service.

Northern Pintails — HP75

Printed by Ashton-Potter (USA) Ltd.

2008 **Litho.** ***Perf. 13¼***

Inscribed "Void after June 30, 2009"

RW75	HP75 $15 **multicolored**	35.00	11.00
	No gum	16.00	
	Inscription block of 4	140.00	
b.	Souvenir sheet of 1	70.00	—
c.	As "b," without artist's signature (error)	*500.00*	

A sheet commemorating the 75th anniversary of Hunting Permit stamps containing one example of No. RW75 and a label with the vignette of No. RW1 sold for $50. Value, $125.

No. RW75b sold for $30 plus a shipping fee. The artist signed No. RW75b on a designated line in the sheet margin. Ten thousand were prepared.

Self-Adhesive

Serpentine Die Cut 10¾

RW75A	HP75 $15 **multicolored**	35.00	11.00
	No gum	25.00	

Long-tailed Duck and Decoy — HP76

Printed by Ashton-Potter (USA) Ltd.

2009 **Litho.** ***Perf. 13¼***

Inscribed "Void after June 30, 2010"

RW76	HP76 $15 **multicolored**	30.00	11.00
	No gum	16.00	
	P# block of 4	130.00	
b.	Souvenir sheet of 1	60.00	
c.	As "b," without artist's signature (error)	*400.00*	

No. RW76b sold for $30 plus a shipping fee. The artist signed No. RW76b on a designated line in the sheet margin. Ten thousand were prepared.

Self-Adhesive

Serpentine Die Cut 11x10¾

RW76A	HP76 $15 **multicolored**	30.00	11.00
	No gum	20.00	

American Wigeon — HP77

Printed by Banknote Corporation of America for Sennett Security Products.

2010 **Litho.** ***Perf. 11¼x11***

Inscribed "Void after June 30, 2011"

RW77	HP77 $15 **multicolored**	30.00	11.00
	No gum	16.00	
	P# block of 4	120.00	
b.	Souvenir sheet of 1, perf. 13¼	55.00	
c.	As "b," without artist's signature (error)	*200.00*	

No. RW77b was sold for $30 plus a shipping fee. The artist signed No. RW77b on a designated line in the sheet margin. Ten thousand were prepared. There is no back inscription on No. RW77b, and the stamp on the sheet is tagged.

Self-Adhesive

Serpentine Die Cut 11x10¾

RW77A	HP77 $15 **multicolored**	30.00	11.00
	No gum	20.00	

White-fronted Geese — HP78

Printed by Ashton-Potter (USA) Ltd.

2011 **Litho.** ***Perf. 13¼***

Inscribed "Void after June 30, 2012"

RW78	HP78 $15 **multicolored**	37.50	11.00
	No gum	16.00	
	P# block of 4	150.00	
b.	Souvenir sheet of 1	60.00	
c.	As "b," without artist's signature (error)	*175.00*	

No. RW78b was sold for $25 plus a shipping fee. The artist signed No. RW78b on a designated line in the sheet margin. Ten thousand were prepared.

Self-Adhesive

Serpentine Die Cut 11x10¾

RW78A	HP78 $15 **multicolored**	40.00	11.00
	No gum	20.00	

Wood Duck — HP79

Printed by Ashton-Potter (USA) Ltd.

2012 **Litho.** ***Perf. 13¼***

Inscribed "Void after June 30, 2013"

RW79	HP79 $15 **multicolored**	37.50	11.00
	No gum	16.00	
	P# block of 4	160.00	
b.	Souvenir sheet of 1	60.00	
c.	As "b," without artist's signature (error)	*1,750.*	

No. RW79b was sold for $25 plus a shipping fee. The artist signed No. RW79b on a designated line in the sheet margin. There is a back inscription on No. RW79b. Five thousand were prepared.

One No. RW79b was signed in red ink as a "surprise" for a random buyer. This was not authorized.

Self-Adhesive

Serpentine Die Cut 11x10¾

RW79A	HP79 $15 **multicolored**	40.00	11.00
	No gum	20.00	

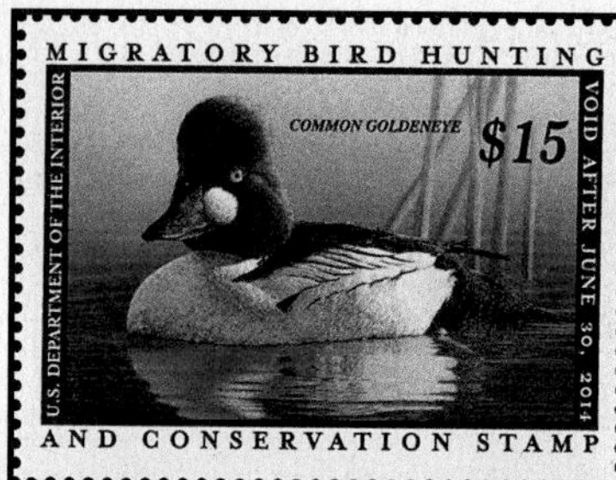

Common Goldeneye — HP80

Printed by Ashton-Potter (USA) Ltd.

2013 Litho. ***Perf. 13¼***

Inscribed "Void after June 30, 2014"

RW80 HP80 $15 **multicolored** 37.50 11.00
No gum 16.00
P# block of 4 150.00
b. Souvenir sheet of 1 80.00
c. As "b," without artist's signature (error) *1,250.*

No. RW80b was sold for $25 plus a shipping fee. The artist signed No. RW80b on a designated line in the sheet margin. There is a back inscription on No. RW80b. Five thousand were prepared.

Self-Adhesive

Serpentine Die Cut 11x10¾

RW80A HP80 $15 **multicolored** 35.00 11.00
No gum 20.00

Canvasbacks — HP81

Printed by Ashton-Potter (USA) Ltd.

2014 Litho. ***Perf. 13¼***

Inscribed "Void after June 30, 2015"

RW81 HP81 $15 **multicolored** 40.00 11.00
No gum 16.00
P# block of 4 160.00

Self-Adhesive

Serpentine Die Cut 11x10¾

RW81A HP81 $15 **multicolored** 40.00 12.50
No gum 20.00

Ruddy Ducks — HP82

Printed by Ashton-Potter (USA) Ltd.

2015 Litho. ***Perf. 13¼***

Inscribed "Void after June 30, 2016"

RW82 HP82 $25 **multicolored** 55.00 12.00
No gum 25.00
P# block of 4 225.00

Self-Adhesive

Serpentine Die Cut 11x10¾

RW82A HP82 $25 **multicolored** 55.00 12.50
No gum 32.50

Trumpeter Swans — HP83

Printed by Ashton-Potter (USA) Ltd.

2016 Litho. ***Perf. 13¼***

Inscribed "Void after June 30, 2017"

RW83 HP83 $25 **multicolored** 90.00 15.00
No gum 40.00
P# block of 4 360.00

Self-Adhesive

Serpentine Die Cut 11x10¾

RW83A HP83 $25 **multicolored** 65.00 12.50
No gum 32.50

Canada Geese — HP84

Printed by Ashton-Potter (USA) Ltd.

2017 Litho. ***Perf. 13¼***

Inscribed "Void after June 30, 2018"

RW84 HP84 $25 **multicolored** 45.00 12.50
No gum 25.00
P# block of 4 190.00

Self-Adhesive

Serpentine Die Cut 11x10¾

RW84A HP84 $25 **multicolored** 40.00 12.50
No gum 32.50

Mallards — HP85

Printed by Ashton-Potter (USA) Ltd.

2018 Litho. ***Serpentine Die Cut 11x10¾***

Inscribed "Void after June 30, 2019"

Self-Adhesive

RW85 HP85 $25 **multicolored** 55.00 12.50
No gum 25.00
P# block of 4 210.00
b. Souvenir sheet of 4 200.00

Sheet of 1

RW85A HP85 $25 **multicolored** 50.00 12.50
No gum 32.50

Inscriptions on the backing paper differ for Nos. RW85, RW85A, and RW85b. Once removed from the backing paper, used examples are considered to be No. RW85.

Wood Duck and Decoy — HP86

Printed by Ashton-Potter (USA) Ltd.

2019 Litho. ***Serpentine Die Cut 11x10¾***

Inscribed "Void after June 30, 2020"

Self-Adhesive

RW86 HP86 $25 **multicolored** 45.00 12.50
No gum 25.00
P# block of 4 190.00

Sheet of 1

RW86A HP86 $25 **multicolored** 45.00 12.50
No gum 32.50

Inscriptions on the backing paper differ for Nos. RW86 and RW86A. Once removed from the backing paper, used examples are considered to be No. RW86.

Black-bellied Whistling Ducks — HP87

Printed by Ashton-Potter (USA) Ltd.

2020 Litho. ***Serpentine Die Cut 11x10¾***

Inscribed "Void after June 30, 2021"

Self-Adhesive

RW87 HP87 $25 **multicolored** 37.50 12.50
No gum 25.00
P# block of 4 160.00

Sheet of 1

RW87A HP87 $25 **multicolored** 37.50 12.50
No gum 32.50

Inscriptions on the backing paper differ for Nos. RW87 and RW87A. Once removed from the backing paper, used examples are considered to be No. RW87.

Lesser Scaup — HP88

Printed by Ashton-Potter (USA) Ltd.

2021 Litho. ***Serpentine Die Cut 11x10¾***

Inscribed "Void after June 30, 2022"

Self-Adhesive

RW88 HP88 $25 **multicolored** 37.50 12.50
No gum 25.00
P# block of 4 160.00

Sheet of 1

RW88A HP88 $25 **multicolored** 37.50 12.50

Inscriptions on the backing paper differ for Nos. RW88 and RW88A. Once removed from the backing paper, used examples are considered to be No. RW88.

Redheads — HP89

Printed by Banknote Corporation of America.

Serpentine Die Cut 11x10¾

2022 Litho., Engr. & Embossed Tagged

Inscribed "Void after June 30, 2023"

Self-Adhesive

RW89	HP89 $25 **multicolored**	37.50	12.50
	No gum	25.00	
	P# block of 4	160.00	

Sheet of 1

RW89A	HP89 $25 **multicolored**	37.50	12.50

Inscriptions on the backing paper differ for Nos. RW89 and RW89A. Once removed from the backing paper, used examples are considered to be No. RW89.

SPECIAL PRINTING

After No. RW51 became void, fifteen uncut sheets of 120 (4 panes of 30 separated by gutters) were overprinted "1934-84" and "50th ANNIVERSARY" in the margins and auctioned by the U.S. Fish and Wildlife Service.

Bids were accepted from September 1 through November 1, 1985. Minimum bid for each sheet was $2,000. The face value of each sheet, had they still been valid, was $900. Each sheet also had the sheet number and pane position printed in the corner of each pane ("01 of 15-1," "01 of 15-2," etc.). Fourteen of the sheets were sold at this and one subsequent auction and one was donated to the Smithsonian.

An individual sheet could be broken up to create these identifiable collectibles: 4 margin overprint blocks of 10; cross gutter block of 4; 6 horizontal pairs with gutter between; 8 vertical pairs with gutter between.

Single stamps from the sheet cannot be distinguished from No. RW51. No used examples can exist.

RW51x $7.50 *Widgeons*

DESIGNERS

1934 — *RW1*	*J.N. Darling*
1935 — *RW2*	*Frank W. Benson*
1936 — *RW3*	*Richard E. Bishop*
1937 — *RW4*	*J.D. Knap*
1938 — *RW5*	*Roland Clark*
1939 — *RW6*	*Lynn Bogue Hunt*
1940 — *RW7*	*Francis L. Jaques*
1941 — *RW8*	*E.R. Kalmbach*
1942 — *RW9*	*A. Lassell Ripley*
1943 — *RW10*	*Walter E. Bohl*
1944 — *RW11*	*Walter A. Weber*
1945 — *RW12*	*Owen J. Bromme*
1946 — *RW13*	*Robert W. Hines*
1947 — *RW14*	*Jack Murray*
1948 — *RW15*	*Maynard Reece*
1949 — *RW16*	*"Roge" E. Preuss*
1950 — *RW17*	*Walter A. Weber*
1951 — *RW18*	*Maynard Reece*
1952 — *RW19*	*John H. Dick*
1953 — *RW20*	*Clayton B. Seagears*
1954 — *RW21*	*Harvey D. Sandstrom*
1955 — *RW22*	*Stanley Stearns*
1956 — *RW23*	*Edward J. Bierly*
1957 — *RW24*	*Jackson Miles Abbott*
1958 — *RW25*	*Leslie C. Kouba*
1959 — *RW26*	*Maynard Reece*
1960 — *RW27*	*John A. Ruthven*
1961 — *RW28*	*Edward A. Morris*
1962 — *RW29*	*Edward A. Morris*
1963 — *RW30*	*Edward J. Bierly*
1964 — *RW31*	*Stanley Stearns*
1965 — *RW32*	*Ron Jenkins*
1966 — *RW33*	*Stanley Stearns*
1967 — *RW34*	*Leslie C. Kouba*
1968 — *RW35*	*C.G. Pritchard*
1969 — *RW36*	*Maynard Reece*
1970 — *RW37*	*Edward J. Bierly*
1971 — *RW38*	*Maynard Reece*
1972 — *RW39*	*Arthur M. Cook*
1973 — *RW40*	*Lee LeBlanc*
1974 — *RW41*	*David A. Maass*
1975 — *RW42*	*James P. Fisher*
1976 — *RW43*	*Alderson Magee*
1977 — *RW44*	*Martin R. Murk*
1978 — *RW45*	*Albert Earl Gilbert*
1979 — *RW46*	*Kenneth L. Michaelsen*
1980 — *RW47*	*Richard W. Plasschaert*
1981 — *RW48*	*John S. Wilson*
1982 — *RW49*	*David A. Maass*
1983 — *RW50*	*Phil Scholer*
1984 — *RW51*	*William C. Morris*
1985 — *RW52*	*Gerald Mobley*
1986 — *RW53*	*Burton E. Moore, Jr.*
1987 — *RW54*	*Arthur G. Anderson*
1988 — *RW55*	*Daniel Smith*
1989 — *RW56*	*Neal R. Anderson*
1990 — *RW57*	*Jim Hautman*
1991 — *RW58*	*Nancy Howe*
1992 — *RW59*	*Joe Hautman*
1993 — *RW60*	*Bruce Miller*
1994 — *RW61*	*Neal R. Anderson*
1995 — *RW62*	*Jim Hautman*
1996 — *RW63*	*Wilhelm Goebel*
1997 — *RW64*	*Robert Hautman*
1998 — *RW65*	*Robert Steiner*
1999 — *RW66*	*Jim Hautman*
2000 — *RW67*	*Adam Grimm*
2001 — *RW68*	*Robert Hautman*
2002 — *RW69*	*Joe Hautman*
2003 — *RW70*	*Ron Louque*
2004 — *RW71*	*Scot Storm*
2005 — *RW72*	*Mark Anderson*
2006 — *RW73*	*Sherrie Russell Meline*
2007 — *RW74*	*Richard Clifton*
2008 — *RW75*	*Joe Hautman*
2009 — *RW76*	*Joshua Spies*
2010 — *RW77*	*Robert Bealle*
2011 — *RW78*	*James Hautman*
2012 — *RW79*	*Joe Hautman*
2013 — *RW80*	*Robert Steiner*
2014 — *RW81*	*Adam Grimm*
2015 — *RW82*	*Jennifer Miller*
2016 — *RW83*	*Joe Hautman*
2017 — *RW84*	*James Hautman*
2018 — *RW85*	*Robert Hautman*
2019 — *RW86*	*Scot Storm*
2020 — *RW87*	*Eddie LeRoy*
2021 — *RW88*	*Richard Clifton*
2022 — *RW89*	*James Hautman*

QUANTITIES SOLD

(Quantities from No. RW65 on are quantities ordered. Quantities sold of these numbers were much less.)

RW1	**635,001**
RW2	**448,204**
RW3	**603,623**
RW4	**783,039**
RW5	**1,002,715**
RW6	**1,111,561**
RW7	**1,260,810**
RW8	**1,439,967**
RW9	**1,383,629**
RW10	**1,169,352**
RW11	**1,487,029**
RW12	**1,725,505**
RW13	**2,016,841**
RW14	**1,722,677**
RW15	**2,127,603**
RW16	**1,954,734**
RW17	**1,903,644**
RW18	**2,167,767**
RW19	**2,296,628**
RW20	**2,268,446**
RW21	**2,184,550**
RW22	**2,369,940**
RW23	**2,332,014**
RW24	**2,355,190**
RW25	**2,176,425**
RW26	**1,626,115**
RW27	**1,725,634**
RW28	**1,344,236**
RW29	**1,147,212**
RW30	**1,448,191**
RW31	**1,573,155**
RW32	**1,558,197**
RW33	**1,805,341**
RW34	**1,934,697**
RW35	**1,837,139**
RW36	**2,072,108**
RW37	**2,420,244**
RW38	**2,445,977**
RW39	**2,184,343**
RW40	**2,094,414**
RW41	**2,214,056**
RW42	**2,237,126**
RW43	**2,170,194**
RW44	**2,196,774**
RW45	**2,216,621**
RW46	**2,090,155**
RW47	**2,045,114**
RW48	**1,907,120**
RW49	**1,926,253**
RW50	**1,867,998**
RW51	**1,913,861**
RW52	**1,780,636**
RW53	**1,794,484**
RW54	**1,663,270**
RW55	**1,402,096**
RW56	**1,415,882**
RW57	**1,408,373**
RW58	**1,423,374**
RW59	**1,347,393**
RW60	**1,402,569**
RW61	**1,471,751**
RW62	**1,539,622**
RW63	**1,560,123**
RW64	**1,697,590**
RW65	**1,195,000**
RW65A	**2,805,000**
RW66	**1,194,000**
RW66A	**2,799,600**
RW67	**1,200,000**
RW67A	**2,800,000**
RW68	**1,194,000**
RW68A	**2,806,000**
RW69	**1,194,000**
RW69A	**2,806,000**
RW70	**1,000,000**
RW71	**1,000,000**
RW71A	**3,000,000**
RW72	**1,000,000**
RW72A	**3,000,000**
RW73	**1,000,000**
RW73A	**3,000,000**
RW74	**500,000**
RW74A	**3,500,000**
RW75	**530,000**
RW75A	**3,509,000**
RW76	**500,000**
RW76A	**3,500,000**
RW77	**200,000**
RW77A	**2,800,000**
RW78	**100,000**
RW78A	**2,060,000**
RW79	**100,000**
RW79A	**2,060,000**
RW80	**100,000**
RW80A	**2,120,000**
RW81	**100,000**
RW81A	**2,500,000**
RW82	**100,000**
RW82A	**2,450,000**
RW83	**30,000**
RW83A	**2,105,000**
RW84	**51,000**
RW84A	**2,390,000**
RW85	**200,000**
RW85b	**12,600**
RW85A	**2,155,000**
RW86	**65,000**
RW86A	**2,365,000**
RW87	**60,000**
RW87A	**2,406,000**
RW88	**60,000**
RW88A	**2,406,000**
RW89	**55,600**
RW89A	**2,387,180**

JUNIOR DUCK STAMPS

As a courtesy to Duck stamp collectors, we list here the Duck stamps issued under the Federal Junior Duck Stamp program, run by the U.S. Fish and Wildlife Service branch of the Department of the Interior and the Federal Duck Stamp Office. The purpose of this program is to teach youth through the medium of art the importance of conserving wetlands and migratory birds.

Students in kindergarden to 12th grade from all 50 states, the District of Columbia, American Samoa and the U.S. Virgin Islands are invited to participate in an annual art competition. The winning entry from each state, district or territory competes for the national championship. The national winner's art appears on that year's Junior Duck stamp, which is sold to raise funds to support the Junior Duck Stamp art and educational program. The United States Postal Service, through its Stamp Fulfillment Services unit, acts as a sales agent for these stamps.

These stamps are not valid for hunting, nor is it required that hunters buy the stamps in order to hunt.

A precursor sheet of nine stamps was released in 1992 as a part of a pilot program instituted before the formal, annual Junior Duck Stamp art competition was begun. The sheet shows stamps from Arkansas, California (2), Florida (2), Illinois (2), Kansas and Vermont. Value, $30.

All issues were printed in panes of 30 with four control/plate numbers. Imperforate examples of Nos. JDS1, JDS2 and JDS3 exist and are believed to be printer's waste.

Catalogue values for all stamps in this section are for stamps with never-hinged original gum.

JD1

1993 **Artist: Jason Parsons (IL)**
JDS1 JD1 $5 *Redhead* 100.00

1994 **Artist: Clark Weaver (PA)**
JDS2 JD1 $5 *Hooded mergansers* *150.00*

1995 **Artist: Jie Huang (MT)**
JDS3 JD1 $5 *Pintail* 425.00

1996 **Artist: Clark Weaver (PA)**
JDS4 JD1 $5 *Canvasbacks* 500.00

1997 **Artist: Scott Russell (CA)**
JDS5 JD1 $5 *Canada geese* 500.00

1998 **Artist: Erik Peterson (MI)**
JDS6 JD1 $5 *Black ducks* *550.00*

1999 **Artist: Ryan Kirby (IL)**
JDS7 JD1 $5 *Wood ducks* 550.00

2000 **Artist: Bonnie Latham (MN)**
JDS8 JD1 $5 *Pintails* 95.00

2001 **Artist: Aremy McCann (MN)**
JDS9 JD1 $5 *Trumpeter swan* 45.00

2002 **Artist: Nathan Closson (MT)**
JDS10 JD1 $5 *Mallards* 30.00

2003 **Artist: Nathan Bauman (PA)**
JDS11 JD1 $5 *Green-winged teal* 25.00

2004 **Artist: Adam Nisbett (MO)**
JDS12 JD1 $5 *Fulvous whistling ducks* 20.00

2005 **Artist: Kerissa Nelson (WI)**
JDS13 JD1 $5 *Ring-necked ducks* 17.50

2006 **Artist: Rebekah Nastav (MO)**
JDS14 JD1 $5 *Redhead* 12.50

2007 **Artist: Paul Willey (AR)**
JDS15 JD1 $5 *Wigeons* 10.00

2008 **Artist: Seokkyun Hong (TX)**
JDS16 JD1 $5 *Hawaiian Nene Geese* 10.00

2009 **Artist: Lily Spang (OH)**
JDS17 JD1 $5 *Wood duck* 10.00

2010 **Artist: Rui Huang (OH)**
JDS18 JD1 $5 *Hooded merganser* 10.00

2011 **Artist: Abraham Hunter (IL)**
JDS19 JD1 $5 *Ring-necked ducks* 10.00

2012 **Artist: Christine Clayton (OH)**
JDS20 JD1 $5 *Northern pintail* 10.00

2013 **Artist: Madison Grimm (SD)**
JDS21 JD1 $5 *Canvasback* 10.00

Type of 1993

2014 **Artist: Si Youn Kim (NJ)**
JDS22 JD1 $5 *King eider* 10.00

Type of 1993

2015 **Artist: Andrew Kneeland (WY)**
JDS23 JD1 $5 *Wood ducks* 10.00

Type of 1993

2016 **Artist: Stacy Shen (CA)**
JDS24 JD1 $5 *Ross's geese* 10.00

Type of 1993

2017 **Artist: Isaac Schreiber (VA)**
JDS25 JD1 $5 *Trumpeter swans* 10.00

Type of 1993

2018 **Artist: Rayen Kang (GA)**
JDS26 JD1 $5 *Emperor goose* 10.00

Type of 1993

2019 **Artist: Nicole Jeon (NY)**
JDS27 JD1 $5 *Harlequin duck* 10.00

Type of 1993

2020 **Artist: Madison Grimm (SD)**
JDS28 JD1 $5 *Wood duck* 10.00

Type of 1993

2021 **Artist: Margaret McMullen (KS)**
JDS29 JD1 $5 *Hooded mergansers* 10.00

Type of 1993

2022 **Artist: Madison Grimm (SD)**
JDS30 JD1 $5 *Green-winged teal* 10.00

STATE HUNTING PERMIT STAMPS

These stamps are used on licenses for hunting waterfowl (ducks, geese, swans) by states and Indian reservations. Stamps which include waterfowl along with a variety of other animals are listed here. Stamps for hunting birds that exclude waterfowl are not listed.

A number of states print stamps in sheets as well as in booklets. The booklets are sent to agents for issuing to hunters. Both varieties are listed. The major listing is given to the sheet stamp since it generally is available in larger quantities and has been the more popularly collected item. In some cases the stamp removed from a booklet, with no tabs or selvage, is identical to a single sheet stamp (see Rhode Island). In these cases the identifiable booklet stamp with tabs and selvage receives an unlettered listing. If the single booklet stamp can be identified by type of perforation or the existence of one or more straight edges, the item receives a lettered listing (see Oregon).

Governor's editions are sold at a premium over the license fee with proceeds intended to help waterfowl habitats. Only those which differ from the regular stamp are listed.

After the period of validity, a number of these stamps were sold at less than face value. This explains the low values on stamps such as Montana Nos. 30, 33, and Flathead Indian Reservation Nos. 2-10.

When used, most stamps are affixed to licenses and signed by the hunter. Values for used stamps are for examples off licenses and without tabs. Although used examples may be extremely scarce, they will always sell for somewhat less than unused examples (two-thirds of the unused value would be the upper limit).

ALABAMA

Printed in sheets of 10.
Stamps are numbered serially.

Catalogue values for all unused stamps in this section are for Never Hinged items.

Artists: Barbara Keel, #1; Wayne Spradley, #2; Jack Deloney, #3; Joe Michelet, #4; John Lee, #5, 25; William Morris, #6, 14; Larry Martin, #7; Danny W. Dorning, #8; Robert C. Knutson, #9, 16, 20; John Warr, #10; Elaine Byrd, #11; Steven Garst, #12; Larry Chandler, #13, 24; James Brantley, #15; Neil Blackwell, #17; Judith Huey, #18; E. Hatcher, #19; Eddie LeRoy, #21, 37; David Sellers, #22, 26, 27; H. Andrew McNeely, #23. Clarence Stewart, #28, #32; David Nix, #29, 33, 39; Jim Denney, #30, 34, 42; John Denney, #31, 36, 38; Steve Burney, #35; Eric Greene, #41

1979-2020

1	$5 Wood ducks, rouletted	12.00	3.00
2	$5 Mallards, *1980*	12.00	3.00
3	$5 Canada geese, *1981*	12.00	3.00
4	$5 Green-winged teal, *1982*	12.00	3.00
5	$5 Wigeons, *1983*	12.00	3.00
6	$5 Buffleheads, *1984*	12.00	3.00
7	$5 Wood ducks, *1985*	12.00	3.00
8	$5 Canada geese, *1986*	12.00	3.00
9	$5 Pintails, *1987*	14.00	3.00
10	$5 Canvasbacks, *1988*	10.00	3.00
11	$5 Hooded mergansers, *1989*	10.00	3.00
12	$5 Aleutian Canada goose, *1990*	10.00	2.50
13	$5 Redheads, *1991*	10.00	2.50
14	$5 Cinnamon teal, *1992*	10.00	2.50
15	$5 Green-winged teal, *1993*	10.00	2.50
16	$5 Canvasbacks, *1994*	10.00	2.50
17	$5 Canada geese, *1995*	10.00	2.50
18	$5 Wood ducks, *1996*	12.00	2.50
19	$5 Snow goose, *1997*	10.00	2.50
20	$5 Barrow's goldeneye, *1998*	10.00	2.50
21	$5 Redheads, *1999*	10.00	2.50
22	$5 Buffleheads, *2000*	10.00	2.50
23	$5 Ruddy duck, *2001*	10.00	2.50
24	$5 Pintail, *2002*	10.00	2.50
25	$5 Wood ducks, *2003*	10.00	2.50
26	$5 Ring-necked ducks, *2004*	10.00	2.50
27	$5 Canada geese, *2005*	10.00	2.50
28	$5 Canvasback, *2006*	10.00	2.50
29	$5 Blue-winged teal, *2007*	10.00	2.50
30	$5 Hooded mergansers, *2008*	10.00	2.50
31	$5 Wood ducks, *2009*	10.00	2.50
32	$5 Pintail, *2010*	10.00	2.50
33	$5 Wigeon, *2011*	10.00	2.50
34	$5 Ring-necked ducks, *2012*	10.00	2.50
35	$5 Canvasbacks, *2013*	10.00	2.50
36	$5 Pintails, *2014*	10.00	2.50
37	$5 Mallards, *2015*	10.00	2.50
38	$10 Wigeons, *2016*	16.00	3.50
39	$10 Canada geese, *2017*	16.00	3.50
40	$10 Blue-winged teal, *2018*	16.00	3.50
41	$10 Wood duck, *2019*	16.00	3.50
42	$10 Pintail, *2020*	16.00	3.50

ALASKA

Printed in sheets of 30.
Stamps are numbered serially on reverse. Booklet pane stamps printed in panes of 5.

Catalogue values for all unused stamps in this section are for Never Hinged items.

1985 Alaska Waterfowl Stamp

Artist: Daniel Smith, #1; James Meger, #2; Carl Branson, #3; Jim Beaudoin, #4; Richard Timm, #5; Louis Frisino, #6; Ronald Louque, #7; Fred Thomas, #8; Ed Tussey, #9; George Lockwood, #10, 13, 23; Cynthia Fisher, #11, 20; Wilhelm Goebel, #12; Robert Steiner, #14, 18, 22, 25; Sherrie Russell Meline, #15; Adam Grimm, #16, 19; Greg Alexander, #17; Don Moore, #21, 24; Sue Steinacher, #26-27; Donna Dewhurst, #28-29; Milo Burcham, #30-33; Declan Troy, #34; Ryan Askren, #35; Jamin Hunter Taylor, #36, 37.

1985-2021

1	$5 Emperor geese	10.00	3.00
2	$5 Steller's eiders, *1986*	10.00	3.00
3	$5 Spectacled eiders, perforated, *1987*	10.00	
a.	Bklt. single, rouletted, with tab	10.00	2.50
4	$5 Trumpeter swans, perforated, *1988*	10.00	
a.	Bklt. single, rouletted, with tab	10.00	2.50
5	$5 Barrow's goldeneyes, perforated, *1989*	10.00	
a.	Bklt. single, rouletted, with tab	10.00	2.50
b.	Governor's edition	*100.00*	

No. 5b was sold in full panes through a sealed bid auction.

6	$5 Old squaws, perforated, *1990*	10.00	
a.	Bklt. single, rouletted, with tab	10.00	2.50
7	$5 Snow geese, perforated, *1991*	10.00	
a.	Bklt. single, rouletted, with tab	10.00	2.50
8	$5 Canvasbacks, perforated, *1992*	10.00	
a.	Bklt. single, rouletted, with tab	10.00	2.50
9	$5 Tule white front geese, perforated, *1993*	14.00	
a.	Bklt. single, rouletted, with tab	14.00	2.50
10	$5 Harlequin ducks, perforated, *1994*	20.00	
a.	Bklt. single, rouletted, with tab	15.00	2.50
b.	Governor's edition	*90.00*	
11	$5 Pacific brant, perforated, *1995*	20.00	
a.	Bklt. single, rouletted, with tab	18.00	2.50
12	$5 Canada geese, *1996*	25.00	
a.	Bklt. single, rouletted, with tab	20.00	2.50
13	$5 King eiders, *1997*	16.00	
a.	Bklt. single, rouletted, with tab	16.00	2.50
14	$5 Barrow's goldeneye, *1998*	12.00	
a.	Bklt. single, with tab	12.00	2.50
15	$5 Pintail, *1999*	12.00	
a.	Bklt. single, with tab	12.00	2.50
16	$5 Common eider, *2000*	18.00	
a.	Bklt. single, with tab	10.00	2.50
17	$5 American wigeon, *2001*	12.50	
a.	Bklt. single, with tab	12.50	2.50
18	$5 Black scoters, *2002*	10.00	
a.	Bklt. single, with tab	10.00	2.50
19	$5 Lesser Canada geese, *2003*	12.00	
a.	Bklt. single, with tab	12.00	2.50
20	$5 Lesser scaup, *2004*	10.00	
a.	Bklt. single, with tab	10.00	2.50
21	$5 Hooded merganser, *2005*	10.00	
a.	Bklt. single, with tab	10.00	2.50
22	$5 Pintails, mallard, green-winged teal, *2006*	10.00	
a.	Bklt. single, with tab	10.00	2.50
23	$5 Northern shovelers, *2007*	10.00	
a.	Bklt. single, with tab	10.00	2.50
24	$5 Northern pintails, *2008*	10.00	
a.	Bklt. single, with tab	10.00	2.50
25	$5 Mallards, *2009*	10.00	
a.	Bklt. single, with tab	10.00	2.50
26	$5 Pintails, *2010*	17.50	
a.	Bklt. single, with tab	12.00	2.50
27	$5 Canada goose, *2011*	10.00	
a.	Bklt. single, with tab	10.00	2.50
28	$5 Harlequin ducks, *2012*	10.00	
a.	Bklt. single, with tab	10.00	2.50
29	$5 White-fronted geese, *2013*	10.00	
a.	Bklt. single, with tab	10.00	2.50
30	$5 White-fronted scoter, *2014*	10.00	
a.	Bklt. single, with tab	10.00	2.50
31	$5 Northern pintail, *2015*	10.00	
a.	Bklt. single, with tab	10.00	2.50
32	$5 Brant, *2016*	10.00	
a.	Bklt. single, with tab	10.00	2.50
33	$10 Wigeon, *2017*	16.00	
a.	Bklt. single, with tab	16.00	3.50
34	$10 Bufflehead, *2018*	16.00	
a.	Bklt. single, with tab	16.00	3.50
35	$10 Emperor goose, *2019*	16.00	
a.	Bklt. single, with tab	16.00	3.50
36	$10 Gadwall, *2020*	16.00	
a.	Bklt. single, with tab	16.00	3.50
37	$10 Ring-necked duck, *2021*	16.00	
a.	Bklt. single, with tab	16.00	3.50

ARIZONA

Printed in booklet panes of 5 with tab and in sheets of 30.
Stamps are numbered serially.

Catalogue values for all unused stamps in this section are for Never Hinged items.

Artists: Daniel Smith, #1; Sherrie Russell Meline, #2, 6-7, 9, 11-18, 21-27; Robert Steiner, #3; Ted Blaylock, #4; Brian Jarvi, #5; Harry Adamson, #8, Larry Hayden, #10; Tom Finley, #19, 20.

1987-2013

No.	Description	Unused	Used
1	$5.50 Pintails, perf. 4 sides	11.00	
a.	Bklt. single, perf. 3 sides, with tab	11.00	3.00
2	$5.50 Green-winged teal, perf. 4 sides, *1988*	12.00	
a.	Bklt. single, perf. 3 sides, with tab	12.00	3.00
3	$5.50 Cinnamon teal, perf. 4 sides, *1989*	11.00	
a.	Bklt. single, perf. 3 sides, with tab	11.00	2.50
b.	$5.50 +$50 Governor's edition	75.00	
4	$5.50 Canada geese, perf. 4 sides, *1990*	12.00	
a.	Bklt. single, perf. 3 sides, with tab	12.00	2.50
b.	$5.50 +$50 Governor's edition	75.00	
5	$5.50 Blue-winged teal, perf. 4 sides, *1991*	10.00	
a.	Bklt. single, perf. 3 sides, with tab	11.00	2.50
b.	$55.50 Governor's edition	75.00	
6	$5.50 Buffleheads, perf. 4 sides, *1992*	10.00	
a.	Bklt. single, perf. 3 sides, with tab	11.00	2.50
b.	$55.50 Governor's edition	75.00	
7	$5.50 Mexican ducks, perf. 4 sides, *1993*	12.00	
a.	Bklt. single, perf. 3 sides, with tab	12.00	2.50
b.	$55.50 Governor's edition	75.00	
8	$5.50 Mallards, perf. 4 sides, *1994*	12.00	
a.	Bklt. single, perf. 3 sides, with tab	12.00	2.50
b.	$55.50 Governor's edition	75.00	
9	$5.50 Wigeon, perf. 4 sides, *1995*	12.00	
a.	Bklt. single, perf. 3 sides, with tab	12.00	2.50
b.	$55.50 Governor's edition	75.00	
10	$5.50 Canvasbacks, perf. 4 sides, *1996*	11.00	
a.	Bklt. single, perf 3 sides, with tab	11.00	2.50
b.	$55.50 Governor's edition	75.00	
11	$5.50 Gadwalls, *1997*	12.00	
a.	Bklt. single, perf 3 sides, with tab	12.00	2.50
b.	$55.50 Governor's edition	75.00	
12	$5.50 Wood duck, *1998*	12.00	
a.	Bklt. single, perf 3 sides, with tab	12.00	2.50
b.	$55.50 Governor's edition	—	
13	$5.50 Snow goose, *1999*	12.00	
a.	Blkt. single, perf. 3 sides, with tab	12.00	2.50
b.	$55.50 Governor's edition	75.00	
14	$7.50 Ruddy duck, *2000*	14.00	
a.	Bklt. single, perf. 3 sides, with tab	14.00	2.50
b.	$55.50 Governor's edition	75.00	
15	$7.50 Redheads, *2001*	14.00	
a.	Bklt. single, perf. 3 sides, with tab	14.00	2.50
b.	$55.50 Governor's edition	75.00	
16	$7.50 Ring-necked ducks, *2002*	14.00	
a.	Bklt. single, perf. 2 sides, with tabs	14.00	2.50
b.	$55.50 Governor's edition	75.00	
17	$7.50 Northern shovelers, *2003*	14.00	
a.	Bklt. single, perf. 2 sides, with tabs	14.00	2.50
b.	$55.50 Governor's edition	75.00	
18	$7.50 Lesser scaup, *2004*	12.00	
a.	Bklt. single, perf. 2 sides, with tabs	12.00	2.50
b.	$55.50 Governor's edition	75.00	—
19	$7.50 Pintails, *2005*	9.50	
a.	Bklt. single, perf. 3 sides, with tabs	10.50	2.50
20	$7.50 Canada geese, *2006*	9.50	
a.	Bklt. single, perf. 3 sides, with tabs	10.50	2.50
b.	$55 Governor's edition	75.00	
21	$8.75 Wood ducks, *2007*	11.00	
a.	Bklt. single, perf. 2 or 3 sides, with tabs	12.00	2.50
b.	$55 Governor's edition	75.00	
22	$8.75 Canvasbacks, *2008*	11.00	
a.	Bklt. single, perf. 2 or 3 sides, with tabs	12.00	2.50
23	$8.75 Hooded mergansers, *2009*	11.00	
a.	Bklt. single, perf. 2 or 3 sides, with tabs	12.00	2.50
24	$8.75 Green-winged teal, *2010*	15.00	
a.	Bklt. single, perf. 2 or 3 sides, with tabs	12.00	2.50
25	$8.75 Bufflehead, *2011*	11.00	
a.	Bklt. single, perf. on 2 or 3 sides, with tabs	12.00	2.50
26	$8.75 Wigeons, *2012*	11.00	
a.	Bklt. single, perf. on 2 or 3 sides, with tabs	12.00	2.50
27	$8.75 Pintail, *2013*	8.00	2.50
a.	Bklt. single, perf. on 2 or 3 sides, with tabs	12.00	2.50

The stamp pictured above, depicting a child's drawing of wigeons in flight, was printed in 2009 in a limited edition of 500 stamps. It was valid for hunting. Value, $175.

The stamp pictured above, depicting a child's drawing of green-winged teal, was printed in 2010 in a limited edition. It was valid for hunting. Value, $135.

The stamp pictured above, depicting a child's drawing of a wood duck, was printed in 2011 in a limited edition. It was valid for hunting. Value, $55.

The stamp pictured above, depicting a child's drawing of a mallard, was printed in a limited edition. It was valid for hunting. Value, $20.

The stamp pictured above, depicting a child's drawing of a fulvous whistling duck, was printed in a limited edition. It was valid for hunting. Value, $15.

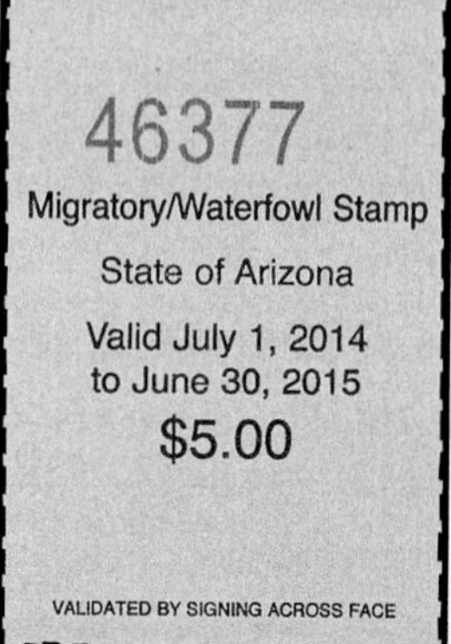

2014-21

No.	Description	Unused	Used
28	$5 black, *light purple, 2014*	35.00	15.00
	On full card with harvest information form	50.00	
29	$5 black, *rose, 2015*	15.00	10.00
	On full card with harvest information form	20.00	
30	$5 black, *blue, 2016*	—	10.00
	On full card with harvest information form	—	
31	$5 black, *tan, 2017*	15.00	10.00
	On full card with harvest information form	20.00	
32	$5 black, *light yellow, 2018*	15.00	10.00
	On full card with harvest information form	20.00	
33	$5 black, *light purple, 2019*	15.00	8.00
	On full card with harvest information form	20.00	
34	$5 black, *yellow green, 2020*	15.00	8.00
	On full card with harvest information form	20.00	
35	$5 black, *rose, 2021*	15.00	8.00
	On full card with harvest information form	20.00	

ARKANSAS

Imperforate varieties of these stamps exist in large quantities. Imperforate examples of Nos. 1 and 2 were sold by the state for $1 each.

No. 1 printed in sheets and booklet panes of 30, others in sheets and booklet panes of 10.

Stamps are numbered serially on reverse.

Catalogue values for all unused stamps in this section are for Never Hinged items.

Artists: Lee LeBlanc, #1; Maynard Reece, #2, 8, 43-44; David Maass, #3, 10, 21; Larry Hayden, #4, 15; Ken Carlson, #5, 13; John P. Cowan, #6; Robert Bateman. #7; Phillip Crowe, #9, 16, 22, 27-27A, 30-30A; Daniel Smith, #11, 14; Jim Hautman, #12, 19, 31-31A, 34-34A, 38-38A, 41-41A; L. Chandler, #17, 20, 25-25A; John Dearman, #18; Zettie Jones, #23; Ralph McDonald, #24-24A. Scot Storm, #26-26A, 32-32B, 36-36A; Cynthie Fisher, #28-28A; Joe Hautman, #29-29A; Milo Burcham, #35-35A; Robert Hautman, #37-37A; Mike Marler, #39-39A; Bruce Miller, #40-40A.

1981-2021

No.	Description	Unused	Used
1	$5.50 Mallards	45.00	12.00
a.	Booklet pane of 30	—	
	Booklet single with top tab, Nos. 110,001-200,000 on back	50.00	
2	$5.50 Wood ducks, *1982*	40.00	9.00
3	$5.50 Green-winged teal, *1983*	55.00	12.00
4	$5.50 Pintails, *1984*	22.50	5.00
5	$5.50 Mallards, *1985*	13.00	4.00
6	$5.50 Black swamp mallards, *1986*	11.00	4.00
7	$7 Wood ducks, *1987*	12.00	4.00

Stamps like Nos. 7 and 8 with $5.50 face values were sold following an order of the state Supreme Court restoring the fee level of 1986. The stamps were sold after the 1988 season had ended. Value, $11 each.

No.	Description	Unused	Used
8	$7 Pintails, *1988*	12.00	4.00

See footnote following No. 7.

No.	Description	Unused	Used
9	$7 Mallards, *1989*	12.00	4.00
10	$7 Black ducks & mallards, *1990*	12.00	4.00
11	$7 Sulphur river wigeons, *1991*	12.00	4.00
12	$7 Shirey Bay shovelers, *1992*	12.00	4.00
13	$7 Grand prairie mallards, *1993*	12.00	4.00
14	$7 Canada goose, *1994*	16.00	4.00

No.	Description	Unused	Used
15	$7 White River mallards, *1995*	14.00	4.00
16	$7 Mallards, black labrador, *1996*	14.00	4.00
17	$7 Labrador retriever, mallards, *1997*	15.00	4.00
18	$7 Labrador retriever, mallards, *1998*	12.00	4.00
19	$7 Wood duck, *1999*	12.00	4.00
20	$7 Mallards and golden retriever, *2000*	11.00	4.00
21	$7 Canvasbacks, *2001*	11.00	4.00
22	$7 Mallards, *2002*	11.00	4.00
23	$7 Mallards & Chesapeake retriever, *2003*	14.00	4.00
24	$7 Mallards, *2004*	11.00	4.00
24A	$20 Mallards, *2004*	30.00	4.00
25	$7 Mallards, Labrador retriever *2005*	12.00	4.00
25A	$20 Mallards, Labrador retriever *2005*	30.00	4.00
26	$7 Mallards, *2006*	12.00	4.00
26A	$20 Mallards, *2006*	30.00	4.00
27	$7 Mallards, Labrador retriever *2007*	12.00	4.00
27A	$20 Mallards, Labrador retriever *2007*	28.00	4.00
28	$7 Mallards, Labrador retriever, *2008*	12.00	4.00
28A	$20 Mallards, Labrador retriever, *2008*	28.00	4.00
29	$7 Hooded mergansers, *2009*	12.00	4.00
29A	$20 Hooded mergansers, *2009*	28.00	4.00
30	$7 Mallards and Black Labrador retriever, *2010*	12.00	4.00
30A	$20 Mallards and Black Labrador retriever, *2010*	35.00	4.00
31	$7 Mallards, *2011*	12.00	4.00
31A	$20 Mallards, *2011*	35.00	4.00

Resident and non-resident fees begin in 2004.

No.	Description	Unused	Used
32	$7 Green-winged teal, *2012*	12.00	4.00
32A	$20 Green-winged teal, *2012*	35.00	4.00
32B	$35 Green-winged teal, *2012 revalued*	55.00	—
33	$7 Mallards, *2013*	12.00	4.00
33A	$35 Mallards, *2013*	45.00	10.00
34	$7 Mallards, *2014*	12.00	4.00
34A	$35 Mallards, *2014*	45.00	10.00
35	$7 Snow geese, *2015*	12.00	4.00
35A	$35 Snow geese, *2015*	45.00	10.00
36	$7 Mallards, *2016*	12.00	4.00
36A	$35 Mallards, *2016*	45.00	10.00
37	$7 Mallards and yellow labrador retriever, *2017*	12.00	4.00
37A	$35 Mallards and yellow labrador retriever, *2017*	45.00	10.00
38	$7 Ring-necked ducks, *2018*	12.00	2.00
38A	$35 Ring-necked ducks, *2018*	45.00	2.00
39	$7 Mallards, *2019*	12.00	2.00
39A	$35 Mallards, *2019*	45.00	2.00
40	$7 Green-winged teal, *2020*	12.00	2.00
40A	$35 Green-winged teal, *2020*	45.00	2.00
41	$7 Mallard, decoy, black Labrador retriever, *2021*	12.00	2.00
41A	$35 Mallard, decoy, black Labrador retriever, *2021*	45.00	2.00

CALIFORNIA

Honey Lake Waterfowl Stamps

Fee $5.00 220 H
STATE OF CALIFORNIA
DEPARTMENT OF FISH AND GAME
SEASONAL PERMIT for
HONEY LAKE
Valid during 1956-57 Waterfowl Season
Stamp must be pasted on back of 1956-57 Hunting License. Owner must validate by signing name across face of Stamp. 41214 8-56 SPO

Required to hunt waterfowl at Honey Lake. Valid for a full season. Stamps are rouletted. Used values are for signed copies. Unsigned stamps without gum probably were used. Values for these stamps are higher than used values, but lower than values shown for gummed unused stamps.

1956-86

No.	Description	Unused	Used
A1	$5 black, *1956-1957*		—
A2	$5 black, *blue green, 1957-1958*		—
A3	$5 black, *dark yellow, 1958-1959*		—
A4	$5 black, *dark yellow, 1959-1960*	900.00	500.00
A5	$5 black, *1960-1961*		1,350.
A6	$5 black, *bluish green, 1961-1962*	—	1,250.
A7	$5 black, *dark yellow, 1962-1963*		950.00
A8	$5 black, *1963-1964*		400.00
A9	$6.50 black, *pink, 1964-1965*	950.00	400.00
A10	$6.50 black, *blue, 1965-1966*		350.00
A11	$6.50 black, *yellow,* Nos. 1-700, printer's information at bottom right, *1966-1967*		375.00
a.	Serial Nos. 701-1050, no printer's information		—
A12	$10 black, *pink, 1967-1968*	—	350.00
A13	$10 black, *blue, 1968-1969*	—	450.00
A14	$10 black, *green, 1969-1970*	—	475.00
A15	$15 black, *dark yellow, 1970-1971*	—	900.00
A16	$15 black, *pink, 1971-1972*		1,750.
A17	$15 black, *blue, 1972-1973*		3,900.
A18	$15 black, *blue, 1973-1974*	—	—
A19	$15 black, *pink, 1974-1975*	40.00	25.00
A20	$15 black, *green, 1975-1976*	125.00	35.00
A21	$15 black, *light yellow, 1976-1977*	125.00	35.00
A22	$20 black, *blue, 1977-1978*	125.00	35.00
A23	$20 blk, *light yel brown, 1978-1979*	125.00	35.00
A24	$20 black, *light yellow, 1979-1980*	125.00	35.00
A25	$15 black, *light blue, 1980-1981*	100.00	30.00
A26	$20 black, *light yellow, 1981-1982*		—
A27	$20 black, *pink, 1982-1983*	90.00	30.00
A28	$20 black, *light green, 1983-1984*	45.00	25.00
A29	$20 black, *dark yellow, 1984-1985*	42.50	25.00
A30	$20 black, *light blue, 1985-1986*	37.50	20.00

Waterfowl Application Stamps

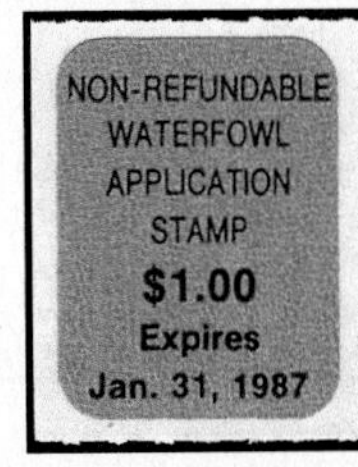

Required to be affixed to hunter's application to hunt, which was printed on a computer punchcard. Hunters were allowed to submit one application for each day during the season, thus increasing their chances to be allowed to hunt for at least one day of the season.

Stamps are die cut and self-adhesive. Applicants were not required to sign stamps.

1986-97

No.	Description	Unused
A31	$1 dark blue & black, *1986-1987*	—
A32	$1 dark green & black, *1987-1988*	—
A33	$1 salmon & black, *1988-1989*	—
A34	$1 pink & black, *1989-1990*	—
A35	$1.05 dark pink & black, *1990-1991*	—
A36	$1.05 green & black, *1991-1992*	850.00
A37	$1.05 blue & black, *1992-1993*	—
A38	$1.05 dark yellow & black, *1993-1994*	750.00
A39	$1.05 pale blue & black, *1994-1995*	600.00
A40	$1.05 yellow & black, *1995-1996*	475.00
A41	$1.05 salmon & black, *1996-1997*	350.00
A42	$1.05 light purple & black, *1997-1998*	250.00

Eighteen $5 black on dark yellow permit stamps were sold for hunting at the state-owned and operated Madeline Plains waterfowl management area for the 1956-57 season. No examples have been recorded.

Statewide Hunting License Validation Stamps

Fees are for resident, junior and non-resident hunters. "No fee" stamps were for disabled veterans. Stamps with special serial numbers for state officials are known for some years. Nos. 2A1-2A3 imperf on 3 sides, rouletted at top. Others die cut.

Stamps are numbered serially.

Used values are for written-upon stamps. Starting with No. 2A4, unused values are for stamps on backing paper.

Remove stamp with this tab. Affix it to application. Tear off tab.
CALIFORNIA HUNTING LICENSE
H 20910-12
(Print this number on tags)
Resident $4.00
Expires June 30, 1963
Date License Issued
Deer Tag No.
Bear Tag No.
Pheasant Tag No.

1962-1963

No.	Description	Unused	Used
2A1	$4 black	400.00	5.00
a.	Ovptd. "NO FEE"	250.00	250.00
2A2	$1 black, *yellow*	1,500.	75.00
2A3	$25 black, *green*	3,750.	175.00

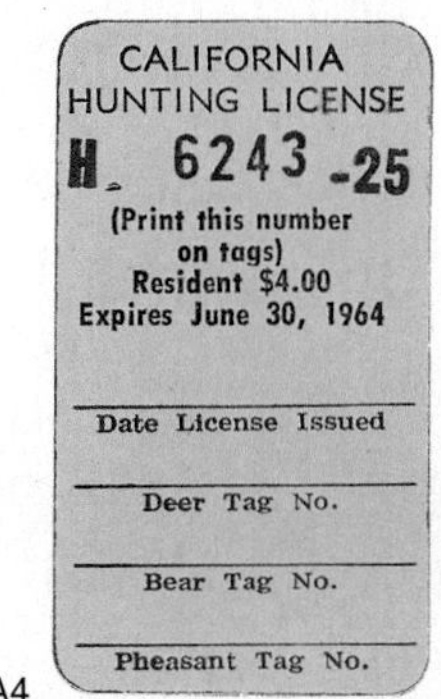

No. 2A4

No.	Description	Unused	Used
1963-1964			
2A4	$4 black, *green*		2.00
a.	Ovptd. "NO FEE"	—	—
2A5	$1 black, *gray*	—	20.00
2A6	$25 black, *yellow orange*		650.00
1964-1965			
2A7	$4 black, *pink*	30.00	1.00
a.	Ovptd. "NO FEE"	250.00	250.00
2A8	$1 black, *yellow brown*	225.00	25.00
2A9	$25 black, *dark gray*		75.00
1965-1966			
2A10	$4 black, *gray*	25.00	1.00
a.	Ovptd. "NO FEE"		—
2A11	$1 black, *yellow gray*		25.00
2A12	$25 black, *ivory*		75.00
1966-1967			
2A13	$4 black, *salmon*	25.00	1.00
a.	Ovptd. "NO FEE"		350.00
2A14	$1 black, *lt blue*	75.00	10.00
2A15	$25 black, *burgundy*		75.00
1967-1968			
2A16	$4 black, *yellow*	20.00	1.00
a.	Ovptd. "NO FEE"		325.00
2A17	$1 black, *green*	45.00	5.00
a.	black, *yellow gray*		—
2A18	$25 black, *brown*	75.00	25.00

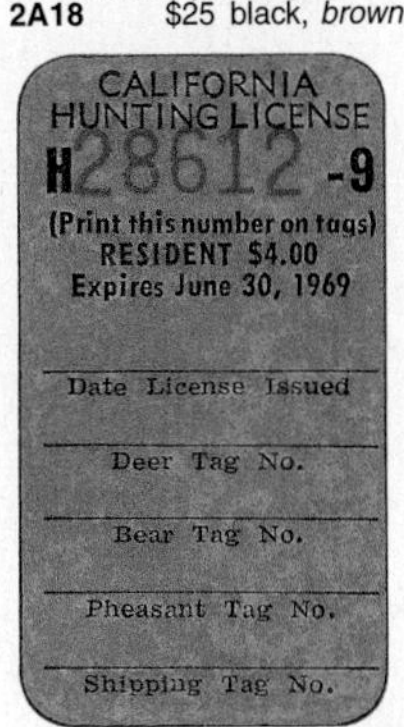

No. 2A19

No.	Description	Unused	Used
1968-1969			
2A19	$4 black, *pink*	55.00	1.00
a.	Ovptd. "NO FEE"		325.00
2A20	$1 black, *blue gray*	175.00	20.00
2A21	$25 black, *light orange*		85.00
1969-1970			
2A22	$4 black	55.00	1.00
a.	Ovptd. "NO FEE"		325.00
2A23	$1 black, *dark pink*	175.00	20.00
2A24	$25 black, *light yellow*	70.00	25.00
1970-1971			
2A25	$4 blue, *manila*	70.00	2.00
a.	Ovptd. "NO FEE"	1,500.	750.00
2A26	$1 black, *blue gray*	75.00	10.00
2A27	$25 black, *gray brown*	100.00	25.00
1971-1972			
2A28	$4 black, *green*	45.00	1.00
a.	Ovptd. "NO FEE"		325.00
b.	Ovptd. "DISABLED VETERANS/NO FEE"		450.00
2A29	$1 black, *lavender*		20.00
2A30	$25 black, *peach*	275.00	35.00
1972-1973			
2A31	$6 black, *pink*		1.00
a.	Ovptd. "DISABLED VETERANS/NO FEE"		450.00
2A32	$2 black, *light yellow*		30.00
2A33	$35 black, *lavender*	225.00	35.00
1973-1974			
2A34	$6 black, *blue*		1.00
a.	Ovptd. "DISABLED VETERANS/NO FEE"		450.00
2A35	$2 black, *lavender*	175.00	20.00
2A36	$35 black, *gray*	275.00	35.00
1974-1975			
2A37	$6 black, *green*	35.00	1.00
a.	Ovptd. "DISABLED VETERANS/NO FEE"		475.00

2A38	$2 black, *orange*		20.00
2A39	$35 black, *reddish purple*	175.00	*25.00*

1975-1976

2A40	$10 red brown, *brown*	40.00	1.00
a.	Ovptd. "DISABLED VETERANS/NO FEE"	—	*500.00*
2A41	$2 black, *dark red*	80.00	20.00
2A42	$35 black, *yellow*	85.00	25.00

1976-1977

2A43	$10 black, *blue*	30.00	1.00
a.	Ovptd. "DISABLED VETERANS/NO FEE"		*800.00*
2A44	$2 black, *gray violet*	*100.00*	20.00
a.	Inscribed "Deer Tag No." instead of "Bear Tag No."		—
2A45	$35 black, *lavender*	85.00	25.00

1977-1978

2A46	$10 black, *red orange*	25.00	1.00
a.	Ovptd. "DISABLED VETERANS/NO FEE"		*450.00*
2A47	$2 black, *yellow green*	95.00	20.00
2A48	$35 black, *pink*	*95.00*	35.00

1978-1979

2A49	$10 black, *yellow*	30.00	1.00
a.	Ovptd. "DISABLED VETERANS/NO FEE"		*425.00*
2A50	$2 black, *red*	70.00	20.00
2A51	$35 black, *light brown*	85.00	25.00

1979-1980

2A52	$10 black, *red*	30.00	1.00
a.	Ovptd. "DISABLED VETERANS/NO FEE"		*425.00*
2A53	$2 black, *yellow green*	70.00	20.00
2A54	$35 black, *dark blue*	85.00	25.00

1980-1981

2A55	$10.25 black, *blue*	25.00	1.00
a.	Ovptd. "DISABLED VETERANS/NO FEE"		*1,100.*
2A56	$2 black, *light brown*	50.00	15.00
2A57	$36.25 black, *tan*	65.00	25.00

1981-1982

2A58	$11.50 black, *dark green*	30.00	1.00
2A59	$2.25 black, *blue*	75.00	20.00
2A60	$40 black, *gray*	*200.00*	*35.00*

1982-1983

2A61	$12.50 black, *pink*	30.00	1.00
2A62	$2.50 black, *brown*	75.00	20.00
2A63	$43.50 black, *orange*	*140.00*	25.00

1983-1984

2A64	$13.25 black, *blue*	50.00	1.00
2A65	$2.75 black, *purple*	*150.00*	20.00
2A66	$46.50 black, *green*	*175.00*	25.00

1984-1985

2A67	$13.25 black, *yellow*	*50.00*	1.00
2A68	$2.75 black, *green*	*150.00*	20.00
2A69	$49.25 black, *brown*	*175.00*	25.00

1985-1986

2A70	$14 black, *blue*	*50.00*	1.00
2A71	$3.50 black, *yellow*	*150.00*	20.00
2A72	$51.75 black, *purple*	*175.00*	25.00

1986-1987

2A73	$18.50 black, *green*		1.00
2A74	$4.50 black, *dark blue*		*15.00*

1987-1988

2A76	$17.50 black, *dark blue*		1.00
2A77	$4.50 black, *purple*		*20.00*

1988-1989

2A79	$19.25 black, *tan*		1.00
2A80	$5 black, *yellow*		*15.00*

1989-1990

2A82	$19.75 black, *blue gray*		1.00
2A83	$5 black, *dark green*		*15.00*

1990-1991

2A85	$21.50 black, *reddish gray*		1.00
2A86	$5.50 black, *yellow*		*15.00*
2A87	$73 black, *pink*		*25.00*

1991-1992

2A88	$23.10 black, *lime green*		1.00
2A89	$5.50 black, *bluish purple*		*15.00*
2A90	$79.80 black, *brown*		*25.00*

1992-1993

2A91	$24.15 black, *yellow*	—	1.00
2A92	$5.80 black, *greenish gold*		*15.00*
2A93	$83.75 black, *mauve*	—	*25.00*

1993-1994

2A94	$24.40 black & white, *green*		1.00
2A95	$5.80 black & white, *light blue*		*15.00*

1994-1995

2A97	$24.95 black & white, *pale yellow*		1.00
2A98	$6.05 black & white, *lavender*		*15.00*
2A99	$86.90 black & white, *gray*		*25.00*

1996-1997

2A100	$25.45 black, *gray brown*		1.00
2A101	$6.30 black, *pink*		*15.00*
2A102	$88.70 black, *pale blue*		*25.00*

Statewide Waterfowl Issues

Nos. 1-24 printed in booklet panes of five, No. 25 in pane of 4.

Issues through 1978 are die cut and self-adhesive. Starting with the 1979 issue, stamps are rouletted. Stamps are numbered serially.

Catalogue values for all unused stamps in this section are for Never Hinged items.

Artists: Paul Johnson, #1-8, 38; Ken Michaelson, #9; Walter Wolfe, #10-11; Robert Steiner, #12, 18-20, 26-35; Robert Richert, #13; Charles Allen, #14; Robert Montanucci, #15; Richard Wilson, #16; Sherrie Russell Meline, #17, 23, 37; Ronald Louque, #21; Larry Hayden, #22; Richard Clifton, #24-25, 43, 44; Richard Radigonda, #36; Harry Adamson, #39; Jeffrey Klinefelter, #40, 51; Tim Taylor, #41; Shari Erickson, #42; John Nelson Harris, #45, 48; Chuck Black, #46; Guy Crittenden, #47, Mark Thone, #49; Frank Dolphens, #50.

Stamps valued with original backing paper. Caution should be used when buying especially Nos. 1 and 2. Both these issues have wider rouletting on the backing paper than Nos. 3-9.

1971-2020

1	$1 Pintails	350.00	65.00
2	$1 Canvasbacks, *1972*	1,100.	150.00
3	$1 Mallards, *1973*	12.50	2.50
4	$1 White-fronted geese, *1974*	3.00	2.50
5	$1 Green-winged teal, backing paper with red wavy lines, *1975*	40.00	8.00
	Waxy backing paper without lines	140.00	

The gum bleeds through the stamp with red wavy lines resulting in a spotted or blotchy effect. Little or no gum bleeds through on stamps with waxy backing paper.

6	$1 Wigeons, *1976*	22.50	2.50
7	$1 Cinnamon teal, *1977*	40.00	9.00
8	$5 Cinnamon teal, *1978*	12.50	2.50
9	$5 Hooded mergansers, *1978*	80.00	15.00
10	$5 Wood ducks, *1979*	9.00	2.50
11	$5 Pintails, *1980*	9.00	2.50
12	$5 Canvasabacks, *1981*	9.00	2.50
13	$5 Wigeons, *1982*	9.00	2.50
14	$5 Green-winged teal, *1983*	12.00	2.50
15	$7.50 Mallard decoy, *1984*	11.00	2.50
16	$7.50 Ring-necked ducks, *1985*	11.00	2.50
17	$7.50 Canada goose, *1986*	11.00	3.00
18	$7.50 Redheads, *1987*	11.00	3.00
19	$7.50 Mallards, *1988*	11.00	3.00
20	$7.50 Cinnamon teal, *1989*	11.00	3.00
21	$7.50 Canada goose, *1990*	11.00	3.00
22	$7.50 Gadwalls, *1991*	11.00	3.00
23	$7.90 White-fronted goose, *1992*	13.00	3.00
24	$10.50 Pintails, *1993*	16.00	4.00

Rouletted Horiz.

25	$10.50 Wood duck, *1994*	15.00	4.00

Perf. Vertically

Birds in flight, denomination at: b, UL. c, UR. d, LL. e, LR.

26	$10.50 Snow geese, booklet pane of 4, #b.-e., *1995*	75.00	
a.	Souvenir sheet of 4, #b.-e. (decorative border)	*275.00*	
b.-e.	Booklet single, each	20.00	4.00

Stamps in No. 26a are perfed on all four sides. No. 26a exists imperf. Value, $350.

Perf. Horizontally

27	$10.50 Mallards, *1996*	16.00	2.50

Issued in panes of 4.

28	$10.50 Pintails, *1997*	16.00	2.50
29	$10.50 Green-winged teal, pair, *1998*	32.50	
a.-b.	a, Female, b, Male, each	15.00	2.50

No. 29 issued in strips of 4 stamps.

30	$10.50 Wood duck, pair, *1999*	40.00	
a.-b.	a, Male, b, Male and female, each	14.00	2.50

No. 30 issued in strips of 2 pairs.

31	$10.50 Canada geese, mallard, wigeon *2000*	16.00	2.50
32	$10.50 Canvasbacks, *2001*	16.00	2.50
33	$10.50 Pintails, *2002*	16.00	2.50
34	$10.50 Mallards, *2003*	20.00	2.50
35	$13.90 Cinnamon teal, *2004*	17.00	2.50

Perf. Vertically

36	$14.20 Pintails, *2005*	17.50	2.50
37	$14.95 White-fronted goose, *2006*	18.50	2.50
38	$16 Pintails, *2007*	35.00	2.50

Perf. Horizontally

39	$16.80 Mallards, *2008*	24.00	2.50

Rouletted at Top

40	$17.85 Shovelers, *2009*	24.00	2.50

Rouletted Horiz.

41	$18.10 Redheads, *2010*	35.00	2.50
42	$18.93 Barrow's goldeneyes, *2011*	95.00	2.50
43	$19.44 Canada geese, *2012*	35.00	2.50
44	$20.01 Wigeons, *2013*	35.00	2.50
45	$20.26 Lesser scaup, *2014*	35.00	2.50
46	$20.52 Green-winged teal, *2015*	35.00	2.50
47	$20.52 Lesser snow geese, *2016*	35.00	2.50
48	$20.52 Ruddy duck, *2017*	35.00	2.50
49	$21.09 Black brants, *2018*	26.00	2.50

Imperf

50	$21.86 Pintails, *2019*	27.50	2.50
51	$22.42 Pintails, *2020*	28.00	2.50

COLORADO

North Central Goose Stamp

Used in an area extending from Ft. Collins to approximately 50 miles east of the city.

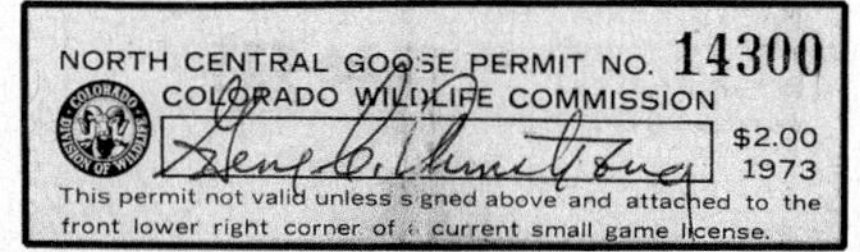

Illustration reduced.

1973

A1	$2 black	—	*1,500.*

No. A1 is die cut and self-adhesive. Unused stamps have glassine backing.

Statewide Issues

Printed in booklet panes of 5 and panes of 30. Stamps are numbered serially.

Imperforate varieties of these stamps are printer's proofs.

Catalogue values for all unused stamps in this section are for Never Hinged items.

Artists: Robert Steiner, #1-2; Charles Allen, #3; Dan Andrews, #4, 29, 32; Sarah Woods, #5; Cynthie Fisher, #6, 9-14, 31; Bill Border, #7; Gerald G. Putt, #8; Jeffrey Klinefelter, #15-16, 18-19. Michael Ashman, #17; Craig Fairbert #20; Richard Clifton, #21-23, 25-26, 28; Charles Black, #24; Guy Crittenden, #27; Michael Sieve, #30.

1990-2021

No.	Description	Unused	Used
1	$5 Canada geese	12.00	
	Bklt. single, with tab, Nos. 80,001-150,000	12.50	3.00
a.	$5 +$50 Governor's edition	60.00	
2	$5 Mallards, *1991*	17.50	
	Bklt. single, with tab, Nos. 80,001-150,000	16.00	3.00
a.	$5 +$50 Governor's edition	60.00	
3	$5 Pintails, *1992*	10.00	
	Bklt. single, with tab, Nos. 80,001-150,000	10.00	3.00
a.	$5 +$50 Governor's edition	60.00	
4	$5 Green-winged teal, *1993*	12.00	
	Bklt. single, with tab, Nos. 80,001-150,000	12.00	3.00
a.	$5 +$50 Governor's edition	60.00	
5	$5 Wood ducks, *1994*	12.00	
	Bklt. single, with tab	12.00	2.50
6	$5 Buffleheads, *1995*	12.00	
	Bklt. single, with tab	12.00	2.50
7	$5 Cinnamon teal, *1996*	12.00	
	Bklt. single, with tab and top selvage	12.00	2.50
8	$5 Wigeons, gold text, *1997*	10.00	
a.	Bklt. single, with tab and top selvage, text in black & white	12.00	2.50
9	$5 Redheads, *1998*	10.00	
a.	Bklt. single, with tab and side selvage	10.00	2.50
10	$5 Blue-winged teal, *1999*	10.00	
a.	Blkt. single, with tab and side selvage	10.00	2.50
11	$5 Gadwalls, *2000*	10.00	
a.	Bklt. single, with tab and side selvage	10.00	2.50
12	$5 Ruddy ducks, *2001*	10.00	2.50
a.	Bklt. single, with tab	*2,150.*	
13	$5 Common goldeneyes, *2002*	10.00	2.50
a.	Bklt. single, with tab	*700.00*	
14	$5 Canvasbacks, *2003*	10.00	2.50
15	$5 Snow geese, *2004*	10.00	2.50
16	$5 Shovelers, *2005*	10.00	2.50
17	$5 Ring-necked ducks, *2006*	10.00	2.50
18	$5 Hooded mergansers, *2007*	10.00	2.50
19	$5 Lesser scaup, *2008*	10.00	2.50
20	$5 Barrow's goldeneye, *2009*	10.00	2.50
21	$5 Pintails, *2010*	10.00	2.50
22	$5 Green-winged teal, *2011*	10.00	2.50
23	$5 Ross's geese, *2012*	10.00	2.50
24	$5 Greater scaups, *2013*	9.00	2.50
25	$5 Canada geese, *2014*	9.00	2.50
26	($7.50) Wood ducks, *2015*	10.00	2.50
27	($10) Mallards, *2016*	15.00	2.50
28	($10) Redheads, *2017*	15.00	2.50
29	($10) Ring-necked ducks, *2018*	13.00	2.50
30	($10) Pintails, *2019*	13.00	2.50
31	($10) Canvasbacks, *2020*	13.00	2.50
32	($10) Canvasbacks, *2021*	13.00	2.50

No. 32 is not required for hunting.

CONNECTICUT

Printed in booklet panes of 10 and sheets of 30.
Stamps are numbered serially.
Imperforate varieties are proofs.

Catalogue values for all unused stamps in this section are for Never Hinged items.

Artists: Thomas Hirata, #1; Robert Leslie, #2, 9; Phillip Crowe, #3; Keith Mueller, #4, 7, 15; Robert Steiner, #5; Joe Hautman, #6; George Lockwood, #8; Robert Richert, #10; Paul Fusco, #11-14; Burt Schuman, #16; Clint Herdman, #17-19; Richard Clifton, #20, John Brennan, #21; Guy Crittenden, #22; Jeffrey Klinefelter, #23, 26; Mark Throne, #24-25; Frank Dolphens, #27; Julia Phillips, #28.

1993-2021

No.	Description	Unused	Used
1	$5 Black ducks	12.00	3.00
	Booklet pane pair with L & R selvage, Nos. 51,001-81,000	24.00	
a.	Sheet of 4	85.00	
b.	$5 +$50 Governor's edition	70.00	
2	$5 Canvasbacks, *1994*	11.00	3.00
	Booklet pair with L & R selvage, Nos. 53,000-up	22.50	
a.	Sheet of 4	55.00	
3	$5 Mallards, *1995*	15.00	3.00
	Booklet pair with L & R selvage	30.00	
4	$5 Oldsquaw ducks, *1996*	16.00	3.00
	Booklet pair with L & R selvage	32.50	
5	$5 Green-winged teal, *1997*	11.00	3.00
a.	$5 +$50 Governor's edition	*150.00*	
6	$5 Mallards, *1998*	12.50	3.00
7	$5 Canada geese, *1999*	15.00	3.00
a.	$5 +$50 Governor's edition	*450.00*	
8	$5 Wood duck, *2000*	10.00	3.00
a.	$5 +$50 Governor's edition	*425.00*	
9	$5 Buffleheads, *2001*	9.00	3.00
a.	$5 +$50 Governor's edition	*425.00*	
10	$5 Greater scaups, *2002*	12.00	3.00
a.	$5 +$50 Governor's edition	*450.00*	

No.	Description	Unused	Used
11	$5 Black Duck, *2003*	10.00	3.00
12	$5 Wood duck, *2004*	25.00	3.00
13	$10 Mallards, *2005*	20.00	3.00
14	$10 Buffleheads, *2006*	25.00	3.00
15	$10 Black duck decoy, *2007*	20.00	3.00
16	$10 Common goldeneyes, *2008*	20.00	3.00

No.	Description	Unused	Used
17	$10 Black duck, *2009*	16.00	3.00

No.	Description	Unused	Used
18	$13 Common goldeneyes, *2010*	25.00	3.00
19	$13 Pintail, *2012*	25.00	3.00
20	$13 Wood ducks, *2013*	25.00	3.00
21	$13 Hooded mergansers, *2014*	25.00	3.00
22	$13 Shovelers, *2015*	21.00	3.00
23	$13 Atlantic brant, *2016*	21.00	3.00
24	$17 Canvasbacks and lighthouse, *2017*	27.50	4.00

Self-Adhesive

No.	Description	Unused	Used
25	$17 Surf scoters and lighthouse, *2018*	27.50	4.00
26	$17 Buffleheads, *2019*	27.50	4.00
27	$17 Wood ducks, *2020*	27.50	4.00
28	$17 Canada goose, *2021*	27.50	4.00

DELAWARE

Printed in sheets of 10.
Starting in 1991, a portion of the printing is numbered serially on the reverse.

Catalogue values for all unused stamps in this section are for Never Hinged items.

Artists: Ned Mayne, #1; Charles Rowe, #2; Lois Butler, #3; John Green, #4; Nolan Haan, #5; Don Breyfogle, #6; Robert Leslie, #7, 10; Bruce Langton, #8; Jim Hautman, #9; Francis Sweet, #11; Ronald Louque, #12; Richard Clifton, #13, 17, 19, 26, 30, 34, 36, 40, 42; Robert Metropulos, #14; Louis Frisino, #15; Michael Ashman, #16, 21; Jeffrey Klinefelter, #18, 24, 35; Russ Duerksen, #20; Brian Blight, #22; George Lockwood, #23, 28; Bonnie Field, #25; Joanna Rivera, #26; John Stewart, #29; Steve Oliver, #31; George LaVanish, #32; Tom Morgan Crain, #33; Dee Dee Murry, #37; Catherine Temple, #38; Daniel Allard, #39; Guy Crittenden, #41.

1980-2021

No.	Description	Unused	Used
1	$5 Black ducks	75.00	20.00
2	$5 Snow geese, *1981*	50.00	20.00
3	$5 Canada geese, *1982*	50.00	20.00
4	$5 Canvasbacks, *1983*	35.00	10.00
5	$5 Mallards, *1984*	15.00	5.00
6	$5 Pintail, *1985*	12.00	3.00
7	$5 Wigeons, *1986*	11.00	3.00
8	$5 Redheads, *1987*	11.00	3.00
9	$5 Wood ducks, *1988*	9.00	3.00
10	$5 Buffleheads, *1989*	9.00	3.00
11	$5 Green-winged teal, *1990*	10.00	3.00
a.	$5 +$50 Governor's edition	85.00	
12	$5 Hooded merganser, no serial number on reverse, *1991*	10.00	
	With serial number on reverse	11.00	3.00
13	$5 Shovelers, no serial number on reverse, *1992*	10.00	
	With serial number on reverse	10.00	2.50
14	$5 Common goldeneye, no serial number on reverse, *1993*	10.00	
	With serial number on reverse	10.00	2.50
15	$5 Blue goose, no serial number on reverse, *1994*	12.00	
	With serial number on reverse	12.00	2.50
16	($6) Scaup, no serial number on reverse, *1995*	11.00	
	With serial number on reverse	11.00	2.50
17	$6 Gadwall, no serial number on reverse, *1996*	12.00	
	With serial number on reverse	12.00	2.50
18	$6 White-winged scoter, no serial number on reverse, *1997*	12.00	
	With serial number on reverse	12.00	2.50
19	$6 Blue-winged teal, *1998*	11.00	2.50
20	$6 Tundra swan, *1999*	11.00	
21	$6 American brant, *2000*	12.00	2.50
22	$6 Oldsquaw, *2001*	11.00	2.50
23	$6 Ruddy ducks, *2002*	11.00	2.50
24	$9 Ring-necked ducks, *2003*	12.00	3.00
25	$9 Black scoters and lighthouse, *2004*	12.00	3.00
a.	$9 +$50 Governor's edition	95.00	
26	$9 Common mergansers and lighthouse, *2005*	12.00	3.00
a.	$9 +$50 Governor's edition	75.00	
27	$9 Red-breasted mergansers, *2006*	12.00	3.00
28	$9 Surf scoters, lighthouse *2007*	12.00	3.00
29	$9 Greater scaup, lighthouse, *2008*	12.00	3.00
30	$9 Black ducks, *2009*	12.00	3.00
31	$9 Canvasback, *2010*	12.00	3.00
32	$9 Hooded mergansers, *2011*	12.00	3.00
33	$9 Lesser scaup, *2012*	12.00	3.00
34	$9 Wigeon, *2013*	12.00	3.00
35	$9 Blue-winged teal, *2014*	12.00	3.00
a.	$9 +$50 Governor's edition	85.00	
36	$9 Black ducks, *2015*	13.00	3.00
37	$9 Green-winged teal, yellow Labrador retriever, *2016*	13.00	3.00
38	$15 Canvasbacks, Chesapeake retriever, *2017*	24.00	4.00
39	$15 Pintails, Golden retriever, *2018*	20.00	4.00
40	$15 Long-tailed duck, black Labrador retriever, *2019*	20.00	4.00
41	$15 Wigeons, chocolate Labrador retriever, *2020*	20.00	4.00
42	$15 Mallard, *2021*	20.00	4.00

FLORIDA

#1-7 issued in booklet panes of 5. Nos. 8-19 in sheets of 10. No. 20 in sheet of 12.

Stamps are numbered serially and rouletted. Serial numbers for stamps with survey tabs attached end in -04.

Catalogue values for all unused stamps in this section are for Never Hinged items.

Illustration reduced.

Artists: Bob Binks, #1, 7; Ernest Simmons, #2; Clark Sullivan, #3; Lee Cable, #4; Heiner Hertling, #5; John Taylor, #6; Robert Steiner, #8; Ronald Louque, #9-10; J. Byron Test, #11; Ben Test, #12; Richard Hansen, #13; Richard Clifton, #14; John Mogus, #15; Antonie Rossini, #16; Kenneth Nanney, #17; Wally Makuchal, #18; M. Frase, #19; Brian Blight, #20; John Harris, #21, 23; Jeffrey Klinefelter, #22; John Nelson Harris, #24.

1979-2003

1 $3.25 Green-winged teal 140.00 20.00
With tab 175.00
2 $3.25 Pintails, *1980* 15.00 5.00
With tab 20.00

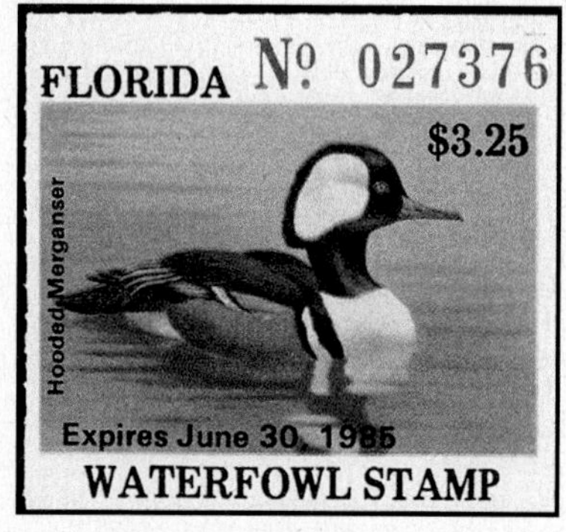

3 $3.25 Wigeon, *1981* 15.00 5.00
With tab 40.00
4 $3.25 Ring-necked ducks, *1982* 22.50 5.00
With tab 30.00
5 $3.25 Buffleheads, *1983* 45.00 5.00
With tab 60.00
6 $3.25 Hooded merganser, *1984* 11.00 3.50
With tab 35.00
7 $3.25 Wood ducks, *1985* 11.00 3.50
With tab 30.00
8 $3 Canvasbacks, *1986* 11.00 3.50
With small tab at top 11.00
With larger survey tab at side and small tab at top 25.00
9 $3.50 Mallards, *1987* 9.00 3.50
With small tab at top 9.00
With larger survey tab at side and small tab at top 25.00
10 $3.50 Redheads, *1988* 8.00 2.50
With small tab at top 8.00
With larger survey tab at side and small tab at top 20.00
11 $3.50 Blue-winged teal, *1989* 8.00 2.50
With small tab at top 8.00
With larger survey tab at side and small tab at top 35.00
12 $3.50 Wood ducks, *1990* 8.00 2.50
With small tab at top 8.00
With larger survey tab at side and small tab at top 35.00
13 $3.50 Northern Pintails, *1991* 9.00 2.50
With small tab at top 9.00
With larger survey tab at side and small tab at top 30.00
14 $3.50 Ruddy duck, *1992* 8.00 2.50
With small tab at top 7.00
With larger survey tab at side and small tab at top 12.00
15 $3.50 American wigeon, *1993* 8.00 2.50
With small tab at top 8.00
With larger survey tab at side and small tab at top 27.50
16 $3.50 Mottled duck, *1994* 9.00 2.50
With small tab at top 9.00
With larger survey tab at side and small tab at top 27.50
17 $3.50 Fulvous whistling duck, *1995* 9.00 2.50
With small tab at top 9.00
With larger survey tab at side and small tab at top 27.50
18 $3.50 Goldeneyes, *1996* 15.00 2.50
With small tab at top 15.00
With larger survey tab at side and small tab at top 27.50
19 ($3.00) Hooded merganser, *1997* 11.00 2.50
With small tab at top 11.00
With larger survey tab at side and small tab at top 27.50

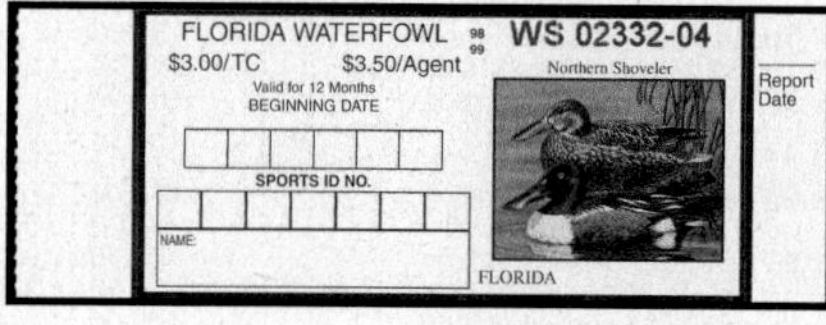

Self-Adhesive

20 $3 Shoveler, *1998* 35.00 2.50

Sold for $3.50 through agents.

21 $3 Pintail, *1999* 12.00 2.50

Sold for $3.50 through agents.

22 $3 Ring-necked duck, *2000* 10.00 2.50

Sold for $3.50 through agents.

23 $3 Canvasback, *2001* 10.00 2.50

Sold for $3.50 through agents.

24 $3 Mottled duck, *2002* 25.00 2.50

Sold for $3.50 through agents. No. 24 with rouletting and with duck facing right come from a special limited reprinting demanded by the artist to correct the appearance of his work. Value, $125.

The 2003 stamp was sold by Florida officials only to the stamp's artist. Values: $125; with small tab at top, $165.

GEORGIA

Not required to hunt waterfowl until 1989.

Nos. 1-4 printed in sheets of 30, others in sheets of 20.

Starting with No 5, stamps are numbered serially.

Catalogue values for all unused stamps in this section are for Never Hinged items.

Artists: Daniel Smith, #1; Jim Killen, #2, 14; James Partee, Jr., #3; Paul Bridgeford, #4; Ralph J. McDonald, #5; Guy Coheleach, #6; Phillip Crowe, #7-8, 11; Jerry Raedeke, #9, 13, 15; Herb Booth, #10; David Lanier, #12.

1985-99

1 $5.50 Wood ducks 15.00
2 $5.50 Mallards, *1986* 9.00
3 $5.50 Canada geese, *1987* 9.00
4 $5.50 Ring-necked ducks, *1988* 9.00
5 $5.50 Duckling & golden retriever puppy, *1989* 14.00 2.50
6 $5.50 Wood ducks, *1990* 9.00 2.50
7 $5.50 Green-winged teal, *1991* 9.50 2.50
8 $5.50 Buffleheads, *1992* 15.00 2.50
9 $5.50 Mallards, *1993* 15.00 2.50
10 $5.50 Ring-necked ducks, *1994* 15.00 2.50
11 $5.50 Wigeons, Labrador retriever, *1995* 32.50 2.50
12 $5.50 Black ducks, *1996* 25.00 2.50
13 $5.50 Lesser scaup, Cockspur Island lighthouse, *1997* 40.00 2.50
14 $5.50 Labrador retriever, ring-necked ducks, *1998* 27.50 2.50
15 $5.50 Pintails, *1999* 22.50 2.50

HAWAII

Required for the hunting of small game. Hunting birds was illegal in Hawaii until 2003. Game bird hunting was permitted beginning July 1, 2003. Game birds that can be hunted include pheasants, francolins, partridges, quail, sand grouses, doves and wild turkeys.

Artists: Patrick Ching, #1, D. Van Zyle, #2; Michael Furuya, #3, 16; Norman Nagai, #4, 7, 10, 13, 14; Marion Berger, #5; Daniel Wang, #6, 15; Joy Keown, #8, 9. Shane Hamamoto, #11. Dan Hoyes, #12; Carol Tredway, #17-18, 20; David Hayes, #19, 23; James Basham, #21; Jessica Onfe, #22; Michael Bailey, #24.

1996-2021

1 $5 Nene goose 9.00
With tab 9.00
a. $5 +$50 Governor's edition 75.00
b. As No. 1, sheet of 4 125.00

No. 1b exists imperf. Value, $175.

2 $5 Hawaiian duck, *1997* 9.00
With tab 12.00
a. As No. 2, sheet of 4 50.00

No. 2a exists imperf. Value, $195.

3 $5 Wild turkey, *1998* 10.00
With tab 12.00
4 $5 Ring-necked pheasant, *1999* 10.00
With tab 12.00
5 $5 Erckel's francolin, *2000* 10.00
With tab 12.00
6 $5 Green pheasant, *2001* 10.00
With tab 12.00
7 $10 Chukar partridge, *2002* 15.00
8 $10 Nene geese, *2003* 15.00
9 $10 Nene geese, *2004* 15.00
10 $10 California quail, *2005* 15.00
11 $10 Black francolin, *2006* 15.00
12 $10 Gray francolin, *2007* 15.00
13 $10 Chukar partridge, *2008* 15.00
14 $10 California quail, *2009* 15.00
15 $10 Green pheasant, *2011* 15.00
16 $10 Wild turkey, *2011* 15.00
17 $10 Mouflon sheep, *2012* 15.00
18 $10 Mouflon sheep, *2015* 16.00
19 $10 Axis deer, *2016* 16.00
20 $10 Pheasant, wild sheep, *2017* 16.00
21 $10 Boar, *2018* 16.00
22 $10 Mouflon sheep, *2019* 16.00
23 $10 Black-tailed deer, *2020* 16.00
24 $10 Hybrid sheep, *2021* 16.00

IDAHO

Printed in booklet panes of 5 and sheets of 30, except No. 5, which was issued in booklets of 10. Numbered serially except for No. 11.

Catalogue values for all unused stamps in this section are for Never Hinged items.

Artists: Robert Leslie, #1; Jim Killen, #2; Daniel Smith, #3; Francis E. Sweet, #4, Richard Clifton, #6, 11; Richard Plasschaert, #7; Sherrie Russell Meline, #8; Bill Moore, #9; David Gressard, #10; T. Smith, #12; Maynard Reece, #13.

1987-98

1	$5.50 Cinnamon teal, perforated	15.00	
a.	Bklt. single, rouletted, with 2-part tab	12.00	3.00
2	$5.50 Green-winged teal, perforated, *1988*	13.00	
a.	Bklt. single, rouletted, with 2-part tab	13.00	3.00
3	$6 Blue-winged teal, perforated, *1989*	10.00	
a.	Bklt. single, rouletted, with 2-part tab	11.00	3.00
4	$6 Trumpeter swans, perforated, *1990*	21.00	
a.	Bklt. single, rouletted, with 2-part tab	21.00	3.00

Die cut self-adhesive

5	$6 green, *1991*	150.00	*35.00*

No. 5 was used provisionally in 1991 when the regular stamps were delayed. Unused value is for stamp, remittance tab and selvage pieces on backing paper.

Designs like No. 1

6	$6 Wigeons, perforated, *1991*	10.00	
a.	Bklt. single, rouletted, with 2-part tab	10.00	2.50
7	$6 Canada geese, perforated, *1992*	10.00	
a.	Bklt. single, rouletted, with 2-part tab	10.00	2.50
8	$6.00 Common goldeneye, perforated, *1993*	12.00	
a.	Bklt. single, rouletted, with 2-part tab	12.00	2.50
9	$6 Harlequin ducks, perforated, *1994*	12.00	
a.	Bklt. single, rouletted, with 2-part tab	12.00	2.50
10	$6 Wood ducks, perforated, *1995*	12.00	
a.	Bklt. single, rouletted, with 2-part tab	12.00	2.50
11	$6.50 Mallard, *1996*	16.00	2.50
12	$6.50 Shovelers, *1997*	22.50	2.50
13	$6.50 Canada geese, *1998*	15.00	2.50

ILLINOIS

Daily Usage Stamps for State-operated Waterfowl Areas.

Date and fee overprinted in black. $2 and $3 stamps were for hunting ducks, $5 stamps for hunting geese and pheasants. 1953-58 had separate pheasant stamps. No duck stamp was printed in 1971.

Some unused stamps have dry gum.

Used stamps have no gum or have staple holes.

Black printing.

Stamps are numbered serially.

1951-1972

A1	$2 yellow, *manila,* imperf., 1951	—	
A2	$2 green, *manila, 1952*	—	
A3	$2 orange, *blue, 1953*	—	—
A4	$2 green, *manila, 1956*	—	—
A5	$2 orange, *light blue green, 1957*	*750.*	*475.*
A6	$2 green, *manila, 1958*	*650.*	*375.*
A7	$3 green, *manila, 1959*	*475.*	*300.*
A8	$5 red brown, *light blue green, 1959*	*475.*	*300.*
A9	$3 red brown, *light blue green, 1960*	*475.*	*300.*
A10	$5 green, *manila, 1960*	*475.*	*300.*
A11	$3 green, *manila, 1961*	*475.*	*300.*
A12	$5 red brown, *light blue green, 1961*	*475.*	*300.*
A13	$3 green, *manila, 1962*	*475.*	*300.*
A14	$5 red brown, *light blue green, 1962*	*475.*	*300.*
A15	$3 orange, *light blue green, 1963*	*475.*	*300.*
A16	$5 green, *manila, 1963*	*475.*	*300.*
A17	$3 green, *manila, 1964*	*475.*	*300.*
A18	$5 red, *light blue green, 1964*	*425.*	*250.*
A19	$3 orange, *light blue green, 1965*	*475.*	*300.*
A20	$5 green, *manila, 1965*	*475.*	*300.*
A21	$3 green, *manila, 1966*	*475.*	*300.*
A22	$5 orange, *light blue green, 1966*	*475.*	*300.*
A23	$3 orange, *light blue green, 1967*	*475.*	*300.*
A24	$5 green, *yellow, 1967*	*475.*	*300.*
A25	$3 green, *yellow, 1968*	*475.*	*300.*
A26	$5 orange, *light blue, 1968*	*475.*	*300.*
A27	$3 orange, *light blue, 1969*	*475.*	*300.*
A28	$5 green, *manila, 1969*	*475.*	*300.*
A29	$3 green, *manila, 1970*	*1,500.*	*900.*
A30	$5 orange, *light blue, 1970*	*1,750.*	*900.*
A31	$5 green, *manila, 1971*	*1,950.*	*1,000.*
A32	$3 orange, *light blue green, 1972*	*9,500.*	
A33	$5 orange, *light blue green, 1972*	*7,500.*	*2,500.*

Catalogue values for unused stamps in this section, from this point to the end, are for Never Hinged items.

No. A34

No. A35

1977-91(?)

A34	black, *light blue,* duck, *1991*	—	—
A35	black, *manila,* goose	—	—

Nos. A34-A35 do not show year or denomination and were used until 1994. No. A34 used before 1991 should exist but has not been reported yet. Separate pheasant and controlled quail and pheasant stamps of a similar design have also been used.

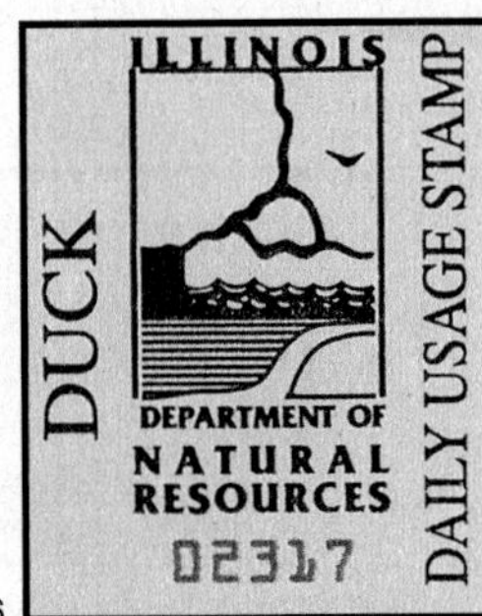

No. A36

No. A37

1996

A36	black, *light blue,* duck	—	—
A37	black, *manila,* goose	—	—

Nos. A36-A37 do not show year or denomination.

Statewide Issues

Nos. 1-10 in sheets of 10. Starting with No. 11, in booklet panes of 5; starting with No. 22, in panes of 10.

Stamps are numbered serially and rouletted.

Catalogue values for all unused stamps in this section are for Never Hinged items.

Artists: Robert Eschenfeldt, #1; Robert G. Larson, #2; Richard Lynch, #3; Everett Staffeldt, #4; John Eggert, #5; Bart Kassabaum, #6, 9, 11, 13; Jim Trindel, #7; Arthur Sinden, #8, 12, 14; George Kieffer, #10; Charles McKay Freeman, #15; John Henson, #16; Phillip Crowe, #17-21; Thomas Hirata, #22-24; Jim Killen, #25-29; Gerald Putt, #30-32. Christina Van Dellen, #33; Karen Latham, #34; Abraham Hunter, #35-36.

1975-2010

1	$5 Mallard	*325.00*	75.00
2	$5 Wood ducks, *1976*	*150.00*	50.00
3	$5 Canada goose, *1977*	100.00	35.00
4	$5 Canvasbacks, *1978*	100.00	22.50
5	$5 Pintail, *1979*	100.00	16.00
6	$5 Green-winged teal, *1980*	100.00	16.00
7	$5 Wigeons, *1981*	85.00	16.00
a.	"Green-winged teal"	*295.00*	
8	$5 Black ducks, *1982*	65.00	12.50
9	$5 Lesser scaup, *1983*	75.00	10.00
10	$5 Blue-winged teal, *1984*	60.00	10.00
11	$5 Redheads, *1985*	16.00	3.00
	With 2-part tab	22.50	
12	$5 Gadwalls, *1986*	12.00	3.00
	With 2-part tab	20.00	
13	$5 Buffleheads, *1987*	12.00	3.00
	With 2-part tab	15.00	
14	$5 Common goldeneyes, *1988*	12.00	2.50
	With 2-part tab	15.00	
15	$5 Ring-necked ducks, *1989*	10.00	2.50
	With 2-part tab	10.00	
16	$10 Lesser snow geese, *1990*	16.00	3.00
	With 2-part tab	17.00	
17	$10 Labrador retriever & Canada goose, *1991*	16.00	3.00
	With 2-part tab	16.00	
a.	Governor's edition with tab	*85.00*	
18	$10 Retriever & mallards, *1992*	25.00	3.00
	With 2-part tab	27.50	
19	$10 Pintail decoys and puppy, *1993*	32.50	3.00
	With 2-part tab	35.00	
20	$10 Canvasbacks & retrievers, *1994*	32.50	3.00
	With 2-part tab	35.00	
21	$10 Retriever, green-winged teal, decoys, *1995*	32.50	3.00
	With 2-part tab	35.00	
22	$10 Wood ducks, *1996*	20.00	2.50
23	$10 Canvasbacks, *1997*	17.50	2.50
24	$10 Canada geese, *1998*	17.50	2.50
25	$10 Canada geese, black Labrador retriever, *1999*	22.50	2.50
a.	Anniversary edition, perforated	*92.50*	
b.	Governor's edition, perforated	*92.50*	
c.	Silver edition, perforated	*92.50*	

Nos. 25a-25c were sold as a set of three.

26	$10 Mallards, golden retriever, *2000*	22.50	2.50
27	$10 Pintails, yellow Labrador retriever, *2001*	22.50	2.50

28	$10 Canvasbacks, Chesapeake retriever, *2002*	22.50	2.50
29	$10 Green-winged teal, Labrador retriever, *2003*	17.50	2.50
30	$10 Wood ducks, *2004*	17.50	2.50
31	$10 Green-winged teals, *2005*	17.50	2.50
32	$10 Northern pintails, *2006*	17.50	2.50
33	$10 Bufflehead, *2007*	17.50	2.50
34	$10 Greater scaup, *2008*	40.00	2.50
35	$10 Common goldeneyes, *2009*	75.00	2.50
36	$15 Blue-winged teal, *2010*	40.00	2.50

INDIANA

Issued in booklet panes of 4 (Nos. 1-10) and booklet panes of 2, starting with No. 11.

Stamps are numbered serially and rouletted.

Catalogue values for all unused stamps in this section are for Never Hinged items.

Artists: Justin H. (Sonny) Bashore, #1-2; Carl (Spike) Knuth, #3; Daniel Renn Pierce, #4; Dean Barrick, #5; Rodney Crossman, #6; George Metz, #7; Kieth Freeman, #8; Lyn Briggs, #9; Rick Pas, #10; Ronald Louque, #11; Susan Hastings Bates, #12.

Bruce Langton, #13, 17; Ann Dahoney, #14; Ken Bucklew, #15, 20, 22, 24, 29, 32; Richard Hansen, #16; Jeffrey Klinefelter, #18, 26, 28, 30, 33, 34-38, 39; Jeffrey Mobley. #19; Charles Riggles, #21, 23, 31; George Lockwood, #25; Biran Blight, 27.

1976-2014

1	$5 Green-winged teal, *1976*	12.00	2.50
2	$5 Pintail, *1977*	10.00	2.50
3	$5 Canada geese, *1978*	10.00	2.50
4	$5 Canvasbacks, *1979*	10.00	2.50
5	$5 Mallard ducklings, *1980*	10.00	2.50
6	$5 Hooded mergansers, *1981*	10.00	2.50
7	$5 Blue-winged teal, *1982*	10.00	2.50
8	$5 Snow geese, *1983*	10.00	2.50
9	$5 Redheads, *1984*	10.00	2.50
10	$5 Pintail, *1985*	10.00	2.50
	With tab	10.50	
11	$5 Wood duck, *1986*	10.00	2.50
	With tab	11.00	
12	$5 Canvasbacks, *1987*	10.00	2.50
	With tab	11.00	
13	$6.75 Redheads, *1988*	12.00	2.50
	With tab	13.00	
14	$6.75 Canada goose, *1989*	12.00	2.50
	With tab	13.00	
15	$6.75 Blue-winged teal, *1990*	12.00	2.50
	With tab	13.00	
16	$6.75 Mallards, *1991*	12.00	2.50
	With tab	13.00	
17	$6.75 Green-winged teal, *1992*	12.00	2.50
	With tab	13.00	
18	$6.75 Wood ducks, *1993*	12.00	2.50
	With tab	13.00	
19	$6.75 Pintail, *1994*	12.00	2.50
	With tab	13.00	
20	$6.75 Goldeneyes, *1995*	12.00	2.50
	With tab	13.00	
21	$6.75 Black ducks, *1996*	12.00	2.50
	With tab	13.00	
22	$6.75 Canada geese, *1997*	12.00	2.50
	With tab	13.00	
23	$6.75 Wigeon, *1998*	12.00	2.50
	With tab	13.00	
24	$6.75 Bluebills, *1999*	12.00	2.50
	With tab	13.00	
25	$6.75 Ring-necked duck, *2000*	12.00	2.50
	With tab	13.00	
26	$6.75 Hooded mergansers, *2001*	12.00	2.50
	With tab	13.00	
27	$6.75 Green-winged teal, *2002*	12.00	2.50
	With tab	13.00	
28	$6.75 Northern shovelers, *2003*	12.00	2.50
	With tab	13.00	
29	$6.75 Wood duck, *2004*	12.00	2.50
	With tab	13.00	
30	$6.75 Buffleheads, *2005*	12.00	2.50
	With tab	13.00	
31	$6.75 Gadwalls, *2006*	12.00	2.50
	With tab	13.00	
32	$6.75 Pintails, *2007*	12.00	2.50
	With tab	13.00	
33	$6.75 Shovelers, *2008*	12.00	2.50
	With tab	13.00	
34	$6.75 Snow geese, *2009*	12.00	2.50
	With tab	13.00	
35	$6.75 Black duck, *2010*	20.00	2.50
	With tab	25.00	
36	$6.75 Wigeon, *2011*	12.00	2.50
	With tab	13.00	
37	$6.75 Canada geese, *2012*	20.00	2.50
	With tab	25.00	
38	$6.75 Wood ducks, *2013*	12.00	2.50
	With tab	13.00	
39	$6.75 Blue-winged teal, *2014*	12.00	2.50
	With tab	13.00	

IOWA

Catalogue values for all unused stamps in this section are for Never Hinged items.

Issued in booklet pane of 5 (No. 1), 10 (others) and sheets of 10 (No. 19).

Artists: Maynard Reece, #1, 6, 22; Thomas Murphy, #2; James Landenberger, #3; Mark Reece, #4; Nick Klepinger, #5, 7; Andrew Peters, #8; Paul Brigford, #9, 12, 15; Brad Reece, #10; Tom Walker, #11; Larry Zach, #13. Jack C. Hahn, #14, 18; John Heidersbach, #16; Mark Cary, #17; Patrick Murillo, #19; Jerry Raedeke, #20; Charlotte Edwards, #21, 26; Dietmar Krumrey, #23, 25, 33; Cynthia Fisher, #24; Sherrie Russell Meline, #27, 29, 35; Mark Anderson, #28; Darren Maurer, #30, 31, 36, 40-41; Neal Anderson, #32, 34; Ronnie Hughes, #37; Mark Kness #38; Tomas Miller, #39; Jeffrey Klinefelter, #42; Jeffrey Hoff, #43; Mike Brown, #44.

1972-98

1	$1 Mallards	100.00	25.00
2	$1 Pintails, *1973*	35.00	7.50
3	$1 Gadwalls, rouletted, *1974*	85.00	7.00
4	$1 Canada geese, *1975*	95.00	9.00
5	$1 Canvasbacks, *1976*	25.00	2.50
6	$1 Lesser scaup, rouletted, *1977*	21.00	2.50
7	$1 Wood ducks, rouletted, *1978*	50.00	5.00
8	$5 Buffleheads, *1979*	250.00	25.00
9	$5 Redheads, *1980*	27.50	6.00
10	$5 Green-winged teal, rouletted, *1981*	27.50	4.00
11	$5 Snow geese, rouletted, *1982*	18.00	2.50
12	$5 Wigeons, *1983*	18.00	2.75
13	$5 Wood ducks, *1984*	35.00	3.00
14	$5 Mallard & mallard decoy, *1985*	20.00	2.50
15	$5 Blue-winged teal, *1986*	15.00	2.50
16	$5 Canada goose, *1987*	15.00	2.50
17	$5 Pintails, *1988*	15.00	2.50
18	$5 Blue-winged teal, *1989*	15.00	2.50
19	$5 Canvasbacks, *1990*	10.00	2.50
20	$5 Mallards, *1991*	10.00	2.50
21	$5 Labrador retriever & ducks, *1992*	10.00	2.50
22	$5 Mallards, *1993*	10.00	2.50
23	$5 Green-winged teal, *1994*	10.00	2.50
24	$5 Canada geese, *1995*	10.00	2.50
25	$5 Canvasbacks, *1996*	10.00	2.50
26	$5 Canada geese, *1997*	10.00	2.50
27	$5 Pintails, *1998*	12.00	2.50

1999

28	Trumpeter swan, *1999*	30.00	2.50

No. 28 not required for hunting. The Department of Natural Resources sent customers No. 28 upon receipt of a postcard given to the customer after paying license fee of $5.

2000

29	Hooded merganser, *2000*	15.00	2.50

No. 29 not required for hunting. The Department of Natural Resources sent customers No. 29 upon receipt of a postcard given to the customer after paying license fee of $5.

2001

30	Snow goose, *2001*	15.00	2.50

No. 30 not required for hunting. The Department of Natural Resources sent customers No. 30 upon receipt of a postcard given to the customer after paying license fee of $5.

2002-15

31	Shovelers, *2002*	17.50	4.00
32	Ruddy duck, *2003*	15.00	4.00
33	Wood ducks, *2004*	14.00	4.00
34	Green-winged teals, *2005*	14.00	4.00
35	Ring-necked duck, *2006*	27.50	4.00
36	Wigeon, *2007*	17.00	4.00
37	Wood duck, *2008*	17.00	4.00
38	Pintail, *2009*	30.00	4.00
39	Green-winged teal, *2010*	30.00	4.00
40	Hooded merganser, *2011*	17.50	4.00
41	Blue-winged teal, *2012*	20.00	4.00
42	Wood ducks, *2013*	20.00	4.00
43	Redhead, *2014*	20.00	4.00
44	Canada geese, *2015*	30.00	4.00

Nos. 31-44 not required for hunting.

The Department of Natural Resources sent customers Nos. 31-38 upon receipt of a postcard given to the customer after paying license fee of $8.50.

Nos. 39-44 were sent to customers upon receipt of a postcard given to the customer after paying license fee of $10.

KANSAS

Marion County Resident Duck Stamps

Wording, type face, border and perforation/roulette differs.

Used values are for stamps without gum.

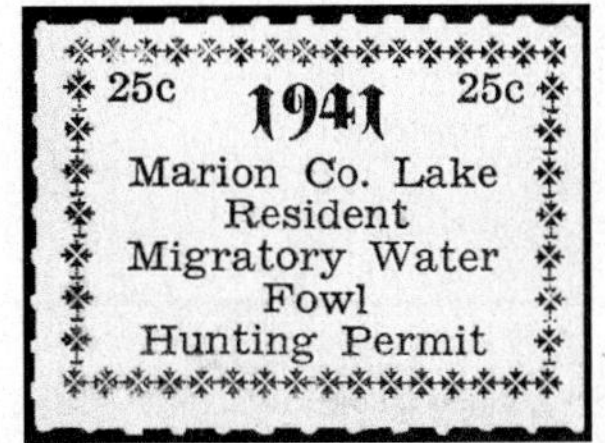

1941-42

A1	25c black		—
A2	25c black, *1942*		—

Remainders from 1941 were rubber stamped "1942" in purple and initialed "J.E.M." by the Park and Lake Supervisor.

No. A3

No. A14

No. A20

Nos. A3-A33 have various designs.

1943-73

A3	25c black, *pink*		—
A4	25c black, *green, 1944*		—
A5	25c green, *1945*		—
A6	25c black, *yellow, 1946*		*27,500.*
A7	25c black, *pink, 1947*		*8,500.*
A8	50c black, *blue, 1948*		*19,500.*
A9	50c black, *1949*		—
A10	50c black, *blue, 1950*		—
A11	50c black, *1951*		—
A12	50c black, *1952*		—
A13	50c black, *blue, 1953*		—
A14	50c black, *pink, 1954*	95.	*65.*
A15	50c black, *green, 1955*	95.	*65.*
A16	50c black, *1956*	110.	*100.*
A17	50c black, *blue, 1957*	85.	*65.*
a.	"1" instead of "I" in "RESIDENT," pos. 3	*1,500.*	*1,250.*
b.	1st 2 lines reversed, pos. 6	*2,000.*	*1,750.*
A18	50c black, *light yellow, 1958*	425.	*250.*
A19	50c black, *1959*	65.	*55.*
A20	50c black, *pink, 1960*	85.	*75.*
a.	Missing ornamental ball, pos. 9	*2,500.*	
A21	50c black, *1961*	125.	*100.*
A22	50c black, *1962*	225.	*150.*
A23	50c black, *pink, 1963*	675.	*400.*
A24	50c black, *pink, 1964*	675.	*400.*
a.	2nd & 3rd lines reversed, pos. 10	—	
A25	50c black, *green, 1965*	475.	*325.*
A26	50c black, *yellow, 1966*	—	—
A27	50c black, *green, 1967*	*7,500.*	*4,500.*
A28	50c black, *pink, 1968*	275.	*200.*
A29	50c black, *yellow, 1969*	275.	*200.*
a.	"Dusk" instead of "Duck," pos. 8	*22,500.*	
A30	50c black, *1970*	450.	*350.*
A31	50c black, *pink, 1971*	*6,500.*	*4,500.*
A32	50c black, *blue, 1972*	*7,500.*	*5,000.*
A33	50c black, *pink, 1973*	*14,500.*	*9,500.*

Statewide Issues

Issued in booklet panes of 10 (Nos. 1-5) and sheets of 30 (starting with No. 2). Starting with No. 11, issued in sheets of 10. No. 1 issued in booklets with one pane of 10 (serial number has prefix "DD") and booklets with two panes of 10 (serial number has prefix "SS").

Nos. 1-4 numbered serially.

Catalogue values for all unused stamps in this section are for Never Hinged items.

Artists: Guy Coheleach, #1; Ann Dahoney, #2, 8; Leon Parson, #3; Wes Dewey, #4; J. Byron Test, #5; Jerry Thomas, #6, 10; Jerry Roedeke, #7; Neal Anderson, #9; Dustin Teasley, #14-18.

1987-96

1	$3 Green-winged teal	10.00	2.50
	Pair from booklet pane with L & R selvage	20.00	
2	$3 Canada geese, *1988*	8.00	2.50
	Pair from booklet pane with L & R selvage	16.00	
a.	Serial number missing	—	
3	$3 Mallards, *1989*	8.00	2.50
	Pair from booklet pane with L & R selvage	16.00	
4	$3 Wood ducks, *1990*	8.00	2.50
	Pair from booklet pane with L & R selvage	16.00	
5	$3 Pintail, rouletted, *1991*	8.00	2.50
	Pair from booklet pane with selvage at L & straight edge at R	16.00	
6	$3 Canvasbacks, *1992*	8.00	2.50
7	$3 Mallards, *1993*	9.00	2.50
8	$3 Blue-winged teal, *1994*	9.00	2.50
9	$3 Barrow's goldeneye, *1995*	9.00	2.50
10	$3 American wigeon, *1996*	10.00	2.50

No. 2a resulted from a drastic misregistration of the serial numbers during printing. Only one example is documented.

Artist: Dustin Teasley.

1997-2004 **Self-Adhesive** ***Die Cut***

11	$3 blue	9.00	2.50
12	$3 green, *1998*	9.00	2.50
13	$3 red, *1999*	8.50	2.50
14	$3 red lilac, *2000*	8.50	2.50
15	$3 orange, *2001*	8.50	2.50
16	$5 blue, *2002*	20.00	2.50
17	$5 green, *2003*	9.50	2.50
18	$5 red, *2004*	9.50	2.50

KENTUCKY

Printed in booklet panes of 5, starting with No. 12 in panes of 30.

Stamps are numbered serially.

Catalogue values for all unused stamps in this section are for Never Hinged items.

Artists: Ray Harm, #1, 7; David Chapple, #2; Ralph J. McDonald, #3, 10; Lynn Kaatz, #4, 15; Phillip Crowe, #5, 9; Jim Oliver, #6; Phillip Powell, #8, 13; Jim Killen, #11; Laurie Parsons Yarnes, #12; Harold Roe, #14, 17; Tim Donovan, #16; Larry Chandler, #18; Ben Burney, #19; Chris Walden, #20-24; Rick Hill, #25.

1985-2009

1	$5.25 Mallards, rouletted	15.00	3.00
	With tab	15.00	
2	$5.25 Wood ducks, rouletted, *1986*	10.00	2.50
	With tab	10.00	
3	$5.25 Black ducks, *1987*	9.00	2.50
	With tab	10.00	
4	$5.25 Canada geese, *1988*	9.00	2.50
	With tab	10.00	
5	$5.25 Retriever & canvasbacks, *1989*	15.00	2.50
	With tab	16.00	
6	$5.25 Wigeons, *1990*	9.00	2.50
	With tab	11.00	
7	$5.25 Pintails, *1991*	9.00	2.50
	With tab	11.00	
8	$5.25 Green-winged teal, *1992*	13.00	2.50
	With tab	15.00	
9	$5.25 Canvasback & decoy, *1993*	20.00	2.50
	With tab	22.50	
10	$5.25 Canada goose, *1994*	16.00	2.50
	With tab	19.00	
11	$7.50 Retriever, decoy, ringnecks, *1995*	25.00	3.00
	With tab	27.50	
12	$7.50 Blue-winged teal, *1996*	13.00	3.00
13	$7.50 Shovelers, *1997*	13.00	3.00
14	$7.50 Gadwalls, *1998*	15.00	3.00
15	$7.50 Common goldeneyes, *1999*	25.00	3.00
16	$7.50 Hooded mergansers, *2000*	19.00	3.00
17	$7.50 Mallards, *2001*	12.00	3.00
18	$7.50 Pintails, *2002*	12.00	3.00
19	$7.50 Snow geese, *2003*	12.00	3.00
20	$7.50 Black ducks, *2004*	17.50	3.00
21	$7.50 Canada geese, *2005*	20.00	3.00
22	$7.50 Mallards, *2006*	12.00	3.00
23	$7.50 Green-winged teal, *2007*	12.00	3.00
24	$7.50 Pintails, *2008*	12.00	3.00
25	$7.50 Snow geese, *2009*	12.00	3.00

Nos. 19-25 not required for hunting.

LOUISIANA

Printed in sheets of 30.

Stamps are numbered serially. Stamps without numbers are artist presentation examples.

Two fees: resident and non-resident.

Catalogue values for all unused stamps in this section are for Never Hinged items.

Artists: David Noll, #1-1A; Elton Louviere, #2-2A; Brett J. Smith, #3-3A; Bruce Heard, #4-4A; Ronald Louque, #5-5A, 8-8A, 11-11A, 25-25A; Don Edwards, #6-6A; John Bertrand, #7-7A; R. Hall, #9-9A; R. C. Davis, #10-10A; Jude Brunet, #12-12A; Edward Butler, #13-13A; Reggie McLeroy, #14-14A; Dale Pousson, #15-15A; Jeffrey Klinefelter, #16-16A, 20-20A, 24-24A; Ken Michaelsen, #17-17A. Edward Suthoff, #18-18A. Tony Bernard, #19-19A, 26-26A; Anthony Padgett, #21-21A; Richard Clifton #22-22A, 29-29A; Wes Dewey, #23-23A; Guy Crittenden, #27-27A, 31-31A; John Nelson Harris, #28-28A, 33-33A; Tim Taylor, #30-30A; Adam Grimm, #32-32A.

1989-2021

1	$5 Blue-winged teal	12.00	2.50
b.	Governor's edition	*100.00*	
1A	$7.50 Blue-winged teal	14.00	2.50
b.	Governor's edition	*150.00*	

Nos. 1b and 2b were available only through a sealed bid auction where sheets of 30 of each denomination with matching serial numbers were sold as a unit.

2	$5 Green-winged teal, *1990*	9.50	2.50
2A	$7.50 Green-winged teal, *1990*	12.00	2.50
3	$5 Wood ducks, *1991*	9.00	2.50
3A	$7.50 Wood ducks, *1991*	13.00	2.50
4	$5 Pintails, *1992*	9.00	2.50
4A	$7.50 Pintails, *1992*	13.00	2.50
5	$5 American wigeon, *1993*	12.00	2.50
5A	$7.50 American wigeon, *1993*	13.00	2.50
6	$5 Mottled duck, *1994*	12.00	2.50
6A	$7.50 Mottled duck, *1994*	13.00	2.50
7	$5 Speckle bellied goose, *1995*	12.00	2.50
7A	$7.50 Speckle bellied goose, *1995*	13.00	2.50
8	$5 Gadwall, *1996*	12.00	2.50
8A	$7.50 Gadwall, *1996*	13.00	2.50
9	$5 Ring-necked ducks, *1997*	10.00	2.50
9A	$13.50 Ring-necked ducks, *1997*	22.50	2.50
10	$5.50 Mallards, *1998*	11.00	2.50
b.	Governor's edition	*150.00*	
10A	$13.50 Mallards, *1998*	22.50	2.50
b.	Governor's edition	*200.00*	
11	$5.50 Snow geese, *1999*	11.00	2.50
11A	$13.50 Snow geese, *1999*	22.50	2.50
12	$5.50 Lesser scaup, *2000*	11.00	2.50
12A	$13.50 Lesser scaup, *2000*	40.00	2.50

No. 12A sold for $25 as stamps were printed before fee increase was finalized.

13	$5.50 Shovelers, *2001*	11.00	2.50
13A	$25 Shovelers, *2001*	35.00	2.50
14	$5.50 Canvasbacks, *2002*	11.00	2.50
14A	$25 Canvasbacks, *2002*	35.00	2.50
15	$5.50 Redheads, *2003*	11.00	2.50
15A	$25 Redheads, *2003*	35.00	2.50
16	$5.50 Hooded mergansers, *2004*	10.00	2.50
16A	$25 Hooded mergansers, *2004*	35.00	2.50
17	$5.50 Pintails, Labrador retriever, *2005*	10.00	2.50
17A	$25 Pintails, Labrador retriever, *2005*	35.00	2.50
18	$5.50 Mallards, Labrador retriever, *2006*	10.00	2.50
18A	$25 Mallards, Labrador retriever, *2006*	35.00	2.50
19	$5.50 Mallards, Labrador retriever, *2007*	10.00	2.50
19A	$25 Mallards, Labrador retriever, *2007*	35.00	2.50
20	$5.50 Wood ducks, Golden retriever, *2008*	10.00	2.50
20A	$25 Wood ducks, Golden retriever, *2008*	35.00	2.50
21	$5.50 Ducks, Chesapeake Bay retriever, *2009*	10.00	2.50
21A	$25 Ducks, Chesapeake Bay retriever, *2009*	35.00	2.50
22	$5.50 Pintails, *2010*	10.00	2.50
22A	$25 Pintails, *2010*	35.00	2.50
23	$5.50 Wood ducks, *2011*	15.00	2.50
23A	$25 Wood ducks, *2011*	35.00	2.50
24	$5.50 Wigeons, *2012*	10.00	2.50
24A	$25 Wigeons, *2012*	35.00	2.50
25	$5.50 Mallards, *2013*	10.00	2.50
25A	$25 Mallards, *2013*	35.00	2.50
26	$5.50 White-fronted geese, *2014*	10.00	2.50
26A	$25 White-fronted geese, *2014*	35.00	2.50
27	$5.50 Blue-winged teal, *2015*	10.00	2.50
27A	$25 Blue-winged teal, *2015*	35.00	2.50
28	$5.50 Gadwalls, *2016*	15.00	2.50
28A	$25 Gadwalls, *2016*	35.00	2.50
29	$5.50 Green-winged teal, *2017*	10.00	2.50
29A	$25 Green-winged teal, *2017*	35.00	2.50
30	$5.50 Canvasbacks, *2018*	15.00	2.50
30A	$25 Canvasbacks, *2018*	30.00	2.50
31	$5.50 Shovelers, *2019*	10.00	2.50
31A	$25 Shovelers, *2019*	30.00	2.50
32	$5.50 Ring-necked duckss, *2020*	10.00	2.50
32A	$25 Ring-necked duckss, *2020*	30.00	2.50
33	$5.50 Mottled duck, *2021*	10.00	2.50
33A	$25 Mottled duck, *2021*	30.00	2.50

Nos.15-33A not required for hunting.

MAINE

Printed in sheets of 10. Nos. 1-10 are numbered serially.

Catalogue values for all unused stamps in this section are for Never Hinged items.

Artists: David Maass, #1-3; Ron Van Gilder, #4; Rick Allen, #5; Jeannine Staples, #6, 10, 15, 18, 20, 23, 25; Thea Flanagan, #7; Patricia D. Carter, #8; Persis Weirs, #9; Susan Jordan, #11; Richard Alley, #12, 19, 16, 21, 24, 33, 36; Paul Fillion, #13; T. Kemp, #14; Darby Mumford, #17; Daniel Cake, #22; Georgette Kanach, #26; Olga Wing, #27; Rebekah LaCourse, #28; Janine Folsom, #29; Richard Alley, Jr., #30; Rebekah Lowell, #31, 34, 37; Michael Loring, #32; Joanna Huffman, #35; Gary Winders, #38.

1984-2021

1	$2.50 Black ducks	20.00	5.00
2	$2.50 Common eiders, *1985*	25.00	5.00
3	$2.50 Wood ducks, *1986*	9.00	2.50
4	$2.50 Buffleheads, *1987*	8.00	2.50
5	$2.50 Green-winged teal, *1988*	8.00	2.50
6	$2.50 Common goldeneyes, *1989*	8.00	2.50
7	$2.50 Canada geese, *1990*	8.00	2.50
8	$2.50 Ring-necked duck, *1991*	8.00	2.50
9	$2.50 Old squaw, *1992*	8.00	2.50
10	$2.50 Hooded merganser, *1993*	8.00	2.50
11	$2.50 Mallards, *1994*	9.00	2.50
12	$2.50 White-winged scoters, *1995*	12.00	2.50
13	$2.50 Blue-winged teal, *1996*	12.00	2.50
14	$2.50 Greater scaup, *1997*	12.00	2.50
15	$2.50 Surf scoters, *1998*	8.00	2.50
16	$2.50 Black duck, *1999*	9.00	2.50
17	$2.50 Common eider, *2000*	8.00	2.50
18	$2.50 Wood duck, *2001*	8.00	2.50
19	$2.50 Buffleheads, *2002*	8.00	2.50
20	$5.50 Green-winged teal, *2003*	12.00	2.50
21	$8.50 Barrow's goldeneye, *2004*	12.00	2.50
22	$8.50 Canada goose, *2005*	12.00	2.50
23	$7.50 Ring-necked ducks, *2006*	12.00	2.50
24	$7.50 Long-tailed ducks, *2007*	12.00	2.50
25	$7.50 Hooded mergansers, *2008*	12.00	2.50
26	$7.50 Mallards, *2009*	12.00	2.50
27	$7.50 Harlequin ducks, *2010*	12.00	2.50
28	$7.50 Wood ducks, *2011*	12.00	2.50
29	$7.50 Ring-necked ducks, *2012*	12.00	2.50
30	$7.50 Greater scaup, *2013*	12.00	2.50
31	$7.50 Wigeon, *2014*	12.00	2.50
32	$7.50 Canvasbacks, *2015*	12.50	2.50
33	$7.50 Blue-winged teal, *2016*	12.00	2.50
34	$7.50 Common eiders, *2017*	12.00	2.50
35	$7.50 Pintails, *2018*	12.00	2.50
36	$7.50 Canada goose, *2019*	12.00	2.50
37	$7.50 Red-breasted mergansers, *2020*	12.00	2.50
38	$7.50 Long-tailed ducks, *2021*	11.50	2.50

MARYLAND

Nos. 1-19 printed in sheets of 10. Starting with No. 20, printed in sheets of 5 with numbered tab at bottom and selvage at top.

Each stamp has tab. Unused value is for stamp with tab. Many used examples have tab attached.

Catalogue values for all unused stamps in this section are for Never Hinged items.

Artists: John Taylor, #1, 6, 24; Stanley Stearns, #2, 5; Louis Frisino, #3, 13, 20; Jack Schroeder, #4, 7; Arthur Eakin, #8; Roger Bucklin, #9; Roger Lent, #10, 16; Carla Huber, #11, 17; David Turnbaugh, #12, 18, 23, 27, 31, 37; Francis Sweet, #14; Christopher White, #15; Will Wilson, #19; Robert Bealle, #21, 30, 35; Charles Schauck, #22; Paul Makuchal, #25, 33, 40, 44; Wally Makuchal, #26, 36; Wilhelm Goebel, #28, 32, 39; James Kinnett, #29; Jim Taylor, #34, 38, 42; Stephen Perrine, #41; Richard Menard Jr., #43; Paul Bridgford, #45; Gersld Putt, #46, Jeffrey Klinefelter, #47; Scott Calpino, #48.

1974-2012

1	$1.10 Mallards	11.00	2.50
2	$1.10 Canada geese, rouletted, *1975*	10.00	2.50
3	$1.10 Canvasbacks, rouletted, *1976*	10.00	2.50
4	$1.10 Greater scaup, *1977*	10.00	2.50
5	$1.10 Redheads, *1978*	10.00	2.50
6	$1.10 Wood ducks, rouletted, *1979*	10.00	2.50
7	$1.10 Pintail decoy, rouletted, *1980*	10.00	2.50
8	$3 Wigeon, rouletted, *1981*	9.00	2.50
9	$3 Canvasback, *1982*	8.00	2.50
10	$3 Wood duck, *1983*	12.00	2.50
11	$6 Black ducks, *1984*	14.00	2.50
12	$6 Canada geese, *1985*	12.00	2.50
13	$6 Hooded mergansers, *1986*	12.00	2.50
14	$6 Redheads, *1987*	13.00	2.50
15	$6 Ruddy ducks, *1988*	12.00	2.50
16	$6 Blue-winged teal, *1989*	12.00	2.50
17	$6 Lesser scaup, *1990*	12.00	2.50
18	$6 Shovelers, *1991*	12.00	2.50
19	$6 Bufflehead, *1992*	12.00	2.50
20	$6 Canvasbacks, *1993*	17.50	2.50
21	$6 Redheads, *1994*	12.00	2.50
22	$6 Mallards, *1995*	42.50	2.50
23	$6 Canada geese, *1996*	45.00	2.50
24	$6 Canvasbacks, *1997*	15.00	2.50
25	$6 Pintails, *1998*	15.00	2.50
26	$6 Wood ducks, *1999*	15.00	2.50
27	$6 Old squaws, *2000*	25.00	2.50
28	$6 Wigeons, *2001*	11.00	2.50
29	$9 Black scoters, *2002*	15.00	2.50
30	$9 Lesser scaup, *2003*	15.00	2.50
31	$9 Pintails, *2004*	15.00	2.50
32	$9 Ruddy duck, *2005*	15.00	2.50
33	$9 Canada geese, *2006*	15.00	2.50
34	$9 Wood ducks, *2007*	15.00	2.50
35	$9 Canvasback, *2008*	15.00	2.50
36	$9 Blue-winged teal, *2009*	15.00	2.50
37	$9 Hooded merganser, *2010*	15.00	2.50
38	$9 Canada geese, *2011*	15.00	2.50
39	($9) Wigeons, *2012*	15.00	2.50

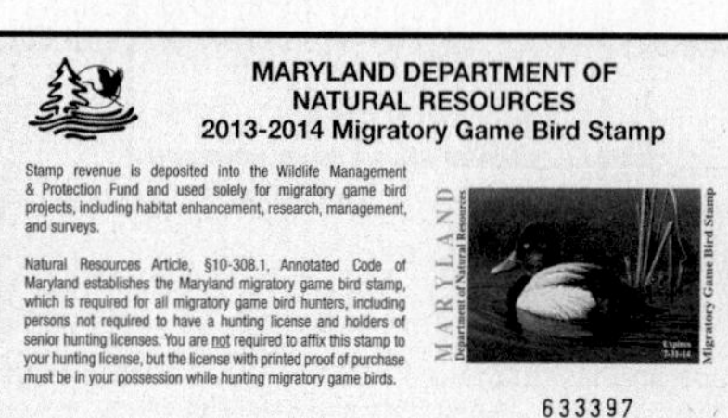

2013-21 ***Die Cut***

Souvenir Sheet
Self-Adhesive

40	($9) Lesser scaup, *2013*	15.00	2.50
41	($9) Ring-necked duck, *2014*	12.00	2.50
42	($9) Canvasbacks, *2015*	12.00	2.50
43	($9) Shovelers, *2016*	12.00	2.50
44	($9) Black ducks, *2017*	17.50	2.50
45	($9) Green-winged teal, *2018*	12.00	2.50
46	($9) Wood ducks, *2019*	12.00	2.50
47	($9) Blue-winged teal, *2020*	12.00	2.50
48	($9) Redheads, *2021*	12.00	2.50

Public Lands Hunting Stamps

Required to hunt waterfowl in state-managed wildlife areas.

Issued in booklet panes of 10.

1975-79

A1	$2 purple	*3,250.*	125.
A2	$2 black, *pink, 1976*	*2,250.*	60.
A3	$2 black, *yellow, 1977*	*1,750.*	60.
A4	$2 black, *1978*	*5,500.*	175.
A5	$2 black, *yellow, 1979*	*1,500.*	50.

MASSACHUSETTS

Printed in sheets of 12.

Catalogue values for all unused stamps in this section are for Never Hinged items.

Artists: Milton Weiler, #1; Tom Hennessey, #2; William Tyner, #3-5; Randy Julius, #6, 8, 10, 12, 19, 27, 33, 38; John Eggert, #7, 9, 24; Joseph Cibula, #11; Robert Piscatori, #13, 15, 25, 30; Peter Baedita, #14, 29; Lou Barnicle, #16; Warren Racket Shreve, #17; Benjamin Smith, #18; Donald Little, #20, 32; Sergio Roffo, #21; David Brega, #22; Christine Wilkinson, #23;

Stephen Badlam #26; Barry Julius, #28, 36; Larry Denton, #31. Matthew Schulz, #34; Gregg Coppolo, #35; Janice Sexton, #37.

1974-2011

No.	Description	Unused	Used
1	$1.25 Wood duck decoy, rouletted	15.00	3.00
2	$1.25 Pintail decoy, *1975*	13.00	3.00
3	$1.25 Canada goose decoy, *1976*	13.00	3.00
4	$1.25 Goldeneye decoy, *1977*	13.00	3.00
5	$1.25 Black duck decoy, *1978*	13.00	3.00
6	$1.25 Ruddy turnstone duck decoy, *1979*	15.00	3.00
a.	Imperf, pair	160.00	
7	$1.25 Old squaw decoy, *1980*	15.00	3.00
8	$1.25 Red-breasted merganser decoy, *1981*	15.00	3.00
9	$1.25 Greater yellowlegs decoy, *1982*	15.00	3.00
10	$1.25 Redhead decoy, *1983*	15.00	3.00
11	$1.25 White-winged scoter decoy, *1984*	15.00	3.00
12	$1.25 Ruddy duck decoy, *1985*	12.00	3.00
13	$1.25 Preening bluebill decoy, *1986*	12.00	2.50
14	$1.25 American wigeon decoy, *1987*	12.00	2.50
15	$1.25 Mallard decoy, *1988*	12.00	2.50
16	$1.25 Brant decoy, *1989*	10.00	2.50
17	$1.25 Whistler hen decoy, *1990*	10.00	2.50
18	$5 Canvasback decoy, *1991*	10.00	2.50
19	$5 Black-bellied plover decoy, *1992*	10.00	2.50
20	$5 Red-breasted merganser decoy, *1993*	10.00	2.50
21	$5 White-winged scoter decoy, *1994*	10.00	2.50
22	$5 Female hooded merganser decoy, *1995*	10.00	2.50
23	$5 Eider decoy, *1996*	10.00	2.50
24	$5 Curlew decoy, *1997*	10.00	2.50
25	$5 Canada goose decoy, *1998*	10.00	2.50
26	$5 Old squaw decoy, *1999*	10.00	2.50
27	$5 Merganser hen decoy, *2000*	10.00	2.50
28	$5 Black duck decoy, *2001*	10.00	2.50
29	$5 Bufflehead decoy, *2002*	10.00	2.50
30	$5 Greenwing teal decoy, *2003*	10.00	2.50
31	$5 Wood duck drake decoy, *2004*	10.00	2.50
32	$5 Old squaw drake decoy, *2005*	10.00	2.50
33	$5 Long-billed curlew decoy, *2006*	18.00	2.50
34	$5 Goldeneye decoy, *2007*	10.00	2.50
35	$5 Black duck decoy, *2008*	10.00	2.50
36	$5 White-winged scoter decoy, *2009*	10.00	2.50
37	$5 Canada goose decoy, *2010*	12.50	2.50
38	$5 Brant decoy, *2011*	18.00	2.50

MICHIGAN

Managed Waterfowl Area Seasonal Passbook Stamps

Required to hunt waterfowl at state-owned and managed waterfowl areas. Stamps were valid for a full season, but permits were available only at district offiices near the hunting sites. Stamps are die cut, self-adhesive and were required to be affixed inside the hunter's passbook.

1986-94

No.	Description	Unused	Used
A1	$10 black & blue, *1986*	—	
A2	$10 green & yellow, *1987*	—	
A3	$10 red & blue, *1988*	—	
A4	$10 black & yellow, *1989*	—	
A5	$10 green & red, *1990*	—	
A6	$10 light green & purple, *1991*	—	
A7	$10 brown & blue, *1992*	—	
A8	$10 blue & red, *1993*	—	
A9	$10 green & gray, *1994*	—	

Managed Waterfowl Area Daily Passbook Stamps

Required to hunt waterfowl at state-owned and managed waterfowl areas. Stamps were valid for a morning hunt or an afternoon hunt on one day. Permits were available only at district offiices near the hunting sites. Stamps are die cut, self-adhesive and were required to be affixed inside the hunter's passbook.

1987-93

No.	Description	Unused	Used
2A2	$3 red & gray, *1987*	—	
2A4	$3 blue & yellow, *1989*	—	
2A5	$3 black & blue, *1990*	—	
2A6	$3 blue & yellow orange, *1991*	—	
2A7	$3 green & light blue, *1992*	—	
2A9	$3 red & pink, *1993*	—	

Nos. 1-5 printed in sheets of 10 with center gutter, rouletted. Printed in sheets of 10 die cut self-adhesives on backing paper (Nos. 6-19), or sheets of 15 (starting with No. 20).

Nos. 1, 3-19 are serially numbered.

Catalogue values for all unused stamps in this section are for Never Hinged items.

Artist: Oscar Warbach.

1976

No.	Description	Unused	Used
1	$2.10 Wood duck	5.00	2.50

Artists: Larry Hayden, #2, 5, 12; Richard Timm, #3; Andrew Kurzmann, #4; Dietmar Krumrey, #6, 14, 23-24, 28, 33; Gjisbert van Frankenhuyzen, #7; Rod Lawrence, #8, 15, 20, 25, 27, 32; Larry Cory, #9, 16; Robert Steiner, #10; Russell Cobane, #11; John Martens, #13; Heiner Hertling, #17; Clark Sullivan, #18; David Bollman, #19; Rusty Fretner, #21; M. Monroe, #22; Kim Diment, #26; Tim McDonald, #29; Christopher Smith, #30, 39, 41, 43, 45; Peter Mathios, #31; Lorna Poulos, #34; J.P. Edwards, #35; Richard Clifton, #36, 38; George Lockwood, #37; Guy Crittenden, #40, 42; Paul Bridgford, #44; John Roberts, #46.

1977-2021

No.	Description	Unused	Used
2	$2.10 Canvasbacks	225.00	35.00
	With numbered tab	295.00	
3	$2.10 Mallards, *1978*	20.00	5.00
	With tab	47.50	
4	$2.10 Canada geese, *1979*	60.00	5.00
	With tab	75.00	
5	$3.75 Lesser scaup, *1980*	17.50	4.00
	With tab	25.00	
6	$3.75 Buffleheads, *1981*	25.00	4.00
7	$3.75 Redheads, *1982*	25.00	4.00

Unused value is for stamp with sufficient margin to show printed spaces for date and time the stamp was sold.

No.	Description	Unused	Used
8	$3.75 Wood ducks, *1983*	25.00	4.00
9	$3.75 on $3.25 Pintails, *1984*	25.00	3.00

No. 9 not issued without surcharge.

No.	Description	Unused	Used
10	$3.75 Ring-necked ducks, *1985*	25.00	3.00
11	$3.75 Common goldeneyes, *1986*	22.00	2.50
12	$3.85 Green-winged teal, *1987*	11.00	2.50
13	$3.85 Canada geese, *1988*	10.00	2.50
14	$3.85 Wigeons, *1989*	10.00	2.50
15	$3.85 Wood ducks, *1990*	10.00	2.50
16	$3.85 Blue-winged teal, *1991*	9.00	2.50
17	$3.85 Red-breasted merganser, *1992*	9.00	2.50
18	$3.85 Hooded merganser, *1993*	9.00	2.50
19	$3.85 Black duck, *1994*	9.00	2.50
20	$4.35 Blue winged teal, *1995*	9.00	3.00
21	$4.35 Canada geese, *1996*	9.00	3.00
22	$5 Canvasbacks, *1997*	20.00	3.00
23	$5 Pintail, *1998*	9.00	3.00
24	$5 Shoveler, *1999*	9.00	3.00

Self-Adhesive Die Cut

No.	Description	Unused	Used
25	$5 Mallards, *2000*	20.00	3.00
26	$5 Ruddy ducks, *2001*	10.00	3.00
27	$5 Wigeons, *2002*	9.00	3.00
28	$5 Redheads, *2003*	9.00	3.00

Rouletted

No.	Description	Unused	Used
29	$5 Wood duck, *2004*	9.00	3.00
30	$5 Blue-winged teals, *2005*	9.00	3.00
31	$5 Wigeon, *2006*	9.00	3.00
32	$5 Pintails, *2007*	8.00	3.00
33	$5 Wood ducks, *2008*	8.00	3.00
34	$5 Canvasbacks, *2009*	10.00	3.00
35	$5 Buffleheads, *2010*	10.00	3.00
36	$5 Mallard, *2011*	8.00	3.00
37	$5 Ring-necked ducks, *2012*	8.00	3.00
38	$5 Black duck, *2013*	8.00	3.00
39	$5 Long-tailed ducks, *2014*	8.00	3.00
40	$6 Common goldeneyes, *2015*	10.00	3.00
41	$6 Green-winged teal, *2016*	10.00	3.00
42	$6 Shovelers, *2017*	10.00	3.00
43	$6 Wigeons and Black Labrador retriever, *2018*	9.00	3.00
44	$6 Pintails, *2019*	9.00	3.00
45	$6 Canada geese, *2020*	9.00	3.00
46	$6 Wood duck, *2021*	9.00	3.00

Nos. 24-46 not required for hunting.

MINNESOTA

License Surcharge Stamps

No. A1 printed in sheets of 10. These stamps served as a $1 surcharge to cover the cost of a license increase.

Nos. A1-A2 issued to raise funds for acquisition and development of wildlife lands.

1957 *Perf. 12½*

No.	Description	Unused	Used
A1	$1 Mallards & Pheasant	85.00	5.00

Cancellation of No. A1 was not required. Value for used stamp is for an example without gum.

1971 MINNESOTA $1.00
Department of Natural Resources
Additional one dollar surcharge to be paid by sportsmen, pursuant to Laws 1971 Chapter 867, for the acquisition and development of wildlife lands.

1971 *Rouletted 9½*

No.	Description	Unused	Used
A2	$1 black, *dark yellow*	*3,500.*	15.00

Cancellation of No. A2 was not required. Value for used stamp is for an example without gum.

Special Canada Goose Season Stamps

Values are for signed copies. No unused stamps are known.

1997 108534
Minnesota Special
Canada Goose Season Permit
Licensee Signature

1997-99

2A1	black, *1997*	95.00
2A2	black, *1998*	75.00
2A3	black, *1999*	75.00

Regular Issues

Printed in sheets of 10.

Catalogue values for all unused stamps in this section are for Never Hinged items.

Artists: David Maass, #1, 3; Leslie Kouba, #2; James Meger, #4; Terry Redlin, #5, 9, Phil Scholer, #6, 17; Gary Moss, #7; Thomas Gross, #8; Brian Jarvi, #10; Ron Van Gilder, #11; Robert Hautman, #12, 16, 25; Jim Hautman, #13, 20; Kevin Daniel, #14, 21; Daniel Smith, #15; Edward DuRose, #18, 40; Bruce Miller, #19; Thomas Moen, #22, 31, 38; John House, #23; Kim Norlien, #24; John Freiberg, #26; Mark Kness, #27, 34; Scot Storm, #28, 33, 39, 45; David Chapman, #29, 37; Joe Hautman, #30; Sara Stack, #32; Kevin Nelson, #35; Stephen Hamrick, #36; Timothy Turenne, #41; Mark Thone, #42; Jim Canturia, #43; Michael Sieve, #44.

1977-2021

1	$3 Mallards	15.00	2.50
2	$3 Lesser scaup, *1978*	12.00	2.50
3	$3 Pintails, *1979*	12.00	2.50
4	$3 Canvasbacks, *1980*	12.00	2.50
5	$3 Canada geese, *1981*	9.50	2.50
6	$3 Redheads, *1982*	12.00	2.50
7	$3 Blue geese & snow goose, *1983*	12.00	2.50
8	$3 Wood ducks, *1984*	12.00	2.50
9	$3 White-fronted geese, *1985*	9.00	2.50
10	$5 Lesser scaup, *1986*	10.00	2.50

Beginning with this issue, left side of sheet has an agent's tab, detachable from the numbered tab.

11	$5 Common goldeneyes, *1987*	11.00	2.50
	With numbered tab	11.00	
	With agent's and numbered tabs	16.00	
12	$5 Buffleheads, *1988*	11.00	2.50
	With numbered tab	11.00	
	With agent's and numbered tabs	17.50	
13	$5 Wigeons, *1989*	11.00	2.50
	With numbered tab	11.00	
	With agent's and numbered tabs	17.50	
14	$5 Hooded mergansers, *1990*	25.00	2.50
	With numbered tab	25.00	
	With agent's and numbered tabs	40.00	
15	$5 Ross's geese, *1991*	10.00	2.50
	With numbered tab	10.00	
	With agent's and numbered tabs	14.00	
16	$5 Barrow's goldeneyes, *1992*	10.00	2.50
	With numbered tab	10.00	
	With agent's and numbered tabs	14.00	
17	$5 Blue-winged teal, *1993*	10.00	2.50
	With numbered tab	10.00	
	With agent's and numbered tabs	14.00	
18	$5 Ringneck duck, *1994*	10.00	2.50
	With numbered tab	10.00	
	With agent's and numbered tabs	13.00	
19	$5 Gadwall, *1995*	10.00	2.50
	With numbered tab	10.00	
	With agent's and numbered tabs	13.00	
20	$5 Greater scaup, *1996*	12.00	2.50
	With numbered tab	12.00	
	With agent's and numbered tabs	18.00	
21	$5 Shovelers, *1997*	11.00	2.50
	With numbered tab	11.00	
	With agent's and numbered tabs	15.00	
22	$5 Harlequins, *1998*	13.00	2.50
	With numbered tab	13.00	
	With agent's and numbered tabs	19.00	
23	$5 Green-winged teal, *1999*	11.00	2.50
	With numbered tab	11.00	
	With agent's and numbered tabs	15.00	

Self- Adhesive Die Cut

24	$5 Red-breasted merganser, *2000*	20.00	2.50

No. 24 is on backing paper affixed to back of license form.

25	$5 Black duck, *2001*	30.00	2.50

No. 25 is on backing paper affixed to back of license form.

26	$5 Ruddy duck, *2002*	15.00	2.50
27	$5 Oldsquaws, *2003*	15.00	2.50
28	$7.50 Common mergansers, *2004*	15.00	2.50
29	$7.50 White-winged scoters, lighthouse, *2005*	15.00	2.50
30	$7.50 Mallard, *2006*	15.00	2.50
31	$7.50 Lesser scaups, *2007*	15.00	2.50
32	$7.50 Ross's geese, *2008*	15.00	2.50
33	$7.50 Common goldeneyes, *2009*	15.00	2.50
34	$7.50 Wood duck, *2010*	15.00	2.50
35	$7.50 Red-breasted merganser, *2011*	15.00	2.50
36	$7.50 Ruddy duck, *2012*	15.00	2.50
37	$7.50 Pintail, *2013*	15.00	2.50
38	$7.50 Canada geese, *2014*	15.00	2.50
39	$7.50 Harlequin duck, *2015*	30.00	2.50
40	$7.50 Wigeon, *2016*	15.00	2.50
41	$7.50 Redheads, *2017*	15.00	2.50
42	$7.50 White-winged scoters, *2018*	15.00	2.50
43	$7.50 Gadwall, *2019*	15.00	2.50
44	$7.50 Snow geese, *2020*	15.00	2.50
45	$7.50 Greater scaup, *2021*	15.00	2.50

Nos. 26-45 are on backing paper affixed to mailing envelopes. Beginning with No. 32, stamps are not required for hunting.

MISSISSIPPI

Starting with No. 2, stamps are printed in sheets of 10. Nos. 2-14 are rouletted. All stamps are numbered serially.

Catalogue values for all unused stamps in this section are for Never Hinged items.

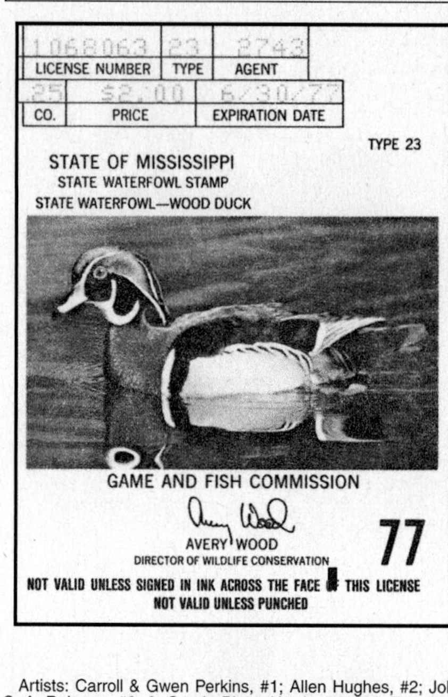

1068063	23	2743
LICENSE NUMBER	TYPE	AGENT

25	$2.00	6/30/77
CO.	PRICE	EXPIRATION DATE

TYPE 23

STATE OF MISSISSIPPI
STATE WATERFOWL STAMP
STATE WATERFOWL—WOOD DUCK

GAME AND FISH COMMISSION

AVERY WOOD
DIRECTOR OF WILDLIFE CONSERVATION

77

NOT VALID UNLESS SIGNED IN INK ACROSS THE FACE OF THIS LICENSE
NOT VALID UNLESS PUNCHED

Artists: Carroll & Gwen Perkins, #1; Allen Hughes, #2; John C. A. Reimers, #3, 6; Carole Pigott Hardy, #4; Bob Tompkins, #5, 13; Jerry Johnson, #7; Jerrie Glasper, #8; Tommy Goodman, #9; Lottie Fulton, #10; Joe Lattl, #11, 17, 22-23; Robert Garner, #12; Debra Aven Swartzendruber, #14; Kathy Dickson, #15; Phillip Crowe, #16; Eddie Suthoff, #18; Emitt Thames, #19-20; James Josey, #21; John MacHudspeth, #24-33B, 36-38B; Joe MacHudspeth, Jr., #34-35B, 39-39B, 42-42B; Lauren Doherty, #40-40B; Paul T. Brown, #41-41B, 45-45B; Bill Stripling, #43-43B; Fred Greenslade, #44-44B; Michael Furtman, #46-46B.

1976 **Without Gum**

1	$2 Wood duck	18.00	5.00
a.	Complete 2-part data processing card	25.00	

1977-2021

2	$2 Mallards	10.00	2.50
3	$2 Green-winged teal, *1978*	10.00	2.50
4	$2 Canvasbacks, *1979*	10.00	2.50
5	$2 Pintails, *1980*	10.00	2.50
6	$2 Redheads, *1981*	10.00	2.50
7	$2 Canada geese, *1982*	10.00	2.50
8	$2 Lesser scaup, *1983*	10.00	2.50
9	$2 Black ducks, *1984*	10.00	2.50
10	$2 Mallards, *1985*	10.00	2.50
a.	Vert. serial No., imperf btwn. serial No. and stamp	150.00	
b.	Horiz. serial No., no vert. silver bar	700.00	
11	$2 Wigeons, *1986*	10.00	2.50
12	$2 Ring-necked ducks, *1987*	10.00	2.50
13	$2 Snow geese, *1988*	10.00	2.50
14	$2 Wood ducks, *1989*	7.00	2.50
15	$2 Snow geese, *1990*	12.50	2.50
16	$2 Labrador retriever & canvasbacks, *1991*	7.50	2.50
17	$2 Green-winged teal, *1992*	7.50	2.50
18	$5 Mallards, *1993*	9.00	2.50
19	$5 Canvasbacks, *1994*	10.00	2.50
20	$5 Blue-winged teals, *1995*	15.00	2.50
21	$5 Hooded merganser, *1996*	17.00	2.50
22	$5 Pintail, *1997*	22.50	2.50
23	$5 Pintails, *1998*	13.00	2.50
24	$5 Ring-necked duck, *1999*	10.00	2.50
24A	$5 Ring-necked duck, self-adhesive, die cut, *1999*	10.00	2.50
25	$5 Mallards, *2000*	10.00	2.50
25A	$5 Mallards, self-adhesive, die cut, *2000*	*1,000.*	
26	$5 Gadwall, *2001*	15.00	2.50
26A	$10 Gadwall, self-adhesive, die cut, *2001*	15.00	2.50
27	$10 Wood duck, *2002*	15.00	2.50
27A	$10 Wood duck, self-adhesive, die cut, *2002*	15.00	2.50
28	$10 Pintail, *2003*	15.00	2.50
28A	$10 Pintail, self-adhesive, die cut, *2003*	15.00	2.50
29	$10 Wood ducks, *2004*	15.00	2.50
29A	$10 Wood ducks, self-adhesive, die cut, *2004*	15.00	2.50
30	$10 Blue-winged teal, *2005*	15.00	2.50
30A	$10 Blue-winged teal, self-adhesive, die cut, *2005*	15.00	2.50
30B	$15 Blue-winged teal, non-resident, self-adhesive, die cut, *2005*	24.00	2.50
31	$10 Labrador retriever, *2006*	15.00	2.50
31A	$10 Labrador retriever, self-adhesive, die cut, *2006*	15.00	2.50
31B	$15 Labrador retriever, non-resident, self-adhesive, die cut, *2006*	24.00	2.50
32	$10 Wood ducks, perf., *2007*	15.00	2.50
32A	$10 Wood ducks, self-adhesive, die cut, *2007*	15.00	2.50
32B	$15 Wood ducks, self-adhesive, die cut, *2007*	24.00	2.50
33	$10 Green-winged teal, perf., *2008*	15.00	2.50
33A	$10 Green-winged teal, self-adhesive, die cut, *2008*	15.00	2.50
33B	$15 Green-winged teal, self-adhesive, die cut, *2008*	24.00	2.50
34	$10 Blue-winged teal, perf., *2009*	15.00	2.50
34A	$10 Blue-winged teal, self-adhesive, die cut, *2009*	15.00	2.50
34B	$15 Blue-winged teal, self-adhesive, die cut, *2009*	24.00	2.50
35	$10 Mallards, perf., *2010*	15.00	2.50
35A	$10 Mallards, self-adhesive, die cut, *2010*	15.00	2.50
35B	$15 Mallards, self-adhesive, die cut, *2010*	24.00	2.50
36	$10 Wood duck, perf., *2011*	15.00	2.50
36A	$10 Wood duck, self-adhesive, die cut, *2011*	15.00	2.50
36B	$15 Wood duck, self-adhesive, die cut, *2011*	24.00	2.50
37	$10 Green-winged teal, perf., *2012*	15.00	2.50
37A	$10 Green-winged teal, self-adhesive, die cut, *2012*	15.00	2.50
37B	$15 Green-winged teal, self-adhesive, die cut, *2012*	24.00	2.50
38	$10 Mallard, perf., *2013*	15.00	2.50
38A	$10 Mallard, self-adhesive, die cut *2013*	15.00	2.50
38B	$15 Mallard, self-adhesive, die cut *2013*	24.00	2.50
39	$10 Wood ducks, perf., *2014*	16.00	2.50
39A	$10 Wood ducks, self-adhesive, die cut *2014*	16.00	2.50
39B	$15 Wood ducks, self-adhesive, die cut *2014*	24.00	2.50
40	$10 Pintail, perf., *2015*	16.00	2.50
40A	$10 Pintail, self-adhesive, die cut, *2015*	16.00	2.50
40B	$15 Pintail, self-adhesive, die cut, *2015*	24.00	2.50
41	$10 Pintail, perf., *2016*	16.00	2.50
41A	$10 Pintail, self-adhesive, die cut, *2016*	16.00	2.50
41B	$15 Pintail, self-adhesive, die cut, *2016*	24.00	2.50
42	$10 Gadwall, perf., *2017*	16.00	2.50
42A	$10 Gadwall, self-adhesive, die cut, *2017*	16.00	2.50
42B	$15 Gadwall, self-adhesive, die cut, *2017*	24.00	2.50
43	$10 Canvasback, perf., *2018*	16.00	2.50
43A	$10 Canvasback, self-adhesive, die cut, *2018*	16.00	2.50
43B	$15 Canvasback, self-adhesive, die cut, *2018*	22.00	2.50
44	$10 Redhead, perf., *2019*	16.00	2.50
44A	$10 Redhead, self-adhesive, die cut, *2019*	16.00	2.50
44B	$15 Redhead, self-adhesive, die cut, *2019*	22.00	2.50
45	$10 Black-bellied whistling duck, perf., *2020*	16.00	2.50
45A	$10 Black-bellied whistling duck, self-adhesive, die cut, *2020*	16.00	2.50
45B	$15 Black-bellied whistling duck, self-adhesive, die cut, *2020*	22.00	2.50
46	$10 Black duck, perf., *2021*	16.00	2.50
46A	$10 Black duck, self-adhesive, die cut, *2021*	16.00	2.50
46B	$15 Black duck, self-adhesive, die cut, *2021*	22.00	2.50

MISSOURI

Issued in booklet panes of five with tab. Nos. 1-8 are rouletted. No. 18 issued in pane of 30.

Catalogue values for all unused stamps in this section are for Never Hinged items.

Artists: Charles Schwartz, #1; David Plank, #2; Tom Crain, #3, 8; Gary Lucy, #4; Doug Ross, #5; Glenn Chambers, #6; Ron Clayton, #7; Ron Ferkol, #9, 13, 18; Bruce Bollman, #10; Kathy Dickson, #11; Eileen Melton, #12; Kevin Guinn, #14; Thomas Bates, #15; Keith Alexander, #16; Ryan Peterson, #17.

1979-96

No.	Description	Unused	Used
1	$3.40 Canada geese	*325.00*	75.00
	With tab	*400.00*	
2	$3.40 Wood ducks, *1980*	*80.00*	18.00
	With tab	*95.00*	
3	$3 Lesser scaup, *1981*	50.00	9.00
	With tab	65.00	
4	$3 Buffleheads, *1982*	50.00	8.00
	With tab	65.00	
5	$3 Blue-winged teal, *1983*	45.00	8.00
	With tab	55.00	
6	$3 Mallards, *1984*	40.00	7.00
	With tab	50.00	
7	$3 American wigeons, *1985*	22.50	3.00
	With tab	25.00	
8	$3 Hooded mergansers, *1986*	12.00	3.00
	With tab	15.00	
9	$3 Pintails, *1987*	9.00	3.00
	With tab	13.00	
10	$3 Canvasback, *1988*	8.00	2.50
	With tab	11.00	
11	$3 Ring-necked ducks, *1989*	8.00	2.50
	With tab	9.25	

All examples of Nos. 12b, 13b, 14b, 15b, 16b, 17b are signed by the governor.

No.	Description	Unused	Used
12	$5 Redheads, *1990*	8.00	2.50
	With two part tab	10.00	
a.	$50 Governor's edition with tab	75.00	
b.	$100 Governor's edition with tab	300.00	
13	$5 Snow geese, *1991*	8.00	2.50
	With two part tab	9.00	
a.	$50 Governor's edition with tab	72.50	
b.	$100 Governor's edition with tab	300.00	
14	$5 Gadwalls, *1992*	8.00	2.50
	With tab	9.00	
a.	$50 Governor's edition with tab	75.00	
b.	$100 Governor's edition with tab	200.00	
15	$5 Green-winged teal, *1993*	8.00	2.50
	With tab	9.00	
a.	$50 Governor's edition with tab	75.00	
b.	$100 Governor's edition with tab	200.00	
16	$5 White-fronted goose, *1994*	8.00	2.50
	With 2-part tab	9.00	
a.	$50 Governor's edition with tab	75.00	
b.	$100 Governor's edition with tab	200.00	
17	$5 Goldeneyes, *1995*	8.00	2.50
	With 2-part tab	9.00	
a.	$50 Governor's edition with tab	75.00	
b.	$100 Governor's edition with tab	200.00	
18	$5 Black ducks, *1996*	8.00	2.50

MONTANA

Bird License Stamps

Required to hunt waterfowl.

Resident ($2, $4, $6), youth ($1, $2), and non-resident ($25, $30, $53) bird licenses. Licenses were no longer produced for youth, beginning in 1985, and non-resident, beginning in 1989.

Nos. 1-33 rouletted.

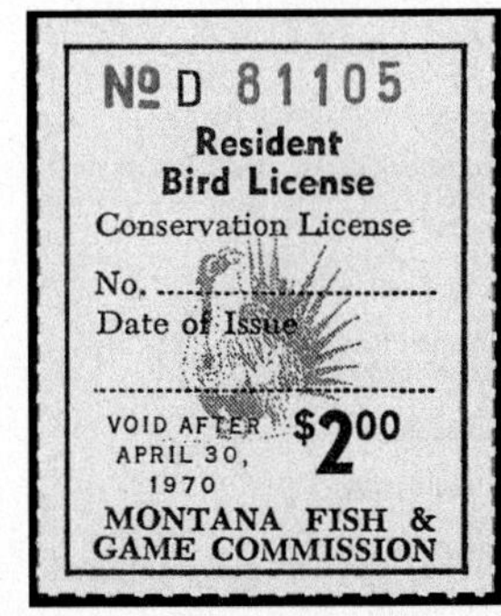

1969

No.	Description	Unused	Used
A1	$2 Sage grouse	425.00	15.00
A2	$1 Sage grouse	425.00	50.00
A3	$25 Sage grouse	425.00	75.00

1970

No.	Description	Unused	Used
A4	$2 Sage grouse	675.00	10.00
a.	Missing "1" in "1971," pos. 10		*650.00*
A5	$1 Sage grouse	*3,250.*	125.00
A6	$25 Sage grouse	—	*350.00*

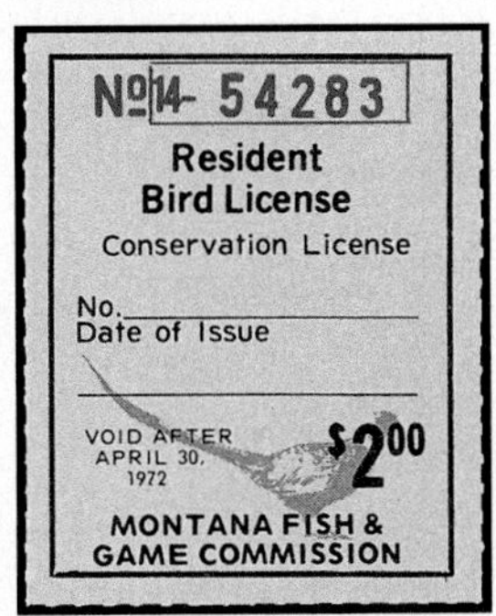

1971

No.	Description	Unused	Used
A7	$2 Pheasant	675.00	10.00
A8	$1 Pheasant	675.00	35.00
A9	$25 Pheasant	675.00	50.00

1972

No.	Description	Unused	Used
A10	$2 Pheasant	675.00	10.00
A11	$1 Pheasant	675.00	35.00
A12	$25 Pheasant	675.00	50.00

1973

No.	Description	Unused	Used
A13	$2 Pheasant	675.00	10.00
A14	$1 Pheasant	675.00	35.00
A15	$25 Pheasant	675.00	50.00

1974

No.	Description	Unused	Used
A16	$2 Pheasant	675.00	10.00
A17	$1 Pheasant	675.00	35.00
A18	$25 Pheasant	675.00	50.00

1975

No.	Description	Unused	Used
A19	$2 Pheasant	675.00	10.00
A20	$1 Pheasant	675.00	35.00
A21	$25 Pheasant	675.00	50.00

1976

No.	Description	Unused	Used
A22	$4 Pheasant	675.00	10.00
A23	$2 Pheasant	675.00	35.00
A24	$30 Pheasant	675.00	50.00

1977

No.	Description	Unused	Used
A25	$4 Pheasant	675.00	10.00
A26	$2 Pheasant	675.00	35.00
A27	$30 Pheasant	675.00	50.00

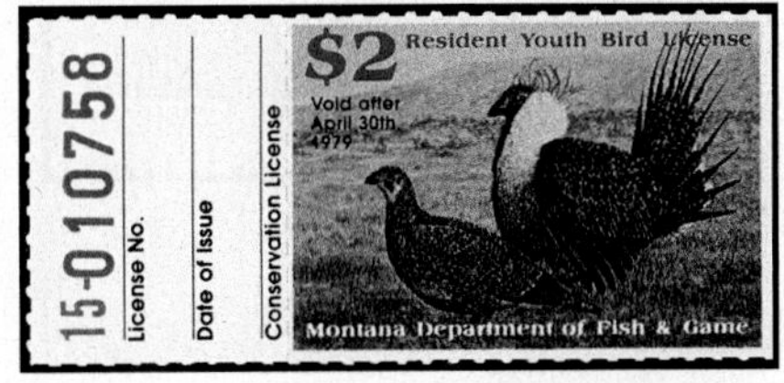

1978

No.	Description	Unused	Used
A28	$4 Sage grouse	9.00	2.00
A29	$2 Sage grouse	9.00	5.00
A30	$30 Sage grouse	9.00	6.50

1979

No.	Description	Unused	Used
A31	$4 Snow geese	9.00	2.00
A32	$2 Snow geese	9.00	5.00
A33	$30 Snow geese	9.00	6.50

1980

No.	Description	Unused	Used
A34	$4 black, *manila*		10.00
A36	$30 black, *gray green*		*35.00*

1982

No.	Description	Unused	Used
A40	$4 black, *yellow*		5.00
A42	$30 black, *light green*		*20.00*

1983

No.	Description	Unused	Used
A43	$4 black, *yellow gray*	*4,250.*	5.00
A44	$2 black, *gray*	*4,250.*	10.00
A45	$30 black, *light blue*	*4,250.*	20.00

1984

No.	Description	Unused	Used
A46	$4 black, *light blue green*	*3,500.*	5.00
A47	$2 black, *light violet*	*3,500.*	10.00
A48	$30 black, *gray*	*3,500.*	20.00

1985

No.	Description	Unused	Used
A49	$4 black, *light blue*	*3,500.*	5.00
A50	$30 black, *lavender*	*3,500.*	20.00

1986

No.	Description	Unused	Used
A51	$4 black, *orange*	*2,900.*	5.00
A52	$30 black, *light blue*	*2,900.*	20.00

1987

No.	Description	Unused	Used
A53	$4 black, *orange brown*	*1,250.*	3.00
A54	$30 black, *tan*	*1,750.*	15.00

1988

No.	Description	Unused	Used
A55	$6 black, *light blue*	*1,100.*	3.00
A56	$53 black, *purple*	*1,750.*	15.00

1989-2000

No.	Description	Unused	Used
A57	$6 black, *rose*	950.00	2.00
A58	$6 black, *lavender, 1990*	450.00	2.00
A59	$6 black, *pale blue, 1991*	350.00	2.00
A60	$6 black, *brown, 1992*	350.00	2.00
A61	$6 black, *blue, 1993*	250.00	1.50
A62	$6 black, *red orange, 1994*	225.00	1.50
A63	$6 black, *blue, 1995*	75.00	1.50
A64	$6 black, *purple, 1996*	50.00	1.00
A65	$6 black, *mauve, 1997*	35.00	1.00
A66	$6 black, *gray, 1998*	15.00	1.00
A66A	$20 black, *light green (non-resident 3-day shooting preserve), 1998*	—	—
A67	$6 black, *green, 1999*	15.00	1.00
A68	$20 black, *red orange (non-resident 3-day shooting preserve), 1999*	—	—
A69	$6 black, *tan, 2000*	12.00	—

Waterfowl Stamps

Issued in booklet panes of 10 and sheets of 30.

Stamps are numbered serially.

Stamps with serial numbers above 31,000 (1986) and above 21,000 (other years) are from booklet panes.

Catalogue values for all unused stamps in this section are for Never Hinged items.

Artist: Joe Thornbrugh, #34, 38, 39, 45, 46, 48; Roger Cruwys, #35, 37, 42; Dave Samuelson, #36; Craig Philips, #40; Darrell Davis, #41; Wayne Dowdy, #43; Jim Borgreen, #44, 50, 51; Cliff Rossberg, #47, 49.

1986-2003

No.	Description	Unused	Used
34	$5 Canada geese	12.00	3.00
	Pair from booklet pane with L & R selvage	*1,750.*	
	Top pair from booklet pane with agent tabs and L & R selvage	—	
35	$5 Redheads, *1987*	15.00	3.00
	Pair from booklet pane with L & R selvage	30.00	
	Top pair from booklet pane with agent tabs and L & R selvage	55.00	
36	$5 Mallards, *1988*	7.00	3.00
	Pair from booklet pane with L & R selvage	25.00	
	Top pair from booklet pane with agent tabs and L & R selvage	40.00	
37	$5 Black Labrador retriever & pintail, *1989*	7.00	3.00
	Pair from booklet pane with L & R selvage	25.00	
	Top pair from booklet pane with agent tabs and L & R selvage	40.00	
a.	Governor's edition	*140.00*	

No. 37a was available only in full sheets only through a sealed bid auction.

No.	Description	Unused	Used
38	$5 Blue-winged & cinnamon teal, *1990*	7.00	2.50
	Pair from booklet pane with L & R selvage	20.00	
	Top pair from booklet pane with agent tabs and L & R selvage	25.00	
39	$5 Snow geese, *1991*	7.00	2.50
	Pair from booklet pane with L & R selvage	20.00	
	Top pair from booklet pane with agent tabs and L & R selvage	25.00	
40	$5 Wood ducks, *1992*	7.00	2.50
	Pair from booklet pane with L & R selvage	20.00	
	Top pair from booklet pane with agent tabs and L & R selvage	25.00	
41	$5 Harlequin ducks, *1993*	7.00	2.50
	Pair from booklet pane with L & R selvage	22.00	
	Top pair from booklet pane with agent tabs and L & R selvage	25.00	
42	$5 Wigeons, *1994*	7.00	2.50
	Pair from booklet pane with L & R selvage	25.00	
	Top pair from booklet pane with agent tabs and L & R selvage	25.00	
43	$5 Tundra swans, *1995*	7.00	2.50
	Pair from booklet pane with L & R selvage	25.00	
	Top pair from booklet pane with agent tabs and L & R selvage	25.00	
44	$5 Canvasbacks, *1996*	7.00	2.50
	Pair from booklet pane with L & R selvage	25.00	
	Top pair from booklet pane with agent tabs and L & R selvage	30.00	
45	$5 Golden retriever, mallard, *1997*	7.00	2.50
	Pair from booklet pane with L & R selvage	25.00	
	Top pair from booklet pane with agent tabs and L & R selvage	30.00	
46	$5 Gadwalls, *1998*	7.00	2.50
	Pair from booklet pane with L & R selvage	25.00	
	Top pair from booklet pane with agent tabs and L & R selvage	30.00	
47	$5 Barrow's goldeneye, *1999*	7.00	2.50
	Pair from booklet pane with L & R selvage	25.00	
	Top pair from booklet pane with agent tabs and L & R selvage	30.00	
48	$5 Mallard decoy, Chesapeake retriever, *2000*	7.00	2.50
	Pair from booklet pane with L & R selvage	25.00	
	Top pair from booklet pane with agent tabs and L & R selvage	30.00	
49	$5 Canada geese, *2001*	7.00	2.50
	Pair from booklet pane with L & R selvage	25.00	
	Top pair from booklet pane with agent tabs and L & R selvage	30.00	
50	($5) Sandhill crane, *2002*	11.00	2.50
51	$5 Mallards, *2003*	75.00	2.50

No. 51 is not required for hunting.

NEBRASKA

Habitat Stamps

Required to hunt waterfowl.
Printed in sheets of 20.

Catalogue values for all unused stamps in this section are for Never Hinged items.

1977-2009

No.	Description	Unused	Used
A1	$7.50 Ring-necked pheasant	12.00	1.50
A2	$7.50 White-tailed deer, *1978*	12.00	1.50
A3	$7.50 Bobwhite quail, *1979*	12.00	1.50
A4	$7.50 Pheasant, *1980*	12.00	1.50
A5	$7.50 Cottontail rabbit, *1981*	12.00	1.50
A6	$7.50 Coyote, *1982*	12.00	1.50
A7	$7.50 Wild turkey, *1983*	12.00	1.50
A8	$7.50 Canada goose, *1984*	12.00	1.50
A9	$7.50 Cardinal, *1985*	12.00	1.50
A10	$7.50 Sharp-tailed grouse, *1986*	12.00	1.50
A11	$7.50 Sandhill crane, *1987*	12.00	1.50
A12	$7.50 Snow geese, *1988*	12.00	1.50
A13	$7.50 Mallards, *1989*	12.00	1.50
A14	$7.50 Pheasants, *1990*	12.00	1.50
A15	$7.50 Canada geese, *1991*	12.00	1.50
A16	$10.00 Raccoon, *1992*	15.00	1.50
A17	$10.00 Fox squirrel, *1993*	15.00	1.50
A18	$10.00 Hungarian partridge, *1994*	15.00	1.50
A19	$10.00 Prairie pronghorns, *1995*	15.00	1.50
A20	$10.00 Ring-necked pheasant, *1996*	15.00	1.50
A21	$10.00 White-tailed deer, *1997*	15.00	1.50
A22	$10.00 Mourning doves, *1998*	15.00	1.50
A23	$10.00 Sandhill cranes, *1999*	15.00	1.50
A24	$10.00 Turkeys, *2000*	15.00	1.50
A25	$10.00 Canada geese, *2001*	15.00	1.50
A26	$13.00 Mountain bluebird, *2002*	18.00	1.50
A27	$13.00 Wigeon, *2003*	18.00	1.50
A28	$13.00 Elk, *2004*	18.00	1.50
A29	$13.00 Deer, *2005*	18.00	1.50
A30	$13.00 Bighorn sheep, *2006*	18.00	1.50
A31	$13.00 Pronghorn antelope, *2007*	18.00	1.50
A32	$13.00 Wood duck, *2008*	18.00	1.50
A33	$13.00 Grouse, *2009*	18.00	1.50

Pictorial Labels

These stamps are not valid for any hunting fees.
Printed in sheets of 10.
Stamps are numbered serially.

Catalogue values for all unused stamps in this section are for Never Hinged items.

Artist: Neal Anderson.

1991-95

No.	Description	Unused
1	$6 Canada geese	11.00
2	$6 Pintails, *1992*	11.00
3	$6 Canvasbacks, *1993*	11.00
4	$6 Mallards, *1994*	11.00
5	$6 Wood ducks, *1995*	11.00

Waterfowl Stamp

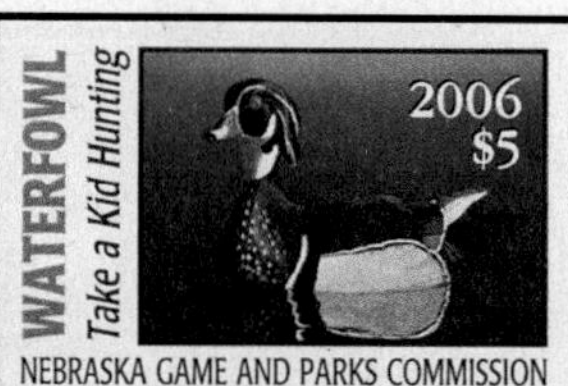

Artist: Brett Cooper

2006-08 ***Rouletted***

No.	Description	Unused	Used
6	$5 Wood duck	10.00	2.50
7	$5 Canvasbacks, *2007*	10.00	2.50
8	$5 Trumpeter swans, *2008*	10.00	2.50

Nos. 6-8 are required for hunting.

Artist: Bethany Cooper

2009 ***Rouletted***

No.	Description	Unused	Used
9	$5 Pintail, *2009*	10.00	2.50

No. 9 is required for hunting.

NEVADA

Printed in booklet panes of 4.
Stamps are rouletted and selvage is found above and below stamps on the pane. The tab portion of the panes in imperforate.
Starting with No. 4 stamps are numbered serially.

Catalogue values for all unused stamps in this section are for Never Hinged items.

Artists: Larry Hayden, #1; Dick Mcrill, #2; Phil Scholer, #3; Richard Timm, #4; Charles Allen, #5; Robert Steiner, #6; Richard Wilson, #7; Nolan Haan. #8, 12; Sherrie Russell Meline, #9, 21, 31; Jim Hautman, #10; Robert Hautman, #11; Tak Nakamura, #13, 17; Richard Clifton, #14, 22; Steve Hopkins, #15; Mark Mueller, #16; Jeffrey Klinefelter, #18, 23, 28, 32, 37; B. Blight, #19; Janie Kreutzjans, #20; Jeff Hoff, #24; David Brevick, #25; Louis Frisino, #26; Adam Oswald, #27, 33. Ken Michaelsen, #29; James Edwards, #30; Gerald Putt, #34; Rebekah Nastav, #35; Jocelyn Beatty, #36; Mark Thorne, #38; Guy Crittenden, #39.

1979-2017

No.	Description	Unused	Used
1	$2 Canvasbacks and decoy	45.00	12.00
	With numbered tab	55.00	

Stamps with tabs without numbers are printer's waste.

No.	Description	Unused	Used
2	$2 Cinnamon teal, *1980*	8.00	3.00
	With tab	10.00	
3	$2 Whistling swans, *1981*	10.00	3.00
	With tab	12.00	
4	$2 Shovelers, *1982*	10.00	3.00
	With tab	12.00	
5	$2 Gadwalls, *1983*	10.50	3.00
	With tab	11.00	
6	$2 Pintails, *1984*	11.00	3.00
	With tab	12.00	
7	$2 Canada geese, *1985*	20.00	3.00
	With tab	25.00	
8	$2 Redheads, *1986*	17.50	2.50
	With tab	25.00	
9	$2 Buffleheads, *1987*	15.00	2.50
	With tab	20.00	
10	$2 Canvasbacks, *1988*	11.00	2.50
	With tab	13.00	
11	$2 Ross's geese, *1989*	12.00	2.50
	With tab	15.00	
12	$5 Green-winged teal, *1990*	11.00	2.50
	With tab	13.00	
13	$5 White-faced ibis, *1991*	11.00	2.50
	With tab	13.00	
14	$5 American wigeon, *1992*	10.00	2.50
	With tab	11.00	
15	$5 Common goldeneye, *1993*	10.00	2.50
	With tab	11.00	
16	$5 Mallards, *1994*	10.00	2.50
	With tab	11.00	
17	$5 Wood duck, *1995*	10.00	2.50
	With tab	11.00	
18	$5 Ring-necked ducks, *1996*	15.00	2.50
	With tab	20.00	
19	$5 Ruddy ducks, *1997*	11.00	2.50
	With tab	13.00	
20	$5 Hooded merganser, *1998*	12.00	2.50
	With tab	15.00	
21	$5 Canvasback decoy, *1999*	11.00	2.50
	With tab	13.00	
22	$5 Canvasbacks, *2000*	15.00	2.50
	With tab	18.00	
23	$5 Lesser Scaups, *2001*	12.00	2.50
	With tab	15.00	
24	$5 Cinnamon teal, *2002*	11.00	2.50
25	$5 Green-winged teal, *2003*	11.00	2.50
	With tab	11.00	
26	$10 Redheads, *2004*	25.00	2.50
	With tab	27.50	
27	$10 Gadwalls, *2005*	14.00	2.50
	With tab	16.00	
28	$10 Tundra swans, *2006*	14.00	2.50
	With tab	16.00	
29	$10 Wood ducks, *2007*	15.00	2.50
	With tab	16.00	

30	$10 Pintail, *2008*	15.00	2.50
	With tab	16.00	
31	$10 Canada goose, *2009*	15.00	2.50
	With tab	16.00	
32	$10 Shovelers, *2010*	15.00	2.50
	With tab	16.00	
33	$10 Green-winged teal, *2011*	15.00	2.50
	With tab	16.00	
34	$10 Wigeon, *2012*	15.00	2.50
	With tab	16.00	
35	$10 Snow goose, *2013*	20.00	2.50
	With tab	20.00	
36	$10 American coots, *2014*	15.00	2.50
	With tab	16.00	
37	$10 White-fronted geese, *2015*	15.00	2.50
	With tab	16.00	
38	$10 Buffleheads, *2016*	15.00	2.50
	With tab	16.00	
39	$10 Ruddy duck, *2017*	15.00	2.50
	With tab	16.00	

NEW HAMPSHIRE

Printed in booklet panes of 1 with 2-part tab and in sheets of 30. Sheet stamps are perf on four sides. Stamps are numbered serially.

Catalogue values for all unused stamps in this section are for Never Hinged items.

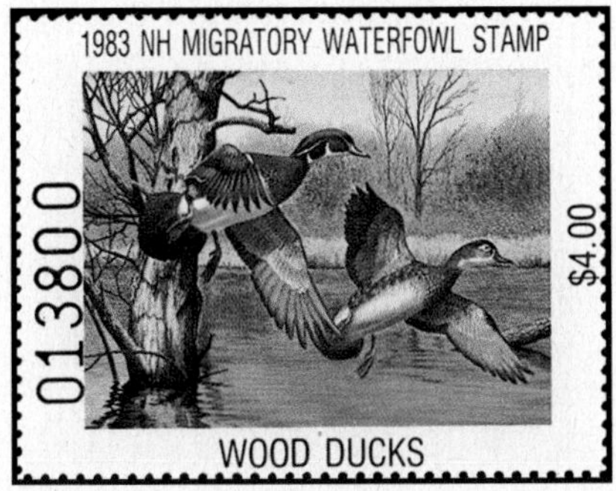

Artists: Richard Plasschaert, #1; Phillip Crowe, #2; Thomas Hirata, #3; Durrant Bell, #4; Robert Steiner, #5-9; Richard Clifton, #10-11, 15; Louis Frisino, #12; Matthew Scharle, #13; Jeffrey Klinefelter, #14; Jim Collins, #16, 20, 23, 24; Bruce Holloway, #17, 21; Susan Knowles Jordan, #18; Charles Freeman, #19; Lindsey Rothe, #22. Kate Kotulak, #25.

1983-2007

1	$4 Wood ducks	110.00	
a.	Booklet single with 2-part tab	135.00	25.00
2	$4 Mallards, *1984*	75.00	
a.	Booklet single with 2-part tab	110.00	20.00
3	$4 Blue-winged teal, *1985*	75.00	
a.	Booklet single with 2-part tab	95.00	20.00
4	$4 Hooded mergansers, *1986*	20.00	
a.	Booklet single with 2-part tab	30.00	6.00
5	$4 Canada geese, *1987*	12.00	
a.	Booklet single with 2-part tab	14.00	4.00
b.	$50 Governor's edition	*200.00*	
6	$4 Buffleheads, *1988*	12.00	
a.	Booklet single with 2-part tab	14.00	3.00
b.	$4 +$46 Governor's edition	50.00	
7	$4 Black ducks, *1989*	11.00	
a.	Booklet single with 2-part tab	12.00	3.00
b.	$4 +$50 Governor's edition	67.50	
8	$4 Green-winged teal, *1990*	11.00	
a.	Booklet single with 2-part tab	12.00	3.00
b.	$4 +$50 Governor's edition	62.50	
9	$4 Golden retriever & mallards, *1991*	15.00	
a.	Booklet single with 2-part tab	17.00	3.00
b.	$4 +$50 Governor's edition	80.00	

Governor's Editions that follow are so inscribed.

10	$4 Ring-necked ducks, *1992*	10.00	
a.	Booklet single with 2-part tab	12.00	3.00
b.	Governor's edition	*275.00*	
11	$4 Hooded mergansers, *1993*	10.00	
a.	Booklet single with 2-part tab	12.00	3.00
b.	Governor's edition	*275.00*	
12	$4 Common goldeneyes, *1994*	10.00	
a.	Bklt. single with 2-part tab	12.00	2.50
b.	Governor's edition	*125.00*	
13	$4 Northern pintails, *1995*	10.00	
a.	Bklt. single with 2-part tab	12.00	2.50
b.	Governor's edition	*100.00*	
14	$4 Surf scooters, *1996*	10.00	
a.	Bklt. single with 2-part tab	12.00	2.50
b.	Governor's edition	100.00	
15	$4 Wood ducks, *1997*	10.00	
a.	Bklt. single with 2-part tab	12.00	2.50
b.	Governor's edition	*125.00*	
16	$4 Canada geese, *1998*	10.00	
a.	Bklt. single with 2-part tab	12.00	2.50
b.	Governor's edition	*130.00*	
17	$4 Mallards, *1999*	11.00	
a.	Bklt. single with 2-part tab	12.00	2.50
b.	Governor's edition	*130.00*	
18	$4 Black ducks, *2000*	11.00	
a.	Bklt. single with 2-part tab	12.00	2.50
b.	Governor's edition	—	
19	$4 Blue-winged teal, *2001*	11.00	
a.	Bklt. single with 2-part tab	12.00	2.50
b.	Governor's edition	—	
20	$4 Pintails, *2002*	8.00	
a.	Bklt. single with 2-part tab	10.00	2.50
b.	Governor's edition	*150.00*	
21	$4 Wood ducks, *2003*	8.00	
a.	Bklt. single with 2-part tab	10.00	2.50
b.	Governor's edition	*125.00*	
22	$4 Wood duck, *2004*	8.00	
a.	Bklt. single with 2-part tab	10.00	2.50
b.	Governor's edition	*125.00*	
23	$4 Old squaws, lighthouse, *2005*	10.00	
a.	Bklt. single with 2-part tab	12.50	
b.	Governor's edition	*125.00*	
24	$4 Common eiders, *2006*	8.00	
a.	Bklt. single with 2-part tab	10.00	2.50
b.	Governor's edition	*125.00*	
25	$4 Black ducks, *2007*	8.00	
a.	Bklt. single with 2-part tab	8.00	2.50
b.	Governor's edition	*125.00*	

NEW JERSEY

Resident and non-resident fees.
Printed in sheets of 30 (starting with No. 1) and booklet panes of 10 (all but Nos. 1A, 2A, 3A, 8b, 8Ad). Sheet stamps are perforated on 4 sides. Stamps are numbered serially.

Catalogue values for all unused stamps in this section are for Never Hinged items.

Artists: Thomas Hirata, #1-1A, 8-8A; David Maass, #2-2A; Ronald Louque, #3-3A; Louis Frisino, #4-4A; Robert Leslie, #5-5A, 9-9A, 14=14A, 25-25A; Daniel Smith, #6-6A; Richard Plasschaert, #7-7A; Bruce Miller, #10-10A; Wilhelm Goebel, #11-11A, 13-13A; Joe Hautman, #12-12A, 17-17A; Phillip Crowe, #15-15A, 21-21A; Richard Clifton, #16-16A; Bob Hautman, #18-18A, 19-19A; Jim Killen, #20-20A; Roger Cruwys, #23-24A.

1984-2008

1	$2.50 Canvasbacks	35.00	
b.	Booklet single, #51,000-102,000	60.00	10.00
1A	$5 Canvasbacks	50.00	10.00
2	$2.50 Mallards, *1985*	15.00	
b.	Booklet single, #51,000-102,000	25.00	6.00
2A	$5 Mallards, *1985*	18.00	5.00
3	$2.50 Pintails, *1986*	15.00	
b.	Booklet single, #51,000-102,000	15.00	3.00
3A	$5 Pintails, *1986*	13.00	3.00
4	$2.50 Canada geese, *1987*	17.00	
b.	Booklet single, #51,000-102,000	17.00	3.00
4A	$5 Canada geese, *1987*	17.00	
c.	Booklet single, #45,001-60,000	17.00	3.00
5	$2.50 Green-winged teal, *1988*	12.00	
b.	Booklet single, #51,000-102,000	12.00	3.00
5A	$5 Green-winged teal, *1988*	12.00	
c.	Booklet single, #45,001-60,000	12.00	3.00
6	$2.50 Snow geese, *1989*	11.00	
b.	Booklet single, #45,001-60,000	11.00	3.00
c.	Governor's edition	*72.50*	
6A	$5 Snow geese, *1989*	11.00	
d.	Booklet single, #45,001-60,000	11.00	3.00
e.	Governor's edition	*140.00*	

Nos. 11b and 12b were available only in sets of sheets of 30 stamps with matching serial numbers through a sealed bid auction.

7	$2.50 Wood ducks, *1990*	12.00	
b.	Booklet single, #45,001-60,000	12.00	3.00
7A	$5 Wood ducks, *1990*	12.00	
c.	Booklet single, #45,001-60,000	12.00	3.00
8	$2.50 Atlantic brant, *1991*	9.00	
b.	Booklet single, #45,001-60,000	9.00	3.00
c.	Atlantic "brandt"	32.50	
8A	$5 Atlantic brant, *1991*	12.00	
d.	Booklet single, #45,001-60,000	12.00	3.00
e.	Atlantic "brandt"	37.50	

Matching serial number sets of Nos. 8c and 8Ae were available for sale only with the purchase of matching serial number sets of Nos. 8 and 8A.

9	$2.50 Bluebills, *1992*	10.00	
b.	Booklet single, #27,691-78,690	10.00	2.50
9A	$5 Bluebills, *1992*	10.00	
c.	Booklet single, #27,691-57,690	10.00	2.50
10	$2.50 Buffleheads, *1993*	10.00	
b.	Booklet single, #27,691-78,690	10.00	2.50
c.	Sheet of 4	*75.00*	
d.	Governor's edition, signed by Florio or Whitman	42.50	
10A	$5 Buffleheads, *1993*	10.00	
e.	Booklet single, #27,691-57,690	10.00	2.50
f.	Sheet of 4	*75.00*	
g.	Governor's edition, signed by Florio or Whitman	82.50	

Nos. 10c and 10Af were available only in sets of sheets with matching serial numbers. The set of sheets sold for $35.

Nos. 10d and 10Ag were available only in sets with matching serial numbers.

11	$2.50 Black ducks, *1994*	12.00	
b.	Bklt. single, perf. 2 or 3 sides	12.00	2.50
11A	$5 Black ducks, *1994*	14.00	
c.	Bklt. single, perf. 2 or 3 sides	14.00	2.50
12	$2.50 Wigeons, lighthouse, *1995*	12.00	
b.	Bklt. single, perf. 3 sides	12.00	2.50
12A	$5 Wigeons, lighthouse, *1995*	14.00	
c.	Bklt. single, perf. 3 sides	14.00	2.50
13	$5 Goldeneyes, lighthouse, *1996*	14.00	
b.	Bklt. single, perf. 2 or 3 sides	14.00	2.50
13A	$10 Goldeneyes, lighthouse, *1996*	16.00	
c.	Bklt. single, perf. 2 or 3 sides	16.00	2.50

The $2.50 was printed but not used as the rate no longer existed. Later they were sold to collectors. Value, unused $10.

14	$5 Old squaws, schooner, *1997*	12.00	
b.	Bklt. single, perf. 2 or 3 sides	12.00	2.50
14A	$10 Old squaws, schooner, *1997*	16.00	
c.	Bklt. single, perf. 2 or 3 sides	16.00	2.50
15	$5 Mallards, *1998*	12.00	
b.	Bklt. single, perf. 2 or 3 sides	12.00	2.50
15A	$10 Mallards, *1998*	15.00	
c.	Bklt. single, perf. 2 or 3 sides	15.00	2.50
16	$5 Redheads, perf. 4 sides, *1999*	12.00	
b.	Bklt. single, perf. 2 or 3 sides	12.00	2.50
16A	$10 Redheads, perf. 4 sides, *1999*	15.00	
c.	Bklt. single, perf. 2 or 3 sides	15.00	2.50
17	$5 Canvasbacks, perf. 4 sides, *2000*	13.00	
b.	Bklt. single, perf. 2 or 3 sides	13.00	2.50
17A	$10 Canvasbacks, perf. 4 sides, *2000*	15.00	
c.	Bklt. single, perf. 2 or 3 sides	15.00	2.50
18	$5 Tundra swans, perf. 4 sides, *2001*	11.00	
b.	Bklt. single, perf. 2 or 3 sides	11.00	2.50
18A	$10 Tundra swans, perf. 4 sides, *2001*	14.00	
c.	Bklt. single, perf. 2 or 3 sides	14.00	2.50
19	$5 Wood ducks, perf. 4 sides, *2002*	11.00	
b.	Bklt. single, perf. 2 or 3 sides	11.00	2.50
19A	$10 Wood ducks, perf. 4 sides, *2002*	14.00	
c.	Bklt. single, perf. 2 or 3 sides	14.00	2.50
20	$5 Pintails, Labrador retriever perf. 4 sides, *2003*	20.00	
b.	Bklt. single, perf. 2 or 3 sides	25.00	2.50
20A	$10 Pintails, Labrador retriever, perf. 4 sides, *2003*	20.00	
c.	Bklt. single, perf. 2 or 3 sides	25.00	2.50
21	$5 Hooded merganser decoy, Labrador retriever, perf. 4 sides, *2004*	10.00	
b.	Bklt. single, perf. 2 or 3 sides	10.00	2.50
21A	$10 Hooded merganser decoy, Labrador retriever, perf. 4 sides, *2004*	15.00	
c.	Bklt. single, perf. 2 or 3 sides	30.00	2.50
22	$5 Canvasback decoys, Chesapeake Bay retriever, perf. 4 sides, *2005*	20.00	
b.	Bklt. single, perf. 2 or 3 sides	15.00	2.50
22A	$10 Canvasback decoys, Chesapeake Bay retriever, perf. 4 sides, *2005*	25.00	
c.	Bklt. single, perf. 2 or 3 sides	17.50	2.50
23	$5 Wood duck decoy, Golden retriever, perf. 4 sides, *2006*	10.00	
b.	Bklt. single, perf. 2 or 3 sides	10.00	2.50
23A	$10 Wood duck decoy, Golden retriever, perf. 4 sides, *2006*	14.00	
c.	Bklt. single, perf. 2 or 3 sides	14.00	2.50
24	$5 Green-winged teal, Labrador retriever, perf. 4 sides, *2007*	8.00	
b.	Bklt. single, perf. 2 or 3 sides	8.00	2.50
24A	$10 Green-winged teal, Labrador retriever, perf. 4 sides, *2007*	14.00	
c.	Bklt. single, perf. 2 or 3 sides	14.00	2.50
25	$5 Canvasbacks, perf. 4 sides, *2008*	8.00	
b.	Bklt. single, perf. 2 or 3 sides	8.00	2.50
25A	$10 Canvasbacks, perf. 4 sides, *2008*	14.00	
c.	Bklt. single, perf. 2 or 3 sides	14.00	2.50

NEW MEXICO

Printed in booklet panes of 5 and sheets of 30. Stamps are numbered serially.

Catalogue values for all unused stamps in this section are for Never Hinged items.

Artist: Robert Steiner.

1991-94

No.	Description	Unused	Used
1	$7.50 Pintails	14.00	
	Booklet single, with large tab and selvage	14.00	5.00
a.	$7.50 +$50 Governor's edition	72.50	
2	$7.50 American wigeon, *1992*	14.00	
	Booklet single, with large tab and selvage	14.00	4.00
a.	$7.50 +$50 Governor's edition	65.00	
3	$7.50 Mallard, *1993*	14.00	
	Booklet single, with large tab and selvage	14.00	4.00
a.	Sheet of 4	60.00	
b.	$7.50 +$50 Governor's edition	65.00	

No. 3a exists imperf. Value, $100.

No. 4: b, Three birds in flight. c, Two birds in flight. d, Two birds flying over land. e, Bird's head close-up.

No.	Description	Unused	Used
4	$7.50 Green-winged teal, sheet of 4, #b.-e., *1994*	95.00	
a.	Souvenir sheet of 4, #b.-e. (decorative border)	195.00	
b.-e.	Bklt. single with large tab and selvage, each	15.00	4.00
f.	Bklt. pane of 4, #b.-e.	85.00	

Stamps in Nos. 4-4a are printed with continuous design and have serial numbers reading down. Stamps in No. 4f have framelines around each design, inscriptions at the top and serial numbers reading up.

No. 4a exists imperf. Value, $225.

NEW YORK

Not required to hunt. Printed in sheets of 30.

Catalogue values for all unused stamps in this section are for Never Hinged items.

Artists: Larry Barton, #1; David Maass, #2; Lee LeBlanc, #3; Richard Plasschaert, #4; Robert Bateman, #5; John Seerey-Lester, #6; Terry Isaac, #7; Anton Ashak, #8; Ron Kleiber, #9; Jerome Hageman, #10; Frederick Szatkowski, #11; Len Rusin, #12; R. Easton, #13; Barbara Woods, #14; Richard Clifton, #15; Rob Leslie, #16; Bruce Miller, #17; Adam Grimm, #18.

1985-2002

No.	Description	Unused	Used
1	$5.50 Canada geese	13.00	
2	$5.50 Mallards, *1986*	9.00	
3	$5.50 Wood ducks, *1987*	9.00	
4	$5.50 Pintails, *1988*	9.00	
5	$5.50 Greater scaup, *1989*	9.00	
6	$5.50 Canvasbacks, *1990*	9.00	
7	$5.50 Redheads, *1991*	11.00	
8	$5.50 Wood ducks, *1992*	11.00	
9	$5.50 Blue-winged teal, *1993*	10.00	
10	$5.50 Canada geese, *1994*	12.00	
11	$5.50 Common goldeneye, *1995*	12.00	
12	$5.50 Common loon, *1996*	11.00	
13	$5.50 Hooded merganser, *1997*	9.00	
14	$5.50 Osprey, *1998*	9.00	
15	$5.50 Buffleheads, *1999*	14.00	
16	$5.50 Wood ducks, *2000*	17.00	
17	$5.50 Pintails, *2001*	9.00	
18	$5.50 Canvasbacks, *2002*	9.00	3.00

NORTH CAROLINA

Not required to hunt until 1988. Printed in sheets of 30. Starting with No. 6, stamps are numbered serially.

Catalogue values for all unused stamps in this section are for Never Hinged items.

Artists: Richard Plasschaert, #1, 10; Jim Killen, #2, 13; Thomas Hirata, #3-4, 16-16A; Larry Barton, #5; Ronald Louque, #6, 18-18A, 19-20A; Louis Frisino, #7; Robert Leslie, #8, 14; Phillip Crowe, #9, 12; Bruce Miller, #11; Wilhelm Goebel, #15-15A, 21-21A; Robert Flowers, #17-17A; Gerald Putt, #25-25A, 27-27A; Scot Storm, #26-26A, 28-28A, 32-32A, 39-39A; Richard Clifton, #29-30A, 35-35A; Jeffrey Klinefelter, #31-31A, 37-37A; Guy Crittenden, #33-33A; Garrett Jacobs, #34-34A, #36-36A; Adam Grimm, #38-38A,

1983-2021

No.	Description	Unused	Used
1	$5.50 Mallards	50.00	
2	$5.50 Wood ducks, *1984*	35.00	
3	$5.50 Canvasbacks, *1985*	25.00	
4	$5.50 Canada geese, *1986*	20.00	
5	$5.50 Pintails, *1987*	15.00	
6	$5 Green-winged teal, *1988*	10.00	3.00
7	$5 Snow geese, *1989*	16.00	3.00
8	$5 Redheads, *1990*	16.00	3.00
9	$5 Blue-winged teals, *1991*	16.00	3.00
10	$5 American wigeons, *1992*	16.00	3.00
11	$5 Tundra swans, *1993*	16.00	3.00
12	$5 Buffleheads, *1994*	16.00	3.00
13	$5 Brant, lighthouse, *1995*	16.00	3.00
14	$5 Pintails, *1996*	16.00	3.00
15	$5 Wood ducks, perf., *1997*	12.00	3.00
15A	$5 Wood ducks, self-adhesive, die cut, *1997*	45.00	
16	$5 Canada geese, perf., *1998*	12.00	3.00
16A	$5 Canada geese, self-adhesive, die cut, *1998*	35.00	
17	$5 Green-winged teal, perf., *1999*	12.00	3.00
17A	$5 Green-winged teal, self-adhesive, die cut, *1999*	25.00	
18	$10 Green-winged teals, perf., *2000*	25.00	3.00
18A	$10 Green-winged teals, self-adhesive, die cut, *2000*	30.00	
19	$10 Black duck, perf., *2001*	17.00	3.00
19A	$10 Black duck, self-adhesive, die cut, *2001*	25.00	
20	$10 Pintails, hunters, dog, perf., *2002*	17.00	3.00
20A	$10 Pintails, hunters, dog, self-adhesive, die cut, *2002*	25.00	
21	$10 Ring-necked ducks, hunters, dog, perf., *2003*	17.00	3.00
21A	$10 Ring-necked ducks, hunters, dog, self-adhesive, die cut, *2003*	35.00	
22	$10 Mallards, perf., *2004*	14.00	3.00
22A	$10 Mallards, self-adhesive, die cut, *2004*	25.00	
23	$10 Green-winged teals, perf., *2005*	14.00	3.00
23A	$10 Green-winged teals, self-adhesive, die cut, *2005*	20.00	
24	$10 Lesser scaups, perf., *2006*	14.00	3.00
24A	$10 Lesser scaups, self-adhesive, die cut, *2006*	15.00	
25	$10 Wood ducks, perf., *2007*	15.00	3.00
25A	$10 Wood ducks, self-adhesive, die cut, *2007*	15.00	
26	$10 Surf scoters, perf., *2008*	15.00	3.00
26A	$10 Surf scoters, self-adhesive, die cut, *2008*	15.00	
27	$10 Wigeons, perf., *2009*	15.00	3.00
27A	$10 Wigeons, self-adhesive, die cut, *2009*	15.00	
28	$10 Snow geese, perf., *2010*	15.00	3.00
28A	$10 Snow geese, self-adhesive, die cut, *2010*	15.00	
29	$10 Canada geese, perf., *2011*	15.00	3.00
29A	$10 Canada geese, self-adhesive, die cut, *2011*	15.00	
30	$10 Redheads, perf., *2012*	15.00	3.00
30A	$10 Redheads, self-adhesive, die cut, *2012*	15.00	
31	$10 Shovelers, perf., *2013*	15.00	3.00
31A	$10 Shovelers, self-adhesive, die cut *2013*	15.00	
32	$10 Hooded mergansers, perf., *2014*	15.00	3.00
32A	$10 Hooded mergansers, self-adhesive, die cut *2014*	15.00	
33	$10 Black ducks, perf., *2015*	15.00	3.00
33A	$10 Black ducks, self-adhesive, die cut, *2015*	15.00	
34	$13 Atlantic brant and lighthouse, perf., *2016*	20.00	3.00
34A	$13 Atlantic brant and lighthouse, self-adhesive, die cut, *2016*	20.00	
35	$13 Gadwalls, perf., *2017*	20.00	3.00
35A	$13 Gadwalls, self-adhesive, die cut, *2017*	20.00	
36	$13 Canvasbacks, perf., *2018*	16.50	2.50
36A	$13 Canvasbacks, self-adhesive, die cut, *2018*	16.50	
37	$13 Ring-necked ducks, perf., *2019*	16.50	2.50
37A	$13 Ring-necked ducks, self-adhesive, die cut, *2019*	16.50	
38	$14 Tundra swans, perf., *2020*	17.50	2.50
38A	$14 Tundra swans, self-adhesive, die cut, *2020*	17.50	
39	$14 Blue-winged teals, perf., *2021*	17.50	2.50
39A	$14 Blue-winged teals, self-adhesive, die cut, *2021*	17.50	

Nos. 21-39A not required for hunting.

NORTH DAKOTA

Small Game Hunting Stamps

Required to hunt small game and waterfowl statewide. Resident and non-resident fees.

Values for 1967-70 non-resident stamps are for examples with staple holes.

Used values are for signed stamps. Unused values for Nos. 12, 16, 18, 20, 22, 24, 26 and 28 are for stamps on backing.

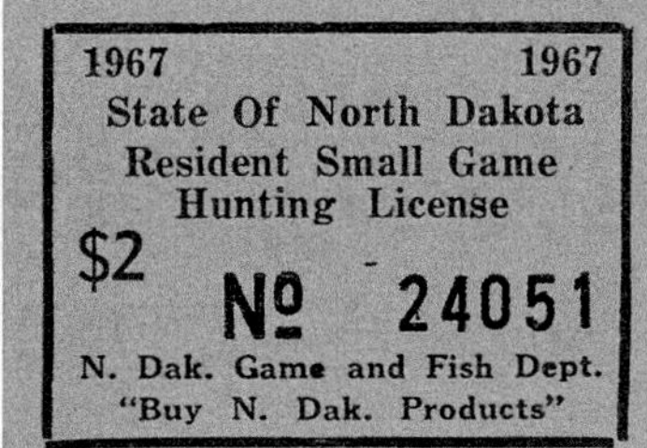

1967-80

No.	Description	Unused	Used
1	$2 black, *green*	*950.00*	60.00
2	$25 black, *green*	*7,500.*	*350.00*
3	$2 black, *pink, 1968*	200.00	20.00
4	$25 black, *yellow, 1968*	*500.00*	*50.00*
5	$2 black, *green, 1969*	190.00	20.00
6	$35 black, *1969*	*450.00*	*50.00*
7	$2 blue, *1970*	160.00	15.00
8	$35 black, *pink, 1970*	*250.00*	*50.00*
9	$2 black, *yellow, 1971*	125.00	10.00
10	$35 black, *1971*		*350.00*
11	$3 black, *pink, 1972*	65.00	5.00
12	$35 red, *1972*	*325.00*	*75.00*
13	$3 black, *yellow, 1973*	65.00	5.00
14	$35 green, *1973*	*2,750.*	*300.00*
15	$3 black, *blue, 1974*	125.00	15.00
16	$35 red, *1974*	*450.00*	*50.00*
17	$3 black, *1975*	95.00	10.00
18	$35 green, *1975*	*225.00*	*40.00*
19	$3 black, *dark yellow, 1976*	55.00	5.00
20	$35 red, *1976*	*125.00*	25.00
21	$3 black, *1977*	90.00	10.00
22	$35 red, *1977*	*100.00*	25.00
23	$5 black, *1978*	45.00	5.00
24	$40 red, *1978*	85.00	20.00
25	$5 black, *1979*	35.00	5.00
26	$40 red, *1979*	45.00	15.00
27	$5 black, *1980*	35.00	5.00
28	$40 green, *1980*	45.00	15.00

Small Game and Habitat Stamps

Required to hunt small game and waterfowl statewide.

Resident ($9), youth ($6) and non-resident ($53) fees.

Resident stamps issued in booklet panes of 5 numbered 20,001-150,000 (1982-86 issues) or 20,001-140,000 (starting with 1987 issue) or sheets of 30 numbered 150,001 and up (1982-86 issues) or 140,001 and up (starting with 1987 issue).

Starting with 1984, resident booklet stamps have straight edges at sides.

Nos. 31, 34, 37, 40 are die cut self adhesives.

Unused values are for stamps on backing.

All youth stamps were issued in booklet panes of 5. Non-resident stamps for 1981, 1982, 1996 and following years were issued in booklet panes of 5.

The 1984-95 non-resident stamps were issued se-tenant with non-resident waterfowl and non-resident general game stamps (rouletted on three sides). The 1994 and 1995 non-resident stamps also were issued se-tenant with only the non-resident general game stamp (rouletted at sides), as well as in booklet panes of 5 (rouletted top and bottom).

Catalogue values for all unused stamps in this section, from this point to the end, are for Never Hinged items.

1981 1981
State of North Dakota
RESIDENT SMALL GAME LICENSE - $6.00
AND HABITAT LICENSE - $3.00
№ 828
N.D. Game and Fish Dept.
NON-TRANSFERABLE

A1

1981

29 A1 $9 black 35.00 3.00
30 A1 $6 black, *blue green* *175.00* 25.00
31 A1 $53 blue 110.00 20.00

A2

Artists: Richard Plaschaert, #32, 73; Terry Radlin, #35; David Maass, #38; Leslie Kouba, #41; Mario Fernandez, #44; Ronald Louque, #47, 75; Louis Frisino, #50; Robert Leslie, #53; Roger Cruwys, #56; Thomas Hirata, #59; Phillip Crowe, #62, 77, 81; Bruce Miller, #65; Darrell Davis, #67; Richard Clifton, #69; Wilhelm Goebel, #71; Jeffrey Klinefelter, #79.

1982

32 A2 $9 Canada geese 85.00
Booklet single with L & R selvage *450.00* 25.00

Serial numbers 1-20,000 are from sheets of 10. Stamps without selvage from booklets sell for considerably less.

33 A1 $6 black, *blue* *175.00* 25.00
34 A1 $53 black 35.00 15.00

1983

35 A2 $9 Mallards 55.00
Booklet single with L & R selvage *1,000.* 25.00

Serial numbers 1-20,000 are from sheets. Stamps without selvage from booklets sell for considerably less.

36 A1 $6 black, *orange* 25.00
37 A1 $53 black *40.00*

1984

38 A2 $9 Canvasbacks 30.00
a. Booklet single, perforated horiz. on 1 or 2 sides *1,250.* 25.00
39 A1 $6 black, *light blue* 25.00
40 A1 $53 black *40.00*

1985

41 A2 $9 Greater scaup 20.00
a. Booklet single, perforated horiz. on 1 or 2 sides *3,250.* 25.00
42 A1 $6 black, *light blue* 25.00
43 A1 $53 black *40.00*

1986

44 A2 $9 Pintails 18.00
a. Booklet single, perforated horiz. on 1 or 2 sides *175.00* 20.00
45 A1 $6 black, *light blue* 25.00
46 A1 $53 black *35.00*

1987

47 A2 $9 Snow geese 15.00
a. Booklet single, perforated horiz. on 1 or 2 sides *45.00* 18.00
48 A1 $6 black, *light blue* — 25.00
49 A1 $53 black *30.00*

1988

50 A2 $9 White-winged scoters 13.00
a. Booklet single, perforated horiz. on 1 or 2 sides 30.00 12.00
51 A1 $6 black, *light blue* — 25.00
52 A1 $53 black *45.00*

Stamps Inscribed "Small Game"

Resident ($6), youth ($3) and non-resident ($50, $75) fees.

1989

53 A2 $6 Redheads 10.00
a. Booklet single, perforated horiz. on 1 or 2 sides 15.00 8.00
54 A1 $3 black, *light blue* — 25.00
55 A1 $50 black 30.00

1990

56 A2 $6 Labrador retriever & mallard 10.00
a. Booklet single, perforated horiz. on 1 or 2 sides 15.00 8.00
57 A1 $3 black, *light blue* 200.00 25.00
58 A1 $50 black 25.00

1991

59 A2 $6 Green-winged teal 9.00
a. Booklet single, perforated horiz. on 1 or 2 sides 13.00 6.00
60 A1 $3 black, *light blue* 200.00 25.00
61 A1 $50 black *350.00* 25.00

1992

62 A2 $6 Blue-winged teal 9.00
a. Booklet single, perforated horiz. on 1 or 2 sides 13.00 6.00
63 A1 $3 black, *light blue* 325.00
64 A1 $50 black 25.00

When supplies of No. 64 ran out, No. 58 was used with the date changed by hand. Unused examples exist. Value, $300.

1993

65 A2 $6 Wood ducks 9.00
a. Booklet single, perforated horiz. on 1 or 2 sides 13.00 6.00
66 A1 $50 black *550.00* 25.00

1994

67 A2 $6 Canada geese 9.00
a. Booklet single, perforated horiz. on 1 or 2 sides 10.00 6.00
68 A1 $75 black, rouletted on 2 adjacent sides *400.00* 20.00
a. Booklet single, rouletted top and bottom —

1995

69 A2 $6 Wigeon 9.00
a. Booklet single, perforated horiz. on 1 or 2 sides 10.00 5.00
70 A1 $75 black, rouletted on 2 adjacent sides *350.00* 20.00
a. Booklet single, rouletted top and bottom —

1996

71 A2 $6 Mallards 9.00
a. Booklet single, perforated horiz. on 1 or 2 sides 10.00 2.50
72 A1 $75 black, rouletted at top and bottom —

1997

73 A2 $6 White-fronted geese 9.00
a. Booklet single, perforated horiz. on 1 or 2 sides 10.00 2.50
74 A1 $75 black, rouletted at top and bottom —

1998

75 A2 $6 Blue-winged teal 9.00
a. Bklt. single, perforated horiz. on 1 or 2 sides 10.00 2.50
76 A1 $75 black, rouletted at top and bottom —

1999

77 A2 $6 Gadwalls 9.00
a. Bklt. single, perforated horiz. on 1 or 2 sides 10.00 2.50
78 A1 $75 black, rouletted at top and bottom —

2000-01

79 $6 Pintails, *2000* 9.00
a. Bklt. single, perforated horiz. on 1 or 2 sides 10.00 2.50
81 A2 $6 Canada geese, *2001* 10.00
a. Bklt. single, perforated horiz. on 1 or 2 sides 10.00 2.50

Expires June 30, 2003
State of North Dakota
Resident Small Game
$6.00
№ 105573
N.D. Game and Fish Dept.
NON-TRANSFERABLE

A3

2002-15

83 A3 $6 black, *green, 2002* 12.00
84 A3 $6 black, *green, 2003* 12.00
85 A3 $6 black, *green, 2004* 12.00
86 A3 $6 black, *green, 2005* 12.00
87 A3 $6 black, *green, 2006* 9.00
88 A3 $6 black, *green, 2007* 9.00
89 A3 $6 black, *green, 2008* 9.00
90 A3 $6 black, *green, 2009* 9.00
91 A3 $6 black, *green, 2010* 9.00
92 A3 $6 black, *green, 2011* 9.00
93 A3 $6 black, *green, 2012* 9.00
94 A3 $6 black, *green, 2013* 9.00
95 A3 $10 black, *green, 2014* 13.00
96 A3 $10 black, *green, 2015* 13.00

Non-Resident Waterfowl Stamps

Required by non-residents to hunt waterfowl only. Unused examples of Nos. A1a, A13a-A19a have no serial number. Used stamps have number written in. Nos. A1-A10 are self-adhesive, die cut. Others are rouletted.

Catalogue values for all unused stamps in this section are for Never Hinged items.

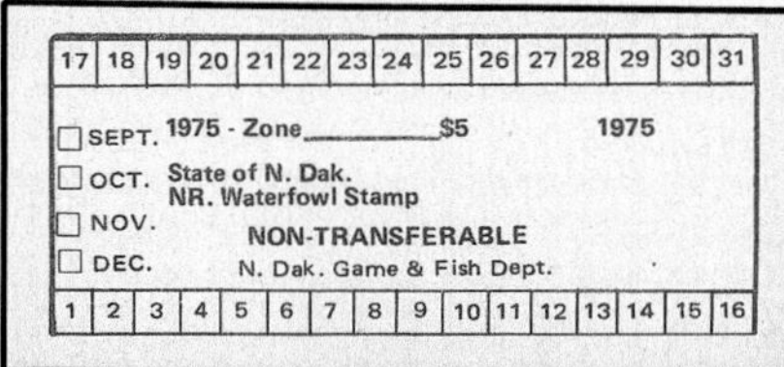

No. A1a

17 18 19 20 21 22 23 24 25 26 27 28 29 30 31
SEPT. 1976 - Zone $5 1976
OCT. State of N. Dak. NR. Waterfowl Stamp № 6355
NOV. NON-TRANSFERABLE
DEC. N. Dak. Game & Fish Dept.
1 2 3 4 5 6 7 8 9 10 11 12 13 14 15 16

No. A2

Illustration reduced.

1975-99

A1 $5 green *225.00*
a. No serial number *225.00* —
A2 $5 red, *1976* *450.00* *100.00*
A3 $5 red, *1977* *250.00* *75.00*
A4 $5 red, *1978* 110.00 25.00
A5 $5 red, *1979* 85.00 20.00
A6 $5 green, *1980* 90.00 20.00
A7 $8 blue, *1981* 225.00 25.00
A8 $8 black, *1982* 35.00 15.00
A9 $8 black, *1983* *65.00*
A10 $8 black, *1984* *65.00*
A11 $8 black, *1985* *65.00*
A12 $8 black, *1986* *55.00*
A13 $8 black, *1987* *50.00*
a. No serial number *650.00* *50.00*
A14 $8 black, *1988* 35.00
a. No serial number *550.00* *50.00*
A15 $8 black, *1989* 550.00 25.00
a. No serial number, light green paper *450.00* *50.00*
A16 $8 black, *1990* 25.00
a. No serial number *425.00* *50.00*
A17 $8 black, *1991* *500.00* 25.00
a. No serial number 350.00 *35.00*
A18 $8 black, *1992* 20.00
a. No serial number *300.00* 35.00

When supplies of No. A18 ran out, No. A16 was used with the date changed by hand. Values, unused $250, used $50.

A19 $10 black, *1993* *450.00* 20.00
a. No serial number *350.00* 30.00
A20 $10 black, rouletted on 2 adjacent sides, *1994* *450.00* 20.00
a. No serial number, rouletted top and bottom 350.00 30.00
A21 $10 black, rouletted on 2 adjacent sides, *1995* *400.00* 20.00
a. No serial number, rouletted top and bottom 175.00 25.00
A22 $10 black, rouletted top and bottom, *1996* *110.00* 20.00
A23 $10 black, rouletted top and bottom, *1997* *100.00* 12.00
A24 $10 black, rouletted top and bottom, *1998* *90.00* 10.00
A25 $10 black, rouletted top and bottom, *1999* *80.00* 10.00
A26 $10 black, rouletted top and bottom, *2000* *70.00* 10.00
A27 $10 black, rouletted top and bottom, *2001* *60.00* 10.00
A28 $10 black, rouletted top and bottom, *2002* *50.00* 10.00

Resident Sportsmen's Stamps

Required to hunt a variety of game, including waterfowl.

Catalogue values for all unused stamps in this section are for Never Hinged items.

1992-2005

2A1	$25 black & purple, *1992-1993*	*3,250.*	*95.00*
2A2	$25 black & purple, *1993-1994*	*1,750.*	*35.00*
2A3	$25 black & purple, *1994-1995*	*450.00*	*25.00*
2A4	$25 black & purple, *1995-1996*	*375.00*	*20.00*
2A5	$25 black & purple, *1996-1997*	*300.00*	*15.00*
2A6	$27 black & purple, *1997-1998*	*150.00*	*12.00*
2A7	$27 black & purple, *1998-1999*	*110.00*	*12.00*
a.	Missing serial number	—	
2A8	$27 black & purple, *1999-2000*	*125.00*	*12.00*
2A9	$27 black & purple, *2000-2001*	*90.00*	*12.00*
2A10	$27 black & purple, *2001-2002*	*90.00*	*12.00*
2A11	$27 black & purple, *2002-2003*	*95.00*	*12.00*
2A12	$27 black & purple, *2003-2004*	*85.00*	*12.00*
2A13	$32 black & purple, *2004-2005*	*95.00*	*12.00*
2A14	$32 black & purple, *2005-2006*	*95.00*	*12.00*

Resident Combination Licenses

2006-15

2A15	$32 black & purple, *2006-2007*	*95.00*	*12.00*
2A16	$32 black & purple, *2007-2008*	*95.00*	*12.00*
2A17	$32 black & purple, *2008-2009*	*95.00*	*12.00*
2A18	$32 black & purple, *2009-2010*	*95.00*	*12.00*
2A19	$32 black & purple, *2010-2011*	*95.00*	*12.00*
2A20	$32 black & purple, *2011-2012*	*95.00*	*12.00*
2A21	$32 black & purple, *2012-2013*	*85.00*	*12.00*
2A22	$32 black & purple, *2013-2014*	*75.00*	*12.00*
2A23	$50 black & purple, *2014-2015*	*80.00*	*10.00*
2A24	$50 black & purple, *2015-2016*	*80.00*	*10.00*

General Game Stamps

Required to hunt a variety of game, including waterfowl.

Catalogue values for all unused stamps in this section are for Never Hinged items.

A7

A8

A9

A10

A11

A12

1983

3A1	A7	$3 black	—	*20.00*
3A2	A8	$3 black, die cut, self-adhesive	—	*35.00*

1984

3A3	A9	$3 Sharp-tailed grouse	*20.00*	
		Booklet single, perforated horiz. on 1 or 2 sides	125.00	15.00

1984-85

3A4	A8	$3 black, die cut, self-adhesive	—	*35.00*

1985

3A5	A9	$3 Ruffed grouse	*18.00*	
		Booklet single, perforated horiz. on 1 or 2 sides	125.00	15.00

1985-86

3A6	A8	$3 black	—	*35.00*

1986

3A7	A9	$3 Male sage grouse	*16.00*	
		Booklet single, perforated horiz. on 1 or 2 sides	100.00	15.00

1986-87

3A8	A8	$3 black	—	*35.00*
3A8A	A10	$3 black, *orange*	—	*25.00*

1987

3A9	A9	$3 Prairie chicken	*15.00*	
		Booklet single, perforated horiz. on 1 or 2 sides	80.00	15.00

1987-88

3A10	A8	$3 black	—	*35.00*
3A10A	A10	$3 black, *orange*	—	*25.00*

1988

3A11	A9	$3 Hungarian partridge	*10.00*	
		Booklet single, perforated horiz. on 1 or 2 sides	55.00	13.00

1988-89

3A12	A8	$3 black	—	*35.00*
3A12A	A10	$3 black, *orange*	*165.00*	*15.00*

1989

3A13	A9	$6 Pheasants	*9.00*	
		Booklet single, perforated horiz. on 1 or 2 sides	35.00	7.00

1989-90

3A14	A11	$6 black	—	*25.00*
3A14A	A12	$6 black, *orange*	*135.00*	*13.00*

1990

3A15	A9	$6 Sandhill crane	*8.00*	
		Booklet single, perforated horiz. on 1 or 2 sides	28.00	6.00

1990-91

3A16	A11	$6 black	—	*25.00*
3A16A	A12	$6 black, *orange*	*135.00*	*13.00*

1991

3A17	A9	$6 Mourning dove	*9.00*	
		Booklet single, perforated horiz. on 1 or 2 sides	25.00	6.00

1991-92

3A18	A11	$6 black	—	*20.00*
3A18A	A12	$6 black, *orange*	*100.00*	*11.00*

1992

3A19	A9	$6 Antelope	*8.00*	
		Booklet single, perforated horiz. on 1 or 2 sides	18.00	5.00

1992-93

3A20	A11	$6 black	—	*20.00*
3A20A	A12	$6 black, *orange*	*95.00*	*9.00*

A13

1993-94

3A21	A13	$6 black, *gray*	*25.00*	*5.00*
3A22	A11	$6 black	—	*20.00*
3A22A	A12	$6 black, *orange*	*90.00*	*8.00*

1994-95

3A23	A13	$6 black	*22.00*	*4.00*
3A24	A11	$6 black	—	*15.00*
3A24A	A12	$6 black, *orange*	*75.00*	*7.00*

1995-96

3A25	A13	$6 black, *gray*	*20.00*	*4.00*
3A26	A11	$6 black	—	*15.00*
3A26A	A12	$6 black, *orange*	*50.00*	*5.00*

1996-97

3A27	A13	$6 black, *gray*	*18.00*	*3.00*
3A28	A12	$6 black, *orange*	*20.00*	*4.00*

1997-98

3A29	A13	$8 black, *gray*	*15.00*	*2.00*
3A30	A12	$8 black, *orange*	*18.00*	*3.00*

1998-99

3A31	A13	$8 black, *gray*	*15.00*	*2.00*
3A32	A12	$8 black, *orange*	*18.00*	*3.00*

1999-2000

3A33	A13	$8 black, *gray*	*15.00*	*2.00*
3A34	A12	$8 black, *orange*	*18.00*	*3.00*

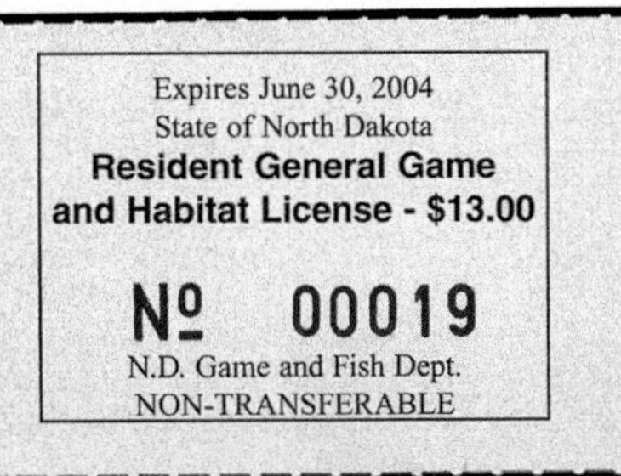

A14

A15

2000-01

3A35	A14 $8 black, *gray*		*15.00*	*2.00*
3A36	A15 $8 black, *orange*		*18.00*	*3.00*

2001-02

3A37	A14 $8 black, *gray*	*15.00*	*2.00*
3A38	A15 $8 black, *orange*	*18.00*	*3.00*

2002-03

3A39	A14 $13 black, *gray*	*18.00*	*2.00*
3A40	A15 $13 black, *orange*	*20.00*	*3.00*

2003-04

3A41	A14 $13 black, *gray*	*18.00*	*2.00*
3A42	A15 $13 black, *orange*	*20.00*	*3.00*

2004-05

3A43	A14 $13 black, *gray*	*18.00*	*2.00*
3A44	A15 $13 black, *orange*	*20.00*	*3.00*

2005-06

3A45	A14 $13 black, *gray*	*18.00*	*2.00*
3A46	A15 $13 black, *orange*	*20.00*	*3.00*

2006-07

3A47	A14 $13 black, *gray*	*18.00*	*2.00*
3A48	A15 $13 black, *orange*	*20.00*	*3.00*

2007-08

3A49	A14 $13 black, *gray*	*18.00*	*2.00*
3A50	A15 $13 black, *orange*	*20.00*	*3.00*

2008-09

3A51	A14 $13 black, *gray*	*18.00*	*2.00*
3A52	A15 $13 black, *orange*	*20.00*	*3.00*

2009-10

3A53	A14 $13 black, *gray*	*18.00*	*2.00*
3A54	A15 $13 black, *orange*	*20.00*	*3.00*

2010-11

3A55	A14 $13 black, *gray*	*18.00*	*2.00*
3A56	A15 $13 black, *orange*	*20.00*	*3.00*

2011-12

3A57	A14 $13 black, *gray*	*18.00*	*2.00*
3A58	A15 $13 black, *orange*	*20.00*	*3.00*

2012-13

3A59	A14 $13 black, *gray*	*18.00*	*2.00*
3A60	A15 $13 black, *orange*	*20.00*	*3.00*

2013-14

3A61	A14 $13 black, *gray*	*18.00*	*2.00*
3A62	A15 $13 black, *orange*	*20.00*	*3.00*

2014-15

3A63	A14 $20 black, *gray*	*25.00*	*2.00*
3A64	A15 $20 black, *orange*	*27.00*	*3.00*

2015-16

3A65	A14 $20 black, *gray*	*25.00*	*2.00*
3A66	A15 $20 black, *orange*	*27.00*	*3.00*

OHIO

Pymatuning Lake Waterfowl Hunting Stamps

Pymatuning Hunting License
Valid when attached to Resident Hunters and Trappers License. Authority H. B. 668.
YEAR 1938 $1.00 NO FEE

1938-45

A1	$1 black, *light yellow*	—
A2	$1 black, *gray, 1939*	—
A3	$1 black, *blue, 1940*	—
A4	$1 black, *pink, 1941*	—
A5	$1 black, *green, 1942*	—
A6	$1 black, *1943*	—
A7	$1 black, *manila, 1944*	—
A8	$1 black, *manila, 1945*	—

Statewide Issues

Nos. 1-18 printed in sheets of 16. Starting with No. 19, stamps are printed in souvenir sheets of 1.

Catalogue values for all unused stamps in this section are for Never Hinged items.

Artists: John Ruthven, #1; Harry Antis, #2; Harold Roe, #3, 6, 15, 17; Ronald Louque, #4; Lynn Kaatz, #5, 8; Cynthie Fisher, #7; Jon Henson, #9; Gregory Clair, #10, 25; Samuel Timm, #11; Kenneth Nanney, #12; Richard Clifton, #13, 26; Ron Kleiber, #14; D. J. Cleland-Hura, #16: Timothy Donovan, #18; Mark Anderson, #19; Brian Blight, #20, 22; Jeffrey Klinefelter, #21, 27, 32, 36, 39; Robert Mertopulos, #23; Adam Grimm, #24, 33, 40; Joel Rogers, #28, 30; Jeffrey Hoff, #29; Tom Morgan Crain, #31; Gunnar Hillard, #34; Christine Clayton, #35; Daniel Allard, #37; Jocelyn Beatty, #38.

1982-2021

1	$5.75 Wood ducks	50.00	10.00
2	$5.75 Mallards, *1983*	35.00	10.00
3	$5.75 Green-winged teal, *1984*	35.00	8.00
4	$5.75 Redheads, *1985*	25.00	6.00
5	$5.75 Canvasback, *1986*	25.00	5.00
6	$6 Blue-winged teal, *1987*	12.00	4.00
7	$6 Common goldeneyes, *1988*	12.00	4.00
8	$6 Canada geese, *1989*	12.00	3.00
9	$9 Black ducks, *1990*	16.00	3.00
10	$9 Lesser scaup, *1991*	16.00	3.00
11	$9 Wood duck, *1992*	16.00	3.00
12	$9 Buffleheads, *1993*	16.00	3.00
13	$11 Mallards, *1994*	21.00	2.50
14	$11 Pintails, *1995*	22.50	2.50
15	$11 Hooded mergansers, *1996*	24.00	2.50
16	$11 Wigeons, *1997*	20.00	2.50
17	$11 Gadwall, *1998*	20.00	2.50
18	$11 Mallard, *1999*	18.00	2.50

Souvenir Sheet

Rouletted

19	$11 Buffleheads, *2000*	25.00	2.50
20	$11 Canvasback, *2001*	22.50	2.50
21	$11 Ring-necked ducks, *2002*	22.50	2.50
22	$11 Hooded mergansers, *2003*	22.50	2.50
23	$15 Tundra swans, *2004*	25.00	2.50
24	$15 Wood duck, *2005*	22.50	2.50
25	$15 Pintail, *2006*	27.50	2.50
26	$15 Canada goose, *2007*	45.00	2.50
27	$15 Green-winged teal, *2008*	22.50	2.50
28	$15 Common goldeneye, *2009*	22.50	2.50
29	$15 Ruddy ducks, *2010*	22.50	2.50
30	$15 Red-breasted merganser, *2011*	40.00	2.50
31	$15 Mallards, *2012*	22.50	2.50
32	$15 Blue-winged teal, *2013*	22.50	2.50
33	$15 Pintail, *2014*	22.50	2.50
34	$15 Shovelers, *2015*	22.50	2.50
35	$15 Wood ducks, *2016*	22.50	2.50
36	$15 Wigeons, *2017*	22.50	2.50
37	$15 Ring-necked ducks, *2018*	19.00	2.50
38	$15 Redheads, *2019*	19.00	2.50
39	$15 Black duck, *2020*	19.00	2.50
40	$15 Mallard, *2021*	19.00	2.50

Nos. 19-40 not required for hunting.

OKLAHOMA

Printed in booklet panes of 10 (Nos. 1-3) and booklet panes of 5 (Starting with No. 4). No. 10 was the first to be printed in a sheet of 30, No. 17 in a sheet of 24.

Catalogue values for all unused stamps in this section are for Never Hinged items.

Artists: Patrick Sawyer, #1; Hoyt Smith, #2, 5, 7, 20; Jeffrey Frey, #3; Gerald Mobley, #4, 6; Rayburn Foster, #8, 12; Jim Gaar, #9; Wanda Mumm, #10; Ronald Louque, #11; Jeffrey Mobley, #13; Jerome Hageman, #14; Richard Kirkman, #15; Richard Clifton, #16, 33; Greg Everhart, #17; Mark Anderson, #18, 24, 38; Jeffrey Klinefelter, #19, 26; Paul Makuchal, #21; Daniel Brevick, #22; Brian Blight, #23; Scot Storm, #25; James Hublick, #27. Jeffrey Hoff, #28; Russell Duerksen, #29; Timothy Turenne, #30; John Brennan, #31, 34; George Lockwood, #32; Shea Meyer, #35; Guy Crittenden, #36; Adam Oswald, #37; Paul Bridgford, #39; John Nelson Harris, #40; Anthony J. Padgett, #41; Kelly Kadlec, #42.

1980-2021

1	$4 Pintails	50.00	10.00
2	$4 Canada goose, *1981*	25.00	8.00
3	$4 Green-winged teal, *1982*	10.00	4.00
4	$4 Wood ducks, *1983*	10.00	10.00
5	$4 Ring-necked ducks, *1984*	10.00	3.00
	With tab	10.00	
6	$4 Mallards, *1985*	8.00	3.00
	With tab	10.00	
7	$4 Snow geese, *1986*	10.00	3.00
	With tab	10.00	
8	$4 Canvasbacks, *1987*	8.00	3.00
	With tab	9.00	
9	$4 Wigeons, *1988*	8.00	3.00
	With tab	9.00	
10	$4 Redheads, *1989*	8.00	3.00
	Booklet single, with tab & selvage at L, selvage at R	9.00	
a.	Governor's edition	*125.00*	

No. 10a was available only in sheets of 30 through a sealed bid auction.

11	$4 Hooded merganser, *1990*	7.50	3.00
	Booklet single, with tab & selvage at L, selvage at R	8.50	
12	$4 Gadwalls, *1991*	7.50	3.00
	Booklet single, with tab & selvage at L, selvage at R	8.50	
13	$4 Lesser scaup, *1992*	7.50	3.00
	Booklet single, with tab & selvage at L, selvage at R	8.50	
14	$4 White-fronted geese, *1993*	7.50	3.00
	Booklet single, with tab & selvage at L, selvage at R	8.50	
15	$4 Blue-winged teal, *1994*	7.50	3.00
	Booklet single, with tab & selvage at L, selvage at R	8.50	
16	$4 Ruddy ducks, *1995*	7.50	3.00
	Booklet single, with tab & selvage at L, selvage at R	8.50	
17	$4 Bufflehead, *1996*	7.50	3.00
	Booklet single, with selvage at L & R	8.50	
18	$4 Goldeneyes, *1997*	7.50	3.00
	Bklt. single, with selvage at L & R	8.50	
19	$4 Shovelers, *1998*	7.50	3.00
	Bklt. single, with selvage at L & R	8.50	
20	$4 Canvasbacks, *1999*	17.50	3.00
21	$4 Pintails, *2000*	8.00	3.00
22	$4 Canada goose, *2001*	8.00	3.00
23	$4 Green-winged teal, *2002*	8.00	3.00
24	$10 Wood duck, *2003*	15.00	3.00
25	$10 Mallard, *2004*	15.00	3.00
26	$10 Snow geese, *2005*	15.00	3.00
27	$10 Wigeons, *2006*	15.00	3.00
28	$10 Redheads, *2007*	15.00	3.00
29	$10 Mallards, Labrador retriever, *2008*	15.00	3.00
30	$10 Gadwalls, *2009*	15.00	3.00
31	$10 Ring-necked duck, *2010*	15.00	3.00
32	$10 Blue-winged teal, *2011*	15.00	3.00
33	$10 White-fronted goose, *2012*	15.00	3.00
34	$10 Common goldeneye, *2013*	15.00	3.00
35	$10 Canvasback, *2014*	15.00	3.00
36	$10 Pintails, *2015*	15.00	3.00

37 $10 Mallard, *2016* 15.00 3.00
38 $10 Green-winged teal, *2017* 15.00 3.00
39 $10 Shovelers, *2018* 15.00 3.00
40 $10 Wood duck, *2019* 14.00 3.00
41 $10 Canada geese, *2020* 14.00 3.00
42 $10 Wigeons, *2021* 14.00 3.00

OREGON

Non-resident fees begin in 1994.
Issued in sheets of 30, except for No. 6. Nos. 2-4 also exist from booklet panes of 5.
Stamps are numbered serially. Nos. 11b, 11c have serial numbers on sheet selvage.
Nos. 10 and 11 were issued on computer form. Unused values are for stamps on form.

Catalogue values for all unused stamps in this section are for Never Hinged items.

Artists: Michael Sieve, #1-3; Dorothy M. Smith, #4; Darrell Davis, #5; Phillip Crowe, #7; Roger Cruwys, #8; Louis Frisino, #9; Kip Richmond, #10; R. Bruce Horsfall, #11; Richard Plasschaert, #12-13; Robert Steiner, #14-37; Harold Cramer Smith, #38; Tim Turene, #39; Robert Andrea, #40; Richard Clifton, #41-42; Guy Crittenden, #43, 45; Jeffrey Klinefelter, #44.

1984-88

1 $5 Canada geese 20.00 7.00
2 $5 Lesser snow goose, *1985* 25.00 10.00
Booklet single, with 3 tabs (2 at left) *350.00*
3 $5 Pacific brant, perf. 4 sides, *1986* 15.00
a. Booklet single, with 2-part tab 15.00 4.00
4 $5 White-fronted geese, perf. 4 sides, *1987* 15.00
a. Booklet single, with 2-part tab 15.00 3.00
5 $5 Great Basin Canada geese, *1988* 15.00 3.00
a. Booklet pane of 1 15.00

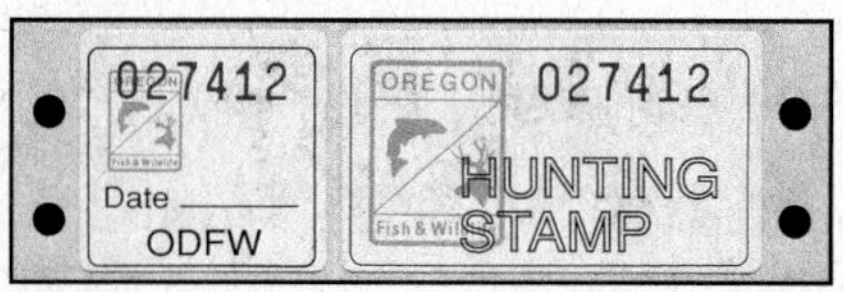

1989-2021 **Die cut self-adhesive**

6 ($5) Red Nos., 16,001 and up 15.00 *6.00*
a. Black Nos., 001-16,000 30.00 *12.50*

This provisional stamp was used in early 1989, when the regular stamps were delayed. Unused value is for stamp and adjacent label with serial number on backing paper.

Designs like No. 1

7 $5 Black Labrador retriever & pintails, *1989* 15.00 2.50
a. Booklet pane of 1 15.00
8 $5 Mallards & golden retriever, *1990* 15.00 2.50
a. Booklet pane of 1 15.00
9 $5 Buffleheads & Chesapeake Bay retriever, perf, *1991* 15.00
a. Rouletted at L 15.00 2.50

No. 9a is straight edged on 3 sides and stamp is attached to paper by selvage. Unused value is for stamp attached to paper.

10 $5 Green-winged teal, *1992* 15.00
a. Die cut, self-adhesive 15.00 2.50
11 $5 Mallards, vert., *1993* 15.00
a. Die cut self-adhesive 15.00 2.50
b. Sheet of 2 22.50
c. $50 Governor's edition sheet of 1 75.00

No. 11b contains No. 11 and the Oregon upland bird stamp. Nos. 11b, 11c exist imperf. Values: No. 11a imperf., $150; No. 11b imperf., $350.

12 $5 Pintails, perf. 4 sides, *1994* 15.00
a. Die cut self-adhesive 15.00 2.50
13 $25 Pintails, diff., die cut self-adhesive, *1994* 40.00 —
14 $5 Wood ducks, *1995* 15.00
a. Booklet pane of 1 15.00 2.50
15 $25 Columbian sharp-tailed grouse, bklt. pane of 1, *1995* 160.00 —
16 $5 Mallards, *1996* 20.00
a. Booklet pane of 1 15.00 2.50
17 $25 Common snipe, booklet pane of 1, *1996* 140.00 —
18 $5 Canvasbacks, *1997* 20.00
a. Booklet pane of 1 15.00 2.50
19 $25 Canvasbacks, booklet pane of 1, *1997* 140.00
20 $5 Pintails, *1998* 20.00
a. Booklet pane of 1 15.00 2.50
21 $25 Pintails, booklet pane of 1, *1998* 37.50
22 $5 Canada geese, *1999* 17.50
a. Booklet pane of 1 15.00 2.50
23 $25 Canada geese, booklet pane of 1, *1999* 65.00
24 $7.50 Canada geese, mallard, wigeon, *2000* 15.00 2.50
a. Booklet pane of 1, no cover 50.00
25 $7.50 Redheads, *2001* 15.00 2.50
a. Booklet pane of 1, no cover 20.00
26 $7.50 American wigeon, *2002* 14.00 2.50
a. Booklet pane of 1, no cover 14.00
27 $7.50 Wood duck, *2003* 14.00 2.50
a. Booklet pane of 1, no cover 14.00
28 $7.50 Ross's goose, *2004* 13.00 2.50
a. Booklet pane of 1, no cover 15.00
29 $7.50 Hooded merganser, *2005* 13.00 2.50
a. Booklet pane of 1, no cover 13.00
30 $7.50 Pintail, mallard, *2006* 12.00 2.50
a. Booklet pane of 1, no cover 12.00
31 $7.50 Wood ducks, *2007* 12.00 2.50
a. Booklet pane of 1, no cover 12.00
32 $7.50 Pintails, *2008* 12.00 2.50
a. Booklet pane of 1, no cover 12.00
33 $7.50 Mallards, *2009* 12.00 2.50
a. Booklet pane of 1, no cover 12.00
34 $9.50 Wood duck, *2010* 16.00 2.50
a. Booklet pane of 1, no cover 16.00
35 $9.50 Canvasback, *2011* 16.00 2.50
a. Booklet pane of 1, no cover 16.00
36 $9.50 Mallard, *2012* 16.00 2.50
a. Booklet pane of 1, no cover 16.00
37 $9.50 Wigeons, *2013* 16.00 2.50
a. Booklet pane of 1, no cover 16.00
38 $9.50 Canada geese, *2014* 16.00 2.50
a. Booklet pane of 1, no cover 16.00
39 $9.50 Pintail, *2015* 16.00 2.50
a. Booklet pane of 1, no cover 16.00
40 $10.50 Common mergansers, *2016* 18.00 2.50
a. Booklet pane of 1, no cover 18.00
41 $10.50 Gadwalls, *2017* 18.00 2.50
a. Booklet pane of 1, no cover 18.00
42 $11 Buffleheads, *2018* 17.00 2.50
a. Booklet pane of 1, no cover 17.00
43 $11 White-fronted geese, *2019* 17.00 2.50
44 $11.50 Redheads, *2020* 17.00 2.50
45 $11.50 Cinnamon teals, *2021* 17.00 2.50

Nos. 27-45 not required for hunting.

PENNSYLVANIA

Not required to hunt.
Printed in sheets of 10.

Catalogue values for all unused stamps in this section are for Never Hinged items.

Artists: Ned Smith, #1, 3; Jim Killen, #2; Robert Knutson, #4; Robert Leslie, #5; John Heldersbach, #6; Ronald Louque, #7; Thomas Hirata, #8, 12; Gerald W. Putt, #9, 14, 16, 18, 20, 23, 25, 27, 29, 31, 33, 36; Robert Sopchick, #10; Glen Reichard, #11; Mark Bray, #13; Clark Weaver, #15, 17, 19; Jocelyn Beatty, #21, 32; Carl Clark, #22; Kerry Holzman, #24; Scott Calpino, #26, 28, 30, 35; Linda Hilgert, #34; Michael Kensinger, #39.

1983-2021

1 $5.50 Wood ducks 10.00
2 $5.50 Canada geese, *1984* 8.00
3 $5.50 Mallards, *1985* 8.00
4 $5.50 Blue-winged teal, *1986* 8.00
5 $5.50 Pintails, *1987* 8.00
6 $5.50 Wood ducks, *1988* 8.00
7 $5.50 Hooded mergansers, *1989* 9.00
8 $5.50 Canvasbacks, *1990* 9.00
9 $5.50 Wigeons, *1991* 9.00
10 $5.50 Canada geese, *1992* 9.00
11 $5.50 Northern shovelers, *1993* 9.00
12 $5.50 Pintails, *1994* 9.00
13 $5.50 Buffleheads, *1995* 9.00
14 $5.50 Black ducks, *1996* 9.00
15 $5.50 Hooded merganser, *1997* 9.00
16 $5.50 Wood ducks, *1998* 9.00
17 $5.50 Ring-necked ducks, *1999* 9.00
18 $5.50 Green-winged teal, *2000* 9.00
19 ($5.50) Pintails, *2001* 9.00
20 $5.50 Snow geese, *2002* 9.00 2.50
21 $5.50 Canvasbacks, *2003* 9.00 2.50
22 $5.50 Hooded mergansers, *2004* 9.00 2.50
23 $5.50 Red-breasted mergansers, *2005* 8.00 2.50
24 $5.50 Pintails, *2006* 8.00 2.50
25 $5.50 Wood ducks, *2007* 8.00 2.50
26 $5.50 Redheads, *2008* 8.00 2.50
27 $5.50 Hooded mergansers, *2009* 8.00 2.50
28 $5.50 Canvasbacks, *2010* 8.00 2.50
29 $5.50 Wigeons, *2011* 8.00 2.50
30 $5.50 Ruddy ducks, *2012* 8.00 2.50
31 $5.50 Black ducks, *2013* 8.00 2.50
32 $5.50 Shoveler, *2014* 8.00 2.50
33 $5.50 Green-winged teal, *2015* 8.00 2.50
34 $5.50 Pintails, *2016* 8.00 2.50
35 $5.50 Buffleheads, *2017* 8.00 2.50
36 $5.50 Mallards, *2018* 8.00 2.50
37 $5.50 Long-tailed ducks, *2019* 8.00 2.50
38 $5.50 Snow geese, *2020* 8.00 2.50
39 $5.50 Wood ducks, *2021* 8.00 2.50

RHODE ISLAND

Issued in booklet panes of 5 and sheets of 30.
Starting with No. 8, the spacing of the reverse text of the booklet stamp differs from the sheet stamp.
Stamps are numbered serially.

Catalogue values for all unused stamps in this section are for Never Hinged items.

Artists: Robert Steiner, #1-7, 9-10, 16; Charles Allen, #8; Keith Mueller, #11-15, 17-20; Miri Kim, #21-23; Jung Kim, #24; Lea Fabre, #25; Eleni Giannopoulos, #26; Joel Dunn, #27; Hope Anderson, #28; Aniena Simone, #29, 31; Kaia Bennett, #30; Inell Chase, #32; Brydie Handfield, #33.

1989-2021

1 $7.50 Canvasbacks 12.00 3.00
Booklet single, with tab 16.00
a. $7.50 +$50 Governor's edition 92.50

No. 1a exists without serial number.

2 $7.50 Canada geese, *1990* 12.00 3.00
Booklet single, with tab 15.00
a. $7.50 +$50 Governor's edition 72.50

No. 2a exists without serial number.

3 $7.50 Wood ducks & Labrador retriever, *1991* 20.00 3.00
Booklet single, with tab 22.50
a. $7.50 +$50 Governor's edition 60.00

No. 3a exists without serial number.

4 $7.50 Blue-winged teal, *1992* 15.00 3.00
Booklet single, with tab 15.00
a. $7.50 +$50 Governor's edition 60.00

No. 4a exists without serial number.

5 $7.50 Pintails, *1993* 13.00 3.00
Booklet single, with tab 13.00
a. Sheet of 4 65.00

No. 5a imperf. is printer's waste.

6 $7.50 Wood ducks, *1994* 17.00 2.50
Booklet single, with tab and selvage 17.00
7 $7.50 Hooded mergansers, *1995* 13.00 2.50
Booklet single, with tab and selvage 13.00
a. Governor's edition *110.00*

No. 7a inscribed "Governor's edition."

8 $7.50 Harlequin, *1996* 22.50 2.50
Booklet single, with tab and selvage 22.50
a. Governor's edition *125.00*

No. 8a inscribed "Governor's edition" and has serial number with "G" prefix.

9 $7.50 Greater scaup, *1997* 13.00 2.50
Booklet single, with tab and selvage 14.00
a. Governor's edition *110.00*

No. 9a inscribed "Governor's edition" and has serial number with "G" prefix.

10 $7.50 Black ducks, *1998* 13.00 2.50
Booklet single, with tab and selvage 14.00
a. Governor's edition *125.00*

No. 11-14 do not have a serial number.

Rouletted

11	$7.50 Common eiders, *1999*	17.00	2.50
	Horiz. pair from booklet pane	60.00	

Booklet pane contains 10 stamps.

12	$7.50 Canvasbacks, *2000*	16.00	2.50
a.	Inscribed "Hunter"	18.00	
a.	Governor's edition	—	
13	$7.50 Mallard, black duck, *2001*	16.00	2.50
a.	Inscribed "Hunter"	17.50	
a.	Governor's edition	*125.00*	
14	$7.50 White-winged scoter, lighthouse, *2002*	13.00	2.50
a.	Inscribed "Hunter"	13.00	
b.	Governor's edition	130.00	—
15	$7.50 Old squaws, *2003*	12.00	2.50
a.	Inscribed "Hunter"	13.00	
b.	Governor's edition	130.00	—
16	$7.50 Canvasbacks, *2004*	11.00	2.50
a.	Inscribed "Hunter"	12.00	
b.	Governor's edition	130.00	—
17	$7.50 Black ducks, lighthouse, *2005*	11.00	2.50
a.	Inscribed "Hunter"	11.00	
18	$7.50 Canvasbacks, lighthouse, *2006*	11.00	2.50
a.	Inscribed "Hunter"	11.00	
b.	Governor's edition	*130.00*	—
19	$7.50 Harlequin decoy, *2007*	11.00	2.50
a.	Inscribed "Hunter"	11.00	
b.	Governor's edition	*130.00*	—
20	$7.50 Mallard decoys, *2008*	12.00	2.50
a.	Inscribed "Hunter"	15.00	
21	$7.50 Hooded merganser, *2009*	12.00	2.50
a.	Inscribed "Hunter"	11.00	
22	$7.50 Red-breasted merganser, *2010*	14.00	2.50
a.	Inscribed "Hunter"	14.00	
23	$7.50 Barrow's goldeneye, *2011*	14.00	2.50
a.	Inscribed "Hunter"	14.00	
24	$7.50 Mallard, *2012*	14.00	2.50
a.	Inscribed "Hunter"	14.00	
25	$7.50 Canvasback, *2013*	14.00	2.50
a.	Inscribed "Hunter"	14.00	
26	$7.50 Canvasbacks, *2014*	14.00	2.50
a.	Inscribed "Hunter"	14.00	
27	$7.50 Green-winged teal, *2015*	14.00	2.50
a.	Inscribed "Hunter"	14.00	
28	$7.50 Wood duck, *2016*	14.00	2.50
a.	Inscribed "Hunter"	14.00	
29	$7.50 Lesser scaup, *2017*	14.00	2.50
a.	Inscribed "Hunter"	14.00	

Self-Adhesive

30	$7.50 Harlequin, *2018*	12.50	2.50
a.	Inscribed "Hunter"	12.50	
31	$7.50 Long-tailed duck, *2019*	12.50	2.50
a.	Inscribed "Hunter"	12.50	
32	$7.50 Canada goose, *2020*	12.50	2.50
a.	Inscribed "Hunter"	12.50	

Die Cut

33	$7.50 Mallard, *2021*	12.50	2.50
a.	Inscribed "Hunter"	12.50	

Nos. 15-33 have no serial number.

SOUTH CAROLINA

Issued in sheets of 30. Stamps with serial numbers were to be issued to hunters.

Catalogue values for all unused stamps in this section are for Never Hinged items.

Artists: Lee LeBlanc, #1; Bob Binks, #2; Jim Killen, #3, 8, 11, 27-33, 39, 40; Al Dornish, #4; Rosemary Millette, #5; Daniel Smith, #6; Steve Dillard, #7; Lee Cable, #9; John Wilson, #10; Russell Cobane, #12; Bob Bolin, #13; Joe Hautman, #14; Rodney Huckaby, #15, 17, 22, 25; D. J. Cleland-Hura, #16, 18; Denise Nelson, #19; Mark Constantine, #20; Jeffrey Klinefelter, #21; James Hublick, #23; Eddie LeRoy, #24; Richard D. Benson, #26; Donnie Hughes, #34; Richard Clifton, #35-36; Scott Storm, #37-38.

1981-2020

1	$5.50 Wood ducks	60.00	15.00

No. 2-22 do not have a serial number.

2	$5.50 Mallards, *1982*	95.00	
a.	Serial number on reverse	*400.00*	25.00
3	$5.50 Pintails, *1983*	95.00	
a.	Serial number on reverse	*350.00*	25.00
4	$5.50 Canada geese, *1984*	65.00	
a.	Serial number on reverse	*150.00*	15.00
5	$5.50 Green-winged teal, *1985*	60.00	
a.	Serial number on reverse	85.00	15.00
6	$5.50 Canvasbacks, *1986*	25.00	
a.	Serial number on reverse	42.50	10.00
7	$5.50 Black ducks, *1987*	20.00	
a.	Serial number on reverse	22.50	5.00
8	$5.50 Wigeon & spaniel, *1988*	20.00	
a.	Serial number on reverse	30.00	5.00
9	$5.50 Blue-winged teal, *1989*	11.00	
a.	Serial number on reverse	14.00	4.00
10	$5.50 Wood ducks, *1990*	10.00	
a.	Serial number on reverse	10.00	4.00
b.	$5.50 +$44.50 Governor's edition	82.50	
c.	$5.50 +$94.50 Governor's edition	190.00	

All examples of No. 10c are signed by the governor.

11	$5.50 Labrador retriever, pintails & decoy, *1991*	11.00	
a.	Serial number on reverse	11.00	4.00
12	$5.50 Buffleheads, *1992*	15.00	
a.	Serial number on front	15.00	3.00
13	$5.50 Lesser scaups, *1993*	15.00	
a.	Serial number on front	15.00	3.00
14	$5.50 Canvasbacks, *1994*	15.00	
a.	Serial number on front	15.00	2.50
15	$5.50 Shovelers, lighthouse, *1995*	15.00	
a.	Serial number on front	15.00	2.50
16	$5.50 Redheads, lighthouse, *1996*	18.00	
a.	Serial number on front	18.00	2.50
17	$5.50 Old squaws, *1997*	18.00	
a.	Serial number on front	18.00	2.50
18	$5.50 Green-winged teals, *1998*	18.00	
a.	Serial number on front	18.00	2.50
19	$5.50 Barrow's goldeneyes, *1999*	18.00	
20	$5.50 Wood ducks, boykin spaniel, *2000*	15.00	2.50
21	$5.50 Mallard, decoy, yellow Labrador retriever, *2001*	15.00	2.50
22	$5.50 Wigeons, chocolate Labrador retriever, *2002*	15.00	2.50
23	$5.50 Green-winged teal, *2003*	15.00	2.50
24	$5.50 Pintails, Labrador retriever, *2004*	15.00	2.50
25	$5.50 Canvasbacks, *2005*	10.00	2.50
26	$5.50 Black ducks, *2006*	10.00	2.50
27	$5.50 Redheads, Golden retriever, *2007*	10.00	2.50
28	$5.50 Blue-winged teal, Labrador retriever, *2008*	10.00	2.50
29	$5.50 Ring-necked duck, Labrador retriever, *2009*	10.00	2.50
30	$5.50 Wood duck and Boykin spaniel, *2010*	10.00	2.50
31	$5.50 Blue-winged teal and Chocolate Labrador retriever, *2011*	10.00	2.50
32	$5.50 Green-winged teal and Golden retriever, *2012*	10.00	2.50
33	$5.50 Black duck and Boykin spaniel, *2013*	10.00	2.50
34	$5.50 Wood ducks, *2014*	10.00	2.50
35	$5.50 Hooded mergansers, *2015*	15.00	2.50
36	$5.50 Mottled ducks, *2016*	10.00	2.50
37	$5.50 Wigeons, *2017*	12.50	2.50
38	$5.50 Pintail, *2018*	12.50	2.50
39	$5.50 Canvasbacks, Boykin spaniel, *2019*	8.50	2.50
40	$5.50 Wood duck, Labrador retriever, *2020*	8.50	2.50

Nos. 23-40 have no serial number.

SOUTH DAKOTA

Resident Waterfowl Stamps

Vertical safety paper (words read up)

1949-50

1	$1 blk, *grn*, vert. safety paper	*1,550.*	85.00
a.	Horizontal safety paper	*2,250.*	*150.00*
2	$1 blk, *lt brn*, vert. safety paper	*1,200.*	65.00
a.	Horizontal safety paper	*2,950.*	*175.00*

Safety paper design of Nos. 1 and 2 washes out if stamp is soaked. Washed out examples sell for considerably less. Used values are for stamps showing safety paper design.

Resident Game Bird Stamp

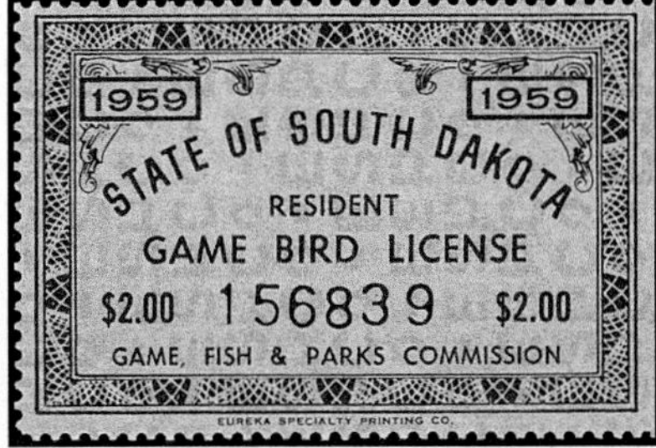

1959

2B	$2 black, *yellow brown*, safety paper	*75.00*	5.00

Safety paper design of No. 2B washes out if stamp is soaked. Washed out examples sell for considerably less. Used values are for stamps showing safety paper design.

Printed in booklet panes of 5.
Stamps are numbered serially.

Catalogue values for all unused stamps in this section, from this point to the end of the Resident Waterfowl stamps, are for Never Hinged items.

Artists: Robert Kusserow, #3; Don Steinbeck, #4; John Moisan, #5; John Wilson, #6, 12; Rosemary Millett, #7, 9; Marion Toillion, #8; John Green, #10, 17; Russell Duerksen, #11, 15-16, 19-20; Mark Anderson, #13, 18, 21, 22; Jeff Reuter, #14; Joshua Spies. #23.

1976-2003

3	$1 Mallards	25.00	3.00
a.	Serial number 4mm high	65.00	10.00
4	$1 Pintails, *1977*	27.50	2.50
5	$1 Canvasbacks, *1978*	13.00	2.50
6	$2 Canada geese, *1986*	8.50	2.50
7	$2 Blue geese, *1987*	7.00	2.50
8	$2 White-fronted geese, *1988*	7.00	2.50
9	$2 Mallards, *1989*	7.00	2.50
10	$2 Blue-winged teal, *1990*	7.00	2.50
11	$2 Pintails, *1991*	7.00	2.50
12	$2 Canvasbacks, *1992*	7.00	2.50
13	$2 Lesser scaup, *1993*	7.00	2.50
14	$2 Redheads, *1994*	7.00	2.50
15	$2 Wood ducks, *1995*	7.00	2.50
16	$2 Canada geese, *1996*	7.00	2.50
17	$2 Wigeons, *1997*	7.00	2.50
18	$2 Green-winged teal, *1998*	7.00	2.50

Migratory Bird Certification Stamps

19	$3 Tundra swan, *1999*	9.00	2.50
20	$3 Buffleheads, *2000*	9.00	2.50
21	$3 Mallards, *2001*	9.00	2.50
22	$3 Canvasbacks, *2002*	9.00	2.50
23	$3 Pintails, *2003*	9.00	2.50

2004-07

No.	Description	Unused	Used
24	$3 purple	9.00	2.50
25	$5 magenta, *2005*	9.00	2.50
26	$5 brown orange, *2006*	9.00	2.50
27	$5 brown, *2007*	9.00	2.50

Non-resident Waterfowl Stamps

Nos. A1-A7, A9 have serial No. in red. Nos. A1-A18 issued in booklet panes of 5. Type faces and designs of Nos. A1-A18 vary.

Unused values are for unpunched stamps. Used values are for signed and punched stamps.

Illustration reduced.

1970-86

No.	Description	Unused	Used
A1	$30 black, *pink*	20.00	
a.	Missing serial number	*8,000.*	
A2	$30 black, *pink, 1971*	10.00	
a.	Overprinted "3"		*450.00*
A3	$30 black, *1972*	4.00	
a.	Overprinted "4"		—
A4	$30 black, *blue, 1973*	8.00	*450.00*
a.	Overprinted "2"	*2,950.*	*450.00*
b.	Overprinted "4"		—
A5	$30 black, *green, 1974*	5.00	
a.	Overprinted "1"	*25.00*	*15.00*
b.	Overprinted "2"	*30.00*	*20.00*
c.	Overprinted "4"	*30.00*	*20.00*
A6	$30 black, *yellow, 1975*	6.00	
a.	Overprinted "UNIT 1"	*45.00*	*25.00*
b.	Overprinted "UNIT 4"	*35.00*	*20.00*
c.	Overprinted "UNIT 3"		*150.00*
A7	$30 black, *yellow, 1976*	5.00	
a.	Overprinted "1"	18.00	*10.00*
b.	Overprinted "2"	35.00	*20.00*
c.	Serial No. 4mm high	*18.00*	
d.	As "c," overprinted "1"	*40.00*	*25.00*
e.	As "c," overprinted "2"	*95.00*	*50.00*
A8	$30 black, *red, 1977*	7.00	
a.	Overprinted "1"	*20.00*	*12.00*
b.	Overprinted "2"	*30.00*	*20.00*
c.	Overprinted "3"	*35.00*	*25.00*
d.	Overprinted "4"	*30.00*	*20.00*
e.	Overprinted "5"	*200.00*	*60.00*
A9	$30 black, *yellow, 1978*	7.00	
a.	Overprinted "1" and 3 strikes of "UNIT 2"	*175.00*	*60.00*
b.	Overprinted "1"		*325.00*
A10	$30 black, *red, 1979*	3.00	
A11	$30 black, *light manila, 1980*	4.00	
a.	Overprinted "1"	6.00	*3.00*
b.	Overprinted "2"	10.00	*6.00*
A12	$30 black, *light yellow, 1981*	4.00	*4.00*
a.	Overprinted "UNIT 1"	6.00	3.00
b.	Overprinted "UNIT 2"	10.00	5.00
A13	$30 black, *blue, 1982*	6.00	
A14	$50 black, *dark yellow, 1982*	7.00	
a.	Overprinted "UNIT 2"		—
A15	$50 black, *red, 1983*	8.00	
a.	Overprinted "AREA 1"	*50.00*	*20.00*
b.	Overprinted "AREA 2"	*65.00*	*30.00*
c.	Serial No. with serifs	*550.00*	
A16	$50 black, *light manila, 1984*	15.00	*15.00*
a.	Overprinted "A"	*325.00*	
b.	Overprinted "B"	*125.00*	
A17	$50 black, *red, 1985*	*3,950.*	*950.00*
A18	$50 black, *1986*	*10.00*	5.00

Bennett County Canada Goose Stamps

Type faces and designs vary. Nos. 2A1-2A2 imperf. Nos. 2A3-2A12 printed in booklet panes of 5, perforated horizontally. Some show vertical perforations.

Nos. 2A1-2A4 were free. No. 2A5 cost $5. Stamps were issued to hunters by means of a drawing.

Used values are for signed stamps.

Illustration reduced.

1974-78

No.	Description	Unused	Used
2A1	black	65.00	45.00
2A2	black, *pink, 1975*	*165.00*	

No.	Description	Unused	Used
2A3	black, *blue, 1976*	30.00	25.00
2A4	black, *yellow, 1977*	25.00	25.00
2A5	black, *greenish blue, 1978*	*900.00*	

West River Unit Canada Goose

Counties handstamped.

Used values are for signed stamps.

1979

No.	Description	Unused	Used
2A6	$2 black, *yellow*	*550.00*	
a.	Bennettt County	*800.00*	200.00
b.	Haakon County	*275.00*	95.00
c.	Jackson County	*275.00*	115.00
d.	Pennington County	*225.00*	85.00

Stamps overprinted for Perkins County exist but may not have been regularly issued. Value, $500 unused.

1980

No.	Description	Unused	Used
2A7	$2 black, *blue*	75.00	
a.	Bennett County	225.00	*75.00*
b.	Haakon County	100.00	*50.00*
c.	Jackson County	110.00	*55.00*
d.	As "c," missing serial number	*6,500.*	
e.	Pennington County	90.00	*45.00*
f.	Perkins County	110.00	*55.00*

Prairie Canada Geese

Counties or Units handstamped.

Used values are for signed stamps.

1981

Perf. 12

No.	Description	Unused	Used
2A8	$2 black, *red*	5.00	
a.	Bennett County	70.00	*35.00*
b.	Haakon County	45.00	*20.00*
c.	Jackson County	45.00	*20.00*
d.	Pennington County	45.00	*20.00*
e.	Perkins County	45.00	*20.00*

1982

No.	Description	Unused	Used
2A9	$2 black, *blue*	120.00	
a.	Bennett County	*1,250.*	*150.00*
b.	Haakon County	*950.00*	*100.00*
c.	Jackson County	*950.00*	*100.00*
d.	Pennington County	*950.00*	*100.00*
e.	Perkins County	*950.00*	*100.00*

1983

Perf. 12

No.	Description	Unused	Used
2A10	$2 black, *yellow*	60.00	
a.	UNIT 2A	70.00	*100.00*
b.	UNIT 31	70.00	*35.00*
c.	UNIT 39	70.00	*35.00*
d.	UNIT 49	70.00	*35.00*
e.	UNIT 53	70.00	*35.00*
f.	UNIT 11, 3mm type	100.00	*50.00*
g.	UNIT 23	100.00	

Rouletted top and bottom

No.	Description	Unused	Used
2A11	$2 black, *yellow*	12.00	
a.	UNIT 2A	65.00	
b.	UNIT 6	45.00	
c.	UNIT 11, 3mm type	60.00	
d.	UNIT 11, 4½mm type	45.00	
e.	UNIT 23	45.00	
f.	UNIT 31	65.00	
g.	UNIT 32	45.00	
h.	UNIT 39	65.00	
i.	UNIT 42	45.00	
j.	UNIT 49	65.00	
k.	UNIT 53, 3mm type	45.00	
l.	UNIT 53, 4½mm type	50.00	

1984

Perf. 12

No.	Description	Unused	Used
2A12	$2 black, *green*	45.00	
a.	UNIT 6	75.00	*30.00*
b.	UNIT 11, 3mm type	85.00	*35.00*
c.	UNIT 11, 4½mm type	75.00	*30.00*
d.	UNIT 23, 3mm type	85.00	*35.00*
e.	UNIT 23, 4½mm type	75.00	*30.00*
f.	UNIT 32	85.00	*30.00*
g.	UNIT 42	75.00	*30.00*
h.	UNIT 47, 3mm type	85.00	*35.00*
i.	UNIT 53, 3mm type	75.00	*30.00*
j.	UNIT 47, 4½mm type		*65.00*
k.	UNIT 53, 4½mm type		*65.00*

1985

Rouletted two adjacent sides

No.	Description	Unused	Used
2A13	$2 black, *red*		
a.	UNIT 47		*85.00*
b.	UNIT 53		*85.00*
c.	UNIT 23		*80.00*
d.	UNIT 32		*100.00*
e.	UNIT 42		*105.00*
f.	UNIT 11		*125.00*

1986

No fee printed on stamp

Imperf. on 3 sides, rouletted at top

No.	Description	Unused	Used
2A14	black		
a.	UNIT 11		*125.00*
b.	UNIT 47		*125.00*
c.	UNIT 53		*125.00*
d.	UNIT 23		*175.00*

105 stamps for hunting whistling swans during the 1984 season exist. The season was canceled. Value, unused $300.

Pheasant Restoration Stamps

Required to hunt all small game, including waterfowl. Printed in booklet panes of 5. No. 3A4 rouletted, others perforated. Stamps are numbered serially.

Catalogue values for all unused stamps in this section, from this point to the end of the Wildlife Habitat stamps, are for Never Hinged items.

1977-88

3A1	$5 Pheasants	13.00	2.50
a.	Rubber-stamped serial number		—
3A2	$5 Pheasants, *1978*	13.00	1.50
3A3	$5 Pheasants, *1979*	13.00	1.50
3A4	$5 Pheasants, *1980*	13.00	2.00
a.	Serial number omitted	65.00	
3A5	$5 Pheasants, *1981*	13.00	2.00
3A6	$5 Pheasants, *1982*	13.00	1.50
a.	Pair, imperf. between	*450.00*	
3A7	$5 Pheasant, *1983*	13.00	1.00
3A8	$5 Pheasant, *1984*	13.00	2.00
3A9	$5 Pheasant, *1985*	13.00	2.00
3A10	$5 Pheasants, *1986*	13.00	2.00
3A11	$5 Pheasants, *1987*	15.00	2.00
3A12	$5 Pheasants, *1988*	13.00	2.00

Wildlife Habitat Stamps

Required to hunt all small game, including waterfowl. Printed in booklet panes of 5. Starting with No. 3A18 stamps are rouletted, others are perforated. Stamps are numbered serially.

1989-99

3A13	$8 Pheasants	13.00	2.00
3A14	$8 White-tailed deer, *1990*	13.00	2.00
3A15	$8 Greater prairie chicken, *1991*	13.00	2.00
3A16	$8 Mule Deer, *1992*	13.00	2.50
3A17	$8 Sharp-tailed grouse, *1993*	13.00	2.00
a.	Pair, imperf. between	*450.00*	
3A18	$8 Turkey, *1994*	13.00	2.00
3A19	$8 Elk, *1995*	13.00	2.00
3A20	$8 Pheasants, *1996*	13.00	1.00
3A21	$8 Antelope, *1997*	13.00	1.00
3A22	$8 Buffalo, *1998*	13.00	1.00
3A23	$8 Buffalo, *1999*	13.00	2.00

Resident Small Game Stamps

Required by residents wishing to hunt small game, including waterfowl. Nos. 4A1, 4A2 issued panes of 10. Others issued in booklet panes of 5. Stamps are numbered serially in red from 1960 to 1967 and 1978. Non-resident small game stamps were not required for hunting.

Catalogue values for all unused stamps in this section are for Never Hinged items.

1960-79

4A1	$2 black, *pink*	15.00	2.00
4A2	$2 black, *blue, 1961*	35.00	3.00
4A3	$2 black, *dark yellow, 1962*	45.00	3.00
4A4	$2 black, *light yellow, 1963*	35.00	3.00
4A5	$2 black, *green, 1964*	35.00	3.00
4A6	$2 black, *1965*	35.00	3.00
4A7	$2 black, *yellow, 1966*	15.00	2.00
4A8	$2 black, *light green, 1967*	35.00	2.00
4A9	$2 black, *light yellow, 1968*	15.00	2.00
4A10	$3 black, *blue, 1969*	35.00	2.00
4A11	$3 black, *light yellow, 1970*	15.00	2.00
4A12	$3 black, *green, 1971*		3.00
4A13	$3 black, *light yellow, 1972*	15.00	2.00
4A14	$3 black, *light yellow, 1973*	15.00	2.00
4A15	$3 black, *1974*	12.00	2.00
4A16	$3 black, *pink, 1975*	15.00	2.00
4A17	$3 black, *gray, 1976*	8.00	1.00
4A18	$3 black, *red, 1977*	6.00	1.00
4A19	$3 black, *1978*	8.00	1.00
4A20	$3 black, *red, 1979*	8.00	1.00

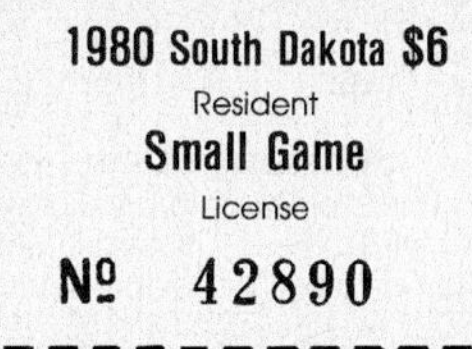

1980-98

4A21	$6 black	10.00	1.00
4A22	$6 black, *light yellow, 1981*	12.00	1.00
4A23	$6 black, *blue, 1982*	6.00	.50
4A24	$6 black, *green, 1983*	13.00	1.00
4A25	$6 black, *light blue, 1984*	*30.00*	1.00
4A26	$6 black, *light blue, 1985*	12.00	1.00
4A27	$6 black, *light blue green, 1986*		2.00
4A28	$6 black, *1987*		2.00
4A29	$6 black, *light green, 1988*	5.00	.50
4A30	$6 black, *1989*		1.00
4A31	$6 black, *light green, 1990*	8.00	.50
4A32	$6 black, *light blue green, 1991*	5.00	.50
4A33	$6 black, *light green, 1992*		1.00
4A34	$6 black, *light pink, 1993*	5.00	.50
4A35	$6 black, *light blue, 1994*	5.00	.50
4A36	$6 black, *yellow, 1995*		1.00
4A37	$6 black, *pink, 1996*	5.00	.50
4A38	$6 black, *light blue, 1997*		.50
4A39	$6 black, *pink, 1998*	8.00	.50

TENNESSEE

Stamps are die cut self-adhesives and are numbered serially.

Cards include both license cost and a fee of 30c (Nos. 1-5), 50c (Nos. 6-13) or $1 (starting with No. 14).

Nos. 3, 5, 7-15 come as 3-part card.

Starting with No. 12, cards come in four parts as well.

1979 and 1980 issues are for resident and non-resident fees.

Unused values are for stamps on original computer card stub.

Catalogue values for all unused stamps in this section are for Never Hinged items.

Artists: Dick Elliott, #1-2; Phillip Crowe, #3-4, 7, 17; Bob Gillespie, #5; Ken Schulz, #6; Allen Hughes, #8; Jimmy Stewart, #9; Ralph J. McDonald, #10, 18; Thomas Hirata, #11, 16; Jim Lamb, #12; Roger Cruwys, #13; Tom Freeman, #14; Richard Clifton, #15, 19; Bob Leslie, #20; Bethany Carter, #21; Beth Ann McMurray, #22; Nick Williamson, #23, 24.; J. Mefford, #25; Joshua Lester, #26-27; Lauren Pollard, #28; Kaydee Hankes, #29-30; Brandon Sharp, #31; Olivia Hughes, #32-33; Joanna Rush, #34, 36; Jet Smith, #35; McKenzie Covrig, #37; Sophie Perry, #38; Mary Alford, #39; Brienna Miller, #40; Erica Brock #42; Joshua Lee, #43.

1979-2021

1	$2 Mallards	75.00	25.00
2	$5 Mallards	*400.00*	*150.00*
3	$2 Canvasbacks, *1980*	45.00	15.00
	3-part card	725.00	
4	$5 Canvasbacks, *1980*	*150.00*	75.00
5	$2 Wood ducks, *1981*	45.00	10.00
	3-part card	—	
6	$6 Canada geese, *1982*	55.00	15.00
7	$6 Pintails, *1983*	50.00	15.00
	3-part card	65.00	
8	$6 Black ducks, *1984*	50.00	12.00
	3-part card	65.00	
9	$6 Blue-winged teal, *1985*	20.00	7.00
	3-part card	45.00	
10	$6 Mallard, *1986*	15.00	5.00
	3-part card	50.00	
11	$6 Canada geese, *1987*	12.00	5.00
	3-part card	25.00	

Card exists with 2/28/88 expiration date rather than correct 2/29 date.

12	$6 Canvasbacks, *1988*	12.00	4.00
	3-part card	20.00	
	4-part card	20.00	
13	$6 Green-winged teal, *1989*	12.00	4.00
	3-part card	20.00	
	4-part card	20.00	
14	$12 Redheads, *1990*	18.00	4.00
	3-part card	25.00	
	4-part card	25.00	
15	$12 Mergansers, *1991*	18.00	4.00
	3-part card	22.00	
	4-part card	22.00	
16	$13 Wood ducks, *1992*	18.00	4.00
	4-part card	22.00	
17	$13 Pintails & decoy, *1993*	20.00	4.00
	4-part card	25.00	
18	$15 Mallard, *1994*	25.00	5.00
	4-part card	30.00	
19	$16 Ring-necked duck, *1995*	30.00	5.00
	4-part card	35.00	
20	$17 Black ducks, *1996*	40.00	5.00
	4-part card	45.00	

Starting With No. 21 Stamps Are Perforated. Not Required For Hunting

21	$10 Mallard, *1999*	15.00	2.50
22	$10 Bufflehead, *2000*	15.00	2.50
23	$10 Wood ducks, *2001*	15.00	2.50
24	$10 Green-winged teal, *2002*	15.00	2.50
25	$10 Canada geese, *2003*	15.00	2.50
26	$10 Wood ducks, *2004*	15.00	2.50
27	$10 Mallards, *2005*	15.00	2.50
28	$10 Canada goose, *2006*	15.00	2.50
29	$10 Harlequin, *2007*	15.00	2.50
30	$10 Wood ducks, *2008*	15.00	2.50
31	$10 Mallards, *2009*	15.00	2.50
32	$10 Wood ducks, *2010*	15.00	2.50
33	$10 Wood ducks, *2011*	16.00	2.50
34	$10 Cinnamon teal, *2012*	16.00	2.50
35	$10 King eiders, *2013*	16.00	2.50
36	$10 Wood ducks, *2014*	16.00	2.50
37	$10 Green-winged teal, *2015*	16.00	2.50
38	$10 Northern shoveler, *2016*	16.00	2.50
39	$10 Cinnamon teal, *2017*	16.00	2.50

No.	Description	Unused	Used
40	$10 Pintails, *2018*	13.50	2.50
41	$10 Shovelers, *2019*	13.50	2.50
42	$10 Redheads, *2020*	13.50	2.50
43	$10 Hooded merganser, *2021*	13.50	2.50

TEXAS

Printed in sheets of 10.
Nos. 1-4 are rouletted.
Stamps are numbered serially.

Catalogue values for all unused stamps in this section are for Never Hinged items.

Artists: Larry Hayden, #1, 12; Ken Carlson, #2, 14; Maynard Reece, #3; David Maass, #4, 9, 15, 26; John Cowan, #5, 8; Herb Booth, #6, 25, 33; Gary Moss, #7, 32; Robert Bateman, #10; Daniel Smith, #11, 16; Jim Hautman, #13, 17, 22, 28; Phillip Crowe, #18; Robert Hautman, #19, 31; Sherrie Russell Meline, #20, 23; John Dearman, #21; Scott and Stuart Gentling, #24; Bruce Miller, #27, 35; Scot Storm, #29; Peter Mathios, #30; Calvin Carter, #34.

1981-2015

No.	Description	Unused	Used
1	$5 Mallards	25.00	8.00
2	$5 Pintails, *1982*	20.00	5.00
3	$5 Wigeons, *1983*	85.00	18.00
4	$5 Wood ducks, *1984*	25.00	5.00
5	$5 Snow geese, *1985*	10.00	3.00
6	$5 Green-winged teal, *1986*	10.00	2.50
7	$5 White-fronted geese, *1987*	10.00	2.50
8	$5 Pintails, *1988*	10.00	2.50
9	$5 Mallards, *1989*	10.00	2.50
10	$5 American wigeons, *1990*	10.00	2.50
11	$7 Wood duck, *1991*	11.00	2.50
12	$7 Canada geese, *1992*	11.00	2.50
13	$7 Blue-winged teal, *1993*	11.00	2.50
14	$7 Shovelers, *1994*	11.00	2.50
15	$7 Buffleheads, *1995*	11.00	2.50

Beginning with No. 16, these stamps were sold only in booklets with other wildlife stamps and were not valid for hunting.

No.	Description	Unused
16	$3 Gadwalls, *1996*	75.00
17	$3 Cinnamon teal, *1997*	65.00
18	$3 Pintail, labrador retriever, *1998*	55.00
19	$3 Canvasbacks, *1999*	40.00
20	$3 Hooded merganser, *2000*	30.00
21	$3 Snow geese, *2001*	20.00
22	$3 Redheads, *2002*	20.00
23	$3 Mottled duck, *2003*	20.00
24	$3 American goldeneye, *2004*	15.00
25	$7 Mallards, *2005*	15.00
26	$7 Green-winged teal, *2006*	20.00
27	$7 Wood duck, *2007*	15.00
28	$7 Pintails, *2008*	15.00
29	$7 Blue-winged teal, *2009*	15.00
30	$7 Wigeons, *2010*	15.00
31	$7 White-fronted geese, *2011*	15.00
32	$7 Canada geese, *2012*	20.00
33	$7 Wood ducks, *2013*	15.00
34	$7 Cinnamon teal, *2014*	15.00
35	$7 Ring-necked duck, *2015*	20.00

No. 23 was issued in booklets with seven other wildlife stamps and was not valid for hunting.

Nos. 25-35 were issued in booklets with five other wildlife stamps and were not valid for hunting.

UTAH

Game Bird Stamps

For hunting game birds, including waterfowl. In 1951 No. A1 or No. 2A1 were required, in 1952 No. A3 or 2A2. No. A1 printed in booklet panes of 25, others in booklet panes of 10. Perforated.

A1

A2

1951

No.	Type	Description	Unused	Used
A1	A1	$3 brown, resident	*20.00*	*7.00*
A2	A1	$15 red, non-resident	*75.00*	—

1952

No.	Type	Description	Unused	Used
A3	A2	$3 red, resident	*65.00*	*10.00*
A4	A2	$15 blue, non-resident	*150.00*	*50.00*

Resident Fishing and Hunting Stamps

For hunting game birds, including waterfowl. Printed in sheets of 40. No. 2A1 printed on linen.

Unused values are for stamps with deer tags attached at left.

No. 2A1

No. 2A2

1951-52

No.	Description	Unused	Used
2A1	$5 blue	5.00	1.00
2A2	$5 green, *1952*	5.00	1.00

Waterfowl Issues

Printed in sheets of 30 or in booklet panes of 5 (starting in 1990). No. 11 issued in sheets of 9. Stamps are numbered serially.

Catalogue values for all unused stamps in this section are for Never Hinged items.

Artists: Leon Parsons, #1; Arthur Anderson, #2; David Chapple, #3; Jim Morgan, #4; Daniel Smith, #5; Robert Steiner, #6-12.

1986-97

No.	Description	Unused	Used
1	$3.30 Whistling swans	10.00	3.00
2	$3.30 Pintails, *1987*	8.00	3.00
3	$3.30 Mallards, *1988*	8.00	2.50
4	$3.30 Canada geese, *1989*	8.00	2.50
5	$3.30 Canvasbacks, perf. 4 sides, *1990*	8.00	
a.	Booklet single, with 2-part tab	8.00	2.50
6	$3.30 Tundra swans, perf. 4 sides, *1991*	12.00	
a.	Booklet single, with 2-part tab	12.00	2.50
7	$3.30 Pintails, perf. 4 sides, *1992*	10.00	
a.	Booklet single, with 2-part tab	10.00	2.50
8	$3.30 Canvasbacks, perf. 4 sides, *1993*	10.00	
a.	Booklet single, with 2-part tab	10.00	2.50
9	$3.30 Chesapeake Retriever and ducks, perf. 4 sides, *1994*	*85.00*	
a.	Booklet single, with 2-part tab	*85.00*	2.50
10	$3.30 Green-winged teal, *1995*	12.00	
a.	Booklet single, with 2-part tab	12.00	2.50
b.	Governor's edition	130.00	
11	$7.50 White-fronted goose, *1996*	16.00	2.50
a.	$97.50 Governor's edition	125.00	

No.	Description	Unused	Used
12	Redheads, pair, *1997*	85.00	
a.-b.	$7.50 Any single	26.00	2.50
c.	$97.50 Governor's Edition	110.00	

No. 12c is No. 12 without the central perforations. The denomination appears only in the upper right corner. The bottom inscription has Governor's Edition plus a serial number.

VERMONT

Printed in sheets of 30.

Catalogue values for all unused stamps in this section are for Never Hinged items.

Artists: Jim Killen, #1-4; Richard Plasschaert, #5-8; Reed Prescott, #9, 11; Robert Mullen, #10; J. Collins, #12; George Lockwood, #13-17; Richard E. Bishop, #18-21; Heather Forcier, #22-25.

1986-2010

No.	Description	Unused	Used
1	$5 Wood ducks	12.00	4.00
2	$5 Common goldeneyes, *1987*	12.00	3.00
3	$5 Black ducks, *1988*	12.00	2.50
4	$5 Canada geese, *1989*	12.00	2.50
5	$5 Green-winged teal, *1990*	12.00	2.50
6	$5 Hooded mergansers, *1991*	12.00	2.50
7	$5 Snow geese, *1992*	12.00	2.50
8	$5 Mallards, *1993*	12.00	2.50
9	$5 Ring-necked duck, *1994*	12.00	2.50
10	$5 Bufflehead, *1995*	12.00	2.50
11	$5 Lesser scaup, *1996*	12.00	2.50
12	$5 Pintails, *1997*	12.00	2.50
13	$5 Blue-winged teal, *1998*	12.00	2.50
14	$5 Canvasbacks, *1999*	12.00	2.50
15	$5 Wigeons, *2000*	10.00	2.50
16	$5 Old squaws, *2001*	10.00	2.50
17	$5 Greater scaups, *2002*	10.00	2.50
18	$5 Mallards, *2003*	10.00	2.50
19	$5 Pintails, *2004*	10.00	2.50
20	$5 Canvasbacks, *2005*	10.00	2.50
21	$5 Canada goose, *2006*	10.00	2.50
22	$5 Ring-necked duck, *2007*	12.00	2.50
23	$7.50 Harlequin, *2008*	12.00	2.50
24	$7.50 Harlequin, *2009*	12.00	2.50
25	$7.50 Wood duck, *2010*	12.00	2.50

No. 26

2011-13 *Die Cut*

Self-Adhesive

No.	Description	Unused	Used
26	$7.50 black + numbered sticker, *2011*	25.00	2.50
27	$7.50 black + numbered sticker, *2012*	13.00	2.50
28	$7.50 black + numbered sticker, *2013*	13.00	2.50

VIRGINIA

Printed in booklet panes of 10 and/or sheets of 30. Stamps are numbered serially.

Catalogue values for all unused stamps in this section are for Never Hinged items.

Artists: Ronald Louque, #1, 24-24A, 34-34A; Arthur LeMay, #2; Louis Frisino, #3; Robert Leslie, #4, 11; Carl Knuth, #5, 12, 17; Bruce Miller, #6; Francis Sweet, #7; Richard Clifton, #8; Wilhelm Goebel, #9; Roger Cruwys, #10; Tim Donovan, #13-14, 19-19A; Jim Wilson, #15-16; Guy Crittenden, #18-18B, 20-20A, 23-23A, 27-27A, 30-30A, 32-32A; Spike Knuth, #21-21A; John Obolewicz, #22-22A, 25-25A, 29-29A; Janet Hong, #26-26A; Brian Murillo, #31-31A; Larry Simons, #33-33A.

1988-2021

No.	Description	Unused	Used
1	$5 Mallards, serial Nos. 1-40,000	13.00	2.50
	Booklet pair with L & R selvage, serial Nos. above 40,000	27.50	
2	$5 Canada geese, serial Nos. 1-40,000, *1989*	12.00	2.50
	Booklet pair with L & R selvage, serial Nos. above 40,000	25.00	
3	$5 Wood ducks, serial Nos. 1-20,000, *1990*	7.00	2.50
	Booklet pair with L & R selvage, serial Nos. above 20,000	24.00	
4	$5 Canvasbacks, serial Nos. 1-20,000, *1991*	7.00	2.50
	Booklet pair with L & R selvage, serial Nos. above 20,000	24.00	
5	$5 Buffleheads, serial Nos. 1-20,000, *1992*	7.00	2.50
	Booklet pair with L & R selvage, serial Nos. above 20,000	24.00	
6	$5 Black ducks, serial Nos. 1-20,000, *1993*	7.00	2.50
	Booklet pair with L & R selvage, serial Nos. above 20,000	24.00	
7	$5 Lesser scaup, *1994*	7.00	2.50
	Booklet pair with L & R selvage	24.00	
8	$5 Snow geese, *1995*	7.00	2.50
	Booklet pair with L & R selvage	24.00	
9	$5 Hooded mergansers, *1996*	12.00	2.50
10	($5) Pintail, Labrador retriever, *1997*	7.00	2.50
11	$5 Mallards, *1998*	12.00	2.50
12	$5 Green-winged teal, *1999*	12.00	2.50
13	$5 Mallards, *2000*	12.00	2.50
14	$5 Blue-winged teal, *2001*	10.00	2.50
15	$5 Canvasbacks, *2002*	10.00	2.50
16	$5 Tundra Swan, *2003*	10.00	2.50
17	$5 American goldeneye, *2004*	10.00	2.50
18	$9.75 Wood ducks, perf. *2005*	13.00	2.50
18A	$9.75 Wood ducks, self-adhesive, die cut *2005*	14.00	2.50
18B	$9.75 Wood ducks, rouletted, with tab *2005*	13.00	2.50
19	$10 Black ducks, perf. *2006*	13.00	2.50
19A	$10 Black ducks, self-adhesive, die cut *2006*	14.00	2.50
20	$10 Canada geese, perf. *2007*	13.50	2.50
20A	$10 Canada geese, self-adhesive, die cut *2007*	13.50	2.50
21	$10 Wigeons, perf., *2008*	13.50	2.50
21A	$10 Wigeons, self-adhesive, die cut, *2008*	13.50	2.50
22	$10 Ring-necked duck, perf., *2009*	13.50	2.50
22A	$10 Ring-necked duck, self-adhesive, die cut, *2009*	13.50	2.50
23	$10 Green-winged teal, perf., *2010*	13.50	2.50
23A	$10 Green-winged teal, self-adhesive, die cut, *2010*	16.00	2.50
24	$10 Redheads, perf., *2011*	16.00	2.50
24A	$10 Redheads, self-adhesive, die cut, *2011*	16.00	2.50
25	$10 Buffleheads, perf., *2012*	16.00	2.50
25A	$10 Buffleheads, self-adhesive, die cut, *2012*	16.00	2.50
26	$10 Hooded mergansers, perf. *2013*	16.00	2.50
26A	$10 Hooded mergansers, self-adhesive, die cut *2013*	16.00	2.50
27	$10 Canvasbacks, perf. *2014*	16.00	2.50
27A	$10 Canvasbacks, self-adhesive, die cut *2014*	16.00	2.50
28	$10 Tundra swans, perf. *2015*	16.00	2.50
28A	$10 Tundra swans, self-adhesive, die cut, *2015*	16.00	2.50
29	$10 Pintails, perf. *2016*	16.00	2.50
29A	$10 Pintails, self-adhesive, die cut, *2016*	16.00	2.50
30	$10 Ring-necked ducks, perf. *2017*	16.00	2.50
30A	$10 Ring-necked ducks, self-adhesive, die cut, *2017*	16.00	2.50
31	$10 Canada goose, perf. *2018*	13.50	2.50
31A	$10 Canada goose, self-adhesive, die cut, *2018*	13.50	2.50
32	$10 Shoveler, perf. *2019*	13.50	2.50
32A	$10 Shoveler, self-adhesive, die cut, *2019*	13.50	2.50
33	$10 Canvasbacks, perf. *2020*	13.50	2.50
33A	$10 Canvasbacks, self-adhesive, die cut, *2020*	13.50	2.50
34	$10 Common goldeneye, perf. *2021*	13.50	2.50
34A	$10 Common goldeneye, self-adhesive, die cut, *2021*	13.50	2.50

Starting with 2005, Virginia stamps are mandatory for hunting.

WASHINGTON

Printed in booklet panes of 1 and sheets of 30. Stamps are numbered serially. Booklet panes starting with No. 7 without staple holes were sold to collectors.

Catalogue values for all unused stamps in this section are for Never Hinged items.

Artists: Keith Warrick, #1; Ray Nichol, #2; Robert Bateman, #3; Maynard Reece, #4; Thomas Quinn, #5; Ronald Louque, #6-7; Phillip Crowe, #8; Fred Thomas, #9, 28; David Hagenbaumer, #10; Cynthie Fisher, #11, 30; Greg Beecham, #12; A. Young, #13; Robert Steiner, #14-16, 22-27; Adam Grimm, #17; Don Nicholson Miller, #18-19; Dan Smith, #20-21; Bart Rulon, #29; Gunnar Hillard, #31; Doug Snyder, #32, Dee Dee Murry, #33; Donnie Hughes, #34; Catherine Temple, #35; Timothy Turenne, #36; Denise Nelson, #37.

1986-2021

No.	Description	Unused	Used
1	$5 Mallards, Nos. 1-60,000	9.00	
	Booklet pane of 1, Nos. 60,001-160,000	12.50	4.00
2	$5 Canvasbacks, Nos. 1-24,000, *1987*	12.00	
	Booklet pane of 1, Nos. 24,001-124,000	12.00	3.00
3	$5 Harlequin, Nos. 1-60,000, *1988*	9.00	
	Booklet pane of 1, Nos. 60,001-160,000	10.00	3.00
4	$5 American wigeons, Nos. 1-60,000, *1989*	9.00	
	Booklet pane of 1, Nos. 60,001-160,000	10.00	2.50
5	$5 Pintails, Nos. 1-60,000, *1990*	9.00	
	Booklet pane of 1, Nos. 60,001-160,000	10.00	2.50
6	$5 Wood duck, Nos. 1-30,000, *1991*	12.00	
	Booklet pane of 1, Nos. above 30,000	12.00	4.00
7	$6 Wood duck, Nos. 100,000-130,000, *1991*	10.00	
	Booklet pane of 1, Nos. above 130,000	10.00	2.50
8	$6 Labrador puppy & Canada geese, Nos. 1-30,000, *1992*	14.00	
	Booklet pane of 1, Nos. above 30,000	14.00	2.50
9	$6 Snow geese, Nos. 1-30,000, *1993*	10.00	
	Booklet pane of 1, Nos. above 30,000	10.00	2.50
10	$6 Black brant, Nos. 1-30,000, *1994*	14.00	
	Booklet pane of 1, Nos. above 30,000	14.00	2.50
11	$6 Mallards, Nos. 1-30,000, *1995*	12.00	
	Booklet pane of 1, Nos. above 30,000	12.00	2.50
12	$6 Redheads, Nos. 1-25,050, *1996*	22.50	
	Booklet pane of 1, Nos. above 25,050	22.50	2.50
13	$6 Canada geese, Nos. 9600001-9625050, *1997*	12.00	
	Bklt. pane of 1, Nos. above 9625050	12.00	2.50
14	$6 Barrow's goldeneye Nos. 1-25,050, *1998*	15.00	
	Bklt. pane of 1, Nos. 25,051-27,050	15.00	2.50
15	$6 Bufflehead, *1999*	15.00	
a.	Bklt. pane of 1	15.00	2.50
16	$6 Canada geese, mallard, wigeon, *2000*	25.00	
a.	Bklt. pane of 1	25.00	2.50
17	$6 Mallards, *2001*	17.50	
a.	Bklt. pane of 1	17.50	2.50
18	$10 Green-winged teal, *2002*	20.00	
a.	Souvenir sheet of 1	20.00	2.50
19	$10 Pintails, *2003*	20.00	
a.	Souvenir sheet of 1	22.50	2.50
20	$10 Canada goose, *2004*	17.50	
a.	Souvenir sheet of 1	17.50	2.50
21	$10 Barrow's goldeneyes, *2005*	17.50	
a.	Souvenir sheet of 1	17.50	2.50
22	$10 Wigeons, mallard, *2006*	15.00	
a.	Souvenir sheet of 1	15.00	2.50
23	$10 Ross's goose, *2007*	15.00	
a.	Souvenir sheet of 1	15.00	2.50
24	$10 Wood ducks, *2008*	15.00	
a.	Souvenir sheet of 1	15.00	2.50
25	$11 Canada goose, *2009*	15.00	
a.	Souvenir sheet of 1	16.00	2.50
26	$10 Pintail, *2010*	40.00	
a.	Souvenir sheet of 1	35.00	2.50
27	$10 Ruddy duck, *2011*	15.00	
a.	Souvenir sheet of 1	25.00	2.50
28	$15 Brant, *2012*	22.00	
a.	Souvenir sheet of 1	25.00	2.50
29	$15 Shovelers, *2013*	22.00	
a.	Souvenir sheet of 1	25.00	2.50

30	$15 Redheads, *2014*	22.00	
a.	Souvenir sheet of 1	25.00	2.50
31	$15 Canvasbacks, *2015*	22.00	
a.	Souvenir sheet of 1	25.00	2.50
32	$15 Hooded merganser, *2016*	22.00	
a.	Souvenir sheet of 1	25.00	2.50
33	$15 Cinnamon teal and yellow Labrador retriever, *2017*	22.00	
a.	Souvenir sheet of 1	25.00	2.50
34	$15 Wood ducks, *2018*	18.50	
a.	Souvenir sheet of 1	18.50	2.50
35	$15 Ring-necked ducks, chocolate Labrador retriever, *2019*	18.50	
a.	Souvenir sheet of 1	18.50	2.50
36	$17 Canada geese, *2020*	21.00	
a.	Souvenir sheet of 1	21.00	2.50
37	$17 Mallards, black Labrador retriever, *2021*	21.00	

Nos. 19-37 not required for hunting. A souvenir sheet containing No. 37 was printed in limited quantities.

WEST VIRGINIA

Printed in sheets of 30 and booklet panes of 5. All booklet stamps have straight edges at sides. Starting in 1990, booklet stamps are numbered serially. Some, but not all, of the 1988 booklet stamps are numbered serially. Stamps from sheets are not numbered serially.

Catalogue values for all unused stamps in this section are for Never Hinged items.

Artists: Daniel Smith, #1-2; Steven Dillard, #3-4; Ronald Louque, #5-6; Louis Frisino, #7-8; Robert Leslie, #9-10; Thomas Hirata, #11-12; Phillip Crowe, #13-14; Richard Clifton, #15-16; Fran Sweet, #17-18; Karl Badgley, #19-20.

1987-96

1	$5 Canada geese, resident	17.50	8.00
	Booklet single with tab at top	65.00	
2	$5 Canada geese, non-resident	16.00	8.00
	Booklet single with tab at top	65.00	
3	$5 Wood ducks, resident, *1988*	10.00	4.00
	Booklet single with tab at top, no serial number	35.00	
a.	Booklet single with serial number on reverse	50.00	4.00
4	$5 Wood ducks, non-resident, *1988*	12.00	4.00
	Booklet single with tab at top, no serial number	35.00	
a.	Booklet single with serial number on reverse	50.00	4.00
5	$5 Decoys, resident, *1989*	13.00	3.00
	Booklet single with tab at top	35.00	
a.	Governor's edition	*65.00*	
6	$5 Decoys, non-resident, *1989*	18.00	3.00
	Booklet single with tab at top	35.00	
a.	Governor's edition	*65.00*	

Nos. 5a and 6a were available only in sheets of 30 through a sealed bid auction.

7	$5 Labrador retriever & decoy, resident, *1990*	20.00	
a.	Booklet single	15.00	3.00
8	$5 Labrador retriever & decoy, non-resident, *1990*	22.00	
a.	Booklet single	15.00	3.00
9	$5 Mallards, resident, *1991*	12.00	
a.	Booklet single	12.00	2.50
10	$5 Mallards, non-resident, *1991*	12.00	
a.	Booklet single	12.00	2.50
b.	Sheet, 3 each #9-10	50.00	

No. 10b is numbered serially; exists imperf. without serial numbers.

11	$5 Canada geese, resident, *1992*	12.00	
a.	Booklet single	12.00	2.50
12	$5 Canada geese, non-resident, *1992*	12.00	
a.	Booklet single	12.00	2.50
13	$5 Pintails, resident, *1993*	12.00	
a.	Booklet single	12.00	2.50
14	$5 Pintails, non-resident, *1993*	12.00	
a.	Booklet single	12.00	2.50
15	$5 Green-winged teal, resident, *1994*	12.00	
a.	Booklet single	12.00	2.50
16	$5 Green-winged teal, non-resident, *1994*	12.00	
a.	Booklet single	12.00	2.50
17	$5 Mallards, resident, *1995*	12.00	
a.	Booklet single	12.00	2.50
18	$5 Mallards, non-resident, *1995*	12.00	
a.	Booklet single	12.00	2.50
19	$5 Wigeons, resident, *1996*	12.00	
a.	Booklet single	12.00	2.50
20	$5 Wigeons, non-resident, *1996*	12.00	
a.	Booklet single	12.00	2.50

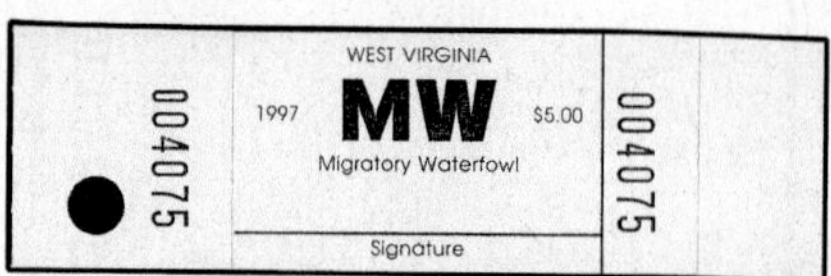

1997-2004

Self-Adhesive

21	$5 black, *1997*	*175.00*	*25.00*
23	$5 light purple and black *1999*	—	*25.00*
28	$5 dark purple and black *2004*	—	

Used values of Nos. 21 and 23 are for signed examples of the stamp portion without the flanking stickers. No. 28 has a clear self-adhesive plastic strip inscribed "2004" affixed to the face of a stamp with a 2002 date, an item which has not been seen by the editors.

WISCONSIN

Printed in sheets of 10. Starting in 1980 the left side of the sheet has an agent tab and a numbered tab, the right side a numbered tab.

Catalogue values for all unused stamps in this section are for Never Hinged items.

Artists: Owen Gromme, #1; Rockne (Rocky) Knuth, #2, 6; Martin Murk, #3; Timothy Schultz, #4, 29; William Koelpin, #5; Michael James Riddet, #7, 15, 26; Greg Alexander, #8, 20; Don Moore, #9, 17, 23; Al Kraayvanger, #10; Richard Timm, #11; Rick Kelley, #12; Daniel Renn Pierce, #13; Terry Doughty, #14, 25, 28, 39; Frank Middlestadt, #16, 22; Les Didier, #18, 21, 24; Sam Timm, #19; Arthur Anderson, #27, 30; Brian Kuether, #31; Robert Leum, #32; Craig Fairgut, #33; James Pieper, #34, 38; John Rickaby, #35, 42; William Millonig, #36; Caleb Metrich, #37, 41, 44; Sara Stack, #40; Robert Metropulos, #43.

1978-2021

1	$3.25 Wood ducks	65.00	9.00
2	$3.25 Buffleheads, rouletted, *1979*	20.00	6.00
3	$3.25 Wigeons, *1980*	12.00	2.50
	With tab	15.00	
4	$3.25 Lesser Scaup, *1981*	10.00	2.50
	With tab	13.00	
5	$3.25 Pintails, *1982*	9.00	2.50
	With numbered tab	9.00	
	With agent's and numbered tab	10.00	
6	$3.25 Blue-winged teal, *1983*	9.00	2.50
	With numbered tab	9.00	
	With agent's and numbered tab	10.00	
7	$3.25 Hooded merganser, *1984*	9.00	2.50
	With numbered tab	9.00	
	With agent's and numbered tab	10.00	
8	$3.25 Lesser scaup, *1985*	12.00	2.50
	With numbered tab	12.00	
	With agent's and numbered tab	15.00	
9	$3.25 Canvasbacks, *1986*	15.00	2.50
	With numbered tab	15.00	
	With agent's and numbered tab	21.00	
10	$3.25 Canada geese, *1987*	9.00	2.50
	With numbered tab	9.00	
	With agent's and numbered tab	10.00	
11	$3.25 Hooded merganser, *1988*	9.00	2.50
	With numbered tab	9.00	
	With agent's and numbered tab	10.00	
12	$3.25 Common goldeneye, *1989*	9.00	2.50
	With numbered tab	9.00	
	With agent's and numbered tab	10.00	
13	$3.25 Redheads, *1990*	9.00	2.50
	With numbered tab	9.00	
	With agent's and numbered tab	10.00	
14	$5.25 Green-winged teal, *1991*	9.00	2.50
	With numbered tab	9.00	
	With agent's and numbered tab	10.00	
15	$5.25 Tundra swans, *1992*	10.00	2.50
	With numbered tab	10.00	
	With agent's and numbered tab	12.00	
16	$5.25 Wood ducks, *1993*	10.00	2.50
	With numbered tab	10.00	
	With agent's and numbered tab	12.00	
17	$5.25 Pintails, *1994*	10.00	2.50
	With numbered tab	10.00	
	With agent's and numbered tabs	12.00	
18	$5.25 Mallards, *1995*	10.00	2.50
	With numbered tab	10.00	
	With agent's and numbered tabs	12.00	
19	($5.25) Green-winged teal, *1996*	10.00	2.50
	With numbered tab	10.00	
	With agent's and numbered tabs	12.00	
20	($7) Canada geese, *1997*	15.00	2.50
	With numbered tab	15.00	
	With agent's and numbered tabs	17.00	
21	$7 Snow goose, *1998*	15.00	2.50
	With numbered tab	15.00	
	With agent's and numbered tabs	17.00	
22	$7 Greater scaups, *1999*	12.00	2.50
23	$7 Canvasbacks, *2000*	12.00	2.50
24	$7 Common goldeneyes, *2001*	14.00	2.50
25	$7 Shovelers, *2002*	11.00	2.50
26	$7 Ring-necked ducks, *2003*	11.00	2.50
27	$7 Pintail, *2004*	11.00	2.50
28	$7 Wood ducks, *2005*	12.50	2.50
29	$7 Green-winged teals, *2006*	12.00	2.50
30	$7 Redheads, *2007*	12.00	2.50
31	$7 Canvasbacks, *2008*	12.00	2.50
32	$7 Wigeons, *2009*	12.00	2.50
33	$7 Wood ducks, *2010*	12.00	2.50
34	$7 Shovelers, *2011*	12.00	2.50
35	$7 Redhead, *2012*	12.00	2.50
36	$7 Long-tailed ducks, *2013*	12.00	2.50
37	$7 Wood duck, *2014*	12.00	2.50
38	$7 Blue-winged teal, *2015*	12.00	2.50
39	$7 Ring-necked ducks, *2016*	12.00	2.50
40	$7 Canvasbacks and lighthouse, *2017*	12.00	2.50
41	$7 Canada geese, *2018*	10.00	2.50
42	$7 Redheads, *2019*	10.00	2.50
43	$7 Wood ducks, *2020*	10.00	2.50
44	$7 Pintails, *2021*	14.00	2.50

Nos. 26-44 not required for hunting. No. 44 sold for $12.

WYOMING

Issued in panes of 5. Required to fish as well as to hunt all small and big game, including waterfowl. Stamps are numbered serially.

Catalogue values for all unused stamps in this section are for Never Hinged items.

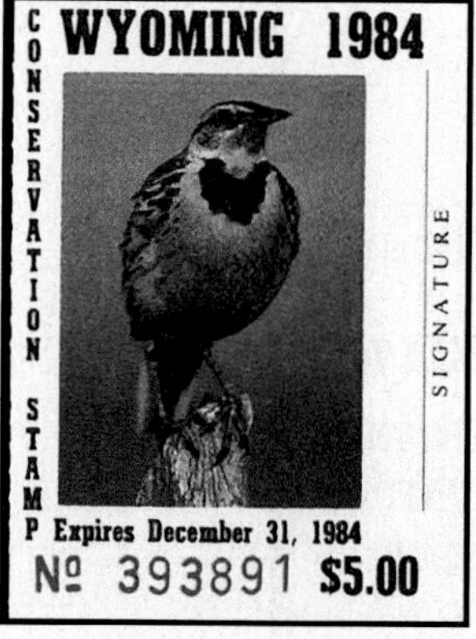

Artists: From photo by Luroy Parker, #1; Robert Kusserow, #2; Dan Andrews, #3, 33; Ted Feeley, #4; Clark Ostergaard, #5; Dave Wade, #6, 8, 10, 13, 17; Connie J. Robinson, #7; Sarah Rogers, #9; James Brooks, #11; Peter Eades, #12; D. Enright, #14; Garth Hegeson, #15; Nick Reitzel, #16; Brent Todd, #18; Paul Kay, #19; Rene Piskorski, #20, 29; Dustin Van Wechel, #21; Ron Staker, #22; Scott Greenig, #23; Art Biro, #24; Jenny Forge, #25; William Smith, #26; Kreig Jacque, #27; Amanda Morton, #28; Karla Mann, #30; Kim Diment, #31, Kip Richmond, #32; Andrew Kneeland, #34; Justin Hayward, #35; Ann Newby, #36; Bill Adair, #37; Justin Hayward, #38.

No. 1 is in vertical format. All others are horizontal.

1984-2021

1	$5 Meadowlark	75.00	6.00
2	$5 Canada geese, *1985*	50.00	5.00
3	$5 Antelope, *1986*	90.00	8.00
4	$5 Grouse, *1987*	85.00	8.00
5	$5 Trout, *1988*	110.00	12.00
6	$5 Mule deer, *1989*	175.00	15.00
7	$5 Bear, *1990*	50.00	5.00
8	$5 Rams, *1991*	45.00	3.50
9	$5 Bald eagle, *1992*	35.00	3.50
10	$5 Elk, *1993*	25.00	3.50
11	$5 Bobcat, *1994*	25.00	3.50
12	$5 Moose, *1995*	22.00	3.50
13	$5 Turkey, *1996*	22.00	3.00
14	$5 Mountain goats, *1997*	22.00	3.00
15	$5 Trumpeter swan, *1998*	20.00	3.00
16	$5 Brown trout, *1999*	20.00	3.00
17	$5 Buffalo, *2000*	20.00	3.00
18	$10 White-tailed deer, *2001*	20.00	5.00

19	$10 River otters, *2002*	20.00	5.00
20	$10 Mountain bluebirds, *2003*	20.00	5.00
21	$10 Mountain lion, *2004*	20.00	5.00
22	$10.50 Burrowing owls, *2005*	20.00	5.00
23	$10.50 Cut-throat trout, *2006*	20.00	5.00
24	$10.50 Blue grouses, *2007*	20.00	5.00
25	$12.50 Black-footed ferret, *2008*	20.00	5.00
26	$12.50 Great gray owl, *2009*	20.00	5.00
27	$12.50 Cinnamon teal, *2010*	20.00	5.00
28	$12.50 Wolverine, *2011*	18.00	5.00
29	$12.50 Black bear, *2012*	18.00	5.00
30	$12.50 Greater short-horned lizard, *2013*	18.00	5.00
31	$12.50 Ruffed grouse, *2014*	18.00	5.00
32	$12.50 Sauger, *2015*	18.00	5.00
33	$12.50 Swift fox, *2016*	18.00	5.00
34	$12.50 Mallard, *2017*	18.00	5.00
35	$12.50 Badger, *2018*	21.00	5.00
36	$12.50 Mule deer, *2019*	21.00	5.00
37	$20 Cutthroat trout *2020*	30.00	5.00
38	$20 Osprey, *2021*	30.00	5.00

Special Goose Management Stamps

$10.00 № 00107 2001
Goose Special Management Permit
This stamp must be in possession while hunting in areas requiring a permit.
Owner must validate by signing on signature line.
Signature of Owner
Expires December 31, 2001

Required to hunt geese at the Springer/Bump Sullivan Wildlife Management Area.

2001-04 *Rouletted Horiz.*

A1	$10 black, *dark yellow, 2001*	—	10.00
A2	$10 black, *light blue, 2002*	25.00	15.00
A3	$10 black, *light green, 2003*	25.00	15.00
A4	$10 black, *grayish tan, 2004*	25.00	15.00

Light Goose Management Stamps

$10.00 2004
LIGHT GOOSE CONSERVATION ORDER
SPECIAL MANAGEMENT PERMIT
Owner must validate by signing on signature line.
Signature of Owner
Expires December 31, 2004 0905

Required to hunt snow geese, blue geese or Ross's geese at the Springer/Bump Sullivan Wildlife Management Area. Unused stamps were issued affixed to a survey card and the survey card was required to be rfilled out and returned to the Wyoming Game and Fish Commission whether or not permit holder hunted or not. Unused values are for unsigned stamps removed from the survey card.

2004-13 *Die Cut*

Self-Adhesive
Serial Number in Red

2A1	$10 blue gray & black, *2004*	—	20.00
2A2	$10.50 green & black, *2005*	25.00	10.00

Serial Number in Black

2A3	$10.50 red & black, *2006*	25.00	10.00
2A4	$10.50 yellow & black, *2007*	25.00	10.00
2A5	$12.50 green & black, *2008*	25.00	10.00
2A6	$12.50 yellow & black, *2009*	25.00	10.00
2A7	$12.50 dark blue & black, *2010*	25.00	10.00
2A8	$12.50 dark blue & black, *2011*	25.00	10.00
2A9	$12.50 blue & black, *2013*	25.00	10.00

INDIAN RESERVATIONS

Stamps for other reservations exist and will be listed after more information is received about them.

CHEYENNE RIVER INDIAN RESERVATION

South Dakota
Birds and Small Game Stamps

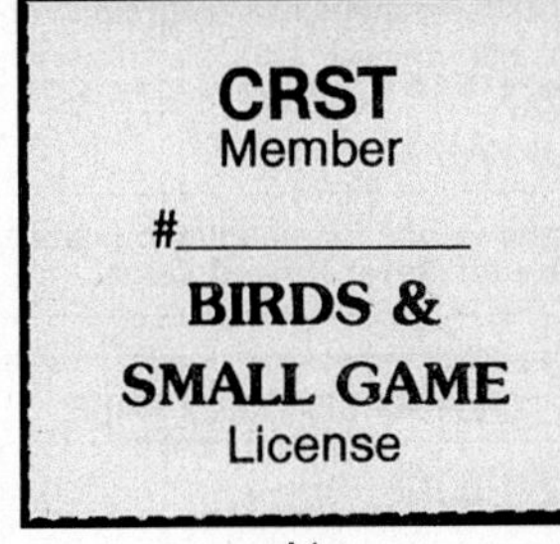

A1

1984?-91 *Rouletted 9.75*

A1 A1	black, *light yellow*, member	*6,500.*	*350.*
a.	Rouletted 6.5	—	850.
A2 A1	black, *yellow*, non-member	*2,500.*	*150.*

Nos. A1-A2 issued in booklet panes of 6 with tab at left. No. A2 printed with diagonal lines on front.

Catalogue values for all unused stamps in this section, from this point to the end, are for Never Hinged items.

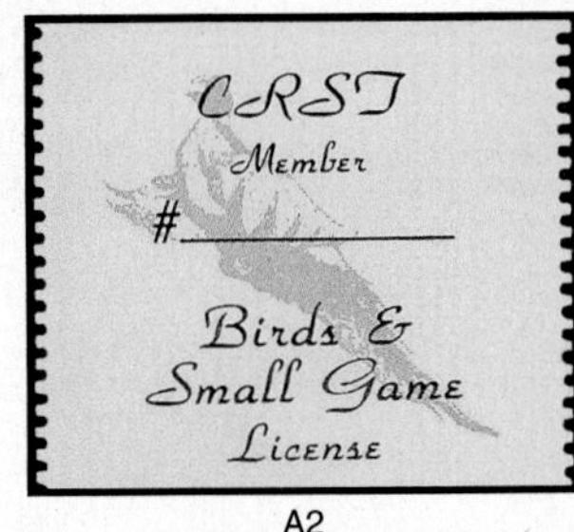

A2

1989-97 **Self-Adhesive** *Perf. 12 Vert.*

A3 A2	black, *yellow*, member	25.00	10.00
A4 A2	black, *yellow*, non-member	45.00	15.00

With Water-Activated Gum

A5 A2	black, *light yellow*, member	13.00	5.00
A6 A2	black, *light yellow*, non-member	27.50	10.00

Rouletted

A7 A2	black, *yellow*, non-member	*150.00*	*45.00*

Nos. A3-A7 issued in booklet panes of 5.

Waterfowl Stamps

Catalogue values for all unused stamps in this section are for Never Hinged items.

1993 *Perf. 12 Vert.*

1	black, *light yellow*, member	15.00	5.00
2	black *light yellow*, non-member	27.50	10.00

Nos. 1-2 issued in panes of 5.

COLVILLE INDIAN RESERVATION

Washington
Bird Stamps

Required by non-tribal members to hunt birds, including waterfowl.

Catalogue values for all unused stamps in this section are for Never Hinged items.

Tribal
Bird
Stamp

A1

1991 Tribal Bird Stamp
Nº 0011
$20.00

A2

1990-91	Self-Adhesive		Die Cut
1 A1	black, *yellow*	—	

Numbered serially in red

2 A2	$20 black, *yellow, 1992*	—	—

CROW INDIAN RESERVATION

Montana
Waterfowl Stamps

Catalogue values for all unused stamps in this section are for Never Hinged items.

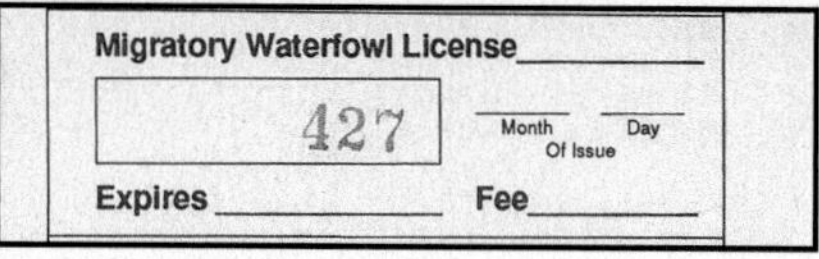

Numbered serially in red

1992	Self-Adhesive	Die Cut	
1	blue	*95.00*	*40.00*
a.	Inscribed "Apr. 30, 199_"	*250.00*	*75.00*

Issued in panes of 5 stamps (4 each No. 1, 1 No. 1a).

Stamps without serial numbers exist. Some may have been issue to hunters during an abbreviated 1993 season.

CROW CREEK SIOUX INDIAN RESERVATION

South Dakota
Non-Indian Small Game Hunting Stamps

Issued 1961-64. The 1961 fee was $2.50. No example is recorded. The 1962 stamps were changed by hand for use in 1963 and 1964. No example of the 1964 stamp is recorded.

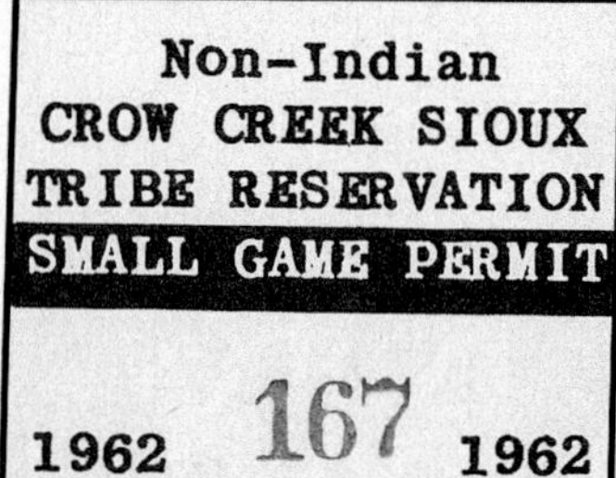

1962-63			
2	$5 black	*22,000.*	—
3	$5 black, *1963*	—	—

Waterfowl Stamps

Fees: $10, reservation resident, non-tribal member; $30, South Dakota resident; $65, non-South Dakota resident.

Catalogue values for all unused stamps in this section, from this point to the end, are for Never Hinged items.

1989-90		Perf. Horiz.	
5	$10 black	*250.*	*150.*
6	$30 black	*9,000.*	*750.*
7	$65 black	*950.*	*350.*
	1990		
8	$10 black, *1990*	175.	*100.*
9	$30 black, *1990*	125.	
10	$65 black, *1990*	550.	*300.*

Fees: $5, tribal member; $15, affiliate, reservation resident; $30 ($35), South Dakota resident/non-resident daily use; $75 ($100), South Dakota resident/non-resident season.

1994 Tribal Member
WATERFOWL
$5
0205

1994		Rouletted Horiz.	
11	$5 green	150.00	15.00
12	$15 blue	225.00	25.00
13	$30 red	225.00	30.00
a.	$25 red (error)	—	
14	$75 red	350.00	55.00

1995-99		Perf. Horiz.	
15	$5 green & multi	100.00	10.00
16	$15 blue & multi	125.00	15.00
17	$30 red & multi	150.00	25.00
18	$75 red & multi	175.00	40.00
19	$5 green & multi, *1996*	30.00	10.00
20	$15 blue & multi, *1996*	45.00	15.00
21	$35 red & multi, *1996*	75.00	20.00
22	$100 red & multi, *1996*	125.00	35.00
23	$5 green & multi, *1997*	12.00	5.00
24	$15 blue & multi, *1997*	35.00	10.00
25	$35 red & multi, *1997*	85.00	20.00
26	$75 red & multi, *1997*	195.00	25.00

No. 25 is inscribed $75, but sold for $35.

27	$5 green & multi, *1998*	12.00	5.00
28	$15 blue & multi, *1998*	35.00	10.00
29	$35 red & multi, *1998*	85.00	20.00
30	$75 red & multi, *1998*	190.00	25.00
31	$5 green & multi, *1999*	12.00	5.00
32	$15 blue & multi, *1999*	35.00	10.00
33	$35 red & multi, *1999*	85.00	20.00
34	$75 red & multi, *1999*	190.00	25.00

Waterfowl Stamps

Fees: $5, tribal member; $15, $20, $30, affiliate; $35, $40, non-resident daily use; $75, $100, non-resident season.

2000-04			
35	$5 green & multi	*75.00*	—
36	$15 blue & multi	*75.00*	—
37	$35 red & multi	*75.00*	—
38	$75 red & multi	*75.00*	—
39	$5 green & multi, *2001*	*100.00*	—
40	$20 blue & multi, *2001*	*100.00*	—
41	$40 red & multi, *2001*	*100.00*	—
42	$100 red & multi, *2001*	*100.00*	—
43	$5 green & multi, *2002*	*125.00*	—
44	$20 blue & multi, *2002*	*125.00*	—
45	$40 red & multi, *2002*	*125.00*	—
46	$100 red & multi, *2002*	*125.00*	—
47	$5 green & multi, *2003*	—	—
48	$30 blue & multi, *2003*	—	—
49	$40 red & multi, *2003*	—	—
50	$100 red & multi, *2003*	—	—
51	$5 green & multi, *2004*	—	—
52	$30 blue & multi, *2004*	—	—
53	$40 red & multi, *2004*	—	—
54	$100 red & multi, *2004*	—	—

In 2001, $15 affiliate, $35 non-resident daily use and $75 non-resident season stamps were printed. It is not known whether these stamps with incorrect fees were sold. Value, set $200.

Twenty-five stamps for 2005 were printed; one example is recorded on license.

Fees: $10, tribal member; $25, affiliate; $40, non-resident daily use; $100, non-resident season.

2006			
59	$10 blue	—	—
60	$25 green	—	—
61	$40 red	—	—
62	$100 red	—	—

Sportsmen's Stamps

For hunting game including waterfowl.

Fees: $10, tribal member; $25, reservation resident, non-tribal member; $100, South Dakota resident; $250, non-South Dakota resident.

Used values are for signed stamps.

Catalogue values for all unused stamps in this section are for Never Hinged items.

1989-90			
A1	$10 black	400.	*100.*
A2	$25 black	1,100.	*300.*
A3	$100 black	350.	*75.*
A4	$250 black	350.	*150.*
A5	$10 black, *1990*	450.	*100.*
A6	$25 black, *1990*	550.	*150.*
A7	$100 black, *1990*	225.	*125.*
A8	$250 black, *1990*	350.	*150.*

Goose Stamps

Fees: $5, tribal member; $10, $15, $20, affiliate; $50, non-resident.

1998-2004			
2A1	$5 green	—	—
2A2	$10 blue	—	—
2A3	$50 red	—	—
2A4	$5 green & multi, *1999*	100.00	—
2A5	$10 blue & multi, *1999*	100.00	—
2A6	$50 red & multi, *1999*	100.00	—
2A7	$5 green & multi, *2000*	60.00	—
2A8	$10 blue & multi, *2000*	60.00	—
2A9	$50 red & multi, *2000*	60.00	—
2A10	$5 green & multi, *2001*	60.00	—
2A11	$10 blue & multi, *2001*	60.00	—
2A12	$50 red & multi, *2001*	60.00	—
2A13	$5 green & multi, *2002*	150.00	—
2A14	$15 blue & multi, *2002*	150.00	—
2A15	$50 red & multi, *2002*	150.00	—
2A16	$5 green & multi, *2003*	—	—
2A17	$20 blue & multi, *2003*	—	—
2A18	$50 red & multi, *2003*	—	—
2A21	$50 red & multi, *2004*	—	—

In 1997, $5 tribal member, $10 affiliate, and $50 non-resident stamps were printed, but the season was canceled. Value, set $400.

Tribal member and affiliate stamps were printed for 2004 but no examples are known. In 2005, 25 stamps were printed.

Fees: $10, tribal member; $25, affiliate; $75, non-resident.

2006			
2A25	$10 blue	—	—
2A26	$25 green	—	—
2A27	$75 red	—	—

FLATHEAD INDIAN RESERVATION

Montana
Bird or Fish Stamps

Catalogue values for all unused stamps in this section are for Never Hinged items.

1987 Bird Stamp Date
№ B# 41946 B
Signature ____________

Numbered serially in Red

1987-90		*Imperf.*	
1	$10 black	750.00	350.00

Confederated Salish & Kootenai Tribes
1988 BIRD OR FISHING STAMP
☐ BIRD ☐ FISHING
$10.00 (Nonrefundable)
Signature ____________
04392

Rouletted 7

1A	$10 black, *1988*, # ends in 0-5	650.00	275.00
b.	Rouletted 5.5, # ends in 8 or 9	950.00	300.00
c.	Rouletted 5.5x7, # ends in 6 or 7	950.00	300.00
	Rouletted 5.5x11		
2	$10 blue, *1989*	8.50	5.00
b.	Rouletted 6.5	20.00	7.50
	Rouletted 6.5 **Self-Adhesive**		
3	$10 blue, *1990*	9.50	5.00

No. 1A printed in booklet panes of 10. Nos. 2-3 printed in booklet panes of 5 stamps se-tenant with 5 stamps marked "Duplicate."

Joint Bird License Stamps

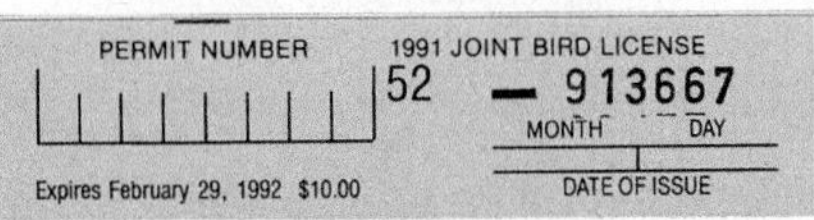

Numbered serially

1991	Self-Adhesive	*Die Cut*	
4	$10 black, *green*	10.50	8.00

Printed in booklet panes of 10.

Bird License Stamps

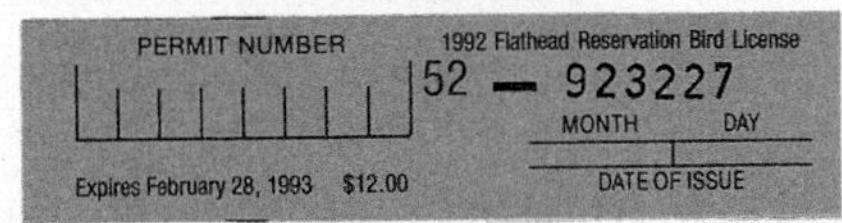

PERMIT NUMBER
1992 Flathead Reservation Bird License
52 — 923227
MONTH
DAY
DATE OF ISSUE
Expires February 28, 1993 $12.00

Numbered serially

1992-2000	Self-Adhesive	*Die Cut*	
5	$12 black, *rose*, season	9.50	5.00
6	$12 black, *salmon*, 3-day	9.00	5.00
7	$12 black, *dark green*, season, *1993*	7.50	4.00
8	$12 black, *dark blue*, 3-day, *1993*	7.00	4.00
9	$12 black, *blue*, season, *1994*	8.00	4.00
10	$12 black, *orange*, 3-day, *1994*	7.00	3.00
11	$12 black, *yellow*, resident, *1995*	9.00	3.00
12	$55 black, *pale blue green*, non-resident, *1995*	15.00	9.00
13	$12 black, *turquoise*, resident, *1996*	9.00	3.00
14	$55 black, *pale orange*, non-resident, *1996*	35.00	15.00
15	$12 black, *pale yellow*, resident, *1997*	8.00	3.00
16	$55 black, *pale blue green*, non-resident, *1997*	15.00	9.00
17	$13 black, *turquoise*, resident, *1998*	8.00	3.00
18	$56 black, *blue*, non-resident, *1998*	12.00	8.00
19	$13 black, *orange*, resident, *1999*	8.00	3.00
20	$56 black, *red*, non-resident, *1999*	10.00	5.00
21	$13 black, *yellow*, reservation, *2000*	12.00	3.00
22	$14 black, *green*, resident, *2000*	12.00	3.00
23	$110 black, *pink*, out-of-state, *2000*	12.00	5.00

Printed in booklet panes of 10.

FORT BELKNAP INDIAN RESERVATION

Montana
Waterfowl Stamps

Catalogue values for all unused stamps in this section are for Never Hinged items.

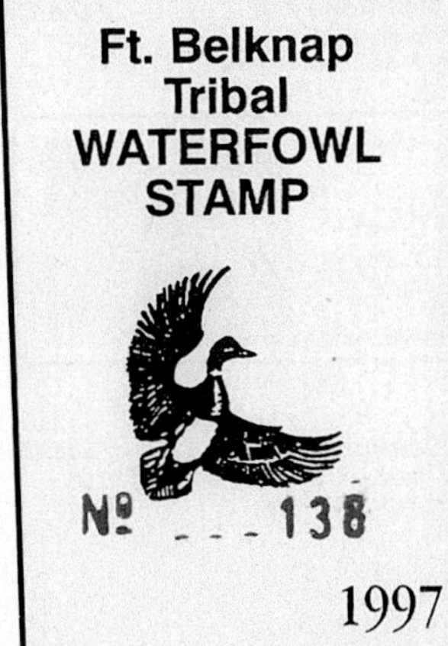

A1

1996-2010	Self-Adhesive	*Die Cut*
1 A1	black	37.50
	Serially Numbered in Red	
2 A1	black, *1997*	67.50
3 A1	green, *1998*	45.00
4 A1	red, *1999*	82.50
5 A1	red, *2000*	160.00
6 A1	dark green, *2001*	160.00
7 A1	maroon, *2003*	135.00
8 A1	blue, *2004*	135.00
9 A1	black, *2005*	135.00
10 A1	green, *2006*	135.00
11 A1	maroon, *yellow, 2007*	135.00
12 A1	blue, *blue, 2008*	135.00
13 A1	red, *yellow, 2009*	135.00
14 A1	green, *2010*	135.00

No. 1 is undated. Nos. 2-14 are dated. No stamp was released in 2002.

Nos. 1-14 were required in addition to a Federal Hunting Permit Stamp.

Hunting licenses on Fort Belknap Reservation cost $10 for residents and $110 for non-residents.

FORT BERTHOLD INDIAN RESERVATION

North Dakota
Small Game Stamps

Stamps issued before 1990 may exist.

Issued in booklet panes of 6 stamps and 6 tabs. Required for hunting small game including waterfowl.

Values are for stamps with tabs. Fees varied, usually $6 for tribe members and $20-$30 for non-members.

Stamps are numbered serially.

Catalogue values for all unused stamps in this section are for Never Hinged items.

1990-98		*Rouletted*	
A6	black, *pink*	85.00	25.00
A7	black, *green, 1991*	80.00	20.00
A8	black, *pink, 1992*	80.00	25.00
A9	black, *blue, 1993*	150.00	75.00
A10	black, *pink, 1994*	70.00	20.00
A11	black, *pink, 1995*	100.00	25.00
A12	black, *green, 1996*	55.00	15.00
A13	black, *light green, 1997*	50.00	12.00
A14	black, *green, 1998*	30.00	12.00
A15	black, *green, 1999*	30.00	12.00
A16	black, *orange, 2000*	25.00	12.00
A17	black, *green, 2001*	25.00	12.00
A18	black, *blue, 2002*	25.00	12.00
A19	black, *pink, 2003*	25.00	12.00
A20	black, *blue, 2004*	25.00	12.00
A21	black, *orange, 2005*	27.50	12.00
A22	black, *orange, 2006*	30.00	12.00
A23	black, *yellow, 2007*	30.00	12.00

Waterfowl Stamps

Stamps issued before 1990 may exist.
Issued in booklet panes of 6 stamps and 6 tabs.
Required for non-member waterfowl hunters only.
Values are for stamps with tabs.
Fees varied, usually $20-$30.
Stamps are numbered serially.

Catalogue values for all unused stamps in this section are for Never Hinged items.

1990-2000		*Rouletted*	
2A6	black	1,750.	450.
2A7	black, *blue, 1991*	500.	200.
2A8	black, *yellow*, #1-60, *1992*	2,950.	550.
2A9	black, *yellow*, #61-120, *1993*	400.	125.
2A10	black, *green*, #1-60, *1994*	375.	100.
2A11	black, *green*, #61-120, *1995*	200.	50.
2A12	black, *green*, #121-198, *1996*	175.	30.
2A13	black, *light green*, #199-276, *1997*	200.	25.
2A14	black, *light green*, #277-334, *1998*	200.	25.
2A15	black, *light green*, #335-432, *1999*	225.	25.
2A16	black, *light green*, #433-588, *2000*	175.	25.
2A17	black, *yellow*, #589-744, *2001*	225.	25.
2A18	black, *red*, #745-900, *2002*	250.	25.
2A19	black, *orange*, #901-1056, *2003*	250.	25.
2A20	black, *pink*, #1057-1212, *2004*	250.	25.

2A21	black, *red*, #1213-1368, *2005*	*250.*	25.
2A22	black, *blue*, #1369-1524, *2006*	*200.*	25.
2A23	black, *pink*, #1525-1680, *2007*	*200.*	25.

Sandhill Crane Stamps

Issued in booklet panes of 6 stamps and 6 tabs.
Required for non-member waterfowl hunters only.
Values are for stamps with tabs.
Fees varied, usually $20-$30.
Stamps are numbered serially.

Catalogue values for all unused stamps in this section are for Never Hinged items.

1997-99 *Rouletted*

3A1	black, *orange*, #1-30	*1,250.*
3A2	black, *orange*, #31-60, *1998*	*1,250.*
3A3	black, *orange*, #61-90, *1999*	*3,500.*

FORT PECK INDIAN RESERVATION

Montana

Stamps issued before 1975 may exist.

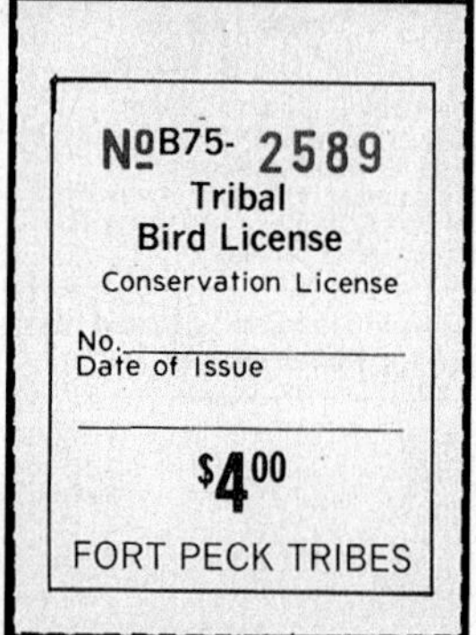

A1

1975-78 *Rouletted*

2	A1 $4 black	*1,250.*	*500.00*
3	A1 $4 black, *1976*	90.	*50.00*
a.	Double impression	*11,500.*	
4	A1 $4 black, *1977*		—
5	A1 $5 black, *orange, 1978*	225.	*100.00*

Waterfowl Stamp

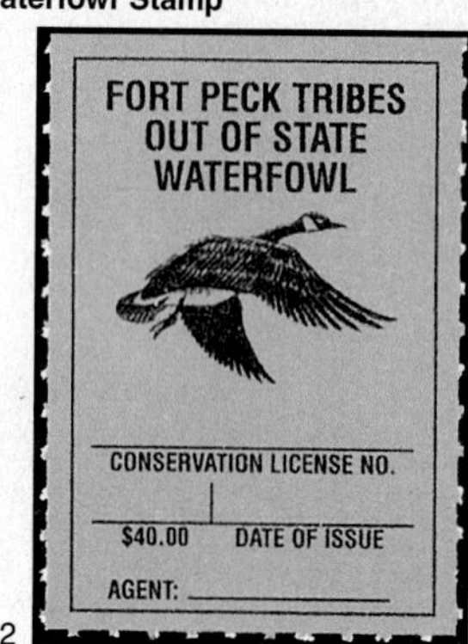

A2

1996 *Rouletted*

6	A2 $10 black, *orange*, resident	20.00
7	A2 $40 black, *green*, out-of-state	30.00

JICARILLA APACHE INDIAN RESERVATION

New Mexico
Wildlife Stamp

Catalogue values for all unused stamps in this section are for Never Hinged items.

A1

A2

1988-96 **Self-Adhesive** *Die Cut*

1 A1 $5 black & gold, *white* 110.00

Rouletted

Water-Activated Gum

2 A2 $5 black & gold, *blue* 12.00

Serial Number Greater than 9000

3 A2 $5 black & gold, *blue,* 80.00

No. 2 was issued in blocks of 4.
No. 2 measures 38.5mm x 64mm. No. 3 is 37mm x 61mm or 66mm.

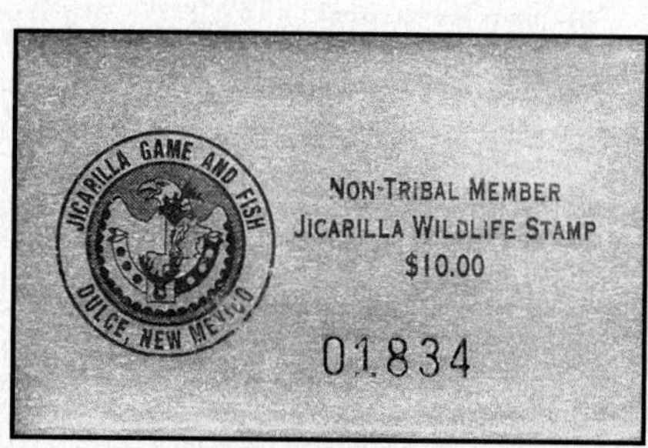

A3

1999-2000 **Self-Adhesive** *Die Cut*

4	A3 $10 blue & black, *gold*, non-tribal	75.00
5	A3 $5 black, *gold*, tribal, *2000*	60.00
6	A3 $10 black, *gold*, non-tribal, *2000*	60.00

A4

2004 **Self-Adhesive** *Die Cut*

7	A4 ($15) brown & multi, tribal	*225.00*
8	A4 ($15) blue gray & multi, non-tribal	*225.00*

A5

2007 **Self-Adhesive** *Die Cut*

9	A5 ($15) green & multi, tribal	*175.00*
10	A5 ($15) brown & multi, non-tribal	*175.00*

Type of 2004

2008-9 **Self-Adhesive** *Die Cut*

11	A4 ($20) red & multi, tribal	*175.00*
12	A4 ($20) yellow & multi, non-tribal	*175.00*
13	A4 ($20) orange & multi, tribal, *2009*	*175.00*
14	A4 ($20) green & multi, non-tribal, *2009*	*175.00*

Nos. 10-11 have a star hand punched to the right of the serial number.

LAKE TRAVERSE (SISSETON-WAHPETON) INDIAN RESERVATION

South Dakota-North Dakota
Waterfowl Stamps

No examples are recorded of stamps from 1987-1990. No. 1 is die cut. Nos. 6, 8-9 are die cut, self-adhesive. No. 7 issued in booklet panes of 5, rouletted, numbered serially in red.

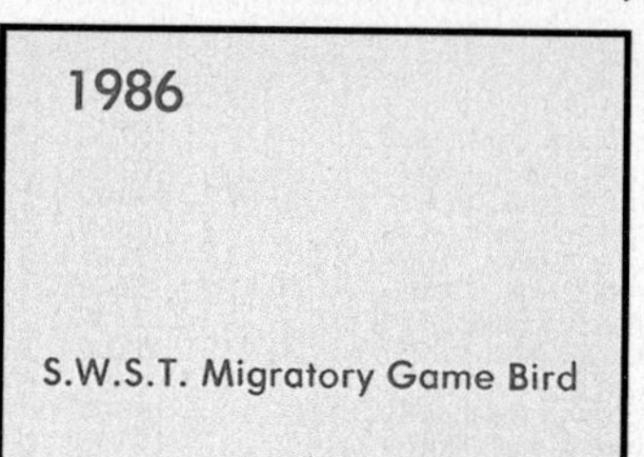

A1

1991 S.W.S.T.
WATERFOWL
License

A2

SISSETON-
WAHPETON 1513

Sioux Tribe
Waterfowl
Stamp
1992

A3

S W D N 1 9 9 4
Lake Traverse
Reservation, SD

A4

1986-2004

1	A1 green	*225.00*	*75.00*

Catalogue values for all unused stamps in this section, from this point to the end, are for Never Hinged items.

6	A2 black, *bright green, 1991*	*125.00*	*25.00*
7	A3 Wood duck, *1992*	15.00	6.00
8	A2 black, *bright red, 1993*	25.00	7.00
9	A4 black, *yellow orange, 1994*	8.00	4.00

Inscribed SWST

10	A4 black, *red orange, 1995*	12.00	5.00
11	A4 black, *blue, 1996*	10.00	4.00
12	A4 black, *bright green, 1997*	11.00	3.00
13	A4 black, *red, 1998*	40.00	7.00
14	A4 black, *orange, 1999*	10.00	4.00
15	A4 black, *yellow green, 2000*	35.00	7.00
16	A4 black, *yellow, 2001*	8.00	4.00
17	A4 black, *orange, 2002*	8.00	4.00
18	A4 black, *blue, 2003*	30.00	7.00
19	A4 black, *yellow, 2004*	25.00	7.00

LOWER BRULE INDIAN RESERVATION

South Dakota Waterfowl Stamps

Serial Nos. are in red. Year and fee are written by hand or typewritten on each stamp. The $5 fee was for for non-members and non-Indians. There was a $2.50 fee for tribal members but no examples of these stamps are recorded.

Numbers have been reserved for the $2.50 stamps.

Since no year is on an unused stamp, they are listed under the first year only.

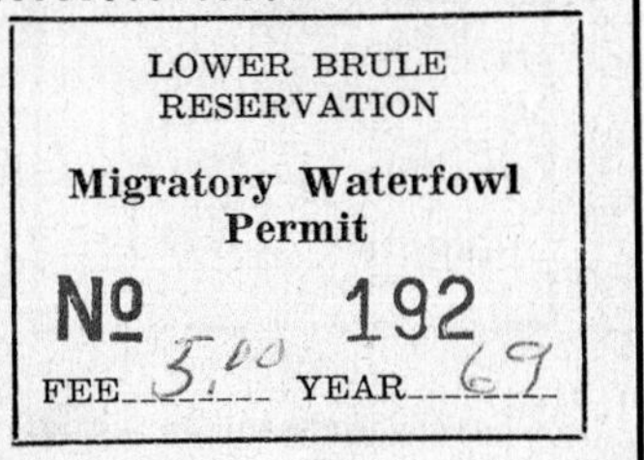

1962-70

2	$5 black	—	
4	$5 black, *1963*		—
6	$5 black, *1964*		*5,000.*
8	$5 black, *1965*		*5,000.*
10	$5 black, *1966*		*4,500.*
12	$5 black, *1967*		*4,000.*
14	$5 black, *1968*		*3,750.*
18	$5 black, *1969*		*3,500.*

LOWER BRULE RESERVATION

Migratory Waterfowl Permit

№ 192

FEE 5.00 YEAR 69

1969-71

20	$5 black	*9,500.*
22	$5 black, *1970*	*6,000.*
24	$5 black, *1971*	—
26	$5 black, *1972*	—

Migratory Bird Hunting and Conservation Stamps

Issued in panes of 20.

All stamps have serial number on reverse.

Catalogue values for all unused stamps in this section, from this point to the end, are for Never Hinged items.

Designs: Nos. 27-31, Birds on the wing. Nos. 32-34, Bison, birds. Nos. 35-37, Deer, birds on the wing. Nos. 38-40, Birds landing, on the ground. Nos. 41-43, Canada geese. No. 44-46, Birds on the wing, diff. Nos. 47-49, Three birds. Nos. 50-51, Elk. Nos. 52-53, Birds on the wing, diff. Nos. 54-55, Canada geese, diff. Nos. 56-57, Eight birds on ground, three in air. Nos. 58-59, Mountains, ducks on water. Nos. 60-61, Goose. Nos. 62-63, Elk, diff.

1995-2008

27	$5 green, tribal member	3.00	9.00
28	$5 orange brown, resident deeded land owner / operator	3.00	9.00
29	$5 blue, resident government employee	3.00	9.00
30	$10 red, non-tribal S.D. resident	5.00	14.00
31	$10 purple, non-resident, out of state	5.00	14.00
32	$5 multi, tribal / resident, *1996*	3.00	9.00
33	$10 multi, non-tribal S.D. resident, *1996*	14.00	5.00
34	$10 multi, non-resident, out of state, *1996*	14.00	5.00
35	$5 multi, tribal / resident, *1997*	9.00	3.00
36	$10 multi, non-tribal S.D. resident, *1997*	14.00	5.00
37	$10 multi, non-resident, out of state, *1997*	14.00	5.00
38	$5 multi, tribal / resident, *1998*	9.00	3.00
39	$10 multi, non-tribal S.D. resident, *1998*	14.00	5.00
40	$10 multi, non-resident, out of state, *1998*	14.00	5.00
41	$5 multi, tribal / resident, *1999*	9.00	3.00
42	$10 multi, non-tribal S. D. resident, *1999*	16.00	5.00
43	$10 multi, non-resident, out of state, *1999*	16.00	5.00
44	$5 multi, tribal / resident, *2000*	11.00	3.00
45	$10 multi, non-tribal S. D. resident, *2000*	24.00	5.00
46	$10 multi, non-resident, out of state, *2000*	24.00	5.00
47	$5 multi, tribal / resident, *2001*	9.00	3.00
48	$10 multi, non-tribal S. D. resident, *2001*	24.00	5.00
49	$10 multi, non-resident, out of state, *2001*	24.00	5.00
50	$5 multi, tribal, *2002*	25.00	10.00
51	$10 multi, non-tribal, *2002*	45.00	10.00
52	$5 multi, tribal, *2003*	35.00	10.00
53	$10 multi, non-tribal, *2003*	55.00	10.00
54	$5 multi, tribal, *2004*	35.00	10.00
55	$10 multi, non-tribal, *2004*	55.00	10.00
56	$5 multi, tribal, *2005*	35.00	10.00
57	$10 multi, non-tribal, *2005*	55.00	10.00
58	$5 multi, tribal, *2006*	35.00	10.00
59	$10 multi, non-tribal, *2006*	55.00	10.00
60	$5 multi, tribal, *2007*	35.00	10.00
61	$10 multi, non-tribal, *2007*	55.00	10.00
62	$5 multi, tribal, *2008*	35.00	10.00
63	$10 multi, non-tribal, *2008*	55.00	10.00

PINE RIDGE (OGLALA SIOUX) INDIAN RESERVATION

South Dakota Waterfowl Stamps

Nos. 1-3 issued in booklet panes of 5, numbered serially in red.

No. 2 perforated, others rouletted.

A1

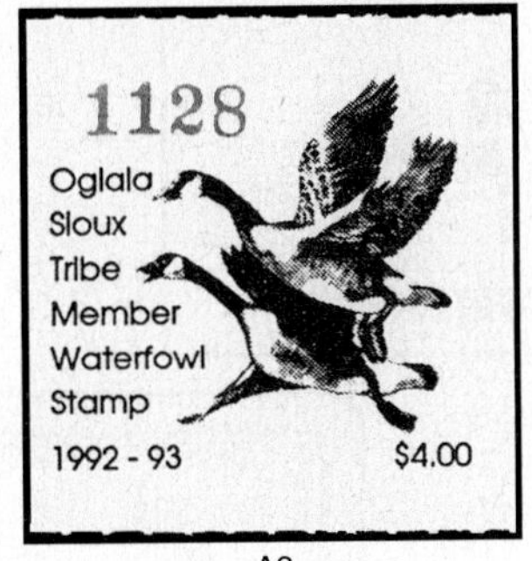

A2

A3

1	A1 $4 black	*275.00*

Earliest known use of No. 1 is 1988.

Catalogue values for all unused stamps in this section, from this point to the end, are for Never Hinged items.

2	A2 $4 black, perforated	15.00	5.00
3	A3 $4 Canada geese, *1992*	11.00	5.00

$6 stamps picturing Canada geese were produced and sold for the 1993 season. The same stamp was rubber handstamped for the 1994 season. However, there was no hunting season those years. Value, each $15.

ROSEBUD INDIAN RESERVATION

South Dakota Tribal Game Bird Stamps

Nos. 1-4 have red serial number. Stamps for 1960, 1964-69 may exist.

Since no year is on an unused stamp, they are listed under the first year only.

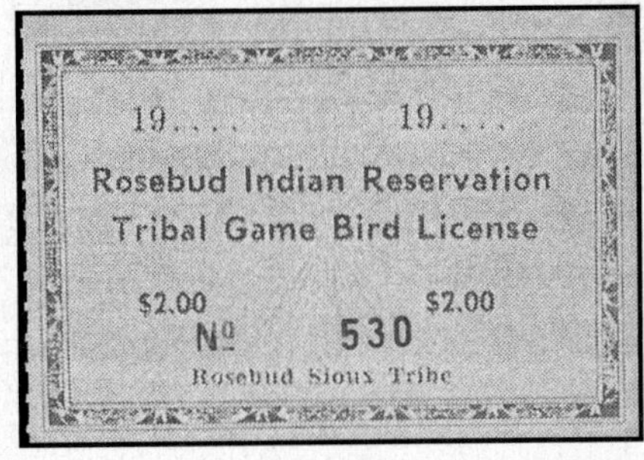

1959-63 ***Rouletted***

1	$2 green, *light green*	—	
2	$2 green, *light green, 1961*		*9,500.*
3	$2 green, *light green, 1962*		*11,000.*
4	$2 green, *light green, 1963*		—

The last two digits of the year date is filled in by hand on Nos. 1-4.

Small Game Stamps

Rosebud Reservation

SMALL GAME

№ 2383

No. 12

Rosebud
Reservation
SMALL GAME

No. 13

1979-80

No.	Description	Unused	Used
12	black	*500.00*	*1,750.*
13	black, *1980*	*65.00*	

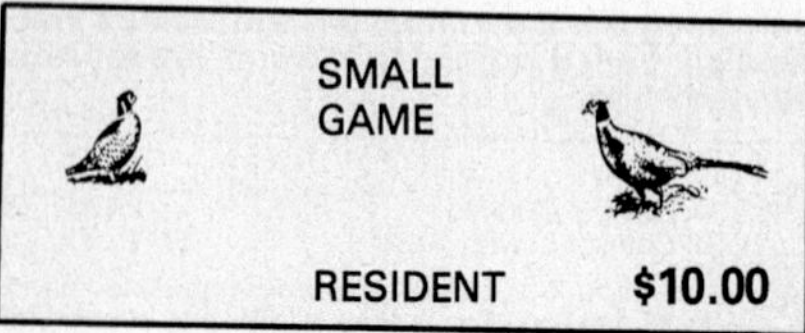

Nos. 14, 15

1988-93 ***Imperf.***

No.	Description	Unused	Used
14	$10 black, resident	25.00	*10.00*
15	$45 black, non-resident, *1989*	125.00	*55.00*

Nos. 16, 17

1990-2000 **Self-Adhesive** ***Die Cut***

No.	Description	Unused	Used
16	$10 black, resident	125.00	*15.00*
a.	Overprinted "RESIDENT" over "Non-resident"	*7,500.*	*1,500.*
17	$45 black, non-resident	650.00	*75.00*
18	black, tribal, *1996*	25.00	15.00
a.	$10 Handwritten value	*900.00*	
19	black, resident, *1996*	75.00	25.00
a.	$50 Handwritten value		
20	black, non-resident, *1996*	225.00	*25.00*
21	$10 red, tribal, *2000*	—	*15.00*
22	$50 red, resident, *2000*	300.00	*15.00*
23	$85 red, non-resident, *2000*	100.00	*25.00*

Unused values for Nos. 16-17 are for never hinged stamps.

No 20 is valued with small faults, usually staple holes. Stamps without faults sell for more.

No. 24

2001 **Die cut, self-adhesive**

No.	Description	Unused	Used
24	$40 black, red & blue, resident	250.00	15.00
25	$40 black, red & blue, non-resident	150.00	

SAN CARLOS INDIAN RESERVATION

Arizona
Habitat Conservation Stamps

Catalogue values for all unused stamps in this section are for Never Hinged items.

A1

1997-2012 **Die cut, self-adhesive**

No.	Description	Unused
1	A1 $5 gold & black, no serial no.	650.00
a.	With handwritten serial no.	650.00
	Serially Numbered in Gray	
2	A1 $5 gold & black, *1998*	12.50
a.	With purple year date handstamp, handwritten serial no.	650.00
b.	With handwritten 2001 year date	67.50
3	A1 $5 gold & black, *1999*	12.50
a.	With handwritten 2001 year date	67.50
4	A1 $5 gold & black, *2000*	12.50
5	A1 $5 red, without serial no., *2001*	55.00
6	A1 $5 blue, narrow date, without serial no., *2002*	22.50
a.	Wide year date	32.50
b.	With handwritten 2003 year date	32.50
	Serially Numbered in Black	
7	A1 $5 green, *2003*	22.50
8	A1 $5 brown, *2004*	22.50
9	A1 $5 brown, wide serial no., *2005*	17.50
a.	Narrow serial no.	85.00
10	A1 $5 green, *2006*	45.00
11	A1 $5 orange, *2007*	22.50
12	A1 $5 purple, *2008*	22.50
13	A1 $5 blue, *2009*	22.50
14	A1 $5 green *2010*	22.50
15	A1 $5 vio blue, *2011*	22.50
16	A1 $5 red, *2012*	22.50

SPIRIT LAKE INDIAN RESERVATION

South Dakota
Waterfowl Stamps

Catalogue values for all unused stamps in this section are for Never Hinged items.

A1

A2

1996-2008 **Die cut, self-adhesive**

No.	Description	Unused
1	A1 black	32.50
2	A1 black, *1997*	45.00
3	A1 black, *1998*	45.00
4	A1 black, *1999*	17.50
5	A1 black, *2000*	22.50
6	A1 black, *2001*	22.50
7	A2 multi, *2001*	12.50
8	A2 multi, *2002*	12.50
9	A2 multi, *2003*	12.50
10	A2 multi, *2004*	12.50
11	A2 multi, *2005*	12.50
12	A2 multi, *2006*	9.00
13	A2 multi, *2007*	9.00
14	A2 multi, *2008*	9.00

STANDING ROCK INDIAN RESERVATION

South Dakota-North Dakota
Waterfowl Stamps

Catalogue values for all unused stamps in this section are for Never Hinged items.

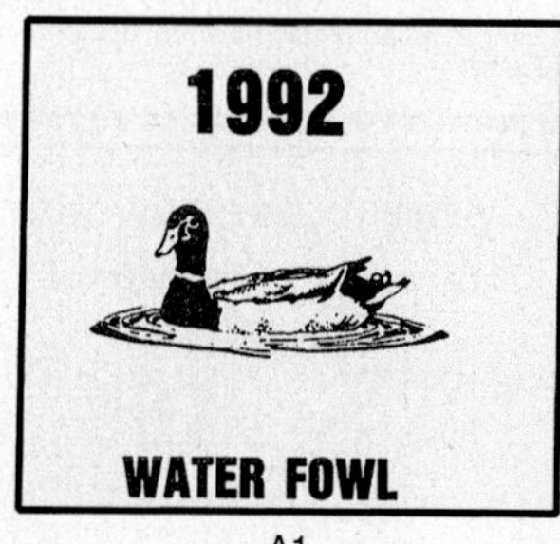

A1

1992-98 **Die cut, self-adhesive**

No.	Description	Unused	Used
1	A1 black	16.00	5.00
2	A1 black, *1993*	10.00	4.00
	Inscribed "SRST"		
3	A1 black, *1994*	8.00	3.00
4	A1 black, *1995*	15.00	5.00
5	A1 black, *1996*	13.00	4.00
6	A1 black, *1997*	9.00	4.00
7	A1 black, *1998*	15.00	5.00

A2

Serially Numbered in Red

1999-2004 ***Rouletted***

No.	Description	Unused	Used
8	A2 black	10.00	5.00
9	A2 black, *2000*	9.00	6.00
10	A2 black, *2001*	9.00	6.00
11	A2 black, *yellow, 2002*	12.50	9.00
12	A2 black, *2003*	9.00	6.00
13	A2 yellow, *2004*	9.00	6.00

WINNEBAGO INDIAN RESERVATION

Nebraska
Migratory Bird Stamps

Catalogue values for all unused stamps in this section are for Never Hinged items.

A1

1997 **Die cut, self-adhesive**

No.	Description	Unused	Used
1	A1 multicolored	9.00	4.50

ZUNI INDIAN RESERVATION

New Mexico
Habitat Stamps

Catalogue values for all unused stamps in this section are for Never Hinged items.

A1

A2

A3

Nos. 2-16 have various native designs. Each has a year date.

Serially Numbered in Red

1995-2010 **Die cut, self-adhesive**

1	A1	multicolored	17.50	9.00

Serially Numbered in Black

2	A2	multicolored, *1996*	20.00	10.00
3	A2	multicolored, *1997*	20.00	10.00
4	A2	multicolored, *1998*	32.50	12.50
5	A2	multicolored, *1999*	18.00	10.00
6	A2	multicolored, *2000*	18.00	10.00
7	A2	multicolored, *2001*	22.50	10.00
8	A2	multicolored, *2002*	22.50	10.00
9	A2	multicolored, *2003*	22.50	10.00
10	A2	multicolored, *2004*	22.50	10.00

Serially Numbered in Red

11	A2	multicolored, *2005*	22.50	10.00
12	A2	multicolored, *2006*	22.50	10.00
13	A2	multicolored, *2007*	22.50	10.00
a.		Plastic coated, no gum	*22.50*	

Plastic Coated Without Gum

14	A2	multicolored, *2008*	*22.50*	
15	A2	multicolored, *2009*	*22.50*	
16	A3	multicolored, *2010*	*22.50*	

SAVINGS STAMPS

"Savings Stamps" is a general philatelic category that includes four slightly different types of stamps issued at different times by either the U.S. Post Office Department or the U.S. Treasury Department. Their common feature was that they all effectively acted as a means for ordinary citizens to save and/or invest incrementally, a little bit at a time. At the same time, the investments effectively were loans to the federal government.

The four types of Savings Stamps are Postal Savings Stamps (issued from 1911-41) and Savings Stamps (1954-61), both issued by the Post Office Department; and War Savings Stamps (1917-45) and a Treasury Savings Stamp (1920), both issued by the Treasury Department.

Postal Savings Stamps were issued in 10c to $5.00 denominations and were redeemable in the form of credits to postal savings accounts. The 1911 10c stamps were available either as stamps or as a stamp imprint on a card to which other stamps could be added. The postal savings system was discontinued March 28, 1966.

Savings Stamps, also issued in 10c to $5.00 denominations, are the savings stamps most familiar to older philatelists. These collectors may remember buying these stamps at school and placing them in booklets. When full, the booklets were redeemable in the form of United States savings bonds. Sale of Savings Stamps was discontinued June 30, 1970.

War Savings Stamps were issued in 25c and $5 denominations (1917-20) and 10c to $5 denominations (1942-45). They were redeemable in the form of United States treasury war certificates, defense bonds or war bonds.

One Treasury Savings Stamp with a $1.00 denomination was issued in 1920. These stamps were redeemable in the form of either war savings stamps or treasury savings certificates.

POSTAL SAVINGS STAMPS

Values for unused Postal Savings stamps are for examples with full original gum. Values for used examples of Nos. PS1, PS4, PS6-PS10 are for stamps with cancels. Values for used examples of Nos. PS11-PS15 and S1-S7 are for stamps without gum.

PS1

Plates of 400 subjects in four panes of 100 each
FLAT PLATE PRINTING

1911, Jan. 3 **Wmk. 191** **Engr.** ***Perf. 12***
Size of design: 18x21½mm

PS1	PS1	10c **orange**	8.50	1.40
		Never hinged	17.50	
		Block of 4, 2mm spacing	37.50	
		Block of 4, 3mm spacing	40.00	
		P# strip of 3, Impt. open star	57.50	
		P# block of 6, Impt. open star	550.00	

Plate Nos. 5504-5507.

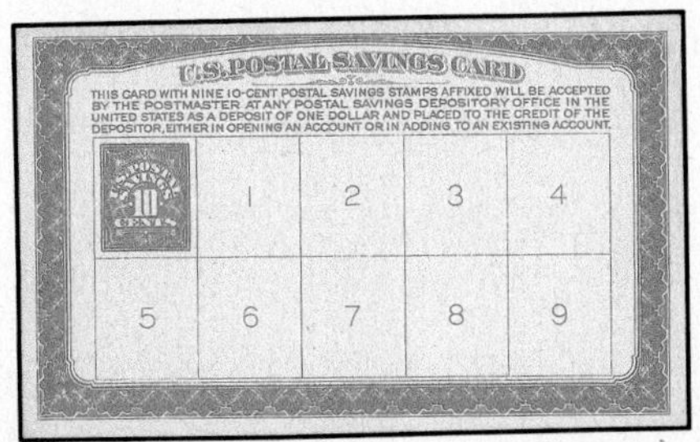

PS1a

Size of design: 137x79mm
Imprinted on Deposit Card

1911, Jan. 3 **Unwmk.**

PS2	PS1a	10c **orange**	300.00	65.00

A 10c deep blue with head of Washington in circle imprinted on deposit card (design 136x79mm) exists, but there is no evidence that it was ever placed in use.

1911, Aug. 14 **Wmk. 190** ***Perf. 12***

PS4	PS1	10c **deep blue**	5.00	1.00
		Never hinged	8.50	
		Block of 4, 2mm spacing	22.50	
		Block of 4, 3mm spacing	25.00	
		P# strip of 3, Impt. open star	30.00	
		P# block of 6, Impt. open star	200.00	
		Never hinged	400.00	

Plate Nos. 5504-5507.

Imprinted on Deposit Card

1911 **Size of design: 133x78mm** **Unwmk.**

PS5	PS1a	10c **deep blue**	*250.00*	40.00

1936 **Unwmk.** ***Perf. 11***

PS6	PS1	10c **deep blue**	3.00	1.25
		violet blue	3.00	1.25
		Never hinged	5.50	
		Block of 4	15.00	
		P# block of 6, Impt. solid star	85.00	
		Never hinged	150.00	

Plate Nos. 21485, 21486.

PS2

PS2a

Plates of 400 subjects in four panes of 100 each
FLAT PLATE PRINTING

1940 **Unwmk.** **Engr.** ***Perf. 11***
Size of design: 19x22mm

PS7	PS2	10c **deep ultramarine,** *Apr. 3*	17.50	6.00
		Never hinged	32.00	
		Block of 4	75.00	
		P# block of 6	190.00	
		Never hinged	325.00	

Plate Nos. 22540, 22541.

PS8	PS2	25c **dark car rose,** *Apr. 1*	20.00	9.00
		Never hinged	36.00	
		Block of 4	85.00	
		P# block of 6	220.00	
		Never hinged	375.00	

Plate Nos. 22542, 22543.

PS9	PS2	50c **dark blue green,** *Apr. 1*	50.00	17.50
		Never hinged	90.00	
		Block of 4	210.00	
		P# block of 6	700.00	
		Never hinged	1,200.	

Plate No. 22544.

PS10	PS2a	$1 **gray black,** *Apr. 1*	140.00	17.50
		Never hinged	250.00	
		Block of 4	575.00	
		P# block of 6	1,500.	
		Never hinged	2,650.	

Plate No. 22545.

Nos. PS11-PS15 redeemable in the form of United States Treasury Defense, War or Savings Bonds.

Catalogue values for unused stamps in this section, from this point to the end, are for Never Hinged items.

Minute Man — PS3

E.E. Plates of 400 subjects in four panes of 100 each
ROTARY PRESS PRINTING

1941, May 1 **Unwmk.** ***Perf. 11x10½***
Size of design: 19x22½mm

PS11 PS3 10c **rose red** .60 .25
a. 10c **carmine rose** .60
Block of 4 2.40
P# block of 4 7.25
b. Bklt. pane of 10, *July 30,* trimmed horizontal edges 50.00
As "b," with Electric Eye marks at left 55.00
c. Booklet pane of 10, perf. horizontal edges 100.00
As "c," with Electric Eye marks at left 115.00

Plate Nos., sheet stamps, 22714-22715, 22722-22723, 148245-148246.
Plate Nos., booklet panes, 147084, 147086, 148241-148242.

PS12 PS3 25c **blue green** 2.00 .25
Block of 4 8.25
P# block of 4 22.50
b. Bklt. pane of 10, *July 30* 60.00
Booklet pane with Electric Eye marks at left 65.00

Plate Nos., sheet stamps, 22716-22717, 22724-22725, 148247-148248.
Plate Nos., booklet panes, 147087-147088, 148243-148244.

PS13 PS3 50c **ultramarine** 7.50 1.00
Block of 4 32.50
P# block of 4 50.00

Plate Nos. 22718-22719, 22726-22727.

PS14 PS3 $1 **gray black** 12.50 2.50
Block of 4 52.50
P# block of 4 75.00

Plate Nos. 22720, 22728.

FLAT PLATE PRINTING
Plates of 100 subjects in four panes of 25 each

Size: 36x46mm ***Perf. 11***

PS15 PS3 $5 **sepia** 42.50 10.00
Block of 4 175.00
P# block of 6 at top or bottom 475.00

Plate Nos. 22730-22737, 22740.

SAVINGS STAMPS

Catalogue values for unused stamps in this section are for Never Hinged items.

Minute Man — S1

E.E. Plates of 400 subjects in four panes of 100 each
ROTARY PRESS PRINTING

1954-57 **Unwmk.** ***Perf. 11x10½***
Size of design: 19x22½mm

S1 S1 10c **rose red,** wet printing, *Nov. 30, 1954* .60 .25
Block of 4 2.40
P# block of 4 3.50
a. Booklet pane of 10, *Apr. 22, 1955* 150.00
Booklet pane with Electric Eye marks at left 165.00
b. Dry printing .40 .25
Block of 4 1.75
P# block of 4 3.00
c. As "b," booklet pane of 10 150.00
Booklet pane with Electric Eye marks at left 165.00

Plate Nos., sheet stamps, 164991-164992 (wet), 165917-165918, 166643-166644, 167089-167090, 168765-168766 (dry).
Plate Nos., booklet panes, 165218-165219 (wet), 165954-165955, 167001-167002 (dry).

S2 S1 25c **blue green,** wet printing, *Dec. 30, 1954* 7.50 1.00
Block of 4 30.00
P# block of 4 35.00
a. Booklet pane of 10, *Apr. 15, 1955* 850.00
Booklet pane with Electric Eye marks at left 875.00
Complete booklet, 4 #S2a *3,750.*
b. Dry printing 7.50 1.00
Block of 4 30.00
P# block of 4 35.00

c. As "b," booklet pane of 10 800.00
Booklet pane with Electric Eye marks at left 825.00

Plate Nos., sheet stamps, 165007-165008 (wet), 165919-165920 (dry), booklet panes, 165220-165221 (wet), 165956-165957 (dry).

S3 S1 50c **ultramarine,** wet printing, *Dec. 31, 1956* 9.00 1.50
Block of 4 37.50
P# block of 4 50.00
a. Dry printing 9.00 1.50
Block of 4 37.50
P# block of 4 50.00

Plate Nos. 165050-165051 (wet), 166741-166742, 166941-166942 (dry).

S4 S1 $1 **gray black,** *Mar. 13, 1957* 25.00 4.00
Block of 4 100.00
P# block of 4 120.00

Plate Nos. 166097-166098, 166683-166684.

Minute Man — S2

FLAT PLATE PRINTING
Plates of 100 subjects in four panes of 25 each

Size: 36x46mm ***Perf. 11***

S5 S2 $5 **sepia,** *Nov. 30, 1956* 110.00 15.00
Block of 4 475.00
P# block of 6 at top or bottom 900.00

Plate No. 166068.

Minute Man and 48-Star Flag — S3

GIORI PRESS PRINTING
Plates of 400 subjects in four panes of 100 each

1958, Nov. 18 **Unwmk.** ***Perf. 11***

S6 S3 25c **dark blue & carmine** 2.00 .25
Block of 4 8.00
P# block of 4 10.00
a. Booklet pane of 10 75.00

Plate Nos.: sheet stamps, 166921, 166925, 166946; booklet panes, 166913, 166916.

Minute Man and 50-Star Flag — S4

Plates of 400 subjects in four panes of 100 each.

1961 **Unwmk.** ***Perf. 11***

S7 S4 25c **dark blue & carmine** 1.50 .25
Block of 4 6.00
P# block of 4 11.00
a. Booklet pane of 10 300.00

Plate Nos.: sheet stamps, 167473, 167476, 167486, 167489, 169089; booklet panes, 167495, 167502, 167508, 167516.

WAR SAVINGS STAMPS

Values for unused War Savings stamps and the Treasury Savings stamp are for examples with full original gum. Nos. WS2 and WS3 are known canceled, but other War Savings stamps were left uncanceled. Examples without gum generally were reomved from savings certificates or booklets. **Caution:** Beware of stamps without gum that have been regummed to appear unused with gum.

WS1

Plates of 300 subjects in six panes of 50 each
FLAT PLATE PRINTING

1917, Dec. 1 **Unwmk.** **Engr.** ***Perf. 11***
Size of design: 28x18½mm

WS1 WS1 25c **deep green** 16.00 2.25
Never hinged 30.00
On document (thrift card) 7.50
Block of 4 70.00
Margin strip of 3, P# 80.00
P# block of 6 1,200.

Plate Nos. 56800, 56810-56811, 56817, 57074-57077, 57149-57152, 57336, 57382, 57395-57396, 57399, 57443, 58801-58804, 59044-59045, 59156, 61207-61210.

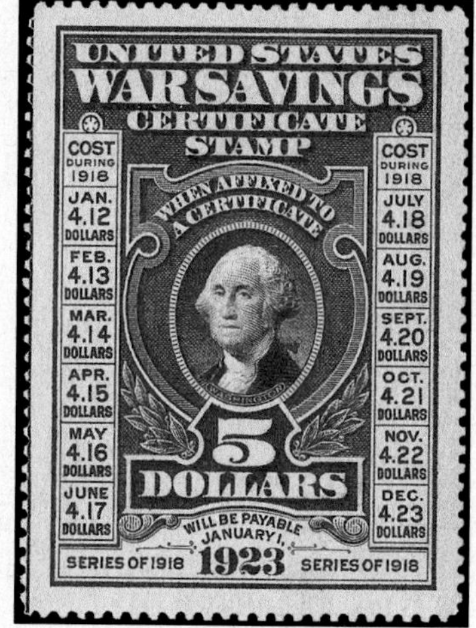

George Washington — WS2

Plates of 80 subjects in four panes of 20 each
FLAT PLATE PRINTING

1917 **Unwmk.** **Engr.** ***Perf. 11***
Size of design: 39x55mm

WS2 WS2 $5 **deep green,** *Nov. 17* 125.00 35.00
Never hinged 250.00
No gum 30.00
On document 45.00
Block of 4 450.00 —
Margin stamp with P# 150.00
P# block of 6 *1,650.*
b. Vert. pair, imperf. horiz. —

Plate Nos. 56914-56917, 57066-57073, 57145-57148, 57169-57176, 57333-57334, 57343-57348, 58431, 58433-58438, 58726-58729, 59071, 60257-60260, 60659-60662, 60665-60668, 60846-60852, 60899, 61203-61206, 61265-61268, 61360-61367, 61388, 61435, 61502.

Rouletted 7

WS3 WS2 $5 **deep green** 1,200. 650.
Never hinged *2,750.*
No gum 475.
On document 700.
Block of 4 5,000.
Margin copy with P# 2,000.

Benjamin Franklin — WS3

Plates of 150 subjects in six panes of 25 each
FLAT PLATE PRINTING

1919, July 3 Unwmk. Engr. ***Perf. 11***
Size of design: 27x36mm

	Unused	Used
WS4 WS3 $5 **deep blue**	325.	
Never hinged	800.	
No gum	160.	
On document		275.
Block of 4	1,350.	
Margin stamp with P#	500.	
Margin stamp with inverted P#	600.	

Plate Nos. 61882-61885, 61910-61913, 61970-61972, 61997-61998, 62007-62013.

George Washington WS4

Plates of 100 subjects in four panes of 25 each
FLAT PLATE PRINTING

1919, Dec. 11 Unwmk. Engr. ***Perf. 11***
Size of design: 36x41½mm

	Unused	Used
WS5 WS4 $5 **carmine**	800.	
Never hinged	2,250.	
No gum	350.	
On document		500.
Block of 4	*3,500.*	
Margin stamp with P#	1,100.	

Plate Nos. 67545-67552, 69349-69352, 69673-69675, 69677-69680, 69829.

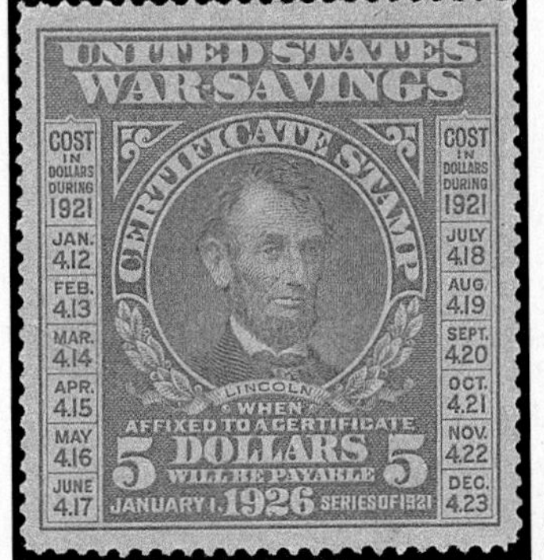

Abraham Lincoln WS5

Plates of 100 subjects in four panes of 25 each
FLAT PLATE PRINTING

1920, Dec. 21 Unwmk. Engr. ***Perf. 11***
Size of design: 39½x42mm

	Unused	Used
WS6 WS5 $5 **orange,** *green*	4,500.	
Never hinged	*12,000.*	
No gum	1,250.	
On document		1,500.
Block of 4		*6,500.*
Margin stamp with P#	5,000.	

Plate Nos. 73129-73136.

Catalogue values for unused stamps in this section, from this point to the end, are for Never Hinged items.

Minute Man — WS6

Plates of 400 subjects in four panes of 100 each
ROTARY PRESS PRINTING

1942 Unwmk. ***Perf. 11x10½***
Size of design: 19x22½mm

	Unused	Used
WS7 WS6 10c **rose red,** *Oct. 29*	.60	.25
a. 10c carmine rose	.60	
Block of 4	2.40	
P# block of 4	6.00	
b. Booklet pane of 10, *Oct. 27*	50.00	
Booklet pane with Electric Eye marks at left	55.00	

Plate Nos., sheet stamps, 149492-149495, 150206-150207, 150706-150707, 155311-155312.
Plate Nos., booklet panes, 149655-149657, 150664.

	Unused	Used
WS8 WS6 25c **dark blue green,** *Oct. 15*	1.10	.25
Block of 4	5.00	
P# block of 4	8.25	
b. Booklet pane of 10, *Nov. 6*	50.00	
Booklet pane with Electric Eye marks at left	55.00	

Plate Nos., sheet stamps, 149587-149590, 150320-150321, 150708-150709, 155313-155314, 155812-155813, 156517-156518, booklet panes, 149658-149660, 150666.

	Unused	Used
WS9 WS6 50c **deep ultra,** *Nov. 12*	4.00	1.25
Block of 4	16.00	
P# block of 4	22.50	

Plate Nos. 149591-149594.

	Unused	Used
WS10 WS6 $1 **gray black,** *Nov. 17*	12.50	3.50
Block of 4	52.50	
P# block of 4	70.00	

Plate Nos. 149595-149598.

WS7

FLAT PLATE PRINTING
Plates of 100 subjects in four panes of 25 each

1945 Unwmk. Size: 36x46mm ***Perf. 11***

	Unused	Used
WS11 WS7 $5 **violet brown**	55.00	17.50
Block of 4	240.00	
P# block of 6 at top or bottom	500.00	

Plate Nos. 150131-150134, 150291.

Type of 1942
Coil Stamps

1943, Aug. 5 Unwmk. ***Perf. 10 Vertically***

	Unused	Used
WS12 WS6 10c **rose red**	2.75	.90
Pair	6.00	
Line pair	10.50	

Plate Nos. 153286-153287.

	Unused	Used
WS13 WS6 25c **dark blue green**	5.00	1.75
Pair	10.50	
Line pair	22.50	

Plate Nos. 153289-153290.

TREASURY SAVINGS STAMP

Alexander Hamilton TS1

FLAT PLATE PRINTING

1920, Dec. 21 Unwmk. Engr. ***Perf. 11***
Size of design: 33½x33½mm

	Unused	Used
TS1 TS1 $1 **red,** *green*	3,750.	
Never hinged	—	
No gum		1,500.
On document		1,750.
Block of 4	*15,000.*	
Margin stamp with P#	*5,000.*	

Plate Nos. 73196-73203.

No. TS1 was not canceled. Examples without gum are considered used, as these generally were removed from savings cards. **Caution:** Beware of stamps without gum that have been regummed to appear unused with gum.

TELEGRAPH STAMPS

These stamps were issued by the individual companies for use on their own telegrams, and can usually be divided into three classes: Free franking privileges issued to various railroad, newspaper and express company officials, etc., whose companies were large users of the lines; those issued at part cost to the lesser officials of the same type companies; and those bearing values which were usually sold to the general public. Occasionally, some of the companies granted the franking privilege to stockholders and minor State (not Federal) officials. Most Telegraph Stamps were issued in booklet form and will be found with one or more straight edges.

Serial numbers may show evidence of doubling, often of a different number. Such doubling is not scarce.

American Rapid Telegraph Company

Organized Feb. 21, 1879, in New York State. Its wires extended as far north as Boston, Mass., and west to Cleveland, Ohio. It was amalgamated with the Bankers and Merchants Telegraph Co., but when that company was unable to pay the fixed charges, the properties of the American Rapid Telegraph Company were sold on Mar. 11, 1891, to a purchasing committee comprised of James W. Converse and others. This purchasing committee deeded the property and franchise of the American Rapid Telegraph Company to the Western Union Telegraph Company on June 25, 1894. Issued three types of stamps: Telegram, Collect and Duplicate. Telegram stamps were issued in sheets of 100 and were used to prepay messages which could be dropped in convenient boxes for collection. Collect and duplicate stamps were issued in alternate rows on the same sheet of 100 subjects. Collect stamps were attached to telegrams sent collect, the receiver of which paid the amount shown by the stamps, while the Duplicate stamps were retained by the Company as vouchers. **Remainders with punched cancellations were bought up by a New York dealer.**

T1

"Prepaid Telegram" Stamps

Engraved and Printed by the American Bank Note Co.

1881 *Perf. 12*

No.	Description	Unused	Used
1T1	T1 1c **black**	20.00	4.75
	Punched		.25
	Block of 4	87.50	
	Punched		1.00
1T2	T1 3c **orange**	50.00	32.50
	Punched		1.50
	Block of 4, punched		10.00
1T3	T1 5c **bister brown**	4.75	1.25
	Punched		.25
	Block of 4	21.00	
	Punched		1.10
a.	5c **brown**	4.75	1.40
	Punched		.25
	Block of 4	21.00	
	Punched		1.00
1T4	T1 10c **purple**	20.00	5.75
	Punched		.25
	Block of 4	85.00	
	Punched		1.00
1T5	T1 15c **green**	8.75	2.50
	Punched		.25
	Block of 4	40.00	
	Punched		1.00
1T6	T1 20c **red**	8.75	2.50
	Punched		.25
	Block of 4, punched		.80
1T7	T1 25c **rose**	12.00	1.75
	Punched		.25
	Block of 4	52.50	
	Punched		1.00
1T8	T1 50c **blue**	32.50	12.50
	Punched		1.50
	Block of 4, punched		8.00

T2

"Collect" Stamps

No.	Description	Unused	Used
1T9	T2 1c **brown**	8.00	5.50
	Punched		.25
1T10	T1 5c **blue**	6.50	4.00
	Punched		.25
1T11	T2 15c **red brown**	6.75	3.25
	Punched		.25
1T12	T2 20c **olive green**	6.50	4.00
	Punched		.25

T3

"Office Coupon" Stamps

No.	Description	Unused	Used
1T13	T3 1c **brown**	14.50	4.40
	Punched		.25
a.	Pair, #1T9, 1T13, punched		2.00
	As "a," block of 4, punched		4.50
1T14	T3 5c **blue**	12.00	5.25
	Punched		.25
a.	Pair, #1T10, 1T14	60.00	
	Punched		3.00
	As "a," block of 4	125.00	
	Punched		7.00
1T15	T3 15c **red brown**	21.00	4.75
	Punched		.25
a.	Pair, #1T11, 1T15	50.00	
	Punched		2.50
	As "a," block of 4	110.00	
	Punched		5.50
1T16	T3 20c **olive green**	21.00	4.75
	Punched		.25
a.	Pair, #1T12, 1T16, punched		2.75
	As "a," block of 4, punched		6.00

Atlantic Telegraph Company

Organized 1884 at Portland, Maine. Its lines extended from Portland, Me., to Boston, Mass., and terminated in the office of the Baltimore and Ohio Telegraph Company at Boston. Later bought out by the Baltimore and Ohio Telegraph Co. Stamps issued by the Atlantic Telegraph Company could also be used for messages destined to any point on the Baltimore and Ohio system. Stamps were printed in panes of six and a full book sold for $10. **Remainders of these stamps, without control numbers, were purchased by a Boston dealer and put on the market about 1932.**

T4

1888 *Perf. 13*

No.	Description	Unused	Used
2T1	T4 1c **green**	6.00	—
	Remainders		2.25
	Pane of 6		—
	Remainders		14.00
2T2	T4 5c **blue**	9.00	—
	Remainders		2.25
	Pane of 6		—
	Remainders		14.00
a.	Horiz. pair, imperf. vert.		—
b.	Vert. pair, imperf. horiz.	25.00	—
2T3	T4 10c **purple brown**	10.00	—
	Remainders		2.25
	Pane of 6		—
	Remainders		14.00
a.	Horiz. pair, imperf. between	40.00	—
2T4	T4 25c **carmine**	7.50	—
	Remainders		2.25
	Pane of 6, remainders		16.00
a.	Vert. pair, imperf. horiz., remainders		—

Baltimore & Ohio Telegraph Companies

"The Baltimore & Ohio Telegraph Co. of the State of New York" was incorporated May 17, 1882. Organization took place under similar charter in 26 other states. It absorbed the National Telegraph Co. and several others. Extended generally along the lines of the Baltimore & Ohio Railroad, but acquired interests in other states. Company absorbed in 1887 by the Western Union Telegraph Co. Stamps were issued in booklet form and sold for $5 and $10, containing all denominations.

T5

Engraved by the American Bank Note Co.

1885 *Perf. 12*

No.	Description	Unused	Used
3T1	T5 1c **vermilion**	110.00	30.00
	Pane of 6	700.00	
3T2	T5 5c **blue**	110.00	40.00
3T3	T5 10c **red brown**	55.00	15.00
	Pane of 6	325.00	
3T4	T5 25c **orange**	95.00	30.00
3T5	T6 **brown**	1.75	
	Pane of 4	12.50	

T6

1886

No.	Description	Unused	Used
3T6	T6 **black**	2.00	*25.00*
	Pane of 4	22.50	

Imprint of Kendall Bank Note Co.

1886 Thin Paper *Perf. 14*

No.	Description	Unused	Used
3T7	T5 1c **green**	8.00	3.00
a.	Thick paper	15.00	.85
b.	Imperf., pair	90.00	
3T8	T5 5c **blue**	5.00	1.25
a.	Thick paper	11.00	4.00
b.	Imperf., pair		55.00
3T9	T5 10c **brown**	8.50	.75
a.	Thick paper	12.50	1.50
3T10	T5 25c **deep orange**	55.00	.75
a.	Thick paper	65.00	1.50

Used examples of Nos. 3T7-3T20 normally have heavy grid cancellations. Lightly canceled stamps command a premium.

Litho. by A. Hoen & Co.

1886 Imprint of firm *Perf. 12*

No.	Description	Unused	Used
3T11	T5 1c **green**	3.00	.65
	Pane of 6	22.50	—
3T12	T5 5c **blue**	9.00	.65
	Pane of 6	60.00	—
a.	Imperf., pair	90.00	
3T13	T5 10c **dark brown**	9.00	.75
	Pane of 6	60.00	—
a.	Vert. pair, imperf. between	60.00	

Wmk. "A HOEN AND CO. BALTIMORE" in double lined capitals in sheet

Perf. 12

No.	Description	Unused	Used
3T14	T5 1c **green**	17.50	1.25
	Pane of 6	115.00	—
3T15	T5 5c **blue**	30.00	1.50
	Pane of 6	190.00	—
a.	Imperf., pair	52.50	—
3T16	T5 10c **dark brown**	20.00	1.25
	Pane of 6	130.00	—

Lithographed by Forbes Co., Boston

1887 Imprint of firm *Perf. 12½*

No.	Description	Unused	Used
3T17	T5 1c **green**	60.00	2.75
3T18	T5 5c **blue**	90.00	6.00
3T19	T5 10c **brown**	90.00	5.50
3T20	T5 25c **yellow**	90.00	8.25
a.	25c **orange**	90.00	5.50

Baltimore & Ohio-Connecticut River Telegraph Companies

The Connecticut River Telegraph Co. ran from New Haven to Hartford. An agreement was entered wherein the Baltimore & Ohio System had mutual use of their lines. This agreement terminated when the Baltimore & Ohio System was absorbed by the Western Union. The Connecticut River Telegraph Company then joined the United Lines. In 1885 stamps (black on yellow) were issued and sold in booklets for $10. In 1887 the Connecticut River Telegraph Co. had extended its lines to New Boston, Mass., and new books of stamps (black on blue) were issued for use on this extension. **Remainders were canceled with bars and sold to a New York dealer.**

T7

1885-87 — *Perf. 11*

No.	Type	Description	Unused	Used
4T1	T7	1c **black**, *yellow*	7.50	6.00
		Remainders		1.25
		Pane of 10	77.50	
		Remainders		6.00
a.		Imperf., pair	40.00	
b.		Vert. pair, imperf. horiz., remainders		—
4T2	T7	5c **black**, *yellow*	5.00	10.00
		Remainders		1.00
		Pane of 10	52.50	
		Remainders		6.00
a.		Horizontal pair, imperf. between, remainders	500.00	400.00
b.		Vert. pair, imperf. between, remainders		35.00
c.		Imperf., pair, remainders		35.00
4T3	T7	1c **black**, *blue* ('87)	12.50	—
		Remainders		4.00
		Pane of 10	130.00	
		Remainders		35.00
4T4	T7	5c **black**, *blue* ('87)	15.00	9.00
		Remainders		4.00
		Pane of 10	160.00	
		Remainders		52.50

California State Telegraph Company

Incorporated June 17, 1854 as the California Telegraph Company and constructed a line from Nevada through Grass Valley to Auburn. Extended to run from San Francisco to Marysville via San Jose and Stockton. Later absorbed Northern Telegraph Co. and thus extended to Eureka. It was incorporated as the California State Telegraph Company on April 6, 1861. At the time of its lease to the Western Union on May 16, 1867 the California State consisted of the following companies which had been previously absorbed:

Alta California Telegraph Co., Atlantic and Pacific States Telegraph Co., National Telegraph Co., Northern California Telegraph Co., Overland Telegraph Co., Placerville and Humboldt Telegraph Co., Tuolumne Telegraph Co. Stamps were issued in booklets, six to a pane. **Remainders of Nos. 5T1 and 5T4 are without frank numbers.**

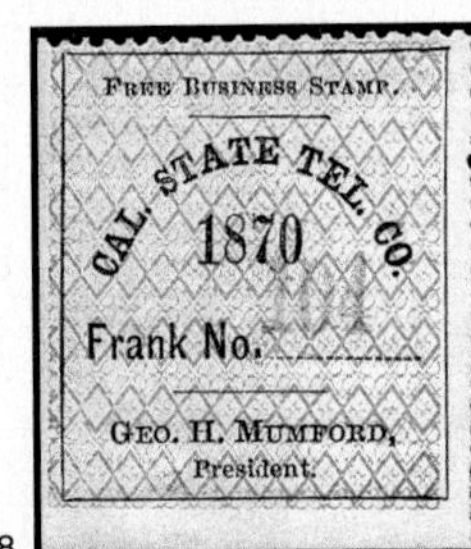

T8

1870 — *Perf. 13½*

No.	Type	Description	Unused	Used
5T1	T8	**black & blue**	500.	—
		Pane of 6	3,250.	
		Without number	1,250.	

T9

1870 — *Perf. 12, 13*

No.	Type	Description	Unused	Used
5T2	T9	**black & red,** without number	390.00	250.00

T10

1871 — Dated "1871"

No.	Type	Description	Unused	Used
5T3	T9	**black & red,** without number	1,250.	
a.		Imperf.	*2,500.*	—
5T4	T10	**black & salmon,** blue number	750.	650.00
		Pane of 6	*4,750.*	
		Without number	1,000.	

1872

No.	Type	Description	Unused	Used
5T5	T10	**green & red,** vert. red number (no year date)	400.00	
		Pane of 6	—	

1873 — Dated "1873"

No.	Type	Description	Unused	Used
5T6	T10	**red & salmon,** blue number	500.00	

1874 — Dated "1874"

No.	Type	Description	Unused	Used
5T7	T10	**blue & salmon,** black number	575.00	
		Pane of 6	—	

1875 — Dated "1875"

No.	Type	Description	Unused	Used
5T8	T10	**brown & green,** black number	475.00	
		Pane of 6	—	

City & Suburban Telegraph Company (New York City and Suburban Printing Telegraph Company)

Organized 1855. Extended only through New York City and Brooklyn. Sold out to the American Telegraph Co. Stamps were sold to the public for prepayment of messages, which could be dropped in convenient boxes for collection. Stamps were issued in sheets of 60 having a face value of $1. These were arranged in six vertical rows of ten, the horizontal rows having the following denominations: 2c, 1c, 1c, 1c, 2c, 3c.

Counterfeits are known both in black and blue, mostly on pelure or hard white paper. Originals are on soft wove paper, somewhat yellowish. Scalloped edge is more sharply etched on the counterfeits.

T11

Typo. — *Imperf.*

No.	Type	Description	Unused	Used
6T1	T11	1c **black**	650.	*750.*
		Pair	—	
		Block of 4	—	
6T2	T11	2c **black**	950.	950.
		Pair	—	
		Pair, 2c + 1c	1,750.	
6T3	T11	3c **black**	1,100.	1,000.
		Pair	—	
		Strip of 3, 1c, 2c & 3c	*7,500.*	

Colusa, Lake & Mendocino Telegraph Company

Was organized in California early in 1873. First known as the Princeton, Colusa and Grand Island Telegraph Co. In May, 1873 they completed their line from Princeton through Colusa, at which point it was connected with the Western Union office, to Grand Island. On Feb. 10, 1875 it was incorporated as the Colusa, Lake & Mendocino Telegraph Co. Its lines were extended into the counties of Colusa, Lake, Mendocino and Napa. Eventually reached a length of 260 miles. Went out of business in 1892. Stamps were issued for prepayment of messages and were sold in books. When sold they were stamped "P.L.W." (the superintendent's initials) in blue. The 5c value was printed 10 to a pane, being two horizontal rows of five. Of the 10c and 25c nothing definite is known about the settings.

T11a

1876 — *Perf. 12*

No.	Type	Description	Unused	Used
7T1	T11a	5c **black**	*1,100.*	—
		Block of 4	*5,000.*	
		Pane of 10	*14,000.*	
		Without "P.L.W."	*2,500.*	
7T2	T11a	10c **black**	*11,000.*	—
7T3	T11a	25c **red**	*12,000.*	—

Commercial Union Telegraph Company

Incorporated in New York State on March 31, 1886. Its lines ran from Albany through Troy to Berlin, N.Y., thence to North Adams, Mass. The lines of this Company, which was controlled by the Postal Telegraph Company, were later extended throughout Northern New York and the States of Massachusetts, Vermont, New Hampshire and Maine. Stamps issued in panes of four.

T12

T13

T14

1891 Lithographed by A. C. Goodwin — *Perf. 12*

No.	Type	Description	Unused	Used
8T1	T12	25c **yellow**	35.00	—
		Pane of 4	150.00	
8T2	T13	25c **green**	35.00	10.00
		Pane of 4	150.00	
a.		Horiz. pair, imperf. vert.	90.00	
8T3	T14	**lilac rose**	75.00	—

Mutual Union Telegraph Company

Incorporated October 4, 1880. Extended over 22 states. Absorbed about 1883 by the Western Union Telegraph Co. Franks issued for use of stockholders, in books, four to a pane.

T15

Engr. by Van Campen Engraving Co., New York

1882-83 — *Perf. 14*

No.	Type	Description	Unused	Used
9T1	T15	**blue**	50.00	20.00
		Pane of 4	225.00	
a.		Vert. pair, imperf. horizontal	140.00	—
b.		Imperf., pair	150.00	
9T2	T15	**carmine**	50.00	—
		Pane of 4	225.00	

North American Telegraph Company

Incorporated October 15, 1885 to run from Chicago to Minneapolis, later being extended into North and South Dakota. Absorbed in 1929 by the Postal System.

Apparently these stamps were not canceled when used. Issued in panes of four.

T15a

1899-1907 *Perf. 12*

10T1	T15a	**violet** (1899)	275.00	
		Pane of 4	1,100.	
10T2	T15a	**green** (1901)	950.00	
10T3	T15a	**dark brown** (1902)	750.00	
10T4	T15a	**blue** (1903)	500.00	
10T5	T15a	**violet** (1904)	350.00	
		Pane of 4	800.00	
a.		Horiz. pair, imperf. vertically	1,500.	
10T6	T15a	**red brown** (1905)	400.00	
a.		Imperf., pair	*2,000.*	—
10T7	T15a	**rose** (1906)	750.00	
10T8	T15a	**green** (1907)	2,250.	

Nos. 10T1 to 10T8 are known imperforate.

Northern Mutual Telegraph Company

Incorporated in New York State as the Northern Mutual Telegraph and Telephone Company on June 20, 1882. Its line, which consisted of a single wire, extended from Syracuse to Ogdensburg via Oswego, Watertown and Clayton, a distance of 170 miles. It was sold to the Bankers and Merchants Telegraph Company in 1883. Stamps were in use for a few days only in April, 1883. Issued in panes of 35 having a face value of $5. Seven horizontal rows of five covering all denominations as follows: 2 rows of 25c, 1 of 20c, 2 of 10c, 2 of 5c. **The remainders and plates were purchased by a New York dealer in 1887.**

T16

1883 *Perf. 14*

11T1	T16	5c **yellow brown**	6.50	—
		Block of 4	30.00	
11T2	T16	10c **yellow brown**	8.50	—
		Block of 4	37.50	
11T3	T16	20c **yellow brown**	20.00	—
		Horizontal pair	45.00	
11T4	T16	25c **yellow brown**	5.50	—
		Block of 4	30.00	
		Pane of 35	375.00	

The first reprints are lighter in color than the originals, perf. 14 and the gum is yellowish instead of white. The pane makeup differs in the reprints. The second reprints are darker than the original, perf. 12. Value $1 each.

Northern New York Telegraph Company

Organized about 1892. Extended from Malone, N.Y. to Massena, N.Y. Re-incorporated as the New York Union Telegraph Co. on April 2, 1896.

T16a

T16b

T16c

Typo. by Charles H. Smith, Brushton, N.Y.

1894-95 ***Rouletted***

12T1	T16a	**green** (overprinted in red "Frank 1894")	45.	
		Pane of 6	290.	
a.		Imperf., pair	50.	
		Pane of 6	160.	
12T2	T16a	**red** (overprinted in black "Frank 1895")	160.	
		Pane of 6	1,500.	
a.		Imperf., pair	50.	
		Pane of 6	160.	
12T3	T16b	1c **yellow** (overprinted in black "One")	80.	
		Pane of 6	525.	
a.		Imperf., pair	50.	
		Pane of 6	160.	
12T4	T16c	10c **blue** (overprinted in red "10")	150.	
		Pane of 6	950.	
a.		Imperf., pair	50.	
		Pane of 6	160.	

Some specialists believe that Nos. 12T1-12T4 were not issued and probably are essays. However, one Northern New York stamp is recorded tied to a piece of a telegraph form by a punch cancel.

Pacific Mutual Telegraph Company

Incorporated in Missouri on June 21, 1883. Operated between St. Louis and Kansas City, Mo., during the years 1884 and 1885. It had 15 offices, 425 miles of poles and 850 miles of wire. The controlling interests were held by the Bankers and Merchants Telegraph Company. The name was changed on Sept. 10, 1910 to Postal Telegraph-Cable Company of Missouri. Stamps were issued in booklets having a face value of $10 and containing 131 stamps as follows: 50-1c, 20-5c, 45-10c, 16-25c. They are not known used.

T17

1883 *Perf. 12*

13T1	T17	1c **black**	40.00	
13T2	T17	1c **slate**	.35	
		Block of 4	1.50	
a.		1c gray	.35	
		Block of 4	1.50	
13T3	T17	5c **black,** *buff*	1.00	
		Block of 4	4.50	
13T4	T17	10c **black,** *green*	.35	
		Block of 4	1.75	
a.		Horiz. pair, imperf. between	—	
13T5	T17	25c **black,** *salmon buff*	1.00	
		Block of 4	4.50	

Pacific Postal Telegraph-Cable Company

The Pacific Postal Telegraph-Cable Company was the Pacific Coast Department of the Postal Telegraph-Cable Company, and was organized in 1886. Its first wire ran from San Francisco to New Westminster, B.C., where it touched the lines of the Canadian Pacific Railway Company, then the only connection between the Eastern and Western Postal systems. Later the Postal's own wires spanned the continent and the two companies were united.

Stamps issued in booklet form in vertical panes of five.

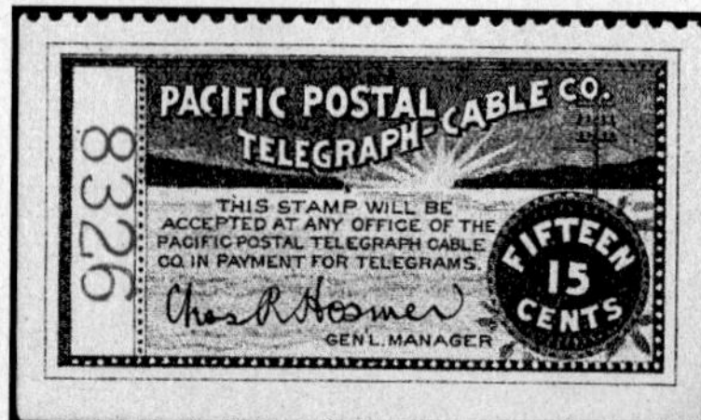
T17a

Perf. 12 Horiz.

14T1	T17a	10c **brown**	160.00	100.00
		Pane of 5	800.00	
14T2	T17a	15c **black**	160.00	100.00
		Pane of 5	800.00	
14T3	T17a	25c **rose red**	160.00	100.00
		Pane of 5	800.00	
14T4	T17a	40c **green**	160.00	100.00
		Pane of 5	800.00	
14T5	T17a	50c **blue**	190.00	100.00
		Pane of 5	950.00	

These stamps were issued with three sizes of frank numbers; large closely spaced, small closely spaced and small widely spaced figures. They also exist without frank numbers.

Postal Telegraph Company

Organized in New York in 1881. Reorganized in 1891 as the Postal Telegraph-Cable Co. The Postal Telegraph Co stamps of 1885 were issued in sheets of 100. **Some years after the reorganization a New York dealer purchased the remainders which were canceled with a purple star.** The Postal Telegraph-Cable Co. issued frank stamps in booklets, usually four stamps to a pane. This company was merged with the Western Union Telegraph Company in 1943.

T18

T19

T20

T21

Engraved by Hamilton Bank Note Co.

1885 *Perf. 14*

15T1	T18	10c **green**	4.00	—
		Remainders		.25
		Block of 4	17.50	
		Remainders		1.25
a.		Horiz. pair, imperf. btwn., remainders		20.00
b.		10c **deep green**	3.50	—
		Remainders		.25
		Block of 4	15.00	
		Remainders		1.25
15T2	T19	15c **orange red**	3.50	—
		Remainders		.60
		Block of 4	15.00	—
		Remainders		3.00
a.		Horizontal pair, imperf. between	37.50	
15T3	T20	25c **blue**	2.00	5.00
		Remainders		.25
		Block of 4	9.00	
		Remainders		.75
a.		Horizontal pair, imperf. between	37.50	—
15T4	T21	50c **brown**	1.75	—
		Remainders		.60
		Block of 4	8.00	
		Remainders		3.00

The 25c in ultramarine and the 50c in black were printed and perforated 16 but are not known to have been issued. Value about $7.50 each.

T22

T22a

Typographed by Moss Engraving Co.

1892-1920 *Perf. 14*

Signature of A.B. Chandler

15T5	T22	**blue gray** (1892)	50.00	
a.		Imperf., pair	120.00	

Perf. 13 to 14½ and Compound

15T6	T22	**gray lilac** (1892)	55.00	
15T7	T22	**red** (1893)	20.00	10.00
		Pane of 4	85.00	

15T8 T22 **red brown** (1893) 6.00 4.00

Perf. 12

15T9 T22 **violet brown** (1894) 6.75
15T10 T22 **gray green** (1894) 4.50
a. Imperf., pair 10.00
Pane of 4 25.00
15T11 T22 **blue** (1895) 50.00
15T12 T22 **rose** (1895) 500.00

Nos. 15T11 and 15T12 are from a new die resembling T22 but without shading under "Postal Telegraph Co."

15T13 T22a **slate green** (1896) 5.50
Pane of 4 25.00
15T14 T22a **brown** (1896) 450.00

Signature of Albert B. Chandler

15T15 T22a **lilac brown** (1897) 1.50 *10.00*
Pane of 4 6.50
15T16 T22a **orange** (1897) 400.00

Typographed by Knapp & Co.

15T17 T22a **pale blue** (1898) 2.25
Pane of 4 10.00
15T18 T22a **rose** (1898) 500.00

Typographed by Moss Engraving Co.

Perf. 12

15T19 T22a **orange brown** (1899) 1.75
Pane of 4 8.25

Perf. 11

15T20 T22a **blue** (1900) 3.00 3.00
a. "I" of "Complimentary" omitted .75 1.00
Pane of 4 3.25

The variety 15T20a represents a different die with many variations in the design.

Perf. 14

15T21 T22a **sea green** (1901) .60 .60
Pane of 4 2.50
a. Horiz. pair, imperf. between —

Signature of John W. Mackay

15T22 T22a **chocolate** (1902) 1.25 .65
Pane of 4 5.50
a. Horiz. pair, imperf. vert. —

Signature of Clarence H. Mackay

15T23 T22a **blue** (1903) 2.75 2.50
Pane of 4 12.50

Perf. 12

15T24 T22a **blue,** *blue* (1904) 4.00 3.00
Pane of 4 17.50
15T25 T22a **blue,** *yellow* (1905) 5.00
Pane of 4 22.50
15T26 T22a **blue,** *light blue* (1906) 5.00 5.00
Pane of 4 22.50
a. Horiz. pair, imperf. vert. —

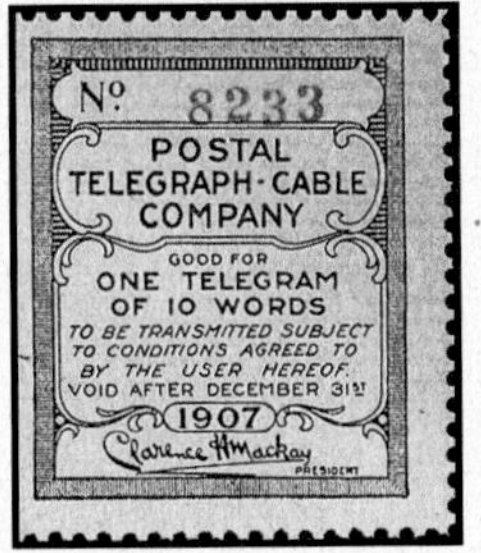

T22b

Perf. 12

15T27 T22b **black,** *yellow* (laid paper) (1907) 80.00
Pane of 4 350.00
15T28 T22b **blue,** *pink* (laid paper) (1907) 50.00
Pane of 4 225.00

"One Telegram of 10 Words" — T22c

15T29 T22c **blue** (1908) 65.00
Pane of 4 275.00
15T30 T22c **yellow** (1908) 550.00
Pane of 4 2,250.
15T31 T22c **black** (1908) 55.00
Pane of 4 225.00
15T32 T22c **brown** (1909) 45.00
Pane of 4 190.00
a. Date reads "1908" *2,350.*
Pair, one #15T32a, one #15T32 *3,000.*
15T33 T22c **olive green** (1909) 25.00
Pane of 4 105.00

15T34 T22c **dark blue** (1910) 40.00
15T35 T22c **dark brown** (1910) 40.00
Pane of 4 170.00
15T36 T22c **violet** (1911) 550.00
15T37 T22c **blue** (1912) 850.00
15T38 T22c **violet** (1913) 1,250.

Perf. 14

15T39 T22c **violet** (not dated) (1914) 550.00
a. Red violet 600.00
Pane of 4 2,250.

"One Telegram"

Perf. 12

15T40 T22c **blue** (1908) 60.00
Pane of 4 260.00
a. Horiz. pair, imperf. between 300.00
15T41 T22c **lilac** (1909) 25.00
Pane of 4 110.00
15T42 T22c **black,** *yellow* (laid paper) (1910) 550.00
a. Date reads "1909" *2,500.*
15T43 T22c **violet** (1910) 15.00
a. **Red violet** 15.00
Pane of 4 —
Pane of 8 140.00
15T44 T22c **dark blue** (1911) 60.00
Pane of 4 260.00
a. Vert. pair, imperf between *1,500.*
15T45 T22c **light violet** (1912) 40.00
Pane of 4 180.00

Perf. 14

15T46 T22c **dark blue** (1913) 175.00
Pane of 8 1,500.
a. Imperf. vertically, pair 260.00
b. Perf. 12 100.00
Pane of 4 425.00
c. Horiz. pair, imperf. between *500.00*
15T47 T22c **dark blue** (not dated) (1914) (no spurs) .25
Pane of 4 2.50
Pane of 8 5.00
a. Dark blue (spurs) .25
Pane of 4 2.50

In panes of four the stamps are 4½mm apart horizontally, panes of eight 5½mm. There are two types of design T22c, one with and one without spurs on colored curved lines above "O" of "Postal" and below "M" of "Company". No. 15T47 comes in both types.

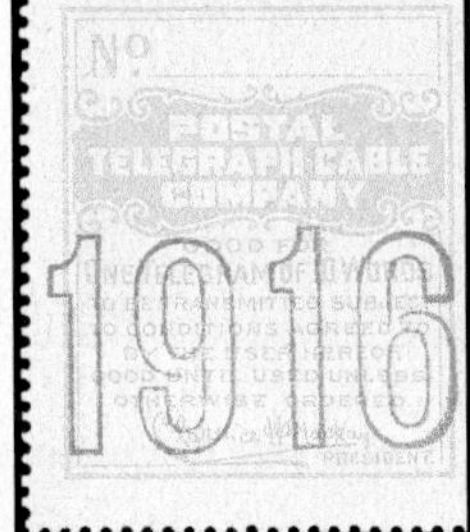

Nos. 15T39 & 15T47 Handstamped, All Four Numerals Complete on Each Stamp

15T47A T22c **violet** (1916) *5,000.*
15T48 T22c **dark blue** (1917) *2,500.*
15T49 T22c **dark blue** (1918) *2,300.*
15T49A T22c **dark blue** (1919) 110.
Pane of 8 975.
15T49B T22c **dark blue** (1920) 90.
Pane of 8 825.

No. 15T49B is handstamped "1920" in small single line numerals.

T22d

1907 *Perf. 12*

15T50 T22d 1c **dark brown** 35.00 20.00
Pane of 4 150.00
15T51 T22d 2c **dull violet** 30.00 20.00
Pane of 4 130.00
15T52 T22d 5c **green** 35.00 22.50
Pane of 4 150.00
15T53 T22d 25c **light red** 37.50 20.00
Pane of 4 160.00

T22e

1931 *Perf. 14*

15T54 T22e 25c **gray blue** (1931) .25
Pane of 6 2.00

No. 15T54 Overprinted "1932" and Control Number in Red

1932

15T55 T22e 25c **gray blue** 110.00
Pane of 6 700.00

Many varieties between Nos. 15T5 and 15T55 are known without frank numbers.

OFFICIAL

Inscribed "Supts."

1900-14 *Perf. 11, 12*

15TO1 T22a **black,** *magenta* 2.00 2.00

"C. G. W." (Chicago, Great Western Railroad) at top

For Use of Railroad Superintendents

Perf. 12

15TO2 T22c **carmine** (1908) 50.00
Pane of 4 240.00
15TO3 T22c **carmine** (1909) 600.00
15TO4 T22c **carmine** (1910) 750.00
15TO5 T22c **carmine** (1911) 600.00
15TO6 T22c **carmine** (1912) 190.00

Perf. 14

15TO7 T22c **carmine** (1913) 600.00
a. Perf. 12 *1,500.*
15TO8 T22c **dull red** (not dated) (1914) .50
Pane of 8 5.00

"E. P." (El Paso and Northeastern Railroad) at top

Perf. 12

15TO9 T22c **orange** (1908) 450.00

"I. C." (Illinois Central Railroad) at top

15TO10 T22c **green** (1908) 80.00
Pane of 4 330.00
15TO11 T22c **yellow green** (1909) 15.00
Pane of 4 —
Pane of 8 130.00
15TO12 T22c **dark green** (1910) 160.00
15TO13 T22c **dark green** (1911) 110.00
Pane of 4 475.00
Pane of 8 950.00
15TO14 T22c **dark green** (1912) 1,250.

Perf. 14

15TO15 T22c **dark green** (1913) 1,500.
15TO16 T22c **dark green** (not dated) (1914) (no spurs) 2.50
Pane of 4 11.00
Pane of 8 22.50
a. **Green** (spurs) 1.25
Pane of 4 7.50
b. Line under "PRESIDENT" (no spurs) 1.00
Pane of 8 12.50

(See note after No. 15T47.)

Both types of design T22c are known of 15TO16.

"O. D." (Old Dominion Steamship Co.) at top

Perf. 12

15TO17 T22c **violet** (1908) *4,000.*

"P. R." (Pennsylvania Railroad) at top

15TO18 T22c **orange brown** (1908) 35.00
Pane of 4 150.00
Pane of 8 300.00
15TO19 T22c **orange brown** (1909) 40.00
Pane of 4 175.00
Pane of 8 375.00
15TO20 T22c **orange brown** (1910) 40.00
Pane of 4 175.00
Pane of 8 375.00
15TO21 T22c **orange brown** (1911) 175.00
15TO22 T22c **orange brown** (1912) 110.00
Pane of 4 *700.00*

Perf. 14

15TO23 T22c **orange brown** (1913) 40.00
Pane of 8 350.00
a. Perf. 12 150.00

"P. R. R." (Pennsylvania Rail Road) at top

15TO24 T22c **orange** (not dated) (1914) 27.50
Pane of 4 125.00
Pane of 8 250.00

"S. W." (El Paso Southwestern Railroad) at top — 15TO26

Perf. 12

15TO25 T22c **yellow** (1909) 850.00
15TO26 T22c **yellow** (1910) 1,500.
15TO27 T22c **yellow** (1911) 500.00
15TO28 T22c **yellow** (1912) 500.00
Pane of 4 2,250.

Nos. 15TO1-15TO17 and 15TO25-15TO28 are without frank numbers.

TO1

1942 **Litho.** **Unwmk.**

15TO29 TO1 5c **pink** 6.50 3.00
Pane of 8 55.00
15TO30 TO1 25c **pale blue** 7.75 4.00
Pane of 8 65.00

The stamps were issued in booklets to all Postal Telegraph employees in the Armed Forces for use in the United States. They were discontinued Oct. 8, 1943. Used stamps normally bear manuscript cancellations.

Western Union Telegraph Company

Organized by consolidation in 1856, eventually extending coverage throughout the United States. Frank stamps were issued regularly since 1871 in booklet form. The large size, early issues, were in panes of four, 1871-1913; the medium size, later issues, were in panes of six, 1914-32; and the final small size issues were in panes of nine, 1933 to 1946.

T23

T24

Engraved by the National Bank Note Co.

1871-94 *Perf. 12*

Signature of William Orton

16T1 T23 **green** (not dated) (1871) 35.00 22.50
16T2 T23 **red** (not dated) (1872) 40.00 20.00
Pane of 4 175.00
16T3 T23 **blue** (not dated) (1873) 45.00 22.50
Pane of 4 200.00
16T4 T23 **brown** (not dated) (1874) 35.00 22.50
Pane of 4 160.00
16T5 T24 **deep green** (1875) 37.50 21.00
16T6 T24 **red** (1876) 40.00
Pane of 4 180.00
16T7 T24 **violet** (1877) 42.50 28.00
16T8 T24 **gray brown** (1878) 40.00

Signature of Norvin Green

16T9 T24 **blue** (1879) 40.00 28.00
Pane of 4 180.00

Engraved by the American Bank Note Co.

16T10 T24 **lilac rose** (1880) 27.50
Pane of 4 120.00
16T11 T24 **green** (1881) 25.00
Pane of 4 110.00
16T12 T24 **blue** (1882) 15.00
Pane of 4 70.00
16T13 T24 **yellow brown** (1883) 27.50
Pane of 4 120.00
16T14 T24 **gray violet** (1884) .60 .30
Pane of 4 3.00
16T15 T24 **green** (1885) 3.25 1.75
Pane of 4 15.00
16T16 T24 **brown violet** (1886) 3.25 2.00
Pane of 4 15.00
a. Imperf pair, without frank numbers —
16T17 T24 **red brown** (1887) 4.50
Pane of 4 22.50
16T18 T24 **blue** (1888) 3.25
Pane of 4 15.00
16T19 T24 **olive green** (1889) 1.75 .80
Pane of 4 8.00
16T20 T24 **purple** (1890) .75 .40
Pane of 4 3.25
16T21 T24 **brown** (1891) 1.50
Pane of 4 6.50
16T22 T24 **vermilion** (1892) 1.75
Pane of 4 8.00
16T23 T24 **blue** (1893) 1.40 .40
Pane of 4 6.25

Signature of Thos. T. Eckert

16T24 T24 **green** (1894) .60 .40
Pane of 4 3.00

T25

Engraved by the International Bank Note Co.

1895-1913 *Perf. 14*

Signature of Thos. T. Eckert

16T25 T25 **dark brown** (1895) .50 .40
Pane of 4 2.50
16T26 T25 **violet** (1896) .50 .40
Pane of 4 2.50
16T27 T25 **rose red** (1897) .50 .40
Pane of 4 2.50
16T28 T25 **yellow green** (1898) .50 .40
Pane of 4 2.50
a. Vertical pair, imperf. between —
16T29 T25 **olive green** (1899) .50 .40
Pane of 4 2.25
16T30 T25 **red violet,** perf. 13 (1900) .50 .45
Pane of 4 3.00
16T31 T25 **brown,** perf. 13 (1901) .50 .40
Pane of 4 2.50
16T32 T25 **blue** (1902) 8.00
Pane of 4 40.00

Signature of R.C. Clowry

16T33 T25 **blue** (1902) 8.00
Pane of 4 40.00
16T34 T25 **green** (1903) .60 .40
Pane of 4 4.00
16T35 T25 **red violet** (1904) .60
Pane of 4 2.75
16T36 T25 **carmine rose** (1905) .60 .50
Pane of 4 2.75
16T37 T25 **blue** (1906) .80 .40
Pane of 4 4.00
a. Vertical pair, imperf. between *200.00*
16T38 T25 **orange brown** (1907) 1.75 .90
Pane of 4 10.00
16T39 T25 **violet** (1908) 2.00 1.00
Pane of 4 9.00
16T40 T25 **olive green** (1909) 2.00
Pane of 4 10.00

Perf. 12

16T41 T25 **buff** (1910) .75 .50
Pane of 4 3.25

Engraved by the American Bank Note Co.

Signature of Theo. N. Vail

16T42 T24 **green** (1911) 14.00
Pane of 4 65.00
16T43 T24 **violet** (1912) 9.00
Pane of 4 42.50

Imprint of Kihn Brothers Bank Note Company

Perf. 14

16T44 T24 **brown** (1913) 10.00
Pane of 4 50.00
a. Vert. pair, imperf. between 35.00
b. Horiz. pair, imperf. between 40.00

T26

Engraved by the E.A. Wright Bank Note Co.

1914-15 Signature of Theo. N. Vail *Perf. 12*

16T45 T26 5c **brown** (1914) 1.10
Pane of 6 8.00
a. Vert. pair, imperf. between —
b. Horiz. pair, imperf. between —
16T46 T26 25c **slate** (1914) 7.00 5.00
Pane of 6 45.00

Signature of Newcomb Carlton

16T47 T26 5c **orange** (1915) 1.50
Pane of 6 10.00
orange yellow 5.00
16T48 T26 25c **olive green** (1915) 4.00
Pane of 6 30.00
a. Vert. pair, imperf. horizontally 45.00

T27

Engraved by the American Bank Note Co.

1916-32

16T49 T27 5c **light blue** (1916) 1.50
Pane of 6 11.00
16T50 T27 25c **carmine lake** (1916) 1.75
Pane of 6 11.00

Engraved by the Security Bank Note Co.

Perf. 11

16T51 T27 5c **yellow brown** (1917) 1.00
Pane of 6 7.50
16T52 T27 25c **deep green** (1917) 3.00
Pane of 6 20.00
16T53 T27 5c **olive green** (1918) .60
Pane of 6 4.50
16T54 T27 25c **dark violet** (1918) 1.75
Pane of 6 14.00
16T55 T27 5c **brown** (1919) 1.25
Pane of 6 9.00
16T56 T27 25c **blue** (1919) 3.25
Pane of 6 22.50

Engraved by the E.A. Wright Bank Note Co.

Perf. 12

16T57 T27 5c **dark green** (1920) .65
Pane of 6 4.25
a. Vert. pair, imperf. between *300.00*
16T58 T27 25c **olive green** (1920) .75
Pane of 6 5.00

Engraved by the Security Bank Note Co.

16T59 T27 5c **carmine rose** (1921) .55
Pane of 6 4.25
16T60 T27 25c **deep blue** (1921) 1.30
Pane of 6 8.50
16T61 T27 5c **yellow brown** (1922) .55
Pane of 6 3.75
a. Horizontal pair, imperf. between 16.00
16T62 T27 25c **claret** (1922) 1.65
Pane of 6 11.50
16T63 T27 5c **olive green** (1923) .65
Pane of 6 4.25
16T64 T27 25c **dull violet** (1923) 1.35
Pane of 6 9.00
16T65 T27 5c **brown** (1924) 1.75
Pane of 6 12.00
16T66 T27 25c **ultramarine** (1924) 4.00
Pane of 6 30.00
16T67 T27 5c **olive green** (1925) .65
Pane of 6 4.25
16T68 T27 25c **carmine rose** (1925) 1.10
Pane of 6 7.00
16T69 T27 5c **blue** (1926) 1.00
Pane of 6 6.50
16T70 T27 25c **light brown** (1926) 2.25
Pane of 6 14.00
16T71 T27 5c **carmine** (1927) .85
Pane of 6 5.75
16T72 T27 25c **green** (1927) 7.25
Pane of 6 47.50

Engraved by the E. A. Wright Bank Note Co.

Without Imprint

16T73 T27 5c **yellow brown** (1928) .75
Pane of 6 4.50
16T74 T27 25c **dark blue** (1928) 1.00
Pane of 6 6.25

Engraved by the Security Bank Note Co.

Without Imprint

16T75 T27 5c **dark green** (1929) .30 .25
Pane of 6 2.00
16T76 T27 25c **red violet** (1929) .85 .50
Pane of 6 5.50
16T77 T27 5c **olive green** (1930) .25 .25
Pane of 6 1.75
16T78 T27 25c **carmine** (1930) .25 .25
Pane of 6 2.00
a. Horiz. pair, imperf. vertically 35.00
16T79 T27 5c **brown** (1931) .25 .25
Pane of 6 1.60
16T80 T27 25c **blue** (1931) .25 .25
Pane of 6 1.60
16T81 T27 5c **green** (1932) .25 .25
Pane of 6 1.60
16T82 T27 25c **rose carmine** (1932) .25 .25
Pane of 6 1.60

T28

Lithographed by Oberly & Newell Co.

1933-40 Without Imprint *Perf. 14x12½*

16T83 T28 5c **pale brown** (1933) .25
Pane of 9 3.25
16T84 T28 25c **green** (1933) .25
Pane of 9 3.25

Lithographed by Security Bank Note Co.

Without Imprint

Perf. 12, 12½

Signature of R. B. White

16T85 T28 5c **lake** (1934) .25
Pane of 9 2.50
16T86 T28 25c **dark blue** (1934) .25
Pane of 9 2.50
16T87 T28 5c **yellow brown** (1935) .25
Pane of 9 2.50
16T88 T28 25c **lake** (1935) .25
Pane of 9 2.50
16T89 T28 5c **blue** (1936) .25 .25
Pane of 9 2.75
16T90 T28 25c **apple green** (1936) .25 .25
Pane of 9 2.50
16T91 T28 5c **bister brown** (1937) .25
Pane of 9 2.50
16T92 T28 25c **carmine rose** (1937) .25
Pane of 9 2.50
16T93 T28 5c **green** (1938) .25 .25
Pane of 9 3.00
16T94 T28 25c **blue** (1938) .30 .25
Pane of 9 3.50
16T95 T28 5c **dull vermilion** (1939) 1.00
Pane of 9 11.50
a. Horiz. pair, imperf. between —
16T96 T28 25c **bright violet** (1939) .50
Pane of 9 6.00
16T97 T28 5c **light blue** (1940) .55
Pane of 9 5.75
16T98 T28 25c **bright green** (1940) .50
Pane of 9 5.50

Samuel F. B. Morse
T29

Plates of 90 stamps.
Stamp designed by Nathaniel Yontiff.
Unlike the frank stamps, Nos. 16T99 to 16T103 were sold to the public in booklet form for use in prepayment of telegraph services.

Engraved by Security Bank Note Co. of Philadelphia

1940 Unwmk. *Perf. 12, 12½x12, 12x12½*

16T99 T29 1c **yellow green** 1.25
Pane of 5 6.50
a. Imperf., pair 50.00
16T100 T29 2c **chestnut** 1.75 1.00
Pane of 5 15.00
a. Imperf., pair 50.00
16T101 T29 5c **deep blue** 3.00
Pane of 5 18.00
a. Vert. pair, imperf. btwn. 65.00
b. Imperf., pair 50.00
16T102 T29 10c **orange** 5.00
Pane of 5 27.50
a. Imperf., pair 50.00
16T103 T29 25c **bright carmine** 4.00
Pane of 5 24.00
a. Imperf., pair 50.00

Type of 1933-40

1941 Litho. *Perf. 12½*

Without Imprint

Signature of R.B. White

16T104 T28 5c **dull rose lilac** .25
Pane of 9 2.50
16T105 T28 25c **vermilion** .60
Pane of 9 6.00

1942 Signature of A.N. Williams

16T106 T28 5c **brown** .30
Pane of 9 3.50
16T107 T28 25c **ultramarine** .30
Pane of 9 3.50

1943

16T108 T28 5c **salmon** .30
Pane of 9 3.50
16T109 T28 25c **red violet** .30
Pane of 9 3.50

1944

16T110 T28 5c **light green** .65
Pane of 9 7.25
16T111 T28 25c **buff** .35
Pane of 9 3.75

1945

16T112 T28 5c **light blue** .40
Pane of 9 5.00
a. Pair, imperf. between —
16T113 T28 25c **light green** .35
Pane of 9 3.75

1946

16T114 T28 5c **light bister brown** 1.25
Pane of 9 15.00
16T115 T28 25c **rose pink** 1.00
Pane of 9 12.00

Many of the stamps between 16T1 and 16T98 and 16T104 to 16T115 are known without frank numbers. Several of them are also known with more than one color used in the frank number and with handstamped and manuscript numbers. The numbers are also found in combination with various letters: O, A, B, C, D, etc.

Western Union discontinued the use of Telegraph stamps with the 1946 issue.

United States Telegraph-Cable-Radio Carriers

Booklets issued to accredited representatives to the World Telecommunications Conferences, Atlantic City, New Jersey, 1947. Valid for messages to points outside the United States. Issued by All America Cables & Radio, Inc., The Commercial Cable Company, Globe Wireless, Limited, Mackay Radio and Telegraph Company, Inc., R C A Communications, Inc., Tropical Radio Telegraph Company and The Western Union Telegraph Company.

TX1

1947 Litho. Unwmk. *Perf. 12½*

17T1 TX1 5c **olive bister** 7.00
Pane of 9 70.00
Pane of 9, 8 5c + 1 10c *900.00*
17T2 TX1 10c **olive bister** 750.00
17T3 TX1 50c **olive bister** 9.00
Pane of 9 90.00

UNLISTED ISSUES

Several telegraph or wireless companies other than those listed above have issued stamps or franks, but as evidence of actual use is lacking, they are not listed. Among these are:

American District Telegraph Co.
American Telegraph Typewriter Co.
Continental Telegraph Co.
Los Angeles and San Gabriel Valley Railroad
Marconi Wireless Telegraph Co.
Mercantile Telegraph Co.
Telepost Co.
Tropical Radio Telegraph Co.
United Fruit Co. Wireless Service.
United Wireless Telegraph Co.

ESSAYS

An essay is a proposed design that differs in some way from the issued stamp.

During approximately 1845-1890, when private banknote engravers competed for contracts to print U.S. postage stamps, essays were produced primarily as examples of the quality of the firms' work and as suggestions as to what their finished product would look like. In most cases, dies were prepared, often with stock vignettes used in making banknotes. These dies were used to print essays for the Post Office Department. Rarely did the competitors go so far as to have essay plates made.

From 1894 onward, virtually all stamps were engraved and printed by the Bureau of Engraving and Printing (BEP). This usually required two types of essays. The first was a model design which was approved — or disapproved — by the Postmaster General. Sometimes preliminary drawings were made by the BEP designers, often in an enlarged size, subsequently photographically reduced to stamp size. An accepted stamp design usually became the engraver's model.

Occasionally during the course of engraving the die, a "progressive proof" was pulled to check the progress of the engraver's work. Because these were produced from an incompletely engraved die, they differ from the final design and are listed here as essays.

During approximately 1867-1870, various experiments were conducted to prevent the reuse of postage stamps. These included experimental grill types, safety papers, water-sensitive papers and inks, coupon essays, and others. These also differed in some way from issued stamps, even if the design was identical. A preliminary listing has been made here.

Because the essays in all their various colors have not been examined by the editors, traditional color names have been retained. Some color names have been taken from *Color Standards and Color Nomenclature,* by Robert Ridgway.

Only essays in private hands have been listed. Others exist but are not available to collectors.

Some essays were produced after the respective stamps were issued. Year dates are given where information is available. The most well known of these posthumous essays are those produced in 1903 for Ernest Schernikow, who purchased the original dies formerly controlled by Joseph R. Carpenter before his death. Schernikow arranged for a minimum of ten sets of die reprints to be made in a range of more than a dozen colors for each die in his possession. Fewer essay reprints were made on colored card, bond and pelure paper. Though the dies were originally engraved for approved stamp production, neither of the companies producing them had anything to do with these subsequent Schernikow reprints. Inasmuch as they are printed from authentic original dies they merit listing for study purposes, but they are not to be confused with original essays produced contemporaneously with stamp production. All of these unauthorized and unofficial essay reprints are presented here in their own sub-sections following Nos. 11-E17b, 72-E5c, 191-E2, 63-E2b, LO1-E1A and are footnoted in the Sanitary Fair section after No. WV13TC1.

Essay papers and cards are white, unless described otherwise.

Values for die essays are for essays showing full die sinkage, on intact card backing, where such are known. Measurements are given where such information is available. Cut-down or faulty examples sell for less, often much less. Examples on full-size original card command a premium. Plate essays are valued in the grade of very fine, where such exist. A number of essays are unique or are reported in very limited quantities. Such items are valued in the conditions in which they issued.

The listings are by manufacturer. Basic stamps may appear in two or more places.

This listing is not complete. Other designs, papers and colors exist. The editors would appreciate reports of unlisted items, as well as photos of items listed herein without illustrations.

POSTMASTERS' PROVISIONALS

NON-CONTIGUOUS LISTINGS

Because many listings are grouped by manufacturer, some catalogue numbers are separated.

No. 5-E1 to 5-E2	**follow 11-E16**
No. 11-E17 to 72-E5	**follow 5-E2**
No. 65-E5 to 72-E8	**follow 72-E5**
No. 63-E13 to 113-E2	**follow 72-E8**
No. 112-E2 to 129-E2	**follow 113-E2**
No. 120-E1 to 122-E5	**follow 129-E2**
No. 115-E3a to 129-E6	**follow 122-E5**
No. 115-E11 to 116-E8	**follow 129-E6**
No. 115-E17 to 148-E1	**follow 116-E8**
No. 145-E2 to 179-E3	**follow 148-E1**
No. 156-E2 to 191-E2	**follow 179-E3**
No. 184-E8	**follows 191-E2**
No. 182-E4 to 190-E3	**follow 184-E8**
No. 184-E17 to 293-E11	**follow 190-E3**
No. 285-E10 to 856-E2	**follow 293-E11**

Albany, N.Y.
Gavit & Co.

1Xa-E1

Design size: 23½x25½mm
Die size: 58x48mm

Benjamin Franklin. With crosshatching about 2mm outside border (usually cut off).

1847

1Xa-E1 5c

a. Die on India die sunk on large card, printed through a mat to eliminate cross-hatching

brownish black	*600.*
scarlet	*600.*
red brown	*600.*
blue	*600.*
green	*600.*

b. Die on India; some mounted on small card

bluish black	325.
scarlet	325.
brown	325.
yellow green	325.
gray blue	325.

c. Die on India cut close

black	250.
blue	250.
red brown	250.
scarlet	250.
green	250.
yellow green	250.
brown violet	250.
rose red	250.

d. Die on bond (1858)

bluish black	375.
scarlet	375.
brown	375.
blue	375.
blue green	375.
violet	375.

e. Die on ivory glazed paper (1905)

black	900.
dark brown	900.
scarlet	900.
blue	900.

New York, N.Y.
Rawdon, Wright & Hatch

9X1-E1

Design 22mm wide
Die size: 50x102mm

Vignette of Washington. Two transfers laid down vertically on the die 22mm apart; top one retouched, with frame around it (this is a proof). Values are for combined transfers. Vignette essay exists cut apart from proof, value $200 each.

1845

9X1-E1 5c

a. Die on India (1879)

black	450.
violet black	450.
gray black	450.

scarlet 450.
dull scarlet 450.
orange 450.
brown 450.
dull brown 450.
green 450.
dull green 450.
ultramarine 450.
dull blue 450.
red violet 450.
b. Die on white bond (1879)
gray black 550.
dull scarlet 550.
dull brown 550.
dull green 550.
dull blue 550.
c. Die on white glazed paper, die sunk (1879)
gray black 700.

POSTAGE STAMPS

1847 ISSUE
Rawdon, Wright, Hatch & Edson

The original model for No. 1 exists, engraved vignette of Franklin mounted on frame, part of frame engraved, rest in pencil, ink and a gray wash. Formerly No. 1-E1, now in the National Postal Museum collection.

Engraved vignette only, matted.

1-E2 5c Die on India (1895), brown *2,500.*

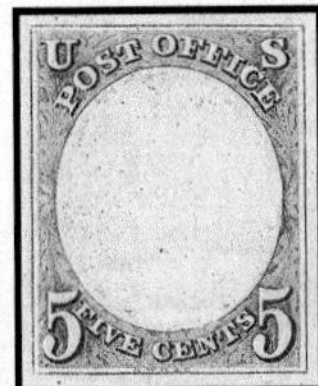

1-E3

Engraved frame only, matted from complete die.

1-E3 5c Die on India (1895), brown 2,500.

The 1895 dates are suppositional.

The original model for No. 2 exists, engraved vignette of Washington mounted (replaced) on frame, "POST OFFICE" and "FIVE CENTS" engraved on former No. 1-E1, "U" and "S" at top and "X" in bottom corners in black ink, rest in pencil and a gray wash. Formerly No. 2-E1, now in the National Postal Museum collection.

2-E1

Incomplete engraving of entire design, area around vignette incomplete, frame lines and "RWH&E" printer's initials not yet added.

2-E1 10c Die on proof paper, affixed to stiff blue laid paper backing, black —

2-E2

Engraved vignette only.

2-E2 10c Die on India (1895)
black *2,500.*
brownish black *2,500.*
brown *2,500.*

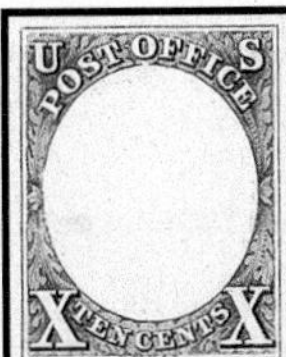

2-E3

Engraved frame only.

2-E3 10c Die on India (1895)
black *4,750.*
brown orange *4,750.*

The 1895 dates are suppositional.

1851 ISSUE
Submitted in Competition for the 1851 Issue Contract
Rawdon, Wright, Hatch & Edson, New York, N.Y.

11-E1

Design size: 18½x23mm
Large 3 in vignette.

11-E1 3c Die on India
black *7,000.*
blue *10,000.*

Submitted in Competition for the 1851 Issue Contract
Henry Benner, Washington, D.C.

11-E2

Design size: 19x24mm
Vignette of Washington.

11-E2 3c
a. Die on India
black *4,000.*
b. Die on proof paper, die sunk on 40x51mm card
black *4,000.*

Submitted in Competition for the 1851 Issue Contract
(Nos. 11-E3 and 11-E4)
John E. Gavit & Co., Albany, N.Y.

11-E3

Design size: 19x23mm
Vignette of Franklin. Three states of die. Second state has double line dash above P of POSTAGE, third state has single dash above P and dot in O of POSTAGE.

11-E3 3c
a. Die on India, die sunk on card
warm black *800.*
scarlet *800.*
red brown *800.*
blue green *800.*
b. Die on India, 41x43mm or smaller
black 300.
greenish black 300.
carmine 300.
scarlet 300.
yellow green 300.
brown 300.
blue green 300.
dull blue 300.
dark blue 300.
c. Die on India, cut to shape
warm black 250.
cool black 250.
black 250.
carmine 250.
orange 250.
brown 250.
dark green 250.
yellow green 250.
olive 250.
light blue 250.
dark blue 250.
violet 250.
scarlet 250.
d. Die on bond
cool black 250.
scarlet 250.
orange brown 250.
brown 250.
green 250.
blue 250.
e. Die on ivory glazed paper
black *700.*
dark brown *700.*
scarlet *700.*
blue *700.*
f. Die on thin card, dusky blue, cut to shape *200.*

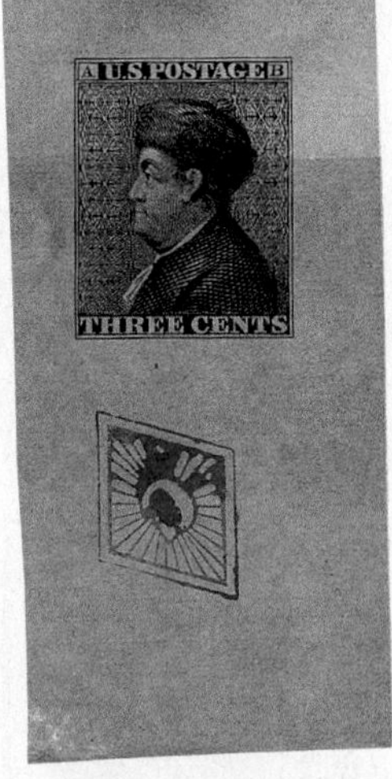

11-E3g

g. Die on Francis Patent experimental paper with trial cancel
black *1,250.*
dark blue *1,250.*
brown *1,250.*

11-E4

Design size: 19x22mm
Die size: 47x75mm
Vignette of Washington. Two states of die. Second state has small diagonal dash in top of left vertical border below arch.

11-E4 3c
a. Die on India, die sunk on card
black *750.*
scarlet *750.*
brown red *750.*
blue green *750.*
b. Die on India, about 30x40mm or smaller
orange 400.
orange brown 400.
brown 400.
dusky yellow brown 400.
yellow green 400.
blue green 400.
dull blue 400.
red violet 400.
deep red orange 400.
black 400.
c. Die on bond (1858)
black 400.
scarlet 400.
brown 400.
green 400.
blue 400.
d. Die on ivory glazed paper (1858)
black *850.*
dark brown *850.*
scarlet *850.*
blue *850.*
e. Die on proof paper (1858)
cool black *475.*
dull red *475.*
dull brown *475.*
dull blue green *475.*
dull blue *475.*

Bradbury, Wilkinson & Co., England

11-E5

Design size: 20½x23½mm
Vignette of Washington.

11-E5 3c
a. On stiff stamp paper about stamp size
black 1,250.
violet red 1,250.
deep carmine 1,250.
dusky carmine 1,250.
deep scarlet 1,250.
orange brown 1,250.
deep green 1,250.
blue 1,250.
ultramarine 1,250.
brown 1,250.
b. On card
violet black 1,250.
dull scarlet 1,250.
blue 1,250.
green 1,250.
brown 1,250.
c. On stiff bond
brown 1,250.
blue 1,250.
violet black 1,250.

Draper, Welsh & Co.

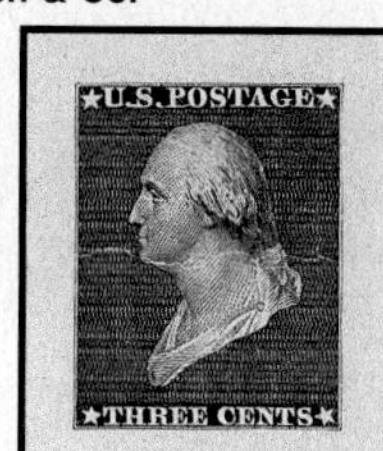

11-E6

Design size: 18x23mm
Vignette of Washington.

11-E6 3c Surface printed on card, black 700.

11-E7

Design size: 17½x24mm
Die size: 44x106mm
Engraved vignette of Washington.

11-E7 3c
a. Die on India, about 44x105mm, die sunk on card, in vert. pair with No. 11-E8
black 1,500.
scarlet 1,500.
brown red 1,500.
green 1,500.
b. Die on India, about 40x45mm or smaller
warm black 400.
cool black 400.
dark carmine 400.
scarlet 400.
brown red 400.
orange brown 400.
brown 400.
yellow green 400.
blue green 400.
blue 400.
dull blue 400.
brown violet 400.
c. Die on India, stamp size
rose 350.
scarlet 350.
red brown 350.
brown 350.
green 350.
cool black 350.
warm black 350.
yellow green 350.
brown violet 350.
ultramarine blue 350.
d. Die on bond
black 400.
scarlet 400.
brown 400.
blue green 400.
blue 400.
e. Die on ivory glazed paper
black 700.
dark brown 700.
scarlet 700.
blue 700.

Submitted in Competition for the 1851 Issue Contract
Draper, Welsh & Co., Philadelphia, Pa.

11-E8

Design size: 19½x24mm
Die size: 44x106mm
On same die 30mm below No. 11-E7
Vignette of Washington.

11-E8 3c
a. Die on India, 28x32mm or smaller
black 300.
dark carmine 300.
scarlet 300.
brown red 300.
red brown 300.
orange brown 300.
brown 300.
yellow green 300.
green 300.
blue green 300.
blue 300.
b. Die on bond, about 32x40mm
black 300.
scarlet 300.
brown 300.
green 300.
blue 300.
c. Die on ivory glazed paper
black 700.
dark brown 700.
scarlet 700.
blue 700.

11-E8D

Design size: 18x23mm
Vignette of Washington.
Washington vignette only. Same head as No. 11-E6 through 11-E8, but with more bust. No gridwork in background.

11-E8D 3c Die on proof paper, mounted on card, black 750.

11-E9c

Design size (No. 11-E9a): 18x33mm
Vignette design size (Nos. 11-E9b, 11-E9c): 18x22mm
As No. 11-E8D, gridwork added to background oval.

11-E9 3c
a. Die on India
black 350.
scarlet 350.
b. Die on India, single line frame
black 300.
blue 300.
dark carmine 300.
orange red 300.
lilac 300.
brown 300.
scarlet 300.
rose violet 300.
deep yellow green 300.
c. Die on India, imprint of Jocelyn, Draper, Welsh & Co., New York
black 300.
blue 300.
dark carmine 300.
orange red 300.
lilac 300.
brown 300.
scarlet 300.
rose violet 300.
deep yellow green 300.

Danforth, Bald & Co.

11-E10

Vignette size: 18x22mm
Design size: 20x26mm
Die size: 57x74mm
Vignette of Washington. Double line frame.

11-E10 3c
a. Die on India, die sunk on card
black 750.
scarlet 750.
red brown 750.
green 750.
b. Die on India, off card, about 33x38mm
black 200.
scarlet 200.
brown 200.
blue 200.
green 200.
dull violet 200.
dull blue 200.
red brown 200.
rose 200.
c. Die on bond, black 350.
d. Die on ivory glazed paper
black 750.
dark brown 750.
scarlet 750.
blue 750.

11-E11

Washington vignette only.

11-E11 3c Die on India
black 325.
dull rose 325.
scarlet 325.
orange 325.
brown orange 325.
brown 325.
green 325.
dark blue 325.
dull violet 325.
rose violet 325.

Submitted in Competition for the 1851 Issue Contract
Danforth, Bald & Co., Phiiladelphia, Pa.

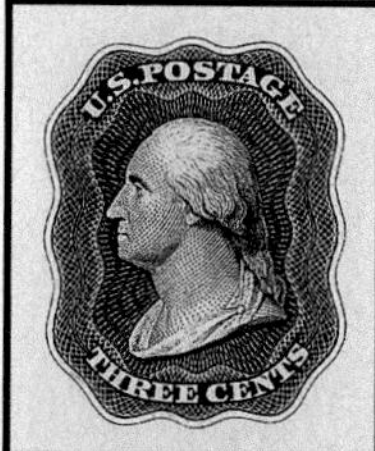

11-E12

Design size: 20x26mm
Die size: 62x66mm
Vignette of Washington. Single line frame. Two states of die. Second state shows scars in lathe lines in front of neck over T, and small dot below design. A third printing has more scars in front of neck.

11-E12 3c
a. Die on India, die sunk on card
black 750.
scarlet 750.
brown red 750.
dusky brown yellow 750.
brown 750.
green 750.
blue 750.
dull blue 750.
b. Die on India, about 43x45mm
black 300.
scarlet 300.

deep scarlet 300.
brown 300.
yellow brown 300.
green 300.
yellow green 300.
blue 300.
dull blue 300.
dark blue 300.
ultramarine blue 300.
orange 300.
red 300.

c. Die on bond
dusky brown yellow 275.
blue 275.

d. Die on ivory glazed paper
black 700.
dark brown 700.
scarlet 700.
blue 700.

e. Plate on thick buff wove
rose 125.
violet brown 125.
orange 125.
dark orange 125.
pink orange 125.

f. Plate on India, dark red orange 150.

g. Plate on ivory wove (head more completely engraved, ruled lines between designs)
black 125.
dark carmine 125.
yellow 125.
blue 125.

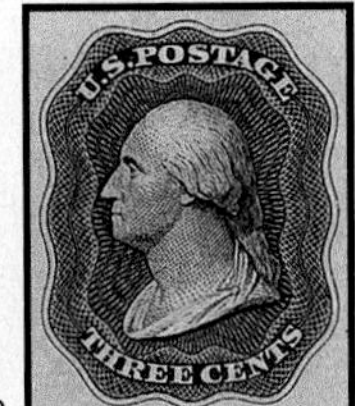

11-E13

Design size: 20x26mm
Die size: 62x66mm
Vignette of Washington. No. 11-E12 reengraved: more dark dots in forehead next to hair, thus line between forehead and hair more distinct.

11-E13 3c
a. Die on India, die sunk on card
black 750.
scarlet 750.
brown red 750.
brown 750.
green 750.

b. Die on ivory glazed paper
black 700.
dark brown 700.
scarlet 700.
blue 700.

Bald, Cousland & Co.

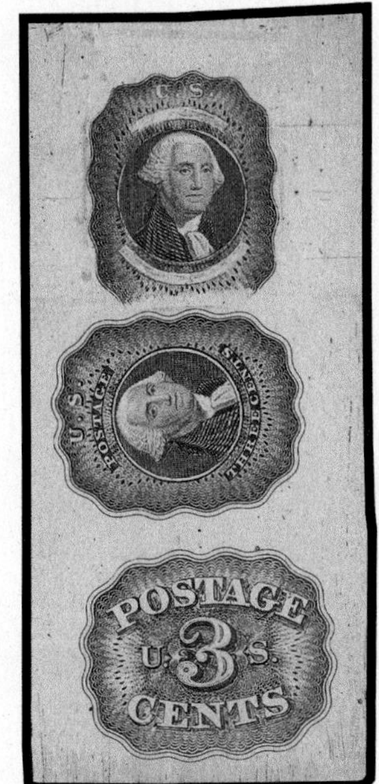

11-E14, 11-E14A, 11-E16

Design size: 22x28mm.
Incomplete design, tablets at top and bottom blank. See No. 11-E14A for listings.

11-E14 3c

Design size: 22x28mm
Die size: 95x43mm
Vignette of Washington. On same die with Nos. 11-E16 and 11-E14. Listings are for the complete triple die essay.

11-E14A 3c
b. Die on India
black 1,000.
scarlet 1,000.
red brown 1,000.
brown 1,000.
yellow green 1,000.
green 1,000.
blue green 1,000.
orange brown 1,000.
rose pink 1,000.
dull blue 1,000.
violet 1,000.

c. Die on bond
black 1,000.
scarlet 1,000.
brown 1,000.
blue green 1,000.
blue 1,000.

d. Die on white glazed paper
black 1,150.

11-E15

Design size: 28x22½mm
POSTAGE / 3 / CENTS in scalloped frame.

11-E15 3c
a. Die on India, die sunk on card
black 750.
scarlet 750.
red brown 750.
green 750.
slate 750.

b. Die on bond, about 40x30mm
black 175.
scarlet 175.
brown 175.
green 175.
blue 175.
slate 275.

c. Die on ivory glazed paper
black 700.
dark brown 750.
scarlet 750.
blue 750.

11-E16

Design size: 28x22½mm
U.S. at sides of 3.

11-E16 3c
a. Die on India, cut small
black 275.
light red 275.
red brown 275.
brown 275.
yellow green 275.
blue green 275.
green 275.
blue 275.
red violet 275.

b. Die on bond, about 40x30mm
black 175.
scarlet 175.
brown 175.
red brown 175.
green 175.
blue green 175.
blue 175.
violet 175.
slate 175.

c. Die on India, Nos. 11-E14A and 11-E16 with albino 11-E14
black 1,000.
scarlet 1,000.
brown 1,000.
green 1,000.
blue green 1,000.
blue 1,000.
red violet 1,000.

d. As "c," die on bond
black 750.
scarlet 750.
brown 750.
green 750.
blue green 750.
gray blue 750.

e. As "c," die on ivory glazed paper, 64x78mm, black 1,150.

f. Die on India, die sunk on card
black 900.
scarlet 900.

Toppan, Carpenter, Casilear & Co.

5-E1

Design size: 20½x26mm
Franklin vignette.

5-E1 1c
a. Die on old proof paper, master die shortened to 18½x22½mm, black 1,250.
b. Die on thick old proof paper, black 1,500.
c. Pair, Nos. 5-E1b, 11-E23, black 2,000.

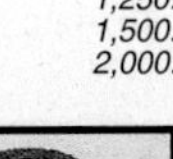

5-E1E

5-E1Ef

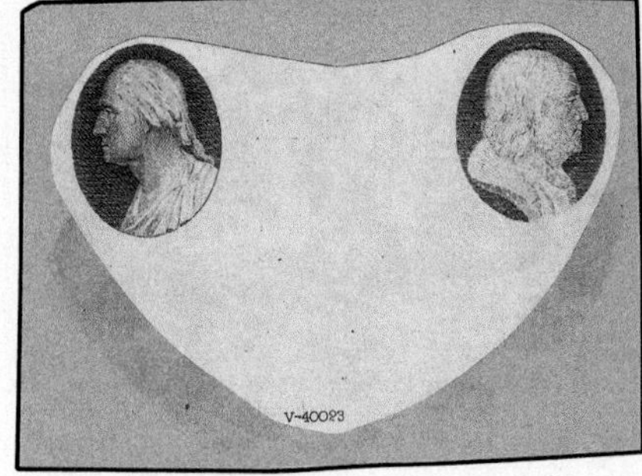

5-E1Eg

Design size: 20x24mm
Similar to No. 5-E1 but with no additional shaded oval border.

5-E1E 1c Die on thin card, black blue —
f. Block of 4 in combination with pair of No. 11-E23, on old proof paper, black 3,500.
g. Pair, No. 5-E1E in combination with No. 11-E23, on old proof paper, die V-40023, cut to shape to show die number and mounted on 75x54mm card 575.
h. Pair, No. 5-E1E in combination with No. 11-E23, die on India, die sunk on card, die V-40023 beneath images, black 5,000.

Nos. 5-E1Eg and 5-E1Eh are essays made by the American Bank Note Co. from the die acquired from Toppan, Carpenter and Company. The die number V-40023 is the new ABNCo. die number. While the essays were produced posthumously, this could prove to be the original die block from which transfers were taken up to be added to bank note designs and later to become the central vignettes for the 1851 postage stamps.

5-E2

Complete design, but with SIX CENTS in value tablet.

5-E2 1c Die on India, black, cut to shape 2,500.

Submitted in Competition for the 1851 Issue Contract (Nos. 11-E17a, 11-E17b, and 11-E18 to 11-E21) Toppan, Carpenter, Casilear & Co., Philadelphia, Pa.

11-E17

Design size: 21½x25mm
Die size: 50½x60mm
Vignette of Washington.

11-E17 3c
a. Die on India, die sunk on card, penciled 'By Casilear at lower left, rose carmine 5,000.
b. Die on old ivory paper
rose carmine *7,250.*
bluish-black *7,250.*

Essay reprints by Schernikow in 1903 from original die (See paragraph eight of the Essay section introduction)

11-E17 3c
c. Die on proof paper, printed through a mat (1903)
black 175.
bright carmine 175.
dull carmine 175.
dark violet red 175.
dull scarlet 175.
dull violet 175.
dull red violet 175.
deep yellow 175.
deep orange 175.
orange brown 175.
dull brown olive 175.
deep green 175.
dark blue green 175.
ultramarine 175.
dark blue 175.
brown 175.
d. Die on colored card (1903)
deep orange, *ivory* 300.
dark blue, *pale green* 300.
orange brown, *light blue* 300.

Toppan, Carpenter, Casilear & Co., Philadelphia, Pa.

11-E18

Design size: 20½x22½mm
Washington. Vignette has solid color background. Crack between N and T of CENTS.

11-E18 3c Die on India, card mounted, 24½x25mm
black *2,000.*
carmine *2,000.*

No. 11-E18A

Design size: 20½x22½mm
Washington. Like No. 11-E18 except background of vignette is clearly engraved horizontal and vertical lines. Crack between N and T of CENTS.

11-E18A 3c Die on India, die sunk on 60x50mm card, carmine *7,000.*
b. As No. 11-E18A, cut down to stamp's size, black *7,000.*
c. As No. 11-E18A, on old ivory paper, cut down to stamp size, rose carmine *7,000.*

No. 11-E19 On Left, No. 11-E20 On Right

No. 11-E19
Design size: 20½x22½mm
Similar to No. 11-E18, with a slightly modified design, vignette background engraved horiz. and vert. lines. In pair with No. 11-E20.

No. 11-E20
Design size: 20x22½mm
Blank curved top and bottom labels. In pair with 11-E19. Also found in pair with 11-E21.

11-E19 3c Die on India, Nos. 11-E19, 11-E20 mounted on card, black *16,500.*

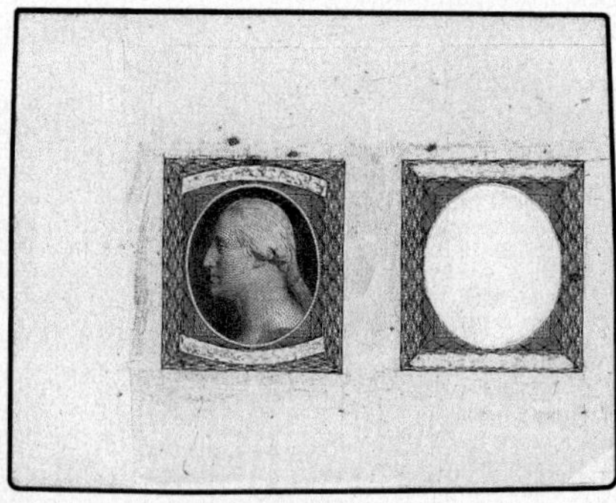
11-E21

Straight labels. Similar to No. 11-E19 but labels erased and vignette cut out. In pair with No. 11-E20.

11-E21 3c Die on India, Nos. 11-E20, 11-E21 mounted on card, black *4,500.*

11-E22

Die size: 37½x46mm

Similar to issued stamp except lathework impinges on colorless oval.

11-E22 3c Die on India
dusky blue *5,000.*
black *5,000.*
With layout lines *10,000.*

Some students consider No. 11-E22 to be proof strikes of the die used to make the "Roosevelt" and Panama-Pacific small die proofs, as the lathework impinges on the colorless oval of Nos. 11P2 and 11P2a as well.

11-E23

Design size: 18x22mm
Washington vignette only. From master die (21½mm high) with more robe and dark background.

11-E23 3c
a. Master die impression, old proof paper, black *900.*
b. Block of 4, 2mm between ovals, thick old ivory paper, black *3,000.*

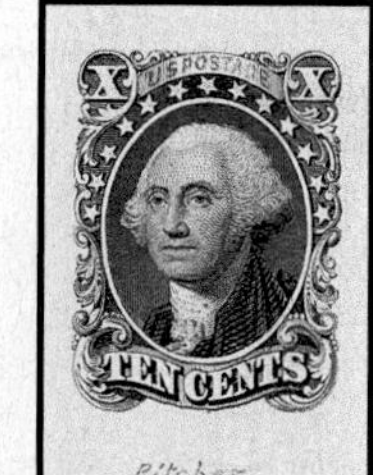

11-E24

Washington vignette only, as No. 11-E23, with outer frame added.

11-E24 3c Die on old proof paper, die v 37991, cut to shape to show die number and mounted on 27x37mm card, black *700.*

No. 11-E24 is an essay made by the American Bank Note Co. from a die acquired from Toppan, Carpenter and Company. The die number V 37991 is the new ABNCo. die number.

13-E1

Design as adopted but top label has pencil lettering only, also no lines in leaf ornaments around Xs in top corners.

13-E1 10c Die on India, black *3,000.*

13-E2

Similar to No. 13-E1 but vert. shading around Xs and lines added in leaf ornaments. No lettering in top label.

13-E2 10c Die on India, black *3,000.*

17-E1

Design size: 19x21½mm
Block sinkage size: 57x49mm
Engine engraved frame without labels or interior shadow lines from straight bands and left side rosettes. No small equilateral crosses in central row of diamonds. Original vignette cut out and replaced by engraved vignette of Washington as adopted.

17-E1 12c Die on India, cut close, mounted on block sunk card, 77x57mm, black *10,000.*

17-E2

Similar to adopted design but no small vertical equilateral crosses in center rows of diamond networks at top, sides and bottom.

17-E2 12c Die on India, brown violet, cut close *900.*
17-E3 12c As No. 17-E2, die on wove, brown violet, cut close *750.*

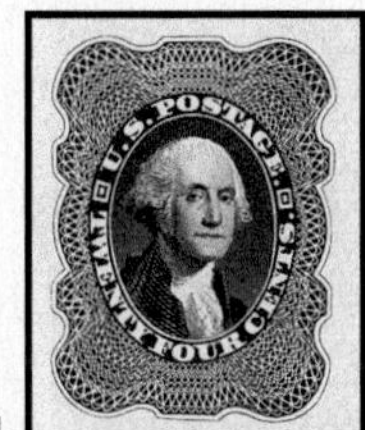

37-E1

Design size: 19½x25½mm
Die size: 46x49mm or larger
Probably not the die used to make the plates. No exterior layout lines. Oval outline recut at bottom of jabot and vignette background etched much darker. Light horizontal lines on stock below chin.

37-E1 24c Die on India, black *2,500.*

37-E2

Incomplete essay for frame only as adopted: no outer frame-line and lathework not retouched.

37-E2 24c Die on India, black *3,500.*

38-E1

Incomplete engraving of entire design, lacking text and numerals at top, bottom and sides.

38-E1 30c Die on India, on 37x45mm card, black *7,000.*

38-E2

Design size: 19x24mm
Incomplete engraving of entire design. Scrolls at each side of 30 have only one outer shading line.

38-E2 30c Die on India, black *2,250.*

39-E1

Design size: 19x24mm
Incomplete engraving of entire design, lacking "U.S. POSTAGE" at top and "NINETY CENTS" at bottom, incomplete curvature lines in top scroll, signed by engraver on card.

39-E1 90c Die on India (45x52mm), mounted on large card (150x215mm), black *4,500.*

1861 ISSUE
Toppan, Carpenter & Co.

For the 1903 Schernikow private reprint essays see section following No. 72-E5.

63-E2b

Franklin vignette with U S POSTAGE at top and ONE CENT at bottom.

63-E2 1c
b. Die on old proof paper, outer line at sides of oval missing (1861), black *1,000.*

63-E3

Side ornaments added.

63-E3 1c
a. Die on old proof paper (1861)
black *1,250.*
blue *1,250.*
b. Die on stiff old ivory paper (1861)
black *1,250.*
blue *1,750.*
f. Die on glazed card, black —

63-E4

With upper and lower right corners incomplete. Serifs of 1s point to right.

63-E4 1c Die on old proof paper (1861), black *2,250.*

63-E4E

As No. 63-E4 but with pencil shading in upper right corner around the "1".

63-E4E 1c Die on old proof paper (1861), black *2,750.*

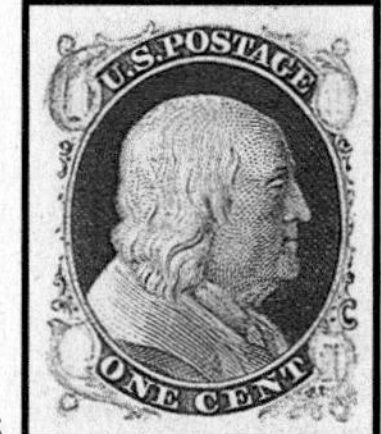

63-E5

With four corners and numerals in pencil (ornaments differ in each corner).

63-E5 1c Die on old proof paper (1861), blue *2,750.*

63-E5A

As No. 63-E5 but ornaments different.

63-E5A 1c Die on old paper (1861), blue *2,750.*

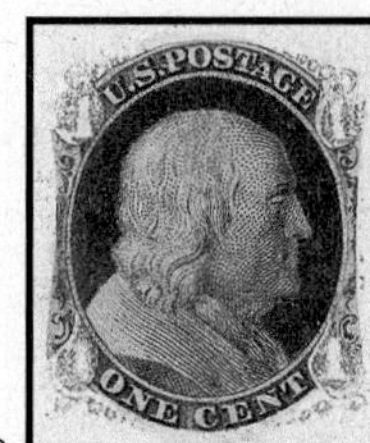

63-E6

As No. 63-E5 but ornaments different.

63-E6 1c Die on old proof paper (1861), blue *3,500.*

63-E7

As Nos. 63-E5 and 63-E6 but ornaments different.

63-E7 1c Die on old proof paper (1861), blue *3,250.*

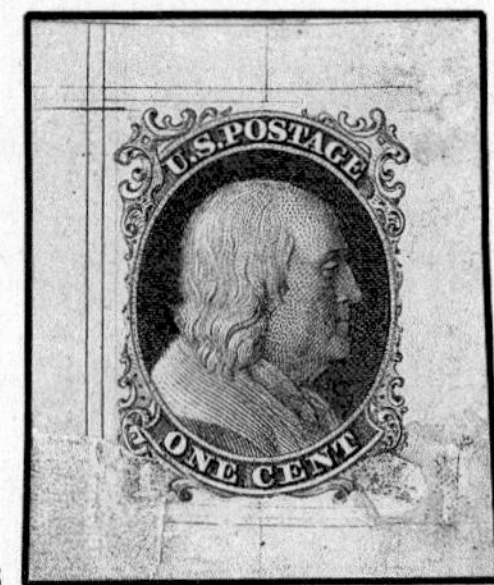
63-E8

Die proof of No. 5 with lower corners cut out of India paper and resketched in pencil on card beneath.

63-E8 1c Die on India, on card (1861), black *2,000.*

63-E9

Completely engraved design.

63-E9 1c
- ***a.*** Die on India, cut to shape (1861)
  - black, on brown toned paper *1,000.*
  - blue *600.*
- ***b.*** Die on India, about 58x57mm, die sunk on card (1861)
  - blue *2,000.*
- ***c.*** Die on old proof paper, about 48x55mm (1861)
  - black *2,000.*
- ***d.*** Die on large old white ivory paper (1861)
  - black *2,000.*
  - blue *2,000.*

65-E2

With tessellated frame, bottom label and diamond blocks. Without rosettes, top label and diamond blocks.

65-E2 3c
- ***a.*** Die on old proof paper (1861)
  - black *1,000.*
  - red *1,000.*
- ***f.*** Die on India
  - black —
  - rose —

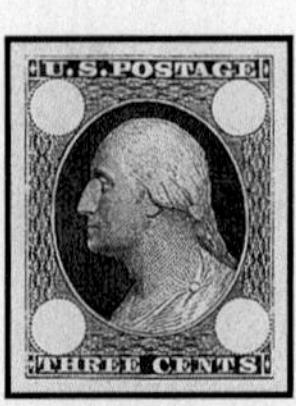
65-E3a

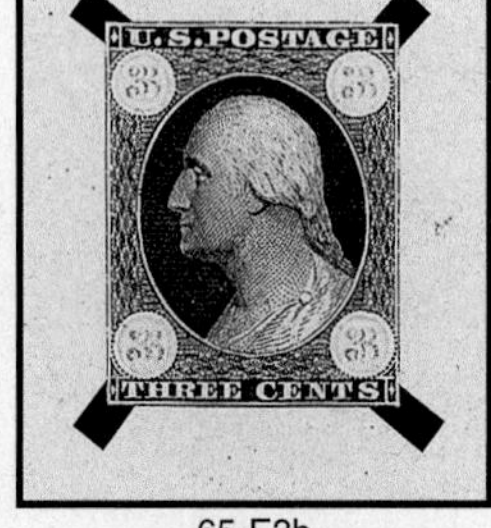
65-E3b

With top label and diamond blocks.

65-E3 3c
- ***a.*** Die on old proof paper (1861)
  - brown red *2,500.*
  - black *2,500.*
- ***b.*** Same as No. 65-E3 with numerals in pencil, Die on old proof paper (1861), black *6,000.*

65-E4

Complete die, with numerals in rosette circles.

65-E4 3c
- ***a.*** Die on India, 75x76mm die sinkage (1861)
  - black *1,500.*
  - carmine *1,500.*
- ***b.*** Die on old proof paper (1861)
  - black *1,500.*
  - dark red *1,500.*
- ***c.*** Die on India, cut to shape (1861)
  - black *1,000.*
  - carmine *1,000.*

67-E1a, Die I

67-E1b, Die II

Vignette size: 13½x16mm
Jefferson vignette only. Two dies: die I incomplete, light background in vignette; die II background essentially complete.

67-E1 5c
- ***a.*** Die I on old proof paper, black (1861) *750.*
- ***f.*** Die I on old thin ivory paper (1861), dark blue *1,000.*
- ***g.*** Die I on old proof paper (1861), dusky ultramarine *1,500.*
- ***h.*** Die II on old ivory paper (1861), navy blue *750.*

67-E2

Vignette die I framed, with spaces for numerals.

67-E2 5c
- ***d.*** Die I on old proof paper (1861), black *2,000.*

67-E3

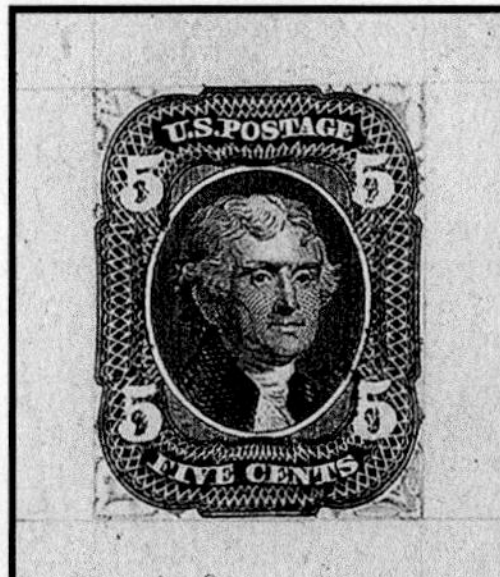
67-E3c

With numerals.

67-E3 5c
- ***b.*** Die I on soft laid paper (1861)
  - black *750.*
  - dark brown *750.*
  - orange brown *750.*
- ***c.*** Die II on old proof paper, pencil designs drawn in corners (1861), black *2,500.*
- ***d.*** Die I on old proof paper, outer lines on corner curves missing (1861), black *500.*

67-E4b

67-E4e

Complete die II design with corner ornaments.

67-E4 5c
- ***a.*** Die II on India, cut to shape (1861), black *500.*
- ***b.*** Die II on brown toned paper (1861), cut to shape
  - black *900.*
  - brown *900.*
- ***c.*** Die II on old proof paper (1861)
  - orange brown *1,500.*
  - black *1,500.*
- ***d.*** Die II on old ivory paper (1861), black *1,500.*
- ***e.*** Die II on old proof paper, additional frameline drawn on curved corners and small circle drawn in each corner (1861), black *2,500.*

69-E1

Vignette size: 15x17mm
Washington vignette only. Die II with more engraving on face, horiz. background lines regularly spaced, outer oval border smudged. Die II known only as 1851 master die.

69-E1 12c
- ***a.*** Die II on old proof paper (1851), black 650.

69-E2b

Curved labels at top and bottom.

69-E2 12c
- ***b.*** Die I on old proof paper (1861)
  - dim red violet *500.*
  - red violet *500.*

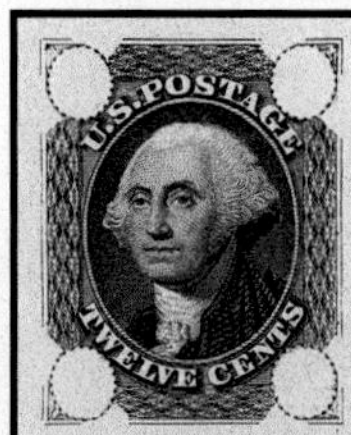
69-E3b

69-E3d

69-E3g

69-E3i

Frame incomplete: all four rosettes blank.

69-E3 12c
- ***b.*** Die on old proof paper (1861)
  - black *1,000.*
  - olive gray *1,000.*
- ***c.*** Die on old ivory, top border and half of rosettes missing (1861), black *1,000.*
- ***d.*** Die on stiff old ivory, top border missing (1861), bluish black *1,000.*
- ***g.*** Die on old proof paper, 1851 die with border lines complete, upper right rosette blank (1861)
  - orange *1,000.*
  - dark green *1,000.*
  - ultramarine *1,000.*
  - violet *1,000.*
- ***h.*** Die I on old proof paper, vignette background incomplete or worn, stock on neck unfinished (1861) —
- ***i.*** Die I on old proof paper, as 69-E3h but both upper rosettes blank (1861), ultramarine *1,000.*

69-E3j

69-E3k

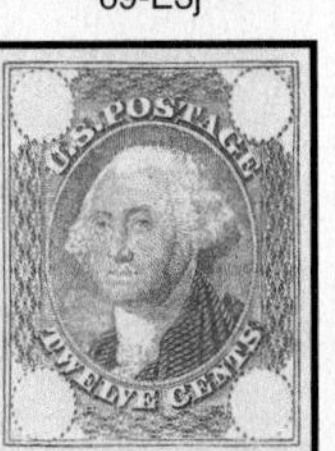

69-E3l

- ***j.*** Die I on old proof paper, as No. 69-E3h but both upper plus lower left rosettes blank (1861), ultramarine *1,000.*
- ***k.*** Die I on old proof paper, as No. 69-E3h but both lower plus upper left rosettes blank, corner borders removed around blank rosettes (1861), ultramarine *1,000.*
- ***l.*** Die I on old proof paper, as No. 69-E3h but all rosettes blank, border lines complete (1861)
  - dim scarlet *750.*
  - orange *750.*
  - green *750.*
  - ultramarine *750.*
  - violet *750.*
- ***m.*** Die I on white wove, as No. 69-E3l (1861), scarlet *750.*
- ***n.*** Die I on old proof paper, complete design (1861)
  - orange *1,000.*
  - dark red *1,000.*
  - orange red *1,000.*
  - ultramarine *1,000.*

69-E4

69-E4d

69-E4e

Original complete design with numerals in corners.

69-E4 12c
- ***a.*** Die on India, card mounted (1861)
  - black *800.*
  - gray black *800.*
- ***b.*** Die on India, cut to shape (1861), black *500.*
- ***c.*** Die on old proof paper (1861), black *500.*
- ***d.*** Die on old proof paper, corners drawn in pencil (1861), black *2,750.*
- ***e.*** Die on old proof paper, as No. 69-E3a but numerals sketched in diagonally and vert. (1861), black *3,500.*
- ***f.*** Die on stiff old ivory paper, as No. 69-E4e but without top border (1861), bluish black *1,500.*
- ***g.*** Die on thin card, black —

70-E2

Washington vignette with oval label. Background complete, eyes retouched.

70-E2 24c
- ***b.*** Die I on old proof paper, background lines incomplete (1861)
  - black *750.*
  - dim red violet *750.*

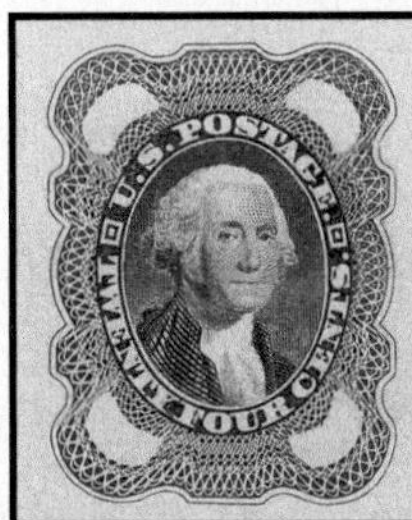

70-E3b

With frame. Blank areas in corners for numerals.

70-E3 24c
- ***b.*** Die on old proof paper (1861), dusky red violet *1,000.*

70-E4

Complete design with numerals in corners.

70-E4 24c
- ***a.*** Die on old proof paper, cut to shape (1861)
  - lilac *400.*
  - black *400.*
  - red violet *400.*
- ***b.*** Die on India, cut close (1861)
  - black *400.*
  - lilac *400.*
  - brown lilac *400.*
- ***c.*** Die on India (1861), dark blue *750.*
- ***d.*** Die on India, mounted on 80x115mm card (1861), lilac *750.*
- ***e.*** On stiff old ivory paper (1861)
  - black *1,000.*
  - lilac *1,000.*

Lower corners of vignette cut out, "NINETY 90 CENTS" in pencil in bottom label.

72-E4 90c Die on India (1861), black *2,000.*

72-E5

Complete design.

72-E5 90c
- ***a.*** Die on India, cut to shape (1861)
  - black *350.*
  - dark blue *350.*
- ***b.*** Die on India, die sunk on card (1861), blue *2,500.*
- ***c.*** Die on India, cut close (1861)
  - black *350.*
  - blue *350.*

Essay reprints by Schernikow in 1903 from original dies (See paragraph eight of the Essay section introduction)

63-E1b

Vignette size: 18½x21½mm
Die size: 49x51mm
Franklin vignette only.

63-E1 1c
- ***a.*** Die on proof paper (1903)
  - black 75.
  - carmine 75.
  - dark carmine 75.
  - scarlet 75.
  - red brown 75.
  - orange 75.
  - yellow brown 75.
  - dark brown 75.
  - violet brown 75.
  - light green 75.
  - green 75.
  - dark blue 75.
  - ultramarine 75.
  - red violet 75.
  - dark violet 75.
  - dusky olive green 75.
- ***b.*** Die on colored card (1903)
  - orange red, *pale yellow* *125.*
  - orange, *pale pink* *125.*
  - yellow brown, *buff* *125.*
  - dark blue, *pink* *125.*
  - dark violet, *pale olive* *125.*
  - dull violet, *blue* *125.*
  - deep green, *pale blue* *125.*
  - violet, *light green* *125.*
- ***c.*** Die on green bond (1903)
  - black *125.*
  - dismal red *125.*
  - green *125.*

63-E2b

Franklin vignette with U S POSTAGE at top and ONE CENT at bottom.

63-E2 1c
- ***a.*** Die on proof paper (1903)
  - black 100.
  - carmine 100.
  - dark carmine 100.
  - scarlet 100.
  - red brown 100.
  - orange 100.
  - yellow brown 100.
  - violet brown 100.
  - gray brown 100.
  - light green 100.
  - green 100.
  - blue 100.
  - red violet 100.
  - ultramarine 100.
  - dusky olive 100.
- ***c.*** Die on green bond (1903)
  - orange *150.*
  - orange brown *150.*
  - violet *150.*
- ***d.*** Die on colored card (1903)
  - deep green, *pale blue* *150.*
  - violet, *light green* *150.*
  - dark orange red, *pale dull green* *150.*
  - olive, *ivory* *150.*
  - brown, *pink* *150.*
  - scarlet, *yellow* *150.*

63-E3

Side ornaments added.

63-E3 1c

c. Die on colored card (1903)

black, *ivory*	*150.*
brown, *pale pink*	*150.*
blue, *blue*	*150.*
orange brown, *pale pink*	*150.*
gray olive, *ivory*	*150.*
gray olive, *buff*	*150.*
scarlet, *pale yellow*	*150.*

d. Die on proof paper (1903)

black	85.
carmine	85.
dark carmine	85.
scarlet	85.
red brown	85.
orange	85.
yellow brown	85.
violet brown	85.
light green	85.
green	85.
blue	85.
violet	85.
red violet	85.
orange brown	85.
dusky olive	85.
ultramarine	85.

e. Die on green bond (1903)

carmine	*150.*
orange	*150.*
violet	*150.*

63-E9

Completely engraved design.

63-E9 1c

e. Die on proof paper, printed through mat (1903)

black	100.
carmine	100.
dark carmine	100.
scarlet	100.
orange	100.
orange brown	100.
yellow brown	100.
light green	100.
green	100.
black blue	100.
violet	100.
red violet	100.
violet brown	100.
gray	100.
blue	100.
ultramarine	100.

f. Die on bond (1903)

orange	*125.*
dismal blue green	*125.*

g. Die on bond, Walls of Troy wmk. (1903)

carmine	*200.*
orange red	*200.*
orange	*200.*
orange brown	*200.*
dark green	*200.*
light ultramarine	*200.*

h. Die on bond, double line of scallops wmk. (1903)

orange red	*200.*
dark green	*200.*

i. Die on green bond (1903)

dismal carmine	*125.*
dismal violet brown	*125.*
dull dark green	*125.*

j. Die on pinkish pelure (1903)

orange red	*300.*
brown red	*300.*
brown orange	*300.*
dull blue green	*300.*
violet	*300.*

k. Die on colored card (1903)

black, *pale blue*	*225.*
carmine, *pale yellow*	*225.*
carmine, *pale pink*	*225.*
brown red, *pale pink*	*225.*
chestnut, *pale olive*	*225.*
dismal olive, *buff*	*225.*
ultramarine, *ivory*	*225.*

l. Die on stiff card (1903), green *250.*

65-E1

Vignette size: 16½x19mm
Die size: 49x50mm
1851 master die of Washington vignette only.

65-E1 3c

a. Die on proof paper (1903)

black	75.
carmine	75.
dark carmine	75.
scarlet	75.
red brown	75.
orange	75.
brown orange	75.
violet brown	75.
dusky olive	75.
light green	75.
green	75.
dark blue	75.
ultramarine	75.
lilac	75.
red violet	75.

b. Die on green bond (1903)

red	*125.*
brown	*125.*
blue	*125.*
olive	*125.*

c. Die on colored card (1903)

carmine, *pale green*	*125.*
scarlet, *yellow*	*125.*
orange, *ivory*	*125.*
olive brown, *blue*	*125.*
dark blue, *pink*	*125.*
violet, *buff*	*125.*
dark green, *pink*	*125.*

65-E2

With tessellated frame, bottom label and diamond blocks. Without rosettes, top label and diamond blocks.

65-E2 3c

b. Die on proof paper, printed through a mat (1903)

black	*85.*
carmine	*85.*
dark carmine	*85.*
scarlet	*85.*
orange	*85.*
yellow	*85.*
yellow brown	*85.*
dusky gray	*85.*
light green	*85.*
green	*85.*
black blue	*85.*
ultramarine	*85.*
lilac	*85.*
dark lilac	*85.*
red violet	*85.*

c. Die on green bond (1903)

black	*150.*
dull orange red	*150.*
orange	*150.*
orange brown	*150.*
blue violet	*150.*
black blue	*150.*
dusky green	*150.*

d. Die on dull pale gray blue thin wove (1903)

dull red	*300.*
orange	*300.*
yellow brown	*300.*
dusky green	*300.*
black blue	*300.*

e. Die on colored card (1903)

black, *light blue*	*150.*
orange red, *yellow*	*150.*
red brown, *ivory*	*150.*
light green, *pink*	*150.*
green, *light green*	*150.*
blue, *buff*	*150.*

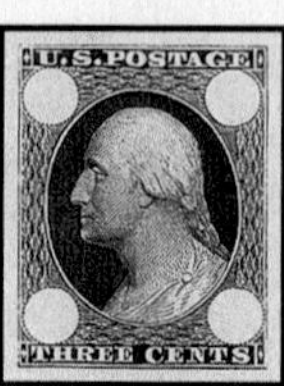

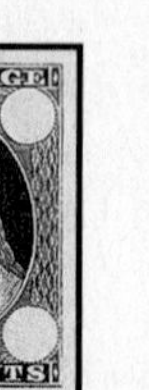

65-E3a 65-E3b

With top label and diamond blocks.

65-E3 3c

c. Die on proof paper, no numerals, printed through a mat (1903)

black	90.
carmine	90.
dark carmine	90.
scarlet	90.
orange	90.
yellow	90.
yellow brown	90.
dusky olive	90.
light green	90.
green	90.
black blue	90.
violet blue	90.
violet brown	90.
lilac	90.
red violet	90.

d. Die on green bond (1903)

dull scarlet	*150.*
dim red	*150.*
orange	*150.*
yellow brown	*150.*
green	*150.*
dusky blue	*150.*
violet	*150.*
black	*150.*

e. Die on colored card (1903)

black, *buff*	*150.*
scarlet, *ivory*	*150.*
orange, *light yellow*	*150.*
brown, *light blue*	*150.*
violet blue, *light pink*	*150.*
violet, *light green*	*150.*

f. Die on pink thin wove (1903)

dull yellow	*300.*
dismal red	*300.*
yellow brown	*300.*
dusky blue green	*300.*
dusky blue	*300.*

67-E1, Die II

Vignette size: 13½x16mm
Jefferson vignette only, Die II, background essentially complete.

67-E1 5c

b. Die II on proof paper (1903)

black	75.
carmine	75.
dark carmine	75.
scarlet	75.
red brown	75.
orange brown	75.
brown	75.
dusky olive	75.
green	75.
dark green	75.
black blue	75.
ultramarine	75.
violet brown	75.
red violet	75.
lilac	75.

c. Die II on colored card (1903)

olive, *buff*	*150.*
carmine, *pale yellow*	*150.*
scarlet, *green*	*150.*
brown, *pink*	*150.*
black, *ivory*	*150.*
ultramarine, *pale blue*	*150.*

d. Die II on green bond (1903)

orange brown	*150.*
dismal red brown	*150.*
dark green	*150.*
violet	*150.*
black blue	*150.*

e. Die II on old thin ivory paper (1903)

green	175.
dark carmine	175.

i. Die II on laid proof paper (1903) —

67-E2

Vignette die II framed, with spaces for numerals.

67-E2 5c
a. Die II on proof paper (1903)
black 95.
carmine 95.
dark carmine 95.
scarlet 95.
red brown 95.
orange 95.
yellow brown 95.
dusky olive 95.
violet brown 95.
light green 95.
dark green 95.
dark blue 95.
ultramarine 95.
red violet 95.
lilac 95.
b. Die II on colored card (1903)
orange brown, *light yellow* *175.*
deep blue, *light pink* *175.*
dusky olive, *light buff* *175.*
dark green, *pale blue* *175.*
red violet, *ivory* *175.*
c. Die II on green bond (1903)
orange brown *160.*
olive green *160.*
violet *160.*
blue *160.*
ultramarine *160.*

67-E3

67-E3 5c
a. Die I on proof paper, printed through a mat (1903)
black 125.
carmine 125.
dark carmine 125.
scarlet 125.
red brown 125.
yellow brown 125.
dark brown 125.
violet brown 125.
light green 125.
green 125.
dark blue 125.
lilac 125.
ultramarine 125.
red violet 125.
dusky olive 125.
e. Die I on colored card (1903)
orange red, *buff* *175.*
orange red, *light yellow* *175.*
olive green, *pale green* *175.*
deep green, *ivory* *175.*
dark blue, *light pink* *175.*
violet brown, *light blue* *175.*
f. Die I on green bond (1903)
black *160.*
scarlet *160.*
brown *160.*
green *160.*
g. Die I on yellow pelure (1903)
scarlet *350.*
brown red *350.*
brown *350.*
dark green *350.*
violet *350.*
blue *350.*
h. Die I on bond, Walls of Troy wmk. (1903)
dark orange *250.*
blue *250.*
carmine *250.*
i. Die I on bond, two line scalloped border wmk. (1903)
dark blue green *250.*
scarlet *250.*

67-E4j

Complete die II design with corner ornaments.

67-E4 5c
f. Die II on proof paper, printed through a mat (1903)
black 125.
carmine 125.
dark carmine 125.
scarlet 125.
orange 125.
brown 125.
yellow brown 125.
dusky olive 125.
light green 125.
green 125.
blue 125.
black blue 125.
violet brown 125.
red violet 125.
lilac 125.
ultramarine 125.
g. Die II on colored card (1903)
red, *light yellow* *150.*
brown, *buff* *150.*
olive green, *light pink* *150.*
dark violet *150.*
violet brown, *pale green* *150.*
dusky yellow green, *dull pale* *150.*
blue green *150.*
brown, *ivory* *150.*
h. Die II on green bond (1903)
black *125.*
dull dark orange *125.*
violet *125.*
i. Die II on bond, Walls of Troy wmk. (1903)
scarlet *250.*
deep red *250.*
dark green *250.*
j. Die II on bond, two-line scalloped border wmk. (1903)
deep orange *250.*
blue *250.*
k. Die II on greenish pelure (1903)
orange *350.*
olive brown *350.*
dark green *350.*
l. Die II on bluish pelure (1903), red brown *450.*

69-E1

Vignette size: 15x17mm
Washington vignette only. Die I incomplete, horiz. background lines irregularly spaced, space occurring about every 2mm. Die I known only on Schernikow reprints.

69-E1 12c
b. Die I on proof paper (1903)
black 60.
carmine 60.
dark carmine 60.
scarlet 60.
red brown 60.
orange 60.
yellow brown 60.
violet brown 60.
gray brown 60.
light green 60.
green 60.
blue 60.
black blue 60.
red violet 60.
lilac 60.
ultramarine 60.
c. Die I on green bond (1903)
black *150.*
red brown *150.*
brown *150.*
d. Die I on colored card (1903)
dark carmine, *ivory* *150.*
dark carmine, *light blue* *150.*
dark olive, *buff* *150.*
dark green, *light yellow* *150.*
dark blue, *pale green* *150.*
violet brown, *light pink* *150.*

69-E2

Curved labels at top and bottom.

69-E2 12c
a. Die II on proof paper, some printed through a mat (1903)
black 75.
carmine 75.
dark carmine 75.
scarlet 75.
orange 75.
yellow 75.
yellow brown 75.
violet brown 75.
gray brown 75.
light green 75.
green 75.
light blue 75.
black blue 75.
red violet 75.
lilac 75.
ultramarine 75.
c. Die I on dull light green bond (1903)
black *150.*
dull red *150.*
dim orange *150.*
yellow brown *150.*
dusky green *150.*
dusky blue *150.*
red violet *150.*
d. Die I on pale yellow thin wove (1903)
dim red *200.*
deep orange red *200.*
yellow brown *200.*
dusky blue *200.*
red violet *200.*
e. Die I on colored card (1903)
dull red, *light pink* *150.*
orange red, *buff* *150.*
brown, *light blue* *150.*
dark olive, *light yellow* *150.*
dull dark blue, *ivory* *150.*
violet, *pale green* *150.*

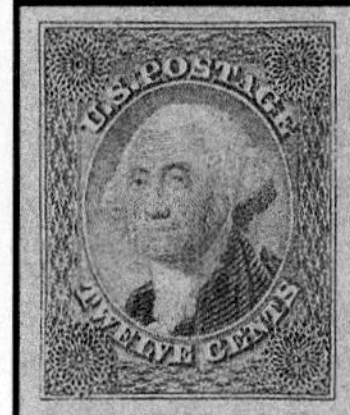

69-E3o

Frame incomplete: all four rosettes blank.

69-E3 12c
a. Die on proof paper (1903)
black 125.
carmine 125.
dark carmine 125.
scarlet 125.
red brown 125.
orange 125.
orange brown 125.
violet brown 125.
light green 125.
green 125.
light blue 125.
black blue 125.
red violet 125.
lilac 125.
ultramarine 125.
e. Die on colored card, top border missing (1903)
orange brown, *light blue* *175.*
deep green, *light yellow* *175.*
deep blue, *light pink* *175.*
violet, *ivory* *175.*
deep yellow orange, *pale yellow green* *175.*
brown, *buff* *175.*
f. Die on green bond, top border missing (1903)
orange *175.*
green *175.*
violet *175.*
o. Die I on pale yellow thin wove (1903), dark red *750.*
p. Die I on pink thin wove (1903), blue *750.*
q. Die I on pale pink (1903), blue *750.*

70-E1

Vignette size: 7x16mm

Washington die II vignette only.

70-E1 24c
a. Die II on proof paper (1903)
black 60.
carmine 60.
dark carmine 60.
scarlet 60.
orange 60.
yellow 60.
yellow brown 60.
violet brown 60.
gray olive 60.
light green 60.
green 60.
light blue 60.
black blue 60.
red violet 60.
lilac 60.
b. Die II on green bond (1903)
black *150.*
red brown *150.*
violet *150.*
orange *150.*
c. Die II on colored card (1903)
dull red, *ivory* *150.*
brown red, *buff* *150.*
brown orange, *light pink* *150.*
dark green, *light yellow* *150.*
blue, *pale green* *150.*
violet, *blue* *150.*

70-E2

Washington vignette with oval label. Background complete, eyes retouched.

70-E2 24c
a. Die II on proof paper (1903)
black 60.
carmine 60.
dark carmine 60.
scarlet 60.
orange 60.
yellow 60.
yellow brown 60.
violet brown 60.
light green 60.
green 60.
light blue 60.
black blue 60.
red violet 60.
lilac 60.
gray olive 60.
ultramarine 60.
c. Die I on colored card (1903)
black, *light pink* *150.*
orange, *buff* *150.*
orange, *light blue* *150.*
dark green, *pale green* *150.*
violet blue, *light yellow* *150.*
violet, *ivory* *150.*
d. Die I on green bond (1903), brown *150.*
e. Die I on dull light blue green bond (1903)
black *150.*
orange red *150.*
orange *150.*
yellow brown *150.*
dusky green *150.*
dull blue *150.*
red violet *150.*
f. Die I on dull pale green blue thin wove (1903)
orange red *300.*
orange *300.*
yellow brown *300.*
dusky green *300.*
dull blue *300.*

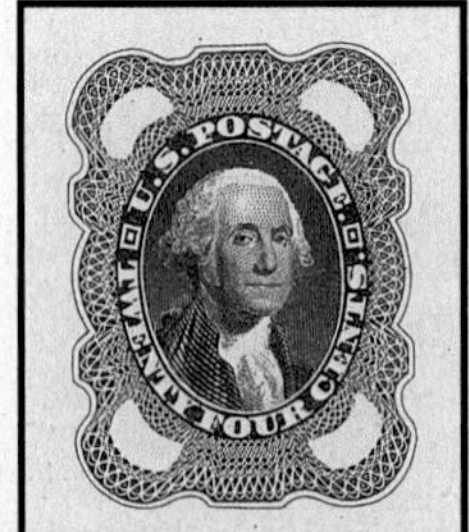
70-EA3

With frame. Blank areas in corners for numerals.

70-E3 24c
a. Die on proof paper (1903)
black 100.
carmine 100.
dark carmine 100.
scarlet 100.
orange 100.
yellow brown 100.
orange brown 100.
violet brown 100.
gray olive 100.
light green 100.
green 100.
light blue 100.
black blue 100.
red violet 100.
lilac 100.
ultramarine 100.
c. Die on colored card (1903)
carmine, *light blue* *175.*
blue, *pale green* *175.*
scarlet, *buff* *175.*
yellow brown, *cream* *175.*
dull violet, *pink* *175.*
dusky green, *light yellow* *175.*
gray olive, *ivory* *175.*
d. Die on green bond (1903)
black *175.*
orange brown *175.*
green *175.*

70-E4

Complete design with numerals in corners.

70-E4 24c
f. Die on proof paper, printed through a mat (1903)
black 125.
carmine 125.
dark carmine 125.
scarlet 125.
red brown 125.
yellow brown 125.
brown 125.
violet brown 125.
gray olive 125.
light green 125.
green 125.
light blue 125.
black blue 125.
red violet 125.
lilac 125.
ultramarine 125.
g. Die on blue pelure (1903)
dark carmine *300.*
scarlet *300.*
orange *300.*
brown *300.*
dusky green *300.*
h. Die on bond (1903)
black *175.*
scarlet *175.*
orange *175.*
dark green *175.*
blue *175.*
i. Die on green bond (1903)
black *250.*
dark red *250.*
green *250.*
j. Die on bond, Walls of Troy wmk. (1903), dark green *300.*
k. Die on bond, double line of scallops wmk. (1903)
deep orange red *300.*
scarlet *300.*
orange *300.*
light blue *300.*
l. Die on colored card, printed through a mat (1903)
dark orange, *ivory* *150.*
dark orange, *light pink* *150.*
brown, *light blue* *150.*
dull dark blue, *pale green* *150.*
violet, *light yellow* *150.*
violet brown, *buff* *150.*

72-E1

Vignette size: 16x17½mm
Washington vignette only.

72-E1 90c
a. Die on proof paper (1903)
black 100.
carmine 100.
dark carmine 100.
scarlet 100.
red brown 100.
orange 100.
orange brown 100.
violet brown 100.
gray olive 100.
light green 100.
green 100.
dark blue 100.
lilac 100.
red violet 100.
yellow brown 100.
ultramarine 100.
b. Die on colored card (1903)
black, *light yellow* *165.*
red brown, *light pink* *165.*
carmine, *buff* *165.*
brown, *pale green* *165.*
dark brown, *light blue* *165.*
ultramarine, *ivory* *165.*
c. Die on dull light blue green bond (1903)
violet brown *165.*
dusky green *165.*
dusky blue *165.*
red violet *165.*

72-E2

Vignette with blank top and bottom labels.

72-E2 90c
a. Die on proof paper (1903)
black 100.
carmine 100.
dark carmine 100.
scarlet 100.
orange 100.
yellow brown 100.
brown 100.
violet brown 100.
gray olive 100.
light green 100.
green 100.
dark blue 100.
red violet 100.
lilac 100.
ultramarine 100.
b. Die on green bond (1903)
dull orange *150.*
dull orange brown *150.*
red violet *150.*
c. Die on colored card (1903)
black, *buff* *185.*
orange red, *light yellow* *185.*
brown, *ivory* *185.*
olive green, *light pink* *185.*
green, *light blue* *185.*
violet brown, *pale green* *185.*

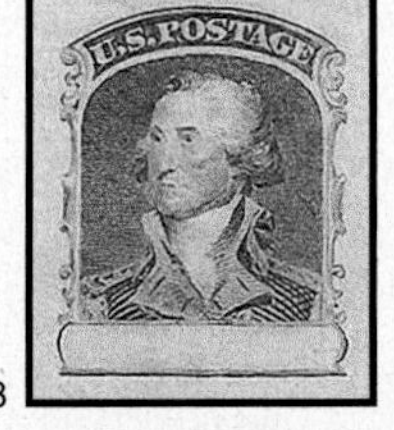

72-E3

U.S. POSTAGE in top label.

72-E3 90c
a. Die on proof paper (1903)
black 125.
carmine 125.
dark carmine 125.
scarlet 125.
orange 125.
yellow 125.
yellow brown 125.
brown 125.
violet brown 125.
gray olive 125.
light green 125.
green 125.
dark blue 125.
lilac 125.
red violet 125.
ultramarine 125.
b. Die on colored card (1903)
orange, *light blue* *185.*
orange red, *light yellow* *185.*
dark blue, *buff* *185.*
violet, *pale green* *185.*
violet brown, *ivory* *185.*
orange brown, *pale pink* *185.*
c. Die on green bond (1903)
black *175.*
brown *175.*
green *175.*
gray olive *175.*

72-E5

Complete design.

72-E5 90c

d. Die on proof paper, printed through a mat (1903)
black 175.
carmine 175.
dark carmine 175.
scarlet 175.
orange 175.
orange brown 175.
yellow brown 175.
brown 175.
violet brown 175.
gray olive 175.
light green 175.
green 175.
dark blue 175.
lilac 175.
red violet 175.
ultramarine 175.

e. Die on colored card (1903)
carmine, *light blue* 250.
dismal brown, *light pink* 250.
orange brown, *buff* 250.
blue, *ivory* 250.
violet, *pale green* 250.
green, *pale yellow* 250.

f. Die on green bond (1903)
dark carmine 225.
red brown 225.
green 225.

g. Die on bond (1903)
brown 250.
orange brown 250.
dark green 250.

h. Die on bond, "Bond No. 1" wmk. (1903), orange brown 350.

i. Die on bond, "Bond No 2" wmk. (1903), orange brown 350.

j. Die on bond, Walls of Troy wmk. (1903)
carmine 300.
scarlet 300.
orange 300.
dark green 300.
ultramarine 300.

k. Die on pink pelure (1903)
brown red 350.
dull yellow 350.
very dark green 350.
dark blue 350.
dull violet 350.

l. Die on bond, Double Scallops wmk. (1903), scarlet 300.

American Bank Note Co.

65-E5

Design size: 19x23½mm
Engraved frame with pencil border, center cut out, mounted over 22x27mm engraved vignette of Washington.

65-E5 3c Die on India, black 3,000.

65-E6

Design size: 19x24½mm
Engraved frame with pencil border, center cut out, mounted over engraved ruled background with engraved Washington vignette mounted on it.

65-E6 Three Cents Die on India, on card about 23x27½mm, black 2,500.

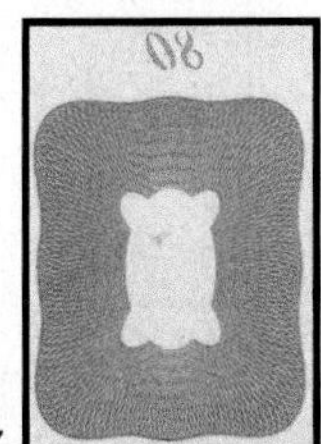
65-E7

Master die No. 80 of frame only.

65-E7 3c Die on India, card mounted
deep orange 2,000.
dark brown 2,000.
green 2,000.
dark blue 2,000.
black 2,000.

65-E7Aa

65-E7Ab

Design size: 19½x24½mm
Engraved lathework frame with Bauld, Cousland & Co. engraved Washington vignette. No denomination.

65-E7A (3c)

a. Die on India (29x35 mm). Engraved frame with pencil border. Blank labels 1,000.

b. Die on India (53x62 mm), die sunk on card. Blank labels and corner tablets
black 1,000.
green 1,000.
brown purple 1,000.

c. As 65-E7Ab, die sunk on card. Top label: American Bank Note. Bottom label: Company. New York. Corner tablets: A, B, N, C. Exists in various states of wear outside the design and off the card, cut down on India
black 1,000.
blue 1,000.
brown 1,000.
brown red 1,000.
red brown 1,000.
orange brown 1,000.
scarlet 1,000.
dark green 1,000.
dull purple 1,000.

d. As No. 65-E7Ac, plate essay, imperf, ungummed. Green on white wove. Complete bottom row of 4 (one recorded) —

e. As No. 65-E7Ac. Loewenberg decal essay, blue (one recorded) —

65-E8

Design size: 19½x24½mm
Engraved lathework frame with Bald, Cousland & Co. engraved Washington vignette and engraved lettered labels and numerals mounted on it.

65-E8 3c Die on India, on 22x27mm card, black 11,000.

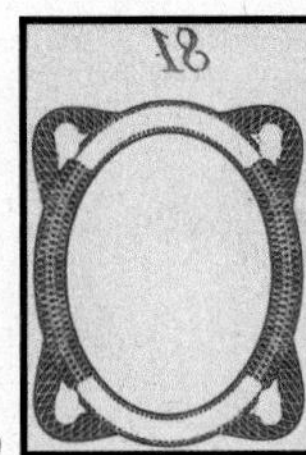
65-E9

Master die No. 81 of frame only.

65-E9 3c Die on India
black 2,750.
brown yellow 2,750.
dark green 2,750.
orange red 2,750.

65-E10

Engraved lathework frame with Bald, Cousland & Co. engraved Washington vignette and engraved lettered labels and numerals mounted on it.

65-E10 3c Die on India, on 28x35mm card, black 7,000.

67-E5

Design size: 21x25mm
Engraved frame used for the 1860 Nova Scotia 5c stamp cut to shape, with engraved lettered labels and Washington vignette No. 209-E7 mounted on it.

67-E5 Five Cents Die on India, on 23x27mm card, black 2,500.

67-E6

Design size: 19x24
Engraved lathework background with Bald, Cousland & Co. engraved Washington vignette and engraved lettered labels and numerals mounted on it.

67-E6 5c Die on India, mounted on 22x26mm card, black 7,000.

67-E7

Design size: 19x24mm
Engraved lathework background with Bald, Cousland & Co. engraved Washington vignette and engraved lettered labels and numerals mounted on it.

67-E7 5c Die on India, mounted on 21x26½mm card, black 7,000.

National Bank Note Co.

The following essays include those formerly listed as Nos. 55-57, 59 and 62 in the Postage section, and the corresponding die and plate essays formerly listed in the Proof section. Former No. 58 is now No. 62B. Former Nos. 60 and 61 are now Nos. 70eTC and 71bTC in the Trial Color Proofs section.

Small die essays from the 1903 Roosevelt albums have "RA" as part of the listing description. Small die essays from the special Panama-Pacific Exposition printings have "PP" as part of the listing description.

63-E10

Frame essay with blank areas for Franklin vignette, labels, numerals, U and S.

63-E10 1c Die on India, black *4,000.*

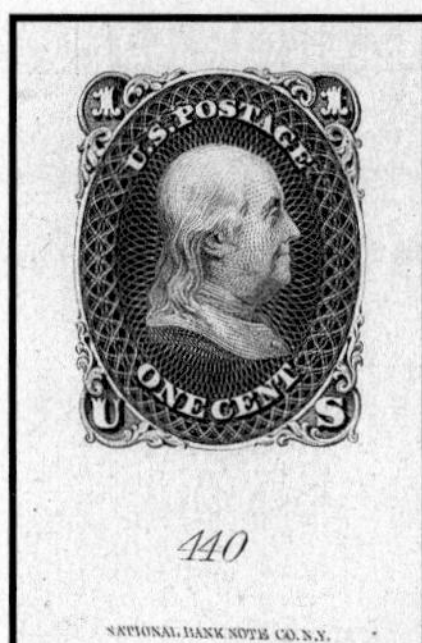

63-E11

Die size: 58x56mm
"Premiere Gravure" die No. 440.

63-E11 1c
a. "Premiere Gravure" die essay on India (formerly Nos. 55P1, 55TC1)
black *4,000.*
indigo *1,500.*
ultramarine *2,750.*
b. RA "Premiere Gravure" small die essay on white wove, 28x31mm (**formerly No. 55P2**), indigo *325.*
c. "Premiere Gravure" plate essay on India (**formerly Nos. 55P3, 55TC3**)
indigo *300.*
blue —
ultramarine *300.*
violet ultramarine —
d. "Premiere Gravure" plate essay on semitransparent stamp paper (**formerly No. 55TC4**), ultramarine *450.*

63-E11e

e. Finished "Premiere Gravure" plate essay on semitransparent stamp paper, perf. 12, gummed (**formerly No. 55**), indigo *50,000.*

No. 63-E11e is valued with perfs cutting slightly into design at top.

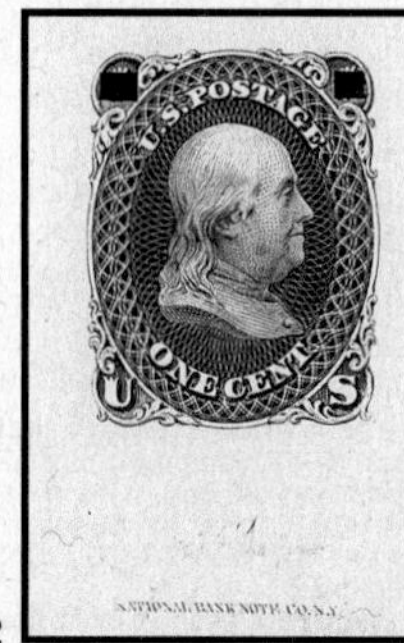

63-E12

Die size: 47x55mm
Apparently complete die except value numerals have been cut out.

63-E12 1c Die on India, die sunk on card, black *1,500.*

65-E11

Die size: 64x76½mm
Washington head only. No die number. NBNC imprint 24 mm below the base of the bust. Vignette similar to No. 65-E14.

65-E11 3c
a. Die on India, on card, carmine (two recorded) *750.*
b. Die on white glazed paper
black (five recorded) *750.*
scarlet (four recorded) *750.*
brown violet *750.*

65-E12

Die size: 78x55mm
Incomplete engraved design, no scrolls outside framelines, no ornaments on 3s, U and S. Vignette: no imprint. No silhouette on top of the head. Thin wispy hair. No gash in the hair around the ear. Well defined chin and lines at the base of the bust.

65-E12 3c Die on India, die sunk on card
black *1,000.*
blue *1,000.*

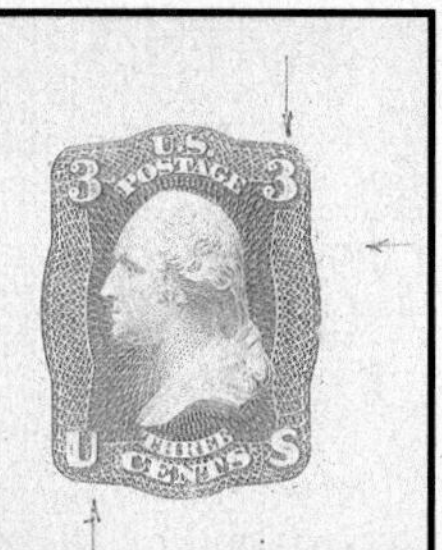

65-E13

As No. 65-E12 but ornaments on 3s, U and S. Shows traces of first border design erased. With imprint and No. 441 below design.

65-E13 3c Die on India, card mounted
scarlet *1,000.*
brown red *1,000.*
ultramarine *1,000.*

65-E14

Die size: 59x55mm
Frame as No. 65-E13 but with scrolls added outside the frame. Vignette: top of head silhouetted. Thick hair lines. Gash in the hair around the ear. Poor definition around the chin and at the base of the bust. No imprint.

65-E14 3c Die on India, die sunk on card
a. Die on India (62 x 74 mm), die sunk on card
black *750.*
scarlet *750.*
pink *1,250.*
brown orange *750.*
deep orange red *750.*
deep red *750.*
b. Die on pelure paper, dim deep red (one recorded) —

65-E15

Washington vignette as No. 65-E12: no silhouette on top of the head, no gash around the ear, well defined lines at the base of the bust; frame as No. 65-E14.

65-E15 3c
a. Die on India, card mounted, deep orange red *1,000.*
b. "Premiere Gravure" die essay on semitransparent stamp paper, 20x25mm-30x37mm
deep orange red *750.*
deep red orange *750.*
dim red *750.*
dim deep red *750.*
dim orange red *750.*
dull pink *750.*
dull violet red *750.*
c. "Premiere Gravure" small die on India (59x55 mm), die sunk on card. Die 441 with NBNC imprint, became the basis of the issued stamp after corner ornaments added (eleven recorded)
red *1,350.*
black *2,000.*
scarlet *2,000.*
pink *2,850.*
orange red *2,000.*
dark orange red *2,000.*
d. RA Small die essay on white wove, 28x31mm altered laydown die of complete design but with outer scrolls removed and replaced by ones similar to "Premiere Gravure" design (1903) (**formerly No. 56P2**), dim deep red *500.*
e. As "c," PP small die essay on pale cream soft wove, 24x29mm (1915) (**formerly No. 56P2a**), deep red *1,250.*
f. "Premiere Gravure" plate No. 2 essay on India (**formerly Nos. 56P3, 56TC3**)
red *250.*
scarlet *350.*
g. "Premiere Gravure" plate essay on semitransparent stamp paper (**formerly Nos. 56aP4, 56TC4**)
red, pair with gum *1,750.*
black *400.*

65-E15h

h. Finished "Premiere Gravure" plate essay on semitransparent stamp paper, perf. 12, gummed (**formerly No. 56)**
brown rose *650.*
orange red *475.*
bright orange red *475.*
dark orange red *475.*
dim deep red *475.*
pink *475.*
deep pink *475.*
P# block of 8, Impt. (any shade) *20,000.*

67-E8

Incomplete impression from die No. 442, border lines and corner scrolls missing.

67-E8 5c Die on India, mounted on 34x50mm card, black *1,750.*

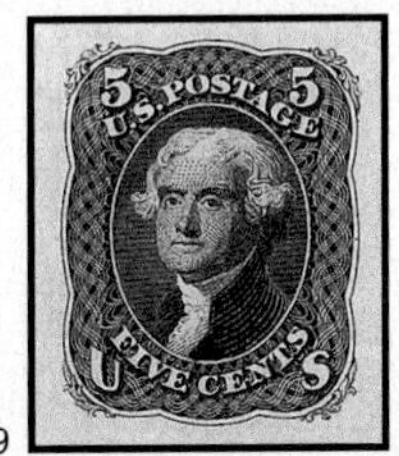

67-E9

Size of die: 58x59mm
"Premiere Gravure" design, with corner scrolls but without leaflets.

67-E9 5c
a. "Premiere Gravure" die essay on India, card mounted (formerly No. 57TC1)
black *2,500.*
scarlet *2,500.*
b. RA Small die essay on white wove, 28x31mm, altered laydown die of complete design but with scrolls removed from corners to resemble "Premiere Gravure" (1903) (**formerly No. 57P2), brown** 400.
c. As "b," PP die essay on pale cream soft wove, 24x29mm (1915) (**formerly No. 57P2a**), brown *1,750.*
d. "Premiere Gravure" plate No. 3 essay on India (**formerly Nos. 57P3, 57TC3)**
brown *350.*
light brown *300.*
dark brown *300.*
red brown *300.*

67-E9e

e. Finished "Premiere Gravure" plate essay on semitransparent stamp paper, perf. 12, gummed (**formerly No. 57**), brown *30,000.*

68-E1

Design size: 14x17½mm
Die size: 26x31mm
Washington vignette only.

68-E1 10c
a. Die on ivory paper, black *1,000.*
b. Die on India *1,000.*

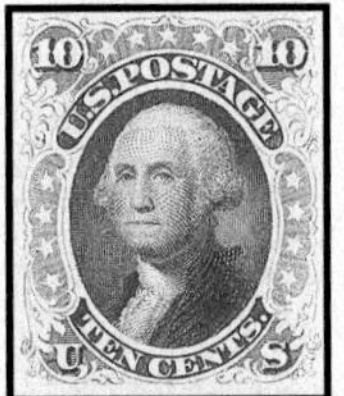

68-E2

Incomplete die No. 443.

68-E2 10c Die on India, 22x26mm, dark green *2,500.*

68-E3

Incomplete die of No. 68P1, thin lines missing on top of frame.

68-E3 10c Die on India
yellowish green *1,100.*
dark green *1,000.*

69-E5

Design size: 12½x16mm
Die size: about 62x65mm
Washington vignette only.

69-E5 12c
a. Die on India, die sunk on card
black *400.*
dark red *400.*
orange red *400.*
b. Die on ivory paper, about 24x28mm
black *500.*
scarlet *500.*
black brown *500.*
blue *500.*

69-E6

Incomplete die No. 444, without corner ornaments.

69-E6 12c
a. "Premiere Gravure" die essay on India, mounted on card (**formerly Nos. 59P1, 59TC1**)
black *2,500.*
scarlet *2,500.*
dark green *2,500.*
b. RA Small die essay on white wove, 29x31mm, altered laydown die of complete design but with scrolls removed from corners to resemble the "Premiere Gravure" (1903) (formerly Nos. 59P2), black *450.*
c. PP "Premiere Gravure" small die essay on pale cream soft wove, 24x29mm (1915) (**formerly No. 59P2a**), black *1,750.*
d. "Premiere Gravure" plate No. 5 essay on India (**formerly No. 59P3**), black *350.*

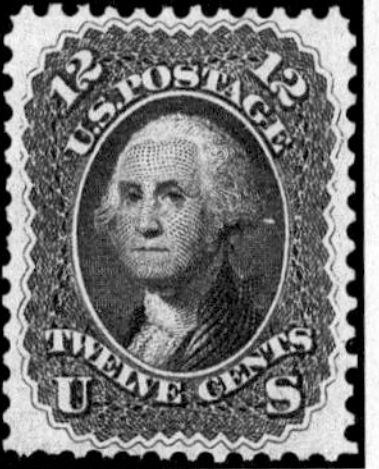

69-E6e

e. Finished "Premiere Gravure" plate essay on semitransparent stamp paper, perf. 12, gummed (**formerly No. 59**), black *90,000.*

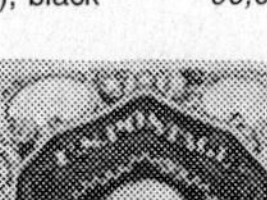

70-E5

Washington vignette in incomplete frame.

70-E5 24c Die on India, black *3,250.*

70-E6

Die size: 56½x56mm

Incomplete die (No. 445): silhouette unfinished, especially scrolls around numerals; shadows over numerals not acid etched.

70-E6 24c Die on India, die sunk on card
black *900.*
violet *900.*
gray violet *900.*
dark violet *900.*
scarlet *900.*
green *900.*
orange *900.*
red brown *900.*
orange brown *900.*
orange yellow *900.*
rose red *900.*
gray *900.*
steel blue *900.*
blue *900.*

For finished "Premiere Gravure" trial color plate proof on semitransparent stamp paper, perf 12, gummed (formerly No. 60), see 70TC6 in the Trial Color, Die and Plate Proof section.

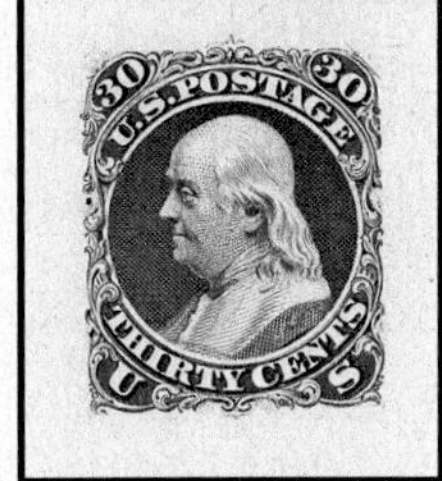

71-E1

Die size: 46x60mm
Incomplete die (No. 446): additional ornaments at top and bottom in pencil, as later engraved.

71-E1 30c Die on India, black *1,750.*

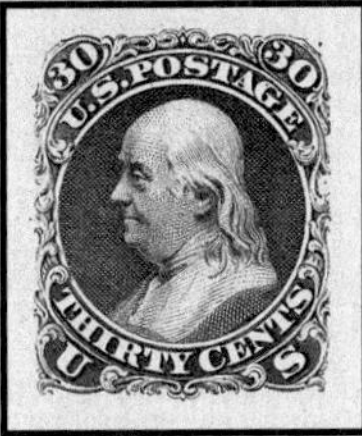

71-E2

"Premiere Gravure" die: left side of frame and silhouette at lower right unfinished.

71-E2 30c
a. "Premiere Gravure" die essay on India, die sunk on card (**formerly No. 61TC1**)
black *1,750.*
green *1,750.*
dull gray blue *1,750.*
violet brown *1,750.*
scarlet *1,750.*
dull rose *1,750.*
b. "Premiere Gravure" plate essay on India (**formerly No. 61P3**), deep red orange *600.*
c. "Premiere Gravure" plate essay on card
black (split thin) *500.*
blue *750.*
d. "Premiere Gravure" plate essay on card, black 12x2mm SPECIMEN overprint, blue *750.*
e. "Premiere Gravure" plate essay on semitransparent stamp paper
deep red orange *1,250.*
yellow orange *1,250.*
lemon yellow *1,250.*
dark orange yellow *1,250.*
dull orange yellow *1,250.*

For finished "Premiere Gravure" trial color proof on semitransparent stamp paper, perf 12, gummed (formerly No. 61), see No. 71TC6 in the Trial Color, Die and Plate Proof section.

72-E6

Die size: 54x63mm
Incomplete die: without thin lines at bottom of frame and in upper left triangle between label and frame, and without leaves at left of U and right of S.

72-E6 90c Die on India, blue (shades) *1,000.*

72-E7

Similar to 72-E6 but lines added in upper left triangle, leaves added at left of U and at right of S. Exists with and without imprint and Die No. 447 added below design.

72-E7 90c
- *a.* Die on India, die sunk on card, black — *1,750.*
- *b.* "Premiere Gravure" die essay on India, thin line under bottom center frame (**formerly Nos. 62P1, 62TC1**)
  - blue — *1,350.*
  - black — *1,750.*
- *d.* PP "Premiere Gravure" small die essay on pale cream soft wove, 24x29mm (1915) (**formerly No. 62P2a**), blue — *1,750.*
- *e.* "Premiere Gravure" plate essay on India, blue — *500.*
- *f.* "Premiere Gravure" plate essay on card, black (split thin) — *500.*
- *g.* "Premiere Gravure" plate essay on semi-transparent stamp paper (**formerly Nos. 62aP4, 62TC4**)
  - blue, pair, gummed — *5,500.*
  - blue green — *275.*

72-E7h

- *h.* Finished "Premiere Gravure" plate essay on semitransparent stamp paper, perf. 12, gummed (**formerly No. 62**), blue — *50,000.*

Die size: 54x63mm
Similar to Nos. 72-E6 and 72-E7 but leaf at left of "U" only, no shading around "U" and "S," leaf and some shading missing at bottom right above "S," shading missing in top label, etc., faint ms. "8" at bottom of backing card.

72-E8 90c Die on India, die sunk on 3¼x3½-inch card, dark blue — —

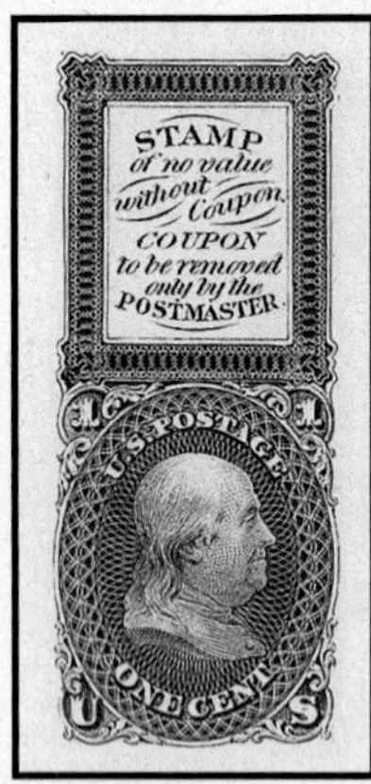

63-E13b

63-E13g

Design size: 20x47mm
Die size: 57x95mm
Bowlsby patent coupon at top of 1c stamp design.

63-E13 1c
- *a.* Die on India, die sunk on card
  - black — *1,750.*
  - red — *1,750.*
  - scarlet — *1,750.*
  - orange — *1,750.*
  - orange brown — *1,750.*
  - brown — *1,750.*
  - yellow brown — *1,750.*
  - blue green — *1,750.*
  - olive green — *1,750.*
  - olive — *1,750.*
  - blue — *1,750.*
  - violet — *1,750.*
  - red violet — *1,750.*
  - gray — *1,750.*
  - gray brown — *1,750.*
  - dull orange yellow — *1,750.*
- *b.* Die on white glazed paper
  - black — *1,750.*
  - dark brown — *1,750.*
  - scarlet — *1,750.*
  - blue — *1,750.*
- *c.* Plate on pelure paper, gummed, red — *300.*
- *d.* Plate on white paper, red — *250.*
- *e.* Plate on white paper, with 13x16mm points-up grill, red — *350.*
  - Split grill — *750.*
- *f.* Plate on white paper, perf. all around and between stamp and coupon
  - red — *200.*
  - blue — *200.*
- *g.* Plate on white paper, perf. all around, imperf. between stamp and coupon
  - red — *200.*
  - blue — *200.*
- *h.* Plate on white paper, perf. all around, rouletted between stamp and coupon
  - red — *300.*
  - blue — *300.*
- *i.* Plate on India paper, black — 750.

1861-66 Essays
Authors Unknown

73-E2

Design size: 21x26mm

73-E2 2c Pencil and watercolor on thick card, bright green — *3,750.*

73-E4

Design size: 21x26mm
Indian vignette. Typographed printings from woodcuts. Plates of three rows of three, one row each of Nos. 73-E3, 73-E4, 73-E5. Listings are of singles.

73-E3

73-E3 2c
- *a.* Plate on white wove
  - red — *30.*
  - scarlet — *30.*
  - violet — *30.*
  - black — *30.*
  - blue — *30.*
  - green — *30.*
- *b.* Plate on mauve wove
  - red — *50.*
  - violet — *50.*
  - black — *50.*
  - blue — *50.*
  - green — *50.*
- *c.* Plate on yellow wove
  - red — *50.*
  - violet — *50.*
  - black — *50.*
  - blue — *50.*
  - green — *50.*
- *d.* Plate on yellow laid
  - red — *50.*
  - violet — *50.*
  - black — *50.*
  - blue — *50.*
  - green — *50.*
- *e.* Plate on pink laid
  - red — *50.*
  - violet — *50.*
  - black — *50.*
  - blue — *50.*
  - green — *50.*
- *f.* Plate on green laid
  - red — *50.*
  - violet — *50.*
  - black — *50.*
  - blue — *50.*
  - green — *50.*
- *g.* Plate on cream laid
  - red — *50.*
  - violet — *50.*
  - black — *50.*
  - blue — *50.*
  - green — *50.*
- *h.* Plate on pale yellow wove
  - red — *50.*
  - green — *50.*
  - blue — *50.*
- *i.* Plate on yellow-surfaced card, violet — *50.*

Design size: 23x26½mm
Small head of Liberty in shield. Typographed printings from woodcuts. On plate with Nos. 73-E3 and 73-E5. Listings are of singles.

73-E4 3c
- *a.* Plate on white wove
  - red — *30.*
  - scarlet — *30.*
  - violet — *30.*
  - black — *30.*
  - blue — *30.*
  - green — *30.*
- *b.* Plate on mauve wove, violet — *50.*
- *c.* Plate on yellow wove
  - red — *50.*
  - violet — *50.*
  - black — *50.*
  - blue — *50.*
  - green — *50.*
- *d.* Plate on yellow laid
  - red — *50.*
  - violet — *50.*
  - black — *50.*
  - blue — *50.*
  - green — *50.*
- *e.* Plate on pink laid
  - carmine — *50.*
  - violet — *50.*
  - black — *50.*
  - blue — *50.*
  - green — *50.*
- *f.* Plate on green laid
  - carmine — *50.*
  - green — *50.*
  - dull violet — *50.*
  - blue — *50.*
- *g.* Plate on cream laid
  - red — *50.*
  - violet — *50.*
  - black — *50.*
  - blue — *50.*
  - green — *50.*
- *h.* Plate on pale yellow wove
  - red — *50.*
  - green — *50.*
  - blue — *50.*
- *i.* Plate on yellow-surfaced card, violet — *50.*
- *j.* Plate on fawn wove, green — *50.*

73-E5

Design size: 22½x25½mm
Large head of Liberty. Typographed impressions from woodcut. On plate with Nos. 73-E3 and 73-E4. Listings are of singles.

73-E5 5c
- *a.* Plate on white wove
  - red — *30.*
  - scarlet — *30.*
  - violet — *30.*
  - black — *30.*
  - blue — *30.*
  - green — *30.*
- *b.* Plate on mauve wove, violet — *50.*
- *c.* Plate on yellow wove
  - red — *50.*
  - violet — *50.*
  - black — *50.*
  - blue — *50.*
  - green — *50.*
- *d.* Plate on yellow laid
  - red — *50.*
  - violet — *50.*
  - black — *50.*
  - blue — *50.*
  - green — *50.*
- *e.* Plate on pink laid
  - red — *50.*
  - black — *50.*
  - blue — *50.*
  - green — *50.*
- *f.* Plate on green laid
  - red — *50.*
  - violet — *50.*
  - black — *50.*
  - blue — *50.*
  - green — *50.*
- *g.* Plate on cream laid
  - red — *50.*
  - black — *50.*
  - blue — *50.*

green 50.
h. Plate on pale yellow wove
red 50.
blue 50.
green 50.
i. Plate on yellow-surfaced card, violet 50.

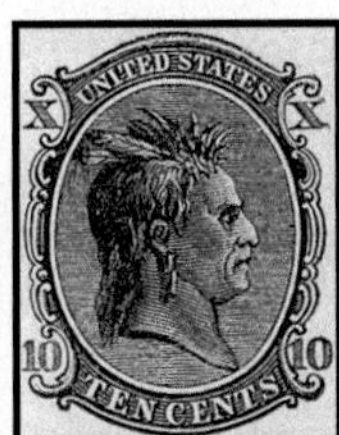
73-E6

Size of design: 21x27mm
Indian vignette. Typographed impressions from woodcut.

73-E6 10c
a. Die on proof paper
black 200.
gray black 200.
carmine 200.
dusky red 200.
brown 200.
green 200.
blue 200.
violet 200.
b. Plate on white paper (pane of 4)
red 600.
violet 600.
brown 600.
black 600.
blue 600.
green 600.
c. Plate on soft cream card (pane of 4)
black 600.
red 600.
blue 600.
green 600.
red violet 600.

1863-64
Henry Loewenberg
Decalcomania and Coated Paper Essays

79-EP

Decalcomania essay pasted to the back of a letter dated Mar. 23, 1863. Written by James MacDonough of the NBNC to the PO's Anthony Zevely. Illustrates Loewenberg's patent 40,489 (granted Nov. 3, 1863). Printed on goldbeaters' skin paper and gummed over the printing. Bottom left corner folded back to prove the concept i.e. that attempts to remove a stamp from an envelope should leave the design behind.

79-EP Shield design. Block of 8, black (one recorded) —

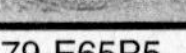
79-E65P5

79-E65P6

79-E66P5

79-E67P5

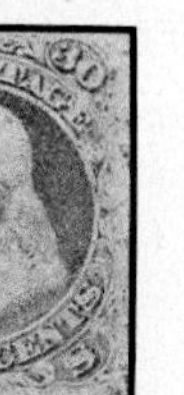
79-E71P5

79-E72P5

79-E73P5

Plate proofs of the 1861 issue printed on goldbeaters' skin paper (Loewenberg patent 40,489). Letters dated Nov. 6 and 28, 1863, in the Brazer archive, indicate that there were at least two printings. The first, before Nov. 6, was mistakenly gummed with NBNC gum. The second was printed between Nov. 6 and 28, and was abandoned half-finished; i.e. probably ungummed.

Values are for essentially sound examples with a very minimal amount of flaking or creasing.

No. 79-E65P6: Based on Loewenberg patent 42,207 (April 5, 1864) for printing on starch-coated paper. Attempts to clean the stamp should result in the coating and the design being wiped from the paper.

79-E65P5 3c
a. Imperforate
rose 50.00
brown lake 50.00
blue 150.00
b. Lake on pale blue 300.00
79-E65P6 3c 3c perforated, rose 75.00
79-E66P5 3c
a. Lake 100.00
b. Lake on pale green 150.00
79-E67P5 5c
brown 75.00
79-E68P5 10c
a. Green 150.00
b. Green on pale rose 250.00
79-E69P5 12c
black 300.00
79-E70P5 24c
a. Lilac 75.00
b. Lilac on pale green 250.00
79-E71P5 30c
a. Orange 100.00
b. Orange on blue-green 250.00
79-E72P5 90c
dark blue 75.00
79-E73P5 2c
a. Black 75.00
b. Black on pale rose 250.00

1867 Essays
Re-use Prevention
Authors Unknown

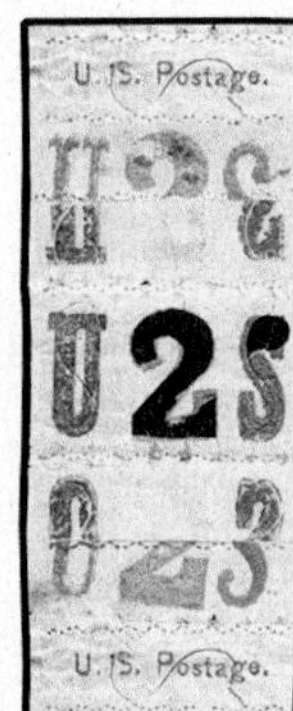

Unfolded — 79-E1

Folded — 79-E1

Design size (folded): 18x23mm
Design size (unfolded): 18x58mm
Folded and scored four times, horiz. crease at center. Bronze overprint U 2 S, (2 punched out). Lower ⅔ gummed below second fold so top ⅓ could be torn off for canceling.

79-E1 2c On white paper, dull red violet *5,000.*

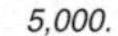

79-E2

Similar to No. 79-E1 but larger and not folded. Pierced with S-shaped cuts as well as punched out 2.

79-E2 2c
a. On white paper, US 7½mm high, bronze, US in dull black *5,000.*
b. On white paper, US 10mm high, bronze, US in violet *5,000.*

79-E3

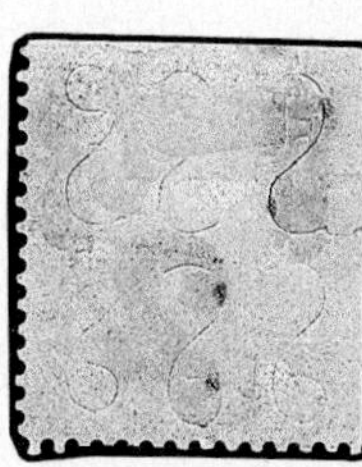
Cuts as on back

U.S. No. 73 as issued but pierced with S-shaped cuts, ovptd. in metallic color.

79-E3 2c Essay on 2c stamp, gold overprint *7,500.*

79-E4a

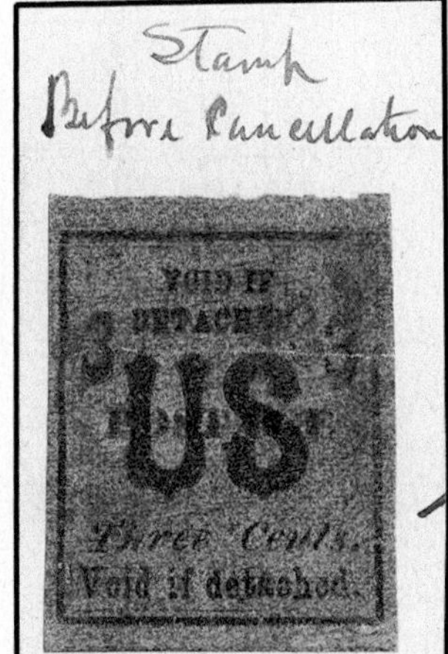

79-E4b

Similar to No. 79-E1 but with punched out 3.

79-E4 3c
a. On white paper, U 3 S black above, bronze below and on face beneath folds 5,000.
b. On green paper, 3 not punched out, 3 black, POSTAGE blue 5,000.

79-E5

Similar to No. 79-E4, with "3 U.S. 3 / Three Cents / Void if detached."

79-E5 3c On green paper, black 3,000.

79-E6

Similar to No. 79-E2 but with punched out 3, gummed.

79-E6 3c
a. On white paper, bronze over violet 3,000.
b. On white paper, U S black, rest bronze 3,000.

79-E7

Vignette map of U.S.

79-E7 3c On thick white paper, rouletted, green, gold 3 on map 8,500.

79-E7A

Similar to 79-E7, without "3" on map.

79-E7A 3c On thick white paper, imperforate block of 9 (unique), black —

1865-66 Essays
Henry Loewenberg

79-E8

Design created by The Loewenberg Stamp Company in 1864. Washington vignette flanked by rod and axe. Printed in reverse on the back of transparent paper, reads correctly from the front. Based on two patents: 40,489 (print first and then gum); and 45,057 (gum first and then print). It is impossible to distinguish between the two without damaging the stamps. Plate essays are from sheets of 25.

79-E8 3c
a. Plate on onionskin paper, imperf., gummed
brown 10.
orange brown 10.
deep orange brown 10.
orange 10.
green 10.
light green 10.
blue green 10.
pale green 10.
red 10.
light red 10.
dark red 10.
violet red 10.
violet 10.
light violet 10.
dull pale violet 10.
blue 10.
dark blue 10.
deep blue 10.
pale blue 10.
dull blue 10.
gold 50.
gray 7.
black 7.
carmine 7.
b. Plate on onionskin paper, perf. 12, gummed
gray black 25.
gray 25.
gray violet 25.
dull violet 25.
brown red 25.
c. Plate on more opaque onionskin paper, imperf.
black 25.
red violet 25.
dull violet 25.
d. Plate on thick transparent paper
gray 25.
black 25.

79-E9

As 79-E8 but printed on the front of the paper. Plate essays are from sheets of 25.

79-E9 3c
a. Plate on white wove, imperf., gummed
blue 10.
red 10.
gray 10.
brown 10.
orange 10.
green 10.
yellow green 10.
b. Plate on clear white paper, imperf.
orange 10.
blue 10.
gray 10.
dark gray 10.
c. Plate on thick wove, fugitive ink, perf., gummed
carmine 10.
violet carmine 10.
pale dull red 10.
gray 10.
pale gray 10.
pale dull tan 10.
green 10.
d. As "c," strip of 3, signed Henry Lowenberg, pale tan 400.

79-E9e

e. Plate on white paper treated with prussiate of potash (Loewenberg patent 53,081, March 6, 1866). The paper turns blue when wet
carmine 10.
Prussian blue 10.
orange 10.
green 10.
brown 10.
black 10.
f. As "e," perf.
carmine 10.
scarlet 10.
orange 10.
blue 10.
green 10.
brown 10.
g. Plate on India
violet brown 10.
green 10.
blue 10.
dark blue 10.
h. Plate on India, signed D.H. Craig, red 350.
i. On white card, 62x72mm, design deeply indented, green 15.
j. On blue wove, red 15.
k. On orange laid
black 15.
gray 15.
l. On blue laid, scarlet 15.
m. On white laid, blue 15.
n. On pink laid, blue 15.
o. On linen cloth. Possibly based on patent 45,468 (Feb. 28, 1865) for embossing linen
green 50.
red 50.
blue 50.
p. On glazed white paper, blue 20.

1867 Essays
John M. Sturgeon

79-E10

Liberty vignette. Curved labels top and bottom. Self-canceling: CANCELLED in colorless sensitive ink, becomes colored when wet. Patented 1867, 1868.

79-E10 10c
a. Die on stiff card, cut close, clearly engraved, not canceled, both labels completely blank, dark carmine 350.
b. Die on wove, rough impression, CANCELLED diagonally each way, dark carmine 450.
c. Die on thick white or tinted paper, gummed, rough impression, about 21x26mm, two lines in upper label, one line in lower label
carmine 200.
dark carmine 200.
very dark carmine 200.
green 200.
dark green 200.
dull red violet 200.
d. As "c," on thick pinkish paper, dark green 250.
g. Single centered in 6-inch wide strip of thick white paper, almost always cut in at top and bottom, dark carmine 400.
h. Horiz. row of five designs on thick white paper, 10mm apart
dark carmine 1,200.
dark purple 1,200.

black 1,200.
i. Single on blue card, ovptd. seal BRITISH CONSULATE, V.R. in center, black 1,250.

American Bank Note Co.

79-E11a

Design size: 16x22mm
Vignette of Columbia. Probably submitted by Charles F. Steel.

79-E11 2c and 3c
a. Engraved die on thick yellowish wove, black —

79-E11b

Design size: 18x22mm
Engraving of frame lines, horiz. shading lines and "3" and "2" added to Columbia vignette, black

b. Engraved die on thick yellowish wove, black —
c. Engraved plate on thick yellowish wove, imperf. (usually found in upper left margin blocks)

rose scarlet	300.
Block of 4	1,250.
blue green	300.
Block of 4	1,250.

79-E11d

d. Engraved plate on stamp paper, perf. 12, gummed

black	175.
rose scarlet	175.
blue green	175.
blue	175.

Author Unknown

79-E12

Design size: 20x26mm
Vignette of Liberty in circle of stars. Vertical color lines outside design to 24x28mm. Curved labels blank. Lithographed.

79-E12 No denomination
a. Die on white paper, dull violet 2,750.
b. Die on bluish paper, blue 2,750.

1865-67 Grill Essays
National Bank Note Co.

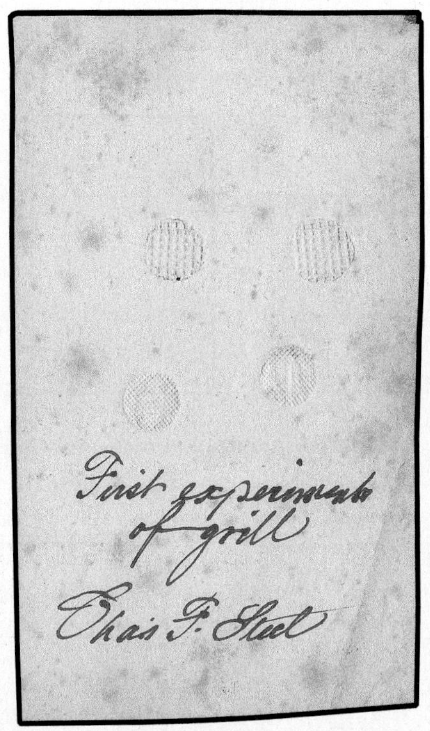

79-E13a

Correspondence in the Brazer archive proves that Charles Steel had produced the first "grill" experiments by late 1865. His patent was registered in 1867.

79-E13
a. Wove paper, 80x140mm, impressed with four diff. seals, crossed lines and flat-bottom square grill, points down, circles 11 or 12mm (two recorded) 9,000.

b. Grills in odd shapes produced by a scratch-like process on white wove, each about 20x25mm (only one of each recorded—do not conform to Steel patent)

cross	1,500.
star in square	1,500.
horizontal lined oval in square	1,500.
diagonal lined oval in square	1,500.

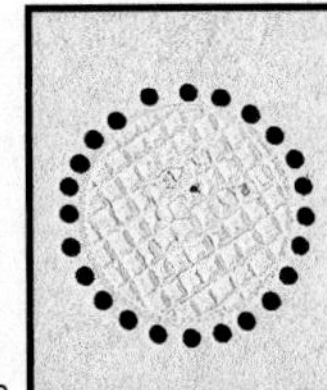

79-E13c

c. White wove, gummed, 15mm circle with points down, flat-bottom square grill, surrounded by 24 perforated holes 1,000.
d. White wove, quadrille batonne watermark, 12mm colored circle with points down grill around 3, roughly grilled colorless 3 below 1,250.

79-E13e

e. White wove, 12mm circle points down, flat-bottom square grill around 3. Grill lines and 3 colored carmine (two recorded) 750.
f. Colorless 15mm points down, flat-bottom square grilled circle on white wove, gummed, perf. 12 500.

79-E14a

79-E14c

79-E14d

Allover pyramid shaped grill with varying degrees of flattening after grilling as called for by Steelc‹cs patent.

79-E14
a. White wove, about 47x26mm, points down pyramid grill, stamped with red 6-digit number, probably to test printing numbers on a grill 750.
b. As "a" but with black scribbles in pen and ink around the number, probably to test pen and ink cancellation on a grill (one recorded) 750.
c. Wove paper with 144x28mm all-over grill with points up as adopted, with manuscript "Ten Thousand Dollars" written across grill area, probably to test ink absorption 1,000.
d. Wove paper in various colors, about 85x40mm, points up grill as adopted

white	200.
pale pink	200.
salmon	200.
light yellow	200.
light gray green	200.
light blue	200.
pale lilac	200.
light gray	200.

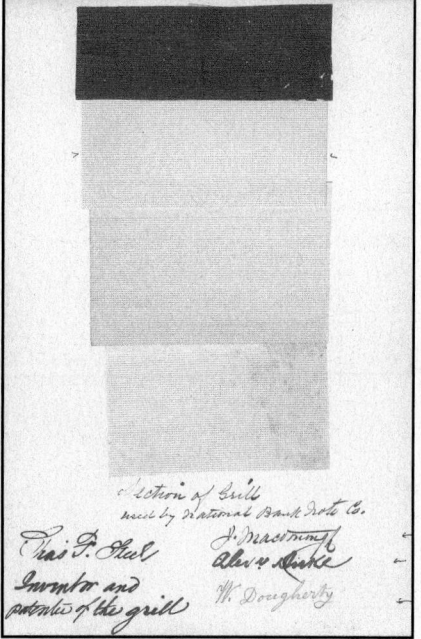

79-E14e, Type I

e.

Type I. As "d". Allover grill. Four blocks stuck to white card (152x228 mm). Signed: Steel, Duke, MacDonough, Dougherty. The essay records Steel's claim to the grill patent — *5,000.*

Type II. As "d". Allover grill. Three large blocks stuck to white card. Only signed by Steel. — *3,000.*

79-E14f

f. Colorless 12mm "3" in pyramid grill circle on tan white wove, gummed, perf. 12 — *200.*

g. As "f," yellow wove — *200.*

h. As "f," white wove, block of 6 with ms. "Subject to a half hour pressure after embossing" — *3,500.*

79-E15

79-E15a

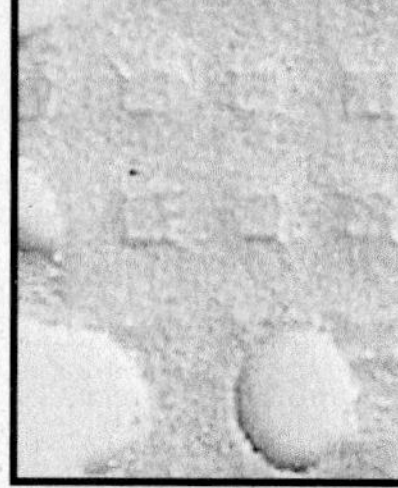

Square Flat Grill

Experimental grills on perf. or imperf. stamps or stamp-size pieces of paper.

Numbers "a" and "b" are allover grills with the square flat shape of the 1865 grill experiments.

No. 79-E15a shows the distinctive square flat grill, enlarged.

79-E15

a. Allover grill of small, flat-bottom squares on stamp paper, points down, 3c rose, imperf, gummed — 350.

perf. 12, gummed — *250.*

perf. 12, cancelled by New York "biscuit" cancel, ungummed (15 recorded) — —

b. As "a" but points up, on 3c stamp, perf. 12, gummed

rose — *200.*

with black handstamp cancel — *600.*

black — *200.*

rose, imperf.— various tests of pen and ink cancels — *200.*

79-E15c

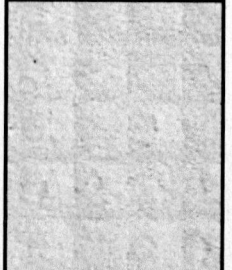

Pyramid Grill

No. 79-E15c has the flattened, pyramid shape that was used for the A grill stamps.

c. points up, imperf. pairs, gummed

3c rose (**formerly No. 79P4**) — *750.*

3c lake (**formerly No. 66aP4**) — *750.*

79-E15d

79-E15e, Type I irregular

79-E15e, Type II regular

Nos. 79-E15d to 79-E15f are allover pinpoint grills (the so-called "Music Box" grill) on various plates.

d. Type I. Points up, irregular pattern, (on plates 11, 34, 52) — *75.*

Type II. Points up, regular pattern (on plates 11, 34, 52) — *75.*

Type III. Points up, canceled on piece (two recorded) — —

e. Type I. Points down, irregular pattern (on plate 11) — *125.*

Type II. Points down, regular pattern (on plate 11) — *125.*

f. 15x16mm grill on stamp size white wove paper, perf. 12, gummed — *125.*

The C grill dates from late 1867 and was required by the Post Office because the allover A pyramid grill, proved too fragile for postal use. The following essays are all C grill experiments.

g. C grill, 13x16mm, points down on stamp size wove paper, perf. 12, gummed

white — *100.*

yellowish — *100.*

pinkish — *100.*

blue — *100.*

h. As "g" but points up, on white wove — *100.*

Nos. 79-E15i through 79-E15n test the C grill on stamps of the 1861 issue. They originate from the archive of papers and stamps retained by Charles F. Steel.

i. C grill on 1c stamp (No. 63), points down (two recorded) — —

j. C grill on 3c stamp (No. 65)

points up (one recorded) — —

points down (one recorded) — —

The 3c C grill essay is almost identical to the issued stamp. There are slight differences in the essay grill which match those on No. 79-E15i and Nos. 79-E15k through 79-E15n.

k. C grill on 5c stamp (No. 76)

points up (one recorded) — —

points down (one recorded) — —

l. C grill on 10c stamp (No. 68)

points up (one recorded) — —

points down (one recorded) — —

m. C grill on 12c stamp (No. 69)

points up (one recorded) — —

points down (one recorded) — —

n. C grill on 30c stamp (No. 71)

points up (one recorded) — —

points down (one recorded) — —

o. C-grill sheet of 100 stamps on stamp paper, imperf., gummed — —

p. Type I. C grill permeability test, "No 1." in pen and ink. Block of 6, imperf., gummed, unflattened — —

Type II. C grill permeability test, "No 2" in pen and ink. Block of 6. Perf. 12, gummed, flattened — —

Type III. C grill block of 6. Flattened, perf. 12, gummed, Signed: MacDonough and Duke — —

The E grill dates from 1868. The following are E grill essays, 11x13mm on white wove stamp paper, perf 12, gummed.

q. Points up — *100.*

r. Points down — *100.*

1867 "Z" grill Experimental Essays

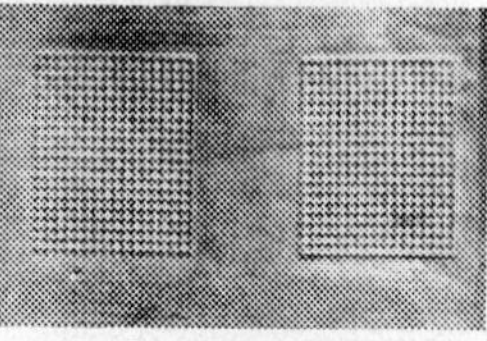

85C-E1

85C-E1 Sheet of white wove stamp paper, imperf., gummed, with experimental "Z" grill impressions, 11x14mm, points down — 175.

85C-E2

85C-E2 Z grill, 11x14mm, points down on stamp size wove paper, perf. 12, partly gummed

white — *200.*

salmon — *200.*

yellow — *200.*

greenish — *200.*

dull violet — *200.*

pale lilac — *200.*

These were made on fully perforated sheet selvage from the 3c and 12c essay panes.

85E-E1 12c Experimental "Z" grill essay, 11x14mm, on heavily horizontally laid paper, gummed, perforated 12

a. On thin transparent paper white paper (not laid), blue — *250.*

b. On salmon paper

black — *250.*

brown — *250.*

green — *250.*

blue — *250.*

c. On deep orange paper

black — *250.*

scarlet — *250.*

brown — *250.*

green — *250.*

blue — *250.*

d. On yellow paper

black — *250.*

brown — *250.*

e. On straw paper

brown — *250.*

green — *250.*

f. On green paper

black — *250.*

scarlet — *250.*

brown — *250.*

green — *250.*

blue — *250.*

g. On lilac paper

black — *250.*

scarlet — *250.*

brown — *250.*

green — *250.*

blue — *250.*

h. On pale rose paper

black — *250.*

scarlet — *250.*

brown — *250.*

green — *250.*

blue — *250.*

Continental Bank Note Co.

White wove paper about 6x9 inches with 7x9½mm grills spaced as they would fall on centers of stamps in a sheet.

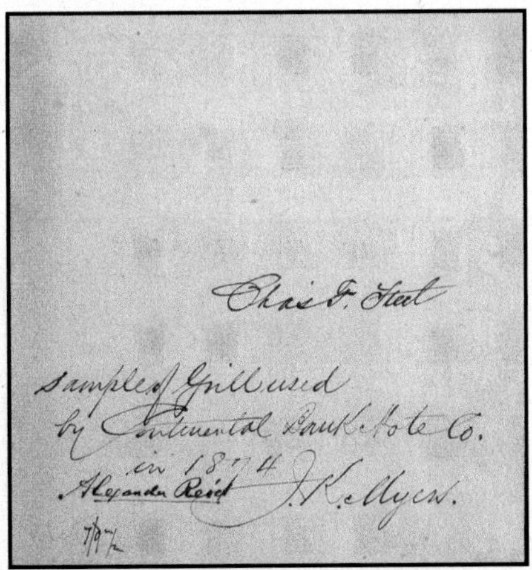

79-E16a

79-E16d

79-E16

- ***a.*** End roller grill at left, ms. "Chas. F. Steel-Sample of Grill used by Continental Bank Note Co. in 1874. Alexander Reid. J.K. Myers." — 3,000.
- ***b.*** Without end roller grill, ms. "Grill of Continental Bank Note Co. Chas. F. Steel." — 3,000.
- ***c.*** End roller grill at right, same inscription as "b" — 3,000.
- ***d.*** On soft card, six grills — 600.

Wilbur I. Trafton

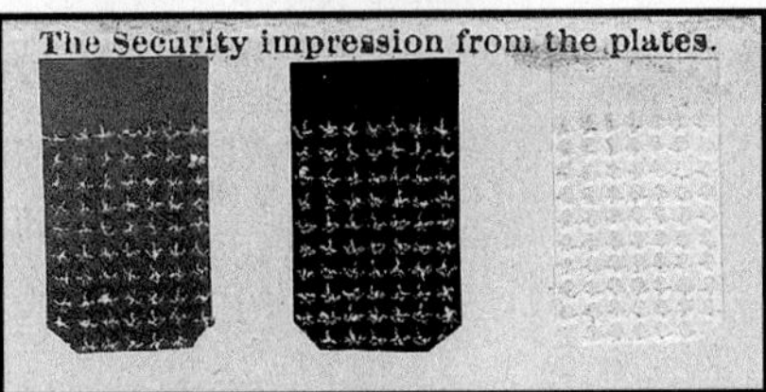

79-E17

Coarse grill in 15mm circle with 7 points up in 11mm, found on 1873 1c, some with 18mm circular cancel, stuck down on printed ad circular along with black, red and albino grill impressions (two each) on paper labeled "The Security Impression from the plates."

79-E17 Entire ad circular with grill examples — *750.*

National Bank Note Co.

On Nov. 6, 1867, MacDonough wrote a letter to Steel in which he asked Steel to bring the design for a "stamp you wish to have made." The following essays almost certainly date from this period. They come closest to what Steel described in his patent as "the ideal stamp."

79-E18

79-E18c

79-E18h

Albino 3 in points down shield-shaped grill in lithographed frame of 3c 1861 stamp.

79-E18 3c

- ***a.*** Die on thick white paper, gummed
  - black — *1,000.*
  - deep pink — *1,000.*
- ***b.*** As "a," with Washington, D.C. Feb. 21 pmk.
  - black — *1,750.*
  - deep pink — *1,750.*
- ***c.*** As "a" but grill with points up, black — *1,000.*
- ***d.*** As "a," perf. 12, gummed, black — *1,000.*
- ***e.*** Die on yellow wove, gummed
  - black — *1,000.*
  - red — *1,000.*
- ***f.*** Die on orange wove
  - black — *1,000.*
  - carmine — *1,000.*
- ***g.*** Die on yellow laid, black — *1,000.*
- ***h.*** Numeral handcolored, dull carmine — *1,500.*
- ***i.*** Frame only, no grill, on grayish wove with pencil "McDonald P.O. Dept. Steel Nature(?)", pale orange brown — *1,500.*

79-E18j

79-E18k

Albino 3 in 13x14mm shield made up of embossed narrow spaced horiz. lines.

- ***j.*** White wove stamp paper, 22x27mm, perf. 12, gummed — 450.

Albino 3 in 13x14mm shield slightly different from No. 79-E18j.

- ***k.*** As "j," different shield — 350.

79-E19a

Illustration reduced.

Typographed impression of frame, lettering and numerals of 3c 1861 stamp with 3 in double lined shield in center. In strip of three about 20mm apart, impression of 3 and shield progressively lighter on impressions two and three.

79-E19 3c

- ***a.*** Engraved (die No. 1570), green — *3,000.*
- ***b.*** Typographed in color on white paper
  - blue green — *2,750.*
  - dark red brown — *2,750.*
- ***c.*** As "b," colored and colorless parts interchanged, on thick paper
  - blue green — *2,750.*
  - dark red brown — *2,750.*

79-E20

Embossed albino shield, uncleared purple ink on rest of die.

79-E20 Shield design, die on card — —

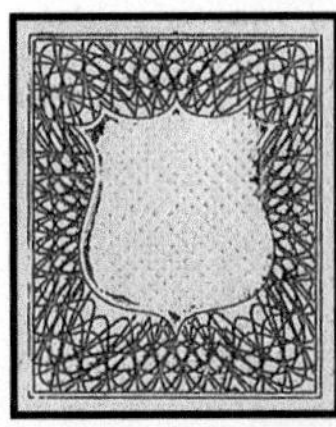
79-E21

Lathework frame with shield shaped vignette cut out, albino 3 in circular grill in center.

79-E21 3c

- ***a.*** Thick paper, perf. 12
  - blue — *500.*
  - carmine — *500.*
- ***b.*** At left in strip of 3 with 2 No. 79-E14e, latter black cancels, carmine — *3,500.*
- ***c.*** Lathework frame on thin wove, allover diagonal grill, imperf., gummed, blue — *1,000.*

79-E22

Lathework frame similar to No. 79-E21 but vignette of 6 horiz. bars with 3 in center printed in glossy ink.

79-E22 3c On pink lilac paper, blue — 3,000.

79-E23

Design of 3c 1861 stamp typographed in relief for surface printing. Single impression lightly block sunk 63x62mm in color. Design has 21x26½mm border inside 23x28½mm colorless rectangle.

79-E23 3c

- ***a.*** Die on 64x75mm ivory paper, black — *400.*
- ***b.*** Die on India, dull violet-red-red — *325.*
- ***c.*** Die on 59x54mm stiff white card, color about 40mm wide (not extending to edges)
  - light red violet — *325.*
  - carmine — *325.*
  - blue — *325.*
- ***d.*** Washington head only, lines on face around eye, on soft card
  - dim blue-green blue — *250.*
  - dim orange-orange red — *250.*

On 17x21mm plain colored rectangle printed through a mat, surrounded by 55x62mm colorless rectangle, vert. 4½mm wide color bands at sides inside 64x62mm die sinkage.

- ***e.*** Washington head with dots around eye, on 17x42mm solid color, on 77x45mm stiff white paper, dull violet-red — *250.*
- ***f.*** India paper on soft white card block sunk 63x62mm, dull violet-red-red with solid color margins — *250.*

Colored India generally cut away outside colorless rectangle 23x28½mm, design heavily embossed through to card beneath.

- ***g.*** As "f," trimmed to shape
  - dark carmine — *350.*
  - orange — *350.*
  - blue green — *350.*
  - red violet — *350.*
- ***h.*** Complete design on India, sunk on card, trimmed to shape
  - blue — *100.*
  - dull green blue — *100.*
- ***i.*** Plate typographed on white wove, imperf., gummed
  - dim red — *50.*
  - dim light orange red — *50.*
  - dim blue green — *50.*
  - dim pale blue — *50.*
  - dim dark blue — *50.*
  - dusky violet red — *50.*

Color outside design generally fills rectangle, design impression shows on back.

- ***j.*** Complete design on glossy sticky paper, deep violet red — *150.*
- ***k.*** As "j," on pelure, perf. 12, gummed, rose — *175.*
- ***l.*** As "k," allover grill, dim red — *150.*
- ***m.*** As "k," 13x16mm grill, gray black — *150.*

79-E24

79-E24c

Block sinkage: 65x76mm
Washington head only.

79-E24 3c

a. Lithographed, face dotted, on 65x76mm solid color background
- black
- red violet 750.
- olive black 750.

b. Typographed, background irregular edge, on card, gray black 1,500.

c. Face lined, on 64x72mm solid color background
- black 750.
- scarlet 750.

Lithographic Essays Derived from the 1861 3c die: Scott 79-E25c-r

79-E25

Plate essays of complete 1861 3c design.

79-E25 3c

a. Plate on hard white transparent wove, dark red 50.

b. Plate on more opaque white wove, dim red 50.

79-E25c

Under Magnification, Surface Cracks Show the Starch Coating

c. Plate on Loewenberg starch coated paper (patent 42,207 of April 5, 1864), generally crinkled. Under magnification, the printed surface can be seen to be cracking
- light pink 25.
- pink 25.
- yellow 25.
- yellow orange 25.
- orange 25.
- brown 25.
- green 25.
- blue 25.
- dark blue 25.
- very light gray 25.
- gray 25.
- black 25.

79-E25d

d. Plate printed with MacDonough fugitive ink (patent 52,869 of Feb. 27, 1866). Glistens in the light. Poorly printed with signs of the ink running during and after printing
- light yellow 20.
- dull olive yellow 20.
- dark olive yellow 20.
- light yellow orange 20.
- yellow orange 20.
- dark yellow orange 20.
- light orange red 20.
- orange red 20.
- dusky violet red 20.

79-E25e

No Surface Cracks Under Magnification

e. Plate on semi-transparent paper. Wyckoff coated paper (patent 53,723 of April 3, 1866). Good quality printing. No cracking to the printed surface
- dull pale blue 25.
- green 25.
- dull orange yellow 25.
- dull orange red 25.

f. Plate on pale green paper, clearly printed, dark g-b green 40.

g. Plate on white wove, 13x16mm points down grill, gummed, dark blue 40.

h. Plate on lilac gray paper, 13x16mm grill, gummed
- dark blue 40.
- dull red 40.
- black 40.

i. Plate on white paper (ungrilled), perf. 12, gummed
- red 25.
- light red 25.
- pale red 25.
- light orange red 25.
- deep yellow orange 25.
- brown 25.
- dark green 25.
- deep blue 25.
- dull g-b blue 25.
- gray black 25.

j. As "h," ms. A or B in UL corner, red 50.

k. Plate on white paper, 13x16mm points down grill, perf. 12, gummed
- black 25.
- gray black 25.
- pale red 25.
- light red 25.
- orange red 25.
- deep orange yellow 25.
- brown 25.
- dark brown 25.
- green 25.
- blue 25.
- dark blue 25.

l. As "j," ms. "s No. 6" on back
- red 50.
- gray black 50.
- dark blue 50.

m. As "j," but grill points up
- red 40.
- pink 40.
- pale rose 40.
- brown 40.
- orange yellow 40.
- deep red orange 40.
- green 40.
- dull blue 40.
- dull light blue 40.

n. As "l," pair with blue oval "American Bank Note Co. April 17, '79", pink 150.

o. Plate on greenish gray chemical paper, 13x16mm grill, perf. 12
- black 50.
- green 50.
- dark blue 50.
- orange red 50.
- light yellow gray 50.
- light red gray 50.

p. As "n," without grill
- red 50.
- rose 50.

q. Plate on pelure, without grill, imperf., gummed, dim red 50.

r. As "p," perf. 12, dim red 50.

Gibson and Harmon Safety Design Overprints: Scott 79-E26

79-E26c

Illustration Reduced.
Plate impressions of 1861 3c stamp overprinted with various safety network designs.

79-E26 3c

a. Vert. pair on 58x80mm India, overprint die 54x71mm or more, small ONE repeated in 41 vert. lines per 40mm, rose pink, overprint deep orange yellow 2,000.

b. As "a," block of 6 inscribed "J. Sangster Pat. 190376, Jan. 6, 1877" 3,500.

c. 65TC3, "VEINTE" overprint, in miniature sheet of 12, perf. 12, black, overprint orange 7,500.

79-E26d

3c 1861 printed in various colors in miniature sheets of 12 with safety overprints based on Gibson's patent 41,118 dated Jan. 5, 1864, for a network overprint in fugitive ink.

Type 1: Big waves. Wavelength = 3.32mm. Amplitude = 3.32mm. Each wave is as high as it is wide.

Two sets of vertical rows. The waves of the second set lie between those of the first, but slightly offset to be higher/lower. The pattern of the wave is illustrated with black dotted lines.

The left hand margin of each sheet has an additional row of waves which lies between the main rows (illustrated in red).

d. Type 1: perforated stamps are gummed, imperf are ungummed
- perf. 12, green, overprint gray tan 550.
- perf. 12, violet, overprint gray tan 550.
- perf. 12, rose red, overprint dull blue 550.
- perf. 12, light red brown, overprint light brown 550.
- imperf., green, overprint greenish tan 550.
- imperf., violet, overprint gray tan 550.
- imperf., rose red, overprint dull blue 550.
- imperf., yellow brown, overprint tan 550.

79-E26e

Type 2: Medium size waves. Wavelength = 3.32mm. Amplitude = 1.66mm. Each wave is half as high as it is wide.

Two sets of vertical rows. The waves of the second set lie between those of the first, but with an approximate 1 mm offset. The two set pattern is illustrated with black dotted lines.

The right hand margin of each sheet has an additional row of waves which lies to the right and above the main pattern (illustrated in red).

e. Type 2: perforated stamps are gummed, imperf are ungummed
perf. 12, dark green, overprinted dull blue — *425.*
perf. 12, violet, overprint gray — *425.*
perf. 12, violet, overprinted gray green — *425.*
perf. 12, violet, overprinted dull blue — *425.*
perf. 12, rose red, overprinted gray blue — *425.*
perf. 12, dull brown red, overprinted olive tan — *425.*
imperf: ultramarine, overprinted tan — *425.*
imperf: violet, overprinted dull blue — *425.*
imperf: violet, overprinted greenish gray — *425.*
imperf: dull rose red, overprinted gray blue — *425.*
imperf: light brown, overprinted light brown — *425.*

Type 3

Type 3: Mesh of waves. Wavelength = 3.32mm. Amplitude = 0.83mm. Each wave is a quarter as high as it is wide.

Three identical sets of waves. One horizontal, two vertical. The waves in the horizontal set are about 0.41mm apart.

Each wave in the vertical sets is about 0.83mm apart. The second set lies between the first with an approximate 0.5mm offset. Black dotted lines illustrate the pattern.

f. Type 3
perf. 12, violet, overprint olive gray — *550.*
perf. 12, violet, overprint greenish gray — *550.*
perf. 12, rose red, overprint gray — *550.*
perf. 12, dull red brown, overprint yellowish tan — *550.*
perf. 12, dull red brown, overprint light brown — *550.*
imperf., violet, overprint olive gray — *550.*
imperf., rose red, overprint gray — *550.*
imperf., rose red, overprint yellowish tan — *550.*
imperf., light brown red, overprint light brown — *550.*

79-E26g

1c blue and 3c rose of 1861 overprinted by a safety network based Harmon's patent 41,105 of Feb. 9, 1864. Overprinted in interlocking circles in colors used for conventional cancellations.

g. 1c blue, perf 12, gummed
red overprint — *2,000.*
h. 3c rose, perf. 12, gummed. Overprinted as #79-E26g
black overprint — *2,000.*
red overprint — *2,000.*
blue overprint — *2,000.*
i. 3c rose, perf. 12, canceled, ungummed
Buffalo patent cancel used from 1863-65, black overprint (two recorded) — *2,000.*
On piece. Washington, DC (March 14). Black overprint (one recorded) — *2,000.*

79-E27

79-E27c

Design size: 20½x26½mm

Engraved in relief for surface printing, large 2 vignette, on same die with No. 79-E28, 20mm apart. Also essayed for envelopes on thick papers.

79-E27 2c
a. Untrimmed die, 30x42mm, on paper with "US" monogram, pale rose — *850.*
b. Die on stiff glazed paper, 63x50mm, black — *600.*
c. Trimmed die on India, on thick soft card, colorless parts in relief
black — *450.*
red — *450.*
orange — *450.*
violet red — *450.*
d. Die on 35x40mm white wove, imperf., gummed
blue — *450.*
albino — *450.*
e. Die on white wove, perf. 12, gummed, smoky violet red — *450.*
f. Untrimmed die on white wove, 61x42mm, black — *550.*

79-E28b

79-E28c

79-E28g

79-E28i

Design size: 21x25½mm

Engraved in relief for surface printing, large 3 in shield vignette, on same die with No. 79-E27, 20mm apart. Also essayed for envelopes on thick papers.

79-E28 3c
a. Untrimmed die on stiff ivory paper, showing color 30x42mm
black — *700.*
rose — *700.*
orange — *700.*
blue — *700.*
b. Untrimmed die on India with No. 79-E27, both embossed, yellow orange — *1,300.*
c. Trimmed die heavily struck on India, card mounted, colorless parts in relief
black — *500.*
red — *500.*
orange — *500.*
d. Die on wide laid paper, "US" monogram, perf. 12, gummed
pale rose — *250.*
dull brown yellow — *250.*
e. Die on greenish wove, 10x12mm points down grill, imperf., gummed, dull brown — *250.*
f. Die on white paper, perf. 12, gummed
smoky violet red — *250.*
green — *250.*
g. Underprinted design only on thin white wove
light blue — *350.*
albino — *350.*
i. "3" within shield, similar to No. 79-E28 but with wide printed margins, paper with vertical scoring, design 30x35mm — *300.*

79-E28H

Illustration reduced.

Design size: 68x38mm

Two compound surface-printed designs, "3" within ornate frame.

79-E28H 3c Untrimmed die on wove paper, green — *2,500.*

79-E29

1861 1c frame only.

79-E29 1c
a. Die on thin crisp paper, safety design underprint, black on dull olive green — *2,750.*
b. Die on pink paper, 18x13mm points down grill, imperf., gummed, red brown — *1,750.*
c. Die on pink "laid" paper, red — *1,750.*
d. Die on pale pink paper, red brown — *1,750.*
e. Die on transparent white paper, red brown — *1,750.*
f. Die on thick yellow paper, red brown — *1,750.*
g. Die on thin transparent white paper, 11x13mm points down grill, perf. 12, gummed, red brown — *1,750.*
h. As "g," imperf. — *2,000.*
i. As "f," with 14x16 points E grill, gummed, red brown — *1,750.*

79-E29j

As No. 79-E29 but with monogram in vignette.

j. Die on transparent white stamp paper, perf. 12, gummed, red brown — *11,000.*

79-E29Xa

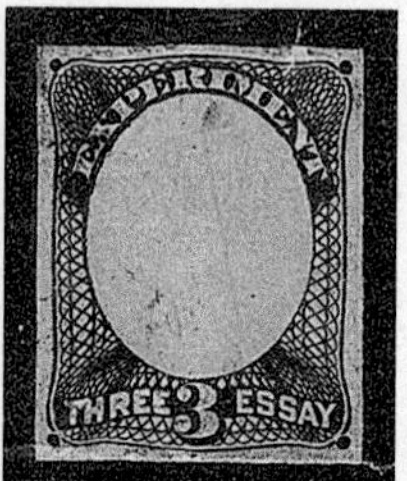

No. 79-E29Xb

Similar to frame design of No. 79-E32, with colors reversed on No. 79-E29Xa, but "normal" on No. 79-E29Xb. "EXPERIMENT" in top label, "THREE 3 ESSAY" in bottom label, blank vignette area, "25868" die number and "EXPERIMENT No. 1" in paper above design on No. 79-E29a, essay cut to shape on No. 79-E29Xb. Each of the listings believed to be unique. American Bank Note Co. essay model.

79-E29X 3c Die on wove, black

a. Colors reversed from "normal" with black lettering and a black outer frame, affixed to tan paper — *2,500.*

b. Colors "normal" with white lettering and a white outer frame, affixed to black card — *2,500.*

79-E30

Design size: 20x26mm
Block size: 64x76 ½mm
Vignette of Liberty. Typographed.

79-E30 3c

a. Colors reversed from "normal" with black lettering and a black outer frame, affixed to tan paper — *2,500.*
black — *850.*
blue green — *850.*

b. Vignette only, on 66x100mm card
black — *750.*
blue green — *750.*
blue — *750.*

c. Vignette only, on proof paper
bright blue — *600.*
blue green — *600.*
black — *600.*

d. Complete design, untrimmed block, colorless 22x27 rectangle around design, broad outer edge in color, on stiff yellowish wove
black — *750.*
blue green — *750.*
violet brown — *750.*
bright violet red — *750.*
red violet — *750.*
buff — *750.*

e. As "d," on proof paper
buff — *750.*
deep blue green — *750.*

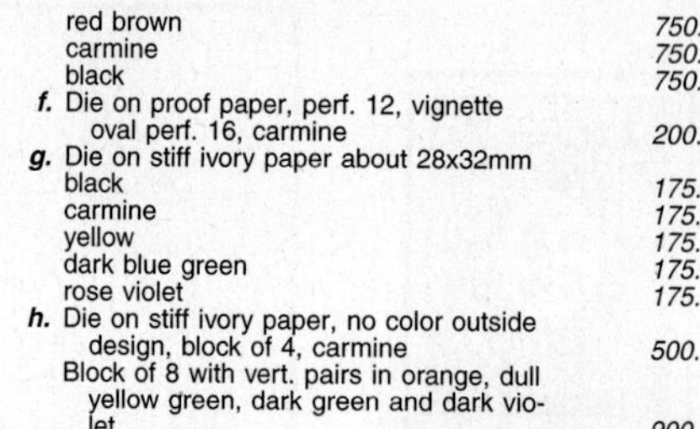

red brown — *750.*
carmine — *750.*
black — *750.*

f. Die on proof paper, perf. 12, vignette oval perf. 16, carmine — *200.*

g. Die on stiff ivory paper about 28x32mm
black — *175.*
carmine — *175.*
yellow — *175.*
dark blue green — *175.*
rose violet — *175.*

h. Die on stiff ivory paper, no color outside design, block of 4, carmine — *500.*
Block of 8 with vert. pairs in orange, dull yellow green, dark green and dark violet — *900.*

79-E30i

i. Die with outer color removed, on 64x90mm white wove stamp paper with imprint below, imperf., gummed
carmine — *175.*
scarlet — *175.*
dim orange red — *175.*
orange — *175.*
dull yellow orange — *175.*
pale dull yellow — *175.*
brown — *175.*
lemon — *175.*
yellow green — *175.*
dull olive green — *175.*
dull greenish gray — *175.*
dim blue green — *175.*
dull blue — *175.*
dull red violet — *175.*
pale red violet — *175.*

j. As "i," tete-beche pairs, each with imprint
carmine, orange — *350.*
buff, pale lilac — *350.*
dark orange brown, yellow — *350.*
dull green gray — *350.*

79-E30k

k. As "i," perf. 12, vignette oval perf. 16 (also found without paper outside perfs.
carmine — *150.*
pale rose — *150.*
dim scarlet — *150.*
dull scarlet — *150.*
dim orange red — *150.*
light red brown — *150.*
dark brown — *150.*
orange — *150.*
dull orange — *150.*
dismal orange — *150.*
dull brown orange — *150.*
pale dull yellow — *150.*
dull brown — *150.*
yellow brown — *150.*
dull olive green — *150.*
dim dark yellow orange — *150.*
light yellow green — *150.*
green — *150.*
dim blue green — *150.*
dark blue green — *150.*
dull greenish gray — *150.*
dull yellowish gray — *150.*
dull blue — *150.*
dim red violet — *150.*
dull red violet — *150.*
pale red violet — *150.*
red violet — *150.*

79-E30l

l. Plate essay on wove, apparently in vertical pairs of designs 7mm apart, in two colors shading into each other, imperf.
red brown to dark orange — *150.*
dark orange to brown red — *150.*
brown olive to red brown — *150.*
red brown to yellow green — *150.*
yellow green to dull carmine — *150.*
dull carmine to yellow green — *150.*
blue green to dull carmine — *150.*
dull carmine to deep blue — *150.*
dull carmine to brown olive — *150.*
brown olive to dull carmine — *150.*
dull carmine to orange — *150.*
orange to deep blue — *150.*
deep blue to orange brown — *150.*
orange brown to dull orange — *150.*

79-E30m Block

Illustration reduced.

m. As "l," on transparent wove, imperf.
red violet to deep violet — *150.*
deep violet to carmine — *150.*
dull scarlet to gold — *150.*
gold to carmine — *150.*
dark violet to blue green — *150.*
blue green to dark violet red — *150.*
violet to yellow green — *150.*
yellow green to red violet — *150.*

n. As "l," plate on stiff yellowish wove, imperf.
dull carmine to orange — *150.*
orange to deep blue — *150.*
brown olive to brown red — *150.*
brown red to yellow green — *150.*
blue green to dull carmine — *150.*
dull carmine to deep blue — *150.*
deep blue to dark brown — *150.*
dark brown to orange — *150.*

o. As "n," outside edge perf. 12
blue green to dull carmine — *150.*
dull carmine to deep blue — *150.*
deep blue to dark brown — *150.*
dark brown to dull orange — *150.*
dull carmine to dull orange — *150.*
dull orange to deep blue — *150.*
yellow green to dull carmine — *150.*
dull carmine to yellow green — *150.*
brown olive to brown red — *150.*
brown red to yellow green — *150.*

p. As "o," plate in single color, outside edge perf. 12, gummed
carmine — *150.*
dull orange — *150.*
orange brown — *150.*
dark brown — *150.*
brown olive — *150.*
dark blue green — *150.*
violet — *150.*

q. As "p," imperf., gummed
brown — *125.*
brown orange — *125.*
dull blue green — *125.*
deep blue — *125.*
carmine — *125.*

r. As "b," heavily stamped on white card, only faint traces of vignette, albino — *125.*

s. As "r," printed design at right, very dark blue green — *250.*

Thorpe Patent Essays

79-E31a

79-E31b

79-E31c

79-E31d

79-E31e

79-E31f

79-E31g

Thorpe's patent 95,624 for double printing was granted on Oct. 5, 1869. His idea was to print every stamp in two inks. Both inks should be insoluble in water. One should be resistant to alkalis and the other to acids. The two printings should be overlaid. Trying to erase a cancel with either an acidic or alkaline solvent, should erase one of the printings, leaving the other exposed.

79-E31 3c Same design as No. 79-E30, black green on white wove paper, underprinted with different designs in various colors, imperf.

a. Red horiz. diamonds *1,400.*
b. Dull yellow green with ONE repeated *1,400.*
c. Red with 2 in circular stars *1,400.*
d. Red with 2 in ovals *1,400.*
e. Red with 3 in diamonds *1,400.*
f. Black with 5 in hexagons *1,400.*
g. Red with X repeated *1,400.*

79-E31i

79-E31j

79-E31k

h. Die on deep orange-surfaced white paper, carmine *150.*
i. As "h," perf. 12, gummed, carmine *150.*
j. Die on tinted wove paper, imperf., carmine
yellow surfaced paper (two blocks of 4 recorded) *150.*
green surfaced paper (one block of 8 recorded) *150.*
k. die on white wove, one color directly over another (gives effect of one color)
black on scarlet *275.*
brown on scarlet *275.*

79-E32

Similar to No. 79-E30f, but perf. vignette removed and frame mounted over 18x23mm Washington vignette.

79-E32 3c Die on 34x40mm white wove, black vignette, blue frame *8,000.*

1868 Essays
Experiments for bicolor printing

79-E33

1c 1861 design, color reversed as adopted. Typographed frame with 43x60mm untrimmed solid color border.

79-E33 1c Die on thin white paper, frame pink, vignette dark blue over pink *1,500.*

79-E35a

79-E35c

79-E35e

79-E35f

Frame lithographed, colored and colorless parts interchanged, vignette engraved and printed in another color.
Die I: colorless vignette oval (Nos. 79-E35a, 79-E35b)
Die II: vignette with horiz. lines (Nos. 79-E35d through 79-E35f)

79-E35 5c
a. Untrimmed die on thin white paper, 40x60mm (values for cut to stamp size)
frame buff, vignette black *2,000.*
frame buff, vignette blue *2,000.*
frame buff, vignette red brown *2,000.*
frame buff, vignette dark brown *2,000.*
frame buff, vignette orange *2,000.*
frame buff, vignette carmine *2,000.*
frame blue green, vignette dark brown *2,000.*
frame blue green, vignette red brown *2,000.*
frame blue green, vignette orange *2,000.*
frame carmine, vignette blue *2,000.*
frame carmine, vignette red brown *2,000.*
frame violet, vignette orange *2,000.*
frame light red, vignette deep orange red *2,000.*
frame light red, vignette yellow orange *2,000.*
b. Die on stiff wove, frame brown, vignette scarlet *2,000.*
c. 45x65mm die impression of lithographed frame only, on ivory paper
black *2,000.*
blue green *2,000.*
d. Die on thin white paper
frame violet, vignette carmine *2,000.*
frame violet, vignette brown *2,000.*
frame violet, vignette red brown *2,000.*
frame carmine, vignette black *2,000.*
e. Vignette only on white glazed paper
black *2,000.*
blue *2,000.*
scarlet *2,000.*
dark brown *2,000.*
f. As "e," without thin outer frameline, on India
lake *2,000.*
red *2,000.*
deep red orange *2,000.*
scarlet *2,000.*
deep green *2,000.*
ultramarine *2,000.*
black *2,000.*

79-E36

Die II vignette as No. 79-E35e, with gothic "United States" above.

79-E36 5c
a. Die on white glazed paper
black *450.*
scarlet *450.*
dark brown *450.*
green *450.*
blue *450.*

79-E37

79-E37a

Die size: 51x63½
5c 1861 design, color reversed as adopted, vignette mounted on typographed frame.

79-E37 5c
a. Die on white card, frame light blue, vignette black *1,000.*
b. Vignette only, die on India, black *350.*

c. Vignette only, die on white glazed paper
blue *350.*
black *350.*
green *350.*

100-E1

Design size: 20½x24½mm
Engraved circular Franklin vignette mounted on 43x75mm white card, engraved Washington head mounted thereon; background, silhouette, etc., retouched in black ink. With engraved frame of No. 71-E1 (vignette cut out) mounted over the double vignette.

100-E1 30c Die on India, 30x34mm, black *16,000.*

1869 ISSUE
George T. Jones

112-E1a

112-E1b

Design size: 24x30mm
U.S. Grant vignette in frame with blank labels, ovals, etc. Paper overprinted with network of fine colored wavy lines in fugitive inks as on beer stamps.

112-E1 No Denomination
a. Die on India cut to stamp size, 1 color
black *2,250.*
blue *2,250.*
b. Die on India cut to stamp size, 2 colors (head in black)
blue, light gray overprint *3,250.*
red, light gray overprint *3,250.*
black, light violet overprint *3,250.*
ocher, pale red violet ovpt. *3,250.*
carmine, gray overprint *3,250.*
blue, yellow overprint *3,250.*

113-E1

Design size: 24x30mm
U.S. Treasury Dept. seal in vignette oval.

113-E1 2c
a. Die on India cut to stamp size, 1 color
carmine *2,500.*
blue *2,500.*
b. Die on India cut to stamp size, 3 colors, black on pale red violet wavy lines and blue green lined vignette *3,750.*

Frame as 112-E1 but with Washington vignette and 2c denomination. Another Washington vignette below but in horiz. lined oval frame.

113-E2 2c Die on 1⅝x3½inch India, black *5,000.*

National Bank Note Co.

All values originally essayed with numerals smaller than adopted. All designs are same size as issued stamps. Sheets of 150 of 1c-12c, sheets of 50 of 24c-90c. Many colors of plate essays exist from one sheet only, some colors from two sheets and a few from three. Some plate essays exist privately perforated.

112-E2

Die size: 40x65mm
Vignette size: 17mm diameter
Vignette of Franklin.

112-E2 1c Die of vignette only on India
orange *900.*
violet brown *900.*
black *900.*

112-E3

Circle of pearls added to vignette, suggestion for frame and 1 in circle at bottom penciled in.

112-E3 1c Die on India, black *1,500.*

112-E4

Complete design as issued but with small value numeral.

112-E4 1c
a. Die on India, die sunk on card
black *1,250.*
violet brown *1,250.*
dark brown *1,250.*
yellow brown *1,250.*
scarlet *1,250.*
carmine *1,250.*
deep violet *1,250.*
blue *1,250.*
green *1,250.*
yellow *1,250.*
b. Plate on stamp paper, imperf., gummed
buff *100.*
deep orange brown *100.*
orange brown *100.*
c. Plate on stamp paper, perf. 12, gummed
buff *100.*
orange brown *100.*
orange *125.*
d. As "c," with 9x9mm grill
buff *110.*
orange brown *110.*
red brown *110.*
chocolate *110.*
black brown *110.*
dull red *110.*
violet *110.*
dark violet *110.*
blue *110.*
deep blue *110.*
green *110.*
yellow *110.*
orange *110.*
rose red *110.*
e. Horiz. pair, one #112-E4c, one #112-E4d *400.*

112-E5

Design size: 23x31mm
Die size: 51x55mm
Design as issued but surrounded by fancy frame with flags and shield. Also essayed for envelopes and wrappers on thick paper.

112-E5 1c
a. Die on stamp paper, perf. 12, gummed, gray *3,000.*
b. Die on white ivory paper
black *2,000.*
black brown *2,000.*
scarlet *2,000.*
blue *2,000.*
c. Die on India
blue *2,000.*
blue green *2,000.*
d. Die on India, cut to shape
carmine *750.*
yellow *750.*

113-E3b

113-E3c

Die size: 41x50mm
Design as issued but with small value numeral. Nos. 113-E3a and 113-Eb have incomplete shading around "UNITED STATES."

113-E3 2c
a. Die on India, die sunk on card
black *1,500.*
yellow *1,500.*
red orange *1,500.*
deep scarlet *1,500.*
brown *1,500.*
green *1,500.*
dusky blue *1,500.*
deep blue *1,500.*
b. Die on India, cut to stamp size
deep orange red *400.*
deep orange yellow *400.*
blue green *400.*
gray black *400.*
light blue *400.*
rose *400.*
c. Complete die on India, die sunk on card
brown *1,500.*
rose *1,500.*
mauve *1,500.*
green *1,500.*
dark chocolate *1,500.*
red brown *1,500.*
d. Plate on stamp paper, perf. 12, gummed
brown *425.*
dark brown *425.*
yellow *425.*
e. As "d," with 9x9mm grill
brown *80.*
dark brown *80.*
orange brown *80.*
dark orange brown *80.*
rose *80.*
brown rose *80.*
copper red *80.*
deep copper red *80.*
green *80.*
deep green *80.*
blue green *80.*
yellow *80.*
orange *80.*
dull yellow orange *80.*
blue *80.*
light violet *80.*
violet *80.*
dark violet *80.*
f. As "e," double grill, orange *300.*
g. Horiz. pair, one #113-E3d, one #113-E3e *1,000.*

113-E4

Original sketch of postrider, printed "NATIONAL BANK NOTE COMPANY. BUSINESS DEPARTMENT. 1868" at top, pencil instructions at bottom, "Reduce to this length" and "2 copies on one plate. Daguerrotype."

113-E4 2c Drawing on paper, black —

114-E3

Die size: 53x47mm

Design nearly as issued: larger motive above and below "POSTAGE" erased, no shading on numeral shield, top leaves and corner leaves do not touch, no dots in lower corners or scrolls beside bottom of shield, no vert. shading lines in "POSTAGE" label. Small value numeral.

114-E3 3c Die on 30x30mm ivory paper, black 1,500.

114-E4

Similar to 114-E3, but smaller motive around "POSTAGE," shield shaded.

114-E4 3c
a. Die on India, die sunk on card
black 1,500.
carmine 1,500.
scarlet 1,500.
orange red 1,500.
yellow orange 1,500.
dull yellow 1,500.
red sepia 1,500.
blue green 1,500.
blue 2,000.
dull red 1,500.
orange brown 1,500.
b. Die on India, cut to stamp size
black 500.
rose 500.
scarlet 500.
chocolate 500.
dull dusky orange 500.
red violet 500.
blackish slate 500.

114-E5

Similar to No. 114-E4 but vert. shading lines added to "POSTAGE" frame.

114-E5 3c Die on India
chocolate 1,500.
dusky yellow orange 1,500.

114-E6

Completed small numeral die essay: leaves at top and sides touch, dots in lower corners added, vert. shading lines in frame around "POSTAGE," shield shaded darker at bottom, scrolls added to bottom of shield.

114-E6 3c
a. Die on India, card mounted
black 1,750.
blue 1,750.
deep orange red 1,750.
b. Plate on stamp paper, imperf., gummed
ultramarine 125.
dark ultramarine 125.
light brown 85.
red brown 85.
dark red brown 85.
pale rose 85.
rose 85.
brown rose 85.
c. Plate on stamp paper, perf. 12, gummed
ultramarine 500.
dark ultramarine 500.
d. As "c," with 9x9mm grill
blue 80.
deep blue 80.
orange brown 80.
black brown 80.
deep black brown 80.
rose red 80.
green 80.
yellow 80.
orange 80.
deep orange 80.
dull violet 80.
deep violet 80.
red violet 80.

114-E7

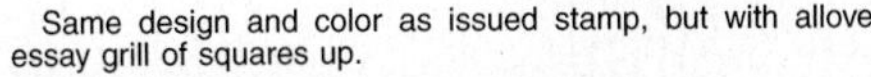

Same design and color as issued stamp, but with allover essay grill of squares up.

114-E7 3c
a. Imperf., gummed, ultramarine 700.
b. As "a," 23mm "NATIONAL BANK NOTE CO. N.Y. SEP 27, 1869" circular pmk., ultramarine 1,100.
c. On thick paper, imperf., gummed, horiz. line defacement, ultramarine 700.
d. Perf. 12, horiz. line defacement, ultramarine 700.

115-E1

Die size: 40x60mm
Vignette of Washington. Design as issued 6c stamp but with 5c denomination. Large lettering, large U and S in corners. Also essayed for envelopes on thick paper.

115-E1 6c
a. Die on India, no frameline, solid vignette background, corner spandrels short at centers
black 700.
carmine 700.
dismal red brown 700.
smoky dusky brown 700.
gray violet 700.
b. Completed die on India, die sunk on card
black 600.
carmine 600.
deep rose 600.
red violet 600.
red brown 600.
deep yellow brown 600.
black brown 600.
dull yellow 600.
orange 600.
dusky blue 600.
dusky slate blue 600.
green 600.
blue green 600.
scarlet 600.
c. Die on proof paper, about 40x65mm
black 600.
carmine 600.
scarlet 600.
red orange 600.
orange 600.
dull yellow 600.
orange brown 600.
olive brown 600.
dusky green 600.
dusky yellow green 600.
light blue 600.
deep blue 600.
red violet 600.
d. Die on pink bond
orange 600.
brown 600.
blue 600.
e. Die on light yellow green bond, black 600.
f. Die on pale olive buff bond
black 600.
carmine 600.
orange 600.
red orange 600.
brown 600.
g. Die on cream wove
black 600.
orange 600.
brown 600.
blue 600.
h. Die on clear white bond
black 600.
blue 600.
orange 600.
red orange brown 600.
i. Die on thick cloudy bond
black 600.
red 600.
orange 600.
orange brown 600.
blue 600.
reddish brown 600.
j. Die on pale lilac bond
dark red orange 700.
orange 700.
blue 700.
k. Die on glazed paper
black 550.
scarlet 550.
yellow 550.

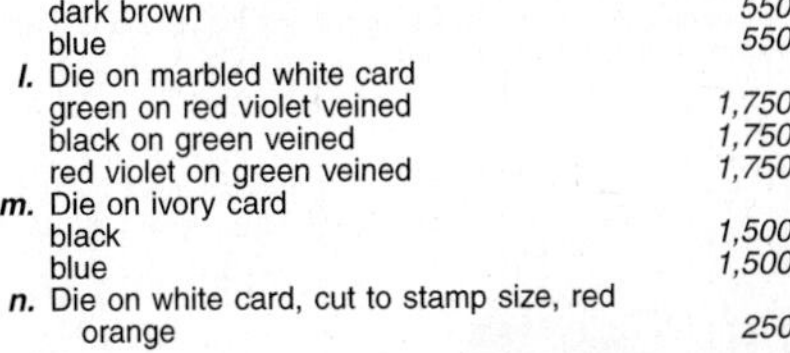

dark brown 550.
blue 550.
l. Die on marbled white card
green on red violet veined 1,750.
black on green veined 1,750.
red violet on green veined 1,750.
m. Die on ivory card
black 1,500.
blue 1,500.
n. Die on white card, cut to stamp size, red orange 250.

115-E2

Die size: 43x63mm
Similar to No. 115-E1 but lettering, U and S smaller.

115-E2 6c
a. Incomplete die on India (incomplete spandrel points, hair on top of head, etc.)
black 750.
dull red brown 750.
b. Complete die on India, die sunk on card
black 750.
blue 750.
dull dusky violet 750.
scarlet 750.
dark orange red 750.
dim dusky red orange 750.
dusky green 750.
dusky green blue green 750.
dusky blue green 750.
c. Plate essay on wove, imperf., gummed
deep ultramarine 150.
orange 150.
dull red violet 80.
deep red violet 80.
red brown 80.
dull red brown 80.
buff 80.
green 80.
d. Plate essay on wove, perf. 12, gummed
orange 200.
blue 200.

115-E3D

Vignette of Washington as used on stamp but with shorter shirt front.

115-E3D 6c Die on India, affixed to card, 35x37mm, black —

115-E3E

As No. 115-E3D, with circle of pearls added around vignette.

115-E3E 6c Die on India, affixed to card, 59x85mm, black 3,000.

116-E1

Oval vignette of Lincoln as on No. 77, but surrounded by double frame line.

116-E1 10c Die on India, 24x24mm, black 1,500.

116-E1D

Die size: 14x18mm

Vignette of Lincoln as on No. 77. As No. 116-E1, but double frame lines removed.

116-E1D 10c Die on India, on card, black *1,150.*

116-E1a

Design size:14x14 ½mm
Round vignette of Lincoln as on No. 77, reduced at bottom.

116-E1a Die on India, on card, black *1,700.*

116-E1b

Design size: about 19 ½x19 ½mm
Die size: 64x68 ½mm
Head as on No. 77 but less bust, large unshaded collar, no cross shading in triangles between labels and fasces, no shading on diamonds at end of value label.

116-E1b Incomplete die on India, on card, black *6,000.*

116-E1c

Small collar, shading on diamonds at end of value label. Also essayed for envelopes on yellow laid paper.

116-E1c Complete die on India, die sunk on card
black *1,100.*
brown black *1,100.*
gray black *1,100.*
carmine *1,100.*
scarlet *1,100.*
brown red *1,100.*
orange *1,100.*
deep orange *1,100.*
deep red *1,100.*
yellow brown *1,100.*
yellow *1,100.*
green *1,100.*
blue green *1,100.*
deep blue *1,100.*
red violet *1,100.*
brown *1,100.*

d. Die on proof paper
black *1,000.*
carmine *1,000.*
bright red *1,000.*
orange red *1,000.*
orange *1,000.*
dark chocolate *1,000.*
dusky yellow brown *1,000.*
green *1,000.*
blue *1,000.*
red violet *1,000.*

e. Die on ivory paper
black *1,000.*
scarlet *1,000.*
black brown *1,000.*
blue *1,000.*

f. Die on clear white thin bond, about 30x35mm
black *1,000.*
red orange *1,000.*
red brown *1,000.*
orange *1,000.*
yellow *1,000.*
blue *1,000.*

g. Die on cloudy cream bond, about 30x35mm
black *1,100.*
light red brown *1,100.*
red orange *1,100.*
blue *1,100.*

h. Die on pink bond, about 39x45mm
red orange *1,000.*
red brown *1,000.*
yellow *1,000.*

i. Die on pale greenish gray bond, about 33x37mm
black *1,050.*
deep carmine *1,050.*
dull scarlet *1,050.*
dark brown *1,050.*
blue *1,050.*

j. Die on marbled white ivory card, about 38x62mm
black on green veined *3,000.*
orange red on green veined *3,000.*
red orange on green veined *3,000.*
dark orange brown on red violet veined *3,000.*

k. Plate on stamp paper, imperf., gummed
deep green *150.*
blue *125.*
ultramarine *125.*
dark ultramarine *125.*
light ultramarine *125.*

l. Plate on stamp paper, perf. 12, gummed
black *1,000.*
orange *200.*

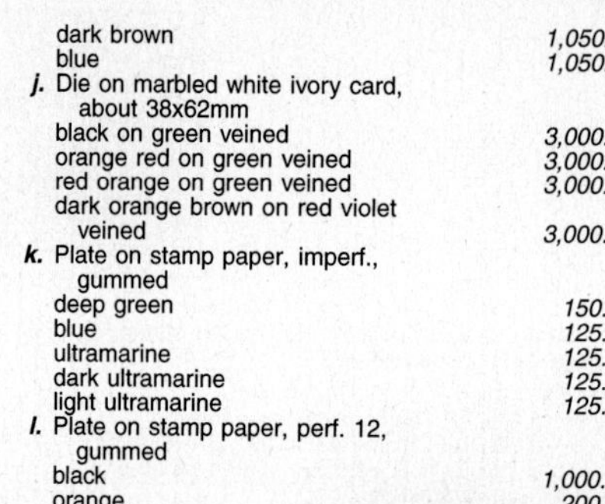

116-E2

Die size: 101x62mm
Vignette of signing the Declaration of Independence as adopted for 24c.

116-E2 10c
a. Die on India, die sunk on card
black *4,250.*
carmine *4,250.*
dim rose *4,250.*
dull scarlet *4,250.*
red orange *4,250.*
orange yellow *4,250.*
red brown *4,250.*
orange brown *4,250.*
green *4,250.*
blue *4,250.*
gray *4,250.*

b. Die on India, cut to stamp size
black *1,500.*
red orange *1,500.*
blue green *1,500.*
dim rose *1,500.*
brown *1,500.*
buff *1,500.*
dull scarlet *1,500.*

Other colors reported to exist.

116-E3

Die size: 63x75mm
Design as adopted for issued stamp, but incomplete shading on bottom ribbon, thin shading lines behind "States," and center of "0" of "10" not filled in.

116-E3 10c Die on India on 61x53mm card, black *2,500.*

116-E4

Similar to No. 116-E3 except shading lines added behind "Ten Cents" and center of "0" of "10" filled in.

116-E4 10c Die on India, die sunk on card
black *2,500.*
orange *2,500.*
blue *2,500.*

117-E1

Die size: 47x51 mm

Similar to No. 117 but with smaller value numerals and blunt tip on arrowhead in triangular element to left of "UNITED STATES POSTAGE". Other subtle differences exist.

117-E1 12c
a. Incomplete die on India, on card, black —

117-E2

Die size: 47x51mm
Design as issued but with smaller value numerals. Sharp tip on arrowhead in triangular element to left of "UNITED STATES POSTAGE". Solid line above dashed line at top of value tablet and curved line added to top-left edge of value tablet. Other subtle differences exist between Nos. 117-E2 and 117-E1.

117-E2 12c
a. Die on card, black *1,600.*
b. Vignette die on India, pencil "Adriatic", black *1,600.*
c. Complete die on India, die sunk on card
black *1,350.*
rose *1,350.*
yellow *1,350.*
scarlet *1,350.*
dark red brown *1,350.*
blue green *1,350.*
blue *1,350.*
dull violet *1,350.*
gray black *1,350.*
orange brown *1,350.*
yellow brown *1,350.*
dull orange red *1,350.*

d. Die on India, cut to stamp size
black *600.*
dusky red orange *600.*
deep orange red *600.*
dim blue *600.*

e. Plate on stamp paper, 9x9mm grill, perf. 12, gummed
green *125.*
rose red *125.*
pale rose red *125.*
yellow brown *125.*
red brown *125.*
orange *125.*
blue *125.*
dull violet *125.*
dull red violet *125.*
yellow orange *125.*

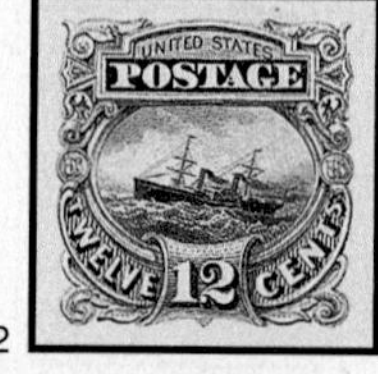

117-E2F

Similar to No. 117-E2, but small numeral not printed, large 12 drawn in pencil.

117-E2F 12c Die on India, black *2,750.*

117-E3

Typographed small numeral design similar to No. 117-E1, relief engraved for surface printing. Heavier lines, upper label with solid background, letters of "UNITED STATES POSTAGE" colorless. Nos. 117-E3a through 117-E3c from untrimmed die, heavily struck with uncolored areas in relief, color covering borders beyond white line exterior of frame. Untrimmed die size: 58x45mm.

117-E3 12c
a. Untrimmed die on card
brown red *750.*
green *750.*
black *750.*
red brown *750.*

b. Untrimmed die on thin pinkish wove
gray black *450.*
dull deep red orange *450.*
dark red orange *450.*

c. Untrimmed die on thick white wove
carmine *600.*
green *600.*

d. Die on white paper, stamp size
carmine *400.*
orange *400.*
brown *400.*
lilac *400.*
green *400.*

e. Die on thin white wove

carmine 400.
gray black 400.
dull deep red orange 400.
deep orange red 400.
g. Die on pinkish wove, perf. 12, gummed, red brown 400.
h. Die on yellow wove, imperf.
gray black 400.
carmine 400.
red brown 400.
dark red violet 400.
i. Die on yellow wove, 11x13mm grill, imperf., red brown 400.
j. Die on white laid
gray 400.
gray black 400.
brown 400.
red brown 400.
k. Die on yellow laid
red brown 400.
brown 400.
dull red violet 400.
carmine 400.
l. Die on salmon laid, red brown 400.
m. Die on pinkish laid
red brown 400.
gray 400.
n. Die on pinkish laid, 11x13mm grill, gummed, red brown 400.
o. Die on dull red violet laid, gray 400.

117-E4

Vignette size: 15x11mm
Untrimmed die size: 63x32mm
Vignette only, similar to No. 117-E3 but lithographed instead of typographed.

117-E4 12c
a. Die on white ivory paper, black 1,000.
b. Complete impression from untrimmed stone in solid color about 63x63mm, on white ivory paper, black 750.
c. Die on glossy-surfaced thin white wove, trimmed to stamp size
carmine 750.
rose pink 750.
yellow 750.
blue green 750.
dim red violet 750.
pale red violet 750.
deep red orange 750.
dull dark red orange 750.
dull dark yellow orange 750.
dark violet red 750.
pale gray 750.
d. Die on thick white wove
yellow 750.
violet red 750.
deep red violet 750.

118-E1

118-E1a

118-E1 15c Die of vignette only on India, mounted on 62x62mm India, die sunk on card, dark blue 3,500.
a. As No. 118-E1, but vignette cut from a plate proof on India, showing framelines on plate, mounted on India, die sunk on card, dark blue —

Type I design but with smaller value numerals.

118-E2 15c Incomplete die (no outer frameline or shading outside frame scrolls) on India, black 4,500.

118-E3

Die size: 62x49mm
Type I design as issued but with smaller value numerals.

118-E3 15c Complete die on India, die sunk on card
black 5,000.
scarlet 5,000.
orange brown 5,000.
green 5,000.
dull violet 5,000.
red brown 5,000.
blue 5,000.

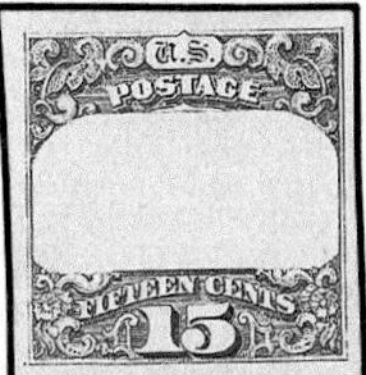
118-E4

Types I and III frame only.

118-E4 15c
a. Die on India, red brown 2,750.
b. Die on India, with vignette mounted in place, blue frame, yellow vignette 3,750.
c. Die on India, with vignette mounted in place, red brown frame, blue vignette 3,500.

118-E5

Type III frame only.

118-E5 15c Die on pink-tinted paper, perforated 3,750.

The type I frame also was used to produce type III stamps, No. 129. On No. 118, the brown fringe lines placed at the sides of the vignette were entered onto the plate one at a time. The lines were not on the die. All positions of the resulting stamp, No. 118, will differ slightly upon close examination.

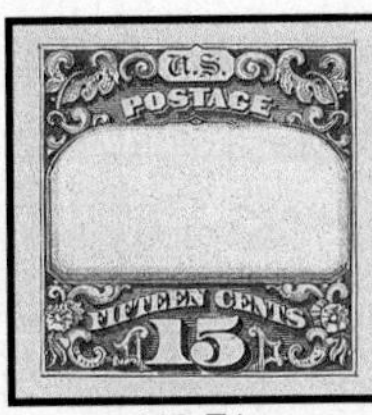
119-E1a

119-E1c

Type II design with large value numerals as issued.

119-E1 15c
a. Type II frame only, die on India
black 3,500.
red brown 3,500.
b. Vignette only, die on India, blue —
c. Type II frame with vignette mounted in place, die on India, red brown frame, blue vignette 7,500.
d. Type II frame with vignette mounted at right, die on India, red brown frame, blue vignette —

129-E1

Die size: 65x49
Type III design as adopted, except in various single colors, large "15" overprint in diff. color.

129-E1 15c
a. Die on India, die sunk on card
orange brown, red overprint 3,500.
blue green, red overprint 3,500.
ultramarine, red overprint 3,500.
violet, red overprint 3,500.
red brown, red overprint 3,500.
b. Die on India, die sunk on card
rose red, ultramarine overprint 3,500.
dull scarlet, ultramarine overprint 3,500.
dark red brown, ultramarine ovpt. 3,500.
c. Die on India, die sunk on card
scarlet, blue green overprint 3,500.
orange brown, blue green overprint 3,500.
dark red brown, blue green overprint 3,500.

129-E2

Similar to No. 129-E1 but without the "15" overprint.

129-E2 Die on India, 34x30mm, dark blue 10,000.

120-E1

Die size: 102x63mm
Design nearly as issued, but shading under leaves at top of frame and ribbon over "TWENTY" are unfinished. Small value numerals. Single color.

120-E1 24c Die on India, black 4,000.

120-E2a

120-E2b

Completed small numeral design in single color. No. 120-E2a has 8mm-high bands of shaded colored lines 31mm long overprinted above and below vignette, printed in various single colors with bands in contrasting color.

120-E2 24c
a. Die on India
black with carmine bands 8,000.
black with violet brown bands 8,000.
black with brown orange bands 8,000.
orange brown with deep dull violet bands 8,000.
orange brown with blue green bands 8,000.
b. Die on India
black 6,500.
scarlet 6,500.
dark red brown 6,500.
blue 6,500.
violet 6,500.
c. Plate on red salmon tinted paper, black 200.
d. Plate on orange buff tinted paper, black 250.
e. Plate on dull yellowish tinted paper, black 250.
f. Plate on blue tinted paper, black 600.
g. Plate on gray tinted paper, black 500.
h. Plate on India, black 300.
j. Plate on card, imperf., black 350.
k. Hybrid die essay on India, small numeral frame, in violet, die sunk on card, red vignette mounted in place, "National Bank Note Co., N.Y." on the India paper at bottom 6,500.

120-E3a

120-E3b

120-E3d

No. 120-E3a bicolor design as issued, except vignette printed separately and mounted in place; No. 120-E3b frame only with

3 border lines around vignette space; No. 120-E3c frame only with 2 border lines around vignette space as issued.

120-E3 24c
- *a.* Die on India, card mounted
  - dull violet frame, green vignette 4,500.
  - violet frame, red vignette 4,500.
  - green frame, violet vignette 4,500.
  - rose frame, green vignette 4,500.
- *b.* Frame die on India, card mounted
  - black 5,000.
  - light green 5,000.
  - dark green 5,000.
- *c.* Frame die on India, block sunk on India, green 5,000.
- *d.* As "b," but frame perforated, and with violet vignette removed and separately die sunk to the right, 108x58mm card 2,000.
- *e.* As "c," but with violet vignette removed from frame and separately die sunk to the right, 88x46mm card. 5,000.

121-E1

Design size: 21½x22mm
Die Size: 71x51mm
Vignette of Surrender of Gen. Burgoyne in ornate frame.

121-E1 30c
- *a.* Die on India, die sunk on card
  - black 800.
  - carmine 800.
  - rose red 800.
  - light brown red 800.
  - red brown 800.
  - brown orange 800.
  - orange 800.
  - red orange 800.
  - yellow green 800.
  - blue 800.
  - dull dark violet 800.
  - yellow brown 800.
  - scarlet 800.
- *b.* Die on stiff ivory paper
  - black 650.
- *c.* Die on India, cut to stamp size
  - dim deep orange red 250.
  - deep yellow orange 250.
  - dim deep blue green 250.
  - dim dusky blue 250.
- *d.* Die on India die sunk on 78x58mm white card
  - dusky blue 1,000.
- *e.* Die on white card, cut to stamp size
  - dim orange 500.
- *f.* Die on proof paper, about 70x50mm
  - black 500.
  - carmine 500.
  - scarlet 500.
  - red orange 500.
  - green 500.
  - violet 500.
- *g.* Die on ivory paper, about 64x50mm
  - black 1,000.
  - dark brown 1,000.
  - scarlet 1,000.
  - blue 1,000.
- *h.* Die on ivory card
  - black 1,000.
  - carmine 1,000.
- *i.* Die on clear white bond, about 33x33mm
  - black 600.
  - blue 600.
  - light red brown 600.
  - orange 600.
- *j.* Die on yellowish cloudy bond, about 34x34mm
  - black 600.
  - orange 600.
  - light red brown 600.
  - blue 600.
- *k.* Die on smoky yellow greenish bond
  - black 600.
  - carmine 600.
  - orange 600.
- *l.* Die on pink bond, about 40x40mm
  - blue 600.
  - dim orange red 600.
  - orange 600.
- *m.* Die on pale olive buff paper
  - black 600.
  - dim orange red 600.
  - orange 600.
- *n.* Die on thick yellowish wove, dim green blue 600.
- *o.* Die on marbled white ivory card, about 40x60mm
  - black on green veined 2,500.
  - black on red violet veined 2,500.
- *p.* Plate essay in black on thin surface-tinted paper
  - *pale gray* 275.
  - *salmon red* 175.
  - *yellow* 175.
  - *orange* 275.
  - *orange buff* 275.

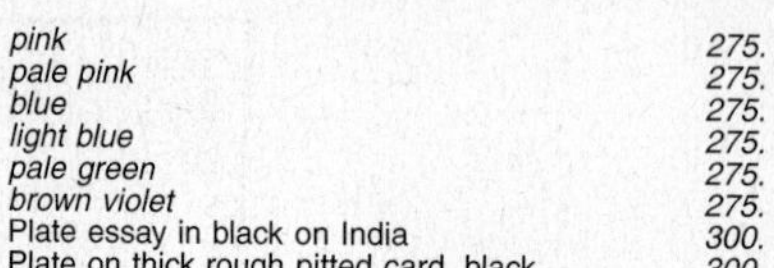
  - *pink* 275.
  - *pale pink* 275.
  - *blue* 275.
  - *light blue* 275.
  - *pale green* 275.
  - *brown violet* 275.
- *q.* Plate essay in black on India 300.
- *r.* Plate on thick rough pitted card, black 300.

121-E1s

- *s.* Plate on bond, red bands overprinted top and bottom as on No. 120-E2a, dull red violet 350.

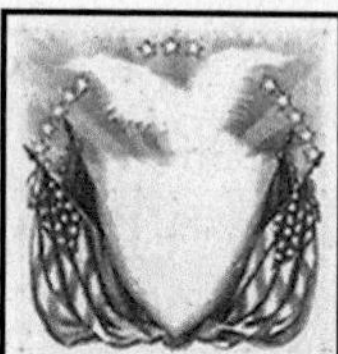
121-E2

Flags, stars and rays only as adopted for issued stamp. Black essay shows traces of vignette also.

121-E2 30c Die on India, mounted on India, block sunk on card
- black 7,500.
- light ultramarine 6,000.
- dark blue 6,000.

121-E3

Eagle, shield and value only as adopted for issued stamp.

121-E3 30c Die on India, card mounted, black 8,500.

122-E1

Die size: 62x69mm
Vignette of Washington in frame similar to that of issued stamp but no shading over U and S in lower corners, small value numerals.

122-E1 90c Die on India, black 3,250.

122-E2

Similar to No. 122-E1 but shading over U and S.

122-E2 90c
- *a.* Die on India, die sunk on card
  - black 2,500.
  - carmine 2,500.
  - scarlet 2,500.
  - red brown 2,500.
  - blue green 2,500.
  - violet 2,500.
- *b.* Plate essay with black vignette on stamp paper, imperf.
  - dull violet 275.
  - red brown 275.
  - orange red 275.
  - pale orange red 275.
  - blue 275.

122-E3

Frame as No. 122-E2, vignette oval with narrow-spaced horiz. lines in same color as frame, but no head.

122-E3 90c Plate on medium India paper, imperf.
- red brown 225.
- blue 225.
- dark blue 225.
- red violet 225.
- dull violet 225.
- dark violet 225.
- rose red 225.
- deep rose red 225.
- yellow 225.
- orange brown 225.
- dark navy blue 225.
- blue green 225.
- deep blue green 225.
- dark blue green 225.
- orange 225.

122-E4

122-E4b

Small numeral frame but with black cut down Lincoln vignette on India from No. 77 mounted in place.

122-E4 90c
- *a.* Die on medium India
  - yellow 3,000.
  - red brown 3,000.
  - rose red 3,000.
  - deep blue green 3,000.
  - dark navy blue 3,000.
  - steel blue 3,000.
  - dull violet 3,000.
- *b.* Plate of Lincoln vignette only, on rough pitted thick gray paper, black 500.
  - Block of 4 2,250.
- *c.* Die on India, Lincoln vignette as used on No. 77, black 2,500.

122-E5

Similar to No. 122-E1, with Washington vignette but with large numerals as on issued stamp.

122-E5 90c
- *a.* Die on India, die sunk on card
  - black 5,000.
  - carmine 5,000.
- *b.* Plate of frame only, 2 lines at top, 3 lines at bottom, on India, mounted on block sunk card, rose red 1,250.
- *c.* As "b," 3 lines at top, 2 lines at bottom
  - rose red 7,750.
  - red brown 1,250.

Safety paper essays, circa 1868-69, on India paper, underprinted with a stable ink with various engraved safety paper designs in another color.

26 different designs found on 5c (No. 115-E), 10c (No. 116-E), 15c (No. 118-E) and 30c (No. 121-E). The number following the "E" in the listing corresponds to the design numbers identified and illustrated, e.g., No. 115-ESP1 identifies the 5c stamp with safety paper design 1, etc. Stamp color given first.

115-ESP1

Design 1: wavy lines

115-ESP1 5c
carmine on scarlet *3,250.*
orange on scarlet *3,250.*
116-ESP1 10c blue on scarlet *5,000.*
121-ESP1 30c carmine on scarlet *3,500.*

121-ESP2

Design 2: banknote type

115-ESP2 5c
carmine on violet *3,250.*
orange on violet *3,250.*
116-ESP2 10c carmine on violet *5,000.*
121-ESP2 30c
carmine on violet *3,500.*
orange on violet *3,500.*
orange on gray *3,500.*

115-ESP3

Design 3: banknote type

115-ESP3 5c
carmine on orange red *3,250.*
carmine on brown *3,250.*
orange on brown *3,250.*
116-ESP3 10c
carmine on orange red *5,000.*
blue on orange and red *5,000.*
121-ESP3 30c
carmine on orange red *3,500.*
orange on brown *3,500.*

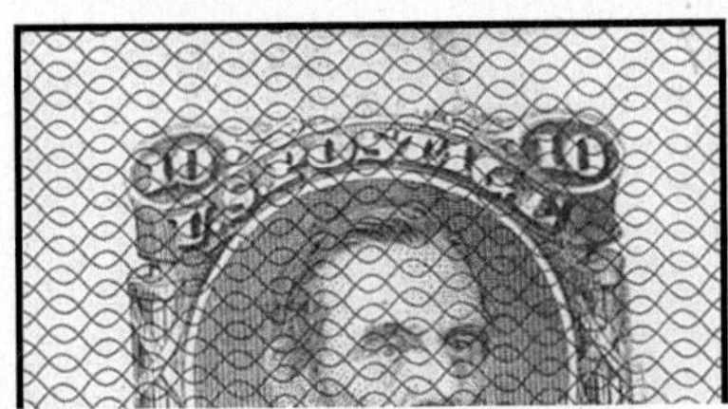
116-ESP4

Design 4: continuous wavy lines

115-ESP4 5c orange on scarlet *3,250.*
116-ESP4 10c
blue on scarlet *5,000.*
carmine on scarlet *5,000.*
121-ESP4 30c black on scarlet *3,500.*

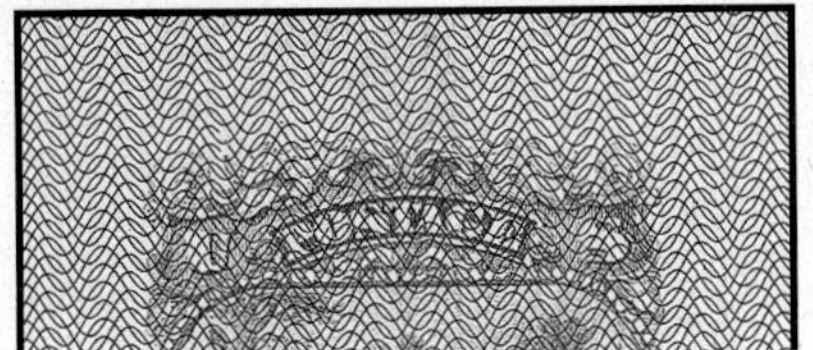
121-ESP5

Design 5: wavy lines

115-ESP5 5c
orange on orange *3,250.*
orange on black *3,250.*
116-ESP5 10c
dark brown on black *5,000.*
orange red on black *5,000.*
carmine on scarlet *5,000.*
121-ESP5 30c
carmine on black *3,500.*
carmine on scarlet *3,500.*

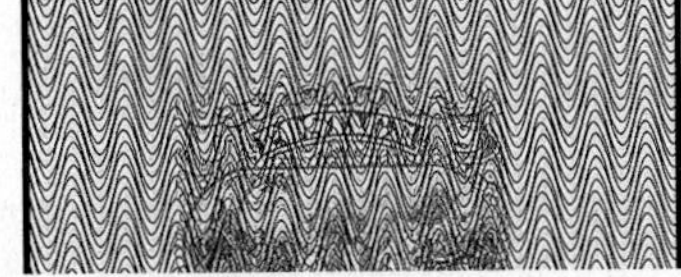
121-ESP6

Design 6: wavy lines

115-ESP6 5c orange on black *3,250.*
116-ESP6 10c blue on black *5,000.*
121-ESP6 30c
carmine on black *3,500.*
orange on black *3,500.*

115-ESP7

Design 7: crossed wavy lines

115-ESP7 5c
carmine on black *3,250.*
orange on black *3,250.*
116-ESP7 10c blue on black *5,000.*
121-ESP7 30c orange on black *3,500.*

116-ESP8

Design 8: wavy lines

115-ESP8 5c carmine on scarlet *3,250.*
116-ESP8 10c
blue on scarlet *5,000.*
carmine on scarlet *5,000.*
orange red on scarlet *5,000.*

118-ESP9

Design 9: wavy lines

118-ESP9 15c
orange brown on orange *3,500.*
blue green on orange *3,500.*
dark blue on orange *3,500.*

118-ESP10

Design 10: continuous whorls

118-ESP10 15c
orange brown on scarlet, horiz. *3,500.*
blue green on scarlet, horiz. *3,500.*
dark blue on scarlet, vert. *3,500.*

118-ESP11

Design 11: banknote type

118-ESP11 15c
orange brown on light scarlet, horiz. *3,500.*
blue green on light scarlet, vert. *3,500.*
dark blue on light scarlet, horiz. *3,500.*

118-ESP12

Design 12: banknote type

118-ESP12 15c
orange brown on deep scarlet *3,500.*
blue green on deep scarlet *3,500.*
dark blue on deep scarlet *3,500.*

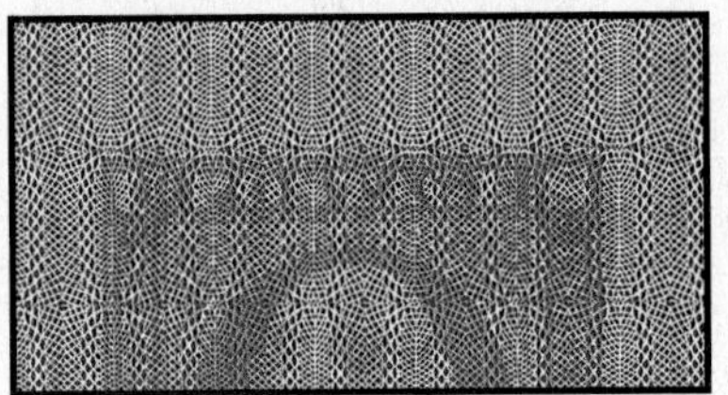
115-ESP13

Design 13: banknote type

115-ESP13 5c orange on brown *3,250.*
116-ESP13 10c
carmine on brown *5,500.*
orange red on brown *5,500.*
blue on brown *5,500.*
121-ESP13 30c carmine on brown *3,500.*

115-ESP14

Design 14: banknote type

115-ESP14 5c
carmine on scarlet *4,500.*
black on scarlet *4,500.*
116-ESP14 10c
carmine on scarlet *5,500.*
orange on scarlet *5,500.*
sepia on scarlet *5,500.*
blue on scarlet *5,500.*
121-ESP14 30c black on scarlet *3,500.*

115-ESP15

Design 15: banknote type

115-ESP15	5c carmine on orange brown	*3,250.*
121-ESP15	30c carmine on deep orange	*3,500.*

116-ESP16

Design 16: multiple rosettes

115-ESP16	5c orange on scarlet	*3,250.*
116-ESP16	10c	
	carmine on scarlet	*5,000.*
	orange red on scarlet	*5,000.*
	sepia on scarlet	*5,000.*
	blue on scarlet	*5,000.*

115-ESP17

Design 17: multiple oval rosettes

115-ESP17	5c carmine on scarlet	*3,250.*
121-ESP17	30c	
	carmine on scarlet	*3,500.*
	orange on scarlet	*3,500.*

115-ESP18

Design 18: negative stars in diagonal lines

115-ESP18	5c	
	black on scarlet	*3,250.*
	carmine on scarlet	*3,250.*
116-ESP18	10c	
	carmine on scarlet	*5,500.*
	sepia on scarlet	*5,500.*
121-ESP18	30c carmine on scarlet	*3,500.*

116-ESP19

Design 19: multiple 6-point stars in lathework

116-ESP19	10c blue on blue green	*7,500.*
121-ESP19	30c carmine on blue green	*3,500.*

116-ESP20

Design 20: banknote type

116-ESP20	10c	
	brown on orange	*5,500.*
	blue on orange	*5,500.*

116-ESP21

Design 21: multiple "ONE"

116-ESP21	10c blue on scarlet	*5,500.*

115-ESP22

Design 22: multiple "TWO"

115-ESP22	5c orange on scarlet	*3,250.*
116-ESP22	10c carmine on scarlet	*5,500.*

115-ESP23

Design 23: multiple "5"s in oval rosettes

115-ESP23	5c black on carmine	*3,250.*

116-ESP24

Design 24: multiple "TEN 10" with gap between rows of arches

116-ESP24	10c	
	carmine on scarlet	*5,500.*
	orange red on scarlet	*5,500.*
	brown on scarlet	*5,500.*
	blue on scarlet	*5,750.*

116-ESP25

Design 25: multiple "TEN 10" with rows of arches touching

115-ESP25	5c	
	orange on scarlet	*3,750.*
	carmine on scarlet	*3,750.*
116-ESP25	10c	
	blue on scarlet	*5,500.*
	carmine on scarlet	*5,500.*

115-ESP26

Design 26: multiple "50"

115-ESP26	5c	
	black on black	*3,250.*
	orange on black	*3,250.*

1870 ISSUE
Continental Banknote Co.
Series 1: Designs derived from concurrent tax paid revenue stamps and essays

145-E1

Vignette of Washington in large ornate "1." Labels and side ornaments not yet engraved.

145-E1	1c engraved die on India, black	*1,850.*

145-E1C

Continental Bank Note Co. Imprint

Design size: 21x24mm.
Die size: 52x52mm
Vignette of Washington in large ornate "1." Die proofs exist on full size 148x231mm card bearing a handstamped imprint as illustrated. These sell for much more.

145-E1C One Cent

d. Engraved die on India, die sunk on card reduced to about die size

black	*1,500.*
scarlet	*1,500.*
green	*1,500.*
ultramarine	*1,500.*
blue	*1,500.*

e. Engraved die essay on India cut close and block sunk on card (about 45x45mm)

scarlet	*1,500.*

146-E1

Design size: 21x25mm
Die size: 46x45mm
Blank vignette in large ornate "2." Die proofs exist on full size 148x231mm card bearing a handstamped imprint as illustrated with No. 145-E1C.

146-E1 Two cent

a. Engraved die on India, die sunk on card reduced to about die size

black	*1,500.*
scarlet	*1,500.*
green	*1,500.*
ultramarine	*1,500.*
blue	*1,500.*

b. Die essay on India cut close and block sunk on card (about 45x45mm)

scarlet	*1,500.*
green	*1,500.*
blue	*1,500.*

147-E1

Design size: 20x25mm

Die size: 43x48mm
Vignette of Lincoln in large ornate "3" with rounded top. Die proofs exist on full size 148x231mm card bearing a handstamped imprint as illustrated with 145-E1C.

147-E1 Three Cent
a. Engraved die on India, die sunk on card reduced to about die size

black	*2,250.*
scarlet	*2,250.*
green	*2,250.*
blue	*2,250.*

b. Die sunk on proof paper 62x68mm

ultramarine	*2,500.*
black (stamp size)	*1,000.*

c. Engraved die on India, cut close and block sunk on card (about 45x45mm)

scarlet	*1,500.*
green	*1,500.*
blue	*1,500.*

148-E1

Design size: 21½x22½mm
Die size: approx. 51x53mm
Blank vignette in large ornate "6."

148-E1 Six Cent
a. Engraved die on India, die sunk on card reduced to about die size

black	*1,500.*
scarlet	*1,500.*
green	*1,500.*
blue	*1,500.*
ultramarine	*1,500.*

b. Die essay on India cut close and block sunk on card (about 45x45mm)

scarlet	*1,650.*
green	*1,650.*
blue	*1,650.*

Series 2: Variations on a three-cent frame pertaining to a vignette of Columbia

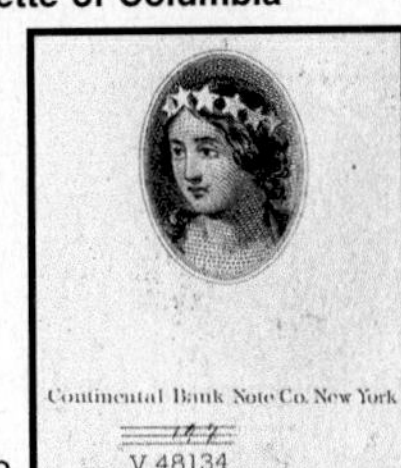

147-E2

Design size: 11½x15½mm
Die size: 47x51mm
Vignette only of Columbia. Continental imprint and die number below design. All known examples have the original die number crossed out by three lines and replaced with V48134 from a reworked die by the American Bank Note Co. Items on Kraft paper are from the archives of the ABNCo.

147-E2
a. Engraved die on India, die sunk on card

black	*1,450.*

b. Die on India reduced and mounted on Kraft paper (from ABNCo. archives)

black	—

Type I: "Flat topped" numeral "3," foliate frame around; 10½x14½ mm oval vignette frame

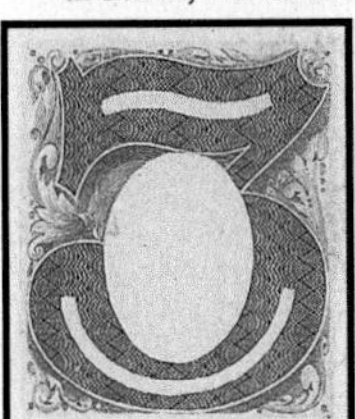
147-E3

Die State 1: blank panels within, no vignette.

147-E3 3c Engraved die on India cut close to design, mounted on India and block sunk on card

black	*2,500.*
green	*2,500.*

147-E3B

No. 147-E2, Columbia vignette in black, cut to shape and mounted in oval.

147-E3B 3c Engraved die on India on card, reduced to approx. 35x41mm

black	*2,750.*
green	*2,750.*

147-E4

Die State 2: As Die State 1 with panels engraved, "THREE CENTS" above, "UNITED STATES POSTAGE" below. Columbia vignette cut to oval shape and pasted in.

147-E4 3c Engraved die on India, die sunk on card

black	*2,250.*
green	*2,000.*

Type II: "Flat topped" numeral; finished panel lettering, 10x14½mm oval vignette frame.

147-E5

Die State 1: numeral only, surrounded by a lined frame 21x25mm without ornamentation.

147-E5 3c Engraved die on India cut close and mounted on card

black	*2,250.*

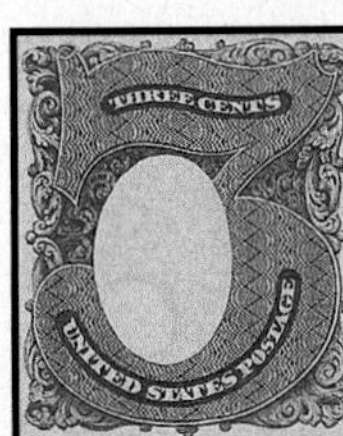
147-E6A

Die State 2: numeral surrounded by scrolled ornamentation, no vignette.

147-E6A 3c Engraved die on India on card, reduced to approx 35x41mm

black	*2,250.*
green	*2,000.*

147-E6B

No. 147-E6A with black Columbia vignette cut to oval and pasted in.

147-E6B 3c Engraved die on India on card, reduced to approx 35x41mm

black	*2,650.*
green	*2,650.*

147-E6C

Die State 3: As Die State 2, but die number "560" added and corrosion marks in vignette frame.

147-E6C 3c Engraved
d. On proof paper reduced to stamp size

black	*1,000.*

e. On India paper reduced to stamp size, on card

green	*2,000.*

f. On India paper, stamp size

green	*750.*

National Banknote Co.

145-E2

Die size: 64x74mm
Engraved vignette of Franklin facing right.

145-E2 1c Die on India, die sunk on card

black (with pencil lines on bust)	*700.*
dull dark orange	*700.*

145-E3

Engraved incomplete Franklin vignette facing right mounted over pencil sketch of frame.

145-E3 1c Die on thin white card, 55x66mm,

black	*2,850.*

145-E4

Incomplete Franklin vignette mounted on more complete pencil sketch of frame.

145-E4 1c Die on thin white card, orange

brown	*2,000.*

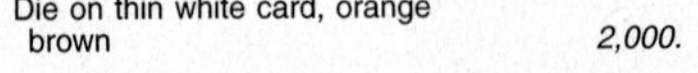

145-E5

Design size: 20x26mm
Engraved vignette mounted on pencil and watercolor frame design, "U.S. POSTAGE" and "ONE CENT" penciled on card.

145-E5 1c Die on thin white card, 45x51mm, dull dark orange *5,750.*

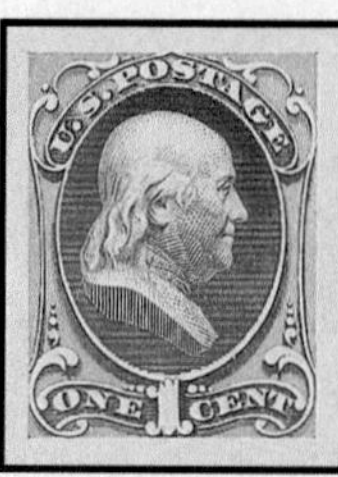

145-E6

Incomplete engraving of entire design; lower edge of bust vert. shading only.

145-E6 1c

a. Die on 64x71mm India, die sunk on card
- ultramarine *475.*
- red *475.*
- orange brown *475.*
- red brown *475.*
- blue green *475.*
- mauve *475.*
- dull lilac *475.*
- black *475.*
- gray *475.*
- carmine *475.*
- carmine rose *475.*
- dull rose *475.*
- dull yellow brown *475.*
- brown violet *475.*
- light green *475.*
- green *475.*
- gray olive *475.*
- yellow *475.*

b. Die on bond, die sunk on card, dark yellow *750.*

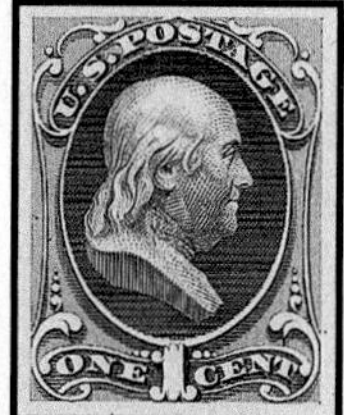

145-E8

Completed die: additional shading lines in background, four horiz. shading lines at top of lower edge of bust.

145-E8 1c

a. Die on India, die sunk on card
- black *475.*
- blue green *475.*
- carmine *475.*
- yellow *475.*
- orange brown *475.*
- orange *475.*
- gray green *475.*
- dull red violet *475.*
- dark blue *475.*

b. Die on ivory glazed paper, 65x72mm
- black *425.*
- black brown *425.*
- scarlet *425.*
- blue *425.*

c. Completed die on thick wove, dismal dusky yellow *425.*

145-E9

Die size: 50½x64mm
Engraved vignette of Franklin facing left, no shading lines at top of bust, etc.

145-E9 1c

a. Die on white glazed paper, black *475.*

b. Die on India, mounted on card stamped "J.I. PEASE.", black *450.*

146-E2

Die size: 62x76mm
Vignette only of Jackson in high stiff collar.

146-E2 2c Die on India, die sunk on card
- black *900.*
- orange brown *900.*

146-E3

Engraved Jackson vignette mounted on watercolor frame.

146-E3 2c Die on thin white card, 46x89mm, black vignette, dark gray frame *5,000.*

146-E4

Engraved Jackson vignette, mounted on watercolor frame (diff. from No. 146-E3).

146-E4 2c Die on thin white card, 46x89mm, black vignette, gray frame *5,000.*

146-E5

Similar to No. 146-E4 but with pencil border around frame.

146-E5 2c Die on thin white card, 45x50mm, dark orange *5,000.*

146-E6

Incomplete die: without shading lines under value ribbon, vert. lines in colorless strips, and broken horiz. lines at top and bottom of frame.

146-E6 2c Die on thin white card, dark orange *2,500.*

146-E7

Die size: 64½x73mm
Completed die of unadopted design.

146-E7 2c

a. Die on India
- carmine *1,000.*
- deep rose *1,000.*
- scarlet *1,000.*
- dim dusky orange orange red *1,000.*
- deep yellow orange *1,000.*
- bone brown *1,000.*
- orange brown *1,000.*
- brown *1,000.*
- canary yellow *1,000.*
- yellow brown *1,000.*
- dark olive green *1,000.*
- green *1,000.*
- dim dusky blue green *1,000.*
- dark blue *1,000.*
- deep ultramarine *1,000.*
- bright blue *1,000.*
- dull violet *1,000.*
- smoky deep red violet red *1,000.*
- gray *1,000.*
- black *1,000.*

b. Die on ivory glazed paper, about 64x77mm
- black *1,000.*
- brown black *1,000.*
- scarlet *1,000.*
- blue *1,000.*

c. Die on thin wove, dark yellow *1,000.*

146-E9

Die size: 62x76mm
Incomplete vignette of Jackson as on issued stamp: incomplete shading in eye and hair in front of ear, right neck tendon on chest not shaded.

146-E9 2c

a. Die on India, on 55x66mm card
- black *750.*
- orange *750.*
- deep yellow orange *750.*
- red brown *750.*
- orange brown *750.*
- dark blue green *750.*
- red violet *750.*

Also known on 87x143mm card showing full die sinkage, pencil inscribed "2c" above and "Jackson" below sinkage area. Value, *$750.*

The red violet shade also is known cut to shape and mounted on card, presumably as a template for a hand-drawn essay for the frame. Value $1,000.

b. Die on glazed paper, die sinkage 50x63mm, black *1,000.*

146-E10

Completed Jackson vignette.

146-E10 2c Die on glazed paper, black *750.*

146-E11

Engraved vignette with pencil and watercolor frame design, labels blank.

146-E11 2c Die on thin white card, 50x60mm, dim dusky bright blue green vignette, dark green frame *6,250.*

146-E12

Die size: 62x75mm
Incomplete engraving of entire design: no leaves on wide bands at sides below vignette, neck tendon and hair in front of ear changed, top of head incomplete, ear hole too dark. This design essayed for envelopes on thick papers.

146-E12 2c Die on India, die sunk on card
- carmine *1,250.*
- orange *1,250.*
- brown orange *1,250.*

brown 1,250.
blue 1,250.
violet 1,250.
green 1,250.

147-E7

Incomplete engraved vignette of Lincoln (horiz. line background), mounted on pencil and watercolor frame design.

147-E7 3c Die on thin white card, black vignette, gray black frame 4,000.

147-E8

Design size: 11x18mm
Incomplete engraving of head only of Washington.

147-E8 3c Die on white glazed paper, black 550.

147-E9

Die size: 16x20mm
Engraved Washington vignette only as adopted.

147-E9 3c Die on white glazed paper, black 650.

Nos. 147-E8 and 147-E9 may have been made from completed dies of No. 147 to produce Nos. 184-E9 and 184-E10.

147-E11

Design size: 20x25½mm
Incomplete engraved vignette (horiz. lined background), mounted on pencil and watercolor frame design.

147-E11 3c Die on thin white card, 45x54mm, carmine vignette, dim light red violet red frame 5,000.

147-E12

Incomplete engraving of entire design: no horizontal lines on nose, parts of hair, chin, collar, forehead unfinished.

147-E12 3c Die on India, die sunk on card
black 575.
deep red 575.
carmine 575.
yellow orange 575.
brown 575.
red brown 575.
dark red brown 575.
yellow brown 575.
ultramarine 575.
dark blue 575.
dark violet blue 575.
blue green 575.
dark red violet 575.

147-E12A

Similar to No. 147-E12 but two sets of horizontal lines in collar area have been lengthened and strengthened; also 11 scored lines cut across thick ink lines of the shoulder cut of vignette.

147-E12A Die on India, dull grayish red —

147-E13

Issued stamp, No. 147, in trial colors, underprinted network in fugitive ink.

147-E13 3c
a. On thick paper, perf. 12, gummed
gray blue, underprinting gray brown 150.
gray blue, underprinting olive gray 150.
green, underprinting olive gray 150.
dim red, underprinting olive gray 150.
dull orange, underprinting olive gray 150.
brown, underprinting olive gray 150.
b. As "a," faint 6mm-high horiz. bar trial cancel
dim red 450.
dull orange 450.
c. As "a," underprinting omitted
gray blue —
dim red —
dull orange —
brown —
d. As "a," imperf, green, underprinting olive gray 325.
Pair 700.
e. As "d," underprinting omitted 325.
Pair 700.
P# block of 10 —

Multiples of the No. 147-E13 varieties can be found with fully or partially underprinted stamps in conjunction with underprinting-omitted stamps.

148-E2

Design size: 19½x25½mm
Die size: 63x76mm
Engraved Lincoln vignette only, hair brushed back, horiz. line background.

148-E2 6c Die on India, die sunk on card
black 1,000.
blue 1,000.

148-E3

Incomplete engraved Lincoln vignette (horiz. lined background) mounted on pencil and watercolor frame with blank labels. Unique.

148-E3 6c Die on thin white card, 45x52mm, dim blue vignette, dim dark blue frame 14,000.

148-E4

Incomplete engraving of entire design: horiz. line background in vignette, lines on cheek and hair unfinished, capital "S" and dotted "i" in "Six" and capital "C" in "Cents," plus ornaments in top corners.

148-E4 6c Die on India, on card, about 50x52mm
carmine 700.
rose 700.
dull rose 700.
red violet 700.
dull violet 700.
deep ultramarine 700.
dark black blue 700.
yellow 700.
green 700.
dark green 700.
dark red brown 700.
deep yellow brown 700.
yellow brown 700.
orange brown 700.

Incomplete engraving of entire design: horiz. line background in vignette, no shading directly under value label, shadows on "SIX CENTS" and shading on ornaments in upper corners unfinished, capital "S" and dotted "i" in "Six" and capital "C" in "Cents," plus ornaments in top corners.

148-E5 6c Die on India, on card
ultramarine 1,000.
carmine 1,250.

148-E6

Similar to No. 148-E5 but with diagonal lines added to vignette background, capital "S" and dotted "i" in "Six" and capital "C" in "Cents," plus ornaments in top corners. (Essay in orange brown has pencil notations for changes.)

148-E6 6c Die on India, die sunk on card
black 1,000.
dull carmine 1,000.
dark rose 1,000.
yellowish black 1,000.
brown 1,000.
gray brown 1,000.
black brown 1,000.
yellow 1,000.
gray olive green 1,000.
dark green 1,000.
ultramarine 1,000.
deep ultramarine 1,000.
dull ultramarine 1,000.
violet 1,000.
dark violet 1,000.
red violet 1,000.
orange brown 1,000.

148-E7

Similar to No. 148-E6 but with dots added to top of hair, capital "S" and dotted "i" in "Six" and capital "C" in "Cents," plus ornaments in top corners.

148-E7 6c Die on India, on card
dark carmine 1,000.
dull rose 1,000.
orange 1,000.
yellow brown 1,000.
dark brown 1,000.

black brown 1,000.
yellow green 1,000.
blue green 1,000.
ultramarine 1,000.
dark red violet 1,000.

148-E8

Similar to No. 148-E7 but die with lines on cheek softened to dots only, capital "S" and dotted "i" in "Six" and capital "C" in "Cents," plus ornaments in top corners.

148-E8 6c Die on India
yellow green 250.
brown 250.
rose 250.

All known examples are much reduced.

148-E9

Incomplete engraving of entire design, similar to No. 148-E10 but with hair brushed forward as on adopted design but shadow under hair in front of ear is round at bottom, not pointed as on approved design. Shading on cheek behind nostril is dotted instead of lined on completed design, undotted "I" in "SIX" and lower case "c" in "cents," plus no ornaments in top corners. Shading extended at sides.

148-E9 6c Die on India, on card, red violet *1,200.*

148-E9A

Similar to No. 148-E9, except recessed shadow sections do not continue above "U.S. POSTAGE" label or at sides.

148-E9A 6c Die on India, on card *2,500.*

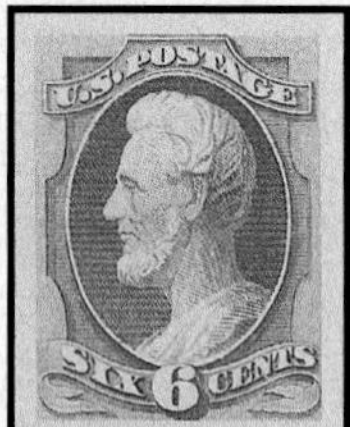
148-E10

Die size: 64x75mm
Frame as adopted, vignette similar to No. 148-E9 but with hair brushed back; lines on cheek. Undotted "I" in "Six" and lower case "c" in "cents," plus no ornaments in top corners. Shading extended at sides.

148-E10 6c
a. Die on India, die sunk on card, deep blue *850.*
b. Die on India, about 30x35mm, carmine *700.*
c. As "a," but no panels above top label, carmine *2,500.*

148-E11

Similar to No. 148-E10a but dots (not lines) on cheek and on lower lip. Shadow under hair in front of ear is rounded at bottom, not pointed as on approved design. Undotted "I" in "Six" and lower case "c" in "cents," plus no ornaments in top corners. Shading extended at sides.

148-E11 6c Die on India, on card
rose pink *700.*
deep rose *700.*
pale rose *700.*
brown rose *700.*
rose carmine *700.*
deep carmine *700.*
brown *700.*
yellow brown *700.*
blue *700.*
red violet *700.*

Die of completed vignette only with hair brushed forward.

148-E12 6c Die on white glazed paper, black *1,500.*

149-E4

Die size: 62x75mm
Vignette of Stanton.

149-E4 7c Die on India, on card, black *1,000.*

149-E4a

Engraved frame of adopted 30c design but with vignette cut out and mounted over Stanton vignette on India No. 149-E4.

149-E4a Stanton vignette with 30c frame on thin, stiff paper mounted on top, black *500.*

The status of No. 149-E4a has been questioned.

149-E6

Design as issued but shading under ear incomplete.

149-E6 7c Die on India, die sunk on card
black *500.*
dark red *500.*
light red *500.*
gray green *500.*
gray black *500.*
yellow brown *500.*
dark brown *500.*
dull yellow brown *500.*
dull red brown *500.*
blue green *500.*
ultramarine *500.*
dim blue *500.*
lilac *500.*
red orange *500.*
yellow orange *500.*

Similar to No. 149-E6 but with dots added on forehead.

149-E7 7c Die on India, brown *1,250.*

150-E1

Design size: 20x25½mm
Incomplete engraved vignette of Jefferson (horiz. line background) mounted on pencil and watercolor frame design with blank labels.

150-E1 10c Die on thin white card, 45x51mm, black vignette, gray frame *3,000.*

150-E2

Design size: 19½x25½mm
Die size: 62x75mm
Jefferson vignette with incomplete engraving of frame: unfinished shading under "TEN" ribbon, under oval at ends of "U.S. POSTAGE," and under shield over ends of value label ribbons.

150-E2 10c Die on India, on card, deep blue green *2,500.*

Similar to No. 150-E2 but showing horizontal shading lines only.

150-E2A 10c Die on India, die sunk on 152x225mm card
blue green *750.*
red violet *750.*

150-E3

Completed engraving of unadopted design.

150-E3 10c
a. Die on India, die sunk on card
carmine *750.*
rose *750.*
gray brown rose *750.*
yellow *750.*
yellow brown *750.*
orange *750.*
orange brown *750.*
brown *750.*
chocolate *750.*
green *750.*
blue green *750.*
greenish gray *750.*
blue *750.*
dull violet *750.*
dull red violet *750.*
dark navy blue *750.*
ultramarine *750.*
deep ultramarine *750.*
dull dusky blue *750.*
navy blue *750.*
slate *750.*
b. Die on bond
dull dusky brown *500.*
brown gray *500.*

All known examples of No. 153-E3b are reduced.

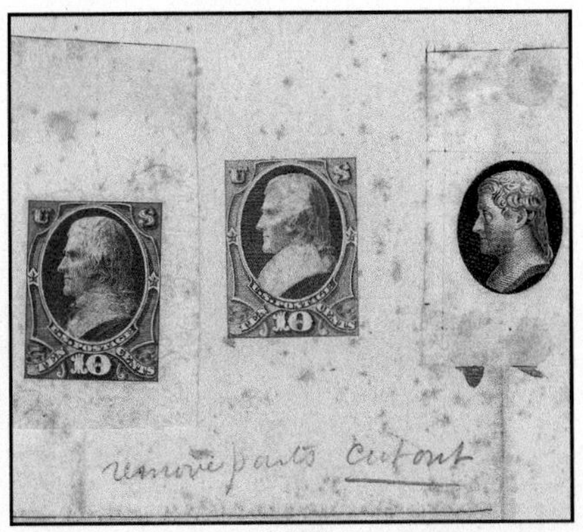

150-E4

Three separate designs. Left one dark blue green, similar to No. 150-E3 but shows engraved attempt to remove coat collar to obtain nude neck (some coat still shows under chin). Middle one brown orange (No. 150-E2) with coat collar and top of hair cut out, neck and bust drawn in. Right one black vignette of head finally adopted (No. 150-E7).

150-E4 10c Dies on India, on card *2,500.*

150-E5

Design size: 19½x25½mm
Same frame as No. 150-E2, but Jefferson vignette has hair arranged differently and bust has no clothing.

150-E5 10c
- ***a.*** Die on India, die sunk on card
  - black *600.*
  - scarlet *600.*
  - brown *600.*
  - blue *600.*
  - green *600.*
- ***b.*** Die on ivory glazed paper, 66x75mm
  - black *500.*
  - black brown *500.*
  - scarlet *500.*
  - blue *500.*
- ***c.*** Die on thin wove, dark yellow *500.*

150-E6

Frame of No. 150-E5 with vignette cut out and replaced by black vignette as adopted.

150-E6 10c Die on India
- deep orange brown *1,750.*
- black *1,500.*

150-E7

Die size: 62x76mm
Vignette of Jefferson as adopted.

150-E7 10c Die on India, die sunk on card
- dark ultramarine *700.*
- yellow *700.*
- brown *700.*

151-E1

Design size: 20x25½mm
Engraved vignette of Washington (No. 79-E37b) mounted on incomplete pencil drawing of frame design.

151-E1 12c Die on India, on 38x47½mm card, black vignette, pencil frame *2,500.*

151-E2

Design size: 20x25½mm
Engraved vignette of Washington (No. 79-E37b) mounted on pencil and watercolor frame design with blank labels.

151-E2 12c Die on card, 46x89mm, black vignette, gray frame *3,000.*

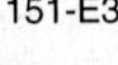

151-E3

Design size: 20x25½mm
Engraved vignette of Washington (No. 79-E37b) mounted on pencil and watercolor frame design with ribbons and blank labels.

151-E3 12c Die on card, 46x89mm, black vignette, gray frame *3,000.*

151-E4

Design size: 20x25½mm
Engraved vignette of Washington (No. 79-E37b) mounted on pencil and watercolor frame design with "U, S, 12" and blank labels.

151-E4 12c Die on card, 46x89mm, black vignette, gray frame *3,000.*

151-E5

Design size: 19½x25½mm
Die size: 62x74mm
Vignette of Henry Clay only.

151-E5 12c Die on India, die sunk on card
- black *600.*
- deep carmine *600.*
- yellow *600.*
- yellow brown *600.*
- brown orange *600.*
- dark orange brown *600.*
- black brown *600.*
- ultramarine *600.*
- dark blue green *600.*
- red violet *600.*

151-E6

Incomplete Clay vignette mounted on watercolor shield-like frame design on gray background, pencil notation "background of stars to be grey."

151-E6 12c Die on card, 53x75mm, blue black vignette, blue frame *4,000.*

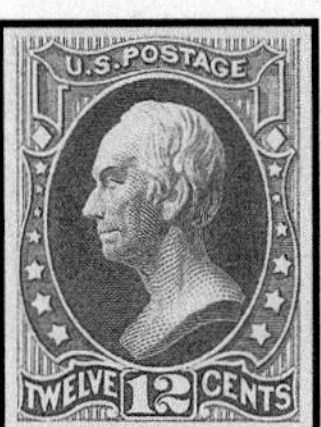

151-E7

Die sinkage size: 63x77mm

Completed die of unadopted design similar to No. 151-E6. This design essayed for envelopes on thick paper.

151-E7 12c
a. Die on India, on card
deep orange brown *900.*
green *900.*
deep ultramarine *900.*
violet *900.*
deep red *900.*
deep orange red *900.*
orange *900.*
dusky red *900.*
b. Die on wove
carmine *700.*
orange *700.*
brown *700.*
orange brown *700.*
ultramarine *700.*
c. Die on card colored yellow, black *700.*

151-E8

Engraved vignette of Washington mounted on partly complete pencil drawing of frame, pencil notation "new border for clay 12c."

151-E8 12c Die on card, black, pencil frame *2,750.*

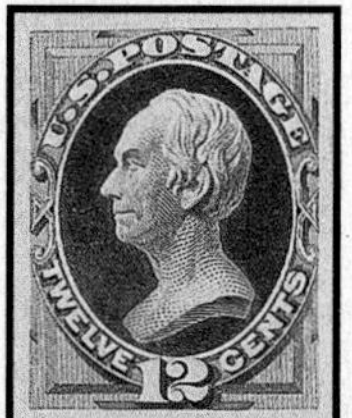

151-E9

Die size: 55x63mm
Incomplete engraving of entire adopted design, without 3 vert. shading lines at left side of lower triangle.

151-E9 12c
a. Die on India, die sunk on card
black *650.*
carmine *650.*
blue green *650.*
blue *650.*
light blue *650.*
orange *650.*
orange brown *650.*
dull red *650.*
brown red *650.*
b. Die on proof paper, about 38x45mm
carmine *650.*
dull carmine *650.*
orange brown *650.*
dull red *650.*
ultramarine *650.*
c. Die on India, on card, about 30x35mm, dark blue *650.*

152-E1

Design size: 19½x25mm
Incomplete vignette of Webster with side whiskers bolder than as adopted, mounted on watercolor frame design with 15 and blank labels.

152-E1 15c Die on white card, 40x61mm, dim red vignette, light red violet frame *2,250.*

152-E2

Design size: 19½x25mm
Die size: 63x76mm
Incomplete engraving of vignette only: missing shading under ear and at back of neck.

152-E2 15c Die on India, die sunk on card, black *750.*

152-E3

Vignette similar to No. 152-E2 but with shading under ear, more shading at back of neck.

152-E3 15c Die on India, die sunk on card
black *700.*
dark orange *700.*
orange *700.*
yellow *700.*
red violet *700.*
ultramarine *700.*
brown *700.*

152-E5

Incomplete engraved design: shading on corner panel bevels incomplete, side whiskers bolder than as adopted. Also essayed for envelopes on thick paper.

152-E5 15c Die on India, die sunk on card, orange brown *750.*

Similar to No. 152-E5 but with pencil marks suggesting shading on corner panels.

152-E6 15c Die on India, orange brown *750.*

152-E7

Similar to No. 152-E5 with engraved shading added to corner panels but white areas incomplete.

152-E7 15c Die on India
orange *650.*
orange yellow *650.*
orange brown *650.*
green *650.*
red violet *650.*
rose carmine *650.*

152-E8

Similar to No. 152-E7 but shading on corner panels complete.

152-E8 15c Die on India, on card, black *1,000.*

153-E1

Design size: 18x23mm
Incomplete engraved vignette of Scott mounted on pencil sketch of partial frame design.

153-E1 24c Die on white card, 33x39mm, dull red violet vignette, pencil frame *1,750.*

153-E2

Design size: 19½x25mm
Complete engraved vignette mounted on pencil and watercolor frame design with "U.S. POSTAGE" in ink.

153-E2 24c Die on white card, 73x110mm, dim blue green *3,250.*

153-E3

Die size: 62x76mm
Incomplete engraved vignette only.

153-E3 24c Die on India, die sunk on card
black *600.*
yellow *600.*
yellow brown *600.*
dark orange brown *600.*
ultramarine *600.*
dark ultramarine *600.*
red violet *600.*

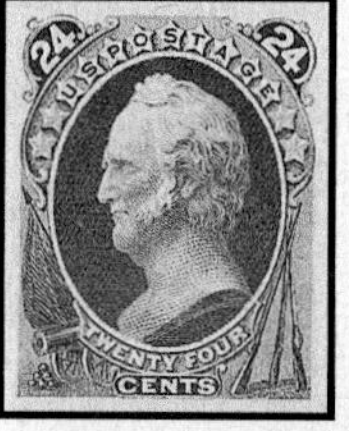

153-E4

Die size: 62x77mm
Incomplete design as adopted: upper corners not squared outside scrolls, no periods after U and S in stars.

153-E4 24c Die on India, die sunk on card
carmine *650.*
orange *650.*
brown orange *650.*
yellow brown *650.*
deep brown *650.*
ultramarine *650.*
dark red violet *650.*
green *650.*

Value off card, cut down, $275.

Previous No. 154-E1 is now No. 149-E4a.

154-E2

Pencil drawing of entire design, labeled "Scott."

154-E2 30c Pencil drawing on white card, 53x92mm *2,400.*

Engraved vignette of Hamilton mounted on pencil drawing of frame.

154-E3 30c Die on card, yellow brown vignette, pencil frame *1,500.*

154-E4

Incomplete engraved vignette of Hamilton.

154-E4 30c Die on India, die sunk on card
- yellow brown *700.*
- dark ultramarine blue *700.*
- orange *700.*

154-E5

Vignette of Hamilton with more engraving on forehead, nose, neck, etc.

154-E5 30c Die on India, die sunk on card
- dark red brown *700.*
- dull carmine *700.*
- ultramarine *700.*

155-E1

Pencil drawing of entire design, labeled "Perry."

155-E1 90c Pencil drawing on white card, 53x92mm *3,000.*

155-E2

Design size: 19½x25mm
Engraved vignette of Perry mounted on pencil and watercolor frame design.

155-E2 90c Die on white card, 73x110mm, dull dark violet vignette, dull red violet frame *3,250.*

155-E3

Die size: 58x79mm
Incomplete engraving of Perry vignette as adopted.

155-E3 90c
- ***a.*** Die on India, die sunk on card
  - black *1,500.*
  - deep yellow orange *600.*
  - orange brown *600.*
  - dark brown *600.*
  - dull carmine *600.*
  - ultramarine blue *600.*
  - dark blue green *600.*
  - dark red violet *600.*
- ***b.*** Die on white ivory paper, black *600.*
- ***c.*** Die on card, carmine *750.*

155-E4

Similar to No. 155-E3 but more lines in hair above forehead.

155-E4 90c Die on India, on card, black *600.*

155-E5

Incomplete engraving of design as adopted: rope above vignette unfinished. Known in black with pencil drawing of rope beneath on the card; value thus, $3,000. Also essayed for envelopes on thick paper.

155-E5 90c Die on India, die sunk on card
- black *750.*
- carmine, off card *325.*
- orange *750.*
- dark orange *750.*
- yellow brown *750.*
- brown *750.*
- deep orange brown *750.*
- deep ultramarine *750.*
- blue green *750.*
- red violet *750.*

Value off card, cut down, $250.

1873 ISSUE
Continental Bank Note Co.

179-E1

Die size: 20x25mm
Vignette of Taylor by Bureau of Engraving and Printing, in engraved frame.

179-E1 Five Cents, Die on India
- black *4,500.*
- blue *4,500.*

179-E2

Design size: 24x29mm
Vignette of Taylor by Bureau of Engraving and Printing, in ornate wash drawing of frame ("FIVE CENTS" black, on shaded ribbon).

179-E2 5c Die on card, black *4,000.*

179-E3

Incomplete vignette: hair, coat, background, etc., unfinished.

179-E3 5c Die on India, violet *2,000.*

George Bowlsby patent

George W. Bowlsby 1873 essay similar in concept to his No. 63-E13 but without coupon attached. It consisted of an unused 1c stamp (No. 156) with horiz. sewing machine perfs. through center, gummed on upper half only, as described in his Dec. 26, 1865 patent. Stamp was meant to be torn in half by postal clerk as cancellation, to prevent reuse.

156-E1 1c blue *250.*
Block of 4 with plate number *1,500.*

1876 - National Safety Paper

Plate designs of 1873-75 issues in normal colors, printed by Continental Bank Note Co. on tinted, thick "pseudo-laid" paper produced by Campbell, Hall and Co. under direction of Samuel Francis. Three paper colors are recorded.

156-E2 1c Blue on:
- pale rose *150.*
- pale yellow *150.*
- pale violet *150.*

158-E1 3c Green on:
- pale rose *150.*
- pale yellow *150.*
- pale violet *150.*

161-E1

161-E1 10c Brown on:
- pale rose *150.*
- pale yellow *150.*
- pale violet *150.*

163-E1 15c Yellow orange on:
- pale rose *200.*
- pale yellow *200.*
- pale violet *200.*

178-E1

178-E1 2c Vermilion on:
pale rose *150.*
pale yellow *150.*
pale violet *150.*

179-E4

179-E4 5c Blue on:
pale rose *300.*
pale yellow *300.*
pale violet *300.*

See No. 147-E13.

The following four listings are known or believed to exist, but they are not on "pseudo-laid" paper and therefore they are not likely on National Safety Paper.

160-E1 7c scarlet vermilion on deep yellow wove —
161-E2 10c brown on deep yellow wove —

165-E1 30c Gray black on:
pale rose —
deep yellow —
pale violet —

166-E1 90c Rose carmine on:
pale rose —
deep yellow —
pale violet —

The editors would like to see evidence of the existence of Nos. 165-E1 and 166-E1.

1876 Joseph Schnoble Patent #171871, Jan 4, 1876

Prior to printing, specially sized paper was top coated on the printing side with an albumin and flycerine "varnish" and allowed to harden. Upon this prepared surface the stamp designs were intaglio printed as usual. Attempts to wash off a cancellation would cause the design to wash off from the layered colored ground.

156-E3

156-E3 1c ultra on dull rose, imperf. 100.
156-E4 1c ultramarine on deep carmine, perf. 12 100.
ultramarine on dull rose, pair, P#229 *250.*
a. Wash-tested strip of 3, ultramarine on dull rose, P#229 —

158-E2

158-E2 3c green on deep carmine, imperf. 100.
green on pale rose, imperf. 100.
green on faint rose, imperf. 100.
158-E3 3c green on deep carmine, perf. 12 100.
green on bright rose, perf. 12 100.
green on pale rose, perf. 12 100.
green on faint rose, perf. 12 100.
a. Wash-tested strip of 4, green on deep carmine, P#257 —
b. Crayon-tested, green on bright rose —

1877 Essays
Philadelphia Bank Note Co.

Die essays for this section were all engraved. The frame-only dies for all values of this series were engraved with two values appearing per die, except the 3c (No. 184-E1) which was engraved alone. In each case the listing is under the lower denomination. The Washington vignette associated with each value of the frames is from engraved master die No. 14. (No. 182-E1).

Except as noted, plate essays in this section are all lithographed from a composite stone plate of two panes. The left pane ("plate 1") consists of horiz. rows of four of the 1c, 3c, 7c, 24c and 90c. The right pane ("plate 2") consists of horiz. rows of four 2c, 6c, 12c and 30c. "Printed by Philadelphia Bank Note Co. Patented June 16, 1876" imprint below 2nd and 3rd designs on each row.

For the 1903 Schernikow private reprint essays see section following No. 191-E2.

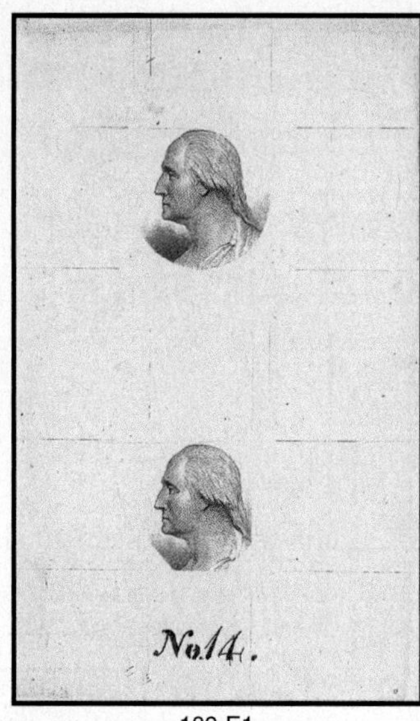

182-E1

Vignette master die "No. 14": two slightly diff. vignettes of Washington, one above the other, bottom one with truncated queue, bust and shading in front of neck.

182-E1
a. Die on old white glazed paper, black *500.*

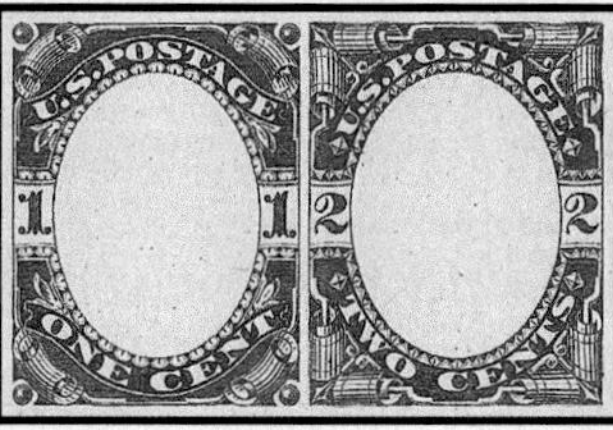
182-E2b

Design size: 20x25mm
Die size: 98x53mm
Frames of 1c and 2c side by side.

182-E2 1c + 2c
a. Die on white pelure
dark carmine *250.*
orange *250.*
brown *250.*
blue green *250.*
blue *250.*
b. Die with vertical line between designs (die size 85x54mm), on India, die sunk on card
dusky red *400.*
deep orange *400.*
orange brown *400.*
dark green *400.*
dark blue *400.*
c. Die on stiff glazed paper, black *400.*
e. Plate sheet of 1c, 2c, 3c, 12c, 24c, 30c, 90c frames only, on card, pale green blue *1,500.*

182-E3b

Complete 1c design, lithographed.

182-E3 1c
a. Plate on stamp paper, imperf., gummed
black *75.*
blue green *75.*
bright ultramarine *75.*
yellow *75.*
b. Plate on stamp paper, perf. 12, gummed
dark red orange *50.*
orange brown *50.*
red brown *50.*
red violet *50.*
violet blue *50.*
ultramarine *50.*
c. Plate 1 "sheet" of 20, complete designs, without imprint, on old glazed paper, imperf., deep brown orange *800.*
d. As "c," with imprint, on old glazed paper, imperf., gummed
black *800.*
dull deep violet red *800.*
ultramarine *800.*
scarlet *800.*
orange *800.*
carmine *800.*
dark carmine *800.*
green *800.*
bluish green *800.*
e. As "d," perf. 12, gummed
dull deep violet red *700.*
ultramarine *700.*
red brown *700.*
violet blue *700.*

Concerning plate 1 sheets of 20, note that composite stone plates also contained the plate 2 sheets of 16 listed as Nos. 183-E2c to 183-E2e. Many such composite sheets remain intact. All separated plate 1 or plate 2 sheets originally were part of a composite sheet.

183-E2b

Complete 2c design, lithographed.

183-E2 2c
a. Plate on stamp paper, imperf.
blue green *60.*
bright ultramarine *60.*
brown *60.*
b. Plate on stamp paper, perf. 12, gummed
bright red orange *35.*
dull red orange *35.*
dark red orange *35.*
red brown *35.*
dark red brown *35.*
dark orange brown *35.*
yellow brown *35.*
dull yellow green *35.*
green *35.*
dull ultramarine *35.*
bright ultramarine *35.*
blue violet *35.*
red violet *35.*
light red violet *35.*
violet red *35.*
c. Plate 2 "sheet" of 16, complete designs, without imprint, on old glazed paper, imperf., deep brown orange *600.*
d. As "c," with imprint, on old glazed paper, imperf., gummed
black *600.*
dull deep violet red *600.*
e. As "d," perf. 12, gummed
dull deep violet red *500.*
deep brown orange *500.*

See note following No. 182-E3e.

184-E1

Design size: 20x25mm
Die size: 54x55mm
Engraved frame of 3c alone on die.

184-E1 3c
a. Die on pelure paper
dark carmine *250.*
dark orange *250.*
orange brown *250.*

bright blue 250.
green 250.
dark green 250.

184-E2a

184-E2a Variety

Built-up model of engraved frame cut to shape inside and out, mounted atop engraved vignette of the same or different color. Warning: fraudulent models combining engraved and lithographed materials exist.

184-E2 3c
a. Die on proof paper
dark scarlet, cut close 250.
blue green, cut close 250.
deep blue, cut close 250.
deep blue frame, dark scarlet vignette 500.
blue green frame, dark scarlet vignette 500.
b. Four examples mounted 2½mm apart on stiff white card, 80x87mm
red 1,000.
orange brown 1,000.
green 1,000.
blue 1,000.
violet 1,000.
green frame, light blue vignette 1,000.

Built-up model as No. 184-E2, vignette as No. 184-E5 with dark background.

184-E3 3c Die on proof paper, scarlet 250.

184-E4

Complete 3c design, vignette with light background.

184-E4 3c
c. Plate lithographed on stamp paper, imperf.
black 75.
carmine 75.
green 75.
dark green 75.
bright ultramarine 75.
orange 75.

No. 184-E4c exists in two plates of 9 tete-beche, in diff. colors, on same piece of paper. Value, $1,400 sheet of 18.

d. Plate lithographed on stamp paper, perf. 12, gummed
dark red orange 50.
red brown 50.
red voilet 50.
brown orange 50.
ultramarine 50.
violet blue 50.
e. Plate sheet of 9 (3x3), imprint below, on stiff white wove
carmine 300.
blue green 300.
f. Plate sheet of 9 (3x3), on glazed thin wove
carmine 300.
blue green 300.
blue 300.
orange 300.
g. Plate sheet of 9 (3x3), on yellowish wove
carmine 300.
blue green 300.
blue 300.
h. Die of complete design on old stiff glazed paper (die size: 55x66mm), black 350.
i. Complete die on glazed wove
deep carmine 200.
scarlet 200.
ultramarine 200.
j. Complete die on India, light orange red 200.

184-E5

Design size: 19x24½mm
Die No. 1 size: about 63x94mm Vignette of Washington slightly diff. from rest of series but with quite diff. frame design.

184-E5 3c
a. Die on glazed paper, about 50x75mm, black 350.
d. Engraved plate of 25 on India, mounted on large card, red brown 750.
f. Plate on proof paper, perf. 12, lithographed
carmine 100.
rose lilac 100.
red orange 100.
h. Plate (printed before plate crack developed) on semiglazed yellowish wove, laid watermark
carmine 30.
dull red 30.
bright orange red 30.
deep orange red 30.
scarlet 30.
deep orange 30.
yellow orange 30.
orange brown 30.
orange yellow 30.
dark yellow green 30.
dusky blue green 30.
dull green blue 30.
violet blue 30.
red violet 30.
black 30.
i. Plate single from sheets of 100 with imprint on yellowish glazed chemically prepared wove, lithographed
black 20.
brown 20.
scarlet 20.
light red 20.
rose pink 20.
carmine 20.
deep carmine 20.
violet rose 20.
deep violet rose 20.
violet red 20.
red violet 20.
violet 20.
blue 20.
pale blue 20.
pale dull blue 20.
yellow 20.
dull brown yellow 20.
orange 20.
red orange 20.

184-E6

Illustration with card margins reduced.
Similar to No. 184-E1 but engraved vignette of Lincoln on India facing ¾ to right. Each design has vignette attached to frame from behind.

184-E6 3c Four examples mounted on 80x89mm card to resemble block of 4
blue 3,000.
green 3,000.

Frame of No. 184-E5 with engraved vignette of Lincoln mounted in place.

184-E7 3c Die on card, brown —

There is some doubt whether No. 184-E7 exists as a genuine essay. The editors would like to see authenticated evidence of its existence.

186-E1a

Design size: 20x25mm
Die size: 92x50mm
Frames of 6c and 7c side by side (6c at right).

186-E1 6c + 7c
a. Die on white pelure, orange 375.
c. Die on white pelure, both 7s reversed on 7c frame, orange 750.
d. Die on old stiff glazed, black 400.

186-E2a

Complete 6c design, lithographed.

186-E2 6c
a. Plate on stamp paper, perf. 12, gummed
bright red orange 35.
dull red orange 35.
dark red orange 35.
red brown 35.
dark red brown 35.
dark orange brown 35.
yellow brown 35.
dull yellow green 35.
green 35.
dull ultramarine 35.
bright ultramarine 35.
blue violet 35.
red violet 35.
light violet red 35.
violet red 35.
b. Plate on stamp paper, gummed
ultramarine 60.
lilac 60.
scarlet 60.
orange 60.
carmine 60.
dark carmine 60.
blue green 60.

186a-E2b

Complete 7c design, lithographed.

186a-E2 7c
a. Plate on stamp paper, imperf.
black 75.
carmine 75.
red orange 75.
yellow orange 75.
green 75.
dark green 75.
dark blue 75.
b. Plate on stamp paper, perf. 12, gummed
red brown 50.
dark red orange 50.
brown orange 50.
red violet 50.
ultramarine 50.
violet blue 50.

188a-E1

Design size: 20x25mm
Die size: 78½x64mm
Frames of 12c and 24c side by side (12c on right).

188a-E1 12c + 24c

a. Die on white pelure	
deep carmine	*300.*
brown orange	*300.*
orange brown	*300.*
blue green	*300.*
blue	*300.*
c. Die on old stiff glazed, black	*400.*

188a-E2a

Complete 12c design, lithographed.

188a-E2 12c

a. Plate on stamp paper, perf. 12, gummed	
bright red orange	*35.*
dull red orange	*35.*
dark red orange	*35.*
red brown	*35.*
dark red brown	*35.*
dark orange brown	*35.*
yellow brown	*35.*
dull yellow green	*35.*
green	*35.*
dull ultramarine	*35.*
bright ultramarine	*35.*
blue violet	*35.*
red violet	*35.*
light red violet	*35.*
violet red	*35.*
b. Plate on stamp paper, gummed	
ultramarine	*60.*
lilac	*60.*
scarlet	*60.*
orange	*60.*
carmine	*60.*
dark carmine	*60.*
blue green	*60.*

189a-E2a

Complete 24c design, lithographed.

189a-E2 24c

a. Plate on stamp paper, perf. 12, gummed	
red brown	*50.*
dark red orange	*50.*
brown orange	*50.*
ultramarine	*50.*
violet blue	*50.*
red violet	*50.*
b. Plate on stamp paper, gummed	
ultramarine	*75.*
lilac	*75.*
scarlet	*75.*
orange	*75.*
carmine	*75.*
dark carmine	*75.*
green	*75.*

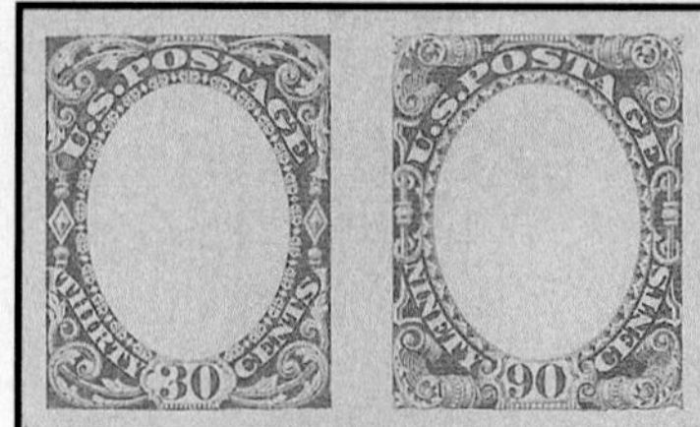

190-E1c

Design size: 20x25mm
Die size: 79x64mm
Frames of 30c and 90c side by side.

190-E1 30c + 90c

a. Die on white pelure	
dark carmine	*300.*
dark red orange	*300.*
dark orange brown	*300.*
brown	*300.*
blue green	*300.*
bright blue	*300.*
b. Die on stiff glazed paper, blue black	*500.*

190-E2a

Complete 30c design, lithographed.

190-E2 30c

a. Plate on stamp paper, perf. 12, gummed	
bright red orange	*35.*
dull red orange	*35.*
dark red orange	*35.*
red brown	*35.*
dark red brown	*35.*
dark orange brown	*35.*
yellow brown	*35.*
dull yellow green	*35.*
green	*35.*
dull ultramarine	*35.*
bright ultramarine	*35.*
blue violet	*35.*
red violet	*35.*
light red violet	*35.*
violet red	*35.*
b. Plate on stamp paper, gummed	
ultramarine	*60.*
lilac	*60.*
scarlet	*60.*
orange	*60.*
carmine	*60.*
dark carmine	*60.*
blue green	*60.*

191-E2

Complete 90c design, lithographed.

191-E2 90c

a. Plate on stamp paper, perf. 12, gummed	
black	*50.*
red brown	*50.*
dark red orange	*50.*
brown orange	*50.*
ultramarine	*50.*
violet blue	*50.*
red violet	*50.*
violet red	*50.*
dark blue green	*50.*
orange brown	*50.*
b. Plate on stamp paper, gummed	
ultramarine	*75.*
lilac	*75.*
scarlet	*75.*
orange	*75.*
carmine	*75.*
dark carmine	*75.*
green	*75.*

Essay reprints by Schernikow in 1903 from original dies (See paragraph eight of the Essay section introduction)

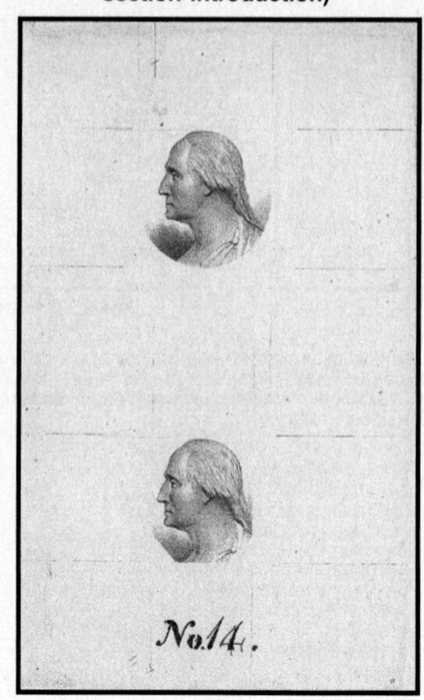

182-E1

Vignette master die "No. 14": two slightly diff. vignettes of Washington, one above the other, bottom one with truncated queue, bust and shading in front of neck.

182-E1

b. Die on proof paper (1903)	
black	*100.*
carmine	*100.*
dull carmine	*100.*
dusky carmine	*100.*
yellow	*100.*
dull scarlet	*100.*
dull orange	*100.*
brown orange	*100.*
brown	*100.*
gray olive	*100.*
blue green	*100.*
dark green	*100.*
black blue	*100.*
ultramarine	*100.*
violet	*100.*
red violet	*100.*

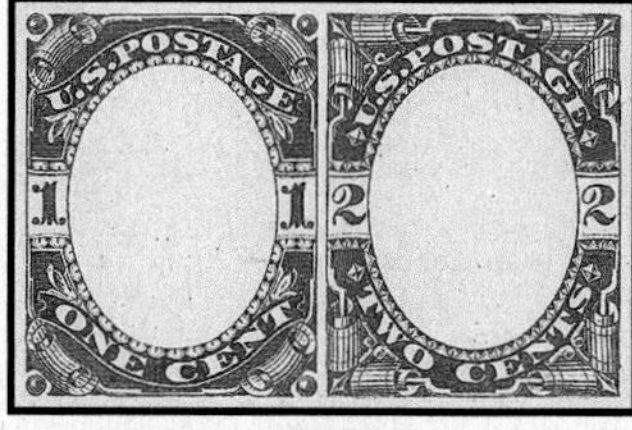

182-E2

Design size: 20x25mm
Die size: 98x53mm
Frames of 1c and 2c side by side.

182-E2 1c + 2c

d. Die on proof paper, printed through a mat (1903)	
black	*100.*
bright carmine	*100.*
dull carmine	*100.*
dim scarlet	*100.*
dark orange	*100.*
dull yellow	*100.*
dark orange brown	*100.*
black olive	*100.*
dark blue green	*100.*
dark blue	*100.*
ultramarine	*100.*
dark navy blue	*100.*
blue violet	*100.*
dull violet	*100.*
red violet	*100.*

184-E1

Design size: 20x25mm
Die size: 54x55mm

Engraved frame of 3c alone on die.

184-E1 3c
b. Die on proof paper (1903)
black 100.
bright carmine 100.
dull carmine 100.
dim scarlet 100.
dark orange 100.
dull yellow 100.
dark orange brown 100.
black olive 100.
dark rose 100.
green 100.
yellow green 100.
dark blue green 100.
dark blue 100.
deep ultramarine 100.
dark navy blue 100.
blue violet 100.
dull violet 100.
red violet 100.

184-E4

Complete 3c design, vignette with light background.

184-E4 3c
k. Complete die on proof paper (1903)
black 75.
bright carmine 75.
dull carmine 75.
dim scarlet 75.
dark orange 75.
dull yellow 75.
dark orange brown 75.
black olive 75.
green 75.
dark blue green 75.
deep ultramarine 75.
dark navy blue 75.
blue violet 75.
dull violet 75.
red violet 75.
l. Complete die on large colored card (1903)
black, *light green* 150.
deep scarlet, *ivory* 150.
red violet, *light blue* 150.
carmine, *pink* 150.

184-E5

Design size: 19x24 ½mm
Die No. 1 size: about 63x94mm Vignette of Washington slightly diff. from rest of series but with quite diff. frame design.

184-E5 3c
b. Die on proof paper (with and without printing through mats) (1903)
black 100.
dark carmine 100.
carmine 100.
bright carmine 100.
brown 100.
red brown 100.
yellow 100.
orange 100.
violet 100.
red violet 100.
violet brown 100.
blue 100.
steel blue 100.
light green 100.
dark green 100.
dull olive 100.
c. Die on colored card, 61x93mm (1903)
scarlet, *yellow* 150.
olive gray, *pale pink* 150.
dull violet, *buff* 150.

Plate proofs printed in sheets of 25 (plate size: 140x164mm). A horiz. crack extends through upper 3s from 2mm back of head on position 11 to vignette on position 12.
All plate essay items valued as singles except No. 184-E5d.

e. Plate on proof paper (1903)
black 15.
blue black 15.
greenish black 15.
dull red violet 15.
dark red violet 15.
dull violet 15.
violet brown 15.
light red brown 15.
orange brown 15.
brown carmine 15.
brown 15.
dim orange 15.
yellow 15.
dull yellow 15.
carmine 15.
light carmine 15.
dark carmine 15.
dull carmine 15.
dull scarlet 15.
dark green 15.
light green 15.
dull olive green 15.
deep ultramarine 15.
g. Plate on green bond, "Crane & Co. 1887" wmk. (1903)
black 25.
carmine 25.
dull carmine 25.
scarlet 25.
brown 25.
brown red 25.
orange brown 25.
red violet 25.
yellow 25.
orange 25.
dark green 25.
light green 25.
yellow green 25.
deep ultramarine 25.
dark navy blue 25.

186-E1

Design size: 20x25mm
Die size: 92x50mm
Frames of 6c and 7c side by side (6c at right).

186-E1 6c + 7c
b. Die on proof paper, printed through a mat (1903)
black 100.
bright carmine 100.
dull carmine 100.
dim scarlet 100.
dark orange 100.
dull yellow 100.
dark orange brown 100.
black olive 100.
green 100.
dark blue green 100.
dark blue 100.
deep ultramarine 100.
dark navy blue 100.
blue violet 100.
dull violet 100.
red violet 100.

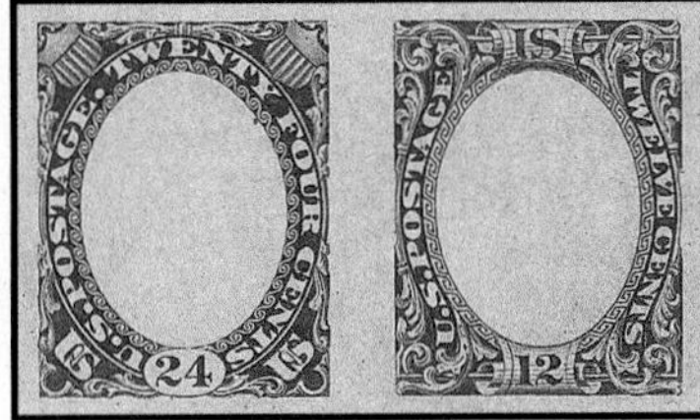

188a-E1

Design size: 20x25mm
Die size: 78 ½x64mm
Frames of 12c and 24c side by side (12c on right).

188a-E1 12c + 24c
b. Die on proof paper, printed through a mat (1903)
black 100.
bright carmine 100.
dull carmine 100.
dim scarlet 100.
dark orange 100.
dull yellow 100.
dark orange brown 100.
black olive 100.
green 100.
dark blue green 100.
dark blue 100.
deep ultramarine 100.
dark navy blue 100.
blue violet 100.
dull violet 100.
red violet 100.

190-E1

Design size: 20x25mm
Die size: 79x64mm
Frames of 30c and 90c side by side.

190-E1 30c + 90c
c. Die on proof paper, printed through a mat (1903)
black 100.
bright carmine 100.
dull carmine 100.
dim scarlet 100.
dark orange 100.
dull yellow 100.
dark orange brown 100.
black olive 100.
green 100.
dark blue green 100.
dark blue 100.
deep ultramarine 100.
dark navy blue 100.
blue violet 100.
dull violet 100.
red violet 100.

1879 Coupon Essay
Azariah B. Harris

184-E8a

Size of coupon design: 25x7 ½mm
A proposed $300 30-year Postal Revenue Bond with 3.65% interest. Daily coupons 3c each, "Receivable for Postage in all parts of the U.S." after date thereon. Entire bond contained six pages of coupons with 16 rows of four (one for each day of two months); 20% bear month and day, others blank.

184-E8 3c
a. Coupon on bond (dated Jan. or Feb.), imperf., black 350.
b. Engraved die on old ivory paper (undated), black 1,000.
c. Single coupon on bond (dated), perf. 12, gummed, blue green 125.
d. Single coupon on bond (undated), perf. 12, gummed, blue green 50.

Continental Bank Note Co.

182-E4

Design size: 18x22mm
Die size: 59x67mm
Engraved vignette of Franklin on white background in unadopted frame.

182-E4 1c
a. Die on India, blue 575.
b. Die on proof paper
black 500.
dull scarlet 500.
dull brown 500.
dull green 500.
dull blue 500.
c. Die on ivory glazed paper
black 750.
black brown 750.
scarlet 750.
blue 750.

All known examples of "b" have reduced margins.

184-E9

Die size: 61½x76½mm
Vignette of Washington on white background in incomplete frame as adopted: no veins in trifoliate ornaments in upper corners.

184-E9 3c Die on India, on card
black 750.
green 750.

184-E10

Similar to No. 184-E9 but completed frame with veins in trifoliate ornaments.

184-E10 3c
a. Die on India, die sunk on card, green 750.
b. Die on proof paper, about 35x40mm
gray black 350.
dull red 350.
dull blue 350.
dull green 350.
dull brown 350.
c. Die on ivory glazed paper
black 600.
black brown 600.
scarlet 600.
blue 600.

Nos. 147-E8 and 147-E9 may have been made from completed dies of No. 147 to produce Nos. 184-E9 and 184-E10.

184-E11

Design size: 17½x21½mm
Die size: 60x75mm
Complete unadopted design with vignette of Liberty on white background.

184-E11 3c
a. Die on India
black 350.
brown red 350.
orange 350.
green 350.
blue 350.
scarlet 350.
b. Die on proof paper
brown 350.
green 350.
gray black 350.
dull red 350.
dull blue 350.
c. Die on ivory glazed paper
black 750.
black brown 750.
scarlet 750.
blue 750.

All known examples of Nos. 184-E11a, 184-E11b have reduced margins.

184-E12

Design size: 19½x24½mm
Die size: 61x71mm

Complete unadopted design with vignette of Washington on white background in frame similar to No. 184-E11 but with numerals of value.

184-E12 3c
a. Die on India, die sunk on card
black 650.
dull scarlet 650.
brown 650.
green 650.
b. Die on white glazed paper
black 500.
black brown 500.
scarlet 500.
blue 500.
c. Plate on India (some adhering to original card backing), imperf.
black 100.
scarlet 100.
orange red 100.
green 100.
d. Plate on white paper, perf. 12, gummed
black 75.
green 75.
blue 75.
brown 75.
red brown 75.
orange 75.
dull scarlet 75.
orange brown 75.
e. Plate on Francis Patent bluish chemical paper, perf. 12, gummed
black 150.
scarlet 150.
red brown 150.
brown 150.
yellow 150.
green 150.
gray 150.
f. Plate on brown chemical paper, perf. 12, gummed
blue 150.
ultramarine 150.
g. Hybrid die on India, mounted on India, block sunk on card, green 400.

184-E13

Design size: 18x22mm
Die size: about 61x62mm
Similar to No. 184-E12 but slightly different frame.

184-E13 3c
a. Die on India, die sunk on card
black 650.
scarlet 650.
green 650.
blue 650.
black brown 650.
blue green 650.
b. Die on ivory glazed paper
black 750.
black brown 750.
scarlet 750.
blue 750.
c. Plate on India, imperf.
black 100.
deep scarlet 100.
green 100.
dark green 100.
dark yellow brown 100.
olive brown 100.
violet brown 100.
orange 100.
d. Plate on stamp paper, perf. 12, gummed
black 75.
dull scarlet 75.
blue green 75.
brown 75.
red brown 75.
dull blue 75.
dark blue 75.
orange 75.
yellow 75.
yellow brown 75.
gray 75.

184-E14

Design size: 19x24½mm
Die size: about 67x71mm

Similar to No. 184-E13 but value label with "THREE" above "CENTS."

184-E14 3c
a. Hybrid die on India mounted on India, block sunk on card
brown red 400.
green 400.
b. Die on ivory glazed paper
black 500.
black brown 500.
scarlet 500.
blue 500.
c. Die on proof paper, about 35x35mm
black 300.
dull scarlet 300.
dull brown 300.
dull green 300.
dull blue 300.
brown red 300.
red brown 300.

184-E15

Design size: 20x25½mm
Die size: 60x73mm
Vignette of Indian maiden in headdress, "PORTAGE" error in top label.

184-E15 3c
a. Hybrid die on India, cut close, mounted on India, block sunk on card
black 900.
dark green 900.
b. Die on proof paper, about 28x35mm
black 600.
dull scarlet 500.
dull brown 500.
dull blue 500.
dull green 500.
c. Die on ivory glazed paper
black 750.
black brown 750.
scarlet 750.
blue 750.
d. Die on India, scarlet —

184-E16

Similar to No. 184-E15 but with spelling corrected to "POSTAGE."

184-E16 3c Die on India, cut close, mounted on India, block sunk on card
black 1,250.
blue 1,250.
steel blue 1,250.
carmine 1,250.
scarlet 1,250.
brown 1,250.
dark green 1,250.

190-E3

Die size: 44½x71½mm
Vignette of Hamilton on white background in frame as adopted.

190-E3 30c
a. Die on proof paper, about 35x48mm
gray black 500.
dull red 500.
dull green 500.
dull brown 500.
dull blue 500.
b. Die on ivory glazed paper
black 750.
black brown 750.
scarlet 750.
blue 750.

American Bank Note Co.

184-E17a

184-E17b

Design size: 22x30mm
Silver photo print of engraved vignette of Washington mounted on pencil and ink frame design.

184-E17 3c
  a. Die on white card, 38x49mm
  light brown vignette, black frame *1,250.*
  b. Die on white card, 38x50mm
  light brown vignette, black frame *1,250.*

On No. 184-E17b, the oval frame lines at the sides and the ornaments at top and bottom extend beyond the rectangular frame lines, and the lettering is less complete than on No. 184-E17a.

1881-82 ISSUE
American Bank Note Co.

205-E1

Die size: 59x74mm
Vignette of Garfield in lined oval.

205-E1 5c Die on India, die sunk on card, black *500.*

205-E2

Die No. C-47 size: 70x83mm
Vignette of Garfield in beaded oval, in plain border of horiz. lines. Found with and without imprint and die number.

205-E2 5c Die on India, die sunk on card
  gray brown *250.*
  gray black *250.*

No. 205-E2 may not be a stamp essay.

205-E3a

205-E3c

Die size: 78x78mm
Vignette of Garfield in beaded oval with cutout at bottom for top of star.

205-E3 5c
  a. Die on India, die sunk on card
  black *750.*
  deep red orange *750.*
  red brown *750.*
  blue *750.*
  green *750.*
  b. Die on ivory glazed paper
  black *750.*
  green *750.*
  blue *750.*
  scarlet *750.*
  red brown *750.*
  c. Negative impression, solid color outside design, die on India, bright red orange *1,000.*

205-E4

Vignette of Garfield as No. 205-E1 in lined oval and finished frame as adopted.

205-E4 5c Die on India, 24x30mm, black *900.*

206-E1

Image of unadopted frame, printed on 40x60mm India paper with text and right "1" cut out.

206-E1 1c Black on India *2,500.*

206-E1B

Image of frame with "DOS CENTAVOS" in upper label and "ONE CENT" pasted on bottom label, affixed to 57x71mm card with additional pencil sketch at right.

206-E1B 1c Black image affixed to card *2,500.*

206-E1C

Design size: 21x26mm
Engraved frame of unadopted design.

206-E1C 1c
  a. Die on white glazed paper, 42x74mm, black *1,000.*
  b. Die on surface-tinted glazed paper, cut close
  green, *buff* *600.*
  black, *orange* *600.*
  brown orange, *blue* *600.*

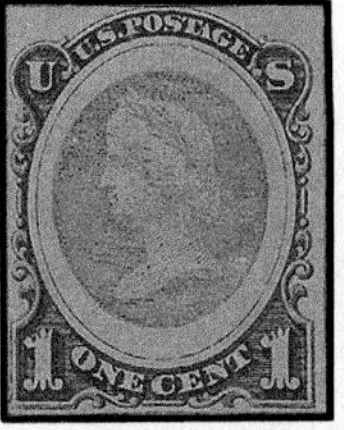

206-E2

Engraved frame almost identical to No. 206-E1C with small typographed vignette of Peace.

206-E2 1c Die on blue surface-tinted ivory paper, cut close, buff vignette, carmine frame *800.*

206-E3

206-E3c

Vignette of Peace only.

206-E3 1c
  a. Engraved vignette
  black *350.*
  dull red violet *350.*
  b. Typographed vignette *350.*
  c. Die on old proof paper, cut to shape to show AMERICAN BANK NOTE CO. and die number V46742, with die number 340 crossed out by etched lines, mounted on card, black *350.*

Nos. 206-E3a and 206-E3c are essays made by the American Bank Note. Co. from a die acquired from toppan, Carpenter and company. The die number V46742 is the new ABNCo. die number.

206-E4

Engraved frame (No. 206-E1C) with typographed vignette of Lincoln mounted on it. Four diff. colors (dull carmine, dull scarlet, dark brown, green) on cream white ivory paper, 22x27mm each, mounted together on 92x114mm thick white card, ms. "American Bank Note Co. N.Y." at lower right.

206-E4 1c Four designs on cream white ivory on card *2,250.*

206-E5

Design size: 18x23½mm

Typographed vignette of Lincoln only.

206-E5 1c Die on white ivory paper
- dull carmine *450.*
- dark yellowish brown *450.*
- dull purple *450.*
- dull dark blue *450.*
- orange *450.*

Do not confuse the listed Lincoln vignette, No. 206-E5, with somewhat similar engravings ca. 1894 by Schlecht for currency.

206-E6

Incomplete engraving of complete design as issued: no shading in upper arabesques.

206-E6 1c
- ***a.*** Die on India
  - gray blue *750.*
  - green blue *750.*
- ***b.*** Die on India, cut close, on India block sunk on card, deep gray blue *350.*

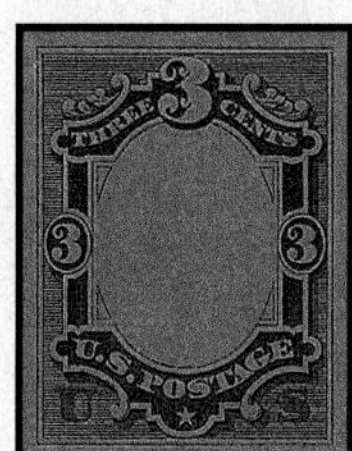

207-E1

Design size: 20½x25½mm

Die size: 49x54½mm

Engraved unadopted frame design with 3's at sides and large 3 at top.

207-E1 3c
- ***a.*** Die on India
  - yellow brown *750.*
  - dull brown *750.*
  - dull blue *750.*
  - green *750.*
- ***b.*** Die on white glazed paper, 32x38mm
  - black *650.*
  - dull dark yellow *650.*
- ***c.*** Die on surface-tinted ivory paper, cut close
  - black, *orange* *500.*
  - green, *buff* *500.*
  - violet blue, *orange* *500.*

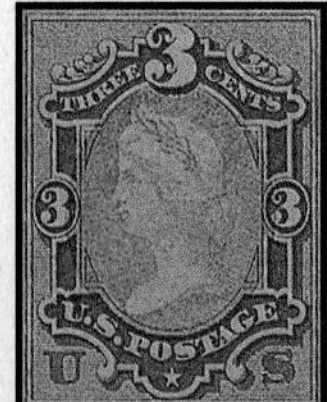

207-E2

Engraved frame as No. 207-E1, with typographed vignette of Peace.

207-E2 3c Die on blue surface-tinted ivory paper, cut close, buff vignette, carmine frame *850.*

207-E3

Engraved frame (No. 207-E1) with typographed vignette of Peace mounted on it. Four diff. color combinations (orange red vignette, dull carmine frame; dull carmine vignette, dull red brown frame; yellow brown vignette and frame; blue green vignette and frame) on cream white ivory paper, 22x27mm each, mounted together on 92x114mm thick white card, ms. "American Bank Note Co. N.Y." at lower right.

207-E3 3c 4 designs on cream white ivory on card *2,500.*

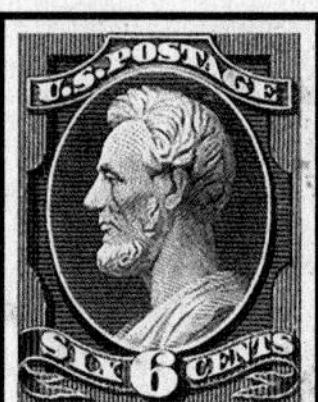

208-E1

Incomplete engraving of design as adopted: unfinished shading on top label and bottom ribbon, four lines between frame sinkage at right and left edges, horiz. line at bottom.

This is a new die engraved by the Bureau of Engraving & Printing for "Roosevelt" proof albums.

208-E1 6c Die on India, on card, black *2,400.*

209-E1

Design size: 20x25mm
Die size: 58x76mm
Engraving of unadopted frame only, no horiz. lines in background.

209-E1 10c Die on thick white card, about 25x33mm
- blue *800.*
- green *800.*

209-E2

Similar to No. 209-E1 but with horiz. lines added to background.

209-E2 10c
- ***a.*** Die on thick white card
  - black *700.*
  - red *700.*
  - green *700.*
  - blue *700.*
- ***b.*** Die on India, on 50x70mm card, black *800.*
- ***c.*** Die on white glazed paper, black *800.*

209-E3

Engraved frame similar to No. 209-E2 with typographed vignette of Peace.

209-E3 10c
- ***a.*** Die on blue surface-tinted glazed paper, cut close, buff vignette, carmine frame *650.*
- ***b.*** Die on orange surface-tinted glazed paper
  - dull carmine vignette, violet frame *650.*
  - dull yellow vignette, violet frame *650.*
  - yellow vignette, green frame *650.*

209-E4

Vignette diameter: 17mm
Engraved Franklin vignette.

209-E4 10c
- ***a.*** Die on India
  - black *575.*
  - dusky carmine *575.*
  - dull scarlet *575.*
  - dim orange *575.*
  - orange brown *575.*
  - yellow green *575.*
  - dim blue green *575.*
  - deep blue *575.*
  - red brown on blue ground *575.*
  - dark red violet *575.*
- ***b.*** Die sunk on glazed paper, approx. 51x69mm
  - dusky carmine *775.*
  - dim scarlet *775.*
  - dim orange *775.*
  - deep blue *775.*
  - dim blue green *775.*
  - dim brown *775.*

209-E5

Design size: 21x26mm
Engraved frame with typographed vignette mounted on it. Four diff. color combinations (dull scarlet vignette, dull carmine frame; dull orange vignette, brown orange frame; yellow brown vignette, dark brown frame; blue green vignette and frame) on cream white ivory paper, 22x27mm each, mounted together on 92x114mm thick white card, ms. "American Bank Note Co. N.Y." at lower right.

209-E5 10c Four designs on cream white ivory on card *2,500.*

209-E6

Vignette diameter: 18mm

Engraved Washington vignette.

209-E6 10c
a. Die on India
black *600.*
dim deep carmine *600.*
dim deep scarlet *600.*
dull orange *600.*
dull brown *600.*
dim blue green *600.*
blue *600.*
dusky red violet *600.*
b. Die sunk on white ivory paper, 55x67mm
dusky carmine *800.*
dull orange *800.*
dull blue green *800.*
scarlet *800.*
dull brown *800.*
red violet *800.*

209-E7

Design size: 21x26mm
Engraved frame with typographed vignette mounted on it. Four diff. color combinations (dull carmine vignette and frame; dull orange vignette, brown orange frame; yellow brown vignette, dark brown frame; blue green vignette and frame) on cream white ivory paper, 22x27mm each, mounted together on 92x114mm thick white card, ms. "American Bank Note Co. N.Y." at lower right.

209-E7 10c
a. Four designs on cream white ivory on card *2,500.*
b. Single composite off card, dull carmine vignette, blue green frame *400.*

Issued stamp, No. 209, in trial color, overprinted network in fugitive ink.

209-E8 10c On thick paper, perf. 12, gummed, sepia, overprint olive gray *150.*

1883 ISSUE
American Bank Note Co.

210-E1

Design size: 20x25½mm
Engraved vignette of Washington (from proof on India of No. 207) with watercolor frame design nearly as adopted but with "TWO" and "CENTS" at an angle, rubber stamp "Feb. 17, 1883" on back.

210-E1 2c Die on white card, 80x90mm, black vignette, gray and white frame *3,000.*

210-E2

Design size: 20x25mm
Engraved vignette of Washington (from proof on India of No. 207) mounted on unadopted watercolor and ink frame design. backstamped "American Bank Note Co. Feb. 27, 1883."

210-E2 2c Die on thick white card, 87x100mm, black and white *3,000.*

210-E3

Design size: 20x25½mm
Engraved vignette of Washington (from proof on India of No. 207) mounted on watercolor frame design as adopted, ms. "2 March 1883 No. 1."

210-E3 2c Die on white card, 80x90mm, black vignette, gray & white frame *6,000.*

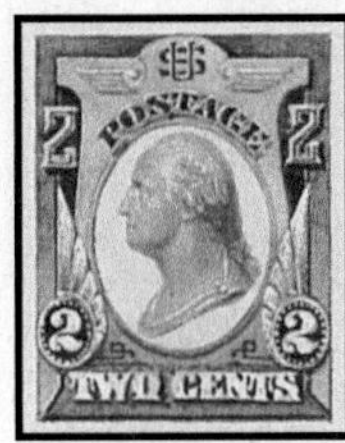

210-E4

Design size: 20x25mm
Engraved vignette of Washington on white background mounted on a brush and pen watercolor drawing of unadopted fancy frame design, backstamped "American Bank Note Co. Mar. 2, 1883" and pencil "No. 2."

210-E4 2c Die on white card, 88x101mm, dusky blue green *5,500.*

210-E5

Design size: 20x25mm
Engraved vignette of Washington (from revenue stamp No. RB17) mounted on wash drawing of unadopted ornate frame design, backstamped "American Bank Note Co. Mar. 2, 1883" and pencil "No. 3."

210-E5 2c Die on white card, 88x101mm, blue violet vignette, black frame *2,500.*

211-E1

Design size: 20x25½mm
Engraved vignette of Jackson mounted on unadopted watercolor frame design.

211-E1 4c Die on white card, 70x70mm, blue green vignette and frame *3,500.*

211-E2

Engraved head of Jackson only.

211-E2 4c Die on India, die sunk on card, black *2,500.*

211-E3

Incomplete engraved vignette of Jackson: lower edge of bust incomplete.

211-E3 4c Die on India, die sunk on card
black *2,500.*
green *2,500.*
red brown *2,500.*

Complete engraved vignette of Jackson.

211-E4 4c Die on India, die sunk on card, blue green *2,500.*

Die size: 60x62mm
Complete design as adopted but with pencil sketch of pedestal top under bust.

211-E5 4c Die on India, die sunk on card, gray black *5,750.*

211-E6

Similar to No. 211-E5 but with incomplete shading engraved on pedestal.

211-E6 4c Die on India, die sunk on card, blue green *2,500.*

1887 ISSUE
American Bank Note Co.

212-E1

Die I, State 1
Die size: 62.5x62.5mm
Incomplete engraved vignette of Franklin facing right; horiz. background lines only.

212-E1 1c Die on 32½x35mm card, India mounted, die sunk on card, black *1,000.*

212-E2

Die 1, State 2
Die size: 62.5x62.5mm
Franklin vignette as on No. 212-E1 but with diagonal lines added to the background shading, sloping downward from right to left.

212-E2 1c Die on India, die sunk on card
black *600.*
ultramarine *600.*

212-E2A

Die II, State 1
Die size: 55x64mm
Incomplete engraved vignette almost exactly like on No. 212-E2, but on a new size die block.

212-E2A 1c Die on India, die sunk on card
black *600.*
ultramarine *600.*

212-E2B

Die II, State 1, marked in pencil
Die size: 55x64mm
As No. 212-E2A, with pencil shading added to mark need for revision.

212-E2B 1c Die on India, die sunk on card, black *850.*

212-E3

Die II, State 2
Die size: 55x64mm
Similar to No. 212-E2A, diagonal shading unchanged, shadows deepened by deeper cut lines per changes suggested by pencil shading on No. 212-E2B.

212-E3 1c Die on India, die sunk on card
black *600.*
ultramarine *600.*

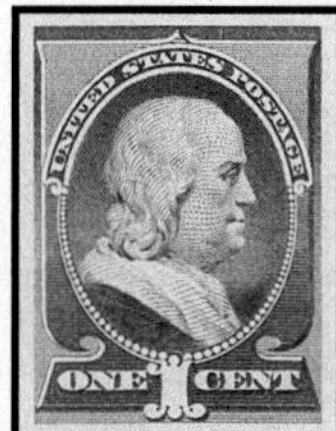
212-E4

Die II, State 3
Die size: 55x64mm
Frame added, very small changes to the vignette, earliest full frame design.

212-E4 1c Die on India, die sunk on card
a. Die on India, die sunk on card, brown (full size) *1,000.*
black *600.*
ultramarine *600.*
b. Die on ivory glazed paper (c. 1893)
black *750.*
black brown *750.*
scarlet *750.*
blue *750.*

212-E5

Die III
Die size: 62.5x62.5mm
New engraving of Franklin vignette facing left; background shading as on No. 212-E2 with diagonal lines sloping downward from right to left.

212-E5 1c Die on India, die sunk on card, ultramarine *600.*

212-E6

Die IV, State 1
Die size: 57x65mm
Frame added as on No. 212-E4, but a few frame elements differ.

212-E6 1c Die on India, die sunk on card, ultramarine 850.

212-E7

Die IV, State 1, marked in pencil
Die size: 57x65mm
Similar to No. 212-E6, with pencil shading added to mark need for revision.

212-E7 1c Die on India, die sunk on card, ultramarine *850.*

212-E8

Die IV, State 2a
Die size: 57x65mm
Similar to No. 212-E6, with some vignette shading lines strenghtened in accordance with pencil markings on No. 212-E7; arc lines on bottom of vignette frame extended from numeral to 8th pearl on right and 13th pearl on left; tablet is unchanged.

212-E8 1c Die on India, die sunk on card
ultramarine *750.*
green *750.*

212-E9

Die 4, State 2b
Die size: 57x65mm
As No. 212-E8 but vignette frame shading lines extend to 21st pearl on right and 22nd pearl on left; deeper shading outside lower right of shield; tablet shading per changes suggested by pencil shading on No. 212-E7.

212-E9 1c Die on India, die sunk on card, ultramarine *750.*

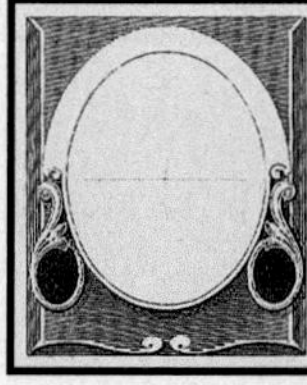
212-E10

Die IV, State 3
Die size: 57x65mm
Deeply cut left background shading extended; pencil lines and notation: "Mr. Jones, Don't you think it would be well to tone off a little of the hard edge of your cut line — This in printing will fill up WMS."

212-E10 1c Die on India, die sunk on card, ultramarine *750.*

1890 ISSUE
American Bank Note Co.

219-E1

Design size: 19x22½mm
Die size: 58x64mm
Engraved die of frame only with blank labels quite similar to adopted design.

219-E1 1c Die on ivory paper, 64x72mm, black *1,750.*

219-E2

Design size: 19x22mm
Engraved Franklin vignette cut down from 1887 1c stamp (No. 212) mounted on watercolor frame design.

219-E2 1c Die on thick light buff card, ultramarine frame *6,000.*

219-E3

Die size: 62x62mm
Engraved Franklin vignette with lettered label above.

219-E3 1c Die on India, die sunk on card, blue *2,000.*

219-E4

Engraved die of vignette only with outer line around the oval.

219-E4 1c Die on India, die sunk on card, 71x70mm, ultramarine *800.*

220-E1

Design size: 19x22mm
Engraved Washington vignette from 3c stamp (from proof on India of No. 184) mounted on watercolor frame design.

220-E1 2c Die on thick white card, 62x66mm, light carmine frame *3,750.*

220-E2

Design size: 19x23mm
Engraved Washington vignette cut from 1887 2c stamp (No. 213) mounted on shield-like watercolor frame design.

220-E2 2c Die on thick light buff card, gray frame *3,000.*

220-E3

Design size: 19x23mm
Engraved Washington vignette cut from 1887 2c stamp (No. 213) mounted on watercolor frame design.

220-E3 2c Die on white card, 105x135mm, gray black frame *6,000.*

220-E4

Design size: 19x22mm
Die size: 56x63mm
Engraved unadopted frame only.

220-E4 2c Die on white ivory paper, black *1,750.*

220-E5

Die size: 61x62mm
Engraved vignette of Washington in oval line frame. Issue 1890 at bottom.

220-E5 2c Die on India, die sunk on card, dark carmine *2,000.*

220-E6

Engraved Washington vignette with lettered label above.

220-E6 2c Die on India, dusky carmine *1,250.*

220-E7

Design size: 19x22½mm
Engraved Washington vignette and lettered top label mounted on pencil drawing of frame design adopted, ms. "J.J.M. — engraved background only without figures or words;" backstamped "Nov. 15, 1889 American Bank Note Co."

220-E7 2c Die on 50x55mm white card, mounted on thick white card, 119x122mm, black vignette, pencil frame *3,000.*

220-E8

Design size: 19x22mm
Die size: 56x63mm
Engraved frame only as adopted with numerals, blank curved top label.

220-E8 2c
- *a.* Die on ivory paper, 64x71mm, black *1,500.*
- *b.* Die on India, 51x62mm

black	*1,500.*
brown black	*1,500.*
dark brown	*1,500.*
dull scarlet	*1,500.*
dark blue green	*1,500.*
dark blue	*1,500.*
red violet	*1,500.*
red orange	*1,500.*

220-E9

Incomplete engraving of entire design as adopted: no dots in rectangular spaces between shading lines on cheek under hair in front of ear and on back of neck.

220-E9 2c Die on India, die sunk on card, lake *1,250.*

(Probably by) The Times, Philadelphia

220-E11

Surface-printed essay for proposed business advertising on stamps.

220-E11 2c Die on India, on card, bright green blue —

American Bank Note Co.

221-E1

Engraved 3c frame as adopted with vignette cut out, mounted over photo of James Madison.

221-E1 3c Die on India, cut close, dark green *2,500.*

221-E2

Engraved vignette of Jackson with lettered label above.

221-E2 3c Die on India, die sunk on card, purple *1,250.*

Design size: 19x22mm
Incomplete engraved design as adopted except Lincoln facing ¾ left: unfinished shading under collar.

222-E1 4c Die on India, die sunk on card, black brown *1,250.*

222-E2

Die No. C-226 size: 62½x62½mm
Completed design with die no. and impt., Lincoln facing ¾ left.

222-E2 4c Die on India, on 25x32mm card, black brown *2,000.*
- *a.* Die number and impt. erased, die sunk on card *2,250.*

222-E3

Incomplete engraving as adopted: no wart on face, no lines on shirt.

222-E3 4c Die on India, die sunk on card, black brown *1,500.*

223-E1

Design size: 19x21½mm
Photo of Seward vignette mounted on watercolor frame design.

223-E1 5c Gray and white on light buff paper in upper right corner of short envelope *7,000.*

223-E2

Design size: 19x22mm
Die size: 63x62mm
Incomplete engraved design as adopted except Grant facing ¾ left: hair neatly combed.

223-E2 5c Die on India, die sunk on card

black	*1,750.*
orange brown	*1,750.*

223-E3

Design size: 19x22mm
Die size: 63x62mm
Incomplete engraving of complete bearded left-facing design: eye pupils not solid color, light shading on right side of face, only one diagonal shading line on left coat shoulder.

223-E3 5c Die on India, die sunk on card, chocolate *1,750.*

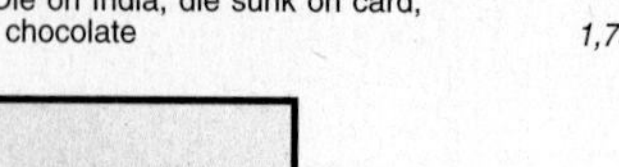

Similar to No. 223-E3 but more complete. Left beard has no diagonal lines and is light at top center.

223-E4 5c Die on India, die sunk on card, chocolate *1,750.*

223-E5

Third state of die: no horiz. lines on left moustache or under lower lip.

223-E5 5c Die on India, die sunk on card, chocolate *1,750.*

223-E6

Completed left-facing design: shows lines omitted from No. 223-E5, several diagonal shading lines on left shoulder of coat.

223-E6 5c Die on India, die sunk on card
black *700.*
chocolate *700.*

223-E7

Design size: 19x22mm
Die size: 62x62mm
Left-facing design with slightly diff. portrait, hair neatly combed. Horiz. shading lines on left coat shoulder, no wash-etched shadows on coat, beard and tie.

223-E7 5c
a. Die on India, die sunk on card
black *700.*
dark brown *700.*
b. Die on glazed paper, impt. and "ESSAY MARCH 1890"
black *750.*
black brown *750.*
scarlet *750.*
blue *750.*

Design size: 19x22mm
Die similar to No. 223-E7 but diagonal shading lines on left coat shoulder, wash-etched shadows on coat, beard and tie.

223-E8 5c Die on India, on card, brown *700.*

223-E9

Die size: 62x63mm
Engraving of right-facing Grant design diff. than adopted: light oval line around vignette, three diagonal lines on shirtfront under tie. Incomplete engraving: right collar unshaded.

223-E9 5c Die on India, dark orange brown *700.*

223-E10

Similar to No. 223-E9 but engraving completed: right collar shaded.

223-E10 5c
a. Die on India, die sunk on card, dark orange brown *700.*
b. Die on ivory paper, impt. and "ESSAY MARCH 1890"
black *750.*
black brown *750.*
scarlet *750.*
blue *750.*

Ferrotype plate 39x51mm of Grant facing ¾ left, outlines engraved, filled with red.

223-E11 5c Metal plate *2,000.*

223-E12

Printing from ferrotype plate, No. 223-E11.

223-E12 5c Die on card, 43x56mm, red *3,000.*

226-E1

Design size: 19x22½mm
Incomplete engraved vignette of Webster with curved label above, mounted on pencil drawing of frame design (includes additional pencil drawings of lower part of frame, value lettering), backstamped "D.S. Ronaldson," frame engraver.

226-E1 10c Die on white card, 51x55mm, black *13,500.*

226-E2

Design size: 19x22½mm
Engraving of unadopted frame design.

226-E2 10c Die on white glazed paper, black *1,000.*

226-E3

Design size: 19x22mm
Engraved 10c frame as adopted, vignette cut out and mounted over photo of John Adams.

226-E3 10c Die on India, cut close, dark green *2,500.*

226-E4

Design size: 19x22mm
Engraved 10c frame as adopted, vignette cut out and mounted over photo of William T. Sherman.

226-E4 10c Die on India, cut close, dark green *2,500.*

227-E1

Design size: 19x22½mm
Engraved vignette of Henry Clay with curved label above, mounted on wash drawing of frame design (includes additional enlarged pencil and wash drawing of frame).

227-E1 15c Die on white card, mounted at left on light buff card, 110x123mm (frame drawing at right), black *7,500.*

228-E1

Design size: 17x18½ mm
Die size: 62x61mm
Incomplete engraved vignette of Jefferson with curved lettered label at top: hair shading incomplete.

228-E1 30c Die on India, die sunk on card, black *750.*

228-E2

Design size: 17x18½mm
Similar to No. 228-E1 but more shading on hair, vert. shading lines on chin.

228-E2 30c Die on India, die sunk on card, black *2,500.*

229-E1

Design size: 17x18½ mm
Die size: 62x62mm
Engraved vignette of Perry with curved lettered label at top.

229-E1 90c Die on India, die sunk on card, red orange *2,500.*

COLUMBIAN ISSUE
Lyman H. Bagg

230-E1

Design sizes: 22x22mm
Left: No. 230-E1 — pencil drawing of Columbus in armor, on paper. "I do not know whether these designs will be of any use to you or not — they are so rough. L.H.B." written at top, "My idea illustrated" at bottom.
Right: No. 237-E1 — pencil drawing of North American continent, on paper.

230-E1 One Cent, Ten Cents, Drawings on 114x72mm white wove, Nos. 230-E1, 237-E1 *6,000.*

American Bank Note Co.

230-E2

230-E3

230-E4

Design size: 33x22mm
Silver print photo vignette of Columbus head mounted on watercolor drawing of unadopted frame design.

230-E2 1c Red violet on stiff white drawing paper *4,500.*
230-E3 1c Blue green on stiff white drawing paper *4,500.*
230-E4 1c Light red on stiff white drawing paper *4,500.*

230-E5

Die size: 57x38mm
Ferrotype metal plate with outline of adopted vignette (reversed) and drawings of Indian man and woman at sides in single line frame 39mm long.

230-E5 1c Metal plate 1,250.

230-E6

Vignette size: 16x15mm
Engraved vignette only as adopted.

230-E6 1c Die on 53x39mm India, on card
yellow brown *2,000.*
black *2,000.*

230-E7

Incomplete engraving of vignette, lettering, value numerals and tablet as issued: without palm tree, incomplete shading on and behind Indian and maiden, on Columbus' head, no shading on scrollwork, etc.

230-E7 1c Die on 39x28mm stiff wove, deep blue *2,000.*

230-E8

Incomplete engraving of entire design as issued: maiden's skirt only lightly engraved, chief's torso and shoulder incompletely engraved, incomplete shading in frame design at top, etc.

230-E8 1c Die on India, die sunk on 99x84mm card, deep blue *1,500.*

231-E1

Design size: 34x22mm
Silver print photo of vignette as adopted, mounted on watercolor drawing of unadopted frame design.

231-E1 2c Die on stiff white drawing paper, red violet *8,500.*

Die size: 74x61½mm
Incomplete engraving of adopted vignette only.

231-E2 2c Die on India, die sunk on card
black *1,500.*
sepia *1,500.*

231-E3

Design size: 35½x22mm
Engraved vignette of Columbus asking aid of Isabella as adopted for 5c, mounted on watercolor drawing of frame design similar to that adopted for 2c.

231-E3 2c Die on stiff white drawing paper, dark brown *4,000.*

231-E4

Vignette size: 29x15mm
Die size: 74x61½mm
Incomplete engraving of vignette as adopted (probably first state of die): cape on back of central figure incomplete, etc.

231-E4 2c Die on India, die sunk on card, black *2,500.*

231-E5

Incomplete engraving of vignette as adopted (probably second state of die): more shading on top right face, etc.; also pencil sketches for lengthening vignette.

231-E5 2c Die on India, die sunk on card,
black *3,250.*

231-E6

Vignette size: 31½x15mm
Die size: 74x61½mm
Incomplete engraving of vignette, longer than Nos. 231-E4 and 231-E5, later shortened as adopted: Columbus' legs, central figure's cape, etc., are incomplete.

231-E6 2c Die on India, die sunk on card,
black *2,500.*

231-E7

Design size: 33x22mm
Die size: 74x61½mm
Incomplete engraving of entire design almost as adopted: figures of value narrower, unfinished crosset shadows in lower corners.

Ridgway numbers used for colors of No. 231-E7.

231-E7 2c
a. Die on India, die sunk on card
13m/4 smoky dusky o-yellow-orange *1,250.*
b. Die on thin white wove card
69o/5 black *800.*
1m/0 dusky red *800.*
3k/2 dull dark orange-red *800.*
5i/0 deep o-orange-red *800.*
5j/1 deep v-deep o-orange-red *800.*
6i/0 deep m. red-orange *800.*
9i/0 deep o-yellow-orange *800.*
9m/0 dusky o-red-orange *800.*
9m/3 dismal dusky o-red-orange *800.*
9m/4 smoky dusky o-red-orange *800.*
9n/2 dull v. dusky o-red-orange *800.*
10k/0 m. dark orange *800.*
11i/0 deep orange *800.*
11k/1 dim dark orange *800.*
13m/1 dim dusky o-yellow-orange *800.*
13m/4 smoky dusky o-yellow-orange *800.*
33m/2 dull dusky g-yellow-green *800.*
37m/1 dim dusky g-blue-green *800.*
43m/2 dull dusky green-blue *800.*
49m/0 dusky blue *800.*
49m/1 dim dusky blue *800.*
55m/2 dull dusky blue-violet *800.*
59m/2 dull dusky violet *800.*
65m/2 dull dusky r-red-violet *800.*
70i/0 deep violet-red-red *800.*

231-E8

Design size: 33x22mm
Incomplete engraving of entire design as adopted: value numerals same as on issued stamp but without thick shading bars at ends of outer frame rectangles, etc.

231-E8 2c Die on India, card mounted, sepia *1,500.*

232-E1

Design size: 33½x22mm
Silver print photo of vignette unadopted for any value (Columbus embarking on voyage of discovery), mounted on watercolor drawing of unadopted frame design.

232-E1 3c Die on stiff white drawing paper,
41x29mm, orange brown *4,000.*

Ferrotype metal plate showing 19x15mm outline of *Santa Maria* (reversed) in 33x15mm vignette frame, outline engraved and filled with red ink.

232-E2 3c Metal plate, 51x30mm *1,250.*

232-E3

Printing from ferrotype plate No. 232-E3.

232-E3 3c Die on stiff white card with rounded corners, 55x42mm, red *1,250.*

232-E4

Vignette size: 30x15mm
Die size: 74x61mm
Incomplete engraving of vignette as adopted: sky composed of horiz. ruled lines, no clouds.

232-E4 3c Die on India, die sunk on card
black *1,250.*
dark yellow-orange *1,250.*
sepia *1,750.*

232-E5

Engraved vignette similar to No. 232-E4 but with "1492 UNITED STATES OF AMERICA 1892" and scrolls around numerals engraved in outline only, pencil outline of frame.

232-E5 3c Die on thick artist's card with beveled edges, 50x38mm, black
brown *3,000.*

233-E1

Design size: 33½x22mm
Silver print photo of wash drawing of vignette as adopted, mounted on watercolor drawing of frame design as adopted but titled "COLUMBUS ON VOYAGE OF DISCOVERY. SHIPS AT SEA."

233-E1 4c Die on stiff white drawing paper,
41x29mm, brown red *4,750.*

233-E2

Design size: 33x22mm
Die size: 74x61½mm
Incomplete engraving of complete design as adopted: unfinished crosset shadows in lower corners.

Ridgway numbers used for some colors of No. 233-E2.

233-E2 4c
a. Die on India, die sunk on card
black *1,250.*
dark yellow orange *1,250.*
b. Die on thin white wove card, die sunk on card
1m/0 dusky red *800.*
3i/1 dim deep orange-red *800.*
3k/2 dull dark orange-red *800.*
5i/0 deep o-orange-red *800.*
9i/0 deep o-red-orange *800.*
9m/1 dim dusky o-red-orange *800.*
11i/0 deep orange *800.*
11k/1 dim dark orange *800.*
11m/2 dull dusky orange *800.*
13k/1 dim dark o-yellow-orange *800.*
13m/2 dull dusky o-yellow-orange *800.*
13k/3 dismal dark o-yellow-orange *800.*
13k/4 smoky dark o-yellow-orange *800.*
13m/4 smoky dusky o-yellow-orange *800.*
15m/2 dull dusky yellow-orange *800.*
33m/2 dull dusky g-yellow-green *800.*
35m/5 gloomy dusky green *800.*
37m/1 dim dusky g-blue-green *800.*
39m/1 dim dusky blue-green *800.*
41m/1 dim dusky b-blue-green *800.*
47m/0 dusky green-blue-blue *800.*
55m/2 dull dusky blue-violet *800.*
63m/2 dull dusky red-violet *800.*
69m/1 dull dusky red-violet-red *800.*
69k/3 dismal dark red-violet-red *800.*
71i/0 deep violet-red-red *800.*
71m/0 dusky violet-red-red *800.*
71o/5 black *800.*
ultramarine *800.*
violet *800.*
red violet *800.*
brown violet *800.*
orange brown *800.*
dark brown *800.*

234-E1

Design size: 38½x22mm
Engraved vignette as adopted, mounted on watercolor drawing of frame design similar to but longer than adopted. Vignette also used on No. 231-E3.

234-E1 5c Die on thick artist's card, block sunk as die essay, black brown *8,500.*

234-E2

Design size: 34x22½mm
Die size: 67x63mm
Engraved vignette as adopted, mounted on watercolor drawing of frame design as adopted, pencil "Oct. 5/92," approval monogram of J.D. Macdonough and ⅞x1 1/32 inches. Vignette also used on No. 231-E3.

234-E2 5c Die on thick artist's card, die sunk,
black brown & white *4,000.*

234-E3

Vignette size: 29½x15mm
Die size: 74x61½mm
Engraved vignette only as adopted.

234-E3 5c Die on India, die sunk on card, sepia *1,250.*

234-E4

Incomplete engraving of entire design: bench at left has horiz. shading only, incomplete shading in Columbus' face, etc.

234-E4 5c Die on 74x60mm India, on card
sepia *1,000.*
blue *1,000.*

235-E1

Ferrotype metal plate with engraved outline design (reversed) of vignette as used on 6c, engraved lines filled with red ink.

235-E1 6c Metal plate, 38x38mm *1,100.*

235-E2

Printing from ferrotype plate No. 235-E1.

235-E2 6c Die on stiff white card with rounded corners, 55x42mm, red *1,250.*

235-E3

Incomplete engraving of frame as adopted: unfinished crosset shadows in lower corners.

235-E3 6c Die on India, black *2,000.*

235-E4

Design size: 34x22mm
Die size: 73x60mm
Incomplete engraving of entire design as adopted: neck and shoulder of horse, side figures in niches, crosset shadows in lower corners all unfinished.

235-E4 6c Die on India, die sunk on card, blue violet *1,500.*

236-E1

Design size: 33½x22mm
Die size: 73x62mm
Design as adopted but frame incompletely engraved: unfinished crosset shadows in lower corners.

236-E1 8c Die on India, on card, black *2,500.*

236-E2

Design as adopted but frame incompletely engraved: unfinished crosset shadows in lower corners, incomplete gown at left and faces at right.

236-E2 8c Die on India, on card, black *1,000.*

237-E2

Ferrotype metal plate with engraved outline design (reversed) of vignette as used on 10c, engraved lines filled with red ink.

237-E2 10c Metal plate, 43x28mm *1,200.*

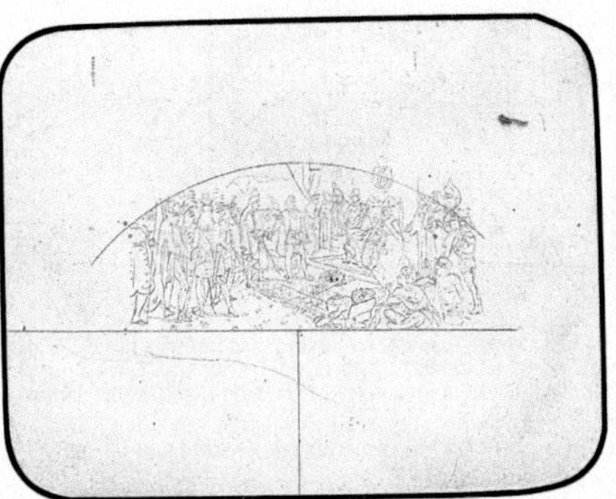

237-E3

Printing from ferrotype plate No. 237-E2.

237-E3 10c Die on stiff white card with rounded corners, 55x42mm, red *1,200.*

237-E4

Design size: 33x22mm
Die size: 74x62mm
Incomplete engraving of entire design as adopted: surroundings of Columbus, floor, etc., three figures behind King Ferdinand, crosset shadows in lower corners all unfinished.

237-E4 10c Die on India, card mounted
black brown *1,000.*
rose carmine *1,000.*

237-E5

Similar to No. 237-E4 but more completely engraved: missing lines on ankle bracelet of Indian, many details in vignette and crosset shadows in lower corners.

237-E5 10c Die on India, die sunk on card
black brown *1,500.*
carmine *1,500.*

238-E1

Design size: 33½x22mm
Silver print photo of vignette unadopted for any value (Columbus relating incidents of voyage to Ferdinand and Isabella), mounted on watercolor drawing of frame design similar to that adopted.

238-E1 15c Die on stiff white drawing paper, 42x30mm, bright ultramarine *5,000.*

238-E2

Vignette size: 30x15mm
Die size: 71x59mm
Incomplete engraving of vignette only as adopted: shading on Columbus' tunic and arms, Isabella's sholder, Ferdinand's robe, seated Indian's robe, robe of kneeling figure in lower left corner, etc., all unfinished.

238-E2 15c Die on India, die sunk on card, black brown *1,500.*

238-E3

Complete engraving of vignette adopted.

238-E3 15c Die on India, black brown *1,500.*

238-E4

Design size: 33½x22mm
Die size: 73½x62mm
Incomplete engraving of complete design as adopted: shading on Isabella's shoulder, Ferdinand's robe, seated Indian's blanket and crosset shadows in lower corners all unfinished.

238-E4 15c Die on India, on card
black brown *1,500.*
blue green *1,500.*

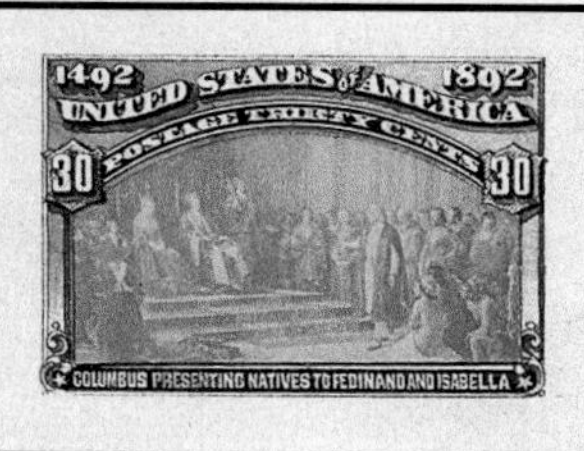
239-E1

Design size: 34½x22½mm
Silver print photo of vignette adopted for 15c, mounted on watercolor and ink drawing of unadopted frame design, titled "COLUMBUS PRESENTING NATIVES TO FERDINAND AND ISABELLA."

239-E1 30c Bluish gray on stiff white drawing paper, 42x30mm *5,000.*

239-E2

Ferrotype metal plate with engraved outline design (reversed) of vignette as used on 30c, engraved lines filled with red ink.

239-E2 30c Metal plate, 39x29mm *1,200.*

239-E3

Printing from ferrotype plate No. 239-E2.

239-E3 30c Die on stiff white card with rounded corners, 55x43mm, red *1,200.*

239-E4

Vignette size: 30x15mm
Die size: 74x62mm
Incomplete engraving of adopted vignette only: table cloth dark at top; horiz. lines on front edge of octagonal footstool, horiz. dots in shadow below windowsill at left, dots on top of head of man standing next to Columbus, etc., all missing.

239-E4 30c Die on India, die sunk on card, black *1,750.*

239-E5

Similar to No. 239-E4 but further engraved: has horiz. lines on front of footstool, etc. Eight pencil instructions for finishing vignette engraving written on large card backing, e.g., "Too much color on table cloth near top."

239-E5 30c Die on India, die sunk on 177x117mm card
black *2,000.*
black brown *2,000.*

239-E6

Design size: 33½x22mm
Die size: 74x63mm
Incomplete engraving of entire design as adopted: table cloth dark at top, diagonal dashes in one direction only between horiz. lines at lower left of vignette, etc.

239-E6 30c Die on India, die sunk on card
black *2,000.*
black brown *2,000.*

239-E7

Similar to No. 239-E6 but diagonal dashes in two directions, more dots on head and hand of man seated at near end of table.

239-E7 30c Die on India, die sunk on card
black brown *1,750.*
orange *1,750.*

239-E8

Incomplete engraving of entire design: window frame, horiz. shading lines on shoulder of man at right, vert. lines on front of table cloth below Columbus all missing. Lighter shading at top of table cloth as on issued stamp.

239-E8 30c Die on India, on card, orange *2,500.*

240-E1

Design size: 34x22mm
Die size: Incomplete engraving of entire design as adopted: unfinished shadows between right arm and body of man on donkey, distant object in front of bowing man's head darker than on issued stamp.

240-E1 50c Die on India, on card, slate blue *1,500.*

240-E2

Incomplete engraving of entire design: missing dots on donkey's flank and long lines on wrist of bowing man, no etching on two riders or their mounts.

240-E2 50c Die on India, on card, slate blue *1,500.*

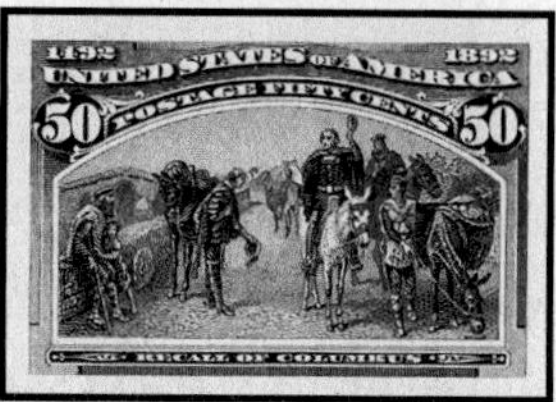
240-E3

Incomplete engraving of entire design: additional engraving on donkey's hindquarters and face of figure to left of Columbus.

240-E3 50c Die on India, on card, slate blue *1,500.*

241-E1

Ferrotype metal plate with engraved outline design (reversed) of vignette as used on $1, engraved lines filled with red ink.

241-E1 $1 Metal plate, 45x29mm *1,200.*

241-E2

Printing from ferrotype plate No. 241-E1.

241-E2 $1 Die on stiff white card with rounded corners, 55½x43mm, red *1,200.*

241-E3

Vignette size: 31x15mm
Die size: 72x59mm
Incomplete engraving of vignette only as adopted (very early state of die): very little shading on Isabella, floor, walls, etc.

241-E3 $1 Die on India, die sunk on card, black brown *2,000.*

241-E4

Incomplete engraving of entire design as adopted: shadow on table cloth, woman in front of table, crosslet shadows at lower corners all unfinished.

241-E4 $1 Die on India, on card, black brown *2,000.*

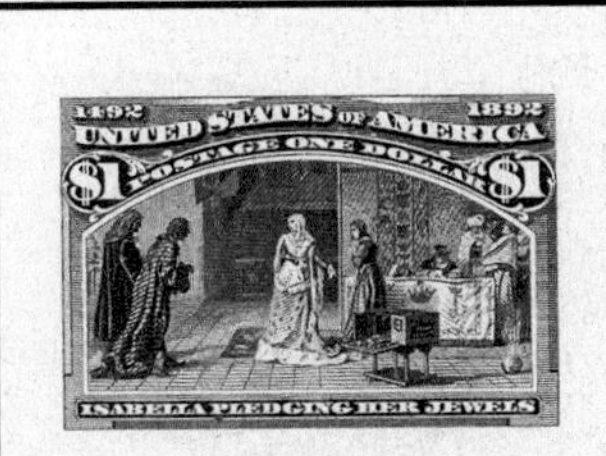
241-E5

Later state of complete design: horiz. lines in rectangle above Isabella missing.

241-E5 $1 Die on India, die sunk on 86x69mm card, black brown *2,000.*

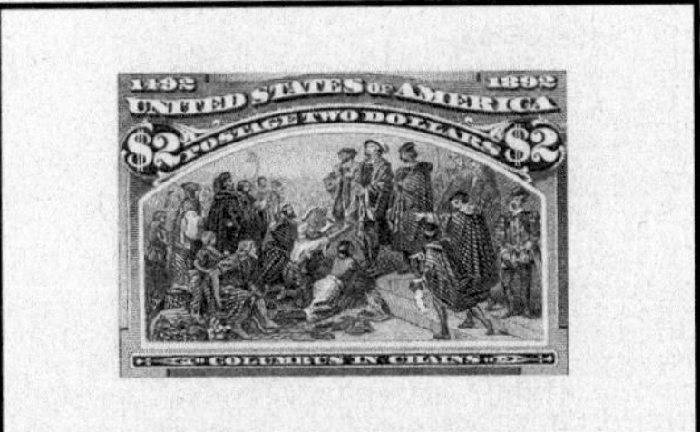
242-E1

Design size: 33½x22mm
Die size: 75x62mm
Incomplete engraving of entire design as adopted: about 12 horiz. lines missing on back of cape of tall man at right, some vert. dashes missing on corselet of soldier at right, incomplete foliage over "C" of "COLUMBUS," etc.

242-E1 $2 Die on India, die sunk on card
dull yellow orange *2,000.*
olive brown *2,000.*

243-E1

Ferrotype metal plate with engraved outline design (reversed) of vignette as used on $3, engraved lines filled with red wax.

243-E1 $3 Metal plate, 45x29mm *1,250.*

243-E2

Printing from ferrotype plate No. 243-E1.

243-E2 $3 Die on stiff white card with rounded corners, 55x43mm, red *1,250.*

243-E3

Design size: 33½x22mm
Incomplete engraving of entire design as adopted: unshaded crossets in lower corners, shading lines on crossets and frame above title label too light. Pencil marks correct these.

243-E3 $3 Die on India, die sunk on card, dark yellow green *1,500.*

243-E4

Incomplete engraving of entire design as adopted, before etching of shadows on Columbus, Ferdinand, backs of chairs, etc.

243-E4 $3 Die on India, on card, dark red *2,000.*

Ferrotype metal plate with engraved outline design (reversed) of Queen Isabella vignette as used on $4, engraved lines filled with red wax.

244-E1 $4 Metal plate, 33x44mm *1,500.*

244-E2

Printing from ferrotype plate No. 244-E1.

244-E2 $4 Die on stiff white card with rounded corners, 43x55mm, red *1,500.*

244-E3

Vignette diameter: 14mm
Incomplete engraving of Isabella head with background of uniform ruled horiz. lines only, blank circle for Columbus vignette at right adjoining.

244-E3 $4 Die on India, on card, black *3,000.*

Similar to No. 244-E3 but background has diagonal shading also.

244-E4 $4 Die on India, on card, black *3,000.*

244-E5

Design size: about 34x21½mm
Die size: 74½x61½mm
Incomplete engraving of vignettes and lettering only: no diagonal shading lines in background of Columbus vignette.

244-E5 $4 Die on India, die sunk on card
black *3,500.*
dark red *4,000.*

244-E6

Design size: 34x22mm
Same engraving as No. 244-E5 but with wash drawing of frame design as adopted.

244-E6 $4 Die on thick artist's card with beveled edges, 50x39mm, gray black *32,000.*

244-E7

Incomplete engraving of entire design as adopted: shadow at top of vert. bar and lines on leaves at bottom between vignettes unfinished; no circular line bordering vignette at Isabella's right shoulder.

244-E7 $4 Die on India, on card, black brown *2,000.*

244-E8

More complete engraving than No. 244-E7 but still missing circular line at Isabella's shoulder; only light shading on Columbus' collar.

244-E8 $4 Die on India, on card
black brown *2,000.*
dark red —

245-E1

Design size: 34½x22½mm
Incomplete engraved vignette as adopted for 1c: missing sky, etc., with pencil drawing of part of frame design.

245-E1 $5 Die on 50x38mm artist's cardboard, on thicker card, 55x43mm, black *4,000.*

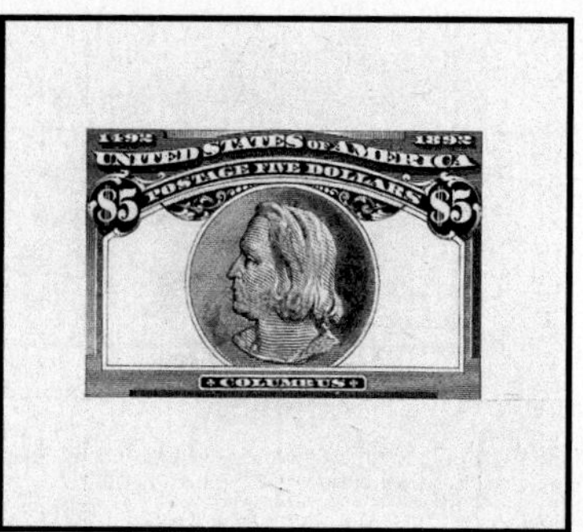

245-E2

Design size: 34x22½mm
Die size: 74½x61½mm
Incomplete engraving of vignette, lettering and frame as adopted (side panels blank): shading unfinished on Columbus' neck, hair and background, and with white and black wash touches.

245-E2 $5 Die on India, die sunk on card, black *3,000.*

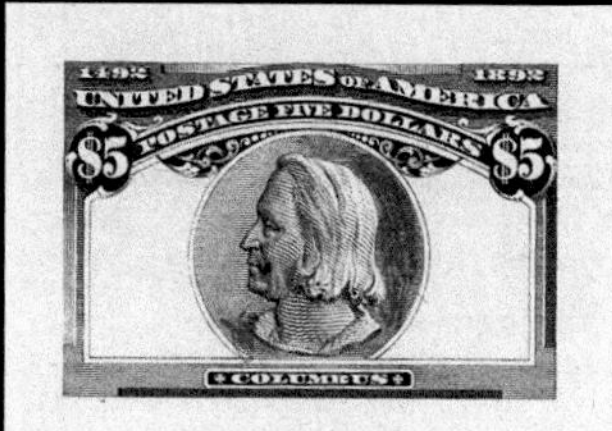

245-E3

Similar to No. 245-E2 but further engraved: shading lines on neck, diagonal lines in background, etc.

245-E3 $5 Die on India, on card, 65x54mm, black *3,000.*

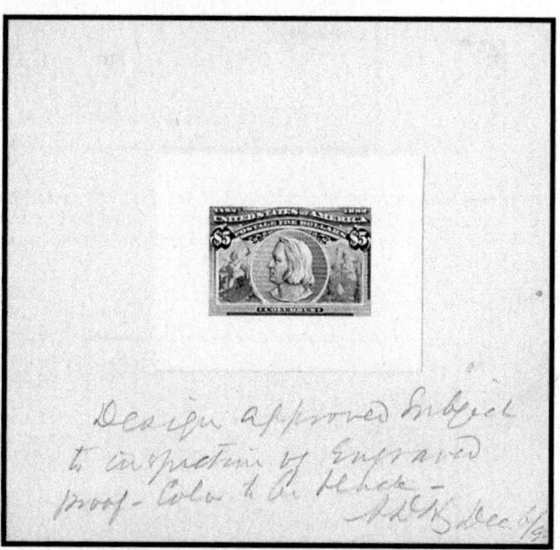

245-E4

Model with photos of female figures mounted each side of vignette, pencil "Design approved subject to inspection of engraved proof, color to be black. A.D.H. Dec. 6 '92" (A.D. Hazen, 3rd asst. PMG).

245-E4 $5 Die on thick white card, on 117x116mm card, black *3,750.*

245-E5

Engraving of No. 245-E3 with retouched photos of side subjects mounted in place.

245-E5 $5 Die on white artist's cardboard, 56½x46mm, die sunk on card, black *2,000.*

245-E6

Design size: 33½x22mm
Incomplete engraving of entire design: one line under "POSTAGE FIVE DOLLARS", no lines outside and no diagonal lines in sky to upper right and upper left of vignette, etc.

245-E6 $5 Die on India, on card, black *2,000.*

245-E7

Similar to No. 245-E2 but with pencil marks to show engraver where to place diagonal shading lines behind head and in front of bust.

245-E7 $5 Die on 65x55mm India, card mounted, black *3,000.*

245-E8

Similar to No. 245-E6 but with pencil marks and white ink suggestions for further engraving.

245-E8 $5 Die on India, die sunk on 83x68mm card, black *2,000.*

245-E9

Similar to No. 245-E6 but further engraved: with diagonal shading above side figures, below numerals and around vignette circle, but still incomplete in arched band above vignette.

245-E9 $5 Die on India, die sunk on 110x83mm card, black *2,000.*

245-E10

Similar to No. 245-E9 but further engraved: with shading lines in arched band above vignette but no shading on pole of liberty cap, object below shield has dotted shading only, spear tip shading incomplete.

245-E10 $5 Die on India, die sunk on 85x70mm card, black *2,000.*

1894 ISSUE
Bureau of Engraving and Printing

The 1c-15c designs of the 1890 issue engraved by the American Bank Note Co. were worked over by the BEP, including the addition of triangles in the upper corners. The 1890 30c was changed to a 50c and the 90c to a $1. Some 1894 essays have American Bank Note Co. imprints below the design.

247-E1

Design size: 18½x22mm
Die size: 61x62mm
Large die engraving of 1890 1c with pencil drawing of UL triangle 3½mm high with straight side next to curved upper label, freehand horiz. ink line at UR.

247-E1 1c Die on India, die sunk on card, black *3,000.*

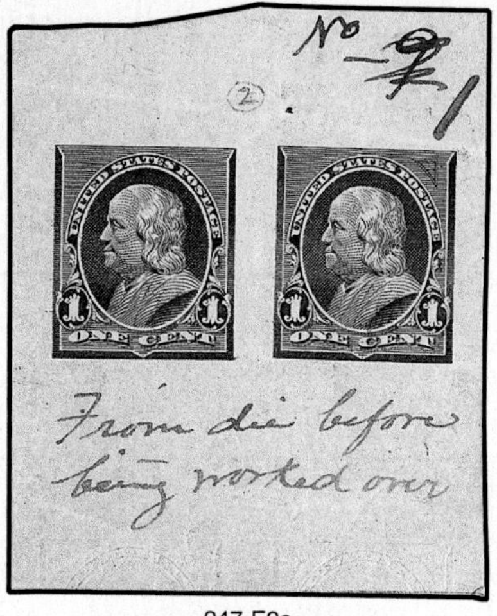

247-E2a

Experimental laydown die with 1890 1c proof 4mm to left of similar design with 15-line high type I triangle in UR corner. Same laydown die also contains two 2c designs 18mm below, 5½mm apart, either uninked or lightly inked in color of 1c (sometimes found separated from 1c designs). No. 247-E2b nearly always found cracked horiz. through designs.

247-E2 1c

a. Die on semiglazed white wove with pencil notations

blue	*1,850.*
ultramarine	*1,850.*

247-E2b

b. Die on white card with pencil notations re color

"1-1 Antwerp, 4 Ultra."	*1,500.*
"2--little lighter--"	*1,500.*
"1 Antwerp blue, 1 Ultra." (not cracked)	*1,750.*
"3 Ul. Blue, 1 Chinese Blue, 2 white"	*1,750.*
"4 Cobalt and Indigo"	*1,500.*
"No 5"	*1,500.*
"No. 6--Antwerp blue"	*1,500.*
"No. 6--with little Antwerp blue"	*1,500.*

247-E3

Die impression of 1890 1c with 15-line high type I triangle in UR corner.

247-E3 1c Die on India, 50x52mm, dusky green *2,500.*

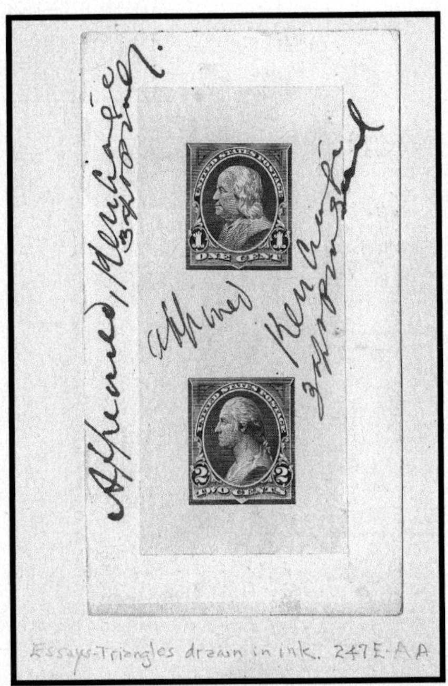

247-E4

Experimental die impression of single 1890 1c with 2c 18mm below, triangles added in ink to upper corners of both designs, ms. "Approved" notations.

247-E4 1c +2c, Die on India, mounted on 57x102mm card, mounted on another card, 144x195mm

green	*4,250.*
dull violet (without added triangles)	*4,000.*

247-E5

Large die engraving of 1890 1c with 18-line high triangle in UL corner (inner lines very thick).

247-E5 1c Die on India, die sunk on card, dusky blue green *1,500.*

247-E6

Similar to No. 247-E5 but inner line of triangle almost as thin as outer line.

247-E6 1c Die on India, die sunk on card, dusky blue green *1,500.*

247-E7

Similar to No. 247-E6 but inner line of triangle same thickness as adopted.

247-E7 1c Die on India, die sunk on card, dusky blue green *1,250.*

247-E8

Incomplete engraving of entire design as adopted including triangles: coat collar, scroll under "U," horiz. lines on frame, oval line of vignette, etc., all unfinished; vignette background not re-etched.

247-E8 1c Die on India, die sunk on card

ultramarine	*1,000.*
blue ("Cobalt 2--Indigo 4")	*1,250.*
dusky blue green	*1,000.*

250-E1

Design size: 18½x22mm
Die size: 61x62½mm
Large die engraving of 1890 2c with pencil drawing of UL triangle 2½mm high.

250-E1 2c Die on India, die sunk on card, black *2,300.*

250-E2

Die width: 92mm
Experimental laydown die with 1890 2c proof 5½mm to left of similar design with 14-line high type I triangles in upper corners (found cut apart from No. 247-E2 and used for trial colors as noted thereon in pencil).

250-E2 2c Die on white card

"1 R&D Lake, 1½P. white"	*2,000.*
"M3 1 white, 7 Gem Lake, ¼ Car. Lake"	*2,000.*
"2 White, 4 Ger. Lake No. 1, ½ R&D Lake"	*2,000.*
"Opal Red"	*2,000.*
"Opal Orange"	*2,000.*
"Opal Maroon"	*2,000.*

250-E3

Die size: 61½x62½mm
American Banknote Co. die No. C-224 annealed, with 18-line high type I triangles engraved in upper corners, ms "No. 1" at lower left of card backing.

250-E3 2c Die on India, die sunk on card

medium deep red	*1,250.*
deep red	*1,250.*
dusky red	*1,250.*
dim red	*1,250.*
medium deep orange-red	*1,250.*
deep o-orange-red	*1,250.*
dusky g-blue-green	*1,250.*
dark medium violet-red-red	*1,250.*

250-E4

Incomplete engraving of entire design: shadows on frame not etched; lines on foliage, front collar and oval line at vignette bottom not recut; dots instead of lines over corner of eye; only one line on truncated scroll at left of right 2 and no line on similar scroll at right of left 2; shadows of TWO CENTS not etched.

250-E4 2c Die on India, die sunk on card

bright red	*1,250.*
light red	*1,250.*
dark red	*1,250.*
deep orange red	*1,250.*

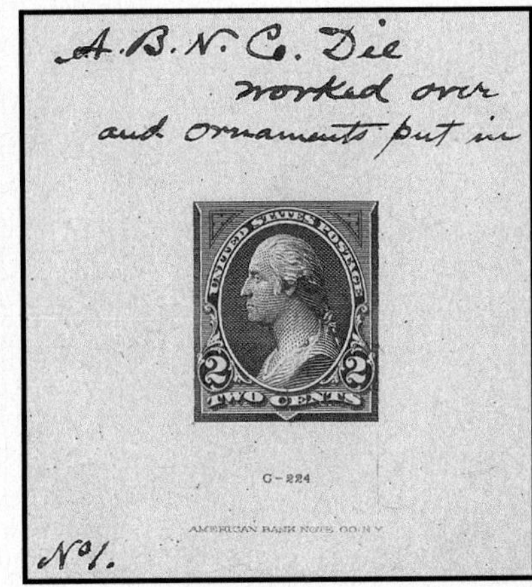

250-E5

Similar to No. 250-E4 but line added to scroll at right of left 2, ms. "A.B.N.Co. Die worked over and ornaments put in" at top, ms. "No. 1" at lower left.

250-E5 2c medium deep red *1,250.*

250-E6

Incomplete engraving of entire design: two lines on truncated scroll at left of right 2 (one later removed), scroll at left of right 2 unfinished, profile of nose and forehead darker than on issued stamp, shadows of "TWO CENTS" not etched, short dashes on inside of outer edge of white oval at lower right, veins on scrolls around 2s not recut. Pencil notations incl. "Old A.B.N.Co. annealed & triangles engraved and rehardened to take up roll for plate."

250-E6 2c Die on India, die sunk on card, medium deep red *1,250.*

250-E7

Incomplete engraving of entire design: bottom of ear still angular and not yet rounded, dots on lobe not yet gathered into two lines, dot shading under corner of eye not yet gathered into four lines, shadows of "TWO CENTS" have been etched.

250-E7 2c Die on India, die sunk on card, medium deep red *1,000.*

251-E1

Die size: 57x76mm
Incomplete engraving of entire design with type II triangles: top of head not silhouetted. Pencil notation "2/ Transfer from roll taken from No. 1 so as to change portrait and make cameo effect. Unfinished."

251-E1 2c Die on India, die sunk on card
dark violet red *1,000.*
light carmine *1,000.*

251-E2

Similar to No. 251-E1 but hair in front of ear unfinished, forehead and hair lightened.

251-E2 2c Die on India, die sunk on card, dusky gray *1,250.*

251-E3

Similar to No. 251-E1, made from hardened die, penciled "(Old) No. 2 / Hard" plus suggestions for strengthening design - drawings of nose and eye.

251-E3 2c Die on India, on 55x73mm card, light carmine *1,000.*

252-E1

Die size: 57x81mm
Incomplete engraving of entire design with type III triangles: top of head not silhouetted, unfinished shadow over eye, etc.

252-E1 2c Die on India, die sunk on card, medium deep red *1,000.*

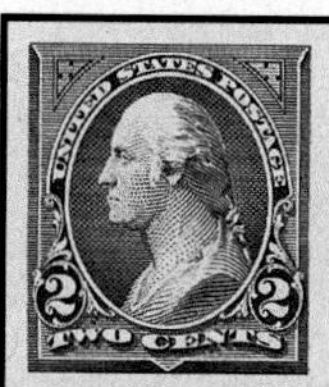

252-E2

Incomplete engraving of entire design with type III triangles: unfinished shadow over eye, etc.

252-E2 2c Die on India, die sunk on card
dusky blue green *2,000.*
dark violet red *1,000.*

252-E3

Design size: 19x22mm
Die size: 56x80½mm
Discarded die, vignette overengraved: too much shading on front hair, cheek, nose, below eye; background too dark; hair in front of ear very prominent.

252-E3 2c Die on India, die sunk on card
light carmine *3,000.*
green, not on card (unique) *3,750.*

253-E1

Die size: 60x63mm
Complete engraved design as adopted but with type II triangles.

253-E1 3c
a. Die on India, die sunk on card
dusky blue green *1,250.*
dark red violet *1,000.*
dusky red violet *1,000.*
b. Die printed directly on card, die sunk on card, violet *1,250.*

254-E1

Design size: about 19x22mm
Die size: 61x63mm
Incomplete engraving of entire design: line under collar wings missing, oval line around vignette not recut; hair, beard, forehead, neck, collar, shirt, etc., all incomplete.

254-E1 4c Die on India, die sunk on card, dark yellow brown *1,500.*

Entire design engraved further than No. 254-E1 but still incomplete: shadows in lettering, etc., not etched, faint lines under collar incomplete, oval around vignette not recut.

254-E2 4c Die on India, die sunk on card, dark yellow brown *1,500.*

254-E3

Entire design engraved further than No. 254-E2 but still incomplete: beard, collar and necktie, etc., unfinished. Some veins recut on foliage under oval label.

254-E3 4c Die on India, die sunk on card, black brown *1,500.*

255-E1

Design size: 19x22mm
Engraved frame of American Bank Note Co. die No. C-227 with triangles, vignette cut out, mounted over engraved vignette of Washington.

255-E1 5c Die on 41x53mm India, on white wove, 48x75mm, black *2,750.*

255-E2

Washington vignette only as on No. 255-E1.

255-E2 5c Die on India, 56-69mm, green *2,000.*

255-E3

Design size: 19x22mm
Engraved frame as adopted with William H. Seward photo mounted on it.

255-E3 5c Die on India, cut close, mounted on 74x84mm white card, black *5,000.*

255-E4

Design size: about 19x22mm
Die size: 62½x75mm
Incomplete engraving of entire design as adopted: no oval border line around vignette.

255-E4 5c Die on India, die sunk on card, orange brown *1,000.*

256-E1

Design size: about 19x22mm
Die size: 62x61½mm
Incomplete engraving of entire design as adopted: white spot on eye and shadows not darkened, diagonal lines missing on beard under mouth, lines on coat unfinished, pencil notations and date "1894" below design.

256-E1 6c Die on India, die sunk on card, dark red *1,250.*

256-E2

Entire design engraved further than No. 256-E1 but still incomplete: diagonal lines on beard under mouth incomplete, lines on coat not as dark as on issued stamp.

256-E2 6c Die on India, die sunk on card, dim dusky red *1,000.*

257-E1

Design size: about 19x22mm
Die size: 58½x60mm
Incomplete engraving of entire design as adopted: lines on coat not recut darker, vignette background not etched darker.

257-E1 8c Die on India, die sunk on card, dusky red violet *1,000.*

258-E1

Design size: about 19x22mm
Die size: 61½x61½mm
Incomplete engraving of entire design as adopted: shading unfinished on cheek, in ear, etc.

258-E1 10c Die on India, die sunk on card, dark brown *1,500.*

Entire design engraved further than No. 258-E1 but still incomplete: unfinished shading on cheek under eye.

258-E2 10c Die on India, die sunk on card, red brown *1,500.*

260-E1

Die impression of 30c No. 228 with "THIRTY CENTS" crossed out by ink, ms "On roll without the head take out ornament."

260-E1 (50c) Die on India (torn before affixing), on 77x77mm card, black *1,500.*

260-E2

Entire design engraved, but without triangles at top corners.

260-E2 50c Die on India, die sunk on 70x115mm card, dark green *2,400.*

261-E1

Design size: 19x22mm
Die size: 50x101mm
Large die engraving of 1890 90c with value label and figure circles blank, no triangles.

261-E1 $1 Die on India, die sunk on card, black *2,250.*

261-E2

Similar to No. 261-E1 but head further re-engraved and background shadows etched deeper.

261-E2 $1 Die on India, die sunk on card, blue green *2,250.*

261-E3

Design size: 19x22mm
Model of engraved Perry vignette mounted on 1890 engraved frame with penciled in triangles, values painted in white and black. Ms. "O.K. July 14/94 TFM" below.

261-E3 $1 Die on India, cut close, mounted on 63x101mm white card, green vignette, black frame *2,000.*

261-E4

Similar to No. 261-E3 but with value lettering and circles added, background of circles unfinished, no triangles.

261-E4 $1 Die on India, die sunk on card, dark indigo blue *2,000.*

261-E4A

Similar to No. 261-E4 but with engraved triangles added, tiny white space above each numeral.

261-E4A $1 Die on India, die sunk on 67x122mm card, deep blue green *3,500.*

261-E5

Incomplete engraving of entire design: hair on top and back of head, whiskers and back of neck, and shading in value circles all unfinished. Triangles are engraved.

261-E5 $1 Die on India, die sunk on card
black 2,000.
orange 2,000.

261-E6

Similar to No. 261-E5 but hair at back of head and whiskers darker, face in front of whiskers darker as on issued stamp. Circular lines extend into colorless vignette oval.

261-E6 $1 Die on India, die sunk on card
black 2,000.
blue green 2,000.

261-E7

Design size: 19x21½mm
Die size: 49x100mm
Incomplete engraving of unadopted dollar value design with portrait of Sen. James B. Beck: value label and numerals blank.

261-E7 $1 Die on India, die sunk on card, black 4,000.

262-E1

Design size: 19x22mm
Die size: 50x101mm
Incomplete engraving of frame only nearly as adopted: smaller $2's.

262-E1 $2 Die on India, die sunk on card, blue green 3,000.

262-E2

Design size: 19x22mm
Die size: 51x112mm
Incomplete engraving of entire design: left value circle blank, right circle engraved $2 outline only, signed by engraver "Lyman F. Ellis."

262-E2 $2 Die on India, die sunk on card, black 3,000.

262-E3

Die size: 51x112mm
Incomplete engraving of entire design: vignette shading unfinished, no veins in leaves around value circles.

262-E3 $2 Die on India, die sunk on card, black 2,500.

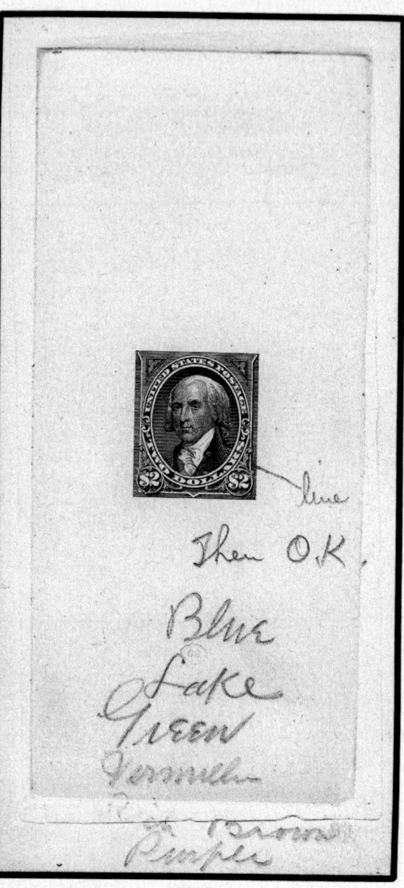

262-E4

Incomplete engraving of entire design: inside of right border line above $2 unfinished, with pencil "line" instruction for border line strengthening, plus penciled "Then O.K./Blue/Lake/Green/Vermilion/Brown/Purple."

262-E4 $2 Die on India, die sunk on 62x128mm card, black 2,500.

Similar to No. 262-E4 but border line complete.

262-E5 $2 Die on India, die sunk on card, black 2,500.

263-E1

263-E1a

Die size: 50x112½mm
Incomplete engraving of entire design: only one line in each scroll at right and left of $5, inner line of right border above $5 unfinished, etc., veins on leaves around right value circle unfinished.

263-E1 $5 Die on India, die sunk on card, black 3,000.
a. With photographic portrait of Marshall affixed as vignette with paper hinge 2,500.

263-E2

Similar to No. 263-E1 but horiz. lines cut into oval line at top and inner oval line above L and R of DOLLARS required retouching as indicated by pencil instructions. Two lines in scrolls around value circles as adopted.

263-E2 $5 Die on India, die sunk on card, black 3,000.

The bicolored essays commonly offered as No. 285-293 bicolored proofs can be found under the following listings: Nos. 285-E8, 286-E8, 287-E9, 288-E5, 289-E4, 290-E4, 291-E8, 292-E6, 293-E7. Values are for full-size cards (approximately 8x6 inches).

TRANS-MISSISSIPPI ISSUE

285-E1

Die size: 79x68mm
Incomplete engraving of vignette only: initial state of die, no lines in sky or water.

285-E1 1c Die on India, die sunk on 151x97mm card, black 2,500.

285-E2

Vignette further engraved: lines in sky and water.

285-E2 1c Die on India, die sunk on card, black *2,500.*

285-E3

Vignette further engraved: more background lines added.

285-E3 1c Die on India, die sunk on card, black *2,500.*

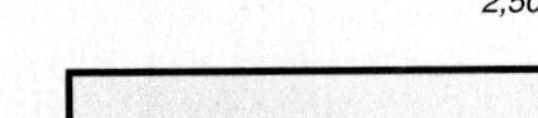

285-E4

Vignette further engraved: Indian at right darker, robe shadow etched.

285-E4 1c Die on India, die sunk on card, black *2,500.*

285-E5

Vignette further engraved: rock in water more complete.

285-E5 1c Die on India, die sunk on card, black *2,500.*

285-E6

Design size: 34x22mm
Die size: 73x62mm
Incomplete bicolor engraving of entire design: no second inner line in numerals.

285-E6 1c Die on India, die sunk on card, orange red & black *2,500.*

Die size: 83x68mm
Incomplete engraving of entire design: vignette unfinished and unetched, frame has second inner line in numerals.

285-E7 1c Die on India, die sunk on card, black *3,500.*

285-E8

Die size: 63x51mm
Complete bicolor engraving of entire design.

285-E8 1c Die with black vignette on India, die sunk on card

dark yellow green ("normal" bicolor)	*750.*
dusky green	*2,000.*
dusky blue green	*2,000.*
brown	*2,000.*

285-E9

Die size: 88x70mm
Incomplete engraving of entire design: corn husks and panels in ends of cartouche unfinished, lines under MARQUETTE and MISSISSIPPI not as thick as on completed die.

285-E9 1c Die on India, die sunk on card, dusky green *2,500.*

285-E10

Unfinished frame in red brown missing second inner line in numerals, with black unfinished "Cattle in the Storm" vignette as used on the $1 value, foreground snow at left incomplete.

285-E10 1c Die on India, red brown & black 3,500.

286-E1

Die size: 78x68mm
Incomplete engraving of Mississippi River Bridge vignette (originally intended for 2c but eventually used on $2): initial state of die, very lightly engraved.

286-E1 2c Die on India, die sunk on card, black *3,750.*

286-E2

Vignette further engraved but no lines on bridge beside two trolley cars.

286-E2 2c Die on India, die sunk on card, black *5,000.*

286-E3

Vignette further engraved but foreground between bridge and boat and foretopdeck incomplete, horse truck visible (later removed).

286-E3 2c Die on India, die sunk on card, black *3,000.*

Complete engraving of vignette only.

286-E4 2c Die on India, die sunk on card, black *3,000.*

286-E5

Design size: 137x88½mm
Pencil sketch by R. Ostrander Smith of 2c frame design as adopted except titled "ST. LOUIS BRIDGE."

286-E5 2c Sketch on tracing paper, 178x120mm *1,500.*

286-E6

Design size: 137x89mm
Complete pencil drawing by R.O. Smith of frame design ("P" of "POSTAGE" in ink), titled "ST. LOUIS BRIDGE."

286-E6 2c Drawing on Whatman drawing board, 1889 wmk., 217x163mm *1,500.*

286-E7

Pencil drawing by R.O. Smith, no title.

286-E7 2c Drawing on 72x61mm tracing paper *1,500.*

286-E7A

Ink and wash drawing of frame, stamp size, similar to adopted design.

286-E7A 2c Drawing on hard, thick paper, black *11,000.*

286-E8

Die size: 63x51mm
Complete bicolor engraving of 2c design but with Mississippi River Bridge vignette as used on $2.

Ridgway numbers used for colors of No. 286-E8.

286-E8 2c Die with black vignette on India, die sunk on card

dark red ("normal" bicolor)	750.
3k/0 dark orange red	2,000.
5k/0 dark o-orange-red	2,000.
5m/1 dim dusky o-orange-red	2,000.
7i/0 deep red orange	2,000.
7m/0 dusky red orange	2,000.
9m/0 dusky o-red-orange	2,000.
9k/2 dull dark o-red-orange	2,000.
13m/3 dismal dusky o-yellow-orange	2,000.
35m/1 dim dusky green	2,000.
49m/1 dim v. dusky blue	2,000.
63m/1 dim dusky red violet	2,000.
71-/0 deep violet-red-red	2,000.

287-E1

Design size: 28x16.5mm
Die No. 259 size: 77x70mm
Initial state of die, very lightly engraved.

287-E1 4c Die on India, die sunk on card, black 3,000.

287-E2

Vignette further engraved: sky lines ruled in.

287-E2 4c Die on India, die sunk on card, black 3,000.

287-E3

Vignette further engraved: more lines added, no right forefoot on bison.

287-E3 4c Die on India, die sunk on card, black 4,500.

287-E4

Shadow under bison incomplete.

287-E4 4c Die on India, die sunk on card, black 3,750.

287-E5

Shadow under bison and foreground penciled in.

287-E5 4c Die on India, die sunk on card, black 3,750.

287-E6

Vignette further engraved: right forefoot added, shadow under bison engraved but not etched.

287-E6 4c Die on India, die sunk on card, black 3,750.

287-E7

Die size: 83x67mm
Incomplete engraving of entire design: no lines in sky, frame shadow etching unfinished.

287-E7 4c Die on India, die sunk on card

black	3,500.
deep orange	3,500.

287-E8

Die size: 63x51mm
Incomplete engraving of entire design: corn husks at lower sides of frame unfinished.

Ridgway numbers used for colors of No. 287-E8.

287-E8 4c Die with black vignette on India, die sunk on card

5k/0 dark o-orange-red	2,000.
5m/0 dusky o-orange-red	2,000.
7m/0 dusky red orange	2,000.
11o/2 dull v. dusky orange	2,000.
13m/3 dismal dusky o-yellow-orange	2,000.
35m/1 dim dusky green	2,000.
39m/1 dim dusky blue green	2,000.
49o/1 dim v. dusky blue	2,000.
61k/1 dim dark violet-red violet	2,000.
63m/1 dim dusky red violet	2,000.
71m/0 dusky violet-red-red	2,000.

287-E9

Die size: 62x51mm
Complete bicolor engraving.

287-E9 4c Die with black vignette on India, die sunk on card

red orange ("normal" bicolor)	550.
deep red orange ("normal" bicolor)	550.

288-E1

Die size: 75x68mm
Initial state of die, very lightly engraved.

288-E1 5c Die on India, die sunk on card, black 3,500.

288-E2

Vignette further engraved: lower clouds at right darkened.

288-E2 5c Die on India, die sunk on card, black 5,500.

288-E3

Vignette further engraved: shading penciled in on figures at right, etc.

288-E3 5c Die on India, die sunk on card, black 3,750.

288-E4

Vignette further engraved but dots in sky at left of flag unfinished.

288-E4 5c Die on India, die sunk on card, black 3,750.

288-E5

Design size: 34x22mm
Die size: 63x51mm
Incomplete bicolor engraving of entire design: unfinished crosshatching at left of "FREMONT," lines against bottom label and frame unfinished, no etching on flag.

Ridgway numbers used for colors of No. 288-E5.

288-E5 5c Die with black vignette on India, die sunk on card

49m/1 dim dusky blue ("normal" bicolor)	750.
49k/1 dim dark blue ("normal" bicolor)	750.
3k/0 dark orange red	2,000.
3m/0 dusky orange red	2,000.
7m/0 dusky red orange	2,000.
7m/1 dim dusky red orange	2,000.
9m/0 dusky o-red-orange	2,000.
11o/2 dull v. dusky orange	2,000.
37m/1 dim dusky g-blue-green	2,000.
39m/1 dim dusky blue green	2,000.
49o/1 dim v. dusky blue	2,000.
63m/1 dim dusky red violet	2,000.
71n/0 medium deep violet-red-red	2,000.
35m/1 dim dusky green	2,000.

288-E7

Die size: 82x68 ½mm
Incomplete engraving of entire design: cornhusks, panels at ends of cartouche, mountains, foreground at sides of title label, sky, etc., all unfinished, figures and mountains not etched dark.

288-E7 5c Die on India, die sunk on card, black 3,250.

Incomplete engraving of vignette: no dots on mountain tops next to right border, unfinished crosshatching at left end of title label.

288-E8 5c Die on India, die sunk on card, black 3,750.

289-E1

Engraved vignette only of mounted Indian, not used for any value.

289-E1 8c Die on India, on card, black *7,500.*

289-E2

Incomplete engraving of vignette only as adopted: blank area for label wider than completed bicolor vignette, knee of kneeling soldier unfinished, etc.

289-E2 8c Die on India, die sunk on card, black *3,000.*

289-E3

Design size: about 33½x21½mm
Incomplete engraving of frame only: shading of sunken center of cartouche at right of vignette unfinished.

289-E3 8c Die on India, 37x26mm, black *3,000.*

289-E4

Incomplete engraving of entire design: top row of distant shrubbery under "ERICA" missing, crosshatching on distant mountains at left, blades of grass at left end of label, some dots against top label all unfinished.

Ridgway numbers used for colors of No. 289-E4.

289-E4 8c Die with black vignette on India, die sunk on card

dark red ("normal" bicolor)	*750.*
dusky red ("normal" bicolor)	*750.*
3m/0 dusky orange red	*2,750.*
5m/0 dusky o-orange-red	*2,750.*
7i/0 deep red orange	*2,750.*
7m/0 dusky red orange	*2,750.*
9m/0 dusky o-red-orange	*2,750.*
11o/2 dull v. dusky orange	*2,750.*
35m/1 dim dusky green	*2,750.*
39m/1 dim dusky blue-green	*2,750.*
49o/1 dim v. dusky blue	*2,750.*
63m/1 dim dusky red violet	*2,750.*
71-/0 deep violet-red-red	*2,750.*

290-E1

Die size: 77x64mm
Incomplete engraving of vignette only: two rows of dots in sky over wagon.

290-E1 10c Die on India, die sunk on card, black *8,500.*

290-E2

Vignette further engraved: three rows of dots in sky over wagon.

290-E2 10c Die on India, die sunk on card, black *3,750.*

290-E3

Vignette further engraved: front of wagon canvas crosshatched.

290-E3 10c Die on India, die sunk on card, black *3,750.*

290-E4

Incomplete bicolor engraving of entire design: cornhusks unfinished, blades of grass to right of girl's feet and some to right of dark horse's feet are missing. Five lines of dots in sky over wagon.

Ridgway numbers used for colors of No. 290-E4.

290-E4 10c Die with black vignette on India, die sunk on card

dull dusky violet blue ("normal" bicolor)	*750.*
dusky blue violet ("normal" bicolor)	*750.*
1i/0 deep red	*2,500.*
3k/0 dark orange red	*2,500.*
5k/0 dark o-orange-red	*2,500.*
5m/0 dusky o-orange-red	*2,500.*
7i/0 deep red orange	*2,500.*
9m/0 dusky o-red-orange	*2,500.*
11o/2 dull v. dusky orange	*2,500.*
35m/1 dim dusky green	*2,500.*
39m/1 dim dusky blue green	*2,500.*
49o/1 dim v. dusky blue	*2,500.*
55m/2 smoky dark v.-blue violet	*2,500.*
63m/1 dim dusky red violet	*2,500.*
71-/0 deep violet-red-red	*2,500.*

290-E6

Incomplete engraving of entire design: cornhusks unfinished, vignette from No. 290-E4 trimmed by engraving to fit frame.

290-E6 10c Die on India, die sunk on card, black brown *3,000.*

Incomplete engraving of entire design: cornhusks and panels at ends of cartouche and both sides and botton of vignette next to border unfinished.

290-E7 10c Die on India, die sunk on card, dull red violet *3,000.*

290-E8

Incomplete engraving of entire design: cornhusks and both sides and bottom of vignette next to border are unfinished, vert. lines on cartouche frame at right of vignette missing.

290-E8 10c Die on India, dull red violet *3,000.*

291-E1

Die size: 76x68mm
Incomplete engraving of vignette only: without sky or mountains.

291-E1 50c Die on India, die sunk on card, black *3,750.*

291-E2

Vignette further engraved: sky ruled in.

291-E2 50c Die on India, die sunk on card, black *3,750.*

291-E3

Vignette further engraved but no shading on distant mountains.

291-E3 50c Die on India, die sunk on card, black *3,750.*

291-E4

Vignette further engraved: light shading on distant mountains.

291-E4 50c Die on India, die sunk on card, black *3,750.*

291-E5

Vignette further engraved: more shading on distant mountains.

291-E5 50c Die on India, die sunk on card, black *3,750.*

291-E6

Vignette further engraved: shadows on miner's hat darker (etched).

291-E6 50c Die on India, die sunk on card, black *3,750.*

291-E7

Vignette further engraved: girth under donkey darkened.

291-E7 50c Die on India, die sunk on card, black *9,000.*

291-E8

Design size: 34x22mm
Die size: 89x71mm
Incomplete bicolor engraving of entire design: shading lines on scroll in LR corner of frame and shrubbery in UL corner of vignette unfinished, sky incomplete.

Ridgway numbers used for colors of No. 291-E8.

291-E8 50c Die with black vignette on India, die sunk on card
dull dusky b-blue-green ("normal" bicolor; die size: 63x51mm) *750.*
dull dusky g-blue-green ("normal" bicolor; die size: 63x51mm) *750.*
1i/0 deep red *2,500.*
3k/0 dark orange red *2,500.*
5m/0 dusky o-orange-red *2,500.*
7m/0 dusky red orange *2,500.*
9i/0 deep o-yellow-orange *2,500.*
9m/0 dusky o-red-orange *2,500.*
11m/2 dull dusky orange *2,500.*
13m/3 dismal dusky o-yellow-orange *2,500.*
35m/1 dim dusky green *2,500.*
39m/1 dim dusky blue green *2,500.*
47n/2 dull v. dusky green-blue blue *2,500.*
49o/1 dim v. dusky blue *2,500.*
61k/1 dim dark violet-red-violet *2,500.*
71m/0 dusky violet-red-red *2,500.*

291-E9

Incomplete engraving of entire design: vignette against top frame unfinished.

291-E9 50c Die on India, die sunk on card
black *3,000.*
deep red orange *3,000.*

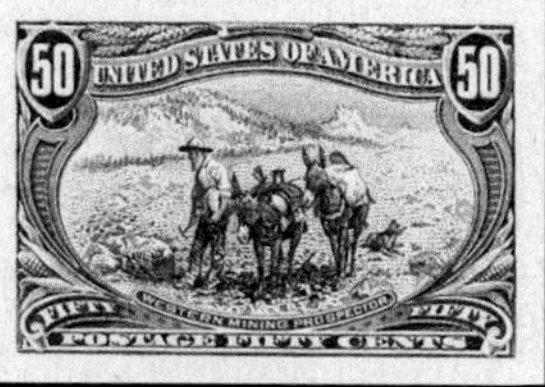

291-E10

Incomplete engraving of entire design: engraving on bottom of miner's pan dots only, not lines as on issued stamp.

291-E10 50c Die on wove, dark green *3,000.*

292-E1

Incomplete engraving of vignette only: initial state of die, lightly engraved.

292-E1 $1 Die on India, die sunk on card, black *6,500.*

292-E2

Vignette further engraved: light shield-shaped vignette outline (later removed.)

292-E2 $1 Die on India, die sunk on card, black *7,500.*

292-E3

Vignette further engraved: left front hoof of lead bull darker.

292-E3 $1 Die on India, die sunk on card, black *3,750.*

Vignette similar to No. 292-E3 but with penciled modeling in snow and among cattle.

292-E4 $1 Die on India, die sunk on card, black *3,750.*

292-E5

Vignette further engraved: foreground snow at left darkened, shield outline removed.

292-E5 $1 Die on India, die sunk on card, black *9,500.*

292-E6

Incomplete engraving of entire bicolored design: right cornhusk and sky against top of frame unfinished, bull's right forefoot does not touch frame, foreground at right end of label unfinished.

Ridgway numbers used for colors of No. 292-E6, where available.

292-E6 $1 Die with black vignette on India, die sunk on card
dull violet blue ("normal" bicolor) *750.*
dull blue ("normal" bicolor) *750.*
dull violet ("normal" bicolor) *3,000.*
3k/0 dark orange red *3,000.*
5m/0 dusky-o-orange-red *3,000.*
7m/0 dusky red orange *3,000.*
9m/0 dusky o-red-orange *3,000.*
9n/3 dismal v. dusky o-red-orange *3,000.*
13n/3 dismal v. dusky o-yellow-orange *3,000.*
35m/1 dim dusky green *3,000.*
43m/1 dim dusky green blue *3,000.*
49m/1 dim dusky blue *3,000.*
57k/4 smoky dark violet-blue violet *3,000.*
63m/1 dim dusky red violet *3,000.*
71-/0 violet-red-red *3,000.*
47n/2 dull dusky green blue *3,000.*
dark brown *3,000.*

292-E7

Incomplete engraving of entire design: left frameline, cornhusks and shading in frame over cornhusks all unfinished.

292-E7 $1 Die on India, die sunk on card, dusky red orange *3,000.*

293-E1

Design size: 34x22mm
Die size: 73x63mm

Vignette of Western mining prospector as used on 50c, but labeled HARVESTING IN THE WEST, frame shows $ same size as numeral 2.

293-E1 $2 Die on India, on card, dusky violet & black *3,500.*

293-E2

Die size: 77x66mm
Incomplete engraving of Farming in the West vignette (originally intended for $2 but eventually used on 2c): initial state of die, very lightly engraved.

293-E2 $2 Die on India, die sunk on card, black *3,000.*

293-E3

Vignette further engraved: four horses shaded.

293-E3 $2 Die on India, die sunk on card, black *3,000.*

293-E4

Vignette further engraved: shading added to background figures and horses, pencil shading above and below half horse at left.

293-E4 $2 Die on India, die sunk on card, black *3,000.*

293-E5

Vignette further engraved: foreground and shadows under horse teams darkened, no shading dots above half horse at left, etc.

293-E5 $2 Die on India, die sunk on card, black *3,000.*

293-E6

Vignette further engraved but foreground in front of plow wheel still unfinished.

293-E6 $2 Die on India, die sunk on card, black *3,000.*

293-E7

Die size: 62x51mm
Incomplete engraving of entire bicolor design: only one plowshare shown, label longer, less foreground than on issued stamp.

Ridgway numbers used for colors of No. 293-E7.

293-E7	$2 Die with black vignette on India, die sunk on card	
	dusky orange red ("normal" bicolor; die size: 63x61mm)	*750.*
	dark red orange ("normal" bicolor; die size: 63x61mm)	*750.*
	1-/0 red	*3,000.*
	3k/0 dark orange red	*3,000.*
	7m/0 dusky red orange	*3,000.*
	35m/1 dim dusky green	*3,000.*
	39m/1 dim dusky blue green	*3,000.*
	45o/1 dim v. dusky blue-green blue	*3,000.*
	45m/2 dull dusky blue-green blue	*3,000.*
	63m/1 dim dusky red violet	*3,000.*
	71i/0 deep violet-red-red	*3,000.*
	47n/2 dull dusky green blue	*3,000.*

The bicolored essays commonly offered as Nos. 285-293 "bicolored proofs" in "original colors," are Nos. 285-E8, 286-E8, 287-E9, 288-E5, 289-E4, 290-E4, 291-E8, 292-E6 and 293-E7. Value, set of nine $6,550.

293-E8

Die size: 82x68mm
Complete engraving with "HARVESTING IN THE WEST" vignette as adopted but from a die not used for the stamp: horses at left vignette border engraved dark up to border line which is solid complete line at both left and right.

293-E8	$2 Die on India, die sunk on card (marked "Proof from 1st die.")	
	black	*2,500.*
	dark orange red	*2,500.*

293-E9

Incomplete engraving of entire design as adopted: black wash over engraving on side of bridge and foreground (engraving under wash unfinished).

293-E9	$2 Die on India, die sunk on card, black	*3,500.*

293-E10

Complete design, vignette further engraved: engraving completed between title label and steamboat and city next to right frame, near side of bridge and smoke shadow on water lighter than on issued stamp.

293-E10	$2 Die on India, die sunk on card, black	*3,500.*

293-E11

Incomplete engraving of entire design: circles in upper corners of vignette next to value ovals, water next to right end of value label, panels at ends of cartouche all unfinished.

293-E11	$2 Die on India, die sunk on card, black	*3,500.*

Edward Rosewater

Rosewater, of St. Louis, was asked by the Post Office Dept. in 1897 to submit proposed designs for the Trans-Mississippi Exposition issue. For that reason, they are listed here.

All are drawings on tracing paper, on 91x142mm buff card.

285-E11

Design size: 62x97mm
Wash drawing of cattle.

285-E11	1c dull orange	*12,500.*

286-E11

Design size: 57x98mm
Wash drawing of mounted Indian saluting wagon train.

286-E11	2c deep orange red	*12,500.*

288-E9

Design size: 61x100mm
Wash drawing of man plowing field.

288-E9	5c dark yellow green	*12,500.*

290-E9

Design size: 62x99mm
Wash drawing of train coming around mountain.

290-E9	Ten Cents, dusky blue	*12,500.*

292-E9

Design size: 60x98mm
Wash drawing of woman holding light, standing on globe.

292-E9 $1 deep orange yellow *12,500.*

PAN-AMERICAN ISSUE
Bureau of Engraving and Printing

294-E1

Design size: 114x82½mm
Preliminary pencil drawing for frame design as adopted.

294-E1 1c Drawing on tracing paper, black *1,750.*

294-E2

Design size: 114x82½mm
Second state of ink drawing for frame design as adopted.

294-E2 1c Drawing on white card, about 6½x5 inches, black *1,750.*

294-E3

Second state of ink drawing for frame design reduced by Bureau of Engraving and Printing to stamp size.

294-E3 1c Reduced drawing on paper, mounted on 59x38mm black card, black —

294-E4

Similar to No. 294-E2, but design reduced to stamp size and with additional details added to columns and elsewhere, "1" denominations made wider (changed back to narrower on final frame engraving).

294-E4 1c Die on India, die sunk on 59x38mm black card, black 1,500.

294-E5

Engraving of vignette only, faint lines especially on the hull of the ship.

294-E5 1c 1c Die on India, die sunk on 107x88mm card, black *1,500.*

294-E6

Engraving of vignette only, various elements such as lines on hull of ship more deeply engraved.

294-E6 1c Die on India, die sunk on 94x78mm card, black 1,500.

294-E7

Engraving of vignette only, lines more deeply engraved than on Nos. 294-E5 and 294-E6, blue die number 10685 on back of card.

294-E7 1c Die on India, die sunk on 201x152mm card, black *1,500.*

294-E8

Die size: 87x68½mm
Engraving of vignette only, still more deeply engraved lines, more smoke from the funnel.

294-E8 1c Die on India, die sunk on card, black *1,500.*

294-E9

Engraving of both frame and vignette, on vignette long lines in the water, ship and sky unfinished

294-E9 1c Die on India, die sunk on 107x88mm card, green and black *1,750.*

295-E1

Design size: 108x82mm
Preliminary pencil drawing of frame similar to that adopted (side ornaments, etc., different); UR corner, etc., unfinished.

295-E1 2c Drawing on tracing paper, black *1,750.*

295-E2

Design size: 114x83mm
Preliminary pencil drawing of frame similar to No. 295-E1 (minor differences) but with UR corner complete.

295-E2 2c Drawing on tracing paper, black *1,500.*

295-E3

Design size: 108x82mm
Preliminary pencil drawing of frame design similar to No. 295-E2 but with minor differences at top, in lettering, etc.

295-E3 2c Drawing on tracing paper, black *1,750.*

295-E4

Design size: 95x70mm
Ink and wash drawing model of frame design as adopted, side torchbearers engraved on India as on U.S. Series of 1901 $10 note.

295-E4 2c Die on white card, about 108x82mm, black *1,750.*

295-E4A

Design size: 88x69mm
Incomplete engraving of vignette only.

295-E4A 2c Die on India, die sunk on card, black *3,500.*

295-E5

Design size: 27x19½mm
Die size: 88x68mm
Complete engraving of frame only as adopted.

295-E5 2c Die on India, die sunk on card, carmine *3,750.*

295-E6

Die size: 88½x69mm
Engraving of entire design with vignette incomplete near frame and on cars.

295-E6 2c Die on India, die sunk on card, carmine & black *2,250.*

296-E1

Preliminary pencil drawing of unadopted frame design.

296-E1 4c Drawing on tracing paper, black *1,750.*

296-E2

Design size: 114x82½mm
Final ink drawing for frame design as adopted.

296-E2 4c Drawing on white card, about 6½x5 inches, black *1,750.*

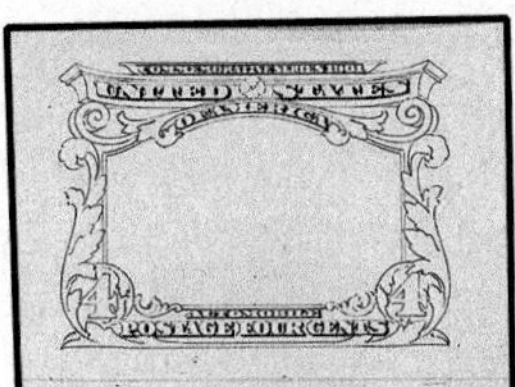
296-E3

Ink drawing of design in No. 296-E2 reduced by Bureau of Engraving and Printing to stamp size.

296-E3 4c Reduced drawing on paper, mounted on 59x38mm black card, black *750.*

296-E4

Design size: 27x19mm
Die size: 88x67mm
Incomplete engraving of entire design as adopted: lines missing at base of capitol dome, above driver's head.

296-E4 4c Die on India, die sunk on card, deep red brown & black *1,750.*

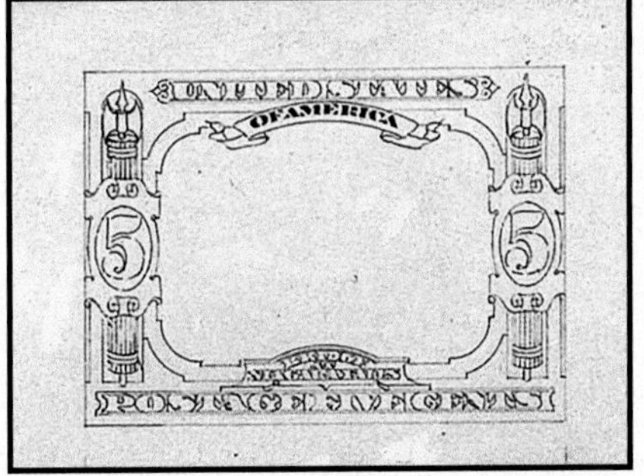
297-E1

Photo reproduction of pencil sketch of unadopted frame design on photosensitive tan paper, reduced to stamp size. Incomplete preliminary pencil drawing of frame design as adopted.

297-E1 5c Photo reproduction on tan paper *1,750.*

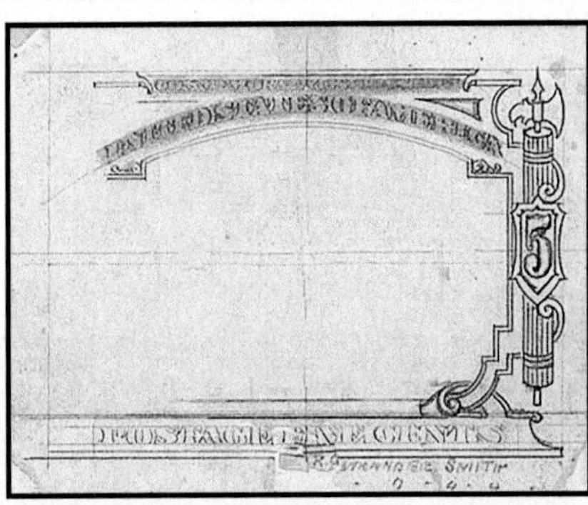
297-E2

Design size: 114x83mm
Incomplete preliminary pencil drawing of frame design as adopted.

297-E2 5c Drawing on tracing paper, black *1,750.*

297-E3

Design size: 114x82½mm
Final ink drawing for frame design as adopted.

297-E3 5c Drawing on white card, about 6½x5 inches, black *1,750.*

297-E4

Photo reproduction of sketch of adopted frame design on photosensitive paper, reduced to stamp size.

297-E4 5c Photo reproduction on tan paper *750.*

297-E5

Die size: 87x68mm
Incomplete engraving of vignette only.

297-E5 5c Die on India, die sunk on card, black *1,500.*

297-E6

Die size: 87x68mm
As No. 297-E5, but more completely engraved.

297-E6 5c Die on India, die sunk on card, black *1,500.*

297-E7

Design size: 27x19 ½mm
Die size: 87x68mm
Incomplete engraving of entire design as adopted: shading at bottom of battleaxes and scrolls at ends of title frame unfinished.

297-E7 5c Die on India, die sunk on card, blue & black *1,750.*

298-E1

Design size:108x82mm
Preliminary pencil drawing of unadopted frame design.

298-E1 8c Drawing on tracing paper, black *1,750.*

298-E2

Design size: 114x83mm
Incomplete preliminary pencil drawing of unadopted frame design.

298-E2 8c Drawing on tracing paper, black *1,750.*

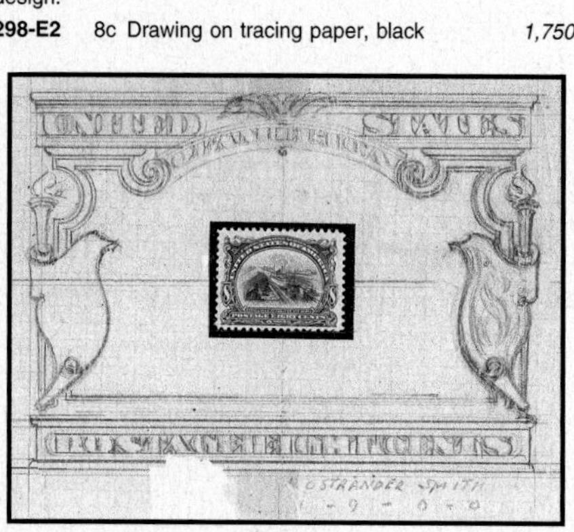

298-E3

Design size: 114x80mm
Preliminary pencil drawing of unadopted frame design.

298-E3 8c Drawing on tracing paper, black *1,500.*

298-E4

Design size: 114x83mm
Preliminary pencil drawing of frame design as adopted.

298-E4 8c Drawing on tracing paper, black *1,500.*

298-E5

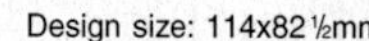

Design size: 114x82 ½mm
Final ink drawing for frame design as adopted. No. 298-E5 has an example of No. 298 mounted in the vignette area.

298-E5 8c Drawing on white card, about 6 ½x5 inches, black *1,750.*

298-E6

Design size: 34x26mm
Photo reproduction of sketch of adopted frame design on photosensitive paper, reduced to stamp size.

298-E6 8c Photo reproduction on tan paper *1,250.*

298-E7

Design size: 27x20mm
Die size: 87x69mm
Incomplete engraving of entire design: shading lines of ornaments, scrolls and ribbons at top unfinished, vignette incomplete at right, no etching on building in left foreground.

298-E7 8c Die on India, die sunk on card, bi-colored *1,750.*

299-E1

Design size: 114x83mm
Preliminary pencil drawing of unadopted frame design (small blank oval at center).

299-E1 10c Drawing on tracing paper, black *1,750.*

299-E2

Design size: 114x82 ½mm
Similar to No. 299-E1 but with outline of eagle and shield in center oval.

299-E2 10c Drawing on tracing paper, black *1,750.*

299-E3

Design size: 114x83mm
Preliminary pencil drawing for frame design as adopted.

299-E3 10c Drawing on tracing paper, black *1,750.*

299-E4

Design size: 114x82 ½mm
Final ink drawing for frame design as adopted.

299-E4 10c Drawing on white card, about 6 ½x9 inches, black *1,750.*

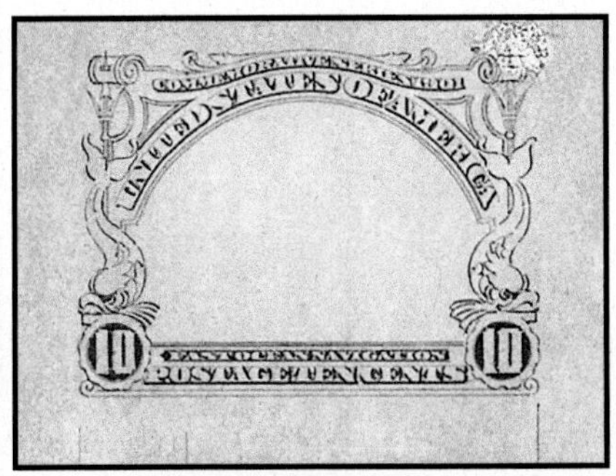

299-E5

Photo reproduction of sketch of adopted frame design on photosensitive paper, reduced to stamp size.

299-E5 10c Photo reproduction on tan paper *750.*

299-E6

Die size: 87x68mm
Incomplete engraving of entire design: frame complete but lines later engraved in the mast, smokestack and sky.

299-E6 10c Die on India, die sunk on card, bi-colored *2,750.*

1902 ISSUE

300-E1

Incomplete engraving of vignette and lower part of frame.

300-E1 1c Die on India, die sunk on card, black *4,000.*

300-E2

Design size: 19x22mm
Die size: 74½x88½mm
Incomplete engraving of entire design: vignette background has horiz. lines only, neckpiece, men at sides, etc., all unfinished.

300-E2 1c Die on India, die sunk on card, black *3,500.*

300-E3

Design size: 136x190mm
Preliminary ink drawing for 5c frame design but later adopted for 1c.

300-E3 1c Drawing on manila paper, blue green, gray blue & black *2,000.*

No. 300-E3 is on the opposite side of the same piece of paper bearing No. 307-E1. Value is for both essays.

300-E4

Design size: 116x135mm
Preliminary pencil and ink drawing for frame design as adopted.

300-E4 1c Drawing on white card, black *3,000.*

301-E1

Design size: 162x188mm
Paper size: 169x214mm
Preliminary pencil drawing of frame design (Raymond Ostrander Smith). Not adopted.

301-E1 2c Drawing on yellowed transparent tracing paper, black *1,500.*

301-E1A

Preliminary pencil and ink drawing of unadopted frame design, on 77x82mm yellowish wove paper, folded vertically and with ink tracing of frame on reverse.

301-E1A 2c Drawing on woven paper, black *2,000.*

301-E1B

Design size: 145x168mm
Preliminary pencil drawing of frame design as adopted.

301-E1B 2c Drawing on tracing paper, black *3,500.*

301-E2

Model with vignette of Houdon bust of Washington, on wash drawing over photo reduced to stamp size for approval by PMG.

301-E2 2c Model mounted on card, black *750.*

301-E3

Design size: 19x22mm
Die size: 75x87½mm
Incomplete engraving of entire design: head unfinished, horiz. background lines only, frame unfinished, lettering either blank or unfinished.

301-E3 2c Die on India, die sunk on card, black *4,000.*

301-E4

Design size: 60x88mm
Preliminary pencil drawing of right numeral 2 design as adopted.

301-E4 2c Drawing on tracing paper, black *500.*

301-E5

Design size: 176x120mm
Preliminary pencil drawing of lower left and upper right design.

301-E5 2c Drawing on tracing paper, black *700.*

301-E6

Design size: 19x22mm
Die size: 74x89mm
Incomplete engraving of entire design: head unfinished, horiz. background lines only, frame almost finished, lettering complete. No. 62057 on back.

301-E6 2c Die on India, die sunk on 153x202mm card, black *3,000.*

302-E1

Design size: 19x22mm
Die size: 74½x88mm
Incomplete engraving of entire design: vignette unfinished, horiz. background lines only, atlantes at sides unfinished. No. 66218 on back.

302-E1 3c Die on India, die sunk on card, black *3,250.*

303-E1

Design size: 19x22mm
Die size: 75x88mm
Incomplete engraving of entire design: vignette unfinished on eyes, hair, beard, etc. No. 58920 on back.

303-E1 4c Die on India, die sunk on card, black *2,500.*

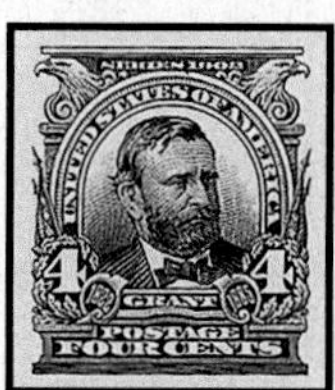
303-E2

Design size: 19x22mm
Incomplete engraving of entire design, shading lines in top of frame unfinished. No. 60085 on back.

303-E2 4c Die on India, die sunk on card, black *2,000.*

303-E3

Photograph of unaccepted design, stamp size, with white wash inside vignette and eagles in corners drawn in pen over portions of photo.

303-E3 4c Retouched photo-sensitive paper, black *900.*

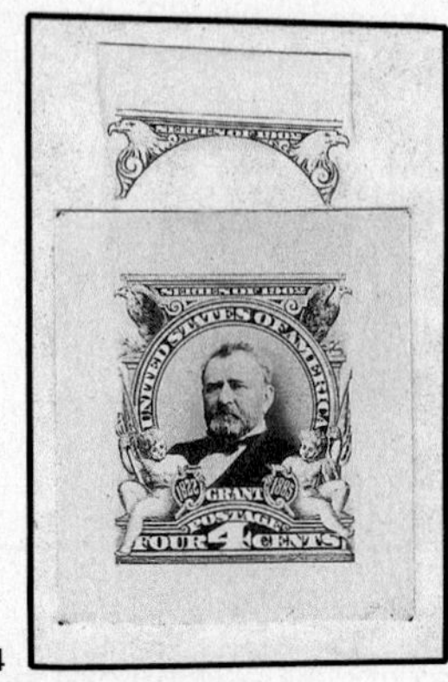
303-E4

Photograph of unaccepted design with additional overlay photo of top portion of frame with eagles similar to those on No. 303-E3.

303-E4 4c Photo-sensitive paper mounted on paper, black *1,100.*

304-E1

Design size: 19x22mm
Die size: 74x87½mm
Rejected die: figure at right poorly draped, blank triangles below "UNITED STATES," no shading in frame around "POSTAGE/FIVE CENTS" except at extreme ends.

304-E1 5c Die on India, die sunk on card, blue *2,300.*

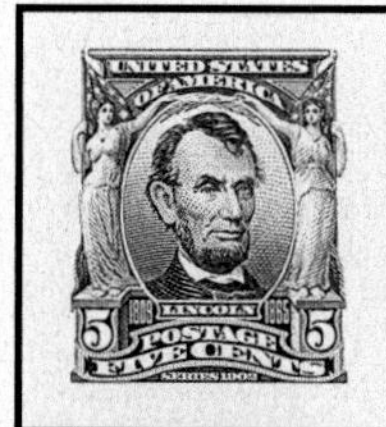
304-E2

Incomplete engraving of entire design: shading on side figures unfinished.

304-E2 5c Die on India, die sunk on card, blue *1,500.*

304-E3

Design size: 107x110mm
Paper size: 141x128mm
Preliminary pencil and ink drawing of unadopted frame design.

304-E3 5c Drawing on onion skin paper, black *1,500.*

Incomplete engraving of entire design as adopted.

305-E1 6c Die on India, lake *1,250.*

305-E2

Design size: 123x210mm
Preliminary ink drawing for unadopted frame design.

305-E2 6c Drawing on kraft paper, black & blue green *4,500.*

Nos. 305-E2, 306-E3 and 308-E2, are all on same piece of kraft paper, with No. 306-E3 on one side and the other two on the other side. Value is for the entire unit of three essays.

306-E1

Design size: 7x3½ inches
Preliminary pencil drawing of left side of frame design as adopted.

306-E1 8c Drawing on tracing paper, black *2,200.*

306-E2

Die size: 76x89mm
Incomplete engraving of vignette and numerals only: head drapery unfinished, horiz. background lines only.

306-E2 8c Die on India, die sunk on card, black *5,000.*

306-E3

Design size: 165x175mm
Preliminary ink drawing for unadopted frame design.

306-E3 8c Drawing on kraft paper, black, blue & green *4,500.*

See note after No. 305-E2.

307-E1

Design size: 135x174mm
Preliminary ink drawing for unadopted frame design.

307-E1 10c Drawing on kraft paper, gray blue *2,000.*

No. 307-E1 is on the opposite side of the same piece of paper bearing No. 300-E3. Value is for both essays.

308-E1

Design size: 19x22mm
Die size: 69x85½mm
Incomplete engraving of entire design: hair, beard, right cheek, eyes and right shoulder all unfinished, horiz. background lines only, name panel blank, ribbon shading unfinished, etc. No. 57796 on back.

308-E1 13c Die on India, die sunk on card, black *3,750.*

308-E2

Design size: 177x220mm
Preliminary ink drawing of 3c frame design but later adopted for 13c.

308-E2 13c Drawing on kraft paper, black & blue green *4,500.*

See note after No. 305-E2.

Design size: 19x22mm
Die size: 75x78mm
Incomplete engravng with complete portrait and initial lines of frame, blue "66439" handstamp on reverse.

309-E1 15c Die on India, die sunk on 153x204mm card, black *4,000.*

310-E1

Design size: 19x22mm
Die size: 74x87½mm
Incomplete engraving of entire design: hair and right cheek unfinished, horiz. background lines only, top of frame and eagles unfinished.

310-E1 50c Die on India, die sunk on card, black *4,000.*

310-E2

Incomplete engraving of entire design, further engraved than No. 310-E1: oval line outside top label thinner at bottom ends than on issued stamp.

310-E2 50c Die on India, die sunk on card, black *4,000.*

312-E1

Design size: 19x22mm
Die size: 76x88mm
Incomplete engraving of entire design: hair, neckpiece, etc., unfinished, horiz. background lines only; top of frame, leaves and numeral surrounds all unfinished.

312-E1 $2 Die on India, die sunk on card, black *4,500.*

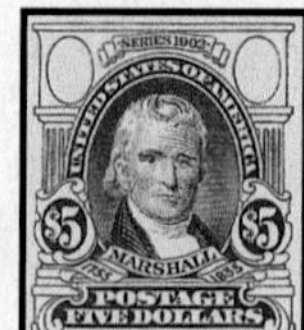

313-E1

Design size: 19x22mm
Die size: 75 ½x87 ½mm
Incomplete engraving of entire design: eyes, cheeks, hair, neckpiece all unfinished, horiz. background lines only, frame engraved in outlines only.

313-E1 $5 Die on India, die sunk on card, dark green *12,000.*

319-E1

Design size: 19 ½x22mm
Die size: 75x87 ½mm
Incomplete engraving of entire design from rejected die (central star between UNITED and STATES, four lines above small lettering, bottom of shield curved): name and date ribbon blank.

319-E1 2c Die on India, die sunk on card, carmine *5,250.*

319-E2

Incomplete engraving of entire design from rejected die: shading on leaves and vignette completed, lettering added to bottom ribbon and started on label above vignette. Blue pencil note on card backing, "May 1903. This die was abandoned at this stage because of crowded condition of lettering above portrait. G.F.C.S." No. 83909 on back.

319-E2 2c Die on India, die sunk on card, carmine *5,250.*

319-E3

Design size: 19 ½x22mm
Die I size: 75 ½x88mm
Incomplete engraving of entire design as adopted (no star between UNITED and STATES, bottom of shield straight): small label above vignette is blank.

319-E3 2c Die on India, die sunk on card, black *5,250.*

LOUISIANA PURCHASE ISSUE

324-E1

Incomplete engraving of entire design: head, hair, eyes, chin, coat all unfinished, horiz. background lines only, bottom label and upper corner labels blank, frame shading unfinished.

324-E1 2c Die on India, die sunk on card, black *3,250.*

325-E1

Incomplete engraving of entire design: head only lightly engraved, horiz. background lines only, laurel leaves unshaded, leaves' background and numeral shields blank.

325-E1 3c Die on India, die sunk on card, black *3,250.*

326-E1

Incomplete engraving of entire design: vignette unfinished, horiz. background lines only, much of frame blank or incomplete.

326-E1 5c Die on India, die sunk on card, black blue *3,250.*

JAMESTOWN ISSUE

328-E1

Incomplete engraving of entire design: vignette, shading on heads in upper corners, numerals and numeral shields all unfinished.

328-E1 1c Die on pale cream soft wove, 30x24mm, dusky green *1,250.*

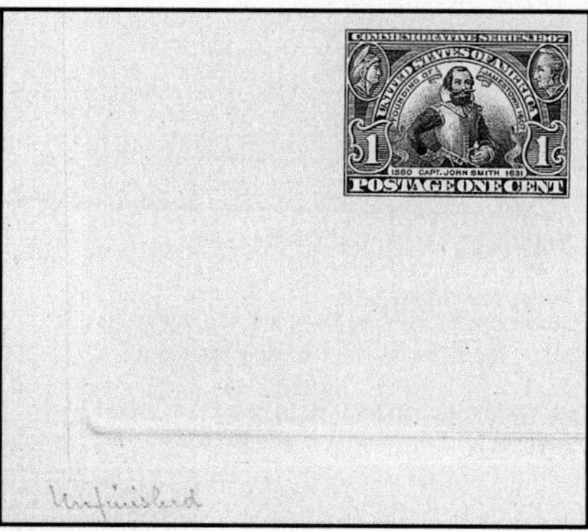

328-E2

Incomplete engraving of entire design: vignette, shading on heads in upper corners, and value tablets unfinished, pencil note "unfinished" at bottom of card.

328-E2 1c Die on India, die sunk on card, 109x94mm, green *2,500.*

330-E1

Incomplete engraving of vignette only: collar, hat, corselet, etc., unfinished. No. 245910 on back.

330-E1 5c Die on India, die sunk on card, 123x132mm, black *2,250.*

330-E2

Incomplete engraving of entire design: no shading in frame background.

330-E2 5c Die on India, die sunk on card, 109x95mm, blue *6,000.*

330-E3

Incomplete engraving of entire design: shading on corselet and arm of Pocahontas unfinished, horiz. background lines only, shading around date and name ribbon unfinished. No. 247606 on back.

330-E3 5c Die on card, 123x175mm, die sunk, blue *4,250.*

Incomplete engraving of entire design: shading on ribbons unfinished.

330-E4 5c Die on India, die sunk on card, 108x98mm, black *5,000.*

1908 ISSUE

331-E1

Photograph of wash drawing of entire design, head and vignette background retouched with black wash. Ms. "GVLM-Sept. 26th-1908" (PMG) in LR corner of backing card.

331-E1 1c Retouched photo on thick gray cardboard, 83x100mm, black *3,750.*

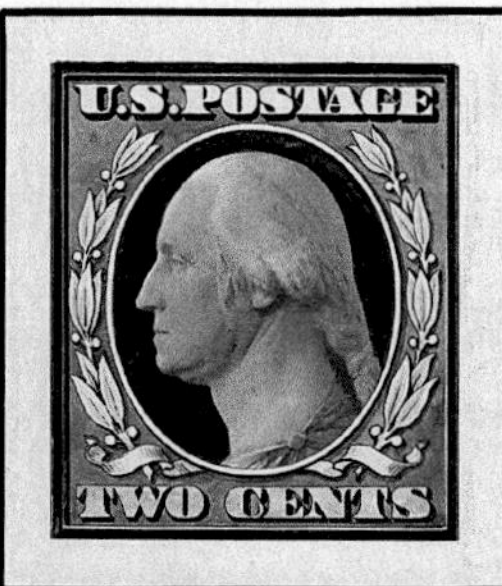

332-E1

Design size: 6 ⅛x7 ¼ inches
Wash drawing of frame design with vignette cut out, mounted over retouched glossy black photo of Houdon bust of Washington.

332-E1 Two Cents, Design on drawing paper, black *1,250.*

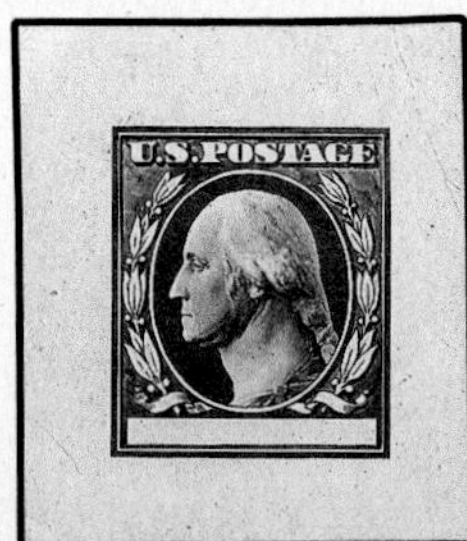

332-E1A

Design size: 19x22mm
Photograph of wash drawing of entire design, denomination blank, part of design hand-painted in black ink and wash.

332-E1A (2c) Retouched photo on 30x34mm card, black *3,250.*

332-E2

Design size: 19x22mm
Photograph of wash drawing of entire design, almost completely retouched with black ink and wash. Pencil "GVLM" (PMG) at top of backing card.

332-E2 Two Cents, Retouched photo on thick gray cardboard, 81x100mm, black *2,000.*

332-E3

Design size: 19x22mm
Incomplete engraving of entire design: shading on leaves at right unfinished. Pencil "Oct 15 - 1908" at LR of backing card.

332-E3 Two Cents, Die on India, die sunk on card, carmine *1,250.*

333-E1

Design size: 18½x22mm
Engraving of design as adopted except "THREE CENTS" at bottom.

333-E1 Three Cents, Die printed directly on card, deep violet *1,250.*

333-E2

Design size: 19x22mm
Photograph of wash drawing of entire design with "3 CENTS 3" drawn in black and white wash. Ms. "Nov. 24/08. J.E.R." (BEP director) in LR corner of backing card.

333-E2 3c Retouched photo on thick gray cardboard, 80x100mm, black *2,000.*

334-E1

Design size: 18½x22mm
Engraving of design as adopted except "FOUR CENTS" at bottom.

334-E1 Four Cents, Die printed directly on card, orange brown *1,250.*

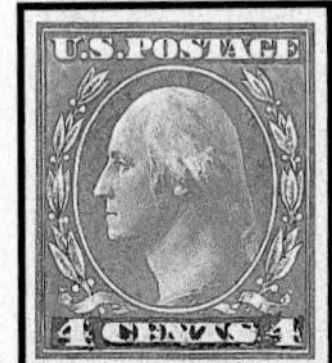
334-E2

Design size: 19x22mm

Photograph of wash drawing of entire design with "4 CENTS 4" drawn in black and white wash. Ms. "Nov. 24/08. J.E.R." (BEP director) in LR corner of backing card.

334-E2 4c Retouched photo on thick gray cardboard, 80x100mm, black *2,000.*

335-E1

Design size: 18½x22mm
Engraving of design as adopted except "FIVE CENTS" at bottom.

335-E1 Five Cents, Die printed directly on card, blue *1,500.*

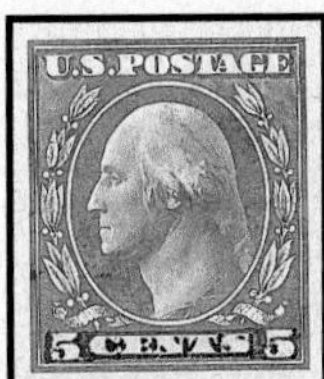
335-E2

Design size: 19x22mm
Photograph of wash drawing of entire design with "5 CENTS 5" drawn in black and white wash. Ms. "Nov. 24/08. J.E.R." (BEP director) in LR corner of backing card.

335-E2 5c Retouched photo on thick gray cardboard, 80x100mm, black *2,000.*

336-E1

Design size: 18½x22mm
Incomplete engraving of design with "SIX CENTS" at bottom.

336-E1 Six Cents, Die on India, on card, red orange *1,250.*

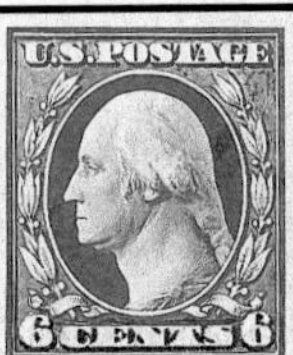
336-E2

Design size: 19x22mm
Photograph of wash drawing of entire design with "6 CENTS 6" drawn in black and white wash. Ms. "Nov. 24/08. J.E.R." (BEP director) in LR corner of backing card.

336-E2 6c Retouched photo on thick gray cardboard, 80x100mm, black *2,000.*

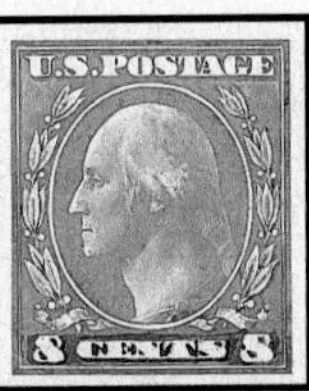
337-E1

Design size: 19x22mm
Photograph of wash drawing of entire design with "8 CENTS 8" drawn in black and white wash. Ms. "Nov. 24/08. J.E.R." (BEP director) in LR corner of backing card.

337-E1 8c Retouched photo on thick gray cardboard, 80x100mm, black *2,000.*

338-E1

Design size: 19x22mm
Photograph of wash drawing of entire design with "10 CENTS 10" drawn in black and white wash. Ms. "Nov. 24/08. J.E.R." (BEP director) in LR corner of backing card.

338-E1 10c Retouched photo on thick gray cardboard, 80x100mm, black *2,000.*

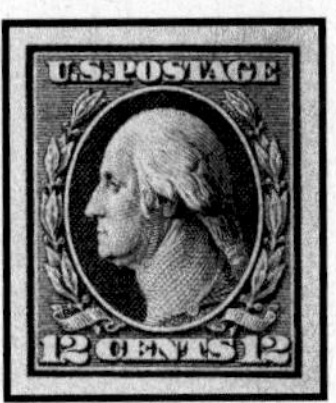
338a-E1

Design size: 18½x22mm
Complete engraving of entire adopted design but a value not issued: "12 CENTS 12" at bottom. Virtually all are stamp size, imperf.

Ridgway numbers used for colors of No. 338a-E1.

338a-E1 12c
- ***a.*** Die on bluish white wove
  - 41n/1 dim v. dusky b-blue-green *900.*
- ***b.*** Die on 1f/1 dim pale red wove
- ***c.*** Die on 7d/1 dim light red orange wove
  - 47m/1 dim dusky g-b. blue *900.*
- ***d.*** Die on 17b/1 dim bright o-y. yellow wove
  - 1i/0 deep red *900.*
  - 5i/0 deep o-orange-red *900.*
  - 27m/0 dusky green yellow *900.*
  - 37m/0 dusky g-blue-green *900.*
  - 41m/0 dusky b-blue-green *900.*
  - 55m/1 dim dusky blue violet *900.*
  - 59m/1 dim dusky violet *900.*
  - 69m/3 dismal dusky r-violet-red *900.*
- ***e.*** Die on 19f/0 pale y-orange yellow wove
  - 1i/0 deep red *900.*
  - 15i/1 dim deep yellow orange *900.*
  - 35m/0 dusky green *900.*
  - 43d/1 dim light green blue *900.*
  - 61m/3 dismal dusky v-red-violet *900.*
  - 69o/5 black *900.*
- ***f.*** Die on 31f/2 dull pale yellow green wove
  - 69o/5 black *900.*
- ***g.*** Die on 42d/1 dim bright green blue wove
  - 41m/1 dim dusky b-blue-green *900.*
- ***h.*** Die on 44-/1 dim medium green blue wove
  - 9k/2 dull dark o-r-orange *900.*
- ***i.*** Die on 45l/1 dim v. dark b-green-blue wove
  - 5i/0 deep o-orange-red *900.*
  - 27m/2 dull dusky green yellow *900.*
- ***j.*** Die on 69g/0 pale r-v. red wove *900.*
- ***k.*** Die on dark blue bond, 69o/5 black *900.*

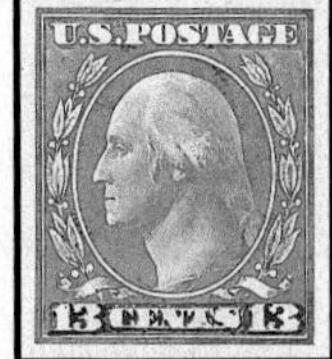
339-E1

Design size: 19x22mm
Photograph of wash drawing of entire design with "13 CENTS 13" drawn in black and white wash. Ms. "Oct. 7-08. J.E.R.-GVLM" (BEP director, PMG) in LL corner of backing card.

339-E1 13c Retouched photo on thick gray cardboard, 80x100mm, black *2,000.*

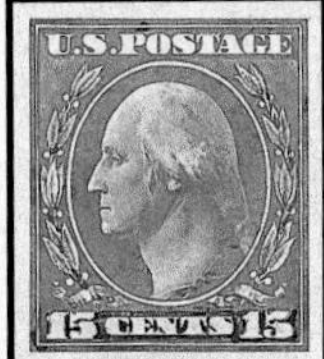
340-E1

Design size: 19x22mm

Photograph of wash drawing of entire design with "15 CENTS 15" drawn in black and white wash. Ms. "Oct. 7-08. J.E.R.-GVLM" (BEP director, PMG) at bottom of backing card.

340-E1 15c Retouched photo on thick gray cardboard, 80x100mm, black *2,000.*

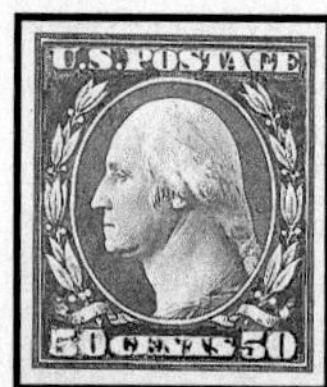

341-E1

Design size: 19x22mm
Photograph of wash drawing of entire design with "50 CENTS 50" drawn in black and white wash. Ms. "Oct. 7-08. J.E.R.-GVLM" (BEP director, PMG) at bottom of backing card.

341-E1 50c Retouched photo on thick gray cardboard, 80x100mm, black *2,000.*

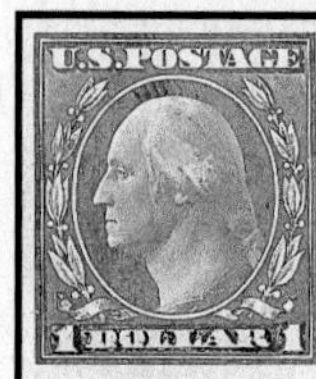

342-E1

Design size: 19x22mm
Photograph of wash drawing of entire design with "1 DOLLAR 1" drawn in black and white wash. Ms. "Oct. 7-08. J.E.R.-GVLM" (BEP director, PMG) at bottom of backing card.

342-E1 $1 Retouched photo on thick gray cardboard, 80x100mm, black *2,000.*

LINCOLN MEMORIAL ISSUE

Design size: 7x8 inches
Photostat of 1908 2c frame design with wash drawing of ribbons and vignette photo of Lincoln's head.

367-E1 Two Cents, Model of Lincoln design, black *1,500.*

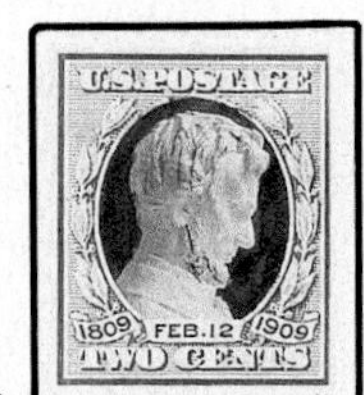

367-E2

Photo of No. 367-E1 reduced to stamp size, retouched to highlight hair and beard, dates added.

367-E2 Two Cents, Retouched photo, black *1,500.*

367-E3

Design size: 19x22mm
Incomplete engraving of entire design: head, background, name/date ribbon all unfinished.

367-E3 Two Cents, Die on India, die sunk on card, 148x201mm, carmine *3,500.*

ALASKA-YUKON-PACIFIC EXPOSITION ISSUE

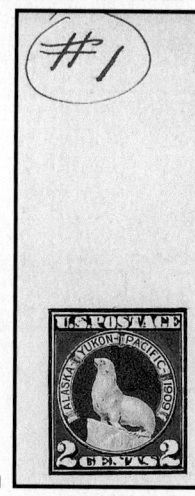

370-E1

Design size: 18½x22mm
Wash drawing of frame similar to 1908 2c design with photo of wash drawing of seal on ice cake as vignette. Ms. "#1" at top of backing card.

370-E1 2c Model on card, about 3x4 inches, black *1,500.*

370-E2

Design size: 18½x22mm
Engraved frame similar to 1908 2c but with wash drawing of "1870 1909" in ribbons and "2 CENTS 2" at bottom, vignette cut out, mounted over engraved vignette of Wm. H. Seward from snuff stamp. Ms. "#2" at UL corner of backing card.

370-E2 2c Model on card, about 3x4 inches, black *1,500.*

370-E3

Design size: 27½x20½mm
Photo of seal on ice cake vignette as originally approved, mounted on ink and wash drawing of frame design as approved. Ms. "#3" at UL corner of backing card, engraved Seward vignette pasted on at bottom, "Approved April 3, 1909 FH Hitchcock Postmaster-General" at right.

370-E3 2c Model on glazed card, 93x70mm, black, white and gray *2,250.*

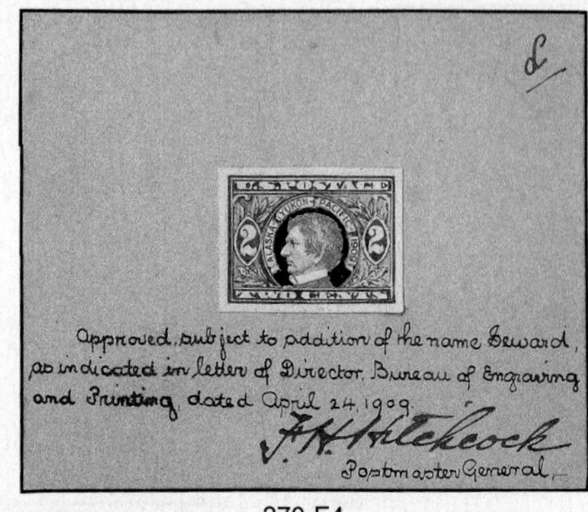

370-E4

Design size: 27½x20mm
Photo of wash drawing of frame and arched ribbon as adopted, vignette cut out, mounted over photo of engraved Seward vignette, background retouched with black wash. Ms. "Approved subject to addition of the name Seward, as indicated in letter of Director, Bureau of Engraving and Printing, dated April 24, 1909. F.H. Hitchcock Postmaster General."

370-E4 2c Model on 93x75mm thick gray card, black *2,250.*

370-E5

Design size: 27x20mm
Retouched photo of wash drawing of adopted frame with seal on ice cake vignette but pencil "WILLIAM H. SEWARD" on white wash ribbon below. Ms. "April 26/09 Approved J.E.R." (BEP director) at LR corner of backing card.

370-E5 2c Retouched photo and pencil on 94x66mm thick gray card, black *2,000.*

Incomplete engraving of entire design: no shading on head or vignette background, no shading lines on ribbons.

370-E6 2c Die on India, die sunk on 8x6 inch card, carmine *2,000.*

370-E7

Design size: 26½x19½mm
Similar to No. 370-E6 but further engraved: face and collar lightly engraved, horiz. background lines only, no shading lines on ribbons.

370-E7 2c Die on wove, 32x26½mm, carmine *2,000.*

372-E1

Wash drawing of adopted vignette design.

372-E1 2c Drawing on artist's cardboard, 11¼x6¾ inches, black *2,000.*

372-E2

Wash drawing of frame design as adopted except "HUDSON-FULTON CENTENARY" at top.

372-E2 2c Drawing on artist's cardboard, 7¾x6¾ inches, black *2,000.*

372-E3

Design size: 33x21½mm

Wash drawing of frame design as adopted with dates "1609-1807" and photo of No. 372-E1 reduced to fit and worked over with wash.

372-E3 2c Model on card, 4x3 inches, black *2,000.*

372-E4

Design size: 33x21½mm

Wash drawing of frame with vignette cut out, mounted over photo of No. 372-E1. Typed/ms. "Approved August 17, 1909 F.H. Hitchcock Postmaster General" and "August 19, 1909 Amend by substituting word 'Celebration' for 'Centenary.' F.H. Hitchcock Postmaster General." Pencil "P.O. 488" in LR corner.

372-E4 2c Model on white card, 129x103mm, black *2,000.*

372-E5

Incomplete engraving of entire design: lettering on flag at masthead of *Clermont* has "N" reversed and no "T."

372-E5 2c Die on wove, 38x27mm, carmine *2,000.*

PANAMA-PACIFIC ISSUE

397-E1

Design size: 27x20mm

Photo of incomplete frame with overlay of circular photo vignette as adopted, with wash drawing of palm trees on each side and "1 CENT 1" in wash. Ms. "Approved July 16, 1912 Frank H. Hitchcock Postmaster General" on backing card.

397-E1 1c Model on card, about 89x77mm, black *1,500.*

Design size: 27x20mm

Photo of incomplete frame with overlay circular photo vignette as adopted, with wash drawing of palm trees on each side and "1 CENT 1" in wash, with "Approved" and signed by the BEP Director J.E. Ralph, but "Opening of Panama Canal 1913" later changed for stamp to "San Francisco 1913."

397-E2 1c Model on thick gray card, 106x86mm, black *1,500.*

398-E1

Design size: about 29½x20mm

Ink and wash drawing of frame design longer than adopted with photo of wash drawing of Golden Gate as eventually used (reduced) on 5c. Backstamp "STAMP DIVISION FEB. 12, 1912 P.O. DEPT" on backing card.

398-E1 2c Model on card, about 4x3 inches, black *2,500.*

398-E2

Design size: 27x20mm

Photo of incomplete frame with photo of wash drawing of vignette as adopted with title "GATUN LOCKS," wash drawing of value numerals. Ms. "Approved Aug. 27, 1912 Frank H. Hitchcock Postmaster General" on backing card.

398-E2 2c Model on thick gray card, 99x72mm, black *1,500.*

Very similar to No. 398-E2 with slightly different wash touch-up and "2"s, with "Approved" and signed by BEP Director J.E. Ralph.

398-E2A 2c Model on thick gray card, 107x86mm, black *1,500.*

398-E3

Completely engraved design as adopted except titled "GATUN LOCKS" in error (design pictures Pedro Miguel locks).

398-E3 2c
- ***a.*** Large die on India, die sunk on card, 202x152mm, carmine *10,000.*
- ***b.*** Small die on India (formerly #398AP2), carmine *6,000.*

398-E4

Design size: 27x20mm

Photo of incomplete engraving (no sky in vignette) with "GATUN LOCKS" in error, ms. "Approved Dec. 17, 1912 Frank Hitchcock Postmaster General" on backing card.

398-E4 2c Model on thick gray card, 97x74mm, black *1,500.*

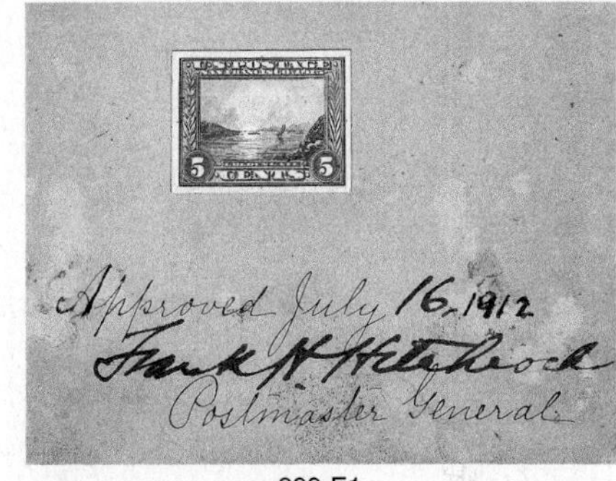

399-E1

Design size: 27x20mm

Photo of wash drawing of frame design as adopted with photo of wash drawing of adopted vignette mounted in place, with additional hand touch-up done in wash on vignette, ms. "Approved July 16, 1912 Frank H., Hitchcock Postmaster General" on backing card.

399-E1 5c Model on 30x22mm white paper, mounted on card, 97x73mm, black *1,500.*

Very similar to No. 399-E1 with slightly different wash touch-up and no steamship below sun, with "Approved" and signed by BEP Director J.E. Ralph.

399-E2 5c Model on thick gray card, 106x86mm, black *1,500.*

400-E1

Design size: 27x20mm

Photo of wash drawing of frame design as adopted with photo of painting adopted for vignette mounted in place, ms. printed "Approved" and dated and signed " Aug. 22, 1912, Frank H. Hitchcock Postmaster General" on backing card.

400-E1 10c Model on 31x34mm white paper, on thick gray card, 98x73mm, black *1,500.*

Very similar to No. 400-E1 with more extensive touching-up of the vignette and frame, with "Approved" and signed by BEP Director J.E. Ralph.

400-E1A 10c Model on thick gray card, 107x86mm, black *1,500.*

400-E2

Design size: 27x20mm
Photo of wash drawing of frame design as adopted with photo of wash drawing of two galleons at anchor in bay, titled "CABRILLO 1542" mounted in place. Backing card marked "II."

400-E2 10c Model on white paper, on 91x85mm thick gray card, black *1,500.*

400-E3

Design size: 27x20mm
Photo of wash drawing of frame design as adopted with photo of Liberty standing among palm fronds, wash touch-up on vignette and "10" denominations drawn in black and white wash, two battleships in bay. Backing card marked "III."

400-E3 10c Model on white paper, on thick gray card, 90x84mm, black *1,500.*

400-E4

Design size: 27x20mm
Similar to No. 400-E3 but steamships replace battleships. Backing card marked "IV."

400-E4 10c Model on white paper, on thick gray card, 90x83mm, black *1,500.*

400-E5

Design size: 27x20mm
Similar to No. 400-E2 but different hand drawn vignette picturing two galleons under full sail in front of snowclad mountains. Backing card marked "V."

400-E5 10c Model on white paper, on thick gray card, 89x83mm, black *1,500.*

1912 ISSUE

Incomplete engraving of entire design, except value tablet area which is '1 CENT 1' at bottom drawn in wash. Ms. "Approved. July 17, 1911 Frank H. Hitchcock. P.M. Gen." on backing card.

405-E1 1c Model on 3½x3¾-inch card, black *6,000.*

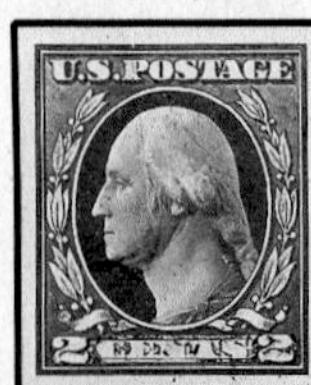

406-E1

Incomplete engraving of entire design, except value tablet area which is '2 CENTS 2' at bottom drawn in wash. Ms. "Approved. July 17, 1911 Frank H. Hitchcock P. M. Gen." on backing card.

406-E1 2c Model on 3⅜x3 11/16-inch card, black —

414-E1

Wash drawing of design as adopted, worked over partial photo with 8 in lower corners drawn in wash. Ms. "Approved. July 17, 1911 Frank H. Hitchcock Postmaster General" on backing card.

414-E1 8c Model on 3½x3¾-inch card, black *2,000.*

414-E2

Vignette of head only without background gridwork, control #490311 on back of card.

414-E2 8c Die on India, die sunk on 152x202mm, olive green *2,250.*

416-E1

Design size: 19x22mm
Photo of wash drawing of generic design with 10 in lower corners drawn in black ink. Ms. "July 17, 1911. (May, 1911 erased) Approved: Frank H. Hitchcock PM Gen" on backing card, backstamped "STAMP DIVISION P.O. DEPT. MAY 15, 1911."

416-E1 10c Model on 87x113mm thick gray card, black *2,000.*

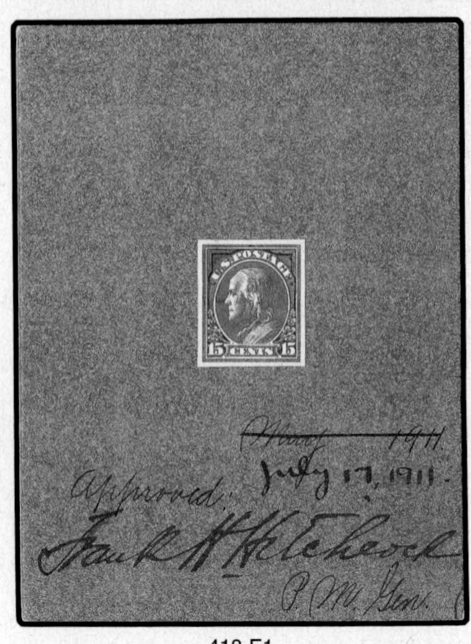

418-E1

Design size: 19x22mm
Photo of wash drawing of generic design with background of frame between oval and outer colorless line in dark gray wash and some colorless retouching, 15 in lower corners drawn in black ink. Ms. "July 17, 1911. (May, 1911 erased) Approved: Frank H. Hitchcock PM Gen" on backing card, backstamped "STAMP DIVISION P.O. DEPT. MAY 15, 1911."

418-E1 15c Model on 87x113mm thick gray card, black *2,000.*

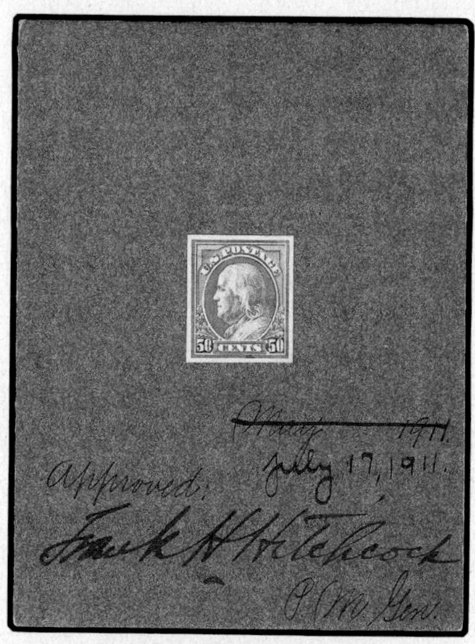

421-E1

Design size: 19x22mm
Photo of wash drawing of generic design with 50 in lower corners drawn in black ink. Ms. "July 17, 1911. (May, 1911 erased) Approved: Frank H. Hitchcock PM Gen" on backing card, backstamped "STAMP DIVISION P.O. DEPT. MAY 15, 1911."

421-E1 50c Model on 77x112mm thick gray card, black *2,000.*

423-E1

Design size: 19x22mm
Photo of wash drawing of generic design with entire value label drawn in black ink. Ms. "July 17, 1911. (May, 1911 erased) Approved: Frank H. Hitchcock PM Gen" on backing card, backstamped "STAMP DIVISION P.O. DEPT. MAY 15, 1911."

423-E1 $1 Model on 87x113mm thick gray card, black *2,000.*

1916 PRECANCEL ESSAYS

499-E1

Design size: 19x22mm
Die size: 90x88mm
"NEW YORK/N.Y." precancel engraved directly onto type I die, printed in one color. Ms. "8/16/22 J.S." in LR corner of backing card on No. 499-E1a. Although dated 1922, records indicate an original proof was pulled in 1916.

499-E1 2c
a. Die on India, die sunk on card, lake —
b. Die on bond paper, 33x36mm, dark carmine —

1918 ISSUE

Complete engraving of Franklin head only as on $2 and $5 values, no shading around head, control #834424 on back of card.

523-E2 $2 Die on India, die sunk on 151x103mm card, black *1,750.*

523-E3

Design size: 16x18¾mm
Complete engraving of vignette only including shading. Pencil control # "837660 May 1917" on back of India paper, pencil "Schofield" at bottom of backing card (#523-E3a), or control #837662 (1917) on back of card (No. 523-E3b).

523-E3 $2
a. Die on 32x33mm India, card mounted, black 1,000.
b. Die on wove, die sunk on card, 203x151mm, black 1,000.

PEACE ISSUE

537-E1

Design size: 21½x18¾mm
Stamp never issued due to World War I.

537-E1 2c
a. Die on India, die sunk on card, deep red 2,250.
b. Die on wove, die sunk on card, 201x138mm, signed on card by Harry S. New 4,000.

537-E2

Die size: 22x19mm
Stamp never issued due to World War I.

537-E2 5c
a. Die on India, die sunk on card, dim dusky g-b-blue 2,000.
b. Die on wove, die sunk on card, 201x138mm, signed on card by Harry S. New 4,000.

SAMUEL F.B. MORSE ISSUE

537-E3

Design size: 21½x18½mm
Incomplete engraving of entire design: vignette and lettering finished but blank spaces beside vignette. Backstamped "932944" and "Jan. 1, 1919" or "932945" and "Jan. 7, 1919". Frame design subsequently used for 3c Victory issue, No. 537, though lettering and value numerals made slightly smaller.

537-E3 3c Die on India, die sunk on card, 141x173mm (#932944) or 151x202mm (#932945), black *3,000.*

VICTORY ISSUE

537-E4

Design size: 21½x18½mm
Die size: 85½x75½mm
Incomplete engraving of entire design: no shading in border and some flags unfinished. Backstamped "936356 Jan. 25, 1919."

537-E4 3c Die on India, die sunk on card, black *3,000.*

PILGRIM ISSUE

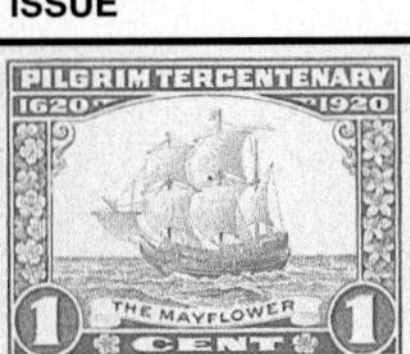

548-E1

Design size: 26x19mm
Incomplete engraving of entire design: sky blank, sails unshaded.

548-E1 1c Die on India, die sunk on card, 201x151mm, green *1,600.*

Almost complete engraving of entire design as adopted, but no crosshatching behind the "1" denominations.

548-E2 1c Die on India, die sunk on card, 203x151mm, green *1,600.*

549-E1

Incomplete engraving of frame only: "CENTS" engraved but numeral circles blank (probably an essay for the 2c and 5c).

549-E1 Die on India, die sunk on card
black *1,600.*
green *1,600.*

549-E2

Design size: 26x19mm
Incomplete engraving of entire design: vignette unfinished, control #1063097 on back of card.

549-E2 2c Die on India, die sunk on card, 202x151mm, black *1,600.*

549-E3

Incomplete engraving of entire design, virtually complete but no crosshatching behind the numeral "2" denominations.

549-E3 2c
a. Die on India, die sunk on card, 202x151mm, control #1063875 on back, black 1,600.
b. Die on India, die sunk on card, 202x151mm, control #1064174 or #1064271 on back, carmine rose 1,600.

1922 ISSUE

551-E1

Design size: 19x22mm
Incomplete engraving of entire design as adopted: name label blank, vignette unfinished. Ms. "Approved--Harry S. New" on backing card on olive brown essay; others not signed but with notation of denomination of stamp for color used ("1c" for green, etc.)

551-E1 ½c Die on India, die sunk on 151x202mm card
olive brown *3,000.*
green *2,500.*
carmine *2,500.*
orange *2,500.*
rose *2,500.*
yellow *2,500.*
blue green *2,500.*
yellow green *2,500.*
carmine rose *2,500.*

Incomplete engraving of entire design but further engraved than No. 551-E1: no lines in white oval over ends of title ribbon and ribbon foldunders not etched as darkly as on issued stamp.

551-E2 ½c Die on India, die sunk on 149x201mm card, olive brown *1,500.*

Nos. 555-E1 Thru 571-E1 Are For Pencil Drawings Of Unadopted Frame Designs, Each On Thin Tissue Paper

555-E1

557-E1

555-E1	3c black	*1,150.*
557-E1	5c black	*1,150.*
557-E2	5c black	*1,150.*
566-E1	15c black	*1,150.*
571-E1	$1 black	*1,150.*

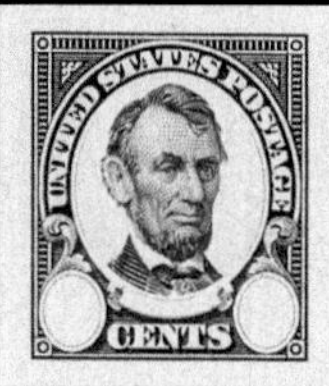

555-E2

Incomplete engraving, no engraving around bust of Lincoln, no denomination.

555-E2 (3c) Die on India, affixed to 5x6¾inch card, black *3,000.*

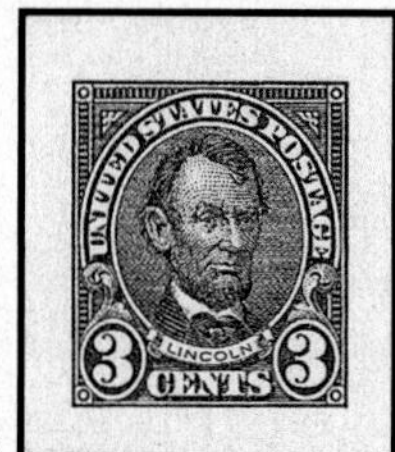

555-E3

Complete engraving with cross-hatched lines surrounding bust of Lincoln.

555-E3 3c Die on India, affixed to card, 26x30mm, violet *3,250.*

560-E1

Complete engraving with background of cross-hatched lines surrounding slightly larger bust of Grant.

560-E1 8c Die on India, die sunk on 97x111mm card, dark olive green *2,000.*

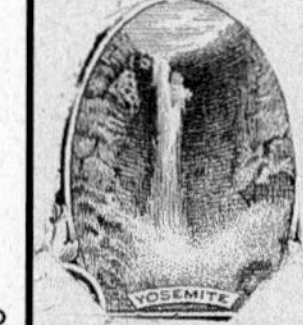

567-E2

Design size: 19x22mm
Engraving of unadopted vignette with unadopted engraved frame cut away.

567-E2 20c Die on India, die sunk on 151x201mm card, cobalt blue *1,750.*

568-E2

Design size: 19x15mm
Die size: 88x75mm
Engraving of adopted vignette with engraved frame cut away.

568-E2 25c Die on India, die sunk on 202x151mm card, green *1,750.*

573-E1

Engraving of accepted vignette.

573-E1 $5 Die on India, affixed to card, 73x87mm, blue *3,750.*

HUGUENOT-WALLOON TERCENTENARY ISSUE

614-E1

Design size: 8½x7¼ inches
Preliminary pencil drawing of *Nieu Nederland* in circular frame. Pencil note: "Reverse — Sailing to America, not away from America — J. B. Stoudt" originally on drawing has been removed.

614-E1 1c black *1,000.*

615-E1

Incomplete engraving of entire design, background of vignette incomplete and central figures only roughed in.

615-E1 2c Die on India, 82x69mm, black *4,500.*

616-E1

Design size: 5½x3⅛ inches
Wash drawing of design adopted for vignette.

616-E1 5c black *1,500.*

617-E1

Almost complete engraving of entire design, lacking strong shading in the foreground of the vignette.

617-E1 1c Die on India, die sunk on card, 126x115mm, green *1,500.*

618-E1

Design size: 36x21mm
Incomplete engraving of entire design as adopted: spaces between letters of "BIRTH OF LIBERTY" not solid color.

618-E1 2c Die on India, die sunk on card, black *1,250.*

618-E2

Design size: 36x21mm
Incomplete engraving of entire design as adopted: numeral circles blank, many shading lines missing in vignette, no shading around "TWO CENTS," etc.

618-E2 2c Die on India, die sunk on 91x71mm card, black *1,500.*

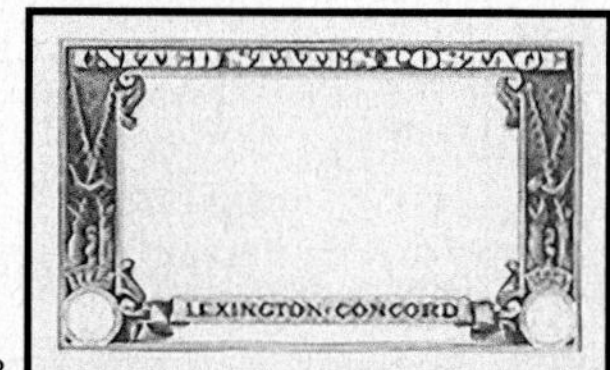

618-E3

Design size: 36x21mm
Engraving of frame only, without vignette or value tablets, control #1317765 on back of card.

618-E3 2c Die on India, die sunk on card, 202x118mm, carmine *1,500.*

NORSE-AMERICAN ISSUE

620-E1

Design size: 21½x19mm
Die essay on wove, vignette complete, frame with blank ribbon and without dates and "CENTENNIAL," hinged onto a 3½ inch square matboard.

620-E1 2c Die essay with frame incomplete, carmine and black *2,500.*

621-E1

Design size: 21½x19mm
Engraving of frame only.

621-E1 5c Die on India, die sunk on card, dark blue *3,000.*

ERICSSON MEMORIAL ISSUE

Wash drawing of design as adopted, stamp size.

628-E1 5c black *750.*

BATTLE OF WHITE PLAINS ISSUE

629-E1

Design size: 8⅜x9 inches
Preliminary ink and watercolor drawing of entire design quite similar to that adopted.

629-E1 2c black & red *750.*

629-E2

Design size: 22x19mm
Card size: 94x66mm
Unfinished engraving of design, vignette, background, foreground, flags and ribbons incomplete, "70010" control number on back.

629-E2 2c Die on India, mounted on card, carmine rose *1,500.*

BURGOYNE CAMPAIGN ISSUE

644-E1

Design size: 22x19mm
Essay size: 25x22mm
Card size: 78x98mm
Photo of wash drawing of unadopted design, on white paper mounted on thick gray card with "Approved" in ink and "May 7, 1927" in pencil subsequently crossed out with "X's."

644-E1 2c black *1,500.*

683-E1

Design size: 13x17 inches
Preliminary ink drawing of design nearly as adopted.

683-E1 2c Drawing on artist's cardboard, black *500.*

American flag and pencil touch-up of outer frame on photo of artist's model with vignette as adopted but entirely different frame.

690-E1 2c black *400.*

702-E1

Engraving of entire design without red cross, engraved cross shows faintly, control #70015 on back of card.

702-E1 2c Die on India, die sunk on 120x142mm card, black *5,000.*

704-E1

Design size: 119x150mm
Preliminary pencil sketch of unadopted ½c design.

704-E1 ½c Drawing on tracing paper, mounted on 195x192mm manila paper, black *2,500.*

718-E1

Design size: 6x7 inches
Watercolor drawing of unadopted design with 2c denomination.

718-E1 2c Drawing on thick artist's card, red *2,500.*

719-E1

Design size: 6x7 inches
Watercolor drawing of entire design similar to that eventually adopted for 5c but with 2c denomination.

719-E1 2c Drawing on thick artist's card, 150x175mm, blue *1,250.*

Engraving of vignette as adopted, within frame, but reversed from final design, without denomination or inscriptions.

742-E1 3c Die on white card, 88x69mm, black *1,750.*

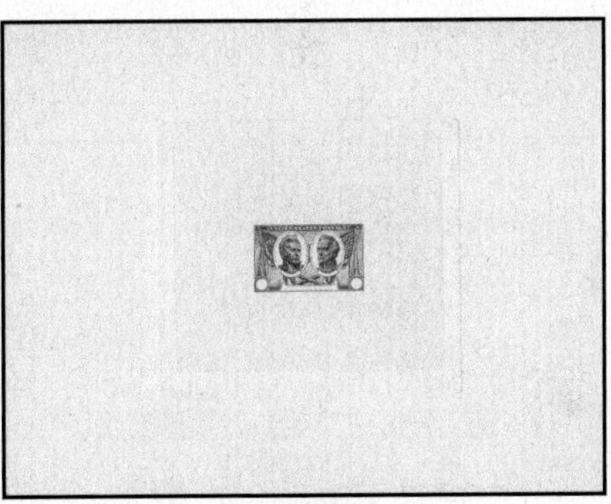
786-E1

Unadopted engraving of entire design without denomination, portraits as adopted but rest of design different from accepted design, control #70027 on back of card.

786-E1 2c Die on wove, die sunk on card, 202x153mm, carmine *1,500.*

791-E1

Engravings of Decatur and MacDonough as adopted, widely spaced.

791-E1 2c Die on wove, die sunk on card, 202x153mm, carmine *1,500.*

791-E2

Engraving of incomplete design without central vignette, control #491747 (1936) on back of card.

791-E2 2c Die on wove, die sunk on card, 198x136mm, carmine *1,500.*

793-E1

Unfinished engravings of three portraits only, control #70031 or 70110 on back.

793-E1 4c Die on wove, die sunk on card, 202x153mm, red brown *2,000.*

PANAMA CANAL ISSUE

856-E1

Design size: 37x21½mm
Essay size: 99x81mm
Card size: 141x117mm
Engraving of unadopted design: "3 CENTS 3" and "25th ANNIVERSARY PANAMA CANAL" changed for final design. "W. O. Marks" at lower right corner, "Engraver's Stock Proof 594256 / Authorized by 'OML'" on reverse.

856-E1 3c Die on India, die sunk on card, deep violet *3,000.*

Unfinished engraving of adopted design, fine horizontal lines in white areas of "FOR DEFENSE" and no dash between "INDUSTRY" and "AGRICULTURE."

899-E1 1c Die on wove, die sunk on card, bright blue green *1,000.*

Engraving of entire design, lacks crosshatching in the shading of background.

899-E2 1c Die on wove, die sunk on card, 140x162mm, green *1,000.*

Engraving of frame as adopted, with "84075" at top and "United States of America" at bottom of die impression, stamped "For Approval" at top of card, signed and dated by four individuals on card.

909-921-E1 5c Die on India, die sunk on card
a. On 227x151mm card, violet *4,000.*
a. On card reduced almost to 89x74mm die size, black *1,500.*

922-E1

Incomplete engraving of entire design, sky unshaded, no smoke from engine, additional background shading missing, blue control number and "MODELING" on reverse of card.

922-E1 3c Die on India, die sunk on card, 200x148mm, violet *2,500.*

As No. 922-E1, with additional background shading added.

922-E2 3c Die on India, die sunk on card, 200x148mm, violet *2,500.*

922-E3

As No. 922-E2, with shading of sky added.

922-E3 3c Die on India, die sunk on card, 200x148mm, violet *2,500.*

922-E4

As No. 922-E3, with additional background and figure shading added.

922-E4 3c Die on India, die sunk on card, 200x148mm, violet *2,500.*

Unadopted design showing steamship under sail, without denomination or background shading, handstamp "Engraver's Stock Proof/Authorized by," initials, "Brooks" (the engraver) in pencil and control #818347A all on back of stamp.

923-E1 3c Die on wove, die sunk on card, 201x152mm, violet *1,500.*

Unfinished engraving of adopted design, lacking smoke from the smokestack and background shading. "Modeling" handstamp and control #818995A on back of card.

923-E2 3c Die on wove, die sunk on card, 201x150mm, violet *1,500.*

Engraved vignette as adopted, "Engraver's Stock Proof/Authorized by," initials, "Brooks" (the engraver) in pencil and control #867263A all on back of stamp.

930-933-E2 Die on wove, die sunk on card, 202x151mm, black *1,500.*

1016-E1

Engraving of adopted design, except "c" cut in design at right where cross should be printed (held in place by tape on back); "Engraver's Stock Proof, Authorized by," initials and blue "103120B" control number on back.

1016-E1 3c Die on wove, die sunk on card, 202x152mm, deep blue *2,500.*

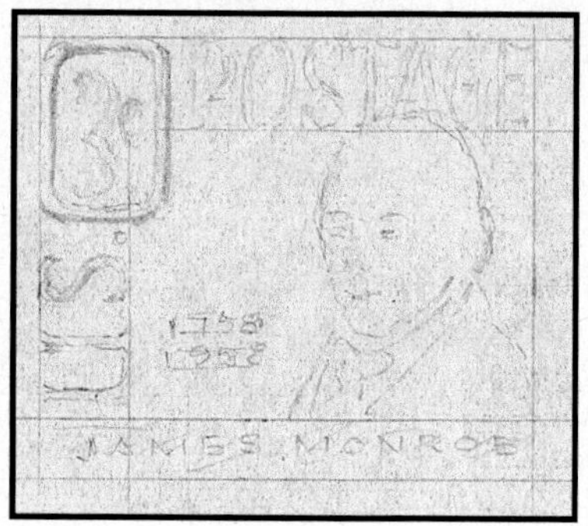

1105-E1

Individual design sizes: 58x33mm; area of 6 designs: 213x87mm

1105-E1 3c Black charcoal on light beige laid artist's paper, irregular 343 x225mm, six hand-drawn designs, note below in blue ink, "First Roughs James Monroe Commemorartive. F. Conley 1957" —

1105-E2

Design size: 43x38mm

1105-E2 3c Pencil drawing of proposed design on tracing paper, irregular 165 x127mm, notes on either side in blue ink, "Trial Layout New Size James Monroe Commemorative." and signed "Frank P. Conley Designer Dec. 1957" —

1105-E3

Design size: 32x37mm

1105-E3 3c Pencil drawing of proposed design on tracing paper, irregular 165 x120mm, notes on either side in blue ink, "Trial Layout New Size Jan. 1958 James Monroe stamp" and signed "Frank P. Conley Designer" —

1105-E4

Design size: 41x35mm

1105-E4 3c Black ink drawing of proposed design in format of issued stamp on tracing paper, 207 x133mm, notes on either side in blue ink, "Trial Layout New Size James Monroe stamp" and signed "Frank P. Conley Designer Jan. 1958" —

1128-E1

Design size: 295x178mm

1128-E1 4c Rough sketch in pencil, black pen and blue artist's crayon on tracing paper 1,500.

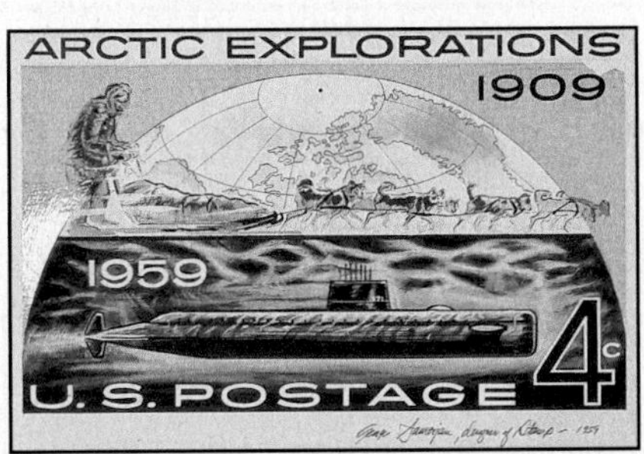

1128-ER2

Design size: 158x95mm

1128-E2 4c Pencil, gray and black watercolor ink, white painted year date, "U.S. Postage," "c" and outline of "4," horizontal background lines on a premade shiny, raised sticker, very close to issued design but with small differences, on white card, signed "George Şamerjan, designer of stamp ¢‹↔› 1959" beneath in black 1,500.

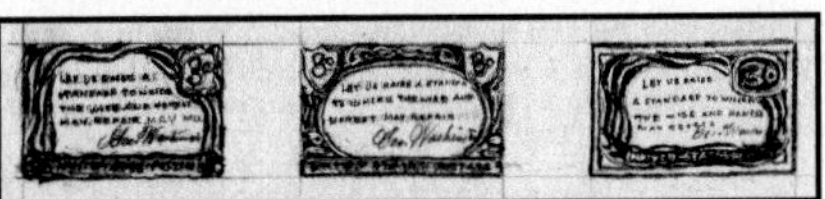

1139-E1

Design size (3): 135x21mm

1139-E1 3c Black charcoal and silver ink rough drawings of three proposed designs on tracing paper, 276 x166mm, no designer notes —

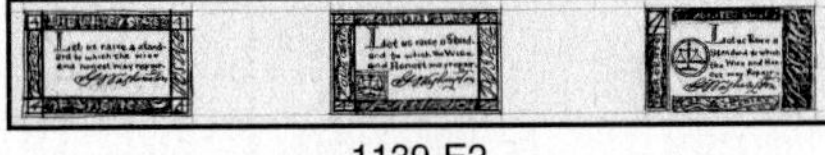

1139-E2

Design size (3): 165x22mm

1139-E2 4c Black and silver ink drawings of three proposed designs on tracing paper, 275x164mm, no designer notes —

E31139

Design size: 35x22mm

1139-E3 4c Dark brown, light brown, dull orange and silver ink handpainted full design on tracing paper, 110 x 92mm, "POSTAGE" on right panel, signed "Frank P. Conley 58" beneath in brown 1,000.

1139-E4

Design size: 35x22mm

1139-E4 4c Dark brown, light brown, dull orange and silver ink handpainted full design on tracing paper, 122 x117mm, "POSTAGE" on right panel, symbol plus other small design differences from #1139-E3, signed "Frank P. Conley '58" beneath in dull orange 1,000.

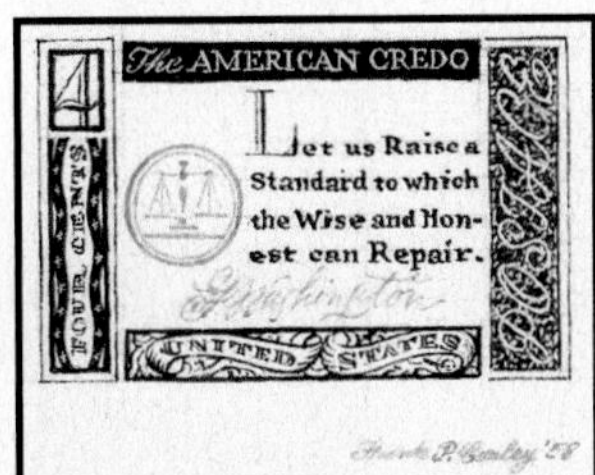

1139-E5

Design size: 35x22mm

1139-E5 4c Dark brown, dull orange and silver ink handpainted full design on tracing paper, 127x216mm, "POSTAGE" on right panel, small design differences from #1139-E3 and 1139-E4, signed "Frank P. Conley '58" beneath in dull orange 1,000.

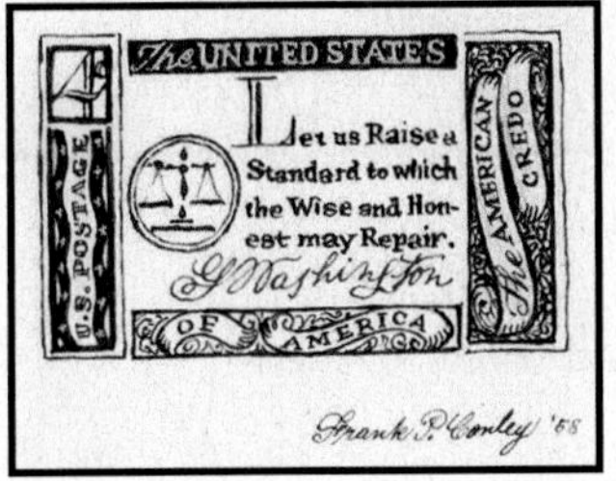

1139-E6

Design size: 35x22mm

1139-E6 4c Brown and silver ink handpainted full design on tracing paper, 274 x152mm, "The AMERICAN CREDO" on right panel, signed "Frank P. Conley '58" beneath in brown 1,000.

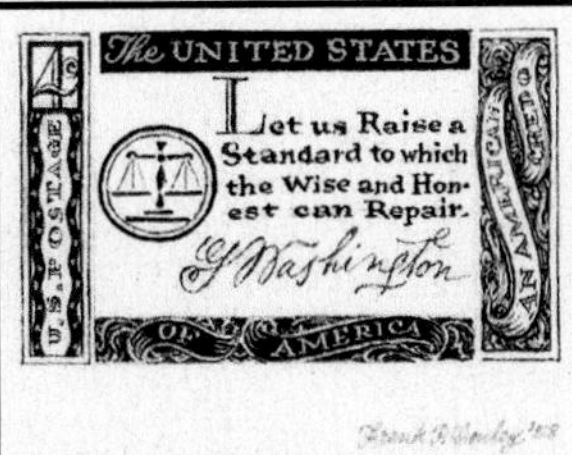

1139-E7

Design size: 35x22mm

1139-E7 4c Dark brown, brown and silver ink handpainted full design on tracing paper, 279 x216mm, "AN AMERICAN CREDO" on right panel, signed "Frank P. Conley '58" beneath in dull orange 1,000.

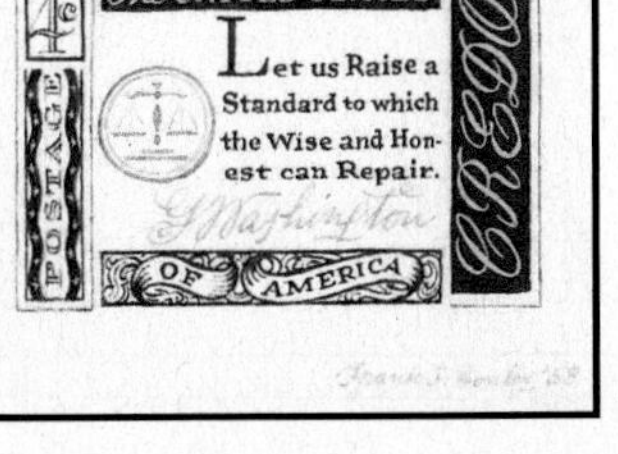

1139-E8

Design size: 35x22mm

1139-E8 4c Dark brown, brown, dull orange and silver ink handpainted full design on tracing paper, 130 x216mm, "CREDO" on right panel, signed "Frank P. Conley '58" beneath in dull orange 1,000.

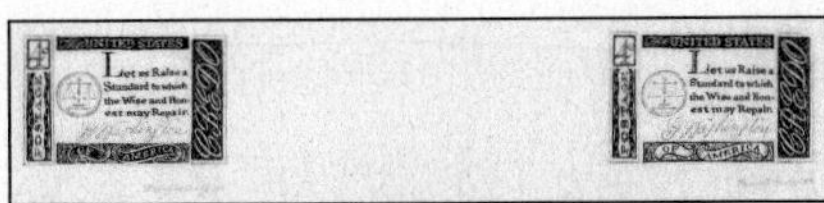

1139-E9

Design size (2): 136x22mm

1139-E9 4c Dark brown, brown, dull orange and silver ink handpainted full designs on tracing paper, 302 x234mm, each with "CREDO" on right panel each with small design differences from #1139-E8, each signed "Frank P. Conley '58" beneath in dull orange —

It is interesting to note that none of the No. 1139 essays contain the text on the center text panel that appears on the issued stamp. Likely, a last-minute change was made.

1140-E1

Design size: 32x21mm

1140-E1 4c Red, blue and silver handpainted full design on tracing paper, 129 x 81mm, similar to issued design but with different symbol at left and different Franklin signature, signed "Frank P. Conley designer" beneath in red 1,000.

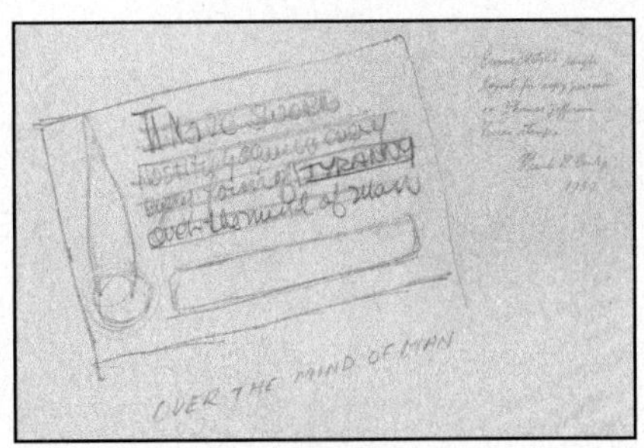

1141-E1

Design size: 125x80mm

1141-E1 4c Rough pencil drawing of proposed design on irregular-sized tracing paper, "Over the mind of man" repeated beneath, "Ervine Metzl's rough layout for copy revision of Thomas Jefferson Credo stamp. Frank P. Conley 1959" at right —

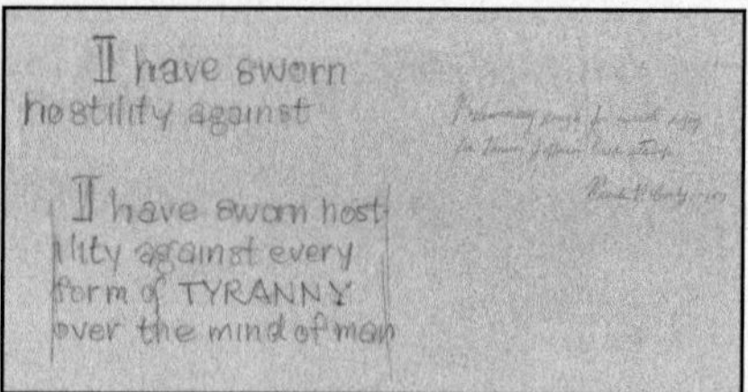

1141-E2

Design size: 90x41mm

1141-E2 4c Rough text only in pencil on irregular-sized tracing paper, part of text repeated above, "Preliminary rough for revised copy for Thomas Jefferson Credo stamp. Frank P. Conley, 1959" at right —

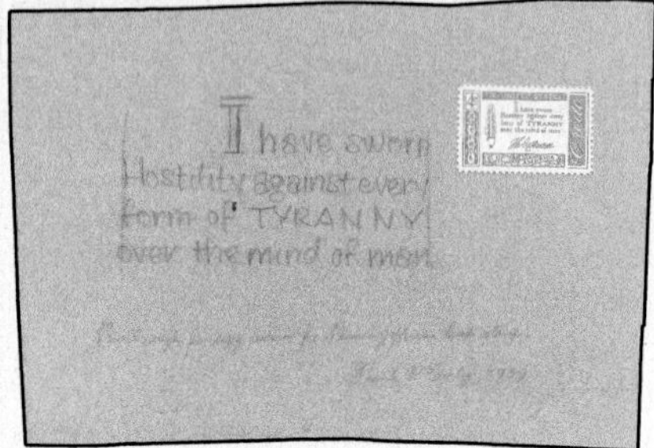

1141-E3

Design size: 98x50mm

1141-E3 4c Rough text only in pencil on tracing paper, 185 x 130mm, "Pencil rough for copy revised for Thomas Jefferson Credo stamp, Frank P. Conley, 1959" beneath —

I have sworn
Hostility against every
form of TYRANNY
over the mind of man.

Trial finished lettering for revised copy for Jefferson Credo stamp.

Frank P. Conley, 1959

1141-E4

Design size: 69x37mm

1141-E4 4c Black India ink sketch of text only on thin wove paper, 280 x 216mm "Trial finished lettering for revised copy for Jefferson Credo stamp. Frank P. Conley, 1959" beneath —

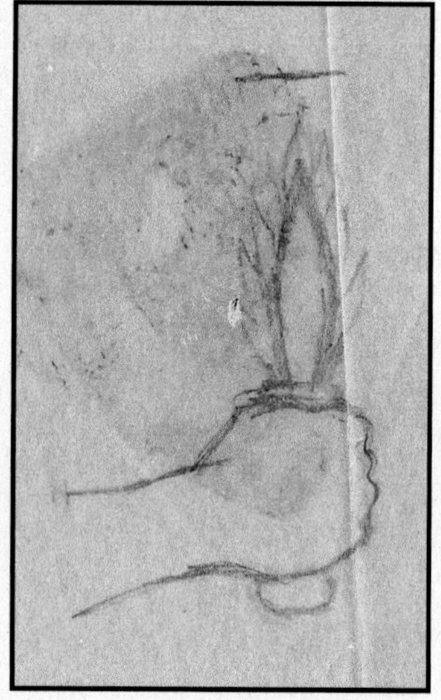

1141-E5

Design size: 33x55mm

1141-E5 4c Pencil sketch of symbol on irregular piece of tracing paper, approximately 220 x110mm, no designer notes —

1141-E6

Design size: 32x55mm

1141-E6 4c Black charcoal sketch of symbol on irregular piece of tracing paper, approximately 200 x120mm, no designer notes —

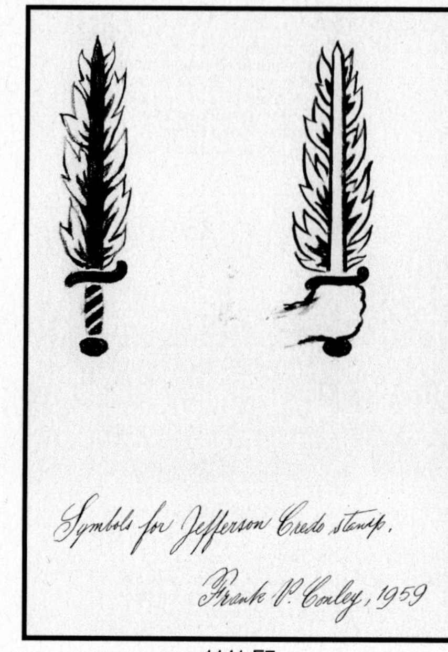

1141-E7

Design size (2): 69x68mm

1141-E7 4c Black charcoal sketches of two symbols on thin wove paper, 280 x216mm, "Symbols for Jefferson Credo stamp, Frank P. Conley, 1959" beneath, in black ink —

1141-E8

Design size (3): 147x68mm

1141-E8 4c Black charcoal sketches of three symbols on thin wove paper, 280 x216mm, "Symbols for Jefferson Credo stamp. Frank P. Conley, 1959" beneath, in black ink —

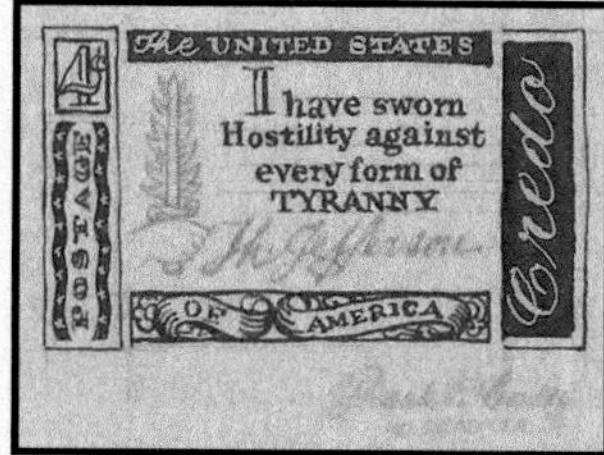

1141-E9

Design size: 37x21mm

1141-E9 4c Dark brown, vermilion and silver handpainted full design on tracing paper, 125 x108mm, signed "Frank P. Conley Designer" beneath in vermilion *1,000.*

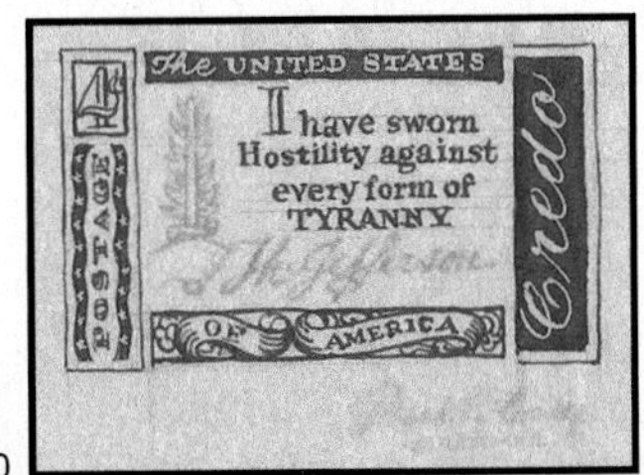

1141-E10

Design size: 37x21mm

1141-E10 4c Dark brown, vermilion and silver handpainted full design on tracing paper, 125 x108mm, different symbol and signature than #1141-E9 or 1141-E11, signed "Frank P. Conley Designer" beneath in vermilion 1,000.

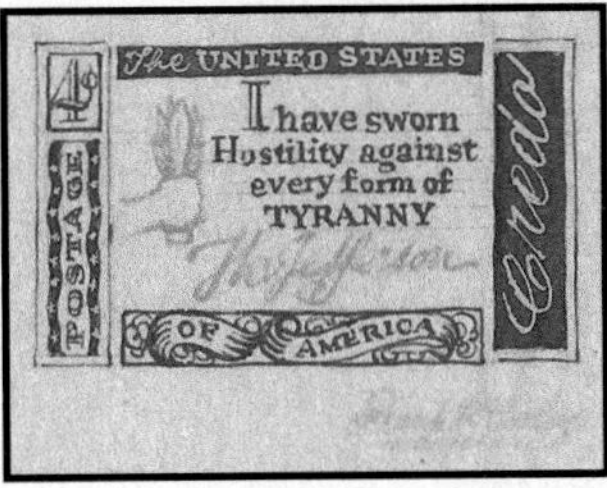

1141-E11

Design size: 37x21mm

1141-E11 4c Dark brown, vermilion and silver handpainted full design on tracing paper, 125 x108mm, different symbol and signature than #1141-E9 or 1141-E10, signed "Frank P. Conley Designer" beneath in vermilion 1,000.

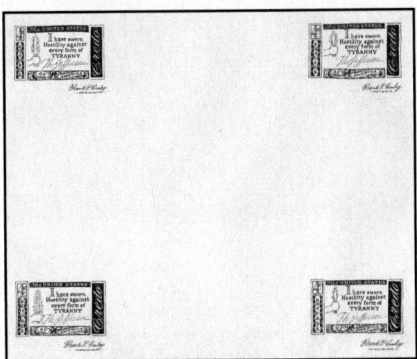

1141-E12

Design size (4 together): 156 x121mm

1141-E12 4c Dark brown, vermilion and silver handpainted full designs on thin wove paper, 280 x 216mm, 4 similar but different essays arranged in a square, each with different symbols and signatures (and each different than those on #1141-E9, 1141-E10 and 1141-E11), each signed "Frank P. Conley Designer" beneath in dark brown —

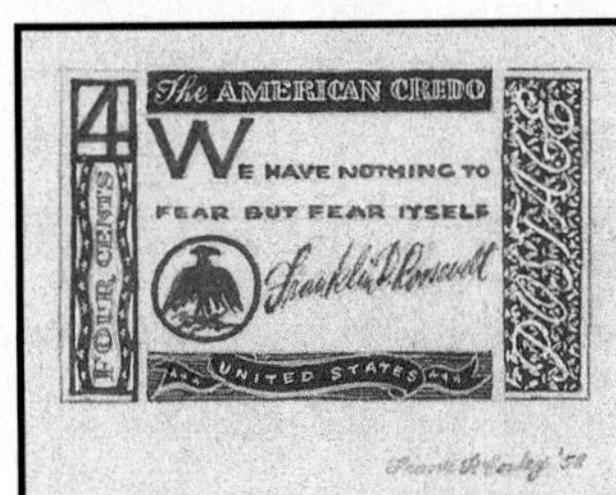

Design size: 36x22mm

1144X-E1 4c Blue, red and silver handpainted full unadopted design on thin wove paper for a proposed Franklin D. Roosevelt Credo series stamp, paper is 135x120mm, signed "Frank P. Conley 1958" beneath in blue —

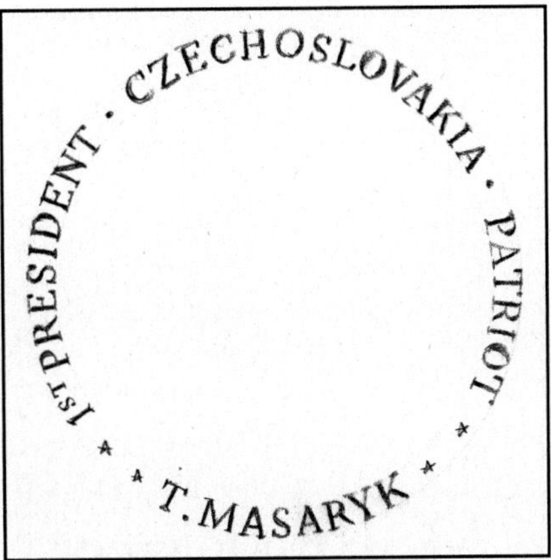

1147-E1

Design size: 157x157mm circle

1147-E1 4c Black charcoal trial design of circular text on medallion on tracing paper, approximately 260 x257mm, double stars before and after name (which does not include middle initial "G"), no dates —

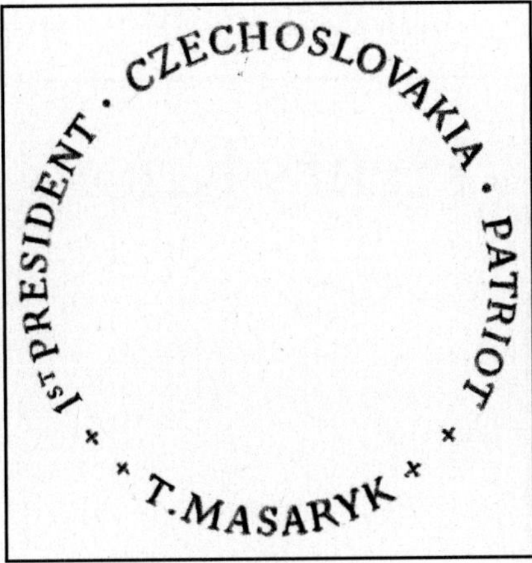

1147-E2

Design size: 159x159mm circle

1147-E2 4c Black charcoal trial design of circular text on medallion on tracing paper, approximately 268 x268mm, double crosses before and after name (which does not include middle initial "G"), no dates —

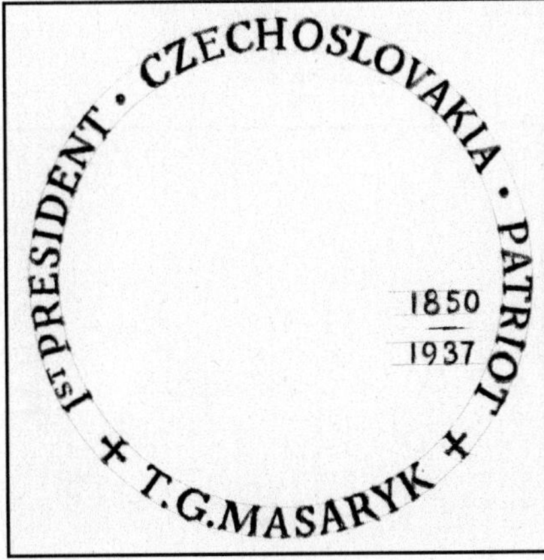

1147-E3

Design size: 159x159mm circle

1147-E3 4c Black charcoal trial design of circular text on medallion on tracing paper, 255 x255mm, large crosses before and after name, "1850/1937" dates instead of "1918/1935" as on issued stamp —

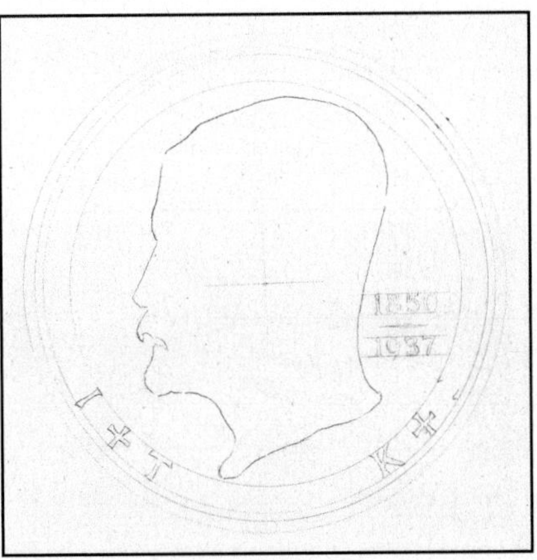

1147-E4

Design size: 173x173mm circle

1147-E4 4c Black pencil design on tracing paper, approximately 250 x290mm with uneven edges, showing circles with outline of Masaryk head, large crosses at bottom before and after name, "1830/1937" dates instead of "1918/1935" as on issued stamp —

1147-E5

Design size: 123x140mm

1147-E5 4c White, tan and black design on 160 x174mm photographic paper with complete design, section showing torch, leaves and ribbons pasted in place, vignette also pasted in place, "1850/1937" dates instead of "1918/1935" as on issued stamp —

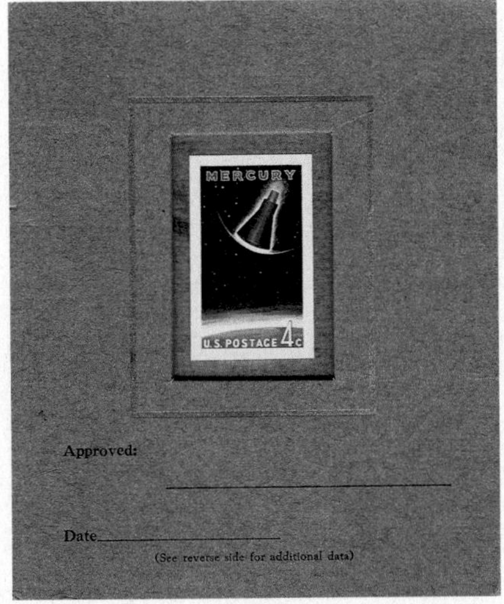

1193-E1

Design size: 21x36mm
Photograph of rejected design model, mounted on thick card, with BEP overleaf calling attention to the "Special Project."

1193-E1 4c Model photo, on 100x120mm card, fold-over overleaf same size, with printed information on back of overleaf *2,500.*

1529-E1

Design size: 183x109mm
Multicolored drawing in colored pencils similar to accepted design on 305x241 sheet of tracing paper, several ink and pencil notes above, at right and below design.

1529-E1 10c Multicolored design —

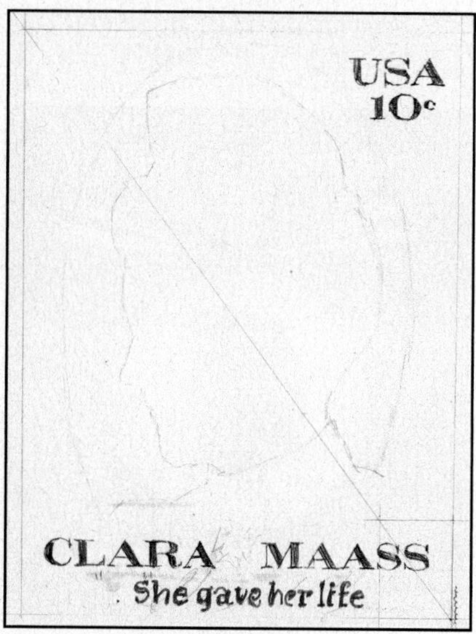

1699-E1

Design size: 166x217mm
Preliminary drawing in pencil and purple ink that matches well the final design, but without detail.

1699-E1 10c Design, text and and head outline on 203x264mm tracing paper —

1799-E1

Design size: 21x25mm
Picture of painting by Gerard David cropped and affixed on picture of simulated stamp with perfs and text, on card with covering gray thin card with cut-out in center to frame the essay; note at top left of covering card says "No (Rejected 3-6-74)," but in fact this is the design that was chosen (with painting cropped slightly differently).

1799-E1 13c Hybrid mock-up of design similar to accepted design —

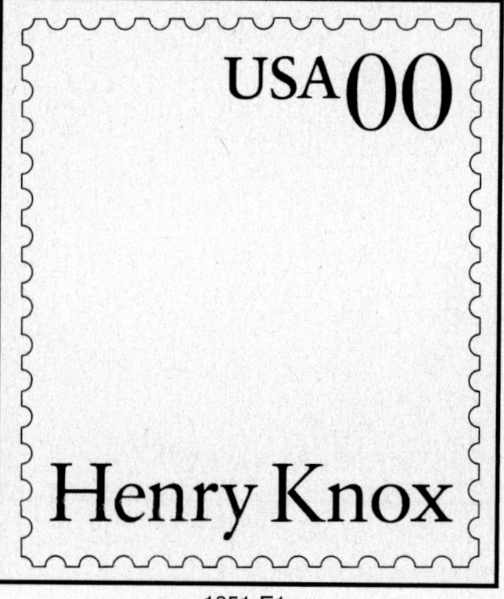

1851-E1

Design size: 109x126mm
Ink drawing of 'USA,' '00' denomination and text; text at bottom.

1851-E1 No denomination, simulated perfs and text on 217x281mm white wove paper, with measurement notes at left, black —

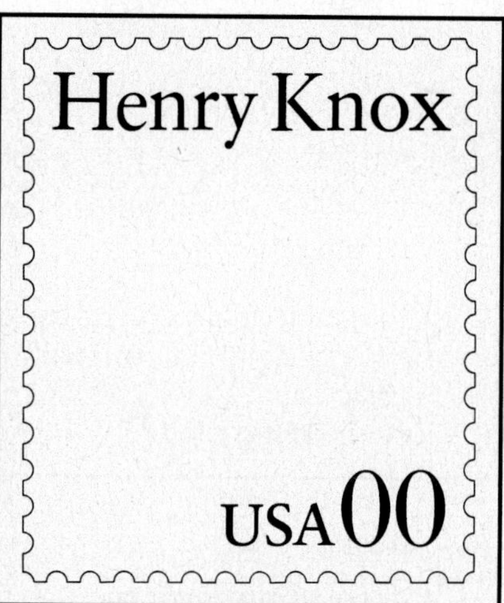

1851-E2

Design size: 109x126mm
Ink drawing of 'USA,' '00' denomination and text; text at top as on issued stamp.

1851-E2 No denomination, simulated perfs and text on 217x281mm white wove paper, with measurement notes at left, black —

2176-E1

Design size: 133x155mm

Pencil trial design (not adopted) on 198x252mm tracing paper, text below design.

2176-E1 4c Pencil design on tracing paper, black —

Incomplete engraving of vignette, no shading or collar.

2179-E1 20c Die on wove, die sunk on card, red brown *600.*

2179-E2

Similar to No. 2179-E1, but with collar added.

2179-E2 20c Die on wove, die sunk on card, red brown *600.*

Similar to issued stamp, but with substantial differences in shading, etc.

2179-E3 20c Die on India, die sunk on thin card, black *650.*

2181-E1

Design size: 106x127mm
Pencil drawing on white board, covered by thick gray paper with center cut-out of design size taped to board at top.

2181-E1 20c Design on white board, covering gray paper marked "B," black —

2181-E2

Design size: 96x115mm
Pencil drawing on white board, covered by thick gray paper with center cut-out of design size taped to board at top.

2181-E2 20c Design on white board, covering gray paper marked "C," black —

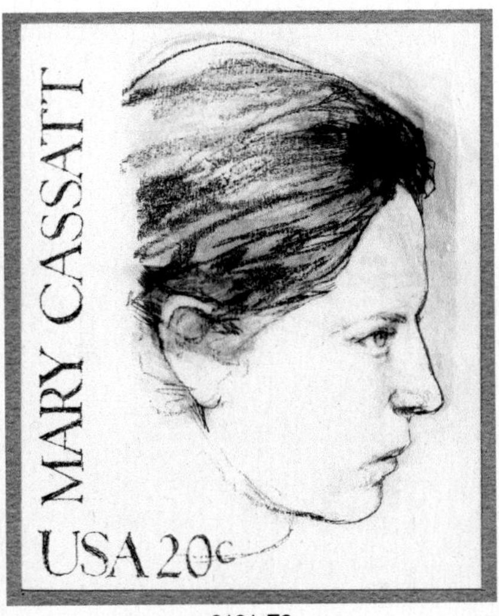

2181-E3

Design size: 106x127mm
Pencil drawing with gray wash in hair and at right on white board, covered by thick gray paper with center cut-out of design size taped to board at top.

2181-E3 20c Design on white board, covering gray paper marked "D," black and gray —

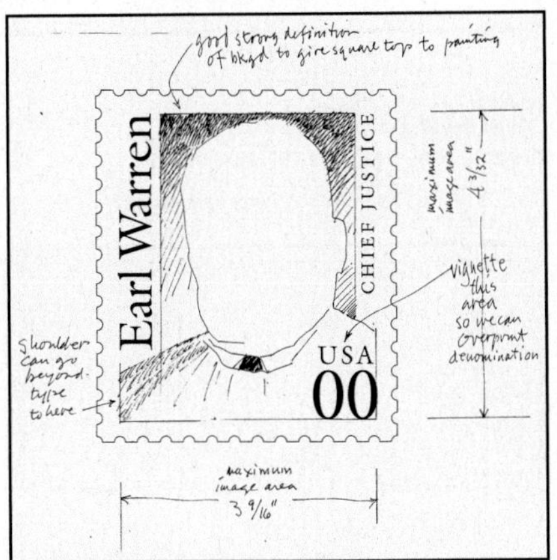

2184-E1

Design size: 108x124
Early version of design on white paper, denomination "00," "Chief Justice" at right, with many black ink notations indicating/suggesting wanted design elements.

2184-E1 No denomination, design and notes on 8½x11 inches white wove paper, black —

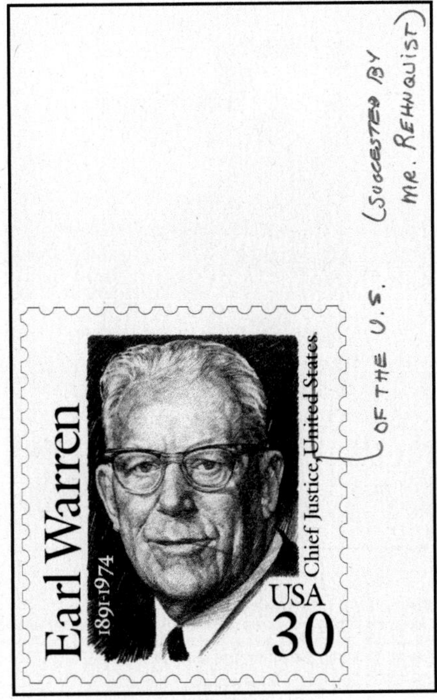

2184-E2

Design size: 112x127mm
Photo essay of early full design, with black felt-tip pen notation at right crossing out "United States" and suggesting it be changed to "OF THE U.S." and "Suggested by Mr. Rehnquist."

2184-E2 30c Design on 8½x11 inches photo paper with handwritten suggestion to change "United States" to "of the U.S.," which suggestion noted as coming from William Rehnquist, Chief Justice of the U.S. Supreme Court, black —

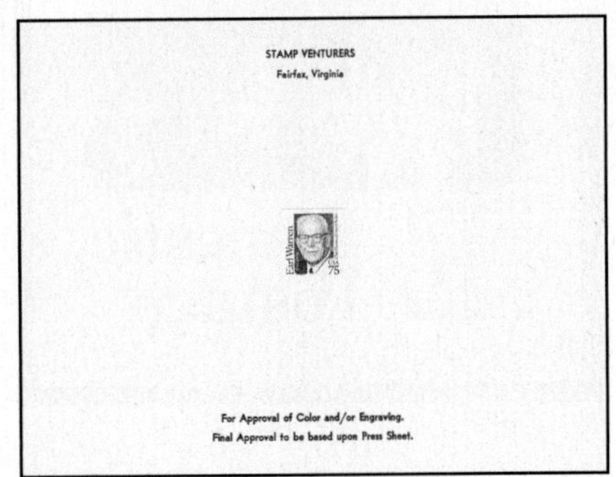

2184-E3

Design size: 18x21mm
Engraving of full design, but denomination shown as 75c and with "Chief Justice, United States" at right.

2184-E3 75c Engraved design cut to 22x24mm size and affixed to 202x152mm card with "STAMP VENTURERS / Fairfax, Virginia" at top and "For Approval of Color and/or Engraving./Final Approval to be based upon Press Sheet.," blue —

2184-E4

Design size: 115x131mm
A 176x204 piece of white wove paper with simulated perforations and 100x115mm cut-out at center inside the perforations, affixed to an 8½x11 inches sheet of white wove paper, prior essay of Warren's face added and correct text at left, dates and denomination blocks affixed, "Chief Justice of the U.S." block replaces previous text at right, signed Chris Calle on backing paper.

2184-E4 29c Photo essay with text, dates and denomination add-ons affixed, black —

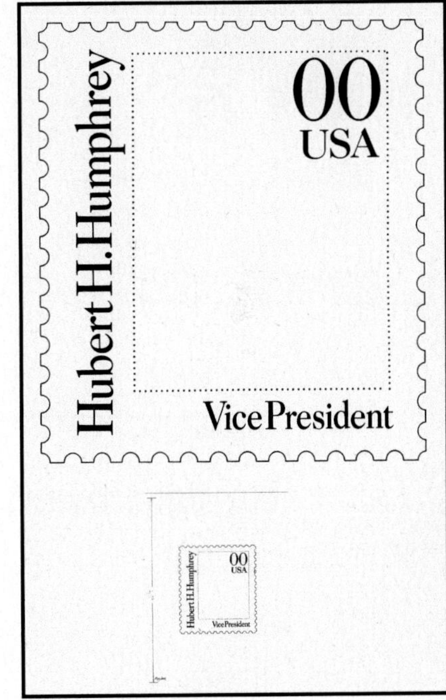

2189-E1

Design size: 111x122mm
Ink drawing of "00" denomination and text.

2189-E1 No denomination, text and simulated perfs on photo paper, measurement notes at left and large image reduced to stamp size affixed below, note on covering tracing paper says "Not Used," black —

2189-E2

Design size: 111x122mm
Ink drawing of "00" denomination and text.

2189-E2 No denomination, text and simulated perfs on white wove paper, measurement notes at left and large image reduced to stamp size affixed below, 8/23/89 handwritten note at lower right, black —

2189-E3

Design size: 98x112mm
Photo of complete essay with handwritten notes indicating that the word "VICE PRESIDENT" at right must be changed to capital and lower case lettering.

2189-E3 25c Essay design on 8½x11 inches white wove paper, black —

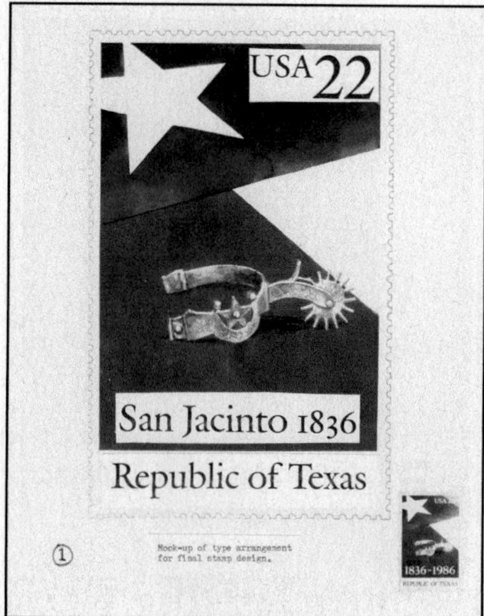

2204-E1

Design size: 129x201mm
Mock-up of text with three corrections on white paper affixed over photo of original essay, with image of original essay reduced to stamp size shown at lower right.

2204-E1 22c Design on photopaper with corrections affixed, multicolored —

2277-E1

Design size: 108x126mm
Black charcoal unadopted trial design of eagle "E" stamp with black ink simulated perforations.

2277-E1 (25c) Design on white wove paper, affixed to 155x205mm thick black card, black —

2284-E1

Design size: each picture 63x73mm plus text underneath. Original multicolored artwork in watercolor and ink affixed to thick white card, names of birds below in black ink.

2284-E1, 2285-E1 25c Two separate designs, each on thin card, affixed to thick white card, printed sticker of artist Chuck Ripper with address at lower right of card, multicolored —

2376-E1

Design size: 108x184mm
Pencil drawing on thin white wove.

2376-E1 (22c) Design on 160x264mm wove paper, "JIM SHARPE" in black ink at lower right corner —

2376-E2

Design size: 108x184mm
Pencil drawing on thin white wove.

2376-E2 (22c) Design on 172x264mm wove paper —

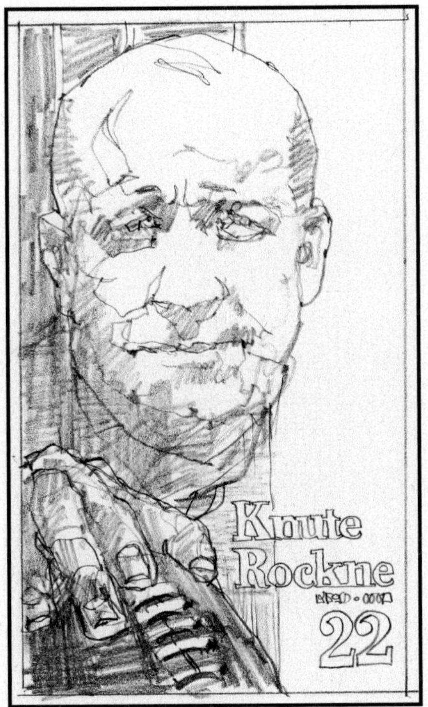

2376-E3

Design size: 109x184mm
Pencil drawing on thin white wove.

2376-E3 (22c) Design on 152x264mm wove paper —

2376-E4

Design size: 109x183mm
Pencil drawing on thin white wove.

2376-E4 (22c) Design on 172x267mm wove paper —

2376-E5

Design size: 113x184mm
Pencil drawing on thin white wove.

2376-E5 (22c) Design on 157x264mm wove paper —

2376-E6

Design size: 113x184mm
Pencil drawing on thin white wove.

2376-E6 (22c) Design on 160x261mm wove paper —

2376-E7

Design size: 108x181mm
Pencil drawing on thin white wove.

2376-E7 (22c) Design on 145x261mm wove paper —

2376-E8

Design size: 108x182mm
Pencil drawing on thin white wove.

2376-E8 (22c) Design on 174x261mm wove paper —

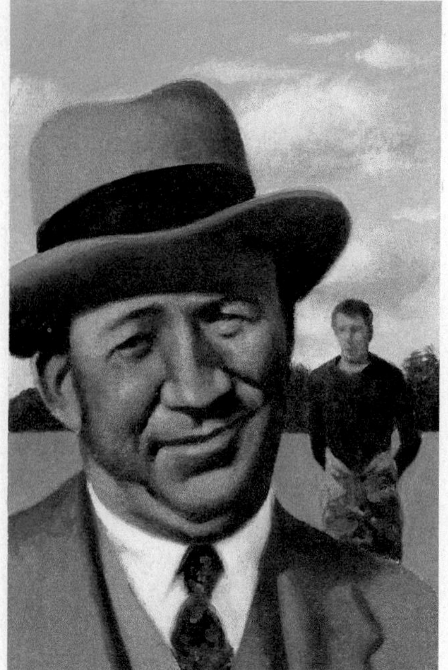

2376-E9

Design size: 115x176mm
Handpainted image on white board, reduced photo of painting mounted below.

2376-E9 (22c) Painting on 202x278mm white board with reduced photo below, small "2" in circle at lower right corner, "Dennis LUZAK" in ink on reverse at top —

2376-E10

Design size: 126-198mm
Photo of design mounted on mock-up photo of stamp perforations and lettering.

2376-E10 (22c) Design mounted beneath cut-out of thin board adhering to 215x278mm thick gray board —

2403-E1

Design size: 36x21mm
Imperforate stamp image as issued except "USA 25" in black instead of white as issued.

2403-E1 25c Near-final image on gummed 211x94mm stamp paper, color bars and "A1111" at left of stamp —

2453-E1

Design size: 110x124mm
Pencil drawing of canoe with black ink lettering and simulated perforations.

2453-E1 12c Design on white wove paper, taped at corners to 207x278mm white wove sheet of paper, stamp-size photo essay of design affixed below on paper with pencil design —

2453-E2

Design size: 110-124mm
Pencil drawing of canoe with black ink lettering and pencil and black ink simulated perforations.

2453-E2 12c Design on white wove paper, taped at corners to 207x278mm white wove sheet of paper, stamp-size photo essay of design affixed below on paper with pencil design, ms. "Punch up, like other one" at top right of large sheet of paper —

Image of pine cone portion of stamp, only.

2491-E1 32c Die on India (?), affixed to card, black —

2538-E1

Design size: 109x176mm
Pencil drawing on thin tracing paper.

2538-E1 No denomination, design on approximately 190x215mm tracing paper, signed "Wolfe" at right bottom beneath design —

2538-E2

Design size: 109x176mm
Photo of No. 2538-E1 with plastic overlay bearing William Soroyan (sic) name at top.

2538-E2 No denomination, photo in black on beige, with plastic overlay in black, all mounted on 8½x11 inch sheet of white wove paper —

2538-E3

Design size: 108x174mm
Pencil drawing on thin tracing paper.

2538-E3 No denomination, design on 171x273mm tracing paper, signed "Wolfe" at right bottom beneath design —

2538-E4

Design size: 108x174mm
Photo of No. 2538-E3 with plastic overlay bearing william Soroyan (sic) name at top.

2538-E4 No denomination, photo in black and beige, with plastic overlay in black, all mounted on 8½x11 inch sheet of white wove paper —

2538-E5

Design size: 108x177mm
Pencil drawing on thin tracing paper.

2538-E5 No denomination, design on 191x215mm tracing paper, signed "Wolfe" at right bottom beneath stamp —

2538-E6

Design size: 108x177mm
Photo of No. 2538-E5 with plastic overlay bearing William Soroyan (sic) name at top.

2538-E6 No denomination, photo in black on beige, plastic overlay in black, all mounted on 8½x11 inch sheet of white wove paper —

2538-E7

Design size: 108x179mm
Pencil drawing on thin tracing paper, includes name Wm Soroyan (sic) at top.

2538-E7 22c Design on 171x260mm tracing paper, signed "Wolfe" at right bottom beneath design —

2538-E8

Design size: 108x179mm
Photo of No. 2538-E7 with plastic overlay changing name at top to William Soroyan (sic).

2538-E8 22c Photo in black on beige, plastic overlay in black, all mounted on 8½x11 inch sheet of white wove paper —

2538-E9

Design size: 109x178mm
Pencil drawing on thin tracing paper.

2538-E9 No denomination, design on tracing paper with no signature (but clearly by Wolfe) —

2538-E10

Design size: 109x178mm
Photo of No. 2538-E9 with plastic overlay bearing William Saroyan (correct spelling) at top.

2538-E10 No denomination, photo in black on beige, plastic overlay in black, all mounted on 8½x11 inch sheet of white wove paper —

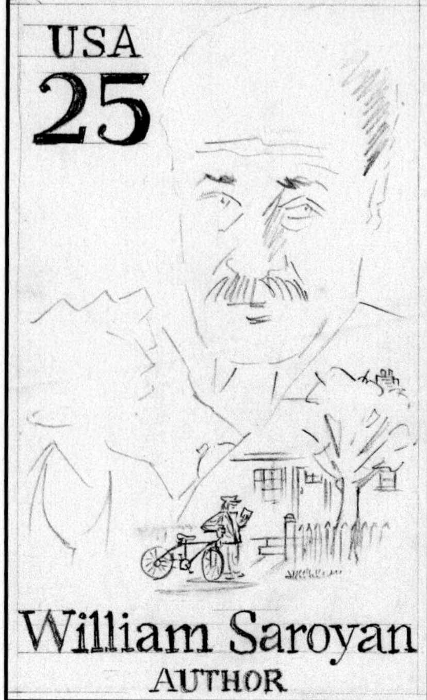

2538-E11

Design size: 106x172mm
Pencil drawing on thin tracing paper, Saroyan spelled correctly.

2538-E11 25c Design on 189x250mm tracing paper —

2538-E12

Design size: 172x110mm
Photo on plastic essay of picture only, with simulated perforations, and "25/USA" and "William Saroyan" on plastic taped to photo.

2538-E12 25c Design on plastic, mounted on 284x191mm white board —

2549-E1

Design size: 73x44mm, "block" size: 161x103mm
Original multicolored art in watercolor and ink.

2545-2549-E1 25c Four separate designs, each on thin card, mounted in block of 4 format on thick brown card, sticker on reverse of "Chuck Ripper/Wildlife Art . . ." —

2551-E1

Design size: 139x216mm
Gray card glued to white card with simulated perforations, picture of service medal carefully cut and glued on gray card, with shading added, "Honoring Those Who Served" and "USA/29" handpainted on gray card in watercolors, plastic overlay taped at top bears the "Desert Shield" and "Desert Storm" wording, PMS310 color choice on tag taped at bottom of overlay, signed "A. Frank/PMG" at right bottom beneath design.

2551-E1 29c Design similar to issued stamp but different in many details —

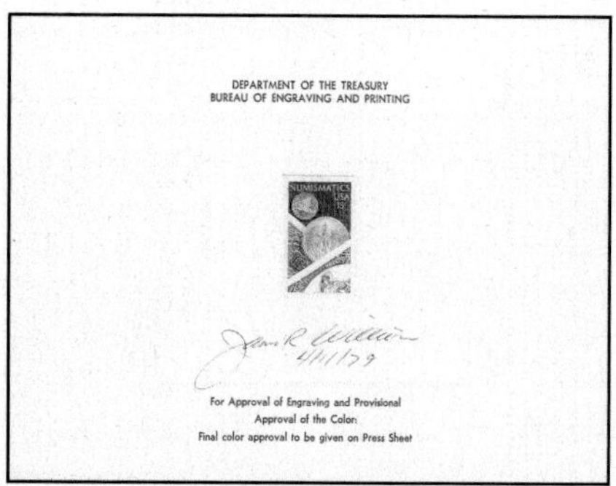

2558-E1

2558-E1 15c Large hybrid die essay, signed "Jack R Williams/ 4/11/79;" while presented in the usual form as a proof on card for approval of engraving and color, this design itself was never approved for stamp —

2602-E1

Design size: 88x97mm
Photo of original Eagle and Shield art with simulated perforations, with artist tracing paper taped overlay with photo of shield

with four stars painted in taped to the overlay, reduced original artwork at right without stars.

2602-E1 (10c) Design in cutout of thin card on 280x216 thick white card —

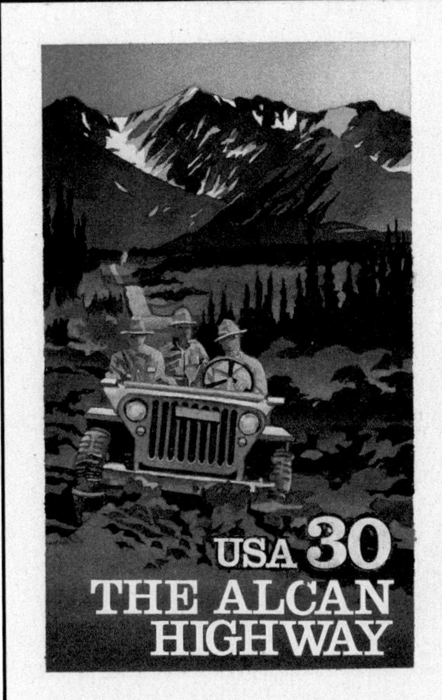

2635-E1

Design size: 111x182mm
Original art from Library of Congress with plastic overlay taped on with "USA 30 / THE ALCAN HIGHWAY" attached to overlay.

2635-E1 30c Design on rough artist's card attached to thick black 175x282mm card, with plastic overlay, description of art beneath design —

2636-E1

Design size: 177x116mm
Design on tracing paper with enhancements in clouds done in pencil, with overlay on tracing paper with further enhancements to clouds done in pencil.

2636-E1 No denomination, 232x161 overlay taped to design of My Old Kentucky Home on 294x210mm underlay —

2636-E2

Design size: 177x116mm
Design of My Old Kentucky Home with cutouts of "30c" attached at upper right and slips of paper glued on to cover "USA" at upper left and "KENTUCKY 1792" at bottom.

2636-E2 Design on 204x191mm white wove paper taped to 290x209mm thin white card —

2646a-E1

Design size of each: 54x93mm; "block" size: 116x193mm
Original multicolored art in watercolor and ink.

2646a-E1 25c Four separate designs, each on thin card, mounted in block of 4 format on white card, mounted on blue backing —

2646a-E2

Design size: 126x199mm
Original art in watercolor and ink.

2646a-E2 25c Multicolored art in watercolor and black ink, bird slightly different than #2646a-E1 —

2646a-E3

Design size: 24x38mm
Original art in watercolor and ink.

2646a-E3 25c Multicolored bird slightly different than #2646a-E1 and #2646a-E2, done in stamp size, mounted on white card —

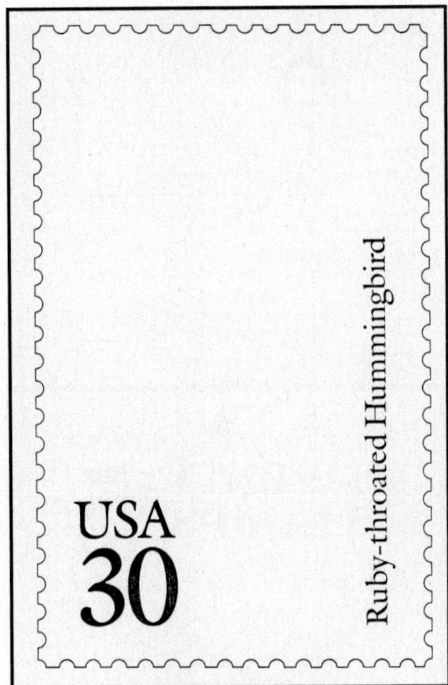

2646a-E4

Design size: 126x198mm
Ink drawing of 30c denomination and text.

2646a-E4 30c Simulated perfs, denomination and text on white card, with measurement notes at left, black —

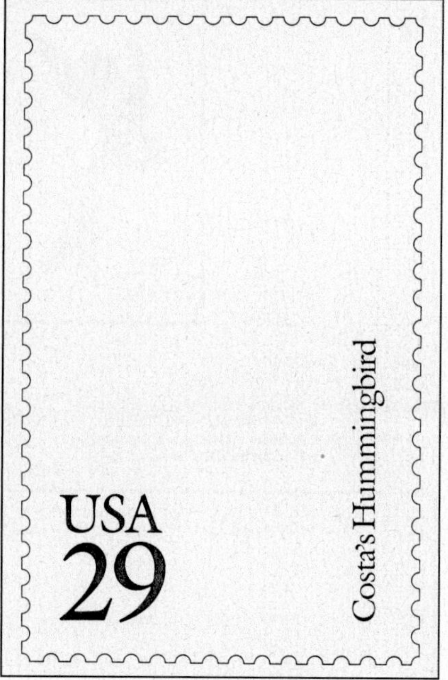

2646a-E5

Design size: 126x198mm
Ink drawing of final 29c denomination and text.

2646a-E5 29c Simulated perfs, denomination and text on white card, with measurement notes at left, black —

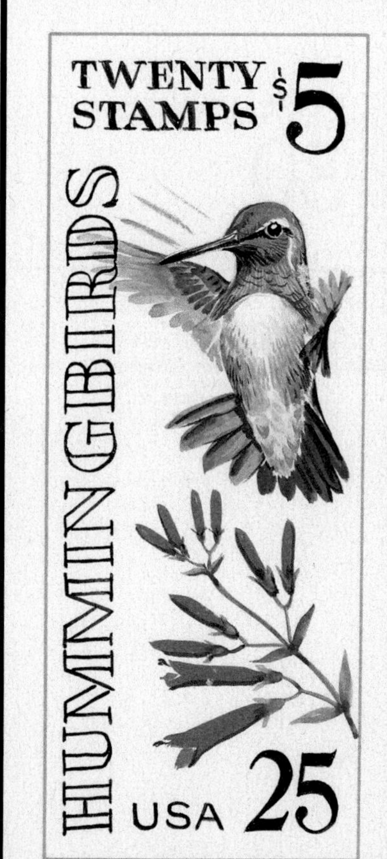

2646a-E6

Design size: 52x129mm; overall size: 65x143mm
Original art in watercolor and black ink.

2646a-E6 25c Multicolored art for proposed booklet cover, later revised, on thin card —

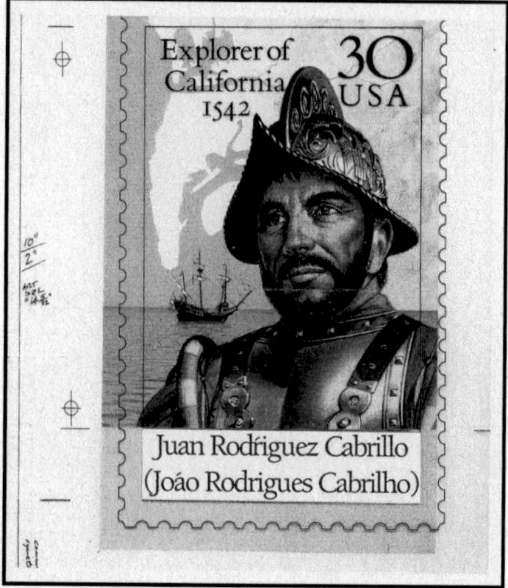

2704-E1

Design size: 94x143mm
Photo of accepted design except with 30c denomination, with plastic overlay with Cabrillo name in both Spanish and Portuguese attached as a possible design alteration (not chosen thus).

2704-E1 Design with Spanish Cabrillo name, overlay in plastic taped at top bearing names in Spanish and Portuguese, underlay 215x278mm —

2746-E1

Design size: 115x178mm
Design in charcoal, 156x28mm slip of paper with identifying verbiage taped beneath design.

2746-E1 No denomination, design on very thin white card attached to thicker 175x229mm white card, "HIGGINS BOND, ILLUSTRATOR . . ." on reverse of card —

2746-E2

Design size: 115x178mm
Design in charcoal, "PERCY LAVON JULIAN" added by hand at top, "29" on very thin card glued on at top left, "Black Heritage USA" on black strip of paper taped to bottom across design.

2746-E2 29c Design on very thin white card attached to thicker 175x229mm white card, "HIGGINS BOND, ILLUSTRATOR . . ." on reverse of card —

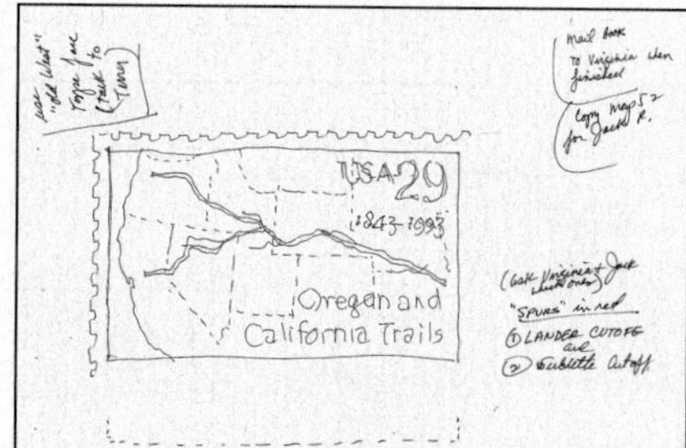

2747-E1

Design size: "stamp" only 151x100mm
Ink drawing of design for Oregon and California trails, with notes and ideas in margins of paper.

2747-E1 29c Hand drawn design on 8½x11 inch white paper from note pad with blue lines, a second very crude drawing on reverse —

2747-E2

Design size: 94x58mm
Ink drawing of design with "Oregon Trail" only text, yellow note paper on back "'Noodling' sketches by Howard Paine" which is certainly also true for No. 2747-E1.

2747-E2 29c Hand drawn design on 8½x11 inch white paper from note pad with blue lines —

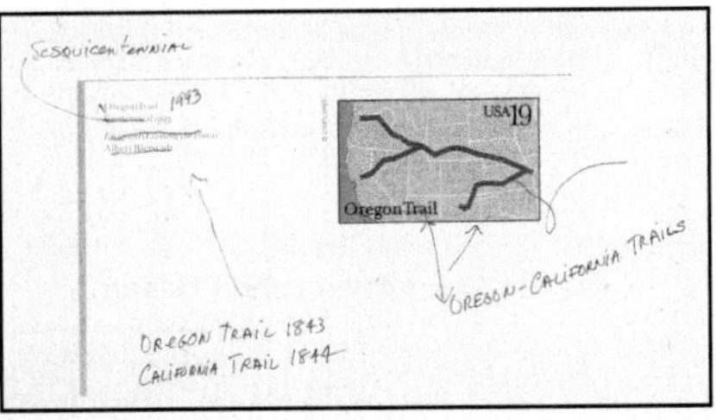

2747-E3

Design size: 57x34mm

Photo of official design showing Oregon, California and New Mexico trails with ink notes indicating New Mexico trail should be omitted and stamp text should say "Oregon-California Trails," plus note indicating this should be called the "Oregon Trail Sesquicentennial 1993."

2747-E3 19c Design and text on 215x146mm white wove paper —

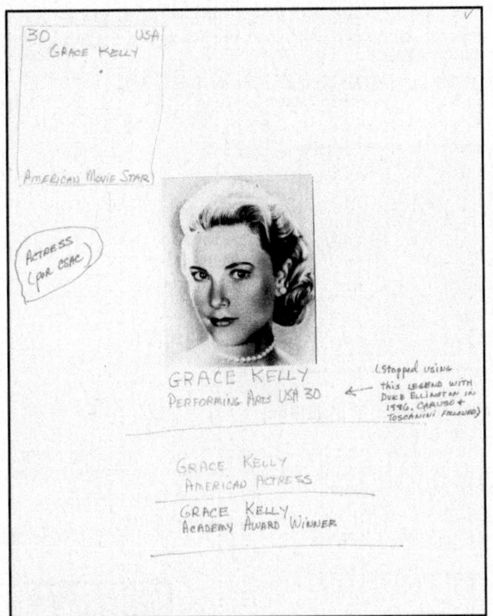

2749-E1

Design size: 69x84mm

Black on white copy of photo of Grace Kelly attached to white paper with notes for several possible texts that could be used (but all ignored on final stamp issue — except name).

2749-E1 30c Photo plus ink and pencil development notes on 8½x11 inch white wove —

Similar to issued stamp, but with noticeable differences in tie, hairline, etc.

2933-E1 32c Die on gummed paper, brown 1,000.

AIR POST STAMPS

1918 ISSUE

Complete engraving of frame only as adopted. Backstamped "626646A ENGRAVER'S STOCK PROOF AUTHORIZED BY" (signature), plus pencil "663" and "Weeks" (?).

C3-E1 24c Die on India, die sunk on card, deep carmine 5,000.

Incomplete engraving of entire design as adopted: unfinished plumes above value numerals and no serial number on biplane.

C3-E2 24c Die on wove, 40x37mm, black vignette, blue frame —

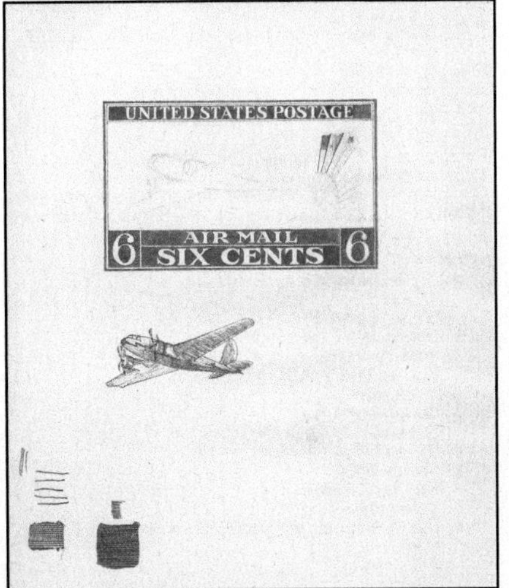

C25-E1

Original pen, ink and wash drawing on thick card for the 1941-44 Transport series of air post stamps, various elements of which were used in the creation of the final accepted design. Size of blue frame is 4⅞x3 inches.

C25-E1 Drawing on thick card, blue and red 3,000.

Engraving of adopted design except without denomination, "C" punch where denominations go, control #722657A (1942) on back of card.

C25-C31-E2 Die on wove, die sunk on card, 201x150mm, black 5,500.

SPECIAL DELIVERY STAMPS

1885 ISSUE
American Bank Note Co.

E1-E1

Incomplete engraving of entire design as adopted: ornaments missing at each side of "SPECIAL," line under messenger is in pencil, shading on left side of messenger tablet missing, leaves and vert. background lines unfinished (latter shaded over with pencil).

E1-E1 10c Die on India, dim dusky g-b. green 2,500.

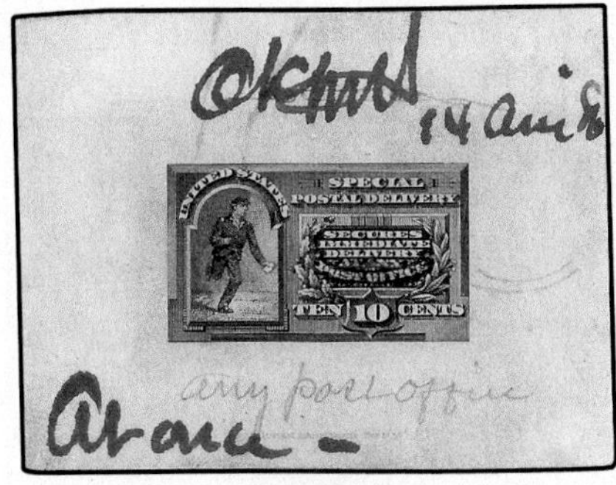

E2-E1

1888 ISSUE

No. E1P1 with "AT ANY OFFICE" drawn in wash on small piece of thin paper and mounted over "AT A SPECIAL / DELIVERY / OFFICE." Pencil "any post office" and ms. "At once O.K. / J.C.M. 14 Aug. 86" (?) on backing card.

E2-E1 10c Die on India, on card, black 2,500.

1908 ISSUE
Bureau of Engraving and Printing

E7-E1

Design size: about 8½x7⅛ inches

Preliminary ink and pencil drawing of entire design somewhat similar to that adopted: ("V.S." for U.S. and other minor changes).

E7-E1 10c Drawing on vellum, black —

E7-E2

Design size: about 8½x7⅛ inches

Preliminary ink and pencil drawing of entire design nearly as adopted: ("V.S." for U.S.)

E7-E2 10c Drawing on white drawing paper, black —

E7-E3

Design size: 213½x179mm

Similar to No. E7-E2 but with "U.S."

E7-E3 10c Drawing on white drawing paper, black 750.

E7-E4

Design size: 26x21½mm

Woodblock size: 45x42mm

Woodblock of entire design as adopted with about 5mm colorless border outside design, solid color beyond, engraved on wood by Giraldon of Paris. (One exists with ms. "Wood cut made in Paris by Mr. Whitney Warren — The cuts and the impression therefrom were turned over to the Director of the Bureau of Engraving & Printing, and by him turned over to the Custodian of Dies, Rolls and Plates and given No. 446. They are now held by the Custodian." Another has typewritten "Prints made in Paris, France, from a wood-cut engraving by an unknown engraver from a design made by Mr. Whitney Warren, architect, of New York City." with ms. "Compliments J.E. Ralph" director of B.E.P. and pencil date "9/7/1917.")

Ridgeway numbers used for colors of Nos. E7-E4 and E7-E5.

E7-E4 10c
- *a.* Woodcut on 19g/2 yellowish wove
  - 43k/1 dim dark green blue *450.*
  - 44m/2 dull dusky m. g-blue *450.*
  - 45j/1 dim v. dark b-g-blue *450.*
  - 45m/1 dim dusky b-g-blue *450.*
- *b.* Woodcut on 19f/2 dull faint y-o-yellow wove
  - 43k/1 dim dark g-blue *450.*
  - 43m/1 dim dusky g-blue *450.*
  - 44k/1 dim dark m. g-blue *450.*
  - 44k/2 dull dark m. g-blue *450.*
  - 45m/1 dim dusky b-g-blue *450.*
  - 45m/2 dull dusky b-g-blue *450.*
- *c.* Woodcut on 19g/2 dull v. faint y-o-yellow wove
  - 43k/1 dim dark g-blue *450.*
  - 43m/1 dim dusky g-blue *450.*

E7-E5

Design size: 26x21½mm
Complete engraving of entire design fairly similar to that adopted but with minor differences.

E7-E5 10c
- *a.* Die on India, die sunk on card, 37m/0 dusky g-b. green blue *750.*
- *b.* Die on soft white wove, 30x35mm, 37m/0 dusky g-blue-green *750.*

REGISTRATION STAMP

F1-E1

Design size: 19x22½mm
Retouched circular photo of vignette mounted on wash drawing of frame design as adopted. Ms. "Approved July 8/11 — Frank H. Hitchcock — Postmaster General" on backing card.

F1-E1 10c Model on white paper, mounted on thick gray cardboard, 81x92mm, black *1,250.*

POSTAGE DUE STAMPS

1879 ISSUE
American Bank Note Co.

J1-E1

Design size: 19½x25½mm
Die size: 54x66½mm
Complete engraving of entire design as adopted except "UNPAID POSTAGE" instead of "POSTAGE DUE" above vignette oval.

J1-E1 1c
- *a.* Die on India, die sunk on card
  - orange brown *850.*
  - slate gray *850.*
  - dark red violet *850.*
  - dull yellow *850.*
  - light orange *850.*
  - red brown *850.*
- *b.* Die on India, cut small (1-4mm)
  - gray black *300.*
  - dull red *300.*
  - dull brown *300.*
  - dull green *300.*
  - dull blue *300.*
- *c.* Die on India, cut close (0-1mm)
  - orange brown *300.*
  - slate gray *300.*
  - dark red violet *300.*
  - dull yellow *300.*
- *d.* Die on ivory glazed paper, die sunk
  - black *700.*
  - black brown *700.*
  - scarlet *700.*
  - blue *700.*

Design size: 19½x25½mm
Die size: 53½x53½mm
Complete engraving of entire design as adopted except "UNPAID POSTAGE" instead of "POSTAGE DUE" above vignette oval.

J2-E1 2c
- *a.* Die on India, die sunk on card
  - dark red violet *850.*
  - black *850.*
- *b.* Die on India, cut small
  - gray black *300.*
  - dull red *300.*
  - dull brown *300.*
  - dull green *300.*
  - dull blue *300.*
- *c.* Die on India, cut close
  - orange brown *300.*
  - dark red violet *300.*
  - slate gray *400.*
- *d.* Die on ivory glazed paper, die sunk
  - black *700.*
  - black brown *700.*
  - scarlet *700.*
  - blue *700.*

Design size: 19½x25½mm
Die size: 53x53mm
Complete engraving of entire design as adopted except "UNPAID POSTAGE" instead of "POSTAGE DUE" above vignette oval.

J3-E1 3c
- *a.* Die on India, die sunk on card, dull yellow *850.*
- *b.* Die on India, cut small
  - gray black *300.*
  - dull red *300.*
  - dull brown *300.*
  - dull green *300.*
  - dull blue *300.*
- *c.* Die on India, cut close, dull yellow *300.*
- *d.* Die on ivory glazed paper, die sunk
  - black *700.*
  - black brown *700.*
  - scarlet *700.*
  - blue *700.*

Design size: 19½x25½mm
Complete engraving of entire design as adopted except "UNPAID POSTAGE" instead of "POSTAGE DUE" above vignette oval.

J4-E1 5c
- *a.* Die on India, die sunk on card, slate gray *850.*
- *b.* Die on India, cut small
  - gray black *300.*
  - dull red *300.*
  - dull brown *300.*
  - dull green *300.*
  - dull blue *300.*
- *c.* Die on India, cut close
  - orange brown *300.*
  - slate gray *300.*
  - dark red violet *300.*
  - dull yellow *300.*
- *d.* Die on ivory glazed paper, die sunk
  - black *700.*
  - black brown *700.*
  - scarlet *700.*
  - blue *700.*

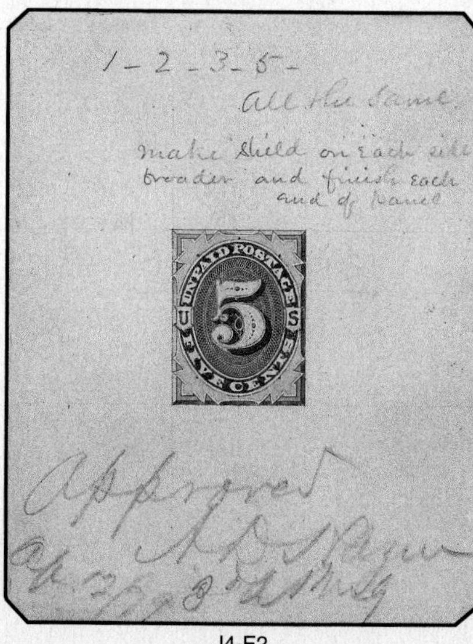

J4-E2

As No. J4-E1 except frame a pencil and wash drawing, vignette engraved numeral and oval lathework numeral cut to shape and pasted over lathework, with design notations.

J4-E2 5c Engraved vignette, frame pencil and wash, on thick card, 70x88mm, brown *4,500.*

1894 ISSUE
Bureau of Engraving and Printing

J31-E1

Design size: 18½x22½mm
Die size: 50x99mm
Incomplete engraving of entire design: no engraved lines on numeral, lathework unfinished on two inclined spots at each side of numeral.

J31-E1 1c Die on India, die sunk on card, deep claret *1,400.*

J31-E2

Design size: 18½x22½mm
Die size: 50x99mm
Incomplete engraving of entire design: engraved lines on numeral but lathework still unfinished on two inclined spots at each side of numeral.

J31-E2 1c Die on India, die sunk on card, claret *1,000.*

J32-E1

Design size: 18½x22½mm
Die size: unknown
Incomplete engraving of entire design: unfinished ornaments by "P" of "POSTAGE" and "E" of "DUE."

J32-E1 2c Die on India, size 26x30mm, deep claret *1,500.*

J33-E1

Incomplete engraving of entire design: blank space for numeral with "3" drawn in pencil.

J33-E1 3c Die on India, die sunk on card, black *1,100.*

J33-E2

Incomplete engraving of entire design: no engraved lines on numeral, bottom lettering in pencil only, no hand retouching of lathework around numeral.

J33-E2 3c Die on India, die sunk on card, black *1,500.*

J33-E3

Incomplete engraving of entire design: no engraved lines on numeral.

J33-E3 3c Die on India, die sunk on card, claret *1,000.*

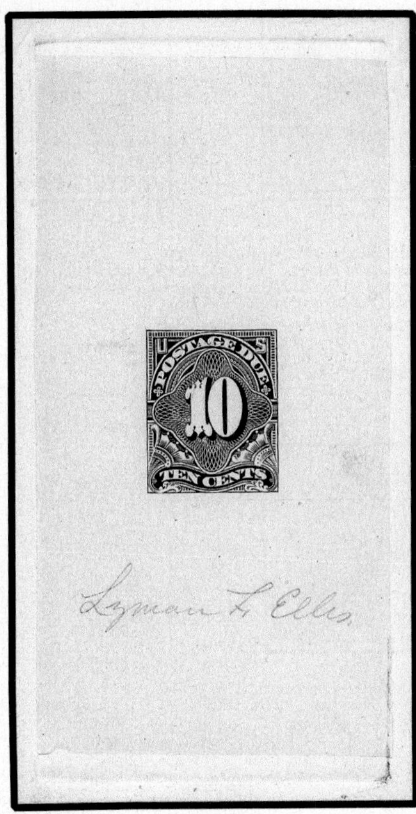

J35-E1

Incomplete engraving of entire design: no engraved lines on numerals, signed by Lyman F. Ellis.

J35-E1 10c Die on India, die sunk on card, black *2,100.*

J36-E1

Incomplete engraving of entire design: no engraved lines on numerals.

J36-E1 30c Die on India, die sunk on card, claret *1,600.*

J37-E1

Incomplete engraving of entire design: 9x9mm blank space for numerals.

J37-E1 50c Die on India, die sunk on card
black *1,600.*
claret *1,600.*

J37-E2

Incomplete engraving of entire design: numerals engraved but hand engraving to retouch lathework around numerals missing.

J37-E2 50c Die on India, die sunk on card, black *2,300.*

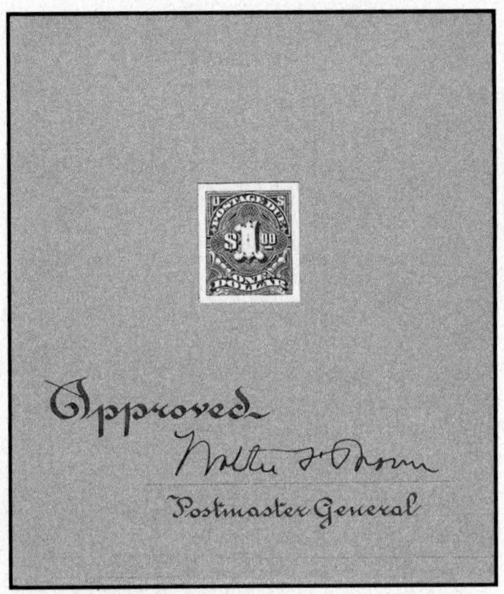

J67-E1

Complete engraving of unissued 1917 denomination with wash drawing in "1" and dollar sign, "Approved / Walter F. Brown (signature) / Postmaster General" below design.

J67A-E1 $1 Die on white card, mounted on gray card, black *21,000.*

OFFICIAL STAMPS

Continental Bank Note Co.
AGRICULTURE

O1-E1

Engraved Franklin vignette with 1 and value label.

O1-E1 1c Die on India, on card (1873), black *2,250.*

O2-E1

Engraved Jackson vignette with 2 and value label.

O2-E1 2c Die on glazed paper (1873), black *2,250.*

O2-E2

Design size: 20x25mm

Engraved vignette, numeral and value label from 1873 2c (No. O2-E1) mounted on pencil and wash drawing for frame design as adopted for Agriculture set. Pencil signature "J. Claxton" on backing card. Frame differs for each dept.

O2-E2 2c Model on yellowish card, 23x30mm, on 90x118mm white card, black vignette, gray black frame *6,500.*

O3-E1

Washington vignette, 3 and value label.

O3-E1 3c Die on India, card mounted (1873), black *2,250.*

O4-E1

Completed vignette with 6 and value label.

O4-E1 6c Die on India, on card (1873), black *2,400.*

O6-E1

Completed Clay vignette with 12 and value label.

O6-E1 12c Die on white glazed paper (1873), black *2,000.*

O7-E1

Vignette of Webster with 15 below.

O7-E1 15c Die on white glazed paper (1873), black *1,250.*

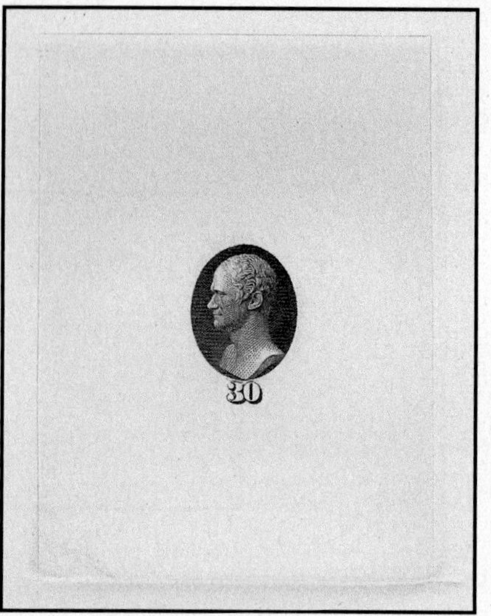

O9-E1

Completed vignette with 30 below.

O9-E1 30c Die on white glazed paper (1873), black *1,500.*

EXECUTIVE

O12-E1

Design size: 20x25mm
See design note for No. O2-E1.

O12-E1 3c Model on yellowish card, 23x30mm, on 90x118mm white card, black *6,000.*

O12-E2

Design size: 19½x25mm
Die size: 64x76mm
Engraving of complete design of No. O12-E1 with "DEP'T" in top label.

O12-E2 3c
  a. Die on India, die sunk on card, green *2,750.*
  b. Die on India, cut close
    black *2,250.*
    green *2,250.*

INTERIOR

O17-E1

Design size: 20x25mm
See design note for No. O2-E1.

O17-E1 3c Model on yellowish card, 23x30mm, on 90x118mm white card, black *9,000.*

JUSTICE

O27-E1

Design size: 20x25mm
See design note for No. O2-E1.

O27-E1 3c Model on yellowish card, 23x30mm, on 90x118mm white card, black *10,000.*

NAVY

O37-E1

Design size: 20x25mm
See design note for No. O2-E1.

O37-E1 3c Model on yellowish card, 23x30mm, on 90x118mm white card, black *4,750.*

O39-E1

Die size: 62x76mm
Completed vignette with 7 and value label.

O39-E1 7c
  a. Die on India, on card (1873), black *1,000.*
  b. Die on white glazed paper, black *1,000.*

POST OFFICE

O47-E1

Design size: 19½x25mm
Complete engraving of entire design as adopted except with Franklin vignette instead of large numeral.

O47-E1 1c
  a. Die on India, mounted on white ivory card
    blue *1,750.*
  b. Die on proof paper
    gray black *1,250.*
    dull scarlet *1,250.*
    dull brown *1,250.*
    dull green *1,250.*
    dull blue *1,250.*
  c. Die on ivory glazed paper
    brown black *1,750.*
    orange red *1,750.*
    blue *1,750.*

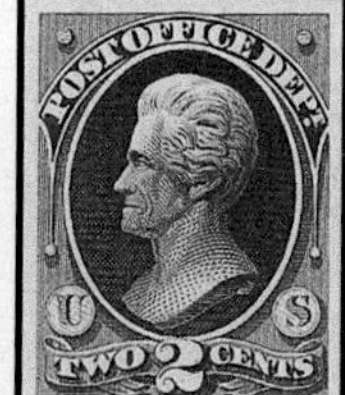

O48-E1

Design size: 19½x25mm
Complete engraving of entire design as adopted except with Jackson vignette instead of large numeral.

O48-E1 2c
  a. Die on India, mounted on white ivory card
    orange brown *1,500.*
  b. Die on proof paper
    gray black *1,250.*
    dull scarlet *1,250.*
    dull brown *1,250.*
    dull green *1,250.*
    dull blue *1,250.*
  c. Die on ivory glazed paper
    black *1,750.*
    brown black *1,750.*
    orange red *1,750.*
    blue *1,750.*

O49-E1

O49-E2

Design size: 20x25mm
Engraved vignette, numeral and value label from 1873 3c (No. 147-E10) mounted on pencil and wash drawing for frame design not adopted for Post Office set.

O49-E1 3c Model on yellowish card, 23x30mm, on 90x118mm white card, black *5,750.*

O49-E2 3c Model on yellowish card, 23x30mm, on 90x118mm white card, black *5,750.*

O49-E3

Design size: 20x25mm
See design note for No. O2-E1.

O49-E3 3c Model on yellowish card, 23x30mm, on 90x118mm white card, black *5,750.*

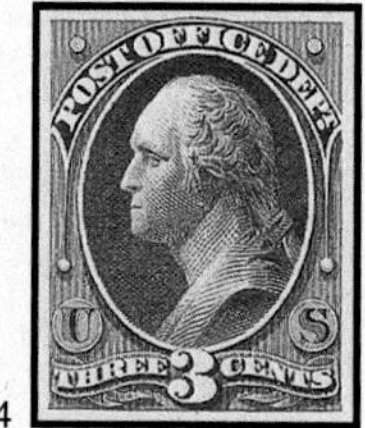

O49-E4

Design size: 19½x25mm
Complete engraving of entire design as adopted except with Washington vignette instead of large numeral.

O49-E4 3c
  a. Die on India, mounted on white ivory card
    green *1,500.*
  b. Die on proof paper
    gray black *1,250.*
    dull scarlet *1,250.*
    dull brown *1,250.*
    dull green *1,250.*
    dull blue *1,250.*
  c. Die on ivory glazed paper
    brown black *1,750.*
    orange red *1,750.*
    blue *1,750.*

O49-E5

Design size: 19½x25mm

As No. O49-E4, but with pencil and watercolor modifications in both top corners.

O49-E5 3c Die on India, black *4,000.*

O49-E6

1870 1c stamp (No. 145) with vignette cut out, "OFFICIAL 3 STAMP" drawn in pencil on envelope on which stamp is mounted. Blue pencil notations on backing envelope "1st design of official stamp for POD" and "Design by Mr. J. Barber for P O Official."

O49-E6 1c Stamp frame mounted on envelope, ultramarine frame, black vignette *7,500.*

O49-E7

Model of engraved frame from No. O49-E4 with hollow oval engraved lathework band with "OFFICIAL / STAMP" drawn in wash mounted in place, numeral drawn in pencil and wash. Ms. "No. 1" on backing card.

O49-E7 3c Model on stiff white card, 50x75mm, green *7,500.*

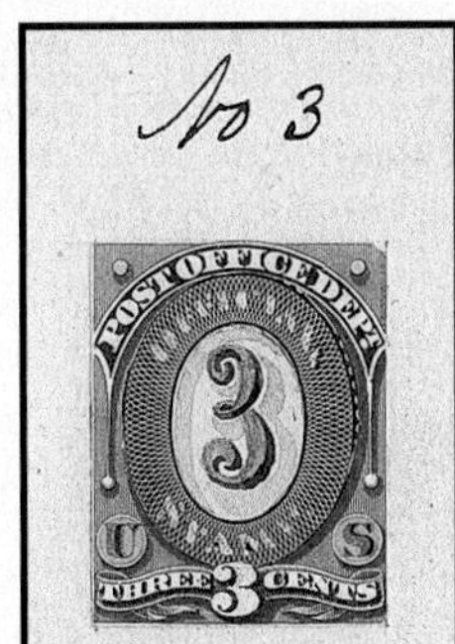

O49-E8

Like No. O49-E6, Ms. "No. 3" on backing card.

O49-E8 3c Model on stiff white card, 50x75mm, green & black *17,500.*

O50-E1

Incomplete engraving of design with Lincoln vignette, without rectangular frame design.

O50-E1 6c Die on white ivory paper, black *4,250.*

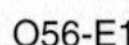
O56-E1

Design size: 19½x25mm

Complete engraving of entire design as adopted except with Perry vignette instead of large numeral.

O56-E1 90c

a. Die on India, mounted on white ivory card

brown	*1,500.*
blue	*1,500.*
orange red	*1,500.*

b. Die on proof paper

gray black	*1,500.*
dull scarlet	*1,500.*
dull brown	*1,500.*
dull green	*1,500.*
dull blue	*1,500.*

c. Die on ivory glazed paper

brown black	*1,750.*
orange red	*1,750.*
blue	*1,750.*

STATE

O59-E1

Design size: 20x25mm

Engraved vignette, numeral and value label from 1873 3c (No. 147-E10) mounted on pencil and wash drawing for frame design as adopted for State set. Pencil signature "J. Claxton" on backing card.

O59-E1 3c Model on yellowish card, 23x30mm, on 90x118mm white card, black *4,750.*

O68-E1

Design size: 25½x40mm

Engraved vignette of Seward mounted in watercolor drawing of adopted frame design. Ms. signatures of J. Claxton and Chas. Skinner on backing card.

O68-E1 Two Dollars, Model on 29x43mm grayish white card, mounted on 96x120mm white card, black *7,500.*

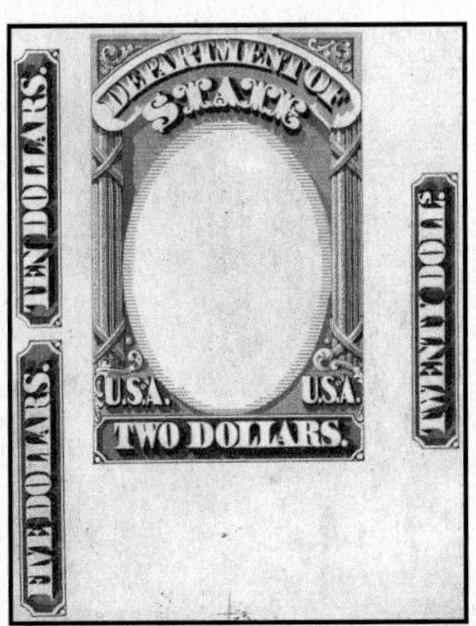

O68-E2

Complete engraving of adopted frame only with "TWO DOLLARS." in value label at bottom. With "FIVE DOLLARS." and "TEN DOLLARS." value labels outside design at left and "TWENTY DOLLs." value tablet at right.

O68-E2 Two Dollars, Die on India, black *15,000.*

O68-E3

Plate engraved frame only (three examples in a block of four with complete bicolor plate proof of $2 at upper left in block).

O68-E3 Two Dollars, Plate essay on India, green *10,000.*

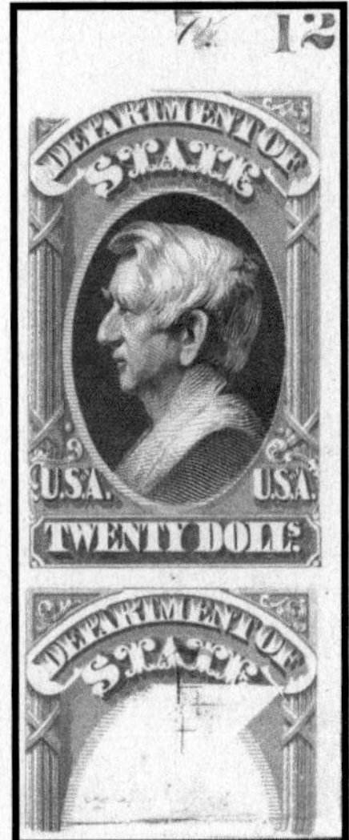

O71-E1

Plate engraving of top half of frame only, paired with $20 plate proof.

O71-E1 Die on India, mounted on card, green *9,000.*

WAR

O85-E1

Design size: 20x25mm

Engraved vignette, numeral and value label from 1873 3c (No. 147-E10) mounted on pencil and wash drawing for frame design as adopted for War set. Pencil signature "J. Claxton" on backing card.

O85-E1 3c Model on yellowish card, 23x30mm, on 90x118mm white card, black *4,750.*

NEWSPAPER AND PERIODICALS

1865 ISSUE
National Bank Note Co.

PR1-E1

Design size: 51x89mm

Typographed design somewhat similar to that adopted but with large Franklin vignette facing left, "PACKAGE" at bottom, other minor differences.

PR1-E1 5c Die on stiff white ivory paper

deep orange red	2,000.
dusky g-b. blue	2,000.
bright blue	2,000.
a. Die on paper with blue ruled lines	
deep orange red	2,000.
carmine	2,000.

1875 ISSUE
National Bank Note Co.

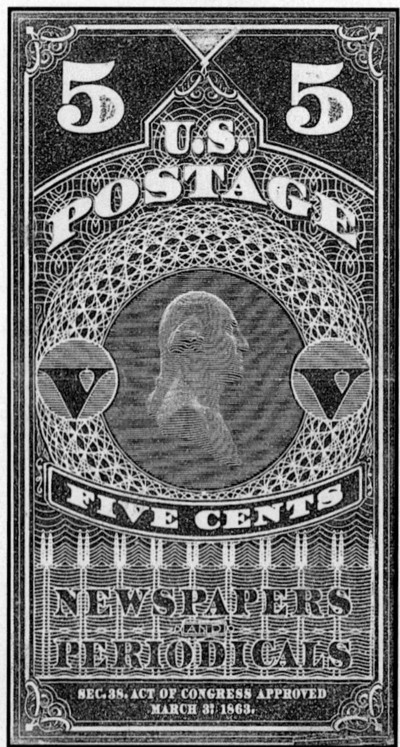

PR5-E1

Design size: 52x96½mm

Typographed design as issued but lacking "National Bank Note Company, New York" imprint at bottom.

PR5-E1 5c Die on wove paper, blue —

1875 ISSUE
Continental Bank Note Co.

PR9-E1

Design size: 19½x25mm

Engraved vignette and numerals (25's) with pencil sketch of unadopted frame design.

PR9-E1 25c Die on India, on card, black *2,750.*

PR9-E2

Design size: 19½x25mm

Complete engraving of unadopted design with "U S" at top and "25 CENTS 25" at bottom.

PR9-E2 25c

a. Die on India, on card	
black	1,350.
scarlet	1,350.
blue	1,350.
green	1,350.
b. Die on white ivory paper	
black	1,350.
black brown	1,350.
scarlet	1,350.
blue	1,350.

PR9-E3

Engraved unfinished die with final design, blank spaces for numerals and value tablets.

PR9-E3 Blank denomination, die on India, mounted on 27x45mm card, black *1,250.*

PR14-E1

Design size: 25x35mm

Wash drawing of complete design as adopted. Backing card signed by both designers, Chas. Skinner and Jos. Claxton.

PR14-E1 9c Drawing on 26x36mm card, on 56x74mm card, black *900.*

Complete engraving except value tablets blank.

PR16-E1 (12c) Die on India, mounted on 26x40mm card, black *1,700.*

PR23-E1

Design size: 24x35½mm

Wash drawing similar to that adopted, backing card signed by designers Skinner and Claxton, also has pencil "$12" and ms. "Continental Bank Note Co."

PR23-E1 96c Drawing on 88x121mm card, black *900.*

PR27-E1

Design size: 24½x35mm

Incomplete engraving of entire design: unshaded (shading pencilled in) inside left, right and bottom framelines, value label, top of "9." Upper corners unfinished.

PR27-E1 $9 Die on India, die sunk on 76x82mm card, black *1,350.*

PR28-E1

Design size: 24½x35mm

Incomplete engraving of entire design: no shading on dollar signs and numerals. No shading on frame around numerals and around value tablet.

PR28-E1 $12 Die on India, die sunk on 66x80mm card, black *1,350.*

PR28-E2

Incomplete engraving of entire design, shading pencilled in around bottom value tablet and top right and left dollar signs and numerals.

PR28-E2 $12 Die on India, die sunk on card, 75x90mm, black *1,150.*

PR29-E1

Design size: 24x35½mm
Wash drawing similar to that adopted but with "U S" in six-pointed stars instead of at top. Backing card signed by designers Skinner and Claxton, also pencil "31/32" and "8 13/32," pencil "Alter" with lines to stars.

PR29-E1 $24 Drawing on 88x121mm card, black *750.*

PR31-E1

Vignette size: 13½x26mm
Engraved vignette only as adopted.

PR31-E1 $48 Die on India, die sunk on card, black *750.*

PR31-E2

Design size: 24x36mm
Wash drawing similar to that adopted, backing card signed by designers Skinner and Claxton, also has pencil "$48" above each value numeral.

PR31-E2 $48 Drawing on 88x121mm card, black *1,350.*

PR32-E1

Design size: 24½x35½mm
Wash drawing similar to that adopted, backing card signed by designers Skinner and Claxton.

PR32-E1 $60 Drawing on 88x121mm card, black *750.*

1885 ISSUE
American Bank Note Co.

PR81-E1

Design size: 23x25mm
Complete engraving of entire design as adopted for 12c-96c.

PR81-E1 1c
- ***a.*** Die on India, die sunk on card
  - black *1,000.*
- ***b.*** Die on white ivory paper
  - black *600.*
  - black brown *600.*
  - scarlet *600.*
  - blue *600.*

1895 ISSUE
Bureau of Engraving and Printing

PR102-E2

Incomplete engraving of entire design: background at upper ends of value label, shading on side lettering and numerals missing.

PR102-E2 1c Die on India, die sunk on card
- black *900.*
- green *1,250.*

Incomplete engraving of entire design but further engraved than No. PR102-E2: shading on PA is light, no shading on PE of NEWSPAPERS or IO of PERIODICALS and shading on OD is light.

PR102-E3 1c Die on India, die sunk on card, black *900.*

Incomplete engraving of entire design but further engraved than No. PR102-E3: shading on PERIODICALS is finished but not on PAPE.

PR102-E4 1c Die on India, die sunk on card, black *900.*

PR103-E1

Design size: 21½x34½mm
Die size: 56x75½mm
Incomplete engraving of entire design: spaces for numerals and value label blank but with pencil outline of lettering.

PR103-E1 2c Die on India, die sunk on card, black *1,250.*

PR103-E2

Incomplete engraving of entire design but further engraved than No. PR103-E1: shading on leaves at ends of value label unfinished, numerals unshaded, unfinished shading on APE of NEWSPAPERS and RIO of PERIODICALS.

PR103-E2 2c Die on India, black *1,250.*

Incomplete engraving of entire design but further engraved than No. PR103-E2: no shading on PE of NEWSPAPERS, unfinished shading on PA of NEWSPAPERS and RIO of PERIODICALS.

PR103-E3 2c Die on India, die sunk on card, black *1,250.*

PR104-E1

Design size: 21½x34½mm
Die size: 57x73mm
Incomplete engraving of entire design: spaces for numerals and value label blank but with pencil outline of lettering.

PR104-E1 5c Die on India, die sunk on card, black *1,500.*

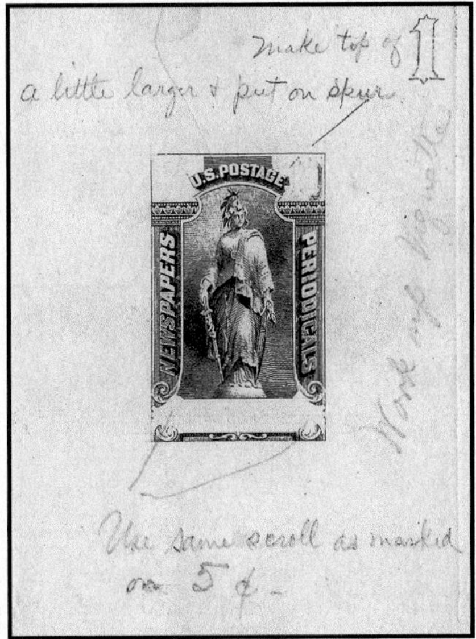

PR105-E1

Design size: 21½x34½mm
Die size: 56x75mm
Incomplete engraving of entire design: spaces for numerals and value label blank but with pencil outline of lettering.

PR105-E1 10c Die on India, die sunk on card, black *1,600.*

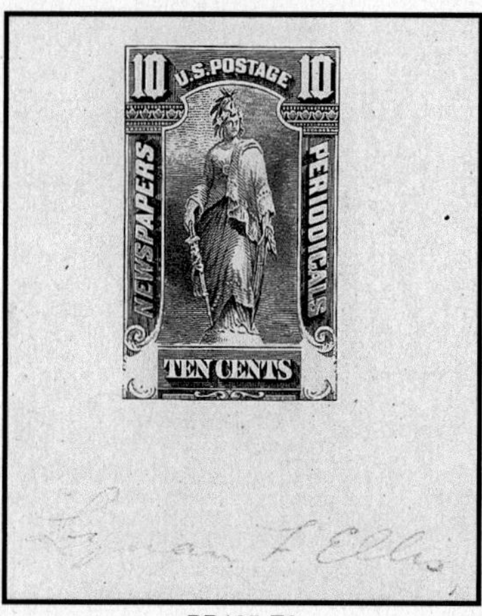

PR105-E2

Incomplete engraving of entire design but further engraved than No. PR105-E1: numerals unfinished, lower corners blank.

PR105-E2 10c Die on India, die sunk on card, black *2,100.*

Incomplete engraving of entire design but further engraved than No. PR105-E2: lower right corner blank.

PR105-E3 10c Die on India, die sunk on card, black *1,250.*

Incomplete engraving of entire design but further engraved than No. PR105-E3: numerals blank, no inner lines.

PR105-E4 10c Die on India, die sunk on card, black *1,250.*

PR105-E5

Design size: 21½x34½mm
Die size: 56x75mm
Incomplete engraving of entire design (early state of die similar to No. PR105-E1) with "10" pencilled in upper right corner and "TEN CENTS" pencilled in at bottom. Pencil notes on India include "Make top of 1 a little larger and put on spur," "Work up Vignette" and "Use same scrolls as marked on 5c-."

PR105-E5 10c Die on India, die sunk on card, black *2,750.*

PR106-E1

Vignette size: 13x25½mm
Die size: 56x72mm
Incomplete engraving of vignette only (transfer of Continental Banknote Co. die for 72c with left side cut off): eagle crest faces front and its right wing is not pointed, shading on left thigh near sword hilt incomplete, bottom of vignette straight instead of curved.

PR106-E1 25c Die on India, die sunk on card
black *3,000.*
deep red *3,000.*

PR106-E2

Design size: about 21x34½mm
Die size: 57½x75mm
Entire design with frame incompletely engraved: vert. lines around CENTS label missing, no shading on TWENTY FIVE, colorless beads under E and FI of same.

PR106-E2 25c Die on India, die sunk on card
black *3,000.*
deep red *3,000.*

PR106-E3

An impression from No. PR106-E2 with pencil shading on TWENTY FIVE and vert. ink lines in spaces around CENTS label, colorless beads also blacked out in ink. Below engraving are three diff. pencil sketches for shape and shading to be engraved.

PR106-E3 25c Die on India, die sunk on card
black *2,750.*
deep red *2,750.*

PR106-E4

An impression from No. PR106-E2 but with shading suggestions from No. PR106-E3 partly engraved except colorless beads have pencil shading only. Below engraving is pencil sketch for corner of CENTS label.

PR106-E4 25c Die on India, die sunk on card
black *2,650.*
deep red *2,000.*

PR106-E5

Design size: 21½x34½mm
Die size: 55x72mm
Large die proof of PR107 with bottom value label cut out and "TWENTY-FIVE CENTS" pencilled in on backing card.

PR106-E5 25c Die on India, die sunk on card, black *1,500.*

PR107-E1

Incomplete engraving of entire design: eagle's head and much of bottom of stamp's design unfinished, top of frame unfinished, value lettering sketched in pencil.

PR107-E1 50c Die on India, die sunk on card, black *1,950.*

PR107-E3

Incomplete engraving of entire design: top of frame and scrolls below FIFTY CENTS unfinished.

PR107-E3 50c Die on India, die sunk on card, black *1,750.*

PR108-E1

Design size: 24½x37mm
Die size: 75x76mm

Incomplete engraving of entire design: vignette and spaces around numerals incomplete, pencil sketch instructions for engraver at top and side for these spaces.

PR108-E1 $2 Die on India, die sunk on card, black *1,650.*

PR108-E2

Design size: 24½x37mm
Die size: 75x76mm
Incomplete engraving of entire design but further engraved than No. PR108-E1: space for ornaments under POSTAGE blank, numerals unshaded.

PR108-E2 $2 Die on India, die sunk on card, scarlet *1,500.*

Further engraved than No. PR108-E2: scrolls under POSTAGE engraved but unfinished.

PR108-E3 $2 Die on India, die sunk on card, black *1,500.*

Incomplete engraving of design, no frame line under "Postage" and other small differences from final design.

PR110-E1 $10 Die on India, green *1,500.*

PR111-E1

Design size (incomplete): 24½x30mm
Die size: 75x84mm
Incomplete engraving of partial design: spaces for stars and 0s of numerals blank, design missing below bottom of vignette.

PR111-E1 $20 Die on India, die sunk on card, black *1,250.*

PR111-E2

Design size: 24½x35½mm
Incomplete lines below denomination at top, only 7 lines below right "0" of "$20" and 8 lines below left "$20" (issued design has 13 lines in both places), die no. "74" at bottom.

PR111-E2 $20 Die on India, 42x54mm, black *1,850.*

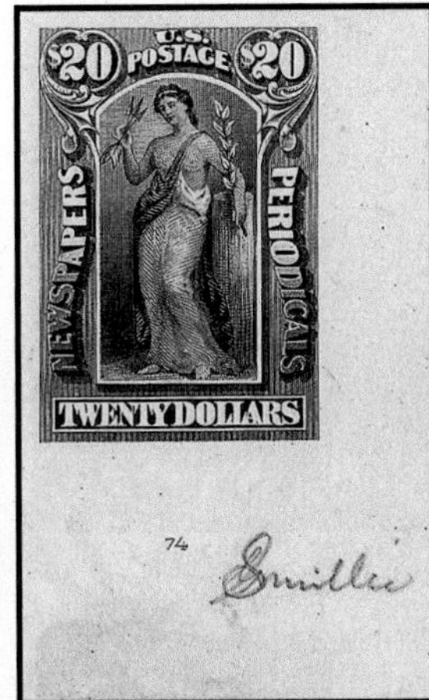
PR111-E3

Design size: 24½x35½mm
Incomplete lines below denomination at top, but with addition of pencil lines of shading to indicate further work needed, die no. "74" at bottom and signed "Smillie" in pencil.

PR111-E3 $20 Die on India, on 71x83mm card, black *1,850.*

PR112-E1

Design size: 24½x35½mm
Die size: 72½x76mm
Incomplete engraving of entire design: upper corners around value numerals unfinished, etc.

PR112-E1 $50 Die on India, on card, black *2,750.*

PR113-E1

Design size: 24½x35½mm
Die size: unknown
Incomplete engraving of entire design: spaces at lower inner corners of value shields blank, shading on numerals and letters at top unfinished.

PR113-E1 $100 Die on India, on card, black *1,850.*

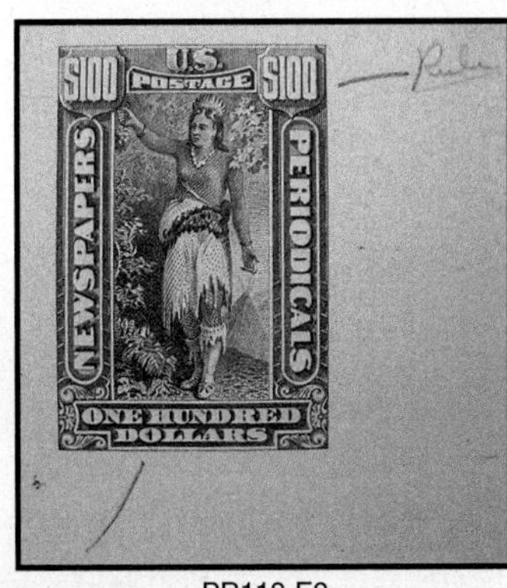
PR113-E2

Design size: 24½x35½mm
Die size: 75x73mm
Further engraved than No. PR113-E1.

PR113-E2 $100 Die on India, die sunk on 80x80mm card, violet *1,750.*

PR113-E3

Further engraved than No. PR113-E2: vignette completed but numerals not shaded, shadows on frame not etched dark.

PR113-E3 $100 Die on India
black *1,750.*
red-violet *1,750.*

Further engraved than No. PR113-E3: numerals shaded, shadows on frame not finally etched, especially above POSTAGE.

PR113-E4 $100 Die on India, black *1,350.*

PARCEL POST STAMPS

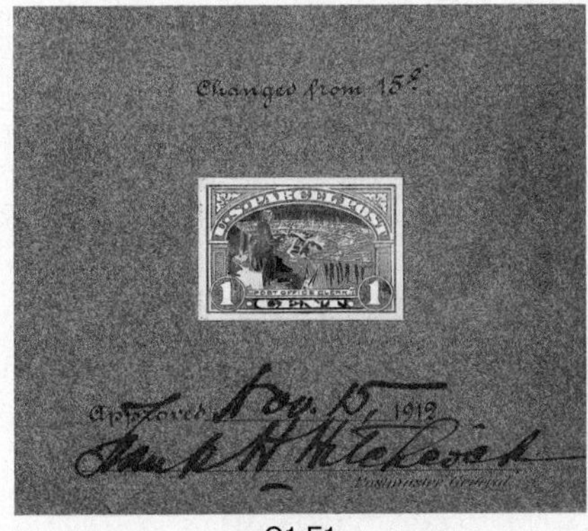
Q1-E1

Design size: 35½x23mm
Photo of wash drawing of frame design with numerals, CENT and POST OFFICE CLERK in black ink, vignette in black wash. Ms. "Changed from 15c" and "Approved Nov. 15, 1912 — Frank H. Hitchcock — Postmaster General" on backing card.

Q1-E1 1c Model on thick gray card, 106x91mm, black *5,500.*

Q2-E1

Design size: 35x23½mm
Photo of wash drawing of frame only as adopted. Ms. "Approved Oct. 10, 1912, for border and size of stamps. Engraving to be ⅞ by 1⅜ inches. Frank H. Hitchcock. Postmaster General" on backing card.

Q2-E1 2c Model on thick gray cardboard, 122x110mm, black *3,500.*

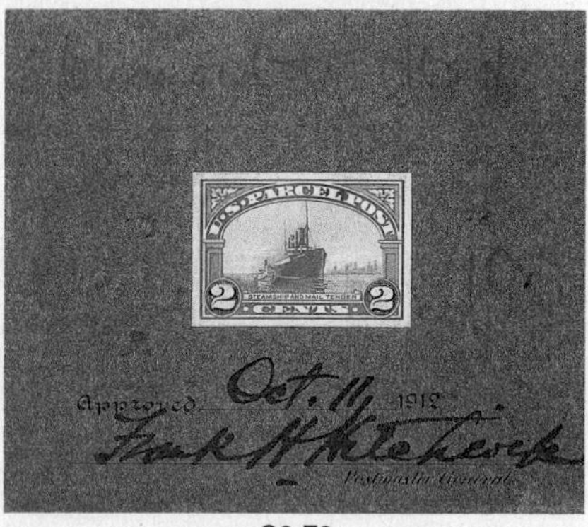

Q2-E2

Design size: 35x23mm
Photo of wash drawing of frame design and retouched photo of ship vignette as eventually used for 10c, numerals and STEAMSHIP AND MAIL TENDER in black ink. Ms. "Changed to 10c" and "Approved Oct. 11, 1912. Frank H. Hitchcock. Postmaster General" on backing card.

Q2-E2 2c Model on thick gray cardboard, 110x83mm, black *8,500.*

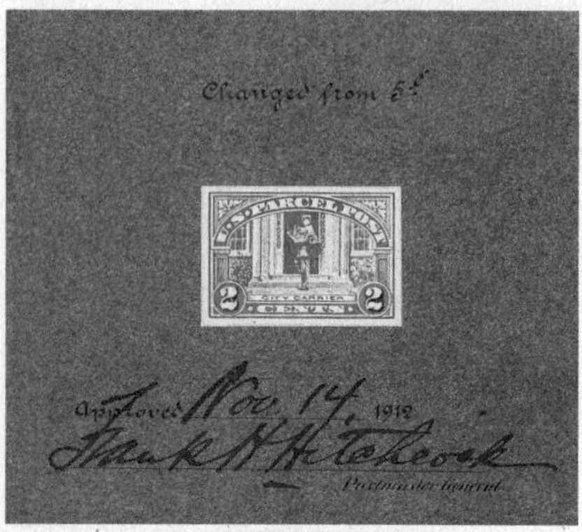

Q2-E3

Design size: 34x22mm
Photo of wash drawing of entire design with adopted vignette, numerals in white wash and CITY CARRIER in black ink. Ms. "Changed from 5c" and "Approved Nov. 14, 1912. Frank H. Hitchcock. Postmaster General" on backing card.

Q2-E3 2c Model on thick gray cardboard, 111x92mm, black *7,500.*

Design size: 34½x22mm
Engraving of adopted design with blank value tablets and "CITY CARRIER" inscription, mail carrier unfinished.

Q2-E4 2c Die on India, sunk on 118x89mm card, black —

Q3-E1

Design size: 35x23mm
Complete engraving of unadopted design: vignette shows mail truck backing up to railroad mail train with clerk about to handle pouches.

Q3-E1 3c Die on white wove, about 43x31mm, carmine *5,000.*

Q3-E2

Design size: 35x22mm
Photo of wash drawing of entire design with adopted vignette (retouched around door to mail car). Ms. "Approved Feb. 22, 1913. Frank H. Hitchcock. Postmaster General" on backing card.

Q3-E2 3c Model on thick gray cardboard, black *5,000.*

Q3-E3

Design size: 35x22mm
Almost complete engraving of adopted design with subtle differences (most evident in shading on windows), on 100x76mm card, affixed with tape to 125x98mm card, small cutout in design, blue control No. 578444 on back.

Q3-E3 3c Die sunk on card, affixed to card, carmine *4,500.*

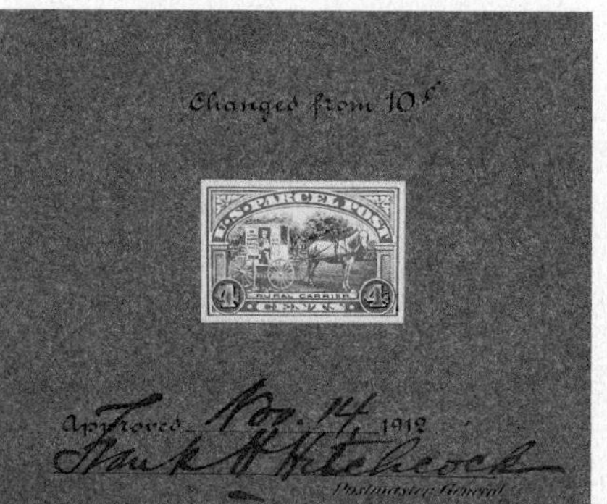

Q4-E1

Design size: 33½x22mm
Photo of wash drawing of entire design with adopted vignette, numerals drawn in white and RURAL CARRIER in black ink. Ms. "Changed from 10c" and "Approved Nov. 14, 1912. Frank H. Hitchcock. Postmaster General" on backing card.

Q4-E1 4c Model on thick gray cardboard, 116x92mm, black *5,500.*

Q5-E1

Design size: 35x23mm

Photo of wash drawing of entire design with vignette (retouched) eventually used for 2c, numerals and CITY LETTER CARRIER in black ink and white wash. Ms. "Changed to 2c.--City Carrier" and "Approved Oct. 10, 1912. Frank H. Hitchcock. Postmaster General" on backing card.

Q5-E1 5c Model on thick gray cardboard, 110x84mm, black *5,500.*

Q5-E2

Design size: 33½x21½mm
Photo of wash drawing of entire design with numerals in gray, unadopted vignette with MAIL TRAIN in black ink, first car retouched with wash. Ms. "Approved . . . 1912 / . . . Postmaster General" on backing card.

Q5-E2 5c Model on thick gray cardboard, 104½x92mm, black *2,750.*

Q5-E3

Design size: 33½x22mm
Photo of wash drawing of entire design with numerals in gray, MAIL TRAIN in black ink, first car retouched with wash. Ms. "Approved . . . 1912 / . . . Postmaster General" on backing card.

Q5-E3 5c Model on thick gray cardboard, 104½x92mm, black *5,500.*

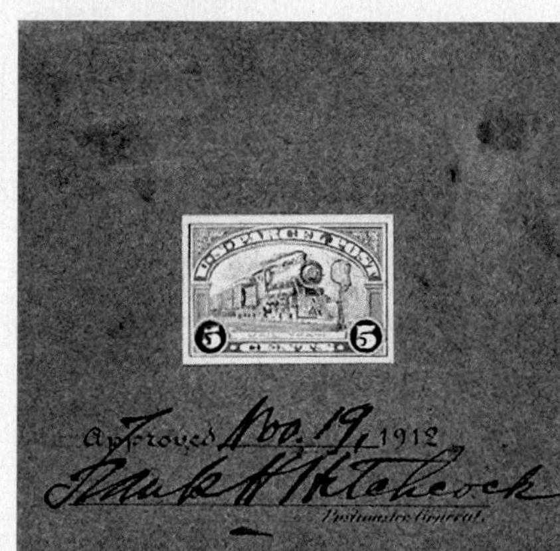

Q5-E4

Design size: 33½x22mm
Photo of wash drawing of entire design with numerals in white with black background, MAIL TRAIN and pouch catcher in black ink. Ms. "Approved Nov. 19, 1912 Frank H. Hitchcock Postmaster General" on backing card.

Q5-E4 5c Model on thick gray cardboard, 94x90mm, black *2,250.*

Q5-E5

Design size: 26x16mm
Complete engraving of accepted vignette (smoke from engine reworked from previous essays).

Q5-E5 5c Die on India, die sunk on card, a square of the India cut away removing the frame and leaving just the vignette *4,600.*

Q6-E1

Design size: 35½x23mm
Photo of wash drawing of entire design with vignette (retouched) eventually used for 4c, numerals and RURAL DELIVERY in black ink and white wash. Ms. "Changed to 4c." and "Approved Oct. 10, 1912. Frank H. Hitchcock. Postmaster General" on backing card.

Q6-E1 10c Model on thick gray cardboard, 111x83mm, black *2,500.*

Q6-E2

Design size: 35x23mm
Photo of wash drawing of entire design with adopted vignette, numerals and STEAMSHIP AND MAIL TENDER in black ink and white wash. Ms. "Changed from 2c." and "Approved Nov. 8, 1912. Frank H. Hitchcock. Postmaster General" on backing card.

Q6-E2 10c Model on thick gray cardboard, 116x92mm, black *2,500.*

Q7-E1

Design size: 33½x22mm
Photo of wash drawing of entire design (redrawn in front of autocar and U S MAIL and STATION A) with AUTOMOBILE SERVICE in black ink. Ms. "Approved . . . 1912 / . . . Postmaster General" on backing card.

Q7-E1 15c Model on thick gray cardboard, 115x93mm, black *1,500.*

Q7-E2

Design size:
Complete engraving of entire design with unadopted title label "COLLECTION SERVICE" instead of the adopted "AUTOMOBILE SERVICE."

Q7-E2 15c Die on white wove, card mounted, carmine *1,500.*

Q8-E1

Design size: 35x22mm
Incomplete engraved design nearly as adopted: aviator wears football helmet, head tilted far forward and one leg dangling over edge of plane, mail bag "No. 1" at his right while another sack hangs loosely out of plane.

Q8-E1 20c Die on white wove, about 37x24mm, carmine *1,500.*

Q8-E2

Design size: 35x22mm
Photo of incomplete engraved design as adopted. Ms. "Approved Nov. 19, 1912. Frank H. Hitchcock. Postmaster General" on backing card.

Q8-E2 20c Model on thick gray cardboard, 98x95mm, black *2,500.*

Q9-E1

Design size: 34½x22½mm
Photo of wash drawing of entire design with numerals and smoke at right painted in. Ms. "Changed from $1.00." and "Approved Nov. 14, 1912. Frank H. Hitchcock. Postmaster General" on backing card.

Q9-E1 25c Model on thick gray cardboard, 112x92mm, black *3,000.*

Q10-E1

Design size: 35x23mm
Photo of drawing of entire design with vignette eventually used for 25c with roof, smokestacks and smoke drawn in. Typed label "Stamp Division / Feb / 21 / 1912 / P.O. Dept" on back of backing paper.

Q10-E1 50c Model on thick white paper, black *1,500.*

Q10-E2

Design size: 33x21½mm
Photo of wash drawing of frame design with vignette cut out, mounted over photo of wash drawing of unadopted vignette design, retouched with wash on cows, etc., with DAIRYING in black ink. Pencil "Original" and ms. "Approved . . . 1912 / . . . Postmaster General" on backing card.

Q10-E2 50c Model on thick gray cardboard, 98x93mm, black *1,500.*

Q10-E3

Design size: 35x23mm
Complete engraving of entire design with unadopted vignette: silo and barns placed closer to front of design.

Q10-E3 50c Die on white wove, about 43x31mm, carmine *3,000.*

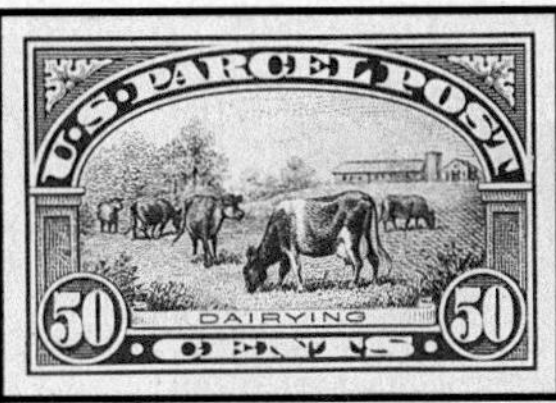

Q10-E4

Design size: 35x22mm
Photo of incomplete engraved design: no vert. lines on frame around corner foliate spandrels or in numeral circles. Ms. "Approved Jan. 8, 1913. Frank H. Hitchcock. Postmaster General" on backing card.

Q10-E4 50c Model on thick gray cardboard, 99x94mm, black *5,500.*

Q11-E1

Design size: 33½x21½mm
Photo of wash drawing of entire design with central horses and thresher retouched. Ms. "Approved Dec. 12, 1912. Frank H. Hitchcock. Postmaster General" on backing card.

Q11-E1 75c Model on thick gray cardboard, 108x89mm, black *5,250.*

Design size: 28x16mm
Complete engraving of accepted vignette.

Q11-E2 75c Die on India, die sunk on card, a square of the India cut away removing the frame and leaving just the vignette —

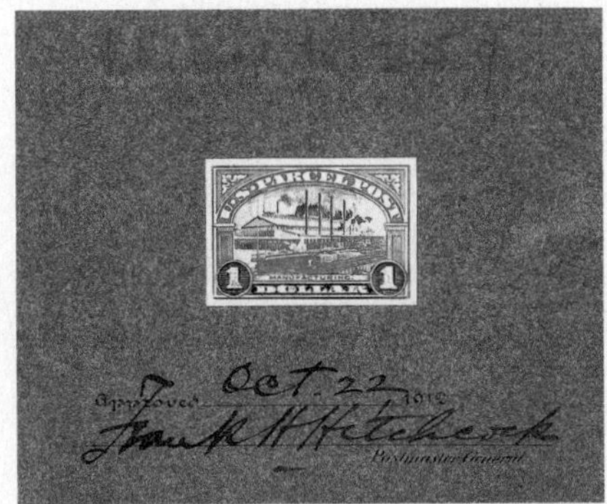

Q12-E1

Photo of wash drawing of entire design with vignette much retouched in black ink, numerals, MANUFACTURING and DOLLAR drawn in black ink and white wash. Ms. "Changed to 25c" and "Approved Oct. 22, 1912. Frank H. Hitchcock. Postmaster General" on backing card.

Q12-E1 $1 Model on thick gray cardboard, 114x86mm, black *5,250.*

Q12-E2

Design size: 35x22mm
Photo of wash drawing of complete design with DOLLAR painted in white and black and FRUIT GROWING in black ink, vignette retouched with wash on fruit pickers. Ms. "Approved . . . 1912 . . . Postmaster General" on backing card.

Q12-E2 $1 Model on thick gray cardboard, 105x94mm, black *5,500.*

Q12-E3

Design size: 36x23½mm
Incomplete engraving of entire design: no shading lines in sky. This may be from a rejected die.

Q12-E3 $1 Die on white wove, about 43x31mm, carmine *4,000.*

Q12a-E1

Engraving of entire design as adopted for 1917 offset Documentary Revenues, etc., but with "U.S. PARCEL POST" around value oval.

Q12a-E1	1c	Die on card, green	*1,500.*
Q12b-E1	2c	Die on card, carmine	*1,500.*
Q12c-E1	3c	Die on card, deep violet	*1,500.*
Q12d-E1	4c	Die on card, brown	*1,500.*
Q12e-E1	5c	Die on card, blue	*1,500.*
Q12f-E1	10c	Die on card, orange yellow	*1,500.*
Q12g-E1	15c	Die on card, gray	*1,500.*
Q12h-E1	20c	Die on wove, carmine rose, affixed to card	*1,500.*

PARCEL POST POSTAGE DUE

Retouched photo of design as adopted, officially dated and approved.

QJQ5-E1a 25c Model, black *1,500.*

CARRIER'S STAMPS

Essays by Toppan, Carpenter, Casilear & Co. in 1851

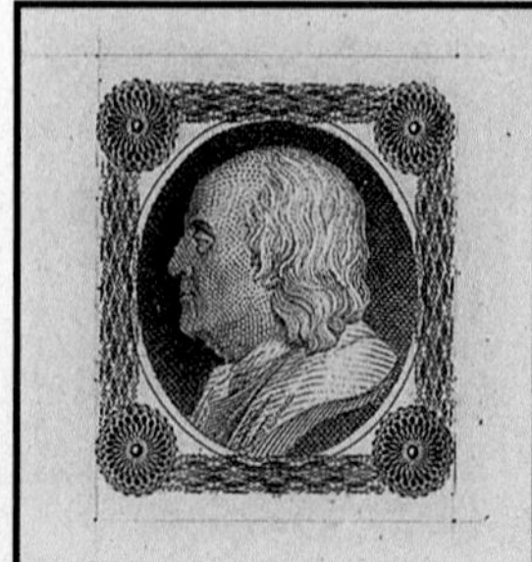

LO1-E1

Die size: 55x50mm
Unfinished die with outer border in a very incomplete state, pencil "For U.S. Carriers Stamp, Vignette 1851, Toppan, Carpenter Casilier & Co."

1851

LO1-E1 (1c) Die on India, die sunk on 96x76mm card, which is mounted on 101x82mm card, black *9,000.*

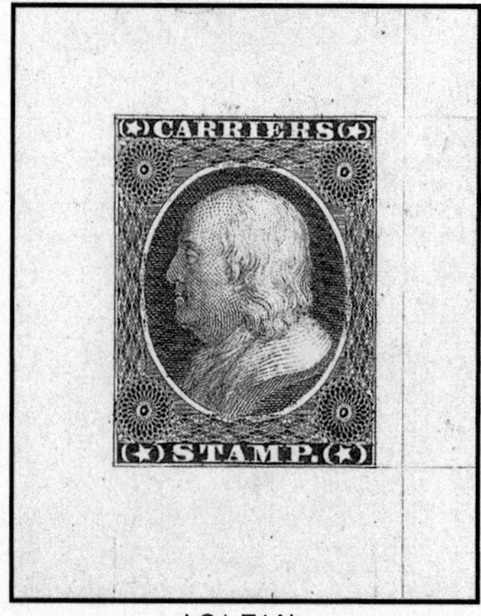

LO1-E1Ab

LO1-E1Ac

LO1-E1Ad

Die size: 57x50mm
Unfinished die with framelines complete at top and bottom, lathework impinging on white oval and rosettes in lower right corner, plus uncleaned horizontal and vertical layout lines.

LO1-E1A (1c)
- ***b.*** Die on 34x42mm, white bond, black *11,000.*
- ***c.*** Die on 60x50mm old ivory paper, die sunk, black *11,000.*
- ***d.*** Die on 62x54mm, pale green bond, red *7,500.*

Essays by Schernikow in 1903 from a new soft steel die made from the original 1851 transfer roll. (See paragraph eight of the Essay section introduction)

LO1-E2

Die size: 50x50mm
Engraving of Franklin vignette only.

1903

LO1-E2 (1c)

a. Die on proof paper

black	*75.*
carmine	*75.*
red	*75.*
light red	*75.*
orange	*75.*
orange brown	*75.*
yellow	*75.*
olive	*75.*
green	*75.*
dark green	*75.*
dark blue	*75.*
violet	*75.*
violet brown	*75.*

b. Die on colored card, about 75x75mm

deep red, *pinkish white*	*175.*
yellow brown, *pale blue*	*175.*
violet brown, *pale green*	*175.*
dark green, *pale pink*	*175.*
dark blue, *pale pink*	*175.*
violet, *pale yellow*	*175.*

c. Die on green bond (die size: 49x50mm)

dull scarlet	*175.*
dull olive	*175.*
dark ultramarine	*175.*

See note above No. 63-E1.

LO1-E3

Design size: 19½x25mm
Die size: 50x50mm
Design as No. LO1-E1, but distinguished by addition of left and right inner frame lines.

1903

LO1-E3 (1c)

a. Die on proof paper

black	*100.*
carmine	*100.*
dark carmine	*100.*
scarlet	*100.*
orange	*100.*
yellow	*100.*
yellow brown	*100.*
olive	*100.*
light green	*100.*
green	*100.*
steel blue	*100.*
violet	*100.*
red violet	*100.*
violet brown	*100.*
ultramarine	*100.*

b. Die on colored card

dull carmine, *pale olive*	*175.*
brown orange, *pink*	*175.*
brown, *pale buff*	*175.*
brown, *pale blue*	*175.*
gray green, *buff*	*175.*
gray green, *yellow*	*175.*
violet, *ivory*	*175.*
dull carmine, *pale blue*	*175.*

c. Die on blue pelure

carmine	*200.*
scarlet	*200.*
orange	*200.*
brown	*200.*
dark green	*200.*

d. Die on green bond

scarlet	*250.*
orange	*250.*
green	*250.*
dull violet	*250.*

e. Die on gummed thick rose paper, cut to stamp size 6,500.

Essays by Clarence Brazer in 1952 using the Schernikow complete die with addition of two diagonal lines in upper right corner.

LO1-E4

Die size: 50x50mm

1952

LO1-E4 (1c) Die on approximately 121x125mm glazed card

scarlet	*650.*
brown	*650.*
green	*650.*
red	*650.*

POST OFFICE SEALS

Registry Seals
1872 ISSUE
National Bank Note Co.

OXF1-E1

Design size: 72x40mm
Block size: 100x56½mm
Design cut on a steel block intended for printing by typography from electrotyped clichés. The design is similar to the adopted design except REGISTERED obliterates other words where it touches them. Apparently only one essay block was made and was not itself altered to produce the die with the adopted image from which electrotypes were made for printing. Accordingly, it is likely that a significant proportion of the impressions from the essay die were made subsequent to the pre-production period. Listed in each category are ink colors that have been seen and are known to be from the essay die; others may exist.

The image for OXF1-E1 was pulled from the essay die as if it were a die for intaglio printing. Accordingly, where the image was intended to print in color, this image is clear; and where the image was intended to print clear, this image is colored. Depsite its appearance, it is from the same die as all OXF1 essays.

OXF1-E1

a. Die on card

chocolate	*1,500.*
black	*1,500.*

OXF1-E2

"Colorless borders." The image was pulled from the essay die as if it were for typographic printing, and the ink from the non-image portion of the die was wiped clean before printing. The images printed on card are often, but not always, on India paper impressed on the card. The images on other surfaces do not use India paper and usually do not show the die block impression.

OXF1-E2

a. Die on card	
green	*1,000.*
carmine (rose)	*1,000.*
red brown	*1,000.*
orange	*1,000.*
orange brown	*1,000.*
yellow	*1,000.*
blue	*1,000.*
blue (left), green (right)	*1,200.*
b. Die on India	
blue	*1,000.*
lavender	*1,000.*
c. Die on bond weight paper	
green	*1,000.*
blue	*1,000.*
d. Die on glossy paper or thin card	
green	*1,000.*

OXF1-E3

"Colored borders." As No. OXf1-E2 except that the non-image portion of the die was not wiped clean before printing. The colored border area is found both completely and partially colored. Most impressions on card do not use India paper.

OXF1-E3

a. Die on card	
green	*1,000.*
rose	*1,000.*
blue	*1,000.*
violet	*1,000.*
brown	*1,000.*
b. Die on India	
green	*1,000.*
red	*1,000.*
rose	*1,000.*
orange brown	*1,000.*
yellow	*1,000.*
blue	*1,000.*
violet	*1,000.*
c. Die on bond weight paper	
blue	*1,000.*
d. Die on glossy paper or thin card	
blue	*1,000.*
brown	*1,000.*

OXF1-E4

As with No. OXF1-E2 except printed on stamp paper, perforated and gummed.

OXF1-E4

a. Die on stamp paper, perf. 12, gummed	
blue	*1,000.*
blue (left), green (right)	*1,200.*

Block size: 80x128mm
Engraving of entire design as adopted but in reverse for making typographed block.

OXF1-E5 Die on white wove, chocolate *1,000.*

Post Office Seals
1877 ISSUE

OX1-E1

Preliminary pen and ink concept design on thick light brown paper. Image size: 44x27mm.

OX1-E1 Black *5,500.*

Value based on 2011 auction realization.

OX1-E2

Design size: 44x27mm
Composite model built up from card proofs of intermediate dies; "Post Obitum," the vignette, and the National Bank Note Company imprint cut out and pasted to card. Hand drawn and water-color additions of frame and lettering, Dated Febry 21, 1877 and signed by "Thos. F. Morris" the designer.

OX1-E2 Brown *5,500.*

Value based on 2011 auction realization.

OX1-E3

Design size: 44x27mm
Progressive die essay on India paper on card. Incomplete engraving of entire design with vignette lacking the cap and background, and border lacking the vertical shading lines (probalby unique).

OX1-E3 Brown *1,250.*

OX1-E4

Design size: 44x27mm.
Progressive die essay on India paper. Lacking the vertical shading lines in the border (probably unique).

OX1-E4 Brown *1,000.*

1861 FIRST DESIGN ESSAYS AND TRIAL COLOR PROOFS

For the convenience of collectors and dealers, the Scott editors present here in one location the important 1861 First Design Essays and Trial Color Proofs. The final "stamps" produced with these designs or colors were at one time listed in the Postage section as Nos. 55-57 and 59-62. These so-called "August" issues or "Premiere Gravure" issues, printed on thin and semitransparent stamp paper, gummed and perforated, were not issued as prepared, but were either engraved further to complete the issued designs (1c, 3c, 5c, 12c and 90c) or issued in slightly revised colors (24c and 30c), and they were therefore appropriately moved to the Essay and Trial Color Proof sections of the U.S. Specialized catalogue in 1991.

The 10c denomination of this First Design series, previously No. 58, was pressed into service as an issued stamp, No. 62B, presumably because the demand for this denomination was greater than could be supplied by the plate or plates in use. Former No. 58 and current No. 62B are the same stamp, and it is listed in the Postage section as No. 62B.

The listings here duplicate the listings in the Essay and Trial Color Proof sections rather than replace them. Their listing here is for the convenience of catalogue users only.

Without Dash Below UL Ornament

Die size: 58x56mm

"Premiere Gravure" die No. 440. No dash under the right tip of the ornament at right of the numeral in upper left corner.

63-E11 1c
- ***a.*** "Premiere Gravure" die essay on India (**formerly Nos. 55P1, 55TC1**)
  - black *4,000.*
  - indigo *1,500.*
  - ultramarine *2,250.*
- ***b.*** RA "Premiere Gravure" small die essay on white wove, 28x31mm (**formerly No. 55P2**), indigo *325.*
- ***c.*** "Premiere Gravure" plate essay on India (**formerly Nos. 55P3, 55TC3**)
  - indigo *300.*
  - blue —
  - ultramarine *300.*
  - violet ultramarine —
- ***d.*** "Premiere Gravure" plate essay on semitransparent stamp paper (**formerly No. 55TC4**), ultramarine *400.*

63-E11e

63-E11e 1c **indigo,** finished "Premiere Gravure" plate essay on semitransparent stamp paper, gummed, perf. 12 **(formerly No. 55)** *50,000.*

No. 63-E11e is valued with perfs cutting slightly into design at top.

Without Corner Ornaments

65-E11

Die size: 64x76½mm

Incomplete engraving of Washington head only.

65-E11 3c
- ***a.*** Die on India, on card, carmine *750.*
- ***b.*** Die on white glazed paper
  - black *750.*
  - scarlet *750.*
  - brown violet *750.*

65-E12

Die size: 78x55mm

Incomplete engraved design, no scrolls outside framelines, no silhouette under chin, no ornaments on 3s, U and S.

65-E12 3c Die on India, die sunk on card
- black *1,000.*
- blue *1,000.*

65-E13

As No. 65-E12 but ornaments on 3s, U and S. Shows traces of first border design erased. With imprint and No. 441 below design.

65-E13 3c Die on India, card mounted
- scarlet *1,000.*
- brown red *1,000.*
- ultramarine *1,000.*

65-E14

Die size: 59x55mm

As No. 65-E13 but with ornaments outside frame.

65-E14 3c Die on India, die sunk on card
- black *750.*
- scarlet *750.*
- pink *1,250.*
- brown orange *750.*
- deep orange red *750.*
- deep red *750.*

"Premiere Gravure" design; no corner ornaments. No imprint or die number on die impression.

65-E15 3c
- ***a.*** Die on India, card mounted, deep orange red *1,000.*
- ***b.*** "Premiere Gravure" die essay on semitransparent stamp paper, 20x25mm-30x37mm
  - deep orange red *750.*
  - deep red orange *750.*
  - dim red *750.*
  - dim deep red *750.*
  - dim orange red *750.*
  - dull pink *750.*
  - dull violet red *750.*
- ***c.*** "Premiere Gravure" die essay on India (**formerly Nos. 56P1, 56TC1**)
  - red *1,350.*
  - black *2,000.*
  - scarlet *2,000.*
  - pink *2,850.*
  - orange red *2,000.*
  - dark orange red *2,000.*
- ***d.*** RA Small die essay on white wove, 28x31mm altered laydown die of complete design but with outer scrolls removed and replaced by ones similar to "Premiere Gravure" design (1903) (**formerly No. 56P2**), dim deep red *325.*
- ***e.*** As "c," PP small die essay on pale cream soft wove, 24x29mm (1915) (**formerly No. 56P2a**), deep red *1,250.*
- ***f.*** "Premiere Gravure" plate No. 2 essay on India (**formerly Nos. 56P3, 56TC3**)
  - red *250.*
  - scarlet *350.*
- ***g.*** "Premiere Gravure" plate essay on semitransparent stamp paper (**formerly Nos. 56aP4, 56TC4**)
  - red, pair with gum *1,750.*
  - black *400.*

65-E15h

65-E15h 3c **brown rose,** finished "Premiere Gravure" plate essay on semitransparent stamp paper, gummed, perf. 12 **(formerly No. 56)** 550.
- orange red 475.
- bright orange red 475.
- dark orange red 475.
- dim deep red 475.
- pink 475.
- deep pink 475.
- P# block of 8, Impt. (any shade) *20,000.*

No Leaflets at Corners

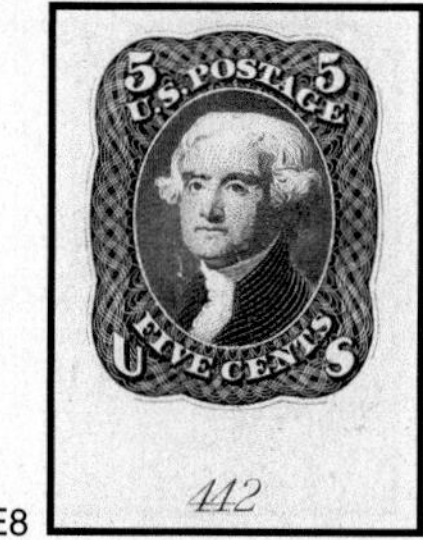

67-E8

Incomplete impression from die No. 442, border lines and corner scrolls missing.

67-E8 5c Die on India, mounted on 34x50mm card, black *1,750.*

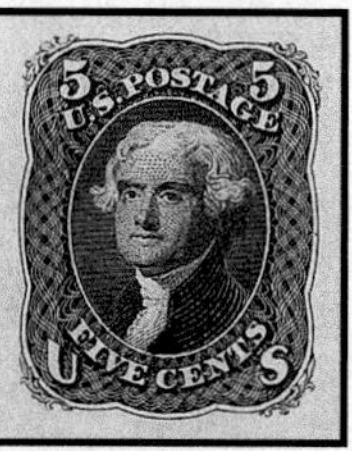

67-E9

Size of die: 58x59mm

"Premiere Gravure" design, with corner scrolls but without leaflets.

67-E9 5c
- ***a.*** "Premiere Gravure" die essay on India, card mounted (formerly No. 57TC1)
  - black *2,500.*
  - scarlet *2,500.*
- ***b.*** RA Small die essay on white wove, 28x31mm, altered laydown die of complete design but with scrolls removed from corners to resemble "Premiere Gravure" (1903) (**formerly No. 57P2), brown** 325.
- ***c.*** As "b," PP die essay on pale cream soft wove, 24x29mm (1915) (**formerly No. 57P2a**), brown *1,750.*

d. "Premiere Gravure" plate No. 3 essay on India (**formerly Nos. 57P3, 57TC3**)
brown *250.*
light brown *300.*
dark brown *300.*
red brown *300.*

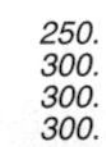

67-E9e

67-E9e 5c **brown,** finished "Premiere Gravure" plate essay on semitransparent stamp paper, gummed, perf. 12 **(formerly No. 57)** *30,000.*

No. 67-E9e is valued with small faults, as all recorded original-gum examples come thus.

One example of No. 67-E9e is known used. It has small faults and a circular datestamp in black.

Without Corner Ornaments

69-E5

Design size: 12½x16mm
Die size: about 62x65mm
Washington vignette only.

69-E5 12c
a. Die on India, die sunk on card
black *400.*
dark red *400.*
orange red *400.*
b. Die on ivory paper, about 24x28mm
black *500.*
scarlet *500.*
black brown *500.*
blue *500.*

Incomplete die No. 444, without corner ornaments.

69-E6 12c
a. "Premiere Gravure" die essay on India, mounted on card (**formerly Nos. 59P1, 59TC1**)
black *2,500.*
scarlet *2,500.*
dark green *2,500.*
b. RA Small die essay on white wove, 29x31mm, altered laydown die of complete design but with scrolls removed from corners to resemble the "Premiere Gravure" (1903) (formerly Nos. 59P2), black *450.*
c. PP "Premiere Gravure" small die essay on pale cream soft wove, 24x29mm (1915) (**formerly No. 59P2a**), black *1,750.*
d. "Premiere Gravure" plate No. 5 essay on India (**formerly No. 59P3**), black *350.*

69-E6e

69-E6e 12c **black,** finished "Premiere Gravure" plate essay on semitransparent stamp paper, gummed, perf. 12 **(formerly No. 59)** *90,000.*

70TC6

No. 70TC6 differs from the issued 1861 24c stamps by its color.

70TC6 24c **dark violet,** finished "Premier Gravure" trial color plate proof on semitransparent stamp paper, gummed, perf. 12 **(formerly No. 60)** *15,000.*

71-E1

Die size: 46x60mm
Incomplete die (No. 446): additional ornaments at top and bottom in pencil, as later engraved.

71-E1 30c Die on India, black *1,750.*

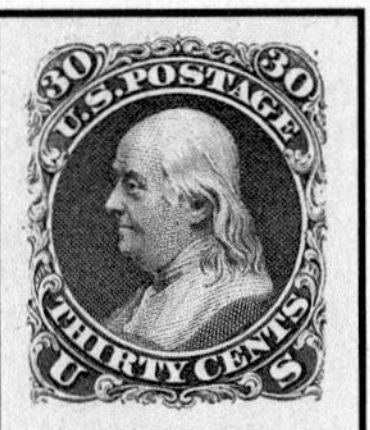

71-E2

"Premiere Gravure" die: left side of frame and silhouette at lower right unfinished.

71-E2 30c
a. "Premiere Gravure" die essay on India, die sunk on card (**formerly No. 61TC1**)
black *1,750.*
green *1,750.*
dull gray blue *1,750.*
violet brown *1,750.*
scarlet *1,750.*
dull rose *1,750.*
b. "Premiere Gravure" plate essay on India (**formerly No. 61P3**), deep red orange *500.*
c. "Premiere Gravure" plate essay on card
black (split thin) *500.*
blue *750.*
d. "Premiere Gravure" plate essay on card, black 12x2mm SPECIMEN overprint, blue *750.*
e. "Premiere Gravure" plate essay on semitransparent stamp paper
deep red orange *1,250.*
yellow orange *1,250.*
lemon yellow *1,250.*
dark orange yellow *1,250.*
dull orange yellow *1,250.*

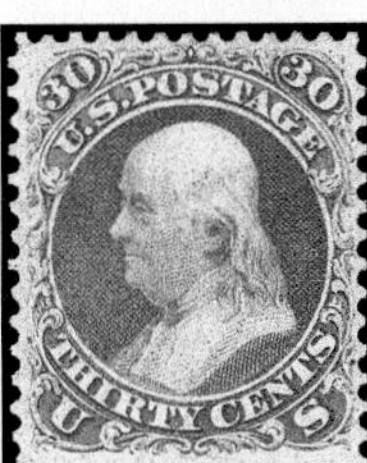

71TC6

No. 71TC6 differs from the issued 1861 30c stamp primarily by its color.

71TC6 30c **red orange,** finished "Premier Gravure" trial color plate proof on semitransparent stamp paper, gummed, perf. 12 **(formerly No. 61)** *40,000.*

No. 71TC6 is valued in the grade of fine.

One example of No. 71TC6 is known used. It has a small repair and is canceled with a quartered cork canel in black.

No Dashes Between the Parallel Angled Lines Above Top Ribbon; No Point of Color at Apex of Lower Angled Line

72-E6

Die size: 54x63mm
Incomplete die: without thin lines at bottom of frame and in upper left triangle between label and frame, and without leaves at left of U and right of S.

72-E6 90c Die on India, blue (shades) *1,000.*

72-E7

Similar to 72-E6 but lines added in upper left triangle, leaves added at left of U and at right of S. Exists with and without imprint and Die No. 447 added below design.

72-E7 90c
a. Die on India, die sunk on card, black *1,750.*
b. "Premiere Gravure" die essay on India, thin line under bottom center frame (**formerly Nos. 62P1, 62TC1**)
blue *1,350.*
black *1,750.*
c. RA "Premiere Gravure" small die essay on white wove, 28x31mm (1903) (**formerly No. 62P2**), blue *500.*
d. PP "Premiere Gravure" small die essay on pale cream soft wove, 24x29mm (1915) (**formerly No. 62P2a**), blue *1,750.*
e. "Premiere Gravure" plate essay on India, blue *500.*
f. "Premiere Gravure" plate essay on card, black (split thin) *500.*
g. "Premiere Gravure" plate essay on semitransparent stamp paper (**formerly Nos. 62aP4, 62TC4**)
blue, pair, gummed *5,500.*
blue green *275.*

72-E7h

72-E7h 90c **blue,** finished "Premiere Gravure" plate essay on semitransparent stamp paper, gummed, perf. 12 **(formerly No. 62)** *50,000.*

Die size: 54x63mm
Similar to Nos. 72-E6 and 72-E7 but leaf at left of "U" only, no shading around "U" and "S," leaf and some shading missing at bottom right above "S," shading missing in top label, etc., faint ms. "8" at bottom of backing card.

72-E8 90c Die on India, die sunk on 3¼x3½-inch card, dark blue —

TRIAL COLOR, DIE AND PLATE PROOFS

PROOFS are known in many styles other than those noted in this section. For the present, however, listings are restricted to die proofs, large and small, and plate proofs on India paper and card, and occasionally on stamp paper or other types of paper. The listings of normal color proofs include several that differ somewhat from the types and/or colors of the issued stamps.

Proofs in other than accepted or approved colors exist in a large variety of shades, colors and papers produced at various times by various people for many different reasons. The field is large. Trial Color Proofs are also listed as die proofs, large and small, and plate proofs on a variety of papers. The listings of Trial Color Proofs also include several that are similar to the colors of the issued stamps.

Some Trial Color Proofs are listed out of sequence. Nos. 156TC2-166TC2, the so-called "Goodall" Small Die Proofs in five colors, follow No. 166P4. Nos. O1TC2-O93TC2, another set of "Goodall" Small Die Proofs, follow No. O123P2a. The last set of "Goodall" Small Die Proofs, Nos. PR9TC2-PR32TC2, follow No. PR113P2a. The "Atlanta" set of Plate Proofs in five colors, Nos. 3TC4-LO2TC4, are listed after QE4aP1.

Large Die Proofs are so termed because of the relatively large piece of paper on which they are printed which is about the size of the die block, 40mm by 50mm or larger. The margins of this group of proofs usually are from 15mm to 20mm in width though abnormal examples prevent the acceptance of these measurements as a complete means of identification.

These proofs were prepared in most cases by the original contracting companies and 19th century issues often show the imprint thereof and letters and numbers of identification. They are listed under Large die (P1). The India paper on which these proofs are printed is of an uneven texture and in some respects resembles hand-made paper. These large die proofs were usually mounted on cards though many are found removed from the card. Large Die Proofs autographed by the engraver or officially approved are worth much more, except for those of the 1922-29 period, which are generally approved and signed proofs.

Values for Large Die Proofs are for the full die proofs mounted on cards unless noted otherwise. Full large die proofs measure 5-6" x 7-8". Cut-down Large Die Proofs sell for less. Values for die proofs of the bicolored 1869 issue are for examples which are completely printed. Occasionally the vignette has been cut out and affixed to an impression of the border.

Die Proofs of all United States stamps of later issues exist. Only those known outside of government ownership are listed.

Hybrids are plate proofs of all issues before 1894, and some from 1989-95, which have been cut to shape, mounted and pressed on large cards to resemble large die proofs. These sell for somewhat less than the corresponding large die proofs.

Small Die Proofs are so called because of the small piece of paper on which they are printed. Proofs of stamps issued prior to 1904 are reprints and not in all cases from the same dies as the large die proofs.

Small Die Proofs (Roosevelt Album, Small die (P2)) — These 302 small die proofs are from sets prepared for 85 ("Roosevelt presentation") albums in 1903 by the Bureau of Engraving and Printing but bear no imprint to this effect. The white wove paper on which they are printed is of a fibrous nature. The margins are small, seldom being more than from 3-5mm in width. Values are for proofs affixed to the original gray card backing from the Roosevelt album. Proofs without the card backing sell for less. Small die proofs from the 1903 Roosevelt albums have "RA" as part of the listing description. Small die proofs before 1904 that do not have "RA" as part of the listing description are not from the 1903 Roosevelt albums.

Small Die Proofs (Panama-Pacific Issue, Small die (P2a)) — A special printing of 413 different small die proofs was made in 1915 for the Panama-Pacific Exposition. These have small margins (2½-3mm) and are on soft yellowish wove paper. They are extremely scarce as only 3-5 of each are known and a few exist only in this special printing. 6-10 exist of No. E6 in two slightly different colors. Panama-Pacific small die proofs have "PP" as part of the listing description.

Plate Proofs are, quite obviously, impressions taken from finished plates and differ from the stamps themselves chiefly in their excellence of impression and the paper on which they are printed. Some of the colors vary.

India Paper is a thin, soft, opaque paper which wrinkles when wet. It varies in thickness and shows particles of bamboo.

Card is a plain, clear white card of good quality, which is found in varying thicknesses for different printings. Plate proofs on card were made in five printings in 1879-94. Quantities range from 500 to 3,200 of the card proofs listed between Scott 3P and 245P.

Margin blocks with full imprint and plate number are indicated by the abbreviation "P# blk. of -."

Numbers have been assigned to all proofs consisting of the number of the regular stamp with the suffix letters "TC" to denote Trial Color or "P" to denote Proof.

Some proofs are not identical to the issued stamps. Some of these are now listed in the Essay section. Others have been left in the proof section to keep sets together at this time.

Values are for items in very fine condition. Most "Panama-Pacific" small die proofs are toned. Values are for moderately toned examples. **Plate proof pairs on stamp paper are valued with original gum unless otherwise noted.**

POSTMASTER PROVISIONAL ISSUES

New York

The die proofs are of the No. 9X1 design. All trial color plate proofs and plate proofs in black are from the small sheet of 9. These latter proofs have minutely different design dimensions.

1845

9X1TC2	5c small die on India paper	
b.	**dull dark violet**	300.
c.	**brown violet**	300.
d.	**deep rose violet**	300.
e.	**deep blue**	300.
f.	**dark green**	300.
g.	**orange yellow**	300.
h.	**brown**	300.
9X1TC5	5c plate on bond paper	
a.	**deep blue**	200.
b.	**dk green**	200.
c.	**brown**	200.
d.	**scarlet**	200.

With "Scar" on Neck

9X1TC2	5c small die on India paper	
i.	**dull blue**	175.
j.	**vermilion**	175.

With "Scar" and dot in "P" of "POST"

9X1TC1d	5c large die on thin glazed card	
e.	**deep ultramarine**	450.
f.	**orange vermilion**	450.
g.	**brown black**	450.
9X1TC2	5c small die on India paper	
k.	**dull gray blue**	300.
l.	**deep green**	300.
m.	**dull dark green**	300.
n.	**dark brown red**	300.
o.	**dull dark brown**	300.
p.	**deep blue,** on bond paper	250.
q.	**deep green,** on bond paper	250.
r.	**dull brown red,** on bond paper	250.
s.	**dull dark brown,** on bond paper	250.

Large die trial color proofs with additional impression of the portrait medallion are listed in the Essay section as Nos. 9X1-E1.

9X1P1	5c **black,** large die on India paper	750.
b.	Dot in "P" of "POST" and scar on neck	525.
c.	As "b," on Bond	525.
d.	As "b," on glazed paper	525.
e.	With scar on neck, on Bond	525.
9X1P2	5c **black,** small die on India paper	350.
b.	With scar on neck	300.
c.	Dot in "P" of "POST" and scar on neck	300.
d.	As "b," on Bond	300.
9X1P3	5c **black,** plate on India paper	—
9X1P4	5c As No. 9X1P2c, plate on card	—

The above listed Large Die varieties have an additional impression of the portrait medallion.

9X1P5	5c **black,** plate on bond paper		
a.	Black on white bond	175.	
b.	Black on blue bond	150.	
	Sheet of 9, either paper	*7,500.*	

Providence, R.I.

10X1TC4	5c plate on card	
a.	**gray blue**	250.
b.	**green**	250.
c.	**brown carmine**	250.
d.	**brown**	250.
10X2TC4	10c plate on card	
a.	**gray blue**	450.
b.	**green**	450.
c.	**brown carmine**	450.
d.	**brown**	450.
	Sheet of 12, any color	3,750.
10X1P4	5c **black,** plate on card	300.
10X2P4	10c **black,** plate on card	500.
	Sheet of 12	3,250.

GENERAL ISSUES

1847

1TC1a	5c large die on India paper	
e.	**violet**	1,000.
f.	**dull blue**	1,000.
g.	**blue green**	1,000.
h.	**dull green**	1,000.
i.	**dark green**	1,000.
j.	**orange yellow**	1,000.
k.	**orange vermilion**	1,000.
l.	**scarlet vermilion**	1,000.
m.	**rose lake**	1,000.
n.	**brown red**	1,000.
o.	**black**	1,000.
1TC1b	5c large die on bond paper	
e.	**deep blue**	800.
f.	**dull blue green**	800.
g.	**orange yellow**	800.
h.	**orange vermilion**	800.
i.	**scarlet vermilion**	800.
j.	**black brown**	800.
k.	**black**	800.
1TC1c	5c large die on wove paper	
e.	**deep blue**	800.
f.	**orange yellow**	800.
g.	**deep yellow**	800.
h.	**orange vermilion**	800.
1TC1d	5c large die on thin glazed card	
e.	**deep ultra**	850.
f.	**scarlet vermilion**	850.
g.	**black brown**	850.
h.	**black**	800.
1TC2	5c small die on India paper	
b.	**deep blue**	625.
c.	**blue green**	625.
d.	**dull green,** on bond	600.
e.	**yellow green**	625.
f.	**orange yellow**	625.
g.	**rose lake,** on bond	625.
h.	**dull rose lake,** on bond	625.
i.	**black**	675.
1TC3	5c plate on India paper	
a.	**orange**	625.
b.	**black**	625.
	Double transfer (80R1)	—
	Double transfer (90R1)	—
1P1	5c **red brn,** large die on India paper	800.
a.	White bond paper	800.
b.	Colored bond paper	1,250.
c.	White laid paper	1,000.
d.	Bluish laid paper	800.
e.	Yelsh wove paper	800.
f.	Bluish wove paper	800.
g.	White wove paper	800.
h.	Card	1,000.
i.	Glazed paper	1,000.
1P3	5c **red brn,** plate on India paper	600.
2TC1a	10c large die on India paper	
e.	**violet**	1,000.
f.	**dull blue**	—
g.	**deep blue**	1,000.
h.	**dark green**	1,000.
i.	**orange yellow**	1,000.
j.	**orange vermilion**	1,000.
k.	**golden brown**	1,000.
l.	**light brown**	1,000.
m.	**dark brown**	1,000.

n. **rose lake** 1,000.
o. **yellow green,** on blue pelure paper 1,000.
2TC1b 10c large die on bond paper
e. **deep blue** 800.
f. **blue green** 800.
g. **dull blue green** 800.
h. **dull green** 800.
i. **orange vermilion** 800.
j. **golden brown** 800.
k. **dark brown** 800.
2TC1c 10c large die on wove paper
e. **deep blue** 800.
f. **dull yellow** 800.
g. **orange yellow** 800.
h. **orange vermilion** 800.
2TC1d 10c large die on thin glazed card
e. **deep blue** 850.
f. **scarlet vermilion** 850.
g. **golden brown** 850.
h. **red brown** 675.
i. **dull red** 675.
j. **black brown** 850.
2TC2 10c small die on India paper
b. **deep blue** 675.
c. **dull gray blue,** on bond paper 625.
d. **yellow green** 675.
e. **orange vermilion** 625.
f. **rose lake** 625.
2TC3 10c plate on India paper
a. **orange** 625.
b. **deep brown** 625.

Original trial color die proofs are often cut down and reduced in size; full-size trial color die proofs sell at higher prices. Reprint proofs with cross-hatching are valued as full-size; cut-down examples sell for less.

Nos. 1TC3 and 2TC3 exist with and without "specimen" overprint. Values are for examples without the overprint. Examples with the overprint are equally as scarce and sell for about the same values.

2P1 10c **black,** large die on India paper 800.
a. White bond paper 800.
b. Colored bond paper 1,250.
c. White laid paper 800.
d. Bluish laid paper 800.
e. Yelsh wove paper 800.
f. Bluish wove paper 800.
g. White wove paper 800.
h. Card 1,000.
i. Glazed paper 1,000.
2P3 10c **black,** plate on India paper 900.
Dbl. transfer (31R1) 1,750.

Original die proofs are generally found cut to stamp size; full size die proofs sell at higher prices. Reprint proofs with cross-hatching are valued as full size; cut down examples sell for less. Plate proofs overprinted "Specimen" sell for about the same as the above values.

Reproductions of 1847 Issue

Actually, official imitations made about 1875 from new dies and plates by order of the Post Office Department.

3TC1a 5c large die on India paper
e. **black** 900.
f. **green** 900.
3TC4 5c plate on card
f. **dull rose lake** 600.
3P1 5c **red brn,** large die on India paper 900.
3P2 5c **red brn,** RA sm die on white wove paper 425.
b. On bond paper 650.
3P2a 5c **red brn,** PP sm die on yelsh wove paper 2,750.
3P3 5c **red brn,** plate on India paper 375.
Block of 4 1,750.
3P4 5c **red brn,** plate on card 250.
Block of 4 1,100.
Plate scratches at UL —
4TC1a 10c large die on India paper
e. **green** 900.
f. 3TC1af and 4TC1ae, **green,** side-by-side composite proof on India paper 11,000.
4TC3 10c plate on India paper
a. **green** 750.
4P1 10c **black,** large die on India paper 1,500.
4P2 10c **black,** RA sm die on white wove paper 425.
b. On bond paper 650.
4P2a 10c **black,** PP sm die on yelsh wove paper 2,750.
4P3 10c **black,** plate on India paper 375.
Block of 4 1,750.
4P4 10c **black,** plate on card 250.
Block of 4 1,100.

1851-60

5TC1a 1c large die on India paper
e. **black** —
5P1 1c **blue,** Type I, large die on India paper *5,000.*
7TC5 1c plate on stamp paper
a. **black** *3,750.*
11TC5 3c plate on stamp paper
a. **black** *3,000.*
11P1 3c **red,** Type I, large die on India paper *5,000.*
11P3 3c **red,** Type I, plate on India paper, brush obliteration 1,000.
Block of 4 5,000.
P# block of 8 *20,000.*
12TC1a 5c large die on India paper
e. **black** *8,500.*
12TC5 5c plate on wove paper
a. **pale brown** 300.
b. **rose brown** 300.
c. **deep red brown** 1,500.
d. **dark olive bister** 300.
e. **olive brown** 300.
f. **olive green** 300.
g. **deep orange** 300.
h. **black** *5,000.*
12P1 5c **brn,** Type I, large die on India paper *7,000.*
12P2a 5c **brn,** Type I, PP sm die on yelsh wove paper *5,000.*
13TC1a 10c large die on India paper
e. **black** *5,000.*
13TC5 10c Plate on wove paper
a. **black** 1,500.
13P1 10c **grn,** Type I, large die on India paper *5,000.*
15TC5 10c plate on wove paper
a. **black** *5,000.*
17P1 12c **black,** large die on India paper *12,500.*
24P3 1c **blue,** Type V (pl. 9), plate on India *1,250.*
Pair *3,000.*
26P3 3c **red,** Type III, plate on India *1,250.*
Pair *3,000.*
30P3 5c **brn,** Type II, plate on India *1,250.*
35P3 10c **grn,** Type V, plate on India *1,250.*
36BP3 12c **blk,** plate III (broken frame lines), plate on India *1,250.*
Block of 4 *5,500.*
36BP5 12c **blk,** plate III (broken frame lines), plate on stamp paper —
Pair —
Block of 4 —
37TC1a 24c large die on India paper
e. **black** *7,000.*
37TC5 24c plate on wove paper
a. **claret brown** 600.
b. **red brown** 600.
c. **orange** 600.
d. **deep yellow** 600.
e. **yellow** 600.
f. **deep blue** 600.
g. **black** —
h. **violet black** 600.
37TC6 24c **red lilac,** on stamp paper, perf 15½, gummed (formerly No. 37b) 1,000.
Block of 4 6,000.
37P1 24c **lilac,** large die on India paper —
37P3 24c **lilac,** plate on India *1,250.*
Pair *3,000.*
37P5 24c **lilac,** plate on stamp paper *1,500.*
Pair *10,000.*
38TC1a 30c large die on India paper
e. **black** *5,000.*
38TC2 30c small die on India paper
b. **black** 1,250.
38TC3 30c plate on India paper
a. **black** 1,400.
Block of 4 9,000.
38TC5 30c plate on wove paper
a. **black** 1,000.
38P1 30c **org,** large die on India paper —
38P2 30c **org,** sm die on white wove paper —
38P3 30c **org,** plate on India *1,250.*
Pair *3,000.*
38P5 30c **org,** plate on stamp paper *1,500.*
Pair *7,750.*
39TC1a 90c large die on India paper
e. **brown orange** *6,000.*
f. **black** *6,000.*
39TC2 90c small die on India paper
b. **black** 1,250.
39TC5 90c plate on wove paper
a. **rose lake** 625.
b. **henna brown** 625.
c. **orange red** 625.
d. **brown orange** 625.
e. **sepia** 625.
f. **dark green** 625.
g. **dark violet brown** 625.
h. **black** 675.

Former Nos. 55-57, 59, 62 are now in the Essay section. Former Nos. 60-61 will be found below as Nos. 70TC3e and 71TC3b, respectively.

39P1 90c **blue,** large die on India paper —
39P2 90c **blue,** sm die on white wove paper —
39P3 90c **blue,** plate on India *1,250.*
Pair *3,000.*
39P5 90c **blue,** plate on stamp paper *4,500.*
Pair *37,500.*

Plate proofs of 24P to 39P are from the original plates. They may be distinguished from the 40P to 47P by the type in the case of the 1c, 3c, 10c and 12c, and by the color in the case of the 5c, 24c, 30c and 90c.

The 3c plate proofs (No. 11) are on proof paper and all known examples have a vertical brush stroke obliteration.

Die proofs of the 30c show full spear point in corners of design.

Reprints of 1857-60 Issue

40TC5 1c plate on wove paper
a. **orange vermilion** 275.
b. **orange** 275.
c. **yellow orange** 275.
d. **orange brown** 275.
e. **dark brown** 275.
f. **dull violet** 275.
g. **violet** 275.
h. **red violet** 275.
i. **gray** 275.
40P1 1c **br blue,** type I, large die on India paper 325.
40P2 1c **br blue,** type I, RA sm die on white wove paper 350.
40P2a 1c **br blue,** type I, PP sm die on yelsh wove paper *2,500.*
40P3 1c **br blue,** type I (new plate), plate on India 90.
Block of 4 550.
40P4 1c **br blue,** type I (new plate), plate on card 50.
Block of 4 220.
40P5 1c **br blue,** type I (new plate), plate on stamp paper 750.
41TC3 3c **red,** plate on India paper —
41P1 3c **scarlet,** type I, large die on India paper 325.
41P2 3c **scarlet,** type I, RA sm die on white wove paper 350.
41P2a 3c **scarlet,** type I, PP sm die on yelsh wove paper *2,500.*
41P3 3c **scarlet,** type I (new plate), plate on India 90.
Block of 4 550.
41P4 3c **scarlet,** type I (new plate), plate on card 75.
Block of 4 330.
41P5 3c **scarlet,** type I (new plate), plate on stamp paper —
42P1 5c **org brn,** type II, large die on India paper 325.
42P2 5c **org brn,** type I, RA sm die on white wove paper 350.
42P3 5c **org brn,** type II (plate II), plate on India
Block of 4 550.
P# blk. of 8 1,450.
42P4 5c **org brn,** type II (plate II), plate on card 50.
Block of 4 220.
P# blk. of 8 —
43P1 10c **grn,** type I, large die on India paper 325.
43P2 10c **grn,** type I, RA sm die on white wove paper 350.
43P2a 10c **grn,** type I, PP sm die on yelsh wove paper *2,500.*
43P3 10c **grn,** type I (new plate), plate on India 90.
Block of 4 550.
43P4 10c **grn,** type I (new plate), plate on card 50.
Block of 4 220.
43P5 10c **grn,** type I (new plate), plate on stamp paper 50.
44P1 12c **greenish blk,** (new die, frame line complete), large die on India paper 325.
44P2 12c **greenish blk,** (new die, frame line complete), RA sm die on white wove paper 350.
44P2a 12c **greenish blk,** (new die, frame line complete), PP sm die on yelsh wove paper *3,500.*
44P3 12c **greenish blk,** (new plate, frame line complete), plate on India 125.
Block of 4 625.
44P4 12c **greenish blk,** (new plate, frame line complete), plate on card 50.
Block of 4 220.
44P5 12c **greenish blk,** (new plate, frame line complete), plate on stamp paper —
45P1 24c **blksh vio,** large die on India paper 325.
45P2 24c **blksh vio,** RA sm die on white wove paper 350.
45P2a 24c **blksh vio,** PP sm die on yelsh wove paper *2,500.*
45P3 24c **blksh vio,** (plate I), plate on India 90.
Block of 4 400.
P# blk. of 8 1,050.
45P4 24c **blksh vio,** (plate I), plate on card 50.
Block of 4 220.
46P1 30c **yel org,** large die on India paper 325.
46P2 30c **yel org,** RA sm die on white wove paper 350.
46P2a 30c **yel org,** PP sm die on yelsh wove paper *2,500.*
46P3 30c **yel org,** (plate I), plate on India 90.
Block of 4 550.
P# blk. of 8 1,450.
46P4 30c **yel org,** (plate I), plate on card 50.
Block of 4 220.
P# blk. of 8 —
47P1 90c **dp blue,** large die on India paper 325.
47P2 90c **dp blue,** RA sm die on white wove paper 350.
47P2a 90c **dp blue,** PP sm die on yelsh wove paper *2,500.*
47P3 90c **dp blue,** (plate I), plate on India 125.
Block of 4 625.
P# blk. of 8 2,000.
47P4 90c **dp blue,** (plate I), plate on card 50.
Block of 4 220.
P# blk. of 8 850.
Nos. 40P4-47P4 (8) 425.00

Nos. 42P2-44P2 were printed from original dies. The 5c shows type I projections at top and bottom. The 12c was printed from a new die and shows complete frame lines.

Nos. 40P1-47P1, large die, exist only as hybrids.

SECOND DESIGNS (Regular Issue)

For "First Designs" see Essay section (former Nos. 55-57, 59, 62), Proofs and Trial Color Proofs (former No. 58) and Trial Color Proofs (former Nos. 60-61).

1861

62BTC1a 10c large die on India paper
e. **black** *2,500.*
62BTC3 10c plate on India paper
a. **green** 300.
b. **light green** 300.
62BP2 10c RA small die proof on white wove paper
b. **Dark green** *325.*
c. **Green** *325.*

Both shades of No. 62BP2 were actually printed from the No. 68 die.

62BP3 10c **dark green,** plate on India *500.*
P# blk. of 8 —
63TC1a 1c large die on India paper
e. **black** *2,500.*

63TC2 1c small die on India paper
b. **black** 750.
c. **red** 750.
d. **brown** 750.
e. **green** —
f. **orange** —
63TC5 1c plate on wove paper, imperf.
a. **rose** 40.
b. **deep orange red** 40.
c. **deep red orange** 40.
d. **dark orange** 40.
e. **yellow orange** 40.
f. **orange brown** 40.
g. **dark brown** 40.
h. **yellow green** 40.
i. **green** 40.
j. **blue green** 40.
k. **gray lilac** 40.
l. **gray black** 40.
m. **slate black** 40.
n. **blue** 40.
o. **light blue** 40.
p. **deep blue** 100.
63TC6 1c plate on wove paper, perf.
a. **rose** 50.
b. **deep orange red** 50.
c. **deep red orange** 50.
d. **dark orange** 50.
e. **yellow orange** 50.
f. **orange brown** 50.
g. **dark brown** 50.
h. **yellow green** 50.
i. **green** 50.
j. **blue green** 50.
k. **gray lilac** 50.
l. **gray black** 50.
m. **slate black** 50.
n. **blue** 50.
o. **light blue** 50.
p. **deep blue** 50.

The perforated 1861 1c trial colors are valued with perfs cutting the design on two sides. Well centered examples are extremely scarce and sell for more.

There are many trial color impressions of the issues of 1861 to 1883 made for experimentation with various patent papers, grills, etc. Some are fully perforated, gummed and with grill.

63P1 1c **blue,** large die on India paper 700.
63P2 1c **blue,** RA sm die on white wove paper 225.
63P2a 1c **blue,** PP sm die on yelsh wove paper 2,750.
b. **indigo** 2,750.
63P3 1c **blue,** plate on India 55.
Block of 4 225.
P# blk. of 8 1,750.
63P4 1c **blue,** plate on card 40.
Block of 4 250.
P# blk. of 8 —
64TC6 3c plate on thin stamp paper, perf 12, gummed
a. **carmine pink** *650.*
64P1 3c **pink,** large die on India paper 3,500.
64P2 3c **pink,** RA sm die on white wove paper —
65TC1a 3c large die on India paper
e. **black** 2,500.
f. **black,** on glazed 2,500.
g. **blue green** 2,500.
h. **orange** 2,500.
i. **brown** 2,500.
j. **dark blue** 2,500.
k. **ocher** 2,500.
l. **green** 2,500.
m. **dull red** 2,500.
n. **slate** 2,500.
o. **red brown** 2,500.
p. **deep pink** 2,500.
q. **rose pink** 2,500.
r. **dark rose** 2,500.
65TC6 3c plate on thin stamp paper, perf 12, gummed
a. **dark carmine** —
65P1 3c **rose,** large die on India paper 1,000.
65P2 3c **rose,** RA sm die on white wove paper —

Specialists have questioned the existence of Nos. 64P2 and 65P2. The editors would like to receive evidence of the existence of either of these proofs.

65P2a 3c **rose,** PP sm die on yelsh wove paper 2,750.
65P3 3c **rose,** plate on India 100.
Block of 4 550.
P# blk. of 8 1,750.
a. **dull red** 100.
65P4 3c **rose,** plate on card 150.
65P5 3c **rose,** plate on stamp paper, pair 1,000.
P# blk. of 8 —
67TC1a 5c large die on India paper
e. **black** 2,500.
f. **dark orange** 2,500.
g. **green** 2,500.
h. **ultramarine** 2,500.
i. **gray** 2,500.
j. **rose brown** —
67TC2 5c small die on India paper
b. **black** —
67P1 5c **buff,** large die on India paper *5,000.*
67P2a 5c **buff,** PP sm die on white wove paper *5,000.*
76P1 5c **brown,** large die on India paper 700.
76P2 5c **brown,** RA sm die on white wove paper 225.
76P2a 5c **brown,** PP sm die on yelsh wove paper 2,750.
76P3 5c **brown,** plate on India 45.
Block of 4 225.
P# blk. of 8 1,750.
76P4 5c **brown,** plate on card 30.
Block of 4 140.
P# blk. of 8 —
68TC1a 10c large die on India paper
e. **orange** 2,500.
f. **red brown** 2,500.
g. **dull pink** 2,500.
h. **scarlet** 2,500.
i. **black** 2,500.
j. **ocher** 2,500.
k. **ultramarine** 2,500.
68TC2 10c small die on India paper
b. **black** 550.
68P1 10c **green,** large die on India paper 650.
68P2 10c **green,** RA sm die on white wove paper 225.
68P2a 10c **green,** PP sm die on yelsh wove paper 2,750.
68P3 10c **green,** plate on India 65.
Block of 4 300.
P# blk. of 8 1,750.
68P4 10c **green,** plate on card 30.
Block of 4 140.
P# blk. of 8 —
69TC1a 12c large die on India paper
e. **scarlet vermilion** 2,500.
f. **brown** 2,500.
g. **red brown** 2,500.
h. **green** 2,500.
i. **orange yellow** 2,500.
69TC2 12c small die on India paper
b. **black** 550.
69P1 12c **black,** large die on India paper 700.
69P2 12c **black,** RA sm die on white wove paper 225.
69P2a 12c **black,** PP sm die on yelsh wove paper 2,750.
69P3 12c **black,** plate on India 65.
Block of 4 300.
P# blk. of 8 1,750.
69P4 12c **black,** plate on card 30.
Block of 4 140.
P# blk. of 8 —
70TC1a 24c large die on India paper
e. **scarlet** 2,500.
f. **green** 2,500.
g. **orange** 2,500.
h. **red brown** 2,500.
i. **orange brown** 2,500.
j. **orange yellow** 2,500.
k. **rose red** 2,500.
l. **gray** 2,500.
m. **steel blue** 2,500.
n. **blue** 2,500.
o. **black** 2,500.
p. **violet** 2,500.
70TC2 24c small die on India paper
b. **violet** 375.
70TC2a 24c PP small die on yelsh wove paper
e. **violet** 2,250.
70TC3 24c plate on India paper
a. **violet** *750.*
Block of 4 *3,250.*
70TC5 24c **gray,** on bluish gray stamp paper 250.
70TC6 24c **dark violet,** semi-transparent stamp paper, perf 12, gummed **(formerly No. 60)** *15,000.*
70P1 24c **red lilac,** large die on India paper —
70P2a 24c **red lilac,** PP sm die on yelsh wove paper 2,750.
70P4 24c **red lilac,** plate on card 500.
78P2 24c **lilac,** RA sm die on white wove paper 225.
78P2a 24c **lilac,** PP sm die on yelsh wove paper 2,750.
78P3 24c **lilac,** plate on India 80.
Block of 4 400.
P# blk. of 8 2,000.
78P4 24c **lilac,** plate on card 80.
Block of 4 400.
P# blk. of 8 —
71TC1a 30c large die on India paper
e. **rose** 2,500.
f. **red orange** 2,500.
71TC2 30c small die on India paper
e. **black** 600.
f. **red orange** 375.
71TC2a 30c PP small die on yelsh wove paper
e. **red orange** 1,250.
71TC6 30c **red orange,** semi-transparent stamp paper, perf 12, gummed **(formerly No. 61)** *45,000.*
71P1 30c **orange,** large die on India paper 500.
71P2 30c **orange,** RA sm die on white wove paper 225.
71P2a 30c **orange,** PP sm die on yelsh wove paper 2,750.
71P3 30c **orange,** plate on India 50.
Block of 4 350.
P# blk. of 8 2,500.
71P4 30c **orange,** plate on card 30.
Block of 4 140.
P# blk. of 8 —
72TC1a 90c large die on India paper
e. **black** 2,500.
f. **ultramarine** 2,500.
g. **bluish gray** 2,500.
h. **violet gray** 2,500.
i. **red brown** 2,500.
j. **orange** 2,500.
k. **yellow orange** 2,500.
l. **scarlet** 2,500.
m. **green** 2,500.
72P1 90c **blue,** large die on India paper 600.
72P2 90c **blue,** RA sm die on white wove paper 225.
72P2a 90c **blue,** PP sm die on yelsh wove paper 2,750.
72P3 90c **blue,** plate on India 60.
Block of 4 400.
P# blk. of 8 2,500.
72P4 90c **blue,** plate on card 30.
Block of 4 140.
P# blk. of 8 —

1861 Gummed Stamp Paper

66TC6 3c **lake,** perf. 12 *2,000.*
Pair *4,500.*
Block of 4 *9,250.*
P# strip of 4 *10,000.*
Double transfer *2,250.*
a. Imperf, pair *1,850.*
P# block of 8 —

John N. Luff recorded the plate number for No. 66TC as 34.

74TC6 3c **scarlet,** perf. 12 *7,000.* 5,000.
Block of 4 *29,000.* 5,000.
With 4 horiz. black pen strokes *5,000.*
With handstamped cancel *10,000.*
a. Imperf, pair *4,000.*

John N. Luff recorded the plate number for No. 74TC as 19.

1861

66TC2 3c **lake,** RA small die on India paper 250.
66TC2a 3c **lake,** PP small die on yelsh wove paper 1,100.
66TC3 3c **lake,** plate on India paper 150.
Block of 4 850.
P# Block of 8 2,250.
74TC1a 3c **scarlet,** large die on India paper 2,250.
74TC2 3c **scarlet,** RA small die on India paper 375.
74TC2a 3c **scarlet,** small die on yelsh wove paper 1,100.
74TC3 3c **scarlet,** plate on India paper 150.
Block of 4 725.
74TC4 3c **scarlet,** plate on card 150.
Block of 4 725.
P# Block of 8 —

1861-67

73TC1a 2c large die on India paper
e. **dull chalky blue** *8,000.*
f. **green** *8,000.*
g. **dull yellow** *8,000.*
h. **dark orange** *8,000.*
i. **scarlet** *8,000.*
j. **dull rose** *8,000.*
k. **brown** *8,000.*
l. **ultramarine** *8,000.*
73TC3 2c plate on India paper
a. **light blue** 250.
b. **dull chalky blue** 500.
c. **green** 250.
d. **olive green** 250.
e. **blue green** *400.*
f. **vermilion** 250.
g. **scarlet** 250.
h. **dull red** 250.
i. **dull rose** 250.
j. **gray black** 250.
Block of 4 *2,500.*
73P1 2c **black,** die I, large die on India paper 10,000.
a. Die II 2,500.
73P2 2c **black,** die II, RA sm die on white wove paper 1,300.
73P2a 2c **black,** die II, PP sm die on yelsh wove paper 8,750.
73P3 2c **black,** die I, plate on India 150.
Block of 4 750.
P# blk. of 8 2,250.
a. Die II 110.
Block of 4 550.
P# blk. of 8 1,750.
73P4 2c **black,** die I, plate on card, P# block of 8 —
a. Die II 75.
Block of 4 400.
P# blk. of 8 —
77TC1a 15c large die on India paper
e. **deep blue** 2,500.
f. **dark red** 2,500.
g. **orange red** 2,500.
h. **dark orange** 2,500.
i. **yellow orange** 2,500.
j. **dark yellow** 2,500.
k. **sepia** 2,500.
l. **orange brown** 2,500.
m. **red brown** 2,500.
n. **blue green** 2,500.
o. **dusky blue** 2,500.
p. **gray black** 2,500.
77TC3 15c plate on India paper
a. **deep blue** 335.
Block of 4 1,650.
77P1 15c **black,** large die on India paper 1,500.
77P2 15c **black,** RA sm die on white wove paper 500.
77P2a 15c **black,** PP sm die on yelsh wove paper 2,750.
77P3 15c **black,** plate on India 55.
Block of 4 250.
P# blk. of 8 3,000.
77P4 15c **black,** plate on card 45.
Block of 4 200.
P# blk. of 8 —
79P5 3c **rose,** A grill, plate on stamp paper, pair *1,500.*
Block of 4 *4,000.*
P# blk. of 8 *10,000.*
83P5 3c **rose,** C grill, plate on stamp paper, pair *1,750.*
94P5 3c **red,** F grill, plate on stamp paper, pair *1,500.*

The listed plate proofs of the 1c (63P), 5c (76P), 10c (68P) and 12c (69P) are from the 100 subject re-issue plates of 1875.

Single proofs of these denominations from the regular issue plates cannot be told apart from the reprints. As the reprint plates had wider spacing between the subjects, multiples can be differentiated. Values are for proofs from the reprint plates. The 2c Die II has a small dot on the left cheek. The 5c has a small notch at the bottom left of the design.

1869

No.	Description	Value
112TC1a	1c large die on India paper	
	e. **black**	2,500.
112P1	1c **buff,** large die on India paper	750.
112P2	1c **buff,** RA sm die on white wove paper	350.
112P2a	1c **buff,** PP sm die on yelsh wove paper	3,000.
112P3	1c **buff,** plate on India	55.
	Block of 4	250.
	P# blk. of 10	950.
112P4	1c **buff,** plate on card	65.
	Block of 4	300.
113TC1a	2c large die on India paper	
	e. **black**	2,500.
113P1	2c **brown,** large die on India paper	750.
113P2	2c **brown,** RA sm die on white wove paper	350.
113P2a	2c **brown,** PP sm die on yelsh wove paper	3,500.
113P3	2c **brown,** plate on India	40.
	Block of 4	175.
	P# blk. of 10	800.
113P4	2c **brown,** plate on card	50.
	Block of 4	225.
	P# blk. of 10	1,000.
114TC1a	3c large die on India paper	
	e. **black**	2,500.
114P1	3c **ultra,** large die on India paper	900.
114P2	3c **ultra,** RA sm die on white wove paper	575.
114P2a	3c **ultra,** PP sm die on yelsh wove paper	*4,000.*
114P3	3c **ultra,** plate on India	45.
	Block of 4	190.
	P# blk. of 10	1,000.
114P4	3c **ultra,** plate on card	85.
	Block of 4	375.
	P# blk. of 10	1,250.
115TC1a	6c large die on India paper	
	e. **deep dull blue**	2,500.
	f. **black**	2,500.
115P1	6c **ultra,** large die on India paper	900.
115P2	6c **ultra,** RA sm die on white wove paper	350.
115P2a	6c **ultra,** PP sm die on yelsh wove paper	3,000.
115P3	6c **ultra,** plate on India	45.
	Block of 4	190.
	P# blk. of 10	1,000.
115P4	6c **ultra,** plate on card	85.
	Block of 4	375.
	P# blk. of 10	1,250.
116TC1a	10c large die on India paper	
	e. **black**	2,500.
	f. **dull dark violet**	2,500.
	g. **deep green**	2,500.
	h. **dull dark orange**	2,500.
	i. **dull rose**	2,500.
	j. **copper red**	2,500.
	k. **chocolate**	2,500.
	l. **dark Prussian blue**	2,500.
116P1	10c **yellow,** large die on India paper	900.
116P2	10c **yellow,** RA sm die on white wove paper	350.
116P2a	10c **yellow,** PP sm die on yelsh wove paper	3,000.
116P3	10c **yellow,** plate on India	45.
	Block of 4	190.
	P# blk. of 10	2,000.
116P4	10c **yellow,** plate on card	55.
	Block of 4	250.
	P# blk. of 10	2,500.
117TC1a	12c large die on India paper	
	e. **black**	2,500.
117P1	12c **green,** large die on India paper	900.
117P2	12c **green,** RA sm die on white wove paper	350.
117P2a	12c **green,** PP sm die on yelsh wove paper	3,000.
117P3	12c **green,** plate on India	45.
	Block of 4	190.
	P# blk. of 10	2,250.
117P4	12c **green,** plate on card	55.
	Block of 4	265.
	P# blk. of 10	2,800.
118TC1a	15c large die on India paper	
	e. **dull dark violet**	2,500.
	f. **deep blue**	2,500.
	g. **dull red brown**	2,500.
	h. **black**	2,500.
	i. **dark blue gray**	2,500.
119P1	15c **brn & bl,** (type II), large die on India paper	550.
119P2	15c **brn & bl,** (type II), RA sm die on white wove paper	450.
119P2a	15c **brn & bl,** (type II), PP sm die on yelsh wove paper	3,000.
119P3	15c **brn & bl,** (type II), plate on India	120.
	Block of 4	600.
	P# blk. of 8	4,000.
129P1	15c **Reissue,** (type III), large die on India paper	550.
129P2	15c **Reissue,** (type III), RA sm die on white wove paper	450.
129P2a	15c **Reissue,** (type III), PP sm die on yelsh wove paper	3,000.
129P3	15c **Reissue,** (type III), plate on India	350.
	Block of 4	1,600.
	P# blk. of 8	4,500.
129P4	15c **Reissue,** (type III), plate on card	140.
	Block of 4	725.
	P# blk. of 8	3,750.
	a. Center inverted *(100)*	*2,750.*
	Block of 4	*15,000.*
	P# blk. of 8	*75,500.*
120TC1a	24c large die on India paper	
	e. **black**	4,500.
120TC3	24c plate on India paper	
	a. **green & reddish lilac**	—
	Block of 4	—
	P# block of 8	6,000.
120P1	24c **grn & vio,** large die on India paper	550.
120P2	24c **grn & vio,** RA sm die on white wove paper	450.
120P2a	24c **grn & vio,** PP sm die on yelsh wove paper	3,000.
120P3	24c **grn & vio,** plate on India	140.
	Block of 4	625.
	P# blk. of 8	6,000.
120P4	24c **grn & vio,** plate on card	140.
	Block of 4	650.
	P# blk. of 8	7,500.
	a. Center inverted *(100)*	*2,750.*
	Block of 4	*15,000.*
	P# blk. of 8	*75,500.*
121TC1a	30c large die on India paper	
	e. **deep blue & deep green**	3,500.
	f. **deep brown & blue**	3,500.
	g. **golden brown & carmine lake**	3,500.
	h. **carmine lake & dull violet**	3,500.
	i. **carmine lake & green**	3,500.
	j. **carmine lake & brown**	3,500.
	k. **carmine lake & black**	3,500.
	l. **dull orange red & deep green**	3,500.
	m. **deep ocher & golden brown**	3,500.
	n. **dull violet & golden brown**	3,500.
	o. **black & deep green**	3,500.
121P1	30c **ultra & car,** large die on India paper	1,250.
121P2	30c **ultra & car,** RA sm die on white wove paper	450.
121P2a	30c **ultra & car,** PP sm die on yelsh wove paper	3,000.
121P3	30c **ultra & car,** plate on India	140.
	Block of 4	625.
	P# blk. of 8	7,500.
121P4	30c **ultra & car,** plate on card	170.
	Block of 4	875.
	P# blk. of 8	—
	a. Flags inverted *(100)*	*2,750.*
	Block of 4	*15,000.*
	P# blk. of 8	*75,500.*
122TC1a	90c large die on India paper	
	e. **brown & deep green**	3,500.
122TC4	90c Plate on card	
	a. **green & black**	1,500.
122P1	90c **car & blk,** large die on India paper	550.
122P2	90c **car & blk,** RA sm die on white wove paper	450.
122P2a	90c **car & blk,** PP sm die on yelsh wove paper	5,000.
122P3	90c **car & blk,** plate on India	180.
	Block of 4	825.
	P# blk. of 8	6,500.
122P4	90c **car & blk,** plate on card	170.
	Block of 4	875.
	P# blk. of 8	8,250.
	a. Center inverted *(100)*	*2,750.*
	Block of 4	*15,000.*
	P# blk. of 8 (unique)	*87,500.*
	Nos. 112P3-117P3, 119P3-122P3 (10)	855.00
	Nos. 112P4-117P4, 120P4-122P4 (9)	875.00

Large die proofs of Nos. 119, 129; 120 and 122 exist only as hybrids.

1880

No.	Description	Value
133P1	1c **dark buff,** large die on India paper	1,000.
133P3	1c **dark buff,** plate on India	100.
	Block of 4	450.
	P# blk. of 10	1,250.

1870-71 National Bank Note Co.

No.	Description	Value
136P5	3c **green,** grill, on stamp paper, pair	*1,200.*
	P# blk. of 12	*14,000.*
145TC1a	1c large die on India paper	
	e. **yellow orange**	600.
	f. **red brown**	600.
	g. **red violet**	600.
	h. **black**	—
	i. **green**	600.
145TC3	1c plate on India paper	
	a. **black**	—
145P1	1c **ultra,** large die on India paper	250.
145P2	1c **ultra,** RA sm die on white wove paper, from new die	175.
145P2a	1c **ultra,** PP sm die on yelsh wove paper	2,500.
145P3	1c **ultra,** plate on India	20.
	Block of 4	90.
	P# blk. of 10	750.
146TC1a	2c large die on India paper	
	e. **black**	600.
146P1	2c **red brn,** large die on India paper	250.
146P3	2c **red brn,** plate on India	20.
	Block of 4	90.
	P# blk. of 12	750.
147TC1a	3c large die on India paper	
	e. **brown**	—
	f. **red brown**	—
	g. **dark red**	—
	h. **light ultramarine**	—
	i. **yellow brown**	—
	j. **dull red violet**	—
	k. **dull grayish red**	—
	l. **yellow orange**	—
	m. **red violet**	—
	n. **green**	—
147TC3	3c plate on India paper	
	a. **brown**	125.
	b. **dark brown**	125.
	c. **red brown**	125.
	d. **orange brown**	125.
	e. **dark red**	125.
	f. **light ultramarine**	125.
	g. **yellow brown**	125.
	h. **dull red violet**	125.
	i. **yellow orange**	125.
	j. **red violet**	125.
147TC5	3c plate on wove paper	
	a. **deep red brown**	125.

Former Nos. 147aTC and 147bTC are now listed in the Essay section as No. 147-E13c.

No.	Description	Value
147P1	3c **green,** large die on India paper	300.
147P3	3c **green,** plate on India	20.
	Block of 4	90.
	P# blk. of 12	750.

The former No. 147Pc4 is now listed in the Essay section as No. 147-E13e.

No.	Description	Value
148TC1a	6c large die on India paper	
	e. **deep magenta**	600.
	f. **ultramarine**	600.
	g. **carmine**	600.
	h. **maroon**	600.
148P1	6c **carmine,** large die on India paper	1,750.
148P3	6c **carmine,** plate on India	35.
	Block of 4	150.
	P# blk. of 12	1,400.
149TC1a	7c large die on India paper	
	e. **black**	550.
149P1	7c **vermilion,** large die on India paper	250.
149P3	7c **vermilion,** plate on India	15.
	Block of 4	70.
	P# blk. of 12	750.
150TC1a	10c large die on India paper	
	e. **blue**	550.
	f. **dull pale blue**	550.
	g. **ultramarine**	550.
	h. **blue green**	550.
	i. **carmine**	550.
	j. **bister**	550.
	k. **dull red**	550.
	l. **red orange**	550.
	m. **yellow brown**	550.
	n. **brown orange**	550.
150P1	10c **brown,** large die on India paper	300.
150P3	10c **brown,** plate on India	40.
	Block of 4	165.
	P# blk. of 12	2,000.
151TC1a	12c large die on India paper	
	e. **orange**	550.
	f. **orange brown**	550.
	g. **brown red**	550.
	h. **dull red**	550.
	i. **carmine**	550.
	j. **blue**	550.
	k. **light blue**	550.
	l. **ultramarine**	550.
	m. **green**	550.
151P1	12c **violet,** large die on India paper	250.
151P3	12c **violet,** plate on India	16.
	Block of 4	70.
	P# blk. of 10	750.
152P1	15c **orange,** large die on India paper	300.
152P3	15c **orange,** plate on India	30.
	Block of 4	135.
	P# blk. of 12	750.
153TC1a	24c large die on India paper	
	e. **dark brown**	550.
153P1	24c **purple,** large die on India paper	300.
153P3	24c **purple,** plate on India	30.
	Block of 4	135.
	P# blk. of 12	750.
154P1	30c **black,** large die on India paper	300.
154P3	30c **black,** plate on India	40.
	Block of 4	170.
	P# blk. of 12	2,250.
155TC1a	90c large die on India paper	
	e. **carmine**	550.
	f. **ultramarine**	550.
	g. **black**	550.
155P1	90c **carmine,** large die on India paper	300.
155P3	90c **carmine,** plate on India	45.
	Block of 4	195.
	P# blk. of 12	2,500.

Secret Marks on 24, 30 and 90c Dies of the Bank Note Issues

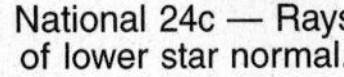

National 24c — Rays of lower star normal.

Continental 24c — Rays of lower star strengthened.

National 30c — Lower line does not join point of shield.

Continental and American 30c — Lower line joins point of shield and bottom line of shield thicker.

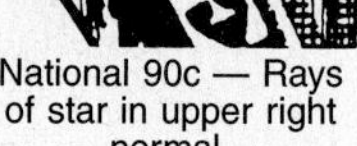

National 90c — Rays of star in upper right normal.

Continental and American 90c — Rays of star in upper right strengthened.

1873 Continental Bank Note Co.

156TC1a	1c large die on India paper	
e.	**scarlet**	*1,500.*
156TC3	1c plate on India paper	
a.	**black**	15.
	Block of 4	65.
156TC4	1c plate on card	
a.	**black**	30.
	Block of 4	140.
156P1	1c **ultra,** large die on India paper	450.
156P3	1c **ultra,** plate on India	55.
	Block of 4	250.
	P# blk. of 14	1,150.
156P4	1c **ultra,** plate on card	300.
157TC1a	2c large die on India paper	
e.	**black**	850.
f.	**dull blue**	850.
g.	**rose**	850.
h.	**deep rose**	850.
157TC3	2c plate on India paper	
a.	**black**	15.
	Block of 4	65.
157P1	2c **brown,** large die on India paper	350.
157P2	2c **brown,** RA sm die on white wove paper	175.
157P2a	2c **brown,** PP sm die on yelsh wove paper	2,500.
157P3	2c **brown,** plate on India	35.
	Block of 4	165.
	P# blk. of 14	1,150.
157P4	2c **brown,** plate on card	20.
	Block of 4	100.
	P# blk. of 14	—
157P5	2c **brown,** plate on stamp paper	—
158TC1a	3c large die on India paper	
e.	**black**	750.
g.	**orange red**	—
158TC3	3c plate on India paper	
a.	**black**	12.
	Block of 4	55.
158P1	3c **green,** large die on India paper	350.
158P2	3c **green,** RA sm die on white wove paper	175.
158P3	3c **green,** plate on India	55.
	Block of 4	220.
	P# blk. of 14	1,150.
158P4	3c **green,** plate on card	150.
158P5	3c **green,** plate on stamp paper, pair	*150.*
a.	On stamp paper, grill, pair	*650.*
158TC4	3c plate on card	
a.	**black**	15.
	Block of 4	75.
	P# block of 12	450.
159TC3	6c plate on India paper	
a.	**black**	30.
	Block of 4	150.
159P1	6c **rose,** large die on India paper	2,000.
159P2	6c **rose,** RA sm die on white wove paper	250.
159P2a	6c **rose,** PP sm die on yelsh wove paper	2,500.
159P3	6c **rose,** plate on India	110.
	Block of 4	525.
	P# blk. of 12	2,000.
159P4	6c **pink,** plate on card	300.
160TC3	7c plate on India paper	
a.	**black**	75.
	Block of 4	325.
160P1	7c **org vermilion,** large die on India paper	250.
160P2	7c **org vermilion,** RA sm die on white wove paper	175.
160P2a	7c **org vermilion,** PP sm die on yelsh wove paper	2,500.
160P3	7c **org vermilion,** plate on India	35.
	Block of 4	165.
	P# blk. of 14	1,150.
160P4	7c **org vermilion,** plate on card	20.
	Block of 4	100.
	P# blk. of 14	—
161P1	10c **brown,** large die on India paper	450.
161P2	10c **brown,** RA sm die on white wove paper	200.
161P3	10c **brown,** plate on India	60.
	Block of 4	300.
	P# blk. of 14	1,300.
161P4	10c **brown,** plate on card	300.
162P1	12c **blackish vio,** large die on India paper	200.
162P2	12c **blackish vio,** RA sm die on white wove paper	175.
162P2a	12c **blackish vio,** PP sm die on yelsh wove paper	2,500.
162P3	12c **blackish vio,** plate on India	38.
	Block of 4	190.
	P# blk. of 14	1,150.
162P4	12c **blackish vio,** plate on card	20.
	Block of 4	100.
	P# blk. of 14	—
162P5	12c **blackish vio,** plate on stamp paper	—
163P1	15c **yel org,** large die on India paper	400.
163P2	15c **yel org,** RA sm die on white wove paper	175.
163P2a	15c **yel org,** PP sm die on yelsh wove paper	2,500.
163P3	15c **yel org,** plate on India	65.
	Block of 4	250.
	P# blk. of 12	1,000.
163P4	15c **yel org,** plate on card	20.
	Block of 4	100.
	P# blk. of 12	—
164P1	24c **violet,** large die on India paper	400.
164P2	24c **violet,** RA sm die on white wove paper	175.
164P2a	24c **violet,** PP sm die on yelsh wove paper	2,500.
164P3	24c **violet,** plate on India	50.
	Block of 4	225.
	P# blk. of 12	1,150.
164P4	24c **violet,** plate on card	30.
	Block of 4	140.
165P1	30c **gray blk,** large die on India paper	400.
165P2	30c **gray blk,** RA sm die on white wove paper	175.
165P2a	30c **gray blk,** PP sm die on yelsh wove paper	2,500.
165P3	30c **gray blk,** plate on India	40.
	Block of 4	200.
	P# blk. of 12	1,150.
165P4	30c **gray blk,** plate on card	20.
	Block of 4	90.
166P1	90c **rose car,** large die on India paper	400.
166P2	90c **rose car,** RA sm die on white wove paper	175.
166P2a	90c **rose car,** PP sm die on yelsh wove paper	2,500.
166P3	90c **rose car,** plate on India	55.
	Block of 4	250.
	P# blk. of 12	1,500.
166P4	90c **rose car,** plate on card	40.
	Block of 4	190.

Die proofs of the 24c, 30c and 90c show secret marks, as illustrated, but as plates of these denominations were not made from these dies, plate proofs can be identified only by color.

Nos. 159TC2-166TC2 are so-called "Goodall" set of Small Die proofs on India Paper of Official Stamps in five colors

159TC2	6c "Goodall" small die on India paper	
b.	**black**	600.
c.	**deep green**	600.
d.	**dull gray blue**	600.
e.	**deep brown**	600.
f.	**dull red**	600.
160TC2	7c "Goodall" small die on India paper	
b.	**black**	600.
c.	**deep green**	600.
d.	**dull gray blue**	600.
e.	**deep brown**	600.
f.	**dull red**	600.
161TC2	10c "Goodall" small die on India paper	
b.	**black**	600.
c.	**deep green**	600.
d.	**dull gray blue**	600.
e.	**deep brown**	600.
f.	**dull red**	600.
162TC2	12c "Goodall" small die on India paper	
b.	**black**	600.
c.	**deep green**	600.
d.	**dull gray blue**	600.
e.	**deep brown**	600.
f.	**dull red**	600.
163TC2	15c "Goodall" small die on India paper	
b.	**black**	600.
c.	**deep green**	600.
d.	**dull gray blue**	600.
e.	**deep brown**	600.
f.	**dull red**	600.
164TC2	24c "Goodall" small die on India paper	
b.	**black**	600.
c.	**deep green**	600.
d.	**dull gray blue**	600.
e.	**deep brown**	600.
f.	**dull red**	600.
165TC2	30c "Goodall" small die on India paper	
b.	**black**	600.
c.	**deep green**	600.
d.	**dull gray blue**	600.
e.	**deep brown**	600.
f.	**dull red**	600.
166TC2	90c "Goodall" small die on India paper	
b.	**black**	600.
c.	**deep green**	600.
d.	**dull gray blue**	600.
e.	**deep brown**	600.
f.	**dull red**	600.

1875

178P5	2c **vermilion,** plate on stamp paper, pair	*600.*
	P# blk. of 12	*12,000.*
179TC1a	5c large die on India paper	
e.	**black**	650.
f.	**scarlet**	1,000.
179TC2	5c "Goodall" small die on India paper	
b.	**black**	550.
c.	**deep green**	550.
d.	**deep brown**	550.
e.	**dull red**	550.
f.	**dull gray blue**	550.
179TC3	5c plate on India paper	
a.	**black**	25.
	Block of 4	125.
179TC4	5c Plate on card	
a.	**black**	45.
	Block of 4	200.

1879 American Bank Note Co.

182TC6	1c plate on stamp paper, gummed, perf. 12	
a.	**ultramarine**	300.
b.	**green**	300.
c.	**deep green**	300.
d.	**vermilion**	300.
e.	**brown**	300.
182P1	1c **gray blue,** large die on India paper	525.
182P3	1c **gray blue,** plate on India	60.
	Block of 4	275.
	P# blk. of 12	1,000.
183TC6	2c plate on stamp paper, gummed, perf. 12	
a.	**ultramarine**	300.
b.	**blue**	300.
c.	**green**	300.
183P1	2c **vermilion,** large die on India paper	300.
183P2	2c **vermilion,** RA sm die on white wove paper	190.
183P2a	2c **vermilion,** PP sm die on yelsh wove paper	2,500.
183P3	2c **vermilion,** plate on India	35.
	Block of 4	160.
	P# blk. of 12	600.
183P4	2c **vermilion,** plate on card	25.
	Block of 4	140.
	P# blk. of 12	—
184TC6	3c plate on stamp paper, gummed, perf. 12	
a.	**ultramarine**	300.
b.	**blue**	300.
c.	**vermilion**	300.
	Block of 4	1,100.
d.	**brown**	300.
184P6	3c **green,** plate on stamp paper, pair	*500.*
	P# blk. of 12	—
185TC6	5c plate on stamp paper, gummed, perf. 12	
a.	**ultramarine**	300.
b.	**green**	300.
c.	**vermilion**	300.
185P1	5c **blue,** large die on India paper	700.
185P2	5c **blue,** RA sm die on white wove paper	225.
185P2a	5c **blue,** PP sm die on yelsh wove paper	2,500.
185P3	5c **blue,** plate on India	70.
	Block of 4	325.
	P# blk. of 12	1,300.
185P4	5c **blue,** plate on card	25.
	Block of 4	140.
	P# blk. of 12	—
186TC6	6c plate on stamp paper, gummed, perf. 12	
a.	**ultramarine**	300.
b.	**blue**	300.
c.	**vermilion**	300.
187TC6	10c plate on stamp paper, gummed, perf. 12	
a.	**ultramarine**	300.
b.	**blue**	300.
c.	**vermilion**	300.
d.	**green**	300.
189TC1a	15c large die on India paper	
e.	**orange vermilion**	1,000.
f.	**orange brown**	1,000.
g.	**chestnut brown**	1,000.
h.	**dark brown**	1,000.
i.	**deep green**	1,000.
j.	**black**	1,000.
189TC1d	15c large die on card	
e.	**orange vermilion**	450.
f.	**orange brown**	450.
g.	**chestnut brown**	450.
h.	**dark brown**	450.
i.	**deep green**	450.
j.	**black**	450.
189TC6	15c plate on stamp paper, gummed, perf. 12	
a.	**ultramarine**	300.
b.	**green**	300.
c.	**vermilion**	300.
d.	**brown**	300.
e.	**dull red**	300.
190TC1a	30c large die on India paper	
e.	**black**	1,000.
f.	**orange vermilion**	1,000.
g.	**dark brown**	1,000.

h. **deep green** 1,000.
i. **dull red brown** 1,000.
j. **green** 1,000.
190TC1d 30c large die on card
e. **orange vermilion** 450.
f. **dark brown** 450.
g. **deep green** 450.
h. **dull red brown** 450.
i. **green** 450.
190TC6 30c plate on stamp paper, gummed, perf. 12
a. **ultramarine** 300.
b. **blue** 300.
c. **green** 300.

See Specimens for No. 189 in deep blue (No. 189S L), No. 209 in green (No. 209S L), No. 210 in pale rose lake (No. 210S L).

190P3 30c **full black,** plate on India —
Block of 4 —
P# block of 10 1,000.
190P4 30c **full black,** plate on card 400.
Block of 4 2,000.
P# blk. of 12 *7,500.*
191TC1a 90c large die on India paper
e. **carmine** 1,000.
f. **dark brown** 1,000.
g. **deep dull orange** 1,000.
h. **indigo** 1,000.
i. **dull red brown** 1,000.
j. **black** 1,000.
191TC1d 90c large die on card
e. **carmine** 450.
f. **dark brown** 450.
g. **deep dull orange** 450.
h. **indigo** 450.
i. **dull red brown** 450.
j. **black** 450.
191P5 90c **car,** plate on stamp paper, pair *2,250.*
P# strip of 5 5,000.
193P4 2c **blk brown,** plate on card 400.
Block of 4 2,000.
P# blk. of 12 7,500.

1881-82 American Bank Note Co.

205TC1a 5c large die on India paper
e. **chestnut brown** 1,000.
f. **deep dull orange** 1,000.
g. **pale ultramarine** 1,000.
h. **deep green** 1,000.
i. **green** 1,000.
j. **carmine** 1,000.
k. **carmine lake** 1,000.
l. **blue black** 1,000.
205TC1d 5c large die on card
e. **chestnut brown** —
f. **pale ultramarine** —
g. **carmine** 450.
h. **black** on glazed card 1,000.
205TC3 5c plate on India paper
a. **green** 200.
b. **carmine lake** 225.
205P1 5c **yel brn,** large die on India paper 250.
205P2 5c **yel brn,** RA sm die on white wove paper 200.
205P2a 5c **yel brn,** PP sm die on yelsh wove paper 2,500.
205P3 5c **yel brn,** plate on India 40.
Block of 4 175.
P# blk. of 12 1,000.
205P4 5c **yel brn,** plate on card 15.
Block of 4 100.
P# blk. of 12 —
Bottom margin P# block of 30 *2,700.*
206TC1a 1c large die on India paper
e. **deep green** 600.
f. **black** 600.
g. **ultramarine** 600.
h. **dark yellow green** 600.
206TC2 1c small die on India paper
b. **deep green** 125.
206TC3 1c plate on India paper
a. **black** 125.
206P1 1c **blue,** large die on India paper 375.
206P2 1c **blue,** RA sm die on white wove paper 200.
206P2a 1c **blue,** PP sm die on yelsh wove paper 2,500.
206P3 1c **blue,** plate on India 40.
Block of 4 175.
P# blk. of 12 1,000.
206P4 1c **blue,** plate on card 20.
Block of 4 120.
P# blk. of 12 —
Bottom margin P# block of 30 *2,700.*
207P1 3c **blue grn,** large die on India paper 375.
207P2 3c **blue grn,** RA sm die on white wove paper 200.
207P2a 3c **blue grn,** PP sm die on yelsh wove paper 2,500.
207P3 3c **blue grn,** plate on India 40.
Block of 4 175.
P# blk. of 12 1,000.
207P4 3c **blue grn,** plate on card 20.
Block of 4 120.
P# blk. of 12 —
Bottom margin P# block of 30 *2,700.*
208TC1a 6c large die on India paper
e. **deep dull orange** 1,000.
f. **indigo** 1,250.
g. **orange vermilion** 1,100.
h. **dark violet** 1,000.
i. **chestnut brown** 1,350.
j. **carmine** 1,250.
208TC1d 6c large die on card
e. **deep dull orange** 450.
f. **orange vermilion** 450.
g. **dark violet** 450.
h. **chestnut brown** 450.
208P1 6c **deep rose,** large die on India paper 2,250.
208P2 6c **deep rose,** RA sm die on white wove paper 200.
208P2a 6c **deep rose,** PP sm die on yelsh wove paper 2,500.
b. **brown red** 2,500.
208P3 6c **deep rose,** plate on India 90.
Block of 4 425.
P# blk. of 12 —
a. **brown red** 100.
208P4 6c **deep rose,** plate on card 60.
Block of 4 240.
P# blk. of 12 —
Bottom margin P# block of 30 *2,700.*
a. **brown red** 50.
209TC1a 10c large die on India paper
e. **carmine** 1,000.
f. **orange brown** 1,000.
g. **orange** 1,000.
h. **deep dull orange** 1,000.
i. **chestnut brown** 1,000.
j. **indigo** 1,000.
k. **pale ultramarine** 1,000.
209TC1d 10c large die on card
e. **carmine** 450.
f. **orange brown** 450.
g. **deep dull orange** 450.
h. **chestnut brown** 450.
i. **indigo** 450.
j. **pale ultramarine** 450.
k. **black,** on glazed card 1,000.
209TC4 10c plate on card
a. **orange brown** 125.
b. **green** 125.
209TC6 10c plate on stamp paper, gummed, perf. 12
a. **green** 300.
209P1 10c **brn,** large die on India paper 800.
209P2 10c **brn,** RA sm die on white wove paper 200.
209P2a 10c **brn,** PP sm die on yelsh wove paper 2,500.
209P3 10c **brn,** plate on India 40.
Block of 4 170.
P# blk. of 12 1,000.
209P4 10c **brn,** plate on card 25.
Block of 4 140.
P# blk. of 12 —
Bottom margin P# block of 30 *2,700.*

1883

210TC1a 2c large die on India paper
e. **red brown** 1,000.
f. **deep dull orange** 1,000.
g. **chestnut brown** 1,000.
h. **violet rose** 1,000.
i. **indigo** 1,000.
j. **black** 1,000.
k. **pale ultramarine** 1,000.
l. **olive green** 1,000.
210TC1d 2c large die on card
e. **brown red** 450.
f. **chestnut brown** 450.
g. **violet rose** 450.
h. **indigo** 450.
i. **olive green** 450.
j. **olive brown** 450.
210TC4 2c plate on card
a. **lake** 140.
b. **rose lake** 140.
c. **deep carmine** 140.
d. **deep red** 140.
210P1 2c **red brn,** large die on India paper 400.
210P2 2c **red brn,** RA sm die on white wove paper 200.
210P2a 2c **red brn,** PP sm die on yelsh wove paper 2,500.
210P3 2c **red brn,** plate on India 40.
Block of 4 180.
P# blk. of 12 1,000.
210P4 2c **red brn,** plate on card 20.
Block of 4 110.
P# blk. of 12 —
Bottom margin P# block of 30 *2,700.*
210P5 2c **red brn,** plate on stamp paper, pair —
211TC1a 4c large die on India paper
e. **green** 1,000.
f. **chestnut brown** 1,000.
g. **orange brown** 1,000.
h. **pale ultramarine** 1,000.
i. **dark brown** 1,000.
j. **black** 1,000.
211TC1d 4c large die on card
e. **green** 450.
f. **chestnut brown** 450.
g. **orange brown** 450.
h. **pale ultramarine** 450.
i. **black** 450.
211P1 4c **grn,** large die on India paper 500.
211P2 4c **grn,** RA sm die on white wove paper 200.
211P2a 4c **grn,** PP sm die on yelsh wove paper 2,500.
211P3 4c **grn,** plate on India 40.
Block of 4 165.
P# blk. of 12 1,000.
211P4 4c **grn,** plate on card 25.
Block of 4 140.
P# blk. of 12 —
Bottom margin P# block of 30 *2,700.*
211P5 4c **green,** plate on stamp paper, pair —

1887-88

212TC1a 1c large die on India paper
e. **indigo** 1,000.
f. **carmine** 1,000.
g. **green** 1,000.
h. **deep green** 1,000.
i. **copper brown** 1,000.
j. **chestnut brown** 1,000.
212TC1d 1c large die on card
e. **green** 450.
f. **deep green** 450.
g. **copper brown** 450.
212P1 1c **ultra,** large die on India paper 650.
212P2 1c **ultra,** RA sm die on white wove paper 200.
212P2a 1c **ultra,** PP sm die on yelsh wove paper 2,500.
212P3 1c **ultra,** plate on India 125.
Block of 4 600.
P# blk. of 12 2,250.
212P4 1c **ultra,** plate on card *2,750.*
Block of 4 *12,500.*
212P5 1c **ultra,** plate on stamp paper, pair —

Examples of No. 212P3 mounted on card are frequently offered as No. 212P4.

213P1 2c **grn,** large die on India paper 500.
213P2 2c **grn,** RA sm die on white wove paper 200.
213P2a 2c **grn,** PP sm die on yelsh wove paper 2,500.
213P3 2c **grn,** plate on India 75.
Block of 4 325.
P# blk. of 12 1,150.
213P4 2c **grn,** plate on card 50.
Block of 4 225.
P# blk. of 12 —
213P5 2c **green,** plate on stamp paper, pair 2,000.
214TC1a 3c large die on India paper
e. **green** 1,000.
f. **dark green** —
g. **dark brown** 1,000.
h. **chestnut brown** 1,000.
i. **dull red brown** 1,000.
j. **deep dull orange** —
214TC1d 3c large die on card
e. **green** 450.
f. **dark green** —
g. **dark brown** 450.
h. **chestnut brown** 450.
i. **dull red brown** 450.
j. **deep dull orange** —
214TC4 3c plate on card
a. **dark green** —
b. **deep orange brown** —
c. **deep dull orange** —

All of 214TC1s above bear inscription "Worked over by new company, June 29th, 1881."

214P1 3c **vermilion,** large die on India paper 500.
214P2 3c **vermilion,** RA sm die on white wove paper 200.
214P2a 3c **vermilion,** PP sm die on yelsh wove paper 2,500.
214P3 3c **vermilion,** plate on India 75.
Block of 4 325.
P# blk. of 12 —
214P4 3c **vermilion,** plate on card 50.
Block of 4 225.
P# blk. of 12 —

Nos. 207P1 & 214P1 inscribed: "Worked over by new company, June 29th, 1881."

215P1 4c **car,** large die on India paper 650.
215P2 4c **car,** RA sm die on white wove paper 200.
215P2a 4c **car,** PP sm die on yelsh wove paper 2,500.
215P3 4c **car,** plate on India 95.
Block of 4 475.
215P4 4c **car,** plate on card 50.
Block of 4 225.
P# blk. of 12 —
216P1 5c **indigo,** large die on India paper 650.
216P2 5c **indigo,** RA sm die on white wove paper 200.
216P2a 5c **indigo,** PP sm die on yelsh wove paper 2,500.
216P3 5c **indigo,** plate on India 75.
Block of 4 325.
216P4 5c **indigo,** plate on card 50.
Block of 4 225.
P# blk. of 12 —
216P5 5c **indigo,** plate on stamp paper, pair *1,500.*
217P1 30c **org brn,** large die on India paper 750.
217P2 30c **org brn,** RA sm die on white wove paper 200.
217P2a 30c **org brn,** PP sm die on yelsh wove paper 2,500.
217P3 30c **org brn,** plate on India 75.
Block of 4 325.
217P4 30c **org brn,** plate on card 50.
Block of 4 225.
P# blk. of 10 —
217P5 30c **org brn,** plate on stamp paper, pair *1,750.*
218P1 90c **purple,** large die on India paper 1,100.
218P2 90c **purple,** RA sm die on white wove paper 200.
218P2a 90c **purple,** PP sm die on yelsh wove paper 2,500.
218P3 90c **purple,** plate on India 90.
Block of 4 400.
218P4 90c **purple,** plate on card 50.
Block of 4 225.
P# strip of 5 *1,500.*
218P5 90c **purple,** plate on stamp paper, pair —

1890-93

219TC1a 1c large die on India paper
e. **green** 600.
f. **dull violet** 600.
219P1 1c **ultra,** large die on India paper 225.
219P2 1c **ultra,** RA sm die on white wove paper 225.
219P2a 1c **ultra,** PP sm die on yelsh wove paper 2,000.
219P3 1c **ultra,** plate on India 25.
Block of 4 110.
P# blk. of 12 500.

219P4	1c **ultra,** plate on card	40.
	Block of 4	180.
	P# blk. of 12	650.
219P5	1c **ultra,** plate on stamp paper, pair	*190.*
219DP1	2c **lake,** large die on India paper	*1,000.*
219DP2	2c **lake,** RA sm die on white wove paper	190.
219DP2a	2c **lake,** PP sm die on yelsh wove paper	2,000.
219DP3	2c **lake,** plate on India	80.
	Block of 4	385.
	P# blk. of 12	1,650.
219DP4	2c **lake,** plate on card	165.
	Block of 4	700.
	P# blk. of 12	*3,250.*
219DP5	2c **lake,** plate on stamp paper, pair	*80.*
	P# blk. of 10	800.
220TC1a	2c large die on India paper	
	e. **dull violet**	600.
	f. **blue green**	600.
	g. **orange,** plate on stamp paper, gummed, pair	250.
220TC5	2c large die on India paper	250.
220P1	2c **car,** large die on India paper	450.
220P2	2c **car,** RA sm die on white wove paper	225.
220P3	2c **car,** plate on India	300.
	Block of 4	1,250.
	P# blk. of 12	*3,850.*
220P4	2c **car,** plate on card	200.
	Block of 4	825.
	P# blk. of 12	*2,500.*
220P5	2c **car,** plate on stamp paper, pair	*125.*
	As No. 220P5, without gum	*60.*
	P# blk. of 12	—
221P1	3c **purple,** large die on India paper	225.
221P2	3c **purple,** RA sm die on white wove paper	225.
221P2a	3c **purple,** PP sm die on yelsh wove paper	2,000.
221P3	3c **purple,** plate on India	35.
	Block of 4	160.
	P# blk. of 12	650.
221P4	3c **purple,** plate on card	25.
	Block of 4	110.
	P# blk. of 12	600.
221P5	3c **purple,** plate on stamp paper, pair	*225.*
222TC1a	4c large die on India paper	
	e. **green**	450.
222TC5	4c plate on stamp paper	
	a. **orange brown**	120.
	b. **yellow brown**	120.
	c. **brown** (shades)	120.
222P1	4c **dk brn,** large die on India paper	550.
222P2	4c **dk brn,** RA sm die on white wove paper	300.
222P2a	4c **dk brn,** PP sm die on yelsh wove paper	2,000.
222P3	4c **dk brn,** plate on India	35.
	Block of 4	160.
	P# blk. of 12	650.
222P4	4c **dk brn,** plate on card	25.
	Block of 4	110.
	P# blk. of 12	725.
222P5	4c **dk brn,** plate on stamp paper, pair	*210.*
223TC1c	5c Large die on glossy wove paper	
	e. **blue**	400.
	f. **dark brown**	400.
223TC5	5c plate on plate on stamp paper	
	a. **bister**	—
	b. **sepia**	—
	c. **brown** (shades)	—
223P1	5c **chocolate,** large die on India paper	225.
223P2	5c **chocolate,** RA sm die on white wove paper	225.
223P2a	5c **chocolate,** PP sm die on yelsh wove paper	2,000.
223P3	5c **chocolate,** plate on India	32.
	Block of 4	135.
	P# blk. of 12	600.
223P4	5c **chocolate,** plate on card	25.
	Block of 4	110.
	P# blk. of 12	625.
223P5	5c **yel brn,** plate on stamp paper, pair	*225.*
224TC1a	6c large die on India paper	
	e. **deep orange red**	400.
224TC5	6c plate on stamp paper	
	a. **orange red**	120.
	b. **violet black**	120.
	c. **yellow**	120.
	d. **olive green**	120.
	e. **purple**	120.
	f. **red orange**	120.
	g. **brown**	120.
	h. **red brown**	120.
	i. **orange brown**	120.
	j. **black brown**	120.
	k. **slate green**	120.
	l. **brown olive**	120.
224P1	6c **brn red,** large die on India paper	225.
224P2	6c **brn red,** RA sm die on white wove paper	225.
224P2a	6c **brn red,** PP sm die on yelsh wove paper	2,000.
224P3	6c **brn red,** plate on India	32.
	Block of 4	135.
	P# blk. of 12	600.
224P4	6c **brn red,** plate on card	20.
	Block of 4	85.
	P# blk. of 12	775.
224P5	6c **brn red,** plate on stamp paper, pair	*225.*
225TC1a	8c large die on India paper	
	e. **yellow orange**	—
	f. **green**	—
225TC1d	8c large die on card	
	e. **dark violet red**	450.
	f. **metallic green**	450.
	g. **salmon**	450.
	h. **orange brown**	450.
	i. **light green**	450.
	j. **blue**	450.
	k. **steel blue**	450.
225P1	8c **lilac,** large die on India paper	600.
225P2	8c **lilac,** RA sm die on white wove paper	225.
225P2a	8c **lilac,** PP sm die on yelsh wove paper	2,000.
225P3	8c **lilac,** plate on India	55.
	Block of 4	250.
	P# blk. of 12	1,100.
225P4	8c **lilac,** plate on card	110.
	Block of 4	500.
	P# blk. of 12	2,000.
225P5	8c **lilac,** plate on stamp paper, pair	*1,000.*
226P1	10c **grn,** large die on India paper	225.
226P2	10c **grn,** RA sm die on white wove paper	225.
226P2a	10c **grn,** PP sm die on yelsh wove paper	2,000.
226P3	10c **grn,** plate on India	45.
	Block of 4	200.
	P# blk. of 12	700.
226P4	10c **grn,** plate on card	40.
	Block of 4	180.
	P# blk. of 12	750.
226P5	10c **grn,** plate on stamp paper, pair	*325.*
227P1	15c **indigo,** large die on India paper	300.
227P2	15c **indigo,** RA sm die on white wove paper	225.
227P2a	15c **indigo,** PP sm die on yelsh wove paper	2,000.
227P3	15c **indigo,** plate on India	45.
	Block of 4	190.
	P# blk. of 12	825.
227P4	15c **indigo,** plate on card	40.
	Block of 4	180.
	P# blk. of 12	875.
227P5	15c **indigo,** plate on stamp paper, pair	*625.*
	P# blk. of 12	*5,000.*
228P1	30c **black,** large die on India paper	300.
228P2	30c **black,** RA sm die on white wove paper	225.
228P2a	30c **black,** PP sm die on yelsh wove paper	2,000.
228P3	30c **black,** plate on India	45.
	Block of 4	190.
	P# blk. of 12	825.
228P4	30c **black,** plate on card	45.
	Block of 4	190.
	P# blk. of 12	875.
228P5	30c **black,** plate on stamp paper, pair	*1,000.*
229P1	90c **orange,** large die on India paper	300.
229P2	90c **orange,** RA sm die on white wove paper	225.
229P2a	90c **orange,** PP sm die on yelsh wove paper	2,000.
229P3	90c **orange,** plate on India	60.
	Block of 4	275.
	P# blk. of 12	1,100.
229P4	90c **orange,** plate on card	50.
	Block of 4	225.
	P# blk. of 12	1,150.
229P5	90c **orange,** plate on stamp paper, pair	*1,450.*

Columbian Issue

1893

230P1	1c **blue,** large die on India paper	900.
230P2	1c **blue,** RA sm die on white wove paper	325.
230P2a	1c **blue,** PP sm die on yelsh wove paper	2,000.
230P3	1c **blue,** plate on India	60.
	Block of 4	300.
	P# blk. of 8	800.
230P4	1c **blue,** plate on card	20.
	Block of 4	130.
	P# blk. of 8	425.
231TC1a	2c large die on India paper	
	e. **sepia**	850.
231TC1d	1c large die on card	
	e. **sepia**	850.
	f. **orange brown**	850.
	g. **deep orange**	850.
	h. **light brown**	850.
	i. **blue green**	850.
	j. **bright rose red**	850.
	k. **rose violet**	850.
231P1	2c **violet,** large die on India paper	1,000.
231P2	2c **violet,** RA sm die on white wove paper	350.
231P2a	2c **violet,** PP sm die on yelsh wove paper	2,500.
231P3	2c **violet,** plate on India	350.
	Block of 4	2,000.
	P# blk. of 8	5,000.
231P4	2c **violet,** plate on card	45.
	Block of 4	260.
	P# blk. of 8	750.
	a. "Broken hat" variety, plate on card	130.
231P5	2c **violet,** plate on stamp paper, pair	*2,000.*

Almost all examples of No. 231P5 are faulty. Value is for pair with minimal faults.

232TC1d	3c large die on card	
	e. **sepia**	850.
	f. **blackish green**	850.
	g. **black**	850.
232TC3	3c plate on India paper	
	a. **blackish green**	800.
232P1	3c **green,** large die on India paper	900.
232P2	3c **green,** RA sm die on white wove paper	325.
232P2a	3c **green,** PP sm die on yelsh wove paper	3,000.
232P3	3c **green,** plate on India	95.
	Block of 4	550.
	P# blk. of 8	1,400.
232P4	3c **green,** plate on card	70.
	Block of 4	425.
	P# blk. of 8	1,100.
233TC1d	4c large die on card	
	e. **sepia**	850.
	f. **deep orange**	850.
	g. **light brown**	850.
	h. **blue green**	850.
	i. **rose red**	850.
	j. **rose violet**	850.
233P1	4c **ultra,** large die on India paper	900.
233P2	4c **ultra,** RA sm die on white wove paper	325.
233P2a	4c **ultra,** PP sm die on yelsh wove paper	3,000.
233P3	4c **ultra,** plate on India	95.
	Block of 4	550.
	P# blk. of 8	1,400.
233P4	4c **ultra,** plate on card	70.
	Block of 4	425.
	P# blk. of 8	1,250.
233aP1	4c **blue,** (error) large die on thin card	*2,750.*
234TC1a	5c large die on India paper	
	e. **black**	850.
	f. **dark violet**	850.
	g. **rose violet**	850.
	h. **red violet**	850.
	i. **brown violet**	850.
	j. **deep blue**	850.
	k. **deep ultramarine**	850.
	l. **black**	850.
	m. **green**	850.
	n. **deep green**	850.
	o. **blue green**	—
	p. **dark olive green**	850.
	q. **deep orange**	850.
	r. **orange red**	850.
	s. **orange brown**	850.
	t. **bright rose red**	850.
	u. **claret**	850.
	v. **brown rose**	850.
	w. **dull rose brown**	850.
	x. **sepia**	850.
	y. **black brown**	—
234TC1d	5c large die on card	
	e. **dark violet**	850.
	f. **rose violet**	850.
	g. **blue green**	850.
	h. **dark olive green**	—
	i. **deep orange**	—
	j. **orange brown**	850.
	k. **claret**	—
	k. **sepia**	850.
	m. **black brown**	—

The 5c trial color proofs differ from the issued stamp.

234P1	5c **choc,** large die on India paper	900.
234P2	5c **choc,** RA sm die on white wove paper	325.
234P2a	5c **choc,** PP sm die on yelsh wove paper	3,000.
234P3	5c **choc,** plate on India	95.
	Block of 4	550.
	P# blk. of 8	1,400.
234P4	5c **choc,** plate on card	65.
	Block of 4	360.
	P# blk. of 8	1,200.
235P1	6c **purple,** large die on India paper	900.
235P2	6c **purple,** RA sm die on white wove paper	325.
235P2a	6c **purple,** PP sm die on yelsh wove paper	3,000.
235P3	6c **purple,** plate on India	95.
	Block of 4	550.
	P# blk. of 8	1,400.
235P4	6c **purple,** plate on card	70.
	Block of 4	425.
	P# blk. of 8	1,300.
236P1	8c **magenta,** large die on India paper	900.
236P2	8c **magenta,** RA sm die on white wove paper	325.
236P2a	8c **magenta,** PP sm die on yelsh wove paper	3,000.
236P3	8c **magenta,** plate on India	95.
	Block of 4	550.
	P# blk. of 8	1,400.
236P4	8c **magenta,** plate on card	150.
	Block of 4	925.
	P# blk. of 8	2,500.
237TC1a	10c large die on India paper	
	e. **bright rose red**	1,250.
	f. **claret**	1,250.
237P1	10c **blk brn,** large die on India paper	900.
237P2	10c **blk brn,** RA sm die on white wove paper	325.
237P2a	10c **blk brn,** PP sm die on yelsh wove paper	3,000.
237P3	10c **blk brn,** plate on India	95.
	Block of 4	550.
	P# blk. of 8	1,400.
237P4	10c **blk brn,** plate on card	70.
	Block of 4	425.
	P# blk. of 8	1,300.
238P1	15c **dk grn,** large die on India paper	900.
238P2	15c **dk grn,** RA sm die on white wove paper	325.
238P2a	15c **dk grn,** PP sm die on yelsh wove paper	3,000.
238P3	15c **dk grn,** plate on India	95.
	Block of 4	550.
	P# blk. of 8	1,400.
238P4	15c **dk grn,** plate on card	80.
	Block of 4	500.
	P# blk. of 8	3,000.
239TC1d	30c large die on card	
	e. **sepia**	1,000.
239TC4	30c plate on card	
	a. **black**	350.

239P1 30c **org brn,** large die on India paper 900.
239P2 30c **org brn,** RA sm die on white wove paper 325.
239P2a 30c **org brn,** PP sm die on yelsh wove paper 3,000.
239P3 30c **org brn,** plate on India 140.
Block of 4 850.
P# blk. of 8 2,400.
239P4 30c **org brn,** plate on card 100.
Block of 4 600.
P# blk. of 8 2,400.
240TC1d 50c large die on card
e. **sepia** 1,000.
240P1 50c **slate bl,** large die on India paper 900.
240P2 50c **slate bl,** RA sm die on white wove paper 325.
240P2a 50c **slate bl,** PP sm die on yelsh wove paper 3,000.
240P3 50c **slate bl,** plate on India 225.
Block of 4 1,300.
P# blk. of 8 3,250.
240P4 50c **slate bl,** plate on card 120.
Block of 4 725.
P# blk. of 8 2,500.
241P1 $1 **salmon,** large die on India paper 1,150.
241P2 $1 **salmon,** RA sm die on white wove paper 450.
241P2a $1 **salmon,** PP sm die on yelsh wove paper 3,000.
241P3 $1 **salmon,** plate on India 250.
Block of 4 1,600.
P# blk. of 8 3,750.
241P4 $1 **salmon,** plate on card 200.
Block of 4 1,200.
242TC1a $2 large die on India paper
e. **sepia** —
f. **red brown** —
242TC3 $2 plate on India paper
a. **blackish brown** 1,000.
242P1 $2 **brn red,** large die on India paper 1,150.
242P2 $2 **brn red,** RA sm die on white wove paper 450.
242P2a $2 **brn red,** PP sm die on yelsh wove paper 3,000.
242P3 $2 **brn red,** plate on India 290.
Block of 4 1,850.
P# blk. of 8 4,250.
242P4 $2 **brn red,** plate on card 175.
Block of 4 1,050.
P# blk. of 8 3,000.
243P1 $3 **yel grn,** large die on India paper 1,150.
243P2 $3 **yel grn,** RA sm die on white wove paper 450.
243P2a $3 **yel grn,** PP sm die on yelsh wove paper 3,000.
243P3 $3 **yel grn,** plate on India 350.
Block of 4 2,100.
P# blk. of 8 5,000.
243P4 $3 **yel grn,** plate on card 225.
Block of 4 1,300.
P# blk. of 8 3,400.
244P1 $4 **crimson lake,** large die on India paper 1,150.
244P2 $4 **crimson lake,** RA sm die on white wove paper 450.
244P2a $4 **crimson lake,** PP sm die on yelsh wove paper 3,000.
244P3 $4 **crimson lake,** plate on India 450.
Block of 4 2,700.
P# blk. of 8 6,250.
244P4 $4 **crimson lake,** plate on card 275.
Block of 4 1,600.
P# blk. of 8 5,500.
245P1 $5 **black,** large die on India paper 1,150.
245P2 $5 **black,** RA sm die on white wove paper 450.
245P2a $5 **black,** PP sm die on yelsh wove paper 3,000.
245P3 $5 **black,** plate on India 525.
Block of 4 3,100.
P# blk. of 8 7,500.
245P4 $5 **black,** plate on card 375.
Block of 4 2,150.
P# blk. of 8 6,750.
Nos. 230P3-245P3 (16) 3,305.
Nos. 230P4-245P4 (16) 2,110.

This set also exists as Large Die proofs, not die sunk, but printed directly on thin card. Set value $7,000. 1c through 50c, $350 each; $1 through $5, $650 each.

Nos. 234P1, 234P2 differ from issued stamp.

1894 Bureau of Engraving and Printing

246TC1a 1c large die on India paper
e. **dusky blue green** —
f. **dark blue** —
246P1 1c **ultra,** large die on India paper 450.
247P1 1c **blue,** large die on India paper 250.
247P2 1c **blue,** RA sm die on white wove paper 250.
247P2a 1c **blue,** PP sm die on yelsh wove paper 2,000.
247P4 1c **blue,** plate on card 100.
Block of 4 450.
P# blk. of 6 2,250.
248P1 2c **pink,** Type I, large die on India paper —
248P4 2c **pink,** Type I, plate on card 100.
Block of 4 475.
P# blk. of 6 2,500.
250P1 2c **car,** Type I, large die on India paper 250.
250P2 2c **car,** Type I, RA sm die on white wove paper 250.
251P1 2c **car,** Type II, large die on India paper 250.
252P1 2c **car,** Type III, 15-subject die (3x5) on India *6,000.*
Single design 350.
Block of 4 1,500.
253TC1a 3c large die on India paper
e. **light red violet** —
f. **dark red violet** —
253P1 3c **purple,** Triangle I, large die on India paper 750.
253P5 3c **purple,** Triangle I, plate on stamp paper, pair *300.*
Block of 4 *625.*
P# blk. of 6 *7,500.*
253AP1 3c **purple,** Triangle II, large die on India paper 325.
253AP2 3c **purple,** Triangle II, RA sm die on white wove paper 250.
253AP2a 3c **purple,** Triangle II, PP sm die on yelsh wove paper 2,000.
254P1 4c **dk brn,** large die on India paper 600.
254P2 4c **dk brn,** RA sm die on white wove paper 250.
254P2a 4c **dk brn,** PP sm die on yelsh wove paper 2,000.
254P5 4c **dk brn,** plate on stamp paper, pair *275.*
Block of 4 *575.*
P# blk. of 6 *7,500.*
255TC1a 5c large die on India paper
e. **black** 1,250.
255P1 5c **choc,** large die on India paper 250.
255P2 5c **choc,** RA sm die on white wove paper 250.
255P2a 5c **choc,** PP sm die on yelsh wove paper 2,000.
255P5 5c **choc,** plate on stamp paper, pair *300.*
Block of 4 *625.*
P# blk. of 6 *9,500.*
256TC1a 6c large die on India paper
e. **dark brown** 1,000.
256P1 6c **brn,** large die on India paper 250.
256P2 6c **brn,** RA sm die on white wove paper 250.
256P2a 6c **brn,** PP sm die on yelsh wove paper 2,000.
256P4 6c **brn,** plate on card 450.
Block of 4 1,900.
P# blk. of 6 *5,500.*
257TC1a 8c large die on India paper
e. **black** 1,250.
257P1 8c **vio brn,** large die on India paper 250.
257P2 8c **vio brn,** RA sm die on white wove paper 250.
257P2a 8c **vio brn,** PP sm die on yelsh wove paper 2,000.
258TC1a 10c large die on India paper
e. **olive** 1,250.
258P1 10c **grn,** large die on India paper 275.
258P2 10c **grn,** RA sm die on white wove paper 250.
258P2a 10c **grn,** PP sm die on yelsh wove paper 2,000.
258P5 10c **grn,** plate on stamp paper, pair *500.*
Block of 4 *1,100.*
P# blk. of 6 *9,500.*
259TC1a 15c large die on India paper
e. **red violet** 1,250.
f. **dark red orange** 1,250.
259P1 15c **dk bl,** large die on India paper 300.
259P2 15c **dk bl,** RA sm die on white wove paper 250.
259P2a 15c **dk bl,** PP sm die on yelsh wove paper 2,000.
260TC1a 50c large die on India paper
e. **black** 1,500.
260P1 50c **org,** large die on India paper 450.
260P2 50c **org,** RA sm die on white wove paper 210.
260P2a 50c **org,** PP sm die on yelsh wove paper 2,000.
261TC1a $1 large die on India paper
e. **lake** 1,500.
f. **orange** 1,500.
261P1 $1 **blk,** large die on India paper 500.
261P2 $1 **blk,** RA sm die on white wove paper 350.
261P2a $1 **blk,** PP sm die on yelsh wove paper 2,000.
262TC1a $2 large die on India paper
e. **black** 1,500.
f. **dull violet** 1,500.
g. **violet** 1,500.
h. **turquoise blue** 1,500.
i. **orange brown** 1,500.
j. **olive green** 1,500.
k. **sepia** 1,500.
l. **greenish black** 1,500.
262P1 $2 **dk bl,** large die on India paper 500.
262P2 $2 **dk bl,** RA sm die on white wove paper 350.
262P2a $2 **dk bl,** PP sm die on yelsh wove paper 2,000.
262P4 $2 **dk bl,** plate on card 450.
Block of 4 2,500.
Margin block of 4, arrow *2,750.*
P# blk. of 6 *6,250.*
263TC1a $5 large die on India paper
e. **black** 1,500.
f. **dark yellow** 1,500.
g. **orange brown** 1,500.
h. **olive green** 1,500.
i. **dull violet** 1,500.
j. **sepia** 1,500.
k. **brown red** 1,500.
263P1 $5 **dk grn,** large die on India paper 650.
263P2 $5 **dk grn,** RA sm die on white wove paper 375.
263P2a $5 **dk grn,** PP sm die on yelsh wove paper 2,000.
263P4 $5 **dk grn,** plate on card 450.
Block of 4 2,500.
Margin block of 4, arrow *2,750.*
P# blk. of 6 *6,500.*

1895 Imperf, with gum

264P5 1c **blue,** plate on stamp paper, pair *275.*
Block of 4 *700.*
P# strip of 3 *850.*
P# blk. of 6 *1,150.*
a. Horiz. P# strip of 3, perf horiz., imperf. vert. *19,000.*
267P5 2c **car,** Type III, plate on stamp paper, pair *200.*
Block of 4 *550.*
P# strip of 3 *650.*
P# blk. of 6 *1,100.*
268P5 3c **purple,** plate on stamp paper, pair *250.*
Block of 4 *700.*
P# strip of 3 *950.*
P# blk. of 6 *2,000.*
269P5 4c **dk brn,** plate on stamp paper, pair *250.*
Block of 4 *700.*
P# strip of 3 *1,250.*
P# blk. of 6 *3,250.*
270P5 5c **choc,** plate on stamp paper, pair *250.*
Block of 4 *700.*
P# strip of 3 *950.*
271P5 6c **dull brn,** plate on stamp paper, pair *275.*
Block of 4 *825.*
P# strip of 3 *1,150.*
272P5 8c **vio brn,** plate on stamp paper, pair *400.*
Block of 4 *1,100.*
P# strip of 3 *1,500.*
P# blk. of 6 *3,100.*
273P5 10c **dk grn,** plate on stamp paper, pair *325.*
Block of 4 *900.*
P# strip of 3 *1,250.*
274P5 15c **dk bl,** plate on stamp paper, pair *1,000.*
Block of 4 *2,750.*
P# strip of 3 *3,750.*
275P5 50c **org,** plate on stamp paper, pair *1,100.*
Block of 4 *3,250.*
P# strip of 3 *4,500.*
276P5 $1 **blk,** Type I, plate on stamp paper, pair *1,450.*
Block of 4 *3,750.*
P# strip of 3 *5,250.*
277P5 $2 **brt bl,** plate on stamp paper, pair *3,250.*
Block of 4 *7,500.*
P# strip of 3 *10,500.*
278P5 $5 **dk grn,** plate on stamp paper, pair *3,250.*
Block of 4 *7,500.*
P# strip of 3 *10,500.*

No. 264P5a exists only as a bottom margin P#24 and imprint strip of 3.

1897-1903

279P1 1c **grn,** large die on India paper 700.
279P2 1c **grn,** RA sm die on white wove paper 375.
279P2a 1c **grn,** PP sm die on yelsh wove paper 2,000.
279BdP2a 2c **org red,** Type IV, PP sm die on yelsh wove paper 2,000.
279BfP1 2c **car,** Type IV, large die on India paper 400.
279BfP2a 2c **car,** Type IV, PP sm die on yelsh wove paper 2,000.
280P1 4c **rose brn,** large die on India paper 700.
280P2a 4c **rose brn,** PP sm die on yelsh wove paper 2,000.
281P1 5c **blue,** large die on India paper 700.
281P2 5c **blue,** RA sm die on white wove paper 375.
281P2a 5c **blue,** PP sm die on yelsh wove paper 2,000.
282P1 6c **lake,** large die on India paper 700.
282P2a 6c **lake,** PP sm die on yelsh wove paper 2,000.
283TC1a 10c large die on India paper
e. **orange** 1,250.
f. **sepia** 1,250.
283P1 10c **org brn,** Type II, large die on India paper 800.
283P2 10c **org brn,** Type II, RA sm die on white wove paper 375.
283P2a 10c **org brn,** Type II, PP sm die on yelsh wove paper 2,000.
283aP1 10c **brn,** Type II, large die on India paper 800.
284TC1a 15c large die on India paper
e. **yellowish olive** *1,500.*
f. **red violet** *1,750.*
g. **deep dull green** *1,750.*
284P1 15c **ol grn,** Type II, large die on India paper 800.
284P2 15c **ol grn,** Type II, RA sm die on white wove paper 375.
284P2a 15c **ol grn,** Type II, PP sm die on yelsh wove paper 2,000.

Trans-Mississippi Issue

1898

285TC1a 1c large die on India paper
e. **black** —
285P1 1c **grn,** large die on India paper 850.
285P2 1c **grn,** RA sm die on white wove paper 750.
285P2a 1c **grn,** PP sm die on yelsh wove paper 3,000.
286TC1a 2c large die on India paper
e. **black** —
286TC4 2c plate on card
a. **purple** 2,500.
b. **black** 2,500.
c. **blue** 2,500.
d. **brown** 2,500.
e. **deep carmine rose** 2,500.
286P1 2c **copper red,** large die on India paper 850.
286P2 2c **copper red,** RA sm die on white wove paper 750.
286P2a 2c **copper red,** PP sm die on yelsh wove paper 3,000.
286P4 2c **copper red,** plate on card *10,000.*
287TC1a 4c large die on India paper
e. **black** —
287P1 4c **org,** large die on India paper 850.
287P2 4c **org,** RA sm die on white wove paper 750.
287P2a 4c **org,** PP sm die on yelsh wove paper 3,000.

288TC1a 5c large die on India paper
e. **black** —
f. **orange brown** *2,500.*
288P1 5c **dull bl,** large die on India paper 850.
288P2 5c **dull bl,** RA sm die on white wove paper 750.
288P2a 5c **dull bl,** PP sm die on yelsh wove paper 3,000.
289TC1a 8c large die on India paper
e. **black** —
289P1 8c **vio brn,** large die on India paper 850.
289P2 8c **vio brn,** RA sm die on white wove paper 750.
289P2a 8c **vio brn,** PP sm die on yelsh wove paper 3,000.
290TC1a 10c large die on India paper
e. **black** 1,500.
290TC2 10c small die on India paper
b. **black** 1,250.
290P1 10c **gray vio,** large die on India paper 850.
290P2 10c **gray vio,** RA sm die on white wove paper 750.
290P2a 10c **gray vio,** PP sm die on yelsh wove paper 3,000.
291TC1a 50c large die on India paper
e. **black** 1,500.
291TC2 50c small die on wove paper
b. **black** 2,400.
291P1 50c **sage grn,** large die on India paper 850.
291P2 50c **sage grn,** RA sm die on white wove paper 750.
291P2a 50c **sage grn,** PP sm die on yelsh wove paper 3,000.
292TC1a $1 large die on India paper
e. **black** —
292P1 $1 **blk,** large die on India paper 1,000.
292P2 $1 **blk,** RA sm die on white wove paper 750.
292P2a $1 **blk,** PP sm die on yelsh wove paper 3,000.
293TC1a $2 large die on India paper
e. **black** 5,000.
293P1 $2 **org brn,** large die on India paper 1,000.
293P2 $2 **org brn,** RA sm die on white wove paper 750.
293P2a $2 **org brn,** PP sm die on yelsh wove paper 3,000.
293P4 $2 **org brn,** plate on card 6,000.
Block of 4 *27,500.*
P# blk. of 6 *35,000.*

The bicolored essays commonly offered as Nos. 285-293 bicolored proofs in "original" colors can be found under the following essay listings: Nos. 285-E8, 286-E8, 287-E9, 288-E5, 289-E4, 290-E4, 291-E8, 292-E6, and 293-E7. Value, set of nine $6,550.

Pan-American Issue

1901

294P1 1c **grn & blk,** large die on India paper 575.
294P1a 1c **grn & blk,** large die on wove paper *1,500.*
294P2 1c **grn & blk,** RA sm die on white wove paper 575.
294P2a 1c **grn & blk,** PP sm die on yelsh wove paper 3,000.
295P1 2c **car & blk,** large die on India paper 575.
295P1a 2c **car & blk,** large die on wove paper *1,500.*
295P2 2c **car & blk,** RA sm die on white wove paper 575.
295P2a 2c **car & blk,** PP sm die on yelsh wove paper 3,000.
b. small die proof on yelsh bond *1,250.*
296P1 4c **choc & blk,** large die on India paper 575.
296P1a 4c **choc & blk,** large die on wove paper *1,500.*
296P2 4c **choc & blk,** RA sm die on white wove paper 575.
296P2a 4c **choc & blk,** PP sm die on yelsh wove paper 3,000.
297P1 5c **ultra & blk,** large die on India paper 575.
297P1a 5c **ultra & blk,** large die on wove paper *1,500.*
297P2 5c **ultra & blk,** RA sm die on white wove paper 575.
297P2a 5c **ultra & blk,** PP sm die on yelsh wove paper 3,000.
298TC2 8c small die on wove
b. **violet & black** *3,250.*
298P1 8c **brn vio & blk,** large die on India paper 575.
298P1a 8c **brn vio & blk,** large die on wove paper *1,500.*
298P2 8c **brn vio & blk,** RA sm die on white wove paper 575.
298P2a 8c **brn vio & blk,** PP sm die on yelsh wove paper 3,000.
299P1 10c **yel brn & blk,** large die on India paper 575.
299P1a 10c **yel brn & blk,** large die on wove paper *1,500.*
299P2 10c **yel brn & blk,** RA sm die on white wove paper 575.
299P2a 10c **yel brn & blk,** PP sm die on yelsh wove paper 3,000.

1902-03

300P1 1c **grn,** large die on India paper 1,750.
300P2 1c **grn,** RA sm die on white wove paper 300.
300P2a 1c **grn,** PP sm die on yelsh wove paper 2,500.
301P1 2c **car,** large die on India paper 1,750.
301P2 2c **car,** RA sm die on white wove paper 300.
301P2a 2c **car,** PP sm die on yelsh wove paper 2,500.
302P1 3c **purple,** large die on India paper 1,750.
302P2 3c **purple,** RA sm die on white wove paper 300.
302P2a 3c **purple,** PP sm die on yelsh wove paper 2,500.
303P1 4c **org brn,** large die on India paper 1,750.
303P2 4c **org brn,** RA sm die on white wove paper 300.
303P2a 4c **org brn,** PP sm die on yelsh wove paper 2,500.
304P1 5c **blue,** large die on India paper 1,750.
304P2 5c **blue,** RA sm die on white wove paper 300.
304P2a 5c **blue,** PP sm die on yelsh wove paper 2,500.
305P1 6c **lake,** large die on India paper 1,750.
305P2 6c **lake,** RA sm die on white wove paper 300.
305P2a 6c **lake,** PP sm die on yelsh wove paper 2,500.
306P1 8c **vio blk,** large die on India paper 1,750.
306P2 8c **vio blk,** RA sm die on white wove paper 300.
306P2a 8c **vio blk,** PP sm die on yelsh wove paper 2,500.
307P1 10c **org brn,** large die on India paper 1,750.
307P2 10c **org brn,** RA sm die on white wove paper 300.
307P2a 10c **org brn,** PP sm die on yelsh wove paper 2,500.
308TC1a 13c large die on India paper
e. **gray violet, type I** 1,000.
308P1 13c **dp vio brn,** large die on India paper 1,750.
308P2 13c **dp vio brn,** RA sm die on white wove paper 300.
308P2a 13c **dp vio brn,** PP sm die on yelsh wove paper 2,500.
309P1 15c **ol grn,** large die on India paper 1,750.
309P2 15c **ol grn,** RA sm die on white wove paper 300.
309P2a 15c **ol grn,** PP sm die on yelsh wove paper 2,500.
310P1 50c **org,** large die on India paper 1,750.
310P2 50c **org,** RA sm die on white wove paper 300.
310P2a 50c **org,** PP sm die on yelsh wove paper 2,500.
311P1 $1 **blk,** large die on India paper 1,750.
311P2 $1 **blk,** RA sm die on white wove paper 300.
311P2a $1 **blk,** PP sm die on yelsh wove paper 2,500.
312P1 $2 **blue,** large die on India paper 2,500.
312P2 $2 **blue,** RA sm die on white wove paper 300.
312P2a $2 **blue,** PP sm die on yelsh wove paper 2,500.
313P1 $5 **grn,** large die on India paper 3,000.
313P2 $5 **grn,** RA sm die on white wove paper 375.
313P2a $5 **grn,** PP sm die on yelsh wove paper 2,500.

1903

319TC1a 2c large die on India paper
e. **black,** type I 3,250.
f. **lake,** type I —
319P1 2c **car,** Type I, large die on India paper 1,500.
319FiP1 2c **car,** Type II, large die on India paper 2,750.
319FiP2 2c **car,** Type II, sm die on white wove paper 1,000.
319FiP2a 2c **car,** Type II, PP sm die on yelsh wove paper 3,500.
b. small die proof on yelsh wove paper *1,000.*

Louisiana Purchase Issue

1904

323P1 1c **grn,** large die on India paper 1,400.
323P2 1c **grn,** sm die on white wove paper 1,000.
323P2a 1c **grn,** PP sm die on yelsh wove paper 3,500.
324P1 2c **car,** large die on India paper 1,400.
324P2 2c **car,** sm die on white wove paper 1,000.
324P2a 2c **car,** PP sm die on yelsh wove paper 3,500.
325P1 3c **vio,** large die on India paper 1,400.
325P2 3c **vio,** sm die on white wove paper 1,000.
325P2a 3c **vio,** PP sm die on yelsh wove paper 3,500.
326TC1d 5c large die on thin glazed card
e. **black** 3,500.
326P1 5c **dk bl,** large die on India paper 1,400.
326P2 5c **dk bl,** sm die on white wove paper 1,000.
326P2a 5c **dk bl,** PP sm die on yelsh wove paper 3,500.
327P1 10c **brn,** large die on India paper 1,400.
327P2 10c **brn,** sm die on white wove paper 1,000.
327P2a 10c **brn,** PP sm die on yelsh wove paper 3,500.

Jamestown Exposition Issue

1907

328P1 1c **grn,** large die on India paper 1,000.
328P2 1c **grn,** sm die on white wove paper 900.
328P2a 1c **grn,** PP sm die on yelsh wove paper 3,000.
329P1 2c **car,** large die on India paper 1,000.
329P2 2c **car,** sm die on white wove paper 900.
329P2a 2c **car,** PP sm die on yelsh wove paper 3,000.
330TC1a 5c large die on India paper
e. **ultramarine** 1,600.
f. **black** 1,700.
330P1 5c **dk bl,** large die on India paper 1,000.
330P2 5c **dk bl,** sm die on white wove paper 900.
330P2a 5c **dk bl,** PP sm die on yelsh wove paper 3,000.

1908-09

331P1 1c **grn,** large die on India paper 1,250.
331P2 1c **grn,** sm die on white wove paper 725.
331P2a 1c **grn,** PP sm die on yelsh wove paper 2,500.
332TC1a 2c large die on India paper
e. **dull violet** 750.
f. **light ultramarine** 750.
g. **bright ultramarine** 750.
h. **light green** 750.
i. **dark olive green** 750.
j. **golden yellow** 750.
k. **dull orange** 750.
l. **rose carmine** 750.
m. **ultramarine** 750.
n. **black** —
o. **dark blue** —
p. **blue** 850.
q. **lilac brown** 850.
r. **lilac** 850.
s. **blue black** 850.
t. **sage green** 850.
u. **lilac black** 850.
v. **brown** 850.
w. **brown black** 850.
x. **purple** —
y. **orange brown** 850.
z. **ultra,** *orange brown* 750.
aa. **ultra,** *green* 750.
ab. **green,** *pink* 750.
ac. **green,** *rose* 750.
ad. **dark green,** *green* 750.
ae. **green,** *orange brown* 750.
af. **purple,** *orange brown* 750.
ag. **blue,** *yellow* 750.
ah. **green,** *yellow* 750.
ai. **brown,** *orange brown* 750.
aj. **brown,** *yellow* 750.
ak. **green,** *amber yellow* —
332P1 2c **car,** large die on India paper 1,250.
a. **carmine,** large die on amber paper —
b. **carmine,** large die on lt blue paper —
332P2 2c **car,** sm die on white wove paper 725.
332P2a 2c **car,** PP sm die on yelsh wove paper 2,500.
333P1 3c **dp vio,** large die on India paper 1,250.
333P2 3c **dp vio,** sm die on white wove paper 725.
333P2a 3c **dp vio,** PP sm die on yelsh wove paper 2,500.
334P1 4c **brn,** large die on India paper 1,250.
334P2 4c **brn,** sm die on white wove paper 725.
334P2a 4c **brn,** PP sm die on yelsh wove paper 2,500.
335TC1a 5c large die on India paper
e. **green,** *pink* —
335P1 5c **blue,** large die on India paper 1,250.
a. **blue,** large die on salmon paper —
335P2 5c **blue,** sm die on white wove paper 725.
335P2a 5c **blue,** PP sm die on yelsh wove paper 2,500.
336TC1a 6c large die on India paper
e. **brown** —
336P1 6c **red org,** large die on India paper 1,250.
336P2 6c **red org,** sm die on white wove paper 725.
336P2a 6c **red org,** PP sm die on yelsh wove paper 2,500.
337TC1a 8c large die on India paper
e. **green (shades),** *yellow* *1,000.*
f. **orange (shades),** *yellow* —
g. **blue,** *buff* —
h. **blue,** *yellow* —
337P1 8c **ol grn,** large die on India paper 1,250.
a. **olive green,** large die on yellow paper —
337P2 8c **ol grn,** sm die on white wove paper 725.
337P2a 8c **ol grn,** PP sm die on yelsh wove paper 2,500.
338TC1a 10c large die on India paper
e. **carmine,** *pale yellow green* —
f. **brown,** *yellow* —
g. **green,** *pink* *1,000.*
h. **orange,** *greenish blue* *1,000.*
i. **brown,** *gray lavender* —
j. **orange,** *orange* —
k. **black,** *pink* —
l. **orange,** *yellow* —
m. **brown** —
n. **carmine** —
o. **blue,** *pink* —
p. **brown,** *pink* *1,000.*
q. **black** —
338P1 10c **yel,** large die on India paper 1,250.
338P2 10c **yel,** sm die on white wove paper 725.
338P2a 10c **yel,** PP sm die on yelsh wove paper 2,500.
339TC1a 13c large die on India paper
e. **blue,** *yellow* —
f. **sea green,** *deep yellow* —
g. **sea green,** *pale blue* —
h. **deep violet,** *yellow* —
339P1 13c **bl grn,** large die on India paper 1,250.
339P2 13c **bl grn,** sm die on white wove paper 725.
339P2a 13c **bl grn,** PP sm die on yelsh wove paper 2,500.
340TC1a 15c large die on India paper
e. **blue,** *pale lilac* 1,000.
f. **blue,** *greenish blue* 1,000.
g. **blue,** *pink* 1,000.
h. **blue,** *yellow* 1,000.
i. **dark blue,** *buff* 1,000.
j. **orange brown,** *yellow* 1,000.
k. **dark purple,** *yellow* 1,000.
l. **orange,** *yellow* 1,000.
m. **violet,** *yellow* 1,000.
n. **black,** *orange* 1,000.
340P1 15c **pale ultra,** large die on India paper 1,250.
340P2 15c **pale ultra,** sm die on white wove paper 725.
340P2a 15c **pale ultra,** PP sm die on yelsh wove paper 2,500.
341TC1a 50c large die on India paper
e. **lilac,** *light blue* *1,000.*
f. **dark violet,** *yellow* *1,000.*
g. **violet,** *yellow* —
h. **orange,** *yellow* —
i. **orange brown,** *yellow* —
341P1 50c **vio,** large die on India paper 1,250.
a. **violet,** large die on pale lilac paper —
b. **violet,** large die on yellow paper —
c. **violet,** large die on greenish paper —
341P2 50c **vio,** sm die on white wove paper 725.
341P2a 50c **vio,** PP sm die on yelsh wove paper 2,500.
342TC1a $1 large die on India paper
e. **brown,** *blue* —
f. **carmine lake** 1,200.
g. **pink** 1,200.
h. **brown,** *blue green* —
i. **violet brown,** *pink* —
j. **violet brown,** *gray* —
342TC2 $1 small die on India paper
b. **carmine lake** 1,100.
c. **pink** 1,100.

342P1 $1 **vio blk,** large die on India paper 1,500.
342P2 $1 **vio blk,** sm die on white wove paper 725.
342P2a $1 **vio blk,** PP sm die on yelsh wove paper 2,500.

Lincoln Memorial Issue

1909

367P1 2c **car,** large die on India paper 1,750.
367P2 2c **car,** sm die on white wove paper 2,000.
367P2a 2c **car,** PP sm die on yelsh wove paper 3,000.

Alaska-Yukon Issue

370P1 2c **car,** large die on India paper 1,100.
370P2 2c **car,** sm die on white wove paper 1,000.
370P2a 2c **car,** PP sm die on yelsh wove paper 3,000.

Hudson-Fulton Issue

372P1 2c **car,** large die on India paper 1,250.
372P2 2c **car,** sm die on white wove paper 1,000.
372P2a 2c **car,** PP sm die on yelsh wove paper 3,000.

Panama-Pacific Issue

1912-13

397P1 1c **grn,** large die on India paper 1,750.
397P2 1c **grn,** sm die on white wove paper 1,500.
397P2a 1c **grn,** PP sm die on yelsh wove paper 3,000.
398P1 2c **car,** large die on India paper 1,750.
398P2 2c **car,** sm die on white wove paper 1,500.
398P2a 2c **car,** PP sm die on yelsh wove paper 3,000.
399P1 5c **blue,** large die on India paper 1,750.
399P2 5c **blue,** sm die on white wove paper 1,500.
399P2a 5c **blue,** PP sm die on yelsh wove paper 3,000.
400TC1a 10c large die on India paper
e. **brown red** 1,750.
400TC2 10c small die on India paper
b. **carmine lake** 1,100.
400P1 10c **org yel,** large die on India paper 1,750.
400P2 10c **org yel,** sm die on white wove paper 1,500.
400P2a 10c **org yel,** PP sm die on yelsh wove paper 3,000.
400AP1 10c **org,** large die on India paper 1,750.
400AP2 10c **org,** sm die on white wove paper 1,500.
400AP2a 10c **org,** PP sm die on yelsh wove paper 3,000.

No. 398P inscribed "Gatun Locks" is listed in the Essay section as No. 398-E3.

1912-19

405P1 1c **grn,** large die on India paper 1,400.
405P2 1c **grn,** sm die on white wove paper 650.
405P2a 1c **grn,** PP sm die on yelsh wove paper 2,500.
406P1 2c **car,** large die on India paper 1,400.
406P1a 2c **car,** large die on white wove paper *2,750.*
406P2 2c **car,** sm die on white wove paper 650.
406P2a 2c **car,** PP sm die on yelsh wove paper 2,500.
407P1 7c **blk,** large die on India paper 1,400.
407P2 7c **blk,** sm die on white wove paper 650.
407P2a 7c **blk,** PP sm die on yelsh wove paper 2,500.
414TC1a 8c large die on India paper
e. **black** 1,750.
414P1 8c **ol grn,** large die on India paper 1,400.
414P2 8c **ol grn,** sm die on white wove paper 650.
414P2a 8c **ol grn,** PP sm die on yelsh wove paper 2,500.
415P1 9c **ol grn,** large die on India paper 1,400.
415P2 9c **ol grn,** sm die on white wove paper 650.
415P2a 9c **ol grn,** PP sm die on yelsh wove paper 2,500.
416P1 10c **org yel,** large die on India paper 1,400.
416P2 10c **org yel,** sm die on white wove paper 650.
416P2a 10c **org yel,** PP sm die on yelsh wove paper 2,500.
434P1 11c **dk grn,** large die on India paper 1,500.
417P1 12c **cl brn,** large die on India paper 1,400.
417P2 12c **cl brn,** sm die on white wove paper 650.
417P2a 12c **cl brn,** PP sm die on yelsh wove paper 2,500.
513TC1a 13c large die on India paper
e. **violet** 650.
f. **lilac** 650.
g. **violet brown** 650.
h. **light ultramarine** 650.
i. **ultramarine** 650.
j. **deep ultramarine** 650.
k. **green** 650.
l. **dark green** 650.
m. **olive green** 650.
n. **orange yellow** 650.
o. **orange** 650.
p. **red orange** 650.
q. **ocher** 650.
r. **salmon red** 650.
s. **brown carmine** 650.
t. **claret brown** 650.
u. **brown** 650.
v. **black brown** 650.
w. **gray** 650.
x. **black** 650.
513P1 13c **apple grn,** large die on India paper 1,500.
418P1 15c **gray,** large die on India paper 1,400.
418P2 15c **gray,** sm die on white wove paper 650.
418P2a 15c **gray,** PP sm die on yelsh wove paper 2,500.
419P1 20c **ultra,** large die on India paper 1,400.
419P2 20c **ultra,** sm die on white wove paper 650.
419P2a 20c **ultra,** PP sm die on yelsh wove paper 2,500.
420P1 30c **org red,** large die on India paper 1,400.
420P2 30c **org red,** sm die on white wove paper 650.
420P2a 30c **org red,** PP sm die on yelsh wove paper 2,500.
421P1 50c **violet,** large die on India paper 1,500.
421P2 50c **violet,** sm die on white wove paper 650.
421P2a 50c **violet,** PP sm die on yelsh wove paper 2,500.
423P1 $1 **vio blk,** large die on India paper 1,400.
423P2 $1 **vio blk,** sm die on white wove paper 650.
423P2a $1 **vio blk,** PP sm die on yelsh wove paper 2,500.

1917-20

502P1 3c **dk vio,** type II, 10-subject die proof (2x5) on India paper, die sunk on card *6,500.*
524TC1a $5 large die on India paper
e. **carmine & black** 1,350.
524P1 $5 **dp grn & blk,** large die on India paper 1,500.
547TC1a $2 large die on India paper
e. **green & black** 1,500.
547P1 $2 **car & blk,** large die on India paper 1,500.

Victory Issue

1919

537P1 3c **violet,** large die on India paper 1,100.
537P2 3c **violet,** sm die on white wove paper 1,500.

Pilgrim Issue

1920

548P1 1c **grn,** large die on India paper 1,250.
548P2 1c **grn,** sm die on white wove paper 1,200.
549P1 2c **car,** large die on India paper 1,250.
549P2 2c **car,** sm die on white wove paper 1,200.
550P1 5c **blue,** large die on India paper 1,250.
550P2 5c **blue,** sm die on white wove paper 1,200.

1922-26

551P1 ½c **ol brn,** large die on India paper 1,500.
551P1a ½c **ol brn,** large die on white wove paper —
551P3 ½c **ol brn,** plate on white wove paper —
551P4 ½c **ol brn,** plate on card —
552TC2 1c small die on thin glazed card
b. **black** —
552P1 1c **dp grn,** large die on India paper 1,000.
552P1a 1c **dp grn,** large die on white wove paper 700.
552P3 1c **dp grn,** plate on white wove paper —
553P1 1½c **yel brn,** large die on India paper 1,000.
553P3 1½c **yel brn,** plate on white wove paper —
554TC2 2c small die on bond paper
b. **black** 1,250.
554P1 2c **car,** large die on India paper 1,000.
554P1a 2c **car,** large die on white wove paper 700.
554P3 2c **car,** plate on white wove paper —
555P1 3c **vio,** large die on India paper 1,250.
555P1a 3c **vio,** large die on white wove paper 1,000.
555P3 3c **vio,** plate on white wove paper —
556P1 4c **yel brn,** large die on India paper 1,200.
556P1a 4c **yel brn,** large die on white wove paper 700.
556P3 4c **yel brn,** plate on white wove paper —
557P1 5c **dk bl,** large die on India paper 1,000.
557P1a 5c **dk bl,** large die on white wove paper 700.
557P3 5c **dk bl,** plate on white wove paper —
558P1 6c **red org,** large die on India paper 1,000.
558P1a 6c **red org,** large die on white wove paper 700.
558P3 6c **red org,** plate on white wove paper —
559P1 7c **blk,** large die on India paper 1,000.
559P1a 7c **blk,** large die on white wove paper 700.
559P3 7c **blk,** plate on white wove paper —
560P1 8c **ol grn,** large die on India paper 1,000.
560P1a 8c **ol grn,** large die on white wove paper 700.
560P3 8c **ol grn,** plate on white wove paper —
561TC1a 9c large die on India paper
e. **red orange** 2,250.
561P1 9c **rose,** large die on India paper 1,000.
561P1a 9c **rose,** large die on white wove paper 700.
561P3 9c **rose,** plate on white wove paper —
562P1 10c **org,** large die on India paper 1,000.
562P1a 10c **org,** large die on white wove paper 700.
562P3 10c **org,** plate on white wove paper —
563TC1a 11c large die on India paper
e. **deep green** 2,250.
563P1 11c **lt bl,** large die on India paper 1,500.
563P1a 11c **lt bl,** large die on white wove paper 700.
563P3 11c **lt bl,** plate on white wove paper —
564P1 12c **brn vio,** large die on India paper 1,000.
564P1a 12c **brn vio,** large die on white wove paper 700.
564P3 12c **brn vio,** plate on white wove paper —
622TC1a 13c large die on India paper
e. **black** 2,250.
622P1 13c **grn,** large die on India paper 1,000.
622P1a 13c **grn,** large die on white wove paper 700.
622P3 13c **grn,** plate on white wove paper —
565TC1a 14c large die on India paper
e. **dark brown** 2,250.
565P1 14c **dk bl,** large die on India paper 1,250.
565P1a 14c **dk bl,** large die on white wove paper 700.
565P3 14c **dk bl,** plate on white wove paper —
566TC1a 15c large die on India paper
e. **black** 2,250.
566P1 15c **grey,** large die on India paper 1,250.
566P1a 15c **grey,** large die on white wove paper 700.
566P3 15c **grey,** plate on white wove paper —
623P1 17c **blk,** large die on India paper 1,000.
623P3 17c **blk,** plate on white wove paper —
567P1 20c **car rose,** large die on India paper 1,000.
567P1a 20c **car rose,** large die on white wove paper 700.
567P3 20c **car rose,** plate on white wove paper —
568P1 25c **dp grn,** large die on India paper 1,000.
568P1a 25c **dp grn,** large die on white wove paper 700.
568P3 25c **dp grn,** plate on white wove paper —
569P1 30c **ol brn,** large die on India paper 1,000.
569P1a 30c **ol brn,** large die on white wove paper 700.
569P3 30c **ol brn,** plate on white wove paper —
570P1 50c **lilac,** large die on India paper 1,250.
570P1a 50c **lilac,** large die on white wove paper 700.
570P3 50c **lilac,** plate on white wove paper —
571P1 $1 **vio brn,** large die on India paper 1,500.
571P1a $1 **vio brn,** large die on white wove paper 700.
571P3 $1 **vio brn,** plate on white wove paper —
572P1 $2 **dp bl,** large die on India paper 2,500.
572P1a $2 **dp bl,** large die on white wove paper 700.
572P2 $2 **dp bl,** small die on India paper —
572P3 $2 **dp bl,** plate on white wove paper —
573P1 $5 **car & dk bl,** large die on India paper 5,000.
573P1b $5 **car & dk bl,** large die on card *1,500.*

Catalogue values for large and small proofs between Nos. 610TC1a and 1193P1 are often based on one-time auction realizations. Because these items range in scarcity from unique to just a few known, actual market prices, when available, may be higher or lower than the values shown.

Harding Memorial Issue

1923-26

610TC1a 2c large die on India paper
e. **green** *4,000.*
610P1 2c large die on India paper 3,000.
610P1a 2c large die on white wove paper 2,000.
610P2 2c small die on white or yelsh wove paper 1,500.

Huguenot Walloon Issue

614P1 1c large die on India paper 3,000.
614P1a 1c large die on white wove paper 2,000.
614P2 1c small die on white or yelsh wove paper 2,000.
615P1 2c large die on India paper 3,000.
615P1a 2c large die on white wove paper 2,000.
615P2 2c small die on white or yelsh wove paper 2,000.
616P1 5c large die on India paper 3,000.
616P1a 5c large die on white wove paper 2,000.
616P2 5c small die on white or yelsh wove paper 2,000.

Lexington Concord Issue

617P1 1c large die on India paper 3,000.
617P1a 1c large die on white wove paper 2,000.
617P2 1c small die on white or yelsh wove paper 2,000.
618TC1a 2c large die on India paper
e. **black** *3,000.*
618P1 2c large die on India paper 3,000.
618P1a 2c large die on white wove paper 2,000.
618P2 2c small die on white or yelsh wove paper 2,000.
619P1 5c large die on India paper 3,000.
619P1a 5c large die on white wove paper 2,000.
619P2 5c small die on white or yelsh wove paper 2,000.

Norse American Issue

620P1 2c large die on India paper 3,000.
620P1a 2c large die on white wove paper 2,000.
620P2 2c small die on white or yelsh wove paper 3,000.
621P1 5c large die on India paper 3,000.
621P1a 5c large die on white wove paper 2,000.
621P2 5c small die on white or yelsh wove paper 3,000.

Sesquicentennial Exposition Issue

627P1 2c large die on India paper 1,500.
627P1a 2c large die on white wove paper 1,000.
627P2 2c small die on white or yelsh wove paper 1,500.

Ericsson Memorial Issue

628TC1a 5c large die on India paper
e. **dull dusky blue** 1,500.
628TC2 5c small die on India paper
b. **gray blue** 1,000.
628P1 5c large die on India paper 1,500.
628P1a 5c large die on white wove paper 1,000.
628P2 5c small die on white or yelsh wove paper 1,500.

Battle of White Plains Issue

629P1 2c large die on India paper 1,500.
629P1a 2c large die on white wove paper 1,000.
629P2 2c small die on white or yelsh wove paper 1,500.

1927-29

Vermont Sesquicentennial Issue

643P1 2c large die on India paper 1,500.
643P1a 2c large die on white wove paper 1,000.
643P2 2c small die on white or yelsh wove paper 1,500.

Burgoyne Campaign Issue

644P1 2c large die on India paper 1,500.
644P1a 2c large die on white wove paper 1,000.
644P2 2c small die on white or yelsh wove paper 1,500.

Valley Forge Issue

645P1 2c large die on India paper 1,500.
645P1a 2c large die on white wove paper 1,000.
645P2 2c small die on white or yelsh wove paper 1,500.

Aeronautics Conference Issue

649P1 2c large die on India paper 1,500.
649P1a 2c large die on white wove paper 1,000.
649P2 2c small die on white or yelsh wove paper 1,500.
650P1 5c large die on India paper 1,500.
650P1a 5c large die on white wove paper 1,000.
650P2 5c small die on white or yelsh wove paper 1,500.

George Rogers Clark Issue

651P1 2c large die on India paper 1,500.
651P1a 2c large die on white wove paper 1,000.
651P2 2c small die on white or yelsh wove paper 1,500.

Electric Lights Golden Jubilee

654P1 2c large die on India paper 1,500.
654P1a 2c large die on white wove paper 1,000.
654P2 2c small die on white or yelsh wove paper 1,500.

John Sullivan

657P1 2c large die on India paper 1,500.
657P1a 2c large die on white wove paper 1,000.
657P2 2c small die on white or yelsh wove paper 1,500.

Battle of Fallen Timbers Issue

680P1 2c large die on India paper 1,500.
680P1a 2c large die on white wove paper 1,000.
680P2 2c small die on white or yelsh wove paper 2,500.

Ohio River Canalization Issue

681P1 2c large die on India paper 1,500.
681P1a 2c large die on white wove paper 1,500.
681P2 2c small die on white or yelsh wove paper 1,500.

1930-31

Massachusetts Bay Colony Issue

682P1 2c large die on India paper 1,500.
682P1a 2c large die on white wove paper 1,000.
682P2 2c small die on white or yelsh wove paper 1,500.

Carolina Charleston Issue

683P1 2c large die on India paper 1,500.
683P1a 2c large die on white wove paper 1,000.
683P2 2c small die on white or yelsh wove paper 1,500.

Harding & Taft

684P1 1½c **brn,** large die on India paper 1,500.
685P1 4c **brn,** large die on India paper 1,500.

Braddock's Field Issue

688P1 2c large die on India paper 1,500.
688P1a 2c large die on white wove paper 1,000.
688P2 2c small die on white or yelsh wove paper 1,500.

Von Steuben Issue

689P1 2c large die on India paper 1,500.
689P1a 2c large die on white wove paper 1,000.
689P2 2c small die on white or yelsh wove paper 1,500.

Pulaski Issue

690P1 2c large die on India paper 1,500.
690P1a 2c large die on white wove paper 1,000.
690P2 2c small die on white or yelsh wove paper 1,500.

Red Cross Issue

702P1a 2c large die on white wove paper 1,000.
702P2 2c small die on white or yelsh wove paper 1,500.

Yorktown Issue

703P1 2c large die on India paper 1,500.
703P1a 2c large die on white wove paper 1,000.
703P2 2c small die on white or yelsh wove paper 1,500.

Washington Bicentennial

1932

704P1 ½c **ol brn,** large die on India paper 1,000.
704P1a ½c **ol brn,** large die on white wove paper 1,000.
704P2 ½c **ol brn,** sm die on white or yelsh wove paper 1,500.
705P1 1c **grn,** large die on India paper 1,000.
705P1a 1c **grn,** large die on white wove paper 1,000.
705P2 1c **grn,** sm die on white or yelsh wove paper 1,500.
706P1 1½c **brn,** large die on India paper 1,000.
706P1a 1½c **brn,** large die on white wove paper 1,000.
706P2 1½c **brn,** sm die on white or yelsh wove paper 1,500.
707P1 2c **car rose,** large die on India paper 1,000.
707P1a 2c **car rose,** large die on white wove paper 1,000.
707P2 2c **car rose,** sm die on white or yelsh wove paper 1,500.
708P1 3c **dp vio,** large die on India paper 1,000.
708P1a 3c **dp vio,** large die on white wove paper 1,000.
708P2 3c **dp vio,** sm die on white or yelsh wove paper 1,500.
709P1 4c **lt brn,** large die on India paper 1,000.
709P1a 4c **lt brn,** large die on white wove paper 1,000.
709P2 4c **lt brn,** small die on white or yelsh wove paper 1,500.
710P1 5c **blue,** large die on India paper 1,000.
710P1a 5c **blue,** large die on white wove paper 1,000.
710P2 5c **blue,** sm die on white or yelsh wove paper 1,500.
711P1 6c **red org,** large die on India paper 1,000.
711P1a 6c **red org,** large die on white wove paper 1,000.
711P2 6c **red org,** sm die on white or yelsh wove paper 1,500.
711P3 6c **red org,** plate proof on wove paper *2,500.*
712P1 7c **blk,** large die on India paper 1,000.
712P1a 7c **blk,** large die on white wove paper 1,000.
712P2 7c **blk,** sm die on white or yelsh wove paper 1,500.
713P1 8c **ol bis,** large die on India paper 1,000.
713P1a 8c **ol bis,** large die on white wove paper 1,000.
713P2 8c **ol bis,** sm die on white or yelsh wove paper 1,500.
714P1 9c **pale red,** large die on India paper 1,000.
714P1a 9c **pale red,** large die on white wove paper 1,000.
714P2 9c **pale red,** sm die on white or yelsh wove paper 1,500.
715P1 10c **org yel,** large die on India paper 1,000.
715P1a 10c **org yel,** large die on white wove paper 1,000.
715P2 10c **org yel,** sm die on white or yelsh wove paper 1,500.

Winter Olympic Games Issue

716P1 2c large die on India paper 1,000.
716P1a 2c large die on white wove paper 1,000.
716P2 2c small die on white or yelsh wove paper 1,500.

Arbor Day Issue

717P1 2c large die on India paper 1,000.
717P1a 2c large die on white wove paper 1,000.
717P2 2c small die on white or yelsh wove paper 1,500.

Summer Olympic Games Issue

718TC1a 3c large die on India paper
e. **carmine** *7,500.*
718P1 3c large die on India paper *10,000.*
718P1a 3c large die on white wove paper 1,000.
718P2 3c small die on white or yelsh wove paper 1,500.
719P1 5c large die on India paper *15,000.*
719P1a 5c large die on white wove paper 1,000.
719P2 5c small die on white or yelsh wove paper 1,500.

Washington Issue

720TC2 3c small die on bond paper
b. **black** 2,750.
720P1 3c large die on India paper 2,000.

William Penn Issue

724P1 3c large die on India paper 1,000.
724P1a 3c large die on white wove paper 1,000.
724P2 3c small die on white or yelsh wove paper 1,500.

Daniel Webster Issue

725P1 3c large die on India paper 1,000.
725P1a 3c large die on white wove paper 1,000.
725P2 3c small die on white or yelsh wove paper 1,500.

Georgia Bicentennial Issue

1933-34

726P1 3c large die on India paper 1,000.
726P1a 3c large die on white wove paper 1,000.
726P2 3c small die on white or yelsh wove paper 1,500.

Peace of 1783 Issue

727P1 3c large die on India paper 1,000.
727P1a 3c large die on white wove paper 1,000.
727P2 3c small die on white or yelsh wove paper 1,500.

Century of Progress Issue

728P1 1c large die on India paper 1,000.
728P1a 1c large die on white wove paper 1,000.
728P2 1c small die on white or yelsh wove paper 1,500.
729P1 3c large die on India paper 1,000.
729P1a 3c large die on white wove paper 1,000.
729P2 3c small die on white or yelsh wove paper 1,500.

National Recovery Act Issue

732P1a 3c large die on white wove paper 1,000.
732P2 3c small die on white or yelsh wove paper 1,500.

Byrd Antarctic Issue

733P1 3c large die on India paper *1,250.*
733P1a 3c large die on white wove paper 1,000.
733P2 3c small die on white or yelsh wove paper 1,500.

Kosciuszko Issue

734P1 5c large die on India paper *1,250.*
734P1a 5c large die on white wove paper 1,000.
734P2 5c small die on white or yelsh wove paper 1,500.

Maryland Tercentenary Issue

736P1 3c large die on India paper *1,250.*
736P1a 3c large die on white wove paper 1,000.
736P2 3c small die on white or yelsh wove paper 1,500.

Mothers of America Issue

737P1 3c large die on India paper 1,000.
737P1a 3c large die on white wove paper 1,000.
737P2 3c small die on white or yelsh wove paper 1,500.

Wisconsin Tercentenary Issue

739P1a 3c large die on white wove paper 1,000.
739P2 3c small die on white or yelsh wove paper 1,500.

National Parks Year

740P1a 1c large die on white wove paper 1,000.
740P2 1c small die on white or yelsh wove paper 1,500.
741P2 2c small die on white or yelsh wove paper 1,500.
742P1a 3c large die on white wove paper 1,000.
742P2 3c small die on white or yelsh wove paper 1,500.
743P2 4c small die on white or yelsh wove paper 1,500.
744P2 5c small die on white or yelsh wove paper 1,500.
745P2 6c small die on white or yelsh wove paper 1,500.
746P1a 7c large die on white wove paper 1,000.
746P2 7c small die on white or yelsh wove paper 1,500.
747P2 8c small die on white or yelsh wove paper 1,500.
748P1a 9c large die on white wove paper 1,000.
748P2 9c small die on white or yelsh wove paper 1,500.
749P2 10c small die on white or yelsh wove paper 1,500.

> For imperforates of the National Parks set, plus other issues, see the lined note following No. 749 in the Postage section.

Connecticut Tercentennary Issue

1935-37

772TC1d 3c Large die on thin glazed card
e. **black** *1,500.*
772P1 3c large die on India paper *1,500.*
772P2 3c small die on white or yelsh wove paper 1,500.

California Pacific Expo Issue

773TC1d 3c Large die on yellow glazed card
e. **orange red** *1,500.*
773P2 3c small die on white or yelsh wove paper 1,500.

Boulder Dam Issue

774P2 3c small die on white or yelsh wove paper 1,500.

Michigan Centenary Issue

775P2 3c small die on white or yelsh wove paper 1,500.

Texas Centennial Issue

776P2 3c small die on white or yelsh wove paper 1,500.

Rhode Island Tercentenary Issue

777P2 3c small die on white or yelsh wove paper 1,500.

Arkansas Centennial Issue

782P1 3c large die on India paper 1,500.
782P1a 3c large die on white wove paper 1,500.
782P2 3c small die on white or yelsh wove paper 1,500.

Oregon Territory Issue

783P1 3c large die on India paper 1,500.
783P1a 3c large die on white wove paper 1,500.
783P2 3c small die on white or yelsh wove paper 1,500.

Susan B. Anthony Issue

784TC1d 3c large die on glazed card
a. Deep lilac 1,750.
784P2 3c small die on white or yelsh wove paper 1,500.

Army Issue

785TC2 1c small die on bond paper
b. **black** 750.
785P1a 1c large die on white wove paper 1,500.
785P2 1c small die on white or yelsh wove paper 1,500.
786P2 2c small die on white or yelsh wove paper 1,500.
787P1 3c large die on India paper 1,500.
787P1a 3c large die on white wove paper 1,500.
787P2 3c small die on white or yelsh wove paper 1,500.
788TC1a 4c large die on India paper
e. **dark brown** 1,500.
788P2 4c small die on white or yelsh wove paper 1,500.
789TC1a 5c large die on India paper
e. **blue** 1,500.
789P1 5c large die on India paper *1,500.*
789P1a 5c large die on white wove paper 1,500.
789P2 5c small die on white or yelsh wove paper 1,500.

Navy Issue

790P2 1c small die on white or yelsh wove paper 1,500.
791P1 2c large die on India paper 1,500.
791P2 2c small die on white or yelsh wove paper 1,500.
792P2 3c small die on white or yelsh wove paper 1,500.
793TC1a 4c large die on India paper
e. **dark brown** 1,500.
793P2 4c small die on white or yelsh wove paper 1,500.
794P2 5c small die on white or yelsh wove paper 1,500.

Ordinance of 1787 Issue

795P2 3c small die on white or yelsh wove paper 1,500.

Virginia Dare Issue

796P1 5c large die on India paper 1,500.
796P2 5c small die on white or yelsh wove paper 1,500.

Society of Philatelic Americans

797P2 10c small die on white or yelsh wove paper 1,500.

Constitution Sesquicentennial Issue

798TC2 3c small die on bond paper
b. **black** 750.
798P1 3c large die on India paper 1,500.
798P2 3c small die on white or yelsh wove paper 1,500.

Territorial Issues

799TC2 3c small die on bond paper
b. **black** 750.
799P1 3c large die on India paper 1,500.
799P2 3c small die on white or yelsh wove paper 1,500.
800TC2 3c small die on India paper
b. **black** 750.
c. **black,** on bond paper 750.
800P2 3c small die on white or yelsh wove paper 1,500.
801TC1a 3c large die on India paper
e. **black** 1,500.
801TC1b 3c Large die on bond paper
e. **black** 1,500.
801TC2 3c small die on bond paper
b. **black** 750.
801P1 3c large die on India paper 1,500.
801P2 3c small die on white or yelsh wove paper 1,500.
802TC2 3c small die on bond paper
b. **black** 750.

802P1	3c large die on India paper	1,500.
802P2	3c small die on white or yelsh wove paper	1,500.

Presidential Issue

1938

803TC1a	½c large die on India paper	
	***e.* black**	*3,000.*
803P1	½c **dp org,** large die on India paper	*2,000.*
803P2	½c **dp org,** small die on white or yelsh wove paper	3,000.
804P2	1c **grn,** small die on white or yelsh wove paper	3,000.
805P2	1½c **bis brn,** small die on white or yelsh wove paper	3,000.
806P1a	2c **rose car,** large die on white wove paper	*1,800.*
806P2	2c **rose car,** small die on white or yelsh wove paper	*3,000.*
807P1	3c **dp vio,** large die on glazed card	—
807P2	3c **dp vio,** small die on white or yelsh wove paper	3,000.
808P2	4c **red vio,** small die on white or yelsh wove paper	3,000.
809P1	4½c **dk gray,** large die on India paper	*1,500.*
809P2	4½c **dk gray,** small die on white or yelsh wove paper	3,000.
810P1	5c **brt bl,** large die on India paper	*1,500.*
810P2	5c **brt bl,** small die on white or yelsh wove paper	3,000.
811P2	6c **red org,** small die on white or yelsh wove paper	3,000.
812P1	7c **sepia,** large die on India paper	*1,750.*
812P2	7c **sepia,** small die on white or yelsh wove paper	3,000.
813P1a	8c **ol grn,** large die on white wove paper	*1,800.*
813P2	8c **ol grn,** small die on white or yelsh wove paper	3,000.
814P1	9c **ol grn,** large die on India paper	*1,800.*
814P1a	9c **ol grn,** large die on white wove paper	*1,800.*
814P2	9c **ol grn,** small die on white or yelsh wove paper	3,000.
815TC1a	10c large die on India paper	
	***e.* sepia**	1,500.
815P1	10c **brn red,** large die on India paper	*2,500.*
815P2	10c **brn red,** small die on white or yelsh wove paper	3,000.
816P2	11c **ultra,** small die on white or yelsh wove paper	3,000.
817P1	12c **brt vio,** large die on India paper	*1,500.*
817P2	12c **brt vio,** small die on white or yelsh wove paper	3,000.
818P2	13c **bl grn,** small die on white or yelsh wove paper	3,000.
819P2	14c **blue,** small die on white or yelsh wove paper	3,000.
820P1	15c **bl gray,** large die on India paper	*1,800.*
820P1a	15c **bl gray,** large die on white wove paper	*1,800.*
820P2	15c **bl gray,** small die on white or yelsh wove paper	3,000.
821P1	16c **blk,** large die on India paper	*1,500.*
821P2	16c **blk,** small die on white or yelsh wove paper	3,000.
822P2	17c **rose red,** small die on white or yelsh wove paper	3,000.
823P2	18c **brn car,** small die on white or yelsh wove paper	3,000.
824P1	19c **brt vio,** large die on India paper	*1,800.*
824P1a	19c **brt vio,** large die on white wove paper	*1,800.*
824P2	19c **brt vio,** small die on white or yelsh wove paper	3,000.
825P1	20c **brt bl grn,** large die on India paper	*1,800.*
825P1a	20c **brt bl grn,** large die on white wove paper	*1,800.*
825P2	20c **brt bl grn,** small die on white or yelsh wove paper	3,000.
826TC1a	21c large die on India paper	
	***e.* black**	*2,000.*
826P2	21c **dull bl,** small die on white or yelsh wove paper	3,000.
827P2	22c **ver,** small die on white or yelsh wove paper	3,000.
828P1	24c **gray blk,** large die on India paper	*1,800.*
828P2	24c **gray blk,** small die on white or yelsh wove paper	3,000.
829TC1a	25c large die on India paper	
	***e.* green**	*2,000.*
829P2	25c **dp red lilac,** small die on white or yelsh wove paper	3,000.
830P2	30c **dp ultra,** small die on white or yelsh wove paper	3,000.
831P1	50c **lt red vio,** large die on India paper	*1,500.*
831P2	50c **lt red vio,** small die on white or yelsh wove paper	3,000.
832P2	$1 **pur & blk,** small die on white or yelsh wove paper	5,000.
833P2	$2 **yel grn & blk,** small die on white or yelsh wove paper	5,000.
834P2	$5 **car & blk,** small die on white or yelsh wove paper	5,000.

Constitution Ratification Issue

1938

835P1	3c large die on India paper	1,500.
835P2	3c small die on white or yelsh wove paper	1,500.

Swedish-Finnish Tercentenary Issue

836TC1a	3c large die on India paper	
	***e.* purple**	1,500.
836P1	3c large die on India paper	1,500.
836P2	3c small die on white or yelsh wove paper	1,500.

Northwest Territory Sesquicentennial

837TC1a	3c large die on India paper	
	***e.* dark purple**	1,500.
837P2	3c small die on white or yelsh wove paper	800.

Iowa Territory Centennial Issue

838P1	3c large die on India paper	*1,500.*
838P2	3c small die on white or yelsh wove paper	1,500.

Golden Gate Intl. Exposition Issue

1939

852P1	3c large die on India paper	*1,800.*
852P2	3c small die on white or yelsh wove paper	1,500.

New York World's Fair Issue

853P1	3c large die on India paper	*1,500.*
853P2	3c small die on white or yelsh wove paper	1,500.

Washington Inauguration Issue

854TC1a	3c large die on India paper	
	***e.* purple**	900.
854P1	3c large die on India paper	*1,500.*
854P2	3c small die on white or yelsh wove paper	1,500.

Baseball Centennial Issue

855TC1a	3c large die on India paper	
	***e.* red violet**	*2,500.*
855P1	3c large die on India paper	*5,000.*
855P1a	3c large die on white wove paper	*2,000.*
855P2	3c small die on white or yelsh wove paper	2,500.

Panama Canal Issue

856P1	3c large die on white wove paper	2,250.
856P2	3c small die on white or yelsh wove paper	1,500.

Printing Trecentenary Issue

857P2	3c small die on white or yelsh wove paper	1,500.

Statehood Issue

858P2	3c small die on white or yelsh wove paper	1,500.

Famous Americans Issue

Authors

1940

859P2	1c small die on white or yelsh wove paper	1,500.
860P2	2c small die on white or yelsh wove paper	1,500.
861P2	3c small die on white or yelsh wove paper	1,500.
862TC1a	5c large die on India paper	
	***e.* dull blue**	1,500.
862P1	5c large die on India paper	1,500.
862P2	5c small die on white or yelsh wove paper	1,500.
863P1	10c large die on India paper	*2,500.*
863P2	10c small die on white or yelsh wove paper	1,500.

Poets

864P1	1c large die on India paper	*1,500.*
864P2	1c small die on white or yelsh wove paper	1,500.
865P2	2c small die on white or yelsh wove paper	1,500.
866TC1a	3c large die on India paper	
	***e.* dark blue violet**	1,500.
866P2	3c small die on white or yelsh wove paper	1,500.
867P1	5c large die on India paper	1,500.
867P2	5c small die on white or yelsh wove paper	1,500.
868P1	10c large die on India paper	*1,500.*
868P2	10c small die on white or yelsh wove paper	1,500.

Educators

869P1	1c large die on India paper	1,500.
869P2	1c small die on white or yelsh wove paper	1,500.
870P2	2c small die on white or yelsh wove paper	1,500.
871P2	3c small die on white or yelsh wove paper	1,500.
872P1	5c large die on India paper	1,500.
872P2	5c small die on white or yelsh wove paper	1,500.
873P1	10c large die on India paper	1,500.
873P2	10c small die on white or yelsh wove paper	1,500.

Scientists

874P1	1c large die on India paper	*1,500.*
874P2	1c small die on white or yelsh wove paper	1,500.
875P1	2c large die on India paper	1,500.
875P2	2c small die on white or yelsh wove paper	1,500.
876P1	3c large die on India paper	1,500.
876P2	3c small die on white or yelsh wove paper	1,500.
877P2	5c small die on white or yelsh wove paper	1,500.
878P1	10c large die on India paper	*1,500.*
878P2	10c small die on white or yelsh wove paper	1,500.

Composers

879P2	1c small die on white or yelsh wove paper	1,500.
880P1	2c large die on India paper	1,500.
880P2	2c small die on white or yelsh wove paper	1,500.
881P2	3c small die on white or yelsh wove paper	1,500.
882P1	5c large die on India paper	1,500.
882P2	5c small die on white or yelsh wove paper	1,500.
883P2	10c small die on white or yelsh wove paper	1,500.

Artists

884P2	1c small die on white or yelsh wove paper	1,500.
885P1	2c large die on wove paper	1,500.
885P2	2c small die on white or yelsh wove paper	1,500.
886P1	3c large die on wove paper	1,500.
886P2	3c small die on white or yelsh wove paper	1,500.
887P1	5c large die on India paper	1,500.
887P2	5c small die on white or yelsh wove paper	1,500.
888P1	10c large die on India paper	1,500.
888P2	10c small die on white or yelsh wove paper	1,500.

Inventors

889P2	1c small die on white or yelsh wove paper	1,500.
890P1	2c large die on India paper	*1,500.*
890P2	2c small die on white or yelsh wove paper	1,500.
891P1	3c large die on wove paper	1,500.
891P2	3c small die on white or yelsh wove paper	1,500.
892P2	5c small die on white or yelsh wove paper	1,500.
893P2	10c small die on white or yelsh wove paper	1,500.

Pony Express Issue

1940

894P1	3c large die on India paper	*1,500.*
894P2	3c small die on white or yelsh wove paper	1,500.

Pan American Union Issue

895P2	3c small die on white or yelsh wove paper	1,500.

Idaho Statehood Issue

896P1	3c large die on India paper	*1,500.*
896P2	3c small die on white or yelsh wove paper	1,500.

Wyoming Statehood Issue

897TC1a	3c large die on India paper	
	***e.* red violet**	1,500.
897P2	3c small die on white or yelsh wove paper	1,500.

Coronado Expedition Issue

898P1	3c large die on India paper	*1,500.*
898P2	3c small die on white or yelsh wove paper	1,500.

National Defense Issue

899P1	1c large die on India paper	*1,500.*
899P2	1c small die on white or yelsh wove paper	1,500.
900P1	2c large die on India paper	*1,500.*
900P2	2c small die on white or yelsh wove paper	1,500.
901P1	3c large die on India paper	*1,500.*
901P2	3c small die on white or yelsh wove paper	1,500.

Thirteenth Amendment Issue

902P1	3c large die on India paper	*1,500.*
902P2	3c small die on white or yelsh wove paper	1,500.

Vermont Statehood Issue

1941-44

903P1	3c large die on wove paper	1,750.
903P2	3c small die on white or yelsh wove paper	1,500.

Kentucky Statehood Issue

904P1	3c large die on India paper	*1,500.*
904P2	3c small die on white or yelsh wove paper	1,500.

Win the War Issue

905P2	3c small die on white or yelsh wove paper	1,500.

China Resistance Issue

906P2	3c small die on white or yelsh wove paper	1,750.

Allied Nations Issue

907P2	2c small die on white or yelsh wove paper	1,500.

Four Freedoms Issue

908P1	1c large die on India paper	*1,500.*
908P2	1c small die on white or yelsh wove paper	1,500.

Overrun Countries Issue

909P2	5c small die on wove paper	*600.*
910P2	5c small die on wove paper	*600.*
911P2	5c small die on wove paper	*600.*
912P2	5c small die on wove paper	*600.*
913P2	5c small die on wove paper	*600.*
914P2	5c small die on wove paper	*600.*
915P2	5c small die on wove paper	*600.*
916P2	5c small die on wove paper	*600.*
917P2	5c small die on wove paper	*600.*
918P2	5c small die on wove paper	*600.*
919P2	5c small die on wove paper	*600.*
920P2	5c small die on wove paper	*600.*
921P2	5c small die on wove paper	*600.*

Transcontinental Railroad Issue

922P1	3c large die on India paper	*1,500.*
922P2	3c small die on white or yelsh wove paper	1,500.

Steamship Issue

923P1	3c large die on wove paper	*1,600.*
923P2	3c small die on white or yelsh wove paper	1,500.

Telegraph Issue

924P1	3c large die on wove paper	*1,5(*
924P2	3c small die on white or yelsh wove paper	1,5

Philippine Issue

925P1	3c large die on India paper	
925P2	3c small die on white or yelsh wove paper	

Motion Picture Issue

926P1	3c large die on India paper	
926P2	3c small die on white or yelsh wove pap	

Florida Statehood Issue

1945-46

927P1 3c large die on India paper 1,500.

927P2 3c small die on white or yelsh wove paper 1,500.

United Nations Conference Issue

928P2 5c small die on white or yelsh wove paper 1,500.

Iwo Jima (Marines) Issue

929TC1a 3c large die on India paper

e. bright purple 2,300.

929P2 3c small die on white or yelsh wove paper 1,500.

Franklin D. Roosevelt Issue

930P2 1c small die on white or yelsh wove paper 1,500.

931P1a 2c large die on wove paper 1,750.

931P2 2c small die on white or yelsh wove paper 1,500.

932P1a 3c large die on wove paper 1,750.

932P2 3c small die on white or yelsh wove paper 1,500.

933P1a 5c large die on wove paper 1,750.

Army & Navy Issues

934P1a 3c large die on wove paper 1,500.

934P2 3c small die on white or yelsh wove paper 1,200.

935P1a 3c large die on wove paper 1,500.

935P2 3c small die on white or yelsh wove paper 1,500.

Merchant Marine Issue

939P1a 5c large die on wove paper 1,500.

Tennessee Statehood Issue

941P1a 3c large die on wove paper 1,500.

Iowa Statehood Issue

942P1a 3c large die on white wove paper 1,500.

Kearny Expedition Issue

944P1a 3c large die on wove paper 1,500.

Thomas A. Edison Issue

1947-50

945P1a 3c large die on wove paper 1,500.

Joseph Pulitzer Issue

946P1a 3c large die on white wove paper 1,500.

Postage Stamp Centenary Issue

947P1a 3c large die on wove paper 1,500.

Doctors Issue

949P1a 3c large die on wove paper 1,500.

Utah Issue

950TC1c 3c large die on wove paper

e. deep brown 1,500.

U.S.S. Constitution Issue

951P1a 3c large die on wove paper 1,500.

Mississippi Territory Issue

955P1a 3c large die on white wove paper 1,500.

Four Chaplains Issue

956P1a 3c large die on wove paper 1,500.

Swedish Pioneers Issue

958P1a 5c large die on wove paper 1,500.

Progress of Women Issue

959TC1b 3c large die on wove paper

e. bright violet 1,750.

959P1a 3c large die on wove paper 1,500.

William Allen White Issue

960P1a 3c large die on wove paper 1,500.

U.S.-Canada Friendship Issue

961TC1b 3c large die on wove paper

e. brown violet 1,500.

Francis Scott Key Issue

962P1a 3c large die on wove paper 1,500.

Youth Issue

963TC1b 3c large die on white wove paper

e. violet 1,500.

Oregon Statehood Issue

964TC1b 3c large die on wove paper

e. dull violet 1,500.

Harlan Fiske Stone Issue

965P1a 3c large die on wove paper 1,500.

Clara Barton Issue

967P1a 3c large die on wove paper 2,000.

Poultry Issue

968TC1b 3c large die on wove paper

e. red brown 1,500.

Volunteer Firemen Issue

971P1a 3c large die on wove paper 1,500.

Indian Centennial Issue

972P1a 3c large die on wove paper 1,500.

Rough Riders Issue

973P1a 3c large die on wove paper 1,500.

Girl Scouts Issue

974P1a 3c large die on white wove paper 1,500.

Will Rogers Issue

975P1a 3c large die on wove paper 1,750.

Fort Bliss Centennial Issue

976P1a 3c large die on wove paper 1,500.

Moina Michael Issue

977P1a 3c large die on white wove paper 1,500.

Minnesota Territory Issue

981P1a 3c large die on white wove paper 1,500.

Puerto Rico Election Issue

983P1a 3c large die on wove paper 1,500.

G.A.R. Issue

985P1a 3c large die on wove paper 1,500.

American Bankers Assoc. Issue

987TC1b 3c large die on wove paper

e. dark green 1,500.

Samuel Gompers Issue

988P1a 3c large die on wove paper 1,500.

National Capital Sesquicentennial Issue

989P1a 3c large die on white wove paper 1,500.

991P1a 3c large die on wove paper 1,500.

992P1a 3c large die on wove paper 1,500.

Boy Scouts Issue

995P1a 3c large die on white wove paper 2,000.

Nevada Centennial Issue

1951-53

999P1a 3c large die on wove paper 1,500.

Landing of Cadillac Issue

1000P1a 3c large die on wove paper 1,500.

Colorado Statehood Issue

1001P1a 3c large die on wove paper 1,500.

American Chemical Society Issue

1002P1a 3c large die on wove paper 1,500.

Battle of Brooklyn Issue

1003P1a 3c large die on wove paper 1,500.

Betsy Ross Issue

1004P1a 3c large die on wove paper 1,500.

4-H Club Issue

1005P1a 3c large die on wove paper 1,500.

B & O Railroad Issue

1006TC1b 3c large die on wove paper

e. deep blue 1,500.

1006P1a 3c large die on wove paper 1,750.

A.A.A. Issue

1007P1a 3c large die on wove paper 1,500.

Grand Coulee Dam Issue

1009P1a 3c large die on wove paper 1,500.

Lafayette Issue

1010P1a 3c large die on wove paper 1,500.

Mt. Rushmore Memorial Issue

1011P1a 3c large die on wove paper 1,500.

Engineering Centennial Issue

1012P1a 3c large die on wove paper 1,500.

Service Women Issue

1013P1a 3c large die on wove paper 1,500.

Red Cross Issue

1016P1a 3c large die on wove paper 3,000.

National Guard Issue

1017P1a 3c large die on wove paper 1,500.

Ohio Statehood Issue

1018P1a 3c large die on wove paper 1,500.

Washington Territory Issue

1019P1a 3c large die on wove paper 1,500.

Louisana Purchase Issue

1020P1a 3c large die on wove paper 1,500.

Opening of Japan Centennial Issue

1021P1a 5c large die on wove paper 2,000.

American Bar Association Issue

1022P1a 3c large die on wove paper 1,500.

Trucking Industry Issue

1025P1a 3c large die on wove paper 1,500.

Gen. George S. Patton Issue

1026P1a 3c large die on wove paper 1,500.

Columbia University Issue

1954-98

1029P1a 3c large die on wove paper 1,500.

Liberty Issue

1030P1a ½c *Franklin,* large die on wove paper 2,500.

1031P1a 1c *Washington,* large die on wove paper 1,500.

1032P1a 1½c *Mt. Vernon,* large die on wove paper 1,500.

1033P1a 2c *Jefferson,* large die on wove paper 1,500.

1036P1a 4c *Lincoln,* large die on wove paper 1,500.

1038P1a 5c *Monroe,* large die on wove paper 1,500.

1039P1a 6c *Roosevelt,* large die on wove paper 1,500.

1044P1a 10c *Independence Hall,* large die on wove paper 1,500.

1047P1a 20c *Monticello,* large die on wove paper 1,500.

1049P1a 30c *Lee,* large die on wove paper 2,000.

1050P1a 40c *Marshall,* large die on wove paper 2,000.

1051P1a 50c *Anthony,* large die on wove paper 2,000.

1052P1a $1 *Henry,* large die on wove paper 2,000.

1053P1a $5 *Hamilton,* large die on wove paper 2,500.

Nebraska Territory Issue

1060P1a 3c large die on wove paper 1,500.

George Eastman Issue

1062P1a 3c large die on wove paper 1,500.

Lewis & Clark Issue

1063P1a 3c large die on wove paper 1,500.

Pennsylvania Academy of Fine Arts Issue

1064P1a 3c large die on wove paper 1,500.

Armed Forces Reserve Issue

1067P1a 3c large die on wove paper 1,500.

New Hampshire Issue

1068P1a 3c large die on wove paper 1,500.

Soo Locks Issue

1069P1a 3c large die on wove paper 1,500.

Ft. Ticonderoga Issue

1071P1a 3c large die on wove paper 1,500.

Benjamin Franklin Issue

1073P1a 3c large die on wove paper 1,500.

Booker T. Washington Issue

1074P1a 3c large die on wove paper 1,500.

FIPEX Souvenir Sheet

1076P1a large die on wove paper 1,500.

Wildlife Conservation Issue

1077P1a 3c large die on wove paper 1,500.

1078P1a 3c large die on wove paper 1,500.

1079P1a 3c large die on wove paper 1,500.

Pure Food & Drug Laws

1080P1a 3c large die on wove paper 1,500.

Wheatland Issue

1081P1a 3c large die on wove paper 1,500.

Labor Day Issue

1082P1a 3c large die on wove paper 1,500.

Nassau Hall Issue

1083P1a 3c large die on wove paper 1,500.

Children's Issue

1085P1a 3c large die on wove paper 1,500.

Alexander Hamilton Issue

1086P1a 3c large die on wove paper 1,500.

Polio Issue

1087P1a 3c large die on wove paper 1,500.

Coast & Geodetic Survey Issue

1088P1a 3c large die on wove paper 1,500.

Steel Industry Issue

1090P1a 3c large die on wove paper 1,500.

Oklahoma Statehood Issue

1092P1a 3c large die on wove paper 1,500.

Civil War Centennial Issue

1178P1 4c Ft. Sumter, large die

a. On white wove paper 1,500.

b. On stiff yellowish bond paper 1,500.

Project Mercury Issue

1193P1a 4c large die on wove paper 1,500.

Antarctic Issue

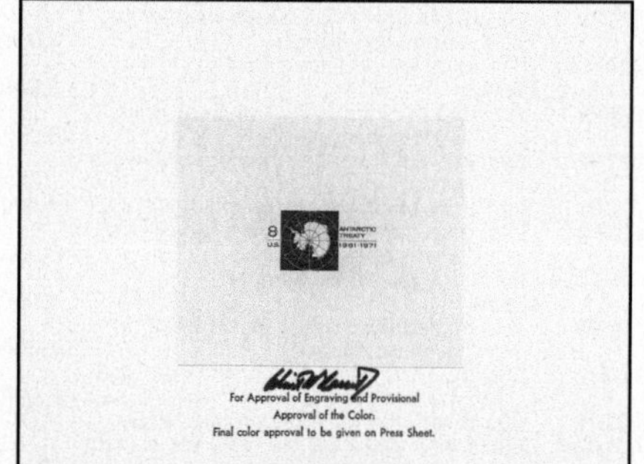

1431P1

1431P1 8c large die on white wove, mounted on card autographed by PMG Winton M. Blount 1,000.

Olympic Games Issue

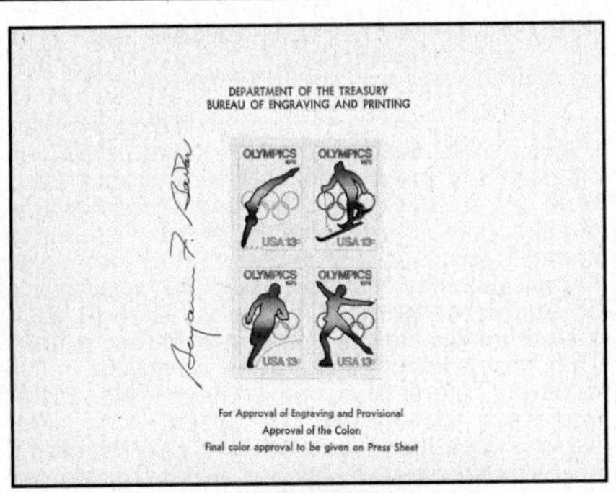

1698aP1

1698aP1 13c large hybrid die proof, mounted on large card imprinted for approval of engraving and color, signed by PMG Benjamin F. Bailar *800.*

Duck Decoy Issue

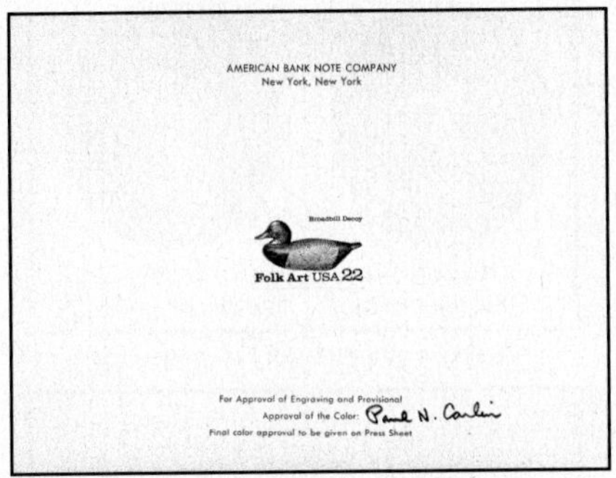

2138P1

2138P1 22c *Broadbill* decoy, large hybrid die proof, mounted on large card imprinted for approval of engraving and color, "Duck Decoys Cylinder Proof," etc. on reverse *240.*

Dennis Chavez Issue

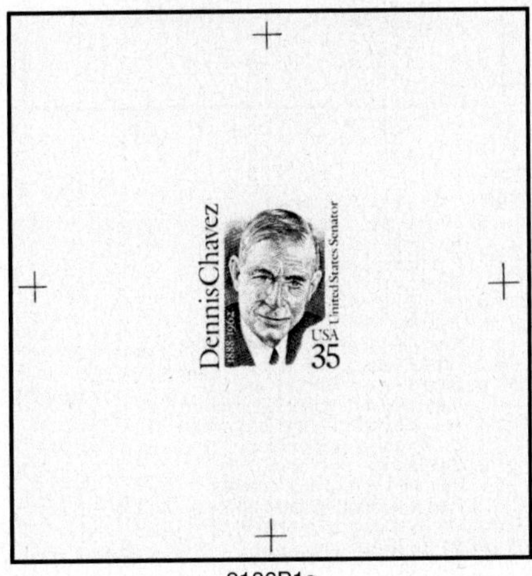

2186P1a

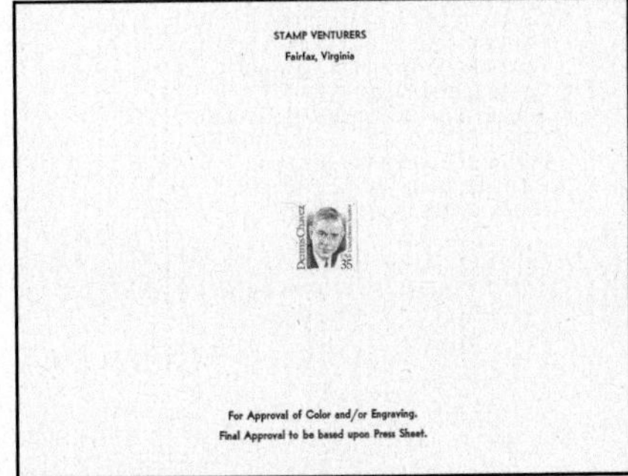

2186P1b

Design size: 13x20mm

2186P1 35c *Dennis Chavez*

a. Engraved large die impression on 114x147mm gummed stamp paper, dated in red "Jan. 30/91," black —

b. Engraved large die impression, cut to stamp size and affixed to large card imprinted for approval of color and/or engraving, black —

Statue of Liberty, 100th Anniversary

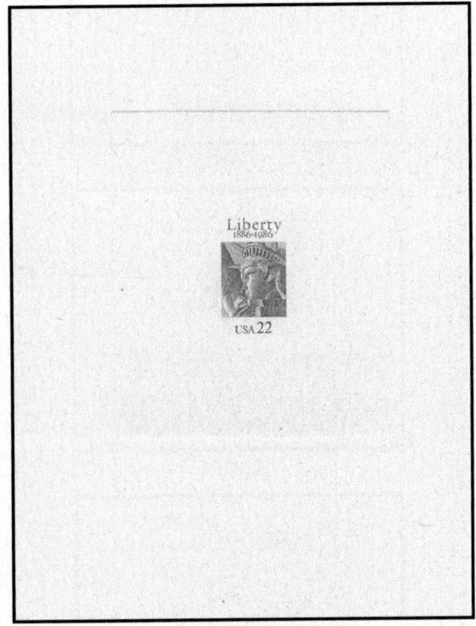

2224TC1

2224TC1e 22c **olive green,** die sunk on card *1,300.*

1988 Winter Olympics, Calgary Issue

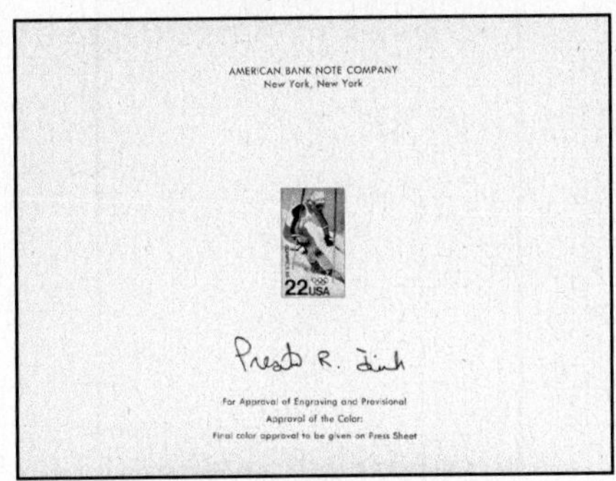

2369P1

2369P1 22c large hybrid die proof, mounted on large card imprinted for approval of engraving and color, "Winter Olympics Stamp From Approved Press Sheet," etc. on reverse *550.*

Moon Landing, 20th Anniversary

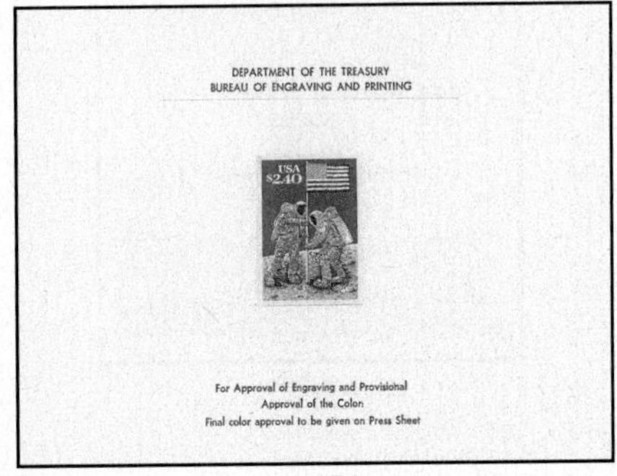

2419P1

2419P1 $2.40 large hybrid die proof, pressed on large card imprinted for approval of engraving and color *2,850.*

Flag and Olympic Rings Issue

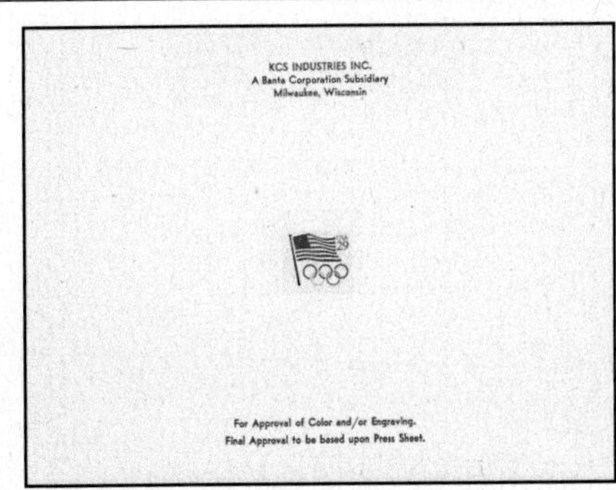

2528P1

2528P1 29c large hybrid die proof, mounted on large card imprinted for approval of engraving and color, "Flag with Olympic Rings Stamp From Approved Press Sheet," etc. on reverse *550.*

Basketball, 100th Anniversary Issue

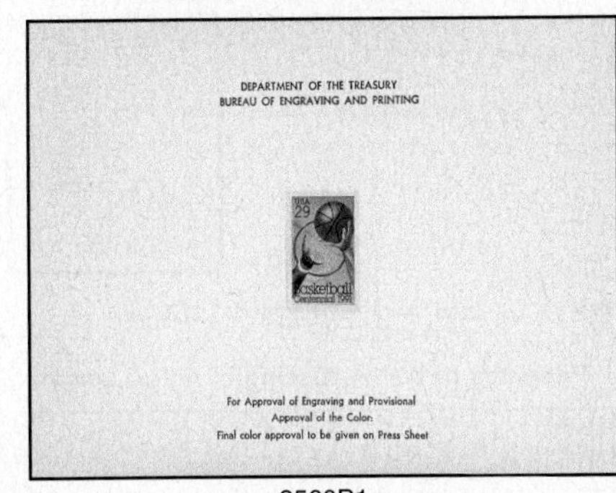

2560P1

2560P1 29c large hybrid die proof, mounted on large card imprinted for approval of engraving and color *950.*

1995

2587P1b 29c **red brown,** die proof on gummed wove paper, ms "7/17/95" and "#3" below design —

Winter Olympics Issue

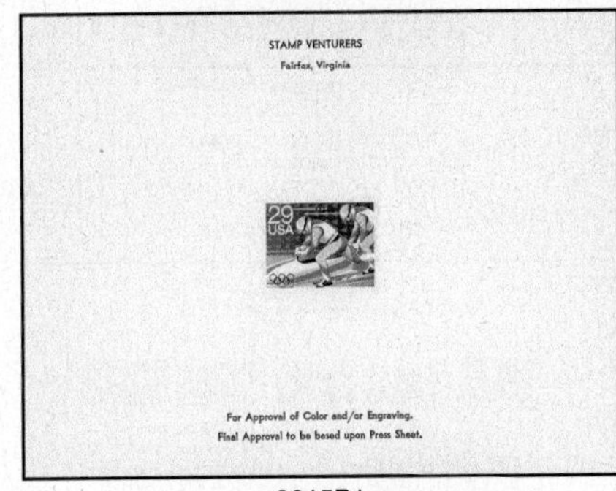

2615P1

2615P1 29c *Bobsledding,* large hybrid die proof, mounted on large card imprinted for approval of engraving and color, "Winter Olympics Stamp from Approved Sheet," etc. on reverse *600.*

Summer Olympics Issue

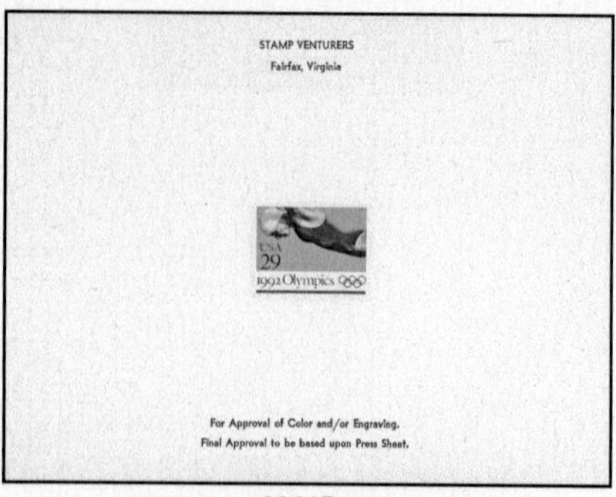

2641P1

2641P1 29c *Swimming,* large hybrid die proof, mounted on large card imprinted for approval of engraving and color, "Summer Olympics Stamp from Approved Sheet," etc. on reverse *500.*

Great Americans — Milton S. Hershey Issue

2933P1a

2933P1a 32c large die on wove, dated "7/3/95" at lower right —

Prisoners of War & Missing in Action Issue

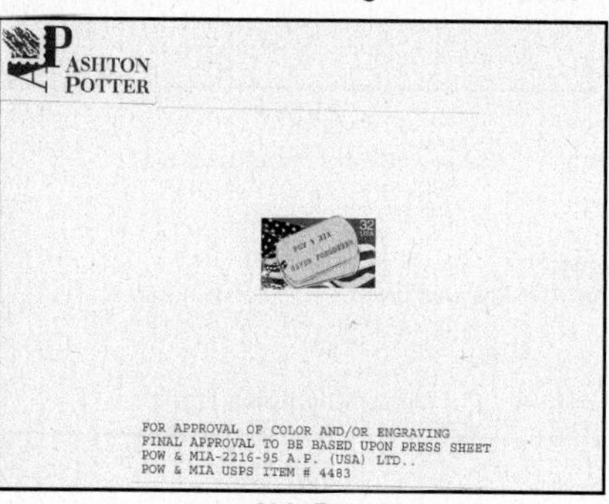

2966P1

2966P1 32c large hybrid die proof, pressed on large card imprinted with Ashton Potter logo and approval information *300.*

World War II Issue

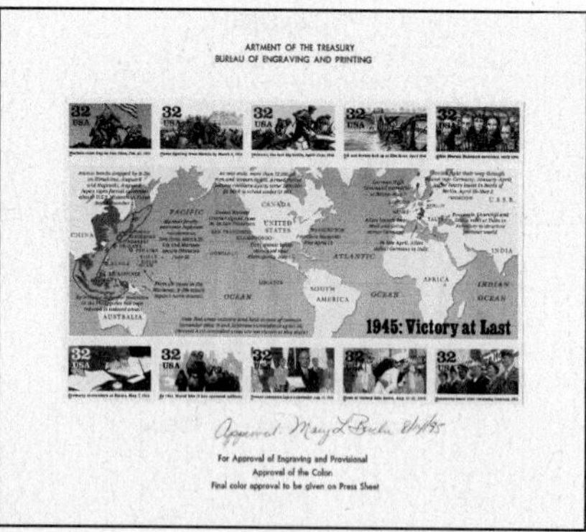

2981P1

2981P1 32c large hybrid die proof, pressed on large card, ms, approved by Mary L. Burke, USPS Production Staff *1,250.*

Space Shuttle Issues

3261P

3262P

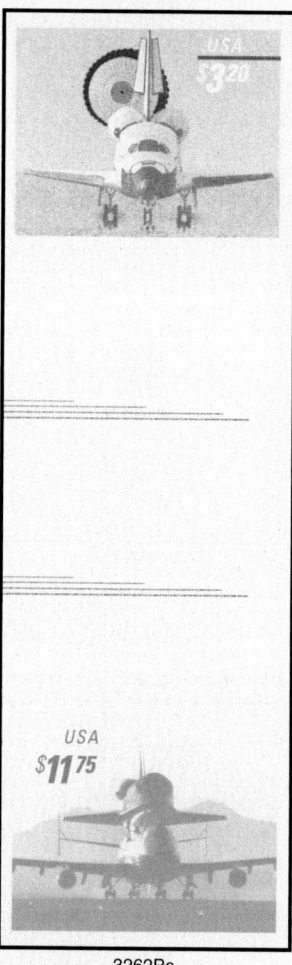

3262Pc

3261P $3.20 **magenta** color only
- ***a.*** On coated paper —
- ***b.*** On uncoated paper *225.*

3262P $11.75 **cyan** color only
- ***a.*** On coated paper —
- ***b.*** On uncoated paper *225.*

- ***c.*** As "a," vertical pair, #3261P and 3262P, with full horiz. gutter between 1,150.
- ***d.*** As "b," vertical pair, #3261P and 3262P, with full horiz. gutter between —

Nos. 1789P through 2788aP, listed below, are all from the proof files of the American Bank Note Co. archives that were sold and are available to collectors. All items listed are on gummed stamp paper and are imperf unless otherwise noted, and they therefore have the appearance of imperf or part-perf stamps, though their source makes clear that they are, in fact, proofs. This group includes progressive proofs in the different colors, plus one variety of No. 2624P and three varieties of No. 2770aP that differ slightly from the issued designs and, therefore, are actually essays. Where single proofs are listed, pairs are worth double the values shown.

1789Pg finished design as issued, pair

1789Pd blue color only, pair

1979

1789P 15c John Paul Jones
- ***a.*** Single, red color ("John Paul Jones") only *50.00*
  - Pair with vert. gutter between —
  - Pair with horiz. gutter between —
  - Cross gutter block of four —
- ***b.*** Single, yellow color only *50.00*
  - Pair with vert. gutter between —
  - Pair with horiz. gutter between —
  - Cross gutter block of four —
- ***c.*** Single, magenta color only 50.00
  - Pair with vert. gutter between —
  - Pair with horiz. gutter between —
  - Cross gutter block of four —
- ***d.*** Single, blue color only *50.00*
  - Pair with vert. gutter between —
  - Pair with horiz. gutter between —
  - Cross gutter block of four —
- ***e.*** Single, black color only *50.00*
  - Pair with vert. gutter between —
  - Pair with horiz. gutter between —
  - Cross gutter block of four —
- ***f.*** Single, tagging blocks only *50.00*
  - Pair with vert. gutter between —
  - Pair with horiz. gutter between —
  - Cross gutter block of four —
- ***g.*** Single, finished design as issued *25.00*
  - Pair *50.00*
  - Pair with vert. gutter between *700.00*
  - Pair with horiz. gutter between *600.00*
  - Cross gutter block of four *3,000.*

2418P

1989

2418P 25c Ernest Hemingway, pair 2,000.
Pair with vert. gutter between —
Pair with horiz. gutter between —
Cross gutter block of four —

2478Pa cross gutter block

Illustration reduced.

1991

2476P 1c Kestrel, pair 150.
Pair with vert. gutter between 200.
Pair with horiz. gutter between 200.
Cross gutter block of four —
a. Perforated
Pair with vert. gutter between 675.
Pair with horiz. gutter between 675.
Cross gutter block of four —

2478P 3c Bluebird, pair 150.
Pair with vert. gutter between 200.
Pair with horiz. gutter between 200.
Cross gutter block of four —
a. Se-tenants, Nos. 2476P and 2478P
Pair, one No. 2476P and one No. 2478P, with vert. gutter between —
Cross gutter block of four, two No. 2476P at left and two No. 2478P at right —
b. Perforated
Pair with vert. gutter between —
Pair with horiz. gutter between —
Cross gutter block of four —
c. Perforated se-tenants
Pair, one No. 2476Pa and one No. 2478Pb, with vert. gutter between —
Cross gutter block of four, two No. 2476Pa at left and two No. 2478Pb at right (unique) —

1990-91

2500aP 25c Olympics, horiz. strip of five 1,500.
Two strips of five with vert. gutter between —
Two strips of five with horiz. gutter between —
Cross gutter block of four strips of five —

2513P 25c Dwight D. Eisenhower, pair 875.

2517P (29c) "F" stamp, perforated
Pair with vert. gutter between —
Pair with horiz. gutter between —
Cross gutter block of four (unique) —

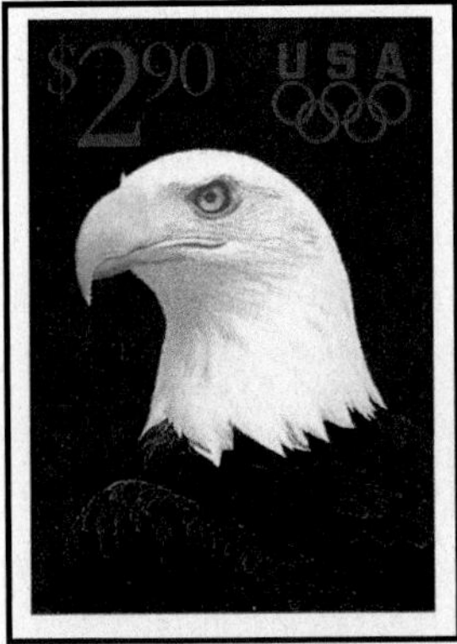

2540Pi with all litho. colors

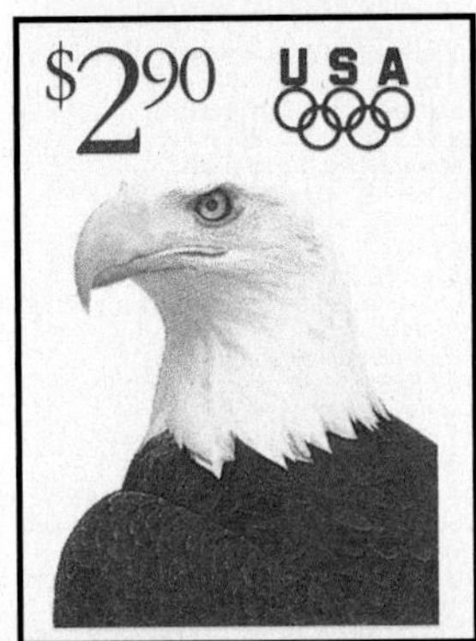

2540Pf magenta, yellow and blue colors only

1991

2540P $2.90 Eagle
a. Single, magenta color only 175.
Pair with vert. gutter between —
Pair with horiz. gutter between —
Cross gutter block of four —
b. Single, yellow color only 175.
Pair with vert. gutter between —
Pair with horiz. gutter between —
Cross gutter block of four —
c. Single, blue color only 175.
Pair with vert. gutter between —
Pair with horiz. gutter between —
Cross gutter block of four —
d. Single, magenta and yellow colors only 175.
Pair with vert. gutter between —
Pair with horiz. gutter between —
Cross gutter block of four —
e. Single, yellow and blue colors only 175.
Pair with vert. gutter between —
Pair with horiz. gutter between —
Cross gutter block of four —
f. Single, magenta, yellow and blue colors only 175.
Pair with vert. gutter between —
Pair with horiz. gutter between —
Cross gutter block of four —
g. Single, black (litho.) color only 175.
Pair with vert. gutter between —
Pair with horiz. gutter between —
Cross gutter block of four —
h. Single, black (litho.) and yellow colors only 175.
Pair with vert. gutter between —
Pair with horiz. gutter between —
Cross gutter block of four —
i. Single, all litho. colors but without black engr. 175.
Pair with vert. gutter between —
Pair with horiz. gutter between —
Cross gutter block of four —
j. Single, finished design as issued 500.
Pair 1,000.
Pair with vert. gutter between —
Pair with horiz. gutter between —
Cross gutter block of four —
k. Perforated, all litho. colors but without black engr. —
Pair with vert. gutter between —
Pair with horiz. gutter between —
Cross gutter block of four —
l. Perforated, finished design as issued
Pair with vert. gutter between —
Pair with horiz. gutter between —
Cross gutter block of four —

2605P, with plate numbers

2605P 23c Flag Presorted First Class Coil, vert. pair, uncut between 250.
Vert. pair, uncut between, with P#A111 —

1992

2624P 1c, 4c and $1 Columbian souvenir sheet 750.
Pair of sheets —
a. As No. 2624P, but with background of No. 2627P (essay) —

2625P 2c, 3c and $4 Columbian souvenir sheet 750.
Pair of sheets —

2626P 5c, 30c and 50c Columbian souvenir sheet 750.
Pair of sheets —

2627P 6c, 8c and $3 Columbian souvenir sheet 750.
Pair of sheets —

2628P 10c, 15c and $2 Columbian souvenir sheet 750.
Pair of sheets —

2629P $4 Columbian souvenir sheet 750.
Pair of sheets —

2646aPi finished design as issued

2646aPe brown color only

Illustrations reduced.

2646aP 29c Hummingbirds booklet pane
b. Pane of five, yellow color only 450.
Two panes of five with vert. gutter between —
Two panes of five with horiz. gutter between —
Cross gutter block of four panes of five —
c. Pane of five, magenta color only 450.
Two panes of five with vert. gutter between —
Two panes of five with horiz. gutter between —
Cross gutter block of four panes of five —
d. Pane of five, blue color only 450.
Two panes of five with vert. gutter between —
Two panes of five with horiz. gutter between —
Cross gutter block of four panes of five —
e. Pane of five, brown color (birds) only 450.
Two panes of five with vert. gutter between —
Two panes of five with horiz. gutter between —
Cross gutter block of four panes of five —
f. Pane of five, brown color ("USA/29") only 450.
Two panes of five with vert. gutter between —
Two panes of five with horiz. gutter between —
Cross gutter block of four panes of five —
g. Pane of five, green color (frames) only 450.
Two panes of five with vert. gutter between —
Two panes of five with horiz. gutter between —
Cross gutter block of four panes of five —
h. Pane of five, orange color (frames) only 450.
Two panes of five with vert. gutter between —
Two panes of five with horiz. gutter between —
Cross gutter block of four panes of five —
i. Pane of five, finished design as issued 450.
Two panes of five with vert. gutter between —
Two panes of five with horiz. gutter between —
Cross gutter block of four panes of five —

2718aPd

2718aPe

Illustrations reduced.

2718aP 29c Christmas Toys booklet pane 600.
Horiz. pair of panes of four 1,500.
Vert. pair of panes of four 1,500.
b. As No. 2718aP, pane of four with two stamps at top from bottom row of normal pane and two stamps at bottom from top row of normal pane 1,000.
c. As No. 2718aP, perforated, pair of panes, uncut horiz. 2,000.
d. Pane of four with two stamps at top from bottom row of normal pane and two stamps at bottom from top row of normal pane, perforated 1,200.
e. Pane of four without red "Greetings" or green denominations 1,200.
f. As No. 2718aPe, two stamps at top from bottom row of "normal" pane and two stamps at bottom from top row of "normal" pane 1,500.
g. Pane of four without green denominations 1,200.
h. As No. 2718aPg, two stamps at top from bottom row of "normal" pane and two stamps at bottom from top row of "normal" pane 1,500.

1993

2737aP 29c American Music booklet pane of eight —
Pair of panes of eight —
c. As No. 2737aP, perforated horiz., uncut vert., pair of panes of eight —
2737bP 29c American Music booklet pane of four 2,000.
d. As No. 2737bP, perforated horiz., uncut vert., pair of panes of four —
e. Pair of panes, one No. 2737aP + one 2737bP —
f. Pair of panes, one No. 2737aPc + one 2737bPd —

2754Pa

2754Pb

Illustration of No. 2754Pa reduced.

2754P 29c Cherokee Strip Land Run, pair 350.
Pair with vert. gutter between 400.
Pair with horiz. gutter between 400.
Cross gutter block of four 1,500.
a. Perforated
Pair with vert. gutter between 250.
Pair with horiz. gutter between 250.
Cross gutter block of four 750.
b. As No. 2754P, without purple inscriptions and black denominations, pair —
Pair with vert. gutter between —
Pair with horiz. gutter between —
Cross gutter block of four —
c. Die proof, signed 11/25/92 for color and/or engraving —
2770aP 29c American Musicals booklet pane of four 1,250.
Pair of panes —
a. Perforated horiz., uncut vert., pair of panes of four —
b. Pane of four, blue color only, with designs slightly different from issued designs (essay) —
c. Pane of four, blue and magenta colors only, with designs slightly different from issued designs (essay) —
d. Pane of four, blue, magenta and yellow colors only, with designs slightly different from issued designs (essay) —
2778aP 29c American Music booklet pane of four
a. Pane of four, yellow color only 300.
On approval card (unique) —
b. Pane of four, pink color only 300.
On approval card (unique) —
c. Pane of four, red color only 300.
On approval card (unique) —
d. Pane of four, blue color only 300.
On approval card (unique) —
e. Pane of four, black color (frames and wording) only 300.
On approval card (unique) —
f. Pane of four, black color (Musicians) only 300.
On approval card (unique) —
g. Pane of four, finished design as issued 1,500.
On approval card (unique) —
h. Pane of four, finished design as issued, on cromalin paper, taped to approval card (unique) —
i. Booklet cover, finished design as issued, on card stock, pair of covers —
j. Booklet cover, finished design as issued, on cromalin paper, taped to approval card (unique) —
k. Perforated horiz., uncut vert., pair of panes of four 1,500.

Some of the sets of progressive proofs are in panes that are 2½ to 3½ stamps tall. These sell for somewhat less than the full panes.

About 20 percent of the examples of No. 2778aPk are split into two pieces. From these pieces come horizontal pairs or blocks of booklet stamps imperf vertically.

2788aP

2788aP 29c Classic Books, block of four 400.
Pair of blocks with vert. gutter between —
Pair of blocks with horiz. gutter between —
Cross gutter block of four blocks —

AIR POST

1918

C1P1 6c **org,** large die on India paper 8,500.
C2P1 16c **grn,** large die on India paper 7,000.
C3P1 24c **car rose & bl,** large die on India paper 8,500.

1923

C4P1 8c **dk grn,** large die on India paper 4,750.
C4P2 8c **dk grn,** small die on white wove paper 5,000.
C5TC1a 16c large die on India paper
e. **dark green** 5,000.
C5P1 16c **dk bl,** large die on India paper 4,750.
C5P2 16c **dk bl,** small die on white wove paper 5,000.
C6P1 24c **car,** large die on India paper 4,750.
C6P2 24c **car,** small die on white wove paper 5,000.

1926-27

C7P1 10c **dk bl,** large die on India paper 3,000.
C8TC1a 15c large die on India paper
e. **orange** 4,750.
C8P1 15c **ol brn,** large die on India paper 3,000.
C9P1 20c **yel grn,** large die on India paper 3,000.

Lindbergh Issue

1927

C10P1 10c **dk bl,** large die on India paper 6,000.
C10P2 10c **dk bl,** small die on white wove paper 7,000.

1928

C11P1 5c **car & bl,** large die on India paper 11,000.

1930

C12P1 5c **vio,** large die on India paper 3,000.

Zeppelin Issue

1930

C13P1 65c **grn,** large die on India paper 17,500.
a. On wove paper 15,000.
C13P2 65c **grn,** small die on white wove paper 25,000.
b. On stamp paper, imperf corner margin plate single —
C14P1 $1.30 **brn,** large die on India paper 17,500.
a. On wove paper 15,000.
C14P2 $1.30 **brn,** small die on white wove paper 25,000.
b. On stamp paper, imperf corner margin plate single —
C15P1 $2.60 **bl,** large die on India paper 17,500.
a. On wove paper 15,000.
C15P2 $2.60 **bl,** small die on white wove paper 25,000.
b. On stamp paper, imperf corner margin plate single —

1932

C17P1 8c **ol bis,** large die on India paper 4,000.

Century of Progress Issue

1933

C18P1 50c **grn,** large die on India paper 17,500.
C18P2 50c **grn,** small die on white wove paper 45,000.

1935-39

C20P2 25c **bl,** small die on white wove paper 3,250.
C21P2 20c **grn,** small die on white wove paper 3,250.
C22P2 50c **car,** small die on white wove paper 3,250.
C23P2 6c **dk bl & car,** small die on white wove paper 7,000.
C24P1 30c **dull bl,** large die on India paper 3,500.
C24P2 30c **dull bl,** small die on white wove paper 2,750.

1941-89

C25P2 6c **car,** small die on white wove paper 3,000.
C26P2 8c **ol grn,** small die on white wove paper 3,000.
C27P1 10c **vio,** large die on white wove paper 5,000.
C27P2 10c **vio,** small die on white wove paper 3,000.
C28P2 15c **brn car,** small die on white wove paper 3,000.
C29P2 20c **brt grn,** small die on white wove paper 3,000.
C30P2 30c **bl,** small die on white wove paper 3,000.
C31P2 50c **org,** small die on white wove paper 3,000.
C32TC1a 5c large die on India paper
e. **blue** 4,750.
C33P1 5c **car,** large die on white wove paper 5,500.
C35TC1a 15c large die on India paper
e. **brown violet** 4,750.
C40P1 6c **car,** large die on white wove paper 5,000.
C44P1 25c **rose car,** large die on white wove paper 5,000.
C44P2 25c **rose car,** small die on white wove paper 3,500.
C45P1 6c **mag,** large die on white wove paper 6,000.
C45P2 6c **mag,** small die on white wove paper 5,000.
C46P1 80c **brt red vio,** large die on white wove paper 5,000.
C46P2 80c **brt red vio,** small die on white wove paper —
C47P1 6c **car,** large die on white wove paper 6,000.
C48P1 4c **brt bl,** large die on white wove paper —

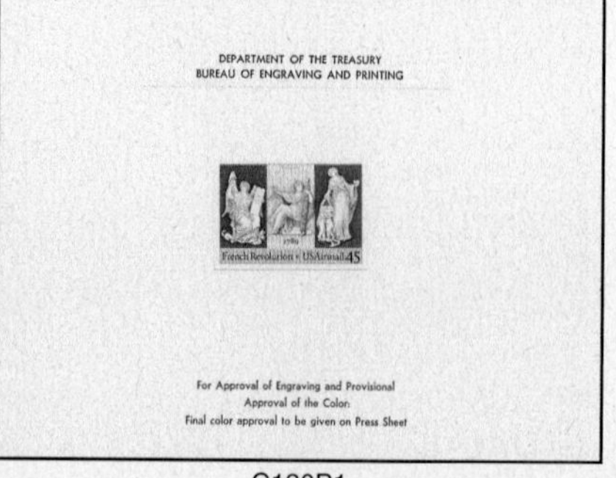

C120P1

C120P1	45c large hybrid die proof, pressed on large card imprinted for approval of engraving and color	1,250.

C128P1

C128P1	50c large hybrid die proof, pressed on large card imprinted for approval of engraving and color	1,250.

AIR POST SPECIAL DELIVERY

1934-36

CE1TC1a	16c large die on India paper	
	e. **black**	4,000.
CE1P2	16c **dk bl**, small die on white wove paper	*4,000.*
CE2P2	16c **red & bl**, small die on white wove paper	*4,000.*

SPECIAL DELIVERY

1885

E1TC1a	10c large die on India paper	
	e. **black**	3,000.
	f. **dark brown**	3,000.
E1TC2	10c small die on wove paper	
	b. **orange yellow**	*2,000.*
E1P1	10c **bl**, large die on India paper	600.
E1P2	10c **bl**, RA sm die on white wove paper	300.
E1P2a	10c **bl**, PP sm die on yelsh wove paper	2,500.
E1P3	10c **bl**, plate on India	35.
	Block of 4	175.
E1P4	10c **bl**, plate on card	30.
	Block of 4	150.
	P# blk. of 8, Impt.	*1,400.*

1888

E2TC1a	10c large die on India paper	
	e. **black**	3,000.
	f. **green**	3,000.
E2TC2	10c small die on India paper	
	b. **olive yellow**	2,000.
E2P1	10c **bl**, large die on India paper	750.
E2P2	10c **bl**, RA sm die on white wove paper	300.
E2P2a	10c **bl**, PP sm die on yelsh wove paper	2,600.
E2P3	10c **bl**, plate on India	35.
	Block of 4	200.
	P# blk. of 8	525.
E2P4	10c **bl**, plate on card	30.
	Block of 4	150.
	P# blk. of 8	—

1893

E3P1	10c **org**, large die on India paper	2,500.
E3P2	10c **org**, RA sm die on white wove paper	300.
E3P2a	10c **org**, PP sm die on yelsh wove paper	4,000.
E3P3	10c **org**, plate on India	75.
	Block of 4	325.
E3P4	10c **org**, plate on card	70.
	Block of 4	310.
	P# blk. of 8, Impt.	1,250.

1894-95

E4P1	10c **bl**, large die on India paper	550.
E4P2	10c **bl**, RA sm die on white wove paper	300.
E4P2a	10c **bl**, PP sm die on yelsh wove paper	3,000.
E4P5	10c **bl**, plate on stamp paper, pair	*6,500.*
E5P5	10c **bl**, plate on stamp paper, pair	*3,500.*
	Block of 4	—
	P# blk. of 6, Impt.	*27,500.*

1902

E6TC1a	10c large die on India paper	
	e. **orange**	3,750.
	f. **black**	3,750.
	g. **rose red**	*3,750.*
E6P1	10c **ultra**, large die on wove paper	*3,500.*
E6P2	10c **ultra**, RA sm die on white wove paper	300.
E6P2a	10c **ultra**, PP sm die on yelsh wove paper	2,500.

1908

E7TC2	10c small die on India paper	
	b. **blue**	*3,500.*
	c. **green**	*3,500.*
E7P1	10c **grn**, large die on India paper	2,750.
E7P2	10c **grn**, sm die on white wove paper	2,000.
E7P2a	10c **grn**, PP sm die on yelsh wove paper	3,000.

1922

E12TC1a	10c large die on India paper	
	e. **black**	3,250.
E12P1	10c **dp ultra**, large die on India paper	2,000.
E12P1a	10c **dp ultra**, large die on white wove paper	2,250.

1925-54

E13P1	15c **dp org**, large die on India paper	2,000.
E13P2	15c **dp org**, small die on white wove paper	*3,000.*
E14P1	20c **blk**, large die on India paper	2,000.
E14P2	20c **black**, small die on white wove paper	1,500.
E14TC1a	20c large die on India paper	
	e. **purple**	4,000.
E17P2	13c **bl**, small die on white or yelsh wove paper	*3,000.*
E20P1	20c **dp bl**, large die on India paper	3,000.

REGISTRATION

1911

F1TC1d	10c Large die on glazed card	
	e. **black**	1,500.
F1P1	10c **ultra**, large die on India paper	10,000.
F1P2	10c **ultra**, sm die on white wove paper	2,000.
F1P2a	10c **ultra**, PP sm die on yelsh wove paper	3,000.

POSTAGE DUE

1879

J1TC1a	1c large die on India paper	
	e. **black**	500.
	f. **gray black**	500.
	g. **ultramarine**	500.
	h. **blue**	500.
	i. **blue green**	500.
	j. **orange**	500.
	k. **red orange**	500.
	l. **olive bister**	500.
J1TC2	1c small die on India paper	
	b. **orange**	100.
J1TC4	1c plate on card	
	a. **black**	50.
J1P1	1c **brn**, large die on India paper	250.
J1P2	1c **brn**, RA sm die on white wove paper	100.
J1P2a	1c **brn**, PP sm die on yelsh wove paper	750.
J1P3	1c **brn**, plate on India	22.
	Block of 4	105.
	P# blk. of 12	450.
J1P4	1c **brn**, plate on card	15.
	Block of 4	90.
J2TC1a	2c large die on India paper	
	e. **black**	500.
	f. **gray black**	500.
	g. **ultramarine**	500.
	h. **blue**	500.
	i. **blue green**	500.
	j. **orange**	500.
	k. **red orange**	500.
	l. **sepia**	500.
J2TC2	2c small die on India paper	
	b. **orange**	100.
J2P1	2c **brn**, large die on India paper	250.
	a. **dk brn**, large die on India paper	—
J2P2	2c **brn**, RA sm die on white wove paper	100.
J2P2a	2c **brn**, PP sm die on yelsh wove paper	750.
J2P3	2c **brn**, plate on India	20.
	Block of 4	90.
	P# blk. of 12	425.
J2P4	2c **brn**, plate on card	15.
	Block of 4	90.
J3TC1a	3c large die on India paper	
	e. **black**	500.
	f. **ultramarine**	500.
	g. **blue**	500.
	h. **blue green**	500.
	i. **orange**	500.
	j. **red orange**	500.
	k. **light brown**	500.
	l. **olive yellow**	—
J3TC2	3c small die on India paper	
	b. **gray black**	100.
	c. **orange**	500.
J3P1	3c **brn**, large die on India paper	250.
	a. **dk brn**, large die on India paper	—
J3P2	3c **brn**, RA sm die on white wove paper	100.
	b. **dk brn**, RA sm die on India paper	—
J3P2a	3c **brn**, PP sm die on yelsh wove paper	750.
J3P3	3c **brn**, plate on India	20.
	Block of 4	90.
	P# blk. of 12	425.
J3P4	3c **brn**, plate on card	15.
	Block of 4	90.
J4TC1a	5c large die on India paper	
	e. **black**	500.
	f. **gray black**	500.
	g. **ultramarine**	500.
	h. **blue**	500.
	i. **blue green**	500.
	j. **orange**	500.
	k. **red orange**	500.
J4TC2	5c small die on India paper	
	b. **orange**	500.
J4P1	5c **brn**, large die on India paper	250.
	a. **dk brn**, large die on India paper	—
J4P2	5c **brn**, RA sm die on white wove paper	100.
J4P2a	5c **brn**, PP sm die on yelsh wove paper	750.
J4P3	5c **brn**, plate on India	20.
	Block of 4	90.
	P# blk. of 12	425.
J4P4	5c **brn**, plate on card	15.
	Block of 4	90.
J5TC1a	10c large die on India paper	
	e. **black**	500.
	f. **gray black**	500.
	g. **blue**	500.
	h. **olive yellow**	500.
	i. **blue green**	500.
	j. **orange**	500.
	k. **red orange**	500.
	l. **olive bister**	500.
	m. **sepia**	500.
	n. **gray**	500.
J5TC2	10c small die on India paper	
	b. **orange**	100.
J5P1	10c **brn**, large die on India paper	250.
	a. **dk brn**, large die on India paper	—
J5P2	10c **brn**, RA sm die on white wove paper	100.
J5P2a	10c **brn**, PP sm die on yelsh wove paper	750.
J5P3	10c **dk brn**, plate on India	32.
	Block of 4	145.
	P# blk. of 12	675.
J5P4	10c **brn**, plate on card	15.
	Block of 4	90.
J6TC1a	30c large die on India paper	
	e. **black**	500.
	f. **gray black**	500.
	g. **blue**	500.
	h. **blue green**	500.
	i. **orange**	500.
	j. **red orange**	500.
	k. **olive bister**	500.
J6TC2	30c small die on India paper	
	b. **olive yellow**	100.
	c. **orange**	100.
	d. **sepia**	100.
J6P1	30c **brn**, large die on India paper	250.
	a. **dk brn**, large die on India paper	—
J6P2	30c **brn**, RA sm die on white wove paper	100.
J6P2a	30c **brn**, PP sm die on yelsh wove paper	750.
J6P3	30c **dk brn**, plate on India	32.
	Block of 4	145.
	P# blk. of 12	675.
J6P4	30c **brn**, plate on card	15.
	Block of 4	90.
J7TC1a	50c large die on India paper	
	e. **black**	500.
	f. **gray black**	500.
	g. **blue**	500.
	i. **blue green**	500.
	j. **orange**	500.
	k. **red orange**	500.
	l. **olive bister**	500.
	m. **sepia**	500.
	n. **gray**	500.
J7TC2	50c small die on India paper	
	b. **blue**	100.
	c. **olive yellow**	100.
	d. **orange**	100.
J7P1	50c **brn**, large die on India paper	250.
	a. **dk brn**, large die on India paper	—
J7P2	50c **brn**, RA sm die on white wove paper	100.
J7P2a	50c **brn**, PP sm die on yelsh wove paper	750.
J7P3	50c **dk brn**, plate on India	32.
	Block of 4	145.
	P# blk. of 12	675.
J7P4	50c **brn**, plate on card	15.
	Block of 4	90.
J1P1-J7P1	1c-50c **brown**, hybrid large die proofs on India paper, cut close and pressed on die sunk card in a "H" pattern	*1,350.*
	Nos. J1P3-J7P3 (7)	178.00
	Nos. J1P4-J7P4 (7)	105.00

1887

J15P2a	1c **red brn**, PP sm die on yelsh wove paper	1,000.
J15P4	1c **red brn**, plate on card	15.
J16P2a	2c **red brn**, PP sm die on yelsh wove paper	1,000.
J16P4	2c **red brn**, plate on card	15.
J17P2a	3c **red brn**, PP sm die on yelsh wove paper	1,000.
J17P4	3c **red brn**, plate on card	20.
J18P2a	5c **red brn**, PP sm die on yelsh wove paper	1,000.
J18P4	5c **red brn**, plate on card	15.
J19P2a	10c **red brn**, PP sm die on yelsh wove paper	1,000.
J19P3	10c **red brn**, plate on India	19.
	Block of 4	90.
	P# blk. of 12	360.
J19P4	10c **red brn**, plate on card	25.
J20P2a	30c **red brn**, PP sm die on yelsh wove paper	1,000.
J20P3	30c **red brn**, plate on India	19.
	Block of 4	90.
	P# blk. of 12	360.
J20P4	30c **red brn**, plate on card	20.
J21P2a	50c **red brn**, PP sm die on yelsh wove paper	1,000.
J21P3	50c **red brn**, plate on India	45.
	Block of 4	210.
	P# blk. of 12	900.
J21P4	50c **red brn**, plate on card	25.
	Nos. J15P4-J21P4 (7)	135.00

1891-93

J22P1	1c **brt cl**, large die on India paper	140.
J22P2	1c **brt cl**, RA sm die on white wove paper	125.
J22P2a	1c **brt cl**, PP sm die on yelsh wove paper	500.
J22P3	1c **brt cl**, plate on India	12.
	Block of 4	65.
J22P4	1c **brt cl**, plate on card	17.
	Block of 4	80.
	P# blk. of 12	—
J22P5	1c **br cl**, plate on stamp paper, pair	*425.*
J23P1	2c **brt cl**, large die on India paper	140.
J23P2	2c **brt cl**, RA sm die on white wove paper	125.
J23P2a	2c **brt cl**, PP sm die on yelsh wove paper	500.
J23P3	2c **brt cl**, plate on India	12.
	Block of 4	65.
J23P4	2c **brt cl**, plate on card	17.
	Block of 4	80.
	P# blk. of 12	—
J23P5	2c **br cl**, plate on stamp paper, pair	*425.*
J24P1	3c **brt cl**, large die on India paper	140.

J24P2 3c **brt cl,** RA sm die on white wove paper 125.
J24P2a 3c **brt cl,** PP sm die on yelsh wove paper 500.
J24P3 3c **brt cl,** plate on India 12.
Block of 4 65.
J24P4 3c **brt cl,** plate on card 17.
Block of 4 80.
P# blk. of 12 —
J24P5 3c **br cl,** plate on stamp paper, pair *425.*
J25P1 5c **brt cl,** large die on India paper 140.
J25P2 5c **brt cl,** RA sm die on white wove paper 125.
J25P2a 5c **brt cl,** PP sm die on yelsh wove paper 500.
J25P3 5c **brt cl,** plate on India 12.
Block of 4 65.
J25P4 5c **brt cl,** plate on card 17.
Block of 4 80.
P# blk. of 12 —
J25P5 5c **br cl,** plate on stamp paper, pair *425.*
J26P1 10c **brt cl,** large die on India paper 140.
J26P2 10c **brt cl,** RA sm die on white wove paper 125.
J26P2a 10c **brt cl,** PP sm die on yelsh wove paper 500.
J26P3 10c **brt cl,** plate on India 12.
Block of 4 65.
J26P4 10c **brt cl,** plate on card 17.
Block of 4 80.
P# blk. of 12 —
J26P5 10c **br cl,** plate on stamp paper, pair *425.*
J27P1 30c **brt cl,** large die on India paper 140.
J27P2 30c **brt cl,** RA sm die on white wove paper 125.
J27P2a 30c **brt cl,** PP sm die on yelsh wove paper 500.
J27P3 30c **brt cl,** plate on India 28.
Block of 4 140.
J27P4 30c **brt cl,** plate on card 17.
Block of 4 80.
P# blk. of 12 —
J27P5 30c **br cl,** plate on stamp paper, pair *500.*
J28P1 50c **brt cl,** large die on India paper 140.
J28P2 50c **brt cl,** RA sm die on white wove paper 125.
J28P2a 50c **brt cl,** PP sm die on yelsh wove paper 500.
J28P3 50c **brt cl,** plate on India 19.
Block of 4 90.
J28P4 50c **brt cl,** plate on card 17.
Block of 4 80.
P# blk. of 12 —
J28P5 50c **br cl,** plate on stamp paper, pair *500.*
Nos. J22P3-J28P3 (7) 107.00
Nos. J22P4-J28P4 (7) 119.00

Values for Nos. J22P5-J28P5 are for pairs with original gum and minor faults.

1894

J31P1 1c **cl,** large die on India paper 165.
J31P2 1c **cl,** RA sm die on white wove paper 120.
J31P2a 1c **cl,** PP sm die on yelsh wove paper 500.
J31P5 1c **cl,** plate on stamp paper, pair *225.*
Block of 4 *500.*
J32P1 2c **brt cl,** large die on India paper 165.
J32P2 2c **brt cl,** RA sm die on white wove paper 120.
J32P2a 2c **brt cl,** PP sm die on yelsh wove paper 500.
J32P4 2c **brt cl,** plate on card 200.
Block of 4 900.
P# blk. of 6 3,500.
J33P1 3c **brt cl,** large die on India paper 165.
J33P2 3c **brt cl,** RA sm die on white wove paper 120.
J33P2a 3c **brt cl,** PP sm die on yelsh wove paper 500.
J34P1 5c **brt cl,** large die on India paper 165.
J34P2 5c **brt cl,** RA sm die on white wove paper 120.
J34P2a 5c **brt cl,** PP sm die on yelsh wove paper 500.
J35P1 10c **brt cl,** large die on India paper 165.
J35P2 10c **brt cl,** RA sm die on white wove paper 120.
J35P2a 10c **brt cl,** PP sm die on yelsh wove paper 500.
J36P1 30c **brt cl,** large die on India paper 165.
J36P2 30c **brt cl,** RA sm die on white wove paper 120.
J36P2a 30c **brt cl,** PP sm die on yelsh wove paper 500.
J37P1 50c **brt cl,** large die on India paper 165.
J37P2 50c **brt cl,** RA sm die on white wove paper 120.
J37P2a 50c **brt cl,** PP sm die on yelsh wove paper 500.

1925

J68P1 ½c **dull red,** large die on India paper *5,750.*

1930-31

J69P1 ½c **dp cl,** large die on India paper 450.
J70P1 1c **dp cl,** large die on India paper 450.
J71P1 2c **dp cl,** large die on India paper 450.
J72P1 3c **dp cl,** large die on India paper 450.
J73P1 5c **dp cl,** large die on India paper 450.
J74P1 10c **dp cl,** large die on India paper 450.
J75P1 30c **dp cl,** large die on India paper 450.
J76P1 50c **dp cl,** large die on India paper 450.
J77P1 $1 **dp cl,** large die on India paper 1,750.
J78P1 $5 **dp cl,** large die on India paper 1,750.

PARCEL POST POSTAGE DUE

1912

JQ1P1 1c **dk grn,** large die on India paper 600.
JQ1P2 1c **dk grn,** sm die on white wove paper 500.
JQ1P2a 1c **dk grn,** PP sm die on yelsh wove paper 750.
JQ2P1 2c **dk grn,** large die on India paper 600.
JQ2P2 2c **dk grn,** sm die on white wove paper 500.
JQ2P2a 2c **dk grn,** PP sm die on yelsh wove paper 750.
JQ3P1 5c **dk grn,** large die on India paper 600.
JQ3P2 5c **dk grn,** sm die on white wove paper 500.
JQ3P2a 5c **dk grn,** PP sm die on yelsh wove paper 700.
JQ4P1 10c **dk grn,** large die on India paper 600.
JQ4P2 10c **dk grn,** sm die on white wove paper 500.
JQ4P2a 10c **dk grn,** PP sm die on yelsh wove paper 700.
JQ5P1 25c **dk grn,** large die on India paper 600.
JQ5P2 25c **dk grn,** sm die on white wove paper 500.
JQ5P2a 25c **dk grn,** PP sm die on yelsh wove paper 700.

Specialists have questioned the existence of genuine examples of Nos. JQ1P2, JQ2P2, JQ3P2, JQ4P2 and JQ5P2. The editors would like to see recent authenticated evidence of their existence.

CARRIERS

1851

LO1TC3 1c plate on India paper
a. **deep green** 250.
Block of 4 1,250.
LO1TC5 1c Plate on wove paper
a. **orange** 350.
LO1P1 1c **bl,** *(Franklin)* large die on India paper 800.
LO1P2 1c **bl,** *(Franklin)* RA sm die on white wove paper 300.
LO1P2a 1c **bl,** *(Franklin)* PP sm die on yelsh wove paper 1,500.
LO1P3 1c **bl,** *(Franklin)* plate on India 50.
Block of 4 210.
Cracked plate —
LO1P4 1c **bl,** *(Franklin)* plate on card 30.
Block of 4 125.
Cracked plate —
LO2TC3 plate on India paper
a. **deep green** 250.
Block of 4 1,250.
LO2TC5 plate on wove paper
a. **orange** 350.
LO2P1 1c **bl,** *(Eagle)* large die on India paper 800.
LO2P2 1c **bl,** *(Eagle)* RA sm die on white wove paper 300.
LO2P2a 1c **bl,** *(Eagle)* PP sm die on yelsh wove paper 1,500.
LO2P3 1c **bl,** *(Eagle)* plate on India 50.
Block of 4 210.
Pl # block of 8 675.
LO2P4 1c **bl,** *(Eagle)* plate on card 30.
Block of 4 125.

Nos. LO1P1 and LO2P1 exist only as hybrids.

LOCALS

1844

5L1P1 5c **blk,** large die on India paper *3,500.*

1855

15L18TC3 (1c) plate on India paper
a. **brown** —
b. **blue** —
c. **green** —
d. **reddish brown** —

OFFICIAL
AGRICULTURE

1873

O1TC1a 1c large die on India paper
e. **black** 500.
O1TC3 1c plate on India paper
a. **black** 75.
O1P1 1c **yel,** large die on India paper 80.
O1P2 1c **yel,** RA sm die on white wove paper 100.
O1P2a 1c **yel,** PP sm die on yelsh wove paper 700.
O1P3 1c **yel,** plate on India 20.
Block of 4 100.
O1P4 1c **yel,** plate on card 10.
Block of 4 50.
P# blk. of 12 225.
O2TC1a 2c large die on India paper
e. **black** 500.
O2TC3 2c plate on India paper
a. **black** 75.
O2P1 2c **yel,** large die on India paper 80.
O2P2 2c **yel,** RA sm die on white wove paper 100.
O2P2a 2c **yel,** PP sm die on yelsh wove paper 700.
O2P3 2c **yel,** plate on India 20.
Block of 4 100.
O2P4 2c **yel,** plate on card 10.
Block of 4 50.
P# blk. of 12 225.
O3TC1a 3c large die on India paper
e. **black** 500.
f. **deep green** 500.
g. **ultra** 500.
O3P1 3c **yel,** large die on India paper 80.
O3P2 3c **yel,** RA sm die on white wove paper 100.
O3P2a 3c **yel,** PP sm die on yelsh wove paper 700.
O3P3 3c **yel,** plate on India 20.
Block of 4 100.
O3P4 3c **yel,** plate on card 10.
Block of 4 50.
P# blk. of 12 225.
O4TC1a 6c large die on India paper
e. **black** 500.
O4TC3 6c plate on India paper
a. **black** 150.
O4P1 6c **yel,** large die on India paper 125.
O4P2 6c **yel,** RA sm die on white wove paper 100.
O4P2a 6c **yel,** PP sm die on yelsh wove paper 700.
O4P3 6c **yel,** plate on India 20.
Block of 4 100.
O4P4 6c **yel,** plate on card 10.
Block of 4 50.
P# blk. of 12 225.
O5TC1a 10c large die on India paper
e. **black** 500.
O5P1 10c **yel,** large die on India paper 80.
O5P2 10c **yel,** RA sm die on white wove paper 100.
O5P2a 10c **yel,** PP sm die on yelsh wove paper 700.
O5P3 10c **yel,** plate on India 20.
Block of 4 100.
O5P4 10c **yel,** plate on card 10.
Block of 4 50.
P# blk. of 12 225.
O6TC1a 12c large die on India paper
e. **black** 500.
O6TC3 12c plate on India paper
a. **black** 75.
O6P1 12c **yel,** large die on India paper 80.
O6P2 12c **yel,** RA sm die on white wove paper 100.
O6P2a 12c **yel,** PP sm die on yelsh wove paper 700.
O6P3 12c **yel,** plate on India 20.
Block of 4 100.
O6P4 12c **yel,** plate on card 10.
Block of 4 50.
P# blk. of 12 225.
O7P1 15c **yel,** large die on India paper 80.
O7P2 15c **yel,** RA sm die on white wove paper 100.
O7P2a 15c **yel,** PP sm die on yelsh wove paper 700.
O7P3 15c **yel,** plate on India 20.
Block of 4 100.
O7P4 15c **yel,** plate on card 10.
Block of 4 50.
P# blk. of 12 225.
O8P1 24c **yel,** large die on India paper 80.
O8P2 24c **yel,** RA sm die on white wove paper 100.
O8P2a 24c **yel,** PP sm die on yelsh wove paper 700.
O8P3 24c **yel,** plate on India 20.
Block of 4 100.
O8P4 24c **yel,** plate on card 10.
Block of 4 50.
P# blk. of 12 225.
O9TC1a 20c large die on India paper
e. **black** 500.
O9P1 30c **yel,** large die on India paper 80.
O9P2 30c **yel,** RA sm die on white wove paper 100.
O9P2a 30c **yel,** PP sm die on yelsh wove paper 700.
O9P3 30c **yel,** plate on India 20.
Block of 4 100.
O9P4 30c **yel,** plate on card 10.
Block of 4 50.
P# blk. of 12 225.
Nos. O1P3-O9P3 (9) 180.00
Nos. O1P4-O9P4 (9) 90.00

EXECUTIVE

O10P1 1c **car,** large die on India paper 100.
O10P2 1c **car,** RA sm die on white wove paper 100.
O10P2a 1c **car,** PP sm die on yelsh wove paper 700.
O10P3 1c **car,** plate on India 20.
Block of 4 100.
O10P4 1c **car,** plate on card 10.
Block of 4 50.
P# blk. of 12 225.
O11TC1a 2c large die on India paper
e. **black** 500.
f. **deep brown** 500.
O11TC3 2c plate on India paper
a. **black** 75.
b. **brown carmine** 75.
O11TC4 2c plate on card
a. **brown carmine** 75.
O11P1 2c **car,** large die on India paper 100.
O11P2 2c **car,** RA sm die on white wove paper 100.
O11P2a 2c **car,** PP sm die on yelsh wove paper 700.
O11P3 2c **car,** plate on India 20.
Block of 4 100.
O11P4 2c **car,** plate on card 10.
Block of 4 50.
P# blk. of 12 225.
Foreign entry of 6c Agriculture (pos. 40) —
O12TC1a 3c large die on India paper
e. **black** 500.
f. **deep green** 500.
O12TC3 3c plate on India paper
a. **black** 75.
O12P1 3c **car,** large die on India paper 100.
O12P2 3c **car,** RA sm die on white wove paper 100.
O12P2a 3c **car,** PP sm die on yelsh wove paper 700.
O12P3 3c **car,** plate on India 20.
Block of 4 100.
O12P4 3c **car,** plate on card 10.
Block of 4 50.
P# blk. of 12 225.
O13TC3 6c plate on India paper
a. **black** 90.
O13P1 6c **car,** large die on India paper 100.
O13P2 6c **car,** RA sm die on white wove paper 100.
O13P2a 6c **car,** PP sm die on yelsh wove paper 700.
O13P3 6c **car,** plate on India 20.
Block of 4 125.
O13P4 6c **car,** plate on card 10.
Block of 4 85.
P# blk. of 12 350.
O14TC3 10c plate on India paper
a. **black** 90.
O14P1 10c **car,** large die on India paper 100.
O14P2 10c **car,** RA sm die on white wove paper 100.
O14P2a 10c **car,** PP sm die on yelsh wove paper 700.
O14P3 10c **car,** plate on India 20.
Block of 4 100.
O14P4 10c **car,** plate on card 10.
Block of 4 50.
P# blk. of 12 225.
Nos. O10P3-O14P3 (5) 100.00
Nos. O10P4-O14P4 (5) 50.00

INTERIOR

No.	Description	Value
O15P1	1c **ver,** large die on India paper	80.
O15P2	1c **ver,** RA sm die on white wove paper	100.
O15P2a	1c **ver,** PP sm die on yelsh wove paper	700.
O15P3	1c **ver,** plate on India	20.
	Block of 4	100.
O15P4	1c **ver,** plate on card	10.
	Block of 4	50.
	P# blk. of 12	225.
O16TC1a	2c large die on India paper	
	e. **black**	500.
	f. **deep brown**	500.
O16P1	2c **ver,** large die on India paper	80.
O16P2	2c **ver,** RA sm die on white wove paper	100.
O16P2a	2c **ver,** PP sm die on yelsh wove paper	700.
O16P3	2c **ver,** plate on India	20.
	Block of 4	100.
O16P4	2c **ver,** plate on card	10.
	Block of 4	50.
	P# blk. of 10	200.
O17TC1a	3c large die on India paper	
	e. **black**	500.
	f. **deep green**	500.
O17TC3	3c plate on India paper	
	a. **black**	90.
O17P1	3c **ver,** large die on India paper	80.
O17P2	3c **ver,** RA sm die on white wove paper	100.
O17P2a	3c **ver,** PP sm die on yelsh wove paper	700.
O17P3	3c **ver,** plate on India	20.
	Block of 4	100.
O17P4	3c **ver,** plate on card	10.
	Block of 4	50.
	P# blk. of 10	225.
O18P1	6c **ver,** large die on India paper	80.
O18P2	6c **ver,** RA sm die on white wove paper	100.
O18P2a	6c **ver,** PP sm die on yelsh wove paper	700.
O18P3	6c **ver,** plate on India	20.
	Block of 4	100.
O18P4	6c **ver,** plate on card	10.
	Block of 4	50.
	P# blk. of 12	250.
O19P1	10c **ver,** large die on India paper	80.
O19P2	10c **ver,** RA sm die on white wove paper	100.
O19P2a	10c **ver,** PP sm die on yelsh wove paper	700.
O19P3	10c **ver,** plate on India	20.
	Block of 4	100.
O19P4	10c **ver,** plate on card	10.
	Block of 4	50.
	P# blk. of 12	225.
O20P1	12c **ver,** large die on India paper	80.
O20P2	12c **ver,** RA sm die on white wove paper	100.
O20P2a	12c **ver,** PP sm die on yelsh wove paper	700.
O20P3	12c **ver,** plate on India	20.
	Block of 4	100.
O20P4	12c **ver,** plate on card	10.
	Block of 4	50.
	P# blk. of 12	225.
O21P1	15c **ver,** large die on India paper	80.
O21P2	15c **ver,** RA sm die on white wove paper	100.
O21P2a	15c **ver,** PP sm die on yelsh wove paper	700.
O21P3	15c **ver,** plate on India	20.
	Block of 4	100.
O21P4	15c **ver,** plate on card	10.
	Block of 4	50.
	P# blk. of 12	225.
O22P1	24c **ver,** large die on India paper	80.
O22P2	24c **ver,** RA sm die on white wove paper	100.
O22P2a	24c **ver,** PP sm die on yelsh wove paper	700.
O22P3	24c **ver,** plate on India	20.
	Block of 4	100.
O22P4	24c **ver,** plate on card	10.
	Block of 4	50.
	P# blk. of 12	225.
O23P1	30c **ver,** large die on India paper	80.
O23P2	30c **ver,** RA sm die on white wove paper	100.
O23P2a	30c **ver,** PP sm die on yelsh wove paper	700.
O23P3	30c **ver,** plate on India	20.
	Block of 4	100.
O23P4	30c **ver,** plate on card	10.
	Block of 4	50.
	P# blk. of 12	225.
O24P1	90c **ver,** large die on India paper	80.
O24P2	90c **ver,** RA sm die on white wove paper	100.
O24P2a	90c **ver,** PP sm die on yelsh wove paper	700.
O24P3	90c **ver,** plate on India	20.
	Block of 4	100.
O24P4	90c **ver,** plate on card	10.
	Block of 4	50.
	P# blk. of 12	225.
	Nos. O15P3-O24P3 (10)	200.00
	Nos. O15P4-O24P4 (10)	100.00

JUSTICE

No.	Description	Value
O25P1	1c **pur,** large die on India paper	80.
O25P2	1c **pur,** RA sm die on white wove paper	100.
O25P2a	1c **pur,** PP sm die on yelsh wove paper	700.
O25P3	1c **pur,** plate on India	20.
	Block of 4	100.
O25P4	1c **pur,** plate on card	10.
	Block of 4	50.
	P# blk. of 12	225.
O26P1	2c **pur,** large die on India paper	80.
O26P2	2c **pur,** RA sm die on white wove paper	100.
O26P2a	2c **pur,** PP sm die on yelsh wove paper	700.
O26P3	2c **pur,** plate on India	20.
	Block of 4	100.
O26P4	2c **pur,** plate on card	10.
	Block of 4	50.
	P# blk. of 12	225.
O27TC1a	3c large die on India paper	
	e. **black**	500.
	f. **deep green**	500.
O27TC3	3c plate on India paper	
	a. **black**	90.
	b. **bister yellow**	90.
	c. **dull orange**	90.
	d. **black violet**	90.
	e. **violet**	90.
	f. **pale violet**	90.
O27P1	3c **pur,** large die on India paper	80.
O27P2	3c **pur,** RA sm die on white wove paper	100.
O27P2a	3c **pur,** PP sm die on yelsh wove paper	700.
O27P3	3c **pur,** plate on India	20.
	Block of 4	100.
O27P4	3c **pur,** plate on card	10.
	Block of 4	50.
	P# blk. of 12	225.
	Plate Scratches	—
O28P1	6c **pur,** large die on India paper	80.
O28P2	6c **pur,** RA sm die on white wove paper	100.
O28P2a	6c **pur,** PP sm die on yelsh wove paper	700.
O28P3	6c **pur,** plate on India	20.
	Block of 4	100.
O28P4	6c **pur,** plate on card	10.
	Block of 4	50.
	P# blk. of 12	225.
O29P1	10c **pur,** large die on India paper	80.
O29P2	10c **pur,** RA sm die on white wove paper	100.
O29P2a	10c **pur,** PP sm die on yelsh wove paper	700.
O29P3	10c **pur,** plate on India	20.
	Block of 4	100.
O29P4	10c **pur,** plate on card	10.
	Block of 4	50.
	P# blk. of 10	225.
O30P1	12c **pur,** large die on India paper	80.
O30P2	12c **pur,** RA sm die on white wove paper	100.
O30P2a	12c **pur,** PP sm die on yelsh wove paper	700.
O30P3	12c **pur,** plate on India	20.
	Block of 4	100.
O30P4	12c **pur,** plate on card	10.
	Block of 4	50.
	P# blk. of 12	225.
O31P1	15c **pur,** large die on India paper	80.
O31P2	15c **pur,** RA sm die on white wove paper	100.
O31P2a	15c **pur,** PP sm die on yelsh wove paper	700.
O31P3	15c **pur,** plate on India	20.
	Block of 4	100.
O31P4	15c **pur,** plate on card	10.
	Block of 4	50.
	P# blk. of 10	225.
O32P1	24c **pur,** large die on India paper	80.
O32P2	24c **pur,** RA sm die on white wove paper	100.
O32P2a	24c **pur,** PP sm die on yelsh wove paper	700.
O32P3	24c **pur,** plate on India	20.
	Block of 4	100.
O32P4	24c **pur,** plate on card	10.
	Block of 4	50.
	P# blk. of 12	225.
	Short transfer (pos. 98)	—
O33P1	30c **pur,** large die on India paper	80.
O33P2	30c **pur,** RA sm die on white wove paper	100.
O33P2a	30c **pur,** PP sm die on yelsh wove paper	700.
O33P3	30c **pur,** plate on India	20.
	Block of 4	100.
O33P4	30c **pur,** plate on card	10.
	Block of 4	50.
	P# blk. of 12	225.
O34P1	90c **pur,** large die on India paper	80.
O34P2	90c **pur,** RA sm die on white wove paper	100.
O34P2a	90c **pur,** PP sm die on yelsh wove paper	700.
O34P3	90c **pur,** plate on India	20.
	Block of 4	100.
O34P4	90c **pur,** plate on card	10.
	Block of 4	50.
	P# blk. of 12	225.
	Nos. O25P3-O34P3 (10)	200.00
	Nos. O25P4-O34P4 (10)	100.00

NAVY

No.	Description	Value
O35TC3	1c plate on India paper	
	a. **black**	90.
O35P1	1c **ultra,** large die on India paper	80.
O35P2	1c **ultra,** RA sm die on white wove paper	100.
O35P2a	1c **ultra,** PP sm die on yelsh wove paper	700.
O35P3	1c **ultra,** plate on India	20.
	Block of 4	100.
O35P4	1c **ultra,** plate on card	10.
	Block of 4	50.
	P# blk. of 12	225.
O36TC1a	2c large die on India paper	
	e. **black**	500.
	f. **deep brown**	500.
O36TC5	2c plate on wove paper, imperf.	
	a. **deep green**	250.
	b. **greenish black**	250.
O36TC6	2c plate on wove paper, perf.	
	a. **deep green** on pinkish wove	250.
	b. **black**	250.
O36P1	2c **ultra,** large die on India paper	80.
O36P2	2c **ultra,** RA sm die on white wove paper	100.
O36P2a	2c **ultra,** PP sm die on yelsh wove paper	700.
O36P3	2c **ultra,** plate on India	20.
	Block of 4	100.
O36P4	2c **ultra,** plate on card	10.
	Block of 4	50.
	P# blk. of 12	225.
O37TC1a	3c large die on India paper	
	e. **black**	500.
	f. **deep green**	500.
O37TC3	3c plate on India paper	
	a. **black**	90.
O37P1	3c **ultra,** large die on India paper	80.
O37P2	3c **ultra,** RA sm die on white wove paper	100.
O37P2a	3c **ultra,** PP sm die on yelsh wove paper	700.
O37P3	3c **ultra,** plate on India	20.
	Block of 4	100.
O37P4	3c **ultra,** plate on card	10.
	Block of 4	50.
	P# blk. of 10	225.
O38P1	6c **ultra,** large die on India paper	80.
O38P2	6c **ultra,** RA sm die on white wove paper	100.
O38P2a	6c **ultra,** PP sm die on yelsh wove paper	700.
O38P3	6c **ultra,** plate on India	20.
	Block of 4	100.
O38P4	6c **ultra,** plate on card	15.
	Block of 4	75.
	P# blk. of 10	350.
O39P1	7c **ultra,** large die on India paper	80.
O39P2	7c **ultra,** RA sm die on white wove paper	100.
O39P2a	7c **ultra,** PP sm die on yelsh wove paper	700.
O39P3	7c **ultra,** plate on India	20.
	Block of 4	100.
O39P4	7c **ultra,** plate on card	10.
	Block of 4	50.
	P# blk. of 10	225.
O40P1	10c **ultra,** large die on India paper	80.
O40P2	10c **ultra,** RA sm die on white wove paper	100.
O40P2a	10c **ultra,** PP sm die on yelsh wove paper	700.
O40P3	10c **ultra,** plate on India	20.
	Block of 4	100.
	P# blk. of 12	—
O40P4	10c **ultra,** plate on card	10.
	Block of 4	50.
	P# blk. of 12	225.
O41P1	12c **ultra,** large die on India paper	80.
O41P2	12c **ultra,** RA sm die on white wove paper	100.
O41P2a	12c **ultra,** PP sm die on yelsh wove paper	700.
O41P3	12c **ultra,** plate on India	20.
	Block of 4	100.
O41P4	12c **ultra,** plate on card	10.
	Block of 4	50.
	P# blk. of 12	225.
O42P1	15c **ultra,** large die on India paper	80.
O42P2	15c **ultra,** RA sm die on white wove paper	100.
O42P2a	15c **ultra,** PP sm die on yelsh wove paper	700.
O42P3	15c **ultra,** plate on India	20.
	Block of 4	100.
O42P4	15c **ultra,** plate on card	10.
	Block of 4	50.
	P# blk. of 12	225.
O43P1	24c **ultra,** large die on India paper	80.
O43P2	24c **ultra,** RA sm die on white wove paper	100.
O43P2a	24c **ultra,** PP sm die on yelsh wove paper	700.
O43P3	24c **ultra,** plate on India	20.
	Block of 4	100.
O43P4	24c **ultra,** plate on card	10.
	Block of 4	50.
	P# blk. of 12	225.
O44P1	30c **ultra,** large die on India paper	80.
O44P2	30c **ultra,** RA sm die on white wove paper	100.
O44P2a	30c **ultra,** PP sm die on yelsh wove paper	700.
O44P3	30c **ultra,** plate on India	20.
	Block of 4	100.
O44P4	30c **ultra,** plate on card	10.
	Block of 4	50.
	P# blk. of 12	225.
O45P1	90c **ultra,** large die on India paper	80.
O45P2	90c **ultra,** RA sm die on white wove paper	100.
O45P2a	90c **ultra,** PP sm die on yelsh wove paper	700.
O45P3	90c **ultra,** plate on India	20.
	Block of 4	100.

O45P4 90c **ultra,** plate on card 10.
Block of 4 50.
P# blk. of 12 225.
Short transfer at upper left (106, pos. 1, 5) —
Nos. O35P3-O45P3 (11) 220.00
Nos. O35P4-O45P4 (11) 115.00

POST OFFICE

O47P1 1c **blk,** large die on India paper 80.
O47P2 1c **blk,** RA sm die on white wove paper 100.
O47P2a 1c **blk,** PP sm die on yelsh wove paper 700.
O47P3 1c **blk,** plate on India 20.
Block of 4 100.
O47P4 1c **blk,** plate on card 10.
Block of 4 50.
P# blk. of 10 225.
O48TC1a 2c large die on India paper
e. **deep brown** 500.
O48P1 2c **blk,** large die on India paper 80.
O48P2 2c **blk,** RA sm die on white wove paper 100.
O48P2a 2c **blk,** PP sm die on yelsh wove paper 700.
O48P3 2c **blk,** plate on India 20.
Block of 4 100.
O48P4 2c **blk,** plate on card 10.
Block of 4 50.
P# blk. of 14 225.
O49TC1a 3c large die on India paper
e. **deep green** 500.
O49P1 3c **blk,** large die on India paper 80.
O49P2 3c **blk,** RA sm die on white wove paper 100.
O49P2a 3c **blk,** PP sm die on yelsh wove paper 700.
O49P3 3c **blk,** plate on India 20.
Block of 4 100.
O49P4 3c **blk,** plate on card 10.
Block of 4 50.
P# blk. of 12 225.
O50TC1a 6c large die on India paper
e. **deep brown** 500.
f. **brown carmine** 500.
O50P1 6c **blk,** large die on India paper 80.
O50P2 6c **blk,** RA sm die on white wove paper 100.
O50P2a 6c **blk,** PP sm die on yelsh wove paper 700.
O50P3 6c **blk,** plate on India 20.
Block of 4 100.
O50P4 6c **blk,** plate on card 10.
Block of 4 50.
P# blk. of 12 225.
O51P1 10c **blk,** large die on India paper 80.
O51P2 10c **blk,** RA sm die on white wove paper 100.
O51P2a 10c **blk,** PP sm die on yelsh wove paper 700.
O51P3 10c **blk,** plate on India 20.
Block of 4 100.
O51P4 10c **blk,** plate on card 10.
Block of 4 50.
P# blk. of 12 225.
O52P1 12c **blk,** large die on India paper 80.
O52P2 12c **blk,** RA sm die on white wove paper 100.
O52P2a 12c **blk,** PP sm die on yelsh wove paper 700.
O52P3 12c **blk,** plate on India 20.
Block of 4 100.
O52P4 12c **blk,** plate on card 10.
Block of 4 50.
P# blk. of 12 225.
O53P1 15c **blk,** large die on India paper 80.
O53P2 15c **blk,** RA sm die on white wove paper 100.
O53P2a 15c **blk,** PP sm die on yelsh wove paper 700.
O53P3 15c **blk,** plate on India 20.
Block of 4 100.
O53P4 15c **blk,** plate on card 10.
Block of 4 50.
P# blk. of 12 225.
O54P1 24c **blk,** large die on India paper 80.
O54P2 24c **blk,** RA sm die on white wove paper 100.
O54P2a 24c **blk,** PP sm die on yelsh wove paper 700.
O54P3 24c **blk,** plate on India 20.
Block of 4 100.
O54P4 24c **blk,** plate on card 10.
Block of 4 50.
P# blk. of 12 225.
O55P1 30c **blk,** large die on India paper 80.
O55P2 30c **blk,** RA sm die on white wove paper 100.
O55P2a 30c **blk,** PP sm die on yelsh wove paper 700.
O55P3 30c **blk,** plate on India 20.
Block of 4 100.
O55P4 30c **blk,** plate on card 10.
Block of 4 50.
P# blk. of 12 225.
O56P1 90c **blk,** large die on India paper 80.
O56P2 90c **blk,** RA sm die on white wove paper 100.
O56P2a 90c **blk,** PP sm die on yelsh wove paper 700.
O56P3 90c **blk,** plate on India 20.
Block of 4 100.
O56P4 90c **blk,** plate on card 10.
Block of 4 50.
P# blk. of 12 225.
Nos. O47P3-O56P3 (10) 200.00
Nos. O47P4-O56P4 (10) 100.00

STATE

O57TC1a 1c large die on India paper
e. **black** 500.
f. **light ultramarine** 500.
O57TC3 1c plate on India paper
a. **black** 90.
O57P1 1c **grn,** large die on India paper 80.
O57P2 1c **grn,** RA sm die on white wove paper 100.
O57P2a 1c **grn,** PP sm die on yelsh wove paper 700.
O57P3 1c **grn,** plate on India 20.
Block of 4 100.
O57P4 1c **grn,** plate on card 10.
Block of 4 50.
P# blk. of 12 225.
O58TC1a 2c large die on India paper
e. **black** 500.
f. **deep brown** 500.
O58P1 2c **grn,** large die on India paper 80.
O58P2 2c **grn,** RA sm die on white wove paper 100.
O58P2a 2c **grn,** PP sm die on yelsh wove paper 700.
O58P3 2c **grn,** plate on India 20.
Block of 4 100.
O58P4 2c **grn,** plate on card 10.
Block of 4 50.
P# blk. of 10 225.
O59TC1a 3c large die on India paper
e. **black** 500.
O59P1 3c **grn,** large die on India paper 80.
O59P2 3c **grn,** RA sm die on white wove paper 100.
O59P2a 3c **grn,** PP sm die on yelsh wove paper 700.
O59P3 3c **grn,** plate on India 20.
Block of 4 100.
O59P4 3c **grn,** plate on card 10.
Block of 4 50.
P# blk. of 10 225.
O60P1 6c **grn,** large die on India paper 80.
O60P2 6c **grn,** RA sm die on white wove paper 100.
O60P2a 6c **grn,** PP sm die on yelsh wove paper 700.
O60P3 6c **grn,** plate on India 25.
Block of 4 125.
O60P4 6c **grn,** plate on card 16.
Block of 4 85.
P# blk. of 12 375.
O61P1 7c **grn,** large die on India paper 80.
O61P2 7c **grn,** RA sm die on white wove paper 100.
O61P2a 7c **grn,** PP sm die on yelsh wove paper 700.
O61P3 7c **grn,** plate on India 20.
Block of 4 100.
O61P4 7c **grn,** plate on card 10.
Block of 4 50.
P# blk. of 12 225.
O61TC3 10c plate on India paper
a. **black** 90.
O62P1 10c **grn,** large die on India paper 80.
O62P2 10c **grn,** RA sm die on white wove paper 100.
O62P2a 10c **grn,** PP sm die on yelsh wove paper 700.
O62P3 10c **grn,** plate on India 20.
Block of 4 100.
O62P4 10c **grn,** plate on card 10.
Block of 4 50.
P# blk. of 12 225.
O62TC3 10c plate on India paper
a. **black** 90.
O63P1 12c **grn,** large die on India paper 80.
O63P2 12c **grn,** RA sm die on white wove paper 100.
O63P2a 12c **grn,** PP sm die on yelsh wove paper 700.
O63P3 12c **grn,** plate on India 20.
Block of 4 100.
O63P4 12c **grn,** plate on card 10.
Block of 4 50.
P# blk. of 12 225.
O64P1 15c **grn,** large die on India paper 80.
O64P2 15c **grn,** RA sm die on white wove paper 100.
O64P2a 15c **grn,** PP sm die on yelsh wove paper 700.
O64P3 15c **grn,** plate on India 20.
Block of 4 100.
O64P4 15c **grn,** plate on card 10.
Block of 4 50.
P# blk. of 12 225.
O65P1 24c **grn,** large die on India paper 80.
O65P2 24c **grn,** RA sm die on white wove paper 100.
O65P2a 24c **grn,** PP sm die on yelsh wove paper 700.
O65P3 24c **grn,** plate on India 20.
Block of 4 100.
O65P4 24c **grn,** plate on card 10.
Block of 4 50.
P# blk. of 12 225.
O66P1 30c **grn,** large die on India paper 80.
O66P2 30c **grn,** RA sm die on white wove paper 100.
O66P2a 30c **grn,** PP sm die on yelsh wove paper 700.
O66P3 30c **grn,** plate on India 20.
Block of 4 100.
O66P4 30c **grn,** plate on card 10.
Block of 4 50.
P# blk. of 12 225.
O67TC1a 90c large die on India paper
e. **black** 500.
O67P1 90c **grn,** large die on India paper 80.
O67P2 90c **grn,** RA sm die on white wove paper 100.
O67P2a 90c **grn,** PP sm die on yelsh wove paper 700.
O67P3 90c **grn,** plate on India 20.
Block of 4 100.
O67P4 90c **grn,** plate on card 10.
Block of 4 50.
P# blk. of 12 225.
O68TC1a $2 large die on India paper
e. **violet & black** 2,500.
f. **brown red & black** 2,500.
g. **orange red & slate blue** 2,500.
O68P1 $2 **grn & blk,** large die on India paper 150.
O68P2 $2 **grn & blk,** RA sm die on white wove paper 125.
O68P2a $2 **grn & blk,** PP sm die on yelsh wove paper 850.
O68P3 $2 **grn & blk,** plate on India 100.
Block of 4 475.
Sheet of 10 *4,000.*
O68P4 $2 **grn & blk,** plate on card 35.
Block of 4 175.
Sheet of 10 *5,000.*
a. Invtd. center *13,500.*
Half sheet of 5 *70,000.*
O69P1 $5 **grn & blk,** large die on India paper 150.
O69P2 $5 **grn & blk,** RA sm die on white wove paper 125.
O69P2a $5 **grn & blk,** PP sm die on yelsh wove paper 850.
O69P3 $5 **grn & blk,** plate on India 100.
Block of 4 475.
Sheet of 10 *4,000.*
O69P4 $5 **grn & blk,** plate on card 35.
Block of 4 175.
Sheet of 10 *5,000.*
a. Invtd. center *9,500.*
Half sheet of 5 *47,500.*
Sheet of 10 *100,000.*
O70P1 $10 **grn & blk,** large die on India paper 150.
O70P2 $10 **grn & blk,** RA sm die on white wove paper 125.
O70P2a $10 **grn & blk,** PP sm die on yelsh wove paper 850.
O70P3 $10 **grn & blk,** plate on India 100.
Block of 4 475.
Sheet of 10 *4,000.*
O70P4 $10 **grn & blk,** plate on card 35.
Block of 4 —
Sheet of 10 *5,000.*
O71P1 $20 **grn & blk,** large die on India paper 150.
O71P2 $20 **grn & blk,** RA sm die on white wove paper 125.
O71P2a $20 **grn & blk,** PP sm die on yelsh wove paper 900.
O71P3 $20 **grn & blk,** plate on India 100.
Block of 4 475.
Sheet of 10 *4,000.*
O71P4 $20 **grn & blk,** plate on card 35.
Block of 4 175.
Sheet of 10 *8,500.*
a. Invtd. center
Block of 4 *40,000.*
Half sheet of 5 *50,000.*
Nos. O57P3-O71P3 (15) 625.00
Nos. O57P4-O71P4 (15) 256.00

Nos. O68P1 to O71P1 Large Dies exist as hybrids only.

TREASURY

O72TC1a 1c large die on India paper
e. **black** 500.
f. **light ultramarine** 500.
O72P1 1c **brn,** large die on India paper 80.
O72P2 1c **brn,** RA sm die on white wove paper 100.
O72P2a 1c **brn,** PP sm die on yelsh wove paper 700.
O72P3 1c **brn,** plate on India 20.
Block of 4 100.
O72P4 1c **brn,** plate on card 10.
Block of 4 50.
P# blk. of 12 225.
O73TC1a 2c large die on India paper
e. **black** 500.
O73P1 2c **brn,** large die on India paper 80.
O73P2 2c **brn,** RA sm die on white wove paper 100.
O73P2a 2c **brn,** PP sm die on yelsh wove paper 700.
O73P3 2c **brn,** plate on India 20.
Block of 4 100.
O73P4 2c **brn,** plate on card 10.
Block of 4 50.
P# blk. of 12 225.
O74TC1a 3c large die on India paper
e. **black** 500.
f. **deep green** 500.
O74P1 3c **brn,** large die on India paper 80.
O74P2 3c **brn,** RA sm die on white wove paper 100.
O74P2a 3c **brn,** PP sm die on yelsh wove paper 700.
O74P3 3c **brn,** plate on India 20.
Block of 4 100.
O74P4 3c **brn,** plate on card 10.
Block of 4 50.
P# blk. of 12 225.
O75TC1a 6c large die on India paper
e. **black** 500.

O75P1	6c **brn,** large die on India paper	80.
O75P2	6c **brn,** RA sm die on white wove paper	100.
O75P2a	6c **brn,** PP sm die on yelsh wove paper	700.
O75P3	6c **brn,** plate on India	20.
	Block of 4	100.
O75P4	6c **brn,** plate on card	15.
	Block of 4	75.
	P# blk. of 12	375.
O76P1	7c **brn,** large die on India paper	80.
O76P2	7c **brn,** RA sm die on white wove paper	100.
O76P2a	7c **brn,** PP sm die on yelsh wove paper	700.
O76P3	7c **brn,** plate on India	20.
	Block of 4	100.
O76P4	7c **brn,** plate on card	10.
	Block of 4	50.
	P# blk. of 12	225.
O77TC1a	10c large die on India paper	
	e. **black**	500.
O77P1	10c **brn,** large die on India paper	80.
O77P2	10c **brn,** RA sm die on white wove paper	100.
O77P2a	10c **brn,** PP sm die on yelsh wove paper	700.
O77P3	10c **brn,** plate on India	20.
	Block of 4	100.
O77P4	10c **brn,** plate on card	10.
	Block of 4	50.
	P# blk. of 12	225.
O78TC1a	12c large die on India paper	
	e. **black**	500.
O78P1	12c **brn,** large die on India paper	80.
O78P2	12c **brn,** RA sm die on white wove paper	100.
O78P2a	12c **brn,** PP sm die on yelsh wove paper	700.
O78P3	12c **brn,** plate on India	20.
	Block of 4	100.
O78P4	12c **brn,** plate on card	10.
	Block of 4	50.
	P# blk. of 12	225.
O79TC1a	15c large die on India paper	
	e. **black**	500.
O79P1	15c **brn,** large die on India paper	80.
O79P2	15c **brn,** RA sm die on white wove paper	100.
O79P2a	15c **brn,** PP sm die on yelsh wove paper	700.
O79P3	15c **brn,** plate on India	20.
	Block of 4	100.
O79P4	15c **brn,** plate on card	10.
	Block of 4	50.
	P# blk. of 12	275.
O80TC1a	24c large die on India paper	
	e. **black**	500.
O80P1	24c **brn,** large die on India paper	80.
O80P2	24c **brn,** RA sm die on white wove paper	100.
O80P2a	24c **brn,** PP sm die on yelsh wove paper	700.
O80P3	24c **brn,** plate on India	20.
	Block of 4	100.
O80P4	24c **brn,** plate on card	10.
	Block of 4	45.
	P# blk. of 12	225.
O81TC1a	30c large die on India paper	
	e. **black**	500.
O81P1	30c **brn,** large die on India paper	80.
O81P2	30c **brn,** RA sm die on white wove paper	100.
O81P2a	30c **brn,** PP sm die on yelsh wove paper	700.
O81P3	30c **brn,** plate on India	20.
	Block of 4	100.
O81P4	30c **brn,** plate on card	10.
	Block of 4	45.
	P# blk. of 12	225.
O82TC1a	90c large die on India paper	
	e. **black**	500.
O82P1	90c **brn,** large die on India paper	80.
O82P2	90c **brn,** RA sm die on white wove paper	100.
O82P2a	90c **brn,** PP sm die on yelsh wove paper	700.
O82P3	90c **brn,** plate on India	20.
	Block of 4	100.
O82P4	90c **brn,** plate on card	10.
	Block of 4	50.
	P# blk. of 12	225.
	Nos. O72P3-O82P3 (11)	220.00
	Nos. O72P4-O82P4 (11)	115.00

WAR

O83TC1a	1c large die on India paper	
	e. **black**	500.
	f. **light ultramarine**	500.
O83TC3	1c plate on India paper	
	a. **black**	80.
O83P1	1c **rose,** large die on India paper	80.
O83P2	1c **rose,** RA sm die on white wove paper	100.
O83P2a	1c **rose,** PP sm die on yelsh wove paper	700.
O83P3	1c **rose,** plate on India	20.
	Block of 4	100.
O83P4	1c **rose,** plate on card	10.
	Block of 4	50.
	P# blk. of 12	225.
O84TC1a	2c large die on India paper	
	e. **black**	500.
	f. **deep brown**	500.
O84TC3	2c plate on India paper	
	a. **black**	80.
O84TC4	2c plate on card	
	a. **black**	75.
O84P1	2c **rose,** large die on India paper	80.
O84P2	2c **rose,** RA sm die on white wove paper	100.
O84P2a	2c **rose,** PP sm die on yelsh wove paper	700.
O84P3	2c **rose,** plate on India	20.
	Block of 4	100.
O84P4	2c **rose,** plate on card	10.
	Block of 4	50.
O85TC1a	3c large die on India paper	
	e. **black**	500.
	f. **deep green**	500.
	g. **chocolate**	675.
	h. **porcelain blue**	675.
	i. **ultra**	675.
O85P1	3c **rose,** large die on India paper	80.
O85P2	3c **rose,** RA sm die on white wove paper	100.
O85P2a	3c **rose,** PP sm die on yelsh wove paper	700.
O85P3	3c **rose,** plate on India	20.
	Block of 4	100.
O85P4	3c **rose,** plate on card	10.
	Block of 4	50.
	Plate flaw at upper left (32R20)	—
O86TC3	6c plate on India paper	
	a. **black**	80.
O86P1	6c **rose,** large die on India paper	80.
O86P2	6c **rose,** RA sm die on white wove paper	100.
O86P2a	6c **rose,** PP sm die on yelsh wove paper	700.
O86P3	6c **rose,** plate on India	20.
	Block of 4	100.
O86P4	6c **rose,** plate on card	10.
	Block of 4	50.
	P# blk. of 12	225.
O87P1	7c **rose,** large die on India paper	80.
O87P2	7c **rose,** RA sm die on white wove paper	100.
O87P2a	7c **rose,** PP sm die on yelsh wove paper	700.
O87P3	7c **rose,** plate on India	20.
	Block of 4	100.
O87P4	7c **rose,** plate on card	10.
	Block of 4	50.
	P# blk. of 10	225.
O88P1	10c **rose,** large die on India paper	80.
O88P2	10c **rose,** RA sm die on white wove paper	100.
O88P2a	10c **rose,** PP sm die on yelsh wove paper	700.
O88P3	10c **rose,** plate on India	20.
	Block of 4	100.
O88P4	10c **rose,** plate on card	10.
	Block of 4	50.
	P# blk. of 10	225.
O89TC3	12c plate on India paper	
	a. **black**	80.
O89P1	12c **rose,** large die on India paper	80.
O89P2	12c **rose,** RA sm die on white wove paper	100.
O89P2a	12c **rose,** PP sm die on yelsh wove paper	700.
O89P3	12c **rose,** plate on India	20.
	Block of 4	100.
O89P4	12c **rose,** plate on card	10.
	Block of 4	50.
	P# blk. of 12	225.
O90P1	15c **rose,** large die on India paper	80.
O90P2	15c **rose,** RA sm die on white wove paper	100.
O90P2a	15c **rose,** PP sm die on yelsh wove paper	700.
O90P3	15c **rose,** plate on India	20.
	Block of 4	100.
O90P4	15c **rose,** plate on card	10.
	Block of 4	50.
	P# blk. of 12	225.
O91P1	24c **rose,** large die on India paper	80.
O91P2	24c **rose,** RA sm die on white wove paper	100.
O91P2a	24c **rose,** PP sm die on yelsh wove paper	700.
O91P3	24c **rose,** plate on India	20.
	Block of 4	100.
O91P4	24c **rose,** plate on card	10.
	Block of 4	50.
	P# blk. of 12	225.
O92P1	30c **rose,** large die on India paper	80.
O92P2	30c **rose,** RA sm die on white wove paper	100.
O92P2a	30c **rose,** PP sm die on yelsh wove paper	700.
O92P3	30c **rose,** plate on India	20.
	Block of 4	100.
O92P4	30c **rose,** plate on card	10.
	Block of 4	50.
	P# blk. of 12	225.
O93P1	90c **rose,** large die on India paper	80.
O93P2	90c **rose,** RA sm die on white wove paper	100.
O93P2a	90c **rose,** PP sm die on yelsh wove paper	700.
O93P3	90c **rose,** plate on India	20.
	Block of 4	100.
O93P4	90c **rose,** plate on card	10.
	Block of 4	50.
	P# blk. of 12	225.
	Nos. O83P3-O93P3 (11)	220.00
	Nos. O83P4-O93P4 (10)	100.00
	Nos. O1P3-O93P3 (92)	1,675.
	Nos. O1P4-O93P4 (92)	1,036.

Nos. O83P-O93P exist in a plum shade.

POSTAL SAVINGS MAIL

1911

O124P1	1c **dk vio,** large die on India paper	1,000.
O124P2	1c **dk vio,** sm die on white wove paper	275.
O124P2a	1c **dk vio,** PP sm die on yelsh wove paper	1,000.
O121TC1a	2c large die on India paper	
	e. **lake**	500.
O121P1	2c **blk,** large die on India paper	1,000.
O121P2	2c **blk,** sm die on white wove paper	275.
O121P2a	2c **blk,** PP sm die on yelsh wove paper	1,000.
O126TC1c	10c Large die on wove paper	
	e. **black**	*1,250.*
O126P1	10c **car,** large die on India paper	1,000.
O126P2	10c **car,** sm die on white wove paper	275.
O126P2a	10c **car,** PP sm die on yelsh wove paper	1,000.
O122P1	50c **dk grn,** large die on India paper	1,000.
O122P2	50c **dk grn,** sm die on white wove paper	275.
O122P2a	50c **dk grn,** PP sm die on yelsh wove paper	1,000.
O123P1	$1 **ultra,** large die on India paper	1,000.
O123P2	$1 **ultra,** sm die on white wove paper	275.
O123P2a	$1 **ultra,** PP sm die on yelsh wove paper	1,000.

The so-called "Goodall" set of Small Die proofs on India Paper of Official Stamps in five colors

AGRICULTURE

O1TC2	1c "Goodall" small die on India paper	
	b. **black**	300.
	c. **deep green**	300.
	d. **dull gray blue**	300.
	e. **deep brown**	300.
	f. **dull red**	300.
O2TC2	2c "Goodall" small die on India paper	
	b. **black**	300.
	c. **deep green**	300.
	d. **dull gray blue**	300.
	e. **deep brown**	300.
	f. **dull red**	300.
O3TC2	3c "Goodall" small die on India paper	
	b. **black**	300.
	c. **deep green**	300.
	d. **dull gray blue**	300.
	e. **deep brown**	300.
	f. **dull red**	300.
O4TC2	6c "Goodall" small die on India paper	
	b. **black**	300.
	c. **deep green**	300.
	d. **dull gray blue**	300.
	e. **deep brown**	300.
	f. **dull red**	300.
O5TC2	10c "Goodall" small die on India paper	
	b. **black**	300.
	c. **deep green**	300.
	d. **dull gray blue**	300.
	e. **deep brown**	300.
	f. **dull red**	300.
O6TC2	12c "Goodall" small die on India paper	
	b. **black**	300.
	c. **deep green**	300.
	d. **dull gray blue**	300.
	e. **deep brown**	300.
	f. **dull red**	300.
O7TC2	15c "Goodall" small die on India paper	
	b. **black**	300.
	c. **deep green**	300.
	d. **dull gray blue**	300.
	e. **deep brown**	300.
	f. **dull red**	300.
O8TC2	24c "Goodall" small die on India paper	
	b. **black**	300.
	c. **deep green**	300.
	d. **dull gray blue**	300.
	e. **deep brown**	300.
	f. **dull red**	300.
O9TC2	30c "Goodall" small die on India paper	
	b. **black**	300.
	c. **deep green**	300.
	d. **dull gray blue**	300.
	e. **deep brown**	300.
	f. **dull red**	300.

EXECUTIVE

O10TC2	1c "Goodall" small die on India paper	
	b. **black**	300.
	c. **deep green**	300.
	d. **dull gray blue**	300.
	e. **deep brown**	300.
	f. **dull red**	300.
O11TC2	2c "Goodall" small die on India paper	
	b. **black**	300.
	c. **deep green**	300.
	d. **dull gray blue**	300.
	e. **deep brown**	300.
	f. **dull red**	300.
O12TC2	3c "Goodall" small die on India paper	
	b. **black**	300.
	c. **deep green**	300.
	d. **dull gray blue**	300.
	e. **deep brown**	300.
	f. **dull red**	300.
O13TC2	6c "Goodall" small die on India paper	
	b. **black**	300.
	c. **deep green**	300.
	d. **dull gray blue**	300.
	e. **deep brown**	300.
	f. **dull red**	300.
O14TC2	10c "Goodall" small die on India paper	
	b. **black**	300.
	c. **deep green**	300.
	d. **dull gray blue**	300.
	e. **deep brown**	300.

f. **dull red** 300.

INTERIOR

O15TC2 1c "Goodall" small die on India paper
b. **black** 300.
c. **deep green** 300.
d. **dull gray blue** 300.
e. **deep brown** 300.
f. **dull red** 300.

O16TC2 2c "Goodall" small die on India paper
b. **black** 300.
c. **deep green** 300.
d. **dull gray blue** 300.
e. **deep brown** 300.
f. **dull red** 300.

O17TC2 3c "Goodall" small die on India paper
b. **black** 300.
c. **deep green** 300.
d. **dull gray blue** 300.
e. **deep brown** 300.
f. **dull red** 300.

O18TC2 6c "Goodall" small die on India paper
b. **black** 300.
c. **deep green** 300.
d. **dull gray blue** 300.
e. **deep brown** 300.
f. **dull red** 300.

O19TC2 10c "Goodall" small die on India paper
b. **black** 300.
c. **deep green** 300.
d. **dull gray blue** 300.
e. **deep brown** 300.
f. **dull red** 300.

O20TC2 12c "Goodall" small die on India paper
b. **black** 300.
c. **deep green** 300.
d. **dull gray blue** 300.
e. **deep brown** 300.
f. **dull red** 300.

O21TC2 15c "Goodall" small die on India paper
b. **black** 300.
c. **deep green** 300.
d. **dull gray blue** 300.
e. **deep brown** 300.
f. **dull red** 300.

O22TC2 24c "Goodall" small die on India paper
b. **black** 300.
c. **deep green** 300.
d. **dull gray blue** 300.
e. **deep brown** 300.
f. **dull red** 300.

O23TC2 30c "Goodall" small die on India paper
b. **black** 300.
c. **deep green** 300.
d. **dull gray blue** 300.
e. **deep brown** 300.
f. **dull red** 300.

O24TC2 90c "Goodall" small die on India paper
b. **black** 300.
c. **deep green** 300.
d. **dull gray blue** 300.
e. **deep brown** 300.
f. **dull red** 300.

JUSTICE

O25TC2 1c "Goodall" small die on India paper
b. **black** 300.
c. **deep green** 300.
d. **dull gray blue** 300.
e. **deep brown** 300.
f. **dull red** 300.

O26TC2 2c "Goodall" small die on India paper
b. **black** 300.
c. **deep green** 300.
d. **dull gray blue** 300.
e. **deep brown** 300.
f. **dull red** 300.

O27TC2 3c "Goodall" small die on India paper
b. **black** 300.
c. **deep green** 300.
d. **dull gray blue** 300.
e. **deep brown** 300.
f. **dull red** 300.

O28TC2 6c "Goodall" small die on India paper
b. **black** 300.
c. **deep green** 300.
d. **dull gray blue** 300.
e. **deep brown** 300.
f. **dull red** 300.

O29TC2 10c "Goodall" small die on India paper
b. **black** 300.
c. **deep green** 300.
d. **dull gray blue** 300.
e. **deep brown** 300.
f. **dull red** 300.

O30TC2 12c "Goodall" small die on India paper
b. **black** 300.
c. **deep green** 300.
d. **dull gray blue** 300.
e. **deep brown** 300.
f. **dull red** 300.

O31TC2 15c "Goodall" small die on India paper
b. **black** 300.
c. **deep green** 300.
d. **dull gray blue** 300.
e. **deep brown** 300.
f. **dull red** 300.

O32TC2 24c "Goodall" small die on India paper
b. **black** 300.
c. **deep green** 300.
d. **dull gray blue** 300.
e. **deep brown** 300.
f. **dull red** 300.

O33TC2 30c "Goodall" small die on India paper
b. **black** 300.
c. **deep green** 300.
d. **dull gray blue** 300.
e. **deep brown** 300.
f. **dull red** 300.

O34TC2 90c "Goodall" small die on India paper
b. **black** 300.
c. **deep green** 300.
d. **dull gray blue** 300.
e. **deep brown** 300.
f. **dull red** 300.

NAVY

O35TC2 1c "Goodall" small die on India paper
b. **black** 300.
c. **deep green** 300.
d. **dull gray blue** 300.
e. **deep brown** 300.
f. **dull red** 300.

O36TC2 2c "Goodall" small die on India paper
b. **black** 300.
c. **deep green** 300.
d. **dull gray blue** 300.
e. **deep brown** 300.
f. **dull red** 300.

O37TC2 3c "Goodall" small die on India paper
b. **black** 300.
c. **deep green** 300.
d. **dull gray blue** 300.
e. **deep brown** 300.
f. **dull red** 300.

O38TC2 6c "Goodall" small die on India paper
b. **black** 300.
c. **deep green** 300.
d. **dull gray blue** 300.
e. **deep brown** 300.
f. **dull red** 300.

O39TC2 7c "Goodall" small die on India paper
b. **black** 300.
c. **deep green** 300.
d. **dull gray blue** 300.
e. **deep brown** 300.
f. **dull red** 300.

O40TC2 10c "Goodall" small die on India paper
b. **black** 300.
c. **deep green** 300.
d. **dull gray blue** 300.
e. **deep brown** 300.
f. **dull red** 300.

O41TC2 12c "Goodall" small die on India paper
b. **black** 300.
c. **deep green** 300.
d. **dull gray blue** 300.
e. **deep brown** 300.
f. **dull red** 300.

O42TC2 15c "Goodall" small die on India paper
b. **black** 300.
c. **deep green** 300.
d. **dull gray blue** 300.
e. **deep brown** 300.
f. **dull red** 300.

O43TC2 24c "Goodall" small die on India paper
b. **black** 300.
c. **deep green** 300.
d. **dull gray blue** 300.
e. **deep brown** 300.
f. **dull red** 300.

O44TC2 30c "Goodall" small die on India paper
b. **black** 300.
c. **deep green** 300.
d. **dull gray blue** 300.
e. **deep brown** 300.
f. **dull red** 300.

O45TC2 90c "Goodall" small die on India paper
b. **black** 300.
c. **deep green** 300.
d. **dull gray blue** 300.
e. **deep brown** 300.
f. **dull red** 300.

POST OFFICE

O47TC2 1c "Goodall" small die on India paper
b. **black** 300.
c. **deep green** 300.
d. **dull gray blue** 300.
e. **deep brown** 300.
f. **dull red** 300.

O48TC2 2c "Goodall" small die on India paper
b. **black** 300.
c. **deep green** 300.
d. **dull gray blue** 300.
e. **deep brown** 300.
f. **dull red** 300.

O49TC2 3c "Goodall" small die on India paper
b. **black** 300.
c. **deep green** 300.
d. **dull gray blue** 300.
e. **deep brown** 300.
f. **dull red** 300.

O50TC2 6c "Goodall" small die on India paper
b. **black** 300.
c. **deep green** 300.
d. **dull gray blue** 300.
e. **deep brown** 300.
f. **dull red** 300.

O51TC2 10c "Goodall" small die on India paper
b. **black** 300.
c. **deep green** 300.
d. **dull gray blue** 300.
e. **deep brown** 300.
f. **dull red** 300.

O52TC2 12c "Goodall" small die on India paper
b. **black** 300.
c. **deep green** 300.
d. **dull gray blue** 300.
e. **deep brown** 300.
f. **dull red** 300.

O53TC2 15c "Goodall" small die on India paper
b. **black** 300.
c. **deep green** 300.
d. **dull gray blue** 300.
e. **deep brown** 300.
f. **dull red** 300.

O54TC2 24c "Goodall" small die on India paper
b. **black** 300.
c. **deep green** 300.
d. **dull gray blue** 300.
e. **deep brown** 300.
f. **dull red** 300.

O55TC2 30c "Goodall" small die on India paper
b. **black** 300.
c. **deep green** 300.
d. **dull gray blue** 300.
e. **deep brown** 300.
f. **dull red** 300.

O56TC2 90c "Goodall" small die on India paper
b. **black** 300.
c. **deep green** 300.
d. **dull gray blue** 300.
e. **deep brown** 300.
f. **dull red** 300.

STATE

O57TC2 1c "Goodall" small die on India paper
b. **black** 300.
c. **deep green** 300.
d. **dull gray blue** 300.
e. **deep brown** 300.
f. **dull red** 300.

O58TC2 2c "Goodall" small die on India paper
b. **black** 300.
c. **deep green** 300.
d. **dull gray blue** 300.
e. **deep brown** 300.
f. **dull red** 300.

O59TC2 3c "Goodall" small die on India paper
b. **black** 300.
c. **deep green** 300.
d. **dull gray blue** 300.
e. **deep brown** 300.
f. **dull red** 300.

O60TC2 6c "Goodall" small die on India paper
b. **black** 300.
c. **deep green** 300.
d. **dull gray blue** 300.
e. **deep brown** 300.
f. **dull red** 300.

O61TC2 7c "Goodall" small die on India paper
b. **black** 300.
c. **deep green** 300.
d. **dull gray blue** 300.
e. **deep brown** 300.
f. **dull red** 300.

O62TC2 10c "Goodall" small die on India paper
b. **black** 300.
c. **deep green** 300.
d. **dull gray blue** 300.
e. **deep brown** 300.
f. **dull red** 300.

O63TC2 12c "Goodall" small die on India paper
b. **black** 300.
c. **deep green** 300.
d. **dull gray blue** 300.
e. **deep brown** 300.
f. **dull red** 300.

O64TC2 15c "Goodall" small die on India paper
b. **black** 300.
c. **deep green** 300.
d. **dull gray blue** 300.
e. **deep brown** 300.
f. **dull red** 300.

O65TC2 24c "Goodall" small die on India paper
b. **black** 300.
c. **deep green** 300.
d. **dull gray blue** 300.
e. **deep brown** 300.
f. **dull red** 300.

O66TC2 30c "Goodall" small die on India paper
b. **black** 300.
c. **deep green** 300.
d. **dull gray blue** 300.
e. **deep brown** 300.
f. **dull red** 300.

O67TC2 90c "Goodall" small die on India paper
b. **black** 300.
c. **deep green** 300.
d. **dull gray blue** 300.
e. **deep brown** 300.
f. **dull red** 300.

O68TC2 $2 "Goodall" small die on India paper
b. **scarlet frame, green center** *3,250.*
c. **scarlet frame, black center** *3,250.*
d. **scarlet frame, blue center** *3,250.*
e. **scarlet frame, brown center** *3,250.*
f. **violet frame, black center** *3,250.*
g. **green frame, brown center** *3,250.*
h. **brown frame, green center** *3,250.*
i. **brown frame, black center** *3,250.*
j. **red brown frame, green center** *3,250.*

TREASURY

O72TC2 1c "Goodall" small die on India paper
b. **black** 300.
c. **deep green** 300.
d. **dull gray blue** 300.
e. **deep brown** 300.
f. **dull red** 300.

O73TC2 2c "Goodall" small die on India paper
b. **black** 300.
c. **deep green** 300.
d. **dull gray blue** 300.
e. **deep brown** 300.
f. **dull red** 300.

O74TC2 3c "Goodall" small die on India paper
b. **black** 300.
c. **deep green** 300.
d. **dull gray blue** 300.
e. **deep brown** 300.
f. **dull red** 300.

O75TC2 6c "Goodall" small die on India paper
b. **black** 300.
c. **deep green** 300.

d. **dull gray blue** 300.
e. **deep brown** 300.
f. **dull red** 300.
O76TC2 7c "Goodall" small die on India paper
b. **black** 300.
c. **deep green** 300.
d. **dull gray blue** 300.
e. **deep brown** 300.
f. **dull red** 300.
O77TC2 10c "Goodall" small die on India paper
b. **black** 300.
c. **deep green** 300.
d. **dull gray blue** 300.
e. **deep brown** 300.
f. **dull red** 300.
O78TC2 12c "Goodall" small die on India paper
b. **black** 300.
c. **deep green** 300.
d. **dull gray blue** 300.
e. **deep brown** 300.
f. **dull red** 300.
O79TC2 15c "Goodall" small die on India paper
b. **black** 300.
c. **deep green** 300.
d. **dull gray blue** 300.
e. **deep brown** 300.
f. **dull red** 300.
O80TC2 24c "Goodall" small die on India paper
b. **black** 300.
c. **deep green** 300.
d. **dull gray blue** 300.
e. **deep brown** 300.
f. **dull red** 300.
O81TC2 30c "Goodall" small die on India paper
b. **black** 300.
c. **deep green** 300.
d. **dull gray blue** 300.
e. **deep brown** 300.
f. **dull red** 300.
O82TC2 90c "Goodall" small die on India paper
b. **black** 300.
c. **deep green** 300.
d. **dull gray blue** 300.
e. **deep brown** 300.
f. **dull red** 300.

WAR

O83TC2 1c "Goodall" small die on India paper
b. **black** 300.
c. **deep green** 300.
d. **dull gray blue** 300.
e. **deep brown** 300.
f. **dull red** 300.
O84TC2 2c "Goodall" small die on India paper
b. **black** 300.
c. **deep green** 300.
d. **dull gray blue** 300.
e. **deep brown** 300.
f. **dull red** 300.
O85TC2 3c "Goodall" small die on India paper
b. **black** 300.
c. **deep green** 300.
d. **dull gray blue** 300.
e. **deep brown** 300.
f. **dull red** 300.
O86TC2 6c "Goodall" small die on India paper
b. **black** 300.
c. **deep green** 300.
d. **dull gray blue** 300.
e. **deep brown** 300.
f. **dull red** 300.
O87TC2 7c "Goodall" small die on India paper
b. **black** 300.
c. **deep green** 300.
d. **dull gray blue** 300.
e. **deep brown** 300.
f. **dull red** 300.
O88TC2 10c "Goodall" small die on India paper
b. **black** 300.
c. **deep green** 300.
d. **dull gray blue** 300.
e. **deep brown** 300.
f. **dull red** 300.
O89TC2 12c "Goodall" small die on India paper
b. **black** 300.
c. **deep green** 300.
d. **dull gray blue** 300.
e. **deep brown** 300.
f. **dull red** 300.
O90TC2 15c "Goodall" small die on India paper
b. **black** 300.
c. **deep green** 300.
d. **dull gray blue** 300.
e. **deep brown** 300.
f. **dull red** 300.
O91TC2 24c "Goodall" small die on India paper
b. **black** 300.
c. **deep green** 300.
d. **dull gray blue** 300.
e. **deep brown** 300.
f. **dull red** 300.
O92TC2 30c "Goodall" small die on India paper
b. **black** 300.
c. **deep green** 300.
d. **dull gray blue** 300.
e. **deep brown** 300.
f. **dull red** 300.
O93TC2 90c "Goodall" small die on India paper
b. **black** 300.
c. **deep green** 300.
d. **dull gray blue** 300.
e. **deep brown** 300.
f. **dull red** 300.

POST OFFICE SEALS

1872

OXF1TC1a large die on India paper
e. **ultramarine** *1,000.*
f. **carmine** *1,000.*
g. **brown** *1,000.*
h. **red violet** *1,000.*
OXF1TC2 small die on glossy bond paper
b. **chocolate** *1,000.*
OXF1TC2 small die on card
c. **blue,** colored border *1,000.*
d. **deep blue,** colored border *1,000.*
e. **green,** colored border *1,000.*
f. **chocolate,** colored border *1,000.*
OXF1P1 **grn,** large die on India paper 275.
a. Wove paper *950.*
b. Glazed paper *190.*
OXF1P3 **green,** plate proof on India —
OXF1P4 **grn,** plate on card —

1877

OX1TC1a large die on India paper
e. **blue** 500.
f. **green** 500.
g. **orange** 500.
h. **red orange** 500.
i. **black** 500.
OX1TC5 plate on bond paper, imperf.
a. **green** 500.
OX1TC6 plate on bond paper, perforated & gummed
a. **green** —
OX1P1 **brn,** plate on India paper *1,750.*
OX1P3 **brn,** plate on India paper *125.*
Block of 4 650.

1879

OX2TC1a large die on India paper
e. **black** —
OX2aP1 **brn,** large die on India paper 2,500.
OX2aP3 **brn,** plate on India paper 125.
Block of 4 650.

1888-94

OX5P1 **choc,** large die on India paper *750.*

1901-03

OX11P1 **red brn,** large die on India paper *750.*

No. OX11P is a hybrid proof sunk on card.

1972

OX41P1 Pane of 5, blue line proof —

POSTAL NOTE STAMPS

PN1TC5 1c **bister,** plate on white wove, imperf. —

NEWSPAPER

1865

PR1TCb 5c large die on thin hard wove
e. **bright red** 600.
f. **deep reddish brown** 2,500.
g. **dark orange** 2,500.
d. **green** 2,500.
PR1P2a 5c **bl,** PP sm die on yelsh wove paper *4,000.*
PR2TC1a 10c large die on India paper
e. **brown** 600.
f. **dull red** 600.
g. **blue** 600.
h. **blue green** 600.
PR2TC5 10c plate on thick cream wove paper
a. **black** 85.
b. **lake** 85.
c. **blue green** 85.
d. **blue** 85.
PR2P1 10c **grn,** large die on India paper 500.
PR2P2 10c **grn,** RA sm die on white wove paper 225.
PR2P2a 10c **grn,** PP sm die on yelsh wove paper *4,000.*
PR2P4 10c **grn,** plate on card 75.
Block of 4 375.
P# blk. of 6 —
PR2P4a 10c **grn,** plate on thin card 85.
Block of 4 425.
PR3TC1a 25c large die on India paper
e. **ocher** 600.
f. **brown** 600.
g. **brick red** 600.
PR3TC1b 25c large die on thin hard paper
e. **carmine** *2,500.*
PR3TC5 25c plate on thick cream wove paper
a. **black** 85.
b. **lake** 85.
c. **blue green** 85.
d. **blue** 85.
PR3P1 25c **org red,** large die on India paper 575.
PR3P2 25c **org red,** RA sm die on white wove paper 225.
PR3P2a 25c **org red,** PP sm die on yelsh wove paper *4,000.*
PR3P4 25c **org red,** plate on card 75.
Block of 4 375.
P# blk. of 6 —
PR3P4a 25c **org red,** plate on thin card 100.
Block of 4 500.
PR4TC1a 5c large die on India paper
e. **blue green,** *greenish* —
PR4TC5 5c plate on thick cream wove paper
a. **black** 85.
b. **lake** 85.
c. **blue green** 85.
d. **blue** 85.
PR4P1 5c **bl,** large die on India paper 500.
PR4P2 5c **bl,** RA sm die on white wove paper 225.
PR4P4 5c **bl,** plate on card 75.
Block of 4 375.
P# blk. of 6 —
PR4P4a 5c **bl,** plate on thin card 85.
Block of 4 425.

1875

PR5P4 5c **dk bl,** plate on card 65.
PR6P4 10c **dp grn,** plate on card 65.
PR7P4 25c **dk car red,** plate on card 65.
PR9TC1a 2c large die on India paper
e. **orange brown** *600.*
f. **black brown** *600.*
g. **blue green** *600.*
PR9TC3 2c plate on India paper
a. **dark carmine** 35.
b. **brown rose** 35.
c. **scarlet** 35.
d. **orange brown** 35.
e. **sepia** 35.
f. **orange yellow** 35.
g. **dull orange** 35.
h. **green** 35.
i. **light ultramarine** 35.
j. **light blue** 35.
k. **dark violet** 35.
l. **violet black** 35.
PR9P1 2c **blk,** large die on India paper 100.
PR9P2 2c **blk,** RA sm die on white wove paper 50.
PR9P2a 2c **blk,** PP sm die on yelsh wove paper 575.
PR9P3 2c **blk,** plate on India paper 15.
Block of 4 65.
P# block of 10 —
PR9P4 2c **blk,** plate on card 12.
Block of 4 55.
P# blk. of 8 —
PR10TC1a 3c large die on India paper
e. **rose lake** *600.*
PR10P1 3c **blk,** large die on India paper 100.
PR10P2 3c **blk,** RA sm die on white wove paper 50.
PR10P2a 3c **blk,** PP sm die on yelsh wove paper 575.
PR10P3 3c **blk,** plate on India paper 15.
Block of 4 65.
Margin block of 8, Impt. and "B" —
PR10P4 3c **blk,** plate on card 12.
Block of 4 55.
P# blk. of 8 —
PR11P1 4c **blk,** large die on India paper 100.
PR11P2 4c **blk,** RA sm die on white wove paper 50.
PR11P2a 4c **blk,** PP sm die on yelsh wove paper 575.
PR11P3 4c **blk,** plate on India paper 15.
Block of 4 65.
PR11P4 4c **blk,** plate on card 12.
Block of 4 55.
PR12P1 6c **blk,** large die on India paper 100.
PR12P2 6c **blk,** RA sm die on white wove paper 50.
PR12P2a 6c **blk,** PP sm die on yelsh wove paper 575.
PR12P3 6c **blk,** plate on India paper 15.
Block of 4 65.
PR12P4 6c **blk,** plate on card 12.
Block of 4 55.
PR13P1 8c **blk,** large die on India paper 100.
PR13P2 8c **blk,** RA sm die on white wove paper 50.
PR13P2a 8c **blk,** PP sm die on yelsh wove paper 575.
PR13P3 8c **blk,** plate on India paper 15.
Block of 4 65.
PR13P4 8c **blk,** plate on card 12.
Block of 4 55.
PR14P1 9c **blk,** large die on India paper 100.
PR14P2 9c **blk,** RA sm die on white wove paper 50.
PR14P2a 9c **blk,** PP sm die on yelsh wove paper 575.
PR14P3 9c **blk,** plate on India paper 15.
Block of 4 65.
PR14P4 9c **blk,** plate on card 12.
Block of 4 55.
PR15P1 10c **blk,** large die on India paper 100.
PR15P2 10c **blk,** RA sm die on white wove paper 50.
PR15P2a 10c **blk,** PP sm die on yelsh wove paper 575.
PR15P3 10c **blk,** plate on India paper 15.
Block of 4 65.
PR15P4 10c **blk,** plate on card 12.
Block of 4 55.
PR16TC1a 12c large die on India paper
e. **brown rose** *600.*
f. **scarlet** *600.*
g. **sepia** *600.*
h. **green** *600.*
i. **light ultramarine** *600.*
j. **dark violet** *600.*
k. **violet black** *600.*
l. **black** *600.*
PR16TC3 12c plate on India paper
a. **dark carmine** 35.
b. **brown rose** 35.
c. **scarlet** 35.
d. **orange brown** 35.
e. **sepia** 35.
f. **orange yellow** 35.
g. **dull orange** 35.
h. **green** 35.
i. **light ultramarine** 35.
j. **light blue** 35.
k. **dark violet** 35.

l.	**violet black**	35.
m.	**black**	35.
PR16P1	12c **rose,** large die on India paper	100.
PR16P2	12c **rose,** RA sm die on white wove paper	50.
PR16P2a	12c **rose,** PP sm die on yelsh wove paper	575.
PR16P3	12c **rose,** plate on India paper	15.
	Block of 4	65.
PR16P4	12c **rose,** plate on card	12.
	Block of 4	55.
PR17TC1a	24c large die on India paper	
e.	**green**	*600.*
f.	**black**	*600.*
PR17TC3	24c plate on India paper	
a.	**black**	35.
PR17P1	24c **rose,** large die on India paper	100.
PR17P2	24c **rose,** RA sm die on white wove paper	50.
PR17P2a	24c **rose,** PP sm die on yelsh wove paper	575.
PR17P3	24c **rose,** plate on India paper	15.
	Block of 4	65.
PR17P4	24c **rose,** plate on card	12.
	Block of 4	55.
PR18TC1a	36c large die on India paper	
e.	**green**	*600.*
f.	**black**	*600.*
g.	**sepia**	*600.*
PR18TC3	36c plate on India paper	
a.	**black**	35.
PR18P1	36c **rose,** large die on India paper	100.
PR18P2	36c **rose,** RA sm die on white wove paper	50.
PR18P2a	36c **rose,** PP sm die on yelsh wove paper	575.
PR18P3	36c **rose,** plate on India paper	15.
	Block of 4	65.
PR18P4	36c **rose,** plate on card	12.
	Block of 4	55.
PR19TC1a	48c large die on India paper	
e.	**green**	*600.*
f.	**black**	*600.*
g.	**sepia**	*600.*
PR19TC3	48c plate on India paper	
a.	**black**	35.
PR19P1	48c **rose,** large die on India paper	100.
PR19P2	48c **rose,** RA sm die on white wove paper	50.
PR19P2a	48c **rose,** PP sm die on yelsh wove paper	575.
PR19P3	48c **rose,** plate on India paper	15.
	Block of 4	65.
PR19P4	48c **rose,** plate on card	12.
	Block of 4	55.
PR20TC1a	60c large die on India paper	
e.	**black**	*600.*
PR20TC3	60c plate on India paper	
a.	**black**	35.
PR20P1	60c **rose,** large die on India paper	100.
PR20P2	60c **rose,** RA sm die on white wove paper	50.
PR20P2a	60c **rose,** PP sm die on yelsh wove paper	575.
PR20P3	60c **rose,** plate on India paper	15.
	Block of 4	65.
PR20P4	60c **rose,** plate on card	12.
	Block of 4	55.
PR21TC1a	72c large die on India paper	
e.	**black**	*600.*
PR21TC3	72c plate on India paper	
a.	**black**	35.
PR21P1	72c **rose,** large die on India paper	100.
PR21P2	72c **rose,** RA sm die on white wove paper	50.
PR21P2a	72c **rose,** PP sm die on yelsh wove paper	575.
PR21P3	72c **rose,** plate on India paper	15.
	Block of 4	65.
PR21P4	72c **rose,** plate on card	12.
	Block of 4	55.
PR22TC1a	84c large die on India paper	
e.	**black**	*600.*
PR22TC3	84c plate on India paper	
a.	**black**	35.
PR22P1	84c **rose,** large die on India paper	100.
PR22P2	84c **rose,** RA sm die on white wove paper	50.
PR22P2a	84c **rose,** PP sm die on yelsh wove paper	575.
PR22P3	84c **rose,** plate on India paper	15.
	Block of 4	65.
PR22P4	84c **rose,** plate on card	12.
	Block of 4	55.
PR23TC3	96c plate on India paper	
a.	**black**	35.
PR23P1	96c **rose,** large die on India paper	100.
PR23P2	96c **rose,** RA sm die on white wove paper	50.
PR23P2a	96c **rose,** PP sm die on yelsh wove paper	575.
PR23P3	96c **rose,** plate on India paper	15.
	Block of 4	65.
PR23P4	96c **rose,** plate on card	12.
	Block of 4	55.
PR24TC1a	$1.92 large die on India paper	
e.	**orange brown**	*600.*
f.	**green**	*600.*
PR24TC3	$1.92 plate on India paper	
a.	**dark carmine**	35.
b.	**brown rose**	35.
c.	**scarlet**	35.
d.	**orange brown**	35.
e.	**sepia**	35.
f.	**orange yellow**	35.
g.	**dull orange**	35.
h.	**green**	35.
i.	**light ultramarine**	35.
j.	**dark violet**	35.
k.	**violet black**	35.
l.	**black**	35.
PR24P1	$1.92 **dk brn,** large die on India paper	100.
PR24P2	$1.92 **dk brn,** RA sm die on white wove paper	50.
PR24P2a	$1.92 **dk brn,** PP sm die on yelsh wove paper	575.
PR24P3	$1.92 **dk brn,** plate on India paper	18.
	Block of 4	80.
PR24P4	$1.92 **dk brn,** plate on card	15.
	Block of 4	70.
PR25TC1a	$3 large die on India paper	
e.	**dark carmine**	*600.*
f.	**orange yellow**	*600.*
g.	**dull orange**	*600.*
h.	**green**	*600.*
i.	**light ultramarine**	*600.*
j.	**dark violet**	*600.*
k.	**violet black**	*600.*
l.	**black**	*600.*
m.	**brown**	—
PR25TC3	$3 plate on India paper	
a.	**dark carmine**	35.
b.	**brown rose**	35.
c.	**scarlet**	35.
d.	**orange brown**	35.
e.	**sepia**	35.
f.	**orange yellow**	35.
g.	**dull orange**	35.
h.	**green**	35.
i.	**light ultramarine**	35.
j.	**light blue**	35.
k.	**dark violet**	35.
l.	**violet black**	35.
m.	**black**	35.
PR25P1	$3 **ver,** large die on India paper	100.
PR25P2	$3 **ver,** RA sm die on white wove paper	50.
PR25P2a	$3 **ver,** PP sm die on yelsh wove paper	575.
PR25P3	$3 **ver,** plate on India paper	18.
	Block of 4	80.
PR25P4	$3 **ver,** plate on card	15.
	Block of 4	70.
PR26TC1a	$6 large die on India paper	
e.	**dark carmine**	*600.*
f.	**brown rose**	*600.*
g.	**scarlet**	*600.*
h.	**sepia**	*600.*
i.	**orange yellow**	*600.*
j.	**dull orange**	*600.*
k.	**green**	*600.*
l.	**light blue**	*600.*
m.	**dark violet**	*600.*
n.	**violet black**	*600.*
o.	**black**	*600.*
PR26TC3	$6 plate on India paper	
a.	**dark carmine**	35.
b.	**brown rose**	35.
c.	**scarlet**	35.
d.	**orange brown**	35.
e.	**dark brown**	35.
f.	**sepia**	35.
g.	**orange yellow**	35.
h.	**dull orange**	35.
i.	**green**	35.
j.	**light ultramarine**	35.
k.	**light blue**	35.
l.	**dark violet**	35.
m.	**violet black**	35.
n.	**black**	35.
PR26P1	$6 **ultra,** large die on India paper	100.
PR26P2	$6 **ultra,** RA sm die on white wove paper	50.
PR26P2a	$6 **ultra,** PP sm die on yelsh wove paper	575.
PR26P3	$6 **ultra,** plate on India paper	18.
	Block of 4	80.
PR26P4	$6 **ultra,** plate on card	15.
	Block of 4	70.
PR27TC1a	$9 large die on India paper	
e.	**dark carmine**	*600.*
f.	**brown rose**	*600.*
g.	**scarlet**	*600.*
h.	**sepia**	*600.*
i.	**orange yellow**	*600.*
j.	**dull orange**	*600.*
k.	**green**	*600.*
l.	**light ultramarine**	*600.*
m.	**dark violet**	*600.*
n.	**violet black**	*600.*
o.	**black**	*600.*
PR27TC3	$9 plate on India paper	
a.	**dark carmine**	35.
b.	**brown rose**	35.
c.	**scarlet**	35.
d.	**orange brown**	35.
e.	**sepia**	35.
f.	**orange yellow**	35.
g.	**dull orange**	35.
h.	**green**	35.
i.	**light ultramarine**	35.
j.	**light blue**	35.
k.	**dark violet**	35.
l.	**violet black**	35.
m.	**black**	35.
PR27P1	$9 **yel,** large die on India paper	100.
PR27P2	$9 **yel,** RA sm die on white wove paper	50.
PR27P2a	$9 **yel,** PP sm die on yelsh wove paper	575.
PR27P3	$9 **yel,** plate on India paper	18.
	Block of 4	80.
PR27P4	$9 **yel,** plate on card	15.
	Block of 4	70.
PR28TC1a	$12 large die on India paper	
e.	**black**	*600.*
f.	**sepia**	*600.*
g.	**orange brown**	*600.*
PR28P1	$12 **bl grn,** large die on India paper	100.
PR28P2	$12 **bl grn,** RA sm die on white wove paper	50.
PR28P2a	$12 **bl grn,** PP sm die on yelsh wove paper	575.
PR28P3	$12 **bl grn,** plate on India paper	18.
	Block of 4	80.
PR28P4	$12 **bl grn,** plate on card	15.
	Block of 4	70.
PR29TC1a	$24 large die on India paper	
e.	**black**	*600.*
f.	**black brown**	*600.*
g.	**orange brown**	*600.*
h.	**green**	*600.*
PR29TC3	$24 plate on India paper	
a.	**black**	35.
PR29P1	$24 **dk gray vio,** large die on India paper	100.
PR29P2	$24 **dk gray vio,** RA sm die on white wove paper	50.
PR29P2a	$24 **dk gray vio,** PP sm die on yelsh wove paper	575.
PR29P3	$24 **dk gray vio,** plate on India paper	18.
	Block of 4	80.
PR29P4	$24 **dk gray vio,** plate on card	15.
	Block of 4	70.
PR30TC1a	$36 large die on India paper	
e.	**dark carmine**	*600.*
f.	**black**	*600.*
g.	**black brown**	*600.*
h.	**orange brown**	*600.*
i.	**sepia**	*600.*
j.	**violet**	*600.*
k.	**green**	*600.*
PR30TC3	$36 plate on India paper	
a.	**black**	35.
PR30P1	$36 **brn rose,** large die on India paper	100.
PR30P2	$36 **brn rose,** RA sm die on white wove paper	50.
PR30P2a	$36 **brn rose,** PP sm die on yelsh wove paper	575.
PR30P3	$36 **brn rose,** plate on India paper	18.
	Block of 4	90.
PR30P4	$36 **brn rose,** plate on card	15.
	Block of 4	70.
PR31TC1a	$48 large die on India paper	
e.	**violet brown**	*600.*
f.	**black**	*600.*
g.	**sepia**	*600.*
h.	**green**	*600.*
PR31TC3	$48 plate on India paper	
a.	**black**	35.
b.	**violet brown**	35.
PR31P1	$48 **red brn,** large die on India paper	100.
PR31P2	$48 **red brn,** RA sm die on white wove paper	50.
PR31P2a	$48 **red brn,** PP sm die on yelsh wove paper	575.
PR31P3	$48 **red brn,** plate on India paper	23.
	Block of 4	100.
PR31P4	$48 **red brn,** plate on card	15.
	Block of 4	70.
PR32TC1a	$60 large die on India paper	
e.	**dark carmine**	*600.*
f.	**brown rose**	*600.*
g.	**scarlet**	*600.*
h.	**sepia**	*600.*
i.	**orange yellow**	*600.*
j.	**dull orange**	*600.*
k.	**green**	*600.*
l.	**light ultramarine**	*600.*
m.	**orange brown**	*600.*
n.	**violet black**	*600.*
o.	**black**	*600.*
PR32TC3	$60 plate on India paper	
a.	**dark carmine**	35.
b.	**brown rose**	35.
c.	**scarlet**	35.
d.	**sepia**	35.
e.	**orange yellow**	35.
f.	**dull orange**	35.
g.	**green**	35.
h.	**light ultramarine**	35.
i.	**orange brown**	35.
j.	**violet black**	35.
k.	**black**	35.
PR32P1	$60 **vio,** large die on India paper	100.
PR32P2	$60 **vio,** RA sm die on white wove paper	50.
PR32P2a	$60 **vio,** PP sm die on yelsh wove paper	575.
PR32P3	$60 **vio,** plate on India paper	25.
	Block of 4	110.
PR32P4	$60 **vio,** plate on card	18.
	Block of 4	85.
	Nos. PR9P3-PR32P3 (24)	399.00
	Nos. PR9P4-PR32P4 (24)	318.00

1879

PR57P1	2c **dp blk,** large die on India paper	100.
PR57P3	2c **dp blk,** plate on India paper	25.
	Block of 4	125.
	P# block of 10, Impt.	—
PR57P4	2c **dp blk,** plate on card	15.
	Block of 4	90.
PR58P1	3c **dp blk,** large die on India paper	100.
PR58P3	3c **dp blk,** plate on India paper	25.
	Block of 4	125.
PR58P4	3c **dp blk,** plate on card	15.
	Block of 4	90.

PR59P1	4c **dp blk,** large die on India paper	100.
PR59P3	4c **dp blk,** plate on India paper	25.
	Block of 4	125.
PR59P4	4c **dp blk,** plate on card	15.
	Block of 4	90.
PR60P1	6c **dp blk,** large die on India paper	100.
PR60P3	6c **dp blk,** plate on India paper	25.
	Block of 4	125.
PR60P4	6c **dp blk,** plate on card	15.
	Block of 4	90.
PR61P1	8c **dp blk,** large die on India paper	100.
PR61P3	8c **dp blk,** plate on India paper	25.
	Block of 4	125.
PR61P4	8c **dp blk,** plate on card	15.
	Block of 4	90.
PR62P1	10c **dp blk,** large die on India paper	100.
PR62P3	10c **dp blk,** plate on India paper	25.
	Block of 4	125.
PR62P4	10c **dp blk,** plate on card	15.
	Block of 4	90.
PR63P1	12c **red,** large die on India paper	100.
PR63P3	12c **red,** plate on India paper	25.
	Block of 4	125.
PR63P4	12c **red,** plate on card	15.
	Block of 4	90.
PR64P1	24c **red,** large die on India paper	100.
PR64P3	24c **red,** plate on India paper	25.
	Block of 4	125.
PR64P4	24c **red,** plate on card	15.
	Block of 4	90.
PR65P1	36c **red,** large die on India paper	100.
PR65P3	36c **red,** plate on India paper	25.
	Block of 4	125.
PR65P4	36c **red,** plate on card	15.
	Block of 4	90.
PR66P1	48c **red,** large die on India paper	100.
PR66P3	48c **red,** plate on India paper	25.
	Block of 4	125.
PR66P4	48c **red,** plate on card	15.
	Block of 4	90.
PR67P1	60c **red,** large die on India paper	100.
PR67P3	60c **red,** plate on India paper	25.
	Block of 4	125.
PR67P4	60c **red,** plate on card	15.
	Block of 4	90.
PR68P1	72c **red,** large die on India paper	100.
PR68P3	72c **red,** plate on India paper	25.
	Block of 4	125.
PR68P4	72c **red,** plate on card	15.
	Block of 4	90.
PR69P1	84c **red,** large die on India paper	100.
PR69P3	84c **red,** plate on India paper	25.
	Block of 4	125.
PR69P4	84c **red,** plate on card	15.
	Block of 4	90.
PR70P1	96c **red,** large die on India paper	100.
PR70P3	96c **red,** plate on India paper	25.
	Block of 4	125.
PR70P4	96c **red,** plate on card	15.
	Block of 4	90.
PR71P1	$1.92 **pale brn,** large die on India paper	100.
PR71P3	$1.92 **pale brn,** plate on India paper	25.
	Block of 4	125.
PR71P4	$1.92 **pale brn,** plate on card	15.
	Block of 4	90.
PR72P1	$3 **red ver,** large die on India paper	100.
PR72P3	$3 **red ver,** plate on India paper	25.
	Block of 4	125.
PR72P4	$3 **red ver,** plate on card	15.
	Block of 4	90.
PR73P1	$6 **bl,** large die on India paper	100.
PR73P3	$6 **bl,** plate on India paper	25.
	Block of 4	125.
PR73P4	$6 **bl,** plate on card	15.
	Block of 4	90.
PR74P1	$9 **org,** large die on India paper	100.
PR74P3	$9 **org,** plate on India paper	25.
	Block of 4	125.
PR74P4	$9 **org,** plate on card	15.
	Block of 4	90.
PR75P1	$12 **yel grn,** large die on India paper	100.
PR75P3	$12 **yel grn,** plate on India paper	25.
	Block of 4	125.
PR75P4	$12 **yel grn,** plate on card	15.
	Block of 4	90.
PR76P1	$24 **dk vio,** large die on India paper	100.
PR76P3	$24 **dk vio,** plate on India paper	25.
	Block of 4	125.
PR76P4	$24 **dk vio,** plate on card	15.
	Block of 4	90.
PR77P1	$36 **Indian red,** large die on India paper	100.
PR77P3	$36 **Indian red,** plate on India paper	25.
	Block of 4	125.
PR77P4	$36 **Indian red,** plate on card	15.
	Block of 4	90.
PR78P1	$48 **yel brn,** large die on India paper	100.
PR78P3	$48 **yel brn,** plate on India paper	25.
	Block of 4	125.
PR78P4	$48 **yel brn,** plate on card	15.
	Block of 4	90.
PR79P1	$60 **pur,** large die on India paper	100.
PR79P3	$60 **pur,** plate on India paper	25.
	Block of 4	125.
PR79P4	$60 **pur,** plate on card	15.
	Block of 4	90.
	Nos. PR57P3-PR79P3 (23)	575.00
	Nos. PR57P4-PR79P4 (23)	345.00

1885

PR81TC1a	1c large die on India paper	
	e. **salmon**	*600.*
PR81TC3	1c plate on India paper	
	a. **scarlet**	120.
	b. **dark brown**	120.
	c. **violet brown**	120.
	d. **dull orange**	120.
	e. **green**	120.
	f. **light blue**	120.
PR81P1	1c **blk,** large die on India paper	100.
PR81P2	1c **blk,** RA sm die on white wove paper	60.
PR81P2a	1c **blk,** PP sm die on yelsh wove paper	600.
PR81P3	1c **blk,** plate on India paper	25.
	Block of 4	125.
	P# blk. of 8	—
PR81P4	1c **blk,** plate on card	15.
	Block of 4	90.
	P# blk. of 8	425.
PR82P2a	12c **car,** PP sm die on yelsh wove paper	600.
PR82P3	12c **car,** plate on India paper	25.
	Block of 4	125.
PR82P4	12c **car,** plate on card	15.
PR83P2a	24c **car,** PP sm die on yelsh wove paper	600.
PR83P3	24c **car,** plate on India paper	25.
	Block of 4	125.
PR83P4	24c **car,** plate on card	15.
PR84P2a	36c **car,** PP sm die on yelsh wove paper	600.
PR84P3	36c **car,** plate on India paper	25.
	Block of 4	125.
PR84P4	36c **car,** plate on card	15.
PR85P2a	48c **car,** PP sm die on yelsh wove paper	600.
PR85P3	48c **car,** plate on India paper	25.
	Block of 4	125.
PR85P4	48c **car,** plate on card	15.
PR86P2a	60c **car,** PP sm die on yelsh wove paper	600.
PR86P3	60c **car,** plate on India paper	25.
	Block of 4	125.
PR86P4	60c **car,** plate on card	15.
PR87P2a	72c **car,** PP sm die on yelsh wove paper	600.
PR87P3	72c **car,** plate on India paper	25.
	Block of 4	125.
PR87P4	72c **car,** plate on card	15.
PR88P2a	84c **car,** PP sm die on yelsh wove paper	600.
PR88P3	84c **car,** plate on India paper	25.
	Block of 4	125.
PR88P4	84c **car,** plate on card	15.
PR89P2a	96c **car,** PP sm die on yelsh wove paper	600.
PR89P3	96c **car,** plate on India paper	25.
	Block of 4	125.
PR89P4	96c **car,** plate on card	15.
	Nos. PR81P3-PR89P3 (9)	225.00
	Nos. PR81P4-PR89P4 (9)	135.00

1895

PR102TC1a	1c large die on India paper	
	e. **deep scarlet**	*600.*
PR102P1	1c **blk,** large die on India paper	125.
PR102P2	1c **blk,** RA sm die on white wove paper	115.
PR102P2a	1c **blk,** PP sm die on yelsh wove paper	600.
PR103P1	2c **blk,** large die on India paper	125.
PR103P2	2c **blk,** RA sm die on white wove paper	115.
PR103P2a	2c **blk,** PP sm die on yelsh wove paper	600.
PR104P1	5c **blk,** large die on India paper	125.
PR104P2	5c **blk,** RA sm die on white wove paper	115.
PR104P2a	5c **blk,** PP sm die on yelsh wove paper	600.
PR105P1	10c **blk,** large die on India paper	125.
PR105P2	10c **blk,** RA sm die on white wove paper	115.
PR105P2a	10c **blk,** PP sm die on yelsh wove paper	600.
PR106TC1a	25c large die on India paper	
	e. **deep carmine**	*600.*
	f. **dark carmine**	*600.*
PR106P1	25c **car,** large die on India paper	125.
PR106P2	25c **car,** RA sm die on white wove paper	115.
PR106P2a	25c **car,** PP sm die on yelsh wove paper	600.
PR107TC1a	50c large die on India paper	
	e. **black**	*600.*
	f. **deep carmine**	*600.*
PR107P1	50c **car,** large die on India paper	125.
PR107P2	50c **car,** RA sm die on white wove paper	115.
PR107P2a	50c **car,** PP sm die on yelsh wove paper	600.
PR108TC1a	$2 large die on India paper	
	e. **deep scarlet**	*600.*
	f. **dark scarlet**	*600.*
PR108P1	$2 **scar,** large die on India paper	125.
PR108P2	$2 **scar,** RA sm die on white wove paper	115.
PR108P2a	$2 **scar,** PP sm die on yelsh wove paper	600.
PR109TC1a	$5 large die on India paper	
	e. **light ultramarine**	*600.*
	f. **dark ultramarine**	*600.*
PR109P1	$5 **bl,** large die on India paper	125.
PR109P2	$5 **bl,** RA sm die on white wove paper	115.
PR109P2a	$5 **bl,** PP sm die on yelsh wove paper	600.
PR110TC1a	$10 large die on India paper	
	e. **black**	*600.*
PR110P1	$10 **grn,** large die on India paper	125.
PR110P2	$10 **grn,** RA sm die on white wove paper	115.
PR110P2a	$10 **grn,** PP sm die on yelsh wove paper	600.
PR111P1	$20 **slate,** large die on India paper	125.
PR111P2	$20 **slate,** RA sm die on white wove paper	115.
PR111P2a	$20 **slate,** PP sm die on yelsh wove paper	600.
PR112TC1a	$50 large die on India paper	
	e. **black**	*600.*
	f. **deep rose**	*600.*
	g. **dark rose**	*600.*
PR112P1	$50 **car,** large die on India paper	125.
PR112P2	$50 **car,** RA sm die on white wove paper	115.
PR112P2a	$50 **car,** PP sm die on yelsh wove paper	600.
PR113TC1a	$100 large die on India paper	
	e. **black**	*600.*
PR113P1	$100 **pur,** large die on India paper	125.
PR113P2	$100 **pur,** RA sm die on white wove paper	115.
PR113P2a	$100 **pur,** PP sm die on yelsh wove paper	600.

The so-called "Goodall" set of Small Die proofs on India Paper of Newspaper Stamps in five colors

PR9TC2	2c "Goodall" small die on India paper	
	b. **black**	150.
	d. **deep green**	125.
	d. **dull gray blue**	125.
	e. **deep brown**	125.
	f. **dull red**	125.
PR10TC2	3c "Goodall" small die on India paper	
	b. **black**	150.
	c. **deep green**	125.
	d. **dull gray blue**	125.
	e. **deep brown**	125.
	f. **dull red**	125.
PR11TC2	4c "Goodall" small die on India paper	
	b. **black**	150.
	c. **deep green**	125.
	d. **dull gray blue**	125.
	e. **deep brown**	125.
	f. **dull red**	125.
PR12TC2	6c "Goodall" small die on India paper	
	b. **black**	150.
	c. **deep green**	125.
	d. **dull gray blue**	125.
	e. **deep brown**	125.
	f. **dull red**	125.
PR13TC2	8c "Goodall" small die on India paper	
	b. **black**	150.
	c. **deep green**	125.
	d. **dull gray blue**	125.
	e. **deep brown**	125.
	f. **dull red**	125.
PR14TC2	9c "Goodall" small die on India paper	
	b. **black**	150.
	c. **deep green**	125.
	d. **dull gray blue**	125.
	e. **deep brown**	125.
	f. **dull red**	125.
PR15TC2	10c "Goodall" small die on India paper	
	b. **black**	150.
	c. **deep green**	125.
	d. **dull gray blue**	125.
	e. **deep brown**	125.
	f. **dull red**	125.
PR16TC2	12c "Goodall" small die on India paper	
	b. **black**	150.
	c. **deep green**	125.
	d. **dull gray blue**	125.
	e. **deep brown**	125.
	f. **dull red**	125.
PR17TC2	24c "Goodall" small die on India paper	
	b. **black**	150.
	c. **deep green**	125.
	d. **dull gray blue**	125.
	e. **deep brown**	125.
	f. **dull red**	125.
PR18TC2	36c "Goodall" small die on India paper	
	b. **black**	150.
	c. **deep green**	125.
	d. **dull gray blue**	125.
	e. **deep brown**	125.
	f. **dull red**	125.
PR19TC2	48c "Goodall" small die on India paper	
	b. **black**	150.
	c. **deep green**	125.
	d. **dull gray blue**	125.
	e. **deep brown**	125.
	f. **dull red**	125.
PR20TC2	60c "Goodall" small die on India paper	
	b. **black**	150.
	c. **deep green**	125.
	d. **dull gray blue**	125.
	e. **deep brown**	125.
	f. **dull red**	125.
PR21TC2	72c "Goodall" small die on India paper	
	b. **black**	150.
	c. **deep green**	125.
	d. **dull gray blue**	125.
	e. **deep brown**	125.
	f. **dull red**	125.
PR22TC2	84c "Goodall" small die on India paper	
	b. **black**	150.
	c. **deep green**	125.
	d. **dull gray blue**	125.
	e. **deep brown**	125
	f. **dull red**	12
PR23TC2	96c "Goodall" small die on India paper	
	b. **black**	
	c. **deep green**	
	d. **dull gray blue**	
	e. **deep brown**	
	f. **dull red**	
PR24TC2	$1.92 "Goodall" small die on India	
	b. **black**	
	c. **deep green**	

d. **dull gray blue** 125.
e. **deep brown** 125.
f. **dull red** 125.

PR25TC2 $3 "Goodall" small die on India paper
b. **black** 150.
c. **deep green** 125.
d. **dull gray blue** 125.
e. **deep brown** 125.
f. **dull red** 125.

PR26TC2 $6 "Goodall" small die on India paper
b. **black** 150.
c. **deep green** 125.
d. **dull gray blue** 125.
e. **deep brown** 125.
f. **dull red** 125.

PR27TC2 $9 "Goodall" small die on India paper
b. **black** 150.
c. **deep green** 125.
d. **dull gray blue** 125.
e. **deep brown** 125.
f. **dull red** 125.

PR28TC2 $12 "Goodall" small die on India paper
b. **black** 150.
c. **deep green** 125.
d. **dull gray blue** 125.
e. **deep brown** 125.
f. **dull red** 125.

PR29TC2 $24 "Goodall" small die on India paper
b. **black** 150.
c. **deep green** 125.
d. **dull gray blue** 125.
e. **deep brown** 125.
f. **dull red** 125.

PR30TC2 $36 "Goodall" small die on India paper
b. **black** 150.
c. **deep green** 125.
d. **dull gray blue** 125.
e. **deep brown** 125.
f. **dull red** 125.

PR31TC2 $48 "Goodall" small die on India paper
b. **black** 150.
c. **deep green** 125.
d. **dull gray blue** 125.
e. **deep brown** 125.
f. **dull red** 125.

PR32TC2 $60 "Goodall" small die on India paper
b. **black** 150.
c. **deep green** 125.
d. **dull gray blue** 125.
e. **deep brown** 125.
f. **dull red** 125.

PARCEL POST

1912-13

Q1P1 1c **car rose,** large die on India paper 1,400.
Q1P2 1c **car rose,** sm die on India paper 1,200.
Q1P2a 1c **car rose,** PP sm die on yelsh wove paper 2,500.
Q2P1 2c **car rose,** large die on India paper 1,400.
Q2P2 2c **car rose,** sm die on India paper 1,200.
Q2P2a 2c **car rose,** PP sm die on yelsh wove paper 2,500.
Q3P1 3c **car rose,** large die on India paper 1,400.
Q3P2 3c **car rose,** sm die on India paper 1,200.
Q3P2a 3c **car rose,** PP sm die on yelsh wove paper 2,500.
Q4P1 4c **car rose,** large die on India paper 1,400.
Q4P2 4c **car rose,** sm die on India paper 1,200.
Q4P2a 4c **car rose,** PP sm die on yelsh wove paper 2,500.
Q5P1 5c **car rose,** large die on India paper 1,400.
Q5P2 5c **car rose,** sm die on India paper 1,200.
Q5P2a 5c **car rose,** PP sm die on yelsh wove paper 2,500.
Q6P1 10c **car rose,** large die on India paper 1,400.
Q6P2 10c **car rose,** sm die on India paper 1,200.
Q6P2a 10c **car rose,** PP sm die on yelsh wove paper 2,500.
Q7P1 15c **car rose,** large die on India paper 1,400.
Q7P2 15c **car rose,** sm die on India paper 1,200.
Q7P2a 15c **car rose,** PP sm die on yelsh wove paper 2,500.
Q8P1 20c **car rose,** large die on India paper 1,400.
Q8P2 20c **car rose,** sm die on India paper 1,200.
Q8P2a 20c **car rose,** PP sm die on yelsh wove paper 2,500.
Q9P1 25c **car rose,** large die on India paper 1,400.
Q9P2 25c **car rose,** sm die on India paper 1,200.
Q9P2a 25c **car rose,** PP sm die on yelsh wove paper 2,500.
Q10P1 50c **car rose,** large die on India paper 1,400.
Q10P2 50c **car rose,** sm die on India paper 1,200.
Q10P2a 50c **car rose,** PP sm die on yelsh wove paper 2,500.
Q11P1 75c **car rose,** large die on India paper 1,400.
Q11P2 75c **car rose,** sm die on India paper 1,200.
Q11P2a 75c **car rose,** PP sm die on yelsh wove paper 2,500.
Q12P1 $1 **car rose,** large die on India paper 1,400.
Q12P2 $1 **car rose,** sm die on India paper 1,200.
Q12P2a $1 **car rose,** PP sm die on yelsh wove paper 2,500.

SPECIAL HANDLING

1925-28

QE1P1 10c **yel grn,** large die on India paper *2,500.*
QE2P1 15c **yel grn,** large die on India paper *2,500.*
QE3P1 20c **yel grn,** large die on India paper *2,500.*
QE4TC1a 25c large die on India paper
e. **apple green** *3,250.*
f. **olive green** *3,250.*
g. **light blue green** *3,250.*
h. **blue** *3,250.*
i. **dark blue** *3,250.*
j. **orange yellow** *3,250.*
k. **orange** *3,250.*
l. **dull rose** *3,250.*
m. **carmine lake** *3,250.*
n. **carmine rose** *3,250.*
o. **brown** *3,250.*
p. **gray brown** *3,250.*
q. **dark violet brown** *3,250.*
r. **gray black** *3,250.*
s. **black** *3,250.*
QE4P1 25c **dp grn,** large die on India paper *2,500.*
QE4aP1 25c **yel grn,** large die on India paper *3,250.*

THE "ATLANTA" SET OF PLATE PROOFS

A set in five colors on thin card reprinted in 1881 for display at the International Cotton Exhibition in Atlanta, Ga. Blocks exist; they are very rare.

1847 Designs (Reproductions)

3TC4 5c Atlanta plate on card
a. **black** 450.
b. **scarlet** 450.
c. **brown** 450.
d. **green** 450.
e. **blue** 450.

4TC4 10c Atlanta plate on card
a. **black** 450.
b. **scarlet** 450.
c. **brown** 450.
d. **green** 450.
e. **blue** 450.

1851-60 Designs

40TC4 1c Atlanta plate on card
a. **black** 120.
b. **scarlet** 100.
c. **brown** 100.
d. **green** 100.
e. **blue** 100.

41TC4 3c Atlanta plate on card
a. **black** 120.
b. **scarlet** 100.
c. **brown** 100.
d. **green** 100.
e. **blue** 100.

42TC4 5c Atlanta plate on card
a. **black** 120.
b. **scarlet** 100.
c. **brown** 100.
d. **green** 100.
e. **blue** 100.

43TC4 10c Atlanta plate on card
a. **black** 120.
b. **scarlet** 100.
c. **brown** 100.
d. **green** 100.
e. **blue** 100.

44TC4 12c Atlanta plate on card
a. **black** 120.
b. **scarlet** 100.
c. **brown** 100.
d. **green** 100.
e. **blue** 100.

45TC4 24c Atlanta plate on card
a. **black** 120.
b. **scarlet** 100.
c. **brown** 100.
d. **green** 100.
e. **blue** 100.

46TC4 30c Atlanta plate on card
a. **black** 120.
b. **scarlet** 100.
c. **brown** 100.
d. **green** 100.
e. **blue** 100.

47TC4 90c Atlanta plate on card
a. **black** 120.
b. **scarlet** 100.
c. **brown** 100.
d. **green** 100.
e. **blue** 100.

1861-66 Designs

102TC4 1c Atlanta plate on card
a. **black** 100.
b. **scarlet** 90.
c. **brown** 90.
d. **green** 90.
e. **blue** 90.

103TC4 2c Atlanta plate on card
a. **black** 175.
b. **scarlet** 175.
c. **brown** 175.
d. **green** 175.
e. **blue** 175.

104TC4 3c Atlanta plate on card
a. **black** 100.
b. **scarlet** 90.
c. **brown** 90.
d. **green** 90.
e. **blue** 90.

105TC4 5c Atlanta plate on card
a. **black** 100.
b. **scarlet** 90.
c. **brown** 90.
d. **green** 90.
e. **blue** 90.

106TC4 10c Atlanta plate on card
a. **black** 100.
b. **scarlet** 90.
c. **brown** 90.
d. **green** 90.
e. **blue** 90.

107TC4 12c Atlanta plate on card
a. **black** 100.
b. **scarlet** 90.
c. **brown** 90.
d. **green** 90.
e. **blue** 90.

108TC4 15c Atlanta plate on card
a. **black** 100.
b. **scarlet** 90.
c. **brown** 90.
d. **green** 90.
e. **blue** 90.

109TC4 24c Atlanta plate on card
a. **black** 100.
b. **scarlet** 90.
c. **brown** 90.
d. **green** 90.
e. **blue** 90.

110TC4 30c Atlanta plate on card
a. **black** 100.
b. **scarlet** 90.
c. **brown** 90.
d. **green** 90.
e. **blue** 90.

111TC4 90c Atlanta plate on card
a. **black** 100.
b. **scarlet** 90.
c. **brown** 90.
d. **green** 90.
e. **blue** 90.

1869 Designs

123TC4 1c Atlanta plate on card
a. **black** 175.
b. **scarlet** 150.
c. **brown** 150.
d. **green** 150.
e. **blue** 150.

124TC4 2c Atlanta plate on card
a. **black** 175.
b. **scarlet** 150.
c. **brown** 150.
d. **green** 150.
e. **blue** 150.

125TC4 3c Atlanta plate on card
a. **black** 175.
b. **scarlet** 150.
c. **brown** 150.
d. **green** 150.
e. **blue** 150.

126TC4 6c Atlanta plate on card
a. **black** 175.
b. **scarlet** 150.
c. **brown** 150.
d. **green** 150.
e. **blue** 150.

127TC4 10c Atlanta plate on card
a. **black** 175.
b. **scarlet** 150.
c. **brown** 150.
d. **green** 150.
e. **blue** 150.

128TC4 12c Atlanta plate on card
a. **black** 175.
b. **scarlet** 150.
c. **brown** 150.
d. **green** 150.
e. **blue** 150.

129TC4 15c Atlanta plate on card
a. **black frame, scarlet center** 375.
b. **black frame, green center** 375.
c. **scarlet frame, black center** 375.
d. **scarlet frame, blue center** 375.
e. **brown frame, black center** 375.
f. **brown frame, green center** 375.
g. **brown frame, blue center** 375.
h. **green frame, black center** 375.
i. **green frame, blue center** 375.
j. **blue frame, black center** 375.
k. **blue frame, brown center** 375.
l. **blue frame, green center** 375.

130TC4 24c Atlanta plate on card
a. **black frame, scarlet center** 375.
b. **black frame, green center** 375.
c. **black frame, blue center** 375.
d. **scarlet frame, black center** 375.
e. **scarlet frame, blue center** 375.
f. **brown frame, black center** 375.
g. **brown frame, blue center** 375.
h. **green frame, black center** 375.
i. **green frame, brown center** 375.
j. **green frame, blue center** 375.
k. **blue frame, brown center** 375.
l. **blue frame, green center** 375.

131TC4 30c Atlanta plate on card
a. **black frame, scarlet center** 375.
b. **black frame, green center** 375.
c. **black frame, blue center** 375.
d. **scarlet frame, black center** 375.
e. **scarlet frame, green center** 375.
f. **scarlet frame, blue center** 375.
g. **brown frame, black center** 375.
h. **brown frame, scarlet center** 375.
i. **brown frame, blue center** 375.
j. **green frame, black center** 375.
k. **green frame, brown center** 375.
l. **blue frame, scarlet center** 375.
m. **blue frame, brown center** 375.
n. **blue frame, green center** 375.

132TC4 90c Atlanta plate on card
a. **black frame, scarlet center** 600.
b. **black frame, brown center** 600.
c. **black frame, green center** 600.
d. **scarlet frame, blue center** 600.
e. **brown frame, black center** 600.
f. **brown frame, blue center** 600.
g. **green frame, black center** *10,000.*
h. **green frame, brown center** 600.
i. **green frame, blue center** 600.
j. **blue frame, brown center** 600.

k. **blue frame, green center** 600.

1873-75 Designs

156TC4 1c Atlanta plate on card
a. **black** 55.
b. **scarlet** 50.
c. **brown** 50.
d. **green** 50.
e. **blue** 50.

157TC4 2c Atlanta plate on card
a. **black** 55.
b. **scarlet** 50.
c. **brown** 50.
d. **green** 50.
e. **blue** 50.

158TC4 3c Atlanta plate on card
a. **black** 60.
b. **scarlet** 55.
c. **brown** 55.
d. **green** 55.
e. **blue** 55.

159TC4 6c Atlanta plate on card
a. **black** 65.
b. **scarlet** 60.
c. **brown** 60.
d. **green** 60.
e. **blue** 60.

160TC4 7c Atlanta plate on card
a. **black** 55.
b. **scarlet** 50.
c. **brown** 50.
d. **green** 50.
e. **blue** 50.

161TC4 10c Atlanta plate on card
a. **black** 55.
b. **scarlet** 50.
c. **brown** 50.
d. **green** 50.
e. **blue** 50.

162TC4 12c Atlanta plate on card
a. **black** 55.
b. **scarlet** 50.
c. **brown** 50.
d. **green** 50.
e. **blue** 50.

163TC4 15c Atlanta plate on card
a. **black** 55.
b. **scarlet** 50.
c. **brown** 50.
d. **green** 50.
e. **blue** 50.

164TC4 24c Atlanta plate on card
a. **black** 55.
b. **scarlet** 50.
c. **brown** 50.
d. **green** 50.
e. **blue** 50.

165TC4 30c Atlanta plate on card
a. **black** 60.
b. **scarlet** 55.
c. **brown** 55.
d. **green** 55.
e. **blue** 55.

166TC4 90c Atlanta plate on card
a. **black** 55.
b. **scarlet** 50.
c. **brown** 50.
d. **green** 50.
e. **blue** 50.

179TC4 5c Atlanta plate on card
a. **black** 80.
b. **scarlet** 75.
c. **brown** 75.
d. **green** 75.
e. **blue** 75.

POSTAGE DUE

J1TC4 1c Atlanta plate on card
a. **black** 55.
b. **scarlet** 50.
c. **brown** 50.
d. **green** 50.
e. **blue** 50.

J2TC4 2c Atlanta plate on card
a. **black** 55.
b. **scarlet** 50.
c. **brown** 50.
d. **green** 50.
e. **blue** 50.

J3TC4 3c Atlanta plate on card
a. **black** 55.
b. **scarlet** 50.
c. **brown** 50.
d. **green** 50.
e. **blue** 50.

J4TC4 5c Atlanta plate on card
a. **black** 55.
b. **scarlet** 50.
c. **brown** 50.
d. **green** 50.
e. **blue** 50.

J5TC4 10c Atlanta plate on card
a. **black** 55.
b. **scarlet** 50.
c. **brown** 50.
d. **green** 50.
e. **blue** 50.

J6TC4 30c Atlanta plate on card
a. **black** 55.
b. **scarlet** 50.
c. **brown** 50.
d. **green** 50.
e. **blue** 50.

J7TC4 50c Atlanta plate on card
a. **black** 55.
b. **scarlet** 50.
c. **brown** 50.
d. **green** 50.
e. **blue** 50.

OFFICIALS

Agriculture

O1TC4 1c Atlanta plate on card
a. **black** 43.
b. **scarlet** 37.
c. **brown** 37.
d. **green** 37.
e. **blue** 37.

O2TC4 2c Atlanta plate on card
a. **black** 43.
b. **scarlet** 37.
c. **brown** 37.
d. **green** 37.
e. **blue** 37.

O3TC4 3c Atlanta plate on card
a. **black** 43.
b. **scarlet** 37.
c. **brown** 37.
d. **green** 37.
e. **blue** 37.

O4TC4 6c Atlanta plate on card
a. **black** 55.
b. **scarlet** 50.
c. **brown** 50.
d. **green** 50.
e. **blue** 50.

O5TC4 10c Atlanta plate on card
a. **black** 43.
b. **scarlet** 37.
c. **brown** 37.
d. **green** 37.
e. **blue** 37.

O6TC4 12c Atlanta plate on card
a. **black** 43.
b. **scarlet** 37.
c. **brown** 37.
d. **green** 37.
e. **blue** 37.

O7TC4 15c Atlanta plate on card
a. **black** 43.
b. **scarlet** 37.
c. **brown** 37.
d. **green** 37.
e. **blue** 37.

O8TC4 24c Atlanta plate on card
a. **black** 43.
b. **scarlet** 37.
c. **brown** 37.
d. **green** 37.
e. **blue** 37.

O9TC4 30c Atlanta plate on card
a. **black** 43.
b. **scarlet** 37.
c. **brown** 37.
d. **green** 37.
e. **blue** 37.

Executive

O10TC4 1c Atlanta plate on card
a. **black** 43.
b. **scarlet** 37.
c. **brown** 37.
d. **green** 37.
e. **blue** 37.

O11TC4 2c Atlanta plate on card
a. **black** 43.
b. **scarlet** 37.
c. **brown** 37.
d. **green** 37.
e. **blue** 37.

O12TC4 3c Atlanta plate on card
a. **black** 43.
b. **scarlet** 37.
c. **brown** 37.
d. **green** 37.
e. **blue** 37.

O13TC4 6c Atlanta plate on card
a. **black** 43.
b. **scarlet** 37.
c. **brown** 37.
d. **green** 37.
e. **blue** 37.

O14TC4 10c Atlanta plate on card
a. **black** 43.
b. **scarlet** 37.
c. **brown** 37.
d. **green** 37.
e. **blue** 37.

Interior

O15TC4 1c Atlanta plate on card
a. **black** 43.
b. **scarlet** 37.
c. **brown** 37.
d. **green** 37.
e. **blue** 37.

O16TC4 2c Atlanta plate on card
a. **black** 43.
b. **scarlet** 37.
c. **brown** 37.
d. **green** 37.
e. **blue** 37.

O17TC4 3c Atlanta plate on card
a. **black** 43.
b. **scarlet** 37.
c. **brown** 37.
d. **green** 37.
e. **blue** 37.

O18TC4 6c Atlanta plate on card
a. **black** 55.
b. **scarlet** 50.
c. **brown** 50.
d. **green** 50.
e. **blue** 50.

O19TC4 10c Atlanta plate on card
a. **black** 43.
b. **scarlet** 37.
c. **brown** 37.
d. **green** 37.
e. **blue** 37.

O20TC4 12c Atlanta plate on card
a. **black** 43.
b. **scarlet** 37.
c. **brown** 37.
d. **green** 37.
e. **blue** 37.

O21TC4 15c Atlanta plate on card
a. **black** 43.
b. **scarlet** 37.
c. **brown** 37.
d. **green** 37.
e. **blue** 37.

O22TC4 24c Atlanta plate on card
a. **black** 43.
b. **scarlet** 37.
c. **brown** 37.
d. **green** 37.
e. **blue** 37.

O23TC4 30c Atlanta plate on card
a. **black** 60.
b. **scarlet** 55.
c. **brown** 55.
d. **green** 55.
e. **blue** 55.

O24TC4 90c Atlanta plate on card
a. **black** 43.
b. **scarlet** 37.
c. **brown** 37.
d. **green** 37.
e. **blue** 37.

Justice

O25TC4 1c Atlanta plate on card
a. **black** 43.
b. **scarlet** 37.
c. **brown** 37.
d. **green** 37.
e. **blue** 37.

O26TC4 2c Atlanta plate on card
a. **black** 43.
b. **scarlet** 37.
c. **brown** 37.
d. **green** 37.
e. **blue** 37.

O27TC4 3c Atlanta plate on card
a. **black** 43.
b. **scarlet** 37.
c. **brown** 37.
d. **green** 37.
e. **blue** 37.

O28TC4 6c Atlanta plate on card
a. **black** 55.
b. **scarlet** 50.
c. **brown** 50.
d. **green** 50.
e. **blue** 50.

O29TC4 10c Atlanta plate on card
a. **black** 43.
b. **scarlet** 37.
c. **brown** 37.
d. **green** 37.
e. **blue** 37.

O30TC4 12c Atlanta plate on card
a. **black** 43.
b. **scarlet** 37.
c. **brown** 37.
d. **green** 37.
e. **blue** 37.

O31TC4 15c Atlanta plate on card
a. **black** 43.
b. **scarlet** 37.
c. **brown** 37.
d. **green** 37.
e. **blue** 37.

O32TC4 24c Atlanta plate on card
a. **black** 43.
b. **scarlet** 37.
c. **brown** 37.
d. **green** 37.
e. **blue** 37.

O33TC4 30c Atlanta plate on card
a. **black** 60.
b. **scarlet** 55.
c. **brown** 55.
d. **green** 55.
e. **blue** 55.

O34TC4 90c Atlanta plate on card
a. **black** 43.
b. **scarlet** 37.
c. **brown** 37.
d. **green** 37.
e. **blue** 37.

Navy

O35TC4 1c Atlanta plate on card
a. **black** 43.
b. **scarlet** 37.
c. **brown** 37.
d. **green** 37.
e. **blue** 37.

O36TC4 2c Atlanta plate on card
a. **black** 43.
b. **scarlet** 37.
c. **brown** 37.
d. **green** 37.
e. **blue** 37.

O37TC4 3c Atlanta plate on card
a. **black** 43.
b. **scarlet** 37.
c. **brown** 37.
d. **green** 37.
e. **blue** 37.

O38TC4 6c Atlanta plate on card
a. **black** 55.
b. **scarlet** 50.
c. **brown** 50.

d. green 50.
e. blue 50.
O39TC4 7c Atlanta plate on card
a. black 43.
b. scarlet 37.
c. brown 37.
d. green 37.
e. blue 37.
O40TC4 10c Atlanta plate on card
a. black 43.
b. scarlet 37.
c. brown 37.
d. green 37.
e. blue 37.
O41TC4 12c Atlanta plate on card
a. black 43.
b. scarlet 37.
c. brown 37.
d. green 37.
e. blue 37.
O42TC4 15c Atlanta plate on card
a. black 43.
b. scarlet 37.
c. brown 37.
d. green 37.
e. blue 37.
O43TC4 24c Atlanta plate on card
a. black 43.
b. scarlet 37.
c. brown 37.
d. green 37.
e. blue 37.
O44TC4 30c Atlanta plate on card
a. black 60.
b. scarlet 55.
c. brown 55.
d. green 55.
e. blue 55.
O45TC4 90c Atlanta plate on card
a. black 43.
b. scarlet 37.
c. brown 37.
d. green 37.
e. blue 37.

Post Office

O48TC4 2c Atlanta plate on card
a. black 43.
b. scarlet 37.
c. brown 37.
d. green 37.
e. blue 37.
O49TC4 3c Atlanta plate on card
a. black 43.
b. scarlet 37.
c. brown 37.
d. green 37.
e. blue 37.
O50TC4 6c Atlanta plate on card
a. black 43.
b. scarlet 37.
c. brown 37.
d. green 37.
e. blue 37.
O51TC4 10c Atlanta plate on card
a. black 43.
b. scarlet 37.
c. brown 37.
d. green 37.
e. blue 37.
O52TC4 12c Atlanta plate on card
a. black 43.
b. scarlet 37.
c. brown 37.
d. green 37.
e. blue 37.
O53TC4 15c Atlanta plate on card
a. black 43.
b. scarlet 37.
c. brown 37.
d. green 37.
e. blue 37.
O54TC4 24c Atlanta plate on card
a. black 43.
b. scarlet 37.
c. brown 37.
d. green 37.
e. blue 37.
O55TC4 30c Atlanta plate on card
a. black 43.
b. scarlet 37.
c. brown 37.
d. green 37.
e. blue 37.
O56TC4 90c Atlanta plate on card
a. black 43.
b. scarlet 37.
c. brown 37.
d. green 37.
e. blue 37.

State

O57TC4 1c Atlanta plate on card
a. black 43.
b. scarlet 37.
c. brown 37.
d. green 37.
e. blue 37.
O58TC4 2c Atlanta plate on card
a. black 43.
b. scarlet 37.
c. brown 37.
d. green 37.
e. blue 37.
O59TC4 3c Atlanta plate on card
a. black 43.
b. scarlet 37.
c. brown 37.
d. green 37.
e. blue 37.
O60TC4 6c Atlanta plate on card
a. black 55.
b. scarlet 50.
c. brown 50.
d. green 50.
e. blue 50.
O61TC4 7c Atlanta plate on card
a. black 43.
b. scarlet 37.
c. brown 37.
d. green 37.
e. blue 37.
O62TC4 10c Atlanta plate on card
a. black 43.
b. scarlet 37.
c. brown 37.
d. green 37.
e. blue 37.
O63TC4 12c Atlanta plate on card
a. black 43.
b. scarlet 37.
c. brown 37.
d. green 37.
e. blue 37.
O64TC4 15c Atlanta plate on card
a. black 43.
b. scarlet 37.
c. brown 37.
d. green 37.
e. blue 37.
O65TC4 24c Atlanta plate on card
a. black 43.
b. scarlet 37.
c. brown 37.
d. green 37.
e. blue 37.
O66TC4 30c Atlanta plate on card
a. black 60.
b. scarlet 55.
c. brown 55.
d. green 55.
e. blue 55.
O67TC4 90c Atlanta plate on card
a. black 43.
b. scarlet 37.
c. brown 37.
d. green 37.
e. blue 37.
O68TC4 $2 Atlanta plate on card
a. scarlet frame, black center 1,000.
b. scarlet frame, blue center 1,000.
c. brown frame, black center 1,000.
d. brown frame, blue center 1,000.
e. green frame, brown center 1,000.
f. blue frame, brown center 1,000.
g. blue frame, green center 1,000.
O69TC4 $5 Atlanta plate on card
a. scarlet frame, black center 1,000.
b. scarlet frame, blue center 1,000.
c. brown frame, black center 1,000.
d. brown frame, blue center 1,000.
e. green frame, brown center 1,000.
f. blue frame, brown center 1,000.
g. blue frame, green center 1,000.
O70TC4 $10 Atlanta plate on card
a. scarlet frame, black center 1,000.
b. scarlet frame, blue center 1,000.
c. brown frame, black center 1,000.
d. brown frame, blue center 1,000.
e. green frame, brown center 1,000.
f. blue frame, brown center 1,000.
g. blue frame, green center 1,000.
O71TC4 $20 Atlanta plate on card
a. scarlet frame, black center 1,000.
b. scarlet frame, blue center 1,000.
c. brown frame, black center 1,000.
d. brown frame, blue center 1,000.
e. green frame, brown center 1,000.
f. blue frame, brown center 1,000.
g. blue frame, green center 1,000.

Treasury

O72TC4 1c Atlanta plate on card
a. black 43.
b. scarlet 37.
c. brown 37.
d. green 37.
e. blue 37.
O73TC4 2c Atlanta plate on card
a. black 43.
b. scarlet 37.
c. brown 37.
d. green 37.
e. blue 37.
O74TC4 3c Atlanta plate on card
a. black 43.
b. scarlet 37.
c. brown 37.
d. green 37.
e. blue 37.
O75TC4 6c Atlanta plate on card
a. black 55.
b. scarlet 50.
c. brown 50.
d. green 50.
e. blue 50.
O76TC4 7c Atlanta plate on card
a. black 43.
b. scarlet 37.
c. brown 37.
d. green 37.
e. blue 37.
O77TC4 10c Atlanta plate on card
a. black 43.
b. scarlet 37.
c. brown 37.
d. green 37.
e. blue 37.
O78TC4 12c Atlanta plate on card
a. black 43.
b. scarlet 37.
c. brown 37.
d. green 37.
e. blue 37.
O79TC4 15c Atlanta plate on card
a. black 43.
b. scarlet 37.
c. brown 37.
d. green 37.
e. blue 37.
O80TC4 24c Atlanta plate on card
a. black 43.
b. scarlet 37.
c. brown 37.
d. green 37.
e. blue 37.
O81TC4 30c Atlanta plate on card
a. black 60.
b. scarlet 55.
c. brown 55.
d. green 55.
e. blue 55.
O82TC4 90c Atlanta plate on card
a. black 43.
b. scarlet 37.
c. brown 37.
d. green 37.
e. blue 37.

War

O83TC4 1c Atlanta plate on card
a. black 43.
b. scarlet 37.
c. brown 37.
d. green 37.
e. blue 37.
O84TC4 2c Atlanta plate on card
a. black 43.
b. scarlet 37.
c. brown 37.
d. green 37.
e. bluc 37.
O85TC4 3c Atlanta plate on card
a. black 43.
b. scarlet 37.
c. brown 37.
Plate flaw at upper left (32R20) —
d. green 37.
e. blue 37.
O86TC4 6c Atlanta plate on card
a. black 55.
b. scarlet 50.
c. brown 50.
d. green 50.
e. blue 50.
O87TC4 7c Atlanta plate on card
a. black 43.
b. scarlet 37.
c. brown 37.
d. green 37.
e. blue 37.
O88TC4 10c Atlanta plate on card
a. black 43.
b. scarlet 37.
c. brown 37.
d. green 37.
e. blue 37.
O89TC4 12c Atlanta plate on card
a. black 43.
b. scarlet 37.
c. brown 37.
d. green 37.
e. blue 37.
O90TC4 15c Atlanta plate on card
a. black 43.
b. scarlet 37.
c. brown 37.
d. green 37.
e. blue 37.
O91TC4 24c Atlanta plate on card
a. black 43.
b. scarlet 37.
c. brown 37.
d. green 37.
e. blue 37.
O92TC4 30c Atlanta plate on card
a. black 60.
b. scarlet 55.
c. brown 55.
d. green 55.
e. blue 55.
O93TC4 90c Atlanta plate on card
a. black 43.
b. scarlet 37.
c. brown 37.
d. green 37.
e. blue 37.

NEWSPAPERS

PR9TC4 2c Atlanta plate on card
a. black 55.
b. scarlet 40.
c. brown 40.
d. green 40.
e. blue 40.
PR10TC4 3c Atlanta plate on card
a. black 55.
b. scarlet 40.
c. brown 40.
d. green 40.
e. blue 40.
PR11TC4 4c Atlanta plate on card
a. black 55.
b. scarlet 40.
c. brown 40.

d. **green** 40.
e. **blue** 40.
PR12TC4 6c Atlanta plate on card
a. **black** 55.
b. **scarlet** 40.
c. **brown** 40.
d. **green** 40.
e. **blue** 40.
PR13TC4 8c Atlanta plate on card
a. **black** 55.
b. **scarlet** 40.
c. **brown** 40.
d. **green** 40.
e. **blue** 40.
PR14TC4 9c Atlanta plate on card
a. **black** 55.
b. **scarlet** 40.
c. **brown** 40.
d. **green** 40.
e. **blue** 40.
PR15TC4 10c Atlanta plate on card
a. **black** 55.
b. **scarlet** 40.
c. **brown** 40.
d. **green** 40.
e. **blue** 40.
PR16TC4 12c Atlanta plate on card
a. **black** 55.
b. **scarlet** 40.
c. **brown** 40.
d. **green** 40.
e. **blue** 40.
PR17TC4 24c Atlanta plate on card
a. **black** 55.
b. **scarlet** 40.
c. **brown** 40.
d. **green** 40.
e. **blue** 40.
PR18TC4 36c Atlanta plate on card
a. **black** 55.
b. **scarlet** 40.
c. **brown** 40.
d. **green** 40.
e. **blue** 40.
PR19TC4 48c Atlanta plate on card
a. **black** 55.
b. **scarlet** 40.
c. **brown** 40.
d. **green** 40.
e. **blue** 40.
PR20TC4 60c Atlanta plate on card
a. **black** 55.
b. **scarlet** 40.
c. **brown** 40.
d. **green** 40.
e. **blue** 40.
PR21TC4 72c Atlanta plate on card
a. **black** 55.
b. **scarlet** 40.
c. **brown** 40.
d. **green** 40.
e. **blue** 40.
PR22TC4 84c Atlanta plate on card
a. **black** 55.
b. **scarlet** 40.
c. **brown** 40.
d. **green** 40.
e. **blue** 40.
PR23TC4 96c Atlanta plate on card
a. **black** 55.
b. **scarlet** 40.
c. **brown** 40.
d. **green** 40.
e. **blue** 40.
PR24TC4 $1.92 Atlanta plate on card
a. **black** 55.
b. **scarlet** 40.
c. **brown** 40.
d. **green** 40.
e. **blue** 40.
PR25TC4 $3 Atlanta plate on card
a. **black** 55.
b. **scarlet** 40.
c. **brown** 40.
d. **green** 40.
e. **blue** 40.
PR26TC4 $6 Atlanta plate on card
a. **black** 55.
b. **scarlet** 40.
c. **brown** 40.
d. **green** 40.
e. **blue** 40.
PR27TC4 $9 Atlanta plate on card
a. **black** 55.
b. **scarlet** 40.
c. **brown** 40.
d. **green** 40.
e. **blue** 40.
PR28TC4 $12 Atlanta plate on card
a. **black** 55.
b. **scarlet** 40.
c. **brown** 40.
d. **green** 40.
e. **blue** 40.
PR29TC4 $24 Atlanta plate on card
a. **black** 55.
b. **scarlet** 40.
c. **brown** 40.
d. **green** 40.
e. **blue** 40.
PR30TC4 $36 Atlanta plate on card
a. **black** 55.
b. **scarlet** 40.
c. **brown** 40.
d. **green** 40.
e. **blue** 40.
PR31TC4 $48 Atlanta plate on card
a. **black** 55.
b. **scarlet** 40.
c. **brown** 40.
d. **green** 40.
e. **blue** 40.
PR32TC4 $60 Atlanta plate on card
a. **black** 55.
b. **scarlet** 40.
c. **brown** 40.
d. **green** 40.
e. **blue** 40.

CARRIERS

LO1TC4 1c Franklin, Atlanta plate on card
a. **black** 120.
b. **scarlet** 110.
c. **brown** 110.
d. **green** 110.
e. **blue** 110.
LO2TC4 1c Eagle, Atlanta plate on card
a. **black** 120.
b. **scarlet** 110.
c. **brown** 110.
d. **green** 110.
e. **blue** 110.

TELEGRAPH

1881 American Rapid Telegraph Co.

1T1TC2 1c small die on India paper
b. **green** 55.
c. **brown** 55.
d. **red** 55.
e. **blue** 55.
f. **bluish green** 55.
1T1P2 1c **blk,** sm die on India paper 80.
1T1P3 1c **blk,** plate on India paper 32.
Pair 68.
1T2P3 3c **org,** plate on India paper 32.
Pair 68.
1T3TC2 5c small die on India paper
b. **green** 55.
c. **black** 55.
d. **red** 55.
e. **blue** 55.
f. **bluish green** 55.
1T3P2 5c **bis brn,** sm die on India paper 80.
1T3P3 5c **bis brn,** plate on India paper 32.
Pair 68.
1T4P1 10c **pur,** large die on India paper *850.*
1T4P3 10c **pur,** plate on India paper 32.
Pair 68.
1T5TC2 15c small die on India paper
b. **red** 55.
c. **black** 55.
d. **brown** 55.
e. **bluish green** 55.
1T5P2 15c **grn,** sm die on India paper 80.
1T5P3 15c **grn,** plate on India paper 32.
Pair 68.
1T6TC2 20c small die on India paper
b. **green** 55.
c. **black** 55.
d. **brown** 55.
e. **blue** 55.
f. **bluish green** 55.
1T6P2 20c **red,** sm die on India paper 80.
1T6P3 20c **red,** plate on India paper 32.
Pair 68.
1T7P2 25c **rose,** sm die on India paper 80.
1T7P3 25c **rose,** plate on India paper 32.
Pair 68.
1T8P3 50c **bl,** plate on India paper 32.
Pair 68.

"Collect"

1T9P3 1c **brn,** plate on India paper 32.
1T10TC2 5c small die on India paper
b. **red** 55.
c. **black** 55.
d. **brown** 55.
e. **green** 55.
f. **bluish green** 55.
1T10P3 5c **bl,** plate on India paper 32.
1T11TC2 15c small die on India paper
b. **red** 55.
c. **black** 55.
d. **brown** 55.
e. **green** 55.
f. **blue** 55.
g. **bluish green** 55.
1T11P3 15c **red brn,** plate on India paper 32.
1T12P1 20c **ol grn,** large die on India paper *850.*
1T12P3 20c **ol grn,** plate on India paper 32.

Office Coupon

1T13P3 1c **brn,** plate on India paper 32.
a. Pair Nos. 1T9P3, 1T13P3 68.
Same, block of 4 145.
1T14TC2 5c small die on India paper
b. **red** 55.
c. **black** 55.
d. **brown** 55.
e. **green** 55.
f. **bluish green** 55.
1T14P3 5c **bl,** plate on India paper 32.
a. Pair Nos. 1T10P3, 1T14P3 68.
Same, block of 4 145.
1T15TC2 15c small die on India paper
b. **red** 55.
c. **black** 55.
d. **brown** 55.
e. **green** 55.
f. **blue** 55.
g. **bluish green** 55.
1T15P3 15c **red brm,** plate on India paper 32.
a. Pair Nos. 1T11P3, 1T15P3 68.
Same, block of 4 145.
1T16P1 20c **ol grn,** large die on India paper *850.*
1T16P3 20c **ol grn,** plate on India paper 32.
a. Pair Nos. 1T12P3, 1T16P3 68.
Same, block of 4 145.

1885 Baltimore & Ohio Telegraph Co.

3T1P3 1c **ver,** plate on India paper 32.
Pair 68.
3T2TC2 5c small die on India paper
b. **dark olive** 65.
3T2P3 5c **bl,** plate on India paper 32.
Pair 68.
3T3P1 10c **red brn,** large die on India paper *900.*
3T3P3 10c **red brn,** plate on India paper 32.
Pair 68.
3T4TC2 25c small die on India paper
b. **dark olive** 65.
3T4P3 25c **org,** plate on India paper 32.
Pair 68.

1886

3T6P3 **blk,** plate on India paper 32.
Pair 68.
3T7P3 1c **grn,** plate on India paper 32.
3T8P3 5c **bl,** plate on India paper 32.
3T9P3 10c **brn,** plate on India paper 32.
3T10P3 25c **org,** plate on India paper 32.

1894-95 Northern New York Telegraph Co.

12T1P4 **green,** plate on card 125.
12T2P4 **red,** plate on card 125.
12T3P4 1c **yellow,** plate on card 40.
12T4P4 10c **blue,** plate on card 40.

1885 Postal Telegraph Co.

15T1TC1a 10c large die on India paper
e. **red** 65.
f. **blue** 65.
g. **black** 65.
15T1TC2 10c small die on India paper
b. **brown red** 65.
15T1TC3 10c plate on India paper
a. **orange** 65.
15T1P2 10c **grn,** sm die on India paper 55.
15T1P3 10c **grn,** plate on India paper 32.
15T2TC1a 15c large die on India paper
e. **red** 65.
f. **blue** 65.
g. **black** 65.
15T2TC2 15c small die on India paper
b. **red** 55.
c. **blue** 55.
15T2TC3 15c plate on India paper
a. **black** 55.
15T2P3 15c **org red,** plate on India paper 32.
15T3TC1a 25c large die on India paper
e. **red** 65.
f. **black** 65.
15T3TC2 25c small die on India paper
b. **brown red** 65.
c. **brown** 55.
15T3TC3 25c plate on India paper
a. **ultramarine** 40.
b. **brown** 40.
15T3P1 25c **bl,** large die on India paper 65.
15T3P3 25c **bl,** plate on India paper 32.
15T4TC1a 50c large die on India paper
e. **red** 65.
f. **blue** 65.
g. **black** 65.
15T4TC2 50c small die on India paper
b. **dull blue** 65.
15T4TC3 50c plate on India paper
a. **black** 40.
15T4P2 50c **brn,** sm die on India paper 65.
15T4P3 50c **brn,** plate on India paper 32.
15T6TC3 plate on India paper
a. **red brown** 40.

Western Union Telegraph Co.

16T1TC3 (1871) plate on India paper
a. **lilac** 20.
Pair 45.
b. **orange** 20.
Pair 45.
c. **black** 20.
Pair 45.
16T1TC4 (1871) plate on card
a. **lilac** 20.
Pair 45.
b. **orange** 20.
Pair 45.
c. **black** 20.
Pair 45.
d. **violet brown** 20.
Pair 45.
e. **light olive** 20.
Pair 45.
f. **brown** 20.
Pair 45.
g. **orange brown** 20.
Pair 45.
h. **blue green** 20.
Pair 45.
16T1P3 (1871) **brn,** plate on India paper 17.
Pair 35.
16T2P3 (1872) **red,** plate on India paper 17.
Pair 35.
16T3P3 (1873) **bl,** plate on India paper 17.
Pair 35.
16T4P3 (1874) **brn,** plate on India paper 17.
Pair 35.
16T5P3 (1875) **dp grn,** plate on India paper 17.
16T6TC3 (1876) plate on India paper
a. **violet blue** 20.

16T6TC4 (1876) plate on card
a. **violet blue** 20.
16T6P3 (1876) **red,** plate on India paper 17.
16T7TC4 (1877) plate on card
a. **orange yellow** 20.
Pair 45.
b. **dark brown** 20.
Pair 45.
c. **black** 20.
Pane of 4 —
16T7P3 (1877) **vio,** plate on India paper —
16T8TC4 (1878) plate on card
a. **dark brown** —
16T8P3 (1878) **gray brn,** plate on India paper 20.
16T9TC4 (1879) plate on card
a. **blue** —
16T9P3 (1879) **bl,** plate on India paper 14.
16T10TC4 (1880) plate on card
a. **violet brown** —
b. **rose** —
16T10P3 (1880) **lil rose,** plate on India paper 16.
16T11P3 (1881) **grn,** plate on India paper 16.
16T12TC3 (1882) plate on India paper
a. **green** —
16T12P3 (1882) **bl,** plate on India paper 20.
16T13P3 (1883) **yel brn,** plate on India paper 16.
16T14P1 (1884) **gray vio,** large die on India paper 250.
16T14P3 (1884) **gray vio,** plate on India paper 20.
16T15P3 (1885) **grn,** plate on India paper 20.
16T16P3 (1886) **brn vio,** plate on India paper 13.
Pair 28.
16T17P3 (1887) **red brn,** plate on India paper 13.
Pair 28.
16T18P3 (1888) **bl,** plate on India paper 13.
Pair 28.
16T19P3 (1889) **ol grn,** plate on India paper 16.
16T22TC4 (1892) plate on card
a. **black** —
16T22P3 (1892) **ver,** plate on India paper 16.
16T30P3 (1900) **red vio,** plate on India paper 28.
16T44TC1a large die on India paper
e. **deep rose** —
f. **carmine lake** —
g. **rose lake** —
h. **deep ultramarine** —
16T44TC1d Large die printed directly on card
e. **dull red** —
f. **orange** —
g. **rose red** —
h. **orange brown** —
i. **ocher** —
j. **dark blue** —
k. **dark ultramarine** —
l. **green** —
m. **brown lake** —
n. **reddish brown** —
o. **sepia** —
p. **sepia,** unsurfaced card —
q. **dull violet** —
r. **slate green** —
s. **slate blue** —
t. **black** —
u. **black,** unsurfaced card —
16T44TC3 Plate on India paper, sheet of 16
a. **deep rose** —
b. **orange** —
c. **dark blue** —
d. **slate green** —
e. **rose lake** —
16T44TC5 Plate on bond paper, sheet of 16
a. **deep rose** —
b. **orange** —
c. **dark blue** —
d. **slate green** —
e. **rose lake** —
f. **sepia** —
16T44P1 (1913) **brn,** large die on India paper —
16T44P2 (1913) **brn,** sm die on India paper —
16T44P3 (1913) **brn,** plate on India paper —
16T99P5 1c **yel grn,** plate on bond 100.
16T100P5 2c **chestnut,** plate on bond 100.
16T101P5 5c **dp bl,** plate on bond 100.
16T102P5 10c **org,** plate on bond 100.
16T103P5 25c **brt car,** plate on bond 100.

REVENUE

1862-68 by Butler & Carpenter, Philadelphia.
1868-75 by Joseph R. Carpenter, Philadelphia.

Several lists of revenue proofs in trial colors have been published, but the accuracy of some of them is questionable. The following listings are limited to items seen by the editors. The list is not complete.

In the following listing the so-called small die proofs on India paper may be, in fact probably are, plate proofs. The editors shall consider them die proofs, however, until they see them in pairs or blocks. Many revenue proofs on India are mounted on card.

First Issue

1862-71

R1P3 1c Express, **red,** plate on India paper 70.
R1P4 1c Express, **red,** plate on card 65.
Block of 4 275.
R2P1 1c Playing Cards, **red,** large die on India paper 600.
R2P3 1c Playing Cards, **red,** plate on India paper 60.
Block of 4 250.
R2P4 1c Playing Cards, **red,** plate on card 65.
Block of 4 275.
R3TC1a 1c **Proprietary,** die on India paper
e. **black** *950.*
R3TC3 1c **Proprietary,** plate on India paper
a. **black** 80.
R3TC4 1c **Proprietary,** plate on card
a. **carmine** 80.
R3TC5 1c **Proprietary,** plate on bond paper
a. **dull red** 125.
b. **orange red** 125.
c. **dull yellow** 125.
d. **violet rose** 125.
e. **deep blue** 125.
f. **red,** *blue* 125.
g. **blue,** perf. & gum 125.
R3TC5 1c **Proprietary,** plate on wove paper
h. **green,** *buff* —
R3P3 1c Proprietary, **red,** plate on India paper 140.
R3P4 1c Proprietary, **red,** plate on card 45.
Block of 4 200.
R4P4 1c Telegraph, **red,** plate on card 28.
Block of 4 125.
R5P2 2c Bank Check, **bl,** sm die on India paper 525.
R5P4 2c Bank Check, **bl,** plate on card 33.
Block of 4 140.
R6P3 2c Bank Check, **org,** plate on India paper 60.
Block of 4 250.
R7TC4 2c **Certificate,** plate on card
a. **ultramarine** 65.
R7P4 2c Certificate, **bl,** plate on card 28.
Block of 4 125.
R8P3 2c Certificate, **org,** plate on India paper 82.
Block of 4 350.
R9P4 2c Express, **bl,** plate on card 28.
Block of 4 125.
R10P1 2c Express, **org,** large die on India paper 600.
R10P3 2c Express, **org,** plate on India paper 60.
Block of 4 250.
R11TC1a 2c **Playing Cards,** die on India paper
e. **black** 500.
R11P4 2c Playing Cards, **bl,** plate on card 38.
Block of 4 160.
R13TC1a 2c **Proprietary,** die on India paper
e. **black** 650.
f. **carmine** 650.
R13TC3 2c **Proprietary,** plate on India paper
a. **black** 75.
R13P2 2c Proprietary, **bl,** sm die on India paper 400.
R13P4 2c Proprietary, **bl,** plate on card 28.
Block of 4 125.
R15TC3 2c **U.S.I.R.,** plate on India paper
a. **black** 110.
R15TC5 2c **U.S.I.R.,** plate on bond paper
a. **violet rose** 110.
b. **light green** 110.
c. **pale blue** 110.
d. **pale rose** 200.
e. **orange,** *blue* —
f. **pale orange,** perf. & gum 110.
R15P3 2c U.S.I.R., **org,** plate on India paper *1,250.*
R16TC5 3c **Foreign Exchange,** plate on bond paper
a. **green,** *blue* 140.
R16TC7 3c **Foreign Exchange,** plate on goldbeater's skin
a. **blue** 110.
R16P1 3c Foreign Exchange, **grn,** large die on India paper 600.
a. R16P1 + R19P1 composite —
R16P3 3c Foreign Exchange, **grn,** plate on India paper 225.
R16P4 3c Foreign Exchange, **grn,** plate on card 38.
Block of 4 160.
R17P1 3c Playing Cards, **grn,** large die on India paper 700.
R17P2 3c Playing Cards, **grn,** sm die on India paper 400.
R17P4 3c Playing Cards, **grn,** plate on card 100.
Block of 4 425.
R18TC1a 3c **Proprietary,** die on India paper
e. **black** 300.
R18P3 3c Proprietary, **grn,** plate on India paper 60.
Block of 4 250.
R18P4 3c Proprietary, **grn,** plate on card 28.
Block of 4 125.
R19P1 3c Telegraph, **grn,** large die on India paper 600.
R19P3 3c Telegraph, **grn,** plate on India paper 225.
R19P4 3c Telegraph, **grn,** plate on card 28.
Block of 4 125.
R20P3 4c Inland Exchange, **brn,** plate on India paper 225.
R20P4 4c Inland Exchange, **brn,** plate on card 28.
Block of 4 125.
R21TC1a 4c **Playing Cards,** die (?) on India paper
e. **black** 300.
R21P2 4c Playing Cards, **vio,** sm die on India paper 400.
R21P4 4c Playing Cards, **vio,** plate on card 95.
Block of 4 400.
R22TC1a 4c **Proprietary,** die on India paper
e. **black** 350.
f. **deep red lilac** 400.
R22TC3 4c **Proprietary,** plate on India paper
a. **black** 110.
R22TC4 4c **Proprietary,** plate on card
a. **red lilac** 110.
R22P1 4c Proprietary, **vio,** large die on India paper 600.
R22P3 4c Proprietary, **vio,** plate on India paper 110.
Block of 4 475.
R22P4 4c Proprietary, **vio,** plate on card 60.
Block of 4 250.
R23P4 5c Agreement, **red,** plate on card 33.
Block of 4 140.
R24TC3 5c **Certificate,** plate on India paper
a. **carmine** 110.
R24P1a 5c R24P1 + R25P1 composite, large die on India paper —
R24P3 5c Certificate, **red,** plate on India paper 95.
Block of 4 400.
R24P4 5c Certificate, **red,** plate on card 110.
R25TC6 5c **Express,** plate on wove paper
a. **pale olive** —
R25P2 5c Express, **red,** sm die on India paper 250.
R25P4 5c Express, **red,** plate on card 33.
Block of 4 145.
R26TC3 5c **Foreign Exchange,** plate on India paper
a. **orange** 110.
R26P4 5c Foreign Exchange, **red,** plate on card 300.
R27P2 5c Inland Exchange, **red,** sm die on India paper 250.
R27P4 5c Inland Exchange, **red,** plate on card 28.
Block of 4 125.
R28TC1a 5c **Playing Cards,** die (?) on India paper
e. **black** 300.
R28P2 5c Playing Cards, **red,** sm die on India paper —
R28P3 5c Playing Cards, **red,** plate on India paper 105.
Block of 4 440.
R28P4 5c Playing Cards, **red,** plate on card 325.
R29TC5 5c **Proprietary,** plate on bond paper
a. **red,** *blue* —
R29P5 5c Proprietary, **red,** plate on blue wove, gummed —
R30TC1a 6c **Inland Exchange,** die on India paper
e. **black** 350.
R30P3 6c Inland Exchange, **org,** plate on India paper 60.
Block of 4 250.
R30P4 6c Inland Exchange, **org,** plate on card 33.
Block of 4 140.
R31TC1a 6c **Proprietary,** die on India paper
e. **black** —
R32TC1a 10c **Bill of Lading,** die on India paper
e. **greenish blue** 350.
f. **dark green,** R32TC1a+R37TC1a composite —
R32P4 10c Bill of Lading, **bl,** plate on card 33.
Block of 4 140.
R33P3 10c Certificate, **bl,** plate on India paper 140.
R33P4 10c Certificate, **bl,** plate on card 33.
Block of 4 140.
R34P4 10c Contract, **bl,** plate on card 33.
Block of 4 140.
R35TC1a 10c **Foreign Exchange,** die (?) on India paper
e. **black** 350.
R35P4 10c Foreign Exchange, **bl,** plate on card 33.
Block of 4 140.
R36P4 10c Inland Exchange, **bl,** plate on card 33.
Block of 4 140.
R37TC1a 10c **Power of Attorney,** die on India paper
e. **greenish blue** 350.
R37P4 10c Power of Attorney, **bl,** plate on card 33.
Block of 4 140.
R38TC1a 10c **Proprietary,** die on India paper
e. **black** 350.
R38P1 10c Proprietary, **bl,** large die on India paper *700.*
R38P3 10c Proprietary, **bl,** plate on India paper 70.
Block of 4 300.
R39P3 15c Foreign Exchange, **brn,** plate on India paper 90.
Block of 4 375.
R39P4 15c Foreign Exchange, **brn,** plate on card 325.
Block of 4 1,600.
R40P3 15c Inland Exchange, **brn,** plate on India paper 120.
R40P4 15c Inland Exchange, **brn,** plate on card 33.
Block of 4 140.
R41P1 20c Foreign Exchange, **red,** large die on India paper 600.
a. R41P1 + R42P1 composite —
R41P3 20c Foreign Exchange, **red,** plate on India paper 90.
Block of 4 375.
R41P4 20c Foreign Exchange, **red,** plate on card 100.
Block of 4 425.
R42P1 20c Inland Exchange, **red,** large die on India paper 600.
R42P2 20c Inland Exchange, **red,** sm die on India paper 250.
R42P3 20c Inland Exchange, **red,** plate on India paper 260.
R42P4 20c Inland Exchange, **red,** plate on card 33.
Block of 4 140.
R43TC4 25c **Bond,** plate on card
a. **carmine** 90.
R43P4 25c Bond, **red,** plate on card 500.
Block of 4 2,500.
R44TC5 25c **Certificate,** plate on bond paper
a. **blue** 300.
b. **green** 300.
c. **orange** 300.
R44P4 25c Certificate, **red,** plate on card 33.
Block of 4 140.
R45TC1a 25c **Entry of Goods,** hybrid die on India paper
e. **black** —
R45P4 25c Entry of Goods, **red,** plate on card 550.
R46TC5 25c **Insurance,** plate on bond paper
a. **dull red** 150.
b. **vermilion** 170.
c. **blue** 170.
d. **dark blue** 155.
R46TC7 25c **Insurance,** plate on goldbeater's skin
a. **dull red** 210.
b. **vermilion** 210.
c. **blue** 215.
d. **dark blue** 215.
e. **green** 215.
R46P3 25c Insurance, **red,** plate on India paper 60.
Block of 4 250.
R46P4 25c Insurance, **red,** plate on card 33.
Block of 4 140.
R47P4 25c Life Insurance, **red,** plate on card 33.
Block of 4 140.
R48P4 25c Power of Attorney, **red,** plate on card 33.
Block of 4 140.

R49P4 25c Protest, **red,** plate on card 33.
Block of 4 140.
R50P4 25c Warehouse Receipt, **red,** plate on card 33.
Block of 4 140.
R51TC3 30c **Foreign Exchange,** plate on India paper
a. **violet** 130.
b. **violet gray** 130.
c. **deep red lilac** 155.
d. **slate blue** 155.
e. **black** 155.
f. **red** 155.
R51P3 30c Foreign Exchange, **lil,** plate on India paper 110.
Block of 4 475.
R51P4 30c Foreign Exchange, **lil,** plate on card 100.
Block of 4 425.
R52TC3 30c **Inland Exchange,** plate on India paper
a. **deep red lilac** 155.
R52P3 30c Inland Exchange, **lil,** plate on India paper 65.
Block of 4 275.
R52P4 30c Inland Exchange, **lil,** plate on card 55.
Block of 4 230.
R53TC1a 40c **Inland Exchange,** hybrid die on India paper
e. **black** —
R53P3 40c Inland Exchange, **brn,** plate on India paper 150.
R53P4 40c Inland Exchange, **brn,** plate on card 75.
Block of 4 325.
R54P2 50c Conveyance, **bl,** sm die on India paper 250.
R54P4 50c Conveyance, **bl,** plate on card 33.
Block of 4 140.
R55TC5 50c **Entry of Goods,** plate on bond paper
a. **orange** 275.
b. **green** 275.
c. **red** 340.
d. **deep blue** —
R55P3 50c Entry of Goods, **bl,** plate on India paper 65.
Block of 4 275.
R55P4 50c Entry of Goods, **bl,** plate on card 45.
Block of 4 190.
R56P3 50c Foreign Exchange, **bl,** plate on India paper 65.
Block of 4 275.
R56P4 50c Foreign Exchange, **bl,** plate on card 45.
Block of 4 190.
R57P3 50c Lease, **bl,** plate on India paper 65.
Block of 4 275.
R57P4 50c Lease, **bl,** plate on card 38.
Block of 4 160.
R58TC3 50c **Life Insurance,** plate on India paper
a. **ultramarine** 85.
R58P3 50c Life Insurance, **bl,** plate on India paper 65.
Block of 4 275.
R58P4 50c Life Insurance, **bl,** plate on card 38.
Block of 4 160.
R59P4 50c Mortgage, **bl,** plate on card 110.
Block of 4 475.
R60TC1a 50c **Original Process,** die (?) on India paper
e. **black** 280.
R60P3 50c Original Process, **bl,** plate on India paper 65.
Block of 4 275.
R60P4 50c Original Process, **bl,** plate on card 38.
Block of 4 160.
R61P4 50c Passage Ticket, **bl,** plate on card 55.
Block of 4 230.
R62P3 50c Probate of Will, **bl,** plate on India paper 65.
Block of 4 275.
R62P4 50c Probate of Will, **bl,** plate on card 55.
Block of 4 230.
R63P4 50c Surety Bond, **bl,** plate on card 55.
Block of 4 230.
R64TC1a 60c **Inland Exchange,** die (?) on India paper
e. **green** —
R64P3 60c Inland Exchange, **org,** plate on India paper 55.
R64P4 60c Inland Exchange, **org,** plate on card 38.
Block of 4 160.
R65TC1a 70c **Foreign Exchange,** die (?) on India paper
e. **orange** —
f. **black** 285.
R65P3 70c Foreign Exchange, **grn,** plate on India paper 120.
R65P4 70c Foreign Exchange, **grn,** plate on card 55.
Block of 4 230.
R66TC3 $1 **Conveyance,** plate on India paper
a. **carmine** 85.
R66P4 $1 Conveyance, **red,** plate on card 45.
Block of 4 190.
R67TC3 $1 **Entry of Goods,** plate on India paper
a. **carmine** 60.
R67P1 $1 Entry of Goods, **red,** large die on India paper 525.
R67P4 $1 Entry of Goods, **red,** plate on card 45.
Block of 4 190.
R68TC3 $1 **Foreign Exchange,** plate on India paper
a. **carmine** 60.
R68P4 $1 Foreign Exchange, **red,** plate on card 33.
Block of 4 140.
R69TC3 $1 **Inland Exchange,** plate on India paper
a. **carmine** 60.
R69P4 $1 Inland Exchange, **red,** plate on card 55.
Block of 4 230.

R70TC3 $1 **Lease,** plate on India paper
a. **carmine** 130.
R70P4 $1 Lease, **red,** plate on card *425.*
R71TC3 $1 **Life Insurance,** plate on India paper
a. **carmine** 75.
R71P4 $1 Life Insurance, **red,** plate on card 33.
Block of 4 140.
R72TC3 $1 **Manifest,** plate on India paper
a. **carmine** 80.
R72P3 $1 Manifest, **red,** plate on India paper 55.
Block of 4 —
R72P4 $1 Manifest, **red,** plate on card 33.
Block of 4 140.
R73TC1a $1 **Mortgage,** hybrid die on India paper
e. **black** —
R73TC3 $1 **Mortgage,** plate on India paper
a. **carmine** 85.
R73P4 $1 Mortgage, **red,** plate on card 55.
Block of 4 230.
R74TC3 $1 **Passage Ticket,** plate on India paper
a. **carmine** 120.
R74P4 $1 Passage Ticket, **red,** plate on card *425.*
Block of 4 *1,850.*
R75TC3 $1 **Power of Attorney,** plate on India paper
a. **carmine** 120.
R75P4 $1 Power of Attorney, **red,** plate on card 100.
Block of 4 425.
R76TC3 $1 **Probate of Will,** plate on India paper
a. **carmine** 60.
R76P4 $1 Probate of Will, **red,** plate on card 33.
Block of 4 140.
R77P1 $1.30 Foreign Exchange, **org,** large die on India paper *700.*
R77P3 $1.30 Foreign Exchange, **org,** plate on India paper 140.
Block of 4 575.
R77P4 $1.30 Foreign Exchange, **org,** plate on card 100.
Block of 4 425.
R78TC1a $1.50 **Inland Exchange,** die on India paper
e. **black** 475.
R78P3 $1.50 Inland Exchange, **bl,** plate on India paper 110.
Block of 4 475.
R78P4 $1.50 Inland Exchange, **bl,** plate on card 45.
Block of 4 190.
R79P3 $1.60 Foreign Exchange, **grn,** plate on India paper 140.
R79P4 $1.60 Foreign Exchange, **grn,** plate on card 100.
Block of 4 425.
R80TC3 $1.90 **Foreign Exchange,** plate on India paper
a. **black** 155.
R80P3 $1.90 Foreign Exchange, **vio,** plate on India paper 140.
Block of 4 575.
R80P4 $1.90 Foreign Exchange, **vio,** plate on card 100.
Block of 4 425.
R81TC4 $2 **Conveyance,** plate on card
a. **carmine** 85.
R81P3 $2 Conveyance, **red,** plate on India paper 120.
R81P4 $2 Conveyance, **red,** plate on card 33.
Block of 4 140.
R82TC4 $2 **Mortgage,** plate on card
a. **carmine** 85.
R82P3 $2 Mortgage, **red,** plate on India paper 120.
Block of 4 —
R82P4 $2 Mortgage, **red,** plate on card 33.
Block of 4 140.
R83TC1a $2 **Probate of Will,** hybrid die on India paper
e. **black** —
R83P4 $2 Probate of Will, **red,** plate on card 110.
Block of 4 —
R84TC1a $2.50 **Inland Exchange,** die (?) on India paper
e. **black** 120.
R84P3 $2.50 Inland Exchange, **vio,** plate on India paper 250.
R84P4 $2.50 Inland Exchange, **vio,** plate on card 250.
Block of 4 —
R85TC4 $3 **Charter Party,** plate on thin card
a. **dark green** —
R85P3 $3 Charter Party, **grn,** plate on India paper 120.
Block of 4 500.
R85P4 $3 Charter Party, **grn,** plate on card 65.
Block of 4 275.
R86P1 $3 Manifest, **grn,** large die on India paper —
R86P2 $3 Manifest, **grn,** sm die on India paper 350.
R86P3 $3 Manifest, **grn,** plate on India paper 180.
R86P4 $3 Manifest, **grn,** plate on card 65.
Block of 4 275.
R87TC1a $3.50 **Inland Exchange,** die on India paper
e. **black** 400.
R87P3 $3.50 Inland Exchange, **bl,** plate on India paper 180.
R87P4 $3.50 Inland Exchange, **bl,** plate on card 140.
Block of 4 575.
R88TC1a $5 **Charter Party,** hybrid die on India paper
e. **black** —
R88TC3 $5 **Charter Party,** plate on India paper
a. **carmine** 85.
R88P3 $5 Charter Party, **red,** plate on India paper 70.
Block of 4 300.
R88P4 $5 Charter Party, **red,** plate on card 55.
Block of 4 230.
R89TC3 $5 **Conveyance,** plate on India paper
a. **carmine** 90.
R89P3 $5 Conveyance, **red,** plate on India paper 450.
R89P4 $5 Conveyance, **red,** plate on card 55.
Block of 4 230.

R90P2 $5 Manifest, **red,** sm die on India paper 300.
R90P4 $5 Manifest, **red,** plate on card 55.
Block of 4 230.
R91TC3 $5 **Mortgage,** plate on India paper
a. **carmine** 90.
R91P3 $5 Mortgage, **red,** plate on India paper 650.
R91P4 $5 Mortgage, **red,** plate on card 55.
Block of 4 230.
R92P2 $5 Probate of Will, **red,** sm die on India paper 300.
R92P4 $5 Probate of Will, **red,** plate on card 55.
Block of 4 230.
R93P3 $10 Charter Party, **grn,** plate on India paper 120.
R93P4 $10 Charter Party, **grn,** plate on card 55.
Block of 4 230.
R94P4 $10 Conveyance, **grn,** plate on card 55.
Block of 4 230.
R95TC4 $10 **Mortgage,** plate on thin card
a. **yellow green** —
R95P4 $10 Mortgage, **grn,** plate on card 55.
Block of 4 230.
R96P1 $10 Probate of Will, **grn,** large die on India paper *700.*
R96P2 $10 Probate of Will, **grn,** sm die on India paper 300.
R96P4 $10 Probate of Will, **grn,** plate on card 75.
Block of 4 325.
R97P2 $15 Mortgage, **dk bl,** sm die on India paper —
R97P3 $15 Mortgage, **dk bl,** plate on India paper 350.
R97P4 $15 Mortgage, **dk bl,** plate on card 180.
Block of 4 800.
R97eP2 $15 Mortgage, **ultra,** sm die on India paper —
R97eP4 $15 Mortgage, **ultra,** plate on card 350.
Block of 4 —
R97fP3 $15 Mortgage, **milky bl,** plate on India paper 290.
R98TC3 $20 **Conveyance,** plate on India paper
a. **red orange** 220.
R98TC4 $20 **Conveyance,** plate on card
a. **red orange** 120.
R98P3 $20 Conveyance, **org,** plate on India paper 220.
Block of 4 900.
R98P4 $20 Conveyance, **org,** plate on card 100.
Block of 4 425.
R99TC4 $20 **Probate of Will,** plate on card
a. **red orange** 275.
b. **black** 275.
R99P4 $20 Probate of Will, **org,** plate on card 220.
Block of 4 —
R100P3 $25 Mortgage, **red,** plate on India paper 220.
R100P4 $25 Mortgage, **red,** plate on card 160.
Block of 4 675.
R101TC1a $50 **U.S.I.R.,** hybrid die on India paper
e. **black** —
R101TC5 $50 **U.S.I.R.,** plate on bond paper
a. **orange** 275.
b. **deep blue** 275.
R101P3 $50 U.S.I.R., **grn,** plate on India paper 220.
R101P4 $50 U.S.I.R., **grn,** plate on card 230.
Block of 4 950.
R102TC3 $200**U.S.I.R.,** plate on India paper
a. **black** —
b. **green & brown red** 2,000.
R102TC4 $200**U.S.I.R.,** plate on card
a. **black & red** 1,600.
R102TC5 $200**U.S.I.R.,** plate on bond paper
a. **gray brown & red** 1,600.
R102P3 $200U.S.I.R., **grn & org red,** plate on India paper 1,400.

Second Issue

1871-72

R104TC5 2c plate on bond paper
a. **pale blue & black** 60.
R105P3 3c **bl & blk,** plate on India paper 20.
Block of 4 90.
R105P4 3c **bl & blk,** plate on card 15.
Block of 4 65.
P# block of 10 —
R109P3 10c **bl & blk,** plate on India paper 20.
Block of 4 90.
R109P4 10c **bl & blk,** plate on card 15.
Block of 4 65.
P# block of 10 —
R111P3 20c **bl & blk,** plate on India paper 20.
Block of 4 90.
R111P4 20c **bl & blk,** plate on card 15.
Block of 4 65.
P# block of 10 —
R112P3 25c **bl & blk,** plate on India paper 20.
Block of 4 90.
R112P4 25c **bl & blk,** plate on card 15.
Block of 4 65.
P# block of 10 —
R115P3 50c **bl & blk,** plate on India paper 50.
Block of 4 225.
R115P4 50c **bl & blk,** plate on card 15.
Block of 4 65.
P# block of 10 —
R119P3 $1.30 **bl & blk,** plate on India paper 50.
Block of 4 225.
R119P4 $1.30 **bl & blk,** plate on card 38.
Block of 4 160.
P# block of 10 —
R120P3 $1.50 **bl & blk,** plate on India paper 28.
Block of 4 120.
R120P4 $1.50 **bl & blk,** plate on card 22.
Block of 4 100.
Double transfer, design of $1 —
R121P3 $1.60 **bl & blk,** plate on India paper 60.
Block of 4 260.
R121P4 $1.60 **bl & blk,** plate on card 60.
Block of 4 260.
P# block of 10 —

R122P3 $1.90 **bl & blk,** plate on India paper 50.
Block of 4 225.
R122P4 $1.90 **bl & blk,** plate on card 38.
Block of 4 170.
P# block of 10 —
R126P3 $3.50 **bl & blk,** plate on India paper 90.
Block of 4 400.
R126P4 $3.50 **bl & blk,** plate on card 100.
Block of 4 425.
P# block of 8 —
R130P3 $25 **bl & blk,** plate on India paper 150.
Block of 4 650.
R130P4 $25 **bl & blk,** plate on card 110.
Block of 4 500.
P# block of 4 —
R131P3 $50 **bl & blk,** plate on India paper 160.
Block of 4 700.
R131P4 $50 **bl & blk,** plate on card 140.
Block of 4 625.
P# block of 4 —

The "small die proofs" formerly listed under Nos. R103P-R131P are plate proofs from the sheets listed under "Trial Color Proofs."

R132TC1a $200 die on India paper
e. **red, green & black** 2,500.
f. **orange,** master die 2,500.
g. **blue,** master die 2,500.
h. **green,** master die 2,500.
R132P1 $200 **red, bl & blk,** large die on India paper 3,500.
R132P2 $200 **red, bl & blk,** sm die on India paper 2,750.
R132P3 $200 **red, bl & blk,** plate on India paper 2,500.
Red (frame) inverted —
R133TC1a $500 die on India paper
e. **yellow, green & black** *5,000.*
f. **bright green, orange brown & black** *5,000.*
g. **black,** master die *10,000.*
R133TC1b $500 die on bond paper
e. **red, green & black** *5,000.*
f. **light green, light brown & black** *5,000.*
g. **blue, scarlet & black** *5,000.*
R133TC1d $500 die on card
e. **light green, light brown & black** *14,500.*
R133P1 $500 **red, org, grn & blk,** large die on India paper *5,500.*
R133ATC1a $5000 die on India paper
e. **yellow orange, green & black** *20,000.*
f. **olive brown, green & black** *20,000.*
g. **orange red, dark green & black** *20,000.*
h. **orange red, dark blue & black** *20,000.*

The master die is the completed stamp design prior to its division into separate color dies.

Full-size die proofs on full-size card bring substantial premiums above the catalogue values listed for R132TC1a, R133TC1a-R133TC1d, R133ATC1a.

R133AP1 $5000 **red org, dk grn & blk,** large die on India paper *7,500.*

No. R133AP was approved in these colors but never issued. Shade differences of the red orange and dark green colors will be found. It comes both with and without manufacturer's imprints to the left and right of the design. One example exists on bond paper mounted on card with "853½" printed on the lower right card margin.

Due to the unusual manufacturing process of printing these tri-color stamps from single impression plates, proofs with imprints could also be considered to be plate proofs. All are extremely scarce or unique, and are valued in the grade, condition and scarcity in which they exist. For other colors see the trial color proofs listings under No. R133ATC.

Third Issue

1871-72

R134TC4 1c plate on card
a. **brown & black** 60.
R134P4 1c **cl & blk,** plate on card 15.
Block of 4 70.
P# block of 10 —
R135P3 2c **org & blk,** plate on India paper 28.
Block of 4 120.
R135P4 2c **org & blk,** plate on card 15.
Block of 4 70.
P# block of 10 —
R136P3 4c **brn & blk,** plate on India paper 33.
Block of 4 140.
R136P4 4c **brn & blk,** plate on card 15.
Block of 4 70.
P# block of 10 —
R137P3 5c **org & blk,** plate on India paper 33.
Block of 4 140.
R137P4 5c **org & blk,** plate on card 15.
Block of 4 70.
P# block of 10 —
R138P3 6c **org & blk,** plate on India paper 33.
Block of 4 140.
R138P4 6c **org & blk,** plate on card 15.
Block of 4 70.
P# block of 10 —
R139P3 15c **brn & blk,** plate on India paper 33.
Block of 4 140.
R139P4 15c **brn & blk,** plate on card 15.
Block of 4 70.
P# block of 10 —
R140P3 30c **brn & blk,** plate on India paper 38.
Block of 4 160.
R140P4 30c **brn & blk,** plate on card 18.
Block of 4 80.
P# block of 10 —
R141P3 40c **brn & blk,** plate on India paper 38.
Block of 4 160.
R141P4 40c **brn & blk,** plate on card 18.
Block of 4 80.
P# block of 12 —
R142P3 60c **org & blk,** plate on India paper 85.
Block of 4 360.
Foreign entry, design of 70c 225.
R142P4 60c **org & blk,** plate on card 50.
Block of 4 225.
P# block of 10 —
Foreign entry, design of 70c 150.
a. Center inverted *2,250.*
Block of 4 *10,000.*
Foreign entry, design of 70c —
R143P3 70c **grn & blk,** plate on India paper 55.
Block of 4 230.
R143P4 70c **grn & blk,** plate on card 38.
Block of 4 170.
P# block of 10 —
R144P3 $1 **grn & blk,** plate on India paper 50.
Block of 4 210.
R144P4 $1 **grn & blk,** plate on card 38.
Block of 4 170.
P# block of 10 —
R145P3 $2 **ver & blk,** plate on India paper 105.
Block of 4 450.
R145P4 $2 **ver & blk,** plate on card 105.
Block of 4 450.
P# block of 8 —
R146P3 $2.50 **cl & blk,** plate on India paper 65.
Block of 4 260.
R146P4 $2.50 **cl & blk,** plate on card 40.
Block of 4 170.
P# block of 8 —
R147P3 $3 **grn & blk,** plate on India paper 85.
Block of 4 360.
R147P4 $3 **grn & blk,** plate on card 70.
Block of 4 300.
P# block of 8 —
R148P3 $5 **ver & blk,** plate on India paper 85.
Block of 4 360.
R148P4 $5 **ver & blk,** plate on card 55.
Block of 4 240.
P# block of 4 —
R149P3 $10 **grn & blk,** plate on India paper 105.
Block of 4 440.
R149P4 $10 **grn & blk,** plate on card 55.
Block of 4 240.
P# block of 4 —
R150P3 $20 **org & blk,** plate on India paper 150.
Block of 4 650.
R150P4 $20 **org & blk,** plate on card 150.
Block of 4 635.
P# block of 4 —

1875 National Bank Note Co., New York City

R152TC1a 2c Liberty, die on India paper
e. **green** 600.
f. **brown** 600.
g. **black** 600.
R152P1 2c **bl,** (Liberty) large die on India paper 450.
R152P3 2c **bl,** (Liberty) plate on India paper 110.
Block of 4 475.

Documentary

1898

R161TC1a ½c large die on India paper
e. **green** 750.
R163TC1a 1c large die on India paper
e. **green** 750.
f. **black** 750.
R165TC2 1c small die on India paper
b. **green** 650.
R169TC1a 25c large die on India paper
e. **green** 650.
R170TC1a 40c large die on India paper
e. **black** 650.
R172TC1a 80c large die on India paper
e. **green** 1,100.
R173P1 $1 **dk grn,** large die on India paper *600.*
R174TC1a $3 die on India paper
e. **black** 650.
R174P1 $3 **dk brn,** large die on India paper *600.*
R175P1 $5 **org red,** large die on India paper *600.*
R176TC1a $10 die on India paper
e. **green** 650.
R176P1 $10 **blk,** large die on India paper *600.*
R177P1 $30 **red,** large die on India paper *600.*
R178P1 $50 **gray brn,** large die on India paper *600.*

1899

R179TC1a $100 die on India paper
e. **dark green & black** 1,250.
R180P1 $500 **car lake & blk,** large die on India paper *1,650.*
R181TC1a $1000 die on India paper
e. **dark blue & black** 1,250.

1914

R195TC2 ½c small die on wove
b. **black** —
R196TC2 1c small die on wove
b. **blue green** —
R197P2 2c **rose,** sm die on India paper —
R198TC2 3c small die on wove
b. **ultramarine** —
R199TC2 4c small die on wove
b. **brown** —
R200TC2 5c small die on wove
b. **blue** —
R201TC2 10c small die on wove
b. **yellow** —
R202TC2 25c small die on wove
b. **dull violet** —
R203TC2 40c small die on wove
b. **blue green** —
R204TC2 50c small die on wove
b. **red brown** —
R205TC2 80c small die on wove
b. **orange** —

1914-15

R226P1 $500 **bl,** large die on India paper *675.*

1917

R246P1 $30 **dp org,** (without serial No.) large die on India paper *650.*

1940

R298P1 50c **car,** (without ovpt.) large die on India paper *700.*
R305P1 $10 **car,** large die on India paper *825.*
Without overprint —
R306AP1 $50 **car,** large die on India paper *825.*
Without overprint —

1952

R597P1 55c **car,** large die on India paper *675.*

Proprietary

1871-75 Joseph R. Carpenter, Philadelphia

RB1TC5 1c plate on bond paper
a. **blue & black** 70.
b. **scarlet & black** 70.
c. **orange & black** 70.
d. **orange & ultramarine,** on granite bond 60.
RB1P3 1c **grn & blk,** plate on India paper —
RB1P4 1c **grn & blk,** plate on card 12.
Block of 4 52.
P# block of 10 *250.*
RB1P5 1c **grn & blk,** plate on bond 12.
Block of 4 52.
P# block of 10 175.
RB2P3 2c **grn & blk,** plate on India paper 175.
RB2P4 2c **grn & blk,** plate on card 12.
Block of 4 52.
RB2P5 2c **grn & blk,** plate on bond, P# block of 10 175.
RB3TC5 3c Plate on bond paper
a. **blue & black,** with gum 60.
b. **blue & black,** *gray* 60.
RB3TC6 3c plate on wove paper
a. **blue & black** —
RB3P3 3c **grn & blk,** plate on India paper 22.
Block of 4 100.
RB3P4 3c **grn & blk,** plate on card 12.
Block of 4 52.
RB3P5 3c **grn & blk,** plate on bond, P# block of 10 175.
RB4P3 4c **grn & blk,** plate on India paper 22.
Block of 4 100.
RB4P4 4c **grn & blk,** plate on card 12.
Block of 4 52.
RB4P5 4c **grn & blk,** plate on bond, P# block of 10 175.
RB5P3 5c **grn & blk,** plate on India paper 22.
Block of 4 100.
RB5P4 5c **grn & blk,** plate on card 12.
Block of 4 52.
RB5P5 5c **grn & blk,** plate on bond, P# block of 10 175.
RB6P3 6c **grn & blk,** plate on India paper 22.
Block of 4 100.
RB6P4 6c **grn & blk,** plate on card 12.
Block of 4 52.
RB6P5 6c **grn & blk,** plate on bond, P# block of 10 175.
RB7P3 10c **grn & blk,** plate on India paper 22.
Block of 4 100.
RB7P4 10c **grn & blk,** plate on card 12.
Block of 4 52.
RB7P5 10c **grn & blk,** plate on bond, P# block of 10 175.
RB8TC1a 50c Die on India paper
e. **green & brown** 675.
f. **green & purple** 675.
g. **green & brown red** 675.
h. **green & violet** 675.
i. **green & dark carmine** 675.
j. **ultramarine & red** 675.
RB8P2 50c **grn & blk,** sm die on India paper 1,400.
RB8P4 50c **grn & blk,** plate on card 1,000.
RB9TC1a $1 die on India paper
e. **green & brown** 675.
f. **green & purple** 675.
g. **green & violet brown** 675.
h. **green & brown red** 675.
i. **green & violet** 675.
j. **green & dark carmine** 675.
RB9P2 $1 **grn & blk,** sm die on India paper 1,600.
RB9P4 $1 **grn & blk,** plate on card 1,250.
RB10P2 $5 **grn & blk,** sm die on India paper 6,000.
RB10P3 $5 **grn & blk,** plate on India paper 4,500.
RB10P4 $5 **grn & blk,** plate on card 2,750.

1875-83 National Bank Note Co., New York City

RB11TC1a 1c die on India paper
e. **brown** 500.
f. **red brown** 500.
g. **blue** 500.
h. **black** 500.
RB11P1 1c **grn,** lg die on India paper 500.
RB11P3 1c **grn,** plate on India paper 65.
Block of 4 325.
RB11P4 1c **grn,** plate on card —
RB12TC1a 2c die on India paper
e. **green** 500.
f. **black** 500.
g. **brown** 500.

	h. **orange brown**	500.
	i. **blue**	500.
RB12P1	2c **brn,** lg die on India paper	500.
RB12P3	2c **brn,** plate on India paper	65.
	Pair	160.
RB12P4	2c **brn,** plate on card	—
RB13TC1a	3c die on India paper	
	e. **brown**	500.
	f. **green**	500.
	g. **blue**	500.
RB13TC3	3c plate on India paper	
	a. **black**	150.
RB13P1	3c **org,** lg die on India paper	500.
RB13P3	3c **org,** plate on India paper	65.
	Pair	160.
RB13P4	3c **org,** plate on card	—
	Pair	—
	Block of 4	—
RB14TC1a	4c die on India paper	
	e. **green**	450.
	f. **black**	450.
	g. **dark brown**	450.
	h. **blue**	450.
RB14TC3	4c plate on India paper	
	a. **black**	150.
RB14P1	4c **red brn,** lg die on India paper	500.
RB14P3	4c **red brn,** plate on India paper	65.
	Pair	160.
RB14P4	4c **red brn,** plate on card	—
	Pair	—
	Block of 4	—
RB15P1	4c **red,** lg die on India paper	500.
RB16TC1a	5c die on India paper	
	e. **green**	450.
	f. **dark slate**	450.
	g. **blue**	450.
RB16P1	5c **blk,** lg die on India paper	500.
RB16P3	5c **blk,** plate on India paper	65.
	Pair	160.
RB16P4	5c **blk,** plate on card	—
	Pair	—
	Block of 4	—
RB17TC1a	6c die on India paper	
	e. **black**	500.
	f. **blue**	500.
	g. **purple**	500.
	h. **dull violet**	500.
	i. **violet**	500.
	j. **violet brown**	500.
	k. **dark brown**	500.
RB17TC3	6c plate on India paper	
	a. **green**	150.
	b. **black**	150.
RB17P1	6c **vio bl,** lg die on India paper	500.
RB17P3	6c **vio bl,** plate on India paper	65.
	Pair	160.
RB18P1	6c **bl,** lg die on India paper	500.
RB18P3	6c **bl,** plate on India paper	175.
	Pair	400.
RB19TC1a	10c die on India paper	
	e. **black**	550.
RB19P1	10c **bl,** lg die on India paper	500.

No. RB19P1 was produced by the Bureau of Engraving and Printing.

SECOND, THIRD AND PROPRIETARY ISSUES

Stamps Nos. R103 to R131, R134 to R150 and RB1 to RB7.

A special composite plate was made and impressions taken in various colors and shades. Although all varieties in all colors must have been made, only those seen by the editors are listed.

CENTERS IN BLACK

1871-75

R103TC3	1c plate on India paper	
	a. **dark purple**	60.
	b. **dull purple**	60.
	d. **brown**	60.
	e. **black brown**	60.
	g. **light blue**	60.
	h. **dark blue**	70.
	i. **ultramarine**	70.
	k. **yellow green**	70.
	n. **green**	65.
	o. **dark green**	65.
	p. **blue green**	65.
	q. **light orange**	65.
	r. **dark orange**	65.
	s. **deep orange**	65.
	t. **scarlet**	65.
	u. **carmine**	65.
	x. **dark brown red**	65.
R103TC7	1c plate on goldbeater's skin	
	a. **dark brown orange**	90.
R104TC3	2c plate on India paper	
	a. **dark purple**	60.
	b. **dull purple**	60.
	d. **brown**	60.
	e. **black brown**	60.
	g. **light blue**	60.
	h. **dark blue**	70.
	i. **ultramarine**	70.
	k. **yellow green**	70.
	l. **dark yellow green**	70.
	n. **green**	65.
	o. **dark green**	65.
	p. **blue green**	65.
	q. **light orange**	65.
	r. **dark orange**	65.
	s. **deep orange**	65.
	t. **scarlet**	65.
	u. **carmine**	65.
	x. **dark brown red**	65.
R104TC7	2c plate on goldbeater's skin	
	a. **dark brown orange**	90.
R105TC3	3c plate on India paper	
	a. **dark purple**	60.
	b. **dull purple**	60.
	d. **brown**	60.
	e. **black brown**	60.
	g. **light blue**	60.
	h. **dark blue**	70.
	i. **ultramarine**	70.
	k. **yellow green**	70.
	n. **green**	65.
	o. **dark green**	65.
	p. **blue green**	65.
	q. **light orange**	65.
	r. **dark orange**	65.
	s. **deep orange**	65.
	t. **scarlet**	65.
	u. **carmine**	65.
	x. **dark brown red**	65.
R105TC7	3c plate on goldbeater's skin	
	a. **dark brown orange**	90.
R106TC3	4c plate on India paper	
	a. **dark purple**	60.
	b. **dull purple**	60.
	d. **brown**	60.
	e. **black brown**	60.
	f. **orange brown**	65.
	g. **light blue**	60.
	h. **dark blue**	70.
	i. **ultramarine**	70.
	k. **yellow green**	70.
	n. **green**	65.
	o. **dark green**	65.
	p. **blue green**	65.
	q. **light orange**	65.
	r. **dark orange**	65.
	s. **deep orange**	65.
	t. **scarlet**	65.
	u. **carmine**	65.
	x. **dark brown red**	65.
R106TC7	4c plate on goldbeater's skin	
	a. **dark brown orange**	90.
R107TC3	5c plate on India paper	
	a. **dark purple**	60.
	b. **dull purple**	60.
	d. **brown**	60.
	e. **black brown**	60.
	f. **orange brown**	65.
	g. **light blue**	60.
	h. **dark blue**	70.
	i. **ultramarine**	70.
	k. **yellow green**	70.
	n. **green**	65.
	o. **dark green**	65.
	p. **blue green**	65.
	q. **light orange**	65.
	r. **dark orange**	65.
	s. **deep orange**	65.
	t. **scarlet**	65.
	u. **carmine**	65.
	v. **dark carmine**	65.
	w. **purplish carmine**	65.
	x. **dark brown red**	65.
R107TC7	5c plate on goldbeater's skin	
	a. **dark brown orange**	90.
R108TC3	6c plate on India paper	
	a. **dark purple**	60.
	b. **dull purple**	60.
	d. **brown**	60.
	e. **black brown**	60.
	f. **orange brown**	65.
	g. **light blue**	60.
	h. **dark blue**	70.
	i. **ultramarine**	70.
	k. **yellow green**	70.
	n. **green**	65.
	o. **dark green**	65.
	p. **blue green**	65.
	q. **light orange**	65.
	r. **dark orange**	65.
	s. **deep orange**	65.
	t. **scarlet**	65.
	u. **carmine**	65.
	v. **dark carmine**	65.
	w. **purplish carmine**	65.
	x. **dark brown red**	65.
R108TC7	6c plate on goldbeater's skin	
	a. **dark brown orange**	90.
R109TC3	10c plate on India paper	
	a. **dark purple**	60.
	b. **dull purple**	60.
	d. **brown**	60.
	e. **black brown**	60.
	g. **light blue**	60.
	h. **dark blue**	70.
	i. **ultramarine**	70.
	k. **yellow green**	70.
	n. **green**	65.
	o. **dark green**	65.
	p. **blue green**	65.
	q. **light orange**	65.
	r. **dark orange**	65.
	s. **deep orange**	65.
	t. **scarlet**	65.
	u. **carmine**	65.
	x. **dark brown red**	65.
R110TC3	15c plate on India paper	
	a. **dark purple**	60.
	b. **dull purple**	60.
	d. **brown**	60.
	e. **black brown**	60.
	f. **orange brown**	65.
	g. **light blue**	60.
	h. **dark blue**	70.
	i. **ultramarine**	70.
	k. **yellow green**	70.
	n. **green**	65.
	o. dark green	65.
	p. **blue green**	65.
	q. **light orange**	65.
	r. **dark orange**	65.
	s. **deep orange**	65.
	t. **scarlet**	65.
	u. **carmine**	65.
	w. **purplish carmine**	65.
	x. **dark brown red**	65.
R111TC3	20c plate on India paper	
	a. **dark purple**	60.
	b. **dull purple**	60.
	d. **brown**	60.
	e. **black brown**	60.
	g. **light blue**	60.
	h. **dark blue**	70.
	i. **ultramarine**	70.
	k. **yellow green**	70.
	n. **green**	65.
	o. **dark green**	65.
	p. **blue green**	65.
	q. **light orange**	65.
	r. **dark orange**	65.
	s. **deep orange**	65.
	t. **scarlet**	65.
	u. **carmine**	65.
	w. **purplish carmine**	65.
	x. **dark brown red**	65.
R111TC7	20c plate on goldbeater's skin	
	a. **dark brown orange**	90.
R112TC3	25c plate on India paper	
	a. **dark purple**	60.
	b. **dull purple**	60.
	d. **brown**	60.
	e. **black brown**	60.
	g. **light blue**	60.
	h. **dark blue**	70.
	i. **ultramarine**	70.
	k. **yellow green**	70.
	l. **dark yellow green**	70.
	n. **green**	65.
	o. **dark green**	65.
	p. **blue green**	65.
	q. **light orange**	65.
	r. **dark orange**	65.
	s. **deep orange**	65.
	t. **scarlet**	65.
	u. **carmine**	65.
	x. **dark brown red**	65.
R112TC7	25c plate on goldbeater's skin	
	a. **dark brown orange**	90.
R113TC3	30c plate on India paper	
	a. **dark purple**	60.
	b. **dull purple**	60.
	d. **brown**	60.
	e. **black brown**	60.
	g. **light blue**	60.
	h. **dark blue**	70.
	i. **ultramarine**	70.
	k. **yellow green**	70.
	n. **green**	65.
	o. **dark green**	65.
	p. **blue green**	65.
	q. **light orange**	65.
	r. **dark orange**	65.
	s. **deep orange**	65.
	t. **scarlet**	65.
	u. **carmine**	65.
	v. **dark carmine**	65.
	w. **purplish carmine**	65.
	x. **dark brown red**	65.
R113TC7	30c plate on goldbeater's skin	
	a. **dark brown orange**	90.
R114TC3	40c plate on India paper	
	a. **dark purple**	60.
	b. **dull purple**	60.
	d. **brown**	60.
	e. **black brown**	60.
	f. **orange brown**	65.
	g. **light blue**	60.
	h. **dark blue**	70.
	i. **ultramarine**	70.
	k. **yellow green**	70.
	n. **green**	65.
	o. **dark green**	65.
	p. **blue green**	65.
	q. **light orange**	65.
	r. **dark orange**	65.
	s. **deep orange**	65.
	t. **scarlet**	65.
	u. **carmine**	65.
	x. **dark brown red**	65.
R115TC3	50c plate on India paper	
	a. **dark purple**	60.
	b. **dull purple**	60.
	d. **brown**	60.
	e. **black brown**	60.
	g. **light blue**	60.
	h. **dark blue**	70.
	i. **ultramarine**	70.
	k. **yellow green**	70.
	n. **green**	65.
	o. **dark green**	65.
	p. **blue green**	65.
	q. **light orange**	65.
	r. **dark orange**	65.
	s. **deep orange**	65.
	t. **scarlet**	65.
	u. **carmine**	65.
	x. **dark brown red**	65.
R116TC3	60c plate on India paper	
	a. **dark purple**	60.
	b. **dull purple**	60.
	d. **brown**	60.
	e. **black brown**	60.
	g. **light blue**	60.
	h. **dark blue**	70.
	i. **ultramarine**	70.
	k. **yellow green**	70.
	n. **green**	65.
	o. **dark green**	65.
	p. **blue green**	65.

q.	**light orange**	65.
r.	**dark orange**	65.
s.	**deep orange**	65.
t.	**scarlet**	65.
u.	**carmine**	65.
v.	**dark carmine**	65.
x.	**dark brown red**	65.
R116TC7	60c plate on goldbeater's skin	
a.	**dark brown orange**	90.
R117TC3	70c plate on India paper	
a.	**dark purple**	60.
b.	**dull purple**	60.
d.	**brown**	60.
e.	**black brown**	60.
g.	**light blue**	60.
h.	**dark blue**	70.
i.	**ultramarine**	70.
k.	**yellow green**	70.
n.	**green**	65.
o.	**dark green**	65.
p.	**blue green**	65.
q.	**light orange**	65.
r.	**dark orange**	65.
s.	**deep orange**	65.
t.	**scarlet**	65.
u.	**carmine**	65.
x.	**dark brown red**	65.
R118TC3	$1 plate on India paper	
a.	**dark purple**	70.
b.	**dull purple**	70.
d.	**brown**	70.
e.	**black brown**	70.
g.	**light blue**	80.
h.	**dark blue**	85.
i.	**ultramarine**	85.
k.	**yellow green**	80.
n.	**green**	75.
o.	**dark green**	75.
p.	**blue green**	75.
q.	**light orange**	75.
r.	**dark orange**	75.
s.	**deep orange**	75.
t.	**scarlet**	80.
u.	**carmine**	80.
w.	**purplish carmine**	80.
x.	**dark brown red**	80.
R118TC7	$1 plate on goldbeater's skin	
a.	**dark brown orange**	90.
R119TC3	$1.30 plate on India paper	
a.	**dark purple**	70.
b.	**dull purple**	70.
d.	**brown**	70.
e.	**black brown**	70.
g.	**light blue**	80.
h.	**dark blue**	85.
i.	**ultramarine**	85.
k.	**yellow green**	80.
n.	**green**	75.
o.	**dark green**	75.
p.	**blue green**	75.
q.	**light orange**	75.
r.	**dark orange**	75.
s.	**deep orange**	75.
t.	**scarlet**	80.
u.	**carmine**	80.
x.	**dark brown red**	80.
R120TC3	$1.50 plate on India paper	
a.	**dark purple**	70.
b.	**dull purple**	70.
d.	**brown**	70.
e.	**black brown**	70.
g.	**light blue**	80.
h.	**dark blue**	85.
i.	**ultramarine**	85.
k.	**yellow green**	80.
n.	**green**	75.
o.	**dark green**	75.
p.	**blue green**	75.
q.	**light orange**	75.
r.	**dark orange**	75.
s.	**deep orange**	75.
t.	**scarlet**	80.
u.	**carmine**	80.
x.	**dark brown red**	80.
R120TC4	$1.50 plate on card	
a.	**bright yellow green**	75.
R121TC3	$1.60 plate on India paper	
a.	**dark purple**	70.
b.	**dull purple**	70.
d.	**brown**	70.
e.	**black brown**	70.
g.	**light blue**	80.
h.	**dark blue**	85.
i.	**ultramarine**	85.
k.	**yellow green**	80.
n.	**green**	75.
o.	**dark green**	75.
p.	**blue green**	75.
q.	**light orange**	75.
r.	**dark orange**	75.
s.	**deep orange**	75.
t.	**scarlet**	80.
u.	**carmine**	80.
x.	**dark brown red**	80.
R122TC3	$1.90 plate on India paper	
a.	**dark purple**	70.
b.	**dull purple**	70.
d.	**brown**	70.
e.	**black brown**	70.
g.	**light blue**	80.
h.	**dark blue**	85.
i.	**ultramarine**	85.
k.	**yellow green**	80.
n.	**green**	75.
o.	**dark green**	75.
p.	**blue green**	75.
q.	**light orange**	75.
r.	**dark orange**	75.
s.	**deep orange**	75.
t.	**scarlet**	80.
u.	**carmine**	80.
x.	**dark brown red**	80.
R122TC4	$1.90 plate on card	
a.	**bright yellow green**	75.
R123TC3	$2 plate on India paper	
a.	**dark purple**	70.
b.	**dull purple**	70.
d.	**brown**	70.
e.	**black brown**	70.
g.	**light blue**	80.
h.	**dark blue**	85.
i.	**ultramarine**	85.
k.	**yellow green**	80.
n.	**green**	75.
o.	**dark green**	75.
p.	**blue green**	75.
q.	**light orange**	75.
r.	**dark orange**	75.
s.	**deep orange**	75.
t.	**scarlet**	80.
u.	**carmine**	80.
w.	**purplish carmine**	80.
x.	**dark brown red**	80.
R123TC4	$2 plate on card	
a.	**bright yellow green**	75.
R123TC7	$2 plate on goldbeater's skin	
a.	**dark brown orange**	90.
R124TC3	$2.50 plate on India paper	
a.	**dark purple**	70.
b.	**dull purple**	70.
d.	**brown**	70.
e.	**black brown**	70.
g.	**light blue**	80.
h.	**dark blue**	85.
i.	**ultramarine**	85.
k.	**yellow green**	80.
n.	**green**	75.
o.	**dark green**	75.
p.	**blue green**	75.
q.	**light orange**	75.
r.	**dark orange**	75.
s.	**deep orange**	75.
t.	**scarlet**	80.
u.	**carmine**	80.
v.	**dark carmine**	80.
x.	**dark brown red**	80.
R125TC3	$3 plate on India paper	
a.	**dark purple**	70.
b.	**dull purple**	70.
d.	**brown**	70.
e.	**black brown**	70.
g.	**light blue**	80.
h.	**dark blue**	85.
i.	**ultramarine**	85.
k.	**yellow green**	80.
n.	**green**	75.
o.	**dark green**	75.
p.	**blue green**	75.
q.	**light orange**	75.
r.	**dark orange**	75.
s.	**deep orange**	75.
t.	**scarlet**	80.
u.	**carmine**	80.
x.	**dark brown red**	80.
R125TC4	$3 plate on card	
a.	**bright yellow green**	75.
R126TC3	$3.50 plate on India paper	
a.	**dark purple**	70.
b.	**dull purple**	70.
c.	**red purple**	75.
d.	**brown**	70.
e.	**black brown**	70.
g.	**light blue**	80.
h.	**dark blue**	85.
i.	**ultramarine**	85.
k.	**yellow green**	80.
n.	**green**	75.
o.	**dark green**	75.
p.	**blue green**	75.
q.	**light orange**	75.
r.	**dark orange**	75.
s.	**deep orange**	75.
t.	**scarlet**	90.
u.	**carmine**	80.
x.	**dark brown red**	80.
R127TC3	$5 plate on India paper	
a.	**dark purple**	70.
b.	**dull purple**	70.
d.	**brown**	70.
e.	**black brown**	70.
g.	**light blue**	80.
h.	**dark blue**	85.
i.	**ultramarine**	85.
k.	**yellow green**	80.
n.	**green**	75.
o.	**dark green**	75.
p.	**blue green**	75.
q.	**light orange**	75.
r.	**dark orange**	75.
s.	**deep orange**	75.
t.	**scarlet**	75.
u.	**carmine**	75.
w.	**purplish carmine**	75.
x.	**dark brown red**	80.
R127TC7	$5 plate on goldbeater's skin	
a.	**dark brown orange**	100.
R128TC	$10 plate on India paper	
a.	**dark purple**	70.
b.	**dull purple**	70.
d.	**brown**	70.
e.	**black brown**	70.
g.	**light blue**	80.
h.	**dark blue**	85.
i.	**ultramarine**	85.
k.	**yellow green**	75.
n.	**green**	75.
o.	**dark green**	75.
p.	**blue green**	75.
q.	**light orange**	75.
r.	**dark orange**	75.
s.	**deep orange**	75.
t.	**scarlet**	75.
u.	**carmine**	80.
x.	**dark brown red**	80.
R128TC4	$10 plate on card	
a.	**bright yellow green**	75.
R129TC3	$20 plate on India paper	
a.	**dark purple**	95.
b.	**dull purple**	95.
d.	**brown**	95.
e.	**black brown**	95.
g.	**light blue**	90.
h.	**dark blue**	90.
i.	**ultramarine**	90.
k.	**yellow green**	85.
m.	**emerald green**	85.
n.	**green**	75.
o.	**dark green**	75.
p.	**blue green**	75.
q.	**light orange**	75.
r.	**dark orange**	85.
s.	**deep orange**	85.
t.	**scarlet**	90.
u.	**carmine**	80.
v.	**dark carmine**	90.
x.	**dark brown red**	80.
R130TC3	$25 plate on India paper	
a.	**dark purple**	100.
b.	**dull purple**	100.
d.	**brown**	100.
e.	**black brown**	100.
g.	**light blue**	90.
h.	**dark blue**	90.
i.	**ultramarine**	90.
k.	**yellow green**	85.
m.	**emerald green**	85.
n.	**green**	75.
o.	**dark green**	75.
p.	**blue green**	75.
q.	**light orange**	75.
r.	**dark orange**	85.
s.	**deep orange**	85.
t.	**scarlet**	90.
u.	**carmine**	80.
w.	**purplish carmine**	90.
x.	**dark brown red**	300.
R130TC7	$5 plate on goldbeater's skin	
a.	**dark brown orange**	100.
R131TC3	$50 plate on India paper	
a.	**dark purple**	95.
b.	**dull purple**	95.
d.	**brown**	95.
e.	**black brown**	95.
g.	**light blue**	90.
h.	**dark blue**	90.
i.	**ultramarine**	90.
k.	**yellow green**	85.
m.	**emerald green**	85.
n.	**green**	75.
o.	**dark green**	75.
p.	**blue green**	75.
q.	**light orange**	75.
r.	**dark orange**	85.
s.	**deep orange**	85.
t.	**scarlet**	90.
u.	**carmine**	80.
x.	**dark brown red**	80.
R131TC4	$50 plate on card	
a.	**bright yellow green**	85.
RB1TC3	1c plate on India paper	
a.	**dark purple**	70.
b.	**dull purple**	70.
d.	**brown**	65.
e.	**black brown**	65.
g.	**light blue**	75.
h.	**dark blue**	75.
i.	**ultramarine**	70.
k.	**yellow green**	70.
l.	**dark yellow green**	70.
n.	**green**	65.
o.	**dark green**	65.
p.	**blue green**	65.
q.	**light orange**	65.
r.	**dark orange**	65.
s.	**deep orange**	65.
t.	**scarlet**	65.
u.	**carmine**	65.
x.	**dark brown red**	65.
RB2TC3	2c plate on India paper	
a.	**dark purple**	70.
b.	**dull purple**	70.
d.	**brown**	65.
e.	**black brown**	65.
g.	**light blue**	70.
h.	**dark blue**	70.
i.	**ultramarine**	70.
k.	**yellow green**	70.
n.	**green**	65.
o.	**dark green**	65.
p.	**blue green**	65.
q.	**light orange**	65.
r.	**dark orange**	65.
s.	**deep orange**	65.
t.	**scarlet**	65.
u.	**carmine**	65.
x.	**dark brown red**	65.
RB2TC4	2c plate on card	
a.	**bright yellow green**	70.
RB3TC3	3c plate on India paper	
a.	**dark purple**	70.
b.	**dull purple**	70.
d.	**brown**	65.
e.	**black brown**	65.
g.	**light blue**	70.
h.	**dark blue**	70.
i.	**ultramarine**	70.
k.	**yellow green**	70.

l. dark yellow green 70.
n. green 65.
o. dark green 65.
p. blue green 65.
q. light orange 65.
r. dark orange 65.
s. deep orange 65.
t. scarlet 65.
u. carmine 65.
x. dark brown red 65.
RB4TC3 4c plate on India paper
a. dark purple 70.
b. dull purple 70.
d. brown 65.
e. black brown 65.
g. light blue 70.
h. dark blue 70.
i. ultramarine 70.
k. yellow green 70.
n. green 65.
o. dark green 65.
p. blue green 65.
q. light orange 65.
r. dark orange 65.
s. deep orange 65.
t. scarlet 65.
u. carmine 65.
x. dark brown red 65.
RB5TC3 5c plate on India paper
a. dark purple 70.
b. dull purple 70.
d. brown 65.
e. black brown 65.
g. light blue 70.
h. dark blue 70.
i. ultramarine 70.
k. yellow green 70.
l. dark yellow green 70.
n. green 65.
o. dark green 65.
p. blue green 65.
q. light orange 65.
r. dark orange 65.
s. deep orange 65.
t. scarlet 65.
u. carmine 65.
x. dark brown red 65.
RB5TC4 5c plate on card
a. bright yellow green 70.
RB6TC3 6c plate on India paper
a. dark purple 70.
b. dull purple 70.
d. brown 65.
e. black brown 65.
g. light blue 70.
h. dark blue 70.
i. ultramarine 70.
k. yellow green 70.
l. dark yellow green 70.
n. green 65.
o. dark green 65.
p. blue green 65.
q. light orange 65.
r. dark orange 65.
s. deep orange 65.
t. scarlet 65.
u. carmine 65.
x. dark brown red 65.
RB7TC3 10c plate on India paper
a. dark purple 70.
b. dull purple 70.
d. brown 65.
e. black brown 65.
g. light blue 70.
h. dark blue 70.
i. ultramarine 70.
k. yellow green 70.
l. dark yellow green 70.
n. green 65.
o. dark green 65.
p. blue green 65.
q. light orange 65.
r. dark orange 65.
s. deep orange 65.
t. scarlet 65.
u. carmine 65.
x. dark brown red 65.

Battleship Type

1898
RB20TC1d ⅛c large die on card
e. light blue *1,000.*
RB20P1 ⅛c yel grn, lg die on India paper *2,000.*
RB21TC1a ¼c large die on India paper
e. dull green 1,300.
RB21P1 ¼c brn, lg die on India paper *2,000.*
RB22TC1a ⅜c large die on India paper
e. dull green 750.
RB22P1 ⅜c dp org, lg die on India paper *2,000.*
RB23P1 ⅝c dp ultra, lg die on India paper *2,000.*
RB24TC1a 1c large die on India paper
e. dull green 750.
RB24P1 1c dk grn, lg die on India paper *2,000.*
RB25P1 1¼c vio, lg die on India paper *2,000.*
RB26TC1a 1⅞c large die on India paper
e. dull green 750.
f. black 750.
RB26P1 1⅞c dull bl, lg die on India paper *2,000.*
RB27TC1a 2c large die on India paper
e. dull green 500.
RB27P1 2c vio brn, lg die on India paper *2,000.*
RB28P1 2½c lake, lg die on India paper *2,000.*
RB29P1 3¾c ol gray, lg die on India paper *2,000.*
RB30P1 4c pur, lg die on India paper *2,000.*
RB31TC1a 5c large die on India paper
e. dull green 500.
RB31P1 5c brn org, lg die on India paper *2,000.*

Stock Transfer

1918-29
RD20TC1a $50 large die on India paper
e. black *2,250.*
f. blue *2,250.*

Wines

1916
RE33P1 3c grn, with "c" punch cancel, lg die on India paper —
RE34P1 4c grn, with "c" punch cancel, lg die on India paper —
RE41P1 20c grn, with "c" punch cancel, lg die on India paper —
RE42TC1a 24c large die on India paper
e. blue —
RE48P1 80c grn, with "c" punch cancel, lg die on India paper —
RE51TC1a $1.60 large die on India paper
e. bister —
RE56P1 $20 grn, lg die on India paper *5,000.*

Playing Cards

1896 **Bureau of Engraving & Printing**
RF1TC1a 2c large die on India paper
e. black, (On hand) *1,500.*
RF2TC1a 2c large die on India paper
e. lake, (Act of) *1,000.*
RF2P1 2c ultra, lg die on India paper *550.*
a. blue *1,100.*
RF23P1 10c light blue, large die on India paper *4,500.*

Silver Tax

1941
RG60P1 3c gray, without overprint, with "c" punch cancel, lg die on India paper *1,500.*
RG61P1 4c gray, without overprint, with "c" punch cancel, lg die on India paper *1,500.*
RG66P1 25c gray, without overprint, with "c" punch cancel, lg die on India paper *1,500.*
RG72P1 $3 gray, without overprint, lg die on India paper *1,500.*
RG77P5 $30 gray, plate on stamp paper, imperf., serial #0000 *900.*

Consular Service Fee

1952
RK40P1a $20 violet, large die on wove, on card —

PRIVATE DIE PROPRIETARY

The editors are indebted to Eric Jackson and Philip T. Bansner for the compilation of the following listing of Private Die Proprietary die and plate proofs as well as the corrresponding trial color proofs. The large die proofs range in size and format from die impressions on India die sunk on cards generally up to 6x9 inches, through die impressions on India on or off card in medium to stamp size. Many individual listings are known in more than one size and format. Values reflect the size and format most commonly seen.

Private Die Match Stamps

1864
RO1TC1a 1c large die on India paper
e. black 210.
f. green 360.
RO1P1 1c bl, lg die on India paper 270.
RO2TC1a 1c large die on India paper
e. black 270.
f. green 360.
RO2P1 1c org, lg die on India paper 600.
RO2P3 1c org, plate on India paper 90.
RO3P1 1c bl, lg die on India paper 270.
RO4P1 1c bl, lg die on India paper 600.
RO5TC1a 1c large die on India paper
e. black 330.
f. blue 600.
RO5P1 1c grn, lg die on India paper 600.
RO6TC1a 1c large die on India paper
e. black 360.
f. green 600.
RO6P1 1c bl, lg die on India paper 210.
RO7TC1a 1c large die on India paper
e. black 360.
f. green 360.
g. dull green 600.
RO7P1 1c bl, lg die on India paper 210.
RO7P3 1c bl, plate on India paper 210.
RO9TC1a 1c large die on India paper 100.
e. blue 270.
f. brown 330.
g. dark green 600.
h. green 360.
RO9P1 1c blk, lg die on India paper 210.
RO10TC1a 1c large die on India paper
e. blue 360.
f. green 600.
RO10P1 1c blk, lg die on India paper 220.
RO11TC1a 3c large die on India paper
e. blue 600.
f. green 600.
RO11P1 3c blk, lg die on India paper 300.
RO12TC1a 1c large die on India paper
e. blue 270.
f. green 600.
RO12P1 1c blk, lg die on India paper 270.
RO13TC1a 3c large die on India paper
e. black 600.
f. blue 1,200.
RO13P1 3c grn, lg die on India paper 1,200.
RO14TC1a 1c large die on India paper
e. blue 270.
f. green 600.
RO14P1 1c blk, lg die on India paper 210.
RO15TC1a 1c large die on India paper
e. black 270.
f. blue 270.
RO15P1 1c grn, lg die on India paper 360.
RO16TC1a 1c large die on India paper
e. black 270.
f. green 360.
RO16P1 1c bl, lg die on India paper 270.
RO16P3 1c bl, plate on India paper 60.
RO17TC1a 1c large die on India paper
e. black 270.
f. green 600.
g. green, composite RO17TC+RO19TC 1,500.
RO17P1 1c bl, lg die on India paper 210.
a. 1c+3c bl, RO17P1+RO19TC1e composite 1,200.
b. 1c+3c blk, RO17TC1e+RO19P1 composite 900.
RO19TC1a 3c large die on India paper
e. blue 300.
f. green 125.
RO19P1 3c blk, lg die on India paper 450.
RO20TC1a 1c large die on India paper
e. black 210.
f. green 600.
RO20P1 1c bl, lg die on India paper 210.
RO21TC1a 3c large die on India paper
e. blue 450.
f. green 450.
RO21P1 3c blk, lg die on India paper 300.
RO22TC1a 1c large die on India paper
e. black 360.
RO23TC1a 1c large die on India paper
e. black 270.
f. blue 270.
g. green 600.
RO23P1 1c org, lg die on India paper 270.
RO24TC1a 1c large die on India paper
e. black 270.
f. blue 270.
g. green 600.
RO24P1 1c brn, lg die on India paper 270.
RO25TC1a 12c large die on India paper
e. black 475.
f. blue 900.
g. green 900.
RO26TC1a 1c large die on India paper
e. black 270.
f. blue 270.
g. dark brown 270.
h. green 360.
i. light brown 360.
RO27TC1a 12c large die on India paper
e. black 475.
f. blue 600.
g. green 900.
RO28TC1a 1c large die on India paper
e. black 210.
f. brown 360.
g. green 360.
RO28P1 1c bl, lg die on India paper 360.
RO28P3 1c bl, plate on India paper 90.
RO29TC1a 1c large die on India paper
e. blue 360.
f. green 360.
RO29P1 1c blk, lg die on India paper 210.
RO30TC1a 1c large die on India paper
e. black 210.
f. blue 270.
g. green 360.
h. red 600.
RO30P1 1c grn, lg die on India paper 210.
RO31TC1a 1c large die on India paper
e. blue 360.
f. green 270.
g. red 600.
RO31P1 1c blk, lg die on India paper 210.
RO32TC1a 4c large die on India paper
e. blue 600.
f. brown 600.
g. orange 600.
h. vermilion 600.
RO32P1 4c blk, lg die on India paper 360.
RO33P1 4c grn, lg die on India paper 270.
RO35TC1a 1c large die on India paper
e. blue 360.
f. green 600.
RO35P1 1c blk, lg die on India paper 210.
RO37TC1a 3c large die on India paper
e. blue 475.
f. green 475.
RO37P1 3c blk, lg die on India paper 270.
RO38TC1a 1c large die on India paper
e. blue 425.
f. dark blue 600.
g. green 450.
h. red 725.
RO38P1 1c blk, lg die on India paper 425.
RO39TC1a 1c large die on India paper
e. black 360.
RO39P1 1c grn, lg die on India paper 600.
RO40P1 1c bl, lg die on India paper 210.
RO41TC1a 1c large die on India paper
e. black 270.
f. green 360.
RO41P1 1c lake, lg die on India paper 270.
RO42TC1a 1c large die on India paper
e. black 360.
f. blue 360.
g. green 600.
RO42P1 1c lake, lg die on India paper 270.
RO43TC1a 1c large die on India paper
e. blue 600.
RO43P1 1c blk, lg die on India paper 270.
RO44P1 1c grn, lg die on India paper 270.
RO45TC1a 1c large die on India paper
e. blue 425.
f. green 900.

No.	Description	Value
RO45P1	1c **blk,** lg die on India paper	270.
RO46TC1a	1c large die on India paper	
	e. **blue**	425.
	f. **dark blue**	600.
	g. **green**	600.
	h. **orange**	360.
RO46P1	1c **blk,** lg die on India paper	360.
RO47TC1a	1c large die on India paper	
	e. **blue**	360.
	f. **green**	600.
RO47P1	1c **blk,** lg die on India paper	270.
RO47P3	1c **blk,** plate on India paper	90.
RO47P4	1c **blk,** plate on card	75.
RO48P1	1c **blk,** lg die on India paper	600.
RO49TC1a	1c large die on India paper	
	e. **blue**	270.
	f. **brown**	600.
	g. **brown red**	360.
	h. **dark blue**	600.
	i. **green**	600.
	j. **red brown**	600.
RO49P1	1c **blk,** lg die on India paper	210.
RO50P1	1c **blk,** lg die on India paper	450.
RO55TC1a	1c large die on India paper	
	e. **blue**	450.
RO55P1	1c **blk,** lg die on India paper	300.
RO56TC1a	1c large die on India paper	
	e. **blue**	900.
	f. **green**	360.
RO56P1	1c **blk,** lg die on India paper	300.
RO57TC1a	1c large die on India paper	
	e. **black**	210.
	f. **blue**	270.
RO57P1	1c **grn,** lg die on India paper	360.
RO58TC1a	1c large die on India paper	
	e. **black**	360.
	f. **blue**	270.
	g. **dark rose**	600.
	h. **green**	600.
	i. **rose**	360.
RO58P1	1c **lake,** lg die on India paper	270.
RO58P3	1c **lake,** plate on India paper	75.
RO59TC1a	1c large die on India paper	
	e. **black**	270.
RO60TC1a	3c large die on India paper	
	e. **blue**	600.
	f. **green**	600.
RO60P1	3c **blk,** lg die on India paper	360.
RO61TC1a	1c large die on India paper	
	e. **black**	210.
	f. **blue**	360.
RO61P1	1c **grn,** lg die on India paper	360.
RO62TC1a	1c large die on India paper	
	e. **black**	210.
	f. **blue**	210.
RO62P1	1c **grn,** lg die on India paper	210.
RO64TC1a	1c large die on India paper	
	e. **black**	270.
	f. **blue**	360.
	g. **green**	360.
RO64P1	1c **lake,** lg die on India paper	270.
RO65TC1a	1c large die on India paper	
	e. **green**	360.
RO65P1	1c **blk,** lg die on India paper	270.
RO66P1	1c **bl,** lg die on India paper	210.
RO67TC1a	1c large die on India paper	
	e. **blue**	270.
	f. **green**	360.
	g. **red**	600.
	h. **rose**	600.
RO67P1	1c **blk,** lg die on India paper	210.
RO68TC1a	1c large die on India paper	
	e. **black**	270.
	f. **blue**	270.
RO68P1	1c **grn,** lg die on India paper	270.
RO69TC1a	1c large die on India paper	
	e. **blue**	360.
	f. **green**	600.
RO69P1	1c **blk,** lg die on India paper	210.
RO71TC1a	1c large die on India paper	
	e. **black**	300.
	f. **green**	475.
RO72TC1a	1c large die on India paper	
	e. **black**	600.
RO72P1	1c **grn,** lg die on India paper	600.
RO73TC1a	1c large die on India paper	
	e. **blue**	270.
	f. **green**	360.
	g. **red**	600.
	h. **red brown**	270.
RO73P1	1c **blk,** lg die on India paper	210.
RO75P1	1c **car,** lg die on India paper	540.
RO76TC1a	1c large die on India paper	
	e. **blue**	600.
	f. **green**	360.
RO76P1	1c **blk,** lg die on India paper	210.
RO77TC1a	1c large die on India paper	
	e. **black**	270.
	f. **green**	360.
RO77P1	1c **bl,** lg die on India paper	270.
RO78TC1a	1c large die on India paper	
	e. **black**	270.
	f. **dark blue**	600.
	g. **green**	600.
RO78P1	1c **bl,** lg die on India paper	270.
RO80TC1a	1c large die on India paper	
	e. **black**	270.
	f. **green**	600.
RO80P1	1c **bl,** lg die on India paper	600.
RO81TC1a	1c large die on India paper	
	e. **blue**	210.
	f. **dark green**	600.
	g. **green**	270.
	h. **lake**	600.
	i. **red**	360.
RO81P1	1c **blk,** lg die on India paper	210.
RO82TC1a	1c large die on India paper	
	e. **blue**	210.
	f. **green**	600.
RO82P1	1c **blk,** lg die on India paper	210.
RO83TC1a	1c large die on India paper	
	e. **black**	210.
	f. **green**	360.
	g. **red**	600.
RO83P1	1c **bl,** lg die on India paper	210.
RO84TC1a	1c large die on India paper	
	e. **blue**	360.
	f. **green**	600.
RO84P1	1c **blk,** lg die on India paper	210.
RO85TC1a	1c large die on India paper	
	e. **black**	300.
	f. **blue**	360.
	g. **green**	425.
	h. **orange**	600.
	i. **vermilion**	600.
RO85P1	1c **brn,** lg die on India paper	360.
RO85P3	1c **brn,** plate on India paper	100.
RO86TC1a	1c large die on India paper	
	e. **blue**	600.
	f. **brown**	600.
	g. **green**	475.
	h. **orange**	600.
	i. **red**	600.
RO86P1	1c **blk,** lg die on India paper	300.
RO86P3	1c **blk,** plate on India paper	125.
RO87TC1a	1c large die on India paper	
	e. **dull rose**	600.
	f. **orange**	600.
RO87P1	1c **blk,** lg die on India paper	600.
RO87P3	1c **blk,** plate on India paper	50.
RO88TC1a	1c large die on India paper	
	e. **blue**	360.
	f. **green**	600.
RO88P1	1c **blk,** lg die on India paper	210.
RO89TC1a	3c large die on India paper	
	e. **blue**	360.
	f. **green**	360.
RO89P1	3c **blk,** lg die on India paper	210.
RO90TC1a	6c large die on India paper	
	e. **blue**	270.
	f. **brown**	600.
	g. **green**	600.
	h. **orange**	600.
RO90P1	6c **blk,** lg die on India paper	210.
RO90P3	6c **blk,** plate on India paper	125.
RO91TC1a	3c large die on India paper	
	e. **blue**	270.
	f. **brown**	600.
	g. **green**	600.
	h. **orange**	600.
	i. **red**	600.
RO91P1	3c **blk,** lg die on India paper	270.
RO91P3	3c **blk,** plate on India paper	125.
RO92TC1a	1c large die on India paper	
	e. **blue**	360.
	f. **green**	600.
RO92P1	1c **blk,** lg die on India paper	210.
RO94TC1a	3c large die on India paper	
	e. **blue**	270.
	f. **brown**	360.
	g. **green**	270.
	h. **orange**	360.
	i. **red**	600.
	j. **vermilion**	600.
RO94P1	3c **blk,** lg die on India paper	210.
RO94P3	3c **blk,** plate on India paper	175.
RO95TC1a	1c large die on India paper	
	e. **black**	210.
	f. **blue**	210.
	g. **brown**	270.
	h. **dark blue**	600.
RO95P1	1c **grn,** lg die on India paper	270.
RO96TC1a	1c large die on India paper	
	e. **black**	210.
	f. **blue**	270.
RO96P1	1c **grn,** lg die on India paper	360.
RO97TC1a	1c large die on India paper	
	e. **blue**	360.
RO97P1	1c **blk,** lg die on India paper	210.
RO98P1	1c **grn,** lg die on India paper	270.
RO99TC1a	1c large die on India paper	
	e. **black**	210.
	f. **blue**	600.
RO99P1	1c **grn,** lg die on India paper	600.
RO100TC1a	1c large die on India paper	
	e. **blue**	600.
RO100P1	1c **grn,** lg die on India paper	270.
RO100P3	1c **grn,** plate on India paper	65.
RO101TC1a	3c large die on India paper	
	e. **black**	210.
	f. **green**	360.
RO101TC3	3c Plate on India paper	
	a. **orange**	75.
RO101P3	3c **car,** plate on India paper	75.
RO102TC1a	1c large die on India paper	
	e. **black**	210.
	f. **blue**	600.
	g. **green**	600.
RO102P3	5c **org,** plate on India paper	75.
RO103TC1a	1c large die on India paper	
	e. **blue**	270.
	f. **rose**	360.
RO103P1	1c **blk,** lg die on India paper	210.
RO104P1	1c **grn,** lg die on India paper	210.
RO105TC1a	1c large die on India paper	
	e. **blue**	360.
	f. **green**	600.
RO105P1	1c **blk,** lg die on India paper	210.
RO105P3	1c **blk,** plate on India paper	100.
RO106TC1a	1c large die on India paper	
	e. **black**	210.
	f. **blue**	270.
RO106P1	1c **grn,** lg die on India paper	360.
RO107TC1a	1c large die on India paper	
	e. **black**	210.
	f. **green**	360.
RO107P1	1c **bl,** lg die on India paper	270.
RO108P1	1c **red,** lg die on India paper	900.
RO109P1	1c **blk,** lg die on India paper	360.
RO110TC1a	1c large die on India paper	
	e. **black**	210.
	f. **blue**	210.
	g. **orange**	600.
	h. **red**	270.
RO110P1	1c **grn,** lg die on India paper	210.
RO112TC1a	1c large die on India paper	
	e. **black**	210.
	f. **green**	600.
RO112P1	1c **bl,** lg die on India paper	270.
RO112P3	1c **bl,** plate on India paper	100.
RO113TC1a	1c large die on India paper	
	e. **blue**	360.
	f. **green**	600.
	g. **orange**	600.
RO113P1	1c **blk,** lg die on India paper	210.
RO114TC1a	1c large die on India paper	
	e. **black**	900.
RO114P1	1c **lake,** lg die on India paper	900.
RO115TC1a	1c large die on India paper	
	e. **black**	210.
	f. **green**	600.
RO115P1	1c **bl,** lg die on India paper	210.
RO116TC1a	1c large die on India paper	
	e. **black**	270.
	f. **green**	360.
RO116P1	1c **bl,** lg die on India paper	210.
RO118TC1a	8c large die on India paper	
	e. **black**	270.
	f. **dark blue**	600.
	g. **green**	600.
RO118P1	8c **bl,** lg die on India paper	600.
RO119TC1a	1c large die on India paper	
	e. **black**	270.
	f. **blue**	270.
RO119P1	1c **grn,** lg die on India paper	360.
RO120TC1a	1c large die on India paper	
	e. **black**	600.
RO120P1	1c+2c **grn,** RO120P1+RS29P1 composite, lg die on India paper	1,500.
RO121TC1a	1c large die on India paper	
	e. **black**	210.
	f. **blue**	360.
RO121P1	1c **grn,** lg die on India paper	600.
RO122TC1a	1c large die on India paper	
	e. **blue**	360.
	f. **green**	600.
RO122P1	1c **blk,** lg die on India paper	210.
RO123TC1a	1c large die on India paper	
	e. **blue**	600.
RO123P1	1c **blk,** lg die on India paper	210.
RO124P1	1c **grn,** lg die on India paper	900.
RO125TC1a	1c large die on India paper	
	e. **black**	270.
RO125P1	1c **bl,** lg die on India paper	360.
RO126P1	1c **blk,** lg die on India paper	210.
RO127TC1a	1c large die on India paper	
	e. **black**	360.
	f. **green**	270.
RO127P1	1c **bl,** lg die on India paper	210.
RO128TC1a	1c large die on India paper	
	e. **black**	270.
	f. **green**	600.
RO128P1	1c **bl,** lg die on India paper	270.
RO130TC1a	1c large die on India paper	
	e. **black**	270.
	f. **green**	360.
RO130P1	1c **bl,** lg die on India paper	600.
RO130P4	1c **bl,** plate on thin card	—
RO131TC1a	1c large die on India paper	
	e. **black**	210.
	f. **green**	270.
	g. **red**	270.
RO131P1	1c **bl,** lg die on India paper	360.
RO132TC1a	1c large die on India paper	
	e. **black**	270.
	f. **green**	600.
RO132P1	1c **bl,** lg die on India paper	270.
RO132P3	1c **bl,** plate on India paper	125.
RO133TC1a	1c large die on India paper	
	e. **blue**	600.
	f. **green**	360.
RO133P1	1c **blk,** lg die on India paper	270.
RO134TC1a	1c large die on India paper	
	e. **black**	360.
	f. **green**	360.
RO134TC3	1c plate on India paper	
	a. **black**	150.
RO134P1	1c **bl,** lg die on India paper	210.
RO134P3	1c **bl,** plate on India paper	75.
RO135TC1a	1c large die on India paper	
	e. **black**	600.
	f. **blue**	360.
	g. **green**	360.
	h. **rose**	270.
RO135P1	1c **lake,** lg die on India paper	600.
RO136TC1a	1c large die on India paper	
	e. **black**	270.
	f. **green**	360.
RO136P1	1c **bl,** lg die on India paper	210.
RO137TC1a	1c large die on India paper	
	e. **black**	210.
	f. **blue**	210.
	g. **green**	600.
RO138TC1a	1c large die on India paper	
	e. **black**	210.
	f. **blue**	600.
RO138P1	1c **grn,** lg die on India paper	210.
RO139TC1a	5c large die on India paper	
	e. **black**	210.
	f. **green**	600.
RO139P1	5c **bl,** lg die on India paper	270.
RO140TC1a	4c large die on India paper	
	e. **black**	270.
	f. **blue**	360.

RO140P1 4c **grn,** lg die on India paper 270.
RO141TC1a 1c large die on India paper
e. **black** 210.
f. **dark blue** 360.
g. **green** 600.
h. **yellow green** 360.
RO141P1 1c **bl,** lg die on India paper 210.
RO142TC1a 1c large die on India paper
e. **black** 210.
f. **blue** 270.
RO142P1 1c **grn,** lg die on India paper 270.
RO143TC1a 3c large die on India paper
e. **black** 210.
f. **blue** 270.
g. **green** 360.
RO143P1 3c **org,** lg die on India paper 270.
RO144TC1a 1c large die on India paper
e. **black** 600.
RO144P1 1c **bl,** lg die on India paper 475.
RO145TC1a 1c large die on India paper
e. **black** 600.
f. **blue** 600.
RO146TC1a 1c large die on India paper
e. **blue** 600.
f. **green** 360.
RO146P1 1c **blk,** lg die on India paper 210.
RO148TC1a 1c large die on India paper
e. **black** 210.
f. **green** 360.
g. **red** 360.
RO148P1 1c **bl,** lg die on India paper 270.
RO148P3 1c **bl,** plate on India paper 100.
RO152TC1a 1c large die on India paper
e. **blue** 360.
f. **green** 360.
RO152P1 1c **blk,** lg die on India paper 210.
RO152P3 1c **blk,** plate on India paper 75.
RO153TC1a 1c large die on India paper
e. **blue** 270.
f. **brown** 360.
g. **green** 270.
h. **orange** 360.
i. **red** 360.
RO153P1 1c **blk,** lg die on India paper 210.
RO153P3 1c **blk,** plate on India paper 75.
RO155TC1a 1c large die on India paper
e. **blue** 270.
f. **green** 600.
RO155P1 1c **blk,** lg die on India paper 210.
RO155P3 1c **blk,** plate on India paper 65.
RO157TC1a 3c large die on India paper
e. **black** 210.
f. **green** 360.
RO157P1 3c **bl,** lg die on India paper 270.
RO157P3 3c **bl,** plate on India paper 80.
RO158TC1a 1c large die on India paper
e. **blue** 360.
f. **green** 600.
RO158P1 1c **blk,** lg die on India paper 210.
RO159TC1a 3c large die on India paper
e. **black** 270.
f. **green** 600.
RO159P1 3c **bl,** lg die on India paper 210.
RO160TC1a 1c large die on India paper
e. **black** 270.
f. **brown** 600.
g. **green** 360.
RO160P1 1c **bl,** lg die on India paper 210.
RO161TC1a 1c large die on India paper
e. **black** 270.
f. **green** 360.
RO161P1 1c **bl,** lg die on India paper 600.
RO163TC1a 1c large die on India paper
e. **blue** 360.
f. **green** 600.
RO163P1 1c **blk,** lg die on India paper 210.
RO164TC1a 1c large die on India paper
e. **black** 600.
RO164P1 1c **lake,** lg die on India paper 600.
RO165TC1a 12c large die on India paper
e. **black** 900.
f. **green** 1,200.
g. **red** 1,200.
RO165P1 12c **bl,** lg die on India paper 900.
RO166TC1a 1c large die on India paper
e. **black** 360.
f. **blue** 270.
g. **green** 600.
h. **red** 210.
RO166P1 1c **ver,** lg die on India paper 270.
RO167TC1a 3c large die on India paper
e. **black** 210.
f. **green** 360.
g. **red** 360.
h. **ultramarine** 360.
RO167P1 3c **bl,** lg die on India paper 210.
RO168TC1a 1c large die on India paper
e. **black** 600.
f. **green** 360.
RO168P1 1c **bl,** lg die on India paper 210.
RO170P1 1c **blk,** lg die on India paper 550.
RO171TC1a 1c large die on India paper
e. **blue** 360.
f. **green** 360.
RO171P1 1c **blk,** lg die on India paper 210.
RO172TC1a 1c large die on India paper
e. **blue** 270.
f. **green** 600.
RO172P1 1c **blk,** lg die on India paper 210.
RO173TC1a 1c large die on India paper
e. **black** 270.
f. **green** 360.
RO173P1 1c **bl,** lg die on India paper 270.
RO173P3 1c **bl,** plate on India paper 75.
RO174TC1a 1c large die on India paper
e. **black** 360.
f. **green** 360.
RO174P1 1c **bl,** lg die on India paper 210.
RO175TC1a 1c large die on India paper
e. **blue** 325.
f. **green** 425.
g. **red** 600.
RO175P1 1c **blk,** lg die on India paper 270.
RO176P1 1c **bl,** lg die on India paper 600.
RO177TC1a 1c large die on India paper
e. **black** 210.
f. **blue** 270.
g. **green** 600.
RO177P1 1c **grn,** lg die on India paper 210.
RO178TC1a 1c large die on India paper
e. **black** 210.
f. **blue** 360.
RO178P1 1c **grn,** lg die on India paper 600.
RO179TC1a 1c large die on India paper
e. **blue** 600.
f. **green** 600.
RO179P1 1c **blk,** lg die on India paper 210.
RO179P3 1c **blk,** plate on India paper 75.
RO179P4 1c **blk,** plate on card 75.
RO180TC1a 1c large die on India paper
e. **blue** 270.
f. **green** 600.
RO180P1 1c **blk,** lg die on India paper 210.
RO180P3 1c **blk,** plate on India paper 80.
RO181TC1a 1c large die on India paper
e. **blue** 600.
f. **green** 360.
RO181P1 1c **blk,** lg die on India paper 210.
RO182TC1a 1c large die on India paper
e. **blue** 360.
f. **green** 360.
RO182P1 1c **blk,** lg die on India paper 210.
RO183TC1a 1c large die on India paper
e. **blue** 775.
f. **green** 775.
RO183P1 1c **blk,** lg die on India paper 600.
RO184TC1a 1c large die on India paper
e. **blue** 270.
f. **brown** 360.
g. **green** 270.
h. **orange** 360.
i. **red** 360.
RO184P1 1c **blk,** lg die on India paper 210.
RO184P3 1c **blk,** plate on India paper 75.
RO185P1 1c+1c **blk,** RO185P1+RO12P1 composite, lg die on India paper 900.
RO186TC1a 1c large die on India paper
e. **black** 210.
RO186P1 1c **bl,** lg die on India paper 270.

Private Die Canned Fruit Stamp

RP1TC1a 1c large die on India paper
e. **black** 475.
RP1P1 1c **grn,** lg die on India paper 475.

Private Die Medicine Stamps

RS1TC1a 1c large die on India paper
e. **blue** 360.
RS1P1 1c **blk,** lg die on India paper 210.
RS1P3 1c **blk,** plate on India paper —
RS4TC1a 1c large die on India paper
e. **green** 600.
RS4P1 1c **blk,** lg die on India paper 270.
RS4P3 1c **blk,** plate on India paper 125.
RS4P4 1c **blk,** plate on card 150.
RS5P1 1c **bl,** lg die on India paper 600.
RS10TC1a 4c large die on India paper
e. **black** 360.
RS10P1 4c **bl,** lg die on India paper 270.
RS10P3 4c **bl,** plate on India paper 125.
RS10P4 4c **bl,** plate on card 150.
RS14TC1a 4c large die on India paper
e. **black** 360.
f. **blue** 360.
RS14P1 4c **grn,** lg die on India paper 600.
RS14P3 4c **grn,** plate on India paper 100.
RS16TC1a 2c large die on India paper
e. **green** 600.
RS16P1 2c **ver,** lg die on India paper 600.
RS18P1 1c **blk,** lg die on India paper 600.
RS18P4 1c **blk,** plate on card 125.
RS19P4 2c **blk,** plate on card 125.
RS20P4 4c **blk,** plate on card 125.
RS21TC1a 1c large die on India paper
e. **blue** 600.
f. **green** 600.
RS21P1 1c **blk,** lg die on India paper 210.
RS21P3 1c **blk,** plate on India paper 125.
RS22TC1a 2c large die on India paper
e. **blue** 600.
f. **green** 600.
RS22P1 2c **blk,** lg die on India paper 270.
RS22P3 2c **blk,** plate on India paper 125.
RS23TC1a 4c large die on India paper
e. **green** 600.
RS23P1 4c **blk,** lg die on India paper 270.
RS23P3 4c **blk,** plate on India paper 125.
RS24TC1a 1c large die on India paper
e. **blue** 600.
f. **green** 600.
RS24P1 1c **blk,** lg die on India paper 210.
RS25TC1a 2c large die on India paper
e. **blue** 600.
f. **green** 600.
RS25P1 2c **blk,** lg die on India paper 210.
RS26TC1a 4c large die on India paper
e. **blue** 600.
f. **green** 600.
RS26P1 4c **blk,** lg die on India paper 210.
RS27TC1a 4c large die on India paper
e. **blue** 270.
f. **green** 600.
RS27P1 4c **blk,** lg die on India paper 210.
RS28TC1a 2c large die on India paper
e. **black** 270.
f. **blue** 270.
RS28P1 2c **grn,** lg die on India paper 210.
RS29TC1a 2c large die on India paper
e. **black,** composite RS29TC + unissued Eugene Jones & Co. essay with "B.J. & Co." added 900.
f. **black** 210.
g. **blue** 210.
h. **dark blue** 600.
i. **green** 600.
j. **red** 360.
RS29P1 2c **grn,** lg die on India paper 270.

For composite proof RO120P1 + RS29P1, see No. RO120P1.

RS30TC1a 1c large die on India paper
e. **black** 210.
f. **blue** 600.
g. **green** 600.
h. **red** 600.
RS30P1 1c **lake,** lg die on India paper 360.
RS31TC1a 1c large die on India paper
e. **black** 600.
f. **blue** 270.
g. **red** 600.
RS31P1 1c **grn,** lg die on India paper 210.
RS31P3 1c **grn,** plate on India paper 100.
RS31P4 1c **grn,** plate on card 100.
RS33P1 1c **blk,** lg die on India paper 210.
RS33P3 1c **blk,** plate on India paper 50.
RS33P4 1c **blk,** plate on card 50.
RS34TC1a 1c large die on India paper
e. **blue** 210.
f. **green** 270.
g. **red** 600.
RS34P1 1c **blk,** lg die on India paper 270.
RS35TC1a 1c large die on India paper
e. **blue** 360.
f. **green** 600.
RS35P1 1c **blk,** lg die on India paper 210.
RS36TC1a 1c large die on India paper
e. **black** 600.
f. **dark blue** 600.
g. **green** 600.
h. **ultramarine** 600.
i. **yellow green** 270.
RS36P1 1c **bl,** lg die on India paper 210.
RS37P1 2c **blk,** lg die on India paper 550.
RS38TC1a 2c large die on India paper
e. **blue** 900.
f. **green** 900.
RS38P1 2c **blk,** lg die on India paper 360.
RS39TC1a 1c large die on India paper
e. **blue** 360.
f. **green** 360.
g. **orange** 600.
RS39P1 1c **blk,** lg die on India paper 210.
RS39P3 1c **blk,** plate on India paper 100.
RS39P4 1c **blk,** plate on card 100.
RS40TC1a 2c large die on India paper
e. **black** 270.
f. **blue** 360.
RS40P1 2c **grn,** lg die on India paper 600.
RS40P3 2c **grn,** plate on India paper 100.
RS40P4 2c **grn,** plate on card 100.
RS41TC1a 4c large die on India paper
e. **black** 270.
f. **blue** 600.
g. **green** 600.
RS41P3 4c **brn,** plate on India paper 125.
RS41P4 4c **brn,** plate on card 125.
RS42TC1a 1c large die on India paper
e. **green** 600.
f. **blue** 600.
RS42P1 1c **blk,** lg die on India paper 210.
RS43TC1a 4c large die on India paper
e. **black** 270.
f. **green** 600.
RS43P1 4c **bl,** lg die on India paper 270.
RS44TC1a 1c large die on India paper
e. **green** 900.
RS44P1 1c **blk,** lg die on India paper 725.
RS46TC1a 4c large die on India paper
e. **blue** 270.
f. **green** 360.
RS46P1 4c **blk,** lg die on India paper 210.
RS47TC1a 4c large die on India paper
e. **blue** 360.
f. **brown** 600.
g. **green** 360.
h. **orange** 600.
i. **red** 600.
RS47P1 4c **blk,** lg die on India paper 210.
RS47P3 4c **blk,** plate on India paper 125.
RS49TC1a 4c large die on India paper
e. **black** 270.
f. **blue** 360.
RS49P1 4c **grn,** lg die on India paper 210.
RS50TC1a 1c large die on India paper
e. **black** 360.
f. **blue** 360.
g. **green** 600.
RS50P1 1c **ver,** lg die on India paper 270.
RS51TC1a 2c large die on India paper
e. **blue** 600.
f. **green** 600.
RS51P1 2c **blk,** lg die on India paper 210.
RS52TC1a 4c large die on India paper
e. **blue** 600.
f. **green** 600.
RS52P1 4c **blk,** lg die on India paper 210.
RS53TC1a 1c large die on India paper
e. **blue** 270.
f. **brown** 360.
g. **green** 270.
h. **orange** 360.
i. **red** 360.

No.	Description	Price
RS53P1	1c **blk,** lg die on India paper	210.
RS53P3	1c **blk,** plate on India paper	125.
RS54TC1a	2c large die on India paper	
	e. **blue**	270.
	f. **brown**	360.
	g. **green**	270.
	h. **orange**	360.
	i. **red**	600.
RS54P1	2c **blk,** lg die on India paper	210.
RS54P3	2c **blk,** plate on India paper	125.
RS55TC1a	4c large die on India paper	
	e. **blue**	270.
	f. **green**	270.
	g. **orange**	270.
	h. **red**	600.
RS55P1	4c **blk,** lg die on India paper	210.
RS55P3	4c **blk,** plate on India paper	125.
RS56TC1a	3c large die on India paper	
	e. **black**	425.
	f. **green**	600.
RS56P1	3c **bl,** lg die on India paper	425.
RS56P3	3c **bl,** plate on India paper	125.
RS57TC1a	6c large die on India paper	
	e. **blue**	270.
	f. **brown**	360.
	g. **green**	270.
	h. **orange**	360.
	i. **red**	360.
RS57P1	6c **blk,** lg die on India paper	210.
RS57P3	6c **blk,** plate on India paper	100.
RS58TC1a	4c large die on India paper	
	e. **blue**	270.
	f. **blue green**	600.
	g. **dark blue**	600.
	h. **green**	270.
	i. **light blue**	600.
	j. **red**	270.
RS58P1	4c **blk,** lg die on India paper	210.
RS59TC1a	1c large die on India paper	
	e. **blue**	360.
	f. **green**	600.
RS59P1	1c **blk,** lg die on India paper	210.
RS60TC1a	1c large die on India paper	
	e. **blue**	600.
RS60P1	1c **blk,** lg die on India paper	210.
RS60P3	1c **blk,** plate on India paper	65.
RS61P1	4c **bl,** lg die on India paper	600.
RS62TC1a	1c large die on India paper	
	e. **brown**	360.
	f. **green**	270.
	g. **orange**	360.
	h. **red**	600.
	i. **vermilion**	600.
RS62P1	1c **blk,** lg die on India paper	270.
RS62P3	1c **blk,** plate on India paper	125.
RS63P1	1c **bl,** lg die on India paper	210.
RS64TC1a	2c large die on India paper	
	e. **blue**	270.
	f. **brown**	360.
	g. **green**	270.
	h. **orange**	360.
	i. **red**	600.
	j. **vermilion**	600.
RS64P1	2c **blk,** lg die on India paper	210.
RS64P3	2c **blk,** plate on India paper	125.
RS65TC1a	4c large die on India paper	
	e. **blue**	600.
	f. **green**	600.
RS65P1	4c **blk,** lg die on India paper	210.
RS66TC1a	1c large die on India paper	
	e. **blue**	360.
	f. **green**	600.
	g. **light green**	600.
	h. **orange**	600.
	i. **rose red**	600.
RS66P1	1c **blk,** lg die on India paper	600.
RS66P4	1c **blk,** plate on card	85.
RS67TC1a	1c large die on India paper	
	e. **green**	600.
RS67P1	1c **blk,** lg die on India paper	210.
RS68P1	2c **blk,** lg die on India paper	210.
RS68P3	2c **blk,** plate on India paper	90.
RS69TC1a	1c large die on India paper	
	e. **blue**	600.
	f. **green**	600.
RS69P1	1c **blk,** lg die on India paper	210.
RS70TC1a	2c large die on India paper	
	e. **blue**	600.
	f. **green**	600.
RS70P1	2c **blk,** lg die on India paper	270.
RS71TC1a	1c large die on India paper	
	e. **blue**	600.
	f. **green**	600.
RS71P1	1c **blk,** lg die on India paper	210.
RS72TC1a	2c large die on India paper	
	e. **blue**	600.
	f. **green**	600.
RS72P1	2c **blk,** lg die on India paper	210.
RS73TC1a	2c large die on India paper	
	e. **black**	600.
	f. **blue**	900.
	g. **red**	1,200.
RS73P1	2c **grn,** lg die on India paper	600.
RS74TC1a	1c large die on India paper	
	e. **blue**	600.
	f. **green**	600.
RS74hTC1a	$100 large die on India paper	
	e. **blue**	600.
	f. **green**	600.
RS74P1	1c **blk,** lg die on India paper	270.
	h. **blk,** $100 instead of $1.00 (error), lg die on India paper	210.
RS75TC1a	1c large die on India paper	
	e. **black**	360.
	f. **green**	600.
RS75P1	1c **bl,** lg die on India paper	210.
RS76TC1a	2c large die on India paper	
	e. **blue**	360.
	f. **green**	360.
RS77P1	2c **blk,** lg die on India paper	270.
RS78P1	2c **dull pur,** lg die on India paper	900.
RS81TC1a	4c large die on India paper	
	e. **black**	270.
	f. **blue**	600.
	g. **green**	600.
RS81P1	4c **brn,** lg die on India paper	270.
RS82P1	2c **blk,** lg die on India paper	210.
RS83TC1a	4c large die on India paper	
	e. **blue**	600.
	f. **green**	600.
RS83P1	4c **blk,** lg die on India paper	270.
RS84TC1a	1c large die on India paper	
	e. **black**	300.
	f. **blue**	425.
	g. **green**	300.
	h. **orange**	775.
	i. **red**	775.
	j. **slate**	775.
RS84P1	1c **lake,** lg die on India paper	600.
RS84P3	1c **lake,** plate on India paper	—
RS84P4	1c **lake,** plate on card	110.
RS85TC1a	4c large die on India paper	
	e. **blue**	330.
	f. **brown**	330.
	g. **green**	360.
	h. **orange**	450.
RS85P1	4c **blk,** lg die on India paper	300.
RS85P3	4c **blk,** plate on India paper	—
RS86TC1a	1c large die on India paper	
	e. **black**	270.
	f. **blue**	270.
RS86P1	1c **grn,** lg die on India paper	210.
RS88TC1a	1c large die on India paper	
	e. **blue**	600.
	f. **green**	600.
RS88P1	1c **blk,** lg die on India paper	270.
RS88P3	1c **blk,** plate on India paper	100.
RS88P4	1c **blk,** plate on card	100.
RS89TC1a	1c large die on India paper	
	e. **green**	360.
RS89P1	1c **blk,** lg die on India paper	600.
RS90P1	1c **bl,** lg die on India paper	270.
RS90P3	1c **bl,** plate on India paper	125.
RS90P4	1c **bl,** plate on card	125.
RS91TC1a	4c large die on India paper	
	e. **blue**	270.
	f. **green**	600.
RS91P1	4c **blk,** lg die on India paper	210.
RS92TC1a	3c large die on India paper	
	e. **blue**	270.
	f. **brown**	360.
	g. **green**	270.
	h. **orange**	360.
	i. **red**	600.
	j. **vermilion**	600.
RS92P1	3c **blk,** lg die on India paper	210.
RS92P3	3c **blk,** plate on India paper	—
RS94TC1a	4c large die on India paper	
	e. **blue**	600.
	f. **green**	600.
RS94P1	4c **blk,** lg die on India paper	210.
RS95TC1a	1c large die on India paper	
	e. **black**	360.
	f. **blue**	270.
RS95TC3	1c plate on India paper	
	a. **dark blue**	90.
RS95P1	1c **grn,** lg die on India paper	270.
RS95P3	1c **grn,** plate on India paper	90.
RS96TC1a	3c large die on India paper	
	e. **blue**	270.
	f. **green**	600.
RS96P1	3c **blk,** lg die on India paper	210.
RS96P3	3c **blk,** plate on India paper	50.
RS97TC1a	1c large die on India paper	
	e. **blue**	360.
	f. **green**	600.
RS97P1	1c **blk,** lg die on India paper	210.
RS98TC1a	1c large die on India paper	
	e. **blue**	270.
	f. **green**	210.
	g. **red**	600.
RS98P1	1c **blk,** lg die on India paper	210.
RS99TC1a	4c large die on India paper	
	e. **blue**	600.
RS99P1	4c **blk,** lg die on India paper	210.
RS100TC1a	6c large die on India paper	
	e. **green**	600.
RS100P1	6c **blk,** lg die on India paper	210.
RS101TC1a	1c large die on India paper	
	e. **blue**	600.
	f. **green**	600.
RS101P1	1c **blk,** lg die on India paper	210.
RS102TC1a	2c large die on India paper	
	e. **black**	210.
	f. **green**	270.
	g. **rose**	270.
RS102P1	2c **bl,** lg die on India paper	210.
RS103TC1a	4c large die on India paper	
	e. **blue**	600.
	f. **green**	600.
RS103P1	4c **blk,** lg die on India paper	210.
RS104P1	3c **blk,** lg die on India paper	900.
RS105P1	3c **brn,** lg die on India paper	725.
RS106TC1a	2c large die on India paper	
	e. **black**	600.
	f. **green**	360.
RS106P1	2c **bl,** lg die on India paper	270.
RS106P3	2c **bl,** plate on India paper	60.
RS107TC1a	3c large die on India paper	
	e. **green,** composite RS107TC+RS109TC	1,500.
	f. **blue**	360.
RS107P1	3c **blk,** lg die on India paper	270.
	a. 3c+6c **blk,** RS107P1+RS109P1 composite, lg die on India paper	1,200.
RS108TC1a	4c large die on India paper	
	e. **blue**	360.
	f. **green**	600.
RS108P1	4c **blk,** lg die on India paper	210.
RS108P3	4c **blk,** plate on India paper	45.
RS109TC1a	6c large die on India paper	
	e. **blue**	360.
RS109P1	6c **blk,** lg die on India paper	270.
RS110TC1a	2c large die on India paper	
	e. **black**	360.
	f. **green**	360.
RS110P1	2c **bl,** lg die on India paper	210.
RS111TC1a	4c large die on India paper	
	e. **blue**	360.
	f. **green**	600.
RS111P1	4c **blk,** lg die on India paper	210.
RS114TC1a	1c large die on India paper	
	e. **green**	360.
RS114P1	1c **blk,** lg die on India paper	270.
	a. 1c+2c **blk,** RS114P1+RS115P1 composite, lg die on India paper	1,200.
RS115P1	2c **bl,** lg die on India paper	270.
RS116TC1a	4c large die on India paper	
	e. **black**	270.
	f. **blue**	360.
	g. **brown**	600.
	h. **green**	600.
	i. **vermilion**	600.
RS116P1	4c **red,** lg die on India paper	270.
RS117TC1a	1c large die on India paper	
	e. **blue**	425.
	f. **green**	900.
RS117P1	1c **blk,** lg die on India paper	300.
RS118TC1a	1c large die on India paper	
	e. **black**	210.
	f. **blue**	270.
	g. **brown red**	360.
	h. **green**	360.
RS118P1	1c **red,** lg die on India paper	360.
RS118P3	1c **red,** plate on India paper	55.
RS118P4	1c **red,** plate on card	50.
RS119P1	1c **blk,** lg die on India paper	270.
RS120TC1a	2c large die on India paper	
	e. **blue**	270.
	f. **brown**	360.
	g. **green**	270.
	h. **orange**	360.
	i. **red**	600.
	j. **vermilion**	600.
RS120P1	2c **blk,** lg die on India paper	210.
RS121TC1a	3c large die on India paper	
	e. **blue**	600.
	f. **green**	600.
RS121P1	3c **blk,** lg die on India paper	270.
RS121P3	3c **blk,** plate on India paper	75.
RS122TC1a	2c large die on India paper	
	e. **blue**	600.
	f. **green**	600.
RS122P1	2c **blk,** lg die on India paper	210.
RS122P3	2c **blk,** plate on India paper	100.
RS123TC1a	4c large die on India paper	
	e. **blue**	270.
	f. **brown**	360.
	g. **green**	270.
	h. **orange**	360.
	i. **red**	600.
	j. **vermilion**	600.
RS123P1	4c **blk,** lg die on India paper	210.
RS123P3	4c **blk,** plate on India paper	125.
RS124TC1a	1c large die on India paper	
	e. **black**	210.
	f. **blue green**	360.
	g. **green**	600.
	h. **orange**	600.
	i. **red**	270.
RS124P1	1c **bl,** lg die on India paper	360.
RS124P3	1c **bl,** plate on India paper	90.
RS124P4	1c **bl,** plate on card	65.
RS126TC1a	1c large die on India paper	
	e. **black**	270.
	f. **blue**	270.
	g. **brown**	360.
	h. **orange**	360.
	i. **red**	600.
	j. **vermilion**	600.
RS126P1	1c **grn,** lg die on India paper	210.
RS127TC1a	4c large die on India paper	
	e. **black**	270.
	f. **blue**	270.
	g. **brown**	270.
	h. **orange**	360.
	i. **red**	600.
	j. **vermilion**	600.
RS127P1	4c **grn,** lg die on India paper	210.
RS127P3	4c **grn,** plate on India paper	65.
RS128TC1a	2c large die on India paper	
	e. **black**	725.
	f. **green**	475.
	g. **pale blue**	600.
RS128P1	2c **bl,** lg die on India paper	330.
RS128P3	2c **bl,** plate on India paper	150.
RS130TC1a	4c large die on India paper	
	e. **black**	330.
	f. **blue**	425.
RS130P1	4c **grn,** lg die on India paper	330.
RS131TC1a	4c large die on India paper	
	e. **blue**	270.
	f. **brown**	600.
	g. **green**	360.
	h. **orange**	360.
	i. **red**	600.
	j. **vermilion**	600.
RS131P1	4c **blk,** lg die on India paper	210.
RS131P3	4c **blk,** plate on India paper	75.
RS132TC1a	4c large die on India paper	
	e. **blue**	600.
	f. **orange**	600.
RS132P4	4c **blk,** plate on card	75.
RS133TC1a	6c large die on India paper	
	e. **blue**	600.
	f. **green**	600.

RS133P1	6c **blk,** lg die on India paper	210.
RS133P3	6c **blk,** plate on India paper	125.
RS134TC1a	4c large die on India paper	
	e. **black**	360.
	f. **green**	360.
	g. **red**	600.
RS134P1	4c **bl,** lg die on India paper	270.
RS137P1	4c **bl,** lg die on India paper	600.
RS138TC1a	1c large die on India paper	
	e. **blue**	360.
	f. **green**	600.
	g. **red**	600.
	h. **yellow green**	600.
RS138P1	1c **blk,** lg die on India paper	210.
RS139TC1a	2c large die on India paper	
	e. **black**	270.
	f. **blue**	600.
	g. **green**	600.
	h. **red**	270.
	i. **rose**	600.
RS139TC4	2c plate on card	
	a. **blackish violet**	90.
RS141TC1a	4c large die on India paper	
	e. **black**	270.
	f. **blue**	360.
RS141P1	4c **grn,** lg die on India paper	360.
RS141P3	4c **grn,** plate on India paper	125.
RS142TC1a	1c large die on India paper	
	e. **blue**	270.
	f. **brown**	360.
	g. **green**	270.
	h. **orange**	360.
	i. **red**	600.
	j. **vermilion**	600.
RS142P1	1c **blk,** lg die on India paper	210.
RS143TC1a	4c large die on India paper	
	e. **black**	270.
	f. **blue**	270.
RS143P1	4c **grn,** lg die on India paper	270.
RS144TC1a	1c large die on India paper	
	e. **black**	600.
	f. **green**	600.
RS144P1	1c **bl,** lg die on India paper	210.
RS144P3	1c **bl,** plate on India paper	100.
RS144P4	1c **bl,** plate on card	100.
RS145TC1a	2c large die on India paper	
	e. **blue**	500.
RS145P1	2c **blk,** lg die on India paper	175.
RS145P3	2c **blk,** plate on India paper	100.
RS145P4	2c **blk,** plate on card	100.
RS146TC1a	4c large die on India paper	
	e. **black**	360.
	f. **blue**	360.
RS146P1	4c **grn,** lg die on India paper	270.
RS146P3	4c **grn,** plate on India paper	100.
RS146P4	4c **grn,** plate on card	100.
RS150TC1a	1c large die on India paper	
	e. **black**	360.
	f. **blue**	210.
	g. **carmine**	600.
	h. **green**	270.
RS150P1	1c **ver,** lg die on India paper	270.
RS150P3	1c **ver,** plate on India paper	100.
RS151TC1a	1c large die on India paper	
	e. **blue**	600.
	f. **carmine**	600.
RS151P1	1c **blk,** lg die on India paper	210.
RS152TC1a	2c large die on India paper	
	e. **black**	210.
	f. **blue**	360.
RS152P1	2c **grn,** lg die on India paper	210.
RS153TC1a	4c large die on India paper	
	e. **blue**	900.
	f. **green**	900.
RS153P1	4c **blk,** lg die on India paper	550.
RS153P3	4c **blk,** plate on India paper	175.
RS153P4	4c **blk,** plate on card	150.
RS154TC1a	4c large die on India paper	
	e. **black**	600.
RS154P1	4c **bl,** lg die on India paper	600.
RS155TC1a	2c large die on India paper	
	e. **black**	360.
	f. **blue**	270.
	g. **red**	600.
RS155P1	2c **grn,** lg die on India paper	210.
RS156TC1a	6c large die on India paper	
	e. **blue**	270.
	f. **green**	270.
	g. **red**	270.
RS156P1	6c **blk,** lg die on India paper	210.
RS157TC1a	2c large die on India paper	
	e. **blue**	270.
	f. **green**	270.
	g. **red**	600.
	h. **vermilion**	360.
RS157P1	2c **blk,** lg die on India paper	210.
RS158TC1a	1c large die on India paper	
	e. **black**	600.
RS158P1	1c **grn,** lg die on India paper	600.
RS159TC1a	4c large die on India paper	
	e. **black**	450.
RS159P1	4c **bl,** lg die on India paper	270.
RS160TC1a	6c large die on India paper	
	e. **blue**	360.
	f. **green**	600.
RS160P1	6c **blk,** lg die on India paper	270.
RS161TC1a	4c large die on India paper	
	e. **blue**	600.
	f. **green**	900.
RS161P1	4c **blk,** lg die on India paper	360.
RS161P3	4c **blk,** plate on India paper	150.
RS162TC1a	1c large die on India paper	
	e. **black**	210.
	f. **green**	360.
	g. **red**	600.
RS162P1	1c **bl,** lg die on India paper	360.
RS163TC1a	4c large die on India paper	
	e. **black**	360.
	f. **green**	725.
	g. **yellow green**	725.
RS163P1	4c **bl,** lg die on India paper	725.
RS164TC1a	1c large die on India paper	
	e. **blue**	270.
	f. **green**	600.
RS164P1	1c **blk,** lg die on India paper	210.
RS165TC1a	4c large die on India paper	
	e. **black**	210.
	f. **blue**	270.
RS165P1	4c **grn,** lg die on India paper	600.
RS166TC1a	1c large die on India paper	
	e. **blue**	360.
	f. **green**	600.
RS166P1	1c **blk,** lg die on India paper	210.
RS169TC1a	4c large die on India paper	
	e. **blue**	270.
	f. **green**	600.
	g. **red**	270.
RS169P1	4c **blk,** lg die on India paper	210.
RS170TC1a	1c large die on India paper	
	e. **blue**	360.
	f. **green**	600.
RS170P1	1c **blk,** lg die on India paper	210.
RS171TC1a	1c large die on India paper	
	e. **black**	270.
	f. **blue**	270.
	g. **brown**	360.
	h. **dull blue**	600.
	i. **green**	270.
	j. **orange**	360.
	k. **red**	600.
	l. **vermilion**	600.
RS171P1	1c **vio,** lg die on India paper	210.
	u. **pur,** lg die on India paper	600.
RS172TC1a	2c large die on India paper	
	e. **blue**	270.
	f. **brown**	360.
	g. **green**	270.
	h. **orange**	270.
	i. **red**	600.
	j. **vermilion**	600.
RS172P1	2c **blk,** lg die on India paper	210.
RS172P3	2c **blk,** plate on India paper	100.
RS173TC1a	1c large die on India paper	
	e. **black**	270.
	f. **green**	270.
	g. **red**	360.
RS173P1	1c **bl,** lg die on India paper	210.
RS174TC1a	1c large die on India paper	
	e. **black**	360.
	f. **dark blue**	600.
	g. **green**	360.
RS174P1	1c **bl,** lg die on India paper	210.
RS175TC1a	2c large die on India paper	
	e. **black**	300.
	f. **blue**	600.
	g. **green**	600.
RS176TC1a	4c large die on India paper	
	e. **blue**	450.
	f. **green**	600.
RS176P1	4c **blk,** lg die on India paper	300.
RS177TC1a	2c large die on India paper	
	e. **blue**	900.
	f. **green**	1,200.
RS177P1	2c **blk,** lg die on India paper	425.
RS178TC1a	6c large die on India paper	
	e. **blue**	360.
	f. **green**	600.
RS178P1	1c **blk,** lg die on India paper	270.
RS179TC1a	2c large die on India paper	
	e. **black**	360.
	f. **blue**	450.
RS179P1	2c **grn,** lg die on India paper	270.
RS180TC1a	3c large die on India paper	
	e. **blue**	360.
	f. **green**	360.
RS180P1	3c **blk,** lg die on India paper	325.
RS180P3	3c **blk,** plate on India paper	125.
RS181TC1a	4c large die on India paper	
	e. **blue**	270.
	f. **green**	600.
RS181P1	4c **blk,** lg die on India paper	270.
RS182TC1a	4c large die on India paper	
	e. **blue**	270.
	f. **green**	270.
	g. **rose**	360.
RS182P1	4c **blk,** lg die on India paper	210.
RS183TC1a	1c large die on India paper	
	e. **black**	600.
	f. **blue**	360.
	g. **green**	600.
	h. **red**	270.
RS183P1	1c **ver,** lg die on India paper	270.
RS183P3	1c **ver,** plate on India paper	85.
RS184TC1a	2c large die on India paper	
	e. **blue**	360.
	f. **brown**	270.
	g. **green**	270.
	h. **orange**	360.
	i. **vermilion**	360.
RS184P1	2c **blk,** lg die on India paper	210.
RS184P3	2c **blk,** plate on India paper	100.
RS185TC1a	1c large die on India paper	
	e. **blue**	360.
RS185P1	1c **blk,** lg die on India paper	210.
RS185P3	1c **blk,** plate on India paper	100.
RS186TC1a	4c large die on India paper	
	e. **blue**	270.
	f. **green**	600.
RS186P1	4c **blk,** lg die on India paper	210.
RS187TC1a	4c large die on India paper	
	e. **blue**	270.
	f. **brown**	360.
	g. **green**	360.
	h. **orange**	600.
	i. **red**	600.
	j. **vermilion**	600.
RS187P1	4c **blk,** lg die on India paper	210.
RS187P3	4c **blk,** plate on India paper	100.
RS188TC1a	1c large die on India paper	
	e. **blue**	600.
	f. **green**	600.
RS188P1	6c **blk,** lg die on India paper	360.
RS189TC1a	1c large die on India paper	
	e. **black**	210.
	f. **blue**	270.
	g. **red**	270.
RS189P1	1c **grn,** lg die on India paper	270.
RS190TC1a	2c large die on India paper	
	e. **blue**	600.
	f. **green**	600.
RS190P1	2c **blk,** lg die on India paper	210.
RS191TC1a	4c large die on India paper	
	e. **blue**	475.
	f. **green**	475.
RS191P1	4c **blk,** lg die on India paper	300.
RS192TC1a	6c large die on India paper	
	e. **blue**	475.
	f. **green**	475.
	g. **rose**	600.
RS192P1	6c **blk,** lg die on India paper	300.
RS192P3	6c **blk,** plate on India paper	125.
RS193TC1a	2c large die on India paper	
	e. **blue**	600.
	f. **green**	600.
RS193P1	2c **blk,** lg die on India paper	210.
RS194TC1a	1c large die on India paper	
	e. **green**	210.
RS194P1	1c **bl,** lg die on India paper	210.
RS195TC1a	2c large die on India paper	
	e. **blue**	600.
	f. **green**	600.
RS195P1	2c **blk,** lg die on India paper	210.
RS196TC1a	1c large die on India paper	
	e. **black**	600.
	f. **green**	270.
RS196P1	1c **bl,** lg die on India paper	210.
RS197TC1a	2c large die on India paper	
	e. **blue**	360.
RS197P1	2c **blk,** lg die on India paper	210.
RS198TC1a	1c large die on India paper	
	e. **green**	360.
	f. **red**	600.
RS198P1	1c **bl,** lg die on India paper	270.
RS199TC1a	2c large die on India paper	
	e. **green**	600.
RS199P1	2c **bl,** lg die on India paper	300.
RS200P1	4c **blk,** lg die on India paper	210.
RS204TC1a	2c large die on India paper	
	e. **blue**	600.
	f. **green**	600.
RS204P1	2c **blk,** lg die on India paper	210.
RS205TC1a	4c large die on India paper	
	e. **blue**	270.
	f. **green**	600.
RS205P1	4c **blk,** lg die on India paper	210.
RS208TC1a	1c large die on India paper	
	e. **black**	270.
	f. **blue**	270.
	g. **orange**	360.
RS208P1	1c **grn,** lg die on India paper	210.
RS208P3	1c **grn,** plate on India paper	100.
RS208P4	1c **grn,** plate on card	95.
RS209TC1a	2c large die on India paper	
	e. **black**	600.
	f. **blue**	600.
RS209P1	2c **grn,** lg die on India paper	270.
RS210TC1a	4c large die on India paper	
	e. **blue**	270.
	f. **green**	270.
	g. **red**	270.
RS210P1	4c **blk,** lg die on India paper	270.
RS212TC1a	1c large die on India paper	
	e. **black**	270.
	f. **blue**	360.
	g. **green**	600.
RS212P1	1c **grn,** lg die on India paper	270.
RS212P3	1c **grn,** plate on India paper	100.
RS213TC1a	6c large die on India paper	
	e. **blue**	600.
	f. **green**	600.
RS213P1	6c **blk,** lg die on India paper	210.
RS213P3	6c **blk,** plate on India paper	100.
RS213P4	6c **blk,** plate on card	150.
RS214TC1a	4c large die on India paper	
	e. **blue**	360.
	f. **brown**	360.
	g. **green**	270.
	h. **orange**	360.
	i. **red**	600.
	j. **vermilion**	600.
RS214P1	4c **blk,** lg die on India paper	210.
RS214P3	4c **blk,** plate on India paper	65.
RS215TC1a	1c large die on India paper	
	e. **black**	360.
	f. **blue**	550.
	g. **dark red**	600.
	h. **green**	600.
RS215P1	1c **lake,** lg die on India paper	360.
RS216TC1a	1c large die on India paper	
	e. **blue**	600.
	f. **green**	600.
RS216P1	1c **blk,** lg die on India paper	210.
RS216P3	1c **blk,** plate on India paper	75.
RS219P1	4c **bl,** lg die on India paper	360.
RS220TC1a	1c large die on India paper	
	e. **blue**	360.
RS220P1	1c **blk,** lg die on India paper	210.
RS220P3	1c **blk,** plate on India paper	50.
RS221TC1a	4c large die on India paper	
	e. **black**	210.
	f. **blue**	270.
RS221P1	4c **grn,** lg die on India paper	270.
RS221P3	4c **grn,** plate on India paper	50.

RS222TC1a 8c large die on India paper
e. **green** 600.
RS222P1 8c **blk,** lg die on India paper 210.
RS223TC1a 1c large die on India paper
e. **blue** 360.
f. **brown** 360.
g. **green** 270.
h. **orange** 360.
i. **vermilion** 360.
RS223P1 1c **blk,** lg die on India paper 210.
RS223P3 1c **blk,** plate on India paper —
RS224TC1a 1c large die on India paper
e. **blue** 600.
f. **brown** 360.
g. **green** 270.
h. **orange** 360.
i. **red** 600.
RS224P1 1c **blk,** lg die on India paper 210.
RS224P3 1c **blk,** plate on India paper —
RS225P1 4c **blk,** lg die on India paper 210.
RS226TC1a 1c large die on India paper
e. **black** 425.
RS226P3 1c **bl,** plate on India paper 350.
RS228TC1a 1c large die on India paper
e. **black** 210.
f. **blue** 270.
g. **brown** 600.
h. **green** 270.
i. **orange** 600.
j. **red** 600.
k. **vermilion** 600.
RS228P1 1c **brn,** lg die on India paper 270.
RS228P3 1c **brn,** plate on India paper —
RS229TC1a 2c large die on India paper
e. **black** 270.
f. **blue** 270.
g. **brown** 360.
h. **green** 270.
i. **orange** 270.
j. **red** 360.
k. **vermilion** 600.
RS229P1 1c **choc,** lg die on India paper 210.
RS229P3 1c **choc,** plate on India paper 75.
RS230TC1a 6c large die on India paper
e. **blue** 270.
f. **brown** 360.
g. **green** 270.
h. **orange** 360.
i. **vermilion** 270.
RS230P1 6c **blk,** lg die on India paper 210.
RS230P3 6c **blk,** plate on India paper —
RS231TC1a 6c large die on India paper
e. **black** 1,200.
f. **blue** 1,200.
g. **green** 1,200.
h. **red** 900.
RS231P1 6c **org,** lg die on India paper 900.
RS231P4 6c **org,** plate on card 750.
RS232P1 8c **org,** lg die on India paper 900.
RS236TC1a 4c large die on India paper
e. **blue** 600.
RS236P1 4c **blk,** lg die on India paper 210.
RS239TC1a 2c large die on India paper
e. **black** 270.
f. **blue** 360.
g. **brown** 600.
h. **green** 270.
i. **orange** 360.
j. **vermilion** 600.
RS239P1 2c **ver,** lg die on India paper 270.
RS239P3 2c **ver,** plate on India paper 100.
RS240TC1a 4c large die on India paper
e. **blue** 210.
f. **blue green** 600.
g. **brown** 600.
h. **green** 270.
i. **orange** 270.
j. **red** 600.
k. **vermilion** 270.
RS240P1 4c **blk,** lg die on India paper 210.
RS240P3 4c **blk,** plate on India paper 125.

Proofs of Nos. RS239 and RS240 exist in black on card with the denominations and "USIR" obliterated. These most likely are proofs made in preparation of private die facsimile labels, not proofs of or in preparation of revenue stamps.

RS241TC1a 4c large die on India paper
e. **green** 600.
RS241P1 4c **red,** lg die on India paper 270.
RS242TC1a 1c large die on India paper
e. **blue** 270.
f. **green** 600.
RS242P1 4c **blk,** lg die on India paper 210.
RS242P3 4c **blk,** plate on India paper 80.
RS242P4 4c **blk,** plate on card 75.
RS243TC1a 4c large die on India paper
e. **blue** 600.
f. **green** 600.
RS243P1 4c **blk,** lg die on India paper 210.
RS244TC1a 6c large die on India paper
e. **blue** 600.
f. **green** 600.
RS244P1 6c **blk,** lg die on India paper 210.
RS245TC1a 1c large die on India paper
e. **blue** 600.
RS245P1 1c **blk,** lg die on India paper 300.
RS250TC1a 6c large die on India paper
e. **blue** 600.
f. **green** 600.
RS250P1 6c **blk,** lg die on India paper 210.
RS250P3 6c **blk,** plate on India paper 100.
RS251TC1a 1c large die on India paper
e. **blue** 270.
f. **brown** 270.
g. **green** 270.
RS251P1 1c **blk,** lg die on India paper 210.
RS252TC1a 1c large die on India paper
e. **black** 270.
f. **blue** 270.
g. **brown** 360.
h. **green** 270.
i. **orange** 600.
j. **red** 600.
k. **rose** 270.
RS252P1 1c **ver,** lg die on India paper 210.
RS252P3 1c **ver,** plate on India paper 100.
RS253TC1a 4c large die on India paper
e. **blue** 600.
f. **green** 600.
RS253P1 4c **blk,** lg die on India paper 210.
RS258TC1a 6c large die on India paper
e. **black** 600.
RS258P1 6c **brn,** lg die on India paper 210.
RS259TC1a 1c large die on India paper
e. **blue** 270.
f. **brown** 360.
g. **green** 270.
h. **orange** 360.
i. **red** 600.
j. **vermilion** 600.
RS259P1 1c **blk,** lg die on India paper 210.
RS259P3 1c **blk,** plate on India paper 90.
RS260TC1a 2c large die on India paper
e. **blue** 210.
f. **brown** 360.
g. **green** 270.
h. **orange** 360.
i. **red** 600.
j. **rose** 600.
k. **vermilion** 270.
RS260P1 2c **blk,** lg die on India paper 270.
RS260P3 2c **blk,** plate on India paper 90.
RS261TC1a 4c large die on India paper
e. **blue** 270.
f. **brown** 360.
g. **green** 270.
h. **orange** 360.
i. **red** 600.
j. **vermilion** 600.
RS261P1 4c **blk,** lg die on India paper 210.
RS261P3 4c **blk,** plate on India paper 100.
RS262TC1a 2c large die on India paper
e. **blue** 600.
f. **green** 600.
RS262P1 2c **blk,** lg die on India paper 210.
RS263P1 4c **blk,** lg die on India paper 270.
RS263P3 4c **blk,** plate on India paper 90.
RS264TC1a 4c large die on India paper
e. **blue** 360.
f. **green** 360.
RS264P1 4c **blk,** lg die on India paper 270.
RS264AP1 4c **blk,** lg die on India paper 360.
RS265TC1a 1c large die on India paper
e. **black** 270.
f. **blue** 600.
RS265P1 1c **grn,** lg die on India paper 270.
RS267TC1a 4c large die on India paper
e. **black** 270.
f. **blue** 600.
g. **green** 360.
RS267P1 4c **lake,** lg die on India paper 270.
RS270TC1a 12c large die on India paper
e. **black** 360.
f. **blue** 600.
g. **green** 360.
h. **red** 270.
RS270P1 12c **bl,** lg die on India paper 210.
RS271TC1a 4c large die on India paper
e. **blue** 3,000.
RS271P1 4c **blk,** lg die on India paper 3,000.
RS272TC1a 1c large die on India paper
e. **black** 360.
f. **blue** 360.
RS272P1 1c **grn,** lg die on India paper 270.
RS273TC1a 2c large die on India paper
e. **blue** 600.
RS273P1 2c **blk,** lg die on India paper 210.
RS274TC1a 1c large die on India paper
e. **black** 270.
RS274P1 1c **grn,** lg die on India paper 270.
RS274P3 1c **grn,** plate on India paper 65.
RS274P4 1c **grn,** plate on card 60.
RS275TC1a 2c large die on India paper
e. **black** 270.
f. **blue** 360.
RS276P1 2c **grn,** lg die on India paper 210.
RS278TC1a 2½c large die on India paper
e. **black** *1,200.*
RS280TC1a ¼c large die on India paper
e. **black** *1,200.*
RS300P1 4⅜c **blk,** lg die on India paper *1,200.*
RS302TC1a 2½c large die on India paper
e. **black** *1,200.*
RS303TC1a ⅝c large die on India paper
e. **black** *1,200.*
RS306P1 1¼c **pink,** lg die on India paper *1,200.*

Private Die Perfumery Stamps

RT1P3 2c **bl,** plate on India paper 125.
RT1P4 2c **bl,** plate on card 125.
RT2TC1a 1c large die on India paper
e. **brown** 475.
f. **green** 475.
g. **orange** 360.
h. **red** 600.
RT2P1 1c **blk,** lg die on India paper 270.
RT2P3 1c **blk,** plate on India paper 95.
RT4P1 1c **bl,** lg die on India paper 270.
RT5TC1a 2c large die on India paper
e. **black** 210.
f. **blue** 270.
g. **green** 600.
h. **orange** 600.
RT5TC3 2c plate on India paper
a. **orange** 125.
RT5P3 2c **ver,** plate on India paper 100.
RT6TC1a 1c large die on India paper
e. **blue** 450.
f. **brown** 600.
g. **green** 450.
h. **orange** 600.
i. **red** 600.
RT6P1 1c **blk,** lg die on India paper 300.
RT6P3 1c **blk,** plate on India paper 150.
RT8P1 2c **blk,** lg die on India paper 600.
RT10TC1a 4c large die on India paper
e. **blue** 450.
f. **brown** 600.
g. **green** 475.
h. **orange** 600.
i. **red** 600.
RT10P1 4c **blk,** lg die on India paper 300.
RT10P3 4c **blk,** plate on India paper 150.
RT12TC1a 1c large die on India paper
e. **black** 270.
f. **blue** 270.
g. **green** 600.
RT12TC4 1c plate on card
a. **black** 90.
RT12P1 1c **ver,** lg die on India paper 270.
RT12P3 1c **ver,** plate on India paper —
RT13TC1a 2c large die on India paper
e. **black** 270.
f. **blue** 360.
g. **green** 360.
h. **red** 270.
RT13TC3 2c plate on India paper
a. **black** 75.
RT14TC1a 3c large die on India paper
e. **blue** 1,200.
RT14P1 3c **blk,** lg die on India paper 600.
RT16TC1a 1c large die on India paper
e. **blue** 210.
f. **green** 270.
RT16P1 1c **blk,** lg die on India paper 210.
RT17TC1a 2c large die on India paper
e. **black** 360.
f. **blue** 360.
g. **green** 360.
h. **orange** 600.
RT17P1 2c **brn,** lg die on India paper 210.
RT18TC1a 3c large die on India paper
e. **black** 210.
f. **blue** 210.
g. **green** 600.
h. **orange** 600.
i. **red** 360.
RT18P1 3c **grn,** lg die on India paper 210.
RT19TC1a 1c large die on India paper
e. **black** 600.
RT19P1 1c **ver,** lg die on India paper 270.
RT20TC1a 1c large die on India paper
e. **black** 270.
f. **blue** 360.
g. **green** 210.
RT20P1 1c **grn,** lg die on India paper 270.
RT21TC1a 2c large die on India paper
e. **black** 600.
f. **green** 600.
RT21P1 2c **bl,** lg die on India paper 210.
RT22TC1a 1c large die on India paper
e. **black** 210.
f. **blue** 360.
g. **green** 360.
h. **red brown** 360.
i. **ultramarine** 600.
RT22P1 1c **bl,** lg die on India paper 270.
RT23TC1a 2c large die on India paper
e. **blue** 270.
f. **green** 600.
RT23P1 2c **blk,** lg die on India paper 210.
RT24TC1a 3c large die on India paper
e. **black** 210.
f. **blue** 270.
g. **green** 360.
h. **red** 270.
RT25TC1a 4c large die on India paper
e. **black** 210.
f. **blue** 270.
RT25P1 4c **grn,** lg die on India paper 210.
RT26TC1a 1c large die on India paper
e. **black** 210.
f. **blue** 270.
g. **brown** 360.
h. **green** 600.
i. **orange** 360.
j. **red** 600.
RT26P1 1c **grn,** lg die on India paper 210.
RT27P3 1c **grn,** plate on India paper 100.
RT28TC1a 2c large die on India paper
e. **black** 270.
f. **brown** 360.
g. **green** 270.
h. **orange** 360.
i. **red** 360.
RT28P1 2c **bl,** lg die on India paper 210.
RT30TC1a 3c large die on India paper
e. **black** 270.
f. **blue** 270.
g. **brown** 360.
h. **green** 270.
i. **orange** 360.
j. **red** 210.
RT30P1 3c **ver,** lg die on India paper 270.
RT32TC1a 4c large die on India paper
e. **black** 270.
f. **blue** 270.
g. **brown** 600.
h. **green** 270.
i. **orange** 270.
j. **red** 360.
RT32P1 4c **brn,** lg die on India paper 210.

Private Die Playing Card Stamps

RU1P1	5c **blk,** lg die on India paper	4,000.
RU2TC1a	2c large die on India paper	
e.	**black**	210.
f.	**blue**	270.
g.	**green**	360.
RU3TC1a	2c large die on India paper	
e.	**blue**	270.
f.	**green**	270.
RU3P1	4c **blk,** lg die on India paper	210.
RU3P3	4c **blk,** plate on India paper	100.
RU4TC1a	5c large die on India paper	
e.	**black**	270.
f.	**green**	360.
RU4P1	5c **bl,** lg die on India paper	210.
RU5TC1a	5c large die on India paper	
e.	**black**	270.
f.	**brown**	360.
g.	**green**	360.
h.	**light brown**	600.
i.	**orange**	600.
j.	**red**	600.
RU5P1	5c **bl,** lg die on India paper	210.
RU6TC1a	10c large die on India paper	
e.	**black**	210.
f.	**green**	360.
RU6P1	10c **bl,** lg die on India paper	600.
RU6P3	10c **bl,** plate on India paper	100.
RU7TC1a	5c large die on India paper	
e.	**blue**	450.
f.	**green**	450.
RU7P1	5c **blk,** lg die on India paper	300.
RU7P3	5c **blk,** plate on India paper	100.
RU7P4	5c **blk,** plate on card	—
RU8TC1a	5c large die on India paper	
e.	**blue**	270.
f.	**green**	270.
g.	**orange**	360.
RU8P1	5c **blk,** lg die on India paper	210.
RU9TC1a	5c large die on India paper	
e.	**blue**	270.
f.	**green**	600.
RU9P1	5c **blk,** lg die on India paper	300.
RU10TC1a	2c large die on India paper	
e.	**black**	240.
f.	**brown**	600.
g.	**green**	600.
RU10P1	2c **bl,** lg die on India paper	210.
RU11TC1a	5c large die on India paper	
e.	**black**	270.
f.	**blue**	270.
g.	**brown**	360.
RU11P1	5c **grn,** lg die on India paper	270.
RU12TC1a	5c large die on India paper	
e.	**blue**	360.
f.	**green**	360.
RU12P1	5c **blk,** lg die on India paper	210.
RU13TC1a	5c large die on India paper	
e.	**green**	210.
RU13P1	5c **bl,** lg die on India paper	360.
RU14TC1a	5c large die on India paper	
e.	**blue**	270.
f.	**brown**	360.
g.	**green**	360.
h.	**light brown**	600.
i.	**orange**	600.
j.	**red**	360.
RU14P1	5c **blk,** lg die on India paper	210.
RU14P3	5c **blk,** plate on India paper	—
RU15TC1a	5c large die on India paper	
e.	**blue**	360.
f.	**green**	360.
RU15P1	5c **blk,** lg die on India paper	400.
RU16P1	5c **blk,** lg die on India paper	600.

Hunting Permit

RW1P1	1934	$1	**bl,** lg die on wove paper	—
RW1P2	1934	$1	**bl,** small die on wove paper	22,500.
RW2P2	1935	$1	**rose lake,** small die on wove paper	12,500.
RW3P1	1936	$1	**brn blk,** lg die on wove paper	8,500.
RW3P2	1936	$1	**brn blk,** small die on wove paper	8,500.
RW4TC1a		$1	large die on India paper	
e.			**light violet**	5,500.
RW4P1	1937	$1	**lt grn,** lg die on wove paper	—
RW4P2	1937	$1	**lt grn,** small die on wove paper	8,500.
RW5P1	1938	$1	**lt vio,** lg die on wove paper	—
RW5P2	1938	$1	**lt vio,** small die on wove paper	8,500.
RW6P2	1939	$1	**choc,** small die on wove paper	7,500.
RW7P2	1940	$1	**sepia,** small die on wove paper	7,500.
RW8P1	1941	$1	**brn car,** lg die on wove paper	7,500.
RW8P2	1941	$1	**brn car,** small die on wove paper	7,500.
RW9P2	1942	$1	**vio brn,** small die on wove paper	7,500.
RW10P1	1943	$1	**dp rose,** lg die on wove paper	7,500.
RW10P2	1943	$1	**dp rose,** small die on wove paper	7,500.
RW11P2	1944	$1	**red org,** small die on wove paper	7,500.
RW12TC1a		$1	large die on India paper	
e.			**light violet**	20,000.
RW12P1	1945	$1	**blk,** lg die on wove paper	7,500.
RW12P2	1945	$1	**blk,** small die on wove paper	7,500.
RW13P1	1946	$1	**red brn,** lg die on wove paper	7,500.
RW13P2	1946	$1	**red brn,** small die on wove paper	7,500.
RW14P1	1947	$1	**blk,** lg die on wove paper	7,500.
RW14P2	1947	$1	**blk,** small die on wove paper	7,500.
RW15P1	1948	$1	**brt bl,** lg die on wove paper	9,500.
RW15P2	1948	$1	**brt bl,** small die on wove paper	7,500.
RW16P2	1949	$2	**brt grn,** small die on wove paper	7,500.
RW17P2	1950	$2	**vio,** small die on wove paper	7,500.
RW18P2	1951	$2	**gray blk,** small die on wove paper	7,500.
RW19P1	1952	$2	**dp ultra,** lg die on wove paper	7,500.
RW20P2	1953	$2	**dp brn rose,** small die on wove paper	7,500.
RW21P2	1954	$2	**blk,** small die on wove paper	7,500.
RW22P2	1955	$2	**dk bl,** small die on wove paper	7,500.
RW23P1	1956	$2	**blk,** lg die on wove paper	12,500.
RW23P2	1956	$2	**blk,** small die on wove paper	7,500.
RW24P2	1957	$2	**emerald,** small die on wove paper	7,500.
RW25P2	1958	$2	**blk,** small die on wove paper	7,500.
RW26P5	1959	$3	**multi,** plate on stamp paper	3,000.
RW27P5	1960	$3	**multi,** plate on stamp paper	3,000.
RW28P5	1961	$3	**multi,** plate on stamp paper	3,000.
RW29P5	1962	$3	**multi,** plate on stamp paper	3,000.
RW30P5	1963	$3	**multi,** plate on stamp paper	3,000.
RW32P5	1965	$3	**multi,** plate on stamp paper	3,000.
RW33P5	1966	$3	**multi,** plate on stamp paper	3,000.
RW34P5	1967	$3	**multi,** plate on stamp paper	3,000.
RW35P5	1968	$3	**multi,** plate on stamp paper	3,000.
RW36P5	1969	$3	**multi,** plate on stamp paper	3,000.
RW37P5	1970	$3	**multi,** plate on stamp paper	3,000.
RW38P5	1971	$3	**multi,** plate on stamp paper	3,000.
RW39P5	1972	$5	**multi,** plate on stamp paper	3,000.
RW40P5	1973	$5	**multi,** plate on stamp paper	3,000.
RW41P5	1974	$5	**multi,** plate on stamp paper	3,000.
RW42P5	1975	$5	**multi,** plate on stamp paper	3,000.
RW43P5	1976	$5	**grn & blk,** plate on stamp paper	3,000.
RW44P5	1977	$5	**multi,** plate on stamp paper	3,000.
RW45P5	1978	$5	**multi,** plate on stamp paper	3,000.
RW46P5	1979	$7.50	**multi,** plate on stamp paper	3,000.
RW47P5	1980	$7.50	**multi,** plate on stamp paper	3,000.
RW48P5	1981	$7.50	**multi,** plate on stamp paper	3,000.
RW49P5	1982	$7.50	**multi,** plate on stamp paper	3,000.
RW50P5	1983	$7.50	**multi,** plate on stamp paper	3,000.

Firearms Transfer

RY3P1	$1	**grn,** with "c" punch cancel, lg die on wove paper	2,000.

POSTAL SAVINGS

1911

PS1P1	10c	**org,** large die on India paper	1,000.
PS1P2a	10c	**org,** PP sm die on yelsh wove paper	750.
PS4P2a	10c	**dp bl,** PP sm die on yelsh wove paper	750.

1940

PS7TC1	10c	**black,** large die on India paper, die sunk on 97x110mm card	—
PS7P2	10c	**dp ultra,** sm die on wove paper	1,200.
PS8P2	25c	**dk car rose,** sm die on wove paper	1,200.
PS9TC1	50c	**black,** large die on India paper	—
PS9P2	50c	**dk bl grn,** sm die on wove paper	1,200.
PS10P2	$1	**gray blk,** sm die on wove paper	1,200.

1941

PS11P2	10c	**rose red,** sm die on wove paper	1,000.
PS12P2	25c	**bl grn,** sm die on wove paper	1,000.
PS13P2	50c	**ultra,** sm die on wove paper	1,000.
PS14P2	$1	**gray blk,** sm die on wove paper	1,000.
PS15P1	$5	**sepia,** large die on wove paper	4,000.
PS15P2	$5	**sepia,** sm die on wove paper	1,000.

WAR SAVINGS STAMP

1942

WS7P1	10c	**rose red,** large die on India paper	1,400.

SPECIMEN STAMPS

These are regular stamps overprinted "Specimen." Each number has a suffix letter "S" to denote "specimen." The Scott number is that of the stamp as shown in the regular listings and the second letter "A," etc., indicates the type of overprint. Values are for items of a grade of fine-very fine, with at least part original gum.

Specimen
Type A; 12mm long

Specimen.
Type B; 17mm long

Specimen.
Type C; 32mm long

SPECIMEN.
Type D; Capital Letters 12mm long

Specimen.
Type E; Initial Capital

Specimen.
Type F; 22mm long

SPECIMEN
Type G; 14mm long

SPECIMEN
Type H; 16mm long

Specimen
Type I; 20mm long

Specimen
Type J; 23½mm long

Overprinted in Black

1851-56

7S	A	1c **blue,** type II	*6,000.*
11S	A	3c **dull red,** type I	*6,500.*

1857-60

21S	A	1c **blue,** type III	*1,500.*
24S	A	1c **blue,** type V	*1,000.*
26S	A	3c **dull red,** type III	*1,100.*
30S	A	5c **orange brown,** type II	*1,000.*
30AS	A	5c **brown,** type II	*1,850.*
35S	A	10c **green,** type V	*1,250.*
36BS	A	12c **black**	*3,500.*
37S	A	24c **lilac**	*1,000.*
38S	A	30c **orange**	*1,000.*
26S	F	3c **dull red,** type III	*2,250.*
26S	I	3c **dull red,** type III	*4,000.*

1861

63S	A	1c **blue**	900.
65S	A	3c **rose**	900.
68S	A	10c **dark green**	900.
70S	A	24c **red lilac**	900.
72S	A	90c **blue**	900.
73S	A	2c **black**	*2,500.*
76S	A	5c **brown**	*3,000.*
78S	A	24c **lilac**	*3,250.*

Type B
Overprint Black, Except As Noted

1861-66

63S	B	1c **blue** *(1300)*	200.
		P# block of 8, Impt.	*3,250.*
		Without period	—
65S	B	3c **rose** *(1500)*	200.
68S	B	10c **dark green** *(1600)*	200.
		P# block of 8, Impt.	—
69S	B	12c **black** (orange) *(1300)*	200.
71S	B	30c **orange** *(1400)*	200.
		P# block of 8, Impt.	*15,000.*
72S	B	90c **blue** *(1394)*	120.
		P# block of 8, Impt.	—
73S	B	2c **black** (vermilion) *(1306)*	350.
		Block of 4	*1,100.*
		Without period	*500.*
		Block of 4, one stamp without period	*1,850.*
		P# block of 8, Impt. (unique)	*12,000.*
76S	B	5c **brown** *(1306)*	200.
		P# block of 8, Impt.	—
77S	B	15c **black** (vermilion) *(1208)*	200.
		Block of 4	*900.*
78S	B	24c **lilac** *(1300)*	250.

1867-68

86S	A	1c **blue**	*1250.*
85ES	A	12c **black**	*1,750.*
93S	A	2c **black**	*1,100.*
94S	A	3c **rose**	*1,000.*
95S	A	5c **brown**	*5,000.*
97S	A	12c **black**	—
98S	A	15c **black**	*1,000.*
99S	A	24c **gray lilac**	*1,250.*
		Split grill	—
100S	A	30c **orange**	*2,500.*

1869

112S	A	1c **buff**	*1,750.*
113S	A	2c **brown**	*1,750.*
115S	A	6c **ultramarine**	*1,750.*
116S	A	10c **yellow**	*1,750.*
116S	H	10c **yellow**	*4,250.*
117S	A	12c **green**	*3,500.*
119S	A	15c **brown & blue**	*4,000.*
120S	A	24c **green & violet**	*5,750.*
	a.	Without grill	—
121S	A	30c **blue & carmine**	*4,000.*
	a.	Without grill	—
122S	A	90c **carmine & black**	*4,500.*
	a.	Without grill	—

1875

123S	B	1c **buff**	*3,500.*
124S	B	2c **brown**	*3,500.*
125S	B	3c **blue** (blue)	*3,500.*
126S	B	6c **blue** (blue)	*3,500.*
127S	B	10c **yellow** (blue)	—
129S	B	15c **brown & blue** (blue)	*8,750.*

1870-71

145S	A	1c **ultramarine**	*1,500.*
146S	A	2c **red brown**	—
	a.	Handstamped "Specimen" plus manuscript "X"	*1,500.*
147S	A	3c **green**	*1,500.*
	a.	Handstamped "Specimen" plus manuscript check mark	*1,500.*
148S	A	6c **carmine**	*1,500.*
	a.	Handstamped "Specimen" plus manuscript "X"	*1,500.*
149S	A	7c **vermilion**	—
	a.	Handstamped "Specimen" plus manuscript "X"	*1,500.*
150S	A	10c **brown**	*1,500.*
	a.	Handstamped "Specimen" plus manuscript "X"	*1,500.*
151S	A	12c **dull violet**	*1,500.*
152S	A	15c **bright orange**	*1,500.*
	a.	Handstamped "Specimen" plus manuscript check mark	*1,500.*
155S	A	90c **carmine**	*1,500.*

At this time, there are no examples of the major numbers 146S A and 149S A recorded. The editors would like to see such examples.

1875

157S	B	2c **brown** (blue)	*1,900.*
158S	B	3c **green** (blue)	*1,900.*
159S	B	6c **dull pink** (blue)	*1,900.*
160S	B	7c **orange vermilion** (blue)	*1,900.*
161S	B	10c **brown** (blue)	*1,900.*
162S	B	12c **blackish violet** (blue)	1,900.
165S	B	30c **greenish black** (blue)	*1,900.*
166S	B	90c **carmine** (blue)	*1,900.*

Overprinted in Red

Type D

1879

189S	D	15c **red orange**	100.
190S	D	30c **full black**	100.
191S	D	90c **carmine,** brownish black ovpt.	100.
	a.	Overprint in red	—

1881-82

205S	D	5c **yellow brown**	100.
206S	D	1c **gray blue**	100.
207S	D	3c **blue green**	100.
208S	D	6c **brown red**	100.
209S	D	10c **brown**	100.

1883

210S	D	2c **red brown**	120.
211S	D	4c **blue green**	120.

Handstamped in Dull Purple

Type E

1890-93

219S	E	1c **dull blue**	250.
220S	E	2c **carmine**	250.
221S	E	3c **purple**	250.
222S	E	4c **dark brown**	250.
223S	E	5c **chocolate**	250.
224S	E	6c **dull red**	250.
225S	E	8c **lilac**	250.
226S	E	10c **green**	250.
227S	E	15c **blue**	250.
228S	E	30c **black**	250.
229S	E	90c **orange**	250.

COLUMBIAN ISSUE

Handstamped in Dull Purple

1893

230S	E	1c **deep blue**	400.
		Double overprint	—
231S	E	2c **violet**	400.
232S	E	3c **green**	400.
233S	E	4c **ultramarine**	400.
234S	E	5c **chocolate**	400.
235S	E	6c **purple**	400.
236S	E	8c **magenta**	400.
237S	E	10c **black brown**	400.
238S	E	15c **dark green**	400.
239S	E	30c **orange brown**	400.
240S	E	50c **slate blue**	400.
241S	E	$1 **salmon**	500.
242S	E	$2 **brown red**	500.
243S	E	$3 **yellow green**	550.
244S	E	$4 **crimson lake**	575.
245S	E	$5 **black**	675.

Overprinted in Dull Purple

Type F

230S	F	1c **deep blue**	550.
232S	F	3c **green**	550.
233S	F	4c **ultramarine**	550.
234S	F	5c **chocolate**	550.
235S	F	6c **purple**	550.
237S	F	10c **black brown**	550.
243S	F	$3 **yellow green**	700.

Overprinted Type H in Black or Red

231S	H	2c **violet** (Bk)	625.
233S	H	4c **ultramarine** (R)	625.
234S	H	5c **chocolate** (R)	625.

Overprinted Type I in Black or Red

231S	I	2c **violet** (R)	625.
232S	I	3c **green** (R)	625.
233S	I	4c **ultramarine** (R)	625.
234S	I	5c **chocolate** (Bk)	625.
235S	I	6c **purple** (R)	625.
236S	I	8c **magenta** (Bk)	625.
237S	I	10c **black brown** (R)	625.
238S	I	15c **dark green** (R)	625.
239S	I	30c **orange brown** (Bk)	625.
240S	I	50c **slate blue** (R)	625.

Handstamped Type E in Purple

1895

264S	E	1c **blue**	90.
267S	E	2c **carmine,** type III	90.
267aS	E	2c **pink,** type III	90.
268S	E	3c **purple**	90.
269S	E	4c **dark brown**	140.
270S	E	5c **chocolate**	90.
271S	E	6c **dull brown**	90.
272S	E	8c **violet brown**	90.
273S	E	10c **dark green**	90.
274S	E	15c **dark blue**	90.
275S	E	50c **orange**	90.
276S	E	$1 **black,** type I	325.
276AS	E	$1 **black,** type II	*4,750.*
277S	E	$2 **dark blue**	300.
278S	E	$5 **dark green**	400.

1897-1903

279S	E	1c **deep green**	90.
279BS	E	2c **light red,** type IV	90.
279BjS	E	2c Booklet pane of 6, **light red,** type IV (Bk)	525.
		Never hinged	750.
		With plate number	1750.
		Never hinged	2,250.
	a.	As No. 279BjS, inverted overprint on all stamps	*12,500.*
	b.	As No. 279BjS, inverted overprint on one stamp	*12,500.*
	c.	As No. 279BjS, double impression of overprint on bottom two stamps	*12,500.*
280S	E	4c **rose brown**	160.
281S	E	5c **dark blue**	80.
282S	E	6c **lake**	80.
282CS	E	10c **brown,** type I	80.
283S	E	10c **brown,** type II	*1,500.*
284S	E	15c **olive green**	80.

Special Printing

In March 1900 one pane of 100 stamps of each of Nos. 279, 279B, 268, 280-282, 272, 282C, 284 and 275-278 were specially handstamped type E "Specimen" in black for displays at the Paris Exposition (1900) and Pan American Exposition (1901). The 2c pane was light red, type IV.

These examples were handstamped by H. G. Mandel and mounted by him in separate displays for the two Expositions. Examples from the panes in addition to those displayed were handstamped "Specimen," but most were destroyed after the Expositions. Examples of all issues that were handstamped are known.

Additional stamps, not from the mounted display panes, do exist with a black "Specimen" handstamp, but it is believed Mandel applied such handstamps to regularly issued stamps from his personal collection. These include Nos. 267, 267a and 279B in pale red.

TRANS-MISSISSIPPI ISSUE

Type F

1898

285S	F	1c **dark yellow green**	850.
289S	F	8c **violet brown**	1,200.

Overprinted in Dull Purple

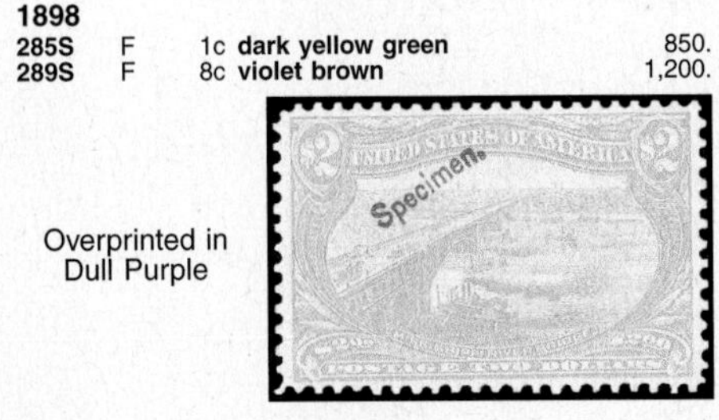

Type E

285S	E	1c **dark yellow green**	250.
286S	E	2c **copper red**	250.
287S	E	4c **orange**	250.
288S	E	5c **dull blue**	250.
289S	E	8c **violet brown**	250.
290S	E	10c **gray violet**	250.
291S	E	50c **sage green**	550.
292S	E	$1 **black**	800.
293S	E	$2 **orange brown**	950.

PAN-AMERICAN ISSUE

1901

294S	E	1c **green & black**	250.
295S	E	2c **carmine**	250.
296S	E	4c **chocolate & black**	250.
	a.	Center inverted	*12,500.*
297S	E	5c **ultramarine & black**	250.
298S	E	8c **brown violet & black**	250.
299S	E	10c **yellow brown & black**	250.

1902

300S	E	1c **blue green**	150.
301S	E	2c **carmine**	150.
302S	E	3c **bright violet**	150.
303S	E	4c **brown**	150.
304S	E	5c **blue**	150.
305S	E	6c **claret**	150.
306S	E	8c **violet black**	150.
307S	E	10c **pale red brown**	150.
308S	E	13c **purple black**	150.
309S	E	15c **olive green**	150.
310S	E	50c **orange**	150.
311S	E	$1 **black**	300.
312S	E	$2 **dark blue**	400.
313S	E	$5 **dark green**	600.

1903

319S	E	2c **carmine**	110.

LOUISIANA PURCHASE ISSUE

1904

323S	E	1c **green**	350.
324S	E	2c **carmine**	350.
325S	E	3c **violet**	350.
326S	E	5c **dark blue**	350.
327S	E	10c **red brown**	350.

SPECIAL DELIVERY STAMPS

Overprinted in Red

Type D

1885

E1S	D	10c **blue**	140.

Handstamped in Dull Purple

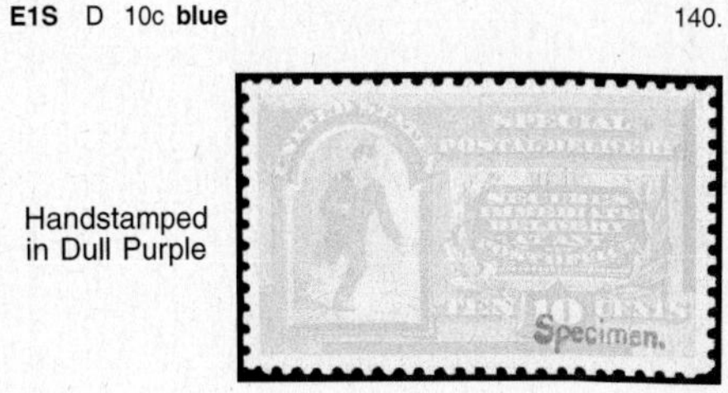

Type E

1888

E2S	E	10c **blue**	150.

1893

E3S	E	10c **orange**	200.

1894

E4S	E	10c **blue**	300.

1895

E5S	E	10c **blue**	175.

1902

E6S	E	10c **ultramarine**	175.

POSTAGE DUE STAMPS

Overprinted in Red

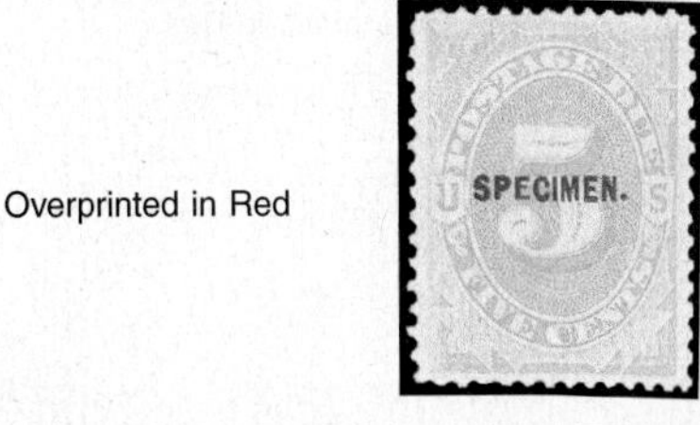

Type D

1879

J1S	D	1c **brown**	250.00
J2S	D	2c **brown**	250.00
J3S	D	3c **brown**	250.0
J4S	D	5c **brown**	250.

1884

J15S	D	1c **red brown**	
J16S	D	2c **red brown**	
J17S	D	3c **red brown**	
J18S	D	5c **red brown**	
J19S	D	10c **red brown**	
J20S	D	30c **red brown**	
J21S	D	50c **red brown**	

Handstamped in Dull Purple

Type E

1895

J38S	E	1c	**deep claret**	85.00
J39S	E	2c	**deep claret**	85.00
J40S	E	3c	**deep claret**	85.00
J41S	E	5c	**deep claret**	85.00
J42S	E	10c	**deep claret**	85.00
J43S	E	30c	**deep claret**	85.00
J44S	E	50c	**deep claret**	85.00

OFFICIAL STAMPS

Special printings of Official stamps were made in 1875 at the time the other Reprints, Re-issues and Special Printings were printed. The Official stamps reprints received specimen overprints, but philatelists believe they most properly should be considered to be part of the special printings. See Official section after No. O120.

NEWSPAPER STAMPS

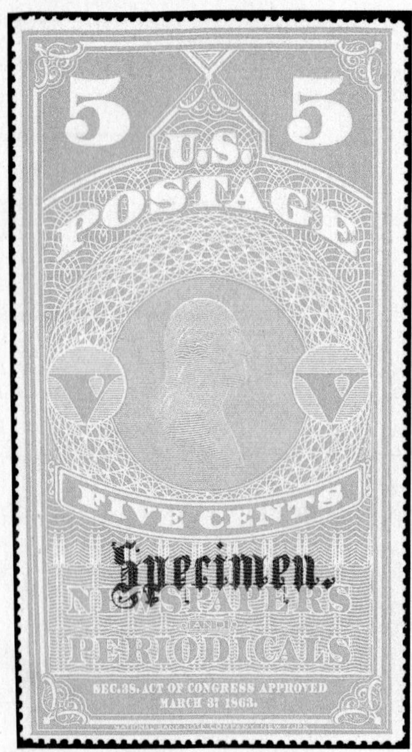

Overprinted in Red

Type C

1865-75

PR2S	C	10c	**blue green**	600.00
PR2bS	C	10c	**blue green,** pelure paper	*600.00*
PR5S	C	5c	**dull blue**	400.00
a.			Triple overprint	900.00
PR6S	C	10c	**dark bluish green**	500.00

Handstamped in Black **Specimen**

Type A

1875

PR9S	A	2c	**black**	750.00
PR11S	A	4c	**black**	750.00
PR12S	A	6c	**black**	750.00
PR16S	A	12c	**rose**	750.00

Overprinted in Black, except as noted

Type B

1875

PR9S	B	2c	**black**	125.00
PR10S	B	3c	**black**	125.00
PR11S	B	4c	**black**	125.00
PR12S	B	6c	**black**	125.00
PR13S	B	8c	**black**	125.00
PR14S	B	9c	**black**	125.00
a.			Overprint in blue	250.00
PR15S	B	10c	**black**	125.00
PR16S	B	12c	**rose**	125.00
a.			Overprint in blue	250.00
PR17S	B	24c	**rose**	125.00
a.			Overprint in blue	250.00
PR18S	B	36c	**rose**	125.00
a.			Overprint in blue	250.00
PR19S	B	48c	**rose**	125.00
a.			Overprint in blue	250.00
PR20S	B	60c	**rose**	125.00
a.			Overprint in blue	250.00
PR21S	B	72c	**rose**	125.00
a.			Overprint in blue	250.00
PR22S	B	84c	**rose**	125.00
a.			Overprint in blue	250.00
PR23S	B	96c	**rose**	125.00
a.			Overprint in blue	250.00
PR24S	B	$1.92	dark brown	125.00
PR25S	B	$3	**vermilion**	125.00
a.			Overprint in blue	250.00
PR26S	B	$6	**ultramarine**	125.00
a.			Overprint in blue	250.00
PR27S	B	$9	**yellow**	125.00
a.			Overprint in blue	250.00
PR28S	B	$12	**dark green**	125.00
a.			Overprint in blue	250.00
PR29S	B	$24	**dark gray violet**	125.00
a.			Overprint in blue	250.00
PR30S	B	$36	**brown rose**	250.00
PR31S	B	$48	**red brown**	250.00
PR32S	B	$60	**violet**	250.00
a.			Overprint in blue	250.00

Overprinted in Red

Type D

1875

PR14S	D	9c	**black**	30.00

1879

PR57S	D	2c	**black**	75.00
PR58S	D	3c	**black**	75.00
PR59S	D	4c	**black**	75.00
PR60S	D	6c	**black**	75.00
PR61S	D	8c	**black**	75.00
PR62S	D	10c	**black**	75.00
a.			Double overprint	*2,000.*
PR63S	D	12c	**red**	75.00
PR64S	D	24c	**red**	75.00
PR65S	D	36c	**red**	75.00
PR66S	D	48c	**red**	75.00
PR67S	D	60c	**red**	75.00
PR68S	D	72c	**red**	75.00
PR69S	D	84c	**red**	75.00
PR70S	D	96c	**red**	75.00
PR71S	D	$1.92	**pale brown**	75.00
PR72S	D	$3	**red vermilion**	75.00
PR73S	D	$6	**blue**	75.00
PR74S	D	$9	**orange**	75.00
PR75S	D	$12	**yellow green**	75.00
PR76S	D	$24	**dark violet**	75.00
PR77S	D	$36	**Indian red**	75.00
PR78S	D	$48	**yellow brown**	75.00
PR79S	D	$60	**purple**	75.00

1885

PR81S	D	1c	**black**	25.00

Handstamped in Dull Purple

Type E

1895 **Wmk. 191**

PR114S	E	1c	**black**	125.00
PR115S	E	2c	**black**	125.00
PR116S	E	5c	**black**	125.00
PR117S	E	10c	**black**	125.00
PR118S	E	25c	**carmine**	125.00
PR119S	E	50c	**carmine**	125.00
PR120S	E	$2	**scarlet**	125.00
PR121S	E	$5	**dark blue**	125.00
PR122S	E	$10	**green**	125.00
PR123S	E	$20	**slate**	125.00
PR124S	E	$50	**dull rose**	125.00
PR125S	E	$100	**purple**	125.00

REVENUE STAMPS

SPECIMEN

Type G & A

1862

R5S	G	2c	Bank Check, **blue** (red)	375.00
R15S	A	2c	U. S. I. R., **orange**	—
R16cS	H	3c	Foreign Exchange, **green** (red)	375.00

Type H

Type H

R16S	H	3c	Foreign Exchange, **green** (red)	375.00
R23S	H	5c	Agreement, **red**	375.00
R34S	H	10c	Contract, **blue** (red)	375.00
R35eS	H	10c	Foreign Exchange, **ultra** (red)	375.00
R36S	H	10c	Inland Exchange, **blue** (red)	375.00
R46S	H	25c	Insurance, **red**	375.00
R52S	H	30c	Inland Exchange, **lilac** (red)	375.00
R53S	H	40c	Inland Exchange, **brown** (red)	375.00
R68S	H	$1	Foreign Exchange, **red**	375.00

Overprinted in Red

Type I & G

1898

R153S	I	1c	**green**	475.00

Type G

R163S	G	1c	**pale blue**	500.00

Type H

Type G

1875 **Overprinted in Red**

RB11S H	1c **green**	300.00
RB20S G	⅛c **green**	500.00

Type J

1918

RC10S J	$1 **green**	475.00

Type J

1926-29

RF20S J	10c **blue**	50.00
	Joint line pair	250.00
RF23S J	10c **light blue**	100.00
	Joint line pair	450.00

PRIVATE DIE MATCH STAMP

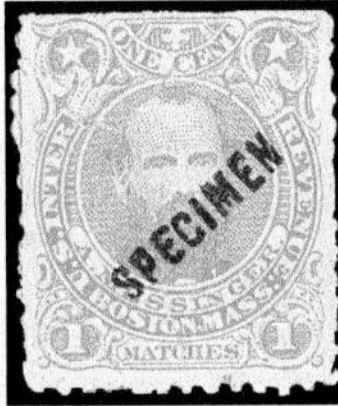

Overprinted with Type G in Red

RO133dS G	1c **black,** A. Messinger	*500.00*

SAVINGS STAMPS

Overprinted Vertically Reading Down in Red

1911

PS4S	10c **deep blue**	250.00

Handstamped in Violet

1917-18

WS1S	25c **deep green**	*500.*
WS2S	$5 **deep green**	*500.*

VARIOUS OVERPRINTS

Overprinted with control numbers in carmine

1861

63S	A24	1c **pale blue** (overprint 9012)	475.
65S	A25	3c **brown red** (overprint 7890)	475.
		Block of 4	*2,150.*
68S	A27	10c **green** (overprint 5678)	475.
69S	A28	12c **gray black** (overprint 4567)	475.
71S	A30	30c **orange** (overprint 2345)	475.
		Block of 4	*2,150.*
72S	A31	90c **pale blue** (overprint 1234)	475.
a.		Pair, one without overprint	—

1863-66

73S	A32	2c **black** (overprint 8901)	475.
		Block of 4	*3,000.*
76S	A26	5c **brown** (overprint 6789)	475.
		Block of 4	*3,500.*
77S	A33	15c **black** (overprint 235)	475.
		Block of 4	*3,500.*
78S	A29	24c **gray lilac** (overprint 3456)	475.

Special Printings Overprinted in Red or Blue

Type K

1889

212S	K A59	1c **ultramarine** (red)	75.00
210S	K A57	2c **red brown** (blue)	75.00
210S	K A57	2c **lake** (blue)	75.00
210S	K A57	2c **rose lake** (blue)	75.00
210S	K A57	2c **scarlet** (blue)	75.00
214S	K A46b	3c **vermilion** (blue)	75.00
211S	K A58	4c **blue green** (red)	75.00
205S	K A56	5c **gray brown** (red)	75.00
208S	K A47b	6c **brown red** (blue)	75.00
		P# strip of 7, Impt.	*600.00*
209S	K A49b	10c **brown** (red)	75.00
		Without overprint	80.00
189S	K A51a	15c **orange** (blue)	75.00
190S	K A53	30c **full black** (red)	75.00
191S	K A54	90c **carmine** (blue)	75.00

Special Printings Overprinted in Red or Blue

Type L

212S	L A59	1c **ultramarine** (red)	75.00
210S	L A57	2c **rose lake** (blue)	75.00
		Without overprint	—
214S	L A46b	3c **purple** (red)	75.00
211S	L A58	4c **dark brown** (red)	75.00
205S	L A56	5c **yellow brown** (blue)	75.00
		Without overprint	—
208S	L A47b	6c **vermilion** (blue)	75.00
209S	L A49b	10c **green** (red)	75.00
		Without overprint	100.00
189S	L A51a	15c **blue** (red)	75.00
		Without overprint	100.00
190S	L A53	30c **full black** (red)	75.00
191S	L A54	90c **orange** (blue)	75.00

Overprinted with Type K Together with "A" in Black Manuscript

191S	M A54	90c **carmine** (blue)	140.00
209S	M A49b	10c **brown** (red)	140.00
211S	M A58	4c **blue green** (red)	140.00

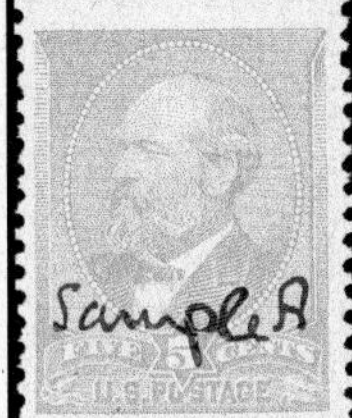

"SAMPLE A" in Manuscript (red or black)

216S	N A56	5c **indigo**	160.00

Regular Issues Overprinted in Blue or Red

125 sets were distributed to delegates to the Universal Postal Congress held in Washington, D. C., May 5 to June 15, 1897.

Type O

1897

264S	O A87	1c **blue**	110.00
267S	O A88	2c **carmine,** type III	110.00
268S	O A89	3c **purple**	110.00
269S	O A90	4c **dark brown**	110.00
270S	O A91	5c **chestnut**	110.00
271S	O A92	6c **claret brown**	110.00
272S	O A93	8c **violet brown**	110.00
273S	O A94	10c **dark green**	110.00
274S	O A95	15c **dark blue**	110.00
275S	O A96	50c **red orange**	110.00
276S	O A97	$1 **black,** type I	350.00
276AS	O A97	$1 **black,** type II	300.00
277S	O A98	$2 **dark blue**	300.00
278S	O A99	$5 **dark green**	350.00

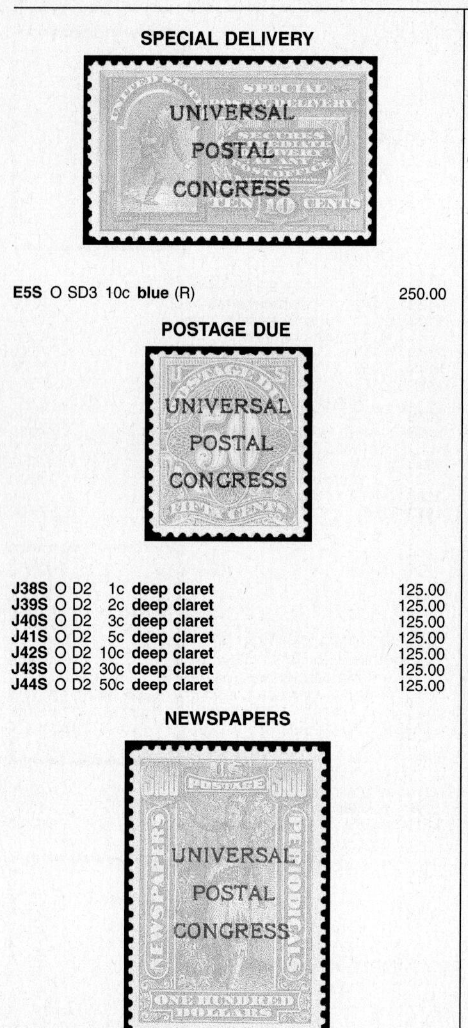

SPECIAL DELIVERY

E5S	O	SD3	10c **blue** (R)	250.00

POSTAGE DUE

J38S	O	D2	1c **deep claret**	125.00
J39S	O	D2	2c **deep claret**	125.00
J40S	O	D2	3c **deep claret**	125.00
J41S	O	D2	5c **deep claret**	125.00
J42S	O	D2	10c **deep claret**	125.00
J43S	O	D2	30c **deep claret**	125.00
J44S	O	D2	50c **deep claret**	125.00

NEWSPAPERS

PR114S	O	N15	1c **black**	225.00
PR115S	O	N15	2c **black**	225.00
PR116S	O	N15	5c **black**	225.00
PR117S	O	N15	10c **black**	225.00
PR118S	O	N16	25c **carmine**	225.00
PR119S	O	N16	50c **carmine**	225.00
PR120S	O	N17	$2 **scarlet**	225.00
PR121S	O	N18	$5 **dark blue**	225.00
PR122S	O	N19	$10 **green**	225.00
PR123S	O	N20	$20 **slate**	225.00
PR124S	O	N21	$50 **dull rose**	225.00
PR125S	O	N22	$100 **purple**	225.00

ENVELOPES

Overprinted

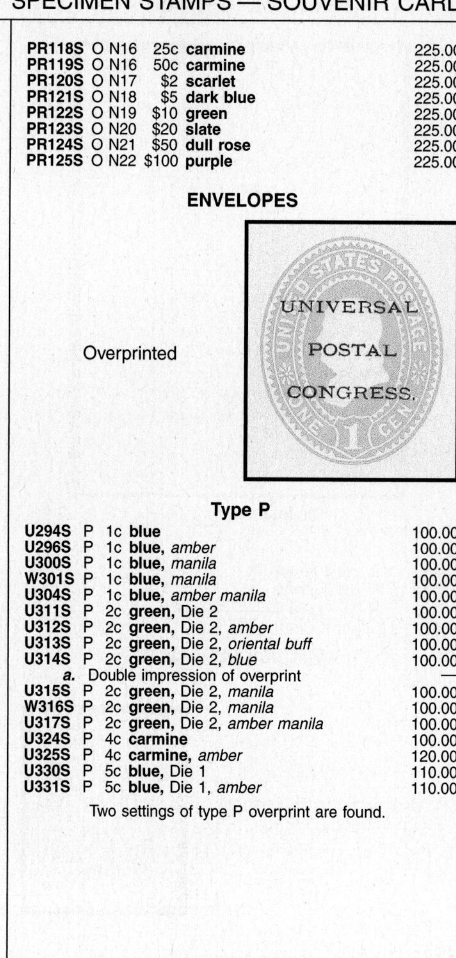

Type P

U294S	P	1c **blue**	100.00
U296S	P	1c **blue,** *amber*	100.00
U300S	P	1c **blue,** *manila*	100.00
W301S	P	1c **blue,** *manila*	100.00
U304S	P	1c **blue,** *amber manila*	100.00
U311S	P	2c **green,** Die 2	100.00
U312S	P	2c **green,** Die 2, *amber*	100.00
U313S	P	2c **green,** Die 2, *oriental buff*	100.00
U314S	P	2c **green,** Die 2, *blue*	100.00
a.		Double impression of overprint	—
U315S	P	2c **green,** Die 2, *manila*	100.00
W316S	P	2c **green,** Die 2, *manila*	100.00
U317S	P	2c **green,** Die 2, *amber manila*	100.00
U324S	P	4c **carmine**	100.00
U325S	P	4c **carmine,** *amber*	120.00
U330S	P	5c **blue,** Die 1	110.00
U331S	P	5c **blue,** Die 1, *amber*	110.00

Two settings of type P overprint are found.

POSTAL CARDS

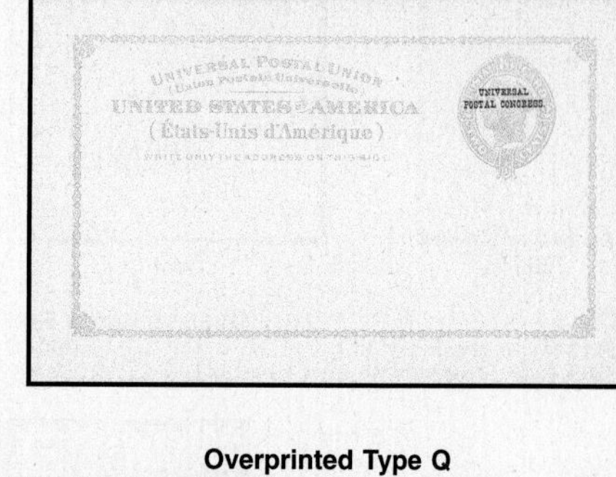

Overprinted Type Q

UX12S	Q	1c **black,** *buff*	600.00
UX13S	Q	2c **blue,** *cream*	600.00

PAID REPLY POSTAL CARDS

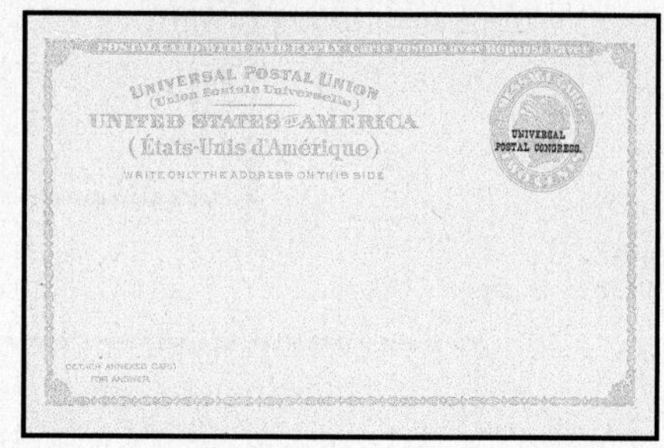

Overprinted Type Q

UY1S	Q	1c **black,** *buff*	600.00
UY2S	Q	2c **blue,** *grayish white*	600.00

As Nos. UY1S-UY2S were made by overprinting unsevered reply cards, values are for unsevered cards.

SOUVENIR CARDS

These cards were issued as souvenirs of the philatelic and numismatic gatherings at which they were distributed by the United States Postal Service (USPS), its predecessor the United States Post Office Department (POD), or the Bureau of Engraving and Printing (BEP). They were not valid for postage. Nos. SC1 and SC3 were produced by members of the trade union now called the International Plate Printers, Die Stampers and Engravers Union. The cards were distributed by the union members.

Listed cards will have a philatelic theme, and most of the cards bear reproductions of United States stamps with the design enlarged, altered by removal of denomination, country name and "Postage" or "Air Mail" or defaced by diagonal bars. The cards are not perforated.

Numismatic cards are listed following the philatelic cards. Cards issued for numismatic shows but showing stamps are listed in the philatelic section. BEP cards having no obvious philatelic or numismatic theme are not listed.

A forerunner of the souvenir cards is the 1939 Philatelic Truck souvenir sheet which the Post Office Department issued and distributed in various cities visited by the Philatelic Truck. It shows the White House, printed in blue on white paper. A total of 730,040 were printed, 173,220 with gum (first printing, many destroyed) and the rest without gum. Value, with gum, $50; without gum, $8. Some of the first printing was made into coil rolls of 500. A joint line pair and a strip of three (both damaged) are known.

Standard abbreviations:
APS — American Philatelic Society
ASDA — American Stamp Dealers Association

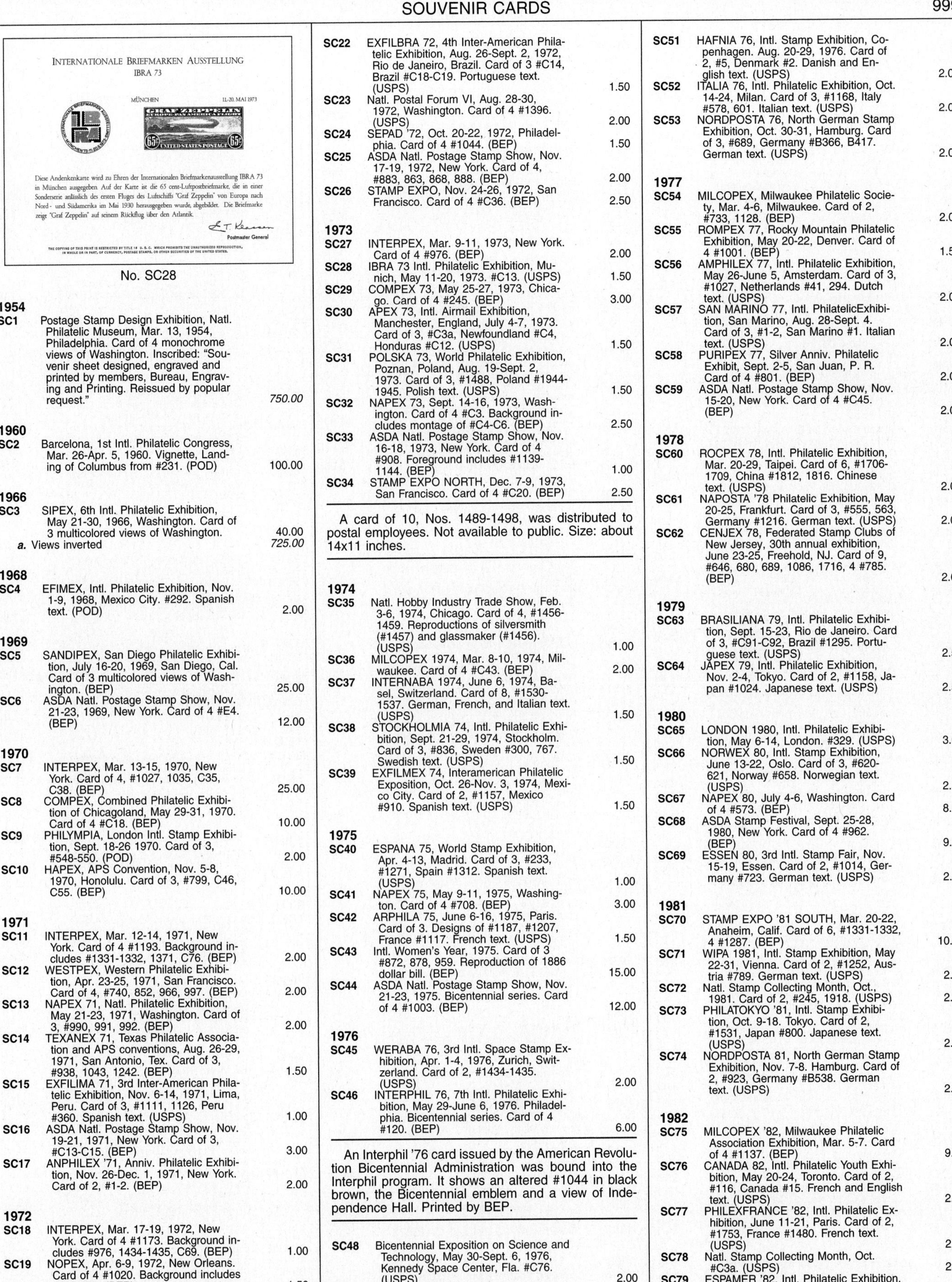

No. SC28

1954

SC1 Postage Stamp Design Exhibition, Natl. Philatelic Museum, Mar. 13, 1954, Philadelphia. Card of 4 monochrome views of Washington. Inscribed: "Souvenir sheet designed, engraved and printed by members, Bureau, Engraving and Printing. Reissued by popular request." *750.00*

1960

SC2 Barcelona, 1st Intl. Philatelic Congress, Mar. 26-Apr. 5, 1960. Vignette, Landing of Columbus from #231. (POD) 100.00

1966

SC3 SIPEX, 6th Intl. Philatelic Exhibition, May 21-30, 1966, Washington. Card of 3 multicolored views of Washington. 40.00
a. Views inverted *725.00*

1968

SC4 EFIMEX, Intl. Philatelic Exhibition, Nov. 1-9, 1968, Mexico City. #292. Spanish text. (POD) 2.00

1969

SC5 SANDIPEX, San Diego Philatelic Exhibition, July 16-20, 1969, San Diego, Cal. Card of 3 multicolored views of Washington. (BEP) 25.00

SC6 ASDA Natl. Postage Stamp Show, Nov. 21-23, 1969, New York. Card of 4 #E4. (BEP) 12.00

1970

SC7 INTERPEX, Mar. 13-15, 1970, New York. Card of 4, #1027, 1035, C35, C38. (BEP) 25.00

SC8 COMPEX, Combined Philatelic Exhibition of Chicagoland, May 29-31, 1970. Card of 4 #C18. (BEP) 10.00

SC9 PHILYMPIA, London Intl. Stamp Exhibition, Sept. 18-26 1970. Card of 3, #548-550. (POD) 2.00

SC10 HAPEX, APS Convention, Nov. 5-8, 1970, Honolulu. Card of 3, #799, C46, C55. (BEP) 10.00

1971

SC11 INTERPEX, Mar. 12-14, 1971, New York. Card of 4 #1193. Background includes #1331-1332, 1371, C76. (BEP) 2.00

SC12 WESTPEX, Western Philatelic Exhibition, Apr. 23-25, 1971, San Francisco. Card of 4, #740, 852, 966, 997. (BEP) 2.00

SC13 NAPEX 71, Natl. Philatelic Exhibition, May 21-23, 1971, Washington. Card of 3, #990, 991, 992. (BEP) 2.00

SC14 TEXANEX 71, Texas Philatelic Association and APS conventions, Aug. 26-29, 1971, San Antonio, Tex. Card of 3, #938, 1043, 1242. (BEP) 1.50

SC15 EXFILIMA 71, 3rd Inter-American Philatelic Exhibition, Nov. 6-14, 1971, Lima, Peru. Card of 3, #1111, 1126, Peru #360. Spanish text. (USPS) 1.00

SC16 ASDA Natl. Postage Stamp Show, Nov. 19-21, 1971, New York. Card of 3, #C13-C15. (BEP) 3.00

SC17 ANPHILEX '71, Anniv. Philatelic Exhibition, Nov. 26-Dec. 1, 1971, New York. Card of 2, #1-2. (BEP) 2.00

1972

SC18 INTERPEX, Mar. 17-19, 1972, New York. Card of 4 #1173. Background includes #976, 1434-1435, C69. (BEP) 1.00

SC19 NOPEX, Apr. 6-9, 1972, New Orleans. Card of 4 #1020. Background includes #323-327. (BEP) 1.50

SC20 BELGICA 72, Brussels Intl. Philatelic Exhibition, June 24-July 9, 1972, Brussels, Belgium. Card of 3, #914, 1026, 1104. Flemish and French text. (USPS) 1.50

SC21 Olympia Philatelie Munchen 72, Aug. 18-Sept. 10, 1972, Munich, Germany. Card of 4, #1460-1462, C85. German text. (USPS) 1.50

SC22 EXFILBRA 72, 4th Inter-American Philatelic Exhibition, Aug. 26-Sept. 2, 1972, Rio de Janeiro, Brazil. Card of 3 #C14, Brazil #C18-C19. Portuguese text. (USPS) 1.50

SC23 Natl. Postal Forum VI, Aug. 28-30, 1972, Washington. Card of 4 #1396. (USPS) 2.00

SC24 SEPAD '72, Oct. 20-22, 1972, Philadelphia. Card of 4 #1044. (BEP) 1.50

SC25 ASDA Natl. Postage Stamp Show, Nov. 17-19, 1972, New York. Card of 4, #883, 863, 868, 888. (BEP) 2.00

SC26 STAMP EXPO, Nov. 24-26, 1972, San Francisco. Card of 4 #C36. (BEP) 2.50

1973

SC27 INTERPEX, Mar. 9-11, 1973, New York. Card of 4 #976. (BEP) 2.00

SC28 IBRA 73 Intl. Philatelic Exhibition, Munich, May 11-20, 1973. #C13. (USPS) 1.50

SC29 COMPEX 73, May 25-27, 1973, Chicago. Card of 4 #245. (BEP) 3.00

SC30 APEX 73, Intl. Airmail Exhibition, Manchester, England, July 4-7, 1973. Card of 3, #C3a, Newfoundland #C4, Honduras #C12. (USPS) 1.50

SC31 POLSKA 73, World Philatelic Exhibition, Poznan, Poland, Aug. 19-Sept. 2, 1973. Card of 3, #1488, Poland #1944-1945. Polish text. (USPS) 1.50

SC32 NAPEX 73, Sept. 14-16, 1973, Washington. Card of 4 #C3. Background includes montage of #C4-C6. (BEP) 2.50

SC33 ASDA Natl. Postage Stamp Show, Nov. 16-18, 1973, New York. Card of 4 #908. Foreground includes #1139-1144. (BEP) 1.00

SC34 STAMP EXPO NORTH, Dec. 7-9, 1973, San Francisco. Card of 4 #C20. (BEP) 2.50

A card of 10, Nos. 1489-1498, was distributed to postal employees. Not available to public. Size: about 14x11 inches.

1974

SC35 Natl. Hobby Industry Trade Show, Feb. 3-6, 1974, Chicago. Card of 4, #1456-1459. Reproductions of silversmith (#1457) and glassmaker (#1456). (USPS) 1.00

SC36 MILCOPEX 1974, Mar. 8-10, 1974, Milwaukee. Card of 4 #C43. (BEP) 2.00

SC37 INTERNABA 1974, June 6, 1974, Basel, Switzerland. Card of 8, #1530-1537. German, French, and Italian text. (USPS) 1.50

SC38 STOCKHOLMIA 74, Intl. Philatelic Exhibition, Sept. 21-29, 1974, Stockholm. Card of 3, #836, Sweden #300, 767. Swedish text. (USPS) 1.50

SC39 EXFILMEX 74, Interamerican Philatelic Exposition, Oct. 26-Nov. 3, 1974, Mexico City. Card of 2, #1157, Mexico #910. Spanish text. (USPS) 1.50

1975

SC40 ESPANA 75, World Stamp Exhibition, Apr. 4-13, Madrid. Card of 3, #233, #1271, Spain #1312. Spanish text. (USPS) 1.00

SC41 NAPEX 75, May 9-11, 1975, Washington. Card of 4 #708. (BEP) 3.00

SC42 ARPHILA 75, June 6-16, 1975, Paris. Card of 3. Designs of #1187, #1207, France #1117. French text. (USPS) 1.50

SC43 Intl. Women's Year, 1975. Card of 3 #872, 878, 959. Reproduction of 1886 dollar bill. (BEP) 15.00

SC44 ASDA Natl. Postage Stamp Show, Nov. 21-23, 1975. Bicentennial series. Card of 4 #1003. (BEP) 12.00

1976

SC45 WERABA 76, 3rd Intl. Space Stamp Exhibition, Apr. 1-4, 1976, Zurich, Switzerland. Card of 2, #1434-1435. (USPS) 2.00

SC46 INTERPHIL 76, 7th Intl. Philatelic Exhibition, May 29-June 6, 1976. Philadelphia. Bicentennial series. Card of 4 #120. (BEP) 6.00

An Interphil '76 card issued by the American Revolution Bicentennial Administration was bound into the Interphil program. It shows an altered #1044 in black brown, the Bicentennial emblem and a view of Independence Hall. Printed by BEP.

SC48 Bicentennial Exposition on Science and Technology, May 30-Sept. 6, 1976, Kennedy Space Center, Fla. #C76. (USPS) 2.00

SC49 STAMP EXPO 76, June 11-13, 1976, Los Angeles. Bicentennial series. Card of 4, #1351, 1352, 1345, 1348. (BEP) 5.00

SC50 Colorado Statehood Centennial, Aug. 1, 1976. Card of 3, #743, 288, 1670. (USPS) 2.00

SC51 HAFNIA 76, Intl. Stamp Exhibition, Copenhagen. Aug. 20-29, 1976. Card of 2, #5, Denmark #2. Danish and English text. (USPS) 2.00

SC52 ITALIA 76, Intl. Philatelic Exhibition, Oct. 14-24, Milan. Card of 3, #1168, Italy #578, 601. Italian text. (USPS) 2.00

SC53 NORDPOSTA 76, North German Stamp Exhibition, Oct. 30-31, Hamburg. Card of 3, #689, Germany #B366, B417. German text. (USPS) 2.00

1977

SC54 MILCOPEX, Milwaukee Philatelic Society, Mar. 4-6, Milwaukee. Card of 2, #733, 1128. (BEP) 2.00

SC55 ROMPEX 77, Rocky Mountain Philatelic Exhibition, May 20-22, Denver. Card of 4 #1001. (BEP) 1.50

SC56 AMPHILEX 77, Intl. Philatelic Exhibition, May 26-June 5, Amsterdam. Card of 3, #1027, Netherlands #41, 294. Dutch text. (USPS) 2.00

SC57 SAN MARINO 77, Intl. PhilatelicExhibition, San Marino, Aug. 28-Sept. 4. Card of 3, #1-2, San Marino #1. Italian text. (USPS) 2.00

SC58 PURIPEX 77, Silver Anniv. Philatelic Exhibit, Sept. 2-5, San Juan, P. R. Card of 4 #801. (BEP) 2.00

SC59 ASDA Natl. Postage Stamp Show, Nov. 15-20, New York. Card of 4 #C45. (BEP) 2.00

1978

SC60 ROCPEX 78, Intl. Philatelic Exhibition, Mar. 20-29, Taipei. Card of 6, #1706-1709, China #1812, 1816. Chinese text. (USPS) 2.00

SC61 NAPOSTA '78 Philatelic Exhibition, May 20-25, Frankfurt. Card of 3, #555, 563, Germany #1216. German text. (USPS) 2.00

SC62 CENJEX 78, Federated Stamp Clubs of New Jersey, 30th annual exhibition, June 23-25, Freehold, NJ. Card of 9, #646, 680, 689, 1086, 1716, 4 #785. (BEP) 2.00

1979

SC63 BRASILIANA 79, Intl. Philatelic Exhibition, Sept. 15-23, Rio de Janeiro. Card of 3, #C91-C92, Brazil #1295. Portuguese text. (USPS) 2.50

SC64 JAPEX 79, Intl. Philatelic Exhibition, Nov. 2-4, Tokyo. Card of 2, #1158, Japan #1024. Japanese text. (USPS) 2.50

1980

SC65 LONDON 1980, Intl. Philatelic Exhibition, May 6-14, London. #329. (USPS) 3.00

SC66 NORWEX 80, Intl. Stamp Exhibition, June 13-22, Oslo. Card of 3, #620-621, Norway #658. Norwegian text. (USPS) 2.50

SC67 NAPEX 80, July 4-6, Washington. Card of 4 #573. (BEP) 8.00

SC68 ASDA Stamp Festival, Sept. 25-28, 1980, New York. Card of 4 #962. (BEP) 9.00

SC69 ESSEN 80, 3rd Intl. Stamp Fair, Nov. 15-19, Essen. Card of 2, #1014, Germany #723. German text. (USPS) 2.00

1981

SC70 STAMP EXPO '81 SOUTH, Mar. 20-22, Anaheim, Calif. Card of 6, #1331-1332, 4 #1287. (BEP) 10.00

SC71 WIPA 1981, Intl. Stamp Exhibition, May 22-31, Vienna. Card of 2, #1252, Austria #789. German text. (USPS) 2.50

SC72 Natl. Stamp Collecting Month, Oct., 1981. Card of 2, #245, 1918. (USPS) 2.50

SC73 PHILATOKYO '81, Intl. Stamp Exhibition, Oct. 9-18. Tokyo. Card of 2, #1531, Japan #800. Japanese text. (USPS) 2.50

SC74 NORDPOSTA 81, North German Stamp Exhibition, Nov. 7-8. Hamburg. Card of 2, #923, Germany #B538. German text. (USPS) 2.50

1982

SC75 MILCOPEX '82, Milwaukee Philatelic Association Exhibition, Mar. 5-7. Card of 4 #1137. (BEP) 9.00

SC76 CANADA 82, Intl. Philatelic Youth Exhibition, May 20-24, Toronto. Card of 2, #116, Canada #15. French and English text. (USPS) 2.50

SC77 PHILEXFRANCE '82, Intl. Philatelic Exhibition, June 11-21, Paris. Card of 2, #1753, France #1480. French text. (USPS) 2.50

SC78 Natl. Stamp Collecting Month, Oct. #C3a. (USPS) 2.50

SC79 ESPAMER '82, Intl. Philatelic Exhibition, Oct. 12-17, San Juan, P.R. Card of 4 #244. English and Spanish text. (BEP) 15.00

SC80 ESPAMER '82, Intl. Philatelic Exhibition, Oct. 12-17, San Juan, P.R. Card of 3, #801, 1437, 2024. Spanish and English text. (USPS) 2.50

1983

SC81 Joint stamp issues, Sweden and US. Mar. 24. Card of 3, #958, 2036, Sweden #1453. Swedish and English text. (USPS) 2.50

SC82 Joint stamp issues, Germany and US. Apr. 29. Card of 2, #2040, Germany #1397. German and English text. (USPS) 2.50

SC83 TEMBAL 83, Intl. Philatelic Exhibition, Mar. 21-29, Basel. Card of 2, #C71, Basel #3L1. German text. (USPS) 2.50

SC84 TEXANEX-TOPEX '83 Exhibition, June 17-19, San Antonio. Card of 5, #1660, 4 #776. (BEP) 12.00

SC85 BRASILIANA 83, Intl. Philatelic Exhibition, July 29-Aug. 7, Rio de Janeiro. Card of 2, #2, Brazil #1. Portuguese text. (USPS) 2.50

SC86 BANGKOK 83, Intl. Philatelic Exhibition, Aug. 4-13, Bangkok. Card of 2, #210, Thailand #1. Thai text. (USPS) 2.50

SC87 Intl. Philatelic Memento, 1983-84. #1387. (USPS) 2.50

SC88 Natl. Stamp Collecting Month, Oct. #293 bicolored. (USPS) 2.50

SC89 Philatelic Show '83, Boston, Oct. 21-23. Card of 2, #718-719. (BEP) 9.00

SC90 ASDA 1983, Natl. Postage Stamp Show, New York, Nov. 17-20. Card of 4 #881. (BEP) 9.00

1984

SC91 ESPANA 84, World Exhibition of Philately. Madrid, Apr. 27-May 6. Card of 4 #241. Enlarged vignette, Landing of Columbus, from #231. English and Spanish text. (BEP) 12.00

SC92 ESPANA 84, Intl. Philatelic Exhibition, Madrid, Apr. 27-May 6. Card of 2, #233, Spain #428. Spanish text. (USPS) 2.50

SC93 Stamp Expo '84 South, Anaheim, CA, Apr. 27-29. Card of 4, #1791-1794. (BEP) 10.00

SC94 COMPEX '84, Rosemont, IL, May 25-27. Card of 4 #728. (BEP) 14.00

SC95 HAMBURG '84, Intl. Exhibition for 19th UPU Congress, Hamburg, June 19-26. Card of 2, #C66, Germany #669. English, French and German text. (USPS) 2.50

SC96 St. Lawrence Seaway, 25th anniv., June 26. Card of 2, #1131, Canada #387. English and French text. (USPS) 3.00

SC97 AUSIPEX '84, Australia's 1st intl. exhibition, Melbourne, Sept. 21-30. Card of 2, #290, Western Australia #1. (USPS) 2.50

SC98 Natl. Stamp Collecting Month, Oct. #2104, tricolored. (USPS) 2.50

SC99 PHILAKOREA '84, Seoul, Oct. 22-31. Card of 2, #741, Korea #994. Korean and English text. (USPS) 2.50

SC100 ASDA 1984, Natl. Postage Stamp Show, New York, Nov. 15-18. Card of 4 #1470. (BEP) 8.00

1985

SC101 Intl. Philatelic Memento, 1985. #2. (USPS) 2.50

SC102 OLYMPHILEX '85. Intl. Philatelic Exhibition, Lausanne. Mar. 18-24. Card of 2, #C106, Switzerland #746. French and English text. (USPS) 2.50

SC103 ISRAPHIL '85. Intl. Philatelic Exhibition, Tel Aviv, May 14-22. Card of 2, #566, Israel #33. Hebrew and English text. (USPS) 2.50

SC104 LONG BEACH '85, Numismatic and Philatelic Exposition, Long Beach, CA, Jan. 31-Feb. 3. Card of 4 #954, plus a Series 1865 $20 Gold Certificate. (BEP) 8.00

SC105 MILCOPEX '85, Milwaukee Philatelic Society annual stamp show, Mar. 1-3. Card of 4 #880. (BEP) 8.00

SC106 NAPEX '85, Natl. Philatelic Exhibition, Arlington, VA, June 7-9. Card of 4 #2014. (BEP) 8.00

SC107 ARGENTINA '85, Intl. Philatelic Exhibition, Buenos Aires, July 5-14. Card of 2, #1737, Argentina #B27. Spanish text. (USPS) 2.50

SC108 MOPHILA '85, Intl. Philatelic Exhibition, Hamburg, Sept. 11-15. Card of 2, #296, Germany #B595. German text. (USPS) 2.50

SC109 ITALIA '85, Intl. Philatelic Exhibition, Rome, Oct. 25-Nov. 3. Card of 2, #1107, Italy #830. Italian text. (USPS) 2.50

1986

SC110 Statue of Liberty Centennial, Natl. Philatelic Memento, 1986. #C87. (USPS) 3.00

SC111 Garfield Perry Stamp Club, Natl. Stamp Show, Cleveland, Mar. 21-23. Card of 4 #306. (BEP) 9.00

SC112 AMERIPEX '86, Intl. Philatelic Exhibition, Chicago, May 22-June 1. Card of 3, #134, 2052, 1474.(BEP) 8.00

SC113 STOCKHOLMIA '86, Intl. Philatelic Exhibition, Stockholm, Aug. 28-Sept. 7. Card of 2, #113, Sweden #253. Swedish text. (USPS) 3.00

SC114 HOUPEX '86, Natl. Stamp Show, Houston. Sept. 5-7. Card of 3, #1035, 1042, 1044A. (BEP) 12.00

SC115 LOBEX '86, Numismatic and Philatelic Exhibition, Long Beach, CA, Oct. 2-5. Long Beach Stamp Club 60th anniv. Card of 4, #291, plus a series 1907 $10 Gold Certificate. (BEP) 15.00

SC116 DCSE '86, Dallas Coin and Stamp Exhibition, Dallas, Dec. 11-14. Card of 4 #550, plus $10,000 Federal Reserve Note. (BEP) 18.00

1987

SC117 CAPEX '87, Intl. Philatelic Exhibition, Toronto, June 13-21. Card of 2, #569, Canada #883. English and French text. (USPS) 3.00

SC118 HAFNIA '87, Intl. Philatelic Exhibition, Copenhagen, Oct. 16-25. Card of 2, #299, Denmark #B52. English and Danish text. (USPS) 3.00

SC119 SESCAL '87, Stamp Exhibition of Southern California, Los Angeles, Oct. 16-18. #798. (BEP) 9.00

SC120 HSNA '87, Hawaii State Numismatic Association Exhibition, Honolulu, Nov. 12-15. #799 and a Series 1923 $5 Silver Certificate. (BEP) 21.00

SC121 MONTE CARLO, Intl. Philatelic Exhibition, Monte Carlo, Nov. 13-17. Card of 3, #2287, 2300, Monaco #1589. French and English text. (USPS) 3.00

1988

SC122 FINLANDIA '88, Intl. Philatelic Exhibition, Helsinki, June 1-12. Card of 2, #836, Finland #768. English and Finnish text. (USPS) 3.00

SC123 STAMPSHOW '88, APS natl. stamp show, Detroit, Aug. 25-28. #835. (BEP) 8.00

SC124 MIDAPHIL '88, Kansas City, Nov. 18-20. #627. (BEP) 9.00

1989

SC125 PHILEXFRANCE '89 intl. philatelic exhibition, Paris, July 7-17. Card of 2, #C120, France #2144. English and French text. (USPS) 4.00

SC126 STAMPSHOW '89, APS natl. stamp show, Anaheim, CA, Aug. 24-27. #565. Various reproductions of the portrait of Chief Hollow Horn Bear from which the stamp was designed. (BEP) 12.00

SC127 WORLD STAMP EXPO '89, Washington, Nov. 17-Dec. 3. Card of 4, #2433a-2433d. Embossed reproductions of Supreme Court, Washington Monument, Capitol and Jefferson Memorial. (USPS) 4.00

1990

SC128 ARIPEX 90, Arizona Philatelic Exhibition, Phoenix, Apr. 20-22. Card of 2, #285 and #285 with black vignette. (BEP) 9.00

SC129 STAMPSHOW '90, APS natl. stamp show, Cincinnati, Aug. 23-26. Card of 2, #286 and essay with frame of #286 in red with vignette of #293 in black. (BEP) 9.00

SC130 STAMP WORLD LONDON 90, London, England, May 3-13. Card of 2, #1, Great Britain #1. (USPS) 4.00

1991

SC131 STAMPSHOW '91, APS natl. stamp show, Philadelphia, Aug. 22-25. Card of 3, #537, Essays #537a-E1, 537b-E1. Embossed figure of "Freedom." (BEP) (card has no year date) 11.00

1992

SC132 World Columbian Stamp Expo, Chicago, May 22-31. Card of 2, #118, 119b. (BEP) 11.00

SC132A OLYMPHILEX '92, Barcelona, Spain, July 30-Aug. 7. Card of 6, #2619, #2637-2641. (USPS) *80.00*

SC133 Savings Bond, produced as gift to BEP employees, available to public. 1954 Savings stamp, Series E War Savings bond. (BEP) 14.00

SC134 STAMPSHOW '92. Oakland, CA (BEP) 12.00

1993

SC135 Combined Federal Campaign, produced as gift to BEP employees, available to public. #1016. Photos of 6 other stamps. (BEP) 12.00

SC136 ASDA stamp show, New York, May 1993. Card of 7 #859, 864, 869, 874, 879, 884, 889 (BEP) 12.00

SC137 Savings Bonds, produced as gift to BEP employees, available to the public Aug. 1993. $200 War Savings Bond, #WS8 (BEP) 18.00

SC138 Omaha Stamp Show, Sept. 1993. Card of 4, #E7, PR2, JQ5, QE4 (BEP) 12.00

SC139 ASDA New York Show, Oct. 1993. Card of 2, #499-E1a and similar with negative New York precancel (BEP) 15.00

1994

SC140 Sandical, San Diego, CA, Feb. 1994. Card of 4 #E4 (BEP) 9.00

SC140A Centennial of U.S. Stamp Production, July 1994, BEP Intaglio Print. Card of 13 Types A87-A99 in black 60.00

SC141 Savings Bonds, produced as a gift to BEP employees, available to the public Aug. 1, 1994. #WS7-WS11. 12.00

SC142 STAMPSHOW '94, APS National Stamp Show Pittsburgh, PA. Card of 3, 1c, 2c and 10c Type D2 11.00

SC143 American Stamp Dealers Association, Nov. 1994, New York, NY. Card of 4, 2c, 12c, $3, $6 Types N4-N5, N7-N8 11.00

1995

SC144 Natl. Exhibition of the Columbus Philatelic Club, Apr. 1995, Columbus, OH. Block of 4 of #261. 11.00

No. 144 was issued folded in half.

SC145 Centennial of U.S. Stamp Production, June 1995, BEP Intaglio Print. Card of 13 of Types A87-A99 in blue 50.00

SC146 Savings Bonds, produced as a gift to BEP employees, available to the public Aug. 1, 1995. Card of 3 #905, 907, 940 12.00

SC147 American Stamp Dealers Association, Nov. 1995, New York, NY. Block of 4, #292 10.00

No. SC147 issued folded in half.

1996

SC148 CAPEX '96, Toronto, Canada, June 1996. Block of 4, #291 12.00

SC149 Olymphilex '96, Atlanta, GA, July-August, 1996, Block of 4, #718 11.00

SC150 Billings Stamp Club, Billings, MT, Oct. 1996, Block of 4, #1130 12.00

1997

SC151 Long Beach Coin & Collectibles Expo, Feb. 1997, Lock Seal revenue stamp 11.00

SC152 PACIFIC 97, May 1997, Process or renovated butter revenue stamp 12.00

SC153 Milcopex, Milwaukee, WI, Sept. 1997, Newspaper Types N15, N16 and N19 12.00

1998

SC154 OKPEX 98, Oklahoma City, OK, May 1998, Block of 4, #922 11.00

SC155 Centennial of Trans-Mississippi Exposition Issue, Sept. 1998, BEP Engraved Print. Card of 9 die impressions in green of designs A100-A108 50.00

1999

SC156 Philadelphia National Stamp Exhibition, Oct. 1999, Card of 4, #RS281, RS284, RS290, RS306 12.00

2003

SC157 Georgia Numismatic Association, Dalton, GA (card of one #C45 in blue gray, without denomination and some inscriptions) 45.00

2005

SC158 ANA Coin, Stamp and Collectibles Show, Las Vegas, Oct. 2005, Card of 7, #999, 1248, RF1, RF11, RF26, 7c essay of #RF11, 5c essay of #RF26 55.00

2006

SC159 ANA World's Fair of Money, Denver, CO, card of #1001 without denomination and some inscriptions, 1908 $10 silver certificate 45.00

SC160 Long Beach Coin, Stamp & Collectible Expo, Long Beach, CA, Sept. 2006, Card of #997 in blue, California state shield, Reverse of Series 1923 $10 United States Note 40.00

SC160A ANA Coin, Stamp and Collectibles Show, Las Vegas, Oct. 2006, Card of 5, #RF17, RF24, RF27, essay type of RF19, USPO vignette (BEP) 50.00

2007

SC160B Jamestown 400th Anniv., May 2007, Card of #328-330 in dark blue 45.00

SC161 Whitman Baltimore Coin and Collectibles Convention, Baltimore, MD, Nov. 2007, Card of #962, 1142 in black 40.00

2008

SC162	Florida United Numismatists, Orlando, FL, Jan. 2008, Card of #Q12, 952	35.00
SC163	ANA World's Fair of Money, Baltimore, MD, Aug. 2008, Card of 1⅜ ounce snuff, $19.20 tobacco, 5 Class A cigars stamps	50.00

2009

SC164	ANA National Money Show, Portland, OR, Mar. 2009, Card of #222	40.00
SC165	Whitman Baltimore Coin and Collectibles Convention, Baltimore, MD, Mar. 2009, Card of #77	35.00
SC166	Texas Numismatic Association 51st Texas State Coin and Currency Show, Fort Worth, TX, May 2009, Card of #821	30.00
SC167	American Numismatic Association World's Fair of Money Show, Los Angeles, CA, August 2009, Card of #555	30.00

2010

SC168	ANA National Money Show, Fort Worth, TX, Mar. 2010, Card of #776, 938	35.00
SC169	ANA World's Fair of Money, Boston, MA, Aug. 2010, Card of #951	35.00

Beginning in 2011, the souvenir cards no longer were issued for specific philatelic shows.

2011

SC170	Franklin Commemorative Series - Postmaster, Aug. 2011, Card of #3139a, LO1	40.00

2015

SC171	Centenary of the Opening of the Panama Canal, Card of #399, 400	50.00
SC172	Centenary of the Opening of the Panama Canal, Card of #397, 398	50.00

The numismatic card No. NSC128 also features stamps.

2018

SC173	The Great War 100th Anniversary, Card of #WS4, WS6, $10,000 bond	40.00

NUMISMATIC SOUVENIR CARDS

Included in this section are cards issued by the Bureau of Engraving and Printing showing fractional currency, paper money or parts thereof, for numismatic shows. Not included are press samples sold or given away only at the shows and other special printings. Cards showing both money and stamps are listed in the preceeding section.

Standard abbreviations:

ANA- American Numismatic Association
IPMS- International Paper Money Show
FUN- Florida United Numismatists

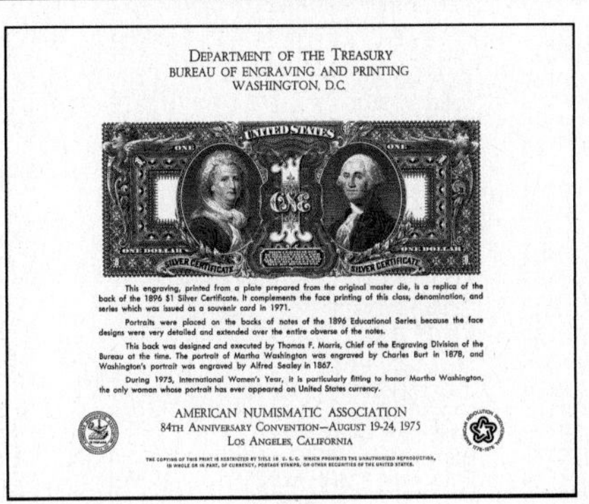

No. NSC8

1969-84

NSC1	ANA	30.00
NSC2	Fresno Numismatic Fair	*100.00*
NSC3	ANA ('70)	35.00
NSC4	ANA ('71)	12.00
NSC5	ANA ('72)	12.00
NSC6	ANA ('73)	15.00
NSC7	ANA ('74)	12.00
NSC8	ANA ('75)	12.00
NSC9	ANA ('76)	12.00
NSC10	ANA ('77)	15.00
NSC11	IPMS ('78)	5.00
NSC12	ANA ('80)	15.00
NSC13	IPMS ('80)	22.00
NSC14	IPMS ('81)	16.00
NSC15	ANA ('81)	14.00
NSC16	IPMS ('82)	14.00
NSC17	ANA ('82)	7.00
NSC18	FUN ('83)	16.00
NSC19	ANA ('83)	14.00
NSC20	FUN ('84)	16.00
NSC21	IPMS ('84)	24.00
NSC22	ANA ('84)	18.00

1985

NSC23	International Coin Club of El Paso	14.00
NSC24	Pacific Northwest Numismatic Assoc.	16.00
NSC25	IPMS	18.00
NSC26	ANA	16.00
NSC27	International Paper Money Convention (IPMC)	16.00

1986

NSC28	FUN	16.00
NSC29	ANA Midwinter	17.00
NSC30	IPMS	12.00
NSC31	ANA	9.00
NSC32	National World Paper Money Convention (NWPMC)	11.00

1987

NSC33	FUN	16.00
NSC34	ANA Midwinter	20.00
NSC35	BEP Fort Worth	18.00
NSC36	IPMS	14.00
NSC37	ANA	12.00
NSC38	Great Eastern Numismatic Association	12.00

1988

NSC39	FUN	10.00
NSC40	ANA Midwinter	18.00
NSC41	IPMS	15.00
NSC42	ANA	20.00
NSC43	Illinois Numismatic Association	14.00

1989

NSC44	FUN	14.00
NSC45	ANA Midwinter	16.00
NSC46	TNA	20.00
NSC47	IPMS	15.00
NSC48	ANA	16.00

1990

NSC49	FUN	15.00
NSC50	ANA Midwinter	14.00
NSC51	Central States Numismatic Society	14.00
NSC52	Dallas Coin and Stamp Exposition	14.00
NSC53	ANA, Seattle, WA	16.00
NSC54	Westex	15.00
NSC55	Hawaii State Numismatic Association (card has no year date)	18.00

1991

NSC56	FUN (card has no year date)	16.00
NSC57	ANA Midwinter, Dallas, Texas (card has no year date)	20.00
NSC58	IPMS (card has no year date)	16.00
NSC59	ANA Convention, Chicago, IL (card has no year date)	20.00

1992

NSC60	FUN	14.00
NSC61	Central States Numismatics Society	20.00
NSC62	IPMS, Memphis, TN	14.00
NSC63	ANA Convention, Orlando, FL	18.00

1993

NSC64	FUN	18.00
NSC65	ANA Convention, Colorado Springs, CO	16.00
NSC66	Texas Numismatic Association Show	16.00
NSC67	Georgia Numismatic Association Show	18.00
NSC68	ANA Convention, Baltimore, MD	18.00
NSC69	IPMS, Memphis, TN	18.00

1994

NSC70	FUN	16.00
NSC71	ANA Convention, New Orleans, LA	22.00
NSC72	European Paper Money Bourse, Netherlands	20.00
NSC73	IPMS, Memphis, TN	20.00
NSC74	ANA Convention, Detroit, MI	16.00

Nos. NSC75-NSC79 were issued folded in half.

1995

NSC75	FUN	22.00
NSC76	New York Intl. Numismatic Convention	18.00
NSC77	IPMS, Memphis, TN	16.00
NSC78	ANA Convention, Anaheim, CA	16.00
NSC79	Long Beach Numismatic/Philatelic Exposition, Long Beach, CA	16.00

1996

NSC80	FUN	18.00
NSC81	Suburban Washington/Baltimore Coin Show	16.00
NSC82	Central States Numismatic Association	22.00
NSC83	ANA Convention, Denver, CO	18.00

1997

NSC84	FUN	22.00
NSC85	Bay State Coin Show	16.00
NSC86	IPMS, Memphis, TN	16.00
NSC87	ANA Convention, New York, NY	22.00

1998

NSC88	FUN	18.00
NSC89	IPMS, Memphis, TN	18.00
NSC90	ANA Convention, Portland, OR	16.00
NSC91	Long Beach Coin & Collectibles Expo, Long Beach, CA	18.00

1999

NSC92	FUN	22.00
NSC93	Bay State Coin Club	22.00
NSC94	IPMS, Memphis, TN	20.00
NSC95	ANA Convention, Rosemont, IL	20.00

2001

NSC96	FUN	18.00
NSC97	IPMS	18.00
NSC98	ANA Convention, Atlanta, GA	20.00
NSC99	Long Beach Coin & Collectibles Expo, Long Beach, CA	18.00

2002

NSC100	FUN	20.00
NSC101	Texas Numismatic Association, Fort Worth	20.00
NSC102	ANA Convention, New York, NY	20.00
NSC103	Long Beach Coin & Collectibles Expo, Long Beach, CA	20.00

2003

NSC104	FUN	40.00

For the 2003 card issued for the Georgia Numismatic Association, Dalton, GA, see No. SC157.

2002

NSC106	ANA Convention, Baltimore, MD	45.00

2003

NSC107	Natl. & World Paper Money Convention, St. Louis, MO	40.00

2004

NSC108	ANA Convention, Portland, OR	50.00
NSC109	ANA Convention, Pittsburgh, PA	35.00

2005

NSC110	FUN	40.00
NSC111	Money Show of the Southwest, Houston, TX	45.00
NSC112	Long Beach Coin & Stamp Expo, Long Beach, CA	45.00
NSC113	ANA National Money Show, Kansas City, MO	40.00
NSC114	ANA World's Fair of Money, San Francisco, CA	35.00

2006

NSC115	ANA National Money Show, Atlanta, GA	45.00
NSC115A	ANA World's Fair of Money, Denver, CO	45.00
NSC115B	Long Beach Coin & Stamp Expo, Long Beach, CA	45.00

2007

NSC116	ANA National Money Show, Charlotte, NC	35.00
NSC117	ANA World's Fair of Money, Milwaukee, WI	35.00

2008

NSC118	ANA National Money Show, Phoenix, AZ	40.00

2009

NSC119	Central States Numismatic Society, Cincinnati, OH	35.00

2010

NSC120	FUN	35.00

Beginning in 2011, the numismatic souvenir cards no longer were issued for specific numismatic shows.

2011

NSC121	Franklin Commemorative Series - Inventor	40.00
NSC122	Franklin Commemorative Series - Statesman	35.00

2014

NSC123	Defenders of Freedom — Army, dated "2014" at top	40.00
NSC124	Defenders of Freedom — Navy, dated "2014" at top	40.00
NSC125	Defenders of Freedom — Marine Corps, dated "2014" at top	40.00

NSC126	Defenders of Freedom — Air Force, dated "2014" at top	40.00
NSC127	Defenders of Freedom — Coast Guard, dated "2014" at top	40.00

2016

NSC128	Defenders of Democracy — Army, inscribed "Since" and year at top	35.00
NSC129	Defenders of Democracy — Navy, inscribed "Since" and year at top	35.00
NSC130	Defenders of Democracy — Marine Corps, inscribed "Since" and year at top	35.00
NSC131	Defenders of Democracy — Air Force, inscribed "Since" and year at top	35.00
NSC132	Defenders of Democracy — Coast Guard, inscribed "Since" and year at top	35.00

2018

NSC133	The Great War 100th Anniversary, Series 1918 $2 Federal Reserve	35.00
NSC134	The Great War 100th Anniversary, back of Series 1918 $1 Federal Reserve Bank Note	35.00

COMMEMORATIVE PANELS

The U.S. Postal Service began issuing commemorative panels September 20, 1972, with the Wildlife Conservation issue (Scott Nos. 1464-1467). Each panel is devoted to a separate issue. It includes unused examples of the stamp or stamps (usually a block of four), reproduction of steel engravings, and background information on the subject of the issue. Values for panels issued through 1993 are for panels without protective sleeves. Values for panels with protective sleeves are 10% to 25% higher, through 1993. See note preceding No. CP431.

No. CP53

1972

CP1	Wildlife Conservation, #1467a	5.50
CP2	Mail Order, #1468	5.50
CP3	Osteopathic Medicine, #1469	11.00
CP4	Tom Sawyer, #1470	11.00
CP5	Pharmacy, #1473	8.00
CP6	Christmas (angel), #1471	7.50
CP7	Santa Claus, #1472	7.50
CP8	Stamp Collecting, #1474	5.00

1973

CP9	Love, #1475	7.00
CP10	Pamphleteers, #1476	5.00
CP11	George Gershwin, #1484	7.00
CP12	Posting a Broadside, #1477	5.00
CP13	Copernicus, #1488	5.00
CP14	Postal Service Employees, #1489-1498	5.00
CP15	Harry S Truman, #1499	7.00
CP16	Postrider, #1478	7.00
CP17	Boston Tea Party, #1483a	17.50
CP18	Electronics Progress, #1500-1502, C86	7.00
CP19	Robinson Jeffers, #1485	5.00
CP20	Lyndon B. Johnson, #1503	3.00
CP21	Henry O. Tanner, #1486	5.00
CP22	Willa Cather, #1487	5.00
CP23	Drummer, #1479	9.00
CP24	Angus and Longhorn Cattle, #1504	7.00
CP25	Christmas (Madonna), #1507	10.00
CP26	Christmas Tree, needlepoint, #1508	9.00

1974

CP27	Veterans of Foreign Wars, #1525	5.00
CP28	Robert Frost, #1526	5.00
CP29	EXPO '74, #1527	7.00
CP30	Horse Racing, #1528	9.00
CP31	Skylab, #1529	10.00
CP32	Universal Postal Union, #1537a	7.00
CP33	Mineral Heritage, #1541a	9.00
CP34	Kentucky Settlement (Ft. Harrod), #1542	5.00
CP35	First Continental Congress, #1546a	7.00
CP36	Chautauqua, #1505	7.00
CP37	Kansas Wheat, #1506	7.00
CP38	Energy Conservation, #1547	5.00
CP39	Sleepy Hollow Legend, #1548	7.00
CP40	Retarded Children, #1549	5.00
CP41	Christmas (Currier-Ives), #1551	7.00
CP42	Christmas (angel), #1550	7.00

1975

CP43	Benjamin West, #1553	7.00
CP44	Pioneer 10, #1556	10.00
CP45	Collective Bargaining, #1558	5.00
CP46	Contributors to the Cause, #1559-1562	7.00
CP47	Mariner 10, #1557	12.00
CP48	Lexington-Concord Battle, #1563	5.00
CP49	Paul Laurence Dunbar, #1554	7.00
CP50	D. W. Griffith, #1555	9.00
CP51	Battle of Bunker Hill, #1564	7.00
CP52	Military Services (uniforms), #1568a	7.00
CP53	Apollo Soyuz, #1569a	11.00
CP54	World Peace through Law, #1576	5.50
CP55	International Women's Year, #1571	5.50
CP56	Postal Service 200 Years, #1575a	5.00
CP57	Banking and Commerce, #1577a	7.00
CP58	Early Christmas Card, #1580	7.00
CP59	Christmas (Madonna), #1579	7.00

1976

CP60	Spirit of '76, #1631a	9.00
CP61	Interphil '76, #1632	8.50
CP62	State Flags, block of 4 from #1633-1682	16.00
CP63	Telephone Centenary, #1683	7.00
CP64	Commercial Aviation, #1684	8.00
CP65	Chemistry, #1685	9.00
CP66	Benjamin Franklin, #1690	8.00
CP67	Declaration of Independence, #1694a	7.00
CP68	12th Winter Olympics, #1698a	9.00
CP69	Clara Maass, #1699	11.00
CP70	Adolph S. Ochs, #1700	8.00
CP71	Christmas (Currier print), #1702	8.00
CP72	Christmas (Copley Nativity), #1701	10.00

1977

CP73	Washington at Princeton, #1704	10.00
CP74	Sound Recording, #1705	27.50
CP75	Pueblo Art, #1709a	70.00
CP76	Lindbergh Flight, #1710	70.00
CP77	Colorado Statehood, #1711	11.00
CP78	Butterflies, #1715a	14.00
CP79	Lafayette, #1716	11.00
CP80	Skilled Hands for Independence, #1720a	12.00
CP81	Peace Bridge, #1721	12.00
CP82	Battle of Oriskany, #1722	11.00
CP83	Energy Conservation-Development, #1723a	12.00
CP84	Alta California, #1725	12.00
CP85	Articles of Confederation, #1726	18.00
CP86	Talking Pictures, #1727	14.00
CP87	Surrender at Saratoga, #1728	16.00
CP88	Christmas (Washington at Valley Forge), #1729	14.00
CP89	Christmas (rural mailbox), #1730	25.00

1978

CP90	Carl Sandburg, #1731	7.50
CP91	Captain Cook, #1732a	10.00
CP92	Harriet Tubman, #1744	10.00
CP93	American Quilts, #1748a	14.00
CP94	American Dance, #1752a	10.00
CP95	French Alliance, #1753	9.00
CP96	Pap Test, #1754	9.00
CP97	Jimmie Rodgers, #1755	10.00
CP98	Photography, #1758	10.00
CP99	George M. Cohan, #1756	14.00
CP100	Viking Missions, #1759	30.00
CP101	American Owls, #1763a	30.00
CP102	American Trees, #1767a	24.00
CP103	Christmas (Madonna), #1768	12.00
CP104	Christmas (hobby-horse), #1769	12.00

1979

CP105	Robert F. Kennedy, #1770	10.00
CP106	Martin Luther King, Jr., #1771	9.00
CP107	Year of the Child, #1772	7.00
CP108	John Steinbeck, #1773	6.00
CP109	Albert Einstein, #1774	9.00
CP110	Pennsylvania Toleware, #1778a	10.00
CP111	American Architecture, #1782a	9.00
CP112	Endangered Flora, #1786a	9.00
CP113	Seeing Eye Dogs, #1787	7.00
CP114	Special Olympics, #1788	7.00
CP115	John Paul Jones, #1789	8.00
CP116	Olympic Games, #1794a	9.00
CP117	Christmas (Madonna), #1799	9.00
CP118	Christmas (Santa Claus), #1800	9.00
CP119	Will Rogers, #1801	9.00
CP120	Viet Nam Veterans, #1802	9.00
CP121	10c, 31c Olympics, #1790, C97	9.00

1980

CP122	Winter Olympics, #1798a	7.00
CP123	W.C Fields, #1803	12.00
CP124	Benjamin Banneker, #1804	7.00
CP125	Frances Perkins, #1821	5.00
CP126	Emily Bissell, #1823	9.00
CP127	Helen Keller, #1824	5.00
CP128	Veterans Administration, #1825	5.00
CP129	Galvez, #1826	5.00
CP130	Coral Reefs, #1830a	8.00
CP131	Organized Labor, #1831	5.00
CP132	Edith Wharton, #1832	5.00
CP133	Education, #1833	5.00
CP134	Indian Masks, #1837a	12.50
CP135	Architecture, #1841a	7.00
CP136	Christmas Window, #1842	9.00
CP137	Christmas Toys, #1843	9.00

1981

CP138	Dirksen, #1874	6.00
CP139	Young, #1875	8.00
CP140	Flowers, #1879a	9.00
CP141	Red Cross, #1910	7.00
CP142	Savings and Loan, #1911	7.00
CP143	Space Achievements, #1919a	12.00
CP144	Management, #1920	5.00
CP145	Wildlife, #1924a	9.50
CP146	Disabled, #1925	5.00
CP147	Millay, #1926	5.00
CP148	Architecture, #1931a	7.00
CP149	Zaharias, Jones, #1932, 1933	31.50
CP150	Remington, #1934	9.50
CP151	18c, 20c Hoban, #1935, 1936	5.00
CP152	Yorktown, Va. Capes, #1938a	5.00
CP153	Madonna and Child, #1939	7.00
CP154	Teddy Bear, #1940	8.00
CP155	John Hanson, #1941	5.00
CP156	Desert Plants, #1945a	9.50

1982

CP157	FDR, #1950	9.50
CP158	Love, #1951	10.00
CP159	Washington, #1952	11.00
CP160	Birds and Flowers, block of 4 from #1953-2002	31.50
CP161	US-Netherlands, #2003	12.00
CP162	Library of Congress, #2004	10.00
CP163	Knoxville World's Fair, #2009a	9.50
CP164	Horatio Alger, #2010	10.00
CP165	Aging, #2011	10.00
CP166	Barrymores, #2012	11.50
CP167	Dr. Mary Walker, #2013	9.50
CP168	Peace Garden, #2014	10.00
CP169	Libraries, #2015	8.00
CP170	Jackie Robinson, #2016	31.50
CP171	Touro Synagogue, #2017	9.50
CP172	Wolf Trap Farm, #2018	11.25
CP173	Architecture, #2022a	10.00
CP174	Francis of Assisi, #2023	10.00
CP175	Ponce de Leon, #2024	10.00
CP176	Puppy, Kitten, #2025	15.00
CP177	Madonna and Child, #2026	14.00
CP178	Children Playing, #2030a	14.00

1983

CP179	Science, #2031	5.00
CP180	Ballooning, #2035a	7.00
CP181	US-Sweden, #2036	5.00
CP182	CCC, #2037	5.00
CP183	Priestley, #2038	5.00
CP184	Voluntarism, #2039	14.00
CP185	German Immigration, #2040	5.00
CP186	Brooklyn Bridge, #2041	9.00
CP187	TVA, #2042	5.00
CP188	Fitness, #2043	5.00
CP189	Scott Joplin, #2044	5.00
CP190	Medal of Honor, #2045	9.50
CP191	Babe Ruth, #2046	24.00
CP192	Hawthorne, #2047	5.00
CP193	13c Olympics, #2051a	6.50

CP194	28c Olympics, #C104a	6.50
CP195	40c Olympics, #C108a	7.00
CP196	35c Olympics, #C112a	8.00
CP197	Treaty of Paris, #2052	6.00
CP198	Civil Service, #2053	6.00
CP199	Metropolitan Opera, #2054	9.50
CP200	Inventors, #2058a	7.00
CP201	Streetcars, #2062a	9.00
CP202	Madonna and Child, #2063	9.50
CP203	Santa Claus, #2064	9.50
CP204	Martin Luther, #2065	7.00

1984

CP205	Alaska, #2066	5.00
CP206	Winter Olympics, #2070a	6.50
CP207	FDIC, #2071	5.00
CP208	Love, #2072	5.00
CP209	Woodson, #2073	6.25
CP210	Conservation, #2074	5.00
CP211	Credit Union, #2075	5.00
CP212	Orchids, #2079a	7.00
CP213	Hawaii, #2080	7.00
CP214	National Archives, #2081	5.00
CP215	Olympics, #2085a	7.00
CP216	World Expo, #2086	5.00
CP217	Health Research, #2087	5.00
CP218	Fairbanks, #2088	7.00
CP219	Thorpe, #2089	7.00
CP220	McCormack, #2090	7.00
CP221	St. Lawrence Seaway, #2091	7.00
CP222	Waterfowl, #2092	10.00
CP223	Roanoke Voyages, #2093	5.00
CP224	Melville, #2094	6.50
CP225	Horace Moses, #2095	5.00
CP226	Smokey Bear, #2096	22.50
CP227	Roberto Clemente, #2097	30.50
CP228	Dogs, #2101a	9.50
CP229	Crime Prevention, #2102	5.00
CP230	Hispanic Americans, #2103	5.00
CP231	Family Unity, #2104	5.00
CP232	Eleanor Roosevelt, #2105	11.25
CP233	Readers, #2106	4.75
CP234	Madonna and Child, #2107	6.00
CP235	Child's Santa, #2108	6.00
CP236	Vietnam Memorial, #2109	11.25

1985

CP237	Jerome Kern, #2110	7.00
CP238	Bethune, #2137	7.00
CP239	Duck Decoys, #2141a	16.00
CP240	Winter Special Olympics, #2142	5.00
CP241	Love, #2143	5.00
CP242	REA, #2144	5.00
CP243	AMERIPEX '86, #2145	5.00
CP244	Abigail Adams, #2146	5.00
CP245	Bartholdi, #2147	9.50
CP246	Korean Veterans, #2152	9.50
CP247	Social Security, #2153	4.75
CP248	World War I Veterans, #2154	6.00
CP249	Horses, #2158a	13.00
CP250	Education, #2159	4.75
CP251	Youth Year, #2163a	11.50
CP252	Hunger, #2164	4.75
CP253	Madonna and Child, #2165	7.00
CP254	Poinsettias, #2166	7.00

1986

CP255	Arkansas, #2167	4.75
CP256	Stamp Collecting booklet pane, #2201a	7.00
CP257	Love, #2202	9.50
CP258	Sojourner Truth, #2203	9.50
CP259	Texas Republic, #2204	7.00
CP260	Fish booklet pane, #2209a	9.50
CP261	Hospitals, #2210	4.75
CP262	Duke Ellington, #2211	10.00
CP263	Presidents Souvenir Sheet No. 1, #2216	7.00
CP264	Presidents Souvenir Sheet No. 2, #2217	7.00
CP265	Presidents Souvenir Sheet No. 3, #2218	7.00
CP266	Presidents Souvenir Sheet No. 4, #2219	7.00
CP267	Arctic Explorers, #2223a	9.00
CP268	Statue of Liberty, #2224	9.50
CP269	Navajo Art, #2238a	11.00
CP270	T.S. Eliot, #2239	6.50
CP271	Woodcarved Figurines, #2243a	9.50
CP272	Madonna and Child, #2244	7.00
CP273	Village Scene, #2245	7.00

1987

CP274	Michigan, #2246	7.00
CP275	Pan American Games, #2247	4.75
CP276	Love, #2248	7.00
CP277	du Sable, #2249	7.00
CP278	Caruso, #2250	9.50
CP279	Girl Scouts, #2251	11.00
CP280	Special Occasions booklet pane, #2274a	6.50
CP281	United Way, #2275	4.75
CP282	Wildlife, #2286, 2287, 2296, 2297, 2306, 2307, 2316, 2317, 2326, 2327	9.50
CP283	Wildlife, #2288, 2289, 2298, 2299, 2308, 2309, 2318, 2319, 2328, 2329	9.50
CP284	Wildlife, #2290, 2291, 2300, 2301, 2310, 2311, 2320, 2321, 2330, 2331	9.50
CP285	Wildlife, #2292, 2293, 2302, 2303, 2312, 2313, 2322, 2323, 2332, 2333	9.50
CP286	Wildlife, #2294, 2295, 2304, 2305, 2314, 2315, 2324, 2325, 2334, 2335	9.50

1987-90

CP287	Delaware, #2336	9.50
CP288	Pennsylvania, #2337	6.50
CP289	New Jersey, #2338	6.50
CP290	Georgia, #2339	6.50
CP291	Connecticut, #2340	6.50
CP292	Massachusetts, #2341	6.50
CP293	Maryland, #2342	6.50
CP294	South Carolina, #2343	6.50
CP295	New Hampshire, #2344	6.50
CP296	Virginia, #2345	6.50
CP297	New York, #2346	6.50
CP298	North Carolina, #2347	6.50
CP299	Rhode Island, #2348	6.50

1987

CP300	U.S.-Morocco, #2349	5.00
CP301	William Faulkner, #2350	5.00
CP302	Lacemaking, #2354a	9.50
CP303	Drafting of the Constitution booklet pane, #2359a	6.50
CP304	Signing of the Constitution, #2360	7.00
CP305	Certified Public Accounting, #2361	38.00
CP306	Locomotives booklet pane, #2366a	9.00
CP307	Madonna and Child, #2367	6.00
CP308	Christmas Ornaments, #2368	5.00

1988

CP309	Winter Olympics, #2369	6.50
CP310	Australia Bicentennial, #2370	9.50
CP311	James Weldon Johnson, #2371	6.50
CP312	Cats, #2375a	9.50
CP313	Knute Rockne, #2376	13.50
CP314	New Sweden, #C117	6.50
CP315	Francis Ouimet, #2377	20.00
CP316	25c, 45c Love, #2378 and #2379	6.50
CP317	Summer Olympics, #2380	6.50
CP318	Classic Automobiles booklet pane, #2385a	9.50
CP319	Antarctic Explorers, #2389a	7.00
CP320	Carousel Animals, #2393a	9.00
CP321	Special Occasions booklet singles, #2395-2398	7.00
CP322	Madonna and Child, Sleigh, #2399, 2400	7.00

1989

CP323	Montana, #2401	6.50
CP324	A. Philip Randolph, #2402	8.00
CP325	North Dakota, #2403	6.50
CP326	Washington Statehood, #2404	6.50
CP327	Steamboats booklet pane, #2409a	9.50
CP328	World Stamp Expo, #2410	5.00
CP329	Arturo Toscanini, #2411	8.00

1989-90

CP330	House of Representatives, #2412	8.00
CP331	Senate, #2413	8.00
CP332	Executive Branch, #2414	8.00
CP333	Supreme Court, #2415	8.00

1989

CP334	South Dakota, #2416	6.50
CP335	Lou Gehrig, #2417	30.00
CP336	French Revolution, #C120	7.00
CP337	Ernest Hemingway, #2418	11.50
CP338	Letter Carriers, #2420	7.00
CP339	Bill of Rights, #2421	7.00
CP340	Dinosaurs, #2425a	15.00
CP341	Pre-Columbian Artifacts, #2426, C121	7.00
CP342	Madonna, Sleigh with Presents, #2427, 2428	8.00
CP343	Traditional Mail Delivery, #2437a	6.50
CP344	Futuristic Mail Delivery, #C125a	9.50

1990

CP345	Idaho, #2439	6.50
CP346	Love, #2440	6.50
CP347	Ida B. Wells, #2442	10.00
CP348	Wyoming, #2444	6.50
CP349	Classic Films, #2448a	16.00
CP350	Marianne Moore, #2449	5.00
CP351	Lighthouses booklet pane, #2474a	16.00
CP352	Olympians, #2500a	11.50
CP353	Indian Headdresses booklet pane, #2505c	10.00
CP354	Micronesia, Marshall Islands, #2507a	6.50
CP355	Sea Creatures, #2511a	14.00
CP356	Grand Canyon & Tropical Coastline, #2512, C127	8.00
CP357	Eisenhower, #2513	8.00
CP358	Madonna and Child, Christmas Tree, #2514-2515	8.00

1991

CP359	Switzerland, #2532	9.50
CP360	Vermont Statehood, #2533	6.50
CP361	Savings Bonds, #2534	5.50
CP362	Love, #2535-2536	8.00
CP363	William Saroyan, #2538	14.00
CP364	Fishing Flies, #2549a	14.00
CP365	Cole Porter, #2550	7.00
CP366	Antarctic Treaty, C130	6.50
CP367	Operations Desert Shield & Desert Storm, #2551	30.00
CP368	Summer Olympics, #2557a	8.00
CP369	Numismatics, #2558	7.00
CP370	World War II, #2559	11.00
CP371	Basketball, #2560	16.00
CP372	District of Columbia, #2561	7.00
CP373	Comedians, #2566c	12.00
CP374	Jan E. Matzeliger, #2567	8.00
CP375	Space Exploration, #2577a	12.00
CP376	Bering Land Bridge, #C131	7.00
CP377	Madonna and Child, Santa in Chimney, #2578-2579	10.00

1992

CP378	Winter Olympics, #2615a	7.00
CP379	World Columbian Stamp Expo '92, #2616	8.00
CP380	W.E.B. DuBois, #2617	12.00
CP381	Love, #2618	7.00
CP382	Olympic Baseball, #2619	30.00
CP383	Voyages of Columbus, #2623a	8.00
CP384	Columbus, #2624-2625	50.00
CP385	Columbus, #2626, 2629	50.00
CP386	Columbus, #2627-2628	50.00
CP387	New York Stock Exchange, #2630	11.50
CP388	Space Accomplishments, #2634a	11.50
CP389	Alaska Highway, #2635	6.50
CP390	Kentucky Statehood, #2636	6.50
CP391	Summer Olympics, #2641a	8.00
CP392	Hummingbirds, #2646a	11.50
CP393	World War II, #2697	12.00
CP394	Wildflowers, #2647, 2648, 2657, 2658, 2667, 2668, 2677, 2678, 2687, 2688	30.00
CP395	Wildflowers, #2649, 2650, 2659, 2660, 2669, 2670, 2679, 2680, 2689, 2690	30.00
CP396	Wildflowers, #2651, 2652, 2661, 2662, 2671, 2672, 2681, 2682, 2691, 2692	30.00
CP397	Wildflowers, #2653, 2654, 2663, 2664, 2673, 2674, 2683, 2684, 2693, 2694	30.00
CP398	Wildflowers, #2655, 2656, 2665, 2666, 2675, 2676, 2685, 2686, 2695, 2696	30.00
CP399	Dorothy Parker, #2698	6.50
CP400	Dr. Theodore von Karman, #2699	11.25
CP401	Minerals, #2703a	13.00
CP402	Juan Rodriguez Cabrillo, #2704	8.00
CP403	Wild Animals, #2709a	11.25
CP404	Madonna and Child, wheeled toys, #2710, 2714a	11.25
CP405	Chinese New Year, #2720	22.50

1993

CP406	Elvis Presley, #2721	24.00
CP407	Space Fantasy, #2745a	14.00
CP408	Percy Lavon Julian, #2746	12.00
CP409	Oregon Trail, #2747	8.00
CP410	World University Games, #2748	8.00
CP411	Grace Kelly, #2749	22.00
CP412	Oklahoma!, #2722	8.00
CP413	Circus, #2753a	10.00
CP414	Cherokee Strip, #2754	8.00
CP415	Dean Acheson, #2755	11.25
CP416	Sports horses, #2759a	11.50
CP417	Garden flowers, #2764a	9.50
CP418	World War II, #2765	12.00
CP419	Hank Williams, #2723	21.00
CP420	Rock & Roll/Rhythm & Blues, #2737b	22.00
CP421	Joe Louis, #2766	27.50
CP422	Broadway Musicals, #2770a	11.25
CP423	National Postal Museum, #2782a	10.00
CP424	American Sign Language, #2784a	9.00
CP425	Country & Western Music, #2778a	21.00
CP426	Christmas, #2789, 2794a	11.25
CP427	Youth Classics, #2788a	11.25
CP428	Mariana Islands, #2804	9.00
CP429	Columbus' Landing in Puerto Rico, #2805	10.00
CP430	AIDS Awareness, #2806	11.00

Starting with No. CP431, panels are shrink wrapped in plastic with cardboard backing. Shrink wrapping is not suitable for philatelic storage, as the plastic will shrink, bending the panels. Values from 1994 on are for panels without the plastic wrapping.

1994

CP431	Winter Olympics, #2807-2811	14.00
CP432	Edward R. Murrow, #2812	9.50
CP434	Love, #2814	11.25
CP436	Dr. Allison Davis, #2816	11.25
CP437	Chinese New Year, #2817	14.00
CP438	Buffalo Soldiers, #2818	12.00
CP439	Silent Screen Stars, #2828a	14.00
CP440	Garden Flowers, #2829-2833	10.00
CP441	World Cup Soccer, #2837	11.50
CP442	World War II, #2838	12.00
CP443	Norman Rockwell, #2839	18.00
CP444	Moon Landing, #2841	20.00
CP445	Locomotives, #2843-2847	12.00
CP446	George Meany, #2848	6.50
CP447	Popular Singers, #2853a	12.00
CP448	Jazz/Blues Singers, block of 10, 2854-2861	16.00

Block of 10 on No. CP448 may contain different combination of stamps.

CP449	James Thurber, #2862	7.00
CP450	Wonders of the Sea, #2866a	12.00
CP451	Cranes, block of 2 #2868a	12.00
CP453	Christmas Madonna and Child, #2871	7.00
CP454	Christmas stocking, #2872	7.00
CP455	Chinese New Year, #2876	12.00

1995

CP456	Florida Statehood, #2950	10.00
CP457	Earth Day, #2954a	10.00
CP458	Richard M. Nixon, #2955	15.00
CP459	Bessie Coleman, #2956	13.00

CP460	Love, #2957-2958	13.00
CP461	Recreational Sports, #2965a	13.00
CP462	Prisoners of War/Missing in Action, #2966	12.00
CP463	Marilyn Monroe, #2967	24.00
CP464	Texas Statehood, #2968	12.00
CP465	Great Lakes Lighthouses, #2973a	13.00
CP466	United Nations, #2974	10.00
CP467	Carousel Horses, #2979a	15.00
CP468	Woman Suffrage, #2980	9.50
CP469	World War II, #2981	14.00
CP470	Louis Armstrong, #2982	16.00
CP471	Jazz Musicians, #2992a	15.00
CP472	Garden Flowers, #2993-2997	9.00
CP473	Republic of Palau, #2999	9.50
CP474	Naval Academy, #3001	11.00
CP475	Tennessee Williams, #3002	11.50
CP476	Christmas, Madonna and Child, #3003	12.00
CP477	Santa Claus, Children with toys, #3007a	12.00
CP478	James K. Polk, #2587	9.50
CP479	Antique Automobiles, 3023a	16.00

1996

CP480	Utah Statehood, #3024	10.00
CP481	Garden Flowers, #3029a	10.00
CP482	Ernest E. Just, #3058	13.00
CP483	Smithsonian Institution, #3059	9.00
CP484	Chinese New Year, #3060	16.00
CP485	Pioneers of Communication, #3064a	12.00
CP486	Fulbright Scholarships, #3065	9.50
CP487	Summer Olympic Games, #3068, 2 pages	31.50

Beginning with No. CP487, some items contain two pages. One has text and engraved illustrations, the second has the stamp(s).

CP488	Marathon, #3067	12.00
CP489	Georgia O'Keeffe, #3069	9.50
CP490	Tennessee Statehood, #3070	9.50
CP491	Indian Dances, #3076a	15.00
CP492	Prehistoric Animals, #3080a	15.00
CP493	Breast Cancer Awareness, #3081	9.50
CP494	James Dean, #3082	15.00
CP495	Folk Heroes, #3086a	14.00
CP496	Olympic Games, Cent., #3087	11.00
CP497	Iowa Statehood, #3088	9.50
CP498	Rural Free Delivery, #3090	9.50
CP499	Riverboats, #3095a	15.00
CP500	Big Band Leaders, #3099a	14.00
CP501	Songwriters, #3103a	14.00
CP502	F. Scott Fitzgerald, #3104	14.00
CP503	Endangered Species, #3105, 2 pages	24.00
CP504	Computer Technology, #3106	14.00
CP505	Madonna & Child, #3107	13.00
CP506	Family Scenes, #3111a	13.00
CP507	Hanukkah, #3118	12.00
CP507A	Cycling, #3119	30.00

1997

CP508	Chinese New Year, #3120	18.00
CP509	Benjamin O. Davis, Sr., #3121	14.00
CP510	Love Swans, #3123-3124	11.50
CP511	Helping Children Learn, #3125	9.50
CP512	PACIFIC 97 Stagecoach & Ship, #3131a	14.00
CP513	Thornton Wilder, #3134	12.00
CP514	Raoul Wallenberg, #3135	11.25
CP515	Dinosaurs, #3136	22.50
CP516	Bugs Bunny, #3137c	18.00
CP517	PACIFIC 97 Franklin, #3139	38.00
CP518	PACIFIC 97 Washington, #3140	38.00
CP519	Marshall Plan, #3141	11.50
CP520	Classic American Aircraft, #3142, 2 pages	22.50
CP521	Football Coaches, #3146a	18.00
CP522	American Dolls, #3151	40.00
CP523	Humphrey Bogart, #3152	13.00
CP524	"The Stars & Stripes Forever!," #3153	11.25
CP525	Opera Singers, #3157a	12.00
CP526	Composers & Conductors, #3165a	14.00
CP527	Padre Felix Varela, #3166	10.00
CP528	Department of the Air Force, #3167	14.00
CP529	Movie Monsters, #3172a	14.00
CP530	Supersonic Flight, #3173	15.00
CP531	Women in Military Service, #3174	12.00
CP532	Kwanzaa, #3175	10.00
CP533	Madonna & Child, #3176a	14.00
CP534	Holly, #3177a	14.00

1998

CP535	Chinese New Year, #3179	12.00
CP536	Alpine Skiing, #3180	11.25
CP537	Madam C.J. Walker, #3181	12.00

Celebrate the Century

1998-2000

CP537A	1900s, #3182, 2 pages	20.00
CP537B	1910s, #3183, 2 pages	20.00
CP537C	1920s, #3184, 2 pages	18.00
CP537D	1930s, #3185, 2 pages	20.00
CP537E	1940s, #3186, 2 pages	24.00
CP537F	1950s, #3187, 2 pages	17.00
CP537G	1960s, #3188, 2 pages	21.00
CP537H	1970s, #3189, 2 pages	18.00
CP537I	1980s, #3190, 2 pages	17.00
CP537J	1990s, #3191, 2 pages	16.00

1998

CP538	Remember the Maine,inscribed "Key West, Florida" #3192	10.00
a.	Inscribed "Scottsdale, Arizona."	16.00
CP539	Flowering Trees, #3197a	12.00
CP540	Alexander Calder, #3202a	11.50
CP541	Cinco de Mayo, #3203	10.00
CP542	Sylvester & Tweety, #3204c	16.00
CP543	Wisconsin Statehood, #3206	11.25
CP544	Trans-Mississippi, #3209-3210, 2 pages	20.00
CP545	Berlin Airlift, #3211	10.00
CP546	Folk Musicians, #3215a	14.00
CP547	Gospel Singers, #3219a	14.00
CP548	Spanish Settlement, #3220	10.00
CP549	Stephen Vincent Benét, #3221	10.00
CP550	Tropical Birds, #3225a	13.00
CP551	Alfred Hitchcock, #3226	13.00
CP552	Organ & Tissue Donation, #3227	12.00
CP553	Bright Eyes, #3234a	12.00
CP554	Klondike Gold Rush, #3235	10.00
CP555	American Art, #3236	21.00
CP556	American Ballet, #3237	13.00
CP557	Space Discovery, #3242a	14.00
CP558	Giving & Sharing, #3243	10.00
CP559	Madonna & Child, #3244a	14.00
CP560	Wreaths, #3252b	11.25
CP561	Breast Cancer Awareness, #B1	17.00

1999

CP562	Chinese New Year, #3272	12.00
CP563	Malcolm X, #3273	11.25
CP564	Love, #3274a	14.00
CP565	Love, #3275	10.00
CP566	Hospice Care, #3276	10.00
CP567	Irish Immigration, #3286	12.00
CP568	Lunt & Fontanne, #3287	9.50
CP569	Arctic Animals, #3292a	10.00
CP570	Sonoran Desert, #3293, 2 pages	14.00
CP571	Daffy Duck, #3306c	15.00
CP572	Ayn Rand, #3308	18.00
CP573	Cinco de Mayo, #3309	9.50
CP574	John & William Bartram, #3314	10.00
CP575	Prostate Cancer, #3315	10.00
CP576	California Gold Rush, #3316	10.00
CP577	Aquarium Fish, #3320a	10.00
CP578	Extreme Sports, #3324a	10.00
CP579	American Glass, #3328a	10.00
CP580	James Cagney, #3329	10.00
CP581	Honoring Those who Served, #3331	10.00
CP582	Famous Trains, #3337a	13.00
CP583	Frederick Law Olmsted, #3338	10.00
CP584	Hollywood Composers, #3344a	12.00
CP585	Broadway Songwriters, #3350a	12.00
CP586	Insects & Spiders, #3351, 2 pages	18.00
CP587	Hanukkah, #3352	10.00
CP588	NATO, #3354	10.00
CP589	Madonna & Child, #3355	10.00
CP590	Deer, #3359a	10.00
CP591	Kwanzaa, #3368	10.00
CP592	Year 2000, #3369	14.00

2000

CP593	Chinese New Year, #3370	10.00
CP594	Patricia Roberts Harris, #3371	13.00
CP595	Los Angeles Class Submarine, #3372	14.00
CP596	Pacific Coast Rain Forest, #3378, 2 pages	18.00
CP597	Louise Nevelson, #3383a	11.25
CP598	Hubble Space Telescope Images, #3388a	14.00
CP599	American Samoa, #3389	10.00
CP600	Library of Congress, #3390	10.00
CP601	Road Runner & Wile E. Coyote, #3391c	12.00
CP602	Distinguished Soldiers, #3396a	13.00
CP603	Summer Sports, #3397	10.00
CP604	Adoption, #3398	12.00
CP605	Youth Team Sports, #3402a	12.00
CP606	The Stars and Stripes, #3403, 2 pages	21.00
CP607	Legends of Baseball, #3408, 2 pages	24.00
CP608	Stampin' the Future, #3417a	12.00
CP609	California Statehood, #3438	10.00
CP610	Deep Sea Creatures, #3443a	13.00
CP611	Thomas Wolfe, #3444	10.00
CP612	White House, #3445	11.25
CP613	Edward G. Robinson, #3446	8.00

2001

CP614	Non-denominated Love Letters, #3496	12.00
CP615	34c Love, #3497	12.00
CP615A	55c Love, #3499	13.00
CP616	Chinese New Year, #3500	14.00
CP617	Roy Wilkins, #3501	17.00
CP618	Nine-Mile Prairie, #C136	12.00
CP618A	American Illustrators, #3502, 2 pages	22.50
CP619	Diabetes Awareness, #3503	11.25
CP620	Nobel Prize, #3504	14.00
CP621	Pan-American Inverts, #3505, 2 pages	24.00
CP622	Mt. McKinley, #C137	13.00
CP623	Great Plains Prairie, #3506, 2 pages	22.50
CP624	Peanuts Comic Strip, #3507	17.00
CP625	Honoring Veterans, #3508	12.00
CP626	Frida Kahlo, #3509	14.00
CP627	Legendary Playing Fields, #3510-3519	27.50

No. CP627 consists of 2 pages. One has text and engraved illustrations. The other consists of the pane of stamps.

CP628	Leonard Bernstein, #3521	14.00
CP629	Lucille Ball, #3523	14.00
CP630	Amish Quilts, #3527a	14.00
CP631	Carnivorous Plants, #3531a	13.00
CP632	Eid, #3532	10.00
CP633	Enrico Fermi, #3533	11.25
CP634	That's All Folks!, #3535c	14.00
CP635	Madonna & Child, #3536	10.00
CP636	Santas, #3540b	11.25
CP637	James Madison, #3545	12.00
CP638	Thanksgiving, #3546	12.00
CP639	Hanukkah, #3547	10.00
CP640	Kwanzaa, #3548	10.00
CP641	57c Love, #3551	12.00

2002

CP642	Winter Olympics, #3555a	12.00
CP643	Mentoring a Child, #3556	12.00
CP644	Langston Hughes, #3557	12.00
CP645	Happy Birthday, #3558	12.00
CP646	Chinese New Year, #3559	16.00
CP647	U.S. Military Academy Bicentennial, #3560	14.00
CP648	Greetings from America, #3610a	34.00
CP649	Longleaf Pine Forest, #3611	26.00

Nos. CP648 and CP649 each consist of 2 pages. One has text and engraved illustrations. The other contains the pane of stamps.

CP650	Heroes of 2001, #B2	16.00
CP651	Masters of American Photography, #3649	30.00

No. CP651 consists of 2 pages. One has text and engraved illustrations. The other consists of the pane of stamps.

CP652	John James Audubon, #3650	13.50
CP653	Harry Houdini, #3651	13.50
CP654	Andy Warhol, #3652	13.50
CP655	Teddy Bears, #3653-3656	11.00
CP656	37c Love, #3657	10.00
CP657	60c Love, #3658	12.00
CP658	Ogden Nash, #3659	12.00
CP659	Duke Kahanamoku, #3660	17.00
CP660	American Bats, #3664a	17.00
CP661	Women in Journalism, #3668a	14.00
CP662	Irving Berlin, #3669	12.00
CP663	Neuter or Spay, #3671a	12.00
CP664	Hanukkah, #3672	11.25
CP665	Kwanzaa, #3673	11.25
CP666	Eid, #3674	10.00
CP667	Madonna & Child, #3675	12.00
CP668	Christmas Snowmen, #3679a	11.00
CP669	Cary Grant, #3692	13.00
CP670	Hawaiian Missionary Stamps, #3694	26.00

No. CP670 consists of 2 pages. One has text and engraved illustrations. The other contains the pane of stamps.

CP671	Happy Birthday, #3695	10.00
CP672	Greetings from America, #3745a	31.50

No. CP672 consists of 2 pages. One has text and engraved illustrations. The other contains the pane of stamps.

2003

CP673	Thurgood Marshall, #3746	12.00
CP674	Chinese New Year, #3747	13.00
CP675	Zora Neale Hurston, #3748	14.00
CP676	Special Olympics, #3771	13.00
CP677	American Filmmaking: Behind the Scenes, #3772	30.00

No. CP677 consists of 2 pages. One has text and engraved illustrations. The other contains the pane of stamps.

CP678	Ohio Statehood, Bicent., #3773	13.00
CP679	Pelican Island National Wildlife Refuge, #3774	14.00
CP680	Old Glory, #3780b	15.00
CP681	Cesar E. Chavez, #3781	12.00
CP682	Louisiana Purchase, #3782	13.00
CP683	First Flight of Wright Brothers, #3783b	14.00
CP684	Audrey Hepburn, #3786	15.00
CP685	Southeastern Lighthouses, #3791a	14.00
CP686	Arctic Tundra, #3802	26.00
CP687	Korean War Veterans Memorial, #3803	13.00
CP688	Mary Cassatt Paintings, #3807a	13.00
CP689	Early Football Heroes, #3811a	17.00
CP690	Roy Acuff, #3812	13.00
CP691	District of Columbia, #3813	13.00
CP692	Reptiles and Amphibians, #3818a	17.00
CP693	Stop Family Violence, #B3	13.00
CP694	Madonna and Child, #3820	13.00
CP695	Christmas Holiday Music Makers, #3824a	13.00

2004

CP696	Pacific Coral Reef, #3831	26.00

No. CP696 consists of 2 pages. One has text and engraved illustrations. The other contains the pane of stamps.

CP697	Chinese New Year, #3832	13.00
CP698	Love, #3833	13.00
CP699	Paul Robeson, #3834	13.00
CP700	Theodor Seuss Geisel (Dr. Seuss), #3835	17.00
CP701	Love (White Lilacs and Pink Roses), #3836	12.00
CP702	Love (Five Varieties of Pink Roses), #3837	12.00
CP703	U.S. Air Force Academy, #3838	13.00
CP704	Henry Mancini, #3839	13.00
CP705	American Choreographers, #3843a	14.00
CP706	Lewis and Clark, #3854	16.00
CP707	Lewis and Clark booklet pane, #3856b	16.00
CP708	Isamu Noguchi, #3861a	12.00
CP709	National World War II Memorial, #3862	14.00
CP710	Summer Olympics, Athens, Greece, #3863	13.00
CP711	Art of Disney, #3868a	16.00

CP712	USS Constellation, #3869	14.00
CP713	R. Buckminster Fuller, #3870	12.00
CP714	James Baldwin, #3871	11.25
CP715	Martin Johnson Heade, #3872	11.25
CP716	Art of the American Indian, #3873	27.50

No. CP716 consists of 2 pages. One has text and engraved illustrations. The other contains the pane of stamps.

CP717	John Wayne, #3876	17.00
CP718	Sickle Cell Disease, #3877	12.00
CP719	Cloudscapes, #3878	26.00

No. CP719 consists of 2 pages. One has text and engraved illustrations. The other contains the pane of stamps.

CP720	Christmas Madonna, #3879	13.00
CP721	Hanukkah, #3880	10.00
CP722	Kwanzaa, #3881	10.00
CP723	Moss Hart, #3882	11.25
CP724	Christmas Ornaments, #3886a	12.00

2005

CP725	Chinese New Year, #3895	27.50

No. CP725 consists of two pages. One has text and engraved illustrations. The other contains the pane of stamps.

CP726	Marian Anderson, #3896	16.00
CP727	Ronald Reagan, #3897	18.00
CP728	Love, #3898	13.00
CP729	Northeast Deciduous Forest, #3899	26.00

No. CP729 consists of two pages. One has text and engraved illustrations. The other contains the pane of stamps.

CP730	Spring Flowers, #3903a	12.00
CP731	Robert Penn Warren, #3904	10.00
CP732	Yip Harburg, #3905	10.00
CP733	American Scientists, #3909a	11.25
CP734	Modern American Architecture, #3910	26.00

No. CP734 consists of two pages. One has text and engraved illustrations. The other contains the pane of stamps.

CP735	Henry Fonda, #3911	10.00
CP736	Disney Characters, #3915a	20.00
CP737	Advances in Aviation, #3916-3925	29.00

No. CP737 consists of two pages. One has text and illustrations. The other contains the pane of stamps.

CP738	Rio Grande Blankets, #3929a	10.00
CP739	Presidential Libraries, #3930	10.00
CP740	Sporty Cars of the 1950s, #3935b	20.00
CP741	Arthur Ashe, #3936	13.00
CP742	To Form a More Perfect Union, #3937	32.50

No. CP742 consists of two pages. One has text and illustrations. The other contains the pane of stamps.

CP743	Child Health, #3938	10.00
CP744	Let's Dance, #3942a	10.00
CP745	Greta Garbo, #3943	16.00
CP746	Jim Henson and the Muppets, #3944	27.50

No. CP746 consists of two pages. One has text and engraved illustrations. The other contains the pane of stamps.

CP747	Constellations, #3948a	20.00
CP748	Christmas, #3952a	10.00
CP749	Distinguished Marines, #3964a	18.00

2006

CP750	Love, #3976	9.50
CP751	Children's Book Animals, #3994a	20.00

No. CP751 consists of two pages. One has text and illustrations. The other contains the pane of stamps.

CP752	2006 Winter Olympics, #3995	10.00
CP753	Hattie McDaniel, #3996	11.25
CP754	Chinese New Year, #3997	20.00

No. CP754 consists of two pages. One has text and illustrations. The other contains the pane of stamps.

CP755	39c Wedding, #3998	10.00
CP756	63c Wedding, #3999	10.00
CP757	Sugar Ray Robinson, #4020	10.00
CP758	Benjamin Franklin, #4024a	10.00
CP759	Disney Characters, #4028a	10.00
CP760	Love Birds, #4029	10.00
CP761	Katherine Anne Porter, #4030	10.00
CP762	Amber Alert, #4031	10.00
CP763	Wonders of America, #4033-4072	31.50

No. CP763 consists of two pages. One has text and illustrations. The other contains the pane of stamps.

CP764	Samuel de Champlain, #4073	10.00
CP765	Washington 2006 World Philatelic Exhibition, #4075	12.00
CP766	Distinguished American Diplomats, #4076	10.00

No. CP766 consists of two pages. One has text and illustrations. The other contains the pane of stamps.

CP767	Judy Garland, #4077	10.00
CP768	Ronald Reagan, #4078	11.25
CP769	Happy Birthday, #4079	10.00
CP770	Baseball Sluggers, #4083a	11.25
CP771	DC Comics Superheroes, #4084	26.00

No. CP771 consists of two pages. One has text and engraved illustrations. The other contains the pane of stamps.

CP772	Motorcycles, #4088a	12.00
CP773	Quilts of Gee's Bend, Alabama, #4098b	11.25
CP774	Southern Florida Wetland, #4099	26.00

No. CP774 consists of two pages. One has text and engraved illustrations. The other contains the pane of stamps.

CP775	Christmas Madonna, #4100	9.50
CP776	Christmas Snowflakes, #4104a	9.50
CP777	Eid, #4117	9.50
CP778	Hanukkah, #4118	9.50
CP779	Kwanzaa, #4119	9.50
CP780	39c Ella Fitzgerald, #4120	9.50
CP781	39c Oklahoma Statehood, #4121	9.50
CP782	39c Love, #4122	9.50
CP783	84c International Polar Year, #4123	9.50
CP784	39c Henry Wadsworth Longfellow, #4124	9.50
CP785	41c Settlement of Jamestown, #4136	25.00

No. CP785 consists of two pages. One has text and illustrations. The other contains the pane of stamps.

CP786	Star Wars, #4143	25.00

No. CP786 consists of two pages. One has text and engraved illustrations. The other contains the pane of stamps.

CP787	Pacific Lighthouses, #4150a	10.00
CP788	41c Wedding Hearts, #4151	10.00
CP789	58c Wedding Hearts, #4152	10.00
CP790	Pollination, #4156d	13.50
CP791	Marvel Comics Super Heroes, #4159	25.00

No. CP791 consists of two pages. One has text and engraved illustrations. The other contains the pane of stamps.

CP792	Vintage Mahogany Speedboats, #4163a	10.00
CP793	Louis Comfort Tiffany, #4165	10.00
CP794	Disney Characters, #4195a	10.00
CP795	Celebrate, #4196	9.50
CP796	James Stewart, #4197	10.00
CP797	Alpine Tundra, #4198	25.00

No. CP796 consists of two pages. One has text and engraved illustrations. The other contains the pane of stamps.

CP798	Gerald R. Ford, #4199	9.50
CP799	Jury Duty, #4200	9.50
CP800	Mendez v. Westminster School District, #4201	9.50
CP801	Eid, #4202	9.50
CP802	Polar Lights, #4204a	10.00
CP803	Yoda, #4205	10.00
CP804	Christmas Madonna, #4206	10.00
CP805	Christmas Holiday Knits #4210a	10.00
CP806	Hanukkah, #4219	9.50
CP807	Kwanzaa, #4220	9.50

2008

CP808	Chinese New Year, #4221	10.00
CP809	Charles W. Chesnutt, #4222	10.00
CP810	Marjorie Kinnan Rawlings, #4223	10.00
a.	With corrected date on panel	10.00
CP811	41c American Scientists, #4227a	10.00
CP812	42c American Journalists, #4252a	10.00
CP813	42c Frank Sinatra, #4265	10.00
CP814	42c Minnesota Statehood, #4266	10.00
CP815	42c Love, #4270	10.00
CP816	42c Wedding Hearts, #4271-4272	10.00
CP817	Charles and Ray Eames, #4333	25.00

No. CP817 consists of two pages. One has text and engraved illustrations. The other contains the pane of stamps.

CP818	Olympic Games, #4334	10.00
CP819	Vintage Black Cinema, #4340a	10.00
CP820	Take Me Out to the Ball Game, #4341	10.00
CP821	Disney Characters - Imagination, #4345a	10.00
CP822	Albert Bierstadt, #4346	10.00
CP823	Latin Jazz, #4349	10.00
CP824	Bette Davis, #4350	10.00
CP825	Great Lakes Dunes, #4352	25.00

No. CP825 consists of two pages. One has text and engraved illustrations. The other contains the pane of stamps.

CP826	Automobiles of the 1950s, #4357a	10.00
CP827	Alzheimer's Disease Awareness, #4358	10.00
CP828	Christmas Madonna, #4359	10.00
CP829	Christmas Nutcrackers, #4363a	10.00

2009

CP830	Alaska Statehood, #4374	10.00
CP831	Chinese New Year, #4375	10.00
CP832	Oregon Statehood, #4376	10.00
CP833	Edgar Allan Poe, #4377	10.00
CP834	44c Abraham Lincoln, #4383a	10.00
CP835	44c Civil Rights Pioneers, #4384	25.00
CP836	44c Bob Hope, #4406	10.00
CP837	44c Anna Julia Cooper, #4408	10.00
CP838	44c Gulf Coast Lighthouses, #4413a	10.00
CP839	44c Early TV Memories, #4414	25.00
CP840	44c Hawaii Statehood, #4415	10.00
CP841	44c Thanksgiving Day Parade, #4420a	10.00
CP842	44c Gary Cooper, #4421	10.00
CP843	44c Supreme Court Justices, #4422	25.00
CP844	44c Kelp Forest, #4423	25.00

2010

CP845	44c Chinese New Year, #4435	10.00
CP846	44c 2010 Winter Olympics, Vancouver, #4436	10.00
CP847	44c Distinguished Sailors, #4443a	10.00
CP848	44c Abstract Expressionists, #4444	25.00
CP849	44c Bill Mauldin, #4445	10.00
CP850	44c Cowboys of the Silver Screen, #4449a	10.00
CP851	44c Animal Rescue, #4460a	10.00
CP852	44c Katharine Hepburn, #4461	10.00
CP853	44c Kate Smith, #4463	10.00
CP854	44c Oscar Micheaux, #4464	10.00
CP855	44c Negro Leagues Baseball, #4466a	10.00
CP856	44c Sunday Funnies, #4471a	10.00
CP857	44c Scouting, #4472	10.00
CP858	44c Winslow Homer, #4473	10.00
CP859	44c Hawaiian Rain Forest, #4474	25.00
CP860	44c Mother Teresa, #4475	10.00
CP861	44c Julia de Burgos, #4476	10.00

2011

CP862	(44c) Chinese New Year, #4492	11.00
CP863	(44c) Kansas Statehood, #4493	11.00
CP864	(44c) Ronald Reagan, #4494	11.00
CP865	(44c) Latin Music Legends, #4501a	11.00
CP866	(44c) Jazz, #4503	11.00
CP867	(44c) Civil War Battles of 1861, #4522-4523	27.00

No. CP867 consists of two pages. One has text and engraved illustrations. The other contains the pane of stamps.

CP868	(44c) Go Green, #4524	27.00

No. CP868 consists of two pages. One has text and engraved illustrations. The other contains the pane of stamps.

CP869	(44c) Helen Hayes, #4525	11.00
CP870	(44c) Gregory Peck, #4526	11.00
CP871	(44c) Mercury Project and Messenger Mission, #4527-4528	11.00
CP872	(44c) Indianapolis 500, #4530	11.00
CP873	(44c) American Scientists, #4544a	11.00
CP874	(44c) Mark Twain, #4545	11.00
CP875	(44c) Pioneers of American Industrial Design, #4546	27.00

No. CP875 consists of two pages. One has text and engraved illustrations. The other contains the pane of stamps.

CP876	(44c) Owney, the Postal Dog, #4547	11.00
CP877	(44c) U.S. Merchant Marine, #4551a	11.00
CP878	(44c) Disney-Pixar Films, Send a Hello, 4557a	11.00
CP879	(44c) Edward Hopper, #4558	11.00
CP880	(44c) Barbara Jordan, #4565	11.00
CP881	(44c) Romare Bearden, 4569a	11.00

2012

CP882	(44c) New Mexico Statehood, #4591	12.00
CP883	(45c) Chinese New Year, #4623	12.00
CP884	(45c) John H. Johnson, #4624	12.00
CP885	(45c) Heart Health, #4625	12.00
CP886	(45c) Arizona Statehood, #4627	12.00
CP887	(45c) Danny Thomas, #4628	12.00
CP888	(45c) Cherry Blossom Centennial, #4652a	12.00
CP889	(45c) William H. Johnson, #4653	12.00
CP890	(45c) Twentieth-Century Poets, #4663a	12.00
CP891	(45c) Civil War Battles of 1862, #4664-4665	27.00

No. CP891 consists of two panes. One has text and engraved illustrations. The other contains the pane of stamps.

CP892	(45c) José Ferrer, #4666	12.00
CP893	(45c) Louisiana Statehood, #4667	12.00
CP894	(45c) Great Film Directors, #4671a	12.00
CP896	(45c) Bicycling, #4690a	12.00
CP897	(45c) Girl Scouts of America, Cent., #4691	12.00
CP898	(45c) Edith Piaf and Miles Davis, #4693a	12.00
CP895	(45c) Mail a Smile, #4681a	12.00
CP899	(45c) Major League Baseball All-Stars, #4697a	12.00
CP900	(45c) Ted Williams, #4694	12.00
CP901	(45c) Larry Doby, #4695	12.00
CP902	(45c) Willie Stargell, #4696	12.00
CP903	(45c) Joe DiMaggio, #4697	12.00
CP904	(45c) Innovative Choreographers, #4701a	12.00
CP905	(45c) Edgar Rice Burroughs, #4702	12.00
CP906	(45c) USS Constitution, #4703	12.00
CP907	(45c) O. Henry, #4705	12.00
CP908	(45c) Earthscapes, #4710	27.00

No. CP908 consists of two panes. One has text and engraved illustrations. The other contains the pane of stamps.

CP909	(45c) Lady Bird Johnson, #4716	27.00

No. CP909 consists of two panes. One has text and engraved illustrations. The other contains the pane of stamps.

2013

CP910	(45c) Emancipation Proclamation, #4721	14.00
CP911	(45c) Chinese New Year, #4726	14.00
CP912	(46c) Rosa Parks, #4742	14.00
CP913	(46c) Muscle Cars, #4747a	14.00
CP914	(46c) Modern Art in America, #4748	29.00

No. CP914 consists of two pages. One has text and engraved illustrations. The other contains the pane of stamps.

CP915	(46c) La Florida, #4753a	14.00
CP916	(46c) Lydia Mendoza, #4786	14.00
CP917	(46c) Civil War Battles of 1863, #4787-4788	14.00

No. CP917 consists of two pages. One has text and engraved illustrations. The other contains the pane of stamps.

CP918	(46c) Johnny Cash, #4789	14.00
CP919	(46c) West Virginia Statehood, #4790	14.00
CP920	(46c) New England Coastal Lighthouses, #4795a	14.00
CP921	(46c) Building a Nation, #4801	29.00

No. CP921,consists of two pages. One has text and engraved illustrations. The other contains the pane of stamps.

CP922	(46c) Althea Gibson, #4803	14.00

CP923 (46c) March on Washington, 50th Anniv., #4804 14.00
CP924 (46c) Battle of Lake Erie, #4805 14.00
CP925 $2 Inverted Jenny sheet, #4806 29.00

No. CP925 consists of two pages. One has text and engraved illustrations. The other contains the pane of stamps.

CP926 (46c) Ray Charles, #4807 14.00
CP927 (46c) Medals of Honor, #4822-4823 29.00

No. CP927 consists of two pages. One has text and engraved illustrations. The other contains the pane of stamps.

CP928 (46c) Harry Potter, #4825-4844 29.00

No. CP928 consists of two pages. One has text and engraved illustrations. The other contains the pane of stamps.

2014

CP929 (46c) Chinese New Year, #4846 14.00
CP930 (49c) Shirley Chisholm, #4856 14.00
CP931 (49c) Charlton Heston, #4892 14.00
CP932 (49c) Vintage Circus Posters, #4905a 29.00

No. CP932 consists of two pages. One has text and engraved illustrations. The other contains the pane of stamps.

CP933 (49c) Harvey Milk, #4906 14.00
CP934 (49c) Nevada Statehood, #4907 14.00
CP935 (49c) Medal of Honor — Korean War, #4822a-4823a 29.00

No. CP935 consists of two pages. One has text and engraved illustrations. The other contains the pane of stamps.

CP936 (49c) Civil War Battles of 1864, #4911a 29.00

No. CP936 consists of two pages. One has text and engraved illustrations. The other contains the pane of stamps.

CP937 (49c) Farmers Markets, #4915a 14.00
CP938 (49c) Janis Joplin, #4916 14.00
CP939 (49c) Bombardment of Fort McHenry, #4921 14.00
CP940 (49c) Celebrity Chefs, #4926a 14.00
CP941 (49c) Batman, #4928-4935 29.00

No. CP941 consists of two pages. One has text and engraved illustrations. The other contains the pane of stamps.

CP942 (49c) Wilt Chamberlain, #4951a 14.00

2015

CP943 (49c) Battle of New Orleans, #4952 14.00
CP944 (49c) Chinese New Year, #4957 14.00
CP945 (49c) Robert Robinson Taylor, #4958 14.00
CP946 (49c) Martín Ramírez, #4972a 14.00
CP947 (49c) From Me to You, #4978 14.00
CP948 (49c) Maya Angelou, #4979 14.00
CP949 (49c) Civil War Events of 1865, #4981a 29.00

No. CP949 consists of two pages. One has text and engraved illustrations. The other contains the pane of stamps.

CP950 (49c) Gifts of Friendship, #4983a 14.00
CP951 (49c) Special Olympics World Games, #4986 14.00
CP952 (49c) Help Find Missing Children, #4987 14.00
CP953 (49c) Medal of Honor, #4988a 29.00

No. CP953 consists of two pages. One has text and engraved illustrations. The other contains the pane of stamps.

CP954 (49c) Coast Guard, #5008 14.00
CP955 (49c) Elvis Presley, #5009 14.00
CP956 (49c) World Stamp Show 2016, #5011a 14.00
CP957 (49c) Ingrid Bergman, #5012 14.00
CP958 (49c) Paul Newman, #5020 14.00

2016

CP959 (49c) Richard Allen, #5056 14.00
CP960 (49c) Chinese New Year, #5057 14.00
CP961 (49c) Sarah Vaughan, #5059 14.00
CP962 (47c) Shirley Temple, #5060 14.00
CP963 (47c) World Stamp Show 2016, #5062-5063 29.00

No. CP963 consists of two pages. One has text and engraved illustrations. The other contains the pane of stamps.

CP964 (47c) Repeal of the Stamp Act, #5064 29.00

No. CP964 consists of two pages. One has text and engraved illustrations. The other contains the pane of stamps.

CP965 (47c) Service Cross Medals, #5068a 14.00
CP966 (47c) Views of Our Planets, #5076a 14.00
CP967 (47c) Pluto Explored, #5078a 29.00

No. CP967 consists of two pages. One has text and engraved illustrations. The other contains the pane of stamps.

CP968 (47c) Classics Forever, #5079 29.00

No. CP968 consists of two pages. One has text and engraved illustrations. The other contains the pane of stamps.

CP969 (47c) National Parks Service, #5080 29.00

No. CP969 consists of two pages. One has text and engraved illustrations. The other contains the pane of stamps.

CP970 (47c) Indiana Statehood, #5091 14.00
CP971 (47c) Jaime Escalante, #5100 14.00
CP972 (47c) Star Trek, #5135a 14.00
CP973 (47c) Wonder Woman, #5152a 14.00

2017

CP974 (47c) Chinese New Year, #5154 16.00
CP975 (49c) Dorothy Height, #5171 16.00
CP976 (49c) Oscar de la Renta, #5173 32.00

No. CP976 consists of two pages. One has text and engraved illustrations. The other contains the pane of stamps.

CP977 (49c) Pres. John F. Kennedy, #5175 32.00

No. CP977 consists of two pages. One has text and engraved illustrations. The other contains the pane of stamps.

CP978 (49c) Nebraska Statehood, #5179 16.00
CP979 (49c) Mississippi Statehood, #5190 16.00
CP980 (49c) Henry David Thoreau, #5202 16.00
CP981 (49c) Sports Balls, #5210a 16.00
CP982 (49c) Total Eclipse of the Sun, #5211 16.00
CP983 (49c) Andrew Wyeth, #5212 32.00

No. CP983 consists of two pages. One has text and engraved illustrations. The other contains the pane of stamps.

CP984 (49c) Disney Villains, #5222a 32.00

No. CP984 consists of two pages. One has text and engraved illustrations. The other contains the pane of stamps.

CP985 (49c) Sharks, #5227a 16.00
CP986 (49c) Protect Pollinators, #5232a 16.00
CP987 (49c) Father Ted Hesburgh, #5241 16.00
CP988 (49c) National Museum of African American History and Culture, #5251 16.00
CP989 (49c) History of Ice Hockey, #5253b, and Canada #3039 32.00

No. CP989 consists of two pages. One has text and engraved illustrations. The other contains the pane of stamps.

2018

CP990 (49c) Chinese New Year, #5254 16.00
CP991 (50c) Lena Horne, #5259 16.00
CP992 (50c) Bioluminescent Life, #5273a 32.00

No. CP992 consists of two pages. One has text and engraved illustrations. The other contains the pane of stamps.

CP993 (50c) Illinois Statehood, #5274 16.00
CP994 (50c) Mister Rogers, #5275 16.00
CP995 (50c) STEM Education, #5279a 16.00
CP996 (50c) U.S. Air Mail Centenary (Blue), #5281 16.00
CP997 (50c) U.S. Air Mail Centenary (Carmine Lake), #5282 16.00
CP998 (50c) Sally Ride, #5283 16.00
CP999 (50c) Flag Act of 1818, Bicent., #5284 16.00
CP1000 (50c) O Beautiful, #5298 32.00

No. CP1000 consists of two pages. One has text and engraved illustrations. The other contains the pane of stamps.

CP1001 (50c) Scooby-Doo, #5299 16.00
CP1002 (50c) World War I, Cent., #5300 16.00
CP1003 (50c) The Art of Magic, #5305a 16.00
CP1004 (50c) Dragons, #5310a 16.00
CP1005 (50c) John Lennon, #5315a 16.00
CP1006 (50c) First Responders, #5316 16.00
CP1007 (50c) Hot Wheels Toy Cars, #5321-5330 32.00

No. CP1007 consists of two pages. One has text and engraved illustrations. The other contains the pane of stamps.

2019

CP1008 (50c) Chinese New Year, #5340 16.00
CP1009 (55c) Gregory Hines, #5349 16.00
CP1010 (55c) Alabama Statehood, #5360 16.00
CP1011 (55c) Marvin Gaye, #5371 16.00
CP1012 (55c) Post Office Murals, #5376a 16.00
CP1013 (55c) Maureen Connolly Brinker, #5377 16.00
CP1014 (55c) Transcontinental Railroad, #5380a 16.00
CP1015 (55c) Wild and Scenic Rivers, #5381 32.00

No. CP1015 consists of two pages. One has text and engraved illustrations. The other contains the pane of stamps.

CP1016 (55c) Art of Ellsworth Kelly, #5391a 16.00
CP1017 (55c) USS Missouri, #5392 16.00
CP1018 (55c) George H. W. Bush, #5393 16.00
CP1019 (55c) Sesame Street, 50th Anniv., #5394 32.00

No. CP1019 consists of two pages. One has text and engraved illustrations. The other contains the pane of stamps.

CP1020 (55c) First Moon Landing, 50th Anniv., #5400a 16.00
CP1021 (55c) State and County Fairs, #5404a 16.00
CP1022 (55c) Military Working Dogs, #5408a 22.00

No. CP1022 consists of two pages. One has text and engraved illustrations. The other contains the block of stamps.

CP1023 (55c) Woodstock Music Festival, 50th Anniv., #5409 16.00
CP1024 (55c) Tyrannosaurus Rex, #5413a 16.00

2020

CP1025 (55c) Chinese New Year, #5428 16.00
CP1026 (55c) Gwen Ifill, #5432 16.00
CP1027 (55c) Arnold Palmer, #5455 16.00
CP1028 (55c) Maine Statehood, #5456 16.00
CP1029 (55c) American Gardens, #5470a 16.00
CP1030 (55c) Voices of the Harlem Renaissance, #5474a 16.00
CP1031 (55c) Enjoy the Great Outdoors, #5479a 16.00
CP1032 (55c) Hip Hop, #5483a 16.00
CP1033 (55c) Bugs Bunny, #5494-5503 32.00

No. CP1033 consists of two pages. One has text and engraved illustrations. The other contains the pane of stamps.

CP1034 (55c) Ruth Asawa, #5504-5513 32.00

No. CP1034 consists of two pages. One has text and engraved illustrations. The other contains the pane of stamps.

CP1035 (55c) Innovation, #5518a 16.00
CP1036 (55c) Woman Suffrage Centenary, #5523 16.00
CP1037 (55c) Mayflower in Plymouth Harbor, #5524 16.00
CP1038 (55c) Drug Free USA, #5542 16.00

2021

CP1039 (55c) August Wilson, #5555 16.00
CP1040 (55c) Chinese New Year, #5556 16.00
CP1041 (55c) Chien-Shiung Wu, #5557 16.00
CP1042 (55c) Star Wars Droids, #5573-5582 32.00

No. CP1042 consists of two pages. One has text and engraved illustrations. The other contains the pane of stamps.

CP1043 (55c) Heritage Breeds, #5583-5592 32.00

No. CP1043 consists of two pages. One has text and engraved illustrations. The other contains the pane of stamps.

CP1044 (55c) Go For Broke, #5593 16.00
CP1045 (55c) Emilio Sanchez, #5597b 16.00
CP1046 (55c) Sun Science, #5607b 16.00
CP1047 (55c) Yogi Berra, #5608 16.00
CP1048 (55c) Tap Dance, #5613b 16.00
CP1049 (55c) Mystery Message, #5614 16.00
CP1050 (55c) Raven Story, #5620 16.00
CP1051 (55c) Mid-Atlantic Lighthouses, #5625b 16.00
CP1052 (55c) Missouri Statehood, #5626 16.00
CP1053 (55c) Backyard Games, #5634b 16.00
CP1054 (58c) Message Monsters, #5639b 16.00
CP1055 (58c) Day of the Dead, #5643b 16.00

2022

CP1056 (58c) Chinese New Year, #5662 18.00
CP1057 (58c) Edmonia Lewis, #5663 18.00
CP1058 (58c) Title IX, #5671b 18.00
CP1059 (58c) Shel Silverstein, #5683 18.00

SOUVENIR PAGES

These are post office new-issue announcement bulletins, including an illustration of the stamp's design and informative text. They bear an example of the stamp, tied by a first day of issue cancellation. Varieties of bulletin watermarks and text changes, etc., are beyond the scope of this catalogue.

Values for Scott Nos. SP1-SP295 are for folded examples. Values for Official Souvenir Pages (Nos. SP296 on) are for examples that never have been folded.

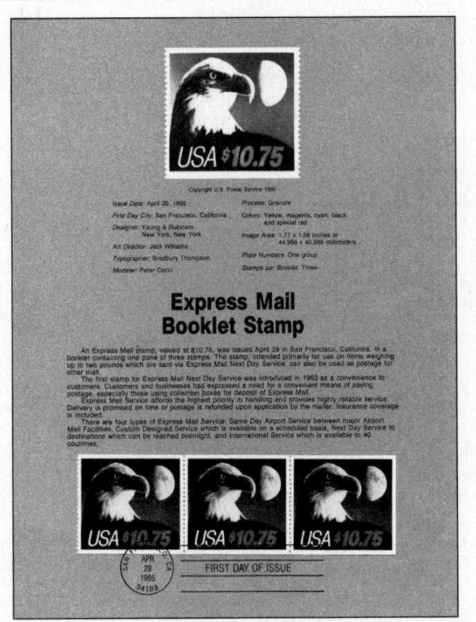

No. SP674a

UNOFFICIAL SOUVENIR PAGES

Liberty Issue

1960-65

SP1	1¼c	Palace of Governors, sheet, coil, #1031A, 1054A	50.00
SP2	8c	Pershing, #1214	30.00
SP3	11c	Statue of Liberty, #1044A	27.50
SP4	25c	Revere coil, #1059A	10.00

1959

SP5	4c	49 Star Flag, #1132	—
SP6	7c	Hawaii Statehood, #C55	—
SP7	4c	Soil Conservation, #1133	—
SP8	10c	Pan American Games, #C56	—
SP9	4c	Petroleum, #1134	—
SP10	4c	Dental Health, #1135	—
SP11	4c, 8c	Reuter, #1136, 1137	—
SP12	4c	McDowell, #1138	—

1960-61

SP13	4c	Washington Credo, #1139	75.00
SP14	4c	Franklin Credo, #1140	75.00
SP15	4c	Jefferson Credo, #1141	75.00
SP16	4c	F.S. Key Credo, #1142	75.00
SP17	4c	Lincoln Credo, #1143	65.00
SP18	4c	P. Henry Credo, #1144	45.00

1961

SP19	4c	Boy Scout, #1145	75.00
SP20	4c	Winter Olympics, #1146	75.00
SP21	4c, 8c	Masaryk, #1147, 1148	75.00
SP22	4c	Refugee Year, #1149	45.00
SP23	4c	Water Consevation, #1150	30.00
SP24	4c	SEATO, #1151	30.00
SP25	4c	American Women, #1152	30.00
SP26	10c	Liberty Bell, #C57	—
SP27	15c	Statue of Liberty, #C58	—
SP28	25c	Lincoln, #C59	—
SP29	4c	50 Star Flag, #1153	50.00
SP30	4c	Pony Express, #1154	50.00
SP31	7c	Jet, carmine, #C60	25.00
SP32	7c	Booklet pane of 6, #C60a	37.50
SP33	7c	Jet coil, #C61	17.50
SP34	4c	Handicapped, #1155	50.00
SP35	4c	Forestry Congress, #1156	50.00
SP36	4c	Mexican Independence, #1157	35.00
SP37	4c	U.S., Japan Treaty, #1158	25.00
SP38	4c, 8c	Paderewski, #1159-1160	40.00
SP39	4c	Sen. Taft, #1161	45.00
SP40	4c	Wheels of Freedom, #1162	45.00
SP41	4c	Boys' Clubs, #1163	45.00
SP42	4c	Automated Post Office, #1164	45.00
SP43	4c, 8c	Mannerheim, #1165-1166	45.00
SP44	4c	Camp Fire Girls, #1167	45.00
SP45	4c, 8c	Garibaldi, #1168-1169	45.00
SP46	4c	Sen. George, #1170	45.00
SP47	4c	Carnegie, #1171	45.00
SP48	4c	Dulles, #1172	45.00
SP49	4c	Echo I, #1173	25.00

1961

SP50	4c, 8c	Gandhi, #1174-1175	18.00
SP51	4c	Range Conservation, #1176	18.00
SP52	4c	Greeley, #1177	18.00

1961-65

SP53	4c	Ft. Sumter, #1178	18.00
SP54	4c	Shiloh, #1179	25.00
SP55	5c	Gettysburg, #1180	8.00
SP56	5c	Wilderness, #1181	8.50
SP57	5c	Appomattox, #1182	8.50

1961

SP58	4c	Kansas, #1183	13.50
SP59	13c	Liberty Bell, #C62	18.00
SP60	4c	Sen. Norris, #1184	12.00
SP61	4c	Naval Aviation, #1185	18.00
SP62	4c	Workmen's Compensation, #1186	18.00
SP63	4c	Remington, #1187	11.00
SP64	4c	Sun Yat sen, #1188	18.00
SP65	4c	Basketball, #1189	18.00
SP66	4c	Nursing, #1190	22.50

1962

SP67	4c	New Mexico, #1191	11.25
SP68	4c	Arizona, #1192	11.25
SP69	4c	Project Mercury, #1193	9.00
SP70	4c	Malaria, #1194	13.50
SP71	4c	Hughes, #1195	19.00
SP72	4c	Seattle World's Fair, #1196	15.75
SP73	4c	Louisiana, #1197	15.75
SP74	4c	Homestead Act, #1198	15.75
SP75	4c	Girl Scouts, #1199	18.00
SP76	4c	McMahon, #1200	15.75
SP77	4c	Apprenticeship, #1201	15.75
SP78	4c	Rayburn, #1202	15.75
SP79	4c	Hammarskjold, #1203	15.75
SP80	4c	Hammarskjold, yellow inverted, #1204	36.00
SP81	4c	Christmas, #1205	45.00
SP82	4c	Higher Education, #1206	11.00
SP83	8c	Capitol, #C64	13.50
SP83a	8c	Capitol sheet, booklet, coil, #C64, C64b, C65	18.00
SP84	8c	Capitol, tagged, #C64a	34.00
SP85	8c	Capitol booklet single, #C64b	22.50
SP86	8c	Capitol coil, #C65	13.50
SP87	4c	Winslow Homer, #1207	13.50
SP88	5c	Flag, #1208	11.25
SP89	1c	Jackson, #1209	11.25
SP90	5c	Washington, #1213	15.75
SP91	5c	Washington booklet pane of 5 + label, #1213a	27.00
SP92	1c	Jackson coil, #1225	15.75
SP93	5c	Washington coil, #1229	15.75
SP94	15c	Montgomery Blair, #C66	—

1963

SP96	5c	Food for Peace, #1231	6.50
SP97	5c	West Virginia, #1232	9.00
SP97A	6c	Eagle, #C67	7.50
SP97B	8c	Amelia Earhart, #C68	18.00
SP98	5c	Emancipation Proclamation, #1233	11.25
SP99	5c	Alliance for Progress, #1234	7.00
SP100	5c	Cordell Hull, #1235	7.00
SP101	5c	Eleanor Roosevelt, #1236	7.00
SP102	5c	Science, #1237	7.00
SP103	5c	City Mail Delivery, #1238	9.00
SP104	5c	Red Cross, #1239	6.25
SP105	5c	Christmas, #1240	8.00
SP106	5c	Audubon, #1241	7.00

1964

SP107	5c	Sam Houston, #1242	11.00
SP108	5c	C.M. Russell, #1243	9.00
SP109	5c	N.Y. World's Fair, #1244	8.00
SP110	5c	John Muir, #1245	11.00
SP111	5c	Kennedy (Boston, Mass.) (At least 4 other cities known), #1246	13.50
SP112	5c	New Jersey, #1247	8.00
SP113	5c	Nevada, #1248	8.00
SP114	5c	Register and Vote, #1249	7.00
SP115	5c	Shakespeare, #1250	8.00
SP116	5c	Mayo Brothers, #1251	9.00
SP117	8c	Goddard, #C69	8.00
SP118	5c	Music, #1252	8.00
SP119	5c	Homemakers, #1253	8.00
SP120	5c	Christmas Plants, #1257b	18.00
SP121	5c	Christmas, tagged, #1257c	80.00
SP122	5c	Verrazano Narrows Bridge, #1258	8.00
SP123	5c	Fine Arts, #1259	8.00
SP124	5c	Amateur Radio, #1260	7.00

1965

SP125	5c	New Orleans, #1261	7.00
SP126	5c	Sokols, #1262	7.00
SP127	5c	Cancer, #1263	7.00
SP128	5c	Churchill, #1264	7.50
SP129	5c	Magna Carta, #1265	7.00
SP130	5c	I.C.Y., #1266	7.00
SP131	5c	Salvation Army, #1267	7.00
SP132	5c	Dante, #1268	7.00
SP133	5c	Hoover, #1269	7.50
SP134	5c	Fulton, #1270	7.00
SP135	5c	Florida, #1271	7.50
SP136	5c	Traffic Safety, #1272	7.00
SP137	5c	Copley, #1273	7.50
SP138	11c	I.T.U., #1274	7.50
SP139	5c	Stevenson, #1275	7.50
SP140	5c	Christmas, #1276	7.00

Prominent Americans

1965-73

SP141	1c	Jefferson, #1278	7.00
SP141a	1c	Jefferson sheet, booklet, coil, #1278, 1278a 1299	6.25
SP142	1c	Jefferson booklet pane of 8, #1278a	7.50
SP143	1¼c	Gallatin, #1279	7.00
SP144	2c	Wright, #1280	5.75
SP145	2c	Wright booklet pane of 5 + label, #1280a	8.50
SP146	3c	Parkman, #1281	7.00
SP147	4c	Lincoln, #1282	5.00
SP148	5c	Washington, #1283	5.00
SP149	5c	Washington, redrawn, #1283B	5.75
SP150	6c	Roosevelt, #1284	5.00
SP151	6c	Roosevelt booklet pane of 8, #1284b	11.50
SP151a	6c	Roosevelt booklet, vert. coil, #1284b, 1298	5.00
SP151b	6c	Roosevelt booklet, horiz. coil, #1284b, 1305	5.00
SP152	8c	Einstein, #1285	9.00
SP153	10c	Jackson, #1286	7.00
SP154	12c	Ford, #1286A	10.00
SP155	13c	Kennedy, #1287	18.00
SP156	15c	Holmes, #1288	9.50
SP157	20c	Marshall, #1289	8.00
SP158	25c	Douglass, #1290	11.00
SP159	30c	Dewey, #1291	27.00
SP160	40c	Paine, #1292	36.00
SP161	50c	Stone, #1293	32.00
SP162	$1	O'Neill, #1294	57.50
SP163	$5	Moore, #1295	135.00
SP164	6c	Roosevelt, vert. coil, #1298	5.00
SP165	1c	Jefferson, coil, #1299	5.75
SP166	4c	Lincoln, coil, #1303	7.00
SP167	5c	Washington, coil, #1304	6.25
SP168	6c	Roosevelt, horiz. coil, #1305	5.75

Nos. 1297, 1305C and 1305E are known on unofficial pages. They are not listed here. For official pages of these issues, see Nos. SP296-SP298.

1966

SP169	5c	Migratory Bird Treaty, #1306	9.50
SP170	5c	ASPCA, #1307	7.00
SP171	5c	Indiana, #1308	7.00
SP172	5c	Circus, #1309	8.00
SP173	5c	SIPEX, #1310	6.25
SP174	5c	SIPEX Souvenir Sheet, #1311	6.50
SP175	5c	Bill of Rights, #1312	7.00
SP176	5c	Poland, #1313	7.00
SP177	5c	National Park Service, #1314	7.00
SP178	5c	Marine Corps Reserve, #1315	5.75
SP179	5c	Women's Clubs, #1316	7.00
SP180	5c	Johnny Appleseed, #1317	7.00
SP181	5c	Beautifcation of America, #1318	7.50
SP182	5c	Great River Road, #1319	7.00
SP183	5c	Savings Bonds Servicemen, #1320	7.00
SP184	5c	Christmas, #1321	6.25
SP185	5c	Mary Cassatt, #1322	7.00

1967

SP186	8c	Alaska, #C70	9.50
SP187	5c	Grange, #1323	6.25
SP188	20c	Audubon, #C71	9.50
SP189	5c	Canada, #1324	6.25
SP190	5c	Erie Canal, #1325	6.25
SP191	5c	Search for Peace, #1326	7.00
SP192	5c	Thoreau, #1327	6.50
SP193	5c	Nebraska, #1328	6.50
SP194	5c	VOA, #1329	6.50
SP195	5c	Crockett, #1330	7.00
SP196	5c	Space, #1332b	22.50
SP197	5c	Urban Planning, #1333	6.50
SP198	5c	Finland, #1334	7.00
SP199	5c	Eakins, #1335	6.50
SP200	5c	Christmas, #1336	6.25
SP201	5c	Mississippi, #1337	6.25

1968-71

SP202	6c Flags, Giori Press, #1338	5.75
SP203	6c Flag, Huck Press, #1338D	5.00
SP204	8c Flag, #1338F	5.75
SP205	6c Flag coil, #1338A	5.50

1968

SP206	10c 50 star Runway, #C72	8.00
SP207	10c sheet, coil, booklet pane of 8, #C72, C72b, C73	22.50
SP207a	10c sheet, booklet single, coil, #C72, C72b, C73	8.00
SP208	10c 50 star Runway coil, #C73	8.00
SP209	6c Illinois, #1339	5.00
SP210	6c HemisFair, #1340	7.00
SP211	$1 Airlift, #1341	57.50
SP212	6c Youth, #1342	5.00
SP213	10c Air Mail Service, #C74	7.50
SP214	6c Law and Order, #1343	5.00
SP215	6c Register and Vote, #1344	5.00
SP216	6c Historic Flags, #1345-1354	80.00
SP217	6c Disney, #1355	18.00
SP218	6c Marquette, #1356	7.00
SP219	6c Daniel Boone, #1357	7.00
SP220	6c Arkansas River Navigation, #1358	7.00
SP221	6c Leif Erikson, #1359	13.50
SP222	6c Cherokee Strip, #1360	8.00
SP223	6c John Trumbull, #1361	7.00
SP224	6c Waterfowl, #1362	8.00
SP225	6c Christmas, #1363	7.00
SP226	6c Chief Joseph, #1364	8.00
SP227	20c USA, #C75	11.00

1969

SP228	6c Beautification, #1368a	18.00
SP229	6c American Legion, #1369	7.00
SP230	6c Grandma Moses, #1370	6.25
SP231	6c Apollo 8, #1371	13.50
SP232	6c W.C. Handy, #1372	9.00
SP233	6c California, #1373	6.25
SP234	6c Powell, #1374	7.00
SP235	6c Alabama, #1375	7.00
SP236	6c Botanical Congress, #1379a	18.00
SP237	10c Man on the Moon, #C76	12.00
SP238	6c Dartmouth, #1380	7.00
SP239	6c Baseball, #1381	36.00
SP240	6c Football, #1382	13.50
SP241	6c Eisenhower, #1383	7.00
SP242	6c Christmas, #1384	7.00
SP243	6c Hope, #1385	6.25
SP244	45c Special Delivery, #E22	31.50
SP245	6c Harnett, #1386	6.25

1970

SP246	6c Natural History, #1390a	36.00
SP247	6c Maine, #1391	8.00
SP248	6c Wildlife Conservation, #1392	11.00

Regular Issue

1970-71

SP249	6c Eisenhower, #1393	5.00
SP249a	6c sheet, booklet, coil stamps, #1393, 1393a, 1401	7.50
SP249b	6c sheet, coil stamps, #1393, 1401	7.00
SP250	6c Eisenhower booklet pane of 8, #1393a	11.25
SP250a	6c booklet, coil, #1393a, 1401	5.00
SP251	6c Eisenhower booklet pane of 5 + label, #1393b	5.00
SP252	8c Eisenhower, #1394	5.00
SP252a	8c sheet, booklet, coil, #1394-1395, 1402	5.00
SP253	8c Eisenhower booklet pane of 8, #1395a	13.50
SP254	8c Eisenhower booklet pane of 8, #1395b	13.50
SP255	8c U.S.P.S., #1396	9.50
SP256	16c Pyle, #1398	8.00
SP257	6c Eisenhower coil, #1401	6.25
SP258	8c Eisenhower coil, #1402	5.00

1970

SP259	6c Masters, #1405	7.00
SP260	6c Suffrage, #1406	6.25
SP261	6c So. Carolina, #1407	6.25
SP262	6c Stone Mountain, #1408	8.00
SP263	6c Ft. Snelling, #1409	7.00
SP264	6c Anti pollution, #1413a	20.00
SP265	6c Christmas Nativity, #1414	11.50
SP266	6c Christmas Toys, #1418b	9.50
SP267	6c Toys, precanceled, #1418c	40.00
SP268	6c U.N., #1419	8.00
SP269	6c Mayflower, #1420	7.00
SP270	6c DAV, Servicemen, #1422a	25.00

1971

SP271	6c Wool, #1423	8.00
SP272	6c MacArthur, #1424	9.00
SP273	6c Blood Donors, #1425	7.00
SP274	8c Missouri, #1426	7.00
SP275	9c Delta Wing, #C77	8.00
SP276	11c Jet, #C78	8.00
SP276a	11c sheet, booklet, coil, #C78, C78a, C82	11.25
SP277	11c Jet booklet pane, #C78a	16.00
SP278	60c Special Delivery, #E23	22.50
SP279	8c Wildlife, #1430a	13.50
SP280	8c Antarctic Treaty, #1431	11.00
SP281	8c Bicentennial Emblem, #1432	13.50
SP282	17c Statue of Liberty, #C80	13.50
SP283	21c USA, #C81	18.00
SP284	11c Jet coil, #C82	9.00
SP285	8c Sloan, #1433	10.00
SP286	8c Space, #1435b	18.00
SP287	8c Dickenson, #1436	11.25
SP288	8c San Juan, #1437	15.75
SP289	8c Drug Abuse, #1438	9.00
SP290	8c CARE, #1439	9.00
SP291	8c Historic Preservation, #1443a	11.25
SP292	8c Adoration, #1444	9.00
SP293	8c Patridge, #1445	9.00

1972

SP294	8c Lanier, #1446	9.50
SP295	8c Peace Corps, #1447	9.50

OFFICIAL SOUVENIR PAGES

In 1972 the USPS began issuing "official" Souvenir pages by subscription. A few more "unofficials" were produced.

Prominent Americans

1970-78

SP296	3c Parkman, coil, #1297	2.90
SP297	$1 O'Neill, coil, #1305C	11.00
SP298	15c Holmes, coil, #1305E	2.90
SP299	7c Franklin, #1393D	3.60
SP300	14c LaGuardia, #1397	80.00
SP301	18c Blackwell, #1399	2.50
SP302	21c Giannini, #1400	2.90

1972

SP303	2c Cape Hatteras, #1451a	65.00
SP304	6c Wolf Trap Farm, #1452	22.50
SP305	8c Yellowstone, #1453	80.00
SP306	11c City of Refuge, #C84	72.00
SP307	15c Mt. McKinley, #1454	15.75
SP308	8c Family Planning, #1455	650.00
	Unofficials exist, value $150.	
SP309	8c Colonial Craftsmen, #1459a	10.00
SP310	Olympics, #1460-1462, C85	7.50
	#1460-1462, C85, with #1460 having broken red ring cylinder flaw	*400.00*
SP311	8c PTA, #1463	4.25
SP312	8c Wildlife, #1467a	4.75
SP313	8c Mail Order, #1468	3.00
SP314	8c Osteopathic, #1469	3.75
SP315	8c Tom Sawyer, #1470	5.00
SP316	8c Christmas, #1471-1472	4.25
SP317	8c Pharmacy, #1473	4.75
SP318	8c Stamp Collecting, #1474	3.60

1973

SP319	8c Love, #1475	4.75
SP320	8c Printing, #1476	3.60
SP321	8c Broadside, #1477	3.60
SP322	8c Postrider, #1478	3.60
SP323	8c Drummer, #1479	2.25
SP324	8c Tea Party, #1483a	3.75
SP325	8c Gershwin, #1484	3.75
SP326	8c Jeffers, #1485	3.60
SP327	8c Tanner, #1486	3.75
SP328	8c Cather, #1487	5.25
SP329	8c Copernicus, #1488	4.00
SP330	8c Postal People, #1489-1498	4.00
SP331	8c Truman, #1499	3.60
SP332	Electronics, #1500-1502, C86	7.00
SP333	8c L.B. Johnson, #1503	3.25

1973-74

SP334	8c Cattle, #1504	2.75
SP335	10c Chautauqua, #1505	2.25
SP336	10c Kansas Winter Wheat, #1506	2.00

1973

SP337	8c Christmas, #1507-1508	4.25

Regular Issues

1973-74

SP338	10c Crossed Flags, #1509	2.50
SP339	10c Jefferson Memorial, #1510	2.50
SP340	10c ZIP, #1511	3.60
SP341	6.3c Liberty Bell coil, #1518	2.90
SP341A	13c Winged Envelope, #C79	2.90
SP341B	13c Airmail, coil, #C83	2.90

1974

SP342	18c Statue of Liberty, #C87	5.25
SP343	26c Mt. Rushmore, #C88	3.75
SP344	10c VFW, #1525	2.25
SP345	10c Robert Frost, #1526	3.75
SP346	10c EXPO '74, #1527	4.25
SP347	10c Horse Racing, #1528	4.25
SP348	10c Skylab, #1529	4.00
SP349	10c UPU, #1537a	4.25
SP350	10c Minerals, #1541a	4.25
SP351	10c Ft. Harrod, #1542	2.25
SP352	10c Continental Congress, #1546a	3.75
SP353	10c Energy, #1547	2.25
SP354	10c Sleepy Hollow, #1548	3.75
SP355	10c Retarded Children, #1549	3.00
SP356	10c Christmas, #1550-1552	3.75

1975

SP357	10c Benjamin West, #1553	2.25
SP358	10c Dunbar, #1554	3.60
SP359	10c D.W. Griffith, #1555	3.75
SP360	10c Pioneer, #1556	4.25
SP361	10c Mariner, #1557	4.25
SP362	10c Collective Bargaining, #1558	2.25
SP363	8c Sybil Ludington, #1559	2.25
SP364	10c Salem Poor, #1560	2.90
SP365	10c Haym Salomon, #1561	2.75
SP366	15c Peter Francisco, #1562	2.75
SP367	10c Lexington & Concord, #1563	2.75
SP368	10c Bunker Hill, #1564	2.75
SP369	10c Military Uniforms, #1568a	4.25
SP370	10c Apollo Soyuz, #1570a	5.25
SP371	10c Women's Year, #1571	2.25
SP372	10c Postal Service, #1575	2.90
SP373	10c Peace through Law, #1576	2.25
SP374	10c Banking and Commerce, #1578a	2.75
SP375	10c Christmas, #1579-1580	2.90

Americana Issue

1975-81

SP376	1c, 2c, 3c, 4c Americana, #1581-1585	2.90
SP377	9c Capitol Dome, #1591	2.25
SP378	10c Justice, #1592	2.25
SP379	11c Printing Press, #1593	2.50
SP380	12c Torch sheet, coil, #1594, 1816	2.50
SP381	13c Eagle and Shield, #1596	3.60
SP382	15c Flag sheet, coil, #1597, 1618C	2.25
SP383	16c Statue of Liberty sheet, coil, #1599, 1619	2.50
SP384	24c Old North Church, #1603	2.50
SP385	28c Ft. Nisqually, #1604	2.90
SP386	29c Lighthouse, #1605	3.60
SP387	30c Schoolhouse, #1606	3.25
SP388	50c "Betty" Lamp, #1608	2.90
SP389	$1 Candle Holder, #1610	3.25
SP390	$2 Kerosene Lamp, #1611	4.25
SP391	$5 R. R. Lantern, #1612	8.00
SP392	1c Inkwell, coil, #1811	2.50
SP393	3.1c Guitar, coil, #1613	4.50
SP394	3.5c Violin, coil, #1813	2.25
SP395	7.7c Saxhorns, coil, #1614	2.25
SP396	7.9c Drum, coil, #1615	2.25
SP397	8.4c Piano, coil, #1615C	2.90
SP398	9c Capitol Dome, coil, #1616	2.25
SP398A	10c Justice, coil, #1617	2.25
SP399	13c Liberty Bell, coil, #1618	2.25
SP400	13c 13 star Flag sheet, coil, #1622, 1625	2.25
SP401	9c, 13c Booklet pane, perf. 10, #1623Bc	13.50

1976

SP402	13c Spririt of '76, #1631a	3.60
SP403	25c, 31c Plane and Globes, #C89-C90	2.50
SP404	13c Interphil 76, #1632	2.75
SP405	13c State Flags, #1633-1642	5.75
SP406	13c State Flags, #1643-1652	5.75
SP407	13c State Flags, #1653-1662	5.75
SP408	13c State Flags, #1663-1672	5.75
SP409	13c State Flags, #1673-1682	5.75
SP410	13c Telephone, #1683	2.50
SP411	13c Aviation, #1684	2.50
SP412	13c Chemistry, #1685	2.50
SP413	13c Bicentennial Souvenir Sheet, #1686	7.00
SP414	18c Bicentennial Souvenir Sheet, #1687	7.00
SP415	24c Bicentennial Souvenir Sheet, #1688	7.00
SP416	31c Bicentennial Souvenir Sheet, #1689	7.00
SP417	13c Franklin, #1690	2.00
SP418	13c Declaration of Independence, #1694a	3.25
SP419	13c Olympics, #1698a	3.25
SP420	13c Clara Maass, #1699	4.50
SP421	13c Adolph Ochs, #1700	2.50
SP422	13c Christmas, #1701-1703	2.75

1977

SP423	13c Washington at Princeton, #1704	2.50
SP424	13c Sound Recording, #1705	2.90
SP425	13c Pueblo Pottery, #1709a	4.75
SP426	13c Lindbergh Flight, #1710	2.90
SP427	13c Colorado, #1711	2.00
SP428	13c Butterflies, #1715a	3.60
SP429	13c Lafayette, #1716	2.00
SP430	13c Skilled Hands, #1720a	3.25
SP431	13c Peace Bridge, #1721	2.50
SP432	13c Oriskany, #1722	2.50
SP433	13c Energy, #1724a	2.50
SP434	13c Alta California, #1725	2.50
SP435	13c Articles of Confederation, #1726	3.00
SP436	13c Talking Pictures, #1727	3.00
SP437	13c Saratoga, #1728	2.25
SP438	13c Christmas, #1729-1730	2.25

1978

SP439	13c Sandburg, #1731	2.90
SP440	13c Capt. Cook, #1732, 1733	3.00
SP441	13c Indian Head Penny, #1734	3.00
SP442	15c A Sheet, coil, #1735, 1743	3.75
SP443	15c Roses booklet single, #1737	2.90
SP444	15c Windmills booklet pane of 10, #1742a	7.00
SP445	13c Tubman, #1744	2.90
SP446	13c Quilts, #1748a	3.60
SP447	13c American Dance, #1752a	4.25
SP448	13c French Alliance, #1753	2.50

SP449	13c Cancer Detection, #1754	3.00
SP450	13c Jimmie Rodgers, #1755	3.00
SP451	15c George M. Cohan, #1756	3.00
SP452	13c CAPEX '78 Souvenir Sheet, #1757	5.00
SP453	15c Photography, #1758	3.60
SP454	15c Viking Missions, #1759	4.75
SP455	15c Owls, #1763a	3.75
SP456	31c Wright Brothers, #C92a	2.90
SP457	15c Trees, #1767a	2.90
SP458	15c Madonna and Child, #1768	2.50
SP459	15c Hobby Horse, #1769	2.50

1979

SP460	15c Robert F. Kennedy, #1770	2.90
SP461	15c Martin Luther King Jr., #1771	3.60
SP462	15c Year of the Child, #1772	2.25
SP463	15c John Steinbeck, #1773	4.50
SP464	15c Einstein, #1774	4.50
SP465	21c Chanute, #C94a	2.90
SP466	15c Toleware, #1778a	3.75
SP467	15c Architecture, #1782a	2.90
SP468	15c Endangered Flora, #1786a	2.90
SP469	15c Seeing Eye Dogs, #1787	2.25
SP470	15c Special Olympics, #1788	2.25
SP471	15c John Paul Jones, #1789	2.25
SP472	10c Olympics, #1790	2.50
SP473	15c Olympics, #1794a	3.60
SP474	31c Olympics, #C97	3.00

1980

SP475	15c Winter Olympics, #1798a	3.75

1979

SP476	15c Madonna and Child, #1799	2.25
SP477	15c Santa Claus, #1800	2.25
SP478	15c Will Rogers, #1801	2.90
SP479	15c Vietnam Veterans, #1802	3.75
SP480	25c Wiley Post, #C96a	3.00

1980

SP481	15c W.C. Fields, #1803	3.60
SP482	15c Benjamin Banneker, #1804	2.90
SP483	15c Letter Writing Week, #1805-1810	2.90
SP484	18c B sheet, coil, #1818, 1820	2.25
SP485	18c B booklet pane of 8, #1819a	2.25
SP486	15c Frances Perkins, #1821	2.25
SP487	15c Dolley Madison, #1822	3.00
SP488	15c Emily Bissell, #1823	3.00
SP489	15c Helen Keller, #1824	2.25
SP490	15c Veterans Administration, #1825	2.25
SP491	15c Galvez, #1826	2.25
SP492	15c Coral Reefs, #1830a	3.75
SP493	15c Organized Labor, #1831	2.90
SP494	15c Edith Wharton, #1832	2.90
SP495	15c Education, #1833	2.50
SP496	15c Indian Masks, #1837a	3.60
SP497	15c Architecture, #1841a	2.90
SP498	40c Mazzei, #C98	2.75
SP499	15c Christmas Window, #1842	2.25
SP500	15c Christmas Toys, #1843	2.90
SP501	28c Blanche Stuart Scott, #C99	2.75
SP502	35c Curtiss, #C100	2.75

Great Americans

1980-85

SP503	1c Dix, #1844	2.50
SP504	2c Stravinsky, #1845	2.75
SP505	3c Clay, #1846	2.50
SP506	4c Schurz, #1847	2.90
SP507	5c Buck, #1848	2.90
SP508	6c Lippmann, #1849	2.90
SP509	7c Baldwin, #1850	2.25
SP510	8c Knox, #1851	2.25
SP511	9c Thayer, #1852	2.25
SP512	10c Russell, #1853	2.25
SP513	11c Partridge, #1854	2.25
SP514	13c Crazy Horse, #1855	2.90
SP515	14c Lewis, #1856	3.75
SP516	17c Carson, #1857	2.25
SP517	18c Mason, #1858	2.25
SP518	19c Sequoyah, #1859	2.25
SP519	20c Bunche, #1860	3.75
SP520	20c Gallaudet, #1861	2.25
SP521	20c Truman, #1862	2.25
SP522	22c Audubon, #1863	2.90
SP523	30c Laubach, #1864	2.25
SP524	35c Drew, #1865	2.25
SP525	37c Millikan, #1866	2.25
SP526	39c Clark, #1867	2.25
SP527	40c Gilbreth, #1868	2.25
SP528	50c Nimitz, #1869	2.90

1981

SP529	15c Dirksen, #1874	2.25
SP530	15c Young, #1875	3.75
SP531	18c Flowers, #1879a	2.90
SP532	18c Animals, #1889a	4.50
SP533	18c Flag sheet, coil, #1890-1891	2.25
SP534	6c, 18c Booklet pane, #1893a	2.25
SP535	20c Flag sheet, coil, #1894-1895	2.25
SP536	20c Flag booklet pane of 6, #1896a	2.25

1982

SP537	20c Flag booklet pane of 10, #1896b	3.00

Transportation Coils

1981-84

SP538	1c Omnibus, #1897	2.25
SP539	2c Locomotive, #1897A	3.00
SP540	3c Handcar, #1898	2.90
SP541	4c Stagecoach, #1898A	2.90
SP542	5c Motorcycle, #1899	4.00
SP543	5.2c Sleigh, #1900	3.25
SP544	5.9c Bicycle, #1901	4.50
SP545	7.4c Baby Buggy, #1902	2.90
SP546	9.3c Mail Wagon, #1903	2.90
SP547	10.9c Hansom Cab, #1904	3.00
SP548	11c Caboose, #1905	2.90
SP549	17c Electric Auto, #1906	2.25
SP550	18c Surrey, #1907	3.25
	a. Surrey page with 17c Auto #1906 affixed (error)	—
SP551	20c Fire Pumper, #1908	3.75

1983

SP552	$9.35 Express Mail single, #1909	67.50
SP552a	$9.35 Express Mail booklet pane of 3, #1909a	125.00

1981

SP553	18c Red Cross, #1910	2.25
SP554	18c Savings and Loan, #1911	2.25
SP555	18c Space Achievements, #1919a	5.00
SP556	18c Management, #1920	2.25
SP557	18c Wildlife, #1924a	2.90
SP558	18c Disabled, #1925	2.25
SP559	18c Millay, #1926	2.25
SP560	18c Alcoholism, #1927	2.25
SP561	18c Architecture, #1931a	3.00
SP562	18c Zaharias, #1932	13.50
SP563	18c Jones, #1933	16.50
SP564	18c Remington, #1934	3.60
SP565	18c, 20c Hoban, #1935-1936	1.75
SP566	18c Yorktown, Va. Capes, #1938a	2.90
SP567	20c Madonna and Child, #1939	2.25
SP568	20c Teddy Bear, #1940	3.25
SP569	20c John Hanson, #1941	2.25
SP570	20c Desert Plants, #1945a	3.00
SP571	20c C sheet, coil, #1946	2.90
SP572	20c C Booklet pane of 10, #1948a	2.75

1982

SP573	20c Bighorn Sheep, #1949a	2.90
SP574	20c FDR, #1950	2.25
SP575	20c Love, #1951	2.25
SP576	20c Washington, #1952	2.90
SP577	20c Birds and Flowers, #1953-1962	10.00
SP578	20c Birds and Flowers, #1963-1972	10.00
SP579	20c Birds and Flowers, #1973-1982	10.00
SP580	20c Birds and Flowers, #1983-1992	10.00
SP581	20c Birds and Flowers, #1993-2002	10.00
SP582	20c US Netherlands, #2003	2.25
SP583	20c Library of Congress, #2004	2.25
SP584	20c Consumer Education, #2005	2.90
SP585	20c Knoxville World's Fair, #2009a	2.25
SP586	20c Horatio Alger, #2010	2.25
SP587	20c Aging, #2011	2.25
SP588	20c Barrymores, #2012	2.90
SP589	20c Dr. Mary Walker, #2013	2.25
SP590	20c Peace Garden, #2014	2.25
SP591	20c Libraries, #2015	2.25
SP592	20c Jackie Robinson, #2016	12.00
SP593	20c Touro Synagogue, #2017	2.25
SP594	20c Wolf Trap Farm, #2018	2.25
SP595	20c Architecture, #2022a	3.00
SP596	20c Francis of Assisi, #2023	2.25
SP597	20c Ponce de Leon, #2024	2.25
SP598	13c Puppy, Kitten, #2025	2.90
SP599	20c Madonna and Child, #2026	2.90
SP600	20c Children Playing, #2030a	3.00

1983

SP601	1c, 4c, 13c Official Mail, #O127-O129	2.90
SP602	17c Official Mail, #O130	2.90
SP603	$1 Official Mail, #O132	3.75
SP604	$5 Official Mail, #O133	9.00
SP605	20c Official Mail coil, #O135	3.00
SP606	20c Science, #2031	2.25
SP607	20c Ballooning, #2035a	2.25
SP608	20c US Sweden, #2036	2.25
SP609	20c CCC, #2037	2.25
SP610	20c Priestley, #2038	2.25
SP611	20c Voluntarism, #2039	2.25
SP612	20c German Immigration, #2040	2.25
SP613	20c Brooklyn Bridge, #2041	2.25
SP614	20c TVA, #2042	2.25
SP615	20c Fitness, #2043	2.25
SP616	20c Scott Joplin, #2044	2.25
SP617	20c Medal of Honor, #2045	4.50
SP618	20c Babe Ruth, #2046	10.00
SP619	20c Hawthorne, #2047	2.25
SP620	13c Olympics, #2051a	2.90
SP621	28c Olympics, #C104a	2.90
SP622	40c Olympics, #C108a	2.90
SP623	35c Olympics, #C112a	2.90
SP624	20c Treaty of Paris, #2052	2.25
SP625	20c Civil Service, #2053	2.25
SP626	20c Metropolitan Opera, #2054	2.75
SP627	20c Inventors, #2058a	2.75
SP628	20c Streetcars, #2062a	3.25
SP629	20c Madonna and Child, #2063	2.25
SP630	20c Santa Claus, #2064	2.25
SP631	20c Martin Luther, #2065	3.75

1984-85

SP632	20c Alaska, #2066	2.25
SP633	20c Winter Olympics, #2070a	2.90
SP634	20c FDIC, #2071	2.25
SP635	20c Love, #2072	2.25
SP636	20c Woodson, #2073	2.90
SP637	14c, 22c D sheet, coil, #O138-O139	2.25
SP638	20c Conservation, #2074	2.25
SP639	20c Credit Union, #2075	2.25
SP640	20c Orchids, #2079a	3.75
SP641	20c Hawaii, #2080	2.75
SP642	20c National Archives, #2081	2.50
SP643	20c Olympics, #2085a	2.90
SP644	20c World Expo, #2086	2.50
SP645	20c Health Research, #2087	2.50
SP646	20c Fairbanks, #2088	3.75
SP647	20c Thorpe, #2089	8.00
SP648	20c McCormack, #2090	3.75
SP649	20c St. Lawrence Seaway, #2091	2.25
SP650	20c Waterfowl, #2092	3.75
SP651	20c Roanoke Voyages, #2093	2.25
SP652	20c Melville, #2094	2.50
SP653	20c Horace Moses, #2095	2.25
SP654	20c Smokey Bear, #2096	7.50
SP655	20c Clemente, #2097	11.00
SP656	20c Dogs, #2101a	3.75
SP657	20c Crime Prevention, #2102	2.75
SP658	20c Hispanic Americans, #2103	2.25
SP659	20c Family Unity, #2104	2.25
SP660	20c Eleanor Roosevelt, #2105	3.00
SP661	20c Readers, #2106	2.25
SP662	20c Madonna and Child, #2107	2.25
SP663	20c Child's Santa, #2108	2.25
SP664	20c Vietnam Memorial, #2109	3.75

1985-87

SP665	20c Jerome Kern, #2110	2.25
SP666	22c D sheet, coil, #2111-2112	2.25
SP667	22c D booklet pane of 10, #2113a	2.90
SP668	33c Verville, #C113	2.25
SP669	39c Sperry, #C114	2.75
SP670	44c Transpacific, #C115	2.25
SP671	22c Flags sheet, coil, #2114-2115	2.25
SP671a	22c Flag "T" coil, #2115b	2.75
SP672	22c Flag booklet pane of 5, #2116a	2.25
SP673	22c Seashells, #2121a	3.75
SP674	$10.75 Express Mail single, #2122	38.00
SP674a	$10.75 Express Mail booklet pane of 3, #2122a	77.50

Transportation Coils

1985-89

SP675	3.4c School Bus, #2123	2.90
SP676	4.9c Buckboard, #2124	2.75
SP677	5.5c Star Route Truck, #2125	2.90
SP678	6c Tricycle, #2126	2.25
SP679	7.1c Tractor, #2127	2.50
SP679a	7.1c Tractor, Zip+4 precancel, #2127b	2.25
SP680	8.3c Ambulance, #2128	2.25
SP681	8.5c Tow Truck, #2129	2.25
SP682	10.1c Oil Wagon, #2130	2.25
SP682a	10.1c Red precancel, #2130a	2.25
SP683	11c Stutz Bearcat, #2131	2.75
SP684	12c Stanley Steamer, #2132	2.90
SP685	12.5c Pushcart, #2133	2.25
SP686	14c Iceboat, #2134	2.90
SP687	17c Dog Sled, #2135	2.25
SP688	25c Bread Wagon, #2136	2.90

1985

SP689	22c Bethune, #2137	3.75
SP690	22c Duck Decoys, #2141a	4.25
SP691	22c Winter Special Olympics, #2142	2.25
SP692	22c Love, #2143	2.25
SP693	22c REA, #2144	2.25
SP694	14c, 22c Official Mail, #O129A, O136	2.25
SP695	22c AMERIPEX '86, #2145	2.25
SP696	22c Abigail Adams, #2146	2.25
SP697	22c Bartholdi, #2147	2.75
SP698	18c Washington coil, #2149	2.90
SP699	21.1c Letters coil, #2150	2.75
SP700	22c Korean Veterans, #2152	2.90
SP701	22c Social Security, #2153	2.25
SP702	44c Serra, #C116	2.25
SP703	22c World War I Veterans, #2154	3.75
SP704	22c Horses, #2158a	4.00
SP705	22c Education, #2159	2.25
SP706	22c Youth Year, #2163a	4.00
SP707	22c Hunger, #2164	2.25
SP708	22c Madonna and Child, #2165	2.25
SP709	22c Poinsettias, #2166	2.25

1986

SP710	22c Arkansas, #2167	2.25

Great Americans

1986-94

SP711	1c Mitchell, #2168	3.75
SP712	2c Lyon, #2169	2.25
SP713	3c White, #2170	2.25
SP714	4c Flanagan, #2171	2.25
SP715	5c Black, #2172	2.90

No.	Description	Price
SP716	5c Munoz Marin, #2173	2.25
SP717	10c Red Cloud, #2175	3.75
SP718	14c Howe, #2176	2.25
SP719	15c Cody, #2177	2.25
SP720	17c Lockwood, #2178	2.90
SP721	20c Apgar, #2179	3.25
SP722	21c Carlson, #2180	2.25
SP723	23c Cassatt, #2181	2.25
SP724	25c London, #2182	2.25
SP724a	25c London, pane of 10, #2182a	4.00
SP725	28c Sitting Bull, #2183	3.25
SP726	29c Warren, #2184	2.75
SP727	29c Jefferson, #2185	2.25
SP728	35c Chavez, #2186	2.90
SP729	40c Chennault, #2187	2.90
SP730	45c Cushing, #2188	2.25
SP731	52c Humphrey, #2189	2.50
SP732	56c Harvard, #2190	2.50
SP733	65c Arnold, #2191	3.00
SP734	75c Willkie, #2192	3.00
SP735	$1 Revel, #2193	2.75
SP736	$1 Hopkins, #2194	2.75
SP737	$2 Bryan, #2195	4.00
SP739	$5 Harte, #2196	9.00
SP740	25c London, #2197a	2.25

1986

No.	Description	Price
SP741	22c Stamp Collecting, #2201a	3.00
SP742	22c Love, #2202	2.90
SP743	22c Sojourner Truth, #2203	3.75
SP744	22c Texas Republic, #2204	2.25
SP745	22c Fish booklet pane of 5, #2209a	4.25
SP746	22c Hospitals, #2210	2.00
SP747	22c Duke Ellington, #2211	4.25
SP748	22c Presidents Sheet #1, #2216	4.00
SP749	22c Presidents Sheet #2, #2217	4.00
SP750	22c Presidents Sheet #3, #2218	4.00
SP751	22c Presidents Sheet #4, #2219	4.00
SP752	22c Arctic Explorers, #2223a	3.75
SP753	22c Statue of Liberty, #2224	2.75

1987

No.	Description	Price
SP754	2c Locomotive, reengraved, #2226	2.25

1986

No.	Description	Price
SP755	22c Navajo Art, #2238a	3.75
SP756	22c T.S. Eliot, #2239	3.75
SP757	22c Woodcarved Figurines, #2243a	3.75
SP758	22c Madonna and Child, #2244	2.25
SP759	22c Village Scene, #2245	2.25

1987

No.	Description	Price
SP760	22c Michigan, #2246	2.75
SP761	22c Pan American Games, #2247	2.25
SP762	22c Love, #2248	2.25
SP763	22c du Sable, #2249	4.50
SP764	22c Caruso, #2250	2.75
SP765	22c Girl Scouts, #2251	4.25

Transportation Coils

1987-88

No.	Description	Price
SP766	3c Conestoga Wagon, #2252	3.00
SP767	5c, 17.5c Milk Wagon, Racing Car, #2253, 2262	3.00
SP768	5.3c Elevator, #2254	2.50
SP769	7.6c Carreta, #2255	2.50
SP770	8.4c Wheelchair, #2256	2.50
SP771	10c Canal Boat, #2257	2.75
SP772	13c Patrol Wagon, #2258	3.75
SP773	13.2c Coal Car, #2259	3.75
SP774	15c Tugboat, #2260	2.75
SP775	16.7c Popcorn Wagon, #2261	2.75
SP776	20c Cable Car, #2263	2.75
SP777	20.5c Fire Engine, #2264	3.25
SP778	21c Mail Car, #2265	3.25
SP779	24.1c Tandem Bicycle, #2266	2.50

1987

No.	Description	Price
SP780	22c Special Occasions, #2274a	3.00
SP781	22c United Way, #2275	2.25

1987-89

No.	Description	Price
SP782	22c Flag and Fireworks, #2276	2.25
SP783	22c Flag, pair from booklet, #2276a	2.25
SP784	(25c) "E" sheet, coil, #2277, 2279	2.50
SP785	(25c) "E" booklet pane of 10, #2282a	2.90
SP786	25c Flag with Clouds, #2278	2.25
SP787	25c Flag with Clouds booklet pane of 6, #2285c	2.75
SP788	25c Flag over Yosemite coil, block tagging, #2280	2.25
SP788a	25c Flag over Yosemite, prephosphored uncoated paper (mottled tagging), #2280a	2.25
SP789	25c Honeybee coil, #2281	3.25
SP790	25c Pheasant, #2283a	3.75
SP791	25c Owl and Grosbeak, #2285b	2.90
SP792	(25c) "E" Official coil, #O140	2.25
SP793	20c Official coil, #O138B	2.25
SP794	15c, 25c Official coils, #O138A, O141	2.25

1987

No.	Description	Price
SP795	22c Wildlife, #2286-2295	5.00
SP796	22c Wildlife, #2296-2305	5.00
SP797	22c Wildlife, #2306-2315	5.00
SP798	22c Wildlife, #2316-2325	5.00
SP799	22c Wildlife, #2326-2335	5.00

Ratification of the Constitution

1987-90

No.	Description	Price
SP800	22c Delaware, #2336	2.75
SP801	22c Pennsylvania, #2337	2.25
SP802	22c New Jersey, #2338	2.75
SP803	22c Georgia, #2339	2.75
SP804	22c Connecticut, #2340	2.75
SP805	22c Massachusetts, #2341	2.75
SP806	22c Maryland, #2342	2.75
SP807	25c South Carolina, #2343	2.25
SP808	25c New Hampshire, #2344	2.25
SP809	25c Virginia, #2345	2.75
SP810	25c New York, #2346	2.25
SP811	25c North Carolina, #2347	2.75
SP812	25c Rhode Island, #2348	2.25

1987

No.	Description	Price
SP813	22c U.S./Morocco, #2349	2.25
SP814	22c William Faulkner, #2350	4.50
SP815	22c Lacemaking, #2354a	4.75
SP816	22c Constitution, #2359a	2.90
SP817	22c Signing of Constitution, #2360	2.25
SP818	22c Certified Public Accounting, #2361	4.25
SP819	22c Locomotives, #2366a	7.00
SP820	22c Madonna and Child, #2367	2.25
SP821	22c Christmas Ornament, #2368	2.25

1988

No.	Description	Price
SP822	22c Winter Olympics, #2369	2.25
SP823	22c Australia Bicentennial, #2370	2.90
SP824	22c James Weldon Johnson, #2371	2.75
SP825	22c Cats, #2375a	4.50
SP826	22c Knute Rockne, #2376	8.00
SP827	44c New Sweden, #C117	2.25
SP828	45c Samuel P. Langley, #C118	2.25
SP829	25c Francis Ouimet, #2377	10.00
SP830	36c Igor Sikorsky, #C119	2.25
SP831	25c Love, #2378	2.25
SP832	45c Love, #2379	2.25
SP833	25c Summer Olympics, #2380	2.25
SP834	25c Classic Automobiles, #2385a	4.25
SP835	25c Antarctic Explorers, #2389a	2.75
SP836	25c Carousel Animals, #2393a	3.75
SP837	$8.75 Express Mail, #2394	20.00
SP838	25c Special Occasions, #2396a	16.50
SP839	25c Special Occasions, #2398a	16.50
SP840	25c Madonna and Child, #2399	2.25
SP841	25c Village Scene, #2400	2.25

1989

No.	Description	Price
SP842	25c Montana, #2401	2.25
SP843	25c A. Philip Randolph, #2402	2.90
SP844	25c North Dakota, #2403	2.25
SP845	25c Washington Statehood, #2404	2.25
SP846	25c Steamboats, #2409a	4.50
SP847	25c World Stamp Expo, #2410	2.25
SP848	25c Toscanini, #2411	3.75

Branches of Government

1989-90

No.	Description	Price
SP849	25c House of Representatives, #2412	2.25
SP850	25c Senate, #2413	2.25
SP851	25c Executive, #2414	2.25
SP852	25c Supreme Court, #2415	2.25

1989

No.	Description	Price
SP853	25c South Dakota, #2416	2.25
SP854	25c Lou Gehrig, #2417	12.00
SP855	1c Official, litho., #O143	2.25
SP856	45c French Revolution, #C120	3.75
SP857	25c Ernest Hemingway, #2418	4.25
SP858	$2.40 Moon Landing, #2419	14.75
SP859	25c Letter Carriers, #2420	2.25
SP860	25c Bill of Rights, #2421	2.25
SP861	25c Dinosaurs, #2425a	5.00
SP862	25c, 45c Pre-Columbian Artifacts, #2426, C121	2.25
SP863	25c Madonna sheet single, booklet pane of 10, #2427, 2427a	4.75
SP864	25c Sleigh single, booklet pane of 10, #2428, 2429a	4.75
SP865	25c Eagle & Shield, #2431	2.25
SP866	90c World Stamp Expo '89, #2433	10.00
SP867	25c Traditional Mail Delivery, #2437a	3.60
SP868	45c Futuristic Mail Delivery, #C126	3.75
SP869	45c Futuristic Mail Delivery, #C125a	3.75
SP870	25c Traditional Mail Delivery, #2438	4.50

1990

No.	Description	Price
SP871	25c Idaho, #2439	2.25
SP872	25c Love single, booklet pane of 10, #2440, 2441a	3.75
SP873	25c Ida B. Wells, #2442	3.75
SP874	15c Beach Umbrella, #2443a	3.75
SP875	25c Wyoming, #2444	2.90
SP876	25c Classic Films, #2448a	7.00
SP877	25c Marianne Moore, #2449	2.90

Transportation Coils

1990-92

No.	Description	Price
SP879	4c Steam Carriage, #2451	2.25
SP880	5c Circus Wagon, #2452	2.75
SP880A	5c Circus Wagon, #2452B	3.75
SP880B	5c Circus Wagon with cent sign, #2452D	3.60
SP881	5c, 10c Canoe, engr., Tractor Trailer, #2453, 2457	2.50
SP882	5c Canoe, photo., #2454	2.75
SP883	10c Tractor trailer, photo., #2458	3.60
SP891	20c Cog Railway, #2463	2.90
SP892	23c Lunch Wagon, #2464	2.75
SP893	32c Ferry Boat, #2466	2.90
SP895	$1 Seaplane, #2468	4.50

1990-94

No.	Description	Price
SP897	25c Lighthouses, booklet pane of 5, #2474a	7.00
SP898	25c Flag, #2475	2.75

Flora and Fauna Series

No.	Description	Price
SP899	1c, 3c, 30c Kestrel, Bluebird, Cardinal, #2476, 2478, 2480	2.50
SP900	1c Kestrel with cent sign, #2477	2.50
SP901	19c Fawn, #2479	2.50
SP902	45c Pumpkinseed Sunfish, #2481	2.75
SP903	$2 Bobcat, #2482	3.75
SP904	20c Blue jay, #2483	2.50
SP905	29c Wood Ducks booklet panes of 10, #2484a, 2485a	10.00
SP906	29c African Violets bklt. pane of 10, #2486a	3.60
SP907	32c Peach & Pear, #2488b, 2493-2494	3.75
SP908	29c Red Squirrel, #2489	2.75
SP909	29c Red Rose, #2490	2.50
SP910	29c Pine Cone, #2491	2.75
SP911	32c Pink rose, #2492	3.75
SP919	25c Olympians, #2496-2500	4.00
SP920	25c Indian Headdresses, #2505a	4.75
SP921	25c Micronesia, Marshall Islands, #2507a	2.25
SP922	25c Sea Creatures, #2511a	4.75
SP923	25c, 45c Grand Canyon, Tropical Coastline, #2512, C127	2.25
SP924	25c Eisenhower, #2513	2.75
SP925	25c Madonna sheet single, booklet pane of 10, #2514, 2514a	4.25
SP926	25c Christmas Tree sheet single, booklet pane of 10, #2515, 2516a	4.25

1991-95

No.	Description	Price
SP927	(29c) "F" Flower single, coil pair, #2517, 2518	2.25
SP928	(29c) "F" Flower booklet panes of 10, #2519a, 2520a	7.75
SP929	(4c) Make-up Rate, #2521	2.25
SP930	(29c) "F" Flag, #2522	2.75
SP931	(29c) "F" Official coil, #O144	2.25
SP932	29c Mt. Rushmore, #2523	2.75
SP933	29c Mt. Rushmore, photo., #2523A	2.25
SP934	29c Flower single, booklet pane of 10, #2524, 2527a	4.50
SP935	29c Flower coil, #2525	2.25
SP936	29c Flower coil, #2526	2.25
SP937	4c Official, #O146	2.50
SP938	29c Flag, Olympic Rings, #2528a	4.50
SP939	19c Fishing Boat coil, #2529	3.75
SP939A	19c Fishing Boat coil reissue, #2529C	2.90
SP940	19c Ballooning, #2530a	3.75
SP941	29c Flags on Parade, #2531	2.50
SP942	29c Liberty Torch, #2531A	2.50
SP943	50c Switzerland, #2532	2.25
SP944	20c Vermont Statehood, #2533	2.50
SP945	50c Harriet Quimby, #C128	2.75
SP946	29c Savings Bonds, #2534	2.25
SP947	29c, 52c Love, #2535, 2536a, 2537	9.00
SP948	40c William T. Piper, #C129	2.25
SP949	29c William Saroyan, #2538	4.25
SP950	Official 19c, 23c, 29c, #O145, O147-O148	2.50
SP951	$1.00 USPS/Olympic Rings, #2539	3.00
SP952	$2.90 Eagle, #2540	10.00
SP953	$9.95 Eagle, #2541	26.00
SP954	$14 Eagle, #2542	34.00
SP955	$2.90 Futuristic Space Shuttle, #2543	9.00
SP956	$3 Challenger Shuttle, #2544	11.25
SP956A	$10.75 Endeavour Shuttle, #2544A	22.00
SP957	29c Fishing Flies, #2549a	15.75
SP958	29c Cole Porter, #2550	2.75
SP959	50c Antarctic Treaty, #C130	2.75
SP960	29c Desert Shield, Desert Storm, #2551	9.00
SP961	29c 1992 Summer Olympics, #2553-2557	4.75
SP962	29c Numismatics, #2558	3.75
SP963	29c World War II, #2559	9.00
SP964	29c Basketball, #2560	5.00
SP965	29c District of Columbia, #2561	2.25
SP966	29c Comedians, #2566a	5.50
SP967	29c Jan E. Matzeliger, #2567	4.25
SP968	29c Space Exploration, #2577a	9.00
SP969	50c Bering Land Bridge, #C131	2.25

SP970	29c	Madonna and Child sheet single, booklet pane of 10, #2578, 2578a	8.00
SP971	29c	Santa Claus sheet and booklet singles, #2579, 2580 or 2581, 2582-2585	12.00
SP973	32c	James K. Polk, #2587	4.75
SP976	$1	Surrender of Gen. Burgoyne, #2590	3.75
SP978	$5	Washington and Jackson, #2592	11.25
SP980	29c	Pledge of Allegiance, #2593a	3.60
SP982	29c	Eagle & Shield self-adhesives, #2595-2597	3.00
SP983	29c	Eagle self-adhesive, #2598	2.50
SP984	29c	Statue of Liberty, #2599	2.50
SP990	(10c)	Eagle and Shield coil, #2602	3.75
SP991	(10c)	Eagle and Shield coils, #2603-2604	3.75
SP993	23c	Stars and Stripes coil, #2605	2.25
SP994	23c	USA coil, #2606	2.90
SP994A	23c	USA coil, #2607	2.25
SP994B	23c	USA coil, #2608	2.50
SP995	29c	Flag over White House, #2609	2.50

1992

SP997	29c	Winter Olympics, #2611-2615	3.75
SP998	29c	World Columbian Stamp Expo '92, #2616	3.00
SP999	29c	W.E.B. DuBois, #2617	4.25
SP1000	29c	Love, #2618	2.25
SP1001	29c	Olympic Baseball, #2619	10.00
SP1002	29c	First Voyage of Columbus, #2623a	3.00
SP1003	1c, 4c, $1	First Sighting of Land souvenir sheet, #2624	6.25
SP1004	2c, 3c, $4	Claiming a New World souvenir sheet, #2625	7.50
SP1005	5c, 30c, 50c	Seeking Royal Support souvenir sheet, #2626	5.75
SP1006	6c, 8c, $3	Royal Favor Restored souvenir sheet, #2627	7.50
SP1007	10c, 15c, $2	Reporting Discoveries souvenir sheet, #2628	7.50
SP1008	$5	Columbus souvenir sheet, #2629	10.00
SP1009	29c	New York Stock Exchange, #2630	2.50
SP1010	29c	Space Accomplishments, #2634a	5.25
SP1011	29c	Alaska Highway, #2635	2.75
SP1012	29c	Kentucky Statehood, #2636	2.50
SP1013	29c	Summer Olympics, #2637-2641	3.75
SP1014	29c	Hummingbirds, #2646a	7.00
SP1015	29c	Wildflowers, #2647-2656	7.00
SP1016	29c	Wildflowers, #2657-2666	7.00
SP1017	29c	Wildflowers, #2667-2676	7.00
SP1018	29c	Wildflowers, #2677-2686	7.00
SP1019	29c	Wildflowers, #2687-2696	7.00
SP1020	29c	World War II, #2697	5.00
SP1021	29c	Dorothy Parker, #2698	2.75
SP1022	29c	Dr. Theodore von Karman, #2699	4.25
SP1023	29c	Minerals strip of 4, #2703a	4.00
SP1024	29c	Juan Rodriguez Cabrillo, #2704	2.75
SP1025	29c	Wild Animals, #2709a	5.25
SP1026	29c	Madonna and Child sheet single, booklet pane of 10, #2710, 2710a	7.00
SP1027	29c	Christmas Toys block of 4, booklet pane of 4 and booklet single, #2714a, 2718a, 2719	4.25
SP1028	29c	Chinese New Year, #2720	8.00

1993

SP1029	29c	Elvis Presley, #2721	12.00
SP1030	29c	Oklahoma!, #2722	2.25
SP1030A	29c	Hank Williams sheet stamp, #2723A	4.25
SP1030B	29c	Rock & Roll/Rhythm & Blues sheet single, booklet pane of 8, #2737b	22.00

No. SP1030B exists with any one of #2724-2730 affixed along with #2737b.

SP1034	29c	Space Fantasy, #2745a	8.00
SP1035	29c	Percy Lavon Julian, #2746	3.75
SP1036	29c	Oregon Trail, #2747	2.25
SP1037	29c	World University Games, #2748	2.25
SP1038	29c	Grace Kelly, #2749	7.00
SP1039	29c	Circus, #2753a	4.25
SP1040	29c	Cherokee Strip, #2754	3.75
SP1041	29c	Dean Acheson, #2755	2.25
SP1042	29c	Sporting Horses, #2759a	4.75
SP1043	29c	Garden Flowers, #2764a	3.75
SP1044	29c	World War II, #2765	7.00
SP1045	29c	Joe Louis, #2766	11.00
SP1046	29c	Broadway Musicals, #2770a	4.25
SP1047	29c	National Postal Museum strip of 4, #2782a	3.00
SP1048	29c	American Sign Language, #2784a	2.25
SP1049	29c	Country & Western Music sheet stamp and booklet pane of 4, #2778a	13.50

No. SP1049 exists with any one of #2771-2774 affixed along with #2778a.

SP1050	10c	Official Mail, #O146A	2.50
SP1052	29c	Classic Books strip of 4, #2788a	2.90
SP1053	29c	Traditional Christmas sheet stamp, booklet pane of 4, #2789, 2790a	4.75
SP1054	29c	Contemporary Christmas booklet pane of 10, sheet and self-adhesive single stamps, #2803	11.25

No. SP1054 exists with any one of #2791-2794, 2798a, 2798b, 2799-2802 affixed along with #2803.

SP1055	29c	Mariana Islands, #2804	2.25
SP1056	29c	Columbus' Landing in Puerto Rico, #2805	2.90
SP1057	29c	AIDS Awareness, #2806, 2806b	4.50

1994

SP1058	29c	Winter Olympics, #2811a	4.75
SP1059	29c	Edward R. Murrow, #2812	3.00
SP1060	29c	Love self-adhesive, #2813	3.00
SP1061	29c, 52c	Love booklet pane of 10, single sheet stamp, #2814a, 2815	6.25
SP1062	29c	Love sheet stamp, #2814C	2.90
SP1063	29c	Dr. Allison Davis, #2816	4.50
SP1064	29c	Chinese New Year, #2817	3.25
SP1065	29c	Buffalo Soldiers, #2818	4.75
SP1066	29c	Silent Screen Stars, #2819-2828	5.00
SP1067	29c	Garden Flowers, #2833a	5.00
SP1068	29c, 40c, 50c	World Cup Soccer, #2834-2836	5.00
SP1069		World Cup Soccer, #2837	5.00
SP1070	29c	World War II, #2838	5.75
SP1071	29c, 50c	Norman Rockwell stamp, souvenir sheet, #2839-2840	12.00
SP1072	29c, $9.95	Moon Landing, #2841-2842	22.50
SP1073	29c	Locomotives, #2847a	7.50
SP1074	29c	George Meany, #2848	2.90
SP1075	29c	Popular Singers, #2853a	7.00
SP1076	29c	Jazz and Blues Singers block of 10, #2854-2861	10.00

Block of 10 on No. SP1076 may contain different combinations of stamps.

SP1077	29c	James Thurber, #2862	3.75
SP1078	29c	Wonders of the Sea, #2866a	4.50
SP1079	29c	Cranes, #2868a	2.90
SP1079A		Legends of the West, #2869	20.00
SP1080	29c	Traditional Christmas sheet stamp, booklet pane of 10, #2871, 2871b	6.25
SP1081	29c	Contemporary Christmas sheet stamp, block of 4 from booklet pane, #2872	4.25
SP1082	29c	Contemporary Christmas self-adhesive stamps, #2873-2874	5.00
SP1083	$2	Bureau of Engraving and Printing Souvenir Sheet, #2875	16.00

1995-96

SP1084	29c	Chinese New Year, #2876	4.25
SP1085	G	make-up rate, G stamps, #2877, 2884, 2890, 2893	3.75
SP1086	G	make-up rate, G stamps, #2878, 2880, 2882, 2885, 2888, 2892	3.75
SP1087	G	stamps, official G stamp, #2879, 2881, 2883, 2889, O152	3.75
SP1088	G	self-adhesive stamps, #2886-2887	7.00
SP1091	32c	Flag Over Porch, #2897, 2913, 2915-2916	4.50
SP1096	(5c)	Butte coil, #2902	4.00
SP1097	(5c)	Mountain coil, #2903, 2904	4.50
SP1099		Butte, Mountain, Juke Box, Auto Tail Fin, Auto, Flag over porch, #2902B, 2904A, 2906, 2910, 2912A, 2915B	4.50
SP1099A		Mountain, Juke Box, Flag Over Porch coil and booklet stamps, #2904B, 2912B, 2915D, 2921b	4.50
SP1100	(10c)	Auto coil, #2905	4.25
SP1102		Eagle & shield, Flag over porch, #2907, 2920D, 2921	4.25
SP1103	(15c)	Auto Tail Fin, #2908-2909	4.25
SP1105	(25c)	Juke Box, #2911-2912	2.90
SP1110	32c	Flag over Field self-adhesive, #2919	4.25
SP1114	(32c)	Non-denominated Love, #2948-2949	2.25
SP1115	32c	Florida Statehood, #2950	2.25

Great Americans Series

1995-99

SP1126	32c	Milton Hershey, #2933	2.25
SP1127	32c	Cal Farley, #2934	2.90
SP1128	32c	Henry R. Luce, #2935	5.00
SP1129	32c	Lila & DeWitt Wallace, #2936	4.00
SP1131	46c	Ruth Benedict, #2938	2.90
SP1133	55c	Alice Hamilton, #2940	2.25
SP1134	55c	Justin S. Morrill, #2941	5.00
SP1135	77c	Mary Breckinridge, #2942	4.50
SP1136	78c	Alice Paul, #2943	2.25

1995

SP1141	32c	Kids Care, #2954a	2.90
SP1142	32c	Richard Nixon, #2955	2.90
SP1143	32c	Bessie Coleman, #2956	3.75
SP1144	1-32c	Official, #O153-O156	2.50
SP1145	32c, 55c	Love (with denominations), #2957-2960	2.90
SP1146	32c	Recreational Sports, #2965a	7.00
SP1147	32c	Prisoners of War/Missing in Action, #2966	3.00
SP1148	32c	Marilyn Monroe, #2967	13.50
SP1149	32c	Texas Statehood, #2968	3.60
SP1150	32c	Great Lakes Lighthouses, #2973a	8.00
SP1151	32c	United Nations, #2974	2.25
SP1152	32c	Civil War, #2975	14.00
SP1153	32c	Carousel Horses, #2979a	4.75
SP1154	32c	Woman Suffrage, #2980	2.25
SP1155	32c	World War II, #2981	6.25
SP1156	32c	Louis Armstrong, #2982	4.00
SP1157	32c	Jazz Musicians, #2992a	7.00
SP1158	32c	Garden Flowers, #2997a	5.75
SP1159	60c	Eddie Rickenbacker, #2998	3.60
SP1160	32c	Republic of Palau, #2999	2.90
SP1161	32c	Comic Strip Classics, #3000	14.00
SP1162	32c	Naval Academy, #3001	3.60
SP1163	32c	Tennessee Williams, #3002	3.60
SP1164	32c	Traditional Christmas sheet stamp, booklet pane of 10, #3003, 3003b	5.00
SP1165	32c	Contemporary Christmas block of 4, self-adhesive stamps, #3007a, 3010-3011	4.25

No. SP1165 may include different combinations of Nos. 3008-3011.

SP1166	32c	Midnight Angel, #3012	3.75
SP1167	32c	Children Sledding, #3013	3.75
SP1168	32c	Antique Automobiles, #3023a	5.50

1996

SP1169	32c	Utah Statehood, #3024	2.90
SP1170	32c	Garden Flowers, #3029a	5.25
SP1171	1, 32c	Flag Over Porch, Love self-adhesives, Kestrel coil, #2920e, 3030, 3044	12.00

Flora and Fauna Series

1996-99

SP1171A	1c	Kestrel, self-adhesive, #3031	5.00
SP1172	2c	Woodpecker, #3032	3.00
SP1173	3c	Bluebird, #3033	3.00
SP1184	$1	Red Fox, #3036	7.00
SP1185	2c	Woodpecker coil, #3045	5.00
SP1187	20c	Bluejay self-adhesive coil, booklet stamps, #3048, 3053	4.00
SP1188	32c	Yellow Rose, #3049	4.25
SP1189	20c	Ring-necked Pheasant, #3050, 3055	5.25
SP1191A	33c	Coral Pink Rose, serpentine die cut 10¾x10½, #3052E	5.25
SP1191	33c	Coral Pink Rose, #3052	5.25
SP1192	32c	Yellow Rose coil, #3054	5.25

1996

SP1197	32c	Ernest E. Just, #3058	4.25
SP1198	32c	Smithsonian Institution, #3059	2.90
SP1199	32c	Chinese New Year, #3060	5.25
SP1200	32c	Pioneers of Communication, #3064a	3.75
SP1201	32c	Fulbright Scholarships, #3065	2.90
SP1202	50c	Jacqueline Cochran, #3066	2.90
SP1203	32c	Marathon, #3067	2.90
SP1204	32c	Olympic Games, #3068	14.75
SP1205	32c	Georgia O'Keeffe, #3069	3.75
SP1206	32c	Tennessee Statehood, #3070	2.90
SP1207	32c	American Indian Dances, #3076a	3.75
SP1208	32c	Prehistoric Animals, #3080a	3.75
SP1209	32c	Breast Cancer Awareness, #3081	4.00
SP1210	32c	James Dean, #3082	5.25
SP1211	32c	Folk Heroes, #3086a	4.50
SP1212	32c	Centennial Olympic Games, #3087	4.00
SP1213	32c	Iowa Statehood, #3088-3089	4.00
SP1214	32c	Rural Free Delivery, #3090	3.00
SP1215	32c	Riverboats, #3095b	57.50
SP1216	32c	Big Band Leaders, #3099a	5.25
SP1217	32c	Songwriters, #3103a	5.25
SP1218	23c	F. Scott Fitzgerald, #3104	3.00
SP1219	32c	Endangered Species, #3105	16.00
SP1220	32c	Computer Technology, #3106	3.00
SP1221	32c	Madonna & Child sheet & booklet stamps, #3107, 3112	5.25
SP1222	32c	Contemporary Christmas block of 4, self-adhesive stamp, #3111a, 3113	5.25

No. SP1222 may contain Nos. 3114-3116 instead of No. 3113.

SP1223	32c	Skaters, #3117	5.25
SP1224	32c	Hanukkah, #3118	4.00
SP1225	32c	Cycling souvenir sheet, #3119	5.25

1997

SP1226	32c	Chinese New Year, #3120	6.00
SP1227	32c	Benjamin O. Davis, Sr., #3121	5.25
SP1228	32c	Statue of Liberty, #3122	4.50
SP1229	32, 55c	Love Swans, #3123-3124	4.50
SP1230	32c	Helping Children Learn, #3125	4.00
SP1231	32c	Merian Botanical Prints, #3126-3129	4.50
SP1232	32c	PACIFIC 97 Triangles, #3131a	5.25
SP1233	(25c), 32c	Flag Over Porch, Juke Box linerless coils, #3132-3133	4.50
SP1234	32c	Thornton Wilder, #3134	4.00
SP1235	32c	Raoul Wallenberg, #3135	4.00
SP1236	32c	Dinosaurs, #3136	16.00
SP1237	32c	Bugs Bunny, #3137	16.00
SP1238	50c	PACIFIC 97 Franklin, #3139	13.00
SP1239	60c	PACIFIC 97 Washington, #3140	13.00
SP1240	32c	Marshall Plan, #3141	4.50
SP1241	32c	Classic American Aircraft, #3142	16.00
SP1242	32c	Football Coaches, #3146a	13.50
SP1242A	32c	Vince Lombardi, #3147	9.00
SP1242B	32c	Bear Bryant, #3148	9.00
SP1242C	32c	Pop Warner, #3149	9.00
SP1242D	32c	George Halas, #3150	9.00
SP1243	32c	Classic American Dolls, #3151	11.50
SP1244	32c	Humphrey Bogart, #3152	5.25
SP1245	32c	The Stars and Stripes Forever!, #3153	5.25
SP1246	32c	Opera Singers, #3157a	8.50
SP1247	32c	Composers & Conductors, #3165a	10.00
SP1248	32c	Padre Felix Varela, #3155	5.25
SP1249	32c	Department of the Air Force, #3167	9.00
SP1250	32c	Movie Monsters, #3172a	11.00
SP1251	32c	Supersonic Flight, #3173	8.50
SP1252	32c	Women in Military Service, #3174	5.25
SP1253	32c	Kwanzaa, #3175	5.00
SP1254	32c	Madonna and Child, #3176	5.75
SP1255	32c	Holly, #3177	5.75
SP1256	$3	Mars Pathfinder, #3178	15.00

1998

SP1257	32c	Chinese New Year, #3179	5.00
SP1258	32c	Alpine Skiing, #3180	5.00
SP1259	32c	Madam C.J. Walker, #3181	5.00

Celebrate the Century

1998-2000

SP1259A	32c	1900s, #3182	13.50
SP1259B	32c	1910s, #3183	13.50
SP1259C	32c	1920s, #3184	13.50
SP1259D	32c	1930s, #3185	13.50
SP1259E	33c	1940s, #3186	13.50
SP1259F	33c	1950s, #3187	13.50
SP1259G	33c	1960s, #3188	13.50
SP1259H	33c	1970s, #3189	13.50
SP1259I	33c	1980s, #3190	13.50
SP1259J	33c	1990s, #3191	13.50

1998

SP1260	32c	"Remember the Maine," #3192	5.00
SP1261	32c	Flowering Trees, #3197a	7.00
SP1262	32c	Alexander Calder, #3202a	7.00
SP1263	32c	Cinco de Mayo, #3203	5.00
SP1264	32c	Sylvester & Tweety, #3204a	7.00
SP1265	32c	Wisconsin Statehood, #3206	5.00
SP1266	(5c), (25c)	Wetlands, Diner Coils, #3207-3208	5.00
SP1266A	(25c)	Diner coil, #3208A	5.00
SP1267	1c-$2	Trans-Mississippi, #3209	15.75
SP1268	$1	Trans-Mississippi, #3209h	11.00
SP1269	32c	Berlin Airlift, #3211	5.00
SP1270	32c	Folk Musicians, #3215a	7.50
SP1271	32c	Gospel Singers, #3219a	6.25
SP1272	32c	Spanish Settlement, #3220	5.00
SP1273	32c	Stephen Vincent Benét, #3221	5.00
SP1274	32c	Tropical Birds, #3225a	8.00
SP1275	32c	Alfred Hitchcock, #3226	5.50
SP1276	32c	Organ & Tissue Donation, #3227	5.00
SP1277	(10c)	Modern Bicycle, #3229	5.00
SP1278	32c	Bright Eyes, #3234a	7.50
SP1279	32c	Klondike Gold Rush, #3235	5.00
SP1280	32c	American Art, #3236	13.50
SP1281	32c	Ballet, #3237	5.00
SP1282	32c	Space Discovery, #3242a	7.00
SP1283	32c	Giving & Sharing, #3243	5.00
SP1284	32c	Madonna & Child, #3244	5.00
SP1285	32c	Wreaths, #3248a, 3252a	7.00
SP1286	(32+8c)	Breast Cancer Awareness, #B1	5.00
SP1287	(1c), (33c)	Weather Vane, Uncle Sam's Hat, #3257-3258, 3260	5.00
SP1288	22c	Uncle Sam, #3259, 3263	5.00
SP1289	$3.20	Space Shuttle Landing, #3261	15.00
SP1290	$11.75	Piggyback Space Shuttle, #3262	22.50
SP1291	(33c)	Uncle Sam's Hat, #3267-3269	5.75
SP1292	(33c)	Uncle Sam's Hat, #3264, 3266	6.25
SP1293	(5c), (10c)	Wetlands, Eagle & Shield, #3207A, 3270-3271	5.00

1999

SP1294	33c	Chinese New Year, #3272	7.00
SP1295	33c	Malcolm X, #3273	8.50
SP1296	33c	Love, #3274	5.00
SP1297	55c	Love, #3275	5.00
SP1298	33c	Hospice Care, #3276	5.00
SP1299	33c	Flag and City, #3279-3280, 3282	5.00
SP1300	33c	Flag Over Chalkboard, #3283	5.00
SP1301	33c	Irish Immigration, #3286	5.00
SP1302	33c	Lunt & Fontanne, #3287	5.00
SP1303	33c	Arctic Animals, #3292a	7.00
SP1304	33c	Sonoran Desert, #3293	12.00
SP1305	33c	Berries, #3294-3297	6.25
SP1306	33c	Daffy Duck, #3306a	7.00
SP1307	33c	Ayn Rand, #3308	5.00
SP1308	33c	Cinco de Mayo, #3309	5.75
SP1309	33c	Tropical Flowers, #3310-3313	6.25
SP1310	48c	Niagara Falls, #C133	5.75
SP1311	33c	John & William Bartram, #3314	5.00
SP1312	33c	Prostate Cancer, #3315	5.00
SP1313	33c	California Gold Rush, #3316	5.00
SP1314	33c	Aquarium Fish, #3317-3320	6.25
SP1315	33c	Extreme Sports, #3321-3324	6.00
SP1316	33c	American Glass, #3328a	6.25
SP1317	33c	James Cagney, #3329	6.25
SP1318	55c	Billy Mitchell, #3330	6.00
SP1319	40c	Rio Grande, #C134	5.00
SP1320	33c	Honoring Those Who Served, #3331	5.00
SP1321	45c	Universal Postal Union, #3332	5.00
SP1322	33c	Famous Trains, #3337a	7.00
SP1323	33c	Frederick Law Olmsted, #3338	5.75
SP1324	33c	Hollywood Composers, #3344a	12.00
SP1325	33c	Broadway Songwriters, #3350a	12.00
SP1326	33c	Insects & Spiders, #3351	15.00
SP1327	33c	Hanukkah, #3352	5.00
SP1328	22c	Uncle Sam, #3353	5.00
SP1329	33c	Official coil, #O157	5.00
SP1330	33c	NATO, #3354	5.00
SP1331	33c	Madonna & Child, #3355	5.00
SP1332	33c	Christmas Deer, #3359a	6.00
SP1333	33c	Kwanzaa, #3368	5.00
SP1334	33c	Year 2000, #3369	5.00

2000

SP1335	33c	Chinese New Year, #3370	7.00
SP1336	60c	Grand Canyon, #C135	5.00
SP1337	33c	Patricia Roberts Harris, #3371	5.00
SP1338	33c	Berries, dated 2000, #3294a-3296a, 3297c	5.00
SP1339	33c	Los Angeles Class Submarine (sheet stamp), #3372	14.00
SP1340	33c	Pacific Coast Rain Forest, #3378	14.00
SP1341	33c	Louise Nevelson, #3383a	6.50
SP1342	33c	Hubble Space Telescope Images, #3388a	6.50
SP1343	33c	American Samoa, #3389	5.00
SP1344	33c	Library of Congress, #3390	5.00
SP1345	33c	Road Runner & Wile E. Coyote, #3391a	8.00
SP1346	33c	Distinguished Soldiers, 3396a	7.00
SP1347	33c	Summer Sports, #3397	5.00
SP1348	33c	Adoption, #3398	8.00
SP1349	33c	Youth Team Sports, #3402a	5.00
SP1350	33c	The Stars and Stripes, #3403	14.00
SP1351	33c	Legends of Baseball, #3408	18.00
SP1352	33c	Stampin' the Future, #3417a	5.50

Distinguished Americans Series

2000-09

SP1355	10c	Gen. Joseph W. Stilwell, #3420	5.00
SP1357	23c	Wilma Rudolph, #3422, 3436	5.00
SP1361	33c	Claude Pepper, #3426	5.00
SP1362	58c	Margaret Chase Smith, #3427	5.25
SP1362A	59c	James A. Michener, #3427A	5.25
SP1363	63c	Dr. Jonas Salk, #3428	5.25
SP1365	75c	Harriet Beecher Stowe, #3430	5.25
SP1366	76c	Hattie Caraway, #3431	5.00
SP1366A	76c	Edward Trudeau, #3432A	5.25
SP1366B	78c	Mary Lasker, #3432B	5.25
SP1367	83c	Edna Ferber, #3432	5.00
SP1368	87c	Dr. Albert Sabin, #3435	5.25

2000

SP1373	33c	California Statehood, #3438	5.00
SP1374	33c	Deep Sea Creatures, #3443a	6.50
SP1375	33c	Thomas Wolfe, #3444	5.00
SP1376	33c	White House, #3445	5.00
SP1377	33c	Edward G. Robinson, #3446	5.00
SP1378	(10c)	New York Public Library Lion, #3447	5.00
SP1379	(34c)	Flag Over Farm, #3448-3450	5.00
SP1380	(34c)	Statue of Liberty, #3451-3453	5.00
SP1381	(34c)	Flowers, #3454-3457	5.00

2001

SP1382	34c	Statue of Liberty self-adhesive coil, #3466	4.50
SP1382A	21c	American Buffalo, #3467, 3484	4.50
SP1383	21c	American Buffalo, #3468, 3475	4.50
SP1383A	23c	George Washington, #3468A, 3475A	5.00
SP1384	34c	Flag over Farm, #3469	4.50
SP1385	34c	Flag over Farm self-adhesive, #3470	4.50
SP1386	55c	Eagle, #3471	5.00
SP1386A	57c	Eagle, #3471A	4.25
SP1387	$3.50	US Capitol, #3472	11.50
SP1388	$12.25	Washington Monument, #3473	23.25
SP1389	34c	Statue of Liberty, #3476, 3477, 3485	5.25
SP1390	34c	Flowers, #3478-3481	5.25
SP1391	20c	George Washington, #3482	4.50
SP1392	34c	Apple and Orange, #3491, 3492	5.00
SP1393	34c	Flag over Farm self-adhesive booklet, #3495	5.00
SP1394	(34c)	Love, #3496	4.50
SP1395	34c, 55c	Love, #3497, 3499	6.25
SP1396	34c	Chinese New Year, #3500	6.00
SP1397	34c	Roy Wilkins, #3501	7.50
SP1398	34c	American Illustrators, #3502	22.00
SP1399	34c	Official, #O158	4.50
SP1400	70c	Nine-Mile Prairie, #C136	5.00
SP1401	34c	Diabetes Awareness, #3503	5.00
SP1402	34c	Nobel Prize, #3504	5.00
SP1403	1c-80c	Pan-American Inverts, #3505	15.00
SP1404	80c	Mt. McKinley, #C137	6.25
SP1405	34c	Great Plains Prairie, #3506	14.00
SP1406	34c	Peanuts Comic Strip, #3507	10.00
SP1407	34c	Honoring Veterans, #3508	7.00
SP1408	60c	Acadia National Park, #C138	5.00
SP1409	34c	Frida Kahlo, #3509	10.00
SP1410	34c	Legendary Playing Fields, #3510-3519	23.00
SP1411	(10c)	Atlas Statue, #3520	4.50
SP1412	34c	Leonard Bernstein, #3521	5.00
SP1413	(15c)	Woody Wagon, #3522	4.50
SP1414	34c	Lucille Ball, #3523	10.00
SP1415	34c	Amish Quilts, #3524-3527	6.00
SP1416	34c	Carnivorous Plants, #3528-3531	6.00
SP1417	34c	Eid, #3532	4.50
SP1418	34c	Enrico Fermi, #3533	5.00
SP1419	34c	That's All Folks!, #3534a	9.00
SP1420	34c	Christmas Madonna, #3536	4.50
SP1421	34c	Christmas Santas, #3537-3540	5.00
SP1422	34c	James Madison, #3545	4.50
SP1423	34c	Thanksgiving, #3546	4.50
SP1424	34c	Hanukkah, #3547	4.50
SP1425	34c	Kwanzaa, #3548	4.50
SP1426	34c	United We Stand booklet and coil, #3549, 3550	10.00
SP1427	57c	Love, #3551	5.25

2002

SP1428	34c	Winter Olympics, #3552-3555	7.00
SP1429	34c	Mentoring a Child, #3556	4.50
SP1430	34c	Langston Hughes, #3557	7.00
SP1431	34c	Happy Birthday, #3558	4.50
SP1432	34c	Chinese New Year, #3559	5.00
SP1433	34c	US Military Academy, Bicent., #3560	5.00
SP1434	34c	Greetings from America, #3561-3610	27.50
SP1435	34c	Longleaf Pine Forest, #3611	13.50
SP1436	5c	Toleware Coffeepot, #3612	4.50
SP1437	3c	Star, #3613-3615	4.50
SP1438	23c	George Washington, #3616-3618	5.25
SP1439	(37c)	Flag, #3620-3623	6.00
SP1440	(37c)	Toy coils, #3626-3629	7.00

2003

SP1440A	37c	Flag, perf. 11 ¼, #3629F	4.50

2002

SP1441	37c	Flag, #3630-3631, 3633, 3635	4.50

2003

SP1441A	37c	Flag, self-adhesive booklet stamp, #3637	5.00

2002

SP1442	37c	Toy coils, #3638-3641	5.00

2003

SP1442A	37c	Antique Toys booklet stamps, #3642a, 3643a, 3644a, 3644f	6.00

2002

SP1443	60c	Coverlet Eagle, #3646	4.50
SP1444	$3.85	Jefferson Memorial, #3647	10.00
SP1445	$13.65	Capitol Dome, #3648	23.00
SP1446	(34c+11c)	Heroes of 2001, #B2	13.50
SP1447	37c	Masters of American Photography, #3649	21.50
SP1448	37c	John James Audubon, #3650	5.00
SP1449	37c	Harry Houdini, #3651	5.00
SP1450	37c	Official coil, #O159	4.75
SP1451	37c	Andy Warhol, #3652	5.00
SP1452	37c	Teddy Bears, #3653-3656	5.00
SP1453	37c, 60c	Love #3657-3658	5.00
SP1454	37c	Ogden Nash, #3659	5.00

SP1455	37c	Duke Kahanamoku, #3660	5.75
SP1456	37c	American Bats, #3661-3664	7.00
SP1457	37c	Women in Journalism, #3665-3668	7.00
SP1458	37c	Irving Berlin, #3669	5.00
SP1459	37c	Neuter and Spay, #3670-3671	5.00
SP1460	37c	Hanukkah, #3672	4.75
SP1461	37c	Kwanzaa, #3673	4.75
SP1462	37c	Eid #3674	4.75
SP1463	37c	Christmas Madonna, #3675	5.00
SP1464	37c	Christmas Snowmen, #3676-3679	5.00
SP1465	37c	Cary Grant, #3692	7.00
SP1466	(5c)	Sea Coast, #3693	5.00
SP1467	37c	Hawaiian Missionary Stamps, #3694	11.00
SP1468	37c	Happy Birthday, #3695	5.00
SP1469	37c	Greetings from America, #3696-3745	31.50

2003

SP1470	37c	Thurgood Marshall, #3746	5.25
SP1471	37c	Chinese New Year, #3747	5.25
SP1472	37c	Zora Neale Hurston, #3748	5.25

American Design Series

2003-14

SP1473	1c	Tiffany Lamp, #3749	4.75
SP1473A	1c	Tiffany Lamp, litho., #3749A	4.25
SP1475	10c	American Clock, #3757	4.75
SP1476	2c	Navajo Necklace, #3751-3752, *2005*	4.75
SP1477	2c	Navajo Necklace, #3753	4.75
SP1478	3c	Silver Coffeepot, #3754	4.75
SP1479	4c	Chippendale Chair, #3755	4.75
SP1480	5c	Toleware, #3756	4.75
SP1481	2c	Navajo Necklace, #3750	4.75
SP1482	1c	Tiffany Lamp coil, #3758	5.25
SP1482A	1c	Tiffany Lamp coil, litho., #3758A	4.25
SP1482Ab	1c	Tiffany Lamp coil, #3758A, dated Apr. 28, 2009	4.25
SP1482C	2c	Navajo Necklace coil, #3758B	5.00
SP1483	3c	Silver Coffeepot coil, #3759	4.75
SP1484	4c	Chippendale Chair coil, #3761	4.75
SP1485	4c	Chippendale Chair coil, dated "2013," #3761A	5.00
SP1486	10c	American Clock coil, #3762	4.75
SP1487	10c	American Clock litho. coil, #3763	4.25
SP1490	$1	Wisdom, #3766	6.25
SP1493	(10c)	New York Public Library Lion, perf. 10 vert, #3769	5.25

2004

SP1494	(10c)	Atlas Statue, #3770	4.75

2003

SP1495	80c	Special Olympics, #3771	5.75
SP1496	37c	American Filmmaking: Behind the Scenes, #3772	11.50
SP1497	37c	Ohio Statehood, Bicent., #3773	5.25
SP1498	37c	Pelican Island National Wildlife Refuge, #3774	5.25
SP1499	(5c)	Sea Coast perforated coil, #3775	5.25
SP1500	37c	Old Glory, #3776-3780	5.00
SP1501	37c	Cesar E. Chavez, #3781	5.25
SP1502	37c	Louisiana Purchase, #3782	5.25
SP1503	37c	First Flight of Wright Brothers, #3783	5.25
SP1504	37c	Purple Heart, #3784	5.25
SP1505	37c	Purple Heart, #3784A	5.25
SP1506	37c	Audrey Hepburn, #3786	5.75
SP1507	37c	Southeastern Lighthouses #3787-3791	6.25
SP1508	(25c)	Eagles, two different stamps from #3792-3801	4.50
SP1508A	(25c)	Eagles, #3792-3801	7.00
SP1508Ab	(25c)	Eagles, dated 2005, #3792a-3801b	7.00
SP1509	37c	Arctic Tundra, #3802	11.25
SP1510	37c	Korean War Veterans Memorial, #3803	5.25
SP1511	37c	Mary Cassatt Paintings, #3804-3807	5.00
SP1512	37c	Early Football Heroes, #3808-3811	8.00
SP1513	37c	Roy Acuff, #3812	4.75
SP1514	37c	District of Columbia, #3813	4.50
SP1515	37c	Reptiles And Amphibians, #3814-3818	7.00
SP1516	(37c+8c)	Stop Family Violence, #B3	5.00
SP1517	37c	Christmas Madonna, #3820	4.50
SP1518	37c	Christmas Holiday Music Makers, 2 sets of #3821-3824	5.25
SP1519	37c	Snowy Egret coil, #3829	4.50

2004

SP1520	37c	Snowy Egret booklet stamp, #3830	4.50
SP1521	37c	Pacific Coral Reef, #3831	14.00
SP1522	37c	Chinese New Year, #3832	5.00
SP1523	37c	Love, #3833	4.50
SP1524	37c	Paul Robeson, #3834	4.25
SP1525	37c	Theodor Seuss Geisel (Dr. Seuss), #3835	5.00
SP1526	37c	Love (White Lilacs and Pink Roses), #3836	4.25
SP1527	60c	Love (Five Varieties of Pink Roses), #3837	4.25
SP1528	37c	US Air Force Academy, #3838	4.50
SP1529	(5c)	Sea Coast coil reprint, serpentine die cut 9½x10, #3785	4.25

A souvenir page containing the original printing of No. 3785 was not prepared as there was no first day cancel applied to that stamp.

SP1530	37c	Henry Mancini, #3839	4.50
SP1531	37c	American Choreographers, #3840-3843	5.00
SP1532	(25c)	Eagles, perforated, #3844-3853	7.00
SP1533	37c	Lewis and Clark sheet stamp, #3854 (11 cancels)	9.00
SP1534	37c	Lewis and Clark booklet stamps, #3855-3856 (11 cancels)	9.00
SP1535	37c	Isamu Noguchi, #3857-3861	5.25
SP1536	37c	National World War II Memorial, #3862	4.25
SP1537	37c	Summer Olympic Games, Athens, #3863	4.25
SP1538	(5c)	Sea Coast coil, perf. 9¾ vert., #3864	4.25
SP1539	37c	Disney Characters, #3865-3868	7.00
SP1540	37c	USS Constellation, #3869	4.25
SP1541	37c	R. Buckminster Fuller, #3870	4.25
SP1542	37c	James Baldwin, #3871	4.25
SP1543	37c	Martin Johnson Heade, #3872	4.25
SP1544	37c	Art of the American Indian, #3873	8.50
SP1547	37c	John Wayne, #3876	7.50
SP1548	37c	Sickle Cell Disease Awareness, #3877	4.25
SP1549	37c	Cloudscapes, #3878	8.50
SP1550	37c	Christmas Madonna, #3879	4.75
SP1551	37c	Hanukkah, #3880	4.25
SP1552	37c	Kwanzaa, #3881	4.25
SP1553	37c	Moss Hart, #3882	4.25
SP1554	37c	Christmas Santa Claus Ornaments, #3883-3894	7.00

2005

SP1555	37c	Chinese New Year double-sided sheet, #3895	16.00

No. SP1555 was sold in a shrink-wrapped package containing the announcement page, a stamp mount, a cardboard backing and one pane of No. 3895 canceled on both sides.

SP1556	37c	Marian Anderson, #3896	4.25
SP1557	37c	Ronald Reagan, #3897	10.00
SP1558	37c	Love, #3898	4.25
SP1559	37c	Northeast Deciduous Forest, #3899	12.00
SP1560	37c	Spring Flowers, #3900-3903	5.25
SP1561	37c	Robert Penn Warren, #3904	4.25
SP1562	37c	Yip Harburg, #3905	4.25
SP1563	37c	American Scientists, #3906-3909	5.25
SP1564	37c	Modern American Architecture, #3910	10.00
SP1565	37c	Henry Fonda, #3911	4.25
SP1566	37c	Disney Characters, #3912-3915	7.50
SP1567	37c	Advances in Aviation, pane of #3916-3925	12.00
SP1568	37c	Rio Grande Blankets, #3926-3929	5.25
SP1568A	37c	Presidential Libraries, #3930	7.00
SP1569	37c	Sporty Cars, #3931-3935	6.00
SP1570	37c	Arthur Ashe, #3936	4.50
SP1571	37c	To Form a More Perfect Union, #3937	7.00
SP1572	37c	Child Health, #3938	4.25
SP1573	37c	Let's Dance, #3939-3942	5.00
SP1574	37c	Greta Garbo, #3943	5.25
SP1575	37c	Jim Henson and the Muppets, #3944	8.00
SP1576	37c	Constellations, #3945-3948	5.25
SP1577	37c	Christmas, #3949-3960	7.00
SP1578	37c	Distinguished Marines, #3961-3964	5.00
SP1579	(37c)	Flag and Statue of Liberty, #3965-3967, 3970, 3972, 3974, 3975	7.00

No. SP1579 consists of two sheets.

2006

SP1580	(39c)	Love, #3976	4.25
SP1582	39c	Flag and Statue of Liberty, #3978, 3981, 3982, 3983, 3985	5.25
SP1583	39c	Flag and Statue of Liberty Coil, perf. 10 vert., #3979	5.25
SP1584	39c	Flag and Statue of Liberty Coil serpentine die cut 11 vert., #3980	4.25
	a.	Like #1584, but dated and canceled 2/8/06, "S" plate number text	4.25
	b.	Like #1584a, but with "V" in plate number text	4.25

No. SP1584 is dated and canceled 1/9/06.

SP1585	39c	Flag and Statue of Liberty, #3985b	4.25
SP1591	39c	Children's Book Animals, #3987-3994	7.00
SP1592	39c	Turin Winter Olympics, #3995	4.25
SP1593	39c	Hattie McDaniel, #3996	4.25
SP1594	39c	Chinese New Year, #3997	8.00
SP1595	63c	Bryce Canyon, #C139	4.25
SP1596	75c	Great Smoky Mountains National Park, #C140	4.25
SP1597	84c	Yosemite National Park, #C141	4.25
SP1598	39c	Official, #O160	4.25
SP1599		Weddings, #3998-3999	5.25
SP1600	24c	Common Buckey Butterfly, #4000-4002	5.25
SP1601	39c	Crops, #4003-4017	9.00
SP1602	$4.05	X-Plane, #4018	8.00
SP1603	$14.40	X-Plane, #4019	20.00
SP1604	39c	Sugar Ray Robinson, #4020	4.25
SP1605	39c	Benjamin Franklin, #4021-4024	5.25
SP1606	39c	Disney Characters, #4025-4028	6.25
SP1607	39c	Love, #4029	4.25
SP1608	39c	Katherine Anne Porter, #4030	4.25
SP1609	39c	Amber Alert, #4031	4.25
SP1610	39c	Purple Heart, #4032	4.25
SP1611	39c	Wonders of America, #4033-4072	34.00
SP1612	39c	Samuel de Champlain, #4073	5.25
SP1613		Samuel de Champlain souvenir sheet, #4074	5.00
SP1614		Washington 2006 World Philatelic Exhibition souvenir sheet, #4075	13.50
SP1615	39c	Distinguished American Diplomats souvenir sheet, #4076	5.25
SP1616	39c	Judy Garland, #4077	4.25
SP1617	39c	Ronald Reagan, #4078	5.00
SP1618	39c	Happy Birthday, #4079	4.25
SP1619	39c	Baseball Sluggers, #4080-4083	5.75
SP1620	39c	DC Comics Superheroes, #4084	12.00
SP1621	39c	Motorcycles, #4085-4088	5.25
SP1622	39c	Quilts of Gee's Bend, Alabama, #4089-4098	7.00
SP1623	39c	Southern Florida Wetland, #4099	9.00
SP1624	$1	Official with solid blue background, #O161	6.25
SP1625	39c	Christmas Madonna, #4100	4.25
SP1626	39c	Christmas Snowflakes, #4101-4116	7.00
SP1627	39c	Eid, #4117	4.25
SP1628	39c	Hanukkah, #4118	4.25
SP1629	39c	Kwanzaa, #4119	4.25

2007-2012

SP1630	39c	Ella Fitzgerald, #4120	4.25
SP1631	39c	Oklahoma Statehood, #4121	4.25
SP1632	39c	Love, #4122	4.25
SP1633	84c	International Polar Year souvenir sheet, #4123	5.75
SP1634	39c	Henry Wadsworth Longfellow, #4124	4.25
SP1635	(41c)	"Forever" stamps, #4125-4128	5.25
SP1635a	(42c)	Forever stamp dated 2008, #4127d	4.25
SP1635b	(42c)	Forever stamps dated 2008, #4125b, 4126b	4.25
SP1635c	(42c)	Forever stamp dated 2008, #4127f	4.25
SP1635d	(44c)	Forever stamp dated 2009, #4127i	4.25
SP1635e	(44c)	Forever stamp dated 2009, #4128b	4.25
SP1635f	(44c)	Forever stamp dated 2009, #4125f, 4126d	5.25
SP1636	(41c)	Non-denominated Flag, #4129-4135	7.00
SP1637	41c	Settlement of Jamestown, #4136	4.25
SP1638	26c	Florida Panther, #4137, 4139, 4141, 4142	5.25
SP1639	17c	Bighorn Sheep, #4138	4.25
SP1640	17c	Bighorn Sheep coil, #4140	4.25
SP1641	41c	Star Wars, #4143	8.00
SP1642	69c	Okefenokee Swamp, #C142	4.25
SP1643	90c	Hagatna Bay, Guam, #C143	4.25
SP1644	$4.60	Air Force One, #4144	9.00
SP1645	$16.25	Marine One, #4145	25.00
SP1646	41c	Pacific Lighthouses, #4146-4150	6.25
SP1647	41c	Official coil, #O162	4.25
SP1648		Love Hearts, #4151-4152	5.25
SP1649	41c	Pollination, #4156b, 4156c	7.00
SP1650	(10c)	Patriotic Banner, #4157-4158	4.25
SP1651	41c	Marvel Comics Superheroes, #4159	13.50
SP1652	41c	Vintage Mahogany Speedboats, #4160-4163	6.25
SP1653	41c	Purple Heart, #4164	4.25
SP1654	41c	Louis Comfort Tiffany, #4165	4.25
SP1655	41c	Flowers, #4166-4185	12.00
SP1656	41c	Flag, #4186-4191	8.00
SP1657	41c	Disney Characters, #4192-4195	7.00
SP1658	41c	Celebrate, #4196	4.50
SP1659	41c	James Stewart, #4197	4.50
SP1660	41c	Alpine Tundra, #4198	9.00
SP1661	41c	Gerald R. Ford, #4199	4.25
SP1662	41c	Jury Duty, #4200	4.25
SP1663	41c	Mendez v. Westminster, #4201	4.25
SP1664	41c	Eid, #4202	4.25
SP1665	41c	Auroras, #4203-4204	4.25
SP1666	41c	Yoda, #4205	5.00
SP1667	41c	Christmas Madonna, #4206	4.25
SP1668	41c	Christmas Knits, #4209, 4210, 4212, 4215	5.25

No. SP1668 appears to have a representative sampling of Nos. 4207-4218, and other examples may show different stamps from the set.

SP1669	41c	Hanukkah, #4219	4.25
SP1670	41c	Kwanzaa, #4220	4.25
SP1671	41c	Chinese New Year, #4221	4.25
SP1672	41c	Charles W. Chesnutt, #4222	4.25
SP1673	41c	Marjorie Kinnan Rawlings, #4223	4.25

2008

SP1674	41c	American Scientists, #4224-4227	5.25
SP1675	41c	Flags, #4230, 4244, 4245, 4247 (lilac sheet)	5.25

No. SP1675 appears to have a representative sampling of Nos. 4228-4231 and Nos. 4244-4247.

SP1676	41c	Flags, #4234, 4236, 4237, 4243 (gray sheet)	5.25

No. SP1676 appears to have a representative sampling of Nos. 4232-4243.

SP1677	42c	American Journalists, #4248-4252	5.25

SP1678	27c	Tropical Fruit, #4253-4262	7.00
SP1679	42c	Purple Heart, #4263-4264	4.25
SP1680	42c	Frank Sinatra, #4265	4.50
SP1681	72c	13-Mile Woods, New Hampshire, #C144	4.25
SP1682	94c	Trunk Bay, St. John, Virgin Islands, #C145	5.00
SP1683	42c	Minnesota Statehood, #4266	4.25
SP1684	62c	Dragonfly, #4267	5.00
SP1685	$4.80	Mount Rushmore, #4268	10.00
SP1686	$16.50	Hoover Dam, #4269	22.50
SP1687	42c	Love, #4270	4.25
SP1688	42c, 59c	Wedding Hearts, #4271-4272	5.25
SP1689	42c	Flags of Our Nation, #4273-4282	8.50
SP1690	42c	Flags of Our Nation, #4283-4292	8.50
SP1691	42c	Flags of Our Nation, #4293-4302	8.50
SP1692	44c	Flags of Our Nation, #4303-4312	9.00
SP1693	(44c)	Flags of Our Nation, #4313-4322	9.00
SP1694	(45c)	Flags of Our Nation, #4323-4332	9.00
SP1695	42c	Charles and Ray Eames, #4333	12.00
SP1696	42c	Summer Olympics, #4334	4.25
SP1697	42c	Celebrate, #4335	4.25
SP1698	42c	Vintage Black Cinema, #4336-4340	5.25
SP1699	42c	Take Me Out to the Ball Game, #4341	4.25
SP1700	42c	Disney Characters - Imagination, #4342-4345	7.00
SP1701	42c	Albert Bierstadt, #4346	4.25
SP1702	42c	Sunflower, #4347	4.25
SP1703	(5c)	Sea Coast coil, litho. #4348	4.25
SP1704	42c	Latin Jazz, #4349	4.25
SP1705	42c	Bette Davis, #4350	4.25
SP1706	42c	Eid, #4351	4.25
SP1707	42c	Great Lakes Dunes, #4352	9.00
SP1708	42c	Automobiles of the 1950s, #4353-4357	5.75
SP1709	42c	Alzheimer's Disease Awareness #4358	4.25
SP1710	42c	Christmas Madonna, #4359	4.25
SP1711	42c	Christmas Nutcrackers, #4362, 4363, 4365, 4368	5.25

No. SP1711 appears to have a representative sampling of Nos. 4360-4371.

SP1712	42c	Hanukkah, #4372	4.25
SP1713	42c	Kwanzaa, #4373	4.25

2009

SP1714	42c	Alaska Statehood, #4374	4.50
SP1715	42c	Chinese New Year, #4375	4.50
SP1716	42c	Oregon Statehood, #4376	4.50
SP1717	42c	Edgar Allan Poe, #4377	4.50
SP1718	$4.95	Redwood Forest, #4378	11.00
SP1719	$17.50	Old Faithful, #4379	25.00
SP1720	42c	Abraham Lincoln, #4380-4383	7.00
SP1721	42c	Civil Rights Pioneers, #4384	5.25
SP1722	(5c)	Patriotic Banner coil, #4385	4.50
SP1723	1c	Official, #O163	4.50
SP1724	61c	Richard Wright, #4386	6.00
SP1725	28c	Polar Bear, Polar Bear coil, #4387, 4389	7.00
SP1726	64c	Dolphin #4388	7.00
SP1727	44c	Purple Heart #4390	5.00
SP1728	44c	Flag, #4391, 4395	5.00
SP1729	44c	Flag, #4392-4394	5.00
SP1730	44c	Flag, #4396	4.50
SP1731	44c, 61c	Wedding Rings, Wedding Cake, #4397-4398	5.75
SP1732	44c	The Simpsons, #4399-4403	7.00
SP1733	44c	Love, #4404-4405	5.75
SP1734	44c	Bob Hope, #4406	5.00
SP1735	44c	Celebrate, #4407	5.00
SP1736	44c	Anna Julia Cooper, #4408	5.00
SP1737	79c	Zion National Park, #C146	7.00
SP1738	98c	Grand Teton National Park, #C147	7.00
SP1739	44c	Gulf Coast Lighthouses, #4409-4413	7.00
SP1740	44c	Early TV Memories, #4414	13.50
SP1741	44c	Hawaii Statehood, #4415	5.00
SP1742	44c	Eid, #4416	5.00
SP1743	44c	Thanksgiving Day Parade, #4417-4420	5.75
SP1744	44c	Gary Cooper, #4421	5.00
SP1745	44c	Supreme Court Justices, #4422	7.00
SP1746	44c	Kelp Forest, #4423	9.00
SP1747	44c	Christmas Madonna, #4424	5.00
SP1748	44c	Christmas, #4425-4432	7.75
SP1749	44c	Hanukkah, #4433	4.50
SP1750	44c	Kwanzaa, #4434	4.50

2010

SP1751	44c	Chinese New Year, #4435	5.00
SP1752	44c	2010 Winter Olympics, #4436	5.00
SP1753	(44c)	Forever stamp, #4437	5.00
SP1754	$4.90	Mackinac Bridge, #4438	11.00
SP1755	$18.30	Bixby Creek Bridge, #4439	27.00
SP1756	44c	Distinguished Sailors, #4440-4443	7.00
SP1757	44c	Abstract Expressionists, #4444	9.50
SP1758	44c	Bill Mauldin, #4445	5.00
SP1759	44c	Cowboys of the Silver Screen, #4446-4449	7.00
SP1760	44c	Love, #4450	5.00
SP1761	44c	Animal Rescue, #4451-4460	9.00
SP1762	44c	Katharine Hepburn, #4461	5.00
SP1763	64c	Monarch Butterfly, #4462	7.00
SP1764	44c	Kate Smith, #4463	5.00
SP1765	44c	Oscar Micheaux, #4464	5.00
SP1766	44c	Negro Leagues Baseball, #4465-4466	7.00
SP1767	44c	Sunday Funnies, #4467-4471	7.00
SP1768	44c	Scouting, #4472	5.00
SP1769	44c	Winslow Homer, #4473	5.00
SP1770	44c	Hawaiian Rain Forest, #4474	9.00
SP1771	44c	Mother Teresa, #4475	5.00
SP1772	44c	Julia de Burgos, #4476	5.00
SP1773	44c	Christmas - Angel with Lute, #4477	5.00
SP1774	44c	Christmas - Evergreens, #4478-4485	9.00
SP1775	(44c)	Statue of Liberty and Flag coils, #4486, 4488, 4491	7.00

No. SP1775 appears to have a representative sampling of Nos. 4486-4491.

2011

SP1776	(44c)	Chinese New Year, #4492	5.00
SP1777	(44c)	Kansas Statehood, #4493	5.00
SP1778	(44c)	Ronald Reagan, #4494	5.00
SP1779	(5c)	Art Deco Bird, #4495	5.00
SP1780	44c	Quill and Inkwell, #4496	7.00
SP1781	(44c)	Latin Music Legends, #4497-4501	9.00
SP1782	(44c)	Celebrate, #4502	5.00
SP1783	(44c)	Jazz, #4503	5.00
SP1784	20c	George Washington, #4504, 4512	5.00
SP1785	29c	Herbs, #4505-4509, 4513-4517	9.00
SP1786	84c	Oveta Culp Hobby, #4510	7.00
SP1787	$4.95	New River Gorge Bridge, #4511	9.00
SP1788	(44c)	Statue of Liberty Reproduction and Flag ATM booklet stamps, #4518-4519	7.00
SP1789	80c	Voyageurs National Park, #C148	7.00
SP1790	(44c)	Wedding Roses, #4520	5.00
SP1791	64c	Wedding Cake, #4521	7.00
SP1792	(44c)	Civil War, #4522-4523	7.00
SP1793	(44c)	Go Green, #4524	9.00
SP1794	(44c)	Helen Hayes, #4525	5.00
SP1795	(44c)	Gregory Peck, #4526	5.00
SP1796	(44c)	Mercury Project and Messenger Mission, #4527-4528	7.00
SP1797	(44c)	Purple Heart, #4529	5.00
SP1798	(44c)	Indianapolis 500, #4530	5.00
SP1799	(44c)	Garden of Love, #4531-4540	9.00
SP1800	(44c)	American Scientists, #4541-4544	7.00
SP1801	(44c)	Mark Twain, #4545	5.00
SP1802	(44c)	Pioneers of Industrial Design, #4546	9.00
SP1803	(44c)	Owney, the Postal Dog, #4547	5.00
SP1804	(44c)	U.S. Merchant Marine, #4548-4551	7.00
SP1805	(44c)	Eid, #4552	5.00
SP1806	(44c)	Disney-Pixar Films - Send a Hello, #4553-4557	9.00
SP1807	(44c)	Edward Hopper, #4558	5.00
SP1808	(44c)	Statue of Liberty Reproduction and Flag convertible booklet stamps, #4559, 4560, 4562, 4563	7.00

No. SP1808 appears to have a representative sampling from Nos. 4559-4564.

SP1809	(44c)	Barbara Jordan, #4565	5.00
SP1810	(44c+11c)	Save Vanishing Species, #B4	5.00
SP1811	(44c)	Romare Bearden, #4566-4569	7.00
SP1812	(44c)	Christmas - Madonna, #4570	5.00
SP1813	(44c)	Christmas - Ornaments, #4571, 4576, 4581, 4582	7.00

No. SP1813 appears to have a representative sampling from Nos. 4571-4582.

SP1814	(44c)	Hanukkah, #4583	5.00
SP1815	(44c)	Kwanzaa, #4584	5.00

2012

SP1816	(25c)	Eagles, #4585-4590	7.00
SP1817	(44c)	New Mexico Statehood, #4591	5.00
SP1818	32c	Aloha Shirts, #4592-4601	9.00
SP1819	85c	Glacier National Park, #C149	7.00
SP1820	65c	Wedding Cake, #4602	7.00
SP1821	65c	Baltimore Checkerspot Butterfly, #4603	7.00
SP1822	65c	Dogs at Work, #4604-4607	9.00
SP1823	85c	Birds of Prey, #4608-4612	9.00
SP1824	45c	Weather Vanes, #4613-4617	7.00
SP1825	$1.05	Amish Buggy, Lancaster County, Pennsylvania, #C150	7.00
SP1826	(45c)	Bonsai, #4618-4622	7.00
SP1827	(45c)	Chinese New Year, #4623	5.00
SP1828	(45c)	John H. Johnson, #4624	5.00
SP1829	(45c)	Heart Health, #4625	5.00
SP1830	(45c)	Love, #4626	5.00
SP1831	(45c)	Arizona Statehood, #4627	5.00
SP1832	(45c)	Danny Thomas, #4628	5.00
SP1833	(45c)	Flags, #4632, 4635, 4637, 4638, 4642, 4644, 4645, 4647	9.00

No. SP1833 appears to have a representative sampling from Nos. 4629-4648.

SP1834	$5.15	Sunshine Skyway Bridge, #4649	9.00
SP1835	$18.95	Carmel Mission, #4650	34.00
SP1836	(45c)	Cherry Blossom Centennial, #4651-4652	7.00
SP1837	(45c)	William H. Johnson, #4653	5.00
SP1838	(45c)	Twentieth Century Poets, #4654-4663	9.00
SP1839	(45c)	Civil War, #4664-4665	7.00
SP1840	(45c)	José Ferrer, #4666	5.00
SP1841	(45c)	Louisiana Statehood, #4667	5.00
SP1842	(45c)	Great Film Directors, #4668-4671	7.00
SP1843	1c	Bobcat, #4672	5.00
SP1844	(45c)	Flags (Avery booklet stamps), #4673-4676	7.00
SP1845	(45c)	Disney-Pixar Films - Mail a Smile, #4677-4681	9.00
SP1846	32c	Aloha Shirts booklet stamps, #4682-4686	9.00
SP1847	(45c)	Bicycling, #4687-4690	7.00
SP1848	(45c)	Girl Scouts of America, Cent., #4691	5.00
SP1849	(45c)	Edith Piaf and Miles Davis, #4692-4693	7.00
SP1850	(45c)	Major League Baseball All-Stars, #4694-4697 (dated July 20)	7.00
SP1851	(45c)	Ted Williams, #4694 (dated July 21)	5.00
SP1852	(45c)	Larry Doby, #4695 (dated July 21)	5.00
SP1853	(45c)	Willie Stargell, #4696 (dated July 21)	5.00
SP1854	(45c)	Joe DiMaggio, #4697 (dated July 21)	5.00
SP1855	(45c)	Innovative Choreographers, #4698-4701	7.00
SP1856	(45c)	Edgar Rice Burroughs, #4702	5.00
SP1857	(45c)	USS Constitution, #4703	5.00
SP1858	(45c)	Purple Heart, #4704	5.00
SP1859	(45c)	O. Henry, #4705	5.00
SP1860	(45c)	Flags (Ashton-Potter ATM booklet stamps), #4706-4709	7.00
SP1861	(45c)	Earthscapes, #4710	13.50
SP1862	(45c)	Christmas - Religious, #4711	5.00
SP1863	(45c)	Christmas - Santa Over Town, #4712-4715	7.00
SP1864	(45c)	Lady Bird Johnson, #4716	7.00
SP1865	$1	Waves of Color, #4717	7.00
SP1866	$2	Waves of Color, #4718	7.00
SP1867	$5	Waves of Color, #4719	11.00
SP1868	$10	Waves of Color, #4720	20.00

2013

SP1869	(45c)	Emancipation Proclamation, #4721	5.00
SP1870	46c	Kaleidoscope Flowers, #4722-4725	7.00
SP1871	(45c)	Chinese New Year, #4726	7.00
SP1872	33c	Apples, #4727-4734	9.00
SP1873	66c	Wedding Cake, #4735	7.00
SP1874	66c	Spicebush Swallowtail Butterfly, #4736	7.00
SP1875	86c	Tufted Puffins, #4737	7.00
SP1876	$5.60	Arlington Green Bridge, #4738	9.00
SP1877	$19.95	Grand Central Terminal, #4739	37.50
SP1878	($1.10)	Earth, #4740	7.00
SP1879	(46c)	Love, #4741	5.00
SP1880	(46c)	Rosa Parks, #4742	5.00
SP1881	(46c)	Muscle Cars, #4742	7.00
SP1882	(46c)	Modern Art in America, #4748	11.00
SP1883	46c	Patriotic Star, #4749	5.00
SP1884	(46c)	La Florida, #4750-4753	7.00
SP1885	(46c)	Vintage Seed Packets, #4754-4763	9.00
SP1886	(46c)	Wedding Flowers, #4764	5.00
SP1887	66c	Flowers and "Yes I Do," #4765	7.00
SP1888	(46c)	Flags For All Seasons, #4769, 4772, 4774, 4775	7.00

No. SP1888 appears to have a representative sampling of Nos. 4766-4777.

SP1889	(46c)	Flags For All Seasons booklet stamps, #4778-4785	9.00
SP1890	(46c)	Lydia Mendoza, #4786	5.00
SP1891	(46c)	Civil War, #4787-4788	7.00
SP1892	(46c)	Johnny Cash, #4789	5.00
SP1893	(46c)	West Virginia Statehood, #4790	5.00
SP1894	(46c)	New England Coastal Lighthouses, #4791-4795	9.00
SP1895	(46c)	Flags For All Seasons booklet stamps (Avery Dennison printing), #4796-4799	9.00
SP1896	(46c)	Eid, #4800	5.00
SP1897	(46c)	Made in America, #4801	36.00

No. SP1897 consists of three pages containing each of the five panes having different margins of No. 4801.

SP1898	1c	Bobcat coil, #4802	5.00
SP1899	(46c)	Flags For All Seasons booklet stamps (Sennett printing with overall tagging), #4782a-4785a	9.00
SP1900	(46c)	Althea Gibson, #4803	5.00
SP1901	(46c)	March on Washington, 50th Anniv., #4804	5.00
SP1902	(46c)	Battle of Lake Erie, #4805	5.00
SP1903	$2	Inverted Jenny pane, #4806	27.00
SP1904	(46c)	Ray Charles, #4807	5.00
SP1905	(10c)	Snowflakes, #4808-4812	5.00
SP1906	(46c)	Christmas - Holy Family, #4813	5.00
SP1907	($1.10)	Christmas - Wreath, #4814	7.00
SP1908	(46c)	Christmas - Virgin and Child, #4815	5.00
SP1909	(46c)	Christmas - Poinsettias, #4816, 4821	7.00
SP1910	(46c)	Christmas - Gingerbread Houses, #4817-4820	9.00
SP1911	(46c)	Navy and Army Medals of Honor, #4822-4823	7.00
SP1912	(46c)	Hanukkah, #4824	5.00
SP1913	(46c)	Harry Potter Characters, #4825-4844	18.00
SP1914	(46c)	Kwanzaa, #4845	5.00

2014

SP1915	(46c)	Chinese New Year, #4846	5.00
SP1916	(46c)	Love, #4847	5.00
SP1917	49c	Ferns, #4848-4852	9.00

No.	Denom.	Description	Price
SP1918	(49c)	Fort McHenry Flag and Fireworks, #4853-4855	7.00
SP1919	(49c)	Shirley Chisholm, #4856	5.00
SP1920	34c	Hummingbird, #4857-4858	7.00
SP1921	70c	Great Spangled Fritillary Butterfly, #4859	7.00
SP1922	21c	Abraham Lincoln, #4860-4861	7.00
SP1923	(49c)	Winter Flowers, #4862-4865	9.00
SP1924	91c	Ralph Ellison, #4866	7.00
SP1925	70c	Wedding Cake, #4867	7.00
SP1926	(49c)	Fort McHenry Flag and Fireworks, #4868-4871	9.50
SP1927	($5.60)	Verrazano-Narrows Bridge, #4872	11.00
SP1928	($19.99)	USS Arizona Memorial, #4873	36.00
SP1929	(49c)	Ferns, #4874-4878	9.00
SP1930	70c	C. Alfred "Chief" Anderson, #4879	7.00
SP1931	(49c)	Jimi Hendrix, #4880	5.00
SP1932	(49c)	Flag For All Seasons booklet stamps, dated "2014," #4782b-4785b	9.00
SP1933	70c	Flowers and "Yes I Do," #4881	7.00
SP1934	(49c)	Songbirds, #4882-4891	11.00
SP1935	(49c)	Charlton Heston, #4892	5.00
SP1936	($1.15)	Global Sea Temperatures Map, #4893	7.00
SP1937	(49c)	Flags, #4894-4897	9.50
SP1938	(49c)	Wedding Flowers, dated "2014," #4764a	5.00
SP1939	(49c)	Circus Posters, #4898-4905	9.00
SP1940		Circus Posters imperforate sheet of 3, #4905c	9.00
SP1941	(49c)	Harvey Milk, #4906	5.00
SP1942	(49c)	Nevada Statehood, #4907	5.00
SP1943	(49c)	Hot Rods, #4908-4909	7.00
SP1944	(49c)	Medal of Honor, dated "2014," #4822a-4823a	7.00
SP1945	(49c)	Civil War, #4910-4911	7.00
SP1946	(49c)	Farmers Markets, #4912-4915	9.00
SP1947	(49c)	Janis Joplin, #4916	5.00
SP1948	(49c)	Christmas - Poinsettia, dated "2014," #4816b	5.00
SP1949	(49c)	Hudson River School Paintings, #4917-4920	9.00
SP1950	(49c)	Fort McHenry, #4921	5.00
SP1951	(49c)	Celebrity Chefs, #4922-4926	9.00
SP1952	($5.75)	Glade Creek Grist Mill, #4927	11.00
SP1953	(49c+11c)	Breast Cancer Research, #B5	5.00
SP1954	(49c)	Batman, #4928-4935	9.00
SP1955	(49c)	Purple Heart, dated "2014," #4704a	5.00
SP1956	($1.15)	Silver Bells Wreath, #4936	7.00
SP1957	(49c)	Winter Fun, #4937-4944	9.00
SP1958	(49c)	Christmas - Magi, #4945	5.00
SP1959	(49c)	Christmas - Rudolph the Red-nosed Reindeer, #4946-4949	9.00
SP1960	(49c)	Wilt Chamberlain, #4950-4951	7.00

2015

No.	Denom.	Description	Price
SP1961	(49c)	Battle of New Orleans, #4952	5.00
SP1962	$1	Patriotic Waves, #4953	7.00
SP1963	$2	Patriotic Waves, #4954	7.00
SP1964	(49c)	Love, #4955-4956	7.00
SP1965	(49c)	Chinese New Year, #4957	5.00
SP1966	(49c)	Robert Robinson Taylor, #4958	5.00
SP1967	(49c)	Rose and Heart, #4959	5.00
SP1968	70c	Tulip and Heart, #4960	7.00
SP1969	1c	Bobcat, dated "2015," #4672a	5.00
SP1970	(10c)	Flags, #4961-4963	7.00
SP1971	(49c)	Water Lilies, #4964-4967	7.00
SP1972	(49c)	Martín Ramírez, #4968-4972	9.00
SP1973	(49c)	Ferns, lithographed coils, #4973-4977, 4973a-4977a	9.00
SP1974	(49c)	From Me to You, #4978	5.00
SP1975	(49c)	Maya Angelou, #4979	5.00
SP1976	(49c)	Civil War, #4980-4981	7.00
SP1977	(49c)	Gifts of Friendship, #4982-4985	9.00
SP1978	(49c)	Special Olympics World Games, #4986	5.00
SP1979	(49c)	Help Find Missing Children, #4987	5.00
SP1980	(49c)	Medals of Honor, dated "2015," #4822b, 4823b, 4988	7.00
SP1981	(22c)	Emperor Penguins, #4989-4990	7.00
SP1982	(35c)	Coastal Birds, #4991-4998	9.00
SP1983	(71c)	Eastern Tiger Swallowtail Butterfly, #4999	7.00
SP1984	(71c)	Wedding Cake, #5000	7.00
SP1985	(71c)	Flowers and "Yes, I Do," #5001	7.00
SP1986	(71c)	Tulip and Heart, #5002	7.00
SP1987	(93c)	Flannery O'Connor, #5003	7.00
SP1988	(49c)	Summer Harvest, #5004-5007	9.00
SP1989	(49c)	Coast Guard, #5008	5.00
SP1990	(49c)	Elvis Presley, #5009	5.00
SP1991	(49c)	World Stamp Show 2016, #5010-5011	7.00
SP1992	(49c)	Ingrid Bergman, #5012	5.00
SP1993	(25c)	Eagles, #5013-5018	7.00
SP1994	(49c)	Celebrate, #5019	5.00
SP1995	(49c)	Paul Newman, #5020	5.00
SP1996	(49c)	Christmas - A Charlie Brown Christmas, #5021-5030	11.00
SP1997	(49c)	Geometric Snowflakes, #5031-5034	9.00

2016

No.	Denom.	Description	Price
SP1998	(49c)	Love, #5036	5.00
SP1999	1c	Albemarle Pippin Apples coil, #5037	5.00
SP2000	5c	Pinot Noir Grapes coil, #5038	5.00
SP2001	10c	Red Pears coil, #5039	5.00
SP2002	$6.45	La Cueva del Indio, #5040	11.00
SP2003	$22.95	Columbia River Gorge, #5041	40.50
SP2004	(49c)	Botanical Art, #5042-5051	11.00
SP2005	(49c)	Flag, #5052-5055	9.00
SP2006	(49c)	Richard Allen, #5056	5.50
SP2007	(49c)	Chinese New Year, #5057	5.50
SP2008	($1.20)	Moon, #5058	7.00
SP2009	(49c)	Sarah Vaughan, #5059	5.00
SP2010	(47c)	Shirley Temple, #5060	5.00
SP2011	(5c)	"USA" and Star, #5061	5.00
SP2012	(47c)	World Stamp Show 2016, #5062-5063	7.00
SP2013	(47c)	Repeal of the Stamp Act, #5064	5.00
SP2014	(47c)	Service Cross Medals, #5065-5068	10.00
SP2015	(47c)	Views of Our Planets, #5069-5076	10.00
SP2016	(47c)	Pluto Explored, #5077-5078	7.50
SP2017	(47c)	Classics Forever, #5079a-5079f	10.00
SP2018	(47c)	National Park Service, #5080	16.00
SP2019	(47c)	Colorful Celebrations, #5081-5090	12.00
SP2020	(47c)	Indiana Statehood, #5091	6.00
SP2021	(47c)	Eid, #5092	6.00
SP2022	(47c)	Soda Fountain Favorites, #5093-5097	10.00
SP2023	(25c)	Star Quilts, #5098-5099	6.00
SP2024	(47c)	Jaime Escalante, #5100	6.00
SP2025	(47c)	Pickup Trucks, #5101-5104	10.00
SP2026	(89c)	Henry James, #5105	7.50
SP2027	(47c)	Pets, #5106-5125	20.00
SP2028	(47c)	Songbirds in Snow, #5126-5129	10.00
SP2029	(47c)	Patriotic Spiral, #5130-5131	7.50
SP2030	(47c)	Star Trek, #5132-5135	10.00
SP2031	(68c)	Eastern Tailed-Blue Butterfly, #5136	7.50
SP2032	(47c)	Jack-O'-Lanterns, #5137-5140	10.00
SP2033	(47c)	Kwanzaa, #5141	6.00
SP2034	(47c)	Diwali, #5142	6.00
SP2035	(47c)	Christmas - Madonna and Child, #5143	6.00
SP2036	(47c)	Christmas - Nativity, #5144	6.00
SP2037	(47c)	Christmas - Holiday Windows, #5145-5148	10.00
SP2038	(47c)	Wonder Woman, #5149-5152	10.00
SP2039	(47c)	Hanukkah, #5153	6.00

2017

No.	Denom.	Description	Price
SP2040	(47c)	Chinese New Year, #5154	6.00
SP2041	(47c)	Love, #5155	6.00
SP2042	$6.65	Lili'uokalani Gardens, #5156	12.50
SP2043	$23.75	Gateway Arch, #5157	47.50
SP2044	(49c)	Flag, #5158, 5160, 5161, 5162	7.50
SP2045	(34c)	Shells, #5163-5170	10.00
SP2046	(49c)	Dorothy Height, #5171	6.00
SP2047	(5c)	"USA" and Star with Blue Frame, #5172	6.00
SP2048	(49c)	Oscar de la Renta, #5173	13.00
SP2049	(21c)	People Wearing Uncle Sam Hats, #5174	6.00
SP2050	(49c)	Pres. John F. Kennedy, #5175	6.00
SP2052	5c	Pinot Noir Grapes, serpentine die cut 11¼x11, #5177	6.00
SP2053	10c	Red Pears, serpentine die cut 11¼x11, #5178	6.00
SP2054	(49c)	Nebraska Statehood, #5179	6.00
SP2055	(49c)	WPA Posters, #5180-5189	12.00
SP2056	(49c)	Mississippi Statehood, #5190	6.00
SP2057	(70c)	Robert Panara, #5191	7.50
SP2058	(49c)	Delicioso (Latin American Dishes), #5192-5197	10.00
SP2059	($1.15)	Echeveria, #5198	7.50
SP2060	(49c)	Boutonniere, #5199	6.00
SP2061	(70c)	Corsage, #5200	7.50
SP2062	3c	Strawberries coil, #5201	6.00
SP2063	(49c)	Henry David Thoreau, #5202	6.00
SP2064	(49c)	Sports Balls, #5203-5210	10.00
SP2065	(49c)	Total Eclipse of the Sun, #5211	6.00
SP2066	(49c)	Andrew Wyeth Paintings, #5212	13.00
SP2067	(49c)	Disney Villains, #5213-5222	12.00
SP2068	(49c)	Sharks, #5223-5227	10.00
SP2069	(49c)	Protect Pollinators, #5228-5232	10.00
SP2070	(49c)	Flowers from the Garden, #5233-5240	12.00
SP2071	(49c)	Father Ted Hesburgh, #5241-5242	7.50
SP2072	(49c)	The Snowy Day, #5243-5246	10.00
SP2073	(49c)	Christmas Carols, #5247-5250	10.00
SP2074	(49c)	National Museum of African American History and Culture, #5251	6.00
SP2075	(49c)	History of Ice Hockey, #5252-5253	7.50
SP2076	(49c+11c)	Alzheimer's Disease Awareness, #B6	7.50

2018

No.	Denom.	Description	Price
SP2077	(49c)	Chinese New Year, #5254	6.00
SP2078	(49c)	Love, #5255	6.00
SP2079	2c	Meyer Lemons, #5256	6.00
SP2080	$6.70	Byodo-In Temple, #5257	12.50
SP2081	$24.70	Sleeping Bear Dunes, #5258	47.50
SP2082	(50c)	Lena Horne, #5259	6.00
SP2083	(50c)	Flag, #5260, 5262	7.50
SP2084	(50c)	Bioluminescent Life, #5264-5273	12.00
SP2085	(50c)	Illinois Statehood Bicent., #5274	6.00
SP2086	(50c)	Mister Rogers, #5275	6.00
SP2087	(50c)	Science, Technology Engineering and Mathematics Education, #5276-5279	7.50
SP2088	(50c)	Peace Rose, #5280	6.00
SP2089	(50c)	Blue Air Mail Centenary, #5281	6.00
SP2090	(50c)	Carmine Lake Air Mail Centenary, #5282	6.00
SP2091	(50c)	Sally Ride, #5283	6.00
SP2092	(50c)	Flag Act of 1818, Bicent., #5284	6.00
SP2093	(50c)	Frozen Treats, #5285-5294	12.00
SP2094	$1	Statue of Freedom, #5295	7.50
SP2095	$2	Statue of Freedom, #5296	10.00
SP2096	$5	Statue of Freedom, #5297	11.00
SP2097	(50c)	O Beautiful, #5298	20.00
SP2098	(50c)	Scooby-Doo, #5299	6.00
SP2099	(50c)	World War I, Cent, #5300	6.00
SP2100	(50c)	The Art of Magic, #5301-5305	10.00
SP2101	(50c)	The Art of Magic souvenir sheet, #5306	7.50
SP2102	(50c)	Dragons, #5307-5310	10.00
SP2103	($1.15)	Poinsettia, #5311	7.50
SP2104	(50c)	John Lennon, #5312-5315	10.00
SP2105	(50c)	First Responders, #5316	6.00
SP2106	(50c)	Birds in Winter, #5317-5320	10.00
SP2107	(50c)	Hot Wheels Toy Cars, #5321-5330	11.00
SP2108	(50c)	Christmas - Madonna, #5331	6.00
SP2109	(50c)	Christmas - Santa Claus booklet stamps, #5332-5335	10.00
SP2110	(50c)	Christmas - Santa Claus souvenir sheet, #5336	6.00
SP2111	(50c)	Kwanzaa, #5337	6.00
SP2112	(50c)	Hanukkah, #5338	6.00

2019

No.	Denom.	Description	Price
SP2113	(50c)	Love, #5339	6.00
SP2114	(50c)	Chinese New Year, #5340	6.00
SP2115	(15c)	People Wearing Uncle Sam's Hat coil stamp, #5341	6.00
SP2116	(55c)	U.S. Flag, #5342-5345	10.00
SP2117	(70c)	California Dogface Butterfly, #5346	7.50
SP2118	$7.35	Joshua Tree, #5347	15.00
SP2119	$25.50	Bethesda Fountain, #5348	50.00
SP2120	(55c)	Gregory Hines, #5349	6.00
SP2121	(55c)	Cactus Flowers, #5350-5359	12.00
SP2122	(55c)	Alabama Statehood, #5360	6.00
SP2123	(55c)	Star Ribbon, #5361-5362	7.50
SP2124	(35c)	Coral Reefs, #5363-5370	10.00
SP2125	(55c)	Marvin Gaye, #5371	6.00
SP2126	(55c)	Post Office Murals, #5372-5376	10.00
SP2127	(55c)	Maureen "Little Mo" Connolly Brinker, #5377	6.00
SP2128	(55c)	Transcontinental Railroad, #5378-5380	7.50
SP2129	(55c)	Wild and Scenic Rivers, #5381	20.00
SP2130	(55c)	Art of Ellsworth Kelly, #5382-5391	12.00
SP2131	(55c)	USS Missouri, #5392	6.00
SP2132	(55c)	George H.W. Bush, #5393	6.00
SP2133	(55c)	Sesame Street, 50th Anniv., #5394	20.00
SP2134	(55c)	Frogs, #5395-5398	10.00
SP2135	(55c)	First Moon Landing, 50th Anniv., #5399-5400	7.50
SP2136	(55c)	State and County Fairs, #5401-5404	10.00
SP2137	(55c)	Military Working Dogs, #5405-5408	10.00
SP2138	(55c)	Woodstock Music Festival, 50th Anniv., #5409	6.00
SP2139	(55c)	Tyrannosaurus Rex, #5410-5413	10.00
SP2140	(85c)	Walt Whitman, #5414	7.50
SP2141	(55c)	Winter Berries, #5415-5418	10.00
SP2142	(55c)	Purple Heart with Frame, #5419	6.00
SP2143	(55c)	Spooky Silhouettes, #5420-5423	10.00
SP2144	(55c)	Christmas Wreaths, #5424-5427	10.00
SP2145	(55c+10c)	Healing Post-traumatic Stress Disorder, #B7	7.50

2020

No.	Denom.	Description	Price
SP2146	(55c)	Chinese New Year, #5428	6.00
SP2147	$7.75	Big Bend, #5429	15.50
SP2148	$26.35	Grand Island Ice Caves, #5430	52.50
SP2149	(55c)	Love, #5431	6.00
SP2150	(55c)	Gwen Ifill, #5432	6.00
SP2151	(10c)	Star and Stripes, #5433	6.00
SP2152	(55c)	Celebrate, #5434	6.00
SP2153	(55c)	Wild Orchids, #5438-5442, 5450-5454	12.00

No. SP2153 appears to have a representative sampling from Nos. 5435-5454.

No.	Denom.	Description	Price
SP2154	(55c)	Arnold Palmer, #5455	6.00
SP2155	(55c)	Maine Statehood Bicentenary, #5456	6.00
SP2156	(55c)	Boutonniere, #5457	6.00
SP2157	(70c)	Corsage, #5458	7.50
SP2158	(55c)	Earth Day, 50th Anniv., #5459	6.00
SP2159	($1.20)	Chrysanthemum, #5460	7.50
SP2160	(55c)	American Gardens, #5461-5470	12.00
SP2161	(55c)	Voices of the Harlem Renaissance, #5471-5474	10.00
SP2162	(55c)	Enjoy the Great Outdoors, #5475-5479	10.00
SP2163	(55c)	Hip Hop, #5480-5483	10.00
SP2164	(55c)	Fruits and Vegetables, #5484-5493	12.00
SP2165	(55c)	Bugs Bunny, 80th Anniv., #5494-5503	12.00
SP2166	(55c)	Wire Sculptures of Ruth Asawa, #5504-5513	12.00
SP2167	(55c)	Innovation, #5514-5518	10.00
SP2168	(55c)	Thank You, #5519-5522	10.00
SP2169	(55c)	Woman Suffrage Centenary, #5523	6.00
SP2170	(55c)	Mayflower in Plymouth Harbor, 400th Anniv., #5524	6.00
SP2171	(55c)	Christmas — Madonna, #5525	6.00
SP2172	(55c)	Christmas — Holiday Delights, #5526-5529	10.00
SP2173	(55c)	Hanukkah, #5530	6.00
SP2174	(55c)	Kwanzaa, #5531	6.00
SP2175	(55c)	Winter Scenes, #5532-5541	12.00
SP2176	(55c)	Drug Free USA, #5542	6.00

2021

SP2177	(55c)	Love, #5543	6.00
SP2178	(20c)	Brush Rabbit, #5544-5545	7.50
SP2179	(36c)	Barns, #5546-5553	10.00
SP2180	$7.95	Castillo de San Marcos, #5554	16.00
SP2181	(55c)	August Wilson, #5555	6.00
SP2182	(55c)	Chinese New Year, #5556	6.00
SP2183	(55c)	Chien-Shiung Wu, #5557	6.00
SP2184	(55c)	Garden Beauty, #5558-5567	12.00
SP2185	(75c)	Colorado Hairstreak Butterfly, #5568	7.50
SP2186	(55c)	Espresso Drinks, #5569-5572	10.00
SP2187	(55c)	Star Wars Droids, #5573-5582	12.00
SP2188	(55c)	Heritage Breeds, #5583-5592	12.00
SP2189	(55c)	Go For Broke, #5593	6.00
SP2190	(55c)	Emilio Sanchez, #5594-5597	10.00
SP2191	(55c)	Sun Science, #5598-5607	12.00
SP2192	(55c)	Yogi Berra, #5608	6.00
SP2193	(55c)	Tap Dance, #5609-5613	10.00
SP2194	(55c)	Mystery Message, #5614	6.00
SP2195	(55c)	Western Wear, #5615-5618	10.00
SP2196	(95c)	Ursula K. Le Guin, #5619	7.50
SP2197	(55c)	Raven Story, #5620	6.00
SP2198	(55c)	Mid-Atlantic Lighthouses, #5621-5625	10.00
SP2199	(55c)	Missouri Statehood Bicentenary, #5626	6.00
SP2200	(55c)	Backyard Games, #5627-5634	12.00
SP2201	(58c)	Happy Birthday, #5635	6.00
SP2202	(58c)	Message Monsters, #5636-5639	10.00
SP2203	(58c)	Day of the Dead, #5640-5643	10.00
SP2204	(58c)	Christmas, #5644-5647	10.00
SP2205	(58c)	Otters in Snow, #5648-5651	10.00

COMPUTER VENDED POSTAGE

1992

SPCVP1	29c	Postage and Mailing Center (PMC) coil strip of 3, #31	4.25

1994

SPCVP2	29c	Postage and Mailing Center (PMC) horiz. coil strip of 3, #32	4.50

1996

SPCVP3	32c	Postage and Mailing Center (PMC) horiz. strip of 3, #33	5.00

INTERNATIONAL REPLY COUPONS

Coupons produced by the Universal Postal Union for member countries to provide for payment of postage on a return letter from a foreign country. Exchangeable for a stamp representing single-rate ordinary postage (and starting with the use of Type D3, airmail postage) to a foreign country under the terms of contract as printed on the face of the coupon in French and the language of the issuing country and on the reverse in four, five or six other languages.

Postmasters are instructed to apply a postmark indicating date of sale to the left circle on the coupon. When offered for exchange for stamps, the receiving postmaster is instructed to cancel the right circle.

Coupons with no postmark are not valid for exchange. Coupons with two postmarks have been redeemed and normally are kept by the post office making the exchange. **Coupons with one postmark are valued here.** Some coupons with a stamp added to pay an increased rate are listed in footnotes.

The following is a list of all varieties issued by the Universal Postal Union for any or all member countries.

Dates are those when the rate went into effect. The date that any item was put on sale in the United States can be very different.

Type A — Face

Wmk. "25c Union Postale Universelle 25c"

1907-20

A1 Face — Name of country in letters 1 ½mm high.
Reverse — Printed rules between paragraphs German text contains four lines.

1907-20

A2 Face — Same as A1.
Reverse — Same as A1 but without rules between paragraphs.

1910-20

A3 Face — Same as A1 and A2.
Reverse — Same as A2 except German text has but three lines.

1912-20

A4 Face — Name of country in bold face type; letters 2mm to 2 ½mm high.
Reverse — Same as A3.

1922-25

A5 Face — French words "le mois d'émission écoulé, deux mois encore."
Reverse — As A3 and A4 but overprinted with new contract in red; last line of red German text has five words.

Wmk. "50c Union Postale Universelle 50c"

1925-26

A6 Face — Same as A5.
Reverse — Four paragraphs of five lines each.

1926-29

A7 Face — French words "il est valable pendant un délai de six mois."
Reverse — As A6 but overprinted with new contract in red; last line of red German text has two words.

Wmk. "40c Union Postale Universelle 40c"

1926-29

A8 Face — Design redrawn. Without lines in hemispheres.
Reverse — Four paragraphs of four lines each.

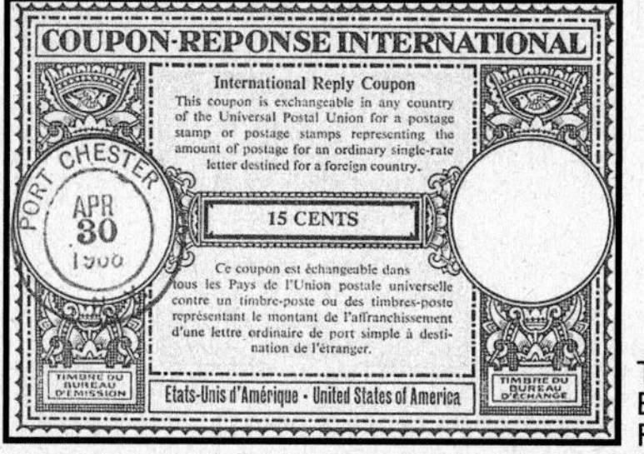

Type B — Face

1931-35 **Wmk. Double-lined "UPU"**

B1 Face — French words "d'une lettre simple."
Reverse — Four paragraphs of three lines each.

1935-36

B2 Face — French words "d'une lettre ordinaire de port simple."
Reverse — Last line of German text contains two words.

1936-37

B3 Face — Same as B2.
Reverse — Last line of German text contains one word.

1937-40

B4 Face — Same as B2 and B3. "Any Country of the Union."
Reverse — German text is in German Gothic type.

1945

B5 Face — "Any Country of the Universal Postal Union."
Reverse — Each paragraph reads "Universal Postal Union."

Type B5 exists without central printing on face.

1950

B6 Face — Same as B5.
Reverse — Five paragraphs (English, Arabic, Chinese, Spanish, Russian).

1954

B7 Face — Same as B5.
Reverse — Six paragraphs (German, English, Arabic, Chinese, Spanish, Russian.)

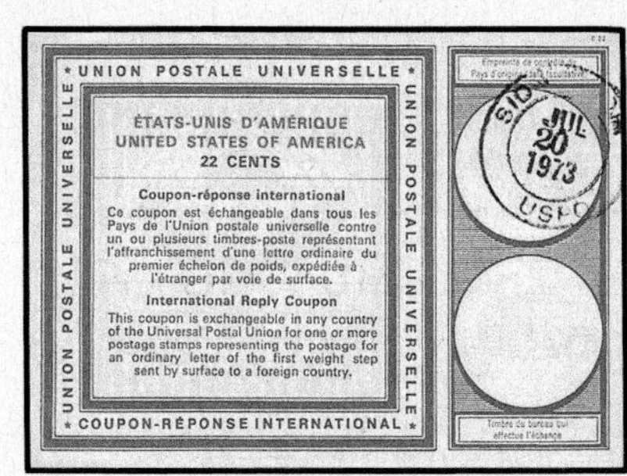

Type C — Face

1968 **Wmk. Single-lined "UPU" Multiple**

C1 Face — French words "d'une lettre ordinaire de port simple."
Reverse — Six paragraphs (German, English, Arabic, Chinese, Spanish, Russian).

Foreign coupons, but not U.S., of type C1 are known with large double-lined "UPU" watermark, as on type B coupons.

1971

C2 Face — French words "d'une lettre ordinaire du premier échelon de poids."
Reverse — Six paragraphs (German, English, Arabic, Chinese, Spanish, Russian).

Type D — Face

1975 **Wmk. Single-lined "UPU" Multiple**

D1 Face — French words "d'une lettre ordinaire, expédiée à l'étranger par voie de surface."
Reverse — Six paragraphs (German, English, Arabic, Chinese, Spanish, Russian).

D2 Face — Left box does not have third line of French and dotted circle.
Reverse — Same as D1.

On D1 and D2 the watermark runs horizontally or vertically.

D3 Face — ....aerienne. Left box as D2 with (faculative) added.
Reverse — As D1, all references are to air service.

D4 Face As D3, "CN 01 / (ancien C22)" replaces "C22."

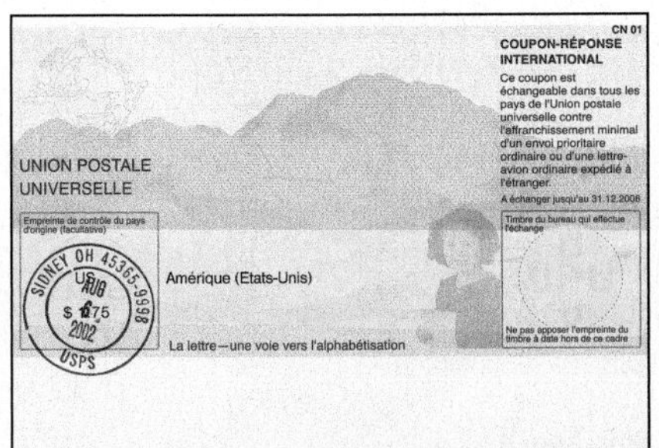

Type E — Face

Wmk. "UPU" in cross & 8-pointed star horiz. across sheet

2002

E1 Face Shown
Reverse Six paragraphs (German, English, Arabic, Chinese, Spanish, Russian), repeating expiration date paragraph in same languages, bar code.

Coupons exist without the validating origination markings. Type E coupons have a bar code on the reverse that identifies the originating country and the date of printing.

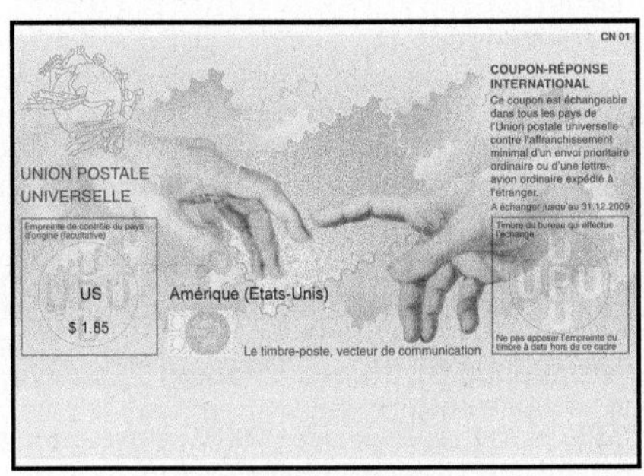

Type F — Face

Wmk. "UPU" in cross & 8-pointed star horiz. across sheet

2006

F1 Face Shown
Reverse Six paragraphs (German, English, Arabic, Chinese, Spanish, Russian), repeating expiration date paragraph in same languages, bar code.

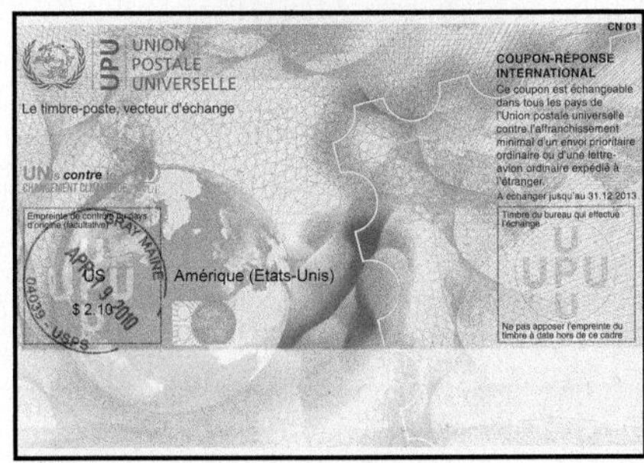

Type G — Face

2009

G1 Face Shown
Reverse Six paragraphs (German, English, Arabic, Chinese, Spanish, Russian), repeating expiration date paragraph in same languages, bar code.

REPLY COUPONS ISSUED FOR THE UNITED STATES

1907, Oct. 1

IRC2 A2 6c **slate green & gray green** 27.50

Rules omitted on reverse.

Earliest documented use: Oct. 10, 1907.

1912

IRC3 A4 6c **slate green & gray green** 32.50

Three line English paragraph on face.

1922, Jan. 1

IRC4 A5 11c **slate green & gray green,** name 81½mm long 25.00
a. Name 88½mm long 25.00

Five line English paragraph on face. Red overprint on reverse.

1925-26

IRC5 A6 11c **slate green & gray green** 22.50

Five line English paragraph on face. No overprint on reverse.

IRC6 A6 9c **slate green & gray green,** *Oct. 1, 1925* 22.50

1926

IRC7 A7 9c **slate green & gray green** 32.50

Four line English paragraph on face. Red overprint on reverse.

IRC8 A8 9c **slate green & gray green** 25.00

Without lines in hemispheres.

1935

IRC9 B2 9c **blue & yellow** 11.00

On reverse, last line of German text contains two words.

1936

IRC10 B3 9c **blue & yellow** 11.00

On reverse, last line of German text contains one word.

1937

IRC11 B4 9c **blue & yellow** 8.00

On reverse, German text in German Gothic type.

1945

IRC12 B5 9c **blue & yellow,** Italian text on reverse in 4 lines 6.00
a. Italian text on reverse in 3 lines 7.50

On face, "Universal Postal Union" replaces "Union."

1948, Oct. 15

IRC13 B5 11c **blue & yellow** 5.00

1950

IRC14 B6 11c **blue & yellow** 6.00

On reverse, text in English, Arabic, Chinese, Spanish, Russian.

1954, July 1

IRC15 B7 13c **blue & yellow** 6.00

On reverse, text in German, English, Arabic, Chinese, Spanish, Russian.
Varieties: period under "u" of "amount" in English text on reverse, and period under "n" of "amount." Also, country name either 47mm or 50mm long.

No. IRC15 Surcharged in Various Manners

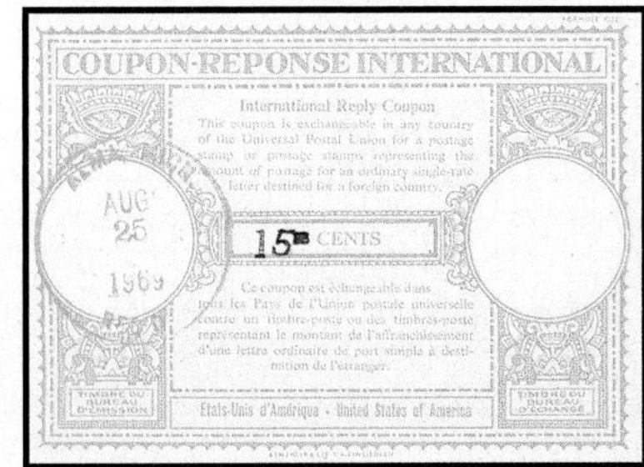

1959, May 2

IRC16 B7 15c on 13c **blue & yellow** 6.00

Individual post offices were instructed to surcharge the 13c coupon, resulting in many types of surcharge in various inks. For example, "REVALUED 15 CENTS," reading vertically; "15," etc.

1959, May 2

IRC17 B7 15c **blue & yellow** 5.00

1964

IRC18 B7 15c **blue & yellow** 5.00
a. Reverse printing 60mm deep instead of 65mm (smaller Arabic characters) 5.00

On face, box at lower left: "Empreinte de contrôle / du Pays d'origine / (date facultative)" replaces "Timbre du / Bureau / d'Emission."

1969

IRC19 C1 15c **blue & yellow** 4.50

1971, July 1

IRC20 C2 22c **blue & yellow** 4.50

No. IRC20 Surcharged in Various Manners

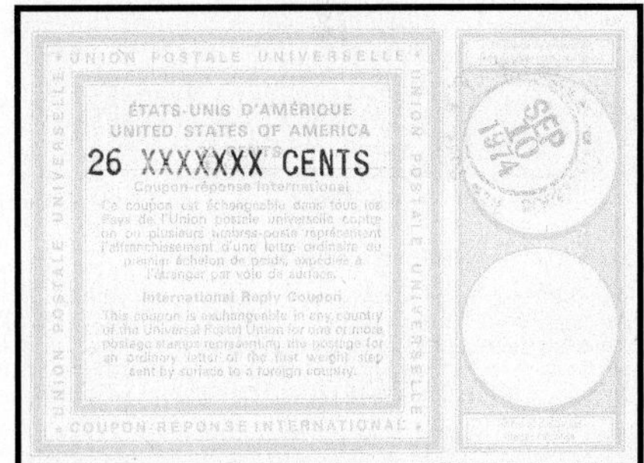

1974, Jan. 5

IRC21 C2 26c on 22c **blue & yellow** 6.50

See note after No. IRC16.

1975, Jan. 2

IRC22 D1 26c **yellow & blue** 4.00

No. IRC22 Surcharged in Various Manners

1976, Jan. 3

IRC23 D1 42c on 26c **yellow & blue** 6.50

See note after No. IRC16. Several post offices are known to have surcharged No. IRC21 (42c on 26c on 22c).

Provisional surcharges on Nos. IRC24-IRC27 were not permitted.

1976, Jan. 3

IRC24 D1 42c **blue & yellow** 4.50

Many foreign countries use non-denominated IRCs. The U.S. has never ordered or used these "generic" items.

1981, July 1

IRC26 D1 65c **blue & yellow** 5.50

1986, Jan. 1

IRC27 D2 80c **blue & yellow** 5.50

1988, Apr. 3

IRC28 D2 95c **blue & yellow** 5.00
IRC29 D3 95c **blue & yellow** 5.00
a. "9.1992" in lower left corner 5.00

Post offices were authorized on July 11, 1995 to revalue remaining stock of 95c IRCs to $1.05 by applying 10c in stamps until new stock (No. 30) arrived. All 95c varieties are known revalued thus.

The date of issue of No. IRC29 is not known. Earliest documented use: Jan. 2, 1992.

No. IRC28 exists with inverted watermark (tops of letters facing right).

1995

IRC30 D4 $1.05 **blue & yellow**, "4.95" in lower left corner 3.75
a. "10.98" in lower left corner 25.00
b. As "a," with "United States of America" in left box 50.00

"1.05" comes 1 ½mm or 3mm high. 3mm height has numerals more widely spaced.

Earliest documented use: July 12, 1995.

Post offices were authorized on Jan. 7, 2001, to revalue remaining stock of $1.05 IRCs to $1.75 by applying 70c in stamps until new stock arrived. All $1.05 varieties are known revalued thus. Value $7.

2002, Jan. 1

IRC31 E1 $1.75 **multicolored** 3.50

Effective Jan. 8, 2006, the rate increased to $1.85. Post offices were authorized to revalue remaining stock of $1.75 IRCs to $1.85 by applying 10c in stamps.

2006, Aug. 17

IRC32 F1 $1.85 **multicolored** 3.75

Effective May 14, 2007, the rate increased to $2. Post offices were authorized to revalue remaining stock of $1.85 IRCs to $2 by applying 15c in stamps or postage validation imprinter labels.

2009, Aug. 4

IRC33 G1 $2.10 **multicolored** 4.25

Effective Jan. 22, 2012, the rate increased to $2.20. Post offices were authorized to revalue remaining stock of $2.10 IRCs to $2.20 by applying 10c in stamps or postage validation meter labels.

The availability of International Reply Coupons ended January 13, 2013, after which they were not supposed to be on sale. They lost their validity December 31, 2013.

POST OFFICE SEALS

Official Seals began to appear in 1872. They do not express any value, having no franking power.

The first seal issued was designed to prevent tampering with registered letters while in transit. It was intended to be affixed over the juncture of the flaps of the large official envelopes in which registered mail letters were enclosed or stamp requisitions were shipped to postmasters and was so used exclusively. Beginning in 1877 (No. OX1 and later), Post Office Seals were used to repair damaged letters, reseal those opened by mistake or by customs inspectors, and to seal letters received by the Post Office unsealed.

Values for unused Post Office Seals are for those without creases. Uncanceled seals without gum will sell for less.

Used Post Office Seals will usually have creases from being applied over the edges of damaged or accidentally opened covers but will have either cancels, precancels or a signature or notation indicating use on the seal. Creased, uncanceled seals without gum are considered used and will sell for less than either an unused or a canceled used seal.

Covers with Post Office Seals are almost always damaged except in cases when the seal was applied to a cover marked "Received Unsealed." The values shown are for covers where the damage is consistent with the application of the seal.

Post Office Seals must be tied or exhibit some auxiliary marking or docketing to qualify for "on cover" values. No. OXF1 must bear a circular date stamp cancel and the cover to which it is affixed must bear the identical cancel to qualify for the "on cover" value.

REGISTRY SEALS

RGS1

National Bank Note Co.

Typographed from copper-faced electrotyped cliches or a plate made from them arranged in a 30-subject format (3x10) cut into two panes of 15 (3x5). A unique pane of 9 (3x3) exists, imperforate and without gum, and perforated and gummed examples of it may may have been distributed to post offices.

1872 Typo. Unwmk. *Perf. 12*
White Wove Paper

OXF1	RGS1	**green**	30.00	10.00
		On cover, Registered Package envelope, Terrell signature		60.00
		On cover, Registered Package envelope, Barber signature		40.00
		On cover, Postage Stamp Agency envelope, Terrell signature		250.00
		On cover, Postage Stamp Agency envelope, Barber signature		150.00
		Block of 4	*500.00*	
		Upper pane of 15	*2,000.*	
		Lower pane of 15 (unique)	*4,250.*	
a.		Pelure paper	*500.00*	275.00
b.		Imperf., pair	*1,250.*	
c.		Horizontally laid paper	*500.00*	
d.		Printed on both sides	*375.00*	
e.		Printed on both sides, back inverted	*400.00*	
f.		Double impression	*450.00*	—
g.		Double impression, one inverted	—	*450.00*

The second impression of Nos. OXF1d and OXF1e are usually faint, and the second impressions on Nos. OXF1f and OXF1g are always faint.

Cancellations

Black	10.00
Clearly readable town, month and day	+10.00
Same, with clearly readable year	+30.00
Blue	+5.00
Red	+15.00
Magenta	+30.00
Panama	—
Shanghai	—

Special Printings

Continental Bank Note Co.
Pane of 30 subjects (5x6)

1875(?) Hard White Wove Paper *Perf. 12*
Without Gum

OXF2 RGS1 **bluish green** *1,000.*
Pane of 30 —

American Bank Note Co.
Plate of 15 subjects (3x5)

1880(?) Soft Porous Paper *Perf. 12*
Without Gum

OXF3 RGS1 **bluish green** *1,250.*

POSTAGE STAMP AGENCY SEALS

Used to seal registered pouches containing stamps for distribution to Post Offices.

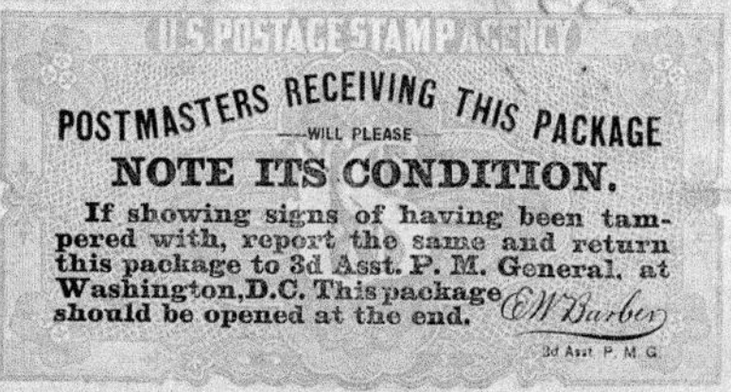

PSA1

Background size: 102x52mm.

Barber Signature

1875-93 Litho. Unwmk. *Die Cut*

OXF4 PSA1 **brown & black** 30.00
On cover 85.00

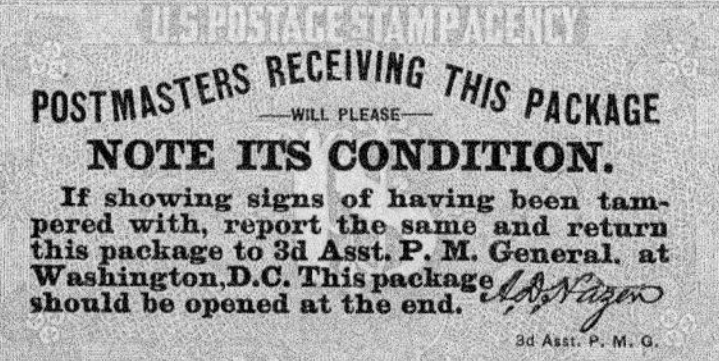

PSA2

Hazen Signature, Text 86mm Wide

OXF5 PSA2 **brown & black,** *1877* 25.00
On cover 60.00

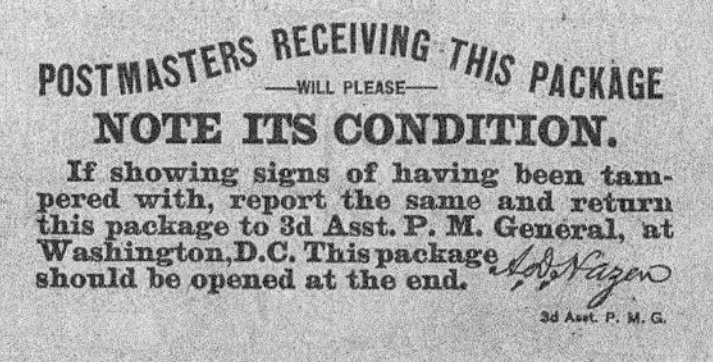

PSA3

Hazen Signature, Text 87mm Wide

OXF6	PSA3	**pink & red,** *1886*	50.00
		On cover	350.00
a.		**Salmon & red**	60.00
		On cover	*400.00*

POSTMASTERS RECEIVING THIS PACKAGE
—WILL PLEASE—
NOTE ITS CONDITIONS.
If showing signs of having been tampered with, report the same and return this package to 3d Asst. P. M. General, at Washington, D.C. This package should be opened at the end. H. R. Harris, 3d Asst. P. M. G.

PSA4

Harris Signature

OXF7 PSA4 **pink & red,** *1887* 45.00
On cover 150.00
a. **Salmon & red,** 55.00
On cover 175.00

POSTMASTERS RECEIVING THIS PACKAGE
—WILL PLEASE—
NOTE ITS CONDITION.
If showing signs of having been tampered with, report the same and return this package to 3d Asst. P. M. General, at Washington, D. C. This package should be opened at the end. A. D. Hazen, 3d Asst. P. M. G.

PSA5

Hazen Signature, Text 90½mm Wide

OXF8 PSA5 **pink & red,** *1889* 45.00
On cover 150.00

POSTMASTERS RECEIVING THIS PACKAGE
—WILL PLEASE—
NOTE ITS CONDITION.
If showing signs of having been tampered with, report the same and return this package to 3d Asst. P. M. General, at Washington, D. C. This package should be opened at the end. Kerr Craige, 3d Asst. P. M. G.

PSA6

Craige Signature

OXF9 PSA6 **pink & red,** *1893* 45.00
On cover 200.00

OPEN AT END.
THE POSTMASTER TO WHOM THIS PACKAGE IS SENT MUST NOTE ITS CONDITION AND CAREFULLY COUNT ITS CONTENTS.
If it shows signs of having been tampered with, the fact should be reported to the THIRD ASSISTANT POSTMASTER-GENERAL.
If the count shows a deficiency in the contents of the package, or an excess, the case must be treated as indicated in Sec. 120 P. L. & R. The Postmaster should not correspond with the Stamp Agent, but with the 3rd Assistant Postmaster-General. See also Sec. 1088 as to misdirected packages. KERR CRAIGE, 3d Asst. P. M. G.

PSA7

Background size: 120½x67mm.

Craige Signature, "3rd Asst. P.M.G."

1894 **Litho.** **Unwmk.** ***Die Cut***
OXF10 PSA7 **pink & black** 60.00
On cover 250.00

OPEN AT END.
THE POSTMASTER TO WHOM THIS PACKAGE IS SENT MUST NOTE ITS CONDITION AND CAREFULLY COUNT ITS CONTENTS.
If it shows signs of having been tampered with, the fact should be reported to the THIRD ASSISTANT POSTMASTER-GENERAL.
If the count shows a deficiency in the contents of the package, or an excess, the case must be treated as indicated in Sec. 120 P. L. & R. The Postmaster should not correspond with the Stamp Agent, but with the Third Assistant Postmaster-General. See also Sec. 1088 as to misdirected packages.
KERR CRAIGE, Third Assistant Postmaster-General.

PSA8

Craige Signature, "Third Assistant Postmaster General"

OXF11 PSA8 **pink & black** 35.00
On cover 150.00
a. **Deep pink & black** 35.00
On cover 150.00
b. Lacking pink background, on cover —

OPEN AT END.
THE POSTMASTER TO WHOM THIS PACKAGE IS SENT MUST NOTE ITS CONDITION AND CAREFULLY COUNT ITS CONTENTS.
If it shows signs of having been tampered with, the fact should be reported to the THIRD ASSISTANT POSTMASTER-GENERAL.
If the count shows a deficiency in the contents of the package, or an excess, the case must be treated as indicated in Sec. 120 P. L. & R. The Postmaster should not correspond with the Stamp Agent, but with the Third Assistant Postmaster-General. See also Sec. 1088 as to misdirected packages.
JOHN A. MERRITT, ~~KERR CRAIGE,~~ Third Assistant Postmaster-General.

PSA9

"John A. Merritt" in Sans-Serif Capitals at Left. Two Horizontal Lines Obliterating "Kerr Craige."

1897
OXF12 PSA9 **pale pink & black** 100.00
On cover *2,500.*

OPEN AT END.
THE POSTMASTER TO WHOM THIS PACKAGE IS SENT MUST NOTE ITS CONDITION AND CAREFULLY COUNT ITS CONTENTS.
If it shows signs of having been tampered with, the fact should be reported to the THIRD ASSISTANT POSTMASTER-GENERAL.
If the count shows a deficiency in the contents of the package, or an excess, the case must be treated as indicated in Sec. 120 P. L. & R. The Postmaster should not correspond with the Stamp Agent, but with the Third Assistant Postmaster-General. See also Sec. 1088 as to misdirected packages.
JOHN A. MERRITT, Third Assistant Postmaster-General.

PSA10

Merritt Signature

1897-1914
OXF13 PSA10 **rose & black** 35.00
On cover 130.00

OPEN AT END.
THE POSTMASTER TO WHOM THIS PACKAGE IS SENT MUST NOTE ITS CONDITION AND CAREFULLY COUNT ITS CONTENTS.
If it shows signs of having been tampered with, the fact should be reported to the THIRD ASSISTANT POSTMASTER-GENERAL.
If the count shows a deficiency in the contents of the package, or an excess, the case must be treated as indicated in Sec. 120, P. L. & R. The Postmaster should not correspond with the Stamp Agent, but with the Third Assistant Postmaster-General. See also Sec. 1088 as to misdirected packages.
EDWIN C. MADDEN, Third Assistant Postmaster-General.

PSA11

Madden Signature

OXF14 PSA11 **rose & black,** *1899* 40.00
On cover 250.00

The first paragraph of text reads: "...MUST NOTE ITS CONDITION AND CAREFULLY COUNT..."

OPEN AT END.
THE POSTMASTER TO WHOM THIS PACKAGE IS SENT MUST NOTE ITS CONDITION AND IMMEDIATELY UPON ITS RECEIPT CAREFULLY COUNT ITS CONTENTS.
If it shows signs of having been tampered with, the fact should be reported to the THIRD ASSISTANT POSTMASTER-GENERAL.
If the count shows a deficiency in the contents of the package, or an excess, the case must be treated as indicated in Sec. 120, P. L. & R. The Postmaster should not correspond with the Stamp Agent, but with the Third Assistant Postmaster-General. See also Sec. 1088 as to misdirected packages.
EDWIN C. MADDEN, Third Assistant Postmaster-General.

PSA12

OXF14A PSA12 **rose & black,** *1899*
On cover *250.00*

The first paragraph of text reads: "...MUST NOTE ITS CONDITION AND IMMEDIATELY UPON.."

OPEN AT END.
THE POSTMASTER TO WHOM THIS PACKAGE IS SENT MUST NOTE ITS CONDITION AND IMMEDIATELY UPON ITS RECEIPT CAREFULLY COUNT ITS CONTENTS.
If it shows signs of having been tampered with, the fact should be reported to the Third Assistant Postmaster General.
INVOICE FOR THIS PACKAGE OF STAMPS WILL BE FOUND WITHIN. Count the stamps carefully, IN THE PRESENCE OF A DISINTERESTED WITNESS, as indicated on stub of invoice, and if an excess or shortage is found, treat the case as directed in Section 333, P. L. & R., notifying the Third Assistant Postmaster General, Division of Stamps. See Section 878, P. L. & R., as to misdirected packages.

PSA13

"Section 878"

OXF15 PSA13 **rose & black,** *1907* 30.00
On cover 140.00

OPEN AT END.
THE POSTMASTER TO WHOM THIS PACKAGE IS SENT MUST NOTE ITS CONDITION AND IMMEDIATELY UPON ITS RECEIPT CAREFULLY COUNT ITS CONTENTS.
If it shows signs of having been tampered with, the fact should be reported to the Third Assistant Postmaster General.
INVOICE FOR THIS PACKAGE OF STAMPS WILL BE FOUND WITHIN. Count the stamps carefully, IN THE PRESENCE OF A DISINTERESTED WITNESS, as indicated on invoice, and if an excess or shortage is found, treat the case as directed in Section 333, P. L. & R., as amended (1912 Postal Guide, page 43), notifying the Third Assistant Postmaster General, Division of Stamps. See Section 878, P. L. & R., as to misdirected packages.

PSA14

OXF15A PSA14 **rose & black,**
On cover *2,500.*

OPEN AT END
THE POSTMASTER TO WHOM THIS PACKAGE IS SENT MUST NOTE ITS CONDITION AND IMMEDIATELY UPON ITS RECEIPT CAREFULLY COUNT ITS CONTENTS.
If it shows signs of having been tampered with, the fact should be reported to the Third Assistant Postmaster General, Division of Stamps.
INVOICE FOR THIS PACKAGE OF STAMPS WILL BE FOUND WITHIN. Count the stamps carefully, IN THE PRESENCE OF A DISINTERESTED WITNESS, as indicated on invoice, and if an excess or shortage is found, treat the case as directed in Section 159, P. L. & R., notifying the Third Assistant Postmaster General, Division of Stamps. See Section 970, P. L. & R., as to misdirected packages.

PSA15

"Section 970"

OXF16 PSA15 **rose & black,** *1912* 35.00
On cover 175.00

OPEN AT END
THE POSTMASTER TO WHOM THIS PACKAGE IS SENT MUST NOTE ITS CONDITION AND IMMEDIATELY UPON ITS RECEIPT CAREFULLY COUNT ITS CONTENTS.
If it shows signs of having been tampered with, the fact should be reported to the Third Assistant Postmaster General, Division of Stamps.
INVOICE FOR THIS PACKAGE OF STAMPS WILL BE FOUND WITHIN. Count the stamps carefully, IN THE PRESENCE OF A DISINTERESTED WITNESS, as indicated on invoice, and if an excess or shortage is found, treat the case as directed in Section 159, P. L. & R., notifying the Third Assistant Postmaster General, Division of Stamps. See Section 970, P. L. & R., as to misdirected packages.

PSA16

OXF17 PSA16 **rose & black,** *1914* 40.00
On cover 175.00

DEAD LETTER OFFICE SEALS

Nos. OXA1-OXA9 were used by general Dead Letter Office personnel. Nos. OXB1-OXB5 appear to have been used only by the Money Division of the Dead Letter Office. Both types were used for forwarding mail and may also have been used to return mail to the sender.

Post Office Department,
Office of Third Assistant Postmaster General,
DIVISION OF DEAD LETTERS,
TO THE PERSON ADDRESSED:
Inform your correspondent of the correct name of your post office.
TO THE POSTMASTER:
If this letter cannot be delivered you will, at the expiration of SEVEN days, stamp the letter with your postmarking stamp, and send it to the Dead Letter Office as "Unmailable," as required by Sec. 443, Postal Regulations.
A. D. HAZEN, Third Assistant P. M. Gen'l.

"Hazen" — DLO1

1884 **Litho.** ***Perf. 10½***
OXA1 DLO1 **black** 55.00
On cover 200.00

Perf. 12

OXA1A DLO1 **black** 25.00
On cover 125.00

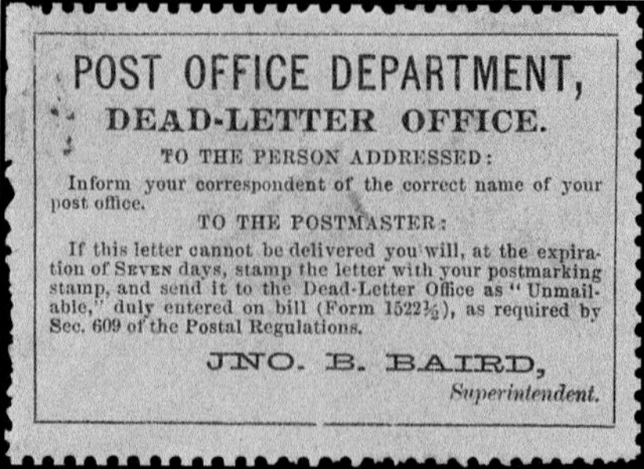
POST OFFICE DEPARTMENT,
DEAD-LETTER OFFICE.
TO THE PERSON ADDRESSED:
Inform your correspondent of the correct name of your post office.
TO THE POSTMASTER:
If this letter cannot be delivered you will, at the expiration of SEVEN days, stamp the letter with your postmarking stamp, and send it to the Dead-Letter Office as "Unmailable," duly entered on bill (Form 1522½), as required by Sec. 609 of the Postal Regulations.
JNO. B. BAIRD,
Superintendent.

"Baird" — DLO2

1887-88 *Perf. 10½*

OXA2 DLO2 **black** 55.00
On cover *350.00*

a. Last line of text reads "the Postal Regulations" instead of "Sec. 609 of the Postal Regulations", on cover —

POST OFFICE DEPARTMENT,
DEAD-LETTER OFFICE.
TO THE PERSON ADDRESSED:
Inform your correspondent of the correct name of your post office.
TO THE POSTMASTER:
If this letter cannot be delivered you will, at the expiration of SEVEN days, stamp the letter with your postmarking stamp, and send it to the Dead-Letter Office as "Unmailable," duly entered on bill (Form 1522½), as required by Paragraph 6 of Sec. 609 of the Postal Regulations.
SUPERINTENDENT.

"Superintendent" — DLO3

1891 *Perf. 10½*

OXA3 DLO3 **black** 35.00
On cover 175.00

Perf. 12

OXA3A DLO3 **black** 30.00
On cover 150.00

POST OFFICE DEPARTMENT,
Office of First Ass't P. M. General,
DEAD-LETTER OFFICE.
TO THE PERSON ADDRESSED:
Inform your correspondent of the correct name of your post office.
TO THE POSTMASTER:
If this letter cannot be delivered you will, at the expiration of SEVEN days, stamp the letter with your postmarking stamp, and send it to the Dead-Letter Office as "Unmailable," duly entered on bill (Form 1522½), as required by Paragraph 6 of Sec. 566 of the Postal Regulations.
5—2807

"5-2807" — DLO4

d it to the Dead-Letter Office as "
ered on bill (Form 1522½), as req
Sec. 609 of the Postal Regulations.
5—2807

OXA4a

1892 *Perf. 12*

OXA4 DLO4 **black** 25.00
On cover 125.00

a. With "Sec. 609 of the Postal Regulations" instead of "Sec. 566" —

POST OFFICE DEPARTMENT,
Office of First Ass't P. M. General,
DEAD-LETTER OFFICE.
TO THE PERSON ADDRESSED:
Inform your correspondent of the correct name of your post office.
TO THE POSTMASTER:
If this letter can not be delivered you will, at the expiration of SEVEN days, stamp the letter with your postmarking stamp, and send it to the Dead-Letter Office as "Unmailable," duly entered on bill (Form 1522½), as required by Paragraph 6 of Sec. 566 of the Postal Regulations.
5—3282

"5-3282" — DLO5

1895 *Perf. 12*

OXA5 DLO5 **black** — 25.00
On cover 150.00

1898(?) *Hyphen hole perf. 7*

OXA6 DLO5 **black** 35.00
On cover 225.00

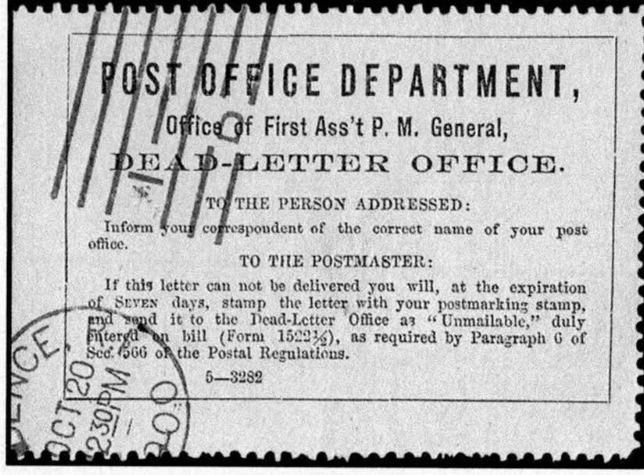
POST OFFICE DEPARTMENT,
Office of First Ass't P. M. General,
DEAD-LETTER OFFICE.
TO THE PERSON ADDRESSED:
Inform your correspondent of the correct name of your post office.
TO THE POSTMASTER:
If this letter can not be delivered you will, at the expiration of SEVEN days, stamp the letter with your postmarking stamp, and send it to the Dead-Letter Office as "Unmailable," duly entered on bill (Form 1522½), as required by Paragraph 6 of Sec. 566 of the Postal Regulations.
5—3282

DLO6

Similar to DLO5 but smaller type used for instructions to the postmasters.

1900 *Perf. 12*

OXA7 DLO6 **black** 45.00
On cover 250.00

POST OFFICE DEPARTMENT,
Office of First Ass't P. M. General,
DEAD-LETTER OFFICE.
TO THE PERSON ADDRESSED:
Inform your correspondent of the correct name of your post office.
TO THE POSTMASTER:
If this letter can not be delivered you will, at the expiration of SEVEN days, stamp the letter with your postmarking stamp, and send it to the Dead-Letter Office as "Unmailable," duly entered on bill (Form 1522½), as required by Sec. 686 of the Postal Regulations.
5—3282

"5-3282" at Right — DLO7

1902(?) 12 *Perf. 12*

OXA8 DLO7 **black** 25.00
On cover 125.00

POST OFFICE DEPARTMENT,
Office of First Ass't P. M. General,
DEAD-LETTER OFFICE.
TO THE PERSON ADDRESSED:
Inform your correspondent of the correct name of your post office.
TO THE POSTMASTER:
If this letter can not be delivered you will, at the expiration of SEVEN days, stamp the letter with your postmarking stamp, and send it to the Dead-Letter Office as "Unmailable," duly entered on bill (Form 1522½), as required by Paragraph 6 of Sec. 566 of the Postal Regulations.
5—3282.

"5-3282" at Center — DLO8

1902(?) *Perf. 12*

OXA9 DLO8 **black** 25.00
On cover 125.00

DEAD LETTER OFFICE RETURN SEALS

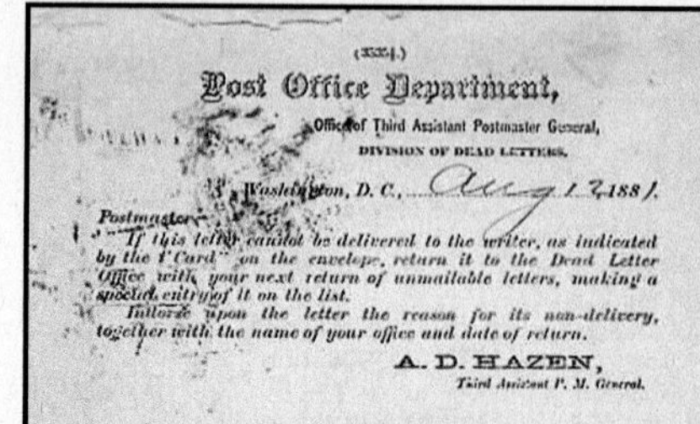
(3534.)
Post Office Department,
Office of Third Assistant Postmaster General,
DIVISION OF DEAD LETTERS,
Washington, D. C., Aug 1 2 188 1
Postmaster:
If this letter cannot be delivered to the writer, as indicated by the "Card" on the envelope, return it to the Dead Letter Office with your next return of unmailable letters, making a special entry of it on the list.
Indorse upon the letter the reason for its non-delivery, together with the name of your office and date of return.
A. D. HAZEN,
Third Assistant P. M. General.

DLO9

Incomplete Year Date ("188 ")

1881-91 *Die Cut*

OXB1 DLO9 **black** —
On cover *1,000.*

(3535.)
Post Office Department,
OFFICE OF THIRD ASSISTANT POSTMASTER GENERAL,
DIVISION OF DEAD LETTERS,
Washington, D. C., May 7, 1883.
If this letter cannot be delivered you will, at the expiration of SEVEN days, stamp the letter with your postmarking stamp, and return it and this circular to the DEAD LETTER OFFICE, with your next RETURN OF UNMAILABLE LETTERS, DULY NUMBERED AND ENTERED ON THE LIST, FORM No. 1522.
A. D. HAZEN,
Third Assistant P. M. General.
To the person addressed: Inform your correspondent of the correct name of your post office.

"1883" — DLO10

Complete Year Date

OXB2 DLO10 **black** (1882) 75.00
On cover *400.00*

OXB3 DLO10 **black** (1883) 75.00
On cover *400.00*

OXB4 DLO10 **black** (1886) 75.00
On cover *400.00*

Post Office Department,
OFFICE OF THIRD ASSISTANT POSTMASTER GENERAL,
DIVISION OF DEAD LETTERS,
Washington, D. C., Nov 16, 188
If this letter cannot be delivered you will, at the expiration of SEVEN days, stamp the letter with your postmarking stamp, and return it and this circular to the DEAD LETTER OFFICE, with your next RETURN OF UNMAILABLE LETTERS, DULY NUMBERED AND ENTERED ON THE LIST, FORM No. 1522.
A. D. HAZEN,
Third Assistant P. M. General.
To the person addressed: Inform your correspondent of the correct name of your post office.

DLO11

Incomplete Year Date ("188")

OXB5 DLO11 **black** *1883*
On cover 600.00

Post Office Department,
DEAD-LETTER OFFICE,
WASHINGTON, D. C., July 20, 1887
Postmaster:
Upon the delivery of this letter, please obtain the envelope, if agreeable to the party addressed, and return it to the Dead-Letter Office. If the letter cannot be delivered you will, at the expiration of SEVEN days, stamp the letter with your postmarking stamp, and return it and this circular to the DEAD-LETTER OFFICE, ~~with your next RETURN OF UNMAILABLE LETTERS, DULY NUMBERED AND ENTERED ON THE LIST, FORM No. 1522.~~
JNO. B. BAIRD,
Superintendent.

DLO12

Incomplete Year Date ("188")

OXB6 DLO12 **black** 75.00
On cover *250.00*

Post Office Department,
DEAD-LETTER OFFICE,
WASHINGTON, D. C., ..., 189
Postmaster:
Upon the delivery of this letter, please obtain the envelope, if agreeable to the party addressed, and return it to the Dead-Letter Office. If the letter can not be delivered, you will, at the expiration of SEVEN days, stamp the letter with your postmarking stamp, and return it and this circular to the DEAD-LETTER OFFICE, with your next RETURN OF UNMAILABLE LETTERS, DULY NUMBERED AND ENTERED ON THE LIST, FORM No. 1522.
5—3194 SUPERINTENDENT.

DLO13

Incomplete Year Date ("189")

OXB7	DLO13 **black** (1891?)	75.00	
	On cover	*500.00*	
a.	Without form number "5-3194" at LL, on cover	*500.00*	

POST OFFICE SEALS

No. OX1 was prepared for use in the Dead Letter Office but was distributed to other offices and used in the same way as later seals. Most on-cover examples are normal Post Office usages from larger East Coast cities. New York and Philadelphia predominate. Very few examples with Dead Letter Office markings are recorded. For that reason, No. OX1 is listed with the other Post Office Seals.

POS1

("Post Obitum" in background.)
National Bank Note Co.
Plate of 50 subjects (5x10)
Silk Paper

1877 Silk Paper Engr. *Perf. 12*

OX1	POS1 **brown**	60.00	35.00
	On cover		*1,000.*
	Block of 4	—	

Earliest documented use: April 15, 1878.

Cancellations

Used (creased, no gum, or marking without town or date)	35.00
With town marking	+40.00
With town marking and year date	+65.00

POS2

American Bank Note Co.

Plates of 50 (5x10 bearing the imprint of the American Bank Note Co. centered on all four sides in the selvage. At least one of the panes used has a reversed "2" to the right of the top imprint. A proof of a plate of 100 (10x10) in two panes of 50 is known to have existed with a single marginal imprint on each pane, but no issued seals have been shown to have been printed from this plate

(Also plates of 50 (5x10) subjects)

1879 Engr. *Perf. 12*

Thin, crisp, semi-translucent paper, yellowish gum

OX2	POS2 **red brown**	5.00	2.00
	On cover		100.00
	Block of 4	45.00	
	Margin block with imprint	75.00	
a.	**Brown**	12.50	5.00
	On cover		225.00
	Block of 4	100.00	
	Margin block with imprint	150.00	

Seal impression can be clearly seen when viewed from the back.

1879(?) Thick, opaque paper

OX3	POS2 **yellow brown**	*150.00*	*150.00*

1881(?)

Thin, hard porous paper, clear transparent gum

OX4	POS2 **deep brown**	60.00	
	Block of 4	300.00	
	Margin block of 4 with imprint (side)	350.00	
	Margin block of 6 with imprint (bottom)	400.00	
	Margin block of 4 with imprint & reversed "2" (top)	450.00	
	Pane of 50	—	

No. OX4 is the so-called "Special Printing." It was produced from a new plate prepared from the original die. It received little usage, but at least two full panes are known to have existed.

Colors

Beginning with OX5, many Official Seals exhibit a wide variety of shades. Minimal care was exercised in their printing. It is not uncommon for seals within a single pane to vary in shade from dark to very light. No attempt is being made here to list all of the various shades separately.

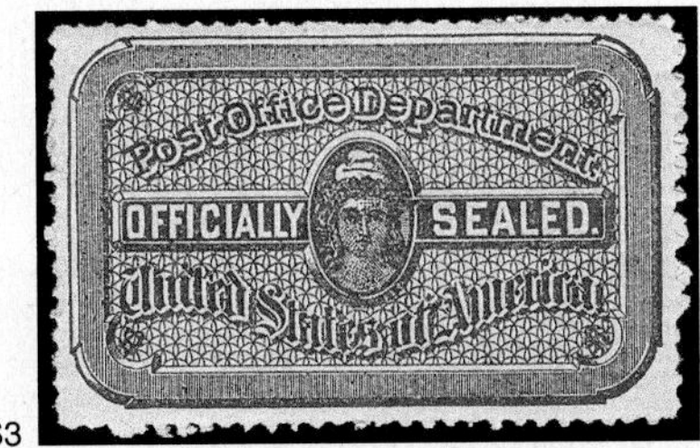

POS3

Without words in lower label.
Outer frame line at top and left is thick and heavy (compare with POS4).
Plate of 72 subjects (8x9)

1888 Typo. *Rough perf. 12*

Medium thick, crisp paper

OX5	POS3 **chocolate** (shades)	2.00	1.00
	On cover		60.00
	Block of 4	12.50	
a.	Imperf, pair	25.00	
	Pane of 72, imperf	*900.00*	

A perforated pane of 72 exists, but lacks three corner seals.

Imperforates

Imperforates of Nos. OX6, OX7, and OX10 are believed to be printer's waste. No seals were issued imperforate, though some may have been sent to post offices.

Plate of 42 subjects (7x6)

1889 *Rough perf. 12*

Thick to extremely thick paper

OX6	POS3 **chocolate** (shades)	2.00	1.00
	On cover		50.00
	Block of 4	12.50	
	Pane of 42	*600.00*	

1890 *Perf. 12*

OX7	POS3 **bister brown** (shades)	5.00	3.00
	On cover		75.00
	Block of 4	25.00	
	Pane of 42	*600.00*	
a.	**Rose brown**	5.00	3.00
	On cover		75.00
	Block of 4	25.00	
	Pane of 42	—	
b.	**Yellow brown**	5.00	3.00
	On cover		75.00
	Block of 4	25.00	
	Pane of 42	—	
c.	Imperf. vertically, pair	50.00	—
d.	Imperf. horizontally, pair	50.00	—
e.	Vertical pair, imperf. between	100.00	
f.	Horizontal pair, imperf. between	100.00	
g.	Double impression		400.00

Cancellation

Puerto Rico	+75.00

Examples of No. OX7 with multiple impressions widely spaced or at angles to each other, are found on normal paper and various documents. These are printer's waste.

1892 *Rouletted 5½*

OX8	POS3 **light brown** (shades)	27.50	20.00
	On cover		*750.00*
	Block of 4	320.00	
	Pane of 42	—	

1895(?) *Hyphen Hole Perf. 7*

OX9	POS3 **gray brown**	8.50	6.00
	On cover		500.00
	Block of 4	200.00	

Earliest documented use: Feb. 3, 1897.

1898(?) Thin soft paper *Perf. 12*

OX10	POS3 **brown** (shades)	10.00	5.00
	On cover		250.00
	Block of 4	80.00	

Cancellation

Cuba	—

POS4

Outer frame line at top and left is thin.
Otherwise similar to POS3.
Printed in sheets of 143 (11x13)

1900 Litho. *Perf. 12*

OX11	POS4 **red brown**	1.00	.50
	On cover		35.00
	Block of 4	5.00	
a.	**Gray brown**	3.00	2.00
	On cover		45.00
	Block of 4	17.50	
b.	**Dark brown**	3.50	2.50
	On cover		85.00
	Block of 4	17.50	
c.	**Orange brown**	2.50	2.50
	On cover		75.00
	Block of 4	15.00	

Most imperfs and part perfs are printers waste. Some genuine perforation errors may have been issued to post offices.

Watermarks

Watermarks cover only a portion of the panes. Many stamps in each pane did not receive any of the watermark. Values for watermarked panes are for examples with at least 50% of the watermark present.

POS4a

Similar to POS3 but smaller.
Design: 38x23mm
Issued in panes of 20 (5x4)

1907 Typo. *Perf. 12*

OX12	POS4a **bright royal blue**	2.00	2.00
	On cover		45.00
	Block of 4	12.50	
	Pane of 20	60.00	
b.	Wmkd. "Rolleston Mills" in sheet	25.00	25.00
	Block of 4	180.00	

Earliest documented use: June 1, 1907.

OX13	POS4a **blue** (shades)	.25	.25
	On cover		25.00
	Block of 4	2.50	
	Pane of 20	20.00	
a.	Wmkd. Seal of U.S. in sheet (2 types)	1.50	1.50
	Block of 4	8.00	
	Pane of 20	50.00	
b.	Wmkd. "Rolleston Mills" in sheet	1.00	1.00
	Block of 4	6.00	
	Pane of 20	40.00	
c.	Wmkd. "Birchwood Superfine" in sheet	—	*180.00*
	Block of 4	—	
	Pane of 20	—	
d.	Pelure paper	*20.00*	*20.00*
e.	Toned paper	*25.00*	*25.00*
f.	Printed on both sides	*250.00*	
	Block of 4	1,400.	

Numerous varieties such as imperf., part perf., tete beche, and double impressions exist. These seem to be from printer's waste. Some genuine perforation errors may have been issued to post offices.

All recorded examples of No. OX13f show the reverse-side impression inverted in relation to the impression on the face.

The earliest uses of No. OX13 are in early 1908; when the cancel or cover date is in 1907 the stamp almost certainly will be No. OX12.

1912 *Hyphen Hole 6½*

OX14	POS4a **blue**	1.75	1.50
	On cover		75.00
	Block of 4	10.00	
	Pane of 20	45.00	
a.	Wmkd. Seal of U.S. in sheet	10.00	10.00
	Block of 4	50.00	
	Pane of 20	300.00	
b.	Wmkd. "Rolleston Mills" in sheet	2.50	2.50
	Block of 4	15.00	
	Pane of 20	80.00	

Panes of 10 were made from panes of 20 for use in smaller post offices. Complete booklets with covers exist.

1913 ***Perf. 12 x Hyphen Hole 6½***

OX15 POS4a **blue** 3.50 3.00
On cover 100.00
Block of 4 20.00
Pane of 20 110.00
a. Hyphen-hole perf 6½ (right) x Perf. 12 (left, top, bottom) 15.00 —
b. Wmkd. Seal of U.S. in sheet 4.50 4.00
Block of 4 40.00
Pane of 20 250.00
c. As "a" and "b" 40.00 —

Nos. OX15a and OX15c come from panes that are perfed between the left selvage and the seals.

1913 ***Hyphen Hole 6½ x Perf. 12***

OX16 POS4a **blue** 5.25 5.25
On cover 400.00
Block of 4 40.00
Pane of 20 250.00
a. Wmkd. Seal of U.S. in sheet 15.00 15.00
Block of 4 60.00
Pane of 20 300.00
b. Wmkd. "Rolleston Mills" in sheet —

1916 ***Perf. 12***

OX17 POS4a **black,** *pink* 2.00 1.50
On cover 75.00
Block of 4 20.00
Pane of 20 100.00
a. Imperf horiz., pane of 20 *500.00*

1917 ***Perf. 12***

OX18 POS4a **black** (shades to gray) .40 .40
On cover 27.50
Block of 4 6.00
Pane of 20 40.00
b. Vert. pair, imperf horizontally 25.00
c. Horiz. pair, imperf vertically 20.00
d. Vertical pair, imperf between 60.00
e. Horizontal pair, imperf between 35.00
f. Imperf, pair 50.00

POS5

Quartermaster General's Office
Issued in panes of 10 (2x5) without selvage.

1919 ***Perf. 12***

OX19 POS5 **indigo** 150.
Block of 4 *700.*
Pane of 10 *1,600.*

Rouletted 7

OX20 POS5 **indigo** — *4,000.*

The pane format of No. OX20 is not known. One of the few reported examples is rouletted on four sides.

Nos. OX19-OX20 were used on mail to and from the Procurement Division of the Quartermaster General's Office. After five weeks of use the seals were withdrawn when the Mail and Records Section became a full branch of the Quartermaster General's Office.

POS6

Issued in panes of 20 (5x4) and 16 (4x4).

Panes of 10 were made from panes of 20 for use in smaller post offices. Panes are valued as having the selvage on the left of the pane. Panes without the selvage sell for less. Pairs of imperforate and partially perforated seals are listed with the most common variety having the same paper type and surviving perforation, if any.

Thin, white, crisp paper

The paper used for Nos. OX21-OX27 is thin enough to allow reading text on the envelope.

1919 ***Perf. 12 (sometimes rough)***

OX21 POS6 **black** (shades) .30 .25
On cover 12.50
Block of 4 3.00
Pane of 20 15.00
a. Imperf, pair 17.50
On cover —
Imperf. pane of 20 250.00
b. Vert. pair, imperf horiz. 12.50
Pane of 20, imperf. horiz. 200.00
c. Horiz. pair, imperf vert. 12.50
Pane of 20, imperf. vert. 200.00
d. Vert. pair, imperf btwn. 25.00
e. Horiz. pair, imperf btwn. 25.00
f. Wmkd. eagle and star in sheet (1936?) 2.00 2.00
Block of 4 15.00
Pane of 20 75.00
g. As "f," imperf, pair 35.00
Imperf. pane of 20 400.00
h. As "f," vert. pair, imperf horiz. 27.50
i. As "f," vert. pair, imperf btwn. 40.00
j. As "f," horiz. pair, imperf. vert. 27.50
Pane of 20, imperf. vert. 2,500.
k. As "f," horiz. pair, imperf. btwn. 40.00
l. Wmkd. "Certificate Bond," "Made in USA," or McElwain logo in sheet (1936?) 10.00 10.00
Block of 4 60.00
Pane of 20 300.00

Earliest documented use: 1920.

1936(?) ***Perf. 12x9***

OX22 POS6 **black** (shades) 7.50 7.50
On cover 85.00
Block of 4 35.00
Pane of 20 200.00
a. Vert. pair, imperf. horiz. 50.00
b. Wmkd. eagle and star in sheet 7.50 7.50
Block of 4 35.00
Pane of 20 200.00
c. As "b," vert. pair, imperf. horiz. 50.00

Earliest documented use: Oct. 1936 (No. OX22 or OX23.)

1936(?) ***Perf. 12x8½***

OX23 POS6 **black** (shades) 2.50 2.50
On cover 40.00
Block of 4 12.50
Pane of 20 75.00
a. Wmkd. eagle and star in sheet 4.00 4.00
Block of 4 20.00
Pane of 20 110.00

1927(?) ***Perf. 12½***

OX24 POS6 **gray black,** on cover —

1936(?) ***Perf. 8½***

OX25 POS6 **gray black** —
a. Wmkd. eagle and star in sheet —

1936(?) ***Perf. 12x9½***

OX26 POS6 **gray black,** pane of 20 —

1935(?) ***Perf. 11½***

OX27 POS6 **gray black** *17.50* *17.50*
On cover 50.00
a. Vert. pair, imperf. btwn. 75.00
Pane of 20, middle row of horiz. perfs. omitted 1,200.

Medium to thick, opaque, egg or cream colored paper

1945(?) ***Perf. 12***

OX28 POS6 **gray black** .40 .40
On cover 25.00
Block of 4 5.00
Pane of 20 30.00
a. Vert. pair, imperf btwn. 25.00

1945(?) ***Perf. 12½***

OX29 POS6 **gray black** .50 .50
On cover 27.50
Block of 4 6.00
Pane of 20 35.00

1945(?) ***Perf. 12½x9***

OX29A POS6 **gray black,** on cover —

1944(?) ***Perf. 12½x8½***

OX30 POS6 **gray black** 1.00 1.00
On cover 32.50
Block of 4 5.00
Pane of 20 30.00

1947(?) ***Perf. 8½***

OX31 POS6 **gray black** 1.00 1.00
On cover 32.50
Block of 4 5.00
Pane of 20 30.00

1947(?) ***Perf. 8½x12***

OX32 POS6 **gray black** —

1947(?) ***Perf. 8½x8***

OX33 POS6 **gray black,** —
On cover —

1947(?) ***Perf. 8x8½***

OX33A POS6 **gray black** —
On cover —

Thick, gray, very soft paper

1948 ***Perf. 12½ (sometimes rough)***

OX34 POS6 **gray black** 1.00 1.00
Block of 4 8.00
On cover 35.00
Pane of 16 45.00

1947 ***Perf. 8½***

OX35 POS6 **gray black** 3.50 3.50
On cover 45.00
Block of 4 15.00
Pane of 20 80.00

1946(?) ***Perf. 12½x8½***

OX36 POS6 **gray black** 27.50 27.50

1948 ***Hyphen Hole Perf. 9½***

OX38 POS6 **gray black** 12.50 12.50
On cover 50.00
Block of 4 50.00
Pane of 16 250.00
a. Pane of 5, imperf at sides, with tab 125.00

Pane of 5 tab inscribed "16-56146-1 GPO." Pane of 5 also known on cream paper. Seals without the tab generally cannot be distinguished from No. OX39.

1950(?) ***Hyphen Hole Perf. 9½ x Imperf***

Medium thick, cream or white paper

Design width: 37½mm

OX39 POS6 **gray black** .25 .25
On cover 12.50
Pane of 5 with tab 1.25
a. Vert. pair, imperf between 12.50
b. Pane of 5, imperf, with tab 20.00
c. Pane of 5, imperf at top & btwn. rows 2 & 3, 4 & 5 30.00

Pane of 5 tab inscribed, "16-56164-1 GPO."
Earliest documented use: Jan. 23, 1950.

1969(?) ***Hyphen Hole Perf. 9½ x Imperf***

Medium thick, white paper

Design width: 38½mm

OX40 POS6 **gray black** .25 .25
On cover 30.00
Pane of 5 with tab 2.25
a. Vert. pair, imperf. btwn. —
b. Pane of 5, Imperf 35.00
c. Double impression —

Tab inscribed, "c43-16-56164-1 GPO"

Earliest documented use: Feb. 11, 1969.

POS7

Design size, Nos. OX41-OX45, 37x21mm.
On Nos. OX41-OX50, tab is inscribed, "LABEL 21, JULY 1971."

1972 **Litho.** ***Rouletted 9½ x Imperf***

OX41 POS7 **black** .25 .25
On cover 12.50
Pane of 5 2.00
a. Imperf, pair 10.00

1972(?) ***Rouletted 6½ x Imperf***

OX42 POS7 **black** .25 .25
On cover 5.00
Pane of 5 2.75

1973(?) **Litho.** ***Hyphen Hole 7 x Imperf***

OX43 POS7 **black** .30 .25
On cover 7.50
Pane of 5 9.00

1976(?) **Litho.** ***Rouletted 8½ x Imperf***

OX44 POS7 **black** .25 .25
On cover 7.50
Pane of 5 2.00

1979(?) **Litho.** ***Perf. 12½ x Imperf***

OX45 POS7 **black** .25 .25
On cover 7.50
Pane of 5 2.25
Small holes .25 .25
On cover 7.50
Pane of 5 2.25

1988(?) **Litho.** ***Die Cut***

Self-Adhesive

OX46 POS7 **black,** 38x21mm, fluorescent paper .25 .25
On cover *7.50*
Pane of 5 3.50

OX47 POS7 **black,** 38x21mm, non-fluorescent paper .25 .25
On cover *7.50*
Pane of 5 3.50

OX48 POS7 **gray** (shades), 37x21mm .25 .25
On cover *7.50*
Pane of 5 3.50

OX49 POS7	**black,** 40x21mm	.50	.50
	On cover		*15.00*
	Pane of 5	10.00	

On No. OX49, BY is 2x1mm, P of POSTAL is left of P in POSTAL of Emblem. Tab inscribed as No. OX41, but 1's have no bottom serif.

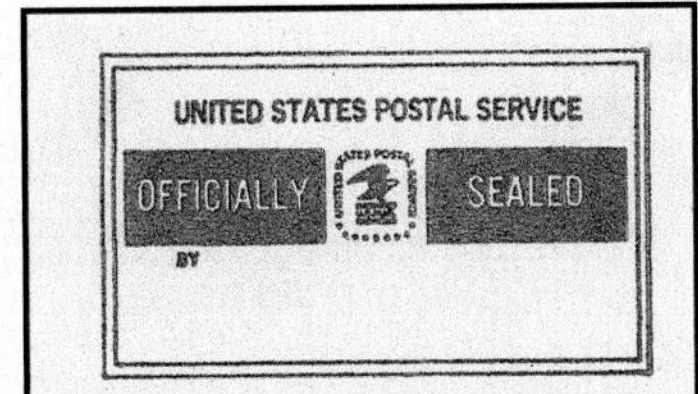

POS7a

Size: 37x21mm

OX50 POS7a	**purple**	—	—
	On cover		—

Earliest documented use: Dec. 2, 1992.

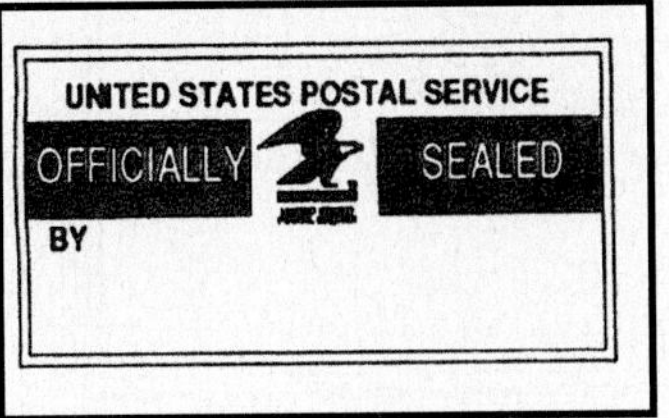

POS8

Tab inscribed "LABEL 21, JAN. 1992."

Size: 44x22mm

1992	**Self-adhesive**		***Die Cut***
OX51 POS8	**black**	1.00	1.00
	On cover		*25.00*
	Pane of 5	10.00	

Earliest documented use: Mar. 1992.

Size: 41x21mm

1992?	**Self-Adhesive**		***Die Cut***
OX52 POS8	**black**	.25	.25
	On cover		*7.50*
	Pane of 5	3.50	

No. OX52 exists on both white and brown backing paper. Those on brown backing paper are worth more.

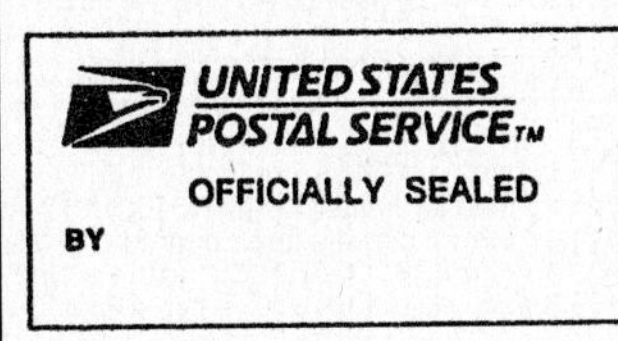

POS9

Tab inscribed "Label 21, April 1994."

1994	**Self-Adhesive**		***Die Cut***
OX53 POS9	**black**	.25	.25
	On cover		*7.50*
	Pane of 5	3.50	

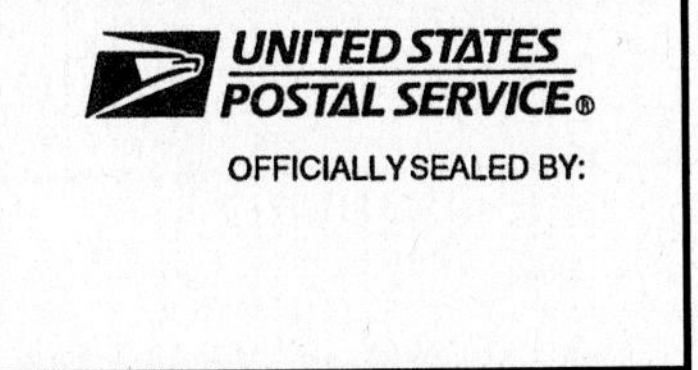

POS10

Tab inscribed "Label 21, August 1996."

1996	**Self-Adhesive**		***Die Cut***
OX54 POS10	**black**	.25	.25
	On cover		*20.00*
	Pane of 5	2.00	
a.	"OFFICALLY"	*.25*	.25
	On cover		7.50
	Pane of 5	*2.00*	

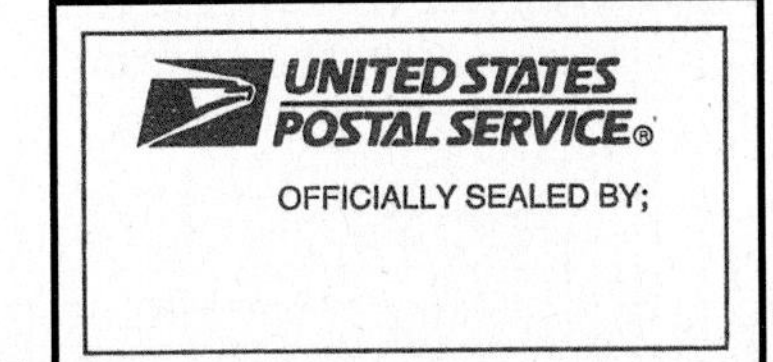

POS11

Tab inscribed "Label 21, August 1996."

1996	**Self-Adhesive**		***Die Cut***
OX55 POS11	**black**	.25	.25
	On cover		7.50
	Pane of 5	3.00	

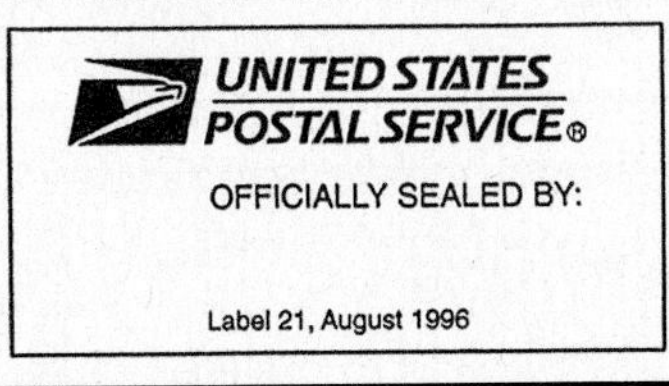

POS12

Seal inscribed "Label 21, August 1996."

2006 (?)	**Self-Adhesive**		***Die Cut***
OX56 POS12	**black**	.25	.25
	On cover		*7.50*
	Pane of 5	3.00	

Although No. OX56 is inscribed "August 1996," it likely was issued in 2006.

SEA POST SEALS

These seals were used by clerks on North German Lloyd ships on the New York-Bremen and New York-Hamburg routes.

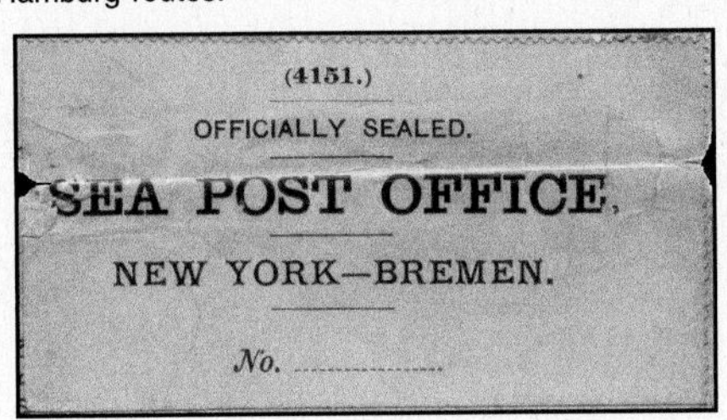

SPS1

1895 (?)		***Perf. 12 on 2 or 3 sides***	
OXSP1 SPS1	**black,** 91x50mm	400.00	400.00
	On cover		*1,750.*

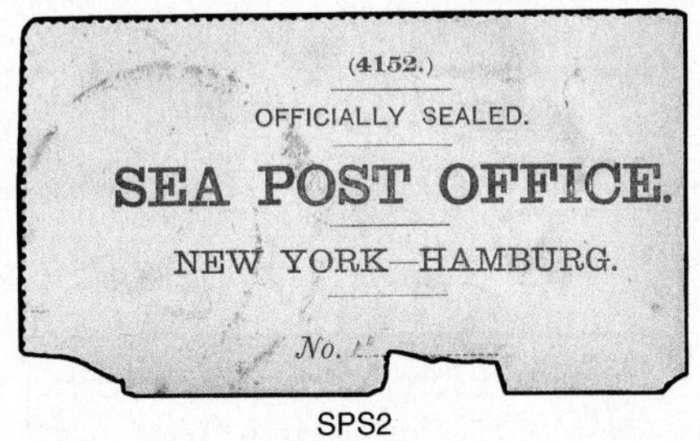

SPS2

1895 (?)		***Perf. 12***	
OXSP2 SPS2	**black,** 91x50mm, with "4152" at top and New York-Hamburg beneath Sea Post Office	450.00	

No. OXSP2 is unique but damaged at bottom, and it is valued thus.

TYPESET SEALS

These seals were privately printed for sale mostly to Fourth Class Post Offices. Many are extremely rare. Unquestioned varieties are listed. Many others exist.

All are imperf or die cut except Nos. LOX7-LOX11 and LOX36.

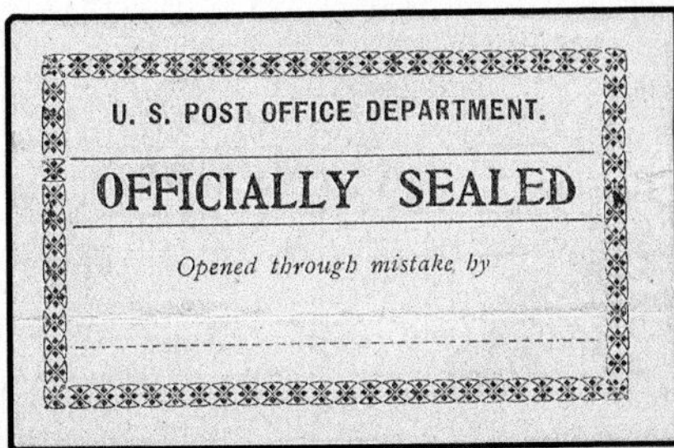

TSS1

LOX1 TSS1	**black**	*350.00*	*350.00*
	On cover		900.00

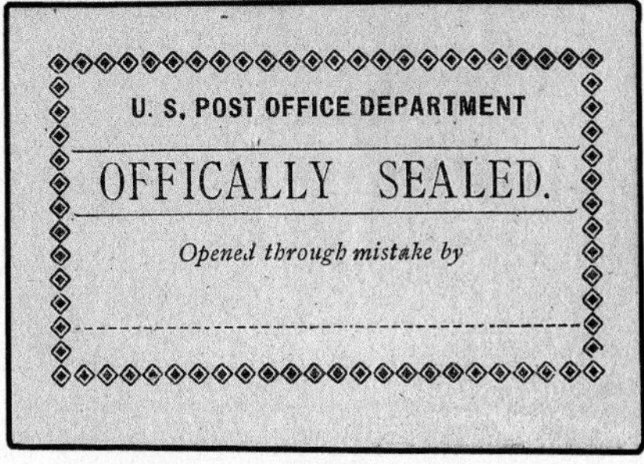

TSS2

LOX2 TSS2	**black,** 15 diamonds vertically in frame	*1,000.*	*1,000.*
a.	14 diamonds vertically		*450.*
b.	14 diamonds vertically, no period after "DEPARTMENT"		*450.*
c.	"OFFICALLY" misspelling, 14 diamonds vertically	*800.*	
	On cover		—

TSS3

LOX3 TSS3	**black**		*1,000.*
	On cover		*1,100.*

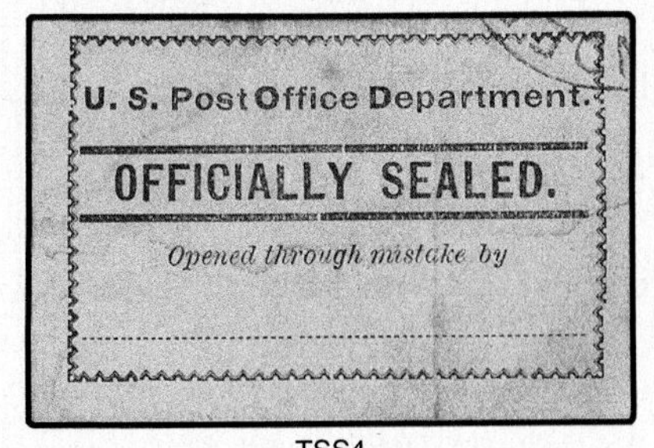

TSS4

LOX4 TSS4	**black,** *pink*		*900.*

No. LOX4 used is valued with minor flaws.

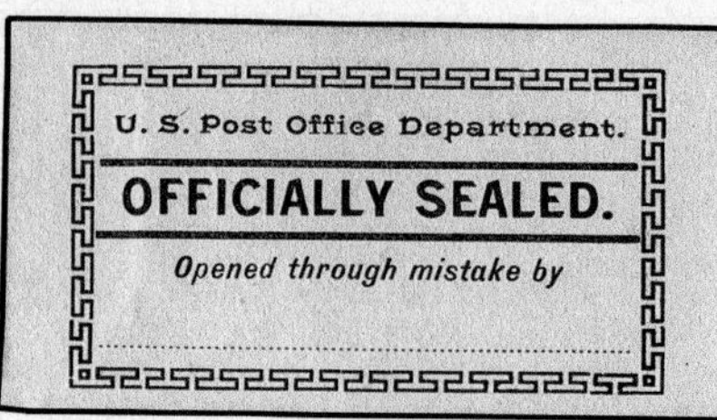

TSS5

LOX5 TSS5 **black** *400. 400.*
LOX5A TSS5 **black,** *pink* *1,000.*

TSS6

LOX6 TSS6 **black** —

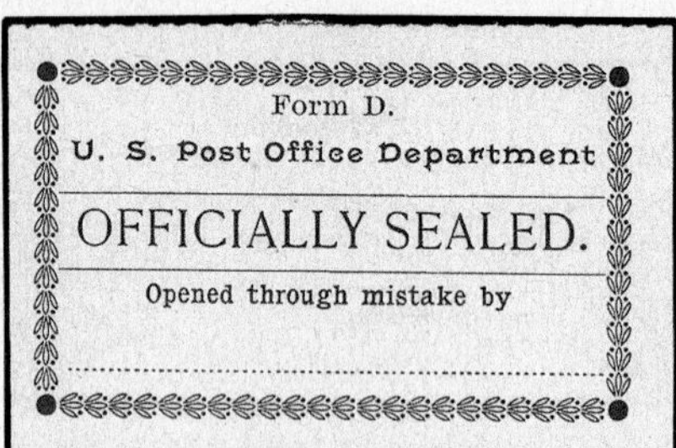

TSS7

Rouletted 9½ horizontally

LOX7 TSS7 **black** *750. 750.*

TSS8

Printed and distributed by Morrill Bros., P.O. Supply Printers, Fulton, N.Y., in panes of 4, two tete beche pairs.

Rouletted 12½ in black at top & side

LOX8 TSS8 **black,** rouletted 11½ 100.00 100.00
Sheet of 4 1,250.
On cover *750.00*
a. **black,** rouletted 12½ 100.00 100.00
c. **black,** rouletted 12½ by 11½ 100.00 100.00
On cover *750.00*
Sheet of 4, 1 each, clockwise, Nos. LOX8, LOX8c, LOX8d, LOX8e *1,000.*
d. **black,** rouletted 11½ and 12½, compounded with 11½ 100.00 100.00
e. **black,** rouletted 11½ and 12½ compound by 12½ 100.00 100.00
On cover 750.00
Sheet of 4, 1 each, clockwise, Nos. LOX8, LOX8e, LOX8d, LOX8c *1,000.*
f. **black,** rouletted 16½ 200.00 200.00
On cover *800.00*
On cover with No. OX5 *1,000.*
g. **black,** rouletted 16½ on 3 sides 300.00

Gauge transition of rouletting on Nos. LOX8d and LOX8e occurs about one-quarter of the way across the top edge of the seal.

TSS9

Solid lines above and below "OFFICIALLY SEALED."

Rouletted 12½, 16½ in black between

LOX9 TSS9 **black** *350.00 350.00*
On cover *1,200.*

TSS10

Dotted lines above and below "OFFICIALLY SEALED."

Rouletted 12½ in black

LOX10 TSS10 **black,** *pink* *300.00 450.00*
a. Dot after "OFFICIALLY" *700.00*

Dyed examples of No. LOX11 are frequently misrepresented as No. LOX10.

Rouletted 11½, 12½ or 16½ in black

LOX11 TSS10 **black,** rouletted 12½ at top and side 2.00 *75.00*
On cover *900.00*
Sheet of 4 15.00
a. Double impression *250.00*
Sheet of 4 —
b. Double impression, one inverted *250.00*
c. Dot after "OFFICIALLY" 4.00 *100.00*
On cover *1,500.*
Sheet of 4, one seal with dot 12.50
d. **black,** rouletted 11½ at top or bottom 200.00 *200.00*
Sheet of 2, both seals with dot *1,250.*
f. **black,** rouletted 11½ at top and side 100.00
Sheet of 4 *750.00*
g. **black,** rouletted 12½ by 11½ *500.00*
h. **black,** rouletted 16½ at top or bottom 200.00 —
On cover 1,000.
Sheet of 2, both seals with dot *1,250.*
i. As "h," sheet of 2, tete beche, both seals with dot *1,250.*
j. **black,** rouletted 16½ at top and side 250.00

New footnote after No. LOX11 and LOX11c off-cover used seals must have unmistakable evidence of use such as a cancel or contemporaneous notation in the signature line.

LOX11E TSS10 **blue,** rouletted 11½ at top or bottom *750.00 750.00*

TSS11

Printed and distributed by The Lemoyne Supply Co., Lemoyne, Pa.

LOX12 TSS11 **black** *200.00*
On cover *800.00*

Outer and inner framelines on No. LOX12 have closed mitered corners. Some examples have damaged top corners. Thick lines above and below "OFFICIALLY SEALED."

TSS11a

LOX12A TSS11a **blue** *1,250.*

Similar to No. LOX12, but with a different setting of the three lines of type. The frameline corners are mitered but slightly open at the top.

TSS11B

LOX13 TSS11B **blue** *500.00*
LOX13A TSS11B **black** *1,100.*

Outer and inner framelines on Nos. LOX13 and LOX13A have narrow spacing at left and right, and have corner of square-ended rules that are open at the corners. Thin lines above and below "OFFICIALLY SEALED."

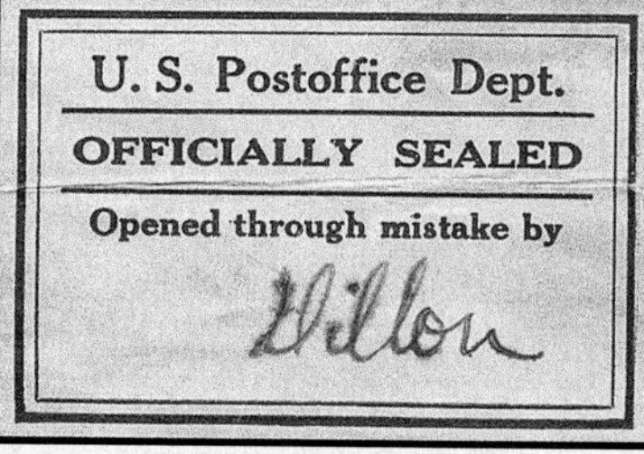

TSS12

LOX14 TSS12 **blue** *1,250. 1,250.*

Outer and inner framelines on No. LOX14 have wide spacing, and the closed corners are mitered like Nos. LOX12 and LOX12A. "OFFICIALLY SEALED" set in a type face with flatter and wider letters and reduced letter spacing.

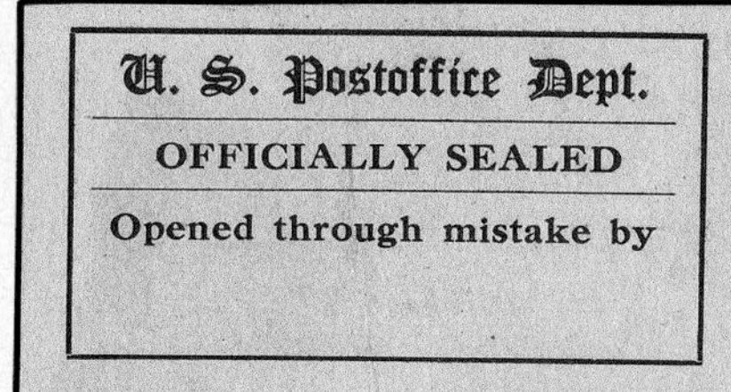

TSS13

LOX15 TSS13 **black** *800.00 600.00*
On cover *1,250.*

No. LOX15 unused is valued with small faults and crease.
See No. LOX29 for a similar design in blue.

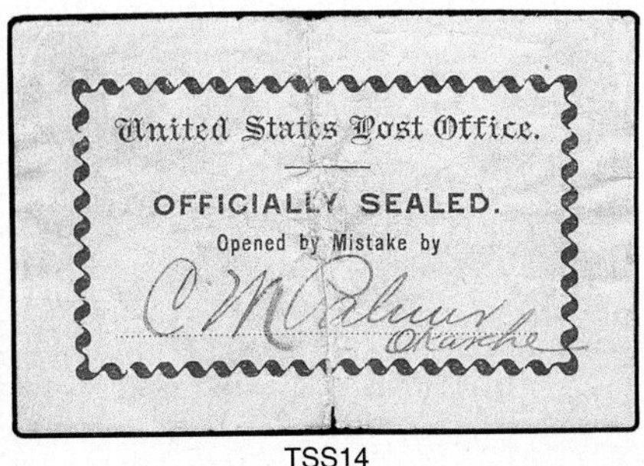

TSS14

LOX16 TSS14 **blue** *1,100.* 650.00

No. LOX16 used is valued with usual crease, thin spots and small tear.

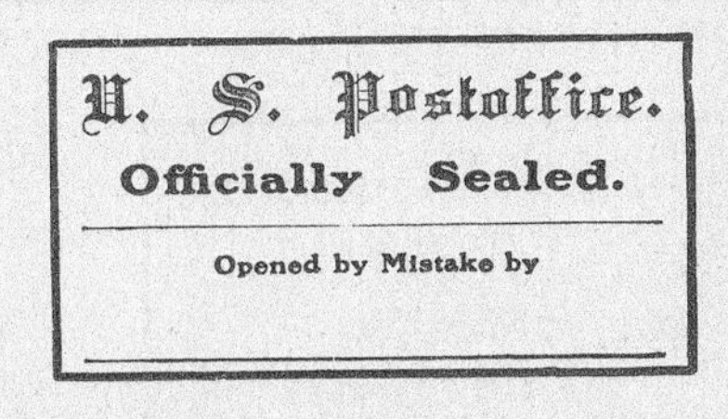

TSS15

Period after "Sealed"; 6mm between "Officially" and "Sealed".

LOX17	TSS15 **dark blue**		125.00	*225.00*
	On cover			*600.00*
a.	Printed on both sides		*750.00*	
LOX18	TSS15 **black**		200.00	—
	On cover			*750.00*

Two types of No. LOX18: Type I (shown) has first "o" of "Post office" upside-down; Type II corrects the inversion. Both types found with approx. equal frequency.

TSS15a

No period after "Sealed"; 2mm between "Officially" and "Sealed".

LOX18A TSS15a **dark blue** 200.00 400.00

TSS16

LOX19 TSS16 **black** *500.00* *500.00*

TSS16a

LOX19A TSS16a **black** *2,000.*

Type I
TSS17

Type II — Bottom line in heavy type face. Period after "Office." Two different types or settings are known. The illustrated type has a dotted line above "BY" that does not show in the illustration.

LOX20 TSS17 **black,** *light green* (Type I), on cover —

LOX20A TSS17 **black,** *light green* (Type II) *1,500.*

No. LOX20 on cover is unique. No. LOX20A also is unique, and it is valued with a major thin at top center.

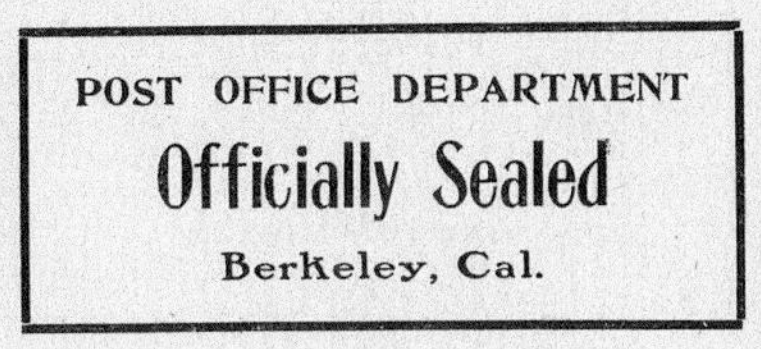

TSS18

LOX21 TSS18 **black** *500.* —

TSS18a

LOX21A TSS18a **black** — *1,000.*
On cover *1,250.*

No. LOX21A unused is valued with crease and small faults.

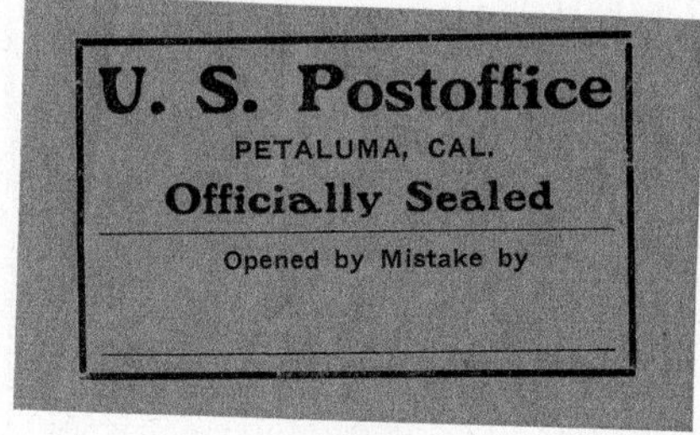

TSS19

LOX22 TSS19 **black,** *blue* *2,150.*

No. LOX22 is unique. It is creased and is valued as such.

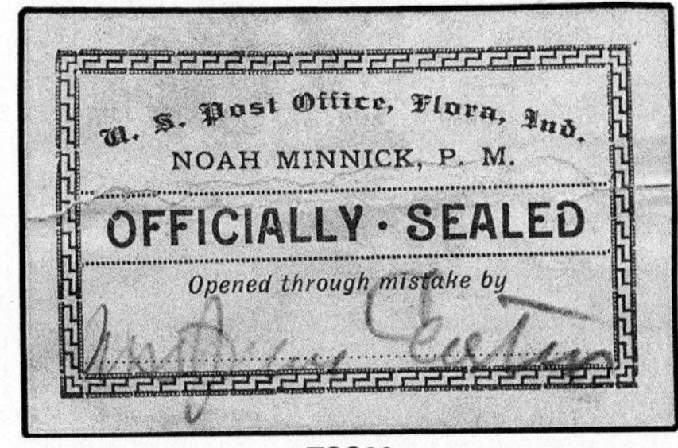

TSS20

LOX23 TSS20 **black** *1,000.*

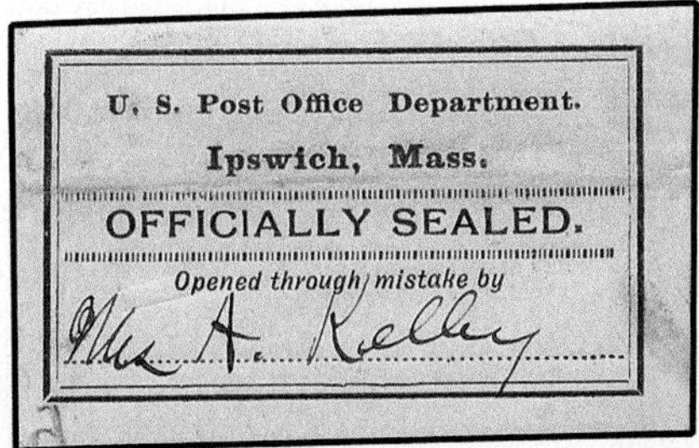

TSS21

LOX24 TSS21 **black,** on cover *2,000.*

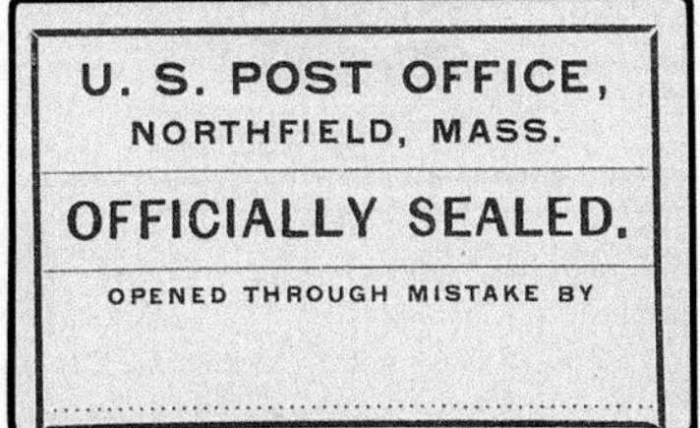

TSS22

LOX25 TSS22 **black** *800.*

At least three examples of No. LOX25 exist. All have faults. Value is for the finest example.

TSS23

LOX26 TSS23 **black** *1,400.*

No. LOX26 used is valued with small fault. It is unique.

TSS24

LOX27 TSS24 **black,** *dark brown red* *1,350.*

No. LOX27 is valued with crease and small flaws.

TSS25

LOX28 TSS25 **black** *1,000.*
On cover *2,000.*

The unique on-cover seal shown was torn in half when the envelope was opened.

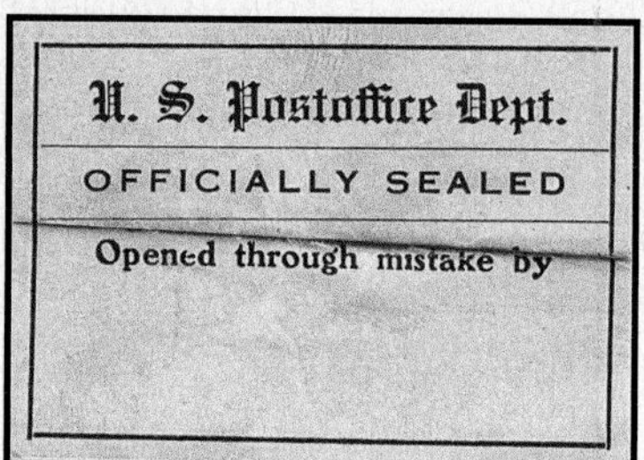

TSS26

LOX29 TSS26 **blue,** on cover *2,000.*

No. LOX29 is unique.

TSS27

LOX30 TSS27 **black,** pair on cover *3,000.*

No. LOX30 is unique. The seals were torn in half when the envelope was opened.

TSS28

LOX31 TSS28 **red,** *cream* *1,500.*

No. LOX31 is unique. It has a thin spot and crease and is valued as such.

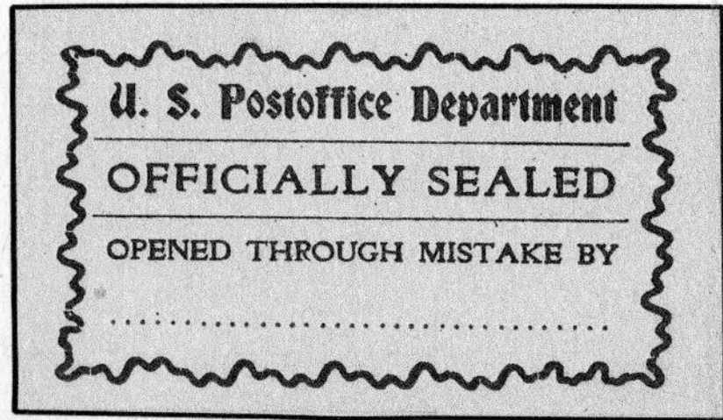

TSS29

LOX32 TSS29 **black** *900.*

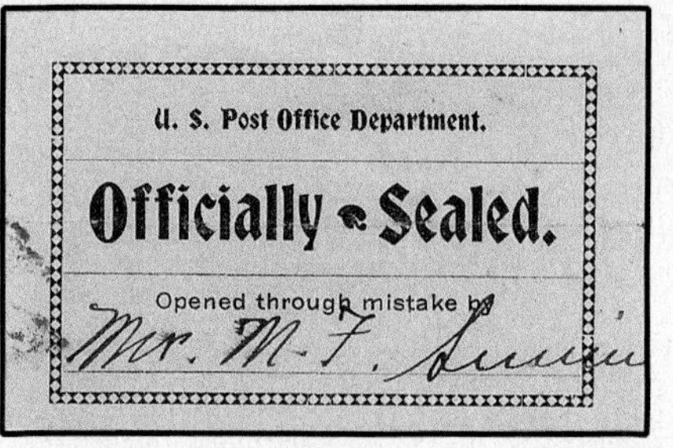

TSS30

LOX33 TSS30 **black** *1,500.*

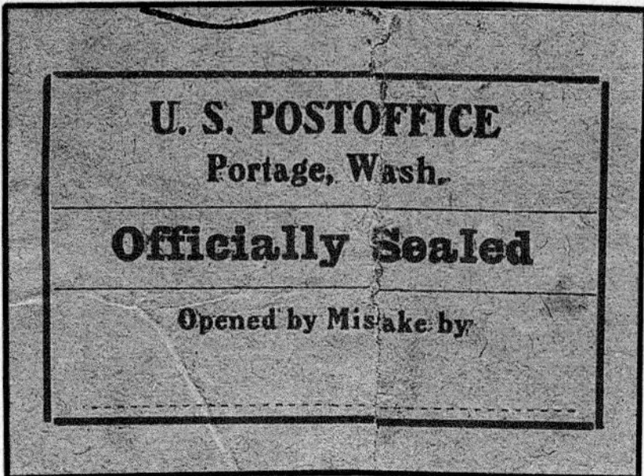

TSS31

LOX34 TSS31 **red,** *rose* *800.*
On cover *1,100.*

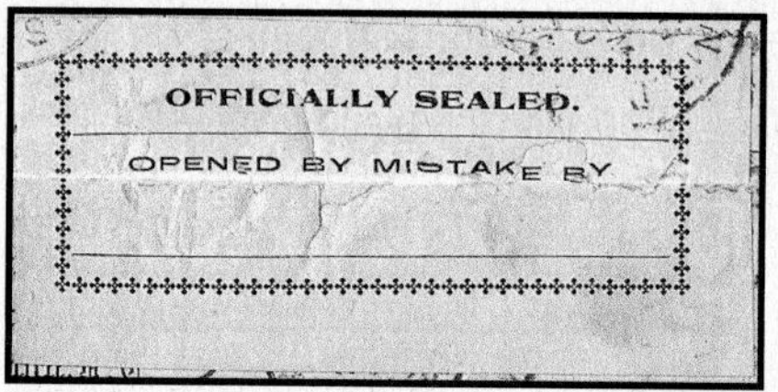

TSS32

LOX35 TSS32 **black,** on cover *1,100.*

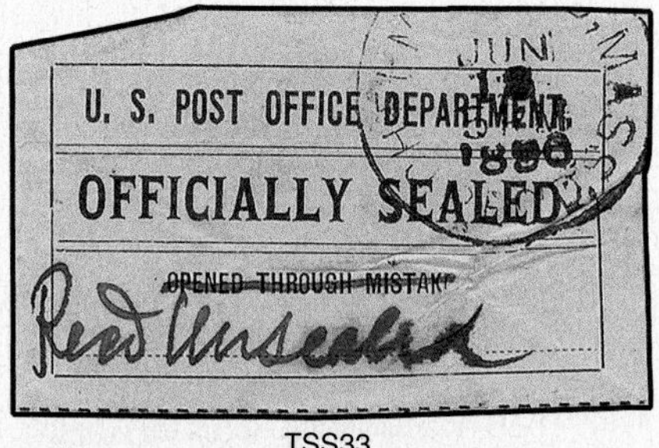

TSS33

Rouletted (at least one side)

LOX36 TSS33 **black** *750.*

U. S. Postoffice.
Officially Sealed.
OPENED BY MISTAKE BY

TSS34

LOX37 TSS34 **green** *1,500.*

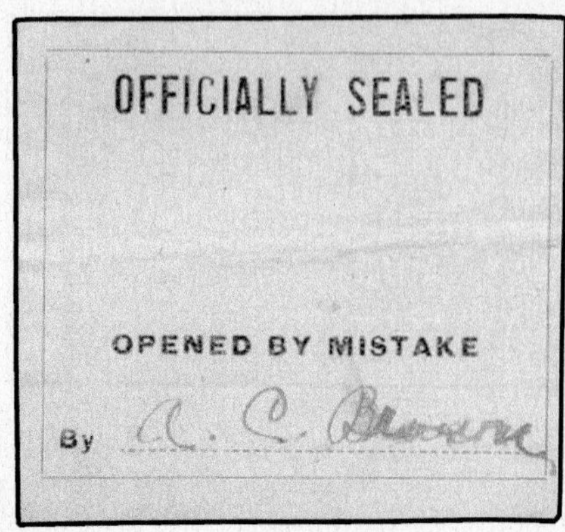

TSS35

LOX38 TSS35 **black,** *tan* *1,000.*

TSS36

LOX39 TSS36 **black,** *tan* *1,250.*

TSS37

LOX40 TSS37 **black,** *tan* *1,200.*

TSS38

LOX41 TSS38 **black** —

No LOX41 is unique.

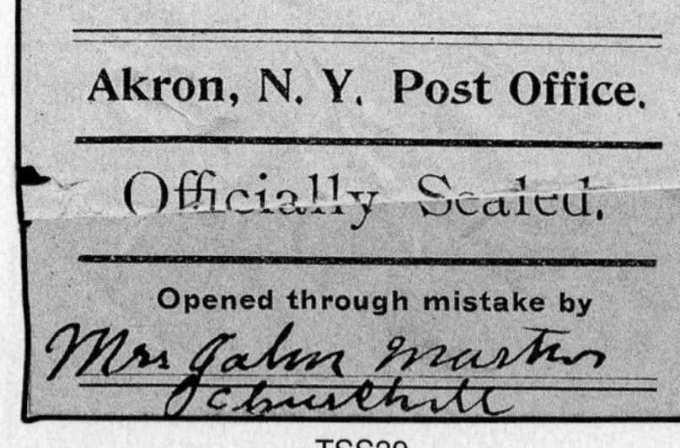

TSS39

LOX42 TSS39 **black,** on cover —

No. LOX42 is unique.

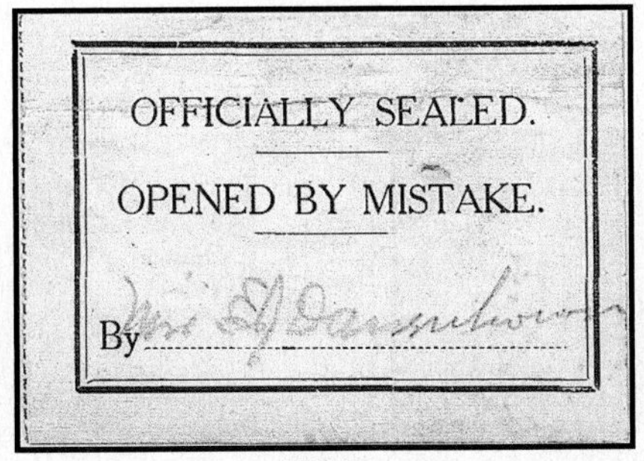

TSS40

LOX43 TSS40 **black** *1,100.*

No. LOX43 is unique.

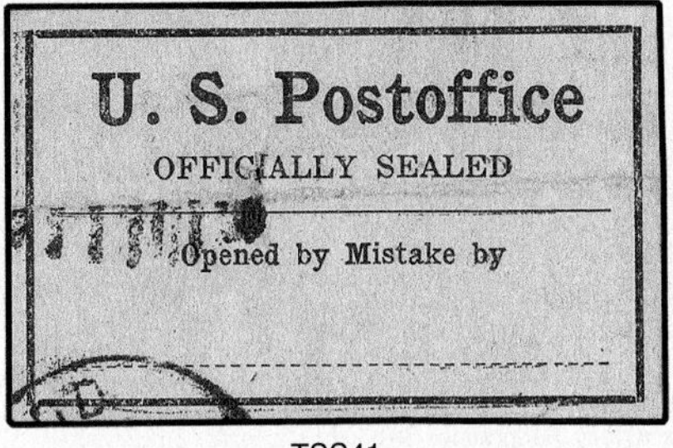

TSS41

LOX44 TSS41 **blue,** *yellow* *1,100.*

No. LOX44 is unique.

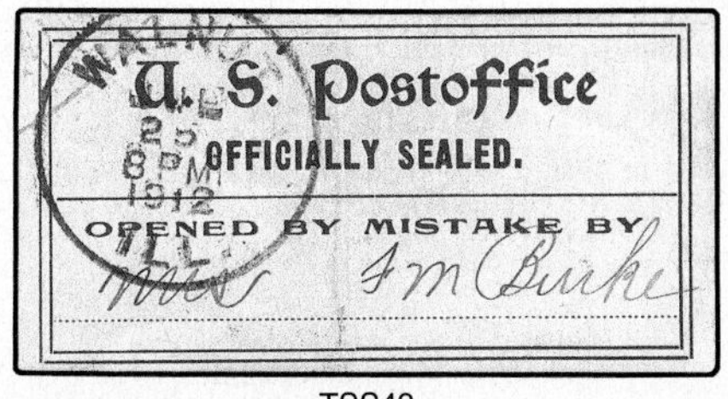

TSS42

LOX45 TSS42 **dark blue** *1,000.*

No. LOX 45 is unique.

TSS43

LOX46 TSS43 **black,** *light pink* —

No. LOX46 currently is unique. It is split in half horizontally and repaired.

POSTAL COUNTERFEITS

While possession of counterfeit stamps remains contrary to law, U.S. postal counterfeits can now be found in philatelic auctions, exhibits, dealer advertising, and current philatelic literature. Neither the Postal Inspection Service nor the U.S. Secret Service have intervened to confiscate these items.

Before purchasing counterfeits, collectors should obtain a certificate of authenticity (that the item in question is a genuine counterfeit) from a recognized expertizing service.

Values for counterfeits on cover are for contemporaneous usage.

The listings in this section follow standard Scott policy. A comparison of the attributes found in the counterfeit listing with those of the genuine stamp will enable collectors to distinguish the real from the spurious. The description field of each listing contains a letter rarity code keyed to the list below.

Numbers that survive in the hands of collectors:

A = Probably in the low thousands.
B = Probably 500-1500.
C = Probably in the low hundreds.
D = Probably equal to or fewer than 250.
E = Probably equal to or fewer than 100.
F = Probably equal to or fewer than 25.
G = 5 or fewer reported.
H = Unique in philatelic hands.
I = None known in philatelic hands.

Genuine No. 250

No. 250(CF1)

No. 250(CF2)

No. 250(CF3)

Size: 19-19.5x22.5-23mm

Thin coarsely woven white paper

COPPER ELECTROTYPE LITHO PLATE OF 5

1895 ***Imperf.***

250(CF1) A88 2c **light rose carmine** *(E)* *225.00*
Full pane of 5 *(G)* 1,500.

Technically, No. 250(CF1) is "unfinished production," not yet perforated as the final product.

No. 250(CF1) has smooth, tending toward brownish gum. Much of the central oval is solid. While No. 250(CF2) is scarce, individual unused examples are not rare. Multiples are very difficult to find.

Genuine examples of No. 250 were printed by recess engraving on smooth white wove paper with smooth, yellowish gum, perf. 12.1. Image size: 19x22mm.

Perf. 11.8

250(CF2) A88 2c **rose carmine** *(C)* *75.00* *150.00*
On cover *(G)* *2,500.*
Strip of 5 *(G)* *800.00*
Block of 4 —

No. 250(CF2) has smooth, tending toward brownish gum. Much of the central oval is solid. Used examples are known on cover. While scarce, individual unused examples are not rare. Multiples are very difficult to find. Each "stamp" in the plate of 5 has minutely different characteristics.

Genuine examples of No. 250 were printed by recess engraving on smooth white wove paper with smooth, yellowish gum, perf. 12.1. Image size: 19x22mm.

Perf. 11.8

250(CF3) A88 2c **light rose carmine** *(C)* *75.00* *150.00*
On official notice from office of third assistant postmaster general to post offices, "stamp" with manuscript or printed "c" *950.00*
On official notice from office of post office inspectors to post offices, "stamp" with punched "c" *950.00*
On cover *(F)* *2,500.*
Strip of 5 *(G)* 750.00

No. 250(CF3) has glossy and whiter gum than Nos. 250(CF1) and 250(CF2).The April 10, 1895, letter used to notify postmasters, describes the color and impression of No.250(CF1) as "the lighter look of more open engraving, but under a magnifying glass, it will be found that this is attributable to the broken lines instead of continuous lines of the genuine steel engraving." Much of the central oval is solid. Used examples are known on cover. While scarce, individual unused examples are not rare.

Multiples are very difficult to find. Each "stamp" in the plate of 5 has minutely different characteristics.

Many surviving examples have been marked "C" by postal authorities.

Genuine No. 252

No. 252(CF1)

Size: 18.5-19x22mm

Thin, see-through white paper

1896	**STONE LITHO PLATES**	***Perf. 12.1***
252(CF1) A88 2c **pink** *(F)*		*1,500. 1,750.*
Block of 4		—

No. 252(CF1) has good detail, but a flat impression. The width of the oval at the mouth is 13mm. The vast majority of No. 252(CF1) were seized. Very few are known.

Genuine examples of No. 252 were printed by recess engraving on smooth white wove paper with smooth, light yellow gum, perf. 12.1. Image size: 19x22-22.5mm. The width of the oval at the mouth is 13.5mm.

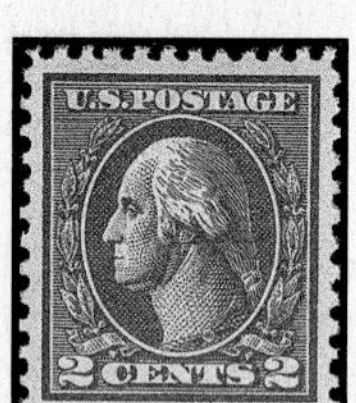

Genuine No. 528

No. 528A(CF1)

Size: approximately 18.5-19x21.6mm

Sheets of 10

ENGRAVING USING A COPPER PLATE

1920	**Unwmk.**	***Perf. 11.9***	
528A(CF1) A140 2c **carmine** simulating offset Type VI, *(C)*		*50.00*	*75.00*
Block of 4		*350.00*	
Complete cliche of 10		*1,000.*	
On cover (Unused) *(G)*		*1,000.*	
On cover (Used) *(F)*			*1,250.*

No. 528A(CF1) appears somewhat brighter than a genuine example and exhibits variable print quality, due to the lack of sufficient lines in the area of the head, especially above the ear. Gum and paper are slightly darker than a genuine example.

Genuine examples of No. 528A were printed by offset lithography and perforated 11. Inking and shading lines are consistently applied across the entire design. Size: 18.5x21.3mm.

Genuine No. 634

No. 634(CF1)

No. 634(CF2)

No. 634(CF3)

Size: 19.5mmx23mm

OFFSET LITHOGRAPHY

1932	**Unwmk.**	***Perf. 11.65***	
634(CF1) A157 2c **carmine** *(C)*		*35.00*	*35.00*
On cover (Used) *(F)*			*2,000.*
Block of 4		*900.00*	

No. 634(CF1) is a fairly crude counterfeit with a heavy, overinked appearance. It does not have an oversized "S" in "Washington." The gum is a thick yellow brown or whitish. The interior oval is 13.5mm across.

Genuine examples of No. 634 were printed by recess engraving. Inking and shading lines are consistent across the entire design. Perforations gauge 11x10.5. There are horizontal gum breakers. The interior oval is 13.5mm across. Size: 19x22.3mm.

Size: 19x22.2mm

1935 or 1936	**Thick Paper**	***Perf. 14.1***	
634(CF2) A157 2c **carmine** *(C)*		*40.00*	*40.00*
On cover *(F)*			*900.00*
Block of 4		*180.00*	
Full pane of 100 (no marginal markings)		*2,250.*	

Size: 18.6-18.8x22.2mm

1936 **Typo.**	**Thick paper**	***Perf. 11.9***	
634(CF3) A157 2c **carmine** *(A)*		*20.00*	*20.00*
On cover *(F)*			*600.00*
Block of 4		*110.00*	

All examples of Nos. 634(CF2) and 634(CF3) have an oversize "S" in "Washington." The interior oval is 13.0mm across, and the bust appears visually smaller. Color is flat and image is coarse compared to genuine examples. They appear flat with the inking of uneven quality. Paper and gum are slightly darker than the genuine, and the gum has no gum breakers. Exact quantities are not known, but these are the most often seen U.S. postal counterfeits, both on and off cover, until modern times.

Genuine No. 807

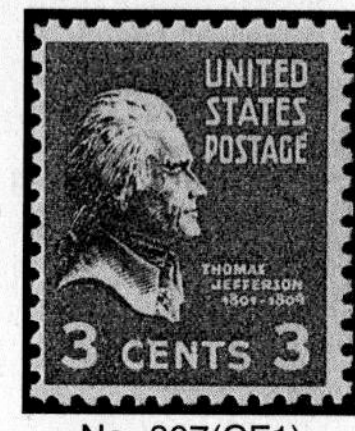

No. 807(CF1)

No. 807(CF2)

Thin, yellowish paper

Size: 19x22.6mm

OFFSET LITHOGRAPHY

1938	**Unwmk.**	***Perf. 11.7***	
807(CF1) A279 3c **deep violet** *(C)*		*40.00*	*30.00*
On cover *(G)*			*300.00*
Block of 4 *(G)*		*250.00*	

Imperf

807(CF2) A279 3c **deep violet,** pair *(B)*		*80.00*	*75.00*
Block of 4 *(F)*		*160.00*	
Full pane of 100 (no marginal markings) *(G)*		*2,500.*	

Nos. 807(CF1) and 807(CF2) are close to the genuine stamp in color, but the background lines are less distinct, often connected by splotches of ink. There are no horizontal gum breakers. Perforations on No. 807(CF1) range from irregular with small holes to clean and regular. Some examples of 807(CF2) are known with incomplete and inconsistent impressions.

Genuine examples of No. 807 were printed by recess engraving, and have distinct and finely engraved background lines. They are perforated 11x10.5, and have horizontal gum breakers.

Genuine No. 1030

No. 1030(CF1)

Size: 19.5x22.25mm

Soft, low-quality white paper

SURFACE PRINTED

1954	**Unwmk.**	***Ragged Perf. 9.9***
1030(CF1) A477 ½c **light orange**		
Pair, on cover *(G)*		*4,000.*

No. 1030(CF1) appears smaller than a genuine example because there is much more margin around the design. Printing is light and indistinct. For example, the lettering of "U.S. Postage" runs together. On-cover examples contain propaganda items from North Korea that were inserted into the South Korean post with a U.S. return address and forged U.S. cancellation, for delivery in Pusan. No off-cover examples are known. Only two covers are known. See No. 1049(CF1).

Genuine examples of No. 1030 are red orange, are perforated 11x10.5, size: 19x22.5mm. The features of the face are clear and each letter of text is distinct.

Genuine No. 1036

No. 1036(CF1)

Size: 19.75x22mm

Thin shiny paper

PHOTOGRAPHIC OFFSET LITHOGRAPHY

1954	**Unwmk.**	***Perf. 12.4***	
1036(CF1) A483 4c **red violet** *(E)*		*75.00*	*50.00*
P# block of 4 (P#26401LL)		*1,000.*	
Pane of 100 (with marginal markings including P#26401 at LL)			*3,500.*

No. 1036(CF1) was produced from photographically prepared plates using coil stamps as the initial model; thus, images of the counterfeit are both shorter and wider than genuine examples. The color is brighter and the design less detailed than the genuine. For example, there is a white space between the shoulders and the background. There is less vertical space between the stamps and more horizontal space. There are no horizontal gum breakers. Perforation holes are very small.

Genuine examples of No. 1036 were printed by recess engraving. The background lines extend all the way to Lincoln's shoulders. Perforations are 11x10.5. Size: 19x22.5mm.

Genuine No. 1044

Size: Unspecified

Slightly yellowish paper

PHOTOGRAPHIC OFFSET LITHOGRAPHY

1954	**Unwmk.**	***Imperf.***
1044(CF1) A491 10c **rose lake** *(I)*		

No. 1044(CF1) has been reported by the Postal Inspection Service, and one unfinished pane of 100 is in their files.

See *Linn's Stamp News* 10/15/90.

Genuine No. 1049

Size: 19.5x22.25mm

Soft, low-quality white paper

SURFACE PRINTED

1954	**Unwmk.**	***Ragged Perf. 9.9***
1049(CF1) A496 30c **black,** pair on cover with pair of #1030(CF1) *(H)*		*9,000.*

No. 1049(CF1) appears smaller than genuine examples because there is much more margin around the design. Printing is light and indistinct. For example, the lettering of "U.S. Postage" runs together. The only known cover contains propaganda items from North Korea that was inserted into the South Korean post with a U.S. return address and forged U.S. cancellation for delivery in Pusan. No off-cover examples are known.

Genuine examples of No. 1049 are black, perforated 11x10.5. The features of the face are clear and each letter of text is distinct. Size: 19x22.5mm.

Genuine No. 1052

Size: Unspecified
Slightly yellowish paper

PHOTOGRAPHIC OFFSET LITHOGRAPHY

1954 Unwmk. *Imperf.*

1052(CF1) A499 $1 **purple** *(I)*

No. 1052(CF1) has been reported by the Postal Inspection Service, and one unfinished pane of 100 is in their files.

See *Linn's Stamp News* 10/15/90.

Genuine No. 1213

Unknown printing method

1962 Unwmk. *Imperf.*

1213(CF1) A650 5c **dark blue grey**

No. 1213(CF1) is mentioned in the March 1982 issue of *The American Philatelist* as existing, but with no details given. No examples have been seen by the editors.

Genuine No. 1284

No. 1284(CF1)

Size: 22.25x19mm

PHOTOGRAPHIC OFFSET LITHOGRAPHY

1966 Unwmk. *Perf. 12.6*

1284(CF1) A716 6c **grey brown***(G)*	*250.00*	
On cover *(H)*	*750.00*	

No. 1284(CF1) is surface printed, and therefore has parts of the design missing their shading lines and lacking definition. Varieties exist of both dull and bright papers, some with rough perforations. The example on cover is a bottom margin single with thin simulated Electric Eye markings.

Genuine examples of No. 1284 were printed by recess engraving and exhibit a complete design. Perforations gauge 10.5x11. Size: 22.5x18.5mm.

Genuine No. 1287

No. 1287(CF1)

No. 1287(CF1A)

No. 1287(CF3)

Size: 19x22.5mm
Thick white or yellowish paper

PHOTOGRAPHIC OFFSET LITHOGRAPHY

1967 Unwmk. *Perf. 11.8*

Untagged

1287(CF1)	A719 13c **red brown** *(B)*	*50.00*	*35.00*
	Block of 4	*225.00*	
	Full pane of 100, no margins	*6,000.*	

Imperf

1287(CF1A)	A719 13c **red brown,** pair *(H)*	*300.00*	
	On cover, pair *(G)*		*500.00*

Nos. 1287(CF1) and 1287(CF1A) have a constant variety, a dot over the "c" of "13c." The portrait is closer to red brown than the brown of a genuine example.

No. 1287(CF1) has smooth dull gum without horizontal gum breakers. The portrait is poorly printed, with a wide vertical white line on left cheek. Most examples are poorly centered.

The No. 1287(CF1A pair is unique, without gum, and shows partial plate number 39293 (not a genuine plate number, thought here is a genuine number 29393).

1287(CF2)	A719 13c **plum** *(C)*	*60.00*	*45.00*
	On cover		*500.00*

Perf. 12.5

1287(CF3)	A719 13c **plum** *(C)*	*50.00*	*35.00*

Nos. 1287(CF2) and 1287(CF3) do not have the "dot over c" variety. They have a darker, more consistent print than No. 1287(CF1), with a thinner white vertical line on left cheek, and very light shading on forehead, upper lip, chin, and around the eyes.

Genuine examples of No. 1287 were printed by recess engraving, with all areas of the face having consistent shading. Color is dark brown. Perforations gauge 11x10.5.

Genuine No. 1288

1968 Unwmk. *Imperf., 12 x imperf., imperf. x 12*

PHOTOGRAPHICALLY PREPARED ALUMINUM OFFSET PLATE

Hard, thin paper with smooth surface

1288(CF1) A720 15c **red,** Type I *(I)*

No. 1288(CF1) has been reported by the Postal Inspection Service, and unfinished panes of 100 are in their files. The counterfeits are reported to be more red than the genuine magenta of No. 1288 and the design is muddy compared to genuine examples. No stamps are fully perforated and some are fully imperf.

See *Linn's Stamp News* 10/18/81.

Genuine examples of No. 1288 were printed by recess engraving, with full and consistent shading throughout the design. Perforations measure 11x10.5.

Genuine No. 1293

1968 Unwmk. *Perf. 11.8*

OFFSET

1293(CF1) A725 50c **rose** *(I)*

No. 1293(CF1) has been reported by the Postal Inspection Service, and unfinished panes of 100 are in their files. Design has less definition and detail than genuine examples.

See *Linn's Stamp News* 2/12/90.

Genuine examples of No. 1293 were printed by recess engraving, so shading is consistent and clear. Perforations gauge 11x10.5.

Geniune No. 1295

No. 1295(CF1)

1966 Offset Unwmk. *Perf. 11.1x10.7*

Medium White Fluorescent Paper, Untagged

Size: 18.7x22.4mm

1295(CF1) A727 $5 black *(H)*	*500.00*	
1295(CF2) A727 $5 black *(H)*		—

No. 1295(CF1) lacks the detail and depth of the original. The perforations match well but appear to have been punched vertically. This counterfeit glows blue under both long wave and short wave ultraviolet light. The gum is white, with no gum breakers.

Genuine examples of No. 1295 were printed by recess engraving on untagged paper. There are tagged and untagged versions, the latter glowing green under short wave ultraviolet light. Perforations measure 11.1x10.6 and size is 18.9x22.5mm.

No. 1295(CF2) is gauge 12 with dry gum and better facial definition.

Genuine No. 1393

No. 1393(CF1)

No. 1393(CF2)

1970 Unwmk. *Perf. 10.3*

PHOTOGRAPHIC OFFSET LITHOGRAPHY

Thin white to yellowish paper

Size: 19x22.5mm

1393(CF1)	A815 6c **blue black** *(B)*	*150.00*	*100.00*
	On cover		*900.00*

Perf. 10.9x10.5

1393(CF2)	A815 6c **blue black** *(E)*	*150.00*	*100.00*
	Zip block of 4	*350.00*	
a.	**dark slate blue**	*200.00*	*150.00*
	P# block of 4 (P#31920 LR)	*900.00*	

On Nos. 1393(CF1) and 1393(CF2) the shading at the top of the head and in the right ear is partially missing. "Eisenhower" and "USA" are filled in and appear solid. There are no horizontal gum breakers.

Genuine examples of No. 1393 were printed by recess engraving. "Eisenhower" and "USA" can be seen under magnification to be made up of closely spaced engraved diagonal lines. No. 1393 is dark blue grey, has gauge 11x10.5 perforations and has horizontal gum breakers.

Genuine No. 1394

No. 1394(CF1)

No. 1394(CF2)

1971 Unwmk. *Perf. 12.3*

PHOTOGRAPHIC OFFSET LITHOGRAPHY

Thin slightly darker paper

Size: 19.5x20.5mm

1394(CF1)	A815a 8c **blk, red & bl grey** *(D)*	*50.00*	*40.00*

Imperf

1394(CF2)	A815a 8c **blk, red & bl grey,** pair *(B)*	*60.00*	*40.00*
	Mail Early block of 6	*375.00*	
	Zip block of 4	*250.00*	
	P# block of 4 (P# 33063LR)	*550.00*	
	Full pane of 100 (with normal marginal markings)	*3,500.*	

Full pane of 100 (with normal marginal markings), horiz. perforations under rows 2, 5 and 8 *(H)* 5,000.

While Nos. 1394(CF1) and 1394(CF2) have higher quality images of Eisenhower than most counterfeits, the printing quality of "Eisenhower" is poor, being light and/or smeared. Black vignette, and blue and red lettering sometimes are misaligned. No. 1394(CF1) has smaller perf holes than genuine examples.

Genuine examples of No. 1394 were printed by recess engraving. Colors are almost always perfectly aligned, and "Eisenhower" and "USA" are clearly and cleanly printed. Perforations gauge 11.

Genuine No. 1474

No. 1474(CF1)

1972 Offset Untagged Unwmk. *Perf. 11.8*
Thin, White Paper
Size: 39x29mm

1474(CF1) A888 8c **multicolored** *(H)*
On cover 750.00

No. 1474(CF1) has the green a good match with the issued stamp, but the brown in the No. 1 design lacks definition and is a darker brown. Paper is whiter, and the ink glows white under short wave ultraviolet light. Known only on cover together with a genuine 29c stamp to make up the 2003 37c rate. Genuine examples of No. 1474 are lithographed (green) and engraved (brown and black). They are perf. 11.1 and tagged, glowing yellow green under short wave ultraviolet light. Size is 36.5x28mm.

Genuine No. 1509

No. 1509(CF2)

1973 Unwmk. *Perf. 12*
PHOTOGRAPHIC OFFSET LITHOGRAPHY
Untagged

1509(CF1) A928 10c **red & bright blue** 40.00

According to press reports, *Linn's Stamp News* 2/12/90, No. 1509(CF1) shares many of the same characteristics as No. 1509(CF2), but has larger perforation holes and poor reproduction of "United States," which is blotchy with excess ink. Although many were used on mail, the bulk were seized by the Postal Inspection Service. The editors have not seen an example of No. 1509(CF1).

Perf. 12.5
Poor quality medium fluorescent white paper

1509(CF2) A928 10c **red & brt blue** *(D)*

No. 1509(CF2) has small-hole, poorly applied line perforations that were applied from the back. Color is bright blue rather than dark blue, and the stars in the field of stars in the left part of the flag are too large and run into one another or are partially filled by excess ink. Reproduces the vertical joint line characteristic of Huck press printing. Gum is shiny white without horizontal gum breakers.

Genuine examples of No. 1509 were printed by recess engraving. They have well defined stars in the left side flag. They are block tagged and bulls-eye perforated 11x10.5. Gum is shiny yellowish with horizontal gum breakers.

Genuine No. 1510

No. 1510(CF1)

No. 1510(CF4)

1973 Unwmk. *Imperf.*
PHOTOGRAPHIC OFFSET LITHOGRAPHY
Thin white paper, gummed
Size: 19x22.5mm
Untagged

1510(CF1) A924 10c **flat grey blue** *(D)* 75.00

No. 1510(CF1) is a lower right margin block of 8, with traces of what may be horizotal perf 12 perforations at right. It has the least definition in shading lines present of any of the 1510(CF) counterfeits.

Thick white paper, gummed

1510(CF2) A924 10c **flat grey blue** *(E)* 100.00

No. 1510(CF2) is missing many of the shading lines in the Jefferson Memorial, especially in the triangular area above the entrance.

Thin white paper, gummed

1510(CF3) A924 10c **deep blue** *(E)* 100.00

No. 1510(CF3) has a deep blue color and the best defined shading lines of all the No. 1510(CF) imperfs.

Perf. 12.5
Heavy paper

1510(CF4) A924 10c **blue** *(H)* 75.00

Large dots form background with some appearing in the text and in the right margin on No. 1510(CF4), unlike Nos. 1510(CF1)-1510(CF3). Size: 19.7x22.7mm.

Genuine examples of No. 1510 were printed by recess engraving, and are perforated 11x10.5. They are tagged, and have horizontal gum breakers. They are a darker blue than any 1510(CF).

Genuine No. 1595

No. 1595(CF1)

1975 Unwmk. *Imperf.*
PHOTOGRAPHIC OFFSET LITHOGRAPHY
Off white medium thickness paper
Size: 19x22mm
Untagged

1595(CF1) A998 13c **brown** *(B)* 50.00 45.00
On cover 400.00
Block of 4 225.00

No. 1595(CF1) reproduces the 13c Liberty Bell design issued in booklet and coil forms only; thus there are straight edges on at least one side of all genuine examples. The counterfeit examples were all produced and sold in strips and sheets that have stamps perforated on all four sides. The bottom of the bell clapper is open, making it look like an "A."

This is the so-called "Boston" counterfeit, printed in sheets of 400, four panes of 100 stamps each.

Genuine No. 1894

1981 Unwmk. *Crude Perf. 9*
PHOTOGRAPHIC OFFSET LITHOGRAPHY
Untagged

1894(CF1) A1281 20c **blk, dk bl & red** *(G)* 100.00

Imperf

1894(CF2) A1281 20c **blk, dk blue & red** *(I)*

Nos. 1894(CF1) and 1894(CF2) have a gap between the field of stars and the short red stripes. The design has a coarse appearance, especially in the Supreme Court building, and the blue is brighter than that of genuine examples. Nos. 1894(CF1) and 1894(CF2) were written up in the philatelic press, *Linn's Stamp News* 7/4/83, noting that 250,000 perforated examples had been used on mailings, but the editors have not seen an example of either. No. 1894(CF2) exists only in the files of the Postal Inspection Service.

Genuine examples of No. 1894 were printed by recess engraving on white gummed paper with light vertical gum breakers. Authentic stamps do not have a large gap between the field of stars and the short stripes, although freak prints of No. 1894 do exist with this variety. Perforations gauge 11.

Genuine No. 1946

No. 1946(CF1)

1981 Unwmk. *Perf. 12.5*
PHOTOGRAPHIC OFFSET LITHOGRAPHY
Off white thin paper
Size: 20x21.5mm
Untagged

1946(CF1) A1332 (20c) **brown,** Pane of 100 *(H)* *2,500.*

Pane of 100 No. 1946(CF1) has marginal markings with the exception of P#; stamps are lined through horizontally. Surface printed on flat-gummed paper with no gloss. Color is flat. Perforations are irregularly spaced.

Genuine examples of No. 1946 were printed by photogravure on white, tagged paper with a light gloss. Perforations gauge 11x10.5. Size: 20x22.75mm.

Genuine No. 2111

1985 Unwmk. *Perf. Unknown*
PHOTOGRAPHIC OFFSET LITHOGRAPHY
Untagged

2111(CF1) A1496 (22c) **gray green** *(I)*

Imperf

2111(CF2) A1496 (22c) **gray green** *(I)*

Discovery of Nos. 2111(CF1) and 2111(CF2) was announced by local law enforcement in Lubbock, Texas, which turned the issues over to the Postal Inspection Service. Images of full panes were subsequently released by the service. They appear to be of better than average quality, but no details are available. See *Linn's Stamp News* 4/23/90.

Genuine examples of No. 2111 were produced by photogravure printing in green, with perfs that gauge 11. Stamps have a yellowish gum, and are tagged. Size: 18x20.5mm.

Genuine No. 2182

No. 2182(CF1)

1986 Unwmk. *Crude Perf. 11.25*
PHOTOGRAPHIC OFFSET LITHOGRAPHY
Glossy label-style paper
Untagged

2182(CF1) A1564 25c **blue**
On cover *(G)* 300.00

Design of No. 2182(CF1) is less detailed and more sketchy than genuine examples of No. 2182 and is composed of a dot pattern, with stripped-in solid lettering. Lighter blue than genuine examples. All examples reported to date are on glossy label-type paper, untagged and on cover.There might have been more than one attempt to counterfeit this stamp.

Genuine examples of No. 2182 were printed by recess engraving on paper with large block tagging. Color is green blue, perforations gauge 11. Size: 18x20.25mm.

Genuine No. 2531

No. 2531(CF1)

1991 UNKOWN PRINTING METHOD Unwmk.

Rouletted 9.5 X 9.25 to simulate perforations

Ungummed white paper with yellowish surface tint

Untagged

2531(CF1) A1883 29c **red, bl & blk** *(B)* 40.00 25.00
On cover *(F)* 200.00
Strip of 6 250.00

Greenish surfaced paper

2531(CF2) A1883 29c **red, bl & blk** *(B)* 40.00 25.00
Strip of 6 250.00

Nos. 2531(CF1) and 2531(CF2) were printed in six-stamp strips on ungummed paper in Taiwan for use with a paper weight. Some migrated to the U.S. and were sold in 1993. The presence of "29c" violated USPS regulations and encouraged fraudulent use. Top of flag poles and shaded areas of flag are made up of patterns of large dots. There are more areas of shading in the flag than on genuine examples of No. 2531.

A press report in *Stamp Collector* 7/17/93, stated that there was also a domestic counterfeiting operation that produced No. 2531(CF2). Though attempts were made to use them in the mails, the great majority were seized by the Postal Inspection Service. There has been no additional information released that would help identify No. 2531(CF2).

Genuine examples of No. 2531 were printed by photogravure on tagged white paper with no tint on the face of the stamps. The top of the flag pole is made up of fine dots in the shape of a triangle. Perforations gauge 11.

Genuine No. 2938

1995 Unwmk. *Perf. Unknown*

PHOTOGRAPHIC OFFSET LITHOGRAPHY

Untagged

2938(CF1) A2253 46c **carmine** *(I)*

No. 2938(CF1) has been reported by the Postal Inspection Service, which holds unfinished panes in their files. Design has less definition and detail than authentic examples of No. 2938. See *Stamp Collector* 6/22/98.

Genuine examples of No. 2938 were printed by recess engraving on white pre-phosphored paper with embedded tagging. Shading is consistent and clear. Perforations gauge 11. Size: 18.5x21mm.

Genuine No. 3281

No. 3281(CF1)

1999 Unwmk. *Imperf.*

OFFSET LITHOGRAPHY

Heavy slick ungummed paper

Untagged

Coil Stamp Size:18x21mm

3281(CF1) A2540e 33c **multicolored,** pair, diagonal black line through "33USA" *(C)* 50.00

3281(CF2) A2540e 33c **multicolored,** pair, without black diagonal line through "33USA" 50.00

The date and background of No. 3281(CF1) are composed of widely spaced dots with an obvious dot pattern. Image size is the same as the genuine No. 3281. There is no backing paper as there is with genuine self-adhesive stamps. These may have been produced for use in refrigerator magnets sold as an ancillary product by the Postal Service.

Genuine examples of No. 3281 were photogravure-printed, are tagged, die cut 9.8 vertically and have a solid "1999" year date. They are self-adhesive on backing paper.

Genuine No. 3622

No. 3622(CF1)

2002 Unwmk. *Serpentine Die Cut 10 Vert.*

OFFSET LITHOGRAPHY

Untagged

Self-Adhesive

Thin, shiny paper on thin backing

Coil Stamp Size:18x21mm

3622(CF1) A2807b (37c) **multicolored** *(A)* 40.00 30.00
On cover *(D)* 45.00

No. 3622(CF1) is dated "2003" instead of the correct "2002." It has a strong dot pattern that includes black dots in both red and white stripes and in the stars. The red is brighter than in genuine examples and there is a yellowish tint to the white stripes. Sold in rolls of 100 with no plate number. Die cut and image size match genuine examples.

3622(CF2) A2807b (37c) **multicolored** *(A)* 40.00 30.00
On cover *(D)* 45.00

No. 3622(CF2) is similar to No. 3622(CF1), but it is die cut 9.6. It has a bluish tint under longwave and shortwave UV light.

Genuine examples of No. 3622 were photogravure printed on thicker paper and dated "2002." The stripes in the flag are white and there are no black dots in the red and white stripes or the stars.

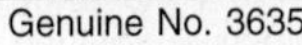

Genuine No. 3635

No. 3635(CF1)

Serpentine Die Cut 11.3 on 2, 3, or 4 Sides

2002 OFFSET LITHOGRAPHY Unwmk.

Untagged

Self-Adhesive

Booklet Stamps Size: 18.25x21mm

3635(CF1) A2812j 37c **multicolored** *(A)* 15.00 30.00
On cover *(D)* 75.00
Booklet Pane of 20 *(C)* 350.00

No. 3635(CF1) lacks microprinting and has shading in the white stripes that has an obvious pattern of dots, giving them a light yellow tint. The paper is slightly darker than genuine examples . All panes seen to date have plate number B5555. Die cut gauge and pattern and image size are similar to genuine examples. Wavy die cuts extend through backing so individual stamps can be separated from the pane with backing intact.

Genuine examples of No. 3635 are yellow-green tagged, have "USPS" microprinted in the top red flag stripe, and are printed by photogravure. The shading in the white stripes looks like the dimpled surface of a paper towel rather than individual dots. Wavy die cuts do not extend through the backing paper.

Genuine No. 3981

No. 3981(CF1)

2006 Unwmk. *Serpentine Die Cut 9.4 Vert.*

OFFSET LITHOGRAPHY

Untagged

Self-Adhesive

Thin, yellowish slick paper, back and front

Coil Stamps Size: 18.5x21mm

3981(CF1) A3040c 39c **multicolored** *(B)* 20.00 30.00

Die Cut 9.5 Vert.

3981(CF2) A3040c 39c **multicolored** *(G)* 20.00 30.00
3981(CF3) A3040c 39c **multicolored** *(B)* 20.00 30.00

Nos. 3981(CF1) and 3981(CF2) have "2006" dates composed of dots and the microprinted "USPS" is only a dark patch, not lettering. The dots of the design are indistinct. While untagged, No. 3981(CF1) gives a medium hi-brite bluish violet-white response under shortwave UV, and No. 3981(CF2) exhibits an even higher level of hi-brite response.

Genuine examples of No. 3981 were photogravure printed, die cut 9.4 and have yellow-green tagging. The dots are distinct and there is a distinct microprinted "USPS" in the top red stripe next to the blue field of stars.

No. 3981(CF3) found June 20, 2020 used on piece. Similar to No. 3981(CF1), but the die cut gauge measures 9.6.

Genuine No. 3982

No. 3982(CF1)

2006 Unwmk. *Serpentine Die Cut 10.5 Vert.*

OFFSET LITHOGRAPHY

Untagged

Self-Adhesive

Thick, slick paper on backing

Coil Stamp Size: 19x20.5mm

3982(CF1) A3040d 39c **multicolored** *(B)* 20.00 *30.00*

No. 3982(CF1) is slightly smaller than genuine examples, has a solid "2006" date and does not react under UV light. The blue sky is a grid pattern with the white background showing through. The inking pattern is distinct. The die cut matches genuine examples.

3982(CF2) A3040d 39c **multicolored** *(G)* 20.00 *30.00*

No. 3982(CF2) has a design size of 17.4x20mm. It has a fuzzy "2006" year date, and the "39USA" is thinner than on the genuine stamp. It does not react under UV light. It has a crude die cut of 10.5.

3982(CF3) A3040d 39c **multicolored** *(F)* 20.00 *30.00*

No. 3982(CF3) is a very good quality counterfeit. The design is 18x20.8mm, and the die cut is 10.2. It shows bluish under shortwave UV light. Under longwave UV light, the paper is hibrite.

3982(CF4) A3040d 39c **multicolored** *(G)* 20.00 *30.00*

No. 3982(CF4) is similar to No. 3982(CF2). The design is 17.3x19.8mm, and the die cut is a very crude 10.6. It has a greenish tint under shortwave UV light, and is hibrite under longwave UV light.

Genuine examples of No. 3982 were photogravure printed with yellow-green tagging and an image size of 19.5x21.5mm. The "2006" date is composed of dots. The blue sky is solid and the inking pattern is less distinct.

Counterfeit examples of United States forever stamps, starting with the 2007 Liberty Bell issue, have increased exponentially. See editorial note after No. 4394(CF2).

Genuine No. 4132

No. 4132(CF1)

2007 Unwmk. *Serpentine Die Cut 9¼ Vert.*

OFFSET LITHOGRAPHY

Untagged

Self-Adhesive

4132(CF1) A3149 (41c) **multicolored** *(G)* — —

No. 4132(CF1) is used on piece. There is no reaction under long wave and shortwave UV light. The die cuts are crude and uneven and measure approximately gauge 9.7. The lettering is made up of black, red and blue dots. The date is solid black. There are light diagonal lines in the field that run from lower left to upper right. The white stripes and stars are clear. The tan stripes include red and blue specs. Red stripes are solid red. Pole has black lines along the left edge for shading.

Genuine No. 4133

No. 4133(CF1)

2007 Unwmk. ***Serpentine Die Cut 11 Vert.***

OFFSET LITHOGRAPHY

Untagged
Self-Adhesive
Coil Stamps

Thin, smooth-backed paper

4133(CF1) A3149d (41c) **multicolored** *(G)* *20.00 30.00*

Among the features that distinguish Nos. 4133(CF1)-4133(CF6) from genuine examples are the short lanyard connecting the UL corner of the flag to the halyard and the shading in the flag pole.

On No. 4133(CF1) the laynard is composed of four straight dots. The red stripes of the flag are a grid of red on white. The tan background has a coarse litho dot overlay. The center of the flag pole is unshaded.

4133(CF2) A3149d (41c) **multicolored** *(A)* *20.00 30.00*

On No. 4133(CF2) the lanyard is composed of three straight dots. The red stripes of the flag are solid with an overlay of tiny black dots. The yellowish background has a fine litho dot overlay. The flag pole has a vertical row of tiny shading dots in the center of the pole.

4133(CF3) A3149d (41c) **multicolored** *(A)* *20.00 30.00*

On No. 4133(CF3) the lanyard is composed of a straight double line of four dots over three dots. The red stripes of the flag are solid with an overlay sprinkling of tiny black dots. The yellowish background has a fine litho dot pattern with large dots interspersed with tiny ones. The flag pole has one unshaded vertical stripe.

4133(CF4) A3149d (41c) **multicolored** *(A)* *20.00 30.00*

On No. 4133(CF4) the lanyard is composed of a straight line of four dots. The red stripes of the flag are a coarse grid of red on white. The yellowish background has a coarse dot pattern. The flag pole has a vertical row of tiny shading dots in the center of the pole.

4133(CF5) A3149d (41c) **multicolored** *(A)* *20.00 30.00*

On No. 4133(CF5) the lanyard is composed of a straight double line of four dots, with a gap between dots two and three, over three dots. The red stripes of the flag are solid overlaid with a few tiny black dots. The background has a pinkish tint arising from a medium dot pattern that includes a grid of red dots. The flag pole is completely shaded.

4133(CF6) A3149d (41c) **multicolored** *(A)* *20.00 30.00*

On No. 4133(CF6) the lanyard is kinked. The red stripes of the flag are solid overlaid with a few tiny black dots. The background has fine dot pattern. The flag pole is completely shaded.

Nos. 4133(CF1)-4133(CF6) were produced on paper that gives a blue-white response under shortwave UV light. The printing of the flag is somewhat embossed into the paper, which shows from the back. Die cutting matches genuine examples. The background is a solid yellow-tan, but overlaid with dots in a pattern that ranges from coarse with large dots to medium to fine with large dots surrounded by tiny ones.

Genuine examples of No. 4133 are tagged yellow-green. The red stripes and tan background are solid. The lanyard is a double line of tiny dots. Shading in the flag pole is uniform both in size of dots and coverage over the pole.

4133(CF7) A3149d (41c) **multicolored** *(H)* *20.00 30.00*

On No. 4133(CF7) Red and black "S111" plate number. (First plate number found on a counterfeit coil stamp.) Red and blue inks also visible. Untagged. The lanyard is composed of three diagonal lines with the red stripes of the flag solid with very faint diagonal white lines. The tan background is composed of a fine lithographed dot overlay. The center of the flag pole is unshaded. The die cuts are uneven at approximately gauge 9.3.

4133(CF8) A3149d (41c) **multicolored** *(H)* *20.00 30.00*

On No. 4133(CF8) Multicolored "S111" plate number using red, blue and black. (First multicolored plate number found on a counterfeit coil stamp). Untagged. The lanyard is composed of two sets of two black dots. The red stripes of the flag are solid with a diagonal white-dot pattern. The yellow background is composed of a coarse lithographed dot overlay. The center of the flag pole is unshaded. The die cuts are uneven and below gauge 8.

Genuine No. 4187

No. 4187(CF1)

2007 Unwmk. ***Serpentine Die Cut 10.2 Vert.***

OFFSET LITHOGRAPHY

Untagged
Self-Adhesive
Coil Stamps

Plasticized paper with shiny back

4187(CF1) A3184a 41c **multicolored** *(A)* *20.00 30.00*

On No. 4187(CF1) the flag lanyard is composed of a double row of alternating dots. The right edge of the flag pole is composed of two columns of alternating dots.

4187(CF2) A3184a 41c **multicolored** *(A)* *20.00 30.00*

On No. 4187(CF2) the lanyard is like No. 4187(CF1). The right side of the flag pole is composed of three columns of alternating dots.

4187(CF3) A3184a 41c **multicolored** *(A)* *20.00 30.00*

On No. 4187(CF3) the lanyard is composed of a single row of dots. The left edge of the flag pole is composed of three columns of alternating dots.

4187(CF4) A3184a 41c **multicolored** *(A)* *20.00 30.00*

On No. 4187(CF4) the lanyard is like No. 4187(CF3). The left edge of the flag pole is composed of four rows of alternating dots.

4187(CF5) A3184a 41c **multicolored** *(A)* *20.00 30.00*

On No. 4187(CF5) the lanyard is composed of a single row of dots linked by an extra dot in the white flag margin to the left of the blue field. The left edge of the flag pole has three rows of alternating dots.

Nos. 4187(CF1)-4187(CF5) have a background of fine dots, and no microprinting. The "41USA" is weakly formed by light blue dots. All give off a blue-white glow under shortwave uv light.

4187(CF6) A3184a 41c **multicolored** *(A)* *20.00 30.00*

On No. 4187(CF6) the background is a coarse, more pronounced grid of dots. The red stripes have a distinct grid of blue dots. "41USA" is darker and stronger than on Nos. 4187(CF1)-4187(CF5).

4187(CF7) A3184a 41c **multicolored** *(G)* 20.00 *30.00*

No. 4187(CF7) has a lanyard made up of sequential double black dots. The red stripes are solid with a diagonal white-dot pattern. The union is covered with a pattern of red and white dots in the background. The tan background is composed of a coarse dot overlay. The denomination is a light blue. The flag pole is unshaded and is made up of a double column of sequential triple black dots. Die cuts are uneven and approximately 10.3.

4187(CF8) A3184a 41c **multicolored** *(A)* 20.00 *30.00*

On No. 4187(CF8), the flag pole, lanyard and color of the denomination and tan background are the same as on No. 4187(CF7), but the red stripes are solid with a diagonal black-dot pattern. The union is covered with a pattern of large red dots in the background. Die cuts are uneven and approximately 10.4.

Genuine examples of No. 4187 are tagged pale green, die cut 11 and have "41USA" printed in solid silver. The background is a solid tan.

Genuine No. 4228

Genuine No. 4229

Genuine No. 4230

Genuine No. 4231

2008 Unwmk. ***Perf. 9.5 Vert.***

OFFSET LITHOGRAPHY

Untagged
Coil Stamps

4228(CF1) A3214 42c **multicolored** *(B)* *30.00 40.00*
4229(CF1) A3215 42c **multicolored** *(B)* *30.00 40.00*
4230(CF1) A3216 42c **multicolored** *(B)* *30.00 40.00*
4231(CF1) A3217 42c **multicolored** *(B)* *30.00 40.00*

Nos. 4228(CF1)-4231(CF1) are known to exist but few specific details are available. The color design size is larger than genuine examples, but the date is not as distinct and the shading dots in the "42" are missing. The perfs match those of genuine examples.

Genuine examples of Nos. 4228-4231 were printed by photogravure.

Genuine No. 4235

No. 4235(CF1)

2008 Unwmk. ***Serpentine Die Cut 9.5 Vert.***

OFFSET LITHOGRAPHY

Untagged
Self-Adhesive

Coil Stamps Size: 17.5x21.25mm

4232(CF1) A3214a 42c **multicolored** *(B)* *30.00 40.00*
4233(CF1) A3215a 42c **multicolored** *(G)* *30.00 40.00*
4234(CF1) A3216a 42c **multicolored** *(B)* *30.00 40.00*
4235(CF1) A3217a 42c **multicolored** *(G)* *30.00 40.00*

Nos. 4232(CF1)-4235(CF1) are offset printed. They are taller than genuine examples because of larger top and bottom margins. The shading of the red strips lack the pattern of genuine examples. There is a backdrop of blue and red dots behind the "2008." The date is also closer to the design than on genuine examples.

4235(CF2) A3217a 42c **multicolored** *(B)* 30.00 *40.00*

No. 4235(CF2) is similar to No. 4235(CF1), but the year date is lower than either No. 4235(CF1) or the genuine stamp. There are large yellow dots on the design and in the margins.

Genuine examples of Nos. 4232-4325 were printed by lithograph, have a clean, crisp "2008" and darker red stripes than Nos. 4232(CF1)-4235(CF1).

Genuine No. 4387

No. 4387(CF1)

2009 Unwmk. ***Serpentine Die Cut 9.4***

OFFSET LITHOGRAPHY

Untagged
Self-Adhesive

4387(CF1) A3340 28c **multicolored** *(G)* — —

No. 4387(CF1) was found in 2018 used on piece. It is nonreactive under shortwave and long wave UV light. The microprinting of "USPS" is missing. The die cuts are crude and uneven that measure approximately gauge 9.4, both horizontally and vertically. The "USA" lettering is crude and not white. The "28" is crude and made up of multicolored dots. The year date is missing.

Genuine No. 4390

No. 4390(CF1)

2009 Unwmk. ***Serpentine Die Cut 11¼x10¾***

OFFSET LITHOGRAPHY

Untagged
Self-Adhesive

4390(CF1) A3341a 44c **multicolored** *(G)* 20.00 *30.00*

On No. 4390(CF1), the die cuts are crude and uneven at 11.3x11.3. The microprinting is a blob. Crude lettering that is mostly black but with red, yellow and blue dots. Paper is hibrite under longwave UV light.

Genuine No. 4392

No. 4392(CF1)

2009 Unwmk. *Serpentine Die Cut 11 Vert.*
OFFSET LITHOGRAPHY
Untagged
Self-Adhesive
Glossy paper
Coil Stamps Size: 18x21mm

4392(CF1) A3342a 44c **multicolored** *(F)* *20.00 30.00*

On No. 4392(CF1), the red stripes are a bright red. There is a coarse litho dot pattern in an obvious grid. The stars have a weak grid of multicolored dots.The numerals in the date are composed of dots, and there is no microprinting. Lettering of "USA" is coarsely outlined. While untagged, the paper on Nos. 4392(CF1)-4392(CF4) does respond purplish-white under shortwave uv light.

4392(CF2) A3342a 44c **multicolored** *(A)* *20.00 30.00*

The red stripes on No. 4392(CF2) are darker than those on No. 4392(CF1), coming close to matching those on genuine examples. The date is less distinct than on No. 4239(CF1) and appears to be narrower. There is no microprinting. Lettering of "USA" is roughly edged with overlying blue dots.

4392(CF3) A3342a 44 **multicolored** *(A)* *20.00 30.00*

The date on No. 4392(CF3) is composed of dots, each of which contains a number of microdots that are visible under 20x magnification, but cannot be resolved by a scanner. The tail of the "9" in the "2009" year date does not extend to the left edge of the digit. There is no microprinting. The lettering of "USA" is coarsely outlined by dots with an overspray of dark blue microdots.

4392(CF4) A3342a 44c **multicolored** *(A)* *20.00 30.00*

On No. 4392(CF4) the numerals of the date are surrounded by a heavy spray of dots. The tail of the "9" in the "2009" year date extends to the left edge of the digit. The numerals of the date are composed of microdots, which appear spray painted under 20x magnification. There is no microprinting. Letters of "USA" are sharply edged with an overlay of dark blue microdots.

Genuine examples of No. 4392 were lithographed with microprinted "USPS" in the top red stripe near the blue field, and have yellow-green tagging on prephosphored matte paper. Letters have sharp black outlining. Date and numerals are solid. There is a fine dot pattern in the red stripes. Stars have a regular grid of blue dots.

Genuine No. 4393

No. 4393(CF1)

2009 Unwmk. *Serpentine Die Cut 9.5 Vert.*
OFFSET LITHOGRAPHY
Untagged
Self-Adhesive
Matte paper
Coil Stamps Size: Variable

4393(CF1) A3342b 44c **multicolored** *(A)* *20.00 30.00*

No. 4393(CF1) is 17.7mm wide. The lettering is coarsely outlined and there is no microprinting. There is cyan under the black in the year date and the tail of the "9" in "2009" extends to the edge of the digit.

4393(CF2) A3342b 44c **multicolored** *(A)* *20.00 30.00*

No. 4393(CF2) is 17.7mm wide. The lettering is coarsely outlined and there is no microprinting. The crossbar on the "A" of "USA" is tilted to the UR. There is no cyan under the black in the year date and the tail of the "9" in "2009" is short and does not extend to the edge of the digit. There is no distinct dot pattern in the white stripes.

4393(CF3) A3342b 44c **multicolored** *(A)* *20.00 30.00*
On cover —

No. 4393(CF3) is 17.7mm wide. The lettering is coarsely outlined and there is no microprinting. The crossbar on the "A" of "USA" is horizontal. There is no cyan under the black in the year date and the tail of the "9" in "2009" is short and does not extend to the edge of the digit. There is no distinct dot pattern in the white stripes.

4393(CF4) A3342b 44c **multicolored** *(A)* *20.00 30.00*
On cover —

No. 4393(CF4) is 17.1mm wide. The lettering is coarsely outlined and there is no microprinting. The crossbar on the "A" in "USA" is horizontal. There is no cyan under the black in the year date and the tail of the "9" in "2009" is short and does not extend to the edge of the digit. There is almost no dot pattern in the white stripes.

4393(CF5) A3342b 44c **multicolored** *(A)* *20.00 30.00*
On cover —

No. 4393(CF5) is 17.3mm wide. The lettering is coarsely outlined and there is no microprinting. The year date is composed of multicolored dots. There is a distinct dot pattern of shading in the white stripes.

4393(CF6) A3342b 44c **multicolored** *(A)* *20.00 30.00*

No. 4393(CF6) is 18mm wide. The lettering is coarsely outlined and there is no microprinting. The year date is composed of multicolored dots. There is a distinct dot pattern of shading in the white stripes.

4393(CF7) A3342b 44c **multicolored** *(G)* *20.00 30.00*

No. 4393(CF7) is 18.5mm wide. The lettering is not outlined and there is microprinting. The black year date is distinct and clear. There are black shading dots in the red stripes.

4393(CF8) A3342b 44c **multicolored** *(F)* *20.00 30.00*
Strip of 20

No. 4393(CF8) is 18.5mm wide. The lettering is not outlined and there is microprinting. The black year date is distinct and clear. There are black shading lines in the red stripe below the microprinting. There is a black dot that appears just below the microprinted "USPS" on every other stamp in a strip of 20.

4393(CF9) A3342b 44c **multicolored** *(G)* 20.00 *30.00*

On No. 4393(CF9), the design is 18mm wide, and the die cut is 9.4 and crude. The year date is very crude, made up of coarse multicolored dots. There is no microprinting. There is no reaction under shortwave UV light; the paper is hibrite under longwave UV light.

4393(CF10) A3342b 44c **multicolored** *(G)* 20.00 *30.00*

On No. 4393(CF10), the design is 18.2mm wide, and the die cut is 9.5, smooth and even. The year date is crude and made up of coarse multicolored dots. There are large yellow dots across the stamp, including the margins. The white stripes are made up of red, yellow and blue dots, with virtually all of the white stripes covered. There is no microprinting. There is no reaction under shortwave UV light; the paper is hibrite under longwave UV light.

Genuine examples of No. 4393 are photogravure printed with a micorprinted "USPS" at the top of the white stripe at the bottom center. They are tagged yellow-green under shortwave UV light. They are 18.5mm wide. The lettering is sharply outlined and the date is solid.

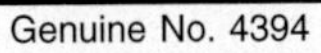
Genuine No. 4394

No. 4394(CF1)

2009 Unwmk. *Serpentine Die Cut 8.5 Vert.*
OFFSET LITHOGRAPHY
Untagged
Self-Adhesive
Glossy paper
Coil Stamps Size: 18.5x21.5mm

4394(CF1) A3342c 44c **multicolored** *(E)* *30.00 40.00*

No. 4394(CF1) is 24.5mm wide, die cut to die cut, about 1.5mm larger than a genuine example, although the image width is the same. The inscription has coarse outlines. Die cut gauge is similar to genuine, but is not consistent along the stamp edge. Untagged, but under flourescent white light, the blue is not as purple as the genuine. The dot pattern in the white stripes is weak and square where it exists. The date is not as close to the design as on the genuine stamp.

4394(CF2) A3342c 44c **multicolored** *(F)* 30.00 *40.00*

On No. 4394(CF2), the die cuts are a crude and uneven 8.3. The stamp and margins are dotted with large yellow dots. The year date is fairly crude. There is no reaction under shortwave UV light, and the paper is hibrite under longwave UV light.

Genuine examples of No. 4394 have an inscription with sharp outline. They are tagged and printed on matte paper. The dots in the white stripes of the flag are in a regular diamond pattern.

Counterfeiting of United States forever stamps has increased exponentially in 2021 with most new issues being faked. Scott catalog editors have noted within the Postage section of this catalog what stamp issues are known to exist as counterfeits and have placed that information in footnotes.

Because of the large number of new counterfeit forever stamps (more than 300 major numbers in the last year), Scott editors have decided to only list denominated and earlier counterfeits in the Scott U.S. Specialized catalog. No forever or nondenominated postcard-rate counterfeits are included in this catalog from the years 2007-date. Plans are in the works to update the Scott U.S. Specialized catalog digital edition with images and information on the new discoveries of counterfeits on a more timely basis starting in fall 2022.

COUNTERFEIT AIR POST STAMPS

Genuine No. C15

No. C15(CF1)

1930 Unwmk. *Perf. 11.5*
ENGRAVED
Thin white paper
Size: 45x19mm

C15(CF1) AP11 $2.60 **blue** *(F)* *1,500. 1,000.*
a. Large die proof **orange red** *(H)* *2,000.*
b. Large die proof **blue** —

While the objective of this counterfeit was to defraud collectors, the Postal Inspection Service did in fact make an attempt to gather up examples in dealer hands. Few were made, and of these a very small number are known either on philatelic mail or are canceled to order. No. C15(CF1), often called the "Panelli forgery," is a darker blue than genuine examples of No. C15, but the paper is a good match. The counterfeits were printed and perforated individually, so centering and perforating range from credible (10.9) to suspicious (irregular 11.4-12.4x11.4). Examples perforated 11.5 exist. Details for the design are generally unclear, including the numbers on the Zeppelin. The top of the "R" in "GRAF" is very thin, and the lettering in the label in the bottom center of the airship is unreadable.

Perforations on genuine examples of No. C15 gauge 11. The details of engraving are clear and distinct. The bar at the top of the "R" in "GRAF" clearly closes the letter. Gum is of higher quality. Size: 46x18.5mm.

Genuine No. C64

1962 Unwmk. *Perf. Unknown*
PRINTING METHOD UNKNOWN

C64(CF1) AP42 8c **carmine** *(I)*

No. C64(CF1) was mentioned in the March 1982 issue of *The American Philatelist*, but with no details provided. No examples have been seen by the editors.

Genuine No. C79

1973 Unwmk. *Perf. Unknown*
PHOTOGRAPHIC OFFSET LITHOGRAPHY
Untagged

C79(CF1) AP55 13c **carmine** *(I)*

No. C79(CF1) has been reported in the March 1982 issue of *The American Philatelist*, with an illustration of a blurry used example on piece, probably obtained from the U.S. Postal Inspection Service, which holds unfinished panes in their files.

Genuine examples of No. C79 were printed by recess engraving. Perforations gauge 11x10.5.

Genuine No. C126a

No. C126a(CF1)

1989 Unwmk. *Imperf.*

LITHOGRAPHED & ENGRAVED

Yellowish bright flourescent paper

Size: 131x82mm

C126(CF1) AP95-AP98 Souvenir sheet of 4, #a-d *(B)* *200.00*

No. C126(CF1) has a distinct beige tone to the gum. It is cut off center with the entire design lower on the sheet than genuine examples of No. C126. The ink at the right edge of the "45" is poorly wiped so that the blue ink runs irregularly out from the numbers, especially the "5." Under magnification, the images are fuzzy. The text is thinner than on genuine examples, and the paper is thicker.

Genuine examples of No. C126 were produced by lithography with the "US Air Mail 45" engraved. There is little to no bleeding of the blue engraved ink from the "45." Paper is white and the gum is whiter than the counterfeit. There is overall phosphor tagging on the front, although tagging omitted examples have been recorded.

COUNTERFEIT POSTAL CARDS

Genuine No. UX12

1894 UNKNOWN PRINTING METHOD

UX12(CF1) PC7 1c **black,** *buff (G)* — —

No. UX12(CF1) has a poor quality image of Jefferson, but printing of genuine postal cards was so poor that it is difficult to authenticate counterfeits; made even more difficult by the lack of any major flaws in the text. However, there are minor flaws: The bottom of the four-petal ornament near the left end of the upper line is cut off. The similar ornament at the middle of the bottom line has a break in the right side of the upper petal. There is a break in the upper line of the farthest left "hairpin" in the line directly under the "NI" of "UNITED." There are only two examples reported, one mint and one used.

Genuine examples of No. UX12 are only marginally better in paper and printing quality.

Genuine No. UX14

No. UX14(CF1)

1897 UNKNOWN PRINTING METHOD

UX14(CF1) PC8 1c **black,** *buff (F)* *1,000. 1,750.*

No. UX14(CF1) is poorly printed but not much worse than the average genuine example. The image of Jefferson is dark and muddy. There is one outstanding flaw on all counterfeits: the bottom of the second "T" in "STATES" lacks serifs. Serifs are also often missing on the outside bottom of the "E" next to the "T." The counterfeit can be further subdivided into at least five types as follows:

Type I: Both "T" and "E" affected. Border line weak below "E" of "UNITED." Small downward bend or break in border line of inscription, directly above center of semicircular ornament. There is a short upward extension of the dot at extreme right end of the inscription panel.

Type II: Both "T" and "E" affected. There are small white spots between tops of "ST" in "STATES," and at the upper-left corner of "O" in "OF." The inner edge of the leaf to the left of the mouth is missing.

Type III: Both "T" and "E" affected. Very small clean break in border line over the second "T" in "STATES." Top of "C" in first "Card" is flattened. The vertical stroke of "T" in "Cent" points down over "E" of "AMERICA."

Type IV: Both "T" and "E" affected. The thin line above the inscription is very weak from the beginning of the first "T" to that of the second "T" in "STATES." There is a slight doubling of the thin oval frameline around the portrait at left, opposite Jefferson's mouth.

Counterfeits are sometimes coated on one or both sides to give the impression of a previous private message and/or address being covered. Prior to the discovery of this counterfeit, this was legal and often done to allow for use of postal cards printed with ads or messaging that were excess and had not been used in the post.

Approximately 25 examples of all types are known.

Mint examples of No. UX14(CF1) have no additional printing beyond the ad and address. Used value is for examples cancelled and used in the mail, which are scarce.

Genuine examples of No. UX14 are generally but not always on lighter cards without the missing serifs identifer.

Genuine No. UX100

1983 UNKNOWN PRINTING METHOD

UX100(CF1) PC74 14c **black and white** *(H)* —

No. UX100(CF1) is an altered version of the multicolored No. UX100. The denomination of No. UX100(CF1) has been altered to 14c from the genuine 13c value. According to a press report in *Linn's Stamp News* 3/18/91, multiple examples were produced, but only a single used example is known.

Color Photocopies of Nos. 3750 and 3784

"Not quite" counterfeits:

Items in this category are either officially or privately made stamp look-alikes. While these items fall outside the scope of the listings above due to the almost individual nature of production, it is important to mention their existence and describe the various types that have occurred.

I. Photocopies of stamps — With the increased quality of photocopying, even color reproduction of genuine stamps is not beyond the technology. However, in the experience of the editors, use of photocopies as U.S. postal counterfeits has, until recently, been used mostly to reproduce stamps that are black and white. See the illustration above.

2. Stamps photocopied onto an envelope.

3. Hand-drawn replicas — Must be done item by item, but can be well done.

4. Paste-on replicas from stamp club spoof sheets — for example a 1970 Wilkinsburg Stamp Club sheetlet, a combination of the 6c Apollo 8 stamp and the 6c Botanical Congress block.

5. Paste-on commercial replicas — Usually occurs with a line through the value.

6. Stamp illustrations clipped from dealer or USPS ads, booklet pane covers, etc.

7. Shaved proofs or stamp illustrations on Bureau souvenir cards.

8. Actual stamp designs, but with no value, used as samples in refrigerator magnets sold by the USPS in Walmarts in 1999.

9. Pieces of genuine margins, or dummy stamp images from production sheets used as stamps. One item that has been seen was created using the label from a Pacific 97 sheet.

10. Tagged margin pieces used to facilitate use of non-tagged low-value stamps, and stamp-like images.

11. USPS stationery, including images of genuine stamps folded to resemble postal stationery.

12. Stamp-like images created by companies such as Pitney-Bowes to use in advertising or for use as props in movies.

NONPOSTAL AND REVENUE COUNTERFEITS

The listings of counterfeits in this section are for non-postal and revenue counterfeits that were created to deprive legal authorities (Treasury Department) of lawful monies due them.

The listings follow standard Scott policy. A comparison of the attributes found in the counterfeit listings with those of genuine stamps will enable collectors to distinguish the real from the spurious. The description field of each listing contains a letter rarity code keyed to the list below.

Numbers that survive in the hands of collectors:
E = Probably equal to or fewer than 100
F = Probably equal to or fewer than 25
G = 5 or fewer reported
H = Unique in philatelic hands

Genuine No. WS4

No. WS4(CF1)

"COUNTERFEIT" handstamp

1919(?) **Engr.** **Unwmk.** ***Perf. 10.6-10.9 Variable***

WS4(CF1) $5 **deep blue**, without handstamp (E) *600.00*
a. With handstamp on gum on reverse *750.00*
b. With handstamp on face *1,000.*

No. WS4(CF1) is a high-quality engraved counterfeit with low-quality perforations, which are variable and somewhat wavering. The paper on the counterfeit is a very light beige, whereas the genuine stamp was printed on white paper and often has an overall blue wash. The counterfeit has flat, white gum. Franklin's head and circular medallion is more finely detailed on the genuine stamp, but overall the counterfeit is very close to the genuine, even in detail. Nos. WS4(CF1) and WS4(CF1b) without gum sell for somewhat less than the values shown, which are for stamps in the grade of very fine and with "original" gum.

Quantities known of the three varieties combined = (E).

Genuine No. R3c

No. R3c(CF1)

1860s **Engr.** ***Perf. 12½***

R3c(CF1) R1 1c **red** (E) *900.00*
a. Vert. strip of 7 (see footnote) —

No. R3c(CF1) is a fairly convincing counterfeit, but the foliate ornamentation at top and bottom, and the engraved lines on Washington's coat, are significantly different.

No. R3ca(CF1) actually is a proof impression printed by the Bureau of Engraving and Printing, with a manuscript note on reverse: "Plate engraved by Hart L. Pierce. Impression from cft. plate taken at the Bureau Eng. and Printing."

Genuine No. R86a

No. R86a(CF1)

No. R86c(CF1)

1860s **Engr.** ***Imperf.***

R86a(CF1) R8 $3 **greeen** (G) *7,500.*

No. R86a(CF1) is a fair counterfeit, but there are myriad small differences in all parts of the design.

Perf.

R86c(CF1) R8 $3 **green** (H) —

Genuine No. REA3

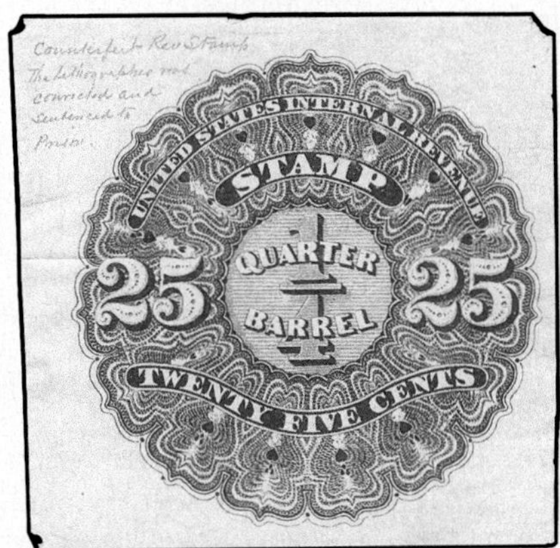

No. REA3(CF1)

1860s **Litho.** ***Imperf.***

REA3(CF1) 25c **blue** (H) *6,000.*

REA3(CF1) is a crude lithographed counterfeit of an engraved stamp. In the upper left margin is written, "Counterfeit

Rev Stamp. The lithographer was convicted and sentenced to Prison."

Genuine No. REA156

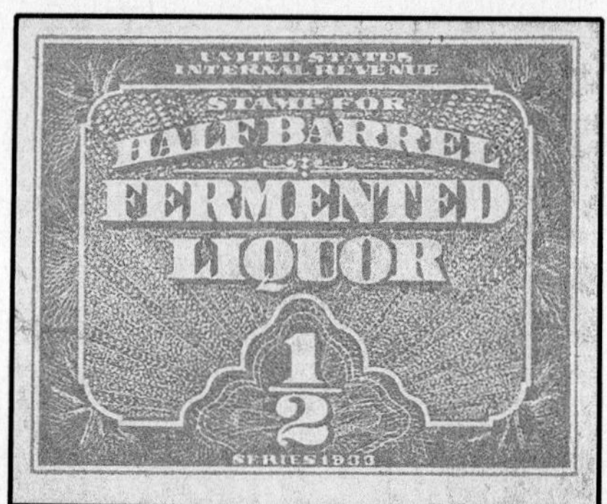

No. REA156(CF1)

1933 **Litho.** ***Imperf.***

REA156(CF1) ½ bbl., **orange**, *light blue* (H) *2,500.*

No. REA156(CF1) is a crude lithographed counterfeit of an engraved stamp. The paper is a much lighter blue than the genuine paper.

Genuine No. RK21

No. RK21(CF1)

1929(?) **Litho.** ***Rough Perfs.***

RK21(CF1) CSF1 10c **orange** (H) *1,750.*

No. RK21(CF1) is a lithographed counterfeit of an engraved stamp. It is canceled by an apparently genuine government handstamp dated Dec. 7, 1920 / Rome Italy.

Genuine No. RO98a

No. RO98a(CF1)

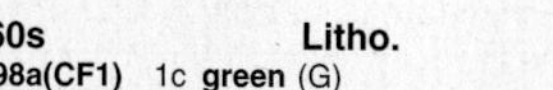

1860s **Litho.** ***Perf. 12¼***

RO98a(CF1) 1c **green** (G) *1,750.*

No. RO98a(CF1) is a crude lithographic counterfeit of an engraved stamp. The most obvious difference, besides the color and uneven perforations, is the background of horizontal lines on No. RO98a(CF1) rather than the lattice-work of diagonal lines on the genuine No. RO98a.

Genuine No. RO112a

No. RO112a(CF1)

1860s **Engr.** ***Perf. 12¼***

RO112a(CF1) 1c **blue** (G) *4,500.*

No. RO112a(CF1) is an engraved counterfeit by Benoni Howard. It differs from the genuine No. RO112a in numerous small details, including the perf. gauge.

TEST STAMPS

Test stamps, also called "dummy stamps," came into being in the late 19th century, and their production continues to the present. These stamps have been printed by both the Bureau of Engraving & Printing and by private companies for use when the Post Office Department, United States Postal Service and other companies wanted to use test stamps rather than accountable paper (i.e., actual stamps that would have to be accounted for).

With the growth of automation and the development of vending equipment in the 20th century, the production and use of test stamps proliferated. A majority are very scarce, as these items generally were not made available to the general public or philatelists.

The test stamps listed here were produced for several purposes:

1. To develop and test production equipment, including printing presses and stamp and booklet manufacturing equipment.
2. To design stamp vending equipment by private companies.
3. To test, adjust and promote stamp affixing equipment by commercial vendors.
4. To test and adjust stamp vending equipment at dispensing sites by the Postal Service and private companies.

The test stamp listings are arranged into two sections, the first being sheet and coil stamps, and the second being booklets. These listings were originally formed by Steven R. Unkrich, in consultation with other leading collectors of test stamps. The listings have since been expanded greatly with the help of the Dummy Stamps Study Group of the United States Stamp Society, headed by Terry Scott. Thanks to Dan Undersander for supplying much of the information in this section's introduction. Those interested in learning more about test (dummy) stamps are invited to join the Dummy Stamps Study Group. Contact Terry Scott at terryrscott@comcast.net.

Blank Design — TE6

Blank Definitive — TE10

Produced by Continental Bank Note Co.

1877-78 **Intermediate Paper** **Unwmk.** ***Perf. 12***

TD6 TE6 blank *150.00*

Block of 4 *600.00*

Prior to 1877, Continental Bank Note Company used "hard" wove paper. In early 1877, they began using an "intermediate" paper. They switched to a "soft" paper in August 1878 that was used until the company merged with American Bank Note Co. in February 1879. American Bank Note Co. only used "soft" paper.

No. TD6 is the large-size blank sheet stamp (TE6). See Nos. TD10, TD11, TD83, TD84A, TD113, TD114 and TD114A for small-size blank sheet test stamps (TE9).

Automatic Postage Stamp Sticker — TE7

1886 ***Perf. 15¾***

TD7 TE7 **red** —

No. TD7 was produced for Hyde & Company of New York for use in their stamp affixing device.

Burt and Tobey's Stamp Battery — TE8

1890 ***Perf. 12***

TD8 TE8 **light green** —

TD8A TE8 **orange brown** —

Perf. 12¼x12

TD8B TE8 **lavender** —

Nos. TD8, TD8A and TD8B have printed simulated perforations in addition to the normal perforations.

The Klein Mfg. Co. — TE9

1890s *Rouletted 11*

TD9 TE9 **red** —

Blank Sheet Test Stamps

Produced by Bureau of Engraving & Printing

1908 **Unwmk.** *Perf. 12*

TD10 TE10 blank 75.00
Block of 4 300.00

On March 7, 1908, the BEP's Director sent a letter to their paper contractor (Jessup & Moore) asking when a previous order for 2,000 sheets of unwatermarked paper for postage stamps would be delivered. It seems likely No. TD10 was given to companies that were developing stamp vending machines after the supply of blank, perforated and gummed double-line watermarked paper (No. TD11) they had been given in 1907 had been exhausted.

Blank Design Type of 1907

Produced by Bureau of Engraving & Printing.

1907 **Wmk. 191** *Perf. 12*

Brownish Gum

TD11 TE10 blank 65.00
Block of 4 260.00

On Oct. 26, 1907, the BEP received an order for "500 sheets of postage stamp paper, perforated and gummed, but not printed." These stamps were given to companies that were developing stamp vending machines for the post office.

No. TD11 is known only on paper with reversed forward-stepping watermark. See explanation before listing for No. 264 in the Postage section. For other blank small-size sheet test stamps, see Nos. TD83, TD84, TD84A, TD113, TD114 and TD114A

TE11

TE12

Mailometer Coil — TE12a

1906-09 **Unwmk.** *Perf. 12*

TD12 TE11 **rose red,** on cover —

Schermack Type III Perforations

TD13 TE12 **red** *450.00*
Pair *900.00*
Pasteup pair —

TD14 TE12a **brown** *150.00*
On cover *525.00*
Pair *350.00*
Guide line pair —
Pasteup pair —
a. Imperf. 100.00
Pair 200.00
b. Pair, No. TD14 + No. TD14a —

Mailometer Type I Perforations

TD14C TE12 **rose red** —
Pair —

A strip of eight No. TD14C is the largest multiple recorded.

TD15 TE12a **brown** *125.00*
Pair *250.00*
Pasteup pair —

Mailometer Type II Perforations

TD15A TE12 **red** —
Pair —
Guide line pair —

TD16 TE12a **brown** —
Pair —
Guide line pair —
Pasteup pair —

Mailometer Type III Perforations

TD17 TE12a **brown** —
Pair —

See Vending and Affixing Machines Perforations section for illustrations of perforation types.

Bureau of Engraving & Printing Test Stamps for Rotary Press Development

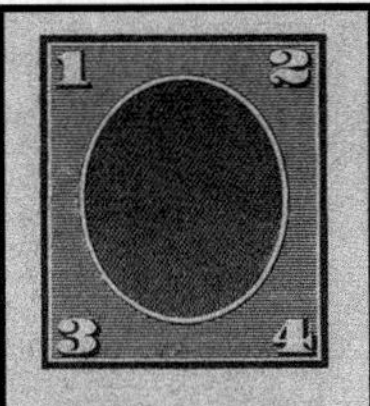

Numerals and Oval — TE13

Numerals and Alexander Hamilton — TE14

Nos. TD18-TD23 were the first test stamps used by the BEP during efforts to develop rotary press printing as a less costly method of stamp production than flat plate printing. Experiments were conducted with intaglio (engraving), letterpress (typography) and offest lithography printing. Engraving was the selected technique. The rotary press was developed under the direction of BEP Director Joseph E. Ralph, but is generally named the Stickney Press after its inventor and patent holder, Benjamin F. Stickney.

1909 **Engr.** *Imperf.*

Ungummed

TD18 TE13 **red** *2,000.*
Block of 9 with pencil inscription on back *14,000.*

Inscription on block of 9 reads "first impression printed from an experimental press designed by J. E. Ralph & B. F. Stickney from intaglio roll JER."

1910 **Ungummed**

TD19 TE14 **red** 200.00
Block of 4 800.00

No. TD19 portrait has facial shading composed of fine lines and dots. Subjects spaced 3½mm horizontally and 2mm vertically.

Typo.

(Letterpress) ***Perf. 12 Vert.***

Ungummed

TD20 TE14 **red** *4,000.*

Perf. 12 Horiz.

Ungummed

TD21 TE14 **red** *1,500.*

Perf. 12

Ungummed

TD22 TE14 **red** —

The portrait on Nos. TD20-TD22 has facial shading composed of fine lines and small squares, open-centered when large.

1910 **Offset (Litho.)** *Perf. 10¼ Horiz.*

TD23 TE14 **red** 400.00
Pair 800.00
Pair, on cover 1,250.

The portrait of No. TD23 has facial shading composed of dots and short lines providing a coarse appearance.

Pairs invariably have one row of perfs cutting slightly into the stamp design and are valued thus. Stamps in pairs alternate 23mm and 25mm tall.

Nos. TD18-TD22 were made by the BEP; No. TD23 was made by an unknown company. The BEP did not buy an offset press until 1914.

Automatic Vending Co. Coil — TE15

TE15a

1909 *Imperf.*

TD24 TE15 **red** *275.00*
Pair *550.00*
Block of 4 *1,250.*
On cover *1,200.*

U.S. Automatic Vending Co. Type 1 separations

TD24A TE15a **red** *200.00*
Vert. pair *425.00*
Vert. pasteup pair *450.00*

Rosback perf 11¾ Vert.

TD24C TE15 **red** *175.00*
Horiz. pair *400.00*
d. Vert. pair, unslit horiz. *350.00*
Block of 4 *1,000.*

Imperf

TD24E TE15 **green** *275.00*
Horiz. pair *1,000.*
Vert. pair *1,150.*

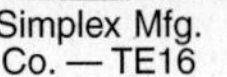
Simplex Mfg. Co. — TE16

TE16a

1909-10 **Solid Background** *Imperf.*

TD25 TE16 **red** 250.00

Horizontal Lines in Background

TD26 TE16a **green** 250.00

Simplex Stamp Affixer — TE17

1909-10 *Imperf.*

TD27 TE17 **red** *500.00*
Vert. pair —

C & R Sales Company, Newark, N.J. — TE17a

Printed by the American Bank Note Co.

1909-11 *Perf. 12 Horiz.*

TD27A TE17a **red** —
Pair —

C & R Sales Co. was incorporated Oct. 22, 1909 and the company name was changed to Postcraft on Feb. 27, 1911. See No. TD66.

"White Stamp Affixer" Coil — TE17b

1910s *Perf. 8½ Horiz.*

TD27B TE17b **red** —
Pair —

Test Stamps for Offset Printing

Minerva Facing Right — TE18

Minerva Facing Left (Text Reversed) — TE19

1910 **Litho.** ***Imperf.***

Design: 30½x34mm

Ungummed White Wove Paper

TD28	TE18	**red**	850.00
	Block of 4		—

Design: 30x33½mm

TD29	TE19	**red**	850.00
	Block of 4		—

Records show Harris approached the BEP in 1908 with an offer to demonstrate their new automatic feeding offset press. Director Ralph turned them down — probably because he and Benjamin Stickney were still working on their rotary press and wanted to avoid any patent lawsuits. Then, in 1910, after Stickney had created the model rotary press that printed No. TD18 (and possibly early versions of No. TD19), and after Marcus Baldwin had created the Typography (letterpress) Hamilton Head die used to create the plate that printed Nos. TD20, TD21 and TD22, Director Ralph told Harris that he was ready to let them demonstrate their offset press. They brought a printing press to Washington, D.C. in June 1910, and set it up inside the BEP to print Nos. TD28 and TD29 offset Minerva test stamps. Nobody has found evidence of who made the Minerva die or when the Minerva offset plate was actually made, but it is likely they were made in 1908. The offset method was not adopted in 1910, but several Harris presses were used to print revenue stamps and the offset issues of 1918-20.

Minerva essays and proofs are listed at the end of the test stamp listings.

"Standard Stamp Affixer" — TE20

1910s ***Perf. 8½ Vert.***

TD30	TE20	**red**	—
	Pair		—

Standard Stamp Affixer Coils

Inscribed "Boston, Mass." — TE21

Inscribed "Everett, Mass." — TE22

Inscribed "Somerville, Mass." — TE23

1910-1930 ***Perf. 10½ Vert.***

TD31	TE21	**green**	—
	Pair		—
TD32	TE21	**red**	20.00
	Pair		50.00
TD33	TE22	**green**	20.00
	Pair		50.00
TD33A	TE22	**red**	—
	Pair		—

Alternating Perf. 8¼ and 8½ Vert.

TD34	TE23	**green**	20.00
	Pair		45.00

Perf. 8½ Vert.

TD35	TE23	**light green**	20.00
	Pair		50.00

Perf. 10½ Vert.

TD36	TE23	**green**	20.00
	Pair		50.00

Alternating Perf. 11 and 10¼ Vert.

TD36A	TE23	**red**	20.00
	Pair		50.00

Multipost Co. Coil — TE24

TE24 Detail

TE24a Detail

1910-1930 ***Perf. 9¾ Vert.***

TD37	TE24	**red**	5.00
	Pair		10.00

Perf. 11½ Vert.

TD37A	TE24	**red**	—
	Pair		*150.00*

Perf. 11¾ Vert.

TD37B	TE24	**red**	—
	Pair		—

Perf. 10¼ Vert.

TD38	TE24a	**red**	20.00
	Pair		50.00

No. TD37 has full shading lines, and No. TD38 has shorter shading lines.

No. TD38 exists precanceled Cleveland/Ohio between lines, in violet.

On some rolls of No. TD38, the design of every other stamp is 1mm taller and 1mm wider than on the adjacent stamp. Every other vertical column of perforations has slightly larger diameter perforation holes.

Midland Supply Co. Coil — TE24b

Perf. 10½ Vert.

TD38A	TE24b	**red**	*350.00*
	Pair		—

Extensive Manufacturing Co. Coils — TE25

1911-13 ***Perf. 8½ Horiz.***

TD39	TE25	**red & blue**	20.00
	Pair		45.00

Perf. 8½ Vert.

TD39A	TE25	**red & blue**	35.00
	Pair		75.00

Perf. 10¼ Vert.

TD40	TE25	**carmine & black**	35.00
	Pair		75.00

Perf. 10¾ Vert.

TD41	TE25	**carmine & black**	35.00
	Pair		75.00

Standard Mailing Machine Co. Coils — TE26

1913 ***Perf. 10½ Vert.***

TD42	TE26	**red**	40.00
	Pair		80.00
TD43	TE26	**red violet**	40.00
	Pair		80.00

Blank Coil Design Type

Blank Coil Design — TE26a

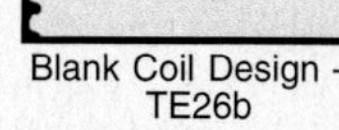
Blank Coil Design — TE26b

1910-27 **Smooth Gum** ***Imperf.***

TD44	TE26a	blank	—
	Pair		—

Expertization is recommended for No. TD44.

Perf. 10½ Vert.

TD45	TE26a	blank	—
	Pair		—

No. TD45 is 25mm tall while No. TD79 is 23.5mm tall.

Perf. 11 Vert.

TD45A	TE26a	blank	10.00
	Pair		20.00

Nos. TD45 and TD45A, and possibly TD44, were produced for General Vending Service Company, Baltimore, MD.

Schermack Type III Perforations

TD46	TE26a	blank	—
	Pair		—
	Paste up pair		—

A paste-up strip of No. TD46 is known with the paste-up at stamp 4 and double perforations between stamps 6 and 7.

Mailometer Type I Perforations

TD47	TE26a	blank	*100.00*
	Pair		*250.00*
	Paste up pair		—

A pair of No. TD47 is known with double perforations at the center of the pair.

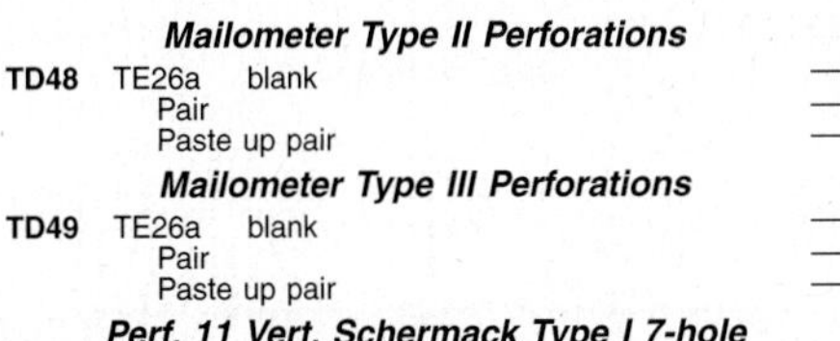

Mailometer Type II Perforations

TD48 TE26a blank —
Pair —
Paste up pair —

Mailometer Type III Perforations

TD49 TE26a blank —
Pair —
Paste up pair —

Perf. 11 Vert. Schermack Type I 7-hole Perforations

TD50 TE26a blank —
Pair —

Perf. 10 Vert. Schermack Type I 7-hole Perforations

TD50A TE26a blank —
Pair —

Illustrations of the different private perforation type test stamps are found in the 'Vending & Affixing Machine Perforations' section of this catalogue.

For other blank coil test stamps see Nos. TD75, TD79, TD106 and TD122.

George Washington — TE27

1912 **Without Gum** ***Imperf.***

TD51 TE27 **brown** 100.00
Block of 4 450.00

No. TD51 tested a photo-etching process by Bruckmann A. G. of Munich, Germany.

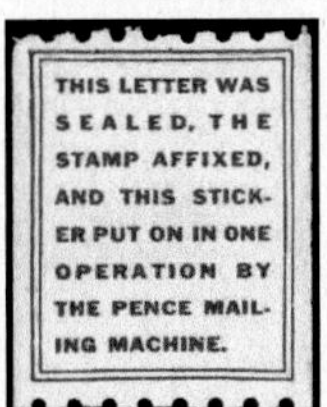

Pence Mailing Machine — TE27a

1914 ***Perf 8½ Horiz.***

TD51A TE27a **red** 100.00
Pair —

New Jersey Vending Machine Co. Coil — TE28

1914-16 ***Perf. 10½ Vert.***

TD52 TE28 **red violet** —
Pair —

National Envelope Sealing and Stamp Manufacturing Coils

Boston, Mass. — TE29

Brattleboro, VT. — TE29a

1911-14 ***Perf. 8½ Horiz.***

TD53 TE29 **red** —
Pair —
TD54 TE29a **red & blue** —
Pair —
TD54A TE29a **red** —
Pair —

U.S. Stamp Distributing and Sales Corporation Coil — TE29b

1919 ***Perf. 11 Horiz.***

Alternating Perf. 8½ and 8¼ Vert.

TD54B TE29b **red** —
Pair —

"Reliable Stamp-O-Matic Corporation" Coil — TE29c

1920s ***Perf. 9½ Vert.***

TD54C TE29c **red** —
Pair —

Mailometer Coils — TE30

TE30a

1922 ***Nine small perforation holes***

TD55 TE30 **red** —
Pair —

Perf. 10¼ Vert. (10 small holes)

TD56 TE30 **violet** —
Pair —
On cover *550.00*

Perf. 12 Vert. (8 small holes)

TD57 TE30 **violet** —
Pair —

Perf. 12 Vert. (9 small holes)

TD57A TE30 **violet** —
Pair —

A strip of four of No. TD57A is known with double perforations at the center of the strip.

Schermack Type III Perforations

TD57B TE30a **violet** —

Perf. 10¼ Vert.

TD58 TE30 **red** —
Pair —
On cover *175.00*

TE30b

Perf. 10½ Vert.

TD59 TE30b **red** —
Pair —

TE30c

Perf. 10½ Vert.

TD60 TE30c **red** —
Pair —

TE30d

Perf. 10½ Vert.

TD60A TE30d **red** *350.00*
Pair *750.00*

Wizard Stamp Affixer Coil — TE31

1915 ***Perf. 10¼ Vert.***

TD61 TE31 **red** —
Pair —

Kendall Stamp Affixer — TE32

1917 ***Perf. 10½ Vert.***

TD61A TE32 **blue** *300.00*
Pair *650.00*

Every other line of vertical perforations alternates between 10.4 and 10.6.

Wizard Stamp Affixer Coil — TE32a

Wizard Stamp Affixer Coil — TE32b

1920s ***Perf. 10 Vert.***

TD62 TE32a **red & blue** —
Pair —

A large version of design TE32a exists with perforating similar to Schermack Type III. It is 28x41mm and is believed to have been used to test a mechanical mattress label applicator.

TD62A TE32b **red & blue** —
Pair —

On No. TD62A, "MADE IN AMERICA" is outlined in red. Several other differences are evident.

Postage Stamp Machine Co. Coil — TE33

1920s ***Perf. 8½ Vert.***

TD63 TE33 **red** —
Pair —

Natural Method Stamp Affixer — TE33a

1910-30 *Perf. 11¾ Vert.*

TD63A	TE33a	**red**	—
	Pair		—

"Security Sealing and Stamping Machine Company" Coil — TE33b

1910-30 *Perf. 8½ Horiz.*

TD63B	TE33b	**red**	—
	Pair		—

Licensed Sanitary Postage Coil — TE34

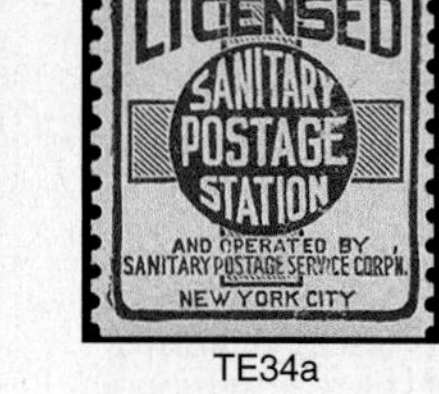

TE34a

1926 *Perf. 10½ Horiz.*

TD64	TE34	**red**	—
	Pair		—

1914 *Perf. 10¾ Vert.*

TD65	TE34a	**red**	17.50
	Pair		35.00

Postcraft Stamp Affixer Coil — TE35

1914 *Perf. 10 Vert.*

TD66	TE35	**red**	—
	Pair		—

Vidaver Mailing Machine Co. Inc. Coil — TE36

1920s *Perf. 10½ Vert.*

TD67	TE36	**red**	90.00
	Pair		180.00

Agnew Auto Mailing — TE37

1920s *Perf. 12*

TD68	TE37	**red brown**	45.00
TD68A	TE37	**red**	—
TD68B	TE37	**dark green**	—

Molyneux Automatic Mailing Machine Coil — TE38

1907 *Perf. 11¾x12*

TD69A	TE38	**light blue green**	—
TD69B	TE38	**orange**	—

Stearns-Daniels Co. Coil — TE39

1920s-30s *Perf. 10¼ Vert.*

TD70	TE39	**green**	—
	Pair		—

RO-TA-RE Stamp Affixer Service Machines Company — TE40

1920s *Perf. 10¼ Vert.*

TD70A	TE40	**blue**	—
	Pair		—

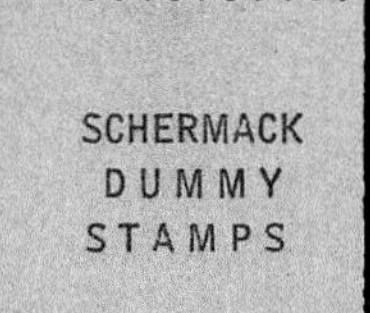

Schermack Dummy Coil — TE41

1920s-30s *Perf. 10½ Horiz.*

TD72	TE41	**red**	—
	Pair		—

National Postal Meter Co., Inc. Coil — TE42

1920s-40s *Perf. 9¾ Vert.*

TD73	TE42	**red**	—
	Pair		—

Postmaster Mfg. for Stampmasters Inc. — TE43

1920s-30s *Perf. 9¾ Vert.*

TD74	TE43	**violet**	15.00
	Pair		30.00

Blank Coil Design Type

Produced by Bureau of Engraving & Printing.

1927-30 *Perf. 9¾ Vert.*

Horiz. Ribbed Gum

TD75	TE26a	blank	.40
	Pair		.85

For other blank coil test stamps, see Nos. TD44, TD45, TD45A, TD46, TD47, TD48, TD49, TD50, TD50A, TD79, TD106 and TD122.

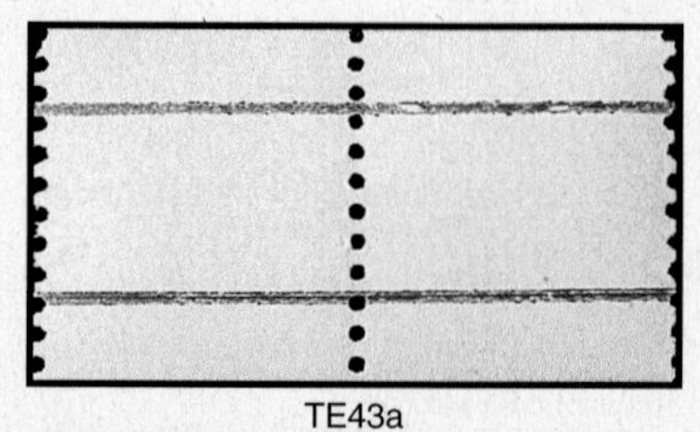

TE43a

With Red Horizontal Lines 13½ mm Apart

TD76	TE43a	blank, *1930-40*	.60
	Pair		1.25
	Pair with gap in precancel-like bars		4.25
	Strip of 10 with wide and narrow gaps in the precancel-like bars		16.00

Gaps appear every six stamps and alternate between wide (3mm) and narrow (2mm) gaps.

Central Machine & Supply Co. Coil — TE44

1930s *Perf. 9¾ Vert.*

TD77	TE44	**red**	—
	Pair		—

Puritan Mailing Machine Co. Coil — TE45

1913 *Perf. 8½ Vert.*

TD78	TE45	**red & black**	—
	Pair		—

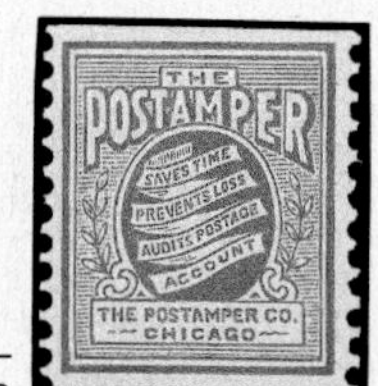

The Postamper Co. Coil — TE45a

1913 *Perf. 10½ Vert.*

TD78A	TE45a	**red**	—
	Pair		—

Peerless Stamp Affixer Coil — TE45b

1914 *Perf. 10½ Vert.*

TD78B	TE45b	**red**	—
	Pair		—

Blank Coil Design Type

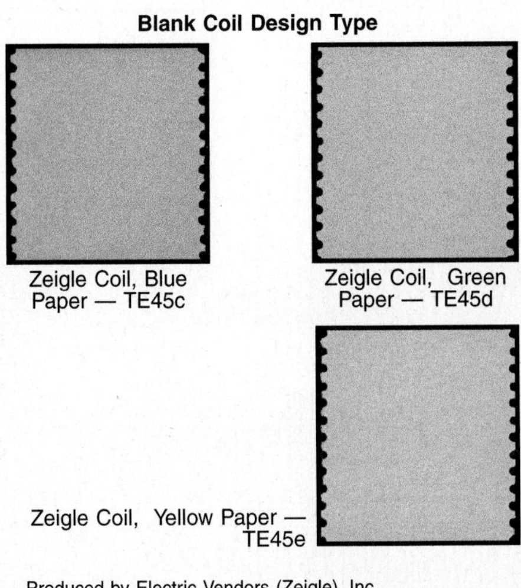

Zeigle Coil, Blue Paper — TE45c

Zeigle Coil, Green Paper — TE45d

Zeigle Coil, Yellow Paper — TE45e

Produced by Electric Vendors (Zeigle), Inc.

1930s ***Perf. 10½ Vert.***

Shiny Smooth Gum

TD79	TE26b blank	7.00
	Pair	15.00
TD80	TE45c *blue*	7.00
	Pair	15.00
TD81	TE45d *green*	7.00
	Pair	15.00
TD82	TE45e *yellow*	7.00
	Pair	15.00

Nos. TD79-TD82 are 23.5mm tall. No. TD79 resembles No. TD45, which is 25mm tall.

Blank Design Type

Produced by Bureau of Engraving & Printing.

1920s-1970 ***Perf. 10***

With Gum Breaker Ridges 5½mm Apart

TD83	TE10 blank, *1920s*	25.00
	Block of 4	100.00
	Vert. pair with horiz. gutter between	—

With Gum Breaker Ridges 11mm Apart

Perf. 11¼x10½

TD84	TE10 blank, *1936*	5.00
	Block of 4	20.00
	Vert. pair with horiz. gutter between	80.00

With Gum Breaker Ridges Alternating Between 5mm and 6½mm Apart

Perf. 11¼x10½

TD84A	TE10 blank, *1956*	4.00
	Block of 4	16.00

Genuine examples of No. TD84A are known with blue, green or red defacement markings, and sell for somewhat less thus.

For other small blank sheet test stamps with different gauge perforations, gum breaker spacings, and/or tagging, see Nos. TD10, TD11, TD83, TD84, TD113, TD114 and TD114A.

Blank Commemorative — TE45g

Stamp Size:40x25mm

With Gum Breaker Ridges Alternating Between 5mm and 6.5mm Apart

Brownish Gum

Perf. 11¼x10½

TD85	TE45g blank, *1950s*	50.00
	Block of 4	200.00

With Gum Breaker Ridges 11mm Apart

TD85A	TE45g blank, *1930s*	50.00
	Block of 4	200.00

Produced by American Bank Note Co.

1943 ***Perf. 12***

TD86	TE45g blank	—

No. TD86 was produced as a test for the Overrun Countries stamps. No. TD86 exists in a pane of 50 with manuscript markings in the margins.

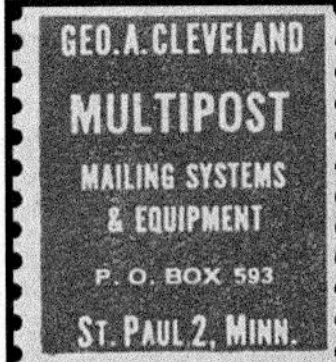

Geo. A. Cleveland Multipost Mailing Systems & Equipment Coil — TE46

1930s-40s ***Perf. 9½ Vert.***

TD87	TE46 **red**	—
	Pair	—

Multipost Co. Walter I. Plant District Agent Coil — TE46a

1930s ***Perf. 11¾ Vert.***

TD87A	TE46a **red**	—
	On cover	—
	Pair	—

Multipost Agents The Office Appliance Co. Coil — TE46b

1930s ***Perf. 11¾ Vert.***

TD87B	TE46b **red**	—
	Pair	—

L.E. Offutt Memphis Multipost Coil — TE46c

1930s ***Perf. 10 Vert.***

TD87C	TE46c **red**	—
	Pair	—

National Postage Service Coil — TE46d

1930s ***Perf. 9¼ Vert.***

TD87D	TE46d **red**	—
	Pair	—

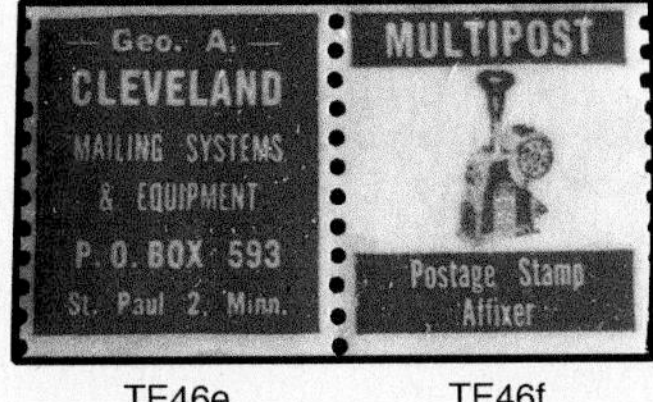

TE46e TE46f

No. TD87E, Geo. A. Cleveland Mailing Systems & Equipment Coil. No. TD87F, Multipost Postage Stamp Affixer Coil.

1930s ***Perf. 10 Vert.***

TD87E	TE46e **red**	—
TD87F	TE46f **red**	—
a.	Pair, #TD87E-TD87F	—

Geo. A. Cleveland N.W. Sales Mgr. Multipost Mailing Machines Coil — TE46g

1930s ***Perf. 9¾ Vert.***

TD87G	TE46g **red**	—

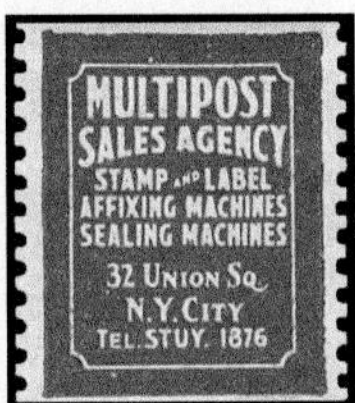

Multipost Sales Agency Coil — TE46h

Perf. 10½ Vert.

TD87H	TE46h **red**	—
	Pair	—

Catalogue values for stamps in this section, from this point to the end, are for Never Hinged items.

Multipost Commercial Controls Coil — TE47

Design size: 18x21mm

1944-49 ***Perf. 9¾ Vert.***

TD88	TE47 **blue**	10.00
	Pair	25.00
TD89	TE47 **black**	10.00
	Pair	25.00
	On cover	75.00
TD90	TE47 **blue black**	10.00
	Pair	25.00

A No. TD90 strip of 4 is known with a "gap" in the stamp printing and then an "overlap" print.

Multipost mailMaster - Commercial Controls Coil — TE48

Multipost mailMaster-Friden Coil — TE49

1944-1957 ***Perf. 9¾ Vert.***

TD91	TE48 **violet**	20.00
	Pair	50.00
TD92	TE48 **red**	30.00
	Pair	50.00
TD93	TE49 **red**	7.00
	Pair	15.00

Framed Rectangle — TE50

Printed by Bureau of Engraving & Printing.

1954-56 ***Perf. 11¼x10½***

TD94	TE50 **carmine**	75.00
	Block of 4	300.00
	P# block of 4, P#141730 or 141731	800.00
a.	Imperf.	110.00

	Pair	225.00
	Block of 4	450.00
	P# block of 4, P#141730 or 141731	850.00
	Horiz. pair, with vert. gutter with EE dashes between stamps	325.00

No. TD94a and TD97a are often confused with each other. No. TD94a is an imperforate rotary press sheet stamp and thus the printed design is slightly narrower and slightly taller (typically 19.0x22.5mm) than No. TD97a, which is an imperforate rotary press coil stamp (typically19.5x22.0mm).

No. TD94 is known with stamps separated horizontally or vertically that were reunited by the BEP using glassine reinforcement strips that are perforated 10½.

Coil Stamps

Perf. 9¾ Vert.

TD95	TE50	**violet**, large holes	5.00
		Pair	10.00
		Joint line pair	30.00
		On cover with "Parade of Postal Progress" cancel	85.00
		Small holes, *1959*	6.00
		Pair	15.00
		Joint line pair	35.00
a.		Imperf., pair	125.00
		Joint line pair	300.00

Misperforated examples of No. TD95 are common and sell for less.

TD96	TE50	**red violet,** small holes	2.00
		Pair	5.00
		Joint line pair	15.00
		Large holes	5.00
		Pair	12.50
		Joint line pair	125.00
		On cover with "Parade of Postal Progress" cancel	85.00
a.		Imperf., vert. pair	*600.00*
		Imperf., horz. pair	*500.00*
		Joint line pair	*950.00*
		Block of 8 with joint line, bottom web margin, P# 165039 and 165940	—

See "large hole" and "small hole" illustrations after No. 1053 in Postage section.

TD97	TE50	**carmine**	200.00
		Pair	400.00
		Joint line pair	600.00
		Vert. pair, unslit horiz.	250.00
		Block of 10 with joint line, top or bottom web margin with P#164564 or 164565, unslit horiz.	*2,500.*
a.		Imperf., vert. pair	300.00
		Imperf., horz. pair	300.00
		Joint line pair	450.00
		Block of 10 with joint line, top or bottom web margin and P#164564 or 164565	*2,500.*

All known examples of No. TD97 have been hand cut from perforated coil web sections. All known examples of No. TD97a are cut from imperforate coil web sections. Examples of Nos. TD97 and TD97a are unknown as BEP-produced coils.

See No. TD94a and its footnote.

Kansas Territorial Centennial Experimental TE51

Printed by Eureka Specialty Printing.

1954 ***Perf. 12x11¾***

TD98	TE51	**brown, red & yellow**	*150.00*
		Block of 4	*600.00*

Nebraska Territorial Centennial Experimental — TE52

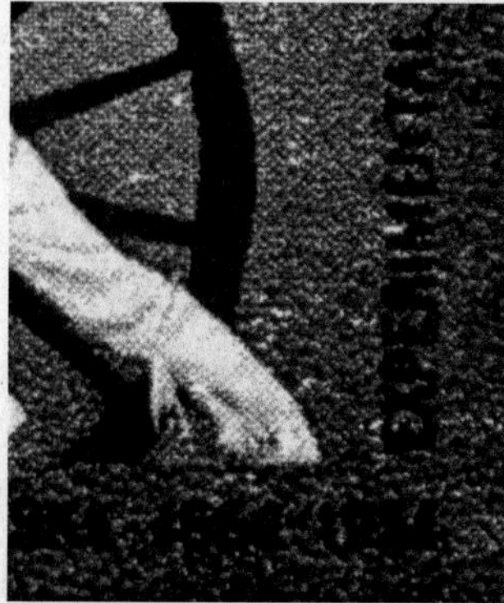

Coarse Impression — TE52 Detail

Fine Impression — TE52a Detail

Printed by Eureka Specialty Printing.

1954 **Solid Background** ***Imperf.***

TD99	TE52	**brown**	*90.00*
		Block of 4	*360.00*
a.		**brown,** *tan*	150.00
		Block of 4	600.00
TD100	TE52	**black**	*15.00*
		Block of 4	*75.00*
a.		**gray**	15.00
		Block of 4	75.00
TD101	TE52	**blue**	*30.00*
		Block of 4	*120.00*
a.		**blue,** *tan*	*150.00*
		Block of 4	600.00

Background of Dots Ungummed

Imperf

TD101B	TE52a	**black**	200.00
		Block of 4	*800.00*

No. TD101B was printed as a sheet of 50 on ungummed paper. The design is similar to No. TD100, but the background printing is a distinct cross-hatching rather than the usual blurred shading, probably due to two different printing processes being used. Nos. TD99, TD100 and TD101 are only known in blocks of four or fewer; one sheet of 50 of No. TD101B is known.

Eureka Specialty Printing Co. — TE52b

Printed by Eureka Specialty Printing.

1954? ***Imperf.***

Design Size: 38x22mm

TD101C	TE52b	**green**	*750.00*
TD101D	TE52b	**blue**	*750.00*
TD101E	TE52b	**brown**	*750.00*
TD101F	TE52b	**pink**	*750.00*

Pitney Bowes Co. — TE53

1958-59 **Tagged** ***Imperf.***

Helecon Paper

TD102	TE53	**carmine**	—
a.		Lumogen paper	—
TD103	TE53	**black**	—

Helecon paper glows orange red under shortwave UV light. Lumogen paper glows bright yellow-green under shortwave UV light.

Stamp-E-Z Postage Stamp Affixer Coil — TE54

1960s ***Imperf.***

TD104	TE54	**red violet**	—
		Pair	—

Perf. 10¼ Vert.

TD104A	TE54	**red violet**	*85.00*
		Pair	*175.00*

Perf. 9¾ Vert.

TD105	TE54	**red**	—
		Pair	—

Blank Coil Design of 1910-27

Produced by Bureau of Engraving & Printing

1960-70s **Overall Tagging** ***Perf. 9¾ Vert.***

Dull Gum

TD106	TE26a	blank	12.50
		Pair	25.00
		Joint line pair	100.00

No. TD106 was produced on an inked press. The ink was wiped, but some stamps have wiping marks and black joint lines.

For Testing Purposes Only Coil — TE55

Produced by Bureau of Engraving & Printing.

1962-86 **Engr.** ***Perf. 9¾ Vert.***

Design Size: Approximately 19½mm Wide

TD107	TE55	**black,** untagged, shiny gum	2.00
		Pair	4.00
		Joint line pair	15.00
a.		Tagged, shiny gum	1.00
		Pair	2.00
		Joint line pair	10.00
b.		Tagged, pebble-surfaced gum	.50
		Pair	1.00
		Joint line pair	5.00
c.		As "b," imperf. pair	250.00
		Joint line pair	750.00
d.		Tagged, dull gum	.50
		Pair	1.00
		Joint line pair	5.00
e.		Untagged, dull gum	1.25
		Pair	2.50
		Joint line pair	10.00

No. TD107 is known on hi-brite fluorescent paper.

No. TD107b is known on slightly yellowish paper.

No. TD107b has been found with red, dark red, rose red, blue, blue green, green, orange, violet, brown, black violet, black, gray black, gray and silver defacement lines, which vary in number and thickness and which have been known to have been forged. Some defacement line colors may all be forgeries.

No. TD107e is known on fluorescent and non-fluorescent papers, as well as on papers with diagonal gum striations or wavy, intermittent gum striations.

TD108	TE55	**carmine,** tagged, *1970*	500.00
		Pair	1,000.
		Joint line pair	*2,500.*

The tagging on Nos. TD108 and TD114 is orange red. All other tagged test stamps except TD102 glow yellow green.

TD109 TE55 **slate green,** untagged, dull gum, *1980* 75.00
Pair 150.00
Joint line pair 400.00
a. Imperf., pair 450.00
Joint line pair 600.00
b. Vert. pair, unslit horiz. 200.00
Block of 12 with joint line, bottom web margin withP#36111 and 36112 *2,000.*

No. TD109 was sent to Germany in large imperf. and part perforate sheets to test coil production equipment.

TD109C TE55 **slate green,** tagged, gray paper, shiny gum 160.00
Pair 325.00
Joint line pair —
TD110 TE55 **orange,** *gray,* tagged, *1975* 1,000.
Pair 2,000.
Joint line pair —
TD111 TE55 **brown,** untagged, *1978* 1.50
Pair 3.00
Joint line pair 30.00

Design Size: Approximately 19mm Wide

TD112 TE55 **black,** untagged, dull gum *1986* .50
Pair 1.00

No. TD107 was printed on the Cottrell press. No. TD112 was printed on the B press. There are no joint lines on these stamps.
See Nos. TD112A, TD126-TD127, TD133, TD133A, TD136-TD137, and TD140.

Printed by Bureau of Engraving & Printing.

1978 Photo. Untagged *Imperf.*

TD112A TE55 **black,** shiny gum 75.00
Pair 150.00
Block of 4 400.00
Block of 6 with bottom web margin, EE dashes and P#173285 —

No. TD112A was printed on the Andreotti press. A bottom web margin block of 18 (9x2) is known with EE dashes, six sets of black color-density bars and P#173285.

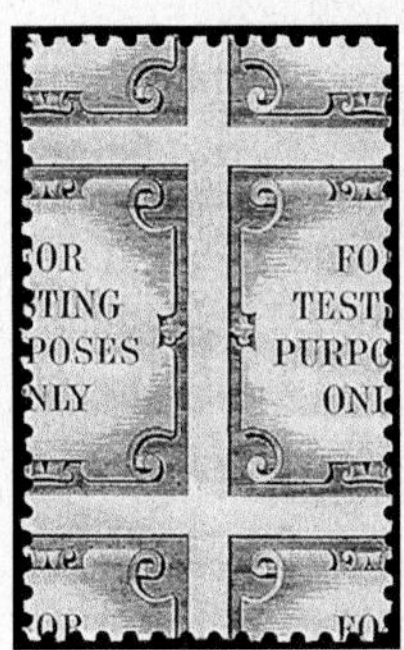

"For Testing Purposes Only" Commemorative Size — TE55a

1970 *Perf. 10½x11¼*

Stamp Size: 25x40mm

Alternating Horizontal Gum Breaker Ridges 4½ and 6½mm Apart

TD112B TE55a **black,** yellow green tagging, shiny pebbled gum —
Block of 4 —

Blank Design Types

Produced by Bureau of Engraving & Printing, with tagging added by Pitney Bowes.

1964-70 *Perf. 11*

TD113 TE10 blank, yellow green tagging 75.00
Block of 4 300.00
TD114 TE10 blank, orange red tagging 75.00
Block of 4 300.00

Nos. TD113-TD114 was produced as a test for Nos. 1254-1257.

With Gum Breaker Ridges 11mm Apart

Perf. 11¼x10½

TD114A TE10 blank, yellow green tagging *1970* 15.00
Block of 4 60.00
Horiz. pair with vert. gutter between 75.00

For other small blank sheet test stamps with different gauge perforations, gum breaker spacings, and/or tagging, see Nos. TD10, TD83, TD85, TD84A, TD113 and TD114.

Blank Commemorative, Light Brown Paper — TE45h

Perf. 11¼x10½

TD114B TE45h blank, *light brown,* yellow green tagging, *1970* 25.00
Block of 4 100.00
Horiz. pair with vert. gutter between 150.00
Vert. pair with horiz. gutter between 250.00

No. TD114B is a commemorative-size blank stamp on the light brown paper used for the bison stamp No. 1392.

Jefferson Memorial Experimental — TE56

Printed by Bureau of Engraving & Printing.

1966 Untagged *Perf. 11*

Engraved (Multicolor Huck Press)

TD114D TE56 **black & orange** 1,000.
Block of 4 4,000.

No. TD114D was produced as a test for No. 1363, the 1968 Christmas stamp. A similar test stamp (without the three lines of text to the left of the design) was made in 1962 to test the BEP's 3-color sheet-fed Giori press. No examples of that test stamp are currently known in collector hands. All known No. TD114D stamps are without gum.

Flag — TE56a

Produced by Avery Products Corp.

1970s *Die Cut*

Self-Adhesive

TD115 TE56a **blue,** on rouletted backing paper *300.00*
Block of 4 *1,200.*
a. On imperforate backing paper —

Jet Fighter Experimental — TE56b

Printed by Bureau of Engraving & Printing

1970 Untagged *Imperf.*

Gravure (7-color Andreotti Press)

TD115B TE56b **multicolored,** white coated paper, smooth shiny gum *225.00*
Block of 4 *900.00*
Block of 12 with bottom sheet margin, EE markings and 6 plate numbers *3,750.*
c. Uncoated paper, ungummed *225.00*
Block of 4 *900.00*
Block of 12 with bottom sheet margin, EE markings and 6 plate numbers *3,750.*

Overall tagging

TD115D TE56b **multicolored,** white coated paper, smooth shiny gum *225.00*
Block of 4 *900.00*
Block of 12 with bottom sheet margin, EE markings and 6 plate numbers *3,750.*
e. White coated paper, pebbled gum *225.00*
Block of 4 *900.00*
Block of 12 with bottom sheet margin, EE markings and 6 plate numbers *3,750.*
f. Cream color coated paper, pebble gum *225.00*
Block of 4 *900.00*
Block of 12 with bottom sheet margin, EE markings and 6 plate numbers *3,750.*

A gravure press, built by Andreotti S.P.A. of Italy, was purchased by the BEP in 1969. It had 7 printing units, one of which was used to apply overall tagging to the web. The 200-subject gravure cylinders used to print these Experimental stamps had plate numbers from the BEP's 6-digit Miscellaneous Series: 171337, 171338, 171339, 171340, 171341 and 171393 (the EE markings and plate number locations match those found on Scott No. 1414). There was no plate number on the cylinder that applied the tagging.
These test stamps were produced in 1970 during performance trials using paper from at least four different manufacturers. Each of the five known sheets of 50 test stamps has a hand written note on the gum side showing the source of the paper: TD115B is on coated paper from Watervliet Paper Co.; TD115Bc is on regular uncoated stamp paper; TD115D is on white coated paper from St. Regis Paper Co.; TD115De is on white coated paper from St. Regis Paper Co.; and TD115Df is on cream colored coated paper from Warren Paper Co. Tagging intensity on TD115Df is greater than on TD115D and TD115De.

Proclaim Liberty TE57

1970s *Perf. 12x11¾*

TD116 TE57 **blue, red & green** 75.00

Christmas Test Stamp TE58

Printed by Bureau of Engraving & Printing for Avery Products Corp. to add die cutting.

1973 *Die Cut*

Self-Adhesive

TD117 TE58 **black,** rouletted backing paper 2.50
Block of 4 with intact matrix 10.00
Pane of 50 150.00
Press sheet of 200 750.00
a. Pair, imperf backing paper —
b. Vert. pair, backing paper rouletted vert. only —

No. TD117 was produced as a test for No. 1552.

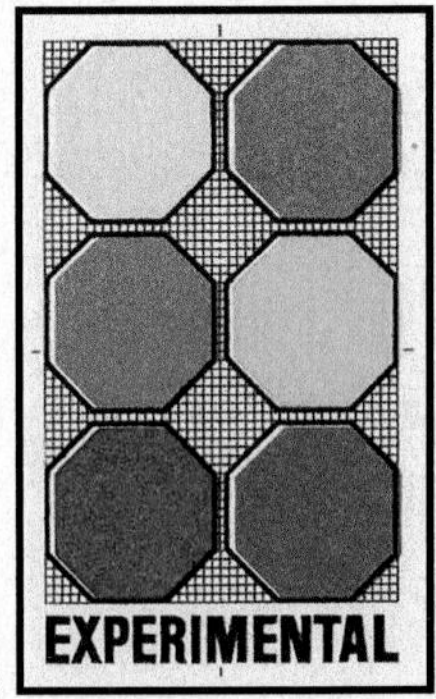

Octagons — TE59

Printed by Bureau of Engraving & Printing.

1979 *Imperf.*

Engr. & Offset

TD118 TE59 **multicolored** 140.00
Block of 4 600.00
Block of 4, black intaglio P# 173404 plus 4 of the 6 offset P#'s 5,000.

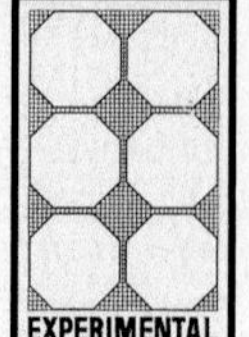

TE59a

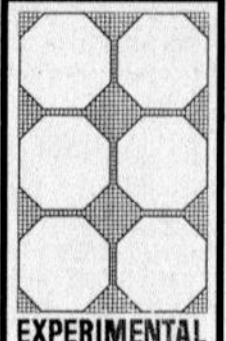

TE59b

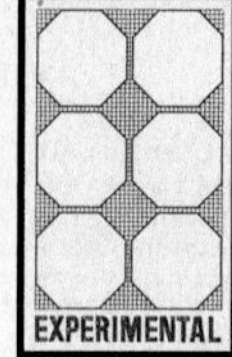

TE59c

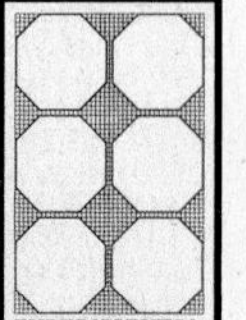

TE59d

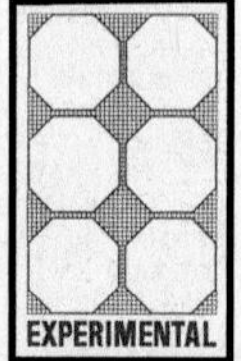

TE59e

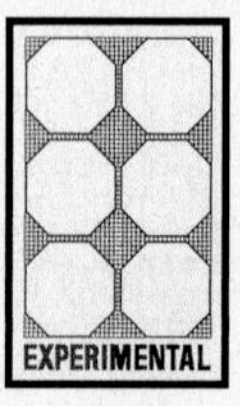

TE59f

Printed by Goebel, GmbH (Germany) from materials supplied by the Bureau of Engraving & Printing.

1979-80			*Imperf.*
TD118A	TE59a	**black**	150.00
TD118B	TE59b	**black and blue**	150.00
TD118C	TE59c	**blue**	150.00
TD118D	TE59d	**blue and red**	150.00
TD118E	TE59e	**red**	150.00
TD118F	TE59f	**red and black**	150.00

A 128-subject web section of Nos. TD118A-TD118F is known to exist. The large bottom margin contains a red EE bar under every other column of No. TD118E (TE59e) solid red stamps. These stamps were printed from a 96-subject plate.

The stamp designs are spaced 23mm apart horizontally and 3mm vertically, whereas the No. TD118 stamp designs are spaced 3mm apart both horizontally and vertically. Nos. TD118A-TD118F were printed from a 96-subject cylinder that has 8 stamps vertically and 12 stamps horizontally. There are no P#'s, but there is a vertical red EE bar in the bottom margin below the center of the No. TD118E solid red stamp.

Flag and Eagle Over Trees Coil — TE60

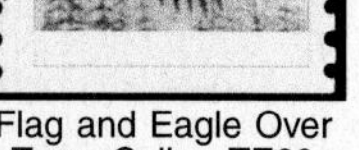
Flag and Eagle Over Trees Coil — TE60a

Printed by Stamp Venturers.

1989			*Perf. 10 Vert.*
TD119	TE60	**gray**	.25
	Pair		.50
	Strip of 5 with counting number on reverse		50.00

Most examples of Nos. TD119 and TD120 come from coils of 100 stamps. Rolls of 3,000 No. TD119 had a four-digit counting number printed on the reverse of every tenth stamp. Back numbers were used to determine the number of stamps remaining on a roll.

Rouletted

TD120	TE60a	**gray**	.25
	Pair		.50

Flag and Eagle Over Trees — TE60b

Printed by Sennett Security Products.

2000			*Perf. Die Cut 10¾ Horiz.*
TD120A	TE60b	**multicolored**	15.00
	Pair		35.00

Most examples of No. TD120A have serpentine die cuts that are slightly misplaced into the top of the design. Because the die cutting is shallow, done from the back and hiding in the design, they can appear to be imperforate, but true imperforate examples are unknown. Values shown are for stamps with misplaced die cuts. Examples with correctly placed die cuts command a higher price.

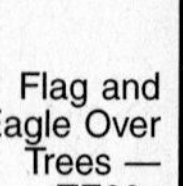

Flag and Eagle Over Trees — TE60c

Printed by Sennett Security Products.

1997		**Untagged**	*Perf. 11¼*
TD120B	TE60c	**multicolored**	—
	P# block of 4		—

The sheet of 20 stamps contains P# S1111 in all four corners UL, UR, LL and LR.

Seal — TE60d

Printed for Battelle Memorial Institute.

Design Size: 28x21½mm

1990		**Tagged**	*Perf. 11*
TD120C	TE60d	**multicolored**	*250.00*
		Horiz. strip of 5	*1,500.*
	d.	Horiz. pair, imperf. vert.	1,000.
		Horiz. strip of 4, imperf. vert.	*1,000.*
		Block of 4, imperf. vert.	*2,000.*

The Seal test stamps were used as part of a 16 month contract between the USPS and Battelle to study water-activated stamp adhesives. Strips of five stamps, each with different gum varieties, were packed in envelopes marked with code letters (only Types E and F are known). While the gums are different, it is difficult to differentiate them unless seen together (Type F gum is slightly yellower than Type E gum; Type E gum is glossier than Type F gum). No. TD120Cd gum is similar to Type F gum. The stamps were tested on sets of five pre-addressed envelopes made with different papers, to evaluate how the stamps stuck to them while going through the mail.

1893 Duryea — TE60e

1894 Haynes — TE60f

1898 Columbia — TE60g

1899 Winton — TE60h

1901 White — TE60i

Water-activated gum

1995		**Photo.**	**Tagged**	*Imperf.*
TD121	TE60e	00c	**multicolored**	200.00
TD121A	TE60f	00c	**multicolored**	200.00
TD121B	TE60g	00c	**multicolored**	200.00
TD121C	TE60h	00c	**multicolored**	200.00
TD121D	TE60i	00c	**multicolored**	200.00
	e.	Vert. or horiz. strip of 5, #TD121-TD121D		1,000.
		Pane of 25		*5,000.*

Self-Adhesive

1995			**Tagged**	*Imperf.*
TD121F	TE60e	00c	**multicolored**	200.00
TD121G	TE60f	00c	**multicolored**	200.00
TD121H	TE60g	00c	**multicolored**	200.00
TD121I	TE60h	00c	**multicolored**	200.00
TD121J	TE60i	00c	**multicolored**	200.00
	k.	Vert. or horiz. strip of 5, #TD121F-TD121J		1,000.
		Pane of 25		*5,000.*

The stamps on the vert. and horiz. strips are in different orders. (Same layout as Nos. 3019-3023).

The left four columns on the sheet format panes of 25 contain "hidden printing" that consists of numbers, text and bar codes. They can only be seen when looking at the stamps at an angle under bright light.

1893 Duryea — TE60j

1894 Haynes — TE60k

1898 Columbia — TE60l

1899 Winton — TE60m

1901 White — TE60n

Water-activated gum

1995	**Tagged**	***Imperf.***
TD121L TE60j 00c **multicolored**		200.00
TD121M TE60k 00c **multicolored**		200.00
TD121N TE60l 00c **multicolored**		200.00
TD121O TE60m 00c **multicolored**		200.00
TD121P TE60n 00c **multicolored**		200.00
q. Vert. strip of 5, #TD121L-TD121P		1,000.
2. Pane of 25		*5,000.*

Nos. TD121L-TD121P are imperf with simulated perforations only.

1995	**Self-Adhesive Tagged**	***Imperf.***
TD121R TE60j 00c **multicolored**		200.00
TD121S TE60k 00c **multicolored**		200.00
TD121T TE60l 00c **multicolored**		200.00
TD121U TE60m 00c **multicolored**		200.00
TD121V TE60n 00c **multicolored**		200.00
w. Vert. strip of 5, #TD121R-TD121V		1,000.
Pane of 25		*5,000.*

Nos. TD121R-TD121V are imperf with simulated perforations only. Vert. strips have stamps in the same order. Horiz. strips contain five identical stamps. The stamps with printed perforations do not have "hidden printing."

The Antique Automobiles test stamps were printed in panes of 25 stamps (5x5). There are no plate numbers or other information to identify the company that produced them, but the designs match known designs for the proposed 32c Antique Auto stamps released by the USPS before changes were made in the placement of dates and names for the 1894 Haynes, 1898 Columbia and 1899 Winton, after which the actual stamps, Nos. 3019-3023, were printed by Stamp Venturers.

There is no die cutting on the self-adhesive stamps. The backing paper on the self-adhesive stamps has a star-SELF-ADHESIVE-letter "A" within circle- DO NOT WET pattern at a 45-degree angle to the printed stamp designs. It is inverted on the stamps with printed perforations and upright on the stamps without printed perforations. This liner-printing design was used by Dittler Brothers printers.

Blank Coil Design Type of 1910-27

Produced by Bureau of Engraving & Printing.

1990s	**Untagged**	***Perf. 9¾ Vert.***
TD122 TE26a blank, coated paper, shiny gum		10.00
Pair		20.00
a. Uncoated paper, shiny gum		10.00
Pair		20.00
b. Coated paper, dull gum		10.00
Pair		20.00
c. Uncoated paper, dull gum		—
Pair		—

No. TD122 with shiny gum is known on hi-brite fluorescent paper.

Stylized Eagle Coil — TE61

Printed by 3M Corp.

Linerless Self-Adhesive

1992	**Tagged**	***Imperf.***
TD123 TE61 29c **multicolored**		15.00
Pair		30.00
P# strip of 5, #1111		325.00

Stamps have printed simulated perforations only. Vertical pairs (or larger) are known cut from the web. Plate number 1111 occurs every 27 stamps.

Flag Over Porch — TE61a

Flag Over Porch — TE61a Detail

Printed by Bureau of Engraving and Printing.

Self-Adhesive

1995	**Tagged(?)**	***Serpentine Die Cut 10.9 Vert.***
	Self-Adhesive	
TD123A TE61a 32c **multicolored**		—
Pair		—
P# strip of 3, #44444		—

No. TD123A looks similar to Scott 2915A and 2915C. All three are self-adhesive Flag Over Porch coils. Scott 2915A has gauge 9.7 serpentine die cuts, while Scott 2915C and TD123A both have gauge 10.9 die cuts. The designs of the three coils are identical except for the year dates printed in the lower left corner of each stamp; Scott 2915A and 2915C both have a red 1996 date whereas No. TD123A has a red 1995 date. No. TD123A was produced in a trial before the BEP officially began producing self-adhesive Flag Over Porch coils. To produce No. TD123A, a roll of self-adhesive paper was run through the Andreotti press that was being used to print water-activated gum Flag Over Porch coils (Scott 2913) from gravure cylinders #44444.

Many of these self-adhesive coil rolls, each containing 100 stamps, were then sent to an outside contractor where multiple tests were performed before it was decided to begin regular production using new gravure cylinders with red 1996 year dates. After the testing was completed, all examples of the self-adhesive coil stamps were supposed to have been returned to the BEP to be destroyed. Scott 2915A and 2915C (the self-adhesive coils with a red 1996 date) were issued on May 21, 1996. Scott 2915C, which has the same gauge die cuts as No. TD123A, is only known with plate #55555, 66666 and 88888 (No. TD123A has plate #44444. Scott 2915A (with the red 1996) exists with plate #44444, but it has a red 1996 date. No self-adhesive Flag Over Porch coils were officially issued with a 1995 date, and thus this coil with the red 1995 date is considered to be a test stamp. Only one coil roll of No. TD123A test stamps is known (it contains five stamps with plate #44444).

Rectangle With Thick Lines Coil — TE62

Reverse "12"

Printed by Bureau of Engraving & Printing.

1996	**Gravure**	***Perf. 9¾ Vert.***
TD124 TE62 **blue,** shiny gum		40.00
Pair		80.00
Strip of 5 with one stamp with crudely etched reversed "2"		1,500.
Strip of 5 with one stamp with crudely etched reversed "12"		1,500.

Reversed numbers appear in the center of every 24th stamp.

Etched "VI"

1994		**Offset**
TD125 TE62 **gray black,** dull gum		100.00
Pair		200.00
a. Shiny gum		100.00
Pair		200.00
Strip of 5, one stamp with etched "VI"		1,250.

The etched "VI" stamps occurs every 24th stamp.

Rectangle With Thin Lines, Water-Activated Coil — TE62a

1998(?)		***Perf. 9¾ Vert.***
TD125B TE62a **blue,** green tagging, dull gum		200.00
Pair		400.00

The same design was used on self-adhesive coils with serpentine die cut perforations. See No. TD130.

For Testing Purposes Only Type of 1962-88

Printed by Bureau of Engraving & Printing (#TD126), Avery-Dennison (#TD127).

1996	**Self-Adhesive**	***Die Cut***
TD126 TE55 **black & light blue**		.25
Pair		.50
P# strip of 5, #1111		5.00

Nos. TD126, TD133 and TD136 appear to be printed on blue paper. Light blue ink was applied in several layers to mask the phosphorescence of the tagged white paper before printing the stamps. A four-digit counting number is on the reverse of the backing paper on every 20th stamp on some rolls. No. TD126 is on backing paper taller than the stamps, with a gap between stamps.

Plate number "1111" occurs every 21 stamps.

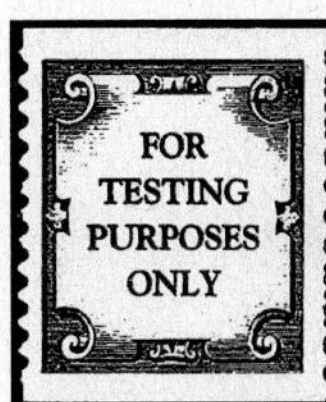

"For Testing Purposes Only" — TE55b

Serpentine Die Cut 11¼ Vert.

TD127 TE55b **black**		.25
Pair		.50
P# strip of 5, #V1		10.00

No. TD127 has printed simulated perforations in addition to serpentine die cutting. Nos. TD127 and TD137 look similar, but No. TD137 does not have the printed simulated perforations. No. TD127 is on backing paper taller than the stamp.

Plate number "V1" occurs every 15 stamps.

Polar Bear Ice Skating — TE62b

Printed by Ashton-Potter (USA) Ltd.

1995	**Tagged**	***Serpentine Die Cut 11½x11¾***
	Self-Adhesive	
TD127A TE62b **multicolored**		650.00
Block of 4		—
Sheetlet of 20		—

The sheetlet of 20 has vertical and horizontal gutters between the stamps with the matrix removed.

Serpentine Die Cut 11x11½

Tagged

TD127B TE62b **multicolored**		750.00
Block of 4		—
Sheetlet of 20		—

The sheetlet of 20 has no vertical or horizontal gutters between the stamps.

Avery Dennison — TE62c

Printed by Avery Dennison.

1996	**Self-Adhesive**	***Serpentine Die Cut 11x11¼***
TD127C TE62c **red**		375.00
Block of 4 with plate position in diagram in selvage		*1,750.*
P# block of 4, #V1		*2,250.*

No. TD127C was printed in sheets of 200 stamps as ten 20-stamp panes. It was a test for the Scott Nos. 3091-3095 Riverboats issue. Only one pane of 20 was known in collectors' hands and it was broken into two blocks and twelve singles. Plate numbers were printed in the upper right and lower left corners of the panes of 20; the pane position diagram was in the lower right corner.

Parrot — TE63

Blank Parrot — TE63a

Parrot — TE63b

Printed by Banknote Corporation of America.

1996 Tagged *Serpentine Die Cut 11¾x11½*

Design Size: 19x26½mm

Self-Adhesive

TD128	TE63	**multicolored**	400.00
		Block of 4	1,750.
TD128A	TE63a	**blank**	40.00
		Block of 4	150.00

Design Size: 23x37mm

Perf. 11½

TD129	TE63b	**multicolored**	—

No. TD128 was printed both in sheets of 50 (10x5) and 20 (54). No. TD128A was produced in panes of 50 (10x5). Both Nos. TD128 and TD128 have die cuts that penetrate the backing paper with horizontal slitting that is approximately 15m long behind each stamp. No. TD128A has horizontal slitting continuous across the backing paper.

No. TD129 was used to test luminescent inks.

Commemorative Size Flower — TE63c

Printed by Dittler Brothers Inc. and American Bank Note Co.

1997 Photo. & Engr. Tagged *Imperf.*

Self-Adhesive

Design Size: 22x36mm

TD129A	TE63c	00c **multicolored**	375.00
TD129B	TE63c	00c **multicolored**	375.00

Nos. TD129A and TD129B were both printed in photogravure and intaglio. No. TD129B has engraved black lines in the flower that do not appear on No. TD129A. See Nos. TDB87-TDB88.

Rectangle With Thin Lines, Self-Adhesive Coil — TE62d

Sideways "2"

Printed by Bureau of Engraving & Printing.

1998 *Serpentine Die Cut 9¾ Vert.*

Self-Adhesive

TD130	TE62d	**blue**	125.00
		Pair	250.00
		Strip of 3 with number "3" printed inside one stamp	*1,500.*
		Strip of 5 with number "2" printed inside one stamp	—

No. TD130 is on backing paper taller than the stamp with a gap between the stamps. A four-digit counting number is known on the reverse of the backing paper.

No. TD130 stamps with numbers printed inside one stamp are spaced 21 stamps apart. A four-digit counting number is known on the reverse of the backing paper every 20 stamps.

For water-activated gum with TE62a design, see No. TD125B.

Star Spangled Banner Coil — TE64a

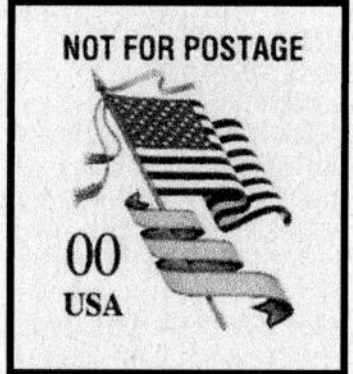

Printing on Liner Paper — TE64b

Printed by Sennett Security Products

1998 Tagged *Serpentine Die Cut 11¼ Vert.*

Self-Adhesive

TD130A	TE64a	00c **multicolored**, with stamp image printed on back of liner paper	35.00
		Horizontal pair, with stamp image (TE64b) on liner	75.00
		Vertical pair, with stamp image (TE64b) on liner	75.00
		Block of 4, with stamp image (TE64b) on liner	150.00
		Envelope with 8 #TD130A on back	75.00
		Single #TD130A removed from envelope (no liner paper)	7.50

No. TD130A was printed from 210-subject gravure cylinders with horizontal and vertical spaces between stamps. The black stamp image (TE64b) printed on the back of the liner paper is not aligned with the stamp image. All known examples of No. TD130A attached to liner paper were hand cut from a partially processed coil web section.

Coil rolls of 3,000 stamps, with liner paper taller than the stamps and with a gap between stamps, were used in a USPS recycling test conducted in December 1998. Stamps without liner paper have been removed from the backs of envelopes used in that test and are worth less than stamps on the original liner paper.

See Nos. TD130B and TD130C for self-adhesive Star Spangled Banner coils that do not have spaces between the stamp designs, and No. TD130D for linerless coils.

Miscut & Misperforated Coil — TE64c

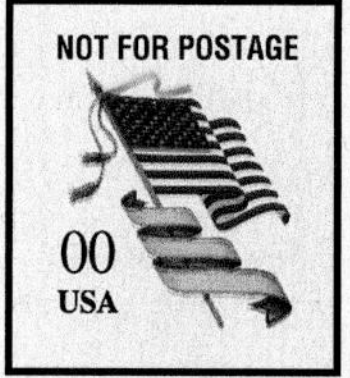

Imperforate Coil — TE64d

Printed by Sennett Security Products

1998 Tagged *Serpentine Die Cut 11¼ Vert.*

Self-Adhesive

TD130B	TE64c	00c **multicolored**	15.00
		Envelope with 8 #TD130B on back	125.00

Imperf.

TD130C	TE64d	00c **multicolored**, with stamp image (TE64b) printed on back of liner paper	50.00
		Pair	100.00
		Block of 4	225.00
		Block of 4 with web margin showing EE markings	300.00

Nos. TD130B and TD130C were printed from 225-subject gravure cylinders without horizontal and vertical spaces between stamps (intended to be processed into coils of 100). Miscut examples of No. TD130B were created when the die cutting mat intended for No. TD130A (with horizontal and vertical spaces between stamps) was used on the imperforate No. TD130C coil web (without spaces between stamps) to make coils containing 3,000 stamps that could be mechanically applied to the back of envelopes in a USPS test.

The black stamp image (TE64b) printed on the back of No. TD130C is not aligned with the stamp image. All known examples of No. TD130C were hand cut from an imperforate coil web section.

See Nos. TD130A and TD130D for other Star Spangled Banner coils.

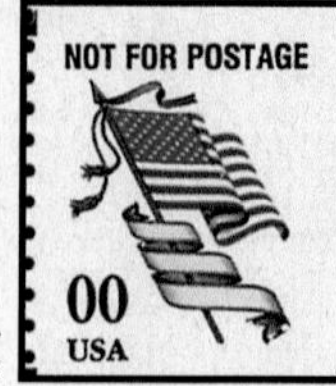

Star Spangled Banner Coil — TE64e

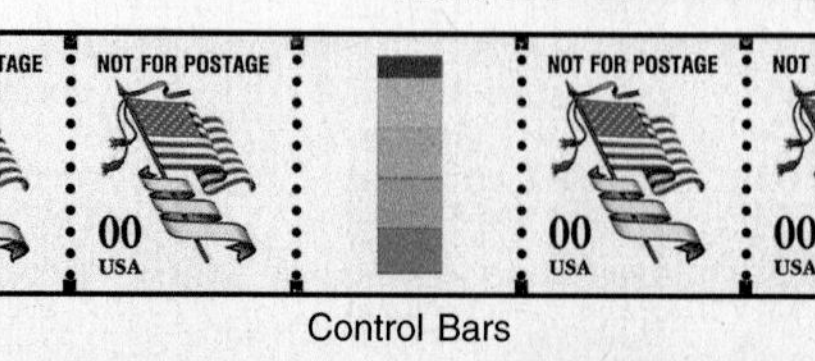

Control Bars

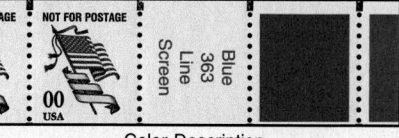

Color Description

Printed by Bureau of Engraving and Printing

1998 Tagged *Perf. 9¾ Vert.*

Linerless Self-Adhesive

TD130D	TE64e	00c **multicolored**	30.00
		Pair	60.00
		P# strip of 5, #11111	300.00
		P# strip of 5, #111 1 (missing blue intaglio)	400.00
		Strip of 5, center stamp with multicolor or offset color control bars (various combinations exist)	*500.00*
		Strip of 11, center stamp with multicolor offset color control bars, 7 stamps with screen density blocks, 1 stamp with color description	*800.00*

It is possible for the strips of 5 with the center stamp having the offset color control bars to have 15 different color combinations. The stamp with the vertical multicolor offset color control bars occurs every 24th stamp in a coil strip. For the strips of 11 with multicolor offset color control bars, the known colors are magenta, yellow, cyan, blue and black.

Plate numbers "1111" or "11111" occur every 24 stamps.

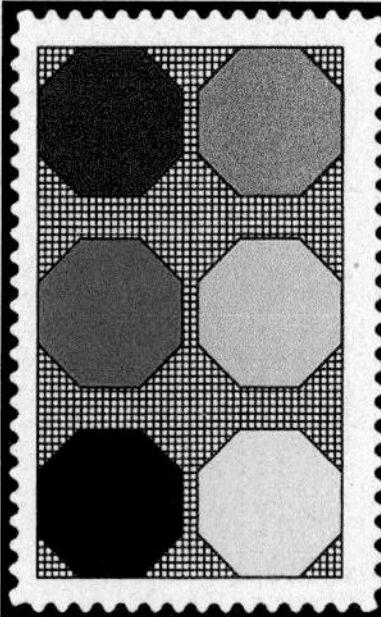

Octagons — TE64f

1998 Tagged *Serpentine Die Cut 12½*

Self-Adhesive

TD130E	TE64f	**multicolored**	20.00
		5 #TD130E affixed to envelope back	100.00

All known examples of No. TD130E were affixed to envelope backs for use in USPS mailing tests.

No. TD130E was printed in sheets of 50. Each of the horizontal rows contained stamps with ten different densities in the octagons, ranging from dark colors in the left column of 5 to a very light color in the right column of 5 stamps.

George Clinton — TE64g

1993 Engr. Tagged *Perf. 11¼x11*

TD130F	TE64g	00c **blue gray**	150.00
		Block of 4	600.00

No. TD130F was produced by American Bank Note Co. using a die supplied by BEP. No. TD130F has semi-glossy water-activated gum and was printed in panes of 100.

Nos. TDB93 and TDB93A have the same design, but No. TDB93 was produced in 18-stamp self-adhesive convertible booklet panes with serpentine die cutting between the stamps.

Full sheets may have what appears to be unprinted stamps at the right in the margin. Such items are part of the unprinted gutter between panes that have been miscut.

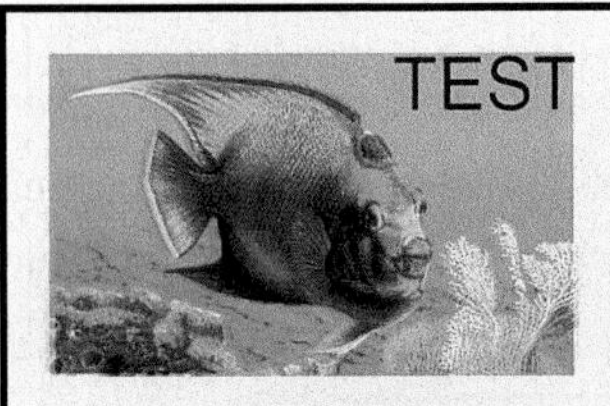

Tropical Fish — TE64h

Printed by Sennett Security Products

1998 **Tagged** ***Imperf.***

Self-Adhesive

TD130G TE64h **multicolored** 150.00
Block of 4 600.00
Block of 4, with either top web margin or bottom EE marks 750.00
Vertical strip of 6 with 2 each normal, 400- and 500-line screen printing with web margin and EE marks *1,200.*

No. TD130G was printed from 84-subject gravure cylinders with three different screen printing intensities on the same sheet. Information printed in the top margin indicates that the top two stamps in the vertical column of 6 stamps were printed with "normal line screens," the middle two were "400 line screens," and the bottom two were "500 line screens." The 500-line screen stamps are noticeably darker than the others. All known examples of No. TD130G were hand cut from an imperforate web section. These test stamps may have been intended to be horizontal coils.

RENA Test Stamp Coil — TE65

1999 ***Die Cut***

Self-Adhesive

TD131 TE65 **blue** 10.00
Pair 20.00

No. TD131 is on backing paper taller than the stamp with a gap between stamps.

Mailbox Coil — TE66

Printed by Avery Dennison.

2000 ***Imperf.***

Linerless Self-Adhesive

TD132 TE66 **bright magenta** 200.00
Vert., pair 400.00
a. Pair with "xxxx" on one stamp 1,500.

Pairs have 1-2mm slit marks between stamps in left and right margins. The "xxxx" was printed under the lower left corner of the stamp at an unknown frequency (the discovery coil roll of 50 stamps had two stamps with the "xxxx").

For Testing Purposes Only Type of 1962-88

Printed by Bureau of Engraving & Printing.

2000 ***Serpentine Die Cut 9¾ Vert.***

Self-Adhesive

TD133 TE55 **black & light blue** .50
Pair 1.00
P# strip of 5, #1111 4.00

Nos. TD126, TD133 and TD136 appear to be printed on blue paper. Light blue ink was applied in several layers to mask the phosphorescence of the tagged white paper before printing the stamps. A four-digit counting number is on the reverse of the backing paper on every 20th stamp on some rolls. No. TD133 is on backing paper taller than the stamps, with a gap between stamps.

Plate numbers appear every 21 stamps, and a vertical white line can occur at either the far right edge of the numbered stamp or the far left edge of the next stamp to the right. Some unnumbered strips without a plate number also are known with a white line at the far edge of one stamp. The white line is an unprinted gap in the blue.

TD133A TE55 **black** 15.00
Pair 30.00
P# strip of 5, #1111 300.00

A four-digit counting number is on the reverse of the backing paper every 20th stamp on some rolls. No. TD133A is on backing paper with no gap between perforation tips.

Plate number "1111" occurs every 24th stamp.

South Carolina Flag Coil — TE67

Printed by Avery Dennison.

2000 ***Serpentine Die Cut 8½ Vert.***

Self-Adhesive

TD134 TE67 **dark blue** *450.00*
Pair *900.00*
P# strip of 5, #V1 *2,750.*
TD135 TE67 **light blue** 20.00
Pair 40.00
P# strip of 5, #V1 250.00

Plate-number examples of Nos. TD134 and TD135 bear a "2000" year date at lower left.Two rolls of No. TD135 are known with a nine-digit accounting number on the back of the P# stamp, at 35-stamp intervals. The examples known are: 000052763-65 and 000052949-51. This accounting number increases by one digit with each revolution of the stamp-printing sleeve. Value, $300.

On Nos. TD134 and TD135 the stamp with the "2000" year date and plate number "VI" occurs every five stamps.

For Testing Purposes Only Type of 1962-88

Printed by Bureau of Engraving & Printing (#TD136), Sennett Security Products (#TD137).

For Testing Purposes Only Coil with Vertical Line Between "N" and "L" of "ONLY" — TE55c

1997 ***Serpentine Die Cut 9¾ Vert.***

Self-Adhesive

TD136 TE55c **black & light blue** .50
Pair 1.00
Strip of 5 with white line on left or right margin of center stamp 6.50

Nos. TD126, TD133 and TD136 apear to be printed on blue paper. Light blue ink was applied in several layers to mask the phosphorescence of the tagged white paper before printing the stamps. A four-digit counting number is on the reverse of the backing paper on every 20th stamps on some rolls. No. TD136 is on backing paper taller than the stamps, with a gap between stamps.

The white line between stamps occurs every 21 stamps.

For Testing Purposes Only Coil with Vertical Line Between "N" and "L" of "ONLY," without light blue — TE55c variety

Serpentine Die Cut 9¾ Vert.

Tagged

Self-Adhesive

TD136A TE55c **black** 7.50
Pair 15.00
Strip of 5 with taller vertical line between the "N" and "L" of "ONLY" on the center stamp 50.00

TE55c variety is similar to TE55c but without the light blue ink applied to mask the phosphorescence of the tagged white paper. The vertical line between the "N" and "L" of "ONLY" is slightly taller every 21 stamps. The stamp to the right of that stamp has the vertical line broken near the bottom. No. TD136A is on backing paper taller than the stamp with a gap between stamps. An inverted four-digit blue counting number is known on the reverse of the backing paper every 20th stamp.

For Testing Purposes Only Coil — TE55d

Serpentine Die Cut 11½ Vert.

TD137 TE55d **black** .50
Pair 1.00
P# strip of 5, #S1 4.00

No. TD137 does not have the printed simulation perforations found on No. TD127, and is on backing paper taller than the stamp with a gap between stamps.

Plate number "S1" occurs every 24th stamp.

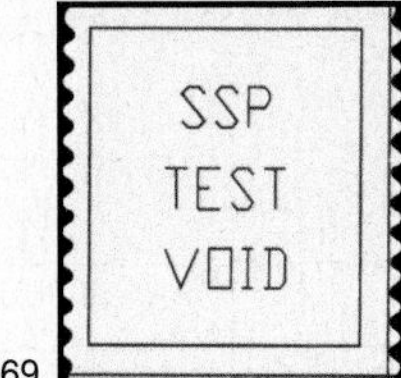

SSP Test Void Coil — TE69

Printed by Sennett Security Products.

2005 ***Serpentine Die Cut 10¼ Vert.***

Self-Adhesive

TD138 TE69 **black** 2.50
Pair 5.00

2000 ***Serpentine Die Cut 11½ Vert.***

Self-Adhesive

TD138A TE69 **black** 10.00
Pair 20.00

Nos. TD138 and TD138A have a horizontal and vertical line printed completely around all stamps. The vertical line is not a joint line. Horizontally mis-slit examples show a continuous horizontal line at either the top or bottom of all stamps.

RENA No Postage Test Stamp Coil — TE70

2006 ***Die Cut***

Self-Adhesive

TD139 TE70 **blue** 2.00
Pair 4.00

No. TD139 is on backing paper taller than the stamp with a gap between stamps.

For Testing Purposes Only Type of 1962-88

Self-Adhesive

Serpentine Die Cut 8¾ Vert.

TD140 TE55 **gray black** 25.00
Pair 50.00
a. Vertical pair, backing paper unslit horiz. *450.00*

The dimensions of the stamp design is slightly larger than other For Testing Purposes Only coils, being 19mm by 22.25mm. No. TD140 is on backing paper taller than the stamp. There are no plate numbers on the No. TD140 stamps.

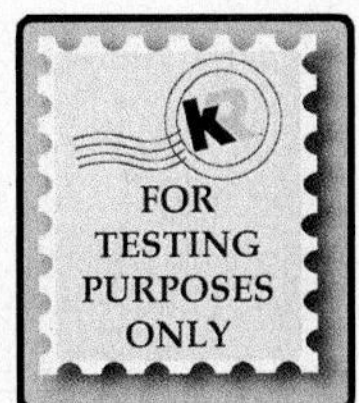

KR For Testing Purposes Only Coil — TE71

Printed for Kirk-Rudy.

2020 ***Straight Line Die Cut***

Self-Adhesive

TD141 TE71 **black on yellow orange** 2.50
Pair 5.00

No. TD141 is on backing paper taller than the stamp, with a 3mm gap.

TEST BOOKLETS: PANES & COVERS

Test booklets normally are collected as complete booklets, and the major listings are for complete booklets. Very often the booklet panes in different booklets are the same or similar. Booklet panes are presented as lettered minor listings. Where similar booklet panes can be differentiated by gum breaker measurements, size measurements, or other factors, they are given separate minor listings. Single stamps from these booklets are not given minor listings.

This test booklet section is divided into four categories: stapled booklets, folded and glued booklets with water-activated gum, folded and glued booklets with self-adhesive gum, and ATM and Convertible Booklet Test Panes.

All perforation measurements are with tab (staples end) at top of 6-subject booklet panes and with tab (stapled end) on left of 8-subject booklet panes.

STAPLED BOOKLETS

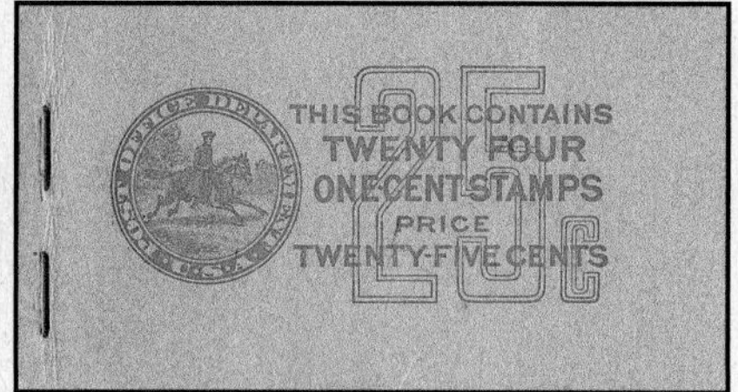

Small Postrider — BC5A

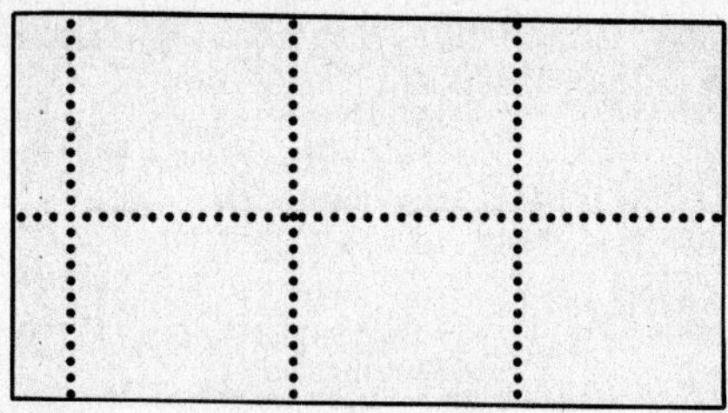

Blank Stamps — TDP1

1927-30 *Perf. 11¼x10½*

TDB1 BC5A 25c **green,** *green,* 4 #TDB1a —
a. TDP1 pane of 6 —

Horiz. gum breakers are 22mm apart on No. TDB1a. No. TDB1 has 5 waxed glassine interleaves, 1 in front of the first pane and 1 behind each pane.

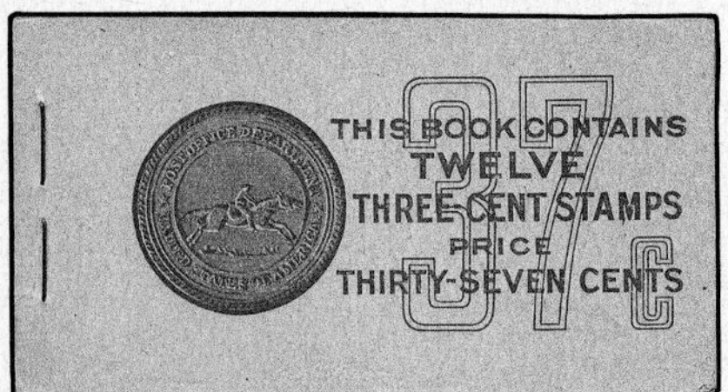

Post Office Seal — BC9A

Blank Stamps—TDP2

1930s

TDB2 BC9A 37c **violet,** *buff,* 2 #TDB2a —
a. TDP1 pane of 6 —
b. Unsevered pair of No. TDB2 booklets containing 2 #TDB2c panes —
c. TDP2 Unsevered pair of TDP1 panes —

No. TDB2b has a double-width cover made up of two unsevered BC9A covers. No. TDB2 has 2 waxed glassine interleaves, 1 behind each pane.

Horiz. gum breakers are 11½mm apart on No. TDB2a.

Framed Rectangles — TDP3

1940

TDB3 BC9A 37c **violet,** *buff,* 2 #TDB3a 500.00
a. TDP3 **violet,** pane of 6, hinged 160.00
Never hinged 225.00

Horiz. gum breakers are 11mm apart on No. TDB3a. No. TDB3 has 2 waxed glassine interleaves, 1 behind each pane.

Earliest documented use: Jan. 13, 1941 (single stamp)

A plate block of 6 (3x2) exists, cut from an untrimmed bottom left plate number 144767 sheet. It is unique.

Catalogue values for booklet panes in this section, from this point to the end, are for Never Hinged items.

Type of 1940

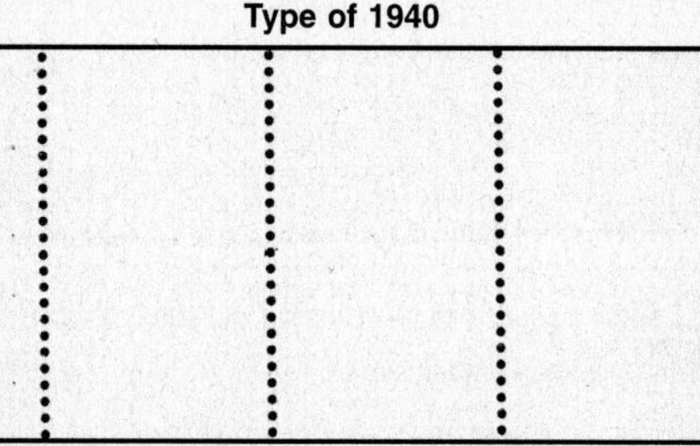

Blank Stamps — TDP4

1940s

TDB4 BC9A 37c **violet,** *buff,* #TDB4a, TDB4b —
a. TDP1 pane of 6 —
b. TDP4 pane of 3, perf. 11¼

Horiz. gum breakers are 6mm apart on Nos. TDB4a and TDB4b. No. TDB4 has 2 waxed glassine interleaves, 1 behind each pane.

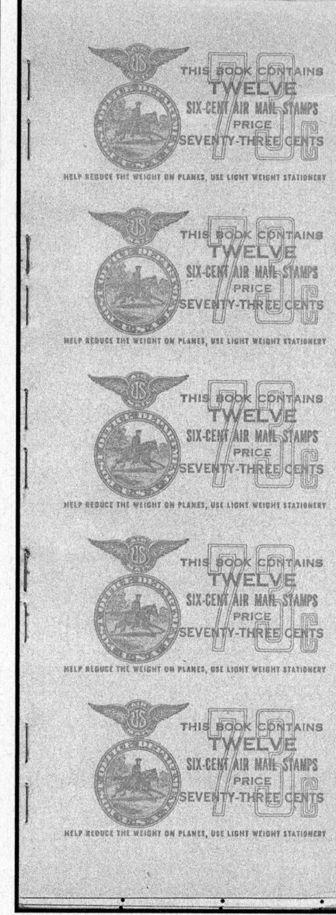

Unsevered Strip of 5 73¢ — BC10

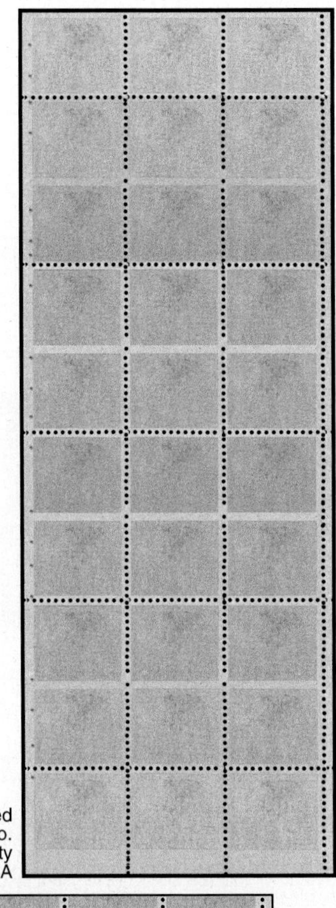

Unsevered Strip of 5 No. 807a Variety — TDP4A

TDP4A Pane of 6

Printed by Bureau of Engraving and Printing

1959 Untagged ***Perf. 11¼x10½***

TDB4C BC10 73c **red,** 4 #TDB4Cd #807a variety —
d. TDP4A Pane of 6 —

No. TDB4C booklets were originally discovered in an unsevered strip of five BC10 booklet covers with four strips of five No. 807a under-inked booklet panes within the covers. The No. 807a printer's waste panes are inverted in relation to the booklet covers with the stapling tab at the opposite end of the stapled booklet covers. No. BC10 73¢ red airmail booklet covers, and No. C39a booklet panes, are narrower than the width of the No. 807a panes, and therefore the stamps in the panes would not align with the covers if cut into individual booklets.

No. TDB4Cd horizontal gum breakers are 5½mm apart, and vertical gum breakers alternate 14mm and 8½mm apart. No. TDB4C has four silicone interleaves, one behind each pane. It is unknown if the discovery strip of five connected booklets is still intact and unsevered.

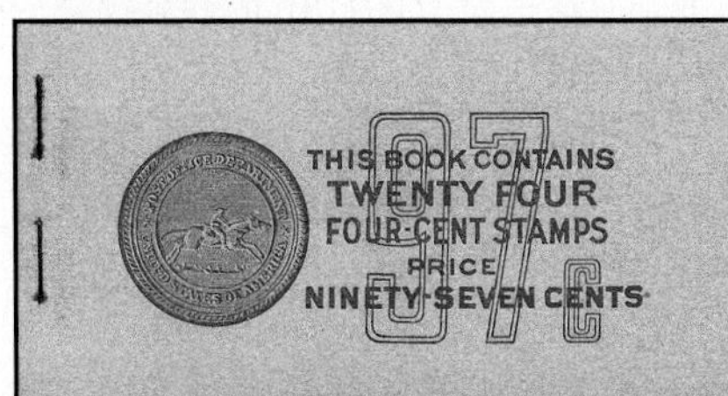

Post Office Seal — BC9H

1959

TDB5 BC9H 97c **blue,** *pink,* 4 #TDB5a 160.00
a. TDP1 pane of 6 —
b. As #TDB5, with silicone interleaves 325.00

Horiz. gum breakers are 5½mm apart, and vert. gum breakers are 21mm apart on No. TDB5a. No. TDB5 has 4 waxed glassine interleaves, and No. TDB5b has 4 silicone interleaves, 1 behind each pane.

U.S. Airmail Wings — BC11C

1959

TDB6 BC11C 85c **blue,** 2 #TDB5a 175.00

Horiz. gum breakers are 5½mm apart on No. TDB6a. Some panes exhibit faint vertical gum breakers, while some panes show no horizontal or vertical gum breakers. No. TDB6 has 2 waxed glassine interleaves, 1 behind each pane.

For Nos. TDB7, TDB8, TDB13, TDB14, TDB15, TDB16, TDB17, TDB18 and TDB19, booklet panes were made from coil stock that had stamp designs rotated 90 degrees from booklet stamps and therefore always appear miscut and misperforated.

Post Office Seal Type of 1959

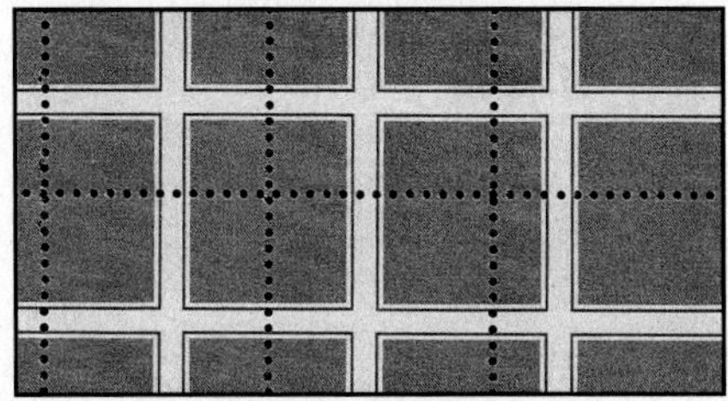

Misperforated and Miscut Framed Rectangles — TDP5

1960-62

TDB7 BC9H 97c **blue,** *pink,* 4 #TDB7a *900.00*
a. TDP5 **red violet,** pane of 6 *200.00*

Horiz. gum breakers are 4½-6½mm apart and vert. gum breakers are 22½mm apart on No. TDB7a. No. TDB7 has 4 glassine interleaves, 1 behind each pane. Some panes show joint lines.

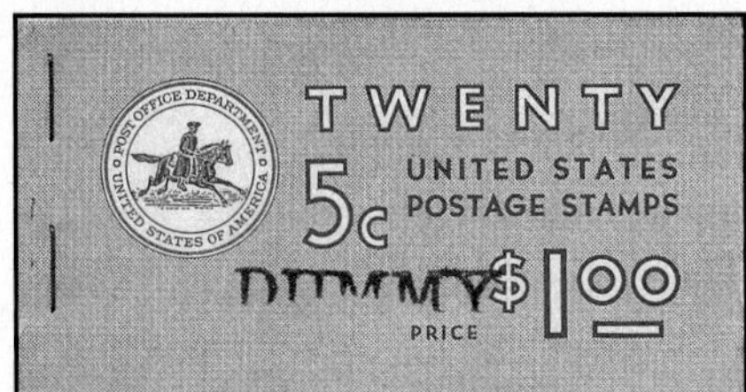

Small Postrider With Shades of Purple to Red Violet "DUMMY" Handstamp — TBC12A

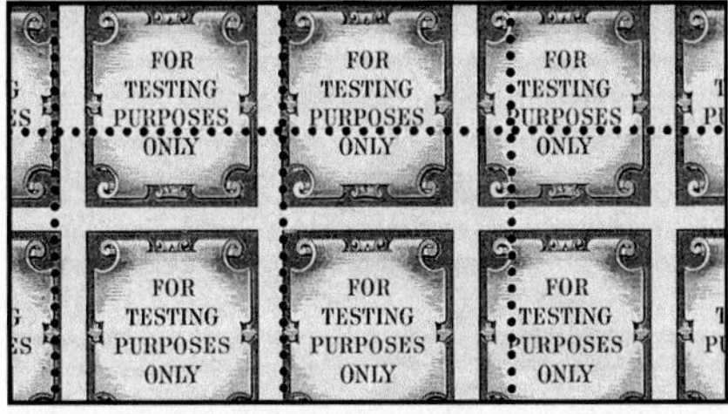

For Testing Purposes Only — TDP6

1962-67 Untagged

Shades of Purple to Red Violet 29½x4½mm "DUMMY" Handstamp

TDB8 TBC12A $1 **blue,** 4 #TDB8a 550.00
a. TDP6 **black,** pane of 6 stamps 100.00

Horiz. gum breakers are 5½mm apart and alternating vert. gum breakers are 22½mm and 8½mm apart on No. TDB8a. No. TDB8 has 4 silicone interleaves, 1 behind each pane, and staples at left. No. TDB8 is the only stapled-cover test booklet containing untagged "For Testing Purposes Only" panes. Some panes show joint lines.

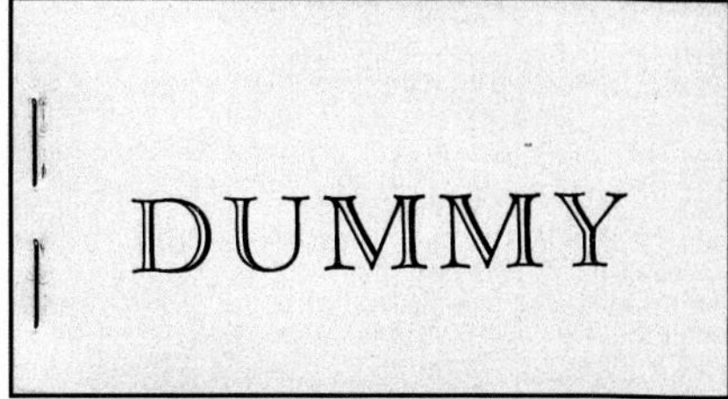

"DUMMY" — TBC12B

1962-67

Black 55x7½mm "DUMMY" Overprint

TDB9 TBC12B **black** 2 #TDB9a 90.00
a. TDP1 pane of 6 4.00

Red 55x7½mm "DUMMY" Overprint

TDB10 TBC12B **red** 2 #TDB9a *1,500.*

Horiz. gum breakers are 11½mm apart, and alternating vert. gum breakers are 14mm and 8½mm apart on No. TDB9a. Nos. TDB9 and TDB10 have 2 glassine interleaves, 1 behind each pane. Two examples of No. TDB10 are recorded. No. TDB9a blank booklet panes are found in Nos. TDB9, TDB10, TDB11 and TDB12.

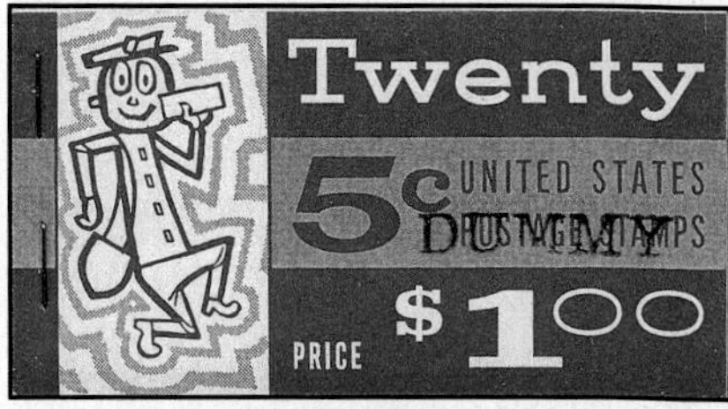

Mr. Zip With "DUMMY" — TBC13A

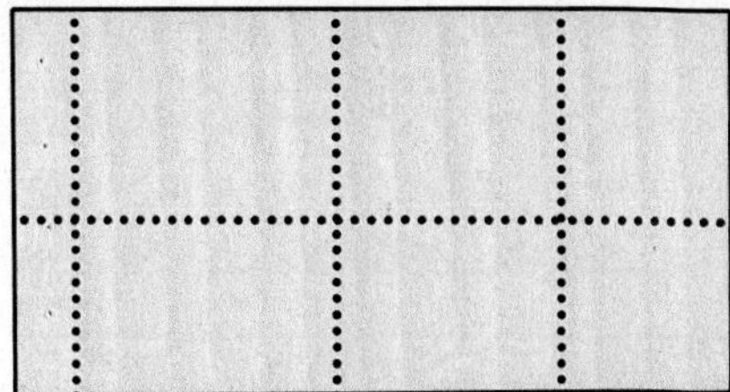

Blank Pane, 3 Sizes of Stamps — TDP1a

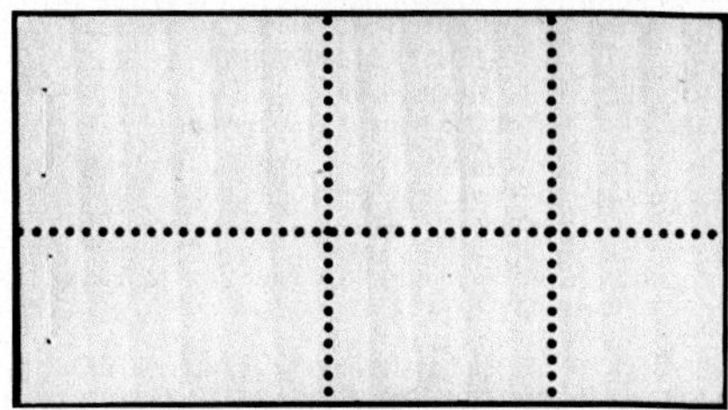

Blank Pane Without Perforated Stapling Tab — TDP1b

1963-66

Shades of Violet to Red Violet 29½x4½mm "DUMMY" Handstamp

TDB11 TBC13A $1 **blue,** 4 #TDB9a 125.00
a. As #TDB11, with 4 #TDB11b 125.00
b. TDP1a pane of 6 25.00
c. As #TDB11, with 4 #TDB11d 225.00
d. TDP1b pane of 6 50.00
e. As No. TDB11, without "DUMMY" handstamp on outside front cover —

Alternating horiz. gum breakers are 4½mm and 6½mm apart, and alternating vert. gum breakers are 14mm and 8½mm apart on Nos. TDB11b and TDB11d.

Mr. Zip with Press-printed "DUMMY" — TBC13B

Red 55x7½mm "DUMMY" Overprint

TDB12 TBC13B $1 **blue,** 4 #TDB9a		50.00
a.	As #TDB12, with different inside front cover	8.00

No. TDB12 has inside front cover reading "Domestic Postage Rates." No. TDB12a has inside front cover reading "Minute Man — Buy — HOLD US Savings Bonds."

Nos. TDB11-TDB12a have 4 silicone interleaves, 1 behind each pane.

An authenticated unexploded booklet exists with the panes inside inverted in relation to the covers (staples at left, tabs on panes at right).

For Nos. TDB13, TDB18, TDB19, TDB20a, TDB21a and TDB21b, the perforation gauge and the gum breaker spacing on the booklet panes are measured with the staple position to the left. The perforation gauge and gum breaker spacing in the small-size booklets (from No. TDB1 to TDB17) are measured with the staple position at the top.

Post Office Seal With Shades of Violet to Red Violet "DUMMY" Handstamp — TBC14A

For Testing Purposes Only — TDP7

1967-68 Tagged *Perf. 11¼x10½*

Shades of Violet to Red Violet 34½x6½mm "DUMMY" Handstamp

TDB13 TBC14A $2 **brown,** 5 #TDB13a		200.00
a.	TDP7 **black,** pane of 8 stamps	35.00

Horiz. gum breakers are 11mm apart and alternating vert. gum breakers are 14mm and 8½mm apart on No. TDB13a. No. TDB13 has 5 silicone interleaves, 1 behind each pane, and staples at left. Some booklets and panes have felt pen markings along the top and bottom edges placed by the technicians for machine adjustments, and are valued less. Some panes show joint lines.

All known No. TDB13 booklet covers are screened at 130 dpi from later 400-subject printings, instead of at 100 dpi from earlier 320-subject printings.

Stamp Silhouette With Purple "DUMMY" Handstamp — TBC15

FTPO Pane Without Perforated Stapling Tab — TDP6a

1960s-72 Tagged *Perf. 11¼x10½*

Purple 34½x6½mm "DUMMY" Handstamp

TDB14 TBC15 $1 **brown,** 4 #TDB14a		150.00
a.	TDP6a **black,** pane of 6 stamps	35.00

Horiz. gum breakers are 11mm apart and vert. gum breakers are 22mm apart on No. TDB14a. No. TDB14 has 4 silicone interleaves, 1 behind each pane, and staples at left. "Dummy" handstamp is 34½x6½mm. All known booklets have a felt pen or other alignment markings on either the front or back covers.

No. TDB14a panes do not have a perforated stapling tab. No. TDB14a panes are found in Nos. TDB14, TDB17 and TDB17b booklets.

TBC15A

Inverted FTPO Pane — TDP6b

Shades of Violet 34½x6½mm "DUMMY" Handstamp

Tagged

TDB15 TBC15A $1 **blue,** 4 #TDB15a		150.00
a.	TDP6b **black,** pane of 6 stamps	35.00
b.	No. TDB15 without "DUMMY" handstamp on outside front cover	*600.00*

Horiz. gum breakers are 11mm apart on No. TDB15a. No. TDB15 has 4 silicone interleaves, 1 behind each pane, and staples at left. Some booklets have felt pen markings on either the front or back covers and are valued less. Some panes show joint lines.

TBC15B

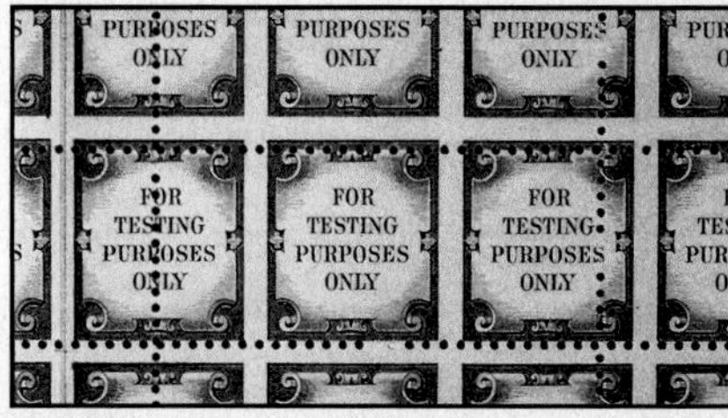

Small FTPO Pane With Perfs. For Large FTPO Pane — TDP6c

Upright FTPO Pane with Stapling at Right, Staples at Left — TDP6d

Shades of Red Violet 29½x4½mm "DUMMY" Handstamp

Tagged

TDB16 TBC15B $1 **claret,** 3 #TDB16a		400.00
a.	TDP6 **black,** pane of 6 stamps	125.00
b.	As #TDB16, with 34½x6½mm "DUMMY" handstamp	400.00
c.	As No. TDB16b, with 3 #TDB16d	*900.00*
d.	TDP6c pane of 6	*300.00*
e.	As #TDB16b, with 3 #TDB16f	—
f.	TDP6d Pane of 6	—

Horizontal gum breakers are 11mm apart on Nos. TDB16a and TDB16d. No. TDB16a has perforations made with a 360-subject perforator (used for booklet panes of 6); No. TDB16d has perforations made with a 400-subject perforator (intended for booklet panes of 8). No. TDB16d panes all have two rows of perforations horizontally with one or two rows of perforations vertically on the pane. No. TDB16d is only known in No. TDB16c. Nos. TDB16, TDB16b, TDB16c and TDB16e have three silicone interleaves, one behind each pane, and staples at left. Some panes show joint lines.

TBC15C

Shades of Violet to Red Violet 29½x5½mm "DUMMY" Handstamp

Tagged

TDB17 TBC15C $1 **red,** 2 #TDB14a		300.00
a.	As No. TDB17, with 2 No. TDB15a	300.00
b.	As #TDB17, with 34¾x7¾mm "DUMMY" handstamp	300.00
c.	As #TDB17a, without "DUMMY" handstamp on outside of front cover	*750.00*

Horizontal gum breakers are 11mm apart, and alternating vertical gum breakers are 14 and 8½mm apart on No. TDB17a. Some panes do not show vertical gum breakers. No. TDB17 has 2 silicone interleaves, 1 behind each pane, and staples at left. Some panes show joint lines.

Eisenhower With Shades of Red Violet "DUMMY" Handstamp — TBC16

1970-71 Tagged *Perf. 11¼x10½*

Shades of Red Violet 29½x4½mm "DUMMY" Handstamp

TDB18 TBC16 $2 **blue,** 5 #TDB13a		325.00
a.	As #TDB18, with 34½x6½mm "DUMMY" handstamp	400.00
b.	As #TDB18 or TDB18b, without "DUMMY" handstamp on outside of front cover	*800.00*

Horiz. gum breakers are 11mm apart and vert. gum breakers are 22mm apart on No. TDB13a. No. TDB18 has 5 silicone interleaves, 1 behind each pane, and staples at left. Some panes show joint lines.

TBC17

Shades of Red Violet to Red 29½x4½mm "DUMMY" Handstamp

TDB19 TBC17 $1.92 **claret,** 3 #TDB13a — 400.00
a. As #TDB19, with shades of red violet to red 34½x6½mm "DUMMY" handstamp — 400.00

No. TDB19 has 3 silicone interleaves, 1 behind each pane, and staples at left. Some panes show joint lines.

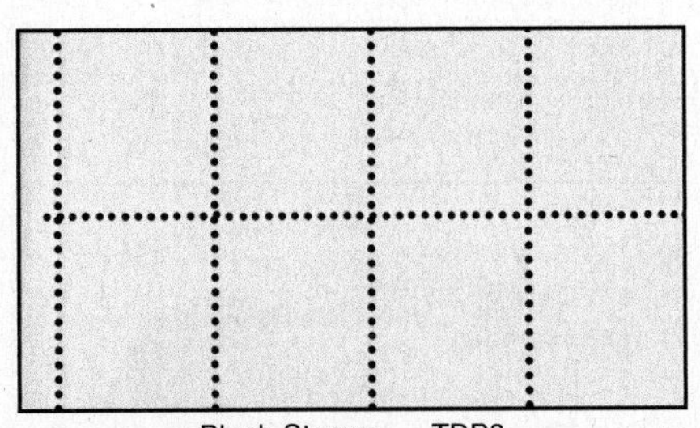

Blank Stamps — TDP8

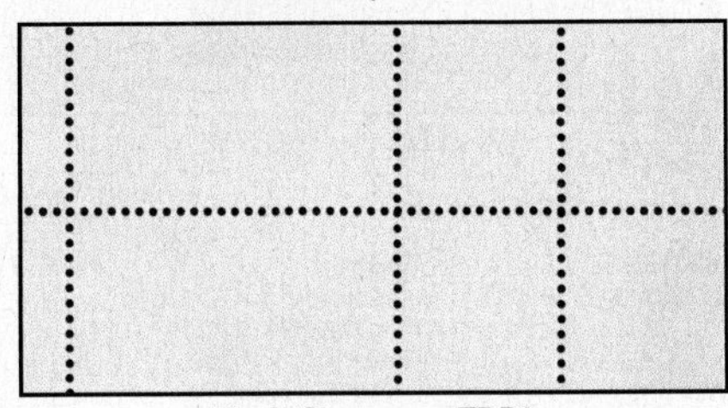

Blank Stamps — TDP9

1970 **Tagged** ***Perf. 11¼x10½***

Shiny Gum with Gum Breaker Ridges 11mm Apart

TDB20a TDP8 pane of 8 stamps, shiny gum, yellow green tagging — —
Horiz. pair of 2 blank panes of 8 — —
Vert. pair of 2 blank panes of 8 — —
Block of 4 blank panes of 8 — —

Some stamps are known with a vertical rejection marking.
The No.TDB20a (TDP8 pane) is the same format as the No. 1393a booklet pane.

1972 **Tagged** ***Perf. 10½x11¼***

Dull DAVAC Gum with Gum Breaker Ridges 11mm Apart

Nashua Paper

TDB21a TDP9 pane of 4 stamps + 2 double-width labels dull gum, yellow green tagging — —
Horiz. pair of 2 blank panes of 4 stamps + 2 labels — —
Vert. pair of 2 blank panes of 4 stamps + 2 labels — —
Block of 4 blank panes of 4 stamps + 2 labels — —

Some stamps are known with a vertical rejection marking.
The No. TDB21a (TDP9) pane is the same format as the No. 1395c booklet pane.

Dull DAVAC Gum with Gum Breaker Ridges 11mm Apart

Nashua Paper

Perf. 10½x11¼

TDB21b TDP8 pane of 7 stamps + label, dull gum, yellow green tagging — —
Horiz. pair of 2 blank panes of 7 stamps + label — —
Vert. pair of 2 blank panes of 7 stamps + label — —
Block of 4 blank panes of 7 stamps + label — —

The No. TDB21b (TDP8) pane is the same format as the No. 1395d booklet pane. No complete booklets containing Nos. TDB20a, TDB21a or TDB21b have been reported.

FOLDED AND GLUED BOOKLETS

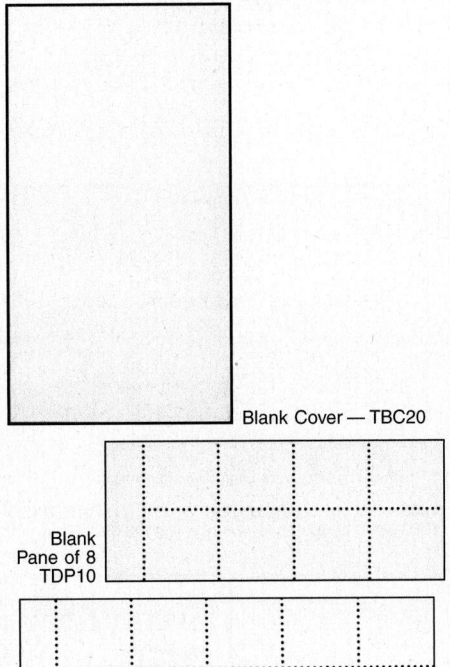

Blank Cover — TBC20

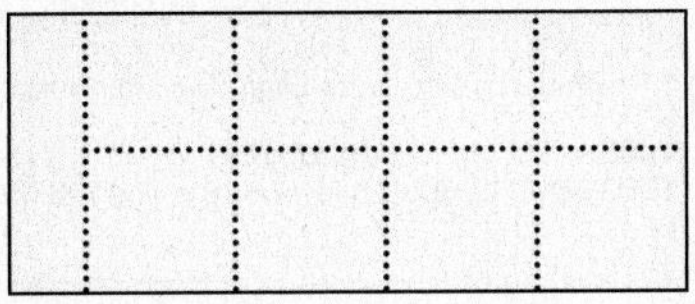

Blank Pane of 8 TDP10

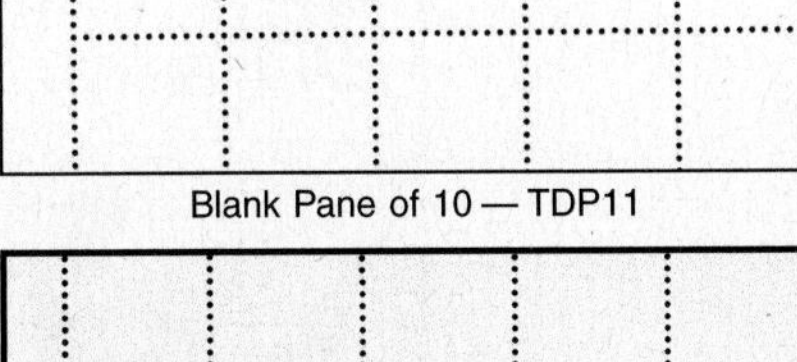

Blank Pane of 10 — TDP11

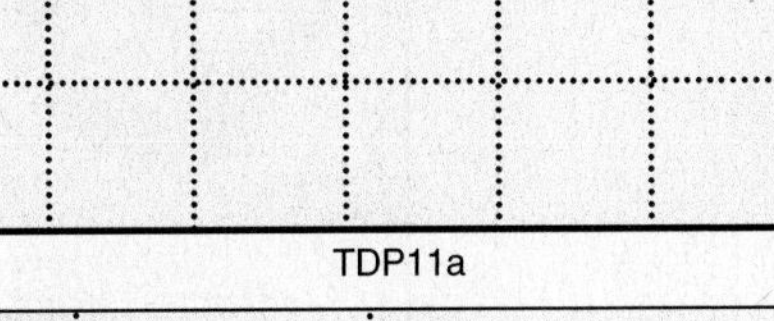

TDP11a

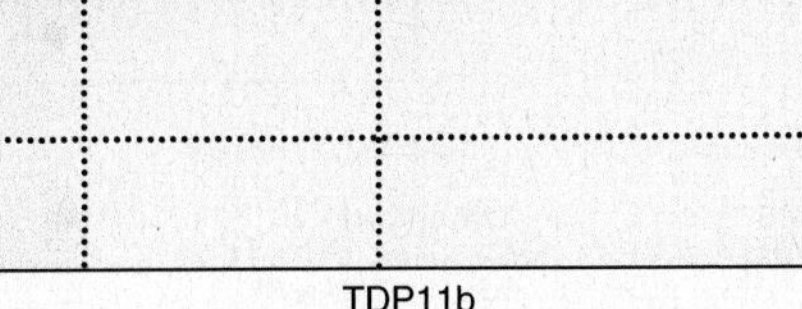

TDP11b

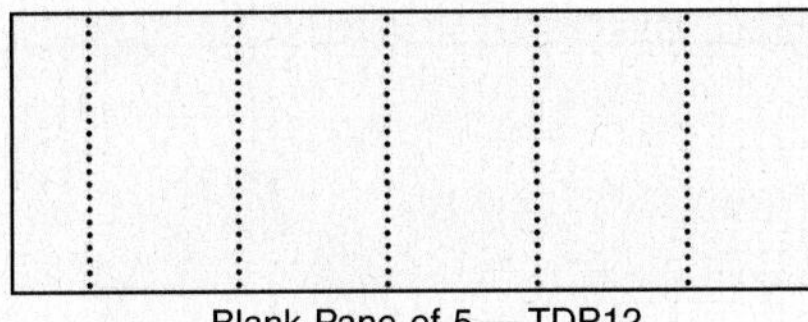

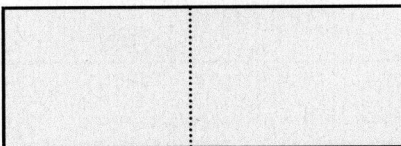

Blank Pane of 5 — TDP12

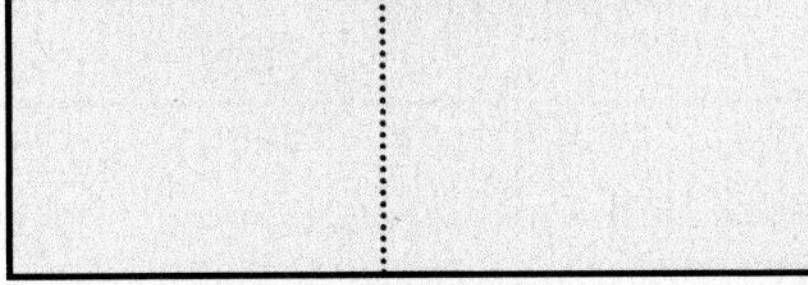

Blank Pane of 2 — TDP12a

Blank Imperf. Pane — TDP12b

Produced by Bureau of Engraving and Printing.

1970s-80s **Untagged** ***Perf. 11x10½***

TDB25 TBC20 blank, #TDB25a — 500.00
a. TDP10 pane of 8, dull gum — —

Perf. 10x9¾

TDB26 TBC20 blank, 2 #TDB26a — 80.00
a. TDP11 pane of 10, shiny gum — 35.00

Perf. 10 Horiz.

TDB27 TBC20 blank, #TDB28a — 40.00
TDB28 TBC20 blank, 2 #TDB28a — 30.00
a. TDP12 pane of 5, dull gum — 12.50
b. As #TDB28, with 2 #TDB28c — 30.00
c. TDP12 pane of 5, shiny gum — 12.50

Produced by KCS Industries

Imperf

TDB29 TBC20 blank, 2 #TDB29a — 50.00
a. TDP12b pane of 1, dull gum — 22.50

Panes in No. TDB29 lack perforations and are attached to each other and the booklet cover with three glue spots. The booklet cover of No. TDB29 is scored at the pane fold location with approximate gauge 6½.

Perf. 11 Horiz.

TDB30 TBC20 blank, 2 #TDB30a — 80.00
a. TDP12a pane of 2, dull gum — 35.00
b. As #TDB30, with inverted pane (perfs unaligned with cover fold) — —

Panes in No. TDB30 are fastened to each other with 3 glue spots and bottom pane is fastened to booklet cover with a 1mm wide glue line. Covers are known with handstamps "A1" (black), "A2" (orange), "B1" (red), or "B2" (violet) on the front and back cover panels.

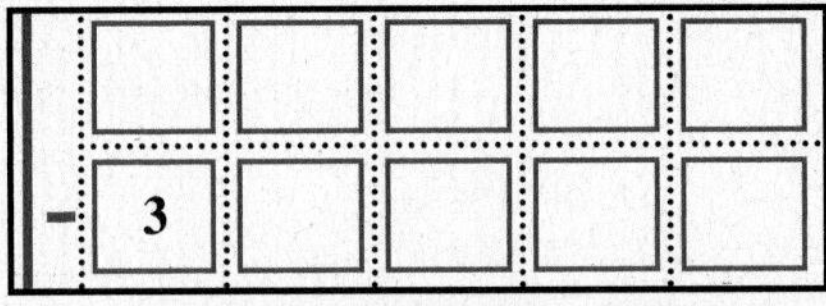

Rectangles and Numeral — TDP13

Made by Goebel, GmbH, Germany, from materials supplied by Bureau of Engraving and Printing

1990s **Untagged** ***Perf. 11x9¾***

TDB30C TBC20 blank, 2 #TDB30Cd — *900.00*
d. TDP13 **blue,** pane of 10, shiny gum — 150.00

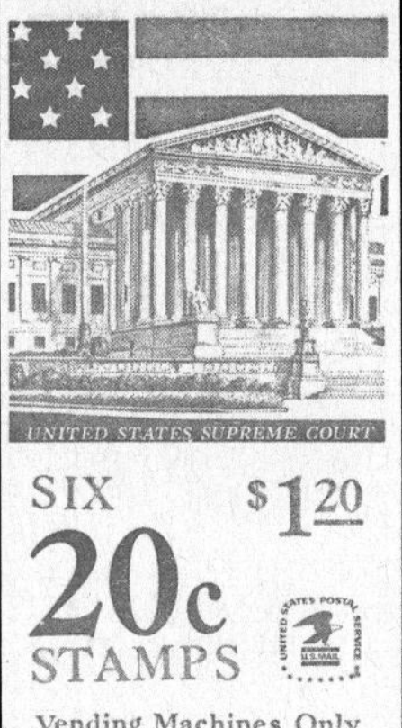

Flag Over Supreme Court — BC29

Produced by Bureau of Engraving & Printing.

1985 **Untagged** ***Perf. 10 Horiz.***

TDB31 BC29 $1.20 **red & blue,** #TDB28a — *1,500.*

Two examples of No. TDB31 are recorded.
The inside cover printing on No. TDB31 is not the same as the printing used on the issued booklet No. BK139. Instead, it has the inside printing found on the $1.10 Flag over Capital booklet No. BK144.

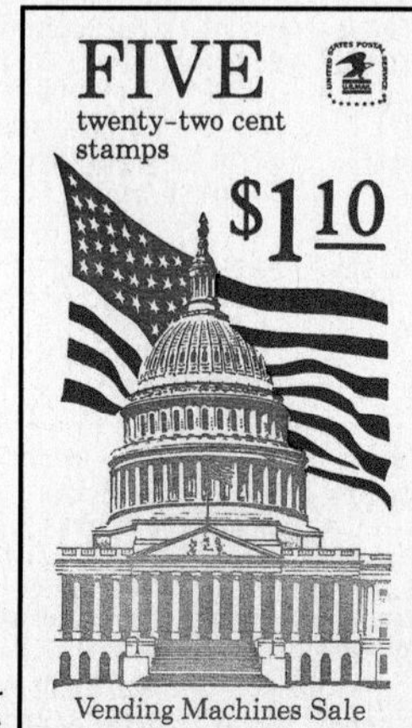

Flag Over Capitol — BC33C

Produced by Bureau of Engraving and Printing.

1985 **Untagged** ***Perf. 10 Horiz.***
TDB32 BC33C $1.10 **red & blue,** #TDB28a 10.00

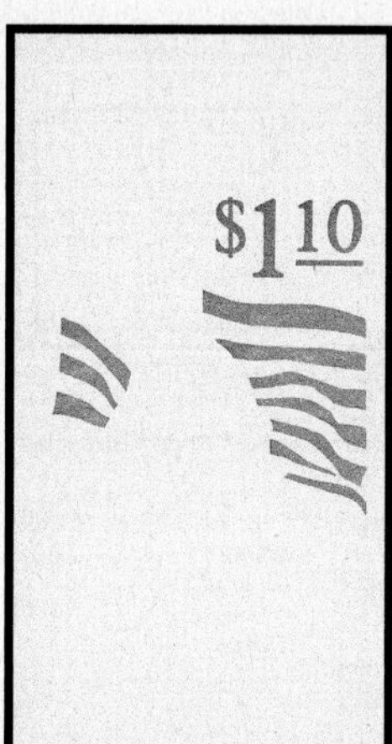

Flag Over Capitol — TBC20A

Produced by Bureau of Engraving and Printing

1985 **Untagged** ***Perf. 10 Horiz.***
TDB32A TBC20A $1.10 **red,** #TDB28a —

Seashells — BC33A

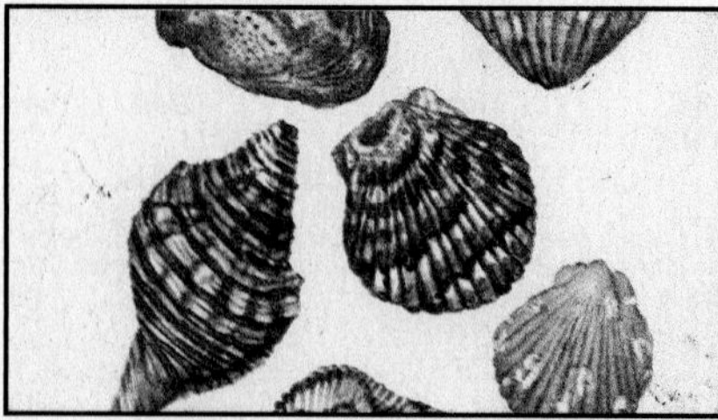
Seashells Without Text — TBC21

Produced by Bureau of Engraving and Printing.

1985 **Untagged** ***Perf. 10x9¾***
TDB33 BC33A $4.40 **multicolored,** 2 #TDB33a *500.00*
a. TDP11 pane of 10, dull gum —

Panes are scored at all horizontal perforation rows. Some booklet covers have a thick irregular horizontal red smudge that was printed on the front cover. It is located above a thin blue horizontal seam line that is found on the front and back covers. These lines resulted from excess ink buildup in the seam where the six offset plates met.

TDB34 TBC21 **multicolored,** 2 #TDB33a *500.00*

Perf. 10 Horiz.

TDB34A TBC21 **multicolored,** 2 #TDB28a *350.00*

No. TDB34A panes are fastened to the inside of the blank back cover, whereas No. TDB33 and TDB34 booklets have the panes fastened to the inside of the front covers with the Seashell illustrations.

Seven consecutive booklet covers are needed to show the complete design of all 25 seashells for Nos. TDB33 -TDB34A.

Seashell — BC33B

Produced by Bureau of Engraving and Printing.

1985 **Untagged** ***Perf. 10x9¾***
TDB35 BC33B $4.40 brown & blue, 2 #TDB33a —

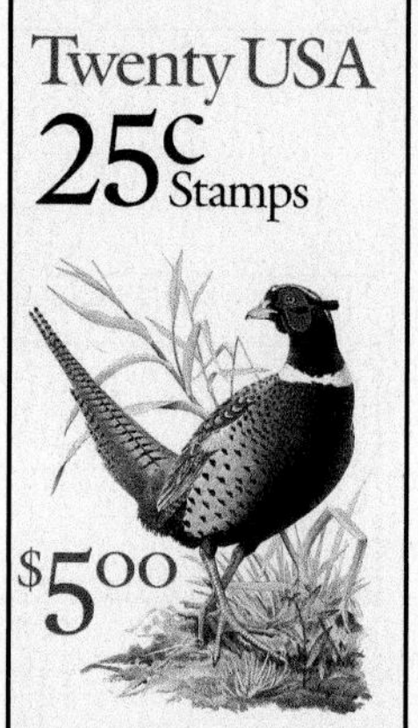

Pheasant — BC41

Produced by American Bank Note Company

1988 **Untagged** ***Perf. 11***
TDB35A BC41 $5 **multicolored,** 2 #TDB35Ab —
b. TDP11b Pane of 4, dull gum —

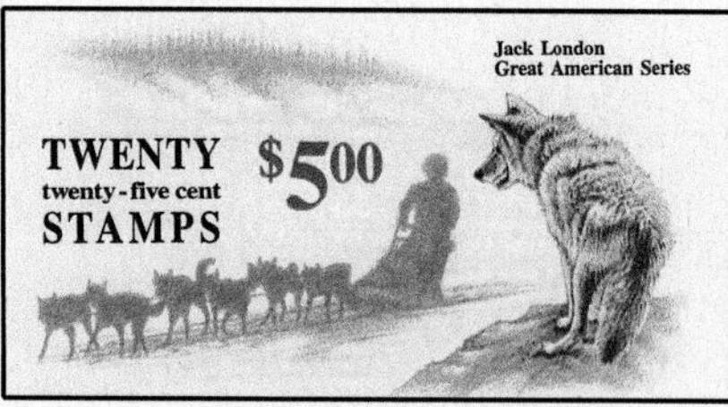

Jack London — BC43

Produced by Bureau of Engraving and Printing

1988 **Untagged** ***Perf. 11¼***
TDB35C BC43 $5 **multicolored,** 2 #TDB35Cd —
d. TDP11 Pane of 10, dull gum —

No. TDB35C booklets were made by hand using the BEP's proprietary process and were sometimes cut at a slight angle, resulting in a trapezoid-shaped booklet that looked like a "chevron" when opened.

Jack London — TBC22

Made by Goebel, GmbH, Germany, from materials supplied by Bureau of Engraving and Printing.

1988 **Untagged** ***Perf. 11x9¾***
TDB36 TBC22 $5 **multicolored,** 2 #TDB30Cd *350.00*

Panes are scored at all horizontal perforation rows. No. TDB36 booklet covers have a small number (1 to 12) in the lower right corner that match the large number on the booklet panes on the inside (also 1-12). No. TDB36 also exists with mismatched pane and cover numbers. Value, $600.

Some booklet covers have red felt pen marks on the outside front cover. An unpublished quote from George Washington is printed on inside front cover and unissued "American Garden" printed on inside back cover.

Wood Duck — BC57B

Produced by KCS Industries.

1991-92 **Tagged** ***Perf. 11***
TDB36A BC57B $5.80 **multicolored,** 1 #TDB36Ab —
b. TDP11a pane of 10, shiny gum —

The discovery copy of TDB36A only contained a single pane. There was no evidence of a second pane having been in the booklet (no disturbance on top of the tab, and no second tab below the pane).

Hummingbird — BC80

Produced by American Bank Note Company.

1994 **Untagged** ***Perf. 11 Horiz.***
TDB37 BC80 $5.80 **multicolored,** 4 #TDB37a —
a. TDP12 pane of 5, shiny gum —

Outside front cover has two green felt pen marks. The panes in Nos. TDB37 and TDB38 are identical except for their width. No. TDB37 panes are just 40mm wide, whereas No. TDB38 panes are 45mm wide.

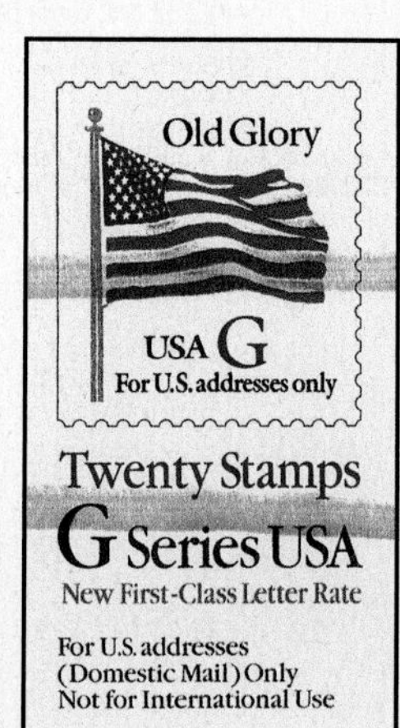

Flag — BC106B

Produced by American Bank Note Company.

1994 Untagged *Perf. 11 Horiz.*

TDB38	BC106B G **multicolored,** 2 #TDB38a	—
a.	TDP12 pane of 5, shiny gum	—

Only two panes remained in the discovery booklet, but the current top pane in that booklet showed evidence that additional pane(s) were once attached to it.

Outside front cover has two aqua felt pen marks. The panes in Nos. TDB37 and TDB38 are identical except for their width. No. TDB37 Hummingbird panes are just 40mm wide, whereas No. TDB38 G Rate panes are 45mm wide.

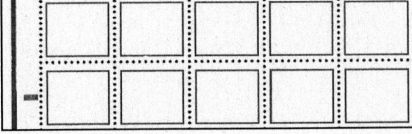

Old Glory
USA G
For U.S. addresses only
Twenty Stamps
G Series USA
New First-Class Letter Rate
For U.S. addresses (Domestic Mail) Only
Not for International Use

Flag — BC106C

Produced by KCS Industries.

1992-1994 Tagged *Perf. 11*

TDB38B	BC106C G **multicolored,** 2 #TDB36Ab	*600.00*
c.	TDP13b pane of 10, shiny gum	—

No. TDB38Bc has "© United States Postal Service 1992 / K" on inside of cover above pane tab.

Daffodils — TBC23

Rectangles, with LRM over left column — TDP14

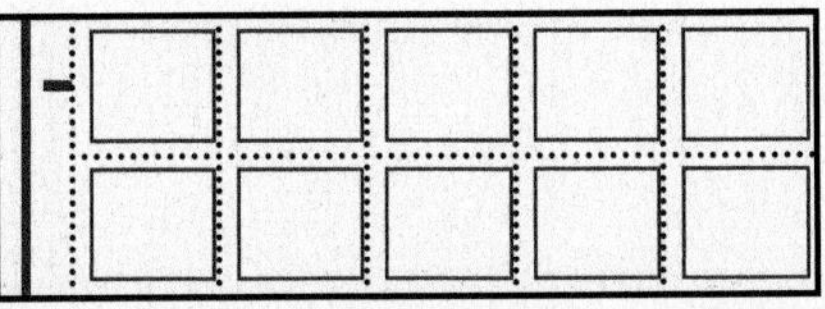

Rectangles, with LRM over right column — TDP14a

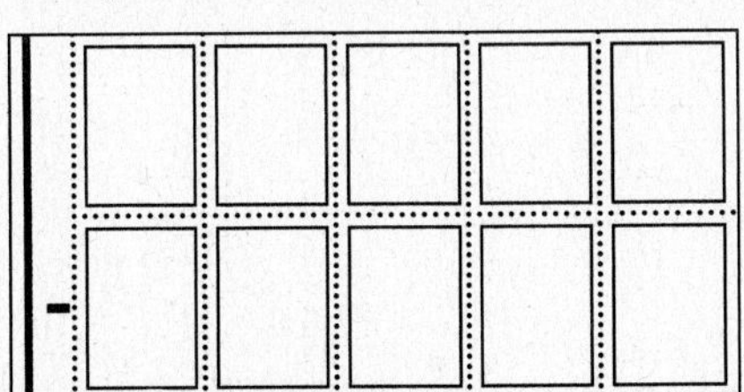

Rectangles (Large Stamps) — TDP15

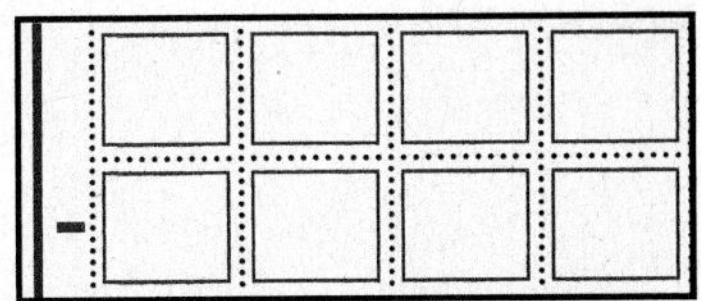

Rectangles (Pane of 8) — TDP16

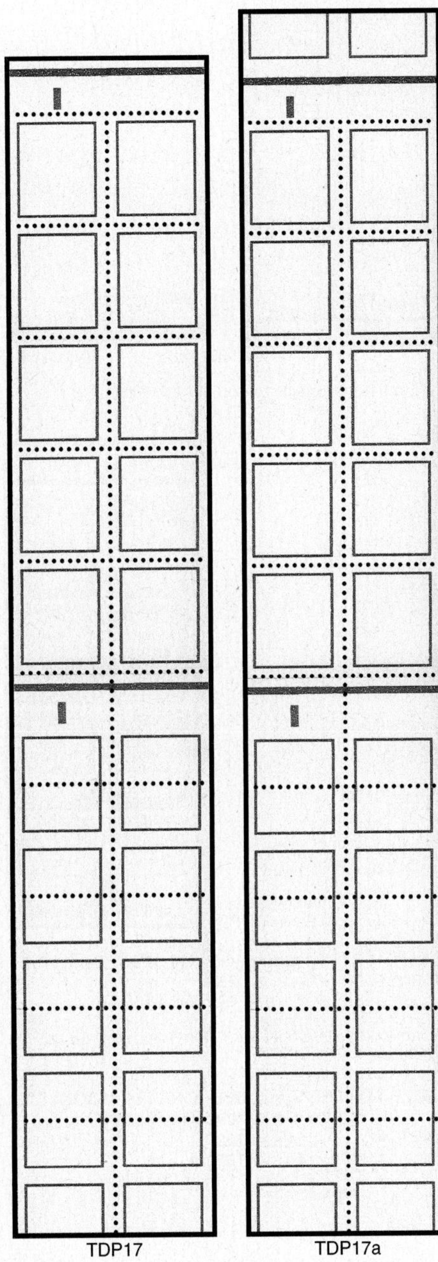

TDP17 TDP17a

Made by Goebel, GmbH, Germany, from materials supplied by Bureau of Engraving and Printing.

1990s Untagged *Perf. 11x9¾*
Shiny Gum

TDB39	TBC23	**multicolored,** 2 #TDB39a	*400.00*
a.		TDP14 **dark blue,** pane of 10, with LRM over the left column	*50.00*
TDB40	TBC23	**multicolored,** 4 #TDB30Cd	—
TDB40A	TBC23	**multicolored,** 2 #TDB30Cd	—
TDB41	TBC23	**multicolored,** 4 #TDB39a	*150.00*
TDB42	TBC23	**multicolored,** 4 #TDB42a	—
a.		TDP14a **dark blue,** pane of 10, with LRM over right column	—
TDB43	TBC23	**multicolored,** 2 #TDB43a, no printing on inside covers	—
a.		TDP15 **black,** pane of 10	60.00
TDB43B	TBC23	**multicolored,** 2 #TDB43a, with printing on inside covers	*150.00*
TDB44	TBC23	**multicolored,** #TDB44a	*150.00*
a.		TDP16 **dark blue,** pane of 8	*100.00*
TDB45	TBC23	**multicolored,** #TDB45a, TDB45b	200.00
a.		TDP17 **dark blue,** pane of 20, 43x257mm, shiny gum	100.00
b.		TDP17a **dark blue,** pane of 20, 43x272mm, shiny gum	100.00

Nos. TDB42 and TDB43 lack printing on inside covers found on Nos. TDB39-TDB41. The numbers on the panes in Nos. TDB40 and TDB40B usually match the numbers on the covers. No. TDB40B also exists with mismatched pane and cover numbers. Value, $900. Numbers on the covers range from 1-12 on Nos. TDB39, TDB40, TDB40B, TDB41, TDB42, and TDB45. Numbers on the covers range from 1-8 on Nos. TDB43 and TDB43b.

No. TDB43b is known with 66.5x84.5mm front covers that show a black EE bar below the Daffodil illustration, and 66.5x81mm front covers that do not show the black EE bar below the Daffodil illustration.

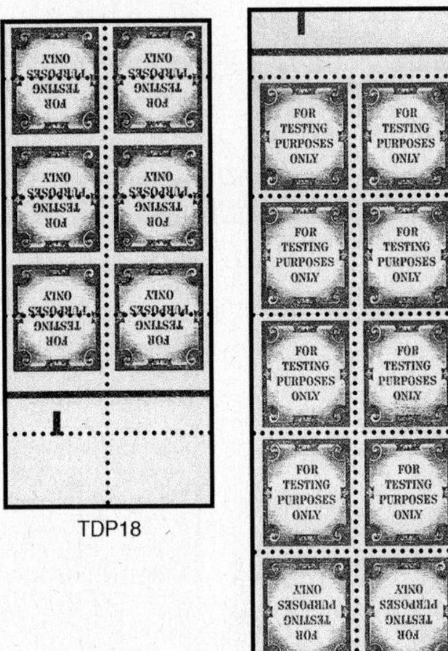

TDP18 TDP19

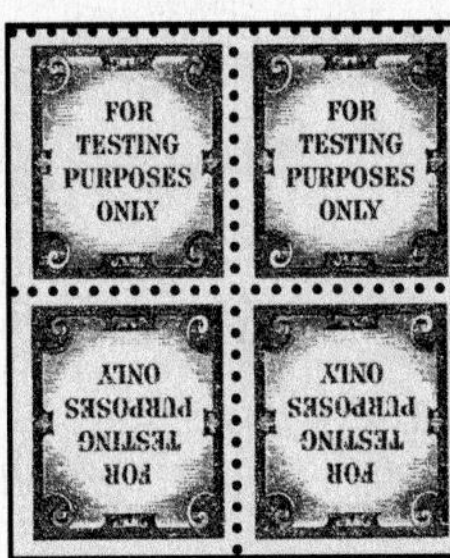

Tete-beche block found in TDP19

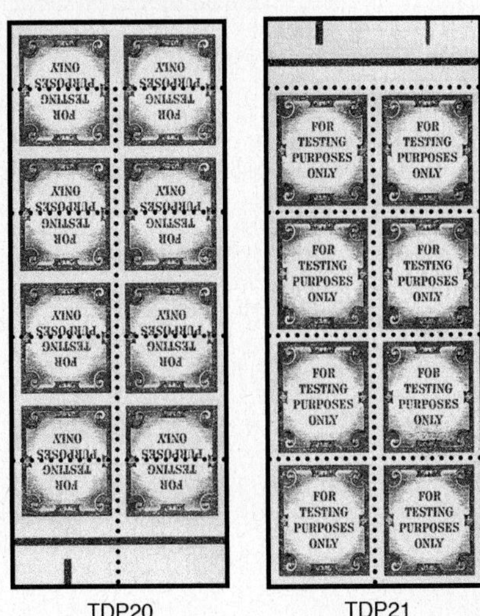

TDP20 TDP21

Made by Goebel, GmbH (Germany) from materials supplied by the Bureau of Engraving and Printing.

Untagged *Perf. 10x9¾*

TDB46 TBC20 blank, #TDB46a, TDB46b, TDB46c, TDB46d *1,200.*
- *a.* TDP18 **black,** pane of 8, 44x100mm, dull gum —
- *b.* TDP19 **black,** pane of 10, 44x135mm, dull gum —
- *c.* TDP20 **black,** pane of 8, 44x111mm, dull gum —
- *d.* TDP21 **black,** pane of 8, 44x111mm, dull gum —

The No. TDB46 booklet panes were printed in gravure by the BEP for use by Goebel GmbH, Germany, to evaluate a new booklet forming machine.

"FRONT COVER" in blue — TBC24

For Testing Purposes Only — TDP22

Perf. 10¾x10½
Overall Tagging

TDB47 TBC24 **red & blue,** #TDB47a *1,200.*
- *a.* TDP22 **black,** pane of 8, 44x110mm, dull gum —

No. TDB47a was cut from the web with horizontal perforations between each row of panes. All known panes thus show a partial row of perforations at bottom.

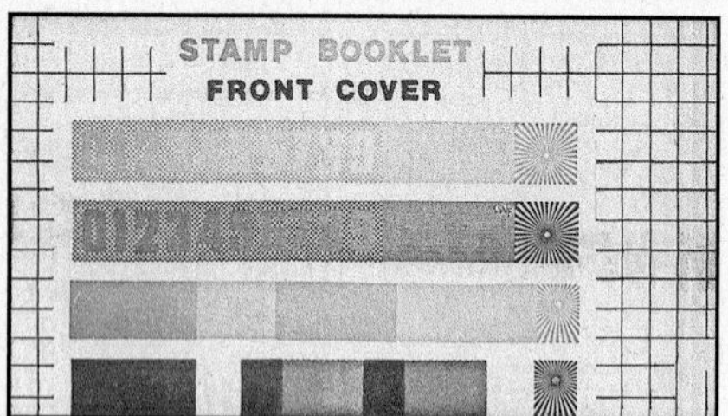

"FRONT COVER" in red — TBC25

For Testing Purposes Only — TDP23

Overall Tagging *Perf. 10x9¾*

TDB48 TBC25 **blue & red,** #TDB48a *750.00*
- *a.* TDP23 **black,** pane of 8, 44x110mm, dull gum —

For Testing Purposes Only — TDP24

Untagged *Perf. Perf. 10x9¾*

TDB49 TBC20 blank, #TDB49a —
- *a.* TDP24 **black,** pane of 8, dull gum, 44x111mm —

No. TDP24 differs from No. TDP21 with narrow EE bar over the left stamp on TDP24.

SELF-ADHESIVE FOLDED & GLUED BOOKLETS
Blank Cover and Pane Types

1990s ? **Untagged** *Perf. 11 Horiz.*

TDB60 TBC20 blank, 2 #TDB60a —
- *a.* TDP12a blank, pane of 2, self-adhesive, 44x132mm —

Stamp Layout TBP25

Pledge of Allegiance TBE25

1990s ***Imperf.***

TDB60B TBE25 29c **multicolored** 100.00
- *c.* TBP25 multicolor (TBC20) pane of 8 1,000.

No. TDB60Bc looks similar to Nos. 2593a and 2594a, both of which are water-activated 29c Pledge of Allegiance booklet panes of 10 stamps. No. TDB60Bc is printed on self-adhesive paper with blue liner printing identical to that found on self-adhesive stamps printed by Sennett Security Products between 1992 and 1996. However, the cross register line (CRL) and length register mark (LRM) found on TDB60Bc were only used by the BEP on booklet panes printed for use on their Goebel booklet forming machine to make booklets with panes glued into the cardboard cover. It is believed TDB60Bc was used in a trial prior to 1996 when the BEP issued BK228 containing self-adhesive panes of No. 2921a, the 32c Flag Over Porch booklet that replaced BK226 that contained water-activated gum panes.

No. TDB60Bc does not have a plate number in the selvage tab, and its CRL and LRM are printed in black rather than blue ink like found on No. 2593a. This shows No. TDB60Bc was printed from experimental plates rather than the same plates used to print No. 2593a, the water-activated gum Pledge of Allegiance booklet pane.

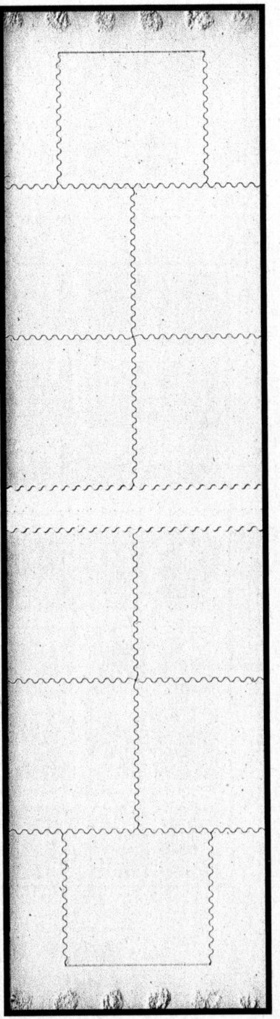
Stamp Layout — TBP61

Blank — TBE39

Serpentine Die Cut 10½x11 on 3 Sides, 10½ on 3 Sides on Stamps at Each End of Pane

1999 Overall Tagging

TDB61 TBC20 blank, self-adhesive blank pane of 10, 8 #TDB61a + 2 #TDB61b 150.00
a. TBE39 Die cut 10½x11 on 3 sides 10.00
b. TBE39 Die cut 10½ on 3 sides 20.00

Stamps in pane have same arrangement as that of the 1999 20c Pheasant booklet, No. BK242A.

All reported No. TDB61 booklets have had the center peel-away strip removed.

ATM and CONVERTIBLE BOOKLET TEST PANES

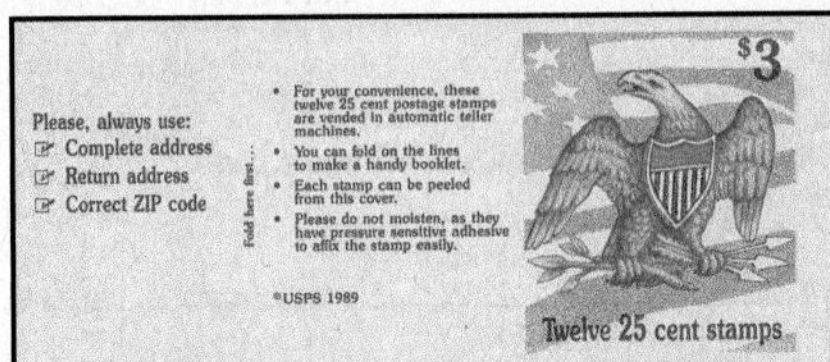

Eagle and Flag Pane Cover — TBC40

Stamp Layout — TBP40

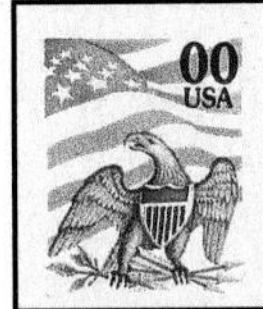

Eagle and Flag — TBE40

Printed by Bureau of Engraving & Printing.

1989 Tagged ***Imperf.***
Self-Adhesive

TDB80 TBE40 00c **multicolored** *125.*
a. TDP40 $3 **red and blue,** (TBC40), pane of 12 slick-surfaced paper on both sides *1,500.*
b. As "a," without cover, piece of printed web containing 24 stamps from four panes, with horizontal and vertical inter-pane gutters *3,000.*
c. As "a," without cover, pair of unsevered panes with vertical inter-pane gutter *4,500.*
d. As "a," slick-surfaced paper on stamp side only *2,250.*

Shiny, Water-Activated Gum

TDB81 TBE40 00c **multicolored** *200.*
a. TBP40 Pane of 12 *2,500.*

The backing paper serves as a booklet cover on No. TDB80a and TDB80d. At least one pane of No. TBD80d exists not fully trimmed, with "Paper Corp" handwritten in the right margin. The liner printing is clearly visible on the thinner No. TDB80a when looking at the stamp side of the pane without backlighting.

No. TDB81 does not have a cover, and does not require backing paper since it is printed on paper with water-activated gum. No. TDB81a panes exist not fully trimmed with colored EE registration markings in the left or right margins.

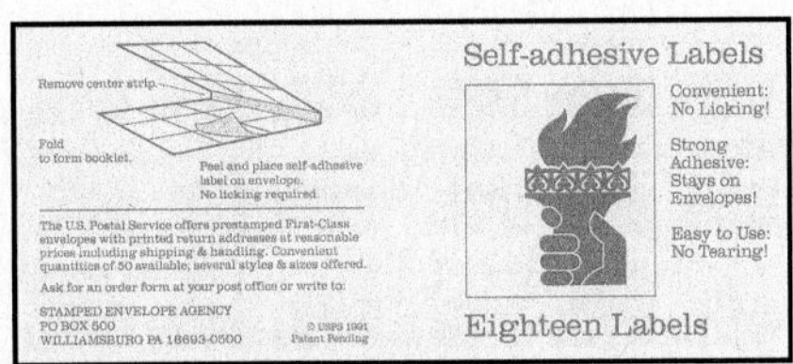

Statue of Liberty Torch Pane Cover — TBC41

Stamp Layout TBP41

Green Liberty Torch TBE41

Printed by Avery Dennison.

1990 Untagged ***Die Cut***
Self-Adhesive

TDB82 TBE41 **green** .50
a. TBP41 *green* (TBC41), pane of 18 10.00

Individual stamps contain different portions of the "ATM TEST / DEMONSTRATION SHEET" text at the left side.

No. TDB82 is similar in design to No. 2531Ae.

Similar to No. 2475a Overprinted in Black "SPECIMEN / FOR ATM TEST" on Each Stamp

Blank Sheetlet Back — TBC42

Flag Pane Cover — TBC43

Stamp Layout — TBP42

Flag — TBE42

Printed by Avery Dennison.

1990 Untagged ***Imperf.***
Printed on Plastic Without Liner Paper

TDB83 TBE42 25c **dark red & dark blue** —
a. TBP42 Pane of 12 with no printing on back (TBC42) —

Die Cut
Printed on Plastic With Self-Adhesive Liner Paper

TDB84 TBE42 25c **dark red & dark blue** —
a. TBP42 Pane of 12 with blue liner writing on back (TBC43) —

A black overprint was applied that reads "SPECIMEN / FOR ATM TEST." The liner writing on the back of No. TDB84a Printed Pane Cover - TBC43 is different than on the issued No. 2475a ATM pane. There are four repeating lines of text that read, "(dot) DO NOT WET (dot / dot) Plastic Stamp (dot) For ATM Use (dot) / (dot) Do not moisten (dot) Self-adhesive (dot) /(dot) (copyright symbol) USPS 1989 (dot) Patent Pending (dot)."

NCR and the United States Postal Service –
A partnership for progress through ATMs

NCR/USPS Flag Sheetlet Back — TBC42A

TDB84B Stamp Layout — TBP42A

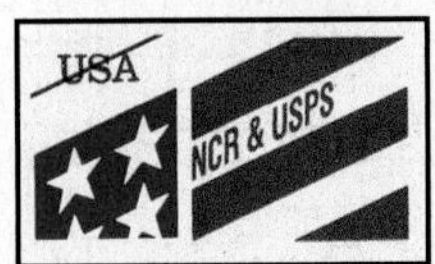

NCR/USPS Flag — TBE42A

Produced by NCR

Without Gum

1990s **Litho.** ***Imperf.***
Untagged

TDB84B TBE42A **red and blue** —
c. TBP42A Pane of 12 with blue printing on back (TBC42A) —

This ATM sheetlet was printed on regular weight plain paper.

NCR Flag Sheetlet Back — TBC42B

TDB84D Stamp Layout — TBP42B

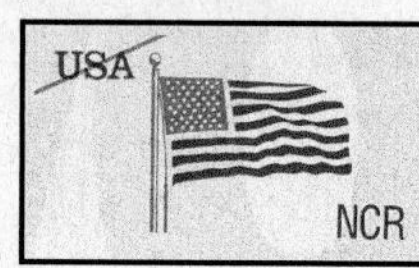

NCR Flag — TBE42B

Produced by NCR

Without Gum

1990s **Litho.** ***Imperf.***
Untagged

TDB84D TBE42B **red and blue** —
e. TBP42B Pane of 12 with red and blue printing on back (TBC42B) —

This ATM sheetlet was printed on regular weight plain paper.

TDB84F Stamp Layout — TBP42C

Red Rose — TBE42C

Without Gum

1990s **Litho.** ***Imperf.***
Untagged

TDB84F TBE42C 29c **red, green and black** —
g. TBP42C Pane of 18 without printing on back (TBC42) —

The No. TDB84Fg ATM pane was printed on regular-weight plain paper.

Stamp Layout — TBP44

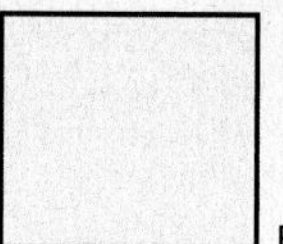
Blank — TBE44

Produced by Dittler Brothers.

1992 **Untagged** ***Die Cut***
Self-Adhesive

TDB85 TBE44 **blank** —
a. TBP44 *blank,* pane of 18 *750.00*
b. As "a," without die cuts 300.00

Nos. TDB85a and TDB85b were produced on thick self-adhesive paper similar to No. 2596a postage stamps, and were used for testing Postal Buddy machines. Backing paper of Nos. TDB85a and TDB85b reads "SELF-ADHESIVE DO NOT WET" on the stamp side of the backing paper. The die cuts on the front of No. TDB85 panes and the roulettes on the liner where the center peel strip was supposed to be located are typically misaligned.

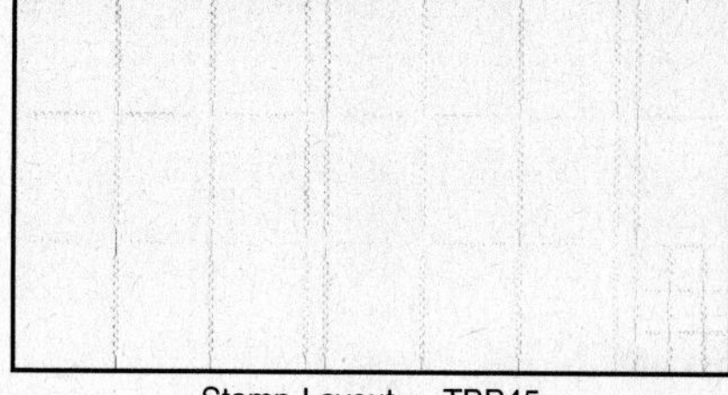
Stamp Layout — TBP45

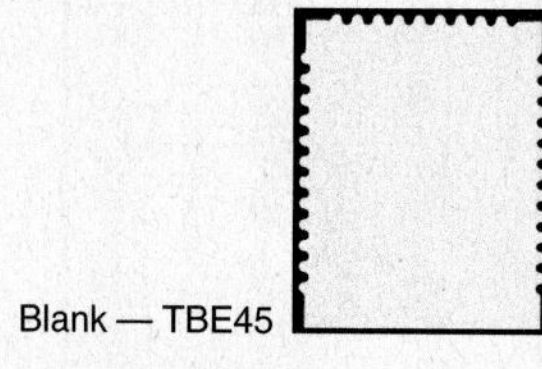
Blank — TBE45

Produced by Bureau of Engraving and Printing.

1996 **Tagged** ***Serpentine Die Cut 10***
Self-Adhesive

TDB86 TBE45 **blank** 30.00
a. TBP45 *blank,* pane of 20 + reorder label (TBC42) 600.00

There is no printing to identify who produced this pane. The "Tic-tac-toe" style of defacement die-cutting in the corner where the reorder label is located on regular panes is only found on Nos. 3112a, 3176a and 3244a convertible booklets produced by the Bureau of Engraving and Printing.

TBC46

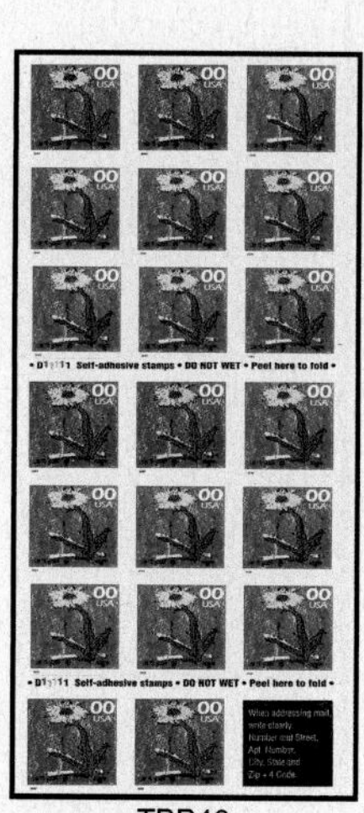
TBP46

TBP47

Flower TBE46

Flower TBE47

Printed in a joint venture of Dittler Brothers and the American Bank Note Co.

Self-Adhesive

1997 **Photo. & Engr.** **Tagged** ***Imperf.***
Design Size: 18x17mm

TDB87 TBE46 00c **multicolored** 375.00

Photo.

TDB88 TBE47 00c **multicolored** 250.00

Nos. TBD87 and TDB88 were printed at the same time on the same web. No. TDB87 was printed from one intaglio and five gravure plates, while Nos. TDB88 was printed from just the five gravure plates. Nos. TDB87 and TDB88 were printed in panes of 20 + reorder label, but all known panes have been cut into singles, pairs, strips of 3 or blocks. The backside printing consists of text and emblems related to Dittler Brothers and the American Banknote Company. No. TBC46 back cover image applies to both Nos. TBP46 and TBP47 stamp layout images. Nos. TBP46 and TBP47 stamp layout images and No. TBC46 back cover image were computer generated by reconstructing partial images found on the front and back of individual stamps cut from the panes.

A press sheet containing just the black intaglio printing exists. It has not been cut up.

See Nos. TD129A-TD129B.

Temple Pane Cover — TBC48

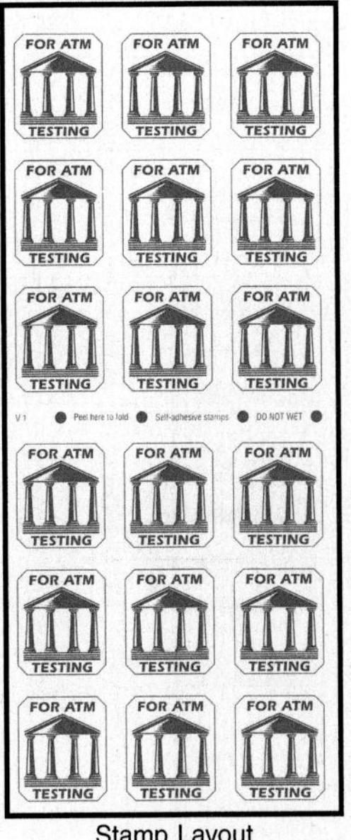

Stamp Layout
TBP48

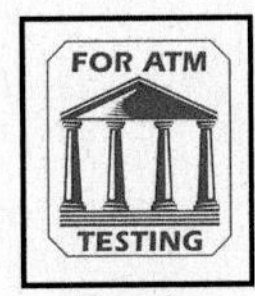

Temple
TBE48

Printed by Avery Dennison.

1997 **Untagged** ***Die Cut***
Self-Adhesive

TDB89	TBE48	**dark blue**	12.50
a.	TBP48	*dark blue* (TBC48), pane of 18	225.00

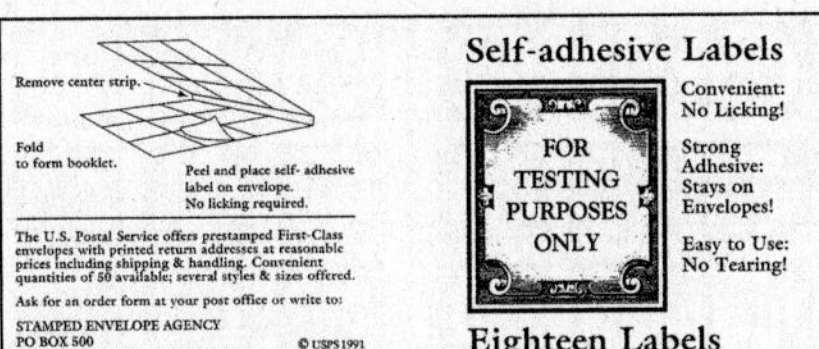

"For Testing Purposes Only" Pane Cover — TBC49

TDB90a, TDB91a, TDB92a
Stamp Layout — TBP49

TBE49

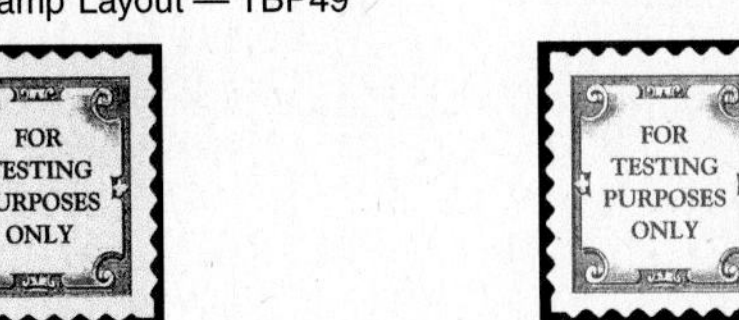

TBE50

TBE51

Printed by Avery Dennison.

1997 **Untagged** ***Die Cut***
Self-Adhesive

TDB90	TBE49	**black**	7.00
a.	TBP49	*black* (TBC49), pane of 18	130.00

Serpentine Die Cut 7¾

TDB91	TBE50	**black**	1.00
a.	TBP49	*black* (TBC49), pane of 18	12.50
TDB92	TBE51	**magenta**	14.00
a.	TBP49	*blue* (TBC49), pane of 18	250.00

George Clinton — TBE52

Stamp Layout
TBP52

Printed by Ashton-Potter (USA) Ltd.

Serpentine Die Cut 11¼x11½
1998 **Engr.** **Tagged**
Self-Adhesive

TDB93	TBE52 00c **blue gray**	10.00
	Envelope with 8 #TDB93 on back	100.00

Imperf.

TDB93A	TBE52 00c **blue gray**	15.00
b.	TBP52 pane of 18 without printing on back (TBC42)	300.00

No. TDB93 was printed in booklet panes of 18 from a 324-subject plate. Full No. TDB93 booklet panes with serpentine die cuts are unknown in collector hands; all known examples of No. TDB93 were affixed to envelope backs for use in USPS mailing tests.

No. TDB93A is an imperforate convertible booklet pane cut from a press sheet. Each of the 18 panes in the press sheet is separated by a gutter. Various registration marks can be found in some margins and gutters.

The 324-subject printing plate for No. TDB93A consists of 6 ATM panes wide by 3 ATM panes tall for a total of 18 ATM panes per plate impression.

See No. TD130F.

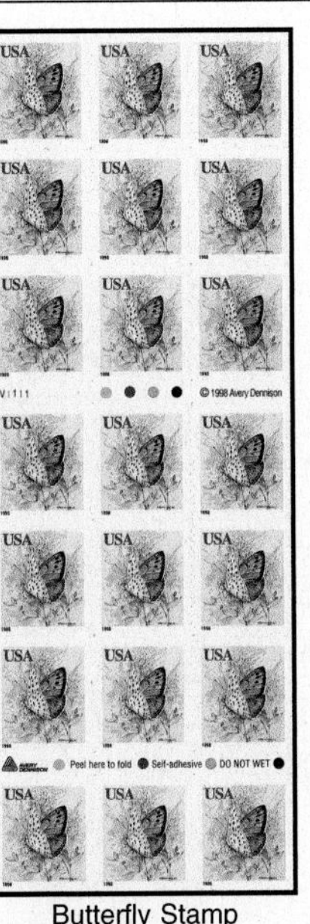

Butterfly Stamp
Layout — TBP53

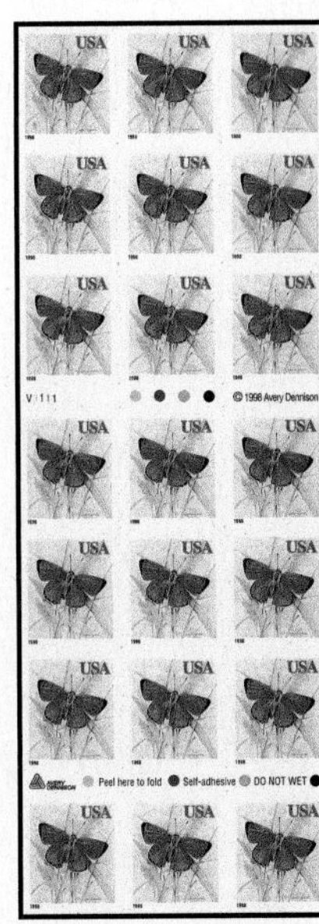

Butterfly Stamp Layout
— TBP53a

Yellow and Violet Butterfly — TBE53

Orange Butterfly — TBE53a

Printed by Avery Dennison.

1998 **Litho.** **Untagged** ***Serpentine Die Cut 11***
Self-Adhesive

TDB94	TBE53	**multicolored** + 1998 date	—
TDB95	TBE53a	**multicolored** + 1998 date	—
a.	TBP53-TBP53a	*multicolored,* double-sided pane of 42, 21 each #TDB94-TDB95	—

No. TDB95a has a 1998 copyright date in the center peel strip and each stamp has a small black "1998" date under the lower left corner of the design. The center peel strip on each side shows the stamps were copyrighted by Avery Dennison.

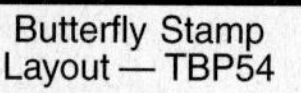
Butterfly Stamp Layout — TBP54

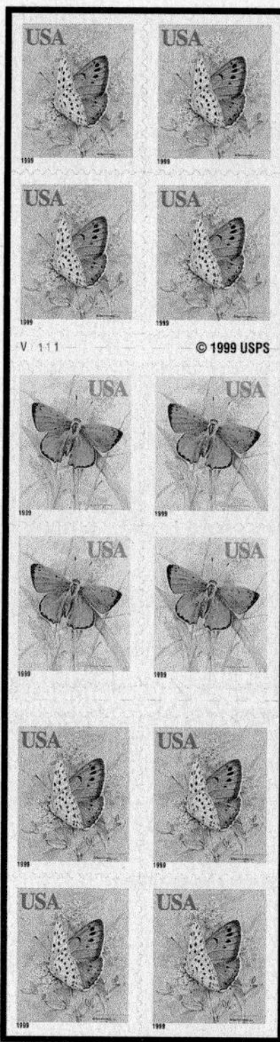

Butterfly Stamp Layout — TBP54a

Printed by Avery Dennison.

1999 Litho. Tagged *Serpentine Die Cut 11*
Self-Adhesive

TDB96 TBE53 **multicolored** + 1999 date —
TDB97 TBE53a **multicolored** + 1999 date —
a. TBP54-TBP54a *multicolored,* double-sided pane of 20, 12 #TDB96, 8 #TDB97 —

No. TDB97a has a 1999 copyright date in the center peel strip and each stamp has a small black 1999 date under the lower left corner of the design. The center peel strip on each side shows these stamps were copyrighted by USPS, rather than Avery Dennison like those on No. TDB95a. The only difference between the TBE53 and TBE53a stamp designs on Nos. TDB95a and TDB97a is the date on the stamps. No. TDB97a is a complete double-sided booklet. Eight stamps plus P# and the booklet cover (TBC54) are printed on one side of the peelable backing paper, and 12 stamps plus P# appear on the other side of the backing paper.

Part of Back Cover TBC55

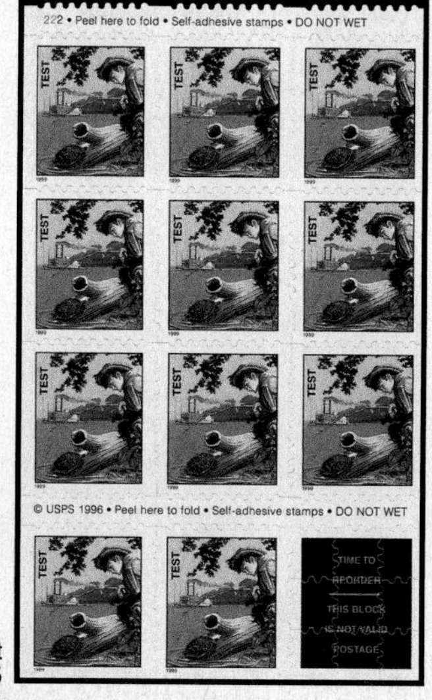

Stamp Layout TBP55

Tom Sawyer — TBE55

Printed by Bureau of Engraving and Printing

1999 Litho. *Serpentine Die Cut 10*
Self-Adhesive

TDB98 TBE55 **multicolored** —
a. TBP55 *multicolored,* (TBC55) pane of 20 plus reorder label —

The only known example of No. TDB98 has plate #2222, indicating it was printed by the BEP. The "tic-tac-toe" style die cutting on the reorder label was only used on BEP produced convertible booklets. No complete panes are known.

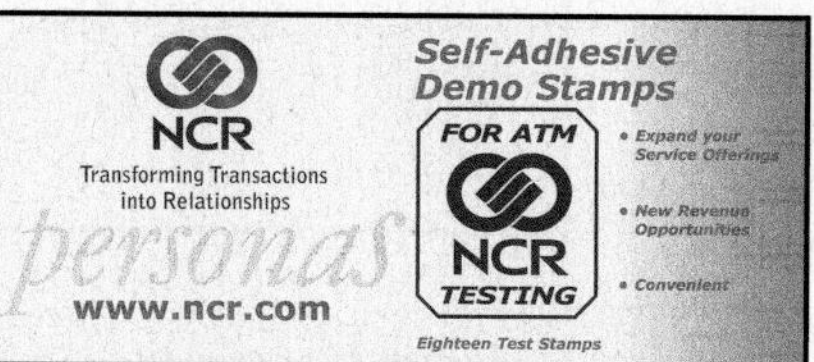

NCR Pane Cover — TBC56

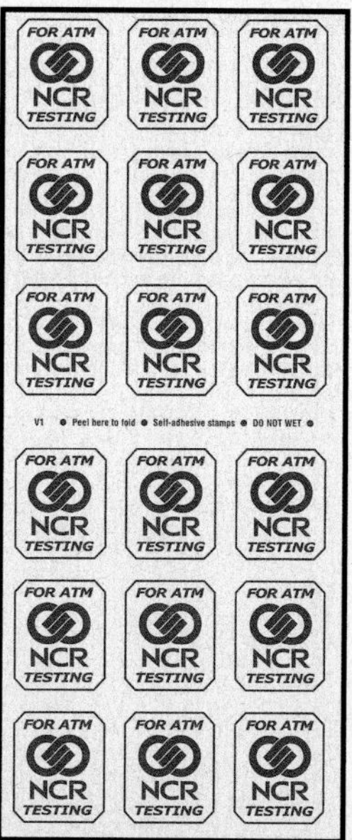

TDB99 Stamp Layout TBP56

NCR Emblem TBE56

Printed by Systemedia for NCR.

2000 Litho. Without Gum *Imperf.*
Untagged

TDB99 TBE56 **black** —
a. TBP56 (TBC56), pane of 18 75.00

This ATM Sheetlet is printed on regular weight plain paper.

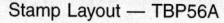

Stamp Layout — TBP56A

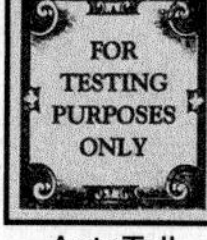

AutoTell Systems — TBE56A

1990s Without Gum *Imperf.*
Untagged

TDB99B TBE56A **black,** *white* —
c. TBP56A pane of 18 with no printing on back (TBC42) —

This ATM sheetlet is printed on regular weight plain white paper.

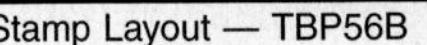

Stamp Layout — TBP56B

Wincor AutoTell LLC — TBE56B

2000 Litho. Without Gum *Imperf.*
Untagged

TDB99D TBE56B **black,** *gray* —
e. TBP56B pane of 18 with no printing on back (TBC42) —

This ATM sheetlet is printed on regular weight plain gray paper made by the Crane Company, using recycled U.S. currency. Some panes show part of the Crane Company watermark that includes the words "OLD MONEY."

Stamp Layout TBP57

"For Test Purposes Only" — TBE57

Printed by Avery Dennison.

2005 Untagged *Serpentine Die Cut 7¾*
Self-Adhesive

TDB100 TBE57 **blue** 7.00
a. TBP57 *black,* (TBC49) pane of 18 110.00

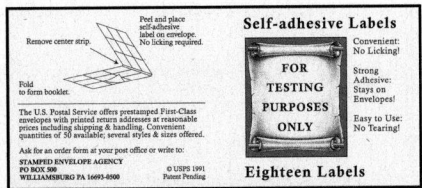

"For Testing Purposes Only" Cover — TBC58

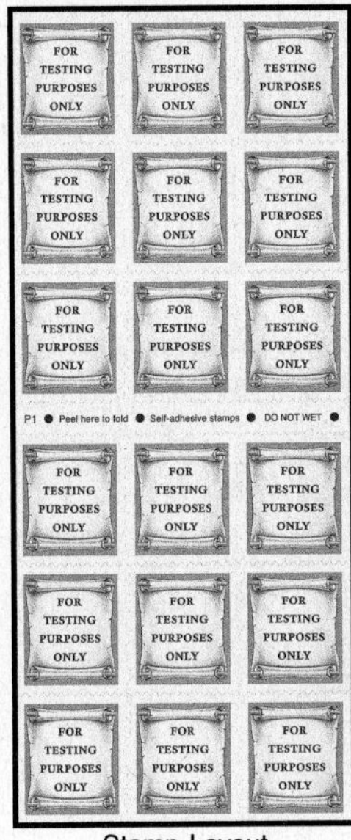

Stamp Layout TBP58

"For Testing Purposes Only" TBE58

Printed by Ashton-Potter (USA) Ltd.

2009 *Serpentine Die Cut 11¼x11*

TDB101 TBE58 **blue** *7.00*
a. TBP58 *black* (TBC58), pane of 18 150.00

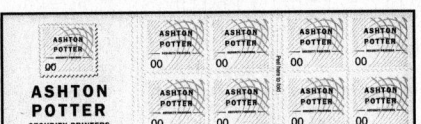

Cover Layout — TBP59

Stamp Layout — TBP59a

Ashton-Potter — TBE59

Printed by Ashton-Potter (USA) Ltd.

2005 Litho. *Serpentine Die Cut 11¼x10¾*
Self-Adhesive

TDB102 TBE59 **multicolored** —
a. TBP59-TBP59a (TBC59), pane of 20 —

No. TDB102 has no plate number in a peel strip. While there is no date printed on the stamps, the panes were likely produced between 2005 and 2007. The peel strips on the side with 8 stamps have 10¾ gauge rouletting, while the peel strips on the side with 12 stamps have no rouletting. The panes were printed on prephosphored paper that was treated to mask the phosphorescence of the yellow green tagging.

TEST STAMP ESSAYS, TRIAL COLOR, AND PLATE PROOFS

TD19P1

Bureau of Engraving & Printing

1910 **Engr.**

TD19P1 **red,** large die on India paper, die sunk on card *2,000.*

No. TD19P1 (199x152mm) has a blue control number "400894" on reverse.

TDP20P1

Bureau of Engraving & Printing

1910 **Typo.**

TD20P1 **black,** large die on thick glazed card *2,000.*

No. TD20P1 (73x83mm) has a control number "420279" and manuscript "first die proof impression of experimental surface die from surface print, JER April 25/10" on reverse.

TDP20P2

Bureau of Engraving & Printing

1910 **Typo.**

TD20P2 **red,** large die on thick glazed card *1,500.*

No. TD20P2 (73x83mm) has manuscript inscription in blue ink "Sample of surface printing from die: Done by Bureau E. & P. 5/20/1910" on front below design, with rubber hand-stamp"420270" on reverse. Another TD20P2 die proof on thick card stock has been cut down to stamp-design size, with control number "420391" (missing last digit) on reverse, Value, $1,000.

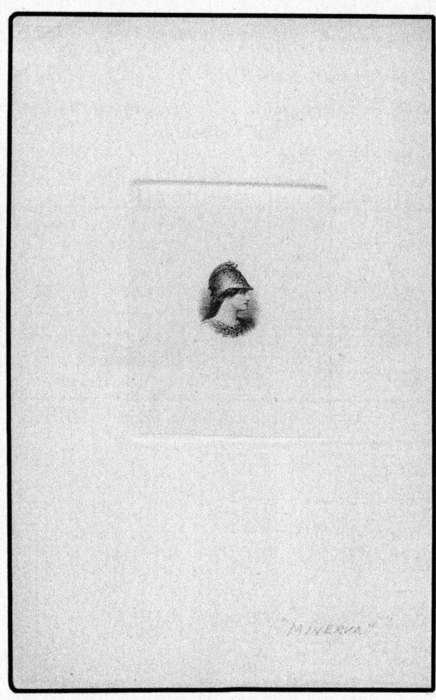
TD28-E1 Minerva Head Essay

No. TD28-E1 (105 x161 mm) is the engraved vignette of Minerva that is found on TD28. The die may have been produced by the Bureau of Engraving and Printing.

1910 **Engr.**

TD28-E1 **black,** large die essay on India, die sunk on card *1,250.*

No. TD28TC1ae

Bureau of Engraving & Printing

TD28TC1a

1910 **Engr.**

TD28TC1a Die on India, die sunk on card

- ***e.*** **blue** *850.*
- ***f.*** **carmine** *850.*
- ***g.*** **dark brown** *850.*
- ***h.*** **dark green** *850.*
- ***i.*** **dark violet brown** *850.*

Nos. TE28TC1ae and TD28TC1ai are known cut down to resemble small die proofs.

TD28TC1d Die on thick glazed card, die sunk, **black** *1,000.*

No. TD28TC1d was probably used in a photo-mechanical process to produce a 192-subject offset plate that was used to print sheets of No. TD28 test stamps on a Harris Offset Printing Press in a June 1910 demonstration at the Bureau of Engraving and Printing.

TD130F-E1

Design size: 18x16½mm
Die size: 112x152mm

1993

TD130F-E1 **black,** large die on wove, die sunk on 133x182mm card *950.00*

Die I. Horizontal lines in lower background are neither continuous nor straight, eyes are dark and squinty, little shading on forehead, nose and chin. Apparently found to be unacceptable and neither improved nor used further.

TD130F-E2

Design size: 18x16½mm
Die size: 80x80mm

TD130F-E2 **black,**large die printed directly on 153x115mm wove paper (top of paper has been trimmed off) *350.00*

Die II. First state of the die. Straight horizontal lines lines in the lower background, hair consists of many short lines, no forehead shading. One example known with thin crosshair lines printed outside the design; one example known with "1st PF R. Baratz" in pencil at bottom right of paper.

TD130F-E3

Design size: 18x16½mm
Die size: 80x80mm

TD130F-E3 **black,** large die printed directly on 153x115mm wove paper *350.00*

As No. TD130F-E2, but with pencil shading added to the background to suggest improvements to be made. One example is known with crosshairs on the die on all four sides.

TD130F-E4

Design size: 18x16½mm
Die size: 80x80mm

TD130F-E4 **black,** large die printed directly on ungummed paper *500.00*

The darker shading lines in the background have been engrvaved further as suggested on No. TD130F-E3. One example is known with thin crosshair lines on the die on all four sides.

TD130F-E5

Design size: 18x16½mm
Die size: 80x80mm

TD130F-E5 **black,** large die on India, die sunk on 228x152mm card *350.00*

Several additions were made to the No. TD139F-E4 die, adding dashed shading lines over Clinton's entire face including cross-hatched lines on the right side of his face, additions to background engraving. One example is known with small holes punched near the outside edge on all four sides. This is the final oval design before it was converted into a round circle design.

TD130F-E6

Design size: 18mm circle
Die size: 80x80mm

1993

TD130F-E6 **black,** large die on wove, die sunk on 228x152mm card *750.00*

Die II oval design converted to a circular, round design. Outline added all around and areas at top and bottom partly engraved to fill in the design. One example known with pencil notation "4/21/94 RB" (R.Baratz) at bottom right.

TD130F-E7

Design size: 18mm circle
Die size: 80x80mm

TD130F-E7 **black,** large die on 80x80mm wove paper *350.00*

Similar to No. TD130F-6, but it has additional engraving added at the bottom to fill in the design. The 80x80mm wove paper may have been removed from a large card after printing. As was the case with Die I, this Die II also was not used to create the engraved final TD130FP1 die proof. Almost nothing on either Die I or Die II matches the details on the vignette of the Die III proof.

TD130F-P1

Design size: 18x23mm Design size of vignette: 18x16½ oval
Die size: 98x90mm

TD130FP1 **blue gray,** large die on India, die sunk on 228x152mm card *750.00*

Engraved complete design as adopted. Both lines of the background grid shading are at an angle. Two examples known with "BEP #1" pencil notation, one known with "BEP-2" pencil notation.

CHRISTMAS SEALS

Issued by the American National Red Cross (1907-1919), the National Tuberculosis Association (1920-1967), the National Tuberculosis and Respiratory Disease Association (1968-1972) and the American Lung Association (1973-).

While the Christmas Seal is not a postage stamp, it has long been associated with the postal service because of its use on letters and packages.

Einar Holboell, an employee of the Danish Post Office, created the Christmas Seal. He believed that seal sales could raise money for charity. The post offices of Denmark, Iceland and Sweden began to sell such seals in the 1904 Christmas season. In the United States, Christmas Seals were first issued in 1907 under the guidance of Emily P. Bissell, following the suggestion of Jacob Riis, social service worker.

Until 1975, all seals (except those of 1907 and 1908 type I) were issued in sheets of 100. The grilled gum (1908) has small square depressions like a waffle. The broken gum (1922), devised to prevent paper curling, consists of depressed lines in the gum, ½mm. apart, forming squares. The vertical and horizontal broken gum (1922, 1923, 1925, 1927-1932) forms diamonds. The perf. 12.00 (1917-1919, 1923, 1925, 1931) has two larger and wider-spaced holes between every 11 smaller holes.

Values are for unused seals with original gum and very-fine centering.

Values for covers are for seals that are tied. Values for 1907-24 are for seals tied on post card or postal card; values for 1925-31 are for seals tied either on card or on cover; values for 1932 to present are for seals tied on envelopes. The 1907-24 seals on cover and 1932+ seals on card sell for more. Values are for non-philatelic and contemporaneous uses. Philatelic and non-contemporaneous uses are worth considerably less.

Seals can be tied by postmark, auxiliary postal marking, private business receiving stamp, offset cancel ink, overlap by canceled stamp or tied seal, or message. Tied seal values are enhanced if the seals are used as postage, tied by meters, used in multiples, used with certain back-of-the-book stamps, used on nonstandard size mailings, double-tied with another organization's seal, to or from a famous individual, to or from a foreign country, with a Christmas seal slogan cancel, or have a nonphilatelic Christmas day cancel.

SEALS ISSUED BY THE DELAWARE CHAPTER OF THE AMERICAN NATIONAL RED CROSS

CS1 (Type I)

Type II — WX2

Designer — Emily P. Bissell.
Nearly $4,000 worth of seals were sold, $3,000 cleared.

Type I — "Merry Christmas" only.
Type II — "Merry Christmas" and "Happy New Year."

1907 ***Perf. 14***

WX1	CS1 Type I	17.50	
	On cover		1,000.
a.	Horiz. pair, imperf. between	1,000.	
b.	Horiz. pair, imperf. vert.	300.00	
c.	Vert. pair, imperf. between	750.00	
	On cover		—
WX2	CS1 Type II	15.00	
	On cover		1,500.
	On cover, both types I and II		*6,750.*
a.	Vert. pair, imperf. between	1,000.	

Types I and II litho. by Theo. Leonhardt & Son, Philadelphia, Pa. The 1st seals were sold Dec. 7, 1907, in Wilmington, Del. Issued in sheets of 228 (19x12). Type II was issued to extend the sale of seals until New Year's Day, 1908. Nos. WX1 and WX2 were sold in only three cities: Wilmington, DE; Philadelphia, PA and Washington D.C. Postmarks from other cities need to be authenticated.

All pairs of No. WX1c also have an imperforate top margin.

Counterfeits of both types exist (perf. 12).

Earliest documented use: No. WX1, Dec. 7, 1907; No. WX2, Dec. 23, 1907.

SEALS ISSUED BY THE AMERICAN NATIONAL RED CROSS

CS2 (Type II)

Designer — Howard Pyle. Sales $135,000.

Type I — frame lines with square corners, small "C" in "Christmas," ear of "8" separate from body of the "8."
Type Ia—frame lines have square corners, small "C" in "Christmas," ear of "8" is joined to the "8."
Type II — frame lines have rounded corners, large "C" in "Christmas," leaves veined.

1908 ***Perf. 14***

WX3	CS2 Type I, perf. 14, smooth gum	35.00	
	On cover		15.00
a.	Perf. 12, smooth gum	45.00	
c.	Perf. 14, grilled gum	100.00	
d.	Perf. 12, grilled gum	50.00	
e.	As #WX3, bklt. pane of 6	500.00	
f.	As "c," bklt. pane of 6	600.00	
g.	As #WX3, bklt. pane of 3	600.00	
	On cover		225.00
l.	Roulette 6¾, without gum	75.00	
	On cover		1,500.

Perf. 12

WX3H	CS2 Type Ia, smooth gum	75.00	
	On cover		15.00
i.	Type Ia, grilled gum	60.00	
j.	Type Ia, perf. 14, smooth gum	55.00	
k.	Type Ia, perf. 14, grilled gum	100.00	
m.	Roulette 6¾, without gum	125.00	
	On cover		500.00
WX4	CS2 Type II	30.00	
	On cover		20.00
a.	Booklet pane of 6	190.00	
b.	Booklet pane of 3	125.00	
	On cover		225.00

Type I litho. by Theo. Leonhardt & Son. Sheets of 250 (14x18), with the 1st space in the 9th and 18th rows left blank.

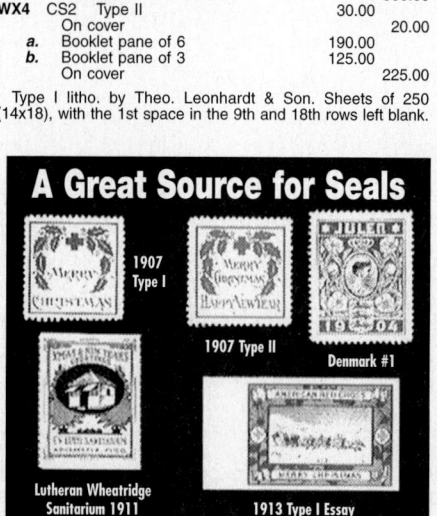

Type II litho. by American Bank Note Co., New York, N.Y. in sheets of 100 (10x10).

Booklet panes have straight edges on 3 sides and perforated on left side where there is a stub, except No. WX4b which is a vert. strip of 3 with stub at top. Panes of 6 were made up in books of 24 and 48 and sold for 25c and 50c, and panes of 3 in books of 9 sold for 10c. The grilled gum has small square depressions like on a waffle.

The 1908 roulette No. WX31 and WX3Hm were provisionals to alleviate shortages. All known postmarks on No. WX31 are from Cincinnati or Pittsburgh and No. WX3Hm was used in Portland, OR. All other postmarks on these seals need to be authenticated.

Earliest document use: No. WX3, Nov. 29, 1908; No. WX3g, Dec. 13, 1908; No. WX3l, Dec. 21, 1908; No. WX3H, Nov. 30, 1908; No. WX3Hm, Dec. 17, 1908; No. WX4, Dec. 2, 1908; No. WX4b, Dec. 2, 1908.

CS3

Designer — Carl Wingate. Sales $250,000.

1909 ***Perf. 12***

WX5	CS3 One type only	1.25	
	On cover		8.00
a.	Overprinted "New Hampshire"	10.00	
	On cover		350.00

Litho. by The Strobridge, Cincinnati, Ohio. Seals with a round punched hole of 3½mm are printers' samples.

"New Hampshire" overprint was created by state's Red Cross with permission of the national office. Overprint is in dark carmine. Counterfeits exist in red and orange red.

Earliest document uses: No. WX5, Nov. 19, 1909; WX5a, Dec. 4, 1909.

CS4

Designer — Frances Thompson. Sales $300,000.

1910 ***Perf. 12***

WX6	CS4 One type only	20.00	
	On cover		8.00
a.	Horiz. pair, imperf. between	—	
b.	Vert. pair, imperf. between	—	

Lithographed by The Strobridge Lithographing Co.
Earliest documented use: Nov. 23, 1910.

SEALS ISSUED BY THE AMERICAN NATIONAL RED CROSS

(But sold by the National Association for the Study and Prevention of Tuberculosis)

"The Old Home Among the Cedars" — CS5 (Type II)

Designer — Anton Rudert under directions of F. D. Millet. Sales $320,000.

Type I — diameter of circle 22mm, solid end in house.
Type II — same circle but thinner, lined end to house.
Type III — diameter of circle 20mm, lined end to house.
Type IV — green windows on house and green berries at bottom.
Type V — design same as types II and III.

1911 ***Perf. 12***

WX7	CS5 Type I	50.00	
	On cover		8.00
WX8	CS5 Type II	120.00	
	On cover		250.00

COIL STAMP

Perf. 8½ Vertically

WX9	CS5 Type III	50.00	
	On cover		2,000.

Rouletted 12 in red x 6 colorless

WX9A	CS5 Type IV	750.00	
	On cover		1,500.

COIL STAMP

WX9B	CS5 Type V	*2,700.*	
	On cover		—

Typo. by Eureka, Scranton, Pa. Type I has name and address of printer and union label in red in top margin. Type II has union label only in green on left margin.

No. WX9B was issued imperforate, but all examples were privately perforated with U.S. Automatic Vending Company type II separations. This is the rarest national seal with only seven documented examples.

Earliest documented use: No. WX7, Nov. 24, 1911; No. WX8, Dec. 11, 1911; No. WX9, Dec. 22, 1911; No. WX9A, Dec. 15, 1911; No. WX9B, no tied examples known.

CS6

Designer — John H. Zeh. Sales $402,256.

1912 ***Perf. 12***

WX10	CS6 One type only	11.00	
	On cover		8.00

Lithographed by The Strobridge Lithographing Co.
Earliest documented use: Nov. 26, 1912.

CS7 (Type I)

Designer — C. J. Budd. Sales $449,505.

Type I — with Poinsettia flowers and green circles around red crosses at either side.
Type II — the Poinsettia flowers have been removed, and the bottom left of the upper ribbon with "American Red Cross" has closed curl filled in green.
Type IIa — the Poinsettia flowers have been removed, and the bottom left of the upper ribbon with "American Red Cross" has open curl filled in red.
Type III — the Poinsettia flowers and green circles have been removed.
Type IV — similar to type IIa, with slight differences (on coarse paper; may have printing on back)

1913 ***Perf. 12***

WX11	CS7 Type I	1,400.	
WX12	CS7 Type II	7.50	
	On cover		1,000.
WX12A	CS7 Type IIa	7.50	
	On cover		1,500.
WX13	CS7 Type III	8.50	
	On cover		8.00

Imperf

WX14	CS7 Type IV	600.00	
	On cover		2,000.

Lithographed by American Bank Note Co.

Only a single sheet of No. WX11 was printed, and it was not sold to the public. Any examples on cover are fakes.

Earliest documented use: No. WX12, Nov. 11, 1913; No. WX12A, Dec. 16, 1913; No. WX13, Nov. 24, 1913; No. WX14; Dec. 24, 1913.

CS8

Designer — Benjamin S. Nash. Sales $555,854.

1914 ***Perf. 12***

WX15	CS8 One type only	10.00	
	On cover		8.00

Lithographed by The Strobridge Lithographing Co.

Earliest documented use: Nov. 26, 1914.

CS9

Designer — Benjamin S. Nash. Sales $760,000.

1915

WX16	CS9	Perf. 12½	10.00	
		On cover		8.00
a.		Perf. 12	65.00	
		On cover		—

Lithographed by Andrew B. Graham Co., Washington, D.C.
Earliest documented use: No. WX16, Nov. 22, 1915.

CS10

Designer — T. M. Cleland. Sales $1,040,810.

1916

WX18	CS10	Perf. 12	5.00	
		On cover		8.00
a.		Perf. 12x12½	6.00	
b.		Perf. 12½x12	15.00	
c.		Perf. 12½	14.00	

Lithographed by the Strobridge Lithographing Co.
Earliest documented use: Nov. 27, 1916.

Seals of 1917-21 are on coated paper.

CS11

Designer — T. M. Cleland. Sales $1,815,110.

1917

WX19	CS11	Perf. 12	2.00	
		On cover		8.00
a.		Perf. 12½	15.00	
c.		Perf. 12x12½	20.00	

Typographed by Eureka Specialty Printing Co.
Perf. 12 has two larger and wider-spaced holes between; every eleven smaller holes.
Sheets come with straight edged margins on all four sides also with perforated margins at either right or left. Perforated margins have the union label imprint in green.
Earliest documented use: Oct. 23, 1917.

SEALS ISSUED BY THE AMERICAN NATIONAL RED CROSS
(Distributed by the National Tuberculosis Association)

CS12

Designer — Charles A. Winter.
These seals were given to members and others in lots of 10, the Natl. Tuberculosis Assoc. being subsidized by a gift of $2,500,000 from the American National Red Cross.
To aid the collector in understanding the complex issues Nos. WX21 and WX22, the following abbreviations are used in the listings:
VM — Varying margins: 1918 Type II booklet panes of 10 (2x5) with varying margins, show perfs. or roulettes on one or both sides of the pane. Cut from press sheets with perf. or rouletted vert. gutters. The cut normally was inaccurate, creating a straight edge on one pane and a tiny perf. or rouletted margin on the next pane.
P4S — Perfed on all four sides, from a sheet of 100 or nonstandard booklet pane.
SE3S — Straight edge on three sides of the booklet pane.
SE4S — Straight edge on all four sides of the booklet pane.
PMT — Perforated margin at top.
PMB — Perforated margin at bottom.
PML — Perforated margin at left.
PMR — Perforated margin at right.

Type I — "American Red Cross" 15mm long, heavy circles between date.
Type II — "American Red Cross" 15½mm long, periods between date.

1918

WX21	CS12	Type I, perf. 11½x12, P4S	7.50	
		On cover		25.00
a.		Perf. 12, P4S	10.00	
		On cover		500.00
b.		Perf. 12, booklet pane of 10, P4S	2.00	
d.		Perf. 12, booklet pane of 10, SE4S	2.00	
WX22	CS12	Type II, perf. 12½xRoulette 9½, from booklet pane	.60	
		On cover		40.00
a.		Perf. 12½, booklet pane of 10 (2x5), SE3S, PMT	2.00	
b.		Perf. 12½x12, bklt. pane of 10 (2x5), SE3S, PMT	—	
d.		Roulette 9½xPerf. 12½, bklt. pane of 10 (2x5), SE3S, PMT	50.00	
e.		Perf. 12½xRoulette 9½, bklt. pane of 10 (2x5), VM, SE at bottom, PMT	25.00	
f.		Perf. 12½, booklet pane of 10 (2x5), VM, SE at bottom, PMT	25.00	
h.		Roulette 9½xPerf. 12½, bklt. pane of 10 (2x5), VM, SE at bottom, PMT	25.00	
i.		Roulette 9½xPerf. 12½ booklet pane of 10 (2x5), VM, roulette 12½ at left, perf. 12½ through the center and at right	—	
j.		Perf. 12½, horiz. booklet pane of 10 (5x2), SE3S, PMR	50.00	
k.		Perf. 12½, except 2nd & 4th vert. rows perf. 12, horiz. bklt. pane of 10 (5x2), SE left & bottom, cut through perfs at right, PMT	—	
l.		Roulette 9½xPerf. 12½, horiz. booklet pane of 10 (5x2), SE3S, PMR	—	
m.		Perf. 12½, booklet pane of 10 (2x5), SE3S, PML	—	
n.		Perf. 12½, booklet pane of 10 (2x5), SE3S, PMB	35.00	

For Perf. 12, see note following No. WX19.
Type I typographed by Eureka Specialty Printing Co.
Booklet panes of 10 (2x5) normally have straight edges on all four sides. They were cut from the sheets of 100 and can be plated by certain flaws which occur on both. Sheets have union label imprint on top margin in brown.
Type II lithographed by Strobridge Lithographing Co.
Booklet panes are the same but normally have a perforated margin at top and stub attached. These too can be plated by flaws.
The seal with "American Red Cross" 17¼mm long is believed to be an essay.
Earliest documented use: No. WX21, Dec. 13, 1918; No. WX21a, Dec. 23, 1918; No. WX22, Dec. 8, 1918.

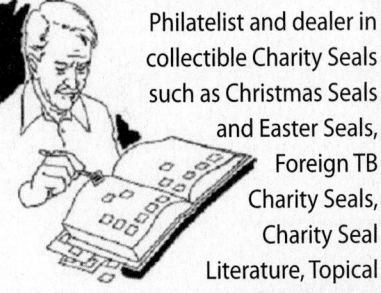

CS13 (Type I)

Designer — Ernest Hamlin Baker. Sales $3,872,534.
Type I — plume at right side of Santa's cap.
Type II — no plume but a white dot in center of band.

1919

WX24	CS13	Type I, perf. 12	.40	
		On cover		8.00
a.		Perf. 12x12	.60	
b.		Perf. 12½x12	.50	
WX25	CS13	Type II, perf. 12½	.40	
		On cover		8.00

For Perf. 12, see note following No. WX19.
This is the first time the double barred cross, the emblem of the National Tuberculosis Association, appeared in the design of the seals. It is also the last time the red cross emblem of the American National Red Cross was used on seals.
Type I typo. by Eureka, and has union label on margin at left in dark blue. Type II litho. by Strobridge.
Earliest documented use: No. WX24, Dec. 1, 1919; No. WX25, Nov. 28, 1919.

SEALS ISSUED BY THE NATIONAL TUBERCULOSIS ASSOCIATION

CS14

Designer — Ernest Hamlin Baker. Sales $3,667,834.

Type I — size of seal 18x22mm.
Type II — seal 18½x23½mm, letters larger & numerals heavier.

1920

WX26	CS14	Type I, perf. 12x12½	.50	
		On cover		8.00
a.		Perf. 12	.60	
b.		Perf. 12½x12	35.00	
c.		Perf. 12½	35.00	
WX27	CS14	Type II, perf. 12½	.50	
		On cover		10.00

Type I typo. by Eureka, and has union label imprint and rings on margin at left in dark blue. Type II litho. & offset by Strobridge.
Earliest documented use: No. WX26, Nov. 16, 1920; No. WX27, Dec. 2, 1920.

CS15

Designer — George V. Curtis. Sales $3,520,303.
Type I — dots in the chimney shading and faces are in diagonal lines, dots on chimney are separate except between the 2 top rows of bricks where they are solid.

Type II — dots in the chimney shading and faces are in horiz. lines.
Type III — as Type I except red dots on chimney are mostly joined forming lines, dots between the 2 top rows of bricks are not a solid mass.

1921

WX28 CS15 Type I, perf. 12½ .65
On cover 8.00
WX29 CS15 Type II, perf. 12½ .50
On cover 8.00
WX29A CS15 Type III, perf. 12 .50
On cover 20.00

Type I typo. by Eureka. Type II offset by Strobridge. Type III typo. by Zeese-Wilkinson Co., Long Island City, N.Y.
Earliest documented use: No. WX28, Nov. 23, 1921; No. WX29, Nov. 27, 1921; No. WX29A, Nov. 23, 1921.

CS16

Designer — T. M. Cleland. Sales $3,857,086.

1922

WX30 CS16 Perf. 12½, broken gum .80
On cover 8.00
a. Perf. 12, broken gum 3.00
b. Perf. 12x12½, broken gum 10.00
c. Perf. 12, smooth gum 3.00
d. Perf. 12½, vertical broken gum 3.00

Typographed by Eureka Specialty Printing Co.
The broken gum, which was devised to prevent curling of paper, consists of depressed lines in the gum ½mm apart, forming squares, or vertical broken gum forming diamonds.
Earliest documented use: Nov. 20, 1922.

CS17

Designer — Rudolph Ruzicka. Sales $4,259,660.

1923

WX31 CS17 Perf. 12½, vertical broken gum .30
On cover 8.00
a. Perf. 12, horizontal broken gum 3.00
b. Perf. 12, vertical broken gum 3.50
c. Perf. 12½x12, vertical broken gum 6.50

For perf 12, see note following No. WX19.
Typographed by Eureka Specialty Printing Co.
The broken gum on this and issues following printed by Eureka consists of very fine depressed lines forming diamonds.
Earliest documented use: Nov. 16, 1923.

CS18

Designer — George V. Curtis. Sales $4,479,656.

1924

WX32 CS18 One type only .30
On cover 8.00

Offset by Strobridge, E.&D., and U.S.P.& L.
Earliest documented use: Nov. 20, 1924.

CS19 (Type II)

Designer — Robert G. Eberhard. Sales $4,937,786.
Type I — red lines at each side of "1925" do not join red tablet below.
Type II — red lines, as in type I, join red tablet below.
Type III — as type I but shorter rays around flames and "ea" of "Health" smaller.

1925 ***Perf. 12½***

WX35 CS19 Type I, vert. broken gum .30
On cover 10.00
a. Perf. 12, vertical broken gum 3.50
b. Perf. 12x12½ vertical broken gum .60
WX36 CS19 Type II .30
On cover 250.00
WX37 CS19 Type III .75
On cover 100.00

For perf 12, see note following No. WX19.
Type I typo. by Eureka. Type II offset by E.&D. Type III litho. by Gugler Lithographing Co., Milwaukee.
Earliest documented use: No. WX35, Nov. 30, 1925; No. WX36, Nov. 9, 1925; No. WX37, Dec. 10, 1925.

CS20

Designer — George V. Curtis. Sales $5,121,872.

1926 ***Perf. 12½***

WX38 CS20 One type only .25
On cover 8.00

Offset by E.&D. and U.S.P.&L.
Printers' marks: E.&D. has a red dot at upper right on seal 91 on some sheets. U.S.P.&L. has a black dot at upper left on seal 56 on some sheets.
Earliest documented use: Nov. 27, 1926.

CS21

Designer — John W. Evans. Sales $5,419,959.

1927

WX39 CS21 Perf. 12, horizontal broken gum .25
On cover 8.00
a. Smooth gum 1.00
WX40 CS21 Perf. 12½, no dot .25
On cover 8.00
WX41 CS21 Perf. 12½, one larger red dot in background 1mm above right post of dashboard on sleigh .25
On cover 8.00

"Bonne Sante" added to design and No. WX39a but with body of sleigh myrtle green instead of green were used in Canada.
Offset: Nos. WX39, WX39a by Eureka. No. WX40 by E.&D. No. WX41 by U.S.P.&L.
Printer's marks: Eureka has no mark but can be identified by the perf. 12. E.&D. has red dot to left of knee of 1st reindeer on seal 92. U.S.P.&L. has 2 red dots in white gutter, one at lower left of seal 46 (and sometimes 41) and the other at upper right of seal 55. The perforations often strike out one of these dots.
Earliest documented use: Nos. WX39-WX41, Nov. 18, 1927.

The Gallant Ship "Argosy" — CS22

Designer — John W. Evans. Sales $5,465,738.

Type I — shading on sails broken, dots in flag regular.
Type II — shading on sails broken, dots in flag spotty.
Type III — shading on sails unbroken, dots in flag regular.

1928 ***Perf. 12½***

WX44 CS22 Type I, vertical broken gum .25
On cover 40.00
WX45 CS22 Type II .25
On cover 60.00
WX46 CS22 Type III .25
On cover 60.00

Seals inscribed "Bonne Annee 1929" or the same as type II but green in water, and black lines of ship heavier and deeper color were used in Canada.
Offset: Type I by Eureka, Type II by Strobridge, Type III by E.&D.
Printers' marks: Type I comes with and without a blue dash above seal 10, also with a blue and a black dash. Type II has 2 blue dashes below seal 100. Type III has red dot in crest of 1st wave on seal 92.
Earliest documented use: Nos. WX44, Nov. 20, 1928; No. WX45, Nov. 15, 1928; No. WX46, Dec. 1, 1928.

CS23

Designer — George V. Curtis. Sales $5,546,147.

1929 ***Perf. 12½***

WX49 CS23 Vertical broken gum .25
On cover 15.00
a. Perf. 12, vertical broken gum .50
b. Perf. 12½x12, vertical broken gum 2.00
c. Overprinted "Air Delivery" 10.00
On cover 250.00
WX50 CS23 Smooth gum .25

Seals inscribed "Bonne Sante 1929" or "Christmas Greetings 1929" were used in Canada.
Offset: Nos. WX49-WX49b by Eureka, No. WX50 by E.&D., U.S.P.&L., and R.R. Heywood Co., Inc., New York, N.Y.
Printers' marks: Eureka is without mark but identified by broken gum. E.&D. has a black dot in lower left corner of seal 92. U.S.P.&L. has blue dot above bell on seal 56. Heywood has a blue dot at lower right corner of seal 100.
No. WX49c was created by the Michigan Anti-tuberculosis Assocation with national approval. A total of 100 panes were overprinted and single panes were dropped via airplane at schools in the state.
Earliest documented use: Nos. WX49-WX50, Nov. 29, 1929.

CS24

Designer — Ernest Hamlin Baker, and redrawn by John W. Evans. Sales $5,309,352.

1930 ***Perf. 12½***

WX55 CS24 Vertical broken gum .25
On cover 10.00
a. Perf. 12, vert. broken gum .50
c. Perf. 12½x12, vertical broken gum 2.50
d. Perf. 12, booklet pane of 10, horiz. broken gum 2.50
e. Perf. 12½, booklet pane of 5 200.00
f. Overprinted "Cambridge Mass." .75
On cover 50.00
WX56 CS24 Smooth gum .25

Seals inscribed "Bonne Sante" or "Merry Christmas" on red border of seal were used in Canada.
Offset: Nos. WX55-WX55d by Eureka, No. WX56 by Strobridge, E.&D. and U.S.P.&L.
Printers' marks: Eureka has a dot between the left foot and middle of "M" of "Merry" on seal 1. Strobridge has 2 dashes below "ALL" on seal 100. E.&D. printed on Nashua paper has dot on coat just under elbow on seal 92, and on Gummed Products Co. paper has the dot on seals 91, 92. U.S.P.&L. has a dash which joins tree to top frame line just under "MA" of "Christmas" on seal 55.
The plate for booklet panes was made up from the left half of the regular plate and can be plated by certain flaws which occur on both.
WX55f overprint created by the Cambridge, Mass., anti-tuberculosis group with national approval.
See WX62f, WX64b.
Earliest documented use: No. WX55 and WX56, Nov. 13, 1930; No. WX55f, June 8, 1931.

CS25

Designer — John W. Evans. Sales $4,526,189.

1931 ***Perf. 12½***

WX61 CS25 Horiz. broken gum (see footnote) 3.00
On cover 10.00
WX62 CS25 Horizontal broken gum .25
On cover 10.00
a. Perf. 12x12½, horiz. broken gum .35
b. Perf. 12x12½, horizontal broken gum 2.50
c. Perf. 12, horizontal broken gum 1.00
d. Perf. 12, vertical broken gum, booklet pane of 10 2.00
f. Overprinted "Cambridge Mass." .50
On cover 50.00
WX63 CS25 Smooth gum .25

For perf 12, see note following No. WX19.

Offset: Nos. WX61-WX62h by Eureka, No. WX63 by Strobridge. No. WX61 has a green dash across inner green frame line at bottom center on each seal in sheet except those in 1st and last vertical rows and the 2 rows at bottom.

Printers' marks: Eureka has none. Strobridge has the usual 2 dashes under seal 100.

The plate for booklet panes was made up from transfers of 60 seals (12x5). The panes can be plated by minor flaws.

WX62f overprint created by the Cambridge, Mass., anti-tuberculosis group with national approval.

Earliest documented uses: Nos. WX61-WX63, Nov. 17, 1931; WX62f, Dec. 24, 1931.

CS26

Designer — Edward F. Volkmann. Sales $3,470,637.

1932

WX64 CS26 Perf. 12½x12¾ .25
On cover 10.00
a. Vertical broken gum .50
b. Overprinted "Cambridge Mass." .75
On cover 50.00
WX65 CS26 Perf. 12 .25
On cover 10.00
WX66 CS26 Perf. 12½ .25
On cover 10.00

Offset: Nos. WX64 by Eureka, No. WX65 by E.&D., No. WX66 by U.S.P.&L., No. WX67 by Columbian Bank Note Co., Chicago. Nos. WX64, WX67 have a little red spur on bottom inner frame line of each seal, at left corner.

Printers' marks: Eureka has a red dash, in each corner of the sheet, which joins the red border to the red inner frame line. E.&D. has a blue dot in snow at lower left on seal 91. U.S.P.&L. has a blue dot on top of post on seal 56. Columbian Bank Note has small "C" in lower part of girl's coat on seal 82.

WX64b overprint created by the Cambridge, Mass., anti-tuberculosis group with national approval.

Earliest documented use: Nos. WX64-WX66, Nov. 14, 1932; WX64b, Dec. 24, 1932.

CS27

Designer — Hans Axel Walleen. Sales $3,429,311.

1933

WX68 CS27 Perf. 12 .25
On cover 40.00
WX69 CS27 Perf. 12½ .25
On cover 40.00

Offset: No. WX68 by Eureka, No. WX69 by Strobridge, U.S.P.&L., and the Columbian Bank Note Co.

Printers' marks; Eureka has rope joining elbow of figure to left on seals 11, 20, 91, 100. Strobridge has the usual 2 dashes under seal 100. U.S.P.&L. has green dot on tail of "s" of "Greetings" on seal 55. Columbian has white "c" on margin, under cross, on seal 93.

Earliest documented use: Nos. WX68-WX69, Oct. 19, 1933.

CS28

Designer — Herman D. Giesen. Sales $3,701,344.

1934

WX72 CS28 Perf. 12½x12¼ .25
On cover 30.00
WX73 CS28 Perf. 12½ (see footnote) .25
On cover 30.00
WX74 CS28 Perf. 12½ (see footnote) .25
On cover 30.00
WX75 CS28 Perf. 12½ (see footnote) .25
On cover 30.00

Offset: No. WX72 by Eureka, No. WX73 by Strobridge, No. WX74 by E.&D. and No. WX75 by U.S.P.&L.

Cutting of blue plate for the under color: Nos. WX72, WX73 (early printing) and WX74 have lettering and date cut slightly larger than ultramarine color. No. WX73 (later printing) has square cutting around letters and date, like top part of letter "T". No. WX75 has cutting around letters and date cut slightly larger.

Printers' marks: Eureka has 5 stars to right of cross on seal 10. Strobridge has 2 blue dashes in lower left corner of seal 91 or in lower right corner of seal 100. E.&D. has a red dot in lower left corner of seal 99. U.S.P.&L. has 5 stars to left of cross on seal 56.

Great Britain issued seals of this design which can be distinguished by the thinner and whiter paper. Sheets have perforated margins on all 4 sides but without any lettering on bottom margin, perf. 12½.

Earliest documented use: Nos. WX72-WX75, Nov. 16, 1934.

CS29

Designer — Ernest Hamlin Baker. Sales $3,946,498.

1935

WX76 CS29 Perf. 12½x12¼ .25
On cover 20.00
WX77 CS29 Perf. 12½ .25
On cover 20.00

Offset: No. WX76 by Eureka, No. WX77 by Strobridge, U.S.P.&L. and Columbian Bank Note Co.

Eureka recut their blue plate and eliminated the faint blue shading around cross, girl's head and at both sides of the upper part of post. U.S.P.& L. eliminated the 2 brown spurs which pointed to the base of cross, in all 4 corners of the sheet.

Printers' marks: Eureka has an extra vertical line of shading on girl's skirt on seal 60. Strobridge has 2 brown dashes in lower right corner of position 100 but sheets from an early printing are without this mark. U.S.P.&L. has a blue dot under post on seal 55. Columbian has a blue "c" under post on seal 99.

The corner seals carry slogans: "Help Fight Tuberculosis," "Protect Your Home from Tuberculosis," "Tuberculosis Is Preventable," "Tuberculosis Is Curable."

Value slogan seal on cover, $50.

Earliest documented use: Nos. WX76-WX77, Nov. 3, 1935.

Printers' marks appear on seal 56 on sheets of 100 unless otherwise noted:

E Eureka Specialty Printing Co.
S Strobridge Lithographing Co. (1930-1958).
S Specialty Printers of America (1975-).
D Edwards & Deutsch Lithographing Co. (E.&D.)
U United States Printing & Lithographing Co. (U.S.P.&L.)
F Fleming-Potter Co., Inc.
W Western Lithograph Co.
B Berlin Lithographing Co. (1956-1969); I. S. Berlin Press (1970-1976); Barton-Cotton (1977-).
R Bradford-Robinson Printing Co.
N Sale-Niagara, Inc.

Seals from 1936 onward are printed by offset.

Seals with tropical gum (dull), starting in 1966, were used in Puerto Rico.

Other printers noted in the listings:
C Cyril Scott (1987-93)
C Connecticut Color (1994-95)
CW Colorform & Webcraft (1995-2000)
M Midland
Mo Moore Response Marketing
V Vertis
WL Wisconsin Label

CS30

Designer — Walter I. Sasse. Sales $4,522,269.

1936 **Pair**

WX80 CS30 Perf. 12½x12 (E) .25
On cover 8.00
WX81 CS30 Perf. 12½ (S,D,U) .25
On cover 8.00

Seals with red background and green cap-band alternate with seals showing green background and red cap-band. The corner seals carry the same slogans as those of 1935.

Value slogan seal on cover, $50.

Two of the three Strobridge printings show vertical green dashes in margin below seal 100, besides "S" on seal 56.

Earliest documented use: Nos. WX80-WX81, Nov. 1, 1936.

CS31

Designer — A. Robert Nelson. Sales $4,985,697.

1937

WX88 CS31 Perf. 12x12½ (E) .25
On cover 8.00
WX89 CS31 Perf. 12½ (S,D,U) .25
On cover 8.00

Positions 23, 28, 73 and 78, carry slogans: "Health for all," "Protect your home," "Preventable" and "Curable."

Value slogan seal on cover, $50.

The "U" printer's mark of U.S.P.&L. appears on seal 55. It is omitted on some sheets.

Earliest documented use: Nos. WX88-WX89, July 20, 1937.

CS32

Designer — Lloyd Coe. Sales $5,239,526.

1938

WX92 CS32 Perf. 12½x12 (E) .25
On cover 8.00
WX93 CS32 Perf. 12½ (S,D,U) .25
On cover 8.00
a. Miniature sheet, imperf. 5.00
On cover 50.00

The corner seals bear portraits of Rene T. H. Laennec, Robert Koch, Edward Livingston Trudeau and Einar Holboll.

No. WX93a contains the 4 corner seals, with the regular seal in the center. It sold for 25¢.

Value portrait seal on cover, $50.

Earliest documented use: Nos. WX92-WX93, Nov. 17, 1938; No. WX93a, Nov. 24, 1938.

CS33

Designer — Rockwell Kent. Sales $5,593,399.

1939

WX96 CS33 Perf. 12½x12 (E) .25
On cover 8.00
a. Booklet pane of 20, perf. 12 2.00
WX97 CS33 Perf. 12½ (S,D,U) .25
On cover 8.00

The center seals, positions 45, 46, 55, 56, carry slogans: "Health to All," "Protect Your Home." "Tuberculosis Preventable Curable" and "Holiday Greetings."

Value slogan seal on cover, $50.
Printers' marks appear on seal 57.
Earliest documented use: Nos. WX96-WX97, Nov. 18, 1939.

CS34

Designer — Felix L. Martini. Sales $6,305,979.

1940

WX100 CS34 Perf. 12½x12 (E) .25
On cover 8.00
WX101 CS34 Perf. 12½x13 (E) .25
On cover 8.00
WX103 CS34 Perf. 12½ (S,D,U) .25
On cover 8.00

Seals 23, 32 and 34 carry the slogan "Protect Us from Tuberculosis." Each slogan seal shows one of the 3 children.
Value slogan seal on cover, $75.
Earliest documented use: Nos. WX100-WX103, Aug. 12, 1940.

CS35

Designer — Stevan Dohanos. Sales $7,530,496.

1941

WX104 CS35 Perf. 12½x12 (E) .25
On cover 8.00
WX105 CS35 Perf. 12½ (S,D,U) .25
On cover 8.00

"S" and "U" printers' marks exist on same sheet.
Earliest documented use: Nos. WX104-WX105, Nov. 3, 1941.

CS36

Designer — Dale Nichols. Sales $9,390,117.

1942

WX108 CS36 Perf. 12x12½ (E) .25
On cover 8.00
WX109 CS36 Perf. 12½ (S,D,U) .25
On cover 8.00

Earliest documented use: Nos. WX108-WX109, Nov. 20, 1942.

CS37

Designer — Andre Dugo. Sales $12,521,494.

Pair

1943

WX112 CS37 Perf. 12½x12 (E) .25
On cover 8.00
WX113 CS37 Perf. 12½ (S,D,U) .25
On cover 8.00

On alternate seals, the vert. frame colors (blue & red) are transposed as are the horiz. frame colors (buff & black).
Seals where "Joyeux Noel" replaces "Greetings 1943" and "1943" added on curtain or the same as No. WX113 but darker colors were used in Canada.
Earliest documented use: Nos. WX112-WX113, Sept. 29, 1943.

CS38

Designer — Spence Wildey. Sales $14,966,227.

1944

WX118 CS38 Perf. 12½x12 (E) .25
On cover 8.00
WX119 CS38 Perf. 12½ (S,D,U) .25
On cover 8.00

Seals with "USA" omitted are for Canada.
Earliest documented use: Nos. WX118-WX119, Sept. 28, 1944.

CS39

Designer — Park Phipps. Sales $15,638,755.

1945 **"USA" at Lower Right Corner**

WX124 CS39 Perf. 12½x12 (E) .25
On cover 8.00
WX125 CS39 Perf. 12½ (S,D,U) .25
On cover 8.00

Seals with "USA" omitted are for Canada.
Earliest documented use: Nos. WX124-WX125, Aug. 6, 1945.

CS40

Designer — Mary Louise Estes and Lloyd Coe. Sales $17,075,608.

1946

WX130 CS40 Perf. 12½x12 (E) .25
On cover 8.00
WX131 CS40 Perf. 12½ (S,D,U) .25
On cover 8.00

Seals with "USA" omitted are for Canada and Bermuda.
Printers' marks are on seal 86.
The center seals (45, 46, 55, 56) bear portraits of Jacob Riis, Emily P. Bissell, E. A. Van Valkenburg and Leigh Mitchell Hodges. Portrait seal tied on cover, value, $50.
Earliest documented use: Nos. WX130-WX131, Oct. 21, 1946.

CS41

Designer — Raymond H. Lufkin. Sales $18,665,523.

1947

WX135 CS41 Perf. 12x12½ (E) .25
On cover 8.00
WX136 CS41 Perf. 12½ (S,D,U) .25
On cover 8.00

Seals with "USA" omitted are for Canada and Great Britain.
The "U" printer's mark of U.S.P.&L. appears on seal 46.
Earliest documented use: Nos. WX135-WX136, July 25, 1947.

CS42

Designer — Jean Barry Bart. Sales $20,153,834.

1948

WX140 CS42 Perf. 12x12½ (E) .25
On cover 8.00
WX141 CS42 Perf. 12½ (S,D,U) .25
On cover 8.00

Seals with "USA" omitted are for Canada and Great Britain.
Earliest documented use: Nos. WX140-WX141, Nov. 22, 1948.

CS43

Designer — Herbert Meyers. Sales $20,226,794.

1949

WX145 CS43 Perf. 12x12½ (E) .25
On cover 8.00
WX146 CS43 Perf. 12½ (S,D,U) .25
On cover 8.00

Seals with "USA" omitted are for Canada & Great Britain.
Earliest documented use: Nos. WX145-WX146, Nov. 19, 1949.

CS44

Designer — Andre Dugo. Sales $20,981,540.

1950

WX150 CS44 Perf. 12½x12 (E) .25
On cover 8.00
WX151 CS44 Perf. 12½ (S,D,U,F) .25
On cover 8.00

Seals with "USA" omitted are for Canada & Great Britain.
Earliest documented use: Nos. WX150-WX151, Nov. 17, 1950.

CS45

Designer — Robert K. Stephens. Sales $21,717,953.

1951

WX155 CS45 Perf. 12½x12 (E) .25
On cover 8.00
WX156 CS45 Perf. 12½ (S,D,U,F) .25
On cover 8.00

Seals with "USA" omitted are for Canada.
Earliest documented use: Nos. WX155-WX156, Nov. 12, 1951.

CS46

Designer — Tom Darling. Sales $23,238,148.

1952

WX159 CS46 Perf. 12½x12 (E) .25
On cover 8.00
WX160 CS46 Perf. 12½ (S,D,U,F) .25
On cover 8.00

For Nos. WX159-WX160 overprinted "Ryukyus" in Japanese characters, see Ryukyu Islands Nos. WX1 and WX1a.

Earliest documented use: Nos. WX159-WX160, Nov. 17, 1952.

CS47

Designers — Elmer Jacobs and E. Willis Jones. Sales $23,889,044.

1953

WX164 CS47 Perf. 13 (E) .25
On cover 8.00
WX165 CS47 Perf. 12½ (S,D,U,F) .25
On cover 8.00

Earliest documented use: Nos. WX164-WX165, Oct. 24, 1953.

CS48

Designer — Jorgen Hansen. Sales $24,670,202.

1954 **Block of 4**

WX168 CS48 Perf. 13 (E) .40
On cover, any single 8.00
WX169 CS48 Perf. 12½ (S,U,F,W) .40
On cover, any single 8.00
WX170 CS48 Perf. 11 (D) .50
On cover, any single 8.00

Earliest documented use: Nos. WX168-WX170, Nov. 4, 1954.

CS49

Designer — Jean Simpson. Sales $25,780,365.

1955 **Pair**

WX173 CS49 Perf. 13 (E) .25
On cover, either single 8.00
WX174 CS49 Perf. 12½ (S,U,F,W) .25
On cover, either single 8.00
WX175 CS49 Perf. 11 (D) .25
On cover, either single 8.00

Earliest documented use: Nos. WX173-WX175, Nov. 17, 1955.

CS50

Designer — Heidi Brandt. Sales $26,310,491.

1956 **Block of 4**

WX178 CS50 Perf. 12½x12 (E) 1.00
On cover, any single 8.00
WX179 CS50 Perf. 12½ (E,S,U,F,W) .50
On cover, any single 8.00
WX180 CS50 Perf. 11 (D,B) .40
On cover, any single 8.00
WX183 CS50 "Puerto Rico," perf. 12½ 3.00

Earliest documented use: Nos. WX178-WX180, Nov. 13, 1956.

CS51

Designer — Clinton Bradley. Sales $25,959,998.

1957 **Block of 4**

WX184 CS51 Perf. 13 (E) .40
On cover, any single 8.00
WX185 CS51 Perf. 12½ (S,U,F,W,R) .40
On cover, any single 8.00
WX186 CS51 Perf. 11 (D,B) .50
On cover, any single 8.00
WX187 CS51 Perf. 10½x11 (D) 1.00
On cover, any single 8.00
WX188 CS51 Perf. 10½ (D) 3.00
On cover, any single 8.00
WX190 CS51 "Puerto Rico," perf. 13 3.00

Earliest documented use: Nos. WX184-WX188, Nov. 15, 1957.

CS52

Designer — Alfred Guerra. Sales $25,955,390.

1958 **Pair**

WX191 CS52 Perf. 13 (E) .25
On cover, either single 8.00
WX192 CS52 Perf. 12½ (S,U,F,W,R) .25
On cover, either single 8.00
WX193 CS52 Perf. 10½x11 (B,D) .50
On cover, either single 8.00
WX194 CS52 Perf. 11 (B,D) .35
On cover, either single 8.00
WX196 CS52 "Puerto Rico," perf. 13 1.50

Earliest documented use: Nos. WX191-WX196, Nov. 10, 1958.

CS53

Designer — Katherine Rowe. Sales $26,740,906.

1959 **Pair**

WX197 CS53 Perf. 13 (E) .25
On cover, either single 8.00
WX198 CS53 Perf. 12½ (F,R,W) .25
On cover, either single 8.00
a. Horiz. pair, imperf. btwn. (D) 1.50
On cover 50.00
WX199 CS53 Perf. 10½x11 (B) .50
On cover, either single 8.00
WX200 CS53 Perf. 11 (B,D) .25
On cover, either single 8.00
WX201 CS53 Perf. 10½ (B) 3.50
On cover, either single 8.00
WX203 CS53 "Puerto Rico," perf. 13 1.50

E.&D. omitted every other vertical row of perforation on a number of sheets which were widely distributed as an experiment. No. WX198a (shown above in illustration) is from these sheets.

Earliest documented use: Nos. WX197-WX198, WX199-WX201, Nov. 16, 1959; No. WX198a Dec. 22, 1959.

CS54

Designer — Philip Richard Costigan. Sales $26,259,030.

1960 **Block of 4**

WX204 CS54 Perf. 12½ (E,F,R,W) .35
On cover, any single 8.00
WX205 CS54 Perf. 12½x12 (E) 2.00
On cover, any single 8.00
WX206 CS54 Perf. 11x10½ (B) .35
On cover, any single 8.00
WX207 CS54 Perf. 11 (D) .35
On cover, any single 8.00
a. As #WX207, block of 4, horiz. imperf. between 4.00
On cover —

Puerto Rico used No. WX204 (E).

Earliest documented use: Nos. WX204-WX207, Nov. 14, 1960.

CS55

Designer — Heidi Brandt. Sales $26,529,517.

1961 **Block of 4**

WX209 CS55 Perf. 12½ (E,F,R,W) .35
On cover, any single 8.00
WX209A CS55 Perf. 12½x12 (E) 2.50
On cover, any single 8.00

WX210 CS55 Perf. 11x10½ (B) .35
On cover, any single 8.00
WX211 CS55 Perf. 11 (D) .35
On cover, any single 8.00

Puerto Rico used No. WX209 (E).
Earliest documented use: Nos. WX209-WX211, Nov. 16, 1961.

CS56

Designer — Paul Dohanos. Sales $27,429,202.

1962 **Block of 4**
WX213 CS56 Perf. 12½ (F,R,W) .35
On cover, any single 8.00
WX214 CS56 Perf. 13 (E) .35
On cover, any single 8.00
WX215 CS56 Perf. 10½x11 (B) .35
On cover, any single 8.00
WX216 CS56 Perf. 11 (D,B) .35
On cover, any single 8.00

Puerto Rico used No. WX214.
Earliest documented use: Nos. WX213-WX216, Nov. 1, 1962.

CS57

Designer — Judith Campbell Piussi. Sales $27,411,806.

1963 **Block of 4**
WX218 CS57 Perf. 12½ (E,F,R,W) .35
On cover, any single 8.00
WX219 CS57 Perf. 11 (B,D) .35
On cover, any single 8.00

Puerto Rico used No. WX218 (E).
Earliest documented use: Nos. WX218-WX219, Nov. 1, 1963.

CS58

Designer — Gaetano di Palma. Sales $28,784,043.

1964 **Block of 4**
WX220 CS58 Perf. 12½ (E,F,R,W) .35
On cover, any single 8.00
WX221 CS58 Perf. 11 (B,D) .35
On cover, any single 8.00

Puerto Rico used No. WX221 (B).
Earliest documented use: Nos. WX220-WX2221, Nov. 9, 1964.

CS59

Designer — Frede Salomonsen. Sales $29,721,878.

1965 **Block of 4**
WX222 CS59 Perf. 12½ (F,W) .35
On cover, any single 8.00
WX223 CS59 Perf. 11 (B,D) .35
On cover, any single 8.00
WX224 CS59 Perf. 13 (E) .35
On cover, any single 8.00

Puerto Rico used No. WX223 (B).
Earliest documented use: Nos. WX222-WX224, Nov. 2, 1965.

CS60

Designer — Heidi Brandt. Sales $30,776,586.

1966 **Block of 8**
WX225 CS60 Perf. 12½ (E,F,W) .65
On cover, any single 8.00
WX226 CS60 Perf. 10½x11 (B) 1.00
On cover, any single 8.00
WX227 CS60 Perf. 11 (D) .65
On cover, any single 8.00

Blocks of four seals with yellow green and white backgrounds alternate in sheet in checkerboard style.
Puerto Rico used No. WX226.
Earliest documented use: Nos. WX225-WX227, Nov. 1, 1966.

Holiday Train — CS61

Designer — L. Gerald Snyder. Sales $31,876,773.
The seals come in 10 designs showing a train filled with Christmas gifts and symbols. The direction of the train is reversed in alternating rows as are the inscriptions "Christmas 1967" and "Greetings 1967." The illustration shows first 2 seals of top row.

1967 **Block of 20 (10x2)**
WX228 CS61 Perf. 13 (E) .65
On cover, any single 8.00
WX229 CS61 Perf. 12½ (F,W) .65
On cover, any single 8.00
WX230 CS61 Perf. 10½ (B) 2.00
On cover, any single 8.00
WX231 CS61 Perf. 11 (D) .75
On cover, any single 8.00
WX232 CS61 Perf. 11x10½ (B) —
On cover, any single —

Puerto Rico used No. WX229 (F).
Earliest documented use: Nos. WX228-WX232, Nov. 6, 1967.

SEALS ISSUED BY NATIONAL TUBERCULOSIS AND RESPIRATORY DISEASE ASSOCIATION

CS62

Designer — William Eisele. Sales $33,059,107.

1968 **Block of 4**
WX233 CS62 Perf. 13 (E) .50
On cover, any single 8.00
WX234 CS62 Perf. 10½x11 (B) 7.50
On cover, any single 8.00
WX234A CS62 Perf. 10½ (B) 2.00
On cover, any single 8.00
WX235 CS62 Perf. 11 (D) .50
On cover, any single 8.00
WX236 CS62 Perf. 12½ (F,W) .50
On cover, any single 8.00

Pairs of seals with bluish green and yellow backgrounds alternate in sheet in checkerboard style.
Puerto Rico used No. WX236 (F).
Earliest documented use: Nos. WX233-WX236, Oct. 31, 1968.

CS63

Designer — Bernice Kochan. Sales $34,437,591.

1969 **Block of 4**
WX237 CS63 Perf. 13 (E) .35
On cover, any single 8.00
WX238 CS63 Perf. 12½ (F,W) .35
On cover, any single 8.00
WX239 CS63 Perf. 10½x11 (B) .50
On cover, any single 8.00
WX240 CS63 Perf. 11 (B) .50
On cover, any single 8.00

Puerto Rico used No. WX238 (F).
Earliest documented use: Nos. WX237-WX240, Nov. 3, 1969.

CS64

Designer — L. Gerald Snyder. Sales $36,237,977.
Sheets contain 100 different designs, Christmas symbols, toys, decorated windows; inscribed alternately "Christmas 1970" and "Greetings 1970." The illustration shows 6 seals from the center of the sheet.

1970 **Sheet of 100 (10x10)**
WX242 CS64 Perf. 12½ (E,F,W) 1.25
On cover, any single 8.00

WX243 CS64 Perf. 11 (B) 1.25
On cover, any single 8.00
WX244 CS64 Perf. 11x10½ (B) 10.00
On cover, any single —

Puerto Rico used No. WX242 (F).
Earliest documented use: Nos. WX242-WX244, Sept. 24, 1970.

CS65

Designer — James Clarke. Sales $36,120,000.

1971 **Block of 8 (2x4)**
WX245 CS65 Perf. 12½ (E,F) .50
On cover, any single 12.00
WX246 CS65 Perf. 11 (B) .50
On cover, any single 12.00

The 4 illustrated seals each come in a 2nd design arrangement: cross at left, inscriptions transposed, and reversed bugler, candle and tree ornaments. Each sheet of 100 has 6 horiz. rows as shown and 4 rows with 2nd designs.
Puerto Rico used No. WX245 (F).
Eureka printings are found with large "E," small "E" and without "E."
Earliest documented use: Nos. WX245-WX246, Oct. 17, 1971.

CS66

Designer — Linda Layman. Sales $38,000,557.
The seals come in 10 designs showing various holiday scenes with decorated country and city houses, carolers, Christmas trees and snowman. Inscribed alternately "1972 Christmas" and "Greetings 1972." Shown are seals from center of row.

1972 **Strip of 10**
WX247 CS66 Perf. 13 (E) .50
On cover, any single 8.00
WX248 CS66 Perf. 12½ (F) .75
On cover, any single 8.00
WX249 CS66 Perf. 11 (B) .50
On cover, any single 8.00

Seal 100 has designer's name. Puerto Rico used No. WX248.
Earliest documented use: Nos. WX247-WX249, Oct. 31, 1972.

SEALS ISSUED BY AMERICAN LUNG ASSOCIATION

CS67

Designer — Cheri Johnson. Sales $36,902,439.

The seals are in 12 designs representing "The 12 Days of Christmas." Inscribed alternately "Christmas 1973" and "Greetings 1973." Shown is block from center of top 2 rows.

1973 **Block of 12**
WX250 CS67 Perf. 12½ (F), 18x22mm .50
On cover, any single 8.00
a. Size 16½x20½mm (E) .50
On cover, any single 8.00
WX251 CS67 Perf. 11 (B,W) .50
On cover, any single 8.00

Seal 100 has designer's name. Puerto Rico used No. WX250 (F).
Earliest documented use: Nos. WX250-WX251, Nov. 15, 1973.

CS68

Designer — Rubidoux. Sales $37,761,745.

1974 **Block of 4**
WX252 CS68 Perf. 12½ (E,F) .35
On cover, any single 8.00
WX253 CS68 Perf. 11 (B) .35
On cover, any single 8.00

Seal 99 has designer's name. Puerto Rico used No. WX252 (F).
Earliest documented use: Nos. WX252-WX253, Oct. 22, 1974.

CS69

Children's paintings of holiday scenes. Different design for each state or territory. Paintings by elementary school children were selected in a nationwide campaign ending in Jan., 1974.
Sales $34,710,107.

1975 **Sheet of 54 (6x9)**
WX254 CS69 Perf. 12½ (S,F) 1.25
On cover, any single 8.00
WX255 CS69 Perf. 11 (B) 2.50
On cover, any single 8.00

Printers' marks are on seal 28 (New Mexico). Specialty Printers' seals (S) carry union labels: "Scranton 4," "Scranton 7," "E. Stroudsburg."
Puerto Rico used No. WX254 (F).
Earliest documented use: Nos. WX254-WX255, Oct. 19, 1975.

CS70

Continuous village picture covers sheet with Christmas activities and Santa crossing the sky with sleigh and reindeer. No inscription on 34 seals. Others inscribed "Christmas 1976," "Greetings 1976," and (on 9 bottom-row seals) "American Lung Association." Illustration shows seals 11-12, 20-21.
Sales $36,489,207.

1976 **Sheet of 54 (9x6)**
WX256 CS70 Perf. 12½ (F,N) 1.25
On cover, any single 8.00
WX257 CS70 Perf. 11 (B) 2.50
On cover, any single 8.00
WX258 CS70 Perf. 13 (S) 1.25
On cover, any single 8.00

Printers' marks (N, B, S) on seal 32 and (F) on seal 23.
Puerto Rico used No. WX256 (F).
Earliest documented use: Nos. WX256-WX258, Nov. 9, 1976.

CS71

Children's paintings of holiday scenes. Different design for each state or territory.
Sales $37,583,883.

1977 **Sheet of 54 (6x9)**
WX259 CS71 Perf. 12½ (F) 1.25
On cover, any single 8.00
WX260 CS71 Perf. 11 (B) 1.25
On cover, any single 8.00
WX261 CS71 Perf. 13 (S) 1.50
On cover, any single 8.00

Printers' marks on seal 28 (Georgia).
Puerto Rico used No. WX259.
Earliest documented use: Nos. WX259-WX261, Oct. 21, 1977.

CS72

Children's paintings of holiday scenes. Different design for each state or territory.

Sales $37,621,466.

1978 **Sheet of 54 (6x9)**

WX262	CS72	Perf. 12½ (F)	1.25	
		On cover, any single		8.00
WX263	CS72	Perf. 11 (B)	1.25	
		On cover, any single		8.00
WX264	CS72	Perf. 13 (S)	1.25	
		On cover, any single		8.00

Printers' marks on seal 29 (New Hampshire).

Puerto Rico used No. WX262.

Earliest documented use: Nos. WX262-WX264, Oct. 13, 1978.

CS73

1979 **Sheet of 54 (6x9)**

WX265	CS73	Perf. 12½ (F)	1.50	
		On cover, any single		8.00
WX266	CS73	Perf. 11 (B)	1.25	
		On cover, any single		8.00
WX267	CS73	Perf. 13 (S)	1.25	
		On cover, any single		8.00

Printer's marks on seal 22 (Virgin Islands). Puerto Rico used No. WX265.

Earliest documented use: Nos. WX265-WX267, Oct. 9, 1979.

From 1980 on, most Christmas seals exist with a one year earlier date. These are design experiments, which began in 1979, and were used in target markets to help select the following year's Christmas seal. These experiments are not listed.

In 1988, Christmas seals branched out into Spring issues, Hanukkah issues in 1997, and Kwanzaa issues in 2001. These seals are not listed.

Starting in 1983, Spanish-text Christmas seals have been used in Spanish-speaking parts of the United States. These seals are listed.

CS74

1980 **Sheet of 54 (6x9)**

WX268	CS74	Perf. 12½ (F)	1.50	
		On cover, any single		8.00
WX269	CS74	Perf. 11 (B)	1.50	
		On cover, any single		8.00
WX270	CS74	Perf. 13 (S)	1.50	
		On cover, any single		8.00

Earliest documented use: Nos. WX268-WX270, Nov. 13, 1980.

CS75

Designer — Norman Rockwell.

1981

WX271	CS75	Perf. 12½ (F)	.25	
		On cover		8.00
WX272	CS75	Perf. 11 (B)	.25	
		On cover		8.00
WX273	CS75	Perf. 13 (S)	.25	
		On cover		8.00

Earliest documented use: Nos. WX271-WX273, Oct. 9, 1981.

CS76

Designer — John Galbreath.

1982 **Block of 12 + 2 Gift Tags**

WX274	CS76	Perf. 12½ (F)	1.00	
		On cover, any single		8.00
a.		Spanish text	2.50	
WX275	CS76	Perf. 11 (B)	1.50	
		On cover, any single		8.00
WX276	CS76	Perf. 13 (S)	1.50	
		On cover, any single		8.00

Earliest documented use: Nos. WX274-WX276, Oct. 5, 1982.

CS77

Designer — Bob Larkin.

1983 **Single Seal + Gift Tag**

WX277	CS77	Perf. 12½ (F)	.30	
		On cover, single		8.00
a.		Spanish text	.50	
WX278	CS77	Perf. 11 (B)	.35	
		On cover, single		8.00
WX279	CS77	Perf. 13 (S)	.30	
		On cover, single		8.00

Earliest documented use: Nos. WX277-WX279, Oct. 6, 1983.

CS78

Designer — Kent Salisbury.

1984 **Block of 12 + 2 Gift Tags**

WX280	CS78	Perf. 11½ (F)	1.00	
		On cover, any single		8.00
a.		Spanish text	1.50	
WX281	CS78	Perf. 11 (B)	.50	
		On cover, any single		8.00
WX282	CS78	Perf. 13 (S)	.50	
		On cover, any single		8.00

Earliest documented use: Nos. WX280-WX282, Oct. 24, 1984.

CS79

Designer — Bob Larkin.

1985 **Single Seal + Gift Tag**

WX283	CS79	Perf. 11½ (F)	1.00	
		On cover, single		8.00
a.		Spanish text	1.50	
WX284	CS79	Perf. 12½, silver foil margins (F)	1.25	
		On cover, single		8.00
WX285	CS79	Perf. 12½, gold foil margins (F)	.50	
		On cover, single		8.00
WX286	CS79	Perf. 11 (B)	.35	
		On cover, single		8.00
WX287	CS79	Perf. 13 (S)	.50	
		On cover, single		8.00
WX288	CS79	Perf. 12½ (M)	.50	
		On cover, single		8.00

Earliest documented use: Nos. WX283-WX288, Oct. 4, 1985.

CS80

Designer — Remo Bramanti.

1986 **Block of 4 + 2 Gift Tags**

WX289	CS80	Perf. 12½ (F, M, S)	1.00	
		On cover, any single		8.00
a.		Spanish text	1.50	
WX290	CS80	Perf. 12½, silver foil margins (F)	1.25	
		On cover, any single		8.00
a.		From sheet of 42 with no horiz. perfs after rows 1, 4 and 5 (F)	1.25	

Earliest documented use: Nos. WX289-WX290, Sept. 18, 1986.

CS81

Designer — Remo Bramanti.

1987 — Block of 4 + 2 Gift Tags

WX292 CS81 Perf. 11½ (F) 1.00
On cover, any single 8.00
a. Spanish text 1.50
WX293 CS81 Perf. 11½, silver foil margins, no horiz. perfs at the folds after rows 1, 4, and 5 (F) 1.50
On cover, any single 8.00
WX294 CS81 Perf. 12½ (S) 1.50
On cover, any single 8.00
WX295 CS81 Perf. 14½ (C) 5.00
On cover, any single 8.00

Earliest documented use: Nos. WX292-WX295, Sept. 21, 1987.

CS82

Designer — Remo Bramanti.

1988 — Block of 4 + 2 Gift Tags

WX296 CS82 Perf. 11½ (F) .50
On cover, any single 8.00
WX297 CS82 Perf. 11½, silver foil margins, no horiz. perfs at the folds after rows 1, 4, and 5 (F) 1.50
On cover, any single 8.00
WX298 CS82 Perf. 12½ (S, C) 1.00
On cover, any single 8.00
a. Spanish text 1.00

Earliest documented use: Nos. WX296-WX298, Sept. 29, 1988.

CS83

Designer — John Clymer.

1989 — Single Seal + Gift Tag

WX299 CS83 Perf. 11½ (F) .35
On cover, single 8.00
a. Spanish text 1.00
WX300 CS83 Perf. 12½, silver foil margins, no horiz. perfs at the folds after rows 1, 4, and 5 (F) .75
On cover, single 8.00
WX301 CS83 Perf. 12½ (S) .35
On cover, single 8.00
WX302 CS83 Self-adhesive, straight die cut over simulated perf. 11½ (printer unknown) .25
On cover, single 8.00

Earliest documented use: Nos. WX299-WX302, Aug. 12, 1989.

CS84

Designer — Maureen Drdak-Jensen.

1990 — Single Seal + Gift Tag

WX303 CS84 Perf. 12¼ (F) .35
On cover, single 8.00
a. Spanish text, perf. 12½ .75
WX304 CS84 Perf. 12¼, silver foil margins, no horiz. perfs at the folds after rows 1, 4, and 5 (F) 1.00
On cover, single 8.00
WX305 CS84 Perf. 12½ (S) .75
On cover, single 8.00
WX306 CS84 Perf. 10½x10 (C) .35
On cover, single 8.00

Earliest documented use: Nos. WX303-WX306, Oct. 2, 1990.

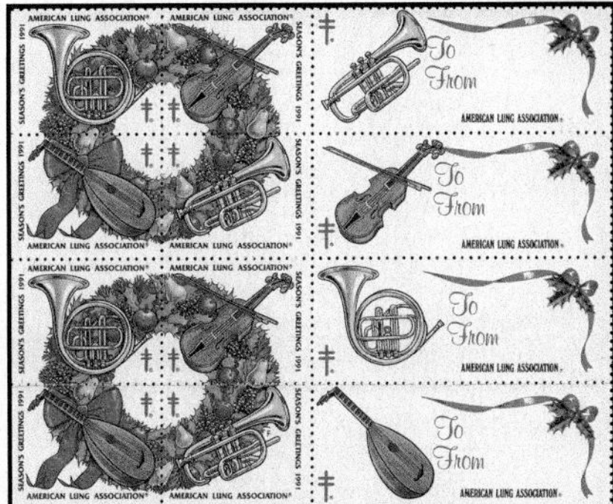

CS85

Designer — David Webster.

1991 — 2 Blocks of 4 + 4 Gift Tags

WX307 CS85 Perf. 10½x11 (F) 1.00
On cover, any single 8.00
a. Spanish text 2.00
WX308 CS85 Perf. 12½, silver foil margins (F) 3.50
On cover, any single 8.00
WX310 CS85 Perf. 12½ (S) 1.00
On cover, any single 8.00
a. Perf. 12½, dull silver ink margins (F) 3.50
On cover, any single 8.00
WX311 CS85 Perf. 11 (C) 1.00
On cover, any single 8.00

Earliest documented use: Nos. WX307-WX311, Sept. 3, 1991.

CS86

Designer — Lynn McKernan.

1992 — Single Seal + Gift Tag

WX312 CS86 10½x10 (F) .35
On cover, single 8.00
a. Spanish text .75
WX313 CS86 Perf. 12½ (S) .35
On cover, single 8.00
WX314 CS86 Perf. 12½, dull silver ink margins (S) .75
On cover, single 8.00
WX315 CS86 Perf. 11 (C) 1.50
On cover, single 8.00

Earliest documented use: Nos. WX312-WX315, Aug. 17, 1992.

CS87

Designer — Mike Chisarik.

1993 — Single Seal + Gift Tag

WX316 CS87 12½ (F) .25
On cover, single 8.00
a. Spanish text .50
WX317 CS87 Perf. 12½, dull silver ink margins (F) .75
On cover, single 8.00
WX318 CS87 Perf. 12¼ (C) .25
On cover, single 8.00

Earliest documented use: Nos. WX316-WX318, Oct. 9, 1993.

CS88

Designer — Linda Figliola.

1994 — Single Seal + Gift Tag

WX319 CS88 12¼, dull silver ink margins (F) .35
On cover, single 8.00
a. Spanish text .35
WX320 CS88 Self-adhesive, straight die cut, dull silver ink margins, roulette at the folds after rows 2, 5 and 8 (unknown printer) .50
On cover, single 8.00
WX321 CS88 Simulated perf. over roulette, dull silver ink margins (unknown printer) 1.25
On cover, single 8.00

Earliest documented use: Nos. WX319-WX321, Oct. 8, 1994.

CS89

1995 — Sheet of 52 + Label

WX322 CS89 12½, dull silver ink margins (F) 2.25
On cover, any single 8.00
WX323 CS89 12¾x12¼, dull silver ink margins (C) 3.00
On cover, any single 8.00
WX324 CS89 Simulated perf. over roulette, seals 27.75x17.5mm, dull silver ink margins (CW) 3.00
On cover, any single 8.00
WX325 CS89 Simulated perf. over roulette, seals 26x17.5mm, dull silver ink margins (CW) 25.00
On cover, any single —
WX326 CS89 Self-adhesive, straight die cut, dull silver ink margins (unknown printer) 3.00
On cover, any single 8.00
a. Horiz. die cutting omitted (error sheets) 15.00

Earliest documented use: Nos. WX322-WX326, Oct. 3, 1995.

CS90

1996 — Sheet of 53 + Label

WX327 CS90 Perf. 11½ (F) 1.50
On cover, any single 8.00
a. Spanish text, perf. 12¼ 7.50
WX328 CS90 Perf. 11½, dull silver ink margins (F) 7.50
On cover, any single 8.00
WX329 CS90 Simulated perf. over roulette (CW) 12.50
On cover, any single —

WX330 CS90 Self-adhesive, straight die cut (CW) 7.50
On cover, any single 8.00

Earliest documented use: Nos. WX327-WX330, Oct. 24, 1996.

CS91

Designer — Lauren J. Haggerty.

1997 Single Seal + Gift Tag

WX331 CS91 Perf. 12¼ (F) .35
On cover, single 8.00
a. Spanish text 2.00
WX332 CS91 Simulated perf. over roulette (CW) .35
On cover, single 8.00
WX333 CS91 Self-adhesive, straight die cut with simulated perfs, except roulette in rows 3, 6 and 9 (printer unknown) .35
On cover, single 8.00
WX334 CS91 Self-adhesive, straight die cut (printer unknown) .40
On cover, single 8.00

Earliest documented use: Nos. WX331-WX334, Oct. 30, 1997.

CS92

Designer — Jill Schellhorn.

1998 Sheet of 36 + 9 Gift Tags

WX335 CS92 Perf. 12¼ (F) 1.75
On cover, any single 8.00
WX336 CS92 Simulated perf. over roulette (CW) 2.00
On cover, any single 8.00
a. Spanish text 15.00
WX337 CS92 Self-adhesive, serpentine die cut (CW) 1.50
On cover, any single 8.00
WX338 CS92 Self-adhesive, straight die cut, except roulette in rows 3, 6 and 9 (CW) 1.50
On cover, any single 8.00

Earliest documented use: Nos. WX335-WX338, Oct. 26, 1998.

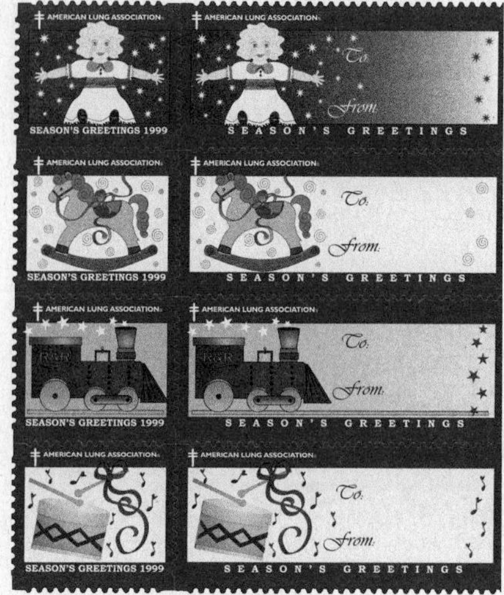

CS93

Designer — Mary Millich Burke.

1999 Block of 4 + 4 Gift Tags

WX339 CS93 Self-adhesive, serpentine die cut (F) 1.25
On cover, any single 8.00
WX340 CS93 Simulated perf. over roulette (CW) .75
On cover, any single 8.00
a. Spanish text (CW) 2.25
WX341 CS93 Perf. 9½ (unknown printer) 7.50
On cover, any single —

Earliest documented use: Nos. WX339-WX341, Oct. 26, 1999.

CS94

Designer — Elaine Verstraete.

2000 Vert. Strip of 4 + 4 Gift Tags

WX342 CS94 Self-adhesive, serpentine die cut, green tinted gift tags (F) 1.75
On cover, any single 8.00
WX343 CS94 Simulated perf. over roulette (CW) 1.25
On cover, any single 8.00
a. Spanish text (CW) 2.25
WX344 CS94 Self-adhesive, serpentine die cut, gift tags not tinted (CW) .75

Earliest documented use: Nos. WX342-WX344, Oct. 1, 2000.

CS95

Designer — Kevin Reid.

2001 Single Seal + Gift Tag

WX345 CS95 Self-adhesive, shallow serpentine die cut, high gloss paper, vignette 22x24mm (F) 2.00
On cover, single 8.00
WX346 CS95 Self-adhesive, shallow angular die cut, vignette 22x22mm (WL) 1.00
On cover, single 8.00
WX347 CS95 Re-moist gum, simulated perf. over roulette (V) .35
On cover, single 8.00
WX348 CS95 Self-adhesive, serpentine die cut, satin paper, vignette 22x24mm (V) .30
On cover, single 8.00
a. Spanish text (V) 3.00

Earliest documented use: Nos. WX345-WX348, Oct. 19, 2001.

CS96

Designer — Barbara Goss.

2002 Vert. Strip of 4 + 4 Gift Tags

WX349 CS96 Self-adhesive, shallow serpentine die cut, vignette 22.5x21mm, with thicker green frame lines (F) 3.50
On cover, any single 8.00
WX350 CS96 Self-adhesive, straight die cut, vignette 22x21mm, with thicker green frame lines (F) 3.50
On cover, any single 8.00
WX351 CS96 Self-adhesive, serpentine die cut, vignette 21.5x21.5mm (Mo) .75
On cover, any single 8.00
a. Spanish text (Mo) —
WX352 CS96 Self-adhesive, serpentine die cut, vignette 22x27mm, silver foil margins (Mo) 1.00
On cover, any single 8.00
WX353 CS96 Self-adhesive, serpentine die cut, vignette 22x26mm, silver foil margins (Mo) 3.00
On cover, any single 8.00
WX354 CS96 Roulette 12½ (Mo) .75
On cover, any single 8.00

Earliest documented use: Nos. WX349-WX354, Nov. 3, 2002.

CS97

Designer — Barbara Goss.

2003 Vert. Strip of 4 + 4 Gift Tags

WX355 CS97 Roulette 12½ 1.25
On cover, any single 8.00
a. Spanish text 7.50
WX356 CS97 Self-adhesive, serpentine die cut 1.25
On cover, any single 8.00
WX357 CS97 Self-adhesive, serpentine die cut, silver foil margins 2.50
On cover, any single 8.00

Earliest documented use: Nos. WX355-WX357, Oct. 9, 2003.

CS98

Designer — Katie Atkinson.

2004 Horiz. Strip of 5

WX358 CS98 Self-adhesive, serpentine die cut, dark blue margins 1.00
WX359 CS98 Self-adhesive, serpentine die cut, silver foil margins .75
On cover, any single 8.00
a. Spanish text 1.50
WX360 CS98 Self-adhesive, serpentine die cut, silver foil margins, gutter between rows 4 and 5, strip of 5 with gift tag at right 2.50

Earliest documented use: Nos. WX358-WX360, Oct. 9, 2004.

All seals from 2005 through 2013 have silver foil margins.

CS99

Designer — Mark Maffin.

2005 Horiz. Strip of 4 + Gift Tag

WX361 CS99 Self-adhesive, serpentine die cut 5.00
On cover, any single 8.00
a. Strip of 4 from sheet of 56 or 64, no gift tag .25
b. Spanish text, strip of 4, no gift tag 1.00

Earliest documented use: No. WX361, Oct. 15, 2005.

CS100

Designer — Debra Jordan Bryan.

2006 Horiz. Strip of 5 + Gift Tag

WX362 CS100 Self-adhesive, serpentine die cut 3.00
On cover, any single 8.00
a. Strip of 5 from sheet of 56 or 64, no gift tag .35
b. Spanish text, strip of 5, no gift tag 1.00

Earliest documented use: No. WX362, Sept. 5, 2006.

CS101

Designer — Karla Dornacher.

2007 Horiz. Strip of 5 + Gift Tag

WX363 CS101 Self-adhesive, serpentine die cut, design 17x23.5mm 4.00
On cover, any single 8.00
a. Self-adhesive, serpentine die cut, design 17x24mm, no gift tag .35
On cover, any single 8.00
b. Spanish text, no gift tag 1.00

Earliest documented use: No. WX363, Oct. 2, 2007.

CS102

Designer — Debra Jordan Bryan.

2008 Horiz. Strip of 5 + Gift Tag

WX364 CS102 Self-adhesive, serpentine die cut 4.00
On cover, any single 8.00
a. Strip of 5 from sheet of 56, no gift tag .35

Earliest documented use: No. WX364, Sept. 23, 2008.

CS103

Designer — Debra Jordan Bryan.

2009 Horiz. Strip of 4 + 4 Gift Tags

WX365 CS103 Self-adhesive, serpentine die cut 4.00
On cover, any single 8.00
a. Strip of 4 from sheet of 56, no gift tags .35

Earliest documented use: No. WX365, Aug. 18, 2009.

CS104

Designer — William Vanderdasson.

2010 Horiz. Strip of 5 + Gift Tag

WX366 CS104 Self-adhesive, serpentine die cut 4.00
On cover, any single 8.00
a. Strip of 5 from sheet of 64, no gift tag .50

Earliest documented use: No. WX366, Aug. 18, 2010.

CS105

Designer — Marcello Corti.

2011 Horiz. Strip of 5 + Gift Tag

WX367 CS105 Self-adhesive, serpentine die cut 4.00
On cover, any single 8.00
a. Strip of 5 from sheet of 56, no gift tag .50

Earliest documented use: No. WX367, Sept. 7, 2011.

CS106

Designer — James Mitchell.

2012 Horiz. Strip of 7 + Gift Tag

WX368 CS106 Self-adhesive, serpentine die cut .40
On cover, any single 8.00
a. Strip of 7 from sheet of 56, no gift tag .75

Earliest documented use: No. WX368, Aug. 31, 2012.

CS107

Designer — Jennifer Brinley.

2013 Horiz. Strip of 7 + Gift Tag

WX369 CS107 Self-adhesive, serpentine die cut 4.00
On cover, any single 8.00
a. Strip of 7 from sheet of 56, no gift tag .75

Earliest documented use: No. WX369, Sept. 6, 2013.

CS108

Designer — John Sloane.

2014 **Horiz. Strip of 6**

WX370 CS108 Self-adhesive, serpentine die cut, green margins .75
On cover, any single 8.00

Earliest documented use: No. WX370, Aug. 30, 2014.

CS109

Designer — Scott Wilson.

2015 **Horiz. Strip of 7**

WX371 CS109 Self-adhesive, serpentine die cut, silver foil margins, design 20x28mm .75
On cover, any single 8.00

WX372 CS109 Self-adhesive, serpentine die cut, silver foil margins, design 21x20mm 1.25
On cover, any single 8.00

Earliest documented use: Nos. WX371-WX372, Sept. 22, 2015.

CS110

Designer — Diane Kater.

2016 **Horiz. Strip of 7**

WX373 CS110 Self-adhesive, serpentine die cut, white margins, design 21x28mm .40
On cover, any single 8.00

WX374 CS110 Self-adhesive, serpentine die cut, white margins, design 18x25mm 1.25
On cover, any single 8.00

Earliest documented use: Nos. WX373-WX374, Sept. 22, 2016.

CS111

Designer — Lisa Alderson.

2017 **Horiz. Strip of 7**

WX375 CS111 Self-adhesive, serpentine die cut, white margins, design 21x28mm .40
On cover, any single 8.00

WX376 CS111 Self-adhesive, serpentine die cut, white margins, design 18x25mm 1.25
On cover, any single 8.00

Earliest documented use: Nos. WX375-WX376, Sept. 12, 2017.

CS112

Designer — Deva Evans.

2018 **Horiz. Strip of 7**

WX377 CS112 Self-adhesive, serpentine die cut, red margins, design 21x28mm .75
On cover, any single 8.00

WX378 CS112 Self-adhesive, serpentine die cut, red margins, design 18x25mm 1.25
On cover, any single 8.00

Earliest documented use: Nos. WX377-WX378, Aug. 30, 2018.

CS113

Designer — Makiko.

2019 **Horiz. Strip of 7**

WX379 CS113 Self-adhesive, serpentine die cut, white margins, design 20x28mm 1.00
On cover, any single 8.00

WX380 CS113 Self-adhesive, serpentine die cut, white margins, design 18x25mm 1.25
On cover, any single 8.00

Earliest documented use: Nos. WX379-WX380, Sept. 26, 2019.

CS114

Designer — Makiko.

2020 **Horiz. Strip of 7**

WX381 CS114 Self-adhesive, serpentine die cut, red margins, design 24x20mm 1.00
On cover, any single 8.00

WX382 CS114 Self-adhesive, serpentine die cut, red margins, design 21x18mm 1.00
On cover, any single 8.00

Earliest documented use: No. WX381-WX382, Sept. 24, 2020.

CS115

Designer — Janet Grace.

2021 **Horiz. Strip of 7**

WX383 CS115 Self-adhesive, serpentine die cut, white margins, design 21x29mm 1.00
On cover, any single 8.00

WX384 CS115 Self-adhesive, serpentine die cut, white margins, design 18x26mm 1.00
On cover, any single 8.00

Earliest documented use: No. WX383-WX384, Oct. 1, 2021.

SANITARY FAIR

The United States Sanitary Commission was authorized by the Secretary of War on June 9, 1861, and approved by President Lincoln on June 13, 1861. It was a committee of inquiry, advice and aid dealing with the health and general comfort of Union troops, supported by public contributions.

Many Sanitary Fairs were held to raise funds for the Commission, and eight issued stamps. The first took place in 1863 at Chicago, where no stamp was issued. Some Sanitary Fairs advertised on envelopes.

Sanitary Fair stamps occupy a position midway between United States semi-official carrier stamps and the private local posts. Although Sanitary Fair stamps were not valid for U.S. postal service, they were prepared for, sold and used at the fair post offices, usually with the approval and participation of the local postmaster.

The Commission undertook to forward soldiers' unpaid and postage due letters. These letters were handstamped "Forwarded by the U.S. Sanitary Commission."

Details about the Sanitary Fair stamps may be found in the following publications:

American Journal of Philately, Jan. 1889, by J. W. Scott
The Collector's Journal, Aug-Sept. 1909, by C. E. Severn
Scott's Monthly Journal, Jan. 1927 (reprint, Apr. 1973), by Elliott Perry

Stamps, April 24th, 1937, by Harry M. Konwiser
Pat Paragraphs, July, 1939, by Elliott Perry
Covers, Aug. 1952, by George B. Wray
Sanitary Fairs, 1992, by Alvin and Marjorie Kantor
The listings were compiled originally by H. M. Konwiser and Dorsey F. Wheless.

SF1

Albany, New York
Army Relief Bazaar
Setting A: narrow spacing, pane of 12.
Setting B: wider spacing, sheet of 25.

1864, Feb. 22-Mar. 30 Litho. *Imperf.*
Thin White Paper

WV1	SF1 10c **rose**	125.	
	Used on cover (tied "Albany")		*9,500.*
	Block of 4, setting A	1,200.	
	Pane of 12, setting A	*10,000.*	
	Block of 4, setting B	500.	
	Sheet of 25, setting B	*3,000.*	
WV2	SF1 10c **black**	700.	
	Block of 5, setting A	*4,500.*	
	Vert. pair, setting B	*2,500.*	

The No. WV1 tied by Albany cancel on cover is unique. One other cover exists in private hands with the stamp uncanceled and slightly damaged.

Vert. pair is only setting B multiple of No. WV2.

Imitations are typographed in red, blue, black or green on a thin white or ordinary white paper, also on colored papers and are:

(a) Eagle with topknot, printed in sheets of 30 (6x5).
(b) Eagle without shading around it.
(c) Eagle with shading around it, but with a period instead of a circle in "C" of "Cents," and "Ten Cents" is smaller.

SF2

Boston, Mass.
National Sailors' Fair

1864, Nov. 9-22 Litho.
Die Cut

WV3	SF2 10c **green**	700.	
	On 3c envelope #U34		*800.*

SF3

Brooklyn, N.Y.
Brooklyn Sanitary Fair

1864, Feb. 22-Mar. 8 Litho. *Imperf.*
Sheets of 25 (WV4)

WV4	SF3 (15c) **green**	1,000.	*4,500.*
	On cover, Fair postmark on envelope		*6,500.*
	Block of 4	*6,500.*	
	Block of 6	*10,000.*	
WV5	SF3 (25c) **black**	*20,000.*	
	On cover, with 1c local #28L2, Fair postmark on envelope		*36,000.*

No. WV4 used is valued canceled by the Fair postmark. Two or more examples also exist with a manuscript cancel. Value with manuscript cancel, $1,100. No. WV5 unused is repaired but unique, and it is valued as such. No. WV5 on cover also is unique.

Fakes exist of No. WV4 on pelure paper.

Imitations: *(a)* Typographed and shows "Sanitary" with a heavy cross bar to "T" and second "A" with a long left leg. *(b)* Is a rough typograph print without shading in letters of "Fair."

SF4

SF5

1863, Dec. Typeset *Imperf.*

WV6	SF4 5c **black,** *rosy buff*	1,000.	*200.*
WV7	SF5 10c **green**	1,100.	
	Tete beche pair	*9,000.*	

No. WV6 used is believed to be unique. It has a manuscript cancel and is faulty. It is valued thus.

SF6

New York, N.Y.
Metropolitan Fair

1864, Apr. 4-27 Engr. *Imperf.*
Thin White Paper

WV8	SF6 10c **blue**	350.
	Sheet of 4	*4,000.*
WV9	SF6 10c **red**	*5,000.*
	Pair	*11,500.*
WV10	SF6 10c **black**	*28,500.*

Engraved and printed by John E. Gavit of Albany, N.Y. from a steel plate composed of four stamps, 2x2. Can be plated by the positions of scrolls and dots around "Ten Cents."

No. WV10 is unique.

SF7

Philadelphia, Pa.
Great Central Fair

1864, June 7-28 Engr. *Perf. 12*
Printed by Butler & Carpenter, Philadelphia
Sheets of 126 (14x9)

WV11	SF7 10c **blue**	40.00	750.00
	On cover tied with Fair postmark		*2,250.*
	On cover with 3c #65, Fair and Philadelphia postmarks		*36,000.*
	On cover with two 2c #73, Fair and Philadelphia postmarks		*25,000.*
	On cover with 3c #65, New York postmark		*42,500.*
	Block of 4	250.00	
WV12	SF7 20c **green**	27.50	600.00
	On cover tied with Fair postmark		*1,500.*
	Block of 4	140.00	
	Block of 12	475.00	
WV13	SF7 30c **black**	35.00	500.00
	On cover tied with Fair postmark		*8,000.*
	Nos. WV11-WV13 on single cover, Fair postmark		*10,000.*
	On cover with pair of 2c #73, Fair and Philadelphia postmarks		*50,000.*
	Block of 4	160.00	
	Block of 6	240.00	

Imprint "Engraved by Butler & Carpenter, Philadelphia" on right margin adjoining three stamps.

Used examples of Nos. WV11-WV13 have Fair cancellation.

The No. WV11 covers used with 3c #65 and with 2c #73 are each unique. The New York usage is on a Metropolitan Fair illustrated envelope. The No. WV13 cover with 2c #73 also is unique.

White and amber envelopes were sold by the fair inscribed "Great Central Fair for the Sanitary Commission," showing picture in several colors of wounded soldier, doctors and ambulance marked "U.S. Sanitary Commission." Same design and inscription are known on U.S. envelope No. U46.

A fake June 23, 1864, postmark is known on No. WV11-WV13 stamps and covers.

Imitation of No. WV13 comes typographed in blue or green on thick paper.

SF8

Springfield, Mass.
Soldiers' Fair

1864, Dec. 19-24 Typo. *Imperf.*

WV14	SF8 10c **lilac**	275.00	
	On unaddressed cover, Fair postmark on envelope		900.00
	Horizontal strip of 4	1,100.	

Design by Thomas Chubbuck, engraver of the postmaster provisional stamp of Brattleboro, Vt.

One cover exists pencil-addressed to Wm. Ingersoll, Springfield Armory; value slightly more than an unaddressed cover.

A fake postmark is known on No. WV14 covers.

Imitations: (a) Without designer's name in lower right corner, in lilac on laid paper. *(b)* With designer's name, but roughly typographed, in lilac on white wove paper. Originals show 5 buttons on uniform.

SF9

Stamford, Conn.
Soldiers' Fair

1864, July 27-29

WV15	SF9 15c **pale brown**	*4,250.*	*6,500.*

Originals have tassels at ends of ribbon inscribed "SOLDIERS FAIR." Imitations have leaning "S" in "CENTS" and come in lilac, brown, green, also black on white paper, green on pinkish paper and other colors.

Twelve examples of No. WV15 are recorded.

ESSAY

Great Central Fair, Philadelphia

1864

WV11-E1	Design as issued but value tablets blank, greenish black on glazed paper (unique)	—

PROOFS

Metropolitan Fair, New York

1864

WV10P4	10c Plate on card	
	a. **black** on white card	900.
	b. **black** on yellow glazed card	—

Great Central Fair, Philadelphia

1864

WV11TC/WV13TC1d	10c and 30c **grnsh blk,** se-tenant, glazed paper, large die	—
WV11P4	10c **blue,** plate on card, imperf.	40.00
	Block of 4	175.00

WV12TC1a 20c Large die on India paper
e. **vermilion** —
f. **bright blue** —
WV12TC1d 20c Large die on glazed paper
e. **greenish black** —
WV12TC5 20c Plate on wove paper, imperf.
a. **vermilion** 40.00
Block of 4 175.00
b. **orange** 40.00
Block of 4 175.00
c. **brown orange,** opaque wove paper 40.00
Block of 4 175.00
d. **black brown** 40.00
Block of 4 175.00
e. **olive** 40.00
Block of 4 175.00
f. **bright blue** 40.00
Block of 4 175.00
g. **lt. ultramarine** 40.00
Block of 4 175.00
h. **purple** 40.00
Block of 4 175.00
i. **claret** 40.00
Block of 4 175.00
j. **black,** opaque wove paper 40.00
Block of 4 175.00
k. **grey black,** experimental double paper, wove, small x pattern 50.00
Block of 4 225.00
l. **grey black,** experimental double paper, wove, large X pattern 50.00
Block of 4 225.00
m. **grey black,** thin opaque paper 40.00
WV12TC6 20c Plate on wove paper, perf. 12
a. **carmine** 40.00
Block of 4 175.00
b. **vermilion** 40.00
Block of 4 175.00
c. **red brown** 40.00
Block of 4 175.00
d. **bright blue** 40.00
Block of 4 175.00
e. **brown black** 40.00
Block of 4 175.00
f. **black** 40.00
Block of 4 175.00
WV12P4 20c **green,** plate on card, imperf. 40.00
Block of 4 175.00
WV12P5 20c Plate on thick wove paper, imperf.
a. **green** 40.00
Block of 4 175.00
WV12P6 20c Plate on thick wove paper, perf. 12
a. **green** 40.00
Block of 4 175.00
WV13TC1a 30c Large die on India paper
e. **blue** *2,500.*

Color shades vary widely.

Schernikow unofficial reprints (1903) exist of WV11TC-WV13TC, se-tenant vertically, large die on glazed white, pink or yellow card and small die on India paper (mounted se-tenant) in carmine, red carmine, vermilion, orange, brown, yellow brown, olive, yellow green, blue green, gray blue, ultramarine, light violet, violet, claret and gray black.

There also exist large die essay reprints on India paper, green bond paper and glazed cardboard without denomination or with 20c. The 20c value has an added line below the center shield.

WV13P4 30c **black,** plate on card, imperf. 40.00
Block of 4 175.00

ENCASED POSTAGE STAMPS

In early 1862, months after the beginning of the American Civil War, people were conserving resources in anticipation of hard times and shortages ahead. Coins were one of the most hoarded resources, and as a result of this hoarding, coins began to command a premium over paper money. The public was reluctant to spend their coins, fearing the premiums for coins might increase, and a loss might result. Many millions of dollars in gold and silver coins, even copper-nickel cents, disappeared into private hands.

The U.S, Mint began coining copper-nickel cents almost exclusively, but could not meet demand. In response, the public turned to postage stamps to meet small obligations, and shopkeepers were forced to accept stamps as change. Envelopes stating the amount of stamps contained within and cards bearing stamps were sometimes used to keep the stamps from sticking and becoming destroyed, and printers sold advertisements on large numbers of these envelopes. By July 1862, the government had authorized the monetizing of postage stamps and began printing stamp impressions on bank note paper.

On August 12, 1862, John Gault was issued a patent for a “Design for Encasing Government Stamps” to be used as the equivalent of currency. Gault's plans called for a postage stamp to have its corners wrapped around a cardboard circle and show through a thin mica covering. An outer metal frame would hold these items secure, and a heavier brass backing would complete the piece. The brass backing would be suitable for advertising purposes. The resulting piece was about the size of a quarter, but much lighter in weight. The stamps placed in the new encased postage were the 1c, 3c, 5c, 10c, 12c, 24c, 30c and 90c stamps of the 1861 issue. Of course, Gault sold his encased postage at a small markup over the value of the stamp enclosed and the cost of production.

On August 21, 1862, the government issued postage currency in 5c, 10c, 25c and 50c denominations, and fractional currency was issued in 1863. These policies, plus the increased production of brass and copper-nickel coinage in 1863, effectively ended Gault's enterprise. Still, encased postage proved very popular, because it solved the major problems of stamp damage and the necessity of opening stamp envelopes to count the contents. More than 30 companies took advantage of the advertising possibilities and had their ads stamped on the brass backing. Perhaps $50,000 or a little more in encased postage eventually was sold and circulated, not nearly enough by itself to solve the nation's small change crisis. Of the approximately 750,000 pieces sold, only 3,500-7,000 are believed to have survived for collectors.

Values are for very fine examples with mica intact, although signs of circulation and handling are to be expected.

Grading encompasses three areas: 1. Case will show signs of wear or handling and signs of original toning. 2. Mica will be intact with no pieces missing. 3. Stamp will be fresh with no signs of toning or wrinkling.

Examples that came with silvered cases and still have some or all of the original silvering will sell for more than the values shown.

The Eight Stamps of the 1861 Issue Used for Encased Postage

Aerated Bread Co., New York

EP1	1c	*7,000.*
EP1A	5c	*15,000.*

No. EP1A is unique.

Ayer's Cathartic Pills, Lowell, Mass.

Varieties with long and short arrows below legend occur on all denominations.

EP2	1c	550.
EP3	3c	475.
EP4	5c	1,000.
EP5	10c	1,500.
EP6	12c	*3,000.*
EP7	24c	*3,500.*
EP7A	30c	*8,000.*

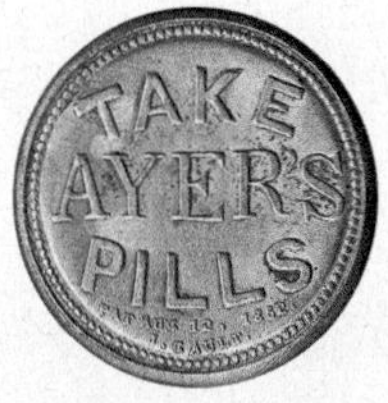

Take Ayer's Pills

EP8	1c	500.
EP9	3c	400.
EP10	5c	1,100.
a.	Ribbed frame	*3,000.*
EP11	10c	1,100.
a.	Ribbed frame	*5,250.*
EP12	12c	*3,000.*
EP12A	30c	*5,000.*

Nos. EP11a and EP12A each are unique.

Ayer's Sarsaparilla

Three varieties: "AYER'S" small, medium or large. Example illustrated is the medium variety.

EP13	1c medium "Ayer's"	450.
a.	Small	750.
EP15	3c medium "Ayer's"	350.
a.	Small	700.
b.	Large	450.
c.	Ribbed frame, medium	2,000.
EP16	5c medium "Ayer's"	2,000.
a.	Large	1,500.
EP17	10c medium "Ayer's"	850.
a.	Ribbed frame, medium	2,000.
b.	Small	1,250.
c.	Large	1,400.
EP18	12c medium "Ayer's"	2,500.
a.	Small	*3,000.*
EP19	24c medium "Ayer's"	1,900.
EP20	30c medium "Ayer's"	*4,500.*

Bailey & Co., Philadelphia

EP21	1c	1,100.
EP22	3c	1,200.
EP23	5c	*2,250.*
EP24	10c	*3,000.*
EP25	12c	*3,000.*

"FANCYGOODS" as one word

"FANCY GOODS" as two words

Joseph L. Bates, Boston

EP26	1c one word	525.
a.	Two words	600.
EP27	3c one word	2,000.
a.	Two words	1,000.
EP28	5c two words	1,250.
a.	One word	1,500.
b.	Ribbed frame, one word	*3,500.*
EP29	10c two words	1,750.
a.	One word	1,500.
b.	Ribbed frame, one word	*3,000.*
EP30	12c two words	*4,250.*

Brown's Bronchial Troches

EP31	1c	2,750.
EP32	3c	650.
EP33	5c	750.
EP34	10c	1,000.
EP35	12c	*3,500.*
EP36	24c	*4,000.*
EP37	30c	*4,500.*

F. Buhl & Co., Detroit

EP38	1c	*2,500.*
EP39	3c	*9,000.*
EP40	5c	*2,250.*
EP41	10c	1,750.
EP42	12c	*5,500.*
EP43	24c	*6,000.*

No. EP39 is unique.

Burnett's Cocoaine Kalliston

EP44	1c	1,000.
EP45	3c	1,000.
EP46	5c	950.
EP47	10c	850.
EP48	12c	*3,750.*
EP49	24c	*5,000.*
EP50	30c	*4,000.*
EP51	90c	*7,500.*

Burnett's Cooking Extracts

EP52	1c	900.
EP53	3c	700.
EP54	5c	750.
EP55	10c	750.
a.	Ribbed frame	*4,000.*
EP56	12c	*2,000.*
EP57	24c	*5,500.*
EP58	30c	*5,750.*
EP58A	90c	*12,500.*

No. EP58A is unique.

A. M. Claflin, Hopkinton, Mass.

EP59	1c	*13,500.*
EP60	3c	—
EP61	5c	*20,000.*
EP62	10c	*10,000.*
EP63	12c	*16,000.*

No. EP60 is unique.

H. A. Cook, Evansville, Ind.

EP64	5c	*4,500.*
EP65	10c	*2,750.*

Dougan, Hatter, New York

EP66	1c	*2,500.*
EP67	3c	*2,500.*
EP68	5c	*3,750.*
EP69	10c	*5,000.*

Drake's Plantation Bitters

EP70	1c	700.
EP71	3c	550.
EP72	5c	600.
a.	Ribbed frame	*2,500.*
EP73	10c	650.
a.	Ribbed frame	*2,500.*
EP74	12c	*2,500.*
EP75	24c	*4,000.*
EP76	30c	*5,000.*
EP77	90c	*11,000.*

Ellis, McAlpin & Co., Cincinnati

EP78	1c	—
EP79	3c	*2,250.*
EP80	5c	1,500.
EP81	10c	1,150.
EP82	12c	*3,500.*
EP83	24c	*3,250.*

Specialists have questioned the existence of No. EP78. The editors would like to see authenticated evidence of this listing.

G. G. Evans, Philadelphia

No.	Denom.	Value
EP84	1c	2,250.
EP85	3c	1,750.
EP86	5c	—
EP87	10c	*9,250.*

No. EP87 is believed to be unique.

Gage Bros. & Drake, Tremont House, Chicago

No.	Denom.	Value
EP88	1c	1,500.
EP89	3c	600.
EP90	5c	750.
EP91	10c	1,100.
a.	Ribbed frame	*4,000.*
EP92	12c	*3,500.*

Only one example of No. EP91a is available to collectors.

J. Gault

No.	Denom.	Value
EP93	1c	750.
a.	Ribbed frame	*7,500.*
EP95	3c	750.
a.	Ribbed frame	1,400.
EP96	5c	650.
a.	Ribbed frame	750.
EP97	10c	900.
a.	Ribbed frame	750.
EP98	12c	1,150.
a.	Ribbed frame	*2,500.*
EP99	24c	2,250.
a.	Ribbed frame	*2,750.*
EP100	30c	*2,750.*
a.	Ribbed frame	*4,250.*
EP101	90c	*12,500.*

L. C. Hopkins & Co., Cincinnati

No.	Denom.	Value
EP102	1c	*6,000.*
EP103	3c	*5,250.*
EP104	5c	*5,500.*
EP105	10c	*5,750.*

Hunt & Nash, Irving House, New York

No.	Denom.	Value
EP106	1c	*2,000.*
EP107	3c	*2,250.*
a.	Ribbed frame	*3,250.*
EP108	5c	1,600.
a.	Ribbed frame	900.
EP109	10c	1,300.
a.	Ribbed frame	1,000.
EP110	12c	*3,250.*
a.	Ribbed frame	*3,250.*
EP111	24c	*3,750.*
a.	Ribbed frame	*4,500.*
EP112	30c	*6,000.*

No. EP112 is unique.

Kirkpatrick & Gault, New York

No.	Denom.	Value
EP113	1c	800.
EP114	3c	900.
EP115	5c	700.
EP116	10c	800.
EP117	12c	*1,350.*
EP118	24c	*1,750.*
EP119	30c	*3,750.*
EP120	90c	*10,000.*

Lord & Taylor, New York

No.	Denom.	Value
EP121	1c	1,500.
EP122	3c	1,500.
EP123	5c	1,050.
EP124	10c	1,250.
EP125	12c	*2,500.*
EP126	24c	*3,250.*
EP127	30c	*4,000.*
EP128	90c	*10,000.*

Mendum's Family Wine Emporium, New York

No.	Denom.	Value
EP129	1c	1,100.
EP130	3c	*2,500.*
EP131	5c	*1,600.*
EP132	10c	*2,750.*
a.	Ribbed frame	*5,000.*
EP133	12c	*3,000.*

B. F. Miles, Peoria

No.	Denom.	Value
EP134	1c	*25,000.*
EP135	5c	*10,000.*

John W. Norris, Chicago

No.	Denom.	Value
EP136	1c	*2,750.*
EP137	3c	*3,750.*
EP138	5c	*3,750.*
EP139	10c	*3,250.*

"INSURANCE" Curved

"INSURANCE" Straight

North America Life Insurance Co., N. Y.

No.	Denom.	Value
EP140	1c Curved	700.
a.	Straight	575.
EP141	3c Straight	800.
a.	Curved	1,750.
EP142	5c Straight	675.
a.	Straight, ribbed frame	1,100.
b.	Curved	*3,000.*
EP143	10c Straight	800.
a.	Straight, ribbed frame	*3,250.*
b.	Curved	1,750.
c.	Curved, ribbed frame	*2,250.*
EP144	12c Straight	*4,000.*
a.	Curved	*4,500.*

No. EP142b is unique. Nos. EP143a and EP144a each may be unique.

Pearce, Tolle & Holton, Cincinnati

No.	Denom.	Value
EP145	1c	*8,000.*
EP146	3c	*3,500.*
EP147	5c	*3,500.*
EP148	10c	*12,000.*
EP149	12c	*9,000.*
EP150	24c	—

No. EP149 is unique.

The existence of No. EP150 has been questioned by specialists. The editors would like to see authenticated evidence of its existence.

Sands' Ale

No.	Denom.	Value
EP151	5c	*5,000.*
EP152	10c	*6,000.*
EP153	12c	—
EP154	30c	—

No. EP154 is unique. The case of the known example has been opened. It is possible that the 30c stamp has been substituted for the original stamp and/or the mica has been replaced.

Schapker & Bussing, Evansville, Ind.

EP155	1c	2,500.
EP156	3c	1,250.
EP157	5c	1,500.
EP158	10c	800.
EP159	12c	*7,500.*

John Shillito & Co., Cincinnati

EP160	1c	*3,000.*
EP161	3c	*1,000.*
EP162	5c	*750.*
EP163	10c	*1,500.*
EP164	12c	*5,500.*

S. Steinfeld, New York

EP165	1c	*3,000.*
EP166	5c	*7,000.*
EP167	10c	*9,500.*
EP168	12c	*6,000.*

No. EP167 may be unique.

N. G. Taylor & Co., Philadelphia

EP169	1c	*3,250.*
EP170	3c	*3,500.*
EP171	5c	*3,750.*
EP172	10c	*3,750.*
EP173	12c	*8,000.*

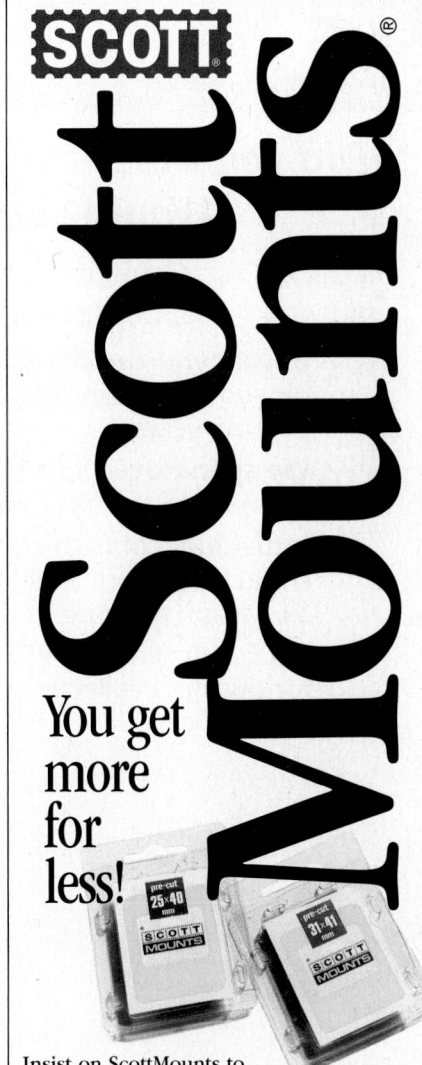

No. EP173 is unique.

Weir and Larminie, Montreal

EP174	1c	*5,500.*
EP175	3c	*12,500.*
EP176	5c	—
EP177	10c	*3,000.*

No. EP176 may be unique.

White, the Hatter, New York

EP178	1c	*2,500.*
EP179	3c	*2,750.*
EP180	5c	*5,000.*
EP181	10c	*5,000.*

POSTAGE CURRENCY

Small coins disappeared from circulation in 1861-62 as cash was hoarded. To ease business transactions, merchants issued notes of credit, promises to pay, tokens, store cards, etc. U.S. Treasurer Francis E. Spinner made a substitute for small currency by affixing postage stamps, singly and in multiples, to Treasury paper. He arranged with the Post office to replace worn stamps with new when necessary.

The next step was to print the stamps on Treasury paper. On July 17, 1862, Congress authorized the issue of such "Postage Currency." It remained in use until May 27, 1863. It was not money, but a means of making stamps negotiable.

On Oct. 10, 1863 a second issue was released. These, and the later three issues, did not show stamps and are called Fractional Currency. In 1876 Congress authorized the minting of silver coins to redeem the outstanding fractional currency.

Values quoted are for notes in crisp, new condition, not creased or worn.
Creased or worn notes sell for 25 percent to 75 percent less.
Items valued with a dash are believed to be unique.

Front Engraved and Printed by the National Bank Note Co.
Back Engraved and Printed in Black by the American Bank Note Co.
"A B Co." on Back

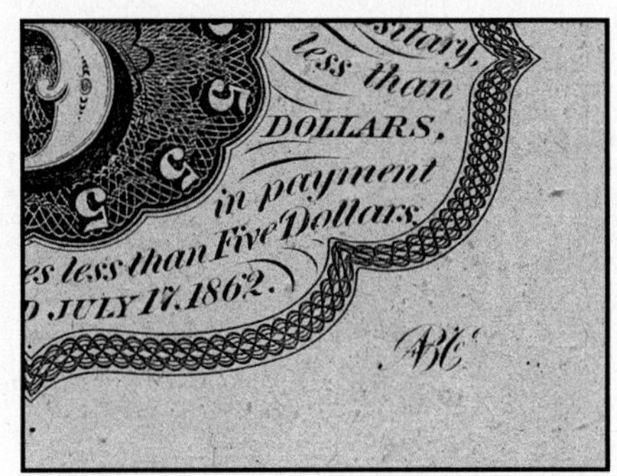

"ABCo." imprint, lower right corner of back (#1-8)

1862, Aug. 21

Perforated Edges-Perf. 12

PC1	5c Bust of Jefferson on 5c stamp, brown	190.00
	a. Inverted back	*950.00*
PC2	10c Bust of Washington on 10c stamp, green	160.00
PC3	25c Five 5c stamps, brown	240.00
PC4	50c Five 10c stamps, green	325.00
	a. Inverted back	*950.00*

Imperforate Edges

PC5	5c Bust of Jefferson on 5c stamp	85.00
	a. Inverted back	*525.00*
PC6	10c Bust of Washington on 10c stamp	85.00
	a. Inverted back	*675.00*
PC7	25c Five 5c stamps	150.00
	a. Inverted back	*600.00*
PC8	50c Five 10c stamps	175.00
	a. Inverted back	*750.00*

No. PC8 exists perforated 14, privately produced.

Front and Back Engraved and Printed by the National Bank Note Co.

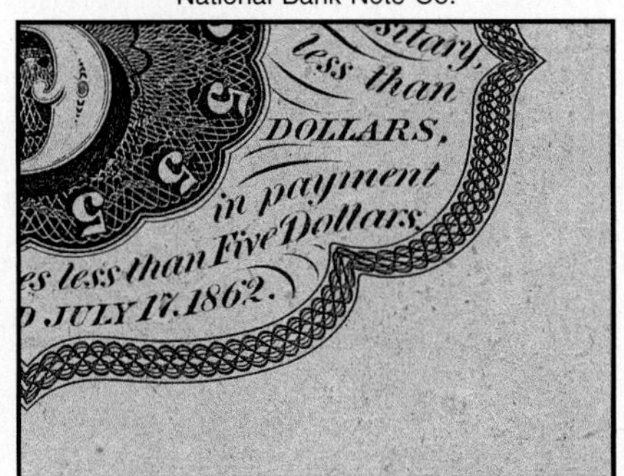

Without "A B Co." on Back

Perforated Edges-Perf. 12

PC9	5c Bust of Jefferson on 5c stamp	230.00
	a. Inverted back	—
PC10	10c Bust of Washington on 10c stamp	275.00
	a. Inverted back	—
PC11	25c Five 5c stamps	340.00
	a. Inverted back	*1,100.*
PC12	50c Five 10c stamps	450.00
	a. Inverted back	—

Imperforate Edges

PC13	5c Bust of Jefferson on 5c stamp	210.00
	a. Inverted back	—
PC14	10c Bust of Washington on 10c stamp	320.00
	a. Inverted back	*1,100.*
PC15	25c Five 5c stamps	425.00
PC16	50c Five 10c stamps	750.00
	a. Inverted back	—

CONFEDERATE STATES OF AMERICA

UNITED STATES STAMPS AND STAMPED ENVELOPES
USED IN THE INDEPENDENT STATES AND IN THE CONFEDERATE STATES

With the secession of South Carolina from the Union on December 20, 1860, a new era began in U.S. history as well as its postal history. Other Southern states quickly followed South Carolina's lead, which in turn led to the formation of the provisional government of the Confederate States of America on February 4, 1861.

President Jefferson Davis' cabinet was completed March 6, 1861, with the acceptance of the position of Postmaster General by John H. Reagan of Texas. The provisional government had already passed regulations that required payment for postage in cash or by the use of the then-current United States stamps and stamped envelopes and that effectively carried over the U.S. 3¢ rate until the new Confederate Post Office Department took over control of the system.

Soon after entering on his duties, Reagan directed the postmasters in the Confederate States and in the newly seceded states to "continue the performance of their duties as such, and render all accounts and pay all moneys (sic) to the order of the Government of the U.S. as they have heretofore done, until the Government of the Confederate States shall be prepared to assume control of its postal affairs."

On May 13, 1861, Postmaster General Reagan issued his proclamation "assuming control and direction of postal service within the limits of the Confederate States of America on and after the first day of June," with new postage rates and regulations. The Federal government suspended operations in the Confederates States (except for western Virginia and the seceding state of Tennessee) by a proclamation issued by Postmaster General Montgomery Blair on May 27, 1861, and June 10 for western and middle Tennessee.

Until the assumption of control by the Confederate Post Office on June 1, 1861, therefore, Southern postmasters continued to use the stamps, stamped envelopes and postal rates of the United States. Stamps soon became scarce in many locations, as the U.S. Post Office was reluctant to re-supply seceded states with additional supplies.

The listings are by Scott number and denomination and, where appropriate, stamps and covers from individual states are indicated. Off-cover stamps are valued in the grade of fine, with the identifying town and date clearly legible. Covers also are valued in the grade of fine, with town and date of use clearly indicated.

TABLE OF SECESSION

	Ordinance of Secession	Admitted to Confederacy	Period for Use of U.S. Stamps: As Independent State	Total to 5/31/1861*
SC	12/20/1860	2/4/1861	46 days	163 days
MS	1/9/1861	2/4/1861	26 days	143 days
FL	1/11/1861	2/4/1861	24 days	142 days
AL	1/11/1861	2/4/1861	24 days	141 days
GA	1/19/1861	2/4/1861	16 days	133 days
LA	1/26/1861	2/4/1861	9 days	126 days
MO	10/31/1861	11/28/1861	—	—
TX	3/2/1861	3/5/1861	3 days	90 days
VA	4/17/1861	5/7/1861	20 days	45 days
AR	5/6/1861	5/18/1861	12 days	26 days
TN	6/8/1861	7/2/1861	24 days	—
NC	5/20/1861	5/27/1861	7 days	12 days

* The use of United States stamps in the seceded States was prohibited after May 31, 1861.

TX — Ordinance of Secession adopted Feb. 1. Popular vote to secede Feb. 23, effective Mar. 2, 1861. Collectors call Texas covers used between Feb. 1 and March 1 inclusive "Transitional Texas Use" covers, and all CSA collectors treat these covers as an integral part of CSA postal history.

Settlers in south Arizona Territory south of the 34th parallel voted to secede 3/16/61 and were accepted into the CSA on Feb. 14, 1862. This was largely symbolic and Confederate forces abanodoned the area in mid-1862.

VA — Ordinance of adopted. Admitted to Confederacy May 7. Scheduled election of May 23 ratified the Ordinance of Secession.

TN — Ordinance passed to "submit to vote of the people a Declaration of Independence, and for other purposes." Adopted May 6. Election took place June 8. General Assembly ratified election June 24.

MO — The Missouri secession vote and admission into the CSA was symbolic, because the Confederacy did not control any part of the state.

KY — Southern sympathizers from a rival government seceded on Nov. 20, 1861. This faction was granted admission to the CSA on Dec. 10, 1861.

Values in the left column are for U.S. stamps and covers bearing U.S. stamps mailed during the dates of Independent Statehood, and values in the right column are for U.S. stamps and covers bearing U.S. stamps mailed during the time after the states were formally admitted to the Confederate States of America.

18	1c Type I, Plate 12	1,000.	1,500.
	On cover	1,500.	1,500.
20	1c Type II, Plate 12	500.	500.
	On cover	1,000.	1,000.
	1c Type II, Plate 11	1,000.	1,000.
	On cover	1,500.	1,500.
21	1c Type III, Plate 12	*5,000.*	*5,000.*
	On cover	7,500.	7,500.
22	1c Type IIIa, Plate 11 or 12	750.	750.
	On cover	1,250.	1,250.
24	1c Type V	150.	150.

On cover

South Carolina	750.	500.
Mississippi	750.	500.
Florida	1,250.	750.
Alabama	750.	500.
Georgia	750.	500.
Louisiana	750.	500.
Texas	1,000.	750.
Virginia	750.	500.
Arkansas	—	**
Tennessee	***	***
North Carolina	**	**

Uses of U.S. Nos. U19//U24 instead of Nos. 18-24 also are known. Values start at $250 more than the values shown for No. 24 for both Independent State use and for Confederate States of America use.

26	3c Type III	50.	50.

On cover

South Carolina	300.	150.
Mississippi	325.	175.
Florida	500.	350.
Alabama	300.	175.
Georgia	300.	175.
Louisiana	300.	175.
Texas	500.	350.
Virginia	300.	200.
Arkansas	*1,250.*	*1,000.*
Tennessee	***	***
North Carolina	*1,200.*	*850.*

Uses of U.S. Nos. U1//U10 and U26-U27 instead of No. 26 also are known. Values start at the same as the values shown for No. 26 for both Independent State use and for Confederate States of America use. While no examples of No. 26 are known used from either independent or CSA Arkansas, the 3¢ star die envelopes (Nos. U26-U27) are known used during Arkansas' CSA period. Value, $1,250.

29	5c Type I	750.	750.
	On cover	1,250.	1,250.
30A	5c Type II	500.	500.
	On cover	1,000.	1,000.
35	10c Type V	200.	200.
	On cover	1,000.	1,000.
36B	12c Type II, Plate 3	500.	500.
	On cover	1,000.	1,000.
37	24c	1,000.	1,000.
	On cover	*5,000.*	*5,000.*
38	30c	1,000.	1,000.
	On cover	*6,500.*	*5,000.*

** = none known

*** = Tennessee did not formally secede until June 8, 1861, after the C.S.A. Post Office had assumed control over the postal system.

The following Scott numbers were replaced by new varieties in 1857-59. They might exist used in an Independent State or in the C.S.A., but to date none has been found: Nos. 19, 23, 25, 25A, 26A, 27, 28, 28A, 30, 31, 32, 33, 34, 36.

Scott 39, the 90¢ blue of 1860, could have been used from New Orleans, but no such use has been found.

CONFEDERATE STATES OF AMERICA

3¢ 1861 POSTMASTERS' PROVISIONALS

As coinage and United States stamps became scarce in the newly seceded states, postal patrons began having problems buying stamps or paying for letters individually. Even though the U.S. Post Office Department was technically in control of the postal system and southern postmasters were operating under Federal authority, the U.S.P.O. began to cut off supplies to the seceded states.

The U.S. government had made the issuance of postmasters' provisionals illegal many years before, but the southern postmasters had to do what they felt was necessary to allow patrons to pay for postage and make the system work. Therefore, a few postmasters took it upon themselves to issue provisional stamps in the 3¢ rate then in effect. Interestingly, these were stamps and envelopes that the U.S. government did not recognize as legal, but they did do postal duty unchallenged in the Confederate States. Yet the proceeds were to be remitted to the U.S. government in Washington! Six authenticated postmasters' provisionals in the 3¢ rate have been recorded.

Because Tennessee did not join the Confederacy until July 2, 1861, the unissued 3¢ Nashville provisional was produced in a state that was in the process of seceding, while the other provisionals were used in the Confederacy before the assumption of control of the postal service by the Confederate States of America on June 1, 1861.

DARLINGTON C.H., S. C.

E1

Handstamped Envelope

8AXU1 E1 3c black *3,500.*

One example of No. 8AXU1 is recorded, used under a pair of C.S.A. No. 7. To be a provisional, the 3¢ marking must be unused or used under Confederate stamps.

FORT VALLEY, GA.

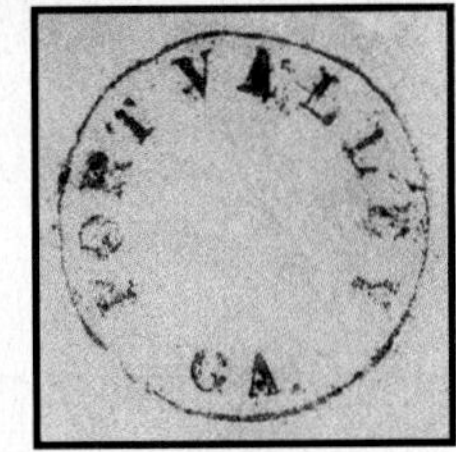

E1 Control

Handstamped Envelope

7AXU1 E1 3c **black** —

HILLSBORO, N.C.

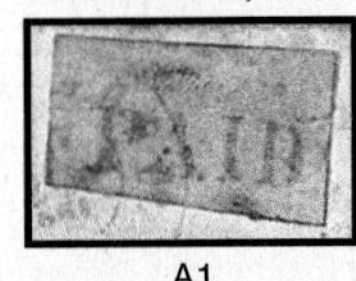

A1

Handstamped Adhesive

1AX1 A1 3c **bluish black,** on cover *8,000.*

No. 1AX1 is unique. This is the same handstamp as used for No. 39X1. 3c usage is determined from the May 27, 1861 circular date stamp.

Cancellation: black town.

JACKSON, MISS.

E1

Handstamped Envelope

2AXU1 E1 3c **black** *3,000.*

See Nos. 43XU1-43XU4.

No. 2AXU1 is unique. It is on a southern patriotic cover.

MADISON COURT HOUSE, FLA.

A1

"CNETS"

Typeset Adhesive

3AX1 A1 3c **gold** — *20,000.*
On cover *120,000.*
a. "CNETS" *22,500.*

No. 3AX1 on cover and No. 3AX1a are each unique.

Cancellations: black town, oblong paid, ms "Paid in Money," manuscript.

See No. 137XU1.

NASHVILLE, TENN.

A1

Typeset Adhesive (5 varieties)

4AX1 A1 3c **carmine** 400.
Horizontal strip of 5 showing all varieties 2,250.

For more than 150 years, it has been believed that No. 4AX1 was prepared by Postmaster McNish with the U.S. rate, but it was not issued. Recent research and historical evidence indicate that this "stamp" most likely is a fantasy rather than a genuine stamp.

Fakes exist of the horizontal strips. Expertization is recommended.

See Nos. 61X2-61XU2.

SELMA, ALA.

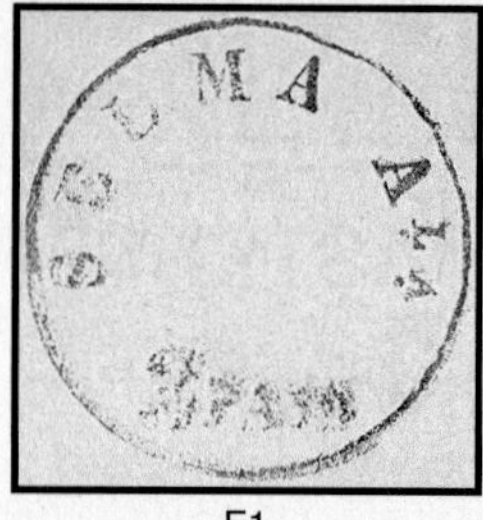

E1

Handstamped Envelope

5AXU1 E1 3c **black** *1,950.*

See Nos. 77XU1-77XU3.

TUSCUMBIA, ALA.

E1

Handstamped Envelope, impression at upper right

6AXU1 E1 3c **dull red,** *buff* *30,000.*

No. 6AXU1 also exists with a 3c 1857 stamp affixed at upper right over the provisional handstamp, tied by black circular "TUSCUMBIA, ALA." town postmark. Value $40,000.

Dangerous forgeries exist of No. 6AXU1.

See Nos. 84XU1-84XU3.

For later additions, listed out of numerical sequence, see:
#7AXU1, **Fort Valley, Ga.**
#8AXU1, **Darlington, C.H., S.C.**

CONFEDERATE POSTMASTERS' PROVISIONALS

These stamps and envelopes were issued by individual postmasters generally during the interim between June 1, 1861, when the use of United States stamps stopped in the Confederacy, and October 16, 1861, when the first Confederate Government stamps were issued. They were occasionally issued at later periods, especially in Texas, when regular issues of government stamps were unavailable.

Canceling stamps of the post offices were often used to produce envelopes, some of which were supplied in advance by private citizens. These envelopes and other stationery therefore may be found in a wide variety of papers, colors, sizes and shapes, including patriotic and semi-official types. It is often difficult to determine whether the impression made by the canceling stamp indicates provisional usage or merely postage paid at the time the letter was deposited in the post office. Occasionally the same mark was used for both purposes.

The *press-printed* **provisional envelopes are in a different category. They were produced in quantity, using envelopes procured in advance by the postmaster, such as those of Charleston, Lynchburg, Memphis, etc.** *The* **press-printed** *envelopes are listed and valued on all known papers.*

The **handstamped** *provisional envelopes are listed and valued according to type and variety of handstamp, but not according to paper. Many exist on such a variety of papers that they defy accurate, complete listing. The value of a handstamped provisional envelope is determined primarily by the clarity of the markings and its overall condition and attractiveness, rather than the type of paper.*

All handstamped provisional envelopes, when used, should also show the postmark of the town of issue.

Most handstamps are impressed at top right, although they exist from some towns in other positions.

Many illustrations in this section are reduced in size.

Values for envelopes are for entires. Values for stamps of provisional issues are for examples with little or no gum; original gum over a large portion of the stamp will increase the value substantially.

ABERDEEN, MISS.

E1

Handstamped Envelopes

1XU1 E1 5c **black** *5,500.*
a. 10c (ms.) on 5c **black** *9,000.*

No. 1XU1a is unique.

ABINGDON, VA.

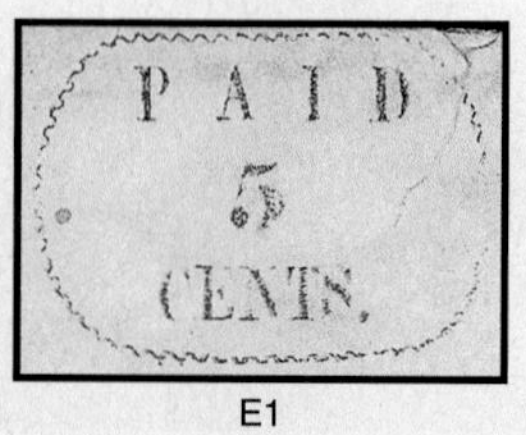

E1

Handstamped Envelopes

2XU1 E1 2c **black** *12,500.*
a. 5c (ms.) on 2c **black** *15,000.*
2XU2 E1 5c **black** *1,500.*
On patriotic cover *3,000.*
2XU3 E1 10c **black** *2,200. 3,500.*

No. 2XU1 is unique. The unused No. 2XU3 is a unique mint example, and the value represents the price realized in a 1997 auction sale. No. 2XU3 used also is unique.

ALBANY, GA.

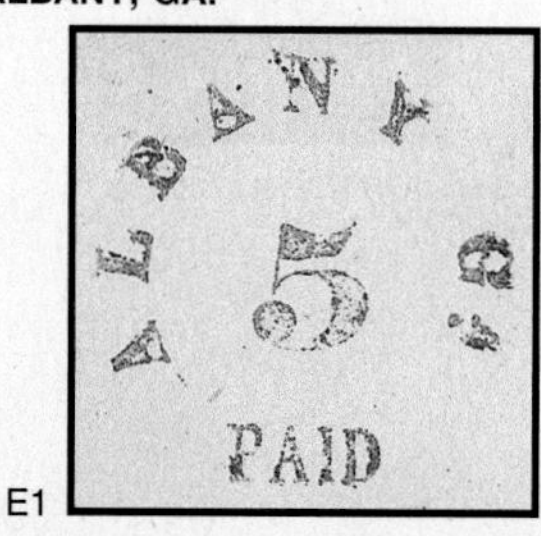

E1

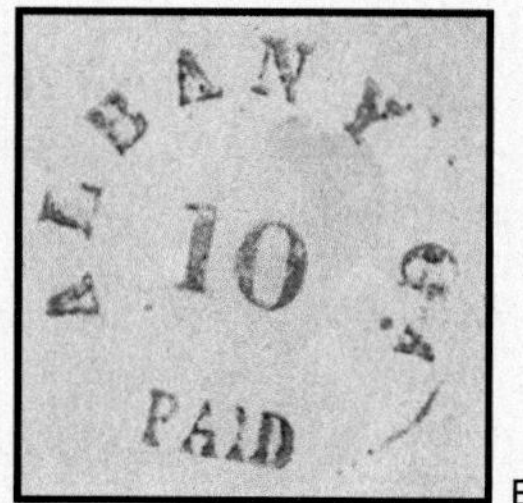

E2

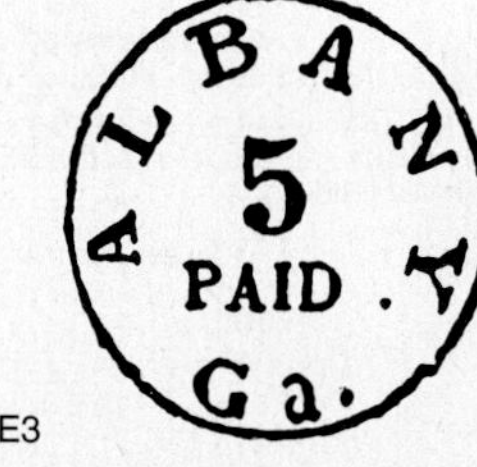

E3

E4

Handstamped Envelopes

3XU1	E1 5c **greenish blue**		1,000.
	On patriotic cover		—
3XU2	E2 10c **greenish blue**		*1,750.*
a.	10c on 5c **greenish blue**		*3,500.*
3XU5	E3 5c **greenish blue**		—
3XU6	E4 10c **greenish blue**		*3,500.*

Only one example each recorded of Nos. 3XU2, 3XU2a and 3XU6. No. 3XU2 is a cover front only and is valued as such. No. 3XU2a is the unique Confederate example of one provisional marking revaluing another.

The existence of No. 3XU5 is in question. The editors would like to see an authenticated example of this marking.

ANDERSON COURT HOUSE, S.C.

E1

E2

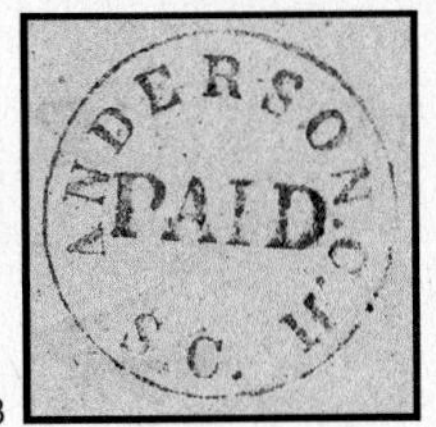

E3

Handstamped Envelopes

4XU1	E1 5c **black**	1,000.	*2,750.*
4XU2	E2 10c (ms.) **black**		*2,500.*
4XU3	E3 (2c) **black,** denomination omitted (circular rate)		*2,250.*

ATHENS, GA

A1 (Type I)

A1 (Type II)

E1

Typographed Adhesives (from woodcuts of two types)

Pairs, both horizontal and vertical, always show one of each type.

5X1	A1 5c **purple** (shades)	1,000.	1,400.
	Pair	—	3,500.
	On cover		2,750.
	Pair on cover		7,000.
	Strip of 4 on cover (horiz.)		*10,000.*
a.	Tete beche pair (vertical)		*7,500.*
	Tete beche pair on cover		*20,000.*
5X2	A1 5c **red, type II**	5,750.	3,000.
	On cover		*12,500.*
	Pair on cover		—

Cancellations in black: grid, town, "PAID."

The colorless ornaments in the four corners of No. 5X2 were recut making them wider than those in No. 5X1.

Dangerous fakes exist of Nos. 5X1 and 5X2. Certificates of authenticity from recognized committees are strongly recommended.

No. 5X2 unused is unique.

The existence of a pair on cover of No. 5X2 is in question. The editors would like to see an example of this usage.

Handstamped Envelopes

5XU1	E1 10c **black,** on patriotic cover	*2,500.*

The markings on No. 5XU1 are the same as those used on stampless envelopes. On the unique listed example of No. 5XU1, there is a handwritten note on the inside of the flap: 'Andrew had these envelopes stamped & I am obliged to use them or loose the postage.' Two or more similar covers from the same correspondence are known, but without the note under the flap. While these also may be provisional use, it cannot be proven, and these covers are considered handstamp paid covers.

ATLANTA, GA.

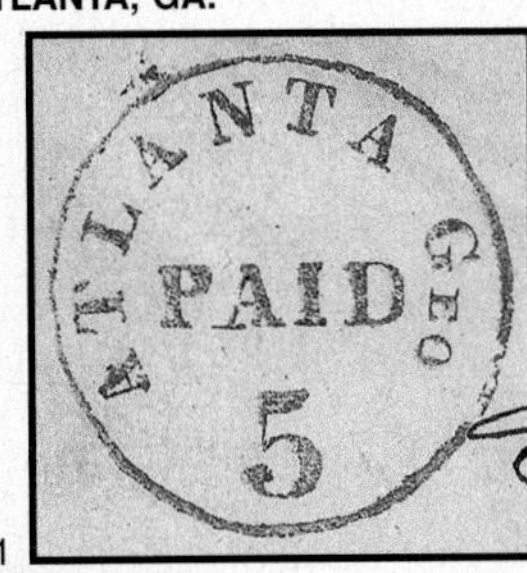

E1

E2

E3

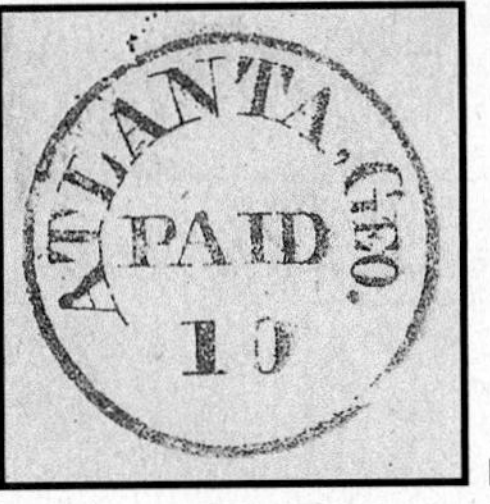

E4

Handstamped Envelopes

6XU1	E1 5c **red**		*5,000.*
6XU2	E1 5c **black**	160.	700.
	On patriotic cover		*3,500.*
a.	10c on 5c **black**		*2,500.*
	On patriotic cover		—
6XU3	E2 PAID, black		*1,000.*
6XU4	E3 2c **black**		*2,750.*
6XU5	E3 5c **black**		1,250.
	On patriotic cover		3,500.
a.	10c on 5c **black**		*2,500.*
6XU6	E4 10c **black**		500.
	On patriotic cover		—

Only one example recorded of No. 6XU1.

E3

Handstamped Envelopes

6XU8	E3 5c **black**	3,500.
6XU9	E3 10c **black** ("10" upright)	3,000.

Only one example recorded of No. 6XU8.

AUSTIN, MISS.

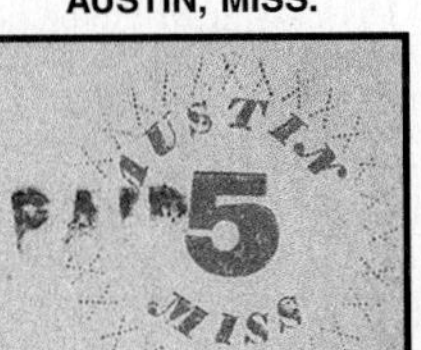

E1

Press-printed Envelope (typeset)

8XU1	E1 5c **red,** *amber*	*75,000.*

One example recorded.

Cancellation: black "Paid."

AUSTIN, TEX.

E1a

Handstamped Adhesive

9X1	E1a 10c **black,** *white* or *buff*	—
	On cover, uncanceled	*18,000.*
	On cover, tied	—

Only one example of No. 9X1 tied on cover is recorded.

Handstamped Envelope

9XU1	E1a 10c **black**	2,500.

Cancellation on Nos. 9X1 and 9XU1: black town.

AUTAUGAVILLE, ALA.

E1

E2

Handstamped Envelopes

10XU1	E1 5c **black**	*20,000.*
10XU2	E2 5c **black**	*20,000.*

No. 10XU2 is unique.

BALCONY FALLS, VA.

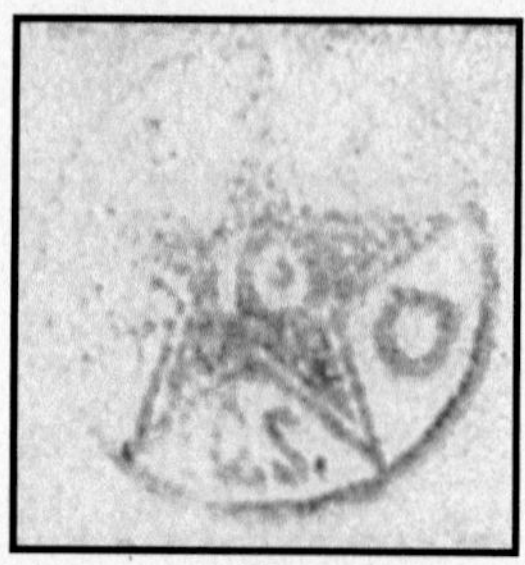

E1

Handstamped Envelope

122XU1 E1 10c **blue** *2,000.*

The use of No. 122XU1 as a provisional marking is in question. The editors would like to see authenticated evidence of its use as a provisional.

BARNWELL COURT HOUSE, S. C.

E1

Handstamped Envelope

123XU1 E1 5c **black** *3,000.*

These are two separate handstamps.

All recorded uses are on addressed covers without postmarks.

BATON ROUGE, LA.

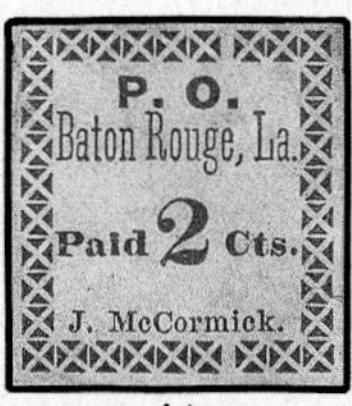

A1

A2

Typeset Adhesives

Ten varieties of each

11X1 A1 2c **green** *8,250. 5,000.*
On cover *50,000.*
a. "McCcrmick" *35,000. 35,000.*
On cover *55,000.*
11X2 A2 5c **green & carmine** (Maltese cross border) *1,500. 1,400.*
On cover *5,000.*
Strip of 3 *7,000.*
Strip of 5 *24,000.*
Canceled in New Orleans, on cover *15,000.*
a. "McCcrmick" *10,000. 3,500.*
On cover *15,000.*

Only one example each is recorded of No. 11X1a unused, used and on cover.

The "Canceled in New Orleans" examples entered the mails in New Orleans after having been placed (uncanceled) on riverboats in Baton Rouge. Two such covers are recorded.

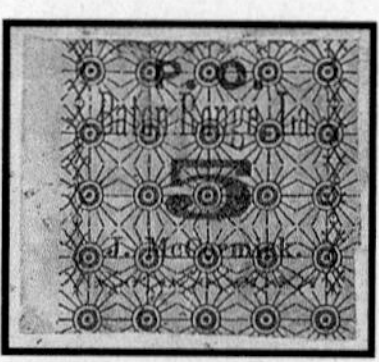

A3

A4

Ten varieties of each

11X3 A3 5c **green & carmine** (crisscross border) *10,000. 4,000.*
On cover *10,000.*
a. "McCcrmick" *32,500.*
11X4 A4 10c **blue** *50,000.*
On cover *75,000.*

Nos. 11X3a and 11X4 on cover are unique.

Cancellation on Nos. 11X1-11X4: black town.

BEAUFORT, S. C.

E1

Handstamped Envelope

150XU1 E1 5c **black** — *3,500.*

To be the No. 150XU1 provisional, the cover must be unused, used under a Confederate stamp, or used from another town. Two examples are recorded.

BEAUMONT, TEX.

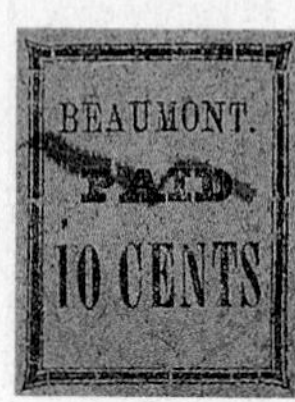

A1

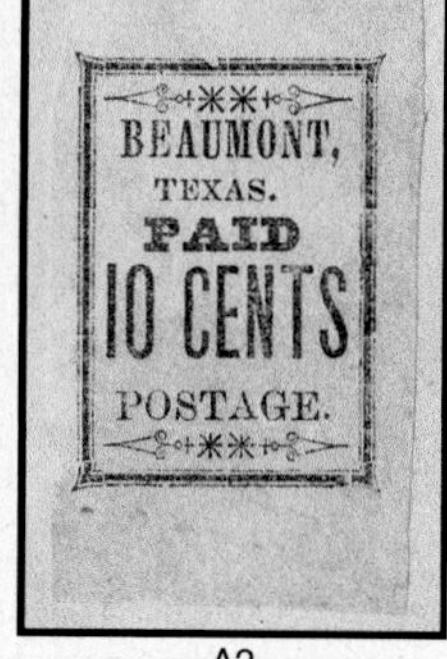

A2

Typeset Adhesives

Several varieties of each

12X1 A1 10c **black,** *yellow* *65,000.*
On cover *75,000.*
12X2 A1 10c **black,** *pink* *40,000.*
On cover *45,000.*

No. 12X1 is smaller than No. 12X2.

12X3 A2 10c **black,** *yellow,* on cover *250,000.*

One example recorded of No. 12X3. Value represents auction realization in 2019.

Cancellations: black pen; black town.

BLUFFTON, S. C.

E1

Handstamped Envelope

124XU1 E1 5c **black** *4,750.*

Only one example recorded of No. 124XU1.

BRIDGEVILLE, ALA.

A1

Handstamped Adhesive in black within red pen-ruled squares

13X1 A1 5c **black & red,** pair on cover *20,000.*

Cancellation is black pen.

CAMDEN, S. C.

E1

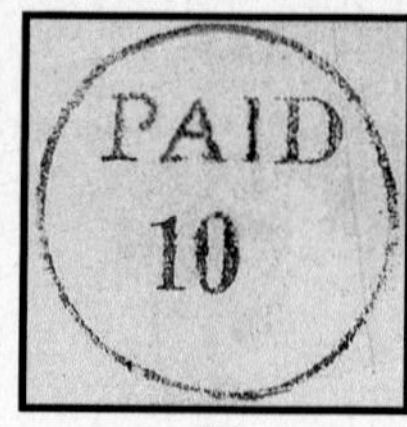

E2

Handstamped Envelopes

125XU1 E1 5c **black** *2,500.*
125XU2 E2 10c **black** *750.*

No. 125XU2 unused was privately carried and is addressed but has no postal markings. No. 125XU2 is indistinguishable from a handstamp paid cover when used.

CANTON, MISS.

E1

"P" in star is initial of Postmaster William Priestly.

Handstamped Envelopes

14XU1 E1 5c **black** *3,500.*
a. 10c (ms.) on 5c **black** *5,000.*

CAROLINA CITY, N. C.

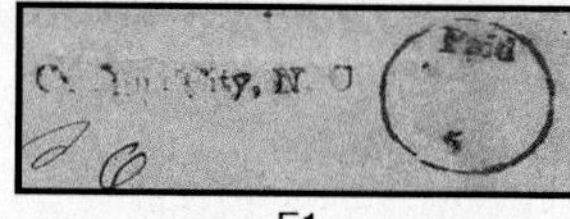

E1

Handstamped Envelope

118XU1 E1 5c **black** *5,000.*

CARTERSVILLE, GA.

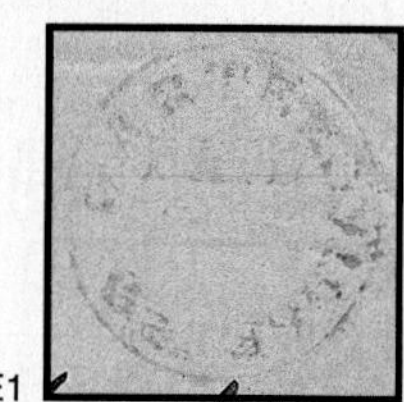

E1

Handstamped Envelope

126XU1 E1 (5c) **red** *1,500.*

CHAPEL HILL, N. C.

E1

Handstamped Envelope

15XU1 E1 5c **black** *4,500.*
On patriotic cover *7,500.*

CHARLESTON, S. C.

A1

E1

E2

Lithographed Adhesive

16X1	A1 5c **blue**	1,400.	800.
	Pair	3,250.	2,200.
	On cover		*2,000.*
	On patriotic cover		*11,500.*
	Pair, on cover		*5,000.*
	On cover with No. 112XU1		*22,500.*
	Used on cover with C.S.A. 5c #6 to make 10c rate		*3,000.*

Values are for stamps showing parts of the outer frame lines on at least 3 sides. The vast majority of this stamp small faults and are valued thus. Completely sound examples are scarce and sell for more.

Cancellation: black town (two types).

Press-printed Envelopes (typographed from woodcut)

16XU1	E1 5c **blue**	1,250.	*1,750.*
16XU2	E1 5c **blue,** *amber*	1,250.	*2,250.*
16XU3	E1 5c **blue,** *orange*	1,250.	*2,250.*
16XU4	E1 5c **blue,** *buff*	1,250.	*1,500.*
16XU5	E1 5c **blue,** *blue*	1,250.	*2,250.*
16XU6	E2 10c **blue,** *orange*		*55,000.*

The No. 16XU6 used entire is unique; value based on 2022 auction sale.

Beware of fakes of the E1 design.

Handstamped Cut Square

16XU7	E2 10c **black**		*2,000.*

There is only one example of No. 16XU7. It is a cutout, not an entire. It may not have been mailed from Charleston, and it may not have paid postage.

CHARLOTTE, N. C.

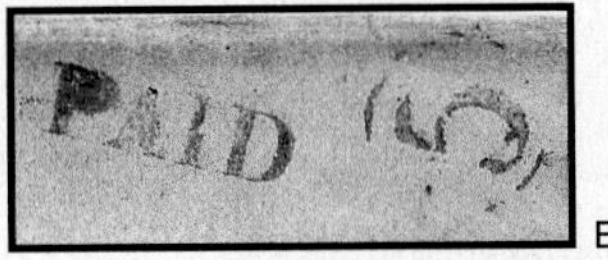
E1

146XU1	E1 5c **blue,** "5" in circle and straight line "PAID"		*3,500.*

CHARLOTTESVILLE, VA.

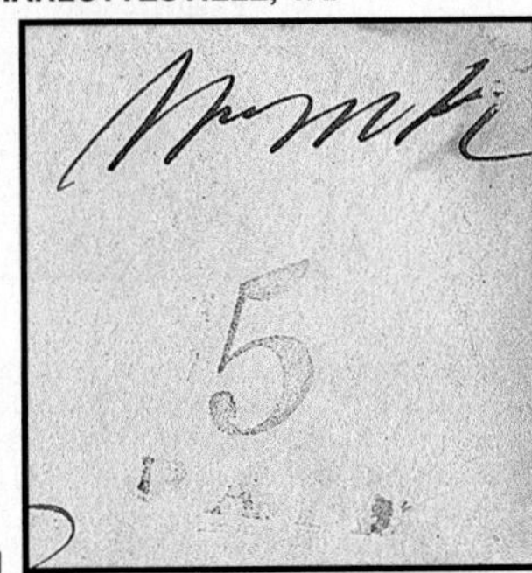
E1

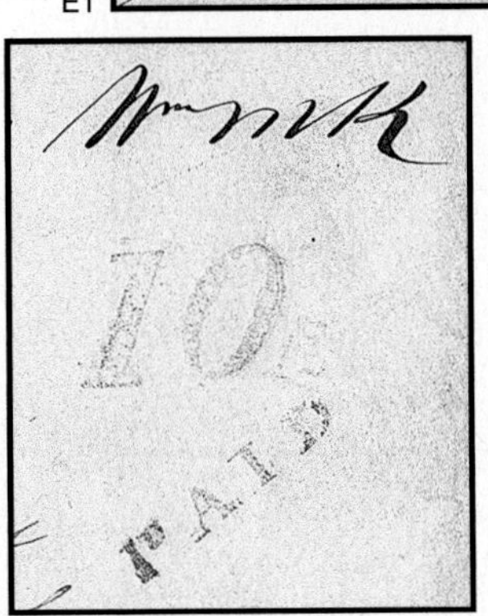
E2

Handstamped Envelopes, Manuscript Initials "WmMK"

127XU1	E1 5c **blue**		*2,250.*
127XU2	E2 10c **blue**		*2,250.*

The control initials appear at the upper right on the front of the envelope.

CHATTANOOGA, TENN.

E1

E2

Handstamped Envelopes

17XU2	E1 5c **black**	1,900.	
17XU3	E2 5c on 2c **black**		*5,000.*

No. 17XU3 is unique.

CHRISTIANSBURG, VA.

E1

Handstamped Envelopes

Impressed at top right

99XU1	E1 5c **black**		*2,250.*
99XU2	E1 5c **blue**		*2,000.*
99XU4	E1 5c **green** on U.S. envelope No. U27		*4,250.*
99XU5	E1 10c **blue**		*3,500.*

The absence of 5c and 10c handstamped paid markings from this town suggests that Nos. 99XU1-99XU5 were used as both provisional and handstamped paid markings.

COLAPARCHEE, GA.

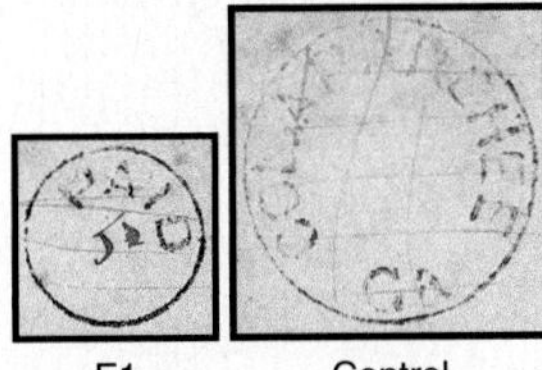
E1 Control

Handstamped Envelope

119XU1	E1 5c **black**		*3,500.*

There are only two recorded examples of No. 119XU1, and both are used from Savannah with a general issue stamp.

The control appears on the front of the envelope.

COLUMBIA, S. C.

Oval Control

Circular Control

E1

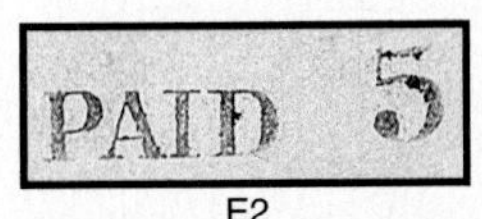

E2

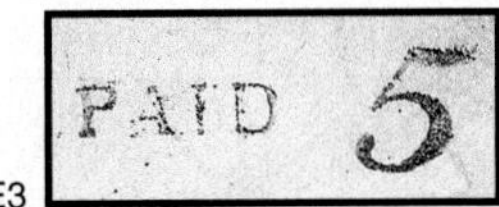

E3

E4

E5

E6

E7

E8

Handstamped Envelopes

18XU1	E1 5c **blue**	550.	*900.*
	Used on cover with C.S.A. 5c #1 or #1c to make 10c rate		*3,000.*
	Used on cover with C.S.A. 5c #7 to make 10c rate		*16,500.*
a.	10c on 5c **blue**		*3,500.*
18XU4	E2 5c **blue,** oval control on front		*2,500.*
a.	Oval control on back		*1,100.*
18XU7	E3 5c **blue,** oval control on back		1,000.
18XU8	E4 5c **blue** oval control on back		1,000.
a.	Circular control on back		2,000.
18XU9	E4 10c **blue** oval control on back		1,250.
18XU10	E5 10c **blue** oval control on back		1,500.
18XU11	E6 5c **blue** oval control on front		*2,500.*
18XU12	E6 10c **blue** oval control on back		1,250.
18XU13	E7 5c **blue** oval control on back		1,000.
a.	Circular control on back		2,000.
18XU14	E8 5c **blue** oval control on back		1,000.
a.	No control (unused)	—	

COLUMBIA, TENN.

E1

Handstamped Envelope

113XU1	E1 5c **red**		*6,000.*

One example recorded.

COLUMBUS, GA.

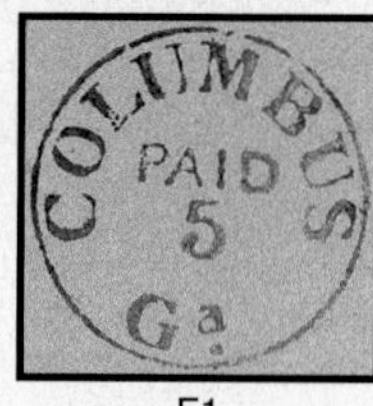

E1

Handstamped Envelopes

19XU1 E1 5c **blue** *900.*
19XU2 E1 10c **red** *3,250.*

COURTLAND, ALA.

E1

Handstamped Envelopes (from woodcut)

103XU1 E1 5c **red** *32,500.*

One example recorded.

CUTHBERT, GA

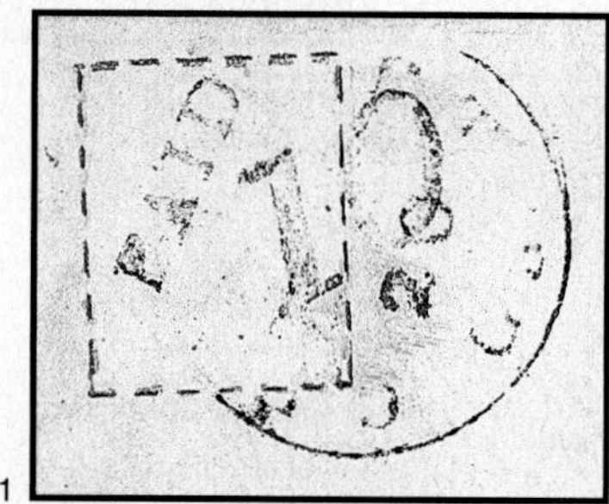

E1

Handstamped Envelope

95XU1 E1 10c **black** *1,000.*

The unique example of No. 95XU1 was used by having a C.S.A. 10c #12c placed over it.

DALTON, GA

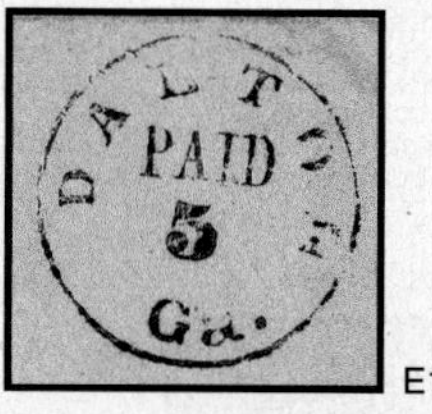

E1

Handstamped Envelopes

20XU1 E1 5c **black** *750.*
a. Denomination omitted (5c rate) *875.*
b. 10c (ms.) on 5c **black** 1,500.
c. 20c (ms.) on 5c **black** —
20XU2 E1 10c **black** 1,250.

DANVILLE, VA.

A1

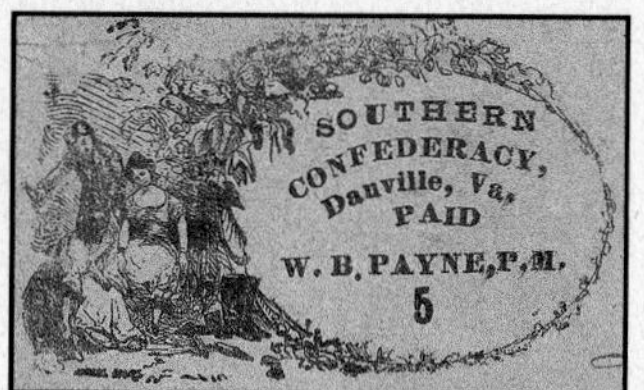

E1

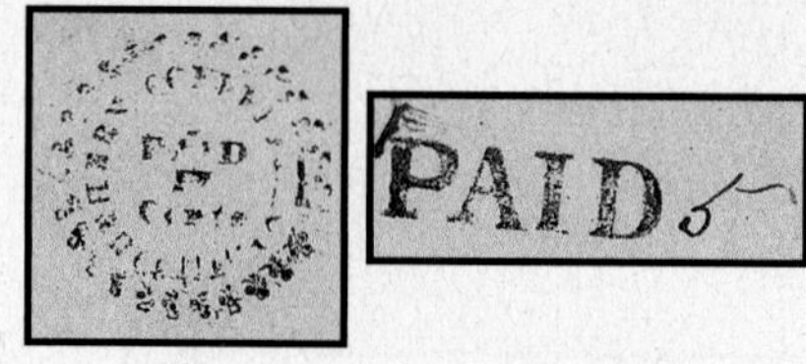

E2

E3

E4

E5

E6

Typeset Adhesive
Wove Paper

21X1 A1 5c **red** *7,500.*
On cover *32,500.*
Cut to shape *6,250.*
On cover, cut to shape *27,500.*

Two varieties known.

Cancellation: blue town.

Laid Paper

21X2 A1 5c **red** *10,000.*

Cancellation: black town.

No. 21X2 is unique.

Press-printed Envelopes (typographed)
Two types: "SOUTHERN" in straight or curved line
Impressed (usually) at top left

21XU1 E1 5c **black** *5,000.*
21XU2 E1 5c **black,** *light yellowish* *5,000.*
21XU3 E1 5c **black,** *dark buff* *5,000.*

Unissued 10c envelopes (type E1, in red) are known. All recorded examples are envelopes that show evidence of added stamps being torn off.

Dangerous forgeries exist of No. 21XU1.

Handstamped Envelopes

21XU3A E2 5c **black** (ms "WBP" initials) *1,000.*
21XU3B E3 5c **black** (ms "WPB" initials) *8,500.*
21XU4 E4 10c **black** *2,500.*
21XU6 E5 10c **black** *2,750.*
21XU7 E6 10c **black** (ms "WBP" initials) —

Types E4 and E5 both exist on one cover.

On No. 21XU3B, the "PAID 5 Cents" handstamp is to the left, and the "PAID" and ms. "5" are toward the right. It is unique.

DEMOPOLIS, ALA.

E1

Handstamped Envelopes, Signature in ms.

22XU1 E1 5c **black** ("Jno. T. Hall") *3,500.*
22XU2 E1 5c **black** ("J. T. Hall") *3,500.*
22XU3 E1 5c (ms.) **black** ("J. T. Hall") *4,000.*

EATONTON, GA.

E1

E2

Handstamped Envelopes

23XU1 E1 5c **black** *3,000.*
a. 10 (ms) on 5c **black** —
23XU2 E2 5c + 5c **black** *5,500.*

EMORY, VA.

A1

Handstamped Adhesives ("PAID" and "5" in circle on selvage of U.S. 1c 1857 issue)
Perf. 15 on three sides

24X1 A1 5c **blue,** on cover, tied *27,500.*
On cover, not tied 22,500.

Also known with "5" above "PAID."

Cancellation: blue town.

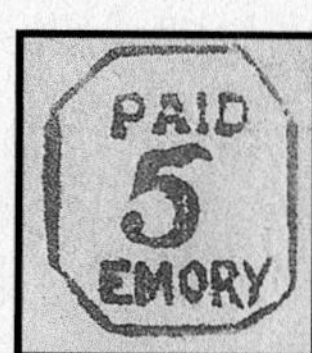

E1

E2

Handstamped Envelopes

24XU1 E1 5c **blue** *4,000.*
24XU2 E2 10c **blue** *5,000.*

One example each recorded of Nos. 24XU1 and 24XU2.

FINCASTLE, VA.

E1

Press-printed Envelope (typeset)

Impressed at top right

104XU1 E1 10c **black** 20,000.

One example recorded of No. 104XU1.

FORSYTH, GA.

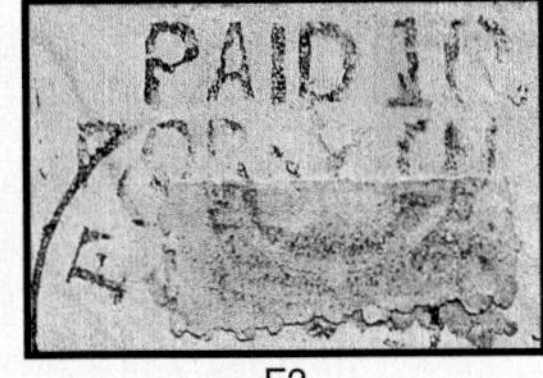

E1 E2

Handstamped Envelope

120XU1 E1 10c **black** 2,000.
120XU2 E2 10c **black** 1,250.

Only one example each recorded of Nos. 120XU1 and 120XU2.

The No. 120XU2 cover has a C.S.A. 10c #11 rouletted used over the provisional marking.

FORT VALLEY, GA.

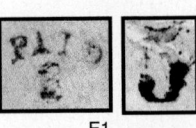

E1 Control

Handstamped Envelope

148XU1 E1 5c on 3c **black** 3,250.

Black circle control on front of envelope. Unique.

FRANKLIN, N. C.

E1

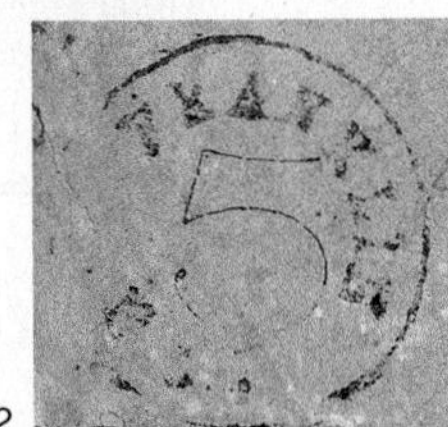

E2

Press-printed Envelope (typeset) (No. 25XU1)

Impressed at top right

25XU1 E1 5c **blue,** *buff* 30,000.
25XU2 E2 5c **black,** large "5" woodcut in 31mm circular town mark 2,500.

The one known No. 25XU1 envelope shows black circular Franklin postmark with manuscript date.

FRAZIERSVILLE, S. C.

E1

Handstamped Envelope, "5" manuscript

128XU1 E1 5c **black** 5,000.

Only one example recorded of No. 128XU1.

FREDERICKSBURG, VA.

A1

Sheets of 20, two panes of 10 varieties each

Typeset Adhesives
Thin bluish paper

26X1	A1 5c **blue,** *bluish*	750.	1,500.
	Block of 4	3,500.	
	Sheet of 20	17,500.	
	On cover		5,000.
	On cover, used to forward Alabama cover to Trevillian's Depot, VA		—
	Pair on cover		12,000.
26X2	A1 10c **red (shades),** *bluish*	2,250.	
	Brown red, *bluish*	1,500.	
	Block of 4	—	

Cancellation: black town.

GAINESVILLE, ALA.

E1

E2

E3

Handstamped Envelopes

27XU1 E1 5c **black** 4,500.
27XU2 E2 5c **black** 5,000.
27XU3 E3 10c ("01") **black** 12,000.

Postmark spells town name "Gainsville."

GALVESTON, TEX.

E1

Handstamped Envelopes

98XU1 E1 5c **black** 500. 1,500.
98XU2 E1 10c **black** 2,500.

E2

E3

Handstamped Envelopes

98XU3 E2 10c **black** 550. 2,750.
98XU4 E2 20c **black** 3,500.
98XU5 E3 5c **black** 4,500.

GASTON, N. C.

E1

Handstamped Envelope

129XU1 E1 5c **black** 6,000.

Only one example recorded of No. 129XU1.

GEORGETOWN, S. C.

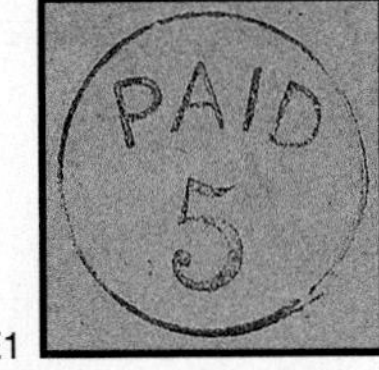

E1

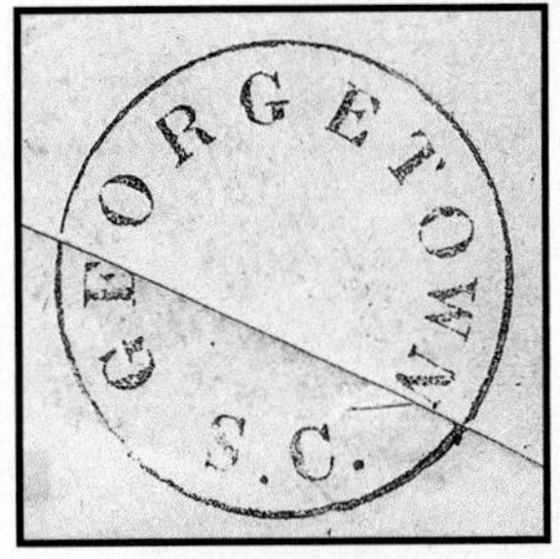

Control

E2

Handstamped Envelopes

28XU1 E1 5c **black** 1,000.
28XU2 E2 5c **black,** separate "5" and straightline "PAID" handstamps, control on reverse — 1,750.

GOLIAD, TEX.

A1

A2

Typeset Adhesives

29X1	A1	5c **black**		*16,500.*
29X2	A1	5c **black,** *gray*		*11,500.*
29X3	A1	5c **black,** *rose*		*12,000.*
		On cover front		*47,500.*
29X4	A1	10c **black**	—	*25,000.*
29X5	A1	10c **black,** *rose*		*12,000.*

Type A1 stamps are signed "Clarke-P.M." vertically in black or red.

29X6	A2	5c **black,** *gray*	*22,500.*
a.		"GOILAD"	*12,000.*
		Pair, left stamp the error	*170,000.*
29X7	A2	10c **black,** *bluish gray*	*12,000.*
		On cover	*50,000.*
a.		"GOILAD"	*15,000.*
		On cover	*30,000.*
29X8	A2	5c **black,** *dark blue,* on cover	*18,000.*
29X9	A2	10c **black,** *dark blue*	*27,500.*

Cancellations in black: pen, town, "Paid"

GONZALES, TEX.

Colman & Law were booksellers when John B. Law (of the firm) was appointed Postmaster. The firm used a small lithographed label on drugs and on the front or inside of books they sold.

A1

Lithographed Adhesives on colored glazed paper

30X1	A1	(5c) **gold,** *dark blue,* pair on cover, *1861*	*15,000.*
30X2	A1	(10c) **gold,** *garnet,* on cover, *1864*	*80,000.*
30X3	A1	(10c) **gold,** *black,* on cover, *1865*	*35,000.*

Cancellations: black town, black pen. No. 30X1 must bear double-circle town cancel as validating control. The control was applied to the labels in the sheet before their sale as stamps. When used, the stamps bear an additional Gonzales double-circle postmark.

GREENSBORO, ALA.

E1

E2

E3

Handstamped Envelopes

31XU1	E1	5c **black**	*3,250.*
31XU2	E1	10c **black**	*3,750.*
31XU3	E2	10c **black**	*6,000.*
31XU4	E3	10c on 5c **black**	*3,000.*

GREENSBORO, N. C.

E1

Handstamped Envelope

32XU1	E1	10c **red**	1,250.

GREENVILLE, ALA.

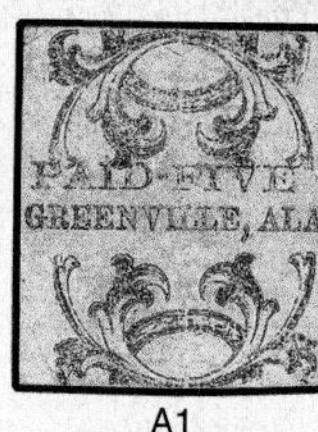
A1

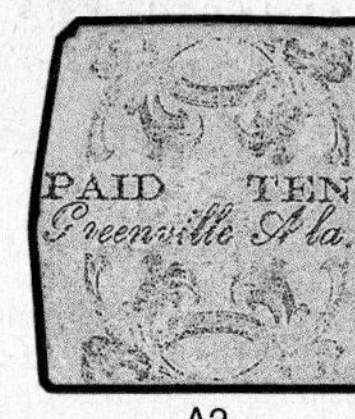
A2

Typeset Adhesives On pinkish surface-colored glazed paper.

33X1	A1	5c **blue & red**	*28,000.*
		On cover	*47,500.*
33X2	A2	10c **red & blue,** on cover	*47,500.*

Two used examples each are known of Nos. 33X1-33X2, and all are on covers. Covers bear a postmark but it was not used to cancel the stamps.

The former No. 33X1a has been identified as a fake.

GREENVILLE, TENN.

E1

144XU1	E1	5c **black**	*5,000.*

Only one example of No. 144XU1 is recorded.

GREENVILLE COURT HOUSE, S. C.

E1

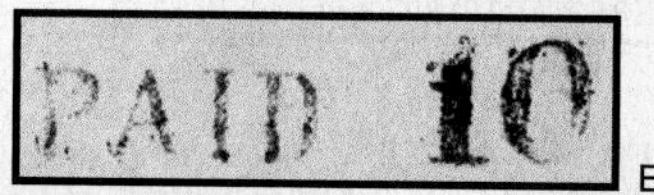
E2

Control A

Control B

Control C

Handstamped Envelopes (Several types)

34XU1	E1	5c **black**	*2,000.*
34XU2	E2	10c **black**	*2,000.*
a.		20c (ms.) on 10c **black**	*3,000.*

Envelopes must bear one of three different postmark controls on the back. When the control postmark is dated, the date must be the same or prior to the date of the postmark on the front of the envelope.

GREENWOOD DEPOT, VA.

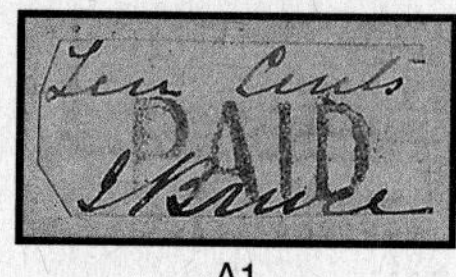
A1

"PAID" Handstamped Adhesive ("PAID" with value and signature in ms.) Laid Paper

35X1	A1	10c **black,** *gray blue,* uncanceled, on cover	*40,000.*
		On cover, tied	—

Six examples recorded of No. 35X1, all on covers. One of these is in the British Library collection. Of the remaining five, only one has the stamp tied to the cover.

Cancellation: black town.

GRIFFIN, GA.

E1

Handstamped Envelopes

102XU1	E1	5c **black**	2,000.
102XU2	E1	10c **black**	*5,000.*

No. 102XU2 is on a large piece of an envelope with July 25 postmark at left. It is unique.

GROVE HILL, ALA.

A1

Handstamped Adhesive (from woodcut)

36X1	A1	5c **black**	*125,000.*
		On cover, tied	*130,000.*

Two examples are recorded. One is on cover tied by the postmark. The other is canceled by magenta pen on a cover front. Value is for the complete cover.

Cancellations: black town, magenta pen.

HALLETTSVILLE, TEX.

A1

Handstamped Adhesive
Ruled Letter Paper

37X1 A1 10c **black,** *gray blue,* on cover *10,000.*

One example known.

Cancellation: black ms.

HAMBURGH, S. C.

E1

Handstamped Envelope

112XU1 E1 5c **black** *8,000.*
On cover with #16X1 (forwarded) —

HARRISBURGH (Harrisburg), TEX.

E1

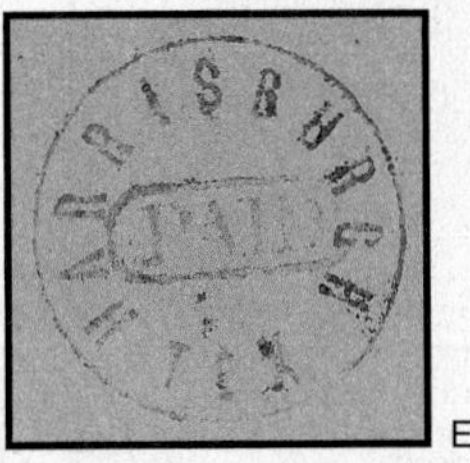

E2

Handstamped Envelope

130XU1 E1 5c **black** *5,500.*
130XU2 E2 10c **black** —

The unused 5c entire is the only example recorded of No. 130XU1

HELENA, TEX.

A1

Typeset Adhesives
Several varieties

38X1 A1 5c **black,** *buff* *22,500. 20,000.*
38X2 A1 10c **black,** *gray* *40,000.*

On 10c "Helena" is in upper and lower case italics.
Used examples are valued with small faults or repairs, as all recorded have faults.

Cancellation: black town.

HILLSBORO, N. C.

A1

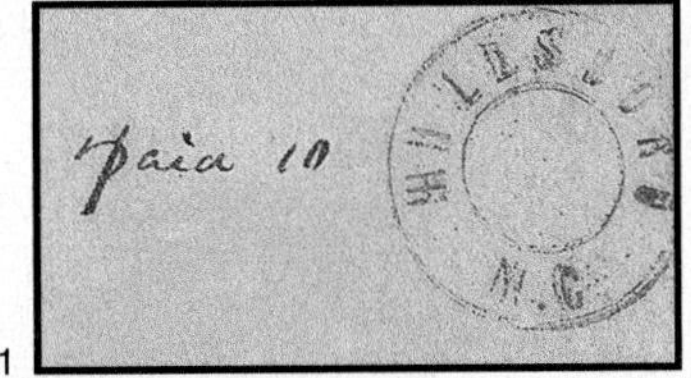

E1

Handstamped Adhesive

39X1 A1 5c **black,** on cover *10,000.*

5c usage is determined by date of June 1, 1861, or later in the dated cancel. No. 39X1 is unique.
See 3c 1861 Postmaster's Provisional No. 1AX1.

Cancellation: black town.

Ms./Handstamped Envelope

39XU1 E1 10c "paid 10" in manuscript with undated blue town cancel as control on face *2,250.*

No. 39XU1 is unique.

HOLLANDALE, TEX.

E1

Handstamped Envelope

132XU1 E1 5c **black** —

HOUSTON, TEX.

E1 No. 40XU1a

Handstamped Envelopes

40XU1 E1 5c **red** — 800.
On patriotic cover —
a. 10c (ms.) on 5c **red** *6,500.*
40XU2 E1 10c **red** — *1,750.*
40XU3 E1 10c **black** *6,750.*
40XU4 E1 5c +10c **red** *2,500.*
40XU5 E1 10c +10c **red** *2,500.*

Nos. 40XU2-40XU5 show "TEX" instead of "TXS."

HUNTSVILLE, TEX.

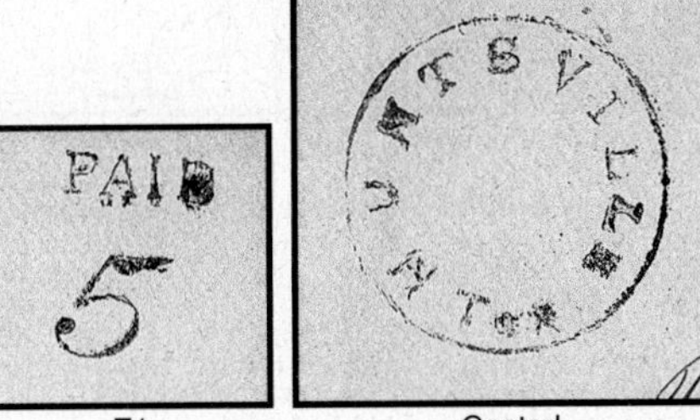

E1 Control

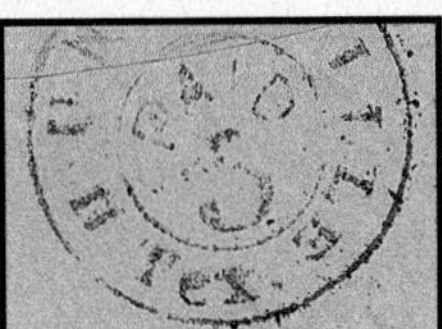

E2

E3

Handstamped Envelope

92XU1 E1 5c **black** *5,000.*
92XU2 E2 5c **black** —
92XU3 E3 10c **black** —

INDEPENDENCE, TEX.

A1

A2

Handstamped Adhesives

41X1 A1 10c **black,** *buff,* on cover, uncanceled, cut to shape *20,000.*
41X2 A1 10c **black,** *dull rose,* on cover —

With small "10" and "Pd" in manuscript

41X3 A2 10c **black,** *buff,* on cover, uncanceled, cut to shape *20,000.*
On cover, uncanceled, cut square —

No. 41X1 is unique.
All known examples of Nos. 41X1-41X3 are uncanceled on covers with black "INDEPENDANCE TEX." (sic) postmark.
The existence of No. 41X2 has been questioned by specialists. The editors would like to see authenticated evidence of the existence of this item.

ISABELLA, GA.

E1

Handstamped Envelope, Manuscript "5"

133XU1 E1 5c **black** *5,000.*

Only one example recorded of No. 133XU1.

IUKA, MISS.

E1

Handstamped Envelope

42XU1 E1 5c **black** *1,750.*
On patriotic cover *4,000.*

JACKSON, MISS.

E1

Handstamped Envelopes
Two types of numeral

43XU1 E1 5c **black** 900.
On patriotic cover *3,000.*
a. 10c on 5c **black** *2,750.*
b. 5c on 3c **black** *1,500.*

43XU2	E1	10c **black**	*2,000.*
a.		5c on 10c **black**	*3,750.*
43XU4	E1	10c on 5c **blue**	*2,750.*

The 5c also exists on a lettersheet.
See 3c 1861 Postmaster's Provisional No. 2AXU1.

JACKSONVILLE, ALA.

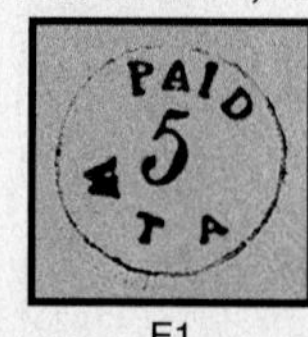

E1

Handstamped Envelope

110XU1	E1	5c **black**	—	*3,000.*

JACKSONVILLE, FLA.

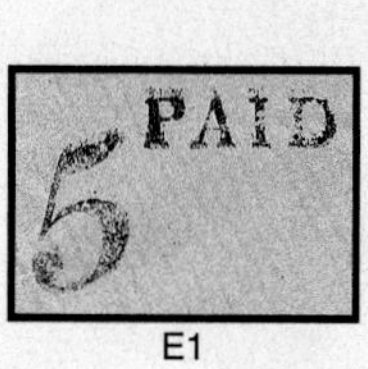

E1

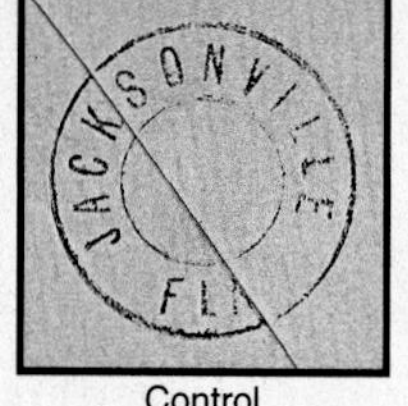

Control

Handstamped Envelope

134XU1	E1	5c **black**	*4,000.*

Undated double circle postmark control on reverse. No. 134XU1 is unique.

JETERSVILLE, VA.

A1

Handstamped Adhesive
("5" with ms. "AHA." initials)
Laid Paper

44X1	A1	5c **black,** vertical pair on cover, uncanceled	*16,000.*

Initials are those of Postmaster A. H. Atwood.

Cancellation: black town.

JONESBORO, TENN.

E1

Handstamped Envelopes

45XU1	E1	5c **black**	*6,000.*
45XU2	E1	5c **dark blue**	*5,000.*

KINGSTON, GA.

E1

E2

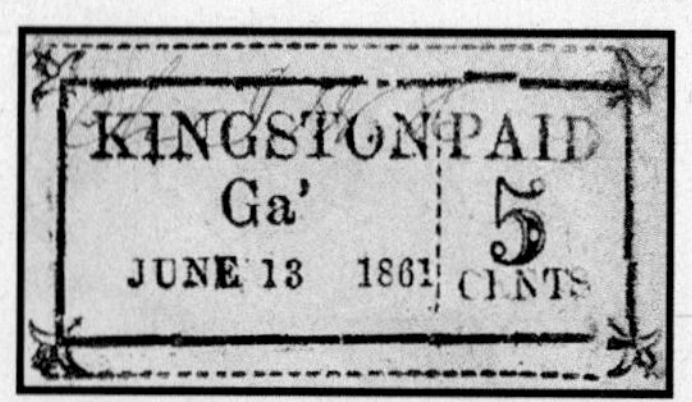

E3

E4

Typeset Envelopes
(design types E1-E2, E4 are handstamps; typeset design E3 probably impressed by hand but possibly press printed)

46XU1	E1	5c **black**	3,000.
46XU2	E2	5c **black**	3,250.
a.		Without "CS" at sides of "5"	*3,500.*
46XU4	E3	5c **black**	*12,500.*
46XU5	E4	5c **black**	*2,000.*

There is only one recorded example of No. 46XU4.

KNOXVILLE, TENN.

A1

Typographed Adhesives
(stereotype from woodcut)
Grayish Laid Paper

47X1	A1	5c **brick red**	*1,750.*	1,400.
		Manuscript cancel		650.
		Horizontal pair	*4,500.*	*3,000.*
		Vertical pair	*4,000.*	
		Vertical strip of 3	*7,000.*	
		On cover, tied by handstamp		*5,000.*
		On cover, manuscript cancel		*2,100.*
		Pair on cover		*7,500.*
47X2	A1	5c **carmine**	*2,750.*	2,250.
		Manuscript cancel		1,250.
		Vertical strip of 3		—
		On cover, tied by handstamp		*7,500.*
		On cover, manuscript cancel		*2,100.*
47X3	A1	10c **green,** on cover		*57,750.*

The #47X3 cover is unique. Value is based on 1997 auction sale.

Cancellations in black: town, bars, pen or pencil.

E1

E2

Press-printed Envelopes (typographed)

47XU1	E1	5c **blue**	*2,500.*
47XU2	E1	5c **blue,** *orange*	*5,000.*
47XU3	E1	10c **red** (cut to shape)	*7,000.*
47XU4	E1	10c **red,** *orange* (cut to shape)	*6,000.*

Only one example each recorded of Nos. 47XU3 and 47XU4. Dangerous fakes exist of Nos. 47XU1 and 47XU2.

Handstamped Envelopes

47XU5	E2	5c **black**	*1,400.*
		On patriotic cover	*3,750.*
a.		10c on 5c **black**	*3,500.*

Type E2 exists with "5" above or below "PAID."

LA GRANGE, TEX.

E1

Handstamped Envelopes

48XU1	E1	5c **black**	—	3,250.
48XU2	E1	10c **black**		3,250.

LAKE CITY, FLA.

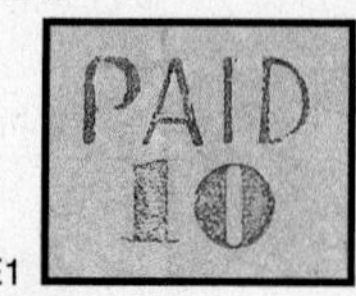

E1

Control Type A

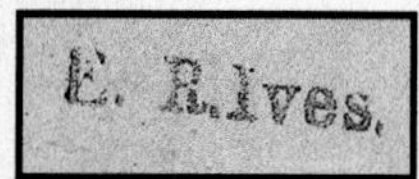

Control Type B

Handstamped Envelope

96XU1	E1	10c **black**	*3,750.*

Envelopes have black circle control mark, or printed name of E. R. Ives, postmaster, on back.

LAURENS COURT HOUSE, S. C.

E1

PAID 5

E2

Control

Handstamped Envelopes

116XU1	E1	5c **black**	*2,000.*
116XU2	E2	5c **black**	*2,000.*

Envelopes have a 25mm undated control mark on reverse. No. 116XU1 is unique.

LENOIR, N. C.

A1

A2

E1

Handstamped Adhesive (from woodcut)
White wove paper with cross-ruled orange lines

49X1 A1 5c **blue & orange** *7,250.* *6,750.*
On cover, pen canceled *8,000.*
On cover, tied by handstamp *17,500.*
a. On paper with narrow-spaced blue vertical lines and no horizontal lines *4,000.*

Cancellations: blue town, blue "Paid" in circle, black pen.

The paper on No. 49X1 has 21-22 vertical orange lines and 3-4 horizontal lines. The paper on No. 49X1a has approximately 53 closely spaced vertical blue lines and no horizontal lines. No. 49X1a is unique, with thins and a repaired tear, and it is valued thus.

Handstamped Envelopes

49XU1 A1 5c **blue** *4,000.*
49XU2 A2 10c (5c+5c) **blue** *25,000.*
49XU3 E1 5c **blue** *4,500.*
49XU4 E1 5c **black** *4,500.*

No. 49XU2 is unique. A variety of No. 49XU3 is recorded with two light strikes of the provisional handstamp, one in blue and one in black.

LEXINGTON, MISS.

E1

Handstamped Envelopes

50XU1 E1 5c **black** *3,750.*
50XU2 E1 10c **black** *5,000.*

Only one example is recorded of No. 50XU2.

LEXINGTON, VA.

E1

Handstamped Envelopes

135XU1 E1 5c **blue** *350.*
Used with 5c #6 to make 10c rate *500.*
135XU2 E1 10c **blue** *350.*

Nos. 135XU1-135XU2 by themselves are indistinguishable from stampless covers when used.

LIBERTY, VA. (and Salem, Va.)

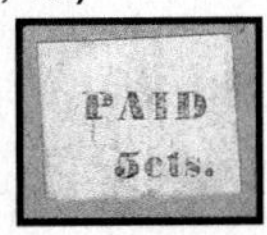

A1

Typeset Adhesive (probably impressed by hand)
Laid Paper

74X1 A1 5c **black,** on cover, uncanceled, with Liberty postmark *25,000.*
On cover, uncanceled, with Salem postmark *25,000.*

Two known on covers with Liberty, Va. postmark; one cover known with the nearby Salem, Va. office postmark.

LIMESTONE SPRINGS, S. C.

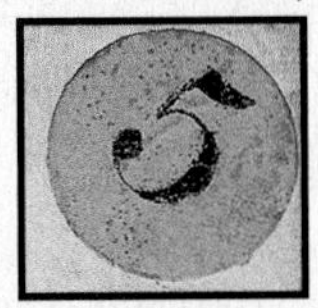

A1

Handstamped Adhesive

121X1 A1 5c **black,** *light blue,* on cover *10,000.*
Two on cover *15,000.*
121X2 A1 5c **black,** *white,* two on cover *32,500.*

Stamps are cut round or rectangular. Covers are not postmarked. The No. 121X2 cover bears the only two recorded examples of this stamp.

LIVINGSTON, ALA.

A1

Lithographed Adhesive

51X1 A1 5c **blue** *10,000.*
On cover *60,000.*
Pair on cover *147,500.*

The pair on cover is unique.

Cancellation: black town.

LYNCHBURG, VA.

A1

E1

Typographed Adhesive
(stereotype from woodcut)

52X1 A1 5c **blue** (shades) *1,800.* *1,500.*
Pair *3,250.*
On cover *4,000.*
Pair on cover *20,000.*

Cancellations: black town, blue town.

Press-printed Envelopes (typographed)
Impressed at top right or left

52XU1 E1 5c **black** *700.00* *3,000.*
52XU2 E1 5c **black,** *amber* *3,000.*
52XU3 E1 5c **black,** *buff* *3,000.*
52XU4 E1 5c **black,** *brown* *3,000.*
On patriotic cover —

MACON, GA.

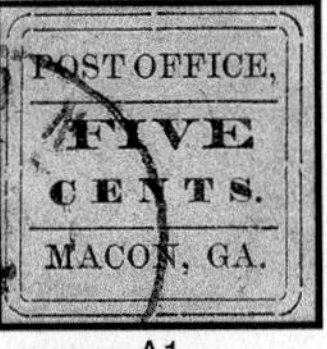

A1

A2

A3

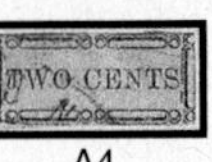

A4

Typeset Adhesives
Several varieties of type A1, 10 of A2, 5 of A3
Wove Paper

53X1 A1 5c **black,** *light blue green* (shades) 1,250. 1,000.
On cover *5,000.*
Pair on cover *14,000.*
Comma after "OFFICE" 950. 1,100.
Comma after "OFFICE," on cover *7,500.*

Warning: Dangerous forgeries exist of the normal variety and the Comma after "OFFICE" variety. Certificates of authenticity from recognized committees are strongly recommended.

53X3 A2 5c **black,** *yellow* 2,500. 1,250.
On cover *6,000.*
Pair on cover *9,000.*
On patriotic cover, single *7,500.*
Pair on patriotic cover *35,000.*
53X4 A3 5c **black,** *yellow* (shades) 3,000. 3,000.
On cover *7,500.*
Pair on cover *11,000.*
a. Vertical tête bêche pair, on cover *60,000.*
53X5 A4 2c **black,** *gray green* —
On cover *50,000.*

Laid Paper

53X6 A2 5c **black,** *yellow* *6,000.* *6,000.*
On cover *8,000.*
53X7 A3 5c **black,** *yellow* *6,000.*
On cover *9,000.*
53X8 A1 5c **black,** *light blue green* 1,750. *2,250.*
On cover *4,500.*

No. 53X4a is unique.

Cancellations: black town, black "PAID" (2 types).

E1

Handstamped Envelope
Two types: "PAID" over "5," "5" over "PAID"

53XU1 E1 5c **black** 250. 650.
On patriotic cover 1,900.

Values are for "PAID" over "5" variety. "5" over "PAID" is much scarcer.

MADISON, GA.

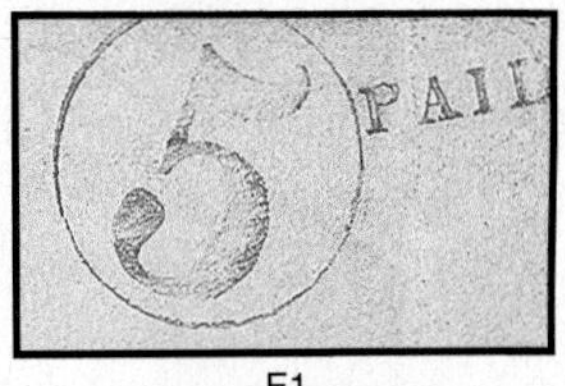

E1

Handstamped Envelope

136XU1 E1 5c **red** *600.*

No. 136XU1 is indistinguishable from a handstamp paid cover when used.

MADISON COURT HOUSE, FLA.

E1

Typeset Envelope

137XU1 E1 5c **black,** *yellow* — *35,000.*

No. 137XU1 is unique.
See 3c 1861 Postmaster's Provisional No. 3AX1.

MARIETTA, GA.

E1

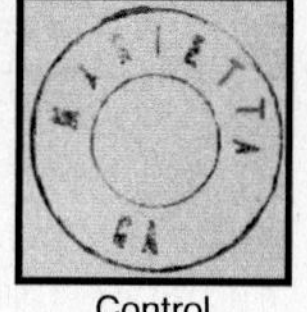

Control

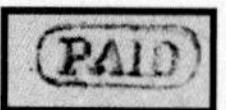

E2

Handstamped Envelopes

54XU1 E1 5c **black** — 500.
a. 10c on 5c **black** — *1,750.*

With Double Circle Control

54XU3 E1 10c **black**
54XU4 E2 5c **black** — *2,000.*

The existence of No. 54XU3 has been questioned by specialists. The editors would like to see authenticated evidence that verifies this listing.

MARION, VA.

A1

Adhesives with Typeset frame and Handstamped numeral in center

55X1 A1 5c **black** — *6,500.*
On cover — *25,000.*
55X2 A1 10c **black** — *10,000.* *10,000.*
On cover — *30,000.*
55X2A A1 10c 10c black, bluish, tied on cover — *15,000.*
55X3 A1 5c **black,** *bluish,* laid paper — — —
55X4 A1 5c **black,** *bluish,* tied on cover — 6,000.

No. 55X2A is unique. It is a sound stamp tied on a cover with some faults. Value is based on 2021 auction sale.

The 2c, 3c, 15c and 20c are believed to be bogus items printed later using the original typeset frame.

Cancellations: black town, black "PAID," black manuscript.

No. 55X4 on cover is believed to be unique. It is tied on a heavily repaired cover and is valued thus.

MARS BLUFF, S. C.

E1

145XU1 E1 5c **black** — *2,000.*

The No. 145XU1 marking is a provisional only when unused, used from another town or used under a general issue.

MEMPHIS, TENN.

A1

56X1a Partial Print

A2

Typographed Adhesives (stereotyped from woodcut)

Plate of 50 (5x10) for the 2c. The stereotypes for the 5c stamps were set in 5 vertical rows of 8, with at least 2 rows set sideways to the right (see Thomas H. Pratt's monograph, "The Postmaster's Provisionals of Memphis").

56X1 A1 2c **blue** (shades) — 100. *1,250.*
Block of 4 — 550.
On cover — *12,500.*
Cracked plate (16, 17, 18) — 250. *1,350.*
Plate scratch across "GALLA" of "MCGALLAWAY" — 200.
a. Partial print — 250. —

On No. 56X1a, a breaking off of the plate at the right edge caused incomplete printing (approximately 2/3 of the stamp) on stamps in positions 5, 10, 15, 20 and 50.

56X2 A2 5c **red** (shades) — 150. *250.*
Pair — *340.* *650.*
Block of 4 — *1,000.* —
On cover — 1,750.
Pair on cover — *4,000.*
Strip of 4 on cover — *9,000.*
On patriotic cover — *11,000.*
Pair on patriotic cover — *12,500.*
a. Tête bêche pair — *1,500.*
Pair on cover — *30,000.*
b. Pair, one sideways — 2,500.
c. Pelure paper — — —

Cancellation on Nos. 56X1-56X2: black town.

Press-printed Envelopes (typographed)

56XU1 A2 5c **red** (shades) — *3,000.*
Used with 5c #56X2 to make 10c rate — *6,000.*
56XU2 A2 5c **red,** *amber* — *3,000.*
Used with C.S.A. 5c #1 to make 10c rate — *8,000.*
Used with #56X2 to make 10c rate — *5,500.*
56XU3 A2 5c **red,** *orange* — *2,500.*
Used with #56X2 — *7,500.*
On patriotic cover — —
56XU4 A2 5c **red,** *cream* — *5,750.*

Only one example of No. 56XU4 is recorded. It is on a cover on which a C.S.A. No. 11 is affixed over the provisional to pay the postage.

MICANOPY, FLA.

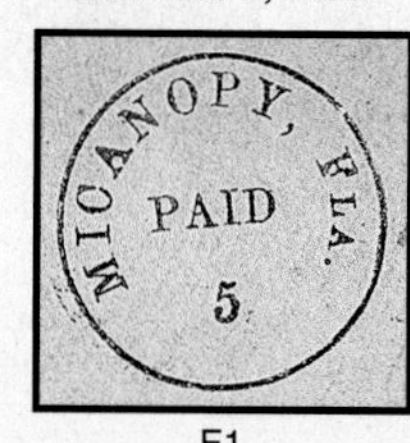

E1

Handstamped Envelope

105XU1 E1 5c **black** — *11,500.*

One example recorded.

MILLEDGEVILLE, GA.

E1

E2

E3

Handstamped Envelopes

Two types of No. 57XU5: Type I, tall, thin "1" and "0" of "10"; Type II, short, fat "1" and "0" of "10."

57XU1 E1 5c **black** — 500.
a. Wide spacing between "I" and "D" of "PAID" — 600.
b. 10c on 5c **black** — 1,000.
57XU2 E1 5c **blue** — 800.
57XU4 E2 10c **black** — 375. 1,200.
a. Wide spacing between "I" and "D" of "PAID" — 1,200.
57XU5 E3 10c **black,** type I — 450. 800.
a. Type II — 1,500.

On No. 57XU4, the "PAID/10" virtually always falls outside the Milledgeville control marking (as in illustration E1).

The existence of No. 57XU2 as a provisional has been questioned by specialists. The editors would like to see authenticated evidence of provisional use of this marking.

MILTON, N. C.

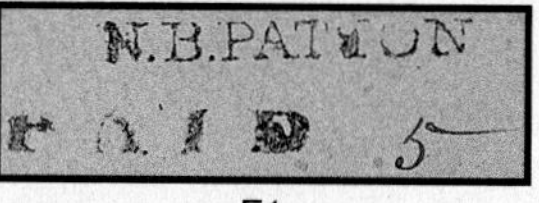

E1

Handstamped Envelope, "5" Manuscript

138XU1 E1 5c **black** — *3,750.*

MOBILE, ALA.

A1

Lithographed Adhesives

58X1 A1 2c **black** — 2,250. 1,200.
Pair — — *2,500.*
On cover — *6,000.*
Pair on cover — *20,000.*
Three singles on one cover — *20,000.*
Five stamps on one cover — *24,000.*
58X2 A1 5c **blue** — 350. 450.
Pair — 900. 1,050.
On cover — 1,750.
On cover, canceled in Claiborne, Ala. — —
On cover, canceled in Montgomery, Ala. — —
Pair on cover — 2,250.
Strip of 3 on cover — *10,000.*
Strip of 4 on cover — *25,000.*
Line through "O" of "Office" (plate scratch) — —

Cancellations: black town, express company.

The existence of a strip of 5 of No. 58X2 has been questioned by specialists. The editors would like to see authenticated evidence of the existence of this strip either on or off cover.

MONTGOMERY, ALA.

E1

E1a

Handstamped Envelopes

59XU1 E1 5c **red** — *1,000.*
a. 10c on 5c **red** — *2,750.*
59XU2 E1 5c **blue** — 400. *1,000.*
59XU3 E1a 10c **red** — *900.*
59XU4 E1a 10c **blue** — *1,250.*
59XU5 E1a 10c **black** — 850.

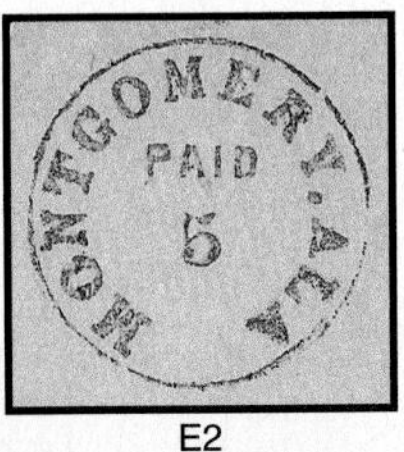

E2

E3

59XU7 E2 2c **red** *2,500.*
59XU7A E2 2c **blue** *3,500.*
59XU8 E2 5c **black** *2,000.*
59XU9 E3 10c **black** *2,000.*
59XU10 E3 10c **red** *1,750.*

The existence of No. 59XU10 is in question. The editors would like to see an authenticated example of this marking.

MOUNT LEBANON, LA.

A1

Woodcut Adhesive (mirror image of design)

60X1 A1 5c **red brown,** on cover *255,000.*

One example known. Value represents sale price at 2009 auction.

Cancellation: black pen.

MOUNT PLEASANT, N. C.

E1

Handstamped Envelope

151XU1 E1 10c **blue** *3,500.*

One example of No. 151XU1 is recorded, posted in January 1866 and covered by a U.S. 3¢ stamp subsequently removed to reveal the provisional.

NASHVILLE, TENN.

A2

Typographed Adhesives (stereotyped from woodcut)

Gray Blue Ribbed Paper

61X2 A2 5c **carmine** (shades) 1,000. 800.
Pair 2,250.
On cover 3,500.
On patriotic cover *5,000.*
Pair on cover *6,000.*
On cover with U.S. 3c 1857 (express) *25,000.*
a. Vertical tête bêche pair *4,000.*
On cover *25,000.*
61X3 A2 5c **brick red** (shades) 900. 850.
Pair 2,250.
On cover 3,500.
On patriotic cover *6,000.*
Pair on cover *7,500.*
On U.S. #U26 (express) *35,000.*
On U.S. #U27 with #26 (express) *25,000.*
a. Vertical tête bêche pair *3,000.*
61X4 A2 5c **gray** (shades) 1,250. 1,500.
On cover *7,500.*
On patriotic cover *12,000.*
Pair on cover *7,500.*
Strip of 5 on cover front *8,750.*
61X5 A2 5c **violet brown** (shades) 1,250. 750.
Block of 4 —
On cover 4,250.
On patriotic cover *35,000.*
Pair on cover *6,000.*
a. Vertical tete beche pair *5,000.* *7,500.*
Pair on cover —
61X6 A2 10c **green** — *3,750.*
On cover *17,500.*
On cover with U.S. 3c 1857 (express) *75,000.*
On U.S. #U26 (express) *90,000.*
On cover with No. 61X2 *27,500.*

Cancellations

Pen Cancel
Blue "Paid"
Blue "Postage Paid"
Blue town
Blue numeral "5"
Blue numeral "10"
Blue express company
Black express company

For the former 61X1, see No. 4AX1 in the 3c 1861 Postmasters' Provisional section.

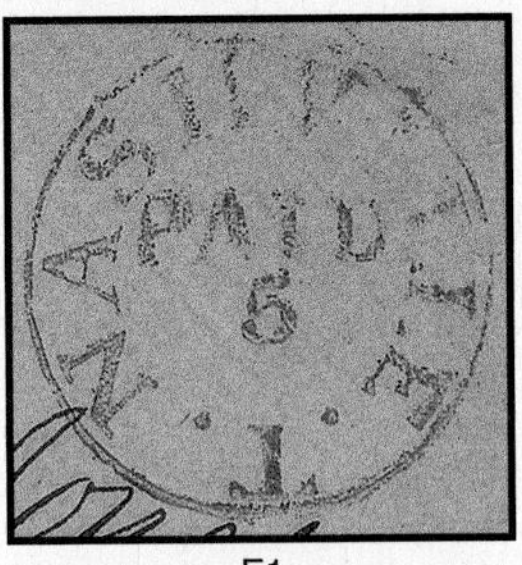

E1

Handstamped Envelopes

61XU1 E1 5c **blue** 900.
On patriotic envelope 2,000.
61XU2 E1 10c on 5c **blue** *2,750.*
On patriotic cover *5,500.*

NEW ORLEANS, LA.

A1

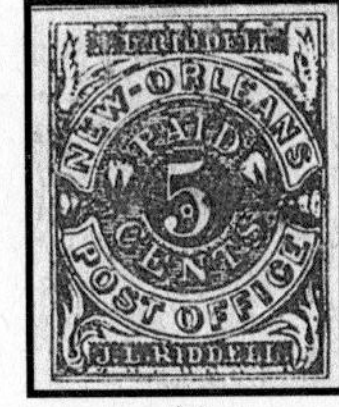

A2

Typographed Adhesives (stereotyped from woodcut)

Plate of 40

62X1 A1 2c **blue,** *July 14, 1861* 225. 800.
Pair 650. *1,650.*
Block of 4 *6,000.*
On cover *5,000.*
On patriotic cover *8,000.*
Pair on cover *7,500.*
Three singles on one cover *20,000.*
Three singles + #62X4, on cover —
Five singles on one cover *12,500.*
Strip of 5 on cover *30,000.*
a. Printed on both sides, on cover *10,500.*
62X2 A1 2c **red** (shades), *Jan. 6, 1862* 190. *1,000.*
Pair 475.
Block of 4 *1,800.*
On cover *17,500.*
62X3 A2 5c **brown,** *white, June 12, 1861* 300. 275.
Pair 800. 575.
Block of 4 2,000.
On cover 475.
On cover from town other than N.O. *5,000.*
On patriotic cover *7,000.*
Pair on cover 900.
Strip of 5 on cover *5,000.*
Pair on cover with U.S. 3c #26 (Southern Letter Unpaid) *170,000.*
On cover with U.S. No. 30A —
a. Printed on both sides *3,750.*
On cover *7,500.*
b. 5c **ocher,** *June 18, 1861* 700. 625.
Pair 1,500.
On cover 2,750.
On patriotic cover *6,000.*
Pair on cover 3,500.
c. 5c **chocolate brown,** *white* *1,500.*

The editors would like to see authenticated evidence of the existence of No. 62X3a on cover.

62X4 A2 5c **red brn,** *bluish, Aug. 22, 1861* 325. 200.
Pair 725. 475.
Horizontal strip of 6 *3,000.*
Block of 4 2,200.
On cover 475.
On patriotic cover *10,000.*
Pair on cover 700.
Block of 4 on cover *5,000.*
Used on cover with C.S.A. 5c #1 to make 10c rate *27,500.*
a. Printed on both sides *3,000.*
On cover *9,000.*
62X5 A2 5c **yel brn,** *off-white, Dec. 3, 1861* 160. *250.*
Pair 350. *525.*
Block of 4 750.
On cover 850.
On patriotic cover *3,000.*
Pair on cover 1,200.
Strip of 5 on cover —
62X6 A2 5c **red** (shades) — *14,000.*
62X7 A2 5c **red** (shades), *bluish* *15,000.*

Cancellations

Black town (single or double circle New Orleans)
Red town (double circle New Orleans)
Town other than New Orleans
Postmaster's handstamp
Black "Paid"
Express Company
Packet boat, cover "STEAM"

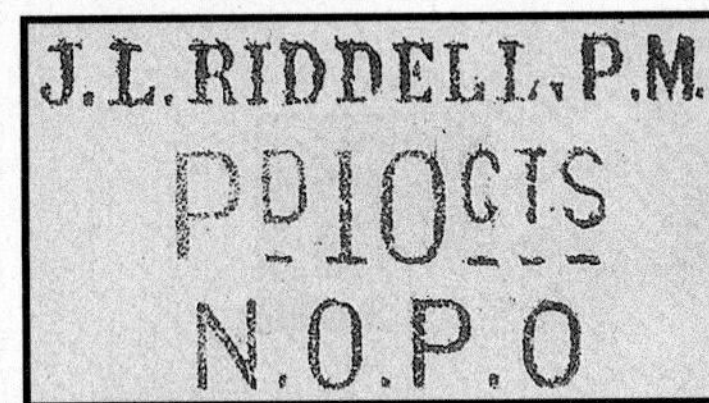

E1

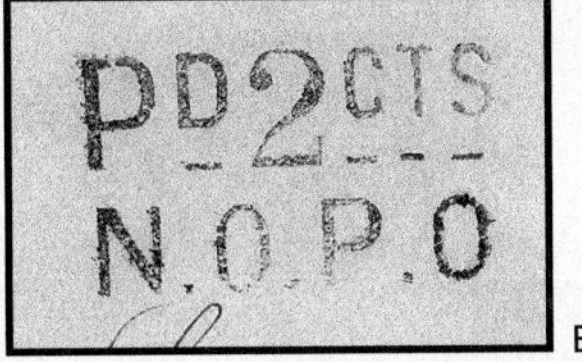

E2

Handstamped Envelopes

62XU1 E1 5c **black** 4,500.
62XU2 E1 10c **black** *11,500.*

"J. L. RIDDELL, P. M." omitted

62XU3 E2 2c **black** *8,500.*

Some authorities question the use of No. 62XU3 as a provisional.

NEW SMYRNA, FLA.

A1

Handstamped Adhesive

On white paper with blue ruled lines

63X1 A1 10c ("O1") on 5c **black** *50,000.*

One example known. It is uncanceled on a postmarked patriotic cover.

NORFOLK, VA.

E1

E2

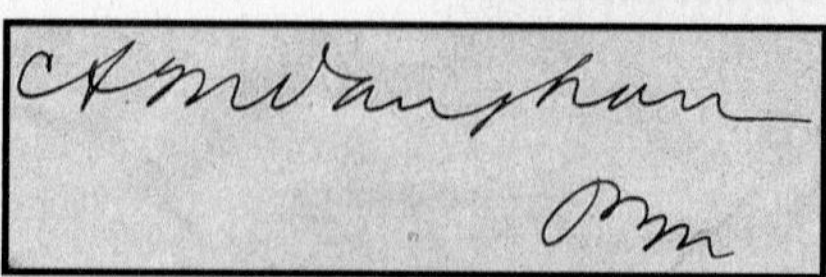

Manuscript Signature

Handstamped Envelopes

Ms Signature on Back

139XU1	E1	5c **blue**	1,000.	*1,750.*
139XU2	E2	10c **blue**		*1,750.*

OAKWAY, S. C.

A1

Handstamped Adhesive (from woodcut)

115X1	A1	5c **black,** on cover		*60,000.*

Two used examples of No. 115X1 are recorded, both on cover. Value represents 2012 auction realization for the cover on which the stamp is tied by manuscript "Paid."

OXFORD, N. C.

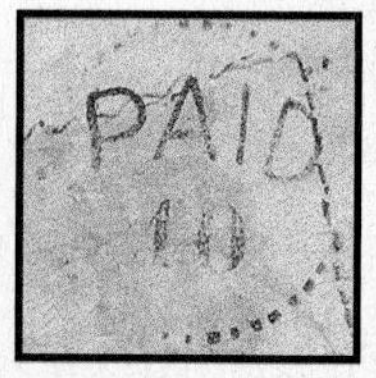

E1

Handstamped Envelope

152XU1	E1	10c **black**	*3,500.*	

One example of No. 152XU1 is recorded, covered by a C.S.A. 10¢ No. 12 that paid the postage.

PATTERSON, N. C.

E1

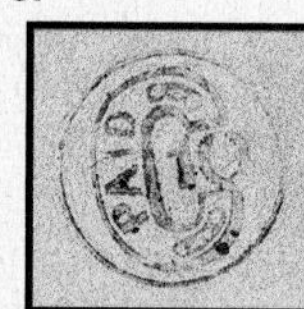

E2

Control

Handstamped Envelopes

149XU1	E1	5c **black**	*750.*	
149XU2	E2	10c **black**		*2,500.*

Nos. 149XU1 and 149XU2 must have an undated postmark on the cover as a control.

PENSACOLA, FLA.

E1

Handstamped Envelopes

106XU1	E1	5c **black**		*5,000.*
a.		10c (ms.) on 5c **black**		*5,250.*
		On patriotic cover		*28,000.*

PETERSBURG, VA.

A1

Typeset Adhesive

Ten varieties

Thick white paper

65X1	A1	5c **red** (shades)	*2,250.*	500.
		Pair	*5,000.*	*1,500.*
		Block of 4	*11,000.*	
		On cover		2,000.
		On patriotic cover		—
		Pair on cover		*12,500.*
		Used on cover with C.S.A. 5c #1 to make 10c rate		*55,000.*

Cancellation: blue town.

PITTSYLVANIA COURT HOUSE, VA.

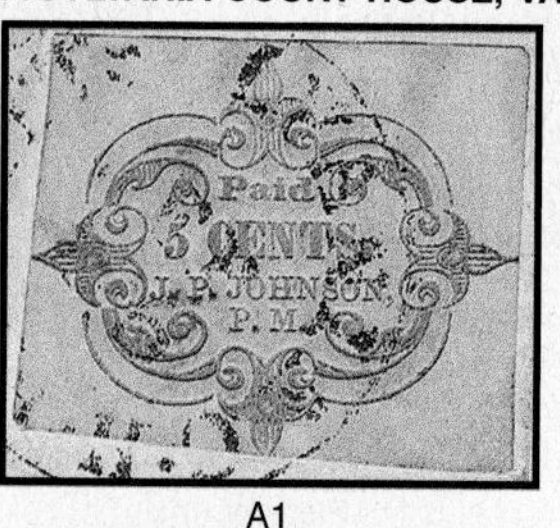

A1

Typeset Adhesives

66X1	A1	5c **dull red,** wove paper	*7,500.*	*9,000.*
		Octagonally cut		*7,500.*
		On cover		*30,000.*
		On cover, octagonally cut		*15,000.*
66X2	A1	5c **dull red,** laid paper		*5,500.*
		On cover		—
		Octagonally cut		*4,500.*
		On cover, octagonally cut		*50,000.*

Cancellation: black town.

PLAINS OF DURA, GA.

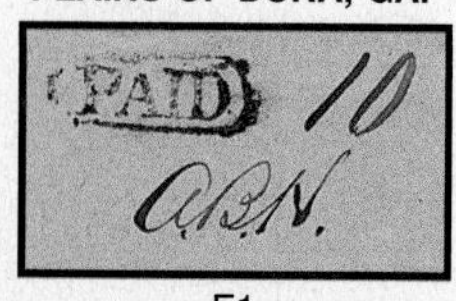

E1

Handstamped Envelopes, Ms. Initials

140XU1	E1	5c **black**		—
140XU2	E1	10c **black**		*5,000.*

No. 140XU2 is unique.

PLEASANT SHADE, VA.

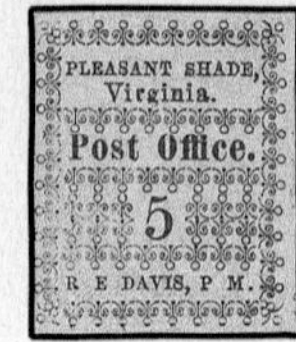

A1

Typeset Adhesive

Five varieties

67X1	A1	5c **blue**	*8,000.*	*15,000.*
		On cover		*35,000.*
		Pair	*13,500.*	
		Pair on cover		*55,000.*
		Block of 6	*42,500.*	

Cancellation: blue town.

PLUM CREEK, TEX.

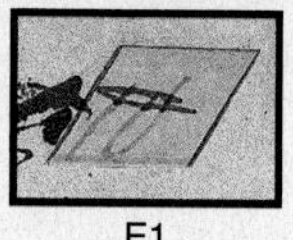

E1

Manuscript Adhesive

141X1	E1	10c **black,** *blue,* on cover		*6,500.*

The stamps have ruled lines with the value "10" in manuscript. Size and shape vary.

PORT GIBSON, MISS.

E1

Manuscript Signature

Handstamped Envelope, Ms Signature

142XU1	E1	5c **black**		—

PORT LAVACA, TEX.

A1

Typeset Adhesive

107X1	A1	10c **black,** on cover		*27,000.*

One example known. It is uncanceled on a postmarked cover.

RALEIGH, N. C.

E1

Handstamped Envelopes

68XU1	E1	5c **red**		500.
		On patriotic cover		5,500.
68XU2	E1	5c **blue**		*4,000.*

RHEATOWN, TENN.

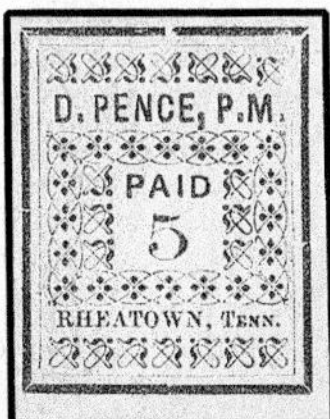

A1

Typeset Adhesive

Three varieties

69X1 A1 5c **red** *6,000.* *6,500.*
On cover, ms. cancel *15,000.*
On cover, tied by handstamp *45,000.*
Pair *15,000.*

Stamps normally were canceled in manuscript. One cover is known with stamp tied by red town postmark.

Cancellations: red town or black pen.

RICHMOND, TEX.

E1

Handstamped Envelopes or Letter Sheets

70XU1 E1 5c **red** 2,250.
a. 10c on 5c **red** *11,750.*
70XU2 E1 10c **red** 2,000.
a. 15c (ms.) on 10c **red** *5,000.*

RINGGOLD, GA.

E1

Handstamped Envelope

71XU1 E1 5c **blue black** *8,500.*

RUTHERFORDTON, N. C.

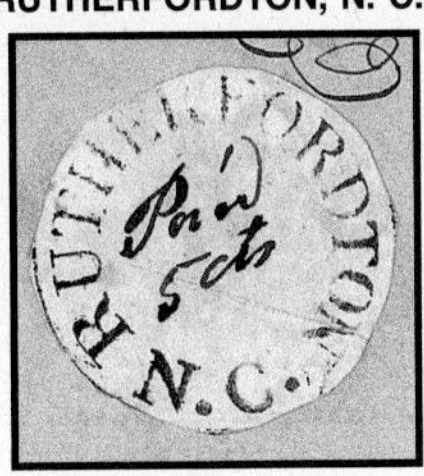

A1

Handstamped Adhesive, Ms. "Paid 5cts"

72X1 A1 5c **black,** cut round, on cover (uncanceled) *60,000.*

No. 72X1 is unique.

SALEM, N. C.

E1

E2

Handstamped Envelopes

73XU1 E1 5c **black** 1,500.
73XU2 E1 10c **black** *3,500.*
73XU3 E2 5c **black** *2,250.*
a. 10c on 5c **black** *2,800.*

Reprints exist on various papers. They either lack the "Paid" and value or have them counterfeited.

Salem, Va.

See No. 74X1 under Liberty, Va.

SALISBURY, N. C.

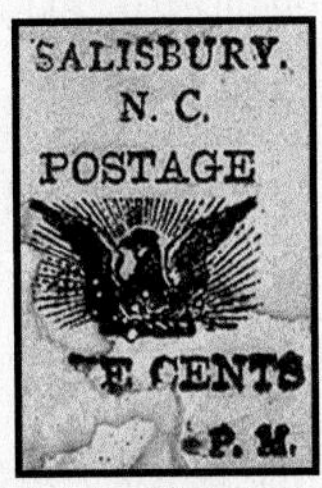

E1

Press-printed Envelope (typeset)

Impressed at top left

75XU1 E1 5c **black,** *greenish* *15,000.*

One example known. Part of the envelope was torn away (now repaired), leaving part of design missing.

SAN ANTONIO, TEX.

E1

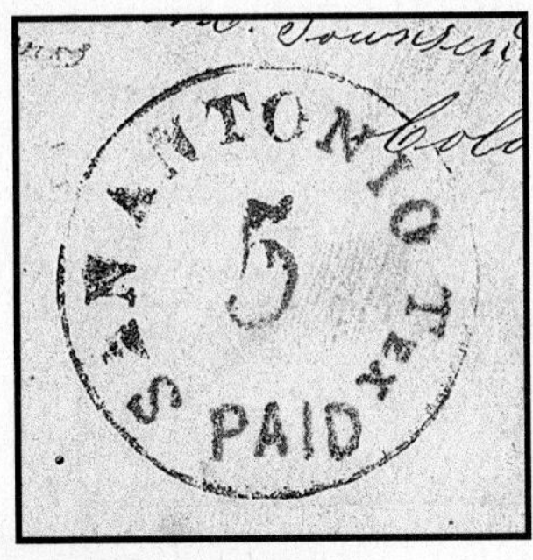

E2

Control

Handstamped Envelopes

76XU1 E1 10c **black** 500. *2,000.*
76XU1A E2 5c **black** *13,000.*
76XU2 E2 10c **black** *2,500.*

Black circle control mark is on front or back.
One example of No. 76XU1A is recorded.

SAVANNAH, GA.

E1

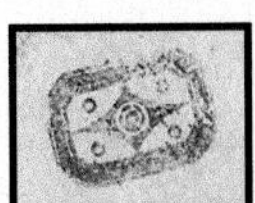

Control

E2

Handstamped Envelopes

101XU1 E1 5c **black** 450.
On patriotic cover *8,000.*
a. 10c on 5c **black** 1,500.
101XU2 E2 5c **black** 600.
a. 20c on 5c **black** *2,000.*
101XU3 E1 10c **black** 750.
101XU4 E2 10c **black** 750.

Envelopes must have octagonal control mark. One example is known of No.101XU2a.

SELMA, ALA.

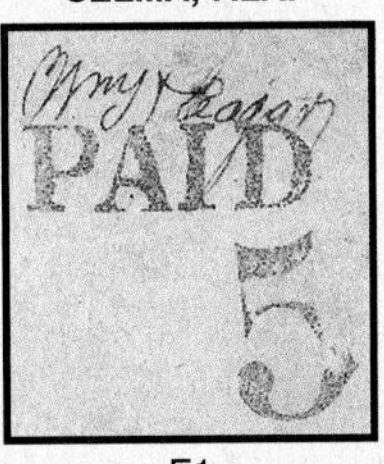

E1

Handstamped Envelopes; Signature in Ms.

77XU1 E1 5c **black** *1,250.*
a. 10c on 5c **black** *3,000.*
77XU2 E1 10c **black** *2,500.*

Signature is that of Postmaster William H. Eagar.
See 3c 1861 Postmaster's Provisional No. 5AX1.

SPARTA, GA.

E1

Handstamped Envelopes

93XU1 E1 5c **red** — 2,250.
93XU2 E1 10c **red** *5,000.*

Only one example recorded of No. 93XU2.

SPARTANBURG, S. C.

A1

A2

Handstamped Adhesives

(on ruled or plain wove paper)

78X1 A1 5c **black,** cut to shape —
Cut square *27,500.*
On cover, cut to shape *9,000.*
Pair on cover *20,000.*
On patriotic cover *50,000.*
a. "Paid" instead of denomination, revalued to 5c with "PAID" and "5" in small circle handstamps, on cover *6,000.*
78X2 A2 5c **black,** *bluish,* on cover *9,000.*
78X3 A2 5c **black,** *brown* *4,000.*
On cover *18,000.*

Among the Nos. 78X1-78X3 stamps, only one sound example of No. 78X1 is recorded cut square (one other stained and defective example is known), and only one No. 78X3 on cover is cut square. All other examples are cut to shape. The only recorded pair of No. 78X1 is on cover. The stamps are cut round, but are still connected. Only one example of No. 78X2 on cover is recorded. Part of the stamp is missing, and the cover is valued thus.

No. 78X1a is unique. Also, only one example of No. 78X2 is recorded; part of the stamp is missing, and the cover is valued thus.

Cancellations: black "PAID," black town.

E1

Control

Handstamped Envelopes

78XU1 E1 10c **black** (control on reverse) *5,000.*

STATESVILLE, N. C.

E1

Handstamped Envelopes

79XU1 E1 5c **black** *1,500.*
a. 10c on 5c **black**, handstamped "10" *3,000.*
b. 10c on 5c **black**, manuscript "10" *2,500.*

There are four identifiable varieties of No. 79XU1. Unused examples of No. 79XU1 are reprints.

SUMTER, S. C.

E1

Handstamped Envelopes

80XU1 E1 5c **black** 500.
a. 10c on 5c **black** *900.*
80XU2 E1 10c **black** 600.
a. 2c (ms.) on 10c **black** *1,100.*

Used examples of Nos. 80XU1-80XU2 are indistinguishable from handstamped "Paid" covers.

TALBOTTON, GA.

E1

Handstamped Envelopes

94XU1 E1 5c **black** 900.
a. 10c on 5c **black** *2,000.*
94XU2 E1 10c **black** 1,250.

TALLADEGA, ALA.

E1

Handstamped Envelopes

143XU1 E1 5c **black** *1,500.* —
143XU2 E1 10c **black** *1,500.* —

These same markings were used on handstamped "Paid" covers.

TELLICO PLAINS, TENN.

A1

Typeset Adhesives

Settings of two 5c and one 10c

Laid Paper

81X1 A1 5c **red** *2,000.* *10,000.*
On cover *15,000.*
81X2 A1 10c **red** *3,750.*
a. Se-tenant pair, Nos. 81X1 and 81X2 *6,250.*
Sheet of 3 (5c+5c+10c) *9,000.*

Cancellation: black pen.

THOMASVILLE, GA.

E1

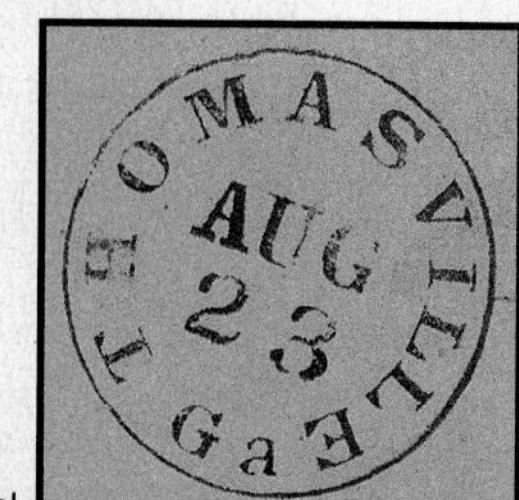

Control

Handstamped Envelopes

82XU1 E1 5c **black** 750.
On patriotic cover *5,000.*

On No. 82XU1, the control is on the reverse of the cover. The dated control is known with five different dates, including June 1, June 13, June 21, and August 23. The patriotic envelope is unique.

E2

82XU2 E2 5c **black** 1,000.

TULLAHOMA, TENN.

E1

Control

Handstamped Envelope

111XU1 E1 10c **black** *5,000.*

The control appears either on the front or the back of the envelope.

TUSCALOOSA, ALA.

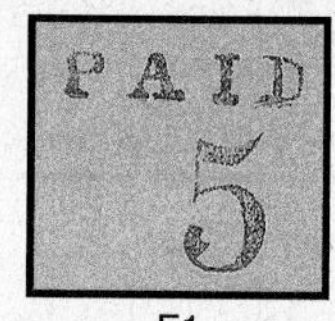

E1

Handstamped Envelopes

83XU1 E1 5c **black** 250.
83XU2 E1 10c **black** 250.

Used examples of Nos. 83XU1-83XU2 are indistinguishable from handstamped "Paid" covers. Some authorities question the use of E1 to produce provisional envelopes.

TUSCUMBIA, ALA.

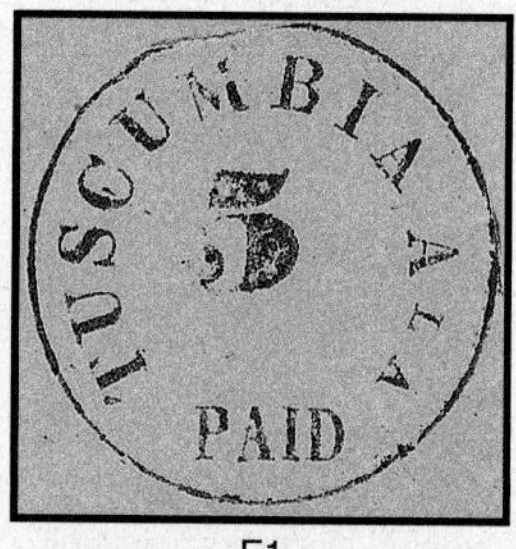

E1

Handstamped Envelopes

84XU1 E1 5c **black** *2,750.*
On patriotic cover *10,000.*
84XU2 E1 5c **red** *5,000.*
84XU3 E1 10c **black** *5,250.*

See 3c 1861 Postmaster's Provisional No. 6AXU1.

UNIONTOWN, ALA.

A1

Typeset Adhesives

(settings of 4 (2x2), 4 varieties of each value)

Laid Paper

86X1 A1 2c **dark blue,** *gray blue,* on cover *65,000.*
86X2 A1 2c **dark blue,** sheet of 4 *30,000.*
86X3 A1 5c **green,** *gray blue* *4,000.* *3,250.*
Pair —
On cover *15,000.*

86X4 A1 5c **green** *4,000. 3,250.*
On cover *15,000.*
Pair on cover *22,500.*
86X5 A1 10c **red,** *gray blue* *10,000.*
On cover *17,500.*

Two examples known of No. 86X1, both on cover (drop letters), one uncanceled and one pen canceled.

The only recorded examples of No. 86X2 are in a unique sheet of 4.

The item listed as No. 86X5 used is an uncanceled stamp on a large piece with part of addressee's name in manuscript. The value for the stamp on cover is for the cover with the stamp pen canceled.

Cancellation on Nos. 86X3-86X5: black town.

UNIONVILLE, S. C.

A1

Handstamped Adhesive
"PAID" and "5" applied separately
Paper with Blue Ruled Lines

87X1 A1 5c **black,** *grayish* *3,500.*
On cover, uncanceled *17,500.*
On cover, tied —
Pair on patriotic cover *32,500.*

The pair on patriotic cover is the only pair recorded.

Cancellation: black town.

VALDOSTA, GA.

E1

Control

E2

Handstamped Envelopes

100XU1 E1 10c **black** *9,000.*
100XU2 E2 5c +5c **black** —

The black circle control must appear on front of the No. 100XU2 envelope and on the back of the No. 100XU1 envelope.

There is one recorded cover each of Nos. 100XU1-100XU2.

VICTORIA, TEX.

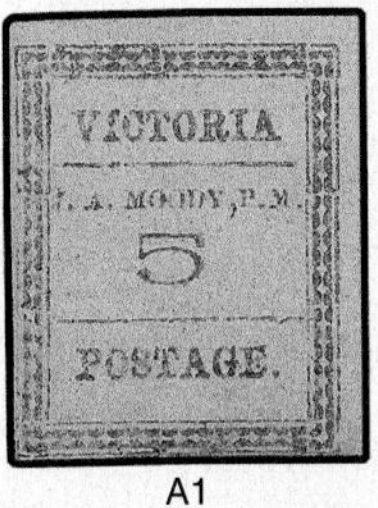

A1

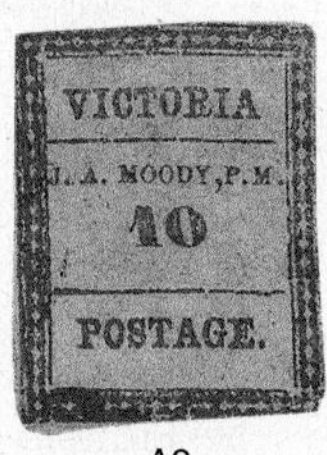

A2

Typeset Adhesives
Surface colored paper

88X1 A1 5c **red brown,** *green* *17,500.*
88X2 A1 10c **red brown,** *green* *22,500.*
On cover *115,000.*
88X3 A2 10c **red brown,** *green,* pelure paper *30,000. 30,000.*

WALTERBOROUGH, S. C.

E1

Handstamped Envelopes

108XU1 E1 10c **black,** *buff* —
108XU2 E1 10c **carmine** *4,000.*

The existence of No. 108XU1 is in question. The editors would like to see authenticated evidence of its existence.

WARRENTON, GA.

E1

Handstamped Envelopes

89XU1 E1 5c **black** *1,500.*
a. 10c (ms.) on 5c **black** *900.*

Fakes of the Warrenton provisional marking based on the illustration shown are known on addressed but postally unused covers.

WASHINGTON, GA.

E1

Handstamped Envelope

117XU1 E1 10c **black** *2,000.*

Envelopes must have black circle postmark control on the back. Examples with the undated control on the front are not considered provisional unless a dated postmark is also present.

WEATHERFORD, TEX.

E1

Handstamped Envelopes
(woodcut with "PAID" inserted in type)

109XU1 E1 5c **black** *2,000.*
109XU2 E1 5c +5c **black** *11,000.*

One example is known of No. 109XU2.

WILKESBORO, N. C.

E1

Handstamped Envelope

147XU1 E1 5c **black,** revalued to 10c *3,500.*

No. 147XU1 is unique.

WILLISTON, S.C.

E1

Handstamped Envelopes

153XU1 E1 10c **brown** *1,250.*

No. 153XU1 is unique. Value is based on 2020 auction sale. This cover must be either unused (as the one recorded example is) or covered by a C.S.A. stamp.

WINNSBOROUGH, S. C.

E1

E2

Control

Handstamped Envelopes

97XU1 E1 5c **black** *2,000.*
On patriotic cover *3,750.*
97XU2 E2 10c **black** *1,000. 2,500.*

Envelopes must have black circle control on front or back.

WYTHEVILLE, VA.

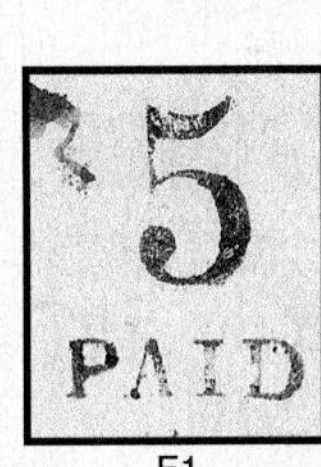

E1

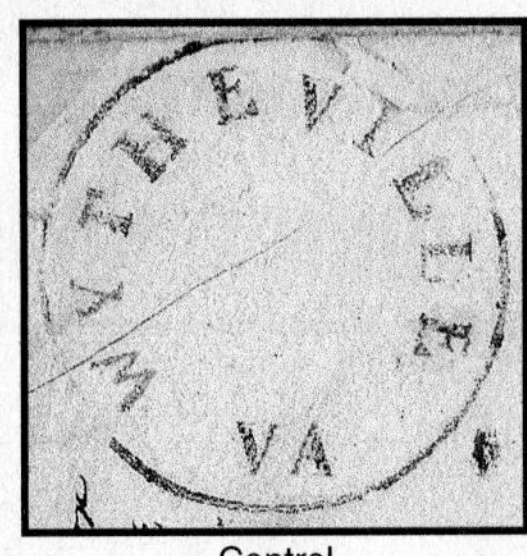

Control

Handstamped Envelope

114XU1 E1 5c **black** 900.

For later additions, listed out of numerical sequence, see:

#74X1, **Liberty, Va.**
#92XU1, **Huntsville, Tex.**
#92XU2, **Huntsville, Tex.**
#92XU3, **Huntsville, Tex.**
#93XU1, **Sparta, Ga.**
#94XU1, **Talbotton, Ga.**
#95XU1, **Cuthbert, GA**
#96XU1, **Lake City, Fla.**
#97XU1, **Winnsborough, S.C.**
#98XU1, **Galveston, Tex.**
#99XU1, **Christiansburg, Va.**
#100XU1, **Valdosta, Ga.**
#101XU1, **Savannah, Ga.**
#102XU1, **Griffin, Ga.**
#103XU1, **Courtland, Ala.**
#104XU1, **Fincastle, Va.**
#105XU1, **Micanopy, Fla.**
#106XU1, **Pensacola, Fla.**
#107X1, **Port Lavaca, Tex.**
#108XU1, **Walterborough, S.C.**
#109XU1, **Weatherford, Tex.**
#110XU1, **Jacksonville, Ala.**
#111XU1, **Tullahoma, Tenn.**
#112XU1, **Hamburgh, S.C.**
#113XU1, **Columbia, Tenn.**
#114XU1, **Wytheville, Va.**
#115X1, **Oakway, S.C.**
#116XU1, **Laurens Court House, S.C.**
#117XU1, **Washington, Ga.**
#118XU1, **Carolina City, N.C.**

#119XU1, **Colaparchee, Ga.**
#120XU1, **Forsyth, Ga.**
#121XU1, **Limestone Springs, S.C.**
#122XU1, **Balcony Falls, Va.**
#123XU1, **Barnwell Court House, S.C.**
#124XU1, **Bluffton, S.C.**
#125XU1, **Camden, S.C.**
#126XU1, **Cartersville, Ga.**
#127XU1, **Charlottesville, Va.**
#128XU1, **Fraziersville, S.C.**
#129XU1, **Gaston, N.C.**
#130XU1, **Harrisburgh, Tex.**
#132XU1, **Hollandale, Tex.**
#133XU1, **Isabella, Ga.**
#134XU1, **Jacksonville, Fla.**
#135XU1, **Lexington, Va.**
#136XU1, **Madison, Ga.**
#137XU1, **Madison Court House, Fla.**
#138XU1, **Milton, N.C.**
#139XU1, **Norfolk, Va.**
#140XU1, **Plains of Dura, Ga.**
#141X1, **Plum Creek, Tex.**
#142XU1, **Port Gibson, Miss.**
#143XU1, **Talladega, Ala.**
#144XU1, **Greenville, Tenn.**
#145XU1, **Mars Bluff, S.C.**
#146XU1, **Charlotte, N.C.**
#147XU1, **Wilkesboro, N.C.**
#148XU1, **Fort Valley, Ga.**
#149XU1, **Patterson, N.C.**
#150XU1, **Beaufort, S.C.**
#151XU1, **Mount Pleasant, N.C.**
#152XU1, **Oxford, N.C.**
#153XU1, **Williston, S.C.**

CONFEDERATE STATES OF AMERICA, GENERAL ISSUES

Due to its tendency to damage the paper and the color of the stamps, the gum on most unused Confederate States stamps very often is removed. Values for unused examples of Nos. 1-5 (the lithographed issues), Nos. 6 and 7 (the typographed issues, but not including No. 6 printed by De La Rue and imported), Nos. 8-10 and 13 (the engraved issues), and both the Keatinge & Ball and Archer & Daly printings of Nos. 11 and 12 are for stamps without gum. The De La Rue printed Nos. 6 and 14 are valued both with original gum and without gum. All Confederate States unused and used stamps are valued in the grade of very fine, with fresh color and no faults. Unused stamps that are valued only without gum will sell for about the same prices if they have original gum and are very fine with fresh color, but stamps with original gum will sell for less if they have paper cracks or creases, staining, or other paper problems caused by gum deterioration.

For explanations of various terms used see the notes at the end of the postage listings.

Due to its tendency to damage the paper and color of the stamps, the gum on most (but not all) Confederate States stamps very often is removed. Except for the De La Rue-printed Nos. 6 and 14, which are valued both with original gum and without gum, unused values for all Confederate States stamps are for stamps without gum. Stamps with original gum sell for about the same prices, if the gum has not deteriorated and damaged the paper or stamp color.

Jefferson Davis — A1

All 5c Lithographs were printed by Hoyer & Ludwig, of Richmond, Va.

Stones A or B — First stones used. Earliest dated cancellation October 16, 1861. Plating not completed hence size of sheets unknown. These stones had imprints. Stamps from Stones A or B are nearly all in the olive green shade. Sharp, clear impressions. Distinctive marks are few and minute.

Stone 1 — Earliest dated cancellation October 18, 1861. Plating completed. Sheet consists of four groups of fifty varieties arranged in two panes of one hundred each without imprint. The first small printing was in olive green and later small printings appeared in light and dark green; the typical shade, however, is an intermediate shade of bright green. The impressions are clear though not as sharp as those from Stones A or B. Distinctive marks are discernible.

Stone 2 — Earliest dated cancellation December 2, 1861. Plating completed. Sheet consists of four groups of fifty varieties arranged in two panes of one hundred each without imprint. All shades other than olive green are known from this stone, the most common being a dull green. Poor impressions. Many noticeable distinctive marks.

1861 Unwmk. Litho. Soft Porous Paper *Imperf.*

Stone 2

1	A1	5c **green** (shades)	300.	175.
		bright green	350.	225.
		dull green	275.	175.
		On cover		300.
		Single on cover (overpaid drop letter)		500.
		On wallpaper cover		*1,800.*
		On prisoner's cover		—
		On prisoner's cover with U.S. #65		—
		On prisoner's cover with U.S. #U34		—
		On patriotic cover		2,500.
		Pair	600.	425.
		Pair on cover		500.
		Block of 4	1,750.	1,300.
		Pair with full horiz. gutter between		—
a.		5c **light green**	275.	175.
b.		5c **dark green**	375.	250.

VARIETIES

Spur on upper left scroll (Pos. 21)	425.	275.
Side margin copy showing initials (Pos. 41 or 50)	—	—
Misplaced transfer (clear twin impressions of lower left scrolls — pos. 1 entered over pos. 10)	—	—
Rouletted unofficially	500.	850.
On cover		*1,750.*
Pair on cover		*3,750.*

Cancellations

Blue town	+10.
Red town	+125.
Violet town	+150.
Green town	+200.
Orange town	+250.
Texas town	+35.
Arkansas town	+100.
Florida town	+110.
Kentucky town	+300.
Blue gridiron	+5.
Red gridiron	+50.
Blue concentric	+5.
Star or flowers	+175.
Numeral	+50.
"Paid"	+50.
"Steamboat"	+150.
Express Co.	+350.
Railroad	+300.
Pen Cancel	60.

Stone 1

1	A1	5c **green**	325.	200.
		bright green	350.	225.
		dull green	300.	200.
a.		5c **light green**	300.	200.
b.		5c **dark green**	375.	250.
c.		5c **olive green**	425.	250.
		On cover		300.
		On patriotic cover		2,500.
		Pair	750.	475.
		Pair on cover		600.
		Block of 4	1,650.	1,250.

VARIETIES

Acid flaw	350.	200.
Arrow between panes	600.	325.
Flaw on "at" of "States" (Pos. 38)	325.	225.

Cancellations

Blue town	+10.
Red town	+80.
Green town	+225.
Texas town	+50.
Arkansas town	+90.
Florida town	+110.
Georgia double straightline town	+350.
Kentucky town	+300.
October, 1861, year date	+40.
Blue gridiron	+5.
Red gridiron	+75.
Blue concentric	+5.
Numeral	+50.
"Paid"	+50.
"Steam"	+150.
"Steamboat"	+150.
Express Company	+350.
Railroad	+300.
Pen Cancel	75.

Stones A or B

1c	A1	5c **olive green**	425.	200.
		On cover		400.
		On patriotic cover		*5,000.*
		Pair	900.	450.
		Pair on cover		700.
		Block of 4	2,250.	1,300.

VARIETIES

White curl back of head	450.	275.
Imprint	775.	475.

Cancellations

Blue town	+10.
Red town	+150.
October, 1861, year date	+50.
Blue gridiron	+5.
Blue concentric	+5.
Numeral	+60.
"Paid"	+50.
"Steam"	+150.
Express Co.	+400.
Pen Cancel	90.

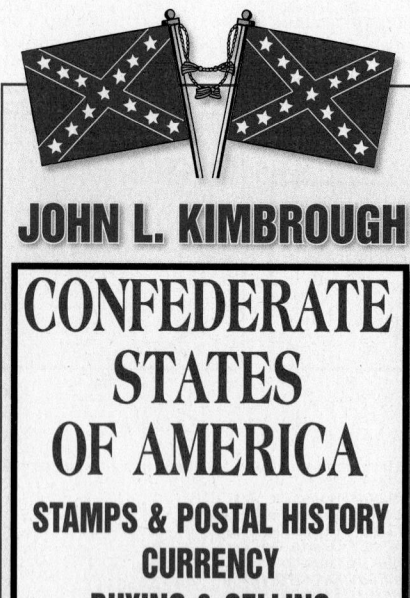

Thomas Jefferson — A2

Hoyer & Ludwig — First stone used. Earliest dated cancellation November 8, 1861. Sheet believed to consist of four groups of fifty varieties each arranged in two panes of one hundred each with imprint at bottom of each pane. Two different imprints are known. Hoyer & Ludwig printings are always in a uniform shade of dark blue. Impressions are clear and distinct, especially so in the early printings. Plating marks are distinct.

J. T. Paterson & Co. — Earliest dated cancellation July 25, 1862. Sheet consists of four groups of fifty varieties each arranged in two panes of one hundred each with imprint at bottom of each pane. Two different imprints are known and at least one pane is known without an imprint. Wide range of shades. Impressions are less clear than those from the Hoyer & Ludwig stone. Paterson stamps show small vertical colored dash below the lowest point of the upper left triangle.

Stone "Y" — Supposedly made by J. T. Paterson & Co., as it shows the distinctive mark of that firm. Plating not completed hence size of sheet unknown. No imprint found. Color is either a light milky blue or a greenish blue. Impressions are very poor and have a blurred appearance. Stone Y stamps invariably show a large flaw at the back of the head as well as small vertical colored dash beneath the upper left triangle.

1861-62 Litho. Soft Porous Paper

Paterson

2	A2 10c **blue**	275.	180.
	On cover		325.
	On wallpaper cover		1,800.
	On patriotic cover		2,250.
	On prisoner's cover with U.S. #65		—
	Pair	650.	425.
	Pair on cover		950.
	Strip of 3 on cover		—
	Block of 4	1,750.	
	Horiz. pair, gutter btwn.	1,500.	
a.	10c **light blue**	300.	200.
b.	10c **dark blue**	700.	300.
c.	10c **indigo**	*5,000.*	*7,500.*
d.	Printed on both sides		*1,750.*

Two examples of No. 2d are recorded. One has a single inverted split impression on the reverse, and the other has a double impression, one inverted, on the reverse.

VARIETIES

Malformed "O" of "POSTAGE" (Pos. 25)	425.	240.
J. T. Paterson & Co. imprint	1,250.	1,250.

Cancellations

Blue town	+10.
Red town	+120.
Green town	+200.
Violet town	—
Texas town	+125.
Arkansas town	+275.
Florida town	+325.
July, 1862, date	+300.
Straight line town	+500.
Blue gridiron	+10.
Red gridiron	+75.
Blue concentric	+10.
Numeral	+80.
"Paid"	+75.
Star or flower	+200.
Railroad	+350.
Express Co.	+300.
Pen Cancel	80.

Hoyer

2b	A2 10c **dark blue**	650.	275.
	On cover		1,000.
	On wallpaper cover		2,000.
	On patriotic cover		3,000.
	On prisoner's cover with U.S. #65		—
	Pair	1,300.	900.
	Pair on cover		*1,700.*
	Strip of 3 on cover		*5,000.*
	Block of 4	2,750.	—
d.	Printed on both sides		—

Specialists have questioned the existence of No. 2bd, the Hoyer & Ludwig printed on both sides. The editors would like to see authenticated evidence of its existence.

VARIETIES

Malformed "T" of "TEN" (Pos. 4)	750.	325.
"G" and "E" of "POSTAGE" joined (Pos. 10)	750.	325.
Circular flaw, upper left star (Pos. 11)	750.	325.
Third spiked ornament at right, white (Pos. 45)	750.	375.
Hoyer & Ludwig imprint	1,000.	850.
Roulletted unofficially		—
On cover		*3,250.*

Cancellations

Blue town	+30.
Red town	+100.
Texas town	+125.
Arkansas town	+275.
Florida town	+325.
Kentucky town	+400.
Nov., 1861, date	+300.
Straight line town	+500.
Blue gridiron	+10.
Red gridiron	+75.
Blue concentric	+10.
Numeral	+75.
"Paid"	+50.
Railroad	+350.
Express Company	+300.
Pen Cancel	95.

Stone Y

2e	A2 10c **light milky blue**	1,250.	325.
	greenish blue	1,400.	375.
	On cover		400.
	On wallpaper cover		1,800.
	On patriotic cover		2,100.
	Pair	3,000.	—
	Block of 4	*10,000.*	2,500.

Cancellations

Blue town	+10.
Red town	+125.
Violet town	+75.
Green town	+300.
Texas town	+125.
Arkansas town	+275.
Florida town	—
Straight line town	+500.
Blue gridiron	+10.
Red gridiron	+75.
Blue concentric	+10.
Numeral	+100.
"Paid"	+100.
Pen Cancel	110.

Andrew Jackson — A3

Sheet consists of four groups of fifty varieties arranged in two panes of 100 each.

One stone only was used. Printed by Hoyer & Ludwig, of Richmond, Va. Issued to prepay drop letter and circular rates. Strips of five used to prepay regular 10c rate, which was changed from 5c on July 1, 1862. Earliest known cancellation, March 21, 1862.

1862 (March?) Soft Porous Paper Litho.

3	A3 2c **green**	1,000.	750.
	light green	1,000.	750.
	dark green	1,000.	800.
	dull yellow green	1,350.	900.
	On cover		*3,500.*
	Pair on cover (double circular rate)		*5,000.*
	Strip of 5 on cover		*13,500.*
	On patriotic cover		—
	Pair	2,100.	—
	Block of 4	6,000.	5,000.
a.	2c **bright yellow green**	*2,000.*	—
	On cover		*4,000.*
	Pair		—

VARIETIES

Diagonal half used as 1c with unsevered pair, on cover (unique)		*15,000.*
Horiz. pair, vert. gutter between	—	—
Pair, mark between stamps (btwn. Pos. 4 and 5)	2,200.	2,100.
Mark above upper right corner (Pos. 30)	1,050.	850.
Mark above upper left corner (Pos. 31)	1,050.	850.
Acid flaw	1,050.	800.

Cancellations

Blue town	+800.
Red town	+800.
Arkansas town	—
Texas town	+1,250.
Blue gridiron	+250.
"Paid"	—
Express Company	—
Railroad	+3,000.
Pen Cancel	375.

1862 Soft Porous Paper Litho.

Stone 2 — First stone used for printing in blue. Plating is the same as Stone 2 in green. Earliest dated cancellation Feb. 26, 1862. Printings from Stone 2 are found in all shades of blue. Rough, coarse impressions are typical of printings from Stone 2.

Stone 3 — A new stone used for printings in blue only. Earliest dated cancellation April 10, 1862. Sheet consists of four groups of fifty varieties each arranged in two panes of one hundred each without imprint. Impressions are clear and sharp, often having a proof-like appearance, especially in the deep blue printing. Plating marks, while not so large as on Stone 2 are distinct and clearly defined.

Stone 2

4	A1 5c **blue**	225.	125.
	light blue	250.	140.
	Pair	625.	450.
	Block of 4	1,300.	*2,000.*
	Horiz. pair, wide gutter between	1,250.	—
	Single on cover (overpaid drop letter)		400.
	Pair on cover		450.
	On wallpaper cover		1,250.
	On patriotic cover		*2,500.*
	On prisoner's cover		—
	On prisoner's cover with U.S. #65		—
a.	5c **dark blue**	275.	175.
b.	5c **light milky blue**	350.	200.

VARIETIES

Spur on upper left scroll (Pos. 21)	250.	150.
Thin hard paper	—	150.
Misplaced transfer (faint twin impression of second lower left scroll at left — pos. 2 entered over pos. 10)		—

Cancellations

Blue town	+20.
Red town	+100.
Orange town	+400.
Texas town	+300.
Arkansas town	+325.
Florida town	+200.
Straight line town	+350.
Blue gridiron	+10.
Red gridiron	+85.
Star or Flowers	+150.
Numeral	+85.
Railroad	—
"Paid"	+50.
"Steamboat"	+400.
Express Company	—
"Way"	+250.
Pen Cancel	65.

Stone 3

4	A1 5c **blue**	750.	250.
a.	5c **dark blue**	800.	275.
b.	5c **light milky blue**	750.	250.
	Pair	1,600.	550.
	Block of 4	3,750.	*2,000.*
	On cover		500.
	Pair on cover		625.
	On patriotic cover		*2,750.*
	Horiz. pair, wide gutter btwn.	—	

Stone 3 stamps can be positively identified by plating only. Color or shade is not a determinant.

VARIETIES

Tops of "C" and "E" of "cents" joined by flaw (Pos. 33)	850.	325.
"Flying bird" above lower left corner ornament (Pos. 19)	850.	325.

Cancellations

Blue town	+40.
Red town	+100.
Texas town	+300.
Arkansas town	+325.
Straight line town	+325.
Blue gridiron	+10.
Star or Flowers	+175.
"Paid"	+50.
Pen Cancel	90.

1862 (March?) Soft Porous Paper Litho.

Settings of fifty varieties repeated.

Printed by Hoyer & Ludwig, of Richmond, Va. One stone used, being the same as that used for the Hoyer & Ludwig 10c value in blue. Color change occured probably in March, 1862.

There are many shades of this stamp. The carmine is a very dark, bright color and should not be confused with the deeper shade of rose.

Earliest known cancellation, March 10, 1862. The earliest date of usage of the carmine shade is May 1, 1862.

5	A2 10c **rose** (shades)	2,400.	400.
	dull rose	2,200.	400.
	brown rose	2,650.	800.
	deep rose	2,500.	750.
	carmine rose	2,650.	850.
	On cover		750.
	On wallpaper cover		*2,000.*
	On patriotic cover		*3,000.*
	On prisoner's cover		*5,500.*
	On prisoner's cover with U.S. #65		—
	Pair	4,900.	1,500.
	Strip of 3	—	*3,000.*
	Block of 4	*12,000.*	*4,500.*
a.	10c **carmine**	*3,750.*	*1,900.*
	On cover		*5,000.*
	On patriotic cover		—

VARIETIES

Malformed "T" of "TEN" (Pos. 4)	2,750.	600.
"G" and "E" of "POSTAGE" joined (Pos. 10)	2,750.	600.
Circular flaw, upper left star (Pos. 11)	2,850.	675.
Third spiked ornament at right, white (Pos. 45)	2,100.	675.
Scratched stone (occurring on Pos. 40, 39, 49 and 48, one pane)	2,100.	925.
Imprint		1,750.
Horiz. pair, vert. gutter between		—

Cancellations

Blue town	+50.
Red town	+125.
Green town	+350.
Texas town	+125.
Arkansas town	—
Straight line town	+700.
April, 1862, year date	—
Blue gridiron	+50.
Black concentric	+50.
Blue concentric	+50.
"Paid"	—

	Railroad		—
	Express Company		—
	Pen Cancel		200.

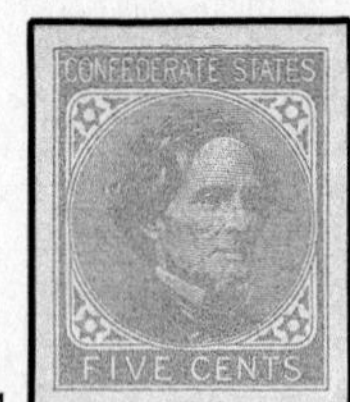

Jefferson Davis — A4

Plate of 400 in four panes of 100 each. No imprint.

No. 6 represents London printings from De La Rue & Co., a number of sheets being sent over by blockade runners. Fine clear impressions. The gum is light and evenly distributed. Exact date of issue unknown. Earliest known cancellation, April 16, 1862.

Typographed by De La Rue & Co. in London, England

1862 (April) Hard Medium Paper

6	A4 5c **light blue**	20.	30.
	No gum	10.	
	Single on cover used before July 1, 1862		150.
	Single on cover (overpaid drop letter)		250.
	Single on patriotic cover used before July 1, 1862		2,000.
	Single on prisoner's cover used before July 1, 1862		—
	On wallpaper cover		1,200.
	On patriotic cover		1,200.
	On prisoner's cover		—
	On prisoner's cover with U.S. #65		—
	Pair	45.	75.
	Pair on cover		100.
	Pair on patriotic cover		*2,000.*
	Block of 4	100.	290.
	Block of 4 on cover		900.

Cancellations

Blue town	+7.
Red town	+55.
Green town	+75.
Texas town	+65.
Arkansas town	+100.
Straight line town	+225.
Blue gridiron	+2.
Red gridiron	+35.
Blue concentric	+7.
Express Company	+350.
Railroad	+250.
"Paid"	+50.

1862 (July) Typo. Thin to Thick Paper

Plate of 400 in four panes of 100 each. No imprint.

Locally printed by Archer & Daly of Richmond, Va., from plates made in London, England, by De La Rue & Co. Printed on both imported English and local papers. Earliest known cancellation, July 13, 1862.

No. 7 shows coarser impressions than No. 6, and the color is duller and often blurred. Gum is light or dark and unevenly distributed.

7	A4 5c **blue** (De La Rue thin paper)	22.	22.
	Single on cover (overpaid drop letter)		200.
	On wallpaper cover		1,200.
	On patriotic cover		1,200.
	On prisoner's cover		—
	On prisoner's cover with U.S. #65		*2,500.*
	Pair	50.	48.
	Pair on cover		300.
	Block of 4	110.	350.
	Block of 4 on cover		800.
	Eight on cover (Trans-Miss. rate)		*4,000.*
a.	5c **deep blue**	28.	35.
b.	Printed on both sides	*2,500.*	*1,400.*
	Pair		*3,000.*
	Pair on cover		*4,000.*

VARIETIES

White tie (UR30), De La Rue paper	200.	250.
Local paper (thick)	50.	55.
White tie (UR30), local paper (thick)	*450.*	*450.*
White tie on cover		400.
Major vert. plate scratch at right (UL 31)	225.	225.
Minor vert. plate scratch at right (UL 41)	100.	100.
Horiz. pair, vert. gutter between, De La Rue thin paper	200.	
Horiz. pair, vert. gutter between, thick local paper	*300.*	

Cancellations

Blue town	+7.
Red town	+75.
Brown town	+30.
Violet town	+110.
Green town	+150.
Texas town	+90.
Arkansas town	+110.
Florida town	+140.
Straight line town	+250.
Blue gridiron	+2.
Red gridiron	+60.
Blue concentric	+7.
Railroad	+250.

Express Company	+400.
Design (stars, etc.)	+75.
"Paid"	+50.

The unissued 10c design A4 was privately printed in various colors for philatelic purposes. (See note below No. 14.)

Counterfeits of the 10c exist.

Andrew Jackson — A5

Sheet of 200 (two panes of 100 each).

One plate. Printed by Archer & Daly of Richmond, Va. Earliest known cancellation. Apr. 21, 1863. Issued to prepay drop letter and circular rates. Strips of five used to prepay regular 10c rate.

1863 (April) Soft Porous Paper Engraved

8	A5 2c **brown red**	75.	*350.*
a.	2c **pale red**	90.	*450.*
	Single on cover, #8 or 8a		*1,500.*
	On prisoner's cover		—
	On prisoner's cover with U.S. #65		—
	Pair	160.	*1,000.*
	Pair on cover		*3,250.*
	On wallpaper cover		—
	Block of 4	375.	—
	Block of 5		—
	Strip of 5 on cover		*4,500.*
	Strip of 5 on wallpaper cover		—
	Strip of 10 on cover		—
	Double transfer	130.	*450.*
	Horiz. pair, vert. gutter between	325.	

Cancellations

Blue town	+35.
Red town	+225.
Violet town	+300.
Army of Tenn.	—
Blue gridiron	+35.
Black numeral	—
Railroad	+325.
Pen cancel	150.

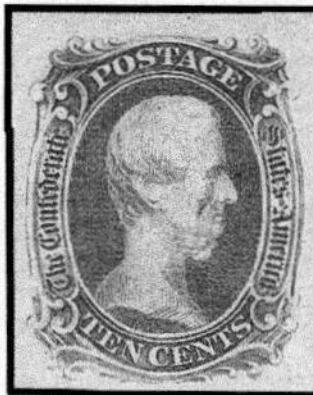

Jefferson Davis "TEN CENTS" — A6

One plate of 200 subjects all of which were probably recut as every example examined to date shows distinct recutting. Plating not completed.

Printed by Archer & Daly of Richmond, Va. First printings in milky blue. First issued in April, 1863. Earliest known cancellation, April 23, 1863.

1863, Apr. Soft Porous Paper Engraved

9	A6 10c **blue**	950.	500.
a.	10c **milky blue** (first printing)	1,050.	550.
b.	10c **gray blue**	1,050.	600.
	On cover		1,500.
	On wallpaper cover		*4,000.*
	On patriotic cover		*4,500.*
	On prisoner's cover		—
	On prisoner's cover with U.S. #65		—
	Pair	2,000.	2,100.
	Pair on cover		*3,000.*
	Block of 4	*5,250.*	
	Curved lines outside the labels at top and bottom are broken in the middle (Pos. 63R)	1,050.	750.
	Double transfer	1,100.	950.
	Damaged plate	1,200.	1,050.

Cancellations

Blue town	+25.
Red town	+150.
Green town	+600.
Violet town	—
Straight line town	+500.
April, 1863, year date	—
Black gridiron	+25.
Blue gridiron	+50.
Red gridiron	+200.
Railroad	+400.
Circle of wedges	+1,250.
Pen Cancel	300.

Frame Line "10 CENTS" — A6a

Printed by Archer & Daly of Richmond, Va.

One copper plate of 100 subjects, all but one of which were recut. Earliest known use April 19, 1863.

Stamp design same as Die A (Pos. 11).

Values are for stamps showing parts of lines on at least 3 of 4 sides. Used stamps showing 4 complete lines sell for 400%-500% of the values given. Unused stamps showing 4 complete lines are exceedingly rare (only two recorded), and the sound example is valued at $35,000.

1863, Apr. Soft Porous Paper Engraved

10	A6a 10c **blue**	5,500.	2,500.
a.	10c **milky blue**	5,500.	2,500.
b.	10c **greenish blue**	6,000.	2,500.
c.	10c **dark blue**	6,000.	2,500.
	On cover		*3,500.*
	On wallpaper cover		*5,500.*
	On patriotic cover		*11,000.*
	On prisoner's cover		*7,500.*
	On prisoner's cover with U.S. #65		—
	Pair	*12,500.*	*6,000.*
	Pair on cover		*7,000.*
	Block of 4	*25,000.*	
	Strip of 4	*25,000.*	
	Strip of 6	—	*22,500.*
	Strip of 7	*47,500.*	
	Double transfer (Pos. 74)	6,250.	2,750.

Cancellations

Blue town	+100.
Red town	+500.
Straight line town	+750.
April, 1863, year date	—
Blue gridiron	+100.
Pen Cancel	1,150.

No Frame Line "10 CENTS" (Die A) — A7

There are many slight differences between A7 (Die A) and A8 (Die B), the most noticeable being the additional line outside the ornaments at the four corners of A8 (Die B).

Stamps were first printed by Archer & Daly, of Richmond, Va. In 1864 the plates were transferred to the firm of Keatinge & Ball in Columbia, S. C., who made further printings from them. Two plates, each with two panes of 100, numbered 1 and 2. First state shows numbers only, later states show various styles of Archer & Daly imprints, and latest show Keatinge & Ball imprints. Archer & Daly stamps show uniformly clear impressions and a good quality of gum evenly distributed (Earliest known cancellation, April 21, 1863); Keatinge & Ball stamps generally show filled in impressions in a deep blue, and the gum is brown and unevenly distributed. (Earliest known cancellation, Oct. 4, 1864). These notes also apply to No. 12.

1863-64 Thick or Thin Paper Engraved

11	A7 10c **blue**	18.	*20.*
	deep blue, Keatinge & Ball ('64)	17.	*35.*
	On cover		125.
	Single on cover (overpaid drop letter)		200.
	On wallpaper cover		1,200.
	On patriotic cover		1,000.
	On prisoner's cover		750.
	On prisoner's cover with U.S. #65		2,500.
	On cover, dp. blue (K. & B.) ('64)		200.
	On wallpaper cover (K. & B.)		1,250.
	On prisoner's cover (K. & B.) with U.S. #65 ('64)		—
	Pair	40.	*45.*
	Pair on cover		275.
	Block of 4	85.	350.
	Strip of 4 on cover (Trans-Mississippi rate)		*4,000.*
	Block of 4 on cover (Trans-Mississippi rate)		*10,000.*
	Margin block of 12, Archer & Daly impt. & P#	600.	
	Margin block of 12, Keatinge & Ball impt. & P#	425.	
a.	10c **milky blue**	55.	60.
b.	10c **dark blue**	25.	30.
c.	10c **greenish blue**	30.	50.
d.	10c **green**	100.	*80.*
e.	Officially perforated 12½ (Archer & Daly printing)	450.	350.
	On cover		*900.*
	On wallpaper cover		—
	Pair	950.	600.
	Pair on cover		*2,750.*
	Block of 4	2,000.	*6,000.*

VARIETIES

Printed on paper with horiz. "textile marks" (lines)	*50.*	*60.*
Horiz. pair, vert. gutter between	125.	
Double transfer	75.	100.
Rouletted unofficially	600.	500.
On cover		800.

Cancellations

Blue town	+5.
Red town	+35.
Orange town	+110.
Brown town	+60.
Green town	+200.
Violet town	+100.
Texas town	+65.
Arkansas town	+125.
Florida town	+200.
Straight line town	+350.
Army of Tenn.	+300.
April, 1863 year date	+75.
"FREE"	+250.
Blue gridiron	+5.
Black concentric circles	+10.
Star	+200.
Crossroads	+150.
"Paid"	+100.
Numeral	+100.
Railroad	+175.
Steamboat	+1,500.

Jefferson Davis (Die B) — A8

Plates bore Nos. 3 and 4, otherwise notes on No. 11 apply. Earliest known use: Archer & Daly — May 1, 1863; Keatinge & Ball — Sept. 4, 1864.

1863-64 Thick or Thin Paper Engraved

12	A8 10c **blue**	22.	25.
	deep blue, Keatinge & Ball ('64)	21.	40.
	On cover		140.
	Single on cover (overpaid drop letter)		200.
	On wallpaper cover		1,200.
	On patriotic cover		1,250.
	On prisoner's cover		750.
	On prisoner's cover with U.S. #65		2,500.
	On cover, dp. blue (K. & B.) ('64)		200.
	Pair	48.	55.
	Pair on cover		200.
	Block of 4	110.	300.
	Strip of 4 on cover (Trans-Mississippi rate)		*4,000.*
	Margin block of 12, Archer & Daly impt. & P#	475.	
	Margin block of 12, Keatinge & Ball impt. & P#	425.	
a.	10c **milky blue**	55.	60.
b.	10c **light blue**	21.	22.
c.	10c **greenish blue**	40.	*50.*
	Strip of 4 on cover (Trans-Mississippi rate)		*4,500.*
d.	10c **dark blue**	24.	25.
e.	10c **green**	150.	140.
f.	Officially perforated 12½ (Archer & Daly printing)	450.	375.
	On cover		*900.*
	Pair	950.	600.
	Pair on cover		—
	Block of 4	2,000.	

VARIETIES

Printed on paper with horiz. "textile marks" (lines)	*50.*	*75.*
Horiz. pair, vert. gutter between	125.	
Double transfer	95.	110.
Rouletted unofficially	—	375.
On cover		850.

Cancellations

Blue town	+5.
Red town	+35.
Brown town	+90.
Green town	+120.
Violet town	+85.
Texas town	+125.
Arkansas town	+150.
Florida town	+200.
Straight line town	+400.
Army of Tenn.	+350.
May, 1863, year date	+60.
Star	+250.
Blue gridiron	+5.
Black concentric circles	+10.
Railroad	+175.

George Washington — A9

One plate which consisted of two panes of 100 each. First printings were from plates with imprint in Old English type under each pane, which was later removed. Printed on paper of varying thickness and in many shades of green. This stamp was also used as currency. Earliest known cancellation, June 1, 1863. Forged cancellations exist.

1863 (June?) Engraved by Archer & Daly

13	A9 20c **green**	45.	*400.*
	On cover		*1,250.*
	On wallpaper cover		*2,000.*
	On patriotic cover		*1,500.*
	On prisoner's cover		*4,000.*
	On prisoner's cover with U.S. #65		*5,000.*
	Pair	100.	*900.*
	Pair on cover (non-Trans-Mississippi rate)		*4,750.*
	Pair on cover (Trans-Mississippi rate)		*4,500.*
	Block of 4	200.	*3,500.*
	Strip of 4 with imprint	425.	
	Block of 8 with imprint	1,050.	
a.	20c **yellow green**	80.	*450.*
b.	20c **dark green**	65.	*500.*
	Short transfer at right	130.	
c.	20c **bluish green**	100.	—
d.	Diagonal half used as 10c on cover		*1,400.*
	Diagonal half on prisoner's cover		—
	Diagonal half on wallpaper cover		*25,000.*
e.	Horizontal half used as 10c on cover		*2,500.*

VARIETIES

Horizontal pair with gutter between	350.	
Double transfer, 20 doubled (Pos. 24L and 35R)	300.	—
"20" on forehead	*3,000.*	—
Rouletted unofficially		*1,100.*
On cover		*3,750.*

Cancellations

Blue town	+50.
Red town	+200.
Violet town	—
Texas town	+100.
Arkansas town	+400.
Tennessee town	+1,000.
Railroad	—

John C. Calhoun — A10

Typographed by De La Rue & Co., London, England

1862

14	A10 1c **orange**	110.
	No gum	60.
	Pair	225.
	Block of 4	475.
a.	1c **deep orange**	145.
	No gum	85.

No. 14 was never put in use.

Upon orders from the Confederate Government, De La Rue & Co. of London, England, prepared Two Cents and Ten Cents typographed plates by altering the One Cent (No. 14) and the Five Cents (Nos. 6-7) designs previously made by them. Stamps were never officially printed from these plates although privately made prints exist in various colors.

Counterfeits

In 1935 a set of 12 lithographed imitations, later known as the "Springfield facsimiles," appeared in plate form. They are in approximately normal colors on yellowish soft wove paper of modern manufacture.

PROOFS

1861

1P5	5c **green,** plate on wove paper	*1,750.*
2TC5	10c Plate on wove paper (stone Y)	
	a. **black**	*4,500.*
2P5	10c **blue,** plate on wove paper	*1,750.*

1862

6TC1c	5c Die on wove paper	
	e. **dark blue**	1,000.
	f. **black**	1,000.
6TC1d	5c Die on glazed card	
	e. **black**	900.
	f. **pink**	*2,000.*
6TC5	5c Plate on wove paper	
	a. **gray blue**	600.
6P1d	5c **light blue,** die on glazed card	600.
	b. 5c **blue** & 1c **orange,** 6P1+14P1 composite die proof on 20x90mm glazed card	*6,500.*
6P5	5c **light blue,** plate on wove paper	150.
	Pair with gutter between	375.
7TC4	5c Plate on thin card	
	a. **carmine**	1,150.
7TC5	5c Plate on wove paper	
	a. **carmine**	1,750.

1863

8TC1c	2c Die on wove paper	
	e. **black**	3,000.
	f. **blue**	3,750.

Nos. 8TC1ab and 8TC1ac have a frame line around the design.

9TC1c	10c Die on wove paper	
	e. **black**	1,500.
11TC1c	10c Die on wove paper	
	e. **black**	—
12P7	10c **deep blue,** plate on thick ribbed paper	750.
13TC1c	20c Die on wove paper	
	e. **red brown**	*4,250.*
13P5a	20c **green,** die on wove paper	*4,000.*

1862

14TC1d	1c Die on glazed card	
	e. **black**	*2,250.*
14TC5	1c Plate on wove paper	
	a. **light yellow brown**	500.
14P1b	1c **orange,** die on glazed card	*2,750.*

SPECIMENS

6s	5c **blue,** "SPECIMEN" diagonal	*7,000.*
14s	1c **orange,** "SPECIMEN" diagonal	*7,000.*
	a. "SPECIMEN" horizontal	—

Nos. 6s and 14s are together on a page originally from the De La Rue archives.

Essay Die Proofs

In working up the final dies, proofs of incomplete designs in various stages were made. Usually dated in typeset lines, they are very rare. Others, of the 10c (No. 12) and the 20c (No. 13) were proofs made as essays from the dies. They are deeply engraved and printed in deep shades of the issued colors, but show only small differences from the stamps as finally issued. All are very rare.

Explanatory Notes

The following notes by Lawrence L. Shenfield explain the various routes, rates and usages of the general issue Confederate stamps.

"Across the Lines"
Letters Carried by Private Express Companies

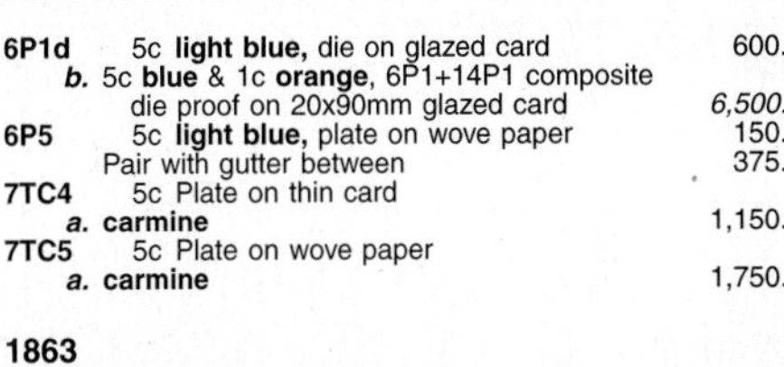

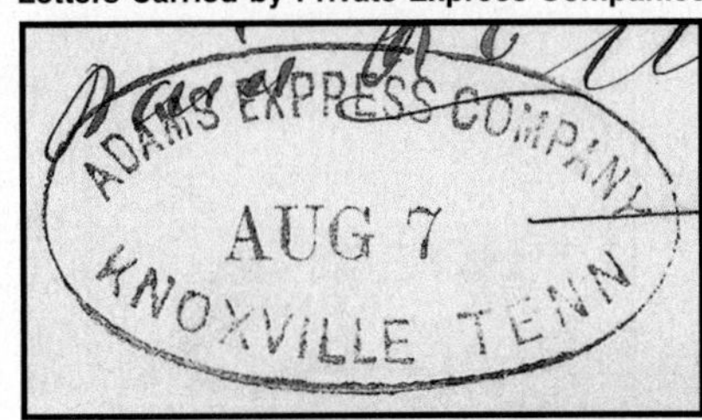

Adams Express Co. and American Letter Express Company Handstamps Used on "Across the Lines" Letters

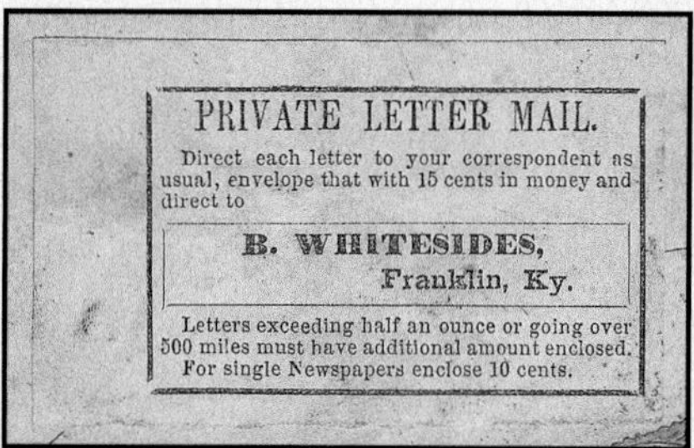

PRIVATE LETTER MAIL.
Direct each letter to your correspondent as usual, envelope that with 15 cents in money and direct to
B. WHITESIDES,
Franklin, Ky.
Letters exceeding half an ounce or going over 500 miles must have additional amount enclosed. For single Newspapers enclose 10 cents.

B. Whitesides Label

About two months after the outbreak of the Civil War, in June, 1861, postal service between North and South and vice versa was carried on largely by Adams Express Company, and the American Letter Express Company. Northern terminus for the traffic was Louisville, Ky.; Southern terminus was Nashville, Tenn. Letters for transmission were delivered to any office of the express company, together with a fee, usually 20c or 25c per ½ ounce to cover carriage. The express company messengers carried letters across the lines and delivered them to their office on the other side, where they were deposited in the Government mail for transmission to addressees, postage paid out of the fee charged. Letters from North to South, always enclosed in 3c U.S. envelopes, usually bear the handstamp of the Louisville office of the express company, and in addition the postmark and "Paid 5" of Nashville, Tenn., indicating its acceptance for delivery at the Nashville Post Office. Letters from South to North sometimes bear the origin postmark of a Southern post office, but more often merely the handstamp of the Louisville express company office applied as the letters cleared through Louisville. The B. Whitesides South to North cover bears a "Private Letter Mail" label. In addition, these covers bear the 3c 1857 U.S. adhesive stamp, cancelled with the postmark and grid of Louisville, Ky., where they went into the Government mail for delivery. Some across-the-lines letters show the handstamp of various express company offices, according to the particular routing the letters followed. On August 26, 1861, the traffic ceased by order of the U.S. Post Office Dept. (Values are for full covers bearing the usual Louisville, Ky., or Nashville, Tenn., handstamps of the express company. Unusual express office markings are rarer and worth more.)

North to South 3c U.S. Envelope, Adams Exp. Co. Louisville, Ky., handstamp	*1,500.*
North to South 3c U.S. Envelope, American Letter Express Co., Ky., handstamp	*2,100.*
South to North 3c 1857, Adams Exp. Co., Louisville, Ky., handstamp	*1,750.*
South to North 3c 1857, American Letter Exp. 250, Nashville, Tenn., handstamp	*2,500.*
South to North 3c 1861, Adams Exp. Co., Louisville, Ky., handstamp	*3,250.*
South to North 3c 1857, B. Whitesides, Franklin, Ky., label	*16,500.*

Blockade-Run Letters from Europe to the Confederate States

Charleston "STEAM-SHIP" in Oval Handstamp

As the Federal Fleet gradually extended its blockade of the Confederate States coastal regions, the South was forced to resort to blockade runners to carry letters to and from outside ports. These letters were all private-ship letters and never bore a foreign stamp if from Europe, nor a Confederate stamp if to Europe. The usual route from Europe was via a West Indies port, Nassau, Bahamas; Hamilton, Bermuda, or Havana, into the Southern ports of Wilmington, N.C. and Charleston, S.C. More rarely such letters came in to Savannah, Mobile and New Orleans. Letters from Europe are the only ones which are surely identified by their markings. They bore either the postmark of Wilmington, N.C., straightline "SHIP" and "12", "22", "32", etc., in manuscript; or the postmark of Charleston, S. C., "STEAMSHIP" in oval, and "12", "22", "32", etc., in manuscript. Very rarely Charleston used a straightline "SHIP" instead of "STEAMSHIP" in oval. All such letters were postage due; the single letter rate of 12c being made up of 2c for the private ship captain plus 10c for the regular single letter Confederate States rate. Over-weight letters were 22c (due), 32c, 42c, etc. A few examples are known on which Confederate General Issue stamps were used, usually as payment for forwarding postage. Covers with such stamps, or with the higher rate markings, 22c, 32, etc., are worth more.

Values are for full covers in fine condition.

Charleston, S.C. "6" handstamp	*2,500.*
Charleston, S.C., postmark, "STEAM—SHIP," and "12" in ms.	*3,000.*
Charleston, S.C., postmark, "SHIP," and "12" in ms.	*3,000.*
Wilmington, N.C., postmark, "SHIP," and "12" in ms.	*3,000.*
Savannah, Ga., postmark "SHIP," and "7" in ms. (*)	*4,000.*
New Orleans, La. postmark, "SHIP" and "10" in ms.	*5,000.*

(* 7c rate: 5c postage before July 1, 1862, plus 2c for ship captain.)

Express Company Mail in the Confederacy

Southern Express Company Handstamps

Shortly after the outbreak of war in 1861, the Adams Express Company divisions operating in the South were forced to suspend operations and turned their Southern lines over to a new company organized under the title Southern Express Company. This express did the bulk of the express business in the Confederacy despite the continued opposition of the Post Office Dept. of the C.S.A. and the ravages of the contending armies upon railroads. Other companies operating in the Confederacy were: South Western Express Co. (New Orleans), Pioneer Express Company, White's Southern Express (only one example known) and some local expresses of limited operation. The first three used handstamps of various designs usually bearing the city name of the office. Postal regulation necessitated the payment of regular Confederate postal rates on letters carried by express companies, express charges being paid in addition. Important letters, particularly money letters, were entrusted to these express companies as well as goods and wares of all kinds. The express rates charged for letters are not known; probably they varied depending upon the difficulty and risk of transmittal. Covers bearing stamps and express company handstamps are very rare.

Prisoner-of-War and Flag-of-Truce Letters

Prison Censor Handstamps

By agreement between the United States and the Confederate States, military prisoners and imprisoned civilians of both sides were permitted to send censored letters to their respective countries. Such letters, if from North to South, usually bore a U.S. 3c 1861 adhesive, postmarked at a city near the prison, to pay the postage to the exchange ground near Old Point Comfort, Va.; and a 10c Confederate stamp, canceled at Richmond, Va. (or "due" handstamp) to pay the Confederate postage to destination. If from South to North, letters usually bore a 10c Confederate stamp canceled at a Southern city (or "paid" handstamp) and a U. S. 3c 1861 adhesive (or "due 3" marking) and the postmark of Old Point Comfort, Va. In addition, prison censor markings, handstamped or manuscript, the name and rank of the soldier, and "Flag of Truce, via Fortress Monroe" in manuscript usually appear on these covers.

Federal prison censor handstamps of various designs are known from these prisons:

Camp Chase, Columbus, O.
David's Island, Pelham, N.Y.
Fort Delaware, Delaware City, Del.
Camp Douglas, Chicago, Ill.
Elmira Prison, Elmira, N.Y.
Johnson's Island, Sandusky, O.
Fort McHenry, Baltimore, Md.
Camp Morton, Indianapolis, Ind.
Fort Oglethorpe, Macon, Ga.
Old Capitol Prison, Washington, D.C.
Point Lookout Prison, Point Lookout, Md.
Fort Pulaski, Savannah, Ga.
Rock Island Prison, Rock Island, Ill.
Ship Island, New Orleans, La.
West's Hospital, Baltimore, Md.
U.S. General Hospital, Gettysburg, Pa.

Several other Federal prisons used manuscript censor markings.

Southern prison censor markings are always in manuscript, and do not identify the prison. The principal Southern prisons were at Richmond and Danville, Va.; Andersonville and Savannah, Ga.; Charleston, Columbia and Florence S.C.; Salisbury, N.C.; Hempstead and Tyler, Tex.

Civilians residing in both the North and the South were also, under exceptional circumstances, permitted to send Flag of Truce letters across the lines. Such covers bore no censor marking nor prison markings, but were always endorsed "via Flag of Truce".

Values will be found under various individual stamps for "on prisoner's cover" and are for the larger prisons. Prisoners' letters from the smaller prisons are much rarer. Only a very small percentage of prisoners' covers bore *both* a U.S. stamp and a Confederate stamp.

The "SOUTHERN LETTER UNPAID" Marking On Northbound Letters of Confederate Origin

By mid-May, 1861, correspondence between the North and South was difficult. In the South, postmasters were resigning and closing their accounts with Washington as the Confederacy prepared to organize its own postal system by June 1. From that date on, town marks and "paid" handstamps (and later postmasters' provisional stamps) were used in all post offices of the seceded states. The three most important Southern cities for clearing mail to the North were Memphis, Nashville and Richmond. The Richmond-Washington route was closed in April; Memphis was closed by June 1st, and mail attempting to cross the lines at these points generally ended up at the dead letter office. However, at Louisville, Kentucky, mail from the South via Nashville continued to arrive in June, July and August. On June 24, 1861, the Post Office Department advised the Louisville post office, "You will forward letters from the South for the Loyal States as unpaid, after removing postage stamps, but foreign letters in which prepayment is compulsory must come to the Dead Letter Office." However, Louisville avoided the task of "removing postage stamps," and instead prepared the "Southern Letter Unpaid" handstamp and special "due 3" markers for use. These markings were applied in the greenish-blue color of the Louisville office to letters of Southern origin that had accumulated, in addition to the usual town mark and grid of Louisville. The letters were delivered in the North as unpaid. Probably Louisville continued to forward such unpaid mail until about July 15. The marking is very rare. Other Southern mail was forwarded from Louisville as late as Aug. 27.

For listings see under U.S. 1857-61 issue, Nos. 26, 35-38. Values shown there are generally for this marking on off-cover stamps. Complete covers bearing stamps showing the full markings are valued from $10,000 upward depending upon the stamps, other postal markings and unusual usages, and condition. Fraudulent covers exist.

Trans-Mississippi Express Mail-the 40c Rate

From the fall of New Orleans on April 24, 1862, the entire reach of the Mississippi River was threatened by the Federal fleets. Late in 1862 the Confederacy experienced difficulty in maintaining regular mail routes trans-Mississippi to the Western states. Private express companies began to carry some mail, but by early 1863 when the Meridian-Jackson-Vicksburg-Shreveport route was seriously menaced, the Post Office Department of the Confederate States was forced to inaugurate an express mail service by contracting with a private company the name of which remains undisclosed. The eastern termini were at Meridian and Brandon, Miss.; the western at Shreveport and Alexandria, La. Letters, usually endorsed "via Meridian (or Brandon)" if going West; "via Shreveport (or Alexandria)" if going East were deposited in any Confederate post office. The rate was 40c per ½ ounce or less. Such Trans-Mississippi Express Mail upon arrival at a terminus was carried by couriers in a devious route across the Mississippi and returned to the regular mails at the nearest terminus on the other side of the river. The precise date of the beginning of the Trans-Mississippi service is not known. The earliest date of use so far seen is November 2, 1863 and the latest use February 9, 1865. These covers can be identified by the written endorsement of the route, but particularly by the rate since many bore no route endorsements.

Strips of four of 10c engraved stamps, pairs of the 20c stamp and various combinations of 10c stamps and the 5c London or Local prints are known; also handstamped Paid 40c marking. No identifying handstamps were used, merely the postmark of the office which received the letter originally. Values for Trans-Mississippi Express covers will be found under various stamps of the General Issues.

A 50c Preferred Mail Express rate, announced in April, 1863, preceded the Trans-Mississippi Express Mail 40c rate. One cover showing this rate is known.

Packet and Steamboat Covers and Markings

Letters carried on Confederate packets operating on coastal routes or up and down the inland waterways were usually handstamped with the name of the packet or marked STEAM or STEAMBOAT. Either United States stamps of the 1857 issue or stamped envelopes of the 1853 or 1860 issues have been found so used, as well as Confederate Postmasters' Provisional and General Issue stamps. Some specially designed pictorial or imprinted packet boat covers also exist. All are scarce and command values from $1,000 upward for handstamped United States envelopes and from $1,500 up for covers bearing Confederate stamps.

The Confederate postal laws did not provide the franking privilege for any mail except official correspondence of the Post Office Department. Such letters could be sent free only when enclosed in officially imprinted envelopes individually signed by the official using them. These envelopes were prepared and issued for Post Office Department use.

The imprints were on United States envelopes of 1853-61 issue, and also on commercial envelopes of various sizes and colors. When officially signed and mailed, they were postmarked, usually at Richmond, Va., with printed or handstamped "FREE". Envelopes are occasionally found unused and unsigned, and more rarely, signed but unused. When such official envelopes were used on other than official Post Office Department business, Confederate stamps were used.

Semi-official envelopes also exist bearing imprints of other government departments, offices, armies, states, etc. Regular postage was required to carry such envelopes through the mails.

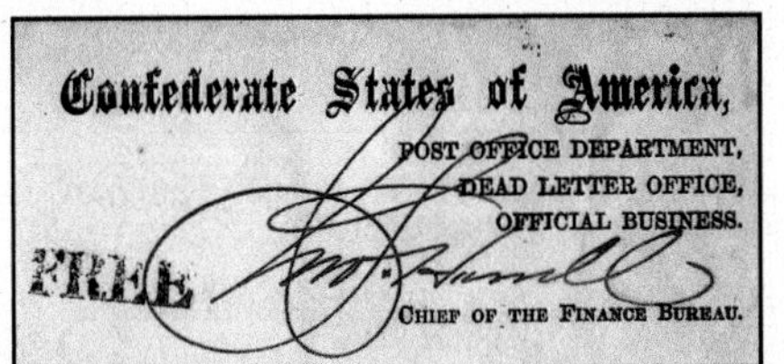

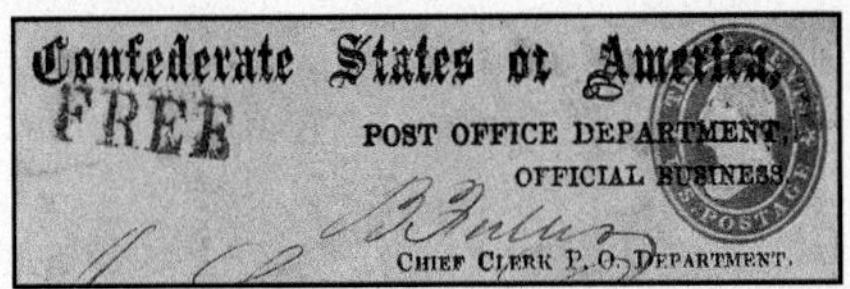

Typical Imprints of Official Envelopes of the Post Office Department. (Many variations of type, style and wording exist.)

Office	Signature
Postmaster General	John H. Reagan
Chief of the Contract Bureau	H. St. Geo. Offutt
Chief of the Appointment Bureau	B. N. Clements
Chief of the Finance Bureau	Jno. L. Harrell
Chief of the Finance Bureau	J. L. Lancaster
Chief of the Finance Bureau	A. Dimitry
Dead Letter Office	A. Dimitry
Dead Letter Office	Jno. L. Harrell
Chief Clerk, P. O. Department	B. Fuller
Chief Clerk	W. D. Miller
Auditor's Office	W. W. Lester
Auditor's Office	B. Baker
Auditor's Office	J. W. Robertson
First Auditor's Office, Treasury Department	J. W. Robertson
First Auditor's Office, Treasury Department	B. Baker
Third Auditor's Office	A. Moise
Third Auditor's Office	I. W. M. Harris
Agency, Post Office Dept. Trans-Miss.	Jas. H. Starr

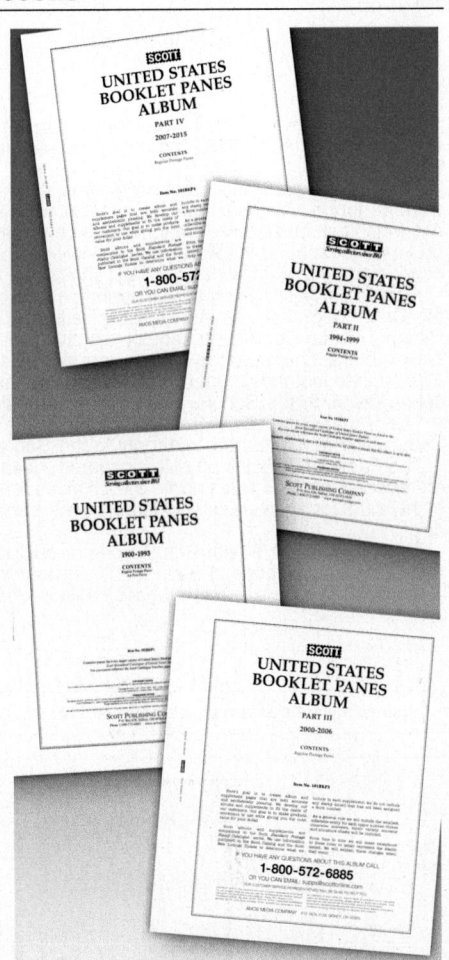

CANAL ZONE

The Canal Zone, a strip of territory with an area of about 552 square miles following generally the line of the Canal, was under the jurisdiction of the United States, 1904-1979, and under the joint jurisdiction of the United States and Panama, 1979-1999, when the Canal, in its entirety, reverted to Panama.

The Canal organization underwent two distinct and fundamental changes. The construction of the Canal and the general administration of civil affairs were performed by the Isthmian Canal Commission under the provisions of the Spooner Act. This was supplanted in April, 1914, by the Panama Canal Act which established the organization known as The Panama Canal. This was an independent government agency which included both the operation and maintenance of the waterway and civil government in the Canal Zone. Most of the quasi-business enterprises relating to the Canal operation were conducted by the Panama Railroad, an adjunct of The Panama Canal.

A basic change in the mode of operations took effect July 1, 1951, under provisions of Public Law 841 of the 81st Congress. This in effect transferred the Canal operations to the Panama Railroad Co., which had been made a federal government corporation in 1948, and changed its name to the Panama Canal Co. Simultaneously the civil government functions of The Panama Canal, including the postal service, were renamed the Canal Zone Government. The organization therefore consisted of two units — the Panama Canal Co. and Canal Zone Government — headed by an individual who was president of the company and governor of the Canal Zone. His appointment as governor was made by the president of the United States, subject to confirmation by the Senate, and he was ex-officio president of the company.

The Canal Zone Government functioned as an independent government agency, and was under direct supervision of the president of the United States who delegated this authority to the Secretary of the Army.

The Panama Canal is 50 miles long from deep water in the Atlantic to deep water in the Pacific. It runs from northwest to southeast with the Atlantic entrance being 33.5 miles north and 27 miles west of the Pacific entrance. The airline distance between the two entrances is 43 miles. It requires about eight hours for an average ship to transit the Canal. Transportation between the Atlantic and Pacific sides of the Isthmus is available by railway, highway or air.

The Canal Zone Postal Service began operating June 24, 1904, when nine post offices were opened in connection with the construction of the Panama Canal. It ceased Sept. 30, 1979, and the Panama Postal Service took over.

Italicized numbers in parentheses indicate quantity issued.

100 CENTAVOS = 1 PESO
100 CENTESIMOS = 1 BALBOA
100 CENTS = 1 DOLLAR

Catalogue values for unused stamps are for Never Hinged items beginning with No. 118 in the regular postage section and No. C6 in the airpost section.

Panama Nos. 72, 72a-72c, 78-79 Handstmped in Violet to Violet-Blue

On the 2c "PANAMA" is normally 13mm long. On the 5c and 10c it measures about 15mm.

On the 2c, "PANAMA" reads up on the upper half of the sheet and down on the lower half. On the 5c and 10c, "PANAMA" reads up at left and down at right on each stamp.

On the 2c only, varieties exist with inverted "V" for "A," accent on "A," inverted "N," etc., in "PANAMA."

1904, June 24 Engr. Unwmk. *Perf. 12*

1	A3	2c **rose**, both "PANAMA" reading up or down *(2600)*	650.	400.
		Single on post card		*1,650.*
		Strip of 3 on cover		*1,300.*
		Block of 4	3,000.	2,000.
		"PANAMA" 15mm long *(260)*	700.	600.
		"P NAMA"	700.	600.
a.		"CANAL ZONE" inverted *(100)*	*1,000.*	850.
		Block of 4	*6,000.*	
b.		"CANAL ZONE" double	*4,250.*	2,000.
c.		"CANAL ZONE" double, both inverted	*20,000.*	
d.		"PANAMA" reading down and up *(52)*	750.	650.
e.		As "d," "CANAL ZONE" invtd.	*9,000.*	*9,000.*
f.		Vert. pair, "PANAMA" reading up on top 2c, down on other	*2,100.*	*2,100.*
g.		As "f," "CANAL ZONE" inverted	*20,000.*	
2	A3	5c **blue** *(7800)*	300.	190.
		On cover		225.
		First day cover		*7,500.*
		Block of 4	1,400.	950.
		Left "PANAMA" 2¼mm below bar *(156)*	575.	500.
		Colon between right "PANAMA" and bar *(156)*	575.	500.
a.		"CANAL ZONE" inverted	775.	600.
		On cover		*800.*
b.		"CANAL ZONE" double	2,250.	1,500.
c.		Pair, one without "CANAL ZONE" overprint	*5,000.*	*5,000.*
d.		"CANAL ZONE" overprint diagonal, reading down to right	800.	700.
3	A3	10c **yellow** *(4946)*	400.	210.
		On cover		325.
		First day cover		*5,000.*
		Block of 4	1,750.	1,100.
		Left "PANAMA" 2¼mm below bar *(100)*	675.	575.
		Colon between right "PANAMA" and bar *(100)*	650.	550.
a.		"CANAL ZONE" inverted *(200)*	775.	600.
		On cover		*800.*
b.		"CANAL ZONE" double		*14,000.*
c.		Pair, one without "CANAL ZONE" overprint	*6,000.*	*5,000.*

Cancellations consist of town and/or bars in magenta or black, or a mixture of both colors.

Nos. 1-3 were withdrawn July 17, 1904.

Forgeries of the "Canal Zone" overprint and cancellations are numerous.

United States Nos. 300, 319, 304, 306 and 307 Overprinted in Black

1904, July 18 Wmk. 191

4	A115	1c **blue green** *(43,738)*	35.00	22.50
		green	35.00	22.50
		On cover		75.00
		Block of 4	150.00	140.00
		P# strip of 3, Impt.	140.00	
		P# block of 6, Impt.	900.00	
5	A129	2c **carmine** *(68,414)*	25.00	25.00
		On cover		75.00
		Block of 4	110.00	125.00
		P# strip of 3, Impt.	100.00	
		P# block of 6, Impt.	1,150.	
a.		2c **scarlet**	32.50	30.00
6	A119	5c **blue** *(20,858)*	85.00	60.00
		On cover		275.00
		Block of 4	375.00	325.00
		P# strip of 3, Impt.	360.00	
		P# block of 6, Impt.	1,450.	
7	A121	8c **violet black** *(7932)*	130.00	85.00
		On cover		500.00
		Block of 4	600.00	450.00
		P# strip of 3, Impt.	575.00	
		P# block of 6, Impt.	3,000.	
8	A122	10c **pale red brown** *(7856)*	120.00	80.00
		On cover		500.00
		Block of 4	500.00	475.00
		P# strip of 3, Impt.	475.00	
		P# block of 6, Impt.	2,500.	
		Nos. 4-8 (5)	395.00	272.50

Nos. 4-8 frequently show minor broken letters.

Cancellations consist of circular town and/or bars in black, blue or magenta.

Beware of fake overprints with non-conforming cancellations and rough overprints. Genuine overprints have crisp lettering.

Stamps of Panama Overprinted in Black

12ovpt

CANAL
ZONE
Regular Type

CANAL
ZONE
Antique Type

The Canal Zone overprint on stamps Nos. 9-15 and 18-20 was made with a plate which had six different stages, each with its peculiar faults and errors. Stage 1: Broken CA-L, broken L, A-L spaced, on Nos. 9, 10, 12-15. Stage 2: broken L, Z, N, E, on Nos. 9, 10, 12-14. Stage 3: same as 2 with additional antique ZONE, on Nos. 9, 11-14, 18. Stage 4: same as 3 with additional antique CANAL on Nos. 9, 12, 13. Stage 5: broken E and letters L, Z, N, and words CANAL and ZONE in antique type on Nos. 12-14, 19, 20. Stage 6: same as 5 except for additional antique Z on stamp which had antique L, on No. 12. The Panama overprints can be distinguished by the different shades of the red overprint, the width of the bar, and the word PANAMA. No. 11 has two different Panama overprints; No. 12 has six; No. 13 five; No. 14 two; and Nos. 15, 18-20, one each. In the "8cts" surcharge of Nos. 14 and 15, there are three varieties of the figure "8." The bar is sometimes misplaced so that it appears on the bottom of the stamp instead of the top.

1904-06 Unwmk.

9	A5	1c **green** *(319,800) Dec. 12, 1904*	2.50	2.00
		On cover		12.50
		Block of 4	11.00	11.00
		Spaced "A L" in "CANAL" *(700)*	110.00	100.00
		"ON" of "ZONE" dropped	300.00	275.00
		On cover		325.00
a.		"CANAL" in antique type *(500)*	90.00	90.00
b.		"ZONE" in antique type *(1500)*	60.00	60.00

c. Inverted overprint 7,500. 6,000.
d. Double overprint 2,750. 2,000.
10 A5 2c **rose** *(367,500) Dec. 12, 1904* 4.00 2.50
On cover 17.50
First day cover *750.00*
Block of 4 19.00 15.00
Spaced "A L" of "CANAL" *(1700)* 85.00 85.00
"ON" of "ZONE" dropped 400.00 400.00
a. Inverted overprint 225.00 275.00
b. "L" of "CANAL" sideways *2,000. 2,250.*

"PANAMA" (15mm long) reading up at left, down at right

Overprint "CANAL ZONE" in Black, "PANAMA" and Bar in Red

11 A3 2c **rose** *(150,000) Dec. 9, 1905* 6.50 4.50
On cover 50.00
Block of 4 30.00 25.00
Inverted "M" in "PANAMA" *(3,000)* 47.50 40.00
"PANAMA" 16mm long *(3000)* 47.50 40.00
a. "ZONE" in antique type *(1500)* 175.00 175.00
b. "PANAMA" overprint inverted, bar at bottom *(200)* 600.00 *675.00*
12 A3 5c **blue** *(400,000) Dec. 12, 1904* 7.50 2.75
On cover 100.00
Block of 4 32.50 20.00
Spaced "A L" in "CANAL" *(300)* 90.00 80.00
"PAMANA" reading up *(2800)* 75.00 70.00
"PAMANA" reading down *(400)* 200.00 180.00
"PANAMA" 16mm long *(1300)* 40.00 37.50
Inverted "M" in "PANAMA" *(1300)* 40.00 37.50
Right "PANAMA" 5mm below bar *(600)* 75.00 70.00
"PANAM" 70.00 65.00
"PAN MA" 75.00 70.00
"ANAMA" 80.00 75.00
a. "CANAL" in antique type *(2750)* 75.00 65.00
b. "ZONE" in antique type *(2950)* 75.00 65.00
c. "CANAL ZONE" double *(200)* 800.00 800.00
d. "PANAMA" double *(120)* 1,100. 1,000.
e. "PANAMA" inverted, bar at bottom 1,000. 1,250.
f. "PANAAM" at right *950.00 850.00*
13 A3 10c **yellow** *(64,900) Dec. 12, 1904* 17.00 12.00
On cover 125.00
Block of 4 100.00 62.50
Spaced "A L" in "CANAL" *(200)* 190.00 180.00
"PANAMA" 16mm long *(400)* 75.00 65.00
"PAMANA" reading down *(200)* 200.00 180.00
Invtd. "M" in "PANAMA" *(400)* 100.00 90.00
Right "PANAMA" 5mm below bar *(398)* 150.00 140.00
Left "PANAMA" touches bar *(400)* 200.00 160.00
a. "CANAL" in antique type *(200)* 180.00 180.00
b. "ZONE" in antique type *(400)* 175.00 160.00
c. "PANAMA" ovpt. double *(80)* 650.00 650.00
d. "PANAMA" overprint in red brown *(5000)* 27.50 22.50
"PANAMA" ovpt. in orange red 32.50 32.50
Nos. 11-13 (3) 31.00 19.25

With Added Surcharge in Red

a

There are three varieties of "8" in the surcharge on Nos. 14-15.

14 A3 8c on 50c **bister brown** *(27,900) Dec. 12, 1904* 25.00 25.00
On cover 200.00
Block of 4 150.00 150.00
Spaced "A L" in "CANAL" *(194)* 160.00 160.00
Right "PANAMA" 5mm below bar *(438)* 200.00 175.00
a. "ZONE" in antique type *(25)* 1,150. 1,150.
b. "CANAL ZONE" inverted *(200)* 450.00 425.00
c. "PANAMA" overprint in rose brown *(6000)* 35.00 35.00
d. As "c," "CANAL" in antique type *(10)* *1,750. 850.00*
e. As "c," "ZONE" in antique type *(10)* *1,750.*
f. As "c," "8 cts" double *(30)* *1,100.*
g. As "c," "8" omitted *4,500.*
h. As "c," "cts 8" —

Nos. 11-14 are overprinted or surcharged on Panama Nos. 77, 77e, 78, 78c, 78d, 78f, 78g, 78h, 79 79c, 79e, 79g and 81 respectively.

On No. 14 with original gum, the gum is almost always disturbed. Unused stamps are valued thus.

Panama No. 74a, 74b Overprinted "CANAL ZONE" in Regular Type in Black and Surcharged Type "a" in Red

Both "PANAMA" (13mm long) Reading Up

15 A3(a) 8c on 50c **bister brown** *(435) Dec. 12, 1904* 2,000. *4,750.*
On cover *10,000.*
Block of 4 *9,000.*
"PANAMA" 15mm long *(50)* 2,400. *5,000.*
"P NAMA" 4,500.
Spaced "A L" in "CANAL" *(5)* 4,500.
a. "PANAMA" reading down and up *(10)* *6,000.* —

On No. 15 with original gum, the gum is almost always disturbed. Unused stamps are valued thus.

Panama Nos. 19 and 21 Surcharged in Black

CANAL ZONE 1 ct. PANAMA PANAMA
a

CANAL ZONE 1 ct. PANAMA PANAMA
b

CANAL ZONE 1 ct. PANAMA PANAMA
c

CANAL ZONE 2 cts. PANAMA PANAMA
d

CANAL ZONE 2 cts. PANAMA PANAMA
e

CANAL ZONE 2 cts. PANAMA PANAMA
f

There were three printings of each denomination, differing principally in the relative position of the various parts of the surcharges. Varieties occur with inverted "V" for the final "A" in "PANAMA," "CA" spaced, "ZO" spaced, "2c" spaced, accents in various positions, and with bars shifted so that two bars appear on top or bottom of the stamp (either with or without the corresponding bar on top or bottom) and sometimes with only one bar at top or bottom.

1906

16 A4 1c on 20c **violet**, type a *(100,000) Mar.* 1.90 1.60
On cover 10.00
Block of 4 8.50 7.50
a. Type b *(100,000) May* 1.90 1.60
On cover 10.00
Block of 4 8.50 7.50
b. Type c *(300,000) Sept.* 1.90 1.50
On cover 10.00
Block of 4 8.50 7.50
Spaced C A 13.00 12.00
c. As No. 16, double surcharge *2,000.*
17 A4 2c on 1p **lake**, type d *(200,000) Mar.* 2.25 2.25
On cover 12.00
Block of 4 12.00 12.00
a. Type e *(200,000) May* 2.25 2.25
On cover 12.00
Block of 4 12.00 12.00
b. Type f *(50,000) Sept.* 20.00 20.00
On cover 75.00
Block of 4 90.00 90.00

Panama Nos. 74, 74a and 74b Overprinted "CANAL ZONE" in Regular Type in Black and Surcharged in Red

b c

1905-06

Both "PANAMA" Reading Up

18 A3(b) 8c on 50c **bister brown** *(17,500) Nov. 1905* 45.00 45.00
On cover 225.00
Block of 4 200.00 230.00
"PANAMA" 15mm long *(1750)* 90.00 80.00
"P NAMA" 125.00 110.00
a. "ZONE" in antique type *(175)* 200.00 180.00
b. "PANAMA" reading down and up *(350)* 160.00 150.00
19 A3(c) 8c on 50c **bister brown** *(19,000) Apr. 23, 1906* 45.00 37.50
On cover 275.00
Block of 4 200.00 200.00
"PANAMA" 15mm long *(1900)* 85.00 70.00
"P NAMA" 90.00
a. "CANAL" in antique type *(190)* 210.00 180.00
b. "ZONE" in antique type *(190)* 210.00 180.00
c. "8 cts" double *1,100. 1,100.*
d. "PANAMA" reading down and up *(380)* 110.00 90.00

On Nos. 18-19 with original gum, the gum is usually disturbed. Unused stamps are valued thus.

Panama No. 81 Overprinted "CANAL ZONE" in Regular Type in Black and Surcharged in Red Type "c" plus Period

"PANAMA" reading up and down

20 A3(c) 8c on 50c **bister brown** *(19,600) Sept. 1906* 35.00 37.50
On cover 200.00
Block of 4 160.00 170.00
"PAMANA" reading up *(392)* 120.00 110.00
a. "CANAL" antique type *(196)* 200.00 180.00
b. "ZONE" in antique type *(196)* 200.00 180.00
c. "8 cts" omitted *(50)* 800.00 800.00
d. "8 cts" double *1,500.*
e. "cts 8" —

Nos. 14 and 18-20 exist without CANAL ZONE overprint but were not regularly issued and are considered printer's waste. Forgeries of the overprint varieties of Nos. 9-15 and 18-20 are known.

On No. 20 with original gum, the gum is usually disturbed. Unused stamps are valued thus.

Fernández de Córdoba — A5

Vasco Núñez de Balboa — A6

Fernández de Córdoba — A7

Justo Arosemena — A8

Manuel J. Hurtado — A9

José de Obaldía — A10

Engraved by Hamilton Bank Note Co.

Overprinted in Black by Isthmian Canal Commission Press.

1906-07 **Unwmk.** ***Perf. 12***

Overprint Reading Up

21 A5 2c **red & black** *(50,000) Oct. 29, 1906* 25.00 25.00
On cover 55.00
Block of 4 125.00 *175.00*
Narrow spacing between "CANAL" and "ZONE" (6¾mm vs. normal 7¼mm (pos. 83) — —
a. "CANAL" only *4,000.*

Overprint Reading Down

22 A6 1c **green & black** *(2,000,000) Jan. 14, 1907* 2.00 .90
dull green & black 2.00 1.00
On cover 5.00
Block of 4 9.00 7.50
"ANA" for "CANAL" *(1000)* 70.00 70.00
"CAN L" for "CANAL" 80.00 80.00
"ONE" for "ZONE" *(3000)* 80.00 80.00
a. Horiz. pair, imperf. btwn. *(50)* 1,100. 1,100.
b. Vert. pair, imperf. btwn. *(20)* *2,000.* *2,000.*
c. Vert. pair, imperf. horiz. *(20)* *2,250.* *1,750.*
d. Inverted overprint reading up *(100)* 550.00 550.00
e. Double overprint *(300)* 275.00 275.00
f. Double overprint, one inverted 1,750. 1,600.
g. Invtd. center, ovpt. reading up *3,500.* *4,500.*
Pair on cover *18,500.*
Block of 4 *17,000.*
h. Horiz. pair, imperf vert. *5,000.*
23 A7 2c **red & black** *(2,370,000) Nov. 25, 1906* 3.00 1.00
scarlet & black, *1907* 3.00 1.00
On cover 6.00
Block of 4 13.00 8.50
"CAN L" for "CANAL" 45.00
a. Horizontal pair, imperf. between *(20)* 2,000. 2,000.
b. Vertical pair, one without overprint 2,500. 2,500.
c. Double overprint *(100)* 600.00 700.00
d. Double overprint, one diagonal 800.00 800.00
e. Double overprint, one diagonal, in pair with normal 2,500.
f. 2c carmine red & black, *Sept. 9, 1907* 5.00 2.75
g. As "f," inverted center and overprint reading up *14,000.*
On cover *17,500.*
h. As "d," one "ZONE CANAL" *4,000.*
i. "CANAL" double *6,500.*
24 A8 5c **ultramarine & black** *(1,390,000) Dec. 1906* 5.75 2.00
light ultramarine & black 5.75 2.00
blue & black, *Sept. 16, 1907* 5.75 2.00
dark blue & black 5.75 2.25
dull blue & black 5.75 2.25
light blue & black 5.75 2.25
On cover 40.00
Block of 4 25.00 20.00
"CAN L" for "CANAL" 60.00
c. Double overprint *(200)* 500.00 400.00
d. "CANAL" only *(10)* *7,000.*
e. "ZONE CANAL" *5,000.*
25 A9 8c **purple & black** *(170,000) Dec. 1906* 20.00 8.00
On cover 100.00
Block of 4 110.00 55.00
a. Horizontal pair, imperf. between and at left margin *(34)* *1,600.* *4,000.*
26 A10 10c **violet & black** *(250,000) Dec. 1906* 20.00 7.00
On cover 100.00
Block of 4 110.00 50.00
a. Dbl. ovpt., one reading up *(10)* *5,000.*
b. Overprint reading up *5,500.*
Nos. 22-26 (5) 50.75 18.90

The early printings of this series were issued on soft, thick, porous-textured paper. A sizeable proportion of some later printings of Nos. 22, 23 and 24 only appear on hard, thinner, smooth-textured paper.

Normal spacing of the early printings is 7¼mm between the words; later printings, 6¾mm. All were printed on soft, porous-textured paper; Nos. 22-24 also printed on hard, smooth-textured paper.

Nos. 22 and 26 exist imperf. between stamp and sheet margin. Nos. 22-25 occur with "CA" of "CANAL" spaced ½mm further apart on position No. 50 of the setting.

The used pair of No. 25a is unique.

No. 23g is valued in sound condition. Almost all examples are faulty to some degree; value with small faults is approximately $6,000.

Córdoba — A11

Arosemena — A12

Hurtado — A13

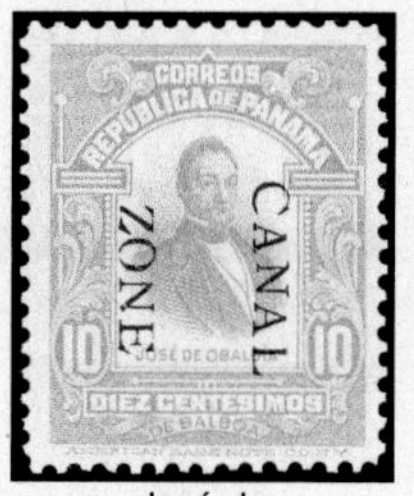

José de Obaldía — A14

Engraved by American Bank Note Co.

1909

Overprint Reading Down

27 A11 2c **vermilion & black** *(500,000) May 11, 1909* 12.00 5.00
On cover 15.00
First day cover 750.00
Block of 4 55.00 27.50
a. Horizontal pair, one without overprint *2,500.*
b. Vert. pair, one without ovpt. *3,250.*
c. Vert. pair, one without "ZONE" —
28 A12 5c **deep blue & black** *(200,000) May 28, 1909* 40.00 12.50
On cover *225.00*
Block of 4 190.00 60.00
29 A13 8c **violet & black** *(50,000) May 25, 1909* 37.50 14.00
On cover 90.00
Block of 4 190.00 82.50
30 A14 10c **violet & black** *(100,000) Jan. 19, 1909* 40.00 14.00
On cover 85.00
Block of 4 200.00 85.00
a. Horizontal pair, one with "ZONE" omitted *3,000.*
b. Vertical pair, one without overprint *4,000.*
Nos. 27-30 (4) 129.50 45.50

Nos. 27-30 occur with "CA" spaced (position 50).

Do not confuse No. 27 with Nos. 39d or 53a.

On No. 30a, the stamp with "ZONE" omitted is also missing most of "CANAL."

Black Overprint Reading Up

Vasco Núñez de Balboa — A15

Engraved, Printed and Overprinted by American Bank Note Co.

Type I

Type I Overprint: "C" with serifs both top and bottom. "L," "Z" and "E" with slanting serifs.

Compare Type I overprint with Types II to V illustrated before Nos. 38, 46, 52 and 55.

1909-10

31 A15 1c **dark green & black** *(4,000,000) Nov. 8, 1909* 4.25 1.25
On cover 5.00
Block of 4 18.00 6.75
a. Inverted center and overprint reading down *22,500.*
c. Bklt. pane of 6, handmade, perf. margins *500.00*
32 A11 2c **vermilion & black** *(4,000,000) Nov. 8, 1909* 4.50 1.25
On cover 5.00
Block of 4 20.00 6.75
a. Vert. pair, imperf. horiz. 1,000. 1,000.
c. Bklt. pane of 6, handmade, perf. margins *800.00*
d. Double overprint (I) *6,000.*
33 A12 5c **deep blue & black** *(2,000,000) Nov. 8, 1909* 17.00 3.50
On cover 40.00
Block of 4 80.00 20.00
a. Double overprint *(200)* 375.00 375.00
On cover *1,000.*
34 A13 8c **violet & black** *(200,000) Mar. 18, 1910* 11.00 5.00
On cover 75.00
Block of 4 50.00 27.50
a. Vertical pair, one without overprint *(10)* *1,750.*
35 A14 10c **violet & black** *(100,000) Nov. 8, 1909* 47.50 20.00
On cover 100.00
Block of 4 210.00 100.00
Nos. 31-35 (5) 84.25 31.00

Normal spacing between words of overprint on No. 31 is 10mm; on No. 32 it is 8½mm, or less frequently 9¼mm; and on Nos. 33 to 35, 8½mm. Spacing variations are known.

A16

A17

1911, Jan. 14

36 A16 10c on 13c **gray** *(476,700)* 6.00 2.00
On cover 50.00
Block of 4 30.00 15.00
a. "10 cts" inverted 325.00 325.00
b. "10 cts" omitted 300.00

The "10 cts" surcharge was applied by the Isthmian Canal Commission Press after the overprinted stamps were received from the American Bank Note Co.

Many used stamps offered as No. 36b are merely No. 36 from which the surcharge has been chemically removed.

1914, Jan. 6

37 A17 10c **gray** *(200,000)* 47.50 11.00
On cover 85.00
Block of 4 200.00 60.00

Black Overprint Reading Up

Type II

Type II Overprint: "C" with serif at top only. "L" and "E" with vertical serifs. "O" tilts to left.

1912-16

38 A15 1c **green & black** *(3,000,000) July 1913* 10.00 3.00
On cover 5.50
Block of 4 45.00 20.00
a. Vertical pair, one without overprint 1,750. 1,750.
On cover *2,250.*
b. Booklet pane of 6, imperf. margins *(120,000)* 575.00
c. Booklet pane of 6, handmade, perf. margins *1,000.*
39 A11 2c **vermilion & black** *(7,500,000) Dec. 1912* 8.00 1.10
orange vermilion & black, *1916* 8.00 1.10
On cover 5.00
Block of 4 40.00 6.50
a. Horiz. pair, right stamp without overprint (20) *1,250.*
b. Horiz. pair, left stamp without overprint (10) *1,500.*
c. Booklet pane of 6, imperf. margins *(194,868)* 550.00
d. Overprint reading down 200.00
e. As "d," inverted center 600.00 *750.00*
On cover *1,000.*
f. As "e," booklet pane of 6, handmade, perf. margins *8,000.*
g. As "c," handmade, perf. margins 900.00 800.00
h. As No. 39, "CANAL" only (1) *2,500.*

40 A12 5c **deep blue & black** *(2,300,000) Dec. 1912*	20.00	2.50
On cover		35.00
Block of 4	95.00	12.00
a. With Cordoba portrait of 2c		*12,500.*
41 A14 10c **violet & black** *(200,000) Feb. 1916*	60.00	7.50
On cover		80.00
Block of 4	250.00	37.50
Nos. 38-41 (4)	98.00	14.10

Normal spacing between words of overprint on the first printing of Nos. 38-40 is 8½mm and on the second printing 9¼mm. The spacing of the single printing of No. 41 and the imperf. margin booklet pane printings of Nos. 38 and 39 is 7¾mm. Minor spacing variations are known.

Map of Panama Canal — A18

Balboa Taking Possession of the Pacific Ocean — A19

Gatun Locks — A20

Culebra Cut — A21

Engraved, Printed and Overprinted by American Bank Note Co.

1915, Mar. 1

Blue Overprint, Type II

42 A18 1c **dark green & black** *(100,000)*	8.75	6.50
On cover		17.50
Block of 4	40.00	30.00
First day cover		200.00
43 A19 2c **carmine & black** *(100,000)*	12.00	4.25
vermilion & black	12.00	4.25
On cover		25.00
First day cover		150.00
Block of 4	50.00	21.00
44 A20 5c **blue & black** *(100,000)*	10.00	5.75
On cover		55.00
Block of 4	45.00	29.00
First day cover		500.00
45 A21 10c **orange & black** *(50,000)*	19.00	11.00
On cover		70.00
Block of 4	80.00	55.00
First day cover		500.00
Nos. 42-45 (4)	49.75	27.50

Normal spacing between words of overprint is 9¼mm on all four values except position No. 61 which is 10mm.

Black Overprint Reading Up

Type III

Type III Overprint: Similar to Type I but letters appear thinner, particularly the lower bar of "L," "Z" and "E." Impressions are often light, rough and irregular, and not centered.

Engraved and Printed by American Bank Note Co.
Overprint applied by
Panama Canal Press, Mount Hope, C.Z.

1915-20

46 A15 1c **green & black,** *Dec. 1915*	175.00	125.00
light green & black, *1920*	250.00	150.00
Single on postcard		175.00
Pair on cover		500.00
Block of 4	775.00	650.00
a. Overprint reading down *(200)*	375.00	
b. Double overprint *(385)*	225.00	
c. "ZONE" double *(2)*	*6,500.*	
d. Double overprint, one reads "ZONE CANAL" *(13)*	2,000.	
47 A11 2c **orange vermilion & black,** *Aug. 1920*	2,750.	60.00
On cover		350.00
Pair on cover		*850.00*
Block of 4	*11,500.*	500.00
48 A12 5c **deep blue & black,** *Dec. 1915*	425.00	130.00
On cover		1,000.
Pair on cover		*2,250.*
Block of 4	*2,100.*	675.00

Spacing between words of overprint on Nos. 46-48 is 9¼mm; spacing varieties are not known. This should not be confused with a fairly common 9¼mm spacing of the 2c value of type I, nor with an uncommon 9¼mm spacing variety of the 5c of type I.

A22

S. S. "Panama" in Culebra Cut — A23

S. S. "Cristobal" in Gatun Locks — A24

Engraved, Printed and Overprinted by American Bank Note Co.

1917, Jan. 23

Blue Overprint, Type II

49 A22 12c **purple & black** *(314,914)*	17.50	5.25
On cover		50.00
First day cover		1,750.
Block of 4	87.50	27.50
50 A23 15c **bright blue & black**	50.00	17.50
On cover		135.00
Block of 4	230.00	95.00
51 A24 24c **yellow brown & black**	35.00	13.00
On cover		325.00
Block of 4	180.00	80.00
Nos. 49-51 (3)	102.50	35.75

Normal spacing between words of overprint is 11¼mm.

Black Overprint Reading Up

Type IV

Type IV Overprint: "C" thick at bottom, "E" with center bar same length as top and bottom bars.

Engraved, Printed and Overprinted by American Bank Note Co.

1918-20

52 A15 1c **green & black** *(2,000,000) Jan. 1918*	32.50	10.00
On cover		12.50
Block of 4	150.00	45.00
a. Overprint reading down	175.00	—
b. Booklet pane of 6 *(60,000)*	600.00	
c. Booklet pane of 6, left vertical row of 3 without overprint	*7,500.*	
d. Booklet pane of 6, right vertical row of 3 with double overprint	*7,500.*	
e. Horiz. bklt. pair, left stamp without overprint	*3,000.*	
f. Horiz. bklt. pair, right stamp with double overprint	*3,000.*	
g. Double overprint, booklet single		3,000.
h. "CANAL" omitted		—
53 A11 2c **vermilion & black** *(2,000,000) Nov. 1918*	110.00	6.00
On cover		10.00
Block of 4	500.00	30.00
a. Overprint reading down	150.00	150.00
b. Horiz. pair, right stamp without ovpt. (from misregistered overprints)	2,000.	
c. Booklet pane of 6 *(34,000)*	1,050.	
d. Booklet pane of 6, left vertical row of 3 without overprint	*15,000.*	
e. Horiz. bklt. pair, left stamp without overprint	*3,000.*	
On cover (unique)		*4,500.*
f. Horiz. sheet pair, left stamp without overprint (2)	*1,750.*	
54 A12 5c **deep blue & black** *(500,000) Apr. 1920*	150.00	32.50
On cover		200.00
Block of 4	825.00	150.00
Nos. 52-54 (3)	292.50	48.50

Normal spacing between words of overprint on Nos. 52 and 53 is 9¼mm. On No. 54 and the booklet printings of Nos. 52 and 53, the normal spacing is 9mm. Minor spacing varieties are known.

No. 53f is in a block of nine containing two such pairs.

Black Overprint Reading Up

Type V

Type V Overprint: Smaller block type 1¾mm high. "A" with flat top.

1920-21

55 A15 1c **light green & black,** *Apr. 1921*	22.50	3.25
On cover		8.00
Block of 4	100.00	16.50
a. Overprint reading down	300.00	225.00
b. Horiz. pair, right stamp without ovpt. (10)	*1,750.*	
c. Horiz. pair, left stamp without ovpt. (21)	1,100.	
d. "ZONE" only	*4,000.*	—
e. Booklet pane of 6	*2,250.*	
f. As No. 55, "CANAL" double (10)	*1,750.*	
g. Vert. pair, one without overprint (2)	3,000.	
h. Vert. pair,one "ZONE" only, one without overprint (1)	*4,000.*	
56 A11 2c **orange vermilion & black,** *Sept. 1920*	8.50	1.75
On cover		7.00
Block of 4	37.50	8.50
a. Double overprint *(100)*	500.00	
b. Double overprint, one reading down *(100)*	600.00	
c. Horiz. pair, right stamp without overprint (11)	1,400.	
d. Horiz. pair, left stamp without overprint (20)	1,000.	
e. Vertical pair, one without overprint	1,500.	
f. "ZONE" double	900.00	

g.	Booklet pane of 6	900.00	
h.	As No. 56, "CANAL" double	800.00	
57	A12 5c **deep blue & black,** *Apr. 1921*	300.00	45.00
	On cover		225.00
	Block of 4	1,350.	200.00
a.	Horiz. pair, right stamp without overprint *(10)*	*2,000.*	
b.	Horiz. pair, left stamp without overprint *(10)*	*2,000.*	
	Nos. 55-57 (3)	331.00	50.00

Normal spacing between words of overprint on Nos. 55-57 is 9½mm. On booklet printings of Nos. 55 and 56 the normal spacing is 9¼mm.

Drydock at Balboa — A25

U.S.S. "Nereus" in Pedro Miguel Locks — A26

1920, Sept.

Black Overprint Type V

58	A25 50c **orange & black**	250.00	160.00
	On cover		*1,000.*
	Block of 4	1,250.	800.00
59	A26 1b **dark violet & black** *(23,014)*	175.00	50.00
	On cover		*1,000.*
	Block of 4	825.00	300.00

José Vallarino — A27

"Land Gate" — A28

Bolívar's Tribute — A29

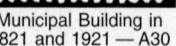

Municipal Building in 1821 and 1921 — A30

Statue of Balboa — A31

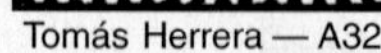
Tomás Herrera — A32

José de Fábrega — A33

Engraved, Printed and Overprinted by American Bank Note Co.

Type V overprint in black, reading up, on all values except the 5c which is overprinted with larger type in red

1921, Nov. 13

60	A27 1c **green**	3.75	1.50
	On cover		6.00
	Block of 4	13.00	7.25
a.	"CANAL" double	*1,900.*	
b.	Booklet pane of 6	*900.00*	
61	A28 2c **carmine**	2.75	1.00
	On cover		15.00
	Block of 4	12.50	4.50
a.	Overprint reading down	200.00	*225.00*
b.	Double overprint	900.00	
c.	Vertical pair, one without overprint	*3,500.*	
d.	"CANAL" double	*1,900.*	
e.	"ZONE" only (1)	*4,000.*	
f.	Booklet pane of 6	*2,000.*	
62	A29 5c **blue** (R)	10.00	3.00
	On cover		30.00
	Block of 4	45.00	18.00
a.	Overprint reading down (R)	65.00	
63	A30 10c **violet**	18.00	7.50
	On cover		60.00
	Block of 4	100.00	35.00
a.	Overprint, reading down	90.00	
64	A31 15c **light blue**	47.50	17.50
	On cover		175.00
	Block of 4	230.00	95.00
65	A32 24c **black brown**	67.50	22.50
	On cover		*600.00*
	Block of 4	360.00	125.00
66	A33 50c **black**	145.00	85.00
	On cover		*600.00*
	Block of 4	700.00	400.00
	Nos. 60-66 (7)	294.50	138.00

Experts question the status of the 5c with a small type V overprint in red or black.

Type III overprint in black, reading up, applied by the Panama Canal Press, Mount Hope, C. Z.

Engraved and printed by the American Bank Note Co.

1924, Jan. 28

67	A27 1c **green**	500.	200.
	Single on postcard		350.
	Pair on cover		750.
	Block of 4	2,250.	900.
a.	"ZONE CANAL" reading down	800.	
b.	"ZONE" only, reading down	*1,900.*	
c.	Se-tenant pair, #67a and 67b	*2,750.*	

Arms of Panama — A34

1924, Feb.

68	A34 1c **dark green**	10.00	4.50
	On cover		12.00
	Block of 4	50.00	24.00
69	A34 2c **carmine**	7.00	2.75
	carmine rose	7.00	2.75
	On cover		15.00
	Block of 4	30.00	12.50

The following were prepared for use, but they were not issued.

A34 5c **dark blue** *(600)*	350.
Block of 4	1,750.
A34 10c **dark violet** *(600)*	350.
Block of 4	1,750.
A34 12c **olive green** *(600)*	350.
Block of 4	1,750.
A34 15c **ultramarine** *(600)*	350.
Block of 4	1,750.
A34 24c **yellow brown** *(600)*	350.
Block of 4	1,750.
A34 50c **orange** *(600)*	350.
Block of 4	1,750.
A34 1b **black** *(600)*	350.
Block of 4	1,750.

The 5c to 1b values were prepared for use but never issued due to abrogation of the Taft Agreement which required the Canal Zone to use overprinted Panama stamps. Six hundred of each denomination were not destroyed, as they were forwarded to the Director General of Posts of Panama for transmission to the UPU which then required about 400 sets. Only a small number of sets appear to have reached the public market.

All Panama stamps overprinted "CANAL ZONE" were withdrawn from sale June 30, 1924, and were no longer valid for postage after Aug. 31, 1924.

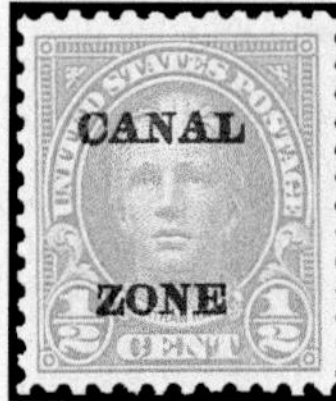

United States Nos. 551-554, 557, 562, 564-566, 569, 570 and 571 Overprinted in Red (No. 70) or Black (all others)

Type A

Letters "A" with Flat Tops

Printed and Overprinted by the U.S. Bureau of Engraving and Printing.

1924-25 Unwmk. *Perf. 11*

70	A154 ½c **olive brown** *(399,500) Apr. 15, 1925*	.25	.70
	Never hinged	.40	
	On cover		4.00
	On cover, single, with 1c additional on 3rd-class cover		20.00
	First day cover		75.00
	Block of 4	1.00	3.25
	P# block of 6	5.00	

No. 71b

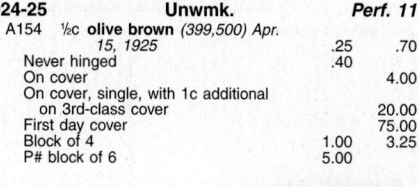

71	A155 1c **deep green** *(1,985,000) July 1, 1924*	1.40	1.00
	Never hinged	2.50	
	On cover		4.00
	First day cover		75.00
	Block of 4	5.75	4.25
	P# block of 6	27.50	
a.	Inverted overprint	500.00	500.00
b.	"ZONE" inverted	350.00	325.00
c.	"CANAL" only *(20)*	1,150.	
d.	"ZONE CANAL" *(180)*	400.00	
e.	Booklet pane of 6 *(43,152)*	80.00	—
f.	Se-tenant pair, #71c and 71d	*1,750.*	
72	A156 1½c **yellow brown** *(180,599) Apr. 15, 1925*	2.00	1.70
	brown	2.00	1.70
	Never hinged	3.25	
	On cover		4.00
	On cover, single franking, on 3rd-class cover		30.00
	First day cover, Nos. 70, 72		80.00
	Block of 4	8.75	9.50
	P# block of 6	37.50	
73	A157 2c **carmine** *(2,975,000) July 1, 1924*	6.75	1.70
	Never hinged	10.50	
	First day cover		80.00
	Block of 4	31.00	8.00
	P# block of 6	160.00	
a.	Booklet pane of 6 *(140,000)*	175.00	
74	A160 5c **dark blue** *(500,000) July 1, 1924*	16.00	7.00
	Never hinged	25.00	
	On cover		20.00
	Block of 4	67.50	37.50
	P# block of 6	300.00	
75	A165 10c **orange** *(60,000) July 1, 1924*	40.00	20.00
	Never hinged	65.00	
	On cover		45.00
	First day cover		500.00
	Block of 4	190.00	105.00
	P# block of 6	875.00	
76	A167 12c **brown violet** *(80,000) July 1, 1924*	32.50	30.00
	Never hinged	62.50	
	On cover		45.00
	First day cover		750.00
	Block of 4	140.00	130.00
	P# block of 6	475.00	
a.	"ZONE" inverted	*3,750.*	*3,000.*

77 A168 14c **dark blue** *(100,000) June 27, 1925* 27.50 22.50
Never hinged 45.00
On cover 50.00
First day cover *500.00*
Block of 4 120.00 140.00
P# block of 6 425.00
78 A169 15c **gray** *(55,000) July 1, 1924* 45.00 37.50
Never hinged 70.00
On cover 52.50
First day cover *500.00*
Block of 4 200.00 190.00
P# block of 6 825.00
79 A172 30c **olive brown** *(40,000) July 1, 1924* 32.50 20.00
Never hinged 52.50
On cover 50.00
Block of 4 140.00 110.00
P# block of 6 600.00
Double transfer (14438 LR79) 600.00
80 A173 50c **lilac** *(25,000) July 1, 1924* 75.00 45.00
Never hinged 150.00
On cover *500.00*
Block of 4 325.00 225.00
P# block of 6 3,000.
81 A174 $1 **violet brown** *(10,000) July 1, 1924* 225.00 95.00
Never hinged 400.00
On cover *1,000.*
Block of 4 1,000. 500.00
Margin block of 4, arrow, top or bottom 1,250.
P# block of 6 *4,250.*
Nos. 70-81 (12) 503.90 282.10

Normal spacing between words of the overprint is 9¼mm. Minor spacing variations are known. The overprint of the early printings used on all values of this series except No. 77 is a sharp, clear impression. The overprint of the late printings, used only on Nos. 70, 71, 73, 76, 77, 78 and 80 is heavy and smudged, with many of the letters, particularly the "A" practically filled.

All examples of Nos. 71b and 76a have a natural straight edge at right.

Booklet panes Nos. 71e, 73a, 84d, 97b, 101a, 106a and 117a were made from 360 subject plates. The handmade booklet panes Nos. 102a, 115c and a provisional lot of 117b were made from Post Office panes from regular 400-subject plates.

United States Nos. 554, 555, 557, 562, 564-567, 569, 570, 571, 623 Overprinted in Red (No. 91) or Black (all others)

Type B

Letters "A" with Sharp Pointed Tops

1925-28 *Perf. 11*

84 A157 2c **carmine** *(1,110,000) May 1926* 27.50 8.00
Never hinged 45.00
On cover 11.00
Block of 4 115.00 37.50
P# block of 6 375.00
P# block of 6 & large 5 point star, side only *2,000.*
a. "CANAL" only *(20)* *2,250.*
b. "ZONE CANAL" *(180)* 425.00
c. Horizontal pair, one without overprint *3,500.*
d. Booklet pane of 6 *(82,000)* 175.00
e. Se-tenant pair, #84a and 84b *3,000.*
85 A158 3c **violet** *(199,200) June 27, 1925* 3.75 3.00
Never hinged 6.00
On cover 6.00
Block of 4 16.50 12.50
P# block of 6 165.00
"CANAL" in wrong font *125.00* *75.00*
"ZONE" in wrong font *175.00* *125.00*
a. "ZONE ZONE" 550.00 550.00
86 A160 5c **dark blue** *(1,343,147) Jan. 7, 1926* 3.50 2.75
Never hinged 6.00
On cover 20.00
Block of 4 15.00 12.00
P# block of 6 165.00
Double transfer (15571 UL 86) — —
"CANAL" in wrong font *175.00* *75.00*
"ZONE" in wrong font *250.00* *125.00*
a. "ZONE ZONE" (LR18) 1,000.
b. "CANAL" inverted (LR7) 950.00
c. Inverted overprint *(80)* 500.00
d. Horizontal pair, one without overprint *3,250.*
e. Overprinted "ZONE CANAL" *(90)* 350.00
f. "ZONE" only *(10)* *2,000.*
g. Vertical pair, one without overprint, other overprint inverted *(11)* *2,000.*
h. "CANAL" only *2,000.*
i. Se-tenant pair, #86e and 86f *2,500.*
87 A165 10c **orange** *(99,510) Aug. 1925* 35.00 12.00
Never hinged 52.50
On cover 40.00
Block of 4 160.00 72.50
P# block of 6 500.00
"CANAL" in wrong font *200.00* *150.00*
"ZONE" in wrong font *325.00* *200.00*
a. "ZONE ZONE" (LR18) *3,000.*
b. "ZONE" only (1) *4,000.*

88 A167 12c **brown violet** *(58,062) Feb. 1926* 20.00 12.50
Never hinged 34.00
On cover 45.00
Block of 4 100.00 57.50
P# block of 6 375.00
"CANAL" in wrong font *600.00* *350.00*
"ZONE" in wrong font —
a. "ZONE ZONE" (LR18) *5,000.*
89 A168 14c **dark blue** *(55,700) Dec. 1928* 27.50 15.00
Never hinged 45.00
On cover 50.00
Block of 4 125.00 70.00
P# block of 6 350.00
90 A169 15c **gray** *(204,138) Nov. 1925* 7.50 4.50
Never hinged 12.00
On cover 15.00
Block of 4 35.00 21.00
P# block of 6 200.00
P# block of 4, large 5 point star, side only *3,000.*
"CANAL" in wrong font *250.00* *175.00*
"ZONE" in wrong font *275.00* *225.00*
a. "ZONE ZONE" (LR18) *5,500.*

It is believed that the four recorded P# blocks of 4 with large 5-point star are the largest known P# multiples from the plate that shows the star.

91 A187 17c **black** *(199,500) Apr. 5, 1926* 4.50 2.75
Never hinged 7.50
On cover 12.50
First day cover *750.00*
Block of 4 19.00 13.00
P# block of 6 190.00
"Z" of "ZONE" under "A" or "L" of "CANAL" 300.00
a. "ZONE" only *(40)* 1,000.
b. "CANAL" only *(11)* 1,900.
c. "ZONE CANAL" *(450)* 275.00
d. Se-tenant pair, #91a and 91c *1,400.*
92 A170 20c **carmine rose** *(259,807) Apr. 5, 1926* 7.25 3.25
Never hinged 12.00
On cover 32.50
First day cover *750.00*
Block of 4 32.50 14.00
P# block of 6 175.00
a. "CANAL" inverted (UR48) *6,500.*
b. "ZONE" inverted (LL76) *4,750.*
c. "ZONE CANAL" (LL91) *4,750.*

Double transfer (14438 LR79)

93 A172 30c **olive brown** *(154,700) Dec. 1925* 5.75 3.75
Never hinged 9.00
On cover 60.00
Block of 4 25.00 19.00
P# block of 6 250.00
Double transfer (14438 LR79) *550.00*
"CANAL" in wrong font *225.00* *150.00*
"ZONE" in wrong font *275.00* *200.00*
94 A173 50c **lilac** *(13,533) July 1928* 230.00 165.00
Never hinged 400.00
On cover *500.00*
Block of 4 1,100. 750.00
P# block of 6 2,350.
"CANAL" in wrong font *375.00* *275.00*
"ZONE" in wrong font *425.00* *350.00*
95 A174 $1 **violet brown** *(20,000) Apr. 1926* 120.00 55.00
Never hinged 250.00
On cover *1,000.*
Block of 4 575.00 250.00
Margin block of 4, arrow, top or bottom 625.00
P# block of 6 2,000.
"CANAL" in wrong font *300.00* *225.00*
"ZONE" in wrong font *350.00* *275.00*
Nos. 84-95 (12) 492.25 287.50

Nos. 85-88, 90 and 93-95 exist with wrong-font "CANAL" and "ZONE." Positions are: Nos. 85-88 and 90, UL51 (CANAL) and UL82 (ZONE); Nos. 93-95, U51 (CANAL) and U82 (ZONE).

Normal spacing between words of the overprint is 11mm on No. 84; 9mm on Nos. 85-88, 90, first printing of No. 91 and the first, third and fourth printing of No. 92; 7mm on the second printings of Nos. 91-92. Minor spacing varieties exist on Nos. 84-88, 90-92.

Overprint Type B on U.S. No. 627

1926

96 A188 2c **carmine rose** *(300,000) July 6, 1926* 4.50 3.75
Never hinged 7.00
On cover 8.00
First day cover 60.00
Block of 4 20.00 18.00
P# block of 6 67.50

On this stamp there is a space of 5mm instead of 9mm between the two words of the overprint.

The authorized date, July 4, fell on a Sunday with the next day also a holiday, so No. 96 was not regularly issued until July 6. But the postmaster sold some stamps and canceled some covers on July 4 for a few favored collectors.

Overprint Type B in Black on U.S. Nos. 583, 584, 591

1926-27 Rotary Press Printings *Perf. 10*

97 A157 2c **carmine** *(1,290,000) Dec. 1926* 45.00 11.00
Never hinged 75.00
On cover 14.00
Block of 4 200.00 50.00
P# block of 4 525.00
a. Pair, one without overprint *(10)* *2,250.*
b. Booklet pane of 6 *(58,000)* 500.00
c. "CANAL" only *(10)* *2,000.*
d. "ZONE" only *2,750.*
98 A158 3c **violet** *(239,600) May 9, 1927* 7.50 4.25
Never hinged 11.00
On cover 12.00
Block of 4 32.50 19.00
P# block of 4 120.00
99 A165 10c **orange** *(128,400) May 9, 1927* 18.00 7.50
Never hinged 27.50
On cover 35.00
Block of 4 82.50 40.00
P# block of 4 225.00
Nos. 97-99 (3) 70.50 22.75

No. 97d is valued in the grade of fine. Very fine examples are not known.

Overprint Type B in Black on U.S. Nos. 632, 634 (Type I), 635, 637, 642

1927-31 Rotary Press Printings *Perf. 11x10½*

100 A155 1c **green** *(434,892) June 28, 1927* 1.75 1.40
Never hinged 2.60
On cover 3.00
Block of 4 7.50 6.75
P# block of 4 14.50
a. Vertical pair, one without overprint *(10)* *3,250.*
101 A157 2c **carmine** *(1,628,195) June 28, 1927* 1.75 1.00
Never hinged 2.50
On cover 3.00
Block of 4 8.00 4.75
P# block of 4 17.50
a. Booklet pane of 6 *(82,108)* 200.00
102 A158 3c **violet** *(1,250,000) Feb., 1931* 4.25 2.75
Never hinged 6.25
On cover 5.00
Block of 4 21.00 13.50
P# block of 4 90.00
a. Booklet pane of 6, handmade, perf. margins *6,500.*
103 A160 5c **blue** *(60,000) Dec. 13, 1927* 25.00 10.00
Never hinged 45.00
On cover 30.00
Block of 4 110.00 42.50
P# block of 4 175.00
104 A165 10c **orange** *(119,800) July, 1930* 17.50 10.00
Never hinged 26.00
On cover 35.00

Block of 4	77.50	45.00
P# block of 4	190.00	
Nos. 100-104 (5)	50.25	25.15

Wet and Dry Printings

Canal Zone stamps printed by both the "wet" and "dry" process are Nos. 105, 108-109, 111-114, 117, 138-140, C21-C24, C26, J25, J27. Starting with Nos. 147 and C27, the Bureau of Engraving and Printing used the "dry" method exclusively. Late dry printings of Nos. 105, 108, 112-114, 117, 138 and 152 also exist with dull gum.

See note on Wet and Dry Printings following U.S. No. 1029.

Maj. Gen. William Crawford Gorgas — A35

Maj. Gen. George Washington Goethals — A36

Gaillard Cut — A37

Maj. Gen. Harry Foote Hodges — A38

Lt. Col. David Du Bose Gaillard — A39

Maj. Gen. William Luther Sibert — A40

Jackson Smith — A41

Rear Adm. Harry Harwood Rousseau — A42

Col. Sydney Bacon Williamson — A43

Joseph Clay Styles Blackburn — A44

Printed by the U. S. Bureau of Engraving and Printing.

Plates of 400 subjects (except 5c), issued in panes of 100. The 5c was printed from plate of 200 subjects, issued in panes of 50. The 400-subject sheets were originally cut by knife into Post Office panes of 100, but beginning in 1948 they were separated by perforations to eliminate straight edges.

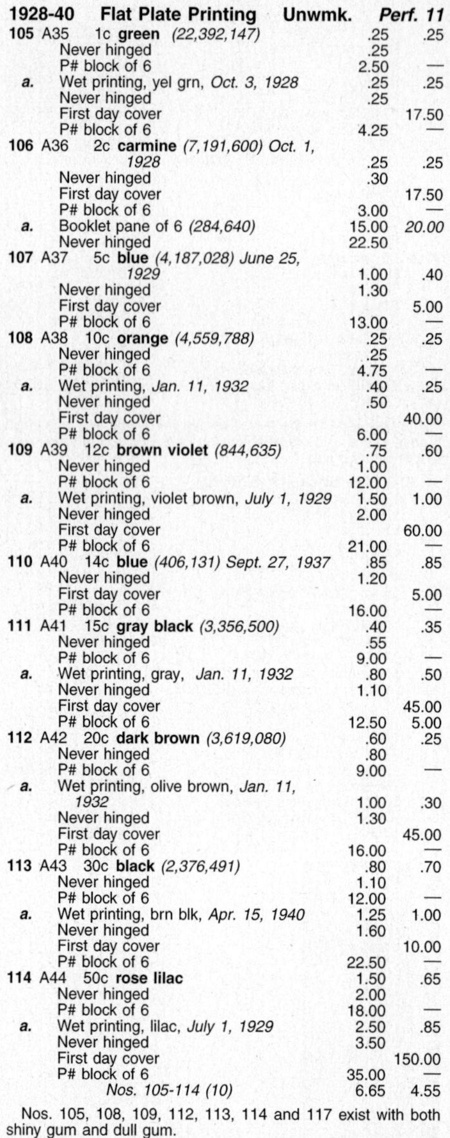

1928-40 Flat Plate Printing Unwmk. *Perf. 11*

105	A35	1c **green** *(22,392,147)*	.25	.25
		Never hinged	.25	
		P# block of 6	2.50	—
a.		Wet printing, yel grn, *Oct. 3, 1928*	.25	.25
		Never hinged	.25	
		First day cover		17.50
		P# block of 6	4.25	—
106	A36	2c **carmine** *(7,191,600) Oct. 1, 1928*	.25	.25
		Never hinged	.30	
		First day cover		17.50
		P# block of 6	3.00	—
a.		Booklet pane of 6 *(284,640)*	15.00	*20.00*
		Never hinged	22.50	
107	A37	5c **blue** *(4,187,028) June 25, 1929*	1.00	.40
		Never hinged	1.30	
		First day cover		5.00
		P# block of 6	13.00	—
108	A38	10c **orange** *(4,559,788)*	.25	.25
		Never hinged	.25	
		P# block of 6	4.75	—
a.		Wet printing, *Jan. 11, 1932*	.40	.25
		Never hinged	.50	
		First day cover		40.00
		P# block of 6	6.00	—
109	A39	12c **brown violet** *(844,635)*	.75	.60
		Never hinged	1.00	
		P# block of 6	12.00	—
a.		Wet printing, violet brown, *July 1, 1929*	1.50	1.00
		Never hinged	2.00	
		First day cover		60.00
		P# block of 6	21.00	—
110	A40	14c **blue** *(406,131) Sept. 27, 1937*	.85	.85
		Never hinged	1.20	
		First day cover		5.00
		P# block of 6	16.00	—
111	A41	15c **gray black** *(3,356,500)*	.40	.35
		Never hinged	.55	
		P# block of 6	9.00	—
a.		Wet printing, gray, *Jan. 11, 1932*	.80	.50
		Never hinged	1.10	
		First day cover		45.00
		P# block of 6	12.50	5.00
112	A42	20c **dark brown** *(3,619,080)*	.60	.25
		Never hinged	.80	
		P# block of 6	9.00	—
a.		Wet printing, olive brown, *Jan. 11, 1932*	1.00	.30
		Never hinged	1.30	
		First day cover		45.00
		P# block of 6	16.00	—
113	A43	30c **black** *(2,376,491)*	.80	.70
		Never hinged	1.10	
		P# block of 6	12.00	—
a.		Wet printing, brn blk, *Apr. 15, 1940*	1.25	1.00
		Never hinged	1.60	
		First day cover		10.00
		P# block of 6	22.50	—
114	A44	50c **rose lilac**	1.50	.65
		Never hinged	2.00	
		P# block of 6	18.00	—
a.		Wet printing, lilac, *July 1, 1929*	2.50	.85
		Never hinged	3.50	
		First day cover		150.00
		P# block of 6	35.00	—
		Nos. 105-114 (10)	6.65	4.55

Nos. 105, 108, 109, 112, 113, 114 and 117 exist with both shiny gum and dull gum.

Coils are listed as Nos. 160-161.

United States Nos. 720 and 695 Overprinted type B

Rotary Press Printing

1933, Jan. 14 *Perf. 11x10½*

115	A226	3c **deep violet** *(3,150,000)*	2.75	.25
		Never hinged	4.00	
		First day cover		12.00
		P# block of 4	35.00	—
a.		"ZONE" only (1)	*4,000.*	
b.		"CANAL" only	*2,600.*	
c.		Booklet pane of 6, handmade, perf. margins	80.00	—
		With plate number	*110.00*	
d.		Vertical pair, one without overprint	—	
e.		Pair without overprint, one with "CANAL ZONE" on reverse, inverted (2)	*3,000.*	
116	A168	14c **dark blue** *(104,800)*	4.50	3.50
		Never hinged	7.00	
		On cover		60.00
		First day cover		20.00
		P# block of 4	60.00	—
a.		"ZONE CANAL" *(16)*	*1,500.*	

Maj. Gen. George Washington Goethals — A45

20th anniversary of the opening of the Panama Canal.

1934 Flat Plate Printing Unwmk. *Perf. 11*

117	A45	3c **red violet**	.25	.25
		Never hinged	.30	
		First day cover		3.00
		P# block of 6	1.00	—
a.		Booklet pane of 6	*12.50*	*32.50*
		Never hinged	*20.00*	
b.		As "a," handmade, perf. margins	160.00	—
c.		Wet printing, violet, *Aug. 15*	.30	.25
		P# block of 6	1.90	—

Coil is listed as No. 153.

Catalogue values for unused stamps in this section, from this point to the end, are for Never Hinged items.

United States Nos. 803 and 805 Overprinted in Black

Rotary Press Printing

1939, Sept. 1 Unwmk. *Perf. 11x10½*

118	A275	½c **red orange** *(1,030,000)*	.25	.25
		Single franking, with 1c additional on third-class cover		50.00
		Single franking, with 1c postal stationery on third-class cover		*150.00*
		First day cover		1.00
		P# block of 4	2.75	—
119	A277	1½c **bister brown** *(935,000)*	.25	.25
		brown	.30	.25
		Single franking on third-class cover		*50.00*
		First day cover		1.00
		P# block of 4	2.25	—

Balboa-Before A46

Balboa-After A47

Gaillard Cut-Before A48

Gaillard Cut-After A49

Bas Obispo-Before A50

Bas Obispo-After A51

Gatun Locks-Before A52

Gatun Locks-After A53

Canal Channel-Before A54

Canal Channel-After A55

Gamboa-Before A56

Gamboa-After A57

Pedro Miguel Locks-Before A58

Pedro Miguel Locks-After A59

Gatun Spillway-Before A60

Gatun Spillway-After A61

25th anniversary of the opening of the Panama Canal.
Withdrawn Feb. 28, 1941; remainders burned Apr. 12, 1941.

Flat Plate Printing

1939, Aug. 15 Unwmk. ***Perf. 11***

120 A46	1c **yellow green** *(1,019,482)*	.60	.30
	On cover		4.00
	First day cover		2.00
	P# block of 6	17.50	—
121 A47	2c **rose carmine** *(227,065)*	.70	.35
	On cover		7.50
	On cover, single franking, on Treaty Rate postcard		40.00
	First day cover		2.00
	P# block of 6	17.50	—
122 A48	3c **purple** *(2,523,735)*	.70	.25
	On cover		12.00
	First day cover		2.00
	P# block of 6	17.50	—
123 A49	5c **dark blue** *(460,213)*	2.00	1.25
	On cover		10.00
	On cover, single franking, on international cover		15.00
	First day cover		2.50
	P# block of 6	30.00	—
124 A50	6c **red orange** *(68,290)*	4.50	3.00
	On cover		12.00
	On cover, single franking, on Steamer/Plane cover to U.S.		25.00
	First day cover		6.00
	P# block of 6	75.00	—
125 A51	7c **black** *(71,235)*	4.75	3.00
	On cover		15.00
	First day cover		6.00
	P# block of 6	75.00	—
126 A52	8c **green** *(41,576)*	7.00	3.25
	On cover		15.00
	First day cover		6.00
	P# block of 6	85.00	—
127 A53	10c **ultramarine** *(83,571)*	5.50	5.00
	On cover		15.00
	On cover, single franking, on airmail cover to Costa Rica or Colombia coast		100.00
	First day cover		6.00
	P# block of 6	85.00	—
128 A54	11c **blue green** *(34,010)*	11.00	8.00
	On cover		35.00
	First day cover		10.00
	P# block of 6	175.00	—
129 A55	12c **brown carmine** *(66,735)*	11.00	7.50
	On cover		12.50
	First day cover		10.00
	P# block of 6	150.00	—
130 A56	14c **dark violet** *(37,365)*	11.00	7.00
	On cover		35.00
	On cover, single uprating of 1c postal stationery on airmail cover to U.S.		125.00
	First day cover		10.00
	P# block of 6	175.00	—
131 A57	15c **olive green** *(105,058)*	14.00	5.75
	On cover		12.50
	First day cover		10.00
	P# block of 6	190.00	—
132 A58	18c **rose pink** *(39,255)*	15.00	8.50
	On cover		20.00
	On cover, single franking, on registered cover to Zone or U.S.		40.00
	First day cover		10.00
	P# block of 6	190.00	—
133 A59	20c **brown** *(100,244)*	17.50	7.00
	On cover		35.00
	First day cover		10.00
	P# block of 6	200.00	—
134 A60	25c **orange** *(34,283)*	27.50	15.00
	On cover		175.00
	First day cover		20.00
	P# block of 6	400.00	—

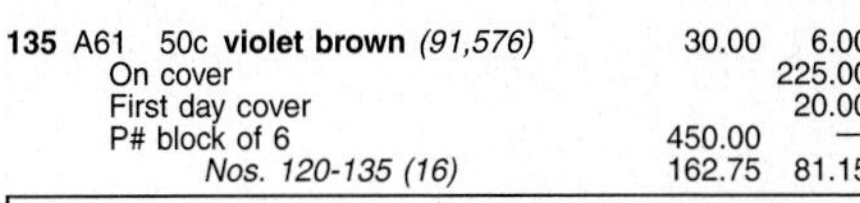

135 A61	50c **violet brown** *(91,576)*	30.00	6.00
	On cover		225.00
	First day cover		20.00
	P# block of 6	450.00	—
	Nos. 120-135 (16)	162.75	81.15

Values for Nos. 120-165 on cover and for single franking usages of these issues are for commercial covers dated near the period of availability of the issue in post offices. Philatelically contrived covers are worth less.

Maj. Gen. George W. Davis — A62

Gov. Charles E. Magoon — A63

Theodore Roosevelt — A64

John F. Stevens — A65

John F. Wallace — A66

1946-49 Unwmk. ***Perf. 11***

Size: 19x22mm

136 A62	½c **bright red** *(1,020,000) Aug. 16, 1948*	.40	.25
	On cover		2.00
	On cover, single, with 1c additional on 3rd-class cover		75.00
	First day cover		1.25
	P# block of 6	3.00	—
137 A63	1½c **chocolate** *(603,600) Aug. 16, 1948*	.40	.25
	On cover		2.00
	On cover, single franking, on 3rd-class cover		100.00
	First day cover		1.25
	P# block of 6	3.00	—
138 A64	2c **light rose carmine** *(6,951,755)*	.25	.25
	P# block of 6	.65	—
a.	Wet printing, rose carmine, *Oct. 27, 1949*	.25	.25
	First day cover		1.00
	P# block of 6	1.00	—
139 A65	5c **dark blue**	.35	.25
	P# block of 6	2.50	—
a.	Wet printing, deep blue, *Apr. 25, 1946*	.60	.25
	First day cover		1.00
	P# block of 6	4.50	—
140 A66	25c **green** *(1,520,000)*	.85	.55
	On cover		20.00
	P# block of 6	7.00	—
a.	Wet printing, yel grn, *Aug. 16, 1948*	3.00	1.00
	First day cover		3.50
	P# block of 6	24.00	—
	Nos. 136-140 (5)	2.25	1.55

See Nos. 155, 162, 164. For overprint, see No. O9.

Map of Biological Area and Coati-mundi A67

25th anniversary of the establishment of the Canal Zone Biological Area on Barro Colorado Island.
Withdrawn Mar. 30, 1951, and remainders destroyed Apr. 10, 1951.

1948, Apr. 17 **Unwmk.** ***Perf. 11***

141 A67 10c **black** *(521,200)* 1.75 1.00
On cover 4.00
On cover, single franking, airmail to Central or S. America 8.00
First day cover 3.00
P# block of 6 15.00 —

"Forty-niners" Arriving at Chagres — A68

Journeying in "Bungo" to Las Cruces — A69

Las Cruces Trail to Panama — A70

Departure for San Francisco — A71

Centenary of the California Gold Rush.
Stocks on hand were processed for destruction on Aug. 11, 1952 and destroyed Aug. 13, 1952.

1949, June 1 **Unwmk.** ***Perf. 11***

142 A68 3c **blue** *(500,000)* .65 .25
On cover 2.00
On foreign postcard 12.00
First day cover 1.00
P# block of 6 6.50 —
143 A69 6c **violet** *(481,600)* .65 .30
On cover 2.00
First day cover 1.00
P# block of 6 6.50 —
144 A70 12c **bright blue green** *(230,200)* 1.75 .90
On cover 8.00
First day cover 2.00
P# block of 6 21.00 —
145 A71 18c **deep red lilac** *(240,200)* 2.00 1.50
On cover 8.00
First day cover 3.25
P# block of 6 20.00 —
Nos. 142-145 (4) 5.05 2.95

Workers in Culebra Cut — A72

Contribution of West Indian laborers in the construction of the Panama Canal.
Entire issue sold, none withdrawn and destroyed.

1951, Aug. 15 **Unwmk.** ***Perf. 11***

146 A72 10c **carmine** *(480,000)* 3.50 1.50
On cover 5.00
On cover, single franking, airmail to Central or S. America 12.50
First day cover 3.00
P# block of 6 27.50 —

Centenary of the completion of the Panama Railroad and the first transcontinental railroad trip in the Americas.

Early Railroad Scene — A73

1955, Jan. 28 **Unwmk.** ***Perf. 11***

147 A73 3c **violet** *(994,000)* 1.00 .60
On cover 5.00
First day cover 1.50
P# block of 6 8.00 —

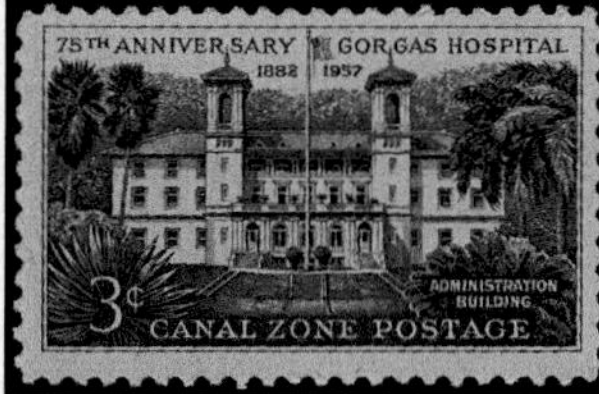

Gorgas Hospital and Ancon Hill — A74

75th anniversary of Gorgas Hospital.

1957, Nov. 17 **Unwmk.** ***Perf. 11***

148 A74 3c **black,** *dull blue green (1,010,000)* .45 .35
Light blue green paper .40 .35
On cover 5.00
On postcard or drop-letter rate after Aug. 1, 1958 10.00
First day cover 1.00
P# block of 4 4.25 —

S.S. Ancon — A75

1958, Aug. 30 **Unwmk.** ***Perf. 11***

149 A75 4c **greenish blue** *(1,749,700)* .40 .30
On cover 4.00
On postcard or drop-letter rate after Jan. 7, 1963 10.00
First day cover 1.00
P# block of 4 3.25 —

Roosevelt Medal and Canal Zone Map — A76

Centenary of the birth of Theodore Roosevelt (1858-1919).

1958, Nov. 15 **Unwmk.** ***Perf. 11***

150 A76 4c **brown** *(1,060,000)* .60 .30
On cover 4.00
First day cover 1.00
P# block of 4 3.50 —

Boy Scout Badge — A77

50th anniversary of the Boy Scouts of America.

Giori Press Printing

1960, Feb. 8 **Unwmk.** ***Perf. 11***

151 A77 4c **dark blue, red & bister** *(654,933)* .55 .40
On cover 4.00
First day cover 1.50
P# block of 4 4.50 —

Administration Building, Balboa Heights — A78

1960, Nov. 1 **Unwmk.** ***Perf. 11***

152 A78 4c **rose lilac** *(2,486,725)* .25 .25
First day cover 1.00
P# block of 4 .90 —

Types of 1934, 1960 and 1946
Coil Stamps

1960-62 **Unwmk.** ***Perf. 10 Vertically***

153 A45 3c **deep violet** *(3,743,959) Nov. 1, 1960* .25 .25
First day cover 1.00
Pair .40 .25
Joint line pair 1.10 —

Perf. 10 Horizontally

154 A78 4c **dull rose lilac** *(2,776,273) Nov. 1, 1960* .25 .25
First day cover 1.00
Pair .40 .25
Joint line pair 1.10 —

Perf. 10 Vertically

155 A65 5c **deep blue** *(3,288,264) Feb. 10, 1962* .25 .25
First day cover 1.00
Pair .50 .50
Joint line pair 1.25 —
Nos. 153-155 (3) .75 .75

Girl Scout Badge and Camp at Gatun Lake — A79

50th anniversary of the Girl Scouts.

Giori Press Printing

1962, Mar. 12 **Unwmk.** ***Perf. 11***

156 A79 4c **blue, dark green & bister** *(640,000)* .40 .30
On cover 4.00
First day cover *(83,717)* 1.25
P# block of 4 2.75 —

Thatcher Ferry Bridge and Map of Western Hemisphere A80

Opening of the Thatcher Ferry Bridge, spanning the Panama Canal.

Giori Press Printing

1962, Oct. 12 **Unwmk.** ***Perf. 11***

157 A80 4c **black & silver** *(775,000)* .35 .25
On cover 4.00
First day cover *(65,833)* 1.00
P# block of 4, 2P# 3.75 —
a. Silver (bridge) omitted *(50)* *8,000.*
Hinged *6,000.*
P# block of 6, black P# only *55,000.*

Goethals Memorial, Balboa — A81

Fort San Lorenzo — A82

1968-71 **Giori Press Printing** ***Perf. 11***

158 A81 6c **green & ultra.** *(1,890,000) Mar. 15, 1968* .30 .30
First day cover 1.00
P# block of 4 2.00 —
159 A82 8c **slate green, blue, dark brown & ocher** *(3,460,000) July 14, 1971* .35 .25
First day cover 1.00
P# block of 4 2.75 —

Types of 1928, 1932 and 1948
Coil Stamps

1975, Feb. 14 Unwmk. *Perf. 10 Vertically*

160 A35 1c **green** *(1,090,958)* .25 .25
First day cover 1.00
Pair .40 .30
Joint line pair 1.00 —
161 A38 10c **orange** *(590,658)* .70 .40
First day cover 1.00
Pair 1.40 .80
Joint line pair 5.00 —
162 A66 25c **yellow green** *(129,831)* 2.75 2.75
First day cover 3.00
Pair 5.50 5.50
Joint line pair 19.00 —
Nos. 160-162 (3) 3.70 3.40

Dredge Cascadas
A83

1976, Feb. 23 Giori Press Printing *Perf. 11*

163 A83 13c **multicolored** *(3,653,950)* .35 .25
On cover 3.00
First day cover 1.00
P# block of 4 2.00 —
a. Booklet pane of 4 *(1,032,400) Apr. 19* 3.00 —

No. 163a exists with and without staple holes in selvage tab.

Stevens Type of 1946

1977 Rotary Press Printing *Perf. 11x10½*
Size: 19x22½mm

164 A65 5c **deep blue** *(1,009,612)* .60 .85
P# block of 4 3.50 —
a. Tagged, dull gum 12.00 15.00
On cover 150.00
P# block of 4 125.00 —

No. 164 exists with both shiny gum and dull gum. Stamps with dull gum exist with and without tagging.

No. 164a exists even though there was no equipment in the Canal Zone to detect tagging.

Value for No. 164a on cover is for covers postmarked prior to Sept. 30, 1979.

Towing Locomotive, Ship in Lock, by Alwyn Sprague
A84

1978, Oct. 25 *Perf. 11*

165 A84 15c **dp grn & bl grn** *(2,921,083)* .35 .25
On cover 4.00
First day cover *(81,405)* 1.00
P# block of 4 2.00 —

No. 165 only exists with dull gum.

AIR POST STAMPS

Values for Nos. C1-C53 on cover and for single franking usages of these issues are for commercial covers dated near the period of availability of the issue in post offices. Philatelically contrived covers are worth less.

Regular Issue of 1928 Surcharged in Dark Blue

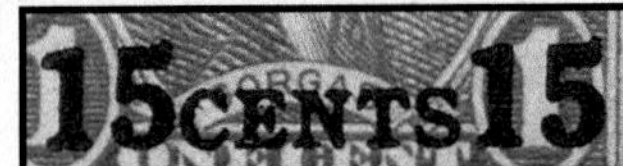

Type I - Flag of "Five" pointing up

Type II - Flag of "5" curved

1929-31 Flat Plate Printing Unwmk. *Perf. 11*

C1 A35 15c on 1c **green,** type I, *Apr. 1, 1929* 7.50 4.75
Never hinged 11.50
On cover 15.00
On cover, single franking, to 15c airmail rate countries (Jamaica, Nicaragua, Ecuador or Colombia coast) 60.00
First day cover 25.00
Block of 4 32.50 25.00
P# block of 6 120.00 —
C2 A35 15c on 1c **yellow green,** type II, *Mar. 1931* 60.00 47.50
Never hinged 120.00
On cover 175.00
Block of 4 300.00 340.00
P# block of 6 900.00 —
C3 A36 25c on 2c **carmine** *(223,880) Jan. 11, 1929* 3.50 2.00
Never hinged 5.25
On cover 15.00
First day cover 17.50
Block of 4 15.00 9.00
P# block of 6 115.00 —
Nos. C1-C3 (3) 71.00 54.25

Nos. 114 and 106 Surcharged in Black

1929, Dec. 31

C4 A44 10c on 50c **lilac** *(116,666)* 8.00 5.75
Never hinged 12.00
On cover 15.00
On cover, single franking, on airmail cover to Costa Rica or Colombia coast 50.00
First day cover 25.00
Block of 4 35.00 25.00
P# block of 6 120.00 —
C5 A36 20c on 2c **carmine** *(638,395)* 4.50 1.25
Never hinged 7.50
On cover 7.50
First day cover 20.00
Block of 4 18.00 6.00
P# block of 6 110.00 —
a. Dropped "2" in surcharge *(7,000)* 85.00 60.00

Catalogue values for unused stamps in this section, from this point to the end, are for Never Hinged items.

Gaillard Cut — AP1

Printed by the U. S. Bureau of Engraving and Printing.

Plates of 200 subjects, issued in panes of 50.

1931-49 Unwmk. *Perf. 11*

C6 AP1 4c **red violet** *(525,000) Jan. 3, 1949* .75 .65
First day cover 2.00
P# block of 6 5.25 —
C7 AP1 5c **yellow green** *(9,935,500) Nov. 18, 1931* .60 .30
green .60 .30
First day cover 10.00
P# block of 6 4.50 —
C8 AP1 6c **yellow brown** *(9,399,500) Feb. 15, 1946* .75 .35
First day cover 2.00
P# block of 6 5.25 —
C9 AP1 10c **orange** *(5,079,000) Nov. 18, 1931* 1.00 .35
First day cover 10.00
P# block of 6 10.00 —
C10 AP1 15c **blue** *(11,072,700) Nov. 18, 1931* 1.25 .30
pale blue 1.25 .30
First day cover 15.00
P# block of 6 11.00 —
C11 AP1 20c **red violet** *(3,184,100) Nov. 18, 1931* 2.00 .25
deep violet 2.00 .30
First day cover 35.00
P# block of 6 20.00 —
C12 AP1 30c **rose lake** *(1,119,500) July 15, 1941* 7.50 1.50
dull rose 7.50 1.50
First day cover 22.50
P# block of 6 60.00 —
C13 AP1 40c **yellow** *(795,600) Nov. 18, 1931* 3.50 1.10
lemon 3.50 1.10
First day cover 75.00
P# block of 6 35.00 —
C14 AP1 $1 **black** *(372,500) Nov. 18, 1931* 10.00 1.60
First day cover 150.00
P# block of 6 95.00 —
Nos. C6-C14 (9) 27.35 6.40

For overprints, see Nos. CO1-CO14.

Douglas Plane over Sosa Hill — AP2

Planes and Map of Central America
AP3

Pan American Clipper and Scene near Fort Amador — AP4

Pan American Clipper at Cristobal Harbor — AP5

Pan American Clipper over Gaillard Cut — AP6

Pan American Clipper Landing — AP7

10th anniversary of Air Mail service and the 25th anniversary of the opening of the Panama Canal.

Withdrawn Feb. 28, 1941, remainders burned Apr. 12, 1941.

Flat Plate Printing

1939, July 15 **Unwmk.** ***Perf. 11***

C15 AP2 5c **greenish black** *(86,576)* 3.75 2.25
On cover 7.50
First day cover 5.00
P# block of 6 45.00 —
C16 AP3 10c **dull violet** *(117,644)* 3.50 3.00
On cover 7.50
On cover, single franking, on airmail cover to Costa Rica or Colombia coast 75.00
First day cover 5.00
P# block of 6 47.50 —
C17 AP4 15c **light brown** *(883,742)* 5.00 1.00
On cover 3.00
First day cover 3.00
P# block of 6 57.50 —
C18 AP5 25c **blue** *(82,126)* 17.50 8.00
On cover 15.00
On cover, single franking, to 25c airmail-rate countries (Peru, the Guianas, Haiti, Dominican Republic, etc.) 45.00
First day cover 17.50
P# block of 6 275.00 —
C19 AP6 30c **rose carmine** *(121,382)* 17.50 6.00
On cover 10.00
First day cover 15.00
P# block of 6 200.00 —
C20 AP7 $1 **green** *(40,051)* 45.00 27.50
On cover 200.00
On cover, single franking, on registered airmail cover to Australasia, Asia or Africa 300.00
First day cover 60.00
P# block of 6 525.00 —
Nos. C15-C20 (6) 92.25 47.75

Globe and Wing — AP8

Flat Plate Printing

1951, July 16 **Unwmk.** ***Perf. 11***

C21 AP8 4c **lt red violet** *(1,315,000)* .75 .35
P# block of 6 7.00 —
a. Wet printing, red violet 1.25 .40
1st day card, Balboa Heights 1.50
P# block of 6 10.00 —
C22 AP8 6c **lt brown** *(22,657,625)* .50 .25
P# block of 6 5.00 —
a. Wet printing, brown .95 .35
1st day cover, Balboa Heights 1.00
P# block of 6 7.50 —
C23 AP8 10c **lt red orange** *(1,049,130)* .90 .35
P# block of 6 8.00 —
a. Wet printing, red orange 2.00 .50
1st day cover, Balboa Heights 2.00
P# block of 6 16.00 —
C24 AP8 21c **lt blue** *(1,460,000)* 8.00 4.00
P# block of 6 75.00 —
a. Wet printing, blue 15.00 5.00
1st day cover, Balboa Heights 7.50
P# block of 6 125.00 —
C25 AP8 31c **cerise** *(375,000)* 9.50 3.75
On cover 25.00
On cover, single franking, on airmail cover to Australasia, Asia or Africa 40.00
1st day cover, Balboa Heights 7.50
P# block of 6 80.00 —
a. Horiz. pair, imperf. vert. *(98)* 1,000. —
C26 AP8 80c **lt gray black** *(827,696)* 6.00 1.50
On cover 100.00
P# block of 6 45.00 —
a. Wet printing, gray black 12.50 1.65
1st day cover, Balboa Heights 12.50
1st day cover, Balboa Heights, #C21-C26 20.00
P# block of 6 115.00 —
Nos. C21-C26 (6) 25.65 10.20

See note after No. 114. Total number of first day covers with one or more of Nos. C21-C26, about 12,000.

Flat Plate Printing

1958, Aug. 16 **Unwmk.** ***Perf. 11***

C27 AP8 5c **yellow green** *(899,923)* 1.00 .60
First day cover *(2,176)* 4.50
P# block of 4 6.00 —
C28 AP8 7c **olive** *(9,381,797)* 1.00 .45
First day cover *(2,815)* 4.50
P# block of 4 6.00 —
C29 AP8 15c **brown violet** *(359,923)* 4.50 2.75
First day cover *(2,040)* 6.00
P# block of 4 37.50 —
C30 AP8 25c **orange yellow** *(600,000)* 12.50 2.75
First day cover *(2,115)* 9.00
P# block of 4 125.00 —
C31 AP8 35c **dark blue** *(283,032)* 9.00 2.75
On cover 30.00
On cover, single franking, on airmail cover to Australasia, Asia or Africa 80.00
First day cover *(1,868)* 11.00
P# block of 4 60.00 —
Nos. C27-C31 (5) 28.00 9.30
Nos. C21-C31 (11) 53.65 19.50

See No. C34.

Emblem of US Army Caribbean School — AP9

US Army Caribbean School for Latin America at Fort Gulick.

Giori Press Printing

1961, Nov. 21 **Unwmk.** ***Perf. 11***

C32 AP9 15c **red & blue** *(560,000)* 1.60 .75
On cover 7.50
On cover, single franking, on foreign postcard or letter to Western Hemisphere 10.00
First day cover *(25,949)* 1.75
P# block of 4 9.50 —

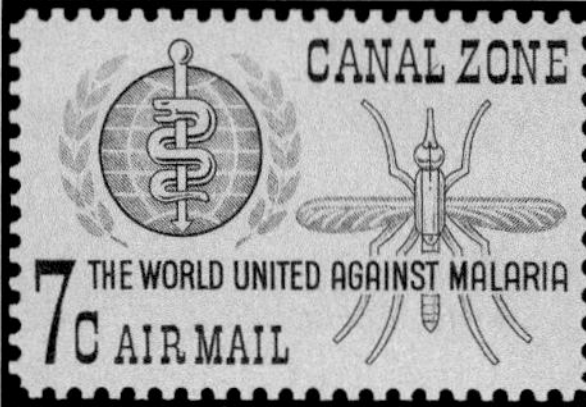

Malaria Eradication Emblem and Mosquito AP10

World Health Organization drive to eradicate malaria.

Giori Press Printing

1962, Sept. 24 **Unwmk.** ***Perf. 11***

C33 AP10 7c **yellow & black** *(862,349)* .50 .40
On cover 5.00
On cover, single franking, airmail to US 10.00
First day cover *(44,433)* 1.00
P# block of 4 3.00 —

Globe-Wing Type of 1951

Rotary Press Printing

1963, Jan. 7 ***Perf. 10½x11***

C34 AP8 8c **carmine** *(5,054,727)* .75 .30
First day cover *(19,128)* 1.00
P# block of 4 4.00 —

Alliance for Progress Emblem AP11

2nd anniv. of the Alliance for Progress, which aims to stimulate economic growth and raise living standards in Latin America.

Giori Press Printing

1963, Aug. 17 **Unwmk.** ***Perf. 11***

C35 AP11 15c **gray, grn & dk ultra** *(405,000)* 1.50 .85
On cover 7.50
On cover, single franking, on foreign postcard or letter to Western Hemisphere 12.50
First day cover *(29,594)* 1.50
P# block of 4 12.50 —

Jet over Canal Zone Views — AP12

50th anniversary of the opening of the Panama Canal. Designs: 6c, Cristobal. 8c, Gatun Locks. 15c, Madden Dam. 20c, Gaillard Cut. 30c, Miraflores Locks. 80c, Balboa.

Giori Press Printing

1964, Aug. 15 **Unwmk.** ***Perf. 11***

C36 AP12 6c **green & black** *(257,193)* .60 .35
On cover 1.50
1st day cover, Balboa 1.50
P# block of 4 3.75 —
C37 AP12 8c **rose red & black** *(3,924,283)* .60 .35
On cover 1.00
1st day cover, Balboa 1.00
P# block of 4 4.00 —
C38 AP12 15c **blue & black** *(472,666)* 1.25 .75
On cover 7.50
On cover, single franking, on foreign postcard 12.50
1st day cover, Balboa 1.00
P# block of 4 9.25 —
C39 AP12 20c **rose lilac & black** *(399,784)* 1.60 1.00
On cover 15.00
On cover, single franking, to Europe or North Africa 40.00
1st day cover, Balboa 2.00
P# block of 4 10.00 —
C40 AP12 30c **reddish brown & black** *(204,524)* 2.75 2.25
On cover 10.00
On cover, single franking, to Australasia, Asia, or sub-Sahara Africa 50.00
1st day cover, Balboa 3.00
P# block of 4 17.50 —
C41 AP12 80c **olive bister & black** *(186,809)* 4.75 3.00
On cover 75.00
1st day cover, Balboa 4.00
1st day cover, Balboa, #C36-C41 10.00
P# block of 4 26.00 —
Nos. C36-C41 (6) 11.55 7.70

There were 57,822 first day covers with one or more of Nos. C36-C41.

Canal Zone Seal and Jet Plane — AP13

Giori Press Printing

1965, July 15 **Unwmk.** ***Perf. 11***

C42 AP13 6c **green & black** *(548,250)* .50 .30
First day cover, Balboa 2.00
P# block of 4 3.25 —
C43 AP13 8c **rose red & black** *(8,357,700)* .45 .25
First day cover, Balboa 1.00
P# block of 4 3.00 —
C44 AP13 15c **blue & black** *(2,385,000)* .75 .25
On cover, single franking, on foreign postcard or letter to Western Hemisphere 8.00
First day cover, Balboa 1.00
P# block of 4 7.00 —
C45 AP13 20c **lilac & black** *(2,290,699)* .80 .30
On cover, single franking, to Europe or North Africa 15.00
First day cover, Balboa 1.25
P# block of 4 4.25 —
C46 AP13 30c **redsh brn & blk** *(2,332,255)* 1.10 .30
On cover, single franking, to Australasia, Asia or sub-Sahara Africa 25.00
First day cover, Balboa 1.25
P# block of 4 6.00 —
C47 AP13 80c **bister & black** *(1,456,596)* 2.50 .75
On cover 15.00
First day cover, Balboa 2.50
First day cover, Balboa, #C42-C47 7.00
P# block of 4 18.00 —
Nos. C42-C47 (6) 6.10 2.15

No. C46 also exists with dull gum.

There were 35,389 first day covers with one or more of Nos. C42-C47.

1968-76

C48 AP13 10c **dull orange & black** *(10,055,000) Mar. 15, 1968* .35 .25
First day cover, Balboa *(7,779)* 1.00
P# block of 4 3.50 —
a. Booklet pane of 4 *(713,390) Feb. 18, 1970* 4.25 —
First day cover, Balboa *(5,054)* 5.00
C49 AP13 11c **olive & black** *(3,335,000) Sept. 24, 1971* .35 .25
First day cover, Balboa *(10,916)* 1.00
P# block of 4 3.50 —
a. Booklet pane of 4 *(1,277,760) Sept. 24, 1971* 3.50 —
First day cover, Balboa *(2,460)* 5.00
C50 AP13 13c **emerald & black** *(1,865,000) Feb. 11, 1974* .85 .25
First day cover, Balboa *(7,646)* 1.00
P# block of 4 5.00 —
a. Booklet pane of 4 *(619,200) Feb. 11, 1974* 6.00 —
First day cover, Balboa *(3,660)* 5.00
C51 AP13 22c **vio & blk** *(363,720) May 10, 1976* 1.10 *2.00*
On cover, single franking, on foreign postcard 15.00
First day cover, Balboa 2.50
P# block of 4 8.00 —
C52 AP13 25c **pale yellow & black** *(1,640,441) Mar. 15, 1968* .80 .70
On cover, single franking, to Western Hemisphere 22.50
First day cover, Balboa 1.00
P# block of 4 5.50 —
C53 AP13 35c **salmon & black** *(573,822) May 10, 1976* 1.25 *2.00*
On cover, single franking, to Europe or North Africa 15.00

First day cover, Balboa		2.50
P# block of 4	10.00	—
Nos. C48-C53 (6)	4.70	*5.45*

No. C50a exists with and without staple holes in selvage tab.
There were 5,047 first day covers with one or more of Nos. C51, C53.
No. C51 and C53 only exist with dull gum.

AIR POST OFFICIAL STAMPS

Beginning in March 1915, stamps for use on official mail were identified by a large "P" perforated through each stamp. These were replaced by overprinted issues in 1941. The use of official stamps was discontinued December 31, 1951. During their currency, they were not for sale in mint condition and were sold to the public only when canceled with a parcel post rotary canceler reading "Balboa Heights, Canal Zone" between two wavy lines.

After having been withdrawn from use, mint stamps (except Nos. CO8-CO12 and O3, O8) were made available to the public at face value for three months beginning Jan. 2, 1952. **Values for used examples of Nos. CO1-CO7, CO14, O1-O2, O4-O9, are for canceled-to-order stamps with original gum, postally used stamps being worth more.** Sheet margins were removed to facilitate overprinting and plate numbers are, therefore, unknown.

Air Post Stamps of 1931-41 Overprinted in Black

Two types of overprint

Type I — "PANAMA CANAL" 19-20mm long

1941-42 Unwmk. *Perf. 11*

CO1	AP1 5c **yellow green** *(42,754) Mar. 31, 1941*	6.50	1.50
	green	6.50	1.50
	On cover		50.00
	Block of 4	27.50	6.00
CO2	AP1 10c **orange** *(49,723) Mar. 31, 1941*	8.50	1.75
	On cover		25.00
	Block of 4	37.50	8.00
CO3	AP1 15c **blue** *(56,898) Mar. 31, 1941*	11.00	1.75
	On cover		25.00
	Block of 4	47.50	15.00
CO4	AP1 20c **red violet** *(22,107) Mar. 31, 1941*	13.00	4.00
	deep violet	13.00	4.00
	On cover		110.00
	Block of 4	62.50	22.50
CO5	AP1 30c **rose lake** *(22,100) June, 4, 1942*	17.50	5.00
	dull rose	17.50	4.50
	On cover		40.00
	Block of 4	80.00	22.50
CO6	AP1 40c **yellow** *(22,875) Mar. 31, 1941*	17.50	7.50
	lemon yellow	17.50	7.50
	On cover		75.00
	Block of 4	80.00	37.50
CO7	AP1 $1 **black** *(29,525) Mar. 31, 1941*	20.00	10.00
	On cover		150.00
	Block of 4	90.00	45.00
	Nos. CO1-CO7 (7)	94.00	31.50

Overprint varieties occur on Nos. CO1-CO7 and CO14: "O" of "OFFICIAL" over "N" of "PANAMA" (entire third row). "O" of "OFFICIAL" broken at top (position 31). "O" of "OFFICIAL" over second "A" of "PANAMA" (position 45). First "F" of "OFFICIAL" over second "A" of "PANAMA" (position 50).

Type II — "PANAMA CANAL" 17mm long

1941, Sept. 22

CO8	AP1 5c **yellow green** *(2,000)*	—	150.00
	On cover		500.00
	Block of 4		925.00
CO9	AP1 10c **orange** *(2,000)*	*1,100.*	260.00
	On cover		400.00
	Block of 4		1,650.
CO10	AP1 20c **red violet** *(2,000)*	—	160.00
	On cover		—
	Block of 4		1,050.
CO11	AP1 30c **rose lake** *(5,000)*	*900.*	60.00
	On cover		125.00
	Block of 4		325.00
CO12	AP1 40c **yellow** *(2,000)*	—	170.00
	On cover		500.00
	Block of 4		1,100.
	Nos. CO8-CO12 (5)		800.00

Type I — "PANAMA CANAL" 19-20mm long

1947, Nov.

CO14	AP1 6c **yellow brown** *(33,450)*	13.00	5.50
	On cover		50.00
	Block of 4	60.00	25.00
a.	Inverted overprint *(50)*		*2,000.*

POSTAGE DUE STAMPS

Prior to 1914, many of the postal issues were handstamped "Postage Due" and used as postage due stamps.

Postage Due Stamps of the United States Nos. J45a, J46a, and J49a Overprinted in Black

1914, Mar. Wmk. 190 *Perf. 12*

J1	D2 1c **rose carmine** *(23,533)*	85.00	15.00
	On cover		275.00
	Block of 4 (2mm spacing)	425.00	70.
	Block of 4 (3mm spacing)	450.00	80.00
	P# block of 6, impt. & star	1,000.	—
J2	D2 2c **rose carmine** *(32,312)*	250.00	42.50
	On cover		275.00
	Block of 4	1,250.	200.00
	P# block of 6	2,000.	—
J3	D2 10c **rose carmine** *(92,493)*	900.00	40.00
	On cover		900.00
	Block of 4 (2mm spacing)	4,000.	170.
	Block of 4 (3mm spacing)	4,000.	170.00
	P# block of 6, Impt. & star	*23,000.*	—

Many examples of Nos. J1-J3 show one or more letters of the overprint out of alignment, principally the "E."
Two examples exist of the plate block of No. J3. The value reflects the 2009 auction sale of the finer of the two.

Blue Overprint, Type II, on Postage Due Stamps of Panama

San Geronimo Castle Gate, Portobelo (See footnote) — D1

Statue of Columbus — D2

Pedro J. Sosa — D3

1915, Mar. Unwmk. *Perf. 12*

J4	D1 1c **olive brown** *(50,000)*	11.00	5.00
	On cover		150.00
	Block of 4	50.00	22.50
J5	D2 2c **olive brown** *(50,000)*	225.00	17.50
	On cover		425.00
	Block of 4	975.00	90.00
J6	D3 10c **olive brown** *(200,000)*	50.00	10.00
	On cover		175.00
	Block of 4	225.00	45.00
	Nos. J4-J6 (3)	286.00	32.50

Type D1 was intended to show a gate of San Lorenzo Castle, Chagres, and is so labeled. By error the stamp actually shows the main gate of San Geronimo Castle, Portobelo.

Surcharged in Red

1915, Nov. Unwmk. *Perf. 12*

J7	D1 1c on 1c **olive brown** *(60,614)*	110.00	14.00
	On cover		160.00
	Block of 4	500.00	65.00
J8	D2 2c on 2c **olive brown**	22.50	7.50
	On cover		225.00
	Block of 4	100.00	37.50
J9	D3 10c on 10c **olive brown** *(175,548)*	22.50	5.00
	On cover		300.00
	Block of 4	100.00	25.00
	Nos. J7-J9 (3)	155.00	26.50

One of the printings of No. J9 shows wider spacing between "1" and "0." Both spacings occur on the same sheet.

D4

Capitol, Panama — D5

1919, Dec.

Surcharged in Carmine by Panama Canal Press, Mount Hope, C. Z.

"Canal Zone" Type III

J10	D4 2c on 2c **olive brown**	40.00	12.50
	On cover		350.00
	Block of 4	170.00	60.00
J11	D5 4c on 4c **olive brown** *(35,695)*	45.00	15.00
	On cover		400.00
	Block of 4	190.00	70.00
a.	"ZONE" omitted	*9,250.*	
b.	"4" omitted	*8,500.*	

Blue Overprint, Type V, on Postage Due Stamp of Panama

1922

J11C	D1 1c **dark olive brown**	—	5.00
d.	"CANAL ZONE" reading down	200.00	

United States Postage Due Stamps Nos. J61, J62b and J65b Overprinted

Type A

Letters "A" with Flat Tops

1924, July 1 *Perf. 11*

J12	D2 1c **carmine rose** *(10,000)*	110.00	27.50
	On cover		100.00
	Block of 4	475.00	125.00
	P# block of 6	1,250.	—
J13	D2 2c **deep claret** *(25,000)*	55.00	15.00
	On cover		110.00
	Block of 4	275.00	65.00
	P# block of 6	775.00	—
J14	D2 10c **deep claret** *(30,000)*	250.00	50.00
	On cover		225.00
	Block of 4 (2mm spacing)	1,250.	210.00
	Block of 4 (3mm spacing)	1,250.	210.00
	Margin block of 6, imprint, star and P#	*3,500.*	—
	Nos. J12-J14 (3)	415.00	92.50

Values for Nos. J12-J29 on cover are for philatelically prepared items. Commercial usages on cover are much more valuable.

United States Nos. 552, 554 and 562 Ovptd. Type A and Additionally Ovptd. at Mount Hope in Red or Blue

1925, Feb. *Perf. 11*

J15	A155 1c **deep green** (R) *(15,000)*	90.00	15.00
	On cover		110.00
	Block of 4	400.00	62.50
	P# block of 6	900.00	—
J16	A157 2c **carmine** (Bl) *(21,335)*	22.50	7.00
	On cover		67.50
	Block of 4	100.00	30.00
	P# block of 6	225.00	—
J17	A165 10c **orange** (R) *(39,819)*	55.00	11.00
	On cover		90.00
	Block of 4	260.00	47.50
	P# block of 6	500.00	—
a.	"POSTAGE DUE" double	800.00	
b.	"E" of "POSTAGE" omitted	750.00	
c.	As "b," "POSTAGE DUE" double	*3,250.*	
	Nos. J15-J17 (3)	167.50	33.00

On U.S. Postage Due Stamps Nos. J61, J62, J65, J65a

Overprinted Type B

Letters "A" with Sharp Pointed Tops

1925, June 24

J18	D2 1c **carmine rose** *(80,000)*	8.00	2.75
	On cover		65.00
	Block of 4	35.00	14.00
	P# block of 6	90.00	—
	"CANAL" in wrong font	*125.00*	*75.00*
	"ZONE" in wrong font	*175.00*	*125.00*
a.	"ZONE ZONE" (LR18)	1,500.	
J19	D2 2c **carmine rose** *(146,430)*	15.00	2.75
	On cover		42.50
	Block of 4	65.00	14.00
	P# block of 6	160.00	—
	"CANAL" in wrong font	*225.00*	*175.00*
	"ZONE" in wrong font	*375.00*	*225.00*
a.	"ZONE ZONE" (LR18)	1,500.	
J20	D2 10c **carmine rose** *(153,980)*	150.00	20.00
	On cover		300.00
	Block of 4, 2mm spacing	650.00	85.00
	Block of 4, 3mm spacing	675.00	90.00
	P# block of 6, Impt. & Star	1,250.	—
	"CANAL" in wrong font	*175.00*	*50.00*
	"ZONE" in wrong font	*200.00*	*100.00*
a.	Vert. pair, one without ovpt. *(10)*	*3,000.*	
	P# block of 6, Impt. & Star	*17,500.*	
b.	10c **rose red**	*250.00*	150.00
	On cover		—
c.	As "b," double overprint	*450.00*	—
	Nos. J18-J20 (3)	173.00	25.50

Nos. J18-J20 exist with wrong font "CANAL" (UL51) and "ZONE" (UL82).

Regular Issue of 1928-29 Surcharged

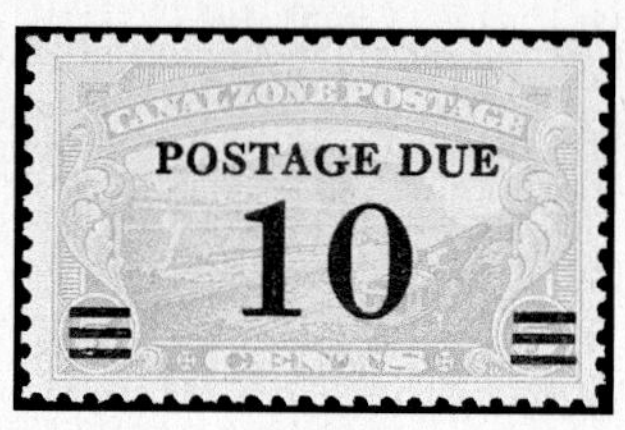

1929-30

J21	A37 1c on 5c **blue** *(35,990) Mar. 20, 1930*	3.75	1.75
	Never hinged	7.50	
	On cover		75.00
	P# block of 6	40.00	—
a.	"POSTAGE DUE" missing *(5)*	*5,500.*	
J22	A37 2c on 5c **blue** *(40,207) Oct. 18, 1930*	6.50	2.50
	Never hinged	13.00	
	On cover		75.00
	P# block of 6	70.00	—
J23	A37 5c on 5c **blue** *(35,464) Dec. 1, 1930*	6.50	2.75
	Never hinged	13.00	
	On cover		125.00
	P# block of 6	70.00	—
J24	A37 10c on 5c **blue** *(90,504) Dec. 16, 1929*	6.50	2.75
	Never hinged	13.00	
	On cover		75.00
	P# block of 6	70.00	—
	Nos. J21-J24 (4)	23.25	9.75

On No. J23 the three short horizontal bars in the lower corners of the surcharge are omitted.

Canal Zone Seal — D6

Printed by the U.S. Bureau of Engraving and Printing.

Plates of 400 subjects, issued in panes of 100.

1932-41 **Flat Plate Printing**

J25	D6 1c **claret** *(378,300) Jan. 2, 1932*	.25	.25
	Never hinged	.30	
	On cover		30.00
	P# block of 6	3.00	—
a.	Dry printing, red violet	.25	.25
	Never hinged	.35	
	On cover		32.50
	P# block of 6	3.00	—
J26	D6 2c **claret** *(413,800) Jan. 2, 1932*	.25	.25
	Never hinged	.30	
	On cover		22.50
	P# block of 6	3.00	—
J27	D6 5c **claret** *Jan. 2, 1932*	.35	.25
	Never hinged	.50	
	On cover		25.00
	P# block of 6	3.50	—
a.	Dry printing, red violet	1.00	.30
	Never hinged	1.40	
	On cover		22.50
	P# block of 6	10.00	—
J28	D6 10c **claret** *(400,600) Jan. 2, 1932*	1.75	1.50
	Never hinged	2.25	
	On cover		32.50
	P# block of 6	15.00	—
J29	D6 15c **claret** *Apr. 21, 1941*	1.25	1.00
	Never hinged	1.60	
	On cover		37.50
	P# block of 6	12.00	—
	Nos. J25-J29 (5)	3.85	3.25

See note after No. J14.

OFFICIAL STAMPS

See note at beginning of Air Post Official Stamps

Regular Issues of 1928-34 Overprinted in Black by the Panama Canal Press, Mount Hope, C.Z.

Type 1

Type 2

Type 1 — "PANAMA" 10mm long
Type 1a — "PANAMA" 9mm long
Type 2 — "PANAMA CANAL" 19-20mm long

1941, Mar. 31 **Unwmk.** *Perf. 11*

O1	A35 1c **yellow green,** type 1 *(87,198)*	2.00	.40
	Never hinged	3.00	
	On cover		70.00
O2	A45 3c **deep violet,** type 1 *(34,958)*	3.75	.75
	Never hinged	5.75	
	On cover		90.00
O3	A37 5c **blue,** type 2 *(19,105)*	*1,000.*	25.00
	On cover		*110.00*
O4	A38 10c **orange,** type 1 *(18,776)*	7.50	1.90
	Never hinged	11.50	
	On cover		200.00
O5	A41 15c **gray black,** type 1 *(16,888)*	15.00	2.25
	Never hinged	22.00	
	gray		2.25
	On cover		140.00
O6	A42 20c **olive brown,** type 1 *(20,264)*	17.50	2.75
	Never hinged	26.00	
	On cover		100.00
O7	A44 50c **lilac,** type 1 *(19,175)*	42.50	5.50
	Never hinged	65.00	
	rose lilac		5.50
	On cover		—
O8	A44 50c **rose lilac,** type 1a *(1000)*		550.00
	Nos. O1-O2,O4-O7 (6)	88.25	13.55

No. O3 exists with "O" directly over "N" of "PANAMA."

No. 139 Overprinted in Black

1947, Feb.

O9	A65 5c **deep blue,** type 1 *(21,639)*	12.50	3.75
	Never hinged	20.00	
	On cover		75.00

POST OFFICE SEALS

POS1

Issued in panes of 8 (2 x 4), without gum, imperforate outer margins.

1907 **Typo.** **Unwmk.** *Perf. 11½*

OX1	POS1 **blue**	35.00	*50.00*
	On cover		*1,500.*
	Block of 4	150.00	
	Pane of 8	*750.00*	

a. Wmkd. seal of U.S. in sheet 75.00 *125.00*
Block of 4 425.00
Pane of 8 *1,250.*

No. OX1 clichés are spaced 3½mm apart both horizontally and vertically.

1910

OX2 POS1 **ultramarine** 50.00 *65.00*
On cover *1,750.*
Block of 4, cliches ½mm apart horiz. and vert. 225.00
Pane of 8 *1,000.*
Block of 4, cliches 1½mm apart horiz., 4mm vert. 275.00
Pane of 8 *1,100.*
a. Wmkd. "Rolleston Mills" in sheet (½mm spacing) 80.00 *100.00*
Block of 4 350.00
b. Wmkd. U.S. Seal in sheet (1½mm x 4mm spacing) 85.00 *100.00*
Block of 4 350.00
Pane of 8 1,500.

POS2

Printed by the Panama Canal Press, Mount Hope, C.Z.

Issued in panes of 25 (5 x 5), without gum, imperforate outer margins at top, bottom, and left.

Rouletted 6 horizontally in color of seal, vertically without color

1917, Sept. 22

OX3 POS2 **slate violet** (shades) 4.00 4.00
On cover 250.00
Block of 4 17.50
Pane of 25 250.00
a. Wmkd. double lined letters in sheet ("Sylvania") 17.50 *25.00*
Block of 4 85.00
Pane of 25 600.00

POS3

Issued in panes of 20 (4 x 5), without gum, imperforate outer margins.

1945 ***Rouletted 6, without color***

OX4 POS3 **deep violet blue** (shades) 7.00 *10.00*
On cover 300.00
Block of 4 35.00
Pane of 20 300.00

POS4

Typographed by the Panama Canal Press.
Issued in panes of 32 (4 x 8), without gum, imperforate margins except at top of pane.

Size: 46x27mm
Seal Diameter: 13mm

1954, Mar. 8 **Unwmk.** ***Perf. 12½***

OX5 POS4 **black** *(16,000)* 5.00 5.00
On cover 200.00
Block of 4 20.00
Pane of 32 200.00
a. Wmkd. Seal of U. S. in sheet 12.50 12.50
Block of 4 60.00
Pane of 32 500.00
b. Double impression 45.00
c. As "a," double impression 75.00

POS5

Seal Diameter: 11½mm

1961, May 16 ***Perf. 12½***

OX6 POS5 **black** (48,000) 3.00 *5.00*
On cover 175.00
Block of 4 12.00
Pane of 32 125.00
a. Wmkd. Seal of U.S. in sheet 7.50 7.50
Block of 4 35.00
Pane of 32 300.00

No. OX6 exists in approximately equal proportions on three types of paper: very thin tissue-like, medium, and heavy opaque.

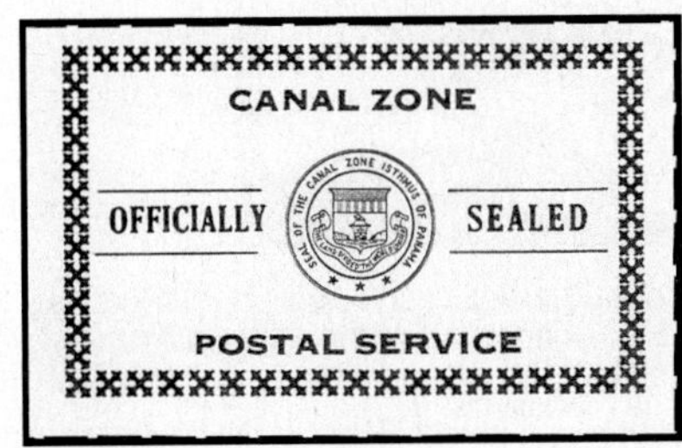

POS6

1974, July 1 ***Rouletted 5***

OX7 POS6 **black** 2.50 *5.00*
On cover 150.00
Block of 4 11.00
Pane of 32 100.00

ENVELOPES

Values for cut squares are for examples with fine margins on all sides. Values for unused entires are for those without printed or manuscript address. A "full corner" includes back and side flaps and commands a premium.

Types of 1909 Panama Stamps Overprinted in Black

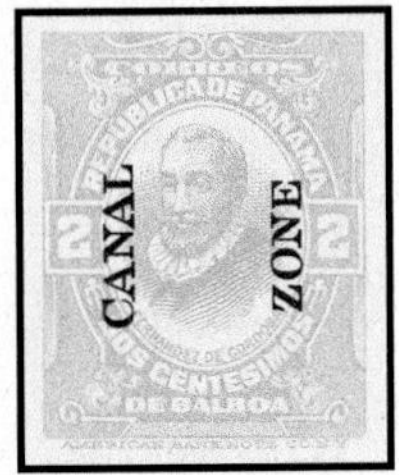

Envelopes of Panama Lithographed and Overprinted by American Bank Note Co.

1916, Apr. 24 **On White Paper**

U1 A18 1c **dk green & black** 14.00 10.00
Entire 90.00 35.00
a. Head and overprint only — —
Entire *1,750.* *2,000.*
b. Frame only — —
Entire *1,500.* *2,500.*
U2 A19 2c **carmine & black** 11.00 4.50
Entire 85.00 25.00
a. 2c **red & black** 12.50 4.50
Entire 85.00 45.00
b. Head and overprint only — —
Entire *750.00* *1,750.*
c. Frame only (red) — —
Entire *850.00* *1,750.*
d. Frame double (carmine) — —
Entire *2,250.* *2,250.*

Types of 1921 Panama Stamps Overprinted in Black

1921, Nov. 13 **On White Paper**

U3 A41 1c **dk green** 140.00 100.00
Entire 700.00 375.00
U4 A42 2c **red** 35.00 20.00
Entire 325.00 125.00

Arms of Panama — U5

Typographed and embossed by American Bank Note Co. with "CANAL ZONE" in color of stamp.

1923, Dec. 15 **On White Paper**

U5 U5 2c **carmine** 55.00 32.50
Entire 200.00 125.00

U.S. Nos. U420 and U429 Overprinted in Black by Bureau of Engraving and Printing, Washington, D.C.

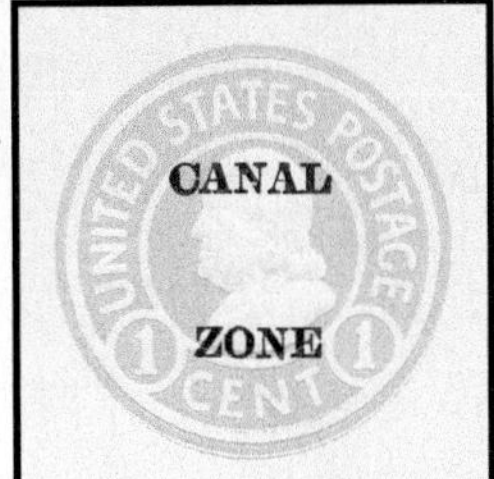

1924, July 1

U6 U92 1c **green** *(50,000)* 3.75 3.00
Entire 25.00 19.00
Entire, 1st day cancel 125.00
U7 U93 2c **carmine** *(100,000)* 5.00 3.00
Entire 35.00 19.00
Entire, 1st day cancel 125.00

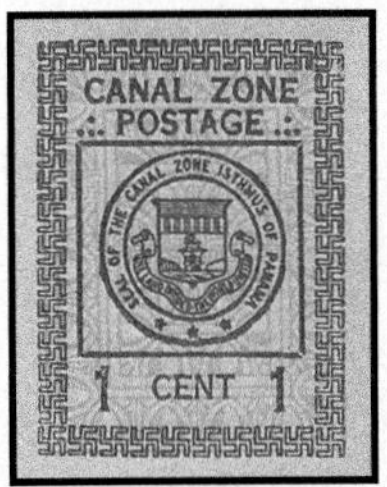

Seal of Canal Zone — U6

Printed by the Panama Canal Press, Mount Hope, C.Z.

1924, Oct. **On White Paper**

U8 U6 1c **green** *(205,000)* 2.00 1.00
Entire 24.00 15.00
U9 U6 2c **carmine** *(1,997,658)* .75 .40
Entire 27.50 15.00

Gorgas — U7

Goethals — U8

Typographed and Embossed by International Envelope Corp., Dayton, O.

1932, Apr. 8

U10 U7 1c **green** *(1,300,000)* .25 .25
Entire 3.00 1.10
Entire, 1st day cancel 35.00
U11 U8 2c **carmine** *(400,250)* .25 .25
Entire 3.50 1.75
Entire, 1st day cancel 35.00

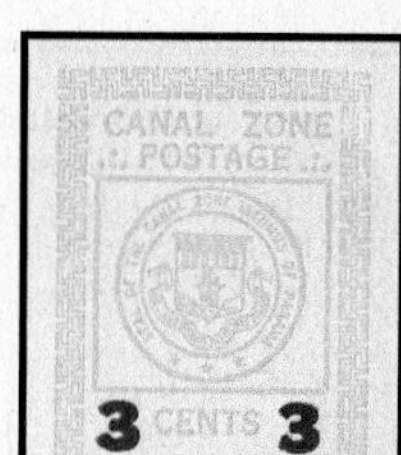

No. U9 Surcharged in Violet by Panama Canal Press, Mount Hope, C.Z. Numerals 3mm high

1932, July 20

U12 U6 3c on 2c **carmine** *(20,000)* 17.50 6.75
Entire 225.00 125.00

No. U11 Surcharged in Violet, Numerals 5mm high

1932, July 20

U13 U8 3c on 2c **carmine** *(320,000)* 2.00 1.00
Entire 25.00 15.00
Entire, 1st day cancel 75.00

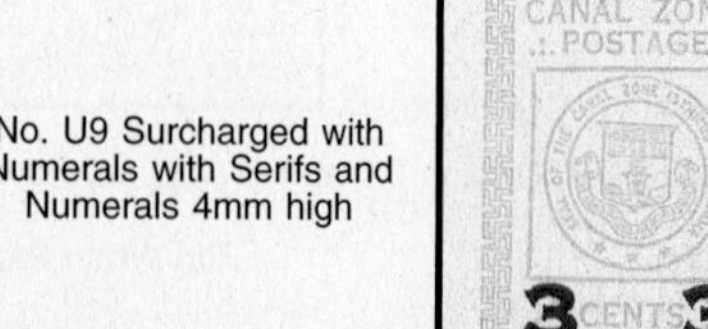

No. U9 Surcharged with Numerals with Serifs and Numerals 4mm high

1934, Jan. 17

U14 U6 3c on 2c **carmine** *(8,000)* 100.00 60.00
Entire 425.00 525.00
U15 U8 3c on 2c **carmine** (Numerals 5mm high) *(23,000)* 25.00 15.00
Entire 250.00 150.00

Typographed and Embossed by International Envelope Corp., Dayton, O.

1934, June 18

U16 U8 3c **purple** *(2,450,000)* .25 .25
Entire 1.20 1.40

1958, Nov. 1

U17 U8 4c **blue** *(596,725)* .25 .25
Entire 1.25 1.25
Entire, 1st day cancel, Cristobal 2.00

Surcharged in Blue

1969, Apr. 28

U18 U8 4c +1c **blue** *(93,850)* .25 *.25*
Entire 1.25 *1.60*
Entire, 1st day cancel 1.50
U19 U8 4c +2c **blue** *(23,125)* .50 *.65*
Entire 2.50 *4.00*
Entire, 1st day cancel 1.50

Ship Passing through Gaillard Cut — U9

Typographed and Embossed by United States Envelope Co., Williamsburg, Pa.

1971, Nov. 17

U20 U9 8c **emerald** *(121,500)* .25 *.30*
Entire .75 .65
Entire, 1st day cancel, Balboa *(9,650)* 1.50

Surcharged in Emerald

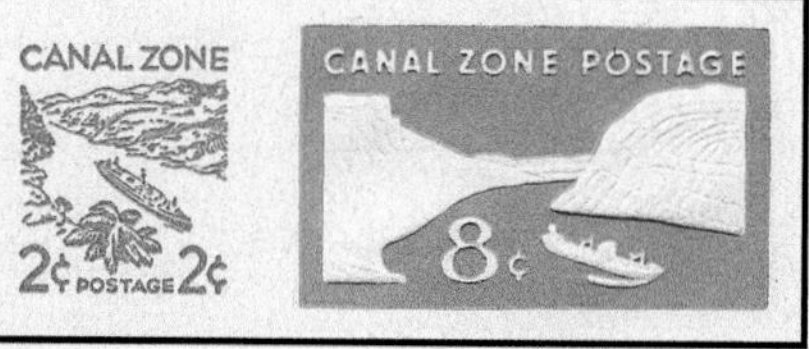

1974, Mar. 2

U21 U9 8c +2c **emerald** .30 *.35*
Entire 1.00 *2.00*
Entire, 1st day cancel 1.25

1976, Feb. 23

U22 U9 13c **violet** *(638,350)* .35 *.40*
Entire .85 .85
Entire, 1st day cancel, Balboa *(9,181)* 1.25

Surcharged at Left of Stamp in Violet as No. UX13

1978, July 5

U23 U9 13c +2c **violet** *(245,041)* .35 *.40*
Entire .85 *2.00*
Entire, 1st day cancel 1.25

AIR POST ENVELOPES

No. U9 Overprinted with Horizontal Blue and Red Bars Across Entire Face and Boxed Inscription in Lower Left with Nine Lines of Instructions

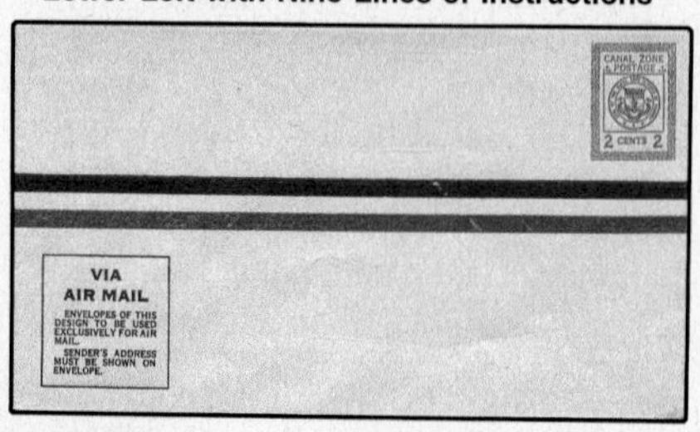

Overprinted by Panama Canal Press, Mount Hope. Additional adhesives required for air post rate.

1928, May 21

UC1 U6 2c **red,** entire *(15,000)* 135.00 65.00
First day cancel 175.00

No. U9 with Similar Overprint of Blue and Red Bars, and "VIA AIR MAIL" in Blue, At Left, No Boxed Inscription

1929

UC2 U6 2c **red,** entire *(60,200)* 65.00 27.50
a. Inscription centered *(10,000) Jan. 11* 325.00 190.00

Earliest known use of No. UC2 is Feb. 6.

DC-4 Skymaster UC1

Typographed and Embossed by International Envelope Corp., Dayton, O.

1949, Jan. 3

UC3 UC1 6c **blue** *(4,400,000)* .25 .25
Entire 4.00 3.50
Entire, 1st day cancel 2.00

1958, Nov. 1

UC4 UC1 7c **carmine** *(1,000,000)* .25 .25
Entire 4.00 3.50
Entire, 1st day cancel 1.50

No. U16 Surcharged at Left of Stamp and Imprinted "VIA AIR MAIL" in Dark Blue

Surcharged by Panama Canal Press, Mount Hope, C.Z.

1963, June 22

UC5 U8 3c + 5c **dp vio** *(105,000)* 1.00 1.00
Entire 6.00 *10.00*
Entire, 1st day cancel 5.00
a. Double surcharge *1,250.*

Jet Liner and Tail Assembly — UC2

Typographed and Embossed by International Envelope Corp., Dayton, O.

1964, Jan. 6

UC6 UC2 8c **deep carmine** *(600,000)* .35 .35
Entire 2.25 2.50
Entire, 1st day cancel, Balboa *(3,855)* 2.25

No. U17 Surcharged at Left of Stamp and Imprinted "VIA AIR MAIL" in Vermilion

Surcharged by Canal Zone Press, La Boca, C.Z.

1965, Oct. 15

UC7 U8 4c + 4c **blue** *(100,000)* .50 .40
Entire 4.50 *9.00*
Entire, 1st day cancel 5.00

Jet Liner and Tail Assembly — UC3

Typographed and Embossed by United States Envelope Co., Williamsburg, Pa.

1966, Feb.

UC8 UC3 8c **carmine** *(224,000)* .50 .45
Entire 5.00 5.00

Earliest known use: Feb. 23.

No. UC8 Surcharged at Left of Stamp as No. UX13 in Vermilion

Surcharged by Canal Zone Press, La Boca, C.Z.

1968, Jan. 18

UC9 UC3 8c + 2c **carmine** *(376,000)* .40 .35
Entire 2.75 *5.00*
Entire, 1st day cancel 4.50

No. UC7 Surcharged at Left of Stamp and Imprinted "VIA AIR MAIL" in Vermilion

Surcharged by Canal Zone Press, La Boca, C.Z.

1968, Feb. 12

UC10 U8 4c + 4c + 2c **blue** *(224,150)* .60 .50
Entire 2.25 *12.50*
Entire, 1st day cancel 5.00

Type of 1966

Typographed and Engraved by United States Envelope Co., Williamsburg, Pa.

1969, Apr. 1

Luminescent Ink

UC11 UC3 10c **ultramarine** *(448,000)* .60 .40
Entire 4.00 *5.00*
Entire, 1st day cancel, Balboa *(9,583)* 2.00

No. U17 Surcharged at Left of Stamp as Nos. UC5 and UX13, and Imprinted "VIA AIR MAIL" in Vermilion

1971, May 17

UC12 U8 4c + 5c + 2c **blue** *(55,775)* .75 .50
Entire 4.00 *12.50*
Entire, 1st day cancel 5.00

No. UC11 Surcharged in Ultramarine

1971, May 17

Luminescent Ink

UC13 UC3 10c + 1c **ultramarine** *(152,000)* .45 .40
Entire 4.00 *8.00*
Entire, 1st day cancel 3.50

Type of 1966

Typographed and Engraved by United States Envelope Co., Williamsburg, Pa.

1971, Nov. 17

UC14 UC3 11c **rose red** *(258,000)* .30 .25
Entire 1.25 1.25
Entire, 1st day cancel, Balboa *(3,451)* 1.50
a. 11c **carmine,** stamp tagged, *(395,000)* .30 .25
Entire 1.25 1.25
Entire, 1st day cancel, Balboa *(5,971)* 1.50

The red diamonds around the envelope edges are luminescent on both Nos. UC14 and UC14a. No. UC14 is size 10, No. UC14a size 6¾.

Surcharged at Left of Stamp in Rose Red as No. UX13

1974, Mar. 2

UC15 UC3 11c + 2c **carmine,** tagged *(305,000)* .35 .30
Entire 1.50 *3.00*
Entire, 1st day cancel 1.25
a. 11c + 2c **rose red,** untagged, *(87,000)* .35 .25
Entire 1.75 2.00

No. U21 with Additional Surcharge in Vermilion and Imprinted "VIA AIR MAIL" in Vermilion

1975, May 3

UC16 U9 8c + 2c + 3c **emerald** *(75,000)* .50 .30
Entire 1.25 *3.00*
Entire, 1st day cancel 1.50

REGISTRATION ENVELOPES

RE1

Panama Registration Envelope surcharged by Panama Canal Press, Mount Hope, C.Z.

1918, Oct. 8mm between CANAL & ZONE

UF1 RE1 10c on 5c **black & red,** *cream (10,000),* entire *1,750. 2,000.*
a. 9¼mm between CANAL & ZONE *(25,000),* entire ('19) *1,300. 2,000.*

Stamped envelopes inscribed "Diez Centesimos," surcharged with numerals "5" and with solid blocks printed over "Canal Zone," were issued by the Republic of Panama after being rejected by the Canal Zone. Parts of "Canal Zone" are often legible under the surcharge blocks. These envelopes exist without surcharge.

POSTAL CARDS

Values are for Entires

Map of Panama — PC1

Panama Card Lithographed by American Bank Note Co., revalued and surcharged in black by the Isthmian Canal Commission.

1907, Feb. 9

UX1 PC1 1c on 2c **carmine,** "CANAL" 15mm *(50,000)* 40. 25.
a. Double surcharge *1,500. 2,000.*
b. Double surcharge, one reading down *2,500.*
c. Triple surcharge, one reading down *3,250.*
d. "CANAL" 13mm *(10,000)* 250. 200.
e. As "d," double surcharge *2,400.*

Balboa — PC2

Panama card lithographed by Hamilton Bank Note Co. Overprinted in black by Isthmian Canal Commission.

At least six types of overprint, reading down.

1908, Mar. 3

UX2 PC2 1c **green & black,** "CANAL" 13mm *(295,000)* 190. 80.
a. Double overprint *1,750. 2,000.*
b. Triple overprint *1,750.* —
c. Period after "ZONE" *(40,000)* 200. 125.
d. "CANAL" 15mm *(30,000)* 200. 125.
e. "ZONE CANAL", reading up *3,500.*
f. Double overprint, one inverted at bottom left *3,000.*

Balboa — PC3

Lithographed by Hamilton Bank Note Co. Overprinted in Black by Panama Canal Press, Mount Hope, C.Z.

1910, Nov. 10

UX3 PC3 1c **green & black** *(40,000)* 190. 70.
a. Double overprint *3,500.*

This card, with overprint reading up, is actually the fourth of seven settings of UX2.

Balboa — PC4

Lithographed and Overprinted by American Bank Note Co.

1913, Mar. 27

UX4 PC4 1c **green & black** *(634,000)* 160. 60.

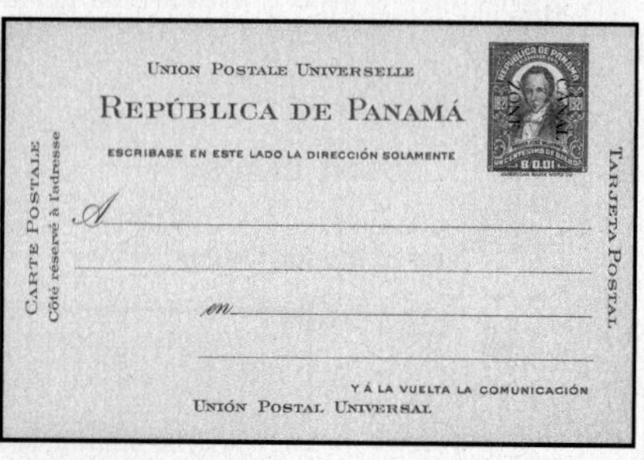

Design of Canal Zone Envelopes Overprinted in black by the American Bank Note Co.

1921, Oct.

UX5 U3 1c **green** 1,000. 450.

Typographed and embossed by American Bank Note Co. with "CANAL ZONE" in color of stamp.

1924, Jan.

UX6 U5 1c **green** 1,050. *1,100.*

U.S. No. UX27 Overprinted by U.S. Gov't. Printing Office at Washington, D.C.

1924, July 1

UX7 PC17 1c **green,** *buff (Jefferson) (50,000)* 80. 35.

Design of Canal Zone Envelope Printed by Panama Canal Press.

1925, Jan.

UX8 U6 1c **green,** *buff (25,000)* 75. 35.
a. Background only *1,800.*

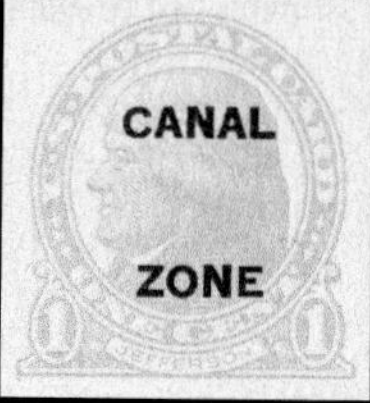

U.S. No. UX27 Overprinted

1925, May

UX9 PC17 1c **green,** *buff (Jefferson) (850,000)* 8.50 5.00

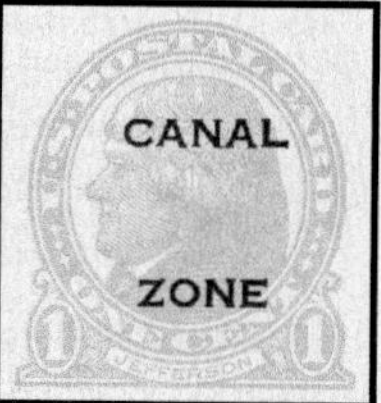

U.S. No. UX27 Overprinted

1935, Oct.

UX10 PC17 1c **green,** *buff (Jefferson) (2,900,000)* 1.80 1.80
a. Double overprint *1,800.*

Used values are for contemporaneous usage without additional postage applied.

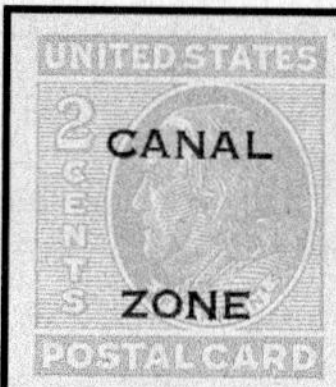

U.S. No. UX38 Overprinted in Black

1952, May 1

UX11 PC22 2c **carmine rose,** *buff (Franklin) (800,000)* 2.00 2.00
1st day cancel, Balboa Heights 3.50

Ship in Lock — PC5

Printed by Bureau of Engraving & Printing, Washington, D.C.

1958, Nov. 1

UX12 PC5 3c **dark blue,** *buff (335,116)* 2.00 *3.00*
First day cancel, Cristobal 1.25

No. UX12 Surcharged at Left of Stamp in Green by Panama Canal Press, Mount Hope, C.Z.

1963, July 27

UX13 PC5 3c + 1c **dark blue,** *buff (78,000)* 4.00 *7.50*
First day cancel 3.50
a. Surcharge inverted at bottom left *750.00*

Ship Passing through Panama Canal — PC6

Printed by Panama Canal Press, Mount Hope, C.Z.

1964, Dec. 1

UX14 PC6 4c **deep violet blue,** *buff (74,200)* 3.75 *7.50*
1st day cancel, Cristobal *(19,260)* 3.50

Ship in Lock (Towing locomotive at right redrawn) — PC7

Printed by Bureau of Engraving & Printing, Washington, D.C.

1965, Aug. 12

UX15 PC7 4c **emerald** *(95,500)* 1.10 *2.00*
1st day cancel, Cristobal *(20,366)* 1.00

No. UX15 Surcharged at Left of Stamp in Green

Surcharged by Canal Zone Press, La Boca, C.Z.

1968, Feb. 12

UX16 PC7 4c + 1c **emerald** *(94,775)* 1.10 *4.00*
First day cancel 1.00

Ship-in-Lock Type of 1965

1969, Apr. 1

UX17 PC7 5c **light ultramarine** *(63,000)* 1.00 *2.50*
1st day cancel, Balboa *(11,835)* 1.00

No. UX17 Surcharged at Left of Stamp in Light Ultramarine as No. UX13

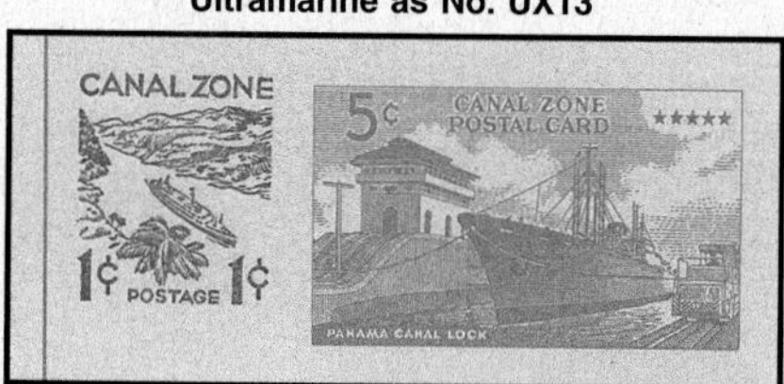

1971, May 24

UX18 PC7 5c + 1c **light ultramarine** *(100,500)* .90 *4.00*
First day cancel 1.00

Ship-in-Lock Type of 1965

Printed by Bureau of Engraving & Printing, Washington, D.C.

1974, Feb. 11

UX19 PC7 8c **brown** *(90,895)* 1.00 *2.00*
1st day cancel, Balboa *(10,375)* 1.00

No. UX19 Surcharged at Left of Stamp in Brown as No. UX13

1976, June 1

UX20 PC7 8c + 1c **brown** *(60,249)* .65 *5.00*
First day cancel 1.00

No. UX19 Surcharged at Left of Stamp in Brown

1978, July 5

UX21 PC7 8c + 2c **brown** *(74,847)* 1.00 *5.00*
First day cancel 1.00

AIR POST POSTAL CARDS

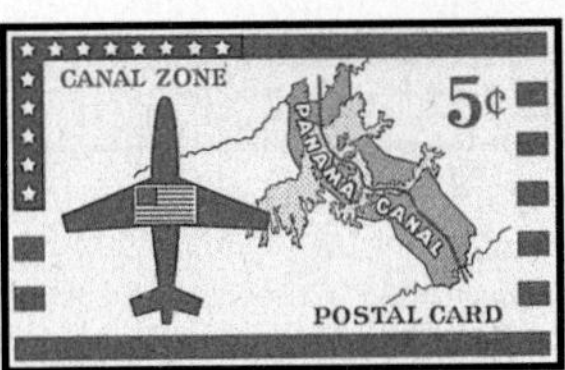

Plane, Flag and Map — APC1

Printed by Bureau of Engraving & Printing, Washington, D.C.

1958, Nov. 1

UXC1 APC1 5c **blue & carmine rose** *(104,957)* 3.00 *7.50*
1st day cancel, Balboa 3.75

No. UXC1 Surcharged at Left of Stamp in Green

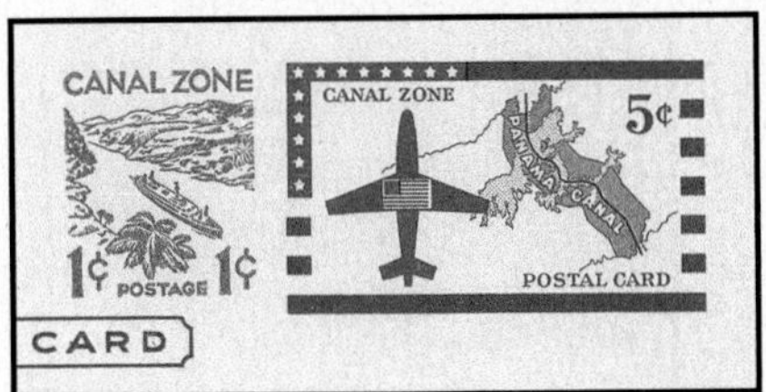

Surcharge by Panama Canal Press, Mount Hope, C.Z.

1963, July 27

UXC2 APC1 5c + 1c **blue & carmine rose** *(48,000)* 8.00 *20.00*
a. Inverted surcharge *1,500.*
First day cancel 5.00

No. UX15 Surcharged at Left of Stamp and Imprinted "AIR MAIL" in Orange Red

1965, Aug. 18

UXC3 PC7 4c + 2c **emerald** *(41,700)* 3.25 *20.00*
First day cancel 6.00

No. UX15 Surcharged at Left of Stamp as No. UC5 and Imprinted "AIR MAIL" in Vermilion by Canal Zone Press, La Boca, C.Z.

1968, Feb. 12

UXC4 PC7 4c + 4c **emerald** *(60,100)* 2.50 *18.00*
First day cancel 6.00

No. UX17 Surcharged at Left of Stamp and Imprinted "AIR MAIL" in Vermilion

1971, May 24

UXC5 PC7 5c + 4c **light ultramarine** *(68,000)* .90 *18.00*
First day cancel 6.00

ESSAYS

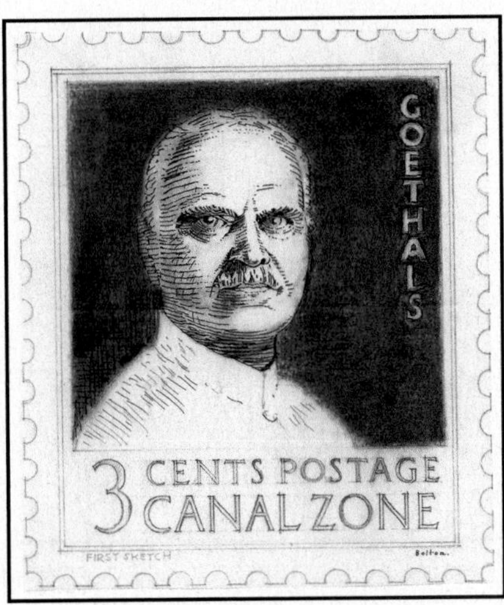

117-E1

Design size: 133 by 153mm
Preliminary pencil, ink and crayon drawing on tracing paper of adopted design.

117-E1 3c Drawing on tracing paper, black *1,000.*

117-E2

Design size: 135 by 145mm
Preliminary pencil, ink and charcoal drawing of adopted design.

117-E2 3c Drawing on tracing paper, black *750.00*

117-E3

Design size: 134 by 157mm
Late pencil, ink and charcol drawing of adopted design with marginal routing notes.

117-E3 3c Drawing on tracing paper, black *1,000.*

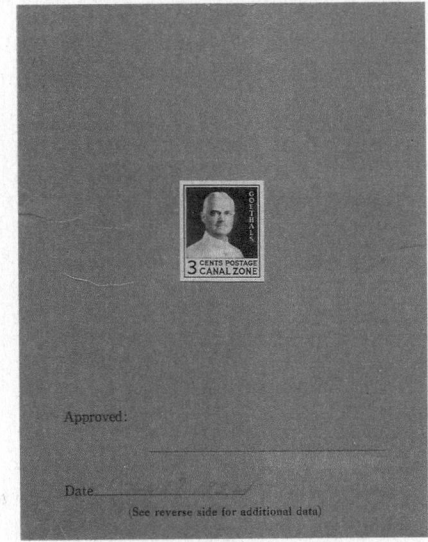

117-E4

Design size: 19 by 22mm, 102 by 128mm card
Photo of wash drawing of adopted design with "Duplicate Model of 3¢ Canal Zone Postage Stamp" on paper covering.

117-E4 3c Model on thick gray card, black *1,000.*

117-E5

Design size: 133 by 153mm
Preliminary pencil drawing of unadopted design.

117-E5 3c Drawing on tracing paper, black —

117-E6

Design size: 19 by 22mm each design
Two rough stamp-sized pencil and ink drawings similar to adopted design on tan cardstock.

117-E6 3c Drawings on tan cardstock, violet *900.00*

120-E1

Design size: 21.5 by 36mm
Reduced photo of composite photo and lettering of unadopted design.

120-E1 1c Model on gray card, black *800.00*

121-E1

Design size: 21.5 by 36mm
Reduced photo of composite photo and lettering of unadopted design.

121-E1 2c Model on gray card, black *800.00*

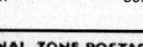

123-E1

Design size: 21.5 by 36mm
Reduced photo of composite photo and lettering of unadopted design.

123-E1 5c Model on gray card, black *800.00*

133-E1

Design size: 21.5 by 36mm
Reduced photo of composite photo and lettering of unadopted design of a steam shovel.

133-E1 20c Model on gray card, black *800.00*

133-E2

Design size: 21.5 by 36mm

Reduced photo of composite photo and lettering of unadopted design showing a ship in the canal.

133-E2 20c Model on gray card, black *800.00*

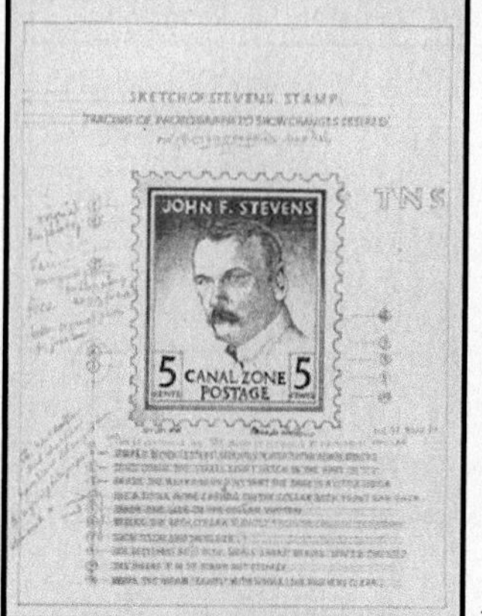

139-E1

Design size: 86 by 102mm
Photostatic working model close to issued design with extensive notes.

139-E1 5c Large model with requested changes *1,500.*

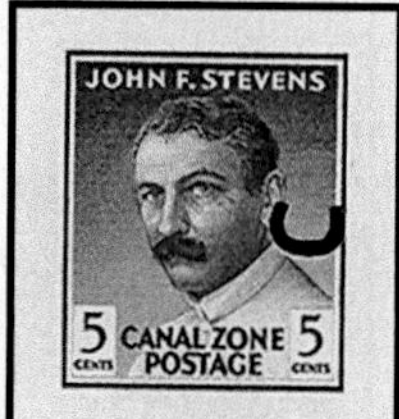

139-E2

Design size: 19 by 22mm
Large die essay of adopted design with more extensive cross hatching and other differences from issued stamp; horse-shoe shaped punch and sunk on card.

139-E2 5c Large die essay *1,500.*

142-E1

Design size: 100 by 120mm
Signed charcoal drawing on paper of close to issued design.

142-E1 3c Drawing on paper, black *600.00*

143-E1

Design size: 100 by 120mm
Signed charcoal drawing on paper of close to issued design.

143-E1 6c Drawing on paper, black *600.00*

144-E1

Design size: 100 by 120mm
Signed charcoal drawing on paper of close to issued design.

144-E1 12c Drawing on paper, black *600.00*

145-E1

Design size: 100 by 120mm
Signed charcoal drawing on paper of close to issued design.

145-E1 18c Drawing on paper, black *600.00*

146-E1

Design size: 100 by 118mm
Drawing of a design similar to issued stamp.

146-E1 5c Drawing —

148-E1

Design size: 108 by 66mm
Drawing on card in shades of green and black of unadopted design.

148-E1 4c Drawing on card, green and black *400.00*

148-E2

Design size: 108 by 71mm
Drawing on card in shades of green and black of unadopted design.

148-E2 4c Drawing on card, green and black *400.00*

148-E3

Design size: 108 by 71mm
Drawing on card in shades of green and black of unadopted design.

148-E3 4c Drawing on card, green and black *400.00*

156-E1

Design size: 71 by 44mm

Drawing in blue, dark green and bister on thin white card; close to adopted design.

156-E1 4c Drawing on card, multicolor *750.00*

ENVELOPES

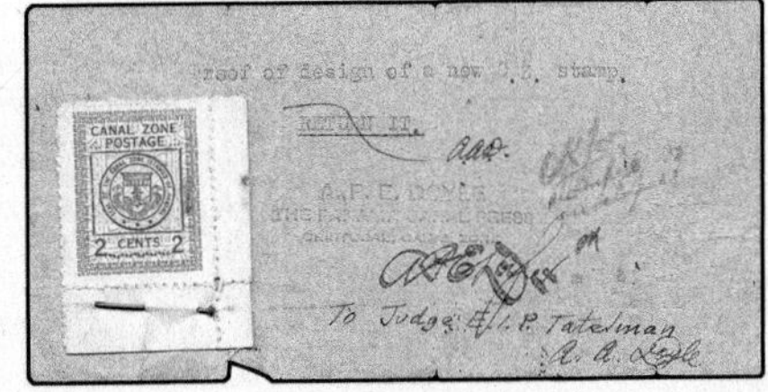

U9-E1

Design size: 21 by 27.5mm
Perforated indicia from issued stamped envelope pinned to card, not adopted.

U9-E1 2c Perforated indicia on pink card, carmine *1,000.*

PROOFS

1928-40

106TC1 2c Large die on India paper
a. **black** *1,300.*
113P2 30c **brn blk,** small die on yellowish wove paper 975.

1934

117P1 3c **dp violet,** large die on India paper *(8)* 475.

1939

120P1 1c **yellow green,** large die on India paper *1,300.*
120P2 1c **yel grn,** small die on yellowish wove paper 875.
121P2 2c **rose car,** small die on yellowish wove paper 875.
122P1 3c **purple,** large die on India paper *1,300.*
122P2 3c **purple,** small die on yellowish wove paper 875.
123P1 5c **dk blue,** large die on India paper *1,300.*
123P2 5c **dk blue,** small die on yellowish wove paper 875.
124P2 6c **red org,** small die on yellowish wove paper 875.
125P2 7c **black,** small die on yellowish wove paper 875.
126P1 8c **green,** large die on India paper *1,300.*
126P2 8c **grn,** small die on yellowish wove paper 875.
127P1 10c **ultra,** large die on India paper *1,300.*
127P2 10c **ultra,** small die on yellowish wove paper 875.
128P1 11c **bl grn,** large die on India paper *1,300.*
128P2 11c **bl grn,** small die on yellowish wove paper 875.
129P1 12c **brn car,** large die on India paper *1,300.*
129P2 12c **brn car,** small die on yellowish wove paper 875.
130P2 14c **dk vio,** small die on yellowish wove paper 875.
131P2 15c **ol grn,** small die on yellowish wove paper 875.
132P2 18c **rose pink,** small die on yellowish wove paper 875.
133P1 20c **brown,** large die on India paper *1,300.*
133P2 20c **brn,** small die on yellowish wove paper 875.
134P1 25c **orange,** large die on India paper *1,300.*
134P2 25c **org,** small die on yellowish wove paper 875.
135P1 50c **violet brown,** large die on India paper *1,300.*
135P2 50c **vio brn,** small die on yellowish wove paper 875.

1946-48

136P1 ½c **brt red,** large die on India paper *1,300.*
137P1 1½c **chocolate,** large die on India paper *1,300.*
139P1 5c **dp blue,** large die on India paper *1,300.*
140P1 25c **yellow green,** large die on India paper *1,300.*
141P1 10c **black,** large die on India paper *825.*

1949

142P1 3c **blue,** large die on India paper *1,150.*
143P1 6c **violet,** large die on India paper *1,150.*
144P1 12c **brt bl grn,** large die on India paper *1,150.*
145P1 18c **dp red lilac,** large die on India paper *1,150.*

1951

146P1 10c **carmine,** large die on India paper *1,500.*

1955

147P1 3c **violet,** large die on India paper *1,500.*

Air Post

1931-49

C6P1 4c **red violet,** large die on India paper *1,600.*
C7P1 5c **lt green,** large die on India paper *1,600.*
C8P1 6c **yel brown,** large die on India paper *1,600.*
C13TC1 40c Large die on India paper
a. **orange** *1,600.*

1939

C15P2 5c **grnsh blk,** small die on yellowish wove paper 925.
C15TC1 5c Large die on India paper
a. **scarlet** *1,300.*
C16P1 10c **dull vio,** large die on India paper *1,300.*
C16P2 10c **dull vio,** small die on yellowish wove paper 925.
C17P1 15c **lt brn,** large die on India paper *1,300.*
C17P2 15c **lt brn,** small die on yellowish wove paper 925.
C18P2 25c **blue,** small die on yellowish wove paper 925.
C19P1 30c **rose car,** large die on India paper *1,300.*
C19P2 30c **rose car,** small die on yellowish wove paper 925.
C20P1 $1 **green,** large die on India paper *1,300.*
C20P2 $1 **grn,** small die on yellowish wove paper 925.

1951

C21P1 4c **red vio,** large die on India paper *1,300.*

Only No. 117P1 has more than two examples reported in private collections.

SPECIMENS

Issues of the American Bank Note Co.

Panama stamps overprinted "CANAL ZONE," handstamped SPECIMEN in three fonts and having a 2.5mm round hole punched in the lower right area.

Where a stamp has more than one type of SPECIMEN overprint, the types are listed chronologically by production dates, not alphabetically.

All SPECIMEN handstamps are red unless otherwise indicated. Almost all examples have a pencil notation on reverse giving the 'F' number (ABNCo. order number), sheet position, and sometimes a sheet designation.

Booklet pane specimens from uncut sheets are usually collected in units of two full panes of six with gutter between or in pairs with gutter between. Because most examples are still in a few large multiples and few have been sold publicly, values for these items are not given.

A few assembled Specimen booklets are known with a red handstamped order number on the front cover. Some examples contain panes that are punched and handstamped; other examples have unmarked panes indistinguishable from those of issued booklets if they are removed from their marked covers.

Uncut booklet covers are known, some with a punched "Specimen A. B. N. Co."

Number in parenthesis after denomination and color is quantity known.

SPECIMEN Type A; 19.8 to 20mm long

SPECIMEN Type B

SPECIMEN Type C; 13.8 to 14.2mm long

Type B subtypes: a, 11.2 to 11.3mm long. b, 13.7 to 13.8mm long. c, 14 to 14.3mm long. d, 15.3mm long.

1909-10 **Portraits Type I**

31S A 1c **dark green & black** *(194)* 25.00
31S C 1c **dark green & black** *(98)* 25.00
32S C 2c **vermilion & black** *(400)* 25.00
33S C 5c **deep blue & black** *(400)* 25.00
34S A 8c **violet & black** *(300)* 25.00
35S A 10c **violet & black** *(100)*

Although known to have existed, the sheet of No. 35S has disappeared. No examples of No. 35S are currently reported in collections.

1911-14 **Maps**

36S C 10c on 13c **gray,** without 10c surcharge *(289)* 35.00
a. Inverted SPECIMEN *(3)* —
b. Double SPECIMEN *(2)* —
37S A 10c **gray** *(299)* 25.00

1912-16 **Portraits Type II**

38S A 1c **green & black** *(100)* 35.00
38S Ba 1c **green & black** *(200)* 25.00
38S Bb 1c **green & black** *(300)* 25.00
38S Bc 1c **green & black** *(300)* 25.00
39S A 2c **vermilion & black,** SPECIMEN in blue *(397)* 25.00
a. Inverted CANAL —
39S A 2c **vermilion & black** *(300)* 25.00
39S Bb 2c **vermilion & black,** SPECIMEN in blue *(300)* 25.00

39S C 2c **vermilion & black** *(300)* 25.00
39S Bc 2c **vermilion & black**, SPECIMEN in blue *(300)* 25.00
39cS Bc 2c **vermilion & black**, SPECIMEN in blue *(74 panes)* —
40S A 5c **deep blue & black** *(400)* 25.00
40S Ba 5c **deep blue & black** *(200)* 25.00
40S C 5c **deep blue & black** *(500)* 25.00
41S Bc 10c **violet & black** *(300)* 25.00

1915-17 Ninth Series Pictorials

42S Bb 1c **dark green & black** *(293)* 30.00
43S Bb 2c **carmine & black** *(293)* 30.00
44S Bb 5c **blue & black** *(293)* 30.00
45S Bb 10c **orange & black** *(293)* 30.00
49S Bc 12c **purple & black** *(300)* 30.00
50S Bc 15c **bright blue & black** *(300)* 30.00
51S Bc 24c **yellow brown & black** *(300)* 30.00

1918-20 Portraits Type IV

52S Bb 1c **green & black** *(300)* 25.00
52S Bc 1c **green & black** *(300)* 25.00
52bS Bc 1c **green & black** *(48 panes)* —
53S Bc 2c **vermilion & black**, SPECIMEN in blue *(600)* 25.00
a. Double SPECIMEN *(1)* —
53cS Bc 2c **vermilion & black**, *(8 panes)* —
a. 13mm different font SPECIMEN *(2)* —
53cS Bb 2c **vermilion & black**, *(24 panes)* —
53cS Bd 2c **vermilion & black**, *(48 panes)* —
a. Missing SPECIMEN *(2)* —
b. Missing punch hole *(1)* —
54S Bb 5c **blue & black** *(300)* 25.00

1920-21 Portraits Type V

55S Bb 1c **light green & black** *(300)* 25.00
55eS Bb 1c **light green & black** *(36 panes)* —
56S Bb 2c **orange vermilion & black** *(400)* 25.00
56S Ba 2c **orange vermilion & black** *(300)* 25.00
56gS Bb 2c **orange vermilion & black** *(48 panes)* —
57S Bb 5c **deep blue & black** *(300)* 25.00
a. Double SPECIMEN *(1)* —

1920 Ninth Series High Value Pictorials

58S Bd 50c **orange & black** *(285)* 60.00
59S Bd $1 **dark violet & black** *(273)* 60.00
a. Double SPECIMEN *(1)* —

1921 Independence Issue

60S Ba 1c **green** *(300)* 35.00
60bS Ba 1c **green** *(46 panes)* —
61S Ba 2c **carmine** *(300)* 35.00
61fS Ba 2c **carmine** *(47 panes)* —
62S Ba 5c **blue** *(300)* 35.00
63S Ba 10c **violet** *(200)* 35.00
64S Ba 15c **light blue** *(200)* 35.00
65S Ba 24c **black brown** *(200)* 35.00
66S Ba 50c **black** *(200)* 35.00

1924 Coat of Arms

68S Ba 1c **dark green** *(300)* 25.00
69S Ba 2c **carmine** *(194)* 25.00

The following unissued stamps have SPECIMEN Type Ba:

A34 1c **dark green** booklet pane *(69 panes)* —
A34 2c **carmine** booklet pane *(71 panes)* —
A34 5c **dark blue** *(300)* 45.00
A34 10c **dark violet** *(300)* 45.00
A34 12c **olive green** *(300)* 45.00
A34 15c **ultramarine** *(300)* 45.00
A34 24c **yellow brown** *(300)* 45.00
A34 50c **orange** *(300)* 45.00
a. Double SPECIMEN *(1)* —
A34 1b **black** *(300)* 45.00
a. Double SPECIMEN *(3)* —

POSTAGE DUES

1915 Blue Overprints

J4S A 1c **olive brown** *(300)* 30.00
J5S Bb 2c **olive brown** *(100)* 35.00
J5S A 2c **olive brown** *(200)* 25.00
J6S Ba 10c **olive brown** *(100)* 60.00

1915 Red Surcharges

J8S Bc 2c on 2c **olive brown** *(300)* 25.00
J8S Bb 2c on 2c **olive brown** *(300)* 25.00
J9S Bc 10c on 10c **olive brown** *(300)* 30.00

The following unissued stamp with a thin "4" surcharge, unlike the thick "4" found on No. J11, has SPECIMEN Type Bb:

D5 4c on 4c **olive brown** *(300)* 25.00

1922 Blue Type V Overprint

J11CS Ba 1c **dark olive brown** *(300)* 25.00

CUBA

After the U.S. battleship "Maine" was destroyed in Havana harbor with a loss of 266 lives in February, 1898, the United States demanded the withdrawal of Spanish troops from Cuba. The Spanish-American War followed. With the peace treaty of Dec. 10, 1898, Spain relinquished Cuba to the United States in trust for its inhabitants. On Jan. 1, 1899, Spanish authority was succeeded by U.S. military rule which lasted until May 20, 1902, when Cuba, as a republic, assumed self-government.

The listings in this catalogue cover the U.S. Administration issue of 1899, the Republic's 1899-1902 issues under U.S. military rule and the Puerto Principe issue of provincial provisionals.

Values for Nos. 176-220 are for stamps in the grade of fine and in sound condition where such exist. Values for Nos. 221-UX2b are for very fine examples.

100 CENTS = 1 DOLLAR

The basic stamps used for overprinting at Puerto Principe are normally poorly centered. Values for Nos. 176-220 are for stamps with fine centering, as typically found. Furthermore, values are for stamps accompanied by certificates issued by competent experts. Convincing fakes and counterfeits are plentiful.

Values for Nos. 221-J4 are for very fine examples.

Puerto Principe Issue

In December, 1898, Puerto Principe, a provincial capital now called Camagüey, ran short of 1c, 2c, 3c, 5c and 10c stamps. The Postmaster ordered Cuban stamps to be surcharged on Dec. 19, 1898.

The surcharging was done to horizontal strips of five stamps, so vertical pairs and blocks do not exist. Five types are found in each setting, and five printings were made. Counterfeits are plentiful.

First Printing

Black Surcharge, 17½mm high

Surcharge measures 17½mm high and is roughly printed in dull black ink.

HABILITADO 2 cents. — Position 1
HABILITADO 2 cents. — Position 2
HABILITADO 2 cents. — Position 3
HABILITADO 2 cents. — Position 4
HABILITADO 2 cents. — Position 5

Position 1 — No serif at right of "t"
Position 2 — Thin numeral except on 1c on 1m No. 176
Position 3 — Broken right foot of "n"
Position 4 — Up-stroke of "t" broken
Position 5 — Broken "DO"

This printing consisted of the following stamps:

176	1c on 1m orange brown, Pos. 1, 2, 3, 4 and 5
178	2c on 2m orange brown, Pos. 1, 3, 4 and 5
179	2c on 2m orange brown, Pos. 2
180	3c on 3m orange brown, Pos. 1, 3, 4 and 5
181	3c on 3m orange brown, Pos. 2
188	5c on 5m orange brown, Pos. 1, 3, 4 and 5
189	5c on 5m orange brown, Pos. 2

Second Printing

Black Surcharge, 17½mm high

This printing was from the same setting as used for the first printing, but the impression is much clearer and the ink quite shiny.

The printing consisted of the following stamps:

179F	3c on 2m orange brown, Pos. 1, 3, 4 and 5
179G	3c on 2m orange brown, Pos. 2
182	5c on 1m orange brown, Pos. 1, 3, 4 and 5
183	5c on 1m orange brown, Pos. 2
184	5c on 2m orange brown, Pos. 1, 3, 4 and 5
185	5c on 2m orange brown, Pos. 2
186	5c on 3m orange brown, Pos. 1, 3, 4 and 5
187	5c on 3m orange brown, Pos. 2
188	5c on 5m orange brown, Pos. 1, 3, 4 and 5
189	5c on 5m orange brown, Pos. 2
190	5c on ½m blue green, Pos. 1, 3, 4 and 5
191	5c on ½m blue green, Pos. 2

Third Printing

Red Surcharge, 20mm high

The same setting as for the first and second was used for the third printing. The 10c denomination first appeared in this printing and position 2 of that value has numerals same as on positions 1, 3, 4 and 5, while position 4 has broken "1" in "10."

The printing consisted of the following stamps:

196	3c on 1c black violet, Pos. 1, 3, 4 and 5
197	3c on 1c black violet, Pos. 2
198	5c on 1c black violet, Pos. 1, 3, 4 and 5
199	5c on 1c black violet, Pos. 2
200	10c on 1c black violet, Pos. 1, 2, 3 and 5
200a	10c on 1c black violet, Pos. 4

Fourth Printing

Black Surcharge, 19½mm high

The same type as before but spaced between so that the surcharge is 2mm taller. Clear impression, shiny ink.

HABILITADO 1 cents. — Position 1
HABILITADO 1 cents. — Position 2
HABILITADO 1 cents. — Position 3
HABILITADO 1 cents. — Position 4
HABILITADO 1 cents. — Position 5

Position 1 — No serif at right of "t"
Position 2 — Broken "1" on No. 177
Position 2 — Thin numerals on 5c stamps
Position 3 — Broken right foot of "n"
Position 4 — Up-stroke of "t" broken
Position 4 — Thin numeral on 3c stamps
Position 5 — Broken "DO"

This printing consisted of the following stamps:

177	1c on 1m orange brn, Pos. 1, 3, 4 and 5
177a	1c on 1m orange brn, Pos. 2
179B	3c on 1m orange brn, Pos. 1, 2, 3 and 5
179D	3c on 1m orange brn, Pos. 4
183B	5c on 1m orange brn, Pos. 1, 3, 4 and 5
189C	5c on 5m orange brn, Pos. 1, 3, 4 and 5
192	5c on ½m blue green, Pos. 1, 3, 4 and 5
193	5c on ½m blue green, Pos. 2

Fifth Printing

Black Surcharge, 19½mm high

HABILITADO 3 cents. — Position 1

HABILITADO 3 cents. — Position 2

HABILITADO 3 eents. — Position 3

HABILITADO 3 cents. — Position 4

HABILITADO 3 cents. — Position 5

Position 1	— Nick in bottom of "e"and lower serif of "s"
Position 2	— Normal surcharge
Position 3	— "eents"
Position 4	— Thin numeral
Position 5	— Nick in upper part of right stroke of "n"

This printing consisted of the following stamps:

201	3c on 1m blue green, Pos. 1, 2 and 5
201b	3c on 1m blue green, Pos. 3
202	3c on 1m blue green, Pos. 4
203	3c on 2m blue green, Pos. 4
203a	3c on 2m blue green, Pos. 3
204	3c on 2m blue green, Pos. 4
205	3c on 3m blue green, Pos. 1, 2 and 5
205b	3c on 3m blue green, Pos. 3
206	3c on 3m blue green, Pos. 4
211	5c on 1m blue green, Pos. 1, 2 and 5
211a	5c on 1m blue green, Pos. 3
212	5c on 1m blue green, Pos. 4
213	5c on 2m blue green, Pos. 1, 2 and 5
213a	5c on 2m blue green, Pos. 3
214	5c on 2m blue green, Pos. 4
215	5c on 3m blue green, Pos. 1, 2 and 5
215a	5c on 3m blue green, Pos. 3
216	5c on 3m blue green, Pos. 4
217	5c on 4m blue green, Pos. 1, 2 and 5
217a	5c on 4m blue green, Pos. 3
218	5c on 4m blue green, Pos. 4
219	5c on 8m blue green, Pos. 1, 2 and 5
219b	5c on 8m blue green, Pos. 3
220	5c on 8m blue green, Pos. 4

Counterfeits exist of all Puerto Principe surcharges. Illustrations have been altered to discourage further counterfeiting.

Regular Issues of Cuba of 1896 and 1898 Surcharged

a

b

Numeral in ( ) after color indicates printing.

Black Surcharge on Nos. 156-158, 160

1898-99

176	(a)	1 cent on 1m **orange brn** (1)	100.00	60.00
177	(b)	1 cents on 1m **org brn** (4)	600.00	115.00
a.		Broken figure "1"	*3,000.*	275.00
b.		Inverted surcharge		*500.00*
d.		Same as "a" inverted		*1,500.*

c

d

178	(c)	2c on 2m **orange brown** (1)	65.00	62.50
a.		Inverted surcharge	500.00	100.00
179	(d)	2c on 2m **orange brown** (1)	82.50	77.50
a.		Inverted surcharge	—	*500.00*

k

l

179B	(k)	3c on 1m **orange brown** (4)	300.	175.
c.		Double surcharge	—	*3,000.*

An unused example is known with "cents" omitted.

179D	(l)	3c on 1m **orange brown** (4)	*1,350.*	*675.00*

e

f

179F	(e)	3c on 2m **orange brown** (2)		*1,500.*

Value is for example with minor faults.

179G	(f)	3c on 2m **orange brown** (2)	—	*2,000.*

Value is for example with minor faults.

180	(e)	3c on 3m **orange brown** (1)	150.	100.
a.		Inverted surcharge		375.
181	(f)	3c on 3m **orange brown** (1)	600.	400.
a.		Inverted surcharge		*750.*

g

h

i

j

182	(g)	5c on 1m **orange brown** (2)	1,000.	165.
a.		Inverted surcharge	—	*1,000.*
183	(h)	5c on 1m **orange brown** (2)	*1,500.*	*1,000.*
a.		Inverted surcharge	—	*1,500.*
184	(g)	5c on 2m **orange brown** (2)	*1,000.*	275.
185	(h)	5c on 2m **orange brown** (2)	1,500.	600.
186	(g)	5c on 3m **orange brown** (2)	1,500.	350.
a.		Inverted surcharge	1,200.	700.
187	(h)	5c an 3m **orange brown** (2)	—	*1,000.*
a.		Inverted surcharge	—	*1,000.*
188	(g)	5c on 5m **orange brown** (1) (2)	145.	230.
a.		Inverted surcharge	—	750.
b.		Double surcharge	—	—
189	(h)	5c on 5m **orange brown** (1) (2)	*3,000.*	425.
a.		Inverted surcharge	*3,000.*	*900.*
b.		Double surcharge	—	—
189C	(i)	5c on 5m **orange brown** (4)		*7,500.*

Values for Nos. 188, 189 are for the first printing.

No. 191

Black Surcharge on No. P25

190	(g)	5c on ½m **blue green** (2)	375.	115.
a.		Inverted surcharge	1,000.	210.
b.		Pair, one without surcharge		500.
191	(h)	5c on ½m **blue green** (2)	1,000.	275.
a.		Inverted surcharge		*1,000.*
192	(i)	5c on ½m **blue green** (4)	*3,000.*	100.
a.		Double surcharge, one diagonal	*3,500.*	—

Value for No. 190b is for pair with unsurcharged stamp at right. One pair with unsurcharged stamp at left is known.

No. 192a is unique.

193	(j)	5c on ½m **blue green** (4)	*900.*	500.

Red Surcharge on No. 161

196	(k)	3c on 1c **black violet** (3)	150.	125.
a.		Inverted surcharge		500.
197	(l)	3c on 1c **black violet** (3)	250.	200.
a.		Inverted surcharge		*1,500.*
198	(i)	5c on 1c **black violet** (3)	92.50	72.50
a.		Inverted surcharge		500.
b.		Vertical surcharge		—
c.		Double surcharge	*600.*	*2,750.*
d.		Double inverted surcharge	—	—

Value for No. 198b is for surcharge reading up. One example is known with surcharge reading down.

199	(j)	5c on 1c **black violet** (3)	150.	115.
a.		Inverted surcharge		*3,000.*
b.		Vertical surcharge	—	—
c.		Double surcharge	*3,000.*	*3,000.*

m

200	(m)	10c on 1c **black violet** (3)	62.50	*92.50*
a.		Broken figure "1"	160.00	*225.00*

Black Surcharge on Nos. P26-P30

201	(k)	3c on 1m **blue green** (5)	350.	350.
a.		Inverted surcharge		450.
b.		"EENTS"	600.	450.
c.		As "b", inverted		850.
202	(l)	3c on 1m **blue green** (5)	1,000.	400.
a.		Inverted surcharge		850.
203	(k)	3c on 2m **blue green** (5)	1,650.	400.
a.		"EENTS"	1,650.	500.
b.		Inverted surcharge		1,500.
c.		As "a," inverted		*2,750.*
204	(l)	3c on 2m **blue green** (5)	*2,750.*	*600.*
a.		Inverted surcharge		*1,500.*

205 (k) 3c on 3m **blue green** (5) 900. 400.
a. Inverted surcharge 750.
b. "EENTS" 1,250. 450.
c. As "b," inverted *2,750.*
206 (l) 3c on 3m **blue green** (5) *1,500.* 550.
a. Inverted surcharge *1,000.*
211 (i) 5c on 1m **blue green** (5) 1,800.
a. "EENTS" — 3,000.
212 (j) 5c on 1m **blue green** (5) — 2,250.
213 (i) 5c on 2m **blue green** (5) 3,000. 1,800.
a. "EENTS" 3,000. 3,000.
214 (j) 5c on 2m **blue green** (5) 3,250. 1,750.
215 (i) 5c on 3m **blue green** (5) 550.
a. "EENTS" 1,000.
216 (j) 5c on 3m **blue green** (5) 3,000. 1,000.
217 (i) 5c on 4m **blue green** (5) *3,000.* 900.
a. "EENTS" *3,000.* 1,500.
b. Inverted surcharge *2,000.*
c. As "a," inverted *3,000.*
218 (j) 5c on 4m **blue green** (5) 3,000. *1,500.*
a. Inverted surcharge *2,000.*
219 (i) 5c on 8m **blue green** (5) *2,500.* 1,250.
a. Inverted surcharge 1,500.
b. "EENTS" 3,000. 2,750.
c. As "b," inverted 2,500.
220 (j) 5c on 8m **blue green** (5) 2,000.
a. Inverted surcharge 2,500.

Puerto Principe pairs, strips and stamps properly canceled on cover are scarce and command high premiums.

Most copies of all but the most common varieties are faulty or have tropical toning. Values are for sound copies where they exist.

United States Stamps Nos. 279, 267, 267b, 279Bf, 279Bh, 268, 281, 282C and 283 Surcharged in Black

1899 **Wmk. 191** ***Perf. 12***

221 A87 1c on 1c **yellow green** 4.50 .40
Never hinged 11.50
On cover 15.00
Block of 4 22.50 4.50
P# strip of 3, Impt. 55.00
P# block of 6, Impt. 290.00
222 A88 2c on 2c **reddish carmine,** type III, *Feb.* 10.00 .75
Never hinged 25.00
On cover 22.50
Block of 4 55.00 8.00
P# strip of 3, Impt. 115.00
P# block of 6, Impt. 650.00
b. 2c on 2c **vermilion,** type III, *Feb.* 10.00 .75
222A A88 2c on 2c **reddish carmine,** type IV, *Feb.* 6.00 .40
Never hinged 15.00
On cover 12.50
Block of 4 30.00 4.50
P# strip of 3, Impt. 65.00
P# block of 6, Impt. 600.00
"CUBA" at bottom *650.00*
"CUPA" (broken letter. pos. 99) 250.00 75.00
c. 2c on 2c **vermilion,** type IV, *Feb.* 6.00 .40
d. As No. 222A, inverted surcharge *5,500.* *4,000.*
223 A88 2½c on 2c **reddish carmine,** type III, *Jan. 2* 6.00 .80
Never hinged 15.00
On cover 20.00
Block of 4 30.00 8.00
P# strip of 3, Impt. 95.00
P# block of 6, Impt. 350.00
b. 2½ on 2c **vermilion,** type III, *Jan. 2* 6.00 .80
223A A88 2½c on 2c **reddish carmine,** type IV, *Jan. 2* 3.50 .50
Never hinged 8.75
On cover 12.50
Block of 4 20.00 4.50
P# strip of 3, Impt. 62.50
P# block of 6, Impt. 250.00
c. 2½c on 2c **vermilion,** type IV, *Jan. 2* 3.50 .50

All 2½c stamps were sold and used as 2 centavo stamps.

224 A89 3c on 3c **purple** 12.00 1.75
Never hinged 30.00
On cover 25.00
Block of 4 57.50 14.00
P# strip of 3, Impt. 110.00
P# block of 6, Impt. 675.00
a. Period between "B" and "A" 40.00 35.00

Two Types of Surcharge

Type I — "3" directly over "P"
Type II — "3" to left over "P"

225 A91 5c on 5c **blue** 12.50 2.00
Never hinged 30.00
On cover 30.00
Block of 4 60.00 15.00
P# strip of 3, Impt. 190.00
P# block of 6, Impt. 800.00
"CUBA" at bottom — —
"CUPA" (broken letter) 80.00 40.00
226 A94 10c on 10c **brown,** type I 25.00 6.00
Never hinged 70.00
On cover 110.00
Block of 4 115.00 45.00
P# strip of 3, Impt. 260.00
P# block of 6, Impt. 1,100.
"CUBA" at bottom 500.00 550.00
b. "CUBA" omitted *7,000.* *4,000.*
226A A94 10c on 10c **brown,** type II *6,000.*
Block of 4 —
Nos. 221-226 (8) 79.50 12.60

No. 226A exists only in the special printing.

The No. 225 "CUPA" variety always has a straight edge at the right.

Special Printing

In March 1900, one pane of 100 each of Nos. 221-225, 226A, J1-J4 and two panes of 50 of No. E1, were specially overprinted for displays at the Paris Exposition (1900) and Pan American Exposition (1901). The 2c pane was light red, type IV. Stamps were handstamped type E "Specimen" in black ink by H. G. Mandel and mounted by him in separate displays for the two Expositions. Additional stamps from each pane were also handstamped "specimen," but most were destroyed after the Expositions. However, because additional stamps that are not Special Printings exist with a black "Specimen" handstamp, expertization by competent authorities is recommended. Nearly all examples remaining bear impression of a dealer's handstamp reading "Special Surcharge" in red ink on the back. Value: Nos. 221-225, each $750; Nos. J1-J4, each $1,500; No. E1, $2,500.

Issues of the Republic under US Military Rule

Statue of Columbus — A20

Royal Palms — A21

Allegory, "Cuba" — A22

Ocean Liner — A23

Cane Field — A24

ORIGINAL RE-ENGRAVED

Re-engraved

The re-engraved stamps issued by the Republic of Cuba in 1905-07 may be distinguished from the Issue of 1899 as follows:

Nos. 227-231 are watermarked U S-C

The re-engraved stamps are unwatermarked.

1c: The ends of the label inscribed "Centavo" are rounded instead of square.

2c: The foliate ornaments, inside the oval disks bearing the numerals of value, have been removed.

5c: Two lines forming a right angle have been added in the upper corners of the label bearing the word "Cuba."

10c: A small ball has been added to each of the square ends of the label bearing the word "Cuba."

Printed by the U.S. Bureau of Engraving and Printing

1899 **Wmk. US-C (191C)** ***Perf. 12***

227 A20 1c **yellow green** 3.50 .25
Never hinged 8.75
On cover 2.00
Block of 4 15.00 1.00
P# block of 10, Impt., type VII 225.00 —
228 A21 2c **carmine** 3.50 .25
Never hinged 8.75
On cover 2.00
Block of 4 15.00 1.00
P# block of 10, Impt., type VII 180.00 —
a. 2c **scarlet** 3.50 .25
b. Booklet pane of 6 *5,500.*
229 A22 3c **purple** 3.50 .30
Never hinged 8.75
On cover 4.00
Block of 4 15.00 2.50
P# block of 10, Impt., type VII 275.00 —
230 A23 5c **blue** 4.50 .30
Never hinged 11.00
On cover 4.00
Block of 4 21.00 2.50
P# block of 10, Impt., type VII 450.00 —
231 A24 10c **brown** 11.00 .80
Never hinged 27.50
On cover 6.50
Block of 4 52.50 5.50
P# block of 10, Impt., type VII 1,200. —
Nos. 227-231 (5) 26.00 1.90

No. 228b was issued by the Republic.

See Nos. 233-237 in Scott Standard Catalogue Vol 2. For surcharge see No. 232.

SPECIAL DELIVERY STAMPS

Issued under Administration of the United States

Special Delivery Stamp of the United States No. E5 Surcharged in Red

1899 **Wmk. 191** ***Perf. 12***

E1 SD3 10c on 10c **blue** 130. 100.
Never hinged 300.
On cover 450.
Block of 4 575.
Margin block of 4, arrow 650.
P# strip of 3, Impt. 1,000.
P# block of 6, Impt. *5,000.*
a. No period after "CUBA" 575. 400.
b. Five dots in curved frame above messenger's head (Pl. 882) *2,500.*

Issue of the Republic under US Military Rule

Special Delivery Messenger SD2

Printed by the US Bureau of Engraving and Printing

1899 **Wmk. US-C (191C)**

Inscribed: "Immediata"

E2 SD2 10c **orange** 52.50 15.00
Never hinged 120.00
On cover 150.00
Block of 4 250.00 —
P# strip of 3, Impt., type VII 300.00
P# block of 6, Impt., type VII 1,000.

Re-engraved

In 1902 the Republic of Cuba issued a stamp of design SD2 re-engraved with word correctly spelled "Inmediata." The corrected die was made in 1899 (See No. E3P). It was printed by the U.S. Bureau of Engraving and Printing.

POSTAGE DUE STAMPS

Issued under Administration of the United States

Postage Due Stamps of the United States Nos. J38, J39, J41 and J42 Srchd. in Black Like Nos. 221-226A

1899 **Wmk. 191** ***Perf. 12***

J1 D2 1c on 1c **deep claret** 45.00 5.25
Never hinged 110.00
Block of 4 210.00 45.00
P# block of 6, Impt. *900.00*
J2 D2 2c on 2c **deep claret** 45.00 5.25
Never hinged 110.00
Block of 4 200.00 30.00
P# block of 6, Impt. *900.00*
a. Inverted surcharge *4,000.*
J3 D2 5c on 5c **deep claret** 42.50 5.25
Never hinged 105.00
Block of 4 210.00 45.00
P# block of 6, Impt. *900.00*
"CUPA" (broken letter) 150.00 140.00
J4 D2 10c on 10c **deep claret** 25.00 2.50
Never hinged 60.00
Block of 4 125.00 27.50
P# block of 6, Impt. *800.00*
Nos. J1-J4 (4) 157.50 18.25

The No. J3 "CUPA" variety always has a straight edge at right.

ENVELOPES

Values are for Cut Squares

US Envelopes of 1887-99 Surcharged

a

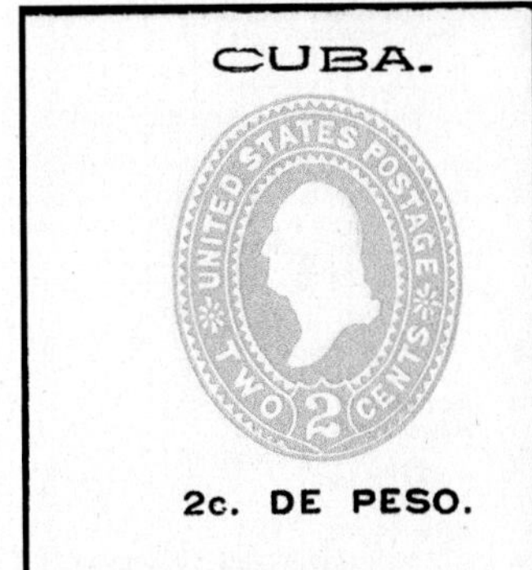

b

1899

U1 U77 (a) 1c on 1c **green,** *oriental buff* (No. U354) 5.00 3.50
Entire 12.00 15.00
U2 U77 (a) 1c on 1c **green,** *blue* (No. U355) 2.50 2.50
Entire 4.00 5.50
a. Double surcharge, entire *5,250.*
U3 U71 (b) 2c on 2c **green** (No. U311) 1.50 1.10
Entire 3.00 3.50
a. Double surcharge, entire *4,500.* *6,500.*
b. Inverted surcharge at lower left, entire — *4,250.*
U4 U71 (b) 2c on 2c **green,** *amber* (No. U312) 2.75 1.65
Entire 5.25 6.00
a. Double surcharge, entire *5,250.*
U5 U71 (a) 2c on 2c **green,** *oriental buff* (No. U313) 17.50 8.00
Entire 47.50 47.50
U6 U79 (a) 2c on 2c **carmine,** *amber* (No. U363) 17.50 17.50
Entire 47.50 47.50
U7 U79 (a) 2c on 2c **carmine,** *oriental buff* (No. U364) 25.00 25.00
Entire 100.00 80.00
U8 U79 (a) 2c on 2c **carmine,** *blue* (No. U365) 3.00 2.00
Entire 7.00 8.00
a. Double surcharge, entire *6,750.*
Nos. U1-U8 (8) 74.75 61.25

In addition to the envelopes listed above, several others are known but were not regularly issued. They are:
1c on 1c green
1c on 1c green, *manila*
2c on 2c carmine
4c on 4c brown
5c on 5c blue

Issue of the Republic under US Military Rule

Columbus — E1

Similar envelopes without watermark on white and amber papers, were issued by the Republic after Military Rule ended in 1902.

1899 **Wmk. "US POD '99" in Monogram**

U9 E1 1c **green** .75 .65
Entire 4.00 4.00
U10 E1 1c **green,** *amber* 1.00 .65
Entire 4.00 4.00
U11 E1 1c **green,** *oriental buff* 17.50 13.00
Entire 85.00 42.50
U12 E1 1c **green,** *blue* 25.00 15.00
Entire 85.00 42.50
U13 E1 2c **carmine** 1.00 .70
Entire 3.75 3.00
U14 E1 2c **carmine,** *amber* 1.00 .70
Entire 3.75 3.00
U15 E1 2c **carmine,** *oriental buff* 9.00 7.75
Entire 35.00 21.00
U16 E1 2c **carmine,** *blue* 25.00 18.00
Entire 60.00 52.50
U17 E1 5c **blue** 3.25 2.25
Entire 5.00 2.75
U18 E1 5c **blue,** *amber* 5.50 5.00
Entire 9.00 6.50
Nos. U9-U18 (10) 89.00 63.70

WRAPPERS

Issue of the Republic under US Military Rule

1899

W1 E1 1c **green,** *manila* 4.00 10.00
Entire 11.00 50.00
W2 E1 2c **carmine,** *manila* 12.00 10.00
Entire 25.00 50.00

POSTAL CARDS

Values are for Entires

U.S. Postal Cards Nos. UX14, UX16 Surcharged

UX1 PC8 1c on 1c **black,** *buff, Jefferson (1,000,000)* 15.00 16.50
a. No period after "1c" 40.00 75.00
b. No period after "Peso" 35.00
c. Surcharge "2c" (error) *6,500.*
UX2 PC3 2c on 2c **black,** *buff, Liberty (583,000)* 15.00 16.50
a. No period after "Peso" 40.00 75.00
b. Double surcharge —

In 1904 the Republic of Cuba revalued remaining stocks of No. UX2 by means of a perforated numeral "1."

PROOFS

1899

227P1 1c **yellow green,** large die on India paper 175.
227P2 1c **yellow green,** RA sm die on white wove paper 160.
227TC1 1c Large die on India paper
a. **blue green** 375.
b. **black** 625.
228P1 2c **carmine,** large die on India paper 175.
228P2 2c **carmine,** RA sm die on white wove paper 160.
228TC1 2c Large die on India paper
a. **black** 625.
229P1 3c **purple,** large die on India paper 175.
229P2 3c **purple,** RA sm die on white wove paper 160.
229TC1 3c Large die on India paper
a. **black** 375.
230P1 5c **blue,** large die on India paper 175.
230P2 5c **blue,** RA sm die on white wove paper 160.
230TC1 5c Large die on India paper
a. **black** 625.
231P1 10c **brown,** large die on India paper 175.
231P2 10c **brown,** RA sm die on white wove paper 160.
231TC1 10c Large die on India paper
a. **gray** 650.
b. **black** 650.

Special Delivery

E2TC1 10c Large die on India paper
a. **blue** 3,750.
E3P1 10c **orange** large die on India paper 600.
E3P2 10c **orange** RA sm die on white wove paper 450.

SPECIMEN STAMPS

Handstamped U.S. Type E in Purple or Black

1899

221S E 1c on 1c **yellow green** 240.
222AS E 2c on 2c **reddish carmine,** type IV 240.
223AS E 2½c on 2c **reddish carmine,** type IV 240.
224S E 3c on 3c **purple** 240.
225S E 5c on 5c **blue** 240.
226S E 10c on 10c **brown,** type I 240.
226AS E 10c on 10c **brown,** type II *6,000.*

See Special Printing Notice following No. 226A for Special Printings with black "Specimen" handstamps, but note that not all stamps with the black "Specimen" handstamp are Special Printings.

1899

227S E 1c **yellow green** 250.
228S E 2c **carmine** 250.
229S E 3c **purple** 250.
230S E 5c **blue** 250.
231S E 10c **brown** 250.

Special Delivery

1899

E1S E 10c on 10c **blue** 1,500.
a. Five dots in curved frame above messenger's head 5,250.
E2S E 10c **orange** 2,100.

Postage Due

1899

J1S E 1c on 1c **deep claret** 525.
J2S E 2c on 2c **deep claret** 525.
J3S E 5c on 5c **deep claret** 525.
J4S E 10c on 10c **deep claret** 525.

See Special Printing Notice following No. 226A for Special Printings with black "Specimen" handstamps, but note that not all stamps with the black "Specimen" handstamp are Special Printings.

DANISH WEST INDIES AND UNITED STATES VIRGIN ISLANDS

Formerly a Danish colony, these islands were purchased by the United States on March 31, 1917 and have since been known as the U.S. Virgin Islands. They lie east of Puerto Rico, have an area of 132 square miles and had a population of 27,086 in 1911. The capital is Charlotte Amalie (also called St. Thomas). Stamps of Danish West Indies were replaced by those of the United States in 1917. However, for the first six months of U.S. ownership, until September 30, 1917, a postal transition period existed. During this period, either U.S., D.W.I. or mixed frankings could be used. The domestic printed matter or postcard rate was 5 bits or 1 cent, and the foreign printed matter or postcard rate was 10 bits, 2 cents, or 5 bits + 1 cent. The domestic minimum weight letter rate was 10 bits, 2 cents, or 5 bits + 1 cent, while the foreign minimum letter rate was 25 bits, 5 cents, or any combination of U.S. and D.W.I. stamps that together totalled 25 bits or 5 cents.

Letters posted to foreign destinations during the transition period are rare because of World War I. Values for covers listed here are for the period before the transition. Transition-period covers, including those with mixed franking, sell for much more.

100 CENTS = 1 DOLLAR
100 BIT = 1 FRANC (1905)

Wmk. 111 — Small Crown

Wmk. 112 — Crown

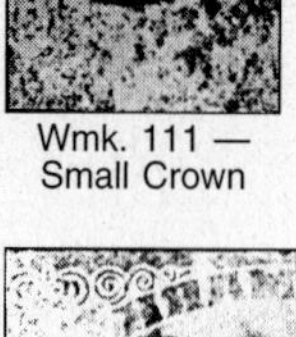

Wmk. 113 — Crown

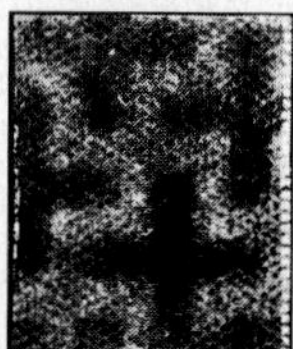

Wmk. 114 — Multiple Crosses

Coat of Arms — A1

1856 **Typo.** **Wmk. 111** ***Imperf.***

1 A1 3c **dark carmine,** brown gum 210. *235.*
Never hinged 625.
On cover 3,000.
Block of 4 1,350.
a. 3c **dark carmine,** yellow gum 350. *375.*
Never hinged 925.
On cover 3,000.
Block of 4 4,400.
b. 3c **carmine,** white gum *3,750.* *3,750.*
On cover —

The brown and yellow gums were applied locally.

Reprint: 1981, carmine, back-printed across two stamps ("Reprint by Dansk Post og Telegrafmuseum 1978"), value, pair, $10.

White Paper

1866 **Yellow Wavy-line Burelage UR to LL**

2 A1 3c **rose** 42.50 *50.*
Never hinged 87.50
On cover 3,000.
Block of 4 210. *275.*
Rouletted 4½ privately 350. 175.
On cover, rouletted 4½ —
Rouletted 9 450. 200.

The value for used blocks is for favor cancel (CTO).

No. 2 reprints, unwatermarked: 1930, carmine, value $100. 1942, rose carmine, back-printed across each row ("Nytryk 1942 G. A. Hagemann Danmark og Dansk Vestindiens Frimaerker Bind 2"), value $50.

1872 ***Perf. 12½***

3 A1 3c **rose** 130. *320.*
Never hinged 265.
On cover *7,500.*
Block of 4 715.

1873 **Without Burelage**

4 A1 4c **dull blue** 325. *700.*
Never hinged 600.
On cover —
Block of 4 1,700.
a. Imperf., pair 775.
b. Horiz. pair, imperf. vert. 575.

The 1930 reprint of No. 4 is ultramarine, unwatermarked and imperf., value $100.

The 1942 4c reprint is blue, unwatermarked, imperf. and has printing on back (see note below No. 2), value $60.

Numeral of Value — A2

Normal Frame Inverted Frame

The arabesques in the corners have a main stem and a branch. When the frame is in normal position, in the upper left corner the branch leaves the main stem half way between two little leaflets. In the lower right corner the branch starts at the foot of the second leaflet. When the frame is inverted the corner designs are, of course, transposed.

Values for inverted frames, covers and blocks are for the cheapest variety.

White Wove Paper, Printings 1-3 Thin, 4-7 Medium, 8-9 Thick
1c Nine printings
3c Eight printings
4c Two printings
5c Six printings
7c Two printings
10c Seven printings
12c Two printings
14c One printing
50c Two printings

1874-79 **Wmk. 112** ***Perf. 14x13½***

5 A2 1c **green & brown red** 35.00 *32.50*
Never hinged 87.50
On cover 250.00
Block of 4 155.00 *260.00*
a. 1c **green & rose lilac,** thin paper 160.00 *190.00*
Never hinged 340.00
b. 1c **green & red violet,** medium paper 50.00 *65.00*
Never hinged 115.00
c. 1c **green & claret,** thick paper 32.50 *26.00*
Never hinged 80.00
e. As "c," inverted frame 40.00 *26.00*
f. As "a," inverted frame *900.00* 1,900.

No. 5 exists with a surcharge similar to the surcharge on No. 15, with 10 CENTS value and 1895 date. This stamp is an essay.

6 A2 3c **blue & carmine** 35.00 18.00
Never hinged 87.50
On cover 225.00
Block of 4 150.00 —
White "wedge" flaw 100.00 100.00
Never hinged 300.00
a. 3c **light blue & rose carmine,** thin paper 45.00 35.00
Never hinged 110.00
b. 3c **deep blue & dark carmine,** medium paper 45.00 25.00
Never hinged 115.00
c. 3c **greenish blue & lake,** thick paper 29.00 18.00
Never hinged 80.00
d. Imperf., pair 325.00 —
Never hinged 475.00
e. Inverted frame, thick paper 45.00 35.00
Never hinged 475.00
f. As "a," inverted frame *800.00* 1,200.

7 A2 4c **brown & dull blue** 23.00 *22.50*
Never hinged 57.50
On cover 225.00
Block of 4 105.00 —
b. 4c **brown & ultramarine,** thin paper 290.00 *250.00*
Never hinged 725.00
c. Diagonal half used as 2c on cover 165.00
d. As "b," inverted frame *1,450.* *2,400.*
Never hinged 3,500.

8 A2 5c **green & gray** 45.00 29.00
Never hinged 95.00
On cover 250.00
Block of 4 195.00 —
a. 5c **yellow green & dark gray,** thin paper 85.00 45.00
Never hinged 225.00
b. Inverted frame, thick paper 37.50 26.00
Never hinged 87.50

9 A2 7c **lilac & orange** 40.00 *135.00*
Never hinged 95.00
On cover 1,100.
Block of 4 200.00 —
a. 7c **lilac & yellow** 120.00 *130.00*
Never hinged 250.00
b. Inverted frame 65.00 *220.00*
Never hinged 200.00

10 A2 10c **blue & brown** 57.50 34.00
Never hinged 140.00
On cover 300.00
Block of 4 265.00 —
a. 10c **dark blue & black brown,** thin paper 85.00 47.50
Never hinged 210.00
b. Period between "t" & "s" of "cents" 72.50 47.50
Never hinged 160.00
c. Inverted frame 26.00 *27.50*
Never hinged 70.00

11 A2 12c **red lilac & yellow green** 60.00 *170.00*
Never hinged 125.00
On cover 1,750.
Block of 4 325.00 —
a. 12c **lilac & deep green** 230.00 *240.00*
Never hinged 575.00

12 A2 14c **lilac & green** 1,050. *1,750.*
Never hinged 2,200.
On cover —
Block of 4 *6,400.*
a. Inverted frame *4,000.* *4,800.*

13 A2 50c **violet,** thin paper 260.00 *390.00*
Never hinged 570.00
On cover 2,500.

	Block of 4	1,850.	
a.	50c **gray violet,** thick paper	310.00	*525.00*
	Never hinged	650.00	

Issue dates: 1c, 3c, 4c, 14c, Jan. 15, 1874. 7c, July 22, 1874. 5c, 10c, 1876; 12c, 1877; 50c, 1879. Colors of major numbers are generally those of the least expensive of two or more shades, and do not indicate the shade of the first printing.

No. 9 Surcharged in Black

a

1887

14 A2 (a)	1c on 7c **lilac & orange**	140.00	*275.00*
	Never hinged	240.00	
	On cover		3,000.
	Block of 4	625.00	—
a.	Double surcharge	350.00	675.00
	Never hinged	650.00	
b.	1c on 7c **lilac & yellow**	190.00	*300.00*
c.	As #14b, double surcharge	325.00	575.00
d.	Inverted frame	175.00	*525.00*
	Never hinged	400.00	

No. 13 Surcharged in Black

b

1895

15 A2 (b)	10c on 50c **violet,** thin paper	45.00	*72.50*
	Never hinged	100.00	
	On cover		275.00
	Block of 4	285.00	—

The "b" surcharge also exists on No. 5, with "10" found in two sizes. These are essays.

1896-1901 *Perf. 13*

16 A2	1c **grn & red vio,** inverted frame ('98)	26.00	*36.50*
	Never hinged	42.50	
	On cover		150.00
	Block of 4	130.00	—
a.	Normal frame	590.00	*735.00*
	Never hinged	1,200.	
17 A2	3c **blue & lake,** inverted frame ('98)	15.50	*17.00*
	Never hinged	29.00	
	On cover		150.00
	Block of 4	70.00	—
	White "wedge" flaw	85.00	*115.00*
	Never hinged	185.00	
a.	Normal frame	400.00	*600.00*
	Never hinged	725.00	
18 A2	4c **bister & dull blue** ('01)	21.50	13.50
	Never hinged	47.50	
	On cover		150.00
	Block of 4	95.00	—
a.	Diagonal half used as 2c on cover		67.50
b.	Inverted frame	85.00	*110.00*
	Never hinged	190.00	
	On cover		250.00
c.	As "b," diagonal half used as 2c on cover		425.00
19 A2	5c **green & gray,** inverted frame	47.50	42.50
	Never hinged	105.00	
	On cover		325.00
	Block of 4	215.00	—
a.	Normal frame	1,375.	*1,700.*
	Never hinged	2,200.	
20 A2	10c **blue & brn** ('01)	110.00	*145.00*
	Never hinged	235.00	
	On cover		1,150.
	Block of 4	650.00	—
a.	Inverted frame	1,550.	*2,925.*
	Never hinged	2,300.	
b.	Period between "t" and "s" of "cents"	155.00	180.00
	Never hinged	305.00	
	Nos. 16-20 (5)	220.50	*254.50*

Two printings each of Nos. 18-19.

Arms — A5

1900

21 A5	1c **light green**	2.60	2.25
	Never hinged	5.25	
	On cover, pair		80.00
	On cover, single franking		300.00
	Block of 4	11.00	9.50
22 A5	5c **light blue**	17.00	*25.00*
	Never hinged	55.00	
	On cover		300.00
	Block of 4	77.50	—

Nos. 6, 17 and 20 Surcharged in Black — c

1902 *Perf. 14x13½*

23 A2	2c on 3c **blue & carmine,** inverted frame	1,075.	*1,450.*
	Never hinged	2,000.	
	On cover		*4,000.*
	Block of 4	*5,000.*	
a.	"2" in date with straight tail	1,200.	*1,600.*
	Never hinged	2,175.	
b.	Normal frame	—	

Perf. 13

24 A2	2c on 3c **blue & lake,** inverted frame	11.50	*32.00*
	Never hinged	16.00	
	On cover		160.00
	Block of 4	52.00	—
	White "wedge" flaw	85.00	115.00
	Never hinged	170.00	
a.	"2" in date with straight tail	30.00	*50.00*
	Never hinged	47.50	
b.	Dated "1901"	1,000.	1,000.
	Never hinged	1,550.	
c.	Normal frame	320.00	*825.00*
	Never hinged	650.00	
d.	Dark green surcharge	3,000.	
e.	As "d" & "a"	—	—
f.	As "d" & "c"	—	

The overprint on No. 24b exists in two types: with "1901" measuring 2.5 mm or 2.2 mm high.

Only one example of No. 24f can exist.

25 A2	8c on 10c **blue & brown**	26.00	*55.00*
	Never hinged	52.50	
	On cover		225.00
	Block of 4	110.00	—
a.	"2" with straight tail	35.00	*65.00*
	Never hinged	65.00	
b.	On No. 20b	55.00	*85.00*
	Never hinged	95.00	
c.	Inverted frame	300.00	*675.00*
	Never hinged	690.00	

Nos. 17 and 20 Surcharged in Black — d

1902 *Perf. 13*

27 A2	2c on 3c **blue & lake,** inverted frame	15.75	*63.00*
	Never hinged	30.00	
	On cover		500.00
	Block of 4	70.00	
	White "wedge" flaw	105.00	*220.00*
	Never hinged	185.00	
a.	Normal frame	415.00	*720.00*
	Never hinged	730.00	
28 A2	8c on 10c **blue & brown**	14.00	15.00
	Never hinged	26.00	
	On cover		175.00
	Block of 4	60.00	—
a.	On No. 20b	26.00	*32.00*
	Never hinged	45.00	
b.	Inverted frame	415.00	*675.00*
	Never hinged	575.00	
	Nos. 23-28 (5)	1,142.	1,615.

1903 **Wmk. 113**

29 A5	2c **carmine**	9.50	*25.00*
	Never hinged	21.00	
	On cover		125.00
	Block of 4	42.00	—
30 A5	8c **brown**	36.00	*62.00*
	Never hinged	90.00	
	On cover		250.00
	Block of 4	150.00	—

King Christian IX — A8

St. Thomas Harbor — A9

1905 **Typo.** *Perf. 13*

31 A8	5b **green**	4.75	3.00
	Never hinged	12.00	
	On cover		35.00
	Block of 4	21.00	—
32 A8	10b **red**	4.75	3.00
	Never hinged	12.00	
	On cover		35.00
	Block of 4	20.00	—
33 A8	20b **green & blue**	9.50	8.00
	Never hinged	24.00	
	On cover		150.00
	Block of 4	43.00	—
34 A8	25b **ultramarine**	9.50	*8.00*
	Never hinged	24.00	
	On cover		85.00
	Block of 4	43.00	—
35 A8	40b **red & gray**	9.50	*7.00*
	Never hinged	24.00	
	On cover		225.00
	Block of 4	43.00	—
36 A8	50b **yellow & gray**	14.00	11.00
	Never hinged	33.00	
	On cover		250.00
	Block of 4	60.00	—

Perf. 12

Wmk. Two Crowns (113)

Frame Typographed, Center Engraved

37 A9	1fr **green & blue**	17.50	*50.00*
	Never hinged	37.50	
	On cover		625.00
	Block of 4	75.00	—
38 A9	2fr **orange red & brown**	32.50	*67.50*
	Never hinged	82.50	
	On cover		1,100.
	Block of 4	160.00	—

39 A9 5fr **yellow & brown**	85.00	315.00
Never hinged	165.00	
On cover		1,750.
Block of 4	410.00	—
Nos. 31-39 (9)	187.00	472.50

On cover values are for commercial usages, usually parcel address cards. Philatelic covers are valued at approximately 25% of these values.

Nos. 18, 22 and 30 Surcharged in Black

1905 **Wmk. 112** ***Perf. 13***

40 A2 5b on 4c **bister & dull blue**	17.50	70.00
Never hinged	43.00	
On cover		250.00
Block of 4	85.00	—
a. Inverted frame	110.00	190.00
Never hinged	195.00	
41 A5 5b on 5c **light blue**	13.00	64.00
Never hinged	35.00	
On cover		250.00
Block of 4	52.00	—

Wmk. 113

42 A5 5b on 8c **brown**	13.00	75.00
Never hinged	35.00	
On cover		250.00
Block of 4	57.50	—
Nos. 40-42 (3)	43.50	209.00

Favor cancels exist on Nos. 40-42. Value 25% less.

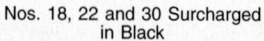

King Frederik VIII — A10

Frame Typographed, Center Engraved

1908 **Wmk. 113** ***Perf. 13***

43 A10 5b **green**	2.75	1.90
Never hinged	7.00	
On cover		22.50
Block of 4	13.50	—
Number block of 6	26.00	
44 A10 10b **red**	2.75	1.90
Never hinged	6.25	
On cover		22.50
Block of 4	13.50	—
Number block of 6	26.00	
45 A10 15b **violet & brown**	5.00	5.75
Never hinged	8.50	
On cover		125.00
Block of 4	25.00	—
Number block of 6	65.00	
46 A10 20b **green & blue**	32.50	27.50
Never hinged	72.50	
On cover		110.00
Block of 4	140.00	—
Number block of 6	300.00	
47 A10 25b **blue & dark blue**	2.25	2.50
Never hinged	4.75	
On cover		35.00
Block of 4	10.50	—
Number block of 6	22.00	
48 A10 30b **claret & slate**	67.50	60.00
Never hinged	120.00	
On cover		350.00
Block of 4	300.00	275.00
Number block of 6	700.00	
49 A10 40b **vermilion & gray**	8.00	11.50
Never hinged	14.50	
On cover		210.00
Block of 4	35.00	—
Number block of 6	75.00	
50 A10 50b **yellow & brown**	8.50	10.00
Never hinged	12.00	
On cover		210.00
Block of 4	37.00	—
Number block of 6	100.00	
Nos. 43-50 (8)	129.25	121.05

Printing numbers appear in the selvage, once per pane, in Roman or Arabic numerals.

King Christian X — A11

Frame Typographed, Center Engraved

1915 **Wmk. 114** ***Perf. 14x14½***

51 A11 5b **yellow green**	5.25	6.25
Never hinged	10.50	
On cover		45.00
Block of 4	23.00	—
Number block of 4	52.50	
52 A11 10b **red**	5.25	110.00
Never hinged	10.50	
On cover		110.00
Block of 4	23.00	—
Number block of 4	52.50	
53 A11 15b **lilac & red brown**	5.25	110.00
Never hinged	10.50	
On cover		300.00
Block of 4	23.00	—
Number block of 4	52.50	
54 A11 20b **green & blue**	5.25	110.00
Never hinged	10.50	
On cover		350.00
Block of 4	23.00	—
Number block of 4	52.50	
55 A11 25b **blue & dark blue**	5.25	16.00
Never hinged	10.50	
On cover		110.00
Block of 4	23.00	
Number block of 4	52.50	
56 A11 30b **claret & black**	5.25	200.00
Never hinged	10.50	
On cover		900.00
Block of 4	23.00	—
Number block of 4	52.50	
57 A11 40b **orange & black**	5.25	200.00
Never hinged	10.50	
On cover		550.00
Block of 4	24.00	—
Number block of 4	52.50	
58 A11 50b **yellow & brown**	5.25	200.00
On cover		650.00
Block of 4	23.00	—
Number block of 4	52.50	
Nos. 51-58 (8)	42.00	952.25

Forged and favor cancellations exist.

Plate identifications 11-D, 50-D or 50-O are located in the selvage in all four corners of the pane. The 50-D is on all denominations. 11-D, all but the 50b, 50-O, all but 15b, 20b, 25b.

POSTAGE DUE STAMPS

Royal Cipher "Christian Rex" — D1

1902 **Litho.** **Unwmk.** ***Perf. 11½***

J1 D1 1c **dark blue**	8.25	45.00
Never hinged	15.75	
On cover		400.00
Block of 4	40.00	
J2 D1 4c **dark blue**	20.00	45.00
Never hinged	40.00	
On cover		350.00
Block of 4	87.50	
J3 D1 6c **dark blue**	40.00	87.50
Never hinged	80.00	
On cover		450.00
Block of 4	175.00	
J4 D1 10c **dark blue**	40.00	87.50
Never hinged	80.00	
On cover		400.00
Block of 4	165.00	
Nos. J1-J4 (4)	108.25	265.00

There are five types of each value. On the 4c they may be distinguished by differences in the figure "4"; on the other values differences are minute.

Used values of Nos. J1-J8 are for canceled stamps. Uncanceled stamps without gum have probably been used. Value 60% of unused. On cover values are for stamps tied by cancellation.

Excellent counterfeits of Nos. J1-J4 exist.

Numeral of value — D2

1905-13 ***Perf. 13***

J5 D2 5b **red & gray**	6.50	8.00
Never hinged	13.50	
On cover		450.00
Block of 4	29.00	—
J6 D2 20b **red & gray**	11.50	14.50
Never hinged	24.00	
On cover		450.00
Block of 4	50.00	—
J7 D2 30b **red & gray**	9.50	14.50
Never hinged	19.00	
On cover		450.00
Block of 4	42.50	—
J8 D2 50b **red & gray**	9.00	36.00
Never hinged	18.00	
On cover		900.00
Block of 4	40.00	—
a. Perf. 14x14½ ('13)	75.00	290.00
Never hinged	115.00	
Block of 4	325.00	—
b. Perf. 11½	475.00	
Never hinged	850.00	
Nos. J5-J8 (4)	36.50	73.00

Nos. J5-J8 are known imperforate but were not regularly issued. Excellent counterfeits exist.

See notes following No. J4 for canceled stamps.

No. J8b is valued in the grade of fine.

ENVELOPES

E1

1877-78 **On White Paper**

U1 E1 2c **light blue** ('78)	5.00	14.00
Entire	20.00	65.00
a. 2c **ultramarine**	20.00	200.00
Entire	100.00	800.00
U2 E1 3c **orange**	5.00	12.50
Entire	20.00	65.00
a. 3c **red orange**	5.50	12.50
Entire	22.50	65.00

Three different Crown watermarks are found on entires of No. U1, four on entires of No. U2. Envelope watermarks do not show on cut squares.

POSTAL CARDS

Values are for entire cards.

Italicized numbers in parentheses indicate quantities issued.

Designs of Adhesive Stamps

"BREV-KORT" at top

1877

Inscription in Three Lines

UX1 A2 6c **violet**	40.00	1,400.

Used value is for card to foreign destination postmarked before April 1, 1879.

1878-85 **Inscription in Four Lines**

UX2 A2 2c **light blue** *(8,800)*	22.50	50.00
UX3 A2 3c **carmine rose** *(17,700)*	17.50	35.00

1888 **Inscription in Five Lines**

UX4 A2 2c **light blue** *(30,500)*	20.00	32.50
UX5 A2 3c **red** *(26,500)*	12.50	22.50

Card No. UX5 Locally Surcharged with type "c" but with date "1901"

1901

UX6 A2 1c on 3c **red** *(2,000)*	50.00	200.00

Card No. UX4 Locally Surcharged with type "c," "1902" date

1902

UX7 A2 1c on 2c **light blue** *(3,000)*	37.50	160.00

Card No. UX5 Surcharged similar to type "c" but heavy letters, "1902" date

1902

UX8 A2 1c on 3c **red** *(7,175)*	12.50	150.00

1903

UX9 A5 1c **light green** *(10,000)*	12.50	30.00
UX10 A5 2c **carmine** *(10,000)*	19.00	70.00

1905

UX11 A8 5b **green** *(16,000)*	12.50	22.50
UX12 A8 10b **red** *(14,000)*	12.50	35.00

1907-08 **Unwmk.**

UX13 A10 5b **green** ('08) *(30,750)*	9.50	27.50
UX14 A10 10b **red** *(19,750)*	12.50	40.00

1913 **Wmk. Wood-grain**

UX15 A10 5b **green** *(10,000)* 90.00 *210.00*
UX16 A10 10b **red** *(10,000)* 100.00 *325.00*

1915-16 **Wmk. Wood-grain**

UX17 A11 5b **yellow green** *(8,200)* 80.00 *250.00*
UX18 A11 10b **red** ('16) *(2,000)* 100.00 —

PAID REPLY POSTAL CARDS

Designs similar to Nos. UX2 and UX3 with added inscriptions in Danish and French: Message Card-Four lines at lower left. Reply Card-Fifth line centered, "Svar. Réponse."

Italicized numbers in parentheses indicate quantities issued.

1883

UY1 A2 2c +2c **light blue,** unsevered *(2,600)* 25.00 *250.00*
m. Message card, detached 12.50 *35.00*
r. Reply card, detached 12.50 *35.00*
UY2 A2 3c +3c **carmine rose,** unsevered 21.00 *150.00*
m. Message card, detached 12.50 *20.00*
r. Reply card, detached 12.50 *25.00*

Designs similar to Nos. UX4 and UX5 with added inscription in fifth line, centered in French: Message Card-"Carte postale avecréponse payée." Reply Card-"Carte postale-réponse."

1888

UY3 A2 2c +2c **light blue,** unsevered *(26,000)* 25.00 *125.00*
m. Message card, detached 10.00 *20.00*
r. Reply card, detached 10.00 *100.00*
UY4 A2 3c +3c **carmine rose,** unsevered *(5,000)* 22.50 *175.00*
m. Message card, detached 11.00 *35.00*
r. Reply card, detached 11.00 *125.00*

No. UY4 Locally Surcharged with type "c" but with date "1901"

1902

UY5 A2 1c on 3c+1c on 3c **carmine rose,** unsevered *(1,000)* 35.00 *300.00*
m. Message card, detached 12.50 *50.00*
r. Reply card, detached 14.00 *75.00*

No. UY4 Surcharged in Copenhagen with type similar to "c" but heavy letters, "1902" date

UY6 A2 1c on 3c+1c on 3c **carmine rose,** unsevered *(975)* 50.00 *350.00*
m. Message card, detached 20.00 *60.00*
r. Reply card, detached 20.00 *75.00*

Designs similar to Nos. UX9 and UX10 with added inscriptions in Danish and English

1903

UY7 A5 1c +1c **light green,** unsevered *(5,000)* 35.00 *75.00*
m. Message card, detached 11.00 *20.00*
r. Reply card, detached 11.00 *25.00*
UY8 A5 2c +2c **carmine,** unsevered *(5,000)* 40.00 *400.00*
m. Message card, detached 15.00 *50.00*
r. Reply card, detached 15.00 *75.00*

Designs similar to Nos. UX11 and UX12 with added inscriptions

1905

UY9 A8 5b +5b **green,** unsevered *(5,000)* 21.00 *75.00*
m. Message card, detached 10.00 *20.00*
r. Reply card, detached 10.00 *30.00*
UY10 A8 10b +10b **red,** unsevered *(4,000)* 30.00 *90.00*
m. Message card 12.50 *25.00*
r. Reply card, detached 15.00 *35.00*

Designs similar to Nos. UX13, UX14 and UX15 with added inscriptions

1908 **Unwmk.**

UY11 A10 5b +5b **green,** unsevered *(7,150)* 25.00 *100.00*
m. Message card, detached 11.00 *30.00*
r. Reply card, detached 11.00 *35.00*
UY12 A10 10b +10b **red,** unsevered *(6,750)* 25.00 *100.00*
m. Message card, detached 12.50 *30.00*
r. Reply card, detached 11.00 *40.00*

1913 **Wmk. Wood-grain**

UY13 A10 5b +5b **green,** unsevered *(5,000)* —
m. Message card, detached —
r. Reply card, detached —

The 10b + 10b red type A10 with wood-grain watermark was authorized and possibly printed, but no example is known.

REVENUE STAMPS

DANISH WEST INDIES DOCUMENTARY TAX

R1

1907 **Litho.** **Wmk. Crown** ***Perf. 12***

R1 R1 10b **red & light green** 2.00 *15.00*
MAK overprint 5.00
U.S. usage *50.00*
a. Inverted watermark 25.00 *50.00*
R2 R1 50b **green** 15.00 *40.00*
U.S. usage *75.00*
a. Inverted watermark — —
R3 R1 1fr **red & gray** 15.00 *40.00*
R4 R1 2fr **black & gray** 2.00 *25.00*
MAK overprint 3.00
a. Inverted watermark 50.00
R5 R1 3fr **red & blue** 30.00 *50.00*
U.S. usage —
R6 R1 5fr **blue** 15.00 *40.00*
U.S. usage *150.00*
R7 R1 7fr **red & yellow** 150.00 *200.00*
U.S. usage *250.00*
R8 R1 10fr **yellow** 20.00 *75.00*
U.S. usage *150.00*
a. Inverted watermark — —
R9 R1 50fr **brown & pink** 300.00 300.00
U.S. usage 300.00
R10 R1 100fr **black & pink** 400.00 400.00

Nos. R2, R4, R5 and R8 Surcharged

1917 ***Perf. & Printing Methods as Before***

R11 R1 10b on 50b (No. R2) *500.00* *600.00*
U.S. usage —
R12 R1 10b on 3fr (No. R5) *500.00*
R13 R1 10b on 10fr (No. R8) *500.00*
R14 R1 50b on 2fr (No. R4) *500.00*
R15 R1 50b on 3fr (No. R5) *500.00*
U.S. usage *600.00*

UNITED STATES VIRGIN ISLANDS DOCUMENTARY TAX

R2

1919 **Litho.** **Unwmk.** ***Perf. 11***

R16 R2 10b **red & light green** 50.00 60.00
R17 R2 50b **green** 60.00 40.00
a. **dark green** — 40.00
R18 R2 1fr **red & gray** — 125.00
R19 R2 2fr **black** — 125.00
a. **gray black** — 125.00
R20 R2 3fr **red & blue** — 150.00
R21 R2 5fr **blue** — 125.00
R22 R2 7fr **red & yellow** 60.00 *100.00*
R23 R2 10fr **orange** — 100.00
a. **dark orange** — 125.00
R24 R2 50fr **brown & pink** — 400.00
R25 R2 100fr **black & pink** — 500.00
a. **black & red** — 500.00

1919 ***Perf. 10***

R27 R2 50b **green** — 50.00
a. **dark green** — 50.00
R28 R2 5fr **blue** 275.00 125.00
R29 R2 10fr **orange** — 125.00

A 10b red & green, perf. 10, also was produced, but currently no examples have been recorded without surcharges.

No. R16 Surcharged in Black

1921 ***Perf. 11***

R30 R2 50b on 10b **red & lt grn** — *1,500.*

No. R28 With Printed Surcharge in Black

R31 R2 10c on 5fr **blue** 500.00 —

R3

1935 ***Perf. 11***

R32 R3 2c **red & green** 7.50 5.00
a. 2c **red & lt yel green** (thin paper) 12.50 7.50
b. 2c **red & yel green** 12.50 6.00
R33 R3 2c **red & apple green** 25.00 15.00
R34 R3 10c **green** 10.00 10.00
R35 R3 20c **red & gray** 25.00 22.50
R36 R3 20c **red & green** 15.00 10.00
a. 20c **red & yellow green** 15.00 10.00
R37 R3 40c **gray** 15.00 10.00
R38 R3 60c **red & milky blue** 20.00 15.00
a. 60c **red & lt blue** 27.50 15.00
R39 R3 60c **red & dp blue** 15.00 15.00
R40 R3 $1 **blue** 35.00 15.00
R41 R3 $1.40 **red & yellow** 40.00 —
R42 R3 $2 **yellow** 32.50 15.00
R43 R3 $10 **reddish brn & pink** 60.00 *100.00*
R44 R3 $20 **black & pink** 95.00 75.00
R45 R3 $100 **red & green** — 75.00

No. R34 With Printed Surcharge in Black

1935 ***Perf. 11***

R47 R3 2c on 10c **green** *600.00*

1965 Unwmk. *Perf. 12½*

No.	Type	Description	Unused	Used
R48	R3	2c **red & yellow green**	4.00	
a.		2c **red & green**	5.00	
R49	R3	10c **green**	15.00	
a.		10c **milky green**	17.50	
R50	R3	20c **red & yellow green**	10.00	
a.		20c **red & green**	10.00	
R51	R3	40c **gray**	10.00	*20.00*
R52	R3	60c **red & light blue**	12.50	
R53	R3	$1 **blue**	15.00	
a.		$1 **milky blue**	15.00	
R54	R3	$2 **yellow**	25.00	*25.00*
R55	R3	$10 **reddish brn & pink**	75.00	
R56	R3	$20 **black & pink**	60.00	
R57	R3	$100 **red & green**	150.00	150.00
R58	R3	$1,000 **green & yellow**		*1,000.*

PLAYING CARDS

Shipments of 10,000 each of Nos. RF1-RF3 were sent to the Virgin Islands on June 17, 1920, Jan. 16, 1926, and Mar. 5, 1934, respectively.

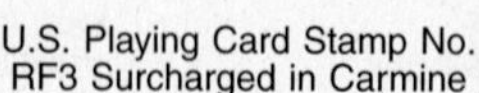

U.S. Playing Card Stamp No. RF3 Surcharged in Carmine

1920 Engr. Wmk. 191R *Rouletted 7*

No.	Description	Unused	Used
RF1	4c on 2c **blue**	225.00	

U.S. Playing Card Stamp No. RF17 Surcharged in Carmine

1926 *Rouletted 7*

No.	Description	Unused	Used
RF2	4c on (8c) **blue**	75.00	

Same Surcharge on U.S. Type RF4

1934 *Perf. 11*

No.	Description	Unused	Used
RF3	4c on (8c) **light blue**	225.00	125.00

The above stamp with perforation 11 was not issued in the United States without the overprint.

TOBACCO TAX

10b Perf. 10 Revenue Handstamp Surcharged in Black

1933 *Perf. 10*

No.	Type	Description	Unused	Used
RJ1	R2	1b on 10b	100.00	75.00
RJ2	R2	2b on 10b	100.00	100.00
RJ3	R2	3b on 10b	—	75.00
RJ4	R2	5b on 10b	100.00	50.00
RJ5	R2	6b on 10b	110.00	90.00
RJ6	R2	7b on 10b	80.00	*110.00*
RJ7	R2	8b on 10b	—	120.00
RJ8	R2	12b on 10b	100.00	—
RJ9	R2	33b on 10b	150.00	—
RJ10	R2	40b on 10b	175.00	—
RJ11	R2	50b on 10b	140.00	—
RJ12	R2	60b on 10b	200.00	—

See footnote following No. R29 concerning the 10b stamp.

10b Perf. 10 Revenue and Nos. R28-R29 with Typed Surcharges in Black

1933 *Perf. 10*

No.	Type	Description	Unused	Used
RJ13	R2	6b on 10b	125.00	75.00
RJ14	R2	6b on 5fr (No. R28)	85.00	75.00
RJ15	R2	6b on 10fr (No. R29)	125.00	125.00
RJ16	R2	7b on 10fr (No. R29)	175.00	—

No. R16 Handstamp Surcharged in Black

1933 *Perf. 11*

No.	Type	Description	Unused	Used
RJ17	R2	2b on 10b **red & lt grn**	—	125.00

Numeral-only Typed Surcharge on No. R16

1933 *Perf. 11*

No.	Type	Description	Unused	Used
RJ18	R2	6 on 10b **red & lt grn**	85.00	—
RJ19	R2	15 on 10b **red & lt grn**	85.00	—
RJ20	R2	40 on 10b **red & lt grn**	125.00	90.00
RJ21	R2	105 on 10b **red & lt grn**	150.00	—

Typed Surcharge in Black on Nos. R16, R21

1933 *Perf. 11*

No.	Type	Description	Unused	Used
RJ22	R2	6b on 10b **red & lt grn**	125.00	—
RJ23	R2	6b on 5fr **blue**	—	—

Numeral-only Handstamp Surcharge in Black on No. R16

1933 *Perf. 11*

No.	Type	Description	Unused	Used
RJ24	R2	5 on 10b **red & lt grn**	75.00	60.00
RJ25	R2	6 on 10b **red & lt grn**	100.00	100.00
RJ26	R2	7 on 10b **red & lt grn**	50.00	50.00
RJ27	R2	8 on 10b **red & lt grn**	100.00	100.00
RJ28	R2	50 on 10b **red & lt grn**	100.00	75.00

No. RF2 Handstamp Surcharged in Black

1933 *Rouletted 7*

No.	Description	Unused	Used
RJ29	1b on 4c on (8c) **blue**		300.00
RJ30	2b on 4c on (8c) **blue**		300.00
RJ31	3b on 4c on (8c) **blue**		350.00
RJ32	5b on 4c on (8c) **blue**		300.00
RJ33	6b on 4c on (8c) **blue**	275.00	—
RJ34	7b on 4c on (8c) **blue**		350.00
RJ35	8b on 4c on (8c) **blue**		375.00
RJ36	12b on 4c on (8c) **blue**	225.00	—
RJ37	33b on 4c on (8c) **blue**	300.00	200.00
RJ38	40b on 4c on (8c) **blue**	—	—

No. RF2 with Typed Surcharge in Black

No.	Description	Unused	Used
RJ39	6b on 4c on (8c) **blue**	250.00	—

ST. CROIX PROVISIONAL TOBACCO TAX

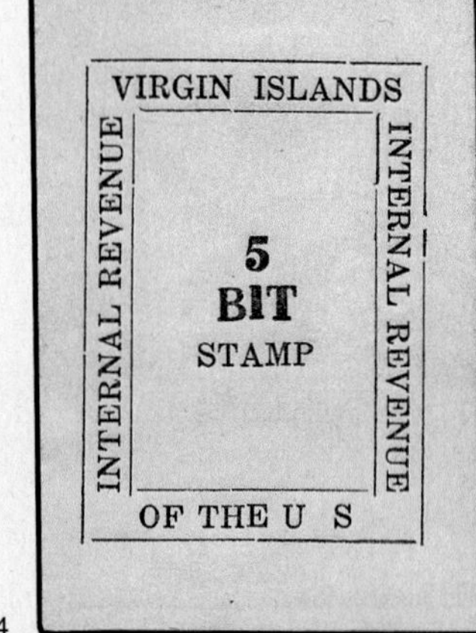

R4

1933-34 Letterpress Without Gum *Imperf.*

No.	Type	Description	Unused	Used
1RJ1	R4	3b **black**	250.00	—
1RJ2	R4	5b **black**	100.00	—
1RJ3	R4	6b **black**	40.00	—
1RJ4	R4	7b **black**	125.00	125.00

A papermaker's watermark appears on some examples of Nos. 1RJ1-1RJ4.

Handstamp Surcharge in Black on Stamps with No Imprinted Denomination

No.	Type	Description	Unused	Used
1RJ5	R4	3b on blank, **black**	250.00	—
1RJ6	R4	7b on blank, **black**	50.00	—
1RJ7	R4	8b on blank, **black**	140.00	—
1RJ8	R4	15b on blank, **black**	160.00	—
1RJ9	R4	40b on blank, **black**		—

Numeral-only Handstamp Surcharge in Black on Nos. 1RJ1-1RJ4

No.	Type	Description	Unused	Used
1RJ10	R4	3 on 6b **black** (#1RJ3)		—
1RJ11	R4	6 on 3b **black** (#1RJ1)	75.00	—
a.		Violet surcharge	200.00	—
1RJ12	R4	6 on 5b **black** (#1RJ2)	250.00	—
1RJ13	R4	6 on 7b **black** (#1RJ4)	100.00	*125.00*
1RJ14	R4	7 on 6b **black** (#1RJ3)	150.00	—
1RJ15	R4	15 on 6b **black** (#1RJ3)	150.00	—

Numeral-only Typed Surcharge in Black on No. 1RJ4

No.	Type	Description	Unused	Used
1RJ16	R4	10 on 7b **black**	300.00	—

On No. 1RJ16, typed "XXXX" obliterates the "7" denomination.

CUSTOMS HOUSE INSPECTION FEE

Danish West Indies Postage Due Stamps of 1905-13 Canceled with the "Toldkammer" Canceling Device in Violet or Black

"Toldkammer" Cancel

Litho. *Perf. 13*

No.	Type	Description	Unused	Used
RL1	D2	5b (on #J5) **red & gray**		—
RL2	D2	20b (on #J6) **red & gray**		*300.00*
RL3	D2	30b (on #J7) **red & gray**		*300.00*
RL4	D2	50b (on #J8) **red & gray**		*100.00*

GUAM

A former Spanish island possession in the Pacific Ocean, one of the Mariana group, about 1,450 miles east of the Philippines. Captured June 20, 1898, and ceded to the United States by treaty after the Spanish-American War. Stamps overprinted "Guam" were used while the post office was under the jurisdiction of the Navy Department from July 7, 1899, until March 29, 1901, when a Postal Agent was appointed by the Post Office Department and the postal service passed under that Department's control. From this date on Guam was supplied with regular United States postage stamps, although the overprints remained in use for several more years.

Italicized numbers in parentheses indicate quantities issued.

Population 9,000 (est. 1899).

100 CENTS = 1 DOLLAR

United States Nos. 279, 279B, 279Bc, 268, 280a, 281, 282, 272, 282C, 283, 284, 275, 275a, 276 and 276A Overprinted

1899 Wmk. 191 *Perf. 12*

Black Overprint

No.	Description	Unused	Used
1	A87 1c **deep green** *(25,000)*	20.00	*25.00*
	Never hinged	40.00	
	On cover		*200.00*
	Block of 4	90.00	*140.00*
	P# strip of 3, Impt.	90.00	
	P# block of 6, Impt.	350.00	

A bogus inverted overprint exists.

No.	Description	Unused	Used
2	A88 2c **red,** type IV, *Dec. (105,000)*	17.50	*25.00*
	light red, type IV	17.50	*25.00*
	On cover		*200.00*
	Never hinged	35.00	
	Block of 4	85.00	*140.00*
	P# strip of 3, Impt.	75.00	
	P# block of 6, Impt.	300.00	—
a.	2c **rose carmine,** type IV, *Aug. 15*	30.00	30.00
	Never hinged	60.00	
	On cover		*225.00*
	Block of 4	125.00	*175.00*
	P# strip of 3, Impt.	100.00	
	P# block of 6, Impt.	375.00	
3	A89 3c **purple** *(5000)*	140.00	*175.00*
	Never hinged	275.00	
	On cover		*400.00*
	Block of 4	600.00	*850.00*
	P# strip of 3, Impt.	575.00	
	P# block of 6, Impt.	1,600.	
4	A90 4c **lilac brown** *(5000)*	125.00	*175.00*
	Never hinged	250.00	
	On cover		*450.00*
	Block of 4	550.00	*825.00*
	P# strip of 3, Impt.	525.00	
	P# block of 6, Impt.	*1,750.*	
	Extra frame line at top (Plate 793 R62)	—	
5	A91 5c **blue** *(20,000)*	32.50	*45.00*
	Never hinged	65.00	
	On cover		*200.00*
	Block of 4	140.00	*250.00*
	P# strip of 3, Impt.	140.00	
	P# block of 6, Impt.	700.00	
6	A92 6c **lake** *(5000)*	125.00	*190.00*
	Never hinged	250.00	
	On cover		*450.00*
	Block of 4	550.00	*1,000.*
	P# strip of 3, Impt.	500.00	
	P# block of 6, Impt.	1,500.	
7	A93 8c **violet brown** *(5000)*	125.00	*160.00*
	Never hinged	275.00	
	On cover		*450.00*
	Block of 4	575.00	*1,000.*
	P# strip of 3, Impt.	575.00	
	P# block of 6, Impt.	1,250.	
8	A94 10c **brown,** type I *(10,000)*	45.00	*55.00*
	Never hinged	90.00	
	On cover		*275.00*
	Block of 4	200.00	*300.00*
	P# strip of 3, Impt.	220.00	
	P# block of 6, Impt.	1,000.	
9	A94 10c **brown,** type II	*2,750.*	—
	Never hinged	*5,500.*	
	Pair	—	
10	A95 15c **olive green** *(5000)*	150.00	140.00
	Never hinged	300.00	
	On cover		*900.00*
	Block of 4	650.00	*875.00*
	P# strip of 3, Impt.	600.00	
	P# block of 6, Impt.	2,200.	
11	A96 50c **orange** *(4000)*	350.00	*400.00*
	Never hinged	700.00	
	On cover		*1,500.*
	Block of 4	1,600.	*2,000.*
	P# strip of 3, Impt.	1,600.	
	P# block of 6, Impt.	4,500.	
a.	50c **red orange**	550.00	—
	Never hinged	1,100.	

Red Overprint

No.	Description	Unused	Used
12	A97 $1 **black,** type I *(3000)*	350.00	*400.00*
	Never hinged	700.00	
	On cover		*3,500.*
	Block of 4	1,750.	*1,750.*
	P# strip of 3, Impt.	1,750.	
	P# block of 6, Impt.	*37,500.*	
13	A97 $1 **black,** type II	*3,750.*	
	Never hinged	—	
	Block of 4	22,500.	
	Nos. 1-8,10-12 (11)	1,480.	*1,790.*

Counterfeits of the overprint exist.

No. 13 exists only in the special printing.

Special Printing

In March 1900, one pane of 100 stamps of each of Nos. 1-8, 10-12 and two panes of 50 stamps of No. E1 were specially overprinted for displays at the Paris Exposition (1900) and Pan American Exposition (1901). The 2c pane was light red, type IV.

Stamps were handstamped type E "Specimen" in black ink by H. G. Mandel and mounted by him in separate displays for the two Expositions. Additional stamps from each pane were also handstamped "Specimen" but most were destroyed after the Expositions. However, becasue additional stamps that are not Special Printings exist with a black "Specimen" handstamp, expertization by competent authorities is recommended.

J. M. Bartels, a stamp dealer, signed some stamps from these panes "Special Surcharge" in pencil on the gum to authenticate them as coming from the "Mandel" Special Printing panes. In 1904 or later, he handstamped additional surviving examples "Special Surcharge" in red ink on the back as his guarantee. Some of these guaranteed stamps had Mandel's "Specimen" handstamp on the face while others did not. Value (with or without "Specimen" handstamp): Nos. 1-8, 10, each $1,000; Nos. 11, E1, each $1,250; No. 12, $2,000.

SPECIAL DELIVERY STAMP

Special Delivery Stamp of the United States, No. E5 Overprinted diagonally in Red

1899 Wmk. 191 *Perf. 12*

No.	Description	Unused	Used
E1	SD3 10c **blue** *(5000)*	150.	*200.00*
	Never hinged	275.	
	On cover		*1,500.*
	Block of 4	650.	
	Margin block of 4, arrow	750.	
	P# strip of 3, Impt.	900.	
	P# block of 6, Impt.	*4,000.*	
a.	Dots in curved frame above messenger (Plate 882)	200.	
	Never hinged	400.	
	P# block of 6, Impt. (Plate 882)	*4,250.*	

Counterfeits of the overprint exist.

The special stamps for Guam were replaced by the regular issues of the United States.

GUAM GUARD MAIL

LOCAL POSTAL SERVICE

Inaugurated April 8, 1930, by Commander Willis W. Bradley, Jr., U.S.N., Governor of Guam, for the conveyance of mail between Agaña and the other smaller towns.

Philippines Nos. 290 and 291 Overprinted

1930, Apr. 8 Unwmk. *Perf. 11*

No.	Description	Unused	Used
M1	A40 2c **green** *(2,000)*	400.	275.
	Never hinged	575.	
	First day cover		600.
	Block of 4	1,700.	
	P# block of 6	—	
M2	A40 4c **carmine** *(3,000)*	225.	150.
	Never hinged	325.	
	First day cover		400.
	Block of 4	950.	
	P# block of 6	—	

Counterfeits of overprint exist.

Seal of Guam — A1

Design size: 19x30mm

1930, July 10 Unwmk. *Perf. 12*

Without Gum

No.	Description	Unused	Used
M3	A1 1c **red & black** *(1,000)*	120.00	150.00
	On cover		225.00
	Block of 4	525.00	
M4	A1 2c **black & red** *(4,000)*	75.00	95.00
	On cover		250.00
	Block of 4	325.00	
a.	Block of 4 with extra impression of vignette covering the intersection of the block	*10,000.*	

Examples are often found showing parts of watermark "CLEVELAND BOND."

Philippines Nos. 290 and 291 Overprinted in Black

1930, Aug. 21 Unwmk. *Perf. 11*

No.	Description	Unused	Used
M5	A40 2c **green** *(20,000)*	2.75	4.50
	Never hinged	4.00	
	On cover		75.00
	Block of 4	12.00	
	P# block of 6	*125.00*	
a.	2c **yellow green**	2.50	4.50

M6	A40 4c **carmine** *(80,000)*	.50	1.75
	Never hinged	1.00	
	On cover		75.00
	Block of 4	2.25	
	P# block of 6	*90.00*	

Same Overprint in Red on Philippines Nos. 290, 291, 292, 293a, and 294

1930, Dec. 29

M7	A40 2c **green** *(50,000)*	.80	2.00
	Never hinged	1.20	
	On cover		50.00
	Block of 4	3.50	
	P# block of 6	*125.00*	
a.	GRAUD (Pos. 63) *(500)*	425.00	
b.	MIAL (Pos. 84) *(500)*	425.00	
M8	A40 4c **carmine** *(50,000)*	.85	1.50
	Never hinged	1.30	
	On cover		50.00
	Block of 4	3.50	
	P# block of 6	*90.00*	
M9	A40 6c **deep violet** *(25,000)*	2.50	4.50
	Never hinged	3.75	
	On cover		60.00
	Block of 4	11.00	
	P# block of 10, Impt.	*250.00*	
M10	A40 8c **orange brown** *(25,000)*	2.50	4.50
	Never hinged	3.75	
	On cover		60.00
	Block of 4	11.00	
	P# block of 10, Impt.	*300.00*	
M11	A40 10c **deep blue** *(25,000)*	2.75	4.50
	Never hinged	4.00	
	On cover		60.00
	Block of 4	11.00	
	P# block of 10, Impt.	*350.00*	

The local postal service was discontinued April 8th, 1931, and replaced by the service of the United States Post Office Department.

ESSAYS

M3-E1

Impression of denomination and inscription only; single impresson in pane of 25.

M3-E1 1c red, on stamp paper with "Cleveland Bond" watermark, perforated vertically *4,000.*

M3-E2

Design size: 15x25mm
Impression of vignette only.

M3-E2	On smooth, thick, off-white paper	
	black	—
	black on thin book paper	—
	green	—
	reddish brown	—
	blue on cream-colored card	—

SPECIMEN STAMPS

Handstamped U.S. Type E in Purple or Black

1899

1S	E	1c **deep green**	175.00
2aS	E	2c **rose carmine,** type IV	175.00
3S	E	3c **purple**	175.00
4S	E	4c **lilac brown**	175.00
5S	E	5c **blue**	175.00
6S	E	6c **lake**	175.00
7S	E	8c **violet brown**	175.00
8S	E	10c **brown,** type I	175.00
10S	E	15c **olive green**	175.00
11S	E	50c **orange**	350.00
12S	E	$1 **black,** type I	350.00
13S	E	$1 **black,** type II	—

Special Delivery

1899

E1S	E	10c **blue**	500.00
E1aS	E	10c **blue**	—

Values for specimen stamps are for fine-very fine appearing examples with minor faults.

See Special Printing notice after No. 13 for Special Printings with black "Specimen" handstamps, but note that not all stamps with the black "Specimen" handstamp are Special Printings.

HAWAII

Until 1893, Hawaii was an independent kingdom. From 1893-1898 it was a republic. The United States annexed Hawaii in 1898, and it became a Territory on June 14, 1900. Hawaiian stamps remained in use through June 13, 1900, and were replaced by U.S. stamps on June 14. In 1959 Hawaii became the 50th State of the Union. Hawaii consists of about 20 islands in the mid-Pacific, about 2,300 miles southwest of San Francisco. The area is 6,434 square miles and the population was estimated at 150,000 in 1899. Honolulu is the capital.

100 CENTS = 1 DOLLAR

Values of Hawaii stamps vary considerably according to condition. For Nos. 1-4, values are for examples with minor damage that has been skillfully repaired.

A1

A2

A3

1851-52 Unwmk. Typeset Pelure Paper *Imperf.*

1	A1 2c **blue**	*625,000.*	*250,000.*
	On cover		*2,250,000.*
2	A1 5c **blue**	*55,000.*	*45,000.*
	On cover		*90,000.*
3	A2 13c **blue**	*37,000.*	*32,500.*
	On cover		*75,000.*
4	A3 13c **blue**	*52,500.*	*42,500.*
	On cover		*80,000.*

Nos. 1-4 are known as the "Missionaries."

Two varieties of each. Nos. 1-4, off cover, are almost invariably damaged.

No. 1 unused and on cover are each unique; the on-cover value is based on a 2013 auction sale.

Values for Nos. 5-82 are for very fine examples. Extremely fine to superb stamps sell at much higher prices, and inferior or poor stamps sell at reduced prices, depending on the condition of the individual example.

King Kamehameha III

A4

A5

Printed in Sheets of 20 (4x5)

1853 Thick White Wove Paper Engr.

5	A4 5c **blue**	1,900.	1,900.
	On cover		*5,000.*
	On cover with U.S. #17		*12,000.*
	Pair	*4,000.*	*4,750.*
a.	Line through "Honolulu" (Pos. 2)	*3,000.*	*3,000.*
6	A5 13c **dark red**	900.	*1,700.*
	On cover		*22,500.*
	On cover with #5		*12,500.*
	On cover with U.S. #11 (pair)		*22,500.*
	On cover with U.S. #17		*32,500.*
	On cover with #5 and U.S. #17		*32,500.*
	On cover with #8 and U.S. #36b		*37,500.*
	Pair	*2,000.*	*4,750.*
	Block of 4	*4,000.*	
	Double transfer	—	

Black Manuscript Surcharge on Scott 6

1857

7	A6 5c on 13c **dark red**	*7,000.*	*10,000.*
	On cover with pair U.S. #7 and 14		*57,500.*
	On cover with pair U.S. #11, 14		*55,000.*
	On cover with U.S. #14		*50,000.*
	On cover with U.S. #14, 20		*57,500.*
	On cover with U.S. #17		*45,000.*

Beware of fake manuscript surcharges. Expertization is strongly recommended.

1857 Thin White Wove Paper

8	A4 5c **blue**	700.	*750.*
	On cover		*2,800.*
	On cover with U.S. #11		—
	On cover with U.S. #7, 15		*6,000.*
	On cover with U.S. #17		*9,000.*
	On cover with U.S. #26		—
	On cover with U.S. #35		*11,000.*
	On cover with U.S. #36		*10,000.*
	On cover with U.S. #69		*12,500.*
	On cover with U.S. #76		—

Pair 1,650. *2,000.*
Pair on cover *15,000.*
a. Line through "Honolulu" (Pos. 2) *1,350.* *1,350.*
On cover with U.S. #17 *6,500.*
b. Double impression *4,250.* *4,750.*

1861 Thin Bluish Wove Paper

9 A4 5c **blue** 400. 400.
On cover *4,500.*
On cover with U.S. #36b *3,250.*
On cover with U.S. #65 *3,000.*
On cover with U.S. #65, 73 *7,750.*
On cover with U.S. #68 *4,250.*
On cover with U.S. #76 *7,000.*
Block of 4 2,000. —
a. Line through "Honolulu" (Pos. 2) *950.* *1,000.*
On cover with U.S. #69 *10,000.*

RE-ISSUE

1868 Ordinary White Wove Paper

10 A4 5c **blue** 27.50
Block of 4 130.
a. Line through "Honolulu" (Pos. 2) 80.
In pair with #10 350.
11 A5 13c **dull rose** 325.
Block of 4 1,400.

Remainders of Nos. 10 and 11 were overprinted "SPECIMEN." See Nos. 10S-11Sb.

Nos. 10 and 11 were never placed in use but stamps (both with and without overprint) were sold at face value at the Honolulu post office.

REPRINTS (Official Imitations) 1889

Original

Reprint

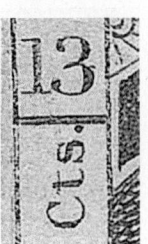

Original

Reprint

5c — Originals have two small dots near the left side of the square in the upper right corner. These dots are missing in the reprints.

13c — The bottom of the 3 of 13 in the upper left corner is flattened in the originals and rounded in the reprints. The "t" of "Cts" on the left side is as tall as the "C" in the reprints, but shorter in the originals.

10R A4 5c **blue** 65.
Block of 4 280.
11R A5 13c **orange red** 300.
Block of 4 1,450.

On August 19, 1892, the remaining supply of reprints was overprinted in black "REPRINT." The reprints (both with and without overprint) were sold at face value.

Quantities sold (including overprints) were 5c-3634 and 13c-1696. See Nos. 10R-S and 11R-S.

Values for the Numeral stamps, Nos. 12-26, are for examples with four reasonably large margins. Unused values are for stamps without gum.

A7

A8

A9

1859-62 Typeset from settings of 10 varieties

12 A7 1c **light blue,** *bluish white* *15,000.* *15,000.*
Pair *37,500.*
a. "1 Ce" omitted *22,500.*
b. "nt" omitted — —

No. 12a is unique.

13 A7 2c **light blue,** *bluish white* *6,250.* *5,000.*
On cover *12,500.*
Block of 4 *27,500.*
a. 2c **dark blue,** *grayish white* *6,750.* *5,000.*
On cover *12,500.*
On cover, both #13 and #13a *40,000.*
b. Comma after "Cents" — *6,750.*
On cover *12,500.*
c. No period after "LETA" — —
14 A7 2c **black,** *greenish blue* ('62) *8,000.* *6,000.*
On cover *10,000.*
a. "2-Cents." —

1859-63

15 A7 1c **black,** *grayish* ('63) 650. *2,750.*
On cover —
Block of 4 3,250.
a. Tête bêche pair *9,000.*
b. "NTER" —
c. Period omitted after "Postage" 850.
d. 1c **black,** *bluish gray* *850.*
Block of 4 —
16 A7 2c **black,** *grayish* 1,000. 850.
On cover *5,000.*
Pair — —
a. "2" at top of rectangle *3,750.* *3,750.*
On cover *13,500.*
b. Printed on both sides — *21,000.*
c. "NTER" *3,250.* *6,500.*
d. 2c **black,** *grayish white* 1,000. 850.
e. Period omitted after "Cents" —
f. Overlapping impressions — —
g. "TAGE" —
17 A7 2c **dark blue,** *bluish* ('63) *12,000.* *8,750.*
Pair *25,000.*
a. "ISL" — —

18 A7 2c **black,** *blue gray* ('63) *3,250.* *6,000.*
On cover *18,000.*
Pair *13,500.*
Thick paper — —

1864-65

19 A7 1c **black** 625. *10,000.*
Pair 1,300.
Block of 4 3,000.
20 A7 2c **black** 775. *1,500.*
On cover *17,500.*
Pair 1,600.
Block of 4 *4,000.*
21 A8 5c **blue,** *blue* ('65) 900. 700.
On cover (pair) *13,000.*
On cover with U.S. #65 —
On cover with U.S. #68 —
On cover with U.S. #76 *8,250.*
Block of 4 *4,500.* —
a. Tête bêche pair *10,500.*
b. 5c **bluish black,** *grayish white* *11,000.* *3,750.*

No. 21b unused is unique. No. 21b used is also unique but defective.

22 A9 5c **blue,** *blue* ('65) 575. *900.*
On cover *13,000.*
On cover with U.S. #76 *9,250.*
On cover with U.S. #63 and 76 —
Block of 4 2,600.
a. Tête bêche pair *18,000.*
b. 5c **blue,** *grayish white* —
c. Overlapping impressions —

1864 Laid Paper

23 A7 1c **black** 300. *2,500.*
On cover with U.S. #76 *12,000.*
Block of 4 1,250.
a. "HA" instead of "HAWAIIAN" *3,500.*
b. Tête bêche pair *6,000.*
c. Tête bêche pair, Nos. 23, 23a *18,000.*
24 A7 2c **black** 350. *1,050.*
Block of 4 1,500.
a. "NTER" *3,250.*
b. "S" of "POSTAGE" omitted *1,500.*
c. Tête bêche pair *7,000.*

A10

1865 **Wove Paper**

25 A10 1c **dark blue** 350.
Block of 4 1,450.
a. Double impression —
b. With inverted impression of No. 21 on face *18,500.*
26 A10 2c **dark blue** 350.
Block of 4 1,500.

Nos. 12 to 26 were typeset and were printed in sheets of 50 (5 settings of 10 varieties each). The sheets were cut into panes of 25 (5x5) before distribution to the post offices.

King Kamehameha IV — A11

1861-63 **Litho.** **Horizontally Laid Paper**

27 A11 2c **pale rose** 350. 350.
On cover *900.*
Pair —
a. 2c **carmine rose** ('63) 3,000. 2,850.

Vertically Laid Paper

28 A11 2c **pale rose** 325. 325.
On cover *1,500.*
Block of 4 1,750. 1,650.
a. 2c **carmine rose** ('63) 400. *450.*
On cover *2,500.*
Block of 4 1,900.

RE-ISSUE

1869 **Engr.** **Thin Wove Paper**

29 A11 2c **red** 45.00 —
Block of 4 240.00

No. 29 was not issued for postal purposes although canceled examples are known. It was sold only at the Honolulu post office, at first without overprint and later with overprint "CANCELLED." See No. 29S.

See note following No. 51.

Princess Victoria Kamamalu — A12

King Kamehameha IV — A13

King Kamehameha V — A14

King Kamehameha V — A15

Mataio Kekuanaoa — A16

1864-86 **Engr.** **Wove Paper** ***Perf. 12***

30 A12 1c **purple** ('86) 11.00 8.00
Never hinged 25.00
On cover 150.00
Block of 4 55.00
a. 1c **mauve** ('71) 60.00 20.00
Never hinged 95.00
On cover, pair 550.00
On cover with #32 *7,000.*
On cover with U.S. #156 600.00
Block of 4 300.00
b. 1c **violet** ('78) 20.00 10.00
Never hinged 45.00
On cover, pair 500.00
On cover with #35 and #36 *6,000.*
Block of 4 160.00 200.00
31 A13 2c **rose vermilion** 65.00 12.50
Never hinged 150.00
On cover 200.00
On cover with #32 *5,000.*
On cover with U.S. #63 and #65 *11,000.*
On cover with U.S. #65 *5,000.*
On cover with U.S. #73 *3,000.*
On cover with U.S. #76 *1,000.*
On cover, pair, with pair U.S. #93 *10,000.*
On cover with #27 and U.S. #76 *15,000.*
On cover with #32 and #33 and U.S. #148 *8,000.*
Block of 4 275.00 *400.00*
a. 2c **vermilion** ('86) 55.00 17.50
Never hinged 130.00
On cover 500.00
b. Half used as 1c on cover with #32 *7,500.*
As "b," with U.S. #117 *18,000.*
32 A14 5c **blue** ('66) 175.00 30.00
Never hinged 375.00
On cover 250.00
On cover with any U.S. issues of 1861-68 *5,000.*
On cover with U.S. #116 *15,000.*
On cover with U.S. #116 and 69 *25,000.*
Block of 4 800.00 175.00
33 A15 6c **yellow green** ('71) 45.00 10.00
Never hinged 100.00
On cover 300.00
a. 6c **bluish green** ('78) 35.00 10.00
Never hinged 85.00
On cover 300.00
On cover with U.S. #179 *1,500.*
On cover with U.S. #183 + #184 *1,750.*
On cover with U.S. #185 *1,250.*
Block of 4 160.00 500.00
b. As "a," horiz. pair, imperf. *2,250.*
34 A16 18c **dull rose** ('71) 100.00 45.00
Never hinged 220.00
On cover 350.00
On cover with No. 36 —
On cover with No. 36 and U.S. No. 179 *2,000.*
On cover with U.S. No. 161 —
On cover with U.S. No. 163 —
On cover with U.S. No. 185 *10,000.*
Block of 4 475.00 —
Nos. 30-34 (5) 396.00 105.50
Set, never hinged 860.00

Half of No. 31 was used with a 5c stamp to make up the 6-cent rate to the United States.

No. 32 has traces of rectangular frame lines surrounding the design. Nos. 39 and 52C have no such frame lines.

King David Kalakaua — A17

Prince William Pitt Leleiohoku — A18

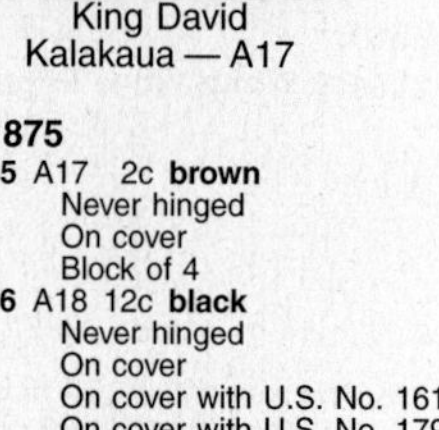

1875

35 A17 2c **brown** 9.00 3.00
Never hinged 22.00
On cover 200.00
Block of 4 45.00 40.00
36 A18 12c **black** 75.00 32.50
Never hinged 165.00
On cover 400.00
On cover with U.S. No. 161 —
On cover with U.S. No. 179b —
Block of 4 350.00 —

Princess Likelike — A19

King David Kalakaua — A20

Queen Kapiolani — A21

Statue of King Kamehameha I — A22

King William Lunalilo — A23

Queen Emma Kaleleonalani — A24

1882

37 A19 1c **blue** 11.00 6.00
Never hinged 27.50
On cover 60.00
Block of 4 55.00 50.00
38 A17 2c **lilac rose** 125.00 47.50
Never hinged 275.00
On cover 150.00
Block of 4 625.00
39 A14 5c **ultramarine** 15.00 3.00
Never hinged 35.00
On cover 27.50
Block of 4 75.00 60.00
a. Vert. pair, imperf. horiz. *5,000.* *6,000.*
40 A20 10c **black** 50.00 25.00
Never hinged 115.00
On cover 160.00
Block of 4 210.00 140.00
41 A21 15c **red brown** 70.00 27.50
Never hinged 150.00
On cover 200.00
Block of 4 325.00 200.00
Nos. 37-41 (5) 271.00 109.00
Set, never hinged 602.50

1883-86

No.		Unused	Used
42	A19 1c **green**	3.00	2.00
	Never hinged	7.00	
	On cover		25.00
	Block of 4	15.00	14.00
43	A17 2c **rose** ('86)	5.00	1.00
	Never hinged	11.00	
	On cover		25.00
	Block of 4	22.50	12.50
a.	2c **dull red**	65.00	22.50
	Never hinged	140.00	
	Block of 4	310.00	
44	A20 10c **red brown** ('84)	40.00	12.00
	Never hinged	90.00	
	On cover		125.00
	Block of 4	190.00	100.00
45	A20 10c **vermilion**	45.00	14.00
	Never hinged	100.00	
	On cover		125.00
	Block of 4	210.00	85.00
46	A18 12c **red lilac**	90.00	40.00
	Never hinged	225.00	
	On cover		425.00
	Block of 4	435.00	250.00
47	A22 25c **dark violet**	160.00	65.00
	Never hinged	350.00	
	On cover		375.00
	Block of 4	725.00	350.00
48	A23 50c **red**	200.00	95.00
	Never hinged	425.00	
	On cover		525.00
	Block of 4	1,050.	
49	A24 $1 **rose red**	325.00	275.00
	Never hinged	675.00	
	On cover		*8,000.*
	Block of 4	1,500.	
	Maltese cross cancellation		150.00
	Nos. 42-49 (8)	868.00	504.00
	Set, never hinged	1,833.	

Other fiscal cancellations exist on No. 49.

Nos. 48-49 are valued used with postal cancels. Canceled-to-order cancels exist and are worth less.

REPRODUCTION and REPRINT

Yellowish Wove Paper

1886-89 **Engr.** ***Imperf.***

No.		Unused
50	A11 2c **orange vermilion**	170.00
	Never hinged	275.00
	Block of 4	825.00
51	A11 2c **carmine** ('89)	35.00
	Never hinged	50.00
	Block of 4	160.00

In 1885, the Postmaster General wished to have on sale complete sets of Hawaii's portrait stamps, but was unable to find either the stone from which Nos. 27 and 28 were printed, or the plate from which No. 29 was printed. He therefore sent an example of No. 29 to the American Bank Note Company, with an order to engrave a new plate like it and print 10,000 stamps therefrom, of which 5000 were overprinted "SPECIMEN" in blue.

The original No. 29 was printed in sheets of fifteen (5x3), but the plate of these "Official Imitations" was made up of fifty stamps (10x5). Later, in 1887, the original die for No. 29 was discovered, and, after retouching, a new plate was made and 37,500 stamps were printed (No. 51). These, like the originals, were printed in sheets of fifteen. They were delivered during 1889 and 1890. In 1892, all remaining unsold in the Post Office were overprinted "Reprint".

No. 29 is red in color, and printed on very thin white wove paper. No. 50 is orange vermilion in color, on medium, white to buff paper. In No. 50 the vertical line on the left side of the portrait touches the horizontal line over the label "Elua Keneta", while in the other two varieties, Nos. 29 and 51, it does not touch the horizontal line by half a millimeter. In No. 51 there are three parallel lines on the left side of the King's nose, while in No. 29 and No. 50 there are no such lines. No. 51 is carmine in color and printed on thick, yellowish to buff, wove paper.

It is claimed that both Nos. 50 and 51 were available for postage, although not made to fill a postal requirement. They exist with favor cancellation. No. 51 also is known postally used. See Nos. 50S-51S.

Queen Liliuokalani — A25

1890-91 ***Perf. 12***

No.		Unused	Used
52	A25 2c **dull violet** ('91)	15.00	1.50
	Never hinged	25.00	
	On cover		25.00
	Block of 4	70.00	12.00
a.	Vert. pair, imperf. horiz.	*3,750.*	
52C	A14 5c **deep indigo**	125.00	150.00
	Never hinged	280.00	
	On cover		500.00
	Block of 4	600.00	*850.00*

Stamps of 1864-91 Overprinted

Three categories of double overprints:
I. Both overprints heavy.
II. One overprint heavy, one of moderate strength.
III. One overprint heavy, one of light or weak strength.

1893 **Overprinted in Red**

No.		Unused	Used
53	A12 1c **violet**	9.00	13.00
	Never hinged	20.00	
	On cover		35.00
	Block of 4	42.50	70.00
a.	"189" instead of "1893"	600.00	—
b.	No period after "GOVT"	*275.00*	*275.00*
f.	Double overprint (III)	*600.00*	
54	A19 1c **blue**	9.00	*15.00*
	Never hinged	21.00	
	On cover		40.00
	Block of 4	45.00	67.50
b.	No period after "GOVT"	*140.00*	*150.00*
e.	Double overprint (II)	*1,500.*	
f.	Double overprint (III)	*400.00*	
55	A19 1c **green**	2.00	*3.00*
	Never hinged	4.00	
	On cover		25.00
	Block of 4	8.00	15.00
d.	Double overprint (I)	*650.00*	*650.00*
f.	Double overprint (III)	*250.00*	*250.00*
g.	Pair, one without ovpt.	*10,000.*	
56	A17 2c **brown**	12.50	*20.00*
	Never hinged	27.50	
	On cover		60.00
	Block of 4	60.00	120.00
b.	No period after "GOVT"	*325.00*	—
57	A25 2c **dull violet**	2.00	1.50
	Never hinged	3.00	
	On cover		25.00
	Block of 4	9.00	6.50
a.	"18 3" instead of "1893"	*900.00*	*900.00*
d.	Double overprint (I)	*1,300.*	*1,000.*
f.	Double overprint (III)	*190.00*	*190.00*
g.	Inverted overprint	*4,000.*	*4,750.*
58	A14 5c **deep indigo**	15.00	*30.00*
	Never hinged	32.00	
	On cover		100.00

Block of 4	72.50	140.00
b. No period after "GOVT"	*275.00*	*275.00*
f. Double overprint (III)	*1,250.*	*675.00*
59 A14 5c **ultramarine**	7.00	3.00
Never hinged	15.00	
On cover		40.00
Block of 4	35.00	22.50
d. Double overprint (I)	*6,500.*	
e. Double overprint (II)	*3,750.*	*3,750.*
f. Double overprint (III)		*600.00*
g. Inverted overprint	*1,500.*	*1,500.*
60 A15 6c **green**	17.50	*25.00*
Never hinged	40.00	
On cover		140.00
Block of 4	85.00	125.00
d. Double overprint (I)	*5,000.*	
e. Double overprint (II)	*1,100.*	
f. Double overprint (III)	400.00	
61 A20 10c **black**	14.00	*20.00*
Never hinged	30.00	
On cover		125.00
Block of 4	65.00	82.50
e. Double overprint (II)	*1,000.*	*900.00*
f. Double overprint (III)	*225.00*	
61B A20 10c **red brown**	*15,000.*	*29,000.*
Never hinged	*25,000.*	
Block of 4	*65,000.*	
62 A18 12c **black**	14.00	*20.00*
Never hinged	30.00	
On cover		150.00
Block of 4	70.00	110.00
d. Double overprint (I)	*1,500.*	
e. Double overprint (II)	*1,100.*	
f. Double overprint (III)	—	
63 A18 12c **red lilac**	175.00	*250.00*
Never hinged	400.00	
On cover		550.00
Block of 4	1,000.	—
64 A22 25c **dark violet**	35.00	*45.00*
Never hinged	70.00	
On cover		225.00
Block of 4	160.00	200.00
Vert. plate scratch at top	90.00	
b. No period after "GOVT"	*350.00*	*350.00*
Never hinged	*600.00*	
f. Double overprint (III)	*1,250.*	
Nos. 53-61,62-64 (12)	312.00	*445.50*
Nos. 53-61, 62-64 never hinged	692.75	

Virtually all known examples of No. 61B are cut in at the top.

Overprinted in Black

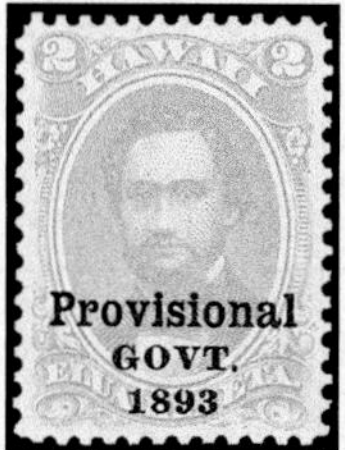

65 A13 2c **vermilion**	85.00	*90.00*
Never hinged	200.00	
On cover		*450.00*
Block of 4	*375.00*	*500.00*
b. No period after "GOVT"	*300.00*	*300.00*
66 A17 2c **rose**	2.50	*2.50*
Never hinged	3.75	
On cover		25.00
Block of 4	11.00	*11.00*
b. No period after "GOVT"	70.00	70.00
d. Double overprint (I)	*4,000.*	
e. Double overprint (II)	*2,750.*	
f. Double overprint (III)	*300.00*	
66C A15 6c **green**	*15,000.*	*29,000.*
On cover		—
Block of 4	*65,000.*	
67 A20 10c **vermilion**	22.50	*30.00*
Never hinged	45.00	
On cover		125.00
Block of 4	110.00	180.00
f. Double overprint (III)	*1,250.*	
68 A20 10c **red brown**	12.00	*13.00*
Never hinged	24.00	
On cover		100.00
Block of 4	57.50	75.00
f. Double overprint (III)	*4,000.*	
69 A18 12c **red lilac**	350.00	*500.00*
Never hinged	575.00	
On cover		950.00
Block of 4	1,600.	*2,400.*
70 A21 15c **red brown**	27.50	*35.00*
Never hinged	55.00	
On cover		300.00
Block of 4	120.00	*150.00*
e. Double overprint (II)	*2,000.*	
71 A16 18c **dull rose**	40.00	40.00
Never hinged	80.00	
On cover		225.00
Block of 4	185.00	*175.00*
a. "18 3" instead of "1893"	*525.00*	*525.00*
b. No period after "GOVT"	*350.00*	*350.00*
d. Double overprint (I)	*650.00*	
f. Double overprint (III)	*275.00*	—
g. Pair, one without ovpt.	*3,500.*	
h. As "b," double overprint (II)	*1,750.*	
72 A23 50c **red**	90.00	*120.00*
Never hinged	180.00	
On cover		600.00
Block of 4	400.00	*500.00*
b. No period after "GOVT"	*500.00*	*500.00*
Never hinged	*775.00*	
f. Double overprint (III)	*1,000.*	
73 A24 $1 **rose red**	160.00	*190.00*
Never hinged	325.00	
On cover		775.00
Block of 4	700.00	*875.00*
b. No period after "GOVT"	*525.00*	500.00
Nos. 65-66,67-73 (9)	789.50	*1,021.*
Nos. 65-66, 67-73 never hinged	1,485.	

Coat of Arms — A26

View of Honolulu — A27

Statue of Kamehameha I — A28

Stars and Palms — A29

S. S. "Arawa" — A30

Pres. Sanford Ballard Dole — A31

1894

74 A26 1c **yellow**	2.00	1.50
Never hinged	4.00	
On cover		25.00
Block of 4	9.00	9.00
75 A27 2c **brown**	2.00	.60
Never hinged	4.00	
On cover		25.00
Block of 4	9.00	7.00
"Flying goose" flaw (48 LR 2)	525.00	475.00
Never hinged	1,100.	
Double transfer	5.00	5.00
76 A28 5c **rose lake**	5.00	2.00
Never hinged	11.00	
On cover		25.00
Block of 4	25.00	15.00
77 A29 10c **yellow green**	8.00	5.00
Never hinged	18.00	
On cover		45.00
Block of 4	35.00	25.00
78 A30 12c **blue**	17.50	*20.00*
Never hinged	37.50	
On cover		150.00
Block of 4	65.00	*80.00*
Double transfer	20.00	20.00
79 A31 25c **deep blue**	22.50	17.50
Never hinged	47.50	
On cover		100.00
Block of 4	100.00	—
Nos. 74-79 (6)	57.00	*46.60*
Set, never hinged	122.50	

Numerous double transfers exist on Nos. 75 and 81.

"CENTS" Added — A32

1899

80 A26 1c **dark green**	2.00	1.50
Never hinged	4.50	
On cover		25.00
Block of 4	9.50	7.00
81 A27 2c **rose**	1.50	1.00
Never hinged	3.50	
On cover		20.00
Block of 4	6.50	6.00
Double transfer	—	—
"Flying goose" flaw (48 LR 2)	350.00	350.00
Never hinged	750.00	
a. 2c **salmon**	1.50	1.50
Never hinged	3.50	
b. Vert. pair, imperf. horiz.	*4,250.*	
82 A32 5c **blue**	8.00	4.00
Never hinged	20.00	
On cover		25.00
Block of 4	40.00	55.00
Nos. 80-82 (3)	11.50	6.50
Set, never hinged	28.00	

OFFICIAL STAMPS

Lorrin Andrews Thurston — O1

1896 Engr. Unwmk. *Perf. 12*

O1 O1 2c **green**	45.00	20.00
Never hinged	90.00	
On cover		400.00
Block of 4	200.00	
O2 O1 5c **black brown**	45.00	20.00
Never hinged	90.00	
On cover		425.00
Block of 4	200.00	
O3 O1 6c **deep ultramarine**	45.00	20.00
Never hinged	90.00	
On cover		—
Block of 4	200.00	
O4 O1 10c **bright rose**	45.00	20.00
Never hinged	90.00	
On cover		475.00
Block of 4	200.00	
O5 O1 12c **orange**	55.00	22.50
Never hinged	110.00	
On cover		—
Block of 4	260.00	
O6 O1 25c **gray violet**	65.00	22.50
Never hinged	130.00	
On cover		—
Block of 4	300.00	
Nos. O1-O6 (6)	300.00	125.00
Set, never hinged	600.00	

Used values for Nos. O1-O6 are for stamps canceled-to-order "FOREIGN OFFICE/HONOLULU H.I." in double circle without date. Values of postally used stamps: Nos. O1-O2, O4, $50 each; No. O3, $125; No. O5, $160; No. O6, $200.

ENVELOPES

Italicized numbers in parentheses indicate quantities issued.
All printed by American Bank Note Co., N.Y.

View of Honolulu Harbor — E1

Envelopes of White Paper, Outside and Inside

1884

U1 E1 1c **light green** *(109,000)*	2.75	3.00
Entire	6.00	*25.00*
a. 1c **green** *(10,000)*	5.00	*15.00*
Entire	15.00	*90.00*
b. 1c **dark green**	10.00	*10.00*
Entire	25.00	*75.00*
c. As No. U1, double impression	*5,250.*	
U2 E1 2c **carmine** *(386,000 including U2a, U2b)*	2.75	4.00
Entire	5.00	*17.50*
a. 2c **red**	2.75	4.00
Entire	5.00	*17.50*
b. 2c **rose**	2.75	4.00
Entire	5.00	*17.50*
c. 2c **pale pink** *(5,000)*	30.00	30.00
Entire	90.00	*100.00*
U3 E1 4c **red** *(18,000)*	15.00	25.00
Entire	50.00	*150.00*
U4 E1 5c **blue** *(90,775)*	6.50	7.50
Entire	17.50	*30.00*
U5 E1 10c **black** *(3,500 plus)*	25.00	37.50
Entire	100.00	*150.00*

Envelopes White Outside, Blue Inside

U6 E1 2c **rose**	175.00	225.00
Entire	425.00	*6,500.*
U7 E1 4c **red**	175.00	225.00
Entire	425.00	*7,500.*
U8 E1 5c **blue**	225.00	250.00
Entire	575.00	*1,250.*
U9 E1 10c **black**	300.00	450.00
Entire	525.00	—
Nos. U1-U9 (9)	927.00	1,227.

Nos. U1, U2, U4 & U5 Overprinted Locally in Red or Black

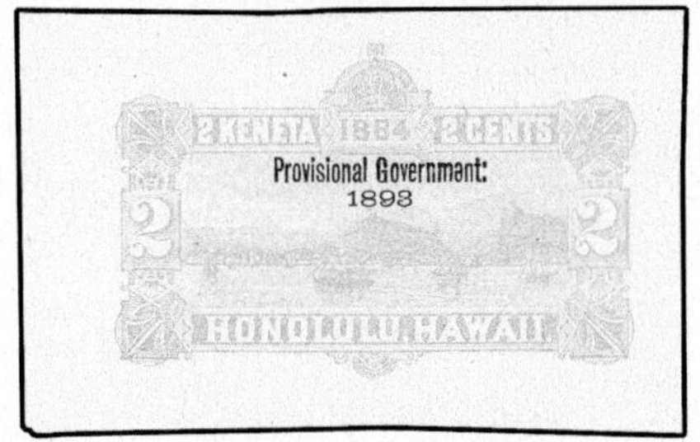

1893

U10 E1 1c **light green** (R) *(16,000)*	6.00	11.00
Entire	12.00	*75.00*
a. Double overprint	*2,000.*	
Entire	*8,000.*	
U11 E1 2c **carmine** (Bk) *(37,000)*	3.00	4.00
Entire	6.00	*20.00*
a. Double overprint	600.00	
Entire	*1,100.*	*1,750.*
b. Double overprint, one inverted, entire	*2,750.*	
c. Double impression	*4,750.*	

No. U11 is known as an unused entire with a triple overprint, two of the overprints being at the bottom right portion of the envelope. Unique. Value, $9,500.

U12 E1 5c **blue** (R) *(34,891)*	4.50	5.00
Entire	10.00	*15.00*
a. Double overprint	375.00	*400.00*
Entire	700.00	*3,000.*
b. Triple overprint, entire		*7,500.*
U13 E1 10c **black** (R) *(17,707 incl. No. U14)*	15.00	20.00
Entire	27.50	*125.00*
a. Double overprint, entire	*2,000.*	*2,000.*
b. Triple overprint, entire	*8,500.*	

Envelope No. U9 Overprinted in Red

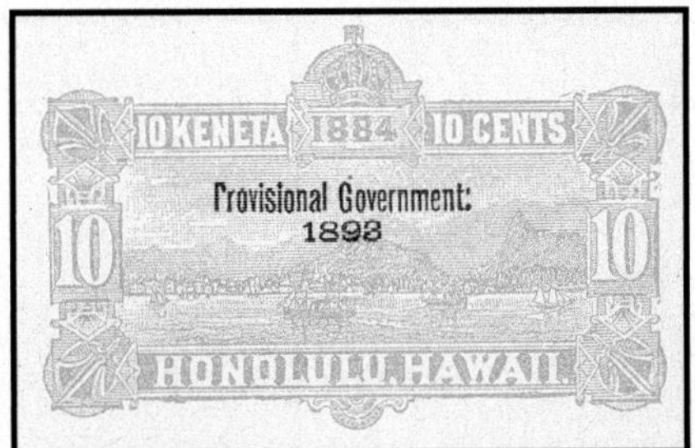

U14 E1 10c **black** (R)	325.	*750.00*
Entire	1,100.	*13,000.*

SPECIAL DELIVERY ENVELOPE

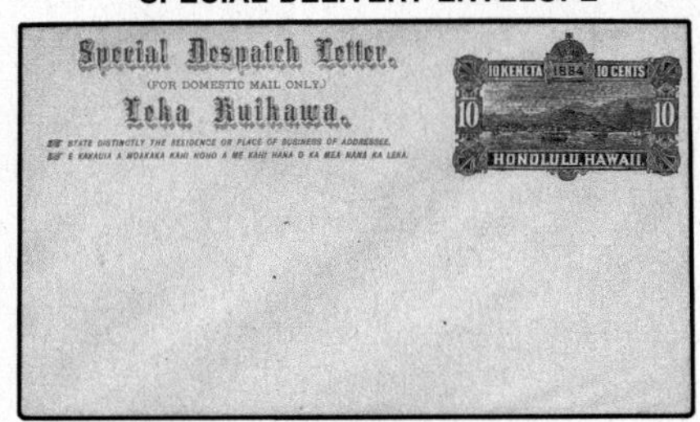

Envelope No. U5 with added inscription "Special Despatch Letter" etc. in red at top left corner
Value is for Entire.

1885

UE1 E1 10c **black** *(2,000)*	175.

Envelope No. UE1 was prepared for use but never issued for postal purposes. Postally used examples exist, but no special delivery service was performed. Favor cancellations exist.

POSTAL CARDS

All printed by American Bank Note Co., N.Y.
Values are for entires.

Queen Liliuokalani — PC1

View of Diamond Head — PC2

Royal Emblems — PC3

1882-92 **Engr.**

UX1 PC1 1c **red,** *buff (125,000)*	30.00	*75.00*
UX2 PC2 2c **black** *(45,000)*	50.00	*90.00*
a. Lithographed ('92)	125.00	200.00
UX3 PC3 3c **blue green** *(21,426)*	67.50	*175.00*

1889 **Litho.**

UX4 PC1 1c **red,** *buff (171,240)*	27.50	*50.00*

Cards Nos. UX4, UX2a and UX3 Overprinted Locally in Red or Black

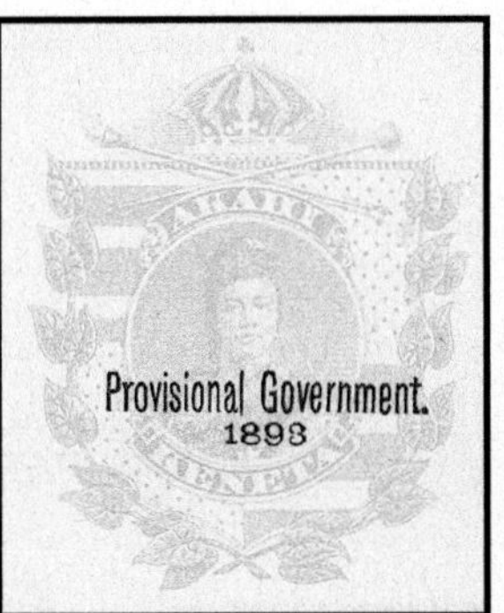

1893

UX5 PC1 1c **red,** *buff* (Bk) *(28,760)*	30.00	*75.00*
a. Double overprint	*4,500.*	*3,500.*
UX6 PC2 2c **black** (R) *(10,000)*	65.00	*95.00*

No. UX6 is known unused with double overprint, one inverted at lower left of card. Unique. Value, $16,000.

UX7 PC3 3c **blue green** (R) *(8,574)*	80.00	*500.00*
a. Double overprint	*18,500.*	

No. UX7a is believed to be unique. The second, full-strength overprint is just above the indicium.

Iolani Palace — PC4

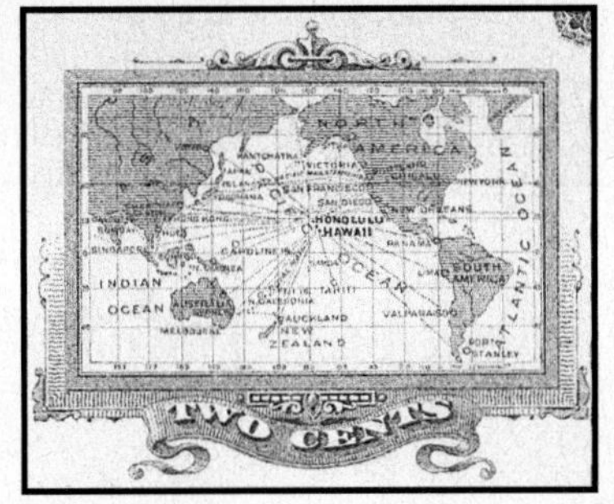

Map of Pacific Ocean, Mercator's Projection — PC5

1894-97 **Litho.**

Border Frame 131½x72½mm

UX8 PC4 1c **red,** *buff (100,000)*	20.00	*40.00*
a. Border frame 132½x74mm ('97) *(200,000)*	20.00	*40.00*
UX9 PC5 2c **green** *(60,000)*	45.00	*80.00*
a. Border frame 132½x74mm ('97) *(190,000)*	45.00	*80.00*

PAID REPLY POSTAL CARDS

Double Cards, Same Designs as Postal Cards With Added Inscriptions

1883 **Litho.**

UY1 PC1 1c +1c **purple,** *buff,* unsevered *(5,000)*	400.00	*450.00*
m. Message card, detached	35.00	*100.00*
r. Reply card, detached	35.00	*100.00*
UY2 PC2 2c +2c **dark blue,** unsevered *(5,000)*	450.00	*500.00*
m. Message card, detached	55.00	*140.00*
r. Reply card, detached	55.00	*140.00*

1889

UY3 PC1 1c +1c **gray violet,** *buff,* unsevered *(5,000)*	450.00	*550.00*
m. Message card, detached	35.00	*110.00*
r. Reply card, detached	35.00	*110.00*

UY4 PC2 2c +2c **sapphire,** unsevered *(5,000)* 450.00 *550.00*
m. Message card, detached 35.00 *90.00*
r. Reply card, detached 35.00 *90.00*

Values for unused unsevered Paid Reply Postal Cards are for cards which have not been folded. Folded cards sell for about 33% of these values.

Detached card used values are for canceled cards with printed messages on the back.

REVENUE STAMPS

R1

R2

R3

R4

R5

R6

Printed by the American Bank Note Co.
Sheets of 70

1877 **Engr.** **Unwmk.** ***Rouletted 8***

R1 R1 25c **green** *(160,000)* 25.00 *20.00*
Never hinged 32.50
R2 R2 50c **yellow orange** *(190,000)* 45.00 20.00
R3 R3 $1 **black** *(580,000)* 45.00 13.00
a. $1 gray 45.00 13.00

Denominations Typo.

R4 R4 $5 **vermilion & violet blue** *(21,000)* 260.00 57.50
R5 R5 $10 **reddish brown & green** *(14,000)* 260.00 65.00
R6 R6 $50 **slate blue & carmine** *(3,500)* *1,050.* *450.00*

No. R6 unused is valued without gum, as all known examples come thus.

Unused values for all revenues except No. R6 are for stamps with original gum. Apparently unused stamps without gum sell for less.

No. R1 Surcharged in Black or Gold

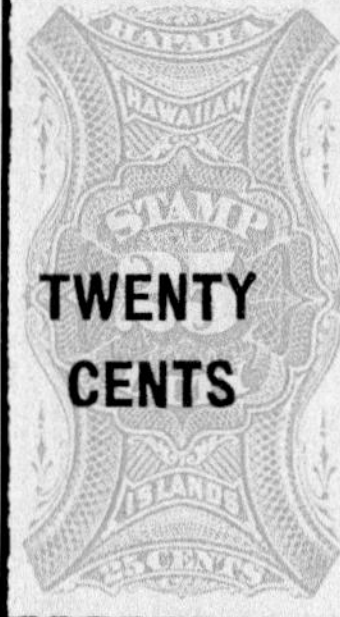

a

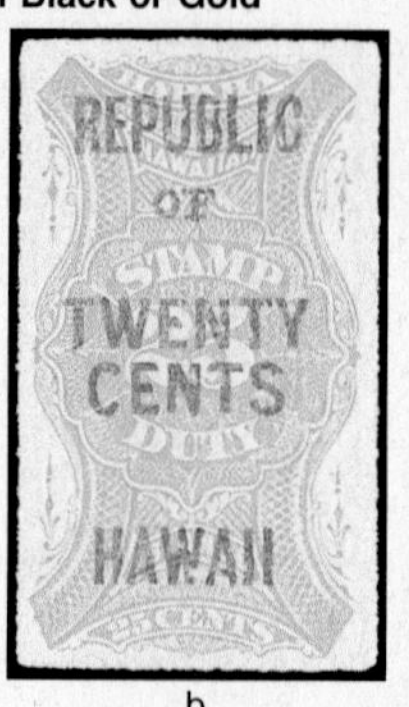

b

1893-94

R7 R1 (a) 20c on 25c **green** 60.00 30.00
Never hinged 80.00
a. Inverted surcharge *1,250.* *900.00*
R8 R1 (b) 20c on 25c **green** (G) 100.00 100.00
Never hinged 175.00
a. Inverted surcharge —
b. Double surcharge — —
c. Double surcharge, one black, one gold — *1,500.*
d. Double surcharge, one gold, one red in different font —
e. Double surcharge, with a single added letter "c" —
f. Double surcharge with two "c" letters added —

On No. R8b, one surcharge is always diagonal. On No. R8c, the black surcharge is 20mm wide, while the normal gold surcharge is 15mm wide.

R7

Sheets of 50

1894 **Litho.** ***Perf. 14***

R9 R7 20c **red** *(10,000)* 375.00 375.00
Never hinged 850.00
a. Imperf. *(25,000)* 575.00 1,200.
Never hinged 1,200.
Pair 1,200.
Never hinged 2,700.

No. R9a is known in an unused pair on paper with "DENNIS" papermaker's watermark.

R10 R7 25c **violet brown** 1,300. 1,000.
Never hinged 2,400.
a. Imperf. 1,900. —
Never hinged 3,800.
Pair 4,250.
Never hinged 7,900.
b. As "a," tete beche pair —

Kamehameha I — R8

Printed by the American Bank Note Co.
Sheets of 100

1897 **Engr.** ***Perf. 12***

R11 R8 $1 **dark blue** *(60,000)* 9.00 9.00
Never hinged 12.50

R9

1901 ***Rouletted 8***

R12 R9 $50 **slate blue & carmine** *(7,000)* 70.00 70.00
Never hinged 120.00

Types of 1877

Printed by the American Bank Note Co.
Sheets of 70

1910-13 **Engr.** ***Perf. 12***

R13 R2 50c **yellow orange** ('13) *(70,000)* 17.50 *30.00*
Never hinged 22.50
R14 R3 $1 **black** ('13) *(35,000)* 22.50 *40.00*
Never hinged 27.50
R15 R4 $5 **vermilion & violet blue** *(14,000)* 45.00 *60.00*
Never hinged 55.00
a. Denomination inverted *10,000.*
R16 R5 $10 **reddish brown & green** *(14,000)* 65.00 *70.00*
Never hinged 75.00

PROOFS

1853

5TC3 5c Plate on wove paper
a. **black** *6,000.*
6TC3 13c Plate on wove paper
a. **black** *6,000.*

1868-89

10TC1a 5c Large die on India paper
e. **orange red** 3,000.
10RTC1a 5c Large die on India paper, on card
e. **orange red** 3,000.
11TC1a 13c Large die on India paper
e. **orange red** 1,000.
11TC3 13c Plate on India paper
a. **orange red** 800.
11RP1 13c **orange red,** large die on India paper 2,500.
11RP3 13c **orange red,** plate on India paper 800.

1861-63

27TC3 2c Plate on India paper
a. **black** 1,100.

1864-71

30P1 1c **purple,** large die on India paper 900.
30P3 1c **purple,** plate on India paper 400.
Block of 4 1,500.
31P1 2c **rose vermilion,** large die on India paper 900.
31P3 2c **rose vermilion,** plate on India paper 400.
Block of 4 —
31P4 2c **rose vermilion,** plate on card 400.
31TC1a 2c Large die on India paper
e. **green** *2,500.*
32P1 5c **blue,** large die on India paper 900.
32P3 5c **blue,** plate on India paper 400.
Block of 4 2,750.
32P4 5c **blue,** plate on card 400.
32TC1a 5c Large die on India paper
e. **black** 1,250.
32TC3 5c Plate on India paper
a. **dark red** 400.
b. **orange red** 400.
c. **orange** 400.
d. **red brown** 400.
Block of 4 1,800.
e. **green** 400.
Block of 4 1,800.
f. **dark violet** 400.
Block of 4 1,800.
33P1 6c **green,** large die on India paper 900.
33P3 6c **green,** plate on India paper 400.
Block of 4 1,800.
34P1 18c **dull rose,** large die on India paper 900.
34P3 18c **dull rose,** plate on India paper 400.
Block of 4 1,800.
34P4 18c **dull rose,** plate on card 400.
34TC1a 18c Large die on India paper
e. **orange red** 900.
f. **dark orange** 900.
34TC3 18c Plate on India paper
a. **orange red** 650.

1875

35P1	2c **brown,** large die on India paper	750.
35P3	2c **brown,** plate on India paper	400.
	Block of 4	1,800.
35P4	2c **brown,** plate on card	400.
35TC1a	2c Large die on India paper	
	e. **black**	*2,600.*
36P1	12c **black,** large die on India paper	900.
36P3	12c **black,** plate on India paper	400.
36P4	12c **black,** plate on card	400.
36TC1a	12c Large die on India paper	
	e. **violet blue**	925.

1882

37P3	1c **blue,** plate on India paper	400.
	Block of 4	1,800.
37TC1a	1c Large die on India paper	
	e. **black**	*3,750.*
39P1	5c **ultramarine,** large die on India paper	900.
39P3	5c **ultramarine,** plate on India paper	400.
40P1	10c **black,** large die on India paper	900.
40P3	10c **black,** plate on India paper	400.
	Block of 4	1,800.
41P3	15c **red brown,** plate on India paper	400.
	Block of 4	1,800.
41P4	15c **red brown,** plate on card	400.

1883-86

42P3	1c **green,** plate on India paper	400.
	Block of 4	1,800.
42P4	1c **green,** plate on card	400.
43P3	2c **rose,** plate on India paper	400.
	Block of 4	1,800.
43P4	2c **rose,** plate on card	400.
47P1	25c **dk violet,** large die on India paper	900.
47P3	25c **dk violet,** plate on India paper	400.
	Block of 4	1,800.
47TC1a	25c Large die on India paper	
	e. **black**	*1,000.*
48P1	50c **red,** large die on India paper	1,000.
48P3	50c **red,** plate on India paper	400.
	Block of 4	1,800.
48TC1a	50c Large die on India paper	
	e. **lake**	*1,700.*
48TC3	50c Plate on India paper	
	a. **lake**	500.
49P1	$1 **rose red,** large die on India paper	*2,100.*
49P3	$1 **rose red,** plate on India paper	400.
	Block of 4	1,800.
49P4	$1 **rose red,** plate on card	500.
49TC1a	$1 Large die on India paper	
	e. **orange red**	1,000.
49TC3	$1 Plate on India paper	
	a. **black**	400.
	b. **orange red**	*1,000.*
	c. **carmine**	*1,000.*
	d. **vermilion**	*1,000.*
	Block of 4	*4,500.*

1886-89

50P1	2c **orange vermilion,** large die on India paper	1,000.
50P3	2c **orange vermilion,** plate on India paper	500.
51P1	2c **carmine,** large die on India paper	1,100.

1890-91

52P1	2c **dull violet,** large die on India paper	*4,000.*
52P3	2c **dull violet,** plate on India paper	500.
52P4	2c **dull violet,** plate on card	500.
52CP3	2c **deep indigo,** plate on India paper	500.

1894

74P1	1c **yellow,** large die on India paper	1,000.
74P3	1c **yellow,** plate on India paper	400.
74P4	1c **yellow,** plate on card	400.
75P1	2c **brown,** large die on India paper	1,000.
75P3	2c **brown,** plate on India paper	400.
75TC1a	2c Large die on India paper	
	e. **dk green**	1,000.
76P1	5c **rose lake,** large die on India paper	1,000.
76P3	5c **rose lake,** plate on India paper	400.
76P4	5c **rose lake,** plate on card	400.
77P1	10c **yellow green,** large die on India paper	1,000.
77P3	10c **yellow green,** plate on India paper	400.
	Block of 4	1,800.
77P4	10c **yellow green,** plate on card	400.
77TC1a	2c Large die on India paper	
	e. **dp blue green**	1,000.
78P1	12c **blue,** large die on India paper	1,000.
78P3	12c **blue,** plate on India paper	400.
78P4	12c **blue,** plate on card	400.
79P1	25c **dp blue,** large die on India paper	1,000.
79P3	25c **dp blue,** plate on India paper	400.
79P4	25c **dp blue,** plate on card	400.

1899

82P3	5c **blue,** plate on India paper	400.
	Block of 4	1,800.
82P4	5c **blue,** plate on card	400.

Official

1896

O1P1	2c **green,** large die on India paper	1,000.
O1P3	2c **green,** plate on India paper	500.
O1P4	2c **green,** plate on card	400.
O2P1	5c **blk brown,** large die on India paper	1,000.
O2P3	5c **blk brown,** plate on India paper	500.
O2P4	5c **blk brown,** plate on card	425.
O3P1	6c **dp ultra,** large die on India paper	1,000.
O3P3	6c **dp ultra,** plate on India paper	500.
O3P4	6c **dp ultra,** plate on card	425.
O4P1	10c **brt rose,** large die on India paper	1,000.
O4P3	10c **brt rose,** plate on India paper	500.
	Block of 4	—
O4P4	10c **brt rose,** plate on card	425.
O4TC1a	2c Large die on India paper	
	e. **black**	1,000.
O5P1	12c **orange,** large die on India paper	1,000.
O5P3	12c **orange,** plate on India paper	500.
O5P4	12c **orange,** plate on card	425.
O5TC1a	12c Large die on India paper	
	e. **black**	1,000.
O6P1	25c **gray violet,** large die on India paper	1,000.
O6P3	25c **gray violet,** plate on India paper	500.
O6P4	25c **gray violet,** plate on card	425.
O6TC1a	25c Large die on India paper	
	e. **black**	1,000.

Envelopes

Uncleared indicia only

1884

U1P1	1c **green,** large die on India paper	*1,000.*
U1TC1a	1c Large die on India paper	
	e. **black**	*750.*
	f. **orange**	*1,000.*
	g. **red**	*1,000.*
	k. **brown,** on bond paper	*1,000.*
U2P1	2c **carmine,** large die on India paper	*1,000.*
U2TC1a	2c Large die on India paper	
	e. **black**	*750.*
	f. **blue**	*1,000.*
	g. **orange**	*1,000.*
U3P1	4c **red,** large die on India paper	*1,000.*
U3TC1a	4c Large die on India paper	
	e. **black**	*750.*
U4P1	5c **blue,** large die on India paper	*1,000.*
U4TC1a	5c Large die on India paper	
	e. **black**	*750.*
U5P1	10c **black,** large die on India paper	*1,000.*
U5TC1a	10c Large die on India paper	
	e. **black**	*750.*

Postal Cards

Large die proofs are of indicia only, India plate proofs are entire card.

1882-95

UX1P1	1c **red,** large die on India paper	*3,500.*
UX1P3	1c **red,** plate on India paper	*2,000.*
UX1TC3	1c Plate on India paper	
	a. **green**	*2,000.*
UX2P3	2c **black,** plate on India paper	*2,000.*
UX3P1	3c **blue green,** large die on India paper	*2,000.*
UX3P3	3c **blue green,** plate on India paper	*2,000.*
UX8TC3	1c Plate on India paper	
	a. **orange**	*3,000.*
	b. **brown**	*3,000.*
UX8TC5	1c Plate on wove paper	
	a. **orange**	*6,000.*

Paid Reply Postal Cards

1889

UY3mTC4	1c **greenish blue,** message card, plate proof on card	*9,500.*
UY3rTC4	1c **greenish blue,** reply card, plate proof on card	*9,500.*

Revenues

1877-97

R1P3	25c **green,** plate on India paper	*600.*
	Block of 4	*2,750.*
R1P4	25c **green,** plate on card	*600.*
R1TC1a	25c Large die on India paper	
	e. **blue green**	*1,150.*
	f. **black**	*1,150.*
	g. **brown red**	*1,150.*
	h. **brown**	*1,150.*
	i. **grayish blue**	*1,150.*
R2P3	50c **yellow orange,** plate on India paper	*600.*
	Block of 4	*2,800.*
R2P4	50c **yellow orange,** plate on card	*600.*
R2TC1a	50c Large die on India paper	
	e. **blue green**	*1,150.*
	f. **black**	*1,150.*
	g. **brown red**	*1,150.*
	h. **brown**	*1,150.*
	i. **grayish blue**	*1,150.*
R3P1	$1 **black,** large die on India paper	*1,150.*
R3P3	$1 **black,** plate on India paper	*600.*
	Block of 4	*2,750.*
R3P4	$1 **black,** plate on card	*600.*
R3TC1a	$1 Large die on India paper	
	e. **blue green**	*1,150.*
	f. **brown red**	*1,150.*
	g. **brown**	*1,150.*
	h. **grayish blue**	*1,150.*
R4P3	$5 **ver. & violet blue,** plate on India paper	*600.*
	Block of 4	*2,750.*
R4P4	$5 **ver. & violet blue,** plate on card	*400.*
R5P3	$10 **reddish brn & grn,** plate on India paper	*600.*
	Block of 4	*2,750.*
R5P4	$10 **reddish brn & grn,** plate on card	*600.*
R6P3	$50 **slate blue & car,** plate on India paper	*600.*
	Block of 4	*2,750.*
R6P4	$50 **slate blue & car,** plate on card	*800.*
R11P1	$1 **dk blue,** Large die on India paper	*1,250.*
R11P3	$1 **dk blue,** plate on India paper	*800.*
R11P4	$1 **dk blue,** plate on card	*700.*

SPECIMEN STAMPS

Overprinted in Black or Red — Type A

1868

10S	A 5c **blue** (R)	25.
	Block of 4	130.
	a. Line through "Honolulu" (Pos. 2)	110.
11S	A 13c **dull rose**	25.
	Block of 4	130.

Overprinted in Black — Type B

11S	B 13c **dull rose**	275.
	Block of 4	1,250.
	a. Double overprint, one as #11S A, one as #11S B	*4,000.*
	b. Period omitted (Pos. 18, 20)	600.

Overprinted in Black — Type C

1889

10RS	C 5c **blue**	65.
	Block of 4	275.
11RS	C 13c **orange red**	250.
	Block of 4	1,100.

Overprinted in Black — Type D

1869

29S	D 2c **red**	55.
	Block of 4	275.

Overprinted in Blue — Type E

1886

50S	E 2c **orange vermilion**	65.
	Block of 4	300.

Overprinted in Black — Type C

1889

No.	Type	Description	Unused	Used
51S	C	2c **carmine**	35.	
		Block of 4	175.	

PHILIPPINES

Following the American occupation of the Philippines, May 1, 1898, after Admiral Dewey's fleet entered Manila Bay, an order was issued by the U. S. Postmaster General (No. 201, May 24, 1898) establishing postal facilities with rates similar to the domestic rates.

Military postal stations were established as branch post offices, each such station being placed within the jurisdiction of the nearest regular post office. Supplies were issued to these military stations through the regular post office of which they were branches.

Several post office clerks were sent to the Philippines and the San Francisco post office was made the nearest regular office for the early Philippine mail and the postmarks of the period point out this fact.

U.S. stamps overprinted "PHILIPPINES" were placed on sale in Manila June 30, 1899. Regular U.S. stamps had been in use from early March, and at the Manila post office Spanish stamps were also acceptable.

The first regular post office was established at Cavite on July 30, 1898, as a branch of the San Francisco post office. The first cancellation was a dated handstamp with "PHILIPPINE STATION" and "SAN FRANCISCO, CAL."

On May 1, 1899, the entire Philippine postal service was separated from San Francisco and numerous varieties of postmarks resulted. Many of the early used stamps show postmarks and cancellations of the Military Station, Camp or R.P.O. types, together with "Killers" of the types employed in the U.S. at the time.

The Philippines became a commonwealth of the United States on November 15, 1935, the High Commissioner of the United States taking office on the same day. The official name of the government was "Commonwealth of the Philippines" as provided by Article 17 of the Constitution. Upon the final and complete withdrawal of sovereignty of the United States and the proclamation of Philippine independence on July 4, 1946, the Commonwealth of the Philippines became the "Republic of the Philippines."

Italicized numbers in parentheses indicate quantities issued.

Authority for dates of issue, stamps from 1899 to 1911, and some quantities issued — "The Postal Issues of the Philippines," by F. L. Palmer (New York, 1912). Authority for quantities issued — "NAPP's Numbers, Volume 2," by Joseph M. Napp (2001).

100 CENTS = 1 DOLLAR
100 CENTAVOS = 1 PESO (1906)

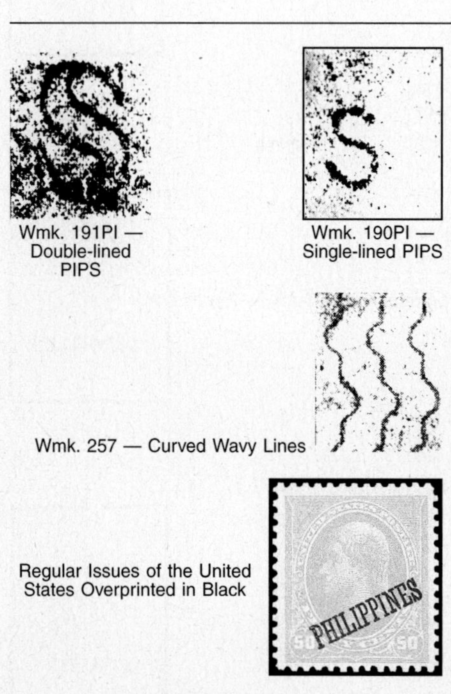

Wmk. 191PI — Double-lined PIPS

Wmk. 190PI — Single-lined PIPS

Wmk. 257 — Curved Wavy Lines

Regular Issues of the United States Overprinted in Black

Printed and overprinted by the U.S. Bureau of Engraving and Printing.

1899, June 30 **Unwmk.** ***Perf. 12***

On U.S. Stamp No. 260

No.	Type	Description	Unused	Used
212	A96	50c **orange**	300.	225.
		Never hinged	775.	
		On cover		—
		Block of 4	1,425.	—
		P# strip of 3, Impt.	1,350.	
		P# block of 6, Impt.	*25,000.*	

On U.S. Stamps Nos. 279, 279B, 279Bd, 279Bj, 279Bf, 279Bc, 268, 281, 282C, 283, 284, 275, 275a

Regular Issues of the United States Overprinted in Black

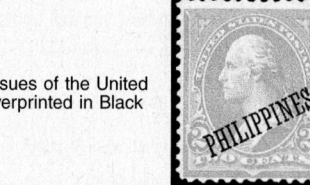

Wmk. Double-lined USPS (191)

No.	Type	Description	Unused	Used
213	A87	1c **yellow green** *(5,500,000)*	3.50	.60
		Never hinged	10.00	
		On cover		10.00
		Block of 4	20.00	5.00
		P# strip of 3, Impt.	40.00	
		P# block of 6, Impt.	225.00	
a.		Inverted overprint	*77,500.*	
214	A88	2c **red,** type IV *(6,970,000)*	1.75	.60
		light red	1.75	.60
		Never hinged	4.25	
		On cover		10.00
		Block of 4	7.00	4.00
		P# strip of 3, Impt.	25.00	
		P# block of 6, Impt.	175.00	
a.		2c **orange red,** type IV, *1901*	1.75	.60
		pale orange red	1.75	.60
		deep orange red, *1903*	1.75	.60
		Never hinged	4.25	
b.		Booklet pane of 6, **red,** type IV *1900*	200.00	*300.00*
		orange red, *1901*	250.00	*300.00*
		Never hinged	450.00	
c.		2c **reddish carmine,** type IV	2.50	1.00
		Never hinged	6.00	
		On cover		12.50
		Block of 4	11.00	7.50
		P# strip of 3, Impt.	35.00	
		P# block of 6, Impt.	225.00	
d.		2c **rose carmine,** type IV	3.00	1.10
		Never hinged	7.25	
		On cover		15.00
		Block of 4	14.00	8.50
		P# strip of 3, Impt.	40.00	
		P# block of 6, Impt.	260.00	
e.		As "d," double ovpt., one albino	750.00	
215	A89	3c **purple** *(673,814)*	9.00	1.25
		Never hinged	21.50	
		On cover		50.00
		Block of 4	42.50	13.50
		P# strip of 3, Impt.	85.00	
		P# block of 6, Impt.	550.00	
216	A91	5c **blue** *(1,700,000)*	9.00	1.00
		Never hinged	21.50	
		On cover		20.00
		Block of 4	42.50	9.00
		P# strip of 3, Impt.	85.00	
		P# block of 6, Impt.	850.00	
a.		Inverted overprint		*6,500.*

No. 216a is valued in the grade of fine.

No.	Type	Description	Unused	Used
217	A94	10c **brown,** type I *(500,000)+*	35.00	4.00
		Never hinged	80.00	
		On cover		100.00
		Block of 4	160.00	55.00
		P# strip of 3, Impt.	175.00	
		P# block of 6, Impt.	700.00	

(+ Quantity includes Nos. 217, 217A)

No.	Type	Description	Unused	Used
217A	A94	10c **orange brown,** type II *(250,000*	110.00	27.50
		Never hinged	275.00	
		On cover		250.00
		Block of 4	525.00	190.00
		P# strip of 3, Impt.	800.00	
		P# block of 6, Impt.	*6,000.*	

No. 217A was overprinted on U.S. No. 283a, vertical watermark. The watermark on No. 217 is horizontal.

No.	Type	Description	Unused	Used
218	A95	15c **olive green** *(200,000)*	40.00	8.00
		light olive green	37.50	8.50
		Never hinged	95.00	
		On cover		110.00
		Block of 4	175.00	52.50
		P# strip of 3, Impt.	200.00	
		P# block of 6, Impt.	3,000.	
219	A96	50c **orange** *(50,000)+*	125.00	37.50
		Never hinged	300.00	
		On cover		*400.00*
		Block of 4	575.00	*250.00*
		P# strip of 3, Impt.	575.00	
		P# block of 6, Impt.	*5,000.*	
a.		50c **red orange**	250.00	55.00
		Never hinged	600.00	
		Block of 4	1,700.	
		Nos. 213-219 (8)	333.25	80.45

(+ Quantity includes Nos. 212, 219, 219a)

Special Printing

In March 1900 one pane of 100 stamps of each of Nos. 213-217, 218, 219 and J1-J5 were specially overprinted for displays at the Paris Exposition (1900) and Pan American Exposition (1901). The 2c pane was light red, type IV.

Stamps were handstampd type E "Specimen" in black ink on the face by H. G. Mandel and mounted by him in separate displays for the two Expositions. Additional stamps from each pane were also handstamped "Specimen" but most were destroyed after the Expositions. However, because additional stamps that are not Special Printings exist with a black "Specimen" handstamp, expertization by competent authorities is recommended.

J. M. Bartels, a stamp dealer, signed some stamps from these panes "Special Surcharge" in pencil on the gum to authenticate them as coming from the "Mandel" Special Printing panes. In 1904 or later, he handstamped additional surviving examples "Special Surcharge" in red ink on the back as his guarantee. Some of these guaranteed stamps had Mandel's "Specimen" handstamp on the face while others did not. Value, each $1,000.

Regular Issue

U.S. Stamps Nos. 280b, 282 and 272 Overprinted in Black

1901, Aug. 30

No.	Type	Description	Unused	Used
220	A90	4c **orange brown** *(404,907)*	35.00	5.00
		Never hinged	80.00	
		On cover		50.00
		Block of 4	160.00	50.00
		P# strip of 3, Impt.	180.00	
		P# block of 6, Impt.	750.00	
221	A92	6c **lake** *(223,465)*	40.00	7.00
		Never hinged	95.00	
		On cover		65.00
		Block of 4	200.00	50.00
		P# strip of 3, Impt.	200.00	
		P# block of 6, Impt.	2,000.	
222	A93	8c **purple brown** *(248,000)*	40.00	7.50
		Never hinged	95.00	
		On cover		50.00
		Block of 4	200.00	55.00
		P# strip of 3, Impt.	200.00	
		P# block of 6, Impt.	1,000.	
		Nos. 220-222 (3)	115.00	19.50

Same Overprint in Red On U.S. Stamps Nos. 276, 276A, 277a and 278

No.	Type	Description	Unused	Used
223	A97	$1 **black,** type I *(3,000)+*	300.00	200.00
		Never hinged	1,000.	
		On cover		800.00
		Block of 4	1,400.	
		P# strip of 3, Impt.	1,500.	
		P# block of 6, Impt.	—	

(+ Quantity includes Nos. 223, 223A)

No.	Type	Description	Unused	Used
223A	A97	$1 **black,** type II	1,500.	750.00
		Never hinged	5,000.	
		On cover		—
		Block of 4	8,750.	—
		P# strip of 3, Impt., one stamp No. 223	16,000.	
b.		Horiz. pair, Nos. 223 and 223A	3,000.	
224	A98	$2 **dark blue** *(1800)*	350.00	325.00
		Never hinged	1,150.	
		On cover		3,250.
		Block of 4	1,600.	—
		P# strip of 3, Impt.	7,000.	
		P# block of 6, Impt.	—	
225	A99	$5 **dark green** *(782)*	500.00	900.00
		Never hinged	1,600.	
		On cover		12,500.
		Block of 4	3,000.	—
		P# strip of 3, Impt.	10,000.	

The existence of a plate block of No. 225 has been questioned by specialists. The editors would like to see evidence of its existence.

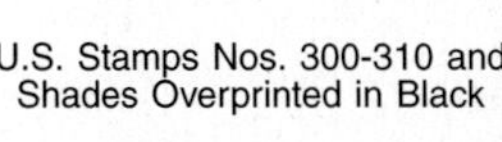
U.S. Stamps Nos. 300-310 and Shades Overprinted in Black

Special Printing

Special printings exist of Nos. 227, 221, 223-225, made from defaced plates. These were made for display at the St. Louis Exposition. All but a few copies were destroyed. Most of the existing copies have the handstamp "Special Printing" on the back. Value: Nos. 227, 221, each $775; No. 223, $1,500; No. 224, $2,000; No. 225, $2,500.

1903-04

No.	Type	Description	Unused	Used
226	A115	1c **blue green** *(9,631,172)*	7.00	.40
		Never hinged	15.50	
		On cover		8.25
		Block of 4	32.50	4.25
		P# strip of 3, Impt.	25.00	
		P# block of 6, Impt.	300.00	
227	A116	2c **carmine** *(850,000)*	9.00	1.10
		Never hinged	20.00	
		On cover		10.00
		Block of 4	42.50	6.00
		P# strip of 3, Impt.	42.50	
		P# block of 6, Impt.	400.00	
228	A117	3c **bright violet** *(14,500)*	67.50	12.50
		Never hinged	150.00	
		On cover		55.00
		Block of 4	275.00	85.00
		P# strip of 3, Impt.	275.00	
		P# block of 6, Impt.	2,000.	
229	A118	4c **brown** *(13,000)*	80.00	22.50
		Never hinged	175.00	
a.		4c **orange brown**	80.00	20.00
		Never hinged	175.00	
		On cover		40.00
		Block of 4	350.00	150.00
		P# strip of 3, Impt.	325.00	
		P# block of 6, Impt.	2,500.	
230	A119	5c **blue** *(1,211,844)*	17.50	1.00
		Never hinged	40.00	
		On cover		22.50
		Block of 4	80.00	7.50
		P# strip of 3, Impt.	70.00	
		P# block of 6, Impt.	1,000.	
231	A120	6c **brnsh lake** *(11,500)*	85.00	22.50
		Never hinged	190.00	
		On cover		65.00
		Block of 4	350.00	150.00
		P# strip of 3, Impt.	350.00	
		P# block of 6, Impt.	3,000.	
232	A121	8c **violet black** *(49,033)*	50.00	15.00
		Never hinged	125.00	
		On cover		300.00
		Block of 4	250.00	100.00
		P# strip of 3, Impt.	275.00	
		P# block of 6, Impt.	2,250.	
233	A122	10c **pale red brown** *(300,179)*	35.00	2.25
		Never hinged	80.00	
		On cover		27.50
		Block of 4	160.00	20.00
		P# strip of 3, Impt.	175.00	
		P# block of 6, Impt.	1,500.	
a.		10c **red brown**	35.00	3.00
		Never hinged	80.00	
		On cover		35.00
		Block of 4	160.00	32.50
		P# strip of 3, Impt.	175.00	
		P# block of 6, Impt.	1,300.	
b.		Pair, one without overprint		1,500.
234	A123	13c **purple black** *(91,341)*	35.00	17.50
		Never hinged	80.00	
a.		13c **brown violet**	35.00	17.50
		Never hinged	80.00	
		On cover		55.00
		Block of 4	150.00	110.00
		P# strip of 3, Impt.	175.00	
		P# block of 6, Impt.	1,850.	
235	A124	15c **olive green** *(183,965)*	60.00	15.00
		Never hinged	135.00	
		On cover		100.00
		Block of 4	275.00	100.00
		P# strip of 3, Impt.	300.00	
		P# block of 6, Impt.	4,750.	
236	A125	50c **orange** *(57,641)*	125.00	35.00
		Never hinged	275.00	
		On cover		300.00
		Block of 4	575.00	275.00
		P# strip of 3, Impt.	575.00	
		P# block of 6, Impt.	35,000.	
		Nos. 226-236 (11)	571.00	144.75
		Set, never hinged	1,285.	

Same Overprint in Red On U.S. Stamps Nos. 311, 312 and 313

No.	Type	Description	Unused	Used
237	A126	$1 **black** *(5617)*	300.00	200.00
		Never hinged	800.00	
		On cover		1,000.
		Block of 4	1,400.	1,850.
		P# strip of 3, Impt.	1,400.	
		P# block of 6, Impt.	8,500.	
238	A127	$2 **dark blue** *(695)*	550.00	800.00
		Never hinged	1,500.	
		Block of 4	3,000.	—
		P# strip of 3, Impt.	3,250.	
		P# block of 6, Impt.	37,500.	
239	A128	$5 **dark green** *(746)*	800.00	2,750.
		Never hinged	2,000.	
		Block of 4	3,750.	—
		P# strip of 3, Impt.	8,500.	
		P# block of 6, Impt.	250,000.	

Same Overprint in Black On U.S. Stamp Nos. 319 and 319c

No.	Type	Description	Unused	Used
240	A129	2c **carmine** *(862,245)*	8.00	2.25
		Never hinged	17.50	
		On cover		3.50
		Block of 4	35.00	15.00
		P# strip of 3, Impt.	45.00	
		P# block of 6, Impt.	600.00	
a.		Booklet pane of 6	1,500.	
b.		2c **scarlet**	8.00	2.75
		Never hinged	19.00	
		On cover		4.00
		Block of 4	35.00	17.50
		P# strip of 3, Impt.	47.50	
		P# block of 6, Impt.	650.00	
c.		As "b," booklet pane of 6	—	

Dates of issue:
Sept. 20, 1903, Nos. 226, 227, 236.
Jan. 4, 1904, Nos. 230, 234, 235, 237, 240a.
Nov. 1, 1904, Nos. 228, 229, 231, 232, 233, 238, 239, 240.

Nos. 212 to 240 were withdrawn from sale on Sept. 8, 1906, the remainders being destroyed.

Special Printing

Two sets of special printings exist of the 1903-04 issue. The first consists of Nos. 226, 230, 234, 235, 236, 237, 240, J6 and J7. These were made for display at the St. Louis Exposition. All but a few stamps were destroyed. Most of the existing examples have the handstamp "Special Surcharge" on the back. Value: No. 237, $1,550; J6, $1,600.; J7, $3,250; others $900.

In 1907 the entire set Nos. 226, 228 to 240, J1 to J7 were specially printed for the Bureau of Insular Affairs on very white paper. They are difficult to distinguish from the ordinary stamps except the Special Delivery stamp which is on U.S. No. E6 (see Philippines No. E2A). Value: No. 237, $1,300; No. 238, $2,600; No. 239, $3,500; others, $1,000.

Regular Issue

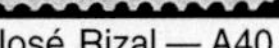
José Rizal — A40

Arms of City of Manila — A41

Printed by the U.S. Bureau of Engraving and Printing.

Plates of 200 subjects in two panes of 100 each.

Booklet panes Nos. 240a, 241b, 242b, 261a, 262b, 276a, 277a, 285a, 286a, 290e, 291b and 292c were made from plates of 180 subjects. No. 214b came from plates of 360 subjects.

Designs: 4c, McKinley. 6c, Ferdinand Magellan. 8c, Miguel Lopez de Legaspi. 10c, Gen. Henry W. Lawton. 12c, Lincoln. 16c, Adm. William T. Sampson. 20c, Washington. 26c, Francisco Carriedo. 30c, Franklin. 2p-10p, Arms of City of Manila.

Wmk. Double-lined PIPS (191PI)

1906, Sept. 8 ***Perf. 12***

No.	Type	Description	Unused	Used
241	A40	2c **deep green** *(51,000,019)*	.40	.25
		Never hinged	1.00	
		P# block of 10, Impt.	40.00	
		Never hinged	65.00	
a.		2c **yellow green** ('10)	.60	.25
		Never hinged	1.50	
		Double transfer		40.00
		P# block of 10, Impt.	30.00	
		Never hinged	50.00	
b.		Booklet pane of 6 *(720,120)*	750.00	800.00
		Never hinged	1,500.	
242	A40	4c **carmine** *(11,000,019)*	.50	.25
		Never hinged	1.25	
		P# block of 10, Impt.	35.00	
		Never hinged	60.00	
a.		4c **carmine lake** ('10)	1.00	.25
		Never hinged	2.50	
		P# block of 10, Impt.	40.00	
		Never hinged	65.00	
b.		Booklet pane of 6*(300,600)*	650.00	700.00
		Never hinged	1,250.	
243	A40	6c **violet** *(1,980,019)*	2.50	.25
		Never hinged	6.25	
		P# block of 10, Impt.	75.00	
		Never hinged	120.00	
244	A40	8c **brown** *(770,019)*	4.50	.90
		Never hinged	11.00	
		P# block of 10, Impt.	140.00	
		Never hinged	225.00	
245	A40	10c **blue** *(5,500,019)*	3.50	.30
		Never hinged	8.75	
		P# block of 10, Impt.	85.00	
		Never hinged	145.00	
a.		10c **dark blue**	3.50	.30
		Never hinged	8.75	
		P# block of 10, Impt.	95.00	
		Never hinged	160.00	
246	A40	12c **brown lake** *(670,019)*	9.00	2.50
		Never hinged	22.50	
		P# block of 10, Impt.	300.00	
		Never hinged	475.00	
247	A40	16c **violet black** *(1,300,019)*	6.00	.35
		Never hinged	15.00	
		P# block of 10, Impt.	325.00	
		Never hinged	475.00	
248	A40	20c **orange brown** *(2,100,019)*	7.00	.35
		Never hinged	17.50	
		P# block of 10, Impt.	275.00	
		Never hinged	450.00	
249	A40	26c **violet brown** *(428,000)*	11.00	3.00
		Never hinged	27.50	
		P# block of 10, Impt.	450.00	
		Never hinged	675.00	
250	A40	30c **olive green** *(1,256,019)*	6.50	1.75
		Never hinged	16.00	
		P# block of 10, Impt.	375.00	
		Never hinged	575.00	

251 A41 1p **orange** *(200,019)* 55.00 17.50
Never hinged 130.00
P# block of 10, Impt. 1,350.
Never hinged 2,000.
252 A41 2p **black** *(100,000)* 50.00 1.75
Never hinged 130.00
P# block of 10, Impt. 1,600.
Never hinged 2,500.
253 A41 4p **dark blue** *(10,000)* 160.00 20.00
Never hinged 375.00
P# block of 10, Impt. 2,750.
Never hinged *5,000.*
254 A41 10p **dark green** *(6,019)* 225.00 80.00
Never hinged 575.00
Block of 4 1,100. 400.00
Nos. 241-254 (14) 540.90 129.15
Set, never hinged 1,316.

1909-13 **Change of Colors**
255 A40 12c **red orange** *(300,000)* 11.00 3.00
Never hinged 27.50
P# block of 10, Impt. 425.00
Never hinged 700.00
256 A40 16c **olive green** *(500,000)* 6.00 .75
Never hinged 15.00
P# block of 10, Impt. 250.00
Never hinged 450.00
257 A40 20c **yellow** *(800,000)* 9.00 1.25
Never hinged 22.50
P# block of 10, Impt. 225.00
Never hinged 375.00
258 A40 26c **blue green** *(250,000)* 3.50 1.25
Never hinged 8.75
P# block of 10, Impt. 250.00
Never hinged 425.00
259 A40 30c **ultramarine** *(600,000)* 13.00 3.50
Never hinged 32.50
P# block of 10, Impt. 400.00
Never hinged 625.00
260 A41 1p **pale violet** *(100,000)* 45.00 5.00
Never hinged 110.00
P# block of 10, Impt. 975.00
Never hinged 1,750.
260A A41 2p **violet brown** ('13) *(50,000)* 100.00 12.00
Never hinged 250.00
P# block of 10, Impt. 1,600.
Never hinged *3,500.*
Nos. 255-260A (7) 187.50 26.75
Set, never hinged 466.25

1911 Wmk. Single-lined PIPS (190PI) ***Perf. 12***
261 A40 2c **green** *(44,000,000)* .75 .25
Never hinged 1.80
On cover 4.00
P# block of 10, Impt. 25.00
Never hinged 40.00
a. Booklet pane of 6 *(896,160)* *800.00 900.00*
Never hinged *1,400.*
262 A40 4c **carmine lake** *(6,000,000)* 3.00 .25
Never hinged 6.75
On cover 6.00
P# block of 10, Impt. 50.00
Never hinged 110.00
a. 4c **carmine** — —
P# block of 10, Impt. 150.00
Never hinged 275.00
b. Booklet pane of 6 *(100,020)* *600.00 700.00*
Never hinged *1,100.*
263 A40 6c **deep violet** *(3,200,000)* 3.00 .25
Never hinged 6.75
P# block of 10, Impt. 90.00
Never hinged 145.00
264 A40 8c **brown** *(1,400,000)* 9.50 .50
Never hinged 21.50
P# block of 10, Impt. 225.00
Never hinged 350.00
265 A40 10c **blue** *(3,700,000)* 4.00 .25
Never hinged 9.00
P# block of 10, Impt. 115.00
Never hinged 180.00
266 A40 12c **orange** *(1,320,000)* 4.00 .45
Never hinged 9.00
P# block of 10, Impt. 235.00
Never hinged 525.00
267 A40 16c **olive green** *(1,000,000)* 4.50 .40
Never hinged 10.00
P# block of 10, Impt. 145.00
Never hinged 225.00
a. 16c **pale olive green** 4.50 .50
Never hinged 10.00
P# block of 10, Impt. 150.00
Never hinged 250.00
268 A40 20c **yellow** *(3,000,000)* 3.50 .25
Never hinged 7.75
P# block of 10, Impt. 140.00
Never hinged 250.00
a. 20c **orange** 4.00 .30
Never hinged 9.00
P# block of 10, Impt. 185.00
Never hinged 300.00
269 A40 26c **blue green** *(249,900)* 6.00 .30
Never hinged 13.50
P# block of 10, Impt. 210.00
Never hinged 375.00
270 A40 30c **ultramarine** *(1,000,000)* 6.00 .50
Never hinged 13.50
P# block of 10, Impt. 175.00
Never hinged 300.00
271 A41 1p **pale violet** *(694,000)* 27.50 .60
Never hinged 62.50
P# block of 10, Impt. 425.00
Never hinged 1,000.
272 A41 2p **violet brown** *(100,000)* 45.00 1.00
Never hinged 100.00
P# block of 10, Impt. 775.00
Never hinged 1,600.
273 A41 4p **deep blue** *(10,000)* 550.00 110.00
Never hinged 1,100.
P# block of 10, Impt. *6,750.*
Never hinged *15,000.*
274 A41 10p **deep green** *(20,000)* 200.00 30.00
Never hinged 400.00
Block of 4 900.00 150.00
Nos. 261-274 (14) 866.75 145.00
Set, never hinged 1,862.

1914
275 A40 30c **gray** *(700,000)* 12.00 .50
Never hinged 27.50
P# block of 10, Impt. 200.00
Never hinged 425.00

1914 ***Perf. 10***
276 A40 2c **green** *(60,000,000)* 3.00 .25
Never hinged 7.00
P# block of 6, no Impt. 25.00
Never hinged 45.00
a. Booklet pane of 6 *(400,080)* *600.00 800.00*
Never hinged *1,250.*
277 A40 4c **carmine** *(2,500,000)* 4.00 .30
Never hinged 9.00
P# block of 6, no Impt. 52.50
Never hinged 90.00
a. Booklet pane of 6 *(56,040)* *600.00*
Never hinged *1,300.*
278 A40 6c **light violet** *(700,000)* 45.00 9.50
Never hinged 100.00
P# block of 10, Impt. 525.00
Never hinged 1,200.
a. 6c **deep violet** 50.00 6.25
Never hinged 110.00
P# block of 10, Impt. 700.00
Never hinged 1,350.
279 A40 8c **brown** *(200,000)* 55.00 10.50
Never hinged 125.00
P# block of 10, Impt. 875.00
Never hinged 2,000.
280 A40 10c **dark blue** *(2,000,000)* 30.00 .25
Never hinged 67.50
P# block of 10, Impt. 375.00
Never hinged 725.00
281 A40 16c **olive green** *(700,000)* 100.00 5.00
Never hinged 225.00
P# block of 10, Impt. *1,200.*
Never hinged *2,500.*
282 A40 20c **orange** *(2,000,000)* 40.00 1.00
Never hinged 85.00
Block of 4 180.00 5.75
283 A40 30c **gray** *(1,300,000)* 60.00 4.50
Never hinged 130.00
P# block of 10, Impt. 1,000.
Never hinged 1,675.
284 A41 1p **pale violet** *(198,000)* 150.00 3.75
Never hinged 350.00
P# block of 10, Impt. *1,800.*
Never hinged *4,000.*
Nos. 276-284 (9) 487.00 35.05
Set, never hinged 1,020.

1918 Wmk. Single-lined PIPS (190PI) ***Perf. 11***
285 A40 2c **green** *(40,000,000)* 21.00 4.25
Never hinged 40.00
P# block of 6, no Impt. 225.00
Never hinged 425.00
a. Booklet pane of 6 *(50,040)* *600.00 800.00*
Never hinged *1,100.*
286 A40 4c **carmine** *(3,000,000)* 26.00 6.00
Never hinged 55.00
P# block of 6, no Impt. 400.00
Never hinged 850.00
a. Booklet pane of 6 *1,350. 2,000.*
287 A40 6c **deep violet** *(1,000,000)* 40.00 6.00
Never hinged 90.00
P# block of 10, Impt. 550.00
Never hinged 1,250.
287A A40 8c **light brown** *(200,000)* 220.00 25.00
Never hinged 400.00
P# block of 10, Impt. *2,750.*
Never hinged *5,000.*
288 A40 10c **dark blue** *(2,000,000)* 60.00 3.00
Never hinged 140.00
P# block of 10, Impt. 650.00
Never hinged 1,400.
289 A40 16c **olive green** *(700,000)* 110.00 10.00
Never hinged 250.00
P# block of 10, Impt. 1,400.
Never hinged *3,200.*
289A A40 20c **orange** *(1,000,000)* 175.00 12.00
Never hinged 400.00
P# block of 10, Impt. 1,950.
Never hinged *4,400.*
289C A40 30c **gray** *(500,000)* 95.00 18.00
Never hinged 215.00
P# block of 10, Impt. 1,500.
Never hinged *3,400.*
289D A41 1p **pale violet** *(200,000)* 100.00 25.00
Never hinged 225.00
P# block of 10, Impt. 1,600.
Never hinged *3,600.*
Nos. 285-289D (9) 847.00 109.25
Set, never hinged 1,815.

1917 Unwmk. ***Perf. 11***
290 A40 2c **yellow green** *(444,746,800)* .25 .25
Never hinged .55
On cover 4.00
P# block of 6, no Impt. 100.00
Never hinged 140.00
a. 2c **dark green** .30 .25
Never hinged .65
green .25 .25
Double transfer — —
P# block of 6, no Impt. 17.50
Never hinged 30.00
b. Vert. pair, imperf. horiz. *2,750.*
c. Horiz. pair, imperf. between *1,500.* —
d. Vertical pair, imperf. btwn. *1,750. 1,000.*
e. Booklet pane of 6 *(3,251,080)* 27.50 *30.00*
Never hinged 60.00
291 A40 4c **carmine** *(50,579,100)* .30 .25
Never hinged .65
On cover 6.00
P# block of 6, no Impt. 15.00
Never hinged 30.00
a. 4c **light rose** .30 .25
Never hinged .65
P# block of 6, no Impt. 15.00
Never hinged 30.00
b. Booklet pane of 6 *(500,820)* 20.00 *22.50*
Never hinged 35.00
292 A40 6c **deep violet** *(8,803,600)* .35 .25
Never hinged .70
P# block of 10, Impt. 22.50
Never hinged 40.00
a. 6c **lilac** .40 .25
Never hinged .80
P# block of 10, Impt. 22.50
Never hinged 40.00
b. 6c **red violet** .40 .25
Never hinged .70
P# block of 10, Impt. 22.50
Never hinged 40.00
c. Booklet pane of 6 *(75)* *550.00 800.00*
Never hinged *900.00*
293 A40 8c **yellow brown** *(6,036,700)* .30 .25
Never hinged .50
P# block of 10, Impt. 25.00
Never hinged 45.00
a. 8c **orange brown** .30 .25
Never hinged .50
P# block of 6, no Impt. 30.00
Never hinged 55.00
294 A40 10c **deep blue** *(15,848,800)* .30 .25
Never hinged .65
P# block of 10, Impt. 19.00
Never hinged 35.00
295 A40 12c **red orange** *(3,396,500)* .35 .25
Never hinged .75
P# block of 10, Impt. 55.00
Never hinged 125.00
296 A40 16c **light olive green** *(3,249,600)* 65.00 .25
Never hinged 130.00
P# block of 10, Impt. 950.00
Never hinged 2,000.
a. 16c **olive bister** 65.00 .50
Never hinged 130.00
P# block of 10, Impt. 1,000.
Never hinged 2,000.
297 A40 20c **orange yellow** *(10,814,600)* .35 .25
Never hinged .75
P# block of 10, Impt. 37.50
Never hinged 85.00
298 A40 26c **green** *(1,595,400)* .50 .45
Never hinged 1.10
P# block of 10, Impt. 47.50
Never hinged 120.00
a. 26c **blue green** .60 .25
Never hinged 1.35
P# block of 10, Impt. 62.50
Never hinged 140.00
299 A40 30c **gray** *(6,031,300)* .55 .25
Never hinged 1.35
P# block of 10, Impt. 52.50
Never hinged 90.00
Dark gray .55 .25
300 A41 1p **pale violet** *(1,173,200)* 40.00 2.00
Never hinged 90.00
P# block of 10, Impt. 375.00
Never hinged 950.00
a. 1p **red lilac** 40.00 2.50
Never hinged 90.00
P# block of 10, Impt. 425.00
Never hinged 1,050.
b. 1p **pale rose lilac** 40.00 1.10
Never hinged 90.00
P# block of 10, Impt. 425.00
Never hinged 1,050.
301 A41 2p **violet brown** *(475,300)* 35.00 1.00
Never hinged 77.50
P# block of 10, Impt. 450.00
Never hinged 1,000.
302 A41 4p **blue** *(541,800)* 32.50 .50
Never hinged 72.50
P# block of 10, Impt. 450.00
Never hinged 1,000.
a. 4p **dark blue** 35.00 .55
Never hinged 77.50
P# block of 10, Impt. 450.00
Never hinged 1,000.
Nos. 290-302 (13) 175.75 6.20
Set, never hinged 377.00

1923-26
303 A40 16c **olive bister** *(Adm. George Dewey) (13,524,300)* 1.00 .25
Never hinged 2.25
P# block of 6, no Impt. 16.50
Never hinged 37.50
a. 16c **olive green** 1.25 .25
Never hinged 2.75
P# block of 6, no Impt. 15.00
Never hinged 35.00
304 A41 10p **deep green** ('26) *(32,400)* 50.00 20.00
Never hinged 110.00
Block of 4 210.00 90.00

Legislative Palace Issue

Issued to commemorate the opening of the Legislative Palace.

Legislative Palace — A42

Printed by the Philippine Bureau of Printing and issued in panes of 50 without plate numbers or imprints.

1926, Dec. 20 **Unwmk.** ***Perf. 12***

319 A42 2c **green & black** *(502,300)*	.50	.25
Never hinged	1.25	
First day cover		3.50
Corner margin block of 4	2.50	1.25
Never hinged	5.00	
a. Horiz. pair, imperf. between	*275.00*	—
b. Vert. pair, imperf. between	*375.00*	
320 A42 4c **carmine & black** *(304,150)*	.55	.40
Never hinged	1.20	
First day cover		3.50
Corner margin block of 4	2.75	1.75
Never hinged	5.50	
a. Horiz. pair, imperf. between	*350.00*	—
b. Vert. pair, imperf. between	*400.00*	
321 A42 16c **olive green & black** *(203,500)*	1.00	.65
Never hinged	2.25	
First day cover		10.00
Corner margin block of 4	5.25	3.25
Never hinged	10.75	
a. Horiz. pair, imperf. between	*250.00*	—
b. Vert. pair, imperf. between	*425.00*	—
c. Double impression of center	*675.00*	
322 A42 18c **light brown & black** *(103,700)*	1.10	.50
Never hinged	2.50	
First day cover		10.00
Corner margin block of 4	5.25	2.50
Never hinged	10.75	
a. Double impression of center *(150)*	*850.00*	
b. Vertical pair, imperf. between	*475.00*	
323 A42 20c **orange & black** *(103,200)*	2.00	1.00
Never hinged	4.50	
Corner margin block of 4	10.00	6.00
Never hinged	22.50	
a. 20c **orange & brown** *(100)*	*600.00*	—
b. As No. 323, imperf., pair *(50)*	*575.00*	*575.00*
c. As "a," imperf., pair *(50)*	*1,750.*	—
d. Vert. pair, imperf. between	*500.00*	
324 A42 24c **gray & black** *(103,100)*	1.00	.55
Never hinged	2.25	
Corner margin block of 4	5.00	3.00
Never hinged	10.50	
a. Vert. pair, imperf. between	*500.00*	
325 A42 1p **rose lilac & black** *(10,800)*	47.50	50.00
Never hinged	70.00	
Corner margin block of 4	225.00	165.00
Never hinged	330.00	
a. Vert. pair, imperf. between	*500.00*	
First day cover, #319-325		400.00
Nos. 319-325 (7)	53.65	53.35
Set, never hinged	83.95	

The existence of No. 321c is questioned by specialists. The editors would like to see evidence of its existence.

No. 322a is valued in the grade of fine.

Rizal Type of 1906

Coil Stamp

Printed by the U.S. Bureau of Engraving and Printing.

1928 **Unwmk.** ***Perf. 11 Vertically***

326 A40 2c **green** *(110,000)*	7.50	*12.50*
Never hinged	19.00	
On cover		100.00
Pair	17.50	*32.50*
Line pair	55.00	*100.00*
Never hinged	140.00	

Types of 1906-1923

1925-31 **Unwmk.** ***Imperf.***

340 A40 2c **yellow green** ('31) *(99,986)*	.50	.50
Never hinged	.90	
P# block of 6, no Impt.	25.00	
Never hinged	37.50	
a. 2c **green** ('25) *(51,000)*	.80	.75
Never hinged	1.80	
P# block of 6, no Impt.	52.50	
Never hinged	77.50	
341 A40 4c **carmine rose** ('31) *(49,855)*	.50	*1.00*
Never hinged	1.00	
P# block of 6, no Impt.	27.50	
Never hinged	42.50	
a. 4c **carmine** ('25) *(25,500)*	1.20	1.00
Never hinged	2.75	
P# block of 6, no Impt.	55.00	
Never hinged	85.00	
342 A40 6c **violet** ('31) *(10,000)*	3.00	3.75
Never hinged	5.00	
P# block of 10, Impt.	115.00	
Never hinged	160.00	
a. 6c **deep violet** ('25) *(5,200)*	12.00	8.00
Never hinged	26.00	
P# block of 10, Impt.	300.00	
Never hinged	400.00	
343 A40 8c **brown** ('31) *(10,000)*	2.00	*5.00*
Never hinged	4.00	
P# block of 10, Impt.	125.00	
Never hinged	180.00	
P# block of 6, no Impt.	120.00	
Never hinged	170.00	
a. 8c **yellow brown** ('25) *(5,200)*	13.00	8.00
Never hinged	26.00	
P# block of 10, Impt.	*320.00*	
Never hinged	425.00	
344 A40 10c **blue** ('31) *(7,000)*	5.00	*7.50*
Never hinged	12.00	
P# block of 10, Impt.	375.00	
Never hinged	500.00	
a. 10c **deep blue** ('25) *(2,200)*	45.00	20.00
Never hinged	100.00	
P# block of 10, Impt.	*900.00*	
Never hinged	1,300.	
345 A40 12c **deep orange** ('31) *(7,000)*	8.00	10.00
Never hinged	15.00	
P# block of 10, Impt.	500.00	
Never hinged	700.00	
P# block of 6, no Impt.	475.00	
Never hinged	675.00	
a. 12c **red orange** ('25) *(2,200)*	60.00	35.00
Never hinged	135.00	
P# block of 10, Impt.	*1,225.*	
Never hinged	1,750.	
P# block of 6, no Impt.	*1,000.*	
346 A40 16c **olive green** *(Dewey)* ('31) *(7,000)*	6.00	7.50
Never hinged	11.00	
P# block of 6, no Impt.	375.00	
Never hinged	550.00	
a. 16c **bister green** ('25) *(2,200)*	42.50	18.00
Never hinged	100.00	
P# block of 6, no Impt.	*750.00*	
Never hinged	1,100.	
347 A40 20c **deep yellow orange** ('31) *(7,000)*	5.00	*7.50*
Never hinged	11.00	
P# block of 10, Impt.	425.00	
Never hinged	600.00	
a. 20c **yellow orange** ('25) *(2,200)*	45.00	20.00
Never hinged	100.00	
P# block of 10, Impt.	*900.00*	
Never hinged	1,300.	
348 A40 26c **green** ('31) *(7,000)*	6.00	*9.00*
Never hinged	11.00	
P# block of 10, Impt.	550.00	
Never hinged	775.00	
P# block of 6, no Impt.	550.00	
Never hinged	775.00	
a. 26c **blue green** ('25) *(2,200)*	45.00	25.00
Never hinged	110.00	
P# block of 10, Impt.	*1,000.*	
Never hinged	1,450.	
349 A40 30c **light gray** ('31) *(7,000)*	8.00	10.00
Never hinged	16.00	
P# block of 10, Impt.	450.00	
Never hinged	650.00	
a. 30c **gray** ('25) *(2,200)*	45.00	25.00
Never hinged	110.00	
P# block of 10, Impt.	*950.00*	
Never hinged	1,400.	
350 A41 1p **light violet** ('31) *(6,395)*	10.00	*15.00*
Never hinged	20.00	
P# block of 10, Impt.	875.00	
Never hinged	1,250.	
a. 1p **violet** ('25) *(2,100)*	200.00	100.00
Never hinged	425.00	
P# block of 10, Impt.	3,700.	
Never hinged	*4,800.*	
351 A41 2p **brown violet** ('31) *(3,612)*	30.00	*45.00*
Never hinged	80.00	
P# block of 10, Impt.	1,600.	
Never hinged	2,200.	
a. 2p **violet brown** ('25) *(600)*	400.00	400.00
Never hinged	675.00	
P# block of 10, Impt.	*5,750.*	
Never hinged	*8,250.*	
352 A41 4p **blue** ('31) *(2,570)*	80.00	90.00
Never hinged	150.00	
Block of 4	350.00	—
P# block of 10, Impt.	—	
a. 4p **deep blue** ('25) *(300)*	2,200.	1,100.
Never hinged	3,500.	
Block of 4	*9,000.*	
353 A41 10p **green** ('31) *(2,208)*	175.00	*225.00*
Never hinged	300.00	
Block of 4	700.00	
a. 10p **deep green** ('25) *(200)*	2,750.	*2,950.*
Never hinged	4,250.	
P# block of 10, Impt., never hinged	*45,000.*	
Nos. 340-353 (14)	339.00	436.75
Set, never hinged	636.90	

Nos. 340a-353a were the original post office issue. These were reprinted twice in 1931 for sale to collectors (Nos. 340-353).

Mount Mayon, Luzon — A43

Post Office, Manila — A44

Pier No. 7, Manila Bay — A45

Vernal Falls, Yosemite Park, California (See Footnote) — A46

Rice Planting — A47

Rice Terraces — A48

Baguio Zigzag — A49

1932, May 3 **Unwmk.** ***Perf. 11***

354 A43 2c **yellow green** *(5,432,000)*	.75	.30
Never hinged	1.25	
First day cover		2.00
P# block of 6	20.00	
Never hinged	25.00	
355 A44 4c **rose carmine** *(1,602,800)*	.75	.30
Never hinged	1.25	
First day cover		2.00
P# block of 6	16.00	
Never hinged	20.00	
356 A45 12c **orange** *(483,000)*	.90	.75
Never hinged	1.30	
First day cover		6.50
P# block of 6	32.50	
Never hinged	40.00	
357 A46 18c **red orange** *(983,400)*	45.00	15.00
Never hinged	72.50	
First day cover		16.00
P# block of 6	350.00	
Never hinged	550.00	
358 A47 20c **yellow** *(441,000)*	1.00	.75
Never hinged	1.60	
First day cover		6.50
P# block of 6	32.50	
Never hinged	40.00	
359 A48 24c **deep violet** *(425,000)*	1.60	1.00
Never hinged	2.75	
First day cover		6.50
P# block of 6	35.00	
Never hinged	45.00	

360 A49 32c **olive brown** *(510,600)* 1.60 1.00
Never hinged 2.75
First day cover 6.50
P# block of 6 27.50
Never hinged 35.00
First day cover, #354-360 50.00
Nos. 354-360 (7) 51.60 19.10
Set, never hinged 83.40

The 18c vignette was intended to show Pagsanjan Falls in Laguna, central Luzon, and is so labeled. Through error the stamp pictures Vernal Falls in Yosemite National Park, California.

For overprints see #C29-C35, C47-C51, C63.

Nos. 302, 302a Surcharged in Orange or Red

1932

368 A41 1p on 4p **blue** (O) *(134,000)* 6.00 1.00
Never hinged 9.75
On cover 1.00
P# block of 10, Impt. 140.00
Never hinged 175.00
a. 1p on 4p **dark blue** (O) 6.00 1.00
Never hinged 9.25
P# block of 10, Impt. 140.00
Never hinged 175.00
369 A41 2p on 4p **dark blue** (R) *(80,000)* 9.00 1.50
Never hinged 15.00
P# block of 10, Impt. 160.00
Never hinged 200.00
a. 2p on 4p **blue** (R) 9.00 1.00
Never hinged 15.00
On cover 2.00
P# block of 10, Impt. 160.00
Never hinged 200.00

Far Eastern Championship

Issued in commemoration of the Tenth Far Eastern Championship Games.

Baseball Players — A50

Tennis Player — A51

Basketball Players — A52

Printed by the Philippine Bureau of Printing.

1934, Apr. 14 **Unwmk.** ***Perf. 11½***

380 A50 2c **yellow brown** *(999,985)* 1.50 .80
brown 1.50 .80
Never hinged 2.25
First day cover 2.00
"T" of "Eastern" malformed 2.00 1.25
381 A51 6c **ultramarine** *(800,000)* .25 .25
pale ultramarine .25 .25
Never hinged .30
First day cover 1.60
a. Vertical pair, imperf. between *700.00*
Never hinged *1,100.*
382 A52 16c **violet brown** *(500,000)* .50 .50
dark violet .50 .50
Never hinged .75
First day cover 2.25
a. Vert. pair, imperf. horiz. *950.00*
Never hinged *1,500.*
Nos. 380-382 (3) 2.25 1.55
Set, never hinged 3.30

José Rizal — A53

Woman and Carabao — A54

La Filipina — A55

Pearl Fishing — A56

Fort Santiago — A57

Salt Spring — A58

Magellan's Landing, 1521 — A59

"Juan de la Cruz" — A60

Rice Terraces — A61

Miguel Lopez de Legaspi and Chief Sikatuna Signing "Blood Compact," 1565 — A62

Barasoain Church, Malolos A63

Battle of Manila Bay, 1898 — A64

Montalban Gorge — A65

George Washington — A66

Printed by U.S. Bureau of Engraving and Printing.

1935, Feb. 15 **Unwmk.** ***Perf. 11***

383 A53 2c **rose** *(62,183,400)* .25 .25
Never hinged .25
First day cover 1.00
P# block of 6 25.00
Never hinged 35.00
384 A54 4c **yellow green** *(14,238,193)* .25 .25
Light yellow green .25 .25
Never hinged .25
First day cover 1.00
P# block of 6 2.00
Never hinged 2.50
385 A55 6c **dark brown** *(1,958,928)* .25 .25
Never hinged .35
First day cover 1.00
P# block of 6 12.00
Never hinged 15.00
386 A56 8c **violet** *(792,000)* .25 .25
Never hinged .35
First day cover 1.60
P# block of 6 16.00
Never hinged 20.00

387 A57 10c **rose carmine** *(341,400)* .30 .25
Never hinged .45
First day cover 1.60
P# block of 6 16.00
Never hinged 20.00
388 A58 12c **black** *(319,500)* .35 .25
Never hinged .50
First day cover 1.60
P# block of 6 16.00
Never hinged 20.00
389 A59 16c **dark blue** *(2,422,778)* .35 .25
Never hinged .55
First day cover 1.60
P# block of 6 16.00
Never hinged 20.00
390 A60 20c **light olive green** *(1,061,400)* .35 .25
Never hinged .45
First day cover 2.25
P# block of 6 20.00
Never hinged 25.00
391 A61 26c **indigo** *(212,000)* .40 .40
Never hinged .60
First day cover 3.00
P# block of 6 16.00
Never hinged 20.00
392 A62 30c **orange red** *(171,200)* .40 .40
Never hinged .60
First day cover 3.00
P# block of 6 20.00
Never hinged 25.00
393 A63 1p **red orange & black** *(80,000)* 2.00 1.25
Never hinged 3.00
First day cover 8.25
P# block of 4, 2 P# 32.50
Never hinged 40.00
394 A64 2p **bister brown & black** *(61,100)* 12.00 2.00
Never hinged 16.00
First day cover 14.00
P# block of 4, 2 P# 65.00
Never hinged 75.00
395 A65 4p **blue & black** *(59,000)* 12.00 4.00
Never hinged 16.00
First day cover
P# block of 4, 2 P# 67.50
Never hinged 85.00
396 A66 5p **green & black** *(54,000)* 25.00 5.00
Never hinged 50.00
First day cover 27.50
P# block of 4, 2 P# 110.00
Never hinged 225.00
Nos. 383-396 (14) 54.15 15.05
Set, never hinged 74.45

USED VALUES

Used values in italics are for postally used examples with cancels of the proper function during the correct period of use.

Issues of the Commonwealth

Commonwealth Inauguration Issue

Issued to commemorate the inauguration of the Philippine Commonwealth, Nov. 15, 1935.

"The Temples of Human Progress" — A67

1935, Nov. 15 Unwmk. *Perf. 11*
397 A67 2c **carmine rose** *(1,531,000)* .25 .25
Never hinged .35
First day cover 1.00
P# block of 6 2.40
Never hinged 3.00
398 A67 6c **deep violet** *(523,000)* .25 .25
Never hinged .35
First day cover 1.00
P# block of 6 3.20
Never hinged 4.00
399 A67 16c **blue** *(313,500)* .25 .25
Never hinged .40
First day cover 1.00
P# block of 6 4.75
Never hinged 6.00
400 A67 36c **yellow green** *(261,000)* .40 .30
Never hinged .65
First day cover 1.40
P# block of 6 6.75
Never hinged 8.50
401 A67 50c **brown** *(218,500)* .70 .55
Never hinged 1.00
First day cover 2.00
P# block of 6 9.50
Never hinged 12.00
Nos. 397-401 (5) 1.85 1.60
Set, never hinged 2.75

Jose Rizal Issue

75th anniversary of the birth of Jose Rizal (1861-1896), national hero of the Filipinos.

Jose Rizal — A68

Printed by the Philippine Bureau of Printing.

1936, June 19 Unwmk. *Perf. 12*
402 A68 2c **yellow brown** *(500,000)* .25 .25
light yellow brown .25 .25
Never hinged .25
First day cover 1.00
403 A68 6c **slate blue** *(300,000)* .25 .25
light slate green .25 .25
Never hinged .25
First day cover 1.00
a. Imperf. vertically, pair *1,000.*
Never hinged *1,500.*
404 A68 36c **red brown** *(200,000)* .50 *.70*
light red brown .50 .70
Never hinged .75
First day cover 2.25
Nos. 402-404 (3) 1.00 1.20
Set, never hinged 1.25

Commonwealth Anniversary Issue

Issued in commemoration of the first anniversary of the Commonwealth.

President Manuel L. Quezon — A69

Printed by U.S. Bureau of Engraving and Printing.

1936, Nov. 15 Unwmk. *Perf. 11*
408 A69 2c **orange brown** *(4,946,816)* .25 .25
Never hinged .30
First day cover 1.00
P# block of 6 6.50
Never hinged 8.00
409 A69 6c **yellow green** *(1,019,900)* .25 .25
Never hinged .30
First day cover 1.00
P# block of 6 6.50
Never hinged 8.00
410 A69 12c **ultramarine** *(527,600)* .25 .25
Never hinged .30
First day cover 1.50
P# block of 6 6.50
Never hinged 8.00
Nos. 408-410 (3) .75 .75
Set, never hinged .90

Stamps of 1935 Overprinted in Black

a

b

1936-37 Unwmk. *Perf. 11*
411 A53(a) 2c **rose,** *Dec. 28, 1936* *(84,092,400)* .25 .25
Never hinged .25
First day cover *35.00*
P# block of 6 12.00
Never hinged 15.00
a. Bklt. pane of 6, *Jan. 15 1937* *(239,492)* 2.50 2.00
Never hinged 4.00
First day cover *40.00*
b. Hyphen omitted 125.00 100.00
412 A54(b) 4c **yellow green,** *Mar. 29, 1937* *(100,000)* .45 *4.00*
Never hinged .70
P# block of 6 35.00
Never hinged 45.00
413 A55(a) 6c **dark brown,** *Oct. 7, 1936* *(2,230,394)* .25 .25
Never hinged .25
On cover .25
P# block of 6 5.50
Never hinged 7.00
414 A56(b) 8c **violet,** *Mar. 29, 1937* *(627,500)* .25 .25
Never hinged .35
On cover .75
P# block of 6 9.50
Never hinged 12.00
415 A57(b) 10c **rose carmine,** *Dec. 28, 1936* *(1,687,550)* .25 .25
Never hinged .25
First day cover 35.00
P# block of 6 4.75
Never hinged 6.00
a. "COMMONWEALT" 20.00 —
Never hinged 30.00
416 A58(b) 12c **black,** *Mar. 29, 1937* *(2,118,600)* .25 .25
Never hinged .30
On cover .75
P# block of 6 9.50
Never hinged 12.00
417 A59(b) 16c **dark blue,** *Oct. 7, 1936* *(597,300)* .25 .25
Never hinged .40
On cover .75
P# block of 6 12.00
Never hinged 15.00
418 A60(a) 20c **lt olive green,** *Mar. 29, 1937* *(100,000)* .90 .40
Never hinged 1.50
On cover .85
P# block of 6 16.00
Never hinged 20.00
419 A61(b) 26c **indigo,** *Mar. 29, 1937* *(100,000)* .80 .35
Never hinged 1.40
On cover .85
P# block of 6 20.00
Never hinged 25.00
420 A62(b) 30c **orange red,** *Dec. 28, 1936* *(836,252)* .45 .25
Never hinged .75
First day cover *35.00*
P# block of 6 9.50
Never hinged 12.00
421 A63(b) 1p **red org & blk,** *Oct. 7, 1936* *(319,250)* .90 .25
Never hinged 1.50
On cover .75
P# block of 4 27.50
Never hinged 35.00
422 A64(b) 2p **bis brn & blk,** *Mar. 29, 1937* *(50,000)* 12.50 4.00
Never hinged 21.00
On cover 6.00
P# block of 4 100.00
Never hinged 130.00
423 A65(b) 4p **blue & blk,** *Mar. 29, 1937* *(30,000)* 45.00 8.00
Never hinged 72.50
On cover *50.00*
P# block of 4 225.00
Never hinged 375.00
424 A66(b) 5p **green & blk,** *Mar. 29, 1937* *(60,500)* 12.50 *25.00*
Never hinged 21.00
On cover *40.00*
P# block of 4 140.00
Never hinged 175.00
Nos. 411-424 (14) 75.00 43.75
Set, never hinged 122.15

Eucharistic Congress Issue

Issued to commemorate the 33rd International Eucharistic Congress held at Manila, Feb. 3-7, 1937.

Map, Symbolical of the Eucharistic Congress Spreading Light of Christianity — A70

FLAT PLATE PRINTING

Plates of 256 subjects in four panes of 64 each.

1937, Feb. 3 Unwmk. *Perf. 11*
425 A70 2c **yellow green** *(4,102,848)* .25 .25
Never hinged .25
First day cover 1.00
P# block of 6 4.00
Never hinged 5.00
426 A70 6c **light brown** *(2,626,240)* .25 .25
Never hinged .25
First day cover 1.00
P# block of 6 4.00
Never hinged 5.00

427 A70 12c **sapphire** *(2,165,440)* .25 .25
Never hinged .25
First day cover 1.00
P# block of 6 4.00
Never hinged 5.00
428 A70 20c **deep orange** *(1,640,640)* .30 .25
Never hinged .50
First day cover 1.00
P# block of 6 5.50
Never hinged 7.00
429 A70 36c **deep violet** *(1,115,840)* .55 .40
Never hinged .80
First day cover 1.40
P# block of 6 8.00
Never hinged 10.00
430 A70 50c **carmine** *(1,115,840)* .70 .35
Never hinged 1.10
First day cover 2.00
P# block of 6 10.00
Never hinged 15.00
Nos. 425-430 (6) 2.30 1.75
Set, never hinged 3.15

Arms of City of Manila — A71

1937, Aug. 27 **Unwmk.** ***Perf. 11***
431 A71 10p **gray** *(70,000)* 5.00 2.00
Never hinged 7.25
P# block of 6 67.50
Never hinged 85.00
432 A71 20p **henna brown** *(90,600)* 4.00 1.40
Never hinged 6.50
First day cover, #431-432 50.00
P# block of 6 65.00
Never hinged 80.00

Stamps of 1935 Overprinted in Black

a

b

COMMONWEALTH

1938-40 **Unwmk.** ***Perf. 11***
433 A53(a) 2c **rose,** *1939 (103,549,959)* .25 .25
Never hinged .25
P# block of 6 8.00
Never hinged 10.00
a. Booklet pane of 6 *(157,176)* 3.50 3.50
Never hinged 5.50
b. As "a," lower left-hand stamp overprinted "WEALTH COMMON-" *(24)* *2,000.*
Never hinged *3,250.*
c. Hyphen omitted 100.00 50.00
434 A54(b) 4c **yellow green,** *1940 (72,500)* 3.00 *30.00*
Never hinged 4.75
P# block of 6 35.00
Never hinged 45.00
435 A55(a) 6c **dark brown,** *May 12, 1939 (4,013,440)* .25 .25
Never hinged .40
First day cover *35.00*
P# block of 6 5.50
Never hinged 7.00
a. 6c **golden brown** .25 .25
Never hinged .40
P# block of 6 5.50
Never hinged 7.00
436 A56(b) 8c **violet,** *1939 (1,583,357)* .25 *1.75*
Never hinged .25
P# block of 6 8.00
Never hinged 10.00
a. "COMMONWEALT" (LR 31) 90.00
Never hinged 140.00
437 A57(b) 10c **rose carmine,** *May 12, 1939 (2,695,242)* .25 .25
Never hinged .25
P# block of 6 8.00
Never hinged 10.00
a. "COMMONWEALT" (LR 31) 65.00 —
Never hinged 100.00

438 A58(b) 12c **black,** *1940 (3,765,000)* .25 *1.00*
Never hinged .25
P# block of 6 8.00
Never hinged 10.00
439 A59(b) 16c **dark blue** *(1,415,700)* .25 .25
Never hinged .25
P# block of 6 16.00
Never hinged 20.00
440 A60(a) 20c **light olive green,** *1939 (1,663,799)* .25 .25
Never hinged .25
P# block of 6 12.00
Never hinged 15.00
441 A61(b) 26c **indigo,** *1940 (597,500)* 1.00 *2.50*
Never hinged 1.50
P# block of 6 16.00
Never hinged 20.00
442 A62(b) 30c **orange red,** *May 23, 1939 (643,100)* 3.00 .70
Never hinged 5.00
P# block of 6 22.50
Never hinged 35.00
443 A63(b) 1p **red org & blk,** *Aug. 29, 1938 (1,065,629)* .60 .25
Never hinged 1.00
First day cover *40.00*
P# block of 4 27.50
Never hinged 35.00
444 A64(b) 2p **bister brown & black,** *1939 (98,000)* 10.00 1.00
Never hinged 15.00
P# block of 4 87.50
Never hinged 110.00
445 A65(b) 4p **blue & black,** *1940 (6,500)* 150.00 250.00
Never hinged 325.00
On cover 500.00
P# block of 4 *700.00*
Never hinged *1,500.*
446 A66(b) 5p **green & black,** *1940 (31,500)* 20.00 8.00
Never hinged 35.00
P# block of 4 200.00
Never hinged 250.00
Nos. 433-446 (14) 189.35 *296.45*
Set, never hinged 414.15

Overprint "b" measures 18½x1¾mm.

No. 433b occurs in booklet pane, No. 433a, position 5; all examples are straight-edged, left and bottom.

All bottom plate blocks of Nos. 433-443 have selvage that was shortened by cutting by the Bureau of Engraving and Printint to set up the proper plate size for positioning the small "COMMON-WEALTH" overprint. This selvage reduction cuts through the plate numbers and is the natural format.

First Foreign Trade Week Issue

Nos. 384, 298a and 432 Surcharged in Red, Violet or Black

a

b

c

1939, July 5
449 A54(a) 2c on 4c **yellow green** (R) *(500,000)* .25 .25
Never hinged .35
First day cover 1.40
P# block of 6 13.50
Never hinged 17.00
450 A40(b) 6c on 26c **blue green** (V) *(166,700)* .25 .50
Never hinged .35
First day cover 2.00
Left arrow block of 4 16.00
Never hinged 20.00
a. 6c on 26c **green** 3.00 1.00
Never hinged 5.00
451 A71(c) 50c on 20p **henna brown** (Bk) *(60,000)* 1.25 1.00
Never hinged 2.00
First day cover 5.00
P# block of 6 27.50
Never hinged 35.00
Nos. 449-451 (3) 1.75 1.75
Set, never hinged 2.70

There are no known reports of plate blocks of Nos. 450 or 450a.

Commonwealth 4th Anniversary Issue (#452-460)

Triumphal Arch — A72

Printed by U.S. Bureau of Engraving and Printing.

1939, Nov. 15 **Unwmk.** ***Perf. 11***
452 A72 2c **yellow green** *(1,562,352)* .25 .25
Never hinged .25
First day cover 1.00
P# block of 6 4.00
Never hinged 5.00
453 A72 6c **carmine** *(1,267,717)* .25 .25
Never hinged .25
First day cover 1.00
P# block of 6 5.50
Never hinged 7.00
454 A72 12c **bright blue** *(971,724)* .25 .25
Never hinged .25
First day cover 1.40
P# block of 6 9.50
Never hinged 12.00
Nos. 452-454 (3) .75 .75
Set, never hinged .75

For overprints see Nos. 469, 476.

Malacañan Palace — A73

1939, Nov. 15 **Unwmk.** ***Perf. 11***
455 A73 2c **green** *(1,578,600)* .25 .25
Never hinged .25
First day cover 1.00
P# block of 6 4.00
Never hinged 5.00
456 A73 6c **orange** *(1,252,859)* .25 .25
Never hinged .25
First day cover 1.00
P# block of 6 6.00
Never hinged 7.50
457 A73 12c **carmine** *(935,800)* .25 .25
Never hinged .25
First day cover 1.40
P# block of 6 9.50
Never hinged 12.00
Nos. 455-457 (3) .75 .75
Set, never hinged .75

For overprint, see No. 470.

President Quezon Taking Oath of Office — A74

1940, Feb. 8 **Unwmk.** ***Perf. 11***
458 A74 2c **dark orange** *(1,572,400)* .25 .25
Never hinged .25
First day cover 1.00
P# block of 6 4.00
Never hinged 5.00
459 A74 6c **dark green** *(1,257,900)* .25 .25
Never hinged .25
First day cover 1.00
P# block of 6 6.00
Never hinged 5.00
460 A74 12c **purple** *(980,779)* .25 .25
Never hinged .30
First day cover 1.40
P# block of 6 9.50
Never hinged 12.00
Nos. 458-460 (3) .75 .75
Set, never hinged .80

For overprints, see Nos. 471, 477.

José Rizal — A75

ROTARY PRESS PRINTING

1941, Apr. 14 **Unwmk.** ***Perf. 11x10½***

Size: 19x22½mm

461 A75 2c **apple green** *(59,915,600)* .25 .50
Never hinged .25
First day cover 1.00
P# block of 4 2.00
Never hinged 2.50

FLAT PLATE PRINTING

1941, Nov. 14 **Unwmk.** ***Perf. 11***

Size: 18¾x22¼mm

462 A75 2c **pale apple green** 1.00 —
Never hinged 1.25
a. Booklet pane of 6 6.00 —
Never hinged 7.50

No. 461 was issued only in sheets. No. 462 was issued only in booklet panes on Nov. 14, 1941, just before the war, and only a few used stamps and covers exist. All examples have one or two straight edges. Mint booklets reappeared after the war. In August 1942, the booklet pane was reprinted in a darker shade (apple green). However, the apple green panes were available only to U.S. collectors during the war years, so no war-period used stamps from the Philippines exist. Value of apple green booklet pane, never hinged, $6.

For type A75 overprinted, see Nos. 464, O37, O39, N1 and NO1.

Stamps of 1935-41
Handstamped in Violet

1944 **Unwmk.** ***Perf. 11, 11x10½***

463 A53 2c **rose** (On 411), *Dec. 3 (168)* *1,250.* *650.00*
a. Booklet pane of 6 *(28)* *12,500.*
463B A53 2c **rose** (On 433), *Dec. 14 (41)* *2,000.* *1,750.*
464 A75 2c **apple green** (On 461), *Nov. 8 (24,400)* 12.50 10.00
Never hinged 22.50
On cover 20.00
P# block of 4 72.50
Never hinged 110.00
a. Pair, one without ovpt. — —
465 A54 4c **yellow green** (On 384), *Nov. 8 (807)* 47.50 *50.00*
Never hinged 80.00
On cover —
466 A55 6c **dark brown** (On 385), *Dec. 14 (64)* *3,250.* *2,000.*
On cover —
467 A69 6c **yellow green** (On 409), *Dec. 3* 300.00 *150.00*
Never hinged *525.00*
On cover —
468 A55 6c **dark brown** (On 413), *Dec. 28 (206)* *4,000.* *825.00*
On cover —
469 A72 6c **carmine** (On 453), *Nov. 8 (235)* *350.00* *125.00*
On cover —
470 A73 6c **orange** (On 456), *Dec. 14 (141)* *1,750.* *725.00*
On cover —
471 A74 6c **dark green** (On 459), *Nov. 8* *500.00* *225.00*
On cover —
P# block of 6 *1,700.*
472 A56 8c **violet** (On 436), *Nov. 8 (1,643)* 17.50 *30.00*
Never hinged 30.00
On cover —
P# block of 6 250.00
a. Pair, one without ovpt. —
473 A57 10c **carmine rose** (On 415), *Nov. 8 (450)* *350.00* *150.00*
On cover —
474 A57 10c **carmine rose** (On 437), *Nov. 8 (358)* *275.00* *200.00*
Never hinged *475.00*
On cover —
475 A69 12c **ultramarine** (On 410), *Dec. 3* *1,100.* *400.00*
On cover —
476 A72 12c **bright blue** (On 454), *Nov. 8 (36)* *7,000.* *2,500.*
On cover —
477 A74 12c **purple** (On 460), *Nov. 8* *500.00* *275.00*
On cover —
478 A59 16c **dark blue** (On 389), *Dec. 3 (122)* *3,000.* —
On cover —
479 A59 16c **dark blue** (On 417), *Nov. 8 (200)* *1,500.* *1,000.*
On cover —
480 A59 16c **dark blue** (On 439), *Nov. 8 (500)* *500.00* *200.00*
On cover —
P# block of 6 *3,500.*
481 A60 20c **light olive green** (On 440), *Nov. 8 (1,401)* 140.00 35.00
Never hinged 230.00
On cover —
482 A62 30c **orange red** (On 420), *Dec. 3 (248)* *450.00* *1,500.*
On cover —
483 A62 30c **orange red** (On 442), *Dec. 3 (200)* *800.00* *375.00*
On cover —
484 A63 1p **red orange & black** (On 443) *Dec. 3 (21)* *6,250.* *4,500.*
On cover —

Nos. 463-484 are valued in the grade of fine to very fine.
No. 463 comes only from the booklet pane. All examples have one or two straight edges.

Types of 1935-37 Overprinted

a

b

c

1945 **Unwmk.** ***Perf. 11***

485 A53(a) 2c **rose,** *Jan. 19 (65,816,000)* .25 .25
Never hinged .25
First day cover 2.50
P# block of 6 4.00
Never hinged 5.00
486 A54(b) 4c **yellow green,** *Jan. 19 (4,986,800)* .25 .25
Never hinged .25
First day cover 2.50
P# block of 6 12.00
Never hinged 15.00
487 A55(a) 6c **golden brown,** *Jan. 19 (4,381,440)* .25 .25
Never hinged .25
First day cover 2.50
P# block of 6 4.00
Never hinged 5.00
488 A56(b) 8c **violet,** *Jan. 19 (535,000)* .25 .25
Never hinged .25
First day cover 3.00
P# block of 6 5.50
Never hinged 7.00
489 A57(b) 10c **rose carmine,** *Jan. 19 (1,060,000)* .25 .25
Never hinged .25
First day cover 3.00
P# block of 6 4.00
Never hinged 5.00
490 A58(b) 12c **black,** *Jan. 19 (3,214,200)* .25 .25
Never hinged .25
First day cover 3.50
P# block of 6 4.00
Never hinged 5.00
491 A59(b) 16c **dark blue,** *Jan. 19 (1,060,000)* .25 .25
Never hinged .30
First day cover 4.00
P# block of 6 4.00
Never hinged 5.00
492 A60(a) 20c **light olive green,** *Jan. 19 (976,800)* .30 .25
Never hinged .40
First day cover 4.25
P# block of 6 9.50
Never hinged 12.00
493 A62(b) 30c **orange red,** *May 1 (535,000)* .50 .35
Never hinged .75
First day cover 2.50
P# block of 6 12.50
Never hinged 16.00
494 A63(b) 1p **red orange & black,** *Jan. 19 (1,434,400)* 1.10 .25
Never hinged 1.60
First day cover 6.50
P# block of 4, 2 P# 16.00
Never hinged 20.00
495 A71(c) 10p **gray,** *May 1 (22,000)* 55.00 13.50
Never hinged 90.00
First day cover 20.00
P# block of 6 375.00
Never hinged 600.00
496 A71(c) 20p **henna brown,** *May 1 (42,500)* 50.00 15.00
Never hinged 75.00
First day cover 25.00
P# block of 6 600.00
Never hinged 750.00
Nos. 485-496 (12) 108.65 31.10
Set, never hinged 169.55

José Rizal — A76

ROTARY PRESS PRINTING

1946, May 28 **Unwmk.** ***Perf. 11x10½***

497 A76 2c **sepia** *(53,560,000)* .25 .25
Never hinged .25
P# block of 4 2.00
Never hinged 2.50

Later issues, released by the Philippine Republic on July 4, 1946, and thereafter, are listed in Scott's Standard Postage Stamp Catalogue, Vol. 5A.

AIR POST STAMPS

Madrid-Manila Flight Issue

Issued to commemorate the flight of Spanish aviators Gallarza and Loriga from Madrid to Manila.

Regular Issue of 1917-26
Overprinted in Red or Violet

Printed by the Philippine Bureau.

1926, May 13 **Unwmk.** ***Perf. 11***

C1 A40 2c **green** (R) *(9,900)* 20.00 25.00
Never hinged 45.00
First day cover 26.00
P# block of 6 725.00
Never hinged 900.00
C2 A40 4c **carmine** (V) *(8,900)* 30.00 35.00
Never hinged 55.00
First day cover 26.00
P# block of 6 400.00
Never hinged 500.00
a. Inverted overprint *(100)* *2,600.* —
C3 A40 6c **lilac** (R) *(5,000)* 60.00 90.00
Never hinged 125.00
First day cover 40.00
Block of 4 325.00
C4 A40 8c **orange brown** (V) *(5,000)* 60.00 85.00
Never hinged 125.00
First day cover 40.00
Block of 4 325.00
C5 A40 10c **deep blue** (R) *(5,000)* 80.00 85.00
Never hinged 140.00
First day cover 40.00
Block of 4 325.00
C6 A40 12c **red orange** (V) *(4,000)* 70.00 95.00
Never hinged 150.00
First day cover 42.50
Block of 4 350.00
C7 A40 16c **light olive green** *(Sampson)* (V) *(300)* *2,800.* *3,250.*
Block of 4 —
C8 A40 16c **olive bister** *(Sampson)* (R) *(100)* *5,000.* *5,000.*
Block of 4 —
C9 A40 16c **olive green** *(Dewey)* (V) *(3,600)* 90.00 125.00
Never hinged 160.00
First day cover 42.50
Block of 4 450.00

C10 A40 20c **orange yellow** (V) *(4,000)* 90.00 125.00
Never hinged 160.00
First day cover 42.50
Block of 4 450.00
C11 A40 26c **blue green** (V) *(3,900)* 90.00 125.00
Never hinged 160.00
First day cover 45.00
Block of 4 450.00
C12 A40 30c **gray** (V) *(4,000)* 90.00 125.00
Never hinged 160.00
First day cover 45.00
Block of 4 450.00
C13 A41 2p **violet brown** (R) *(900)* 500.00 600.00
Never hinged 1,100.
On cover 800.00
Block of 4 —
C14 A41 4p **dark blue** (R) *(700)* 800.00 900.00
Never hinged 1,300.
On cover —
Block of 4 —
C15 A41 10p **deep green** (V) *(500)* 1,000. 1,350.
On cover —
Block of 4 —

Same Overprint on No. 269
Wmk. Single-lined PIPS (190)
Perf. 12

C16 A40 26c **blue green** (V) *(100)* *5,000.*
Block of 4 —

Same Overprint on No. 284
Perf. 10

C17 A41 1p **pale violet** (V) *(2,000)* 300.00 250.00
Never hinged 450.00
On cover —
First day cover *225.00*
Block of 4 1,300.
Bottom margin block of 4, P# *1,750.*

Overprintings of Nos. C1-C6, C9-C15 and C17 were made from two plates. Position No. 89 of the first printing shows broken left blade of propeller.

Plate blocks do not exist for Nos, C3-C16 because the Bureau of Engraving & Printing cut off all selvage from these sheets.

London-Orient Flight Issue

Issued Nov. 9, 1928, to celebrate the arrival of a British squadron of hydroplanes.

Regular Issue of 1917-25 Overprinted in Red

1928, Nov. 9 **Unwmk.** ***Perf. 11***

C18 A40 2c **green** *(101,200)* 1.00 1.00
Never hinged 2.00
First day cover 7.75
P# block of 6 40.00
Never hinged 50.00
C19 A40 4c **carmine** *(50,500)* 1.25 1.50
Never hinged 2.00
First day cover 9.50
P# block of 6 40.00
Never hinged 50.00
C20 A40 6c **violet** *(12,600)* 5.00 3.00
Never hinged 10.00
On cover 4.00
P# block of 6 60.00
Never hinged 70.00
C21 A40 8c **orange brown** *(10,000)* 5.00 3.00
Never hinged 10.00
On cover 5.00
C22 A40 10c **deep blue** *(10,000)* 5.00 3.00
Never hinged 10.00
On cover 5.00
C23 A40 12c **red orange** *(8,000)* 8.00 4.00
Never hinged 12.00
On cover 6.00
C24 A40 16c **olive green** (No. 303a) *(12,600)* 8.00 4.00
Never hinged 12.00
On cover 6.00
C25 A40 20c **orange yellow** *(8,000)* 8.00 4.00
Never hinged 12.00
On cover 6.00
C26 A40 26c **blue green** *(7,000)* 20.00 8.00
Never hinged 35.00
On cover 12.00
C27 A40 30c **gray** *(7,000)* 20.00 8.00
Never hinged 35.00
On cover 12.00

Same Overprint on No. 271
Wmk. Single-lined PIPS (190)
Perf. 12

C28 A41 1p **pale violet** *(6,000)* 55.00 30.00
Never hinged 90.00
On cover 34.00
Block of 4 800.00
Never hinged *1,000.*
Nos. C18-C28 (11) 136.25 69.50
Set, never hinged 230.00

Von Gronau Issue

Commemorating the visit of Capt. Wolfgang von Gronau's airplane on its round-the-world flight.

Nos. 354-360 Overprinted

Printed by the Philippine Bureau.

1932, Sept. 27 **Unwmk.** ***Perf. 11***

C29 A43 2c **yellow green** *(100,000)* .90 .60
Never hinged 1.40
First day cover 2.00
P# block of 6 12.00
Never hinged 15.00
C30 A44 4c **rose carmine** *(80,000)* .90 .40
Never hinged 1.40
First day cover 2.00
P# block of 6 16.00
Never hinged 20.00
C31 A45 12c **orange** *(55,000)* 1.25 .65
Never hinged 2.00
On cover 1.00
P# block of 6 12.00
Never hinged 15.00
C32 A46 18c **red orange** *(25,305)* 5.00 5.00
Never hinged 8.00
On cover 7.00
P# block of 6 75.00
Never hinged 95.00
C33 A47 20c **yellow** *(30,000)* 3.50 3.50
Never hinged 5.75
On cover 6.00
P# block of 6 24.00
Never hinged 30.00
C34 A48 24c **deep violet** *(30,000)* 3.50 4.00
Never hinged 5.75
On cover 6.00
P# block of 6 24.00
Never hinged 30.00
C35 A49 32c **olive brown** *(30,000)* 3.50 3.00
Never hinged 5.75
On cover 7.00
First day cover, #C29-C35 35.00
P# block of 6 24.00
Never hinged 30.00
Nos. C29-C35 (7) 18.55 17.15
Set, never hinged 31.55

Rein Issue

Commemorating the flight from Madrid to Manila of the Spanish aviator Fernando Rein y Loring.

Regular Issue of 1917-25 Overprinted in Black

1933, Apr. 11

C36 A40 2c **green** *(95,000)* .75 .45
Never hinged 1.10
First day cover 1.60
P# block of 6 120.00
Never hinged 150.00
C37 A40 4c **carmine** *(75,000)* .90 .45
Never hinged 1.40
First day cover —
P# block of 6 145.00
Never hinged 180.00
C38 A40 6c **deep violet** *(65,000)* 1.10 .80
Never hinged 1.75
First day cover 3.00
P# block of 10, Impt. 80.00
Never hinged 100.00
C39 A40 8c **orange brown** *(35,000)* 3.75 2.00
Never hinged 5.75
P# block of 10, Impt. 120.00
Never hinged 150.00
C40 A40 10c **dark blue** *(35,000)* 3.75 2.25
Never hinged 5.75
P# block of 10, Impt. 120.00
Never hinged 150.00
C41 A40 12c **orange** *(35,000)* 3.75 2.00
Never hinged 5.75
P# block of 10, Impt. 120.00
Never hinged 150.00
C42 A40 16c **olive green** *(Dewey)* *(35,000)* 3.50 2.00
Never hinged 5.25
P# block of 6 160.00
Never hinged 200.00
C43 A40 20c **yellow** *(35,000)* 3.75 2.00
Never hinged 5.75
P# block of 10, Impt. 160.00
Never hinged 200.00
C44 A40 26c **green** *(35,000)* 3.75 2.75
Never hinged 5.75
a. **26c blue green** 4.00 2.00
Never hinged 6.00

C45 A40 30c **gray** *(30,000)* 4.00 3.00
Never hinged 6.00
First day cover, #C36-C45 40.00
Nos. C36-C45 (10) 29.00 17.70
Set, never hinged 44.25

Stamp of 1917 Overprinted

Printed by the Philippine Bureau.

1933, May 26 **Unwmk.** ***Perf. 11***

C46 A40 2c **green** *(500,000)* .65 .40
Never hinged 1.00
P# block of 6 12.00
Never hinged 15.00

Regular Issue of 1932 Overprinted

C47 A44 4c **rose carmine** *(799,878)* .30 .25
Never hinged .45
P# block of 6 16.00
Never hinged 20.00
C48 A45 12c **orange** *(500,000)* .60 .25
Never hinged .90
P# block of 6 20.00
Never hinged 25.00
C49 A47 20c **yellow** *(500,000)* .60 .25
Never hinged .90
P# block of 6 20.00
Never hinged 25.00
C50 A48 24c **deep violet** *(500,000)* .65 .25
Never hinged 1.00
P# block of 6 24.00
Never hinged 30.00
C51 A49 32c **olive brown** *(500,000)* .85 .35
Never hinged 1.40
First day cover, #C46-C51 35.00
P# block of 6 24.00
Never hinged 30.00
Nos. C46-C51 (6) 3.65 1.75
Set, never hinged 5.65

Transpacific Issue

Issued to commemorate the China Clipper flight from Manila to San Francisco, Dec. 2-5, 1935.

Nos. 387, 392 Overprinted in Gold

1935, Dec. 2 **Unwmk.** ***Perf. 11***

C52 A57 10c **rose carmine** *(500,000)* .40 .25
Never hinged .60
First day cover 2.00
P# block of 6 16.00
Never hinged 20.00
C53 A62 30c **orange red** *(300,000)* .60 .35
Never hinged .90
First day cover 3.00
P# block of 6 22.50
Never hinged 28.00

Manila-Madrid Flight Issue

Issued to commemorate the Manila-Madrid flight by aviators Antonio Arnaiz and Juan Calvo.

Nos. 291, 295, 298a, 298 Surcharged in Various Colors

Printed by the Philippine Bureau.

1936, Sept. 6

C54 A40 2c on 4c **carmine** (Bl) *(2,000,000)* .25 .25
Never hinged .25
First day cover 1.00

P# block of 6 12.00
Never hinged 15.00
C55 A40 6c on 12c **red orange** (V) *(500,000)* .25 .25
Never hinged .30
First day cover 3.00
P# block of 6 20.00
Never hinged 25.00
C56 A40 16c on 26c **blue green** (Bk) *(300,000)* .25 .25
Never hinged .40
First day cover 5.00
a. 16c on 26c **green** 2.00 .70
Never hinged 3.00
Nos. C54-C56 (3) .75 .75
Set, never hinged .95

Air Mail Exhibition Issue

Issued to commemorate the first Air Mail Exhibition, held Feb. 17-19, 1939.

Nos. 298a, 298, 431 Surcharged in Black or Red

Printed by the Philippine Bureau.

1939, Feb. 17
C57 A40 8c on 26c **blue green** (Bk) *(200,000)* 2.00 2.00
Never hinged 4.00
First day cover 3.50
a. 8c on 26c **green** (Bk) 10.00 4.00
Never hinged 16.00
C58 A71 1p on 10p **gray** (R) *(30,000)* 8.00 4.00
Never hinged 12.00
First day cover 8.00
P# block of 6 160.00
Never hinged 200.00

Moro Vinta and Clipper — AP1

Printed by the US Bureau of Engraving and Printing.

1941, June 30 Unwmk. *Perf. 11*
C59 AP1 8c **carmine** *(210,000)* 2.00 .60
Never hinged 2.75
First day cover 2.00
P# block of 6 19.00
Never hinged 24.00
C60 AP1 20c **ultramarine** *(25,000)* 3.00 .50
Never hinged 4.00
First day cover 2.50
P# block of 6 24.00
Never hinged 30.00
C61 AP1 60c **blue green** *(50,000)* 3.00 1.00
Never hinged 4.00
First day cover 3.50
P# block of 6 36.00
Never hinged 45.00
C62 AP1 1p **sepia** *(1,110,000)* .70 .50
Never hinged 1.00
First day cover 2.25
P# block of 6 12.00
Never hinged 15.00
Nos. C59-C62 (4) 8.70 2.60
Set, never hinged 11.75

For overprint see No. NO7. For surcharges see Nos. N10-N11, N35-N36.

No. C47 Handstamped in Violet

1944, Dec. 3 Unwmk. *Perf. 11*
C63 A44 4c **rose carmine** *(122)* *3,750. 2,750.*
On cover —

SPECIAL DELIVERY STAMPS

U.S. No. E5 Overprinted in Red

a

Printed by U.S. Bureau of Engraving & Printing

Wmk. Double-lined USPS (191)

1901, Oct. 15 *Perf. 12*
E1 SD3 10c **dark blue** *(14,998)* 100. 80.
Never hinged 185.
On cover 350.
Block of 4 500.
P# strip of 3, Impt. 500.
P# block of 6, Impt. *4,000.*
a. Dots in curved frame above messenger (Pl. 882) *175. 160.*
P# block of 6, Impt. (Pl. 882) *6,000.*

Special Delivery Messenger SD2

Wmk. Double-lined PIPS (191PI)

1906, Sept. 8 *Perf. 12*
E2 SD2 20c **deep ultramarine** *(40,019)* 45.00 8.00
Never hinged 90.00
On cover 17.50
P# block of 6, Impt. 2,400.
Never hinged *3,000.*
b. 20c **pale ultramarine** 35.00 8.00
Never hinged 70.00
On cover 17.50
P# block of 6, Impt. 2,600.
Never hinged *3,200.*

See Nos. E3-E6. For overprints see Nos. E7-E10, EO1.

SPECIAL PRINTING

U.S. No. E6 Overprinted in Red

1907 Wmk. Double-lined USPS (191) *Perf. 12*
E2A SD4 10c **ultramarine** *3,250.*
Block of 4 *13,500.*
P# block of 6, Impt. *145,000.*

This stamp was part of the set specially printed for the Bureau of Insular Affairs in 1907. See note following No. 240.

There is only one intact plate block of No. E2A. It is fine and is valued thus.

Wmk. Single-lined PIPS (190PI)

1911, Apr. *Perf. 12*
E3 SD2 20c **deep ultramarine** *(200,000)* 22.00 1.75
Never hinged 42.00
On cover 12.50
P# block of 6 1,600.
Never hinged 2,000.

1916 *Perf. 10*
E4 SD2 20c **deep ultramarine** *(200,000)* 175.00 150.00
Never hinged 275.00
On cover 200.00
P# block of 6 2,000.
Never hinged 2,500.
pale ultramarine —
P# block of 6 *4,400.*
Never hinged *5,500.*

Early in 1919 the supply of Special Delivery stamps in the Manila area was exhausted. A Government decree permitted the use of regular issue postage stamps for payment of the special delivery fee when so noted on the cover. This usage was permitted until the new supply of Special Delivery stamps arrived.

1919 Unwmk. *Perf. 11*
E5 SD2 20c **ultramarine** *(4,195,862)* .60 .25
Never hinged .90
On cover 5.00
P# block of 6 120.00
Never hinged 150.00
a. 20c **pale blue** .75 .25
Never hinged 1.00
On cover 5.25
P# block of 6 160.00
Never hinged 200.00
b. 20c **dull violet** .60 .25
Never hinged .90
On cover 5.00
P# block of 6 160.00
Never hinged 200.00

Type of 1906 Issue

1925-31 Unwmk. *Imperf.*
E6 SD2 20c **dull violet** ('31) *(6,500)* 27.50 *75.00*
Never hinged 40.00
On cover 250.00
P# block of 6 275.00
Never hinged 400.00
a. 20c **violet blue** ('25) *(2,100)* 50.00 —
Never hinged 80.00
On cover —
P# block of 6 525.00
Never hinged 750.00

Type of 1919 Overprinted in Black

1939, Apr. 27 Unwmk. *Perf. 11*
E7 SD2 20c **blue violet** *(1,253,250)* .25 .25
Never hinged .40
First day cover 35.00
P# block of 6 80.00
Never hinged 100.00

Nos. E5b and E7 Handstamped in Violet

1944 Unwmk. *Perf. 11*
E8 SD2 20c **dull violet** (On E5b) *(138)* *1,400. 550.00*
On cover —
Block of 4 *6,000.*
E9 SD2 20c **blue violet** (On E7), *Nov. 8* *(600)* *550.00 250.00*
On cover —
P# block of 6 *4,250.*

Type SD2 Overprinted "VICTORY" As No. 486

1945, May 1 Unwmk. *Perf. 11*
E10 SD2 20c **blue violet** *(578,600)* .70 .55
Never hinged 1.10
First day cover 10.00
P# block of 6 20.00
Never hinged 25.00
a. "IC" close together 3.25 2.75
Never hinged 4.75

Some plate blocks of E10 contain No. E10a. These are very rare.

SPECIAL DELIVERY OFFICIAL STAMP

Type of 1906 Issue Overprinted

1931 **Unwmk.** ***Perf. 11***
EO1 SD2 20c **dull violet** *(46,750)* 3.00 *75.00*
Never hinged 4.50
P# block of 6 150.00
Never hinged 190.00
a. No period after "B" 50.00 *250.00*
Never hinged 75.00
b. Double overprint —

It is strongly recommended that expert opinion be acquired for Nos. EO1 and EO1a used.

POSTAGE DUE STAMPS

U.S. Nos. J38-J44 Overprinted in Black

Printed by the U.S. Bureau of Engraving and Printing.

Wmk. Double-lined USPS (191)

1899, Aug. 16 ***Perf. 12***
J1 D2 1c **deep claret** *(340,892)* 7.50 2.50
Never hinged 15.00
On cover 30.00
On cover, used as regular postage 110.00
P# strip of 3, Impt. 125.00
P# block of 6, Impt. *650.00*
J2 D2 2c **deep claret** *(306,983)* 7.50 2.50
Never hinged 15.00
On cover 37.50
P# strip of 3, Impt. 125.00
P# block of 6, Impt. *650.00*
J3 D2 5c **deep claret** *(34,565)* 15.00 2.50
Never hinged 30.00
On cover *70.00*
P# strip of 3, Impt. 200.00
P# block of 6, Impt. *2,000.*
J4 D2 10c **deep claret** *(15,848)* 19.00 5.50
Never hinged 37.50
On cover 100.00
P# strip of 3, Impt. 175.00
P# block of 6, Impt. *1,500.*
J5 D2 50c **deep claret** *(3,216)* 250.00 100.00
Never hinged 425.00
On cover —
P# strip of 3, Impt. 1,100.
P# block of 6, Impt. *18,000.*

No. J1 was used to pay regular postage Sept. 5-19, 1902.

1901, Aug. 31
J6 D2 3c **deep claret** *(14,885)* 17.50 7.00
Never hinged 35.00
On cover 60.00
P# strip of 3, Impt. 175.00
P# block of 6, Impt. *1,250.*
J7 D2 30c **deep claret** *(2,140)* 250.00 110.00
Never hinged 415.00
On cover —
P# strip of 3, Impt. 1,000.
P# block of 6, Impt. *21,500.*
Nos. J1-J7 (7) 566.50 230.00
Set, never hinged 882.50

Post Office Clerk — D3

1928, Aug. 21 **Unwmk.** ***Perf. 11***
J8 D3 4c **brown red** *(948,054)* .25 .25
Never hinged .25
P# block of 6 14.00
Never hinged 17.50
J9 D3 6c **brown red** *(255,490)* .30 .75
Never hinged .45
P# block of 6 14.00
Never hinged 17.50
J10 D3 8c **brown red** *(508,621)* .25 .75
Never hinged .35
P# block of 6 14.00
Never hinged 17.50
J11 D3 10c **brown red** *(254,195)* .30 .75
Never hinged .45
P# block of 6 14.00
Never hinged 17.50
J12 D3 12c **brown red** *(407,457)* .25 .75
Never hinged .35
P# block of 6 14.00
Never hinged 17.50
J13 D3 16c **brown red** *(253,215)* .30 .75
Never hinged .45
P# block of 6 14.00
Never hinged 17.50
J14 D3 20c **brown red** *(259,665)* .30 .75
Never hinged .45
P# block of 6 14.00
Never hinged 17.50
Nos. J8-J14 (7) 1.95 4.75
Set, never hinged 2.75

No. J8 Surcharged in Blue

1937, July 29 **Unwmk.** ***Perf. 11***
J15 D3 3c on 4c **brown red** *(250,000)* .25 .25
Never hinged .35
First day cover 35.00
P# block of 6 18.00
Never hinged 22.50

See note after No. NJ1.

Nos. J8-J14 Handstamped in Violet

1944, Dec. 3 **Unwmk.** ***Perf. 11***
J16 D3 4c **brown red** *(306)* *150.00* —
On cover —
P# block of 6 1,500.
J17 D3 6c **brown red** *(390)* *100.00* —
On cover —
P# block of 6 1,500.
J18 D3 8c **brown red** *(379)* *110.00 350.00*
On cover —
P# block of 6 1,000.
J19 D3 10c **brown red** *(405)* *100.00* —
On cover —
P# block of 6 1,000.
J20 D3 12c **brown red** *(423)* *100.00* —
On cover —
P# block of 6 1,000.
J21 D3 16c **brown red** *(425)* *100.00* 350.00
On cover —
P# block of 6 1,500.
a. Pair, one without ovpt. —
J22 D3 20c **brown red** *(375)* *110.00* —
On cover —
P# block of 6 1,000.
Nos. J16-J22 (7) *770.00*

OFFICIAL STAMPS

Official Handstamped Overprints

"Officers purchasing stamps for government business may, if they so desire, surcharge them with the letters O.B. either in writing with black ink or by rubber stamps but in such a manner as not to obliterate the stamp that postmasters will be unable to determine whether the stamps have been previously used." C.M. Cotterman, Director of Posts, December 26, 1905.

Beginning January 1, 1906, all branches of the Insular Government used postage stamps to prepay postage instead of franking them as before. Some officials used manuscript, some utilized the typewriting machines but by far the larger number provided themselves with rubber stamps. The majority of these read "O.B." but other forms were: "OFFICIAL BUSINESS" or "OFFICIAL MAIL" in two lines, with variations on many of these.

These "O.B." overprints are known on U.S. 1899-1901 stamps; on 1903-06 stamps in red and blue; on 1906 stamps in red, blue, black, yellow and green.

"O.B." overprints were also made on the centavo and peso stamps of the Philippines, per order of May 25, 1907.

Beginning in 1926 the Bureau of Posts issued press-printed official stamps, but many government offices continued to handstamp ordinary postage stamps "O.B." The press-printed "O.B." overprints are listed below.

During the Japanese occupation period 1942-45, the same system of handstamped official overprints prevailed, but the handstamp usually consisted of "K.P.", initials of the Tagalog words, "Kagamitang Pampamahalaan" (Official Business), and the two Japanese characters used in the printed overprint on Nos. NO1 to NO4.

Legislative Palace Issue of 1926 Overprinted in Red

Printed and overprinted by the Philippine Bureau of Printing.

1926, Dec. 20 **Unwmk.** ***Perf. 12***
O1 A42 2c **green & black** *(90,500)* 3.00 1.00
Never hinged 4.50
On cover 2.00
Block of 4 13.00 5.50
O2 A42 4c **carmine & black** *(90,450)* 3.00 1.25
Never hinged 4.50
On cover 2.00
First day cover 10.00
Block of 4 13.00 5.50
a. Vertical pair, imperf. between 550.00
O3 A42 18c **light brown & black** *(70,000)* 8.00 4.00
Never hinged 12.00
On cover 6.50
Block of 4 36.00 20.00
O4 A42 20c **orange & black** *(70,250)* 7.75 1.75
Never hinged 11.50
On cover 3.00
Block of 4 36.00 8.25
First day cover, #O1-O4 50.00
Nos. O1-O4 (4) 21.75 8.00
Set, never hinged 32.50

Regular Issue of 1917-26 Overprinted

Printed and overprinted by the U.S. Bureau of Engraving and Printing.

1931 **Unwmk.** ***Perf. 11***
O5 A40 2c **green** *(22,940,100)* .40 .25
Never hinged .65
P# block of 6 20.00
Never hinged 25.00
a. No period after "B" 17.50 17.50
Never hinged 27.50
b. No period after "O" 40.00 30.00
O6 A40 4c **carmine** *(5,377,000)* .45 .25
Never hinged .70
P# block of 6 20.00
Never hinged 25.00
a. No period after "B" 40.00 20.00
Never hinged 60.00
O7 A40 6c **deep violet** *(616,500)* .75 .25
Never hinged 1.25
P# block of 10, Impt. 40.00
Never hinged 50.00
O8 A40 8c **yellow brown** *(706,700)* .75 .25
Never hinged 1.25
P# block of 6 32.00
Never hinged 40.00
P# block of 10, Impt. 40.00
Never hinged 50.00
O9 A40 10c **deep blue** *(1,006,800)* 1.20 .25
Never hinged 1.90
P# block of 10, Impt. 32.00
Never hinged 40.00
O10 A40 12c **red orange** *(158,050)* 2.00 .25
Never hinged 3.00
P# block of 6 65.00
Never hinged 80.00
P# block of 10, Impt. 80.00
Never hinged 95.00
a. No period after "B" 80.00 80.00
Never hinged 120.00
O11 A40 16c **light olive green** *(Dewey)* *(824,400)* 1.00 .25
Never hinged 1.50
P# block of 6 24.00
Never hinged 30.00
a. 16c olive bister 2.00 .25
Never hinged 3.00
P# block of 6 20.00
Never hinged 25.00
O12 A40 20c **orange yellow** *(509,050)* 1.25 .25
Never hinged 1.90
P# block of 10, Impt. 75.00
Never hinged 95.00
a. No period after "B" 80.00 80.00
Never hinged 120.00

O13 A40 26c **green** *(68,600)* 2.00 1.00
Never hinged 3.25
P# block of 6 120.00
Never hinged 150.00
a. 26c blue green 2.50 1.50
Never hinged 4.00
P# block of 6 130.00
Never hinged 165.00
O14 A40 30c **gray** *(199,400)* 2.00 .25
Never hinged 3.25
P# block of 10, Impt. 80.00
Never hinged 100.00
Nos. O5-O14 (10) 11.80 3.25
Set, never hinged 18.65

Many collectors prefer to collect the plate blocks of 6 of Nos. O5-O6, O8, O10-O11a and O14 as blocks of 10 so they fit aesthetically with the other plate blocks of 10 with imprints.

Regular Issue of 1935 Overprinted in Black

1935 **Unwmk.** ***Perf. 11***
O15 A53 2c **rose** *(7,927,800)* .25 .25
Never hinged .30
P# block of 6 4.75
Never hinged 6.00
a. No period after "B" 15.00 10.00
Never hinged 22.50
b. No period after "O" — —
O16 A54 4c **yellow green** *(5,079,266)* .25 .25
Never hinged .30
P# block of 6 4.00
Never hinged 5.00
a. No period after "B" 15.00 *40.00*
Never hinged 22.50
O17 A55 6c **dark brown** *(786,896)* .25 .25
Never hinged .40
P# block of 6 8.00
Never hinged 10.00
a. No period after "B" 35.00 35.00
Never hinged 52.50
O18 A56 8c **violet** *(656,200)* .30 .25
Never hinged .45
P# block of 6 9.50
Never hinged 12.00
O19 A57 10c **rose carmine** *(756,100)* .30 .25
Never hinged .45
P# block of 6 8.00
Never hinged 10.00
O20 A58 12c **black** *(104,500)* .75 .25
Never hinged 1.10
P# block of 6 8.00
Never hinged 10.00
O21 A59 16c **dark blue** *(254,800)* .55 .25
Never hinged .85
P# block of 6 8.00
Never hinged 10.00
O22 A60 20c **light olive green** *(203,079)* .60 .25
Never hinged .90
P# block of 6 12.00
Never hinged 15.00
O23 A61 26c **indigo** *(67,750)* .90 .25
Never hinged 1.50
P# block of 6 20.00
Never hinged 25.00
O24 A62 30c **orange red** *(83,500)* .80 .25
Never hinged 1.20
P# block of 6 20.00
Never hinged 25.00
Nos. O15-O24 (10) 4.95 2.50
Set, never hinged 7.40

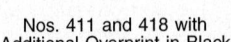

Nos. 411 and 418 with Additional Overprint in Black

1937-38 **Unwmk.** ***Perf. 11***
O25 A53 2c **rose,** *Apr. 10, 1937 (11,580,800)* .25 .25
Never hinged .30
First day cover 50.00
P# block of 6 8.00
Never hinged 10.00
a. No period after "B" 25.00 25.00
Never hinged 45.00
b. Period after "B" raised (UL 4) 150.00
O26 A60 20c **light olive green,** *Apr. 26, 1938 (174,929)* .70 .50
Never hinged 1.10
P# block of 6 20.00
Never hinged 25.00

Regular Issue of 1935 Overprinted In Black

a

b

1938-40 **Unwmk.** ***Perf. 11***
O27 A53(a) 2c **rose** *(23,239,872)* .25 .25
Never hinged .30
P# block of 6 4.75
Never hinged 6.00
a. Hyphen omitted 10.00 10.00
Never hinged 15.00
b. No period after "B" 20.00 *30.00*
Never hinged 30.00
O28 A54(b) 4c **yellow green** *(85,000)* .75 1.00
Never hinged 1.10
P# block of 6 24.00
Never hinged 30.00
O29 A55(a) 6c **dark brown** *(393,549)* .30 .25
Never hinged .45
P# block of 6 12.00
Never hinged 15.00
O30 A56(b) 8c **violet** *(82,000)* .75 .85
Never hinged 1.10
P# block of 6 9.50
Never hinged 12.00
O31 A57(b) 10c **rose carmine** *(1,188,735)* .25 .25
Never hinged .30
P# block of 6 16.00
Never hinged 20.00
a. No period after "O" 50.00 40.00
Never hinged 75.00
O32 A58(b) 12c **black** *(340,000)* .30 .25
Never hinged .45
P# block of 6 12.00
Never hinged 15.00
O33 A59(b) 16c **dark blue** *(490,000)* .30 .25
Never hinged .45
P# block of 6 16.00
Never hinged 20.00
O34 A60(a) 20c **light olive green** ('40) *(162,000)* .55 .85
Never hinged .85
P# block of 6 16.00
Never hinged 20.00
O35 A61(b) 26c **indigo** *(77,000)* 1.50 *2.00*
Never hinged 2.25
P# block of 6 12.00
Never hinged 15.00
O36 A62(b) 30c **orange red** *(82,000)* .75 .85
Never hinged 1.10
P# block of 6 16.00
Never hinged 20.00
Nos. O27-O36 (10) 5.70 6.80
Set, never hinged 8.25

All bottom plate blocks have the plate numbers cut in half. See note after No. 446.

No. 461 Overprinted in Black — c

ROTARY PRESS PRINTING

1941, Apr. 14 **Unwmk.** ***Perf. 11x10½***
O37 A75(c) 2c **apple green** *(21,087,900)* .25 *.40*
Never hinged .30
First day cover 3.50
P# block of 4 2.00
Never hinged 2.50

Nos. O27, O37, O16, O29, O31, O22 and O26 Handstamped in Violet

1944 **Unwmk.** ***Perf. 11, 11x10½***
O38 A53 2c **rose** (On O27) *(128)* *375.00 200.00*
Never hinged *750.00*
On cover —
P# block of 6 *4,000.*
Never hinged *5,000.*
O39 A75 2c **apple green** (On O37) *(13,100)* 15.00 *20.00*
Never hinged 20.00
On cover *25.00*
P# block of 4 160.00
Never hinged 200.00
O40 A54 4c **yellow green** (On O16) *(2,634)* 45.00 *30.00*
Never hinged 80.00
On cover —
P# block of 6 600.00
Never hinged 750.00
O40A A55 6c **dark brown** (On O29) *8,000.* —
Block of 4 —
O41 A57 10c **rose carmine** (On O31) *(665)* *500.00*
Block of 4 *2,100.*
a. No period after "O" *4,000.*
O42 A60 20c **light olive green** (On O22) *8,000.*
O43 A60 20c **light olive green** (On O26) *1,750.*
Block of 4 —

No. 497 Overprinted Type "c" in Black

1946, June 19 **Unwmk.** ***Perf. 11x10½***
O44 A76 2c **sepia** *(10,470,000)* .25 .25
Never hinged .25
P# block of 4 2.00
Never hinged 2.50
a. Vertical pair, bottom stamp without ovpt. —

POST OFFICE SEALS

POS1

1906 **Litho.** **Unwmk.** ***Perf. 12***
OX1 POS1 **light brown** 75.00 75.00
On cover *1,750.*

Wmk. "PIRS" in Double-lined Capitals

1907 ***Perf. 12***
OX2 POS1 **light brown** 95.00 95.00
On cover *2,250.*

Hyphen-hole Perf. 7

OX3 POS1 **orange brown** 40.00 *45.00*

1911 ***Hyphen-hole Perf. 7***
OX4 POS1 **yellow brown** 40.00 *45.00*
On cover *1,750.*
OX5 POS1 **olive bister** 75.00 75.00
On cover *1,750.*
a. Unwatermarked —
OX6 POS1 **yellow** 75.00 75.00
On cover *1,750.*

1913 **Unwmk.** ***Hyphen-hole Perf. 7***
OX7 POS1 **lemon yellow** 3.00 *15.00*
On cover *250.00*

Perf. 12

OX8 POS1 **yellow** 150.00 *200.00*
On cover *2,000.*

Wmk. "USPS" in Single-lined Capitals
Hyphen-hole Perf. 7

OX9 POS1 **yellow** 80.00 50.00
On cover *1,500.*
a. Rouletted 4½ — —

1934 **Unwmk.** ***Roulette***
OX10 POS1 **dark blue** 3.00 1
On cover

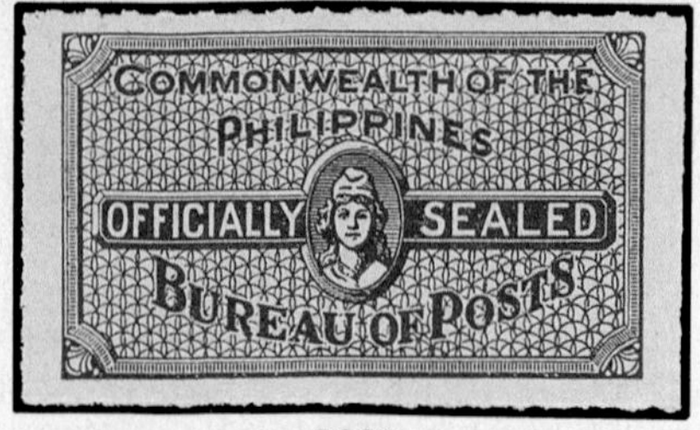

POS2

OX11	POS2	**dark blue**	6.00	*7.50*
		On cover		*300.00*

POS3

1938 ***Hyphen-hole Perf. 7***

OX12	POS3	**dark blue**	3.00	*4.00*
		On cover		*175.00*

ENVELOPES

U.S. Envelopes of 1899 Issue Overprinted below stamp in color of the stamp, except where noted

Note: Many envelopes for which there was no obvious need were issued in small quantities. Anyone residing in the Islands could, by depositing with his postmaster the required amount, order any envelopes in quantities of 500, or multiples thereof, provided it was on the schedule of U.S. envelopes.

Such special orders are indicated by a plus sign after the quantity.

1899-1900

U1	U77	1c	**green** (#U352) *(370,000)*	3.00	2.00
			Entire	8.75	9.50
U2	U77	1c	**green,** *amber* (#U353) *(1,000)+*	18.00	14.00
			Entire	40.00	40.00
U3	U77	1c	**green,** *amber* (#U353) red overprint *(500)+*	22.50	20.00
			Entire	60.00	57.50
U4	U77	1c	**green,** *oriental buff* (#U354) *(1,000)+*	14.00	14.00
			Entire	30.00	30.00
U5	U77	1c	**green,** *oriental buff* (#U354) red overprint *(500)+*	35.00	35.00
			Entire	72.50	*72.50*
U6	U77	1c	**green,** *blue* (#U355) *(1,000)+*	9.00	9.00
			Entire	30.00	30.00
U7	U77	1c	**green,** *blue* (#U355) red overprint *(500)+*	20.00	19.00
			Entire	72.50	67.50
U8	U79	2c	**carmine** (#U362) *(1,180,000)*	1.50	1.50
			Entire	4.00	3.00
U9	U79	2c	**carmine,** *amber* (#U363) *(21,000)*	5.25	5.00
			Entire	15.00	12.50
U10	U79	2c	**carmine,** *oriental buff* (#U364) *(10,000)*	5.25	4.75
			Entire	17.00	13.50

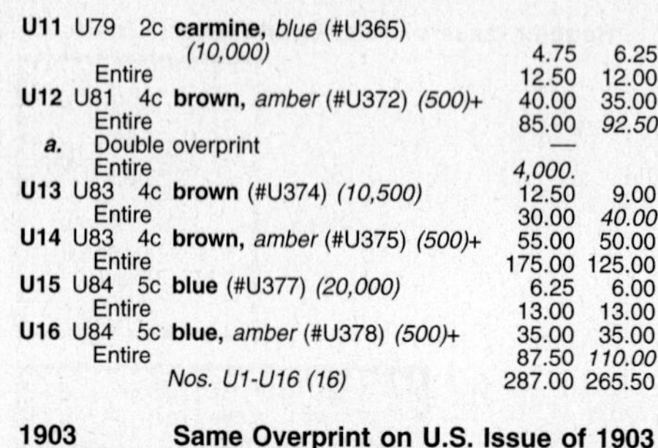

U11	U79	2c	**carmine,** *blue* (#U365) *(10,000)*	4.75	6.25
			Entire	12.50	12.00
U12	U81	4c	**brown,** *amber* (#U372) *(500)+*	40.00	35.00
			Entire	85.00	*92.50*
a.			Double overprint		—
			Entire	*4,000.*	
U13	U83	4c	**brown** (#U374) *(10,500)*	12.50	9.00
			Entire	30.00	*40.00*
U14	U83	4c	**brown,** *amber* (#U375) *(500)+*	55.00	50.00
			Entire	175.00	125.00
U15	U84	5c	**blue** (#U377) *(20,000)*	6.25	6.00
			Entire	13.00	13.00
U16	U84	5c	**blue,** *amber* (#U378) *(500)+*	35.00	35.00
			Entire	87.50	*110.00*
			Nos. U1-U16 (16)	287.00	265.50

1903 **Same Overprint on U.S. Issue of 1903**

U17	U85	1c	**green** (#U379) *(300,000)*	1.50	1.25
			Entire	4.25	4.25
U18	U85	1c	**green,** *amber* (#U380) *(1,000)+*	12.50	12.00
			Entire	22.50	*25.00*
U19	U85	1c	**green,** *oriental buff* (#U381) *(1,000)+*	14.50	12.50
			Entire	26.00	*24.00*
U20	U85	1c	**green,** *blue* (#U382) *(1,500)+*	12.00	11.00
			Entire	26.00	*26.00*
U21	U85	1c	**green,** *manila* (#U383) *(500)+*	20.00	20.00
			Entire	45.00	*47.50*
U22	U86	2c	**carmine** (#U385) *(150,500)*	5.00	3.50
			Entire	7.50	7.00
U23	U86	2c	**carmine,** *amber* (#U386) *(500)+*	17.50	14.00
			Entire	35.00	42.50
U24	U86	2c	**carmine,** *oriental buff* (#U387) *(500)+*	17.50	*25.00*
			Entire	45.00	—
U25	U86	2c	**carmine,** *blue* (#U388) *(500)+*	17.50	17.50
			Entire	40.00	
U26	U87	4c	**chocolate,** *amber* (#U391) *(500)+*	55.00	*75.00*
			Entire	140.00	*190.00*
a.			Double overprint, entire	*7,000.*	
U27	U88	5c	**blue,** *amber* (#U394) *(500)+*	55.00	—
			Entire	125.00	125.00
			Nos. U17-U27 (11)	228.00	191.75

Same Overprint on Re-cut U.S. Issue of 1904

1906

U28	U89	2c	**carmine** (#U395)	42.50	27.50
			Entire	150.00	125.00
U29	U89	2c	**carmine,** *Oriental buff* (#U397)	67.50	*110.00*
			Entire	225.00	*275.00*

Rizal —E1

E2, McKinley.

1908

U30	E1	2c	**green**	.50	.25
			Entire	.85	1.50
U31	E1	2c	**green,** *amber*	4.00	2.25
			Entire	9.00	8.00
U32	E1	2c	**green,** *oriental buff*	5.00	3.00
			Entire	9.00	9.00
U33	E1	2c	**green,** *blue*	5.00	3.00
			Entire	9.00	9.00
U34	E1	2c	**green,** *manila (500)*	7.25	—
			Entire	15.00	20.00
U35	E2	4c	**carmine**	.50	.25
			Entire	1.40	1.25
U36	E2	4c	**carmine,** *amber*	4.00	2.50
			Entire	9.00	7.00
U37	E2	4c	**carmine,** *oriental buff*	4.25	3.50
			Entire	9.00	17.00
U38	E2	4c	**carmine,** *blue*	4.00	3.00
			Entire	8.50	8.50
U39	E2	4c	**carmine,** *manila (500)*	9.00	—
			Entire	20.00	30.00
			Nos. U30-U39 (10)	43.50	17.75

Rizal — E3

1927, Apr. 5

U40	E3	2c	**green**	11.50	9.50
			Entire	30.00	25.00
			Entire, 1st day cancel		*37.50*

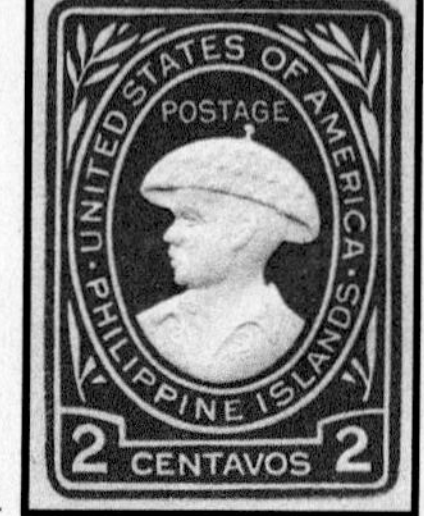

"Juan de la Cruz" — E4

1935, June 19

U41	E4	2c	**carmine**	.35	.25
			Entire	1.25	.75
U42	E4	4c	**olive green**	.50	.30
			Entire	1.65	1.10

For surchages see Nos. NU1-NU2.

Nos. U30, U35, U41 and U42 Handstamped in Violet

1944

U42A	E1	2c	**green** (On U30), entire		—
U43	E4	2c	**carmine** (On U41)	17.50	14.00
			Entire	47.50	*80.00*
U44	E2	4c	**carmine,** *McKinley* (On U35)	—	—
			Entire	950.00	*950.00*
U45	E4	4c	**olive green** (On U42)	82.50	70.00
			Entire	140.00	175.00

WRAPPERS

U.S. Wrappers Overprinted in Color of Stamp

1901

W1	U77	1c	**green,** *manila* (No. W357) *(320,000)*	1.50	1.25
			Entire	5.00	*10.00*

1905

W2	U85	1c	**green,** *manila* (No. W384)	9.00	9.00
			Entire	22.50	*25.00*
a.			Double overprint, entire	*4,500.*	
W3	U86	2c	**carmine,** *manila* (No. W389)	11.00	10.50
			Entire	22.50	*27.50*

Design of Philippine Envelopes

1908

W4	E1	2c	**green,** *manila*	2.00	2.00
			Entire	11.00	*15.00*

POSTAL CARDS

Values are for Entires.
U.S. Cards Overprinted in Black below Stamp

a

1900, Feb.

UX1	(a)	1c **black** (Jefferson) (UX14) *(100,000)*	17.50	15.00
a.		Without period	47.50	75.00
UX2	(a)	2c **black** (Liberty) (UX16) *(20,000)*	40.00	30.00
a.		With double "PHILIPPINES" overprint	*10,000.*	*20,000.*

b

1903, Sept. 15

UX3	(b)	1c **black** (McKinley) (UX18)	*1,250.*	*1,150.*
UX4	(b)	2c **black** (Liberty) (UX16)	*800.*	*700.*

c

1903, Nov. 10

UX5	(c)	1c **black** (McKinley) (UX18)	47.50	40.00
UX6	(c)	2c **black** (Liberty) (UX16)	60.00	55.00

d

1906

UX7	(d)	1c **black** (McKinley) (UX18)	*275.*	*300.*
UX8	(d)	2c **black** (Liberty) (UX16)	*1,750.*	*1,000.*

Designs same as postage issue of 1906

1907

UX9	A40	2c **black,** *buff* (Rizal)	10.00	8.00
UX10	A40	4c **black,** *buff* (McKinley)	25.00	20.00

Color changes

1911

UX11	A40	2c **blue,** *light blue* (Rizal)	8.00	8.00
a.		2c blue on white	20.00	20.00
UX12	A40	4c **blue,** *light blue* (McKinley)	25.00	25.00

An impression of No. UX11 exists on the back of a U.S. No. UX21.

1915

UX13	A40	2c **green,** *buff* (Rizal)	3.00	2.00
UX14	A40	2c **yellow green,** *amber*	3.50	1.50
UX15	A40	4c **green,** *buff* (McKinley)	20.00	15.00

Design of postage issue of 1935

1935

UX16	A53	2c **red,** *pale buff* (Rizal)	2.50	1.60

No. UX16 Overprinted at left of Stamp **COMMONWEALTH**

1938

UX17	A53	2c **red,** *pale buff*	2.50	1.60

No. UX16 Overprinted

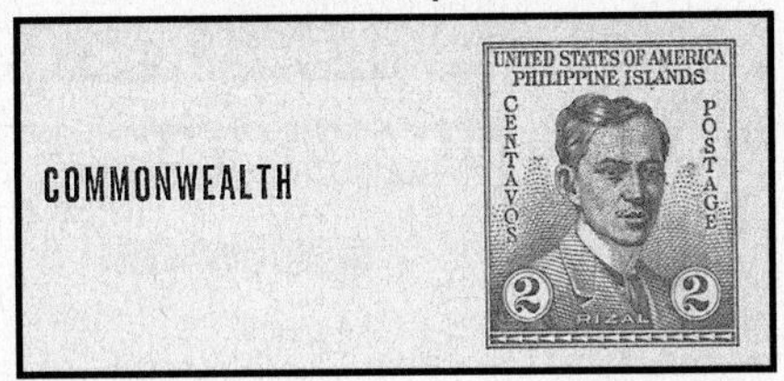

UX18	A53	2c **red,** *pale buff*	45.00	45.00

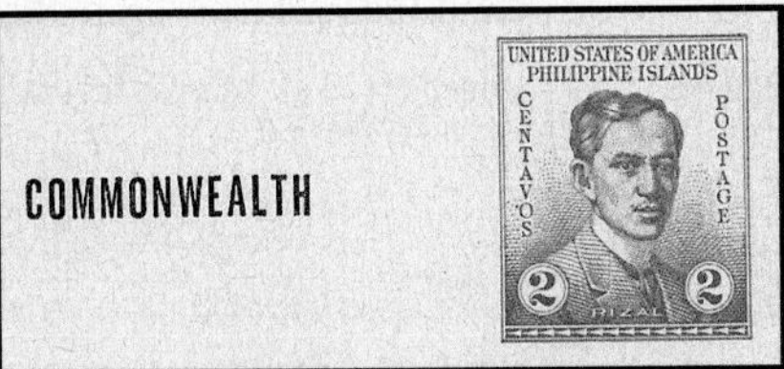

No. UX16 Overprinted

UX19	A53	2c **red,** *pale buff*	4.00	4.00

Nos. UX13, UX18 and UX19 Handstamped in Violet

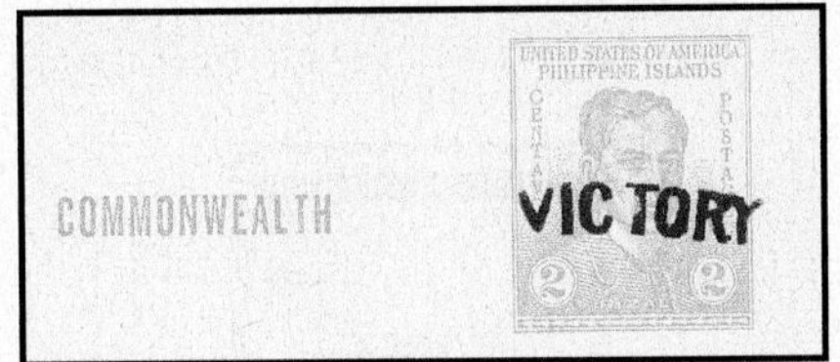

1944

UX20	A40	2c **green,** *buff, Rizal* (On UX13)	*250.00*	*250.00*
UX21	A53	2c **red,** *pale buff* (On UX18)	*900.00*	—
UX22	A53	2c **red,** *pale buff* (On UX19)	*425.00*	*550.00*

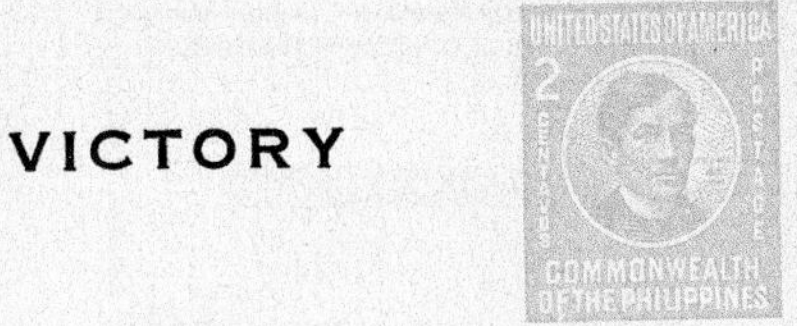

Overprinted in Black at left

1945, Jan. 19

UX23	A76	2c **gray brown,** *pale buff*	1.25	.75
		First day cancel		3.25
a.		"IC" of "Victory" very close	5.00	3.00

This card was not issued without overprint.

PAID REPLY POSTAL CARDS

U.S. Paid Reply Cards of 1892-93 issues

PM1

PR1

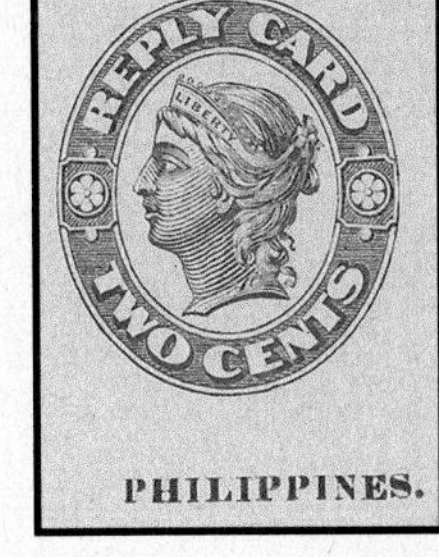

1900, Feb.

UY1	2c +2c **blue,** unsevered *(5,000)*	160.00	375.00
m.	PM1 Message card, detached	27.50	50.00
r.	PR1 Reply card, detached	27.50	50.00
s.	As No. UY1, double impression of overprint on message card		—

Overprinted Type "c" In Black

PM2

PR2

1903

UY2	1c + 1c **black,** *buff,* unsevered *(20,000)*	150.00	375.00
m.	PM2 Message card, detached	22.50	25.00
r.	PR2 Reply card, detached	22.50	25.00

Overprinted Type "c" in Black

PM3

PR3

UY3 2c + 2c **blue,** unsevered *(20,000)* 300.00 *700.00*
m. PM3 Message card, detached 55.00 50.00
r. PR3 Reply card, detached 55.00 50.00

OFFICIAL CARDS

Overprinted at Left of Stamp

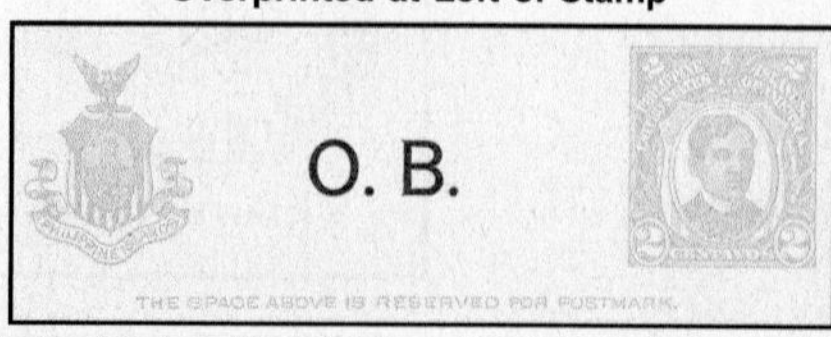

1925 **On postal card No. UX13**
UZ1 A40 2c **green,** *buff* (Rizal) 35.00 35.00

Overprinted at Left of Stamp

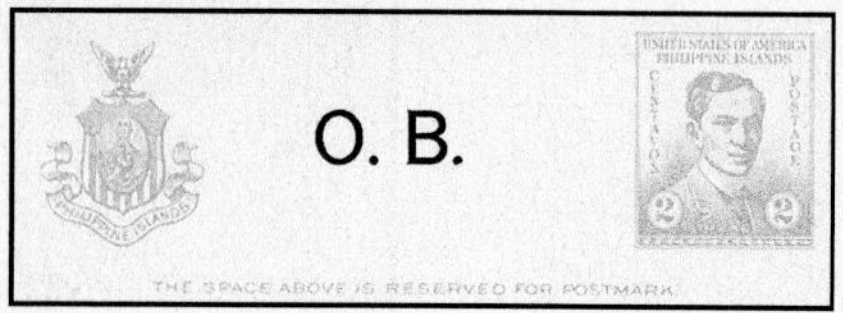

1935 **On postal card No. UX16**
UZ2 A53 2c **red,** *pale buff* 14.00 *17.50*

Overprinted at Left of Stamp

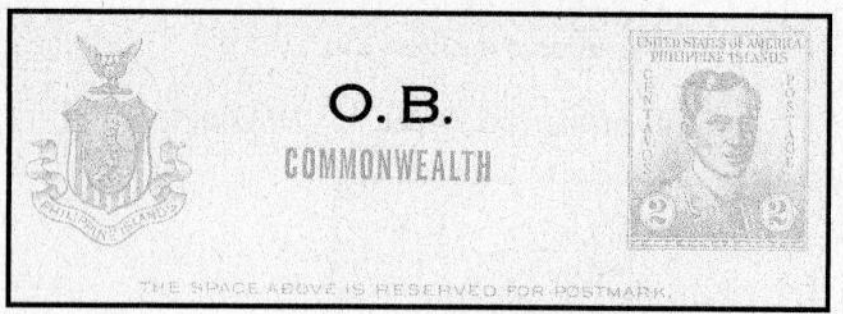

1938 **On postal card No. UX19**
UZ3 A53 2c **red,** *pale buff* 13.00 *17.50*

Overprinted Below Stamp

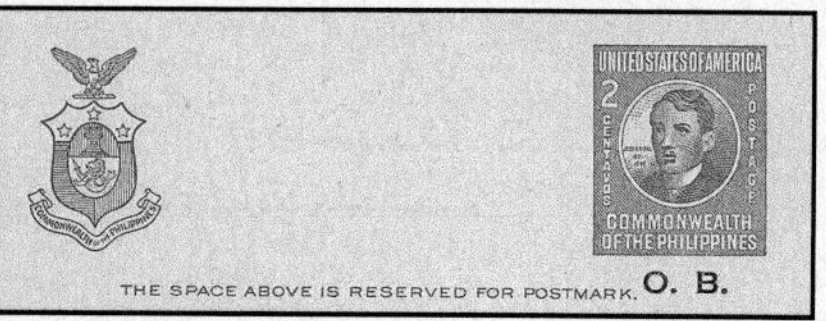

1941 **Design of postage issue of 1941**
UZ4 A75 2c **light green,** *pale buff* 160.00 *200.00*

This card was not issued without overprint.

Postal Card No. UX19 Overprinted at Left of Stamp

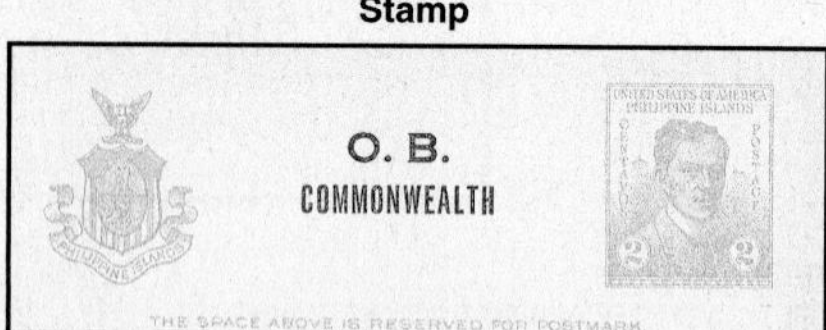

1941
UZ5 A53 2c **red,** *pale buff* 20.00 *25.00*

OCCUPATION STAMPS

Issued Under Japanese Occupation

No. 461 Overprinted in Black

No. 438 Overprinted in Black

No. 439 Overprinted in Black

1942-43 **Unwmk.** ***Perf. 11x10½, 11***

N1 A75 2c **apple green,** *Mar. 4, 1942 (3,000,000)* .25 *1.00*
Never hinged .30
P# block of 4 2.00
Never hinged 2.50
a. Pair, one without overprint —
N2 A58 12c **black,** *Apr. 30, 1943 (310,000)* .25 *2.00*
Never hinged .40
P# block of 6 12.00
Never hinged 15.00
N3 A59 16c **dark blue,** *Mar. 4, 1942 (160,000)* 5.00 3.75
Never hinged 7.50
P# block of 6 37.50
Never hinged 55.00
Nos. N1-N3 (3) 5.50 6.75
Set, never hinged 8.20

Nos. 435a, 435, 442, 443, and 423 Surcharged in Black

a

b

c

d

Type I

Type II

Two types of 50c surcharge
Type I: Center of "A" is a triangle.
Type II: Center of "A" is a pin hole.

1942-43 ***Perf. 11***

N4 A55(a) 5(c) on 6c **golden brown** *Sept. 1, 1942 (800,000)* .25 *.75*
Never hinged .35
First day cover, Manila 4.00
P# block of 6 15.00
Never hinged 20.00
a. Top bar shorter and thinner *(200,000)* .25 *1.00*
Never hinged .35
P# block of 6 50.00
Never hinged 60.00
b. 5(c) on 6c **dark brown** .25 *.85*
Never hinged .35
c. As "b," top bar shorter and thinner .25 *1.00*
Never hinged .35
d. Double surcharge, on cover —
N5 A62(b) 16(c) on 30c **orange red,** *Jan. 11, 1943 (210,000)* .25 *.60*
Never hinged .45
First day cover 5.00
P# block of 6 8.00
Never hinged 10.00
N6 A63(c) 50c on 1p **red orange & black,** type II surcharge, *Apr. 30, 1943 (20,000)* .75 *1.25*
Never hinged 1.10
P# block of 4, 2 P# 16.00
Never hinged 20.00
a. Double surcharge *300.00*
b. Type I surcharge 100.00 90.00
Never hinged 125.00
P# block of 4 500.00
Never hinged 600.00
N7 A65(d) 1p on 4p **blue & black,** *Apr. 30, 1943 (19,975)* 100.00 *150.00*
Never hinged 155.00
Inverted "S" in "PESO," position 4 175.00 *225.00*
P# block of 4 525.00
Never hinged 700.00
Nos. N4-N7 (4) 101.25 152.60
Set, never hinged 156.90

On Nos. N4 and N4b, the top bar measures 1½x22½mm. On Nos. N4a and N4c, the top bar measures 1x21mm and the "5" is smaller and thinner.

Bottom plate blocks of Nos. N2 and N3 have selvage reduced through the plate number. See note after No. 446.

The used value for No. N7 is for postal cancellation. Used stamps exist with first day cancellations. They are worth somewhat less.

No. 384 Surcharged in Black

1942, May 18

N8 A54 2(c) on 4c **yellow green** *(100,000)* 4.00 5.00
Never hinged 8.75
First day cover 6.00
P# block of 6 47.50
Never hinged 60.00

Issued to commemorate Japan's capture of Bataan and Corregidor. The American-Filipino forces finally surrendered May 7, 1942. No. N8 exists with "R" for "B" in BATAAN.

No. 384 Surcharged in Black

1942, Dec. 8
N9 A54 5(c) on 4c **yellow green** *(400,000)* .50 *1.00*
Never hinged .75
First day cover 3.00
P# block of 6 20.00
Never hinged 35.00

1st anniversary of the "Greater East Asia War."

Nos. C59 and C62 Surcharged in Black

1943, Jan. 23
N10 AP1 2(c) on 8c **carmine** *(400,000)* .25 *1.00*
Never hinged .35
P# block of 6 20.00
Never hinged 25.00
N11 AP1 5c on 1p **sepia** *(300,000)* .50 *1.50*
Never hinged .75
First day cover, #N10-N11 4.00
P# block of 6 24.00
Never hinged 30.00

1st anniv. of the Philippine Executive Commission.

Nipa Hut — OS1

Rice Planting — OS2

Mt. Mayon and Mt. Fuji — OS3

Moro Vinta — OS4

The "c" currency is indicated by four Japanese characters, "p" currency by two. Nos. N12-N27 were printed in Japan and sheets have marginal inscriptions but no plate numbers.

Engraved; Typographed (2c, 6c, 25c)

1943-44 **Wmk. 257** ***Perf. 13***
N12 OS1 1c **deep orange,** *June 7, 1943* .25 .40
Never hinged .30
Margin block of 6, inscription 2.40
Never hinged 3.00
N13 OS2 2c **bright green,** *Apr. 1, 1943* .25 .40
Never hinged .30
Margin block of 6, inscription 2.40
Never hinged 3.00
N14 OS1 4c **slate green,** *June 7, 1943* .25 .40
Never hinged .30
Margin block of 6, inscription 2.40
Never hinged 3.00
N15 OS3 5c **brown,** *Apr. 1, 1943* .25 .40
Never hinged .30
Margin block of 6, inscription 2.40
Never hinged 3.00
N16 OS2 6c **red,** *July 14, 1943* .25 .60
Never hinged .30
Margin block of 6, inscription 2.40
Never hinged 3.00
N17 OS3 10c **blue green,** *July 14, 1943* .25 .40
Never hinged .30
Margin block of 6, inscription 2.40
Never hinged 3.00
N18 OS4 12c **steel blue,** *July 14, 1943* 1.00 1.50
Never hinged 1.50
Margin block of 6, inscription 11.00
Never hinged 14.00
N19 OS4 16c **dark brown,** *July 14, 1943* .25 .40
Never hinged .30
Margin block of 6, inscription 2.40
Never hinged 3.00
N20 OS1 20c **rose violet,** *Aug. 16, 1943* 1.25 1.75
Never hinged 1.90
Margin block of 6, inscription 15.00
Never hinged 19.00
N21 OS3 21c **violet,** *Aug. 16, 1943* .25 .40
Never hinged .35
Margin block of 6, inscription 2.40
Never hinged 3.00
N22 OS2 25c **pale brown,** *Aug. 16, 1943* .25 .40
Never hinged .35
Margin block of 6, inscription 2.40
Never hinged 3.00
N23 OS3 1p **deep carmine,** *June 7, 1943* .75 1.25
Never hinged 1.15
Margin block of 6, inscription 9.50
Never hinged 12.00
N24 OS4 2p **dull violet,** *Sept. 16, 1943* 6.50 6.50
Never hinged 10.00
First day cover *14.00*
Margin block of 6, inscription 60.00
Never hinged 75.00
N25 OS4 5p **dark olive,** *Apr. 10, 1944* 16.00 18.00
Never hinged 25.00
First day cover *14.00*
Margin block of 6, inscription 110.00
Never hinged 175.00
Nos. N12-N25 (14) 27.75 32.80
Set, never hinged 42.00

Map of Manila Bay Showing Bataan and Corregidor — OS5

1943, May 7 **Photo.** **Unwmk.**
N26 OS5 2c **carmine red** .25 *.75*
Never hinged .30
Margin block of 6, inscription 4.00
Never hinged 5.00
N27 OS5 5c **bright green** .25 *1.00*
Never hinged .35
Margin block of 6, inscription 6.50
Never hinged 8.00
Colorless dot after left "5" 4.00 —
First day cover, #N26-N27, Manila 4.00

1st anniversary of the fall of Bataan and Corregidor.

No. 440 Surcharged in Black

1943, June 20 **Engr.** ***Perf. 11***
N28 A60 12(c) on 20c **light olive green** *(350,000)* .25 *.75*
Never hinged .35
First day cover 6.00
P# block of 6 11.00
Never hinged 15.00
a. Double surcharge —

350th anniversary of the printing press in the Philippines. "Limbagan" is Tagalog for "printing press."

Rizal Monument, Filipina and Philippine Flag — OS6

1943, Oct. 14 **Photo.** **Unwmk.** ***Perf. 12***
N29 OS6 5c **light blue** .25 *.90*
Never hinged .30
a. Imperf. .25 .90
N30 OS6 12c **orange** .25 *.90*
Never hinged .30
a. Imperf. .25 *.90*
N31 OS6 17c **rose pink** .25 *.90*
Never hinged .30
First day cover, #N29-N31, Manila 3.00
a. Imperf. .25 *.90*
First day cover, #N29a-N31a, Manila 3.00
Nos. N29-N31 (3) .75 *2.70*
Set, never hinged .90

"Independence of the Philippines." Japan granted "independence" Oct. 14, 1943, when the puppet republic was founded.

The imperforate stamps were issued without gum.

Nos. N29-N31 were printed locally and have no plate markings in the selvage.

José Rizal — OS7

Rev. José Burgos — OS8

Apolinario Mabini — OS9

1944, Feb. 17 **Litho.** **Unwmk.** ***Perf. 12***
N32 OS7 5c **blue** .25 *1.00*
Never hinged .30
a. Imperf. .25 *2.00*
Never hinged .35
N33 OS8 12c **carmine** .25 *1.00*
Never hinged .30
a. Imperf. .25 *2.00*
Never hinged .35
N34 OS9 17c **deep orange** .25 *1.00*
Never hinged .30
First day cover, #N32-N34, Manila 1.00
a. Imperf. .25 *2.00*
Never hinged .35
First day cover, #N32a-N34a, *Apr. 17,* Manila 3.00
Nos. N32-N34 (3) .75 *3.00*
Set, never hinged .90

See No. NB8.

Nos. N32-N34a were printed locally and have no plate markings in the selvage.

Nos. C60 and C61 Surcharged in Black

1944, May 7 **Unwmk.** ***Perf. 11***
N35 AP1 5(c) on 20c **ultramarine** .50 1.00
Never hinged .75
P# block of 6 32.50
Never hinged 40.00
N36 AP1 12(c) on 60c **blue green** *(165,000)* 1.75 1.75
Never hinged 2.50
P# block of 6 42.50
Never hinged 52.50
First day cover, #N35-N36 4.00

2nd anniversary of the fall of Bataan and Corregidor.

José P. Laurel — OS10

1945, Jan. 12 **Litho.** **Unwmk.** ***Imperf.***
Without Gum
N37 OS10 5c **dull violet brown** .25 *.50*
Never hinged .30

N38 OS10 7c **blue green** .25 *.50*
Never hinged .30
N39 OS10 20c **chalky blue** .25 *.50*
Never hinged .30
First day cover, #N37-N39 3.00
Nos. N37-N39 (3) *.75 1.50*
Set, never hinged .90

Issued belatedly on Jan. 12, 1945, to commemorate the first anniversary of the puppet Philippine Republic, Oct. 14, 1944. "S" stands for "sentimos."

The special cancellation devices prepared for use on Oct. 14, 1944, were employed on "First Day" covers Jan. 12, 1945.

Nos. N37-N39 were printed locally and have no plate markings in the selvage.

OCCUPATION SEMI-POSTAL STAMPS

Woman, Farming and Cannery — OSP1

1942, Nov. 12 Litho. Unwmk. *Perf. 12*

NB1 OSP1 2c + 1c **pale violet** .25 *.60*
Never hinged .30
NB2 OSP1 5c + 1c **brt grn** .25 *1.00*
Never hinged .30
NB3 OSP1 16c + 2c **orange** 25.00 *32.50*
Never hinged 42.00
First day cover, #NB1-NB3 37.50
Nos. NB1-NB3 (3) 25.50 34.10
Set, never hinged 42.60

Issued to promote the campaign to produce and conserve food. The surtax aided the Red Cross.

Nos. NB1-NB3 were printed locally and have no plate markings in the selvage.

Souvenir Sheet

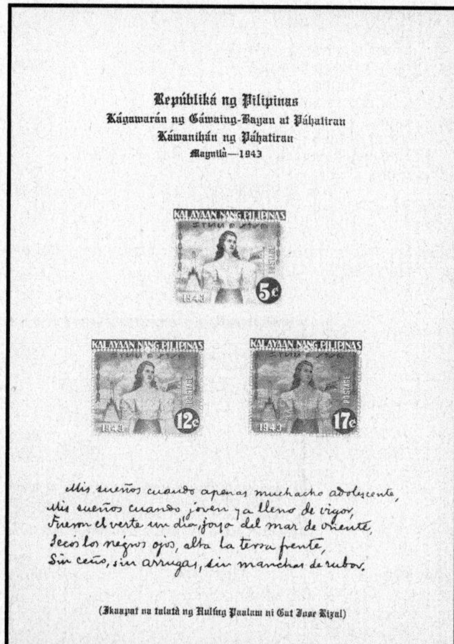

OSP2

Illustration reduced.

1943, Oct. 14 Without Gum *Imperf.*

NB4 OSP2 Sheet of 3 60.00 *17.50*
Sheet with first day cancel and cachet, Manila 17.50
First day cover, Manila —

"Independence of the Philippines."

No. NB4 contains one each of Nos. N29a-N31a. Marginal inscription is from Rizal's "Last Farewell." Sold for 2.50p.

The value of No. NB4 used is for a sheet from a first day cover. Commercially used sheets are extremely scarce and worth much more.

Nos. N18, N20 and N21 Surcharged in Black

1943, Dec. 8 Wmk. 257 *Perf. 13*

NB5 OS4 12c + 21c **steel blue** .25 *1.50*
Never hinged .30
Margin block of 6, inscription 4.00
Never hinged 5.00
NB6 OS1 20c + 36c **rose violet** .25 *1.50*
Never hinged .30
Margin block of 6, inscription 4.00
Never hinged 5.00
NB7 OS3 21c + 40c **violet** .25 *2.00*
Never hinged .30
Margin block of 6, inscription 4.75
Never hinged 6.00
First day cover, #NB5-NB7 2.50
Nos. NB5-NB7 (3) .75 *5.00*
Set, never hinged .90

The surtax was for the benefit of victims of a Luzon flood. "Baha" is Tagalog for "flood."

Souvenir Sheet

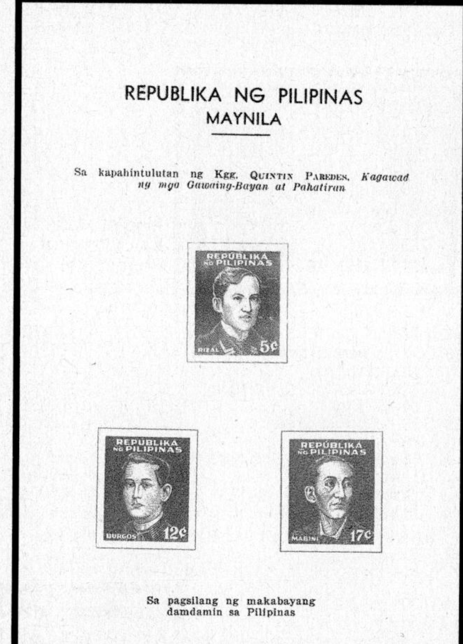

OSP3

Illustration reduced.

1944, Feb. 9 Litho. Unwmk. *Imperf.*
Without Gum

NB8 OSP3 Sheet of 3 6.50 3.50
First day cover *4.00*

No. NB8 contains 1 each of Nos. N32a-N34a.

Sheet sold for 1p, surtax going to a fund for the care of heroes' monuments.

The value for No. NB8 used is for a stamp from a first day cover. Commercially used examples are worth much more.

OCCUPATION POSTAGE DUE

No. J15 Overprinted in Blue

1942, Oct. 14 Unwmk. *Perf. 11*

NJ1 D3 3c on 4c **brown red** *(40,000)* 25.00 *35.00*
Never hinged 37.50
First day cover *35.00*
Double bar — —
Right side P# block of 6 200.00
Never hinged 350.00

On examples of No. J15, two lines were drawn in India ink with a ruling pen across "United States of America" by employees of the Short Paid Section of the Manila Post Office to make a provisional 3c postage due stamp which was used from Sept. 1, 1942 (when the letter rate was raised from 2c to 5c) until Oct. 14 when No. NJ1 went on sale. Value on cover, $175.

Bottom plate blocks of 6 of No. NJ1 are much scarcer than the right side plate blocks. Value $325 hinged, $450 never hinged.

OCCUPATION OFFICIAL STAMPS

Nos. 461, 413, 435, 435a and 442 Overprinted or Surcharged in Black with Bars and

1943-44 Unwmk. *Perf. 11x10½, 11*

NO1 A75 2c **apple green,** *Apr. 7, 1943 (200,000)* .25 *.75*
Never hinged .30
P# block of 4 6.75
Never hinged 8.50
a. Double overprint *400.00*
Never hinged *600.00*
On cover (double overprint) *1,250.*
NO2 A55 5(c) on 6c **dark brown** (On No. 413), *June 26, 1944 (23,049)* 40.00 *45.00*
Never hinged 55.00
First day cover *125.00*
P# block of 6 290.00
Never hinged 375.00
NO3 A55 5(c) on 6c **golden brown** (On No. 435a), *Apr. 7, 1943 (250,000)* .25 *.90*
Never hinged .35
P# block of 6 14.00
Never hinged 17.50
a. Narrower spacing between bars *(249,951)* .25 *.90*
Never hinged .35
b. 5(c) on 6c dark brown (On No. 435) .25 *.90*
Never hinged .35
c. As "b," narrower spacing between bars .25 *.90*
Never hinged .35
d. Double overprint —
NO4 A62 16(c) on 30c **orange red,** *Apr. 7, 1943 (100,000)* .30 *1.25*
Never hinged .45
P# block of 6 20.00
Never hinged 25.00
a. Wider spacing between bars .30 *1.25*
Never hinged .45
First day cover, Nos. NO1, NO3-NO4 *35.00*
b. Surcharged on No. 420 —
Nos. NO1-NO4 (4) 40.80 47.90
Set, never hinged 56.10

On Nos. NO3 and NO3b the bar deleting "United States of America" is 9¾ to 10mm above the bar deleting "Common." On Nos. NO3a and NO3c, the spacing is 8 to 8½mm.

On No. NO4, the center bar is 19mm long, 3½mm below the top bar and 6mm above the Japanese characters. On No. NO4a, the center bar is 20½mm long, 9mm below the top bar and 1mm above the Japanese characters.

"K.P." stands for Kagamitang Pampamahalaan, "Official Business" in Tagalog.

Nos. 435 and 435a Surcharged in Black

1944, Aug. 28 Unwmk. *Perf. 11*

NO5 A55 (5c) on 6c **golden brown** *(500,000)* .30 *.40*
Never hinged .45
P# block of 6 20.00
Never hinged 25.00
a. 5(c) on 6c **dark brown** .30 *.40*
Never hinged .45
P# block of 6 20.00
Never hinged 25.00

Nos. O34 and C62 Overprinted in Black

a

b

NO6 A60(a) 20c **light olive green** *(200,000)* .40 *.50*
Never hinged .60
P# block of 6 12.00
Never hinged 15.00
NO7 AP1(b) 1p **sepia** *(100,000)* .90 *1.00*
Never hinged 1.45
P# block of 6 20.00
Never hinged 25.00
First day cover, #NO5-NO7 4.00
Nos. NO5-NO7 (3) 1.60 1.90
Set, never hinged 2.05

Bottom plate blocks of Nos. NO3-NO6 have selvage reduced through the plate number. See note after No. 446.

OCCUPATION ENVELOPES

No. U41 Surcharged in Black

1943, Apr. 1
NU1 E4 5c on 2c **carmine** .50 .30
Entire 3.00 3.00
Entire, 1st day cancel 4.00

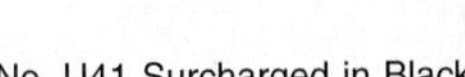

No. U41 Surcharged in Black

1944, Feb. 17
NU2 E4 5c on 2c **carmine** .75 .50
Entire 3.50 *5.00*
Entire, 1st day cancel 7.50
a. Inverted surcharged —
b. Double surcharge —
c. Both 5's missing —

OCCUPATION POSTAL CARDS

Values are for entire cards.
Nos. UX19 and UZ4 Overprinted

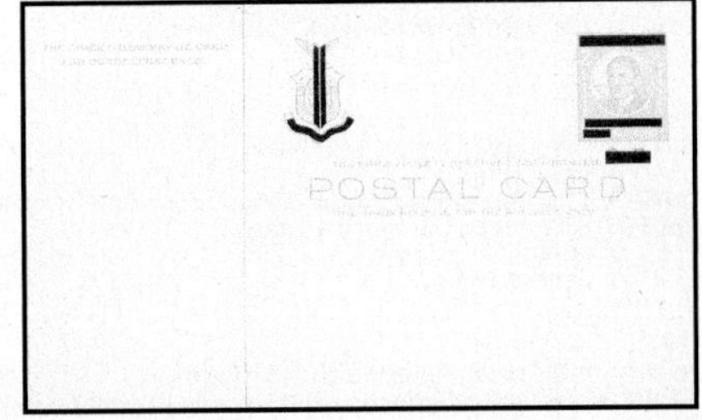

1942
NUX1 A53 2c **red,** *pale buff, Mar. 4, 1942* 15.00 15.00
First day cancel *85.00*
a. Vertical obliteration bars reversed *140.00*
NUX2 A75 2c **light green,** *pale buff, Dec. 12, 1942* 3.00 2.00
First day cancel 6.00

Rice Planting — A77

1943, May 17
NUX3 A77 2c **green** 1.00 *1.00*
First day cancel, Manila 2.00

OCCUPATION OFFICIAL CARDS

Nos. UX19, UX17 and UX18 Overprinted in Black with Bars and

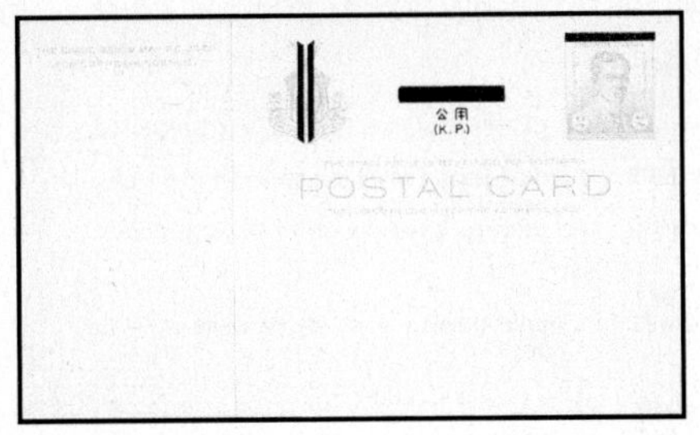

1943, Apr. 7
NUZ1 A53 2c **red,** *pale buff* 5.00 5.00
First day cancel 100.00
a. On No. UX17 — —
b. On No. UX18 *500.00* —

No. NUX3 Overprinted in Black

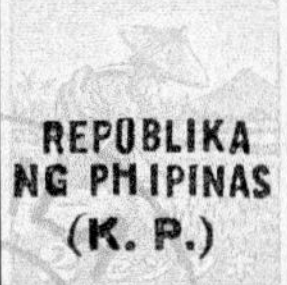

1944, Aug. 28
NUZ2 A77 2c **green** 1.50 *1.00*
First day cancel 2.00
a. Double overprint *700.00*

FILIPINO REVOLUTIONARY GOVERNMENT

Following the defeat of the Spanish fleet by U.S. Commodore Dewey in Manila on May 1, 1898, which essentially ended the Spanish-American War in the Philippines, postal services were disrupted throughout the Philippines. Postal service was reestablished through U.S. Army military stations, beginning in June 1898 near Manila, continuing province by province until culminating at Zamboanga and other cities in the southern areas in late 1899.

Provisional stamps were prepared for use in the central part of the island of Luzon at Malolos in late 1898 under the leadership of General Emilio Aguinaldo, who had proclaimed the Philippine Republic on June 12, 1898. Later, other provisional stamps were prepared by local Filipino insurgents at Iloilo (Panay Island), Bohol, Cebu and Negros, and Spanish period stamps were overprinted and/or surcharged for use by postal officials at Zamboanga and La Union.

The most familiar of these provisionals were the "Aguinaldo" issues of the Filipino Revolutionary Government in central Luzon near Manila. The letters "KKK," the initials of the revolutionary society, "Kataastaasang, Kagalang-galang Katipunan nang Mañga Anak nang Bayan," meaning "Sovereign Worshipful Association of the Sons of the Country," readily identify the Aguinaldo provisionals. Hostilities broke out between the Aguinaldo regime and the occupying American administration in February 1899, and the Filipino-American War continued until the American capture of Aguinaldo on March 23, 1901.

The Aguinaldo regular postage, registration, revenue, newspaper and telegraph stamps were in use in Luzon as early as November 10, 1898, and continued in use through early 1901. Although the postal regulations specified that these stamps be used for their inscribed purpose, they were commonly used interchangeably.

POSTAGE ISSUES

A1

A2

Coat of Arms — A3

1898-99 **Unwmk.** ***Perf. 11½***
Y1 A1 2c **red** 250.00 300.00
On cover *1,500.*
a. Double impression *325.00*
Y2 A2 2c **red** .30 4.00
On cover 350.00
b. Double impression —
d. Horiz. pair, imperf. between —
e. Vert. pair, imperf. between *225.00*
Y3 A3 2c **red** 150.00 *300.00*
On cover *2,000.*

Imperf pairs and pairs, imperf horizontally, have been created from No. Y2e.

REGISTRATION STAMP

RS1

YF1 RS1 8c **green** 5.00 *30.00*
On cover with #Y2 *3,500.*
a. Imperf., pair 400.00
b. Imperf. vertically, pair —

NEWSPAPER STAMP

N1

YP1	N1	1m **black**	2.00	*20.00*
	a.	Imperf., pair	5.00	*20.00*

PROOFS

1906

241P2	2c **yellow green,** small die on white wove paper	500.
241P2a	2c **yellow green,** PP sm die on yelsh wove paper	750.
242TC1	4c **black,** large die on India paper	*1,600.*
242P1	4c **carmine lake,** large die on India paper	*1,000.*
242P2	4c **carmine lake,** small die on white wove paper	500.
242P2a	4c **carmine lake,** PP sm die on yelsh wove paper	750.
243P1	6c **violet,** large die on India paper	*1,000.*
243P2	6c **violet,** small die on white wove paper	500.
243P2a	6c **violet,** PP sm die on yelsh wove paper	750.
244P1	8c **brown,** large die on India paper	*1,000.*
244P2	8c **brown,** small die on white wove paper	500.
244P2a	8c **brown,** PP sm die on yelsh wove paper	750.
245P2	10c **dark blue,** small die on white wove paper	500.
245P2a	10c **dark blue,** PP sm die on yelsh wove paper	750.
246P2	12c **brown lake,** small die on white wove paper	500.
246P2a	12c **brown lake,** PP sm die on yelsh wove paper	750.
247P1	16c **violet black,** large die on India paper	*1,000.*
247P2	16c **violet black,** small die on white wove paper	500.
247P2a	16c **violet black,** PP sm die on yelsh wove paper	750.
248P2	20c **orange brown,** small die on white wove paper	500.
248P2a	20c **orange brown,** PP sm die on yelsh wove paper	750.
249P2	26c **violet brown,** small die on white wove paper	500.
249P2a	26c **violet brown,** PP sm die on yelsh wove paper	750.
250P1	30c **olive green,** large die on India paper	*1,000.*
250P2	30c **olive green,** small die on white wove paper	500.
250P2a	30c **olive green,** PP sm die on yelsh wove paper	750.
251P2	1p **orange,** small die on white wove paper	500.
251P2a	1p **orange,** PP sm die on yelsh wove paper	750.
252P2	2p **black,** small die on white wove paper	500.
252P2a	2p **black,** PP sm die on yelsh wove paper	750.
253P2	4p **dark blue,** small die on white wove paper	500.
253P2a	4p **dark blue,** PP sm die on yelsh wove paper	750.
254P2	10p **dark green,** small die on white wove paper	500.
254P2a	10p **dark green,** PP sm die on yelsh wove paper	750.

1909-13

255P2	12c **red orange,** small die on white wove paper	600.
255P2a	12c **red orange,** PP sm die on yelsh wove paper	625.
256P2	16c **olive green,** small die on white wove paper	600.
256P2a	16c **olive green,** PP sm die on yelsh wove paper	625.
257P2	20c **yellow,** small die on white wove paper	600.
257P2a	20c **yellow,** PP sm die on yelsh wove paper	625.
258P2	26c **blue green,** small die on white wove paper	600.
258P2a	26c **blue green,** PP sm die on yelsh wove paper	625.
259P2	30c **ultramarine,** small die on white wove paper	600.
259P2a	30c **ultramarine,** PP sm die on yelsh wove paper	625.
260P2	1p **pale violet,** small die on white wove paper	600.
260P2a	1p **pale violet,** PP sm die on yelsh wove paper	625.
260AP2	2p **violet brown,** small die on white wove paper	600.
260AP2a	2p **violet brown,** PP sm die on yelsh wove paper	625.
275P2	30c **gray,** small die on white wove paper	600.
275P2a	30c **gray,** PP sm die on yelsh wove paper	625.

1923

303TC1	16c Large die on India paper	
	a. **olive green**	450.
303P1	16c **olive bister,** large die on India paper	450.

1926

322P4	18c **light brown & black,** plate on glazed card	350.

1932

357TC1	18c Large die on India paper	
	a. **orange red**	450.
357P1	18c **red orange,** large die on India paper	450.
360TC1	32c Large die on India paper	
	a. **green**	450.
	b. **olive green**	450.

1935

383P1	2c **rose,** large die on India paper	600.
384P1	4c **yellow green,** large die on India paper	600.
385P1	6c **dk brown,** large die on India paper	600.
386P1	8c **violet,** large die on India paper	600.
387P1	10c **rose carmine,** large die on India paper	600.
388P1	12c **black,** large die on India paper	600.
389P1	16c **dk blue,** large die on India paper	600.
390TC1	20c Large die on India paper	
	a. **black**	—
390P1	20c **lt olive green,** large die on India paper	600.
391P1	26c **indigo,** large die on India paper	600.
392P1	30c **orange red,** large die on India paper	600.
393P1	1p **red org & blk,** large die on India paper	600.
394P1	2p **bis brn & blk,** large die on India paper	600.
395P1	4p **blue & blk,** large die on India paper	600.
396P1	5p **grn & blk,** large die on India paper	600.

1936

408TC1	2c Large die on India paper	
	a. **yellow green**	450.
408P1	2c **orange brown,** large die on India paper	450.

1937

425P2	2c **yellow green,** small die on white wove paper	500.

1939

452P1	2c **yellow green,** large die on India paper	*750.*
452P2	2c **yellow green,** small die on white wove paper	500.
453P2	6c **carmine,** small die on white wove paper	500.
454P2	12c **bright blue,** small die on white wove paper	500.
455P1	2c **green,** large die on India paper	750.
455P2	2c **green,** small die on white wove paper	500.
456P2	6c **orange,** small die on white wove paper	500.
457P2	12c **carmine,** small die on white wove paper	500.

1940

458P1	2c **dk orange,** large die on India paper	1,000.
458P2	2c **dk orange,** small die on white wove paper	600.
459P2	6c **dk green,** small die on white wove paper	600.
460P2	12c **purple,** small die on white wove paper	600.

1941

461P2	2c **apple green,** small die on white wove paper	600.

1946

497P1	2c **sepia,** large die on India paper	—

AIR POST

1941

C59P2	8c **carmine,** small die on white wove paper	500.
C60P2	20c **ultramarine,** small die on white wove paper	500.
C61P2	60c **blue green,** small die on white wove paper	500.
C62P2	1p **sepia,** small die on white wove paper	500.

SPECIAL DELIVERY

1906

E2TC1	20c **black,** large die on India paper	—
E2P1	20c **ultramarine,** large die on wove paper	2,000.
E2TC2	20c Small die on India paper	
	a. **green**	1,000.
E2P2	20c **ultramarine,** small die on wove paper	1,000.
E2P2a	20c **ultramarine,** PP small die on yelsh wove paper	850.

POSTAGE DUE

1899

J1P2	1c **deep claret,** small die on wove paper	2,750.
J2P2	2c **deep claret,** small die on wove paper	2,750.
J3P2	5c **deep claret,** small die on wove paper	2,750.
J4P2	10c **deep claret,** small die on wove paper	2,750.
J5P2	50c **deep claret,** small die on wove paper	2,750.

1901

J6P2	3c **deep claret,** small die on wove paper	2,750.
J7P2	30c **deep claret,** small die on wove paper	2,750.

SPECIMEN STAMPS

Handstamped US Type E in Purple or Black

1899

213S E	1c **yellow green**	175.00
214dS E	2c **rose carmine,** type IV	175.00
215S E	3c **purple**	175.00
216S E	5c **blue**	175.00
217S E	10c **brown,** type I	175.00
218S E	15c **olive brown**	175.00
219S E	50c **orange**	175.00

See "Special Printings" notice after No. 219 for Special Printings with black "Specimen" handstamp, but note that not all stamps with the black "Specimen" handstamp are Special Printings.

Overprinted Type R in Black

1917-25

290S R	2c **green**	40.00
291S R	4c **carmine**	40.00
292S R	6c **deep violet**	40.00
293S R	8c **yellow brown**	40.00
294S R	10c **deep blue**	40.00
295S R	12c **red orange**	40.00
297S R	20c **orange yellow**	40.00
298S R	26c **green**	40.00
299S R	30c **gray**	40.00
300S R	1p **pale violet**	40.00
301S R	2p **violet brown**	40.00
302S R	4p **blue**	40.00

1923-26

303S R	16c **olive bister**	40.00
304S R	10p **deep green**	40.00

1911

269S T	26c **blue green**	—
272S T	2p **violet brown**	—
274S T	10p **deep green**	—

1918

287AS T	8c **light brown**	—

1917

290S T	2c **green**	—
291S T	4c **carmine**	—
294S T	10c **deep blue**	—
295S T	12c **red orange**	—
296S T	16c **light olive green**	—
297S T	20c **orange yellow**	—
299S T	30c **gray**	—
300S T	1p **violet**	—
302S T	4p **dark blue**	—

Overprinted Type R in Red

1926

319S R	2c **green & black**	65.00
320S R	4c **carmine & black**	65.00
321S R	16c **olive green & black**	65.00
322S R	18c **light brown & black**	65.00
323S R	20c **orange & black**	65.00
324S R	24c **gray & black**	65.00
325S R	1p **rose lilac & black**	65.00

Overprinted Type S in Red

1926

319S S	2c **green & black**	65.00
320S S	4c **carmine & black**	65.00
321S S	16c **olive green & black**	65.00
322S S	18c **light brown & black**	65.00
323S S	20c **orange & black**	65.00
324S S	24c **gray & black**	65.00
325S S	1p **rose lilac & black**	65.00

Imperforate examples of this set, on glazed cards with centers in brown, are known with the "Cancelled" overprint. Value, $2,250 for set.

Handstamped in Red Capitals, Type T

Handstamp size: 13x3mm

1925

340aS T	2c **green**	75.00
341aS T	4c **carmine**	75.00
342aS T	6c **deep violet**	75.00
343aS T	8c **yellow brown**	100.00
344aS T	10c **deep blue**	100.00
345aS T	12c **red orange**	100.00
346aS T	16c **bister green**	100.00
347aS T	20c **yellow orange**	100.00
348aS T	26c **blue green**	100.00
349aS T	30c **gray**	100.00
350aS T	1p **violet**	100.00
351aS T	2p **violet brown**	100.00
352aS T	4p **deep blue**	150.00
353aS T	10p **deep green**	250.00

The 1925 Specimens are only known without gum.

1931

340S T	2c **yellow green**	—
341S T	4c **carmine rose**	—
342S T	6c **violet**	—
343S T	8c **brown**	—
344S T	10c **blue**	—
345S T	12c **deep orange**	—
346S T	16c **olive green**	—
347S T	20c **deep yellow orange**	—
348S T	26c **green**	—
349S T	30c **light gray**	—
350S T	1p **light violet**	—
351S T	2p **brown violet**	—
352S T	4p **blue**	—
353S T	10p **green**	—

SPECIAL DELIVERY

Overprinted Type R in Black

1919

E5S R	20c **ultramarine**	200.00
E5bS R	20c **dull violet**	—

Overprinted Type T in Purple

E5aS T	20c **pale blue**	—

Handstamped in Red

Handstamp size: 13x3mm, Type T

1925

E6aS T	20c **violet blue**	300.00

1931

E6S T	20c **dull violet**	—

POSTAGE DUE

Overprinted US Type E in Black

1899

J1S E	1c **deep claret**	500.00
J2S E	2c **deep claret**	500.00
J3S E	5c **deep claret**	500.00
J4S E	10c **deep claret**	500.00
J5S E	50c **deep claret**	500.00

OFFICIAL

1926 **Overprinted Type R in Red**

O1S R	2c **green & black**	30.00
O2S R	4c **carmine & black**	30.00
O3S R	18c **light brown & black**	30.00
O4S R	20c **orange & black**	30.00

1926 **Overprinted Type S in Red**

O1S S	2c **green & black**	30.00
O2S S	4c **carmine & black**	30.00
O3S S	18c **light brown & black**	30.00
O4S S	20c **orange & black**	30.00

PUERTO RICO

(Porto Rico)

United States troops landed at Guanica Bay, Puerto Rico, on July 25, 1898, and mail service between various points in Puerto Rico began soon after under the authority of General Wilson, acting governor of the conquered territory, who authorized a provisional service early in August, 1898. The first Military Postal Station was opened at La Playa de Ponce on August 3, 1898. Control of the island passed formally to the United States on October 18, 1898. Twenty-one military stations operating under the administration of the Military Postal Service were authorized in Puerto Rico after the Spanish-American war. After the overprinted provisional issue of 1900, unoverprinted stamps of the United States replaced those of Puerto Rico.

Name changed to Puerto Rico by Act of Congress, approved May 17, 1932.

Italicized numbers in parentheses indicate quantities issued.

100 CENTS = 1 DOLLAR.

LOCAL ISSUES

Ponce Issue

A11

1898 **Unwmk.** **Handstamped** ***Imperf.***

200 A11 5c **violet** —

No. 200 is a violet handstamp and control mark used on envelopes. Some examples have no control mark. There are three types of circular markings known, and two control marks. Uses on 2¢ U.S. stamps on cover were strictly as a cancellation, not as local postage. Because genuine usage is extremely difficult to authenticate with certainty, certification by competent authorities is essential.

Coamo Issue

A12 — Setting of 10

Types of "5":

I — Curved flag. Pos. 2, 3, 4, 5.

II — Flag turns down at right. Pos. 1, 9, 10.

III — Fancy outlined "5." Pos. 6, 7.

IV — Flag curls into ball at right. Pos. 8.

Typeset, setting of 10

1898, Aug. **Unwmk.** ***Imperf.***

201 A12 5c **black,** Type I	700.	*1,250.*
Type II	700.	*1,300.*
Type III	775.	*1,400.*
Type IV	850.	*1,550.*

Irregular "block" of 4 showing one of each type	3,750.	
Sheet of 10	10,000.	
On cover		*27,500.*
Pair on cover		—

Blocks not showing all four types and pairs normally sell for 10-20% over the value of the individual stamps.

The stamps bear the control mark "F. Santiago" in violet. About 500 were issued.

Dangerous forgeries exist.

Regular Issue

United States Nos. 279, 279Bf, 281, 272 and 282C Overprinted in Black at 36 degree Angle

1899 **Wmk. 191** ***Perf. 12***

210 A87 1c **yellow green,** *Mar. 15*	6.00	1.40
Never hinged	13.00	
On cover		50.00

	First day cover		—
	Block of 4	30.00	10.00
	P# strip of 3, Impt.	52.50	
	P# block of 6, Impt.	300.00	
a.	Overprint at 25 degree angle	8.00	2.25
	Never hinged	17.50	
	Pair, 36 degree and 25 degree angles	27.50	
	"PORTO RICU"	37.50	25.00
211	A88 2c **reddish carmine,** type IV, *Mar. 15*	5.00	1.25
	Never hinged	11.00	
	On cover		50.00
	Block of 4	25.00	10.00
	P# strip of 3, Impt.	40.00	
	P# block of 6, Impt.	350.00	
	"FORTO RICO" (pos. 77)	—	
a.	Overprint at 25 degree angle, *Mar. 15*	6.50	2.25
	Never hinged	14.00	
	On cover		50.00
	First day cover		—
	Block of 4	30.00	17.50
	P# strip of 3, Impt.	42.50	
	P# block of 6, Impt.	275.00	
	Pair, 36 degree and 25 degree angles	27.50	
	P# strip of 3, Impt.	100.00	
	P# block of 6, Impt.	700.00	
	"PORTU RICO" (pos. 46)	52.50	20.00
	"PORTO RICU" (pos. 3)	—	
	"PURTO RICO"	—	
	"FURTU RICO"	—	
212	A91 5c **blue**	12.50	2.50
	Never hinged	27.50	
	On cover		50.00
	Block of 4	55.00	27.50
	P# strip of 3, Impt.	70.00	
	P# block of 6, Impt.	350.00	
213	A93 8c **violet brown**	40.00	17.50
	Never hinged	90.00	
	On cover		125.00
	Block of 4	180.00	110.00
	P# strip of 3, Impt.	260.00	
	P# block of 6, Impt.	*5,000.*	
	"FORTO RICO"	95.00	60.00
a.	Overprint at 25 degree angle	45.00	19.00
	Never hinged	100.00	
	Pair, 36 degree and 25 degree angles	110.00	
c.	"PORTO RIC"	150.00	110.00
214	A94 10c **brown,** type I	22.50	6.00
	Never hinged	50.00	
	On cover		120.00
	Block of 4	100.00	45.00
	P# strip of 3, Impt.	150.00	
	P# block of 6, Impt.	1,500.	
	"FORTO RICO"	87.50	70.00
	Nos. 210-214 (5)	86.00	28.65

Misspellings of the overprint on Nos. 210-214 (PORTO RICU, PORTU RICO, FORTO RICO) are actually broken letters.

United States Nos. 279 and 279B Overprinted in Black

1900

215	A87 1c **yellow green**	7.50	1.40
	Never hinged	17.50	
	On cover		50.00
	Block of 4	32.50	10.00
	P# strip of 3, Impt.	30.00	
	P# block of 6, Impt.	175.00	
216	A88 2c **red,** type IV, *Apr. 2*	5.50	2.00
	Never hinged	12.50	
	On cover		50.00
	Block of 4	25.00	15.00
	P# strip of 3, Impt.	32.50	
	P# block of 6, Impt.	175.00	
b.	Inverted overprint		*12,500.*

Special Printing

In March 1900 one pane of 100 stamps of each of the 1c (No. 215), 2c (No. 216) and 5c, 8c and 10c values, as well as 1c, 2c and 10c postage due stamps were specially overprinted for displays at the Paris Exposition (1900) and Pan American Exposition (1901). These last six items were never regularly issued with the PUERTO RICO overprint and therefore have no Scott catalogue number. The 2c pane was light red, type IV.

Stamps were handstampd type E "Specimen" in black ink by H. G. Mandel and mounted by him in separate displays for the two Expositions. Additional stamps from each pane were also handstamped "Specimen," but most were destroyed after the Expositions. However, because additional stamps that are not Special Printings exist with a black "Specimen" handstamp, expertizaton by competent authorities is reommmended.

J. M. Bartels, a stamp dealer, signed some stamps from these panes "Special Surcharge" in pencil on the gum to authenticate them as coming from the "Mandel" Special Printing panes. In 1904 or later, he handstamped additional surviving examples "Special Surcharge" in red ink on the back as his guarantee. Some of these guaranteed stamps had Mandel's "Specimen" handstamp on the face while others did not. Value, each $2,000.

No Special Printing panes overprinted "Porto Rico" were produced by the government. Stamps do exist with a black type E "Specimen" handstamp, but it is believed that H. G. Mandel applied such handstamps to regularly issued overprinted "Porto Rico" stamps from his personal collection. Examples are known of the 2c type IV, in reddish carmine, 25 degree angle.

AIR POST

In 1938 a series of eight labels, two of which were surcharged, was offered to the public as "Semi-Official Air Post Stamps", the claim being that they had been authorized by the "Puerto Rican postal officials." These labels, printed by the Ever Ready Label Co. of New York, were a private issue of Aerovias Nacionales Puerto Rico, operating a passenger and air express service. Instead of having been authorized by the postal officials, they were at first forbidden but later tolerated by the Post Office Department at Washington.

In 1941 a further set of eight triangular labels was prepared and offered to collectors, and again the Post Office Department officials at Washington objected and forbade their use after September 16, 1941.

These labels represent only the charge for service rendered by a private enterprise for transporting matter outside the mails by plane. Their use did not and does not eliminate the payment of postage on letters carried by air express, which must in every instance be paid by United States postage stamps.

POSTAGE DUE STAMPS

United States Nos. J38, J39 and J42 Overprinted in Black at 36 degree Angle

1899 **Wmk. 191** ***Perf. 12***

J1	D2 1c **deep claret**	22.50	5.50
	Never hinged	50.00	
	On cover		125.00
	Block of 4	100.00	35.00
	P# strip of 3, Impt.	120.00	
	P# block of 6, Impt.	*625.00*	
a.	Overprint at 25 degree angle	22.50	7.50
	Never hinged	50.00	
	Pair, 36 degree and 25 degree angles	65.00	
	P# strip of 3, Impt.	150.00	
	P# block of 6, Impt.	*750.00*	
J2	D2 2c **deep claret**	20.00	6.00
	Never hinged	45.00	
	On cover		250.00
	Block of 4	80.00	37.50
	P# strip of 3, Impt.	120.00	
	P# block of 6, Impt.	*800.00*	
a.	Overprint at 25 degree angle	20.00	7.00
	Never hinged	45.00	
	Pair, 36 degree and 25 degree angles	60.00	
	P# strip of 3, Impt.	140.00	
	P# block of 6, Impt.	*900.00*	
J3	D2 10c **deep claret**	180.00	55.00
	Never hinged	375.00	
	On cover		—
	Block of 4	800.00	—
a.	Overprint at 25 degree angle	160.00	75.00
	Never hinged	330.00	
	Pair, 36 degree and 25 degree angles	650.00	
	P# strip of 3, Impt., 36 degree and 25 degree angles	*1,250.*	
	P# block of 6, Impt., 36 degree and 25 degree angles	*7,250.*	
	Nos. J1-J3 (3)	222.50	66.50

ENVELOPES

U.S. Envelopes of 1887 Issue Ovptd. in Black

20mm long

Note: Some envelopes for which there was no obvious need were issued in small quantities. Anyone residing in Puerto Rico could, by depositing with his postmaster the required amount, order any envelope in quantities of 500, or multiples thereof, provided it was on the schedule of U.S. envelopes. Such special orders are indicated by a plus sign, i. e., Nos. U15 and U18, and half the quantities of Nos. U16 and U17.

1899-1900

U1	U71 2c **green** (No. U311) *(3,000)*	16.00	*20.00*
	Entire	40.00	*350.00*
a.	Double overprint, entire	*3,500.*	
U2	U74 5c **blue** (No. U330) *(1,000)*	20.00	20.00
	Entire	55.00	*350.00*
a.	Double overprint, entire		—
b.	Triple overprint, entire		—

U.S. Envelopes of 1899 Overprinted in color of the stamp

PORTO RICO.

21mm long

U3	U79 2c **carmine** (No. U362) *(100,000)*	3.00	3.00
	Entire	10.00	*12.00*
U4	U84 5c **blue** (No. U377) *(10,000)*	8.00	*9.00*
	Entire	17.50	*32.50*

Overprinted in Black

19mm long

U5	U77 1c **green,** *blue* (No. U355) *(1,000)*		750.
	Entire		1,900.
U6	U79 2c **carmine,** *amber* (No. U363), Die 2 *(500)*	450.	*500.*
	Entire	1,100.	1,100.
U7	U79 2c **carmine,** *oriental buff* (No. U364), Die 2 *(500)*		500.
	Entire		1,100.
U8	U80 2c **carmine,** *oriental buff* (No. U369), Die 3 *(500)*		600.
	Entire		1,300.
U9	U79 2c **carmine,** *blue* (No. U365), Die 2		
	Entire		*4,000.*
U10	U83 4c **brown** (No. U374), Die 3 *(500)*	200.	*500.*
	Entire	500.	*900.*

U.S. Envelopes of 1899 Issue Ovptd.

23mm long

U11	U79 2c **carmine** (No. U362) red overprint *(100,000)*	4.00	3.00
	Entire	10.00	*11.00*
U12	U79 2c **carmine,** *oriental buff* (No. U364), Die 2, black overprint *(1,000)*	—	325.00
	Entire	*1,000.*	*1,200.*

U13 U80 2c **carmine,** *oriental buff* (No. U369), Die 3, black overprint *(1,000)* 375.00
Entire *1,750.*
U14 U84 5c **blue** (No. U377) blue overprint *(10,000)* 14.00 14.00
Entire 45.00 *50.00*

Overprinted in Black PUERTO RICO.

U15 U77 1c **green,** *oriental buff* (No. U354) *(500)+* 20.00 *50.00*
Entire 75.00 *80.00*
U16 U77 1c **green,** *blue* (No. U355) *(1,000)+* 25.00 *50.00*
Entire 95.00 *125.00*
U17 U79 2c **carmine,** *oriental buff* (No. U364) *(1,000)+* 20.00 *50.00*
Entire 95.00 *135.00*
U18 U79 2c **carmine,** *blue* (No. U365) *(500)+* 20.00 *50.00*
Entire 75.00 *135.00*

There were two settings of the overprint, with minor differences, which are found on Nos. U16 and U17.

WRAPPER

U.S. Wrapper of 1899 Issue Ovptd. in Green

PORTO RICO.

21mm long

W1 U77 1c **green,** *manila* (No. W357) *(15,000)* 8.00 *35.00*
Entire 20.00 *110.00*

POSTAL CARDS

Values are for Entires.

Imprinted below stamp

1899-1900 **U.S. Postal Card No. UX14**

UX1 PC8 1c **black,** *buff,* imprint 21mm long 165. *175.*
b. Double imprint 2,250.

Imprinted below stamp

UX1A PC8 1c **black,** *buff,* imprint 20mm long 1,200. *1,300.*

Imprinted below stamp

UX2 PC8 1c **black,** *buff,* imprint 26mm long 165. *190.*

Imprinted below stamp

UX3 PC8 1c **black,** *buff* 150. *200.*
a. Double overprint —

REVENUE STAMPS

U.S. Revenue Stamps Nos. R163, R168-R169, R171 & Type of 1898 Srchd. in Black or Dark Blue

a

PORTO RICO
1 c.
Excise Revenue

b

1901	**Wmk. 191R**	***Hyphen-hole Roulette 7***		
R1	R15(a)	1c on 1c **pale blue** (Bk)	10.00	8.75
R2	R15(a)	10c on 10c **dark brown**	12.50	10.00
R3	R15(a)	25c on 25c **purple brown**	15.00	11.00
R4	R15(a)	50c on 50c **slate violet**	25.00	16.50
R5	R16(b)	$1 on $1 **pale greenish gray**	62.50	22.50
R6	R16(b)	$3 on $3 **pale greenish gray**	70.00	32.50
R7	R16(b)	$5 on $5 **pale greenish gray**	85.00	37.50
R8	R16(b)	$10 on $10 **pale greenish gray**	120.00	70.00
R9	R16(b)	$50 on $50 **pale greenish gray**	325.00	160.00
		Nos. R1-R9 (9)	725.00	368.75

Lines of 1c surcharge spaced farther apart; total depth of surcharge 15¾mm instead of 11mm.

RECTIFIED SPIRITS

U.S. Wine Stamps of 1933-34 Ovptd. in Red or Carmine

Overprint Lines 14mm Apart, Second Line 25mm Long

1937	**Offset Printing**	**Wmk. 191R**	***Rouletted 7***
RE1	RE5	2c **green**	17.50
RE2	RE5	3c **green**	60.00
RE3	RE5	4c **green**	20.00
RE4	RE5	5c **green**	17.50
RE5	RE5	6c **green**	20.00

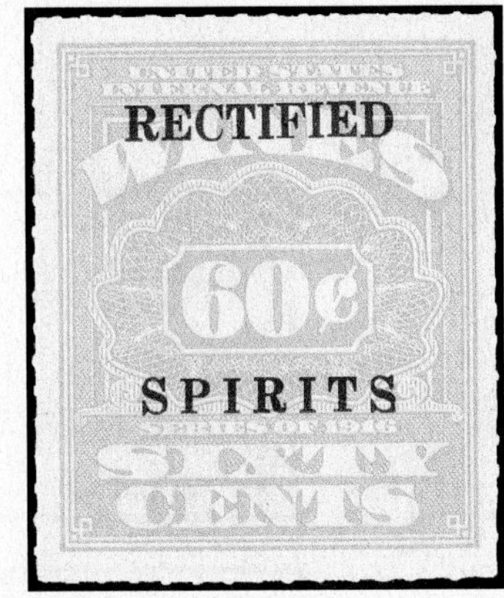

Overprint Lines 21½mm Apart, Second Line 23½mm Long

RE6	RE2	50c **green**	30.00
RE7	RE2	60c **green**	27.50

Handstamped overprints are also found on U.S. Wine stamps of 1933-34.

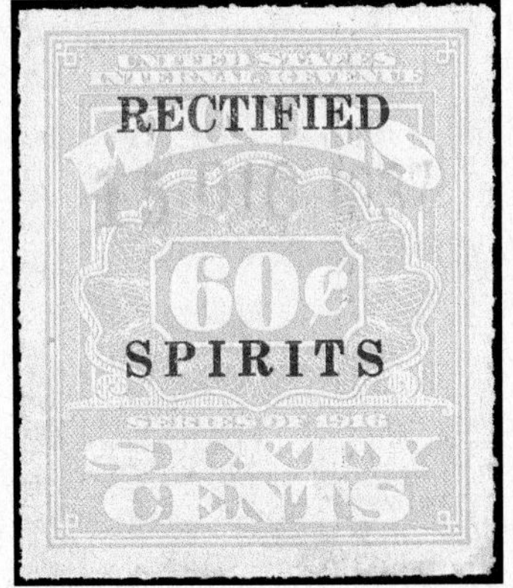

Overprint Lines 18½mm Apart, Second Line 23½mm Long

RE7A RE2 60c **green** —

Examples of No. RE7A are all known with faults.

U.S. Wine Stamps of 1933-34 Ovptd. in Black

a

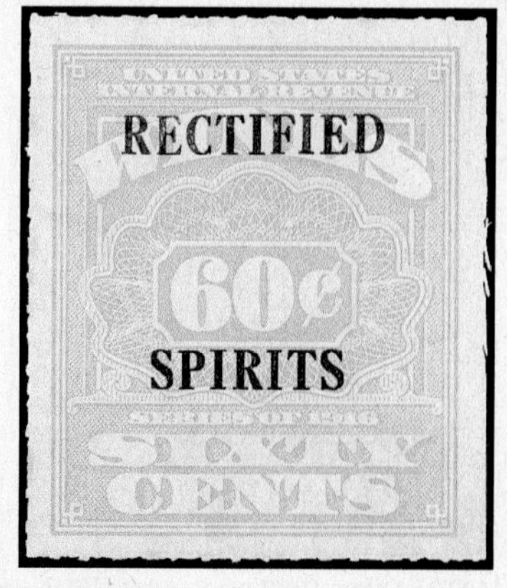

b

1937	Offset Printing	Wmk. 191R	Rouletted 7
RE8	RE5(a)	1c green	22.50
RE9	RE5(a)	2c green	12.50
RE10	RE5(a)	3c green	60.00
RE11	RE5(a)	5c green	12.50
RE12	RE5(a)	6c green	15.00
RE12A	RE2(b)	36c green	—
RE13	RE2(b)	50c green	17.50
RE14	RE2(b)	60c green	15.00
RE15	RE2(b)	72c green	75.00
RE16	RE2(b)	80c green	40.00

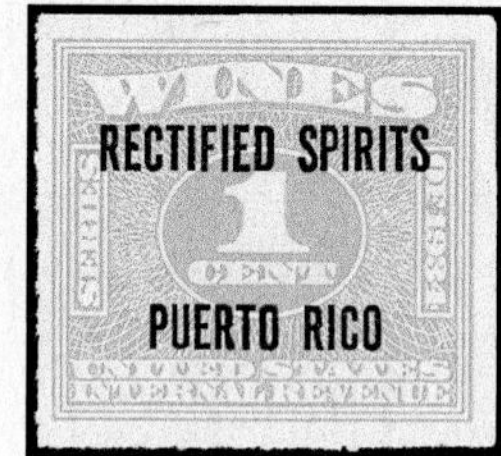

U.S. Wine Stamps of 1933-34 Ovptd. in Black

No. RE19a

Overprint Lines 9mm Apart

1938	Offset Printing	Wmk. 191R	Rouletted 7	
RE17	RE5	½c green		2.50
RE18	RE5	1c green	42.50	.60
RE19	RE5	2c green	42.50	.50
a.		Overprint lines 5.3mm apart	—	
RE20	RE5	3c green	100.00	3.25
RE21	RE5	4c green	—	.65
RE22	RE5	5c green	50.00	1.00
RE23	RE5	6c green	50.00	1.10
RE24	RE5	10c green	100.00	3.50
RE25	RE5	30c green		30.00

Overprint Lines 12½mm Apart

RE26	RE2	36c green		6.00
RE27	RE2	40c green	150.00	5.00
RE28	RE2	50c green	140.00	2.50
RE29	RE2	60c green	105.00	.45
a.		Inverted overprint	—	
RE30	RE2	72c green	150.00	4.00
RE31	RE2	80c green	150.00	4.00
RE32	RE2	$1 green	175.00	7.50

George Sewall Boutwell

Engr. (8c & 58c); Litho.
1942-57 Wmk. 191 *Rouletted 7*
Without Gum

RE33	R1	½c carmine	3.50	1.25
RE34	R1	1c sepia	8.25	3.50
RE35	R1	2c bright yellow green	1.10	.25
RE36	R1	3c lilac	70.00	35.00
RE37	R1	4c olive	2.25	.50
RE38	R1	5c orange	5.00	1.00
RE39	R1	6c red brown	4.00	1.25
RE40	R1	8c bright pink ('57)	8.25	3.50
RE41	R1	10c bright purple	12.50	5.00
RE41A	R1	30c vermilion	160.00	
RE42	R1	36c dull yellow	250.00	70.00
RE43	R1	40c deep claret	20.00	7.00
RE44	R1	50c green	11.00	4.00
RE45	R1	58c red orange	110.00	7.00
RE46	R1	60c brown	1.25	.25
RE47	R1	62c black	3.00	.70
RE48	R1	72c blue	40.00	1.00
RE49	R1	77½c olive gray	11.00	3.50
RE50	R1	80c brownish black	14.00	6.00
RE51	R1	$1 violet	75.00	25.00
		Nos. RE33-RE51 (20)	810.10	175.70

The 30c is believed not to have been placed in use.

SPECIMEN STAMPS

Handstamped U.S. Type E in Purple or Black

1899			
210S	E	1c yellow green	200.00
211S	E	2c reddish carmine, type IV	200.00
212S	E	5c blue	200.00
213S	E	8c violet brown	200.00
214S	E	10c brown	200.00

Postage Due

1899			
J1S	E	1c deep claret	500.00
J2S	E	2c deep claret	500.00
J3S	E	10c deep claret	500.00

See note after No. 216 for Special Printings with black "Specimen" handstamp, but note that not all stamps with the black "Specimen" handstamp are Special Printings.

Revenue

R1S	E	1c on 1c pale blue	40.00
R2S	E	10c on 10c dark brown	40.00
R3S	E	25c on 25c purple brown	40.00
R4S	E	50c on 50c state violet	40.00
R5S	E	$1 on $1 pale greenish gray	40.00
R6S	E	$3 on $3 pale greenish gray	40.00
R7S	E	$5 on $5 pale greenish gray	40.00
R8S	E	$10 on $10 pale greenish gray	40.00
R9S	E	$50 on $50 pale greenish gray	40.00

RYUKYU ISLANDS

rē-ˈyü-ˌkyü ˈī-ləndz

LOCATION — Chain of 63 islands between Japan and Formosa, separating the East China Sea from the Pacific Ocean.
GOVT. — Semi-autonomous under United States administration.
AREA — 848 sq. mi.
POP. — 945,465 (1970)
CAPITAL — Naha, Okinawa

The Ryukyus were part of Japan until American forces occupied them in 1945. The islands reverted to Japan May 15, 1972.

100 Sen = 1 Yen
100 Cents = 1 Dollar (1958)

In the Provisional Issues and Postal Stationery sections, italicized numbers in parentheses indicate quantity sold.

Values for First Day Covers are for unaddressed, cacheted covers. Values are for official cachets for Scott 1-26, C1-C3 and E1; and for commercial cachets for all others. Early cachets from the Japanese Philatelic Society command substantial premiums.

Catalogue values for unused stamps are for Never Hinged items beginning with Scott 1 in the regular postage section, Scott C1 in the air post section, Scott E1 in the special delivery section, Scott R1 in the revenue section, Scott 91S in the specimen section and Scott RQ1 in the unemployment insurance section.

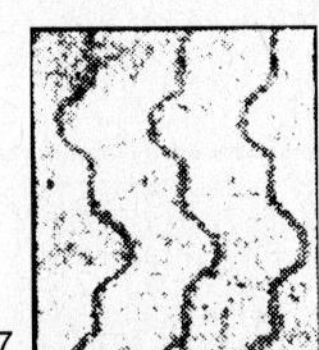

Wmk. 257

Cycad — A1

Lily — A2

Sailing Ship — A3

Farmer — A4

1948-49 Typo. Wmk. 257 ***Perf. 13***

Second Printing, July 18, 1949

1	A1 5s **magenta**	2.00	2.00
	Imprint block of 10	30.00	
2	A2 10s **yellow green**	5.00	5.00
	Imprint block of 10	75.00	
3	A1 20s **yellow green**	3.00	3.00
	Imprint block of 10	42.50	
4	A3 30s **vermilion**	1.25	1.25
	Imprint block of 10	18.00	
5	A2 40s **magenta**	1.25	1.25
	Imprint block of 10	18.00	
6	A3 50s **ultramarine**	5.00	*4.00*
	Imprint block of 10	75.00	
7	A4 1y **ultramarine**	5.00	5.00
	Imprint block of 10	75.00	
	Nos. 1-7 (7)	22.50	21.50

First Printing, July 1, 1948

1a	A1 5s **magenta**	3.00	*3.50*
	First day cover		—
	Imprint block of 10	45.00	
2a	A2 10s **yellow green**	2.00	*2.00*
	First day cover		—
	Imprint block of 10	30.00	
3a	A1 20s **yellow green**	2.00	*2.00*
	First day cover		—
	Imprint block of 10	30.00	
4a	A3 30s **vermilion**	4.00	*3.50*
	First day cover		—
	Imprint block of 10	45.00	
5a	A2 40s **magenta**	50.00	50.00
	First day cover		—
	Imprint block of 10	850.00	
6a	A3 50s **ultramarine**	4.00	4.00
	First day cover		—
	Imprint block of 10	55.00	
7a	A4 1y **ultramarine**	400.00	325.00
	First day cover		1,000.
	Imprint block of 10	*6,250.*	
	Nos. 1a-7a (7)	465.00	390.00

First printing: thick yellow gum, dull colors, rough perforations, grayish paper. Second printing: white gum, sharp colors, clean-cut and rough perforations, white paper. Third printing (Sept. 28, 1950): 5s to 50s denominations, white gum, clean-cut perforations, cream paper (same values as second printings).

A5

Designs: 50s, Tile rooftop and Shisa. 1y, Ryukyuan girl. 2y, Main hall of Shuri Castle. 3y, Female dragonhead statue. 4y, Two women. 5y, Sea shells.

1950, Jan. 21 Photo. Unwmk. ***Perf. 13x13¼***

Off-white Paper

8	A5 50s **dark carmine rose**	.25	.25
	First day cover		20.00
	Imprint block of 6	2.00	
a.	White paper, third printing, *Sept. 6, 1958*	.50	.50
	First day cover		27.50
	Imprint block of 10	6.50	
b.	"White Sky" variety (pos. 76)	3.50	3.50
9	A5 1y **deep blue**	3.25	3.00
	First day cover		20.00
	Imprint block of 6	30.00	
10	A5 2y **rose violet**	9.00	6.00
	First day cover		20.00
	Imprint block of 6	80.00	
11	A5 3y **carmine rose**	22.50	11.00
	First day cover		20.00
	Imprint block of 6	200.00	
12	A5 4y **greenish gray**	11.00	11.00
	First day cover		20.00
	Imprint block of 6	90.00	
13	A5 5y **blue green**	6.50	6.00
	First day cover		20.00
	Imprint block of 6	50.00	
	First day cover, #8-13		200.00
	Nos. 8-13 (6)	52.50	37.25

The original first two printings (No. 8) were printed on off-white paper with yellowish gum and a 5-character imprint in the sheet margin. The first printing is a deep carmine red or dark red, and the second printing a dark carmine rose. The first printing was issued Jan. 21, 1950; the second printing received in Naha Sept. 22, 1950; and the third printing (No. 8a) Sept. 6, 1958. Quantities: first printing: 300,000; second printing: 3,000,000; and third printing: 300,000. The first printing unused is much scarcer than the second printing because most of the first printing was used as postage.

No. 8a has colorless gum and an 8-character imprint in the sheet margin. The color is a deep red.

For No. 8b, a defect in position 76 of the plates used resulted in the sky above the roof being predominantly white in the second printing, whereas in the first printing the 'white sky' is not as pronounced. The master negative and plate were reworked for the third printing, so position 76 in this printing does not have the "white sky" variety.

For surcharges see Nos. 16-17.

Ryukyu University and Female Dragonhead Statue — A6

1951, Feb. 12 ***Perf. 13½x13¼***

14	A6 3y **red brown**	45.00	25.00
	First day cover		60.00
	Imprint block of 6	375.00	

Opening of Ryukyu University, Feb. 12.

Ryukyuan Pine Tree — A7

1951, Feb. 19 ***Perf. 13¼***

15	A7 3y **dark green**	40.00	22.50
	First day cover		60.00
	Imprint block of 6	360.00	

Reforestation Week, Feb. 18-24.

No. 8 surcharged in Black

16A Type I 16 Type II 16B Type III

There are three types of 10y surcharge:

Type I: narrow-spaced rules, "10" normal spacing, "Kai Tei" characters in 9-point type. First printing, Jan. 1, 1952.

Type II: wide-spaced rules, "10" normal spacing, "Kai Tei" characters in 9-point type. Second printing, June 5, 1952.

Type III: rules and "10" both wide-spaced, "Kai Tei" characters in 8-point type. Third printing, Dec. 8, 1952.

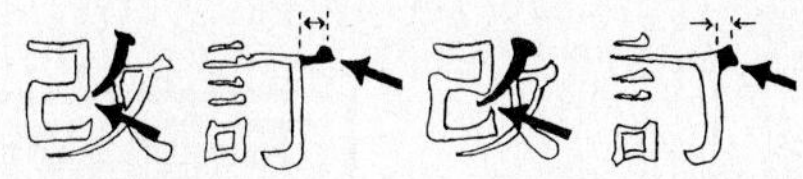

9 Point Kai Tei 8 Point Kai Tei

Both eight and nine point type were used in overprinting Nos. 16-17. In the varieties listed below, the first number indicates the size of the "Kai" character, and the second number is the size of the "Tei" character.

1952 ***Perf. 13½x13***

16	A5 10y on 50s **dark carmine rose** (II)	8.00	8.00
	Imprint block of 6	80.00	
	Top imprint block of 4, *Higa Seal* (pos. 8, 9, 18, 19)	70.00	

c. 8/8 point Kai Tei 8.00 8.00
d. 9/8 point Kai Tei 80.00 80.00
e. 9/9-9/8-8/8 se-tenant (horiz. strip of all 3 varieties) 140.00 140.00
8/8-9/9 horiz. se-tenant pair 30.00 30.00
9/9-8/8 horiz. se-tenant pair 30.00 30.00
f. Surcharge transposed 900.00 —
g. Legend of surcharge only (no obliteration bars) 1,200.
h. Wrong font for "0" (pos. 59) 150.00 150.00
i. Wrong font for "Yen" symbol (pos. 69) 150.00 150.00
j. Surcharge on "white sky" variety (No. 8b) (pos. 76) 150.00 150.00

On No. 16e, the entire obliteration-bars portion of the surcharge normally under the 10 Yen must be visible at the top of the stamp. Ten examples of No. 16e exist (pos. 91-100) with the full obliteration bars also in the bottom selvage.

Forgeries to defraud the Postal Agency of revenue are known, used only, at the Gusikawa Post Office. Two types. Value, $500 each.

16A A5 10y on 50s **dark carmine rose** (I) 30.00 30.00
Imprint block of 6 280.00
a. 8/8 point Kai Tei 30.00 30.00
8/8-9/9 horiz. se-tenant pair (pos. 23-24) 190.00 240.00
9/9-8/8 horiz. se-tenant pair 110.00 110.00
b. Bottom two bars inverted (pos. 17) 150.00 150.00
c. Wrong font for "0" (pos. 73) 250.00 250.00
d. Surcharge on "white sky" variety (No. 8b) (pos. 76) 250.00 250.00
e. Wide spaced obliterating bars (pos. 72) 150.00 150.00
f. Wide spaced bottom obliterating bars (pos. 86, 95) 80.00 80.00

16B A5 10y on 50s **dark carmine rose** (III) 45.00 35.00
Imprint block of 6 400.00
a. Wrong font for "Yen" symbol (pos. 25, 35, 85) 200.00 200.00
b. Wrong font for "Tei" (pos. 26) 350.00 350.00
c. Asterisk missing (pos. 54) — —
d. "Kai Tei" 1.25mm above asterisk (pos. 54) 350.00 350.00
e. "Kai" omitted (pos. 71) —
f. Narrow spaced "10" (pos. 96) 350.00 350.00
Strip of 3, narrow spaced "10" in center (pos. 95-97) 450.00
g. Surcharge on "white sky" variety (No. 8b) 350.00 350.00
h. Extra wide spaced "10" (pos. 60) 200.00 200.00
i. Asterisk within 2.0mm of "Kai Tei" (pos. 87) 200.00 200.00

The Kai Tei of the third printing measures the same as the 8-point type in the earlier printings but has differing characteristics. The Top curved line of the Kai is shorter and the lower curved line is also much shorter.

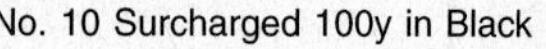
No. 10 Surcharged 100y in Black

17 A5 100y on 2y **rose violet,** Kai Tei characters in 9/9-point type, June 16, 1952 2,000. 1,400.
Hinged 1,600.
Imprint block of 6 17,500.
Top imprint block of 4, *Higa Seal* (pos. 7, 8, 17, 18) 9,500.
a. 8/8 point Kai Tei 2,000. 1,400.
b. 9/8 point Kai Tei 3,250. 3,250.
9/9-9/8-8/8 se-tenant (horiz. strip of all 3 varieties) *9,500. 9,500.*
8/8-9/9 horiz. se-tenant pair *4,750. 4,750.*
9/9-8/8 horiz. se-tenant pair *6,500. 6,500.*
c. Center "0" in wrong font, stamp with 9/9 Kai Tei (pos. 42) 4,000. 4,000.
d. Center "0" in wrong font, stamp with 8/8 Kai Tei (pos. 67, 86) 3,500. 3,500.
e. Center "0" in wrong font, stamp with 9/8 Kai Tei (pos. 53) 5,000. 5,000.
f. Wrong font for last "0" (pos. 59) 5,000. 5,000.
g. Wrong font for "yen" symbol (pos. 69) 5,000. 5,000.
h. "Tei" in wrong font (pos. 9) *4,000. 4,000.*

Varieties of shifted and damaged surcharge characters exist, most notably a damaged ("clipped") Kai (pos. 26, 85).

The "Tei" on No. 17h is the character used on Nos. 16 and 16A.

See note after 16B to differentiate between 8-point and 9-point characters.

Surcharge forgeries are known. Authentication by competant experts is recommended.

Dove, Bean Sprout and Map — A8

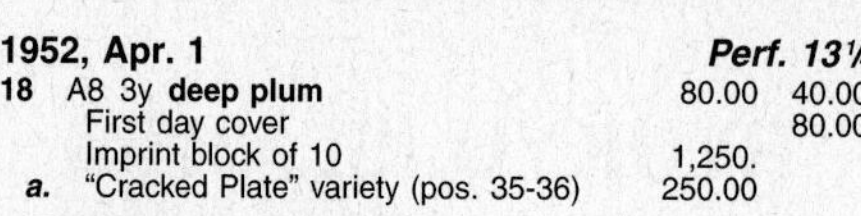

1952, Apr. 1 *Perf. 13¼*
18 A8 3y **deep plum** 80.00 40.00
First day cover 80.00
Imprint block of 10 1,250.
a. "Cracked Plate" variety (pos. 35-36) 250.00

Establishment of the Government of the Ryukyu Islands (GRI), April 1, 1952.

Madanbashi Bridge — A9

Designs: 2y, Main Hall, Shuri Castle. 3y, Shureimon Gate. 6y, Stone Gate, Sogen-ji Temple, Naha. 10y, Benzaiten-do Temple. 30y, Sonohyan Utaki (altar) at Shuri Castle. 50y, Tamaudun (royal mausoleum). Shuri. 100y, Stone Bridge, Hojo Pond, Enkaku Temple.

1952-53 *Perf. 13x13¼*
19 A9 1y **red,** *Nov. 20, 1952* .30 .30
Imprint block of 10 4.50
20 A9 2y **green,** *Nov. 20, 1952* .40 .40
Imprint block of 10 6.00
21 A9 3y **aquamarine,** *Nov. 20, 1952* .50 .50
First day cover, #19-21 40.00
Imprint block of 10 7.50
22 A9 6y **blue,** *Jan. 20, 1953* 2.00 2.00
First day cover 27.50
Imprint block of 10 34.00
23 A9 10y **crimson rose,** *Jan. 20, 1953* 2.50 1.00
First day cover 47.50
Imprint block of 10 45.00
24 A9 30y **olive green,** *Jan. 20, 1953* 9.00 7.50
First day cover 75.00
Imprint block of 10 160.00
a. 30y **light olive green,** *1958* 50.00
Imprint block of 10 750.00
25 A9 50y **rose violet,** *Jan. 20, 1953* 12.50 9.00
First day cover 125.00
Imprint block of 10 175.00
26 A9 100y **claret,** *Jan. 20, 1953* 15.00 5.00
First day cover 190.00
Imprint block of 10 210.00
First day cover, #22-26 550.00
Nos. 19-26 (8) 42.20 25.70

Reception at Shuri Castle — A10

Perry and American Fleet in Naha Port — A11

1953, May 26 *Perf. 13x13¼*
27 A10 3y **deep magenta** 12.00 6.50
Imprint block of 6 105.00
28 A11 6y **chalky blue** 1.25 1.50
First day cover, #27-28 15.00
Imprint block of 6 10.00

Centenary of the arrival of Commodore Matthew Calbraith Perry at Naha, Okinawa.

Chofu Ota and Pencil-shaped Matrix — A12

1953, Oct. 1 *Perf. 13¼x13*
29 A12 4y **orange brown** 11.00 5.00
First day cover 20.00
Imprint block of 10 140.00

Third Newspaper Week, Oct. 1-7.

Shigo Toma and Pen — A13

1954, Oct. 1
30 A13 4y **blue** 10.00 7.50
First day cover 25.00
Imprint block of 10 135.00

Fourth Newspaper Week, Oct. 1-7.

A14

A14a

Ryukyu Pottery — A14b

Designs: 4y, Dachibin (sake or water flask). 15y, Tsuikin lacquerware tray. 20y, Kajimayaa pattern on Kijoka-bashofu textile.

1954-55 **Photo.** *Perf. 13x13¼*
31 A14 4y **brown,** *June 25, 1954* .90 .50
First day cover 10.00
Imprint block of 10 10.00
32 A14a 15y **vermilion,** *June 20, 1955* 3.50 3.50
First day cover 12.50
Imprint block of 10 55.00
33 A14b 20y **yellow orange,** *June 20, 1955* 2.25 2.25
First day cover 12.50
Imprint block of 10 35.00
First day cover, #32-33 35.00
Nos. 31-33 (3) 6.65 6.25

For surcharges see Nos. C19, C21, C23.

Noguni Shrine and Sweet Potato Plant — A15

1955, Nov. 26 *Perf. 13¼*
34 A15 4y **blue** 10.00 7.00
First day cover 22.50
Imprint block of 10 125.00

350th anniv. of the introduction of the sweet potato to the Ryukyu Islands.

Stylized Trees — A16

1956, Feb. 18 *Perf. 13*

35	A16 4y **blue green**	10.00	6.00
	First day cover		20.00
	Imprint block of 6	85.00	

Arbor Week, Feb. 18-24.

Yanaji (Willow) Dance — A17

8y, Munjuru (Straw Hat) Dance. 14y, Nido Tichiuchi Dance.

1956, May 1 *Perf. 13x13¼*

36	A17 5y **rose lilac**	1.00	.60
	First day cover		6.50
	Imprint block of 10	15.00	
37	A17 8y **dk vio blue**	2.00	2.00
	First day cover		6.50
	Imprint block of 10	32.50	
38	A17 14y **reddish brown**	2.50	2.50
	First day cover		6.50
	Imprint block of 10	37.50	
	First day cover, #36-38		35.00
	Nos. 36-38 (3)	5.50	5.10

For surcharges see Nos. C20, C22.

Telephone A18

1956, June 8

39	A18 4y **violet blue**	12.50	8.00
	First day cover		20.00
	Imprint block of 6	110.00	

Establishment of dial telephone system.

Garland of Pine, Bamboo and Plum — A19

1956, Dec. 1 *Perf. 13¼*

40	A19 2y **multicolored**	1.60	1.60
	First day cover		3.50
	Imprint block of 10	22.50	

New Year, 1957.

Map of Okinawa and Pencil Rocket — A20

1957, Oct. 1 **Photo.** *Perf. 13*

41	A20 4y **deep violet blue**	1.00	1.00
	First day cover		6.00
	Imprint block of 10	12.50	

Seventh Newspaper Week, Oct. 1-7.

Phoenix — A21

1957, Dec. 1 *Perf. 13x13¼*

42	A21 2y **multicolored**	.25	.25
	First day cover		1.50
	Imprint block of 10	3.50	

New Year, 1958.

Ryukyu Stamps — A22

1958, July 1 *Perf. 13½*

43	A22 4y **multicolored**	.80	.80
	First day cover		1.25
	Imprint block of 4	4.00	

10th anniv. of 1st Ryukyu stamps.

Yen Symbol and Dollar Sign — A23

Perf. 10.3, 10.8, 11.1 & Compound

1958, Sept. 16 **Typo.**

Without Gum

44	A23 ½c **orange**	.80	.80
	Imprint block of 6	7.25	
a.	Imperf., pair	*1,500.*	
b.	Horiz. pair, imperf. between	225.00	
c.	Vert. pair, imperf. between	575.00	
d.	Vert. strip of 4, imperf. between	800.00	
45	A23 1c **yellow green**	1.25	1.25
	Imprint block of 6	10.00	
a.	Horiz. pair, imperf. between	200.00	
b.	Vert. pair, imperf. between	150.00	
c.	Vert. strip of 3, imperf. between	650.00	
d.	Vert. strip of 4, imperf. between	800.00	
e.	Block of 4, imperf. btwn. vert. & horiz.	*10,000.*	
46	A23 2c **gray blue**	2.00	2.00
	Imprint block of 6	16.00	
a.	Horiz. pair, imperf. between	200.00	
b.	Vert. pair, imperf. between	*2,200.*	
c.	Horiz. strip of 3, imperf. between	450.00	
d.	Horiz. strip of 4, imperf. between	700.00	
47	A23 3c **deep carmine**	1.50	1.50
	Imprint block of 6	12.00	
a.	Horiz. pair, imperf. between	200.00	
b.	Vert. pair, imperf. between	150.00	
c.	Vert. strip of 3, imperf. between	400.00	
d.	Vert. strip of 4, imperf. between	750.00	
e.	Block of 4, imperf. btwn. vert. & horiz.	*10,000.*	
48	A23 4c **lt blue grn**	2.00	2.00
	Imprint block of 6	16.00	
a.	Horiz. pair, imperf. between	*400.00*	
b.	Vert. pair, imperf. between	175.00	
49	A23 5c **orange brown**	4.00	3.75
	Imprint block of 6	32.50	
a.	Horiz. pair, imperf. between	200.00	
b.	Vert. pair, imperf. between	*850.00*	
50	A23 10c **aquamarine**	5.25	4.75
	Imprint block of 6	37.50	
a.	Horiz. pair, imperf. between	200.00	
b.	Vert. pair, imperf. between	150.00	
c.	Vert. strip of 3, imperf. between	750.00	
51	A23 25c **bright violet blue**	7.50	6.00
	Imprint block of 6	57.50	
a.	Gummed paper, perf. 10.3 ('61)	15.00	15.00
	Imprint block of 6	95.00	
b.	Horiz. pair, imperf. between	*2,200.*	
c.	Vert. pair, imperf. between	*5,000.*	
d.	Vert. strip of 3, imperf. between	900.00	
52	A23 50c **gray**	15.00	10.00
	Imprint block of 6	120.00	
a.	Gummed paper, perf. 10.3 ('61)	15.00	15.00
	Imprint block of 6	150.00	
	First day cover, #51a-52a		35.00
b.	Horiz. pair, imperf. between	*1,750.*	
53	A23 $1 **reddish purple**	11.00	5.50
	Imprint block of 6	90.00	
a.	Horiz. pair, imperf. between	450.00	
b.	Vert. pair, imperf. between	*2,250.*	
	Nos. 44-53 (10)	50.30	37.55

Printed locally. Perforation, paper and shade varieties exist. Nos. 51a and 52a are on off-white paper and perf 10.3.

First day covers come with various combinations of stamps: Nos. 44-48, 49-53, 44-53 etc. Values $20 for short set of low values (Nos. 44-48) to $60 for full set on one cover.

Perforation and Paper Varieties of Ryukyu Islands Scott 44-53

Perforation	Perf. ID#	1/2¢ (No. 44) Paper Type				1¢ (No. 45) Paper Type				2¢ (No. 46) Paper Type				3¢ (No. 47) Paper Type				4¢ (No. 48) Paper Type				5¢ (No. 49) Paper Type				10¢ (No. 50) Paper Type				25¢ (No. 51) Paper Type				50¢ (No. 52) Paper Type				$1 (No. 53) Paper Type			
		1	2	3	4	1	2	3	4	1	2	3	4	1	2	3	4	1	2	3	4	1	2	3	4	1	2	3	4	1	2	3	4	1	2	3	4	1	2	3	4
11.1 x 11.1	M	*			*	*	*			*			*	*	*		*	*	*			*	*		*	*	*	*		*		*		*				*		*	
11.1 x 10.8	N	*			*	*	*			*			*	*	*		*	*	*		∞	*	?		*	*	*			*		*		*				*		*	
11.1 x 10.3	O	*			*	?	*			*			*	*	*			*				*	*			*				*		*		*				*			
10.8 x 11.1	P	*			*	*	*			*			*	*	*			*	*			*	*		*	*	*			*		*		*				*		*	
10.8 x 10.8	Q	*			*	*	*			*			*	*	*			*	*			*			*	*	*			*	*	*		*				*		*	
10.8 x 10.3	R	*			*	*	*			*			*	?	*			*	*			*				*	*			*				*							
10.3 x 11.1	S	*				*	*			*			*	*	*		*	?	*			*	*		*		*			*								*			
10.3 x 10.8	T	*			*	*	*			*			*	*	*		*		*			*	*			*	*	*										*		*	
10.3 x 10.3	U	*				?	*			*			*	?	*							*	*		*	?	*			\		*		\							

Paper Legend: 1= off-white; 2= white; 3= ivory; 4= thick

Specialists use a shorthand to refer to perf. and paper types: e.g., 50M3 =10¢ stamp, perf. 11.1 x 11.1, ivory paper.

Notes:

* = Verified variety
? = Reported in literature, but unverified variety.
∞ = 48N4 is unknown; however, a single example of 48N exists on a thick white paper unknown used for any other issue.
\ = These particular perf/paper combinations are known only in stamps of the Second (1961) Printing (51a and 52a)

The following are known unused only: 45R1, 45T2, 47O1, 48N4, 53O1.

The following are known used only: 47N4, 47T4, 50M3, 50Q2, 50R2, 50T2, 51P3, 51S1, 53T3.

Chart classifications and data supplied by courtesy of the Ryukyu Philatelic Specialist Society.

Gate of Courtesy — A24

1958, Oct. 15 Photo. *Perf. 13x13¼*

54 A24 3c **multicolored** 1.25 1.25
First day cover 1.50
Imprint block of 4 6.25

Restoration of Shureimon, Gate of Courtesy, on road leading to Shuri City.

Imitations of this stamp were distributed in 1972 to discourage speculation in Ryukyuan stamps. The imitations were printed without gum and have a lengthy message in light blue printed on the back. A second type exists, with printed black perforations and three Japanese characters on the back ("Mozo Hin" — imitation) in black. Value, sheet of 10 $15.

Lion Dance — A25

1958, Dec. 10 *Perf. 13¼x13*

55 A25 1½c **multicolored** .30 .30
First day cover 1.50
Imprint block of 6 2.00

New Year, 1959.

Trees and Mountains — A26

1959, Apr. 30 *Perf. 13¼*

56 A26 3c **blue, yellow green, green & red** .70 .60
First day cover 1.00
Imprint block of 6 5.50
a. Red omitted 400.00 —

"Make the Ryukyus Green" movement.

Yonaguni Moth — A27

1959, July 23 Photo. *Perf. 13x13¼*

57 A27 3c **multicolored** 1.20 1.00
First day cover 1.50
Imprint block of 6 9.00

Meeting of the Japanese Biological Education Society in Okinawa.

Hibiscus — A28

琉球郵便
Inscribed

Designs: 3c, Fish (Moorish idol). 8c, Sea shell (Phalium bandatum). 13c, Butterfly (Kallinia inachus eucerca), denomination at left, butterfly going up. 17c, Jellyfish (Dactylometra pacifera Goette).

1959, Aug. 10 *Perf. 12¾x13*

58 A28 ½c **multicolored** .30 .25
Imprint block of 10 3.50
59 A28 3c **multicolored** .75 .40
Imprint block of 10 9.00
60 A28 8c **light ultramarine, black & ocher** 10.00 5.50
Imprint block of 10 180.00
61 A28 13c **light blue, gray & orange** 1.75 1.75
Imprint block of 10 28.50
62 A28 17c **dp ultra, org red & yel** 20.00 9.00
Imprint block of 10 330.00
First day cover, #58-62 17.50
Nos. 58-62 (5) 32.80 16.90

Four-character inscription measures 10x2mm on ½c; 12x3mm on 3c, 8c; 8½x2mm on 13c, 17c. See Nos. 76-80.

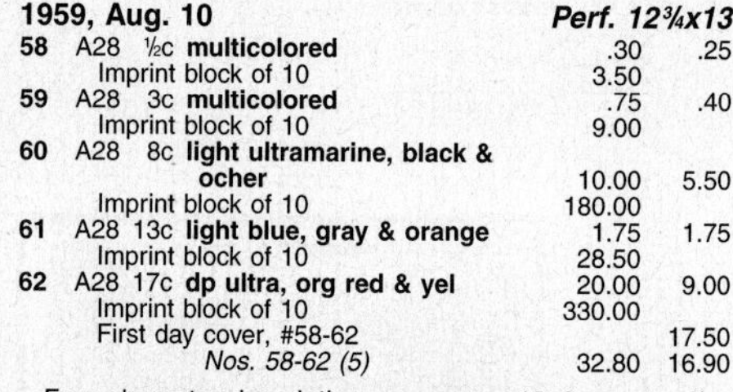

Toy (Yakaji) — A29

1959, Dec. 1 *Perf. 13x13¼*

63 A29 1½c **gold & multicolored** .55 .45
First day cover 1.50
Imprint block of 10 8.00

New Year, 1960.

University Badge A30

1960, May 22 Photo.

64 A30 3c **multicolored** .95 .75
First day cover 1.25
Imprint block of 6 7.25

10th anniv. opening of Ryukyu University.

Straw Hat Folk Dancer — A31

Designs: 2½c, Nufwabushi. 5c, Hatumabushi. 10c, Hanafu.

1960, Nov. 1 **Photo.** ***Perf. 13¼***

Dark Gray Background

65	A31	1c **yellow, red & violet**	2.00	.80
		Imprint block of 10	22.00	
66	A31	2½c **crimson, blue & yellow**	3.00	1.00
		Imprint block of 10	37.50	
67	A31	5c **dark blue, yellow & red**	1.00	.50
		Imprint block of 10	11.00	
68	A31	10c **dark blue, yellow & red**	1.00	.70
		Imprint block of 10	12.00	
		First day cover, #65-68		5.50
		Nos. 65-68 (4)	7.00	3.00

See Nos. 81-87, 220.

Torch and Nago Bay — A32

Runners at Starting Line — A33

1960, Nov. 8 **Litho.** ***Perf. 13x13¼***

72	A32	3c **lt blue, dp bluish grn & ver**	5.00	3.00
		First day cover		3.50
		Imprint block of 6	37.50	
73	A33	8c **orange & dp bluish grn**	1.00	.75
		First day cover		1.50
		Imprint block of 6	7.50	
		First day cover, #72-73		5.00

8th Kyushu Inter-Prefectural Athletic Meet, Nago, Northern Okinawa, Nov. 6-7.

Little Egret and Rising Sun — A34

1960, Dec. 1 **Photo.**

74	A34	3c **reddish brown**	5.00	3.50
		First day cover		4.00
		Imprint block of 6	37.50	

National census.

Okinawa Bull Fight — A35

1960, Dec. 10

75	A35	1½c **bister, dark blue & red brown**	1.50	1.50
		First day cover		2.00
		Imprint block of 6	11.00	

New Year, 1961.

Type of 1959 With Japanese Inscription Redrawn

A28a

1960-61 **Photo.**

76	A28a	½c **multicolored,** *Oct. 1961*	.60	.45
		Imprint block of 10	6.50	
77	A28a	3c **multicolored,** *Aug. 23, 1961*	1.00	.35
		First day cover		1.50
		Imprint block of 10	11.50	
78	A28a	8c **light ultramarine, black & ocher,** *July 1, 1960*	1.25	.80
		Imprint block of 10	14.50	
79	A28a	13c **lt blue & multi,** *July 1, 1960*	1.50	.90
		Imprint block of 10	16.00	
80	A28a	17c **dp ultra, brn rose & yellow,** *July 1, 1960*	12.50	6.00
		Imprint block of 10	130.00	
		First day cover, #78-80		15.00
		Nos. 76-80 (5)	16.85	8.50

Size of Japanese inscription on Nos. 78-80 is 10½x1½mm. On No. 79 the denomination is at right, butterfly going down.

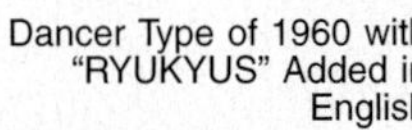

Dancer Type of 1960 with "RYUKYUS" Added in English

Designs: 20c, Shudun. 25c, Haodori. 50c, Nubui Kuduchi. $1, Koteibushi.

1961-64 ***Perf. 13¼***

81	A31	1c **multicolored,** *Dec. 5, 1961*	.25	.25
		First day cover		1.00
		Imprint block of 10	2.00	
82	A31	2½c **multicolored,** *June 20, 1962*	.25	.25
		Imprint block of 10	2.25	
83	A31	5c **multicolored,** *June 20, 1962*	.25	.25
		Imprint block of 10	3.00	
84	A31	10c **multicolored,** *June 20, 1962*	.45	.40
		First day cover, #82-84		1.50
		Imprint block of 10	5.75	
84A	A31	20c **multicolored,** *Jan. 20, 1964*	3.00	1.40
		First day cover		2.50
		Imprint block of 10	35.00	
85	A31	25c **multicolored,** *Feb. 1, 1962*	1.00	.90
		First day cover		2.00
		Imprint block of 10	13.00	
86	A31	50c **multicolored,** *Sept. 1, 1961*	2.50	1.40
		Imprint block of 10	32.50	
87	A31	$1 **multicolored,** *Sept. 1, 1961*	5.50	.25
		Imprint block of 10	62.50	
		First day cover, #86-87		35.00
		Nos. 81-87 (8)	13.20	5.10

Pine Tree — A36

1961, May 1 **Litho.**

88	A36	3c **yellow green & red**	1.75	1.25
		First day cover		1.50
		Imprint block of 6	14.00	

"Make the Ryukyus Green" movement.

Naha, Steamer and Sailboat A37

1961, May 20 **Photo.**

89	A37	3c **aquamarine**	2.25	1.50
		First day cover		1.75
		Imprint block of 6	18.00	

40th anniv. of Naha.

White Silver Temple — A38

1961, Oct. 1 **Typo.** **Unwmk.** ***Perf. 10¾, 10¾x10¼***

90	A38	3c **red brown**	2.50	2.00
		First day cover		2.00
		Imprint block of 6	18.00	
a.		Horiz. pair, imperf. between	*1,000.*	
b.		Vert. pair, imperf. between	*700.00*	

Merger of townships Takamine, Kanegushiku and Miwa with Itoman.

A 3-cent stamp to commemorate the merger of two cities, Shimoji-cho and Hirara-shi of Miyako Island, was scheduled to be issued on Oct. 30, 1961. However, the merger was called off and the stamp was never issued. It features a white chaplet on Kiyako linen on a blue background.

Books and Bird — A39

1961, Nov. 12 **Litho.** ***Perf. 13¼***

91	A39	3c **multicolored**	1.10	.90
		First day cover		1.25
		Imprint block of 6	10.00	

Book Week, 10th anniversary.

Rising Sun and Eagles — A40

1961, Dec. 10 **Photo.**

92	A40	1½c **gold, vermilion & black**	2.00	2.00
		First day cover		3.00
		Imprint block of 6	16.00	

New Year, 1962.

Symbolic Steps, Trees and Government Building — A41

Design: 3c, Government Building.

1962, Apr. 1 ***Perf. 13½***

93	A41	1½c **multicolored**	.60	.60
		Imprint block of 6	4.75	
94	A41	3c **bright green, red & gray**	.80	.80
		Imprint block of 6	6.50	
		First day cover, #93-94		2.00

10th anniv. of the Government of the Ryukyu Islands (GRI).

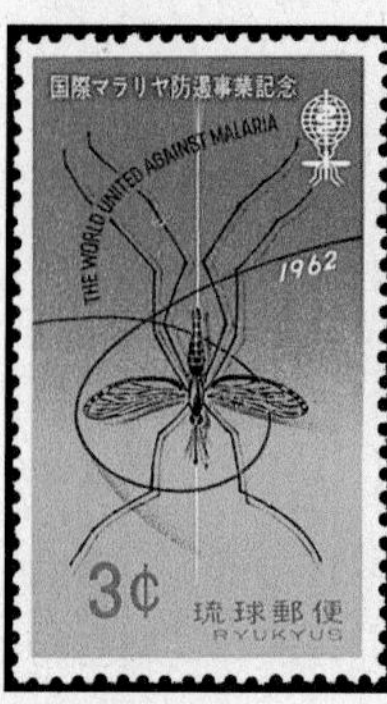

Anopheles Hyrcanus Sinensis — A42

Design: 8c, Malaria eradication emblem and Shurei gate.

1962, Apr. 7 ***Perf. 13¼x13***

95 A42 3c **multicolored** .60 .60
Imprint block of 6 4.50
96 A42 8c **multicolored** .90 .75
Imprint block of 6 7.50
First day cover, #95-96 2.25

World Health Organization drive to eradicate malaria.

Dolls and Toys — A43

1962, May 5 ***Perf. 13x13¼***

97 A43 3c **red, black, blue & buff** 1.10 1.00
First day cover 1.50
Imprint block of 6 9.00

Children's Day, 1962.

Linden or Sea Hibiscus — A44

Flowers: 3c, Deigo tree (Erythrina variegata var. orientealis). 8c, Iju (Schima liukiuensis Nakal). 13c, Touch-me-not (Impatiens balsamina). 17c, Shell flower (Alpinia speciosa).

1962, June 1 **Photo.** ***Perf. 13¼***

98 A44 ½c **multicolored** .35 .25
Imprint block of 10 4.00
99 A44 3c **multicolored** .30 .25
Imprint block of 10 4.50
100 A44 8c **multicolored** .55 .45
Imprint block of 10 6.25
101 A44 13c **multicolored** .75 .60
Imprint block of 10 8.50
102 A44 17c **multicolored** 1.25 .80
Imprint block of 10 14.00
First day cover, #98-102 3.75
Nos. 98-102 (5) 3.20 2.35

See Nos. 107 and 114 for 1½c and 15c flower stamps. For surcharge see No. 190.

Akae (Earthenware) A45

1962, July 5

103 A45 3c **multicolored** 3.50 2.50
First day cover 2.75
Imprint block of 6 26.00

Philatelic Week, July 5-12.

Japanese Fencing (Kendo) A46

1962, July 25 ***Perf. 13¼x13***

104 A46 3c **multicolored** 3.50 2.50
First day cover 3.50
Imprint block of 6 26.00

All-Japan Kendo Meeting in Okinawa, July 24-25, 1962.

Rabbit Playing near Water, Bingata Cloth Design — A47

1962, Dec. 10 ***Perf. 13¼***

105 A47 1½c **gold & multicolored** 1.00 .80
First day cover 1.50
Imprint block of 10 12.50

New Year, 1963.

Young Man and Woman, Stone Relief — A48

1963, Jan. 15 **Photo.**

106 A48 3c **gold, black & blue** .90 .80
First day cover 1.50
Imprint block of 6 6.75

Adult Day.

Gooseneck Cactus (Epiphyllum strictum) — A49

1963, Apr. 5 ***Perf. 13x13¼***

107 A49 1½c **dark blue green, yellow & pink** .25 .25
First day cover 1.25
Imprint block of 10 1.40

Trees and Wooded Hills — A50

1963, Mar. 25 ***Perf. 13¼***

108 A50 3c **ultramarine, green & red brown** 1.00 .80
First day cover 1.25
Imprint block of 6 7.00

"Make the Ryukyus Green" movement.

Map of Okinawa — A51

1963, Apr. 30

109 A51 3c **multicolored** 1.25 1.00
First day cover 1.50
Imprint block of 6 9.00

Opening of the Round Road on Okinawa.

Hawks over Islands — A52

1963, May 10 **Photo.**

110 A52 3c **multicolored** 1.10 .95
First day cover 1.50
Imprint block of 6 9.00

Bird Day, May 10.

Shioya Bridge — A53

1963, June 5

111 A53 3c **multicolored** 1.10 .95
First day cover 1.40
Imprint block of 6 8.25

Opening of Shioya Bridge over Shioya Bay.

Tsuikin-wan Lacquerware Bowl — A54

1963, July 1 ***Perf. 13¼***

112 A54 3c **multicolored** 2.75 2.50
First day cover 2.75
Imprint block of 6 20.00

Philatelic Week.

Map of Far East and JCI Emblem — A55

1963, Sept. 16 **Photo.**

113 A55 3c **multicolored** .70 .70
First day cover 1.25
Imprint block of 6 6.00

Meeting of the International Junior Chamber of Commerce (JCI), Naha, Okinawa, Sept. 16-19.

Hamaomoto (Crinum asiaticum var. japonica) — A56

1963, Oct. 15 *Perf. 13x13¼*

114 A56 15c **multicolored** 1.25 .80
First day cover 1.25
Imprint block of 10 17.50

Site of Nakagusuku Castle — A57

1963, Nov. 1 *Perf. 13¼*

115 A57 3c **multicolored** .60 .60
First day cover 1.25
Imprint block of 6 4.75

Protection of national cultural treasures.

Flame — A58

1963, Dec. 10

116 A58 3c **red, dark blue & yellow** .65 .60
First day cover 1.25
Imprint block of 6 5.00

15th anniv. of the Universal Declaration of Human Rights.

Dragon (Bingata Pattern) — A59

1963, Dec. 10 **Photo.**

117 A59 1½c **multicolored** .55 .50
First day cover 1.50
Imprint block of 10 7.00

New Year, 1964.

Carnation — A60

1964, May 10 *Perf. 13¼*

118 A60 3c **blue, yellow, black & carmine** .40 .35
First day cover 1.25
Imprint block of 6 3.00

Mothers Day.

Pineapples and Sugar Cane — A61

1964, June 1

119 A61 3c **multicolored** .40 .35
First day cover 1.25
Imprint block of 6 3.00

Agricultural census.

Minsah Obi (Sash Woven of Kapok) — A62

1964, July 1 *Perf. 13¼*

120 A62 3c **deep blue, magenta & ocher** .50 .50
First day cover 2.25
Imprint block of 6 4.25
a. 3c **deep blue, deep carmine & ocher** .65 .65
First day cover 2.75
Imprint block of 6 5.00

Philatelic Week.

Girl Scout and Emblem — A63

1964, Aug. 31 **Photo.**

121 A63 3c **multicolored** .45 .40
First day cover 1.25
Imprint block of 6 3.00

10th anniv. of Ryukyuan Girl Scouts.

Shuri Relay Station — A64

Parabolic Antenna and Map — A65

1964, Sept. 1 **Unwmk.**

Black Overprint

122 A64 3c **deep green** .65 .65
Imprint block of 6 5.50
a. Figure "1" inverted 30.00 30.00
b. Overprint inverted *1,500.*
c. Overprint missing *3,500.*
d. Overprint inverted and figure "1" inverted *5,000.*

123 A65 8c **ultramarine** 1.25 1.25
Imprint block of 6 10.00
First day cover, #122-123 4.75
a. Overprint missing *3,500.*

Opening of the Ryukyu Islands-Japan microwave system carrying telephone and telegraph messages. The overprints indicate the system was not actually opened until 1964.

Many of the stamps with overprint errors listed above are damaged. The values listed here are for stamps in very fine condition.

A number of different overprint shifts also exist with the shifts to greater and lesser degrees.

Gate of Courtesy, Olympic Torch and Emblem — A66

1964, Sept. 7 **Photo.** *Perf. 13¼*

124 A66 3c **ultramarine, yellow & red** .30 .25
First day cover (Sept. 7) 1.25
First day cover (Sept. 6 & 7) 25.00
Imprint block of 6 2.50

Relaying the Olympic torch on Okinawa en route to Tokyo.

Torch arrival was scheduled for Sept. 6. A typhoon delayed arrival until Sept. 7. A small number of covers received both Sept. 6 and 7 cancels.

"Naihanchi," Karate Stance — A67

"Makiwara," Strengthening Hands and Feet — A68

"Kumite," Simulated Combat — A69

1964-65 **Photo.**

125 A67 3c **dull claret, yel & blk,** *Oct. 5, 1964* .50 .45
First day cover 1.25
Imprint block of 6 3.25
126 A68 3c **yel & multi,** *Feb. 5, 1965* .40 .40
First day cover 1.25
Imprint block of 6 3.00
Incomplete vertical stroke in "cent" sign 17.50 17.50
First day cover 25.00
127 A69 3c **gray, red & blk,** *June 5, 1965* .40 .40
First day cover 1.25
Imprint block of 6 3.00
Nos. 125-127 (3) 1.30 1.25

Karate, Ryukyuan self-defense sport.

Miyara Dunchi — A70

1964, Nov. 1

128 A70 3c **multicolored** .30 .25
First day cover 1.25
Imprint block of 6 2.25

Protection of national cultural treasures. Miyara Dunchi was built as a residence by Pei-chin Miyara Touen in 1819.

Snake and Iris (Bingata) — A71

1964, Dec. 10 **Photo.**

129 A71 1½c **multicolored** .30 .25
First day cover 2.00
Imprint block of 10 4.00

New Year, 1965.

Boy Scouts — A72

1965, Feb. 6 ***Perf. 13¼***

130 A72 3c **light blue & multi** .45 .40
First day cover 1.50
Imprint block of 6 4.00

10th anniv. of Ryukyuan Boy Scouts.

Main Stadium, Onoyama A73

1965, July 1 ***Perf. 13x13¼***

131 A73 3c **multicolored** .25 .25
First day cover 1.00
Imprint block of 6 2.00

Inauguration of the main stadium of the Onoyama athletic facilities.

Samisen of King Shoko — A74

1965, July 1 **Photo.** ***Perf. 13¼***

132 A74 3c **buff & multicolored** .45 .40
First day cover 1.25
Imprint block of 6 3.25

Philatelic Week.

Kin Power Plant — A75

1965, July 1

133 A75 3c **green & multi** .25 .25
First day cover 1.00
Imprint block of 6 2.00

Completion of Kin power plant.

ICY Emblem, Ryukyu Map — A76

1965, Aug. 24 **Photo.**

134 A76 3c **multicolored** .25 .25
First day cover 1.00
Imprint block of 6 1.75

20th anniv. of the UN and International Cooperation Year, 1964-65.

Naha City Hall — A77

1965, Sept. 18

135 A77 3c **blue & multicolored** .35 .25
First day cover 1.00
Imprint block of 6 1.75

Completion of Naha City Hall.

Chinese Box Turtle (Cyclemys flavomarginata) A78

Turtles: No. 137, Hawksbill turtle (Eretochelys imbricata bissa) (denomination at top, country name at bottom). No. 138, Asian terrapin (Geoemyda japonica) (denomination and country name at top).

1965-66 **Photo.** ***Perf. 13¼***

136 A78 3c **golden brown & multi,** *Oct. 20, 1965* .30 .30
First day cover 1.00
Imprint block of 6 2.50

137 A78 3c **multi,** *Jan. 20, 1966* .30 .30
First day cover 1.00
Imprint block of 6 2.50

138 A78 3c **multicolored,** *Apr. 20, 1966* .30 .30
First day cover 1.00
Imprint block of 6 2.50
Nos. 136-138 (3) .90 .90

Horse (Bingata) — A79

1965, Dec. 10 **Photo.**

139 A79 1½c **multicolored** .25 .25
First day cover 1.50
Imprint block of 10 2.25
a. Gold omitted *2,000. 2,000.*

New Year, 1966.

There are 92 unused and 2 used examples of No. 139a known.

NATURE CONSERVATION ISSUE

Noguchi's Okinawa Woodpecker (Dendrocopus noguchii) — A80

Sika Deer (Cervus nippon var. keramae) — A81

Design: No. 142, Dugong (Dugong dugong).

1966 **Photo.**

140 A80 3c **blue green & multi,** *Feb. 15* .25 .25
First day cover 1.00
Imprint block of 6 1.65

141 A81 3c **blue, red, black, brown & green,** *Mar. 15* .25 .25
First day cover 1.00
Imprint block of 6 1.75

142 A81 3c **blue, yellow green, black & red,** *Apr. 20* .25 .25
First day cover 1.00
Imprint block of 6 1.75
Nos. 140-142 (3) .75 .75

Ryukyu Bungalow Swallow (Hirundo tahitica) — A82

1966, May 10 **Photo.** ***Perf. 13¼***

143 A82 3c **sky blue, black & brown** .25 .25
First day cover 1.00
Imprint block of 6 1.10

4th Bird Week, May 10-16.

Lilies and Ruins A83

1966, June 23 *Perf. 13*
144 A83 3c **multicolored** .25 .25
First day cover 1.00
Imprint block of 6 1.00

Memorial Day, end of the Battle of Okinawa, June 23, 1945.

University of the Ryukyus A84

1966, July 1
145 A84 3c **multicolored** .25 .25
First day cover 1.00
Imprint block of 6 1.00

Transfer of the University of the Ryukyus from U.S. authority to the Ryukyu Government.

Chinkin Ukuhan Lacquerware, 18th Century — A85

1966, Aug. 1 *Perf. 13¼*
146 A85 3c **gray & multicolored** .25 .25
First day cover 1.50
Imprint block of 6 1.30

Philatelic Week.

Tile-Roofed House and UNESCO Emblem — A86

1966, Sept. 20 **Photo.**
147 A86 3c **multicolored** .25 .25
First day cover 1.00
Imprint block of 6 1.10

20th anniv. of UNESCO.

Government Museum and Dragon Statue — A87

1966, Oct. 6
148 A87 3c **multicolored** .25 .25
First day cover 1.00
Imprint block of 6 1.00

Completion of the GRI (Government of the Ryukyu Islands) Museum, Shuri.

Tomb of Nakasone-Toyomiya Genga, Ruler of Miyako — A88

1966, Nov. 1 **Photo.**
149 A88 3c **multicolored** .25 .25
First day cover 1.00
Imprint block of 6 1.00

Protection of national cultural treasures.

Ram in Iris Wreath — A89

1966, Dec. 10 **Photo.** *Perf. 13¼*
150 A89 1½c **dark blue & multicolored** .25 .25
First day cover 1.50
Imprint block of 10 1.10

New Year, 1967.

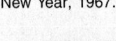

Clown Fish (Amphiprion frenatus) — A90

Fish: No. 152, Young boxfish (Ostracion cubicus) (white numeral at lower left). No. 153, Forceps fish (Forcipiger longirostris) (pale buff numeral at lower right). No. 154, Spotted triggerfish (Balistoides conspicillum) (orange numeral at upper right). No. 155, Saddleback butterflyfish (Chaetodon ephippium) (carmine numeral, lower left).

1966-67
151 A90 3c **orange red & multi,** *Dec. 20, 1966* .25 .25
First day cover 1.00
Imprint block of 6 1.75
152 A90 3c **orange yellow & multi,** *Jan. 10, 1967* .25 .25
First day cover 1.00
Imprint block of 6 1.75
153 A90 3c **multicolored,** *Apr. 10, 1967* .40 .25
First day cover 1.00
Imprint block of 6 2.75
154 A90 3c **multicolored,** *May 25, 1967* .35 .25
First day cover 1.00
Imprint block of 6 2.25
155 A90 3c **multicolored,** *June 10, 1967* .30 .25
First day cover 1.00
Imprint block of 6 1.90
Nos. 151-155 (5) 1.55 1.25

A 3-cent stamp to commemorate Japanese-American-Ryukyuan Joint Arbor Day was scheduled for release on March 16, 1967. However, it was not released. The stamp in light blue and white features American and Japanese flags joined by a shield containing a tree.

Tsuboya Urn — A91

1967, Apr. 20
156 A91 3c **yellow & multicolored** .25 .25
First day cover 1.25
Imprint block of 6 1.65

Philatelic Week.

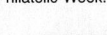

Episcopal Miter (Mitra mitra) — A92

Seashells: No. 158, Venus comb murex (Murex pecten). No. 159, Chiragra spider (Lambis chiragra). No. 160, Green turban (Turbo marmoratus). No. 161, Bubble conch (Euprotomus bulla).

1967-68 **Photo.** *Perf. 13¼*
157 A92 3c **light green & multi,** *July 20, 1967* .25 .25
First day cover 1.00
Imprint block of 6 1.25
158 A92 3c **greenish blue & multi,** *Aug. 30, 1968* .25 .25
First day cover 1.00
Imprint block of 6 1.75
159 A92 3c **brt grn & multi,** *Jan. 18, 1968* .25 .25
First day cover 1.00
Imprint block of 6 1.65
160 A92 3c **light blue & multi,** *Feb. 20, 1968* .30 .25
First day cover 1.00
Imprint block of 6 1.65
161 A92 3c **bright blue & multi,** *June 5, 1968* .60 .50
First day cover 1.00
Imprint block of 6 4.00
Nos. 157-161 (5) 1.65 1.50

Red-tiled Roofs and ITY Emblem — A93

1967, Sept. 11 **Photo.**
162 A93 3c **multicolored** .25 .25
First day cover 1.00
Imprint block of 6 1.25

International Tourist Year.

Mobile TB Clinic Bus — A94

1967, Oct. 13 **Photo.**
163 A94 3c **lilac & multicolored** .25 .25
First day cover 1.00
Imprint block of 6 1.25

15th anniv. of the Anti-Tuberculosis Society.

Hojo Bridge, Enkaku Temple, 1498 — A95

1967, Nov. 1

164 A95 3c **blue green & multi** .25 .25
First day cover 1.00
Imprint block of 6 1.50

Protection of national cultural treasures.

Monkey (Bingata) — A96

1967, Dec. 11 **Photo.** ***Perf. 13¼***

165 A96 1½c **silver & multi** .25 .25
First day cover 1.50
Imprint block of 10 3.00

New Year, 1968.

TV Tower and Map — A97

1967, Dec. 22

166 A97 3c **multicolored** .25 .25
First day cover 1.00
Imprint block of 6 1.50

Opening of Miyako and Yaeyama television stations.

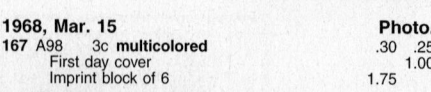

Dr. Kijin Nakachi and Helper — A98

1968, Mar. 15 **Photo.**

167 A98 3c **multicolored** .30 .25
First day cover 1.00
Imprint block of 6 1.75

120th anniv. of the first vaccination in the Ryukyu Islands, by Dr. Kijin Nakachi.

Pill Box (Inro) — A99

1968, Apr. 18

168 A99 3c **gray & multicolored** .45 .45
First day cover 1.25
Imprint block of 6 3.50

Philatelic Week.

Young Man, Library, Book and Map of Ryukyu Islands — A100

1968, May 13

169 A100 3c **multicolored** .30 .25
First day cover 1.00
Imprint block of 6 1.75

10th International Library Week.

Mailmen's Uniforms and Stamp of 1948 A101

1968, July 1 **Photo.** ***Perf. 13¼***

170 A101 3c **multicolored** .30 .25
First day cover 1.00
Imprint block of 6 1.75

First Ryukyuan postage stamps, 20th anniv.

Main Gate, Enkaku Temple — A102

1968, July 15 **Photo. & Engr.**

171 A102 3c **multicolored** .30 .25
First day cover 1.00
Imprint block of 6 1.75

Restoration of the main gate Enkaku Temple, built 1492-1495, destroyed during World War II.

Kagiyadefu Old Man's Dance — A103

1968, Sept. 15 **Photo.**

172 A103 3c **gold & multicolored** .30 .25
First day cover 1.00
Imprint block of 6 2.00

Old People's Day.

Mictyris Longicarpus A104

Crabs: No. 174, Uca dubia stimpson. No. 175, Baptozius vinosus. No. 176, Cardisoma carnifex. No. 177, Ocypode ceratophthalma pallas.

1968-69 **Photo.** ***Perf. 13¼***

173 A104 3c **blue, ocher & black,** *Oct. 10, 1968* .30 .25
First day cover 1.25
Imprint block of 6 2.50

174 A104 3c **light blue green & multi,** *Feb. 5, 1969* .35 .30
First day cover 1.25
Imprint block of 6 2.75

175 A104 3c **light green & multi,** *Mar. 5, 1969* .35 .30
First day cover 1.25
Imprint block of 6 2.75

176 A104 3c **light ultra & multi,** *May 15, 1969* .45 .40
First day cover 1.25
Imprint block of 6 3.25

177 A104 3c **gray blue & multi,** *June 2, 1969* .45 .40
First day cover 1.25
Imprint block of 6 3.25

Nos. 173-177 (5) 1.90 1.65

Saraswati Pavilion (Benzaitan-do Temple) — A105

1968, Nov. 1 **Photo.**

178 A105 3c **multicolored** .30 .25
First day cover 1.00
Imprint block of 6 2.00

Restoration of the Sarawati Pavilion (in front of Enkaku Temple), destroyed during World War II.

Tennis Player — A106

1968, Nov. 23 **Photo.**

179 A106 3c **green & multi** .40 .35
First day cover 1.00
Imprint block of 6 3.25

35th All-Japan East-West Men's Soft-ball Tennis Tournament, Naha City, Nov. 23-24.

Cock and Iris (Bingata) — A107

1968, Dec. 10

180 A107 1½c **orange & multi** .25 .25
First day cover 1.50
Imprint block of 10 3.50

New Year, 1969.

Boxer — A108

1969, Jan. 3

181 A108 3c **gray & multi** .40 .30
First day cover 1.00
Imprint block of 6 2.75

20th All-Japan Amateur Boxing Championships held at the University of the Ryukyus, Jan. 3-5.

Ink Slab Screen — A109

1969, Apr. 17 **Photo.** ***Perf. 13¼x13***

182 A109 3c **salmon, indigo & red** .40 .35
First day cover 1.50
Imprint block of 6 2.75

Philatelic Week.

Box Antennas and Map of Radio Link — A110

1969, July 1 **Photo.**

183 A110 3c **multicolored** .30 .25
First day cover 1.00
Imprint block of 6 2.25

Opening of the UHF (radio) circuit system between Okinawa and the outlying Miyako-Yaeyama Islands.

Gate of Courtesy and Emblems — A111

1969, Aug. 1 **Photo.**

184 A111 3c **Prussian blue, gold & vermilion** .30 .25
First day cover 1.00
Imprint block of 6 2.25

22nd All-Japan Formative Education Study Conf., Naha, Aug. 1-3.

FOLKLORE ISSUE

Tug of War Festival A112

Hari Boat Race A113

Izaiho Ceremony, Kudaka Island A114

Mortar Drum Dance (Ushideiku) A115

Sea God Dance (Ungami) A116

1969-70 **Photo.** ***Perf. 13¼x13***

185 A112 3c **multicolored**, *Aug. 1, 1969* .30 .25
First day cover 1.50
Imprint block of 6 2.25
186 A113 3c **multicolored**, *Sept. 5, 1969* .35 .30
First day cover 1.50
Imprint block of 6 2.25
187 A114 3c **multicolored**, *Oct. 3, 1969* .35 .30
First day cover 1.50
Imprint block of 6 2.25
188 A115 3c **multicolored**, *Jan. 20, 1970* .50 .45
First day cover 1.50
Imprint block of 6 3.50
189 A116 3c **multicolored**, *Feb. 27, 1970* .50 .45
First day cover 1.50
Imprint block of 6 3.50
Nos. 185-189 (5) 2.00 1.75

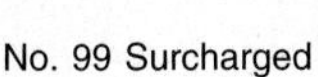

No. 99 Surcharged

1969, Oct. 15 **Photo.** ***Perf. 13¼***

190 A44 ½c on 3c **multicolored** 1.00 1.00
First day cover 3.00
Imprint block of 10 13.50
a. "1/2c" only surcharge 950.00

No. 190a are right margin stamps from a pane with a leftward misregistration of the surcharging plate.

Nakamura-ke Farm House, Built 1713-51 — A117

1969, Nov. 1 **Photo.** ***Perf. 13¼x13***

191 A117 3c **multicolored** .25 .25
First day cover 1.00
Imprint block of 6 1.50

Protection of national cultural treasures.

Statue of Kyuzo Toyama, Maps of Hawaiian and Ryukyu Islands — A118

1969, Dec. 5 **Photo.** ***Perf. 13¼***

192 A118 3c **light ultra & multi** .50 .50
First day cover 1.50
Imprint block of 6 3.75
a. Without overprint *3,000.*
b. Wide-spaced bars *700.00 500.00*

70th anniv. of Ryukyu-Hawaii emigration led by Kyuzo Toyama.

The overprint "1969" at lower left and bars across "1970" at upper right was applied before No. 192 was issued.

Dog and Flowers (Bingata) — A119

1969, Dec. 10 ***Perf. 13¼x13***

193 A119 1½c **pink & multicolored** .25 .25
First day cover 1.50
Imprint block of 10 2.75

New Year, 1970.

Sake Flask Made from Coconut (Yashi-gwa) A120

1970, Apr. 15 **Photo.** ***Perf. 13¼***

194 A120 3c **multicolored** .25 .25
First day cover 1.25
Imprint block of 6 1.75

Philatelic Week, 1970.

CLASSIC OPERA ISSUE

"The Bell" (Shushin Kaneiri) — A121

Child and Kidnapper (Chunusudu) A122

Robe of Feathers (Mekarushi) A123

Vengeance of Two Young Sons (Nidotichiuchi) A124

The Virgin and the Dragon (Kokonomaki) A125

1970 Photo. *Perf. 13¼*

195 A121 3c **dull blue & multi,** *Apr. 28* .60 .40
First day cover 1.75
Imprint block of 6 4.00
a. Souvenir sheet of 4 4.00 4.00
First day cover 5.00

196 A122 3c **light blue & multi,** *May 29* .60 .40
First day cover 1.75
Imprint block of 6 4.00
a. Souvenir sheet of 4 4.00 4.00
First day cover 5.00

197 A123 3c **bluish green & multi,** *June 30* .60 .40
First day cover 1.75
Imprint block of 6 4.00
a. Souvenir sheet of 4 4.00 4.00
First day cover 5.00

198 A124 3c **dull blue green & multi,** *July 30* .60 .40
First day cover 1.75
Imprint block of 6 4.00
a. Souvenir sheet of 4 4.00 4.00
First day cover 5.00

199 A125 3c **multicolored,** *Aug. 25* .60 .40
First day cover 1.75
Imprint block of 6 4.00
a. Souvenir sheet of 4 4.00 4.00
First day cover 5.00
Nos. 195-199 (5) 3.00 2.00
Nos. 195a-199a (5) 20.00 20.00

Underwater Observatory and Tropical Fish — A126

1970, May 22

200 A126 3c **blue green & multi** .30 .25
First day cover 1.25
Imprint block of 6 2.00

Completion of the underwater observatory of Busena-Misaki, Nago.

Noboru Jahana (1865-1908), Politician — A127

Portraits: No. 202, Saion Gushichan Bunjaku (1682-1761), statesman. No. 203, Choho Giwan (1823-1876), regent and poet.

1970-71 Engr.

201 A127 3c **rose claret,** *Sept. 25, 1970* .50 .45
First day cover 2.50
Imprint block of 6 3.50

202 A127 3c **dull blue green,** *Dec. 22, 1970* .75 .65
First day cover 2.50
Imprint block of 6 6.00

203 A127 3c **black,** *Jan. 22, 1971* .50 .45
First day cover 2.50
Imprint block of 6 3.50
Nos. 201-203 (3) 1.75 1.55

Map of Okinawa and People — A128

1970, Oct. 1 Photo.

204 A128 3c **red & multicolored** .25 .25
First day cover 1.00
Imprint block of 6 1.75

Oct. 1, 1970 census.

Great Cycad of Une — A129

1970, Nov. 2 Photo. *Perf. 13¼*

205 A129 3c **gold & multicolored** .25 .25
First day cover 1.00
Imprint block of 6 1.75

Protection of national treasures.

Japanese Flag, Diet and Map of Ryukyus — A130

1970, Nov. 15 Photo.

206 A130 3c **ultramarine & multicolored** .80 .75
First day cover 2.00
Imprint block of 6 6.00

Citizen's participation in national administration to Japanese law of Apr. 24, 1970.

Wild Boar and Cherry Blossoms (Bingata) — A131

1970, Dec. 10 *Perf. 13¼x13*

207 A131 1½c **multicolored** .25 .25
First day cover 1.50
Imprint block of 10 2.40

New Year, 1971.

Low Hand Loom (Jibata) — A132

Farmer Wearing Palm Bark Raincoat (Shurunnui) and Kuba Leaf Hat (Kubagasa) A133

Fisherman's Wooden Box (Yutui) and Scoop (Umi-fujo) — A134

Designs: No. 209, Woman running a filature (reel). No. 211, Woman hulling rice with cylindrical "Shiri-ushi."

1971 Photo. *Perf. 13¼*

208 A132 3c **light blue & multi,** *Feb. 16* .30 .25
First day cover 1.25
Imprint block of 6 2.00

209 A132 3c **pale green & multi,** *Mar. 16* .30 .25
First day cover 1.25
Imprint block of 6 2.00

210 A133 3c **pale blue & multi,** *Apr. 30* .35 .30
First day cover 1.25
Imprint block of 6 2.25

211 A132 3c **yellow & multi,** *May 20* .40 .35
First day cover 1.25
Imprint block of 6 3.00

212 A134 3c **gray & multi,** *June 15* .35 .30
First day cover 1.25
Imprint block of 6 2.25
Nos. 208-212 (5) 1.70 1.45

Water Carrier (Taku) — A135

1971, Apr. 15 Photo.

213 A135 3c **blue green & multicolored** .35 .30
First day cover 1.50
Imprint block of 6 2.75

Philatelic Week.

Old and New Naha, and City Emblem A136

1971, May 20 *Perf. 13¼x13*

214 A136 3c **ultramarine & multicolored** .25 .25
First day cover 1.00
Imprint block of 6 1.75

50th anniv. of Naha as a municipality.

Madder (Sandanka) — A137

Design: 3c, Ogocho (Caesalpinia pulcherrima).

1971 **Photo.** ***Perf. 13¼***

215 A137 2c **gray blue & multicolored,** *Sept. 30* .25 .25
First day cover 1.00
Imprint block of 10 3.00

216 A137 3c **gray grn & multicolored,** *May 10* .25 .25
First day cover 1.00
Imprint block of 10 3.00

GOVERNMENT PARK SERIES

View from Mabuni Hill — A138

Mt. Arashi from Haneji Sea — A139

Yabuchi Island from Yakena Port — A140

1971-72

217 A138 3c **green & multi,** *July 30, 1971* .25 .25
First day cover 1.25
Imprint block of 6 1.50

218 A139 3c **blue & multi,** *Aug. 30, 1971* .25 .25
First day cover 1.25
Imprint block of 6 1.50

219 A140 4c **multicolored,** *Jan. 20, 1972* .25 .25
First day cover 1.25
Imprint block of 6 1.75
Nos. 217-219 (3) .75 .75

For the 4-cent unissued "stamp" picturing Iriomote Park, originally planned for issue in 1971 but never released, see the note after No. RQ8.

Dancer (Nu-fwa-bushi) — A141

1971, Nov. 1 **Photo.** ***Perf. 13¼***

220 A141 4c **Prussian blue & multicolored** .25 .25
First day cover 1.00
Imprint block of 10 2.50

Deva King (Misshaku Kongo), Torin-ji Temple — A142

1971, Dec. 1

221 A142 4c **deep blue & multicolored** .25 .25
First day cover 1.00
Imprint block of 6 1.50

Protection of national cultural treasures.

Rat and Chrysanthemums — A143

1971, Dec. 10 ***Perf. 13¼x13***

222 A143 2c **brown orange & multi** .25 .25
First day cover 1.50
Imprint block of 10 2.50

New Year, 1972.

Student Nurse — A144

1971, Dec. 24 ***Perf. 13¼***

223 A144 4c **dp mauve & multicolored** .25 .25
First day cover 1.00
Imprint block of 6 1.50

Nurses' training, 25th anniversary.

A145

A147

Coral Reef — A146

1972 **Photo.**

224 A145 5c **bright blue & multi,** *Apr. 14* .40 .35
First day cover 1.25
Imprint block of 6 2.75

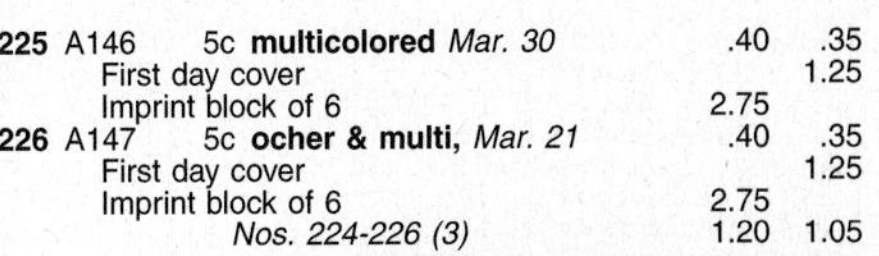

225 A146 5c **multicolored** *Mar. 30* .40 .35
First day cover 1.25
Imprint block of 6 2.75

226 A147 5c **ocher & multi,** *Mar. 21* .40 .35
First day cover 1.25
Imprint block of 6 2.75
Nos. 224-226 (3) 1.20 1.05

Dove, U.S. and Japanese Flags — A148

1972, Apr. 17 **Photo.**

227 A148 5c **bright blue & multi** .80 .80
First day cover 1.50
Imprint block of 6 5.50

Ratification of Ryukya Islands Reversion Agreement.

Antique Sake Container (Yushibin) — A149

1972, Apr. 20

228 A149 5c **ultramarine & multicolored** .60 .60
First day cover 1.25
Imprint block of 6 4.50

Philatelic Week.

Ryukyu stamps were replaced by those of Japan after May 15, 1972.

AIR POST STAMPS

Catalogue values for all unused stamps in this section are for Never Hinged items.

Dove and Map of Ryukyus — AP1

1950, Feb. 15 **Photo.** **Unwmk.** ***Perf. 13x13¼***

C1 AP1 8y **bright blue** 110.00 40.00
First day cover 35.00
Imprint block of 6 1,050.

C2 AP1 12y **lt green** 17.50 17.50
First day cover 35.00
Imprint block of 6 180.00

C3 AP1 16y **rose carmine** 9.00 9.00
First day cover 35.00
Imprint block of 6 80.00
First day cover, #C1-C3 200.00
Nos. C1-C3 (3) 136.50 66.50

Heavenly Maiden AP2

1951-54 ***Perf. 13¼x13***

C4 AP2 13y **chalky blue,** *Oct. 1, 1951* 2.00 2.00
First day cover 60.00
Imprint block of 6, 5-character 300.00
Imprint block of 6, 8-character 30.00

C5	AP2	18y **green,** *Oct. 1, 1951*	3.00	3.00
		First day cover		60.00
		Imprint block of 6, 5-character	45.00	
		Imprint block of 6, 8-character	35.00	
C6	AP2	30y **cerise,** *Oct. 1, 1951*	4.50	1.50
		First day cover		60.00
		First day cover, #C4-C6		250.00
		Imprint block of 6, 5-character	55.00	
		Imprint block of 6, 8-character	120.00	
C7	AP2	40y **purple,** *Aug. 16, 1954*	6.50	6.50
		First day cover		35.00
		Imprint block of 6	72.50	
C8	AP2	50y **orange red,** *Aug. 16, 1954*	7.50	7.50
		First day cover		35.00
		Imprint block of 6	82.50	
		First day cover, #C7-C8		125.00
		Nos. C4-C8 (5)	23.50	20.50

Heavenly Maiden Playing Flute — AP3

1957, Aug. 1 **Engr.** ***Perf. 13x13¼***

C9	AP3	15y **deep blue green**	7.50	4.00
		Imprint block of 6	55.00	
C10	AP3	20y **scarlet**	9.00	7.00
		Imprint block of 6	67.50	
C11	AP3	35y **yellow green**	10.00	8.00
		Imprint block of 6	85.00	
a.		35y **light yellow green,** *1958*	*125.00*	
C12	AP3	45y **reddish brown**	14.00	10.00
		Imprint block of 6	100.00	
C13	AP3	60y **gray & blk**	16.00	12.00
		Imprint block of 6	135.00	
		First day cover, #C9-C13		45.00
		Nos. C9-C13 (5)	56.50	41.00

On one printing of No. C10, position 49 shows an added spur on the right side of the second character from the left. Value unused, $175.

Surcharged in Scarlet, Light Ultramarine & Carmine Red

1959, Dec. 20 **Engr.**

C14	AP3	9c on 15y **blue green** (S)	2.50	2.00
		Imprint block of 6	20.00	
a.		Inverted surcharge	*800.00*	
		Imprint block of 6	*5,750.*	
b.		Pair, one without surcharge	*25,000.*	
C15	AP3	14c on 20y **scarlet** (L.U.)	3.00	3.25
		Imprint block of 6	22.50	
C16	AP3	19c on 35y **yellow green** (CR)	7.00	6.00
		Imprint block of 6	52.50	
C17	AP3	27c on 45y **reddish brown** (L.U.)	12.50	6.00
		Imprint block of 6	110.00	
C18	AP3	35c on 60y **gray** (CR)	11.00	9.00
		Imprint block of 6	95.00	
		First day cover, #C14-C18		35.00
		Nos. C14-C18 (5)	36.00	26.25

No. C15 is found with the variety described below No. C13. Value unused, $125.

Nos. 31-33, 36 and 38 Surcharged in Black, Brown, Red, Blue or Green

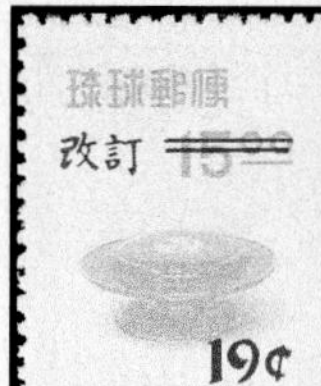

1960, Aug. 3 **Photo.**

C19	A14	9c on 4y **brown**	2.50	1.00
		Imprint block of 10	40.00	
a.		Surcharge inverted and transposed	*12,500.*	*12,500.*
b.		Inverted surcharge (legend only)	*10,000.*	
c.		Surcharge transposed	*800.00*	
d.		Legend of surcharge only	*3,500.*	
e.		Vert. pair, one without surcharge	*11,000.*	

Nos. C19c and C19d are from a single sheet of 100 with surcharge shifted downward. Ten examples of No. C19c exist with "9c" also in bottom selvage. No. C19d is from the top row of the sheet.

No. C19e is unique, pos. 100, caused by paper foldover.

C20	A17	14c on 5y **rose lilac** (Br)	3.00	3.00
		Imprint block of 10	45.00	
C21	A14	19c on 15y **vermilion** (R)	2.50	3.00
		Imprint block of 10	37.50	
C22	A17	27c on 14y **reddish brown** (Bl)	7.00	2.50
		Imprint block of 10	110.00	
C23	A14	35c on 20y **yellow orange** (G)	5.00	5.00
		Imprint block of 10	72.50	
		First day cover, #C19-C23		25.00
		Nos. C19-C23 (5)	20.00	14.50

Wind God — AP4

Designs: 9c, Heavenly Maiden (as on AP2). 14c, Heavenly Maiden (as on AP3). 27c, Wind God at right. 35c, Heavenly Maiden over treetops.

1961, Sept. 21 ***Perf. 13¼***

C24	AP4	9c **multicolored**	.30	.25
		Imprint block of 6	2.25	
C25	AP4	14c **multicolored**	.60	.75
		Imprint block of 6	5.00	
C26	AP4	19c **multicolored**	.70	.85
		Imprint block of 6	5.50	
C27	AP4	27c **multicolored**	3.00	.60
		Imprint block of 6	22.00	
C28	AP4	35c **multicolored**	2.00	1.25
		Imprint block of 6	16.00	
		First day cover, #C24-C28		35.00
		Nos. C24-C28 (5)	6.60	3.70

AP5

AP6

1963, Aug. 28 ***Perf. 13x13¼***

C29	AP5	5½c **multicolored**	.25	.25
		First day cover		1.00
		Imprint block of 10	3.00	
C30	AP6	7c **multicolored**	.30	.30
		First day cover		1.00
		First day cover, #C29-C30		2.50
		Imprint block of 10	3.50	

SPECIAL DELIVERY STAMP

Catalogue value for the unused stamp in this section is for a Never Hinged item.

Sea Horse and Map of Ryukyus — SD1

1950, Feb. 15 **Unwmk.** **Photo.** ***Perf. 13¼***

E1	SD1	5y **bright blue**	25.00	17.50
		First day cover		100.00
		Imprint block of 6	300.00	

QUANTITIES ISSUED

Regular Postage and Commemorative Stamps

Cat. No.	*Quantity*	*Cat. No.*	*Quantity*
1	90,214	*87*	3,019,000
2	55,901	*88*	298,966
3	94,663	*89*	298,966
4	55,413	*90*	398,901
5	76,387	*91*	398,992
6	117,321	*92*	1,498,970
7	291,403	*93*	598,989
1a	61,000	*94*	398,998
2a-4a	181,000	*95*	398,993
5a	29,936	*96*	298,993
6a	99,300	*97*	398,997
7a	46,000	*98*	9,699,000
8	2,559,000	*99*	10,991,500
8a	300,000	*100*	1,549,000
9	1,198,989	*101*	799,000
10	589,000	*102*	1,299,000
11	479,000	*103*	398,995
12	598,999	*104*	298,892
13	397,855	*105*	1,598,949
14	499,000	*106*	348,989
15	498,960	*107*	10,099,000
16	199,197	*108*	348,865
16A	199,900	*109*	348,937
16B	39,900	*110*	348,962
17	9,800	*111*	348,974
18	299,500	*112*	398,974
19	3,014,427	*113*	398,911
20	3,141,777	*114*	1,199,000
21	2,970,827	*115*	398,948
22	191,917	*116*	398,943
23	1,118,617	*117*	1,698,912
24	276,218	*118*	550,000
24a	ca. 1,300	*119*	549,000
25	231,717	*120*	749,000
26	220,130	*121*	799,000
27	398,993	*122*	389,000
28	386,421	*123*	319,000
29	498,854	*124*	1,999,000
30	298,994	*125-127*	999,000
31	4,768,413	*128*	799,000
32	1,202,297	*129*	1,699,000
33	500,059	*130-131*	799,000
34	298,994	*132*	849,000
35	199,000	*133*	799,000
36	455,896	*134*	1,299,000
37	160,518	*135*	1,099,000
38	198,720	*136*	1,299,000
39	198,199	*137-138*	1,598,000
40	599,000	*139*	3,098,000
41	598,075	*140-142*	1,598,000
42	1,198,179	*143-148*	2,498,000
43	1,625,406	*149*	2,298,000
44	994,880	*150*	3,798,000
45	997,759	*151*	2,298,000
46	996,759	*152-156*	1,998,000
47	2,705,955	*157-158*	1,698,000
48	997,542	*159-160*	1,298,000
49	996,609	*161*	898,000
50	996,928	*162*	1,498,000
51	499,000	*163-164*	1,298,000
52	249,000	*165*	3,998,000
52a	78,415	*166-167*	1,298,000
53	248,700	*168*	998,000
54	1,498,991	*169-179*	898,000
55	2,498,897	*180*	3,198,000
56	1,098,972	*181-189*	898,000
57	998,918	*190*	1,773,050
58	2,699,000	*191*	898,000
59	2,499,000	*192*	864,960
60	199,000	*193*	3,198,000
61	499,000	*194*	898,000
62	199,000	*195-199*	598,000
63	1,498,931	*195a-199a*	124,500
64	798,953	*200-206*	898,000
65-68	999,000	*207*	3,198,000
72	598,912	*208-210*	1,098,000
73	398,990	*211-212*	1,298,000
74	598,936	*213*	1,098,000
75	1,998,992	*214*	1,298,000
76	1,000,000	*215-216*	4,998,000
77	2,000,000	*217*	1,498,000
78	500,000	*218-219*	1,798,000
79-80	400,000	*220*	2,998,000
81	12,599,000	*221*	1,798,000
82	11,979,000	*222*	4,998,000
83	6,850,000	*223*	1,798,000

Cat. No.	*Quantity*	*Cat. No.*	*Quantity*
84	5,099,000	*224-226*	2,498,000
84A	1,699,000	*227*	2,998,000
85	4,749,000	*228*	3,998,000
86	2,099,000		

AIR POST STAMPS

Cat. No.	*Quantity*	*Cat. No.*	*Quantity*
C1-C3	198,000	*C18*	96,650
C4	1,952,348	*C19*	1,033,900
C5	331,360	*C19a*	100
C6	762,530	*C20*	230,000
C7	76,166	*C21*	185,000
C8	122,816	*C22*	191,000
C9	708,319	*C23*	190,000
C10	108,824	*C24*	17,199,000
C11	164,147	*C25*	1,999,000
C12	50,335	*C26*	1,250,000
C13	69,092	*C27*	3,499,000
C14	597,103	*C28*	1,699,000
C15	77,951	*C29*	1,199,000
C16	97,635	*C30*	1,949,000
C17	98,353		

SPECIAL DELIVERY STAMP

Cat. No.	*Quantity*
E1	198,804

Stamps of Japan Overprinted by Postmasters in Four Island Districts

PROVISIONAL ISSUES

Trading Ship — A82

Rice Harvest — A83

Gen. Maresuke Nogi — A84

Admiral Heihachiro Togo — A86

Garambi Lighthouse, Taiwan — A88

Meiji Shrine, Tokyo — A90

Plane and Map of Japan — A92

Kasuga Shrine, Nara — A93

Mount Fuji and Cherry Blossoms — A94

Horyu Temple, Nara — A95

Miyajima Torii, Itsukushima Shrine — A96

Great Budda, Kamakura — A98

War Factory Girl — A144

War Worker & Planes — A147

Aviator Saluting & Japanese Flag — A150

Mt. Fuji and Cherry Blossoms — A152

Garambi Lighthouse, Taiwan — A154

Golden Pavilion, Kyoto — A97

Kamatari Fujiwara — A99

Hyuga Monument & Mt. Fuji — A146

Palms and Map of "Greater East Asia" — A148

Torii of Yasukuni Shrine — A151

Torii of Miyajima — A153

Sun & Cherry Blossoms — A161

Sunrise at Sea & Plane — A162

Coal Miners — A163

Yasukuni Shrine — A164

"Thunderstorm below Fuji," by Hokusai — A167

KUME ISLAND

Values are for unused stamps. Used stamps sell for considerably more, should be expertized and are preferred on cover or document.

A1

Mimeographed

Seal Handstamped in Vermilion

1945, Oct. 1 Without Gum Unwmk. ***Imperf.***

1X1 A1 7s **black,** *cream (2,400)* 2,750. 2,500.

On cover —

a. "7" & "SEN" one letter space to left 3,250.

Printed on legal-size U.S. military mimeograph paper and validated by the official seal of the Kume Island postmaster, Norifume Kikuzato. Valid until May 4, 1946.

Cancellations "20.10.1" (Oct. 1, 1945) or "20.10.6" (Oct. 6, 1945) are by favor. See proofs section for stamps on white watermarked U.S. official bond paper.

AMAMI DISTRICT

Inspection Seal ("Ken," abbreviation for *kensa zumi,* inspected or examined; five types and five colors)

Stamps of Japan 1937-46 Handstamped in Black, Blue, Purple, Vermilion or Red

Typographed, Lithographed, Engraved

1947-48 Wmk. 257 ***Perf. 13, Imperf***

2X1 A82 ½s **purple,** #257 1,000.

a. Double seal —

2X2 A83 1s **fawn,** #258 —

2X3 A144 1s **orange brown,** #325 *1,750.*

2X4 A84 2s **crimson,** #259 600.

a. 2s **vermilion,** #259c —

b. Double seal —

2X5 A84 2s **rose red,** imperf., #351 2,000.

2X6 A85 3s **green,** #260 *1,900.*

2X7 A84 3s **brown,** #329 —

2X8 A161 3s **rose carmine,** imperf., #352 *1,300.*

a. Double seal —

2X9 A146 4s **emerald,** #330 700.

a. Double seal —

2X10 A86 5s **brown lake,** #331 700.

2X11 A162 5s **green,** imperf., #353 *1,500.*

2X12 A147 6s **light ultramarine,** #332 —

2X13 A86 7s **orange vermilion,** #333 *1,250.*

2X14 A90 8s **dark purple & pale violet,** #265 *1,500.*

2X15 A148 10s **crimson & dull rose,** #344 600.

2X16 A152 10s **red orange,** imperf., #355 *(48)* *2,500.*

No.	Type	Description	Unused	Used
2X17	A93	14s **rose lake & pale rose,** #268		—
2X18	A150	15s **dull blue,** #336	600.	
2X19	A151	17s **gray violet,** #337	*1,750.*	
2X20	A94	20s **ultramarine,** #269	*1,750.*	
2X21	A152	20s **blue,** #338	600.	
a.		Double seal	—	
2X22	A152	20s **ultramarine,** imperf., #356 *(48)*	*1,750.*	
2X23	A95	25s **dark brown & pale brown,** #270	900.	
2X24	A151	27s **rose brown,** #339	—	
2X25	A153	30s **bluish green,** #340	—	
2X26	A153	30s **bright blue,** imperf., #357	*2,000.*	
2X27	A88	40s **dull violet,** #341	*1,750.*	
2X28	A154	40s **dark violet,** #342	*1,750.*	
2X29	A97	50s **olive & pale olive,** #272	—	
2X30	A163	50s **dark brown,** imperf., #358 *(48)*	*2,000.*	
2X31	A164	1y **deep olive green,** imperf., #359	*2,500.*	
2X32	A167	1y **deep ultramarine,** imperf., #364	—	
2X33	A99	5y **deep gray green,** #274	—	
2X34	A99	5y **deep gray green,** imperf., #360	—	

Nos. 2X5, 2X8, 2X11, 2X16, 2X22, 2X26, 2X30, 2X31, 2X32 and 2X34 were issued without gum.

MIYAKO DISTRICT

Personal Seal of Postmaster Jojin Tomiyama

Stamps of Japan 1937-46 Handstamped in Vermilion or Red

Typographed, Lithographed, Engraved

1946-47 **Wmk. 257** ***Perf. 13***

No.	Type	Description	Unused	Used
3X1	A144	1s **orange brown,** #325	125.	
a.		Double seal	—	
3X2	A84	2s **scarlet,** #259	80.	—
a.		2s **vermilion** #259c ('47)	100.	
b.		2s **pink** #259b ('47)	550.	
c.		Horiz. pair, one without seal	*1,200.*	
d.		Double seal	—	
3X3	A84	3s **brown,** #329	75.	—
3X4	A86	4s **dp green,** #261	40.	—
a.		Double seal	—	
3X5	A86	5s **brown lake,** #331	550.	—
		On cover with #3X17		—
a.		Double seal	—	
3X6	A88	6s **orange,** #263	40.	—
a.		Double seal	—	
3X7	A90	8s **dull violet,** #265	40.	—
a.		Double seal	—	
3X8	A148	10s **crimson & dull rose,** #334	40.	—
		On cover with #3X15		*6,250.*
a.		Double seal	—	
b.		Triple seal	—	
3X9	A152	10s **red orange,** imperf., #355 ('47) *(1,000)*	100.	
3X10	A92	12s **indigo,** #267	40.	—
a.		Double seal	—	
3X11	A93	14s **rose lake & pale rose,** #268	40.	—
a.		Double seal	—	
3X12	A150	15s **dull blue,** #336	40.	—
a.		Double seal	—	
b.		Triple seal	—	
3X13	A151	17s **gray violet,** #337	40.	—
a.		Double seal	—	
3X14	A94	20s **ultramarine,** #269	—	
3X15	A152	20s **blue,** #338	40.	—
a.		Double seal	—	
3X16	A152	20s **ultramarine,** imperf., #356 ('47)	125.	
a.		Double seal	—	
3X17	A95	25s **dark brown & pale brown,** #270	50.	—
a.		Horiz. pair, one without seal	*300.*	
b.		Double seal	—	
3X18	A153	30s **bluish green,** #340	40.	—
a.		Double seal	—	
3X19	A88	40s **dull violet,** #341	250.	—
b.		Horiz. pair, one without seal	—	
3X20	A154	40s **dark violet,** #342	50.	—
a.		Double seal	—	
3X21	A97	50s **olive & pale olive,** #272	50.	—
a.		Double seal	—	
b.		Triple seal	—	
c.		Quadruple seal	—	
3X22	A163	50s **dark brown,** #358 ('47) *(750)*	150.	—
a.		Pair, one without seal	*1,200.*	
b.		Double seal	—	
c.		Triple seal	—	
3X23	A98	1y **brown & pale brown,** #273	—	*9,000.*
3X24	A167	1y **deep ultramarine,** #364 ('47) *(500)*	*1,500.*	*600.*

Nos. 3X9, 3X16, 3X22 and 3X24 were issued without gum.

Nos. 3X22 and 3X24 have sewing machine perf.; No. 3X16 exists with that perf. also.

Nos. 3X1-3X2, 3X2a, 3X3-3X5, 3X8 Handstamp Surcharged

1946-47

No.	Type	Description	Unused	Used
3X25	A144	1y on 1s **orange brown**	120.	—
a.		Double seal	—	
3X26	A84	1y on 2s **crimson**	—	
3X27	A84	1y on 3s **brown** ('47)	3,000.	
3X28	A84	2y on 2s **scarlet**	130.	—
a.		2y on 2s **vermilion** ('47)	130.	—
b.		Double seal	—	
c.		As No. 3X28a, double seal	—	
3X29	A86	4y on 4s **deep green**	100.	—
a.		Double seal	—	
3X30	A86	5y on 5s **brown lake**	100.	—
a.		Double seal	—	
3X31	A148	10y on 10s **crimson & dull rose**	100.	—
a.		Double seal	—	

The overwhelming majority of used examples of Miyako District stamps were used on Bulk Mailing Records documents and Letter Content Certification Records documents. Stamps affixed to such documents command a substantial premium above off-document used stamps.

Cancellation: black Miyako cds.

Some time after mid-1964, Tomiyama Jojin, Postmaster of the Miyako District, prepared several "Display Sheets," each containing 29 genuine provisionals used between Feb. 1, 1946, and June 30, 1948. The stamps were from remainder stock. The stamps are canceled "23.6.30," which was backdated to indicate the last day of normal use (June 30, 1948). Six such Display Sheets are recorded at present. Value, $6,000.

OKINAWA DISTRICT

Personal Seal of Postmaster Shiichi Hirata

R1

Japan Nos. 355-356, 358, 364 Overprinted in Black

1947, Nov. 1 **Wmk. 257** **Litho.** ***Imperf.***

Without Gum

No.	Type	Description	Unused	Used
4X1	A152	10s **red orange** *(13,997)*	1,200.	*1,000.*
		On cover, strip of 3		*9,500.*
		On cover with #4X2		*7,500.*
4X2	A152	20s **ultramarine** *(13,641)*	600.	*1,000.*
		On cover, strip of 3		—
a.		Block of 4, one with double seal, one without seal	*3,000.*	
b.		Pair, one without seal	—	
c.		Double seal	—	
4X3	A163	50s **dark brown** *(6,276)*	900.	*700.*
a.		Double seal	—	
4X4	A167	1y **deep ultramarine** *(1,947)*	1,750.	*1,000.*
a.		Double seal	—	

On Revenue Stamp of Japan

No.	Type	Description	Unused	Used
4X5	R1	30s **brown** *(14,000)*	*3,500.*	*3,500.*
		On cover		*7,500.*

No. 4X5 is on Japan's current 30s revenue stamp. The Hirata seal validated it for postal use.

Nos. 4X1-4X5 are known with rough sewing machine perforations, full or partial. These are scarce to rare.

YAEYAMA DISTRICT

Personal Seal of Postmaster Kenpuku Miyara

Stamps of Japan 1937-46 Handstamped in Black

Typographed, Engraved, Lithographed

1948 **Wmk. 257** ***Perf. 13***

No.	Type	Description	Unused	Used
5X1	A86	4s **deep green,** #261	1,200.	
5X2	A86	5s **brown lake,** #331	1,200.	
5X3	A86	7s **orange vermilion,** #333	800.	
5X4	A148	10s **crimson & dull rose,** #334	*5,000.*	
5X5	A94	20s **ultramarine,** #269	150.	
		On cover with 2 #5X8		—
a.		Double seal	*600.*	
5X6	A96	30s **peacock blue,** #271	1,000.	
		On cover		—
a.		Double seal	—	
5X7	A88	40s **dull violet,** #341	70.	
a.		Double seal	—	
b.		Triple seal	—	
5X8	A97	50s **olive & pale olive,** #272	75.	
a.		Double seal	—	
5X9	A163	50s **dark brown,** imperf., #358 *(250)*	1,350.	
5X10	A99	5y **deep gray green,** #274	2,000.	
a.		Pair, one without seal	—	
b.		Double seal	—	

No. 5X9 was issued without gum.

This handstamp exists double, triple, inverted and in pair, one stamp without overprint.

Provisional postal stationery of the four districts also exists.

LETTER SHEETS

Values are for entires.

Stylized Deigo Blossom — US1

Typographed by Japan Printing Bureau.
Stamp is in upper left corner.

Designer: Shutaro Higa

1948-49

No.	Type	Description	Unused	Used
U1	US1	50s **vermilion,** *cream, July 18, 1949 (250,000)*	50.00	60.00
		First day cancel		—
a.		50s **orange red,** *gray, July 1, 1948 (1,000)*	1,500.	—

Banyan Tree — US2

Designer: Ken Yabu

1950, Jan. 21

No.	Type	Description	Unused	Used
U2	US2	1y **carmine red,** *cream (250,000)*	40.00	50.00
		First day cancel		—

AIR LETTER SHEETS

DC-4 Skymaster and Shurei Gate — UC1

Designer: Chosho Ashitomi

"PAR AVION" (Bilingual) below Stamp

Litho. & Typo. by Japan Printing Bureau

1952-53

No.	Type	Description	Unused	Used
UC1	UC1	12y **light rose,** *pale blue green, Mar. 9, 1953 (76,000)*	20.00	12.50
a.		12y **dull rose,** *pale blue green, Nov. 1, 1952 (50,000)*	30.00	15.00
		First day cancel, No. UC1a		80.00

No. UC1a is on tinted paper with colorless overall inscription "RYUKYU FOREIGN AIRMAIL," repeated in parallel vertical lines, light and indistinct. Dull rose ink of imprinted design and legend "AIR LETTER" appears to bleed. No. UC1 has overall inscription darker and more distinct. Light rose ink of design and legend does not bleed. Model: U.S. No. UC16.

UC2

Litho. & Typo. by Nippon Toppan K.K.
"AEROGRAMME" below Stamp

1955, Sept. 10

UC2 UC2 15y **blue & red,** *pale yellow green (89,300)* 30.00 15.00
First day cancel 60.00
a. 15y **violet blue & dull red,** *pale blue green, Oct. 1957 (33,742)* 45.00 25.00

Printing on the envelope stamp is heavier on No. UC2a than on No. UC2.

No. UC2 Surcharged in Red

"13" & "¢" aligned at bot.; 2 thick bars — a

"¢" raised; 2 thick bars — b

"13" & "¢" as in "a"; 4 thin bars — c

"¢" raised; 4 thin bars — d

Printers: Type "a," Nakamura Printing Co., "b" and "d," Okinawa Printing Co., "c," Sun Printing Co.

1958-60

UC3 UC2 13c on 15y type "a," *Sept. 16, 1958 (60,000)* 20.00 18.00
First day cancel 60.00
a. Type "b," on No. UC2, *June 1, 1959 (2,000)* 40.00 30.00
b. Type "b," on No. UC2a *(7,000)* 50.00 30.00
c. Type "c," on No. UC2, *Sept. 22, 1959 (1,000)* 80.00 80.00
d. As "c," small wrong font "¢" sign 1,400. —
e. Type "c," on No. UC2a *(1,000)* 80.00 80.00
f. As "e," double surcharge, one on reverse *3,250.*
g. Type "b" and No. 46 on No. UC2a, *Aug. 22, 1960 (1,000)* 550.00 —
h. Type "d" and Nos. 55, 58 on No. UC2, *Oct. 1, 1960 (1,000)* 450.00 450.00
i. Type "d" and Nos. 55, 58 on No. UC2a *(2,000)* 300.00 300.00

For Nos. UC3g, UC3h and UC3i, additional stamps have been affixed to make up the 15c rate.

UC3

Lithographed by Japan Printing Bureau

1959, Nov. 10

UC4 UC3 15c **dark blue,** *pale blue (560,000)* 4.00 2.50
First day cancel 10.00

POSTAL CARDS

Deigo Blossom Type
Values are for entire cards.

Nos. UX1-UX9 are typo., others litho.
Printed by Japan Printing Bureau unless otherwise stated.
Quantities in parentheses; "E" means estimated.

Designer: Shutaro Higa

1948, July 1

UX1 US1 10s **dull red,** *grayish tan (100,000)* 50.00 *60.00*

1949, July 1

UX2 US1 15s **orange red,** *gray (E 175,000)* 40.00 *70.00*
First day cancel —
a. 15s **vermilion,** *tan (E 50,000)* 110.00 *125.00*

Banyan Tree Type

Designer: Ken Yabu

1950, Jan. 21

UX3 US2 50s **carmine red,** *light tan (E 200,000)* 10.00 10.00
First day cancel 60.00
a. Grayish tan card (E 25,000) 25.00 *50.00*

Nos. UX2, UX2a Handstamp Surcharged in Vermilion

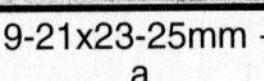
19-21x23-25mm — a

22-23x26-27mm — b

20-21x24-24½mm — c

22-23½x25-26mm — d

1951

UX4 US1 (c) 15s + 85s on #UX2 *(E 35,000)* 100. 100.
a. Type "c" on #UX2a *(E 5,000)* 150. 150.
b. Type "a" on #UX2 *(E 39,000)* 75. *100.*
c. Type "a" on #UX2a *1,500.* —
d. Type "b" on #UX2 *1,500.* *1,500.*
e. Type "d" on #UX2 *(E 4,000)* 150. *200.*
f. Type "d" on #UX2a *(E 1,000)* 250. *300.*

Type "a" exists on the 15s cherry blossom postal card of Japan. Value $100.

Crown, Leaf Ornaments

Naha die 21x22mm
PC3

Tokyo die 18½x19mm
PC4

Designer: Masayoshi Adaniya Koshun Printing Co.

1952

UX5 PC3 1y **vermilion,** *tan, Feb. 8 (400,600)* 50.00 30.00
UX6 PC4 1y **vermilion,** *off-white, Oct. 6 (1,295,000)* 25.00 14.00
a. Tan card, coarse *(50,000)* 30.00 20.00
b. Tan card, smooth *(16,000)* 500.00 150.00

Naminoue Shrine

Naha die 23x25½mm — PC5

Tokyo die 22x24½mm — PC6

Designer: Gensei Agena

1953-57

UX7 PC5 2y **green,** *off-white, Dec. 2, 1953 (1,799,400)* 60.00 20.00
First day cancel 80.00
a. Printed both sides *500.00*
UX8 PC6 2y **green,** *off-white, 1955 (2,799,400)* 15.00 6.00
a. 2y **deep blue green,** *1956 (300,000)* 30.00 16.50
b. 2y **yellow green,** *1957 (2,400,000)* 12.50 3.50
c. As "a," printed on both sides *500.00*
d. As "b," printed on both sides *500.00*

Stylized Pine, Bamboo, Plum Blossoms — PC7

1956 New Year Card

Designer: Koya Oshiro Kotsura and Koshun Printing Companies

1955, Dec. 1

UX9 PC7 2y **red,** *cream* 100.00 45.00
First day cancel 125.00

No. UX9 was printed on rough card (43,400) and smooth-finish card (356,600).

Sun — PC8

1957 New Year Card

Designer: Seikichi Tamanaha Kobundo Printing Co.

1956, Dec. 1

UX10 PC8 2y **brown carmine & yellow,** *off-white (600,000)* 6.00 3.75
First day cancel 10.00

Temple Lion — PC9

1958 New Year Card

Designer: Shin Isagawa Fukuryu Printing Co.

1957, Dec. 1

UX11 PC9 2y **lilac rose,** *off-white (1,000,000)* 1.75 *2.25*
First day cancel 4.00
a. "1" omitted in right date 75.00 75.00
b. Printed on both sides 250.00 *300.00*

Nos. UX8, UX8a and UX8b "Revalued" in Red, Cherry or Pink by Three Naha Printeries

a

b

c

1958-59

UX12 PC6 1½c on 2y **green,** type "a," *Sept. 16 (600,000)* 5.00 5.00
First day cancel 10.00
a. Shrine stamp omitted *750.00* *1,000.*
b. Bar of ½ omitted, top of 2 broken 75.00 *100.00*
c. Type "b," *Nov. (1,000,000)* 10.00 *12.50*
d. Type "c," *1959 (200,000)* 15.00 *22.50*
e. Wrong font "¢," type "c" 30.00 *45.00*
f. "¢" omitted, type "c" *1,500.* 1,500.
g. Double surcharge, type "c" *1,000.* —

Multicolor Yarn Ball — PC10

1959 New Year Card

Designer: Masayoshi Adaniya Kobundo Printing Co.

1958, Dec. 10

UX13 PC10 1½c **black, red, yellow & gray blue,** *off-white (1,514,000)* 1.50 *1.90*
First day cancel 2.00
a. Black omitted —

Toy Pony — PC11

Designer: Seikichi Tamanaha Kobundo Printing Co.

1959, June 20 **Size: 19½x23mm**

UX14 PC11 1½c **dark blue & brown** *(1,140,000)* 1.50 1.25
First day cancel 1.50
a. Dark blue omitted 500.00

Toy Carp and Boy — PC12

1960 New Year Card

Designer: Masayoshi Adaniya

1959, Dec. 1

UX15 PC12 1½c **violet blue, red & black,** *cream (2,000,000)* 1.25 *1.50*
First day cancel 1.75

Toy Pony — PC13

1959, Dec. 30 **Size: 21x25mm**

UX16 PC13 1½c **gray violet & brown,** *cream (3,500,000)* 3.00 .75
First day cancel 2.75

Household Altar — PC14

1961 New Year Card

Designer: Shin Isagawa

1960, Nov. 20

UX17 PC14 1½c **gray, carmine, yellow & black,** *off-white (2,647,591)* 1.50 1.50
First day cancel 1.50

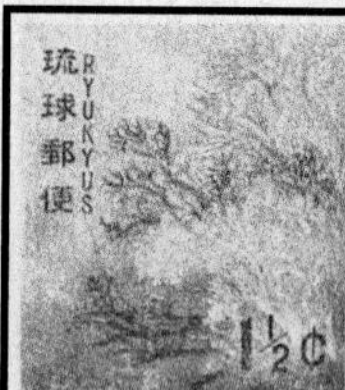

Coral Head — PC15

Summer Greeting Card

Designer: Shinzan Yamada Kidekuni Printing Co.

1961, July 5

UX18 PC15 1½c **ultramarine & cerise,** *off-white (264,900)* 2.25 *3.75*
First day cancel 4.00

Tiger — PC16

1962 New Year Card

Designer: Shin Isagawa

1961, Nov. 15

UX19 PC16 1½c **ocher, black & red,** *off-white (2,891,626)* 1.50 *2.50*
First day cancel 1.65
a. Red omitted 750.00 —
b. Red inverted *500.00* —
c. Red omitted on face, inverted on back *500.00* —
d. Double impression of red, one inverted *500.00* —
e. Double impression of ocher & black, red inverted *500.00* —
f. Double impression of ocher & black, one inverted *500.00* —

Inscribed "RYUKYUS" — PC17

Designer: Seikichi Tamanaha

1961-67

UX20 PC17 1½c **gray violet & brown,** *white ('67) (18,600,000)* 1.00 .50
a. Off-white card ('66) *(4,000,000)* 1.50 .75
b. Cream card, *Dec. 23 (12,500,000)* 1.00 .50
First day cancel 1.35

Ie Island — PC18

Summer Greeting Card

Designer: Shinzan Yamada Sakai Printing Co.

1962, July 10

UX21 PC18 1½c **bright blue, yellow & brown,** *off-white (221,500)* 1.50 *2.50*
First day cancel 3.00
Square notch at left 40.00 *45.00*

New Year Offerings — PC19

1963 New Year Card; Precanceled

Designer: Shin Isagawa Sakai Printing Co.

1962, Nov. 15

UX22 PC19 1½c **olive brown, carmine & black** *(3,000,000)* 1.50 *3.00*
First day cancel 2.25
a. Yellow brown background —
b. Brown ocher background —

Ryukyu Temple Dog and Wine Flask Silhouette PC20

International Postal Card

Designer: Shin Isagawa

1963, Feb. 15

UX23 PC20 5c **vermilion, emerald & black,** *pale yellow (150,000)* 1.75 *5.00*
First day cancel 1.65
a. Black & emerald omitted 450.00

Water Strider — PC21

Summer Greeting Card

Designer: Seikichi Tamanaha

1963, June 20

UX24 PC21 1½c **Prussian green & black,** *off-white (250,000)* 4.00 *4.25*
First day cancel 3.50

Princess Doll — PC22

1964 New Year Card; Precanceled

Designer: Koya Oshiro

1963, Nov. 15

UX25 PC22 1½c **orange red, yellow & ultra,** *off-white (3,200,000)* 2.00 2.00
First day cancel 2.00

Bitter Melon Vine — PC23

Summer Greeting Card

Designer: Shinzan Yamada

1964, June 20

UX26 PC23 1½c **multicolored,** *off-white (285,410)* 1.40 *2.25*
First day cancel 1.75

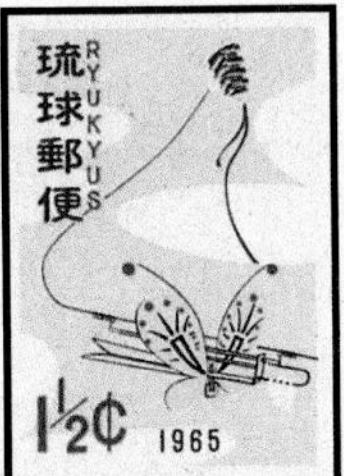

Fighting Kite with Rider — PC24

1965 New Year Card; Precanceled

Designer: Koya Oshiro

1964, Nov. 15

UX27 PC24 1½c **multicolored,** *off-white (4,876,618)* 1.25 *1.75*
First day cancel 2.00

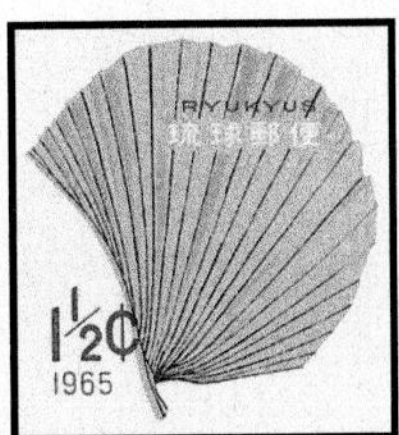

Palm-leaf Fan — PC25

Summer Greeting Card

Designer: Koya Oshiro

1965, June 20

UX28 PC25 1½c **multicolored,** *off-white (340,604)* 1.40 *2.50*
First day cancel 1.65

Toy Pony Rider — PC26

1966 New Year Card; Precanceled

Designer: Seikichi Tamanaha

1965, Nov. 15

UX29 PC26 1½c **multicolored,** *off-white (5,224,622)* 1.25 *1.75*
First day cancel 1.40
a. Silver (background) omitted 250.00

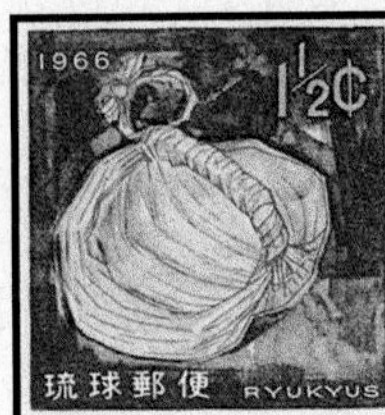

Fan Palm Dipper — PC27

Summer Greeting Card

Designer: Seikichi Tamanaha

1966, June 20

UX30 PC27 1½c **multicolored,** *off-white (339,880)* 1.25 *2.00*
First day cancel 1.40

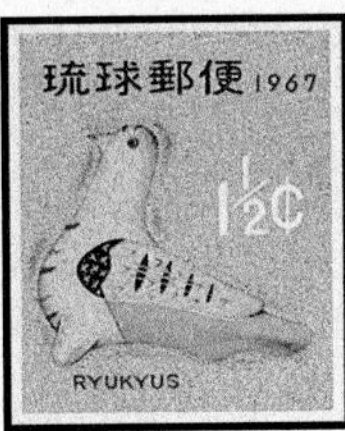

Toy Dove — PC28

1967 New Year Card; Precanceled

Designer: Seikichi Tamanaha

1966, Nov. 15

UX31 PC28 1½c **multicolored,** *off-white (5,500,000)* 1.25 *1.75*
First day cancel 1.65
a. Silver (background) omitted *500.00*
b. Gray blue & green omitted *750.00*

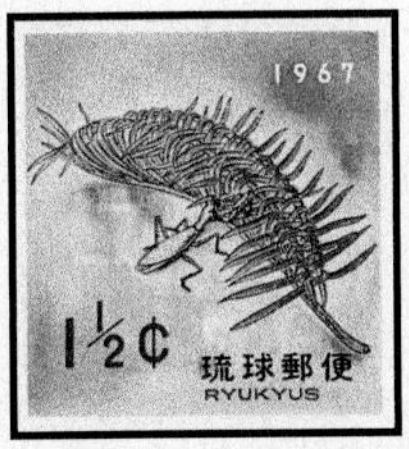

Cycad Insect Cage and Praying Mantis — PC29

Summer Greeting Card

Designer: Shin Isagawa

1967, June 20

UX32 PC29 1½c **multicolored,** *off-white (350.000)* 1.50 *2.50*
First day cancel 1.75

Paper Doll Royalty — PC30

1968 New Year Card; Precanceled

Designer: Shin Isagawa

1967, Nov. 15

UX33 PC30 1½c **multicolored,** *off-white (6,200,000)* 1.10 *1.50*
First day cancel 1.75
a. Gold omitted 500.00

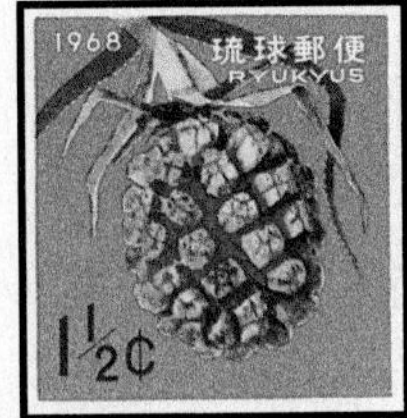

Pandanus Drupe — PC31

Summer Greeting Card

Designer: Seikan Omine

1968, June 20

UX34 PC31 1½c **multicolored,** *off-white (350,000)* 1.25 *2.25*
First day cancel 1.75

Toy Lion — PC32

1969 New Year Card; Precanceled

Designer: Teruyoshi Kinjo

1968, Nov. 15

UX35 PC32 1½c **multicolored,** *off-white (7,000,000)* 1.10 *1.50*
First day cancel 1.50

Ryukyu Trading Ship — PC33

Summer Greeting Card

Designer: Seikichi Tamanaha

1969, June 20

UX36 PC33 1½c **multicolored,** *(349,800)* 1.25 *2.25*
First day cancel 1.75

Toy Devil Mask — PC34

1970 New Year Card; Precanceled

Designer: Teruyoshi Kinjo

1969, Nov. 15

UX37 PC34 1½c **multicolored** *(97,200,000)* 1.10 *1.50*
First day cancel 1.25

Ripe Litchis — PC35

Summer Greeting Card

Designer: Kensei Miyagi

1970, June 20

UX38 PC35 1½c **multicolored** *(400,000)* 1.40 *2.25*
First day cancel 1.50

Thread-winding Implements for Dance — PC36

1971 New Year Card; Precanceled

Designer: Yoshinori Arakai

1970, Nov. 16

UX39 PC36 1½c **multicolored** *(7,500,000)* 1.10 *1.50*
First day cancel 1.25

Ripe Guavas — PC37

Summer Greeting Card

Designer: Kensei Miyagi

1971, July 10

UX40 PC37 1½c **multicolored** *(400,000)* 1.25 *2.25*
First day cancel 1.25

Pony Type of 1961

Zip Code Boxes in Vermilion

1971, July 10

UX41 PC17 1½c **gray violet & brown** *(3,000,000)* 1.25 *3.50*
First day cancel 2.00

No. UX41 Surcharged below Stamp in Vermilion

"Revalued 2¢" applied by Nakamura Printing Co.

1971, Sept. 1

UX42 PC17 2c on 1½c **gray violet & brown** *(1,699,569)* 1.10 *2.25*
First day cancel 2.00
a. Inverted surcharge *500.00*
b. Double surcharge *500.00*
c. Surcharge on back *500.00*
e. Surcharge on back, inverted *500.00*

1972 New Year Card; Precanceled

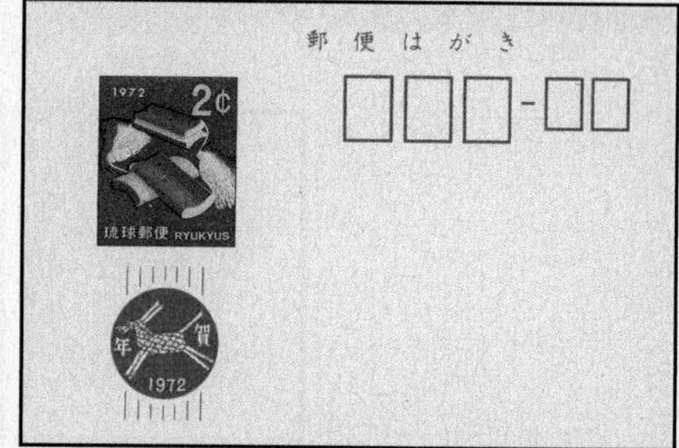

Tasseled Castanets — PC38

Zip Code Boxes in Vermilion

Designer: Yoshinori Arakaki

1971, Nov. 15

UX43 PC38 2c **multicolored** *(8,000,000)* 1.00 *1.50*
First day cancel 1.25

Type of 1961

Zip Code Boxes in Vermilion

1971, Dec. 15

UX44 PC17 2c **gray violet & brown** *(3,500,000)* 1.25 *1.75*
First day cancel 1.65

PAID REPLY POSTAL CARDS

Sold as two attached cards, one for message, one for reply. The major listings are of unsevered cards except Nos. UY4-UY6.

Message

Reply

1948, July 1

UY1 US1 10s + 10s **dull red,** *grayish tan (1,000)* 2,000. —
m. Message card 600. 1,000.
r. Reply card 600. 1,000.

1949, July 18

UY2 US1 15s + 15s **vermilion,** *tan (E 150,000)* 30.00 *40.00*
a. Gray card *(E 75,000)* 75.00 —
First day cancel —
m. Message card 8.00 *16.50*
r. Reply card 8.00 *16.50*

1950, Jan. 21

UY3 US2 50s + 50s **carmine red,** *gray cream (E 130,000)* 25.00 *40.00*
a. Double impression of message card — —
b. Light tan card *(E 96,000)* 15.00 —
First day cancel —
m. Message card 3.50 *13.50*
r. Reply card 3.50 *13.50*

No. UY2a Handstamp Surcharged in Vermilion

1951

UY4 US1 1y (15s+85s) message, type "b" *(E 3,000)* 350. 350.
a. Reply, type "b" *(E 3,000)* 350. 350.
b. Message, type "a" *(E 300)* 600. —
c. Reply, type "a" *(E 300)* 600. —
d. Message, type "d" *(E 200)* 500. —
e. Reply, type "d" *(E 200)* 500. —
f. Message, UY2, type "a" *(E 3,000)* 150. *225.*
g. Reply, UY2, type "a" *(E 3,000)* 150. *225.*
h. Message, UY2, type "b" *(E 2,500)* 275. 275.
i. Reply, UY2, type "b" *(E 2,500)* 275. 275.
j. Message, UY2, type "d" *(E 2,800)* 150. *250.*
k. Reply, UY2, type "d" *(E 2,800)* 150. *250.*
l. 1y + 1y unsevered, type "b" *850.*
m. 1y + 1y unsevered, type "a" *1,450.*
n. 1y + 1y unsevered, type "d" *1,200.*
o. 1y + 1y unsevered, UY2, type "a" *360.*
p. 1y + 1y unsevered, UY2, type "b" *650.*
q. 1y + 1y unsevered, UY2, type "d" *360.*
r. 1y + 1y unsevered, UY2, type "c" *3, 500.*
s. Message, UY2, type "c," —
t. Reply, UY2, type "c" —
u. Message, type "c" —
v. Reply, type "c" —
w. As "n," surcharge omitted on reply card —
x. As "q," surcharge omitted on reply card —
y. As "q," double strike of surcharge on message card —

Types are illustrated above No. UX4.

e

f

g

50 SEN
別 納
琉 球
郵 政 局

h

Typographed Surcharge in Vermilion on No. UY2a

UY5 US1 1y (15s+85s) message, type "f" *(E 20,000)* 125. 125.
a. Reply, type "f" *(E 20,000)* 125. 125.
b. Message, type "e" *(E 12,500)* 225. 225.
c. Reply, type "e" *(E 12,500)* 225. 225.
d. Message, type "g" *(E 500)* — —
e. Reply, type "g" *(E 500)* *1,250.* —
f. Message, UY2, type "e" *(E 15,000)* 125. 125.
g. Reply, UY2, type "e" *(E 15,000)* 125. 125.
h. Message, UY2, type "f" *(E 9,000)* 125. 125.
i. Reply, UY2, type "f" *(E 9,000)* 125. 125.
j. Message, UY2, type "g" *(E 500)* *2,000.*
k. Reply, UY2, type "g" *(E 500)* *1,000.* *1,500.*
l. 1y + 1y unsevered, type "e" *1,000.*
m. 1y + 1y unsevered, UY2, type "e" *375.*

Typographed Surcharge Type "h" in Vermilion on No. UY3

UY6 US2 1y (50s+50s) message *(E 35,000)* 125.00 *150.00*
a. Reply *(E 35,000)* 125.00 *150.00*
b. Message, UY3b *(E 10,000)* 125.00 *150.00*
c. Reply, UY3b *(E 10,000)* 125.00 *150.00*

No. UY6 is unknown as a joined card.

Smooth or Coarse Card

1952, Feb. 8

UY7 PC3 1y + 1y **vermilion,** *gray tan (60,000)* 120.00 *140.00*
First day cancel 250.00
m. Message card 25.00 *50.00*
r. Reply card 25.00 *50.00*

1953

UY8 PC4 1y + 1y **vermilion,** *tan (22,900)* 30.00 *40.00*
First day cancel —
a. Off-white card *(13,800)* 40.00 *50.00*
m. Message card 7.50 *19.00*
r. Reply card 7.50 *26.50*

Off-white or Light Cream Card

1953, Dec. 2

UY9 PC5 2y + 2y **green** *(50,000)* 100.00 90.00
First day cancel 150.00
m. Message card 15.00 *25.00*
r. Reply card 15.00 *35.00*

1955, May

UY10 PC6 2y + 2y **green,** *off-white (280,000)* 10.00 —
a. Reply card blank 500.00
m. Message card 3.25 *11.00*
r. Reply card 3.25 *15.00*

No. UY10 Surcharged in Red

1958, Sept. 16

UY11 PC6 1½c on 2y, 1½c on 2y *(95,000)* 8.00 —
First day cancel 22.50
a. Surcharge on reply card only *500.00* —
b. Surcharge on message card only *500.00* —
c. Reply card double surcharge *750.00* —
d. Reply card stamp omitted (surcharge only) *1,000.* —
m. Message card 2.75 *10.00*
r. Reply card 2.75 *16.50*

Surcharge varieties include: "1" omitted; wrong font "2".

Pony Types

1959, June 20

UY12 PC11 1½c + 1½c **dark blue & brown** *(366,000)* 3.50 —
- First day cancel 4.00
- ***m.*** Message card .65 *3.50*
- ***r.*** Reply card .65 *3.50*

1960, Mar. 10

UY13 PC13 1½c + 1½c **gray violet & brown,** *(150,000)* 7.00 —
- First day cancel 5.00
- ***m.*** Message card 1.50 *5.00*
- ***r.*** Reply card 1.50 *5.00*

International Type

1963, Feb. 15

UY14 PC20 5c + 5c **vermilion, emerald & black,** *pale yellow (70,000)* 2.50 —
- First day cancel 3.00
- ***m.*** Message card .75 *5.00*
- ***r.*** Reply card .75 *5.00*

Pony ("RYUKYUS") Type

1963-69

UY15 PC17 1½c + 1½c **gray violet & brown,** *cream, Mar. 15, (800,000)* 2.00 —
- First day cancel 2.50
- ***a.*** Off-white card, *Mar. 13, 1967 (100,000)* 2.25 —
- ***b.*** White card, *Nov. 22, 1969 (700,000)* 1.75 —
- ***m.*** Message card detached .40 *4.00*
- ***r.*** Reply card detached .40 *4.00*

No. UY14 Surcharged below Stamp in Vermilion

1971, Sept. 1

UY16 PC17 2c on 1½c + 2c on 1½c **gray violet & brown** *(80,000)* 2.00 —
- First day cancel 2.25
- ***m.*** Message card .50 *2.50*
- ***r.*** Reply card .50 *2.50*

Pony ("RYUKYUS") Type

Zip Code Boxes in Vermilion

1971, Nov. 1

UY17 PC17 2c + 2c **gray violet & brown** *(150,000)* 2.00 —
- First day cancel 2.50
- ***m.*** Message card .50 *2.50*
- ***r.*** Reply card .50 *2.50*

OFFICIAL STAMPS ELECTION POSTAL CARDS

Official election free-mail postal cards were authorized by the United States Civil Administration of the Ryukyus, Ordinance 57, Dec. 18, 1951, as a measure to ensure equal access to voters for each candidate standing in district or general elections in the islands. Under the terms of the ordinance and the local enabling legislation, each candidate, on request, could receive a fixed number of cards per election, which were serviced with no mailing costs to the candidate.

Until the issuance of No. UZE15 in 1960, cards were processed without canceling; beginning with that issue, they were treated as regular postal cards and canceled.

With the exception of pieces bearing emergency handstamp or machine-cancel indicia, the cards were special-order printings (incorporating the election indicium) of designs and types of postal cards concurrently in use as regular postal cards (though at times in different colors).

ELECTION INDICIA

Type I

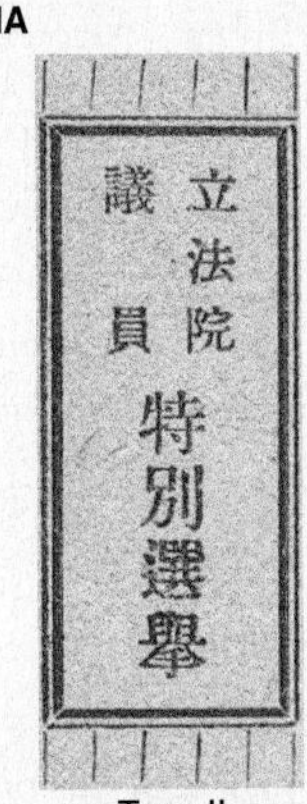

Type II

Type I: Typographed, Size: 18x45mm
Type II: Typographed, Size: 17½x48-49mm

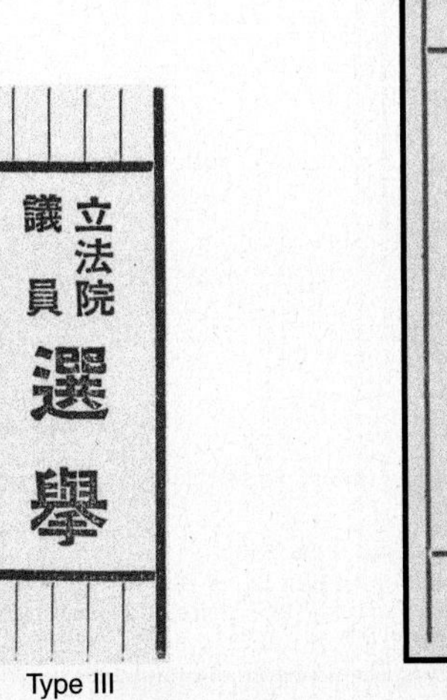

Type III Type IV

Type III: Typographed, Size: 17½x49-51mm
Type IV: Typographed, Size: 16½x62mm

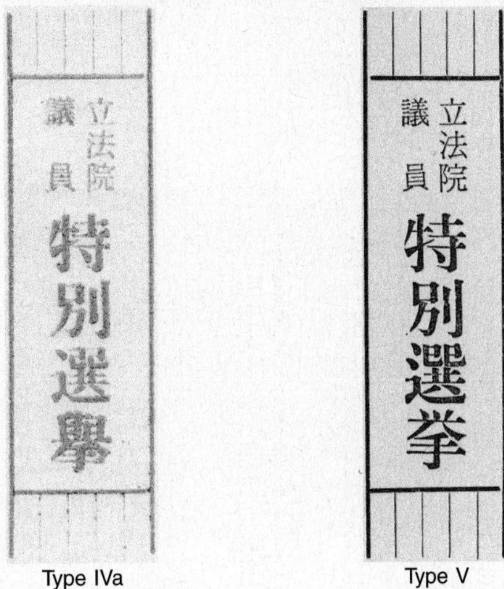

Type IVa Type V

Type IVa: Like Type IV but with second character from bottom ("SEN") having one stroke at upper left instead of two

Type V: Typographed, Size: 16-17x61-63mm (similar to Type IV, but with different bottom character)

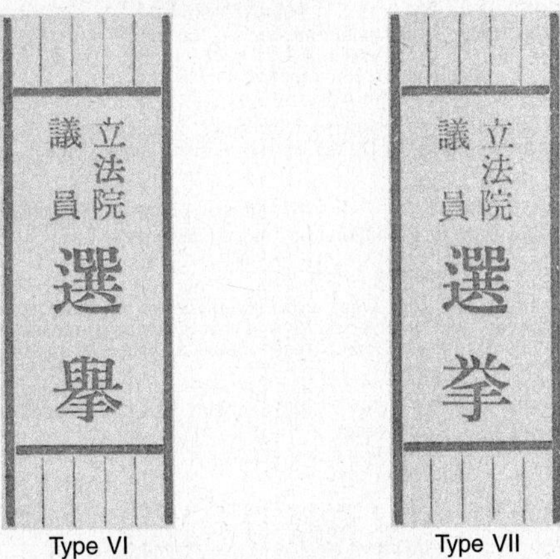

Type VI Type VII

Type VI: Typographed, Size: 17½x51-52mm

Type VII: Typographed, Size: 17½x51-52mm (similar to Type VI, but with different bottom character)

Type VIII

Type IX

Type VIII: Typographed, Size: 17¼-17½x 52mm (similar to Type VII but with second character from bottom ("SEN") having one stroke at upper left instead of two)

Type IX: Handstamped, Size: 17½x51mm

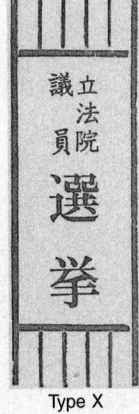

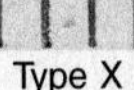
Type X

Type XI

Type X: Typographed, Size: 17½x51-51½mm (similar to Type VIII, but with different appearance of five smaller characters at top)

Type XI: Typographed, Size: 10x31½mm

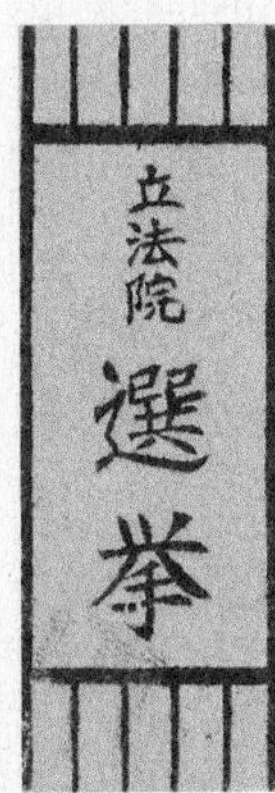

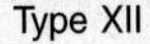
Type XII

Type XIII

Type XII: Handstamped, Size: 17½-18x49½-51½mm, Thick characters

Type XIII: Handstamped, Size: 17½-18x50¼-51mm, Thin characters

Type XIIIa

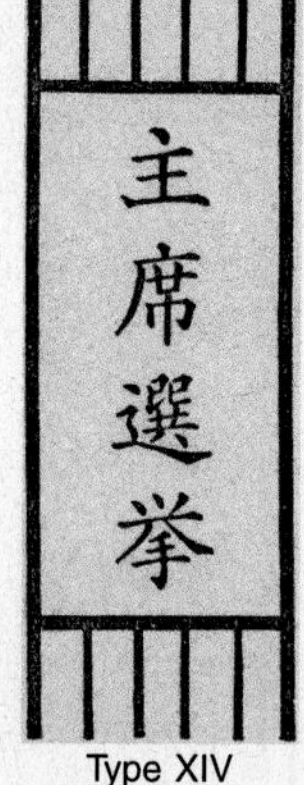

Type XIV

Type XIIIa: Handstamped, Size: 17½-18x50¼x51mm, Thick characters, with shorter lvertical line at lower left.
Type XIV: Typographed, Size: 18x50-50½mm

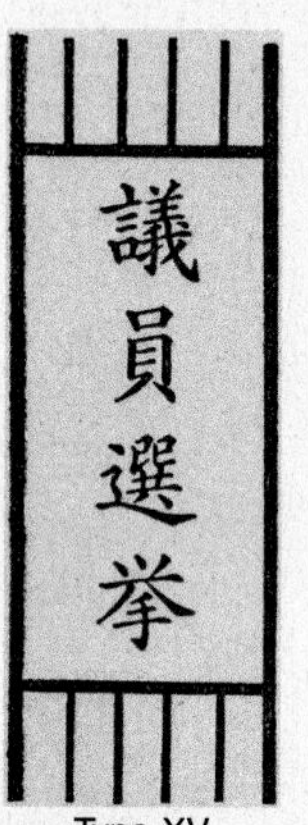

Type XV

Type XVI

Type XV: Typographed, Size: 18x50-50½mm
Type XVI: Machine cancel, Circle diameter: 20mm, Height of legend box: 23½mm

Type XVIa

Type XVII

Type XVIa: Machine cancel, Circle diameter: 20mm, Height of legend box: 20½-22mm
Type XVII: Typographed, Size: 18½x48½-50mm

Type XVIII

Type XVIII: Machine cancel, Circle diameter: 20mm, Height of legend box: 20½-22 mm

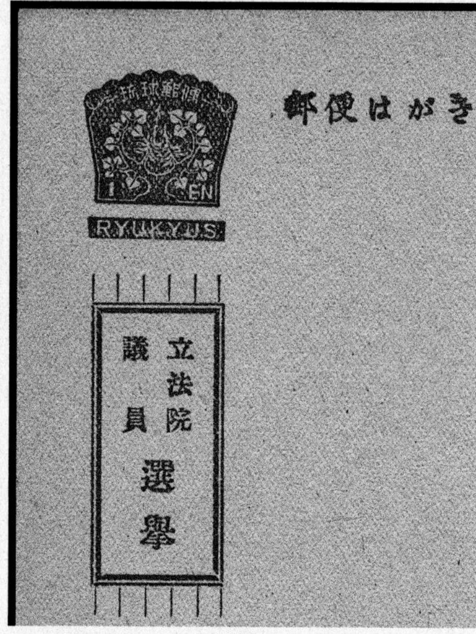

UZE1

1952, Feb. 2 — First General Election

UZE1 PC3 1y **vermilion,** *tan* coarse (Naha die) + Type I *(345,000)* 300.00 500.00
a. Postmarked (error) —

1952, July 26 — 1st District Special Election

UZE2 PC3 1y **vermilion,** *tan* coarse (Naha die) + Type II *(est. 25,000)* — —
a. 2nd character from bottom in indicium (SEN) inverted — —

Used cards or unused with campaign messages must have reference to the 1st District (Kasari, Amami Gunto) election.

1953, Mar. 3 — 4th District Special Election

UZE3 PC4 1y **vermilion,** *tan* coarse (Tokyo die) + Type II *(est. 10,000)* —
a. Postmarked (error) —

Identifiable only when postmarked (in error, with dates between Mar. 3-Mar.31, 1953) and/or with campaign message in reference to 4th District election (Motobu, Okinawa Gunto).

1953, Mar. 27 — 3rd District Special Election

UZE4 PC4 1y **vermilion,** *tan* coarse (Tokyo die) + Type II *(est. 10,000)* 50.00 —
a. Postmarked (error) —

Identifiable only when postmarked (in error, with dates between Mar. 27-Apr. 1953) and/or with campaign message in reference to 3rd District election (Yagaji, Okinawa Gunto).

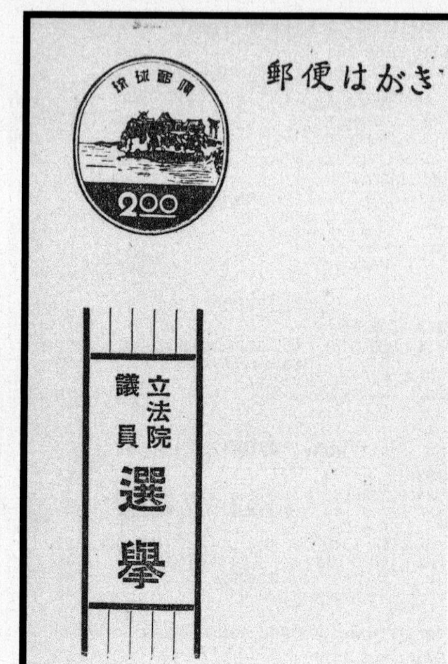

UZE5

1954, Feb. 23 — Second General Election

UZE5 PC5 2y **rose red,** *off white* (Naha die) + Type III *(70,000)* 45.00 —
a. Postmarked (error) —

1954, Nov. 19 — 18th District Special Election

UZE6 PC6 2y **red,** *off white* (Tokyo die) + Type IV 500.00 —
a. Postmarked (error) —
UZE6A PC6 2y **red,** *off white* (Tokyo die) + Type V 500.00 —
a. Postmarked (error) —

Postal records show receipt of 4,000 total cards of Nos. UZE6 and UZE6A, undefined as to type.

1955, Feb. 15 — 20th District Special Election

UZE7 PC6 2y **dark purple,** *off white* (Tokyo die) + Type IV *(2,000)* 500.00

1955, Mar. 8 — 23rd District Special Election

UZE8 PC6 2y **turquoise blue,** *off white* (Tokyo die) + Type V *(2,000)* 500.00 —
a. Postmarked (error) —

1955, June 28 — 22nd District Special Election

UZE9 PC6 2y **dull brown,** *gray cream* (Tokyo die) + Type V *(3,030)* 240.00
a. Postmarked (error) —

1956, Feb. 20 — Third General Election

UZE10 PC6 2y **pale blue green,** *off white* (Tokyo die) + Type VI 75.00 150.00
a. Postmarked (error) —
UZE10A PC6 2y **pale blue green,** *off white* (Tokyo die) + Type VII 75.00 150.00
a. Postmarked (error) —

Postal records show receipt of 65,000 total cards of Nos. UZE10 and UZE10A, undefined as to type.

1956, Oct. 26 — 25th District Special Election

UZE11 PC6 2y **brown red,** *off white* (Tokyo die) + Type IV 300.00
UZE11A PC6 2y **brown red,** *off white* (Tokyo die) + Type V 140.00 350.00

Postal records show a total quantity of 3,030 examples of Nos. UZE11 and UZE11A prepared, unidentified as to type, of which 2,000 were issued.

1957, Aug. 5 — 18th District Special Election

UZE12 PC6 2y **lilac,** *off white* (Tokyo die) + Type IVa *(3,030)* 175.00 —

1958, Feb. 25 — Fourth General Election

UZE13 PC6 2y **deep blue,** *off white* (Tokyo die) + Type VI (bold face print) 130.00 70.00
d. Postmarked (error) —
UZE13A PC6 2y **deep blue,** *off white* (Tokyo die) + Type VI (light face print) 130.00 70.00
b. Postmarked (error) —
UZE13B PC6 2y **deep blue,** *off white* (Tokyo die) + Type VII (bold face print) 130.00 70.00
a. Postmarked (error) —

UZE13C PC6 2y **deep blue,** *off white* (Tokyo die) + Type VII (light face print) 90.00 70.00
a. Postmarked (error) —

Postal records show a total of 140,300 cards of Nos. UZE13-UZE13C prepared in two printings, undefined as to types.

UZE14

1959, July 23 — 26th District Special Election

UZE14 PC6 1½c on 2y **lemon,** *white* (Tokyo die) + Type VIII *(4,100)* 450.00

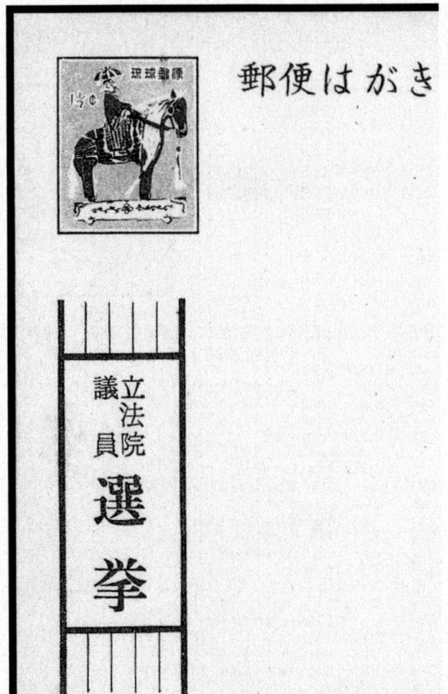

UZE15

1960, Oct. 24 — Fifth General Election

UZE15 PC11 1½c **indigo & claret brown,** *white* (Naha die) + Type VIII *(150,000)* 50.00 50.00
UZE16 PC13 1½c **violet gray & claret brown,** *cream* (Tokyo die) + Type IX in LL corner *(10,000)* 350.00 *650.00*

1962, Oct. 22 — Sixth General Election

UZE17 PC17 1½c **violet gray & claret brown,** *cream* + Type VIII 30.00 50.00
b. Election indicium inverted at right side of card —
UZE17A PC17 1½c **violet gray & claret brown,** *cream* + Type X 30.00 50.00

Postal records show a total of 116,000 cards of Nos. UZE17-UZE17A prepared, undefined as to type.

1962, Oct. 22
Sixth General Election Emergency Issue

UZE18 PC17 1½c **violet gray & claret brown,** *cream* + Type IX *(6,000)* 250.00 —
a. Indicium inverted —

1965, Oct. 25 — Seventh General Election

UZE19 PC17 1½c **violet gray & claret brown,** *cream* + Type XI *(134,000)* 17.50 90.00

1966, Aug. 1 — 3rd District Special Election

UZE20 PC17 1½c **violet gray & claret brown,** *cream* + Type XI *(est. 3,800)* 500.00

No. UZE20 is a remainder copy of No. UZE19 identifiable only when canceled at the Nakijin Post Office or Nago Central Post Office with verification that the card was delivered to a registered voter of Nakijin between Aug. 1 and Aug. 20, 1966.

1966, Aug. 11
3rd District Special Election Emergency Issue

UZE21 PC17 1½c **violet gray & claret brown,** *cream* + Type XII *(est. 200 for #UZE21 and #UZE22)* 425.00
UZE22 PC17 1½c **violet gray & claret brown,** *cream* + Type XIII 150.00
a. Double strike of indicium —

1968, Oct. 21 — First Chief Executive Election

UZE23 PC17 1½c **violet gray & claret brown,** *white* + Type XIV *(300,000)* 20.00 25.00

1968, Oct. 21 — Eighth General Election

UZE24 PC17 1½c **violet gray & claret brown,** *white* + Type XV *(142,000)* 20.00 35.00

1970, Oct. 12 — 1st District Special Election

UZE25 PC17 1½c **violet gray & claret brown,** *white* + Type XV *(4,000)* 350.00

No. UZE25 is a remainder card of No. UZE24, identifiable only when canceled at the Higashi, Kunigami, Ogimi or Oku Post Offices between Oct. 12-Oct. 31, 1970.

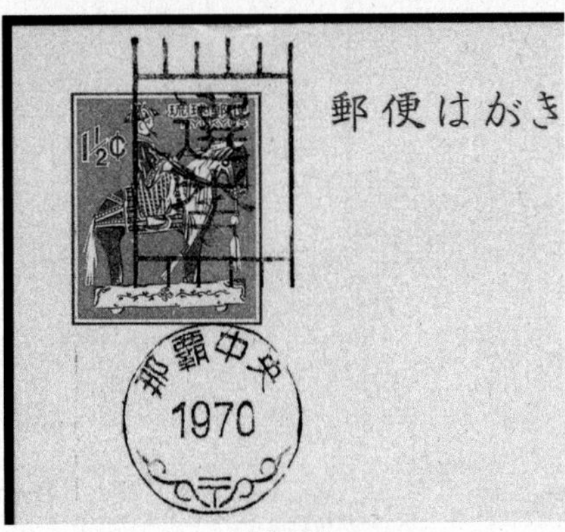

UZE26A

First General Election for Coucilors and Representatives to the Japanese Diet

1970, Oct. 23

UZE26 PC17 1½c **violet gray & claret brown,** *white* + Type XVI *(300,000)* 250.00 20.00
UZE26A PC17 1½c **violet gray & claret brown,** *white* + Type XVIa *(300,000)* 250.00 20.00

Postal records show a total of 171,000 examples of Nos. UZE26-UZE26A prepared, undefined as to type.

Emergency Commercial Card Issue for First General Japanese Diet Election

UZE27 *white or light gray blue* + Type XVI — 20.00
UZE27A *white or light gray blue* + Type XVIa — 20.00

Postal records show a total of 79,000 commercial cards were acquired for official issue as Nos. UZE27-UZE27A after validating. Some of the cards show an imprinted black square, while others show nothing.

1970, Nov. 16 — 21st District Special Election

UZE28 PC17 1½c **violet gray & claret brown,** *white* + Type XVII *(8,000)* 130.00

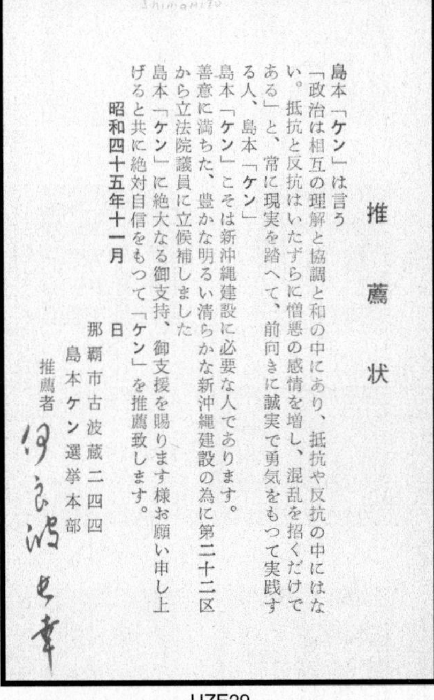
推薦状

島本「ケン」は言う
「政治は相互の理解と協調と和の中にあり、抵抗や反抗の中にはない。抵抗と反抗はいたずらに憎悪の感情を増し、混乱を招くだけである」と、常に現実を踏へて、前向きに誠実で勇気をもって実践する人、島本「ケン」
島本「ケン」こそは新沖縄建設に必要な人であります。
善意に満ちた、豊かな明るい清らかな新沖縄建設の為に第二十二区から立法院議員に立候補しました
島本「ケン」に絶大なる御支持、御支援を賜ります様お願い申し上げると共に絶対自信をもって「ケン」を推薦致します。

昭和四十五年十一月　日

那覇市古波蔵二四四
島本ケン選挙本部
推薦者

UZE29

1970, Nov. 16 — 22nd District Special Election

UZE29 PC17 1½c **violet gray & claret brown,** *white* + Type XVII *(2,000)* 350.00

No. UZE29 is a remainder card of No. UZE28, identifiable only with the imprinted message shown above of candidate Shimamoto Ken.

UZE30 PC17 1½c **violet gray & claret brown,** *white* + Type XIII 300.00
UZE30A PC17 1½c **violet gray & claret brown,** *white* + Type XIIIa 300.00

Postal records show a total of 2,000 of Nos. UZE30-UZE30A prepared, undefined as to type.

1971, Feb. 15 — 7th District Special Election

UZE31 PC17 1½c **violet gray & claret brown,** *white* + Type XV *(4,000)* 250.00

Remainders of No. UXE24 were used for this special election.

1971, June 4
Second General Election for Coucilors and Representatives to the Japanese Diet

UZE32 PC17 1½c **violet gray & claret brown,** *white* + Type XVIII *(25,000)* — 27.50

Emergency Commercial Card Issue for Second General Japanese Diet Election

UZE33 *white* + Type XVIII, 100x148mm *(25,000)* — 17.50
b. Double strike of election indicium, one inverted in LR corner — —
c. Double strike of election indicium, one in lower left corner —
d. Election indicium on front and reverse —
UZE33A *white* + Type XVIII, 104x150mm *(25,000)* — 30.00

REVENUE STAMPS

Upon its establishment Apr. 1, 1952, the government of the Ryukyu Islands assumed responsibility for the issuing of and the profit from revenue stamps. The various series served indiscriminately as evidence of payment of the required fees for various legal, realty and general commercial transactions.

1 yen — R1

1

3

5

10

50

100

500

1000

Designer: Eizo Yonamine

Litho. by Japan Printing Bureau.

1952-54		Wmk. 257		Perf. 13x13½	
R1	R1	1y	**brown rose**	15.00	10.00
R2	R1	3y	**rose red**	20.00	12.00
R3	R1	5y	**blue green**	25.00	15.00
R4	R1	10y	**blue**	25.00	20.00
R5	R1	50y	**purple**	30.00	25.00
R6	R1	100y	**brown yellow**	50.00	30.00
R7	R1	500y	**gray green**	350.00	100.00
R8	R1	1,000y	**vermilion**	200.00	150.00
			Nos. R1-R8 (8)	715.00	362.00

Issued: #R1-R6, July 15, 1952; #R7-R8, Apr. 16, 1954.

Denomination Vertical

"CENT"

"DOLLAR"

Litho. by Kobundo Printing Co., Naha

Perf. 10, 10½, 11 and combinations

1958, Sept. 16			Without Gum	Unwmk.	
R9	R1	1c	**red brown**	30.00	25.00
a.			Horiz. pair, imperf. between	500.00	
R10	R1	3c	**red**	40.00	35.00
a.			Horiz. pair, imperf. between	500.00	
R11	R1	5c	**emerald**	50.00	45.00
R12	R1	10c	**blue**	70.00	65.00
a.			Horiz. pair, imperf. between	450.00	
R13	R1	50c	**purple**	135.00	120.00
R14	R1	$1	**brown yellow**	200.00	175.00
R15	R1	$5	**gray green**	400.00	350.00
R16	R1	$10	**carmine**	450.00	400.00
			Nos. R9-R16 (8)	1,375.	1,215.

R2

R3

R4

Litho. by Japan Printing Bureau.

1959-69		Wmk. 257		Perf. 13x13½	
R17	R2	1c	**red brown**	3.00	1.90
R18	R2	3c	**red**	3.00	1.10
R19	R2	5c	**violet**	5.50	3.25
R20	R2	10c	**bluish green**	10.00	6.00
R21	R2	20c	**orange brown** ('69)	80.00	55.00
R22	R2	30c	**sepia** ('69)	100.00	65.00
R23	R2	50c	**ultramarine**	40.00	14.00
			Engr.		
R24	R3	$1	**olive**	45.00	12.50
R25	R3	$2	**vermilion** ('69)	250.00	50.00
R26	R3	$3	**purple** ('69)	450.00	60.00
R27	R3	$5	**orange**	120.00	45.00
R28	R3	$10	**dark green**	180.00	60.00
R29	R4	$20	**carmine** ('69)	1,500.	200.00
R30	R4	$30	**blue** ('69)	1,750.	*1,250.*
R31	R4	$50	**black** ('69)	2,000.	*1,750.*
			Nos. R17-R28 (12)	1,287.	373.75

UNEMPLOYMENT INSURANCE

These stamps, when affixed in an official booklet and canceled, certified a one-day contract for a day laborer. They were available to employers at certain post offices on various islands.

Dove — RQ1

Shield — RQ2

Lithographed in Naha

1961, Jan. 10		Without Gum	Unwmk.	Roulette	
RQ1	RQ1	2c	**pale red**	800.00	—
RQ2	RQ2	4c	**violet**	60.00	60.00

Redrawn

Lithographed by Japan Printing Bureau

1966, Feb.		Unwmk.		Perf. 13x13½	
RQ3	RQ1	2c	**pale red**	—	—
RQ4	RQ2	4c	**violet**	25.00	25.00

Redrawn stamps have bolder numerals and inscriptions, and fewer, stronger lines of shading in background.

Cycad — RQ3

Lithographed by Japan Printing Bureau

1968, Apr. 19		Wmk. 257		Perf. 13x13½	
RQ5	RQ3	8c	**brown**	30.00	30.00

Nos. RQ3-RQ4 Surcharged

1967-72					
RQ6	RQ1	8c on 2c	**pale red**	60.00	60.00
RQ7	RQ2	8c on 4c	**violet** ('72)	30.00	30.00
RQ8	RQ2	12c on 4c	**violet** ('71)	25.00	25.00

A 4-cent "stamp" picturing Iriomote Park was originally planned for postage in 1971. Its use was changed, and it became a label that was used on the "Ryukyu Islands Emergency Conversion Confirmation Certificate." Value, $250 unused, $225 on document.

PROVISIONAL ISSUES MIYAKO

Stamps of Japan 1938-42 Handstamped in Black, Red or Orange

1948		Typo., Litho., Engr.	Wmk. 257	Perf. 13
3XR1	A84	3s **brown,** #329	60.00	—
a.		Double overprint	—	
3XR2	A86	5s **brown lake,** #331	60.00	—
a.		Horiz. pair, one without revenue overprint	*1,500.*	—
b.		Double overprint	—	
c.		Triple overprint	—	
d.		Quadruple overprint	—	
3XR3	A152	20s **blue,** #338 (R)	40.00	—
a.		Double overprint	—	
b.		Pair, one without overprint	—	
3XR4	A95	25s **dark brown & pale brown,** #270 (R)	40.00	—
a.		Black overprint	600.00	—
b.		Double overprint	—	
c.		Black double overprint	—	
3XR5	A96	30s **bluish green,** #271 (R)	40.00	—
a.		Double overprint	—	
b.		Triple overprint	—	
3XR6	A154	40s **dark violet,** #342 (R)	40.00	—
a.		Double overprint	—	
3XR7	A97	50s **olive & pale olive,** #272 (R)	120.00	
a.		Orange overprint	*500.00*	—
b.		Double overprint	—	

Doubled handstamps are known on all values and pairs with one stamp without handstamp exist on the 5s and 20s.

PROVISIONAL ISSUES YAEYAMA

In addition to the continued use of the then-current Japanese revenue stamps in stock from the wartime period, the varying authorities of the Yaeyama Gunto issued three district-specific revenue series, with a total of 28 values. Only those values at present verified by surviving examples are indicated. Numbers are reserved for other values believed to have been issued, but as yet not seen and verified.

No. 5XR2 — R5

No. 5XR3 — R6

No. 5XR5 — R7

No. 5XR27 — R8

1946 (?) **Without Gum** ***Imperf.***

Value printed, frame handstamped

5XR1 R5 3s **vermilion & black** —
5XR2 R5 10s **vermilion & black** — —

Validating handstamp below

5XR3 R6 1y **vermilion & black** — —

Civil Administration Issues
Value printed, frame handstamped
Cream Paper

1947 (?) **Without Gum** ***Imperf.***

5XR5 R7 10s **vermilion & black** —
5XR6 R7 50s **vermilion & black** — —

Gunto Government Issues
Value printed, frame handstamped
Cream Paper

1950 (?) **Without Gum** ***Imperf.***

5XR17 R8 10s **vermilion & black** —
5XR18 R8 50s **vermilion & black** —
a. 50s **vermilion & blue** —
5XR20 R8 1.50y **vermilion & black** —
5XR22 R8 5y **vermilion & black** —
5XR24 R8 20y **vermilion & black** — —
5XR27 R8 100y **vermilion & black** —

Nos. 5XR17-5XR27 are known with rough perforations, full or partial.

SPECIMEN STAMPS

Regular stamps and postal cards of 1958-65 overprinted with three cursive syllabics *mi-ho-n* ("specimen").

Type A

1961-64 **Overprinted in Black**

91S 3c (B) **multicolored** *(1,000)* 200.00
118S 3c (A) **multicolored** *(1,100)* 400.00
119S 3c (A) **multicolored** *(1,100)* 350.00

Type B

1964-65 **Overprinted in Red or Black**

120aS 3c (B) **deep blue, deep carmine & ocher** (R) *(1,500)* 180.00
121S 3c (B) **multicolored** (R) *(1,500)* 160.00
124S 3c (B) **ultra, yel & red** (R) *(5,000)* 30.00
125S 3s (B) **dull claret, yel & black** *(1,500)* 65.00
126S 3c (B) **yellow & multi** *(2,000)* 55.00
127S 3c (B) **gray, red & black** *(2,000)* 55.00
128S 3c (B) **multicolored** *(1,500)* 65.00
129S 1½c (B) **multicolored** (R) *(1,500)* 65.00
130S 3c (B) **light blue & multi** (R) *(1,500)* 180.00
131S 3c (B) **multicolored** (R) *(1,500)* 55.00
132S 3c (B) **buff & multicolored** *(2,000)* 55.00
133S 3c (B) **green & multi** (R) *(2,000)* 45.00
134S 3c (B) **multicolored** *(2,000)* 45.00
135S 3c (B) **blue & multicolored** *(2,000)* 45.00
136S 3c (B) **golden brown & multi** *(2,000)* 45.00
139S 1½c (B) **multicolored** (R) *(2,500)* 45.00

POSTAL CARDS

1964-65

Overprinted Type A or B in Black or Red

UX26S A 1½c **multicolored** *(1,000)* 450.00
UX27S B 1½c **multicolored** *(1,000)* 325.00
UX28S A 1½c **multicolored** *(1,000)* 275.00
UX29S A 1½c **multicolored** *(1,100)* 225.00

See also Nos. 46TCS and 48TCS following Proofs and Trial Color Proofs.

PROOFS AND TRIAL COLOR PROOFS

1948

1aP2 5s **magenta,** sm die on salmon paper, imperf., without gum —
2aP2 10s **yellow green,** sm die on salmon paper, imperf., without gum —
3aP2 20s **yellow green,** sm die on salmon paper, imperf., without gum —
5aP2 40s **magenta,** sm die on salmon paper, imperf., without gum —
6aP2 50s **ultramarine,** sm die on salmon paper, imperf., without gum —
7aP2 1y **ultramarine,** sm die on salmon paper, imperf., without gum —

Nos. 1aP2-7aP2 are each unique and with stamp-size margins. They may be plate proofs.

Between the printing of Nos. 1a-7a and Nos. 1-7, essay sheets of the series were prepared in Tokyo and overprinted with a swirl-pattern of blue or red dots. These essays sell for about $800 each.

Except for No. 12TC5 4y olive, the proofs and trial color proofs of Nos. 8-13, 18, C1-C3 and E1 are from special plates of 9 subjects.

1950

8TC5 50s plate on soft white paper, imperf., without gum
a. **rose** 1,500.
b. **green** 1,500.
8P5 50s **dark carmine rose,** plate on gummed soft white paper, imperf. 1,250.
9TC5 1y plate on soft white paper, imperf., without gum
a. **rose** 1,500.
b. **green** 1,500.
9P5 1y **deep blue,** plate on gummed soft white paper, imperf. 1,250.
10TC5 2y plate on soft white paper, imperf., without gum
a. **rose** 1,500.
b. **green** 1,500.
10P5 2y **rose violet,** plate on gummed soft white paper, imperf. 1,250.
11TC5 3y plate on soft white paper, imperf., without gum
a. **rose** 1,500.
b. **green** 1,500.
11P5 3y **carmine rose,** plate on gummed soft white paper, imperf. 1,250.
12TC5 4y plate on soft white paper, imperf., without gum
a. **rose** 1,500.
b. **olive** 1,500.
12P5 4y **greenish gray,** plate on gummed soft white paper, imperf. 1,250.
13TC5 5y plate on soft white paper, imperf., without gum
a. **rose** 1,500.
b. **green** 1,500.
13P5 5y **blue green,** plate on gummed soft white paper, imperf. 1,250.

1951 **From plates of 50**

14P5 3y **red brown,** plate on soft white paper, imperf., without gum 750.

From plates of 80

15P5 3y **dark green,** plate on soft white paper, imperf., without gum 550.

1952 **From plates of 18**

18TC5 3y plate on whitish paper, imperf, with gum
a. **pale salmon** 1,500.
b. **scarlet** 1,500.
c. **red orange** 2,000.

Perforated, gummed proof sheets of Nos. 18, 27 and 28 with oversized, untrimmed selvage were printed for display purposes.

The sheets no longer exist. The imprint block of No. 18 exists, plus one single each (with mihon marking) of Nos. 27 and 28.

1958 **From plates of 100**

46TC5 2c **black,** plate on off white paper, imperf., without gum 700.
48TC5 4c **black,** plate on off white paper, imperf., without gum 700.

AIR POST

1950

C1TC5 8y plate on soft white paper, imperf., without gum
a. **rose** 1,500.
b. **light green** 1,500.
C1P5 8y **bright blue,** plate on gummed soft white paper, imperf. 1,250.
C2TC5 12y plate on soft white paper, imperf., without gum
a. **rose** 1,500.
b. **light green** 1,500.
C2P5 12y **green,** plate on gummed soft white paper, imperf. 1,250.
C3TC5 16y plate on soft white paper, imperf., without gum
a. **rose** 1,500.
C3P5 16y **rose carmine,** plate on gummed soft white paper, imperf. 1,250.

1951 **From plates of 50**

C4P5 13y **blue,** plate on soft white paper, imperf., without gum 850.
C5P5 18y **green,** plate on soft white paper, imperf., without gum 850.
C6P5 30y **cerise,** plate on soft white paper, imperf., without gum 700.

SPECIAL DELIVERY

1950

E1TC5 5y plate on soft white paper, imperf., without gum
a. **rose** 1,500.
b. **green** 1,500.
E1P5 5y **bright blue,** plate on gummed soft white paper, imperf. 1,250.

Official proof folders contain one each of Nos. 8P5-13P5, 12TC5b, C1P5-C3P5 and E1P5. The stamps are securely adhered to the folder. Value, $9,000.

Similar folders exist containing photographs of die proofs in black of the same issues and mockups of Nos. U2, UX3 and UY3.

KUME ISLAND

Plate on U.S. Official Watermarked White Bond Paper

1945 **Imperf., Without Gum**

Seal Handstamped in Vermilion

1X1P5 7s **black** *3,500.*
a. "7" and "SEN" one letter space to left, pos. 8 *4,500.*

SPECIMEN OVERPRINTS ON TRIAL COLOR PROOFS

1961 **Overprinted in Vermillion**

46TCS5 2c **black** *(100)* *750.*
48TCS5 4c **black** *(100)* *750.*

Cursive type used for these two trial color proofs is different from the mihon overprints.

TUBERCULOSIS PREVENTION SEALS

Issued by the Ryukyu Tuberculosis Prevention Association (1952-71) in panes of 100 (Nos. WX1 and WX5) and 20 (Nos. WX2-WX4 and WX6-WX20). The sale of seals provided income beyond government funding for treatment. Seals were sold by the pane for the price of 1 Yen (1952-58) or 1¢ (1959-71) per seal.

Nos. WX1 and WX1a are overprinted U.S. Christmas seals (Nos. WX159-WX160). Nos. WX2-WX20 were printed for the Ryukyu Tuberculosis Prevention Association by the Japan Printing Bureau. Nos. WX2-WX20 bear a year date and the word "GREETINGS." Nos. WX2-WX4 show "RYUKYUS" in kanji, and Nos. WX5-WX20 show "RYUKYUS" in both kanji and English.

Nos. WX1-WX20 were printed on unwatermarked paper. Values are for unused seals with original gum.

Designer — Tom Darling.

1952 Overprinted in Black *Perf. 12½x12*

WX1	CS46 **green, red, yellow & black** *(600,000)*	4.00
	Pane of 100	450.00
	Imprint single	10.00
	Imprint block of 4	25.00
a.	Perf 12½	4.50
	Pane of 100	500.00
	Imprint single	20.00
	Imprint block of 4	35.00

Lithographed by Eureka Specialty Co. (No. WX1) and United States Printing and Lithographing Co. (No. WX1a).

Panes of the 1952 Christmas seals (U.S. Nos. WX159 and WX160) were donated by the National Tuberculosis Association and overprinted "Ryu-Kyu" in kanji by the Koshun Insatsusho in Naha. Printer's marks appear on seal 56 in each pane of 100: "E" for Eureka Specialty Printing Co.; "U" for United States Printing and Lithographing Co. Panes printed by the Strobridge Lithographing Co. ("S"), Edwards & Deutch Lithographing Co. ("D") and the Fleming-Potter Co., Inc. ("F") may also have been overprinted, but these have not been verified.

Imprint appears in selvage below seal 100; imprint of Union Local No. 41 on No. WX1, and imprint of Union Local No. 1 on No. WX1a.

TBS1

Designer — Adaniya Masayoshi.

1953 *Perf. 13x13¼*

WX2	TBS1 **green, red, & buff** *(780,000)*	2.00
	On cover	—
	Pane of 20, perf through top and bottom selvage	30.00
	Imprint single, type I	5.00
	Imprint block of 6	15.00
	Pane of 20, perf through top selvage only	30.00
	Imprint single, type I	5.00
	Imprint block of 6	15.00
a.	Imperf *(20,000)*	100.00
	Pane of 20	2,250.
	Imprint single, type I	150.00
	Imprint block of 6	750.00

Imprint appears in selvage below seal 19.

TBS2

Designer — Adaniya Masayoshi.

1954

WX3	TBS2 **light green, red, & black** *(780,000)*	2.00
	Pane of 20, perf through top and bottom selvage	30.00
	Imprint single, type I	5.00
	Imprint block of 6	15.00
	Pane of 20, perf through top selvage only	30.00
	Imprint single, type I	5.00
	Imprint block of 6	15.00
a.	Imperf *(20,000)*	
	Pane of 20	
	Imprint single, type I	
	Imprint block of 6	

Imprint appears in selvage below seal 19.
Editors would like to see examples of No. WX3a.

TBS3

Designer — Adaniya Masayoshi.

1955

WX4	TBS3 **carmine red, apple green & black** *(1,180,000)*	2.00
	Pane of 20, perf through top and bottom selvage	20.00
	Imprint single, type I	5.00
	Imprint block of 6	10.00
	Pane of 20, perf through top selvage only	20.00
	Imprint single, type I	5.00
	Imprint block of 6	10.00
a.	Imperf *(20,000)*	3.00
	Pane of 20	50.00
	Imprint single, type I	5.00
	Imprint block of 6	20.00

Imprint appears in selvage below seal 19.

TBS4

Designer — Adaniya Masayoshi.

1956

WX5	TBS4 **cobalt, carmine red, yellow & black** *(1,460,000)*	2.00
	Pane of 100, perf through top and bottom selvage	150.00
	Imprint single, type I	5.00
	Imprint block of 10	40.00
	Control No. strip of 3	15.00
a.	Imperf *(40,000)*	5.00
	Pane of 100	300.00
	Imprint single, type I	20.00
	Imprint block of 10	80.00
	Control No. strip of 3	50.00

Imprint appears in selvage below seal 98. Five-digit control number appear in right selvage next to seals 20 and 30, or 20, 30 and 40.

Two types of Marginal Imprint on Nos. WX6-WX20

大蔵省印刷局製造
Type I

GOVERNMENT PRINTING BUREAU, TOKYO
Type II

TBS5

Designer — Yamazato Keiichi.

1957

WX6	TBS5 **orange yellow, black, red & light blue** *(1,750,000)*	1.00
	Pane of 20, perf through top and bottom selvage	15.00
	Imprint single, type I	2.00
	Imprint block of 4, type I	4.00
	Imprint single, type II	2.00
	Imprint block of 4, type II	4.00
a.	Imperf *(50,000)*	2.00
	Pane of 20	20.00
	Imprint single, type I	4.00
	Imprint block of 4, type I	10.00
	Imprint single, type II	4.00
	Imprint block of 4, type II	10.00

Imprint type I appears in selvage below seal 20; imprint type II appears in selvage below seal 17. Legend printed in Japanese in right selvage.

TBS6

Designer — Adaniya Masayoshi.

1958 *Perf. 13¼x13*

WX7	TBS6 **yellow, blue, carmine red & black** *(1,900,000)*	.50
	Pane of 20, perf through left and right selvage	8.00
	Imprint single, type I	2.00
	Imprint block of 4, type I	3.00
	Imprint single, type II	2.00
	Imprint block of 4, type II	3.00
a.	Imperf *(80,000)*	2.00
	Pane of 20	20.00
	Imprint single, type I	4.00
	Imprint block of 4, type I	10.00
	Imprint single, type II	4.00
	Imprint block of 4, type II	10.00
b.	Perf 11*(20,000)*	10.00
	Pane of 20	200.00
	Imprint single, type I	25.00
	Imprint block of 4, type I	75.00
	Imprint single, type II	25.00
	Imprint block of 4, type II	75.00

Imprint type I appears in selvage below seal 20; imprint type II appears in selvage below seal 16. Legend printed in Japanese in top selvage. A total of 1,000 imperforate sheets were later perforated (No. WX7b), by order of the Ryukyu Tuberculosis Prevention Association.

TBS7

Designer — Tamanaha Seikichi.

1959 *Perf. 13x13¼*

WX8	TBS7 **vermilion, mauve, ultramarine & indigo** *(2,100,000)*	.50
	Pane of 20, perf through top and bottom selvage	8.00
	Imprint single, type I	2.00
	Imprint block of 4, type I	3.00
	Imprint single, type II	2.00
	Imprint block of 4, type II	3.00
a.	Imperf *(200,000)*	2.00
	Pane of 20	20.00
	Imprint single, type I	4.00
	Imprint block of 4, type I	10.00
	Imprint single, type II	4.00
	Imprint block of 4, type II	10.00

Imprint type I appears in selvage below seal 20; imprint type II appears in selvage below seal 17. Legend printed in Japanese in right selvage.

TBS8

Designer — Oshiro Kohya.

1960 *Perf. 13¼x13*

WX9	TBS8 **scarlet, orange, cobalt, bright blue & black** *(2,450,000)*	.50
	Pane of 20, perf through left and right selvage	8.00
	Imprint single, type I	2.00
	Imprint block of 4, type I	3.00
	Imprint single, type II	2.00
	Imprint block of 4, type II	3.00
a.	Imperf *(50,000)*	2.00
	Pane of 20	20.00
	Imprint single, type I	4.00
	Imprint block of 4, type I	10.00
	Imprint single, type II	4.00
	Imprint block of 4, type II	10.00

Imprint type I appears in selvage below seal 20; imprint type II appears in selvage below seal 16. Legend printed in Japanese in top selvage.

TBS9

Designer — Omine Seikan.

1961 *Perf. 13x13¼*

WX10	TBS9 **multicolored** *(3,450,000)*	.30
	Pane of 20, perf through top and bottom selvage	6.00
	Imprint single, type I	.80
	Imprint block of 4, type I	2.00
	Imprint single, type II	.80
	Imprint block of 4, type II	2.00
a.	Imperf *(50,000)*	1.00
	Pane of 20	12.00
	Imprint single, type I	3.00
	Imprint block of 4, type I	6.00
	Imprint single, type II	3.00
	Imprint block of 4, type II	6.00

Imprint type I appears in selvage below seal 20; imprint type II appears in selvage below seal 17. Legend printed in Japanese in right selvage.

TBS10

Designer — Kabira Choshin.

1962 *Perf. 13¼*

WX11	TBS10 **multicolored** *(3,450,000)*	.30
	Pane of 20, perf through top and bottom selvage	5.00
	Imprint single, type I	.60
	Imprint block of 6, type I	1.50
	Imprint single, type II	.60
	Imprint block of 6, type II	1.50
a.	Imperf *(50,000)*	.50
	Pane of 20	7.00
	Imprint single, type I	1.00
	Imprint block of 6, type I	2.50
	Imprint single, type II	1.00
	Imprint block of 6, type II	2.50

Imprint type I appears in selvage below seal 19; imprint type II appears in selvage below seal 17. Legend printed in English in left selvage and in Japanese in right selvage.

TBS11

Designer — Kabira Choshin.

1963 *Perf. 13x13¼*

WX12	TBS11 **multicolored** *(3,450,000)*	.30
	Pane of 20, perf through top and bottom selvage	5.00
	Imprint single, type I	.60
	Imprint block of 4, type I	1.50
	Imprint single, type II	.60
	Imprint block of 4, type II	1.50
a.	Imperf *(50,000)*	.50
	Pane of 20	7.00
	Imprint single, type I	1.00
	Imprint block of 4, type I	2.50
	Imprint single, type II	1.00
	Imprint block of 4, type II	2.50

Imprint type I appears in selvage below seal 20; imprint type II appears in selvage below seal 17. Legend printed in Japanese in right selvage.

TBS12

Designer — Kabira Choshin.

1964

WX13	TBS12 **multicolored** *(3,650,000)*	.30
	Pane of 20, perf through top and bottom selvage	5.00
	Imprint single, type I	.60
	Imprint block of 4, type I	1.50
	Imprint single, type II	.60
	Imprint block of 4, type II	1.50
a.	Imperf *(50,000)*	.50
	Pane of 20	7.00
	Imprint single, type I	1.00
	Imprint block of 4, type I	2.50
	Imprint single, type II	1.00
	Imprint block of 4, type II	2.50

Imprint type I appears in selvage below seal 20; imprint type II appears in selvage below seal 17. Legend printed in English in left selvage and in Japanese in right selvage.

TBS13

Designer — Oyama Masaru.

1965 *Perf. 13¼x13*

WX14	TBS13 **dark blue, light green, carmine & pink** *(3,700,000)*	.30
	Pane of 20, perf through left and right selvage	5.00
	Imprint single, type I	.60
	Imprint block of 4, type I	1.50
	Imprint single, type II	.60
	Imprint block of 4, type II	1.50
a.	Imperf *(100,000)*	.50
	Pane of 20	7.00
	Imprint single, type I	1.00
	Imprint block of 4, type I	2.50
	Imprint single, type II	1.00
	Imprint block of 4, type II	2.50

Imprint type I appears in selvage below seal 20; imprint type II appears in selvage below seal 16. Legend printed in English in top selvage and in Japanese in top and bottom selvage.

TBS14

Designer — Kabira Choshin.

1966 *Perf. 13x13¼*

WX15	TBS14 **dark green, yellow & carmine** *(3,700,000)*	.30
	Pane of 20, perf through top and bottom selvage	5.00
	Imprint single, type I	.60
	Imprint block of 4, type I	1.50
	Imprint single, type II	.60
	Imprint block of 4, type II	1.50
a.	Imperf *(100,000)*	.50
	Pane of 20	7.00
	Imprint single, type I	1.00
	Imprint block of 4, type I	2.50
	Imprint single, type II	1.00
	Imprint block of 4, type II	2.50

Imprint type I appears in selvage below seal 20; imprint type II appears in selvage below seal 17. Legend printed in English in left selvage and in Japanese in right selvage.

TBS15

Designer — Kabira Choshin.

1967

WX16	TBS15 **blue, carmine, yellow & black** *(4,100,000)*	.30
	Pane of 20, perf through top and bottom selvage	5.00
	Imprint single, type I	.60
	Imprint block of 4, type I	1.50
	Imprint single, type II	.60
	Imprint block of 4, type II	1.50
a.	Imperf *(100,000)*	.50
	Pane of 20	7.00
	Imprint single, type I	1.00
	Imprint block of 4, type I	2.50
	Imprint single, type II	1.00
	Imprint block of 4, type II	2.50

Imprint type I appears in selvage below seal 20; imprint type II appears in selvage below seal 17. Legend printed in English in left selvage and in Japanese in right selvage.

TBS16

Designer — Kabira Choshin.

1968

WX17	TBS16 **blue, carmine & black** *(4,400,000)*	.30
	Pane of 20, perf through top and bottom selvage	5.00
	Imprint single, type I	.60
	Imprint block of 4, type I	1.50
	Imprint single, type II	.60
	Imprint block of 4, type II	1.50
a.	Imperf *(100,000)*	.50
	Pane of 20	7.00
	Imprint single, type I	1.00
	Imprint block of 4, type I	2.50
	Imprint single, type II	1.00
	Imprint block of 4, type II	2.50

Imprint type I appears in selvage below seal 20; imprint type II appears in selvage below seal 17. Legend printed in English in left selvage and in Japanese in right selvage.

TBS17

Designer — Oshiro Kohya.

1969

WX18	TBS17 **multicolored** *(4,600,000)*	.30
	Pane of 20, perf through top and bottom selvage	5.00
	Imprint single, type I	.60
	Imprint block of 4, type I	1.50
	Imprint single, type II	.60
	Imprint block of 4, type II	1.50
a.	Imperf *(100,000)*	.50
	Pane of 20	7.00
	Imprint single, type I	1.00
	Imprint block of 4, type I	2.50
	Imprint single, type II	1.00
	Imprint block of 4, type II	2.50

Imprint type I appears in selvage below seal 20; imprint type II appears in selvage below seal 17. Legend printed in English in left selvage and in Japanese in right selvage.

TBS18

Designer — Kabira Choshin.

1970

WX19	TBS18 **multicolored** *(4,650,000)*	.30
	Pane of 20, perf through top and bottom selvage	5.00
	Imprint single, type I	.60
	Imprint block of 4, type I	1.50
	Imprint single, type II	.60
	Imprint block of 4, type II	1.50
a.	Imperf *(50,000)*	.50
	Pane of 20	7.00
	Imprint single, type I	1.00
	Imprint block of 4, type I	2.50
	Imprint single, type II	1.00
	Imprint block of 4, type II	2.50

Imprint type I appears in selvage below seal 20; imprint type II appears in selvage below seal 17. Legend printed in English in left selvage and in Japanese in right selvage.

TBS19

Designer — Ashimine Kinsei.

1971

WX20	TBS19 **multicolored** *(4,650,000)*	.30
	Pane of 20, perf through top and bottom selvage	5.00
	Imprint single, type I	.60
	Imprint block of 4, type I	1.50
	Imprint single, type II	.60
	Imprint block of 4, type II	1.50
a.	Imperf *(50,000)*	.50
	Pane of 20	7.00
	Imprint single, type I	1.00
	Imprint block of 4, type I	2.50
	Imprint single, type II	1.00
	Imprint block of 4, type II	2.50

Imprint type I appears in selvage below seal 20; imprint type II appears in selvage below seal 17. Legend printed in English in left selvage and in Japanese in right selvage.

Glossary of philatelic terms

This glossary defines nearly 300 terms frequently encountered by stamp collectors and cover collectors. Precise definitions for many philatelic terms do not exist. One collector, dealer or society may define a term in one way, while others will use the term in a slightly different way.

A

Accessories: Various products and tools commonly used by the stamp collector, including hinges, mounts, stamp tongs, perforation gauges, stock books and magnifiers. Stamp albums, catalogs and philatelic literature can also be regarded as accessories.

Adhesive: 1) The gum on the back of a stamp or label. Some stamps have been issued with no adhesive. Stamp adhesive may be water-activated or pressure-sensitive (self-adhesive). 2) A word generally referring to a stamp that may be affixed to an article to prepay postal fees, in contrast to a design printed directly on an article, as with postal stationery. An adhesive can also refer to a registration label or other label added to a cover.

Admirals: A nickname for three British Commonwealth definitive series, those of Canada, 1912-25 (Scott 104-34); New Zealand, 1926 (182-84); and Rhodesia, 1913-19 (119-38). These stamps depict King George V of Great Britain in naval uniform.

Aerogram: A postage-paid airletter sheet with gummed flaps that is written on and then folded to form an envelope. Aerograms are normally carried at less than the airmail letter rate. No enclosures are permitted.

Aerophilately: A specialized area of collecting concentrating on stamps or covers transported by air.

Agency: 1) An extraterritorial post office maintained at various times by a government within the territory of another government. Examples are the post offices maintained by many European powers in the Turkish Empire until 1923. 2) An organization authorized to publicize or sell new issues of stamps on behalf of a stamp-issuing entity.

Air labels: Air labels, or etiquettes, are used by Universal Postal Union member nations to denote airmail carriage. They are inscribed "Par Avion" (French for "By Airmail"). The text usually includes the same message in the language of the country of origin. Air labels also are adhesives issued by private organizations for specific, unofficial flights.

Airmail: The carriage of mail by air. The first regular airmail service began in 1870, when mail was carried from Paris-then besieged by German forces-over enemy lines by balloon. Many countries have issued postage stamps, stamped envelopes, postal cards and aerograms specially designated for airmail use. The first airmail stamp was issued by Italy in 1917 (Italy Scott C1).

Albino: An uninked impression made by a printing plate. Such errors are scarce on stamps. They are found more frequently on postal stationery.

Album: A binder and pages designed for the mounting and display of stamps or covers. Many early albums were permanently bound books. Albums come in many sizes, styles and themes. See the Album section in this almanac.

Album weed: In general, a forged stamp. It also refers to unusual items that resemble postage stamps but were not intended to pay postage, like publicity labels and bogus issues. Album Weeds is the title of a reference book series on forged stamps, written by the Rev. Robert Brisco Ear E.

Aniline: Ink with a coal-tar base. Aniline inks are very sensitive and may dissolve in water or other liquids or chemicals. To prevent the erasure of cancellations and reuse of stamps, aniline inks were used to print some stamps.

Approvals: Priced selections of stamps or covers sent to collectors by mail. The collector purchases the items he chooses, returning the rest to the approval dealer with payment for the purchased items.

Army Post Office: An official United States post office established for use by U.S. military units abroad. An army post office (APO) or military post office is set up to distribute mail to and from military personnel. The APO is indicated by numbers during wartime to prevent revealing personnel locations. The locations become generally known after the conflict ends.

Arrow: On many sheets of stamps, V-shaped arrowlike markings appear in the selvage, generally serving as guides for cutting the sheets into predetermined units. Some collectors save stamps or blocks displaying these marks.

As is: A term written in auction descriptions, or spoken or written during a retail transaction. It indicates that an item or lot is sold without guarantee or return privilege. Stamps are usually sold "as is" when they are damaged or are possibly not genuine.

ATM: 1) In the United States, panes of self-adhesive stamps on a liner the approximate size and shape of U.S. currency, designed for dispensing from automatic teller machines. 2) "Automatenmarken," automatic stamps produced individually by a machine; see also Frama.

Auction: A sale of stamps, covers and other philatelic items where prospective purchasers place bids in an attempt to obtain the desired items. The highest bidder for each lot (described item or items) makes the purchase. Auctions are generally divided into mail sales, where bids are accepted by mail, and public sales, where mail bids are combined with live bidding from individuals present at the auction or participating by telephone.

Authentication mark: A marking, such as initials, placed on the reverse of a stamp examined and certified to be genuine by an expert. Such markings do not detract from the value of the stamps when they represent the endorsement of recognized authorities.

APO: Army Post Office. An official United States post office established for use by U.S. military units abroad. An army post office or military post office is set up to distribute mail to and from military personnel. The APO is indicated by numbers during wartime to prevent revealing personnel locations. The locations become generally known after the conflict ends.

B

Backprint: Printing on the reverse of a stamp. Some stamps have numbers, symbols, advertising or information about the stamp subject printed on the reverse of the stamp.

Backstamp: A postmark applied to mail by the receiving post office or by a post office handling the piece while it is in transit. Backstamps are usually on the back of a cover, but they can be on the front.

Bank mixture: A high-quality mixture of stamps. It generally represents clippings from the mail of banks or other businesses with extensive overseas correspondence, and thus includes a relatively high proportion of foreign stamps of high face value. See also Mission mixture.

Bantams: The nickname of the South African definitive series of 1942-43 (Scott 90-97). Wartime economy measures prompted the manufacture of stamps of small size to conserve paper.

Batonne: A wove or laid paper with watermarklike lines deliberately added in the papermaking process and intended as a guide for handwriting.

Bicolor: Printed in two colors.

Bilingual: Inscribed in two languages. Most Canadian stamps include both English and French text. South African stamps from 1926-49 were printed alternately with English and Afrikaans inscriptions in the same sheet.

Bisect: A stamp cut or perforated into two parts, each half representing half the face value of the original stamp. Officially authorized bisects have often been used during temporary shortages of commonly used denominations. Unauthorized bisects appear on mail from some countries in some periods. Bisects are usually collected on full cover with the stamp tied by a cancel. At times, some countries have permitted trisects or quadrisects.

Bishop mark: The earliest postmark, introduced by Henry Bishop in England circa 1661. A Bishop mark was used to indicate the month and day that a letter was received by a post office. It encouraged prompt delivery by letter carriers.

Black Jack: The nickname of the United States 2¢ black Andrew Jackson stamp issued between 1863 and 1875.

Blind perforation: Intended perforations that are only lightly impressed by the perforating pins, leaving the paper intact, but cut or with a faint impression. Some stamps that appear to be imperforate really are not if they have blind perfs. Stamps with blind perfs are minor varieties carrying little, if any, price premium over normally perforated copies.

Block: A unit of four or more unsevered stamps, including at least two stamps both vertically and horizontally. Most commonly a block refers to a block of four, or a block of stamps two high and two wide, though blocks often contain more stamps and may be irregularly configured (such as, a block of seven consisting of one row of three stamps and one row of four stamps).

Bluenose: The nickname for Canada Scott 158, the 50¢ issue of 1929, picturing the schooner Bluenose.

Bogus: A fictitious stamplike label created for sale to collectors. Bogus issues include labels for nonexistent countries, nonexistent values appended to regularly issued sets and issues for nations or similar entities without postal systems.

Booklet: A unit of one or more small panes or blocks (known as booklet panes) glued, stitched or stapled together between thin card covers to form a convenient unit for mailers to purchase and carry. The first officially issued booklet was produced by Luxembourg in 1895. For some modern booklets of self-adhesive stamps the liner (backing paper) serves as the booklet cover.

Bourse: A meeting of stamp collectors and/or dealers, where stamps and covers are sold or exchanged. A bourse usually has no competitive exhibits of stamps or covers. Almost all public stamp exhibitions include a dealer bourse, though many bourses are held without a corresponding exhibition.

Bull's-Eyes: 1) The nickname for the 1843 first issue of Brazil, Scott 1-3. The similar but smaller issues are called goat's eyes. 2) A bull's-eye cancel refers to a "socked-on-the-nose" postmark with the impression centered directly on the stamp so that the location and date of mailing are shown on the stamp.

Burelage: A design of fine, intricate lines printed on the face of security paper, either to discourage counterfeiting or to prevent the cleaning and reuse of a stamp. The burelage on some stamps is part of the stamp design.

Burele: Adjective form for burelage, meaning having a fine network of lines. Some stamps of Queensland have a burele band on the back. Also called moir.

C

Cachet: In French, cachet means a stamp or a seal. On a cover, the cachet is an added design or text, often corresponding to the design of the postage stamp, the mailed journey of the cover, or some type of special event. Cachets appear on modern first-day covers, first-flight covers and special-event covers.

Canceled-to-order: Stamps are "canceled to order," usually in full sheets, by many governments. The cancels may be printed on the stamps at the same time that the stamp design is printed. A stamp with a cancel and with full gum is likely a CTO stamp, as CTOs do not see actual postal use. CTO stamps are sold to stamp dealers at large discounts from face value. Most catalogs say whether they price CTO stamps or genuinely used stamps.

Cancel: A marking intended to show a stamp has been used and is no longer valid as postage. Modern cancels usually include the name of the original mailing location or a nearby sorting facility and the date of mailing. Most cancellations also include a section of lines, bars, text or a design that prints upon the postage stamp to invalidate it. This part of a cancel is called the killer.

Cantonal stamps: Issues of Switzerland's cantons (states) used before the release of national stamps. The cantonal issues of Basel (1845), Geneva (1843-50) and Zurich (1843-50) are among the classics of philately.

Cape Triangles: Common name for the triangular Cape of Good Hope stamps of 1853-64, the first stamps printed in triangular format. The distinctive shape helped illiterate postal clerks distinguish letters originating in the colony from those from other colonies.

Catalog: A comprehensive book or similar

compilation with descriptive information to help identify stamps. Many catalogs include values for the listed items. An auction catalog is published by the auction firm in advance of a planned sale to notify potential customers of the specific items that will be offered.

Catalog value: The value of a stamp as listed in a given catalog for the most common condition in which the stamp is collected. Some catalogs list stamps at a retail value, though actual dealer prices may vary substantially for reasons of condition, demand or other market factors. Most catalogs have a set minimum value for the most common stamps.

Censored mail: A cover bearing a handstamp or label indicating that the envelope has been opened and the contents inspected by a censor.

Centering: The relative position of the design of a stamp in relation to its margins. Assuming that a stamp is undamaged, centering is generally a very important factor in determining grade and value.

Certified mail: A service of most postal administrations that provides proof of mailing and delivery without indemnity for loss or damage.

Chalky paper: A chalk-surfaced paper for printing stamps. Any attempt to remove the cancel on a used chalky-paper stamp will also remove the design. Immersion of such stamps in water will cause the design to lift off. Touching chalky paper with silver will leave a discernible, pencil-like mark and is a means of distinguishing chalky paper.

Changeling: A stamp whose color has been changed-intentionally or unintentionally-by contact with a chemical or exposure to light.

Charity seals: Stamplike labels that are distributed by a charity. They have no postal validity, although they are often affixed to envelopes. United States Christmas seals are one example.

Charity stamp: see Semipostal.

Cinderella: A stamplike label that is not a postage stamp. Cinderellas include seals and bogus issues, as well as revenue stamps, local post issues and other similar items.

Classic: An early issue, often with a connotation of rarity, although classic stamps are not necessarily rare. A particularly scarce recent item may be referred to as a modern classic.

Cleaning (stamps): Soiled or stained stamps are sometimes cleaned with chemicals or by erasing. The cleaning is usually done to improve the appearance of a stamp. A cleaned stamp can also mean one from which a cancellation has been removed, making a used stamp appear unused.

Cliché: The individual unit consisting of the design of a single stamp, combined with others to make up the complete printing plate. Individual designs on modern one-piece printing plates are referred to as subjects.

Coil: Stamps processed in a long single row and prepared for sale in rolls, often for dispensing from stamp-vending and affixing machines. Some coils, including most U.S. coils, have a straight edge on two parallel sides and perforations on the remaining two parallel sides. Some coils are backprinted with sequence or counting numbers.

Collateral material: Any supportive or explanatory material relating to a given stamp or philatelic topic. The material may be either directly postal in nature (post office news releases, rate schedules, souvenir cards, promotional items) or nonpostal (maps, photos of scenes appearing on stamps).

Combination cover: Cover bearing the stamps of more than one country when separate postal charges are paid for the transport of a cover by each country. Also stamps of the same country canceled at two different times on the same cover as a souvenir.

Commatology: Specialized collecting of postmarks. This term was invented before World War II to describe postmark collecting. It is rarely used. Usually, collectors refer to postmark collecting or marcophily.

Commemorative: A stamp printed in a limited quantity and available for purchase for a limited time. The design may note an anniversary associated with an individual, an historic event, or a national landmark. See also Definitive.

Compound perforations: Different gauge perforations on different sides of a single stamp. The sides with the different gauge measurements are usually perpendicular.

Condition: The overall appearance and soundness of a stamp or cover. Positive condition factors include fresh full color, full original gum on unused stamps, and so on. Damage such as creases, tears, thinned paper, short perforation teeth, toning and so on negatively affect condition.

Controlled mail: A system in which the mailer selects philatelically desirable issues for outgoing mail, arranges for a specific manner of cancellation and secures the stamps' return by the addressee. In some cases such controlled mail operations may provide rare examples of specific rate fulfillment, or other similar postal use.

Copyright block: Block of four or more United States stamps with the copyright notice marginal marking of the United States Postal Service. The copyright marking was introduced in 1978 and replaced the Mail Early marking.

Corner card: An imprinted return address, generally in the upper-left corner of an envelope, from a commercial, institutional or private source, similar to business card or letterhead imprints.

Counterfeit: Any stamp, cancellation or cover created for deception or imitation, intended to be accepted by others as genuine. A counterfeit stamp is designed to deceive postal authorities.

Cover: An envelope or piece of postal stationery, usually one that has been mailed. Folded letters that were addressed and mailed without an envelope and the wrappers from mailed parcels are also covers.

Crash cover: A cover that has been salvaged from the crash of an airplane, train, ship or other vehicle. Such covers often carry a postal marking explaining damage or delay in delivery.

Crease: A noticeable weakening of the paper of a stamp or cover, caused by its being folded or bent at some point. Creases substantially lower a stamp's value. Creases particularly affect cover values when they extend through the attached stamp or a postal marking. Stamp creases are visible in watermark fluid.

Cut cancellation: A cancellation that intentionally slices into the stamp paper. Often a wedge-shaped section is cut away. On many issues, such cancellations indicate use of postage stamps as fiscals (revenues) or telegraph stamps rather than as postage. Cut cancellations were used experimentally on early United States postage stamps to prevent reuse.

Cut square: A neatly trimmed rectangular or square section from a stamped envelope that includes the imprinted postage stamp with ample margin. Collectors generally prefer to collect stationery as entire pieces rather than as cut squares. Some older stationery is available only in cut squares.

Cut-to-shape: A nonrectangular stamp or postal stationery imprint cut to the shape of the design, rather than cut square. Cut-to-shape stamps and stationery generally have lower value than those cut square. One of the world's most valuable stamps, the unique 1856 British Guiana "Penny Magenta" (Scott 13), is a cut-to-shape stamp.

Cylinder: A curved printing plate used on a modern rotary press. The plate has no seams. For United States stamps, cylinders are used to print gravure stamps. See also Sleeve.

Cancellation: A marking intended to show a stamp has been used and is no longer valid as postage. Modern cancels usually include the name of the original mailing location or a nearby sorting facility and the date of mailing. Most cancellations also include a section of lines, bars, text or a design that prints upon the postage stamp to invalidate it. This part of a cancel is called the killer.

CTO: Canceled-to-order. Stamps are "canceled to order," usually in full sheets, by many governments. The cancels may be printed on the stamps at the same time that the stamp design is printed. A stamp with a cancel and with full gum is likely a CTO stamp, as CTOs do not see actual postal use. CTO stamps are sold to stamp dealers at large discounts from face value. Most catalogs say whether they price CTO stamps or genuinely used stamps.

Charity stamp: A stamp sold at a price greater than postal value, with the additional charge dedicated for a special purpose. Usually recognized by the presence of two (often different) values, separated by a "+" sign, on a single stamp.

D

Dead country: A former stamp-issuing entity that has ceased issuing its own stamps. Also, the old name of an active stamp-issuing entity that has changed its name, so that the old name will no longer be used on stamps.

Definitive: Stamp issued in a large indefinite quantity and for an indefinite period, usually several years or more. The United States Presidential issue of 1938 and the 1995 32› Flag Over Porch stamps are examples. Definitive stamp designs usually do not honor a specific time-dated event.

Deltiology: Picture postcard collecting.

Denomination: The face value of a stamp, usually indicated by numerals printed as part of the design. Some modern U.S. stamps produced for rate changes are denominated with a letter. A numerical value is assigned when the letter stamps are issued. An example of this is the H-rate Hat stamp of 1998, which represented the first-class rate of 33¢.

Die: The original engraving of a stamp design, usually recess-engraved in reverse on a small flat piece of soft steel. In traditional intaglio printing, a transfer roll is made from a die and printing plates are made from impressions of the transfer roll. When more than one die is used in the production of an issue, distinctive varieties are often identifiable.

Die cut: A form of separation usually employed on self-adhesive stamps. During processing, an edged tool (die) completely penetrates the stamp paper on all sides of the printed stamp, making the removal of the individual stamps from the liner possible. Die cuts may be straight, shaped in wavy lines to simulate perforation teeth, or take other forms.

Directory markings: Postal indication of failed delivery attempt, stating the reason for failure. Examples are "No Such Number," "Address Unknown" and "Moved."

Duck stamp: Popular name for the United States Migratory Bird Hunting and Conservation stamp, issued for use on hunting licenses. Each annual stamp depicts waterfowl. Also used to describe similar issues from the various states for use by hunters or for sale to collectors.

Dummy stamp: Officially produced imitation stamp used to train employees or to test automatic stamp-dispensing machines. Dummy stamps are usually blank or carry special inscriptions, blocks or other distinguishing ornamentation. They are not valid for postage, nor are they intended to reach the hands of stamp collectors. Some do by favor of postal employees.

Duplex cancel: A two-part postal marking consisting of a canceler and a postmark. The canceler voids the stamp so it cannot be reused. The postmark notes the date and place of mailing.

Duplicate: An additional copy of a stamp that one already has in a collection. Beginners often consider stamps to be duplicates that really are not, because they overlook perforation, watermark or color varieties.

E

Earliest known use: The cover or piece that documents the earliest date on which a stamp or postal stationery item is known to be used. New discoveries can change an established EKU. The EKU for a classic issue may be after the official issue date. Because of accidental early sales, the EKU for modern stamps is often several days before the official first day.

Embossing: The process of giving relief to paper by pressing it with a die. Embossed designs are often found on the printed stamps of postal stationery (usually envelopes and wrappers). Selected stamps of certain countries have been embossed.

Encased postage stamp: A stamp inserted into a small coin-size case with a transparent front or back. Such stamps were circulated as legal coins during periods when coins were scarce.

Entire: An intact piece of postal stationery, in contrast to a cutout of the imprinted stamp. This term is sometimes used in reference to an intact cover or folded letter.

Error: A major mistake in the production of a stamp or postal stationery item. Production errors include imperforate or imperforate-between varieties, missing or incorrect colors, and inversion or doubling of part of the design or overprint. Major errors are usually far scarcer than normal varieties of the same stamp and are highly valued by collectors.

Essay: The artwork of a proposed design for a stamp. Some essays are rendered photographically. Others are drawn in pencil or ink or are painted. Most essays are rejected. One becomes the essay for the accepted design.

Etiquette: A gummed label manufactured for application to an envelope to designate a specific mail service. Airmail etiquettes are most common.

Europa: The "United Europe" theme celebrated annually on stamps of western European nations since 1956. The original Europa stamps were issued by the nations in the European coal and steel association. Today, European nations that are members of the postal and telecommunications association (CEPT) issue Europa stamps. Expertization: The examination of a stamp or cover by an acknowledged expert to determine if it is genuine. As standard procedure, an expert or expertizing body issues a signed certificate, often with an attached photograph, attesting to the item's status.

Exploded: A stamp booklet that has been separated into its various components, usually for purposes of display. Panes are removed intact: individual stamps are not separated from the pane.

Express mail: Next-day mail delivery service in the United States, inaugurated in 1977.

EKU: The cover or piece that documents the earliest date on which a stamp or postal stationery item is known to be used. New discoveries can change an established EKU. The EKU for a classic issue may be after the official issue date. Because of accidental early sales, the EKU for modern stamps is often several days before the official first day.

F

Face: The front of a stamp; the side bearing the design.

Face value: The value of a stamp as inscribed on its face. For letter-denominated or nondenominated stamps, the understood postal value of the stamp.

Facsimile: A reproduction of a genuine stamp or cover. Such items are usually made with no intent to deceive collectors or postal officials. Catalog illustrations may also be considered facsimiles. Fake: A stamp, cover or cancel that has been altered or concocted to appeal to a collector. In a broad sense, fakes include repairs, reperforations and regummed stamps, as well as painted-in cancels, bogus cancels or counterfeit markings. Sometimes entire covers are faked.

Fancy cancel: A general term to describe any pictorial or otherwise unusual obliterating postmark. More specifically, the term is used to describe elaborate handmade pictorial cancels of the 19th century, such as the Waterbury "Running Chicken" of 1869 or the many intricate geometric shapes used during that period in post offices around the country.

Farley's Follies: During 1933-34, U.S. Postmaster General James A. Farley supplied a few imperforate sheets of current commemorative issues to Pres. Franklin D. Roosevelt and other government officials. The resulting uproar from U.S. collectors forced the government to release for public sale 20 issues in generally imperforate and ungummed sheets. They are United States Scott 752-771. Numbers 752-753 are perforated.

Fast colors: Inks resistant to fading.

Field Post Office: A military postal service operating in the field, either on land or at sea. Frequently abbreviated FPO.

Find: A new discovery, usually of something that was not known to exist. It can be a single item or a hoard of stamps or covers.

First-day cover: A cover bearing a stamp tied by a cancellation showing the date of the official first day of issue of that stamp.

Fiscal: A revenue stamp or similar label denoting the payment of tax. Fiscals are ordinarily affixed to documents and canceled by pen, canceler or mutilation. Because of their similarity to postage stamps, fiscals have occasionally been used either legally or illegally to prepay postage. See also Postal fiscal, Revenues.

Flat plate: A flat metal plate used in a printing press, as opposed to a curved or cylindrical plate.

Flaw: A defect in a plate that reproduces as an identifiable variety in the stamp design.

Fleet Post Office (FPO): An official United States post office for use by U.S. military naval units abroad. Frequently abbreviated FPO.

Forerunner: A stamp or postal stationery item used in a given location prior to the issuing of regular stamps for that location. Turkish stamps before 1918 canceled in Palestine are forerunners of Israeli issues. So are the various European nations' issues for use in Palestine, and the subsequent issues of the Palestine Mandate. The term "forerunner" is also used to describe a stamp issued before another stamp or set, if the earlier issue may have influenced the design or purpose of the later issue.

Forgery: A completely fraudulent reproduction of a postage stamp. There are two general types of forgeries: those intended to defraud the postal authorities (see also Counterfeit), and those intended to defraud the collectors (see also Bogus).

Frama: A general name used for an automatic stamp, derived from the name of the Swiss firm, Frama AG, an early producer of such issues. Automatic stamps are produced individually by a machine on demand in a denomination selected by the customer. There normally is no date on the stamp, as there is on a meter stamp. Also called ATM, from the German word Automatenmarken.

Frame: The outer portion of a stamp design, often consisting of a line or a group of panels.

Frank: An indication on a cover that postage is prepaid, partially prepaid or that the letter is to be carried free of postage. Franks may be written, hand-stamped, imprinted or affixed. Free franking is usually limited to soldiers' mail or selected government correspondence. Postage stamp and postage meter stamps are modern methods of franking a letter.

Freak: An abnormal, usually nonre-petitive occurrence in the production of stamps that results in a variation from the normal stamp, but falls short of producing an error. Most paper folds, overinking and perforation shifts are freaks. Those abnormalities occurring repetitively are called varieties and may result in major errors.

Front: The front of a cover with most or all of the back and side panels torn away or removed. Fronts, while desirable if they bear unusual or uncommon postal markings, are less desirable than an intact cover.

Fugitive inks: Printing inks used in stamp production that easily fade or break up in water or chemicals. To counter attempts at forgery or the removal of cancellations, many governments have used fugitive inks to print stamps.

FPO: Field Post Office. A military postal service operating in the field, either on land or at sea. Also Fleet Post Office. An official United States post office for use by U.S. military naval units abroad.

FDC: First-day cover. A cover bearing a stamp tied by a cancellation showing the date of the official first day of issue of that stamp.

Franking: An indication on a cover that postage is prepaid, partially prepaid or that the letter is to be carried free of postage. Franks may be written, hand-stamped, imprinted or affixed. Free franking is usually limited to soldiers' mail or selected government correspondence. Postage stamp and postage meter stamps are modern methods of franking a letter.

G

Ghost tagging: The appearance of a faint image impression in addition to the normal inked impression. This is caused by misregistration of the phosphor tagging in relation to the ink. Sometimes, a plate number impression will have an entirely different number from the ink plate, giving the impression of an error: one dark (normal) number and one light (ghost) number.

Glassine: A thin, semitransparent paper that is moderately resistant to the passage of air and moisture. Envelopes made of glassine are commonly used for temporary stamp storage. Glassine is also used in the manufacture of stamp hinges.

Goldbeater's skin: A thin, tough, translucent paper. The 1886 issue of Prussia was printed in reverse on goldbeater's skin, with the gum applied over the printing. These stamps are brittle and virtually impossible to remove from the paper to which they are affixed.

Granite paper: A paper with small colored fibers added when the paper is made. This paper is used as a deterrent against forgery.

Gravure: A printing process utilizing an intaglio printing plate created by photographic and chemical means, rather than by hand engraving. See also Intaglio.

Grill: A pattern of parallel lines (or dots at the points where lines would cross) forming a grid. A grill is usually: 1) the impressed breaks added to stamps as a security measure (United States issues of 1867-71 and Peru issues of 1874-79); or 2) a grill-like canceling device used on various 19th-century issues.

Gum: The mucilage applied to the backs of adhesive postage stamps, revenue stamps or envelope flaps. Gum is an area of concern for stamp collectors. It may crack and harm the paper of the stamp itself. It may stain or adhere to other stamps or album pages under certain climatic conditions. Many collectors are willing to pay extra for 19th- and some 20th-century stamps with intact, undisturbed original gum.

Gutter: The selvage separating panes on a sheet of stamps. The gutter is usually discarded during processing. The gutter may be unprinted, or bear plate numbers, accounting or control numbers, advertising or other words or markings.

Gutter snipe: One or more stamps to which is attached the full gutter from between panes, plus any amount of an adjoining stamp or stamps. This term is typically used in reference to U.S. stamps. Gutter snipes are freaks caused by misregistration of the cutting device or paper foldover.

H

Handstamp: Cancellation or overprint applied by hand to a cover or to a stamp.

Highway Post Office (HPO): Portable mail-handling equipment for sorting mail in transit on highways (normally by truck). The last official U.S. HPO ran June 30, 1974.

Hinge: Stamp hinges are small, rectangular-shaped pieces of glassine paper, usually gummed on one side. Folded with the gummed side out, the hinge is used to mount stamps. Most modern hinges are peelable. Once dry, they may be easily removed from the stamp, leaving little trace of having been applied.

HPO: Highway Post Office. Portable mail-handling equipment for sorting mail in transit on highways (normally by truck). The last official U.S. HPO ran June 30, 1974.

I

Imperforate: Refers to stamps without perforations or rouletting between the individual stamps in a pane. The earliest stamps were imperforate by design, but after about 1860 most stamps were perforated. Modern imperforates are usually errors or are produced specifically for sale to stamp collectors.

Impression: Any stamped or embossed printing.

Imprimatur: Latin for "let it be printed." The first sheets of stamps from an approved plate, normally checked and retained in a file prior to a final directive to begin stamp production from a plate.

India paper: A thin, tough opaque printing paper of high quality used primarily for striking die proofs.

Indicium: The stamp impression of a postage meter or the imprint on postal stationery (as opposed to an adhesive stamp), indicating prepayment and postal validity. Plural: indicia.

Inscription: The letters, words and numbers that are part of a postage stamp design.

Intaglio: Italian for "in recess." A form of printing in which the inked image is produced by that portion of the plate sunk below the surface. Line engraving and gravure are forms of intaglio printing.

International Reply Coupon: A redeemable certificate issued by member nations of the Universal Postal Union to provide for return postage from recipients in other countries. IRCs are exchangeable for postage at a post office.

Invert: The term generally used to describe any error where one portion of the design is inverted in relation to the other portion(s). An overprint applied upside down is also an invert.

Inverts: The term generally used to describe any error where one portion of the design is inverted in relation to the other portion(s). An overprint applied upside down is also an invert.

IRC: International Reply Coupon. A redeemable certificate issued by member nations of the Universal Postal Union to provide for return postage from recipients in other countries. IRCs are exchangeable for postage at a post office.

J

None

K

Keytype: A basic stamp design utilized for the issues of two or more postal entities, usually differing in the country name and inscription of value. Many of the earlier colonial issues of Britain, France, Spain, Germany and Portugal are keytypes.

Kiloware: A stamp mixture consisting of miscellaneous postally used stamps on envelope corner paper from various sources. Kiloware is sometimes sold by the kilogram (about 2.2 pounds).

L

Label: Any stamplike adhesive that is not a postage stamp or revenue stamp.

Laid paper: One of the two basic types of paper used in stamp printing. Laid paper is distinguished from wove paper by the presence of thin, parallel lines visible when the paper is held to light. The lines are usually a few millimeters apart. See also Batonne.

Letterpress: Printing done directly from the inked, raised surface of the printing plate.

Line engraving: Printing done from an intaglio plate produced from a hand-engraved die and transfer roll rather than by photographic or chemical means. See also Gravure.

Line pair: A pair of coil stamps with a printed line between them. Stamps produced on a flatbed press have a line from the guideline between panes. Stamps produced on a rotary press have a joint line from the space where ink collects between the sections of curved rotary plates.

Liner: Coated paper used as a backing for mint self-adhesive stamps. The liner allows the release of the stamp, which may then be applied with pressure to envelope paper.

Linerless: An experimental form of self-adhesive coil stamp that requires no liner. The mint stamps are rolled upon each other in a manner similar to adhesive tape. See United States Scott 3132, 3133.

Lithography: Printing from a flat surface with a design area that is ink-receptive. The area that is not to print is ink-repellant. The process is based on the principle that an oil-based design surface will attract oily ink.

Locals: Stamps valid within a limited area or within a limited postal system. Local post mail requires the addition of nationally or internationally valid stamps for further service. Locals have been produced both privately and officially.

M

Machin: The name given to a well-known series of British definitive stamps first issued in 1967. The design of the stamp depicts a plaster portrait of Queen Elizabeth II created by artist Arnold Machin.

Mail Early block: U.S. marginal marking block with the selvage bearing the inscription "Mail Early (in the Day)." This first appeared on U.S. marginal selvage in 1968. It was subsequently replaced by the copyright notice. ME blocks typically consist of four or six stamps.

Makeshift booklets: U.S. stamp booklets manufactured using stamps normally issued in individual panes, packaged in generic blue cardboard covers and dispensed by vending machines.

Marcophily: Postmark collecting.

Margin: 1) The selvage surrounding the stamps in a sheet, often carrying inscriptions of various kinds. 2) The unprinted border area around the stamp design. The collectible grades of stamps are determined by the position of the design in relation to the edge of the stamp as perforated or, in the case of imperforate stamps, as cut from the sheet.

Mat: A hard rubber plate used to apply overprints on postage stamps.

Maximaphily: Maximum card collecting.

Maximum card: A picture postcard, a cancel, and a stamp presenting maximum concordance. The stamp is usually affixed to the picture side of the card and is tied by the cancel. Collectors of maximum cards seek to find or create cards with stamp, cancel and picture in maximum agreement, or concordance. The statutes of the International Federation of Philately (FIP) give specific explanatory notes for the postage stamp, the picture postcard, the cancel, concordance of subject, concordance of place and concordance of time. (See Exhibiting chapter.)

Meter: The mechanical or digital device that creates a valid denominated postage imprint known as a meter stamp. Postage is prepaid to the regulating postal authority. Meters were authorized by the UPU in 1920. They are used today by volume mailers to cut the cost of franking mail.

Microprinting: Extremely small letters or numbers added to the designs of selected United States stamps as a security feature. In most cases, 8-power magnification or greater is needed to read microprinting.

Miniature sheet: A smaller-than-normal pane of stamps issued only in that form or in addition to full panes. A miniature sheet is usually without marginal markings or text saying that the sheet was issued in conjunction with or to commemorate some event. See also Souvenir sheet.

Mint: A stamp in the same state as issued by a post office: unused, undamaged and with full original gum (if issued with gum). Over time, handling, light and atmospheric conditions may affect the mint state of stamps.

Mirror image: An offset negative or reverse impression.

Mission mixture: The lowest grade of stamp mixture, containing unsorted but primarily common stamps on paper, as purchased from missions or other institutions. See also Bank mixture.

Missionaries: The first stamps of Hawaii, issued 1851-52, considered among the great classics of philately.

Mixed perforation: See Compound perforation.

Mixed postage: The franking on a cover bearing the stamps of two or more stamp-issuing entities, properly used.

Mixture: A large group of stamps, understood to contain duplication. A mixture is said to be unpicked or picked. A picked mixture may have had stamps removed by a collector or dealer.

Mobile Post Office: Portable mail-handling equipment and personnel, generally in railroad cars, streetcars, trucks or buses.

Mount: Acetate holders, clear on the front and with some sort of adhesive on the back. Collectors use mounts to affix stamps or covers to album or exhibit pages.

Multicolor: More than two colors.

Multiple: An unseparated unit of stamps including at least two stamps, but fewer than the number included in a full pane.

ME block: U.S. marginal marking block with the selvage bearing the inscription "Mail Early (in the Day)." This first appeared on U.S. marginal selvage in 1968. It was subsequently replaced by the copyright notice. ME blocks typically consist of four or six stamps.

MPO: Mobile Post Office. Portable mail-handling equipment and personnel, generally in railroad cars, streetcars, trucks or buses.

N

Native paper: Crude, handmade paper produced locally, as opposed to finer, machine-made paper.

Never hinged: A stamp without hinge marks. A never-hinged (NH) stamp usually has original gum, but this is not always the case.

New issue service: A dealer service that automatically supplies subscribers with new issues of a given country, area or topic. The issues provided are determined by a prearranged standing order that defines the quantity and types of issues.

Newspaper stamps: Stamps issued specifically for the prepayment of mailing rates for newspapers, periodicals and printed matter.

Nondenominated: A stamp with no numerical inscription designating the face value. The value of some nondenominated stamps are marked by a designated letter. Others may have a service inscription that indicates the rate the stamp fulfills.

NH: Never Hinged. A stamp without hinge marks. A never-hinged (NH) stamp usually has original gum, but this is not always the case.

O

Obliteration: 1) A cancellation intended solely to deface a stamp-also called a killer. 2) An overprint intended to deface a portion of the design of a stamp, such as the face of a deposed ruler.

Obsolete: A stamp no longer available from post offices, although possibly still postally valid.

Occupation issue: An issue released for use in territory occupied by a foreign power.

Off-center: A stamp design that is not centered in relation to the edges of the stamp. Generally, off-center stamps are less desirable than stamps more nearly centered in relation to the edges. Stamps that are extremely off-center may be added to collections as production freaks.

Offices abroad: At various times, many nations have maintained post offices in other countries, usually because of the unreliability of the local postal system. In China and the Turkish Empire, especially, many foreign nations maintained their own postal systems as part of their extraterritorial powers. Usually, special stationery and stamps were used by these offices. Most consisted of overprints on the regular issues of the nations maintaining the offices.

Official: Stamp or stationery issued solely for the use of government departments and officials. In many countries such items may be available to collectors in unused condition from the postal authority.

Offset: 1) A printing process that transfers an inked image from a plate to a roller. The roller then applies the ink to paper. 2) The transfer of part of a stamp design or an overprint from one sheet to the back of another, before the ink has dried (also called set off). Such impressions are in reverse (see Mirror image). They are different from stamps printed on both sides.

OHMS: Abbreviation for On His (or Her) Majesty's Service. Used in perfins, overprints or franks to indicate Official use in the British Commonwealth.

Omnibus issue: An issue released by several postal entities to celebrate a common theme. Omnibus issues may or may not share a keytype design.

On paper: Stamps (usually postally used) that are affixed to portions of original envelope or wrapper. Often used to describe stamps prior to soaking.

On piece: A stamp on a portion of the original envelope or wrapper showing all or most of the cancel. Stamps on piece are usually saved that way.

Original gum (OG): The adhesive coating on a mint or unused stamp or envelope flap applied by a postal authority or security printer, usually before the item was issued. Upon request of stamp collectors, postal authorities have at times offered to add gum to items first issued ungummed. See also Regummed.

Overprint: Any printing over the original completed design of a stamp. An overprint that changes the value of a stamp is also called a surcharge.

Oxidation: Darkening of the ink on certain stamps caused by contact with air or light. Some inks used to print stamps, especially oranges, may in time turn brown or black.

P

Packet: 1) A presorted selection of all-different stamps, a common and economical way to begin a general collection; 2) a ship operating on a regular schedule and contracted by a government or post office to carry mail.

Packet letter: A letter carried by a ship operating on a regular schedule and carrying mail by contract with a government or a post office.

Pair: Two unseparated stamps.

Pane: The unit into which a full press sheet is divided before sale at post offices. What a post office customer may refer to as a "sheet of stamps" is more properly called a pane. Most United States full sheets are divided into four or more regular panes or many more booklet panes before they are shipped to post offices.

Paquebot: Cancellation indicating an item was mailed aboard a ship.

Par Avion: A French phrase meaning "By

Air," it appears on airmail etiquettes of most countries, along with a similar phrase in the predominant language of the country of origin.

Parcel post stamps: Special stamps created for payment of parcel post fees.

Part-perforate: A stamp with all perforations missing on one or more sides, but with at least one side perforated.

Paste-up: The ends of rolls of coiled stamps joined together with glue or tape.

Pelure paper: A strong, thin paper occasionally used in stamp printing. Pelure paper is translucent and resembles a slightly dark, thin onion-skin paper.

Pen canceled: Stamps canceled with an ink pen or marker pen rather than a handstamp or machine cancel. Many early stamps were routinely canceled by pen. A pen cancel may also indicate that a stamp was used as a fiscal. Modern stamps may be pen canceled if a sorting clerk or delivery carrier notices a stamp has been missed by a canceling machine.

Penny Black: The black 1-penny British stamp issued May 6, 1840, bearing the portrait of Queen Victoria. It is the world's first adhesive stamp issued for the prepayment of postage.

Perfins: Stamps perforated through the face with identifying initials, designs or holes in coded positions. Perfins are normally used by a business or government office to discourage pilferage or misuse of stamps by employees. Perfins may be either privately or officially produced.

Perforation: The punching out of holes between stamps to make separation easy. 1) Comb perforation-three sides of a stamp are perforated at once, with the process repeated in rows. 2) Harrow perforation-the entire sheet or unit of stamps is perforated in one operation. 3) Line perforation-holes are punched one row at a time. Line perforations are distinguished by the uneven crossing of perforation lines and irregular corners. Comb and harrow perforations usually show alignment of holes at the corners. Some forms of perforation may be difficult to distinguish.

Perforation gauge: A scale printed or designed on metal, transparent or opaque plastic, cardboard or other material to measure the number of perforation holes or teeth within the space of 2 centimeters.

Permit: Franking by the imprint of a number and additional information that identifies a mailer's prepaid postage account, thereby eliminating the need to affix and cancel stamps on large mailings. The mailer must obtain a document (permit) that authorizes his use of this procedure.

Phantom philately: The collection of bogus stamps. The name is derived from Frederick Melville's book Phantom Philately, one of the pioneer works on bogus issues.

Philatelic cover: An envelope, postal card or other item franked and mailed by a stamp collector to create a collectible object. It may or may not have carried a personal or business message. A nonphilatelic cover is usually one that has carried business or personal correspondence and has had its stamps applied by a noncollector. Some stamps are known only on collector-created covers. It is impossible to say whether some covers are philatelically inspired or not. See also Used and Postally used.

Philately: The collection and study of postage stamps, postal stationery and postal history.

Phosphor: A chemical substance used in the production of selected stamps to activate machines that automatically cancel mail. The machines react to the phosphor under ultraviolet light. In 1959, Great Britain began to print phosphor lines on some of its stamps. See also Tagging.

Photogravure: A modern stamp-printing process that is a form of intaglio printing. Plates are made photographically and chemically, rather than by hand engraving a die and transferring it to a plate. The ink in this process rests in the design depressions. The surface of the printing plate is wiped clean. The paper is forced into the depressions and picks up the ink, in a manner much like the line-engraved printing process.

Pictorial: Stamp bearing a picture of some sort, other than a portrait or coat of arms.

Plate: The basic printing unit on a press used to produce stamps. Early stamps were printed from flat plates. Curved or cylindrical plates are used for most modern stamps. See also Cylinder and Sleeve.

Plate block: A block of stamps from the corner or side of a pane including the selvage bearing the number(s) of the plate(s) used to print the sheet from which the pane was separated. Some stamp production methods, like booklet production, normally cut off plate numbers. In the United States, plate number blocks are collected normally as blocks of four to 20 stamps, depending on the press used to print the stamps. When each stamp in a pane is a different design, the entire pane is collected as the plate block.

Plate number: Numerals or an alphanumeric combination that identifies the printing plate used to print postage stamp images. In the United States, plate numbers on sheet stamps often appear in corner margin paper or side margin paper. Plate numbers on coil stamps were commonly trimmed off until about 1980; since then the number appears on stamps at specific intervals. Booklet plate numbers are often found on selvage attached to the pane.

Plating: The reconstruction of a stamp pane by collecting blocks and individual stamps representing various positions. This is possible for many older issues, but most modern issues are too uniform to make the identification of individual positions possible.

Plebiscite issue: A stamp issue promoting a popular vote. After World War I, a number of disputed areas were placed under temporary League of Nations administration, pending plebiscites to determine which nation the populace wished to join. Special issues note the upcoming vote in several of these areas; among them, Allenstein, Carinthia, Eastern Silesia, Marienwerder, Schleswig and Upper Silesia.

PNC: 1) A plate number coil stamp; that is, a stamp from a coil that is inscribed with a plate number. The abbreviations PNC3 and PNC5 identify strips of three or five coil stamps with the PNC located in the center position of the strip. 2) A philatelic-numismatic combination: a cover bearing a stamp and containing a coin, medal or token. The coin and stamp are usually related in such cases; often the cover is canceled on the first day of use of the coin.

Pneumatic post: Letter distribution through pressurized air tubes. Pneumatic posts existed in many large cities in Europe, and special stamps and stationery were often produced for the service.

Postage dues: Stamps or markings indicating that insufficient postage has been affixed to the mailing piece. Postage dues are usually affixed at the office of delivery. The additional postage is collected from the addressee.

Postal card: A government-produced postcard bearing a stamp imprint in the upper-right corner representing prepayment of postage.

Postal fiscal: Revenue or fiscal stamps used postally.

Postal history: The study of postal markings, rates and routes, or anything to do with the history of the posts.

Postal stationery: Stationery bearing imprinted stamps, as opposed to adhesive stamps. Postal stationery includes postal cards, lettercards, stamped envelopes, wrappers, aerograms, telegraph cards, postal savings forms and similar government-produced items. The cost to the mailer is often the price of postage plus an additional charge for the stationery item.

Postally used: A stamp or cover that has seen legitimate postal use, as opposed to one that has been canceled-to-order or favor-canceled. The term "postally used" suggests that an item exists because it was used to carry a personal or business communication, without the sender thinking of creating an item to be collected.

Postcard: A small card, usually with a picture on one side and a space for a written message on the other. Postcards have no imprinted stamp, so the mailer must also purchase postage to mail the postcard. See also Postal card.

Postmark: Any official postal marking. The term is usually used specifically in reference to cancellations bearing the name of a post office of origin and a mailing date.

Precancel: Stamp with a special overprint cancellation allowing it to bypass normal canceling. In some cases the precancel also designates a specific mail-handling service, such as "Presorted First-Class." Other precancels may include the city and state of the issuing post office. Precanceled stamps are used by volume mailers who hold a permit to use them. U.S. precancels fall into two categories: 1) Locals have the mark or text applied by a town or city post office; 2) Bureaus have the mark or text applied by the U.S. Bureau of Engraving and Printing. See also Service inscribed.

Prestamp covers: Folded letters or their outer enclosures used before the introduction of adhesive postage stamps or postal stationery.

Prestige booklet: A stamp booklet with oversized panes, descriptive information and stamp issues commemorating a special topic. Prestige booklets often include panes with no stamps that instead bear labels or additional information, along with panes bearing stamps.

Prexies: The nickname for the U.S. 1938-54 Presidential definitive series, Scott 803-34, 839-51.

Printer's waste: Misprinted, misperforated or misgummed stamps often created during the normal process of stamp production. Printer's waste is supposed to be destroyed, but such material enters the philatelic market through carelessness and theft.

Printing: The process of imprinting designs on paper from an inked surface.

Processing: Steps that finish a printed stamp sheet. Processing includes perforation, trimming, dividing the sheet into individual panes, and packaging for distribution.

Pro Juventute: Latin, meaning for the benefit of youth. Switzerland has issued Pro Juventute semipostals nearly every year since 1913.

Proofs: Trial impressions from a die or printing plate before actual stamp production. Proofs are made to examine a die or plate for defects or to compare the results of using different inks.

Provisional: A postage stamp issued for temporary use to meet postal demands until new or regular stocks of stamps can be obtained.

Plate number block: A block of stamps from the corner or side of a pane including the selvage bearing the number(s) of the plate(s) used to print the sheet from which the pane was separated. Some stamp production methods, like booklet production, normally cut off plate numbers. In the United States, plate number blocks are collected normally as blocks of four to 20 stamps, depending on the press used to print the stamps. When each stamp in a pane is a different design, the entire pane is collected as the plate block.

Press sheet: A complete unit of stamps as printed. Stamps are usually printed in large sheets and are separated into two or more panes before shipment to post offices.

Q

Quadripartition: A block or strip of four stamps that together complete a single entire design. See United States Scott 1448-51, the 1972 Cape Hatteras National Seashore issue.

R

Railway Post Office: Portable mail-handling equipment for sorting mail in transit on trains. The last official U.S. RPO ran June 30, 1977. RPOs were used in many countries. See also Mobile Post Office.

Receiving mark: A postmark or other postal marking applied by the receiving, rather than the originating, post office. See also Backstamp.

Redrawn: A stamp design that has been slightly altered yet maintains the basic design as originally issued.

Re-engraved: A stamp with an altered design as the result of a change made to a transfer roll or printing plate prior to a later printing, thereby distinguishing it from the original die.

Regional: Stamp sold or valid in a specific area of a stamp-issuing entity. Great Britain has issued stamps for the regions of Guernsey, Jersey, Isle of Man, Northern Ireland, Scotland and Wales. Regionals are usually sold only in a given region but are often valid for postage throughout a country.

Registered mail: First-class mail with a numbered receipt, including a valuation of the registered item, for full or limited compensation if the mail is lost. Some countries have issued registered mail stamps. Registered mail is signed for by each postal employee who handles it.

Registration labels: Adhesive labels indicating the registry number and, often, the city of origin for registered articles sent through the mail.

Regummed: A stamp bearing adhesive from an unauthorized source.

Reissue: An official reprinting of a stamp from an obsolete or discontinued issue. Reissues are valid for postage. See also Reprint.

Remainders: Stocks of stamps remaining unsold at the time that an issue is declared obsolete by a post office. Some countries have sold remainders to the stamp trade at substantial discounts from face value. The countries normally mark the stamps with a distinctive cancel. Uncanceled remainders usually cannot be distinguished from stamps sold over the counter before the issue was invalidated.

Repaired stamp: A damaged stamp that has been repaired in some way to reinforce it or to make it resemble an undamaged stamp.

Replica: A reproduction of a stamp or cover. In the 19th century, replica stamps were sold as stamp album space fillers. Replica stamps are often printed in one color in a sheet containing a number of different designs. Replicas can sometimes deceive either a postal clerk or collectors.

Reprint: A stamp printed from the original plate, after the issue has ceased to be postally valid. Official reprints are sometimes made for presentation purposes or official collections. They are often distinguishable in some way from the originals: different colors, perforations, paper or gum. Private reprints, on the other hand, are usually produced strictly for sale to collectors and often closely resemble the original stamps. Private reprints normally sell for less than original copies. Reprints are not valid for postage. See also Reissue.

Retouch: The repairing of a damaged plate or die, often producing a minor, but detectable, difference in the design of the printed stamps.

Revenues: Stamps representing the prepayment or payment of various taxes. Revenues are affixed to official documents and to merchandise. Some stamps, including many issues of the British Commonwealth, are inscribed "Postage and Revenue" and were available for either use. Such issues are usually worth less fiscally canceled than postally used. In some cases, revenues have been used provisionally as postage stamps. See also Fiscal.

Rocket mail: Mail flown in a rocket, even if only a short distance. Many rocket mail experiments have been conducted since 1931. Special labels, cachets or cancels usually note that mail was carried on a rocket.

Rotary plate: A curved or cylindrical printing plate used on a press that rotates the plate to make continuous impressions. Flat plates make single impressions.

Rouletting: The piercing of the paper between stamps to make their separation more convenient. No paper is actually removed from the sheet, as it is in perforating. Rouletting has been made by dash, sawtooth or wavy line.

Rural Free Delivery: System for free home delivery of mail in rural areas of the United States, begun just prior to the turn of the 20th century.

Rust: A brown mold resembling the rust in iron. Rust affects stamp paper and gum in tropical regions.

RPO: Railway Post Office. Portable mail-handling equipment for sorting mail in transit on trains. The last official U.S. RPO ran June 30, 1977. RPOs were used in many countries. See also Mobile Post Office.

RFD: Rural Free Delivery. System for free home delivery of mail in rural areas of the United States, begun just prior to the turn of the 20th century.

S

SASE: A self-addressed, stamped envelope. An unused envelope bearing the address of the sender and sufficient return postage. Enclosed with correspondence to make answering easy.

Secret mark: A minute alteration to a stamp design added to distinguish later printings from earlier printings by a different firm. Secret marks may positively distinguish genuine stamps from counterfeits.

Seebeck: The nickname for various Latin American issues produced 1890-99 in contract with Nicholas Frederick Seebeck, the agent for the Hamilton Bank Note Co. of New York. Seebeck agreed to provide new issues of stamps and stationery each year at no charge, in return for the right to sell remainders and reprints to collectors. The resulting furor destroyed Seebeck and blackened the philatelic reputations of the countries involved.

Self-adhesive: Stamp gum that adheres to envelope paper by the application of pressure alone. Most self-adhesive stamps are sold on a coated paper release liner. See also Liner, Linerless, Water-activated.

Selvage: The marginal paper on a sheet or pane of stamps. Selvage may be unprinted or may contain printer's markings or other information.

Semipostal: A stamp sold at a price greater than postal value, with the additional charge dedicated for a special purpose. Usually recognized by the presence of two (often different) values, separated by a "+" sign, on a single stamp.

Series: A group of stamps with a similar design or theme, issued over a period of time. A series may be planned or may evolve.

Service inscribed: A stamp with wording as part of the initial printed design that identifies the mail-handling service for which the stamp is intended, such as "Presorted First-Class." See also Precancel.

Set: Stamps sharing common design elements, often issued at one time and usually collected as a group.

Se-tenant: French for "joined together." Two or more unseparated stamps of different designs, colors, denominations or types.

Shade: The minor variation commonly found in any basic color. Shades may be accorded catalog status when they are very distinctive.

Sheet: A complete unit of stamps as printed. Stamps are usually printed in large sheets and are separated into two or more panes before shipment to post offices.

Ship letter: Mail carried by private ship.

Short set: An incomplete set of stamps, usually lacking either the high value or one or more key values.

Sleeper: Stamp or other collectible item that seems to be underpriced and may have good investment potential.

Sleeve: 1) A seamless cylindrical printing plate used in rotary intaglio printing. 2) A flat transparent holder, often specifically for protecting and storing a cover.

Soaking: Removal of stamps from envelope paper. Most stamps may be safely soaked in water. Fugitive inks, however, will run in water, and chalky-surfaced papers will lose their designs entirely, so some knowledge of stamps is a necessity. Colored envelope paper should be soaked separately.

Souvenir card: A philatelic card, not valid for postage, issued in conjunction with some special event. The souvenir card often illustrates the design of a postage stamp.

Souvenir page: An announcement of a new United States stamp issue created by the U.S. Postal Service, bearing a copy of the new stamp tied by a first day of issue cancellation.

Souvenir sheet: A small sheet of stamps, including one value or a set of stamps. A souvenir sheet usually has a wide margin and an inscription describing an event being commemorated. Stamps on a souvenir sheet may be perforated or imperforate.

Space filler: A stamp in poor condition used to fill the designated space in a stamp album until a better copy can be found.

Special delivery: A service providing expedited delivery of mail. Called Express by some nations.

Special handling: A U.S. service providing expeditious handling for fourth-class material.

Special printing: Reissue of a stamp of current or recent design, often with distinctive color, paper or perforations.

Specialist: A stamp collector who intensively studies and collects the stamps and postal history of a given country, area, or time period, or who has otherwise limited his collecting field.

Special stamps: Regular postage stamp issues that fall outside the traditional definitions of commemorative and definitive stamps. In the United States, holiday issues such as Contemporary Christmas, Traditional Christmas, Hanukkah and the like are considered special stamps. They are printed in substantially greater quantities than commemorative stamps, and sometimes return to press for additional printings. Love stamps are also considered special stamps.

Specimen: Stamp or stationery item distributed to Universal Postal Union members for identification purposes and to the philatelic press and trade for publicity purposes. Specimens are overprinted or punched with the word "SPECIMEN" or its equivalent, or are overprinted or punched in a way to make them different from the issued stamps. Specimens of scarce stamps tend to be less valuable than the actual stamps. Specimens of relatively common stamps are more valuable.

Speculative issue: A stamp or issue released primarily for sale to collectors, rather than to meet any legitimate postal need.

Splice: The repair of a break in a roll of stamp paper, or the joining of two rolls of paper for continuous printing. Stamps printed over a splice are usually removed and destroyed before the normal stamps are issued.

Stamp: An officially issued postage label, often adhesive, attesting that payment has been rendered for mail delivery. Initially used as a verb, meaning to imprint or impress; as in, to stamp a design.

Stampless cover: A folded sheet or envelope carried as mail without a postage stamp. This term usually refers to covers predating the requirement that stamps be affixed to all letters (in the United States, 1856).

Stock book: A specially manufactured blank book containing rows of pockets on each page to hold stamps.

Straight edge: Flat-plate or rotary-plate stamps from the margins of panes where the sheets were cut apart. Straight-edge stamps have no perforations on one or two adjacent sides. Sometimes straight-edge stamps show a guideline.

Strip: Three or more unseparated stamps in a row, vertically or horizontally.

Surcharge: An overprint that changes or restates the denomination of a stamp or postal stationery item.

Surface-colored paper: Paper colored on the surface only, with a white or uncolored back.

Surtax: The portion of a semipostal stamp purchase price exceeding the postage value. The surtax is designated for donation to a charity or some other purpose.

Sweatbox: A closed box containing dampened spongelike material, over which stuck-together unused stamps are placed on a grill. Humidity softens the gum, allowing separation of stamps. In some cases, the sweatbox may be used to help remove a postally used stamp from envelope paper.

T

T: Abbreviation for the French "Taxe." Handstamped on a stamp, the T indicates the stamp's use as a postage due. Handstamped on a cover, it indicates that postage due has been charged. Several countries have used regular stamps with a perforated initial T as postage dues.

Tagging: Phosphor material on stamps used to activate automatic mail-handling equipment. This may be lines, bars, letters, part of the design area or the entire stamp surface. The tagging may also permeate the stamp paper. Some stamps are issued both with and without tagging. Catalogs describe them as tagged or untagged.

Teeth: The protruding points along the outer edge of a perforated postage stamp when it has been removed from the pane.

Telegraph stamp: Label used for the prepayment of telegraph fees. Telegraph stamps resemble postage stamps.

Tete-beche: French for "head to tail." Two or more unsevered stamps, one of which is inverted in relation to the other.

Thematic: A collection of stamps or covers relating to a specific topic. The topic is expanded by careful inquiry and is presented as a logical story. See also Topical.

Tied: A stamp is said to be tied to a cover when the cancel extends over both the stamp and the envelope paper. Stamps can also be tied by the aging of the mucilage or glue that holds them to the paper.

Tong: Tweezerlike tool with rounded, polished tips, used to handle stamps. Tongs prevent stamps from being soiled by dirt, oil or perspiration.

Topical: 1) Stamp or cover showing a given subject. Examples are flowers, art, birds, elephants or the Statue of Liberty. 2) The collection of stamps by the topic depicted on them, rather than by country of origin. See also Thematic.

Transit mark: A postal marking applied by a post office between the originating and receiving post offices. It can be on the front or back of a cover, card or wrapper.

Triptych: A se-tenant strip of three related stamps forming one overall design. See United States Scott 1629-31, the 1976 Spirit of 76 issue.

Type: A basic design of a stamp or a set. Catalogs use type numbers or letters to save space. Catalogs show a typical design of one type rather than every stamp with that design or a similar design.

U

Underprint: A fine printing underlying the design of a stamp, most often used to deter counterfeiting.

Ungummed: A stamp without gum. Ungummed stamps are either stamps issued without gum or an uncanceled gummed stamp that has had its gum soaked off. Many countries in tropical climates have issued stamps without gum.

Unhinged: A stamp without hinge marks, but not necessarily with original gum.

Universal Postal Union: An international organization formed in Bern, Switzerland, in 1874, to regulate and standardize postal usage and to facilitate the movement of mail between member nations. Today, most nations belong to the UPU. (See UPU section of this almanac.)

Unused: An uncanceled stamp that has not been used but has a hinge mark or some other characteristic or defect that keeps it from being considered a mint stamp. Uncanceled stamps without gum may have been used and missed being canceled, or they may have lost their gum by accident.

Used: A stamp or stationery item that has been canceled by a postal authority to prevent its reuse on mail. In general, a used stamp is any stamp with a cancel or a precanceled stamp without gum. See also Postally Used and Philatelic Cover.

UPU: Universal Postal Union. An international organization formed in Bern, Switzerland, in 1874, to regulate and standardize postal usage and to facilitate the movement of mail between member nations. Today, most nations belong to the UPU.

V

Variety: A variation from the standard form of a stamp. Varieties include different watermarks, inverts, imperforates, missing colors, wrong colors and major color shifts. See also Freak, Error.

Vignette: The central part of a stamp design, usually surrounded by a border. In some cases the vignette shades off gradually into the surrounding area.

W

Want list: A list of needed stamps or covers, identified by catalog number or some other description, submitted by a collector to a dealer, usually including requirements on condition and price.

Water-activated adhesive: Stamp gum designed to adhere to envelope paper only if the gum is moistened. All gummed stamps before 1963 used water-activated adhesive.

Watermark: A deliberate thinning of paper during its manufacture to produce a semitranslucent pattern. Watermarks appear frequently in paper used in stamp printing or envelope manufacture. See also Batonne.

Web: A continuous roll of paper used in stamp printing.

Wing margin: Early British stamps from the side of a pane with selvage attached. British sheets printed before 1880 were perforated down the center of the gutter, producing oversized margins on one side of stamps adjacent to the gutter. Such copies are distinctive and scarcer than normal copies.

Wove paper: A paper showing few differences in texture and thickness when held to light. In the production of wove paper, the pulp is pressed against a very fine netting, producing a virtually uniform texture. Wove paper is the most commonly used paper in stamp production.

Wrapper: A flat sheet or strip open at both ends that can be folded and sealed around a newspaper or periodical. Wrappers can have an imprinted stamp or have a stamp attached.

X

None

Y

None

Z

Zemstvo: A local stamp issued by Russian municipal governments or zemstvos, in accordance with an imperial edict of 1870.

Zeppelins: The stamps issued for, or in honor of, zeppelin flights. Cacheted covers carried on such flights are Zeppelin covers.

ZIP block: U.S. marginal marking block with the selvage bearing the image of the "Mr. ZIP" cartoon character and/or an inscription urging the use of ZIP code. This first appeared on U.S. marginal selvage in 1964. Typically a ZIP block is a block of four stamps.

ZIP code: The U.S. numerical post code used to speed and mechanize mail handling and delivery. The letters stand for Zoning Improvement Plan.

INDEX TO ADVERTISERS – 2023 U.S. SPECIALIZED

ADVERTISER — PAGE

– B –

JIM BARDO 65, 115

– C –

C & H STAMPS....1106

CANAL ZONE STUDY GROUP 1107

MARTIN M. CASSITY....69

CENTURY STAMPS 37

ALAN E. COHEN 29, 39, 45, 53, 423

CUBAN PHILATELIC SOCIETY OF AMERICA INC. 1127

– D –

HJW DAUGHERTY....713

JOHN DENUNE 1062

– E –

EASTERN AUCTIONS, LTD. 7

– F –

RICHARD A. FRIEDBERG 711

– G –

HENRY GITNER PHILATELISTS, INC.....59

– H –

HB PHILATELICS....797

HAWAIIAN ISLANDS STAMP & COIN 1138

– J –

ERIC JACKSON REVENUE STAMPS....715

MICHAEL JAFFE 796, 831

– K –

WALTER KASELL 38, 51

PATRICIA A. KAUFMANN....1083

KELLEHER & ROGERS LTD..... 7A

JOHN L. KIMBROUGH....1100

WILLIAM J. KOZERSKY, PHILATELIST 1063

– L –

LITTLETON COIN COMPANY 1080

– M –

MARKEST STAMP CO. INC. ....Inside Front Cover

ALAN MILLER STAMPS.... 2A

MILLER'S STAMP COMPANY 63

MOUNTAINSIDE STAMPS 479

MYSTIC STAMP CO. .... Back Cover

– P –

PACIFIC MIDWEST CO.....1137

THE PHILATELIC FOUNDATION....1A

PHILATELIC STAMP AUTHENTICATION & GRADING, INC..... 23

– R –

WAYNE ROOT 13

SCHUYLER J. RUMSEY PHILATELIC AUCTIONS 11

– S –

SAM HOUSTON....795

ROBERT A. SIEGEL AUCTION GALLERIES, INC. 9

JAY SMITH....1131

SOUTHWEST STAMPS 5

– T –

DAVID R. TORRE....805

– U –

UNITED POSTAL STATIONERY SOCIETY.... 649, 697

UNITED STATES STAMP SOCIETY....159

– V –

VIDIFORMS COMPANY, INC. 401

VOGT STAMPS....1139

VOLOVSKI RARITIES....43

– W –

LAURENCE L. WINUM....49

2023
UNITED STATES SPECIALIZED DEALER DIRECTORY YELLOW PAGE LISTINGS

This section of your Scott Catalogue contains advertisements to help you conveniently find what you need, when you need it...!

Stamp Stores

New Jersey

BERGEN STAMPS & COLLECTIBLES
306 Queen Anne Rd.
Teaneck, NJ 07666
PH: 201-836-8987
bergenstamps@gmail.com

TRENTON STAMP & COIN
Thomas DeLuca
Store: Forest Glen Plaza
1804 Highway #33
Hamilton Square, NJ 08690
Mail: PO Box 8574
Trenton, NJ 08650
PH: 609-584-8100
FAX: 609-587-8664
TOMD4TSC@aol.com
www.trentonstampandcoin.com

New York

CHAMPION STAMP CO., INC.
432 West 54th St.
New York, NY 10019
PH: 212-489-8130
FAX: 212-581-8130
championstamp@aol.com
www.championstamp.com

CK STAMPS
42-14 Union St. # 2A
Flushing, NY 11355
PH: 917-667-6641
ckstampsllc@yahoo.com

Ohio

HILLTOP STAMP SERVICE
Richard A. Peterson
PO Box 626
Wooster, OH 44691
PH: 330-262-8907 (0)
PH: 330-201-1377 (H)
hilltop@bright.net
hilltopstamps@sssnet.com
www.hilltopstamps.com

Supplies

BROOKLYN GALLERY COIN & STAMP, INC.
8725 4th Ave.
Brooklyn, NY 11209
PH: 718-745-5701
FAX: 718-745-2775
info@brooklyngallery.com
www.brooklyngallery.com

Topicals - Columbus

MR. COLUMBUS
PO Box 1492
Fennville, MI 49408
PH: 269-543-4755
David@MrColumbus1492.com
www.MrColumbus1492.com

United Nations

BRUCE M. MOYER
Box 12031
Charlotte, NC 28220
PH: 908-237-6967
moyer@unstamps.com
www.unstamps.com

United States

ACS STAMP COMPANY
2914 W 135th Ave
Broomfield, Colorado 80020
303-841-8666
www.ACSStamp.com

BROOKMAN STAMP CO.
PO Box 90
Vancouver, WA 98666
PH: 360-695-1391
PH: 800-545-4871
FAX: 360-695-1616
info@brookmanstamps.com
www.brookmanstamps.com

MILLER'S STAMP COMPANY
P.O. Box 1011
Niantic, CT 06357
www.millerstamps.com
PH: 860-908-6200

U.S. - Classics

MILLER'S STAMP COMPANY
P.O. Box 1011
Niantic, CT 06357
www.millerstamps.com
PH: 860-908-6200

U.S. Classics/Moderns

BARDO STAMPS
PO Box 7437
Buffalo Grove, IL 60089
PH: 847-634-2676
jfb7437@aol.com
www.bardostamps.com

U.S.-Collections Wanted

DUTCH COUNTRY AUCTIONS
The Stamp Center
4115 Concord Pike
Wilmington, DE 19803
PH: 302-478-8740
FAX: 302-478-8779
auctions@dutchcountryauctions.com
www.dutchcountryauctions.com

DR. ROBERT FRIEDMAN & SONS STAMP & COIN BUYING CENTER
2029 W. 75th St.
Woodridge, IL 60517
PH: 800-588-8100
FAX: 630-985-1588
stampcollections@drbobstamps.com
www.drbobfriedmanstamps.com

U.S. Postal History

DON TOCHER, US CLASSICS
Boulder, CO
PH: 617-686-0288
dontocher@earthlink.net
www.postalnet.com/dontocher

Wanted - Worldwide Collections

DUTCH COUNTRY AUCTIONS
The Stamp Center
4115 Concord Pike
Wilmington, DE 19803
PH: 302-478-8740
FAX: 302-478-8779
auctions@dutchcountryauctions.com
www.dutchcountryauctions.com

Wanted - U.S. Collections

BROOKMAN STAMP CO.
PO Box 90
Vancouver, WA 98666
PH: 360-695-1391
PH: 800-545-4871
FAX: 360-695-1616
info@brookmanstamps.com
www.brookmanstamps.com

Websites

ACS STAMP COMPANY
2914 W 135th Ave
Broomfield, Colorado 80020
303-841-8666
www.ACSStamp.com

Worldwide

GUILLERMO JALIL
Maipu 466, local 4
1006 Buenos Aires
Argentina
guillermo@jalilstamps.com
philatino@philatino.com
www.philatino.com (worldwide stamp auctions)
www.jalilstamps.com (direct sale, worldwide stamps)

Worldwide-Collections

DR. ROBERT FRIEDMAN & SONS STAMP & COIN BUYING CENTER
2029 W. 75th St.
Woodridge, IL 60517
PH: 800-588-8100
FAX: 630-985-1588
stampcollections@drbobstamps.com
www.drbobfriedmanstamps.com